f
mL
105
I55
2003

International WHO'S WHO in

2003

Popular

MUSIC

International WHO'S WHO in

2003

Popular
MUSIC

Fifth Edition

Europa Publications
Taylor & Francis Group

LONDON AND NEW YORK

First published 1996

ISBN: 1 85743 1766
ISSN: 1740-0163

Series Editor: Elizabeth Sleeman

Associate Editor: Alison Neale

Technology Editor: Ian Preston

Freelance Editorial Team: Kate Bomford, Justin Lewis, Jenifa Sharif

Editorial Co-ordinator: Mary Hill

Administrative Assistant: Haydon Lawrence

Typeset by Bibliocraft Ltd, Dundee

Printed and bound by St Edmundsbury Press, Bury St Edmunds

FOREWORD

The Fifth edition of the INTERNATIONAL WHO'S WHO IN POPULAR MUSIC provides biographical information on over 5,000 prominent people from pop, rock, folk, jazz, rap, dance, world, blues, gospel and country music, including instrumentalists, singers, writers, producers and managers. The biographies include, where available, personal and contact details, information on career, recordings, compositions, publications and honours.

For each edition existing entrants are given the opportunity to make necessary amendments and additions to their biographies, while potential new entrants are asked to complete a questionnaire, providing biographical details. Supplementary research is done by the Europa Publications editorial department in order to ensure that the book is as up to date as possible on publication.

In addition to the biographical information, the directory section provides appendices of record companies, management companies, booking agents and promoters, music publishers, music festivals and events, and music organizations.

Readers are referred to the book's companion title, the INTERNATIONAL WHO'S WHO IN CLASSICAL MUSIC 2003, for a comprehensive collection of information on the most prominent people in the fields of classical and light classical music.

The assistance of the individuals and organizations included in this publication in providing up-to-date material is invaluable, and the editors would like to take this opportunity to express their appreciation.

March 2003

ALPHABETIZATION KEY

The list of names is alphabetical, with the entrants listed under surnames. If part of an entrant's first given name is in parentheses, this will not affect his or her alphabetical listing.

All names beginning Mc or Mac are treated as Mac, e.g. McDevitt before MacDonald.

Names with Arabic prefixes are normally listed after the prefix, except when requested otherwise by the entrant.

In the case of surnames beginning with De, Des, Du, van or von the entries are normally found under the prefix.

Names beginning St are listed as if they began Saint, e.g. St Germain before Salamun.

As a general rule Chinese and Korean names are alphabetized under the first name.

In the case of an entrant whose name is spelt in a variety of ways, who is known by a pseudonym or best known by another name, a cross reference is provided.

CONTENTS

ABBREVIATIONS

AA   Associate in Arts
AB   Alberta
ABC   Australian Broadcasting Corporation
Acad.   Academy
ACLS   American Council of Learned Societies
ACT   Australian Capital Territory
Admin.   Administrator, Administrative
AFofM   American Federation of Musicians
AG   Aktiengesellschaft (Joint Stock Company)
AIDS   acquired immunodeficiency syndrome
AK   Alaska
aka   also known as
AL   Alabama
ALCS   Authors' Lending and Copyright Society
AM   amplitude modulation
A.M.   Member of the Order of Australia
A.O.   Officer of the Order of Australia
Apdo   Apartado (Post Box)
approx.   approximately
Apt   Apartment
apto   apartamento
A & R   Artists and Repertoire
AR   Arkansas
ASCAP   American Society of Composers, Authors and Publishers
Asscn   Association
Assoc.   Associate
Asst   Assistant
ATD   Art Teacher's Diploma
Aug.   August
Avda   Avenida (Avenue)
Ave   Avenue
AZ   Arizona

b.   born
BA   Bachelor of Arts
BAC&S   British Academy of Composers and Songwriters
BAFTA   British Academy of Film and Television Arts
BArch   Bachelor of Architecture
BASCA   British Association of Songwriters, Composers and Authors (now BAC&S)
BBC   British Broadcasting Corporation
BC   British Columbia
BCL   Bachelor of Civil Law
BD   Bachelor of Divinity
Bdwy   Broadway
BE   Bachelor of Engineering; Bachelor of Education
BEd   Bachelor of Education
BEng   Bachelor of Engineering
BFA   Bachelor in Fine Arts
BFI   British Film Institute
BJ   Bachelor of Journalism
Bldg   Building
BLitt   Bachelor of Letters
BLS   Bachelor in Library Science
Blvd   Boulevard
BM   Bachelor of Medicine; Bachelor of Music
BMI   Broadcast Music, Inc
BMus   Bachelor of Music
BP   Boîte postale (Post Box)
BPhil   Bachelor of Philosophy
bros   brothers
BS   Bachelor of Science; Bachelor of Surgery
BSc   Bachelor of Science

BSE   Bachelor of Science in Engineering (USA)
BSFA   British Science Fiction Association
BTh   Bachelor of Theology
BTI   British Theatre Institute

c.   circa; child, children
CA   California
CBC   Canadian Broadcasting Corporation
C.B.E.   Commander of (the Order of) the British Empire
CBS   Columbia Broadcasting System
CD   Compact Disc
CD-ROM   compact disc read-only memory
CEO   Chief Executive Officer
Chair.   Chairman, Chairwoman
Cia   Companhia
Cía   Compañía
Cie   Compagnie
circ.   circulation
CMA   Country Music Association
C.M.G.   Companion of (the Order of) St Michael and St George
CNRS   Centre National de la Recherche Scientifique
c/o   care of
Co   Company; County
CO   Colorado
Col.   Colonia, Colima
COO   Chief Operating Officer
Corpn   Corporation
CP   Case Postale; Caixa Postal; Casella Postale (Post Box)
Cres.   Crescent
Ct   Court
CT   Connecticut
C.V.O.   Commander of the Royal Victorian Order
CWA   Crime Writers' Association

d.   daughter(s)
D.B.E.   Dame Commander of (the Order of) the British Empire
DC   District of Columbia; Distrito Central
DD   Doctor of Divinity
Dd'ES   Diplôme d'études supérieures
DE   Delaware
Dec.   December
DEd   Doctor of Education
demo   demonstration
Dept   Department
D. ès L.   Docteur ès Lettres
D. ès Sc.   Docteur ès Sciences
devt   development
DF   Distrito Federal
DFA   Doctor of Fine Arts; Diploma of Fine Arts
DHL   Doctor of Hebrew Literature
DipEd   Diploma in Education
DipTh   Diploma in Theology
Dir   Director
DJ   Disc Jockey
DJur   Doctor of Law
DLitt   Doctor of Letters
DMus   Doctor of Music
DN   Distrito Nacional
DPhil   Doctor of Philosophy
dpto   departamento
Dr(a)   Doctor(a)

ABBREVIATIONS

Dr.	Drive	L. ès L.	Licencié ès Lettres
DSc	Doctor of Science	L. ès Sc.	Licencié ès Sciences
DSocSci	Doctor of Social Science	LHD	Doctor of Humane Letters
DTh	Doctor of Theology	LLB	Bachelor of Laws
		LLD	Doctor of Laws
E	East(ern)	LL.L	Licentiate of Laws
EC	European Community	LLM	Master of Laws
Ed.	Editor	LP	Long Playing record
Edif.	Edificio (Building)	LRCP	Licenciate, Royal College of Physicians, London
edn	edition	LRSM	Licenciate, Royal Schools of Music
e.g.	exempli gratia (for example)	LSO	London Symphony Orchestra
ENO	English National Opera	LTCL	Licenciate of Trinity College of Music, London
EP	Extended Play	Ltd	Limited
esq.	esquina (corner)	LW	long wave
etc.	et cetera	LWT	London Weekend Television
EU	European Union		
eV	eingetragener Verein	m.	married; million
Exec.	Executive	MA	Massachusetts; Master of Arts
		Man.	Manager; Managing
f.	founded	MAT	Master of Arts and Teaching
fax	facsimile	MB	Manitoba
Feb.	February	MBA	Master of Business Administration
FL	Florida	M.B.E.	Member of (the Order of) the British Empire
FM	frequency modulation	MC	master of ceremonies
FMA	Florida Music Association	MD	Maryland; Music Director
fmr(ly)	former(ly)	MDiv	Master in Divinity
		ME	Maine
GA	Georgia	MEd	Master in Education
Gdns	Gardens	mem.	member
Gen.	General	MEngSc	Master of Engineering
GmbH	Gesellschaft mit beschränkter Haftung (Limited Liability Company)	MFA	Master of Fine Arts
		MHRA	Modern Humanities Research Association
GMT	Greenwich Mean Time	MI	Michigan
Gov.	Governor	MLA	Modern Language Association
GP	General Practitioner	MLitt	Master in Letters
GPO	General Post Office	MLS	Master in Library Science
		MM	Master of Music
h.c.	honoris causa	MMus	Master of Music
HHD	Doctor of Humanities	MN	Minnesota
HI	Hawaii	MO	Missouri
HIV	human immunodeficiency virus	MOBO	Music of Black Origin
HM	His (or Her) Majesty	MP	Member of Parliament
Hon.	Honorary; Honourable	MPh	Master of Philosophy
Hons	Honours	MRCS	Member, Royal College of Surgeons of England
HRH	His (or Her) Royal Highness	MS	Mississippi; Master of Science
HS	Heraldry Society	MSA	Memphis Songwriters' Association
Hwy	Highway	MSc	Master of Science
		Mt	Mount
IA	Iowa	MT	Montana
IBA	Independent Broadcasting Authority	MTh	Master of Theology
ID	Idaho	MTV	Music Television
i.e.	id est (that is to say)	MW	medium wave
IL	Illinois		
IN	Indiana	N	North(ern)
Inc	Incorporated	NABOB	National Association of Black Owned Broadcasters
incl.	including		
int.	international	NARAS	National Academy of Recording Arts & Sciences
IPC	Institute of Professional Critics		
ITA	Independent Television Authority	NAS	National Academy of Songwriters
ITN	Independent Television News	NB	New Brunswick
ITV	Independent Television	NBC	National Broadcasting Company
		NC	North Carolina
Jan.	January	ND	North Dakota
JD	Doctor of Jurisprudence	NDD	National Diploma in Design
JP	Justice of the Peace	NE	Nebraska; North-east(ern)
Jr	Junior	NEA	National Endowment for the Arts
		NF	Newfoundland
K.B.E.	Knight Commander, Order of the British Empire	NH	New Hampshire
		NJ	New Jersey
km	kilometre(s)	NM	New Mexico
KS	Kansas	NME	New Musical Express
KY	Kentucky	no.	number
		Nov.	November
LA	Louisiana	nr	near
LAMDA	London Academy of Music and Dramatic Art		
Lic. en Let.	Licenciado en Letras		

ABBREVIATIONS

NS	Nova Scotia	RSPB	Royal Society for Protection of Birds
NSAI	Nashville Songwriters' Association International	RTS	Royal Television Society
NSW	New South Wales	S	South(ern); San
NT	Northwest Territories; Northern Territory	s.	son(s)
NU	Nunavut Territory	SA	Société Anonyme, Sociedad Anónima (Limited Company); South Australia
NV	Nevada		
NW	North-west(ern)	SC	South Carolina
NY	New York	SD	South Dakota
		SE	South-east(ern)
O.B.E.	Officer of (the Order of) the British Empire	Sec.	Secretary
Oct.	October	Sept.	September
Of.	Oficina (Office)	SFWA	Science Fiction and Fantasy Writers of America
OH	Ohio	SGA	Songwriters' Guild of America
OK	Oklahoma	SK	Saskatchewan
ON	Ontario	SL	Sociedad Limitada
OR	Oregon	Sq.	Square
org.	organization	Sr	Senior
OST	Original Soundtrack	St	Street; Saint
		Sta	Santa
p.	page	STB	Bachelor of Sacred Theology
PA	Pennsylvania	STD	Doctor of Sacred Theology
PBS	Public Broadcasting Service	Ste	Sainte
PE	Prince Edward Island	STL	Reader or Professor of Sacred Theology
PEN	Poets, Playwrights, Essayists, Editors and Novelists (Club)	STM	Master of Sacred Theology
		str	strasse
PETA	People for the Ethical Treatment of Animals	SVSA	South West Virginia Songwriters' Association
Pf	Postfach (Post Box)	SW	South-west(ern); short wave
PGCE	Post Graduate Certificate of Education		
PhB	Bachelor of Philosophy	tel.	telephone
PhD	Doctor of Philosophy	TLS	Times Literary Supplement
PhL	Licenciate of Philosophy	TN	Tennessee
Pkwy	Parkway	trans.	translated; translation; translator
Pl.	Place	Treas.	Treasurer
PLC	Public Limited Company	TV	television
PMB	Private Mail Bag	TX	Texas
PO Box	Post Office Box		
PR(O)	Public Relations (Officer)	u.	utca (street)
Pres.	President	UHF	ultra-high frequency
Prod.	Producer; Produced	UK	United Kingdom
Prof.	Professor	ul.	ulitsa (street)
promo	promotional	UN	United Nations
pt.	part	UNESCO	United Nations Educational, Scientific and Cultural Organization
Pty	Proprietary		
Publ.(s)	Publication(s)	UNICEF	United Nations Children's Fund
		Urb.	Urbanización (urban district)
QC	Québec	US(A)	United States (of America)
Qld	Queensland	USSR	Union of Soviet Socialist Republics
Q.S.O.	Queen's Service Order	UT	Utah
q.v.	quod vide (to which refer)		
		VA	Virginia
RADA	Royal Academy of Dramatic Art	VC	Victoria Cross
R&B	Rhythm and Blues	VHF	very high frequency
Rd	Road	VI	(US) Virgin Islands
Rep.	Republic	Vic.	Victoria
retd	retired	Vol.(s)	Volume(s)
rev. edn	revised edition	VT	Vermont
RGS	Royal Geographical Society		
RI	Rhode Island	W	West(ern)
RNLI	Royal National Life-boat Institution	WA	Western Australia; Washington (state)
ROC	Rock Out Censorship	WI	Wisconsin
rpm	revolutions per minute	WV	West Virginia
RSA	Royal Society of Arts	WY	Wyoming
RSC	Royal Shakespeare Company		
RSL	Royal Society of Literature	YT	Yukon Territory

INTERNATIONAL TELEPHONE CODES

To make international calls to telephone and fax numbers listed in the book, dial the international code of the country from which you are calling, followed by the appropriate code for the country you wish to call (listed below), followed by the area code (if applicable) and telephone or fax number listed in the entry.

	Country code	+ or − GMT*
Afghanistan	93	+4½
Albania	355	+1
Algeria	213	+1
Andorra	376	+1
Angola	244	+1
Antigua and Barbuda	1 268	−4
Argentina	54	−3
Armenia	374	+4
Australia	61	+8 to +10
Australian External Territories:		
Australian Antarctic Territory	672	+3 to +10
Christmas Island	61	+7
Cocos (Keeling) Islands	61	+6½
Norfolk Island	672	+11½
Austria	43	+1
Azerbaijan	994	+5
The Bahamas	1 242	−5
Bahrain	973	+3
Bangladesh	880	+6
Barbados	1 246	−4
Belarus	375	+2
Belgium	32	+1
Belize	501	−6
Benin	229	+1
Bhutan	975	+6
Bolivia	591	−4
Bosnia and Herzegovina	387	+1
Botswana	267	+2
Brazil	55	−3 to −4
Brunei	673	+8

	Country code	+ or − GMT*
Bulgaria	359	+2
Burkina Faso	226	0
Burundi	257	+2
Cambodia	855	+7
Cameroon	237	+1
Canada	1	−3 to −8
Cape Verde	238	−1
The Central African Republic	236	+1
Chad	235	+1
Chile	56	−4
China, People's Republic	86	+8
Special Administrative Regions:		
Hong Kong	852	+8
Macao	853	+8
China (Taiwan)	886	+8
Colombia	57	−5
Comoros	269	+3
Congo, Democratic Republic	243	+1
Congo, Republic	242	+1
Costa Rica	506	−6
Côte d'Ivoire	225	0
Croatia	385	+1
Cuba	53	−5
Cyprus	357	+2
'Turkish Republic of Northern Cyprus'	90 392	+2
Czech Republic	420	+1
Denmark	45	+1
Danish External Territories:		
Faroe Islands	298	0
Greenland	299	−1 to −4

INTERNATIONAL TELEPHONE CODES

	Country code	+ or − GMT*		Country code	+ or − GMT*
Djibouti	253	+3	Hungary	36	+1
Dominica	1 767	−4	Iceland	354	0
Dominican Republic	1 809	−4	India	91	+5½
Ecuador	593	-5	Indonesia	62	+7 to +9
Egypt	20	+2	Iran	98	+3½
El Salvador	503	−6	Iraq	964	+3
Equatorial Guinea	240	+1	Ireland	353	0
Eritrea	291	+3	Israel	972	+2
Estonia	372	+2	Italy	39	+1
Ethiopia	251	+3	Jamaica	1 876	−5
Fiji	679	+12	Japan	81	+9
Finland	358	+2	Jordan	962	+2
Finnish External Territory:			Kazakhstan	7	+6
Åland Islands	358	+2	Kenya	254	+3
France	33	+1	Kiribati	686	+12 to +13
French Overseas Departments:			Korea, Democratic People's		
French Guiana	594	−3	Republic (North Korea)	850	+9
Guadeloupe	590	−4	Korea, Republic (South Korea)	82	+9
Martinique	596	−4	Kuwait	965	+3
Réunion	262	+4	Kyrgyzstan	996	+5
French Overseas Collectivités Territoriales:			Laos	856	+7
Mayotte	269	+3	Latvia	371	+2
Saint Pierre and Miquelon	508	−3	Lebanon	961	+2
French Overseas Territories:			Lesotho	266	+2
French Polynesia	689	−9 to −10	Liberia	231	0
Wallis and Futuna Islands	681	+12	Libya	218	+1
French Overseas Country:			Liechtenstein	423	+1
New Caledonia	687	+11	Lithuania	370	+2
Gabon	241	+1	Luxembourg	352	+1
Gambia	220	0	Macedonia, former Yugoslav		
Georgia	995	+4	republic	389	+1
Germany	49	+1	Madagascar	261	+3
Ghana	233	0	Malawi	265	+2
Greece	30	+2	Malaysia	60	+8
Grenada	1 473	−4	Maldives	960	+5
Guatemala	502	−6	Mali	223	0
Guinea	224	0	Malta	356	+1
Guinea-Bissau	245	0	Marshall Islands	692	+12
Guyana	592	−4	Mauritania	222	0
Haiti	509	−5	Mauritius	230	+4
Honduras	504	−6	Mexico	52	−6 to −7

	Country code	+ or − GMT*		Country code	+ or − GMT*
Micronesia, Federated States	691	+10 to +11	Rwanda	250	+2
Moldova	373	+2	Saint Christopher and Nevis	1 869	−4
Monaco	377	+1	Saint Lucia	1 758	−4
Mongolia	976	+7 to +9	Saint Vincent and the		
Morocco	212	0	Grenadines	1 784	−4
Mozambique	258	+2	Samoa	685	−11
Myanmar	95	+6½	San Marino	378	+1
Namibia	264	+2	São Tomé and Príncipe	239	0
Nauru	674	+12	Saudi Arabia	966	+3
Nepal	977	+5¾	Senegal	221	0
Netherlands	31	+1	Seychelles	248	+4
Netherlands Dependencies:			Sierra Leone	232	0
Aruba	297	−4	Singapore	65	+8
Netherlands Antilles	599	−4	Slovakia	421	+1
New Zealand	64	+12	Slovenia	386	+1
New Zealand's Dependent and			Solomon Islands	677	+11
Associated Territories:			Somalia	252	+3
Tokelan	690	−10	South Africa	27	+2
Cook Islands	682	−10	Spain	34	+1
Niue	683	−11	Sri Lanka	94	+6
Nicaragua	505	−6	Sudan	249	+2
Niger	227	+1	Suriname	597	−3
Nigeria	234	+1	Swaziland	268	+2
Norway	47	+1	Sweden	46	+1
Norwegian External Territory:			Switzerland	41	+1
Svalbard	47	+1	Syria	963	+2
Oman	968	+4	Tajikistan	992	+5
Pakistan	92	+5	Tanzania	255	+3
Palau	680	+9	Thailand	66	+7
Palestinian Autonomous			Timor-Leste	670	+9
Areas	970	+2	Togo	228	0
Panama	507	−5	Tonga	676	+13
Papua New Guinea	675	+10	Trinidad and Tobago	1 868	−4
Paraguay	595	−4	Tunisia	216	+1
Peru	51	−5	Turkey	90	+2
The Philippines	63	+8	Turkmenistan	993	+5
Poland	48	+1	Tuvalu	688	+12
Portugal	351	0	Uganda	256	+3
Qatar	974	+3	Ukraine	380	+2
Romania	40	+2	United Arab Emirates	971	+4
Russian Federation	7	+2 to +12	United Kingdom	44	0

INTERNATIONAL TELEPHONE CODES

	Country code	+ or − GMT*		Country code	+ or − GMT*
United Kingdom Crown			Puerto Rico	1 787	−4
Dependencies	44	0	United States External Territories:		
United Kingdom Overseas Territories:			American Samoa	1 684	−11
Anguilla	1 264	−4	Guam	1 671	+10
Ascension Island	247	0	United States Virgin		
Bermuda	1 441	−4	Islands	1 340	−4
British Virgin Islands	1 284	−4	Uruguay	598	−3
Cayman Islands	1 345	−5	Uzbekistan	998	+5
Diego Garcia (British			Vanuatu	678	+11
Indian Ocean Territory) .	246	+5	Vatican City	39	+1
Falkland Islands	500	−4	Venezuela	58	−4
Gibraltar	350	+1	Viet Nam	84	+7
Montserrat	1 664	−4	Yemen	967	+3
Pitcairn Islands	872	−8	Yugoslavia	381	+1
Saint Helena	290	0	Zambia	260	+2
Tristan da Cunha	2 897	0	Zimbabwe	263	+2
Turks and Caicos Islands .	1 649	−5			
United States of America . . .	1	−5 to −10			
United States Commonwealth Territories:					
Northern Mariana Islands .	1 670	+10			

* The times listed compare the standard (winter) times in the various countries. Some countries adopt Summer (Daylight Saving) Time—i.e. +1 hour—for part of the year.

PART ONE

Biographies

A

AALTONEN, Juhani 'Junnu'; b. 12 Dec. 1935, Finland. Musician (saxophone, flute). *Education:* Flute, Sibelius Academy, Helsinki; Berklee College of Music, Boston, USA, 1970. *Career:* Played with drummer Edward Vesala, 1965–; Played with Arils Andersen's quartet, 1970s; Work in radio, television and studio recordings; Featured soloist, Suomi (jazz suite), Heikki Sarmanto; Crossing, Jukka Linkola; Played in reed section, UMO (New Music Orchestra), 1975–; Former member, jazz rock group Tasavallan Presidentti; Concentrated on flute, as beneficiary of government grant, late 1980s–; Duo with pianist-composer Heikki Sarmanto; Recital of solo improvizations on flute, Tampere Biennale, 1990. *Recordings:* Several with Arild Andersen, 1970s; Nana, Edward Vesala, 1970; with Heikki Sarmanto: Hearts, 1995; Solo: Springbird, 1979. *Honours:* Yrjö Award, Finnish Jazz Federation, 1968. *Address:* Kukintie 10, 01620 Vantaa, Finland.

AARONSON, Paul; b. 16 March 1955, Queens, NY, USA. Sales and Marketing Dir. m. Sharon Stern, 14 Aug. 1994. *Education:* BA, University of Florida, 1976; MBA, St John's University, 1981. *Career:* Salesman, Record Shack, New York, 1978–81; Sales Man., Important Record Distributors, 1981–86; Owner, One Up Promotions, 1987–90; Dir of Marketing, Domino Records, 1991–92; Dir, Sales and Marketing, Viceroy Music, 1992. *Recordings:* with John Mooney: Testimony, 1992; with Cowboy Mouth: Mouthing Off, 1993; with Sunset Heights: Texas Tea, 1994; with Savoy Brown: Bring It Home, 1995; Rattlesnake Guitar, The Music Of Peter Green, 1995. *Current Management:* c/o Viceroy Music Group, 547 W 27th St, Sixth Floor, New York, NY 10001, USA.

ABA YAZEED, Mohamed Mounir; b. 10 Oct. 1954, Aswan, Egypt. Vocalist; Actor. *Education:* Faculty of Applied Arts (Cinematography). *Career:* Films: Bitter Day, Sweet Day; An Egyptian Story; Destiny (total of 11 films); Stage: The King is the King; King of the Beggars; Goodnight Egypt; Television film: Tales of the Stranger. *Recordings include:* Windows; Talk; In The Middle Of The Circle; From First Touch. *Publications:* Windows, 1981; Talk, 1985; In the Middle of the Circle, 1987; From First Touch, 1996. *Honours:* Second Prize, Festival of Arab Television, 1995–96. *Membership:* Syndicate of Musicians; Syndicate of Actors. *Address:* 13 Fl-Bergass St, Garden City, Cairo, Egypt.

ABADIE, Claude; b. 15 Jan. 1920, Paris, France. Musician (clarinet); Bandleader. m. Chantal Bertin, 8 Oct. 1958, two s., one d. *Education:* Engineer. *Career:* Leader, first Dixieland Revival Band, France, early 1940s; Modern jazz musician, late 1960s; Leader, own jazz tentette. *Recordings:* Albums: Blues Pour Boris; Revival New Orleans Sur Seine; Vivement Le 15 Novembre. *Publications:* Le Jazz: Comment Ça Fonctionne, 1994. *Membership:* Union des Musicians de Jazz. *Address:* 16 Domaine des Hocquettes, 92150 Suresnes, France.

ABATÉ, Gregory; b. 31 May 1947, Fall River, MA, USA. Musician (saxophone, flute). m. Denise Marie Forcina, 10 April 1988, two s., one d. *Education:* Berklee College of Music, Boston, USA. *Career:* Major tours of USA and Europe; Radio appearances on some 200 stations throughout USA; Selmer Saxophone Clinician. *Recordings:* with Greg Abaté Quartet: Bop City Live At Birdland; Straight Ahead; Bird Lives; with Greg Abaté Quintet: Live At Chans, featuring Richie Cole; Bop Lives with Kenny Barron Trio and Claudio Roditi; Happy Samba; It's Christmastime, 1995; My Buddy, 1996; Boulevard Of Broken Dreams, the Greg Abate Quintet, 1996; As sideman: Samba Manhattan Style, with Claudio Ruditi, 1996; Blue Chip Jazz, with Mark Soskin, Harvie Swartz. *Publications:* Jazz Times; Penguin Guide To Jazz; Sax Journal; Other trade and national newspapers. *Honours:* Arts International Grant, 1992. *Membership:* International Asscn of Jazz Adjudicators. *Current Management:* Abby Hoffer Enterprises, 223 E 48th St, New York, NY 10017, USA; Entertainment Exclusives, 403 Commonwealth, Boston, MA 02215, USA. *Address:* 70 Fairway Dr., Coventry, RI 02816, USA. *Website:* www.1201music.com.

ABBEY, John E; b. 8 July 1945, London, England. Record Co Exec. *Career:* Editor and founder, Blues and Soul Magazine, London, 1966–85; Pres. and founder, Contempo Records, London, 1971–78; Pres. and co-founder, Ichiban Records Inc, 1985–. *Current Management:* Ichiban Records Inc, PO Box 724677, Atlanta, GA 31139, USA.

ABBOTT, Jacqueline; b. 10 Nov. 1973, Whiston, Merseyside, England. Vocalist. *Career:* Member: The Beautiful South, 1994–; Numerous television appearances, live gigs and festival appearances. *Recordings:* Singles: Good As Gold, 1994; Everybody's Talkin', 1994; One Last Love Song, 1994; Pretenders To The Throne, 1995; Rotterdam (Or Anywhere), 1996; Don't Marry Her, 1996; Liar's Bar, 1997; Perfect 10, 1998; Dumb, 1999; How Long's A Tear Take To Dry, 1999; The River, 2000; Albums: Miaow, 1994; Carry On Up The Charts (compilation), 1994; Blue Is The Colour, 1996; Quench, 1998; Painting It Red, 2000; Solid Bronze: Great Hits (compilation), 2001. *Address:* The Beautiful South, PO Box 87, Hull, East Yorkshire HU5 2NR, England. *Website:* www.beautifulsouth.co.uk.

ABDOU, Saabou; b. 28 Dec. 1963, Maradi, Niger. Musician. m. Hassana, 5 s., 2 d. *Career:* Live concerts. *Compositions:* Saadou; Bori; Carnaval; Tchoun Koussouma. *Recordings:* Carnaval; Tchoun Koussouma. *Honours:* Best Musician of the Year, 1998; Certificate of Honour, 1997. *Membership:* ANACIM. *Current Management:* Band Leader, Carnaval Maradi, Niger.

ABDUL, Paula; b. 19 June 1963, Los Angeles, CA, USA. Vocalist; Dancer; Choreographer. m. (1) Emilio Estevez, 1992, divorced 1994, (2) Brad Beckerman, 1996. *Education:* Television and Radio Studies, Northridge College, California State University. *Career:* Choreographer, LA Laker basketball cheerleaders, several bands, including: Duran Duran, Toto, The Pointer Sisters, ZZ Top; Scenes in films: Bull Durham, Coming To America, The Waiting Game, The Doors; Appeared in a Saturday Night Live sketch with David Duchovny; Choreographer, pop videos including: The Jacksons and Mick Jagger: Torture; George Michael: Monkey; with Janet Jackson: Control; Nasty; When I Think Of You; What Have You Done For Me Lately; City of Crime video (from film Dragnet); Dolly Parton Christmas Special (TV); Tracey Ullman Show (TV), 1989; Fitness video, Cardio Dance; World-wide performances as singer include: Tours throughout USA, UK, Japan and Far East; Prince's Trust Rock Gala, London Palladium, 1989; America Has Heart (earthquake and hurricane benefit concert), 1989; LIFEbeat's Counteraid (AIDS benefit concert), 1993; Own dance company, Co Dance; Judge, American Idol: The Search for a Superstar (TV series), 2002. *Recordings:* Albums: Forever Your Girl (No. 1, USA), 1989; Shut Up And Dance (The Dance Mixes), 1990; Spellbound (No. 1, USA), 1991; Head Over Heels, 1995; Greatest Hits, 2000. Singles: Straight Up (No. 1, USA), 1988; Forever Your Girl (No. 1, USA), 1988; Cold Hearted (No. 1, USA); Opposites Attract (No. 1, USA); Rush Rush (No. 1, USA); The Promise Of A New Day (No. 1, USA); Will You Marry Me, 1992; Head Over Heels, 1995; features on: For Our Children (Disney charity album), 1991. *Honours:* MTV Video Award, Best Choreography, Janet Jackson's Nasty, 1987; Emmy, Best Choreography, for Tracey Ullman Show, 1989; Rolling Stone Awards, Best Female Singer, 1989; American Music Awards, Favourite Pop/Rock Female Vocalist, 1989, 1992; Billboard Magazine, Top Female Pop Album, 1990; Grammy, Best Music Video, Opposites Attract, 1991; Star on Hollywood Walk of Fame, 1993; Humanitarian of the Year, Starlight Foundation, Los Angeles, 1992; Numerous Gold and Platinum discs. *Address:* c/o Third Rail Entertainment, Tri-Star Bldg, 10202 W Washington Ave, Suite 26, Culver City, CA 90232, USA.

ABERCROMBIE, John; b. 16 Dec. 1944, Portchester, NY, USA. Jazz Musician (guitar). *Education:* Berklee School of Music, Boston, USA. *Career:* Musician with Johnny 'Hammond' Smith; Dreams (with Michael and Randy Brecker); Chico Hamilton Band; Gil Evans; Gato Barbieri; Billy Cobham's Spectrum; Founder, own trio Timeless; Founder, trio Gateway (with Jack DeJohnette and Dave Holland), 1975; Leader, own quartet, 1978; Also worked with: Ralph Towner; Michael Brecker; Jan Garbarek; Jack DeJohnette's New Directions; Jan Hammer. *Recordings:* Albums include: Timeless, 1974; Gateway, 1975; Characters, 1977; Night, 1984; Current Events, 1985; Getting There, 1988; While We're Young, 1992; Speak Of The Devil, 1993; Gateway: Homecoming, 1994; Farewell, 1995; Tactics Live, 1996; Open Land, 1999; Cat 'N' Mouse, 2002. *Address:* c/o ECM Records, Pasinger Str. 94, 82166 Gräfelfing, Germany.

ABILDGAARD, Bertel; b. 2 April 1955, Soborg, Denmark. Entertainer; Actor; Songwriter; Musician. m. 14 July 1984, 1 s., 2 d. *Career:* Member: cabaret group, 5XKAJ, 1982–; Main character, Tony, in comedy, Room Service; Many television, radio appearances, radio plays; Solo artiste, 1995. *Recordings:* Kajsynger Pop, 1984; Agte Kærlighed, 1987; Alle Bornene, 1991; Krumme Tær-sang, 1992; Films include: Kajs Fosdeldag, 1990. *Honours:* Se Og Hors Humor Pris, 1988. *Membership:* DPA (Danske Populærautorer). *Current Management:* Erik Morbo/Vagn Moller, Dansk Dirma Og Hotel, Underholding Aps, Rosenyparken 81, 2670 Greve, Denmark.

ABORG, Carl Anders; b. 24 March 1952, Malmö, Sweden. Musician; Journalist; Radio Prod; Teacher; Divorced, 2 s., 1 d. *Education:* Degree in Ethnology, Swedish and Media Communication. *Career:* Member: Aston Reymers Rivaler, 1979–85; Drompojkarna, OJJ!600, Prins Lätt; Television: Own show, 1981; Nygammalt, 1982; Stage: Roskilde, 1982; Film: Alska mig, 1984; Numerous radio. *Compositions:* Sambo; Hall mig hart; Vi bygger om; Rosa-Lill; Grannens Fru. *Recordings:* With Aston Reymers Rivaler: Fran Myggjagare till fotrata, 1979; Kraal, 1980; Tval, 1981; Aston!, 1983; I grodornas land, 1984; Masterverk, 1995; With Drompojkarna: Drompojkarna, 1978; With OJJ!600: OJJ!600, 1986; With Prins Lätt: Nåt att guaga på, 1999.

Honours: Munich Youth Prize for Film Animation, 1988. *Address:* Mariestadsvägen 17, 12150 Johanneshov, Sweden.

ABRAHAMS, Mick; b. 7 April 1943, Luton, Bedfordshire, England. Musician (guitar). *Career:* Guitarist with Neil Christian; Dickie Pride; Toggery Five; McGregor's Engine; Member: Jethro Tull, 1967–69; Concerts include: Support to Pink Floyd, Hyde Park, 1968; Sunbury Jazz and Blues Festival, 1968; Founder, Blodwyn Pig; Solo artiste, 1971–; Financial consultant, 1970s–80s; Re-formed Blodwyn Pig, 1988. *Recordings include:* with Jethro Tull: This Was, 1968; Love Story, 1969; with Blodwyn Pig: Ahead Rings Out, 1969; Getting To This, 1970; All Said And Done, 1991; Lies (A New Day), 1993; Solo albums: Mick Abrahams, 1971; A Musical Evening With Mick Abrahams, 1971; At Last, 1982. *Current Management:* Serious Bob Promotions, 250 W 85th St, Suite 11D, New York, NY 10024, USA.

ACE, (Martin Ivor Kent); b. 30 March 1967, Cheltenham, Gloucestershire, England. Musician (guitar). *Career:* Founder mem., Skunk Anansie, 1994–2001; Signed to indie label One Little Indian, 1994, Virgin Records, 1996; Numerous headlining tours, festival appearances, television and radio shows; Solo artiste, 2001–, working on solo album. *Recordings:* Albums: Paranoid And Sunburnt, 1995; Stoosh, 1996; Post Orgasmic Chill, 1999. Singles: Little Baby Swastikkka, 1994; Selling Jesus, 1995; I Can Dream, 1995; Charity, 1995; Weak, 1996; All I Want, 1996; Twisted (Everyday Hurts), 1996; Hedonism, 1997; Brazen (Weep), 1997; Charlie Big Potato, 1999; Secretly, 1999; Lately, 1999. *Address:* c/o Virgin Records America Inc, 338 N Foothill Rd, Beverly Hills, CA 90210, USA. *Website:* www.acesounds.com.

ADA, Paul; b. 22 Feb. 1962, Istanbul, Turkey. Composer; Vocalist; Musician (piano); Songwriter. *Education:* Academy of Music of Anderlecht, Brussels, Belgium. *Career:* Composer and singer, Rever D'Aventures, Spirou and Fanfasio; Working partners: Ralph Benatar, Serge Frances (lyrics), Michel de Neve (producer). *Compositions:* Songs for: Paul Severs (Belgium); Yasmine Art Sulivan (Belgium); Caroline Jokris (Belgium); Maria Mouzon (Africa); Evy Furman (Germany); Garcia del Valle (Spain). *Recordings:* Maryel Epps: Sing For Me; Curro Savoy: Songs for Whistle; Marc Garcia del Valle: Pienso enti. *Publications:* Music of the Ballet; King Solomon and the Queen of Sheba, 1997; Music and Dreams: The Musical, 1995. *Address:* Rue Limnander 37, 1070, Brussels, Belgium.

ADAM F, (Adam Fenton); b. 8 Feb. 1972, Liverpool, England. Prod; Remixer; DJ. *Career:* Started career in a funk band; Produced drum and bass for Lucky Spin Records, London; Released debut album, 1997; Worked with US rappers, producing Hip Hop, 2000; Collaborations: Redman; M.O.P.; Everything But The Girl. *Recordings:* Albums: Colours, 1997; Kaos, 2001; Singles: Circles, 1995; F-Jam, Metropolis, 1996; Music In My Mind, 1998; Smash Sumthin' (with Redman), Stand Clear (with M.O.P.), 2001. *Honours:* MOBO Award, Best Album, Colours, 1997. *Address:* c/o EMI Records, EMI House, 43 Brook Green, London W6 7EF, England.

ADAMS, Ben, (Benjamin Anthony Edward Stevens); b. 22 Nov. 1981, Middlesex, England. Vocalist; Musician (piano, violin, oboe); Songwriter. *Career:* Former head chorister, St Margaret's, Westminster Abbey; Sang solos on two albums and performed in front of Pope John Paul II and Queen Elizabeth II; Joined A1 pop group; Signed recording contract, 1999; Sell-out theatre tours of South-East Asia and UK, 2000–01. *Recordings:* Albums: Here We Come, 1999; The A List, 2000; Make It Good, 2002. Singles: Be The First To Believe, Summertime Of Our Lives, Ready Or Not/Everytime, 1999; Like A Rose, Take On Me, Same Old Brand New You, 2000; No More, 2001; Caught In The Middle, 2002. *Honours:* BRIT Award, Best Newcomer, 2001; Honoured at MTV Mandarin Music Awards. *Current Management:* c/o Byrne Blood Ltd. *Website:* www.a1-online.com.

ADAMS, Bob; b. 10 March 1922, Dalkeith, Scotland. Musician (saxophone, clarinet, bass clarinet, flute). m. Audrey Mason, 30 April 1948, 2 s. *Education:* Choir boy, Duke of Buccleuch's Private Chapel. *Career:* Geraldo Orchestra, 1947–55; Jack Parnell Orchestra, ATV 1956–63; Emigrated to South Africa, 1963–80; MD, Guys and Dolls, Fiddler On The Roof, Cabaret (Johannesburg); Conductor for many visiting artistes, including: Englebert Humperdinck, Marlene Deitrich, Frankie Laine, Johnny Mathis, Jerry Lewis, Eartha Kitt, Kenneth McKellar. *Compositions:* Scored four films for 20th Century Fox Studios, South Africa; When I See A Rainbow, chosen for World Song Festival, Tokyo, 1975. *Recordings:* Switched On Sax; Let's Party With Bob; Upon A Time; Tales For Children. *Membership:* Musicians' Union. *Address:* 50 Brick Farm Close, Richmond, Surrey TW9 4EG, England.

ADAMS, Bryan; b. 5 Nov. 1959, Kingston, ON, Canada. Vocalist; Songwriter; Musician (guitar). *Career:* International recording artiste; Numerous world-wide tours; Album sales exceed 40m. copies. *Recordings:* Albums: Bryan Adams, 1980; You Want It You Got It, 1981; Cuts Like A Knife, 1983; Reckless, 1984; Into The Fire, 1987; Waking Up The Neighbours, 1991; So Far So Good, 1993; Live! Live! Live!, 1995; 18 'Til I Die, 1996; MTV Unplugged, 1987; On A Day Like Today, 1998; Best Of Me, 2001; Singles include: Summer Of '69, 1985; Heaven, 1985; Run To You, 1985; Can't Stop

This Thing We Started, 1991; There Will Never Be Another Tonight, 1991; It's Only Love (with Tina Turner); Everything I Do, I Do It For You (theme from Robin Hood, Prince Of Thieves film), 1991; All I Want Is You, 1992; Please Forgive Me, 1993; All For Love (with Sting and Rod Stewart), 1993; Have You Ever Really Loved A Woman, 1995; I Finally Found Someone (with Barbra Streisand), 1996; Star, 1996; The Only Thing That Looks Good On Me Is You, 1996; Let's Make A Night To Remember, 1996; On A Day Like Today, 1998; When You're Gone (with Melanie C.), 1998. *Honours:* Longest standing No. 1 in UK singles chart, 16 weeks, Everything I Do, I Do It For You, 1991; 15 Canadian Juno Awards; Grammy Award; American Music Award. *Address:* c/o Press Dept, A&M Records, 136–144 New King's Rd, London SW6 4LZ, England.

ADAMS, (David) Ryan; b. 5 Nov. 1974, Jacksonville, NC, USA. Vocalist; Musician (guitar, piano); Songwriter. *Career:* Mem., Patty Duke Syndrome; Mem., alternative country band, Whiskeytown, 1994–97; With Emmylou Harris, tribute album to Gram Parsons; Solo artiste, 2000–. *Recordings:* Albums: with Whiskeytown: Faithless Street, 1996; Strangers Almanac, 1997; Rural Free Delivery (with Emmylou Harris), 1997; Pneumonia, 2001; Solo: Heartbreaker, 2000; Gold, 2001; Demolition, 2002; Answering Bell, 2002. Singles: with Whiskeytown: Angels, 1995; Bloodshot Singles, 1997; Car Songs, 1997; Solo: New York, New York, 2001; Nuclear, 2002; features on: Real: The Tom T. Hall Project, 1998; Return Of The Grievous Angel, 1999; Timeless: Hank Williams Tribute, 2001. *Honours:* NME Award, Best Solo Artist, 2003. *Current Management:* FCC Management, 209 10th Ave S, Nashville, TN 37203, USA. *Address:* c/o Lost Highway Records, 2220 Colorado Ave, Santa Monica, CA 90404, USA. *Website:* www.ryan-adams.com.

ADAMS, Faye Ann; b. 24 March 1952, Allentown, PA, USA. Certified Music Specialist in Voice; Musical Instructor (piano, band and orchestral). m. Ronald G. Adams, 19 Oct. 1974, 2 d. *Education:* BSc; MEd, Kutztown State University; Mansfield State University School of Music. *Career:* Soprano; Piano accompanist; Proprietor and instructor, Willing Hearts, Hands and Voices Music Studio; Former head music specialist, Reading City School District; Solo vocalist in Pennsylvania German dialect, German Festival (Heemt Fescht). *Publications:* Events at Allemangel: Historic Research on Berks County History, 1995. *Honours:* Zeswitz Music Award for Music Achievement, 1973, 1974. *Address:* 42 George Rd, Lenhartsville, PA 19534, USA.

ADAMS, Michael; b. 20 May 1951, Birmingham, AL, USA. Musician. m. Marsha Adams, 1 s., 2 d. *Education:* BS, Music Education, Tennessee State University; MM, Percussion, Roosevelt University, Chicago, IL. *Career:* Played with Skokie Valley Symphony, Chicago Civic Orchestra, New York City Ballet, Merit Music Program, Lyric Opera of Chicago, Von Freeman (jazz). *Compositions:* Sonata Ico for Marimba Quintet. *Recordings:* Misled, song on album Mirror Town, Ronnie Laws. *Contributions to:* Chicago Sun Times, 1989. *Membership:* Sinfonia; Percussive Arts Society. *Address:* 15505 Cottage Grove, Dolton, IL 60419, USA.

ADAMS, Oleta; b. Seattle, WA, USA. Vocalist. *Career:* Leader, own trio, 1980s; Cabaret singer, Kansas; Singer with Tears For Fears, album and tours, 1987; Solo artiste, 1990–. *Recordings:* Albums: Circle Of One, 1990; Evolution, 1993; Never Knew, 1995; Movin' On, 1995; Come Walk With Me, 1997; The Very Best Of…, 1998; All The Love, 2001; Singles: Rhythm Of Life, 1990; Get Here, 1991; Circle Of One, 1991; Don't Let The Sun Go Down On Me, 1992; I Just Had To Hear Your Voice, 1993; With Tears For Fears: Woman In Chains, Badman's Song, on album The Seeds Of Love, 1989. *Current Management:* Morey Management Group, 335 N Maple Dr., Suite 351, Beverly Hills, CA 90210, USA.

ADDISON, Ben; Musician (drums). *Career:* Former Member, Boys Wonder; Formed Corduroy, for one-off gig; Decided to continue and obtained record deal; Several UK top ten hits. *Recordings:* Singles: Something in My Eye; The Frighteners; London, England; The Joker is Wild; Overhauls; Albums: Dad Man Cat, 1992; High Havoc, 1993; Out Of Here, 1994; The New You, 1997.

ADDISON, Scott; Musician (keyboards); Vocalist. *Career:* Former Member, Boys Wonder; Member, Corduroy; Played one-off gig as Corduroy, decided to continue; Obtained record deal; Several UK top ten hits. *Recordings:* Singles: Something in My Eye; The Frighteners; London, England; The Joker is Wild; Albums: Dad Man Cat, 1992; High Havoc, 1993; Out Of Here, 1994; The New You, 1997.

ADE, King Sunny; b. 1 Sept. 1946, Oshogbo, Nigeria. Vocalist. *Career:* Played with semi-professional juju bands, Nigeria; Lead guitarist, Rhythm Dandies, 1964; Also played with Tunde Nightingale; Formed the Green Spots, 1966; Renamed the African Beats, late 60s; Formed own label, Sunny Alade Records, 1975; Established the Ariya, own juju nightclub, Lagos, Nigeria; Also owns an oil firm, a mining company and a film and video production company; Founded the King Sunny Ade Foundation for young musicians and performers, Lagos; Formed supergroup, The Way Forward, 1996; Tours include UK, USA and Japan; African Beats dissolved; Currently playing in Nigeria, with new group Golden Mercury; Appeared in films: Juju Music,

1988; Live At Montreux, 1990; Roots of Rhythm, 1997. *Recordings:* Numerous albums include: Alanu Loluwa, 1967; Sunny Ade Live Play, 1976; In London, 1977; Festac 77, 1978; The Message, 1981; Ariya Special, 1982; Conscience, 1982; Juju Music, 1982; Synchro System, 1983; Aura, 1984; Otito, 1985; Saviour, 1986; Funmilayo, 1989; Live At The Hollywood Palace, 1992; E Dide, 1995; Odu, 1998; Singles include: Challenge Cup, 1967. *Address:* c/o Atomic Communications Group, 6226 1/2 Manchester Ave, Los Angeles, CA 90045, USA.

ADEDAYO, Shola, (Olu-Shola); b. 27 April 1964, Nigeria. Vocalist. *Education:* Trained as nurse. *Career:* Many ventures with African band Leke Leke, 1990–93; Member, all-girl dance band Orage; Managing Director, recording company. *Recordings:* Album: with Leke Leke: Leke Leke; Single: with Orage: Body And Soul. *Membership:* Musicians' Union; BAC&S; Music of Black Origin. *Current Management:* Taurus Records (UK). *Address:* 12 Queen Adelaide Rd, Penge, London SE20 7DX, England. *Telephone:* (20) 8778-1471. *Fax:* (20) 8778-1471. *E-mail:* Mbsenen7@yahoo.co.uk.

ADEJUMO, Shade; b. 12 Aug. 1963, Paddington, London, England. Vocalist; Songwriter. *Career:* Backing vocalist with: Carroll Thompson; Lavine Hudson; Take That; Mica Paris; Sting; Yazz; David Grant; Television appearances: Richard Littlejohn Show; Michael Ball Show; The White Room; The South Bank Show; The BRIT Awards; Concerts include: Wembley Arena; The Grand; The Marquee; The London Palladium; Radio broadcast: BBC2. *Membership:* Musicians' Union. *Address:* 32 Red Post Hill, Herne Hill, London SE24 9JQ, England.

ADKINS, Trace (Tracy Deryl); b. 13 Jan. 1962, Sarepta, Louisiana, USA. Country Vocalist; Musician (guitar). 2 d. *Education:* Petroleum Technology, Louisiana Technical University; Music studies. *Career:* After graduation worked on an oil rig for several years before deciding to pursue musical career; Joined gospel quartet the New Commitments; Solo career, early 1990s; Signed to Capitol Nashville by label president Scott Hendricks; Made steady progress on both Billboard's country album and singles charts, including a no. 1 single (This Ain't) No Thinkin' Thing, 1997; Television appearances: AM Nashville; CNN; Fox News Channel; Prime Time Country; Talk of the Town; TNN Country News; WNAB Mornings; WGN Morning Show; Good Morning Dallas; Grand Ole Opry; Film appearance: Square Dance, 1986. *Recordings:* Albums: with New Commitments: The New Commitment Quartet, 1979; The Best Of The New Commitment Quartet, 1980; Solo: Dreamin' Out Loud, 1996; Big Time, 1997; More, 1999; Chrome, 2001. Singles: Solo: Every Light In The House Is On, 1996; (This Ain't) No Thinkin' Thing, 1997; I Left Something Turned On At Home; The Rest Of Mine, 1997; Lonely Won't Leave Me Alone, 1998; Contributions to film soundtrack, Baydu Sunrise, Square Dance, 1986. *Honours:* People's Choice Ark-La-Tex, Male Gospel Vocalist of the Year, 1980; Wild Turkey Battle of the Bands, 1985; Terry Award Dance Band of the Year, 1987; Academy of Country Music, New Male Vocalist, 1997. *Address:* c/o The Country Music Asscn, 1 Music Circle S., Nashville, TN 37203, USA. *Website:* www.traceadkins.com.

ADLER, Richard; b. 3 Aug. 1921, New York, NY, USA. Composer; Lyricist; Prod. *Career:* Collaborator with Jerry Ross, music and lyrics for musicals: Pajama Game, 1954; Damn Yankees, 1955; Composer, lyricist, Kwamina, 1961; Television productions: Little Women, 1959; Gift of The Magi, 1959; Produced White House shows, salutes and galas for President Kennedy and President Johnson, 1962–65; Composer, lyricist, producer: A Mother's Kisses, 1968; Revival of Pajama Game, 1973; Rex, 1976; Commissions include: Wilderness Suite, for Dept of Interior; The Lady Remembers, Retrospectrum, for Statue of Liberty/Ellis Island; Eight By Adler, for Chicago City Ballet; Chicago (ballet), for City of Chicago; Fanfare and Overture, US Olympic Festival, for Olympic Committee, 1987; Producer of several Broadway shows. *Honours:* Variety Critics Poll Winner, The Pajama Game, 1954; Inducted into Songwriters Hall of Fame, 1984. *Membership:* Dramatists Guild; Songwriters Guild of America; Trustee, John F Kennedy Center For The Performing Arts, 1964–77.

ADOLFSSON, Jorgen; b. 14 March 1951, Hallingeberg, Sweden. Musician; Composer. m. Vered Adolfsson Mann, 13 April 1994, 1 s., 1 d. *Education:* Art and Film History, Stockholm University; Classical Violin, 1961–69. *Career:* Member, Archimedes Badkar, Ramlosa Kvallar, Iskra, Vargavinter, Bitter Funeral Beer Band, Karl Brothers, Uroboro; Performer of Music for Modern Choreographers including Kenneth Kvarnstrom, Cristina Caprioli, Bogdan Szyber, Carina Reich, Greta Lindholm, Efva Lilja; Television and Radio Productions; Performed with Don Cherry, Mongezi Feza, Johnny Dyani, Jon Rose, Lars Gullin, Raymond Strid, Tommy Adolfsson. *Compositions:* Grodsymfonin, 1976; Ancient Evenings, Future Mornings, 1984; Exhibo Suite, 1990; Syrinx Svit, 1991; Music in Sand, 1991; Fem Danser, 1995; Digger Dog, 1995. *Recordings:* With Iskra, Allemansratt, Besvarjelser, Fantasies; Luft; With Bitter Funeral Beer Band, Bitter Funeral Beer; With Karl Brothers, Air Change; With Vargavinter, S/T, Roster Fran Alla Land; With Archimedes Badkar, II, Tre, Afro 70; with Per Tjernberg: Universal Riddim. *Honours:* Grand Prix, International Video Danse/Carina Ari, 1992. *Membership:* STIM; FSJ; SKAP; Fylkingen. *Current Management:* Musikcentrum,

Chapmansgatan 4, 11236 Stockholm, Sweden. *Address:* Selmedalsringen 8 4 tr, 129 36 Hagersten, Sweden.

ADOLFSSON, Tommy C; b. 21 Oct. 1953, Ljusdal, Halsingland, Sweden. m. Cecilia Johansson, 1 d. *Education:* Trumpet Studies, Music School, 1963–70; Economy College, 1969–72; Trumpet Studies, Stockholm Music Conservatory, 1970–74; Development Studies, Sussex University, England, Sweden, Tanzania, Malawi, Zambia, Madagascar, 1976–78; Music Studies, England, 1976; Music Studies, Senegal, Tanzania, 1976; Music Studies, Theory and Ensemble play, Birkagarden Music College, 1980–82; Music Studies, Bali and Java, 1983; Music Studies, India, 1984; Japanese Taiko Drum music studies, 1990; Marketing courses for artists, 1991, 1995. *Career:* Archimedes Bathtube, world music group, 1974–82; ISKRA, free improvised music, 1980–85; Bitter Funeral Beer Band, afro-jazz, 1980–86; Half Nelson, brassband, 1985–88; DAST, Quartet, South African music and poetry, 1985–90; Kenneth Kvarnstrom Danscompany, modern ballet, 1989–91; Swedish Radio jazz group, 1990–94; Peter Bryngelsson Project, 1992; Cristina Caprioli Danscompany, 1992–93; Tuomo Hapaalas Waterorchestra, Stockholm Waterfestival, 1994; Jazz group Krakatau, Finland, 1995–96. *Compositions:* Wet Fantasy, ISKRA; Three Voices on a White Line; Echoes Beyond Joy and Despair; Baptismal Song; IA; Syrinx Suite, CD, Karl Brothers; Ballet Music: 1989–91: XXX; Exhibo; Trio, Duo, Solo; 1992: Ubergang; Damp; Luege, 1993; Theatre Music: 1996: The Jurt, A Stormy History; The Dolphin. *Recordings:* Archimedes Bathtube, Three, 1975–78; Bitter Funeral Beer Band, 1981; ISKRA, Fantasies, 1984; Bitter Funereal Beer Band 2, Praise Drumming, 1986; Karl Brothers, Air Change, 1994. *Honours:* Academy of Art Awards, 1985, 1991, 1993, 1994, 1997; STIM Award, 1995. *Membership:* STIM; SAMI; SKAP. *Address:* Torkel Knutssonsgatan 39, 2 tr, 118 49 Stockholm, Sweden.

ADSHEAD, Christopher John; b. 3 April 1966. Musician (Bass guitar). 1 d. *Career:* Joined RAF Central Band, 1984; QEII World Cruise, 1990; Summer season in Devon, 1991; Moved to London, worked at Talk of London nightclub, played in shows including Cats at the New London Theatre and the Cats British tour, 1993–95; Played in Joseph and the Amazing Technicolour Dreamcoat with Phillip Schofield at Hammersmith Apollo, 1995–96; Played on Grease British tour with Shane Ritchie, 1996–97; Played in Boogie Nights with Shane Ritchie, 1997–99; Television credits include Pebble Mill at One, Richard and Judy Tonight, The Six O'clock Show, Talking Telephone Numbers, Going Live/Live and Kicking, Night Fever; Radio credits include Paul Jones Blues Night, Friday Night is Music Night; Concerts include The Monaghan Blues Festival with Out of the Blue. *Recordings:* Marilla Ness: From Where I Stand; Shane Ritchie: The Album; Boogie Nights: Cast Album. *Address:* 72 Clarkes Dr., Uxbridge, Middlesex UB8 3UL, England.

AERTS, Raymond Benedict Charles; b. 12 April 1966, Amsterdam, Netherlands. Theatre and Concert Prod; Artiste Agent and Man. m. Sarah Frances Kate Reÿs-Smith, 1 Aug. 1992. *Education:* Marketing Communications; School of Music, piano. *Career:* with Charles Aerts Theatre Productions International, concert and theatre productions for: Liza Minelli; Ray Charles; Shirley Bassey; Bold and Beautiful In Concert; Lionel Hampton; Don McLean; Oklahoma!; Elvis; Annie Get Your Gun; Maria de Lourdes; Artists represented include: Charles Aznavour; Gilbert Bécaud; Nana Mouskouri; Julien Clerc; Lionel Hampton; Maria Callas; Don McLean; Shirley Bassey. *Honours:* with Charles Aerts Theatre Productions International: Ridder, Orde van Oranje Nassau, Netherlands; Chevalier, Ordre des Arts et des Lettres, France; Vecta Mem. of Honour; Cultural awards and honours from: Brazil; Hungary; Bulgaria; Indonesia. *Membership:* Vecta.

AFANASIEFF, Walter; Prod; Musician (keyboards); Songwriter; Partner, 1 c. *Career:* Played keyboards with violinist Jean-Luc Ponty; Formed band, The Warriors, with Joaquin Lievano; Became prod. for Sony Music; Worked with: All-4-One, Allure, Marc Anthony, Babyface, Regina Belle, George Benson, Michael Bolton, Boyz II Men, Mariah Carey, Coco, Céline Dion, Kenny G., Whitney Houston, Michael Jackson, Trey Lorenz, Ricky Martin, *NSYNC, Aaron Neville, New Kids on the Block, Lionel Ritchie, Savage Garden, Barbra Streisand, Luther Vandross, Narada Michael Walden. *Honours:* Grammy Award, Producer of the Year. *Address:* c/o Sony Music Entertainment Inc, 550 Madison Ave, New York, NY 10022-3211, USA.

AGERSKOV, Flemming Michael; b. 29 Sept. 1963, Holstebro, Denmark. 2 d. *Education:* Studied Classical Trumpet, Conservatory in Århus, 1983–85; Japanese Music, Kyoto, Japan, 1985–86. *Career:* Played with Marc Johnson, Eliane Elias, Marilyn Mazur, Jonas Johansen, Jon Balke, Martin France, Joakim Milder, Fredrik Lundin; Ray Charles; Iain Ballamy; Josefine Cronholm; Kresten Osgood; Egberto Gismonti; Formed own group, Face to Face, with Martin France, Julian Argüelles; Jesper Nordenstroem and Hans Andersson, 1997. *Compositions:* Arctic Views; With Closed Eyes. *Recordings:* CV Joergensen: Sjaelland; Fraklip fra det fjrrne; Kim Kristensen: A Jazzpar 93 Project on Storyville; Flemming Agershov: Face to Face, 1999; Josefine Cronholm/Ibis: Wild Garden; Peter Danemo: Alive. *Publications:* The Two Rooms, 2000. *Honours:* Trumpet Player of the Year, 1991; Danish Music Award, Push To Participate, Takuan, 2001. *Address:* Holbergsgade 18, 1 TV, 1057 Copenhagen K, Denmark. *E-mail:* agerskov@email.dk. *Website:* www.face2face.dk.

AGHILI, Shadmehr; b. 1972, Iran. Vocalist; Musician; Actor. *Career:* Singer and writer of popular songs; Film appearance: Par e Parvaz (also composed soundtrack). *Recordings include:* Mosafer; Dehati; Bahar e Man. *Address:* c/o Radio Network 1 (Voice of the Islamic Republic of Iran), Tehran, Iran.

AGUILAR, Pepe; b. San Antonio, Texas. Vocalist. *Career:* Son of Antonio Aguilar and Flor Silvestre; Began singing, aged 3; Collaborations include: Rocio Durcal; Vikki Carr; Has produced for Jose Julian; Guadalupe Pineda; Antonio Aguilar. *Recordings:* Recuerdame Bonito, 1992; Chiquilla Bonita, 1995; Con Tambora, 1995; Que Bueno Mariachi, 1995; Exitos Con Banda, 1997; Por Mujeres Como Tu, 1998; Por El Amor De Siempre, Por Una Mujer Bonita, 1999; Grande De Los Grande, 2000; Mejor De Nosotros, Tambora 2: Cautiva Y Triste, 2001. *Website:* www.pepeaguilar.com.

AGUILERA, Christina Maria; b. 18 Dec. 1980, Staten Island, NY, USA. Vocalist. *Career:* Appeared on US Star Search TV talent show aged 8; Joined cast of Orlando-based TV show The New Mickey Mouse Club aged 12; Intensive world-wide promotional touring since 1997; Signed recording contract in 1998 following inclusion on Disney's Mulan OST; Numerous TV appearances including Christmas At The White House spectacular, 1999 and Super Bowl 2000 half-time show. *Recordings:* Albums: Christina Aguilera, 1999; Mi Reflejo, 2000; My Kind Of Christmas, 2000; Stripped, 2002. Singles: All I Wanna Do (with Keizo Nakanishi), 1997; Reflection (from Mulan), 1998; Genie In A Bottle, 1999; What A Girl Wants, 1999; Come On Over Baby (All I Want Is You), 2000; I Turn To You, 2000; Lady Marmalade (with Lil' Kim, Mya and Pink), 2001. *Honours:* Grammy, Best New Artist, 2000; ALMA Award, Best New Entertainer, 2000; Billboard Award, Female Vocalist of the Year, 2000; Billboard Latin Music Award, Best Pop Album of the Year, Mi Reflejo, 2001. *Address:* c/o Irving Azoff, 3500 W Olive Ave, Suite 600, Burbank, CA 91505, USA.

AHLIN, Tina; b. 6 July 1967, Stockholm, Sweden. Musician (piano); Vocalist; Arranger; Composer. *Career:* Several big pop acts and pop tours around Scandinavia; Lisa Wilsson, Orup, Tomas Dileva; Musician, lots of records; worked with several television productions and television orchestra; Written arrangements to Swedish Radio Symphony Orchestra, Choirs, Big Bands; Work with lots of Jazz and Pop Concerts. *Address:* Ehrensvardsg 2, 3 tr, 112 35 Stockholm, Sweden.

AHROLD, Robert Liam (Robbin); b. 29 Sept. 1943, Washington, USA. Copyright Exec. m. Kyle Warren, 20 March 1972, 2 d. *Education:* BSc, Foreign Service School, Georgetown University. *Career:* Reporter, Time Magazine, 1967–71; Various positions, Home Box Office, including Director, Special Programming; Director, Corporate Public Relations, 1974–82; Producer, Executive producer, Celebration, first pay television Rock Series, 1975; Vice-President, Corporate Relations, RCA Records, 1982–87; Various pay television music specials for HBO including: Country In New York, 1976; Vice-President, Corporate Relations, Broadcast Music Inc, 1987–. *Publications:* Editor, publisher, Musicworld (quarterly membership magazine for BMI). *Honours:* Vice-President, Board of Governors, New York Chapter, NARAS; NATAS; Country Music Asscn; Gospel Music Asscn; National Academy Popular Music. *Address:* c/o Broadcast Music Inc, 320 W 57th St, New York, NY 10019, USA.

AHVENLAHTI, Olli; b. 6 Aug. 1949, Finland. Composer; Musician (piano, keyboards). *Education:* Piano from age 7; Sibelius Academy from age 11; Berklee College of Music, Boston, USA; Musicology, English Philology, Helsinki University, 1968–73. *Career:* First jazz concert, Hasse Walli-Make Lievonen Sextet, 1969; Collaborated with Mike Koskinen, Pekka Pöyry, Esko Rsnell; Founding member, The Group, 1970s; Represented Finland, Nordring radio contest; Formed quintet with trumpeter Markku Johansson, 1970s; Chief conductor, TV1, Finnish Broadcasting Company, 1990–; Pianist, backing singer Vesa-Matti Loiri. *Compositions:* Composer, arranger for UMO (New Music Orchestra); Music for theatre, film, television dramas; Piece based on texts from Herman Hesse's Glass Bead Game. *Honours:* Yrjö Award, Finnish Jazz Federation, 1975.

AINLAY, Chuck; Engineer; Prod. *Career:* Partner, BackStage Studio, Nashville; Worked with: The Blue, Mark Knopfler, Roy Orbison. *Address:* c/o BackStage Studio, Sound Stage Studios, 10 Music Circle S, Nashville, TN 32703, USA. *Website:* www.soundstagestudios.com.

AIREY, Don; b. 21 June 1948, Sunderland, England. Musician (Keyboards); Arranger; Conductor. m. Doris, 25 March 1977, 2 s., 1 d. *Education:* Nottingham University; Royal Manchester College of Music. *Career:* Member of Groups: Colosseum II, 1975–78; Rainbow, 1978–81; Ozzy Osbourne, 1982–85; Jethro Tull, 1986–87; Whitesnake, 1988–90; Gary Moore Blues Band, 1990–91; Session Player, Arranger, 1992–95, ELO, 1996–97; Conducted winning entry, Eurovision Song Contest. *Compositions:* Numerous co-writes on various heavy metal albums. *Recordings:* Down to Earth, Rainbow; Blizzard Of Oz, Ozzy Osbourne; Whitesnake 87, Whitesnake; Still Got The Blues, Gary Moore; Variations, Andrew Lloyd Webber; 20 Years Of Jethro Tull, Jethro Tull, 1988; Back To The Light, Brian May, 1993; Solo album, K2, Tales Of Triumph And Tragedy, Don Airey. *Honours:* Eurovision 97.

Membership: BAC&S; PRS. *Current Management:* Sound Evision Enterprises Ltd. *Address:* 4 Hardwick Rd Ind Pk, Gt Gransden, Sandy, Bedfordshire SG19 3BJ, England.

AITKEN, Matt; b. 25 Aug. 1956. Songwriter; Prod. *Career:* Member, pop band Agents Aren't Aeroplanes, with Mike Stock and Pete Waterman, 1980s; Member, songwriting/production team Stock Aitken Waterman (SAW), 1984–93; Co-founder, PWL label, 1988; Co-producer with Mike Stock, Love This Records, 1994–. *Recordings:* Albums: Hit Factory, 1987; Hit Factory, Vol. 2, 1988; Hit Factory, Vol. 3, 1989; The Best Of Stock Aitken And Waterman, 1990; Single: Roadblock, 1987; As co-writer, producer, hit singles include: You Spin Me Round, Dead Or Alive (No. 1, UK), 1984; So Macho, Sinitta, 1986; Respectable, Mel and Kim (No. 1, UK), 1987; Never Gonna Give You Up, Rick Astley, 1987; Got To Be Certain, 1988; The Locomotion, 1988; Hand On Your Heart (No. 1, UK), 1989; Better The Devil You Know, 1990; with Robson Green and Jerome Flynn: Unchained Melody (No. 1, UK), 1995; I Believe/Up On The Roof (No. 1, UK), 1995; What Becomes Of The Broken Hearted (No. 1, UK), 1996; Other recordings with: Jason Donovan; Sonia; Brother Beyond; Big Fun; Donna Summer; Divine; Hazell Dean. *Honours:* BRIT Award, Best Producer, Stock Aitken Waterman, 1988. *Address:* c/o Love This Records, Hundred House, 100 Union St, London SE1 0NL, England.

AJAO, Steven John; b. 1 Oct. 1952, Birmingham, England. Musician (blues guitar, saxophone). 1 s. *Education:* Moseley School of Art, Lanchester Polytechnic (Art). *Career:* Mainly blues guitarist to 1981; Started to play alto and tenor saxophone; Numerous jazz club appearances; Played with: Red Rodney, Brighton, 1987; Bude Jazz Festival, 1988; Le Puy Peace Festival, 1989; Recorded sessions for Ali Campbell (UB40); Slade; Mickey Greaney. *Current Management:* Bob Lamb. *Address:* 122a Highbury Rd, Kings Heath, Birmingham B14 7QP, England.

AKABU. See: LEE, Dave.

AKENDENGUE, Pierre Claver; b. 25 April 1943, Aouta, Gabon. Psychologist; Musician. m. Michelle Ossouach, 31 Aug. 1997, 6 s., 3 d. *Education:* Physiotherapy, 1968–69; PhD, Psychology, Sorbonne, 1987; Musicology; Ethnomusicology. *Career:* Many compositions and recordings; Concerts world-wide including Africa, Europe, Canada, West Indies, Japan. *Compositions:* Nandipo Nkere, Powe; Owende; Africa Obota; Awana; Silence; Maladalite; Piroguier Lambarena. *Recordings:* Nandipo, 1974; Africa Obota, 1976; Awana, 1982; Silence, 1990; Lambarena, 1995; Maladilite, 1995; Espoir A Soweto, 1997; Passe Compose, 1997. *Honours:* Prize, Young Singers, SACEM, 1976; Best Film Music Award, FESCAPO, 1985; RFI Trophy, 1989. *Membership:* Founder, Gabonese Asscn of Artists and Performers. *Current Management:* Melodie, 50 rue Stendhal, 75020 Paris, France. *Address:* PO Box 13, 305 Libreville, Gabon.

AKIYOSHI, Toshiko; b. 12 Dec. 1929, Dairen, Manchuria, People's Republic of China. Musician (piano); Composer. m. (1) Charlie Mariano; (2) Lew Tabackin. *Education:* Classically-trained piano; Berklee College of Music, Boston, USA. *Career:* Successful jazz pianist, Japan; Recorded for Norman Granz; Moved to USA; Member, various groups including Charlie Mariano; Charles Mingus; Became composer, especially for big bands; Worked with saxophonist (later her husband) Lew Tabackin, Los Angeles, early 1970s; Leader own small group; Subject, documentary film Toshiko Akiyoshi, Jazz Is My Native Language, 1984. *Recordings:* Toshiko's Piano, 1953; Amazing Toshiko Akiyoshi, 1954; The Toshiko Trio, 1954; Jam Session For Musicians III: The Historic Mocambo Session '54, 1954; Toshiko Her Trio, 1956; Toshiko Her Quartet, 1956; The Many Sides Of Toshiko, 1957; United Nations, 1958; Toshiko Meets Her Old Pals, 1961; Country And Western Jazz Pianos (with Steve Kühn), 1963; Mariano-Toshiko Quartet, 1963; Toshiko Akiyoshi, 1965; Toshiko At The Top Of The Gate, 1968; Toshiko Akiyoshi Quartet Vols I–III, 1970–71; Solo Piano, 1971; Dedications, 1976–77; Plays Billy Strayhorn, 1978; Finesse, 1978; Interlude, 1987; Remembering Bud, Cleopatra's Dream, 1990; Carnegie Hall Concert Live, 1991; Albums with Lew Tabackin: Kogun, 1974; Long Yellow Road, 1974–75; Tales Of A Courtesan, 1975; Road Time, 1976; Insights, 1976; March Of The Tadpoles, 1977; Dedications II, 1977; Live At Newport '77, 1977; Sumi-e, 1979; Farewell To Mingus, 1980; From Toshiko With Love, 1981; Tanuki's Night Out, 1981; European Memoirs, 1982; Carnegie Hall Concert Live, 1991; Live At Maybeck Recital Hall, 1995.

AKKERMAN, Jan; b. 24 Dec. 1946, Amsterdam, Netherlands. Musician (guitar, lute); Composer; Arranger. *Education:* Gradutate, Music Lyceum, Amsterdam. *Career:* Member, groups including: Johnny and The Cellar Rockers, 1958; The Hunters; Brainbox, 1969; Focus, 1969–76; Solo artiste, 1973–; Periodic reunions with Focus; Member, side project Forcefield, with Ray Fenwick and Cozy Powell, 1988–89. *Recordings:* Albums: with Focus: In And Out Of Focus, 1971; Moving Waves, 1971; Focus III, 1972; At The Rainbow, 1973; Hamburger Concerto, 1974; Mother Focus, 1975; Focus Con Proby, 1977; House Of The King, 1983; Pass Me Not, 1995; Solo albums: Profile, 1973; Tabernakel, 1974; Eli, 1977; Jan Akkerman, 1978; Arunjuez, 1978; Live, 1979; 3, 1980; It Could Happen To You, 1985; Can't Stand Noise, 1986; Pleasure Point, 1987; The Noise Of Art, 1990; Heartware, 1998; with

Forcefield: The Talisman, 1988; To Oz And Back, 1989; Singles: with Focus: House Of The King, 1971; Hocus Pocus, 1971; Sylvia, 1972. *Honours:* Melody Maker Poll Winner, Best Guitarist, 1973. *Address:* c/o Bert Bijlsma, P/A Hamrikkerweg 4, 9943 TB, NW Scheemda, Netherlands.

AKYUZ, Osman Refik; b. 16 June 1974, Istanbul, Turkey. Recording Engineer; Prod; Musician (vocals, bass guitar, keyboards). *Education:* Capital University; The Recording Workshop, USA; Ulster County College; Timur Selcuk Music School. *Career:* Video Clips, Happy, Let Me Be, Major Radio Stations in Turkey; Süüpeermeen; Numerous TV and radio jingles. *Compositions:* Happy; Aydede; Let Me Be; Sunday Morning; The Land of Sand; Ascend; A Sail To Sky. *Recordings:* Atonall; Iksir. *Address:* Zergerdan SOK, No. 22 80850 Emirgan, Istanbul, Turkey. *Telephone:* (212) 277-6369. *E-mail:* ora@oramusic.net. *Website:* www.atonall.com.

ALAKOTILA, Timo Pekka; b. 15 July 1959, Finland. Musician (piano, harmonium); Composer; Arranger; Prod. *Education:* Conservatory of Helsimes. *Career:* Mem., JPP, 1982–; Teacher of composition and music theory, Helsinki Pop and Jazz Conservatory; Teacher, Folk Music Dept, Sibelius Academy; Mem., Maria Kalaniemi's Aldargaz ensemble, 1994–; Mem., Troka; Mem., Luna Nova; Numerous tours world-wide; Worked with: Värttinä, Hannu Ilmolahti, Järvelän Näppärit, Feeniks, Tallari, Hannu Seppänen, Burlakat, Loituma, Kaira, Halo. *Compositions:* Folkmoods West; Having Myself A Time, 1998. *Recordings:* Albums: with JPP: Laitisen Mankeliska; JPP; I've Found A New Tango; Pirun Polska; Kaustinen Rhapsody; String Tease; History; with Aldargaz: IHO; AHMA; Harmonia Mundi; with Troka: Troka; Smash. *Honours:* with JPP: Folk Music Group Championship, 1982; Band of the Year, Kastinen Festival, 1986; Finnish Radio Tunnustus Prize, 1988; Album of the Year, Helsingin Sanomat, 1988; with Aldargaz: Prize of Finland, Award for Artistic Achievement, 1996. *Current Management:* Hoedown, Laivurinrinne 2, 00120 Helsinki, Finland. *Website:* www.hoedown.com.

ALAN, Mark; b. 14 Sept. 1939, Elizabeth, New Jersey, USA. Personal Man; Agent. 1 s, 1 d. *Education:* BSc, Masters, Speech and Theatre. *Career:* Premier Talent Agency, New York City, 1965–68; President, New Beat Management, New York City, 1968–71; Artists included: Tommy James and the Shondells; The Illusion; Robin McNamara; The Sidekicks; Exile; Worked with Jeff Barry and Tommy James; Manager, Andre Cymone; Airkraft; Zwarte; President and owner, National Talent Associates, Minneapolis; President, Mark Alan Agency, 1988–; Manager for Illerazzum, Every Mother's Nightmare and Peter Phippen. *Recordings:* As manager include: The Dance Electric, Andre Cymone; Did You See Her Eyes, The Illusion; Lay A Little Lovin' On Me, Robin McNamara; with Tommy James: Draggin The Line; Come to Me; Ball And Chain; She; Ball Of Fire; Sweet Cherry Wine; Crimson And Clover; Crystal Blue Persuasion; with Zwarte: Zwarte; Hit The Road; Easy Street; with Peter Phippen: Book Of Dreams; Albums: with The Illusion: The Illusion; Together (As A Way Of Life); with How Does It Feel; Tommy James: Crimson And Clover; Best Of Tommy James And The Shondells; Travelin'; Tommy James; LP, Tommy James; with Robin McNamara: Lay A Little Lovin' On Me; with Andre Cymone: AC. *Current Management:* Mark Alan Agency, PO Box 21323, St Paul, MN 55121, USA.

ALBARN, Damon; b. 23 March 1968, Whitechapel, London, England. Vocalist; Songwriter. *Education:* Drama School, Stratford East, one year; Part-time music course, Goldsmith's College. *Career:* First solo concerts, Colchester Arts Centre; Mem., Blur, 1989–; Mem., Gorillaz, 2000–; Numerous television and radio appearances, include: Later With Jools Holland; Top of the Pops; Loose Ends, Radio 4; Later With... Britpop Now; Extensive tours, concerts include: Alexandra Palace, Reading Festival, 1993; Glastonbury, 1994; Mile End, 1995; V97, 1997; UK Arena Tour, 1997; Glastonbury, 1998; T in the Park, 1999; Reading and Leeds Festival, 1999; Actor, film, Face, 1997. *Recordings:* Albums: with Blur: Leisure, 1991; Modern Life Is Rubbish, 1993; Parklife, 1994; The Great Escape, 1995; Blur, 1997; 13, 1999; The Best Of Blur, 2000; with Gorillaz: Gorillaz, 2001; G-Sides, 2002; Phase One: Celebrity Take Down, 2002; Solo: Mali Music (various contributors), 2002. Singles: with Blur: She's So High, 1990; There's No Other Way, 1991; Bang, 1991; Popscene, 1992; For Tomorrow, 1993; Chemical World, 1993; Sunday Sunday, 1993; Girls And Boys, 1994; To The End, 1994; Parklife, 1994; End Of A Century, 1994; Country House, 1995; The Universal, 1995; Stereotypes, 1996; Charmless Man, 1996; Beetlebum, 1997; Song 2, 1997; On Your Own, 1997; MOR, 1997; Tender, 1999; Coffee And TV, 1999; No Distance Left To Run, 1999; Music Is My Radar, 2000; with Gorillaz: Clint Eastwood, 2001; 19–2000, 2001; Rock The House, 2001; Solo: Original film scores: Ravenous (with Michael Nyman), 1998; Ordinary Decent Criminal, 1999; 101 Reykjavík (with Einar Örn Benediktsson), 2000. *Honours:* Platinum discs, incl. for Parklife; BRIT Awards, Best Single, Video, Album and Band, 1995; Q Awards, Best Album, 1994, 1995. *Current Management:* CMO Management, Unit 32, Ransomes Dock, 35–37 Parkgate Rd, London SW11 4NP, England. *Website:* www.blur.co.uk; www.gorillaz.com.

ALBERTO, José, (José Alberto Justiniano); b. 22 Dec. 1958, Santo Domingo, Dominican Republic. Vocalist; Bandleader. *Education:* Studied music at Antilles Military Academy, Puerto Rico. *Career:* Club circuit singer, New York; Recording artiste, 1976–; Known as 'El Canario' (The Canary); Member, Tipica 73, 1978–81; Bandleader, 1984–; Appearances include: Debut UK performance, with Celia Cruz, 1978; New Orleans Jazz and Heritage Festival, with Celia Cruz, 1990; New York Salsa Festival, Madison Square Garden, 1990. *Recordings:* Albums: with Tito Rodríguez II: Curious?, 1976; with Tipica 73: Salsa Encendida, 1978; Tipica 73 En Cuba, Intercambio Cultural, 1979; Charangueando Con La Tipica 73, 1980; Into The 80s, 1981; Solo: Tipicamente, 1984; Canto Canario, 1985; Latino Style, 1986; Sueño Contigo, 1988; Mis Amores, 1989; Dance With Me, 1991. *Current Management:* Ralph Mercado Management, 568 Broadway, Suite 806, New York, NY 10012, USA.

ALBERTS, Al, (Al Albertini); b. 19 Aug. 1922, Philadelphia, USA. Musician; Television Presenter. m. Stella Zippi, 6 June 1953, 2 s. *Education:* BS, Temple University, 1951. *Career:* Lead singer, The Four Aces, 1946–58, 1975–85; President, Alstel Television Productions Inc, Chester, Pennsylvania, 1958–; Executive producer, television host, Al Alberts Showcase Station, Philadelphia, 1968–; President, Al Alberts Onstage Ltd, Chester, 1988–. *Recordings include:* It's No Sin; Tell Me Why; Stranger In Paradise; Three Coins In The Fountain; Love Is A Many Splendoured Thing; Mr Sandman; Dream; Heart And Soul; A Woman In Love; Heart Of My Heart; Garden In The Rain; It's A Woman's World; Lazy, Hazy, Crazy Days Of Summer. *Honours:* Inducted into Music Hall of Fame, 1988. *Address:* Al Alberts Onstage Ltd, 15 E Eighth St, Chester, PA 19013, USA.

ALBINI, Steve; b. USA. Vocalist; Musician (guitar); Record Prod. *Career:* Founder, Big Black, 1982–88; Founder, Rapeman, 1988; Record producer, for artists including The Pixies; The Wedding Present; Tad; The Breeders; Formed Shellac with Bob Weston and Todd Trainer, 1993; Toured with Shellac 1993–95. *Recordings include:* Albums: with Big Black: Racer X, 1985; Atomizer, 1986; The Hammer Party, 1986; Sound Of Impact, 1987; Big Black, Live, 1989; Rich Man's Track, 1989; Pigpile, 1992; with Rapeman: Two Nuns And A Pack Mule, 1988; with Shellac: At Action Park, 1994; Terraform, 1998; 1000 Hurts, 2000; As producer include: Surfer Rosa, The Pixies; Pod, The Breeders; Salt Lick, Tad; Seamonsters, The Wedding Present; Bush; Storm And Stress; Melt Banana; PW Long.

ALBURO, Francisco; b. 19 July 1953, Legaspi City, Philippines. Vocalist; Musician (keyboards). m. Minerva de Leon, 7 May 1977, 2 s., 2 d. *Education:* Course, Melody School of Music, Stamford House, London. *Career:* Formed group, The Spider's Webb (first Phillipino band), 1973; Member, PI Sea Dust, 1976–82; Partime singer, Memoza Club, 1983; Bass guitar, Pula't Asul Band, 1990; Solo singer, 1991–95.

ALDRIDGE, Chris, (B. B./Beebé Aldridge); b. 14 March 1976, Walsall, England. Musician (saxophone, flute); Composer; Teacher. *Education:* University of Wolverhampton, Music, BA (Hons); Apprentice Lead Alto Saxophonist: Walsall Jazz Orchestra; Midland Youth Jazz Orchestra. *Career:* Performed at London Marathon, 1997; London Jazz Festival, Reading Rock Festival, 1998; Montreux Jazz Festival, 1989; sell-out appearances at Ronnie Scott's and Rock City; Played on Intimate with a Stranger film soundtrack; Collaborations include: Bud Shank; John Dankworth; Kenny Baker; Victor Mendoza; Bobby Shew; Roy Wood; Hot Chocolate; The Christians; Various musical instrument manfacturer endorsements. *Compositions:* Original music for The Biome Dome (prize-winning entry at BBC Gardeners World Live, 2000). *Recordings include:* Waddaman by Mother; Home Turf by Gold Blade; 1000 Nudes by Divine Sounds; Stereoman by Bizarre Inc; Solo: Chris Aldridge, 1997; featured soloist on Montreux Jazz Festival compilation, 1999; Holy Island (as Beebé), 2001. *Honours:* Lead Alto Saxophonist of BBC Big Band Competition Winners, Walsall Jazz Orchestra, 1995. *Membership:* Musicians' Union. *Address:* 19 Bransdale Rd, Swingbridge Park, Clayhanger, Brownhills, West Midlands, WS8 7SD, England. *Website:* www.big-it-up.com; www.beebeplanet.com.

ALDRIDGE, Roger Merle; b. 18 Sept. 1946, Kansas City, Missouri, USA. Jazz Composer; Sr Risk Man. m. Nancy Sherwood, 9 Jan. 1999, 1 s., 2 d. *Education:* Jazz Studies, Berklee College of Music, Boston, 1964–68; Advanced Composition Studies, Washington University, 1969; BA, Music Composition, McKendree College, 1972; MA, Music Composition, Highlands University, 1974; CSP, Institute for the Certification of Computer Professionals, 1985. *Career:* Performed with Smokey Robinson, Diahann Carroll, 1970–72; Composed multimedia theatre music and jazz works, 1972–77; Instructor of Music, Fontbonne Colege, 1974–77; Adjunct Professor, Montgomery College, 1988–99; Composed many works including contemporary jazz pieces, rags, blues and traditional style fiddle tunes, 1989–. *Compositions include:* Farewell to the Goslings; Atlantic Flyway; Winter's Woods; October Morn; Treasure the Chesapeake; Appalachian Twilight; Autumn Walk; Anne's Lullaby; Spring Beauties; Young Henry's Wild Ride; Buzzards in Love; Appalachian Awakening; Desperate Measures; Salt Marsh Rag; Spirit Journeys Suite; Blues for Lester, Connecticut Avenue SUVs. *Recordings include:* Earth's Essence; A Celtic Portrait; Michigan's Heritage; Buzzards in Love, Appalachian Awakening; Spirit Journeys. *Honours:* Research Grant, Institute of Scientific Studies, 1973; Montie Award, Best Music in a Video, 1992; Award and Grant, Fannie Mae Foundation,

1994; Award, Chesapeake Bay Foundation, 1995. *Membership:* BMI; American Music Center; Chesapeake Bay Foundation. *Address:* 4205 Gelding Lane, Olney, MD 20832, USA.

ALEMAÑY, Jesús, (Jesús Alemañy Castrillo); b. 14 Oct. 1962, Guanabacoa, Cuba. Musician (Trumpet); Composer. *Education:* Conservatoire Guillermo Tomas, Guanabacoa. *Career:* began studying trumpet at the Conservatoire, aged 13; Invited to join Sierra Maestra, Cuba's leading contemporary ensemble specializing in the roots style of salsa known as son, featuring the trumpet as solo instrument, aged 16; Played with Sierra Maestra for over a decade, recording 11 albums; Relocated to London, 1992; Organized (with Paris-based Cuban pianist Akfredo Rodriguez) a Descarga jam session in Paris to honour percussionist Patato Váldez, 1994; Impressed Hannibal Records boss Joe Boyd; Both musicians invited to record in Cuba with some of the top Cuban musicians; Project became the band ¡Cubanismo!; Remains as band leader after Rodriguez's departure; Subsequent releases were a straight Latin album, Reencarnación, and a collaboration with New Orleans musicians, Mardi Gras Mambo. *Recordings:* Albums include: with ¡Cubanismo!: Jesús Alemañy's ¡Cubanismo!, 1996; Malembe, 1997; Reencarnación, 1998; Mardi Gras Mambo, 2000; with Sierra Maestra: Son Highlights From Cuba, 1993; ¡Dundunbanza!, 1994; features on: Wild Mood Swings, The Cure, 1996; Cuba Linda, Alfredo Rodriguez, 1997; Curtains, Tindersticks, 1997. *Website:* www.jesusalemany.com.

ALESSANDRO; b. 26 Nov. 1959, Venice, Italy. Vocalist; Musician (guitar); Entertainer. *Education:* Cosmologist; Linguist. *Career:* With Los Primos, tour of Japan, 1988; With Ole, Italy, 1989; Australia; Singapore; Hong Kong; Russia; Canada; Presently touring UK with solo show Passion, Grace, Fire; Television appearances: Wogan; Just For Laughs; Edinburgh Nights; Television commercials: Canale 5. *Recordings:* Wrote and performed Lorca's Women, for RSC; with Los Primos: Paul's Lurking Grapefruit, Latino-comedy. *Honours:* Time Out Magazine, Pick of The Fringe, 1989; Winner, Covent Garden Street Festival, 1989; British Gas Best Newcomer, Edinburgh Festival, 1992. *Membership:* Musicians' Union. *Current Management:* Wizard Entertainments, 102 Euston St, London NW1 2HA. *Address:* 14B Vicarage Grove, London SE5 7LW, England.

ALEXANDER, Dennis; b. 7 May 1953, Fyvie, Aberdeenshire, Scotland. Entertainer; Musician (acoustic guitar). m. Isobel, 3 Aug. 1974, 1 s., 1 d. *Education:* Member, Ist Purchase and Supply, Hand Promotions Events Management. *Career:* Lead singer, Crooked Jack; Writer, producer, Crooked Jack's Giant Jeely Piece Show; Appearances, Edinburgh Festival Fringe; Major folk festivals in Scotland. *Recordings:* Tomorrow Must Wait; The Giant Jeely Piece Show (video); An Audience with Crooked Jack. *Membership:* Musicians' Union. *Current Management:* Crooked Jack Promotions. *Address:* 222 High St, Kirkcaldy, Fife KY1 1JT, Scotland.

ALEXANDER, Gregg; b. 4 May 1970, Grosse Point, MI, USA. Vocalist; Musician (guitar); Songwriter; Prod. *Career:* Solo artiste; Mem. and lead singer, The New Radicals, 1998–99; Songwriter; Songs recorded by: Danielle Brisebois, Geri Halliwell, Ronan Keating, Rod Stewart. *Recordings:* Albums: Solo: Save Me From Myself; Michigan Rain; Intoxifornication, 1992; with The New Radicals: Maybe You've Been Brainwashed Too, 1998.

ALEXANDER, John Eric; b. 10 Feb. 1962, Elizabeth, New Jersey, USA. Composer. m. Ellen Greiss, 3 Aug. 1986, 1 s. *Education:* BFA, Parsons School of Design, 1983. *Career:* Associate Producer, Iris Films Inc, New York, 1975–83; Producer, Sam Alexander Productions, New York, 1983–86; John Eric Alexander Music Inc, New York, 1986–. *Compositions:* Composer, music producer, film soundtracks: The Fly, 1986; Red Heat, 1987; Predator, 1987; The Mosquito Coast, 1987; Witches of Eastwick, 1988; Flatliners, 1990; Lethal Weapon II, 1990; Bird On A Wire, 1990; Die Hard II, 1990; Silence of The Lambs, 1991; Point Break, 1991; Ricochet, 1991. *Honours:* Cannes Film Festival Award, Witches of Eastwick, 1988. *Membership:* AFofM.

ALEXANDER, Otis Douglas; b. 1 June 1949, Virginia, USA. Musician (French horn, piano). *Education:* BA, MS, University of the District of Columbia; MLS, Ball State University; Norfolk State University; University of Toledo; Studied French horn with Hermann Suehs, piano with Hildred Roach, voice with Nelda Ormond, Robert Porter, opera with Gloria Amos. *Career:* Original choreography in tribute to world-renowned poet, Andre Lorde, Brooklyn Academy of Music; Danced in Oscar Brown, Jr and Lonnie Levister's, Slave Song; Performed principal role in William Grant Still's opera, Highway I; Recitalist, Whim Great House Museum; Recitalist, Cuttington University College and Harrison Opera House. *Compositions:* Queen Mary (folk play with music). *Publications:* Virgin Islands and Caribbean Communities: An Afro Treasure Chest. *Honours:* Plaque and Certificate, Outstanding Musical Performance and Directing, 1996. *Address:* PO Box 8052, Christiansted, St Croix, VI 00823, USA.

ALEXANDER, Van; b. 2 May 1915, New York, NY, USA. Music Arranger; Composer; Conductor; Author. m. Beth Baremore, 22 Sept. 1938, 2 d. *Education:* Columbia University; Studied with Otto Cesana, New York City; with Mario Tedsco, California; (orchestration, conducting, composition).

Career: Worked with Chick Webb at The Savoy Ballroom, New York; Benny Goodman; Paul Whiteman; Les Brown; Formed own band, played on radio, The Fitch Bandwagon; Morey Amsterdam's Laugh and Swing Club; Played ballrooms, theatres throughout USA, including: New York Paramount, Loews State; Capitol, New York; Earle, Philadelphia; The Stanley, Pittsburg; Arranger/conductor for Dinah Shore; Doris Day; Dean Martin; Gordon and Sheila MacRae; Kay Starr; Peggy Lee; Dakota Staton; Patty Andrews. *Compositions include:* 22 feature films; Co-writer, arranger, A-Tisket-A-Tasket, hit for Ella Fitzgerald; Hundreds of television segments include; The Wacky World of Jonathan Winters; Gene Kelly's Wonderful World of Girls; The Goldiggers Chevy Show; Composer, conductor, NBC's 50th Anniversary Show, A Closer Look; Dom De Luise specials; 1969 Emmy Awards; The Guy Mitchell Show Series; Scoring credits: Hazel; I Dream of Jeanie; Bewitched; Donna Reed; Dennis The Menace. *Recordings:* Swing Staged For Stereo; Savoy Stomp; The Last Dance; Numerous albums with Gordon MacRae; Kay Starr; Dakota Staton; Dorothy Kirsten (all on Capitol Records). *Publications:* First Arrangement (a learning method for the novice arranger). *Honours:* Irwin Kostal Award, 1995; NARAS Hall of Fame Award, for A-Tisket-A-Tasket, 1986; Los Angeles Jazz Society, Composer/Arranger Award, 1997; Pacific Pioneer Broadcasters, Diamond Circle Award, 1996. *Membership:* ASCAP; ASMAC; NARAS; Big Band Academy of America; Academy of Motion Picture Arts and Sciences; Hon. mem. of SPERDVAC (Society to Preserve and Encourage Radio Drama), Variety and Comedy, 1993; National Sheet Music Society, 1988.

ALFORD, Clem; b. 2 Oct. 1945, Glasgow, Scotland. Musician. Divorced. *Career:* Major Recitals, Radio in India; Toured Europe, Far East, including Japan; Major concert appearances with Lakshmi Shankar, Royal Albert Hall; Many Sessions with Major Musical Personalities, Lulu, Maurice Jarre, John Williams. *Compositions:* The Electronic Sitar of Clem Alford; Magic Carpet; Sangeet Sagar; Pop Explosion, Sitar Style; K.P.M.; One More Magic Carpet II; Akasa, Staying On. *Recordings:* The Electronic Sitar Of Clem Alford; Magic Carpet; Sangeet Sagar; Pop Explosion, Sitar Style; K.P.M.; One More Magic Carpet II; Monsoon, Akasa, Jewell in The Crown; Mirror Image, 1974; Once Moor, 1996. *Publications:* The Sitar Manual; The Sitar Book. *Honours:* Jr Sangeet Ratnakar, West Bengal; Sangeet Sudhakar, Kolkata; Sur-Mani, Mumbai. *Membership:* PRS; MCPS; PAMRA; Indian Music Congress. *Address:* 9 Tavistock Mansions, 16 Tavistock Pl., London WC1H 9RA, England.

ALIFANTIS, Nicu; b. 31 May 1954, Braila, Romania. Vocalist; Composer; Musician (guitar). *Career:* Wrote music for theatre, 10 film soundtracks; 19 recitals; 5000 concerts, tours: Romania; Bulgaria; Czechoslovakia; Germany; Israel; England; Italy; Hungary; Holland. *Recordings:* 3 singles; 6 albums; 2 CDs, 1 in France, produced by Radio France International; 8 albums with other singers. *Honours:* 3 awards, Theatre Music, 1986, 1991, 1993; First awards for Singer of the Year, 1993. *Membership:* Romanian Union of Composers; International Union of Theatre, UNIMA. *Current Management:* Aurel Mitram, PO Box 26–54, Bucharest, Romania.

ALLDIS, Dominic William; b. 15 April 1962, London, England. Musician (piano); Vocalist; Composer. *Career:* Debut at Purcell Room, London, 1985; Recitals at major festivals with Midi grand piano, 1986–89; Performances at jazz clubs, jazz festivals, 1990–; Formed trio, 1996; Teaching Staff, Royal Acad. of Music, 1993; Gives presentations to companies and businesses using music as metaphor for business concerns, 1998–. *Recordings:* Night Music, original composition for piano and synthesizers, 1989; Turn Out The Stars: The Songs Of Bill Evans, 1996; If Love Were All: The Songs Of Noël Coward, 2002; Watch What Happens: The Songs Of Michel Legrand. *Publications:* A Classical Approach to Jazz Piano. *Honours:* Royal Acad. of Music, hon. assoc. *Membership:* Asscn of British Jazz Musicians; Musicians' Union. *Current Management:* Canzona Music. *Address:* 122 Dawes Rd, Fulham, London SW6 7EG, England. *E-mail:* dominic@dominicalldis.com. *Website:* www.dominicalldis.com.

ALLEN, Duane David; b. 29 April 1943, Taylortown, Texas, USA. Vocalist; Songwriter. m. Norah Lee Stuart, 22 Sept. 1969, 2 s. *Education:* BS, Music, East Texas University, 1965. *Career:* Radio DJ, Paris, Texas, 1963–65; Lead singer, US gospel/country group Oak Ridge Boys, 1966–; Co-owner, president, Silverline/Goldline Music Publishing; Owner, president, Superior Sound Studios. *Compositions:* He Did It All For Me; Here's A Song For The Man; How Much Further Can We Go; I Will Follow The Sun. *Recordings:* Singles include: Praise The Lord And Pass The Soup; I'll Be True To You; Y'All Come Back Saloon; Elvira; Bobbie Sue; Leavin' Louisiana In The Broad Daylight; Trying To Love Two Women; American Made; Make My Life With You; I Guess It Never Hurts To Hurt Sometime; Come On In; Albums include: International, 1971; Light, 1972; Hymns, 1973; Street Gospel, 1973; Gospel Gold Heartwarming, 1974; Oak Ridge Boys, 1974, Super Gold, 1974; Sky High, 1975; Old Fashioned…, 1976; Y'All Come Back Saloon, 1977; Room Service, 1978; The Oak Ridge Boys Have Arrived, 1979; Together, 1980; Greatest Hits, 1980; Fancy Free, 1981; Bobbie Sue, 1982; Oak Ridge Boys Christmas, 1982; Friendship, 1983; American Made, 1983; The Oak Ridge Boys Deliver, 1984; Greatest Hits II, 1984; Step On Out, 1985; Seasons, 1985; Christmas Again, 1986; Where The Fast Lane Ends, 1986; Monongahela,

1987; New Horizons, 1988; American Dreams, 1989; Greatest Hits III, 1989; Unstoppable, 1991; The Long Haul, 1992. *Publications:* Co-author, The History of Gospel Music, 1971. *Honours:* Grammy Awards, 1970–77; 12 Gospel Music Asscn Dove Awards; American Music Award, Best Country Group of the Year, 1982; Country Music Asscn Award, Vocal Group of the Year, 1978; Academy of Country Music Awards, Best Vocal Group 1977, 1979; Numerous Gold discs. *Membership:* CMA; Gospel Music Asscn; AFTRA; National Academy Recording Arts and Sciences; Academy of Country Music. *Current Management:* Don Light Talent. *Address:* PO Box 120308, Nashville, TN 37212, USA.

ALLEN, Geri; b. 1957, Detroit, Michigan, USA. Jazz Musician (piano). *Education:* Jazz Studies Degree, Howard University, Washington, 1979; Masters Degree, Ethnomusicology, University of Pittsburgh, 1982; Studied piano with Kenny Barrow. *Career:* Formed own trio with Ron Carter, Tony Williams; Also played with: Ornette Coleman; Wallace Roney; Jack DeJohnette; Betty Carter; Dave Holland; Marcus Belgrave; Steve Coleman; Lester Bowie. *Recordings:* The Printmakers; Twilight Time; The Nurturer; Maroons; Twenty One; Etudes And Segments (with Charlie Haden, Paul Motian); Feed The Fire (with Betty Carter, Jack DeJohnette, Dave Holland); Solo: Sound Museum, 1996; Gathering, 1998. *Honours:* Howard University Alumni Award; SESAE Special Achievement Award; Eubie Blake Award; Downbeat Critics Poll, Talent Deserving Wider Recognition, 1993, 1994. *Current Management:* Blue Note. *Address:* 1290 Avenue of the Americas, 35th Floor, New York, NY 10104, USA.

ALLEN, Henry Kaleialoha; b. 11 June 1933, Honolulu, HI, USA. Master Artist, Hawaiian Steel Guitar; Recording Artiste; Show Prod. m. Sherron Allen, 1971, 1 s., 2 d. *Education:* Studied Jazz, Los Angeles, Music Theory, Composition, Johnny Smith, Alex Keck; Hawaiian Music Institute, Teaching Hawaiian Steel Guitar for County of Maui, Hawaii. *Career:* Music parts in films; Hawaiian Eye; Blue Hawaii; Barnaby Jones; Mama's Family; Regular guest on Home Shopping Channel Network; QVC and produces Hawaiian shows and music for their 50th state tours; Show Producer, own shows; Music is played, inflight, American Airlines; Opened up Planet Hollywood with Music in Maui, 1995; Own record label, Rainbow Records. *Compositions include:* Lahaina; Walking in the Sand; Hookipa (Jazz) Noalani; Koele Mist; We Say Aloha; Goodbye; Lanikai; Hawaii, Islands in the Sky; Kalele; Swinging. *Recordings:* Albums: Memories Of Hawaii; Magic Of Steel Guitar; Blue Hawaii. *Publications:* Learning to Play the Hawaiian Way, 1991; Book of Songs, Hawaiian Steel Guitar, 1993. *Honours:* Awards, State Foundation/ Culture and the Arts, 1995, 1996; Master Artist Grants; ASCAP Awards, 1996, 1997; County of Maui Grant for Music Work Musicians Asscn of Hawaii (Lifetime Mem.); ASCAP Mem.; HSGA Mem. *Current Management:* Own Manager, Polynesian Promotions, Rainbow Records. *Address:* 5161-D, Kohi St, Lahaina, Maui, Hawaii 96761, USA.

ALLEN, Peter Raymond; b. 23 Nov. 1954, Newbury, Berkshire, England. *Career:* Formed Pete Allen Jazz Band, 1978; Regular television and radio shows followed including: Pebble Mill at One, BBC Television; Jazzin Around, HTV Series; Most BBC Radio Two Programmes including five broadcasts for Friday Night is Music Night and own six week series for Radio Two. *Compositions:* Beau Sejour; Mystic Gypsy; St Louis Street Stomp; Riverside Rag; Springtime Swing; Black Lion Rag; At the Upton Mardi Gras. *Recordings:* Turkey Trot, 1978; Down in Honky Tonk Town, 1979; Gonna Build A Mountain, 1980; Beau Sejour, 1987; Big Chief, Loose Tie, 1996; All Aboard for Alabama, 1997; Oh Play That Thing, 1998; Reeds 'n' Rhythm, 1998; Movin' On, 1999. *Honours:* World Wide All Stars, Sacramento, USA, 1984; Hon. Citizenship of New Orleans, 1992; European Top Eight Jazz Band, Germany. *Membership:* Performing Rights Soc; Lions International. *Address:* PO Box 505, Chippenham, Wiltshire SW15 3WS, England.

ALLEN, Rick; b. 1 Nov. 1963, Sheffield, England. Musician (drums). *Career:* Drummer, Def Leppard, 1978–; Concerts include: Support tours to Sammy Hagar; AC/DC; Ted Nugent; Reading Rock Festival, 1980; Lost left arm in car crash, 1984; Returns to perform with custom-built electronic drum kit, 1985; Monsters of Rock festivals, including Castle Donington, 1986; Royal Albert Hall, 1989; Freddie Mercury Tribute Concert, Wembley Stadium, 1992; Television interview, Fighting Back, BBC1, 1992. *Recordings:* Albums: On Through The Night, 1980; High 'n' Dry, 1981; Pyromania, 1983; Hysteria, 1987; Adrenalize, 1992; Retroactive, 1993; Vault 1980–95, 1995; Slang, 1996; Euphoria, 1999; X, 2002. Singles include: Hello America, 1980; Photograph, 1983; Rock Of Ages, 1983; Foolin', 1983; Animal, 1987; Pour Some Sugar On Me, 1987; Armageddon It, 1988; Love Bites (No. 1, USA), 1988; Rocket, 1989; Let's Get Rocked (No. 2, UK), 1992; Make Love Like A Man, 1992; Have You Ever Needed Someone So Bad, 1992; Heaven Is, 1993; Two Steps Behind (featured in film soundtrack The Last Action Hero), 1993; Action, 1994; When Love And Hate Collide (No. 2, UK), 1995; All I Want Is Everything, 1996; Promises, 1999; Now, 2002. *Honours:* American Music Awards: Favourite Heavy Metal Album, Favourite Heavy Metal Artists, 1989. *Current Management:* Q-Prime Inc. *Address:* 729 Seventh Ave, 14th Floor, New York, NY 10019, USA. *Website:* www.defleppard.com.

ALLEN, Terry, (Terry L. Comp); b. 1 Sept. 1947, Niles, Michigan, USA. Entertainer; Vocalist; Musician (bass, rhythm guitar). m. Barbara Sweets, 23 April 1995, 4 s., 4 d. *Education:* Aircraft Maintenance Diploma. *Career:* Tours USA and Canada, playing private and public clubs and military bases; Numerous television and radio appearances, state and county fairs, 1969–81; Currently, Director of Marketing for Gf Mac Management Inc. *Recordings:* CB Duck; A Little Love, 1978; Time Has; Footprints; Good Old Days, 1989. *Honours:* NE Country Music Hall of Fame, Achievement and Performance Award, 1987. *Current Management:* Blackhawk International, Dalton Fuller Management. *Address:* Rt1 Box 200, Rising City, NE 68658, USA.

ALLEYNE, Cheryl Louise; b. 4 Sept. 1963, North London, England. *Education:* College of Arts and Technology, Newcastle upon Tyne, England, 1984–87. *Career:* Freelance Drummer; Appeared On BBC Television, Mad About Music, Blue Peter, Top of the Pops, MTV Spring Break Jams; Interviewed On Jazz FM, Women's Hour, Radio 4. *Compositions:* Solar Breeze. *Recordings:* Include, The Human Groove, 1989; Chameleon, 1993; Magic Of Olmec, 1995; Gail Thompson's Jazz Africa, 1995; Somewhere Out There, 1996; Tomorrows Path, 1997. *Publications:* Best of British Publications; Best of British Women. *Honours:* Most Promising Musician of the Year, 1986. *Address:* 9 Croxford Gardens, Wood Green, London N22 5QU, England.

ALLISON, Bernard; b. 26 Nov. 1965, Chicago, Illinois, USA. Musician (Guitar); Vocalist; Arranger; Composer. 1 d. *Career:* Documentary Film, The Next Generation; France, Grand de Sable, Paris Premier; Live at the New Morning. *Recordings:* The Next Generation; Hang On; Low Down And Dirty; Playin' A Losin' Game; No Mercy; Funkifino; Born With The Blues; Times Are Changing. *Honours:* New Artist of the Year, Atlanta, Georgia, 1998. *Membership:* SCEM. *Current Management:* Blue Sky Artists World-wide. *Address:* 761 Washington Ave N, Minneapolis, MN 55401, USA.

ALLISON, Jim (James H.); b. 13 Feb. 1959, Gettyburg, Pennsylvania, USA. Songwriter; Music Publisher; Prod. *Education:* Master's Penn State University, Gettysburg College, BA. *Career:* Began writing songs aged 13; High school English teacher for 2 years; Musician and bandleader for 20 years; Set up own music publishing and production company, 1985; Studio owner and producer; Recorded and helped launch country music career of Billy Ray Cyrus. *Compositions:* What Am I Gonna Do About You, Reba McEntire; Fade To Blue, LeAnn Rimes; Cowboys Don't Cry, Daron Norwood. *Recordings:* Razzy Bailey; Earl Thomas Conley; Mickey Gilley; Brenda Lee; Jo Dee Messina; Del Reeves; Connie Smith; Jett Williams; Lee Ann Womack. *Publications:* 1001 Song Ideas Vols 1 and 2, 1999; Million Dollar Ideas: Inventions Creations and Opportunities, 2000. *Honours:* Nashville Songwriters Asscn award, What Am I Gonna Do About You, 1987; Billboard Song Contest, Nobody Loves Me Like The Blues, Winner, 1992. *Membership:* CMA. *Current Management:* AlliSongs Inc. *Address:* 1603 Horton Ave, Nashville, Tennessee 37212, USA. *Website:* www.allisongs.com.

ALLISON, Mose; b. 11 Nov. 1927, Tippo, Mississippi, USA. Vocalist; Jazz/ Blues Musician (piano); Lyricist; Composer. *Education:* Chemical engineering; English; Philosophy. *Career:* Influenced by Louis Jordan, Louis Armstrong and Nat 'King' Cole, started out playing trumpet then switched to piano; After college and the army, appeared professionally for the first time, 1950; Returned to college shortly after; Recorded with Al Cohn and Bobby Brookmeyer for Prestige Records, 1956; Signed own deal, 1957; Joined Columbia in 1960 for 2 years before a 14-year stint with Atlantic; After a 6-year recording hiatus re-emerged briefly on Elektra before current deal with Blue Note; Tours extensively throughout North America, Britain and Europe. *Compositions include:* Ain't You A Mess; Certified Senior Citizen; Ever Since I Stole The Blues; The Fool Killer; Gimcracks and Gewgaws; How Does It Feel To Be Good Looking?; Natural Born Malcontent; Parchman Farm; What Do You Do After You Ruin Your Life?; You're Mind Is On Vacation. *Recordings:* Albums include: Back Country Suite, 1957; I Love The Life I Live, 1960; I Don't Worry About A Thing, 1962; I've Been Doin' Some Thinkin', 1968; Your Mind Is On Vacation, 1976; Middleclass White Boy, 1982; Gimcracks And Gewgaws, 1997; The Mose Chronicles #1, 2000; The Mose Chronicles #2, 2001. *Current Management:* The Blues Agency, 323 Beale St, Suite 2000, Memphis, Tennesee, USA.

ALLMAN, Gregg; b. 8 Dec. 1947, Nashville, Tennessee, USA. Musician. m. Cher Bono, 1975, divorced 1979, 1 c. *Career:* Co-founder, Hour Glass; Support to Eric Burdon and the Animals, 1967; Co-founder, singer, Allman Brothers (with brother Duane), 1969–76, 1978–81, 1989–; Solo artiste, 1973–; Also recorded with wife Cher, 1976–79; Appearances include: Atlanta International Pop Festival, with Jimi Hendrix, Jethro Tull, B. B. King, 1979; Fillmore East, New York, 1971; Mar Y Sol Festival, Puerto Rico, 1972; Watkins Glen Raceway, with Grateful Dead and the Band (largest-ever concert of 600,000), 1973; Knebworth Festival, 1974; New Orleans Jazz and Heritage Festival, 1993; Actor, film Rush, 1991. *Recordings:* Albums with Hour Glass: Hour Glass, 1967; Power Of Love, 1968; with The Allman Brothers: Allman Brothers Band, 1970; At Fillmore East, 1971; Eat A Peach, 1972; Brothers And Sisters, 1973; Win Lose Or Draw, 1975; The Road Goes On Forever, 1976; Wipe The Windows, Check The Oil, Dollar Gas, 1976;

Enlightened Rogues, 1979; Brothers Of The Road, 1981; The Best Of The Allman Band, 1981; Dreams, 1989; Seven Turns, 1989; Shades Of Two Worlds, 1991; Second Set, 1995; Fantastic Allman Brothers Original Hits, 1999; Solo albums: Laid Back, 1973; The Gregg Allman Tour, 1974; Playin' Up A Storm, 1977; I'm No Angel, 1987; Just Before The Bullets Fly, 1988; Searchin' For Simplicity, 1997; with Cher: Allman And Woman, 1976; Two The Hard Way, 1977.

ALLOUCHE, Joël; b. 6 Nov. 1960, Bougie, Algeria. Musician (drums, percussion). m. 24 Dec. 1988, 1 s., 1 d. *Career:* Professional with pop bands, singers, 1975–; Jazz, 1980–; Played in Japan; Canada; USA; Africa; England; India; Worked with musicians incl.: John Surman; Kenny Wheeler; Palle Danielsson; Enrico Rava; Urs Leimgruber; Don Friedman; Maurice Magnoni; Palle Danielsson; Marc Ducret; François Jeanneau; Michel Portal; Doudou Gouirand; Don Cherry; Antonello Salis; Concerts, festivals with Coincidence, the Llabador brothers group; International concerts with trio of guitarist Philippe Caillat, in Berlin, Copenhagen, Hamburg, Hungary; Mem., Reflexionen, 1983, Maurice Magnoni Quintet, 1987, Marc Ducret Trio, 1988, Pandémonium, François Jeanneau Quartet, Michel Portal's New Unit, 1990; Master classes, conservatoires and music schools. *Recordings:* French Connection, Philippe Caillat, 1981; Fire Brigade, Philippe Caillat, 1982; with J. P. Llabador: Coincidence, 1984; Brussels, 1987; Forgotten Tales, Doudou Gouirand, with Don Cherry, 1985; with Urs Leimgruber: Reflexionen, 1986; Live, 1986; Remember To Remember, 1987; Andata Senza Ritorno, Maurice Magnoni, 1988; Superbe Déménagement, 1989; Gris, Marc Ducret, 1990; Lato Sensu, Philippe Gareil, 1991; Beatles Stories, Gérard Pansanel/Antonello Salis, 1992; Maloya Transit, François Jeanneau And Trio Tambours, 1992; Paolo Damiani, with Kenny Wheeler, 1992; Nguyên Lê, with Art Lande, Paul McCandless, 1992; Dominique Pifarely, with Ricardo del Fra, F. Couturier, 1993; Birds Can Fly, J. P. Llabador, 1995; Orchestra Improvista, Nino Rota-Fellini (Gouirand, Pansanel), 1995; Tales From Vietnam, Nguyen Lê, 1996; Few Notes, Jean Bardy, 1998; Tamborea, Engergypsy, 1999; Soniba Kuyate; Kanakassi, W. P. Fresu, 1999. *Address:* 8 bis rue du Professeur Lombard, 34000 Montpellier, France.

ALLPASS, Soma; b. 9 July 1968, Copenhagen, Denmark. Musician (cello, piano, guitar); Vocalist; Songwriter; Arranger. *Education:* Private lessons in Cello, 10 years; Royal Academy of Music, Copenhagen, 5 years; Lessons in piano and singing. *Career:* Cellist and backing singer, Trains and Boats and Trains, rock band, 1989–94; Co-arranger, Roskilde Festival, 1992, 1993, 1994; Tours in Denmark, Norway, Sweden, Germany, England, Finland and New York; New Music Seminar, 1992. *Recordings:* Albums: Trains And Boats And Trains, 1990; Hum (mini album), 1990; Engulfed, 1991; Minimal Star, 1992. Singles: I Like Cars, 1992. *Honours:* Rodovre Music Prize, 1996. *Membership:* KODA; Danish Musicians' Union. *Current Management:* Jim Holm, Klarboderne 3, 1001, Copenhagen K, Denmark. *Address:* Brofogedvej 2, 2th, 2400 Copenhagen NV, Denmark.

ALL-STAR FRESH; b. 1 Aug. 1965, Amsterdam, Netherlands. Prod; Rap Artiste; Remixer; Composer. *Career:* Leader, producer, King Bee. *Compositions include:* (co-writer) Cappella: Move On Baby; Move Your Body; U and Me. *Recordings:* Back By Dope Demand; Must Be The Music. *Honours:* Dance Artist Award, 1991, 1992. *Current Management:* Hans Van Pol Management.

ALLWRIGHT, (Sydney) Graeme; b. 7 Nov. 1926, Lyall Bay, New Zealand. Vocalist; Author; Composer. m. Catherine Dasté, 8 June 1951, 3 s., 1 d. *Career:* 30 years professional stage work, television, radio; Concerts include: Nyons Festival, Switzerland; Le Printemps de Bourges; Les Francofolies à la Rochelle, France; L'Olympia, Palais des Sports. *Recordings:* 19 albums. *Publications:* Song books. *Membership:* SACEM; ADAMI. *Current Management:* Claire Bataille. *Address:* 13 Pl. D'Aligre, 75000 Paris, France.

ALMEIDA, Joaquim; b. 24 July 1931. Vocalist; Composer; Musician (trumpet). m. Alice Almeida, 2 s., 1 d. *Education:* Music Conservatoire. *Career:* Starlet in San Vicente; Singing and playing in clubs; Performed in Adega Machadol; Founded, Vozde Cadoverde, toured around Europe, Africa. *Compositions include:* Cretchu Di Cei; Amorde Mai; Wibovente Year 2000. *Recordings include:* Un Creole In France. *Honours:* Prize of Recognition for Best Cabovermnteau Artist. *Membership:* SACEM. *Current Management:* Edition 4, Paris. *Address:* 3 Allee Maurice Chevalier, 93100 Montreuil, France.

ALMOND, Peter Marc; b. 9 July 1959, Southport, Lancashire, England. Vocalist; Lyricist. *Education:* College, Southport; Fine Arts, Leeds Polytechnic. *Career:* Founded Soft Cell, with David Ball, 1979–84, re-formed 2001; Also recorded as Marc' and the Mambas; Solo artiste, 1984–; Major concerts include: Future 2 Science Fiction Music Festival, 1980; Terrence Higgins Trust benefit concert, 1990; Red Hot and Dance AIDS benefit concert, Barcelona, 1991; Royal Albert Hall, London; Philharmonic Hall, Liverpool, 1992. *Recordings:* Albums: with Soft Cell: Some Bizarre Album, 1981; Non-Stop Erotic Cabaret, 1981; Non-Stop Ecstatic Dancing, 1982; The Art Of Falling Apart, 1983; as Marc and the Mambas: Untitled, 1982; Torment And Toreros, 1983; This Last Night In Sodom, 1984; Wasted, 1995; Cruelty Without Beauty, 2002; Compilations: The Singles Album, 1986; Memorabilia,

The Singles (remixed by Ball), 1991; The Very Best Of, 2002; as Marc Almond and the Willing Sinners: Vermin In Ermine, 1984; Solo: Mother Fist And Her Five Daughters, 1987; Enchanted, 1990; Tenement Symphony, 1991; 12 Years Of Tears, Live At The Albert Hall, 1993; Fantastic Star, 1996; Live In Concert, 1998; Open All Night, 1999; Stranger Things, 2001. Singles: with Soft Cell: Tainted Love (No. 1, UK), 1981; Bedsitter; Say Hello Wave Goodbye; Torch; Soul Inside; Solo: I Feel Love (medley), with Bronski Beat; Something's Gotten Hold Of My Heart; Jacky; My Hand Over My Heart; The Days Of Pearly Spencer; Adored And Explored; Glorious. *Honours:* Best Selling Single of the Year, for Tainted Love, 1981; BRIT Award, Best British Single, for Tainted Love, 1982; Billboard Magazine, New Wave Band of the Year, 1982. *Website:* www.marcalmond.co.uk.

ALMQVIST, 'Howlin' Pelle (Peter); b. 1979. Vocalist. *Career:* Mem., lead singer, Swedish band, The Hives, 1993–; Signed to Universal Music, 2001. *Recordings:* Albums: Barely Legal, 1997; Veni Vidi Vicious, 2000; Your New Favourite Band (compilation, UK only), 2001. Singles: Oh, Lord! When? How? (EP), 1996; aka I.D.I.O.T. (EP), 1998; Hate To Say I Told You So; Main Offender; Supply & Demand. *Honours:* NME Award, Best International Band, 2003. *Address:* The Hives, c/o Pelle Almqvist, Regnbågsvägen 46, 737 43 Fagersta, Sweden. *E-mail:* hives@innocent.com. *Website:* www.hives.nu.

ALPERT, Herb; b. 31 March 1935, Los Angeles, California, USA. Musician (trumpet); Songwriter; Arranger; Record Co Exec. m. Lani Hall, 1 s., 2 d. *Education:* University of Southern California. *Career:* Three television specials; Leader, own group Tijuana Brass; Multiple world tours; Owner, Dore Records; Manager, Jan and Dean; Co-founder with Jerry Moss, A & M Records (formerly Carnival), 1962–89; Artists have included: The Carpenters; Captain and Tennille; Carole King; Cat Stevens; The Police; Squeeze; Joe Jackson; Bryan Adams. *Compositions include:* Wonderful World, Sam Cooke (co-writer with Lou Adler). *Recordings:* The Lonely Bull; A Taste Of Honey; Spanish Flea; Tijuana Taxi; Casino Royale; This Guy's In Love With You, 1968; Rise (No. 1, USA), 1979; Albums include: The Lonely Bull, 1963; Tijuana Brass, 1963; Tijuana Brass Vol. 2, 1964; South Of The Border, 1965; Whipped Cream And Other Delights, 1965; Going Places, 1966; SRO, 1967; Sounds Like Us, 1967; Herb Alpert's Ninth, 1968; The Best Of The Brass, 1968; Warm, 1969; Rise, 1979; Keep Your Eyes On Me, 1979; Magic Man, 1981; My Abstract Heart, 1989; Midnight Sun, 1992; Second Wind, 1996; Passion Dance, 1997; Colors, 1999; Definitive Hits, 2001. *Honours:* Numerous Grammy Awards. *Current Management:* c/o Kip Cohen, La Brea Tours, Inc, 1414 Sixth St, Santa Monica, CA 90401, USA.

ALQUERES, Gabriela; b. 1 Sept. 1972, Sao Paulo, Brazil. Musician (guitar); Songwriter. m. Pete Whittard, 23 Nov. 1992. *Education:* The Guitar Institute. *Career:* Played with David McAlmont supporting Cyndi Lauper; Venues played include the Royal Albert Hall; Radio appearances include GLR. *Membership:* Musicians' Union. *Address:* 7 Cambridge Gardens, Muswell Hill, London N10 2LL, England.

ALSOU, (Alsou Tenisheva); b. 27 June 1983, Bugulma, Tatarstan, Russia. Vocalist. *Career:* Relocated to Moscow, Russia, aged 9; Educated in and resident of England from age 13; Discovered by manager Valeriy Belotserkovsky, 1998; Russia's most popular teen star by end of 1999; Many Russian concerts throughout 2000–01; Became first Russian pop artiste ever to sign with international record company following appearance at Eurovision Song Contest, 2000. *Recordings:* Albums: Alsou, 1999; Greatest Hits, Alsou (world-wide release), 2001; Singles: Winter Dream, 1999; Solo, You're My No. 1 (with Enrique Iglesias), 2000; Before You Love Me, 2001. *Honours:* Eurovision Song Contest, second place, Solo, 2000; Presented with award for largest Russian single sales ever, You Are My Number One (136,000 copies), 2001. *Address:* c/o Universal Music Group, Russia. *Website:* www.alsouonline.com.

ALSTON, Andy; Musician (accordion, keyboards). 2 c. *Career:* Mem., Del Amitri, 1987–. *Recordings:* Albums: Waking Hours, 1989; Change Everything, 1992; Twisted, 1995; Some Other Sucker's Parade, 1997; Hatful Of Rain/ Lousy With Love, 1998; Can You Do Me Good?, 2002. Singles: Nothing Ever Happens, 1990; Move Away Jimmy Blue, 1990; Spit In The Rain, 1990; Always The Last To Know, 1992; Be My Downfall, 1992; Just Like A Man, 1992; When You Were Wrong, 1993; Here And Now, 1995; Driving With The Brakes On, 1995; Roll To Me, 1995; Tell Her This, 1996; Not Where It's At, 1997; Don't Come Home Too Soon, 1998; Cry To Be Found, 1998; Just Before You Leave, 2002. *Address:* c/o A & M Records Inc, 595 Madison Ave, New York, NY 10022, USA. *Website:* www.delamitri.com.

ALTERHAUG, Bjorn; b. 3 June 1945, Mo i Rana, Norway. Asst Prof; Jazz Musician (bass). m. Anne-Lise Alterhaug, 1 Jan. 1968, 1 s., 1 d. *Education:* University. *Career:* Played as jazz soloist with: Ben Webster; Lucky Thompson; Chet Baker; Clark Terry; Numerous television and radio performances; Festival composer, Silver Jubilee of North Norway Festival, 1989. *Compositions:* For big band and symphony-setting. *Recordings:* Solo albums: Moments, 1979; A Ballad, 1986; Constellations, 1991. *Publications:* Articles on improvisation and communication. *Honours:* Buddy Award,

Norwegian Jazz Federation (highest honour). *Membership:* Norwegian Jazz Federation; NOPA.

ALTMAN, John Neville Rufus; b. 5 Dec. 1949, London, England. Composer; Conductor; Arranger; Orchestrator; Musician (saxophone). m. Rita Pukacz, 30 Oct. 1977, 3 s., 1 d. *Education:* BA Hons, University of Sussex; Birkbeck College, London. *Career:* Recorded as keyboard player with Eric Clapton; Sting; Phil Collins; Saxophonist with Muddy Waters; Little Richard; Ben E King; Jimmy Page; John Lennon; Dr John; Slim Gaillard; Musical Director for Van Morrison, late 1970s; Regular conductor, Royal Philharmonic Orchestra. *Compositions:* Films include: Funny Bones; Bhaji On The Beach; Hear My Song; Bad Behaviour; Devlin; Camilla; Titanic; RKO 281; The Lost Empire; Fidel; Beautiful Joe; Television includes: Peak Practice; Miss Marple; Shadowlands; First and Last; Comic Relief, 1995; By The Sword Divided; Composer, arranger, producer of over 3000 commercials including: British Airways; ATandT; Pan Am; General Motors; Stella Artois; Rover; Intercity; British Telecom; Films as arranger, orchestrator, conductor include: Monty Python's Life of Brian; Erik The Viking; Just A Gigolo; Foreign Bodies; The Sheltering Sky; Leon (aka The Professional); Golden Eye; Little Voice. *Recordings:* Arranger, conductor, producer: Singles: Downtown Train, Rod Stewart; Kissing A Fool, George Michael; That Ole Devil Called Love, Alison Moyet; Always Look On The Bright Side Of Life, Monty Python; Walking In The Air, Aled Jones; Love Is On Our Side, Tom Jones; It's Oh So Quiet, Björk; Albums: Streetfighting Years, Simple Minds; Hey Manhattan, Prefab Sprout; A Very Special Season, Diana Ross; Wildest Dreams, Tina Turner; Closing credits, song for film: Innocent Lies, Patricia Kaas. *Honours:* TRIC Award, 1995; Primetime Emmy Award, Outstanding Music Composition for a Drama or Miniseries, RKO 281, 2000. *Membership:* PRS; ASCAP; BAC&S; ASMAC. *Current Management:* SMA, 8938 Keith Ave, West Hollywood, CA 90069, USA.

ALU, Steve; b. 13 July 1957, Beckenham, Kent, England. Front of House Sound Engineer; Tour Man; Studio Sound Engineer. *Career:* 15 years practical experience engineering, production and tour management; Credits: One The Juggler; AirHead; Bolshoi; Eddie and The Hotrods; N-Joi; Senser; OMD; Jason Rebello; Bush Telegraph; Phil Manzanera; Louise Goffin; Royal Festival Ballet; Limelight/Hippodrome clubs; Concorde Agency; Elevator Man. *Address:* Flat F, 78 Deptford High St, Deptford, London SE8 4RT, England.

AMA, Shola, (Mathurin Campbell); b. 8 March 1979, Willesden, London, England. Vocalist. *Career:* Solo recording artiste, 1997–; Television appearances including Top of the Pops; Tour with Fugees, 1997; Tour with Jamiroquai's Jam in the Park; UK Rhythm Nation tour. *Recordings include:* Albums: Much Love, 1997; In Return, 1999; Singles: You Might Need Somebody, 1997; You're The One That I Love, 1997; Who's Loving My Baby, 1997; Much Love, 1998; Taboo (with Glamma Kid), 1999; Imagine, 2000. *Honours:* MOBO Awards, Best R&B Artist, Best Newcomer, 1997; BRIT Award, Best Female, 1998. *Current Management:* 1 2 One Management. *Address:* c/o 20 Damien St, London E1 2HX, England.

AMBROSE, Edmund David; b. 11 Dec. 1945, Highgate, London, England. Record Co Exec; Musician (bass). m. Angela, 3 Sept. 1975, 2 s., 1 d. *Education:* Brymshaw College of Art; London College of Printing. *Career:* Musician with: Shotgun Express; Julie Driscoll; Brian Auger and Trinity; Arthur Brown; Cat Stevens; Numerous television and radio appearances; Concerts include: Royal Albert Hall and Fairfield Hall; Director of Planet 3 Records; Publishing for: Sex Pistols; Vapors; Dexy's Midnight Runners; Duran Duran; Pet Shop Boys; Transvision Vamp; Love City Groove. *Recordings:* with Shotgun Express: Shotgun Express, 1969; with Brian Auger and The Trinity: Open, 1967; Definitely What, 1968; Steetnoise, 1968; Befour, 1970; Genesis, 1975. *Honours:* Brightest Hope, Best Record with Brian Auger and The Trinity. *Membership:* Chelsea Arts Club; Rye Art Gallery. *Address:* 71 Finlay St, Fulham, London SW6 6HF, England.

AMENT, Jeff; b. 10 March 1963. Rock Musician (bass). *Career:* Musician in Seattle SubPop scene, 1980s; Member, Green River, 1987–89; Mother Love Bone, 1989; Pearl Jam, 1990–; Concerts with Pearl Jam: Support to Alice In Chains, 1991; Lollapalooza Festival 92 tour, 1992; Drop In The Park concert, Seattle, 1992; European tour, 1992; Bridge School Benefit, with Neil Young, Elton John, Sammy Hagar, James Taylor, 1992; Support to Keith Richards and The Expensive Winos, New York, 1992; Concert appearances with Neil Young; Group appearance in film Singles, 1992; Also member, Temple of The Dog project, 1991. *Recordings:* Albums: with Green River: Rehab Doll (EP), 1988; with Mother Love Bone: Shine (EP), 1989; Apple, 1990; with Pearl Jam: Ten (No. 2, USA), 1991; Vs. (No. 1, USA), 1993; Vitalogy, 1994; No Code, 1996; Live On Two Legs, 1998; Yield, 1998; Riot Act, 2002; with Temple Of The Dog: Temple Of The Dog, 1991; Singles: with Pearl Jam: Alive, 1992; Even Flow, 1992; Jeremy, 1992. *Honours:* American Music Award: Favourite New Artist, 1993; Rolling Stone Readers' Awards, Best New American Band, Best Video, 1993; 4 MTV Awards, 1993; Highest 1-week album sales total in history, Vs., 1993. *Current Management:* Curtis Management, 1423 34th Ave, Seattle, WA 98122, USA.

AMES, Roger; b. 1949, Trinidad. Record Co Exec. *Career:* EMI UK, 1975–79; A & R dept, Phonogram, PolyGram UK, 1979–83; Gen. Man., London Records, 1983, purchased back catalogue of Factory Records, signed New Order; Man. Dir, London Records; Chair. and CEO, PolyGram UK, 1991–94; Group Exec. Vice-Pres., PolyGram International Ltd, and Pres., PolyGram Music Group, 1996–99; Pres., Warner Music International, 1999; Chair. and CEO, Warner Music Group, 1999–. *Address:* Warner Music Group, 75 Rockefeller Plaza, New York, NY 10019, USA. *Website:* www.wmg.com.

AMIGO, Vicente; b. 25 March 1967, Guadalcanal, Sevilla, Spain. *Career:* Paris Guitar Festival; International Festival of Cordoba; First on David Bowie Spanish tour, USA; L'Ete de Nimes, France; Legends of Guitar Festival, Sevilla; International Guitar Festival, La Habana; Mestres Da Guitarra, Paco de Lucia, John McLaughlin. *Compositions:* De mi corazón al aire, 1991; Poeta, Concierto flamenco para un marinero en tierra, orchestra; Vivencias imaginadas, 1995. *Honours:* Icaro, 1991; Ateneo de Cordoba, 1992; Best Flamenco Guitarist (Guitar Player), 1993. *Current Management:* Intercambio de Cultura y Arte (ICARI). *Address:* c/o Carretas, 14-5-I-5, 28012 Madrid, Spain.

AMOS, Tori, (Myra Ellen Amos); b. 22 Aug. 1963, Newton, NC, USA. Vocalist; Songwriter; Musician (piano). m. Mark Hawley, 1998, 1 d. *Education:* Scholarship, Peabody Institute, Baltimore, USA. *Career:* Singer, piano bars as teenager; Solo recording artiste, 1987–; Numerous tours, television and radio appearances. *Recordings:* Albums: Y Kant Tori Read, 1988; Little Earthquakes, 1991; Under The Pink, 1994; Boys For Pele, 1995; From The Choirgirl Hotel, 1998; Star Profile, 1998; To Venus And Back, 1999; Maximum Tori, 2000; Strange Little Girls, 2001; Scarlet's Walk, 2003. Singles: Me And A Gun (EP), 1991; Precious Things, 1991; Silent All These Years, 1991; Crucify, 1992; Winter, 1992; China, 1992; Little Drummer Boy, 1992; God, 1993; Cornflake Girl, 1994; Pretty Good Year, 1994; Tea With The Waitress, 1994; Past The Mission, 1994; Caught A Lite Sneeze, 1996; In The Springtime Of His Voodoo, 1996; Professional Widow (No. 1, UK) 1997; Talula, 1998; Spark, 1998; Raspberry Swirl, 1998; Jackie's Strength, 1999; Bliss, 1999; 1,000 Oceans, 1999; Concertina, 2000; featured track on: Tower Of Strength (Leonard Cohen tribute), 1995; Contributions to many film soundtracks. *Honours:* Q Award, Best New Act, 1992. *Current Management:* Spivak Entertainment, 11845 W Olympic Blvd, Suite 1125, Los Angeles, CA 90064, USA. *Website:* www.toriamos.com.

AMRAM, David Werner; b. 17 Nov. 1930, Philidelphia, USA. Composer; Conductor; Musician. m. Loralee Ecobelli, 1 s., 2 d. *Education:* Oberlin Conservatory Music, 1948–49; Manhattan School of Music, 1955–56; BA, George Washington University, 1952; LLD, Moravian College, PA, 1979; MusD, Muhlenberg College, 1988; University Hartford, 1989; DMus, St Lawrence University, 1994. *Career:* Head Free Schooltime Concert Series, Philharmonic Orchestra, 1971–; Leo Block Chair, Arts and Humanities, University; Conductor, Soloist with 14 orchestras; Composer, incidental music for productions, Broadway plays, films and television; Recording Artiste; Conductor; Composer; Multi Instrumentalist; Music Director, International Jewish Arts Festival. *Compositions include:* (for orchestras) Ode to Lof Buckley; (Opera) The Final Ingredient, 12th Night. *Publications:* Vibrations: Adventures and Musical Times of David Amram; At Home Around The World. *Honours:* Include, Obie Award. *Current Management:* Ed Keane Associate, 32 Saint Edward Rd, Boston, MA 02128, USA.

AMSALLEM, Franck; b. 25 Oct. 1961, Oran, Algeria. Musician (piano); Composer; Prod. *Education:* Nice Conservatory of Music; Berklee College of Music; Manhattan School of Music. *Career:* Performed with Gerry Mulligan, Charles Lloyd, Bobby Watson, Joe Chambers, Harry Belafonte, Blood Sweat and Tears, Bob Belden, Tim Ries, Peter King, Didier Lockwood; Featured on French National Radio. *Compositions:* Out A Day; Chanson Triste; After; Running After Eternity; Nuits, 1994. *Recordings:* Out A Day; Regards; Is That So; Years Gone By; New York Stories; On Second Thoughts, 2000. *Honours:* Fondation de la Vocation, 1989; NEA Competition Fellowship, 1990; Ascap Award for Young Composers, 1991. *Current Management:* FRAM Music. *Address:* 100 Ocean Parkway #6K, Brooklyn, NY 11218, USA. *E-mail:* sallemjazz@yahoo.com.

AMSTELL, Billy; b. 20 Aug. 1911, London, England. Musician (saxophone, clarinet); Composer; Author. m. Tessa, 19 June 1938. *Education:* Two Certificates for Piano, Royal College of Music. *Career:* 11 years with Ambrose Orchestra; Two years with Geraldo Orchestra, radio and records; Eight years with Stanley Black on BBC Radio shows: Much Binding In The Marsh; The Goon Show; Ray's A Laugh; Life With The Lyons; With wife, presented to HRH Princess Anne; Played twice at Buckingham Palace; Sergeant i/c Station Band, RAF Wittering, Lincs. *Compositions:* At least 30 compositions (Peter Maurice, Music Coy, Keith Prowse, Bosworth). *Recordings:* Over 1000 with: Ambrose; Geraldo; Stanley Black; Geoff Love; Video: Don't Fuss, Mr Ambrose. *Publications:* Memoirs: Don't Fuss, Mr Ambrose. *Honours:* Guild of Freeman of the City of London; Hon. Citizen of New Orleans (USA). *Membership:* Musicians' Union (Hon); PRS; Academy of Songwriters and Authors; Hon. mem. of the Clarinet and Saxophone Society of Great Britain; Life Mem., Bomber Command Asscn; Associate Hon. Mem., Pathfinders Asscn. *Address:*

Billy Amstell, 40 Ebrington Rd, Kenton, Harrow, Middlesex HA3 0LT, England.

AMURO, Namie; b. 20 Sept. 1977, Naha City, Okinawa, Japan. Vocalist. m. Sam Maruyama, 1997, 1 s. *Education:* Okinawa Stage School. *Career:* Formed group, Super Monkeys, with four friends; Released single Mr USA, 1992; After brief time away from group, rejoined in 1994 to release other successful singles; Solo artiste, 1995–; Appeared in many commercials. *Recordings:* Albums: Solo: Sweet 19 Blues, 1996; Concentration 20, 1997; 181920, 1998; Genius 2000, 2000. Singles: with Super Monkeys: Mr USA, 1992; Paradise Train, 1994; Try Me, 1995; Solo: Body Feels Exit, 1995; Respect The Power Of Love; Toi Et Moi, 1999. *Address:* c/o Avex Trax, Room 3608-10, Windsor House, 311 Gloucester Rd, Causeway Bay, Hong Kong. *Website:* www.amuro.com.

AMYOT, Robert; b. 25 July 1953, Montréal, Canada. French Bagpipes. 2 d. *Education:* Traditional Singing French State Diploma. *Career:* Played with Jean Blanchard and Evelyne Girardon in Beau-Temps-Sur-La-Province; La Grande Bande de Cornemuse; Le Quintette deCornemuse; Major folk festivals around the world, St-Chartier. *Compositions:* Le Brandevin; Le Loriot de Baltimore; Le Harfang des Neiges; Marie Miville; L'Anniversaire. *Recordings:* Sur La Vignolon; Trappeur Courtois; Le Grand Festin; La Grande Bande de Cornemuse; Le Quintette de Cornemuse. *Publications:* Cornemuse; Souffles Infinis Souffles Continus, collection Moda, article, 1991. *Honours:* First Prize, Cornemuse in Anost, France, 1987; President, St-Chartier Jury, 1990–96. *Membership:* APMT, France. *Current Management:* Cie du Beau Temps, 20 Cours Suchet, 69002 Lyon, France. *Address:* Le Bourgeal Dessous, 74130 Brizon, France.

ANANDA PROJECT. See: BRANN, Chris.

ANASTACIA, (Anastacia Newkirk); b. 17 Sept. 1973, Chicago, USA. Vocalist; Songwriter. *Education:* Professional Children's School, Manhattan, graduate. *Career:* Cabaret singer father and musical theatre actress mother; Worked as a dancer on pop videos and TV prior to being discovered as vocalist on MTV talent show The Cut; Career developed in Europe prior to USA success; Performed alongside Michael Jackson at historic United We Stand benefit concert, 2001. *Compositions:* Boom, chosen as official song of World Cup, 2002. *Recordings:* Albums: Not That Kind, 2000; Freak of Nature, 2001; Singles: I'm Outta Love, Not That Kind, 2000; Cowboys and Kisses, Made For Lovin' You, Paid My Dues, 2001; One Day In Your Life, 2002. *Honours:* World Music Award, Best New International Artist, 2001; MTV Europe Music Award, Best Pop Act, 2001. *Current Management:* Lisa Braude, Braude Management, PO Box 7249, San Diego, CA 92167, USA. *Website:* www.anastacia.com.

ANCHEV, Emil; Vocalist. *Career:* Founder member, lead vocalist, Concurant, 1986; Numerous concerts, television and radio programmes, Bulgaria. *Recordings:* Rock For Peace, 1988; Rock Festival In Mitchurin, 1989; The Black Sheep (rock collection), 1992; Something Wet (best-selling album, Bulgaria), 1994; The Best Of Bulgarian Rock, 1995. *Honours:* First prizes: Top Rock Band, Youth Festival Vidin, 1989; Rock Ring, Sofia, 1990; Top Rock Composition: The Cavalry, 1991; Top Rock Singer, Bulgaria, 1994; Group of the Year, The Darik Radio Countdown, 1994. *Address:* 40 St Stambolov Blvd, 1202 Sofia, Bulgaria.

ANDERSEN, Arild; b. 27 Oct. 1945, Oslo, Norway. Jazz Musician (bass); Bandleader; Composer. *Education:* Studied music with Karel Netolicka and George Russell. *Career:* Touring musician with George Russell, Jan Garbarek, Karin Krog, Edward Vesala, 1966–73; Also worked with Don Cherry; Stan Getz; Sam Rivers; Paul Bley; Bandleader, own quartet, 1974; Member, Norwegian quintet Masquelero, 1983–. *Compositions include:* Sagn (series of works based on traditional folk songs), premiered at Vossajazz Festival, 1990. *Recordings:* Albums: Clouds In My Head, 1975; Shimri, 1976; Green Shading Into Blue, 1978; Lifelines, 1980; A Molde Concert, 1981; Sagn, 1990; Masquelero, 1983; Bande A Part, 1985; If You Look Far Enough (with Nana Vasconcelos, Ralph Towner), 1993; Kritin Lavransdatter, 1995; Hyperborean, 1997.

ANDERSEN, Torfinn Nergaard; b. Norway. Music Co-Exec. *Career:* Director, Groovy Management; Owner, Record label, Rec 90 (Norway); Manager for Butterfly Garden (Norway). *Membership:* FONO. *Current Management:* Groovy Management, PO Box 1291, 5001 Bergen, Norway.

ANDERSON, Beth; b. 3 Jan. 1950, Kentucky, USA. Composer, Musician (piano). m. Elliotte Rusty Harold. *Education:* BA, University of California; MFA, MA, Mills College. *Career:* Wrote music for, off off Broadway musicals: Nirvana Manor; Elizabeth Rex: Or The Well Bred Mother Goes To Camp; Fat Opera. *Compositions:* Minnesota Swale; Trio: Dream In 'D'; Net Work. *Recordings:* Belgian Tango; Revel. *Publications:* Beauty is Revolution; The Internet for Women In Music. *Honours:* National Endowment for the Arts; National Public Radio Satellite Program Development Fund Grant. *Membership:* New York Women Composers; International Alliance of Women in Music; Poets and Writers. *Address:* 135 Eastern Parkway, #4D, Brooklyn, NY 11238, USA.

ANDERSON, Bill (James William III); b. 1 Nov. 1937, Columbia, South Carolina, USA. Country vocalist; Songwriter; Musician (guitar, harmonica); Actor; Presenter. *Career:* Began career as sports writer; Later DJ in Commerce, Georgia; After early writing success, signed by Decca Records as a performer, 1958; Joined the Grand Ole Opry, 1961; US country and pop successes for five decades as both writer and performer; Written hits for artists including: Ivory Joe Hunter; Jerry Lee Lewis; Dean Martin; Ray Price; Collin Raye; Debbie Reynolds; Connie Smith; Porter Wagoner; Steve Wariner; Lawrence Welk; Kitty Wells; Faron Young; Ken Dodd; As artist, over 80 Billboard country chart singles, 1958–91; Movie appearances include: Forbidden Island, 1959; Gold Guitar, 1966; Las Vegas Hillbillies, 1966; Forty Acre Feud, 1968; From Nashville With Love, 1969; Hosted own TV show, 1966; Also US TV game shows: The Better Sex, 1977–78; Fandango, 1983–89; Host, Opry Backstage; Idiosyncratic monologues on record earned the nickname Whispering Bill. *Compositions include:* Cincinnati Ohio; City Lights; Eight By Ten; Face To The Wall; Five Little Fingers; Get A Little Dirt On Your Hands; Happy Birthday To Me; Happy State of Mind; I Can't Remember; I Don't Love You Anymore; I Get The Fever; I Love You Drops; I May Never Get To Heaven; I Missed Me; I Never Once Stopped Loving You; I've Enjoyed As Much of This As I Can Stand; If It's All The Same To You; Losing Your Love; Mama Sang A Song; My Life (Throw It Away If I Want To); Nobody But A Fool Would Love You; Once A Day; Peel Me A Nanner; Po' Folks; River Boat; Saginaw Michigan; Still; That's What It's Like To Be Lonesome; Then and Only Then; Tip of My Fingers; Two Teardrops; Walk Out Backwards; We All Missed You; When Two Worlds Collide; Wild Weekend; Wish You Were Here; You and Your Sweet Love. *Recordings include:* Mama Sang A Song, 1962; Still, 1963; I Get The Fever, 1966; For Loving You (with Jan Howard), 1967; My Life (Throw It Away If I Want To), 1969; Where Have All Our Heroes Gone, 1970; Always Remember, 1971; World Of Make Believe, 1973; Sometimes (with Mary Lou Turner), 1975; I Can't Wait Any Longer, 1978; Albums: I Love You Drops, 1966; Greatest Hits, 1967; For Loving You (with Jan Howard), 1968; My Life/But You Know I Love You, 1969; Sometimes (with Mary Lou Turner), 1976. *Publications:* I Hope You're Living As High On The Hog As The Pig You Turned Out To Be (anecdotes), 1983; Whispering Bill (autobiography), 1989. *Honours:* Nashville Songwriters Hall of Fame, 1975; Georgia Music Hall of Fame, 1985; Vocal Event of the Year, Too Country (with Brad Paisley, George Jones and Buck Owens), 2001; Country Music Hall of Fame, 2001. *Address:* c/o Sony/ATV Tree Music, 8 Music Sq. W, Nashville, TN 37203, USA.

ANDERSON, Billy (William John); b. 5 March 1946, Colinsburgh, Fife, Scotland. Musician (piano accordion); Radio Presenter; Tutor. m. Elizabeth W Hannah, 12 Aug. 1966, 3 s., 1 d. *Education:* Piano-accordion as a boy. *Career:* Composer; Arranger; Producer; Broadcast with BBC Radio, television, 1969–; Freelance presenter with Radio Tay, Dundee, 1984–; Tours: USA; Canada; United Arab Emirates; Oman; Brunei; North Malaysia; Germany; Netherlands; Italy; Australia. *Recordings:* Seven albums with Albany (own group); Sonas, 1999; Origins, 2002. *Publications:* 5 compositions published. *Membership:* Musicians' Union; PRS. *Address:* 4 Kingsloan Court, Largoward, Leven, Fife KY9 1JH, Scotland. *E-mail:* billy.anderson@ukonline.co.uk.

ANDERSON, Brett; b. 29 Sept. 1967, Haywards Heath, London, England. Vocalist; Songwriter. *Career:* Founder member: Geoff, 1985; Suave and Elegant, 1989; Suede, 1989–; Television appearances include: Top of the Pops, BBC1; BRIT Awards, Alexandra Palace, London, 1993; The Beat, ITV; Later With Jools Holland, BBC2; The Tonight Show, NBC Television; Concerts include: Phoenix Festival; Glastonbury Festival; Tours, Europe, America and Japan. *Recordings:* Albums: Suede (No. 1, UK), 1993; Dog Man Star, 1994; Coming Up, 1996; Sci-Fi Lullabies, 1997; Head Music, 1999; Sessions CD (fan club release), 2000; A New Morning, 2002. Singles: The Drowners, 1992; Metal Mickey, 1992; Animal Nitrate, 1993; So Young, 1993; Stay Together, 1994; We Are The Pigs, 1994; The Wild Ones, 1994; New Generation, 1995; Trash, 1996; Beautiful Ones, 1996; Saturday Night, 1997; Lazy, 1997; Filmstar, 1997; Electricity, 1999; She's In Fashion, 1999; Everything Will Flow, 1999; Can't Get Enough, 1999; Positivity, 2002; Obsessions, 2002; Contributor, Shipbuilding, to War Child charity album, 1995. *Honours:* Mercury Music Prize, 1993; Q Award, Best New Act, 1993. *Current Management:* Interceptor Enterprises, The Greenhouse, 34–38 Provost St, London N1 7NG, England. *Address:* c/o Sony Music Entertainment, European Regional Office, 10 Great Marlborough St, London W1F 7LP, England. *Website:* www.suede.net.

ANDERSON, Carleen; b. 10 May 1957, Houston, Texas, USA. Vocalist; Songwriter. 1 s. *Education:* Music Education Studies, University of Southern California; Graduate, Music Performance, Los Angeles City College. *Career:* Country and Western session singer, 1976–79; Joined Black Widow as lead singer, 1976–77; Joined Family Funkton, lead singer, 1978; Worked as bank teller and office clerk; Singer and Songwriter, Young Disciples, 1990–92; Solo work; Work with Paul Weller, Bryan Ferry, Doctor John; Joined Brand New Heavies, 1999. *Recordings:* Singles: Apparently Nothin' (with Young Disciples), 1991; Mama Said, 1993; Nervous Breakdown, True Spirit, 1994; Let It Last, 1995; Maybe I'm Amazed, Woman In Me, 1998; Apparently Nothing (with Brand New Heavies), 2000; Albums: True Spirit, 1994; Blessed Burden, 1998.

ANDERSON, Chris(topher William); b. 22 Sept. 1956, Los Angeles, California, USA. Musician (guitar); Vocalist; Songwriter. m. Sharon Ann Cooper, 11 May 1991, 1 s., 1 d. *Career:* Leader, own Chris Anderson Band; Tours with artists including: Allman Brothers; Stevie Ray Vaughan; Double Trouble; Lynyrd Skynyrd; Bad Company; Government Mule; Outlaws; Marshall Tucker; Charlie Daniels; Wet Willie; Concerts include: Radio City Music Hall; Television: Throw, Fox Television; Commercials: Bush Radio; Budweiser; Videos: Srascle, Outlaws. *Recordings:* Old Friend, Chris Anderson Band; Trouble On The Tracks, Double Trouble; Right On Time, Grinder Switch; Floyd Miles. *Honours:* Inducted into Rock and Roll Hall of Fame. *Membership:* AFTRA; AFofM. *Current Management:* Doc Field, Creative Action Music Group. *Address:* 865 Bellevue Rd, Suite E-12; Nashville, TN 37221, USA.

ANDERSON, Dave; b. 21 Nov. 1949, Essex, England. Musician (bass); Studio Owner; Record Co Owner; Record Prod; Engineer. 1 s, 2 d. *Career:* Worked with Arid, Bob Calvert, Edwyn Collins, Amon Düül II, David Gray, Groundhogs, Hawkwind, Nick Lowe, Ocean Colour Scene, The Sundays, Superstar, Space Ritual.net; Library Music for Chappell Music Publishers. *Recordings:* Albums with the above artists. *Membership:* PRS; MCPS; PPL. *Current Management:* Stephen Budd Management Ltd, 109b Regents Park Rd, Primrose Hill, London NW1 8UR, England. *Address:* Foel Studio, Llanfair Caeeinion, Powys SY21 0DS, Wales.

ANDERSON, Emma Victoria Jane; b. 10 June 1967, Wimbledon, London, England. Musician (guitar); Songwriter. *Education:* BA (Hons) Humanities, Ealing College of Higher Education, 1986–90. *Career:* Bass player, The Rover Girls, 1986–88; Lead guitarist, songwriter, Lush, 1988–96; Signed to 4AD Records; World-wide tours include rock festival tour Lollapalooza, 1992; Guitarist, Songwriter, Sing-Sing, 1998–. *Recordings:* Singles: with Lush: Mad Love (EP), 1990; Sweetness And Light, 1990; For Love, 1992; Single Girl, 1996; Ladykillers, 1996; 500 (Shake Baby Shake), 1996; with Sing-Sing: Feels Like Summer, 1998; I'll Be, 2000; Tegan, 2001; Albums: with Lush: Scar (mini album), 1989; Gala, 1990; Spooky, 1992; Split, 1994; Lovelife, 1996; Ciao! Best Of Lush, 2000; with Sing-Sing: The Joy Of Sing-Sing, 2001. *Membership:* PRS; Musicians' Union; PAMRA. *Current Management:* Ifan Thomas, 23 Management, 1308 Factory Pl., Studio 504, Los Angeles, CA 90013, USA. *E-mail:* ifan@23-studios.com.

ANDERSON, Ian; b. 26 July 1947, Weston-Super-Mare, England. Writer; Broadcaster; Musician (guitar, slide guitar). m. Hanitra Rasoanaivo, 2 May 1990, 1 step-d. *Career:* Solo musician, 1967–72; Member of duo Hot Vultures, 1972–79; English Country Blues Band, 1979–83; Tiger Moth, 1983–89; Editor of Folk Roots Magazine, 1979–; Radio presenter, BBC and ILR, 1984–. *Recordings:* 5 solo albums include: Stereo Death Breakdown, 1969; 3 albums with Hot Vultures include: Up The Line, 1979; 2 albums with English Country Blues Band, compiled as Unruly, 1993; 2 albums with Tiger Moth, compiled as Mothballs, 1995. *Publications:* Folk Roots Magazine. *Current Management:* Folk Music Services. *Address:* c/o Folk Music Services, PO Box 337, London N4 1TW, England.

ANDERSON, Ian Scott; b. 10 Aug. 1947, Dunfermline. Musician; Songwriter. m. Shona, 1 s., 1 d. *Career:* 30 years, 60m. albums, countless radio and television appearances. *Compositions include:* Living In The Past; Aqualung; Thick As A Brick. *Recordings:* Numerous including Living In The Past; Aqualung: Thick As A Brick; Minstrel In The Gallery; The Best Of Jethro Tull; Songs From The Wood; Heavy Horses; Celtic Experience. *Honours:* Grammy Award, 1988. *Membership:* PRS; Composers Guild. *Address:* Jethro Tull Production Ltd, PO Box 159, Witney, Oxon OX8 6JP, England.

ANDERSON, James Noel; b. 23 Dec. 1951, Butler, Pennsylvania, USA. Recording Engineer; Prod; Radio Consultant. m. Phoebe Ferguson, 10 Oct. 1982, 2 s. *Education:* BS, Music Education, Duquesne University, 1973; Postgraduate, 1974; Postgraduate, Eastman School of Music, 1976; Postgraduate, Audio Engineering, Berlin, 1978. *Career:* Audio engineer, radio stations, Pittsburgh, Washington, 1973–80; President, James Anderson Audio (radio consultant), New York, 1980; Radio programmes: Taylor Made Piano, with Billy Taylor, 1981; Co-producer, Segovia! (radio documentary), 1983 Television programme: Segovia At The White House, with Andres Segovia, 1980. *Recordings:* Albums as recording engineer: Live At Fat Tuesdays, Pepper Adams, 1983; Sweet And Lovely, James Moody, 1989; Uptown/ Downtown, McCoy Tyner, 1989. *Honours:* Peabody Award, Taylor-Made Piano, 1982; EBU Prix Futura Award, 1986. *Membership:* Audio Engineering Society; NARAS; Audio Independents in Radio.

ANDERSON, John, (John David Alexander); b. 13 Dec. 1954, Orlando, Florida, USA. Country vocalist; Songwriter; Musician (guitar, harmonica). *Career:* Formed bands the Weed Seeds and the Living End during teens; Moved to Nashville and sang with sister Donna, 1972; Staff writer for Al Gallico Music; First recorded for Ace of Hearts, 1974; Signed to Warner Bros Records, 1977; Over 50 country chart entries for Warner Bros, MCA, BNA and Mercury include: Black Sheep, co-written by film-maker Robert Altman; Swingin', biggest selling country single in Warner Bros history (1.4m.).

Compositions include: Swingin'; Goin' Down Hill; I Wish I Could've Been There. *Recordings:* Wild And Blue, 1982; Black Sheep, Swingin', 1983; Money In The Bank, 1993; Straight Tequila Night, 1991; Albums: Wild And Blue, 1982; All The People Are Talkin', 1983; Eye Of A Hurricane, 1984; Seminole Wind, 1992. *Honours:* CMA, Horizon Award, 1983; CMA, Single of the Year, Swingin', 1983. *Address:* c/o The Bobby Roberts Company Inc, 909 Meadowlark Lane, Goodlettsville, TN 37072, USA.

ANDERSON, Jon; b. 25 Oct. 1944, Accrington, Lancashire, England. Vocalist. *Career:* Member, The Warriors, late 1960s; Co-founder, UK progressive rock group Yes, 1968–80; 1991–; Duo with Vangelis as Jon and Vangelis, 1980–; Concerts include: Support to Cream, Royal Albert Hall, 1968; Support to Janis Joplin, Royal Albert Hall, 1969; Montreux Television Festival, 1969; Support to The Nice, Royal Festival Hall, 1970; Tours, UK and USA, 1970–; Reading Festival, 1975; Evening of Yes Music, US tour, 1989; Yesshows '91, Round The World In 80 Dates tour, 1991. *Recordings:* Albums: with Yes: Yes, 1969; Time And A Word, 1970; Fragile, 1971; Close To The Edge, 1972; Yessongs, 1973; Tales From The Topographic Oceans, 1973; Relayer, 1974; Yesterdays, 1975; Going For The One, 1977; Tormato, 1978; 90125, 1983; 9012 Live, The Solos, 1986; Union, 1991; Yesstory, 1991; Symphonic Music Of Yes, 1993; History Of The Future, 1993; Open Your Eyes, 1999; Ladder, 1999; with Jon and Vangelis: Short Stories, 1980; Jon And Vangelis, 1980; Private Collection, 1983; The Best Of Jon And Vangelis, 1984; Solo albums: Olias Of Sunhillow, 1976; Song Of Seven, 1980; Animation, 1982; Three Ships, 1985; Change We Must, 1994; The More You Know, 1998; Simply Christmas, 2001; with Anderson Bruford Wakeman Howe: Anderson Bruford Wakeman Howe, 1989; Contributor, Shine, Mike Oldfield; Legend, Tangerine Dream; Wintertime Is On, Whole World Band (proceeds to Down's Syndrome Association, Sickle Cell Society). Singles: with Yes include: Roundabout, 1972; Wondrous Stories, 1977; Owner Of A Lonely Heart (No. 1, USA), 1983; Leave It, 1984; with Vangelis: I Hear You Now, 1980; I'll Find My Way Home, 1982; Whatever You Believe, with Steve Harley, Mike Batt (charity single), 1988. *Honours:* Gold Ticket, Madison Square Garden, 1978; Grammy Award, Best Rock Instrumental Performance, Cinema, 1985. *Current Management:* Big Bear Management, 9 Hillgate St, London W8 7SP, England.

ANDERSON, Laurie P; b. 5 June 1947, Illinois, USA. Performance Artist; Musician (keyboards, violin). *Education:* MFA, Columbia University; BA, Barnard College. *Career:* Major performances: Stories From The Nerve Bible; Voices From The Beyond; Empty Places; Talk Normal; Natural History; United States; Films, videos: Carmen; Personal Service Announcements; Beautiful Red Dress; Talk Normal; Alive From Off Center; What You Mean We?; Language Is A Virus; Home of The Brave; This Is The Picture; Sharkey's Day; O Superman; Dear Reader; Puppet Motel (CD ROM), 1995. *Recordings include:* O Superman, 1981; Big Science, 1982; Mister Heartbreak, 1984; United States Live, 1985; Home Of The Brave, 1986; Strange Angels, 1989; Bright Red, 1994; The Ugly One With The Jewels And Other Stories, 1995; Live At Town Hall, New York City, 2002; Film scores: Swimming To Cambodia; Monster In A Box. *Publications:* Stories From The Nerve Bible, 1994; Empty Places; Postcard Book; United States; Words In Reverse. *Honours:* Distinguished Alumna Award, Columbia School of The Arts; Hon. Doctorates, Art Institute of Chicago, Philadelphia College of the Arts. *Current Management:* Original Artists, 853 Broadway, Suite 1901, New York, NY 10003, USA.

ANDERSON, Lynn Rene; b. 26 Sept. 1947, Grand Forks, North Dakota, USA. Country Vocalist. m. (1) Glenn Sutton, 1968, divorced; (2) Harold Stream III, divorced. *Career:* Former success as horse rider; Solo artiste, 1966–; Television appearances include: Lynn Anderson specials; Resident guest, Lawrence Welk Show, 1967–70; Grand Ole Opry; Ed Sullivan Show. *Recordings:* US Country No. 1 hit singles: Rose Garden; You're My Man; How Can I Unlove You?; Keep Me In Mind; What A Man My Man Is; Other hits include: If I Kiss You (Will You Go Away); That's A No No; Top Of The World; Rocky Top; Encore; Duets include: with Gary Morris: You're Welcome To Tonight; with Ed Bruce: Fool For Each Other; with Billy Joe Royal: Under The Boardwalk; Numerous albums include: Ride Ride Ride, 1967; With Love From Lynn, 1969; No Love At All, 1970; Cry, 1972; Singing My Song, 1973; Smile For Me, 1974; All The King's Horses, 1976; From The Inside, 1978; Lynn Anderson Is Back, 1983; What She Does Best, 1988; Greatest Hits, 1992; Cowboy's Sweetheart, 1993. *Honours:* Gold discs; Over 700 horse riding trophies. *Current Management:* Anders Productions. *Address:* 4925 Tyne Valley Blvd, Nashville, TN 37220, USA.

ANDERSON, Moira; b. 5 June 1940, Kirkintilloch, Scotland. Vocalist. *Career:* Singer, traditional Scottish folk music; Also interpretations of popular standards and light operatic works; Regular UK television appearances, especially religious programmes. *Recordings:* Numerous albums include: Moira Anderson's Scotland, 1970; This Is Moira Anderson, 1971; The Auld Scotch Songs, 1975; Someone Wonderful, 1978; Golden Memories, 1981; The Love Of God, 1986; A Land For All Seasons, 1988; 20 Scottish Favourites, 1990. *Honours:* O.B.E., Services to music industry. *Address:* International Artistes Ltd, Mezzanine Floor, 235 Regent St, London W1R 8AX, England.

ANDERSON, Roger Lee; b. 6 Jan. 1955, Peoria, Illinois, USA. Musician (Keyboards); Songwriter. m. Pegeen Conners, 10 June 1996. *Education:* Bradley University, Peoria, Illinois, two years. *Recordings:* Eargazm, album; Tumblin' Dice, cassette; Knight Crawler, CD. *Honours:* Best Pop Artist, Prairie Sun Midwest Readers' Poll, 1983; Best Keyboardist, Twin Cities Blues News Readers' Poll, 1997. *Membership:* Minnesota Music Movement; NARAS. *Current Management:* Artist Representation and Management. *Address:* 1257 Arcade St, St Paul, MN 55106, USA.

ANDERSON, Terry Randall; b. 25 Dec. 1956, Louisberg, North Carolina, USA. Songwriter; Musician (drums, guitar). m. Grace Brummett, 29 April 1989, 1 s. *Education:* 2 years college, Sandhills Community College, Southern Pines, North Carolina, USA. *Career:* Two European tours; Drums with: Don Dixon; Marti Jones. *Compositions:* Battleship Chains, recorded by Georgia Satellites; I Love You Period; Co-wrote 4 songs on Dan Baird's solo record. *Recordings:* Solo record on ESD (Minn, Minn). *Membership:* ASCAP. *Current Management:* Harry Simmons, Simmons Management. *Address:* 5214 Western Blvd, Raleigh, NC 27606, USA.

ANDERSSON, Göran Bror Benny; b. 16 Dec. 1946, Stockholm, Sweden. Composer; Musician (keyboards). m. (1) Frida Lyngstad, 1978, divorced 1981, (2) Mona Nörklit, Dec. 1981, 2 s., 1 d. *Career:* Songwriter with Björn Ulvæus, 1966–; Duo with Ulvæus as The Hootenanny Singers; Partner in production with Ulvæus at Polar Music, 1971; Mem., Swedish pop group, Abba, 1973–82; Winner, Eurovision Song Contest, 1974; World-wide tours; Concerts include: Royal Performance, Stockholm, 1976; Royal Albert Hall, London, 1977; UNICEF concert, New York, 1979; Wembley Arena, six sell-out performances, 1979; Reunion with Abba, Swedish TV's This Is Your Life, 1986; The Story of Abba (Channel 4), 1991; Film: Abba: The Movie, 1977; Continued writing and producing with Ulvæus, 1982–; Produced musical Mamma Mia!, with Andersson, West End, London, 1999–. *Compositions include:* Abba songs (with Ulvaeus); Musicals: Chess (with lyrics by Tim Rice), 1983; Mamma Mia! (with Ulvaeus), 1999; Composer, Kristina Från Duvemåla, musical based on Vilhelm Moberg's epic novels, Utvandrarna. *Recordings:* Albums: with Ulvaeus: Happiness, 1971; with Abba: Waterloo, 1974; Abba, 1976; Greatest Hits, 1976; Arrival, 1977; The Album, 1978; Voulez-Vous, 1979; Greatest Hits Vol. 2, 1979; Super Trouper, 1980; The Visitors, 1981; The Singles: The First Ten Years, 1982; Thank You For The Music, 1983; Absolute Abba, 1988; Abba Gold, 1992; More Abba Gold, 1993; Forever Gold, 1998; The Definitive Collection, 2001. Singles include: with Abba: Ring Ring, 1973; Waterloo (No. 1, UK), 1974; Mamma Mia (No. 1, UK), 1975; Dancing Queen (No. 1, UK and USA), 1976; Fernando (No. 1, UK), 1976; Money Money Money, 1976; Knowing Me Knowing You (No. 1, UK), 1977; The Name Of The Game (No. 1, UK), 1977; Take A Chance On Me (No. 1, UK), 1978; Summer Night City, 1978; Chiquitita, 1979; Does Your Mother Know?, 1979; Angel Eyes/Voulez-Vous, 1979; Gimme Gimme Gimme (A Man After Midnight), 1979; I Have A Dream, 1979; The Winner Takes It All (No. 1, UK), 1980; Super Trouper (No. 1, UK), 1980; On And On And On, 1981; Lay All Your Love On Me, 1981; One Of Us, 1981; When All Is Said And Done, 1982; Head Over Heels, 1982; The Day Before You Came, 1982; Under Attack, 1982; Thank You For The Music, 1983. *Honours:* with Abba: Gold discs; Best-selling group in history of popular music, Guinness Book of Records, 1979; World Music Award, Best Selling Swedish Artist, 1993; Ivor Novello Award, Special International Award (with Björn Ulvaeus), 2002. *Address:* Södra Brobänken 41A, 111 49 Stockholm, Sweden. *Website:* www.abbasite.com.

ANDERSSON, Mats Lennart; b. 2 Jan. 1964, Stockholm, Sweden. Drums. *Education:* Member, bob hund, 1991; More than 300 gigs in Scandinavia; Played at famous Roskilde, Lollipop, Ruisrock, Quartfestivalen and Hultsfred. *Compositions:* I Stället för Musik: Förvirring, 1996; Düsseldorf, 1996. *Recordings:* bob hund, 1993; Edvin Medvind, 7, 1994; I Stället för Musik: förvirring, 1996; Omslag: Martin Kann, 1996; Düsseldorf 3:53, 1996; Ett fall och en lösning, 1997; Nu är det väl revolution på gång?, 1998; Jag rear ut min själ! Allt skal bort!!!, 1998; Helgen V.48, 1999; Sover aldrig, 1999. *Honours:* Grammy, best live act, 1994; Grammy, best lyrics, 1996. *Membership:* STIM; SAMI. *Address:* c/o bob hunds förlag, Råsundavägen 150, 169 36 Solna, Sweden.

ANDRE, Peter; b. 1973, England. Vocalist. *Career:* Moved to Australia, aged 10; Solo artiste, 1990–; Australian tours as support act to Madonna and Bobby Brown; Collaborations: Coolio; Montell Jordan; Brian McKnight; Fugees. *Recordings:* Albums: Natural, 1996; Time, 1997; Peter Andre, 1999; The Very Best Of Peter Andre, 2002. Singles: Turn It Up, 1995; Mysterious Girl, 1995; Only One, 1996; Flava (No. 1, UK), 1996; I Feel You (No. 1, UK), 1996; Lonely, 1997; All About Us, 1997; Natural, 1997; All Night All Right (with Warren G.), 1998; Kiss The Girl, 1998. *Honours:* Winner, talent contest to win recording contract, Australia, 1990; Best Australian Pop Dance release, Aria Awards, 1993. *Address:* c/o Mushroom Records, 1 Shorrolds Rd, London SW6 7TR, England. *Website:* www.peterandre.com.

ANDREA, Mihallaq; b. 17 July 1949, Korce, Albania. Musician (Guitar, Organ); Composer. m. Irena Cironaku, 21 Nov. 1988, 1 s., 1 d. *Career:* Appearances at National Festivals, Kenget e Stines (The Songs of the Season); The Geologist; Appearance, Serenata Korcare Festival.

Compositions: Margarita; Serenata; Kitare E Dashur (My Dearly Beloved Guitar); Eja, Eja (Come, Come); Ne Kinema (At The Cinema). *Recordings:* The above; Fatkeqesia (The Misfortune). *Honours:* First Place, the music of the drama, The Geologist, 1984; First Place, Serenata Korcare Festival, 1999. *Membership:* Chair, Musical Society, Serenata Korcare. *Address:* Petro Saro, No. 9 Lagjja 3, Korce, Albania.

ANDREA, Nanni; b. 20 May 1963, Porretta Terme, Italy. Prod; Promoter. m. Cristina Baisi, 27 April 1998. 1 c. *Career:* Music Producer, mainly Soul, Funk and R&B; Recordings for many labels. *Address:* Via Giardini 81, 41026 Pavullo, Modena, Italy.

ANDREASSEN, Preben; b. 23 Aug. 1944, Ålborg, Denmark. Organist; Choir Dir. m., 2 s. *Education:* Royal Danish Music Academic, Copenhagen; Diploma Degree, Church Organ and Choir Direction, 1974. *Career:* Concerts in Germany, Sweden, Norway, Holland, Greece, USA Los Angeles and Denmark; Television: Danich Channe 1, Before Sunday, 1992, 1993, 1998; Youth Services, 1991, 1995; Christmas Services, 1993; Gospel Services, 1998, 2000. *Compositions:* Choir works at Publisher Edition EGTVED: Before Sunday, 1992; Christmas Songs, 1994; New Danish Hymnbook, 1994; Music for Meditation, 1998; Hymns in different collection. *Recordings:* Christmas Music, 1982; Before Sunday, MC, VCR; CD Life is Living, 1992; Gospel Music, 1997, 1998. *Publications:* Brondbyvester Church Organ History, 1987; Christmas Songs, edition EGTVED, 1994. *Honours:* Intl Choir Fest, Veldhoven, Holland, First Prize, 1989. *Membership:* Danich Organist Society; Danich Director Society. *Address:* Brondbyvester Church as Organist, Pianist, Choir Director and Composer, started in 1975.

ANDREWS, Bob 'Derwood'; b. 17 June 1959, Fulham, London, England. Musician (guitar); Songwriter. *Career:* Guitarist, punk band Generation X, 1976–79; Formed Empire, early 80s; Formed Westworld, 1986; Tours with Generation X; Westworld; Appeared on Top of the Pops, and reached No. 11, UK charts, with both bands; Formed Moondogg, 1994; Album due 1995. *Recordings:* Albums: with Generation X: Generation X; Valley Of The Dolls; Unreleased third album; with Westworld: Where The Action Is; Beatbox Rock 'N' Roll; with Empire: Expensive Sound; with Jimmy Pursey: Imagination Camouflage. *Membership:* PRS. *Current Management:* Moondogg. *Address:* PO Box 163, Cave Creek, AZ 85331, USA.

ANDREWS, Dame Julie, (Julia Wells); b. 1 Oct. 1935, Walton-on-Thames, Surrey, England. Vocalist; Actress. m. (1) Tony Walton, 10 May 1959, divorced 1968, 1 d., (2) Blake Edwards, 1969, 1 step-s., 1 step-d., 2 adopted d. *Education:* Voice lessons with Lillian Stiles-Allen. *Career:* As actress: Debut, Starlight Roof, London Hippodrome, 1947; Appeared: Royal Command Performance, 1948; Broadway production, The Boyfriend, New York, 1954; My Fair Lady, 1956–60; Camelot, 1960–62; Putting It Together, 1993; Victor, Victoria, 1995/96; Films: Mary Poppins, 1963; The Americanization of Emily, 1964; The Sound of Music, 1964; Hawaii, 1965; Torn Curtain, 1966; Thoroughly Modern Millie, 1966; Star!, 1967; Darling Lili, 1970; The Tamarind Seed, 1973; 10, 1979; Little Miss Marker, 1980; S.O.B., 1980; Victor/Victoria, 1981; The Man Who Loved Women, 1983; That's Life!, 1986; Duet For One, 1986; The Sound of Christmas (TV), 1987; Our Sons (TV), 1991; Relative Values, 1999; The Princess Diaries, 2001; Television: High Tor (debut), 1956; Host, The Julie Andrews Hour, 1972–73; Great Performances Live in Concert, 1990; Julie (comedy series), ABC Television, 1992. *Recordings:* Albums: A Christmas Treasure, 1968; The Secret Of Christmas, 1977; Love Me Tender, 1983; Broadway's Fair, 1984; Love Julie, 1989; Broadway: The Music Of Richard Rogers, 1994; Here I'll Stay, 1996; Nobody Sings It Better, 1996; with Carol Burnett: Julie And Carol At Carnegie Hall, 1962; At The Lincoln Center, 1989; Cast and film soundtracks: My Fair Lady (Broadway cast), 1956; Camelot (Broadway cast), 1961; Mary Poppins (film soundtrack), 1964; The Sound Of Music (film soundtrack), 1965; The King And I (studio cast), 1992. *Publications:* Mandy (as Julie Edwards), 1972; The Last of the Really Great Whangdoodles, 1974. *Honours:* Academy Award, Best Actress, 1964; Three Golden Globe Awards, 1964, 1965; Emmy Award, 1987; BAFTA Silver Mask, 1989; D.B.E.; Kennedy Center Honor, 2001. *Address:* Triad Artists, 10100 Santa Monica Blvd, 16th Floor, Los Angeles, CA 90067, USA. *Telephone:* (252) 716-7000.

ANDREWS, Patti; b. 16 Feb. 1920, Minnesota, Louisiana, USA. Vocalist. *Career:* Lead singer, vocal group The Andrews Sisters (with sisters Laverne and Maxene), 1938–53; Occasional reunions until Laverne's death, 1967; Solo artiste, 1953–; Film appearances include: Argentine Nights, 1940; Buck Privates; Hollywood Canteen, 1944; Stage appearances include: Broadway musical, Over Here, 1974; Currently singing with Glenn Miller Orchestra. *Recordings:* Hits include: with The Andrews Sisters: Bei Mir Bist Du Schon; Hold Tight, Hold Tight; Roll Out The Barrel; Boogie Woogie Bugle Boy; Says My Heart; Say Si Si; I'll Be With You At Apple Blossom Time; Three Little Sisters; Strip Polka; Collaborations with: Bing Crosby; Burl Ives; Les Paul; Ernest Tubbs; Carmen Miranda; Solo hit: I Can Dream, Can't I? (No. 1, USA), 1949; Albums include: with The Andrews Sisters: Curtain Call, 1956; By Popular Demand, 1957; Dancing Twenties, 1958; The Andrews Sisters Present, 1963; The Andrews Sisters Go Hawaiian, 1965; with Maxene

Andrews: Over Here (cast recording), 1974; Numerous compilations and greatest hits collections.

ANDRIES, Alexandru Braesti; b. 13 Oct. 1954, Brasov, Romania. Vocalist; Songwriter; Musician (electric guitar, acoustic guitar, keyboards, harmonica); Architect; Lecturer. *Education:* Graduate, Institute of Architecture, 1980; PhD in progress. *Career:* Guest, most Romanian jazz festivals including: Sibiu; Costinesti; Cluj; Constanta; Bucharest, 1979–; Tours throughout Romania; Concerts include: Palace Hall, Bucharest; Polivalenta Hall, Bucharest; Special guest, concerts at American Cultural Center, Bucharest; Guest, British Council, 1989; Appearances, most jazz and blues clubs in Romania: Club A, Bucharest; Constanta; Timisoara; Tirgu-Mures; Iasi; Special guest star, Golden Stag Festival, Brasov, Romania, with Kylie Minogue, Dionne Warwick, 1993; Guest, most Romanian radio stations: ProFM; Contact; Total; Independent television stations. *Recordings:* Albums: Interiors 1, 1984; Interiors 2, 1985; Country And Western Greatest Hits, 1986; Rock 'N' Roll, 1987; On Distance, 1988; Three Mirrors, 1989; Censored, 1990; Today, 1991; Appetite Rises Eating, 1992; My She-Neighbours 1, 2, 3, 1992; How Far Away, 1993; Nothing New On The Eastern Front, 1993; Slow Burning Down, 1994; Alexandru Andries, 1994; Hocus Pocus, 1995; White Album, 1996; Home, 1996; Ungra, 1996; Silence Of The Heart, 1996; In Concert, 1997; All By Myself, 1997; Bluntly, 1998; Secret Colours, 1998; Black And White, 1999; Texteriors, 1999; Songs For The Princess, 1999; Bad Weather, 2000; Live, 2001; Singles: Waiting For Maria, 1990; Wait 'Til Tomorrow, 1992; Dream With Angels, 1994; Watercolours, 1999; Bingo Romania, 2000; Videos: How Far Away, 1992; 21 Decembrie 1995/Teatrul Bulandra, 1996; In Concert, 1997; Blues Alive, The Most Beautiful Day, 2000; Live, 2001. Publicatons: Home Alone, short stories, 1992; Waiting For Maria, 1990; Happy Birthday Mr Dylan (Romanian translations from Bob Dylan's songs), 1991. *Honours:* Voted Best Singer/Songwriter, Vox, Pop, Rock (Romanian musical newspaper), 1990–; Golden Record Award, 1991; Best Singer, 1992; The Pro FM Contact Radio Awards, Best Singer, Songwriter, 1994. *Membership:* Romanian Union of Composers; Romanian Union of Writers; Romanian Union of Architects; The Mickey Mouse Club, 1993. *Current Management:* Aurel Mitran Management, Calea Victorei 48–50, Sc.B, Apt 73, Sector 1, Bucharest 70102, Romania. *Address:* Soseaua Stefan Cel Mare 26, Blvd 24A, Apt 26, Sector 2, Bucharest 71158, Romania.

ANDRST, Lubos; b. 26 July 1948, Prague, Czech Republic. Musician; Jazz and Blues Musician (guitar); Composer. 2 c. *Education:* Autodidact. *Career:* Musician with J. Stivín, E. Viklicky, R. Dasek, M. Svoboda, M. Misik, M. Prokop, among others; Founder, Energit, 1973; Founder, Lubos Andrst Blues Band, 1980; Founder, Lubos Andrst Group, 1993; Accompanied Paul Jones, Katy Webster, 1998, 2000; Special guest of B. B. King; Teaches course in jazz music, Conservatory, Prague. *Compositions:* Some 80 compositions incl. Capricornus, November, Ikebana, La Bodeguita Dez Medio, Imprints, Encountering, White Landscape, Follow Your Heart, Europe Blues, Wide-Open Door. *Recordings:* 35 albums incl.: Energit 1975; Piknik, 1978; Capricornus, 1981; Plus-Minus Blues, 1988; Imprints, 1992; L. Andrst With Friends, 1996; Acoustic Set, 1996; Blues Time, 1998; Man With A Guitar, 1999. *Publications:* Jazz Rock Blues, 1988; Redaction, 1995. *Current Management:* ARTA Music, Lublanska 57, 120 00 Prague 2, Czech Republic. *Telephone:* (222) 511858. *E-mail:* 2hp@arta.cz. *Address:* Matousova 6, 150 00 Prague 5, Czech Republic. *E-mail:* jazzblues@seznam.cz. *Website:* www.lubosandrst.cz.

ANDRUSZKOW, Lfe; b. 22 Sept. 1955, Copenhagen, Denmark. Vocalist; Composer; Musician (guitar, multi-instrumentalist). m., 2 c. *Education:* Private lessons in classical music on trumpet and cornet by conductor Jorgen Clausen and piano by Professor Anker Blyme; Private lessons in vocal by tutor Jens Christian Smith (Denmark), tutor Ian Adams (London), and by various tutors at Musicians' Institute, London. *Career:* Performed with pop-rock bands since 1979: The Law, Art Exist, The Act and Life; Performed on Ringe Festival, 1984 and Roskilde Festival, 1985. *Recordings:* Albums: Europe After The Rain, 1996; Promises, 1998. Singles: Aubaude Dolorose, 1985; Videos: Heaven Cries For No One, 1988; Dreams Without Reality, 1988; Tones Of An Outsider, 1989; Dancing In Burning Silhouettes, 1990; Promises, 1998; Scores: Sincerely (radio play), 1984; Images (musical), 1986; Film soundtrack: Vertical, 1995; Lyrics for Michael Westwood: Bromskij Garden, 1994; Live For It All, 1996; My Living Dawn, 1998. *Current Management:* Out of Eden Records, Sankt Pauls Gade 42, DK 1313 Copenhagen K, Denmark.

ANGELOPULO, Charles; b. 8 Dec. 1954, Pretoria, South Africa. Vocalist; Composer. m. 6 May 1978, 1 s., 1 d. *Career:* Title role, Jesus Christ Superstar, 1990; Lead singer: Web; Cafe Society; Blasé. *Compositions:* Over 65 recorded and released titles include: Helen of Troy, The Rock Opera; I Love Africa; Good Time Girl; When You Gonna Love Me; Nothing Anybody Can Say. *Honours:* Finalist, South African Music Awards, 1995. *Membership:* SAMRO; ASAMI. *Address:* 433 16th Ave, Rietfontein, Pretoria 0084, South Africa.

ANGER, Darol; b. 7 May 1953, Seattle, Washington, USA. Musician (violin, mandolin, guitar); Publisher; Author; Educator. *Education:* UC at Santa Cruz; Informal music study with David Grisman; David Baker. *Career:* Member, Montreux Band, 1984; Founding member, David Grisman Quintet (DGQ);

Played with artists including Stéphane Grappelli; Bela Fleck; Tony Rice; Mark O'Connor; Vassar Clements; Bill Keith; Richard Greene; Mike Marshall; Tony Trischka; Todd Phillips; Leader, Turtle Island String Quartet; Co-leader (with Mike Marshall), Psychograss; Co-founded the Anger/Marshall Band; Works with the Heritage Folk Music Project; Continues appearances with previous groups; Works as a producer and arranger for other artists; Featured soloist on film soundtracks, including Best Offer; A Shock To The System; Country; Annual seminars at US colleges; Instructor at Mark O'Connor Fiddle Camps. *Recordings include:* with Montreux Band: Sign Language; Let Them Say; Montreux Retrospective; with David Grisman: The David Grisman Quintet; Hot Dawg; Acoustic Christmas; with Turtle Island String Quartet: Turtle Island String Quartet; Metropolis; Skylife; On The Town; Spider Dreams; A Night In Tunisia, A Week In Detroit; By The Fireside; with Psychograss: Like Minds; Anger/Marshall and Psychograss; with Mike Marshall: The Duo; Chiaroscuro; with Barbara Higbie: Tideline; Live At Montreux; Solo albums include: Fiddlistics; Jazz Violin Celebration; Also appears on: Harvest, 1996; When No One's Around, 1997; Heritage, 1998; View From Here, 1998; Heritage, 1999; With A Little Luck, 1999; Featured on recordings by: Suzanne Vega; Thomas Dolby; Henry Kaiser; Bela Fleck; Tony Trischka; John Gorka. *Publications:* Grant Wood and Street Stuff; Songs For Turtle Island; The Turtle Island Workbook; Darol Anger Originals; Fiddle Tunes. *Membership:* NARAS; String Chair, International Asscn of Jazz Educators (IAJE); Sonneck Society. *Current Management:* BZ Productions, PO Box 19297, Oakland, CA 94619, USA.

ANGGUN, (Anggun Cipta Sasmi); b. 29 April 1974, Jakarta, Indonesia. Vocalist. m. Michel Georgea. *Career:* Daughter of singer and prod. Darto Singo; At seven years old recorded album of children's songs; At 12 years old recorded successful rock album, Dunia Aku Punya (World Of Mine); Extensive touring through Asia; Moved to France, 1994, worked with French musician and prod. Erick Benzi on album, Au Nom De La Lune, 1997; Lilith Fair tour, 1998; Appeared in Christmas concert, Vatican City, 2000. *Recordings:* Albums: Dunia Aku Punya, 1986; Anak Putih Abu Abu, 1991; Nocturno, 1992; Anggun C. Sasmi… Lah!!!, 1993; Yang Hilang, 1994; Au Nom De La Lune (aka Anggun), 1997; Snow On The Sahara, 1998; Desirs Contraires, 2000; Chrysalis, 2000. Singles: La Neige Au Sahara, 1997. *Address:* c/o Sony Music Europe, A&R, Ricardo Fernandez, 10 Great Marlborough St, London W1V 2LP, England. *Website:* www.anggun.com.

ANGUS, Colin; b. 24 Aug. 1961, Aberdeen, Scotland. Musician. *Education:* Aberdeen University. *Career:* Member: Alone Again Or; Founder member: The Shamen, 1986–. *Recordings:* Albums: Drop, 1987; In Gorbechev We Trust, 1989; Phorward, 1989; En-Tact, 1990; Progeny, 1991; Boss Drum, 1992; SOS, 1993; Axis Mutatis, 1995; Hempton Manor, 1996; UV, 1998; On Air, The BBC Sessions (compilation), 1998; Singles include: Christopher Mayhew Says, 1987; Jesus Loves Amerika, 1988; Pro Gen, 1990; Move Any Mountain (Pro Gen '91), 1991; L.S.I., 1992; Ebeneezer Goode (No. 1, UK), 1992; Boss Drum, 1992; Phorever People, 1992; Destination Eschaton, 1995; Hemp, 1996; Universal, 1998; U Nations, 1998. *Current Management:* Moksha Management, PO Box 102, London E15 2HH, England.

ANKA, Paul; b. 30 July 1941, Ottowa, Ontario, Canada. Vocalist; Composer. m. Marie Ann Alison de Zogheb, 16 Feb. 1963, 5 d. *Career:* Live and television appearances world-wide, 1956–; Actor, films: Girls Town; The Private Lives of Adam and Eve; Look In Any Window; The Longest Day. *Compositions include:* It Doesn't Matter Any More, for Buddy Holly, 1959; Co-writer (with Johnny Carson), Theme for Tonight Show, NBC Television, 1962–; My Way, for Frank Sinatra, 1969; She's A Lady, for Tom Jones, 1971. *Recordings:* Numerous singles include: Diana; I Love You Baby; You Are My Destiny; Crazy Love; (All Of A Sudden) My Heart Sings; Lonely Boy; Put Your Head On My Shoulder; It's Time To Cry; Puppy Love; My Home Town; Summer's Gone; The Story Of My Love; Tonight My Love Tonight; Dance On Little Girl; Love Me Warm And Tender; A Steel Guitar And A Glass Of Wine; Eso Beso (That Kiss!); Albums include: Paul Anka Sings His Big 15, 1960; Anka At The Copa, 1960; Young Alive And In Love!, 1962; Let's Sit This One Out, 1962; Golden Hits, 1963; Goodnight My Love, 1969; Life Goes On, 1969; Paul Anka, 1972; Jubilation, 1972; Paul Anka Gold, 1974; Feelings, 1975; Times Of Your Life, 1976; The Painter, 1976; The Music Man, 1977; Listen To Your Heart, 1978; Both Sides Of Love, 1978; Walk A Fine Line, 1983; Paul Anka Five Decades, 1992; A Body Of Work, 1998; Christmas With Paul Anka, 2000. *Honours:* Numerous BMI Awards, for Most Performed Songs and Over 1 Million Plays; 15 Gold discs; Inducted, Songwriters Hall of Fame, 1993. *Membership:* BMI. *Address:* c/o Paul Anka Productions, 10573 W Pico Blvd, Suite 159, Los Angeles, CA 90064, USA.

ANNIES, Nicholas Charles; b. 23 Jan. 1971, Kettering, England. Photographer; Graphic Artist. m. Lauren Kelly Behan, 4 Aug. 1996, 1 d. *Career:* Manager, record labels: Reality Recordings, c. 1990; ADI Records, 1991; Paradise Records, 1992; Co-manager, Village of Experimental Sound Studios, Cambridge; PA Engineer, including Caister Weekenders, 1987–91; Graphic Designer; Professional website designer; Managing Director: Once Click Solutions Ltd. *Recordings:* Singles: Armageddon (12), co-produced by Shades Of Rhythm, 1991; with 39 Orbits: 2 12 releases, 1993–94; Music For A Mono Nation, due 2002. *Publications:* Underworld, monthly magazine,

Peterborough City, 1990–93. *Membership:* Musicians' Union; Society of Amateur Artists; Media Records Italy.

ANNISETTE, (Annisette Hansen); b. 29 Aug. 1948, Denmark. Vocalist; Songwriter; Composer; Lyricist. m. Thomas Koppel, 1971, 2 d. *Career:* Lead Singer, The Savage Rose, 1967–; Numerous tours: Denmark; Europe; USA; Middle East; Newport Festival, 1969; Numerous international television appearances; Title role in her own musical drama with Thomas Koppel, Bella Vita, 1997; Vocal Soloist on the occasion of the 50th Anniversary of Denmark's Liberation from Nazi Army, 1995, in Symphony 2 by Thomas Koppel. *Compositions:* Several songs, Savage Rose; Lyrics for: Bella Vita, Thomas Koppel, 1993; Symphony No2, Thomas Koppel, 1995; Script for musical drama Bella Vita, 1996–97. *Recordings:* Savage Rose, 18 albums; Triumph Of Death (ballet), Thomas Koppel, Bella Vita, 1993; Black Angel, 1995. *Honours:* Several Gold, Platinum and Double Platinum Awards, 1968–97; Prize of Honour, Danish Songwriters; Union, 1995; Grammy, 1996. *Membership:* Danish Artist's Union; Danish Jazz, Beat and Folk Authors' Society; Authors' Union. *Current Management:* South Harbor Productions, Frederikshíj 114, 2450 Copenhagen SV, Denmark.

ANSELMO, Phil; b. USA. Rock Vocalist; Songwriter. *Career:* Lead vocalist, lyricist, US heavy rock group Pantera, 1986–; Also, lead vocalist with side-project Down, 1995–. *Recordings:* Albums with Pantera: Power Metal, 1988; Cowboys From Hell, 1990; A Vulgar Display Of Power, 1992; with Down: Nola, 1995; Singles with Pantera include: Cowboys From Hell; Mouth For War. *Current Management:* Concrete Management, 301 W 31st St, Suite 11-D, New York, NY 10019, USA.

ANSEMS, Tony; b. 9 March 1940, Tilburg, Netherlands. Musician (guitar); Songwriter. m. Rita, 8 April 1964, 3 s. *Education:* American College, Bryn Mawr, Pennsylvania. *Career:* Guitarist with Breakaway; Songwriter; President, Songwriters of Wisconsin. *Compositions:* with Danny Mack: Old Rockers Never Die. *Membership:* NSA; NAS; ASCAP. *Address:* PO Box 1027, Neenah, WI 54957–1027, USA.

ANSTICE-BROWN, Sam; b. 24 July 1963, Sherborne, Dorset, England. Musician (drums); Arranger. *Education:* BMus, Berklee College of Music, Boston, USA. *Career:* Tours, gigs with: Georgie Fame; Barbara Thompson; Mornington Lockett; Guy Barker; Jean Toussant; Iain Ballamy; Tony Wjan; John Etheridge; Bobby Wellins; Dick Morissey; Don Weller; Dave Newton; Alan Skidmore; Bobby Wellins. *Recordings:* Take It Or Leave It, Giladatzmon; Back To Square One, Organix. *Membership:* Musicians' Union. *Address:* 2 Church St, Kingsbury, Martock, TA12 6AU, England. *Website:* www.sambrown.co.uk.

ANT, Adam, (Stuart Leslie Goddard); b. 3 Nov. 1954, Marylebone, London, England. Vocalist; Songwriter; Actor. m. (1), (2), 1 c. *Career:* Founder, lead singer, Adam and the Ants, 1977–82; Early tours with Siouxsie and The Banshees; X-Ray Spex; Desolation Angels; The Slits; Regular British tours, 1979–; Solo artiste, 1982–86, 1992–; Appeared at Live Aid, Wembley Stadium, 1985; Numerous television and radio appearances; Member, all-star Peace Choir, 1991; Actor, 15 films, including World Gone Wild; Sunset Heat; Numerous television series including: Northern Exposure; The Equalizer. *Compositions:* Numerous songs with co-writer Marco Pirroni; Songs covered by: Elastica; Nine Inch Nails. *Recordings:* Albums: with Adam and the Ants: Dirk Wears White Sox, 1979; Kings Of The Wild Frontier, 1980; Prince Charming, 1981; Solo: Friend Or Foe, 1982; Strip, 1983; Vive Le Rock, 1985; Hits, 1986; Manners And Physique, 1990; Wonderful, 1995; Antbox (career box set), 2001; Singles include: Ant Music; Dog Eat Dog; Kings Of The Wild Frontier (No. 2, UK); Stand And Deliver (No. 1, UK); Prince Charming (No. 1, UK); Ant Rap (No. 3, UK); Goody Two Shoes (No. 1, UK); Puss In Boots; Apollo 9; featured tracks on film soundtracks including: Jubilee; Metropolis. *Honours:* Ivor Novello Award, Songwriters of Year, with Pirroni, 1982; BRIT Award, Best British Album, Kings Of The Wild Frontier, 1982. *Current Management:* UK/LA Management, Bugle House, 21a Noel St, London W1V 3PD, England. *Website:* www.adam-ant.net.

ANTHONY, Marc, (Marco Antonio Muniz); b. 16 Sept. 1968, New York, NY, USA. Vocalist; Songwriter. *Career:* Sang back-up on demos and TV commercials, aged 12; Started writing songs in high school including Boy I've Been Told, a hit for SaFire, 1988; Starred in the film East Side Story, 1988; Teamed up with composer of the film score, Louie Vega; Resulting album When The Night Is Over, 1990; Release featured many Latin musicians, awakening interest in salsa; Signed to Sony and released first solo album, Otra Nota, 1993; Starred in Paul Simon's Broadway musical The Capeman, 1998. *Recordings:* Otra Nota, 1993; Todo A Su Tiempo, 1995; Contra La Corriente, 1997; Marc Anthony, 1999; Libre, 2000. *Honours:* Latin Grammy Award, Song of the Year, Dimelo (I Need To Know), 2000. *Website:* www.marcanthony.net.

ANTHONY, Michael; b. 20 June 1955, Chicago, Illinois, USA. Musician (bass). *Career:* Member, Snake; Bass player, US rock group Van Halen, 1974–; Support tours with UFO; Santana; Black Sabbath; Regular US and world-wide tours; Major concerts: California Music Festival, 1979; US Festival, 1982; 1983; Monsters of Rock Festival, Castle Donington, 1984;

Monsters of Rock US tour (with Metallica, Scorpions), 1988; Texxas Jam, 1988; Co-host, radio show with Sammy Hagar, Radio Westwood One, 1992. *Recordings:* Albums: Van Halen, 1978; Van Halen II, 1979; Women And Children First, 1980; Fair Warning, 1981; Diver Down, 1982; 1984, 1984; 5150 (No. 1, USA), 1986; OU812 (No. 1, USA), 1988; For Unlawful Carnal Knowledge (No. 1, USA) 1991; Right Here Right Now, 1993; Balance, 1995; Van Halen III, 1998; Van Halen 1978–84 (retrospective box set), 2000; Singles include: You Really Got Me, 1978; Running With The Devil, 1978; Dance The Night Away, 1979; And The Cradle Will Rock, 1980; (Oh) Pretty Woman, 1981; Dancing In The Street, 1982; Jump (No. 1, USA), 1984; Panama, 1984; I'll Wait, 1984; Hot For Teacher, 1984; Why Can't This Be Love, 1986; Dreams, 1986; Love Walks In, 1986; When It's Love, 1988; Finish What Ya Started, 1988; Feels So Good, 1989; Poundcake, 1991; Top Of The World, 1991; Right Now, 1992; Appears on: Heart Of Stone, Cher, 1989; Trash, Alice Cooper, 1989; Fresh Outta P University; 1997; R, R Kelly, 1998; I Do, Blaque, 1999; Ain't Talkin' Bout Dub, Apollo Four Forty; Post-Mersh Vol. 3, Minutemen. *Honours:* Platinum discs; Grammy Award, Best Hard Rock Performance, 1992; MTV Music Video Awards, 1984, 1992; Band awarded Gold Ticket, Madison Square Garden, 1988; American Music Award, Favourite Album, 1992. *Current Management:* SRO Management Inc, 189 Carlton St, Toronto, ON M5A 2K7, Canada.

ANTILL, Danny Terrance; b. 8 Sept. 1959, Johannesburg, South Africa. Musician (keyboards, flute); Prod; Arranger. m. 6 Feb. 1982, 1 s., 2 d. *Education:* Eighth Grade classical piano, flute, Royal Academy of Music. *Career:* Toured with Stingray throughout South Africa; Appeared on national television 1, 2, 3; Solo piano albums released throughout Europe; Playlisted on German national radio. *Recordings:* Stingray; Danny Antill, 3 solo albums released throughout Europe; Amaduduzo, Siyabamukela; Amaduduzo, Exotic Voices And Rhythms; Producer, arranger, 17 Gold records; Composer, theme song for local blockbuster film Boetie Gaan Bordertoe. *Honours:* 17 Gold records; Top 5 3 years consecutively. *Membership:* SAMRO. *Current Management:* Brettian Productions. *Address:* Brettian Productions, PO Box 96395, Brixton 2019, Johannesburg, South Africa.

ANTOINE THE SWAN. See: **KIEDIS, Anthony.**

APACHE INDIAN, (Steven Kapoor); b. Birmingham, England. Vocalist. *Career:* Solo artiste, 1992–; International tours include Middle East, India, Japan. *Recordings:* Albums: No Reservations, 1992; Make Way For The Indian, 1995; Real People, 1998; Wild East, 1998; Best Of Apache Indian, 2000; Karma, 2002. Singles: Boom-Shack-A-Lack, 1993; Arranged Marriage; features on Wreck Shop, Wreckx 'N' Effect, 1993. *Address:* c/o Island Records, 22 St Peters Sq., London W6 9NW, England.

APELBAUM, Morris Moishe; b. 13 July 1957, Haifa, Israel. Prod; Engineer. m. 1 s. *Education:* BSc; BA; DipEd; Dip Admin. *Recordings:* Producer: Oliver Jones: Many Moods; Lights Of Burgundy; Tim Brady: Scenarios; Imaginary Guitars; Inventions; Double Variations. *Honours:* Juno Award. *Membership:* CARAS; SOCAN. *Current Management:* Silent Sound. *Address:* 3880 Clark St, Montréal, QC H2W 1W6, Canada.

APHEX TWIN, (Richard D. James), (Polygon Window, AFX, Caustic Window, Powerpill); b. 18 Aug. 1971, Republic of Ireland. Prod; Remixer; DJ. *Career:* Based in Cornwall, started producing tracks on own custom-made equipment; First recordings (including Analogue Bubblebath) released on Exeter's Mighty Force Records; Debut album on Belgium's R & S Records; Subsequent releases on Warp Records; Collaborations: Mike Paradinas; Luke Vibert; LFO; Remixed: Baby Ford; Saint Etienne; Beck; Wagon Christ. *Recordings:* Albums: Selected Ambient Works 85–92, 1993; Surfing On Sine Waves (as Polygon Window), 1993; Selected Ambient Works II, 1994; I Care Because You Do, 1995; Richard D James LP, 1996; Drukqs, 2001; Singles: Analogue Bubblebath, 1991; Digeridoo, 1992; Pac-Man (as Powerpill), 1992; Quoth (as Polygon Window), 1993; Gak (as Gak), 1994; Donkey Rhubarb, 1995; Ventolin EP, 1995; Come To Daddy, 1997; Windowlicker, 1999. *Address:* c/o Warp Records, Spectrum House, 32–34 Gordon House Rd, London NW5 1LP, England. *Website:* www.drukqs.net.

APHROHEAD. See: **FELIX DA HOUSECAT.**

APOLLO. See: **BUKEM, LTJ.**

APPLE, Fiona, (Fiona Apple Maggart); b. 13 Sept. 1977, New York, NY, USA. Vocalist. *Career:* Obtained recording contract; Numerous television appearances and live dates. *Recordings:* Singles: Criminal, 1998; Shadowboxer, 1998; Paper Bag, 1999; Fast As You Can, 2000; Albums: Tidal, 1996; When The Pawn Hits…, 2000. *Honours:* Best New Artist, MTV Video Music Awards, 1997.

APPLESEED. See: **SEATE, Tshepo.**

APPLETON, Nicole Marie; b. 7 Dec. 1974, Canada. Vocalist. *Career:* Mem., female vocal group, All Saints, 1995–2001; Feature film, Honest, released 2000; Mem., Appleton, with sister Natalie, 2001–. *Recordings:* Albums: with

All Saints: All Saints, 1997; Saints And Sinners, 2000; All Hits (compilation), 2001; with Appleton: Everything's Eventual, 2003. Singles: with All Saints: I Know Where It's At, 1997; Never Ever (No. 1, UK), 1997; Under The Bridge (No. 1, UK), 1998; Lady Marmalade (No. 1, UK), 1998; Bootie Call (No. 1, UK), 1998; War Of Nerves, 1998; Pure Shores (No. 1, UK), 2000; Black Coffee (No. 1, UK), 2000; All Hooked Up, 2001; with Appleton: Fantasy, 2002. *Publications:* Together (autobiography), 2002. *Honours:* BRIT Award, Best Single, Never Ever, 1998. *Current Management:* John Benson. *Address:* c/o Universal Music Group, 100 Universal City Plaza, Universal City, CA 91608, USA. *Website:* www.natalieandnicoleappleton.com.

APPLETON-HOWLETT, Natalie Jane; b. 14 May 1973, Toronto, Canada. Vocalist. *Career:* Mem., female vocal group, All Saints, 1995–2001; Feature film, Honest, released 2000; Mem., Appleton, with sister Nicole, 2001–. *Recordings:* Albums: with All Saints: All Saints, 1997; Saints And Sinners, 2000; All Hits (compilation), 2001; with Appleton: Everything's Eventual, 2003. Singles: with All Saints: I Know Where It's At, 1997; Never Ever (No. 1, UK), 1997; Under The Bridge (No. 1, UK), 1998; Lady Marmalade (No. 1, UK), 1998; Bootie Call (No. 1, UK), 1998; War Of Nerves, 1998; Pure Shores (No. 1, UK), 2000; Black Coffee (No. 1, UK), 2000; All Hooked Up, 2001; with Appleton: Fantasy, 2002. *Publications:* Together (autobiography), 2002. *Honours:* BRIT Award, Best Single, Never Ever, 1998. *Current Management:* John Benson. *Address:* c/o Universal Music Group, 100 Universal City Plaza, Universal City, CA 91608, USA. *Website:* www.natalieandnicoleappleton.com.

APRIL, Johnny; b. 27 March 1965, Enfield, Connecticut, USA. Musician (bass guitar). *Career:* Former cook and car repair man; Gained rock group experience with Maniax and Mostly Holy prior to appointment as bassist with Staind; First gig with Staind, 1995; Released self-financed debut album, 1996; Album sold 4000 copies; Discovered by Fred Durst, 1997; Signed to Flip/Elektra; Presented to rock cognoscenti at Limp Bizkit gold record party for Three Dollar Bill Y'All $, 1998; Major breakthrough with unscheduled smash US No. 1 radio hit Outside; Appeared on bill for Korn-founded Family Values tours, 1999 and 2001; Headlined MTV's Return Of The Rock tour, 2000. *Recordings:* Albums: Tormented, 1996; Dysfunction, 1999; Break The Cycle, 2001; Singles: Mudshovel, Just Go, 1999; Home, Outside, 2000; It's Been Awhile, Fade, 2001. *Honours:* Break The Cycle certified quadruple platinum by RIAA; It's Been Awhile topped Billboard Modern Rock Singles Chart for record-equalling 16 weeks; VH-1 Award, Your Song Kicked Ass But Was Played Too Damn Much prize, 2001. *Address:* c/o The Firm, Inc, 9100 Whilshire Blvd, Suite 400W, Beverly Hills, CA 90212, USA. *Website:* www.staind.com.

AQUAMANDA, (Amanda Greatorex); b. Matlock, Derbyshire, England. Vocalist; Musician (keyboards); Writer; Prod. *Education:* BA Hons, Fashion Textile Design (Fashion Designer), Leicester. *Career:* Vocalist, lyricist, Knights of The Occasional Table; Breathe track on compilation album Shamanarchy In The UK; Album and cover design, Knees Up Mother Earth, 1993; Session on John Peel, 1994; Now solo as Aquamanda; Runs record label Fairy Cake Universe with partner Dr Tony Hare. *Compositions:* Lyricist, vocalist, composer, Knees Up Mother Earth. *Recordings:* Album: Knights Of The Occasional Table, 1993; Solo single: Free Your Spirit (12 vinyl), 1995. *Membership:* PRS; MCPS; PPL; Musicians' Union. *Current Management:* Dr Tony Hare, FCU Records. *Address:* Fairy Cake Universe, PO Box LB621, London W1A 5EB, England.

ARAGAO, Monique Cavalcanti de; b. 10 Nov. 1960, Rio de Janeiro, Brazil. Composer; Musician (piano); Arranger. m. David Ganc, 1 s. *Education:* BA, Music, University of Rio de Janeiro; Piano with Undine de Mello and Linda Bustani and voice with Carol McDavit, Clarice Szajmbrum. *Career:* Television: Monique Aragao Special, TVE, 1990; Special, Dentro and Fora do Compasso, TVE, 1994; Guest appearance, New Year's Eve special, TV Globe, 1993; Radio: Radio Roquete Pinto; Radio Mec; Radio Journal do Brasil; Radio Nacional. *Recordings:* Solo: Monique Aragao, 1991; Canoas, 1993; Ventos do Brasil, 1995; Original soundtracks for theatre, films, ballet. *Publications:* Coral Hoje; Choral Pieces. *Honours:* Contests Alcina Navarro, 1970; Liddy Mignone, Lucia Branco, 1976; Sharp Prize, 1992. *Membership:* AMAR (RJ). *Current Management:* Zillion Artistic Productions.

ARATA, Tony; b. Savannah, GA, USA. Songwriter. m. Jaymi. *Education:* Journalism, Georgia Southern University. *Career:* Songs recorded by: Suzy Bogguss, Garth Brooks, Philip Claypool, Patricia Conroy, Helen Darling, Chris Gaines, Jim Glaser, Emmylou Harris, Sylvia Hutton, Michael James, Hal Ketchum, Dave Koz, Patty Loveless, Ruby Lovett, Delbert McClinton, Reba McIntire, Barra MacNeils, Oak Ridge Boys, Lee Roy Parnell, Ronna Reeves, Allen Reynolds, Dan Seals, David Slater, Jo-El Sonnier, Randy Travis, Tanya Tucker, Clay Walker, Don Williams, George Winston, Trisha Yearwood. *Recordings:* Albums: Solo: Songwriters On Beale Street; Changes; The Names Behind The Artist; Way Back When. *Compositions include:* Anonymous; Black And White And Blue; The Change; The Dance; Don't Forget Who You're Talking To; Don't Let Her See Me Fall; Dreaming With My Eyes Open; Everybody's Equal; Face To Face; Fairytale; Handful of Dust; Here I Am; I Don't Want To Go Out Wondering; I Hear A Call; I Used To Worry; I Wish Hearts Would Break; I've Been Down Too Long; I'll Be Your

Fool Tonight; I'm Holding My Own; In The Wink Of An Eye; Kickin' And Screamin'; Long Stretch Of Lonesome; Love Every Time; Love Is Stronger; The Man In The Mirror; Nothing But Love; One Of My Reasons; Part Of Me; Pretend; Right Where It Hurts; Same Old Story; Satisfied Mind; Slower; Someday I Will Lead The Parade; Stand By The Road; Standing By The River; Tell The Truth; That's The Way I Remember It; This Is My Prayer For You; What Else Can I Do; Why Ain't I Running; You Can't Get There From Here; You Were Gone. *Honours:* Acad. of Country Music, Song of the Year, for The Dance. *E-mail:* tony@tonyarata.com. *Website:* www.tonyarata.com.

ARCARI, Dave; b. 14 Aug. 1964, Glasgow, Scotland. Musician (guitar); Prod; Publicist. m. Anne, 5 Feb. 1993. *Education:* Fife College. *Career:* Ex-member, band Summerfield Blues; Numerous live sessions for BBC Radio; Television appearances, European Cable Shows; Member of the Radiotones. *Compositions:* Ain't Crying, 1993; 24 Hours, 1993; Uncle Jack, 1995; Journeytime is Over, 1997; You Oughta Know, 1997; Good Friend Blues, 1998; Gravel Road, 1998; Pomegranate Heart, 1998; Devil Got My Woman, 1998; Don't Stop, 1999; Close To The Edge, 2000; She's Gone, 2000; Wherever I Go, 2000; No More Mister Nice Guy, 2000; One Side Blind, 2000; Day Job, 2000; Bring My Baby Back, 2001; Born To Ride, 2002; Bunker, 2002. *Recordings:* with Summerfield Blues: Devil And The Freightman; Let's Scare The Posh People; Little Miss Behavin'; with Denim Elliots: Gooseberry Rain; with Radiotones: Whiskey'd Up. *Honours:* Scottish Blues Band of the Year, 1993. *Membership:* Musicians' Union; MMF; AIM. *Current Management:* Buzz Artist Management, Perth, Scotland. *Address:* 14 Corsiehill Rd, Perth, PH2 7BZ, Scotland.

ARCH, David; b. 25 Oct. 1962, Watford, England. Composer; Musician (keyboards); Arranger. m. Katherine, 2 Jan. 1991, 1 s., 1 d. *Education:* King James College, Henley; Guildhall School of Music, GGSM. *Career:* In NYJO whilst at college; MD for Dash, Hot Shoe Show (Wayne Sleep); Session keyboard player, many films, television, album projects; Started composing, joined Joe and Co, 1988; Now writing, mainly advertisements and television music. *Compositions:* GMTV logos; LWT logos; Numerous commercials. *Recordings:* Played on soundtracks for Notting Hill, Return Of The Jedi, The Avengers, An Ideal Husband, Goldeneye, The Saint. *Membership:* PRS; MCPS; Academy of Composers and Songwriters. *Current Management:* Joe and Co. *Address:* Denholm House, Pinner Hill, Pinner, Middlesex HAS 3XX, England.

ARCHER, Gem; Musician (guitar); Vocalist. *Career:* Singer and guitarist, Heavy Stereo; Numerous tours; Joined Oasis as guitarist, 1999; Concert, Finsbury Park, London, 2002. *Recordings:* Albums: with Heavy Stereo: Deja Voodoo; with Oasis: Familiar To Millions (Live), 2001; Heathen Chemistry, 2002. Singles: with Heavy Stereo: Sleep Freak, 1995; Mouse In A Hole, 1996; Smiler, 1996; with Oasis: Stop Crying Your Heart Out, 2002; Little By Little/She Is Love, 2002; The Hindu Times, 2002. *Honours:* NME Awards, Best UK Band, Artist of the Year, 2003. *Current Management:* Ignition Management, 54 Linhope St, London NW1 6HL, England. *Website:* www.oasisnet.com.

ARCHER, Martin Walker; b. 9 March 1957, Sheffield, England. Musician (saxophone, electronics, composer). *Education:* Law degree, Nottingham University, 1978. *Career:* Leader, Composer, Hornweb, 1983–93; Current member, Transient v Resident, ASK, Closed Order; Owner of Discus Record Label. *Recordings:* Albums: with Hornweb Saxophone Quartet: Kinesis, 1986; Sixteen, 1987; Universe Works, 1989; Solo recordings: Wild Pathway Favourites, 1988; Ghost Lily Cascade, 1994; 88 Enemies, 1998; Winter Pilgrim Arriving, 2000; With Transient v Resident: Electrical Shroud, 1995; Dharma Day, 1998; WKCR, 1999; Medulla, 1999; With Simon H Fell: Pure Water Construction, 1998; with Geraldine Monk: Angel High Wires, 2001; Compiler Of The Network miniatures series: Vol. I, 1994; Vol. II, 1995; The Music is Silent, 1996; Sound Gallery, 1997. *Honours:* Wire Magazine World Top 25 album, Wild Pathway Favourites, 1988. *Membership:* Sonic Arts Network; Society for Promotion of New Music. *Current Management:* Discus. *Address:* Discus, PO Box 658, Sheffield S10 3YR, England.

ARCHER, Tasmin Angela; b. 3 Aug. 1963, Bradford, England. Vocalist; Songwriter. *Career:* Solo artiste, 1992–; Tours of USA, United Kingdom, Europe. *Recordings:* Singles: Sleeping Satellite (No. 1, UK), 1992; In Your Care; Lords Of The New Church; Arriene; Shipbuilding; One More Goodnight With The Boys; Albums: Great Expectations, 1992; Bloom, 1995; Premium Gold Collection (compilation), 2000. *Honours:* BRIT Award, Best Newcomer, 1993. *Membership:* Musicians' Union. *Current Management:* Ian McAndrew, Wildlife Entertainment. *Address:* 21 Heathmans Rd, Parsons Green, London SW6 4TJ, England.

ARDEN-GRIFFITH, Paul; b. 18 Jan. 1952, Stockport, England. Opera, Music-Theatre, Concert, Cabaret Vocalist (tenor). *Education:* Royal Manchester College of Music; Cantica Voice Studio. *Career:* Concert, theatre singer, 1971–; Opera singer, 1973–; Major operas include: Midsummer Night's Dream; The Rake's Progress; Of Mice and Men; Carmina Burana; The Barber of Seville; Music, theatre performances include: The Merry Widow; Phantom of The Opera; The Legendary Lanza; Babes In The Wood; Gilbert and Sullivan to Lloyd Webber: The Great British Musicals; German production of

Sunset Boulevard; Die Fledermaus; Music Theatre: That Old Minstrel Magic; Concerts, cabarets include: London: Dorchester Hotel; Hyde Park Intercontinental; Picadilly Theatre; The Belfry Club; Savoy Hotel; Tramshed; Theatre Royal Drury Lane; The Limelight Club; Internationally: Wexford (Eire); Hong Kong; Sydney; Singapore; Palm Springs (California); Phoenix (AZ); Television appearances include: Wozzeck; A Christmas Carol; The Cleopatras; The Comic Strip; The Bill; Pebble Mill At One; Save The Children Christmas Special. *Recordings:* Paul Arden Griffith, The Song Is You, 1986; Phantom Of The Opera (original cast album), 1987; An Evening With Alan Jay Lerner, 1987; Minstrel Magic (Black and White Minstrel cast album), 1993; A Minstrel On Broadway, 1994; Encore!, Paul Arden-Griffith In Concert, 1995; The Classic Collection, 1995; Accolade!, 1996; Video: On Stage At The Hackney Empire, 1989. *Honours:* Gwilym Gwalchmai Jones Scholarship For Singing, 1974. *Membership:* British Actors Equity Asscn; Musicians' Union; Barezzi Theatre School, president; Concert Artistes' Asscn (CAA). *Address:* c/o Ken Spencer Personal Management, 138 Sandy Hill Rd, London SE18 7BA, England.

ARENA, Tina; b. 1 Sept. 1967, Melbourne, Australia. Vocalist. *Career:* Former member, Young Talent Time, Australia; Other performances include: Nine, 1987; Soul Dynamite, 1989; Joseph and His Amazing Technicolour Dreamcoat, 1992. *Recordings:* Albums: Tiny Tina, 1977; Strong As Steel, 1990; Don't Ask, 1995; In Deep, 1997; Singles: Chains, 1995; Heaven Help My Heart, 1995; Show Me Heaven, 1995; Sorrento Moon (I Remember), 1996; Burn, 1997; If I Didn't Love You, 1997; Now I Can Dance, 1997; I Want To Know What Love Is, 1998; If I Was A River, 1998; Whistle Down The Wind, 1998; I Want To Spend My Lifetime Loving You, 1998; Live For The One I Love, 2000. *Honours:* Performer and Rock Performer of the Year MO Awards, 1996; 1995 Aria Best Pop Release, Chains, 1995 Aria Song the Year, Chains; Aria Female Artist of the Year, 1995; Aria Album of the Year, Don't Ask, 1995; Variety Club Entertainer of the Year, 1995; Advance Australia Foundation Award, 1996; APRA Song of the Year, Wasn't It Good, 1996; World Music Award for World's Highest Selling Female Artist, Highest Selling Female Artist in Australian History, 1996. *Address:* c/o RCM International, Lennox House, 229 Lennox St, Richmond, Vic 3121, Australia.

ARGENT, Rod; b. 14 June 1945, St Albans, Hertfordshire, England. Musician (keyboards); Vocalist. *Career:* Founder, The Zombies, 1963–69; Founder, own group Argent, 1970s; Also solo artiste and record producer; Appearances include: New York, 1964; British tour, with Dusty Springfield, The Searchers, 1965; Caravan of Stars US tour, 1965; Production partnerships with Chris White and Peter Van Hooke, 1980s. *Recordings:* Albums: with the Zombies: The Zombies, 1965; Begin Here, 1965; Odyssey And Oracle, 1967; with Argent: Argent, 1970; Ring Of Hands, 1971; All Together Now, 1972; In Deep, 1973; Nexus, 1974; Encore, 1974; Circus, 1975; Counterpoints, 1975; Anthology, 1976; Hold Your Head Up, 1978; Rock Giants, 1982; Music From The Spheres, 1991; Solo: Moving Home, 1978; Ghosts, 1982; Shadowshow, 1985; Red House, 1988; Rescue, 1991; with Nanci Griffith: Late Night Grande Hotel, 1991; MCA Years, 1993; also: Into The West, 1993; Painted Desert Serenade, 1993; Sun Ain't Gonna Shine Anymore, 1994; Healing Bones, 1994; On Nights Like This, 1996; Martyrs And Madmen, 1997; Dick Bartley Presents.., 1998; Salty Heaven, 1999; Singles include: with the Zombies: She's Not There (No. 2, USA), 1964; Tell Her No, 1965; with Argent: Hold Your Head Up, 1971; God Gave Rock And Roll To You, 1973; with Colin Blunstone: Sanctuary, 2001; Co-producer, debut album by Tanita Tikaram, 1988.

ARGÜELLES, Julian; b. 28 Jan. 1966. Musician (saxophones, various woodwinds); Composer. *Education:* Trinity College of Music. *Career:* Various youth bands; Loose Tubes, including a Proms performance; Mike Gibbs Orchestra; Kenny Wheeler Big Band; Chris McGregor's Brotherhood of Breath; The Very Big Carla Bley Band; Hermeto Pascoal; Django Bates' Delightful Precipice; Performed Concerto for piano, percussion and saxophone, by Mario Lagina. *Recordings:* with Julian Argüelles Quartet: Phaedrus; Home Truths; Scapes, 1996; Skull View, 1997; Escapade, 1999; Various recordings with: Steve Argüelles, Django Bates, Kenny Wheeler, Mike Gibbs, Mario Laginha. *Honours:* Pat Smyth Award; Various BBC Awards; Commission by BBC Radio 3 for Octet; Jazz Composers Alliance, Julius Hemphill Award (USA), 1999. *Address:* 12B Balchier Rd, London SE22 0QN, England.

ARMAOU, Lyndsay Gael Christian; b. 18 Dec. 1980, Athens, Greece. Vocalist; Musician (piano, guitar). *Career:* Member, B*Witched; Numerous tours and television appearances; Several hit singles. *Recordings:* Singles: C'est La Vie, 1998; Rollercoaster, 1998; To You I Belong, 1998; Blame It On The Weatherman, 1998; Jesse Hold On, 1999; Albums: B*Witched, 1998; Awake And Breathe, 1999.

ARMATAGE, John Sinclair; b. 5 Aug. 1929, Newcastle Upon Tyne, England. Musician (drums). m. Ann Johnston, 9 May 1975. *Career:* Member, Wally Fawkes Band; Bruce Turner Jump Band; Alan Elsdon Band; Pete Allen Band; Terry Lightfoot Band; Tours with Don Byas; Ben Webster; Earl Hines; Red Allen; Pee Wee Russell; Films: Living Jazz; Plenty; Television and radio appearances. *Recordings:* Albums with: Bruce Turner; Alan Elsdon; Bud Freeman; Terry Lightfoot. *Current Management:* Ann Armatage. *Address:* 1 Keable Rd, Wrecclesham, Farnham, Surrey GU10 4PW, England.

ARMATRADING, Joan; b. 9 Dec. 1950, Basseterre, St Kitts. Vocalist; Songwriter; Musician (guitar). *Career:* Songwriting, performing partnership, with Pam Nestor, 1969–73; Solo artiste, 1973–; Appearances include: Regular international tours; Concerts include: Prince's Trust Gala, Wembley Arena, 1986; Nelson Mandela's 70th Birthday Tribute, Wembley Stadium, 1988; Numerous world tours, 1973–96. *Compositions include:* Down To Zero; Willow, 1977. *Recordings:* Singles: Love And Affection, 1976; Rosie, 1980; Me Myself I, 1980; All The Way From America, 1980; I'm Lucky, 1981; Drop The Pilot, 1983; Perfect Day, 1997; Albums include: Whatever's For Us, 1973; Joan Armatrading, 1976; Show Some Emotion, 1977; Stepping Out, 1979; Me Myself I, 1980; Walk Under Ladders, 1981; The Key, 1983; Track Record, 1983; The Shouting Stage, 1988; The Very Best Of…, 1991; What's Inside, 1995; Living For You; Greatest Hits, 1996; Love And Affection, 1997; 20th Century Masters, The Millennium Edition (compilation), 2000; The Collection (compilation), 2001; Also appears on: Listen To The Music: 70s Females, 1996; Carols Of Christmas Vol. 2, 1997; Prince's Trust 10th Anniversary Birthday, 1997; Film soundtrack, The Wild Geese, 1978. *Honours:* BASCA Ivor Novello Award for Outstanding Contemporary Collection, 1996. *Address:* c/o F Winter and Co, Ramillies House, 2 Ramillies St, London W1V 1DF, England.

ARMSTRONG, Billie Joe; b. 17 Feb. 1972, San Pablo, CA, USA. Vocalist; Musician (guitar). m. Adrienne Nesser, 1994, 2 s. *Career:* Founding mem., Sweet Children, renamed Green Day, 1989–; Numerous tours and television appearances; Side projects, Pinhead Gunpowder and Screeching Weasel; Gained major label deal; Provided track for soundtrack to film Godzilla; Appeared in cartoon King of the Hill as The Stubborn Stains. *Recordings:* Albums: 39/Smooth, 1990; Kerplunk, 1991; Dookie, 1994; Insomniac, 1994; Nimrod, 1997; Foot in Mouth, 1998; Warning, 2000; International Superhits (compilation), 2001; Shenanigans, 2002. Singles: Sweet Children (EP), 1987; 1,000 Hours (EP), 1989; Slappy (EP), 1990; Live Tracks (EP), 1994; Welcome To Paradise, 1994; Longview, 1994; Basket Case, 1994; When I Come Around, 1994; Geek Stink Breath, 1995; Stuck With Me, 1995; Bowling Bowling Bowling Parking Parking (EP), 1996; Foot In Mouth (EP), 1996; Brain Stew/ Jaded, 1996; Hitchin' A Ride, 1997; Time Of Your Life, 1997; Redundant #1, #2, 1998; Minority, 2000; Warning, 2001; Waiting, 2001. *Address:* c/o Reprise Records, Warner Bros Records Inc, 3300 Warner Blvd, Burbank, CA 91505, USA. *Website:* www.greenday.com.

ARMSTRONG, Craig; b. 1959, Shettleston, Scotland. Composer. *Education:* Composition and Piano, Royal Acad. of Music, 1981. *Career:* Resident student composer, London Contemporary Dance Theatre, 1980; Music and dance specialist, Strathclyde Council, 1982; Founder, Performance music, theatre and dance group, 1988; Former mem., Hipsway, The Big Dish, The Kindness of Strangers, Texas; Worked with Björk, Evan Dando, Massive Attack, Madonna, McAlmont, Luciano Pavarotti, Tina Turner, U2. *Recordings:* Albums: Hope (with others), 1993; The Space Between Us, 1998; As If To Nothing, 2002. Singles: Wake Up In New York, 2002. *Compositions:* for film: Daddy's Gone, 1994; Close, 1995; Fridge, 1995; A Good Day for the Bad Guys, 1995; Romeo and Juliet, 1996; Romeo and Juliet Vol. II, 1996; Orphans, 1997; Best Laid Plans, 1998; Plunkett & Macleane, 1998; One Day in September (documentary), 1999; The Bone Collector, 1999; Moulin Rouge, 2000; Kiss of the Dragon, 2001; The Quiet American, 2002. *Contributions to:* Mission Impossible, Goldeneye, Batman Forever, 1995–96; for television: Encounters (BBC2), 1991; Tartan Shorts (STV), 1994; London Bridge (Carlton), 1995; Classical music: 7 Stations, 1985; String Quartet, 1988; Crow, 1988; Losing Alec, 1988; score to Macbeth (Tron Theatre), 1993; score to The Broken Heart (RSC, Barbican), 1994; If Time Must Pass, 1999; When Morning Turns To Light, 2000; My Grandmother's Love Letters, 2000; Visconti, 2001. *Honours:* GLAA Young Jazz Musician of the Year, 1980; Ivor Novello Award, for Romeo and Juliet, 1996; Anthony Asquith Award, for Romeo and Juliet, 1996; BAFTA Award, for Romeo and Juliet, 1996; ASCAP Award, for The Bone Collector, 1999; Golden Globe, Best Original Music, for Moulin Rouge, 2001; World Soundtrack Award, Discovery of the Year, 2001; IF Award, for Moulin Rouge, 2001; American Film Institute Award, Composer of the Year, 2001. *Address:* c/o Melankolic Records, Astralwerks Records, 104 W 29th St, Fourth Floor, New York, NY 10001, USA. *Website:* www.craigarmstrong.com.

ARMSTRONG, Gerry; b. 28 Oct. 1929, Detroit, Michigan, USA. Folk Vocalist. m. George D Armstrong, 24 April 1954, (deceased 1993), 2 d. *Career:* I Come For To Sing, weekly programme with Studs Terkel, Big Bill Broonzy and others, 1953–; Folk clubs, festivals, churches, schools, radio and television, films, 1960s–70s; Sometimes play with 3 generations of Armstrong family on stage together, 1990s. *Recordings:* Simple Gifts, Folkways (now Smithsonian); Wheel Of The Year, Flying Fish (now Rounder); Golden Ring; Five Days Singing, Vols 1 and 2 (Folk-legacy); My Singing Bird (tape); Once Upon A Time… (tape of stories); Music in My Mother's House, CD. *Publications:* 3 children's books: The Magic Bagpipe; The Boat On The Hill; The Fairy Thorn; Many stories in school readers, Cricket magazine. *Membership:* Old Town School of Folk Music; The Aural Tradition; Sacred Harp Singers. *Address:* 1535 Lake Ave, Wilmette, IL 60091–1637, USA.

ARMSTRONG, Roland. See: **ROLLO.**

ARMSTRONG, Tim (Timothy Lockwood); b. 1966. Vocalist; Musician (guitar). m. Brody, March 1998. *Career:* Member, Operation Ivy; Joined Downfall; Started Rancid, with Matt Freeman; Numerous live shows; Started own record label, Hellcat Records, 1996. *Recordings:* Singles: Rancid, 1993; Radio, Radio, Radio, 1994; Roots Radicals, 1995; Time Bomb, 1995; Ruby Soho, 1996; Bloodclot, 1998; Hooligans, 1998; Brad Logan, 1998; Albums: Rancid, 1993; Let's Go, 1994; And Out Come The Wolves, 1995; Life Won't Wait, 1998.

ARMSTRONG, Timothy Paul; b. 10 Feb. 1961, Birmingham, England. Vocalist; Songwriter. 2 s., 1 d. *Education:* Two years piano, SC Music. *Career:* Member, band The Politicians, 1981–86; Appearances: Telethons, 1981–85; Shazam Television Special, 1985; NZ Today, 1992–93. *Recordings:* Singles: Down In Baghdad, 1983; Energy, 1985; Christmas Day/Photograph, 1986; Albums: Relationships, 1992; Breaking Hearts, 1993; Wondering Why, 1995. *Honours:* Waikato Rock Awards: Best Male Vocalist, Best Recorded Work. *Current Management:* Tim Armstrong. *Address:* 11 Beatrice Pl., Hamilton, New Zealand.

ARNESEN, Dag S; b. 3 May 1950, Bergen, Norway. Musician (piano); Composer. m. Wenche Gausdal, 17 Oct. 1986. *Education:* Teacher training (Music); Classical piano, Music Conservatory, Bergen. *Career:* Norwegian television (NRV) appearances: with own group: Ny Bris; with project for Vossa Jazz, 8 piece band includes Elvin Jones, drums, Jon Surman, saxophone, Palle Danielson, bass; with Joe Henderson, Woody Shaw Quintet. *Recordings:* Albums: Ny Bris, 1982; Renascent, 1984; The Day After, 1990; Photographs, 1992; Movin', 1994; Wandering Around Grieg, 1996; Inner Lines, 1998. *Honours:* The Vossa Jazz Prize, 1992; The Grieg Prize, 1994. *Membership:* FNJ; NOPA; GRAMART. *Address:* Gutenbergs V6 18, 5035 B6 Sandviken, Norway.

ARNOLD, Cheryl Christine; b. 23 April 1951, Seattle, Washington, USA. Country Vocalist. m. 23 June 1979, Michael Stipek, 3 s. (triplets). *Education:* Washington University, 1970–73. *Career:* Country singer, 1980–; Support act for country artistes including: Lorrie Morgan, 1982; Hoyt Axton, 1984; Loretta Lynn, 1984; Ricky Nelson, 1985; Johnny Cash, 1988; Reba McEntire, 1989; Glen Campbell, 1990. *Membership:* ACM; CMA.

ARNOLD, David; b. 1962, Luton, England. Composer. *Compositions:* The Young Americans, 1993; Stargate, 1994; Last of the Dogmen, 1995; Independence Day, 1996; Stargate SG-1 (TV theme), 1997; The Visitor (TV theme), 1997; A Life Less Ordinary, 1997; Tomorrow Never Dies, 1997; Godzilla, 1998; Wing Commander (theme only), 1999; The World is Not Enough, 1999; Randall & Hopkirk (Deceased) (TV), 2000; Shaft, 2000; Baby Boy, 2001; The Musketeer, 2002. *Honours:* Grammy Award, for Independence Day, 1996. *Current Management:* Blue Focus Management, 15233 Ventura Blvd, Suite 200, Sherman Oaks, CA 91403, USA.

ARNOLD, David Michael; b. 21 April 1958, Maidstone, Kent, England. Vocalist; Composer. 1 s. *Education:* Technical School; Hackney and Hastings Colleges. *Career:* Various radio appearances, 1980–94; Formed own record label, appearances, 1980–94; Meridian Television, 1993, 1995. *Recordings:* High Upon The Rhythm; Hallelujah; Valentine; National Health Tender. *Publications:* Various (International). *Membership:* PRS; MCPS. *Current Management:* Happy House; Dead Happy Records. *Address:* 3B Castledown Ave, Hastings, East Sussex TN34 3RJ, England.

ARNOLD, Eddy (Richard Edward); b. 15 May 1918, Madisonville, Tennessee, USA. Country Vocalist. m. Sally Arnold, 28 Nov. 1941, 1 s., 1 d. *Career:* Member, Pee Wee King's Golden West Cowboys, 1940–43; Radio appearances: WSM Radio, Nashville, as solo artist The 'Tennessee Plowboy'; Co-host, Grand Ole Opry, 1943–48; Host, Checkerboard Square, 1947–55; Television appearances: Milton Berle Show, 1949; Host, Eddy Arnold Time, 1950s; Guest on all major shows including Ed Sullivan; Jackie Gleason; Johnny Carson; Dean Martin; Television specials: Profile From The Land, 1968; Kraft Music Hall Specials, 1967–71; Appeared films: Feudin' Rhythm, 1949; Hoedown, 1950: One of first country artists to play Carnegie Hall, 1966; Performed with symphony orchestras of Hartford; Nashville; Memphis, 1960s. *Recordings:* Record sales total over 80m. (one of most successful artists in history); Over 145 country hits including 21 US Country No. 1s, 1945–55; Hits include: Please Stay Home With Me; That's How Much I Love You; Bouquet Of Roses; Anytime; I'll Hold You In My Heart; Just A Little Lovin' Will Go A Long Way; Cattle Call; Tennessee Stud; What's He Doing In My World?; Make The World Go Away; The Last Word In Lonesome Is Me; Misty Blue; Turn The World Around; Albums: Memories Are Made Of This, 1995; Christmas Time, 1997; Songs I Love To Sing; Then You Can Tell Me Goodbye; I Need You All The Time. *Publications:* It's A Long Way From Chester Country, 1969. *Honours:* Inducted into Country Music Hall of Fame, 1966; Entertainer of the Year, 1967; Pioneer Award, Academy of Country Music, 1984; President's Award Songwriter's Guild, 1987. *Current Management:* Gerald W. Purcell Associates. *Address:* 964 Second Ave, New York, NY 10022, USA.

ARNOLD, Kristine; b. California, USA. Vocalist. m. Leonard Arnold, 2 d. *Career:* Member, duo Sweethearts of The Rodeo with sister Janis Gill; Signed to Columbia Records; Sugar Hill Records; Winners, Wrangler Country Showcase, 1985. *Recordings:* Sweethearts Of The Rodeo, 1986; Top 20 hits include: Since I Found You; Midnight Girl/Sunset Town; Satisfy You; Chains Of Gold, 1987; Rodeo Waltz, 1993; Video: Things Will Grow. *Honours:* CMA's Vocal Duo, 9 consecutive years; Music City News Award, Best Vocal Duo; TNN Viewers Choice Awards, Favourite Group; NAIRD Award, Best Country Album, 1994. *Current Management:* M Hitchcock Management. *Address:* PO Box 159007, Nashville, TN 37214, USA.

ARNOLD, P. P, (b. Patricia Ann Cole); b. 1946, Los Angeles, CA, USA. Soul Vocalist. m. David Arnold, 1 s., 1 d. *Career:* Singer, church choirs; Mem., Ike and Tina Turner's backing group, the Ikettes, 1966; Mem., backing trio, the Nice, 1966; Signed to Immediate Records, 1967; Appearances in musicals: Catch My Soul, 1969; Jesus Christ Superstar, 1970; Starlight Express, 1984; Once on this Island, 1994; Television appearances include: Quincy, Fame, Knots Landing, T. J. Hooker, St Elsewhere; Contributed to film soundtrack, Electric Dreams, 1984; Toured as session singer with: the Beatmasters, Dr John, Freddie King, Nils Lofgren, Oasis, Ocean Colour Scene, Primal Scream, Small Faces, Roger Waters, Paul Weller; Solo artiste, formed Band of Angels, 1999; Played, Jazz Café, London, 1999. *Recordings:* Albums: First Lady Of Immediate, 1967; Kafunta, 1968; Body Talk, 1981; In The Heat Of The Night, 1982; Night Dubbing, 1983; Scandalous, 1983; Imagination, 1989. *Current Management:* Elizabeth H. McLean, 6 Homedale Place, Prudhoe, Northumberland NE42 5AZ, England. *Website:* www.pparnold.com.

ARRIALE, Lynne; b. 29 May 1957, Milwaukee, Wisconsin, USA. Composer; Jazz Musician (piano). *Education:* BMus, MMus, Classical Piano. *Career:* Tour of Japan with 100 Golden Fingers (featuring 10 great jazz pianists); Tours of Europe and North America with the Lynne Arriale Trio. *Recordings:* Albums: The Eyes Have It; When You Listen; With Words Unspoken, 1996; Long Road Home, 1997; Melody, 1999; Live At The Montreux Jazz Festival (Lynne Arriale Trio), 2000; Inspiration, 2002. *Honours:* First Prize, Great American Jazz Piano Competition, 1993; Great American Piano Competition, winner. *Membership:* International Asscn of Jazz Educators. *Current Management:* Suzi Reynolds and Assocs, 200 Rector Pl. 7H, New York, NY 10280, USA; Promotion Aktiv, Gerold Merkle, Zirbenweg 52, 87448 Waltenhoffen, Germany. *E-mail:* promotionaktiv.jazzgentur@online.de.

ARROYO, Joe (Alvaro José); b. 1955, Cartagena, Colombia. Vocalist; Songwriter. *Career:* Nightclub singer from age 12; Formed La Protesta, 1970; Singer, Fruko Y Sus Tesos, 1971–81; South American and US tours; Numerous hits; Formed own group, La Verdad (15 piece band), 1981–; Concerts include: Empire Leicester Square, London 1992; Founder, own band, Son Caribeno (the Caribbean Sound). *Recordings:* Hit singles: with Fruko y sus Tesos: Manyoma; Tania; El Ausente; with La Verdad: Tumbatecho, 1986; Rebelión (considered all-time Latin classic), UK release 1991; Numerous hit albums with La Verdad include: En Acción; Musa Original; Toque de Clase; Fire in my Mind; Fuego; Reinando en Vida; Deja que te Cante; Cruzando el Milenio; Noche. *Honours:* Over 100 music awards; Conga de Oro, Barranquila Carnival; 13 Golden Bongo Awards. *Address:* c/o Jenny Adlington, World Circuit Records, 106 Cleveland St, London W1P 5DP, England.

ARSON, Nicholaus, (Nicholaus Almqvist); b. 1977. Musician (guitar). *Career:* Mem., Swedish band, The Hives, 1993–; Signed to Universal Music, 2001. *Recordings:* Albums: Barely Legal, 1997; Veni Vidi Vicious, 2000; Your New Favourite Band (compilation, UK only), 2001. Singles: Oh, Lord! When? How? (EP), 1996; aka I.D.I.O.T. (EP), 1998; Hate To Say I Told You So; Main Offender; Supply & Demand. *Honours:* NME Award, Best International Band, 2003. *Address:* The Hives, c/o Pelle Almqvist, Regnbågsvägen 46, 737 43 Fagersta, Sweden. *E-mail:* hives@innocent.com. *Website:* www.hives.nu.

ARTHUR, Davey; b. 24 Sept. 1954, Donegal, Ireland. Musician (multi-instrumentalist); Vocalist. *Career:* Mem., The Buskers; Mem., Tam Linn; Appeared at the Cambridge Folk Festival; Later became the Fureys and Davey Arthur, 1980–. *Recordings:* The Cisco Special, 1960; Songs Of Woody Guthrie, 1961; I Ain't Got No Home, 1962; The Sound Of The Fureys And Davey Arthur, 1981; When You Were Sweet Sixteen, 1982; Steal Away, 1983; In Concert, 1984; Golden Days, 1984; At The End Of A Perfect Day, 1985; The First Leaves Of Autumn, 1986; The Fureys Finest, 1987; The Fureys Collection, 1989; The Scattering, 1989; The Very Best Of, 1991; The Winds Of Change, 1992; Singles include: When You Were Sweet Sixteen, 1981. *Current Management:* PAKT Events Agency, Coventry, England. *Telephone:* (0)24 7667 5573. *Website:* www.daveyarthur.com.

ARTHURS, Paul 'Bonehead'; b. 23 June 1965, Manchester, England. Musician (guitar). *Career:* Founder mem., Rain, with Paul McGuigan and Tony McCarroll; Joined by Liam Gallagher and changed band name to Oasis; Joined by Noel Gallagher; Debut performance, Boardwalk, Manchester, 1991; Numerous support slots, to The Milltown Brothers, BMX Bandits, The Verve, Liz Phair, The Real People, Dodgy; Signed to Creation Records, 1993; Numerous tours and television appearances; Festival dates; Left band, 1999, during recordings for 2000 album Standing On The Shoulder Of Giants.

Recordings: Albums: Definitely Maybe, 1994; What's The Story (Morning Glory), 1995; Be Here Now, 1997; The Masterplan, boxed set, 1999; Standing On The Shoulder Of Giants (No. 1, UK), 2000. Singles: Supersonic, 1994; Whatever, 1994; Cigarettes And Alcohol, 1994; Shakermaker, 1994; Live Forever, 1994; Some Might Say (No. 1, UK, 1995); Wonderwall, 1995; Roll With It, 1995; Champagne Supernova, 1995; Don't Look Back in Anger (No. 1, UK, 1996); D'You Know What I Mean (No. 1, UK, 1997); Stand By Me; All Around The World (No. 1, UK, 1998); Go Let It Out (Number 1, UK), 2000; Who Feels Love?, 2000; Sunday Morning Call, 2000. *Honours:* BRIT Awards, Best British Newcomer, 1995; Best British Group, Best British Album, 1996.

ARTIST, (THE). See: **PRINCE.**

AS ONE. See: **DEGIORGIO, Kirk.**

ASHANTI, (Ashanti Douglas); b. 13 Oct. 1980, Glen Cove, NY, USA. Hip Hop/ R&B Vocalist; Songwriter. *Career:* Signed to Jive Records when 14 years old; Epic Records when 17 years old; Appearance, Polly (television musical film); Signed to Murder Inc Records; Guest vocals, duets, songwriter; Solo artiste, 2002–; Worked with: Big Punisher, Ja Rule, J. Lo, Big Pun, Fat Joe, Notorious B.I.G. *Recordings:* Albums: Ashanti, 2002; Foolish/Unfoolish: Reflections on Love, 2002. Singles: Happy, 2002; Foolish, 2002. *Honours:* MOBO Award, Best R&B Act, 2002; American Music Awards, Best New Pop/ Rock Artist, Best New Hip Hop/R&B Artist, 2003. *Address:* c/o Murder Inc Records, 2220 Colorado Ave, Santa Monica, CA 90404, USA. *Website:* www.ashantimusic.net.

ASHCROFT, Richard; b. 11 Sept. 1971. Vocalist; Songwriter; Musician (guitar). m. Kate Radley, 1 s. *Career:* Vocalist, The Verve, 1988–2000; Concerts include: Lollapalooza Tour, USA, 1994; British tours, 1994–95; Support to Oasis, Paris, 1995; Glastonbury Festival, 1995; Solo career, 2000–; UK tour, 2002. *Compositions include:* On Your Own; Drive You Home; History; No Knock On My Door. *Recordings:* Albums: with The Verve: A Storm In Heaven, 1993; A Northern Soul, 1995; Urban Hymns, 1997; Solo: Alone With Everybody, 2000; Human Conditions, 2002. Singles: with The Verve: This Is Music, 1995; On Your Own, 1995, 1995; History, 1995; Bitter Sweet Symphony, 1997; The Drugs Don't Work, 1997; Sonnet, 1998; Lucky Man, 1998; Solo: Song For The Lovers, 2000; Money To Burn, 2000; C'mon People (We're Making It Now), 2000; Check The Meaning, 2002. *Honours:* BRIT Awards: Best British Group; Best British Album (Urban Hymns), 1998. *Current Management:* Larrikin Management, 8391 Beverly Blvd #298, Los Angeles, CA 90048, USA. *Website:* www.richardashcroft.com.

ASHER, James; b. 4 Sept. 1950, Eastbourne, Sussex, England. Composer; Prod; Musician (keyboard, drums). *Education:* Grade VI violin. *Career:* Sound engineer, R G Jones studio, London. *Compositions:* Wrote and recorded over 20 albums library music; Films and television include: La Filiere Chinoise, Cinema Euro Group; Gems, Thames Television; The Boat Show, BBC2; The Plant, Screen One; Television station idents for: Central; Granada; MTV, USA; Future Television, Lebanon; European Superchannel; Television themes for: Ulster Television news; Channel 4 rugby programme. *Recordings:* Single: Peppermint Lump (produced by Pete Townshend); Albums: The Great Wheel; Globalarium (used by The Clothes Show, BBC1); Dance Of The Light; Rivers Of Life; Feet In The Soil; Tigers Of The Raj; Tigers Of The Remix; Raising The Rhythms; Colours Of Trance, with harpist Madeleine Doherty; As drummer: Empty Glass, Pete Townshend; Producer for: Ritchie; John 'Rabbit' Bundrick; Ritchie; Asha. *Membership:* APC; REPRO. *Address:* 34 Starfield Rd, London W12 9SW, England.

ASHER, Peter; b. 22 June 1944, London, England. Man; Record Prod; Vocalist; Musician (guitar). m. Wendy Worth, 20 May 1983, 1 d. *Education:* Philosophy, King's College, London University. *Career:* Member, duo, Peter and Gordon, 9 top records, 3 Gold discs, 1964–68; Head of A & R, Apple Records, 1968–70; Produced, signed, James Taylor; Founder, Peter Asher Management, USA; Began management of Linda Ronstadt; Today represents: Peter Blakeley; Chicano Soul'n Power; Iris DeMent; The Innocence Mission; Little Feat; Kirsty MacColl; Maria Fatal; Mariachi Los Campaneros de Nati Cano; Randy Newman; Over The Rhine; Linda Ronstadt; Laura Satterfield; James Taylor; Williams Brothers; Warren Zevon; Department for management of major record producers, engineers, including Phil Ramone, George Massenburg. *Recordings:* Albums produced include: with 10,000 Maniacs: In My Tribe, 1987; Blind Man's Zoo, 1989; with Linda Ronstadt: Canciones de mi padre, 1987; Cry Like A Rainstorm, Howl Like The Wind, 1989; Frenesi, 1992; with Mary's Danish: American Standard, 1992; with Neil Diamond: The Christmas Album, 1992; The Christmas Album, Vol. 2, 1994; with Randy Newman: Faust, 1995; Albums or tracks for: Paul Jones; Barbara Keith; Tony Kosinec; Jo Mama; John Stewart; Kate Taylor; Tony Joe White; Andrew Gold; John David Souther; Bonnie Raitt; Ronin; Cher; Peter Blakeley; Maria McKee; Williams Brothers; Diana Ross; Julia Fordham; Ringo Starr; Olivia Newton-John; Laura Satterfield; Dixie Chicks. *Honours:* 31 Gold, 19 Platinum albums, USA; 8 Grammy winning records; 2 Grammys, Producer of the Year, 1978, 1989. *Address:* 644 N Doheny Dr., Los Angeles, CA 90069, USA.

ASHER, Phil; b. 3 Jan. 1966, London, England. Prod; Remixer; DJ. *Career:* World-wide DJ; Compiler of Jazz In The House album series for Kickin' Music; Member: Restless Soul, Pascal's Bongo Massive, Two Shiny Heads, Electric Soul; Collaborations: Orin Walters, Luke McCarty, Nathan Haine. *Recordings:* Albums: Sound Travels (with Nathan Haines), 2001; Singles: Pascal's Bongo Massive Vol. 1, 1991; Vol. 2, 1992; Vol. 3, 1993; Let Go (with Two Shiny Heads), 1992; Dub House Disco (with Two Shiny Heads), 1992; Mama (with Restless Soul), 1997; Psykodelik (with Restless Soul), 1997; Phlash 3000 Parts 1 and 2 (as Phlash), 2000; Earth Is The Place (with Nathan Haines), 2001. *Current Management:* c/o Phlash Music, Suite B, 2 Tunstall Rd, London SW9 2DA, England.

ASHFORD, Nickolas (Nick); b. 4 May 1942, Fairfield, South Carolina, USA. Songwriter; Musician; Vocalist. m. Valerie Simpson, 1974. *Career:* Member, performing, recording, songwriting duo with Valerie Simpson; Later joined by Jo Armstead. *Compositions:* Co-writer, Never Had It So Good, Ronnie Milsap; One Step At A Time, Maxine Brown, The Shirelles; Let's Go Get Stoned, Ray Charles; Songs: Ain't No Mountain High Enough; You're All I Need To Get By; Reach Out and Touch Somebody's Hand; Remember Me. *Recordings:* with Valerie Simpson: Keep It Comin', 1973; Gimme Something Real, 1973; I Wanna Be Selfish, 1974; Come As You Are, 1976; So, So Satisfied, 1977; Send It, 1977; Is It Still Good To Ya?, 1978; Stay Free, 1979; A Musical Affair, 1980; Performance, 1981; Street Opera, 1982; High-Rise, 1983; Solid, 1984; Real Love, 1986; Love Or Physical, 1989; I'm On Your Side, 1991; Live Wire! The Singles, 1993; Emperors Of Soul, 1994; Best Of Smokey Robinson And The Miracles, 1995; Best Of Diana Ross And The Supremes, 1995; Ultimate Collection, Gladys Knight, 1997; Hit singles: It Seems To Hang On, 1978; Found A Cure, 1979; Solid, 1984; Babies, 1985. *Current Management:* Hopsack and Silk Productions, 254 W 72nd St, Suite 1A, New York, NY 10023, USA.

ASHILAAKO BILANSO MBO, Djonimbo; b. 3 July 1969, Bolobo, Congo. Country Vocalist; Musician (guitar, flute); Composer; Interpreter; Artist. 2 s. *Education:* Degree in secondary studies. *Career:* Numerous appearances on national television and radio, 1984–; Playing character in stories for the Francohone Photo Magazine, Amina; Singer with Planete Lolingo Band, 1976; Tout Grand Nania Band, 1979; Credo Band, 1980; Fa-Sol Band, 1983–. *Compositions:* Si Bonne, Si Belle, Si Compliquée... La Vie, 1989; Bosso Bikali, 1993. *Recordings:* La Vie est Belle et Compliquée, 1996. *Honours:* First Prize, Radio Challenge for Family Planning, 1986; Third Prize, poetry and song challenge, Goethe Institute, 1987; First Prize, National Song Festival, 1991; Second Prize, Song Festival, French Embassy, 1998. *Membership:* National Society of Artists. *Address:* B P 18525 Kinshasa 13, Democratic Republic of the Congo.

ASHLEY, Steve (Stephen Frank); b. 9 March 1946, Perivale, London, England. Vocalist; Songwriter; Musician (guitar, bouzouki, harmonica, whistle). m. Elizabeth Mary Holborow, 1 d., 1 s. *Education:* DipAD (Hons), Maidstone. *Career:* Founder member, Albion Country Band, 1972; Formed Ragged Robin, 1973; Solo tours of Europe and USA; Television and radio appearances, 1974–79, including Family Album (performed with members of Fairport Convention); Peace Songs for CND; Formed Steve Ashley Band, 1983; Tours of Europe, including festivals at Glastonbury, Cambridge and Cropredy. *Compositions:* Songs: Fire and Wine; Duke of Cambridge; The Rough With The Smooth; Once in a While; Say Goodbye; Gog and Magog; Original music: Ballad of the Ten Rod Plot, 1991; Stable Lads, for Anglia Television, 1993. *Recordings:* Albums: Stroll On, 1974; Speedy Return, 1975; Demo Tapes, 1980; Family Album, 1981; More Demo Tapes, 1983; Mysterious Ways, 1990; The Test Of Time, 1999; Stroll on Revisited, 1999; Everyday Lives, 2001. *Honours:* Contemporary Folk Album of the Year, for Stroll On, Folk Review, 1974. *Membership:* MCPS; PRS; PAMRA. *Current Management:* Elizabeth Jones Entertainments. *Address:* 87 Prestbury Rd, Cheltenham, Gloucestershire GL52 2DR, England.

ASHTON, Bill (William Michael); b. 6 Dec. 1936, Blackpool, Lancashire, England. Musician (saxophones, clarinet); Composer; Bandleader; Songwriter; Journalist. *Education:* St Peter's College, Oxford; Degree, Modern Languages, DipEd. *Career:* Founder, University Dance Band The Ambassadors; OU Big Band; Founder, secretary, OU Modern Jazz Club; Taught in France, 1960–61; Played US bases with The Stardust Combo, Caveau Des Fouleurs, Chateaudun, France; Worked in Red Bludd's Bluesicians, London; Co-founder with Pat Evans, The London Schools Jazz Orchestra, later renamed The London Youth, then The National Youth Jazz Orchestra (NYJO); Worked full-time with NYJO, 1973–; With NYJO, played world-wide, made numerous television appearances, and recorded over 30 albums; Royal Variety Performance, 1978; Toured twice with Shorty Rogers, John Dankworth, John Williams, and many singers; Formed own publishing company, Stanza Music, 1967; Numerous compositions for NYJO. *Recordings:* with National Youth Jazz Orchestra, Live at London Weekend Television, 1975; These Are The Jokes, 1996; View From The Hill, 1996; In Control, 1999; also; Live At The Blue Note, with Irvin Mayfield and Chico Freeman, 1999. *Honours:* MBE; Inter-University Jazz Band Competition Award, 1962; Critics Choice, 1992, 1995; British Jazz Award, Best British Big Band, 1993, 1995; BBC Radio 2

Award, Services to Jazz, 1995; Fellow, Leeds College of Music, 1995. *Address:* NYJO Records, 11 Victor Rd, Harrow, Middlesex HA2 6PT, England.

ASHWORTH, Stephanie; Musician (bass guitar). *Career:* Resides in Australia; Joined group Sandpit, 1995; Replaced bassist Toby Ralph in Melbourne-based trio Something For Kate, 1998; Band gradually broke nationally, then internationally with first USA/Japan tour, 2000; Big sell-out Australian shows including Mythology and Echo-la-la-lalia tours plus Powderfinger support slots, 2001; Group subject of JJJ radio station special, 2001. *Recordings:* Albums: with Sandpit: On Second Thought (compilation), 1998; with Something For Kate: Beautiful Sharks, 1999; QandA With Dean Martin (compilation), 2000; Echolalia, 2001; Singles: with Sandpit: Lessons In Posture (EP), 1995; Tyranny Of Creeps (EP), 1997; Along The Moors, 1998; with Something For Kate: Harpoon/Clint, 1998; Electricity, Hallways, Whatever You Want, 1999; The Astronaut, 2000; Monsters, Three Dimensions, Twenty Years, 2001. *Honours:* Australian Music Industry Critics Awards, Album of the Year, 2000; Australian Live Music Awards, Best Live Act, 2000; JJJ Listeners' Poll, Best Album, 2001. *Current Management:* Carlene Albronda, Catapult Management, Sydney, Australia. *E-mail:* carlene@presto.net.au. *Website:* www.somethingforkate.com.

ASQUITH, Stuart Andrew; b. 23 Sept. 1971, Wakefield, England. Songwriter; Entertainer; Musician (keyboard). *Education:* Piano lessons, 4–8 years old; Keyboard lessons. *Career:* Made White Label dance record, under name, Mind Vacation, 1992; Changed name of band to Lost In Process; Made demos, signed to Ouch! Records, 1995. *Recordings:* Aint We Funky/Sustain The Pressure; Pacemaker/We Can Do This; Rock On; Made In Rio; All recorded 1995. *Membership:* Musicians' Union.

ASTBURY, Ian; b. 14 May 1962, Heswall, Merseyside, England. Vocalist. *Career:* Founder, Southern Death Cult, 1982; Re-named Death Cult, 1983; Re-named The Cult, 1984–95; Formed Holy Barbarians, 1996–99; Re-formed The Cult, 1999–; Headline tours include: UK, Europe, North America, Japan; Also tours with: Bauhaus, 1983; Big Country, 1984; Billy Idol, 1987; Guns N' Roses, 1987; Metallica, 1989; Lenny Kravitz, 1991; Major concerts include: Futurama Festival, Leeds, 1983; A Gathering of The Tribes Festival, California, 1990; Kick Out The Jams Festival, Detroit, 1992; Cult In The Park '92 Festival, Finsbury Park, London, 1992; Guns N' Roses concert, Milton Keynes, 1993; Vocalist for The Doors reunion tour, 2002–03. *Recordings:* Albums: Southern Death Cult, 1983; Dreamtime, 1984; Love, 1985; Electric, 1987; Sonic Temple, 1989; Ceremony, 1991; Pure Cult (No. 1, UK), 1993; The Cult, 1994; Ghost Dance, 1996; High Octane Cult, 1996; Cream, 1996; Celebrity Deathmatch, 1999; Zen Mafia, 1999; Best Of Rare Cult (compilation), 2000; Beyond Good And Evil, 2001; Singles include: Fat Man, 1983; Spiritwalker, 1984; She Sells Sanctuary, 1985; Rain, 1985; Love Removal Machine, 1987; Lil' Devil, 1987; Wild Flower, 1987; Fire Woman, 1989; Edie (Ciao Baby), 1989; Sweet Soul Sister, 1990; Wild Hearted Son, 1990; Rise, 2001. *Current Management:* Deluxe Entertainment, 12750 Ventura Blvd, Suite 202, Studio City, CA 91604, USA.

ASTLEY, Jon; b. 22 Jan. 1951, Manchester, England. Record Prod. 2 d. *Career:* Producer, 1978–; 2 own records released as solo artist, songwriter, 1986, 1988. *Recordings:* Producer for: The Who; Eric Clapton; Phil Collins; Corey Hart; The Rolling Stones; Debbie Harry; The Eagles; Pete Townsend; LSO and LPO; Loz Netto; Johnny Be Good; Orphan; Own recordings; Remixing and remastering extensive catalogues: The Who; Eric Clapton; Bob Dylan; Joni Mitchell; Pete Townsend; Tropicana; Tori Amos. *Membership:* MCPS; PRS. *Current Management:* A-Sharp Publishing Co. *Address:* 2 Embankment, Twickenham, TW1 3DH, England.

ASTLEY, Rick; b. 6 Feb. 1966, Warrington, Cheshire, England. Vocalist; Songwriter. *Career:* Drummer, school band, Give Way, 1982; Lead singer, FBI, 1984; Apprenticeship, Stock/Aitken/Waterman, 1985; Tape Operator, PWL Studios, 1986; Solo artiste, 1987–; Numerous concerts include: Far East/ Australian tour, 1988; Prince's Trust Concert, Royal Albert Hall, 1988; World tour, 1988–89; US tour, 1989. *Recordings:* Albums: Whenever You Need Somebody (No. 1, UK), 1987; Hold Me In Your Arms, 1988; Free, 1991; Body And Soul, 1992; Keep It Turned On, 2001. Singles include: Never Gonna Give You Up (No. 1, UK, USA, 15 other countries), 1987; When I Fall In Love, 1987; Together Forever (No. 1, USA), 1988; It Would Take A Strong Man, 1988; She Wants To Dance With Me, 1988; Take To Your Heart, 1988; Cry For Help, 1991; Hopelessly, 1993; The Ones You Love, 1994. *Honours:* BRIT Award, Best British Single, Never Gonna Give You Up, 1988; Two Billboard Awards, 1988.

ASTON, Michael Philip; b. 22 Aug. 1957, Bridgend, South Wales. Musician; Artist; Vocalist. m. Margaret La Guardia, 23 June 1992. *Career:* Lead vocalist: Gene Loves Jezebel; Toured: USA; Europe; world; MTV Live At Ritz, NY; MTV New Year's Eve Ball; John Peel sessions; Joan Rivers Show (Fox); Television: Japan; Italy; France; Argentina; Songs, various films; Film Role: She's Having A Baby, by John Hughes, 1986. *Recordings:* Gene Loves Jezebel: Promise; Immigrant; Discover; House Of Dolls; From The Mouth Of Babes; Love Lies Bleeding; Voodoo Dollies; Albums: Edith Grove, 1995; Why Me Why This Why Now, 1995. *Publications:* Gothic Rock (Black book); Various A–Z

Rock. *Honours:* T J Martel MVP, 1995; Song of Year, Desire, College USA, 1986. *Current Management:* William Morris (USA). *Address:* 1419 N Hayworth Ave, Los Angeles, CA 90046, USA.

ASTRAUSKAS, Rimantas; b. 9 April 1954, Kaunas, Lithuania. Ethnomusicologist; Prod. *Education:* Kaunas J. Gruodis Higher Music School, 1973; MA, Lithuanian State Conservatoire, 1978; Dr of Humanities, Musicology, Lithuanian Academy of Music, 1993. *Career:* Producer, Lithuanian State Television and Radio Committee, 1978–88; Lecturer, Lithuanian Academy of Music, 1988–; Associate Professor of Ethnomusicology, 1994–; Chair., Council for the Protection of Ethnic Culture, Lithuanian Parliament, 2000–02. *Compositions:* Author, over 500 television and radio broadcasts on various musical topics and events; Co-author, Documentary Film, Išaudes Šokio Rašta. *Publications:* Typological Classification of Tunes (ed.), 1996; Ritual and Music (ed.), 1999; Folk Culture at the Beginning of the Third Millennium (ed.), 2001; Over 30 articles on Lithuanian Traditional Music. *Honours:* Special Award, Best Broadcast at International Contest of Musical Broadcasts in Kishinew, 1982. *Membership:* International Organization of Folk Art; International Council for Traditional Music; European Seminar in Ethnomusicology; Lithuanian Composers' Union. *Address:* V. Grybo 1/29–11, 2055 Vilnius, Lithuania. *Telephone:* (5) 2711106. *Fax:* (5) 2120093. *E-mail:* astram@delfi.it.

ATB, (Andre Tanneberger); b. 1973, Freiberg, Germany. Prod; Remixer; DJ. *Career:* Resident DJ at Tarm Center, Bochum, Germany; World-wide DJ; Collaborations with York; Remixes for Moby, Rank 1, Sash, Blank and Jones, Enigma. *Recordings:* Albums: Movin' Melodies, 2000; Two Worlds, 2001; Singles: 9PM (Till I Come), 1999; Don't Stop, 2000; Killer, 2000; Fields Of Love (with York), 2001; Let U Go, 2001. *Current Management:* c/o Ministry of Sound Recordings Ltd, 103 Gaunt St, London SE1 6DP, England.

ATKINS, Bobby Lee; b. 22 May 1933, Surrey Country, USA. Musician (guitar); Vocalist. m. Judy Smit, 4 April 1961, 6 s., 1 d. *Career:* Began with Bill Monroe and the Bluegrass Boys; Played with Charlie Monroe, Flint Hill Playboys; Played with Joe Stone for 15 years; Played with Joe and the Dixie Mountaineers all over USA; Formed own band, Bobby Atkins and The Countrymen, 1967; Rated among the ten best banjo players in the world; Songwriter; Composer; Arranger; Music Publisher, Bob's Special Music Publishing Co; 2 film scores; Performed on stage with: Mac Wiseman; Clyde Moody; Jim Fanes; Radio with: Flatt and Scruggs; Don Reno; Red Smiley. *Recordings:* over 60 albums and two film scores including: Crimes Of The Heart; Gold Hill Gold; The Best Of Bobby Atkins, Mark Albin And The Country; The Country Side Of Bobby Atkins. *Honours:* Songwriter of the Year, Hawaii; Represented in Bluegrass Hall of Fame, Nashville, Tennessee; Top Male Vocal, Top Band, Top Musician; Top Songwriter; Living Legend Award, 1995; Country Music Organisation of America, Songwriter of the Year, Male Vocalist and Album of the Year, Vallejo. *Membership:* Country and Bluegrass Music Asscn; Wall of Fame, New York, New York. *Current Management:* c/o Jolene Caudill, 1109 Cleburne St, Greensboro, NC 27408, USA. *Address:* PO Box 251, Summerfield, NC 27358, USA.

ATKINS, Juan, (Model 500, Infiniti); b. 12 Sept. 1962, Detroit, Michigan, USA. Prod; Remixer; DJ. *Career:* Techno innovator; credited with inventing the Techno genre as part of the Belleville Three (with Derrick May and Kevin Saunderson); Member: Cybotron; Collaborations: Derrick May, Kevin Saunderson, Maurizio. *Recordings:* Albums: Enter (with Cybotron), 1983; Sonic Sunset, 1994; Deep Space, 1995; Skynet (as Infiniti), 1998; Mind And Body, 1999; Singles: Clear (with Cybotron), 1983; as Model 500: No UFO's, 1985; Night Drive (Thru Babylon), 1985; Technicolor, 1986; Sound Of Stereo, 1987; Interference, 1988; The Chase, 1989; Ocean To Ocean, 1990; Jazz Is The Teacher, 1993; The Flow, 1995; I Wanna Be There, 1996; Be Brave, 1999; Game One (as Infiniti), 1996. *Current Management:* c/o Metroplex Records, Detroit, Michigan, USA.

ATLAS, Natacha; b. 20 March 1964, Brussels, Belgium. Vocalist; Dancer. *Career:* Singer, various bands in Northampton, England; Returned to Belgium and worked in Arabic and Turkish nightclubs; Singer with Mandanga, Belgian salsa band; Singer on projects with ¡Loca! and Jah Wobble, 1991–; Mem., Trans-Global Underground (TGU); Appearances at Glastonbury, WOMAD, Reading and Phoenix festivals and at Brixton Acad., London; many international festivals; Worked with musicians including: Apache Indian, Peter Gabriel, David Arnold; Contributed to film soundtracks including Stargate. *Recordings:* Albums: with Trans-Global Underground: International Times; Solo: Diaspora, 1995; Halim, 1998; Gedida, 1999; The Remix Collection, 2000; Ayeshteni, 2001. Singles: with ¡Loca!: Timbal, 1991; with Jah Wobble's Invaders of the Heart: Rising Above Bedlam, 1991. *Honours:* Nuit de Clip Award for the video of Amulet, Tunisia. *Address:* c/o Trans-Global Underground, c/o Lisa Richards, 28 Winchester St, Brighton BN1 4NX, England.

AUBUT, Lise; b. 29 Aug. 1943, Lévis, Québec, Canada. Songwriter; Impresario. *Education:* CEGEP. *Career:* Songwriter, 15 musical albums and over 150 songs. *Compositions include:* Hit songs: Paquetville, sung by Edith Butler; Un Million de Fois Je T'aime. *Honours:* 3 Felix Awards; 3 Platinum discs. *Membership:* SPACQ; SODRAC; SACEM. *Address:* 86 Côte Ste Catherine, Outremont, QC H2V 2A3, Canada.

AUCH, Greg; b. 28 Jan. 1967, Charlotte, NC, USA. Country Musician (drums); Vocalist. m. Linda Auch, 3 s. *Career:* Mem., The Moody Brothers, 1987–98; Played guitar and drums, Disneyland Paris, 1992–98; On Stage for TNN; Sang At The White House for George Bush, Take Pride In America Campaign. *Membership:* National Academy of Recording Arts and Sciences. *Address:* 5900 Oakwielde Ct, Charlotte, NC 28227, USA.

AUGER, Brian Albert Gordon; b. 18 July 1939, London, England. Musician (organ, piano); Composer; Prod. m. Ella Natale, 14 Nov. 1968, 1 s., 2 d. *Education:* One year, College of Marin, San Francisco, CA. *Career:* Professional musician, 1963–; Performed with: Brian Auger Trinity; Brian Auger's Oblivion Express; Eric Burdon/Brian Auger Band; World-wide tours; Major television shows in UK; Europe; USA; Japan; Czechoslovakia; Hungary; Greece; Radio appearances world-wide. *Recordings:* No. 1 single: This Wheel's On Fire, 1968; Albums: Brian Auger Trinity And Julie Driscoll: Open, 1967; Definitely What, 1968; Streetnoise, 1969; Brian Auger Trinity: Befour, 1970: Brian Auger's Oblivion Express: Oblivion Express, 1970; A Better Land, 1971; Second Wind, 1972; Closer To It, 1973; Straight Ahead, 1974; Reinforcements, 1975; Live Oblivion, Vol. 1, 1975; Vol. II, 1976; Happiness Heartaches, 1977; Encore, 1978; Planet Earth Calling, 1981; Here And Now, 1983; Keys To The Heart, 1987; Eric Burdon/Brian Auger Band: Access All Areas, 1993; The Best Of Brian Auger, 1997; Voices Of Other Times, 2000. *Honours:* Poll Winner, Jazz Piano and New Star categories, UK Melody Maker magazine, 1963; German Rock and Folk Best Jazz and Best Rock Organist, 1970; Best Jazz Organist, USA Keyboard Magazine, 1976, 1977. *Current Management:* Steve Zelenka, Resource Management, 1341 Ocean Ave #456, Santa Monica, CA 90401, USA.

AUSTEN, Ed, (Edward John Roberts); b. 22 Dec. 1942, London, England. Musician (guitar, bass, mandolin); Vocalist. *Education:* One year classical guitar. *Career:* Worked with: The Who; Free; Derek and The Dominoes; Eric Clapton; The Hollies; Dave Dee; Cliff Bennett; Robert Fripp; Andy Summers; Many artistes on country music circuit. *Membership:* Musicians' Union. *Address:* 417 Wimbourne Rd E, Ferndown, Dorset BH22 9L2, England.

AUSTIN, Dallas; Prod; Songwriter; *Recordings include:* Troop, Attitude, musician, producer, 1989; Ooooooooh... On The TLC Tip, arranger, producer, 1992; White Men Can't Jump, producer, drummer, 1992; DJ Jazzy Jeff And The Fresh Prince, Code Red, composer, producer, 1993; Hi Five, Faithful, producer, 1993; Joi, Pendulum Vibe, vocalist, producer, 1994; Madonna, Bedtime Stories, producer, 1994; Berry Gordy, Music, The Magic, The Memories, producer, 1995; Michael Jackson, History: Past, Present And Future, keyboards, producer, 1995; Boyz II Men, II: Yo Te Voy A Amar, producer, 1995; Fishbone, Chim Chim's Bad Ass Revenge, producer, 1996; Nutty Professor soundtrack, producer, 1996; Indigo Girls, Shaming Of The Sun, vocals, 1997; Michael Jackson, Blood On The Dance Floor, keyboards, producer, 1997; Aretha Franklin, Rose Is Still A Rose, arranger, producer, 1998; Brandy, Never Say Never, producer, 1998; N'Dea Davenport, producer, 1998; Monica, Boy is Mine, producer, 1998; TLC, Fanmail, arranger, vocals, 1999.

AUSTIN, Patti; b. 10 Aug. 1948, California, USA. Vocalist. *Career:* Child performer from age 3; Appearances included Sammy Davis, Jr television show; Theatre performances: Lost In The Stars; Finian's Rainbow; Tours with Quincy Jones, age 9; Harry Belafonte, age 16; Recording debut, age 17; Singer, television jingles, session work, 1970s; Worked with: Paul Simon; Billy Joel; Frankie Valli; Joe Cocker; George Benson; Roberta Flack; Marshall Tucker; Steely Dan; The Blues Brothers; Continued to work with Quincy Jones. *Recordings:* Albums: End Of A Rainbow, 1976; Havana Candy, 1977; Live At The Bottom Line, 1979; Body Language, 1980; Every Home Should Have One, 1981; Patti Austin, 1984; Gettin' Away With Murder, 1985; The Real Me, 1988; Love's Gonna Get You, 1990; Carry On, 1991; Live, 1992; That Secret Place, 1994; In And Out Of Love, 1998; Street Of Dreams, 1999; On The Way To Love, 2001; For Ella, 2002. Singles: Family Tree, 1969; Every Home Should Have One; Razzmatazz (with Quincy Jones), 1981; The Dude, 1982; with James Ingram: Baby Come To Me, theme for television series General Hospital (No. 1, USA), 1983; Film themes: Two Of A Kind, 1984; Shirley Valentine, 1988; Soldier Boy, 1991; Givin' In To Love, 1991; Reach, 1994; I'll Keep Your Dreams Alive, 1995; Why You Wanna Be Like That?, 1998; Guest vocalist, album George Gershwin songs, Hollywood Bowl Orchestra, 1992. *Honours:* Grammy Award, The Dude, 1982.

AVALON, Frankie, (Francis Avallone); b. 18 Sept. 1939, Philadelphia, Pennsylvania, USA. Vocalist; Musician (trumpet); Actor. m. Kay Avalon, 4 s., 4 d. *Career:* Began playing trumpet with Rocco and The Saints; Television appearances include: Patti Duke Show; Ed Sullivan Show; Pat Boone Show; Perry Como Show; Milton Berle Show; American Bandstand; Hullaballoo; Steve Allen Show; Dinah Shore Show; Film appearances include: Jamboree, 1957; Guns of The Timberland, 1960; The Alamo, 1960; Sail A Crooked Ship, 1962; Voyage To The Bottom of The Sea, 1962; Beach Party, 1963; Bikini Beach, 1964; Muscle Beach Party, 1964; The Carpetbaggers, 1964; Beach

Blanket Bingo, 1965; I'll Take Sweden, 1965; Sergeant Deadhead, 1966; Fireball 500, 1966; How To Stuff A Wild Bikini, 1966; Skidoo, 1968; The Take, 1974; Grease, 1978; Back To The Beach, 1987; Appearances include: Alan Freed's New York Christmas Rock 'n' Roll Spectacular, 1959; Saturday Night At The London Palladium, ITV, 1967; American Bandstand's 20th Anniversary Special, ABC, 1973; Easy Does It, Starring Frankie Avalon, CBS, 1976. *Recordings include:* De De Dinah, 1957; Venus, 1959; Bobby Sox To Stockings, 1959; A Boy Without A Girl, 1959; Just Ask Your Heart, 1959; Why (No. 1, USA), 1960; When The Good Guys Used To Win, 1999; Albums include: Swingin' On A Rainbow, 1960; A Whole Lotta Frankie, 1961; Frankie Avalon's Christmas Album, 1962; Venus, 1978; Fabulous Frankie Avalon, 1991; Good Guys, 1999; The EP Collection, 2000. *Honours:* Star on Hollywood Walk of Fame, 1992. *Current Management:* Fox Entertainment, 1650 Broadway, Suite 503, New York, NY 10019, USA.

AVELLA, Vicente G; b. 27 Nov. 1970, Caracas, Venezuela. Composer; Musician (Piano). m. Kirsten Sollek-Avella, 27 Dec. 1996. *Education:* BM, Piano Performance, Indiana University, 1995; MM, Composition, Eastman School of Music, 1998. *Career:* Score to animations, A Spring Day, 1997, Up The Tree, 1999, by Glenn Ehlers; Outdone, by Dan Pejril; Score to independent film, A Night Less Ordinary, by John Rockefeller, 1999; Score to industrial video by The Greater Rochester Visitors Association; Performances by ALEA III, Boston, 1997, and Academic Octet of Caracas, Venezuela, 1998; Score to animation by Val Perkins, Bibbily Bobbily Job, 2000; Score to animation by Shaun Forster, The Diestmobile, 2000; Score to short film by E. Hannois, The Shell, 2001. *Compositions:* Different Beginnings, concerto for 2 drums and orchestra, 1998; Vegetaciones and In the Forestial Depths of the Day, songs for mezzosoprano and chamber ensemble; String Quartet; Winter's Cold Light, for brass quintet; Songs of Sand, a set of songs for mezzosoprano and piano, 2000. *Honours:* Second Place, 15th International Composition Competition for Young Composers, 1997; Bernard and Rose Sernoffsky Competition Prize, 1998. *Membership:* ASCAP; The Society of Composers and Lyricists. *Current Management:* Westwood Entertainment Group. *Address:* 162 Chestnut St, Suite 2, Rutherford, New Jersey, NJ 07070, USA.

AVON, Alan; b. 25 Dec. 1945, England. Vocalist; Actor; Songwriter. *Education:* Private Music; Drama Tuition. *Career:* Backing and session vocalist, London, 1960s; Lead vocalist, Hedgehoppers Anonymous; Toured Europe, Southern Africa, UK, 1965–72; Solo artiste, 1972–; Numerous radio, television, and record apperances; Now presenter, commercial radio. *Recordings:* Hit single: Good News Week, Hedgehoppers Anonymous, 1965; Compositions featured on other artists' albums. *Honours:* 3 SARI Awards: Best Male Vocalist; Best Album; Best British Group, 1972. *Membership:* Equity; British Academy of Songwriters, Composers and Authors. *Current Management:* Dinosaur Promotions. *Address:* 5 Heyburn Cres., Westport Gardens, Stoke On Trent, Staffordshire ST6 4DL, England.

AYALA, Jose (Joey); b. 1 June 1956, Philippines. Songwriter; Performer; Musician. m. Maria Jessie G Sorongon, 2 s. *Education:* AB, Economics. *Career:* School Based Theatre Artist; Independent, Alternative Album Production; Entertainment World, Neo-Ethnic Icon. *Compositions:* modern dance, Encantada, 1992; Noche Buena, 1995; I Hotel/The Fall, 1997. *Recordings:* Panganay Ng Umaga, 1982; Magkabilaan, 1986; Mga Awit ng Tanod-lupa, 1991; Lumad Sa S'yudad, 1992; Lupa't Langit, 1997. *Honours:* Ten Outstanding Young Men, 1991; Awit Awards, 1992, 1993, 1997; Katha Award, 1997; Datu Bago Citation, 1998. *Current Management:* Ma Jessie S Ayala, Bagong Lumad Productions. *Address:* 11 St Lucia St, Rosalia Compound, Tandang Sora, QCMM, Philippines.

AYERS, Nigel; b. 3 July 1957, Tideswell, Derbyshire, England. Composer; Visual Artist. *Education:* BA Hons, Fine Art, Sculpture, 1977. *Career:* Founder pioneering multimedia performance group Nocturnal Emissions, 1978; Business ventures: Record labels: Sterile Records, 1978; Earthly Delights, 1987–; Tours: Europe; USA; Canada, including performances with Butch Dance Company: Poppo and the GoGo Boys; Exhibitions of video work in Tate Gallery and ICA, London; Soundtracks for film work by Charlotte Bill. *Recordings include:* Tissue Of Lies, 1978; Drowning In A Sea Of Bliss, 1982; Viral Shedding, 1983; Befehlsnotstand, 1984; Spiritflesh, 1988; Magnetized Light, 1993; Glossalalia, 1994; Imaginary Time, 1995. *Publications:* Network News, Vegetation Flesh, 1995. *Honours:* Meet The Composer, New York City, 1992. *Membership:* MCPS; PRS; PPL. *Current Management:* Earthly Delights. *Address:* PO Box 2, Lostwithiel, Cornwall PL22 OYY, England.

AYERS, Roy; b. 10 Sept. 1940, Los Angeles, California, USA. Musician (vibraphone). m. Argerie J Ayers, 20 July 1973, 2 s., 1 d. *Career:* Appeared on Merv Griffin, Johnny Carson, Jay Leno and most Jazz festivals throughout the world; Live on BBC Hammersmith Odeon London, many times; Live film, Ronnie Scott's Jazz House London. *Compositions:* Everybody Loves The Sunshine; Running Away; Love Will Bring Us Back; Searching; Most Sampled Composer, by most major Rap Groups, 1988–97. *Recordings:* Recorded 80 albums including: Wayne Henderson, 1980; Music Of Many Colors, 1980; Pre-Mixture, 1981; Center Of The World, 1981; Feeling Good, 1982; Lots Of Love, 1983; Silver Vibrations, 1983; Drivin' On Up, 1983; In The Dark, 1984; You Might Be Surprised, 1985; I'm The One, 1987; Searchin',

1991; Drive, 1992; Vibesman Live At Ronnie Scott's, 1995; Essential Groove Live, 1996; Spoken Word, 1998; Singles include: Get On Up Get On Down, 1978; Heat Of The Beat (with Wayne Henderson), 1979; Don't Stop The Feeling, 1980; Poo Poo La La, 1984; Expansions (with Scott Grooves), 1998. *Publications:* Leonard Feather, Encyclopedia of Jazz, second edition, 1960–65. *Honours:* New Star on Vibes Downbeat Mag, 1966; American Music Award, 1977; Louis Armstrong Award, 1978; Best Song of Year, Get Money, 1997. *Membership:* ASCAP; Local 802; American Federation of Musicians. *Current Management:* Roy Ayers, PO Box 1219, New York, NY 10023, USA.

AYRES, Ben; Musician (multi-instrumentalist); Songwriter. *Career:* Mem., General Havoc, –1991; Founding mem., Cornershop, 1992–; Mem., Clinton; Founder, owner, Meccico label, 1998–. *Recordings:* Albums: with Cornershop: Hold On It Hurts, 1994; Woman's Gotta Have It, 1995; When I Was Born For The 7th Time, 1997; Handcream For A Generation, 2002; with Clinton: Disco And The Halfway To Discontent, 1998. Singles: with Cornershop: In The Days Of Ford Cortina (EP), 1993; Lock Stock & Double Barrel (EP), 1993; Readers' Wives (EP), 1993; Born Disco, Died Heavy Metal, 1994; Jullander Shere, 1995; Wog (The Western Oriental Mixes), 1996; Butter The Soul, 1996; Good Ships, 1997; Brimful Of Asha, 1997; Sleep On The Left Side, 1998; Lessons Learned From Rocky I To Rocky III, 2002; with Clinton: Jam Jar, 1995; Superloose, 1996; Superloose (The Automator Remixes), 1997; David D. Chambers; Buttoned Down Disco; People Power In The Disco Hour. *Address:* c/o Oasis Productions, 36 W 20th St, New York, NY 10011, USA. *Website:* www.cornershop.com.

AYICK, Paul; b. 28 May 1947, Paterson, New Jersey, USA. Musician (trumpet); Composer. m. Rose Marie Kissel, 6 Jan. 1984, 1 d. *Education:* New York College of Music, 1967–69; New York University, 1969–71. *Career:* Trumpeter with Ray Fernandez, 1972–75; Hugh Brodie, 1975–78; Leader, Paul Ayick Quintet, 1978–88; Co-leader with Ira Sullivan, 1990; Also appeared with: Les Elgant; Ray Anthony; John Spider Martin; Little Anthony; Paul Cohen; Gene Krupa Band. *Recordings:* Currently recording project for trumpet, synthesizer. *Publications:* Photographer, contributor, journals and magazines. *Membership:* AFofM. *Current Management:* Gemini Productions. *Address:* 4800 SW 70th Terrace, Davie, FL 33314, USA.

AYRES, Mark Richard; b. 28 Dec. 1960, London, England. Composer. m. Nicola Jane, 11 Sept. 1993, 2 s. *Education:* BSc, Music, Electronics, University of Keele. *Career:* Composer of music for films including: The Innocent Sleep; Television including: Doctor Who, BBC Television, 1988–89. *Compositions:* Soundtracks: The Innocent Sleep, for soprano, orchestra; Doctor Who; Numerous arrangements of film, television themes, for album release. *Membership:* British Academy of Composers and Songwriters; Musicians' Union; PRS; MCPS.

AZNAVOUR, Charles, (Varenagh Aznavourian); b. 22 May 1924, Paris, France. Vocalist; Actor. m. (1) Micheline Rugel, 1946, (2) Evelyene Plessis, 1955, (3) Ulla Thorsel, 1967, 5 c. (1 deceased). *Education:* Ecole Centrale de TSF. *Career:* Centre de Spectacle, Paris; Jean Dasté Company, 1941; Les Fâcheux, Arlequin, 1944; Numerous film appearances, 1964–. *Compositions include:* Songs: Il Pleut; Le Feutre Tropez; Jezebel (all recorded by Edith Piaf); Hier Encore (Yesterday When I Was Young); The Old Fashioned Way; She (theme for ITV series, The Seven Faces of Woman); What Makes A Man; Happy Anniversary. *Recordings:* Albums include: Charles Aznavour Sings, 1963; Qui, 1964; Et Voici, 1964; Sings His Love Songs In English, 1965; Encore, 1966; De T'Avoir Aimée, 1966; Désormais, 1972; Chez Lui A Paris, 1973; A Tapestry Of Dreams, 1974; I Sing For You, 1975; In Times To Be, 1983; Aznavour, 1990; En Espanol, Vols I–III, 1991; The Old Fashioned Way, 1992; Jezabel, 1993; Toi Et Moi, 1994; Il Faut Savior, 1995; Paris Palais Des Congres, 1996; Jazznavour, 1999. *Honours:* Chevalier Légion d'Honneur, Des Arts et Lettres; Grand Prix National de la Chanson, 1986. *Address:* c/o Lévon Sayan, 76–78 Ave des Champs Elysées, Bureau 322, 75008 Paris, France.

AZRAK, Janice; b. 12 Dec. 1951, Brooklyn, New York, USA. Record Co Exec. *Career:* Publicist, MCA Records, New York, 1971–76; SIR Productions, New York, 1976–77; Vice-president, Creative Services/Artist Development, Warner Brothers Records, Nashville, 1977–. *Membership:* Vice-President, Board of Directors, Academy of Country Music, 1985–86. *Address:* c/o Warner Brothers Records, 20 Music St E, Nashville, TN 37203, USA.

AZZI, María Susana; b. 12 Oct. 1952, Buenos Aires, Argentina. Social Anthropologist. *Education:* Licenciada en Ciencias Antropòlógicas, Universidad de Buenos Aires, 1987; Columbia University, New York, 1986; MBA, Escuela Superior de Economía y Administración de Empresas, Buenos Aires; Piano Lessons with Teresa Eichelbaum, 1984–92, Vera Anosova, 1992–95. *Career:* Professor, Board Member, Academia Nacional del Tango, Buenos Aires; Lecturer on the Tango and Astor Piazzolla in Argentina, USA, Europe, Australia, Mexico and Korea; Television and radio appearances in Argentina and UK; Consultant work for: Sony Classical (USA), Dance Perspectives Foundation and Metropolitan Museum of Art, Metropolitan Museum of Art, New York; Smithsonian Institution, Washington DC; Fundación Astor Piazzolla and Instituto Nacional de Antropología, Buenos Aires, Argentina. *Publications include:* Italian Immigration and Their Impact On The Tango In Argentina, 1997; Tango Album by Yo-Yo Ma, 1997; Tango Argentino, 1998; Asphalt, by Paolo Ziegler, liner notes, 1998; Tango Ballad, by Gidon Kremer, liner notes, 1999; Le Grand Tango: A Biography of Astor Piazzola, forthcoming. *Membership:* Academia Nacional del Tango; Society for Ethnomusicology; American Anthropological Asscn; International Council for Traditional Music; International Asscn for the Study of Popular Music. *Address:* Posadas 1612 8°, Buenos Aires 1112, Argentina.

B

BABULJAK, Karel; b. 5 Oct. 1957, Prague, Czech Republic. Musician (keyboards, zither, guitar, drums); Composer; Poet. m. (1) Barbora, 1982, (2) Tereza, 22 June 1996, 2 s., 1 d. *Career:* Broadrange Musician and Composer, rock reggae, new age, made demonic experiments; Founder Member of Groups: Relaxace, 1979; Ma'ma Bubo, 1983; Vopruz, 1983; Sajkedelik Sraml Band, 1992; Karel Babuljak and His Band of Dreams, 1999; Member of groups: Babalet, 1983–; Hypnotix, 1988–90; Boothill 1998–; Cooperation with Theatre Prague 5. *Recordings include:* Solo Albums: A Mass Of Lany; Billiard Blues; Bubol's Shouts from Darkness; A Man With a Knapsack; Albums with groups: Mama Bubo: Ball-Shapedness, 1983–85; Planet Haj, 1985; So That They Love One Another; Relaxace: Dhjana, 1991; Kadael, 1993; Flower Reggae, 1995; Sound and Silence, 1996; Boothill: Sister, 1999. *Current Management:* Lubos Fendrych, Nad Koulkon 21, 15000 Prague 5 Czech Republic. *Address:* Na'drazni 213, 33805 My'to v Cecha'ch, Czech Republic. *E-mail:* karelbabuljak@netscape.net.

BABY SPICE. See: **BUNTON, Emma.**

BACA, Susana; b. Chorrillos, Lima, Peru. Vocalist. m. Ricardo Pereira. *Career:* Formed experimental group combining poetry and song; Researched Afro-Peruvian tradition and formed the Instituto Negrocontinuo with husband; first US performance in Brooklyn, 1995; One US and six European tours. *Recordings:* Albums: Susana Baca, 1997; Del Fuego Y Del Agua, 1999; Eco De Sombras, 2000; Lamento Negro (earlier Cuban recordings), 2001; Espiritu Vivo, 2002. *Publications:* The Cultural Importance of Black Peruvians (with Richard Pereira), 1992. *Honours:* Latin Grammy Award, Best Folk Album, for Lamento Negro, 2002. *Address:* c/o Iris Musique, 5 Passage St-Sebastien, 75011 Paris, France.

BACAR, Zena; b. Ilha de Mocambique, Mozambique. Vocalist; Songwriter. *Career:* Fisher woman; Founding mem. and lead singer, Eyuphuro, 1981; Recorded the first international release for a Mozambican group, Mama Mosambiki, 1989; Toured Europe, late 1980s–early 1990s; Disbanded shortly after; Re-formed, 1998. *Recordings:* Albums: Parado De Sucessos; Mama Mosambiki, 1990; Yellela, 2001. *Address:* c/o World Music Network/Riverboat Records, 6 Abbeville Mews, 88 Clapham Park Rd, London SW4 7BX, England. *E-mail:* post@worldmusic.net. *Website:* www.worldmusic.net.

BACCHUS, Brian Michel; b. 8 Aug. 1957, New York, NY, USA. Record Co Exec; Record Prod. *Education:* AB, Syracuse University, 1980. *Career:* National Jazz Promotions Co-ordinator, Polygram Records, New York, 1986–87; Manager, National Jazz Promotions, 1987–88; Director, Jazz Promotion, 1988–90; Director, Antilles Records/Island Records, New York, 1990–. *Recordings:* Producer of albums: Remembrance, The Harper Brothers, 1990; Music Inside, Joyce, 1990; Amazon Secrets, Ricardo Silveira, 1990; Kenny Drew Jr, 1991; with Randy Weston: Spirits Of Our Ancestors, 1991; Volcano Blues, 1993; Khepara, 1998; Sanctified Shells, Steve Turre, 1992; Ann Dyer and The No Good Time Fairies, 1995; Timepeace, Terry Callier, 1998. *Honours:* Billboard Award, Top Jazz Album, Remembrance, 1990. *Address:* c/o Antilles Records, 825 Eighth Ave, New York, NY 10019, USA.

BACCINI, John; b. 31 March 1947, Luton, Bedfordshire, England. Musician. *Career:* Played electric bass guitar in clubs and pubs, 1960–; First recording at Abbey Road studios; Played in Germany, 1964; Played in clubs and on radio and television, 1966–70; Numerous BBC radio sessions and shows with various bands, also performing backing and lead vocals; Over 40 records for major labels, to date; Engineer, up to 4000 sessions, from rhythm section work to orchestral and 60 piece choir, all musical styles; Producer, 1970–; Music Publisher, 1973–; Songwriter. *Membership:* PRS; MCPS. *Current Management:* Everyday Music, 14–15 Cam Sq., Wilbury Way, Hitchin, Hertfordshire SG4 0TZ, England.

BACH, Sebastian, (Sebastian Bierk); b. 3 April 1968, Bahamas. Rock Vocalist; Lyricist. m. Maria Aquinar, 1992. *Career:* Lead singer, US rock group Skid Row, 1986–98; Major appearances include: Support to Bon Jovi, US tour, 1988; Support to Guns N' Roses, US tour, 1991; European tour, 1991; US tour, 1992; Earth Pledge Concert, Central Park, New York, 1992; South American tour, 1992; Monsters of Rock Festival, Castle Donington, 1992; Japanese tour, 1992; Took title role in Broadway production of Jekyll and Hyde, 2000. *Recordings:* Albums: Skid Row, 1989; Slave To The Grind (No. 1, USA), 1991; B-Sides Ourselves, 1992; Subhuman Race, 1995; Scream, 1996; Working Man, 1996; 12 Picks, 1997; Forty Seasons..., 1998; Loaded Deck, 1998; Bring 'Em Bach Alive, 1999; Singles: Youth Gone Wild, 1989; 18 and Life, 1989; I Remember You, 1990; Monkey Business, 1991; Slave To The Grind, 1991; Wasted Time, 1991. *Honours:* Gold discs; American Music Awards, Favourite New Hard Rock Artist, 1990. *Current Management:* Doc McGhee, McGhee Entertainment, 8730 Sunset Blvd, Suite 175, Los Angeles, CA 90069, USA.

BACH YEN, , (Bach Yen Tran, Blanche Hirondelle); b. 12 June 1942, Soc Trang, Viet Nam. Pop and Folk Vocalist. m. Tran Quang Hai, 17 June 1978, 1 d. *Career:* Started performing in Paris, 1961, in the style of Edith Piaf; Tour of Europe including Belgium, Germany and Austria; Visited USA, 1965; Appeared on Ed Sullivan TV Show; Appearances on other television shows and appearances with Bing Crosby, Joey Bishop, Mike Douglas, Pat Boone; Toured in 46 US states and also visited Canada, Mexico, Caracas, Panama, Bogotá, Curaçao, alongside Jimmy Duranti, Liberace and Frankie Avalon; Sang for John Wayne film, The Green Berets; Returned to Paris; Met Musician and Ethnomusicologist Tran Quang Hai and worked with traditional Vietnamese folk music; Performed in over 2,000 concerts. *Recordings:* Recorded 7 albums with Tran Quang Hai. *Honours:* Grand Prix du Disque, Académie Charles Cros in 1983. *Address:* 12 rue Gutenberg, 94450 Limeil Brevannes, France.

BACHARACH, Burt; b. 12 May 1928, Kansas City, Missouri, USA. Composer; Arranger; Conductor; Musician (piano). m. (1) Paula Stewart, (2) Angie Dickinson, (3) Carole Bayer Sager, 1982, 1 s., 1 d. *Education:* Composition and Theory, McGill University, Montréal; Music Academy West, Santa Barbara. *Career:* Jazz musician, 1940s; Accompanist, arranger, conductor, various artists including Vic Damone; Marlene Dietrich; Joel Gray; Steve Lawrence. *Compositions:* Popular songs, film music and stage musicals; Regular collaborations with Hal David, 1962–70; Carole Bayer Sager, 1981–; Numerous hit songs as co-writer include: with Hal David: The Story of My Life, Marty Robbins; Magic Moments, Perry Como; Tower of Strength, Frankie Vaughan; Wives and Lovers, Jack Jones; 24 Hours From Tulsa, Gene Pitney; What The World Needs Now Is Love, Jackie DeShannon; Walk On By; Trains and Boats and Planes; Do You Know The Way To San Jose?; Alfie (all by Dionne Warwick); Anyone Who Had A Heart, Cilla Black; There's Always Something There To Remind Me, Sandie Shaw; Make It Easy On Yourself, Walker Brothers; What's New Pussycat?, Tom Jones; This Guy's In Love With You, Herb Alpert; Raindrops Keep Fallin' On My Head, Sacha Distel; Close To You, The Carpenters; Numerous film scores include: The Man Who Shot Liberty Valence; Wives and Lovers; What's New Pussycat?; Alfie; Casino Royale; Butch Cassidy and The Sundance Kid; with Carole Bayer Sager: Making Love, Roberta Flack; Heartlight, Neil Diamond; That's What Friends Are For, Dionne Warwick and Friends (AIDS charity record); On My Own, Patti Labelle and Michael McDonald; with Carole Bayer Sager, Peter Allen and Christopher Cross: Arthur's Theme, Christopher Cross. *Recordings:* Albums include: Hit Maker, 1965; Reach Out, 1967; Make It Easy On Yourself, 1969; Burt Bacharach, 1971; Portrait In Music, 1971; Living Together, 1973; Greatest Hits, 1974; Futures, 1977, 1999; Woman, 1979; Walk On By, 1989; Butch Cassidy and The Sundance Kid, 1989. *Publications:* Numerous song books. *Honours:* Entertainers of the Year, with Hal David, Cue Magazine, 1969; 3 Academy Awards; 4 Grammy Awards; 2 Emmy Awards; 1 Tony Award. *Address:* c/o McMullen and Co, Hollywood, CA, USA.

BACHCHAN, Amitabh Harivanshrai; b. 11 Oct. 1942, Alahabad, India. Vocalist; Actor. m. Jaya Bhaduri. *Career:* Indian film actor but, unusually, does much of own singing; First film, Saat Hindustani, later became one of the most popular Indian film actors; Retired from acting and became involved in politics; Returned to film as head of prod. co; Acting comeback, 1997; Named the Superstar of the Millennium by BBC Online poll, defeating many Hollywood legends such as Alec Guinness and Marlon Brando, 1999; Host, quiz show Kaun Banega Crorepati (Indian version of Who Wants To Be A Millionaire?); Critically acclaimed role in film, Mohabbatein, 2000; Became first living Asian to have a statue of his likeness installed in Madame Tussaud's waxwork museum, London. *Recordings include:* It's My Choice (compilation), 1997; Bachchan Blast (remixes), 2000. *Honours:* Filmfare, Lifetime Achievement Award, 1991; BBC, Superstar of the Millennium, 1999; Filmfare, Star of the 20th Century, 2000.

BACHMAN, Randy; b. 27 Sept. 1943, Winnipeg, Manitoba, Canada. Vocalist; Musician (guitar); Songwriter. *Career:* Father of singer-songwriter Tal Bachman; Member, Guess Who; Founder member, Brave Belt; Re-formed as Bachman-Turner Overdrive, 1972–76; Solo career, 1977–79; Founder member, Ironhorse, 1979; Union, 1981; Solo artist, 1981–; Tours with re-formed Guess Who, 1984. *Compositions include:* You Ain't Seen Nothing Yet. *Recordings:* with Bachman-Turner Overdrive: Singles: Let It Ride, 1974; Takin' Care Of Business, 1974; You Ain't Seen Nothing Yet (No. 1, USA), 1974; Roll On Down The Highway, 1975; Hey You, 1975; Albums: Bachman-Turner Overdrive, 1973; Bachman-Turner Overdrive 2, 1974; Not Fragile (No. 1, USA), 1974; BTO As Brave Belt, 1975; Four-Wheel Drive, 1975; Head On, 1976; The Best Of BTO (So Far), 1976; Bachman-Turner Overdrive, 1984; Solo albums: Axe, 1972; Survivor, 1978; Any Road (featuring Neil Young), 1993; with Ironhorse: Ironhorse, 1979; Everything Is Grey, 1979; with Union: on Strike, 1981; CD, Merge, 1996; Randy Bachman Song book, 1999. *Honours:* Prairie Music Hall of Fame, Manitoba, Canada, 1999. *Current Management:*

c/o Marty Kramer Bachman Headquarters, 10331 Steveston Hwy, Richmond, BC V7A 1N3, Canada.

BACKER, Matthew De Bracey; b. New Orleans, Louisiana, USA. Musician (guitar); Vocalist; Songwriter. m. Elisa Richards, 5 Jan. 1994. *Education:* BA Hons, University of Warwick; Berklee College of Music, Boston, USA. *Career:* Recordings, performances, television appearances with: Sinéad O'Connor; Elton John; Marcella Detroit; Aimee Mann; Emmylou Harris; Mica Paris; Joe Cocker; Swing Out Sister; Beautiful South; Sarah Jane Morris; Michael Ball; Suzanne Rhatigan; Jools Holland; Kate Saint John; Daniel Cartier; Soundtrack work for television programmes including Equinox; Cracker; Spitting Image; Knowing Me Knowing You; Rory Bremner; Solo and collaborative singing/songwriting, and session work. *Membership:* Musicians' Union.

BADALAMENTI, Angelo, (Andy Badale, Angelo Bagdelamenti); b. 22 March 1937, New York, NY, USA. Composer. *Education:* Eastman School of Music. *Career:* Composed some pop songs (under name Andy Badale); Collaborations with artistes including Julee Cruise, Jocelyn West, Tim Booth, Marianne Faithfull, the Pet Shop Boys; Worked as orchestrator and conductor on many movies; Some cameo appearances in films and television. *Compositions:* For film: Gordon's War (as Andy Badale), 1973; Law and Disorder (as Andy Badale), 1974; Blue Velvet, 1986; A Nightmare on Elm Street 3: Dream Warriors, 1987; Weeds, 1987; Tough Guys Don't Dance, 1987; Parents, 1989; Cousins, 1989; National Lampoon's Christmas Vacation, 1989; Wait Until Spring, Bandini, 1989; Wild at Heart, 1990; The Comfort of Strangers, 1990; Twin Peaks: Fire Walk With Me, 1992; Naked in New York, 1994; La cité des enfants perdus, 1995; Lost Highway, 1997; The Blood Oranges, 1997; Arlington Road, 1999; song Who Will Take My Dreams Away?, for La fille sur le pont, 1999; The Straight Story, 1999; Holy Smoke, 1999; Forever Mine, 1999; Story of a Bad Boy, 1999; The Beach, 2000; A Piece of Eden, 2000; Julie Johnson, 2001; Mulholland Drive, 2001; Cet amour-là, 2001; Suspended Animation, 2001; Secretary, 2002; L'Adversaire, 2002; Cabin Fever, 2002; Auto Focus, 2002; Resistance, 2002; Mysteries of Love, 2002; Darkened Room, 2002. For television: Twin Peaks, 1990; Industrial Symphony No. 1: The Dream of the Broken Hearted, 1990; On the Air, 1992; David Lynch's Hotel Room, 1993; Witch Hunt, 1994; Inside the Actor's Studio (as Angelo Bagdelamenti), 1994; Profiler, 1996; Cracker (aka Fitz), 1997; Mario Puzo's The Last Don, 1997; Lathe of Heaven, 2002.

BADLEY, Bill; b. Wiltshire, England. Musician (guitar, banjo, mandolin, lute); Vocalist. *Education:* Medieval Studies, Exeter University; Lute, Royal College of Music. *Career:* Played with: The Consort of Musicke; The New London Consort; The Dufay Collective; Own group, Arcadia; Film work includes: Lady Jane; Caravaggio; Member, The Carnival Band, 1984–; First performance, Burnley Canalside Festival, 1984; Play material from: Sweden; Croatia; USA; Bolivia; Spain; UK; France; Appearances include: festivals, arts theatres and centres; Barbican Centre; Glasgow Cathedral; Birmingham Symphony Hall; Assistant producer, Thames Television. *Recordings include:* Album with Maddy Prior: Christmas Carols. *Current Management:* c/o Jim McPhee, Acorn Entertainments. *Address:* Winterfold House, 46 Woodfield Rd, Kings Heath, Birmingham B13 9UJ, England.

BADLY DRAWN BOY, (Damon Gough); b. 2 Oct. 1970, Bolton, England. Vocalist; Musician (guitar, keyboards); Songwriter. *Career:* Collaborated with UNKLE, 1998; Runs Twisted Nerve record label with Andy Votel. *Recordings:* Albums: The Hour Of Bewilderbeast, 2000; About A Boy OST, 2002; Have You Fed The Fish?, 2002. Singles: EP1, 1997; EP2, EP3, 1998; It Came From The Ground, Once Around The Block, 1999; Another Pearl, Disillusion, 2000; Pissing In The Wind, 2001; Silent Sigh, 2002; Something To Talk About, 2002. *Honours:* Mercury Music Prize, The Hour of Bewilderbeast, 2000. *Current Management:* Big Life Management, 67–69 Chalton St, London NW1 1HY, England. *Address:* c/o XL-Recordings, 17–19 Alma Rd, London SW18 1AA, England. *Website:* www.badlydrawnboy.co.uk.

BADU, Erykah; b. 26 Feb. 1972, Dallas, Texas, USA. Vocalist; Songwriter. 1 s. *Education:* Graduated in Theatre, Grambling State University, Louisiana. *Career:* Performances with cousin Free, in Erykah Free; Turned solo, obtained recording deal; Appeared in interview in numerous publications including Time and Rolling Stone; Support slots to numerous artists including Wu Tang Clan; Collaborations: Omar; OutKast; Guru. *Recordings:* Singles: Next Lifetime, 1997; Tyrone, 1997; Apple Tree, 1997; On and On, 1997; Southern Girl, 1999; You Got Me (with The Roots), 1999; Bag Lady, 2000; Didn't Cha Know, 2001; Albums: Baduizm, 1997; Live, 1997; Heartache, 1998; Mama's Gun, 2000. *Honours:* Grammy Award, Best Rap Performance By Duo Or Group, You Got Me (with The Roots), 2000.

BAEZ, Joan Chandos; b. 9 Jan. 1941, Staten Island, New York, USA. Vocalist. m. David Harris, 26 March 1968, divorced 1974, 1 s. *Education:* Boston University, 1958; Dr Humane Letters, Antioch University, 1980; Rutgers University, 1980. *Recordings:* Albums include: Joan Baez, 1960; Joan Baez, Vol. 2, 1961; In Concert, part 2, 1963; 5, 1964; Farewell Angelina, 1965; Noel, 1966; Joan, 1967; Baptism, 1968; Any Day Now, 1968; David's Album, 1969; One Day At A Time, 1969; First Ten Years, 1970; Carry It On

(soundtrack), 1971; Ballad Book, 1972; Come From The Shadows, 1972; Where Are You Now My Son?, 1973; Hits, Greatest and Others, 1973; Gracias A La Vida, 1974; Contemporary Ballad Book, 1974; Diamonds and Rust, 1975; From Every Stage, 1976; Gulf Winds, 1976; Blowin' Away, 1977; Best Of, 1977; Honest Lullaby, 1979; Very Early Joan, 1982; Recently, 1987; Diamonds and Rust In The Bullring, 1989; Speaking Of Dreams, 1989; Play Me Backwards, 1992; Rare Live and Classic, 1993; Ring Them Bells, 1995; Gone from Danger, 1997; Dreams, 1997; Best Of..., 1997; 20th Century Masters: The Millennium, 1999. *Publications:* Joan Baez Song Book, 1964; Daybreak, 1968; Coming Out (with David Harris), 1971; And Then I Wrote (song book), 1979; And A Voice To Sing With: A Memoir, 1987. *Honours:* 8 Gold albums; 1 Gold single; Joan Baez Day In Atlanta, Georgia, 2 Aug. 1975; Thomas Merton Award, 1976; Public Service, Third Annual Rock Music, 1977; Best Female Vocalist, Bay Area Music, 1978, 1979; ACLU Awards, 1979, 1989; Jefferson Award, 1980; Lennon Peace Tribute, 1982; ADA Award, 1982; Sane Education Fund Peace, 1983; Chevalier, Legion of Honour, France, 1983; Academy Charles Cros (France), 1983; Death Penalty Focus, California, 1992. *Membership:* Founder, Institute Study Nonviolence, 1965; Founder, President, Humanitas International Human Rights Committee, 1979–92. *Address:* PO Box 1026, Menlo Park, CA 94026, USA.

BAGGE, Nigel; b. 6 June 1953, London, England. Musician (guitar); Vocalist; Songwriter. *Career:* Extensive gigging, bands include: Cold Comfort, 1970s; Highway 61, 1985–90; Duck Soup, 1990–; Bag Band, 1992–93; Juice On The Loose, 1990; Nicky Moore's Blues Corporation, 1993–97; Angela Brown and The Mighty 45s, 1997–; Various session work. *Recordings:* Albums: Cold Comfort: In The Can; Highway 61: Talk To Me; Further Up The Road; Nicky Moore's Blues Corporation: I Just Got Back; Holding On; Angela Brown and the Mighty 45s: Thinking Out Loud. *Membership:* Musicians' Union. *Current Management:* A.R.M., PO Box 177, New Malden, Surrey KT3 6YT, England.

BAHRI, Mamdouh; b. 31 July 1957, Sfax, Tunisia. Musician (guitar). m. Geva Nouyrit, 24 July 1993, 1 s., 1 d. *Education:* Swiss Jazz School; Seminars with Joe Diorio, Jim Hall, John Abercrombie. *Career:* Festival Jazz D'0-Beziers, 1989; Bastia Festival, 1990; Carthage Music Festival, Tunisia, 1991; New Yok, Blue Note, 1992, 95; Romans Festival, 1993; Pori Jazz Festival, Finland, 1995; Sweet Basil, 1995; Appearances in USA: New York; Alabama; Connecticut; Maryland. *Recordings:* From Tunisia With Love, The Spirit Of Life Ensemble, 1992; Mamoudh Bahri, Nefta, 1993; Inspirations, 1993; Feel The Spirit, 1994; Live At The S Spot, 1995. *Membership:* SACEM; SPEDIDAM; ADAMI. *Address:* 4 Lot Bonnier D'Alco, 34990 Juvignac, France.

BAIKIE, Pete; b. 17 April 1957, Edinburgh, Scotland. Composer; Writer; Comedian; Musician (guitar, piano), Actor. *Education:* Edinburgh University. *Career:* Actor, writer, BBC Radio 4 series In Other Words... The Bodgers, 1985; Actor, singer/musician, BBC Radio 4 series Bodgers, Banks and Sparkes, 1986; Actor, singer, musician, writer, CH4 television series, Absolutely, 1989–93; Actor, writer, CH4 television series, Squawkie Talkie, 1995; Actor, role of Bandleader, Swing Kids (Disney film); Producer, HTV/Paramount television series Barry Welsh Is Coming, 1996–; Bandleader/musician, Channel 5 UK television series The Jack Docherty Show, 1997; Co-presenter, BBC Radio 2 series Saturday Night Jack, 2000–01; Co-founder, Absolutely Productions, 1989–. *Compositions:* Television themes for: It's Only TV But I LIke It (BBC1), Vic and Bob's Shooting Stars, Two Fat Ladies, Bang Bang It's Reeves and Mortimer, Stressed Eric (all BBC2); Barbara, 2DTV (both ITV1); Absolutely; mr don and mr george; Squawkie Talkie; Teenage Health Freak (all CH4); Radio themes for: Labour Exchange; If You're So Clever; The Preventers, BBC Radio 4. *Membership:* Musicians' Union; BAC&S. *Address:* c/o Absolutely Productions, 226 Craven House, 121 Kingsway, London WC2B 6PA, England. *Website:* www.absolutely-uk.com.

BAILEY, Derek; b. 29 Jan. 1930, Sheffield, Yorkshire, England. Musician (guitar). 1 s. *Education:* Music with C H C Biltcliffe; Guitar with George Wing, Jack Duarte, and others. *Career:* Orchestral guitarist, 1951–65; Soloist, 1965–; Performed solo concerts in most of world's cultural centres; Played with most of the musicians associated with freely improvised music. *Recordings:* Recorded over 100 albums on many labels; Recorded with: Company; Cecil Taylor; Han Bennink; Anthony Braxton; Steve Lacy. *Publications:* Improvisation, Its Nature and Practice. *Current Management:* Incus Records. *Address:* 14 Downs Rd, London E5 8DS, England.

BAILEY, Jim; b. 10 Jan. 1948, Philadelphia, USA. Vocalist; Actor; Entertainer. *Education:* Voice, piano, Philadelphia Conservatory of Music. *Career:* Concerts world-wide include: Carnegie Hall, Las Vegas; Top casinos; London Palladium; Specials: Superbowl; Olympics; Peoples Choice Awards; Royal Variety (twice); Television shows: about 40 include: Here's Lucy; Vegas; Rockford Files; Carol Burnett Show; Ed Sullivan; Tonight Show; Des O'Connor; Russell Harty; Pebble Mill. *Recordings:* Jim Bailey Live At Carnegie Hall; Jim Bailey Sings, 1998; Also performed for three US Presidents. *Honours:* Las Vegas Entertainer of the Year, 4 times; People's Choice Award; IPA Award, 2 times; Many theatre awards. *Current Management:* Stephen Campbell Management. *Address:* 350 N Crescent Dr., Suite 105, Beverly Hills, CA 90210, USA.

BAILEY, Philip; b. 8 May 1951, Denver, Colorado, USA. Vocalist; Musician (percussion); Prod. *Career:* Musical director, gospel group The Stovall Sisters; Member, Friends and Love; Member, Earth Wind and Fire, 1972–84, 1987–; Solo recording artiste, 1983–86; Peformances include: Opened for Sly and The Family Stone, Madison Square Gardens, 1974; Featured as rock band in film, Shining Star, 1975; Tours, USA, Europe, Asia, 1979; Music for UNICEF Concert, UN, New York, 1979; Earth Pledge Concert, Central Park, New York, 1992. *Recordings:* Albums: Last Days and Time, 1972; Head To The Sky, 1973; Open Our Eyes, 1973; That's The Way Of The World, 1975; Gratitude, 1976; Spirit, 1976; All 'N' All, 1978; The Best Of, Vol. 1, 1979; I Am, 1979; Faces, 1980; Raise, 1981; Powerlight, 1983; Chinese Wall, 1985; The Wonders Of His Love, 1984; Inside Out, 1986; Triumph, 1986; Wonders Of Love, 1988; Family Affair, 1990; Philip Bailey, 1994; Dreams, 1999; Singles include: Getaway, 1976; Saturday Nite, 1977; Serpentine Fire, 1978; Fantasy, 1978; Got To Get You Into My Life, 1978; September, 1979; Runnin', 1979; Boogie Wonderland, 1979; After The Love Has Gone, 1979; Star, 1979; Let's Groove, 1981; Here With Me, 1994; Solo: Easy Lover (duet with Phil Collins, No. 1, UK), 1985. *Honours:* American Music Awards, Favourite Band, Soul/ Rhythm and Blues, 1977, 1979; Grammy, Best R&B Vocal Performance, All 'N' All, 1979; After The Love Has Gone, 1980; Best R&B Instrumental, Boogie Wonderland, 1980; Gold Ticket, Madison Square Garden, 1979; MTV Music Video, 1985; Ivor Novello Award, Easy Lover, 1986; Grammy Award, Best Gospel Performance, 1987. *Current Management:* Bob Cavallo, Third Rail Entertainment. *Address:* 9169 Sunset Blvd, Los Angeles, CA 90069, USA.

BAILEY, Roy; b. 20 Oct. 1935, London, England. Folk Vocalist; Musician (guitar); Academic. m. Val Turbard, 10 Aug. 1963, 1 s., 1 d. *Education:* BA Hons, Social Science. *Career:* Professional singer, 1960–; Radio, television, tours, in: UK; Switzerland; Canada; USA; Australia; Appearances include festivals in: UK; Canada; Switzerland; Belgium; Australia; Professor of Sociology and Social Work, Sheffield Hallam University, 1988. *Recordings:* Smoke and Dust Where The Heart Should Have Been, 1965; Oats and Beans and Kangaroos, 1966; Cobweb Of Dreams, 1967; Roy Bailey, 1970; That's Not The Way It's Got To Be (with Leon Rosselson), 1975; New Bell Wake, 1976; Love Loneliness and Laundry (with Leon Rosselson) 1977; If I Knew Who The Enemy Was (with Leon Rosselson) 1978; Hard Times, 1982; Freedom Peacefully, 1985; Leaves From A Tree, 1989; Why Does It Have To Be Me, 1990; Never Leave A Story Unsung, 1992; What You Do With What You've Got, 1993; Business As Usual, 1994; Rhythm and Reds (with Band of Hope), 1994; New Directions in the Old, 1997; Past Masters, 1998. *Publications:* Contemporary Social Problems in Britain (with Jock Young), 1973; Radical Social Work (with Mike Brake), 1975; Radical Social Work and Practice (with Mike Brake), 1980; Theory and Practice In Social Work (with Phil Lee), 1982. *Honours:* Fellow, Royal Society of Arts, 1989; Emeritus Professor, Sheffield Hallam University, 1990. *Current Management:* Brass Tacks Music Agency, PO Box 1162, Sheffield S8 9JY, England.

BAIN, Aly; b. 15 May 1946, Lerwick, Shetland, Scotland. Musician (violin). *Education:* Began playing aged 11; Taught by Tom Anderson. *Career:* Member, Boys of The Lough, 1988; Television includes: Presenter, Down Home, series on spread of fiddle music from Scotland and Ireland to North America, BBC, 1991; Series, The Shetland Set, BBC, 1991. *Recordings:* Aly Bain-Mike Whelans, 1971; The Silver Bow (with Tom Anderson), 1976; Shetland Folk Fiddling Vol. 2 (with Tom Anderson), 1978; Aly Bain, 1985; Down Home Vol. 1, 1986; Down Home Vol. 2, 1986; Aly Meets The Cajuns, 1988; The Pearl, 1995; Follow The Moonstone, 1996; Lonely Bird, 1996; Ruby, 1998.

BAIYEWU, Tunde; b. London, England. Vocalist. *Education:* Newcastle University. *Career:* Singer, The Lighthouse Family, 1994–; Television includes: Top of the Pops. *Recordings:* Albums: Ocean Drive, 1995; Postcards From Heaven, 1997; Whatever Gets You Through The Day, 2001; Singles: Lifted, 1995; Ocean Drive (for film soundtrack Jack and Sarah), 1995; Goodbye Heartbreak, 1996; Loving Every Minute, 1996; Raincloud, 1997; High, 1998; Lost In Space, 1998; Question Of Faith, 1998; Free/One, 2001. *Current Management:* Kitchenware, 7 The Stables, St Thomas St, Newcastle upon Tyne, Tyne and Wear NE1 4LE, England.

BAJTALA, Janos; b. 5 Dec. 1944, Budapest, Hungary. Vocalist; Composer; Arranger; Musician (piano). 1 s. *Education:* Diploma, Jazz Academy, Budapest. *Career:* Formed Jazz/Soul Trio, 1965; Television and radio shows in Hungary, 1965–71; Tours with soul bands The Bandwagon, Foundation, 1974; Co-arranger, West End hit musical, The Black Mikado, 1975–76; Tours with reggae group Chosen Few, 1981–88; Tours with Boney M, 1991–98; Tours with Jimmy Ruffin (Motown), 1999–; First appearance in 24 years in Hungary, broadcast on national television, 1995. *Recordings:* Gipsy Girl (own composition), charted in Hungary, 1968; Keyboards, Black Mikado cast album, 1975; Keyboards on album Bad Weathers, Vivian Weathers, 1980; Various recordings with Chosen Few, 1981–88. *Honours:* First prize, nationwide pop and jazz contest, 1967; Best soloist, Hugarian International Jazz Festival, 1971. *Membership:* PRS. *Address:* 176 Weedington Rd, London NW5 4QQ, England. *Telephone:* (20) 7482-3570. *E-mail:* janosbajala@hotmail.com.

BAKALA, Bretislav; b. 18 June 1957, Brno, Czech Republic. Musician (keyboard). m. Marta Srvtova, 8 Sept. 1984, 1 s., 1 d. *Education:* Diploma, College of Technology, Brno, Faculty of Electronics; Folk Art School. *Career:* Keyboard in Jazz Duo Brno; Good Company, Dancing 19, in Norway, Germany, Switzerland, Mallorca, Austria, 1987–97; Immerwieder, 1 CD, Just Friends, 2 CD, Composer, Keyboards, Sound Studio. *Compositions:* Warum Lieb'ich Dich Allein; Lift Me Up; You're Crossing My Life; New Day; Zeit, Du Heilst Wunden. *Recordings:* Immer Wieder, CD, 1994; Just Friends, CD, 1996. *Current Management:* Good Sound CZ. *Address:* 2a Gymnaziem 2448, 39701 Pisek, Czech Republic.

BAKER, Anita; b. 20 Dec. 1957, Detroit, USA. Vocalist. m. Walter Bridgforth, 24 Dec. 1988, 1 s. *Career:* Lead vocalist, soul group Chapter 8, 1976–80; Solo singer, 1983–; Appearances include: Nelson Mandela International Tribute, Wembley, 1990; Radio City Music Hall, 1990; Compositions tour, 1990; Television appearances include: Christmas in Washington, NBC, 1991; A Call To Action In The War Against AIDS, ABC, 1992. *Recordings:* Albums: with Chapter 8: Chapter 8; Solo albums: The Songstress, 1983; Rapture (No. 1, USA R&B chart), 1986; Giving You The Best That I Got (No. 1, USA), 1988; Compositions, 1990; Rhythm Of Love, 1994; Singles: No More Tears; Angel; You're The Best Thing Yet; Sweet Love; Caught Up In The Rapture; Same Ole Love; No One In The World; Just Because; Giving You The Best That I Got; Talk To Me; Soul Inspiration; Fairy Tales; Live In London; Body and Soul; I Apologize; It's Been You; When You Love Someone; featured on: Rubáiyát (Elektra Records 40th Anniversary compilation), 1990; Barcelona Gold, 1992. *Honours:* Grammy Awards: 5 consecutive Best Female R&B Vocal Performances, 1987–91; Best R&B Song, Sweet Love, 1987; Giving The Best That I Got, 1989; Best Soul/Gospel Performance, 1988; Soul Train Awards: Best Single, Female, 1987; Best R&B Single, Best R&B Album, Best R&B Song, 1989; American Music Awards: Favourite Female Soul/R&B Artist, 1988, 1990; Favourite Female Soul/R&B Album, 1988; NAACP Image Award, Best Female Artist, 1990. *Current Management:* Sterling/Winters Co, 1640 Ave of the Stars, Los Angeles, CA 90067, USA.

BAKER, Arthur; Prod; Remixer. *Career:* Worked with as Prod.: Afrika Bambaataa, Ash, Lee Coombs, Felix da Housecat, Mansun, Timo Mass, New Order, Senser. Worked with as Remixer: David Bowie, Bob Dylan, Fleetwood Mac, Morcheeba, The Pet Shop Boys, Rolling Stones, Bruce Springsteen, Talking Heads. *Address:* c/o Stephen Budd Management Ltd, 109b Regents Park Rd, Primrose Hill, London NW1 8UR, England. *Website:* www.record-producers.com.

BAKER, Carroll Anne; b. 4 March 1949, Nova Scotia, Canada. Country Vocalist; Songwriter. *Career:* British tour with Slim Whitman; Recorded duets with daughter Candace; Eddie Eastman; Jack Scott; Roger Whittaker; Concert with Canada Pops Orchestra; Television includes: 3 Carroll Baker super specials, CBC; Mini-series, 7 half-hour shows, CBC; Guest appearances: Hee Haw; New Country; Nashville Now; The Tommy Hunter Show; Lifetime; Canada AM; Headlined for Regent Holiday Tours, Carroll Baker's Country Cruise, 1989. *Compositions include:* I'm An Old Rock and Roller (Dancin' To A Different Beat). *Recordings:* I Should Have Put A Hold On Love (Canadian Country No. 2), 1990. *Honours:* Entertainer of the Year, Country Award, Canada; 3 Platinum, 6 Gold albums; 5 Gold Singles; JUNO Awards: 1975–78; Big Country Awards, 1975–81; 1987; BMI Award, 1977; RPM Programmer Award, 1978, 1981; Procan Award, 1983; 14 consecutive No. 1 singles, Canadian country charts, 1975–81; Top Country Female, Canadian Country Music, 1985; Martin Guitar Award, 1989; Lifetime Achievement, Canadian Country Music Awards, 1991; Inductee, Canadian Country Music Hall of Honour, 1992. *Membership:* AFofM; ACTRA; SOCAN. *Current Management:* John Beaulieu, Carroll Baker Enterprises Inc. *Address:* 210 Dimson Ave, Guelph, ON N1G 3C8, Canada.

BAKER, Ginger (Peter); b. 19 Aug. 1939, Lewisham, London, England. Musician (drums). *Career:* Drummer with Terry Lightfoot; Acker Bilk; Alexis Korner's Blues Incorporated, 1962; Graham Bond Organisation, 1963; Member, Cream, 1966–68; Blind Faith, 1969; Airforce, 1970–72; Salt (Nigeria); Baker-Gurvitz Army; Energy; Short spells with Atomic Rooster and Hawkwind; Ginger Baker's Nutters; Solo recording artiste, and leader of own trio (with Bill Frisell and Charlie Haden); Collaboration with Masters of Reality, 1993; Performances include: with Cream: Jazz and Blues Festival, Windsor, 1966, 1967; 2 US tours, 1967; Madison Square Garden, New York, 1968; Royal Albert Hall, London, 1968; with Blind Faith: Hyde Park, London, 1969; Madison Square Garden, New York, 1969. *Recordings:* Albums: with Cream: Fresh Cream, 1967; Disraeli Gears, 1967; Wheels Of Fire, 1968; Goodbye, 1969; The Best Of Cream, 1969; Live Cream, 1970; Live Cream Vol. 2, 1972; Heavy Cream, 1972; 20th Century Masters (compilation), 2000; with Blind Faith: Blind Faith (No. 1, UK and USA), 1969; with Airforce: Airforce, 1970; Airforce 2, 1972; Solo: The Best Of, 1973; 11 Sides Of Baker, 1977; From Humble Origins, 1983; Horses and Trees, 1987; In Concert, 1987; African Force, 1980s; In Concert, 1987; Middle Passage, 1992; The Album, 1992; The Alternative Album, 1992; Unseen Rain, 1993; with Ginger Baker Trio: Going Back Home, 1995; Falling Off The Roof, 1995; Do What You Like, 1998; Coward Of The County, 1999; Singles with Cream include: I Feel Free, 1967;

Strange Brew, 1967; Sunshine Of Your Love, 1968; White Room, 1968. *Current Management:* Kron Management, 41489 Frontier Rd, Parker, CO 80134, USA.

BAKER, Ronald; b. 21 Nov. 1968, Baltimore, Maryland, USA. Musician (trumpet); Vocalist. m. Patricia Labeau, 26 Feb. 1994, 1 d. *Education:* BA, Music Education. *Career:* Appearances on Radio France; Played in film, Le Nouveau Monde; Opened concerts for: André Ceccarelli; Black Label; Roy Haynes; Benny Waters; Major festivals include: Montlouis; Montpellier; Orléans; Concert at Virgin Megastore. *Recordings:* Oberlin Jazz Ensemble; Perry-Boulanger Duo; Oppossum Gang. *Address:* 1 Passage Des Grillons, 37390 La Membrolle, France.

BAKER, Toni; b. 24 Feb. 1949, Littleborough, Lancashire, England. Musician (keyboards); MD; Arranger. m. Stephanie, 12 Dec. 1986, 1 s., 1 d. *Education:* Piano lessons, aged 5–14. *Career:* Played American bases, in soul music apprenticeship; Television shows include: Opportunity Knocks, 1971–76; Formed: Shabby Tiger, pop/rock band; No. 1 hits in Denmark, Netherlands, Belgium; Session work, freelance; Played with The Dakotas. *Compositions:* Eat You Up (No. 3, Japan); 5 album tracks for Shabby Tiger include: Nancy; Shabby Tiger; 20th Century Cowboy. *Membership:* Musicians' Union; Equity.

BALD HEAD SLICK. See: **GURU.**

BALDAN, Bebo; b. 16 April 1966, Venice, Italy. Prod., Musician (drums, percussion, electronics); Composer. *Education:* Studied with Percussione Ricerca Ensemble, Conservatory of Venice, Nana Vasconcelos, Trilok Gurtu. *Career:* Played in: Italy (Interzone Festival, RAI Television, Videomusic Television); France (Sacre du Printemps); England; Switzerland; Brazil; New York (and KPEL Radio, Berkeley, California); Tallinn Jazz Festival, Estonia; Tour of Mexico, Venezuela and Scandinavia; Played with Eugenio Bennato, DMA, Max M'Bass Ado, Andrea Braido, Luis Rizzo, Estasia, Duck Baker, Tolo Marton, Stephen James, Eddy C Campbell, Pitura Freska. *Compositions:* The Armenian Island, 1999; Soundtracks: Macbeth, film by Claudio Misculin; Aqua Nostra Igniset, film by Anselmo de Filippis. *Recordings:* As composer: Bebo Baldan: Vapor Frames; with Stephen James: Soniasikri-Sub Rosa, 1992; with David Torn: Diving Into The World, 1995; Earthbeat, 1995; Tantra, featuring David Torn, 1999; Jaya, 1998; Maya, 2000. *Publications:* Ethnos, featuring Gilberto Gil, 1999; Passion of Scotland; Anima, Private Music, Light from the Abyss by P Zennaro and Carolyn Carlson, 1999. *Membership:* SIAE. *Current Management:* Exit. *Address:* Via Antelao, 18 Mestre, Venice, Italy.

BALDASSARI, Butch (Jerome Donald); b. 12 Nov. 1952, Scranton, Pennsylvania, USA. Musician (Mandolin). m. L Sinclair Dickey, 19 March 1993, 1 s. *Education:* Studied Guitar and Violin privately, Pennsylvania and Nevada; 1 Semester, Berklee School of Music, Boston. *Career:* Appearances, CBS, This Morning, Prairie Home Companion, CNN Showbiz, Tennessee Crossroads; Adjunct Associate Professor, Mandolin, Blair School of Music. *Compositions:* What's Doin'; Jack Rabbit Trail; Old Town; Slocum Hollow; Consider This; It's Raining the Blues; King Wilkie. *Recordings:* Gifts, Plectrasonics and All the Rage, with Nashville Mandolin Ensemble; Travellers, Reflections, Cantabile, New Classics, American Portraits, Old Town, Evergreen, solo. *Publications:* You Can Play Bluegrass Mandolin, Vols 1 and 2 (Video); 30 Fiddle Tunes for Mandolin. *Honours:* Co-Producer, Recorded Event of the Year, IBM, 1994. *Membership:* BMI; IBMA; CMSA; NARAS.

BALDOUS, Bernard; b. 12 Dec. 1951, Montpellier, France. Musician (acoustic bass). *Education:* Conservatoire de Musique, Montpellier, 1977; Berklee College of Music, Boston, USA, 1979. *Career:* Plays bass with: R Anouillez; S Baldous; J Blanton; J Benayoun; V Espi-nieto; Fanfan Sanchez; E Goldstein; M Levine; A Marcos; C McBride; J Neves; F Nicolas; J Peiffer; V Perez; P Pellegati; D Ragot; G Reilles; P Rosengoltz; Sega Seck; P Torreglosa; F Urtado; S Wilson; A Woygnet. *Compositions:* Fantome; Gigi; BB Blues. *Recordings:* Bernard Baldous Trio, 1993; Concerto for Jazz Band and Symphony Orchestra, 1994; Instant Jazz Quintet, 1995. *Membership:* Jazz Action Montpellier. *Address:* 3 Pl. Coluche, 34670 Baillargues, France.

BALDRY, Long John; b. 12 Jan. 1941, Haddon, Derbyshire, England. Vocalist. *Career:* Member, R&B groups: Cyril Davies' All-Stars; Ramblin' Jack Elliot; Member, Alexis Korner's Blues Incorporated, 1961; Worked with Horace Silver Quintet, Cyril Davies' R&B All-Stars, 1962; Founder, the Hoochie Coochie Men, 1964; British tour, with Chuck Berry, Moody Blues, 1965; National Jazz and Blues Festival, 1965; Member, Steampacket, 1965–66; Member, Bluesology, 1966–67; Soloist, Rolling Stones '66, 1966; Solo artiste, 1967–; Becomes manager of Stuart A Brown (Bluesology), 1968; First US tour, 1971; Moved to Canada, 1980. *Recordings:* Hit singles include: Let The Heartaches Begin (No. 1, UK), 1967; When The Sun Comes Shinin' Thru, 1968; Mexico, 1968; It's Too Late Now, 1969; Albums: with Alexis Korner: R&B From The Marquee, 1962; with The Hoochie Coochie Men: Long John's Blues, 1964; Solo: It Ain't Easy, 1971; Everything Stops For Tea, 1971; Out!, 1979; Silent Treatment, 1986; It Still Ain't Easy, 1991; The Best Of Long John Baldry, 1991; On Stage Tonight, 1994; Let Rock The Heartaches Begin, 1995;

A Thrill's A Thrill, 1996; With The Best, 1996; Right To Sing The Blues, 1996. *Current Management:* S L Feldman, 1505 W Second Ave, Suite 200, Vancouver, BC V6H 3Y4, Canada.

BALKE, Jon Georg; b. 7 June 1955, Hamar, Norway. Musician (piano, keyboards); Composer. *Career:* Started professional career with Arild Andersen's quartet, 1974; Tours of Europe; Recordings for ECM Records; Later established as composer for groups such as Oslo 13; Masqualero; Jokleba; Magnetic North Orchestra; Also composer of chamber music and theatre. *Recordings:* Albums: Nonsentration, 1992; Further, 1994; Rotor, 1998; Solarized, 1999; Saturation, 1998; Kyanos, 2002. *Honours:* Buddy Award, Norwegian Jazz Federation, 1985; Jazz Musician of Year, 1994; Edvard prize for composition, 2000. *Membership:* Norwegian Composers Asscn; Norwegian Jazz Forum.

BALL, Daryl; b. 9 May 1974, Ballymena, Co Antrim, Northern Ireland. Songwriter; Musician (guitar, bass). *Career:* Started playing guitar aged 15 with school band; Joined The Norwegians; Formed Stripped; Regulars on local radio throughout Ireland and numerous international stations; Television appearance, The Next Big Thing (USA). *Recordings:* The Norwegians, Turn it On, 1991; With Stripped: 4 Walls, 1998; The Girl With Cartoon Eyes, 1999; Compilations: Burbs, 1999. *Honours:* Finalist, Fourth Annual Song for Peace, 1999. *Membership:* Musicians' Union. *Address:* 37 Mount St, Ballymena, Co Antrim BT43 6BW, Northern Ireland.

BALL, David; b. 3 May 1959, Blackpool, Lancashire, England. Musician (synthesizer); Composer. m. Ginny. *Career:* Formed Soft Cell, with Marc Almond, 1979–84, re-formed 2001; Concerts include: Futurama 2 Festival, Leeds, 1980; British tours, 1982–84; Mem., The Grid, with Richard Norris, 1990–; Written and produced for: Kylie Minogue; Billie Ray Martin. *Compositions:* Score for stage musical, Suddenly Last Summer, 1983. *Recordings:* Albums: with Soft Cell: Non-Stop Erotic Cabaret, 1981; Non-Stop Ecstatic Dancing, 1982; The Art Of Falling Apart, 1983; The Last Night In Sodom, 1984; Wasted, 1995; Cruelty Without Beauty, 2002; Compilations: The Singles Album, 1986; Memorabilia, The Singles (remixed by Ball), 1991; The Very Best Of, 2002; Solo: In Strict Tempo, 1983; Singles: with Soft Cell: Tainted Love (World-wide No. 1), 1981; Bedsitter, 1981; Say Hello Wave Goodbye, 1982; Torch, 1982; What, 1982; with The Grid: Floatation, 1990; Beat Called Love, 1990; Texas Cowboys, 1993; Swamp Thing, 1994; Rollercoaster, 1994; Diablo, 1995. *Honours:* Billboard Award, New Wave Band of the Year, 1981; BRIT Award, Best British Single, for Tainted Love, 1982.

BALL, Ian E; b. 1974, Southport, England. Musician (guitar, bass, percussion, harmonica); Vocalist. *Career:* Founding mem., Gomez, 1996–; Numerous concerts, festival, radio and television appearances. *Recordings:* Albums: Bring It On, 1998; Liquid Skin, 1999; Abandoned Shopping Trolley Hotline, 2000; In Our Gun, 2002. Singles: 78 Stone Wobble, 1998; Whippin' Piccadilly, 1998; Get Myself Arrested (EP), 1998; Bring It On, 1999; Rhythm And Blues Alibi, 1999; We Haven't Turned Around (in soundtrack to film, American Beauty), 1999; Machismo (EP), 2000; Collaboration: Hobotalk, Beauty In Madness, 2000. *Honours:* Mercury Music Prize, 1998. *Address:* c/o Hut Records, Kensal House, 553–579 Harrow Rd, London W10 4RH, England. *Website:* www.gomez.co.uk.

BALL, Kenny Daniel; b. 22 May 1930, Ilford, Essex, England. Jazz Musician (trumpet). m. Michelle, 28 Dec. 1984, 1 s., 4 d. *Career:* Played with Charlie Galbraith; Sid Phillip; Eric Delaney; George Chisholm; Terry Lightfoot; Al Fairweather; Formed own dixieland band, Kenny Ball's Jazzmen, 1958–; Film debut, Live It Up (with Gene Vincent), 1963; Film, Trad Dad; Television appearances: Easy Beat, 3 series; Morcambe and Wise, 6 series; Saturday Night at the Mill, 4 series; Numerous foreign tours; UK concerts with: Acker Bilk; Kenny Baker; Lonnie Donegan; George Chisholm; Played at wedding reception, HRH the Prince and Princess of Wales, 1981. *Compositions:* Midnight in Moscow, arrangement. *Recordings:* Albums include: Kenny Ball and His Jazzmen, 1961; The Kenny Ball Show, 1962; The Big Ones, Kenny Ball Style, 1963; Jazz Band Ball, 1964; Trubute To Tokyo, 1964; The Sound Of Kenny Ball, 1968; King Of The Swingers, 1969; At The Jazz Band Ball, 1970; Fleet Street Lightning, 1970; Saturday Night With Kenny Ball and His Band, 1970; Pixie Dust (A Tribute To Walt Disney), 1971; My Very Good Friend… Fats Waller, 1972; Have A Drink On Me, 1972; Let's All Sing A Happy Song, 1973; A Friend To You, 1974; Titillating Tango, 1976; In Concert, 1978; Way Down Yonder, 1977; Soap, 1981; Ball, Barber and Bilk Live At The Royal Festival Hall (with Chris Barber and Acker Bilk), 1984; Kenny Ball and His Jazzmen Play The Movie Greats, 1987; On Stage, 1988; Dixie, 1989; Kenny Ball Plays British, 1989; Jazz Classics, 1990; Kenny Ball Now, 1990; The Ultimate! (with Chris Barber and Acker Bilk), 1991; Singles include: Samantha; Midnight In Moscow; March Of The Siamese Children; The Green Leaves Of Summer; Sukiyaki. *Honours:* 3 Carl Alan Awards; Billboard Best Band. *Membership:* PRS; MCPS; BAC&S; MU. *Current Management:* John Martin Promotions. *Address:* Warmans Farm, Burton End, Stansted, Essex CM24 8UQ, England.

BALL, Malcolm; b. 8 Aug. 1953, Ilford, England. Musician (percussion, keyboards); Composer. *Education:* Royal College of Music, London. *Career:*

Specializing in contemporary music of all kinds; BBC Radio broadcasts with Geoff Warren Quartet for Jazz in Britain, Jazz Today; Arts Council tours of Hungary, Yugoslavia; Workshops with Graham Collier; Head of Percussion, London Borough of Redbridge; Examiner for GSM, London; Writer for Avant, contemporary music magazine; Author, articles on Stockhausen on the Internet. *Compositions:* Close Your Eyes and See, for orchestra, 1995; Many used for library music; O-taiko-Do, Terror Nova, for percussion ensemble. *Recordings:* Close Your Eyes and See, in New British Music, Vol. 1. *Publications:* Percussive Perspectives (IMP). *Honours:* Licentiate, Royal Academy of Music, London. *Membership:* Royal Society of Musicians of Great Britain; Musicians' Union; Stockhausen Society; British Harry Partch Society. *Address:* 79 Chalgrove Cres., Ilford, Essex IG5 0LX, England.

BALL, Michael Ashley; b. 27 June 1962, Bromsgrove, Hereford and Worcester, England. Vocalist; Entertainer. Partner, Cathy McGowan. *Education:* Plymouth College; Guildford School of Music and Drama, 1981–84. *Career:* The Pirates of Penzance, 1984; Les Miserables, West End, 1985; Phantom of the Opera, West End, 1987; Aspects of Love, West End and New York, 1989–90; Represented UK, Eurovision Song Contest, 1992; British tours, 1992, 1993, 1994, 1996, 1999; Television apperances: Host, own series, Michael Ball, 1993, 1994; Film appearance, England My England, 1995; Chitty Chitty Bang Bang, West End, 2002. *Recordings:* Albums: Michael Ball, 1992; Always, 1993; West Side Story, 1993; One Careful Owner, 1994; The Best Of Michael Ball, 1994; First Love, 1996; Michael Ball: The Musicals, 1996; The Movies, 1998; Singles include: Love Changes Everything; The First Man You Remember; It's Still You; One Step Out Of Time; Sunset Boulevard; From Here to Eternity; The Lovers We Were; Wherever You Are; Something Inside So Strong; Appears on cast albums: Les Miserables; Aspects Of Love; Encore!, Andrew Lloyd Webber collection; West Side Story; Passion; Sang on Rugby World Cup album. *Honours:* 10 Gold albums; 1 Platinum album; Variey Club of Great Britain, Recording Artiste of 1998; Theatre Goers Club of Great Britain Award, Most Popular Muscial Actor over the last 21 years, 1999. *Current Management:* Michael Ball Enterprises, PO Box 173, Hampton, TW12 1HF, England. *E-mail:* mbe@michaelball.co.uk. *Website:* www.michaelball.co.uk.

BALL, Tom; b. 24 Oct. 1950, Los Angeles, California, USA. Vocalist; Musician (harmonica, guitar); Writer. m. Laurie Linn, 2 Oct. 1983, 1 d. *Education:* Santa Monica College. *Career:* Singer, harmonica player, Yerba Buena Blues Band, 1965–67; Freelance musician, 1968–79; Member duo, Tom Ball and Kenny Sultan, 1979–; Business Venture: Good Time Blues Pub (BMI); Studio work on 150 recordings, films, television shows. *Recordings:* Albums: Confusion, 1981; Who Drank My Beer, 1983; Bloodshot Eyes, 1986; Guitar Music, 1988; Too Much Fun, 1990; Filthy Rich, 1993; Double Vision, 1996; 20th Anniversary—Live!, 2000; 18 Pieces for Solo Steel-string Guitar, 2003. *Publications:* Author: Blues Harmonica, 1993; Nasty Blues, 1995; Sonny Terry Licks, 1997; Little Walter/Big Walter Licks, 2000; The Marty Macgraw Book, 2002; Dropped D Tuning, 2003. *Honours:* Telly Award Winner, 1994. *Membership:* NARAS; AFTRA; AFofM; Folk Alliance. *Current Management:* Mercer Management. *Address:* PO Box 20156, Santa Barbara, CA 93120, USA. *Website:* www.tomballkennysultan.com.

BALLAMY, Iain Mark; b. 20 Feb. 1964, Guildford, Surrey, England. Musician (saxophone); Composer. *Education:* City and Guilds Musical Instrument Technology; Piano lessons as child. *Career:* Worked with groups including: Loose Tubes; Delightful Precipice; Human Chain; Bill Bruford's Earthworks; Balloon Man; Dewey Redman; Gil Evans; Hermeto Pascoal, 1982–; Karnatica College of Percussion, Voice of God; Tours: USA; Canada; Japan; Hong Kong; India; Europe; Scandinavia; Morocco; Turkey; Toronto; Saskatoon; Brecon; Glasgow; Edinburgh; Willisau; Leverkusen; Soho; Cork; Festivals: Berlin; Montreux; Frankfurt; Monterey; Montréal; Copenhagen; Molde; Istanbul; World-wide television and radio broadcasts and appearances including The Tube, Bergerac, Right to Reply and Wogan; Performances at Ronnie Scott's, Knitting Factory, Royal Festival Hall, Royal Albert Hall, Barbican and most international jazz festivals; Appeared in Out There, musical theatre production, 1995–96. *Compositions:* Commissions for Apollo Saxophone Quartet, Salford College, Birmingham Jazz, Food Cheltenham Jazz Festival, Bath International Festival. *Recordings:* All Men Amen; Balloon Man; with Django Bates: Summer Fruits; Winter Truce; 4 albums with Bill Bruford's Enthusiasts; Appeared on 45 CDs. *Honours:* John Dankworth Cup, 1985; BT British Jazz Award, best ensemble, 1995. *Membership:* Musicians' Union; PRS; MCPS; GVL. *Address:* 4 Old Queen Anne House, London, England.

BALLARD, Glen; b. 1953, Natchez, MS, USA. Songwriter; Record Prod; Arranger; Musician (piano, guitar); Programmer; Screenwriter. *Education:* BA, English, Political Science and Journalism, University of Mississippi. *Career:* Joined Elton John's organization, Los Angeles; Songwriter, MCA Music Publishing, 1978; Independent songwriter, late 1980s; Formed Java Records, 1996, later part of Island/Def Jam; Producer, co-writer, soundtrack to film Titan A.E., 2000; As prod. and songwriter, worked with: Paula Abdul, Aerosmith, Anastacia, Backstreet Boys, Philip Bailey, George Benson, Natalie Cole, Dave Matthews Band, Céline Dion, Earth Wind & Fire, Sheena Easton, Aretha Franklin, Michael Jackson, Al Jarreau, Quincy Jones, Alanis Morissette, No Doubt, K. T. Oslin, Wilson Phillips, Pointer Sisters, Seal, Shakira, George Strait, Curtis Stigers, Barbra Streisand, Van Halen, Jack Wagner. *Honours:* Five Grammy Awards, incl. Best Rock Song, 1990, Best Rock Album, Album of the Year, Best Video of the Year; National Acad. of Songwriters, Songwriter of the Year, 1997; ASCAP Songwriter of 1997; NARAS Governor's Award, 1997. *Address:* c/o Java Records, Universal Music Publishing Ltd, Elsinore House, 77 Fulham Palace Rd, London W6 8JA, England. *Website:* www.javarecords.com.

BALLARD, Kaye; b. 20 Nov. 1926, Cleveland, Ohio, USA. Actress; Vocalist. *Career:* Television: The Mothers-in-Law; Perry Como Show; Doris Day Show; over 150 performances on the Tonight Show; Films: The Ritz; The Girl Most Likely; House Is Not A Home; Eternity; Which Way To The Front; Modern Love; Tiger Warsaw; Falling In Love Again; Freaky Friday; Concerts include: 2 Royal Command Performances; Hello Dolly; Nymph Errant; Stage performances include: Nunsense; Gypsy; Annie Get Your Gun; High Spirits; Odd Couple; Ziegfield Follies (touring companies); Top Bananas; Three To Make Ready; Touch and Go; Wonderful Town; She Stoops To Conquer; Golden Apple; Carnival; Molly (Broadway); One woman shows: Working 42nd Street At Last; Hey Ma. *Recordings include:* Nymph Errant; Songs From Hey Ma; Fanny Brice; Then and Again; Unsung Sondheim; Ladies Who Wrote The Lyrics; Long Time Friends; Golden Apple; Gershwin Rarities; Follies; Peanuts. *Membership:* SAG; AFTRA; Equity. *Current Management:* Mark Sendroff c/o Gottlier, Schiff, Bonsee and Sendroff. *Address:* c/o Lee S Mimms, 2644 E Chevy Chase Dr., Glendale, CA 91206, USA.

BALTAZANIS, Kostas; b. 20 Feb. 1965, Patras, Greece. Musician (guitar); Music Educator; Writer. *Education:* BMus, Performance; Professor Music, Berklee College of Music, Boston, USA. *Career:* Artistic Director, Nakas Conservatory, Athens, Greece; Studio musician, clinician for Berklee College of Music; Writer of music education books. *Publications:* Jazz Harmony; Music Theory and Ear Training; Electric Guitar. *Address:* 25 25th Martiou Str, 16233 Athens, Greece.

BANDY, Moe (Marion); b. 12 Feb. 1944, Meridian, Mississippi, USA. Country vocalist; Musician (guitar). *Career:* Played guitar in father's band The Mission City Playboys, San Antonio, Texas; Rodeo rider; Debut single Lonely Lady, Satin Records, 1964; Regular on San Antonio TV show Country Corner, 1973; Signed to GRC Records, 1974; Many Billboard country hits mostly on Columbia Records, including some with Joe Stampley, 1974–89; Moe and Joe collaborations included controversial parody of Boy George, Where's The Dress, 1984; Americana, 1988, used by George Bush Sr as presidential theme song; Opened own 900 seater Moe Bandy Americana Theatre in Branson, Missouri. *Recordings:* Hank Williams You Wrote My Life, 1975; Just Good Ol' Boys (with Joe Stampley), I Cheated Me Right Out Of You, It's A Cheatin' Situation, 1979; She's Not Really Cheatin' (She's Just Getting' Even), 1982. *Honours:* CMA, Vocal Duo of the Year (with Joe Stampley), 1980. *Address:* c/o The Moe Bandy Americana Theatre, Branson, MO, USA; c/o The Bobby Roberts Company Inc, 909 Meadowlark Lane, Goodlettsville, TN 37072, USA.

BANGALTER, Thomas; b. 1 Jan. 1975, Paris, France. Prod; Remixer; DJ. *Career:* Formed Daft Punk with school friend Guy Manuel De Homem Christo, 1992; Debut single released on Scotland's Soma Records, 1994; Found commercial success with the release of Da Funk; Signed to Virgin Records and released debut album Homework; Founder: Roule Records; Collaborations: Bob Sinclair; Alan Braxe; Remixed: Gabrielle; Ian Pooley; Chemical Brothers. *Recordings:* Albums: Homework, 1996; Discovery, 2001; Alive 1997, 2001; Singles: Da Funk, 1995; Musique, Trax On Da Rocks, 1996; Around The World, Burnin', 1997; Revolution 909, Music Sounds Better With You (with Stardust), 1998; One More Time, 2000; Aerodynamic, 2001; Harder Better Faster Stronger, 2001. *Address:* c/o Virgin Records, Kensal House, 553–579 Harrow Rd, London W10 4RH, England.

BANKS, Mike; b. Detroit, Michigan, USA. Musician (bass guitar); Prod. *Career:* Former session bass guitarist with Parliament; Founder: Underground Resistance (techno collective and label), Submerge Distribution and record shop in Detroit; Collaborations: Jeff Mills, Robert Hood, Suburban Knight, Octave One; Member: Members of The House, L'Homme Van Renn. *Recordings:* Albums: Sonic Destroyer (as X101), 1991; BXA (as X102), 1992; Interstellar Fugitives (with Underground Resistance), 1998; Singles: As Underground Resistance: Final Frontier, 1991; Nation To Nation, 1991; Living For The Night (featuring Yolanda Reynolds), 1991; Riot EP, 1991; World To World, 1991; Galaxy 2 Galaxy, 1992; Codebreaker, 1997; Turning Point, 1998; Hardlife, 2001. *Current Management:* c/o Submerge Distribution, 2030 Grand River, Detroit, Michigan, USA.

BANKS, Nick; b. 28 July 1965, Rotherham, Yorkshire, England. Musician (drums). *Career:* Mem., Pulp, 1987–; Numerous tours, television appearances and festival dates; Contribution to film soundtrack, Mission Impossible, 1996. *Recordings:* Albums: Freaks, 1987; Separations, 1992; His 'N' Hers, 1994; Different Class (No. 1, UK) 1995; This Is Hardcore (No. 1, UK), 1998; We Love Life, 2001; Hits, 2002. Singles: Master Of The Universe, 1987; My Legendary Girlfriend, 1990; Countdown, 1991; OU, 1992; Babies, 1992;

Razzmatazz, 1993; Lipgloss, 1993; Do You Remember The First Time?, 1994; The Sisters (EP), 1994; Common People (No. 2, UK), 1995; Sorted For E's and Whizz/Misshapes (No. 2, UK), 1995; Disco 2000, 1995; Something Changed, 1996; Help The Aged, 1997; This Is Hardcore, 1998; A Little Soul, 1998; Party Hard, 1998; The Trees/Sunrise, 2001; Bad Cover Version, 2002. *Honours:* Mercury Music Prize, 1995; BRIT Award, 1996. *Address:* c/o Island Records, 825 Eighth Ave, New York, NY 10019, USA. *Website:* www.pulponline.com.

BANKS, Paul; b. 1973, England. Musician (guitar). *Career:* Member, Shed Seven; Numerous television appearances and live tours. *Recordings:* Singles: Mark, 1994; Dolphin, 1994; Speakeasy, 1994; Ocean Pie, 1994; Where Have You Been Tonight?, 1995; Getting Better, 1996; Bully Boy, 1996; On Standby, 1996; Chasing Rainbows, 1996; She Left Me On Friday, 1998; The Heroes, 1998; The Devil In Your Shoes, 1998; Disco Down, 1999; Cry For Help, 2001; Albums: Change Giver, 1996; A Maximum High, 1996; Let It Ride, 1998; Going For Gold, The Best Of Shed Seven, 1999; Truth Be Told, 2001.

BANKS, Tony; b. 27 March 1950. Musician (keyboards). *Career:* Musician, Genesis, 1970–; Solo artiste, 1979–; Numerous world-wide tours, include concerts at: Philharmonic Hall, New York; Giants Stadium, New York; Madison Square Gardens, New York; L A Forum; Rainbow Theatre, London; Wembley Arena; World tour, played to 3m. people, 1987. *Recordings:* Albums: with Genesis: Foxtrot, 1972; Selling England By The Pound, 1973; Genesis Live, 1973; The Lamb Lies Down On Broadway, 1974; Trick Of The Tail, 1976; Wind and Wuthering, 1977; Seconds Out, 1977; And Then There Were Three, 1980; Duke, 1980; Abacab, 1981; Three Sides Live, 1982; Genesis, 1983; Invisible Touch, 1986; We Can't Dance, 1991; Genesis Live, 1992; Calling All Stations, 1997; Archives Vol. 1, 1998; Not About Us, 1998; Demo Mix Down On Broadway, 1998; Turn It On Again, 1999; Archive Vol. 2, 2001; Solo: A Curious Feeling; The Fugitive; The Wicked Lady; Soundtracks; Bankstatement; Still; with Mike and The Mechanics: Living Years, 1988; Singles: with Genesis: Abacab; Follow You Follow Me; Mama; Illegal Alien; Invisible Touch; Land Of Confusion; Tonight Tonight Tonight; That's All; Turn It On Again. *Honours:* Golden Ticket, Madison Square Gardens, 1986; First group with 5 US Top 5 singles from one album, 1986; Band of Year, Rolling Stone Readers Poll, 1987. *Current Management:* Hit and Run Music, 30 Ives St, London SW3 2ND, England.

BANNISTER, Brian; Vocalist; Musician (banjo, mandolin, harmonica). *Career:* Founder member, Salty Dog; Winner, Birmingham songwriting competition; Performed official Olympic bid record; Resident topical songwriter for John Tainton Show, BBC; Member, The Debonairs, including television and radio appearances; Founder member, Mack and The Boys, 1989; Member, The New Bushbury Mountain Daredevils, 1992–; Work includes: Backing vocalist, Slade album; Producer, songwriter, dance artists. *Recordings:* with The Debonairs: Hoochey Coochey Man; with Sub Zero: Out Of The Blue; with The Balti Brothers: Balti; with Mack and The Boys: Mack and The Boys; Downtime Love; with The New Bushbury Mountain Daredevils: Bushwacked; The Yellow Album; Bushbury Mountain. *Current Management:* c/o Jim McPhee, Acorn Entertainments. *Address:* Winterfold House, 46 Woodfield Rd, Kings Heath, Birmingham B13 9UJ, England.

BANTON, Pato, (Patrick Murray); b. Birmingham, England. Reggae Vocalist; Songwriter. *Career:* Tours throughout USA and South America with own eight-piece group The Reggae Revolution; Now solo recording artiste. *Recordings:* Albums include: Never Give In, 1987; Visions Of The World, 1989; Wize Up!, 1990; Mad Professor Recaptures Pato Banton, 1990; Live and Kickin' All Over America, 1991; Universal Love, 1992; Collections, 1995; Stay Positive, 1996; Time Come, 1999; Go Pato, 2000; Live In Brazil, 2000; Singles include: Hello Tosh; Baby Come Back, with UB40 (No. 1, UK); Pato and Roger Come Again; Beams Of Light; Tudo de Bom; Spirits In The Material World; Cowboy Song, with Sting; Bubbling Hot; Legalise It!. *Current Management:* Atomic Communications Group, 10553 W Jefferson Blvd, Culver City, CA 90232, USA.

BARBEAU, Mark Jerome; b. 20 Sept. 1961, San Francisco, California, USA. Event Production; Production Consultant; Screen Writer; Graphic Artist. *Education:* San Francisco City College. *Career:* Personal manager for: Anton Barbeau, pop singer; Produced touring scenery for Primus, Fishbone, Babes In Toyland, during Lollapalooza '93 tour; Formerly Account Executive for FM Productions on tours for: U2; Pink Floyd; Metallica; Guns N' Roses; ZZ Top; Rolling Stones; Currently Operations Manager, Key Events, and runs own company Runlikehell Productions, San Francisco, focussing on artist management and tour production; Currently personal manager for San Francisco Rock Band, Handfullaflowers. *Publications:* Pop artist in The Art of Rock, edited by Paul Gruskin. *Address:* 2269 Chestnut St, PMB #143, San Francisco, CA 94123, USA.

BARBER, (Daniel) Chris(topher); b. 17 April 1930, Welwyn Garden City, Hertfordshire, England. Jazz Musician (trombone, trumpet, horn, double bass); Bandleader; Composer. *Education:* Trombone, bass, Guildhall School of Music. *Career:* Leader, various amateur jazz bands; Formed first band with Lonnie Donegan, Monty Sunshine, 1940s; Leader, Chris Barber Jazzband (later changed to Chris Barber Jazz and Blues Band), 1954–; International

tours and concerts include: 1954 line-up re-formed for 40th Anniversary concerts: Royal Festival Hall, 100 Club, Netherlands, Germany, 1994; Also played with Ken Colyer; Joe Harriott; Wild Bill Davis; Mac Rebenneck; Helped promote US artists in UK, including Brownie McGhee; Muddy Waters; Louis Jordan. *Compositions:* Numerous works with Richard Hill, including Jazz Elements; Concerto For Jazz Trombone (both premiered in Berlin). *Recordings:* Numerous albums include: Ragtime, 1960; Getting Around, 1963; Live In East Berlin, 1968; Sideways, 1974; Take Me Back To New Orleans, 1980; Everybody Knows, 1987; Stardust, 1988; Essential Chris Barber, 1990; Get Yourself To Jackson Square, 1990. *Honours:* O.B.E., 1991. *Current Management:* Vic Gibbons, Cromwell Management, 4/5 High St, Huntingdon, Cambridgeshire PE18 6TE, England.

BARBER, Tony; b. 20 April 1963, Edmonton, London, England. Musician (guitar, bass, drums, synthesizer); Prod. m. Nathalie, 1 d. *Career:* Musician with Lack of Knowledge, 1979–85; Boys Wonder, 1987–88; Buzzcocks, 1992–; Solo recordings as Airport; Appeared on records by other artists, 1986–. *Compositions:* Sirens are Back, with Lack of Knowledge, 1984; Lift Off with Airport, as Airport, 2000. *Recordings:* Wandering Sickness, 1979; Sirens Are Back, 1984; Goodbye James Dean, 1987; Pied Piper Of Feedback, 1990; Trade Test Transmissions, 1993; Troublemaker, 1995; Denim On Ice, 1996; Powersurge, 1996; Modern, 1999; Instant Wigwam and Igloo Mixture, 1999; Lift Off With Airport, 2000. *Membership:* PRS; PAMRA; PPL. *Current Management:* 26 Charlton Rd, Edmonton, London N9 8EJ, England; Damage Productions, 130 Seigel St, Fourth Floor, Brooklyn, NY 11206, USA.

BARBIER, Denis; b. 22 April 1954, Paris, France. Composer; Musician (flute). 1 d. *Education:* Conservatories, Montréal, Vincennes. *Career:* Flute soloist, National French Jazz Orchestra; US tour, with Big Band Lumière, 1991; Tour, Europe, with Gil Evans and Big Band Lumière, 1986; Concerts on Radio France with Lumière; National French Orchestra; Chute Libre; Moravagine; France Culture with Shi Pei Pou (Peking). *Compositions include:* Music for theatre; Jazz on the Moon, for symphonic orchestra and solo alto saxophone, 1996. *Recordings:* Piece Pour Voix, Cordes Et Hautbois, 1998; Sous Le Signe Du Cheval (wind quintet and piano), 1995; Work For 30 Musicians and Rhythm Section In 4 Movements, 1995; Film music: L'Alibi En Or, with Charles Aznavour, 1993; Fausto (A La Mode, USA), 1993; Bosna, 1994; Milice, Film Noir, 1996; Slogans, 2001; Music for television serial, 1984–; Documentaries: From the Sea to the Land, for two harps, with Serge Moati, 1996; Brook par Brook, 2002; Television films: Barbe Bleue, with Samy Frey; Jazz records: PRAO with Mino Cinelu and Brothers; Denis Barbier Jazz Group; Chute Libre and Moravagine with Mino Cinelu; National French Jazz Orchestra. *Membership:* SACEM; SACD. *Current Management:* Éditions des Alouettes. *Address:* 8 rue Jules Vallés, 75011 Paris, France.

BARBIERI, Richard; b. 30 Nov. 1957. Musician (keyboards). *Career:* Member, Japan, 1977–83; Member, The Dolphin Brothers (with Steve Jansen), 1987; Member, Rain Tree Crow (with 3 former members of Japan), 1992; Member, The Porcupine Tree, 1993–; British tours include: Support to Blue Öyster Cult, 1978; Backing musician, No-Man, 1992; Record producer, Swedish group Lustans Lakejer, 1982. *Recordings:* Albums with Japan: Adolescent Sex, 1978; Obscure Alternatives, 1978; Life In Tokyo, 1979; Quiet Life, 1980; Gentlemen Take Polaroids, 1980; Assemblage, 1981; Tin Drum, 1981; Oil On Canvas, 1983; Exorcising Ghosts, 1984; with The Dolphin Brothers: Catch The Fall, 1987; with Rain Tree Crow: Rain Tree Crow, 1991; with Steve Jansen: Stone To Flesh, 1995; Changing Hands, 1998; with Porcupine Tree: Signify, 1997; Stupid Dream, 1999; Singles include: The Art Of Parties, 1981; Quiet Life, 1981; Visions Of China, 1981; Ghosts, 1982; Cantonese Boy, 1982; Life In Tokyo, 1982; Night Porter, 1982; Canton, 1982.

BARBOSA, Chris; Prod; Remixer. *Career:* Produced or performed production remixes for many artists including: Shannon; Robin Gibb; Billy Idol; George Michael; New Kids on the Block; The Spinners; Lisa Fischer; George Lammond; Nolan Thomas; Andru Donalds; Safire; Cynthia; Judy Torres; Monet; Alisha. *Recordings include:* Bad Of The Heart, George Lamond, 1978; Hot Power Mixes, 1987; I Wasn't Born Yesterday, Safire, 1990; No More Games, New Kids On The Block, 1991; Best Of Freestyle, 1992; Bass Bomb: Latin Hip Hop, 1993; Freestyle Greatest Hits, 1994; Essential, Shannon, 1995; Wherever The Rhythm Takes Me, Alisha, 1996; Absolutely: The Very Best Of..., 1997; Freestyle Explosion, 1998. *Honours:* ASCAP Pop Award. *Address:* CBM Entertainment Corp, 185 Ardsley Loop, Suite 1B, Brooklyn, NY 11239, USA.

BARCODE; b. 6 Dec. 1971, Barcelona, Spain. Programmer; Songwriter; Musician (keyboards, synthesizers). *Career:* Numerous concerts with band HED include: Phoenix Festival, 1994; Glastonbury Festival, 1995; Les Confort Moderne, 10th anniversay, Poitiers, France, 1995; Strawberry Fayre Festival, Cambridge, 1995; Megatropolis, London, 1995. *Recordings:* HED: Reigndance, 1994; Reigndance remix, Unity compilation album, 1994; Folklaw, 1995; New Dance, 1996; New Dance Remix, 1997; Beerserk, 1999; Hardcore, 2002. *Membership:* Musicians' Union. *Current Management:* Diehard Records.

BARD, Alexander; b. 17 March 1961, Vaestra Ny, Sweden. Artist; Record Prod; Songwriter. *Education:* Masters Degree, Economics, Geography.

Recordings: with Army of Lovers: Disco Extravaganza, 1990; Massive Luxury Overdose, 1991; The Gods Of Earth and Heaven, 1993; Glory Glamour and Gold, 1994; Les Greatest Hits, 1995; Crucified, 1999; with Vacuum: The Plutonium Cathedral, 1997; Seance At The Chaebol, 1998; Also: Abba A Tribute, 1999. *Membership:* Co-owner, Stockholm Records. *Current Management:* Tra La La Productions. *Address:* c/o Tra La La Productions, Naerkesgatan 1, 11640 Stockholm, Sweden.

BARDY, Jean; b. 3 March 1957, Soisy, Montmorency, France. Musician (bass, guitar, trumpet); Composer. *Education:* Conservatoire de Musique d'Eubonne. *Career:* Professional jazz bass player, playing Be-Bop in clubs including: River Bop; Petit Opportun; Cardinal Paf; Throughout France; Played with artists including: Guy Lafitte; René Urtreger; Martial Solal; Laurent Cugny; Barney Wilen; Laurent de Wilde; Pepper Adams; Roy Haynes; Steve Grossman; Sonny Stitt; Chet Baker (1 year in France, Europe); Nat Adderley; Johnny Griffin; Harold Danko; Dee Dee Bridgwater. *Compositions:* Received grant: Léonard de Vinci, from French government to write original music while in the USA. *Recordings:* Live In Paris, Antoine Hervé; Sud, Antoine Illouz; Naif; Rhythm-A-Ning, Laurent Cugny, Gil Evans, 1987; Samya Cynthia, François Chassagnite; César Le Chien; Chansons, Jean Bardy, 1991; Anna Livia Plurabelle, André Hodeir. *Honours:* Prix Django Reinhardt for: Live In Paris; Rhythmning; Prix de l'Academie du Disque. *Address:* 7 rue de l'Elysic-Ménilmontant, 75020 Paris, France.

BARE, Bobby (Robert Joseph); b. 7 April 1935, Ironton, Ohio, USA. Country Vocalist; Songwriter. *Career:* Prolific recording artist, 1955–; Club, television and radio station appearances; Television includes: Grand Ole Opry; Host, Bobby Bare and Friends; Film appearance, A Distant Trumpet, 1964. *Recordings:* Singles include: All American Boy; Detroit City; 500 Miles Away From Home; Miller's Cave; A Dear John Letter; Come Sundown; Please Don't Tell Me How The Story Ends; Marie Laveau; Daddy What If; The Jogger; Tequila Sheila; Numbers; Numerous albums include: Detroit City, 1963; 500 Miles Away From Home, 1963; The Travelling Bare, 1964; Tender Years, 1965; Talk Me Some Sense, 1966; Folsom Prison Blues, 1968; Lincoln Park Inn, 1969; This Is Bare Country, 1970; I'm A Long Way From Home, 1971; What Am I Gonna Do, 1972; Memphis Tennessee, 1973; Lullabys, Legends and Lies, 1974; Cowboys and Daddys, 1975; The Winner and Other Losers, 1978; Bare, 1979; Down and Dirty, 1980; Drunk and Crazy, 1980; As Is, 1981; Ain't Got Nothing To Lose, 1982; Bobby Bare-The Mercury Years 1970–72, 1987; Country Store, 1988; I Love An Old Fashioned Christmas, 1995; Hard Time Hungrys, 1998; Live At Gilley's, 1999; with Skeeter Davis: Tunes For Two, 1965; Your Husband, My Wife, 1970; with The Hillsiders: The English Countryside, 1967; with Norma Jean and Liz Anderson: The Game Of Triangles, 1967. *Honours:* Grammy, Detroit City, 1963. *Current Management:* Bare Enterprises, PO Box 2422, Hendersonville, TN 37077, USA.

BARKER, Aaron G, Sr; b. 3 May 1953, San Antonio, Texas, USA. Songwriter; *Compositions:* for George Strait: Baby Blue, 1988; Love Without End, 1990; Easy Come, Easy Go, 1990; I Know She Still Loves Me, 1995; I'd Like To Have That One Back, 1995; I Can Still Make Cheyene, 1997; for Doug Supernaw: Honky Tonkin' Fool, 1993; Not Enough Hours, 1995; for Clay Walker: Watch This, 1997; You're Beginning to Get to Me, 1998; for George Strait: Peace of Mind, 1998; Christmas Cookie, 1999; Old Time Christmas, 1999; I Am a Cowboy, for Bill Enquall, 1998; What About Now, for Lonestar, 1998; I'm Leaving, 1998. *Recordings:* Feelin' Like Freedom. *Honours:* Voted No. 1 in all three trades, Cash Box, 1988; Songwriters Award, Music City News, 1990. *Membership:* Country Music Asscn; NSAI; Academy of Country Music. *Current Management:* OTex Music, 1000 18th Ave S, Nashville, TN 37212, USA.

BARKER, Guy; b. 26 Dec. 1957, London, England. Jazz Musician (trumpet). *Education:* Royal College of Music. *Career:* Member, National Youth Jazz Orchestra; Major concerts include: Cleveland Jazz Festival, 1978; South Bank Jazz Festival, 1989; Leader, own quintet, British tour, 1978; Also played with: Gil Evans; John Dankworth; Chris Hunter; Stan Tracey's Hexad; Hubbard's Cubbard; Ornette Coleman; Peter King; Jim Mullen; Jack Sharpe Big Band; Featured soloist, London Symphony Orchestra; Played in backing groups with artists including: Sammy Davis Jr; Mel Tormé; Liza Minnelli; Lena Horne; British tour with Frank Sinatra, 1991; Far East tour with Georgie Fame; Tribute tours to Chet Baker and Bix Beiderbecke. *Recordings:* Albums include: Holly J, 1989; Isn't It, 1991; with Hubbard's Cubbard: Hubbard's Cubbard, 1983; Nip It In The Bud, 1985; with Clark Tracey: Suddenly Last Tuesday, 1986; Stiperstones, 1987; with Peter King: Brother Bernard, 1988; Soundtrack, 2002; Featured on soundtracks: Insignificance, 1985; Absolute Beginners, 1986; The Living Daylights, 1987; Also featured on recordings with Paul McCartney; Grace Jones; Joan Armatrading; XTC; Sting; Erasure; The The; The Beautiful South.

BARKER, Paul; b. 8 Feb. 1950, Palo Alto, California, USA. Musician (Bass, Keyboards). *Career:* Member, Ministry, 1986–; Numerous side projects including Pigface, including Steve Albini, Jello Biafra, Chris Connelly and Dwayne Goettell; Numerous tours including Lollapalooza; Covered the Grateful Dead's song Friend of the Devil for the Neil Young Bridge School Benefits album. *Recordings:* Halloween Remix, 1987; Stigmata, 1988; Burning

Inside, 1989; Jesus Built My Hotrod, 1991; N.W.O., 1992; Just One Fix, 1992; The Fall, 1995; Lay Lady Lay, 1996; Bad Blood, 1995; Albums: Twitch, 1985; The Land Of Rape and Honey, 1988; The Mind Is a Terrible Thing to Taste, 1989; In Case You Didn't Feel Like Showing Up (Live), 1990; Psalm 69: The Way To Succeed and the Way to Suck Eggs, 1992; Filth Pig, 1996; Dark Side Of the Spoon, 1999.

BARKER, Travis Landon; b. 14 Nov. 1975, Fontana, California, USA. Musician (drums). *Career:* Former member of punk-pop groups The Vandals and The Aquabats; Replaced Scott Raynor as Blink-182 drummer, 1998–; Numerous TV appearances and concerts world-wide including: The Enema Strikes Back '99 tour, released on CD as The Mark Tom and Travis Show; 11-week US Summer tour, 2001; Cameo appearance with group in American Pie film, 1999. *Recordings:* Albums: Enema Of The State, 1999; The Mark Tom and Travis Show (live), 2000; Take Off Your Pants and Jacket, 2001; Singles: What's My Age Again, All The Small Things, 1999; Adam's Song, Man Overboard, 2000; The Rock Show, Stay Together For The Kids, 2001. *Honours:* World-wide sales of 1999 album in excess of 7m. *E-mail:* travis@loserkids.com. *Website:* www.blink182.com.

BARLOW, Eric; Vocalist; Musician (guitar). *Education:* Classical training. *Career:* Member, The New Bushbury Mountain Daredevils, 1992–; Backing vocals, Slade; Producer, songwriter for various dance artists; Topical songs for radio. *Compositions include:* Songs recorded by artists including: Jaki Graham; Asia Blue; Several songs at number 1, Europe and Africa, including: Heartbreaker, Rozalla. *Recordings:* Solo: You Betta Run; with Rozalla: Heartbreaker; Sunny; The Perfect Kiss; Spirit Of Africa; with Mack and The Boys: The Unknown Legends; with The New Bushbury Monutain Daredevils: Bushwacked; The Yellow Album; Bushbury Mountain; Banjo Spiders, 1999. *Current Management:* c/o Jim McPhee, Acorn Entertainments. *Address:* Winterfield House, 46 Woodfield Rd, Kings Heath, Birmingham B13 9UJ, England.

BARLOW, Gary; b. 20 Jan. 1971, Fradham, Cheshire, England. Vocalist; Songwriter; Prod. *Career:* Songwriter, singer, prod., UK all-male vocal group, Take That, 1991–96; Tours of UK, Europe, Asia, Pacific, 1992–95; Television appearances with Take That included: Take That and Party (Channel 4), 1993; Take That Away documentary, BBC2, 1993; Take That in Berlin, 1994; Solo artiste, 1996–. *Recordings:* Albums: with Take That: Take That and Party, 1992; Everything Changes, 1993; Nobody Else, 1995; Greatest Hits, 1996; Solo: Open Road, 1997; Twelve Months Eleven Days, 1999. Singles include: with Take That: Do What U Like, 1991; Promises, 1991; It Only Takes A Minute, 1992; I Found Heaven, 1992; A Million Love Songs, 1992; Once You've Tasted Love, 1992; Could It Be Magic, 1993; Why Can't I Wake Up With You, 1993; Pray (No. 1, UK), 1993; Relight My Fire (with Lulu, No. 1, UK), 1993; Babe (No. 1, UK), 1993; Everything Changes (No. 1, UK), 1993; Love Ain't Here Anymore, 1994; Sure (No. 1, UK), 1994; Back For Good (No. 1, UK), 1995; Never Forget (No. 1, UK), 1995; How Deep Is Your Love (No. 1, UK), 1996; Solo: Forever Love, 1996; Love Won't Wait, 1997; So Help Me Girl, 1997; Open Road, 1997; For All That You Want, 1999; Stronger, 1999. *Publications:* Numerous videos, books, magazines. *Honours:* Nordoff Robbins Silver Clef Award for best band; Golden Camera Award, Berlin, Germany; Golden Otto Award for best band; MTV Award for Best Group in Europe; Seven Smash Hit Awards, 1992; Two BRIT Awards, incl. Best British Single, 1994; Ivor Novello Awards for Most Performed Work and Best Selling Song, 1996; Gold and Platinum discs. *Current Management:* Simon Fuller, 19 Management, Unit 32, Ransomes Dock, 35–37 Parkgate Rd, London SW11 4NP, England.

BARLOW, Thomas; b. 30 Sept. 1961, Manila, Philippines. Musician (saxophone). *Education:* BA Hons, University of Kent; PGCE, De Montfort University. *Career:* Founder member, The Larks; Aztec Camera, UK, Europe tour, 1988; Tommy Barlow Quartet; Butterfield 8; Founder member, Deptford Dance Orchestra (later Jools Holland Big Band); Matt Bianco; Holly Johnson; Swordfish. *Recordings:* 3 singles, 1 EP, with The Larks; Recording sessions with: Aztec Camera (No. 3 UK charts), 1988; Jools Holland; Deptford Dance Orchestra; BBC Education Programme; Swordfish. *Membership:* Musicians' Union; PRS. *Address:* 161A Southampton Way, Camberwell, London SE5 7EJ, England.

BARNACLE, Gary; b. 3 April 1959, Nicosia, Cyprus. Musician (saxophone, flute); Songwriter. *Career:* Toured with The Ruts; Elvis Costello; Soft Cell; Marc Almond; Tina Turner; Level 42; Jamiroquai; Played at various Prince's Trust concerts; Nelson Mandela Tribute, Wembley Stadium; Midge Ure's All Star Band; Numerous television, radio appearances in UK and abroad, include 40 Top of the Pops. *Compositions:* Co-writer, Jazzmasters album; Space Clav, Jamiroquai; Leisure Process Tracks; Ruts D C tracks. *Recordings:* Gold and Platinum discs with artists including: Tina Turner (4 albums); Phil Collins; Paul McCartney; David Bowie; The Clash; Swing Out Sister; The Beautiful South; Jamiroquai (2 albums); Björk (2 albums); Soul II Soul; James Brown; Five Star; Yazz; T'Pau (including hit single China In Your Hand); Elvis Costello; Pet Shop Boys; Massive Attack. *Membership:* MCPS; PRS; Musicians' Union; GVL (Germany); SENA (Netherlands). *Address:* 160 Queenstown Rd, Battersea, London SW8 3QE, England.

BARNACLE, Steve; b. 27 Sept. 1956, Aldershot, Hampshire, England. Musician (bass guitar, guitar); Composer; Prod. m. Lesley Lacey-Smith, 10 July 1989, 1 s., 2 d. *Career:* Numerous world tours; Most television and radio shows with artists including: Tina Turner; Pete Townshend; Deborah Harry; Spear of Destiny; Rick Wakeman; Julien Clerc (France only). *Compositions:* Co-writer, co-producer, Beat Boy album, Visage; Co-writer: Dream City, Samantha Fox; Juanita, Iron Maiden; Numerous writing and production credits. *Membership:* PRS; Musicians' Union; MCPS. *Address:* 65 Natal Rd, Streatham, London SW16 6JA, England.

BARNARD, Robert Graeme; b. 24 Nov. 1933, Melbourne, Australia. m. Danielle Ann Barnard, 22 July 1993, 2 s., 1 d. *Career:* Regular appearances on variety television; Co-Compere for ABC Television Jazz Programme; Featured Soloist, Queensland Symphony Orchestra; Tours extensively. *Compositions:* Many pieces recorded over the years. *Recordings:* Lord Of The Rings, with John Sangster; Many with Graeme Bell; About 300 under own name including: Bob Barnard-With Strings. *Honours:* Order of Australia, 1990; Advance Australia Award, 1991; Received prestigious, MO Award, 1993, 1997. *Membership:* Professional Musicians Club. *Address:* 8/9 Hume St, Crows Nest, Sydney, 2065, Australia.

BARNES, Alan Leonard; b. 23 July 1959, Altrincham, Cheshire, England. Musician (Saxophone, Clarinet). m. Clare Hirst, 31 July 1995, 1 s., 1 d. *Education:* Leeds Music College, First Class Diploma in Jazz and Light Music, 1977–80. *Career:* Pasadena Roof Orchestra, 1980–82; Tommy Chase Quartet, 1983–86; Coled Jazz Renegades, 1986–88; Humphrey Lyttelton Band, 1988–92; Freelance Musician with bands by Mike Westbrook, Kenny Baker, Don Weller, Warren Vache, Freddie Hubbard, John Dankworth; Own quartet and duo with David Newton; Founder, own Jazz label, Woodville Records, 2003. *Compositions:* Blues on the Beach; The Hawk; Side-Steppin'; Freedom Samba; Below Zero; The Sherlock Holmes Suite, 2002. *Recordings:* Below Zero, with David Newton Trio; Like Minds; Thirsty Work; Days Of Wine and Roses, with Tony Coe; A Dotty Blues; Shine, with Warren Vaché; Memories Of You; Manhattan, with Conte Candoli; If You Could See Me Now, with the Jim Watson Trio. *Honours:* British Jazz Awards: Alto Sax, 1995, 1997, 1999, 2001 Clarinet, 1994, 1996, 1998, Baritone Sax, 1998, 2000, 2002; BBC Jazz Instrumentalist of the Year, 2001. *Address:* 146 Kings Ave, London SW12 0BA, England.

BARNES, Jimmy; b. Scotland. Musician (guitar); Vocalist. *Career:* Lead singer, Australian group, Cold Chisel, 1979–83; Solo artiste, 1984–. *Recordings:* with Cold Chisel: Breakfast At Sweethearts, 1979; East, 1980; Circus Animals, 1982; The Last Wave Of Summer, 1998; Solo albums: Body Swerve, 1984; Jimmy Barnes, 1985; Freight Train Heart, 1987; Barnestorming, 1988; Two Fires, 1990; Heat, 1993; Psychlone, 1995; Hits: The Best Of Jimmy Barnes, 1996. *Current Management:* Michael Long Management, PO Box 136, Double Bay 2028, New South Wales, Australia.

BARNES, John; b. 15 May 1932, Manchester, England. Musician (Saxophone, Clarinets); Vocalist. m. Patricia Ann Barnes, 1 March 1958. *Recordings:* Alex Welsh Band; Humphrey Lyttelton Band. *Honours:* 10 times Winner, British Jazz Awards, Baritone Saxophone, 1987–99; Winner, Baritone, Downbeat Magazine, 1966. *Address:* 16 Worton Rd, Isleworth, Middlesex TW7 6HN, England.

BARNES, Neil; b. 6 Aug. 1960, London, England. Prod; Remixer. *Career:* Co-founder Hard Hands Records with Paul Daley; World-wide DJ; Member of Leftfield, split 2002; Collaborations: Djum Djum, Afrika Bambaataa, Roots Manuva, John Lydon. *Recordings:* Albums: Leftism, 1995; Rhythm and Stealth, 1999; Singles: Not Forgotten, 1990; Release The Pressure, 1992; Song Of Life, 1992; Open Up (with John Lydon) 1993; Original, 1995; Afrika Shox (with Afrika Bambaataa), 1999. *Current Management:* c/o Hard Hands Recordings, The Courtyard, Saga Centre, 326 Kensal Rd, London W10 5BZ, England.

BARNHOLDT, Ole; b. 14 Feb. 1958, Hvorup, Denmark. Composer. *Education:* Graduate, Film Music Composition, Dick Grove School of Music, Los Angeles, USA, 1988; Masters degree, Music, University of Ålborg, Denmark, 1990. *Career:* Scored various film, television, video projects, 1988–. *Compositions:* For Denmark's Radio Symphony Orchestra: Valley Heart; Siciliano For Maria. *Publications:* Music Design. *Membership:* KODA (Denmark). *Current Management:* Whiteheart Music Ltd. *Address:* Whiteheart Music Ltd, 100 Edenbridge Rd, Enfield EN1 2HT, England.

BARRATT, Bob; b. 22 March 1938, Croydon, Surrey, England. Record Prod. m. Annette Key, 24 Sept. 1960, 3 d. *Career:* Wrote songs as child; Office boy, EMI Records, 1959; Trained as record producer by Norman Newell and Norrie Paramor; Artist roster included: Max Boyce; Pam Ayres; Wurzels; Basil Brush; King's Singers; Fivepenny Piece; Gene Vincent; Chris Barber; Vince Hill (Edelweiss); Ran own label, Grasmere Records, featuring specialist music, 1984–. *Compositions:* 400 songs and instrumentals; 7 songs used in films; Many used by recorded libraries; 450 recordings of own compositions made by artists including: Gene Vincent; Dick Haymes; Roger Whittaker; King's Singers; Big Daddy; Brigitte Bardot. *Recordings:* Produced hundreds of records including: We All Had Doctor's Papers, Max Boyce (number 1 album, UK charts); Combine Harvester, Wurzels (number 1 single, UK charts). *Honours:* 4 Gold discs, 12 Silver discs; Twice winner of Gibraltar Song Festival, as songwriter.

BARRET, Eric; b. 5 May 1959, Le Havre, France. Musician (saxophone); Composer. *Career:* Played with J P Mas, A Ceccarelli, 1983; Barret, Romano Texier, 1985; Orchestre National de Jazz, 1986; D Humair, 1988; Quartet with M Ducret, 1988; Also played with: A Hervé, R Urtreger, S Swallow, J Griffin, K Wheeler, A Farmer, L Bennett, S Grossman, F Hubbard; Professor, Bagneux Music Conservatory, 1991–; Member, Roy Haynes 4tet, 1997; Orchestre National de Jazz, 1997. *Recordings:* Barret, Romano Texier, 1987; Eric Barret Quartet, 1989; L'Echappe Belle, 1992. *Publications:* Etudes Jazz Pour Saxophone, 2 Vols; Gammes Et Arpèges Pour Le Jazz, 1987. *Honours:* Boris Vian Price; Bien débuter le saxophone, 1997. *Current Management:* Hélène Manfredi, Atout Jazz. *Address:* 118 rue du Chateau des Rentiers, 75013 Paris, France.

BARRETT, Andrew; b. 19 Aug. 1953, Oceanside, New York, USA. Musician (keyboards); Arranger; Composer. m. Kathleen Anna McGinley, 22 Sept. 1980. *Education:* Mus B, Indiana University, 1975. *Career:* Musician, arranger for various artists including: Diana Ross; Irene Cara; Sister Sledge, 1981–82; Consultant, Cats Shubert Organization, 1982–; Synthesizer consultant, New York stage productions including: Cats, 1987; Me and My Girl, 1987; Les Miserables, 1988; Phantom of The Opera, 1988; Miss Saigon, 1989. *Compositions:* Contributor, film soundtracks: Nightmare On Elm Street, Part II, 1987; National Lampoon's Christmas Vacation, 1990; Shattered, 1991. *Membership:* ASCAP; NARAS.

BARRETT, Brian; b. 9 Feb. 1968, Murfreesboro, Tennessee, USA. Recording Artist; Songwriter. m. Katrina Startin Barrett. *Education:* Hardin-Simmons University, Abilene, Texas. *Career:* Appearances: Concert of The Age Tour; Television includes: TBN (Gospel America with Pat Boone); Carman's Time 2, TBN; Z-TV; TNN; CCM TV (Family Channel); ACTS TV Network; Nashville's Talk of The Town (WTVF CBS Affiliate); Radio: CCM Radio; Dawson McAllister's Praise Him In Your Youth; 20: The Countdown Magazine; The Best Country Countdown. *Recordings:* Albums: Brian Barrett, 1993; Nailed In Stone, 1995; Also appeared on: Child's Christmas, Revel Players, 1993; Tribute: The Songs Of Andrae Crouch, 1996; Should've Been Gone, Empty Grave, 1999. *Honours:* CCM Readers Awards, Favourite Country Artist, Favourite Country Album. *Membership:* Gospel Music Assn; Alpha Psi Omega (Theatrical Society). *Current Management:* Michael Smith and Associates. *Address:* 1024 17th Ave S, Nashville, TN 37212, USA.

BARRETT, James Charles; b. 4 Dec. 1970, London, England. Musician (Bass guitar, programming); Career: Co-Founder, Member, Rock/dance group Senser, 1989–99; Numerous television and radio appearances including The Word (Channel 4), The Beat (Channel 4), Raw Soup, Naked City, MTV's Most Wanted, Glastonbury Live, Chart Show, numerous European shows; John Peel session on Radio 1; Toured extensively throughout Europe, USA, Japan; Numerous festivals. *Recordings:* Singles: Eject; The Key/No Comply; Switch; Age Of Panic; Adrenalin; Breed; Harry Moss Mix; Albums: Stacked Up; Asylum. *Current Management:* Space Management. *Address:* 24 Gibson Gardens, Stoke Newington London N16 7HB, England.

BARRETT, Mark Vincent; b. 27 Jan. 1959, Bishops Stortford, England. Musician (guitar); Sound Engineering. 1 s., 1 d. *Education:* Fine Art Degree, Stourbridge College of Art; Acton Guitar Institute. *Career:* Member, East Orange, 1983; Q Lazzarus, 1988; Guitarist for Janey Lee Grace; Radio broadcasts: GLR; Regional BBC stations; Various US stations; Major US tour; Television, Tricks and Tracks, BBC. *Recordings:* with Q Lazzarus: Don't Let Go; Goodbye Horses, from film The Silence Of The Lambs; Mexico 70; Albums: Dust Has Come To Stay; Sing When You're Winning; Singles: Everywhere; Worthless. *Membership:* Musicians' Union. *Current Management:* Diamond Sounds Management. *Address:* Fox and Punch Bowl, Burfield Rd, Old Windsor, Berkshire, England.

BARRETT, Paul; b. 8 Aug. 1954, Dublin, Ireland. Prod; Musician Arranger (Keyboards, Brass); Composer. *Education:* Trinity College, Dublin (Mus B); Royal Irish Academy of Music. *Career:* Trombone, RTE Symphony Orchestra, 1970–74; Musical Arranger, EMI Records, 1975–76; Keyboards, arranger, composer, trombonist, RTE Television, radio, 1975–89; Founder, bands: Sleepless Knights, 1976–77; Metropolis, 1979–82; Junta, 1982; Founder, STS, 1983; 24 track studio with Fairlight CMI; Performed with artists including: U2; Marianne Faithfull; The Edge; Sinead O'Connor; Brian Eno; Tom Robinson; Bono; Hazel O'Connor; Steve Lillywhite; Luka Bloom; Flood; Hothouse Flowers; Bill Whelan; Christy Moore; Now composing film music; Producing records for U2; Hazel O'Connor; Hothouse Flowers; Luka Bloom; Bono; The Stars of Heaven; Carole King; Coosh; Equation; Quincy Jones; Boyzone. *Recordings:* with U2: Desire; Joshua Tree; Unforgettable Fire; Rattle and Hum; Achtung Baby; Night and Day; Passengers; Best Of, 1980–90; with Hothouse Flowers: Home; with Hazel O'Connor: Private Wars; with Frank Sinatra and Bono: I've Got You Under My Skin; Contributed to recordings for: Quincy Jones; Frank Sinatra; Jim Sheridan; Stevie Wonder;

Marvin Gaye; Johnny Cash; Ray Charles; Leonard Cohen; Willie Nelson. *Honours:* Platinum discs, Desire; Rattle and Hum; Joshua Tree; Unforgettable Fire; Gold disc, Home. *Membership:* PRS; MCPS; AYIC; PAMRA. *Current Management:* STS. *Address:* c/o STS, Ballyward Stud, Oldcourt, Manor Kilbride, Co Wicklow, Ireland.

BARRETT, Paul Frank Stalin; b. 14 Dec. 1940, Blackwood, Wales. Booking Agent; Promoter; Personal Man. m. Lorraine Jayne Booth, 27 July 1972, 1 s., 1 d. *Career:* Owner, Paul Barrett Rock 'n' Roll Enterprises; 30 years as promoter, booking agent, personal manager, representing among others: The Jets; Crazy Cavan and the Rhythm Rockers; Freddie 'Fingers' Lee and His Trio; Matchbox; Jean Vincent; Earl Jackson and The Jailbreakers; Wee Willie Harris; The Rimshots; Jack Scott; Tommy Sands; Numerous personal appearances, television, radio; Film appearances: Blue Suede Shoes; Bloody New Year. *Recordings:* Spirit Of Woodstock; I Told You So; Punk; Girl Please Stay; Solo vocals, Superstar, featured on Gold album. *Honours:* Bop Cat of High Standing, Carl Perkins Fan Club. *Membership:* PRS; MCPS. *Address:* 16 Grove Pl., Penarth CF64 2ND, South Wales.

BARRETT, Tina Ann; b. 16 Sept. 1976, West London, England. Vocalist; Actor. *Education:* Classical ballet, Arts Educational School, London. *Career:* Appeared in fashion shows, pantomimes and TV advertisements; Danced professionally in UK and overseas for various pop artistes; Mem., S Club 7, 1998–; Group quickly achieved international success, following sales of TV series Miami 7, 1999, LA 7, 2000, and Hollywood 7, 2001, featuring the band's music, to nearly 100 countries; Also made nature TV series, S Club 7 Go Wild, 2000, and various TV specials; First British tour with S Club 7, 2001; Band renamed S Club, 2001. *Recordings:* Albums: S Club, 1999; 7 (No. 1, UK), 2000; Sunshine, 2001; Seeing Double, 2002. Singles: Bring It All Back (No. 1, UK), 1999; S Club Party, 1999; Two In A Million/You're My Number One, 1999; Reach, 2000; Natural, 2000; Never Had A Dream Come True (No. 1, UK), 2000; Don't Stop Movin' (No. 1, UK), 2001; Have You Ever (No. 1, UK), 2001; You, 2002. *Honours:* BRIT Awards, Best British Newcomer, 2000, Best British Single, for Don't Stop Movin', 2002; Record of the Year Award, for Don't Stop Movin', 2001. *Current Management:* 19 Management, Unit 32, Ransomes Dock, 35–37 Parkgate Rd, London SW11 4NP, England. *Website:* www.sclub.com.

BARRON, Andy; b. 4 June 1962, Doncaster, England. Musician (drums). m. Anne Braymand, 22 Aug. 1992. *Education:* College; Doncaster Youth Jazz Orchestra. *Career:* Played, recorded or toured with Dominic Miller; Nigel Kennedy; Mark King; Mike Lindup; Julia Fordham; Kenny Wheeler; John Scofield; Rick Margitza; Kenny Werner; Stan Sultzman; Marcia Maria; Eurojazz; ORJ (Orchestra Regional de Jazz Rhone Alpes); John Surman; Pierre Drevet; Mario Stantchev; London Contemporary Dance. *Membership:* ORJ; AIMRA. *Address:* 50 rue de la Convention, 38200 Vienne, France; Garden Flat 27, Rye Hill Park, London SE15 3JN, England.

BARRON, Chris; b. 1968. Vocalist. *Education:* Music theory, New York's New School College. *Career:* Founder member, funk/rock group The Spin Doctors, 1988–; Tours, performances include: Horizon of Blue Developing Everywhere tour, 1992; Saturday Night Live, 1992; MTV Drops The Ball '93, 1992; Late Night Show With David Letterman, CBS Television, 1993. *Recordings:* Singles include: Little Miss Can't Be Wrong, 1992; Two Princes, 1993; Albums: Homebelly Groove, 1990; Pocket Full Of Kryptonite, 1992; Turn It Upside Down, 1994; You've Got To Believe In Something, 1996; Here Comes The Bride, 1999; Just Go Ahead Now (compilation), 2000; Can't Be Wrong, 2001; Solo: Shag, 2001. *Address:* c/o DAS Communications, 83 Riverside Dr., New York, NY 10024, USA.

BARRON, Christine Angela; b. 9 May 1949, Birmingham, England. Composer; Musician; Author; Music Teacher; Adjudicator. *Education:* Moseley School of Art, Birmingham; School of Contemporary Pop and Jazz. *Career:* Began as freelance percussionist, including work with Birmingham Symphony Orchestra; Theatre, cabaret musician with top entertainers including: Bruce Forsyth; Des O'Connor; Leslie Crowther; Val Doonican; Part-time lecturer, percussion and composition; North Warwickshire and Hinkley College of Technology and Art, Nuneaton, Warwickshire; Well known in the UK for innovative percussion workshops and master classes featuring percussion; Adjudicator and Member, British and International Federation of Festivals for Music, Dance and Speech. *Compositions include:* Television signature tunes: Shut That Door (also released as single); Where Are They Now; Commissioned by Chappell Music Library for album, short pieces as jingles, theme, incidental music for television, radio, films (distributed world-wide); Collaboration with Boosey and Hawkes Music Publishers on albums, including album recorded by Royal Philharmonic Orchestra; Also wrote for their educational catalogue under pseudonyms: Chris Barron, Christine Barron. *Publications:* 2 comprehensive tutors with cassette for Learn As You Play series: Learn As You Play Drums; Learn As You Play Tuned Percussion and Timpani; Learn As You Play Drums Cassette. *Membership:* The British Academy of Composers and Songwriters; British Federation of Festivals for Music, Dance and Speech; International Federation of Festivals for Music, Dance and Speech. *Current Management:* Boosey and Hawkes Music

Publishers Ltd. *Address:* 27 Madeira Croft, Coventry, Warwickshire CV5 8NX, England.

BARRON, Jay; b. 24 Feb. 1957, Yokusuka, Japan. Artist Man; Concert Tour Prod. m. Leann Barron, 2 May 1990, 1 d. *Career:* Artist manager; International concert tour producer, Barron Entertainment. *Membership:* CMA; ACM; AFofM; NARAS. *Address:* Barron Entertainment, 1600 Linden Ave, Nashville TN 37212, USA.

BARROW, Geoff; b. 9 Dec. 1971, Walton in Gordano, Bristol, England. Musician (keyboards, drums, programming); Prod; Arranger; Songwriter. *Career:* Tape Operator, Coach House Studio, Bristol; Worked on Massive Attack's Blue Lines; Wrote track for Neneh Cherry's Home Brew album; Remixed work for Primal Scream, Paul Weller, Depeche Mode; Massive Attack; Earthling; Mem., Portishead, 1991–; Joined with Adrian Utley and Dave McDonald; Signed to Go!Beat Records; Short Feature Film, To Kill A Dead Man shown at cinemas and projected on the MI5 building in London, 1995; Glastonbury Festival appearance, 1995; Internet concert broadcast, New York, 1997. *Recordings:* Albums: Dummy, 1994; Herd Of Instinct, 1995; Portishead, 1997; PNYC, 1998, Glory Times, 1998; Roseland, New York (DVD), 2002. Singles: Numb (EP), 1994; Sour Times, 1994; Glory Box, 1995; All Mine, 1997; Cowboys (EP), 1997; Over, 1997; Only You, 1998. *Honours:* Mercury Music Prize, Best Album, 1995. *Address:* c/o Go Beat Records, The Fulham Palace, Bishops Ave, London SW6 6EA, England. *Website:* www.portishead.co.uk.

BARRY, Daemion; b. 20 Nov. 1960, London, England. Musician; Composer. 1 s. *Education:* First Class Hons degree, Exeter University. *Compositions:* Television credits: Signs and Wonders, BBC; The English Wife, Meridian; Chandler and Co, BBC; My Good Friend, Anglia; A Woman's Guide To Adultery, Carlton Television; Friday On My Mind, BBC; Thicker Than Water, BBC; Reportage, BBC2; Go Wild, ITV; Gamesmaster, CH4; The Farm, TVE; Cinema credits: The Duke of Edinburgh Award Scheme; Commercial: Robinsons Orange Drinks; McCallum; Dalziel and Pasco. *Honours:* BAFTA Award, Best Original Music Score, Friday On My Mind; Golden Gate Award (USA), Friday On My Mind. *Membership:* PRS; British Songwriters; BAFTA; Groucho. *Current Management:* Soundtrack Music Associates, 22 Ives St, Chelsea, London SW3 2ND, England.

BARRY, James M; b. 16 Jan. 1952, Chicago, Illinois, USA. Songwriter. m. Emma Fontes, 1 July 1992, 1 s., 1 d. *Education:* Illinois Wesleyan University, BFA Theatre Cum Laude; Musical Theatre. *Compositions:* Colors of Grey, for award winning CBS documentary; If I Could Only Say Goodbye, David Hasselhoff, Baywatch; Step By Step, Groove U. *Publications:* Hear The Quiet. *Membership:* EMI Music Publishing; ASCAP; Songwriters Guild of America. *Address:* 389 S Many Lakes Dr., Kalispell, MT 59901, USA.

BARRY, John, (Jonathan Barry Prendergast); b. 3 Nov. 1933, York, Yorkshire, England. Composer. *Career:* Leader, John Barry Seven, 1957–62; Stage musical, Billy, 1974; Arranger, What Do You Want (for Adam Faith), 1959; Composer, film scores, 1959–. *Recordings:* Albums: Elizabeth Taylor In London, 1963; Sophia Loren In Rome, 1965; Eternal Echoes, 2001. Singles: with John Barry Seven: Hit and Miss (theme for Juke Box Jury, BBC), 1960; Walk Don't Run, 1960. *Compositions:* Beat Girl, 1959; Drumbeat, 1959; Stringbeat, 1961; Man In The Middle, 1962; Dr No, 1962; It's All Happening, 1963; Zulu, 1963; From Russia With Love, 1963; The Man In The Middle, 1964; Goldfinger, 1964; King Rat, 1965; Four In The Morning, 1965; Passion Flower Hotel, 1965; Thunderball, 1965; The Wrong Box, 1966; The Chase, 1966; The Quiller Memorandum, 1966; You Only Live Twice, 1967; The Lion In Winter, 1968; On Her Majesty's Secret Service, 1969; Midnight Cowboy, 1969; Lolita My Love, 1971; Mary Queen of Scots, 1971; The Persuaders, 1971; Alice's Adventures In Wonderland, 1971; Diamonds Are Forever, 1971; A Doll's House, 1973; The Man With The Golden Gun, 1974; Robin and Marian, 1976; King Kong, 1976; The Deep, 1977; Moonraker, 1979; Frances, 1982; Body Heat, 1983; Out of Africa, 1985; Jagged Edge, 1985; A View To A Kill, 1985; Peggy Sue Got Married, 1986; Howard The Duck, 1986; The Living Daylights, 1987; Dances With Wolves, 1990; Ruby Cairo; Indecent Proposal; Chaplin; Moviola II-Action and Adventure, 1995; The Scarlet Letter, 1995; King Rat, 1995; Beyondness of Things, 1999; Playing By Heart, 2000; The Last Valley, 2001. *Honours:* Academy Awards, Best Original Song, Born Free, 1967, Best Original Score, Born Free, 1967, Midnight Cowboy, 1969, Out of Africa, 1985, Dances With Wolves, 1990; Golden Globe, Best Original Score, Out of Africa, 1985; O.B.E., 1999. *Current Management:* Blue Focus Management, 15233 Ventura Blvd, Suite 200, Sherman Oaks, CA 91403, USA. *Address:* c/o Decca UK, 22 St Peter's Sq., London W6 9NW, England.

BARRY, Mark Anthony Luke; b. 26 Oct. 1978, Manchester, England. Vocalist; Songwriter. *Career:* Co-founder: BBMak pop group, 1996; Signed to UK company Telstar; Gained large US popularity after licence deal with Hollywood/Disney; Performed to over 100m. US viewers through group's own TV specials; Supported Britney Spears on sell-out US tour followed by 28-date first headline US tour, 2000; UK shows with The Corrs, 2001. *Recordings:* Albums: Sooner Or Later, 2000; Singles: Back Here, Still On Your Side, 2000; Ghost Of You and Me, 2001. *Honours:* Debut LP sales of over 1m. copies.

Address: c/o Diane Young. *E-mail:* DaytimeENT@aol.com. *Website:* www.bbmak.co.uk.

BARTHOLOMEW, Simon James; b. 16 Oct. 1965, Woolwich, London, England. Musician (rhythm, lead guitar). *Education:* BA (Hons) Fine Art, Polytechnic of East London. *Career:* Guitarist, The Brand New Heavies; The Akimbo Band; Session musician for Mother Earth; Jamiroquai; Samuel Purdey; Mr X. *Recordings:* Albums: with The Brand New Heavies: The Brand New Heavies; The Heavy Rhyme Experience; Brother Sister; Akimbo on Top; Shelter. *Honours:* Platinum disc, Brother Sister album. *Membership:* Musicians' Union; MCPS; PRS. *Current Management:* Wildlife Entertainment. *Address:* Unit F, 21 Heathmans Rd, Parsons Green, London, England.

BARTON, Bart; b. USA. Songwriter; Record Prod; Man. m. Pat McKool, 9 Oct. 1975. *Education:* College; Vocal Education; Piano. *Career:* Songwriter; Record Producer; President, Canyon Creek Records; President, Nashville Bekool Music; Owner, Lemonsquare Music and Friends of the General Music. *Recordings:* She's Sitting Pretty, 1989; Contributed to Super Country 89 Album, 1989; Co-Producer and writer of four songs on album, A Tribute to the American Veterans. *Honours:* Canadian Country Music Asscn, Outstanding International Support Award. *Membership:* CMA; CCMA; GMA; CARAS; NARAS. *Address:* 23 Music Sq. E, Suite 101, Nashville, TN 37203, USA.

BARTON, James L; b. 12 June 1948, Memphis, Tennessee, USA. Musician (trumpet, flugel horn, piccolo trumpet, cornet); Musical Dir; Arranger. m. Lorraine McKenna, 8 Dec. 1990, 2 s. *Education:* MSE, BSE, University of Michigan, Ann Arbor, 1966–72; De Anza College, Cupertino, California, 1974–76; Private music instruction with Claude Gordon, 1974–80. *Career:* Played with The Platters; Little Anthony; The Shirells; Tommy Rowe; K. C. and The Sunshine Band; Bo Diddley; Musicals, London's West End: Cats; Sophisticated Ladies; Grease; Starlight Express; Into The Woods; Also performed in Assassins, Ronnie Scott's, London. *Compositions:* Looking Back, 1989. *Honours:* John Phillips Sousa Award, 1966, 1969, 1970. *Membership:* AFofM; Musicians' Union (UK). *Current Management:* Musical Director, West End Theatres, London. *Address:* Flat 2, 56 Upper Berkeley St, London W1H 7PP, England.

BARTON, Lou Ann; b. 17 Feb. 1954, Fort Worth, Texas, USA. Vocalist. *Career:* Live concerts for television: MTV; Austin City Limits; Texas Connection; Member of bands: Fabulous Thunderbirds, 1975; Triple Threat Review and Double Trouble (both as lead singer with Stevie Ray Vaughan), 1977–80; Solo artist, Lou Ann Barton Band, 1981–95; Featured vocalist with Jimmie Vaughn supporting Eric Clapton, Royal Albert Hall, 1993. *Recordings:* Old Enough, 1982; Austin Rhythm and Blues Christmas, 1983; Forbidden Tones, 1988; Read My Lips, 1989; Dreams Come True with Angela Strehli, Marcia Ball, 1990; Sugar Coated Love, 1998. *Honours:* 4 times winner, Austin Chronicle Music Awards include 3 years Female Vocalist of Year; Inducted Texas Hall of Fame, 1992. *Current Management:* Davis McLarty Agency. *Address:* PO Box 3156, Austin, TX 78764, USA.

BARTON, Tim; b. 27 March 1959, Melbourne, Australia. Vocalist; Musician; Comedian. m. Jane O'Brien, 30 Aug. 1992. *Education:* Grade 5 guitar, Bruce Clarke Jazz School, Australia. *Career:* Tours: INXS; Men At Work; Midnight Oil; Concerts: Rolf Harris; Yothu Yindi; Jeff St John; Television: Touralla Telefon; Tours: Europe; Australia; Radio: Gary Crowley Show, GLR; Currently touring extensively with Tim Barton's All Star Six. *Recordings:* with Tim Bartons's All Star Six: T-BASS; Solo: So Called Thing Called Love. *Membership:* PRS; Musicians' Union. *Current Management:* Job Management. *Address:* 71a Penwith Rd, London SW18 4PX, England.

BARZEN, Dietmar; b. 18 Oct. 1958, Oberhausen, Germany. Prod; Composer. m. 31 May 1994, 1 d. *Education:* Dipl-kfm, Dr rer pol in Business Administration and Marketing; Composer. *Compositions:* Songs into the Light, Chris Sutton; Friday Night, Kent; Sky High, Far Side Gallery; Piano Dreams, David Warwick; Number One, SES. *Recordings:* Approximately 150 published and released titles. *Membership:* Marketing Club. *Address:* Mail Box 4502241, 50877 Cologne, Germany.

BASA, Andrej; b. 10 Feb. 1950, Ljubljana, Croatia. Composer; Musician (keyboards); Prod; Arranger. m. 27 Nov. 1977, 1 s. *Education:* Academy of Music, Ljubljana. *Career:* Australia; America; Canada; 25 years on television; More than 1200 compositions, 2000 arrangements. *Recordings:* Suite for orchestra; Music for 3 films; Album: Between The Sky and The Earth (instrumental music); As producer, arranger, sound engineer: over 180 albums with various artists. *Honours:* Eurovision Song Contest, 1993; 6 Festival awards. *Membership:* HDS, Croatia. *Address:* 51215 Kastav, Rubesi 139A, Croatia.

BASIA, (Basia Trzetrzelewska); b. Jaworzno, Poland. Vocalist; Songwriter. *Career:* Singer, Matt Bianco, –1986; Solo artiste, 1986–; Concerts include: Broadway. *Recordings:* Albums: Solo: Time And Tide; London, Warsaw, New York; The Sweetest Illusion; Basia On Broadway; Clear Horizon—The Best Of Basia, 1998. Singles: with Matt Bianco: Half A Minute; Get Out Of Your Lazy

Bed, 1984; Solo: Until You Come Back; Time And Tide; Drunk On Love; Third Time Lucky; Contributor, Pret-A-Porter (film soundtrack). *Current Management:* What Music Ltd, 59 Swains Lane, London N6 6QL, England.

BASS, Lance (James Lansten); b. 4 May 1979, Laurel, MI, USA. Vocalist. *Career:* Aged 11 joined local community choir; First engagement with the Mississippi Show Stoppers; Toured USA with Attache choir; Mem., *NSYNC vocal quintet, 1995–; Signed to BMG Ariola Munich, 1997; First headline US tour, 1998; Created own pop and country record label, Free Lance Entertainment, 2000; Released own film production, On The Line, 2001. *Recordings:* Albums: *NSYNC, 1998; No Strings Attached, 2000; Celebrity, 2001. Singles include: I Want You Back, 1997; Tearin' Up My Heart, 1997; Let The Music Heal Your Soul (various artists charity single credited to Bravo All Stars), 1999; Music Of My Heart (with Gloria Estefan), 1999; Bye, Bye, Bye, 2000; I'll Never Stop, 2000; It's Gonna Be Me, 2000; This I Promise You, 2000; Pop, 2001; Gone, 2001. *Honours:* Presented with keys to City of Orlando, 2000; American Music Award, Favorite Pop/Rock Band, Duo or Group, 2002. *Address:* c/o Wright Entertainment Group, PO Box 590009, Orlando, FL 32859–0009, USA. *Website:* www.nsync.com.

BASSEY, Dame Shirley; b. 8 Jan. 1937, Tiger Bay, Cardiff, Wales. Vocalist; Entertainer. m. (1) Kenneth Hume; (2) Sergio Novak. *Career:* Variety and revue singer, 1950s; Headlined concerts in New York, Las Vegas, early 1960s; Concerts and regular television appearances world-wide; Semi-retirement, 1981–. *Recordings:* Hit singles include: Banana Boat Song; Kiss Me Honey Honey, Kiss Me; As I Love You (No. 1, UK), 1959; As Long As He Needs Me; Big Spender; You'll Never Know; I'll Get By; (I) Who Have Nothing; Bond film themes: Goldfinger; Diamonds Are Forever; Moonraker; Numerous albums include: The Bewitching Miss Bassey, 1959; Fabulous Shirley Bassey, 1960; Shirley, 1961; Shirley Bassey, 1962; Let's Face The Music, 1962; Shirley Bassey Belts The Best!, 1965; I've Got A Song For You, 1966; Twelve Of Those Songs, 1968; Live At The Talk Of The Town, 1970; Something, 1970; Something Else, 1971; Big Spender, 1971; It's Magic, 1971; What Now My Love, 1971; I Capricorn, 1972; And I Love You So, 1972; Never, Never, Never, 1973; Live At Carnegie Hall, 1973; Broadway, Bassey's Way, 1973; Nobody Does It Like Me, 1974; Good Bad and Beautiful, 1975; Love Life and Feelings, 1976; Thoughts Of Love, 1976; You Take My Heart Away, 1977; The Magic Is You, 1979; As Long As He Needs Me, 1980; As Time Goes By, 1980; I'm In The Mood For Love, 1981; Love Songs, 1982; All By Myself, 1984; I Am What I Am, 1984; Playing Solitaire, 1985; I've Got You Under My Skin, 1985; Sings The Songs From The Shows, 1986; Born To Sing The Blues, 1987; Let Me Sing and I'm Happy, 1988; Her Favourite Songs, 1988; Keep The Music Playing, 1991; New York, New York, 1991; Love Album, 1994; Songs Of Andrew Lloyd Webber, 1995; Birthday Concert, 1997; Power Of Love, 1998; Let Me Sing and I'm Happy, 1998; Sings The Movies, 1998; Great Shirley Bassey, 1999; Greatest Hits, 2001; Various compilations; Collaborations with: Yello (The Rhythm Divine, 1987), Propellerheads (History Repeating, 1997). *Honours:* 20 Gold discs; 14 Silver discs; TV Times Award, Best Female Singer, 1972; Britannia Award, Best Female Solo Singer In The Last 50 Years, 1977; American Guild of Variety Artists Award, Best Female Entertainer, 1976. *Current Management:* c/o Stan Scottland, JKES Services, 404 Park Ave S, 10th Floor, New York, NY 10016, USA.

BASTOS, Waldemar; b. 1954, Sao Salvador do Congo, Angola. Vocalist; Songwriter. *Career:* Began performing, 1961; Formed Jovial in Kabinda; Fled Angola, 1982; Now based in Lisbon. *Recordings:* Estamos Juntos (featuring Chico Buarque and Martinho da Vila), 1983; Angola Minha Namorada (featuring Jorge Degas), 1990; Pitanga Madura, 1992; Pretaluz, 1998. *Website:* www.luakabop.com.

BATES, Django Leon; b. 2 Oct. 1960, Beckenham, Kent, England. Musician (keyboards, horn); Composer. m. Beverley Hills, 26 Aug. 1988 1 s., 1 d. *Education:* CYM/Full time Young Musicians (Morley College). *Career:* Formed Human Chain, 1981; Co-founder, Loose Tubes, 1983; Formed Delightful Precipice, 1992; Toured over 30 countries with these bands and others: Europe; USA; South America; Japan; Scandinavia; Television includes: 1 In A Million, BBC Television, 1996. *Compositions include:* Writing commissions for Evelyn Glennie; J McGregor; London Sinfonietta. *Recordings:* Summer Fruits/ Unrest; Autumn Fires/Green Shoots; Winter Truce/Homes Blaze; Spring Is Here/Shall We Dance? Good Evening… Here Is The News; Like Life; Quiet Nights; Contributor, All Men Amen, Iain Ballamy, 1995. *Publications:* Quarterly newsletter, available from management. *Honours:* 3 UK Wire Awards, All Music, 1987; German Stern Des Jahres, 1993; French Academie Du Jazz, 1994. *Current Management:* Peter Luxton, Partnerships.

BATES, Simon Dominic; b. 24 Aug. 1964, London, England. Musician (saxophone, clarinet, flute, wind synthesizer); Programmer. *Education:* BA Hons, Colchester Institute; LGSM (Jazz), Guildhall SMD. *Career:* Yamaha Saxophone; Wind Synthesizer endorsee and clinician; Musician with: Simon Bates Quartet; Sax Appeal; Peter Erskine; Chaka Khan; Lulu; Billy Ocean; D:ream; Eddie Floyd; Tony Remy; The Great Googly Moogly; The Diplomats; Zig Zag; Dominic King. *Recordings:* Television, radio, library sessions; Albums and singles with: D:ream; The Diplomats; EKO; Sasha/Brian Transeau.

Membership: Musicians' Union. *Address:* 1 Erin Close, Bromley, Kent BR1 4NX, England.

BATES, Stuart; b. 19 Sept. 1967, Orpington. Musician. *Education:* Canterbury Cathedral Choir School; Lancing College Music School; Royal Holloway and Bedford New College; University of London. *Career:* Hammond, keyboards, accordion, The Divine Comedy, 1996–; Shows across Europe and Japan, collaboration and performances with Michael Nyman, 1997, with Ronnie Spectre, 1999; Trombone with Elvis Da Costa and The Imposter, 1996; Hammond trombone, The Full Hundred, 2002–; Television includes Top of the Pops, TFI Friday, Later with Jools Holland, The Big Breakfast, The Late Late Show; The Hot Press Awards; Radio includes, Radio 1, Capital Radio, GLR, Virgin Radio, Radio France. *Recordings:* Casanova; A Short Album About Love; Fin De Siecle; Theme to television series, Tomorrow's World; A Secret History; Regeneration (The Divine Comedy); Reload (Tom Jones); Punishing Kiss (Ute Lemper). *Membership:* Musicians' Union. *Current Management:* Divine Management, Top Floor, 1 Cowcross St, London EC1M 6DR, England.

BATSFORD, Richard; b. 25 Oct. 1969, Birmingham, England. Musician; Promoter; Journalist. *Education:* Durham University. *Career:* Singer, National Youth Choir, City of Birmingham Symphony Orchestra; Singer, keyboard player, Gides Park and the Beach Bums; Vocalist; Session Keyboard Player. *Membership:* Musicians' Union. *Current Management:* The GAG Club. *Address:* 2 Valentine Court, Valentine Rd, Kings Heath, Birmingham, B14 7AN, England.

BATT, Mike; b. 6 Feb. 1950. Songwriter; Composer; Prod; Arranger; Vocalist. *Career:* Began as A & R man for Liberty/UA Records, producing Groundhogs, Big Joe Williams, leaving to pursue independent career as Artist, Writer Producer; Produced Linda Lewis, Steeleye Span (All Around My Hat), Elkie Brooks (Lilac Wine), David Essex (Oh What a Circus); Wrote, sang and produced The Wombles (8 UK hits, 4 gold albums) and solo albums Schizophonia, Tarot Suite and others; Produced and composed for Vanessa Mae's album The Violin Player, 1995; Worked with Bond and Becky Taylor, 2000–01. *Compositions include:* Caravans, film score; Bright Eyes, for Art Garfunkel, (No 1, UK); A Winter's Tale, David Essex; I Feel Like Buddy Holly, Alvin Stardust; Please Don't Fall in Love, Cliff Richard; Solo hit singles: Summertime City; The Ride to Agadir; Lady of the Dawn; The Winds of Change; Theatrical project The Hunting of the Snark, starring Cliff Richard, Roger Daltrey, Deniece Williams, John Hurt, Sir John Gielgud, Captain Sensible, Art Garfunkel; Produced Phantom of the Opera hit (Steve Harley and Sarah Brightman); Composer of many commissioned pieces, incl. the opening of the Channel Tunnel for HM the Queen, also for HM the Queen's Golden Wedding Anniversary, 1997; One Minute Silence, 2002. *Membership:* PRS, council; Vice-President, BAC&S. *Address:* c/o Artbeat Ltd, PO Box 214, Farnham, Surrey GU10 5XZ, England.

BATTEUX, Slim; b. 11 July 1949, La Fère, Aisne, France. Backing Vocalist; Vocalist; Musician (Hammond B3). Divorced, 2 d. *Career:* Backing singer for: Diane Tell; Eddy Mitchell; Michel Jonasz; Patricia Kaas; Bill Deraime; Johnny Halliday; Jean-Jacques Goldman; Dicks Rivers; Francis Cabrel; Florent Cagny; Hughes Aufrey; Veronique Samson; Percy Sledge; Billy Paul; Recordings with most of the above artists. *Recordings include:* Ellis Island: Voices of America; Ray Charles; Garry Christian. *Publications:* Je parle Sioux-Lakota. *Membership:* SPEDIDAM; ADAMI; SACEM. *Address:* 9 bis, rue Descombes, 75017 Paris, France.

BATTLE, Nicholas Nigel; b. 14 Aug. 1957, Dartmouth, Devon, England. Music Publisher; Musician; Man. m. Lynn, 12 Aug. 1989. *Education:* Classical violin, led Sheffield Youth Orchestra. *Career:* Bass player, After The Fire; Bass player, Writz; Also worked with Godley and Creme, Kajagoogoo; Gen. Man., Windswept Pacific Music Ltd. *Recordings:* Songs recorded by Cliff Richard: First Date; Front Page; Producer, Falling In Love Again, Techno Twins. *Membership:* PRS; BAC&S; MPA Pop Publishers Committee; IPA Council. *Address:* c/o Windswept Music Ltd, Hope House, 40 St Peter's Rd, London W6 9BH, England.

BAUER, Johannes; b. 22 July 1954, Halle, East Germany. Musician. *Education:* Trombone Studies, Berlin, 1971–77. *Career:* Freelance Improvisational Musician, 1979–; Duo with Barry Gay, Trio with Annick Nozati and Fred Van Hove Doppelmoppel (with Konrad Bauer, Joe Sachse, Uwe Kropinski) Slawterhaus (with Dietmar Diesner, Jon Rose, Peter Hellinger), Ulrich Gumpert Trio, Peter Brötzmann Alarm Orchester, März Combo, Tony Oxleys Contemporary Music Ensemble, Globe Unity Orchestra, Derek Baileys Company, Cecil Taylor European Big Band; Leader of Various Workshop Bands. *Recordings:* Round About Mittweida; ALARM; Nr.12; Cecil Taylor in Berlin '88; Slawterhaus Live a Victoriaville; Organo Pleno; Bauer Bauer; In The Tradition; The Wild Man's Band. *Address:* Dannecker Str 6, Berlin 10245, Germany.

BAUER, Judah; b. 1973, Appleton, WI, USA. Musician (guitar, harmonica). *Career:* Mem., Twenty-Miles; Mem., Jon Spencer Blues Explosion, 1990–. *Recordings:* Albums: Jon Spencer Blues Explosion, 1992; Crypt Style, 1992;

Extra Width, 1993; Mo' Width, 1994; Orange, 1994; Experimental Remixes, 1995; Now I Got Worry, 1996; Controversial Negro, 1997; Rocketship, 1997; ACME, 1998; Magical Colours, 2000; Plastic Fang, 2002. Singles: The Sound Of The Future Is Here Today, 1992; Shirt-jac, 1992; Son Of Sam, 1992; Big Yule Log Boogie, 1992; Train 3, 1993; Bellbottoms, 1995; Get With It, 1996; 2 Kindsa Love, 1996; Wail, 1997; Rocketship, 1997; Talk About The Blues, 1998. *Address:* c/o Mute Records, 136 W 18th St, New York, NY 10011, USA.

BAUER, William Henry (Billy); b. 14 Nov. 1915, Bronx, New York, USA. Musician (banjo, guitar). m. Marion V Cos, 15 March 1941, 1 s., 1 d. *Education:* Harmony and theory in college. *Career:* Woody Herman, 1942–45; Lennie Tristano, 1946–49; Teacher, Conservatory of Modern Music, 1946–49; NBC Staff Musician, 1950–58; Benny Goodman, 1958; Brussels Worlds Fair, Sherwood Inn, 1960–62; Ice Capades, 1963–67; Broadway Theatre, 1968–69; Billy Bauer Guitar School, 1970–. *Recordings:* Freelance recording musician for about 10 years; Guitar solos recorded: Blue Mist; Purple Haze; Short Stories; Greenway; Impressions; Pam, for Woody Herman; Marionette; Blue Boy, both for Lennie Tristano; Duet for saxophone and guitar recorded by Lee Konitz. *Publications:* Jazz Lines, by Lennie Tristano, Lee Konitz, Warne Marsh; Author, Guitar Instructor Series; Sideman: Autobiography of Billy Bauer, 1997. *Honours:* Metronome All Star Poll, 1947–51; Down Beat Award, 1949–50. *Membership:* ASCAP. *Current Management:* William H Bauer Inc.

BAY, Hans Henrik; b. 26 Dec. 1963, Copenhagen, Denmark. Musician (guitar); Composer. m. Susanne Bechmann, 1 s., 1 d. *Education:* Rhythmic Music Conservatory, Copenhagen. *Career:* Tour in Denmark with Jorgen Emborg, 1988–89; Tour in Denmark with Ensemble NEW and Billy Cobham, 1997; Played with James Moody, Ed Neumeister, Jukkis Outtila, Tomas Franck, Bob Rockwell and Jesper Lundgaard. *Compositions:* Crescent 434, 6/8, In the Bar. *Recordings:* Jorgen Emborg Septet: Keyword, 1989; Ensemble New with Billy Cobham, 1998. *Membership:* Danish Music Union; Danish Jazz Beat Folk Autorer. *Current Management:* Ole Cristensen, vendersgade 28, 7000 Fredericia, Denmark. *Address:* Bredager 32, 7120 Vejle O, Denmark.

BAYLIS, Christopher Edward; b. 7 July 1954, Reading, Berkshire, England. Prod; Musician (guitar). *Education:* BSc, University of Surrey. *Career:* Founder mem., Siam, 1980; Formed The Guitar Orchestra, 1989; Production credits include: Maddy Prior; Davey Arthur; Automatic Dlamini. *Recordings:* The Guitar Orchestra, 1991; Interpretations, The Guitar Orchestra, 1994. *Membership:* PRS; MCPS; Musicians' Union. *Current Management:* Park Records. *Address:* PO Box 651, Oxford OX2 9RB, England.

BAYNE, Iain; b. 22 Jan. 1960, St Andrews, Fife, Scotland. Musician (drums, percussion, piano). *Career:* Member, Scottish folk group Runrig, 1980–; International concerts include: Canada, 1987; Support to U2, Murrayfield Stadium, Edinburgh, 1987; Royal Concert Hall, Glasgow; Open-air concert, Loch Lomond. *Recordings:* Albums: Play Gaelic, 1978; Highland Connection, 1979; Recovery, 1981; Heartland, 1985; The Cutter and The Clan, 1987; Once In A Lifetime, 1988; Searchlight, 1989; The Big Wheel, 1991; Amazing Things, 1993; Transmitting Live, 1995. *Current Management:* Marlene Ross Management, 55 Wellington St, Aberdeen AB2 1BX, Scotland.

BAYNHAM, Frank; b. 29 May 1942, Warrington, England. Musician (English concertina, bodhran). m. Sherry, 5 Jan. 1972, 3 s. *Education:* BEd, Hons, Lancaster University, Art, Music. *Career:* Founder member, Wigan Folk Club; Played solo and with various individuals, bands; Formed current band Kings of Puck, 1993. *Honours:* Guinness Best Entertainment of Puck Fair, Killorglin, Co Kerry, Ireland, with Steve Ashton, Dave Mann, 1993. *Membership:* Musicians' Union. *Current Management:* Ricky McCabe Entertainments Ltd. *Address:* 26 Crosby Rd N, Waterloo, Liverpool L22 4QF, England.

BAYNTON-POWER, David; b. 29 Jan. 1961, England. Musician (drums). *Career:* Mem., James, 1990–2001; Numerous tours, festival dates and television appearances; Farewell 'Getting Away With It' concert, Manchester Evening News Arena, Dec. 2001. *Recordings:* Albums: Gold Mother, 1990; Seven, 1992; Laid, 1993; Wah Wah, 1994; Whiplash, 1997; The Best Of James, 1998; Millionaires, 1999; B-Sides Ultra, 2001; Pleased To Meet You, 2001; Getting Away With It, 2002. Singles incl.: How Was It For You, 1990; Come Home, 1990; Lose Control, 1990; Sit Down, 1991; Sound, 1991; Born Of Frustration, 1992; Ring The Bells, 1992; Seven, 1992; Sometimes, 1993; Laid, 1993; Say Something/Jam J, 1994; She's A Star, 1997; Tomorrow, 1997; Waltzing Along, 1997; Destiny Calling, 1998; Runaground, 1998; Sit Down (remix), 1998; I Know What I'm Here For, 1999; Fred Astaire, 1999; We're Gonna Miss You, 1999; Getting Away With It (All Messed Up), 2001. *Current Management:* Rudge Management, 1 Star St, London W2 1QD, England.

BAYSHAW, Debbie; b. 5 Feb. 1958, Chapeau, Québec, Canada. Vocalist. m. Peter Komisar Jr, 1 s., 3 d. *Education:* 4 years classical guitar. *Career:* Performed coast to coast, Canada; Appeared several major television shows; Host, 3 part variety mini series, CBC, Toronto. *Recordings:* Albums: Time To Move Along; Mixed Emotions. *Honours:* Winner, Canadian Open Country Singing Contest; CBC TV Contest, Look Out World Here We Come.

Membership: AFofM. *Current Management:* Big Peach Records. *Address:* RR2, Grand Valley, Ontario L0N 1G0, Canada. *Telephone:* (519) 928-2257.

BEACHILL, Peter C; b. 1 Feb. 1961, Barnsley, Yorkshire, England. Musician (trombone). *Education:* Leeds College of Music. *Career:* Studio musician; Various television shows: Royal Variety; Barrymore; BAFTA Awards; BBC, LWT Shows; Tours with James Last; Natalie Cole; Shirley Bassey; Pete Townsend; Cliff Richard; Chris Rea; Eric Clapton; Oasis. *Recordings:* Albums with: Paul McCartney; Sting; Pet Shop Boys; Diana Ross; Rod Stewart; James Last; Shirley Bassey; Cliff Richard; Peter Gabriel; Eric Clapton; Grace Jones; Pink Floyd; Led Zeppelin; Pete Townshend. *Honours:* BBC Don Lusher Trombone Award. *Membership:* Royal Society of Musicians. *Address:* 16 Coniston Rd, Muswell Hill, London N10 2BP, England.

BEAKER, Norman; b. 21 June 1950, Manchester, England. Musician (guitar, piano); Vocalist; Composer; Prod. m. Sept. 1977, divorced 1985, 1 s. *Education:* College of Music (Northern). *Career:* Concerts with Alexis Korner; Eric Clapton; Jack Bruce; B. B. King; Lowell Fulsom; Graham Bond; Buddy Guy; Television and radio appearances include: Old Grey Whistle Test; The Tube; So It Goes; Radio 1 in Concert; Paul Jones R&B Show Radio 2; Capital Radio with Jack Bruce; First blues band to tour East Germany, 1977. *Recordings:* Into The Blues, Norman Beaker Band; Modern Days Lonely Nights; I Was Once A Gambler (Phil Guy); Theme music, World In Action; Theme music, Stand Up. *Publications:* Freelance writer on R&B, various magazines and journals. *Honours:* Blues Guitarist of the Year, 1989. *Membership:* PRS; MCPS. *Current Management:* Actual Music.

BEANS; Vocalist. *Career:* Released cassette-only recordings on Anti-Pop Recordings label; Mem., The Anti-Pop Consortium, 1997–2002; Supported DJ Shadow's US tour, 2002; Solo artiste, 2002–; Collaborations with Arto Lindsey, Vernon Reid. *Recordings:* Albums: Tragic Epilogue, 2000; Arrhythmia, 2002. Singles: Diagonal Ryme Gargantua (EP), 2000; What Am I?, 2000; Lift, 2000; The Ends Against The Middle (EP), 2001; Ghostlawns, 2002. *Current Management:* Amaechi Uzoigwe, Ozone Music. *Address:* c/o Warp Records Ltd, Spectrum House, 32–34 Gordon House Rd, London NW5 1LP, England. *Website:* www.warprecords.com.

BEARD, Frank; b. 11 June 1949, Frankston, Texas, USA. Musician (drums). *Career:* Joined The Warlocks, 1967; Band name changed to The American Blues, 1968; Founder member, ZZ Top, 1970–; Toured regularly, 1970–; Tours include Eliminator tour, 1984; Afterburner tour, 1985–87; Recycler tour, 1990; Rock The Bowl '91, Milton Keynes, 1991. *Recordings:* Albums include: 2 with The American Blues, 1968; with ZZ Top: ZZ Top's First Album, 1970; Rio Grande Mud, 1972; Tres Hombres, 1973; Fandango, 1975; Tejas, 1977; The Best Of, 1978; Deguello, 1979; El Loco, 1981; Eliminator, 1983; Afterburner, 1985; Recycler, 1990; Greatest Hits, 1992; Antenna, 1994; XXX, 1999; Singles include: La Grange, 1974; Tush, 1975; Gimme All Your Lovin', 1983; Sharp Dressed Man, 1983; Legs, 1984; Sleeping Bag, 1985; Stages, 1986; Rough Boy, 1986; Velcro Fly, 1986; Doubleback, from film Back To The Future Part III, 1990; Viva Las Vegas, 1992. *Honours:* Several MTV Video Awards; ZZ Top Day, Texas, 1991; Silver Clef Award, Nordoff-Robbins Music Therapy Foundation, 1992. *Current Management:* Lone Wolf Management, PO Box 163690, Austin, TX 78716, USA.

BEARD, Susan Stephanie (Sue); b. 25 Feb. 1961, London, England. Jazz Vocalist; Songwriter; Actress; Writer; Stand-up Comic; Musician (piano, oboe, ukelele). *Education:* Bristol University postgraduate certificate in film; BA Hons, Music, York University, 1983. *Career:* Comic/satirical jazz singer; Television appearances: Les Dawson Show, BBC1; Pebble Mill, BBC1; The Happening, with Jools Holland, CH4 Television; Numerous radio broadcasts include: Loose Ends; Pick of The Week, BBC Radio 4; BBC Radio 2; JFM; Many commercial stations; Concerts include: Live at London's Comedy Store; Ronnie Scott's; Pizza On The Park; Astoria; One Woman Show Tour including Edinburgh Festival; Kuala Lumpur; Arezzo, Paris. *Compositions:* Spooks! (children's musical), 1995; Composer, performer, many topical, satirical and jazz songs for radio, television, live performances. *Current Management:* Nick Young, Crawfords. *Address:* 2 Conduit St, London W1R 9TG, England.

BÉART, Guy; b. 16 July 1930, Cairo, Egypt. Vocalist; Composer; Engineer; Author. 2 d. *Education:* Ecole Nationale des Ponts et Chaussées. *Career:* Cabaret, recitals and concerts, Paris; Author, producer, television series Bienvenue, 1966–72. *Compositions:* Songs for artists including: Zizi Jeanmaire; Juliette Greco; Patachou, Maurice Chevalier; Film music includes: L'Eau Vive; Pierrot La Tendresse; La Gamberge. *Honours:* Chevalier, Légion d'Honneur; Officier, Ordre National du Mérite; Commandeur des Arts et des Lettres; Grand Prix, Academy du Disque, 1957; Academy Charles Cros, 1965; Grand Prix de la Chanson, SACEM, 1987; Prix Balzac, 1987. *Address:* Editions Temporel, 2 rue du Marquis de Morès, 92380 Garches, France.

BEASLEY, Walter; b. California, USA. Musician (alto/soprano saxophones); Songwriter. *Career:* Jazz Explosion's Just The Sax tour. *Recordings:* Albums: Walter Beasley, 1988; Just Kickin' It, 1989; Intimacy, 1992; Private Time, 1995; Live and More, 1996; Tonight We Love, 1997; For Your Pleasure, 1998; Won't You Let Me Love You, 2000; Rendez Vous, 2002; Call Me; I'm So

Happy; Jump On It; Nothin' But A Thang; On The Edge; Tenderness; Where; Singles: You Are The One; If You Ever Loved Someone; Don't Say Goodbye. *Current Management:* c/o Preston Powell, Jazzateria Inc, 112 W 72nd St, #2F, New York, NY 10023, USA.

BEAUFORD, Carter; b. 2 Nov. 1957, USA. Musician (drums). *Education:* Shenandoah Conservatory, Winchester, Virginia, studied occupational therapy. *Career:* Son of a jazz trumpeter; Attended schools in North Carolina prior to becoming full-time musician; Resides in Charlottesville, California; Moonlights as session player including guest appearance on a Carlos Santana album; First gig with jazz-fusion outfit led by local luminary Big Nick Nicholas, aged 9; Played with Secrets band 1984–90; Four year residency as pianist on Ramsey Lewis' BET On Jazz show; Drummer for The Dave Matthews Band, 1991–; Rapid growth of fanbase through touring schedules; First album released on group's own Bama Rags label certified gold by RIAA; First national US tour in support of RCA debut album, 1994; Many worldwide concerts and festival appearances since including 2001 album tour; Group permits fans to tape-record shows for personal use; I Did It single officially released through Napster, 2001. *Recordings:* Albums: Remember Two Things (live), 1993; Under The Table and Dreaming, 1994; Crash, 1996; Live At Red Rocks 8–15–95, 1997; Before These Crowded Streets, 1998; Listener Supported (live), 1999; Everyday, Live In Chicago 12–19–98, 2001; Singles: Recently (EP), 1994; What Would You Say, Jimi Thing, Ants Marching, 1995; So Much To Say, Too Much, 1996; Don't Drink The Water, 1997; Satellite, Crash Into Me, Crush, 1998; I Did It, The Space Between, Everyday, 2001. *Honours:* Grammy Awards: Best Rock Performance By A Duo Or Group With Vocal, 1997; VH-1 Awards: Favourite Group; Must Have Album; Song of the Year, 2001; Top-grossing touring band in USA, 2000. *Address:* c/o Red Light Communications, 3305 Lobban Pl., Charlottesville, VA 22903, USA. *E-mail:* info@rlc.net. *Website:* www.dmband.com.

BEAUPRE, Jhan; b. 29 April 1950, Dallas, Texas, USA. Songwriter; Musician (Guitar). m. Joyce Ann Beaupre, 10 July 1983, 6 d. *Education:* Degree in Nursing, Southwestern Union College, 1978. *Career:* Founded The Sound System, age 15; Played with various bands for 7 years; Business venture, Sound Illusions, promoting and recording new artists and songwriters. *Compositions include:* She Can Make A Man Cry; A Good Guitar; There's A Flame. *Honours:* Semi-finalist, Austin Songwriters; Placed 2 times, Wisconsin Songwriters. *Membership:* BMI; Austin Song Writers Group; Secretary, Johnson County Asscn; Song Writers of Wisconsin; Fort Bend S W Group. *Current Management:* Davis and Davis Music, 5755 June Lane, Winston-Salem, NC 27127, USA.

BEAUSSIER, Daniel Gérard Jacques; b. 2 June 1957, Valenciennes, Nord, France. Musician; Composer; Teacher; Prod. m. Aesa Sigurjonsdottir, 22 Aug. 1987, 3 s., 1 d. *Education:* Engineer, ICAM. *Career:* Tour, Europe, with Carla Bley, 1988; with Nana Vasconcellos, Paris Jazz Festival, 1991; Hozan Yamamato, 1995; Monica Passos; Charlélie Couture; Shiro Daimon; Astrolab Collectif; Correspondances with D Beaussier (150 concerts). *Recordings:* Fleur Carnivore, Carla Bley; Lueurs Bleues, Daniel Goyone, Trilok Gurtu; Sans(e)krit, Daniel Beaussier; Casamento, Monica Passos; Chambre 13, Lydia Domancich; You Are Here, Uman. *Publications:* Analysis of solos in Findings, My Experience With Saxophone, by Steve Lacy. *Honours:* First prize, CNR, Lille, France. *Membership:* UMJ; FNEIJ; IAJS; Director, EDIM, Creative Music School, Paris. *Current Management:* EDIM Productions. *Address:* 24 Ave d'Alembert, 92160 Antony, France.

BEAVERS, Les; b. 23 Nov. 1934, Manchester, England. Musician (guitar). m. Terry Burton, 23 Jan. 1963. *Career:* Played at various ballrooms, 1956–59; Played with BBC Northern Dance Orchestra, 1959–68; Bob Sharples, Thames Television, 1963–78; Appearances on Granada Television and sessions on STV, among others; Also theatre tours. *Membership:* Musicians' Union. *Address:* 7 Sandown Rd, Sunny Bank, Bury, Lancashire BL9 8HN, England.

BEBEK, Zeljko; b. 16 Dec. 1945, Sarajevo, Croatia. Vocalist. m. Sandra Bebek, 2 Oct. 1982, 2 d. *Education:* University of Civil Rights. *Career:* Hundreds of concerts and television shows, over 20 years; 2m. recordings; Many concerts of Townsends and Townsends Peoples in Zagreb, Sarajevo; Tours: Europe; USA; Canada. *Recordings:* (Singing in Croatian language) Bosanac; Selma; Na Zadnjem Sjedistu; Da Je Srece Bilo; Dabogda Te Voda Odnijela; Sta Je Meni Ovo Trebalo; A Svemir Miruje; Odlazim; Tijana. *Membership:* Hrvatska Glazbewa Unija (HGU). *Current Management:* Song Agency, Split, Croatia. *Address:* Crnciceva 41, 41000 Zagreb, Croatia.

BECK, (Beck Hansen); b. 8 July 1970, Los Angeles, CA, USA. Musician; Vocalist. *Career:* Early performances at local parties in Los Angeles; Worked with producers Karl Stephenson, and later the Dust Brothers; Numerous tours and live appearances including Glastonbury Festival, England, 1997; Collaborated with Snoop Doggy Dogg; Air; Remixed: Air; Jon Spencer Blues Explosion; Bjork; David Bowie; Covered Bowie's Diamond Dogs for Moulin Rouge OST, 2001. *Recordings:* Singles: Loser, 1994; Beercan EP, 1994; Devil's Haircut (remixed by Noel Gallagher), 1996; Where It's At, 1996; The New Pollution, 1997; Jack Ass, 1997; Sissyneck, 1997; Deadweight, 1998; Tropicalia, 1999; Nobody's Fault But My Own EP, 1999; Sexxlaws, 1999;

Mixed Bizness, 2000; Albums: Mellow Gold, 1994; One Foot in the Grave, 1994; Stereopathic Soul Manure, 1994; Odelay, 1996; Mutations, 1998; Midnite Vultures, 1999; Sea Change, 2002. *Honours:* Grammy Award, Alternative Music Performance (Mutations), 2000; BRIT Award, Best International Male, 1997, 1999, 2000. *Address:* c/o Geffen Records, 2220 Colorado Ave, Santa Monica, CA 90404, USA. *Website:* www.beck.com.

BECK, Jeff; b. 24 June 1944, Surrey, England. Musician (guitar); Composer; Vocalist. *Education:* Wimbledon Art College. *Career:* Member, Screaming Lord Sutch; The Tridents; Guitarist, The Yardbirds, 1965–66; Appearances include: Tours with the Kinks, 1965; The Beatles, Paris, 1965; Manfred Mann, 1965; Rolling Stones '66 tour, 1966; Leader, Jeff Beck Group, 1967–; Concerts include: National Jazz and Blues Festival, 1967, 1968; Newport Jazz Festival, 1969; Secret Policeman's Other Ball, London (Amnesty benefit), 1981; Prince's Trust Rock Gala, Royal Albert Hall, 1983; US tour with Stevie Ray Vaughan, 1989. *Recordings:* Hit singles include: with the Yardbirds: Heart Full Of Soul; For Your Love; Evil Hearted You/Still I'm Sad; Shapes Of Things; Over Under Sideways Down; with Jeff Beck Group: Hi-Ho Silver Lining; Tallyman; Love Is Blue; Albums include: with the Yardbirds: For Your Love, 1965; Having A Rave Up With The Yardbirds, 1965; The Yardbirds with Sonny Boy Williamson, 1966; Yardbirds, 1966; Over Under Sideways Down, 1966; with Jeff Beck Group/solo: Truth, 1968; Beck-Ola, 1969; Rough and Ready, 1971; Jeff Beck Group, 1972; Jeff Beck, Tim Bogert and Carmine Appice, 1973; Blow By Blow, 1975; Wired, 1976; Jeff Beck With The Jan Hammer Group Live, 1977; There and Back, 1980; Flash, 1985; Jeff Beck's Guitar Shop With Terry Bozzio and Tony Hymas, 1989; Crazy Legs, 1993; Up, 1995; The Best Of Beck, 1995; Blow By Blow, 1995; Shapes Of Things, 1998; Who Else! 1999; You Had It Coming, 2001; Beck-Ola Cosa Nostra; Contributor, film soundtracks: The Pope Must Die, 1991; Honeymoon In Vegas, 1992; Contributor, Blaze Of Glory, Jon Bon Jovi, 1990; Amused To Death, Roger Waters, 1992; Tribute To Muddy Waters, 1993; Stone Free: A Tribute To Jimi Hendrix, 1993. *Honours:* Grammy Awards, Best Rock Instrumental Performance, 1986, 1990, 2002; BAFTA Award, Best Original Television Music, Frankie's House, with Jed Leiber, 1993. *Current Management:* c/o Ernest Chapman, Equator Music, 17 Hereford Mansions, Hereford Rd, London W2 5BA, England.

BECKER, Irene; b. 30 March 1951, Ålborg, Denmark. Musician (piano); Composer. m. Pierre Dorge, 24 Aug. 1985. *Education:* Cand Phil. in Music, University of Copenhagen. *Career:* Member, Pierre Dorge's New Jungle Orchestra, 1980–; Member, Trio: Dorge, Becker, Carlsen; Performs with singer Sainkho Namtclylak, Austria; Composer, film music. *Recordings:* Albums: New Jungle Orchestra, 10 albums; Dancing On The Island, Irene Becker and Sainkho. *Membership:* DJBFA; Danish Musicians' Union. *Current Management:* Copenhagen Concerts, Holmbladsgade 35, 2300 Copenhagen S, Denmark.

BECKER, Jason; Rock Musician (guitar). *Education:* Classical guitar. *Career:* Guitarist, US rock group Cacophony (with Marty Friedman), 1986–90; Also solo artiste; Guitarist, David Lee Roth, 1991–. *Recordings:* Albums: with Cacophony: Speed Metal Symphony, 1987; Go Off, 1989; Solo: Perpetual Burn, 1988; Perspective, 1996; Raspberry Jams, 1999; with David Lee Roth: A Little Ain't Enough, 1991.

BECKER, Walter; b. 20 Feb. 1950, New York, USA. Musician (guitar, bass); Record Prod. 1 s., 2 step-s. *Career:* Founder member, Steely Dan, 1972–81, 1993–; Record producer, 1980–; Solo recording artiste; Tours of USA; Japan; Europe; Australia. *Recordings:* Albums: Can't Buy A Thrill, 1973; My Sportin' Life, 1973; Countdown To Ecstasy, 1973; Pretzel Logic, 1974; Katy Lied, 1975; The Royal Scam, 1976; Aja, 1978; Greatest Hits, 1979; Metal Leg, 1980; Gaucho, 1981; Reelin' In The Years, 1985; Do It Again, 1987; Remastered: The Best Of Steely Dan, 1993; Citizen Steely Dan 1972–80, 1993; Alive In America, 1995; Two Against Nature, 2000; Solo: 11 Tracks Of Whack, 1995; Singles include: Dallas; Show Biz Kids; My Old School; Black Friday; Kid Charlemagne; Haitian Divorce; Deacon Blues; FM (No Static At All); Rikki Don't Lose That Number; As producer: Flaunt The Imperfection, China Crisis, 1985; Flying Cowboys, Rickie Jones, 1989; Jazz recordings for: LeeAnn Ledgerwood; Andy Laverne; Jeff Beal; Jeremy Steig; David Kikosi; Lorraine Feather; Sam Butler; Donald Fagen. *Honours:* Platinum disc; Grammy Awards, Aja, 1978; Two Against Nature, 2001; Inducted into Hollywood's Rock Walk, 1993. *Current Management:* HK Management, 8900 Wilshire Blvd, Suite 300, Beverly Hills, CA 90211, USA.

BECKERS, (Ludo) Lazy Lew; b. 27 March 1957, Molenstede, Belgium. Musician (Harmonica). m. 27 March 1981, 1 s., 1 d. *Education:* Jazz Theory Lessons, Halewÿnstichting, Antwerp, Belgium. *Career:* Harmonica Player (sometimes Singer), The Zoots, 1984–86; The Sultans, 1987; Medford Slim Band, 1990–94; Brothers in Blues, 1990–96; European Tours with Zora Young, R L Burnside, Big Lucky Carter, Calvin Jackson. *Recordings:* The Zoots and Louisiana Red; The Sultans; Medford Slim Band; P Vansant. *Membership:* SABAM. *Address:* 77 Te Boelaarlei, 2140 Borgerhout, Belgium.

BECKETT, Steve; Record Co Exec. *Career:* Mem., punk band with Rob Mitchell; Opened record store with Mitchell (deceased, 2001), Warp Records, in Sheffield, England, 1987; Co-founded Warp Records label for electronic music, 1989; First release, WAP 001, Track With No Name, by Forgemasters, 1989; Released compilations of various artistes, 1993–; Artistes signed include: Anti-Pop Consortium, Aphex Twin, Autechre, Black Dog, Boards of Canada, Broadcast, LFO, Nightmares on Wax, Plaid, Plone, Red Snapper, Sabres of Paradise, Squarepusher. *Address:* Warp Records Ltd, Spectrum House, 32–34 Gordon House Rd, London NW5 1LP, England. *Website:* www.warprecords.com.

BECKHAM, Victoria, (Posh Spice); b. 17 April 1974, Cuffley, England. Vocalist. m. David Beckham, 4 July 1999, 2 s. *Education:* Jason Theatre School, Laine Arts Theatre College. *Career:* Mem., Touch, later renamed Spice Girls, 1993–; Numerous tours, concerts, television and radio appearances; Film, Spiceworld: The Movie, 1997; World tour incl. UK, Europe, India, USA; Solo artiste, 2000–. *Recordings:* Albums: with Spice Girls: Spice (No. 1, UK), 1996; Spiceworld (No. 1, UK), 1997; Forever, 2000; Solo: Victoria Beckham, 2001. Singles: with Spice Girls: Wannabe (No. 1, UK and USA), 1996; Say You'll Be There (No. 1, UK), 1996; 2 Become 1 (No. 1, UK), 1996; Mama/ Who Do You Think You Are (No. 1, UK), 1997; Step To Me, 1997; Spice Up Your Life (No. 1, UK), 1997; Too Much (No. 1, UK), 1997; Stop, 1998; (How Does It Feel To Be) On Top Of the World, with England United, 1998; Move Over/Generation Next, 1998; Viva Forever (No. 1, UK), 1998; Goodbye (No. 1, UK), 1998; Holler/Let Love Lead The Way (No. 1, UK), 2000; Solo: Out Of Your Mind (with True Steppers/Dane Bowers), 2000; Not Such An Innocent Girl, 2001; A Mind Of Its Own, 2002. *Publications:* Learning to Fly (autobiography), 2001. *Honours:* BRIT Awards, Best Video, for Say You'll Be There, Best Single, for Wannabe, 1997, Outstanding Contribution, 2000; Two Ivor Novello songwriting awards, 1997; Smash Hits Award, Best Band, 1997; Three American Music Awards, 1998; Special BRIT Award for International Sales, 1998. *Address:* c/o The Outside Organisation, Butler House, 177–178 Tottenham Court Rd, London W1T 7NY, England. *Telephone:* (20) 7436-3633. *Fax:* (20) 7436-3632. *Website:* www.victoriabeckham.net.

BEDER, Mark; b. 16 Nov. 1959, London, England. Record Prod; Music Publisher; Artist Man. 1 s., 1 d. *Career:* A & R Dept, Carlin Music Publishers; A & R Manager, Polydor and Virgin Records; Currently Managing Director for Pumphouse Music; Pumphouse Sounds; Pumphouse Songs; FXU Records; Manager of: D:ream; X-Avia; Tri; Siren; D J Peer; Recordings by artists listed above. *Honours:* Best Newcomers; Best Dance Act; Radio One Tune of the Year, 1992; Official Labour Party Anthem, Things Can Only Get Better. *Membership:* PRS; MCPS; MPA; IMF. *Address:* FXU, G T Studios, 97 Scrubs Lane, London NW10 6QU, England.

BEEBY, John; b. 18 Nov. 1945, Nuneaton, Warwickshire, England. Musician (guitar); Songwriter; Prod. m. 16 Nov. 1974, 1 s. *Career:* Tour, Germany, 1963–64; The Zephyrs, 1964; Toured with: Del Shannon; Jerry Lee Lewis; Billy Fury; Pretty Things; Count Prince Miller, 1968; Tony Gregory; Horace Faith; Television appearances include: Ready Steady Go; Top of the Pops; Scene At 6.30; Wogan; Pebble Mill; Film appearances: Be My Guest (with Jerry Lee Lewis, Steve Marriot); Primitive London; Ice Cream Dream; Business Ventures: John Beeby's Music Place, 1975; Worked freelance with various artists; Worked with Eurythmics' Dave Stewart as songwriter, producer, 1980s; Co-writer, Dreamtime, with Daryl Hall, 1986; Co-writer, producer, with Brian Hodgson, Why Do I Always Get It Wrong (UK entry, Eurovision Song Contest), No. 2, 1989; Worked in Nashville, USA, with various artists including Robert Ellis Orral, Larry Henley, Roger Cook, 1989. *Recordings:* She's Lost You, 1964; Wonder What I'm Gonna Do, 1965; A Little Bit Of Soap, 1965; Dreamtime, 1986; Why Do I Always Get It Wrong, 1989; Take A Chance On Me, 1989. *Honours:* BMI Dreamtime, USA; BMI Dreamtime, UK. *Membership:* PRS; BAC&S. *Address:* Crouch End, London N8, England.

BEECHER, Franny; b. Philadelphia, Pennsylvania, USA. Musician (guitar). *Education:* Worked with Benny Goodman. *Career:* Original member, Bill Haley's Comets, 1952–62; Invented rock 'n' roll music; First rock band to headline a film; Worked with Buddy Grecco. *Recordings:* Rock Around The Clock; See You Later Alligator; Crazy Man Crazy; Shake Rattle and Roll; Rock The Joint; Mabo Rock; Rudy's Rock; Florida Twist; Skinnie Minnie; Capitol 50th Anniversary Jazz Box; Undercurrent Blues; From The Original Master Tapes; Back To A Better Time; Decca Years and More; Bring Back The Music; Rock-A-Billy Son. *Publications:* Rock Around The Clock; Stage Clear; We're Gonna Party; Never Too Old To Rock. *Honours:* Best Vocal Group, 1954; Best Instrumental Group, 1956; Best Guitar Player; Rock and Roll Hall of Fame; Gold Records. *Address:* Rock It Concerts, Bruno Mefer Platz 1, 80937 Munich, Germany.

BEEDLE, Ashley, (Daddy Ash, Black Jazz Chronicles, Delta House of Funk); b. 25 Nov. 1962, Hemel Hempstead, England. Prod; Remixer; DJ. *Career:* Worked in record shops Black Market and Flying Records in London; Formed X-Press 2 with Rocky and Diesel, 1993; Signed to Junior Boy's Own label; Member: Ballistic Brothers; Black Science Orchestra; Disco Evangelists; Founder: Afro Art Records; Collaborations: David Holmes; Marc Woolford; Remixed: Fatboy Slim; River Ocean; Richard Blackwood; D-Influence; Gabrielle; East 17. *Recordings:* Albums: Walter's Room (with Black Science Orchestra), 1994; Ballistic Brothers vs The Eccentric Afros, 1995; London

Hooligan Soul (with Ballistic Brothers), 1995; Future Juju (as Black Jazz Chronicles), 1998; Muzikizum, 2002. Singles: Where Were You (with Black Science Orchestra), 1992; Muzik X-Press, London X-Press, 1993; Altered States EP (with Black Science Orchestra), Rock 2 House, 1994; The Sound, 1995; Tranz Euro Express, 1996; Blacker (with Ballistic Brothers), 1997; AC/DC, 2000; Smoke Machine, Muzikizum, 2001; Lazy (featuring David Byrne), 2002. *Honours:* Muzik Awards, Best Producers, X-Press 2, 2001. *Membership:* MCPS/PRS. *Address:* c/o Skint Records, 73A Middle St, Brighton, Sussex BN1 4BA, England.

BEGGS, Nick; b. 15 Dec. 1961, Winslow, Bucks, England. Musician (bass guitar, chapman stick); Prod; Writer; Arranger. 1 d. *Career:* Kajagoogoo; Ellis Beggs and Howard Iona; Belinda Carlisle. *Compositions:* White Feathers; Islands; Crazy People's Right to Speak; Homelands; The Book of Kells; Beyond These Shores. *Recordings:* Big Bubbles No Troubles, Ellis Beggs and Howard; A Woman and A man, Belinda Carlisle; The Thunderthief, John Paul Jones, 2001. *Publications:* Too Shy, Kajagoogoo, 1983. *Membership:* Musicians' Union; MCPS; PPL; PRS. *Address:* 61 Atheldene Rd, London SW18 3BN, England.

BEGLEY, Seamus; b. Dingle, County Kerry, Ireland. Vocalist; Musician (button accordion). *Career:* Brother of Eilin Begley, Maire Begley, Seosaimhin Ni Bheaglaoich and Breandan Begley; Started playing for local dances, aged 14; Long-term collaboration with Steve Cooney. *Recordings:* Albums include: An Ciarraioch Mallaithe (with sister Maire), 1972; Plancstai Bhaile Na Buc (with Maire), 1989; features on Vinnie Kilduff, 1990; Meiteal (with Steve Cooney), 1997; Water From The Well, The Chieftains, 2000. *Honours:* Ireland National Entertainment Awards, Most Popular Traditional Act (with Steve Cooney), 1997.

BEIJBOM, Lars; b. 1 Aug. 1950, Sweden. Composer; Arranger; Drums. 1 s. *Education:* Berklee College of Music, composition, arranging diploma, 1975. *Career:* Composer and arranged music for large number of radio/television programmes; Big Bands Symphony Orchestra's, Pop/Rock/Jazz; Played, arranged and composed music for artists including: George Russell, Dorothy Donegan, Tomas Ledin, Maritza Horn, Tre Damer, The Swedish Radio Jazz Group, The Danish Radio Big Band, NDR-band; Musical Arranger, Danish star Stig Rossen, 1997–. *Compositions:* Three for Daniel; The Swinging Triangle; In the Long Run; Eat Your Heart Out; Up Your Alley; The Goose is Out; Sweet Sadness; The Fire Within; Alpha and Omega; 11 Peterborough Street. *Recordings:* Subway Baby, 1977; White Orange, 1980; Bright Orange: The Goose is Out, 1983; Beijbom Kroner Big Band, Live in Copenhagen, 1996; Beijbom Kroner Big Band, Opposites Attract, 1998; Tredamer, Duke, We Love You Madly, 1999. *Honours:* Jazz CD of the Year, Danish Jazz Special Critics Choice, for Live in Copenhagen, 1997. *Membership:* STIM; SKAP; SAMI. *Address:* Flygelv 4, 22472 Lund, Sweden.

BEINS, Burkhard; b. 22 Oct. 1964, Celle, Germany. Musician (percussion). *Career:* Various punkbands and experimental music for taped material and percussion, 1980–90; Concerts, Festivals: Second LMC Festival, London; Musique Action, Vendoeuvre; Symposium For Contemporary Music, Kopenhagen; 2:13 Club Festival, Berlin; Recordings with contemporary improvised and composed music; Currently active groups: Activity Center, NUNC, Yarbles, 2:13 Ensemble, Das Kreisen, Sowari, Perlon; Worked With Keith Rowe, John Butcher, Fred Frith, Maggie Nicols, John Bisset, Sven Ake Johansson. *Recordings:* Relay III; NUNC; Yarbles; Activity Center; Perlon. *Current Management:* 2:13 Music, 139 Gibson Gardens, London N16 7HH. *Address:* Ackerstr 2, 10115 Berlin, Germany.

BELAFONTE, Harry (Harold George); b. 1 March 1927, Harlem, New York, USA. Vocalist; Actor; Prod; Human Rights Activist. m. (1) Marguerite, 1948; (2) Julie Robinson, 1957, 1 s., 3 d. *Education:* Dramatic Workshop of The New School For Social Research. *Career:* Member, American Negro Theater, late 1940s; Performer, New York clubs, early 1950s; Singer, actor, Broadway, 1953; Recording artist, actor, 1954; World-wide tours: UK; Europe; USA; Canada; Australia; New Zealand; Jamaica; Cuba; Actor, films: Bright Road, 1952; Carmen Jones (television version), 1955; Island In The Sun, 1957; Odds Against Tomorrow, 1959; Buck and The Preacher, 1971; Uptown Saturday Night, 1974; First Look, 1984; The Player, 1992; Television appearances include: A Time For Laughter, 1967; Harry and Lena (with Lena Horne), 1969; Tonight With Belafonte, 1960; As producer: Strolling Twenties; Beat Street; Producer, stage: To Be Young Gifted and Black, 1969; Performer, co-ordinator, We Are The World, USA For Africa charity recording, 1985. *Recordings:* Songs include: Banana Boat Song; Matilda; Island In The Sun; Mary's Boy Child; Numerous albums include: Calypso, 1956; Porgy and Bess (with Lena Horne), 1959; Streets I Have Walked, 1963; Don't Stop The Carnival, 1972; Belafonte '89, 1989; Also recorded with Miriam Makeba; Nana Mouskouri. *Honours:* Tony Award, John Murray Anderson's Almanac, Broadway, 1953; Emmy Award (first black recipient), Tonight With Belafonte, 1960; Grammy Award, We Are The World, 1985; American Music Award, We Are The World, 1985; Cultural adviser, Peace Corps (first entertainer chosen), 1988; National Conference of Black Mayors Tribute, 1991; UNICEF's Danny Kaye Award, 1989; Mandela Courage Award (Inaugural presentation), 1990;

UNICEF Goodwill Ambassador, 1987. *Address:* c/o William Morris Agency, 1325 Avenue of the Americas, New York, NY 10019, USA.

BELASCO, Pete; b. 1 July 1966, Queens, NY, USA. Vocalist; Songwriter; Saxophonist. m. 3 Oct. 1991, 1 d. *Education:* Rutgers University, New Jersey. *Career:* Today, show appearance with Kim Carnes. *Compositions:* Lap of Luxury, sung by Diane Wild-Island. *Recordings:* Get it Together. *Membership:* BMI. *Current Management:* Avenue Management Group, Bruce Garfield, 250 W 57th St Suite 407, New York, NY 10019, USA.

BELCHEV, Mikhail Ivanov; b. 13 Aug. 1946, Sofia, Bulgaria. Vocalist; Composer; Lyricist; Musician (guitar); Dir. m. Christina Konstantinova Belcheva, 15 April 1988, 1 s. *Education:* Hons degrees in: Mining, Geology Engineering; Theatre Directing; Television Directing; Bodra Smyana Bulgarian National Youth Choir. *Career:* Solo artiste since 1967–; Tours: Italy, 1970; Spain, 1982; France, 1983; West Berlin, 1986; USA, 1987; Canada, 1988; USSR; Germany; Poland; Czechoslovakia; Romania. *Recordings:* Albums: Where Are Your Friends, 1972; Counterpart, 1977; Re-Qualification, 1988; Cricket On The Pavement, 1993; Man To Hug (lyrics by Mikhail Belchev) 1994; Television biographical musical films: Where Are You Friends, 1973; Counterpart, 1977. *Publications:* Poetry: At First Cock-Crow, 1987; A Man To Hug, 1994. *Honours:* Cyril and Methodius Order Highest degree, Golden Orpheus Festival, many awards; Awards, Bratislava and Sopot Festivals. *Membership:* Bulgarian Artiste Asscn; The Music Author Board of Directors.

BELEW, Adrian; Musician (guitar); Vocalist; Songwriter; Prod. *Career:* Session musician, 1980s; Singer, guitarist, King Crimson, 1981–84, 1993–; Solo artiste, 1982–; Founder, The Bears, 1986; Producer, Jars of Clay, 1966. *Recordings:* Albums: Solo: Lone Rhino, 1982; Twang Bar King, 1983; Mr Musichead, 1989; Young Lions, 1990; Inner Revolution, 1990; Desire Caught By The Tail, 1991; The Acoustic Adrian Belew, 1995; with King Crimson: Discipline, 1981; Beat, 1982; Three Of A Perfect Pair, 1984; Vroom, 1995; Thrak, 1995; B'Boom, 1995; with The Bears: The Bears, 1987; As session musician: with Laurie Anderson: Mister Heartbreak, 1984; Home Of The Brave, 1986; with David Bowie: Stage, 1978; Lodger, 1979; Another Face, 1981; with Talking Heads: Remain In Light, 1980; The Name Of This Band Is, 1982; with Frank Zappa: In New York, 1978; Sheik Yerbouti, 1979; Yer Are What You Is, 1982; You Can't Do That On Stage Anymore, 1988; The Key, Joan Armatrading, 1983; The Catherine Wheel, David Byrne, 1981; Maybe It's Live, Robert Palmer, 1982; Zoolook, Jean-Michel Jarre, 1984; True Colors, Cyndi Lauper, 1986; Strange Little Girls, Tori Amos, 2001. *Current Management:* Umbrella Artists, PO Box 8385, 2612 Erie Ave, Cincinnati, OH 45208, USA.

BELL, Andy; b. 25 April 1964. Vocalist; Songwriter. *Career:* Vocalist, Void; Lead vocalist, pop duo, Erasure, with Vince Clarke, 1985–; Numerous UK and international tours, television appearances. *Recordings:* Albums: Wonderland, 1986; The Circus, 1987; The Two-Ring Circus, 1987; The Innocents (No. 1, UK), 1988; Wild! (No. 1, UK), 1989; Chorus (No. 1, UK), 1991; Pop!—The First 20 Hits (No. 1, UK), 1992; I Say I Say I Say (No. 1, UK), 1994; Erasure, 1995; Cowboy, 1997; Loveboat, 2000; Other People's Songs, 2003. Singles: Who Needs Love..., 1985; Heavenly Action, 1985; Oh L'amour, 1986; Sometimes, 1986; It Doesn't Have..., 1987; Victim Of Love, 1987; The Circus, 1987; Ship Of Fools, 1988; Chains Of Love, 1988; A Little Respect, 1988; Crackers... (EP), 1988; Drama!, 1989; You Surround Me, 1989; Blue Savannah, 1990; Star, 1990; Chorus, 1991; Love To Hate You, 1991; Am I Right? (EP), 1991; Breath Of Life, 1992; Abba-Esque (EP, No. 1, UK), 1992; Who Needs Love..., 1992; Always, 1994; Run To The Sun, 1994; I Love Saturday (EP), 1994; Stay With Me, 1995; Fingers & Thumbs..., 1995; Rock Me Gently, 1996; In My Arms, 1997; Don't Say Your..., 1997; Rain, 1997; Freedom, 2000; Moon & The Sky, 2000; Solsbury Hill, 2003; Contributor to: Red Hot and Blue (AIDS benefit record); Tame Yourself (animal rights benefit record). *Honours:* BRIT Award, Best British Group, 1989; Ivor Novello Award, Most Performed Work of 1990, Blue Savannah, 1991. *Address:* c/o Mute Records, 429 Harrow Rd, London W10 4RE, England. *Website:* www.erasureinfo.com.

BELL, Andy (Andrew Piran); b. 11 Aug. 1970, Cardiff, Wales. Musician (guitar); Songwriter. m. Idha Övelius, 12 Feb. 1992. *Education:* Banbury Art School, 1988–89. *Career:* Singer, songwriter and lead guitarist, rock band Ride, 1988–96; Session musician with Idha, 1992–; Mem., Hurricane #1, 1997–99; Mem., Oasis, 1999–; Concert, Finsbury Park, London, 2002. *Recordings:* Albums: with Ride: Nowhere, 1990; Going Blank Again, 1992; Carnival Of Light, 1994; Tarantula, 1996; OX4, 2001; with Idha: Melody Inn, 1994; with Hurricane #1: Hurricane #1, 1997; Only The Strongest Will Survive, 1999; with Oasis: Familiar To Millions (Live), 2001; Heathen Chemistry, 2002. Singles: with Oasis: Stop Crying Your Heart Out, 2002; Little By Little/She Is Love, 2002; The Hindu Times, 2002. *Honours:* NME Awards, Best UK Band, Artist of the Year, 2003. *Current Management:* Ignition Management, 54 Linhope St, London NW1 6HL, England. *Website:* www.oasisnet.com.

BELL, Chris; b. 26 Aug. 1960, London, England. Musician (drums). *Career:* Joined Thompson Twins, 1979–82; Tour with King Trigger, 1982; Joined Spear of Destiny, 1982–83; Work with Specimin, 1985; Joined Gene Love Jezebel, 1986–91; Tour, USA, Japan, 1986; Television includes: MTV Awards, Joan Rivers Show, 1986; Tours: UK/Europe, USA, Japan, South America, UK, 1988; USA, supporting Echo and The Bunnymen, New Order, 1987; USA, Europe, UK, supporting Billy Idol, 1990; USA, 1990; Tours, recordings, television, with Big Country, 1991–92; Tour, recording, Nan Vernon, 1992; Tours with Hugh Cornwell, UK, Europe, 1993; France, 1994; UK, 1994; Live work with Phantom Chords, 1994–95; Various sessions, 1995; Live work with Gene Loves Jezebel, 1995. *Recordings:* Albums with Thompson Twins: A Product Of, 1981; Set, 1982; Single: In The Name Of Love; Grapes Of Wrath, Spear Of Destiny, 1982; Single: Ain't That Always The Way, Edwyn Collins, 1985; with Gene Loves Jezebel, The Immigrant, 1985; House Of Dolls; Kiss Of Life, 1989; Album with Nan Vernon, 1993; Album with Hugh Cornwell, 1995. *Address:* 2 Bolingbroke Rd, London W14 OAL, England.

BELL, Colin Stewart; b. 11 Sept. 1952, Carrickfergus, County Antrim, Northern Ireland. Record Co Exec. *Education:* BA Hons Drama. *Career:* Publicist, Rogers and Cowan; Manager, Tom Robinson Band; Head of Press, Phonogram UK Ltd; Managing Director, London Records, 1991–98; Manager, Elton John. *Honours:* Leslie Perrin P R Award; Music Week Marketing Award. *Address:* c/o Elton John Management, 7 King St Cloisters, Clifton Walk, London W6 0GY, England.

BELL, Dennis Lawrence; b. 4 Dec. 1941, New York, NY, USA. Record Prod; Musician (keyboard); Music Educator; Personal Man; Arranger; Conductor; Composer. m. Claudette Washington, 28 April 1979, 1 s., 3 d. *Education:* BM, NYU; Master of Arts, Composition, Queens College; Piano, arranging, composition, conducting with variety of teachers. *Career:* Television appearances include: Joan Rivers; BBC, One World One Voice; Top of the Pops; with U2: Madison Square Garden; Carnegie Hall; Rattle and Hum; Commercials: Pizza Hut with Aretha Franklin; Roy Rogers; Drakes Company; Give Peace A Chance; Keep Rising To The Top; Videos. *Recordings:* with Tom Browne; Dave Valentine; Doug E. Fresh; U2; Celia Cruz; Give Peace A Chance; Touché; Lee Ritenour; Scrooged film soundtrack. *Publications:* Music Alive. *Honours:* Boystown for Public Service; Bronx Boro President's Award for Community Service. *Membership:* BMI; National Asscn of Jazz Educators.

BELL, Eric; b. 3 Sept. 1947, Belfast, Northern Ireland. Musician (guitar); Vocalist; Songwriter. *Career:* Musician with Van Morrison, Northern Ireland, 1967; Founder member, rock group Thin Lizzy, 1969–74; Co-arranger, Whiskey In The Jar; Television appearance: Top of the pops; Joined Noel Redding Band, 1976–78. *Recordings:* with Thin Lizzy: Whiskey In The Jar; The Rocker; Collection; Soldier Of Fortune; Dedication: The Very Best... ; Remembering. *Honours:* Gold album, The Adventures of Thin Lizzy; Silver single, Whiskey In The Jar. *Address:* 115 Pembroke Ave, Enfield, Middlesex EN1 4EZ, England.

BELL, Mark, (Fawn, Clarke); b. Leeds, West Yorkshire, England. Prod; Remixer. *Career:* Formed LFO with production partner Gez Varley, 1990; Signed to Warp Records; Released debut album, 1991; Collaborations: Bjork; Depeche Mode; Richie Hawtin; Remixed: Art of Noise; Yellow Magic Orchestra; Erasure; Radiohead. *Recordings:* Albums: Frequencies, 1991; Advance, 1996; Singles: LFO, 1990; What Is House, 1991; Tied Up, 1995; Lofthouse EP (as Clarke), 1996. *Address:* c/o Warp Records, Spectrum House, 32–34 Gordon House Rd, London NW5 1LP, England.

BELL, Philip; b. 21 May 1965, Finsbury Park, London, England. Musician (guitar, bass). *Education:* Guitar Institute of Technology, Wapping, London. *Career:* Guitarist, Brothers Like Outlaw; European Tour supporting Arrested Development, 1993; Also festivals including: Fest'in Bahia, Salvador, Brazil, 1992; Citta D'ella Musica, Bari, Italy, 1992; Metropolis, Rotterdam, Netherlands, 1992; Jazz In Sardinia, 1992; Radio and television: Chart Show, 1993; BBC Radio 1 session; Member, Vibe Tribe; Concerts include Phoenix Festivals, UK, 1993–94; with The Filberts, Glastonbury Festival, 1993; Television: TXT, 1994; with Leena Conquest: European Tour supporting Bryan Ferry, 1994. *Recordings:* with Vibe Tribe: Johnny; Our Purpose, 1993; with FM Inc: Call Me Anytime, 1992; Fresh 'n' Funky; Chill Me, 1993; African Wonderland, 1996. *Publications:* Music Journalist, Sounds, 1980–84. *Membership:* Musicians' Union; PRS; MCPS. *Address:* 17A Northbrook Rd, London N22 4YQ, England.

BELL, Thom; b. Philadelphia, PA, USA. Prod; Songwriter; Arranger; Musician (keyboards). *Career:* Mem., Gamble's Romeos, MFSB (Mother, Father, Sister, Brother) band; Prod. and arranger, Cameo records, –1968; Philly Groove, 1968–69; Formed songwriting team with Linda Creed; Independent prod., arranger, songwriter; Worked with: Delfonics, Ronnie Dyson, Phyllis Hyman, Elton John, Johnny Mathis, O'Jays, Showstoppers, Spinners, Stylistics, Deniece Williams. *Compositions include:* Betcha By Golly Wow; Break Your Promise; Could It Be I'm Falling In Love; Didn't I Blow Your Mind This Time; Ghetto Child; I'm Stone In Love With You; La-La Means I Love You.

BELLAMY, David; b. 16 Sept. 1950, Darby, Florida, USA. Vocalist; Songwriter. *Career:* Played R&B clubs, backing Eddie Floyd, Percy Sledge, Little Anthony and the Imperials; Played throughout Southeast USA, with own band, Jericho; Wrote Spiders and Snakes for Jim Stafford, 3m. sales world-wide; Cut demos with Neil Diamond's band; Formed Bellamy Brothers with brother Howard; Most successful duo in country music history; Tours with Loggins and Messina; Doobie Brothers; Beach Boys; Conway Twitty; Collaborated as songwriter with Costas, Don Schlitz and Bobby Braddock; Formed Bellamy Brothers Records; Initiated annual Snake Rattle and Roll Jam, 1989, major charity fundraiser. *Compositions include:* Spiders and Snakes; Sugar Daddy; Do You Love As Good As You Look; Old Hippie; Kids of The Baby Boom. *Recordings:* Singles include: Let Your Love Flow, 1976 (No. 1 in charts in ten countries); If I Said You Had A Beautiful Body Would You Hold It Against Me, 1979; Sugar Daddy, Dancin' Cowboys, 1980; Do You Love As Good As You Look, 1981; For All The Wrong Reasons, 1982; Redneck Girl, 1982; When I'm Away From You, 1983; I Need More Of You, 1985; Feelin' The Feelin,' 1985; Too Much Is Not Enough, 1986; Kids Of The Baby Boom, 1986; Crazy From The Heart, 1987; Rip Off The Knob, 1993; Dancin', 1996; Lonely Planet, 1999; The 25 Year Collection Vols 1 and 2 (compilations), 2001; 22 albums, 1976–94. *Honours:* Platinum albums, UK, Scandinavia; Gold albums, USA, Austria, Germany, UK, Norway, Sweden; Record of the Year, If I Said You Had A Beautiful Body, England, 1979; Independent Video of Year, Cowboy Beat, CMT. *Membership:* ASCAP; AFTRA; AFofM. *Current Management:* Refugee Management International. *Address:* 209 10th Ave S, Suite 347, Nashville, TN 37203, USA.

BELLAMY, Howard; b. 2 Feb. 1946, Darby, Florida, USA. Vocalist; Songwriter. m. Ilona. *Career:* Played R&B Clubs, backing Eddie Floyd, Percy Sledge, Little Anthony and the Imperials; Played Southeast USA with own band, Jericho; Became Jim Stafford's road manager; Cut demos with Neil Diamond's band; Formed The Bellamy Brothers with brother David; Most successful duo in country music history; Toured USA with Loggins and Messina; Doobie Brothers; Beach Boys; Conway Twitty; 14 number 1 singles in US country charts; Collaborated with Costa, Don Schlitz and Bobby Braddock; Formed Bellamy Brothers Records; Initiated annual benefit concert, Snake Rattle and Roll Jam, 1989, major local charity fundraiser. *Recordings:* Singles include: Let Your Love Flow, 1976 (No. 1 in charts in ten countries); If I Said You Had A Beautiful Body Would You Hold It Against Me, 1979; Sugar Daddy, 1980; Dancin' Cowboys, 1980; Do You Love As Good As You Look, 1981; For All The Wrong Reasons, 1982; Redneck Girl, 1982; When I'm Away From You, 1983; Old Hippie, 1985; I Need More Of You, 1985; Feelin' The Feelin', 1985; Too Much Is Not Enough, 1986; Kids Of The Baby Boom, 1986; Crazy From The Heart, 1987; You'll Never Be Sorry, 1989; Rip Off The Knob, 1993; Dancin', 1996; Lonely Planet, 1999; The 25 Year Collection Vols 1 and 2 (compilations), 2001; 22 albums, 1976–94. *Honours:* Platinum albums, England, Scandinavia; Gold albums, USA, Austria, Germany, UK, Norway, Sweden; Record of the Year, If I Said You Had A Beautiful Body, UK, 1979; Independent Video of 1992, Cowboy Beat, CMT. *Membership:* ASCAP; AFTRA; AFofM. *Current Management:* Refugee Management, 209 10th Ave S, Suite 347, Nashville, TN 37203, USA.

BELLAMY, Matthew James; b. 9 June 1978. Vocalist; Musician (guitar). *Career:* Formed group Gothic Plague in adopted hometown of Teignmouth, aged 13; Group became Fixed Penalty then Rocket Baby Dolls before finally settling on name Muse; Released two 1,000-copy EPs on UK independent label Dangerous; Signed to Madonna's US label Maverick following lauded UK In The City '98 and New York CMJ festival appearances; Rapid rise to fame followed; Live shows include: Ill-fated Woodstock '99 US festival; Headline slots at UK's Leeds, Reading and T In The Park festivals, 2000; European tours, 2001. *Recordings:* Albums: Showbiz, 1999; Origin Of Symmetry, 2001; Hullabaloo, 2002. Singles: Muse EP, 1998; Muscle Museum EP, Uno, Cave, 1999; Sunburn, Unintended, 2000; Plug In Baby, New Born, Bliss, Hyper Music/Feeling Good, 2001; Dead Star In Your World, 2002. *Honours:* NME Award, Best Newcomer, 2000; Kerrang! Award, Best British Band, 2001. *Current Management:* Taste Media/SJP Management, 263 Putney Bridge Rd, London SW15 2PU, England. *Website:* www.muse-official.com.

BELLEST, Christian; b. 8 April 1922, Paris, France. Musician (trumpet); Arranger. m. Sally Pearce, 9 Jan. 1962, 1 s. *Education:* CEP; Musical studies, harmony, counterpoint, fugas. *Career:* Accompanist, arranger, for singers including Edith Piaf; Yves Montand; Michel Berger; Veronique Sanson; Paul Anka; Television series and films. *Recordings:* Django Reinhardt; Aux Combelle; Jazz de Paris; Jacques Helian. *Publications:* Co-author, Le Jazz for collection Que Sais-Je; Articles for Les Cahiers Du Jazz. *Membership:* Academie Du Jazz. *Address:* 9 rue Victorien Sardou, 75016 Paris, France.

BELLOW, Roger David; b. 15 April 1950, Chicago, Illinois, USA. Musician (guitar, violin, mandolin, banjo, bass); Teacher. m. Judy Golombeck, 25 Sept. 1977, divorced. *Education:* BA University of Tennesse; Antioch College; Foreign study, Bogotá, Colombia; Old Town School of Folk Music, Chicago. *Career:* Cas Walker, TV Show, Knoxville, Tennessee, 1968–70; Kennedy Center Concert, Washington, DC, 1976; Kaustinen International Folk Festival, Finland, 1981; Belize Tour, 1983; University of Chicago, Folk

Festival, 1986; Faculty of Augusta Heritage Center, Elkins, W Virginia, 1989–; SC Arts Comm Resident Artist, 1987–; Host, Vintage Country Radio Program, public radio, 1987–2001; Japan Tour, 1993; University of Chicago Folk Festival, 1999; Performing at the Encuentro de Dos Tradiciones in Mexico, March 2000; Performance on Radio México, 2001. *Recordings:* with Revonah: Get In Line Brother, 1980; with Flying Fish: Success Street, 1988; On The Road To Prosperity, 1991; (Japanese recording) The Bay Quintet, 1993; with Augusta Faculty Band: Zombies Of Swing, 1994; Allons a Grand Kaplan, with Paul Dudley Kershaw, 1998; Cross Country Swing, with Paul Anastasio, 1999; Sentimental Journey, with Ann Caldwell, 2001. *Publications:* Research published in Bluegrass Unlimited and Journal of Country Music. *Honours:* South Carolina Folk Heritage Award, 1995; SC Grant for Research in Country Music. *Membership:* AFofM; ROPE (Reunion of Professional Entertainers). *Current Management:* Town and Country Music.

BELLULA, Faudel. See: **CHEB FAUDEL.**

BELMONDO, Lionel; b. 19 Aug. 1963, Hyères, France. Musician (saxophones, flute). *Education:* Jazz, Piano and saxophone studies, Conservatory de Toulon. *Career:* Director, School of Music, Centre Vas; Professor in other schools, 1982–90; Moved to Paris, 1990; Sideman for concerts with Michel Legrand; Phil Woods; Toots Thielemans; Dee Dee Bridgewater; Horace Silver; Lew Tabackin; Own quintet with brother Stéphane; Leader, Belmondo Big Band, with brother Stéphane; Television: Belmondo In Concert, on Jazz 6, at M6, 1995. *Recordings include:* Belmondo Quintet; For All Friends, Belmondo Quintet; Love and Peace, Dee Dee Bridgewater; Face The Challenge In Music, 1996; Cyclades, Jean-Loup Longnon, 1996; Jazz Singers 1919–94, 1998. *Honours:* Prix Django Reinhardt, Best French Musician (with brother Stéphane), 1994. *Current Management:* KSM (Karen Strugg Management). *Address:* 17 rue des Ecoles, 75005 Paris, France.

BELMONDO, Stéphane; b. 8 July 1967, Hyères, France. Musician (trumpet, flugelhorn). m. Elisabeth Kontomanou, 1 s. *Education:* Conservatory, Toulon, Marseilles. *Career:* Member, Big Band Lumiere, conducted by Gil Evans; Sideman and concerts with Michel Legrand Big Band; Chet Baker; Tom Harrell; David Liebman; Dee Dee Bridgewater; Horace Silver; Own quintet with brother Lionel Belmondo; Own Belmondo Big Band, with brother Lionel; Television: Belmondo In Concert, Jazz 6 at M6, 1995. *Recordings:* Belmondo Quintet JAR; For All Friends, Belmondo Quintet; Sideman: Big Band Band Lumiere with Gil Evans; Love and Peace, Dee Dee Bridgewater; Parapluies de Cherbourg, 1996; Face The Challenge In Music, 1996; Cyclades, Jean-Loup Longnon, 1996; Soley Glase, Ziskakan, 1997; Jazz Singers 1919–94, 1998; Moon and Sand, Tom Harrell. *Honours:* Django Reinhardt Award, Best French Musician, with brother Lionel, 1994. *Current Management:* KSM (Karen Strugg Management). *Address:* 17 rue des Ecoles, 75005 Paris, France.

BELTRAMI, Marco; b. 1968, Fornese, Italy. Composer. *Education:* Yale School of Music; Composer scholarship with Jerry Goldsmith. *Compositions:* Death Match, 1994; The Bicyclist, 1994; Land's End (TV), 1995; The Whispering, 1996; The Incorporated, 1996; Scream, 1996; Stranger in My Home (TV), 1997; Mimic, 1997; Scream 2, 1997; Halloween H20: Twenty Years Later (additional music), 1998; The Faculty, 1998; Nightwatch (additional music), 1998; 54, 1998; David and Lisa (TV), 1998; The Minus Man, 1999; The Florentine, 1999; Deep Water (TV), 1999; Scream 3, 1999; The Crow: Salvation, 2000; The Watcher, 2000; Dracula 2000, 2001; Angel Eyes, 2001; Joy Ride, 2001; Blade 2: Bloodlust, 2002; Resident Evil (with others), 2002; I Am Dina, 2002. *Membership:* BMI. *Current Management:* Greenspan Artist Management, 6777 Hollywood Blvd, Suite 514, Los Angeles, CA 90028, USA.

BEN, Besiakov; b. 27 Oct. 1956, Copenhagen, Denmark. Musician (piano, organ). 1 s. *Compositions:* Choo Choo, with Lennart Ginman and Mike Clark. *Recordings:* You Stepped Out Of a Dream, 1990; Raney, with Doug Raney, 1996; The Red Light, with Bent Jaedig, 1996; When Granny Sleeps, with Dave Liebman, 1995; Human Beat Boxer, with Niclas Knudsen and Adam Nussbaum, 1997; Aviation, with George Garzone, Billy Hart, Ray Drummond and Jens Winther, 1999; Hey Why Don't We Play, with George Garzone, 2001. *Honours:* Ben Webster Prize, 1990; Jasa Prize, 1993. *Membership:* Danish Musicians Asscn. *Address:* GL Vartov Vej 21, 2900 Hellerup, Denmark.

BEN, Jorge, (Jorge Duílio Menezes, Jorge Ben Jor); b. 1940, Rio de Janeiro, Brazil. Vocalist; Musician (guitar); Composer; Songwriter. *Career:* Fuses different musical traditions, both Brazilian and international; Music is rhythmically very creative with an African feel combined with rock, samba, baião (music based on northeastern Brazilian folkloric forms) and maracatu (an Afro-Brazilian processional dance); Career started in the early 1960s, when bossa nova was the dominant music, but gained more recognition during MPB (Música Popular Brasileira) era when experimentation and fusing of styles was more accepted; First big hit Mas Que Nada in 1963 covered by Sergio Mendes, who had US hit with the song; Mas Que Nada revived and entered UK chart when the Tamba Trio's recording was used in Nike advertisement during soccer World Cup, 1998; Had many hits in Brazil which firmly established career, 1969–72; Toured internationally many times

and has worked with artists including: King Sunny Ade; Os Mutantes; Timbalada. *Compositions:* Mas Que Nada. *Recordings:* Single: Mas Que Nada, 1963; Albums include: Samba Esquema Novo, 1963; Sacundin Ben Samba, 1964; O Bidú, 1967; Jorge Ben, 1969; Forca Bruta, 1970; Ben, 1972; Dez Anos Depois, 1973; A Tabú De Esmerelda, 1974; Samba Nova, 1975; Africa Brasil, 1976; A Banda Do Ze Pretinho, 1978; Salve Simpatia, 1979; Alo Alo Como Vai?, 1980; Dadiva, 1983; Benjor, 1989; Ao Vivo No Rio, 1992; 23, 1993; Homo Sapiens, 1995; Musicas Para Tocar Em Elevador, 1997; Puro Suingue, 2000.

BENATAR, Pat, (Patricia Andrzejewski); b. Brooklyn, New York, USA. Vocalist. m. (1) Dennis Benatar, 1972, divorced 1979; (2) Neil Geraldo, 20 Feb. 1982, 1 d. *Education:* Studied health education; Brief training opera singer. *Career:* Singer, Holiday Inns, Virginia, 1972–74; Singing waitress in New York Club, Catch A Rising Star; Solo artiste, 1979–. *Recordings:* Singles include: Heartbreaker; You Better Run; Treat Me Right; Love Is A Battlefield; Hell Is For Children; Invincible (soundtrack to film Legend of Billie Jean); Hit Me With Your Best Shot; Sex As A Weapon; We Belong; All Fired Up; Albums include: In The Heat Of The Night, 1979; Crimes Of Passion, 1980; Precious Time, 1981; Get Nervous, 1982; Live From Earth, 1983; Tropico, 1984; Seven The Hard Way, 1985; Wide Awake In Dreamland, 1988; True Love, 1991; Gravity's Rainbow, 1993; Best Of Pat Benatar Vols 1 and 2, 2001; Christmas In America, 2001. *Honours:* 4 Grammy Awards, Best Female Rock Vocal Performance, 1981–84; Numerous Gold discs. *Current Management:* Lookout Management, 2644 30th St, First Floor, Santa Monica, CA 90405, USA.

BENBOW, Steve (Stephen George); b. 29 Nov. 1931, London, England. Vocalist; Musician (guitar). m. Sandra Estelle Benbow, 10 Feb. 1976. *Career:* Television appearances on BBC Focus, Blue Peter, Late Night Line Up, Muses with Milligan and Plectrum; Radio appearances on BBC Guitar Club, Saturday Skiffle Club, Saturday Club, Easy Beat, Radio Luxembourg series Have Guitar Will Travel; Stage Show, Spike Milligan meets Steve Benbow, Lyric Theatre, London. *Compositions:* You Can Have Him; Madrid; Pickin' and Grinnin'; I Travel the World. *Recordings:* Admiral Benbow, 1962; I Travel the World, 1963; This, That and the Other, 1964; Irish Songs, double album, 1965; Of Situations and Predicaments, 1967; Friendly Folk, 1971. *Publications:* Guitar Tutor, Folk Music Accompaniment for Guitar, 1965. *Membership:* Equity; PRS; PAMRA; Musicians' Union. *Address:* 55 St Marks Rd, Old Hanwell, London W7 2PN, England.

BENDIX, Nicky; b. 22 March 1969, Odense, Denmark. Musician (piano, keyboard); Music Teacher; Composer; Arranger. *Education:* Piano lessons. *Career:* Started composing and playing at age 15; Performed in Jazz/fusion settings with the Danish Radio Big Band, Rudi Smith, Jorge Degas, Uffe Markussen, Henrik Bolberg and Bent Jædig; Own composition, Suite for Mankind, performed on TV2, Denmark in Sept. 1997; Since 1993 has composed and performed music for contemporary dance and multimedia events; Multimedia performer, The Pillar of Shame, 1997; Composed and recorded the music score for the film En Sidste gang, by Jesper Bernt. *Recordings:* Trancework, 1994; with Sunset Yellow: Sunset Yellow, 1995; with Sunzet: Sunzet, 1998. *Honours:* Jazz Musician of the Year, FYN, Denmark, 1995. *Membership:* Dansk Musiker Forbund. *Current Management:* NB Music. *Address:* Andekæret 160, 5300 Kekteminde C, Denmark.

BENEDETTI, Peter Sergio (Pepe); b. 15 July 1938, Greenock, Scotland. Jazz Blues Vocalist; Musician (tenor saxophone, clarinet). m. Lorna Magner, 14 Feb. 1980, divorced 1983, 1 d. *Education:* College Commerce, 1988–89; Mabel Fletcher School of Music and Drama, Liverpool, 1990. *Career:* Musician, Robert Bros Circus, 6 months, 1978; Promotional tour, London, Tony Conn Rockabilly Artiste, 1979; Support Jack Bruce Tour, 1985; Played for: The Undertakers, Liverpool, Played 3 day concerts, Hamburg, West Germany, 1990–91; 6 week tour, Sonny Curtis, Denmark, 1991. *Compositions:* Songwriting: Country/rock; Blues; Rock 'n' roll. *Honours:* Elgin Music Festival (Jazz), Best Male Singer, 1958. *Membership:* Musicians' Union. *Current Management:* Rock/Fairisle Music.

BENET, Eric; b. Milwaulkee, Wisconsin, USA. Vocalist. *Career:* Began career as part of Gerard in the late '80s; Formed Benet and released debut album, 1992; Solo career, 1999–; Collaborations: Faith Evans; Tamia; Roy Ayers; Me'Shell Ndegeocello. *Recordings:* Albums: Benet (with Benet), 1992; True To Myself, 1996; A Day In The Life, 1999; Singles: Spiritual Thang, 1996; Georgy Porgy, Why You Follow Me, Spend My Life With You, 1999. *Address:* c/o Warner Music, The Warner Building, 28 Kensington Church St, London W8 4EP, England.

BÉNEY, Jean-Christophe; b. 2 Oct. 1969, Boulogne, Billancourt, France. Jazz Musician (saxophone). *Education:* Conservatoire National Supérieure de Musique, Paris. *Career:* Le Pom (Scene et Marnaise de Création Musicale); Orchestra co-directed by François Jeanneau, Patrice Caratini; Philippe Macé; Andy Emler; Jean-Christophe Béney Quartet (Pierre de Bethmann, Jules Bikoko; Benjamin Hénocq); Laurent Coq Quartet; Belmonder Big Band; Antoine Heuve Big Band; Nicolas Folmer Quintet. *Recordings:* Hard Scores, Patrice Caratini, 1996; Le Pom, 1997; Sérénade, Philippe Sellam, 1997; Le Pom, 1997; Tenor Joke, with Jean-Christophe Béney Quartet, 1998; Jaywalker, with Laurent Coq Quartet, 1998. *Honours:* Prix de Soloiste,

Concours National de Jazz de la Défense, 1995. *Membership:* SACEM; ADAMI; SPEDIDAM. *Current Management:* C C PRoduction, 70 Ave du 11 novembre, 94170 Le Perreux-sur-Marne, France. *Address:* 2 rue Cyrano de Bergerac, 75018 Paris, France.

BENHAMOU, Lionel; b. 27 Aug. 1956, Paris, France. Musician (guitar). m. Helene Ruyer, 30 Oct. 1987, 1 s., 1 d. *Education:* Music school, harmony with Mr Weber. *Career:* Tours with: Gil Evans; Martial Solal; Bernard Lubat; Many festivals in Europe; Plays with Orchestre National de Jazz, directed by Laurent Cugny. *Recordings:* with Lionel Benhamou Trio: Fruits Cuits, Fruits Crus; 5 albums with Orchestre National de Jazz; Yestenow, conducted by Laurent Cugny; Rhythm-A-Ning, with Gil Evans; Santander, Laurent Cugny; Golden Hair, Gil Evans; 20 Ans de Jazz En France. *Publications:* 10 Themes et Improvisations Pour Le Saxophone. *Membership:* UMJ. *Address:* 75 rue de Turenne, 75003 Paris, France.

BENNETT, Allan Charles; b. 12 March 1968, London, England. Musician (tenor, soprano saxophones); Vocalist; Songwriter. 1 d. *Education:* Grade 5 Practical, Grade 5 Theory, Music O Level; Sound Engineering Foundation Course. *Career:* Waltham Forest Assembly Hall, oboist, Waltham Forest Intermediate Band, 1976; Saxophonist, community reggae band Reality, 1987; Lead saxophonist, reggae band Jimmy Mac, 1991; Polish Club Manchester; Palm Tree Club, Tottenham; Singer, songwriter, saxophonist, Tusu, 1989; Marquee; Porter House, Nottinghamshire; Lead saxophonist, Tribal Union, 1994; Sydenham Wells Park; Amersham Arms the gig; Allan B Promotions and live shows, 1992–; Solo saxophonist, Allan and Lea, 1994; Kingshead Theatre Pub. *Recordings:* with Jimmy Mac: Little Bit Of Your Time, 1991; with Tusu: August The Two (songs include: Dream Crazy; Catch 66; Fascination); Slipping Away, 1992; Gone To Earth: Be The Dub, 1994; Humanoia: Nothing More, Nothing Less, 1992. *Membership:* Musicians' Union. *Address:* 22 Gaitskill House, The Drive, Walthamstow, London E17 3DD, England.

BENNETT, Brian Laurence; b. 9 Feb. 1940, London, England. Musician (drums); Composer. m. Margaret Tuton, 2 s., 1 d. *Career:* Backed Gene Vincent, Eddie Cochran on tour; Drummer, Cliff Richard and The Shadows, 1961–; Session drummer, 1970s–80s; Composer of film and television music; Arranger, producer; Brian Bennett Band support to Cliff Richard, UK, Japan, USSR, 1970s; Played with Hank Marvin as The Shadows, Knebworth, 1990; British tour, joined by Hank Marvin, also son Warren Bennett on keyboards. *Compositions include:* Film themes: Summer Holiday; Wonderful Life; Finders Keepers; The Harpist, 1997; Score: The Boys; Soundtrack: French Dressing; The American Way; Terminal Choice; Television soundtracks: Dallas; Knots Landing; Ruth Rendell Mysteries; Nomads of The Wind, BBC2; Pulaski; The Knock; The Sweeney; Minder; Global Sunrise, BBC, 1997; Living Britain, BBC 2; Dirty Work, 2000. *Honours:* 3 Ivor Novello Awards: Summer Holiday, 1962; 25 Years in British Music, 1983; Best TV Theme, Ruth Rendell Mysteries, 1989. *Membership:* PRS; MCPS; APC; MPA; SODS. *Address:* 91 Tabernacle St, London EC2A 4JN, England.

BENNETT, Easther; Vocalist. m. Shane Lynch, 1998. *Career:* Singer, UK all-female vocal group Eternal, 1992–. *Recordings:* Albums: Always and Forever, 1993; Power Of a Woman, 1995; Before The Rain, 1997; Greatest Hits, 1998; Eternal, 1999; Essential Eternal (compilation), 2001; Singles: Stay, 1993; Power Of a Woman, 1995; I Am Blessed, 1995; Good Thing, 1996; Secrets, 1996; Don't You Love, 1997; I Wanna Be The Only One (No. 1, UK), 1997; Angel Of Mine, 1997; What'cha Gonna Do, 1999; Mind Odyssey. *Honours:* Smash Hits Award; International Dance Award, Dance Act of the Year, 1995; Only UK act to have 6 Top 15 hits from debut album.

BENNETT, Phil; b. 28 Sept. 1958, Singapore. Vocalist; Songwriter; Musician (keyboards). m. Fifi, 4 July 1992. *Career:* Band Member: Helicopters, mid 1980s; Love Bites, 1990s; Witness, 1997; Support shows with: Duran Duran, Elvis Costello, Joe Jackson, Wreckless Eric, Sandi and the Sunsets, Midnight Oil, Church, Gang Gajang, Models, Jimmy Barnes; Member, PillBox, 1998. *Compositions:* Eyewitness, 1997; Carved in Stone, 1997. *Recordings:* Albums: The Helicopters, 1982; Great Moments in Aviation, 1984; Never Seen Eyes, solo, 1990; Kiss the Feet, 1995; Stories from the South, Witness, 1998; Singles: Eyewitness, Lovebites, 1997; Eyewitnes, Witness, 1998; Carved in Stone, Witness, 1998. *Honours:* Sonics Magazine on Cue Award, 1990; Australia Day Award, 1993. *Membership:* Australian Performing Rights Asscn. *Current Management:* Mischief Management, 8 Michael Court, Shelley 6148, WA, Australia.

BENNETT, Rex; b. 16 Dec. 1920, Victoria, London. Musician (Drums). m. Olive Rosa Bennett, 1 May 1946, 1 d. *Recordings:* Sandie Shaw; Brotherhood Of Man; Crispin St Peter; Ray Conniff in Britain; Singalong with Max; Bring Me Sunshine, Morecambe and Wise; Dave Dee Dozy Mick and Tich; Jonathan King; Anita Harris; Everly Bros; Kenny Ball; Acker Bilk; Johnny Halliday; Mike Batt; Harold Geller; Vince Hill; Shirley Bassey; Maynard Ferguson with Strings; Matt Monro; Tony Blackburn; Cliff Richard; George Martin; Madmovies for Bob Monkhouse; Numerous backing tracks for most American jazz musicians. *Address:* 1 Ellery Close, Cranleigh, Surrey, GU6 8DF, England.

BENNETT, Richard; b. 1951, Chicago, IL, USA. Musician (Guitar); Prod; Arranger; Writer. *Education:* Taught by Forrest Skaggs. *Career:* Record Producer, Musician, session and touring; Recording and touring with Neil Diamond in Los Angeles, 1971–88. *Recordings:* The Red Road, Bill Miller, 1994; Raven In the Snow, Bill Miller, 1995; A Native Suite, Bill Miller, 1995; Kim Richey, Kim Richey, 1995; Silvertone, Steve Earle, 1995; Capitol, High and Dry, Marty Brown; Wild Kentucky Skies, Marty Brown; Cryin', Lovin', Leavin', Marty Brown; Hillbilly Rock, Marty Stuart; Tempted, Marty Stuart; This One's Gonna Hurt You, Marty Stuart; Come on Joe, Jo-El Sonnier; Have A Little Faith, Joe-El Sonnier; Lost and Profound, Lost and Profound; Memory Thieves, Lost and Profound; A Joyful Noise, The Sullivan's; Music Makin' Mama, Jim Silvers; Everybody Knows, Prairie Oyster; Plectrasonics, Nashville Mandolin Ensemble; Sessions: Billy Pilgrim, 1994; Mark Knopfler and Neil Diamond, 1995. *Current Management:* Dennis Muirhead, Muirhead Management, 202 Fulham Rd, Chelsea, London SW10 9PJ, England.

BENNETT, Tony (Anthony Dominick Benedetto); b. 3 Aug. 1926, Queens, New York, USA. Vocalist; Entertainer. m. (1) Patricia Beech, 1952, divorced 1971, 2 c., (2) Sandra Grant, 1971, divorced 1984, 2 d. *Education:* High School of Industrial Arts, Manhattan; Vocal Studies, American Theater Wing School; DMus, University of Berkeley. *Career:* Debut in nightclub, 1946; Spotted by Bob Hope; Numerous live and television appearances; owner and recording artist with Improv Records; Paintings exhibited at Butler Institute of American Art, Youngstown, Ohio, 1994. *Recordings:* Albums: All-Time Greatest Hits, 1950; Forty Years: The Artistry Of Tony Bennett, 1950; Jazz, 1954; Beat Of My Heart, 1957; Chicago, 1959; I Left My Heart In San Francisco, 1962; I Wanna Be Around, 1963; Who Can I Turn To, 1964; If I Ruled The World: Songs for the Jet Set, 1965; Movie Songs, 1966; Snowfall: Christmas Album, 1968; Very Thought Of You, 1971; Bill Evans & Tony Bennett, 1975; My Best To You, 1982; 16 Most Requested Songs, 1986; Art Of Excellence, 1986; Bennett/Berlin, 1987; Astoria: Portrait Of The Artist, 1990; Basie Swings Bennett Sings, 1990; Good Life, 1990; Tony Bennett, 1990; Perfectly Frank, 1992; Essence Of, 1993; Steppin' Out, 1993; MTV Unplugged, 1994; Here's To The Ladies, 1995; Something, 1995; Classic Tony Bennett, Vol. 1, 1995, Vol. 2, 1996; On Holiday, 1996; All-Time Hall Of Fame Hits, 1997; Tony Bennett At Carnegie Hall, 1997; Hollywood And Broadway, 1998; Playground, 1998; Songs From The Heart, 1998; This Is Jazz No. 33, 1998; Forever Gold, 1999; Hot & Cool: Bennett Sings Ellington, 1999; Rodgers & Hart Songs, 1999; Together Again, 1999; Classic Tony Bennett, 2000; Good Life, 2000; High Profile, 2000; Tony Bennett With Count Basie, 2000; Ultimate Tony Bennett, 2000; Magic Of, 2001; Playing With My Friends, 2001; Tony Bennett Collection, 2001; As Time Goes By, 2002; Essential Tony Bennett, 2002; Have You Met Miss Jones, 2002; Wonderful World, 2002. *Publications:* What My Heart Has Seen, paintings, 1996; The Good Life, autobiography, 1998. *Honours:* Eight Grammy Awards, incl. Best Traditional Pop Vocal Performance, 1990, 1992, 1994, 1998, Album of the Year, 1994; Emmy Award; Cable Ace Award for television special; Gold disc for recordings of Because of You, I Left My Heart in San Francisco. *Membership:* Save the Rainforest; Project for Walden Woods; Juvenile Diabetes Foundation; American Cancer Society. *Address:* 130 W 57th St, Apt 9D, New York, NY 10019, USA. *Website:* www.tonybennett.net.

BENNETT, Vernie; b. 1972. Vocalist. *Education:* Studied law. *Career:* Singer, UK all-female vocal group Eternal, 1992–. *Recordings:* Albums: Always and Forever, 1993; Power Of a Woman, 1995; Greatest Hits, 1997; Before The Rain, 1997; Power Of a Woman, 1998; Eternal, 1999; Essential Eternal (compilation), 2001; Singles: Stay, 1993; Power Of a Woman, 1995; I Am Blessed, 1995; Secrets, 1996; Good Thing, 1996; Angel Of Mine, 1997; Don't You Love, 1997; I Wanna Be The Only One (No. 1, UK), 1997; What'cha Gonna Do, 1999. *Honours:* Smash Hits Award; Only UK act to have 6 top 15 hits from debut album.

BENNETT, Warren; b. 4 July 1962, Palmers Green, London, England. Composer; Musician. m. Jane Catherine, 18 May 1991, 2 d. *Career:* Music for television includes Wuthering Heights, London's Burning, Ambassador, The Knock, Staying Alive, Birds of a Feather; Arranger, Hank Marvin albums Into the Light, Heartbeat, Plays Cliff, Plays Holly, Plays Lloyd Webber and Tim Rice; Arranger, Darren Day album Summer Holiday; Concert tours with Hank Marvin, 1994, 1995, 1997, 1998. *Recordings:* Solo: Secrets Of The Heart; Pathways To Love; Close to the Hedge, with Mark Griffiths; Classical Guitar Moods, with Mirage. *Address:* Waffles Music Ltd, 91 Tabernacle St, London EC2A 2BA, England.

BENNETT, Willie P; b. 26 Oct. 1951, Toronto, Ontario, Canada. Songwriter; Musician (harmonica, mandolin, guitar). *Career:* Radio appearances: CBC Radio National, Toronto: The Entertainers; Morningside; Prime Time; Six Days On the Road; Swingin' On a Star, Murray Mclaughlin; Touch The Earth; CFTO TV: Lifetime; CFPL TV: Morning Break; CBC-TV: Ninety Minutes Live, Peter Gzowsky; Festivals: Ontario: Canadian Music; Carlisle Bluegrass; Festival of Friends; Home Country Folk; Mariposa Folk; Northern Lights; Northwinds; Ottawa Folk; Summerfolk; Alberta: Calgary Folk; Edmonton Folk; Northwest Territories: Folk On The Rocks; Saskatchewan: Redberry Folk and Country; British Columbia: Vancouver Folk; Manitoba: Winnipeg Folk. *Recordings:* As artist: Trying To Start Out Clean; Blackie and

The Rodeo King; Hobo's/Taunt; The Lucky Ones; Collectibles; Take My Own Advice; As musician with artists: Fred J Eaglesmith; Robert Atyeo; Joe Hall; The Dixie Flyers; Also appears on: Slightly Haunted, 1996; She and She and She, 1996; Flying Jenny, 1997; Lipstick, Lies and Gasoline, 1997; Painter Passing Through, 1998; Industrial Lullaby, 1998. *Honours:* CCMA Award Song of the Year: Hello, So Long Goodbye, 1990. *Membership:* AFofM; ACTRA; Canadian Country Music Asscn. *Current Management:* Dark Light Music Ltd. *Address:* 51 Bulwer St, Toronto, ON M5T 1A1, Canada.

BENNINGTON, Chester; b. 20 March 1976, Phoenix, AZ, USA. Vocalist. m. Samantha. *Career:* Vocalist, Grey Daze; Joined Xero; Renamed Hybrid Theory and signed to Warner Bros, Spring 2000; Further name change to Linkin Park prior to first record releases; Numerous international appearances; Live shows include: Family Values, Ozzfest tours, KROQ Acoustic Christmas Concert 2001; TV specials include: Live At The Fillmore; Reverb. *Recordings:* Albums: with Grey Daze: Wake Me, 1994; No Sun Today, 1997; with Linkin Park: Hybrid Theory, 2000; Reanimation, 2002. Singles: with Linkin Park: Hybrid Theory (EP), 2000; One Step Closer, 2001; Crawling, 2001; Papercut, 2001; In The End, 2001; Pts.Of.Athrty, 2002. *Honours:* Billboard Award, Best Modern Rock Artist, 2001; Rock Bear Awards, Best International Band, Best International Album, 2001; Kerrang! Award, Best International Newcomer, 2001; Rolling Stone Award, Best Hard Rock/Metal Band, 2001; MTV Awards, Best Group, Best Hard Rock, 2002. *Current Management:* Andy Gould Management, 8484 Wilshire Blvd #425, Beverly Hills, CA 90211, USA. *Website:* www.linkinpark.com.

BENOIT, Blue Boy, (Benoît Billot); b. 24 May 1946, Paris, France. Vocalist; Musician (harmonica, guitar). 2 d. *Education:* Ecole Des Beaux Arts, Paris. *Career:* Harmonica with: Stevie Wonder; Carole King; James Taylor; Albert King; 1970–72; Plays with Zachery Richard, 1972; First band: Benoît Blue Boy and The Tortilleurs, 1978. *Recordings:* Benoît Blue Boy, 1978; Original, 1979; Le Blues du Vendeur de Blues, 1981; Plaisir Simple, 1982; Tortillage, 1986; BBB et les Toit Cleurs, 1988; Parlez Vouz Français?, 1990; Plus Tard Dans La Soirée, 1992; Couvert de Bleus, 1994. *Membership:* SACEM; ADAMI. *Current Management:* Denis Leblond. *Address:* c/o Musiques Bleues, 16 rue Jacquemunt, 75017 Paris, France.

BENOIT, Tab; b. 17 Nov. 1967, Baton Rouge, Louisiana, USA. Blues/Rock Vocalist; Musician (guitar, harmonica). *Career:* Guitarist, various country, rock and blues bands, Houma, Louisiana, 1986–89; Solo Career, New Orleans, Louisiana, 1990–; Appears on Strike a Deep Chord compilation CD, 1991; TV Debut on Baywatch Nights, 1993; Songs featured on TV in Melrose Place, Party of Five, Northern Exposure, Beverly Hills 90210, Baywatch. *Recordings:* Strike a Deep Chord: Blues Guitars for the Homeless, 1991; Nice and Warm, 1992; What I Live For, 1994; Standing on the Bank, 1995; Live: Swampland Jam, 1997; Homesick for the Road, 1999. *Membership:* Screen Actors Guild. *Current Management:* Thunderbird Management Group LLC. *Address:* c/o 1245 Park Ave, Suite 10 E, New York, NY 10128, USA.

BENSON, George; b. 22 March 1943, Pittsburgh, Pennsylvania, USA. Musician (guitar); Vocalist. *Career:* Session musician, Pittsburgh; Guitarist with Brother Jack McDuff; Session work with Herbie Hancock, Wes Montgomery, 1966; Solo artist, 1966–; Regular world-wide tours; Major concerts include: Rock In Rio Festival, 1983; JVC Jazz Festival, Newport, USA, 1990; North Sea Jazz Festival, Netherlands, 1991; Guitar Legends, Seville, Spain, 1991. *Recordings:* Singles include: This Masquerade; Nature Boy; Give Me The Night; Love X Love; Turn Your Love Around; On Broadway; Love Ballad; Moody's Mood; In Your Eyes; Love All The Hurt Away (duet with Aretha Franklin); Never Give Up On A Good Thing; The Greatest Love Of All; Lady Love Me; Feel Like Makin' Love; Shiver; Albums: Its Uptown, 1966; Benson Burner, 1966; Giblet Gravy, 1967; Tell It Like It Is, 1969; The Other Side Of Abbey Road, 1970; Beyond The Blue Horizon, 1972; Good King Bad, 1973; Bad Benson, 1974; Supership, 1975; Breezin' (No. 1, USA), 1976; Benson and Farrell (with jazz flautist Joe Farrell), 1976; George Benson In Concert: Carnegie Hall, 1977; In Flight, 1977; Weekend In LA, 1978; Livin' Inside Your Love, 1979; Give Me The Night, 1981; George Benson Collection, 1981; In Your Eyes, 1983; 20/20, 1985; The Love Songs (No. 1, UK), 1985; While The City Sleeps, 1986; Collaboration, 1987; Twice The Love, 1988; Tenderly (No. 1, USA Jazz chart), 1989; Big Boss Band, 1990; Midnight Moods: The Love Collection, 1991; Love Remembers, 1993; The Most Exciting New Guitarist On The Jazz, 1994; Take Five, 1995; Live and Smokin', 1995; California Dreamin', 1996; That's Right, 1996; Lil' Darlin', 1996; Talkin' Verve, 1997; Essentials, 1998; Standing Together, 1998; Masquerade, 1998; Masquerade Is Over, 1999; Love and Jazz, 1999; Live At Casa Caribe, 2000; Absolute Benson, 2000; All Blues, 2001; Guest musician, Back On The Block, Quincy Jones, 1991. *Honours:* Grammy Awards: Best R&B Instrumental, 1976, 1980; Record of the Year, 1976; Best Pop Instrumental, 1976, 1984; Best R&B Male Vocal Performance, 1978, 1980; Best Jazz Voval Performance, 1980; Best Jazz Instrumental Performance, 1991. *Current Management:* Ken Fritz Management, 648 N Robertson Blvd, Los Angeles, CA 90069, USA.

BENSON, Ray; b. 16 March 1951, Philadelphia, Pennsylvania, USA. Musician (guitar); Vocalist; Record Prod; Actor; Man. m. Diane Carr, 27 March 1983, 2 s. *Education:* 1 year Antioch College. *Career:* Leader, lead

singer, Asleep At The Wheel, for 25 years; Producer, 9 Asleep At The Wheel albums, 1973–93; Also producer for George Strait; Ricky Van Shelton; Sweethearts of the Rodeo; k d lang; Aaron Neville and Rob Wasserman; Bruce Hornsby and Willie Nelson; Darden Smith; Don Walser; 8 film scores; Commercials include: Anheuser-Busch products, Coors, Delta Airlines, Pepsi Cola, Levi's Jeans; Actor, 4 music videos; Numerous television appearances include: Austin City Limits, with band Asleep At The Wheel; Wild Texas Wind; Nashville Now; Johnny Carson; Executive Director and Co-Producer, Texas Festival, Kennedy Centre, 1991. *Recordings:* Albums: Coming Right At Ya, 1973; Asleep At The Wheel, 1974; Texas Gold, 1975; The Wheel, 1977; Served Live, 1979; Framed, 1980; Drivin', 1980; Pasture Prime, 1985; Asleep At The Wheel 10, 1987; Western Standard Time, 1988; Keepin' Me Up Nights, 1990; Live and Kickin', 1992; Route 66, 1992; The Swingin' Best Of Asleep At The Wheel, 1992; Tribute To The Music Of Bob Wills and The Texas Playboys, 1993; Still Swingin', 1994; The Wheel Keeps On Rollin', 1995; Minstrel Man From Georgia, 1996; Texas Top Hand, 1996; Way Out West, 1996; Swing, 1997; Live Back to the Future Now, 1997; Down At The Sky-Vue Drive In, 1998; Horse Whisperer, 1998; Songs Of Forbidden Love, 1998; Fiddle Fire, 1998; Global Voices, 1998; More, 1999. *Honours:* Academy of Country Music Award, 1977; Buddy Award, 1985; 4 Grammy Awards; Western Swing Society Hall of Fame, 1994. *Membership:* Trustee, NARAS; Board Mem., R&B Foundation. *Current Management:* Bismeaux Productions, PO Box 463, Austin, TX 78767, USA.

BENSUSAN, Pierre; b. 30 Oct. 1957, Oran, French Algeria. Musician (guitar); Vocalist; Composer. m. Doatea Cornu, 22 June 1985, 1 s. *Career:* Festivals include: Montreux, Nyon, (Switzerland); Musiques Métisses d'Angouleme (France); Jazz Festivals: Montréal; Edmonton (Canada); Brussels; Guitar Festivals: Liege, Grand, (Belgium); Milwaukee (USA): Tel-Aviv (Israel); Paris, Nice (France); Festival Inter-Celtic de Lorient (France); Zenith-Paris (as Jacques Higelin's guest); Boston; Germany (Stockfish tour); Bern; Lanzburg; Eppalinges (Switzerland); Summer Banks Festival, London; Vancouver, Toronto (Canada); Polymusicales de Bollene; Bergamo (Italy); Rotterdam (Netherlands); Flanders Festival, Grand (Belgium); Appeared with or played with artistes including: Suzanne Vega; Jacques Higelin; Paco de Lucia; Carla Bley; Larry Coryell; Philip Catherine; Doc Watson; John Renbourn and David Bromberg; Nana Vasconcelos; Oregon; Uzeb; Taj Mahal; Alan Stivell; Al Stewart; Bobby Thomas; Didier Malherbe. *Recordings:* Près de Paris; Pierre Bensusan 2; Musiques; Solilai; Spices; Wu Wei; Live an New Morning; Nice Feeling. *Publications:* The Guitar Book; Dagad Music; 3 videos: The Guitar of Pierre Bensusan, Vol. 1 and 2; Pierre Bensusan in Concert, A World of Celtic Fingerstyle Guitar. *Honours:* Grand Prix du Disque, Montreux Festival, 1976. *Address:* B P 232, 02406 Chateau Thierry Cedex, France.

BENTZON, Nikolaj; b. 21 Feb. 1964, Copenhagen, Denmark. Jazz Musician (piano); Composer. m. Agnethe Koch, 3 July 1993, 1 s., 2 d. *Education:* Performance Diploma, Berklee College of Music, Boston, USA. *Career:* Member of Danish Radio Jazz Orchestra, 1990–; Leader of Nikolaj Bentzon Trio, 1989; Nikolaj Bentzon and The Scandinavian Connection, 1992–; The Nikolaj Bentzon Brotherhood, 1995; Nikolai Bentzon Constitution, 1997 with Herbie Hancock Headhunters' rhythm section Paul Jackson (bass) and Mike Clarke (drums); 3 years with Ernie Wilkin's Almost Big Band; Debut performance of Bob Brookmeyer's November Music, written for Nikolaj Bentzon, 24 Nov. 1994, Radio House, Copenhagen. *Recordings:* Albums: with Nikolaj Bentzon Trio: Pianoforte, Between Us, Triskelos, Nexus; 1 album with Nikolaj Bentzon and The Scandinavian Connection; 1 album with Nikolaj Bentzon Brotherhood; 1 album featuring Mike Clark and Paul Jackson; Bentzon album featuring Headhunter greats Paul Jackson, Mike Clarke, 1998. *Honours:* Best soloist, Dunkerque Jazz Festival, 1983; Jacob Gade Award, 1983; Oscar Peterson Jazz Award, 1985; Danish Society for Jazz, Rock and Folk Music Hon. Award, 1991. *Current Management:* Anders Tidemann, Word of Mouth. *Address:* Grundtvigsvej 27B, suite 4mf, 1864 Copenhagen, Denmark.

BERAUD, Marie Laure; b. 22 Jan. 1959, Lyon, France. Vocalist. 2 s. *Education:* Degree Languages and History of Arts, University, Paris. *Career:* Four-month tour including France; Belgium; Netherlands; Germany; Switzerland; USA (Ballroom Club, New York), 1992; Television apperances include: Nulle Part Ailleurs, with Antoine de Gaunes, 1992. *Recordings:* Album: Turbigo 12–12, 1992; Singles: Viens Simon; Les Immortelles; Macadam Ramdam, 1992. *Honours:* Academie Charles Cros First Album Prize, 1992. *Membership:* SACEM. *Current Management:* Cyril Prieur, Talent Sorcier. *Address:* Talent Sorcier, 3 rue des Petites Écuries, 75010 Paris, France.

BERENGUER, José; b. 21 Oct. 1955, Barcelona, Spain. Musician (guitar). *Education:* PhD, Clinical Psychology, Medicine; Composer, computer, electroacoustical music. *Career:* Autumno Musicale, Como, Italy; Internationale Fenienkurse-Danmstadt, Germany; Synthèse, Bourges, France; Festival International de Músicadel Segle XX, Barcelona, Spain; Puntope En Cuentro, Madrid, Spain; Para Lelo Madrid. *Recordings:* Klängé, 1993; Antropometria Don Quichotte; Spira; Constellacions; Silence. *Honours:* TIME of CIM/UNESCO; Electroacoustic Music Prize, Bourges. *Membership:* Chairman of Ascociacion de Musica Electroacoustica de Espana; Vice-chairman of Associaó Catacana de Compositors; International Electroacoustic Music Academy of Bourges. *Current Management:* Côchlea. *Address:* Sardeeva 516 6e 2a, 08024 Barcelona, Spain.

BERESFORD, Steve; b. 6 March 1950, Wellington, Shropshire. Musician (Piano). *Education:* BA, York University. *Career:* Worked on a large number of film soundtracks, concerts, recordings. *Compositions:* I Was There; Unremarkable; Thanks to Minnie; My Hawaiian Bath Tub Melody; Pentimento; Avril Brisé. *Recordings:* Cue Sheets; Short in the UK; The Bath Of Surprise; Museum Of Towing and Recovery; Fish Of the Week. *Membership:* PRS; MCPS; PAMRA; MU. *Address:* 62 Oxford Gardens, London W10 5UN, England.

BERG, Shelton Glen; b. 18 Aug. 1955, Cleveland, OH, USA. Musician (piano); Educator; Composer; Arranger. *Education:* MM, Piano Performance, University of Houston, 1979; BM, Piano Performance, University of Houston, 1977. *Career:* Chair, Jazz Studies, University of Southern California, 1991–; Composer: Fudge, ABC Television Series, A League of Their Own, CBS Television; Orchestra for Film: Edwards and Hunt; President: International Association of Jazz Education, 1996–98. *Compositions:* Numerous compositions for Jazz Combos, Chorus and Big Band. *Recordings:* as Pianist: The Joy, with Bill Watrons; A Time for Love; Space Available. *Publications:* Jazz Improvisation: The Goal-Note Method, 1989; Numerous articles in Jazz Educators Journal and Piano and Keyboard Magazines. *Honours:* Finalist, 1988 Great American Jazz Piano Competition; Commission: Theme Song of 1986 US Olympia Festival. *Membership:* IAJE; MENC. *Current Management:* Open Door Management. *Address:* 3545 Downing Ave, Glendale, CA 91208, USA.

BERG, Terje; b. 24 Jan. 1972, Trondheim, Norway. Musician (bass). *Education:* College. *Career:* Started Hedge Hog, 1989; Toured Europe, 1994, 1995. *Recordings:* Erase, 1992; Surprise, 1992; Primal Gutter, 1993; Mercury Red, 1994; Mindless, 1994; The Healing EP, 1995; Thorn Cord Wonder, 1995. *Current Management:* Martin Aam, Hedge Hogment. *Address:* Hedge Hog, PO Box 683, 7001 Trondheim, Norway.

BERGE, Svein; b. Tromso, Norway. Musician. *Career:* Mem., Röyksopp, 2002–. *Recordings:* Album: Melody AM, 2002. Singles: Easy, 2002; Remind Me, 2002; Poor Leno, 2003. *Address:* c/o Astralwerks Records, 104 W 29th St, Fourth Floor, New York, NY 10001, USA. *Website:* www.astralwerks.com/royksopp/.

BERGGREN, Jonas 'Joker'; b. 21 March 1967, Sweden. Musician (keyboards); Songwriter; Vocalist. *Career:* Member, Ace of Base, 1990–. *Recordings:* Albums: Happy Nation, 1993; The Bridge, 1995; Made In Sweden, 1996; Cruel Summer, 1998; Flowers, 1999; Greatest Hits, 2000; Singles: Wheel Of Fortune; All That She Wants (No. 1, UK), 1993; Lucky Love; The Sign, Don't Turn Around, Cruel Summer, Life Is A Flower, Always Have Always Will; No. 1 records in UK; USA; Canada; Australia; New Zealand; Israel; Argentina; Europe. *Honours:* Platinum discs world-wide. *Current Management:* Siljemark Production AB, Gårdsvägen 4, 171 52 Solna, Sweden.

BERGGREN, Linn (Malin); b. 1970, Sweden. Vocalist. *Career:* Singer, Ace of Base, 1990–. *Recordings:* Albums: Happy Nation, 1993; The Bridge, 1995; Made In Sweden, 1996; Cruel Summer, 1998; Flowers, 1999; Greatest Hits, 2000; Singles: Wheel Of Fortune; All That She Wants (No. 1, UK), 1993; Lucky Love; The Sign, Don't Turn Around, Cruel Summer, Life Is A Flower, Always Have Always Will; No. 1 records in UK; USA; Canada; Australia; New Zealand; Israel; Argentina; Europe. *Honours:* Platinum discs world-wide. *Current Management:* Siljemark Production AB, Gårdsvägen 4, 171 52 Solna, Sweden.

BERGH, Totti; b. 5 Dec. 1935, Oslo, Norway. Musician (tenor, soprano, alto saxophones). m. Laila Dalseth, 1 June 1963, 2 d. *Career:* Jazz artist; Television and radio appearances in Scandinavia; Concerts include: Playboy Jazz Festival; Sacramento Jazz Festival; Caribbean Cruises; Molde Jazz Festival; Oslo Jazz Festival; Jakarta Jazz Festival; Currently fronting own group with singer (wife) Laila Dalseth. *Recordings:* with Bengt Hallberg's Swinging Swedes: We Love Norway, 1977; with Laila Dalseth/Louis Stewart Quintet: Daydreams, 1984; I Hear A Rhapsody, 1985; with Al Cohn: Tenor Gladness, 1986; with George Masso, Major Holley: Major Blues, 1990; with Plas Johnson: On The Trail, 1992; with Joe Cohn: Remember, 1995; with Laila Dalseth/Philip Catherine Sextet: A Woman's Intuition, 1995.

BERGMAN, Alan; b. Brooklyn, New York, USA. Lyricist; Writer. m. Marilyn Keith, 2 d. *Education:* BA, Music, University of North Carolina. *Career:* Collaborated with Marilyn Bergman; Michel Legrand; Dave Grusin; Marvin Hamlisch; Henry Mancini; Johnny Mandel; John Williams; David Shire: Neil Diamond; James Newton Howard; Quincy Jones; Lew Spence; Sammy Fain; Billy Goldenberg; Lalo Schifrin; Norman Luboff; Sergio Mendes. *Compositions:* Songs include: That Face; Yellow Bird; Nice 'n' Easy; The Windmills of Your Mind; The Way We Were; The Summer Knows; What Are You Doing The Rest of Your Life?; Summer Me, Winter Me; So Many Stars;

You Must Believe In Spring; Places That Belong To You; You Don't Bring Me Flowers; Little Boy Lost; In The Heat of The Night; The Hands of Time; I Love To Dance; I Believe In Love; Sweet Gingerbread Man; The Last Time I Felt Like This; I'll Never Say Goodbye; Make Me Rainbows; Like A Lover; The Island; All His Children; Marmalade, Molasses and Honey; If We Were In Love; It Might Be You; How Do You Keep The Music Playing; Papa Can You Hear Me? The Way He Makes Me Feel; Ordinary Miracles; Where Do You Start? Most of All You; The Girl Who Used To Be Me; Michel Legrand Album; Live At Donte's; Broadway scores: Something More; Ballrooom; Film/TV scores: Yentl; Queen of The Stardust Ballroom; Sybil; TV themes: Maude; Good Times; Alice; Brooklyn Bridge; The Powers That Be. *Honours:* 3 Academy; 2 Emmy; 2 Golden Globe; 2 Grammy; Inducted into Songwriters Hall of Fame, 1979. *Membership:* ASCAP; AMPAS; Songwriters Guild of America; Society of Composers and Lyricists. *Current Management:* Gorfaine Scwartz. *Address:* 3301 Barham Blvd #201, Los Angeles, CA 90068, USA.

BERGMAN, Barry; b. 24 Aug. 1944, New York, USA. Artist Man; Music Publisher. *Education:* BS, New York University, 1966. *Career:* Vice-President, Marks Music, 1975–79; Vice-President, Creative Affairs, United Artists Music, 1979–81; Owner, Barry Bergman Management, 1982–; Ellymax Music, 1985–, Wood Monkey Music, 1986–; Artist manager for: Keven Jordan; Marc Ribler; Rob Friedman; Kings Country; Publisher of music by: Cher; Kiss; Michael Bolton; Kathy Mattea. *Contributions to:* Billboard Magazine, Narm Sounding Board. *Honours:* ASCAP Pop Award, 1989. *Membership:* ASCAP; Broadcast Music Inc; Founder, President, International Managers Forum, USA. *Current Management:* Barry Bergman Management, 350 E 30th St, Suite 4D, New York, NY 10016, USA.

BERGMAN, Marilyn; b. Brooklyn, New York, USA. Lyricist; Writer. m. Alan Bergman, 1 d. *Education:* New York University; High School of Music and Art. *Career:* Collaborators: Alan Bergman; Michel Legrand; Dave Grusin; Marvin Hamlisch; Henry Mancini; Johnny Mandel; John Williams; David Shire; Neil Diamond; James Newton Howard; Quincy Jones; Lew Spence; Sammy Fain; Billy Goldenberg; Lalo Schifrin; Norman Luboff; Sergio Mendes. *Compositions include:* Yellow Bird; Nice 'n' Easy; The Windmills of Your Mind; The Way We Were; The Summer Knows; What Are You Doing For The Rest of Your Life?; Summer Me Winter Me; So Many Stars; You Must Believe In Spring; Places That Belong To You; You Don't Bring Me Flowers; Little Boy Lost; In The Heat of The Night; The Hands of Time; I Love To Dance; I Believe In Love; Sweet Gingerbread Man; The Last Time I Felt Like This; I'll Never Say Goodbye; Make Me Rainbows; Like a Lover; The Island; All His Children; Marmalade, Molasses and Honey; If We Were In Love; It Might Be You; How Do You Keep The Music Playing; Papa Can You Hear Me?; The Way He Makes Me Feel; Ordinary Miracles; Where Do You Start?; Most of All You; The Girl Who Used To Be Me; Portrait Edition; Michel Legrand Album; Live At Donte's; Broadway scores: Something More; Ballroom; Film/TV scores, Yentl; Queen of The Stardust Ballroom; Sybil. *Honours:* 3 Academy; 2 Golden Globe; 2 Emmy; 2 Grammy; Inducted into Songwriters Hall of Fame, 1979; Crystal Award, Women In Film, 1986. *Membership:* (Chairman) ASCAP; AMPAS; Society of Composers and Lyricists; Songwriters Guild of America. *Current Management:* Gorfaine/Scwartz.

BERGSTEIN, Scott; b. 8 June 1952, Midland, Michigan, USA. Record Co Exec. m. Elisa Fegarido, 18 Nov. 1989, 1 s. *Education:* BA Communications, American University, Washington DC. *Career:* Head Buyer, Wherehouse Records; International Operations Manager, Casablanca Records; Director of Artist Development, Allegiance Records; Marketing Manager, Chameleon Music Group; Senior Vice-President, Higher Octave Music. *Membership:* NARAS; NARM; AFIM. *Address:* 23852 Pacific Coast Hwy #2C, Malibu, CA 90265, USA.

BERLIOZ, Gérard; b. 15 March 1943, Paris, France. Musician (percussion, tympanon, cymbalum); Music Educator. m. 11 April 1964, 1 s., 1 d. *Education:* Prix de Percussion du Mans; Prix de Percussion, Conservatoire National Supérieur de Music de Paris. *Career:* Professor, several conservatoires in Paris region; Worked with symphony orchestras: Radio-France; Radio-Moscow; Leningrad; Prague; Music Hall concerts at Moulin Rouge; Casino de Paris; Olympia; Theatres, operas, ballet companies include: Paris; Rouen; Vichy; Nice; Toulouse; Grenoble (others in France); Monte Carlo; Canada; Japan; Festivals all over France; International tours with: Mikis Theodorakis; Lorin Maazel; Jerry Lewis (Europe, North Africa, South Africa, USA, Canada, Japan, Thailand, South America, Israel, Australia); Musician accompanying: Claude Bolling; Tom Jones; Ginger Rogers; Ray Charles; Charles Aznavour; Gilbert Bécaud; Mireille Mathieu; Catherine Ribeiro; Music for films, musical comedies and recordings with: Michel Legrand; Maurice Jarre; Claude Nougaro; Mikis Theodakaris; Jean Claude Naude; Guy Defatto; Mireille Mathieu; Catherine Ribeiro. *Publications:* Director, Percussion Collection; Chronicler, Journal: Tam Tam Percussion; Author, several instruction manuals; Author, numerous articles on percussion. *Membership:* L'Ordre National Des Musiciens.

BERNARD, Alain; b. 8 Sept. 1952. Jazz Musician (piano, synthesizer); Arranger. *Education:* English studies, Paris University, 1971–72; Private music lessons until 1985; CIM Diploma, orchestration, arrangement, composition. *Career:* Musician, 1977–; Sideman for French musicians including: R Guérin; Gérard Badini Swing Machine; Ornicar big-band; American musicians include: F Foster; E L Davis; Joe Henderson; J Newman; Dee Dee Bridgewater; Jazz festivals at Nice and Dresden; Founder, own trio, 1987; Plays in France and Germany. *Recordings:* Mais Où Est Donc Ornicar, with Joe Henderson; Mr Swing Is Still Alive, Gérard Badini Super Swing Machine; Jazz Cartoon; L'Incroyable Huck. *Membership:* SACEM; SPEDIDAM; ADAMI. *Address:* 6 rue de l'Ile Irus, Tourlarec, 56870 Baden, France. *Telephone:* (2) 97580043.

BERNARD, Claude Camille; b. 5 Oct. 1945, Paris, France. Musician (alto saxophone); Bandleader. Widower, 2 s., 2 d. *Education:* Conservatoire Artistique Cardinal Lemoine; Jean Ledieu, Professor, alto saxophone, soloist, Conservatoire National, Nancy. *Career:* Festivals: Chateauvallon, 1976; Vansovin, 1977; Suse den Netherlands; Yugoslavia, Turkey, 1994; People's Republic of China, Africa, 1995; Played with: Steve Lacy; Michael Smith; Lavelle; Mickey Baker; Wei Wei; Specializes in improvisation, solo and accompanied. *Recordings:* Quebella Promenade; Brin de Laine; Facett'vega. *Publications:* Olympic Games Atlanta centennial with Wei Wei and Michael Smith Band, 1996. *Membership:* Syndicat des Chefs d'Orchestre; SACEM; SACD; Centre International de Musicotherapie. *Address:* 48 Ave du Maréchal Foch, 78400 Chatou, France.

BERNSTEIN, Elmer; b. 4 April 1922, New York, NY, USA. Composer; Conductor. m. (1) Pearl Glusman, 21 Dec. 1946, 2 s., (2) Eve Adamson, 25 Oct. 1965, 2 d. *Education:* Studied composition with Israel Citkowitz, Roger Sessions, Ivan Langstroth and Stefan Wolpe; New York University. *Career:* US Army Air Corps, arranger and composer for the Armed Forces Radio Service; Concert Pianist, 1946–50; Composer and conductor for films; Founder of Film Music Collection, 1974. *Compositions:* How Now, Dow Jones (musical), 1967; Three orchestral suites; Chamber music and songs; Many film scores including: The Man With the Golden Arm, 1955; The Ten Commandments, 1956; Desire Under the Elms, 1958; The Magnificent Seven, 1960; Walk on the Wild Side, 1963; To Kill a Mocking Bird, 1963; Hawaii, 1966; Thoroughly Modern Millie, 1967; The Bridge at Remagen, 1969; The Trial of Billy Jack, 1974; Airplane!, 1980; Ghostbusters, 1984; My Left Foot, 1989; The Grifters, 1991; The Age of Innocence, 1993; Search and Destroy, 1995; Devil in a Blue Dress, 1995; Bulletproof, 1996; Buddy, 1997; Hoodlum, 1997; The Rainmaker, 1997; Concerto for Guitar and Orchestra for Two Christophers, 2001. *Honours:* Star on the Hollywood Walk of Fame, 1996. *Membership:* Acad. of Motion Picture Art and Sciences, first vice-pres., 1963–73; Composers and Lyricists Guild of America, pres., 1970–82; Film Music Society, pres., 1995–. *Current Management:* Blue Focus Management, 15233 Ventura Blvd, Suite 200, Sherman Oaks, CA 91403, USA. *Address:* c/o ASCAP, ASCAP Bldg, 1 Lincoln Plaza, New York, NY 10023, USA.

BERRY, Bill; b. 31 July 1958, Hibbing, Minnesota, USA. Musician (drums). *Career:* Member, R.E.M., 1980–97; World-wide tours; Member, side project, Hindu Love Gods, 1986–90. *Recordings:* Albums: with R.E.M.: Chronic Town (mini album), 1982; Murmur, 1983; Reckoning, 1984; Fables Of The Reconstruction, 1985; Life's Rich Pageant, 1986; Dead Letter Office, 1987; Document, 1987; Eponymous, 1988; Green, 1988; Out Of Time, 1991; The Best Of REM, 1991; Automatic For The People, 1992; Monster, 1995; with Hindu Love Gods: Hindu Love Gods, 1990; Also appears on: Beat The Retreat, 1994; I'll Sleep When I'm Dead, 1996; Live On Letterman, 1997; Singles: with R.E.M.: The One I Love, 1987; Stand, 1989; Orange Crush, 1989; Losing My Religion, 1991; Shiny Happy People, 1991; Near Wild Heaven, 1991; Radio Song, 1991; Drive, 1992; Man On The Moon, 1992; The Sidewinder Sleeps Tonite, 1993; Everybody Hurts, 1993; Crush With Eyeliner; Nightswimming; What's The Frequency Kenneth?; Tracks featured on film soundtracks: Batchelor Party, 1984; Until The End Of The World, 1991; Coneheads, 1993; Recordings with: Indigo Girls; Warren Zevon; Love Tractor; Contributor, albums: Tom's Album; I'm Your Fan. *Honours:* Earth Day Award, 1990; Numerous MTV Music Video Awards; Billboard Awards: Best Modern Rock Artists, Best World Album, 1991; BRIT Awards: Best International Group, 1992, 1993, 1995; Grammy Awards, Best Pop Performance, Alternative Music Album, Music Video, 1992; Atlanta Music Awards: Act of the Year, Rock Album, Video, 1992; IRMA, International Band of the Year, 1993; Rolling Stone Critics Awards: Best Band, Best Album; Q Awards: Best Album, 1991, 1992; Best Act In The World, 1991, 1995. *Current Management:* REM/Athens Ltd, 250 W Clayton St, Athens, GA 30601, USA.

BERRY, Chuck, (Charles Edward Anderson Berry); b. 18 Oct. 1926, San Jose, California, USA. Rock 'n' Renamed Chuck Berry Trio; Established Berry Park, Wentzville, Missouri (home and country club); Owner, nightclub The Bandstand, St Louis; Hundreds of world-wide concerts including: Newport Jazz Festival, 1958; New York Folk Festival, 1965; Toronto Rock 'n' Roll Revival, 1969; UK Rock 'n' Roll Revival, Wembley, 1972; White House concert, for President Carter, 1979; 60th Birthday concert, Fox Theatre, St Louis, 1986; Film appearances: Rock Rock Rock, 1956; Jazz On A Summers Day, 1958; Go Johnny Go, 1959; American Hot Wax, 1978; Hail! Hail! Rock 'n' Roll!, 1987. *Recordings:* Numerous albums include: Chuck Berry, 1963; Chuck Berry On Stage, 1963; His Latest and Greatest, 1964; Chuck Berry's Greatest Hits, 1964; St Louis To Liverpool, 1965; Chuck Berry In London, 1965; Chuck

Berry's Golden Decade, 1968; Back Home, 1970; St Louis To Frisco To Memphis, 1972; Golden Decade Vol. 2, 1973; Motorvatin', 1977; Rock! Rock! Rock 'N' Roll, 1980; Chuck Berry: The Chess Box, 1990; Anthology, 2000; Singles include: Maybellene, 1955; Roll Over Beethoven, 1956; School Day, 1957; Rock and Roll Music, 1957; Sweet Little Sixteen, 1958; Johnny B Goode, 1958; Memphis Tennessee, 1963; Nadine (Is It You?), 1964; No Particular Place To Go, 1964; You Never Can Tell, 1964; My Ding A Ling, 1972. *Publications:* Chuck Berry: The Autobiography, 1988. *Honours:* Grammy, Lifetime Achievement Award, 1985; Inducted into Rock and Roll Hall of Fame, 1986; Hollywood Walk of Fame, 1987; Inducted into Songwriters Hall of Fame, 1986; Maybellene inducted into NARAS Hall of Fame, 1988; St Louis Walk of Fame, 1989; Johnny B Goode, featured on Voyager Interstellar Record, NASA's Voyager satellite, 1989; Roll Over Beethoven inducted into NARAS Hall of Fame, 1990. *Current Management:* Ira Okun Enterprises, 211 S Beverly Dr., Suite 103, Beverly Hills, CA 90212, USA.

BERRY, Dave; b. 6 Feb. 1941, Sheffield, England. Vocalist. m. Marthy Van-Lopik, 20 Feb. 1967, 1 d. *Career:* Tours with Rolling Stones, 1964–65; Television: Top of the Pops; Ready Steady Go; Lucky Stars; Song Festival, Knokke, Belgium; Gran Gala, Netherlands; Concert tours, 60s package with other artists, 1985–95. *Recordings:* Memphis Tennessee, 1963; Crying Game, 1964; Baby Its You, 1964; This Strange Effect, 1965; Little Things, 1965; Mama, 1966; Albums: Dave Berry, 1964; Can I Get It From You, 1965; A Dozen Berry's, 1966; Special Sound Of, 1968; 68, 1968; Remembering, 1976; The Crying Game, 1983; This Strange Effect, 1986; A Totally Random Evening With, 1992; The Very Best Of, 1999. *Honours:* Press Prize, Knokke, Belgium. *Current Management:* Brian Gannon Management. *Address:* PO Box 106, Rochdale, England.

BERRY, Jan; b. 3 April 1941, Los Angeles, California, USA. Vocalist. m. Gertie Filip, 1991. *Career:* Member, duo Jan and Dean (with Dean Torrence), 1957–66; 1973–; Career interrupted by serious accident, 1966; Performances include: Dick Clark's stage show, Michigan State Fair, with Frankie Avalon, Duane Eddy, The Coasters, 1959; American Bandstand, ABC TV, 1964; New York, with The Animals, Chuck Berry, Del Shannon, 1964; California Surfer's Stomp Festival, 1973; Subject of biopic, Dead Man's Curve, ABC TV, 1978. *Recordings:* Albums: Jan and Dean Take Linda Surfin', 1963; Surf City and Other Swinging Cities, 1963; Drag City, 1964; Dead Man's Curve/The New Girl At School, 1964; The Little Old Lady From Pasadena, 1964; Ride The Wild Surf (film soundtrack), 1964; Command Performance/Live In Person, 1965; Jan and Dean Meet Batman, 1966; One Summer Night: Live, 1982; Various compilations; Live. *Recordings include:* Center Stage, 2000; Surf City, 2001; Singles include: with Jan and Dean: Linda, 1963; Surf City (No. 1, USA), 1963; Honolulu Lulu, 1963; Dead Man's Curve, 1964; The Little Old Lady (From Pasadena), 1964; Ride The Wild Surf, 1964; Catch A Wave, 1964; You Really Know How To Hurt A Guy, 1965; Solo albums: Mother Earth, 1972; Don't You Just Know It, 1972; Tinsel Town, 1974. *Current Management:* Bill Hollingshead Productions, 1720 N Ross St, Santa Ana, CA 92706, USA.

BERRY, John; b. 14 Sept. 1959, Aiken, South Carolina, USA. Vocalist; Songwriter. m. Robin Calvert, 2 s., 1 d. *Career:* Moved to Nashville, 1990; Tours, concerts with own band; Television includes: Music City Tonight; The Ralph Emery Show; CBS This Morning; NBC Weekend Today; Entertainment Tonight; The Road; Exclusively Leeza; Conan O'Brian. *Recordings:* Albums: John Berry, 1995; Standing On The Edge, 1995; O Holy Night, 1995; Faces, 1996; Better Than A Biscuit, 1998; Wildest Dreams, 1999; All The Way To There, 2002. Singles: Your Love Amazes Me (No. 1); Standing On The Edge Of Goodbye; I Think About It All The Time; If I Had Any Pride Left At All, 1995; Change My Mind, 1996; She's Takin' A Shine, 1997. *Honours:* 2 Gold albums; 1 Platinum album, John Berry, 1995; Platinum single, Your Love Amazes Me; Grammy Awards: Best Male Country Performance, 1995, 1996. *Membership:* AFofM; CMA; NARAS; ACM. *Current Management:* Corlew-O'Grady Management. *Address:* 1503 17th Ave S, Nashville, TN 37212, USA.

BERRY, Mark, (Bez); b. 18 April 1964, Manchester, England. Musician (percussion); Dancer. *Career:* Mem., Happy Mondays, 1985–93; Tours, UK, Europe, USA; Support tours to: New Order, UK, 1987; Jane's Addiction, USA, 1990; Concerts include: Glastonbury Festival, 1990; Great British Music Weekend, Wembley, 1990; Feile Festival, Tipperary, 1990; Cities In The Park Festival, Prestwich, 1990; Founder mem., Black Grape, 1993–98; Numerous live concerts and festival appearances; Re-formed Happy Mondays, 1999. *Recordings:* Albums: with Happy Mondays: Squirrel And G-Man Twenty-Four Hour Party People Plastic Face Carnt Smile (White Out), 1986; Bummed, 1988; Pills 'N' Thrills and Bellyaches (No. 1, UK), 1990; Live, 1991; ...Yes Please!, 1992; Loads, 1995; Happy Mondays Greatest Hits, 1999; with Black Grape: It's Great When You're Straight... Yeah!, 1995; Stupid, Stupid, Stupid, 1997. Singles: with Happy Mondays: Twenty-Four Hour Party People, 1987; WFL (Wrote For Luck), 1988; Madchester Rave On (EP), 1989; Step On, 1990; Kinky Afro, 1990; Loose Fit, 1991; Judge Fudge, 1991; The Boys Are Back In Town, 1999; with Black Grape: Reverend Black Grape, 1995; In The Name of The Father, 1995; Kelly's Heroes, 1995; England's Irie, 1996; Fat Neck, 1996; Get Higher, 1997; Marbles, 1998. *Publications:* Freaky Dancin'. *Honours:* Best

Indie Act, DMC World DJ Awards, 1991. *Address:* c/o London Records, PO Box 1422, Chancellors House, Chancellors Rd, London W6 9SG, England. *Website:* www.londonrecords.co.uk.

BERRYMAN, Guy; b. 12 April 1978, Fife, Scotland. Musician (bass guitar); Songwriter. *Education:* University College, London. *Career:* Mem., Coldplay, 1998–. *Recordings:* Albums: Parachutes, 2000; A Rush Of Blood To The Head, 2002. Singles: The Safety EP, 1998; Brothers and Sisters, The Blue Room EP, 1999; Shiver, 2000; Yellow, 2000; Trouble, 2000; Don't Panic, 2001; In My Place, 2002; A Rush Of Blood To The Head, 2002; The Scientist, 2002. *Honours:* BRIT Awards, Best Album, 2001, Best British Group, Best British Album, 2003; Grammy Award, Best Alternative Album, for Parachutes, 2001; MTV Award, Best UK and Ireland Act, 2002; Billboard Group of the Year, 2002; NME Award, Best Album, 2003. *Current Management:* Phil Harvey. *Address:* c/o Parlophone Records, 43 Brook Green, London W6 7EF, England. *Website:* www.coldplay.com.

BERRYMAN, Peter Anthony; b. 22 June 1945, Redruth, Cornwall, England. Musician (Guitar); Composer; Teacher. 2 s., 1 d. *Career:* Tours With Famous Jug Band, 1969–71; Mormos, Africa, 1973; Julie Felix, Australasia, 1974; Bridget St John, UK, 1976; Brenda Wootton, France, 1985–90; Blue Ticket, 1987–93; Solo, UK, Europe, 1972–; Radio Includes, John Peel; Andy Kershaw; Television Includes Old Grey Whistle Test, BBC2; Festivals, Cambridge; Hyde Park; Glastonbury; L'Orient; Womad; Guitar Teacher, 1982–; Music for Kneehigh Theatre; Theatre Rotto; The Barneys. *Recordings:* Spiral Staircase, 1968; Sunshine Possibilities, 1969; Chameleon, 1970; Legendary Me; Magical Flight; Sky In My Pie; Past, Present and Future; Under A Summer Sky; Best Of British Folk; Picture Rags; The Electric Muse; Duet, with Adrian O'Reilly, 1999. *Publications:* Silver Harvest, 1998. *Membership:* PRS. *Address:* Hill Cottage, Lanwithan Rd, Lostwithiel, Cornwall PL22 0LA, England.

BERT, Eddie; b. 16 May 1922, Yonkers, New York, USA. Musician (trombone). m. Mollie Petrillo, 21 Aug. 1940, 3 d. *Education:* Manhattan School of Music, Bachelor and Master of Music. *Career:* Orchestras include: Illinois Jacquet's Big Band; Thelonius Monk; Charles Mingus; Elliot Lawrence; Lionel Hampton; Stan Kenton; Benny Goodman's Orchestra; Charlie Barnet; Woody Herman; Red Norvo; Broadway shows include: Bye Bye Birdie, 1960; How To Succeed In Business, 1961; Golden Boy, 1964; Pippin, 1972–77; Ain't Misbehavin', 1978–82; Human Comedy, 1984–85; Uptown It's Hot, 1986; Films: Jam Session With Charlie Barnet Orchestra, 1943; The French Connection; School Daze (Spike Lee), 1987; Television: Dick Cavett Show, 1968–72; Associate Professor, Essex College, 1981–82; Bridgeport University, 1984–86; Tours include: USSR, France, Denmark, 1975; Spain, 1986; Netherlands, 1987; Italy, 1987; Japan, with Walt Levinsky's Great American Swing Band, 1988–89; Five Continents with Gene Harris-Philip Morris Superband, 1989; Performances: Dick Gibson's Jazz Party, Denver, Colorado, 1979, 1981; Florida Jazz Festival, 1981, 1982; Carnegie Hall Jazz Festival, 1980–84. *Recordings include:* As Eddie Bert: Like Cool, 1955; East Coast Jazz, 1955; Encore, 1955; Musician Of the Year, 1955; Kaleidoscope, 1987; The Human Factor, Eddie Bert Sextet, 1987; Live At Birdland, Eddie Bert Quintet, 1991; Also appears on: Ellington Masterpieces, 1988; Just A-Settin' and A-Rockin', 1990; Music Of Jimmie Lunceford, 1992; Monk On Monk, 1997; This Is Living!, 1997; Complete Blue Note 50s Sessions, 1998; Star Wars and Other Galactic Funk, 1999. *Publications:* Eddie Bert Trombone Method; Eddie Bert Lead Sheet Book. *Honours:* Brass Conference Salute, Hotel Roosevelt, New York City, 1990. *Membership:* NARAS.

BERTHELSEN, Claus Gymoese; b. 28 Sept. 1958, Copenhagen, Denmark. Songwriter; Author; Vocalist. 1 d. *Education:* Bachelor of Economics; Copenhagen Boys Choir. *Career:* Founder, own group Nave; Several gigs in Denmark including: The Roskilde Festival (twice); Numerous Danish television appearances with Nave; Actor in Gangway I Tyrol. *Compositions:* Songs: Carry On; Marble Afternoon. *Recordings:* Albums: with Nave: Fish; Careless; Absolution Music. *Membership:* DJBFA. *Current Management:* Allan Graunkjaer, Record Music Denmark. *Address:* Wilkensvej 25, 2000 Frederiksberg, Denmark.

BERTRAM, Dominique; b. 8 Aug. 1954, Alger, Algeria. Musician (electric bass). m. Florence Faisan, 6 Nov. 1991, 1 s., 1 d. *Career:* Worked with singers: Michael Jonasz; Veronique Sanson; Catherine Lara; Patrick Bruel; Al Jarreau. *Recordings:* Michael Jonasz; Veronique Sanson; Dominique Bertram: Chinese Paradise, 1985; Bass Now, 1992. *Publications:* Method Up Bass, 1990; Jouer de la Basse C'est Facile, 1994. *Membership:* SACEM; Spedidam; ADAMI. *Address:* 101 rue de Mont-Cenis, 75018 Paris, France.

BERTRAM, Hans-Dieter 'Sherry'; b. 20 May 1936, Leipzig, Germany. Musician (drums, percussion). m. Dagmar, 16 Sept. 1969, 2 s. *Education:* Study of Engineering, Berlin, 1959; Berlin Conservatory, 1959–65. *Career:* Freelance Musician; Graphic Designer; Moderator for Rias Radio Station, 1957–89; Concerts and recordings, Berlin Philarmonic Orchestra, 1962; Deutsche Oper Berlin, 1962, 1967, 1972, 1993–95; Musicals and music for theatre; Studio musician for television, radio, films, jingles, records, Rias Live

Talk Show, 1969–89; CA 1000 Programs; Jazz drummer with own groups, bigbands; Percussion teacher at Leo-Borchard Music School. *Membership:* Landesmusikrat Berlin, Jazz Department. *Current Management:* Orchester Bertram GmbH. *Address:* Rudolstaedter Strasse 123, 10713 Berlin, Germany.

BERTRAND, Plastic; b. 24 Feb. 1954, Brussels, Belgium. Vocalist; Composer; Writer; Prod. m. Evelyne Van Daele, 1979, 1 s., 1 d. *Education:* Conservatoire Royal de Musique de Bruxelles (university level musical High School). *Career:* Singer, drummer, punk band: Hubble Bubble, 1975; Solo career, 1977–; 8 albums; International tours world-wide; Appears in own television shows: France (TF Jackspot); Italy (Due per tutti); Belgium (Supercool). *Recordings:* Wrote, produced: Ça Plane Pour Moi; Tout Petite La Planète; Stop Ou Encore; Sentimentale-Moi; Hula Hoop; Slave To The Beat; Plastic Hits (compilation), 1995. *Honours:* 15 Gold, 5 Platinum records world-wide; Billboard Award; Grand Prix de l'Académie Française Du Disque. *Membership:* SABAM. *Current Management:* MMD, Broodthaers Pierrette. *Address:* 38 rue Fernand Bernier, 1060 Brussels, Belgium.

BESEMANN, Robyn; b. 19 Jan. 1954, Reed City, Michigan, USA. Vocalist; Songwriter; Public Speaker; Author. m. Ivan L Besemann, 1 s., 1 d. *Career:* Gospel recording artist signed with Incubator Records for 2 years; Executive Director, co-founder of LIFE Aerobics, 1980–88; Franklin Graham Crusades; Regular tours. *Recordings:* In His Name, 1993; For His Glory, 1995. *Membership:* Gospel Music Asscn (GMA).

BEST, Matthew; b. 26 Jan. 1961, London, England. Musician (drums, keyboards); DJ; Record Prod. *Education:* West London Institute of HE. *Career:* Studio drummer, Captain Sensible, 1977–80; Formed Carcrash International, 1983–84; Played live for UK Subs and Anti-Nowhere League; Formed Urban Dogs; Pressure Point (featuring P P Arnold); Simultaneously member of Psychic TV, 1986–; Formed Greedy Beat Syndicate; Play live with techno band Yum Yum. *Recordings:* 2 albums, Urban Dogs; 12 albums, Psychic TV; 2 albums, Greedy Beat Syndicate. *Membership:* Musicians' Union. *Current Management:* Colleen Sanders, 1–7 Boundary Row, London SE1, England. *Address:* 19 Irving St, London WC2H 7AU, England.

BETTENCOURT, Nuno; b. 20 Sept. 1966, Azores, Portugal. Musician (guitar); Prod. *Career:* Member, Sinful; Guitarist, US funk/rock group Extreme, 1985–; Played Boston club circuit, 1985–88; World-wide appearances include: British tour, 1991; A Concert For Life, Tribute to Freddie Mercury, Wembley, 1992; American Dream concerts, London, 1992; Support to Bryan Adams, European tour, 1992. *Recordings:* Singles include: Get The Funk Out, 1991; More Than Words (No. 1, USA), 1991; Decadence Dance, 1991; Hole-Hearted, 1991; Song For Love, 1992; Stop The World, 1992; Albums: Extreme, 1989; Extreme II Pornograffitti, 1991; III Sides To Every Story, 1992; Very Special Christmas Vol. 2, 1992; Shaved and Dangerous, 1993; Ultimate Rock Vol. 1, 1993; There Is No God, 1994; Kiss My Ass, 1994; Honey, 1994; Waiting For The Punchline, 1995; Flesh, 1995; Schizophonic, 1997; Mourning Widows, 1999. *Honours:* Boston Music Awards: Act of Year; Outstanding Rock Single, Hole Hearted; Outstanding Pop Single; Outstanding Song/Songwriter, More Than Words; Outstanding Instrumentalist, 1992. *Current Management:* Andon Artists, 79 Fairview Farm Rd, West Redding, CT 06896, USA.

BETTIS, John; b. 24 Oct. 1946, Long Beach, California, USA. Lyricist. *Career:* Co-founder, The Carpenters; 38 songs recorded by them, 1970–; Other artists: Michael Jackson; Madonna; Whitney Houston; Diana Ross; 180m. records sold. *Compositions include:* Top of The World; Yesterday Once More; Only Yesterday; Goodbye To Love; Human Nature; Crazy For You; Slow Hand; One Moment In Time; When You Tell Me That You Love Me. *Honours:* Academy Award; Golden Globe; Emmy.

BEVAN, Alonza; b. 24 Oct. 1970, London, England. Musician (bass guitar). *Career:* Founding mem., The Objects of Desire, with Crispian Mills and Paul Winterhart, renamed The Kays; Founding mem., Kula Shaker, with Jay Darlington, 1995–99; Mem., Johnny Marr's Healers, 2000–; Numerous TV appearances and appearances at rock festivals. *Recordings:* Albums: K, 1996; Peasants, Pigs and Astronauts, 1999. Singles: Tattva, 1996; Hey Dude, 1996; Govinda, 1996; Hush, 1997; Sound Of Drums, 1998.

BEVAN, Bev(erley); b. 24 Nov. 1946, Birmingham, England. Musician (drums). *Career:* Member, groups: Carl Wayne and The Vikings; Denny Laine and The Diplomats; Danny King and The Mayfair Set; Drummer, The Move, 1966–72; Appearances include: National Jazz and Blues Festival, 1966; Support to The Rolling Stones, Paris, 1967; Art Festival Ball, Brighton, 1967; Isle of Wight Festival, 1968; Reading Festival, 1972; Drummer, Electric Light Orchestra (ELO), 1972–; Concerts include: Heartbeat '86 benefit, Birmingham, 1986; Brief spell, drummer, Black Sabbath, including Reading Festival, 1983. *Recordings:* Albums: with the Move: Move, 1968; Shazam, 1970; Looking On, 1970; Message From The Country, 1971; Great Move: The Best Of The Move, 1993; with ELO: Electric Light Orchestra, 1972; On The Third Day, 1973; Eldorado, 1974; The Night The Light Went On In Long Beach, 1974; Face The Music, 1975; Olé ELO, 1976; A New World Record, 1976; Out Of The Blue, 1977; Discovery (No. 1, UK), 1979; ELO's Greatest

Hits, 1979; Xanadu (film soundtrack), 1980; Time, 1981; Secret Messages, 1983; Balance Of Power, 1986; Greatest Hits, 1989; Afterglow, 1990; Electric Light Orchestra, 1991; Moment Of Truth, 1994; One Night Live In Australia, 1997; Live At Wembley '78, 1998; Flashback 2000; Also appears on: Twang! A Tribute, 1996; Supernatural Fairy Tails, 1996; Under Wheels Of Confusion, 1996; Singles: with the Move include: I Can Hear The Grass Grow; Flowers In The Rain; Fire Brigade; Blackberry Way (No. 1, UK); Hello Susie; Curly; Brontosaurus; California Man; with ELO: Roll Over Beethoven; Showdown; Can't Get It Out Of My Head; Strange Magic; Evil Woman; Lovin' Thing; Rockaria!; Do Ya; Telephone Line; Turn To Stone; Mr Blue Sky; Wild West Hero; Shine A Little Love; Don't Bring Me Down; Xanadu (No. 1, UK); Hold On Tight; Rock 'n' Roll Is King; Calling America; Solo: Let There Be Drums. *Honours:* Outstanding Contribution to British Music, Ivor Novello Award, 1979.

BEX, Emmanuel Jean; b. 8 June 1959, Caen, France. Musician (Hammond organ). m. Sophie Simon, 31 Aug. 1991, 1 s., 1 d. *Education:* Conservatory of Caen; Conservatory of Paris. *Career:* Member, quintet The Bex'tet, 1991; Sideman with: Babick Reinhardt; Barney Wilen; Philippe Catherine; New Group, Steel Bex, with E Bex and Steel Band, 1997; New Group, Bex Machine, E Bex Quartet, 1997; New Group, Bex, with Philip Catherine and Aldo Romano, 1998; New Group, Bex, with Glenn Ferris and Simon Goubert, 2000. *Recordings:* Bex and Jouvelet In Public, 1983; with Ray Lema: Bwana Zoulu, 1987; with Bex, Pino, Teslard: Triple Idiome, 1988; with Xavier Jouvelet: Blues Congo, 1988; with La Bande à Badauld: Vacances Au Soleil, 1988; Caravanserail, 1989; with Bertrand Renaudin: Interplay, 1990; Miscellaneous Song, 1991; with Carl Schlosser: Texas Sound, 1992; with Babick Reinhardt: Histoire Simple, 1992; with Marais, Bex, Romano: Poissons Nageurs, 1993; with Bex'tet: Enfance, 1991; Organique, 1993; Rouge Et Or, 1995; with Barney Wilen: Nitty Gritty, 1993; Steel Bex, Emmanuel Bex, 1996; Due des Lowbards, Christian Escoudé Trio, 1997; '3' with trios: Bex/Romano/ Catherine, Bex/Huchard/Barthelmy, Bex/Ceccareli/Lagrene, 1997; Mauve, 2000; Here and Now, Bex/Ferris/Goubert, 2001. *Honours:* Prix Django Reinhardt, Academy of Jazz, 1995. *Current Management:* Sophie Simon Management. *Address:* 8 Impasse Chanut, 93200 Saint Denis, France.

BEZ. See: **BERRY, Mark.**

BFC. See: **CRAIG, Carl.**

BHAMRAH, Kulwant Singh; b. 11 Feb. 1955, India. Bhangra Vocalist; Songwriter. m. Satvinder Bhamrah, 3 March 1979, 1 s., 1 d. *Education:* Civil engineer. *Career:* Singer, Bhangra Folk Panjabi band Apna Sangeet; Performed in: UK; Kenya; Tanzania; Canada; America; Singapore; India; Television appearances include: BBC; ITV; CH4; TV Asia; Star TV; Appeared on all official Asian broadcasting radio stations. *Compositions:* Writes own songs. *Recordings:* Albums include: Toor India; Mera Yaar; Chack Dey Phattay; Desi Rytham; Musicblasters; Mini Blasters; Mister Blasters; Hi-Kiddaw. *Honours:* Asian Pop Awards, Best Band, 1988; Best Songwriter, 1992; Best Live Band, 1994. *Membership:* PRS; MCPS; Musicians' Union; British Actor Equity.

BHATIA, Anjali; b. 15 Oct. 1968, Chiswick, London, England. Vocalist; Musician (guitar, drums); Songwriter. *Education:* Kingsway Princeton College, BTec, Art and Design; Goldsmiths College, degree in textiles design, Art and critical theory; Certificate in Music Technology, Islington Music Workshop; Classical guitar training, Grade 4. *Career:* Festivals: Reading, Phoenix; Radio: 3 John Peel sessions, Solo Artist, Producer and Engineer. *Recordings:* Singles: Supermodel/Superficial; Kenuweehead; f is for fame; Eat The Gems; Album: Chocolate Revenge; Sheer Witchery, singles compilation, 1999. *Membership:* PRS; Musicians' Union. *Address:* c/o Beggars Banquet/ Wiija Records, 17–19 Alma Rd, London SW18 1AA, England.

BHEAGLAOICH, Seosaimhín Ní; b. West Kerry, Gaeltacht, Ireland. Vocalist; Broadcaster. *Education:* BA (Mod) Hons Trinity College Dublin. *Career:* Presenter, television series The Mountain Lark, RTE; Broadcaster with Raidio-Na-Gaeltachta; Numerous television appearances, RTE, Ireland; Presenter, As I Roved Out, BBC Ulster. *Recordings:* Solo album: Taobh Na Gréine (Under The Sun), Gael-Linn; Sings title track: Mná Na h-Éireann, on Macalla, all-woman group's first album; Also sings on Macalla 2. *Current Management:* Gael-Linn. *Address:* Gael-Linn, 26 Cearnóg Mhuirfean, Bac 2, Ireland.

BHOSLE, Asha; b. 8 Sept. 1933, Sangli, Maharashtra, India. Vocalist; Composer. *Career:* Indian film playback singer; Daughter of actor and singer Dinanath Mangeshkar, sister of Lata Mangeshkar; Has recorded over 12,000 songs in 18 languages; First film Chunaria, 1948; First solo number in Raat Ki Rani, 1949; Sang in styles influenced by Latin American and American Big Band Jazz; Worked extensively with Kishore Kumar in the 1970s; Numerous tours and performances world-wide. *Recordings include:* Albums: soundtracks: Dus Lakh, 1967; Shikhar, 1968; Hare Rama Hare Krishna, 1972; Naina, 1973; Pran Jaye Par Vachan Na Jaye, 1974; Don, 1977; Umrao Jaan, 1981; Ijazat, 1986; Dilwale Dulhania Le Jayeng, 1995; Rangeela, 1996; Solo: Songs Of My Soul: Rare and Classic Vol. 1, Songs Of My Soul: Rare and Classic Vol. 2,

2001. *Honours:* Filmfare Award, 1967, 1968, 1971, 1972, 1973, 1974, 1977, 1996; Filmfare Special Award, Rangeela Re, 1996; Filmfare Lifetime Achievement Award, 2001; National Award, 1981, 1986; Nightingale of Asia, 1987; Lata Mangeshkar Award, Madhya Pradesh Govt, 1989; Maharashtra Govt, 1999; Screen Videocon Award, 1997; MTV Contribution to Music Award, 1997; Five Channel V Awards; Singer of the Millennium, Dubai, 2000; Kolhapuri Bhushan Award, 2000; Sangli Bhushan Award, 2000; Omega Excellence Lifetime Achievement Award, 2000; Dada Saheb Phalke Award, 2001; Dayawati Modi Award, 2001; Hon. Doctorates, University of Amravati, University of Jalgaon.

BICKERSTETH, John Dennis; b. 27 June 1954, Constantine, Cornwall, England. Musician (piano, keyboards); Vocalist; Composer; Entertainer. *Education:* Choral Scholar, Truro Cathedral; Organ, piano, John Winter and Guillaume Ormond. *Career:* Member of: Cruiser; Ian and The Muscletones; The Barneys; Ian Dunlop's Babylon Babies; Daniel Rovai and Friends; Ton and Kirschen Theatre (Potsdam); Chip Bray Show (Amsterdam Lido); MD, Back On Stage, UFA Fabrik, Berlin; MD, Stewart and Ross; Live television: Japan; Ireland; Germany; M'Toto; J B Band; Botticelli Angels. *Recordings:* Album: Ian and The Muscletones. *Membership:* Musicians' Union. *Current Management:* Wouter de Boer, Streetwise, Oosterburger voorstraat 88, 1018 MR Amsterdam, The Netherland. *Address:* Tregarth, Bissoe, Truro, Cornwall TR4 8RJ, England.

BICKERTON, Wayne; b. 11 July 1941, Rhyl, Wales. Songwriter; Music Publisher; Prod. m. Carole Da-Silva. *Career:* Lee Curtis and the All Stars; Pete Best Four; Songwriting in partnership with Tony Waddington, hits with: Bing Crosby; Jose Feliciano; The Bachelors; Tom Jones; Andy Williams; Decca Records, producer/head of DERAM, 1967–70; Polydor/Polygram, Divsional Manager, 1970–74; Odyssey Group/State Records and State Music, Founder, 1974–78; Performing Rights Society, Chairman and Acting Chief Executive, 1978–96; SESAC, Consultant, 1996; SESAC, Chairman, 1997; Reliable Source Music, Chairman and Managing Director. *Recordings:* Singles (as producer/co-writer): Sugar Baby Love, Rubettes, 1974; Juke Box Jive, Rubettes, 1974; Sugar Candy Kisses, Mac and Katie Kissos, 1975; I Can Do It, Rubettes, 1975. *Honours:* Songwriter of the Year (joint), Ivor Novello Awards, 1975; Top British Record Producer by British Phonographic Industry, 1976; Fellow of Liverpool University, 1996; Dr of Laws LL.D (Hons), 1997; Ambassador for Merseyside, 1997. *Membership:* PRS, Chairman, 1993; MCPS; BAC&S (UK); ASCAP; BMI (USA). *Current Management:* Reliable Source Music. *Address:* 6 Kenrick Pl., London W1H 3FF, England. *Website:* www.reliable-source.co.uk.

BICKNELL, Robert David; b. 7 Dec. 1957, Jersey, St Helier, Channel Islands. Singing Teacher. *Career:* Tosca, Aida, Carmen, Hello Dolly, Rocky Horror Show, Godspell, Many pantomimes; TV, Robin Hood, Lenny Henry Show, Doctor Who, Saturday Night Live; TV as Singing Coach, Big Breakfast Show, 16 months; Richard and Judy; Ozone; This Morning; Musical Director, Royal Albert Hall, Wembley Arena; Teacher: Redroofs Theatre School; Goldsmiths University of London. *Recordings:* Love Can Build a Bridge; Film, The Matchmaker. *Contributions to:* Daily Mail. *Honours:* BMus, London. *Membership:* Equity; British Voice Asscn; Incorporated Society of Musicians. *Address:* 69 Lower Flat, Acre Lane, London SW2 5TN, England.

BIDDLE, Elizabeth Rosina; b. 29 April 1952, Pontypridd, South Wales. Record Prod; Music Agent; Musician (bassoon). *Education:* Aberystwth University, BA Hons Music; Guildhall School of Music and Drama, City University, MA Music Performance Studies. *Career:* Director of Music, Comprehensive School, 1984; Bassoon tutor at Christs Hospital, Horsham, 1984–99; Founded Upbeat Management, 1986; Founded Upbeat Recordings, 1989. *Recordings:* Producer for The Temperance Seven; Terry Lightfoot; Ken Colyer; Carey Blyton. *Publications:* Writer for Musical Opinion for 3 years. *Membership:* IAMA; BPI. *Address:* 6 Carleton Ave, Wallington, Surrey SM6 9LN, England.

BIET, Remi; b. 1 Oct. 1958, Dieppe, France. Musician (saxophones, flute). m. Brigitte Tailleux, 2 d. *Education:* Ecole Normale d'Instituteurs. *Career:* Tours: USA (New Orleans, San Francisco, Chicago); Italy; Madagascar; Sicily; Germany; Television: Syria; Jordan; France; Italy. *Recordings:* ONJ: Badault; A Plus Tard, 1991; Mingus, Monk Ellington, 1992; Bouquet Final, 1993. *Membership:* UMJ. *Address:* 7 Parc de l'Andelle, 76130 Mt St Aignan, France.

BIG BOI, (Antoine Patton); b. 1 Feb. 1975, Savannah, GA, USA. Rap Artiste. *Education:* Tri-City High School, Atlanta. *Career:* Mem., Outkast, with Dre; Signed to LaFace Records; Designed Outkast Clothing line. *Recordings:* Albums: Southernplayalisticadillacmuzik, 1994; ATLiens, 1996; Aquemini, 1998; Stankonia, 2000; Dungeon Family... Even In The Darkness, 2001; Big Boi And Dre Present..., 2002. Singles: Player's Ball (No. 1, USA), 1994; Elevators (Me & You), 1996; Ms Jackson (No. 1, USA). *Honours:* Platinum disc; American Music Award, Best Hip Hop/R&B Group, 2003. *Address:* LaFace Records, A & R Dept, 1 Capital City Plaza, 3350 Peachtree Rd, Suite 1500, Atlanta, GA 30326, USA. *Website:* www.outkast.com.

BIG YOUTH, (Manley Augustus Buchanan); b. 19 April 1949, Jamaica. Reggae DJ; Record Co Owner. *Career:* Former cab driver and mechanic;

Leading reggae DJ, Kingston, 1970s; Founder, Negusa Nagast and Augustus Buchanan record labels, 1973. *Recordings:* Albums: Screaming Target, 1973; Reggae Phenomenon, 1974; Dreadlocks Dread, 1975; Natty Cultural Dread, 1976; Hit The Road Jack, 1976; Isaiah First Prophet Of Old, 1978; Everybody Skank: the Best Of Big Youth, 1980; Some Great Big Youth, 1981; The Chanting Dread Inna Fine Style, 1983; Live at Reggae Sunsplash, 1984; A Luta Continua, 1985; Manifestation, 1988; Jamming In the House Of Dread, 1991; Higher Ground, 1997; Also appears on: Escape Artist, 1981; Holy Ground, 1990; Legends Of Reggae Music, 1998. *Address:* c/o Zoe Productions, 450 Broome St, Eighth Floor, New York, NY 10013, USA.

BIKEL, Theodore; b. 2 May 1924, Vienna, Austria. Actor; Lecturer; Musician (Guitar, singer). m. Rita Bikel, 2 s. *Education:* Royal Academy of Dramatic Art. *Career:* Theatre and Film Including Fiddler On The Roof, Le Gazza Ladra. *Compositions:* My Side of The Mountain. *Recordings:* 20 Albums. *Publications:* Folk songs and Footnotes; Theo. (Autobiography). *Honours:* Hon. Doctorate, University of Hartford; Emmy Award, 1988. *Membership:* American Federation of Musicians; Actors Equity; Screen Actors Guild; AFTRA; AGMA; Asscn of Actors and Artists of America. *Current Management:* Honeyhill Productions Inc, 94 Honey Hill Rd, CT 06897, USA. *Address:* Associated Actors and Artists of America, Suite 500, 165 W 46th St, New York, NY 10036, USA.

BÍLÁ, Lucie (Hana Zanáková); b. 7 April 1966, Otvovice, Czechoslovakia. Vocalist; Actress. 1 s. *Career:* Co-owner, Theatre Ta Fantastika, Prague; Toured throughout Western Europe; Performed in charity concerts in Czech Republic; Theatre includes: Les Misérables, 1992; Dracula, 1995; Rat-Catcher, 1996; Joan of Arc, 2000; Film: King Ubu. *Recordings:* Albums: Missariel, 1993; Lucie Bílá, 1994; Binoculars, 1995; Stars As Stars, 1998. *Publications:* Nyní jiz to vim (Now I Know it Already), 1999. *Honours:* Czech Grammy Awards, 1992–96; Most Popular Singer, Czech Republic, 1994–97; Czech Musical Acad. Prize, 1997; Czech Nightingale Trophies, 1996, 1997, 1998, 1999, 2000, 2001; Thalia Prize, for Joan of Arc, 2000. *Address:* Theatre Ta Fantastika, Karlova ul. 8, 110 00 Prague 1, Czech Republic. *Telephone:* (2) 24-23-25-32.

BÍLÁ, Vera; b. 22 May 1954, Rokycany, Czechoslovakia. 1 s. *Career:* Appeared on 8pm TV News, France 2, Canal and RAI; Theatre Des Bouffes Du Nord, Paris, France, 6 days; Festivals, Jazz, Montréal, Bourges, Paleo-Nyon, Arezzo, Rennes; Womad, USA, UK, Germany, Spain, Czech Republic; Concerts include: Hollywood Bowl 1999; Cenral Park, New York 2000; Barbican Centre, London, 2001; Cinque d'Hiver, Paris, 2002. *Compositions:* E Daj Nasval'i on compilation of festivals: Transmusical Rennes, 1996; Arezzo Wave, 1997. *Recordings:* CDRom Pop, 1996; Kake Kolore, 1998; Rovana, 2001. *Publications:* Article in Liberation; Article in Les Inrockuptibles. *Honours:* Record of the Year, 1996. *Address:* c/o Jiri Smetana, Vinohradska 168, 13000 Prague, Czech Republic. *Telephone:* (2) 603179344. *Fax:* (2) 71733567. *E-mail:* jiri.smetana@volny.cz.

BILAL, (Bilal Sayeed Oliver); b. Philadelphia, Pennsylvania, USA. Vocalist. *Education:* Mannes Music Conservatory, New York City, classically-trained. *Career:* Approached by Moyo Entertainment, moved to Brooklyn and started gigging; Demo tape heard by Erykah Badu; Contributed to her Mama's Gun album; Released debut album on Interscope Records, 2001; Member of the Soulaquarians collective which includes: Talib Kweli; D'Angelo; Jill Scott; Questlove; James Poyser; Collaborations: Common; Erykah Badu; Mos Def; Guru. *Recordings:* Albums: First Born Second, 2001; Singles: Soul Sista, 2001. *Address:* c/o Interscope Records, 825 Eighth Ave, New York, USA. *Website:* www.bilal-the-man.com.

BILEZIKJIAN, John; b. 1 Feb. 1948, California, USA. Musician; Composer. m. Helen Louise Bilezikjian. *Education:* AA, Los Angeles Valley College, 1968; BA, Northridge, 1970. *Career:* Mission Impossible; I Spy; Apples Way; KPFK; KCRW; KFAC; The Postman Aways Rings Twice; Anastasia; Schindlers List; The Prince of Egypt. *Compositions:* Preludio Primo; Jemilleh; Eastern Fantasy; Ansial; Taksim Opus 10; Taksim Opus 20; The Land of Noah's Ark; I Love You Baby; Music for Film, Television and Stage. *Recordings:* America's Oud Virtuoso; the Art Of The Oud; The Neo Classical Oud; The Magic Of John Bilezikjian; Music Of the Armenian Diaspora; Dantz Fever; Armenian Connection; Moonlight Sonata; 1001 Nights; Dream Of Scheherazade; Sirocco; Tapestry Of the Dance. *Publications:* Thesis, Gail Schwartz. *Honours:* Gen Awards, 1994, 1995; Most Outstanding Musician. *Membership:* Musicians' Union.

BILK, Acker (Bernard Stanley); b. 28 Jan. 1929, Pensford, Somerset, England. Musician (clarinet); Composer; Bandleader. m. Jean, 1 s., 1 d. *Career:* Began playing clarinet in Royal Engineers, 1948; Clarinet, Ken Colyer's Band; Formed Bristol Paramount Jazz Band; Freelance artiste; Guest musician on numerous records; Collaborated with artistes incl. Van Morrison, Chris Barber, Humphrey Lyttelton, Stan Tracey, Leon Young, Norrie Paramour; Tours world-wide, now with Paramount Jazz Band; Played with Reunion Paramount Jazz Band, Isle of Bute Jazz Festival, 1995; Owner 2 publishing companies. *Recordings:* Singles include: Summer-Set; Aria; Stranger On The Shore (No. 1, USA and UK, 1961); Albums include: The One For Me; Sheer Magic; Evergreen; Chalumeau: That's My Home; Three In The

Morning (with Humphrey Lyttelton, John Barnes, Dave Green, Dave Cliff, Bobby Worth); Giants Of Jazz (with Paramount Jazz Band, Kenny Ball and his Jazzmen, Kenny Baker Don Lusher All Stars); Chris Barber and Acker Bilk, That's It Then!; Clarinet Moods With Acker Bilk, Acker Bilk with string orchestra; Acker Bilk: The Oscars; Clarinet Moods with Acker Bilk; All the Hits and More; The Christmas Album; Acker Bilk and His Paramount Jazz Band; Acker Bilk In Holland; It Looks Like A Big Time Tonight; Hits Blues and Class; Great Moments; Best Of Acker Bilk. *Honours:* M.B.E., 2001. *Current Management:* Pamela Frances Sutton. *Address:* Acker's International Jazz Agency, 53 Cambridge Mansions, Cambridge Rd, London SW11 4RX, England. *Telephone:* (20) 7978-5885. *Website:* www.ackersmusicagency.co.uk.

BILLINGTON, Scott Thomas; b. 27 Oct. 1951, Melrose, MA, USA. Record Prod; Musician (harmonica). 1 d. *Career:* Produced over 100 albums of roots-orientated music for labels including: Rounder; Columbia; Sire; Real World; Vice-Pres. of A&R, Rounder Records. *Recordings include:* Alright Again, Clarence Gatemouth Brown; Pictures and Paintings, Charlie Rich; Voodoo, The Dirty Dozen Brass Band; Turning Point, Buckwheat Zydeco; Johnny Adams, One Foot in the Blues, 1996; Beau Jocque and the Zydeco Hi-Rollers, 1996; Bill Morrissey, You'll Never Get to Heaven, 1996; Ruth Brown, R&B = Ruth Brown, 1997; Irma Thomas, The Story Of My Life, 1997; Irma Thomas, Marcia Ball and Tracy Nelson, Sing It!, 1998; Davell Crawford, The B-3 and Me, 1998; Ruth Brown, A Good Day for the Blues, 1999. *Honours:* Two Grammy Awards; Grand Prix Du Disque; Two W. C. Handy Awards; Producer of the Year, Offbeat Magazine, New Orleans, 1997; Keeping the Blues Alive Award for Producer, The Blues Foundation. *Membership:* NARAS; BMI. *Address:* 47 Forrester St, Newburyport, MA 01950, USA.

BILOUS, Edward; Composer; Conductor. *Education:* BM, Composition and Conducting, Manhattan School of Music; MM DMA, Composition, Juilliard School. *Career:* After graduation, joined Juilliard School, Music, Drama, Liberal Arts Department, Lincoln Center Institute; Co-chairman of Literature, Music Department at Juilliard; Artistic Director of Music Advancement Program; Director, Consultant of Music Education programme by Juilliard and Berkley Learning Technologies. *Compositions:* Film, television music: Sleepaway Camp; Le Bain; Tribeca; Anna Sorror; Urban Fairy Tales; The Last Romantic; Theme for Monaco Film Festival, 1993; Mixing Nia by Ethan Coen, 1998; Orchestrator, arranger for: Carnegie Hall Tribute to Pete Townshend (with Roger Daltrey, Alice Cooper, Sinead O'Connor, The Spin Doctors, Eddie Vedder); CD-ROM tour of Beauborg Museum, Pompidou Center, Paris; Juilliard Music Adventure; Educational Adventure Game; Circus!. *Honours:* Joseph Machlis Award for Excellence, Juilliard School; Best Public Service Announcement Award (Elephant Slaughter), Cannes, 1989. *Current Management:* SESAC. *Address:* 55 Music Sq. E, Nashville, TN 37203, USA.

BILY, Antonin; b. 7 May 1939, Prague, Czech Republic. Composer; Arranger; Musician (piano). m. Jitka Bila, 31 Aug. 1972, 2 s. *Education:* Conservatory of Prague and J. Jezek Conservatory. *Career:* Pianist and Composer, Traditional Jazz Studio, Prague, 1960–; Teacher and Head of Composition/Conducting Section, J. Jezek Conservatory, Prague, 1986–. *Compositions:* Metamorphoses of Time, 1986; Modus Vivendi, 1991; Fine Stagione; A Town So Strange; On the Seventh Floor. *Recordings:* CCA 20 albums with Traditional Jazz Studio, some recorded with Benny Waters, Tonny Scot, Albert Nicholas, Beryl Breyden. *Honours:* First prize, Jazz Festival Düsseldorf, 1968; First prize, International Contest of Composition for Jazz Bigband, Barga, Italy, 1989. *Membership:* Asscn of Music Artists and Scientists; Czech Music Society; Czech Jazz Society. *Address:* Severovychodni IV, č 12, 14100 Prague 4, Czech Republic.

BINDING, Philip Robert; b. 20 March 1960, Barry, South Wales. Composer; Prod; Writer; Musician (piano, synthesizer). m. Helen Garnett, 23 Nov. 1990, 1 d. *Education:* Ravensbourne Art College, 1978–80; Piano, Theory. *Career:* Sound Engineer, 1980–91; Formed Boom Productions with Simon Moore, producing music for TV, film, 1991. *Compositions:* TV themes; Incidental music includes Gladiators; International Gladiators; You Bet; Pop Quiz; What's My Line; ITV Sport; Missing; Expert Witness; Strange But True; Beadle's About; Love and Marriage; ITV Promotions; World Cup '98 theme tune; C5 News; Moment of Truth; Gladiators; Survivor; HTV News. *Membership:* Musicians' Union; BAC&S; PRS; MCPS. *Address:* Boom! Music Ltd, Tanglewood, 16 Blackwood Close, West Byfleet, Surrey KT14 6PP, England.

BINDZI, Lucien; b. Cameroon. Artist Man; Music Promoter. *Education:* Industrial Electricity Diploma. *Career:* Service Leader, Director, Kilo Brother; Rhénaly Péchiney, Alsace; Radio Host and nightclub DJ, Brittany; Founder, President, producer of shows of African music, dance and culture, Africa Music International, 1986–; F. Bindzi Mibolo Schools of Art, 1997–; Manager, group The Veterans, specialising in traditional Bikutsi music; Numerous tours throughout Africa; Frequent No. 1 hits, African charts. *Recordings:* Albums with The Veterans include: Min Sounga Mi Kabard, 1975; Me Ne Ngon Oyap, 1983; Wa Dug Ma, 1984; Au Village, 1985; Traditions, 1986; Les Veterans Presentent Ahanda, 1988; Toss Difference, 1993. *Address:* Africa Music International, 15 rue Charles Gounod, 56100 Lorient, France.

BINNS, Henry; b. 1971, London, England. Prod; Remixer. *Career:* Started as studio engineer; Began remixing with partner, Sam Hardaker, under the name Zero 7; Produced own material as Zero 7; Collaborations: Sia Furler; Sophie Barker; Mozez; Remixed: Terry Callier; Radiohead; Lenny Kravitz; Lambchop, NERD. *Recordings:* Albums: Simple Things, 2001. Singles: EP 1, 1999; EP 2, 2000; Destiny (featuring Sia and Sophie), 2001; I Have Seen (featuring Mozez), 2001; In the Waiting Line (featuring Sophie) 2001; Distractions (featuring Sia), 2002. *Honours:* Muzik Award, Best New Artist, 2001. *Membership:* PRS. *Address:* c/o Solar Management Ltd, 42–48 Charlbert St, London NW8 7BU, England. *Telephone:* (20) 7722-4175. *Fax:* (20) 7722-4072. *E-mail:* info@solarmanagment.co.uk. *Website:* www.solarmanagement.co.uk.

BIRCH, Rob, (Rob B.); b. 11 June 1961, Nottingham, England. Vocalist; Rap Artiste. *Career:* Founded Gee Street Studio and Record Label; Formed Stereo MCs; Gigs on indie dance scene including support to Happy Mondays; Live shows with extended band and extra vocalists; Numerous remixes including U2, PM Dawn, Queen Latifah, Disposable Heroes of Hiphoprisy, Monie Love, Electronic, Madonna, Frozen, Jungle Brothers. *Recordings:* Singles: Elevate My Mind, 1990; Lost In Music, 1991; Connected, 1992; Step It Up, 1993; Creation, 1993; Deep Down and Dirty, 2001; We Belong In This World Together, 2001; Albums: Supernatural, 1990; Connected, 1992; Stereo MCs, 1993; Deep Down and Dirty, 2001. *Honours:* BRIT Awards: Best British Group; Best British Album, Connected, 1994.

BIRGÉ, Jean-Jacques Gaston; b. 5 Nov. 1952, Paris, France. Composer; Musician (synthesizer); Film Dir. 1 d. *Education:* IDHEC Diploma, National Film School. *Career:* Live music on 24 silent films including: Caligari; Fall of The House of Usher; Jeanne d'Arc; The Man With The Camera; J'Accuse; Le K (with Richard Bohringer); Il Etait Une Fois La Fête Fotaine; The Extraordinary Museum, Japan; Jours de cirque, Monaco; EuroPrix, Austria; The Alphabet, CD-ROM, 1999. *Recordings:* Trop D'Adrénaline Nuit, 1977; Rideau!, 1980; A Travail Égal Salaire Égal, 1981; Carnage, 1985; L'Hallali, 1988; Qui Vive?, 1990; Kind Lieder, 1991; Urgent Meeting, 1992; Opération Blow Up, 1993; Sarajevo Suite, 1994; Carton, enhanced CD, 1997; Machiavel, enhanced CD, 1998. *Publications:* The Sniper. *Honours:* British Academy Award for TV Arts, 1994; Video Grand Prize at Locarno Festival for Sarajevo, A Street Under Siege (collective); For Alphabet: Grand Prix Möbies Interna-Visual, 2000; Prix Multimedia SACD, 2000; First Prize, CineKid, Netherlands, 2000; Giga Maus, Germany, 2000; First Prize, MMCA, Japan, 2000; For Le cielest bleu: SCAM Prize, Best Internet Site, 2001–02; Narrow Cast Award, 2002; For Flying Puppet: Prix Spécial Centre Pompidou, Flash Festival 2002. *Membership:* Un Drame Musical Instantané; Les allumés du jazz. *Address:* 60 rue René Alazard, 93170 Bagnolet, France. *E-mail:* jjbirge@wanadoo.fr. *Website:* www.hyptique.com/drame/; www.flyingpuppet.com; www.lecielestbleu.com.

BIRGE, Jodle (Birge Lonquist); b. 6 Nov. 1945, Sebbersund, Denmark. Musician (guitar). m. Inger-Lise, 1 s., 1 d. *Education:* Butcher. *Career:* Concerts incl.: Wembley Arena, London, England; Jonkobing Ice-stadium, Sweden; Tivoli Gardens, Copenhagen, Denmark; Fan Fair, Nashville, USA; Spruce Meadows, Calgery, Canada; Television shows in: Denmark, USA, Canada; First Dane to perform at Grand Ole Opry at Nashville, 1998. *Recordings:* Rigtige Venner (Best Buddies); Tre Hvide Duer, (Three White Doves); Tusinde Rode Roser (Garden Full Of Roses); 98 albums released in Denmark, sales of more than 2m. *Honours:* Silver, Gold, Platinum discs. *Current Management:* Calle Nielsen, CB and Ole B Booking Aps, Denmark. *Address:* Jordsmonnet 4, PO Box 224, 8900 Randers, Denmark.

BIRGISSON, Jön Por (Jönsi); b. Iceland. Vocalist; Musician (guitar). *Career:* Founding mem., lead singer, Icelandic band, Sigur Rös, 1994–; Signed to MCA/Universal, USA, FatCat Records, UK; Music featured in film, Vanilla Sky, 2001; North American tour, 2001; European tour, 2002. *Recordings:* Albums: Von; Agoetis Byrjun, 2000; ( ), 2002. Singles: Ny Batteri, 2000; Svefn-G-Englar, 2001; Contributed to: Angels of the Universe (soundtrack), 2001. *Honours:* Shortlist Music Prize, 2001. *Address:* c/o FatCat Records, PO Box 3400, Brighton BN1 4WG, England. *Website:* www.sigur-ros.com.

BIRKBY, Peter Richard; b. 30 Nov. 1957, England. Composer; Musician (percussion). *Education:* Leeds College of Music. *Career:* BBC Radio; Television from Pebble Mill; Tours with Shirley Bassey; Vic Damone; Gene Pitney; Dave Willetts; Jesus Christ Superstar. *Recordings:* Three Movements for Orchestra, Queen Elizabeth Hall, 1994; With own group, Legends: Special Edition, 1986. *Publications:* Over 80 pieces for Percussion (solo and ensemble); 6 for Orchestra; 20 for Jazz Orchestra. *Membership:* PRS; MCPS; Musicians' Union. *Address:* PO Box 7, South Kirkby, Pontefract, West Yorkshire WF9 3XJ, England.

BIRKETT, Chris; b. 14 April 1953, Aldershot, Hampshire, England. Record Prod; Composer; Musician (guitar); Vocalist. m. Janet Susan Hewett, 25 Jan. 1981, 1 s., 1 d. *Career:* Guitarist with: Ann Peebles; Rufus Thomas; Gene Knight; Love Affair; Singer with Omaha Sherif; Producer: Sinead O'Connor; Buffy Sainte-Marie; Talitha MacKenzie; Television, radio: Wogan; Pebble Mill; BBC News; Radio: Radio1; GLR; Capital. *Compositions include:* The

album: Men From The Sky. *Recordings:* As producer/mixer/writer: Sinead O'Connor: Nothing Compares 2U; Album: I Do Not Want; Kiss Of Life, Mandinka/Put 'Em On Me; Siedah Garrett; Copperhead Road, Steve Earle; with Five Star: Silk and Steel; Luxury Of Life; Love Letters/That Old Devil, Alison Moyet; Nothing But Flowers, Talking Heads; Movements, Osibisa; Johnny Come Lately, Pogues; Holding Up Half The Sky: Voices Of Celtic Women; Also with artists: Sting; Buffy Sainte-Marie; Laurie Freelove; Darden Smith; Cry Sisco; The Bible; Randy Remet; Hernandez; Mango Grove; Mr Big; Ice Cold In Alice; Richard Jon Smith; John Otway; Roman Holiday; Precious Wilson; John Kongos; Siobhan McCarthy; Mondino; The Soul Brothers; Talitha MacKenzie; Guo Yue and Joji Hirota. *Publications:* Articles in Billboard, Studio Engineer. *Honours:* Ampex Golden Reel Awards: Gold Star and Mango Grove; Platinum discs: Nothing Compares 2U, Sinead O'Connor. *Membership:* PRS; MCPS; Musicians' Union. *Current Management:* Einstein Brothers, Toronto, Canada.

BIRKIN, Jane; b. 14 Dec. 1946, London, England (French, b. British, citizen). Actress; Vocalist. m. John Barry, divorced, 1 d., 1 d. with Serge Gainsbourg, 1 s. with Jacques Doillon. *Career:* Theatre includes: Carving a Statue, 1964; Passion Flower Hotel, 1965; La Fausse suivante, 1985; L'Aide-Mémoire, 1993; Créatrice et Interprète de Oh! pardon tu dormais, 1999; Films include: The Knack, 1965; Blow Up, 1966; Les Chemins de Katmandou, 1969; Je t'aime moi non plus, 1976; Mort sur le Nil, 1978; Jane B par Agnès V, 1988; Noir comme le souvenir, 1995; La fille d'un soldat ne pleure jamais, 1999; The Last September, 2000; Ceci est mon corps, 2001. *Recordings include:* C'est la vie qui veut ça; La Baigneuse de Brighton; Je t'aime moi non plus; Di doo dah; Le Canari est sur le balcon; Baby Song; Si ça peut te consoler; Tu n'es pas le premier garçon; Lolita Go Home; Love for Sale; La Ballade; Ex-fan des sixties; Baby Alone in Babylone. *Honours:* Gold Leaf Award, Canada, 1968; Triomphe du cinéma, 1969, 1973; Le Métier trophy, 1970; Victoire de la musique, for best female singer, 1992; Grand Prix du disque, Acad. Charles-Cros; Chevalier des Arts et des Lettres. *Address:* VMA, 10 ave George V, 75008 Paris, France.

BIRO, Daniel Andrew; b. 29 Jan. 1963, Johannesburg, South Africa. Composer; Songwriter; Musician (piano). *Education:* 8 years, Jazz Conservatory, Monaco; 3 years Nice University, France. *Career:* As keyboard player, World tours with: The Truth, 1987; Big Bam Boo, 1989; Bandleader, songwriter with L'Orange, 1993–; Arranger, musicals by Henry Lewis include: Joan of Kent; The End of The World Show; Co-founder, Lust, multi-arts performance organization; Business venture, record label, Sargasso Records, (Experimental New Music). *Compositions:* For dance: Beauty and The Beast, 1992; Desert, 1995; For film: Lessons In How To Wear Red, 1994; Mu, 1995; For lust: Through The Mirror, 1993; The Pinocchio Tapes, 1994; Beba In White, 1995. *Recordings:* Albums: Soho Square, 1993; The Comparative Anatomy Of Angels, 1996; Elegant Enigmas, 1999. *Membership:* Musicians' Union; SACEM (France); SPNM. *Address:* PO Box 10565, London N1 8SR, England.

BIROSIK, P. J; b. 2 Sept. 1956, New York, NY, USA. Music Industry Consultant. *Education:* MA, Columbia, 1977. *Career:* Formed Musik International Corporation, 1977; Services offered include: Market planning; Media promotion; Media relations; A & R/label development; Previous clients include: Ozzy Osbourne; Black Sabbath; Van Halen; Nils Lofgren; Paul McCartney and Wings; Kiss; Uriah Heep; Blondie; David Soul; Virgin; Lol Creme and Kevin Godley; Fleetwood Mac; Rod Stewart; Stevie Nicks; Herbie Hancock; Sony Records; Guns N' Roses; Journey; Japan; David Sylvian; Amii Stewart; Studio 54; The Doobie Brothers; Rickie Lee Jones; Art of Persuasion; Max Million; Chuck E; New World Music; Earth Wave Productions; New Earth Records. *Publications:* Monthly columns in magazines and newspapers. *Honours:* Gold records, Independent Promotion: Journey: Look Into The Future; Al Wilson: Show and Tell; Billboard Magazine: Best College Station, 1977; First Place, Inland Empire Awards: Best Jazz Programming, 1977. *Membership:* Voting mem., NARAS, 1980–95; NAIRD, 1994, 1995; Judge, NAIRD Indie Awards, 1993–95; Founder, New Age Music Network; International Platform Asscn; CMC; IMA: ED; ABA. *Current Management:* Musik International. *Address:* 154 Betasso Rd, Boulder, CO 80302, USA.

BIRTLES, Gary; b. 10 June 1955, Leicester, England. Musician (saxophone); Vocalist. 2 s. *Career:* Singer, own band, The Swinging Laurels; 2 UK support tours with Culture Club; Saxophone session player for Funboy 3; Member, brass section, The Beautiful South, 1990–; Currently singer, Country/Pop band Yellowbelly; Television appearances include: Top of the Pops, with Funboy 3 and The Beautiful South. *Recordings:* Singles: with The Swinging Laurels: Peace Of Mind, 1980; Rodeo, 1982; Lonely Boy, 1983; Zoom, 1984. *Membership:* PRS. *Address:* 138 Howard Rd, Leicester LE2 1XJ, England.

BISCUIT BOY. See: HEATON, Paul David.

BISHOP, Michael Joseph; b. 14 June 1951, Santa Monica, California, USA. Recording Engineer; Record Prod. m. Wendy LaTessa, 22 Sept. 1979, 2 d. *Career:* Record producer, recording engineer, 1972–. *Recordings:* As recording engineer: Play That Funky Music, Wild Cherry, 1986; Live At Carnegie Hall, Liza Minnelli, 1987; The Sound Of Music, Cincinnati Pops Orchestra, 1988; Big Band Hit Parade, Dave Brubeck/Cab Calloway/Gerry Mulligan/Doc

Severensen, 1988; To Diz with Love, Dizzy Gillespie, 1992; The Great Fantasy Adventure Album, Cincinnati Pops Orchestra, 1995; Seven Steps to Heaven, Ray Brown Trio, 1996; Come On In This House, Junior Wells, 1996; Live at Buddy Guys, Junior Wells, 1997; Copland: Music Of America, Cincinnati Pops Orchestra, 1997; Tribute at Town Hall, Oscar Peterson, 1996; So What's New?, Dave Brubeck, 1998. *Honours:* Grammy Award. *Membership:* Audio Engineering Society; NARAS; MPGA; ASCAP; AQHA; NRHA. *Address:* Telarc International Corp, 23307 Commerce Park Rd, Cleveland, OH 44122, USA.

BISMUT, Michel; b. 20 April 1954, Tunis, Tunisia. Composer; Musician (contrebass). m. Agnes Berger, 17 Oct. 1992, 1 s., 1 d. *Education:* Engineer, Computer Science and Management; Classic Conservatoire, Avignon-France. *Career:* Jazz festivals and clubs throughout France; Also UK; Germany; Spain; Israel; Appearances, French local television and national radio. *Recordings:* Socco, 1991; UR, 1996. *Membership:* SACEM (French Composers' Society). *Current Management:* Condorcet Productions. *Address:* 21 rue Tour Gayraud, 34000 Montpellier, France.

BISSET, John; b. 3 Nov. 1960, Stockport, England. Musician (Guitar). 2 s. *Education:* Fine Art Degree, Ravensbourne College of Art. *Career:* Improviser, Composer and Arranger; Work with London Electric Guitar Orchestra; Toured England with Billy Jenkins; Appearances at Relay, live shows; Performances at 2:13 Club run with Burkhard Beins, 1994098; Brush 'n' Strings with Rhodri Davies and Marcus Heesch, improvised music with live painting; Tha Arc, English tour, 1999; Go! daily radio show for children compiled by John Bisset and presented with children; Arranger and Performer, Happy Happy; Arranger of Purcell for dance piece Vivre d'Amour; Invited Artist, Real Time Music Meeting, Hamburg, 1998; Tours with Burkhard Beins on drums; Fairplay '98 Festival. *Recordings:* Flying Fish (without wings); Funny Old World; Ralay OOO Random Play 2; Kneel Down Like A Saint Gorilla and Stop; Dervish; Holly; 13 Lumps Of Chease, with London Electric Guitar Orchestra. *Membership:* PRS. *Address:* 139 Gibson Gardens, London N16 7HH, England.

BJELLAND, Kat; b. Woodburn, Oregon, USA. Vocalist; Musician (guitar). *Career:* Member, bands with Courtney Love (Hole) and Jennifer (L7); Founder, all-girl rock group Babes In Toyland, 1987–97. *Recordings:* Albums: With Babes In Toyland: Spanking Machine, 1990; To Mother (mini album), 1991; Fontanelle, 1992; Peel Sessions, 1992; Painkiller, 1993; Nemesisters, 1995; Devil (compilation), 2000; Also appears on: Teriyaki Asthma, 1991; Fast Track To Nowhere, 1994; Spirit Of '73, 1995; Reading '95, 1995; Screwed, 1996; Honky, 1997; Songs Of The Witchblade, 1998; River Of Song, 1998. *Address:* c/o Pinnacle Entertainment Inc, 83 Riverside Dr., New York, NY 10024, USA.

BJÖRK, (Björk Gudmundsdóttir); b. 21 Nov. 1965, Reykjavík, Iceland. Vocalist; Songwriter. m. Thór Eldon, divorced, 1 s. *Career:* Solo release, aged 11; Singer, various Icelandic groups including: Exodus; Tappi Tikarras; Singer, Kukl, later The Sugarcubes, 1987–92; Solo artiste, 1992–; Recent appearances include Reading Festival, 1995; Film appearance, Dancer in the Dark, 2000. *Recordings:* Albums: with The Sugarcubes: Life's Too Good, 1988; Here Today Tomorrow Next Week, 1989; Stick Around For Joy, 1992; It's It, 1992; Solo: Björk, 1977; Debut, 1993; Post, 1995; Telegram, 1996; Homogenic, 1997; Selmasongs, 2000; Vespertine, 2001; Greatest Hits, 2002; Family Tree, 2002. Singles: with The Sugarcubes: Birthday; Solo: Venus As A Boy; Violently Happy; Human Behaviour; Big Time Sensuality; Play Dead; Army Of Me; Isobel; Blow A Fuse (It's Oh So Quiet); Possibly Maybe; I Miss You/ Cover Me; Hyperballad; Hunter; Bachelorette; All Is Full Of Love; Alarm Call; Pagan Poetry; Selmasongs, 2000; Other recordings: Gling-Go, Trio Gudmundar Ingolfssonar, 1990; Ex-El, Graham Massey, 1991; Tank Girl, 1995; Mission Impossible, 1996; Nearly God, 1996; Archive, 1997; Tibetan Freedom Concert, 1997; Not For Threes, 1998; Great Crossover Potential, 1998; Y2K Beat The Clock Version 1, 1999; Family Tree (favourite songs), 2002. *Honours:* BRIT Awards: Best International Newcomer, 1994; MTV European Music Award, Best International Female Artist, 1994, 1996, 1997; Platinum and Gold records; Palme d'Or, Cannes, for Dancer in the Dark, 2000. *Current Management:* Insane Artists Management, 7218 Beverly Blvd, Los Angeles, CA 90036, USA. *Address:* c/o One Little Indian Records, 250 York Rd, London SW11 3SJ, England.

BJÖRKENHEIM, Raoul Melvin; b. 11 Feb. 1956, Los Angeles, California, USA. Musician (guitar). m. Päivi Björkenheim (Määttä), 1 s. *Education:* Helsinki Conservatory, 1977–78; Berklee College of Music, Boston, USA, 1978–81. *Career:* Founder member, own jazz groups Arbuusi and Roommushklahn, 1980–83; Member, Edward Vesala's Sound and Fury, 1984–86; with Sielun Veljet, 1989; Member, Krakatau, 1987–; Tours throughout Finland with above. *Compositions:* For big band: Other Places; Some; Primal Mind; For symphony orchestra: Whales; Ballando; For electric guitar orchestra: Apocalypso. *Recordings:* with Edward Vesala: Bad Luck Good Luck; Kullervo; Lumi; with Krakatau: Ritual, 1988; Alive, 1990; Volition, 1992; Matinale, 1994. *Honours:* Yrjö Award, Finnish Jazz Federation, 1984; Emma Prize, Best Jazz Record, Volition, 1993. *Current Management:* Gunnar Pfabe. *Address:* Heinsbergstrasse 30, 50674 Cologne, Germany.

BJORNS, Siggi; b. 26 June 1955, Iceland. Musician (guitar, harmonica). *Career:* Former fisherman, 14 years; Professional musician, 1988–; Performed in clubs and halls in more than 20 countries; Television apperances in Denmark and Iceland; Radio broadcasts in Denmark, Iceland, Norway and New Zealand. *Compositions:* Bubbinn; Kotturinn; Beitningartremmi; One Gentle Touch. *Recordings:* Albums: Blues On Both Sides, 1993; Live At Sorens, 1993; Bisinn a Trinidad, 1994; Smoke 'n' Perfume, 1995; Road, 1998. *Membership:* Dansk Musikerforbund (Danish Musicians' Union); KODA; GRAMEX; DJBIA. *Current Management:* Tusund Tjalir, Iceland. *Address:* Brammersgade 2A-3, 8000 Århus C, Denmark.

BLACHMAN, Thomas; b. 2 April 1963, Copenhagen, Denmark. Musician (drums); Composer; Bandleader; Prod; Label Man. *Education:* Jazz Composition, Berklee College of Music, Boston, USA. *Career:* Co-founder, jazz quintet Page One; Tours of Europe, USA, 1986–90; Played drums for Lee Konitz, Joe Henderson; Solo artist, 1991–. *Recordings:* Albums: with Page One: Beating Bop Live, 1988; Live At Ronnie Scott's, 1989; Solo albums: Love Boat, 1991; Blachman Meets Al and Remee, 1994; Blachman Introduces Standard Jazz and Rap Vol. 1, Billie Koppel, 1995; Caroline Henderson, 1995. *Honours:* 3 Grammy Awards, 1991, 1995. *Current Management:* Mega Records. *Address:* Capella India Kaj 1, Frihavnen, 2100 Copenhagen O, Denmark.

BLACK, Barry; b. 1 July 1950, Newcastle upon Tyne, England. Musician (drums, percussion). m. Barbara Ann, 1 s., 1 d. *Education:* Personal tutors, aged 10–16; Further studies for LTCL, LGSM. *Career:* Member, John Miles Band, 1973–83; Tours: Europe, USA, Canada; Support tours with: Elton John; Fleetwood Mac; Aerosmith; Jethro Tull; Tour with Beckett (later renamed Back Street Crawler); 2 albums, with Splinter; Television appearances: Top of the Pops; Magpie; Blue Peter; Mike Mansfield television specials; Tonite Show. *Compositions:* Do It Anyway, John Miles; Madness Money and Music, Sheena Easton; Take My Love and Run, The Hollies. *Recordings:* All John Miles albums and singles, up to early 1980s; Also: Barry Black, 1995; Tragic Animal Stories, 1997. *Membership:* PRS; Equity; Musicians' Union.

BLACK, Charlie; b. Cheverly, Maryland, USA. Country Music Songwriter. *Career:* Staff Writer, Terrace Music, Nashville, 1970–; Songwriter, Warner Chappell Music, 1977–88; Own company, Five-Bar-B Songs, 1989–; Songs recorded by: Roy Orbison; Anne Murray; Paul Anka; Dan Seals; Kenny Rogers; K T Oslin; Eddy Raven; Bobby Bare; Bellamy Brothers; Charlie Rich. *Compositions:* No. 1 Country Hit Singles: Anne Murray: Shadows In The Moonlight; A Little Good News; Blessed Are The Believers; Reba McEntire: You Lie; K T Oslin: Come Next Monday; T G Shepard: Slow Burn; Strong Heart; Bellamy Brothers: Do You Love As Good As You Look; Tommy Overstreet: I Don't Know You Anymore; Earl Thomas Conley: Honor Bound; Gary Morris: 100% Chance of Rain; Also appears on: At Last, Dirk Hamilton, 1977; Simple Little Words, Cristy Lane, 1979; Twist of Fate, Cee Cee Chapman, 1988; More I Learn, Ronna Reeves, 1992. *Honours:* Country Music Writer of Year, SESAC, 1979; Country Music Writer of Year, ASCAP 1983, 1984; Elected to NSAI Songwriters Hall of Fame, 1991. *Membership:* ASCAP Southern Advisory Board. *Current Management:* Poker Productions. *Address:* 1618 16th Ave S, Nashville, TN 37212, USA.

BLACK, Clint; b. 4 Feb. 1962, USA. Vocalist; Songwriter; Prod. m. Lisa Hartman Black, 20 Oct. 1991. *Career:* Film: Maverick; Television: Wings episode; Half-time performance, Superbowl XXXVIII; Performed National Memorial Day Celebration, Washington DC, 1994. *Recordings:* Killing Time, 1989; Put Yourself In My Shoes, 1990; The Hard Way, 1992; No Time To Kill, 1993; One Emotion, 1994; Nothin' But the Taillights, 1997; D'Lectrified, 1999. *Honours:* CMA's Horizon Award, 1989; CMA's Top Male Vocalist, 1990; AMA's Favourite New Country Artist, 1990; Music City News: Star of Tomorrow, Album of the Year, 1990; ACM's Album of the Year, Single of the Year; Best New Vocalist; Best Male Vocalist, 1990. *Current Management:* Mark Hartley. *Address:* c/o Fitzgerald/Hartley, 50 W Main St, Ventura, CA 93001, USA.

BLACK, Don, (Donald Blackstone); b. 21 June, 1938. Lyricist; Comedian. m. Shirley Berg, 7 Dec. 1958, 2 s. *Career:* Writer, NME, 1955; Lyric writer, 1960–; Worked with: Charles Aznavour, John Barry, Elmer Bernstein, Ron Grainer, Marvin Hamlisch, Maurice Jarre, Quincy Jones, Michel Legrand, Andrew Lloyd Webber, Henry Mancini, Charles Strouse, Jule Styne. *Compositions:* Songs: April Fool; Walk Away; Ben (with Walter Scharf), 1972; Musicals: Billy, 1974; Tell Me On Sunday, 1980; The Little Prince and the Aviator, 1982; Song and Dance, 1982; Aspects of Love, 1989; Sunset Boulevard, 1993; The Goodbye Girl, 1997; Bombay Dreams, 2001; Romeo and Juliet, 2002; Dracula, 2002; Title songs to films: Thunderball, 1965; Born Free, 1966; To Sir With Love, 1967; True Grit, 1969; Diamonds Are Forever, 1971; The Man With The Golden Gun, 1974; Tomorrow Never Dies; The World Is Not Enough. *Honours:* Acad. Award, for Born Free, 1966; Golden Globe; Five Ivor Novello Awards; Two Tony Awards, Sunset Boulevard, 1995; O.B.E., 1999; Platinum, Gold, Silver discs. *Membership:* Chair., BAC&S, 1986–. *Address:* c/o John Cohen, Clintons Solicitors, 55 Drury Lane, London WC2B 5SQ, England.

BLACK, Frances; b. 25 June 1960, Dublin, Ireland. Vocalist. m. Brian Allen, 1 s., 1 d. *Education:* Rathmines College. *Career:* Member of Arcady, Woman's Heart Tour; Toured with Kieran Goss; Solo career; Tours in USA, Australia, England, Ireland. *Recordings:* Albums with The Black Family: The Black Family, 1986; Time For Touching Home, 1988; What A Time, 1996; With Arcady: After the Ball, 1991; With Kieran Goss: Black and Goss, 1994, 1995; Solo: Talk to Me, 1994; The Sky Road, 1995; Smile on Your Face, 1996; Don't Get Me Wrong, 1998; Also appears on: Woman's Heart, 1994; Celtic Twilight Vol. 3, 1996; Loving Time, 1997; Songs Of The Irish Whistle Vol. 2, 1999; Holding Up Half The Sky, 1999; Singles/EPs: Fear Is The Enemy Of Love and Children, 1994; Stranger On The Shore, 1996; Love Me Please, 1997. *Honours:* Most Popular Irish Entertainer; National Entertainment Awards, 1995; Best Female, 1995, 1996, IRMA. *Current Management:* Pat Egan/Brian Allen. *Address:* c/o Merchants Court, 24 Merchants Quay, Dublin, Ireland.

BLACK, Frank, (Black Francis, Charles Michael Kitteridge Thompson IV); b. 1965, Long Beach, CA, USA. Vocalist; Songwriter; Musician (guitar). *Education:* Studied Anthropology, University of Massachusetts. *Career:* Formed The Pixies; Early support slots with Throwing Muses; Numerous tours and festival dates; Some television appearances; Support on U2's Zoo TV tour; Band disbanded, 1993; Some solo releases and live gigs, with band The Catholics. *Recordings:* with The Pixies: Singles: Gigantic; Monkey Gone To Heaven; Here Comes Your Man; Velouria; Dig For Fire; Planet Of Sound; Alec Eiffel; Head On; Debaser; Albums: Come On Pilgrim, 1987; Surfer Rosa, 1988; Doolittle, 1989; Bossanova, 1990; Trompe Le Monde, 1991; Death To The Pixies (boxed set), 1997; Pixies At The BBC (sessions), 1998; Complete B-Sides, 2001; solo: Singles include: Hang On To Your Ego, 1993; Headache, 1994; Albums: Frank Black, 1993; Teenager Of The Year, 1994; The Cult Of Ray, 1996; Frank Black and The Catholics, 1998; Pistolero, 1999; Dog In The Sand, 2001; Black Letter Days (with The Catholics), 2002; Devil's Workshop (with The Catholics), 2002.

BLACK, Mary; b. 23 May 1955, Dublin, Ireland. Vocalist. *Career:* Folk singer, Dublin folk clubs; Member, De Dannan; Also solo career; Appearance, television series Bringing It All Back Home, with Emmylou Harris, Dolores Keane, Nashville; Also with Van Morrison on Celtic Heartbeat; Tours, USA, UK, Japan. *Recordings:* Mary Black, 1983; Collected, 1984; Without The Fanfare, 1985; The Black Family, with the Black Family, 1986; By The Time It Gets Dark, 1987; Time For Touching Home (with the Black Family), 1989; No Frontiers, 1989; Babes In The Wood (No. 1, Ireland), 1991; The Best Of Mary Black, 1991; The Collection, 1992; The Holy Ground, 1993; Circus, 1995; Looking Back, 1995; One and Only, 1997; Shine, 1997; Song For Ireland, 1999; Songs Of The Irish Whislte, 1999; Speaking With The Angel, 2000. *Honours:* Best Female Artist, Irish Rock Music Awards Poll, 1987, 1988. *Current Management:* Dara Management, Dublin.

BLACK JAZZ CHRONICLES. See: **BEEDLE, Ashley.**

BLACK SHELLS. See: **TOMIIE, Satoshi.**

BLACKBURN, Paul; b. 1974, Southport, England. Musician (guitar, bass, percussion, omnichord). *Career:* Founding mem., Gomez, 1996–; Numerous concerts, festival, radio and television appearances. *Recordings:* Albums: Bring It On, 1998; Liquid Skin, 1999; Abandoned Shopping Trolley Hotline, 2000; In Our Gun, 2002. Singles: 78 Stone Wobble, 1998; Whippin' Piccadilly, 1998; Get Myself Arrested (EP), 1998; Bring It On, 1999; Rhythm And Blues Alibi, 1999; We Haven't Turned Around (on soundtrack to film, American Beauty), 1999; Machismo (EP), 2000. *Honours:* Mercury Music Prize, 1998. *Address:* c/o Hut Records, Kensal House, 553–579 Harrow Rd, London W10 4RH, England. *Website:* www.gomez.co.uk.

BLACKMORE, Ritchie (Richard Hugh); b. 14 April 1945, Weston-Super-Mare, Avon, England. Rock Musician (guitar); Composer. *Education:* Thompson School of Music, 1 year. *Career:* Musician, toured with: Mike Dee and The Jaywalkers, 1961–62; Screaming Lord Sutch and His Savages, 1962; Gene Vincent; Jerry Lee Lewis; The Outlaws; The Musketeers; The Dominators; The Wild Boys, 1964; Neil Christian's Crusaders; The Roman Empire; Mandrake Root, 1967; Founder member, UK rock group Deep Purple, 1968–75; Founder, Ritchie Blackmore's Rainbow, 1975–84; Re-formed Deep Purple, 1984–. *Recordings:* Albums: with Deep Purple: Shades Of Deep Purple, 1968; The Book Of Taliesyn, 1969; Deep Purple, 1969; Concerto For Group and Orchestra, 1970; Deep Purple In Rock, 1970; Fireball, 1971; Machine Head, 1972; Made In Japan, 1972; Purple Passages, 1972; Who Do You Think We Are?, 1973; Burn, 1974; Stormbringer, 1974; 24 Carat Purple, 1975; Come Taste The Band, 1975; Made In Europe, 1976; Last Concert In Japan, 1977; Perfect Strangers, 1985; House Of Blue Light, 1987; Nobody's Perfect, 1988; Slaves and Masters, 1990; Stranger In Us All, 1995; with Rainbow: Ritchie Blackmore's Rainbow, 1975; Rainbow Rising, 1976; Live On Stage, 1977; Long Live Rock and Roll, 1978; Live In Germany, 1976, 90; Down To Earth, 1979; Difficult To Cure, 1981; Straight Between The Eyes, 1982; Bent Out Of Shape, 1983; Finyl Vinyl, 1986; Blackmore's Night: Shadow Of the Moon, 1996; Under a Violet Moon, 1999; Fires At Midnight, 2001. *Honours:* Numerous magazine poll wins, as Best Band; Best Guitarist; Best Album; Best Song. *Membership:* ASCAP; BMI; PRS. *Current Management:*

Carole Stevens at Minstrel Hall Music. *Address:* PO Box 735, Nesconset, NY 11767, USA.

BLACKSTOCK, Narvel Wayne; b. 31 Aug. 1956, Fort Worth, Texas, USA. Artist Man; Entertainment Co Exec. m. Reba McEntire, 3 June 1989, 4 c. (3 from previous marriage). *Career:* Personal Manager: President, Starstruck Entertainment, Nashville, 1988–; Clients include: Reba McEntire. *Membership:* NARAS; Country Music Asscn; Academy of Country Music. *Address:* Starstruck Entertainment, 40 Music Sq. W, Nashville, TN 37203, USA.

BLACKWELL, Chris; b. 22 June 1937, London, England. Record Co Exec. *Career:* Founder, chairman, Island Records, 1962–97; Issued masters from Jamaican producers; Signings to Island include: Jimmy Cliff; Bob Marley; Millie Small (My Boy Lollipop, sold 6m. copies); Spencer Davis Group; Steve Winwood; John Martyn; Robert Palmer; Nick Drake; Cat Stevens; Free; Mott The Hoople; Spooky Tooth; Fairport Convention; B-52's; Toots and The Maytals. *Address:* c/o Island Records, 400 Lafayette St, New York, NY 10003, USA.

BLACKWOOD, Sarah; b. Halifax, England. Vocalist. *Career:* Singer, Dubstar, 1994–2000; British tour, 1996. *Recordings:* Albums: Disgraceful, 1995; Goodbye, 1997; Make It Better, 2000; Singles: Stars, 1995; Anywhere, 1995; Not So Manic Now, 1996; Elevator Song, 1996; Cathedral Park, 1997; I Will Be Your Girlfriend, 1997; No More Talk, 1997; Anxious, 1998; I (Friday Night), 2000. *Address:* c/o Food Records, 43 Brook Green, London W6 7EF, England.

BLADES, Jack; Vocalist; Musician (bass guitar). *Career:* Member, Night Ranger, 1981–88; Concerts include: supports to Santana; Judas Priest; Doobie Brothers; Member, Damn Yankees, 1989–; US tour with Bad Company, 1990; Member, side project Shaw Blades (with Tommy Shaw), 1995. *Recordings:* Albums: with Night Ranger: Dawn Patrol, 1982; Midnight Madness, 1983; Seven Wishes, 1985; Big Life, 1987; Man In Motion, 1988; Live In Japan, 1990; Neverland, 1997; Seven, 1998; with Damn Yankees: Damn Yankees, 1991; Don't Tread, 1992; with Shaw Blades: Hallucination, 1995; with Tommy Shaw: 7 Deadly Zens, 1998; Singles: with Night Ranger: Sister Christian; Sentimental Street; with Damn Yankees: Coming Of Age; High Enough; Come Again; Where You Goin' Now; Silence Is Broken, from film Nowhere To Run, 1993. *Honours:* Motor City Music Award, Outstanding National Rock Pop Single, 1992. *Current Management:* Madhouse Management, PO Box 15108, Ann Arbor, MI 48106, USA.

BLADES, Rubén; b. 16 July 1948, Panama City, Panama. Vocalist; Bandleader; Composer; Actor. *Education:* University of Panama; Harvard Law School, USA. *Career:* Vocalist, groups Conjunto Latino, Los Salvjes del Ritmo, 1966–69; Lawyer, National Bank of Panama, 1969–74; Joined Ray Barretto's band, 1974; Renamed Guarare, 1975; Member, Fania All-Stars, 1976–80; Songwriter, numerous Latin artistes, 1970s; Subject of television documentary, The Return of Rubén Blades, 1986; Leader, group Seis del Solar, 1984–; Film appearances include: Crossover Dreams, 1985; Critical Condition, 1987; The Milagro Beanfield War, 1988; The Lemon Sisters; The Two Jakes; Dead Man Out, 1989. *Recordings:* Albums include: with Pete Rodríguez, De Panama a Nuevo York, 1970; with Ray Barretto: Barretto, 1975; Barretto Live: Tomorrow, 1976; with Fania All-Stars: Tribute To Tito Rodríguez, 1976; with Larry Harlow: La Raza Latina, 1977; with Louie Ramírez: Louie Ramírez y Sus Amigos, 1978; with Willie Colón: The Good, The Bad, The Ugly, 1975; Metiendo Mano!, 1977; Siembra, 1978; Maestra Vida (parts 1 and 2), 1980; Canciones del Solar de los Aburridos, 1981; The Last Fight, 1982; Solo: El Que La Hace La Paga, 1983; Buscando America, 1984; Mucho Mejor, 1984; Crossover Dreams (film soundtrack), 1985; Escenas, 1985; Agua de Luna, 1987; Doble Filo, 1987; Nothing But The Truth, 1988; Antecedente, 1988; Rubén Blades y Son del Solar... Live!, 1990; Caminando, 1991. *Honours:* Gold discs; Grammy Award, Antecedente, 1988; ACE Award, Dead Man Out, 1989; Composer of the Year, Latin NY magazine, 1976. *Current Management:* Morra, Brezner, Steinberg and Tenenbaum, 345 N Maple Dr., Suite 200, Beverly Hills, CA 90210, USA.

BLAKE, Adam James Wyndham; b. 30 July 1960, Lincoln, England. Vocalist; Songwriter; Musician (guitar, bass); Teacher. m. Catherine Ramage, 31 Aug. 1991, 1 d. *Career:* Played with many groups including: The Cannibals; Treatment; Mumbo-Jumbo; The Hipshakers; Raw, 1976–; Bassist, Natacha Atlas; Guitarist, Errol Linton. *Recordings:* Restless; Put You Behind Me; Waiting For Love; Even If You Hadn't; Friends. *Publications:* Numerous articles published in periodicals. *Membership:* PRS; Musicians' Union; PAMRA. *Address:* 77 Linden Gardens, London W2 4EU, England.

BLAKE, Ian; b. 9 Dec. 1955, London, England. Composer; Prod; Musician (Woodwinds, Keyboards, Bass). *Education:* Degree Course, London University; Member of London Boy Singers, 1968–71; Piano, organ, clarinet and lute lessons. *Career:* Tours and recording with Pyewackett, 1980–88; with Mike Jackson, 1988–93; Backing Musician for June Tabor, Michelle Shocked, Eric Bogle; Musician, National Theatre, London, 1987; Tours with Mellstock Band, 1988; Writer and Musician, The Crusades, Barossa Festival, 1992.

Compositions: Persephone, 1995; Spirit of Place, 1996; The Gathering of the Animals, 1998. *Recordings:* Producer and Musician, Eric Bogles' Small Miracles, 1997; Writer, Producer, Musician, over 20 children's albums; Contributor, albums by Martin Simpson, Andrew Cronshaw, June Tabor. *Publications:* The Really Easy Cello Book, 1989. *Honours:* Gold Disc, 1995. *Membership:* APRA; Musicians' Union of Australia. *Current Management:* Serpentine Productions, PO Box 1750, Canberra, ACT 2601, Australia. *Address:* 4 Rudall St, Latham, ACT 2615, Australia.

BLAKE, Karl Antony; b. 5 Dec. 1956, Reading, Berkshire, England. Musician; Filmaker; Lyricist. *Education:* BA Hons, Fine Art and Mixed Media, 1991–94. *Career:* Formed Lemon Kittens, 1978; Joined as duo by Danielle Dax, 1979–82; Formed Shock Headed Peters, 1982–87; Formed British Racing Green, 1987; Formed Evil Twin with David Mellor; Re-formed Shock Headed Peters, 1990–; Currently member of all 3 groups; Small roles in films, Chariots of Fire, Caravaggio, Voice of Silence. *Recordings:* with Lemon Kittens: 2 EPs; 2 albums: We Buy A Hammer For Daddy; The Big Dentist; with Shock Headed Peters: 3 EPs; 5 albums: Not Born Beautiful; Fear Engine; Several Headed Enemy; Fear Engine II; Tendercide, 1996; 2 EPs as member, Alternative TV with Mark Perry, 1985–86; Solo: 1 EP, 1 album as The Underneath, 1986–87; 9 short films, poetry in compilation; 2 solo archive albums as Karl Blake. *Address:* BM Swarf, London WC1N 3XX, England.

BLAKE, Norman; b. 20 Oct. 1965, Bellshill, Scotland. Musician (guitar); Vocalist. 1 d. *Career:* Member, The Boy Hairdressers; Founder member, Teenage Fanclub, 1989–. *Recordings:* Albums: A Catholic Education, 1990; Bandwagonesque, 1991; Thirteen, 1993; Grand Prix, 1995; Mobile Safari, 1995; Sharks Patrol These Waters, 1995; Life Goes On, 1995; Reading '95 Special, 1995; Songs From Northern Britain, 1997; Howdy, 2000. *Address:* c/o Creation Records, 109 Regents Park Rd, London NW1 8UR, England.

BLANCHARD, Pierre; b. 24 May 1956, Saint-Quentin, France. Musician (violin); Composer; Arranger. 1 s. *Education:* Conservatoire de St Quentin; Université Musicale International de Paris; 6 months study in New York. *Career:* Lived in Paris, 1977–; Professor CIM, 1979–81; Violinist, Martial Solal's Big Band, 1981–86; Played throughout Europe; Played with Stéphane Grappelli, Antibes and Paris Festivals, 1988; Formed Gulf String, 1989; Director of Jazz class, CNR D'Aubervilliers: La Courneuve, 1992–; Formed Quintette A Cordes de Pierre Blanchard, 1994; Other festivals include: Halle That Jazz, 1993; Presences, 1994; Banlieues Bleues, 1995; Also worked with: Bernard Lubat, Jacques Thollot, Rene Urtreger. *Recordings:* Solo albums: Each One Teach One, 1985; Music For String Quartet, Jazz Trio, Violin and Lee Konitz, 1987; Gulf String, 1993; 2 albums with Martial Solal Big Band; with Raphael Fays: Voyages, 1988; Gipsy Touch, 1991; with Pierre Michelot: Bass and Bosses, 1989; Other albums with René Urtreger, Eric Le Lann, Post Image, Jazzogene Big Band; Also appears on: Compact Jazz, 1992; Turtle's Dream, 1994; Voyage Aux Amériques, 1995; Ca Va Ca Va, 1996; Lagoa, 1998. *Honours:* Stéphane Grappelli donated the violin of M Warlop, 1984. *Current Management:* Claudette de San Isidoro. *Address:* 93 bis rue de Montreux, 75011 Paris, France.

BLANCHARD, Terence; b. 13 March 1962, New Orleans, LA, USA. Musician. *Education:* Studied jazz with Ellis Marsalis, classical trumpet with George Jensen, 1978; Graduated, New Orleans Center of Creative Arts; Attended, Rutgers University, 1980. *Career:* Toured with Lionel Hampton, 1980; Joined Art Blakey and the Jazz Messengers, world-wide tours, 1982; Formed Harrison-Blanchard, 1990; Worked on Spike Lee's film Malcolm X, made first screen appearance; Tours throughout USA, Canada, Japan and Europe, 1991; Artistic Dir, Thelonius Monk Institute of Jazz Performance, University of Southern California. *Compositions:* Film scores: Caveman's Valentine, 2001; Original Sin, 2001; Glitter, 2001; Jim Brown—All American, 2002; People I Know, 2002; Barbershop, 2002; The 25th Hour, 2002; Dark Blue, 2003. *Recordings include:* with Art Blakey: Dr Jeckyle, 1992; New Year's Eve At Sweet Basil, 1992; Art Blakey's Jazz Messengers: Live In Leverkeusen, 1995; as Harrison-Blanchard: New York Second Line, 1985; Discernment, 1986; Crystal Stair, 1987; Black Pearl, 1988; Solo: Mo' Better Blues, 1990; Terence Blanchard, 1991; Simply Stated, 1992; Malcolm X Jazz Suite, 1993; Malcolm X (film score), 1993; Billie Holliday Songbook, 1994; Romantic Defiance, 1995; Clockers (film score), 1995; The Heart Speaks, 1995; Summer Of Sam (film score), 1999; Jazz In Film, 1999; Let's Get Lost, 2001; Wandering Moon, 2001. *Contributions to:* Articles in professional journals and magazines. *Honours:* Grand Prix du Disque, 1984. *Current Management:* Burgess Management, 3225 Prytania St, New Orleans, LA 70115, USA.

BLAND, Bill; b. 6 Feb. 1962, Wirral, Merseyside, England. Musician (African and Latin percussion). *Education:* Anthropology, School of Oriental and African Studies, London; Studied Cuban percussion with Oscar Valdes and African percussion with Emmanuel Tagoe. *Career:* Radio and TV appearances with Ebo Iye, with Peter Badejo, 1991; Roberto Plas's Latin Ensemble, 1992; Orquesta la Clave featuring Jesus Alemany, 1993; London Afro Blok, Commonwealth Games, Canada, 1994; Palenke, 1996; Yoruba Jazz People, 1998; Kevin Haynes Grupo Elegoua, 1999. *Recordings:* Alex Wilson, Afro Saxon. *Address:* 33 Macbeth House, Ivy St, Hoxton, London N1 5JG, England.

BLAND, Bobby (Robert); b. 27 Jan. 1930, Rosemark, Tennessee, USA. Vocalist. *Career:* Former valet for B. B. King, 1949; Member, The Beale Streeters; Gospel and blues vocalist; Early recordings with Ike Turner, 1952; Performances on US R&B circuit, 1957–; Ann Arbor Jazz and Blues Festival, 1973; First British tour, 1982; Regular tours with B. B. King, 1990s. *Recordings:* Hits include: Farther Up The Road, 1957; I'll Take Care Of You, 1960; I Pity The Fool, 1961; Don't Cry No More, 1961; Turn On Your Love Light, 1962; Stormy Monday Blues, 1962; Call Me / That's The Way Love Is, 1963; Sometimes You Gotta Cry A Little, 1963; Ain't Nothing You Can Do, 1964; This Time I'm Gone For Good, 1974; Albums include: Here's The Man, 1962; Call On Me/That's The Way Love Is, 1963; Ain't Nothing You Can Do, 1964; His California Album, 1974; Dreamer, 1974; Together For The First Time... Live (with B. B. King), 1974; Get On Down With Bobby Bland, 1975; Together Again... Live (with B. B. King), 1976; Reflections In Blue, 1977; Come Fly With Me, 1978; I Feel Good, I Feel Fine, 1979; You've Got Me Loving You, 1984; Members Only, 1985; After All, 1986; Blues You Can Use, 1988; Midnight Run, 1989. *Honours:* Inducted into Rock and Roll Hall of Fame, 1992. *Address:* It's Happening Now Presents, PO Box 8073, Pittsburg, CA 94565, USA.

BLANDAMER, Oscar Stewart Van; b. 8 May 1947, Weymouth, England. Songwriter; Musician (saxophone, guitar). m. Dianne Harrington, 16 July 1966, 1 s., 1 d. *Education:* 1 year saxophone lessons. *Career:* Member: Orphesians, 1963–66; Jimmy James and the Vagabonds, 1969–72; Curly, 1973–75; Flirtations, Johnny Wakelin, 1976–78; Q-Tips, 1978–81; Adam Ant, 1981–83; Funk Bros, 1984–. *Compositions:* Darling, recorded by over 30 artists (3 No. 1 singles, US country chart); Songs covered by: Kim Wilde; Q-Tips; Paul Young; Tom Jones; Cliff Richard; Phil Everly. *Recordings:* with: Status Quo, 1973; Stiff Little Fingers, 1979; Wishbone Ash, 1979; Ray Minnhinnett's Bluesbusters, 1990; Video with Paul McCartney, 1984. *Honours:* 3 ASCAP Awards. *Membership:* Musicians' Union; BAC&S; PRS; MCPS. *Current Management:* Hyperfunk Productions.

BLANT, David; b. 21 Nov. 1949, Burton-On-Trent, England. Musician (bass guitar, accordion); Teacher. m. Jennifer Gow, 27 March 1971, 1 s., 1 d. *Education:* Dartington College of Arts. *Career:* Various bands from age 13; Member of: Yeah Jazz (Indie band); R Cajun and the Zydeco brothers, 1985–; Number of appearances, BBC Radio 2. *Recordings:* with R Cajun: Pig Sticking; In Arcadia; Out Of The Swamp; Don't Leave The Floor; No Known Cure; That Cajun Thing. *Membership:* Musicians' Union; PRS. *Current Management:* Swamp Management. *Address:* PO Box 94, Derby DE22 1XA, England.

BLATNY, Pavel; b. 14 Sept. 1931, Brno, Czech Republic. m. Danuse Spirková, 19 June 1982, 1 s., 1 d. *Education:* Musicology, University of Brno, 1958; Berklee School of Music, USA, 1968. *Career:* Composer; Conductor; Pianist; Chief, Music Department, Czech Television, to 1992; Professor, Janácek's Academy, Brno, to 1990. *Compositions include:* Concerto for Jazz Orchestra, 1962–64; Roll-call; Willow; Christmas Eve; Noonday Witch; Bells; Twelfth Night, based on Shakespeare's play, 1975; Two Movements for Brasses, 1982; Signals for Jazz Orchestra, 1985; Prologue for mixed choir and jazz orchestra, 1984; Per organo e big band, 1983; Ring a Ring o' Roses, for solo piano, 1984; Confrontation, 1995; Play Jazz, Rock, New Music, 1997; Meditation, 1999. *Honours:* Prize of Leos Jánácek, 1984; Antiteatro D'Argento for the whole work, Nepal, Italy, 1988. *Membership:* President, Club of Moravian Composers. *Address:* 62400 Brno, Absolonova 35, Czech Republic.

BLATT, Melanie; b. 25 March 1975. Vocalist. *Career:* Founding member, female vocal group All Saints, 1993–2000; Film, Honest, released 2000; Collaboration, Artful Dodger. *Recordings:* Singles: Silver Shadow; I Know Where It's At, 1997; Never Ever (No. 1, UK), 1997; Under The Bridge (No. 1, UK), 1998; Lady Marmalade (No. 1, UK), 1998; Bootie Call (No. 1, UK), 1998; War Of Nerves, 1998; Pure Shores (No. 1, UK), 2000; Black Coffee (No. 1, UK), 2000; All Hooked Up, 2001; Albums: All Saints, 1997; Band Alert, 1998; Saints and Sinners, 2000; All Hits (compilation), 2001. *Honours:* BRIT Award, Best Single, Never Ever, 1998. *Current Management:* John Benson.

BLAZEVIĆ, Kresimir; b. 27 Jan. 1958, Slavonski Brod, Croatia. Prof. of Literature; Musician (guitar); Composer; Lyricist; Singer; Concert Hall Programme Man. m. Matea Banoza, 18 May 1991, 1 d. *Education:* University, Ethnology and Literature; Primary musical school, violin, guitar. *Career:* Mem., The Animatori, –1999; Over 500 concerts; Over 100 television and radio appearances; Solo artiste, 1999–; Composer, music for documentary films. *Compositions:* 60 published works, music and lyrics; Girls in City Clothes, 1996. *Recordings:* Eight albums with The Animatori incl.: The Dream Book; Reanimatori, 1995; K. B. & The Footballers, 1998; There's Plenty Of Time, 1999; with Branko Bogunović: B. B. Twang. Hit singles include: Summer's Back To Town; I'll Stay Always Young; Summer Rendevous; Angels Asking Us To Take Away Their Wings. *Publications:* Since I'm Lying the Whole Day in the Shadow. *Contributions to:* Newspapers and magazines, about music, literature, theology, ethnology. *Membership:* HGU (Croatian Musical Union); Croatian Composers Society; Sec., Matrix Croatica, Zagreb. *Address:* 10000 Zagreb, Buzanova 14, Croatia.

BLEY, Carla Borg; b. 11 May 1938, Oakland, California, USA. Composer; Arranger. m. (1) Paul Bley, 27 Jan. 1959, divorced 1967; (2) Michael Mantler, 29 Sept. 1967, divorced 1992, 1 d. *Career:* Freelance jazz composer, 1956–; Pianist, Jazz Composers Orchestra, New York, 1964–; European concert tours, Jazz Realities, 1965–66; Founder, WATT, 1973–; Toured Europe with Jack Bruce Band, 1975; Leader, Carla Bley Band, touring USA, Europe, 1977–. *Compositions:* Composed and recorded: A Genuine Tong Funeral (with Charlie Haden), 1967; Liberation Music Orchestra, 1969; Escalator Over The Hill (opera), 1970–71; Tropic Appetites, 1973; Composer, Chamber Orchestra 3/4, 1974–75; Film score, Mortelle Randonée, 1983. *Recordings:* Dinner Music, 1976; with The Carla Bley Band: European tour, 1977; Musique Mecanique, with Nick Mason, 1979; Fictitious Sports, 1980; Social Studies, 1980; Carla Bley Live!, 1981; Heavy Heart, 1984; I Hate To Sing, 1985; Night Glo, 1985; Sextet, 1987; Duets, 1988; Fleur Carnivore, 1989; The Very Big Carla Bley Band, 1991; Go Together, 1993; Big Band Theory, 1993; Songs With Legs (with Andy Sheppard), 1995; Goes to Church, 1996; Fancy Chamber Music, 1998; Are We There Yet?, 1999; 4x4, 2000; Looking For America, 2003. *Honours:* Guggenheim Fellowship, 1972; Oscar du Disque de Jazz, 1973; Composition grants, 1970s; New York Jazz Award, Arranger, 1979; Deutscher Schallplattenpreis, 1985; Downbeat Poll, Best Composer, 1980s; Jazz Times, Composer, 1990; Hi Fi Vision, Jazz Musician of Year, 1990; Prix Jazz Moderne, 1991; Downbeat Poll, Composer/Arranger, 1990–94. *Membership:* NARAS. *Current Management:* Watt Works Inc. *Address:* c/o Watt Works Inc, PO Box 67, Willow, NY 12494, USA. *Website:* www.wattxtrawatt.com.

BLEY, Paul; b. 10 Nov. 1932, Montréal, Québec, Canada. Musician (piano, synthesizer); Bandleader; Composer; Record Prod. m. (1) Carla Bley, (2) Annette Peacock. *Career:* Leader, own trio and quintet (latter included Ornette Coleman, Don Cherry, Charlie Haden, Billy Higgins); Also played with: Pat Metheny; Jaco Pastorius; Charlie Parker; Jackie McLean; Donald Byrd; Art Blakey; Charles Mingus; Bill Evans; Don Ellis; Jimmy Giuffre; John Gilmore; Formed own label, IAI, 1970s. *Recordings:* Albums include: Introducing Paul Bley, 1954; Paul Bley, 1955; Solemn Meditation, 1958; Footloose, 1963; Barrage, 1965; Closer, 1966; Touching, 1966; Ramblin', 1967; Blood, 1967; Paul Bley In Haarlem, 1967; Mr Joy, 1968; The Fabulous Paul Bley Quintet, 1969; Paul Bley Trio In Canada, 1969; Ballads, 1970; The Paul Bley Synthesizer Show, 1971; Improvise, 1971; Dual Unity, 1972; Paul Bley and Scorpio, 1973; Open To Love, 1973; Paul Bley/NHOP, 1974; Alone Again, 1975; Copenhagen and Haarlem, 1975; Turning Point, 1975; Virtuosi, 1975; Bley, Metheney, Pastorius, Ditmus, 1975; Japan Suite, 1976; Axis, 1978; Sonor, 1983; Tango Palace, 1983; Tears, 1984; Questions, 1985; Hot, 1986; My Standard, 1986; Fragments, 1986; The Paul Bley Quartet, 1988; Solo, 1988; Solo Piano, 1988; Floater Syndrome, 1989; The Nearness Of You, 1990; Bebop, 1990; Rejoicing, 1990; Blues For Red, 1991; Live At Sweet Basil, 1991; Indian Summer, 1991; Right Time Right Place, 1991; Memoirs, 1990; Changing Hands, 1991; Lyrics, 1991; In The Evenings Out There, 1991; Plays Carla Bley, 1991; If We May, 1993; Fabulous Paul Bley Quintet, 1994; Modern Chant, 1994; Speachless, 1995; Chaos, 1998; Not Two, Not One, 1999; Also recorded with Annette Peacock; Paul Motian; Jesper Lundgaard; Chet Baker; Jimmy Giuffre; Gary Peacock; As producer: albums for artists including Sun Ra; Marion Brown; Sam Rivers.

BLICHFELDT, Anders; b. 9 Nov. 1963, Copenhagen, Denmark. Vocalist; Musician (guitar). m. Marina, 20 Aug. 1988, 2 s. *Education:* Piano Tuner. *Career:* Lead singer, Big Fat Snake; Approximately 300 concerts, 1991–94 including Roskilde Festival, 1991, 1994; Midfyn Festival, 1991, 1992, 1994; Skanderborg Festival, 1991, 1992; Several national television and radio shows, 1991–94. *Recordings:* Big Fat Snake, 1991; Born Lucky, 1992; Beautiful Thing, 1994; Midnight Mission, 1995. *Membership:* DJBFA; Dansk Artist Forbund. *Current Management:* Århus Musikkontor. *Address:* Mindegade 10, 8000, Århus C, Denmark.

BLIGE, Mary J; b. 11 Jan. 1971, New York, USA. Vocalist. *Career:* Solo recording artiste; Numerous tours, appearances. *Recordings:* Albums: What's The 411?, 1992; What's The 411? (Remix), 1993; My Life, 1994; Mary Jane, 1995; Share My World, 1997; The Tour, 1998; Mary, 1999; No More Drama, 2001; Ballads, 2001. Singles: What's The 411, 1992; Sweet Thing, 1993; My Love, 1994; You Bring Me Joy, 1995; All Night Long, 1995; Not Gon' Cry, 1996; Love Is All We Need, 1997; Everything, 1997; Seven Days, 1999; All That I Can Say, 1999; As (with George Michael), 1999; No More Drama, 2002; Also appears on: Father's Day, 1990; Changes, 1992; Close To You, 1992; Panther, 1995; Show, 1995; MTV Party To Go, 1995; Waiting To Exhale, 1995; Nutty Professor, 1996; Case, 1996; Ironman, 1996; Love and Consequences, 1998; Miseducation Of Lauryn Hill, 1998; Nu Nation Project, 1998. *Honours:* American Music Award, Best Female Hip Hop/R&B Artist, 2003. *Address:* c/o MCA Records, 2220 Colorado Ave, Santa Monica, CA 90404, USA. *Website:* www.mjblige.com.

BLIZARD, H. Ralph; b. 5 Dec. 1918, Kingsport, Tennessee, USA. Musician (fiddle). 2 s. *Career:* Smithsonian Institute Festival; Kingsport Symphony Orchestra; American Festival of Fiddle Tunes; Swannond Gathering, Asheville, North Carolina; Augusta Heritage Festival; Hudson River Clearwater Revival Festival, Croton, New York; Festival, American Fiddle Tunes, Port Townsend, Washington; Tampa Center, Performing Arts, Tampa,

Florida; Good Morning America, ABC; PBS Appearances; Charles Karult, Sunday Morning, CBS; Library of Congress. *Recordings:* Blizard Train; Ralph Blizard Fiddles; Blue Highway; Green Grass Cloggers: Through The Ears; Southern Ramble; Old Time Music On The Air; American Fogies. *Honours:* Mount Airy Fiddle Championship, 3 years. *Membership:* Appointed by Governor to Tennessee Arts Committee, 1987–92. *Address:* 1084 State Route #37, Blountville, TN 37617, USA.

BLOMSTROM, John Paul, Sr; b. 19 April 1949, Miami, Oklahoma, USA. Artist Agent; Musician (drums). m. Cheryl Ann Byrd, 28 Dec. 1978, 1 s., 2 d. *Career:* Artist manager for The Tonyans (family group), 1970s; Vince Vance and the Valiants; Lic and Stiff, 1980; First promoter to bring Pat Benatar to Houston; Also promoter of artists including Muddy Waters; Hall and Oates; Prince; The Police; Agent for artists including Madam X; Appeared in film, Robocop II. *Publications:* Writer for Music News. *Current Management:* American Bands Management. *Address:* PO Box 840607, Houston, TX 77284–0607, USA. *Telephone:* (713) 785-3700.

BLONDIN, Ludivine (Josette Edmee); b. 10 Oct. 1958, Lyon, France. Actress; Vocalist; Model. Partner, John Phil Wayne, 1 d. *Career:* Singer, musical act/films: L'Art de la Fugue with Bernard Haller and Maurice Biraud; William Tell with Will Lyman; Drole D'Endroit Pour Une Rencontre, with Gerard Depardieu; La Petite Maison Dans La Prairie, with Michael Landon; Interview of John Phil Wayne for France 3 TV and TLM TV; Introduction portrait of John Phil Wayne as video. *Recordings:* Fairy Tales For Fauve; Recording for French radio and television as animator: Les Jeux de 20 Heures; Les Jeux Du Dimanche; La Soupiere a Des Oreilles; Maurice Bejart à Arles. *Membership:* AZ Production, France. *Current Management:* Longsongs Music Ltd, 21–23 Greenwich Market, London SE10 9HZ, England.

BLONDY, Alpha; b. 1953, Dimbokoro, Côte d'Ivoire. Reggae Vocalist; Bandleader. *Education:* Columbia University, USA, 1980–81. *Career:* Leading West African reggae vocalist and bandleader, 1980s. *Recordings:* Albums: Cocody Rock, 1984; Jah Glory, 1985; Jerusalem, 1986; Revolution, 1987; Apartheid Is Nazism, 1987; The Prophets, 1989; SOS Tribal War, 1991; Masada, 1992; Live Au Zenith, 1992; Dieu, 1994; Yitzhak Rabin, 1998; Merci, 2002. *Current Management:* MA Chetata Management, 105 W 28th St, Third Floor, New York, NY 10001, USA.

BLOOM, Eric; b. 1 Dec. 1944. Vocalist; Musician (guitar, keyboards). *Career:* Singer, guitarist, keyboard player, US rock group Blue Öyster Cult, 1971–; Regular US tours including support to Alice Cooper, 1972; World tour, 1978; Monsters of Rock Festival, Castle Donington, 1981; British tour, 1989. *Recordings:* Albums: Blue Öyster Cult, 1972; Tyranny and Mutation, 1973; Secret Treaties, 1974; Live On Your Feet Or On Your Knees, 1975; Agents Of Fortune, 1976; Spectres, 1978; Some Enchanted Evening, 1978; Mirrors, 1979; Cultosaurus Erectus, 1980; Fire Of Unknown Origin, 1981; ETL (Extra-Terrestrial Live), 1982; The Revolution By Night, 1983; Club Ninja, 1986; Imaginos, 1988; Career Of Evil: The Metal Years, 1990; Bad Channels, 1992; Live 1976, 1994; Cult Classic, 1994; Summerdaze, 1997; Singles include: (Don't Fear) The Reaper, 1976; In Thee, 1979; Burnin' For You, 1981; Film soundtrack, Bad Channels, 1992. *Honours:* Platinum disc, (Don't Fear) The Reaper. *Current Management:* Steve Schenck, 415 Madison Ave, New York, NY 10017, USA.

BLUE, Barry; b. 4 Dec. 1950, London, England. Songwriter; Prod; Vocalist. m. Lynda Blue, 20 May 1974, 1 s., 2 d. *Career:* First television appearance: Stubby Kaye's Silver Star Show, age 11; First major concert: Split Festival, Yugoslavia singing his own composition, 1969; First radio appearance: Bassist, Spice (later became Uriah Heep), John Peel Show; First major tour: Solo artist singer with Queen and Status Quo, 1973; Staff Producer, CBS Records, 1976–; Producer, composer numerous hit records for artists including: Bananarama; Five Star; Heatwave; Diana Ross; Céline Dion; Opened Aosis Recording Studios, where albums produced for artists include: Sinead O'Connor, Bronski Beat, Depeche Mode, Fine Young Cannibals, 1984–88; Owner of Escape Records. *Recordings include:* Dancin' On A Saturday Night (sold 1m.); Sugar Me, Lynsey de Paul; Boogie Nights, Heatwave; Always and Forever, Heatwave; Over 30 UK Chart singles as singer, producer and writer. *Honours:* Carl Allan Award, 1973; Producer of the Year, 1977; 6 BMI, ASCAP Awards. *Membership:* Councillor, BAC&S; PRS. *Current Management:* The Escape Artist Company. *Address:* PO Box 31, Bushey, Hertfordshire WD2 2PT, England.

BLUE, Sam, (Simon Blewitt); b. 21 Aug. 1959, Newcastle upon Tyne, England. Vocalist; Songwriter; Actor. 1 s., 1 d. *Education:* Technical College. *Career:* Backing artists: Lulu; Michael Ball; 1991–93; Giant Killers, 1995; Sang on many television, radio, cinema commercials; Toured Britain, Europe, former USSR, with Ya-Ya, 1987–89; Ultravox, 1993–95; Also television, radio with these groups; Appeared (acting) in Spender, television series; Co-wrote Hollywood Men theme tune for Carlton TV, 1996. *Recordings:* Emerson single: Something Special, 1984; Lead singer, Ya-Ya album, 1988; Ultravox: Ingenuity, 1994–95; Live, 1995; Eternal 12 single: So Good, 1994; GTS: Tracks From The Dust Shelf, 1995; GTS, Time Stood Still, 1996; Chorus work on Evita, film and soundtrack; Solo single: For The Life You Don't Yet Know,

1997; Backing Vocalist on Montserrat Caballe album, Friends for Life, 1997. *Membership:* PRS; MCPS. *Current Management:* Christine Poundford, Hobsons Singers. *Address:* 62 Chiswick High Rd, London W4 1SY, England.

BLUMBERG, Stuart Lester; b. 27 Oct. 1947, Detroit, Michigan, USA. Musician (trumpet). m. Dorothy Ebeling, 1 s. *Education:* AA, Los Angeles Valley College, 1969; California State University, Northridge. *Career:* Toured with Don Ellis; Louis Bellson; First trumpet, numerous Broadway performances; Music Contractor, Shubert Theatre, Los Angeles, 1991; Recorded numerous television and radio commercials, film soundtracks. *Recordings:* with various artists including: Frank Sinatra; Barbra Streisand; Lou Rawls; Lionel Richie; The Osmonds; Joe Cocker; Dionne Warwick; The Rolling Stones; Barry Manilow; Beach Boys; The Commodores; The Pointer Sisters; Steppenwolf; Jermaine Jackson; Carly Simon; Talking Heads; Air Supply; Blood, Sweat and Tears. *Membership:* NARAS.

BLUMENTHAL, Laurent Pierre; b. 21 Dec. 1964, Paris, France. Musician (saxophone). m. Marianne, 11 Aug. 1992, 2 d. *Education:* Diploma, CNR Lyons (saxophone, harmony), 1983; 2 months at Eastman School of Music, Rochester, New York, 1986. *Career:* Concerts and tours: with La Velle and Orj: Tour of USSR, 1991; with Tourmaline: Tour of Québec, 1991; Festival de Montréal, 1992; with L'Orchestre National de Jazz: Germany; Italy; Portugal; France, 1993–94; with Dimitrinaiditch / Laurent Blumenthal Duo: Tour of Germany, 1995; Played all French jazz festivals, 1990–; Performed with own quintet, septet, and artistes including: Johnny Griffin; Ernie Watts; Michel Colombier; ORJ; Henri Texier; Daniel Humair; Mario Stanchev; L'Orchestre National de Jazz, with Denis Badault (ONJ Badault); Also performed with Tito Puente; Nicole Croisille; Louis Sclavis. *Recordings:* Il Était Une Fois La Révolution, ORJ, 1988; Shakok, Shakok, 1989; Johnny Griffin et l'ORJ, ORJ, 1990; Sozopol, Mario Stanchev, 1990; Parcours, Aira Works, 1990; Kaleidodscope, Mario Stanchev, 1992; Monk Mingus Ellington, ONJ Badault, 1993; Bouquet Final, ONJ Badault, 1994. *Honours:* First prize, National Saxophone Competition, 1987; First Prize, Festival de Vienne, with Shakok, 1988; First prize, Festival de Sorgues, 1993; Second prize (soloist), Third prize (group), with Dimitri Naiditch, Concours de la Défense, 1993. *Current Management:* Dominique Camard. *Address:* 12 rue Justin Godart, 69004 Lyon, France.

BLUNSTONE, Colin; b. 24 June 1945, Hatfield, Hertfordshire, England. Vocalist. *Career:* Singer, the Zombies, 1963–67; Solo career, 1969–; Re-formed the Zombies, 1991; Appearances include: with The Shangri-Las, The Nashville Teens, USA, 1964; with Dusty Springfield, The Searchers, UK, 1965; Support to Herman's Hermits, US Caravan of Stars tour, 1965; Film appearance, Bunny Lake Is Missing, 1966. *Recordings:* Albums: with the Zombies: The Zombies, 1965; The Zombies: Begin Here, 1965; Odyssey and Oracle, 1967; New World, 1991; Solo: One Year, 1971; Ennismore, 1973; Journey, 1974; Planes, 1976; Never Even Thought, 1978; Late Nights In Soho, 1979; I Don't Believe In Miracles, 1982; Sings His Greatest Hits, 1991; Echo Bridge, 1995; Live At The BBC, 1996; Light Inside, 1998; Other albums include: Walk On Water, Mae McKenna, 1977; Tarot Suite, Mike Batt, 1979; Exiled, Exiled, 1980; Keats, Keats, 1984; Greatest Show On Earth, Martin Darville and Friends, 2000; Singles: with the Zombies: She's Not There (No. 2, USA), 1964; Tell Her No, 1965; with the Alan Parsons Project: Pyramid, 1978; Eye Of The Sky, 1982; Ammonia Avenue, 1984; Vulture Culture, 1985; Definitive Collection, 1997. *Current Management:* Rhino Management, Third Floor, Compass House, 30–36 East St, Bromley Kent BR1 1QU, England. *Website:* www.colinblunstone.co.uk.

BLUNT, Martin; b. May 1964. Musician (bass guitar). *Career:* Fmr mem., Makin' Time; Founding mem., The Charlatans, 1990–; Signed to Beggars Banquet Records, later Universal Records; Numerous tours, festivals, television and radio appearances. *Recordings:* Albums: Some Friendly (No. 1, UK), 1990; Between 10th And 11th, 1992; Up To Our Hips, 1995; The Charlatans (No. 1, UK), 1995; Tellin' Stories (No. 1, UK), 1997; Melting Pot: The Best Of The Charlatans, 1998; Us And Us Only, 1999; Songs From The Other Side, 2000; Wonderland, 2001; Live It Like You Love It, 2002. Singles: Indian Rope, 1990; The Only One I Know, 1990; Then, 1990; Me In Time, 1991; Over Rising, 1991; Weirdo, 1992; Tremelo Song, 1992; Can't Get Out Of Bed, 1994; Autograph, 1994; I Never Want An Easy Life If Me And He Were Ever To Get There, 1994; Jesus Hairdo, 1994; Crashin' In, 1994; Just Lookin', 1995; Just When You're Thinkin' Things Over, 1995; One To Another, 1996; North Country Boy, 1997; How High, 1997; Tellin' Stories, 1997; My Beautiful Friend, 1999; Forever, 1999; Impossible, 2000; Love Is The Key, 2001; A Man Needs To Be Told, 2001; You're So Pretty—We're So Pretty, 2002. *Honours:* Gold, Silver and Platinum discs. *Address:* The Charlatans, PO Box 134, Sandbach, Cheshire CW11 1YS, England. *E-mail:* cat@thecharlatans.net. *Website:* www.thecharlatans.net.

BOBEK, Pavel; b. 16 Sept. 1937, Prague, Czech Republic. Vocalist; Musician. m. Marta Pokorna, 10 Oct. 1978, 1 s., 1 d. *Education:* Architecture, Prague Institute of Technology, 1961; Private Lessons, Piano. *Career:* Member, Olympic Rock and Roll Group, 1963–66; Actor, Singer, The Prague Semafor Theatre, 1967–90; Solo Singer, Founder of Band, 1982–. *Recordings:* First Singles, 1963; Six albums, 1975–93; Seven compilation albums; The Best

Of Pavel Bobek Vols I and II. *Honours:* Platinum Record, 1993. *Membership:* OSA; SAI. *Current Management:* Venkow Records, Ovenecka 6, 170 00 Prague 7, Czech Republic. *Address:* ul 8 Listopadu 45, 169 00 Prague 6, Czech Republic.

BOBINEC, Ivica; b. 16 Sept. 1937, Zagreb, Croatia. Radio Station Exec. m. Visnja Kolina, 1 July 1961, 1 s., 1 d. *Education:* Graduated ethnologist, University of Zagreb; Musical Academy, Zagreb. *Career:* Singer, bass guitar player, Combo 5 (orchestra), 1973–86; International concert tours across Europe, 1966–95; Split Festival, Zagreb Festival of Popular Music, 1971–77; Radio and television appearances 1958–95, including Eurovision Song Contest, Luxembourg, 1984; Bergen, Norway, 1986; General Manager, Cibona Radio Station. *Compositions:* Cibona (music and lyrics), anthem of Croatian National Basketball Team, 1990. *Recordings:* Solo: Pijem Da Zaboravim Nju, 1973. *Membership:* Glazbena Unija (Music Society of Croatia). *Current Management:* Agency Estrada Zagreb, Croatia.

BOCK, Jerry (Jerrold Lewis); b. 23 Nov. 1928, New Haven, Connecticut, USA. Composer. m. Patricia Faggen, 1950, 1 s., 1 d. *Education:* University of Wisconsin. *Career:* Composer, scores for high school and college musicals; Author for television, 1951–54; Member, New York board Educiradio broadcasts, 1961–. *Compositions:* Film score: Wonders of Manhattan, 1956; Music for show Mr Wonderful, 1956; with Sheldon Harnick: The Body Beautiful, 1958; Fiorello, 1959; Tenderloin, 1960; She Loves Me, 1963; Fiddler On The Roof, 1964; The Apple Tree, 1966; The Rothschilds, 1970; Jerome Robbins Broadway, 1989. *Honours:* Songwriters Hall of Fame, 1990; Theatre Hall of Fame, 1990. *Membership:* Broadcast Music Inc.

BOCKER, Ingemar; b. 6 May 1934, Stockholm, Sweden. Jazz Musician; Transcriber. 1 d. *Education:* Musicology Degree, Stockholm University. *Career:* Toured Sweden Extensively; Toured American Forces Clubs in West Germany, 1953–55, 1960–62; Toured with Rock and Rhythms Blues Groups; Joined Swedish Folk Rockband Kebnekaise 1972; Archivist, Swedish Centre for Folk Music Research, 1987–; Tour of Sweden with Stan Hasselgard Story, 1998. *Compositions:* Comanche Spring; Ballad of Blackberries and Melon; Galliarde Moderne; Wet Paint. *Recordings:* Kebnekaise II and III; Electric Mountain. *Publications:* Lars Gullin 8 Compositions Transcribed by I Bocker, 1998; Several articles in professional journals and magazines. *Membership:* Swedish Jazz Musicians Organization; Lars Gullin Society; SKAP; STIM-NCB. *Address:* Tenstavagen 94, 16365 Spanga, Sweden.

BOCOUM, Afel; b. 1955, Niafunke, Mali. Musician (guitar); Vocalist; Composer. *Career:* Played with Ensemble Niafunké; Formed band, Alkibar, 1999; Supported Ensemble Niafunké on international tour, 2000. *Recordings:* Albums: with Ensemble Niafunké: Radio Mali; The Source, 1991; Solo: Alkibar, 1999. Contribution to: Mali Music, 2002. *Address:* c/o World Circuit Records, 138 Kingsland Rd, London E2 8DY, England.

BODDIE, Don O'Mar; b. 22 Nov. 1944, St Louis, Missouri, USA. m. Paula R Boddie, 27 July 1991, 4 s., 2 d. *Education:* BS, Management, 1988; BS, Business Administration, 1988; BA, Music Arts, St Louis Musical Institute, 1968; BA, Music Management, JR College District, St Louis, Missouri, 1974; MBS, Music Production, 1975. *Career:* Super Sonic Attractions; Stars Spectacular; Salem Spirit Festival; Vocal Music Director, Martin Luther King Middle School, 1992–93; Clay CEC, 1997–98. *Compositions:* Can't Stop the Fire, 1982; Passing Fancy. *Recordings:* Two Piece Love; True Love; Dreams; Lets Be Lovers; Satisfaction; Legend Of O'Mar the Grand Master; Lover Pt 1 and 2; As I Go, 1997; Clay School Song, 1997; Clay Code Of Honor, 1997. *Publications:* Lets Be Lovers, 1982, released, 1988; Can't Stop the Fire, 1992; Dreams, 1997. *Membership:* Friends of Black Music Society; MAM of Missouri.

BODILSEN, Jesper Vejbaek; b. 5 Jan. 1970, Haslev, Denmark. Bass Player (double bass/electric bass). *Education:* Rhythmical Diploma Degree, Royal Academy of Music, Århus; Played Cornet in Balleskolens Brass Band, 1980–89; Lessons in Big Band Arranging, Line Writing. *Career:* Pori Jazz, Beijing Jazz Festival, Scandinavian Jazz Quartet, 1994; Concerts with Ed Thigpen, Duke Jordan, Janusz Carmello, Bent Jaedig, 1994; James Moody, 1996; Fred Wesley, 1996; Horace Parlan, 1996; Ulf Wakenius, 1997; Tours with Beibom/Kroner Big Band, 1996–97; Katrine Madsen, 1998; Stig Rossen, 1997; Member, Ed Thigpen Trio, 1997; Jazzpar Concerts with Erling Kroner, Dino Saluzzi, 1998. *Compositions:* Dedication, 1994. *Recordings:* Contributor, albums: Come Rain Or Come Shine, Hanne Romer, 1994; New Deal, Scandinavian Jazz Quartet, 1994; A Night in Bilbao, Scandinavian Jazz Quartet, 1996; Giving It Away, Helle Hansen, 1995; Red Letter Days, Harvest Moon, 1995; I'm Old Fashioned Katrine Madsen, 1996; Dream Dancing, Katrine Madsen, 1997. *Address:* Godthaabsvej 36 B, 2 TV, 2000 Frederiksberg, Denmark.

BODINAT, Henri de; b. 15 July 1948, Paris, France. Co Pres. m. Clèmence de Lasteyrie, 12 Sept. 1989, 2 s., 2 d. *Education:* Masters, Social Sciences; PhD, Economy, Harvard Business School. *Career:* Chief Executive Officer, Sony Music, France, 1985–94; Managing Director, Club Mediterrannée, 1994–94; Executive, Sony Software Europe, 1994; President, Musisoft SA,

1997–. *Publications:* Influence in the Multinational Corporation, 1977; The State: A Parenthesis in History?, 1996. *Address:* Musisoft, 85 rue Fondary, 75015 Paris, France.

BOGGUSS, Suzy Kay; b. 30 Dec. 1956, Aledo, Illinois, USA. Country vocalist. *Education:* Art degree. *Career:* Country singer, 1986–. *Recordings:* Songs include: I Want To Be A Cowboy's Sweetheart; Night Rider's Lament; I Don't Want To Set The World On Fire; Somewhere Between, 1989; Moment Of Truth, 1990; Aces, 1991; Voices In The Wind, 1992; Sorry Seems To Be The Hardest Word, 1994; Give Me Some Wheels, 1996; No Way Out, 1996; Somebody To Love, 1998; Albums: Somewhere Between, 1988; Moment Of Truth, 1990; Aces, 1991; Voices In The Wind, 1992; Somethin' Up My Sleeve, 1993; Simpatico, 1994; Nobody Love, Nobody Gets Hurt, 1998; It's A Perfect Day, 1999; Greatest Hits Vols 1 and 2 (compilations), 2001; Other recordings: Happy Trails, with Michael Martin Murphey, 1990; Hopelessly Yours, with Lee Greenwood. *Honours:* CMA Horizon Award, Most Promising Artist, 1992. *Address:* Left Bank Organization, 1018 17th Ave S, Suite 10, Nashville, TN 37212, USA.

BOGLE, Eric; b. 23 Sept. 1944, Peebles, Scotland. Songwriter; Musician (guitar). m. Carmel, 29 Jan. 1972. *Career:* Accountant until 1980; Full-time musician, 1980–; Various tours, television appearances. *Recordings:* The Band Played Waltzing Matilda; The Green Fields Of France/No Man's Land; Albums include: Scraps Of Paper, 1981; When The Wind Blows, 1985; Singing In The Spirit Home, 1987; Something Of Value, 1988; Song Book, 1990; Voices In The Wilderness, 1991; I Wrote This Song, 1995; Hard Hard Times, 1997; Emigrant and The Exile, 1997; Small Miracles, 1998. *Publications:* Five song books, 12 CDs, 1980–. *Honours:* United Nations Peace Medal, 1986; APRA Gold Award, 1986; Order of Australia Medal, 1987. *Membership:* Full mem., APRA. *Address:* PO Box 529, Magill, Adelaide, South Australia 5072, Australia.

BOGLIUNI, Mario; b. 24 May 1935, Svetvincenat-Pula, Croatia. Composer; Musician (piano); Arranger. m. Maria Adler, 24 Aug. 1973, 1 s. *Education:* Conservatorium of Music Art. *Career:* Concerts and tours, Croatia; European countries; Australia, 1969; USA, 1970; Russia, 1974; Editor, several series on pop music; Compositions for theatre and film. *Compositions:* Songs: Running Out of World; Why Do I Love You; Sailors Cha Cha Cha; Three Friends; Serenade. *Honours:* 25 Croatian and international festival awards. *Membership:* Music Asscn of Croatia (DHS). *Current Management:* Mr Finderle Vigor, Agency Adriatic, Opatijska 45, 51000 Rijeka, Croatia. *Address:* Sestinski Dol 121 A, 41000 Zagreb, Croatia.

BOIC, Drazen; b. 11 April 1931, Zagreb, Croatia. Musician (piano); Composer; Arranger. m. Anita, 23 Sept. 1967, 1 s., 1 d. *Education:* Dr of Medicine; Secondary Music School, Zagreb. *Career:* 45 years, love for jazz, playing jazz, commercial music; Leader, own trio, quartet, quintet, sextet; Croatian Zagreb Radio Orchestra, 1954–58; Playing for US Air Forces, 1957–64; Tours in Russia, 1967–80; Pianist, ballet school, Zagreb, 1980–90; Piano player, Hotel Esplanade, Zagreb, 1980–. *Compositions include:* Tiho i Mirno; Ljetni Ritam; Anita Fedor; Petra. *Membership:* Croatian Musicians' Union, Zagreb. *Address:* Cvijica 17, Zagreb, Croatia.

BOIC, Fedor; b. 17 Oct. 1968, Zagreb, Croatia. Composer; Prod; Musician (keyboards). *Career:* Playing in theatre, Komedija; With Tereda Kesouija: ITD Band; Aerodrom; Novi Fosili; Many Croatian television and radio shows; Currently playing keyboards in Prijavo Kazaliste; Producer, sound engineer, JM Sound Studio-Zagreb on over 30 LPs for artists including: ITD Band; Jasna Zlokic; Sanja Dolezal; Novi Fosili; Jasmin Stauros; Venera; Vesna Ivic; Duka Caic; Prljavo Kazaliste. *Publications:* Suzy; Jugoton; Ofej. *Honours:* 3 Gold records; 1 Gold CD; 10 Silver records; Porin. *Membership:* HDS, Croatian Composer Society; HGU, Croatian Musician Society. *Current Management:* Branko Paic, Crno Bijeli Suijet CBS Croatia. *Address:* Brace Cvijica 17, 41000 Zagreb, Croatia.

BOJSEN-MOLLER, Cai; b. 7 March 1966, Copenhagen, Denmark. Composer; Musician (Drums, Keyboards, Composer). m. Anna Reumert, 20 April 1986, 1 s., 1 d. *Career:* Musician, Gangway; Musician for Busstop, Paris-Paris, Naive, Lisa Nilsson and Louise Hoffsten; Composer, Solo Performer, 1990; International concerts in England, Japan and Germany; Performed Roskilde Festival, 1997. *Compositions:* Solo albums: A Bit of Something, 1997; Super Sonic Jazzy Session, 1998; Singles: A Night in the Pit, 1996; Revertrhythm, 1996; Bits, 1997. *Recordings:* Compilations: Get Lost, 1996; Past, Present and Future, 1997; Further Adventures in Techno Soul, 1998. *Publications:* Film/Art Videos: Talk Like Whales, 1994; Pets, 1995. *Honours:* 4 Grammy Awards, Gangway, 1993.

BOLAM, Frank; b. 22 April 1949, Glasgow, Scotland. Musician (guitars). m. Jeanette Morrison, 13 May 1967, 1 s., 1 d. *Education:* Studied under Iain McHaffie and Ron Moore, main guitar teachers in Scotland. *Career:* Professional since age 21; Major productions, theatre, musicals including: Hair, Glasgow Metropole Theatre; West Side Story; Chess; Television appearances include: Ronnie Scott's The Jazz Series; Radio. *Recordings include:* The Jazz Train; Extensive professional and session work; Full time

teacher, Glasgow schools; Teacher, lecturer, Strathclyde University. *Publications:* Complete guitar courses (all styles and levels) for exam syllabus for Glasgow and Renfrew Education Department, commissioned by Strathclyde Education Department. *Membership:* Glasgow Society of Musicians; Musicians' Union; EIS. *Address:* 47 Coltmuir St, Glasgow G22 6LU, Scotland.

BOLGER, Leslie; b. 11 Aug. 1947, Liverpool, England. Musician (guitar); Lecturer. m. Claire Holland, 21 April 1970, 3 d. *Education:* Certificate in Education (with distinction), University of Manchester; Studied with world renowned jazz guitarist George Gola, Australia. *Career:* Jazz performances with artistes including: Martin Taylor; Louis Stewart; Ike Isaacs; Gary Potter; Kenny Baker; Don Rendal; Many television and radio broadcasts; Arranger, Music Adviser, Granada Television; Session guitarist, Arranger, Piccadilly Radio and Radio Merseyside; Backing guitarist for many top cabaret artists including: Russ Abbott; Joe Longthorne; Bob Monkhouse; Vince Hill. *Honours:* Many first places with honours or distinction for Les Bolger Jazz Guitar Ensemble. *Membership:* Musicians' Union. *Current Management:* Claire Bolger. *Address:* 12 Firbank Close, Daresbury View, Runcorn, Cheshire WA7 6NR, England.

BOLLING, Claude; b. 10 April 1930, Cannes, France. Jazz Musician (piano); Composer; Bandleader; Orchestra Conductor. m. Irène Dervize-Sadyker, 1959, 2 s. *Education:* Private teachers including Bob Colin, Earl Hines, Willie The Lion Smith; Maurice Duruflé. *Career:* As jazz pianist worked with: Dizzy Gillespie; Stéphane Grappelli; Rex Stewart; Roy Eldridge; Sidney Bechet; Albert Nicholas; Lionel Hampton; The Ellingtonians; Carmen McRae; Jo Williams; Formed group Les Parisiennes; Claude Bolling Big Band; Many jazz and variety shows. *Compositions include:* Sonatas 1 and 2 for two pianists; Suites for flute, violin, cello, chamber orchestra; Guitar Concerto; Picnic Suite; Toot Suite; More than 100 film soundtrack scores include: Le Jour et l'Heure; Borsalino; Lucky Luke; Le Magnifique; Willie and Phil; California Suite; La Mandarine; L'Homme en Colère; Flic Story; Le Mur de l'Atlantique; On Ne Meurt Que Deux Fois; Television: Jazz Memories; Le Brigades du Tigre; Chantecler. *Honours:* Gold Records, Canada, USA; Medaille d'Or Maurice Ravel; Officier Arts et Lettres; Chevalier Ordre Nationale du Mérite; Chevalier de la Légion d'Honneur; Los Angeles and New Orleans Honour Citizen; SACEM, Gold Medal and Grand Prix, 1984. *Address:* 20 Ave de Lorraine, 92380 Garches, France.

BOLO, Yammie, (Roland Maclean); b. 1970, Kingston, Jamaica. Reggae Vocalist. *Career:* Began as Singer with Sugar Minott's Youth Promotion sound system; Solo singer, 1985–; Founder, Yam Euphony record label, 1992. *Recordings:* Numerous singles include: When A Man's In Love, 1985; Jah Made Them All, 1986; Roots Pon Mi Corner, 1986; Free Mandela, 1987; Ransome Of a Man's Life, 1987; Tell Me Why Is This Fussing and Fighting, 1988; Love Me With Feeling, 1989; Poverty and Brutality, 1989; Poor Man's Cry, 1990; Struggle in Babylon, 1990; Turbo Charge, 1991; Blood A Run, 1991; Iniquity Worker, 1991; Jah Jah Loving, 1991; It's Not Surprising, 1992; Joe the Boss, 1992; Be Still, 1992; Revolution; Bowl Mus Fall; Albums: Ransom, 1989; Jah Made Them All, 1989; Who Knows It Feels It, 1991; Up Life Street, 1992; Cool and Easy, 1993; with Lloyd Hemmings: Meets Lloyd Hemmings, 1993. *Address:* c/o Free World Music Inc, 230 12th St, Suite 117, Miami Beach, FL 33139–4603, USA.

BOLTON, Michael, (Michael Bolotin); b. 26 Feb. 1953, New Haven, Connecticut, USA. Vocalist; Songwriter; Prod. 3 d. *Career:* Singer, US rock group Blackjack, 1978–82; Collaborator, Glasnost album as member of US songwriting team in Moscow, 1988; Solo recording artiste, formerly under name Michael Bolotin; Appearances include: Support to Heart, USA, 1988; Support to Ozzy Osbourne, USA, 1988; US tour with Kenny G, 1990; US tour with Céline Dion, 1992; Songwriter for Barbra Streisand, Cher, KISS, Kenny G and Peabo Bryson; World Tour, 1993–95; Christmas in Vienna, 1997; Numerous television appearances include TV special, This Is Michael Bolton, NBC, 1992. *Compositions include:* How Am I Supposed To Live Without You, Laura Branigan, 1983; I Found Someone, Cher, 1988; Co-writer (with Paul Stanley), Forever, Kiss, 1990; Co-writer (with Bob Dylan), Steel Bars, 1992. *Recordings:* Singles include: That's What Love's All About, 1987; Dock Of The Bay, 1988; How Am I Supposed To Live Without You, 1990; How Can We Be Lovers, 1990; When I'm Back On My Feet Again, 1990; Georgia On My Mind, 1990; Love Is A Wonderful Thing, 1991; Time, Love and Tenderness, 1991; When A Man Loves A Woman, 1991; Missing You Now, with Kenny G, 1992; Steel Bars, 1992; To Love Somebody, 1993; Drift Away, 1993; Said I Loved You... But I Lied, 1993; A Love So Beautiful, 1995; Can I Touch You... There, 1995; The Best Of Love, 1997; Safe Place From The Storm, 1998; Reach Out I'll Be There, 1999; Albums include: Michael Bolton, 1983; Everybody's Crazy, 1985; The Hunger, 1987; Soul Provider, 1989; Time Love and Tenderness (No. 1, USA), 1991; Timeless: The Classics (No. 1, USA), 1992; The One Thing, 1993; All That Matters, 1997; My Secret Passion, 1998; Timeless Vol. 2, 1999; Greatest Hits 1985–95, 1995; Contributor, Pavarotti and Friends (charity record for Bosnia relief), 1996; Go The Distance, theme from Disney film Hercules; This Is The Time: The Christmas Album, 1996; All That Matters, 1997; My Secret Passion, 1998; Timeless: The Classics Vol. 2, 1999; Live From Catania, 2001; Only A Woman Like You, 2002. *Publications:* The Secret of the

Lost Kingdom, children's book, 1997. *Honours:* New York Music Award, Best R&B Vocalist, 1988; ASCAP Airplay Awards, 1989; Pollstar Tour of the Year, 1990; Grammy Awards: Best Pop Vocal Performance, 1990, 1992; American Music Awards: Favourite Male Pop/Rock Artist, Favourite Album, 1992, 1993; BMI Song of the Year, 1991; Gold and Platinum discs; Hitmakers Award, National Songwriters Hall of Fame, 1995; Five times winner, BMI Million Performance Song Award. *Membership:* BMI. *Current Management:* Louis Levin Management, 130 W 57th St #10-B, New York, NY 10019, USA.

BOLVIG, Palle P. S; b. 25 Nov. 1932, Copenhagen, Denmark. Musician (trumpet, flugelhorn); Composer; Arranger. m. Jytte, 12 July 1969, 1 s., 3 d. *Career:* Member, Ib Glindemann Orchestra, 1951–61; Member, International Band, Newport Festival, 1958; Member, Danish Radio Big Band, 1964–. *Compositions:* Easy Mood, 1961; Gosty Day, 1970; Zabacoot, 1970; Portrait of Cordoba, 1971; Back To Tenderness, 1971; Child of Pain, 1985; Blue January, 1999. *Recordings:* Newport International Band, 1958; Brownsville Trolley Line, Danish Radio Big Band, 1969; Ben Webster and the Danish Radio Big-Band, 1970; Thad Jones and the Danish Radio Big-Band, 1978; Ernie Wilkins Almost Big-Band, 1981; Aura, Miles Davis, 1985; with the Danish Radio Band: Little Bit Of Duke, 1994; First British tour, 1995; Suite For Jazz Band, 1995; Also: Captain Coe's Famous Racearound, 1996; Like Life, Django Bates, 1998; Impulsive, the Danish Radio Jazz Orchestra, 1997; Ways Of Seeing, the Danish Radio Jazz Orchestra, 1999; Blues, Blues and All That Jazz, Allan Bo Bard, 1999. *Honours:* Selected, Newport International Jazz Band, 1958. *Membership:* The Danish Trumpet Societies. *Address:* Danmarks Radio P2 Jazz, 1999 Frederiksberg C, Denmark.

BOM-BANE, Jane (Bayley); b. 11 Sept. 1953, Leek, Staffordshire, England. Vocalist; Composer; Lyricist; Musician (harmonium). m. André Schmidt, 20 Dec. 1982, divorced, 1 s. *Education:* BA Hons, French, Cultural Studies, PGCE, English, French, Spanish, Warwick University; History of Music (part of degree); Piano lessons as child. *Career:* Appearances include: Bracknell Festival, 1993; Edinburgh Fringe Festival, 1994, 1995; Glasgow Mayfest, GFT, 1995; Television and radio includes: Usual Suspects, BBC Radio Scotland, 1994; Don't Look Down, STV, 1994; We Stayed In With Jungr and Parker, BBC Radio 2, 1994; Russian State television. *Recordings:* Away/ Mantovani, The Swinging Cats, 1980; Boy/Yob, The Round-a-way Wrong Chamber, 1984; Solo albums: Round-a-way Wrong Songs, 1993; It Makes Me Laugh, 1995; Soundtrack: The Man From Porlock, 1995. *Membership:* Musicians' Union; PRS. *Current Management:* Round-a-way Wrong Music. *Address:* PO Box 8416, London SW9 92B, England.

BON JOVI, Jon, (John Bongiovi); b. 2 March 1962, Sayreville, New Jersey, USA. Vocalist; Songwriter; Musician (guitar). m. Dorothea Hurley, May 1989, 1 s., 1 d. *Career:* Singer, local bands: Raze; Atlantic City Expressway; Singer, founder member, US rock group Bon Jovi, 1984–; 40m. albums sold world-wide to date; Numerous world-wide tours, including USA, UK, Europe, USSR, South America, Australia, Japan, 1984–; Support tours with Kiss; Scorpions; .38 Special; Headliners, Donington Monsters of Rock Festival, 1987; Moscow Music Peace Festival, 1989; Numerous television, radio and video appearances world-wide; Own management company, BJM; Own record label Jambco. *Recordings:* US No. 1 singles include: You Give Love A Bad Name, 1986; Living On A Prayer, 1987; Bad Medicine, 1988; I'll Be There For You, 1989; Solo: Blaze Of Glory, 1990; Destination Anywhere, 1997; Midnight In Chelsea Pt 1, 1997; Real Life Pt 1, 1999; Real Life Pt 2, 1999; Numerous other hits include: Wanted Dead Or Alive; Lay Your Hands On Me; Living In Sin; Born To Be My Baby; Keep The Faith; In These Arms; I'll Sleep When I'm Dead; Bed Of Roses; Always; I Believe; Someday I'll be Saturday Night; This Ain't A Love Song; Lie To Me; These Days; Hey God; One Road Man; Albums: Bon Jovi, 1984; 7800° Fahrenheit, 1985; Slippery When Wet (13m. copies sold), 1986; New Jersey, 1988; Keep The Faith, 1991; Crossroad (Best Of), 1994; These Days, 1995; Crush, 2000; One Wild Night 1985–2001 (live compilation), 2001; Solo album: Blaze Of Glory (film soundtrack, Young Guns II); Contributor, Stairway To Heaven/Highway To Hell charity record, 1989; Two Rooms (Elton John/Bernie Taupin tribute album), 1991. *Honours:* American Music Awards, Favourite Pop/Rock Band, 1988; Favourite Pop/Rock Single, 1991; Bon Jovi Day, Sayreville, 1989; Silver Clef, Nordoff-Robbins Music Therapy, 1990; All albums Gold or Platinum status; Golden Globe, Best Original Song, Blaze of Glory, 1991; Best Selling Album of Year, Crossroad, 1994; BRIT Award, Best International Group, 1996. *Current Management:* c/o BJM, 809 Elder Circle, Austin, TX 78733, USA.

BONDS, Gary 'US', (Gary Anderson); b. 6 June 1939, Jacksonville, Florida, USA. Vocalist; Songwriter; Prod. *Career:* Member, group The Turks; Solo artiste, 1960–; Co-writer, producer with Bruce Springsteen and Steve Van Zandt, 1978–; Appearances include: British tour, 1962; Richard Nader's second Rock 'n' Roll Revival concert, with Bill Haley, Jackie Wilson, 1969; Nuclear Disarmament rally, with Bruce Springsteen, James Taylor, Linda Ronstadt, Jackson Browne, Central Park, New York, 1982; Radio City Music Hall, New York, WCBS Radio's 20th Anniversary Concert, 1992. *Recordings:* Singles include: New Orleans, 1960; Quarter To Three (No. 1, USA), 1961; School Is Out, 1961; Dance Til Quarter To Three, 1961; Dear Lady Twist, 1962; Twist, Twist Señora, 1962; This Little Girl (written by Bruce

Springsteen), 1981; Out Of Work (also written by Springsteen), 1982; Albums: Dedication, 1978; On The Line, 1982; Standing In The Line Of Fire, 1984; Take Me Back To New Orleans, 1995; King Biscuit Flower Hour Presents Gary US Bonds Live, 2001; Producer for artistes including: Johnny Paycheck; ZZ Hill.

BONE, Greg; b. 21 Jan. 1962, Hartlepool, England. Musician (guitar). 1 s. *Career:* Played with Terry Ronald; Support tours with Hall and Oates, 1990; Robert Palmer, 1991; Television: Harry (drama series); Performances with Bros on Wogan; Top of the Pops; Going Live; Polish Music Festival; Radio sessions with One Word and Terry Ronald; Numerous television and radio appearances with Band of Thieves (now known as Thieves Like Us). *Recordings:* with the Pet Shop Boys: Discography, 1991; Was It Worth It? 1991; DJ Culture, 1991; Bilingual, 1996; Clive Griffin, Clive Griffin, 1993; Nobody Else, Take That, 1995; Sole Purpose, Secret Life, 1995; Warehouse Grooves Vol. 5, 1998; Love and The Russian Winter, Simply Red, 1999; Reload, Tom Jones, 1999; Killing Time, Tina Cousins, 2000; Steptacular, Steps, 2000. *Membership:* Musicians' Union.

BONET, Maria Del Mar; b. 27 April 1947, Palma, Majorca, Spain. Vocalist; Songwriter; Musician (guitar). *Career:* Began singing with Els Setze Jutges, Barcelona, 1967; Performed in: France; Denmark; England; Switzerland; Venezuela; Mexico; Argentina; Chile; Portugal; Poland; Italy; Sweden; Germany; Greece; Tunisia; Netherlands; Belgium; Former USSR; Japan; Annual concerts, Plaça del Rei, Barcelona; Recorded and toured, France and Spain, with Ensemble de Musique Traditionelle de Tunís, 1985; Toured Spain, with Brazilian Milton Nascimiento, 1986; Presented Arenal, with choreographer, dancer, Nacho Duato, 1988; International Peralada Music Festival, 1992; Performed show, The Greece of Theodorakis, 1993; Performed in Cants d'Abelone, 1994; Performed show, Merhaba, Summer Festival, Barcelona, 1994; Edinburgh International Festival, 1995. *Recordings include:* Maria del Mar Bonet, 1974; A L'Olympia, 1975; Maria del Mar Bonet, 1976; Cançons de Festa, 1976; Alenar, 1977; Saba de Terrer, 1979; Quico-Maria del Mar, 1979; Cançons de la Nostra Mediterranea, 1980; L'Aguila Negra, 1981; Jardi Tancat, 1981; Sempre, 1981; Breviari d'Amor, 1982; Maria del Mar Bonet, 1983; Anells d'Aigua, 1985; Gavines i Dragons, 1987; Ben A Prop, 1989; Bon Viatge Faci la Cadernera, 1990; Coreografies, with Nacho Duato, 1990; Ellas, Maria del Mar Bonet Canta a Theodorakis, 1993; Salmaia, 1995; El Cor el Temps, 1997; Cavall de Foc, 1999. *Publications:* Antologia de la Nova Cançó Catalana, 1968; Maria del Mar Bonet, 1976; La Nova Cançó, 1976; Tretze que Cantan, 1982; Veinte Años de Canción en España, 1984; Una Història de la Cançó, 1987; 25 Anys de Cançó a Mallorca, 1987; Secreta Veu (poems and watercolours), 1987; Maria del Mar Bonet (biography), Joan Manresa, 1994; Quadern de Viatge, poems and watercolours, 1998. *Honours:* Spanish Gold disc, 1971; French Government Charles Cross Academy Award, Best Foreign Record, 1984; Cross of St George, Catalan Government Prize, 1984; Catalan Government National Prize, 1992. *Membership:* Societat General d'Autors i Editors (SGAE); Associació de Cantants i Intèrprets Professionals en Llangua Catalana (ACIC). *Current Management:* Jordi de Ramon. *Address:* Sepúlveda, 147–149 Principal 1a, 08011 Barcelona, Catalonia, Spain.

BONFILS, Tony; b. 27 Jan. 1948, Nice, France. Musician (bass guitar, double bass); Vocalist. 3 s., 1 d. *Education:* Licence de Psychologie; Prix de Contre Basse; Medaille de Solfege. *Career:* Bass player with: Dee Dee Bridgewater; Sacha Distel; Charles Aznavour; Also studio musician.

BONGA, Ntshukumo (Ntshuks); b. 1 Oct. 1963, Johannesburg, South Africa. Musician (alto saxophone, clarinet); Engineer. *Education:* BSc (Hons), Aeronautical Engineering and Design. *Career:* Appearances include: Reithalle, Berne, Switzerland; Purcell Room, South Bank Centre; London Jazz Festival, 1994; London ICA, 1996; WOMAD Festival, 1997; Performances with Robyn Hitchcock; Radio broadcasts: Interview BBC World Service, Network Africa, 1993; Interview, session, BBC Radio 3, Impressions, 1994; PM Live, Radio South Africa. *Recordings:* Album: Urban Ritual, Ntshuks Bonga's Tshisa; Moss Elixir, Robyn Hitchcock. *Honours:* Debut Album, Urban Ritual, voted No 6, Wire magazine Jazz/Improvised Music Poll, 1995. *Membership:* Musicians' Union; PRS; London Musicians Collective. *Address:* 22 Norcott Rd, Stoke Newington, London N16 7EL, England.

BONHAM, Jason; b. 1967, England. Musician (drums, percussion). m. Jan Charteris, 5 May 1990. *Education:* Played drums from age 4; Taught by father, John Bonham. *Career:* Member, Airrace, 1984; Founder member, Virginia Wolf, 1986; Worked with members of Led Zeppelin, 1987–88; Concert, Atlantic Records 40th Anniversary concert, Madison Square Garden, 1988; US tour with Jimmy Page, 1988; Founder, own group, Bonham, 1990–. *Recordings:* Albums: with Airrace: Shaft Of Light, 1984; with Virginia Wolf: Virginia Wolf, 1986; with Jimmy Page: Outrider, 1988; with Bonham: The Disregard Of Timekeeping, 1989; Madhatter, 1992; with Motherland: Peace For Me, 1994; with Red Blooded Blues: Red Blooded Blues, 1995; Also contributed to: Rock Star OST, 2001; Solo Albums: In The Name Of My Father Zepset, 1997; When You See The Sun, 1997. *Current Management:* Part Rock Management, Suite 318, 535 Kings Rd, London SW10 0SZ, England.

BONIN, Nathalie; b. 17 Nov. 1971, San Francisco, USA. Musician (violin). *Education:* Aaron Copland School of Music, 1985–86; McGill University, 1987–88, 1993. *Career:* Composer Director, Ca Se Soigne, 1998; Producer Co-ordinator, String Festival 1998; Duke Ellington Tribute Concert, 1998; Valentino Orchestra, 1998; Said Mesnaoui, Arabic Violin and Percussion, 1998. *Recordings:* Moist; Excentricus; Cineparc; Clair de Lune; Mendelssohn: Concerto for Violin Nos 1 and 2; Beethoven Symphony No. 3; Verismo; Enfants Retour; Prokofieff: Pierre et le Loup; Korngold. *Honours:* Québec Arts Council Grant; Deans Honour List, McGill; First Prize Winner, Darius Milhaud Competition; Winner Canadian Music Competition; First Prize Winner, CW Post Summer Chamber Music Festival Concerto Competition. *Membership:* AFM; SOCAN. *Address:* 6410 Chabot St, Montréal, QC H2G 2TZ, Canada.

BONN, Stanley; b. 3 Feb. 1924, Freeport, Illinois, USA. Owner, Record Label/Publishing Co; Prod; Dir. m. Eva L Bonn, 5 Aug. 1947, 1 s., 1 d. *Career:* Owner, ESB Records, Gather Round Music, Bonnfire Publishing; Worked with Bobby Lee Caldwell, John P Swisshelm, Rob Lynn, Jeff Ashbaker, Eddie Sheppard. *Compositions:* The Sounds of the Universe. *Recordings:* The Gold in this Ring; Janie's Song; Highway 44; She's a Dance Hall Lady; Don't Watch Me Fall Apart; West Texas Lady; Ten Minutes After Five; The Sounds Of the Universe; All the Tears; Toe Tappin' Country Man; Three Reasons; 2nd Wind; First Date Blues. *Honours:* Song of the Year, five times; Record Label of the Year, 1991, 1992, 1994; Golden Eagle Award, California Country Music Asscn, 1994. *Membership:* Country Music Asscn of America; California Country Music Asscn; Greater Southern Country Music Asscn. *Address:* ESB Records, PO Box 6429, Huntington Beach, CA 92615–6429, USA.

BONNEY, Simon; b. 3 June 1961, Sydney, Australia. Vocalist; Songwriter. m. 15 June 1984, 1 s., 1 d. *Career:* Performed in film Wings of Desire (Wim Wenders), with Crime and the City Solution; Contributor to film scores: To The Ends of The World (Wim Wenders); Faraway So Close (Wim Wenders); Gas Food and Lodgings (Alison Anders); Underworld (Roger Christian); Also appeared on MTV Road Hog. *Recordings:* Albums with Crime and the City Solution: Just South Of Heaven, 1985; Room Of Lights, 1986; Shine, 1988; The Bride Ship, 1989; Paradise Discotheque, 1990; The Adversary: Live; Solo albums: Forever, 1992; Everyman, 1995; Also featured on film soundtrack albums: Wings Of Desire; To The Ends Of The World; Faraway So Close; Underworld. *Membership:* PRS. *Current Management:* c/o Ted Gardner, Larrkin Management, 8391 Beverly Blvd #298, Los Angeles, CA 90048, USA.

BONO, (Paul Hewson); b. 10 May 1960, Dublin, Ireland. Vocalist; Lyricist. m. Alison, 2 d., 1 s. *Career:* Founder member, lead singer, rock group U2, 1978–; Regular national, international and world-wide tours; Major concerts include: US Festival, 1983; The Longest Day, Milton Keynes Bowl, 1985; Live Aid, Wembley, 1985; Self Aid, Ireland, 1986; A Conspiracy of Hope (Amnesty International US tour), 1986; Smile Jamaica (hurricane relief concert), 1988; Very Special Arts Festival, White House, 1988; New Year's Eve Concert, Dublin (televised throughout Europe), 1989; Yankee Stadium, New York (second concert ever), 1992; Group established own record company, Mother Records. *Compositions include:* Co-writer, Jah Love, Neville Brothers; Lyrics, Misere, Zucchero and Pavarotti; Screenplay, Million Dollar Hotel. *Recordings:* Albums: with U2: Boy, 1980; October, 1981; War (No. 1, UK), 1983; Under A Blood Red Sky, 1983; The Unforgettable Fire (No. 1, UK), 1984; Wide Awake In America, 1985; The Joshua Tree (No. 1, UK and USA), 1987; Rattle and Hum, also film (No. 1, USA), 1988; Achtung Baby (No. 1, USA), 1991; Zooropa (No. 1, UK and USA), 1993; Passengers (film soundtrack), with Brian Eno, 1995; Pop, 1997; The Best Of 1980–90 (compilation), 1998; All That You Can't Leave Behind, 2001; The Best Of 1990–2000 (compilation), 2002. Hit singles include: Out Of Control (No. 1, Ireland), 1979; Another Day (No. 1, Ireland), 1980; New Year's Day, 1983; Two Hearts Beat As One, 1983; Pride (In The Name Of Love), 1984; The Unforgettable Fire, 1985; With Or Without You (No. 1, USA), 1987; I Still Haven't Found What I'm Looking For (No. 1, USA), 1987; Where The Streets Have No Name, 1987; Desire (No. 1, UK), 1988; Angel Of Harlem, 1988; When Love Comes To Town, with B. B. King, 1989; All I Want Is You, 1989; The Fly (No. 1, UK), 1991; Mysterious Ways, 1992; One, 1992; Even Better Than The Real Thing, 1992; Who's Gonna Ride Your Wild Horses, 1992; Stay, 1993; Hold Me, Thrill Me, Kiss Me (from film soundtrack Batman Forever), 1995; Discotheque (No. 1, UK), 1997; Staring At The Sun, 1997; If God Will Send His Angels, 1998; Sweetest Thing, 1998; Beautiful Day (No. 1, UK), 2000; Stuck In A Moment You Can't Get Out Of, 2001; Walk On, 2001; Electrical Storm, 2002; Contributor, Do They Know It's Christmas?, Band Aid, 1985; Sun City, Little Steven, 1985; In A Lifetime, Clannad, 1986; Mystery Girl, Roy Orbison, 1988; Special Christmas, charity album, 1987; Folkways: A Vision Shared (Woody Guthrie tribute), 1988; Live For Ireland, 1989; Red Hot + Blue (Cole Porter tribute), 1990; Tower Of Song (Leonard Cohen tribute), 1995; Pavarotti and Friends, 1996; Forces Of Nature, 1999. *Honours:* Grammy Awards, Album of the Year, for The Joshua Tree, 1987, Best Rock Album, for All That You Can't Leave Behind, 2001, Best Alternative Music Album, for Zooropa, 1993, Song of the Year, for Beautiful Day, 2000, Record of the Year, for Beautiful Day, 2000, for Walk On, 2001, Best Rock Performance By A Duo Or Group With Vocal, for The Joshua Tree, 1987, for Desire, 1988, for Achtung Baby, 1992, for Beautiful Day, 2000, for Elevation, 2001, Best Pop Performance By A Duo Or Group

With Vocal, for Stuck In A Moment You Can't Get Out Of, 2001, Best Music Video, Long Form, for Zoo TV: Live From Sydney, 1994, Best Performance Music Video, for Where The Streets Have No Name, 1988; BRIT Awards: Best International Group, 1988–90, 1992, 1998, 2001; Best Live Act, 1993; Outstanding Contribution To The British Music Industry, 2001; World Music Award, Irish Artist of the Year, 1993; Juno Award, International Entertainer of the Year, 1993; Q Awards, Best Act In The World, 1990, 1992, 1993; Merit Award, 1994; American Music Award, Favorite Internet Artist of the Year, 2002; Ivor Novello Award, Best Song Musically and Lyrically, for Walk On, 2002; Golden Globe, Best Original Song, for The Hands That Built America (from film Gangs of New York), 2003; Numerous poll wins and awards, Billboard and Rolling Stone magazines; Gold and Platinum discs. *Current Management:* Principle Management, 30–32 Sir John Rogersons Quay, Dublin 2, Ireland. *Website:* www.u2.com.

BONSALL, Joseph Sloan, Jr; b. 18 May 1948, Philadelphia, Pennsylvania, USA. Vocalist. m. Barbara Holt, 1969. *Career:* Member, gospel singing groups, 1966–73; Member, gospel/country group The Oak Ridge Boys, 1973–; Co-owner, Silverline/Goldline Music Publishing. *Recordings:* Singles: Y'All Come Back Saloon; I'll Be True To You; Leavin' Louisiana In The Broad Daylight; Trying To Love Two Women; Elvira; Bobbie Sue; American Made; Love Song; I Guess It Never Hurts To Hurt Sometime; Come On In; Make My Life With You; Albums: Oak Ridge Boys, 1974; Sky High, 1975; Old Fashioned..., 1976; Live, 1977; Y'All Come Back Saloon, 1977; Room Service, 1978; The Oak Ridge Boys Have Arrived, 1979; Together, 1980; Greatest Hits, 1980; Fancy Free, 1981; Bobbie Sue, 1982; Christmas, 1982; Very Best, 1982; American Made, 1983; The Oak Ridge Boys Deliver, 1983; Friendship, 1983; Greatest Hits II, 1984; Seasons, 1985; Step On Out, 1985; Where The Fast Lane Ends, 1986; Christmas Again, 1986; Monogahela, 1987; New Horizons, 1988; American Dreams, 1989; Greatest Hits III, 1989; Unstoppable, 1991; The Long Haul, 1992. *Honours:* Numerous Gospel Music Asscn Dove Awards; Grammy Awards, 1970–77; CMA Vocal Group of the Year, 1978; ACM Awards, Best Vocal Group, 1977, 1979; American Music Award, Best Country Group, 1982; Gold discs. *Membership:* Academy of Country Music; NARAS; AFTRA; Country Music Asscn. *Current Management:* Don Light Talent, PO Box 120308, Nashville, TN 37212, USA.

BOO, Betty, (Alison Moira Clarkson); b. 6 March 1970, Kensington, London, England. Rap Artiste; Vocalist; Songwriter. *Career:* Mem., rap group the She-Rockers; Duo, Hit 'n' Run; Guest singer with Beatmasters; Solo artiste, 1990–; Songwriter for artistes incl.: Hear' Say, Louise, Tweenies. *Compositions:* co-writer: Pure and Simple (No. 1 UK hit for Hear' Say. *Recordings:* Albums: Boomania, 1990; Grrr... It's Betty Boo!, 1992. Singles: with Beatmasters: Hey DJ (I Can't Dance To That Music You're Playing), 1989; Solo: Doin' The Do, 1990; Where Are You Baby, 1990; 24 Hours, 1990; Let Me Take You There, 1992; I'm On My Way, 1992. *Honours:* Numerous dance music awards. *Current Management:* Big Life Management, 67–69 Chalton St, London NW1 1HY, England.

BOOHORISHVILI, Mehab; b. 15 June 1972, Batumi, Georgia. Folk Vocalist; Musician (guitar). *Education:* Batumi Music College. *Career:* Turkey Folklore Festival, 1995; Eshme, group, Spain; Legames International Folklore Festival, 1997; GIEZA International Folk Festival, Spain, 1997; Bravo Festival, Tblisi, Georgia, 1998; Ariola, Otello, Turker; Festival of Arpendos; Leader, Folk Song Trio; Member, Batume folk song group; Singer, Batumi State Opera. *Recordings:* Interpretations of major Georgian folk songs with Batami State folk song group. *Honours:* Prize, GIEZA Festival, Spain, 1997; Prize, Spara Festival, 1997. *Address:* S Khimstiashvili St No. 6 Apt 11, Batumi, Georgia.

BOONE, Debby (Deborah Ann); b. 22 Sept. 1956, Hackensack, New Jersey, USA. Vocalist; Actress. m. Gabriel Ferrer, 1979, 2 s., 2 d. *Career:* singer with (father) Pat Boone and family group, 1970–; Recording artist, 1977–; Numerous television appearances include: Sins of The Past, ABC TV, 1984; Stage performances: Seven Brides For Seven Brothers, national tour, 1981–82; Sound of Music, national tour, 1987–88. *Recordings:* You Light Up My Life (No. 1, USA), 1977; Midstream, 1978; Love Has No Reason, 1980; Friends For Life, 1987; Reflections, 1988; Choose Life, 1992; Surrender, 1992; With My Song, 1992; Home For Christmas, 1993; Greatest Hymns, 2000; You Light Up My Life: Greatest Inspirational Songs, 2001. *Publications:* Debby Boone: So Far; Bedtime Hugs For Little Ones (children's book), 1988; Co-author, Tomorrow Is A Brand New Day, 1989. *Honours:* American Music Award, Song of the Year; Grammy Awards: Best New Artist, 1977; CMA Best New Country Artist, 1977; Singing Star of Year, AGVA, 1978; Dove Awards, 1980, 1984; Best Inspirational Performance, 1980; Best Gospel Performance, Keep The Flame Burning, 1984; Best New Personality, National Asscn Theatre Owners. *Current Management:* c/o Sparrow Communications Group, 101 Winners Circle, Brentwood, TN 37024, USA.

BOONE, Pat; b. 1 June 1934, Jacksonville, Florida, USA. Vocalist; Actor. m. Shirley Foley, 14 Nov. 1953, 4 d. *Education:* North Texas State Teachers' College; David Liscomb College; Gradute magna cum laude, Columbia, 1958. *Career:* Appearances include: Ted Mack TV Show, 1953; Arthur Godfrey Show, CBS, 1954–55; Own television show, 1957; Numerous other television appearances include: Moonlighting; Co-host, Wish You Were Here, Nashville Network, 1988–; Film appearances include: Bernadine, 1957; April Love, 1957; Mardi Gras, 1958; Journey To The Centre of The Earth, 1959; All Hands On Deck, 1961; State Fair, 1962; Main Attraction, 1962; Yellow Canary, 1963; Greatest Story Ever Told, 1965; Perils of Pauline, 1967; The Cross and The Switchblade, 1971; Owner, Lamb and Lion Records. *Publications include:* Twixt Twelve and Twenty, 1958; Between You Me and The Gatepost, 1960; The Real Christmas, 1961; Care and Feeding of Parents, 1967; A New Song, 1971; Joy, 1973; A Miracle A Day Keeps The Devil Away; My Faith, 1976; Pat Boone Devotional Book, 1977; The Honeymoon Is Over, 1977; Together: 25 Years With The Boone Family, 1979; Pray To Win: God Wants You To Succeed, 1980. *Honours:* Listed in Top Ten Attractions, 1957; Listed in Top Fifteen Namepower Stars, 1959. *Current Management:* Tim Swift, Cossette Productions. *Address:* 8899 Beverly Blvd, Los Angeles, CA 90048, USA.

BOOTH, Tim; b. 4 Feb. 1960, Leeds, England. Vocalist; Lyricist. 1 s. *Education:* University of Manchester. *Career:* Founder mem., lead singer, James, 1982–2001; Numerous tours, festival dates and television appearances; Farewell 'Getting Away With It' concert, Manchester Evening News Arena, Dec. 2001. *Recordings:* Albums: with James: Stutter, 1986; Strip Mine, 1988; One Man Clapping, 1989; Gold Mother, 1990; Seven, 1992; Laid, 1993; Wah Wah, 1994; Whiplash, 1997; The Best Of James, 1998; Millionaires, 1999; B-Sides Ultra, 2001; Pleased To Meet You, 2001; Getting Away With It, 2002; Solo: Booth And The Bad Angel (with Angelo Badalamenti), 1996. Singles incl.: with James: Jimone (EP), 1983; Jim 2 (EP), 1985; How Was It For You, 1990; Come Home, 1990; Lose Control, 1990; Sit Down, 1991; Sound, 1991; Born Of Frustration, 1992; Ring The Bells, 1992; Seven, 1992; Sometimes, 1993; Laid, 1993; Say Something/Jam J, 1994; She's A Star, 1997; Tomorrow, 1997; Waltzing Along, 1997; Destiny Calling, 1998; Runaground, 1998; Sit Down (remix), 1998; I Know What I'm Here For, 1999; Fred Astaire, 1999; We're Gonna Miss You, 1999; Getting Away With It (All Messed Up), 2001. *Current Management:* Rudge Management, 1 Star St, London W2 1QD, England.

BORDEN, David; b. 25 Dec. 1938, Boston, Massachusetts, USA. Composer; Musician (Piano, Synthesizer)., m. (2) Rebecca Godin, 12 Aug. 1994, 1 s. *Education:* BM, Eastman School of Music; MM, ESM, MA, Music Composition, Harvard University; Fulbright Student, Hochschule für Musik, Berlin, Germany. *Career:* WBAI Free Music Store, The Kitchen, The Knitting Factory, Dance Theatre Workshop, Town Hall, Lincoln Center, New York City; Tivoli Konzert Halle, Copenhagen; Barbican Centre, London; Portsmouth Festival, England; New Music America, Montréal, Canada. *Compositions:* The Continuing Story of Counterpunt; Easter, Enfield in Winter; The Birthday Variations; Variations on a Theme of Philip Glass; Angels. *Recordings:* The Continuing Story Of Counterpunt; Place, Times and People; Cayuga Nightmusic; Another Mallard's Portable Masterpiece. *Membership:* American Music Center. *Address:* PO Box 842, Ithaca, NY 14851, USA.

BORLAND, Wes; b. 7 Feb. 1975, Nashville, USA. Musician (guitar). m. Heather McMillan, April 1998. *Education:* Learnt blues/country guitar at father's church; Douglas Anderson School of The Arts, studied jazz guitar for three years. *Career:* Sang and played guitar for own band in Jacksonville; Joined Limp Bizkit, 1994; Signed to Flip/Interscope on strength of demo tape; Striking live shows at concerts and festivals; Group spearheaded 'nu-metal' breakthrough in Europe, 2001; Worked with side-project group Big Dumb Face whilst member of Limp Bizkit; Left Limp Bizkit, October 2001. *Recordings:* Albums: Three Dollar Bill, Y'All $, 1997; Significant Other, 1999; Chocolate Starfish and The Hot Dog Flavored Water, 2000; New Old Songs (remix album), 2001; Duke Lion Fights The Terror (with Big Dumb Face), 2001; Singles: Faith, 1997; Nookie, Rearranged, 1999; Break Stuff, Take A Look Around (from Mission Impossible 2 OST), My Generation, 2000; Rollin', My Way, Boiler, 2001. *Honours:* Second and third albums both debuted at #1 on US chart; Significant Other sales in excess of 6m.; American Music Award, Favourite Alternative Artist, 2002. *Address:* c/o Geffen Records, USA. *Website:* www.geffen.com; www.limpbizkit.com.

BORUM, Stefan; b. 21 Aug. 1954, Viborg, Denmark. Composer; Musician (piano). 2 s., 1 d. *Education:* 1 term, Creative Music Studio, Woodstock, New York, USA, 1980. *Career:* Member: Blue Sun, 1975–78; Concerts include: Roskilde Festival, 1977; Member, Lost Kids, 1979–80; Created Sun Quartet; Concerts include: Italian tour, 1984–85; First Prize winner, Jazz On The Oder, 1987; Jazz Jamboree, Warsaw, 1987; Autumn Rhythms, Leningrad, 1988; Member, Shades of Blue, 1987–; Concerts include: Djurs Bluesland, 1988, 1990, 1992; Notoddon Blues Festival, 1991. *Recordings:* It's All Money Johnny, Blue Sun, 1976; Sun Quartet, Sun Quartet, 1987; On A Mission From Muddy Waters, Shades of Blue, 1992. *Membership:* DMF (Danish Musicians' Union); DJFBA.

BOSCO, João, (Joao Bosco De Freitas Mucci); b. 1946, Ponte Nova, Minas Gerais, Brazil. Vocalist; Musician (guitar); Composer. *Education:* Ouro Preto University, Civil Engineering, 1972. *Career:* From musical family: mother, violinist; father, samba singer; sister, concert pianist; brother,

composer; University collaboration with lyricist Vinicius de Morais; Began long association with ex-psychiatrist Aldir Blanc, late 1970s–late 1980s; Supplied Elis Regina with much of her best material; After her early death, became known as a performer of own material; Struggled with censorship during military dictatorship in Brazil; 1977 composition O Bebaido e a Equilibrista (The Drunkard and the Tightrope Walker) became Amnesty International theme song; Influenced by many styles including: samba; jazz; African; Cuban; rock; In addition to Portuguese, lyrics use languages including: English; French; Spanish; Yoruban; International stage appearances include: Lee Ritenour, 1988; Montreux Jazz Festival; First major tour of USA, early 1990s. *Recordings:* João Bosco, 1973 Caca A Raposa, 1975; Galos De Briga, 1976; Tiro De Misericordia, 1977; Linha De Passe, 1979; Bandalhismo, 1980; Essa E A Sua Vida, 1981; Comissão De Frente, 1982; Ao Vivo 100th Apresentacao, 1983; Gagabirô, 1984; Cabeca De Nego, 1986; AiAiAi De Mim, 1986; Na Onda Que Balanca, 1987; Bosco, 1989; Zona De Fronteira, 1991; Afrocanto, 1992; Da Licenca Men Senhor, 1996; Benguele OST, 1998; Na Esquinha, 2000; features on: Festival, Lee Ritenour, 1988.

BOSÉ, Miguel Dominguín; b. 3 April 1956, Aries, Panama. Vocalist; Songwriter; Actor. *Career:* Solo artiste; Film appearances: Gli Eroi, 1972; Vera, un Cuento Cruel, 1973; Retrato de Familia, 1976; Oedipus Orca, 1976; Giovannino, 1976; Garofano Rosso, 1976; Suspiria, 1977; La Gabbia, 1977; California, 1977; Sentados al Borde de la Mañana con los Pies Colgando, 1978; En Penumbra, 1985; El Caballero del Dragón, 1985; Shangay Lily, 1989; L'Avaro, 1989; Lo Más Natural, 1990; Tacones Lejanos, 1991; La Nuit Sacrée, 1993; Mazeppa, 1993; Enciende mi Pasión, 1994; La Reine Margot, 1994; Gazon Maudit, 1995; Amor Digital, 1996; Libertarias, 1996; Oui, 1996; La Mirada del Otro, 1998. *Recordings:* Albums: Soy, 1975; Es Tan Fácil, 1976; Linda, 1977; Miguel Bosé, 1978; La Misa Campesina, 1979; Chicas, 1979; Miguel, 1980; Madrid, 1980; Cosas De Niños, 1980; Más Allá, 1981; Bravo Muchachos, 1982; Made In Spain, 1983; Bandido, 1984; Salamandra, 1986; XXX, 1987; De Bandido A Duende, 1988; Los Chicos No Lloran, 1990; Directo '90, 1990; Querido Miguel, 1993; Bajo El Signo De Cain (aka Under The Sign Of Cain), 1994; De Partisano A Duende, 1994; Pedro Y El Lobo, 1994; Laberinto, 1995; Personalidad, 1996; Mordre Dans Ton Coeur, 1997; 11 Maneras De Ponerse Un Sombrero, 1998; Sereno, 2002. *Address:* c/o Warner Music Latina Inc, Discos de Centroamerica, SA, PO Box 50-F, Guatemala City, Guatemala.

BOSKOV, Ole; b. 31 Aug. 1963, Copenhagen, Denmark. Musician (piano, acoustic guitar, keyboards); Vocalist; Songwriter. m. Tina, 5 Sept. 1992. *Education:* Piano lessons for 16 years, organ lessons for 2 years, and guitar lessons for 4 years. *Career:* No. 1 hit single in Denmark with Danish version of MC Hammer's Can't Touch This; Debut album of own compositions, 1996. *Compositions include:* Listen To The Wind; Pennsylvania; Going Crazy. *Recordings:* Backing vocals for Ester Brohus; Solo albums: Listen To The Wind, 1996; Mr Romance, 1998. *Membership:* Danish Songwriters Guild. *Address:* Rolfsvej 22 st th, 2000 Frederiksberg, Denmark.

BOSS, (THE). See: **MORALES, David.**

BOSTIC, Earl; b. 4 June 1947. Musician (Bass). m. Maria Kottmair, 2 d. *Education:* BA, Wayne State University, Detroit, Michigan, USA, 1971. *Career:* Leo Wright Quartet, 1980–84; Played with Sarah Leander at Theater des Westens, 1980; Played with Eartha Kitt at the Groschenoper, Frankfurt, Germany, 1988; Rudy Stevenson Band, 1994–98; Harry's Freilach, 1994–98; Bregenz Music Festival in Porgy and Bess Stageband, 1997, 1998. *Recordings:* Wayne Martin: Hometown Boy; Klesmer Tov; Lia Ander: This Masquerade. *Address:* Karlsruherstr 16, 10711 Berlin, Germany.

BOSTOCK, Chris; b. 23 Nov. 1959, Hillingdon, London, England. Songwriter; Prod; Musician (bass, keyboards). *Career:* Songwriter and Bassist with Vic Godard's Subway Sect, 1981–82 and JoBoxers, 1983–86; 3 hit singles, 1 hit album; Touring in UK, USA, Canada, Australia, New Zealand and with Dave Stewart and Spiritual Cowboys, 1990–92; 2 albums; Touring in Europe; Sessions for OMD, Shakespears Sister, Style Council, Sandie Shaw; Produced albums for Savage World, 1993; Clint Bradley, 1997; Film soundtracks: Bad Girl, with Jane Horrocks, 1992; Dad Savage, with Patrick Stewart, 1998. *Compositions:* Hit Singles: Just Got Lucky; Johnny Friendly; Is This Really the First Time. *Recordings:* Boxerbeat, 1983; Just Got Lucky, 1983; Johnny Friendly, 1983; Is This Really the First Time, 1985; Spiritual Cowboys and Honest albums by Dave Stewart and the Spiritual Cowboys; Goodbye Cruel World, Shakespears Sister; Cafe Bleu, album, Style Council. *Membership:* Re-Pro; PRS; Musicians' Union. *Current Management:* Clive Banks Ltd, 1 Glenthorne Mews, 115a Glenthorne Rd, London W6 0JL, England.

BOTH, Robert Allen; b. 10 Nov. 1952, Montclair, New Jersey, USA. Recording Engineer; Prod; Musician. m. Karen Sue Cody, 2 March 1987, 1 s. *Education:* Art School, Ridgewood; Guitar and piano lessons. *Career:* A & R, Polydor Records, New York City, 1971–72; A & R Director, Recording engineer, producer, James Brown Enterprises, New York City, 1972–76; Staff engineer, Delta Recording, 1976–77; Staff engineer, Quad Recording, 1979; Owner, Chief engineer, Twain Recordings, New Jersey, 1976–; Audio instructor, Ramapo College of New Jersey, 1993; Audio Instructor, William Paterson University, New Jersey, 1995–; Audio Instructor, County College of Morris, New Jersey, 1997–. *Recordings:* with The JB's: Doin' It, 1973; with Maceo Parker, USA, 1974; with James Brown: Get On The Good Foot, 1972; Reality, 1974; The Payback, 1974; Hell, 1974; Sex Machine Today, 1975; Hot, 1975; with Lyn Collins: Check Me Out, 1975; with The JB's Damn Night, 1974; Breakin' Bread, 1974; Hustle with Speed, 1975; JB's Reunion, 1999; Soul Of the Funky, 1999. *Publications:* Articles in the music press. *Honours:* 3 RIAA Gold Records Awards for work with James Brown. *Membership:* Music Producers Guild of America. *Address:* Twain Recording, 18 Hiawatha Pass, West Milford, NJ 07480, USA. *E-mail:* bobboth@warwick.net.

BOTSCHINSKY, Allan; b. 29 March 1940, Copenhagen, Denmark. Musician (trumpet, flugelhorn); Composer. *Education:* Royal Danish Conservatory at age 14; Studied trumpet under Cecil Collins at the Manhattan School of Music, New York; Private studies of classical composition with Professor Svend Erik Werner and Bo Holten. *Career:* Professional at age 16, playing in leading groups of Copenhagen's Jazz Scene, with, among others, Oscar Pettiford, Stan Getz, Dexter Gordon and Ben Webster; Member of Jazz Quintet '60 and the Danish Radio Jazz Group; Played with and conducted The Danish Radio Big Band, whose guest conductors included Thad Jones, Oliver Nelson, Stan Kenton, Dizzy Gillespie, Maynard Ferguson and George Russell; Regular tours and recordings with Peter Herbolzheimer's Rhythm Combination and Brass and Ali Haurand's European Jazz Ensemble and European Trumpet Summit. *Compositions:* Numerous compositions and arrangements include: Sentiments, prizewinning suite for large orchestra and voice; Exercises For Jazz Orchestra; Synergy, piece for string quartet and jazz quintet; A Jazz Sonata, for trumpet and piano; Jazz-Antiphony, brass octet; Fantasia, piece for solo trumpet and symphony orchestra. *Recordings include:* Duologue, 1987; The Night, 1988; Jazzpar 95, 1995; Last Summer, 1992; I've Got Another Rhythm, 1995; Also appears on: Conversations, Sahib Shihab, 1963; Ben Webster Plays Duke Ellington, 1967; Akili, Akili, 1987; She Touched Me, Thomas Clausen, 1988; Lee Konitz and The Jazzpar All Stars, 1992; Axen, Bent Axen, 1996. *Honours:* Ben Webster Prize, 1983; Special television tribute entitled The Music of Allan Botschinsky, 1984. *Address:* 64 Gilbey House, 38–46 Jamestown Rd, London NW1 7BY, England.

BOTTUM, Roddy; b. 1 July 1963, Los Angeles, California, USA. Musician (keyboards). *Education:* Classically-trained pianist. *Career:* Member, US rock group Faith No More, 1980–98; Leader, alternative pop band Imperial Teen, 1994–; Appearances include: Brixton, London (recorded for live video), 1990; Reading Festival, 1990; Monsters of Rock Festivals, Italy and France, 1990; Supported Robert Plant, USA, 1990; Day On The Green, San Francisco, 1991; Rock In Rio II Festival, Brazil, 1991; Phoenix Festival, 1993, 1995. *Recordings:* Singles include: with Faith No More: We Care A Lot, 1988; Epic, 1990; Falling To Pieces, 1990; From Out Of Nowhere, 1990; Midlife Crisis, 1992; A Small Victory, 1992; Everything's Ruined, 1992; I'm Easy, 1993; Falling, 1994; Ricochet, 1995; Evidence, 1995; Ashes To Ashes, 1997; I Started A Joke, 1998; Albums: with Faith No More: Faith No More, 1985; Introduce Yourself, 1987; The Real Thing, 1989; Live At Brixton Academy, 1991; Angel Dust, 1992; King For A Day… Fool For A Lifetime, 1995; Album Of the Year, 1997; with Imperial Teen: Seasick, 1996; What Is Not To Love, 1998; Additional work: with Fenix TX, Lechuza, 2001. *Honours:* Bammy Awards: Outstanding Group, Best Keyboardist, 1991; MTV Video Award, Best Special Effects, 1991; Bay Area Award, Outstanding Keyboardist, 1993. *Current Management:* Warren Entner Management, 5550 Wilshire Blvd, Suite 302, Los Angeles, CA 90036, USA.

BOUBLIL, Alain Albert; b. 5 March 1941, Tunis, Tunisia. Author; Dramatist. *Career:* Author, dramatist and lyricist. *Publications:* Wrote libretto and lyrics for: La Révolution Française, 1973; Les Misérables, 1980; Abbacadabra, 1984; Miss Saigon, 1989; Le Journal d'Adam et Eve (play), 1994; Martin Guerre, 1996. *Honours:* 2 Tony Awards, 2 Grammy Awards, 2 Victoire de la Musique Awards, Molière Award (all for Les Misérables); Evening Standard Drama Award (for Miss Saigon); Laurence Olivier Award (for Martin Guerre). *Address:* c/o Cameron Mackintosh Ltd, 1 Bedford Sq., London WC1B 3RA, England.

BOUCOUM, Afel; b. 1955, Niafunke, Mali. Vocalist; Musician (guitar); Songwriter. *Education:* Won scholarship to study at government agricultural college in Mali. *Career:* Began by accompanying father to his performances; At 13 joined Ali Farka Toure's band, ASCO, 1968; Agricultural advisor by profession; Joined Orchestre Diaba Regional, 1982; Toured internationally with Toure since 1991; Formed Alkibar, early 1980s; Involved in Damon Albarn's Mali Music project. *Recordings:* The Source, Ali Farka Toure, 1992; Alkibar, 1999; The Rough Guide To The Music Of Mali and Guinea, 2000; The Music Of Mali, 2001. *Honours:* Mali's Biennale, second place, 1972. *Address:* c/o World Circuit Ltd, 138 Kingsland Rd, London E2 8DY, England.

BOULIANE, Daniel G; b. 26 Oct. 1963, Hull, Québec, Canada. Prod; Composer; Musician (keyboards, drums, percussion); Vocalist. m. Lise Roy, 1981, 1 s., 1 d. *Education:* Université du Québec; College Alexandre. *Career:* Soundtracks for NFB documentaries; Soundtracks for TV series; Soundtracks for Moving the Mountain; Soundtracks for many national ads. *Compositions:*

for Nadia: Free Free; Live on Love; Shine On; Beatman; for Roxxy: Love Set Us Free; I Feel You; For Us to Be; for Nathalie Page: This is the Time. *Recordings:* New World, 1994; Nomad, 1996; Remember, 1998; Image Compilation, 1992. *Publications:* Titles of Dak: New World, 1994; Nomad, 1996; Remember, 1998. *Membership:* Academic of Canadian Cinema and Television.

BOURASSA, Francois; b. 26 Sept. 1959, Montréal, Canada. Jazz Musician (piano). *Education:* Bachelor's Degree, Composition, McGill University; Master's Degree, Jazz, Academic Honours and Distinction in Performance, New England Conservatory of Music, Boston. *Career:* Concerts in Canada, USA, Europe (France, Belgium, Spain), Korea, Moscow, Mexico; Canadian tours of jazz festivals; Concert with Dave Brubeck; Celebration of Charles Dutoit's birthday, Radio France, Radio Canada. *Compositions:* Reflet 1; Jeune Vieux Jeune; Echo; Tour of France. *Recordings:* Reflet 1, 1986; Jeune Vieux Jeune, 1993; Echo, 1996; Cactus, 1998; Trio François Bourassa et André LeRoux: Live, 2001. *Honours:* Canada and Québec Arts Council Compositions Grants; Winner, 1985 Montréal International Jazz Festival's Competition. *Current Management:* Fleming Artists Management, 4102 St Urbain, Montréal, QC H2W IV3, Canada.

BOURDE, Hervé; b. 12 July 1951, Marseilles, France. Musician (saxophone, flute, piano); Composer. 1 d. *Career:* Tours, France and Europe, 15 years; Concepts for jazz festivals. *Recordings:* 6 solo records; 10 as soloist, composer. *Honours:* First prize, City of Marseilles Conservatoire. *Membership:* SPEDIDAM; ADAMI.

BOURDON, Rod; b. 20 Jan. 1979, Calabasas, CA, USA. Musician (drums). *Career:* Founding mem., Xero; Renamed Hybrid Theory and signed to Warner Bros, Spring 2000; Further name change to Linkin Park prior to first record releases; Numerous international appearances; Live shows include: Family Values, Ozzfest tours, KROQ Acoustic Christmas Concert 2001; TV specials include: Live At The Fillmore; Reverb. *Recordings:* Albums: Hybrid Theory, 2000; Reanimation, 2002. Singles: Hybrid Theory (EP), 2000; One Step Closer, 2001; Crawling, 2001; Papercut, 2001; In The End, 2001; Pts.Of.Athrty, 2002. *Honours:* Billboard Award, Best Modern Rock Artist, 2001; Rock Bear Awards, Best International Band, Best International Album, 2001; Kerrang! Award, Best International Newcomer, 2001; Rolling Stone Award, Best Hard Rock/Metal Band, 2001; MTV Awards, Best Group, Best Hard Rock, 2002. *Current Management:* Andy Gould Management, 8484 Wilshire Blvd #425, Beverly Hills, CA 90211, USA. *Website:* www.linkinpark.com.

BOURGOIN, Patrick G; b. 16 Dec. 1948, Paris, France. Musician (saxophones, flute, clarinet, EWI). *Education:* Autodidacte. *Career:* Has played with many French artists including Gino Vanelli in Paris and Manu Dibango on world tour, 1971–. *Recordings include:* With many French artists; Music for films; 1 album with Duran Duran. *Membership:* SACEM; SPEDIDAM. *Address:* 80 Bd Gambetta, 94130 Nogent sur Marne, France.

BOUSSAGUET, Pierre-Michel-André; b. 12 Nov. 1962, Albi, France. Jazz Musician (string bass player); Composer; Arranger. Divorced, 2 d. *Career:* with Guy Lafitte, 1986–; Tours, world-wide with artists including: Wynton Marsalis; Joe Pass; Didier Lockwood; Monty Alexander. *Compositions:* Impressions III, Creation for symphonic orchestra and jazz quartet; Symphonic and jazz pieces, 1997. *Recordings:* 2 Bass hits (with Ray Brown), 1988–; P Boussaguet Quintet featuring Tom Harrell, 1992; Charme, 1998; duet with Guy Lafitte, Crossings, 1999; current trio featuring H Sellin and A Queen, Charme, 1999. *Membership:* SACEM; UMJ. *Current Management:* B Hopper Management. *Address:* 52 rue Pierre Mourgues, 81000 Albi, France.

BOVA, Jeffrey Stephen; b. 22 June 1953, District of Columbia, USA. Musician (keyboards); Composer. *Education:* Berklee College of Music, 1971–72; Manhattan School of Music, 1972–75. *Career:* Musician, composer, 1975–; Assistant composer, arranger, Herbie Hancock, 1987–88; Cyndi Lauper, 1987–89; Ryuichi Sakamoto, 1988–89; Musician, composer, Distance, 1988–. *Compositions:* Composer, arranger, film soundtracks: Colors, 1989; The Handmaid's Tale, 1990; Pretty Woman, 1990. *Recordings:* Keyboard player on numerous albums including: The Bridge, Billy Joel, 1986; True Colors, Cyndi Lauper, 1986; Love, Aztec Camera, 1987; The Hunger, Michael Bolton, 1987; Cher, Cher, 1987; Foreign Affair, Tina Turner, 1989; Journeyman, Eric Clapton, 1989; Bat Out Of Hell II: Back Into Hell, Meat Loaf, 1993; Welcome To The Neighbourhood, Meat Loaf, 1995; Falling Into You, Céline Dion, 1996; Still Waters, The Bee Gees, 1997; Other recordings by Average White Band; Ian Hunter; Robert Hart; Hall and Oates; Mick Jones. *Honours:* Numerous Platinum discs. *Membership:* ASCAP.

BOVEE, Bob (Robert); b. 17 Feb. 1946, Omaha, Nebraska, USA. Musician (guitar, harmonica, banjo, autoharp); Vocalist. m. Gail A Heil, 8 Dec. 1988. *Education:* BA, History, University of Nebraska, 1969. *Career:* Six tours, Western Europe; Regular tours USA, 1971–; Iowa Public TV; Prairie Home Companion; River City Folk; Rural Route 3; Other syndicated radio shows; Festival of American Fiddle Tunes; Merlefest, Augusta Heritage Center; Roots Festival, San Diego. *Recordings:* Pop Wagner and Bob Bovee, 1977; The Roundup, 1979; For Old Time's Sake, 1985; Behind The Times, 1986; Come

All You Waddies, 1988; Rebel Voices, 1988; Come Over and See Me, 1991; Rural Route 2, 1996; When the Cactus is in Bloom, 2000. *Publications:* Numerous articles, reviews, American traditional music. *Address:* 18287 Gap Dr., Spring Grove, MN 55974, USA.

BOWEN, Lorraine; b. 31 Oct. 1961, Gloucestershire, England. Musician; Performer; Songwriter. *Education:* BMus (Hons) Surrey University. *Career:* Singing teacher to Billy Bragg; Writer, singer, The Lorraine Bowen Experience; Songwriter; International songwriter and performer of lounge hits and comedy songs. *Compositions:* Julie Christie; Crumble Song; Bicycle Adventure; I Love London; Space; Spinach. *Recordings:* with The Dinner Ladies: These Knees Have Seen The World, 1989; with Billy Bragg: The Internationale, 1990; Don't Try This At Home, 1991; William Bloke, 1997; with The Lorraine Bowen Experience: Greatest Hits Vol. I, 1995; Vol. II, 1998; Bossy Nova, 2001; Oh! What A Star!, 2002; Songs from the Living Room, 2002. *Membership:* MCPS; Musicians' Union; PRS. *Current Management:* Sequin Skirt Management. *Address:* c/o 6 Stannard Rd, London E8 1DB, England.

BOWIE, David, (David Jones); b. 8 Jan. 1947, Brixton, London, England. Vocalist; Actor. m. (1) Angela Barnet, divorced, 1 s., (2) Iman, 24 April 1992. *Career:* Solo recording artist, 1970–; Lead singer, Tin Machine, 1989–91; Actor, films, 1976–; World tours, concerts, television and radio appearances, many as Ziggy Stardust and Aladdin Sane; Performances include: Beckenham Free Festival (also organizer), 1969; Glastonbury Festival, 1971; Carnegie Hall, 1972; Royal Festival Hall, 1972; Earls Court, 1973; Madison Square Garden, 1978; Live Aid, Wembley, 1985; Dodger Stadium, Los Angeles, 1990; A Concert For Life (Freddie Mercury Tribute), 1992; Film appearances include: The Man Who Fell To Earth, 1976; Christiane F, 1980; Cat People, 1982; The Hunger, 1983; Merry Christmas Mr Lawrence, 1983; Ziggy Stardust, 1983; Labyrinth, 1986; Absolute Beginners, 1986; The Last Temptation of Christ, 1988; Theatre includes: The Elephant Man, 1980; Founded Bowieart.com online art dealer. *Recordings:* Numerous solo albums include: David Bowie, 1969; The Man Who Sold The World, 1971; Hunky Dory, 1971; The Rise and Fall Of Ziggy Stardust. . ., 1972; Aladdin Sane (No. 1, UK), 1973; Pin-Ups (No. 1, UK), 1973; Diamond Dogs (No. 1, UK), 1974; David Live, 1974; Young Americans, 1975; Station To Station, 1976; Low, 1977; Heroes, 1977; Lodger, 1979; Scary Monsters (No. 1, UK), 1980; Let's Dance (No. 1, UK), 1983; Ziggy Stardust The Motion Picture, 1983; Tonight (No. 1, UK), 1984; Never Let Me Down, 1987; Changesbowie (compilation; No. 1, UK), 1990; Black Tie White Noise (No. 1, UK), 1993; The Singles Collection (compilation), 1993; Outside, 1995; Earthling, 1997; Hours, 1999; Bowie At The Beeb (compilation of radio sessions and concerts), 2000; Heathen, 2002; with Tin Machine: Tin Machine, 1989; Tin Machine II, 1991; Numerous solo hit singles include: Space Oddity, 1969 (No. 1, UK, 1975); The Man Who Sold The World, 1971; Starman, 1972; The Jean Genie, 1972; Drive-In Saturday, 1973; Life On Mars?, 1973; Sorrow, 1973; Rebel Rebel, 1974; Diamond Dogs, 1974; Young Americans, 1975; Fame (No. 1, USA), 1975; Golden Years, 1975; Sound and Vision, 1977; Heroes, 1977; Boys Keep Swinging, 1979; Ashes To Ashes (No. 1, UK), 1980; Fashion, 1980; Wild Is The Wind, 1981; Cat People, 1982; Let's Dance (No. 1, UK and USA), 1983; China Girl, 1983; Modern Love, 1983; Blue Jean, 1984; Absolute Beginners, 1986; Fame 90, 1990; Real Cool World, 1992; Jump They Say, 1993; The Heart's Filthy Lesson, 1995; Strangers When We Meet/The Man Who Sold The World, 1995; Hallo Spaceboy, 1996; Little Wonder, 1997; Dead Man Walking, 1997; Seven Years In Tibet, 1997; I Can't Read, 1998; Growin' Up; Pretty Things Are Going To Hell, 1999; Thursday's Child, 1999; Seven, 2000; Everyone Says 'Hi', 2002; with Bing Crosby: Peace On Earth/Little Drummer Boy, 1977 (UK hit, 1982); with Mick Jagger: Dancing In The Street (No. 1, UK), 1985; with Queen: Under Pressure (No. 1, UK), 1981; with Pat Metheny Group: This Is Not America, 1985; Other projects include: Theme for When The Wind Blows, 1986; Music for The Buddha Of Suburbia (BBC TV), 1993; Other collaborators include: Goldie, Lou Reed, Nine Inch Nails, Iggy Pop. *Honours:* Music Video Awards; Silver Clef Award for Outstanding Achievement, 1987; Ivor Novello Awards include: Outstanding Contribution To British Music, 1990; Q Magazine Inspiration Award (with Brian Eno), 1995; BRIT Award, Outstanding Contribution To Music, 1996. *Current Management:* Isolar Enterprises, 641 Fifth Ave, Suite 22Q, New York, NY 10022, USA. *Website:* www.davidbowie.com.

BOWLS, Richard John (Ric); b. 13 July 1950, Rantoul, Illinois, USA. Recording Engineer; Musician (violin, guitar, keyboards). *Education:* Graduate, University of California, Riverside; Private music lessons from age 8; Also played in numerous orchestras. *Career:* Touring musician, 1975–77; Independent sound engineer, 1977–; Sound engineer, Total Expereince Records, 1986–88; Sound engineer, programmer, MIDI Studio Systems, 1988–; Technical consultant, Music Suite, 1992–; Designer, builder, various recording studios and keyboard systems; Guest speaker, lecturer on Electronic music; Owner/designer, Sendit Electronics; Owner, It's Only Plastic, music recording studios, 1999; Chief Engineer, Studio 56 Entertainment, 2001–; Recording engineer, films: Apocalypse Now; Darkman; Halloween; The Fog; Television credits as engineer and/or synth programming include: War and Remembrance; Knots Landing; Dallas; The Incredible Hulk; Little House On The Prairie; Wonder Woman; Love Boat; Hawaii 5–0; Moonlighting;

Baywatch; Star Trek: The Next Generation; Mission Impossible; Brady Bunch; Recordings and/or live credits include: Giorgio Moroder (11 albums); Donna Summer (5 albums); Cher; Michael Nesmith; Berlin; Gap Band; Oingo Boingo; Ahmad Jamal; Yarborough and Peoples; ELO; Deniece Williams; Earth Wind and Fire; The Crusaders; Frank Zappa; Stephen Stills; Barbra Streisand; George Clinton; David Bowie; Carl Palmer; Jean Luc-Ponty; Aretha Franklin; Peter Frampton; Sly Stone; Tom Jones; Lalo Schifrin; Cityscrapes film score; Co-productions with Carmine Appice. *Honours:* Academy Award, Apocalypse Now; Platinum disc, Donna Summer; 2 Gold discs, Cher; Grammy Award, Best Music Video, Michael Nesmith; Emmy Award, Golden Globe, People's Choice Award, all for War and Remembrance, 1989. *Membership:* NARAS. *Current Management:* Neil Scotti and Associates, 415 N Camden Dr, Beverly Hills, CA 90210, USA. *Address:* 1722 Rogers Pl. #25E, Burbank, CA 91504–3668, USA.

BOWN, Alan; b. 21 July 1942, Slough, Berkshire, England. Musician (trumpet); Man. m. Jean, 7 March 1964, 1 s., 1 d. *Education:* S/M/RAF School of Music; RAF bandsman, 1956–60. *Career:* Started playing with The John Barry Seven; Recorded 5 albums over 10 years with own band The Alan Bown; Tours with: The Who; Yes; Moody Blues; Cream; Television appearances: Top of the Pops; Ready Steady Go; Old Grey Whistle Test. *Recordings:* All compositions on own albums: Live At The Marquee, 1963 (first album); Outward Bown; Listen. *Membership:* PRS. *Address:* 71 Shaggy Calf Lane, Slough, Berks SL2 SHN, England.

BOWN, Andrew Steven; b. 27 March 1946, City of London, England. Musician (keyboards, bass guitar, guitar, harmonica); Vocalist. m. Caroline Attard, 4 June 1971, 1 s., 1 d. *Education:* Piano, Grade 6; Recorder to Grade 6. *Career:* Musician with: The Herd; Status Quo; Pink Floyd; Appearances include: Live Aid; Knebsworth Festival; Prince of Wales Trust; Last Tattoo in Berlin for HM Queen. *Compositions:* with Status Quo: Burning Bridges; Come On You Reds; Whatever You Want. *Recordings:* The Herd, Paradise Lost, 1968; The Final Cut, Pink Floyd, 1983; All albums with Status Quo, 1970–; Recordings with other artistes include: Jerry Lee Lewis; Roger Waters; Tim Hardin; Lesley Duncan; Johnny Halliday; Paul McCartney; Wendy James; Dusty Springfield. *Honours:* Silver Clef, 1981; Ivor Novello Award, 1983; BRIT Award, 1991. *Membership:* Musicians' Union; PRS; Equity. *Address:* c/o Universal Music Group, Universal Studios, 100 Universal City Plaza, Universal City, CA 91608, USA.

BOX, Mick; b. 8 June 1947, Walthamstow, London, England. Vocalist; Musician (guitar). *Career:* Founder member, UK rock band, Uriah Heep, 1970–; Extensive international tours; First western heavy rock group to perform in Moscow, 1987. *Recordings:* Albums: Very 'Eavy, Very 'Umble, 1970; Salisbury, 1971; Look At Yourself, 1971; Demons and Wizards, 1972; The Magician's Birthday, 1972; Uriah Heep Live, 1973; Sweet Freedom, 1973; Wonderworld, 1974; Return To Fantasy, 1975; High and Mighty, 1976; The Best Of Uriah Heep, 1976; Firefly, 1977; Innocent Victim, 1978; Fallen Angel, 1978; Conquest, 1980; Abnominog, 1982; Head First, 1983; Equator, 1985; Anthology, 1986; Live In Moscow, 1988; Raging Silence, 1989; The Uriah Heep Story, 1990; Still 'Eavy, Still Proud, 1990; Different World, 1991; Rarities, 1991; Sea Of Light, 1995; Time Of Revelation, 1996; Classic Heep, 1998; Spellbinder, 1999; Future Echoes Of The Past, 2001; Electrically Driven (with Ian Anderson), 2001.

BOY GEORGE, (George O'Dowd); b. 14 June 1961, Eltham, Kent, England. Vocalist; Songwriter; DJ. *Career:* Singer, Bow Wow Wow (under name Lieutenant Lush); Founder member, singer, Culture Club, 1982–89, re-formed 1998; Solo artiste, 1987–; Numerous tours world-wide, including Artists Against Apartheid, 1988; Composed, appeared in musical, Taboo (West End), 2002. *Compositions:* Numerous collaborations with John Themis. *Recordings:* Albums: with Culture Club: Kissing To Be Clever, 1982; Colour By Numbers (No. 1, UK and USA), 1983; From Luxury To Heartache, 1986; Don't Mind If I Do, 1998; Culture Club Box Set, 2002; Solo: Sold, 1987; Tense Nervous Headache, 1988; High Hat, 1989; Martyr Mantras, 1991; Cheapness and Beauty, 1995; U Can Never B 2 Straight, 2001. Hit singles: with Culture Club: Do You Really Want To Hurt Me; (No. 1, UK), 1982; Church Of The Poisoned Mind, 1983; Karma Chameleon (No. 1, UK and USA), 1983; Victims, 1983; It's A Miracle, 1984; Move Away, 1986; Solo: Il Adore; The Crying Game (film theme) with Pet Shop Boys, 1992; Everything I Own (No. 1, UK), 1987; When Will You Learn, 1999. *Publications:* Take It Like A Man (autobiography). *Honours:* BRIT Awards: Best British Newcomer, 1983; Best British Group, 1984. *Current Management:* Wedge Music, 63 Grosvenor St, London W1X 9DA, England.

BOYD, Brandon; b. 15 Feb. 1976, Van Nuys, California, USA. Vocalist; Musician (percussion). *Career:* Formed group Incubus with school friends in Calabasas, California, 1991; Initially played small parties, graduating to support slots in Hollywood, California; Circulated demo tapes of Closet Cultivation and Incubus before independent album release, 1995; Group signed by Immortal/Epic; Built US and European following support slots on tours with: Sugar Ray; Black Sabbath; Korn; Drive reached #1 on US Modern Rock Chart, 2001; First Japanese and Australian live dates, 2001. *Recordings:* Albums: Fungus Amongus, 1995; S.C.I.E.N.C.E., 1997; Make Yourself, 1999;

Morning View, 2001; Singles: Enjoy Incubus EP, 1997; Pardon Me, 1999; Stellar, When Incubus Attacks Vol. 1 EP, 2000; Drive, Wish You Were Here, 2001. *Honours:* Make Yourself album certified double platinum by RIAA; Billboard Award, Modern Rock Single of the Year, 2001. *Current Management:* Steve Rennie, REN Management, California, USA. *Website:* www.enjoyincubus.com.

BOYLAN, John Patrick; b. 21 March 1941, New York, USA. Prod. *Education:* BA, Bard College. *Career:* Executive Producer, CBS Records, 1976–80; Vice-President, CBS, 1980–86; President, Great Eastern Music Co, 1986–. *Recordings:* Producer for numerous acts including: Boston; The Charlie Daniels Band; Linda Ronstadt; Little River Band; Nelson; Carly Simon; As producer, film soundtracks: Nightshift; Urban Cowboy; Footloose; Born On The Fourth Of July; The Simpsons Sing The Blues. *Honours:* Numerous Platinum and Gold discs. *Membership:* NARAS; AFTRA; AFofM. *Address:* Great Eastern Music Co, 5750 Wilshire Blvd, Los Angeles, CA 90036, USA.

BOYLE, Dee (Diarmuid); b. Rotherham, England. Musician (drums). *Career:* Member, Chakk, 1985–88; The Longpigs; Left band, 1999. *Recordings:* Singles: Happy Again; She Said, 1995/1996; Jesus Christ, 1995; Far, 1996; On and On, 1996; Lost Myself, 1996; Blue Skies, 1999; Albums: The Sun Is Often Out, 1996; Mobile Home, 1999.

BOZIC, Petar Vedran; b. 21 May 1947, Zadar, Croatia. Vocalist; Musician (guitars, piano, harp). m. Majstorovic-Bozic Nada, 9 Sept. 1972, 1 s. *Education:* Studied mathematics; Musical schools, 10 years. *Career:* Played piano, amateur groups, 1963; Played guitar professionally, 1965; Played in famous Croatian groups: Gresnici, Roboti, Wheels of Fire, MI, BP Convention, Time, Boomerang, Parni Valjak; Countless stage, TV, radio appearances; Toured all over Europe; Studio Musician, Telephon Blues Band (formerly Call 66). *Compositions:* Several. *Recordings:* Studio Musician, recorded over 200 LPs or CDs, 1972–. *Honours:* HGU (Croatian Musicians' Union), Status prize for Best Guitar Player of the Year, 2000; Stari Macak (critics award), Lifetime Achievement in Rock and Roll Music, 2001. *Membership:* HGU. *Address:* Livadarskiput 3, 10000 Zagreb, Croatia.

BRAAM, Michiel; b. 17 May 1964, Nijmegen, Netherlands. Musician (piano); Composer; Bandleader. *Education:* Conservatory Hogeschool Voor de Kunsten Arnhem. *Career:* Leader, Pianist, Composer, Bik Bent Braam, Bentje Braam, Trio Braamdejoodevatcher; All Kinds of Projects In The Field of Modern Jazz and Improvised Musicians; Many television and radio appearances. *Compositions:* Het XYZ Der Bik Bent Braam; The Second Coolbook; The Hobbit. *Recordings:* Bik Bent Braam-Howdy; Bentje Braam: Playing The Second Coolbook; Trio Braamdejoodevatcher: Monk Materials and Colors; Solo-Oeps; Bik Bent Goes Bansai; Black/White; Het XYZ Der Bik Bent Braam. *Publications:* Tetterettet, 1996; New Dutch Swing, 1998. *Honours:* Dutch Most Important Encouragement Prize, 1989, 1996, 1997. *Membership:* Dutch Union of Improvising Musicians. *Current Management:* St Bik Bent Braam. *Address:* Prinseneiland 97bg, NL 1013, Amsterdam, Netherlands. *Telephone:* (20) 6129801. *E-mail:* bbbraam@xs4all.nl. *Website:* www.michielbraam.com.

BRADFIELD, James Dean; b. 21 Feb. 1969, Newport, Gwent, Wales. Musician (guitar); Vocalist. *Career:* Formed Betty Blue, became Manic Street Preachers; Numerous sell-out tours, many festival appearances; TV and radio appearances; First Western group to play concert in Cuba since 1979, February 2001. *Recordings:* Singles: New Art Riot EP, 1990; You Love Us, 1991; Motorcycle Emptiness, 1992; Theme From M.A.S.H., 1992; From Despair To Where, 1993; La Tristessa Durera, 1993; Roses in the Hospital, 1993; Faster/PCP, 1994; She Is Suffering, 1994; A Design for Life, 1996; Everything Must Go, 1996; Kevin Carter, 1996; Australia, 1996; If You Tolerate This Your Children Will Be Next (No. 1, UK), 1998; The Everlasting, 1998; You Stole The Sun From My Heart, 1999; Tsunami, 1999; The Masses Against The Classes (No. 1, UK), 2000; So Why So Sad, 2001; Found That Soul, 2001; Ocean Spray, 2001; Let Robeson Sing, 2001; Albums: Generation Terrorists, 1992; Gold Against the Soul, 1993; The Holy Bible, 1994; Everything Must Go (No. 1, UK), 1996; This Is My Truth, Tell Me Yours (No. 1, UK), 1998; Know Your Enemy, 2001; Forever Delayed, 2002; Also featured on: Lopez (with 808 State), 1997; I'm Left, You're Right, She's Gone (duet with Tom Jones), 1999; Producer for Northern Uproar, 1996; producer and co-writer, Some Kind Of Bliss, Kylie Minogue, 1997. *Honours:* BRIT Awards: Best British Group, 1997, 1999; Best British Album, 1997, 1999. *Current Management:* Martin Hall. *Address:* c/o Epic Records, 550 Madison Ave, New York, NY 10022-3211, USA. *Website:* www.manics.co.uk.

BRADFIELD, Marian; b. 31 Dec. 1953, Waterford, Ireland. Vocalist; Songwriter; Musician (guitar). m. Robert Bradfield, 17 Aug. 1974, 2 d. *Career:* Began career with Young Generation Choir, Waterford; Formed own group Peace; Performed at George Doherty's Folk Club, Donegal; Support concerts with: Mary Black; The Fureys; Davey Arthur; Concert with Sharon Shannon and Mick Hanley, Forum, Waterford, 1994; Performed with Altan, Belfast Festival; Showcase in Austin, Texas; Numerous television appearances include: Kenny Live, RTE; Bibi Show; Anderson On The Box, BBC; Mike Moloney; Alan Corcoran; Numerous radio appearances on FM 2, BBC Ulster

and local radio (Christmas Eve Special). *Recordings:* Albums: Marian, 1993; Tonight Is Just For Us, 1994; The Emperor's Field, 1998. *Honours:* Voted one of Ireland's Top 10 singers, Hot Press Readers, 1993.

BRADLEY, Stuart; b. 23 Sept. 1965, London, England. Musician (bass guitar, double bass); Teacher. m. Elizabeth Allen, 1 April 1995. *Education:* Studied violin with father, Desmond Bradley, composition with John Thomas and double bass with Clive Brown and Kevin Rundell; LRSM, DipMus, Open University; LTCL, MusEd, 1998. *Career:* Major tours with Take That, Gary Glitter, Roger Taylor and The London Philharmonic Orchestra; West End work on Taboo; Numerous television and radio appearances; Principal Bass Instructor, Acad. of Contemporary Music until 1996; Mem., Rockschool Ltd examiner panel, 1993–; Senior Music Examiner, –2002. *Compositions:* Brass Septet, 1997; Piece for Chamber Orchestra, 1998. *Recordings:* Why Can't I Wake Up With You?, Take That; Happiness, Roger Taylor; Piaf, Elaine Paige; Up And Over, Edwin Starr. *Membership:* Musicians' Union; PAMRA; Driving Instructors' Asscn; Register of Approved Driving Instructors; Institute of Advanced Motorists. *Address:* 65 Spring Rd, Lower Feltham, Middlesex TW13 7JA, England. *Telephone:* (20) 8893-7089. *E-mail:* stuartbradley@openlink.org.

BRADY, Paul; b. 19 May 1947, Strabane, County Tyrone, Northern Ireland. Folk Vocalist; Songwriter; Musician (multi-instrumentalist). *Career:* Member, The Kult; Planxty; Duo with Andy Irvine; Solo artiste, 1978–; Tours, including support to Dire Straits; Eric Clapton; Recent performance, Cambridge Folk Festival, 1995. *Compositions:* Songs include: Crazy Dreams (recorded by Roger Chapman, Dave Edmunds); Night Hunting Time (recorded by Santana); Steel Claw; Paradise Is Here (both recorded by Tina Turner); Film soundtrack, Cal, with Mark Knopfler; 2 tracks, Luck of The Draw, Bonnie Raitt, 1991. *Recordings:* Albums: Andy Irvine/Paul Brady, 1976; The High Part Of The Road (with Tommy Peoples), 1976; Welcome Here Kind Stranger, 1978; Hard Station, 1981; True For You, 1983; Full Moon, 1984; Back To The Centre, 1986; Molloy, Brady, Peoples (with Matt Molloy, Tommy Peoples), 1986; Primitive Dance, 1987; Paradise Is Here, 1989; Trick Or Treat, 1991; Spirits Colliding, 1995; Oh What A World, 2001; Singles include: Crazy Dreams (No. 1, Ireland); Theme music, UK television series, Faith In The Future, 1995. *Current Management:* c/o Ed Bicknell, Damage Management, 16 Lambton Pl., London W11 2SH, England.

BRADY, Philip; b. 4 March 1939, Liverpool, England. Vocalist; Musician (guitar). m. Barbara Ann Shaw, 6 March 1942, 1 s., 1 d. *Career:* Tommy Collins tour, Bill Clifton Show, 1963; Ernest Tubb Record Shop, Porter Waggonmaster Show, 1968; Jeannie Sealey, Hank Cochran tour, Germany; First Country Music Awards Show, Wembley Stadium; Bill Anderson, Loretta Lynn, Conway Twitty, George Hamilton IV; Buck Owens Tour, Liverpool Empire; London Palladium, Country Meets Folk, 1969; Hank Snow, Willie Nelson tour, Liverpool Empire, Bellevue Manchester, Lyceum Ballroom London, 1970; Nightride BBC; Slim Whitman Tour, all ABC theatres nationwide, 1972; Tours: Germany; Italy; Norway; Netherlands; Saudi Arabia. *Recordings:* Singles: American Sailor At The Cavern/Sidetracked; Little Rosa/One More Time; Rambling Boy; Lonesome For You; Let The Whole World Sing It With Me; Brady Country; Songs Of Nashville; A Little Bit Country; Live At Gunton Hall; Bobby McGee and Other Favourites; 7 albums. *Honours:* BCMA Award, presented by Roy Orbison, 1970. *Membership:* Equity. *Current Management:* Mike Hughes Entertainment. *Address:* 96 Bold St, Liverpool, England.

BRAGG, Billy; b. 20 Dec. 1957. Vocalist; Songwriter; Musician (guitar). *Recordings:* Singles include: Between The Wars, 1985; Levi Stubbs Tears, 1986; She's Leaving Home (with Cara Tivey; No. 1, UK), 1988; Sexuality, 1991; Albums include: Life's A Riot With Spy vs Spy, 1983; Brewing Up With Billy Bragg, 1984; Talking With The Taxman About Poetry, 1986; Back To Basics, 1987; Workers Playtime, 1988; The Internationale, 1990; Don't Try This At Home, 1991; William Bloke, 1996; Mermaid Avenue (with Wilco), 1998; Mermaid Avenue Vol. 2 (with Wilco), 2000; Also collaborated with: Kirsty MacColl, Beats International. *Current Management:* Sincere Management. *Address:* 421 Harrow Rd, London W10 4RD, England.

BRAKE, Marita; b. Springfield, Illinois, USA. Vocalist; Songwriter; Musician (guitar). m. Gil Moore, 11 Sept. 1982. *Education:* BS, Theatre, Illinois State University; Private music lessons, seminars, workshops. *Career:* Community concerts tour; Carnegie Hall; Canterbury Festival, Canterbury, England; Television broadcasts on BBC and PBS. *Compositions:* The Marita Brake In Concert Song Book, 1997. *Recordings:* Albums: The Road I Took To You, 1989; Gypsy Moon, 1996. *Publications:* Contributor of articles in magazines and reviews. *Honours:* Performance for Presidential Inauguration, 1997; Woman of Distinction Award for Excellence in the Arts. *Membership:* Nashville Songwriters Asscn; Folk Alliance; Gospel Music Asscn.

BRAMERIE, Thomas; b. 18 Sept. 1965, Bergerac, France. Musician (acoustic bass). m. Edith Vuillon, 22 Aug. 1992. *Education:* Various private lessons. *Career:* Sideman with various international jazz musicians in Europe, 1987–; Played with: Chet Baker; Toots Thielemans; Johnny Griffin; Frank Wess; Tom Harrell; Joshua Redman; European tour, with Jimmy Scott, 1994; Festival appearances: Nice; Montreux; Newport; Northsea; Permanent member, Belmondo Quintet; Michele Hendricks Quintet; Dédé Ceccarelli Quartet; Regular member of Dee Dee Bridgewater's Band, 1997; Several world tours, Japan, Europe, South America, USA, Canada. *Recordings:* Live In Paris, Teddy Edwards Quartet, 1994; For All Friends, Belmondo Quintet, 1994; From The Heart, Dédé Ceccarelli Quartet, 1996; Ted Nash European Quartet, 1996. *Address:* 641 E 11th St, Suite 4A, New York, NY 10009, USA.

BRAMLETT, Paul Kent; b. 31 May 1944, MS, USA. Attorney; Vocalist; Record Prod. m. Shirley, 2 s. *Education:* BA, David Lipsund University, 1966; JD, University of MS, 1969. *Career:* Performed on Stage as Singer, USA, European Countries. *Recordings:* 2 Albums, 1984, 1991. *Honours:* BA Hons; Special Guest Student, Niville Symphony, 1966. *Address:* PO Box 150734, Nashville, TN 31215 0734, USA.

BRANCH, Alan; b. 22 Jan. 1962, London, England. Sound Engineer; Musician (guitar); Prod; Programmer. m. 4 May 1988, 2 d. *Education:* City and Guilds, and Advanced City and Guilds Carpentry, Lime Grove College; Goldsmiths University, General Musicianship. *Career:* Live, session guitarist; Student; Tape operator at Topic Records; Engineer at The Works Studio; Engineer at Roundhouse Studios; Chief Engineer, Roundhouse Recording Studios. *Recordings:* Artists: M People; De La Soul; D:ream; Jamiroquai; Living Colour; Ruby Turner; Boy George; Omar; On U Sound; Adrian Sherwood; Primal Scream; Lighthouse Family; Eternal; Simply Red; Depeche Mode; Nine Inch Nails; Sinead O'Connor; The Popes; Various other artists. *Membership:* Musicians' Union. *Address:* 69 Lateward Rd, Brentford, Middlesex TW8 0PL, England.

BRAND, Oscar; b. 7 Feb, Winnipeg, Manitoba, Canada. Composer; Folk Vocalist; Musician (guitar); Writer. m. Karen Grossman, 14 June 1970, 3 s., 1 d. *Education:* BS Brooklyn College, 1942; Laureate History, Fairfield University, 1974. *Career:* Presenter, Folksong Festival, New York Public Radio, (oldest continuous radio show in history), 1945–; On credits of 75 documentary films; Hundreds of radio and television shows include: Host, Let's Sing Out, Canadian series; Music Director, Sunday Show, NBC; Exploring; Treasure Chest; Host, composer, First Look; Spirit of '76, NBC; Performer for children on television, records and film; Member, advisory panel which created television programme Sesame Street; Curator of Songwriters Hall of Fame; President, Gypsy Hill Music; Lecturer on Dramatic Writing, Hofstra University, Hempstead, New York; Artistic Director, Project America, 1998–2000. *Compositions include:* Songs for: Doris Day; Ella Fitzgerald; Harry Belafonte; The Smothers Brothers; Mormon Tabernacle Choir; Scripted, scored ballets for Agnes DeMille and Michael Bennett; Commercials include: Maxwell House; Oldsmobile; Log Cabin; Rival; Songs in films: The Fox; Sybil; The Long Riders; Blue Chips; Music for: In White America; Score for: How To Steal An Election; Music and lyrics with Paul Nassau for Broadway shows: A Joyful Noise; The Education of Hyman Kaplan; Wrote, scored Kennedy Center's Bicentennial musical, Sing America Sing; 2 new musicals in progress: Thunder Bay; Fun and Games. *Recordings:* Over 90 albums, latest being: I Love Cats, 1994; Get A Dog, 1995; Campaign Songs 1789–1996, 1999. *Publications:* Author, several best-selling books including: When I First Came To This Land; The Ballad Mongers (autobiography); Party Songs; Singing Holidays; Bawdy Songs; Songs of '76; Western Guitar; Celebrate; Bridge of Hope. *Honours:* Laureate, Fairfield University, 1972; Peabody Awards, 1982, 1996; Hon. PhD, University of Winnipeg, 1989; Radio Pioneers of America, 1991; Awards for film credits: Venice, Edinburgh, Golden Reel, Valley Forge, Freedoms Foundation; Scholastic; Golden Lion; Peabody; Ohio State; Edison; Emmy. *Membership:* SAG; AFTRA; ACTRA; Dramatists Guild; AFofM.

BRANDY, (Brandy Norwood); b. 11 Feb. 1979, McComb, Mississippi USA. Vocalist. *Education:* Major in Psychology and Music, Pepperdine University, California, USA. *Career:* Began singing when a child in the local church; Competed in numerous talent shows; Obtained record deal aged 14; Numerous live appearances and TV appearances; Many acting TV roles, incl. sitcom Moesha. *Recordings:* Albums: De Faida Cortita, 1995; Brandy, 1995; Never Say Never, 1998; Full Moon, 2002. Singles: Make it Right, 1990; Sittin' Up in My Room, 1995; Missing You, 1996; Top Of the World, 1998; The Boy is Mine (with Monica; No. 1, USA), 1998; Have You Ever, 1999; Almost Doesn't Count, 1999; What About Us, 2002; Also appears on: Michael Jackson, Invincible, 2001; Big Punisher, Endangered Species, 2001.

BRANHAM, (Robert) Shon; b. 27 Dec. 1960, Orange, Texas, USA. Maintenance Engineer. m. JoAnn LaPointe, 27 Oct. 1984, 2 d. *Career:* Appearances on local TV station; Won Male Vocalist from Texas; Appeared in Las Vegas in national contest, for Country Music Association of America. *Recordings:* Albums: This Country Boy Is Green, 1994; Two Steppin' Heaven, 1995; Shon, 2002. *Honours:* Male Vocalist from Texas, CMAA, 1993. *Membership:* International Fan Club Organization, Nashville. *Address:* Rt 1, Box 186, Kirbyville, TX 75956, USA.

BRANN, Chris, (P'Taah, Feral, Ananda Project); b. Atlanta, Georgia, USA. Prod; Remixer; DJ. *Career:* Formed Wamdue Kids, 1994; Has recorded for many labels including Strictly Rhythm; Collaborations: Gaelle Adisson; Remixed: Boney James; Bebel Gilberto; Everything But The Girl. *Recordings:*

Albums: Resource Toolbox Vol. 1 (with Wamdue Kids), 1996; These Branching Moments (with Wamdue Kids), 1997; Program Yourself (with Wamdue Kids), 1998; Release (as Ananda Project), 2001; Singles: Deep Dreams (with Wamdue Kids), 1996; King Of My Castle (UK No. 1 with Wamdue Project), 1997; Cascades Of Color (as Ananda Project), 1999; You're The Reason (with Wamdue Project), 1999; Glory Glory (as Ananda Project), 2000. *Address:* c/o Nite Grooves, 115 W 30th St, #306, New York, NY 10001, USA.

BRAUN, Rick; b. 6 July 1955, Allentown, Pennsylvania, USA. Musician (trumpet); Composer; Prod. m. Laura Hunter, 18 Oct. 1992. *Education:* Eastman School of Music, Rochester, New York. *Career:* Montreux Jazz Festival, 1979; 3 world tours with Rod Stewart, 1989–90; 1991–92; 1995; Tonight Show, 1991; Featured soloist with Sade, 1994. *Compositions:* Co-writer, Here With Me, REO Speedwagon, 1989. *Recordings:* Intimate Secrets, 1993; Christmas Present, 1994; Nightwalk, 1994; Beat Street, 1995; Body and Soul, 1996; Full Stride, 1998; Best Of Braun, 1999; Featured soloist; Album, Tina Turner, 1994; Born A Rebel, Tom Petty, 1984. *Honours:* BMI Top 100 Songs of the Year, Here With Me, 1990. *Membership:* BMI; AFofM. *Current Management:* Chapman and Co Management. *Address:* PO Box 5549, Santa Monica, CA 90409, USA.

BRAXTON, Anthony; b. 4 June 1945, Chicago, Illinois, USA. Jazz Musician (alto saxophone, clarinet). *Education:* Wilson Jr College. *Career:* Played clarinet and alto saxophone, US Army; Joined musician's co-operative, AACM, Chicago, 1966; Formed own group, The Creative Construction Company (CCC), 1968; Co-founder, Circle (with Chick Corea, Dave Holland, Barry Altschul), 1970; Played in France with various European improvisers; Member, Globe Unity Orchestra; Performed at Derek Bailey's Company Festivals; Performed with own quartet; Duo with drummer Max Roach, 1970s; Teacher, Wesleyan College, Connecticut, 1980s–. *Compositions:* Approximately 400 include: Series of 12 operas, Trillium; Quartet (London), 1985; Quartet (Birmingham), 1985; Quartet (Willisau), 1991. *Recordings:* Over 70 albums as bandleader; Appeared on numerous other recordings by artistes including Joseph Jarman; George Lewis; Max Roach; Derek Bailey; Muhal Richard Abrams; CCC; ROVA Saxophone Quartet; London Jazz Composers Orchestra. *Publications:* Tri-axium Writings, 1985; Composition Notes (5 vols), 1988.

BRAXTON, Toni; b. 1969, Philadelphia, Pennsylvania, USA. Vocalist. *Career:* Member of female vocal group with sisters Tamar, Trin and Tavanda, 1990; Solo recording artiste. *Recordings include:* Solo albums: Toni Braxton, 1993, Secrets, 1996; The Heat, 2000; Snowflakes, 2001; Hit singles: Breathe Again, 1994; Another Sad Love Song, 1994; Unbreak My Heart (No. 1, USA), 1996; You're Making Me High (No. 1, USA), 1996; I Don't Want To, 1997; How Could An Angel Break My Heart (with Kenny G), 1997; He Wasn't Man Enough, 2000; Spanish Guitar, 2000. *Honours:* Grammy Award, Best Female R&B Vocal Performance, He Wasn't Man Enough, 2001. *Address:* c/o Stiefel Entertainment, Suite 6120, 9255 Sunset Blvd, Los Angeles, CA 90069, USA.

BRAZIER, Graham Philip (The Brazz); b. 6 May 1952, Auckland, New Zealand. Vocalist; Composer; Musician (guitar, saxophone, harmonica). m. Alexandra, 13 Nov. 1993, 1 s., 1 d. *Career:* Appearances, national New Zealand and Australian television on video clips, interviews, Film: Queen City Rocker; Played support to Dire Straits; Eurythmics; Fleetwood Mac; Bryan Ferry; Marianne Faithfull; Canned Heat; Bo Diddley; Gerry Harrison; Many major Australian acts. *Recordings:* Albums include: 4 Hello Sailor studio albums; 2 solo albums; 1 live album; Numerous compilations, EPs and singles. *Honours:* Vocalist of Year; Best Song; Runner-up for APRA Silver Scroll 3 times. *Membership:* APRA (voting mem.). *Current Management:* James Rowe (Strawberry Fields), PO Box, Raglan, New Zealand. *Address:* 13 Taupata St, Mt Eden, Auckland 3, New Zealand.

BRAZIER, Roy; b. 28 Jan. 1965, Walthamstow, London, England. Bandleader; Musician (saxophone, blues harp); Vocalist. *Career:* Founder member, Darktown, 1987, for parties, functions; Performed for Williams Grand Prix Engineering; Concerts supporting Mud; The Troggs; Desmond Dekker; Jools Holland; Television and video appearances: Ridin' High, Robert Palmer (full length album video); Television commercial for News of The World, Greystoke Productions; Performed 309 gigs, 1994; Television advertisement for Cross and Blackwell, 1996; Television appearance on Top Gear, BBC TV, 1997. *Recordings:* with Darktown: Blues, Jazz and Other Animals. *Honours:* Voted in Top Ten Blues Harp players, UK, 1995; Certificate of Excellence for Blues Harmonica at the European Harmonica Festival, Germany, 1996. *Membership:* Musicians' Union. *Address:* 227 Monks Walk, Buntingford, Hertfordshire SG9 9DY, England.

B-REAL, (Louis Freeze); b. 2 June 1970, South Gate, Los Angeles, USA. Vocalist; Rap Artiste. *Career:* Member, Cypress Hill; Numerous tours including Lollapalooza; Collaboration with Pearl Jam on soundtrack to film Judgement Night, 1993; Remix of Insane the Brain by Jason Nevins, 1999. *Recordings:* Singles include: Phunky Feel One, 1991; Hand On The Pump, 1991; Latin Lingo, 1991; Insane In The Brain, 1993; We Ain't Goin' Out Like That EP, 1995; Throw Your Set In The Air, 1995; Boom Biddy Bye Bye, 1996; Unreleased and Revamped, 1996; Illusions, 1996; Tequila Sunrise, 1998; Rap

Superstar, 2000; Albums: Cypress Hill, 1991; Black Sunday, 1993; Cypress Hill III, Temples Of Boom, 1995; IV, 1998; solo: The Psycho Realm; additional collaborations: Eat At Whitey's (with Everlast), 2000; No Retreat (with Dilated Peoples), 2000; Xplosion (with OutKast), 2000; Deadly Assassins (single; with Everlast), 2001.

BRECHIN, Sandy; b. 20 April 1969, Edinburgh, Scotland. Musician; Composer; Label Owner. *Education:* MA, Languages, Edinburgh University; Private accordion and piano lessons. *Career:* Toured all over the world with the bands, Burach, Seelyhoo and the Sandy Brechin Band, as well as a variety of solo, teaching and session work; Many appearances on BBC TV and Radio, STV and Channel 4, including, The Lottery Show Live: A Song for Britain, 1997; Also several appearances on European TV and Radio and in the USA and Far East; Scottish Folk Festival Tour of Germany, 1996 with Aly Bain and Phil Cunningham; Recent appearances: STV's Boxed Set, 2000, with Donnie Munro and Karen Mathieson; Channel 4's Tartan Jam, 2000, with Martyn Bennet and Natalie Macmaster; Toured USA, Canada, South America, Scandinavia, Iceland, Spain, France, Netherlands, Italy, Germany, Czech Republic, Turkey, Hong Kong, Thailand and Middle East; Owner, Brechin All Records. *Recordings:* With Burach: The Weird Set, 1995; Born Tired, 1997; Deeper, 2000; With Seelyhoo: The First Caul, 1995; Leetra, 1998; Solo Albums: Out Of His Box, 1996; Out Of His tree, 1999; On the West Side, Donnie Munro, 2000; Also appears on over 30 other albums and compilations; Tuitional Video: Learn Scottish Accordion with Sandy Brechin, 2000. *Publications:* How to Get (The Best) Out of Your Box, book of own compositions, 2000. *Membership:* Musicians' Union; Equity; MCPS/PRS; TMSA. *Current Management:* Brechin All Records. *Address:* 5 The Square, Kirkliston, West Lothian, EH29 9AX, Scotland.

BRECKER, Michael; b. 29 March 1949, Philadelphia, PA, USA. Musician (saxophone, horns); Bandleader. *Career:* Member, Billy Cobham's band, 1970s; Founder, group Dreams; The Brecker Brothers (with Randy Brecker); Bandleader, 1987–; Also played with Horace Silver; James Taylor; Yoko Ono; David Sancious; Prolific session musician. *Recordings:* Albums: with Billy Cobham: Crosswinds, 1974; Total Eclipse, 1974; Shabazz, 1975; A Funky Thide To Sings, 1975; Inner Conflicts, 1978; with The Brecker Brothers: The Brecker Brothers, 1975; Back To Back, 1976; Don't Stop The Music, 1977; Heavy Metal Be-Bop, 1978; Detente, 1980; Straphangin', 1981; Blue Montreux, 1989; Collection, Vol. I, 1990; Vol. II, 1992; Big Idea, 1992; Return Of The Brecker Brothers, 1992; Out Of The Loop, 1994; Solo albums: City Scape, 1983; Mike Brecker, 1987; Don't Try This At Home, 1989; Now You See It, Now You Don't, 1991; Tales from Hudson, 1997; Two Blocks from the Edge, 1998; Time Is Of The Essence, 1999; Nearness Of You: The Ballad Book, 2001; with Randy Brecker: Toe To Toe, 1990; In The Idiom, 1991; Score, 1993; with Herbie Hancock: The New Standard, 1996; Directions In Music (also with Roy Hargrove), 2002; Also recorded with numerous artists including: Dreams; Steps Ahead; Charles Mingus; John Lennon; Eric Clapton; Paul Simon; Pat Metheny; John Abercrombie. *Publications:* Michael Brecker Artist Transcription Books, Vols I and II. *Honours:* 7 Grammy Awards including Best Jazz Instrumental Performance, 1996, 1997, Best Jazz Instrumental Solo, 1996, 1997. *Current Management:* Depth of Field Management, 1501 Broadway, Suite 1304, New York, NY 10036, USA.

BRECKER, Randy (Randall Edward); b. 27 Nov. 1945, Philadelphia, Pennsylvania, USA. Musician (trumpet, saxophone, horns); Arranger. m. Eliane Elias, 1 d. *Education:* Indiana University, 1963–66; Classical trumpet studies at school. *Career:* Professional trumpeter, 1966–; Prolific freelance musician; Played with: Blood, Sweat and Tears; Horace Silver; Art Blakey; Clark Terry; Janis Joplin; Stevie Wonder; James Brown; Larry Coryell; Billy Cobham; Charles Mingus; Lew Tabakin; Bandleader/arranger, 1975–; Formed Dreams with brother Michael; The Brecker Brothers (also with Michael); Leader, Randy Brecker Band; Arranger for numerous artists include: George Benson; Diana Ross; Chaka Khan; Clinician, National Association of Jazz Educators. *Recordings:* Albums: with The Brecker Brothers: The Brecker Brothers, 1975; Back To Back, 1976; Don't Stop The Music, 1977; Heavy Metal Be-Bop, 1978; Detente, 1980; Straphangin', 1981; Blue Montreux, 1989; Collection, Vol. I, 1990; Collection, Vol. 2, 1992; Big Idea, 1992; Return Of The Brecker Brothers, 1992; Out Of The Loop, 1994; Solo albums: Toe To Toe, 1989; In The Idiom, 1991; Live At Sweet Basil, 1992; Score, 1993; Into The Sun, 1995; Hanging In The City, 2001; with Horace Silver: You Gotta Take A Little Love, 1969; with Billy Cobham: Crosswinds, 1974; Total Eclipse, 1974; Shabazz, 1975; A Funky Thide To Sings, 1975; Inner Conflicts, 1978; with Charles Mingus: Me, Myself and Eye, 1978; Also on albums by numerous artists including: George Benson; Carla Bley; Eric Clapton; Dire Straits; Billy Joel; Elton John; Rickie Lee Jones; B. B. King; Manhattan Transfer; John Mayall; Lou Reed; Diana Ross; Todd Rundgren; Carly Simon; Paul Simon; Bruce Springsteen; Steely Dan; James Taylor; Tina Turner; Luther Vandross; Steve Winwood; Frank Zappa. *Membership:* AFofM. *Current Management:* Depth of Field Management. *Address:* 1501 Broadway, Suite 1304, New York, NY 10036, USA.

BREGVADZE, Nani Georgievna; b. 21 July 1938, Georgia. Vocalist. *Education:* Tbilisi Conservatoire (pianoforte class under Machutadze). *Career:* Soloist with Georgian State Philharmonia, 1959–, with Georgian popular orchestra 'Rero', 1959–64, with 'Orera', 1964–80; Specializes in Georgian music and Russian romances; Has toured abroad on numerous occasions. *Honours:* People's Artist of USSR, 1983; Hon. Citizen of Tbilisi, 1995; Order of Honour, 1995; People's Artist of Georgia, 1996; State Prize of Georgia, 1997. *Address:* Irakly Abashidze str. 18A, Apt 10, 380079 Tbilisi, Georgia. *Telephone:* (32) 22-37-22.

BRENNAN, Dave; b. 24 Dec. 1936, Rotherham, England. Bandleader; Musician (banjo, guitar, parade drums); Vocalist; Master of Ceremonies; Broadcaster. m. (1) 2 s., (2) Val Hudson, 28 Sept. 1996. *Education:* CEng; M I MechE. *Career:* Own jazz programme, BBC Radio Sheffield, 17 years; Bandleader, 1960–; Leader: Jubilee Jazz Band; Jubilee New Orleans Brass Band; Heritage New Orleans Brass Band; Big Easy New Orleans Parade Band; Toured widely including: USSR (twice), Russia and Siberia; Toured Europe with the International Jazz Band, 1997. *Recordings:* Mardi Gras in New Orleans; Take Me To The Mardi Gras; Rags, Stomps and Dreamy Melodies; Inn Swinger; Amazing Grace; Bouncing Around; Let's Get This Show On The Road with Alton Purnell; Swinging At Swinden, with Louis Nelson; International Jazz Band; Several recordings with Chris Blount Jazz Band, Ken Colyer and Sarah Spencer's Rue Conti Jazz Band. *Membership:* Musicians' Union; MI Mech E; Labour Party; SIMA. *Address:* Tanglewood, Marcliff Lane, Wickersley, Rotherham, S66 2AZ, England.

BRENNAN, John Wolf; b. 1954, Dublin, Ireland. Musician (piano, organ); Composer; Conductor. m. Béatrice, 2 d. *Education:* Musicology, Film and Literature, University of Fribourg; Piano (with Eva Serman), Lucerne Conservatory; Organ, Conducting, Academy of School and Church Music; Composition (with Karl Berger), CMS Woodstock/New York and (with James Wilson) Royal Irish Academy of Music, Dublin; Masterclasses with Edison Denisov, Ennio Morricone, Klaus Huber and Heinz Holliger. *Career:* Concert tours in Western and Eastern Europe, Russia, Japan, Canada and USA; Recording projects include: Pago Libre (pan-European jazz quartet with Arkady Shilkloper, Tscho Theissing and Daniele Patumi); Trio Aurealis (with Robert Dick and Daniele Patumi); Pipelines (with Hans Kennel and Marc Unternährer); Momentum (with Gene Coleman, Christian Wolfarth and Alfred Zimmerlin); Entropology (with Eddie Prévost and Simon Picard); HeXtet (with Julie Tippetts, Evan Parker, Chris Cutler, Paul Rutherford and Peter Whyman); Nisajo (with Nicky Heinen and Alexander Alexandrov); Many other collaborations include: Alex Cline; Gabriele Hasler; Norma Winstone; Christy Doran; Urs Leimgruber; Corin Curschellas; Lindsay Cooper; Margrit Rieben; Reto Senn; Member of Swiss composers' group, Groupe Lacroix; Has composed for piano; glockenspiel; chamber ensemble; a capella choir; choir, orchestra and alphorn. *Compositions include:* The Well-Prepared Clavier; Silly Blooze; Sonata Pentatonica; KLA4; Zigfing; Frictions; Euratorium; Bestiarium; Through The Ear of a Raindrop; Sculptural Sonorities; Morgenstern Hat Gold Im Mund; Epithalamium; Alef Bet: An Ori-ental Peace Piece; A Golly Gale's Way To Galway Bay; Nearly Charming; The Age of Anxiety. *Recordings include:* Aurealis, 1997; Through the Ear Of a Raindrop, 1998; The Well-Prepared Clavier, 1998; Brink Man Ship, 1998; Minute Age, 1999; Momentum, 1999; Entropology: The Science Of Sonic Poetry, 2000; Pipelines, 2000; Momentum 2, 2000; Cinémagique, 2001. *Honours:* Werkjahr, Dienemann Foundation, Lucerne, 1989; Förderpreis, Sarna Jubilee Foundation, 1991; Stipendium of BINZ39 Art Foundation Zurich, 1993; Prize, National Flute Asscn, USA, 1993; Award, Jubilee Foundation of Union Bank of Switzerland, 1994; Miglior Disco Del Anno, Jazzpoll of MusicaJazz, Milano, 1994; Album of the Year, Jazzthetik, 1996; Invitation by Hindemith Foundation to write octet, 1997; London Fellowship, Zuger Kulturstiftung Landis and Gyr, 1997; Markant Foundation Fellowship and opera commission, 2000. *Membership:* AIC; CMC; STV; SMS. *Current Management:* Musaic Artist Management, Claudia Julina, 1016 S B St, San Mateo, CA 94401, USA. *Address:* Hofmattstrasse 5, 6353 Weggis, Lucerne, Switzerland. *E-mail:* johnwolf@brennan.ch. *Website:* www.brennan.ch.

BRENNAN, Maire, (Maire Ni Bhraonain); b. 4 Aug. 1952, Dublin, Ireland. Vocalist; Musician (harp). *Career:* Founder member, singer, harpist, folk group Clannad, 1970–; Regular Irish and international tours include: Germany, 1975; USA, 1979; Europe, 1983; UK, 1986, 1991; Concerts include: Cambridge Folk Festival, 1991; Scottish Fleadh, Glasgow, 1992; Fleadh '92, Finsbury Park, London, 1992; Royal Albert Hall, 1993; Television includes: Clannad In Donegal, CH4 documentary, 1991; Hostage: Tribute To Brian Keenan, BBC, 1991; The Tonight Show, NBC, 1993. *Compositions include:* Television and film music: Harry's Game, ITV, 1982 (also used in film soundtrack Patriot Games and Volkswagen television commercial); Robin of Sherwood, ITV, 1984; The Atlantic Realm, BBC1, 1988. *Recordings:* Albums: Magical Ring, 1983; Legend, 1984; Macalla, 1986; Sirius, 1987; Atlantic Realm, 1989; Pastpresent, 1989; Clannad The Collection, 1989; Anam, 1993; Banba, 1993; Lore, 1996; Landmarks, 1998; Solo albums: Maire, 1992; Misty-Eyed Adventures, 1995; Perfect Time, 1998; Whisper To The Wild Water, 1999; Solo album: Maire, 1992; Singles include: Theme From Harry's Game, 1982; Robin (The Hooded Man), 1984; In A Lifetime, 1986; Both Sides Now, with Paul Young (used in film soundtrack Switch), 1991. *Honours:* Ivor Novello Award, Best Theme From A Television Or Radio Production, Theme From Harry's Game, 1983; British Academy Award, Best Soundtrack of Year, Robin of Sherwood, 1985. *Current Management:* Upfront Management, 4 Windmill Lane, Dublin 2, Ireland.

BRESLIN, Paul; b. 27 June 1950. Vocalist; Composer; Lyricist; Musician (guitar). m. Cathy Liegeois, 14 Feb. 1989, 1 s. *Education:* Reed College. *Career:* Bandleader, on stage and live television, for Percy Sledge, 1994–95; Bandleader for Billy Paul, Europe, 1995; Played all major French jazz festivals with Eddy Louiss (Hammond organ). *Compositions:* Music and lyrics for Ray Charles: Separate Ways; Good Thang. *Recordings:* Solo albums: Hot Lunch; Rikitikitak; Musician on recordings by: Gilbert Becaud; Serge Gainsbourg; Michel Columbier; Françoise Hardy; Catherine Deneuve; Eddy Louiss; France Gall; Michel Berger. *Current Management:* Delabel-Chrysalis. *Address:* 24 Pl. des Voges, 75003 Paris, France.

BRETT, Martin; b. 29 March 1959, Dorking, Surrey, England. Musician (bass guitar, guitar, piano). 2 s. *Career:* Bass guitar, Voice of the Beehive; World-wide tours; Television includes: Top of the Pops; Songwriting partnership with Voice of the Beehive for new album and singles; Formed own music production company, Brett Dempsey Music, with Michael Dempsey (former Cure mem.); Studio in Sussex; Composer for films, television and commercials. *Recordings:* Albums: Let It Bee; Honey Lingers; Sex and Misery. Singles include: Don't Call Me Baby; Monsters and Angels; Angel Come Down. *Membership:* PRS; PAMRA; Musicians' Union; MCPS. *E-mail:* info@bdmmusic.com. *Website:* www.bdmmusic.com.

BREWER, Neil; b. 15 July 1952, Berkhamsted, England. Musician (guitar, bass guitar); Vocalist. *Career:* Several major tours and radio shows: Television appearance with band Druid, Old Grey Whistle Test, 1975; Currently solo artist, guitarist and lead vocalist, with self-programmed/arranged computerised backing. *Recordings:* Albums: Toward The Sun, 1975; Fluid Druid, 1976; Druid 1; Singles: Modern Women, Splash; 2 singles, Frame By Frame. *Membership:* Musicians' Union; PRS. *Address:* 45 Melsted Rd, Boxmoor, Hemel Hempstead, Hertfordshire HP1 1SX, England.

BREWER, Teresa; b. 7 May 1931, Toledo, Ohio, USA. Vocalist. m. Bob Thiele, 24 Oct. 1972, 4 d. (previous marriage). *Career:* Played with: Count Basie; Duke Ellington; Benny Carter; Stéphane Grappelli; Earl Hines; Ruby Braff; Dizzy Gillespie; Television appearances: Co-host, Summertime USA, with Mel Tormé, 1953; Co-host, Perry Presents, with Tony Bennett, 1959; Ed Sullivan Show, 39 times; Film appearances include: Those Redheads From Seattle, 1953; Concerts include: Carnegie Hall, New York City, 1978; Montreux Jazz Festival, Switzerland, 1983. *Recordings:* 75 albums and 125 singles; Recorded over 600 songs; 43 songs in US charts including: Music! Music! Music!; Till I Waltz Again With You; Ricochet; A Sweet Old Fashioned Girl; Let Me Go Lover!; A Tear Fell; The Original Sound Of Miss Music! Music! Music!, 2001. *Honours:* 6 Gold records. *Membership:* Society of Singers. *Current Management:* Bob Thiele. *Address:* c/o Bill Munroe, 584 Prospect St, New Haven, CT 06511, USA.

BREWIS, David; b. 3 June 1957, Sunderland, England. Musician (guitar, bass, keyboards); Record Prod; Songwriter. *Education:* Newcastle College (diploma). *Career:* Member, Kane Gang; UK and European tours; Television appearances include Solid Gold (USA); Top of the Pops; Whistle Test; The Tube; Co-writer of theme for BAFTA Award-winning children's series Byker Grove (Zenith for BBC TV, 1988–). *Recordings:* Albums: with the Kane Gang: Bad and Lowdown World, 1985; Miracle, 1987; Hit singles: Small Town Creed, 1984; Closest Thing To Heaven, 1984; Respect Yourself, 1984; Gun Law, 1985; Motortown, 1987; Don't Look Any Further (US Billboard No. 1), 1988; As Producer: Prefab Sprout albums: Swoon, 1984; tracks for compilation Life Of Surprises, 1992; As Guitarist: Andromeda Heights, Prefab Sprout album, 1997; Ocean Drive, Lighthouse Family album, 1995. *Membership:* PRS; BMI. *Address:* Soul Kitchens, St Thomas Workshops, Newcastle Upon Tyne NE1 4LE, England.

BREWSTER, Cori; b. 1960, Canada. Musician (guitar); Vocalist. *Career:* Major Canadian festivals, television shows. *Recordings:* Album: One More Mountain, 1994. *Current Management:* Horton Management and Publishing. *Address:* PO Box 48165, 595 Burrard St, Vancouver, BC V7X 1N8, Canada.

BREZOVSKY, Ali; b. 26 Feb. 1940, Slovakia. Composer. m. Vlasta Brezovska, 8 Dec. 1963, 1 s., 1 d. *Education:* Faculty of Pedagogy, Bratislava, Slovakia. *Career:* Various projects including scores to Slovak films, Smoliari, 1978; Losers, Zázracny Autobus, 1981; Magic Bus; Scores to theatre plays, many songs (pop and rock) and instrumental compositions. *Compositions:* Rozpravkovi Stopari, fairy-tale; Hitchhikers (children's); Cengá Do Triedy (School Bell is Ringing); Let/Flight: Songs for LP of a popular Slovak Rock Group. *Recordings:* CD, original soundtracks Of Ali Brezovsky, 1996. *Honours:* Third Place, International Music Festival, Bratislavska, Lyra, 1974, 1985; Award for Original Soundtrack, 1978; Smoliari; Summer Film Festival. *Membership:* Slovak Music Asscn; Soza/Slovak Union of Authors.

BRIGHT, Anna Lia; b. 25 Feb. 1952, West Palm Beach, Florida, USA. Songwriter; Vocalist; Poet. *Education:* Studied under Napoleon Bright and Bengt Lindskog. *Career:* Appearances on Danish television and radio; Singer

in piano bars, clubs, cafés and concert halls in Holland, Spain, Scandinavia and the Canary Islands; Currently Songwriter for various artists; Tours schools with her show Stand Up Poetry (poetry, song and storytelling). *Recordings:* As songwriter, Wind and Fire, by Frank Ryan, You Better Believe, by Zapp Zapp and Walk The Walk; As singer and songwriter, That's Lambada; To This Planet. *Publications:* Undiscovered Days, poetry, 1996. *Honours:* Editors Choice Award for OutstandingAchievement in Poetry, National Library of Poetry, 1997; Hon. Mention for short stories entered in Daily City Short Story Contest; Certificate of Achievement, university song contest for Border Line Affair. *Membership:* KODA; NCB; DJBFA. *Address:* Mosedalvej 9 2 th, 2500 Valby, Copenhagen, Denmark.

BRIGHTMAN, Sarah; b. 14 Aug. 1961, London, England. Vocalist; Actress; Dancer. m. Andrew Lloyd Webber, 1984, divorced 1990; partner Frank Peterson. *Career:* Former mem., Pan's People and Hot Gossip groups; Concerts world-wide, including tour, The Music of Andrew Lloyd Webber; Performances include: Cats, 1981; Masquerade, 1982; Song and Dance (TV), 1984; The Merry Widow (operatic debut, Sadlers Wells, London), 1985; Requiem, 1985; The Phantom of the Opera (West End and Broadway), 1986; Aspects of Love (West End and Broadway), 1991–92; I and Albert; The Nightingale, 1982; Trelawney of the Wells, 1993; Relative Values, 1993; Dangerous Obsession; The Innocents. *Recordings:* Albums: The Trees They Grow So High, 1986; The Songs That Got Away, 1989; As I Came Of Age, 1990; Sings The Music Of Andrew Lloyd Webber, 1992; Dive, 1993; Surrender: Unexpected Songs, 1995; Fly, 1996; Timeless, 1997; Eden, 1998; In Concert, 1999; La Luna, 2000; Very Best Of 1990–2000, 2001; Whiter Shade Of Pale/ Question Of Honour, 2001; Encore, 2002. Singles: I Lost My Heart To A Starship Trooper (with Hot Gossip), 1978; Pie Jesu (with Paul Miles-Kingston), 1985; The Phantom Of The Opera (with Steve Harley), 1986; All I Ask Of You (with Cliff Richard), 1986; Wishing You Were Somehow Here Again, 1986; Amigos Para Siempre (Olympic anthem, with José Carreras), 1991; Time To Say Goodbye (with Andrea Bocelli), 1997. *Address:* c/o Sunhand Ltd, 63 Grosvenor St, London W1X 9DA, England. *Telephone:* (20) 7493-7831. *Website:* www.sarah-brightman.com.

BRIMLEY, Robert George; b. 11 March 1943, Kent, England. Musician (jazz guitar, piano, keyboards). m. Indra, 1989, 2 s. *Education:* Technical College; Classical music training, since 9 years of age. *Career:* Played most jazz venues, jazz festivals. *Compositions:* Music written for television documentary Corporate Video work; Jingles; Kitty To The Cape; Aldabra Underwater Documentary; Air Ambulance Theme; Lands End Theme; Film including: A Year In Cornwall; Geeyor Tin Mine; Songs Loving You; Love With A Stranger. *Membership:* PRS; BAC&S; Musicians' Union. *Current Management:* Cot Valley Music. *Address:* Cot Valley Lodge, Cot Valley, St Just, Penzance, Cornwall, England.

BRINCK, Lars; b. 30 March 1957, Copenhagen, Denmark. Musician (keyboards); Composer; Arranger. m. Karen-Lis Kristensen, 18 Aug. 1984, 4 s. *Education:* Royal Academy of Music, Århus, Denmark. *Career:* Keyboard player for: Arvid Hunter; Gary Snider; Poul Krebs; Jette Torp; Tomas Kellerup; Erik Grip; Lene Siel; Television appearances, Denmark, 1989–91. *Recordings:* Arvid Hunter, 1989; Tomas Kellerup, 1990–92; Gary Snider, 1992; Erik Grip, 1993; Lene Siel, 1994; Jette Torp, 1995; Lars Brinck Jam Session, 1997. *Publications:* Numerous piano teaching manuals. *Honours:* Royal Academy Annual Award, three times. *Membership:* DJBFA; Gramex. *Address:* c/o LB Productions, Ludvig Holbergsvej 13, 8230 Åbyhoej, Denmark.

BRISLIN, Kate (Young); b. 19 Feb. 1946, Portsmouth, Ohio, USA. Vocalist. m. (1) Tom Brislin, 8 June 1968; (2) Jody Stecher, 29 July 1987. *Education:* BA, English, University of Guam. *Career:* Appearance, Prairie Home Companion, May 1994; As backing singer: with Laurie Lewis: Restless Rambling Heart, 1986; Earth and Sky, 1997; Third Annual Farewell Reunion, Mike Seeger, 1994; Pieces of My Heart, Alice Gerrard, 1994; with Jody Stecher: Going Up On The Mountain, 1976; Rasa, 1980; Out On The Rolling Sea, 1994; Heartsong, 1997; Oh The Wind and The Rain, 1999. *Recordings:* with Arkansas Sheiks: Whiskey Before Breakfast, 1975; with The Blue Flame Stringband, 1982; with the Any Old Time Stringband, 1978; I Bid You Goodnight, 1996; with Any Old Time: Ladies Choice, 1980; Duets with Jody Stecher: A Song That Will Linger, 1989; Blue Lightning, 1991; Our Town, 1993; Stay Awhile, 1995; Duet with Katy Moffatt: Sleepless Nights, 1996; Heart Songs, 1997; Also appears on: Young Fogies Vol. 2, 1995; Use A Napkin, 1995; American Fogies Vol. 2, 1996; Rounder Bluegrass Guitar, 1996. *Membership:* IBMA; North American Folk Alliance. *Address:* 133 Lake St, San Francisco, CA 94118, USA.

BRITT, Michael Wayne; b. 15 June 1966, Fort Worth, Texas, USA. Country vocalist; Musician (guitar). *Education:* University of Texas, Pharmacy and English. *Career:* Received first guitar, aged 15; Played in various school bands; Joined Santa Fe and had minor hits on independent label 16th Avenue as member of Canyon, 1988–90; Formed Texasee with Dean Sams, Keech Rainwater, Richie McDonald and John Rich, 1992; Group became resident house band at the Wildhorse Saloon, Nashville; After subsequent name change to Lonestar, came to the attention of BMG and were signed to their BNA subsidiary; Released promotional six-track live CD, recorded at the

Wildhorse; First country chart entry No News/Tequila Talkin' from debut album Lonestar, 1996; Single, Amazed, from third album became huge international hit and career record to date, 1999; By early 2000s, Lonestar estimated to be the most successful country group in the world. *Compositions include:* Runnin' Away With My Heart. *Recordings include:* No News, Tequila Talkin', 1996; Come Cryin' To Me, You Walked In, 1997; Say When, Everything's Changed, 1998; Amazed, Smile, 1999; I'm Already There, 2002; Albums include: Lonestar, 1995; Crazy Nights, 1997; Lonely Grill, 1999; I'm Already There, 2001. *Address:* c/o Country Music Asscn, 1 Music Circle S, Nashville, TN 37203, USA.

BRITTON, Reginald L; b. 19 Nov. 1964. Musician (Drums). 3 c. *Education:* School marching bands; Bellville Black Knight Drum Corps. *Career:* Young Americans; Tash and Country Magic; Eddie Snow's Snow Flakes; G Sharp Band; Tom Irwin Band; Oysters Rockefeller. *Compositions:* 63 Blues; Mind My Own Business; Hooked on Something; Too Stupid; Little Bit Crazy; Every Now and Then; Gone to Long; Loving Ways. *Recordings:* Past and Present; Oysters Rockefeller. *Publications:* 63 Blues, 1996; Mind Your Own Business, 1998; Hooked on Something, 1998; Every Now and Then, 1998. *Membership:* Central Illinois Blues Club; American Federation of Musicians. *Current Management:* Oyster Sound Management and Record Corp. *Address:* PO Box 20656 Springfield, IL 62708, USA.

BRITTON, Simon, (Balance); b. 22 Jan. 1971, Bristol, England. Record Prod; Re-Mixer; Vocalist; Musician (keyboards). *Education:* Trained vocalist; Studied classical music. *Career:* Vocalist under name 'Balance', major recording success in Europe; Featured vocalist, several Top 10 UK Dance Music hits; Producer, several Dance Music hits; Featured vocalist with Black Box (major Italian production team). *Recordings:* Backing vocalist for artists including Tears For Fears; Scritti Politti; Massive Attack. *Membership:* Musicians' Union. *Current Management:* Leisure UK. *Address:* Suite 404, Victory House, Somers Rd N, Portsmouth, Hampshire PO1 1PJ, England.

BROCHET, Marc; b. 3 April 1956, Soissons, Aisne, France. Composer; Musician; Teacher. m. Dominique Hemard, 11 Dec. 1981, 1 s., 2 d. *Education:* First Prize d'Harmonie; Orchestration; Conservatoire Superieur de Paris. *Career:* Concerts with vocal jazz group Vox Office; Festivals include: Nice; Vienna; Tel Aviv; Televised concert for M6; Teacher in musical writings, Conservatoire National d'Enseignement Superieur de Poitiers. *Compositions:* Music for theatre and dance. *Recordings:* Boppin' In French, Vox Office. *Publications:* for television and radio.

B-ROCK. See: **LITRELL, Brian Thomas.**

BROCK, Dave; b. Isleworth, Middlesex, England. Vocalist; Musician (guitar). *Career:* Founder member, UK rock group Hawkwind, 1969–; Regular UK and US tours; Concerts include: Glastonbury Fayre, 1971, 1981; Reading Festival, 1975, 1977, 1986; Futurama Festival, Leeds, 1979; Stonehenge Festival, 1981, 1984; Monsters of Rock, Castle Donington, 1982. *Recordings:* Albums: Hawkwind, 1970; In Search Of Space, 1971; Doremi Fasol Latido, 1972; Space Ritual, 1973; Hall Of The Mountain Grill, 1974; Warrior On The Edge Of Time, 1975; Astounding Sounds and Amazing Music, 1976; Road Hawks, 1976; Masters Of The Universe, 1977; Quark Strangeness and Charm, 1977; 25 Years On, 1978; PXR-5, 1979; Live 1979, 1980; Levitation, 1980; Sonic Attack, 1981; Church Of Hawkwind, 1982; Choose Your Masques, 1982; Zones, 1983; The Chronicle Of The Black Sword, 1985; Angels Of Death, 1987; Spirit Of The Age, 1988; The Xenon Codex, 1988; Space Bandits, 1990; Stasis, 1990; Electric Tepee, 1992; It Is The Business Of The Future, 1993; The Business Trip, 1994; New World's Fair, 1995; Alien 4, 1996; In Your Area, 1999; Weird Tapes Vols 1–6, 2000; Spacebrock, 2001; Singles include: Silver Machine, 1972; Urban Guerilla, 1973. *Current Management:* Doug Smith Associates, PO Box 2098, London W12 9RZ, England.

BRODERICK, Michael; b. 21 April 1941, Dumfries, Scotland. Folk Vocalist; Musician (bodhran). m. Irene Masia, 3 Sept. 1976, 1 s., 1 d. *Career:* Founder member of folk group The Whistlebinkies; Appearances include: John Cage's Scottish Circus, 1991; Toured extensively including: France, Germany, Italy, Sweden and People's Republic of China; Played at numerous festivals including Edinburgh International Festival and The Hong Kong Folk Festival; Television appearances: Celtic Weave, 1994; Celtic Connection, 1994. *Recordings:* The Whistlebinkies 1–5; Anniversary (compilation); Inner Sound. *Membership:* Equity; PRS. *Address:* Eddie McGuire, 13 Lawrence St, Glasgow G11 5HH, Scotland.

BRODY, Lane (Lynn Connie Voorlas); b. Oak Park, Illinois, USA. Vocalist; Songwriter. m. Edward H Bayers Jr, 14 Nov. 1994. *Education:* Private study. *Career:* Singer; Commercials include: Wrigley's; Johnson Wax; McDonalds; Tours world-wide with: John Anderson; Willie Nelson; Steve Wariner; Tom Bresh; Lee Greenwood; Television appearances: Taxi; Heart of The City; OSO TV Special; Lee Greenwood TV Special; Today Show; Austin City Limits. *Compositions include:* Tough Enough; Hottest Night of the Year, Anne Muray (co-wrote); All The Unsung Heroes; Yellow Rose (co-wrote). *Recordings:* Tender Mercies theme; The Gift Of Life theme; Country Gold soundtrack; Yellow Rose title track; All The Unsung Heroes title song; Tough

Enough, title track. *Honours:* BMI Award, Yellow Rose; American Film Festival Video Documentary of the Year; Numerous awards, Military and Charity organizations. *Membership:* SAG; AFTRA; NARAS; CMA; ACM. *Current Management:* Lane Brody Global Fan Club. *Address:* PO Box 24775, Nashville, TN 37202, USA.

BROFSKY, Howard; b. 2 May 1927, New York, USA. Musician; Musicologist. m. Robin Westen, 2 s., 1 d. *Education:* PhD, New York University. *Career:* Assistant Professor, University of Chicago, 1960–67; Professor, Queens College, Graduate School, City University of New York, 1967–92; President, Vermont Jazz Center. *Recordings:* Georgie Johnson, Paris, 1955; Larry Rivers and The East 13th Street Band, 1985. *Publications:* The Art of Listening: Developing Musical Perception. *Honours:* Fulbright Fellowship, 1953, 1972. *Membership:* IAJE; AMS; International Musicological Society.

BROKENSHIRE, Frederick; b. 21 April 1952, Toronto, Ontario, Canada. Music Industry Exec. 2 s., 1 d. *Education:* 2 years, Memorial University of Newfoundland. *Career:* Entered music business, 1972; President, majority shareholder, The Duckworth Group; Atlantica Music and Distribution Ltd; Duckworth Distribution Ltd; Latitude Records Inc; FRB Productions; Wildshore Music Inc; Atlantica Musique et Distribution Ltee; Fred's Records Ltd; Atlantic Canada's leading music companies; Engaged in record production, distribution, artist management, concert promotion, retail, with offices in: St John's; Halifax; Moncton; Toronto; Canada. *Membership:* Founding mem., president, Music Industry Asscn, Newfoundland; Director, East Coast Music Asscn; Mem., regional representative, Canadian Country Music Asscn; Canadian Academy Recording Arts and Sciences; Mem., Music Industry Asscn of Nova Scotia. *Address:* The Duckworth Music Group, 198 Duckworth St, St John's, Newfoundland A1C 1G5, Canada.

BROKOP, Lisa; b. 6 June 1973, Surrey, British Columbia, Canada. Vocalist; Songwriter; Musician (guitar, keyboards). *Career:* Singer, Rhythm guitarist, keyboardist, Marty Gillan and the Sweetwater Band, 1988; Formed own band, 1989; Toured with Clay Walker and George Strait; Film role: Harmony Cats; Performed CCMA Awards Show, Canada, and CMA Awards Show Nashville, 1992. *Recordings:* Albums: Every Little Girl's Dream, 1994; Lisa Brokop, 1995; Singles: Give Me A Ring Sometime, 1994; Take That, 1994; Who Needs You, 1995; She Can't Save Him, 1995; Before He Kissed, 1996; How Do I Let Go, 1998; When You Get To Be You, 1998. *Honours:* Horizon Award (Best New Artist), Gospel Performer of Year, British Columbia Country Music Asscn (BCCMA), 1990; Princess Margaret Order of Lion, Special Ambassador, 1991; CKWX Songwriter's Contest, 1991; Female Vocalist of Year, BCCMA, 1992; Youth Achievement Award, Vocal Excellence, YTV, 1992; Female Vocalist of Year, International Achievement Award, BCCMA, 1993; Vocal Collaboration Award with Johner Brothers, Saskatchewan Country Music Asscn, 1994; Worldfest Houston Gold Award, 1994; Female Vocalist of Year, International Achievement Award, Single of Year, BCCMA, 1994. *Membership:* SOCAN; CCMA; CMA; ACM; AFofM. *Current Management:* Mascioli Entertainment Corporation. *Address:* 11 Music Circle S, First Floor, Nashville, TN 37203, USA.

BROM, Gustav; b. 22 May 1921, Velké Leváre, Czech Republic. Jazz Band Conductor; Musician (violin, clarinet, saxophone). m. Marie Bromová-Gergelová, 1 s., 1 d. *Education:* Music school; Private study. *Career:* Jazz band leader, 5 years; 300 concerts home and abroad; Jazz festivals; Rated among 10 best world jazz bands in world. *Recordings:* 175 albums; About 100 singles; About 30 CDs; 20 own compositions. *Publications:* My Life With Jazzband. *Honours:* Czechoslovak State Award. *Address:* Preslova 28, 602 00 Brno, Czech Republic.

BROM, Rafael; b. 13 Aug. 1952, Prague, Czech Republic. Vocalist; Musician (multi-instrumentalist); Composer; Prod; Performer. *Education:* Graphic Art; Fine Art; Computer Graphics. *Career:* Appearances: Radio stations, USA, Canada; 9 albums, 2 singles. *Recordings:* Albums: Rafael Brom 1, 1983; Lord Hamilton-Padre Pio, 1985; Peace Of Heart, 1986; The Sounds Of Heaven, 1989; Dance For Padre Pio, 1991; The True Measure of Love, 1992; Music For Peace Of Mind, 1993; The Christmas Songs; You'll Never Walk Alone; Angelophany; All My Love To You Jesus. *Honours:* ASCAP Special Award. *Membership:* ASCAP. *Current Management:* Cosmotone Records. *Address:* PMB 412, 3350-A Hwy 6, Sugarland, TX 77478, USA. *Website:* www.marianland.com/music02.

BRON, Gerry; b. 1 March 1933, London, England. Man; Prod; Co Dir. m. 8 July 1982, 2 s. *Education:* Clarinet, Harmony, Composition, Trinity College of Music, London. *Career:* Family Business, 1949; Manager: Gene Pitney; Manfred Mann; Uriah Heep; Formed Bronze Records, 1971; Built Roundhouse Recording Studios, 1974. *Recordings:* Productions include: Manfred Mann; Bonzo Dog Doo Dah Band; Colosseum; Juicy Lucy; Osibisa; Gene Pitney; Uriah Heep. *Address:* 17 Priory Rd, London NW6 4NN, England.

BRONZE, David; b. 2 April 1952, Billericay, Essex, England. Musician (bass). m. Julie, 1 s., 1 d. *Career:* Mem., Procul Harum, Robin Trower Band, Dr Feelgood, Art of Noise, Duane Eddy Band, Barbara Dickson Band, Mickey

Jupp Band, Chris Farlowe and The Thunderbirds, Eric Clapton Band, Paul Carrack Band. *Recordings:* with Dr Feelgood, as prod., mixer, musician: Down At The Doctors, 1994; On The Road Again, 1996; As musician: with Eric Clapton: From The Cradle, 1994; Pilgrim, 1998; with Procol Harum: Prodigal Stranger, 1991; with Paul Carrack: Beautiful World, 1997; with Gary Barlow: Open Road, 1997; with Nik Kershaw: 1997, 15 Minutes, 1999; To Be Frank, 2001; with Eric Bibb: Home To Me, 1997; Painting Signs, 2001; Natural Light (also prod.), 2003; with S.A.S. Band: Show, 2001; with Gordon Haskell: Shadows On The Wall, 2002; Many sessions with various artistes. *Honours:* Blueprint magazine, Best UK Bassist, 2000, 2001, 2002. *Membership:* PRS; Musicians' Union; PAMRA. *Address:* c/o 107A High St, Canvey Island, Essex, England.

BROOKES, Jon; Musician (drums). *Career:* Founding mem., The Charlatans, 1990–; Signed to Beggars Banquet Records, later Universal Records; Numerous tours, festivals, television and radio appearances. *Recordings:* Albums: Some Friendly (No. 1, UK), 1990; Between 10th And 11th, 1992; Up To Our Hips, 1995; The Charlatans (No. 1, UK), 1995; Tellin' Stories (No. 1, UK), 1997; Melting Pot: The Best Of The Charlatans, 1998; Us And Us Only, 1999; Songs From The Other Side, 2000; Wonderland, 2001; Live It Like You Love It, 2002. Singles: Indian Rope, 1990; The Only One I Know, 1990; Then, 1990; Me In Time, 1991; Over Rising, 1991; Weirdo, 1992; Tremelo Song, 1992; Can't Get Out Of Bed, 1994; Autograph, 1994; I Never Want An Easy Life If Me And He Were Ever To Get There, 1994; Jesus Hairdo, 1994; Crashin' In, 1994; Just Lookin', 1995; Just When You're Thinkin' Things Over, 1995; One To Another, 1996; North Country Boy, 1997; How High, 1997; Tellin' Stories, 1997; My Beautiful Friend, 1999; Forever, 1999; Impossible, 2000; Love Is The Key, 2001; A Man Needs To Be Told, 2001; You're So Pretty—We're So Pretty, 2002. *Honours:* Gold, Silver and Platinum discs. *Address:* The Charlatans, PO Box 134, Sandbach, Cheshire CW11 1YS, England. *E-mail:* cat@thecharlatans.net. *Website:* www.thecharlatans.net.

BROOKLYN FRIENDS. See: **MORALES, David.**

BROOKS, Anthony Lewis; b. 20 April 1956, Treorchy, Rhondda, Wales. Prod; Composer; Performer. 1 s. *Education:* Electrical Engineering, Nayland Technical College; Piano, Brass, Percussion, Bass, University of Wales; Music Degree, IRCAM; Sound Design Degree, Institute of Research Computers and Music, Paris. *Career:* Executives, British tours, Artatak, British tours, Television and Radio; ICA London Performance, 1975; Europe, USA Tours with Various Groups; Darts 2, British tours; Olympic Culture Event, Centre for Performing Arts, Atlanta, 1996; Danish Television, Tony Brooks Is Orchestra Soundscapes; Culture City Europe, Copenhagen, 1996; The World Is One Festival, Seoul, 1996; The Oedipus Production, Seoul, 1997; Designed Coil Interactive Sound and Image Room installation, leading museums for modern art, Scandinavia, 1998–99; Performance for Danish Institute for Electroacoustic Music, 1998; Performed at Malmö, Sweden Statensteater, 1997; Performed and composed Oedipus Trilogy, Seoul, Republic of Korea; Performed, Exit Festival, Sweden, 1999; Behind the Wall, International Århus Festival, Denmark, 1999; Danish Newave and New York Festival, 1999. *Compositions:* Heaven People; Earth Tribe, 1, 2, and 3. *Recordings:* Tony Brooks Is Earth Tribe, 1, 2, and 3; Heaven People. *Membership:* Danish Music Union; Danish Jazz Beat and Folk Authors; IRCAM, Paris. *Current Management:* Pappagallo, Schleppegrellesgade 8, 8000 Århus, Denmark. *Address:* Heibergsgade 21 kld, 800 Århus C, Denmark.

BROOKS, Clyde Scott; b. 16 Jan. 1948, Milwaukee, USA. Musician (percussion, drums); Record Prod. m. Geri Brooks, 13 May 1988. *Education:* Berklee College of Music, Boston, 1968–70. *Career:* Session musician for: Dolly Parton; Kenny Rogers; Ronnie Milsap; Don Henley; Oak Ridge Boys; Johnny Winter; Jerry Lee Lewis; Barbara Mandrell; George Strait; Ted Nugent; Little Richard; B J Thomas. *Recordings:* Record producer for recordings by: Nancy Brooks; Lynn Anderson; The Headlights; B B Watson; Ronna Reeves. *Publications:* Author, The Recording Drummer, 1974. *Membership:* AFTRA; Country Music Asscn; AFofM.

BROOKS, David John; b. 6 June 1951, Sheffield, England. Vocalist; Songwriter; Musician (guitar, keyboards). m. Anthia Stephens, 19 Feb. 1985. *Education:* Wells Cathedral School. *Career:* Opening solo act for many bands on various tours including: Fairport Convention; Georgie Fame; Chris Farlowe; Steve Gibbons Band; Ronnie Lane's Slim Chance. *Compositions:* Theme and incidental music, BBC television series: The Family, 1974; Story of Ruth, 1978; Romers Egypt, 1980; Breakaway Girls, 1978; Vox Pop, 1983; One Day, 1988; In Solidarity, 1989; Forty Minutes, 1993. *Recordings:* Family Theme, 1974; Vox Pop, 1983. *Membership:* BAC&S; PRS; Musicians' Union. *Current Management:* Anthia Brooks. *Address:* 82 Lambton Rd, London SW20 0LP, England.

BROOKS, Elkie, (Elaine Bookbinder); b. 25 Feb. 1946, Salford, Manchester, England. Vocalist. *Career:* Toured with Eric Delaney Band, 1960s; Joined jazz-rock act Dada (later became Vinegar Joe), 1970–74; Solo artiste, 1974–. *Recordings:* Albums: Rich Man's Woman, 1975; Two Days Away, 1977; Shooting Star, 1978; Live and Learn, 1979; Pearls, 1981; Pearls II, 1982; Minutes, 1984; Screen Gems, 1984; No More The Fool, 1986; The

Very Best Of Elkie Brooks, 1986; The Early Years 1964–66, 1987; Bookbinder's Kid, 1988; Inspiration, 1989; Round Midnight, 1993; Pearls III, 1993; Circles, 1995; Nothin' But The Blues, 1996; Round Midnight, 1996; From The Heart, 1996; Pearls Concert Live, 1999; We've Got Tonight, 2000; Singles include: Hello Stranger; The Way You Do The Things You Do; Pearl's A Singer, 1977; Sunshine After Rain, 1977; Fool If You Think It's Over, 1982; Nights In White Satin, 1982; No More The Fool, 1986. *Address:* c/o Barry Collings Entertainments, 21a Clifftown Rd, Southend-on-Sea, Essex SS1 1AB, England.

BROOKS, Kix (Leon Eric III); b. 12 May 1955, Shreveport, Louisiana, USA. Country vocalist; Musician (guitar); Songwriter. *Career:* Member, Brooks and Dunn (with Ronnie Dunn). *Compositions include:* Brand New Man; I'm Only In It For The Love; My Next Broken Heart; That Ain't No Way To Go; Whiskey Under The Bridge; You're Gonna Miss Me When I'm Gone. *Recordings:* solo: Baby When Your Heart Breaks Down, 1983; Sacred Ground, 1989: as Brooks and Dunn: Brand New Man, 1991; My Next Broken Heart, 1991; Neon Moon, 1992; Boot Scootin' Boogie, 1992; Hard Workin' Man, 1993; We'll Burn That Bridge, 1993; She Used To Be Mine, 1993; Rock My World (Little Country Girl), 1993; That Ain't No Way To Go, 1994; She's Not The Cheatin' Kind, 1994; Little Miss Honky Tonk, 1995; You're Gonna Miss Me When I'm Gone, 1995; Whiskey Under The Bridge, 1995; My Maria, 1996; I Am That Man, 1996; A Man This Lonely, 1996; He's Got You, 1997; Honky Tonk Truth, 1997; How Long Gone, 1998; Husbands and Wives, 1998; I Can't Get Over You, 1999; You'll Always Be Loved By Me, 2000; Ain't Nothing 'Bout You, 2001; Only In America, 2001; The Long Goodbye, 2002; Albums include: Brand New Man, 1991; Hard Workin' Man, 1993; Waitin' On Sundown, 1994; Borderline, 1996; The Greatest Hits Collection, 1997; If You See Her, 1998; Tight Rope, 1999; Steers and Stripes, 2001. *Honours:* various including: CMA, Vocal Duo of the Year, 1993–98. *Website:* www.brooks-dunn.com.

BROOKS, Meredith; b. Corvallis, Oregon, USA. Vocalist; Songwriter; Musician (guitar). *Career:* Member, all-female group The Graces, 1990; Solo recording artist, 1991–. *Recordings include:* Albums: Blurring The Edges, 1997; See It Through My Eyes, 1997; Deconstruction, 1999; Hit Singles: Bitch, 1997; What Would Happen, 1998. *Current Management:* Lori Leve Management, 151 N Almont Dr., Suite 305, Beverly Hills, CA 90211, USA.

BROOKS, Nikki (Nichola Jane); b. Bristol, England. Musician (keyboards, bass guitar, clarinet); Vocalist. *Education:* BPharm, Degree; All grades Theory and Practical, Guildhall School of Music, Associate and Licentiate, London College of Music Diplomas. *Career:* ECT, Ch4, 1985; Lead vocalist, McCoy, 1985; Lead vocalist, Wild!, 1986–87; Lead and backing vocalist, bass, keyboards in various covers bands; Currently in Adam and The Ants covers band, and session musician; Played with members of: Gillan; Iron Maiden; UFO; Wild Horses; Pat Travers Band; Gary Moore Band; Tours, festivals in UK and Europe; Vocal sessions include: Dreamboys, LA Centrefold Videos; Currently writing material with songwriting partner. *Recordings:* Wrote and recorded 4 song session for BBC Radio 1 Rock Show (Tommy Vance). *Honours:* Prize for Grade 3 Guildhall Practical Piano. *Membership:* Musicians' Union; PRS. *Address:* Flat C, 49 Roxborough Park, Harrow-On-The-Hill, Middlesex HA1 3BA, England.

BROOKS, (Troyal) Garth; b. 7 Feb. 1962, Tulsa, Oklahoma, USA. Country vocalist; Songwriter; Musician (guitar). m. Sandra Mahl, 1986, 2 d. *Education:* BS, Journalism and Advertising, Oklahoma State University, 1985. *Career:* Television specials include: This Is Garth Brooks, 1992; This Is Garth Brooks Too!, 1994; Garth Brooks: The Hits, 1995; Best selling country album ever, No Fences (over 13m. copies). *Recordings:* Albums: Garth Brooks, 1989; No Fences, 1990; Ropin' The Wind, 1991; The Chase, 1992; Beyond The Season, 1992; In Pieces, 1993; The Hits, 1994; Fresh Horses, 1995; Sevens, 1997; In The Life Of Chris Gaines, 1999; The Colors Of Christmas, 1999; Scarecrow, 2001; Singles: If Tomorrow Never Comes, 1989; Tour EP, 1994; To Make You Feel My Love, 1998; One Heart At A Time, 1998; Lost In You, 1999. *Honours:* Grammy Award; CMA Horizon Award, Video of the Year, 1990; CMA Awards: Best Single, Best Album 1991; Music City News/TNN Award, Video of Year, 1991; CMA Entertainer of the Year, 1991–92; Numerous ACM Awards include: Music Entertainer of the Year, 1991–94, Best Single 1991, Best Album 1991; ASCAP Voice of Music Award, 1992; 9 People's Choice Awards; American Music Awards, Favourite Country Male Artist, Favourite Country Album, for Double Live, 2001, Special Award of Merit, 2002; Top-selling solo artist in American music history, RIAA. *Membership:* Inducted into Grand Ole Opry; ASCAP; CMA; ACM. *Current Management:* Scott Stern, GB Management Inc, 1111 17th Ave S, Nashville, TN 37212, USA.

BROSCH, Christopher; b. 9 April 1957, Munich, Germany. Promoter; Agent. m. Kerstin Estherr Brosch, 20 June 1991, 1 d. *Education:* Law studies, Cologne. *Career:* Freelance tour manager for various German tour promoters, 1980–85; Talent Booker for Peter Rieger Koncertagentur, Cologne, acts include: Peter Gabriel; Joe Cocker; Run-DMC; Beastie Boys; Changed to Hamburg based company, Blinffish Promotion, as talent booker for new bands; Started own company: Bizarre Productions, 1992; Acts promoted include: Beastie Boys; Portishead; Hole; Cocteau Twins; Oasis; Foo Fighters;

Daft Punk; New talent outdoor festival in the summer. *Address:* Buelaustr 8, 20099 Hamburg, Germany.

BROUDIE, Ian; b. 4 Aug. 1958. Vocalist; Songwriter; Musician (guitar); Prod. *Career:* Member, Original Mirrors, late 1970s; Member, Big In Japan, 1977; Member, duo, Care, mid-1980s; Founder, The Lightning Seeds, 1990–; Record producer, 1980s–; Numerous television and radio appearances; Concerts include: Glastonbury Festival, 1995. *Recordings:* Albums: Cloudcuckooland, 1991; Sense, 1992; Jollification, 1994; Dizzy Heights, 1996; Like You Do... The Best Of, 1997; Tilt, 1999; Singles: with The Lightning Seeds: Pure, 1989; Joy, 1990; Life Of Riley, 1992; Sense, 1992; Lucky You, 1994; Change, 1995; Marvellous, 1995; Perfect, 1995; Ready Or Not, 1996; What If, 1996; Sugar Coated Iceberg, 1997; You Showed Me, 1997; What You Say, 1997; Life's Too Short, 1999; Singer, songwriter, Three Lions (Official England Squad's Euro '96 theme) with David Baddiel and Frank Skinner (No. 1, UK), 1996/1998; Record producer, numerous artists include: Echo and The Bunnymen; The Fall; Wah!; Icicle Works; The Primitives; Alison Moyet; Frank and Walters; Dodgy; Sleeper. *Current Management:* JPR Management, The Powerhouse, 70 Chiswick High Rd, London W4 1SY, England.

BROUGHTON, Bruce; b. 8 March 1945, Los Angeles, CA, USA. Composer. *Education:* University of Southern California. *Compositions:* For film: The Ice Pirates, 1984; Young Sherlock Holmes, 1985; Silverado, 1985; The Boy Who Could Fly, 1986; Sweet Liberty, 1987; Square Dance, 1987; The Monster Squad, 1987; Harry and the Hendersons, 1987; Cross My Heart, 1987; Big Shots, 1987; The Rescue, 1988; The Presidio, 1988; Last Rites, 1988; Moonwalker, 1988; Jacknife, 1989; Narrow Margin, 1990; Betsy's Wedding, 1990; The Rescuers Down Under, 1990; All I Want for Christmas, 1991; Tiny Toon Adventures: How I Spent My Vacation, 1992; From Time to Time, 1992; Honey, I Blew Up the Kid, 1992; Stay Tuned, 1992; So I Married an Axe Murderer, 1993; Homeward Bound: The Incredible Journey, 1993; For Love or Money, 1993; Tombstone, 1993; Holy Matrimony, 1994; Baby's Day Out, 1994; Miracle on 34th Street, 1994; Infinity, 1996; Homeward Bound II: Lost in San Francisco, 1996; Carried Away, 1996; House Arrest, 1996; Shadow Conspiracy, 1997; True Women, 1997; A Simple Wish, 1997; One Tough Cop, 1998; Krippendorf's Tribe, 1998; Lost in Space, 1998; For television: Hawaii Five-O, 1968; Barnaby Jones, 1973; Dirty Sally, 1974; Police Woman, 1974; Khan!, 1975; Three for the Road, 1975; Spencer's Pilots, 1976; Quincy, 1976; The Andros Targets, 1977; Logan's Run, 1977; The Oregon Trail, 1977; How the West Was Won, 1978; Dallas, 1978; The Runaways, 1978; The Paradise Connection, 1979; Hart to Hart, 1979; Buck Rogers in the 25th Century, 1979; The Return of Frank Cannon, 1980; Desperate Voyage, 1980; Skag, 1980; Killjoy, 1981; The Girl, the Gold Watch & Dynamite, 1981; One Shoe Makes It Murder, 1982; Desperate Lives, 1982; The Blue and the Gray, 1982; This Girl for Hire, 1983; M.A.D.D.: Mothers Against Drunk Driving, 1983; Cowboy, 1983; Two Marriages, 1983; Passions, 1984; The Master of Ballantrae, 1984; The First Olympics: Athens 1896, 1984; The Cowboy and the Ballerina, 1984; Stormin' Home, 1985; Amazing Stories, 1985; The Thanksgiving Promise, 1986; George Washington II: The Forging of a Nation, 1986; Sorry, Wrong Number, 1989; Tiny Toon Adventures, 1990; The Old Man and the Sea, 1990; Capitol Critters, 1992; O Pioneers!, 1992; JAG (theme), 1995; Glory & Honor, 1998; Night Ride Home, 1999; Jeremiah, 1999; The Ballad of Lucy Whipple, 1999. *Honours:* Emmy Awards, for Dallas, Buck Rogers, The First Olympics, Tiny Tune Adventures, O Pioneers!, Glory and Honor. *Membership:* ASCAP. *Current Management:* Blue Focus Management, 15233 Ventura Blvd, Suite 200, Sherman Oaks, CA 91403, USA. *Website:* www.brucebroughton.com.

BROUWER, Leovigildo; b. 1939, La Habana, Cuba. Orchestra Conductor; Composer; Musician (guitar, violoncello, clarinet, piano, percussion). *Education:* Guitar with Isaac Nicola; Peyrellade Conservatoire, La Habana; Juilliard School of Music, New York; Hartford University. *Career:* Directed Music Department, Instituto Cubano, 1960; Created the Experimentacion of Sounds with Silvio Rodriguez and Pablo Milanes, 1968; Composed music for more than 100 films all around the world. *Compositions:* Conductor, Orquesta de Cuba. *Honours:* Hon. Mem., Cim of UNESCO, 1987. *Current Management:* Intercambio de Cultura y Arte. *Address:* Carreteras, 14–5-I-5, 28012 Madrid, Spain.

BROWN, Alex; b. 17 Jan. 1967, Glynde, England. Vocalist; Musician (piano, trumpet, guitar, drums). *Education:* Grade 8 trumpet; Music and Drama at college. *Career:* Lead singer, Macho Frog, 1985–88; UK (South East) tour, 1987; Signed to Brown Bear Records; *Tours:* Austria, Germany, 1991; Belgium, England; Appearances at: Radio 1 FM Roadshows; Atlantic 252 Roadshows; BBC Children In Need Show. *Recordings:* That's What It Takes, 1993; Supernatural Love, 1994; Life Is Just Worth Living, 1994; Halfway To Heaven, 1994; Too Far Away, 1995; What I Like, 1995; I've Been Missing You, 1995. *Membership:* PRS; Musicians' Union; PPL; VPL; Umbrella. *Current Management:* Brown Bear Records. *Address:* 123A Wilton Rd, Victoria, London SW1V 1JZ, England.

BROWN, Andy; b. 1 Nov. 1968, Auckland, New Zealand. Vocalist; Songwriter. *Career:* Mainstage NZ Festival, 1991; Shelterbelt Festival, 1992; New Zealand Tour; Australian Tour, 1993; Parachute Music Festivals, 1992, 1994, 1995; New Zealand tour, 3 months; Tear Fund, Hope and Justice Tour,

1995; World Tour, Europe and USA, 1996. *Recordings:* Albums: Surge, 1991; Nice Moon, 1994; Merge, 1996; Pakajam, 1998. *Honours:* Nice Moon, 10 Best of '94, Audio Video magazine, NZ. *Membership:* Australasian Performing Rights Asscn. *Current Management:* Mantis Productions, c/o Rowdy Disc, PO Box 16298, Sandringham, Auckland, New Zealand.

BROWN, Angie; b. 13 June 1963, Clapham, London, England. Vocalist; Actor. *Education:* Private drama lessons; 4 years intensive singing lessons with Annette Batram. *Career:* Solo singer; Television appearances include: Jonathan Ross, 1990; America's Top Ten, 1992; Dance Energy, 1993; Top of the Pops, 3 times, 1992–93; Big World Cafe, 1990; The Beat; Dublin Two; Pebble Mill; Currently vocalist of Ramona 55. *Compositions:* Took My Love. *Recordings:* Singles: with Bizarre Inc (No. 2, UK) 1992; I'm Gonna Get You (No. 3, UK), 1992; Took My Love, 1993; You Got It; Album: An Album I Thought I Could Only Dream Of!, with Ramona 55, 1994; Also appears on: Bizarre Inc, Energique, 1992; Midge Ure, If I Was, 1993; Mark Morrison, Return Of The Mack (No. 1, UK), 1996; Anthony Thistlethwaite, Crawfish and Caviar, 1997; Other session work includes: Heaven 17, Sarah Cracknell, Holly Johnson, Londonbeat, Freak Power. *Membership:* Equity; Performing Rights Society; Musicians' Union; PAMRA. *Current Management:* Laurie Jay. *Address:* LJE, 32 Willesden Lane, Kilburn, London NW6 7ST, England.

BROWN, Bobby; b. 5 Feb. 1969, Roxbury, Massachusetts, USA. Vocalist. m. Whitney Houston, 18 July 1992, 1 d. *Career:* Founder member, New Edition, 1981–85, re-formed 1995; Solo artiste, 1985–; Film appearance, Ghostbusters II, 1989; Established Bosstown recording studio and record label. *Recordings:* New Edition singles include: Candy Girl (No. 1, UK), 1983; Cool It Now, 1984; Mr Telephone Man, 1985; Solo albums: King Of Stage, 1986; Don't Be Cruel (No. 1, USA), 1989; Dance... Ya Know It!, 1989; Bobby, 1992; B Brown Posse, 1993; NBA Jam Session, 1993; Remixes N The Key Of B, 1993; Forever, 1997; Greatest Hits, 2000; Singles include: Girlfriend, 1986; Girl Next Door, 1987; Don't Be Cruel, 1988; My Prerogative (No. 1, USA), 1989; Roni, 1989; Every Little Step, 1989; On Our Own, from film Ghostbusters II, 1989; Rock Wit' Cha, 1989; Humpin' Around, 1992; Good Enough, 1992; Get Away, 1993; That's The Way Love Is, 1993; Two Can Play That Game, 1995; Feelin' Inside, 1997; with Glenn Medeiros: She Ain't Worth It (No. 1, USA), 1990; Contributor, Voices That Care charity single (for Red Cross Gulf Crisis). *Honours:* various including: Regular winner, SKC Boston Music Awards, 1989–; Soul Train Music Award, Best R&B/Urban Contemporary Album of the Year; Regular winner, American Music Awards, 1990–; Grammy, Best Male R&B Vocal Performance, Every Little Step, 1990; Coca-Cola Atlanta Music Award, Outstanding Male Vocalist, 1992. *Current Management:* Tommy Brown, 2160 N Central Rd, Fort Lee, NJ 08014, USA. *Address:* c/o MCA Records, 2220 Colorado Ave, Santa Monica, CA 90404, USA.

BROWN, Chris; b. Stockport, Cheshire, England. Recording Engineer; Record Prod. *Career:* Senior Engineer, Abbey Road Studios, London. *Current Management:* Townhouse Management. *Address:* 150 Goldhawk Rd, London W12 8HH, England.

BROWN, Chris (Christopher M.); b. 1 July 1954, Evanston, Illinois, USA. Composer; Prod; Recording Engineer. *Education:* Oberlin College Conservatory of Music. *Career:* Long affiliation with Paul Winter and The Winter Consort, 26 albums in nearly 20 years; Scores for: television; film; industrial videos; Recorded, edited or mixed numerous albums, CDs, films and video scores. *Recordings include:* Prayer for the Wild Things, Paul Winter, 1995. *Honours:* Grammy Award, 1995. *Membership:* NARAS; AFofM. *Current Management:* Image-Net, Goshen, CT, USA. *Address:* 1401 Rt 35, South Salem, NY 10590, USA.

BROWN, Errol; b. 12 Nov. 1948, Kingston, Jamaica. Vocalist; Songwriter. *Career:* Lead vocalist, Hot Chocolate, 1969–87; Solo artiste, 1987–; Mixing Engineer and Producer 1980s–90s. *Compositions:* Think About Your Children, Mary Hopkin; Bet Yer Life I Do, Herman's Hermits; Hits for Hot Chocolate include: Every 1's A Winner; Girl Crazy; It Started With A Kiss; Tears On The Telephone. *Recordings:* Albums with Hot Chocolate: Cicero Park, 1974; Hot Chocolate, 1975; Man To Man, 1976; Hot Chocolate's Greatest Hits, 1976; Every 1's A Winner, 1978; Going Through The Motions, 1979; 20 Hottest Hits, 1979; Class, 1980; Mystery, 1982; Love Shot, 1983; The Very Best Of Hot Chocolate, 1987; Their Greatest Hits, 1993; Solo albums: That's How Love Is, 1989; Secret Rendevous 1992; Still Sexy, 2000; 30 hit singles with Hot Chocolate include: Love Is Life, 1970; I Believe (In Love), 1971; Brother Louie (No. 1, USA), 1973; Emma, 1974; Disco Queen, 1975; A Child's Prayer, 1975; You Sexy Thing, 1976; Don't Stop It Now, 1976; Man To Man, 1976; Heaven In The Back Seat Of My Cadillac, 1976; So You Win Again (No. 1, UK), 1977; Put Your Love In Me, 1977; Every 1's A Winner, 1979; No Doubt About It, 1980; Girl Crazy, 1982; It Started With A Kiss, 1982; Tears On The Telephone, 1983; I Gave You My Heart (Didn't I), 1984. *Current Management:* Richard Martin Management, Agency House, 6 The Steyne, Worthing, West Sussex BN11 3DS, England.

BROWN, Foxy, (Inga Marchand); b. 6 Sept. 1979, Brooklyn, NY, USA. Rap Artiste. *Career:* Contributed to songs, I Shot Ya, LL Cool J, 1995; Guest appearances on songs by BLACKstreet, Toni Braxton, Case, Jay-Z, Method

Man, Total; Signed to Def Jam Records, 1996; Appeared in film, Woo, 1998. *Recordings:* Albums: Ill Na Na, 1996; Chyna Doll (No. 1, USA), 1998; Broken Silence, 2001. *Address:* c/o Def Jam Records, 2220 Colorado Ave, Santa Monica, CA 90404, USA.

BROWN, Ian George; b. 20 Feb. 1963, Ancoats, Greater Manchester, England. Vocalist; Songwriter; Musician (bass guitar). *Career:* Formed Patrol, 1980; Name changed to English Rose, 1983; Became the Stone Roses, 1984–96; Numerous tours world-wide with the Stone Roses; Solo artiste, 1997–. *Recordings:* Albums: with the Stone Roses: The Stone Roses, 1989; Turn Into Stone, 1992; Second Coming, 1994; The Very Best Of The Stone Roses, 2002; Solo: Unfinished Monkey Business, 1998; Golden Greats, 1999; Music Of The Spheres, 2001; Remixes Of The Spheres, 2002. Singles: with the Stone Roses: Made Of Stone, 1989; She Bangs The Drums, 1989; Fool's Gold/ What The World Is Waiting For, 1989; Elephant Stone, 1990; One Love, 1990; I Wanna Be Adored, 1991; Waterfall, 1992; I Am The Resurrection, 1993; Love Spreads, 1994; Ten Storey Love Song, 1995; Begging You, 1995; Solo: My Star, 1998; Corpses, 1998; Can't See Me, 1998; Love Like A Fountain, 1999; Dolphins Were Monkeys, 2000. *Address:* c/o Polydor (UK), 72 Black Lion Lane, London W6 9BE, England. *Website:* www.ianbrown-online.co.uk.

BROWN, James; b. 3 May 1928, Barnwell, South Carolina, USA. Soul Vocalist; Broadcasting Exec. m. (1) Deidre Jenkins, (2) Adrienne Brown, deceased 1996. *Career:* Singer with, then leader of own backing group Famous Flames, 1956–68; Solo performer, recording artist, 1969–; President, JB Broadcasting Ltd, 1968–; James Brown Network, 1968–; Film appearances include: Ski Party, 1964; Come To The Table, 1974; The Blues Brothers, 1980; Concerts include: The Biggest Show of Stars tour, 1963; The TAMI Show, 1964; Newport Jazz Festival, 1969; Festival of Hope, Garden City, 1972; Grand Ole Opry, Nashville, 1979; Montreux Jazz Festival, 1981; Coca-Cola Music Festival, Essex, 1992; Pori Jazz, Finland, 1995; Owner, several US radio stations; Co-owner, Brown Stone Records, 1992–. *Compositions include:* Film scores: Black Caesar, 1972; Slaughter's Big Rip Off, 1972. *Recordings:* Over 75 albums include: Live At The Apollo, 1963; I Can't Stand Myself, 1968; Hot Pants, 1971; The Payback, 1974; I'm Real, 1988; Universal James, 1992; Try Me, 1996; I'm Back, 1998; Hit singles include: Please, Please, Please, 1956; Out Of Sight, 1964; Papa's Got A Brand New Bag, 1965; I Got You (I Feel Good), 1966; It's A Man's Man's Man's World, 1966; Cold Sweat, 1967; I Got The Feelin', 1968; Say It Loud, 1968; Give It Up Or Turn It Loose, 1969; Get Up, I Feel Like Being A Sex Machine, 1970; Super Bad, 1970; Get On The Good Foot, 1972; Get Up Offa That Thing, 1976; Living In America (used in film Rocky IV), 1986; I'm Real, 1988; Soul Jubilee, 1990; Love Over-Due, 1991; Love Power Peace, 1992; Funky Christmas, 1995; Hookedonbrown, 1996; Say It Live and Loud, 1998; On Stage Live, 1999. *Honours:* Inducted, Rock 'n' Roll Hall of Fame, 1986; Grammy Awards: Best R&B Recording, 1965; Best R&B Performance, 1987; 44 Gold discs; Award of Merit, American Music Awards, 1992; NARAS Lifetime Achievement Award, 1992; Lifetime Achievement Trophy, Rhythm and Blues Foundation Pioneer Awards, 1993; Lifetime Achievement Award, National Asscn of Black Owned Broadcasters' Awards, 1993. *Current Management:* Brothers Management Associates. *Address:* 141 Dunbar Ave, Fords, NJ 08863, USA.

BROWN, James Kofi; b. 15 Feb. 1949, Kumasi, Kwadaso, Ghana. Musician (guitar); Vocalist; Composer; Arranger. m. Comfort Peprah Aman Fo, 4 April 1992, 3 s. *Career:* Many concerts in Ghana and 2 in Paris, France; Various radio and television appearances including: TV 5, Radio France International, Radio Africa No 1, Radio GBC 2, Ghana Broadcasting Corporation. *Recordings:* Time Is So Hard; Riot (That's Too Bad); I'm In The Mood For Love; Life Is A Stage; Be My Girl; I've Found A New Lover (Georgina); Let's Be Together. *Honours:* Best video clip, festival in Paris, France. *Membership:* SACEM; SDRM French Musical Society. *Address:* 229 Ave D'Argenteuil, 92270 Bois Colombes, France.

BROWN, James Lee; b. 7 Oct. 1953, Rocky Mt, North Carolina, USA. Musician (alto, tenor and soprano saxophones, keyboards). m. Angela Y Brown, 8 Aug. 1982, 2 s., 2 d. *Education:* 2 years college; Peabody study. *Career:* Appearances: WSMU TV Nashville, Tennessee; Howard University WHUR-Radio; WEAA Radio Morgan State University. *Recordings:* Saxophonic Praises; Manifestation. *Honours:* ASCAP Award for Songwriting. *Current Management:* Saxophonic Praises Inc. *Address:* 4714 Keppler PL, Temple Hills, MD 20748, USA.

BROWN, Jim Ed (James Edward); b. 1 April 1934, Sparkman, Arkansas, USA. Country vocalist; Songwriter; Musician (guitar). *Career:* Featured on own radio show on KCLA, Pine Bluff, Arkansas with elder sister Maxine, late 1940s; Won talent contest on Barnyard Frolics, KLRA radio, Little Rock, Arkansas, early 1950s; Five singles on Fabor Records from 1954 onwards; Joined by sister Bonnie and became the Browns, 1955; Eighteen hits for RCA including number one pop and country hit The Three Bells, 1959; Recorded solo as Jim Edward Brown, 1965–67; Changed recording name to Jim Ed Brown, 1967–; Hit singles for RCA (including many with singer Helen Cornelius) until 1981; Host of TV shows: You Can Be A Star; Going Our Way (with wife Becky); Continued appearances on Grand Ole Opry; Opened The Jim Ed Brown Theater in Nashville, late 1980s. *Compositions include:*

Looking Back To See. *Recordings include:* I Don't Want To Have To Marry You (with Helen Cornelius), 1976; Lying In Love With You, 1979; Saying Hello–Saying I Love You–Saying Goodbye (with Helen Cornelius), 1976; Pop A Top, 1967; Fools, 1979; Albums: Alone With You, 1966; I Don't Want To Have To Marry You (with Helen Cornelius), 1976. *Honours:* CMA, Duo of the Year, 1976; Music City News, Album of the Year, I Don't Want To Have To Marry You, 1976. *Membership:* Grand Ole Opry, 1983. *Address:* c/o Billy Deaton Talent, 1300 Division, Suite 102, Nashville, TN, 37203, USA.

BROWN, Kevin John; b. 19 July 1960, Nottingham, England. Musician (saxophone). *Career:* Member, The Beautiful South; Numerous tours: UK, Ireland, Europe, USA, Canada, Japan, 1989–94; Television appearances: Wogan; Top of the Pops; The Word; MotorMouth; Dennis Miller Show; Live performances recorded for television/video include: Feile Festival Live, Ireland, 1992, 1994; Bourges Festival Live, France; Live session, The Kelly Show, Ireland; Phoenix Festival, Stratford Upon Avon; Later with Jools Holland; Radio appearances include: Live session, Emma Freud, Radio 1; The Secret Gig, Radio 1. *Recordings:* Albums: with The Beautiful South: Choke, 1990; 0898, 1992; Carry On Up The Charts, 1994 (No. 1, UK); Rubaiyat (Elektra Records 40th anniversary), 1990; with The Miracle Drug: Imperial 66, 1993. *Honours:* Platinum Discs, Choke, Carry On Up The Charts; Gold Disc, 0898. *Membership:* Musicians' Union. *Address:* 136B Portland Rd, Hucknall, Nottingham NG15 7SA, England.

BROWN, Lester Valentine; b. 27 Feb. 1958, Jamaica. Songwriter. 3 s., 2 d. *Education:* Singing; Music business training (NBT). *Career:* Various public appearances, overseas tours (Caribbean); Own independent record label: Black Nation Music Productions. *Recordings:* I Want You To Want Me, cover of My Love Is True. *Membership:* Musicians' Union. *Current Management:* Broad Lane Music and Artist Management. *Address:* 14 St Peters House, Cunningham Rd, London N15 4DT, England.

BROWN, Melanie Janice, (Melanie B., later Melanie G., Scary Spice); b. 29 May 1975, Leeds, England. Vocalist. m. Jimmy Gulzar, 12 Sept. 1998, divorced, 1 d. *Career:* Mem., Touch, later renamed Spice Girls, 1993–; Numerous tours, concerts, television and radio appearances; Film, Spiceworld: The Movie, 1997; World tour incl. UK, Europe, India, USA; Solo artiste, 1998–; Presenter, This Is My Moment (ITV1), 2001. *Recordings:* Albums: with Spice Girls: Spice (No. 1, UK), 1996; Spiceworld (No. 1, UK), 1997; Forever, 2000. Singles: with Spice Girls: Wannabe (No. 1, UK and USA), 1996; Say You'll Be There (No. 1, UK), 1996; 2 Become 1 (No. 1, UK), 1996; Mama/Who Do You Think You Are (No. 1, UK), 1997; Step To Me, 1997; Spice Up Your Life (No. 1, UK), 1997; Too Much (No. 1, UK), 1997; Stop, 1998; (How Does It Feel To Be) On Top Of The World, with England United, 1998; Move Over/Generation Next, 1998; Viva Forever (No. 1, UK), 1998; Goodbye (No. 1, UK), 1998; Holler/Let Love Lead The Way (No. 1, UK), 2000; Solo: I Want You Back, featuring Missy 'Misdemeanour' Elliott (No. 1, UK), 1998; Word Up, 1999; Tell Me, 2000; Lullaby, 2001; Feels So Good, 2001; Hot, 2002. *Honours:* BRIT Awards, Best British Single, 1997, Bestselling British Album Act, 1998, Outstanding Contribution, 2000. *Address:* c/o Virgin Records Ltd, 553–79 Harrow Rd, London W10 4RH, England. *Website:* c3.vmg.co.uk/spicegirls.

BROWN, Michael; b. 29 April 1968, Grimsby, South Humberside, England. Songwriter; Musician (saxophone, bass guitar, keyboards). *Career:* Saxophonist, Illustrious GY, 1988–93; Signed major recording contract, Arista, 1991; Toured nationally as support act with Arista, 1991; Television appearances on: Going Live (BBC), Mar 1993; Live and Kicking (BBC), 1993; Played acoustically, Steve Wright Show (BBC Radio 1), 1993; Illustrious GY disbanded, 1994; Formed new band: Giant Killers, as songwriter; Signed record contract with MCA, and publishing deal with Windswept Pacific, 1995. *Recordings:* Illustrious GY: Twenty Questions, 1993; Anytime At All, 1993; I'm Ugly, 1993; Album: No, No, No, 1993. *Membership:* Musicians' Union. *Current Management:* Jonathon Cooke, Fat Cat Management. *Address:* 81 Harley House, Marylebone Rd, London NW1 5HT, England.

BROWN, Norman; b. Shreveport, Louisiana, USA. Musician (guitar). *Education:* Musicians Institute, Hollywood, California, USA. *Career:* World-wide touring, world-wide radio airplay. *Recordings:* Albums: Just Between Us; After The Storm; Better Days Ahead; Celebration. *Honours:* Soul Train Award: Best Jazz Album, BMI, 1995. *Current Management:* Bruce Kramer, Anchor Entertainment, 3522 Moore St, Los Angeles, CA 90066, USA.

BROWN, Robert Jackson; b. 17 Oct. 1935, Framingham, Massachusetts, USA. Prod; Composer; Lyricist; Arranger; Vocalist; Musician (piano, string bass). m. Belva Rousseau, 12 May 1956, divorced 1971, 1 s., 1 d. *Education:* Kimball Union Academy (College Preparation); Colby College; Piano lessons from age 7; Violin, clarinet, voice, music courses, Colby College, Boston Conservatory of Music; Harvard University. *Career:* Founded Upstarts, vocal/ instrumental quintet, 1961; Studio singer, jingle writer, vocal arranger, lounge performer, Boston, 1961–64; New York City, 1964–86; Creative Producer, Mark Century Corporation, 1966–69; Music Director, Herb Mendelsohn Associates, New York City, 1969–71; President, Creative Director, Hunter Productions Inc; BMK Productions; BMK Records, Inc; Badito Productions Inc, 1970–78, all in New York City; Owner, Chief

Engineer, Brownsound Recording Studios, New York City, 1978–83; Formed the Badito Brothers Band, 1974; Lead singer, conductor, music director, The Four Lads vocal group, 1983–86; Lounge performer, Tampa Bay area, Florida, 1986–; Music director, Russ Byrd Music and Entertainment, St Petersburg, Florida, 1989–91; Singer, Pied Pipers vocal group, pianist, Warren Covington Orchestra, 1993–94; Pianist, The Jimmy Dorsey Orchestra, 1995; Music Director, First United Methodist Church, Largo, 1997–98; Music Director, St Paul's Lutheran Church, Clearwater, 1998; 9-week concert tour with the Pied Pipers vocal group, with the Jimmy Dorsey Orchestra, 1999. *Publications:* Talking To Joscelynne, National Library of Poetry, 1995. *Honours:* Editor's Choice Award, National Library of Poetry, 1995. *Membership:* Screen Actors Guild; American Federation of Television and Radio Artists. *Address:* PO Box #5253, Largo, FL 33779–5253, USA.

BROWN, Sam; b. 7 Oct. 1964, Stratford, London, England. Vocalist; Musician (keyboards). 1 s., 1 d. *Career:* Backing Vocalist, In the Shade, Small Faces, 1976; Numerous sessions as backing vocalist and keyboardist; Recording deal with A&M, 1986; Numerous tours and promotional activities; Released second album independently, 1993; Backing Vocalist, The Division Bell, Pink Floyd, and world tour, 1994, appeared on live album, P.U.L.S.E.; Worked with Jools Holland's Big Band; Duet with Fish on new album; Appeared on Nordoff-Robbins Rock Therapy record, and contributed Hammond organ, 1996; Numerous shows with Jools Holland R&B orchestra, 1996; Performed with Joe Brown (father) on The Subway Soopa Stringz, 1996. *Recordings:* Singles: Stop!, 1988 (reissued 1989); This Feeling, 1989; Can I Get A Witness, 1989; With a Little Love, 1990; Kissing Gate, 1990; Albums: Stop!, 1988; April Moon, 1990; 43 Minutes..., 1992; Box, 1997; Reboot, 2001; Appearances on: Before I Forget, Jon Lord, 1982; Too Rye Ay, Dexy's Midnight Runners, 1982; About Face, David Gilmour, 1984; Lowdown, Kane Gang, 1985; CD Of JB, James Brown, 1985; Break Every Rule, Tina Turner, 1986; Division Bell, Pink Floyd, 1994; Pulse, 1995; Blood Brother, Tom Robinson, 1997; 56 and Taller Than You Think, Joe Brown, 1997; Prince's Trust 10th Anniversary Birthday Album; Small World Big Band, Jools Holland's Rhythm 'n' Blues Orchestra, 2001.

BROWN, Selwyn 'Bumbo'; Musician (keyboards). *Career:* Mem., Steel Pulse; Signed to Island Records, Elektra Records, MCA Records, Tuff Gong International; Television appearances include: Arsenio Hall, The Tonight Show with Jay Leno, Late Night with Conan O'Brien, The Keenan Ivory Wayans Show; Performed at the inauguration of President Bill Clinton, Washington, DC, 1993; Extensive world-wide tours; Band mems vary, currently nine-piece band; Performances with: Bob Dylan, Herbie Hancock, INXS, Bob Marley & the Wailers, Robert Palmer, Santana, Sting, The Stranglers, Peter Tosh, Stevie Wonder. *Recordings:* Albums: Handsworth Revolution, 1978; Tribute To The Martyrs, 1979; Caught You (aka Reggae Fever), 1980; True Democracy, 1982; Earth Crisis, 1984; Reggae Refreshers, 1985; Babylon The Bandit, 1985; State of Emergency, 1988; Victims, 1991; Rastafari Centennial, 1992; Smash Hits, 1993; Vex, 1994; Rastanthology, 1996; Rage & Fury, 1997; Sound System: The Island Anthology, 1996; Living Legacy, 1999. *Honours:* Grammy Award, for Babylon The Bandit. *Address:* Steel Pulse, 42 Upper Dean St, Digbeth, Birmingham, West Midlands B5 4SG, England. *E-mail:* info@steel-pulse.com. *Website:* www.steel-pulse.com.

BROWN, T. Graham (Anthony Graham); b. 1954, Arabi, Georgia, USA. Country Vocalist; Songwriter. *Career:* Founder, Rio Diamond, 1976; Founder, T Graham Brown's Rock of Spam, 1979; Demo singer, Nashville, 1982; Recorded commercials for Budweiser; McDonalds; Solo artiste, 1985–. *Recordings:* Hit singles: US Country No. 1 hits: Hell Or High Water; Don't Go To Strangers; Darlene; Albums include: I Tell It Like It Used To Be, 1986; Brilliant Conversationalist, 1987; Come As You Were, 1988; Bumper To Bumper, 1990; You Can't Take It With You, 1991. *Current Management:* Starbound Management, 128 Volunteer Dr., Hendersonville, TN 37075, USA.

BROWN, Tony Ersic; b. 11 Dec. 1946, Greensboro, North Carolina, USA. Record Co Exec; Songwriter; Prod; Musician (keyboards). m. (1) Janie Breeding (divorced), (2) Gina Morrison, 19 April 1979. *Career:* Songwriter, Silverline Music, 1972; Musician with: Oak Ridge Boys, 1972–75; Elvis Presley, 1975–77; Emmylou Harris, 1977–80; Roseanne Cash, 1980–83; A&R Executive, RCA Records, 1978–84; A&R Executive, MCA Records, 1984–. *Recordings:* Albums include: with Emmylou Harris: Blue Kentucky Girl, 1979; Christmas Album, 1979; Evangeline, 1981; Cimarron, 1981; White Shoes, 1983; with Guy Clark: Better Days, 1983; Also appears on: Guitar Town, 1986; Pontiac, 1987; Little Love Affairs, 1988; Lyle Lovett and His Large Band, 1989; Hardin County Line, 1990; For My Broken Heart, 1991; Love and Danger, 1992; Reba McEntire Greatest Hits Vol. 2, 1993; 8 Seconds, 1994; Strait Out Of The Box, 1995; Step Right Up, 1996; Horse Whisperer, 1998. *Honours:* Dove Award, Gospel Music Assn, 1972; Grammy Awards, 1980, 1983, 1985; Producer of the Year, NARAS, 1991. *Membership:* NARAS; Nashville Entertainment Assn; CMA; ACM; Gospel Music Assn. *Address:* c/o MCA Records, 60 Music Sq. E, Nashville, TN 37203, USA.

BROWNE, Jackson; b. 9 Oct. 1948, Heidelberg, Germany. Vocalist; Songwriter; Musician (guitar, piano). *Career:* Brief spell with Nitty Gritty Dirt Band, 1966; Solo singer, songwriter, musician, 1967–; Tours and concerts

with Joni Mitchell; The Eagles; Bruce Springsteen; Neil Young; Trisha Yearwood; Major concerts include: Musicians United For Safe Energy (MUSE), Madison Square Garden (instigated by Browne and Bonnie Raitt), 1979; Glastonbury Festival, 1982; Montreux Jazz Festival, 1982; US Festival, 1982; Benefit concerts for: Amnesty International, Chile, 1990; Christie Institute, Los Angeles, 1990; Victims of Hurricane Inki, Hawaii, 1992; Various concerts for other environmental causes; Nelson Mandela Tributes, Wembley Stadium, 1988, 1990; Sang with Bonnie Raitt and Stevie Wonder, memorial service for Stevie Ray Vaughan, Dallas, Texas, 1990. *Compositions:* Songs recorded by Tom Rush; Nico; Linda Ronstadt; The Eagles; Co-writer with Glenn Frey, Take It Easy. *Recordings:* Albums: Jackson Browne, 1972; For Everyman, 1973; Late For The Sky, 1974; The Pretender, 1976; Running On Empty, 1978; Hold Out (No. 1, USA), 1980; Lawyers In Love, 1983; Lives In The Balance, 1987; World In Motion, 1989; I'm Alive, 1993; Looking East, 1996; The Next Voice You Hear: The Best Of Jackson Browne, 1997; The Naked Ride Home, 2002; Also featured on No Nukes album, 1980; Sun City, Artists United Against Apartheid, 1985; For Our Children, Disney AIDS benefit album, 1991; Singles include: Doctor My Eyes, 1972; Here Come Those Tears Again, 1977; Running On Empty, 1978; Stay, 1978; That Girl Could Sing, 1980; Somebody's Baby, used in film Fast Times At Ridgemont High, 1982; Tender Is The Night, 1983; You're A Friend Of Mine, with Clarence Clemons, 1986; For America, 1987. *Current Management:* Donald Miller, 12746 Kling St, Studio City, CA 91604, USA.

BROWNE, Michael Jerome; b. 9 April 1960, Indiana, USA. Vocalist; Musician (guitar, banjo, fiddle, mandolin, harmonica). *Career:* Solo artiste, coffee houses and street corners, Canada, USA, UK, 1974–84; Lead singer, guitarist, Stephen Barry Band, 1984–99; Accompanist, Vann Walls and visiting blues artistes. *Compositions:* (co-written with B. A. Markus): Blacktop; You're For Me; Children; The Path You Leave Behind; May You Come And Stay; Cancer Ward Blues; Guitar Mama. *Recordings:* In The Evening (with Vann Walls), 1997; Michael Jerome Browne, 1998; Drive On, 2001. *Honours:* Real Blues Award, Best Canadian Acoustic Blues Artist, 1998; Maple Blues Award, Acoustic Artist of the Year, 2001. *Membership:* American Federation of Musicians. *Address:* 5454 Waverly St, Montréal, QC H2T 2X9, Canada.

BRUBECK, David Warren; b. 6 Dec. 1920, Concord, California, USA. Jazz Musician; Composer. m. Iola Whitlock, 1942. 5 s., 1 d. *Education:* BA, University of Pacific; Composition with Darius Milhaud, Mills College. *Career:* Leader, Dave Brubeck Octet, Trio, Quartet, 1946–; Formed Dave Brubeck Quartet, 1951; Played colleges, festivals, clubs, symphony orchestras; 3 month tour, Middle East, Europe, for State Department; Frequent tours, Europe, Australia, Japan, USSR. *Compositions:* Ballets; Points On Jazz; Glances; Orchestral; Elementals; They All Sang Yankee Doodle; Flute and Guitar; Tritonis; Piano; Reminiscences Of The Cattle Country; Four By Four; Oratorios; The Light In The Wilderness; Beloved Son; Voice of The Holy Spirit; Cantatas; Gates of Justice; Truth; La Fiesta de la Posada; Chorus and Orchestra; Pange Lingua Mass; To Hope; I See; Satie; Four New England Pieces; Lenten Tryptich; Over 100 jazz. *Compositions:* Blue Rondo A La Turk; In Your Own Sweet Way; The Duke. *Recordings include:* Stardust, 1951; Jazz At Oberlin, 1953; Time Out, 1959; Time Further Out, 1961; The Dave Brubeck Quartet At Carnegie Hall (live), 1963; The Last Time We Saw Paris, 1967; Brubeck and Desmond Duets, 1975; Paper Moon, 1981; One Alone, 2000. *Honours:* Hon. doctorates from: University of Pacific; Fairfield University; University of Bridgeport; Mills College; Niagara University; BMI Jazz Pioneer Award, 1985; Compostela Humanitarian Award, 1986; Connecticut Arts Council Award, 1987; American Eagle Award, National Music Council, 1988; Duke Ellington Fellow, Yale University. *Current Management:* Derry Music Company. *Address:* PO Box 216, Wilton, CT 06897, USA.

BRUCE, Hal Nelson; b. 27 May 1952, Halifax, Nova Scotia, Canada. Musician (guitars, piano, harmonica, bass, percussion); Vocalist (lead and harmony); Songwriter. 1 s., 1 d. *Education:* Cartography (mapping). *Career:* Began playing in first rock 'n' roll band aged 14; Full-time player, 1982–; Entertained 3 years running on Canadian Country Awards Show; Opened for Beach Boys 1989, Parlee Beach, Canada, 70,000 people; Performed in Halifax, Vancouver, Nashville, USA and London, UK; Three consecutive performances as only solo performer, International Beatle Week, Liverpool, UK. *Recordings:* The First Time, 1988; Goin' Home, 1992; Cover-Up, 1995; On Our Way, 1998; In My Life, 2002; Penhorn Promotional Christmas Album, 2002. *Honours:* Male Vocalist of the Year, 1991, Nova Scotia; Winner, talent search, Nova Scotia; Winner, Entertainer, Male Vocalist, Band, Video, Songwriter of the Year, Nova Scotia Country Music Awards; Vocalist and Band of the Year, CHFX Radio; Best of Texas Award for Songwriting. *Membership:* Atlantic Federation of Musicians; Nova Scotia Country Music Assn; Songwriters Assn of Nova Scotia; Canadian Country Music Assn; Music Industry Assn of Nova Scotia. *Address:* 18 Bellefontaine Court, Lawrencetown, NS B2Z 1L3, Canada. *Telephone:* (902) 435-7410. *E-mail:* halbruce@halbruce.com. *Website:* www.halbruce.com.

BRUCE, Jack; b. 14 May 1943, Glasgow, Scotland. Musician (bass); Vocalist. *Education:* Piano, Royal Scottish Academy of Music. *Career:* Member, Alexis Korner Blues Incorporated, 1962; Graham Bond Organisation, 1963; John

Mayall's Bluesbreakers, 1965; Manfred Mann, 1965–66; Founder member, Cream (with Ginger Baker, Eric Clapton), 1966–68; Solo artiste, 1969–; Played in Tony Williams' Lifetime; Member, West Bruce and Laing; Leader, Jack Bruce and Friends (with Larry Coryell and Mitch Mitchell); Member, John McLaughlin's Mahavishnu Orchestra; Jack Bruce Band; Collaboration with Robin Trower, Bill Lordan, in BLT, 1981; Performances include: with Cream: National Jazz and Blues Festival, Windsor, 1967; Madison Square Garden, 1968; Royal Albert Hall, London, 1968. *Recordings:* Albums: with Cream: Fresh Cream, 1967; Disraeli Gears, 1967; Wheels Of Fire, 1968; Goodbye, 1969; Live Cream, 1970; Live Cream, Vol. 2, 1972; Heavy Cream, 1972; Solo albums: Songs For A Tailor, 1969; Things We Like, 1970; Harmony Row, 1971; Jack Bruce At His Best, 1972; Out Of The Storm, 1974; How's Tricks, 1977; I've Always Wanted To Do This, 1980; Greatest Hits, 1980; Truce, 1982; Automatic, 1987; Willpower, 1989; A Question Of Time, 1990; with West Bruce and Laing: Why Dontcha, 1972; with Jack Bruce and Friends: Live At The Bottom Line, 1992; Something Else, 1993; Cities Of The Heart, 1994; And Friends, 1994; Monkjack, 1995; Sitting On Top Of The World, 1997; Shadows In The Air, 2001; Singles: with Cream: Wrapping Paper, 1966; I Feel Free, 1967; Strange Brew, 1967; Sunshine Of Your Love, 1968; Anyone For Tennis (theme for film The Savage Seven), 1968; White Room, 1968.

BRUEL, Patrick; b. 14 May 1959, Tlemcen, Algeria. Actor; Vocalist. *Career:* Solo artiste; Actor, films include: Le Coup de Sirocco, 1979; Ma femme s'appelle reviens, 1982; Les Diplômés du dernier rang, 1982; Le Bâtard, 1983; Le Grand carnaval, 1983; Marche à l'ombre, 1984; La Tête dans le sac, 1984; P.R.O.F.S., 1985; Suivez mon regard, 1986; La Mémoire tatouée, 1986; Attention bandits, 1987; Un homme amoureux, 1987; La Maison assassinée, 1988; L'Union sacrée, 1989; Force majeure, 1989; Il y a des jours... et des lunes, 1990; Toutes peines confondues, 1992; Profil Bas, 1993; Sabrina, 1995; Les Cent et une nuits, 1995; Hommes femmes mode d'emploi, 1996; Le Jaguar, 1996; K, 1997; Paparazzi, 1998; Hors jeu, 1998; The Misadventures of Margaret, 1998; Lost and Found, 1999; Le Lait de la tendresse humaine, 2001; Les Jolies choses, 2001; Many television appearances. *Recordings:* Albums: Deux Faces, 1986; A Tout A L'heure (live), 1987; Alors Regarde, 1989; Tour '91–Si Ce Soir... (live), 1991; Trois, 1994; Tour '95–On S'etait Dit... (live), 1995; Juste Avant, 1999; Rien Ne S'efface (live), 2001; Entre Deux, 2002. *Address:* c/o BMG France, 4–6 place de la Bourse, 75002 Paris, France. *Website:* www.patrickbruel.com.

BRUFORD, Bill; b. 17 May 1949, Sevenoaks, Kent, England. Musician (drums, percussion). m. Carolyn, 2 March 1973, 2 s., 1 d. *Education:* Leeds University; Lessons from Lou Pocock, Royal Philharmonic Orchestra. *Career:* Mem., Yes; Genesis; UK; King Crimson; Gong; Sideman to USA and Japanese leaders; Solo career as bandleader with Bill Bruford's Earthworks; World-wide tours, 1968–. *Compositions:* 160 shared or solo; Writer for BBC TV and Buddy Rich Orchestra. *Recordings:* Over 80 album releases, 1968–; Solo albums include: Feels Good To Me, 1978; One Of A Kind, 1978; The Bruford Tapes, 1980; Gradually Going Tornado, 1980; Earthworks, 1987; Dig?, 1989; All Heaven Broken Loose, 1991; Heavenly Bodies, 1997; If Summer Had Its Ghosts, 1997; A Part And Yet Apart, 1999; Sound Of Surprise, 2001; Upper Extremities, 2001; Footloose And Fancy Free, 2002. *Publications:* When In Doubt, Roll; numerous magazine articles. *Honours:* Modern Drummer Magazine Hall of Fame; Gold records. *Membership:* Percussive Arts Society; PRS; BAC&S.

BRUN, Christian; b. 24 Dec. 1965, Antibes, France. Musician (guitar); Composer. *Education:* Masters degree, Physics; Music school, lessons with Tal Farlow. *Career:* Performances with Lou Bennett; Turk Mauro; Big Band 31 and Dee Dee Bridgewater; Andre Villeger; Daniel Huck; Performed at festivals: Marciac; Albijazz; Jazz sur son 31; Jazz Sous les Pommiers. *Recordings:* Houseful; Samantha's Dance, with Steve Mabry; Brooklyn Session, with D Kikoski, L Plaxico, T Campbell. *Honours:* Winner, Radio France Concourse, 1991. *Membership:* SACEM; SPEDIDAM. *Address:* Les Campanules, 29 rue des Boulets, 75011 Paris, France.

BRUNBORG, Tore; b. 20 May 1960, Trondheim, Norway. Jazz Musician (tenor, soprano saxophone). 1 s., 1 d. *Education:* Music Conservatory in Trondheim. *Career:* Toured, recorded, with Masqualero, 1982–92. *Compositions:* Comission for Vossa Jazz, 1989; Music for big band, small groups. *Recordings:* 3 recordings with Masqualero; Also with: Bo Stieff; Rita Marcotulli; Jon Balke; Arild Anderson; Anders Jormin; Chick Lyall; Appears on: Bande A Part, 1985; Aero, 1988; Re-enter, 1991; Nonsentration, 1992; Hyperborean, 1997; North Story, 1998. *Honours:* Reenskaugprisen; Spelemannsprisen (3 times with Masqualero). *Membership:* Norwegian Musicians' Union. *Address:* Billingstadveien 52, 1362 Billingstad, Norway.

BRUNDTLAND, Torbjörn; b. Tromso, Norway. Musician. *Career:* Mem., Röyksopp, 2002–. *Recordings:* Album: Melody AM, 2002. Singles: Easy, 2002; Remind Me, 2002; Poor Leno, 2003. *Address:* c/o Astralwerks Records, 104 W 29th St, Fourth Floor, New York, NY 10001, USA. *Website:* www.astralwerks.com/royksopp/.

BRUNEAU, Thierry; b. 28 July 1949, Paris, France. Musician (alto saxophone, bass clarinet, bassoon, flute, tenor and baritone saxophones). m. Päivi Hernala, 30 Oct. 1971. *Education:* Anthropology; Ethnomusicology; CIM (jazz school); Private lessons with Allen Eager, Buddy Collette, Chris Woods; Conservatoire of Music (bassoon, flute). *Career:* Member, Big Bands: Alan Silva Celestrial Communication Orchestra; Laurent Cugny Big Band Lumiere; Quintet with Charles Tyler, 1987; Tours: Scandinavia, 1989–90; Japan, 1989; Europe with local rhythm sections, Mal Waldron, 1988–93; Ken McIntyre, 1990–92, 1996; Anthony Ortega, 1991–92, 1995; Concerts with: Richard Davis, 1990; Dennis Charles, 1994; Also played with: Duke Jordan; Han Bennink; Frank Lowe; Scriptwriter, actor, composer, film Last Date (Hans Hylkema's film about Eric Dolphy); Founder, own record label, Serene, 1989; Released some Eric Dolphy material (the Uppsala Concert); Played festivals at: Turku, Finland; Gothenburg, Sweden; Vienne, Tourcoing, Montpellier, TBB, Jazz Valley (France). *Recordings:* Live At De Kave, Thierry Bruneau Quartet featuring Mal Waldron; Tribute, Ken McIntyre/Thierry Bruneau Quintet featuring Richard Davis; Anthony Ortega/Thierry Bruneau: 7 Standards and A Blues, Anthony Ortega. *Publications:* Book on Eric Dolphy in preparation. *Address:* Saincy, 77510 Bellot, France.

BRUNET, Alain; b. 6 March 1947, Saint Sorlin, Drome, France. Musician (trumpet). *Education:* MA, Literature; Musicology, Sorbonne University, Paris National Conservatory. *Career:* Founder, Module, 1974; Founder, Alain Brunet Quartet; Played with: Martial Solal; René Utreger; Jean-Louis Chautemps; Lee Konitz; Sonny Stitt; Georges Wein; Swing Limited Corporation; Machi-oul Big Band; Michel Graillier; Richard Raux; Al Grey; Stéphane Grappelli; Bernard Lubat; Didier Lockwood; Festivals: Vienna, 1983; Paris, 1984; Montpellier, 1988–90; Nevers, 1988; Nice, 1989–90, 1992–93; Montreux, 1992; New Orleans, 1992; Midem, 1993; Halle That Jazz Paris, 1993; Montréal, 1993; Newport, Saratoga, 1993; Invited to numerous international festivals include: East Africa; Tunisia; Greece; Belgium; Germany; Italy; Russia; Poland; Finland; Appearances on French television, 1975–; Hosted with Eve Ruggieri, Musiques Au Coeur (Jazz News), France 2 TV; Adviser to President, Fifth TV Channel; Tour, USA includes: Boston, San Francisco, Los Angeles, 1995; Appeared Midem, Cannes, 1994. *Recordings:* with Machi-oul Big Band, 1975; Module, 1982; Rominus, with Didier Lockwood, 1991; Alain Brunet Plays Serge Gainsbourg, 1993; French Melodies in LA, Alain Brunet, 1997. *Membership:* SACEM. *Current Management:* Azimuth, 14 rue Bleue, 75009 Paris, France.

BRUNNING, Bob; b. 29 June 1943, Bournemouth, Dorset, England. Musician (bass); Writer. m. Halina, 8 Aug. 1977, 2 s., 1 d. *Education:* College of St Mark and St John, Chelsea, 3 year course qualified teacher, 1967; Now headteacher. *Career:* Began in Bournemouth with Tony Blackburn; College band, 1964–67; Fives Company (3 singles); Member, Fleetwood Mac, 1967; Savoy Brown, 1967; Own bands: Brunning Sunflower Blues Band, 1968–71; Tramp, 1971–74; The DeLuxe Blues Band, 1981–95. *Recordings:* 26 albums with all above, several recordings with visiting blues legends; Latest recording, DeLuxe Blues Band; Other collaborations include: Jo Ann Kelly, Memphis Slim. *Publications:* Blues: The British Connection; Behind The Mask: Biography of Fleetwood Mac; Blues In Britain: The 50s To The 90s. *Current Management:* BB Management. *Address:* 55 Cavendish Rd, Colliers Wood, London SW19 2ET, England.

BRUNTON, Gary; b. 9 March 1968, Burnley, Lancashire, England. Jazz Musician (double bass). m. Beatrice Welter, 18 Sept. 1993. *Education:* Modern Languages, Business Studies, University College, Swansea; Bass, double bass, CIM; Classical bass with Thierry Barbé; Private studies with: Henri Texier; Pierre Michelot; Ray Brown; Dave Holland; Gary Peacock, Paris Conservatory. *Career:* with Upper Space Group: Duc des Lombards; Sunset; Festival de Django Reinhardt, 1995; with Edouard Ferlet Trio: Petit Opportun; Festival de Jazz de Parthenay, 1994; Hotel Adagio; Hotel Lutecia; Trilogie: Salle André Marechal, 1994; with Guitar Hell: Tours, Germany, 1994, 1995; Sunset; Hot Club de Lyon; La Tour Rose; Performances with: Trio Bojan Zulfikarpasic: Radio France Inter; with Trio Michel Grailler: Le Petit Journal Montparnasse; Le Houdon; with Jonathan Lewis Quartet: Jazz Parade, BBC Radio; Brecon Jazz Festival, Tour, Britain, 1990; Elizabeth Kontamanu Quartet, Rumanian tour, 1992; Stephanie Crawford Quartet; Michelle Hendricks; Paulo Fresu; Stéphane Belmondo; François Théberge; Pete Osbourne; Jeannot Rabeson; Patrice Galas; Philippe Soirat; Simon Goubert; Sangoma Everett; Olivier Hutman; Charles Bellonzi; Craig Handy. *Recordings:* Lucide Beausonge; Laure Milena; Bruno Joubrel; Patrick Husson; Commercial television; Film track, Tom Est Tout Seul, La Bande Son, Canal+. *Membership:* UMJ (Union Musiciens de Jazz). *Address:* 37 Bld Ornano, 75018 Paris, France.

BRUNTON, Richard McNaughton; b. 3 Oct. 1949, Newcastle upon Tyne, England. Musician (guitars, keyboards); Composer. 1 s., 2 d. *Education:* Piano lessons age 8–12. *Career:* Own R&B band, Newcastle, 1964–68; Moved to London, freelance guitarist, 1969; Recorded over 200 records for artists including: Gerry Rafferty; Dr John; Barbara Dickson; Greg Lake; Pete Sinfield; Numerous television and film soundtracks. *Recordings include:* Pete Sinfield, Still, 1973; with Gerry Rafferty: Night Owl, 1979; Snakes and Ladders, 1980; Best Of..., 1989; with Steve Jolliffe: Journeys Out Of The

Body, 1982; Doorways To The Soul, 1988; Richard Thompson, Sweet Talker, 1992; Supernatural Fairy Tales, 1996; Greg Lake, From The Beginning, 1997; BBC television soundtracks: The Grass Arena; Life and Loves Of a She-Devil. *Membership:* Musicians' Union; PRS; BAC&S.

BRYAN, Kelle; b. 1976. Vocalist. *Career:* Singer, UK all-female vocal group, Eternal, 1992–98. *Recordings:* Albums: with Eternal: Always and Forever, 1993; Power Of a Woman, 1995; Before The Rain, 1997; Greatest Hits, 1998; Essential Eternal (compilation), 2001; solo: Breakfast In Bed, 2000; Singles: with Eternal: Stay, 1993; Power Of a Woman, 1995; I Am Blessed, 1995; Good Thing, 1996; Secrets, 1996; Don't You Love, 1997; I Wanna Be The Only One (No. 1, UK), 1997; Angel Of Mine, 1997; solo: Higher Than Heaven, 1999; I Wanna Know, 2000. *Honours:* Smash Hits Award; International Dance Award, Dance Act of the Year, 1995; Only UK act to have 6 Top 15 hits from debut album. *Current Management:* First Avenue Management, The Courtyard, 42 Colwith Rd, London W6 9EY, England.

BRYANT, Colin; b. 20 Nov. 1936, Poole, Dorset, England. Musician (clarinet, saxophones). m. (1) 1 s., 2 d., (2). *Education:* Privately taught; Later, Royal Marines School of Music. *Career:* Professional musician since leaving school; Principal clarinet, Band of Royal Marines, 1950s; Clarinet saxophone with Nat Gonnella, late 1950s; Toured with Louis Armstrong All Stars, 1962; Tours, performances, throughout Europe; Featured in film with Joe Darensburg (Louis Armstrong's clarinetist); Jazzband leader, The Hot Rhythm Orchestra, Cunard QE2, 1975–97; Cruises every year for 21 years; Many BBC Radio and ITV performances; Only jazzband invited to play at The Houses of Parliament; Director of Entertainment Agency; Numerous recordings on own Hot Rhythm label. *Honours:* Melody Maker Poll Winner, Best Jazz Clarinet, 1963. *Membership:* Musicians' Union. *Current Management:* C B Entertainments. *Address:* 24 Bushmead Dr., Ringwood, Hants BH24 2HU, England.

BRYANT, Dana; b. 2 May 1965, New York, NY, USA. Spoken word artist. *Education:* BA, Brandeis University. *Career:* Jazz festivals: Vienna, 1992; Berlin Jazz, 1992; Brighton Jazz Bop, 1993; Television: The Charlie Rose Show, 1992; Fighting Wordz, MTV, 1992; Spoken Word Unplugged, 1993; The South Bank Show, Ch 4, 1994; The Girlie Show, London, Ch 4, 1996. *Recordings:* Dominican Girdles Heat, 1993; Wishing From The Top, 1996; Also appears on: Quiet Revolution, 1993; Time and Love, 1997; Adventures Of Bread and Butter, 1998; Jazzonia, 1998. *Publications:* Song of The Siren, 1995. *Membership:* ASCAP. *Current Management:* Knitting; Fencing; Cycling. *Address:* c/o The Groove Academy, 62 White St, Suite 312, New York, NY 10013, USA.

BRYANT, Gerry; b. 30 April 1965, Portsmouth, England. Musician (bass guitar). *Education:* Technical Colleges. *Career:* Bass guitarist, group Mega City Four, touring throughout Europe including Scandinavia, Japan, USA and Canada, 1988–; Appeared on Peel Sessions, 1988–93; The Word, Ch4, 1992; Concerts include: Reading Festival, 1990–92; Glastonbury Festival, 1993; Phoenix Festival, 1994; Sound Engineer and Tour Manager, 1996–2001; Tours of: USA; New Zealand; Australia; Europe/UK; Director: The Rooms Rehearsal Studios Ltd. *Recordings:* with Mega City Four: Tranzophobia, 1988; Who Cares Wins, 1989; Terribly Sorry Bob, 1990; Sebastopol Road, 1992; Inspiringly Titled... (live album), 1992; Magic Bullets, 1993; Soulscraper, 1996; with Serpico: Everyone Vs Everyone, 2001. *Publications:* Tall Stories and Creepy Crawlies, Mega City Four biography, 1994. *Membership:* Musicians' Union. *Current Management:* Paul Bolton, ICM/Fair Warning. *Address:* 12 Orwell Close, Farnborough, Hnats, GU14 9LR, England.

BRYANT, Teri; b. 2 May 1961, Walgrave, Northamptonshire, England. Musician (drums, percussion). m. Juliet, 3 Oct. 1992, 1 d. *Career:* Mem., group Iona, 1992–; Toured, recorded with artists from UK and USA including: Steve Taylor; Cliff Richard; Darrell Mansfield; Sheila Walsh; Lies Damned Lies; Ben Okafor; Graham Kendrick; Ishmael; Phil and John (The Woodthieves); Iona; Richard Darbyshire; Martin Smith; Noel Richards; Dave Bilbrough; Adrian Snell; Paul Field; Others including 6 years with Peter Murphy (ex-Bauhaus), including 3 albums, extensive tours, USA, Japan, Israel, Europe. *Recordings:* Love Hysteria, 1987; Deep, 1989; Don't Look Now, 1989; Iona, 1990; Holy Smoke, 1991; Book Of Kells, 1992; Beyond These Shores, 1994; Journey Into The Morn, 1995; Heaven's Bright Sun, 1997; Arms Of Mercy, 1998; Solo: Psalm, 1995; Timbrel, 1999. *Honours:* GMA International Artist Award: The Book of Kells, 1993. *Membership:* Musicians' Union. *Address:* c/o Psalm Drummers, St Barnabas Church, Istead Rise, Gravesend, Kent DA13 9DA, England.

BRYCE, Owen; b. 8 Aug. 1920, Woolwich, London, England. Musician (trumpet, piano); Writer; Lecturer. m. Iris Edith, 22 Dec. 1945, 1 s., 3 d. *Career:* Founder mem., George Webb's Dixielanders, many records, broadcasts; Own band, 1956–; Many broadcasts, appearances include Savoy Hotel; Lecturer for many organizations, county councils, colleges, summer schools; First speaker on Jazz on BBC Schools Service; Teacher, pupils include Chris Barber; Cy Laurie. *Publications:* Let's Play Jazz 1–4; The George Webb Dixielanders... My Part, 2002. *Honours:* Diploma Polish Music Festival; Freeman of New Orleans. *Membership:* Musicians' Union. *Address:*

58 Pond Bank, Blisworth, Northants NN7 3EL, England. *Telephone:* (1604) 858192. *E-mail:* owen-iris@bryceo.fsnet.co.uk. *Website:* mysite.freeserve.com/bryceandjazz/.

BRYDON, Mark; b. Sheffield, England. Prod; Arranger; Remixer; Composer; Musician (multi-instrumentalist). *Career:* Mem., Cloud 9; Mem., Moloko, with Roisin Murphy, 1995–. *Recordings:* Albums: Do You Like My Tight Sweater?, 1995; I Am Not A Doctor, 1998; Things To Make And Do, 2000; All Back To Mine, 2001. Singles: Where Is The What If The What Is The Why; Fe Fi Fo Fun For Me; The Moloko EP, 1995; Fun For Me, 1995; Dominoid, 1996; The Flipside, 1998; Sing It Back, 1999; The Time Is Now, 2000; Pure Pleasure Seeker, 2000; Indigo, 2000. *Address:* c/o Echo Records, Chrysalis Group PLC, The Chrysalis Bldg, Bramley Rd, London W10 6SP, England. *Website:* www.moloko.co.uk.

BRYDOY, Eivind; b. 20 June 1964, Levanger, Norway. Artist Man. *Education:* MBA, Norwegian School of Economics; University of New Orleans; UMIST, Manchester, England. *Career:* Stageway, 3 years; Controller, Stageway Record Company, 1 year; Agency Dept, Stageway, 2 years; Manager, Artistpartner, own company, 4 years. *Publications:* Eureka Collaborative Agreements, 1992. *Membership:* General Secretary, International Managers Forum, Norway. *Current Management:* Cecilia, Ephemera Cornflakes, Baba Nation, Trang Fodsel, Di Derre. *Address:* Grini Naeringspark 17, 1345 Osteraas, Norway.

BRYNGELSSON, Hans Inge Peter; b. 17 Sept. 1955, Vetlanda, Sweden. Musician; Composer. m. Anita Malmguist Bryngelsson, 11 Dec. 1986, 1 s. *Education:* Vallehilde Folkhojskole Dramatic Institute; Private courses in composition. *Career:* Leader of the Band Ragnarö, 1972–84, 4 albums; Leader, Triangulus, 1985–89, 2 albums; Guitarsis, Music for 10 guitars, Urban Turban, 1993–; Composed music for film, theatre, expositions, radio and TV. *Compositions:* Via, 1990; Happy Starr, 1992; Sound of Glass, 1995; Guitarrsis, Music for 10 guitarists; Katabasis, Music for 5 bass instr. *Recordings:* Ragnarö, 1976; King Tung, 1979; Via, 1990; Urban Turban, 1994; Urban Turban Overtime, 1996; Astro Turf, 1998. *Publications:* Ode to the Stone, TV-film, 1991; The Other Shore Michael Wiström, TV-film, 1992; Snalast, TV-film, 1997. *Honours:* STIM's Musical Prize, SKAPs Musical Prize. *Membership:* STIM; SKAP; SAMI.

BRYSON, David; b. 5 Oct. 1961, San Francisco, California, USA. Musician (Guitar). *Career:* Formed acoustic duo with Adam Duritz; Became Counting Crows; Numerous headlining tours and TV appearances including MTV. *Recordings:* Singles: Round Here, 1994; Mr Jones, 1994; Rain King, 1994; Angels Of the Silence (live), 1996; Albums: August and Everything After, 1993; Recovering the Satellites, 1996; Across a Wire: Live in New York, 1998; Long December, 1999; Daylight Fading, 1999; Hard Candy, 2002; Guest Appearances: Steve Walsh, Schemer-Dreamer, 1980; Wild Flowers, Tales Like These, 1990; Faith No More, Angel Dust, 1992; Steve Taylor, Squint, 1993; Sordid Humor, Light Music for Dying People, 1994; Train: Train, 1998, Meet Virginia, 1999; Better Days, Leaving The Blue, 2001; Blue Druids, Roadsigns Towards Antiquity, 2001.

BRYSON, (Robert) Peabo; b. 13 April 1951, Greenville, South Carolina, USA. Soul Vocalist; Prod. *Career:* Former member, Moses Dillard; Tex-Town Display; Michael Zager's Moon Band, 1976–78; Solo artiste, 1979–. *Recordings:* Albums: Reaching For The Sky, 1978; Crosswinds, 1978; We're The Best Of Friends (with Natalie Cole), 1979; Live–and More (with Roberta Flack), 1980; Paradise, 1980; I Am Love, 1981; Turn The Hands Of Time, 1981; Don't Play With Fire, 1982; Born To Love (with Roberta Flack), 1983; The Peabo Bryson Collection, 1984; Straight From The Heart, 1984; Quiet Storm, 1986; Take No Prisoners, 1987; Positive, 1988; All My Love, 1989; Can You Stop The Rain, 1991; Tonight I Celebrate My Love, 1992; Through The Fire, 1994; Peace On Earth, 1997; Family Christmas, 1998; Unconditional Love, 1999; Singles: Closer Than Close; Lost In The Night; Shower You With Love; Why Goodbye; How Wonderful We Are; Light The World; with Michael Zager's Moon Band: Reaching For The Sky; I'm So Into You; Solo: If Ever You're In My Arms Again, 1984; Duets: Gimme Some Time, with Natalie Cole, 1979; Tonight I Celebrate My Love, with Roberta Flack (No. 2, UK), 1983; Beauty and The Beast, with Céline Dion, 1992; Other duets with Melissa Manchester; Regina Belle; Other collaborations include: Kenny G, Barry Mann, Minnie Riperton; Contributor, Color and Light: Jazz Sketches On Sondheim, 1995. *Current Management:* David M. Franklin and Associates, 999 Peachtree St, Suite 2680, Atlanta, GA 30309, USA.

BRYSON, William Shields; b. 10 Nov. 1946, Evanston, Illinois, USA. Musician (bass); Vocalist. m. Anne Jeanine Bailey, 24 July 1976. *Career:* Bass player, Bluegrass Cardinals; Country Gazette; Doug Dillard Band; The Long Riders with Ry Cooder, 1980–84; The Desert Rose Band, 1984–. *Recordings:* Albums include: What A Way Earn A Living, Country Gazette, 1977; Long Riders (film soundtrack), Ry Cooder, 1980; Jackrabbit, Doug Dillard, 1980; Home Coming and Family Reunion, The Dillards, 1980; with The Desert Rose Band: The Desert Rose Band, 1987; Running, 1988; Pages Of Life, 1990; True Love, 1991; A Dozen Roses, 1991. *Honours:* ACM Awards: Bass Player of the

Year, 1990; Touring Band of the Year, Desert Rose Band, 1988–90. *Membership:* Screen Actors Guild; AFTRA; AFofM.

BRZEZICKI, Mark; b. 21 June 1957, Slough, Berkshire, England. Musician (drums, percussion). *Education:* City and Guilds, HNC, Aircraft Engineering, Brooklands Technical College. *Career:* Member of Big Country, 1981–; Tours include: Fish, 1990–91; Midge Ure, 1991–92; Procol Harum, USA 1991, Europe, 1992; Major concerts include: Mandela Concert, Wembley Stadium, 1989; Annual Prince's Trust Rock Galas, 1985–88; Procol Harum European Festivals, 1992; Chieftains, Midge Ure, Roger Daltrey show, 1994; Television appearances include: Children in Need, 1989, BBC; ITV Telethon Live, 1992; BBC Breakfast Time; Phil Collins' This Is Your Life; Appearances with Sting; Nils Lofgren; Procol Harum; The Cult; Tears For Fears; Fish; Midge Ure; Big Country. *Recordings:* Big Country albums including: The Crossing, 1983; Steeltown (No. 1, UK), 1984; The Seer, 1986 and 7 others; also 5 albums with Pete Townshend; 3 with Midge Ure; 4 Prince's Trust Rock Gala Compilations; Also appeared on albums by artists including: Roger Daltrey; Simon Townshend; Procol Harum; Love and Money; The Cult; Fish; Nils Lofgren; Joan Armatrading; Ultravox; Howard Jones; Nik Kershaw; Steve Harley; Go West; Tom Robinson; Played on film soundtracks: Quick Silver Lightning; Rambo 3; Restless Natives; White City. *Honours:* Invited Special Guest, World Drum Festival, Canada, 1987; Zildjian Musician Poll, Best Rock/Pop mainstream drummer UK, 1988–90; Making Music Poll, 1988; Pearl Drummers Club, Best UK Rock/Pop drummer, 1990; Prince's Trust Award, 1984; Numerous Platinum, Gold and Silver records. *Membership:* Prince's Trust; GISM; PRS. *Current Management:* Ian Grant Management. *Address:* Owl House, Byers Lane, South Godstone, Surrey RH9 8JL, England.

BT, (Brian Transeau), (Libra, Elastic Chakra); b. Washington DC, USA. Prod; Remixer. *Education:* Berklee School of Music, Boston, USA. *Career:* Played synthesizer on a Salt 'N 'Pepa album; Started producing for Deep Dish's label; Signed to Perfecto, 1995; Began remixing, notably on his reworking of Tori Amos' Blue Skies; Collaborations: Deep Dish; Sasha; Tsunami One; Remixed: Billie Ray Martin; Madonna; Seal; Mike Oldfield. *Address:* c/o Pioneer Entertainment, Pioneer House, Hollybush Hill, Stoke Poges, Slough, SL2 4QP, England.

BUARQUE, Chico; b. 1944, Rio de Janeiro, Brazil. Vocalist; Musician (guitar); Songwriter. *Career:* Brother of vocalist Miucha, uncle of Bebel Gilberto; Dropped out of University of Sao Paulo to absorb local Bossa Nova scene and began writing songs; Came to prominence when compositions recorded by vocalist Nara Leao; Made first record Pedro Pedriero, 1965; Wrote and scored the play Roda Vida, 1968; Recorded Construction, containing more political works, 1971; Subsequently forced to submit work to government censorship board; Virtually all compositions rejected by 1975; Freely performs, records, writes songs, books and plays as well as scoring films, 1980s–. *Compositions:* Pedro Pedreiro; A Banda; Carolina; Roda Viva; Saiba; Construcao; Folhetim; Vai Passar. *Recordings:* Albums include: Chico Buarque De Hollanda, 1966; Construcao, 1971; Vida, 1980; Chico Buarque, 1984; Caetano E Chico Juntos E Ao Vivo, 1993; Chico Buarque En Espanol, 1997; As Cidades, 1999; Chico Buarque Song Book #8, 2001. *Website:* www.uol.com.br/chicobuarque.

BUCHANAN, Keisha; b. 30 Sept. 1984, London, England. Vocalist. *Career:* Founding mem., Sugababes, 1998–; Signed to London-Sire Records, 2000; Signed to Island Records, 2001. *Recordings:* Albums: One Touch, 2000; Angels With Dirty Faces, 2002. Singles: Overload, 2000; New Year, 2000; Run For Cover, 2001; Soul Sound, 2001; Freak Like Me, 2002; Round Round, 2002. *Honours:* Q Award, for Freak Like Me, 2002; BRIT Award, Best Dance Act, 2003. *Address:* c/o Island Records, 825 Eighth Ave, New York, NY 10019, USA. *Website:* www.sugababes.com.

BUCHANAN, Margo; b. 3 Feb. 1955, Lanark, Scotland. Vocalist. m. Paul Wickens, 31 Jan. 1992. *Career:* Television: European promotional tour, Billy Idol, 1986; Concert By The Lake, with Eric Clapton, Phil Collins, Steve Winwood, 1988; Amnesty International Concert, with Dave Gilmour, Seal, Tom Jones, 1990; Concert with Billy Bragg, Hugh Cornwell, London Palladium, 1990; The Great Music Experience, with Joni Mitchell, Bob Dylan, Bon Jovi, 1994. *Recordings:* with Tina Turner: Break Every Rule, 1987; with Mink Deville: Silver Bullets; Recording/writing with Sam Brown: This Feeling; Your Love Is All; It Makes Me Wonder; With A Little Love; As One; with Jools Holland: No-One's To Blame. *Membership:* Musicians' Union; Equity. *Current Management:* One Management, 43 St Albans Ave, London W4 5JS, England.

BUCHANAN, Wallis; b. 27 Nov. 1965, London, England. Musician (didgeridoo, vibraphone). *Career:* Member, Jamiroquai; Numerous tours and TV appearances. *Recordings:* Singles: When You Gonna Learn, 1993; Too Young To Die, 1993; Blow Your Mind, 1993; Emergency On Planet Earth, 1993; Space Cowboy EP, 1994; Half The Man, 1994; Stillness In Time, 1995; Virtual Insanity, 1996; Cosmic Girl, 1996; Light Years, 1996; Alright, 1997; Deeper Underground (No. 1, UK), 1998; High Times, 1997; Canned Heat, 1999; Little L, 2001; Albums: Emergency on Planet Earth (No. 1, UK), 1993;

Travelling Without Moving, 1996; Synkronized, 1999; A Funk Odyssey, 2001. *Honours:* Gold and Platinum Albums; Several MTV Video Music Awards.

BUCHANAN-HINDLEY, Aileen; b. 26 July 1964, Kippen, Stirlingshire, Scotland. Musician (accordion). m. Guy Hindley, 6 July 1996. *Education:* Accordion lessons with W Campbell. *Career:* Lead Accordion with Carousel Ceilidh Band, 1997–; Winter season work with Inversnaid Hotel, Loch Lomond, Scotland, 1977. *Address:* 32 Tuxford Rd, Ansdell, Lytham St Annes, Lancashire FY8 4BH, England.

BUCHWALD, Martyn Jerel; b. 30 Jan. 1942, Cincinnatti, USA. m. Karen Deal, Aug. 1989, 2 d. *Compositions:* Miracles; Count On Me; Runaway; Atlanta Lady; Comin Back To Me. *Recordings:* Airplane; Starship; PKA Marty Balin. *Honours:* Rock and Roll Hall of Fame; BAM Award; BMI Award. *Membership:* AFM; AFTRA; SAG. *Address:* 436 Bevedere St, San Francisco, CA 94117, USA.

BUCK, Gary Ralph; b. 21 March 1940, Thessalon, Ontario, Canada. Vocalist; Record Prod; Songwriter. m. Deb Way, 2 s., 3 d. *Career:* Singer, most major Country Music television and radio shows, USA and Canada; Tours throughout USA, Canada (Calgary Exhibition promotion), England, New Zealand (Miss NZ Pageant); Publisher, composer, songwriter for Calgary's Olympic bid; Music for commercials include: Pepsi, Molson's Export Ale, Kelloggs' Raisin Bran, Mastercard, Ford; Television appearances include: Gary Buck Show, CKCO TV, 1965–67; Host, Maritime Telethon, 3 times; Founder, President, Canadian Country Music Hall of Fame; Manager, Capitol Records Publishing Division, 3 years; Started Broadland Publishing Co; Became Broadlands International Records, 1991; International Director, Country Music Association, Nashville, 10 years; Founding Director, Academy of Country Music Entertainment, now known as Canadian Country Music Association; Literary Agent for Hank Snow; Producer of over 100 albums, launched careers of Wayne Rostad; Family Brown; Dallas Harms; Lee Roy Anderson; Currently producer for Gene Watson; Billie Jo Spears; George Hamilton IV. *Honours:* Top Male Singer, Canada, 5 times; Top Country Record Producer, 1975; Medal of Merit, City of Sault Ste Marie, for contributions to music industry, 1990.

BUCK, Peter; b. 6 Dec. 1956. Musician (guitar); Prod. *Career:* Member, R.E.M., 1980–; International tours; Also member, side-project, Hindu Love Gods, 1986–90. *Recordings:* Albums: with R.E.M.: Chronic Town (mini album), 1982; Murmur, 1983; Reckoning, 1984; Fables Of The Reconstruction, 1985; Life's Rich Pageant, 1986; Dead Letter Office, 1987; Document, 1987; Eponymous, 1988; Green, 1988; Out Of Time (No. 1, UK and USA), 1991; The Best Of R.E.M., 1991; Automatic For The People (No. 1, UK), 1992; Monster (No. 1, UK), 1994; New Adventures In Hi-Fi, (No. 1, UK) 1996; Up, 1998; Star Profiles, 1999; Reveal (No. 1, UK), 2001; with Hindu Love Gods: Hindu Love Gods, 1990; Singles include: with R.E.M.: It's The End Of The World As We Know It (and I Feel Fine), 1987; The One I Love, 1987; Finest Worksong, 1988; Stand, 1989; Orange Crush, 1989; Losing My Religion, 1991; Shiny Happy People, 1991; Near Wild Heaven, 1991; Radio Song, 1991; Drive, 1992; Man On The Moon, 1992; The Sidewinder Sleeps Tonite, 1993; Everybody Hurts, 1993; Nightswimming, 1993; What's The Frequency, Kenneth?, 1994; Bang and Blame, 1994; Crush With Eyeliner, 1995; Strange Currencies, 1995; Tongue, 1996; E-Bow The Letter, 1996; Bittersweet Me, 1996; Electrolite, 1996; Daysleeper, 1998; Lotus, 1998; At My Most Beautiful, 1999; The Great Beyond, 2000; Imitation Of Life, 2001; All The Way To Reno (You're Gonna Be A Star), 2001; Tracks featured on film soundtracks: Bachelor Party, 1984; Until The End Of The World, 1991; Coneheads, 1993; Man On The Moon, 1999; Other recordings: with Indigo Girls; Warren Zevon; Billy Bragg; The Dream Academy; eels; Robyn Hitchcock; Liz Phair; Contributor, albums: Tom's Album; I'm Your Fan; Time Inbetween; Producer, albums by Uncle Tupelo; Vigilantes Of Love. *Honours:* Earth Day Award, 1990; Numerous MTV Music Video Awards; Billboard Awards; Best Modern Rock Artist, Best World Album, 1991; BRIT Awards: Best International Group, 1992, 1993, 1995; Grammy Awards: Best Pop Performance, Alternative Music Album, Music Video, 1992; Atlanta Music Awards: Act of the Year, Rock Album, Video, 1992; IRMA, International Band of the Year, 1993; Rolling Stone Critics Awards: Best Band, Best Album, 1993; Q Awards: Best Album, 1991, 1992; Best Act In The World, 1991, 1995. *Current Management:* REM/Athens Ltd, 250 W Clayton St, Athens, GA 30601, USA.

BUCKETHEADS, (THE). See: **GONZALEZ, Kenny.**

BUCKINGHAM, Lindsey; b. 3 Oct. 1947. Musician (guitar); Vocalist; Songwriter. *Career:* Member, rock band Fritz, 1960s; Duo, Buckingham Nicks (with Stevie Nicks), 1971–74; Member, Fleetwood Mac, 1975–87; Solo artiste, 1981–; Appearances include: Regular US tours; Madison Square Garden; US Festival, 1982. *Compositions:* with Fleetwood Mac: Second Hand News; Tusk; Go Your Own Way; Big Love; Oh Diane. *Recordings:* Albums: with Buckingham Nicks: Buckingham Nicks, 1973; with Fleetwood Mac: Fleetwood Mac, 1975; Rumours, 1977; Tusk, 1979; Live, 1980; Mirage (also producer), 1982; Tango In The Night, 1987; Behind The Mask, 1990; Time, 1995; Dance, 1997; Solo albums: Law and Order, 1981; Go Insane, 1984; Out Of The Cradle, 1992; Singles with Fleetwood Mac: Over My Head; Rhiannon (Will

You Ever Win); Say You Love Me; Dreams; You Make Loving Fun; Tusk; Sara; Think About Me; Trouble; Gypsy; Solo singles: Soul Drifter, 1992; Countdown, 1992; Don't Look Down, 1993; Also appears on: Building The Perfect Beast, Don Henley, 1984; Behind The Sun, Eric Clapton, 1985; Songs and Music, Tom Petty, 1996; Unchained, Johnny Cash, 1996; Show Must Go On, Leo Sayer, 1996; Guilty: 30 Years Of Randy Newman, 1998; Trouble In Shangri-La, Stevie Nicks, 2001. *Honours:* Grammy Award, Fleetwood Mac, Rumours, 1977; American Music Awards: Favourite Pop/Rock Group, Favourite Album, 1978. *Current Management:* Michael Brokaw Management, 2934 Beverly Glen Circle #383, Bel Air, CA 90077, USA.

BUCKLAND, Jonny; b. 11 Sept. 1978, Mold, Wales. Musician (guitar); Songwriter. *Education:* University College, London. *Career:* Mem., Coldplay, 1998–. *Recordings:* Albums: Parachutes, 2000; A Rush Of Blood To The Head, 2002. Singles: The Safety EP, 1998; Brothers and Sisters, The Blue Room EP, 1999; Shiver, 2000; Yellow, 2000; Trouble, 2000; Don't Panic, 2001; In My Place, 2002; A Rush Of Blood To The Head, 2002; The Scientist, 2002. *Honours:* BRIT Awards, Best Album, 2001, Best British Group, Best British Album, 2003; Grammy Award, Best Alternative Album, for Parachutes, 2001; MTV Award, Best UK and Ireland Act, 2002; Billboard Group of the Year, 2002; NME Award, Best Album, 2003. *Current Management:* Phil Harvey. *Address:* c/o Parlophone Records, 43 Brook Green, London W6 7EF, England. *Website:* www.coldplay.com.

BUCKLEY, Steve; b. 6 Jan. 1959, Orpington, Kent, England. Musician (saxophones, bass clarinet, tin whistle). *Education:* Leeds University degree; Classical clarinet tuition at school. *Career:* Tours, recordings with Loose Tubes; Delightful Precipice; Human Chain; Numerous television and radio appearances with these bands; Long association with South American, African London-based bands; Recent projects incl. BBC Award-winning 'Big Air', co-led by Chris Batchelor and featuring Myra Melford, Jim Black and Owen Marshall. *Recordings:* Open Letter, Loose Tubes; Third Policeman, Django Bates; Summer Fruits, Delightful Precipice; Winter Truce, Delightful Precipice; Whole and The Half, Buckley Batchelor; Pyrotechnics, Human Chain; Live At Bad Gleichenberg; Noble, Marshall, Buckley Bud Moon; Noble Marshall Buckley; Life as We Know It, Buckley Batchelor; Barrel Organ Far From Home, Huw Warren. *Address:* 140 Amelia St, London SE17 3AR, England.

BUDD, Stephen; b. 25 Dec. 1958, London, England. m. 6 June 1986, 1 d., 1 s. *Career:* Started Torch Records, age 20, 1979; Signed: The Sound; The Cardiacs; Big Sound Authority; Manager: The Sound, Big Sound Authority; Sally Oldfield, 1980–85; Managed producers, Tony Visconti, Arthur Baker, 1985–88; Started Stephen Budd Management, managing producers: Martyn Ware; Mike Hedges; Rick Nowels; Rafe McKenna; Arthur Baker, Steve Levine, Charlie Rapino, Gary Katz and others 1988–; Formed Morrison Budd Music Publishing, with partner Bryan Morrison, 1993–; Formed Supervision Management with Paul Craig, for artists Lloyd Cole, Heaven 17, The Webb Brothers, Dark Flower, Seventh Son, Screaming Orphans, Sherena Dugani, 1999–. *Honours:* Numerous Gold, Platinum discs. *Membership:* Board mem., International Managers Forum; Chairman, Producer Managers Group. *Current Management:* Stephen Budd Management, 109B Regents Park Rd, London NW1 8UR, England.

BUDDE, Martin; b. 25 Oct. 1966, Århus, Denmark. Musician (drums, organ). *Career:* Drummer, Godless Wicked Creeps, 1991–; Organist, The Defectors, 1997–. *Recordings:* with Godless Wicked Creeps: Victim Of Science; Hellcoholic; Hystereo; Smile; with The Defectors: Allright Girl; Albums: Let Me; Baby Gimme Love. *Membership:* Danish Music Society. *Address:* Laessoesgade 53 2th8000 Århus, Denmark.

BUDTS, Danny; b. 12 May 1958, Wilrijk, Belgium. Musician (guitar, synthesizer); Vocalist; Songwriter; Composer; Producer. m. Machteld de Muynck, 6 Nov. 1982, 2 s. *Career:* Lead Guitar, Cold Turkey, 1970s; Syndromeda, own midi studio, 1990; Different interviews on local radios. *Recordings:* Mind Trips, 1997; Circles Of Life, 1997; The Legacy Of God, 1998; Birth Of a Black Hole, 1999; The Alien Abduction Phenomenon, 2001; In Touch With The Stars, 2001; Creatures From The Inner, 2003; Tracks on: Truth or Dare; Movements; Sequences 14, 19 and 27. *Honours:* Movements, CD, composition contest, 1997. *Current Management:* Synth Music Direct/New Harmony, PO Box 592, Sheffield S35 0FF, England. *Address:* Pastoryveld 28, 2180 Ekeren, Belgium. *E-mail:* syndromeda@antwerpen.be. *Website:* www.syndromeda.bewoner.antwerpen.be.

BUDWEISEROVA, Irena; b. 8 Nov. 1957, Rokycany, Czech Republic. Vocalist. m. Pavel Barta, 4 Jan. 1986, 1 d. *Education:* Conservatoire. *Career:* Member, Folk/Jazz group, Spiritual Kvintet, 1980–; Own Band, Budweiserova and Friends, Jazz, Blues, Soul, 1988–; Performed in 4 musicals, 2 on stage in Prague, 1993–; Speak About the Music, Czech Radio, 1997–98; Professor, Conservatoire of Jaroslav Jezek, Prague, 1998–; Concerts with Classical Guitar, Jan Zacek, Germany; Jazz concerts; Tour of Europe, Canada, USA, South America, Australia. *Recordings:* 15 albums with Spiritual Kvintet; With own group: Blue Soul, 1993; Moment, 1995; Taking Of the Skin, 1996; Crustaceans Of The Time, 2000; Guest on: Walking and Talking, Josef

Vejvoda Big Band, The Raven with ASPM Group; 2 albums with Rangers; 2 albums from musicals Bastard and Babylon. *Honours:* Female Vocalist of the Year, 1983; Prize, Thalia, 1998. *Membership:* Federation of Authors in Interprets; Czech Jazz Company. *Current Management:* Pavel Barta Agency. *Address:* Varsavska 29/882, 120 00 Prague 2, Czech Republic. *Telephone:* (2) 22519808. *E-mail:* pavel.barta@volny.cz; pbag@cbox.cz.

BUENA, Mutya; b. 21 May 1984, London, England. Vocalist. *Career:* Founding mem., Sugababes, 1998–; Signed to London Records, 2000; Signed to Island Records, 2001. *Recordings:* Album: One Touch, 2000; Angels With Dirty Faces, 2002. Singles: Overload, 2000; New Year, 2000; Run For Cover, 2001; Soul Sound, 2001; Freak Like Me, 2002; Round Round, 2002. *Honours:* Q Award, for Freak Like Me, 2002; BRIT Award, Best Dance Act, 2003. *Address:* c/o Island Records, 825 Eighth Ave, New York, NY 10019, USA. *Website:* www.sugababes.com.

BUFFETT, Jimmy; b. 25 Dec. 1946, Pascagoula, Mississippi, USA. Country Vocalist; Songwriter. m. Jane Slagsvol, 27 Aug. 1977. *Education:* BS, History, Journalism, University of Southern California, 1969. *Career:* Former freelance journalist, Inside Sports Outside magazine; Billboard magazine; Solo artiste, 1970s–; Formed Coral Reef Band, 1975. *Compositions include:* Railroad Lady (recorded by Merle Haggard); He Went To Paris (recorded by Waylon Jennings); Margaritaville; Come Monday; Cheeseburger In Paradise. *Recordings:* Albums: Down To Earth, 1972; High Cumberland Jubilee, 1972; A White Sport Coat and A Pink Crustacean, 1973; Living and Dying In 3/4 Time, 1974; A1A, 1974; Rancho Deluxe (film soundtrack), 1975; Havana Daydreaming, 1976; Changes In Latitudes, Changes In Attitudes, 1977; Son Of a Son Of a Sailor, 1978; You Had To Be There, 1978; Volcano, 1979; Coconut Telegraph, 1980; Somewhere Over China, 1981; One Particular Harbour, 1983; Riddles In The Sand, 1984; Last Mango In Paris, 1985; Songs You Know By Heart, 1986; Floridays, 1986; Hot Water, 1988; Off To See The Lizard, 1989; Live Feeding Frenzy, 1991; Before The Beach, 1993; Fruitcakes, 1994; Margaritaville Cafe, 1995; Barometer Soup, 1995; Late Night Gumbo, 1995; Banana Wind, 1996; Christmas Island, 1996; Don't Stop The Carnival, 1998; Biloxi, 1998; Beach House On The Moon, 1999. *Publications:* Tales From Margaritaville, 1989. *Honours:* Platinum and Gold discs. *Membership:* Hon. director, Greenpeace; Founder mem., Cousteau Society. *Current Management:* Howard Kaufman, HK Management, 8900 Wilshire Blvd, Suite 300, Beverly Hills, CA 90211, USA.

BUHRER, Rolf Marcel; b. 28 June 1932, Zurich, Switzerland. Musician (valve-bone, upright string bass). 1 s. *Career:* Member of bands: Laferrière; Claude Luter; Mixim Saury; Played with: Albert Nicolas; Mezz Mezzrow; Harry 'Sweets' Edison; Eddie Davis; Moustache; Tours: France, Germany, North Africa; Numerous recordings. *Membership:* UMJ (Union Musician de Jazz).

BUIRETTE, Michele Jeanne; b. 4 March 1949, Boulogne Sur Seine, France. Musician (accordion). 1 d. *Education:* Maitrise de Psychologie. *Career:* Jazz Festivals: Le Mans; Berlin; Grenoble; Tours, Europe: Germany; Netherlands; Switzerland; Italy; Croatia; Slovenia. *Recordings:* with Pied de Poule: Indiscretion; Café Noir; Jamais Tranquille!; Solo: La Mise En Plis. *Membership:* SACEM. *Current Management:* Edna Fainaru. *Address:* 63 Blvd de Ménilmoutant, 75011 Paris, France.

BUKEM, LTJ, (Danny Williamson), (Apollo); b. 1967, Watford, Hertfordshire, England. Prod; Remixer; DJ. *Career:* Started career as DJ, late 1980s; Got break playing at the Biology raves; Founder: Good Looking Records; Promoter: Logical Progression and Speed club nights in London; World-wide DJ; Club residency at The End, London; Collaborations: MC Conrad; Peshay; Remixed: Jodeci; The Shamen; Grace; Michelle Gayle. *Recordings:* Albums: Journey Inwards, 2000; LTJ Bukem: Producer, 2001; Singles: Demon's Theme, 1993; Music, 1994; Horizons, 1995; Rhodes To Freedom, 1999; Sunrain, 2000. *Membership:* PRS. *Address:* c/o Good Looking Records, 84 Queen's Rd, Watford, Hertfordshire, WD17 2LA, England. *Website:* www.thegoodlookingorganisation.co.uk.

BUKOVSKY, Petr; b. 1 April 1947, Prague, Czech Republic. Musician (guitar, piano). Divorced, 1 s., 1 d. *Career:* Songwriter, Radio, TV, Gramophone Companies (Pop, Rock, Brass and Dance Music), 1970–. *Recordings:* The Angel Ship, 1970; The Lime, The Lime My, 1974; Today We Will Polka Play to You, 1974; Lidice Warns, 1975; The Easter Rod, 1975; The Gamekeeper's Lodge, 1982; I Know, 1995; Today For the Last Time, 1997; I Can't Call You, 1997; The Caravan, 1998; I Have the Cottage, 1998; We Dance Tango, 1998. *Honours:* Today We Will Polka Play to You, 1974; The Easter Rod, 1975. *Membership:* OSA, Czech Republic. *Address:* Bukovsky Petr, Vitosska 3415/11, 14300 Prague 4, Modrany, Czech Republic.

BULOW, Harry Timothy; b. 19 Feb. 1951, Des Moines, Iowa, USA. Composer; Conductor; Musician (Saxophone). m. Ellen Bulow, 18 June 1992, 1 s., 1 d. *Education:* BA, Music, San Diego State University, 1975; MA, 1978, PhD, 1983, University of California at Los Angeles. *Career:* Composer of film scores, popular songs and jazz. *Compositions:* Film music: The Burglar, 1979–80; Popular songs: Touch My Life; He Is The Lord; All The Love I Had

For You; I Don't Know Why; It's Jesus; Jazz: Kickback; Crystal Cove; Milpas Street Blues; Sola Street Strut; Hilo Bay; Distant Memory. *Recordings:* Numerous. *Honours:* Henry Mancini Award for Film Music Composition, 1980. *Membership:* ASCAP; Society of Composers; Southeastern Composers League, USA. *Address:* PO Box 806, Mooresville, NC 28117, USA.

BUNDRICK, John Douglas, (Rabbit); b. 21 Nov. 1948, Baytown, Texas, USA. Musician (keyboards, piano, hammond organ); Composer. m. Susan Elizabeth Vickers, 17 Sept. 1989. *Education:* Piano lessons, age 7; School and college music. *Career:* Musical Director, composer, Johnny Nash, Sweden, 1971; Moved to UK, 1971; Member, Free, 1972; Eric Burdon, 1975; Co-founder, Crawler, 1976–79; The Who, 1979–; Concerts include Live Aid Concert, Wembley, 1985; Pete Townshend, US tour, 1993; Roger Daltrey, Carnegie Hall Concert, US tour, 1994; Television: Garth Brooks, BBC TV; Jay Leno Show, Los Angeles; Prolific session musician. *Recordings:* Numerous albums include: with The Who: Face Dances; Who's Better Who's Best; The Singles; Join Together; Live Aid; with Johnny Nash: I Can See Clearly Now; Celebrate Life; Here Again; My Merry Go Round; with Free: Heartbreaker; Free Story; The Best Of Free; with Pete Townshend: Rough Mix; Empty Glass; Psychoderelict; White City; with Andy Fairweather-Low: La Booga Rooga; Be Bop 'N' Holla; with Rabbit: Dream Jungle; Broken Arrows; Dark Saloon; Run For Cover; Same Old Story; Solo albums include: Moccasin Warrior, 1997, Moccasin Warrior II, 1998; Echoes Of Africa, 1999; The Fairy Garden, 1999; Welcome To America, 2001; Other. *Recordings include:* Catch A Fire, Bob Marley; Solid Air, John Martyn; Show Some Emotion, Joan Armatrading; Catfish Rising, Jethro Tull; Back Street Crawler, Paul Kossoff; Cosmic Wheels, Donovan; Survivor, Eric Burdon; Highway To The Sun, Snowy White; A Celebration: The Music Of Pete Townshend, Roger Daltrey; She's The Boss, Mick Jagger; Bebop The Future, David Essex; Live At The Albert Hall, David Gilmore; Amused To Death, Roger Waters; Other recordings with artistes including Tom Robinson; Backstreet Crawler; Claire Hamill; Sandy Denny; Suzi Quatro; Toots and the Maytals; Russ Ballard; Peter Frampton; Hank Wangford; Bill Wyman; Richard Thompson; Barbara Dickson; Boo Hewerdine; Kossoff, Kirke, Tetsu and Rabbit; Film soundtracks: Rocky Horror Picture Show; King Ralph; McVicar; Bad Timing. *Membership:* PRS; Musicians' Union. *Address:* c/o David Clayton, 39 Staverton Rd, Bilborough, Nottingham NG8 4ET, England.

BUNFORD, Huw, (Bunf); b. 15 Sept. 1967, Cardiff, Wales. Musician (guitar). *Career:* Member, Super Furry Animals; Early releases on small indie label; Obtained major indie label deal; Numerous international tours, and many festival appearances. *Recordings:* Singles: Llanfairpwllgwyngyllgogerychwyndrobwl... EP, 1995; Moog Droog EP, 1995; God! Show Me Magic, 1996; If You Don't Want Me To Destroy You, 1996; The Man Don't Give A Fuck, 1996; Hometown Unicorn, 1996; Something 4 The Weekend, 1996; The International Language Of Screaming, 1997; Hermann Loves Pauline, 1997; Demons, 1997; Play It Cool, 1997; Ice Hockey Hair, 1998; Northern Lights, 1999; Fire In My Heart, 1999; Do Or Die, 2000; Juxtaposed With You, 2001; Albums: Fuzzy Logic, 1996; Radiator, 1997; Outspaced (compilation), 1998; Guerrilla, 1999; Mwng, 2000; Rings Around The World, 2001.

BUNN, Roger; b. Norwich, England. Vocalist; Musician (guitars, bass guitars); Composer; Music Exec; Lyricist; Journalist; Activist. *Career:* Lead guitar, The Toffs, Wee Willie Harris (at Star Club), The Bluebottles; Guitar and electric bass, Ken Stevens Big Band; Guitar and double bass, Val Merrill Orchestra; Double bass, Denny Mann Orchestra, Cave Club Heidelburg, The Blue Notes, The Spontaneous Music Ensemble, for Marianne Faithfull, for Graham Bond, Roger Bunn's UFO Avant Ensemble (resident, UFO Club, London), The Giant Sun Trolley; Mem., close harmony jazz ensemble, Don Riddell Four, The London Beat Poets; Founder mem., close harmony group, Djinn; Founder musician, Jazz Against Apartheid, 1990–; Various stage and touring shows; Dir, Music Industry Human Rights Asscn; Patron, Professional Golfers Asscn European Tour; Editor, Tiger Alert (golf e-mail magazine). *Compositions include:* Worked with: Graham Bell, Eddie Gomez, Tim Hardin, Pete Brown. *Recordings:* Albums: Solo: Piece Of Mind, 1969; played on: The Arts School Dance; Roger Bunn's Endjin; Open Door, Kieran White; All That Moody, Davey Graham; Stagecoach; Roxy Music; Woman, Mike McGear; Almost Comercially Viable, Peggy Seeger. Singles: Got To Be Your Lover (video soundtrack), Billy Idol. *Honours:* Hon. Chief, African National Congress. *Address:* 192 Chiswick Village, London W4 3DG, England. *Telephone:* (20) 8742-2803.

BUNTON, Emma Lee, (Baby Spice); b. 21 Jan. 1976, London, England. Vocalist. *Career:* Actress, including appearances in EastEnders; Mem., Touch, later renamed Spice Girls, 1993–; Numerous tours, concerts, television and radio appearances; Film, Spiceworld: The Movie, 1997; World tour incl. UK, Europe, India, USA; Presenter on TV and radio including BBC Radio 1 and satellite TV show; Solo artiste, 1999–; Solo appearance, Breast Cancer Awareness concert. *Recordings:* Albums: with Spice Girls: Spice (No. 1, UK), 1996; Spiceworld (No. 1, UK), 1997; Forever, 2000; Solo: A Girl Like Me, 2001. Singles: with Spice Girls: Wannabe (No. 1, UK and USA), 1996; Say You'll Be There (No. 1, UK), 1996; 2 Become 1 (No. 1, UK), 1996; Mama/Who Do You Think You Are (No. 1, UK), 1997; Step To Me, 1997; Spice Up Your Life (No.

1, UK), 1997; Too Much (No. 1, UK), 1997; Stop, 1998; (How Does It Feel To Be) On Top Of The World, 1998; Move Over/Generation Next, 1998; Viva Forever (No. 1, UK), 1998; Goodbye (No. 1, UK), 1998; Holler/Let Love Lead The Way (No. 1, UK), 2000; Solo: What I Am (with Tin Tin Out), 1999; What Took You So Long? (No. 1, UK), 2001; Take My Breath Away, 2001; We're Not Gonna Sleep Tonight, 2001. *Honours:* BRIT Awards, Best British Single, Wannabe, 1997, Bestselling British Album Act, 1998, Outstanding Contribution, 2000. *Address:* c/o Virgin Records Ltd, 553–79 Harrow Rd, London W10 4RH, England. *Website:* c3.vmg.co.uk/spicegirls.

BURCH, Bruce; b. Georgia, USA. Musician (guitar); Songwriter. m. Cindy. *Education:* College degree, University of Georgia. *Career:* Football Coach, Gainsville High School; Signed to Combine Music, Nashville, to develop songwriting, then Famous Music; Co-founder, Burch Brothers Music (with brother David). *Compositions:* Hits include: Reba McEntire: Rumor Has It; T Graham Brown: The Last Resort; Billy Joe Royal: Out of Sight and On My Mind; Other songs recorded by: Reba McEntire; Aaron Tippin; George Fox; Dan Seals; Barbara Mandrell; Oak Ridge Boys. *Membership:* SESAC. *Address:* c/o SESAC, 55 Music E, Nashville, TN 37203, USA.

BURDON, Eric; b. 11 May 1941, Walker, Newcastle, Tyne and Wear, England. Vocalist. *Education:* Newcastle College of Art and Industrial Design. *Career:* Member, The Pagans; Member, The Animals, 1963–67; Became Eric Burdon and The New Animals, 1968; Eric Burdon and War, 1970; Solo artiste, 1971–; Also, leader, Eric Burdon Band; Tours world-wide; Major concerts include: Monterey Pop Festival, 1967; Reading Festival, 1973; Film appearances: Top Gear, 1965; Stranger In The House, 1967; Joe Vs The Volcano, 1990. *Recordings:* Hit singles include: with The Animals: House Of The Rising Sun (No. 1, UK and USA), 1964; I'm Crying, 1964; Don't Let Me Be Misunderstood, 1965; Bring It On Home To Me, 1965; We've Gotta Get Out Of This Place, 1965; It's My Life, 1965; Inside Looking Out, 1966; Don't Bring Me Down, 1966; Good Times, 1967; San Franciscan Nights, 1967; Albums: with the Animals: The Animals, 1964; Animal Tracks, 1965; The Animals On Tour, 1965; The Best Of The Animals, 1966; The Most Of The Animals, 1966; Animalisms, 1966; Animalization, 1966; Help Me Girl, 1967; When I Was Young, 1967; Best Of (Vol. 2), 1967; Winds Of Change, 1967; The Twain Shall Meet, 1968; Every One Of Us, 1968; Love Is, 1969; Before We Were So Rudely Interrupted, 1977; Ark, 1983; Rip It To Shreds, 1984; with Eric Burdon and War: Eric Burdon Declares War, 1970; Black Man's Burdon, 1971; Solo/Eric Burdon Band: Eric Is Here, 1967; Guilty, 1971; Ring Of Fire, 1974; Sun Secrets, 1975; Stop (with Jimmy Witherspoon), 1975; Survivor, 1978; Gotta Find My Baby, 1979; Last Drive, 1980; Live, 1982; Comeback, 1982; I Used To Be An Animal, 1988; Wicked Man (with Jimmy Witherspoon), 1988; Crawling King Snake, 1992; Lost Within The Halls Of Fame, 1995; Misunderstood, 1995; Soldier Of Fortune, 1997; The Ultimate Comeback, 2001. *Publications:* Autobiography, I Used To Be An Animal, But I'm All Right Now, 1986. *Current Management:* c/o Denis Vaughan, Bond St House, 14 Clifford St, London W1X 2JD, England.

BURGESS, John Edward; b. 8 March 1932, London, England. Record Prod; Studio Owner. m. Jean Horsfall, 5 Sept. 1964, 3 s. *Career:* Press, promotion, publicity, EMI Records, 1951; Production assistant to Norman Newell; Founder member, AIR Group of Companies with George Martin, 1965; AIR Studios opened 1969; Merged with Chrysalis, 1974; Managing Director, Air Studios, Montserrat, West Indies, 1979; Managing Director, Air Studios, London, 1969–90, Lyndhurst, 1990–. *Recordings:* Producer for: Adam Faith; Manfred Mann; Peter and Gordon; Freddie and the Dreamers; John Barry Seven; Cast albums: Barnum; Guys and Dolls. *Address:* 2 Sudbury Hill, Harrow on the Hill, Harrow, Middlesex HA1 3SB, England.

BURGESS, Tim; b. 30 May 1967, Salford, Manchester, England. Vocalist. *Career:* Fmr mem., Electric Crayons; Founding mem., lead singer, The Charlatans, 1990–; Signed to Beggars Banquet Records, later Universal Records; Numerous tours, festivals, television and radio appearances. *Recordings:* Albums: Some Friendly (No. 1, UK), 1990; Between 10th And 11th, 1992; Up To Our Hips, 1995; The Charlatans (No. 1, UK), 1995; Tellin' Stories (No. 1, UK), 1997; Melting Pot: The Best Of The Charlatans, 1998; Us And Us Only, 1999; Songs From The Other Side, 2000; Wonderland, 2001; Live It Like You Love It, 2002. Singles: Indian Rope, 1990; The Only One I Know, 1990; Then, 1990; Me In Time, 1991; Over Rising, 1991; Weirdo, 1992; Tremelo Song, 1992; Can't Get Out Of Bed, 1994; Autograph, 1994; I Never Want An Easy Life If Me And He Were Ever To Get There, 1994; Jesus Hairdo, 1994; Crashin' In, 1994; Just Lookin', 1995; Just When You're Thinkin' Things Over, 1995; One To Another, 1996; North Country Boy, 1997; How High, 1997; Tellin' Stories, 1997; My Beautiful Friend, 1999; Forever, 1999; Impossible, 2000; Love Is The Key, 2001; A Man Needs To Be Told, 2001; You're So Pretty—We're So Pretty, 2002; with Saint Etienne: I Was Born On Christmas Day, 1993; with The Chemical Brothers: Life Is Sweet, 1995. *Honours:* Gold, Silver and Platinum discs. *Current Management:* Steve Harrison Management, 2 Witton Walk, Northwich, Cheshire CW9 5AT, England. *Address:* The Charlatans, PO Box 134, Sandbach, Cheshire CW11 1YS, England. *E-mail:* cat@thecharlatans.net. *Website:* www.thecharlatans.net.

BURGH, Steven Lawrence; b. 17 Dec. 1950, Trenton, New Jersey, USA. Record Prod; Musician (guitar). m. Jamie Reisch, 26 Feb. 1983, 1 s., 1 d. *Career:* Musician with: Phoebe Snow; Steve Forbert; Gladys Knight; Billy Joel; Producer, engineer, Baby Monster Studios, New York, 1986–. *Recordings:* As musician: with Phoebe Snow: Phoebe Snow, 1974; It Looks Like Snow, 1976; Never Letting Go, 1978; with Billy Joel: 52nd Street; with Steve Forbert: Alive In Arrival, 1978; Steve Forbert, 1982; Film soundtrack, Tender Mercies, 1982. *Honours:* Grammy, 52nd Street, 1978; Academy Award, Tender Mercies, 1982.

BURKE, Solomon; b. 1936, Philadelphia, PA, USA. Soul Vocalist. *Career:* Own radio show, Solomon's Temple; Wonder Boy Preacher; Toured in Soul Clan revival with Wilson Pickett, Ben E. King, Don Covay, Joe Tex; Owner, mortuary business; First UK appearance in 15 years, Barbican Centre, 2002. *Recordings:* Albums: The Best Of Solomon Burke, 1965; Proud Mary, 1968; Soul Alive, 1981; A Change Is Gonna Come; Cry To Me, 1984; Greatest Hits; If You Need Me; Rock 'N' Soul; The Bishop Rides South, 1988; The Definition Of Soul, 1997; Don't Give Up On Me, 2002. Singles include: Be-Bop Grandma, 1959; Just Out Of Reach (Of My Two Empty Arms), 1961; Cry To Me, 1962; If You Need Me, 1963; Goodbye Baby (Baby Goodbye), 1964; Everybody Needs Somebody To Love, 1964; The Price; Got To Get You Off My Mind, 1965. *Address:* c/o Frank Riley, High Rd, 751 Brigdeway, Third Floor, Sausalito, CA 94965, USA. *Website:* www.fatpossum.com.

BURLEY, Philip George (Pip); b. 31 Dec. 1943, Croydon, Surrey, England. Musician (keyboards) Composer; Television Prod. m. Christine Komaromy, 10 June 1974, 3 d. *Career:* Freelance keyboard player, composer, arranger; Played with: Sydney Lipton; Joe Loss; Ken Mackintosh; Cabaret with The Semitones; Television producer, 1987–; Credits include: Darling Buds of May; A Touch of Frost; Pride of Africa. *Compositions:* Music for television includes: Musicround; Darling Buds of May; Score for Romeo and Juliet, 1993; The Comedy of Errors, 1995. *Honours:* Ivor Novello Award, 1991. *Membership:* PRS; Chief Barker, Variety Clubs of Great Britain, 1999–. *Address:* Heathwoods, Dorking Rd, Tadworth, Surrey KT20 7TJ, England.

BURMAKA, Maria; b. 16 June 1970, Kharkiv, Ukraine. m. Dmytro Nebesiftchuk, 27 Nov. 1993, 1 d. *Education:* Kharkiv State University; Music School. *Career:* Won Grand Prix, all Ukrainian festivals: Oberig; Chervona Ruta; Many concerts in Ukraine; Concerts: France; Germany, 1992; Canada; Poland; USA, 1989–93; Songs at MB top national hit parade 7 times, 1993–94. *Recordings:* Cassette: Don't Blossom Spring, 1990; CD, Maria, 1992; CD: Hope Remains, 1994. *Honours:* Laureate, Ukrainian festivals, 1989–93; Album, Hope Remains, Best In Ukraine, Council of New Stars of Old Year Festival, 1993–94. *Current Management:* Dmytro Nebesijtchuk. *Address:* Schuseva St 36, #12, 254060 Kiev, Ukraine.

BURN, Chris; b. 13 March 1955, Epping, Essex, England. Musician (piano). *Education:* Surrey University, BMus, MMus. *Career:* British tours, 1985, 1987, 1990, 1992, 1994; Festivals: Bochum; Berlin: Copenhagen; Ulrichsberg; Cologne; Victoriaville, 1996; Radio 3 broadcasts: 1989, 1992, 1994; WDR TV, radio. *Recordings:* A Fountain Replete; Ensemble; A Henry Cowell Concert; Music for Three Rivers. *Publications:* Various articles. *Honours:* ACGB, 1988, 1990, 1992, 1994. *Membership:* PRS; MCPS. *Current Management:* ACTA. *Address:* 11 Marits Ave, Ongar, Essex CM5 9AY, England.

BURNEL, Jean-Jacques; b. 21 Feb. 1952, London, England. Vocalist; Musician (bass). *Education:* History degree, Bradford University. *Career:* Founder member, UK rock group The Stranglers, 1976–; Headline tours, Europe; UK; USA; Canada; International concerts include: Support to Patti Smith, 1976; Climax Blues Band, 1977; Loch Lomond Festival, 1979; Reading Rock Festival, 1983; Alexandra Palace, 1990; Support to Simple Minds, 1991; Dartmoor Prison (first band ever to do so), 1992. *Recordings:* Albums include: Rattus Norvegicus, 1977; No More Heroes, 1978; Black and White, 1978; Live (X Cert), 1979; The Raven, 1979; Themeninblack, 1981; La Folie, 1982; The Collection, 1982; Feline, 1983; Aural Sculpture, 1984; Dreamtime, 1986; All Live and All Of The Night, 1988; 10, 1990; Greatest Hits, 1991; In The Night, 1992; Saturday Night, Sunday Morning, 1993; About Time, 1995; Written In Red, 1997; The Hit Men (singles compilation), 1997; 5 Live 01, 2001; Solo album: Euroman Cometh, 1979; with Dave Greenfield, Fire and Water, 1983; Hit singles include: Peaches, 1977; Something Better Change, 1977; No More Heroes, 1977; Five Minutes, 1978; Nice 'n' Sleazy, 1978; Duchess, 1979; Golden Brown (No. 2, UK), 1982; Strange Little Girl, 1982; European Female, 1983; Skin Deep, 1984; Always The Sun, 1986; All Day and All Of The Night, 1987. *Honours:* Ivor Novello Award, Most Performed Work of 1982, Golden Brown, 1983. *Current Management:* Cruisin' Music. *Address:* c/o 21 Gay St, Bath BA1 2PD, England.

BURNETT, T-Bone (John Henry); b. 18 Jan. 1945, St Louis, Missouri, USA. Musician (guitar); Songwriter; Prod; Vocalist. *Career:* Touring musician with Delaney and Bonnie; B-52s; Bob Dylan's Rolling Thunder Revue, 1970s; Founder, Alpha Band, 1976–79; Solo recording artiste, 1972, 1980–; Worked with Richard Thompson; Elvis Costello, 1980s. *Recordings:* Albums: J Henry Burnett, 1972; Truth Decay, 1980; Proof Through The Night, 1983; Behind The Trap Door, 1984; T-Bone Burnett, 1986; The Talking Animals, 1988; The

Criminal Under My Own Hat, 1992; with Alpha Band: Alpha Band, 1977; Spark In The Dark, 1977; Statue Makers Of Hollywood, 1978; with Bob Dylan: Hard Rain, 1976; Blowin' In The Wind, 1985; with Los Lobos: How Will The Wolf Survive, 1984; By The Light Of The Moon, 1987; La Pistola Y El Corazon, 1988; with Roy Orbison: In Dreams, 1987; Mystery Girl, 1989; Friends: Black and White Night, 1988; Other recordings with: Willie Dixon; Kinky Friedman; Emmylou Harris; Golden Palaminos; Producer, albums with Bruce Cockburn; Leo Kottke; Bo Deans; Nitty Gritty Dirt Band; Elvis Costello, Spike, 1989; Counting Crows, August and Everything After, 1993; Gillian Welch, Revival, 1996; Wallflowers, Bringing Down The Horse, 1996; Natalie Merchant, Motherland, 2001. *Current Management:* Addis, Wechsler and Associates. *Address:* 955 S Carillo Dr., Third Floor, Los Angeles, CA 90048, USA.

BURNS, Christian Anthony; b. 18 Jan. 1976, Liverpool, England. Vocalist; Musician (guitar); Songwriter. *Career:* Co-founder of BBMak pop group, 1996; Signed to UK company Telstar; Gained large US popularity after licence deal with Hollywood/Disney; Performed to over 100m. US viewers through group's own TV specials; Supported Britney Spears on sell-out US tour followed by 28-date first headline US tour, 2000; UK shows with The Corrs, 2001. *Recordings:* Albums: Sooner Or Later, 2000; Singles: Back Here, Still On Your Side, 2000; Ghost Of You and Me, 2001. *Honours:* Debut LP sales of over 1m. copies. *Address:* c/o Diane Young. *E-mail:* DaytimeENT@aol.com. *Website:* www.bbmak.co.uk.

BURNS, Patty; b. 16 Aug. 1967, Köln, Cologne, Germany. *Career:* Belgian support act for Scorpions; Performing alongside Marillion, Magnum, Erasure, Kent Festival, England, Sopot Festival, Poland, Bregenz Festival, Austria, Jurmala Festival, Russia. *Compositions:* Fast Traveller; Too Late; Explode Your Nature; Reach the Sky. *Recordings:* Just Remember (Trust Me); Ready for Duty, CD; Evening News, CD; These Boods, CD. *Honours:* Winner, Belgian National Rock Meeting; Graduate, Jurmala Festival and Bregenz. *Current Management:* Life for Music, Belgium. *Address:* 96 Basilique Ave, 1089 Brussels, Belgium.

BURNS, Robert Beverley; b. 16 May 1923, Toronto, Ontario, Canada. Musician (saxophones, clarinets). m. Enid Lambert Burns, 30 Oct. 1991, 1 s., 2 d. *Education:* Toronto Conservatory; Tuition with William Matthews ARCM; Hiram and Walter Lear, London, Bournemouth. *Career:* One of few jazz and classical musicians; RCAF HQ Band, Europe; Returned Canada, 1946; Played with Maynard Ferguson, Ellis McClintock, Mart Kenney, and studio work, Toronto; Returned to England, 1948; Played, recorded with Ted Heath, Ambrose, Lew Stone, Jack Parnell's first band; Theatre, studio freelancing until 1989; Led jazz groups, productions at the National Theatre; Played Triparte by Robert Farnon, commissioned by Musicians' Union for May Day Concert at Festival Hall, Concerto for 3 saxophones played by 1 player; Toured with Tony Bennett, recorded at Albert Hall; Tours, 4 times with Benny Goodman, Ireland, Europe; Soloist, film tracks: The Spy Who Came In From The Cold; Dance With A Stranger; Shot In The Dark; Two For The Road. *Compositions:* Love theme, I Believe In You; Small jazz groups for Frank Cordell film music. *Recordings include:* with Benny Goodman: Today; London Date; Directions In Jazz, Bill Le Sage; Great Jazz Solos Revisited, Bernie Cash; As House Band, HMV Studios titles include: When I'm Sixty-Four; Albums with Robert Farnon; Frank Chacksfield; Eric Rogers; Frank Sinatra In London, Robert Farnon; 25 years recording ITV artists including: Lena Horne; Ella Fitzgerald; Peggy Lee; Vic Damone; Vera Lynn; Petula Clark; Barbra Streisand; Also many classical recordings with the four major orchestras; Films and music as soloist with Bill McGuffie; House band with major labels; Albums with The Beatles including solo on When I'm Sixty-Four; Albums with Vanessa Redgrave and Noel Coward. *Honours:* Winner, All Canadian Jazz Poll (saxophone), ARCM. *Membership:* Musicians' Union, Canada, England. *Address:* 124 Pearl St, Sarnia, ON N7T 5G5, Canada.

BURNS, Robert George Henry; b. 24 Feb. 1953, London, England. Musician (bass guitar); Composer; Educator. m. Elizabeth Chennells, 14 Jan. 1991, 1 s. *Education:* Guildhall School of Music and Drama; Brunel University College; Rhodesian College of Music. *Career:* Tours, live dates, recordings with: Sam and Dave; Edwin Starr; Lene Lovich; Isaac Hayes; Pete Townshend; Eric Burdon; David Gilmour; Albert Lee; James Burton; Jerry Donahue; Viv Stanshall; Zoot Money; Formed Robert Burns Music, 1987. *Compositions:* Soundtracks for clients including: Lonrho; Sunday Times; IBM; MTV; P & O. *Recordings:* Television: Red Dwarf; Mr Bean; 2 Point 4 Children; Alas Smith and Jones; Lenny Henry; Blackadder III; Not The Nine O'Clock News; Three Of a Kind. *Publications:* The Rock File; Columnist for Bassist and Musician magazines; Syllabus for Trinity/Rockschool graded exams for bass guitar, 1992. *Honours:* Appointed Principal Examiner, Bass Guitar, Trinity College of Music, 1992; Head, Bass Guitar Studies, BASStech/Thames Valley University, 1994. *Address:* Crouch End, London N8, England.

BURNSTEIN, Cliff; b. 1953. Man. Exec. *Career:* Joint founder and head, with Peter Mensch, Q-Prime Management; Managed artistes and groups incl.: AC/DC, Tal Bachman, Crazy Town, Def Leppard, Dokken, Fountains of Wayne, Garbage, Nina Gordon, Hole, Bruce Hornsby, Ivy, Madonna, Metallica, Queensryche, Red Hot Chili Peppers, Rush, Shania Twain,

Smashing Pumpkins, Tesla, Vercua Salt, Warrior Soul; Q-Prime Management acquired part-ownership, with Zomba Music Publishing, of Volcano Records, 1998. *Address:* Q-Prime Management, Third Floor, 9000 Sunset Blvd, Los Angeles, CA, USA.

BURONFOSSE, Marc; b. 6 May 1963, Soissons, France. Musician (upright acoustic bass). m. Jennifer Forse, 22 May 1993, 1 d. *Education:* 3 year degree, Sound Engineering. *Education:* Prize, Union Des Conservatoires de Paris. *Career:* Japanese tour with Las Solistes de Versailles (chamber orchestra); Fellowship to study at the New School of Music, New York; Tour of Central Africa with Sylvain Kassap Quartet; European tours with Sylvain Kassap Quartet and Bojan Z Quartet; Television and radio appearances. *Recordings:* Sylvain Kassap Quartet Quixote; Bojan Z Quartet. *Honours:* First prize, Concours de la Défense, 1992; Concours Etrechy, 1995. *Membership:* ADAMI; SACEM; SPEDIDAM.

BURRELL, Boz; b. 1 Aug. 1946, Holbeach, England. Musician (bass guitar); Vocalist. *Career:* King Crimson; founder member, UK Rock Group Bad Company, 1973–83; founder member, Snape; toured world-wide; concerts include: Madison Square Gardens with Bad Company; headlined Hyde Park Gig with King Crimson, 1971. *Compositions:* Include: Smokin'45; Whiskey Bottle; Gone, Gone, Gone. *Recordings:* Albums: with King Crimson, Islands, 1971; Earthbound, 1972; Accidentally Born in New Orleans, 1972; Live At Jackson; Young Boys Guide to King Crimson, 1976; BBC Sessions, 1994; Beginners' Guide To The King Crimson Collectors' Club, 2000; with Amazing Blundle: Albums: Blundle, 1973; Musgrave Street, 1974; with Bad Company: Albums: Bad Company, 1974; Straight Shooter, 1975; Run With The Pack, 1976; Burnin' Sky, 1977; Desolation Angels, 1979; Rough Diamonds, 1982; 10 From 6, 1985; Fame and Fortune, 1986; with Snape and Alexis Korner: Album: On The Move, 1996; The 'Original' Bad Company Anthology, 1999; Singles: Can't Get Enough; Feel Like Makin' Love; Young Blood; Movin' On; Hey Hey; Hammer Of Love; also played with: Graham Bond; Gary Brooker; Eric Burdon; Roger Chapman; Dick Heckstall-Smith; Tim Hinkley (Hinkley's Heroes); Ronnie Lane; Alvin Lee; Lulu; Zoot Money; Esther Phillips; Pete Townsend; Ruby Turner; Ronnie Wood; currently playing with Tam White/ Boz Burrell Band. *Honours:* Gold, Platinum Albums with Bad Company; Grammy Award, 1975; Hon. Col of Louisiana, with Bad Company, 1977. *Membership:* Musicians' Union. *Address:* c/o Gremlin Productions, PO Box 216, Diss, Norfolk IP22 2TY, England.

BURRELL, Kenny; b. 31 July 1931, Detroit, Michigan, USA. Jazz Musician (guitar). *Education:* Classical guitar, 1952–53; BMus, Wayne University, Detroit, 1955. *Career:* Played with Candy Johnson Sextet; Yusef Lateef; Tommy Flanagan; Dizzy Gillespie, 1951; Oscar Peterson Trio, 1955; Hampton Hawes Trio, 1956; Benny Goodman, 1957; Association with organist Jimmy Smith; Recorded with John Coltrane, Sonny Rollins, Coleman Hawkins; Leader, own trio. *Recordings:* Albums include: The Cats, 1957; Kenny Burrell–John Coltrane, 1958; At The Five Spot Cafe Vol. 1, 1959; Midnight Blue, 1960s; Live At The Village Vanguard, 1960s; Guitar Forms, 1965; For Charlie Christian and Benny Goodman, 1967; Handcrafted, 1978; Kenny Burrell In New York, 1981; Night Song, 1982; Listen To The Dawn, 1983; Bluesin' Around, 1984; A La Carte, 1986; Generations, 1987; Blue Lights Vols 1 and 2, 1989; Togethering, 1989; Recapitulation, 1989; Guiding Spirit, 1989; Sunup To Sundown, 1991; Soulero, 1996; Love Is The Answer, 1998. *Current Management:* Tropix International. *Address:* 163 Third Ave, Suite 206, New York, NY 10003, USA.

BURROUGHS, Gary Stuart; b. 3 April 1953, Doncaster, England. Musician (drums, percussion, multi-instrumentalist); Vocalist; Songwriter; Prod; Engineer. m. Lyn Acton, 26 Nov. 1976, 1 s. *Education:* Hull Technical College; Lead tenor, school, 1961; Tenor horn, cornet, Askern Siver Prize Band, 1963. *Career:* Drummer with: Soul Image; The Pink; Listen; The Weazles; Johnny Duncan and the Bluegrass Boys; Rock and Roll Circus; Rock Orchestrals; Johnny Johnson and the Bandwagon; Snake Eye; The Killers; Jackal; Buster Crab; Sarah Gordans All American Soul Show; Sheer Elegance; Roy Wood: Wizzo; Christie; Nosmo King; Luggage; Export; Earthman Liberation; What Katy Did Next; Tiffanys; Gimmex; Stork Club; Bertice Redding; Lionel Bart; Simon Townshend; Resistdance; Marino; NGO; Fila Brazillia; Derek Bailey; Naked Orange, 1968–; Tour Manager, Limmie and The Family Cookin', 1976; Sound Engineer, Fairview Music, 1979; Derek Bailey; Lead singer with: Techno Pop; Marino; Listen; Blitzkrieg; The Weazles; The Choirboys; NGO; Drummer with: American Sweet Sound Tour; Simon Townshend; Support, West Coast Tour, Pretenders; Support, Duran Duran World tour, 1984; Television: Saturday Superstore, BBC1; Lift Off with Ayshea; Regional television, BBC2; Televised live concerts: Syracuse, USA; Seattle, USA; Baltimore, USA; Producer for: Smash live, Top of the Pops, BBC1, 1994; Various radio; Business ventures: DIG for music, Midem, 1991; Wall 2 Wall Records, 1990; Wall 2 Wall Studios, 1992. *Recordings:* Single: Year Of The Tiger, 1975; Session drummer, vocalist, various singles, 1976–98; As solo artist: Single: Paint It Black, 1980; Album: Sacred Places; with Marino: Blues For Lovers, 1991. *Honours:* Blues Album of the Year, Paris, France, 1992. *Membership:* PRS; Equity. *Current Management:* Wall 2 Wall.

BURTON, Gary; b. 23 Jan. 1943, Anderson, Indiana, USA. Jazz Musician (vibraphone, piano). *Education:* Berklee College of Music, Boston. *Career:* Member, George Shearing's Group, 1963; Played with Stan Getz, 2 years; Formed own bands, 1960s–; Leader, various bands featuring artists including: Larry Coryell; Roy Haynes; Pat Metheny; Eberhard Weber; Also recorded with Stéphane Grappelli; Carla Bley; Keith Jarrett; Chick Corea; Michael Brecker; Peter Erskine; Teacher, Berklee College of Music, 1971–. *Recordings include:* Albums: Duster, 1967; Lofty Fake Anagram, 1967; Country Roads and Other Places, 1968; Green Apple, 1969; Hotel Hello, 1974; Matchbook, 1974; Dreams So Real, 1975; Easy As Pie, 1980; Picture This, 1983; Real Life Hits, 1984; Whiz Kids, 1986; Times Like These, 1988; Cool Nights, 1990; Six Pack, 1993; Live In Cannes, 1996; Astor Piazzolla Reunion, 1996; Departure, 1997; Like Minds, 1998; Libertango: The Music Of Astor Piazzolla, 2000; For Hamp, Red, Bags and Cal, 2001; Selected Recordings, 2002; with Carla Bley: A Genuine Tang Funeral, 1968; with Stéphane Grappelli: Paris Encounter, 1969; with Keith Jarrett: Gary Burton and Keith Jarrett, 1970; with Eberhard Weber, Ring, 1974; Passengers, 1976; with Chick Corea: Crystal Silence, 1972; Duet, 1978; with Ralph Towner: Slide Show, 1976; with Pat Metheny: Reunion, 1989; with Paul Bley: Right Time Right Place, 1991; with Makoto Ozone: Face To Face, 1995. *Current Management:* Ted Kurland Associates, 173 Brighton Ave, Boston, MA 02134, USA.

BURTON, Paddy (Patrick Henry); b. 19 Aug. 1961, Stockport, Cheshire, England. Musician (percussion); Musical Instrument Maker (slitdrums, multiplayer giant xylophones). 2 s. *Education:* Newcastle University. *Career:* Musical Director for theatre companies; Performing musician with local bands, 1978–86; Musician in Residence, City of Edinburgh District Council, 1990–92; Player with Amadeus, 1993–; Jack Drum Arts; Dodgy Clutch; The Fabulous Salami Brothers. *Recordings:* Trashcan Gamelan Edinburgh, 1992; Black Diamonds, Black Gold, 1993; Fish Xylophone, 1994. *Membership:* Musicians' Union; Sound Sense; Equity. *Address:* 43–44 Gladstone Terrace, Sunniside, Bishop Auckland, County Durham DL13 4LS, England.

BURWELL, Carter; b. 18 Nov. 1955, New York, NY, USA. Composer; *Compositions:* For television: Framed (additional music), 1990; And the Band Played On, 1993; Children Remember the Holocaust, 1995; For film: Blood Simple, 1984; A Hero of Our Time, 1985; Psycho III, 1986; Raising Arizona, 1987; Pass the Ammo, 1988; It Takes Two, 1988; The Beat, 1988; Checking Out, 1989; Miller's Crossing, 1990; Scorchers, 1991; Doc Hollywood, 1991; Barton Fink, 1991; Waterland, 1992; Buffy the Vampire Slayer, 1992; Storyville, 1992; A Dangerous Woman, 1993; Kalifornia, 1993; This Boy's Life, 1993; Wayne's World 2, 1993; The Hudsucker Proxy, 1994; Airheads, 1994; It Could Happen to You, 1994; The Celluloid Closet, 1995; Bad Company, 1995; Rob Roy, 1995; A Goofy Movie, 1995; Two Bits, 1995; The Chamber, 1996; Fargo, 1996; Fear, 1996; Joe's Apartment, 1996; The Spanish Prisoner, 1997; Picture Perfect, 1997; The Locusts, 1997; Girls Night Out, 1997; Assassins, 1997; Conspiracy Theory, 1997; The Jackal, 1997; Velvet Goldmine, 1998; Gods and Monsters, 1998; The Big Lebowski, 1998; Being John Malkovich, 1999; The Corruptor, 1999; The General's Daughter, 1999; The Hi-Lo Country, 1999; Mystery, Alaska, 1999; What Planet Are You From?, 2000; Hamlet, 2000; O Brother, Where Art Thou?, 2000; Book of Shadows: Blair Witch 2, 2000; A Knight's Tale, 2001. *Membership:* ASCAP. *Current Management:* Creative Artists Agency (CAA), 9830 Wilshire Blvd, Beverly Hills, CA 90212-1825, USA.

BUSH, John; b. 24 Aug. 1963, Los Angeles, California, USA. Vocalist. *Career:* Lead Singer, Anthrax, 1992–; Lead Singer, Armored Saint; Appeared with Anthrax on episode of TV Show, News Radio; Recorded with Armored Saint in film Hellraiser 3. *Compositions:* With Anthrax: Only; Black Lodge; Fueled; Inside Out; With Armored Saint: Can U Deliver; Over the Edge; Reign of Fire. *Recordings:* Albums: with Anthrax: Sound Of White Noise, 1993; Stomp 442, 1995; Vol. VIII: The Threat Is Real, 1998; Madhouse: The Very Best Of Anthrax, 2001; with Armored Saint: March Of The Saint, 1984; Delirious Nomad, 1985; Symbol Of Salvation, 1991. *Membership:* AFTRA. *Current Management:* Concrete Management. *Address:* 10074 Sully Dr., Sun Valley, CA 91352, USA.

BUSH, Kate (Catherine); b. 30 July 1958, Bexleyheath, Kent, England. Vocalist; Songwriter. *Education:* Voice, dance and mime lessons. *Career:* Limited live performances include: Tour of Life, Europe, 1979; Secret Policeman's Third Ball, London, 1987; Television appearances include: Bringing It All Back Home documentary, 1991; Writer, dir, actress, film The Line, The Cross and The Curve, 1994. *Recordings:* Albums: The Kick Inside, 1978; Lionheart, 1978; Never For Ever (No. 1, UK), 1980; The Dreaming, 1982; Hounds Of Love (No. 1, UK), 1985; The Whole Story (No. 1, UK), 1986; The Sensual World (No. 2, UK), 1989; This Woman's Work, 1990; The Red Shoes (No. 2, UK), 1993; Contributor, Games Without Frontiers, Peter Gabriel, 1980; Two Rooms: Celebrating The Songs Of Elton John And Bernie Taupin, 1991. Singles include: Wuthering Heights (No. 1, UK), 1978; The Man With The Child In His Eyes, 1978; Wow, 1979; Breathing, 1980; Babooshka, 1980; Army Dreamers, 1980; Sat In Your Lap, 1981; Running Up That Hill, 1985; Cloudbusting, 1985; Hounds Of Love, 1986; Experiment IV, 1986; Don't Give Up (duet with Peter Gabriel), 1986; This Woman's Work (from film soundtrack She's Having A Baby), 1988; The Sensual World, 1989; Moments Of Pleasure, 1993; Rubberband Girl, 1993; Man I Love, 1994; The Red Shoes, 1994. *Honours:* Ivor Novello Awards, Outstanding British Lyrics, The Man With The Child In His Eyes, 1979, Outstanding Contribution to British Music, 2002; BRIT Award, Best British Female Artist, 1987; Q Award, Inspiration Award, 2001. *Current Management:* c/o Reluctant Management, 10603 Rochester Ave, Los Angeles, CA 90024, USA.

BUSHWACKA!, (Matthew Stuart Benjamin); b. 2 Aug. 1972, London, England. Prod; Remixer; DJ. *Career:* DJ with Ratpack; Resident DJ at The End, London; Engineer at Mr C's Watershed Studio, London; Mem., Makesome Breaksome, Mashupheadz; Collaborations: Layo Paskin, Nathan Coles; Co-founder Plank/Oblong Records with Lewis Copeland. *Recordings:* Albums: Wak'd (as Plantastik), 1998; Low Life (with Layo), 1999; Cellar Dwellas, 2000; Night Works (with Layo), 2002. Singles: Deep South (with Layo), 1999; Monster, 2000; Healer, 2000. *Current Management:* c/o End Recordings, 18 W Central St, London WC1A 1JJ, England.

BUSSCHOTS, Patrick Eugéne; b. 18 Dec. 1953, Mortsel, Belgium. Man.-Dir. m. Lydia, 28 Oct. 1978, 2 d. *Education:* Jeweller; Various business courses. *Career:* Retail, wholesale, production, publishing; Currently holding, grouping all activities with ARS Productions. *Recordings:* with Technotronic: Pump Up The Jam; Material with: Faith No More; Gipsy Kings. *Honours:* World Music Award, Monte Carlo, 1990. *Membership:* IFPI. *Address:* ARS Productions, Singel 5, 2150 Kontich, Belgium.

BUSTA RHYMES, (Trevor Smith); b. 1972, Brooklyn, New York, USA. Rap Artiste; Prod. 2 s., 1 deceased. *Career:* Co-founder, Leaders of the New School; Obtained record deal; Guest artist on albums by artists including Boyz II Men, Mary J Blige, TLC and A Tribe Called Quest; Involvement in various film projects including Higher Learning; Began to release solo recordings; Formed own record company, Flipmode Entertainment; Started own clothing line, Bushi; Provided voice of Reptar in Rugrats film, and contributed one song, On Your Marks, Get Set, Ready, Go, to soundtrack; Duets with Ozzy Osbourne and Janet Jackson on third album; Appeared in remake of film Shaft, 2000; Several tours. *Recordings:* Singles: Woo Hah Got You All In Check, 1996; It's a Party, 1996; Put Your Hands Where My Eyes Could See, 1997; Dangerous, 1997; Turn It Up, 1998; One/Rhymes Galore, 1998; What's It Gonna Be, 1999; Gimme Some More, 1999; Get Out, 2000; Fire, 2000; Break Ya Neck, 2001; As I Come Back, 2001; Albums: The Coming, 1996; When Disaster Strikes, 1997; Extinction Level Event, 1998; Anarchy, 2000; Genesis, 2001.

BUTCHER, John Bernard; b. 25 Oct. 1954, Brighton, England. Musician (saxophone). *Education:* PhD, Theoretical Physics. *Career:* Worked mainly in jazz, late 1970s; Improvisation and new-music, early 1980s; Regular groups include: News From The Shed; Embers; Frisque Concordance; Ensemble; Festival appearances include: Berlin Total Music Meeting; Du Maurier Jazz (Canada); Knitting Factory (New York); Company (London); Head of ACTA Records. *Recordings:* Fonetiks, 1985; Conceits, 1987; News From The Shed, 1989; Cultural Baggage, 1990; Thirteen Friendly Numbers, 1992; Spellings, 1993; Respiritus, 1995; Concert Moves, 1995; London and Cologne, 1998. *Address:* 28 Aylmer Rd, London W12 9LQ, England.

BUTCHER, Simon David; b. 21 Dec. 1975, Mansfield, Nottinghamshire. Vocalist; Musician (guitar, violin, keyboards). *Career:* Professional musician; Interviewed and played on Trent FM, BBC Radio Nottingham, Sherwood Radio, Radio Mansfield, BBC Radio Cambridge, Radio Hallam, BBC Radio Sheffield, Ashfield Community Radio; BBC East Midland Television performing Buzzer; Clarendon Cable Television, NTL Cable 7, acoustic set and interview, XFM Demo Call. *Compositions:* Soon You Will; Next Stage; Roadrunner. *Recordings:* Dual Carriageway; Bitch; Indignant; Soon You Will; Next Stage; Roadrunner. *Honours:* Delirium Win Band of the Year, 1995. *Membership:* PRS; MCPS; PPL; Musicians' Union; BAC&S; IMF; AURA. *Current Management:* First Step Management, David Butcher, 96 George St, Mansfield, Nottinghamshire NG19 6SB, England.

BUTINA, Roman; b. 5 Aug. 1937, Zagreb, Croatia. Musician (organ, keyboards); Composer. m. Ljerka Miladinov, 4 June 1960, 1 s., 1 d. *Education:* Dr of Medicine; Dip, Intermediate Music School. *Career:* Member, Dalmatia vocal group, 12 years; Tours former Yugoslavia, Eastern, Western Europe; Leader, organist, The Blue Stars group, 1970–72; Performer, Hammond Organ, Electric Piano, Laguna Hotel, occasionally Zagreb-Intercontinental Hotel, 1973. *Compositions:* recorded and published, numerous popular tunes and songs. *Publications:* As Editor: With Song Through Zagorje, 1960; Greetings Tyrol, 1969; Ancient Croatian Songs, 1972; World Folk Songs, 1975. *Honours:* Second Prize, Zagreb Festival, 1971. *Membership:* Croatian Composers Asscn; Union of Artists of Croatia, Zagreb. *Address:* Turopolska 36, 10000 Zagreb, Croatia.

BUTLER, Bernard; b. 1 May 1970, Stamford Hill, London, England. Musician (guitar, keyboards); Songwriter. m. Elisa. *Education:* History, Queen Mary College, London, 1 year; Studied violin and piano. *Career:* Mem., Suede, 1992–95; Television appearances include: Top of the Pops, BBC1;

BRIT Awards; Later With Jools Holland, BBC2; The Tonight Show, NBC; Concerts include Glastonbury Festival; Tours, Europe, America, Japan; Mem., duo McAlmont and Butler (with David McAlmont), 1994–95, 2001–; Solo artiste. *Recordings:* Albums: with Suede: Suede (No. 1, UK), 1993; Dog Man Star, 1994; with McAlmont and Butler: The Sound Of McAlmont And Butler, 1995; Bring It Back, 2002; Solo: People Move On, 1998; Friends and Lovers, 2000. Singles include: with Suede: The Drowners, 1992; Metal Mickey, 1992; Animal Nitrate, 1993; So Young, 1993; Stay Together, 1994; We Are The Pigs, 1994; Wild One, 1994; New Generation, 1995; with McAlmont and Butler: Yes, 1995; You Do, 1995; Solo: Stay, 1998; Not Alone, 1998; I'd Do It Again If I Could, 2000; Also recorded with Bryan Ferry; Edwyn Collins; Aimee Mann; Sparks; Eddi Reader; Neneh Cherry. *Honours:* Mercury Music Prize, 1993. *Current Management:* Geoff Travis. *Address:* c/o EMI Group PLC, 4 Tenterden St, Hanover Sq., London W1A 2AY, England. *E-mail:* infobb@bernardbutler.com. *Website:* www.bernardbutler.com.

BUTLER, Clara G; b. 28 Oct. 1938, Greenville, South Carolina, USA. Songwriter; Dancer; Record Co Exec. m. Jojo St Mitchell, 18 May 1993, 1 s., 1 d. *Education:* 1 year college; 7 years with management team and songwriting team. *Career:* Arthur Murray Dance Awards; Dancing Instructor; CEO of record company, Notary Public; Music publisher and songwriter; Real estate owner; Executive producer of recording artists. *Compositions:* Songs I Must Be Gettin' Older Now; It's You For Me; Executive Producer for groups: Destination Unknown; Safari. *Honours:* Business Leader; Ballroom Dancing Awards. *Membership:* Broadcast Music Inc; Antithesis Music. *Current Management:* The Amethyst Group Ltd.

BUTLER, Edith; b. 27 July 1942, Paquetville, New Brunswick, Canada. Vocalist; Musician (guitar). *Education:* BA, Arts, Pedagogie; MA, Literature. *Career:* Tours: Canada; USA; Japan; Olympia Theatre of Paris, France; Place des Arts, Montréal; All major television and radio shows, Canada, France, last 25 years. *Recordings:* 25 albums; 250 songs. *Honours:* 3 Platinum records; 3 Gold records; 3 Felix Awards; Nelly Award; Charles-Cros Award; Ordre National du Mérite, France, 1998; Helen Creighton Acheivement Award. *Membership:* SOCAN; SACEM; SODRAC. *Current Management:* Lise Aubut. *Address:* 86 Côte Ste Catherine, Montréal, QC H2V 2A3, Canada.

BUTLER, Geezer (Terry); b. 17 July 1949, Birmingham, England. Musician (bass). *Career:* Bass player, UK heavy rock group Black Sabbath, 1967–; Numerous concerts world-wide include: Madison Square Garden, New York, 1975; Live Aid, Philadelphia, 1985. *Recordings:* Singles include: Paranoid; Iron Man; War Pigs; Never Say Die; Albums: Black Sabbath, 1969; Paranoid, 1970; Masters Of Reality, 1971; Sabbath Bloody Sabbath, 1973; Sabotage, 1975; Technical Ectasy, 1976; Never Say Die, 1978; Heaven and Hell, 1980; Mob Rules, 1981; Live Evil, 1983; Born Again, 1983; Seventh Star, 1986; The Eternal Idol, 1987; Headless Cross, 1990; Tyr, 1990; Dehumanizer, 1992; Cross Purposes, 1994; Ozzmosis, 1995; Alive and Dead, 1996; Black Science, 1997; Reunion, 1998; Contributed to Big Country albums Driving To Damascus, 1999; One In A Million, 2001; Numerous compilations. *Current Management:* Gloria Butler Management, PO Box 2686, Knowle B94 5NQ, England.

BUTLER, Jonathan Kenneth; b. 10 Oct. 1961, Cape Town, South Africa. Musician (guitar); Vocalist; Songwriter. m. Barenese Vanessa, 28 Jan. 1983, 2 d. *Career:* Three-month US tour with Whitney Houston; Three weeks with Eric Clapton, Albert Hall; Extensive touring in own right of USA, Japan, Europe, South America, South Africa; Television: Carson; Jay Leno; David Letterman; Top of the Pops; Mandela Birthday Concert, Wembley. *Recordings:* Albums: Introducing Jonathan Butler, 1977; Jonathan Butler, 1987; More Than Friends, 1988; Heal Our Land, 1990; Head To Head, 1994; Do You Love Me? 1997; Story Of Life, 1999; The Source, 2000; EP: Deliverance; Singles: with Ruby Turner, If You're Ready (Come Go With Me), 1986; Solo: Lies, 1987; Sarah, Sarah, 1989; Sing Me Your Love, 1990; I'm On My Knees, 1994; Can We Start All Over Again, 1995; Lost To Love, 1998; features on: Millie Jackson, Tide Is Turning, 1988; Marcus Miller, Sun Don't Lie, 1993; Will Downing, Invitation Only, 1997; George Duke, Is Love Enough?, 1997; Rachelle Ferrell, Individuality, 2000. *Honours:* NAACP Award; 5 ASCAP Awards. *Membership:* Musicians' Union; PRS; AFTRA. *Current Management:* Running Dog Management. *Address:* Minka, Lower Hampton Rd, Sunbury, Middlesex TW16 5PR, England.

BUTLER, Nigel; Songwriter; Prod; Programmer. *Career:* Worked with, as Prod. and Songwriter: Bardot, B*Witched, Hear'say, Steps, theaudience; Worked with as Programmer: Alisha's Attic, The Charlatans, Erasure, Patricia Kass, Manic Street Preachers, The Orb, Travis. *Address:* c/o Stephen Budd Management Ltd, 109b Regents Park Rd, Primrose Hill, London NW1 8UR, England. *Website:* www.record-producers.com.

BUXTON, Felix; b. England. DJ; Prod; Songwriter. *Career:* Mem., Basement Jaxx, 1994–; Co-founder, owner, Atlantic Jaxx records, 1994–; Remixes for acts, incl. Pet Shop Boys, Roger Sanchez, Lil' Mo Yin Yang; Worked with vocalist Corrina Josephs; Numerous gigs and television appearances. *Recordings:* Albums: Atlantic Jaxx (compilation), 1997; Remedy, 1999; Rooty, 2001. Singles: Samba Magic, 1995; Fly Life, 1997; Same Old Show/Automatic,

1998; Red Alert, 1999; Rendez-vu, 1999; Jump 'n' Shout, 1999; Bingo Bango, 2000; Jus 1 Kiss, 2001; Romeo, 2001; Where's Your Head At?, 2001; Get Me Off, 2002. *Honours:* BRIT Award, Best British Dance Act, 2002. *Address:* c/o Astralwerks Records, 104 W 29th St, Fourth Floor, New York, NY 10001, USA. *Website:* www.basementjaxx.co.uk.

BYERS, Rodney; Musician (guitar). *Career:* Mem., The Specials; Early tours supporting The Clash; Formed own record label, 2-Tone; Debut album produced by Elvis Costello; Numerous tours and television appearances. *Recordings:* Albums include: The Specials, 1979; More Specials, 1980; The Singles Collection, 1991; Too Much Too Young, 1993; Today's Specials, 1996; Guilty 'Til Proved Innocent, 1998; Blue Plate Specials Live, 1999; More Specials, 2002. Singles: Gangsters; A Message to You, Rudi; Too Much Too Young; Rat Race; Stereotype; Do Nothing; Ghost Town; Racist Friend; Free Nelson Mandela.

BYFORD, Bill; b. 24 May 1955, Castleford, West Yorkshire, England. Music Publisher; Songwriter; Musician (guitar). m. Honor Mary Eastwood, 29 Aug. 1977, 1 d. *Education:* MA, Film and Media; BEd (Hons). *Career:* Publisher and Managing Director, Palace of Fun Music, 1980–; Member, songwriter with The Rhythm Sisters, 1986–92; Currently working with Steve Tilston and Maggie Boyle; Featured artist on film soundtracks including: Patriot Games; Before The Fall; Music journalist with NME; Melody Maker; The Guardian, 1973–. *Membership:* BAC&S; PRS; MPS. *Current Management:* Palace of Fun Management. *Address:* 16 Elm View, Huddersfield Rd, Halifax, West Yorkshire HX3 0AE, England.

BYRD, Donald; b. 9 Dec. 1932, Detroit, Michigan, USA. Jazz Musician (trumpet); Educator. *Education:* Studied trumpet and composition. *Career:* Recorded with John Coltrane; Sonny Rollins; Art Blakey; Dexter Gordon; Kenny Clarke; Pepper Adams; Educator, Rutgers University and Howard University. *Recordings:* Long Green, 1955; Two Trumpets, 1956; The Young Bloods, 1956; September Afternoon, 1957; At Newport, 1957; X-tacy, 1957; Jazz Eyes, 1957; Byrd In Paris, Vols 1 and 2, 1958; 10 To 4 At The 5 Spot, 1958; Off To The Races, 1958; Byrd In Flight, 1960; Royal Flush, 1961; Chant, 1961; Groovin' For Nat, 1962; Mustang, 1966; The Creeper, 1967; Electric Byrd, 1970; Black Byrd, 1973; Street Lady, 1974; Steppin' Into Tomorrow, 1975; Places and Spaces, 1975; Caricatures, 1977; Thank You… For F U M L (Funking Up My Life), 1978; Love Byrd, 1981; Words Sounds Colours Shapes, 1982; Harlem Blues, 1987; Getting Down To Business, 1989; A City Called Heaven, 1991; Jazz Lab, 1995; with Kenny Clarke: Bohemia After Dark, 1955; with Art Blakey: The Jazz Messengers, 1956; with John Coltrane: Lush Life, 1958; with Dexter Gordon: One Flight Up, 1964; with Kenny Burrell and Herbie Hancock, A New Perspective, 1964. *Address:* c/o Department of Music, Rutgers University, New Brunswick, NJ 08903, USA.

BYRNE, David; b. 14 May 1952, Dumbarton, Scotland. Vocalist; Songwriter; Composer; Film Dir; Photographer. m. Adelle Lutz, 1987. *Education:* Rhode Island School of Design, 1970–71; Maryland Institute College of Art, 1971–72. *Career:* Co-founder, singer, songwriter, Talking Heads, 1974–88; Recorded 10 albums, numerous world-wide concerts, television and radio appearances; Solo artiste, producer, composer, 1980–; Founder, Luaka Bop record label, 1988; Also artist, stage and lighting designer, album covers/posters designer. *Compositions include:* Film/stage scores: The Knee Plays, 1984; Alive From

Off Center, 1984; Sounds From True Stories, 1986; The Forest, 1986; Something Wild, 1986; The Catherine Wheel, 1988; The Last Emperor, 1988; The Giant Woman and The Lightning Man, 1990; A Young Man's Dream and A Woman's Secret, 1990. *Recordings include:* with Talking Heads: Talking Heads '77, 1977; More Songs About Buildings and Food, 1978; Fear Of Music, 1979; Remain In Light, 1980; The Name Of This Band Is Talking Heads, 1982; Speaking In Tongues, 1983; Stop Making Sense, 1984; Little Creatures, 1985; True Stories, 1986; Naked, 1988; Popular Favourites: Sand In The Vaseline, 1992; with Brian Eno: My Life In The Bush Of Ghosts, 1981; Solo albums: The Forest, 1988; Rei Momo, 1989; Uh-Oh, 1992; David Byrne, 1994; Feelings, 1997; Look Into The Eyeball, 2001; Solo singles: Forestry, 1991; Angels, 1994; As producer: Mesopotamia, B-52's; Waiting, Fun Boy 3; Elegibo, Margareth Menezes (2 tracks). *Honours:* Academy Award, Golden Globe, and Hollywood Foreign Press Asscn Award, Best Original Score, The Last Emperor, 1987; Film Critics Award, Best Documentary, 1985; MTV's Video Vanguard Award, 1985; Music Video Producers Asscn, 1992. *Membership:* Musicians' Union; Screen Actors Guild. *Address:* PO Box 652, Cooper Station, New York, NY 10276, USA.

BYRNE, Nicholas Bernard James Adam; b. 9 Oct. 1978, Dublin, Ireland. Vocalist. *Career:* Mem., Westlife, 1999–; Numerous tours, festivals and television appearances. *Recordings:* Albums: Westlife, 1999; Coast To Coast (No. 1, UK), 2000; World Of Our Own (No. 1, UK), 2001; Where Dreams Come True, 2001; Unbreakable: The Greatest Hits, 2002. Singles: Swear It Again (No. 1, UK), 1999; If I Let You Go, 1999; Flying Without Wings (No. 1, UK), 1999; I Have A Dream (No. 1, UK), 1999; Fool Again (No. 1, UK), 2000; Against All Odds (with Mariah Carey, No. 1, UK), 2000; My Love (No. 1, UK), 2000; What Makes A Man, 2000; Uptown Girl (for Comic Relief charity, No. 1, UK), 2001; Queen Of My Heart (No. 1, UK), 2001; World Of Our Own (No. 1, UK), 2002; Bop Bop Baby, 2002; Westlife Unbreakable, 2002. *Honours:* BRIT Awards, Best Pop Act, 2001, 2002. *Address:* c/o RCA Records, 1540 Broadway, New York, NY 10036, USA. *Website:* www.westlife.co.uk.

BYUL-BYUL OGLU, Polad; b. 4 Feb. 1945, Baku, Azerbaijan. Composer; Vocalist; Film Actor. *Education:* PhD, Azerbaijan State Conservatory. *Career:* Head of pop-music ensembles, 1975–87; Head, Azerbaijan State Philharmonic, 1987–88; Minister of Culture, 1988–; Mem., Milli-Medjlis, 1995–; Dir.-Gen., int. org. TURKSOI, 1994; Hon. Prof., Azerbaijan University of Culture and Arts; Prof., Int. Humanitarian Acad. *Recordings:* Symphonic works, chamber and instrumental music, musical, vocal cycles, incidental music, pop songs. *Honours:* People's Artist of Azerbaijan. *Address:* c/o Ministry of Culture, Azadlyg Sq. 1, 370016 Baku, Azerbaijan.

BYWATER, Richard; Musician (string bass). *Career:* Founder member, Mack and The Boys, tours throughout Europe, 1990–93; Headlined Birmingham's largest ever concert, 100,000 audience; Member, The New Bushbury Mountain Daredevils, 1992–; Backing vocals for Slade; Production, songwriting for dance artists; Topical songs for radio. *Recordings:* with Mack and The Boys: Mack and The Boys; Downtime Love; The Unknown Legends; with The New Bushbury Mountain Daredevils: Bushwacked; The Yellow Album; Bushbury Mountain. *Current Management:* Jim McPhee, Acorn Entertainments. *Address:* Winterfold House, 46 Woodfield Rd, Kings Heath, Birmingham 0B13 9UJ, England.

C

CABBLE, Lise; b. 10 Jan. 1958, Copenhagen, Denmark. Songwriter; Vocalist; Musician (guitar). *Career:* Founder member, all-girl punk band Clinic Q, 1981; Founder member, singer, guitarist, songwriter, rock band Miss B Haven, 1986; Tours: England; France; Netherlands; Germany; Denmark. *Recordings:* with Miss B Haven: Ice On Fire, 1987; On Honeymoon, 1988; Nobody's Angel, 1990; Miss B Haven, 1991; Suk and Stads, 1994. *Honours:* Danish songwriter and singer awards; Several awards with Miss B Haven. *Current Management:* Ernst Mikael Jorgensen, PDH. *Address:* Katrinebjerg 10, Morkov, Denmark.

CABLE, Stuart; b. 19 May 1970, Aberdare, Wales. Musician (drums). *Career:* Ex-school caterer and bulding site worker; Member of King Katwalk before joining Tragic Love Company, 1991; Name changed to Stereophonics prior to joining Richard Branson's newly-formed V2 records, 1996; Toured UK, Europe and USA supporting acts including: Manic Street Preachers; Ocean Colour Scene; The Who; Aerosmith; Headlined various UK gigs and festivals including: Hillsborough Benefit Concert, 1997; Cardiff Castle, 1998; Reading Leeds and Glasgow Festivals, 2000; Donington, Chepstow, T In The Park, 2001; Host of television series, Cable TV (BBC 2 Wales), 2002. *Recordings:* Albums: Word Gets Around, 1997; Performance and Cocktails, 1999; Just Enough Education To Perform, 2001; Vegas Two Times, 2002. Singles: Looks Like Chaplin, 1996; Local Boy In The Photograph, More Life In A Tramp's Vest, A Thousand Trees, Traffic, 1997; The Bartender and The Thief, 1998; Just Looking, Pick A Part That's New, I Wouldn't Believe Your Radio, Hurry Up and Wait, 1999; Mama Told Me Not To Come (with Tom Jones), 2000; Mr Writer, Have A Nice Day, Step On My Old Size Nines, Handbags and Gladrags, 2001. *Honours:* BRIT Award, Best Newcomer, 1998; Kerrang: Best New Band, 1998; Best Band, Best Album, 1999; Q Awards, Best Live Act, 1999; BAFTA Cymru, Best Music Programme, Stereophonics – Live At Morfa, 1999. *Current Management:* Marsupial Management Ltd, Unit 3, Home Farm, Welford, nr Newbury, Berkshire RG20 8HR, England. *E-mail:* marsupial@btinternet.com. *Website:* www.stereophonics.com.

CACCI, Neil 'Guitar Man', (Neil Cacciottolo); b. 9 Nov. 1953, Evergreen Park, IL, USA. Studio Musician; Arranger; Business Rep. *Education:* Three years, Southwest College; Media Communications and Journalism, Omega School of Communications; Graduate, Carnvale School of Music, Chicago. *Career:* Prepares budgets, various recording projects; Supervisor, all aspects of studio production; Public relations services, major and independent artistes; Studio musician, involved with recording background music, demo production for song catalogues, commercial recordings; Professional career, 1969–. *Recordings:* Part Time Love; Rhonda Lee; Bye Bye Baby; Lonely Highway; Love's Touch; Enchanted Meadow; Country Life; The Happy Traveller; Melinda. *Publications:* The Do's and Don'ts of the Music Industry. *Honours:* CMA Record Promoter and Company of the Year Award, 1992; International Indie Gold Record Awards. *Membership:* AFofM; Production Signatory; CMA; GMA; NARAS; ASCAP (writer and publisher); Publisher, Harry Fox Agency. *Current Management:* Central Management, Nashville, TN, USA. *Address:* PO Box 660, Palos Park, IL 60464-0660, USA. *Telephone:* (708) 371-9533. *Fax:* (708) 371-9535. *E-mail:* sunsetpromogrp@inetmail.atl.net.

CACIA, Paul Scott; b. 20 June 1956, Santa Ana, California, USA. Musician (trumpet); Bandleader; Prod. m. Janine Cameo, 1978, 2 d. *Education:* Studied with Claude Gordon, 1970–74. *Career:* Musician with: Calvin Jackson, 1972; Louis Bellson Big Band, 1973; Stan Kenton College Neophonic, 1974; Buddy Miles Express, 1975; Don Ellis Electric Orchestra, 1976; Ray Anthony, 1978; Al Hirt Big Band, 1979; Independent musician and producer, 1979–84; Bandleader, The New Age Orchestra, 1984–; Director, Don Ellis Estate, 1984–87; Lecturer, Besson trumpets, 1984–; Chairman, Stan Kenton Scholar Fund. *Recordings:* Albums include: Unbelieveable, 1977; Big Band Portrait, 1979; All In Good Time, 1982; Believe It!, Mormon Tabernacle Choir, 1983; Hardcore Jazz, Shelley Manne and Phil Woods, 1986; Alumni Tribute To Stan Kenton, 1987. *Membership:* AFofM.

CADBURY, Richard (Dik) Benjamin; b. 12 June 1950, Selly Oak, Birmingham, England. Musician (bass, guitar); Vocalist; Composer. m. Barbara, 21 March 1979, 2 d. *Education:* Violin to Grade 5; School Chorus and Church choral singing. *Career:* Toured, recorded with Decameron, 1973–76; Member, Steve Hackett (bass and vocals), 1978–80; Tours include: Reading Festival, 1979; UK; Europe; North America, 1980; Owner, Millstream Recording Studio, 1978–88. *Compositions include:* Saturday, for Third Light (with Dave Bell). *Recordings:* Albums: with Decameron, Mammoth Special; Tomorrow's Pantomime, Third Light; with Steve Hackett: Spectral Mornings, Defector; First solo album: About Time, 1999. *Membership:* Musicians' Union; PRS. *Address:* c/o Voiceatility, Hilcot House, Stanley Rd, Cheltenham, Glos GL52 6PF, England.

CAENS, Thierry-Gerard; b. 24 Sept. 1958, Dijon, France. Musician (trumpet). m. Noëlle Diebold, 15 Sept. 1984, 2 s., 1 d. *Education:* Paris National Superior Conservatory with Maurice André. *Career:* Former solo trumpet with Lyon Orchestra; Former solo cornet with Paris Opera Orchestra; Tours of Japan; Creator, William Sheller Trumpet Concerto, Pleyel, Paris, 1992; Soloist, Cyrano, B O Music by Jean-Claude Petit; Duo with Jean Guillou, Organ. *Recordings:* Tangos and Milongas; Haydn; Bach Brandenburg Concerts; Haydn; Jericho. *Publications:* Leduc-Hamelle publishers in Paris. *Honours:* First prize, Paris Conservatory; Victoires de la Musique. *Membership:* Artistic Director, Camerata de Bourgogne; Music Festival of Great Wine of Burgundy. *Current Management:* Jacques Thelen; Salle Pleyel.

CAFFEY, Charlotte; b. 21 Oct. 1953, Santa Monica, CA, USA. Vocalist; Musician (guitar). *Career:* Mem., the Go-Go's (formerly The Misfits), 1978–85; Backing singer for Belinda Carlisle; Formed the Graces, with Meredith Brooks and Gia Campbell; The Go-Go's re-formed briefly for PETA benefit concert, 1990; Mem., re-formed Go-Go's, 1994, Shows in Las Vegas; The Go-Go's re-formed, 2000–, for an album and tours, including US tour with B-52's; Founder, owner, Five Foot Two Records, 2002. Albums: Beauty And The Beat (No. 1, USA), 1981; Vacation, 1982; Talk Show, 1984; Return To The Valley Of The Go-Go's, 1994; God Bless The Go-Go's, 2001; Contributor, Tame Yourself (animal rights benefit album), 1991; with the Graces: Perfect View, 1989; Other: Soundtrack to film Clueless. *Current Management:* c/o Left Bank Management, 9255 Sunset Blvd, West Hollywood, CA 90069, USA. *E-mail:* gogos@beyondmusic.com. *Website:* www.gogos.com.

CAFFREY, Leon; Musician (drums). *Career:* Member, The Farm; Hunkpapa; Played with Squeeze and China Crisis; Joined Space, 1998; Numerous tours and television appearances. *Recordings:* Singles: The Ballad of Tom Jones (with Cerys Matthews), 1998; Begin Again, 1998; Bad Days, 1998; Diary of a Wimp, 2000; Album: Tin Planet, 1998; Greatest Hits, 2002.

CAIN, Jonathan; b. 26 Feb. 1950, Chicago, Illinois, USA. Musician (keyboards); Songwriter; Prod. *Career:* Member, The Babys; Member, US rock group Journey, 1981–87; Member, Bad English, 1988–91; Member, Hardline, 1992–; Concerts include: Mountain Aire Festival, 1981, 1986; Support to Rolling Stones, US tour, 1981; Concert, Oakland Alameda County Coliseum, with Santana, The Tubes, Toto, 1982; US tour, supported by Bryan Adams, 1983. *Recordings:* Albums: with Journey: Escape, 1981; Frontiers, 1983; Raised On Radio, 1986; Greatest Hits, 1989; Trial By Fire, 1996; When You Love A Woman, 1996; Remember Me, 1998; Arrival, 2001; with Bad English: Bad English, 1989; Backlash, 1991; Solo albums: Back To The Innocence, 1995; Piano With A View, 1995; Body Language, 1997; For A Lifetime, 1998; Singles: with Journey: Still They Ride; Who's Crying Now; Separate Ways (Worlds Apart); Faithfully; After The Fall; Send Her My Love; Be Good To Yourself; Suzanne; Girl Can't Help It; I'll Be Alright; with Bad English: When I See You Smile (No. 1, USA) 1990; Straight To Your Heart, 1991. *Address:* c/o Hemming Morse, 650 California St, Suite 900, San Francisco, CA 94108, USA.

CAINES, Ronald Arthur; b. 13 Dec. 1939, Bristol, England. Artist; Musician (saxophonist). m. Susan Weaver, 21 April 1958, 1 s., 2 d. *Education:* West of England College of Art. *Career:* Worked extensively in Europe, especially France, Switzerland, UK college circuit; Played in Keith Tippett's Big Band, Ark; Also with: Julie Tippett; Evan Parker; in 1970s; Played improvised and Latin based music, led modern jazz quartet. *Compositions include:* Northern Hemisphere; Bathers of Lake Balaton; Isadora; Music for film Laughter In The Dark, 1969. *Recordings:* Mercator Projected; SNAFU; The World of East of Eden. *Membership:* PRS; Musicians' Union (Delegate). *Current Management:* Ben Williams, Vital Communications. *Address:* 15 Highbury Villas, Kingsdown, Bristol B52 8BX, England.

CAIRNS, Andy; b. Ireland. Vocalist; Musician (guitar). *Career:* Singer, musician, Irish rock group Therapy?, 1989–; Appearances include Top of the Pops, BBC1. *Recordings:* Albums: Baby Teeth, 1991; Pleasure Death (mini album), 1992; Nurse, 1993; Troublegum, 1994; Infernal Love, 1995; Semi-Detached, 1998; Shameless, 2001; EPs: Shortsharpshock, 1993; Face The Strange, 1993; Opal Mantra, 1993; Singles: Die Laughing, 1994; Nowhere, 1994; Trigger Inside, 1994; Stories, 1995; Loose, 1995; Diane, 1995; Church of Noise, 1998; Lonely, Cryin' Only, 1998; Hate Kill Destroy, 2000. *Current Management:* DCG Management, 89 Upper Georges St, Dun Laoghaire, Dublin, Ireland.

CALAZANS, Teca; b. 27 Oct. 1940, Vitoria, Espirito Santo, Brazil. Composer; Vocalist. m. Philippe Lesage, 15 June 1991, 1 d. *Career:* Former actress; Moved to France, 1970; Recorded 6 discs, performed at Olympia, with Claude Nougaro, return to Brazil, 1979–88; 5 solo albums, compère television show, 3 years; Appearances include: Festival de Jazz de Vienne, 1991; 60

Villes pour les jeunesses Musicales de France, 1992; Festival de la Guitare, 1992; Festival de Chateauvallon, 1992; Festival de Jazz Zurich au Moods, 1994; Passage Du Nord Ouest, Paris, 1994; Soiree Jazz 94, Nice Jazz Festival, 1995; Guitar master de Paul, 1995; Tournée, Japan, 2000; Festival Avante, Lisbon, Portugal, 2000; Cantoria Brasileira, Rio de Janeiro, Minas Gerais, 2002. *Compositions:* Côco Verde; Gabriel; Caíco (sung by Milton Nascimento); Firuliu (sung by Nara Leâo); Atras da luminosidade (sung by Gal Costa). *Recordings:* Musigues et Chants du Brasil, 1974; Caminho das Aguas, 1975; Cade o Povo, 1975; Desafio de Viola, 1978; Povo Daqui, 1980; Eu Nao Sou Dos, 1981; Teca Calazans, 1982; Mário Trezentos, 350, 1983; Jardin Exotique, 1983; Mina do Mar, 1985; Teca Calazans Chante Villa Lobos, 1990; Pizindim, 1991; Intuiçao, 1993; O Samba dos Bambas, 1994; Firoliu, 1997; Forro de Cara Nova, 1998; Alma De Tupi, 2000; Cantoria Brasileira (with Elomar, Xangai, Pena Brance, Renato Teixeira). *Publications:* Nordeste' Song, 2002; Brazil: Cantadores and Repentistas, 2002. *Current Management:* Rita Sá Rego, Cirandas. *Address:* 3 Ave Mathilde, 95210 Saint Gratien, France. *Telephone:* (1) 39-64-16-53. *Fax:* (1) 39-89-75-18. *E-mail:* tecalazans@ wanadoo.fr.

CALDER, Clive; b. South Africa. Music Co Exec. *Career:* Founder, CCP Records, South Africa, 1972; Founder, Chair. and CEO, Zomba Music Group, mid-1970s–2002; Founder, Jive Records, Zomba Books, Zomba Management, Zomba Music Publishers; Sold Zomba Music Group to BMG Music, 2002, remained in advisory role to the co. *Address:* c/o Zomba Music Group, BMG Music, Times Sq., 1540 Broadway, New York, NY 10036, USA.

CALE, J. J. (John Weldon); b. 5 Dec. 1938, Oklahoma City, Oklahoma, USA. Vocalist; Songwriter; Musician (guitar). *Career:* Singer, songwriter, pioneer of 'Tulsa sound'; Leader, Johnny Cale and the Valentines; Toured briefly with Grand Ole Opry road company; Backing musician to Red Sovine, Little Jimmy Dickens; Studio engineer, guitarist, Los Angeles, 1964; Played with artists including: Leon Russell; Delaney and Bonnie. *Compositions include:* Crazy Mama; Cajun Moon; Travelin' Light; Don't Cry Sister; Don't Go To Strangers; Songs covered by other artists include: After Midnight; Cocaine; I'll Make Love To You (all recorded by Eric Clapton); Mr Breeze (Johnny Cash, Lynyrd Skynyrd, The Allman Brothers); Clyde (Waylon Jennings); Bringing It Back (Kansas, Lynyrd Skynyrd); Same Old Blues (Bryan Ferry, Captain Beefheart); Magnolia (Deep Purple, Poco, Chris Smither, Jose Feliciano); The Sensitive Kind (John Mayall, Santana); Film scores include: La Femme de Mon Pote (My Best Friend's Girl), 1984. *Recordings:* Albums: A Trip Down Sunset Strip (recorded under the name The Leathercoat Minds), 1967; Naturally, 1972; Really, 1973; Okie, 1973; Troubadour, 1976; #5, 1979; Shades, 1981; Grasshopper, 1982; #8, 1983; Special Edition, 1984; Travel Log, 1989; #10, 1992; Closer To You, 1994; Guitar Man, 1996; Anyway the Wind Blows: The Anthology, 1997; The Very Best of J. J. Cale, 1998; Universal Masters Collection, 2000; Live, 2001; 20th Century Master Series, The Best of J. J. Cale, 2002; DVDs, Videos: J. J. Cale Live, 2002; The Lost Session, with Leon Russell, live, 2002; Producer, albums by John Hammond: Got Love If You Want It; Trouble No More; Contributor, Rhythm of The Saints, Paul Simon, 1990; The Tractors, The Tractors, 1994; Fish Tree Water Blues, 1999. *Current Management:* The Rosebud Agency, PO Box 170429, San Francisco, CA 94117, USA.

CALE, John; b. 9 March 1942, Garnant, Wales. Vocalist; Musician (bass, keyboards, viola); Prod. *Education:* Classical music training. *Career:* Member, The Dream Syndicate; Founder member, The Velvet Underground, 1964–68, 1993; Solo artiste, 1970–; Residency, Café Bizarre, Greenwich Village, 1966; House band, Andy Warhol's Factory arts collective, New York, 1966; Reunion, with Lou Reed, Nico, 1972; Reunion with Velvet Underground, European Tour, 1993; Production includes: Nico: The Marble Index, 1969, Desert Shore, 1970, The End, 1974; Iggy Pop: The Stooges, 1969; Patti Smith: Horses, 1975; Jonathan Richman: Modern Lovers, 1975; Squeeze: Squeeze, 1977; Happy Mondays: Squirrel and G Man, 1987; Siouxsie and The Banshees: Rapture, 1995. *Recordings:* Albums: with The Velvet Underground: The Velvet Underground and Nico, 1967; White Light, White Heat, 1968; Live MCMXCIII, 1993; Solo albums include: Vintage Violence, 1970; Church of Anthrax, 1971; Academy in Peril, 1972; Paris 1919, 1973; Fear, 1974; June 1 1974, 1974; Slow Dazzle, 1975; Helen of Troy, 1975; Guts, 1977; Animal Justice, 1977; Sabotage, 1979; Honi Soit, 1981; Music For A New Society, 1982; Caribbean Sunset, 1984; Comes Alive, 1984; Artificial Intelligence, 1985; Words For The Dying, 1989; Fragments of a Rainy Season, 1992; Walking on Locusts, 1996; Dance Music, 1998; Le Vent de la Nuit, 1999; Close Watch, 1999; with Lou Reed: Songs For Drella, 1990; with Brian Eno: Wrong Way Up, 1991; with Bob Neuwirth: Last Day On Earth, 1994; Collaborated on: Small World, Big Band, Jools Holland's Rhythm 'n' Blues Orchestra, 2001; Film scores: Sid and Nancy, 1982; Paris S'Eveille, 1991; La Naissance de l'Amour, 1993; Antartida, 1995; N'oublie pas que tu vas mourir, 1996; I Shot Andy Warhol, 1997; Eat and Kiss, 1997. *Honours:* Inducted into Rock 'n' Roll Hall of Fame (with Velvet Underground), 1996; Honor Fellow, Goldsmiths College, London, 1997. *Current Management:* Firebrand Management, Suite 1.3, 12 Rickett St, London SW6 1RU, England.

CALHOUN, Dave; b. 11 Feb. 1969, Whitehaven, Cumbria, England. Musician (guitar); Vocalist; Songwriter. *Career:* Played guitar alongside Dave Fenton of The Vapors, 1990; Played with Moondigger at many London venues including the Marquee, 1993–96; Currently writing and recording with Zenshoppers. *Recordings:* 423, Moondigger, 1993; Guitarist Of The Year Album, 1994; Sorrows Wedding, single, Zenshoppers; Relax, album, Brian Green. *Publications:* Currently working on two guitar tuition books. *Honours:* Guitarist of the Year, 1994–95. *Membership:* Musicians' Union; PRS; MCPS. *Current Management:* John Glover, 34 Lotts Rd, Chelsea, London SW10, England. *Address:* 15 Broughton Rd, Thornton Heath, Surrey CR7 6AG, England.

CALHOUN, William; b. 22 July 1964, Brooklyn, New York, USA. Musician (Drums). *Career:* Member, Living Colour, 1984–95; Backed Mick Jagger on Primitive Cool album, 1986; Demo produced by Mick Jagger obtained them record deal; Support slots to live dates with Rolling Stones. *Recordings:* Singles: Cult of Personality, 1988; Glamour Boys, 1988; Type, 1990; Love Rears Its Ugly Head, 1990; Solace of You, 1991; Talkin' Loud and Sayin' Nothing, 1991; Auslander, 1993; Bi, 1993; Sunshine of Your Love, 1994; Albums: Vivid, 1988; Time's Up, 1990; Biscuits, 1993; Stain, 1993; Pride (compilation), 1995; Also collaborated with: B. B. King; Cynthia Jane.

CALLE, Ed (Eduardo Joaquin); b. 10 Aug. 1959, Caracas, Venezuela. Musician (saxophone); Composer; Arranger; Teacher. *Education:* Senior Mathematics Major; Masters degree Music, University of Miami. *Career:* Sony recording artist; Recorded and toured with international artistes including Frank Sinatra; Gloria Estefan; Vicki Carr; Julio Iglesias; Arturo Sandoval; Regina Belle. *Recordings:* Solo albums (original compositions and arrangements): Nightgames, 1985; Double-talk, 1996; Sunset Harbor, 1999. *Publications:* Working on books for the saxophone; Many published arrangements. *Membership:* NARAS. *Current Management:* Carl Valldejulli, Turi's Music/Quiet Storm. *Address:* Turi's Music, 103 Westward Dr., Miami Springs, FL 33166, USA.

CALLIS, Jo; b. 2 May 1955, Rotherham, Yorkshire, England. Musician; Songwriter. *Education:* Edinburgh College of Art. *Career:* Member of bands including: The Human League; The Rezillos; Shake; Boots For Dancing; Co-writer with many other artistes. *Recordings:* Albums: with The Human League: Dare (No. 1, UK), 1981; Love and Dancing, 1982; Hysteria, 1984; Octopus, 1995; with The Rezillos: Can't Stand The Rezillos; Singles: with The Human League: Don't You Want Me (No. 1, UK and USA), 1981; Open Your Heart, 1981; Mirror Man, 1982; (Keep Feeling) Fascination, 1983; The Lebanon, 1984; Life On Your Own, 1984; Louise, 1984; with The Rezillos: Top of the Pops, 1978. *Honours:* ASCAP Awards, Don't You Want Me, (Keep Feeling) Fascination. *Membership:* BAC&S. *Address:* 3A Rochester Terrace, Edinburgh EH10 5AA, Scotland.

CALZADO, David, (Sergio David Calzado Almenares); b. 1957, Cuba. Vocalist; Musician (violin); Songwriter; Prod. *Education:* Escuela Nacional de Arte, Cuba, 1978. *Career:* Born into a musical family; Grandfather was a Trovador and father was a member of the Orquesta Estrellas Cubana; After graduating in music, played with father's band and Orquesta Ritmo Oriental; Produced records for Cuban record company Egrem; Became first violin at the Tropicana in Havana where approached to form a band for the summer season at the Sporting Club of Monaco; Band became La Charanga Habanera; During five years of summer stints in Monaco, supported stars including: Whitney Houston; Barry White; Charles Aznavour; Band had classic charanga line-up of flutes, violins, bass piano and percussion but re-launched with brass and reduced violin section, 1993; Spectacular live show included elaborate costumes and choreography; Charanga Habanera split, 2000; Retained right to the act name and put together a younger group under the same name.

CAMARA DE LANDA, Enrique Guillermo; b. 3 May 1951, Buenos Aires, Argentina. Enthomusicologist. *Education:* Philosophy Doctorate, University of Valladolid, Spain, 1994; Degree in Musical Pedagogy, 1977, Degree in Musicology, 1979, Argentinian Catholic University, Buenos Aires; Piano degree, 1972. *Career:* Currently Professor of Ethnomusiclogy at the Universidad de Valladolid, Spain. *Publications:* Tango de ida y vuelta, 1992; Argentina: Charnada y chamamé, 1992; Argentina: Carnaval, 1994; L'arrivée du tango en Italie, 1995; Proyecciones de la baguala, 1996; Erkencho, 1995. *Membership:* Vice-President, SIbE (Sociedad Ibérica de Etnomusicología); SEdEM (Sociedad Española de Musicología); IASPM; AAM (Asociación Argentina de Musicología). *Address:* Azorin 5, 4°A, 47005 Valladolid, Spain.

CAMBUZAT, François R; Vocalist; Musician (guitar); Composer; *Recordings:* With the Kim Squad: Young Bastards, 1988; Solo: Notre-Dame des Naufragés, 1988; Uccidiamo Kim, 1990; With Il Gran Teatro Amaro: Port-Famine, 1991; Hôtel Brennesel, 1993; Piazza Orphelins, 1995; With F R Cambuzat et les Enfants Rouges: Swinoujscie-Tunis, 1995; Reus-Ljubljana, 1998; Taurisano-Cajarc, 1998; L'Enfance Rouge: Davos-Legros, 1999; Rostock-Mamur, 2001; Various compilations. *Membership:* ATTAC. *Current Management:* L'Enfance Rouge. *Address:* 43 allée des Cigales, 06600 Antibes, France. *Telephone:* (347) 3603427. *Website:* www.enfancerouge.org.

CAMERON, Chris; b. England. Musician (keyboards); Arranger; Prod. *Career:* Worked with: Hot Chocolate; Wham!; George Michael (also his musical director); Stevie Nicks; Terence Trent D'Arby; Breathe; Take That; Presumptos Implicados; Pepsi and Shirlie; A1; Gary Barlow; Joe Cocker; Randy Crawford, Chris De Burgh, Will Downing; Stephen Duffy; Elton John; John Martyn; 911; Pet Shop Boys; Steps; Tina Turner. *Current Management:* The Liaison and Promotion Co. *Address:* 70 Gloucester Pl., London W1H 3HL, England.

CAMERON, John Allan; b. 16 Dec. 1938, Inverness, Cape Breton, Nova Scotia, Canada. Vocalist; Songwriter; Musician. *Education:* BEd, St Francis Xavier University, Antignoish, Nova Scotia, Canada. *Career:* Professional, 1968; Toured and performed throughout world from Arctic to Middle East; Appeared in Las Vegas and on Grand Ole Opry; Toured with Anne Murray for several years; Hosted TV shows, CBC and CTV Networks. *Recordings:* Here Comes John Allan Cameron, 1968; Get There By Dawn, 1975; Lord of the Dance, 1977; Weddings, Wakes and Other Things, 1979; Free Born Man, 1987; Good Times, 1990; Wind Willow, 1991; Glencoe Station, 1996. *Honours:* East Coast Music Ascn's Lifetime Achievement Award, 1995; Hon. Dr of Letters, University College, Cape Breton, 1998. *Membership:* AFofM; SOCAN. *Current Management:* Joella Foulds, Rave Entertainment Inc. *Address:* Rave Entertainment Inc, 363 Charlotte St, Suite 1, Sydney, NS, B1P 1E1, Canada.

CAMERON, Kate; b. 14 Nov. 1965, Hemel Hempstead, Hertfordshire, England. Vocalist; Songwriter; Entertainer; Musician (piano, French horn). *Education:* Theory, Grade V; French Horn, Grade VIII; Piano, Grade VII; O and A Level, Grade A. *Career:* Lead vocalist, backing vocalist, vocal arranger, writer with GMT, 1990–92; Worked with Doug Wimbish, Bob Jones, John Waddell, Q; Host of Singers Nightclub; Musical Director, Minx, all-female cabaret acapella group, 1993–95; Session singer for artists including Norman Cook, 1994. *Recordings:* P.A.S.S.I.O.N.; Jon of The Pleased Wimmin, 1995; with Freak Power (backing vocals): Rush; Get In Touch, 1994. *Membership:* Musicians' Union; Variety Artiste's Association. *Current Management:* The Vocal Agency. *Address:* 43 Windsor Dr., East Barnet, Herts EN4 8UE, England.

CAMERON, Matt; b. 28 Nov. 1962, San Diego, CA, USA. Musician (drums). *Career:* Appeared in film Attack of the Killer Tomatoes, 1970s; Mem., US heavy rock group, Soundgarden, 1986–97; Mem., Temple of the Dog, 1992; Mem., Hater, 1993; Mem., Wellwater Conspiracy, 1997–; Mem., Pearl Jam, 2000–; Numerous tours and festival appearances. *Recordings:* with Soundgarden: Singles: Nothing to Say, 1987; Flower, 1989; Loud Love, 1990; Hands All Over/Get On the Snake EP, 1990; Jesus Christ Pose, 1992; Outshined, 1992; Rusty Cage, 1992; Spoonman, 1994; The Day I Tried to Live, 1994; Black Hole Sun, 1994; Fell on Black Days, 1995; Pretty Noose, 1996; Burden in My Hand, 1996; Blow Up the Outside World, 1996; Ty Cobb, 1996; Bleed Together, 1996; Albums: Ultramega OK, 1988; Louder than Love, 1989; Badmotorfinger, 1991; Superunknown (No. 1, USA), 1994; Down on the Upside, 1996; A-Sides, 1997; with Temle of The Dog: Album: Temple of The Dog, 1992; with Hater: Single: Circles, 1993; Album: Hater, 1993; with Wellwater Conspiracy: Albums: Declaration of Conformity, 1997; Brotherhood of Electric: Operational Directives, 1999; Scroll and Its Combinations, 2001; with Pearl Jam: Albums: Binaural, 2000; Live 2000 (series of live albums), 2000; Riot Act, 2002. *Honours:* Grammy Award for Black Hole Sun, 1994. *Address:* c/o A&M Records, Interscope Records, 2220 Colorado Ave, Santa Monica, CA 90404, USA. *Website:* www.soundgardenonline.co.uk.

CAMILLERI, Claude Anthony Paul Francis Xavier; b. 9 Nov. 1963, Malta. Audio Engineering and Production Lecturer; Engineering Prod. m. Sharon, 16 June 1988, 1 s., 2 d. *Education:* Maynooth University, Ireland, 1984; Piano and guitar; Synthesis / Music Technology. *Career:* Considered leading pioneer in training audio engineers and producers, 1986–; Lectures, various universities and colleges world-wide; Founder, Alchemea; Work for Sony; Polygram; Virgin; EMI; Chrysalis; Acid-Jazz; Motor-Germany; Various productions for independent labels. *Recordings:* Producer for various record labels; Own albums on own label; Various collaborations. *Publications:* Various papers on production and sound/audio engineering; Two books due for publication in 1996. *Honours:* National Training Award for Achievements in field of training and education. *Membership:* APRS; Producer's Guild. *Current Management:* c/o Hari Voyantzis, Alchemea Records. *Address:* The Windsor Centre, Windsor St, The Angel, Islington, London N1 8QH, England.

CAMILO, Michel; b. 4 April 1954, Santo Domingo, Dominican Republic. Jazz Musician (piano); Composer; Conductor. m. Sandra Camilo, 22 Feb. 1975. *Education:* Universidad Autonoma de Santo Domingo (VASD); National Conservatory, Dominican Republic; Juilliard School of Music; Mannes School of Music. *Career:* Appearances include: Carnegie Hall debut, 1986; Berlin Jazz Festival, 1987; Musical director, Heineken Jazz Festival, Dominican Republic, 1987–; Newport Jazz Festival; North Sea Jazz Festival; Pori Jazz Festival; Grande Parade du Jazz; Copenhagen Jazz Festival; New Orleans Jazz Festival; Madrid and Barcelona Jazz Festivals; San Sebastian and Andorra Jazz Festival; Lugano Jazz Festival; Film: Two Much, 1996. *Recordings:* Why Not, 1986; Suntan/Michel Camilo in trio, 1987; Michel Camilo, 1988; On Fire, 1991; On The Other Hand, 1991; Rendezvous, 1993; One More Once, 1994;

Two Much (soundtrack), 1996; Rhapsody For Two Pianos and Orchestra, 1992; Thru My Eyes, 1996; Triangulo, 2002. *Honours:* Emmy Award, 1986; Voted among Top Jazz Artists of Year, Billboard magazine, 1989, 1991; Hon. Professorship (VASD), 1992; Dr h.c. (Utesa), 1993. *Membership:* AFofM; RMA; American Music Center. *Current Management:* Sandra Camilo, Redondo Music. *Address:* PO Box 216, Katonah, NY 10536, USA.

CAMISON, Mathias (Mat); b. 5 Aug. 1941, Algeria. Composer; Arranger; Musician (keyboard). *Education:* Conservatory. *Career:* Musician on tour: All French stars; Artists including Jimmy Cliff; The Four Tops; Film (France): Black and White In Color; Many hits, England, USA as Pepper Box; Television music for: Canal; Sport; Music on France 1; Horse races. *Recordings include:* Hits with Pepper Box; Love Me Baby, Sheila B Devotion; We've Got A Feeling, with Chris Waddle and B Boli. *Honours:* Academy Award; Molière. *Membership:* SACEM; SPEDIDAM; ADAMI. *Address:* 5 rue de la Tuilierie, 92150 Suresnes, France.

CAMOZZI, Christopher Alan; b. 1 May 1957, Burlingame, California, USA. Musician (guitar). *Education:* Private musical study. *Career:* Musician for Michael Bolton tours: Soul Provider; Time, Love and Tenderness; Timeless, The Classics; The One Thing tours; Television: Tonight Show; Arsenio Hall; Billboard Music Awards; American Music Awards; VH-1 Honours; Oprah Winfrey Show; Donahue; NBC TV; Specials; VH2 Unplugged; with Mariah Carey: Grammy Awards; Tonight Show. *Recordings:* with Michael Bolton: Soul Provider; Time, Love and Tenderness; Timeless, The Classics; with Mariah Carey: Mariah Carey; with Barbra Streisand: Greatest Hits and More; with Whitney Houston: I'm Your Baby Tonight. *Publications:* Guitar Player; Peavey Monitor. *Membership:* Musicians' Union. *Address:* 3341 Abbey Lane, Palmdale, CA 93551, USA.

CAMP, Manel; b. 20 April 1947, Manresa, Barcelona, Spain. Musician (piano); Arranger; Composer; Concert and Recording Dir. *Education:* Professional diploma, piano; Contemporary composition, orchestration, Language and methodology of Jazz, Berklee College of Music, Boston. *Career:* As solo pianist: International festivals: Grenoble, France; Brirstonas, Lithuania; Cheboksari and Yaroslav, Russia; Buenos Aires, Argentina; Caracas, Venezuela; Boston, USA; Barcelona, Madrid, San Sebastian and Granada, Spain. *Compositions:* Petita Suite; Simbols; Canigo; Ressorgir; El Llibre de les Besties. *Recordings:* Minorisa, Fusion; Poesia Secreta; Primer Viatge; La Meva Petita Terra; Escàndols; El Complot Dels Anells; Viu; Ben A Prop; Diàlegs; Ressorgir; Duets; Contrast; Coratge; Rosebud; Complicitats; Canço; Canigo; L'Ultime Frontera. *Publications:* Scores of first two albums. *Honours:* Best Recording Composition, Generalitat de Catalunya, 1985; Best Musical Performance, Radio Nacional, 1988; Best Soloist, International Festival Jazz, San Sebastian, 1986; National Cinematographyc Award, Generalitat, 1992; Premi Altaveu, 1996; Premi, Iniciativa, 1997. *Membership:* Associació Catalana de Compositors; Associació de Musica de Jazz de Catalunya. *Current Management:* Madma. *Address:* c/o de la Mel, 23, 2n, 08240 Manresa, Barcelona, Spain.

CAMP, Richard; b. 16 April 1956, Ipswich, Suffolk, England. Vocalist; Musician (guitar). *Career:* Lead singer, guitarist, with Blind Dog Beerbelly Blues Band; Live performances include: Diana Luke Show, Greater London Radio, 1994; Guitarist with groups: Click Click; Savage Bees; World Circus; Eclipse. *Recordings:* Single: Leave Well Alone, Savage Bees, 1978; EP: Reanimate, Click Click, 1983; Album: Blue Guitar, Blind Dog Beerbelly Blues Band, 1996. *Membership:* Musicians' Union. *Address:* PO Box 4039, Dunstable, Bedfordshire LU5 4DG, England.

CAMPBELL, Ali (Alistair); b. 15 Feb. 1959, Birmingham, England. Vocalist; Musician (guitar). *Career:* Member, UK reggae group, UB40, 1979–; Also solo artiste; Concerts include: Tour with the Pretenders, 1980; Support to The Police, Rockatta De Bowl, Milton Keynes, 1980; Nelson Mandela's 70th Birthday Tribute, Wembley Stadium, 1988; Film, Dance With The Devil, 1988; Television film: UB40 – A Family Affair (Channel 4), 1991. *Recordings:* Albums: with UB40: Signing Off, 1980; Present Arms, 1981; The Singles Album, 1982; UB44, 1982; UB40 Live, 1983; Labour of Love (No. 1, UK), 1983; Geffrey Morgan, 1984; Baggariddim, 1985; Rat In The Kitchen, 1986; CCCP – Live In Moscow, 1987; The Best of UB40 Vol. 1, 1987; Labour of Love II, 1990; Promises and Lies (No. 1, UK), 1993; Anansi, 1995; Guns In The Ghetto, 1997; Labour of Love III, 1998; Very Best of UB40, 2000; Solo: Big Love, 1995; Singles include: King/Food For Thought, 1980; My Way of Thinking, 1980; The Earth Dies Screaming, 1980; One In Ten, 1981; Love Is All Is Alright, 1982; Red Red Wine (No. 1, UK), 1983 (also No. 1, USA, 1988); Please Don't Make Me Cry, 1983; Many Rivers To Cross, 1983; Cherry Oh Baby, 1984; If It Happens Again, 1984; I Got You Babe, duet with Chrissie Hynde (No. 1, UK), 1985; Don't Break My Heart, 1985; Sing Our Own Song, 1986; Rat In Mi Kitchen, 1987; Maybe Tomorrow, 1987; Breakfast In Bed, duet with Chrissie Hynde, 1988; Homely Girl, 1989; Kingston Town, 1990; I'll Be Your Baby Tonight, with Robert Palmer, 1990; The Way You Do The Things You Do, 1990; Here I Am (Come and Take Me), 1991; Can't Help Falling In Love, used in film soundtrack Sliver (No. 1, UK and USA), 1993; Higher Ground, 1993; Bring Me Your Cup, 1993; Way You Do The Things You Do, 1993; C'est La Vie, 1994; Come Back Darling, 1998; Train Is Coming,

1999; Light My Fire, 2000; Solo: That Look In Your Eyes, 1995. *Current Management:* David Harper, What Management, 12B South Bar, First Floor, Banbury, Oxon OX16 9AA, England.

CAMPBELL, David; b. 22 Oct. 1969, Glasgow, Scotland. Musician (drums, percussion); Songwriter; Musical Arranger; Prod. *Education:* Clydebank College. *Career:* Drummer, percussionist, writer, arranger, producer with: Parksorch, 1987–88; Kiss 'N' Tell, 1988–92; Ragged Laughter, 1992–94; Raglin Street Rattle, 1994–; Concerts and tours include: Beat The Clyde, 1987; Prince of Wales Gala Concert, 1989; Solo American tour of Southern states, 1993; US Coast to Coast tour, 1994; TV Special, Live at The Festival, 1988. *Compositions include:* Need A Lover, 1992; State of Confusion, 1993, On Brilliant Wings, 1994, She Called My Name, 1995; Seize the Day, Moment in White, 1999. *Recordings include:* Cava Sessions, 1988; The Word Is Out... The Time Is Now, 1992; Raglin Street Rattle, 1995; Dog on Wheels, EP, with Belle and Sebastian, 1996; Year Zero, 1999. *Honours:* Premier Student of the Year, Clydebank College, 1990. *Membership:* PRS. *Address:* 8 Whitslade St, Provanhall, Glasgow G34 9PY, Scotland.

CAMPBELL, Eddie; b. 6 July 1965, Scotland. Musician (Keyboards). *Career:* Member, Texas; Numerous tours, festival appearances and TV appearances. *Recordings:* Singles include: I Don't Want a Lover, 1989; Tired of Being Alone, 1993; Say What You Want, 1997; Halo, 1997; Put Your Arms Around Me, 1997; Black Eyed Boy, 1997; In Our Lifetime, 1999; Summer Son, 1999; In Demand, 2000; Inner Smile, 2001; Albums: Southside, 1989; Mother's Heaven, 1991; Rick's Road, 1993; White on Blonde (No. 1, UK), 1997; The Hush (No. 1, UK) 1999; The Greatest Hits (No. 1, UK), 2000.

CAMPBELL, Glen Travis; b. 22 April 1936, Delight, Arkansas, USA. Vocalist; Musician (guitar). *Career:* Member, Dick Bills Band, 1954; Founder, Glen Campbell and The Western Wranglers, 1958; Session musician, Los Angeles; Replaced Brian Wilson touring with the Beach Boys; Television work; Film appearances include: True Grit, 1969; Norwood, 1970; Duets with Anne Murray, Rita Coolidge, Tanya Tucker; Tours, television appearances, late 1970s. *Recordings:* Hit singles include: Gentle On My Mind; By The Time I Get To Phoenix; Wichita Lineman; Galveston; Rhinestone Cowboy; Southern Nights; Albums include: Too Late To Worry, Too Late To Cry, 1963; The Astounding 12-String Guitar of Glen Campbell, 1964; Gentle On My Mind, 1967; By The Time I Get To Phoenix, 1967; Hey Little One, 1968; A New Place In The Sun, 1968; Galveston, 1969; Try A Little Kindness, 1970; Oh Happy Day, 1970; Norwood (soundtrack), 1970; The Last Time I Saw Her, 1971; Anne Murray/Glen Campbell, 1971; I Knew Jesus (Before He Was A Star), 1973; Reunion (The Songs of Jimmy Webb), 1974; Rhinestone Cowboy, 1975; Bloodline, 1976; Southern Nights, 1977; Basic, 1978; Somethin' About You Baby I Like, 1980; It's The World Gone Crazy, 1981; Old Home Town, 1983; Letter To Home, 1984; Just A Matter of Time, 1986; No More Night, 1988; Still Within The Sound of My Voice, 1988; Walkin' In The Sun, 1990; Unconditional Love, 1991; Favourite Hymns, 1992; Somebody Like That, 1993; Phoenix, 1994; Christmas with Glen Campbell, 1995; Branson City Limits, 1998; In Concert (Live), 1999. *Honours:* Grammy, Best Country and Western Recording, Gentle On My Mind, 1967. *Current Management:* Girsey, Schneider and Co, 10351 Santa Monica Blvd #300, Los Angeles, CA 90025, USA.

CAMPBELL, Isobel; b. 27 April 1976. Vocalist; Musician (cello); Songwriter. *Career:* Mem., Belle and Sebastian, 1996–; The Gentle Waves 1998–; Collaborations: Arab Strap; Snow Patrol; Curated Bowlie Weekend Festival with other Belle and Sebastian band members, 1999. *Recordings:* Albums: with The Gentle Waves: The Green Fields of Foreverland, 1999; Swansong For You, 2000; with Belle and Sebastian: Tigermilk, If You're Feeling Sinister, 1996; The Boy With The Arab Strap 1998; Fold Your Hands Child – You Walk Like A Peasant, 2000; Storytelling, 2002; Solo: Ghost Of Yesterday (with Bill Wells), 2002. Singles: with The Gentle Waves: Weathershow, 1999; Falling From Grace, 2000; with Belle and Sebastian: Dog On Wheels EP, Lazy Line Painter Jane EP, 3–6–9 Seconds of Light EP, 1997; This Is Just A Modern Rock Song EP, 1998; Legal Man, 2000; Jonathan David, I'm Waking Up To Us, 2001. *Honours:* BRIT Award, Best Newcomer, 1999. *Current Management:* Banchory Management, PO Box 25074, Glasgow G2 6YL, Scotland. *Website:* www.belleandsebastian.co.uk.

CAMPBELL, John; b. 16 April 1953, Reigate, Surrey, England. Music Publisher; Artist Man. m. Sue, 7 April 1984. *Career:* Chairman JC Music; Publisher, Manager for: Richard Feldman; Nick Trevisick; Jeff Paris; Michael Graves; Mike Moran; Howard New; Lowcraft; Akure; Santessa; Bachelor Number One; Mikey Graham; Artist Manager for: Marcella Detroit; Shakespears Sister; Lena Fiagbe; Oui 3; Clementines; Nut. *Recordings:* Stay, Shakespears Sister (No. 1, 8 weeks, UK charts); Gotta Get It Right, Lena Fiagbe; I Believe, Marcella Detroit. *Membership:* Pegs Club; Liberal Party; Groucho Club. *Address:* 84 Strand on the Green, (Studio at rear), London W4 3PU, England.

CAMPBELL, Junior (William); b. 31 May 1947, Glasgow, Scotland. Composer; Arranger; Musician; Vocalist; Conductor. m. (1) Margaret Hutcheson, 7 Jan. 1967, (2) Susan Chibnall, 18 March 1989, 1 s., 1 d. *Education:* Studied orchestration, composition, conducting with Eric Gilder and Max Saunders, RCM. *Career:* Founder member, Gaylords, 1961; Later became Marmalade, many hits, 1968–71; Solo artist, singer, 1972–74; Record producer, songwriter, 1974–80; Produced many artists including Barbara Dickson; Film and television composer including Bafta Award drama: Taking Over The Asylum; Composer on 104 Thomas The Tank Engine Films. *Recordings:* with Marmalade: Lovin' Things, 1968; Ob-La-Di Ob-La-Da (No. 1, UK), 1969; Reflections of My Life, 1970; Rainbow, 1970; Compilation: Reflections of The Marmalade, 2001; Solo: Hallelujah Freedom, 1972; Sweet Illusion; Second Time Around, 2001. *Membership:* BAC&S; PRS; MCPS. *Address:* Greyfriars Lodge, Greyfriars Dr., Ascot, Berks SL5 9JD, England.

CAMPBELL, Rita; b. 28 Sept. 1968, London, England. Vocalist; Songwriter. *Career:* Backing singer for: D:ream, Take That tour; Kenny Thomas, British tour; Act of Faith, British tour; Brand New Heavies, European tour; Billie Ray Martin; China Black; Carleen Anderson; X-Avia; Ronnie Simon; Bell Curtis; Angie Brown; Mary Pearce; Dream Academy; Rin Tin Tin; Cindy Jackson; Perception; Television includes: Smash Hits Awards; Dance Energy; In The Air Tonight (Virgin's 21st); Top of the Pops; The James Whale Show; Later with Jools Holland; TFI Friday; Songwriter for group, Steps. *Recordings:* with: Pauline Henry; Sly and Robbie; Bizarre Inc; Odyssey; Act of Faith; Glamma Kid; Kavana; Cleopatra; Dream Academy; Perception; Medalling Thieves; Steps; Westlife; Samantha Mumba; Jools Holland; George Harrison; Bonnie Tyler; Paul Weller; Commercials: Ribena Spring; Audi; American Airlines; Gordons Gin; Heineken Beer; Pepsi; Sugar Puffs. *Membership:* Musicians' Union. *Current Management:* Hobsons Singers; Session Connection; Simon Harrison. *Address:* 21 Ruckholt Close, Leyton, London E10 5NX, England.

CAMPBELL, Robin; b. 25 Dec. 1954, Birmingham, England. Musician (guitar); Vocalist. *Career:* Lead guitarist, vocalist, UK reggae group, UB40, 1979–; Concerts include: Tour with the Pretenders, 1980; Support to The Police, Rockatta De Bowl, Milton Keynes, 1980; Nelson Mandela's 70th Birthday Tribute, Wembley Stadium, 1988; Film, Dance With The Devil, 1988; Television film: UB40 – A Family Affair (Channel 4), 1991. *Recordings:* Albums: with UB40: Signing Off, 1980; Present Arms, 1981; The Singles Album, 1982; UB44, 1982; UB40 Live, 1983; Labour of Love (No. 1, UK), 1983; Geffrey Morgan, 1984; Baggariddim, 1985; Rat In The Kitchen, 1986; CCCP – Live In Moscow, 1987; The Best of UB40 Vol. 1, 1987; Labour of Love II, 1990; Promises and Lies (No. 1, UK), 1993; Anansi, 1995; Guns In The Ghetto, 1997; Labour of Love III, 1998; Very Best of UB40, 2000; Singles include: King/Food For Thought, 1980; My Way of Thinking, 1980; The Earth Dies Screaming, 1980; One In Ten, 1981; Love Is All Is Alright, 1982; Red Red Wine (No. 1, UK), 1983 (also No. 1, USA, 1988); Please Don't Make Me Cry, 1983; Many Rivers To Cross, 1983; Cherry Oh Baby, 1984; If It Happens Again, 1984; I Got You Babe, duet with Chrissie Hynde (No. 1, UK), 1985; Don't Break My Heart, 1985; Sing Our Own Song, 1986; Rat In Mi Kitchen, 1987; Maybe Tomorrow, 1987; Breakfast In Bed, duet with Chrissie Hynde, 1988; Homely Girl, 1989; Kingston Town, 1990; I'll Be Your Baby Tonight, with Robert Palmer, 1990; The Way You Do The Things You Do, 1990; Here I Am (Come and Take Me), 1991; Can't Help Falling In Love, used in film soundtrack Sliver (No. 1, UK and USA), 1993; Higher Ground, 1993; Bring Me Your Cup, 1993; Way You Do The Things You Do, 1993; C'est La Vie, 1994; Come Back Darling, 1998; Train Is Coming, 1999; Light My Fire, 2000. *Current Management:* David Harper, What Management, 12B South Bar, First Floor, Banbury, Oxon OX16 9AA, England.

CAMPBELL, Simon John; b. 9 Jan. 1958, Bury, Lancashire, England. Musician (guitar); Vocalist; Prod. m. Angela Mary Campbell, 5 Sept. 1982, 2 s. *Education:* BSc, Chemistry. *Career:* Tours, 1 single, 1 EP with rock band Whitefire, 1975–81; National tours with R&B band Roadrunner, 1981–85; Tours with pop band Gilt Edge, Cutting Edge, 1985–86; International tours, 1 album with pop band Little Brother, 1986–89; 1 album with Disciples, 1990–92; with The Method, 1992–94; with Simon Campbell Band, 1994–95; Featured artist with The 1995 7. *Membership:* Musicians' Union. *Current Management:* Music Business Management, International House, Drake St, Rochdale OL16 1PN, England.

CAMPBELL, Vivian; b. 25 Aug. 1962, Belfast, Northern Ireland. Rock musician (guitar). *Career:* Guitarist, Dio, 1983–87; Whitesnake, 1987–88; Guitarist, Trinity; Riverdogs; Guitarist, Shadow King, 1991; Def Leppard, 1992–; Major international tours and concerts include Freddie Mercury Tribute Concert, Wembley Stadium, 1992. *Recordings:* Albums: with Dio: Holy Diver, 1983; The Last In Line, 1984; Sacred Heart, 1985; with Whitesnake: Whitesnake, 1987; with Shadow King: Shadow King, 1991; with Def Leppard: Adrenalize (No. 1, UK and USA), 1992; Retroactive, 1993; Vault 1980–95, 1995; Slang, 1996; Euphoria, 1999; X, 2002. Singles: with Def Leppard: Let's Get Rocked (No. 2, UK), 1992; Make Love Like A Man, 1992; Have You Ever Needed Someone So Bad, 1992; Stand Up (Kick Love Into Motion), 1992; Heaven Is, 1993; Tonight, 1993; Two Steps Behind, used in film soundtrack The Last Action Hero, 1993; When Love and Hate Collide (No. 2, UK), 1995; Slang, 1996; All I Want Is Everything, 1996; Now, 2002; Guest musician, Long Hard Look, Lou Gramm, 1989; Brunel's LA Zoo, with Bunny Brunel, 1998; Fear of Flying, with PJ Smith, 2001. *Current*

Management: Q-Prime Inc, 729 Seventh Ave, 14th Floor, New York, NY 10019, USA. *Website:* www.defleppard.com.

CAMPI, Ray; b. 20 April 1934, New York, NY, USA. Musician (guitar, bass, dobro steel). *Education:* BFA, University of Texas, Austin, TX, USA, 1957. *Career:* Austin City Limits, national public TV; Tomorrow Show, NBC TV; Texas Saturday Night, BBC II TV, 1991, BBC Radio, 1977; Echo's Show. *Compositions:* Rockin' At the Ritz; Caterpillar; A Little Bit of Heartache; Kick Da Bukkit. *Recordings:* Over 50 albums on Rollin' Rock Records, 1956–96. *Publications:* Rolling Stone, 1980; Dynamite, 1995; Now Dig This, 1996. *Membership:* Austin Federation of Musicians. *Current Management:* Paul Barrett, Rock 'n' Roll Enterprises. *Address:* 2872½ W Ave 35, Los Angeles, CA 90065, USA. *Website:* www.electricearl.com; www.rockabillyhall.com.

CANAPE, Jean-François; b. 1 Dec. 1945, Lagny, France. Jazz Musician (trumpet, key bugle, flute). m. Bathany Jeanne, 26 March 1988, 1 s. *Education:* Versailles Conservatory. *Career:* Several international festivals and tours: Montreux; Newport; Paris; Berlin; Babylon; Tokyo; Brazaville; India; Boulogne (played with Dave Liebman); Member, Orchestre National de Jazz, 1989–91; Played and composed for cinema, theatre, contemporary and classical music. *Recordings:* KONPS, Jean-François Canape Trio; Participated in: Jack-Line; Claire, with ONJ; Katchinas, Gerard Marais. *Current Management:* Sylvie Caqué. *Address:* 18 rue des Plantes, 75014 Paris, France.

CANIBOL, Heinz; b. 3 July 1951, Gelsenkirchen, Germany. Man.-Dir. m. Brigitte Canibol, 3 Feb. 1984. *Education:* Degree in Economics. *Career:* Product Manager and Marketing Director, CBS Records, Germany, 1977–89; Managing Director, Sony Music, Austria, 1989–91; Managing Director and Vice-President G/A/S, MCA Music Entertainment, Germany, 1992–. *Address:* c/o MCA Music Entertainment, Winterhuder Weg 27, 22085 Hamburg, Germany.

CANN, Judith Leonie; b. 3 April 1958, Perth, Western Australia. Composer; Musician (keyboard). m. David George Hunt, 14 June 1986, 1 s., 1 d. *Education:* BA, film making; One year, Australian Film and TV School; Exchange student, National Film School, UK.; Post-graduate diploma in conducting (Surrey University). *Career:* Composed, performed synthesized scores and music for use in the film, television, video industry. *Recordings:* 25 library tracks with Chappell; 175 library tracks with Carlin; Scored music for 1492 The Shattered Utopia (short film); Making Ends Meet; Network Europe; Channel Tunnel videos; Television series: A Tale of 4 Market Towns; World In Action; Laser, video, fireworks display in People's Republic of China. *Publications:* Article in APV magazine, Videomaker. *Honours:* Stemra Award, Netherlands, Most Impressive Use of Library Music, 1994. *Membership:* PRS; Musicians' Union. *Address:* 82 Bushey Hall Rd, Bushey, Herts WD2 2EQ, England.

CANO, José María; b. 21 Feb. 1959, Madrid, Spain. Composer; Arranger; Songwriter; Musician (guitar); Prod. *Career:* Mem., Mecano, with Ana Torroja and brother, Nacho Cano, 1980–; Simultaneous solo career, 1992–; Music prod. *Recordings:* Albums: with Mecano: Mecano, 1982; ¿Dónde Está El País De Las Hadas?, 1983; Ya Viene El Sol, 1984; En Concierto, 1985; Lo Ultimo De Mecano, 1986; Entre El Cielo Y El Suelo, 1986; Descanso Dominical, 1988; Aidalai, 1991; Ana José Nacho, 1998; Solo: Luna (opera), 1997; José Cano, 2000. *Address:* c/o Sony Music Entertainment, European Regional Office, 10 Great Marlborough St, London W1F 7LP, England. *E-mail:* mecanoweb@mecanoweb.com. *Website:* www.mecanoweb.com; www.josecano.com.

CANO, Nacho; b. 26 Feb. 1963, Madrid, Spain. Composer; Arranger; Songwriter; Musician (keyboards, synthesizer); Prod. *Career:* Mem., Mecano, with Ana Torroja and brother, José Cano, 1980–; Simultaneous solo career, 1992–; Music prod. *Recordings:* Albums: with Mecano: Mecano, 1982; ¿Dónde Está El País De Las Hadas?, 1983; Ya Viene El Sol, 1984; En Concierto, 1985; Lo Ultimo De Mecano, 1986; Entre El Cielo Y El Suelo, 1986; Descanso Dominical, 1988; Aidalai, 1991; Ana José Nacho, 1998; Solo: Un Mundo Separado Por El Mismo Dios, 1994; El Lado Femenino, 1996; Amor Humor, 1999. *Address:* c/o Sony Music Entertainment, European Regional Office, 10 Great Marlborough St, London W1F 7LP, England. *E-mail:* mecanoweb@mecanoweb.com. *Website:* www.mecanoweb.com; www.nachocano.com.

CANONGE, Mario-Laurent; b. 5 Sept. 1960, Fort-de-France, Martinique. Musician (Piano, Keyboards). 2 d. *Education:* BA, Musicology; Classical Music, Conservatoire Haute de Seine, 2 years. *Career:* Formed group, Ultramarine, 1983; Solo artiste; Television: Sur le Pont des Artistes; Rien a Cine, France Inter; Top Live, Europe I; Cerde de Minuit, Pintenne 2; Jazz 2, Jazz a Vienne; Concerts: New Morning, Zenith de Paris; Bataclan; Casino de Paris. *Compositions:* Pei Mwen Jodi; Pogo; Yélé Congo; L'esé; Palé; Si on sa Révé; Vidé Bo Kay; Echapaya; Dimanoua; Non Muoia; Sé Kon Ca; Bam Ti Bonjou. *Recordings:* Albums: Retour Aux Sources, 1991; Trait D'Union, 1993; Hommage A Marius Cultier, 1994; Aromes Caraibes, 1995; Carte Blanche, 2001. *Honours:* Best Pianist, Prix de la Défense, 1983; Best Album, Best Composer, SACEM Martinique, 1992–94, Best Album, Best Music, 1996; Musical Research Prize, 1995. *Current Management:* c/o François Post, Vivienne Sicnasi Promotion, 6 Pl. George Sand, 91130, Ris Orangis, France.

CANOVILLE, Katherine; b. 13 Jan. 1965, Hillingdon, Middlesex, England. Co Dir; Group Man. m. Stephen Carrington, 7 July 1995. *Career:* Concert promoter, 1979–81; Artist Manager, 1981–95; Managing Director, Buzz Magazine, 1986–89; Co-founder, Nation Records, 1988; Managing Director, Nation Records, 1990–; Sole Trader, QFM Promotions, 1994. *Publications:* Ex-writer for Oracle/Teletext World Music Page, until 1992. *Membership:* BMIA BRIT Award Committee.

CANTRELL, Jerry; b. 18 March 1966, Tacorna, WA, USA. Musician (guitar); Vocals. *Career:* Member, Alice in Chains; Numerous tours and TV appearances including MTV Unplugged session. *Recordings:* Singles: Sap EP, 1992; Would?, 1993; Them Bones, 1993; Angry Chair, 1993; Down In A Hole, 1993; Grind, 1995; I Stay Away, 1995; Heaven Beside You, 1996; Fear The Voices, 1999; Bank Heist, 1999; Again, 2001; Albums: Facelift, 1990; Dirt, 1992; Sap, 1992; Jar of Flies (No. 1, USA), 1994; Alice in Chains (No. 1, USA), 1995; I Stay Away, 1995; Unplugged, 1996; Nothing Safe, 1999; Music Bank, 1999; Live, 2000; Greatest Hits, 2001; Solo Album: Boggy Depot, 1998; Degradation Trip, 2002.

CAPALDI, Jim; b. 2 Aug. 1944, Evesham, Herefordshire, England. Musician (drums); Vocalist. *Career:* Member, The Helions; Deep Feeling; Traffic, 1967–69, 1970–74, re-formed 1994; Also solo artiste. *Recordings:* Albums: with Traffic: Mr Fantasy, 1968; Traffic, 1968; Last Exit, 1969; Heaven Is In Your Mind, 1969; Best of Traffic, 1969; John Barleycorn Must Die, 1970; Low Spark of High-Heeled Boys, 1971; Welcome To The Canteen, 1971; Shoot Out At The Fantasy Factory, 1973; When The Eagle Flies, 1974; Far From Home, 1994; Feelin' Alright (The Very Best of Traffic), 2000; Solo albums: Oh How We Danced, 1972; Whale Meat Again, 1974; Short Cut Draw Blood, 1976; Fierce Heart, 1983; Some Came Running, 1989; Prince of Darkness, 1995; Let Thunder Cry, 1999; Singles with Traffic include: Paper Sun, 1967; Hole In My Shoe, 1967; Here We Go Round The Mulberry Bush (film title theme), 1967; No Name No Face No Number; Solo single: Love Hurts, 1975; Guest, Alone Together, Dave Mason, 1970. *Address:* c/o Freedom Songs, PO Box 272, London N20 0BY, England.

CAPLIN, Arnold Stewart; b. 8 May 1929, New York, USA. Record Co Exec; Record Prod. m. Barbara Stein, 29 June 1950, 2 s. *Career:* President, Biograph Records, 1964–; Consultant, advisor, Historic Records. *Recordings:* Albums: As producer for Thad Jones; George Gershwin; Scott Joplin; James P Johnson; Mel Lewis; Benny Goodman. *Membership:* ASCAP; Broadcast Music Inc; NARAS (fellow); NAIRD; World Jazz Federation. *Address:* c/o Biograph Records, 35 Medford St, Somerville, MA 02143–4242, USA.

CAPONE, Franco; b. 11 Jan. 1968, Rome, Italy. Author; Composer; Musician (guitar); Arranger; Language Teacher. m. Rita Tenan, 7 Sept. 1991. *Education:* Masters of Arts, Languages; PGCE Education. *Career:* Founder, French group, Melody, 1987–88; Moved to England, 1989; Worked on first album, 1991; Founded group, Open Arms, 1992; Recorded two albums, tours, Scotland, Ireland, Italy, Belgium, 1992–95; New album due 1996. *Recordings:* The World My Home, 1991; with Open Arms: Walking With Us, 1992; Back To The World, 1994. *Membership:* Musicians' Union. *Current Management:* PPS Communications/Culture-Music, Villaverla, Italy.

CAPTAIN HOLLYWOOD, (Tony Harrison); b. 9 Aug. 1962, Newark, New Jersey, USA. Vocalist; Rap Artiste; Prod. *Career:* Choreographer, major German television programme; Artist, performing and producing: The Mixmaster; Twenty 4 Seven, 1986–90; Captain Hollywood Project, 1991–. *Recordings:* Albums: Love Is Not Sex, 1993; Singles: More and More, 1991; All I Want, 1993; Only With You, 1993; Rhythm of Life, 1994. *Publications:* Grand Piano; I Can't Stand It; More and More. *Honours:* 14 Gold records; 1 Diamond award; 1 Platinum. *Membership:* GEMA, Germany. *Current Management:* Susanne Foecker, D-Town Management. *Address:* Schündelnhöfe 8, 41751 Viersen, Germany.

CAPTAIN SENSIBLE, (Ray Burns); b. 24 April 1954, Croydon, Surrey, England. Vocalist; Musician (lead guitar, bass). *Career:* Invented punk as member of The Damned; Many tours; Numerous television appearances include several on Top of the Pops. *Compositions:* Writes most of own material. *Recordings:* Albums: Solo albums, 1982– include: Women and Captain First, 1982; The Power of Love, 1983; Sensible Singles, 1984; Revolution Now, 1989; Live At The Milky Way (Amsterdam), 1995; Meathead, 1995; The Universe of Geoffrey Brown, 1998; Singles include: Happy Talk (No. 1, UK), 1982; Wot (No. 1, France, 7 weeks), 1982 ; Glad It's All Over, 1984; Come On Down, 1985; Revolution Now, 1987; Smash It Up Part 4, 1990; Wot 93, 1994. *Membership:* PRS; Musicians' Union. *Current Management:* Forward Agency Booking (FAB). *Address:* Humbug Records, Suite 4N, Leroy House, Essex Rd, Islington, London, England.

CARA, Irene; b. 18 March 1959, Bronx, New York, USA. Vocalist; Actor; Dancer. *Career:* Stage appearances: Maggie Flynn, Broadway, 1968; The Me Nobody Knows, 1970; Via Galactica, New York, 1972; Got To Go Disco, 1979; Ain't Misbehavin'; Film appearances: Aaron Loves Angela, 1975; Sparkle, 1976; Fame, 1980; DC Cab, 1980; City Heat, 1984; A Certain Fury, 1985; Busted Up, 1986; Killing 'Em Softly, 1985; The Man In 5-A; Collaborations:

George Duke; The Brecker Brothers; Oleta Adams; Giorgio Moroder. *Recordings:* Singles: Fame (No. 1, UK), 1980; Flashdance... What A Feeling (No. 1, USA); Why Me, 1983; Out Here On My Own; The Dream, from film DC Cab, 1984; Breakdance, 1984; All My Heart, 1996; Albums: Anyone Can See, 1982; What A Feelin', 1983; Carasmatic, 1987. *Honours:* Obie Award; Academy Awards: Best Song, Fame; Best Song, Flashdance... What A Feeling. *Membership:* Equity; Screen Actors Guild. *Address:* c/o Talent Consultants International Ltd, 1560 Broadway, Suite 1308, New York, NY 10036, USA.

CARCELES RUIZ, Lola; b. 8 June 1960, Murcia, Spain. Vocalist. m. 25 May 1978, 2 s., 1 d. *Education:* 5 years at conservatory. *Career:* Performed throughout Spain, 10 years; Television and radio work; Performed in USA, 1995. *Honours:* First Prize, Spanish Song Contest. *Current Management:* Francisco Ferrer Montoya. *Address:* c/o Augustin Lara N, 10, 5°B, Vistalegre, Murcia, Spain.

CAREY, Mariah; b. 22 March 1970, Long Island, New York, USA. Vocalist; Songwriter. m. Tommy Mottola, 5 June 1993, divorced. *Career:* Backing singer, Brenda K Starr, New York, 1988; Solo recording artiste, 1988–; 80m. albums sold to date; Concerts world-wide; Numerous television appearances include: Tonight Show; Arsenio Hall Show; Saturday Night Live; Top of the Pops; Wogan; Movie: Glitter, 2001. *Recordings:* Albums: Mariah Carey (No. 1, USA), 1990; Emotions, 1991; MTV Unplugged EP, 1992; Music Box (No. 1, USA and UK), 1993; Merry Christmas, 1994; Daydream (No. 1, UK), 1995; Butterfly, 1997; #1s, 1998; Rainbow, 1999; Glitter, 2001; Greatest Hits, 2001; Charmbracelet, 2002. Singles: Vision of Love (No. 1, USA), 1990; Love Takes Time (No. 1, USA), 1990; Someday (No. 1, USA), 1991; I Don't Wanna Cry (No. 1, USA), 1991; Emotions (No. 1, USA), 1991; Can't Let Go, 1992; Make It Happen, 1992; I'll Be There (No. 1, USA), 1992; Dreamlover (No. 1, USA), 1993; Hero (No. 1, USA), 1993; Without You (No. 1, UK), 1994; Anytime You Need A Friend, 1994; Endless Love (with Luther Vandross), 1994; All I Want For Christmas Is You, 1994; Fantasy (No. 1, USA), 1995; One Sweet Day (with Boyz II Men; No. 1, USA), 1995; Always Be My Baby (No. 1, USA), 1995; Open Arms, 1996; Honey (No. 1, USA), 1997; Butterfly, 1997; Breakdown, 1997; My All (No. 1, USA), 1998; When You Believe (Prince of Egypt) (with Whitney Houston), 1998; I Still Believe, 1999; Heartbreaker, 1999; Thank God I Found You, 2000; Can't Take That Away, 2000; Against All Odds (with Westlife; No. 1, UK), 2000; Loverboy, 2001; Never Too Far, 2001. *Honours:* Grammy Awards: Best Female Pop Vocal, Best Artist, 1991; Rolling Stone Award, Best Female Singer, 1991; Three Soul Train Awards, 1991; Six Billboard Music Awards, 1991–92; Four American Music Awards, 1992–93, Special Award of Achievement, 2000; Three Citations, BMI Pop Awards, 1993; International Dance Music Award, Best Solo Artist, 1996; Numerous platinum and gold discs. *Current Management:* Hoffman Entertainment, 20 W 55th St, 11th Floor, New York, NY 10022, USA. *Address:* c/o Island/Def Jam Records, 825 Eighth Ave, New York, NY 10019, USA. *Website:* www.mariahcarey.com.

CARLISLE, Belinda; b. 17 Aug. 1958, Hollywood, CA, USA. Vocalist. m. Morgan Mason, 12 April 1986, 1 s. *Career:* Mem., Black Randy, Metro Squad; Founder mem., lead singer, all-girl group The Go-Go's (formerly The Misfits), 1978–85; Numerous tours world-wide; Solo artiste, 1986–94; Support to Robert Palmer, US tour, 1986; Solo tour, USA and Canada, 1988; The Go-Go's re-formed briefly for a PETA benefit concert, 1990; Mem., re-formed Go-Go's, 1994, Shows in Las Vegas; The Go-Go's re-formed, 2000–, for an album and tours, including US tour with B-52's; Television includes: Late Night With David Letterman; Top of the Pops; Summer Scene; The O-Zone; Stage performance, Grease, 1983; Film appearance, Swing Shift, 1984; Model, Almay Cosmetics. *Recordings:* Albums: with the Go-Go's: Beauty and The Beat (No. 1, USA), 1981; Vacation, 1982; Talk Show, 1984; Return To The Valley of The Go-Go's, 1994; God Bless The Go-Go's, 2001; Contributor, Rainbow Warriors, 1989; Tame Yourself (animal rights benefit album), 1991; Solo: Belinda, 1986; Heaven On Earth, 1987; Runaway Horses, 1989; Live Your Life Be Free, 1991; Greatest Hits, 1992; Real, 1993; A Woman and A Man, 1996; Runaway Live, 2000. Singles: with the Go-Gos: Our Lips Are Sealed; We Got The Beat; Head Over Heels; The Whole World Lost Its Head; Solo: Mad About You, 1986; Heaven Is A Place On Earth (No. 1, UK and USA), 1987; I Get Weak (No. 2, USA), 1988; Circle In The Sand, 1988; I Feel Free, 1988; World Without You, 1988; Leave A Light On, 1989; Summer Rain, 1990; Runaway Horses, 1990; We Want The Same Thing, 1990; Live Your Life Be Free, 1991; Do You Feel Like I Feel, 1991; It's Too Real, 1993; Band of Gold, 1996; All God's Children, 1999. *Address:* Virgin Records Inc, 338 N Foothill Rd, Beverly Hills, CA 90210, USA. *E-mail:* gogos@beyondmusic.com. *Website:* www.gogos.com.

CARLOTTI, Jan-Mari; b. 23 June 1948, Meknès, Morocco. Vocalist; Musician (guitar); Writer; Composer. *Education:* Medieval History; Ethnology; Sanskrit. *Career:* Singer, solely in Occitan (Provençal language); Formed Mont Jóia, 1974–83; Solo artist, 1983; Also worked with Anita/Anita, Michel Marre. *Recordings:* 5 albums with Mont Jóia; 6 albums as solo artist or in other groups; Latest: Chants des Troubadours, with Michel Marre, 1995. *Publications include:* Anthologie De La Nouvelle Chanson Occitaine, 1984. *Honours:* Grand Prix, Academie Charles Cros, 1978, 1994; First Prize,

International Artist, Turin Folk Competition, 1989; Best Solo Artist, Trad Magazine, 1991. *Current Management:* Ass Mont Jóia, Ostau de Provença, Parc Jourdan, 13100 Aix, France. *Address:* 2 bis Imp Fleury-Proudhon, 13200 Arles, France.

CARLSTROEM, Vigilante; b. 1977. Musician (guitar). *Career:* Mem., Swedish band, The Hives, 1993–; Signed to Universal Music, 2001. *Recordings:* Albums: Barely Legal, 1997; Veni Vidi Vicious, 2000; Your New Favourite Band (compilation, UK only), 2001. Singles: Oh, Lord! When? How? (EP), 1996; a.k.a I.D.I.O.T. (EP), 1998; Hate To Say I Told You So; Main Offender; Supply & Demand. *Honours:* NME Award, Best International Band, 2003. *Address:* The Hives, c/o Pelle Almqvist, Regnbågsvägen 46, 737 43 Fagersta, Sweden. *E-mail:* hives@innocent.com. *Website:* www.hives.nu.

CARLYLE, Mary Theresa, (Mary McLeish); b. 18 March 1938, Glasgow, Scotland. Musician (piano); Entertainer; Vocalist; Songwriter. m. Dick Le Claire, 15 Feb. 1968, 5 s. *Education:* Privately, Frank McLeish, MA, ARCM; Violet Stewart, LRAM, ARCM. *Career:* Carroll Levis Discoveries, age 16; Variety; Moss Empires Tour, Scotland; Concert Parties; Rep; Reviews; BBC TV STV Drama, variety; Summer season Jersey's Sunshine Hotel, 1960; Winter, Manchester Clubland; US Forces Club Piani/bar, Frankfurt; Return Jersey, Formed trio, 1964; Played residencies, main hotels, clubs, also solo work; One of original (and current) resident musicians, Blue Note Club, Jersey. *Compositions include:* Jersey Suite, co-writer, Jack Duff; All I Got Was You; Jersey (all profits to J A Monday Club, children's charity); I'll Think of You This Christmas; The Faceless Face; I'll Never Cry; How Can I Write A Song For You?. *Membership:* Equity; Musicians' Union. *Current Management:* Dick Ray Organisation Ltd, Jersey. *Address:* 40 Seaton Pl., St Helier, Jersey JE2 3QL, Channel Islands.

CARMEN, Eric; b. 11 Aug. 1949, Cleveland, Ohio, USA. Vocalist; Songwriter. *Education:* Classical singing, Cleveland Institute of Music. *Career:* Singer, various groups, Cleveland, 1960s; Lead singer, The Choir, 1968; Name changed to Raspberries, 1971–75; Solo recording artiste, 1975–80, 1985–; Over 15m. record sales. *Recordings include:* Albums with: The Raspberries: The Raspberries, 1971; Fresh, 1972; Side 3, 1973; Starting Over, 1975; Solo albums: Eric Carmen, 1975; Boats Against The Current, 1977; Change of Heart, 1978; Tonight You're Mine, 1980; Eric Carmen, 1985; The Best of Eric Carmen, 1988; Winter Dreams, 1998; Someone That You Loved Before, 1998; All By Myself (compilation), 2000; Singles: with The Raspberries: Go All the Way, 1972; Overnight Sensation, 1974; All By Myself (No. 2, USA); Never Gonna Fall In Love Again, 1976; Sunrise, 1976; Change of Heart, 1978; It Hurts Too Much, 1980; I Wanna Hear It From Your Lips, 1985; Solo: Hungry Eyes, used in film soundtrack Dirty Dancing, 1988; Make Me Lose Control, 1988; Reason To Try (used for Olympics Games coverage, NBC TV), 1988; My Heart Stops, 1992; All By Myself, 1993; Make Me Lose Control, 1993. *Current Management:* QBQ Entertainment Inc, 341 Madison Ave, 14th Floor, New York, NY 10017, USA.

CARMICHAEL, Anita; b. 17 Sept. 1964, Upminster, Essex, England. Musician (saxophone, alto); Vocalist. m. Michael Tanousis, 27 Aug. 1993, 1 s. *Education:* Guildhall School of Music. *Career:* Tours with: The Communards; Jonathan Butler; Fay Weldon; Imagination; M-People; Television, radio: Woman's Hour (BBC Radio 4); BBC World Service; TV: Pebble Mill; Cue The Music; Women's Jazz Archive (BBC GLR); Concerts: Antibes Festival; Brecon; Glastonbury; Jakarta; Montreux; Ronnie Scott's Club; Jazz Cafe; Red Sea; JVC Capital Jazz; Live TV and BBC Radio 2, 3, 5. *Recordings:* Live At The Premises (EP), 1993; The Unadulterated, 1994; Plays Dinner Jazz (EP), 1995; Saxotronix, 1995; Lipstick On My Reed, 1996; Video: Sax Skills With Anita Carmichael, 1995. *Honours:* Wire magazine, Newcomer of the Year, 1987. *Membership:* Musicians' Union; PRS; MCPS; Ronnie Scott's. *Current Management:* Saxology Records. *Address:* 49E St Pauls Rd, London N1 2LT, England.

CARMICHAEL, Jim; b. 21 Feb. 1971, Sevenoaks, Kent, England. Musician (drums); Songwriter; Prod. *Education:* Design and Communication; Berklee College of Music, Boston, USA, 1989. *Career:* Principal percussionist in winning orchestra at National Festival For Youth, 1988; Drummer, acid jazz group, K-Creative, 1991–93; Member: Freak Power; Every Day People (EDP), 2000–; Played with Les Rhythmes Digitales, Barry Adamson, Mandalay, Regular Fries, Izit, K-Creative. *Compositions:* QED, with K Creative, 1992. *Recordings:* with K-Creative: QED, 1992; with Izit: The Whole Affair, 1993; Imaginary Man, 1995; with Freak Power: Drive Thru Booty, 1994; More of Everything for Everybody, 1996; Carmichael's Crunchy Nut Loops, 1997; Mandalay: Empathy, 1998; with EDP: Sweet Music, 2001. *Address:* Flat 2, 3 College Terrace, Brighton BN2 2EE, England.

CARNEIRO, Fernando (Nando); b. 26 June 1953, Belo Horizonte, Brazil. Nora Kholki, 10 July 1997, 2 s. *Education:* Classical Guitar; Classical Piano; Composition and Orchestration. *Career:* A Barca Do Sol, own group; Recordings with singers: Olivia Byington and Beth Goulart; World tours with E Gismonti, 1986, 1990, 1991, 1993, 1994, 1995, 1996. *Compositions:* Kiss of the Spider Woman, soundtrack, Co-writer. *Recordings:* Topazio, Visom; Infancia, Gismonti; Zig-Zag, Gismonti; Glimpse, T Gurtu; Brassileiro, Brassil.

Honours: Fiat Prize, Os Povos Da Floresta, 1989. *Current Management:* Maquinando Music. *Address:* Igarapaua, 59–301 Leblon, Rio de Janeiro, RJ, Brazil.

CARNES, Kim; b. 20 July 1945, Los Angeles, California, USA. Vocalist; Songwriter. m. Dave Ellington. *Career:* Member, New Christy Minstrels, 1960s; Solo artiste; Success as songwriter with husband Dave Ellington. *Compositions include:* Songs recorded by artists including Frank Sinatra; Barbra Streisand; Kenny Rogers. *Recordings:* Albums: Rest On Me, 1972; Kim Carnes, 1975; Sailin', 1976; St Vincent's Court, 1979; Romance Dance, 1980; Mistaken Identity, 1981; Voyeur, 1982; Cafe Racers, 1983; Lighthouse, 1986; View From The House, 1988; Gypsy Honeymoon – The Best Of, 1993; Crazy In The Night, 1990; Back To Back, 1998; Mistaken Identity Collection; King Biscuit Flower Hour, 1998; Sweet Love Song of My Soul, 1999; Singles: Bette Davis Eyes (No. 1, USA); Draw of The Cards; What About Me (with Kenny Rogers, James Ingram), 1984; Make No Mistake He's Mine (with Barbra Streisand); Speed of The Sound of Loneliness (with Lyle Lovett, 1988); Contributor, We Are The World, USA For Africa, 1985. *Address:* c/o William Morris Agency, 2100 West End Ave, Suite 1000, Nashville, TN 37203, USA.

CARPENTER, Mary Chapin; b. 21 Jan. 1958, Princeton, New Jersey, USA. Country / Folk vocalist; Musician (guitar); Songwriter. *Education:* Degree, American civilization. *Career:* Winner, numerous local music competitions; Solo recording artiste, 1986–. *Compositions:* Songs recorded by Tony Tice; Joan Baez. *Recordings:* Singles include: Right Now, 1991; I Feel Lucky, 1992; Albums: Home Town Girl, 1987; State of The Heart, 1989; Shooting Straight In The Dark, 1990; Come On Come On, 1992; Stones In The Road, 1994; A Place In The World, 1996; Party Doll and Other Favourites, 1999; Time Sex Love, 2001; Also appears on recordings by: Joan Baez; Roseanne Cash; The Chieftains; Shawn Colvin; Indigo Girls; Patty Loveless; Dolly Parton; The Rankin Family; Ricky Skaggs; Dusty Springfield; Pam Tillis; Trisha Yearwood. *Honours:* 5 Washington Area Music Awards; CMA Vocalist of the Year, 1992. *Current Management:* Studio One Artists, 7010 Westmoreland Ave #100, Takoma Park, MD 20912, USA.

CARPENTER, Richard Lynn; b. 15 Oct. 1946, New Haven, Connecticut, USA. Vocalist; Composer; Arranger; Musician (piano). m. Mary Rudolph, 1984, 2 s. *Career:* Co-member, The Carpenters (with sister Karen), 1969–83; Group demise with death of Karen, 1983; Composer, numerous hits; World-wide tours, countless television, radio appearances; Advisor, television film The Karen Carpenter Story. *Recordings:* Singles include: (They Long To Be) Close To You (No. 1, USA), 1970; We've Only Just Begun, 1971; Rainy Days and Mondays, 1971; Goodbye To Love, 1972; Yesterday Once More, 1973; Top of The World (No. 1, USA), 1973; Please Mr Postman (No. 1, USA), 1975; Calling Occupants of Interplanetary Craft, 1977; Albums: Offering (aka Ticket To Ride), 1969; Close To You, 1970; Carpenters, 1971; A Song For You, 1972; Now and Then, 1973; Horizon, 1975; A Kind of Hush, 1976; Live At The Palladium, 1977; The Singles 1974–78, 1978; Christmas Portrait, 1978; Made In America, 1979; Voice of The Heart, 1983; Yesterday Once More, 1984; An Old Fashioned Christmas, 1985; Lovelines, 1990; Christmas Portrait, 1991; From The Top, 1991; Only Yesterday, 1993; Solo albums: Time, 1987; Pianist Arranger Composer Conductor, 1998. *Honours:* Numerous gold discs; Group of Year, 1971; 3 Grammy Awards; American Music Award, 1973. *Membership:* ASCAP; National Academy of Songwriters; NARAS. *Address:* PO Box 1084, Downey, CA 90240, USA.

CARR, Andy; b. 6 Dec. 1967, Kirkcaldy, Fife, Scotland. Musician (bass guitar, guitar); Vocalist; Songwriter. *Education:* Fife College of Further and Higher Education. *Career:* Lead vocalist and bass guitar with Summerfield Blues with live sessions on Annie Webster Show for BBC Scotland, on BBC Radio Tweed and on various independent radio stations. *Recordings:* with Summerfield Blues: Devil and The Freightman, Let's Scare The Posh People (EP) and Little Miss Behavin'. *Honours:* Scottish Blues Band of the Year, 1993–94. *Membership:* PRS; Musicians' Union. *Current Management:* Dave Arcari. *Address:* 192 Glasgow Rd, Perth, Scotland.

CARR, Budd; b. 5 Sept. 1945, Jersey City, New Jersey, USA. Music Supervisor. m. Jeanne, 4 Oct. 1970, 2 s., 1 d. *Education:* BA, MA, University of Illinois. *Career:* Began as music agent with CMA; Acts handled include: James Taylor; Bob Seger; Blind Faith; Carole King; Crosby Stills and Nash; Moved to IFA, acts handled: Eric Clapton Comeback Tour; Queen; Jefferson Starship; Stephen Stills; Left agency, signed band Kansas; Became personal manager, started management company, 1980; Joined forces with Wil Sharpe in Carr/Sharpe Entertainment Services, 1990; Clients include: Slaughter; Boxing Gandhis; The Buddah Heads; Eric Gales Band; John Wetton; After 25 films as a music supervisor, joined Joel Sill, Windswept Pacific Entertainment, whose catalogue includes: John Mellencamp; Rod Stewart; Willie Nelson; Numerous hits songs of 50s, 60s, 70s; Film credits include: Music consultant: The Terminator, 1984; Return of The Living Dead, 1985; Music supervisor: Salvador, 1986; Platoon, 1986; Wall Street, 1987; Talk Radio, 1988; Alien Nation, 1988; Born On The Fourth of July, 1989; Executive Music Producer: The Doors, 1991; JFK: 1991; Heaven and Earth, 1993; Natural Born Killers, 1994; Copycat, 1995; Nixon, 1995; Twister, 1996; Speed 2, 1997; I Know What You Did Last Summer, 1997; Stigmata, 1999. *Address:*

Carr Sharpe Entertainment, 9320 Wilshire Blvd, Suite 200, Beverly Hills, CA 90212, USA.

CARR, Ian (Henry Randell); b. 21 April 1933, Dumfries, Scotland. Musician (trumpet); Composer; Author; Broadcaster. m. (1) Margaret B Bell, 28 June 1963 (deceased 1967), 1 d, (2) Sandra L Major, 9 Dec. 1972 (divorced 1993). *Education:* BA Hons, English Language and Literature, King's College, Newcastle on Tyne, 1952–56. *Career:* Emcee Five, 1960–62; Rendell-Carr Quintet, 1962–69; Ian Carr's Nucleus, 1969–88; Ian Carr Group, 1989–92; United Jazz and Rock Ensemble, 1975–; Many international radio and television appearances. *Compositions:* Solar Plexus, 1970; Labyrinth, 1973; Out of The Long Dark, 1978; Awakening, 1980; Old Heartland, 1988; Sounds and Sweet Airs, 1992; Shhh, 1995; Fyace, 1997. *Recordings:* Numerous professional recordings. *Publications:* Music Outside, 1973; Miles Davis, A Critical Biography, 1982; Keith Jarrett, The Man and His Music, 1991; Co-author, Rough Guide to Jazz, 1995. *Contributions to:* Jazz Feature Writer for BBC Music Magazine, 1992–. *Honours:* Italian Calabria Award for Outstanding Contribution in the Field of Jazz, 1982. *Membership:* Royal Society of Musicians of Great Britain; Professor, Guildhall School of Music; PRS; APC. *Current Management:* Barbara Levy, England. *Address:* Flat 1, 34 Brailsford Rd, London SW2 2TE, England.

CARR, Martin; b. 29 Nov. 1968, Thurso, Scotland. Musician (guitar); Songwriter. *Career:* Member, The Boo Radleys, 1989–99; Televison includes: Top of the Pops; With the Boo Radleys; White Room; The Word; Solo artiste, as Brave Captain, 2002–. *Compositions include:* Lazarus, 1993; Wake Up Boo, 1994; Ride the Tiger, 1995. *Recordings:* Albums: with Boo Radleys: Ichabod and I, 1989; Everything's Alright Forever, 1992; Giant Steps, 1993; Learning To Walk, 1994; Sharks Patrol These Waters, 1995; Wake Up, 1995; C'mon Kids, 1996; with Eggman, First Fruits, 1996; King Size, 1998; Solo: Advertisements For Myself, 2002. Hit single: with Boo Radleys: Wake Up Boo, 1995. *Publications:* Front cover of Melody Maker, 3 times, 1995; Front cover of NME, 1993, 1995. *Honours:* NME Brat Award, 1994; Select Magazine, Best Album of the Year, 1994; Liverpool Echo, Album of the Year, 1995. *Address:* c/o Creation Records, 10 Westgate St, London E8 3RN, England.

CARR, Vikki, (Florencia Bisenta De Casillas Martinez Cardona); b. 19 July 1941, El Paso, Texas, USA. Vocalist; Actress. *Career:* Appearances include: Television shows with: Dean Martin; Ed Sullivan; Jackie Gleason; Jerry Lewis; Carol Burnett; Bob Hope; Danny Kaye; Glen Campbell; Johnny Carson; Hostess of Tonight Show, several times; 5 TV specials; Concerts in USA, Europe, Australia, Japan; Stage actress, South Pacific, Kansas City; Unsinkable Molly Brown, Ohio; I'm Getting My Act Together and Taking It On The Road, St Louis; Hostess, Mrs America Pageant, 1981–87; Mrs World Pageant, 1984–87; Founder and Chairman, Vikki Carr Scholarship Foundation, 1971; TV appearances in Baywatch; Bilingual TV special, Memorias, Memorias, 1998. *Recordings:* Albums include: It Must Be Him, 1967; For Once In My Life, 1969; Nashville By Carr, 1970; Vikki Carr Y El Amore, 1980; Cosas Del Amor, 1990; Reta Manda Y Provoca, 1998; Memorias Memorias, 1999; Vikki Carr Christmas Album, 2000; contribution to album, Standards, 2002. *Honours:* Hon. doctorates: St Edwards University, 1974; University of San Diego, 1975; Woman of Year, LA Times, 1970; Visiting Entertainer of Year, Mexico City, 1972; Singer of the Year, American Guild Variety Artists, 1972; Woman of The World, 1974; Humanitarian Award, Nosotros, 1981; Woman of the Year, League United Latin American Citizens, 1983; Hispanic Woman of the Year, 1984; Grammy Award, Best Mexican-American Performance, 1985; Silver Achievement, YWCA, 1989; Golden Eagle, Nosotros, 1989; 3 times Grammy Winner, 1985, 1992, 1995; Founder of Hope Award, City of Hope, Los Angeles, 1990; Career Achievement Award, Asscn of Hispanic Critics, 1990; Key Girl Scouts of America Award, 1991; Hispanic Heritage Award, Washington CD. *Current Management:* Vi-Car Entertainment Inc. *Address:* c/o Peter Shukat, 111 W 57th St, Suite 1120, New York, NY 10019, USA.

CARRACK, Paul; b. 22 April, 1951, Sheffield, Yorkshire, England. Vocalist; Songwriter; Musician (keyboards). *Career:* Member: Ace; Squeeze, 1980–81; Mike and The Mechanics, 1986–; Concerts include: Prince's Trust Rock Gala, Birmingham, 1989; Also solo artiste, 1980–; Collaborations: Nick Lowe; Carlene Carter; John Hiatt; Phil Manzanera; The Pretenders; Roxy Music; Elvis Costello; The Undertones; The Smiths; Eric Clapton; Elton John; Roger Waters. *Recordings:* Albums include: with Squeeze: East Side Story, 1981; with Mike and The Mechanics: Mike and The Mechanics, 1986; The Living Years, 1988; Word of Mouth, 1991; Beggar On A Beach of Gold, 1995; Hits, 1996; solo: The Nightbirds, 1980; Suburban Voodoo, 1982; One Good Reason, 1987; Ace Mechanic, 1987; Carrack Collection, 1988; Groove Approved, 1989; Carrackter Reference, 1991; Blue Views, 1996; Beautiful World, 1997; Satisfy My Soul, 2000; Singles include: with Squeeze: Labelled With Love, 1981; with Mike and The Mechanics: Silent Running, 1986; All I Need Is A Miracle, 1986; The Living Years (No. 1, USA), 1989; Over My Shoulder, 1995; solo: How Long?, 1996. *Current Management:* Alan Wood. *Telephone:* (1142) 580338. *E-mail:* paul@carrack-uk.com. *Website:* www.carrack-uk.com.

CARRASCO, Joe 'King', (Joe Teutsch); b. 6 Dec. 1953, Dumas, Texas, USA. Musician (guitar). Divorced, 1 s. *Education:* University of Texas, 1972. *Career:* Son of Stiff tour, 1980; Saturday Night Live, 1981; Austin City Limits, 1981. *Recordings:* Albums include: Bandido Rock, 1988; Tales From The Crypt (with The Crowns), 2000. *Honours:* Mem. of Texas Music Hall of Fame. *Membership:* ASCAP. *Current Management:* IKC Productions. *Address:* PO Box 12233, Austin, TX 78711, USA.

CARRINGTON, Terri Lyne; b. 4 Aug. 1965, Medford, Massachusetts, USA. Musician (drums); Songwriter; Vocalist; Prod. *Education:* Berklee College of Music, Boston. *Career:* Original house drummer, Arsenio Hall Show; Toured with: Al Jarreau; Herbie Hancock; David Sanborn; Joe Sample; Stan Getz; Wayne Shorter; Gerald Albright; Lalah Hathaway. *Compositions:* Reach For Your Dreams, for 1996 Olympics; Josa Lee, for Dianne Reeves; Whatcha Gonna Do, Patrice Rushen. *Recordings:* Albums: As a leader: Real Life Story; Solo: Jazz Is A Spirit, 2002. *Honours:* Boston Music Award, 1989, 1990. *Membership:* NARAS. *Address:* 366 W California Ave #1, Glendale, CA 91203, USA.

CARROLL, Dina; b. 21 Aug. 1968, Cambridge, England. Vocalist; Songwriter. *Career:* Lead vocalist, Quartz, 1990; Solo artiste, 1992–; British tours, 1993, 1994; Concerts include: Support to Luther Vandross, Wembley, 1993. *Compositions:* Co-writer with producer, Nigel Lowis. *Recordings:* Albums: So Close, 1993; Only Human, 1996; Very Best Of, 2001; Singles: with Quartz: It's Too Late, 1991; solo: Ain't No Man, 1992; Special Kind of Love, 1992; So Close, 1992; This Time, 1993; Express, 1993; Don't Be A Stranger, 1993; The Perfect Year (co-written by Andrew Lloyd Webber), 1993; Escaping, 1996; Only Human, 1996; One Two Three, 1998. *Honours:* First-ever million-selling debut album for UK female, So Close, 1993; BRIT Award, Best Female Artist, 1994; Mercury Music Prize, 1993; 3 International Dance Awards, 1994; Great Britain Variety Award, Best Performing Artist; Silver Clef Award, Best Newcomer, 1994. *Current Management:* First Avenue Management, The Courtyard, 42 Colwith Rd, London W6 9EY, England.

CARRON-SMITH, Patricia; b. 3 April 1952, Llantrisant, Wales. Vocalist; Musician. *Career:* Member, Welsh traditional music group Swansea Jack, 1977–78; Member, Welsh traditional group Calennig, 1978–; Television includes: Torth y Fara, S4C, 1982; Folk On The Move, HTV, 1983; Trade Winds, BBC Wales, 1985; Fastest To Frisco, BBC Wales, 1986; Evening News, Dunedin, New Zealand, 1990; Celtic Magic, HTV, 1990; Gwerin y Werin, S4C, 1995. *Recordings:* with Swansea Jack: The Seven Wonders, 1978; with Calennig: Songs and Tunes From Wales, 1980; You Can Take a White Horse Anywhere, 1983; Dyddiau Gwynion Ionawr, 1985; Dwr Glan, 1990; Trade Winds, 1994; A Gower Garland, 2000; Numerous compilations. *Membership:* Equity; Musicians' Union; PRS; PAMRA; CDdWC; COTC. *Address:* 1 Ty Clwyta Cottages, Cross Inn, Llantrisant Cynon Raf CF72 8AZ, Wales.

CARSON, Jeff; b. 16 Dec. 1963, Tulsa, Oklahoma, USA. Vocalist; Songwriter; Musician (guitar, harmonica). m. Kim Cooper, 14 Dec. 1987. *Recordings:* Albums: Jeff Carson, 1995; Butterfly Kisses, 1997; Shine On, 1998; Singles: Yeah Buddy, 1995; Not On Your Love, 1995; The Car, 1995; Holdin' On to Something, 1996; That Last Mile, 1996; Do It Again, 1997; Butterfly Kisses, 1997; Here's the Deal, 1997; Shine On, 1998. *Honours:* Academy of Country Music, Video of the Year, The Car, 1996. *Current Management:* Marv Dennis and Associates. *Address:* 1002 18th Ave S, Nashville, TN 37212, USA.

CARSTEA, Elena; b. 26 Feb. 1963, Agnita, Sibiu County, Romania. Musician (guitar). *Education:* Classic Singing. *Career:* Television shows include: Golden Orpheus, 1993; Stars Duel, 1993; Mamaia Festival; Five O'Clock Tea; Golden Stag; Radio and television concerts. *Recordings:* Your Eyes, 1988; Tomorrow; Some Day, 1990; Ballad For Sandra, 1994. *Honours:* Public Prize for Composition, Your Eyes, 1983; Best Vocal Soloist of the Year, 1994. *Membership:* Radio Contact. *Current Management:* Doru Costea. *Address:* 61 Buzesti St A6, Third Floor, Apt 18, Sector 1, Bucharest, Romania.

CARTER, Benny (Bennett Lester); b. 8 Aug. 1907, New York, NY, USA. Musician (saxophone, clarinet, trumpet); Composer; Conductor. *Career:* Musician, arranger, with bands including: Charlie Johnson, Fletcher Henderson, Chick Webb, Horace Henderson, 1925–32; Leader, own band, 1932–35, 1938–46; Arranger, BBC studio orchestra, 1936–38; Film appearance: Snows of Kilimanjaro, 1952; Conductor, workshops, US universities, 1970–; Member, music advisory panel, NEA, 1976–79; Artist in residence, Rutgers University, 1986. *Compositions include:* Film scores: Stormy Weather, 1943; As Thousands Cheer, 1943; Panic In The Streets, 1950; Snows of Kilimanjaro, 1952; The Five Pennies, 1959; Guns of Navarone, 1961; A Man Called Adam, 1966; Buck and The Preacher, 1972; Cosmic Eye, 1985. *Recordings:* Albums include: Ridin' In Rhythm, 1933; Jazz Giant, 1957; Further Definitions, 1961; The Benny Carter 4: Montreux '77, 1977; Central City Sketches, 1987; In The Mood For Swing, 1987; Over The Rainbow, 1989; All That Jazz, 1990; All of Me, 1991; Song Book, 1995; Advanced Swing, 1996. *Honours:* Silver Award, Esquire, 1943; Gold award, 1946; Grammy Lifetime Achievement Award, 1987; Aggie Award, Songwriters Guild, 1988; Downbeat

Awards; ASMAC Golden Score Award. *Address:* PO Box 870, Hollywood, CA 90028, USA.

CARTER, Carlene, (Rebecca Carlene Smith); b. 26 Sept. 1955, Nashville, Tennessee, USA. Country vocalist; Songwriter. m. (1) Joe Simpkins, divorced, 1 d., (2) Jack Routh, divorced, 1 s., (3) Nick Lowe, divorced. *Education:* Piano lessons; Guitar lessons with Carl Perkins. *Career:* Country singer, 1974–; Concerts include: Wembley Country Music Family, with Carter family, 1981; Film appearance: Too Drunk To Remember, London Film Festival; Stage performance: Pump Boys and Dinettes, with Kiki Dee, Paul Jones, London, 1985. *Compositions:* Easy From Now On; Appalachian Eyes; Guardian Angel. *Recordings:* Albums: Carlene Carter, 1978; Two Sides To Every Woman, 1979; Musical Shapes, 1980; Blue Nun, 1981; C'est Bon, 1983; I Fell In Love, 1990; Little Acts of Treason, 1995; Hindsight 20/20, 1996; Contributor, The Junkie and The Juicehead Minus Me, Johnny Cash, 1974; Lost Dogs and Mixed Blessings, John Prine, 1995; Also recorded with members of Squeeze; Dave Edmunds; Kiki Dee; Albert Lee; Jim Kettner. *Current Management:* Fitzgerald-Hartley Co, 1212 16th Ave S, Nashville, TN 37203, USA.

CARTER, Deana; b. 1964, Nashville, Tennessee, USA. Vocalist; Songwriter; Musician (guitar). *Career:* British tour support to Jimmy Nail, 1995; Recording Artists, extensive tours of USA and Canada. *Recordings:* Debut album, Did I Shave My Legs For This?, 1995; Did I Shave My Legs For This, 1996; Everything's Gonna Be Alright, 1998; Father Christmas (with Fred Carter Jr), 2001. *Honours:* Did I Shave My Legs for This, Quadruple Platinum album; Everything's Gonna Be Alright, Gold Album; CMA Single of the Year, for Strawberry Wine, 1997; Orville H Gibson Award, Best Country Guitarist, 1999. *Membership:* Country Music Assen; ASCAP. *Current Management:* The Left Bank Organization, 6609 Currywood Dr., Nashville, TN 37205, USA.

CARTER, Derrick, (Sound Patrol, Tone Theory, Oneiro, The Unknown); b. 21 Oct. 1969, Chicago, Illinois, USA. Prod; Remixer; DJ. *Career:* Started to DJ, aged 9; Worked for Curtis Jones' Cajual label; First release, 1987; First break with Symbols and Instruments, 1989; Co-founder, Classic Records (with Luke Solomon), 1996–; World-wide DJ; Club residency at The End, London; Collaborations: Mark Farina; Chris Nazuka; Basement Jaxx; Cajmere; Remixes: Blaze; Tortoise; Slam; Modjo. *Recordings:* Albums: Sweetened – No Lemon (as Sound Patrol), 1995; Squaredancing In A Roundhouse, 2002. Singles: Mood (with Symbols and Instruments), 1989; Dream States (with Cajmere), 1993; Tripping Amongst The Stars (as Sound Patrol), 1995; Limbo of Vanished Possibilities (as Tone Theory), 1995; Wear A Pair, 1996; Mo Pschidt EP, 2000; Shh! (as Oneiro), 2001. *Current Management:* Mumbo Jumbo Management, 2A Southam St, London W10 5PH, England.

CARTER, Kent; b. 12 June 1939, Hanover, New Hampshire, USA. m. June 1981, 4 s. *Education:* Berklee School of Music, Boston; Private study, piano, cello, bassoon (as child), bass. *Career:* Participated in October Revolution, New York, early 1960s; Performed with Jazz Composers Guild Orchestra; Toured, recorded with artistes including: Paul Bley; Carla Bley; Michael Mantler; Steve Lacy; Don Cherry; Gato Barbieri; Alan Silva; Mal Waldron; Michael Smith; Bobby Bradford; Max Roach; Enrico Rava; Roswell Rudd; Derek Bailey; John Stevens; Trevor Watts; Steve McCall, 1964–; Member, co-founder, Tok Trio, including tours, Europe and Japan; Member, Steve Lacy Quintet, including tour, USA, 1970–81; Most major European jazz festivals; Radio WDR Köln, Germany; Radio France; Radio RAI, Italy; Founder, leader, chamber group Kent Carter String Trio, with Carlos Zingaro, Francois Dreno; Played major music festivals, Europe; Collaboration with Michala Marcus (dance) in productions including Dance Music Image, 1975–. *Compositions include:* Collaboration with choreographer Jean Pomares in ballet Paysages Avec Couple. *Recordings:* Beauvais Cathedral; Kent Carter Solo With Claude Bernard; Suspensions; La Contrebasse; Album: The Willisau Suites, 1999. *Address:* Riviere, 16320 Juillaguet, France.

CARTER, Mel; b. 22 April 1939, Cincinnati, Ohio, USA. Vocalist. *Education:* Cincinnati Conservatory of Music. *Career:* Leading soloist, Assistant Director, Greater Cincinnati Youth and Young Adult Choral Union; Moved to Hollywood, 1960; Appearances include: Ciro's, with Dinah Washington; The Crescendo, with Bessie Griffin's Gospel Pearls; Guest on Ed Sullivan Show; Opened at The Flamingo, Las Vegas, with Damita Jo; First hit single led to touring with Dick Clark Caravan of Stars, sharing bill with Sonny and Cher, Tom Jones, others; Headlined nightclubs across USA, Canada; Appearances include: Slate Brothers, Hollywood; Cocoanut Grove; La Fiesta, Mexico; Hotel Americana, New York; Fairmont, Dallas; Played Sportin' Life in concert of Porgy and Bess; Starred in Glitter Palace; Successful actor, films include: Prime Time; No Way Out; Television includes: American Bandstand; Hullaballoo; Tonight Shows; New Love American Style; CHiPs; Many commercials; TV and film soundtracks; Tour of Japan; Engagements: Trump Castle; Taj Mahal; Merv Griffin's Resorts Casino Hotel, Atlantic City; Performance in Fly Blackbird Revisited, early 1990s. *Recordings include:* Albums: When A Boy Falls In Love; My Heart Sings; Hold Me, Thrill Me, Kiss Me; Enter Laughing; Easy Listening; Be My Love; This Is My Life; Willing; Raise The World/ The Album of Life – Title Song; Live In Hollywood; The Best

Of; Hit singles include: When A Boy Falls In Love, 1963; Hold Me, Thrill Me, Kiss Me, 1965; All of a Sudden My Heart Sings, 1965; Band of Gold, 1966; You, You, You, 1966; Take Good Care of Her, 1966. *Honours:* LA Weekly's La Wee Award; Gold disc.

CARTER, Nick(olas Gene); b. 28 Jan. 1980, Jamestown, NY, USA. Vocalist; Musician (drums). *Career:* Brother of vocalist Aaron Carter; Acted in commercials on TV; Vocalist for Tampa Buccaneer's pre-game show; Mem., Backstreet Boys, 1993–; Numerous tours and television appearances. *Recordings:* Albums: with Backstreet Boys: Backstreet Boys, 1996; Live in Concert, 1998; Backstreet's Back, 1998; Millennium, 1999; Black And Blue, 2000; Greatest Hits Chapter 1, 2001; Solo: Now Or Never, 2002. Singles: with Backstreet Boys: We've Got It Goin' On, 1995; Quit Playing Games, 1998; I'll Never Break Your Heart, 1998; Everybody, 1998; As Long As You Love Me, 1998; Anywhere for You, 1998; All I Have to Give, 1998; I Want It That Way (No. 1, UK), 1999; Larger Than Life, 1999; Show Me The Meaning of Being Lonely, 2000; The One, 2000; Shape of My Heart, 2000; Drowning, 2001; The Call, 2001. *Honours:* MTV European Music Award, Best Pop Act, 1997, Best Group, 1999; Billboard Music Awards, Best Group, Best Adult Contemporary Group, 1998, Album of the Year, Artist of the Year, 1999; MTV Music Video Awards, Best Group Video, 1998, Viewer's Choice, for I Want It That Way, 1999; World Music Awards, Best-Selling Pop Group, 1999, 2000, Best-Selling R&B Group, 1999, 2000, Best-Selling Dance Group, 1999, 2000, Best American Group, 2000; American Music Awards, Favorite Pop/Rock Band, Duo or Group, 2000, 2001. *Website:* www.backstreetboys.com; www.nickcarter.com.

CARTER, Ronald; b. 4 May 1937, Ferndale, Michigan, USA. Jazz Musician (bass); Educator. m. Janet Hosbrouck, 7 June 1958, 2 s. *Education:* BMus, Eastman School of Music, 1959; MusM, Manhattan School of Music, 1962. *Career:* Bass player, college orchestras; Bass player for Chico Hamilton Quintet; Don Ellis; Cannonball Adderley; Thelonious Monk; Eric Dolphy; Miles Davis, 1963–68; Wynton Marsalis; Formed own quartet, 1975; Also prolific freelance musician for numerous artists including George Benson; Sonny Rollins; VSOP Band (with Herbie Hancock and Tony Williams); McCoy Tyner; Freddie Hubbard; George Duke; Aretha Franklin; Lena Horne; Jazz teacher, universities in Buffalo, St Louis, New York. *Recordings:* Albums: Out Front, 1966; Uptown Conversation, 1970; Blues Farm, 1973; All Blues, 1974; Magic, 1975; Spanish Blue, 1975; Anything Goes, 1975; Yellow and Green, 1976; Pastels, 1977; Song For You, 1977; Parade, 1979; New York Slick, 1980; Patrao, 1980; Heart and Soul, 1982; Etudes, 1983; Live At Village West, 1984; All Alone, 1989; with Eric Dolphy: Out There, 1960; with Don Ellis: How Time Passes, 1960; with Miles Davis: Seven Steps To Heaven, 1963; Miles In The Sky, 1968; with Herbie Hancock: Maiden Voyage, 1965; Also on numerous recordings by: Roy Ayers; Gato Barbieri; George Benson; Billy Cobham; Chick Corea; Larry Coryell; Miles Davis; Roberta Flack; The Four Tops; Freddie Hubbard; Billy Joel; Quincy Jones; Manhattan Transfer; Diana Ross; Tom Rush; Paul Simon; Grace Slick; Jimmy Smith. *Publications:* Author, books on jazz and classical bass. *Honours:* Downbeat Critics Award, International Jazz Bassist of Year, 1965; Readers Poll Winner, 1973–75, 1983; Detroit Free Press, Jazz Bassist of Decade, 1966; Japan All-Star Jazz Poll Winner, 1969–70; Grammy, Best Jazz Instrumental Composition, 1987. *Membership:* Jazz Musicians' Asscn. *Current Management:* c/o JoAnne Jimenez, The Bridge Agency, 110 Salem Rd, Pound Ridge, NY 10576, USA.

CARTHY, Eliza Amy Forbes; b. 23 Aug. 1975, Scarborough, England. Musician (violin); Folk vocalist; Songwriter. *Career:* Pro, sang with Watersons Cambridge Festival, 1988; Waterdaughters Vancouver Folk Music Festival, 1989; Tours of USA, Australia, England, Germany; TV appearances: Secombe on Sunday, TV Ballads, London Cable 1, later with Jools Holland; ABC Arts Show, Australia; Mountain Stage, USA; Headlined Sidmouth Folk Festival, 1999; Signed major recording deal, 1998. *Compositions:* By Then; The Wrong Favour; Time In the Sun; Peggy; Accordion Song, 1998; Russia, 1998; Red Rice, 1998; Fallen Leaves, 1998. *Recordings:* Albums: Eliza Carthy and Nancy Kerr, 1993; Waterson: Carthy, 1994; Heat, Light and Sound, 1995; Norma Waterson, 1996; Common Tongue, 1997; Eliza Carthy and the Kings of Calicutt, 1997; Red Rice, 1998; Angels and Cigarettes, 2000; On Reflection (with Nancy Kerr), 2002; Anglicana, 2002. *Membership:* Musicians' Union; PRS; Labour Party. *Current Management:* Nigel Morton, Moneypenny Management, 35 Britannia Row, London, England. *Address:* c/o Mrs Casey Music, PO Box 296, Matlock, Derbyshire DE4 3XU, England.

CARTHY, Martin; b. 21 May 1940, Hatfield, Hertfordshire, England. Vocalist; Musician (guitar). m. Norma Waterson. *Career:* Member, skiffle group, The Thameside Four; solo folk artiste, 1963–; Resident musician, Troubadour folk club, London; Member, Three City Four; regular recordings, tours, with Dave Swarbrick; Member, Steeleye Span, 1969–72; Member, Brass Monkey; The Watersons; Keith Hancock Band. *Recordings:* Solo albums: Martin Carthy, 1965; Second Album, 1966; Byker Hill, 1967; But Two Came By (with Dave Swarbrick), 1968; Prince Heathen (with Dave Swarbrick), 1969; Landfall, 1971; This Is Martin Carthy, 1972; Sweet Wivelsfield, 1974; Shearwater, 1975; Crown of Horn, 1976; Because It's There, 1979; Out of The Cut, 1982; Right of Passage, 1989; Life and Limb (with Dave Swarbrick),

1990; Skin and Bone (with Dave Swarbrick), 1992; Kershaw Sessions, 1995; Signs of Life, 1999; Both Ears and The Tail, 2001.

CARTWRIGHT, Deirdre Josephine; b. 27 July 1956, London, England. Musician (guitar); Composer; Author; Teacher. 1 d. *Career:* Guitar Presenter of both series of BBC TV's Rockschool, shown world-wide; Toured 17 countries with guest stars, national tours with own group Deirdre Cartwright Group, 1994–95; Arts Council tour with her eight-piece band, 1996; Concerts, Germany, Switzerland, 1996–97; Co-runs weekly jazz club, Blow the Fuse, at Vortex, North London; Presents new record releases for Jazz Notes, Radio 3; Advisory Panel, Jazz Services. *Recordings:* with The Guest Stars: The Guest Stars; Out At Night; Live In Berlin; One Night Stands, as featured artist, jazz compilation; Debut by with The Deirdre Cartwright Group; Play, second solo CD with Steve Lodder, Annie Whitehead, 1998. *Publications:* Rockschool Books; Rock Guitar Method; The Rockschool Sessions; The Rockfile. *Honours:* Arts Council Composition Award, 1991; Arts Council funded commission, 1996. *Membership:* Musicians' Union; PRS. *Current Management:* Blow The Fuse Records.

CARTY, John; b. 7 Jan. 1962, London, England. Musician (Fiddle, Banjo, Flute). m. Maureen Brennan, 23 May 1987, 1 s., 1 d. *Education:* Taught by Brendan Mulkere, traditional Irish music. *Career:* Moved to Ireland, 1991; First album on banjo, 1994, led to three-album deal; Fiddle release, Last Night's Fun, multi-instrumentalist playing fiddle, banjo and flute; Leading member of band, At the Racket. *Compositions:* Jimmy Batty's, recorded on The Cat That Ate the Candle; Seanamhas Tube Station, recorded on At the Racke. *Recordings:* Albums: The Cat That Ate The Candle, 1994; Last Night's Fun, 1996; At The Racket, 1997. *Current Management:* Racket Management. *Address:* Knockroe, Boyle, Co Roscommon, Ireland.

CASABLANCAS, Julian; b. 23 Aug. 1978, New York, NY, USA. Vocalist; Songwriter. *Education:* L'Institut Le Rosey, Switzerland; Dwight School, Manhattan. *Career:* Mem., The Strokes, 1998–; Band headlined, Reading Festival, 2002. *Recordings:* Albums: Is This It, 2001. Singles: The Modern Age, 2001; Hard To Explain/New York City Cops, 2001; Last Nite/When It Started, 2001. *Honours:* NME Awards, Band of the Year, Best New Act, Album of the Year, 2001; BRIT Award, Best International Newcomer, 2002. *Current Management:* Ryan Gentles, Wiz Kid Management. *Address:* c/o RCA Records, 1540 Broadway, New York, NY 10036, USA. *Website:* www.thestrokes.com.

CASADY, Jack (John); b. 13 April 1944, Washington DC, USA. Musician (bass). *Education:* Montgomery College, Maryland. *Career:* Member, The Triumphs; Member, Jefferson Airplane, 1966–72, 1992; Also member, side project, Hot Tuna, 1968–78; Member, Kantner Balin Casady (KBC) Band, 1985–88, 1992–; Performances include: Berkeley Folk Festival, 1966; Monterey Jazz Festival, 1966; Monterey Pop Festival, 1967; Newport Pop Festival, 1968; Isle of Wight Festival, 1968; Atlantic City Pop Festival, 1969; Woodstock Music and Art Fair, 1969; Altamont Speedway, with Rolling Stones, 1969; Bath Festival, 1970. *Recordings:* Albums: with Jefferson Airplane: Jefferson Airplane Takes Off, 1966; After Bathing At Baxter's, 1968; Crown of Creation, 1968; Volunteers, 1969; Blows Against The Empire, 1970; Bark, 1970; Jefferson Airplane, 1989; Jefferson Airplane Loves You, 1992; with Hot Tuna: Burgers, 1972; The Phosphorescent Rat, 1974; America's Choice, 1975; Yellow Fever, 1975; Hopkorov, 1976; Double Dose, 1977; Pair A Dice Found, 1990; Live At Sweetwater, 1992; Best Of, 1998; And Furthermore, 1999; with KBC Band: KBC Band, 1986; with Jefferson Starship: Deep Space, 1995; Windows of Heaven, 1999; Ignition, 2001; Guest musician: If Only I Could Remember My Name, David Crosby, 1972. *Current Management:* Bill Thompson Management, 2051 Third St, San Francisco, CA 94107, USA.

CASALS, Manu; b. 9 May 1970, France. Sound Engineer; Technical Man. *Education:* University of Nantes; University of Brest. *Career:* Sound Engineer, Live Concerts, Calvin Russel, Denez Prigent, Festival des Vieilles Charrues, Les Fiestas des Hesperides Festival; Sound Engineer, Studio. *Recordings:* Denez Prigent Albums; Philmarie, Matmathah albums; Major Mix in Festival. *Current Management:* La Chapelle and GAM Recording Studio. *Address:* 5 rue du Bac, 4950 Waimes, Belgium and 50 rue des Châlets, 72000 Le Mans, France.

CASEY, Al (Albert A); b. 15 Sept. 1915, Louisville, Kentucky, USA. Musician (guitar). m. Athena Casey, 18 Sept. 1937, 1 s. *Education:* 2 Years at musical school. *Career:* Guitarist for artists including: Fats Waller, Teddy Wilson, King Curtis. *Honours:* Esquire Magazine Award, 1943–44. *Membership:* AFofM, New York City. *Current Management:* Al Wolman, New York, USA. *Address:* 404 W 54th St, Apt 3J, New York, NY, USA.

CASEY, Harry Wayne; b. 31 Jan. 1951, Hialeah, Florida, USA. Musician (keyboards); Vocalist; Prod; Arranger. *Career:* Founder member (as KC), KC and the Sunshine Band, 1973; Writer, arranger, producer, KC and the Sunshine Band; George McCrae; Career interrupted by severe injuries in car crash, 1982. *Recordings:* Albums: Do It Good, 1974; KC and The Sunshine Band, 1975; The Sound of Sunshine, 1975; Part Three, 1976; I Like To Do It,

1977; Who Do Ya Love, 1978; Do You Wanna Go To Party, 1979; Greatest Hits, 1980; Painter, 1981; All In A Night's Work, 1983; The Best Of, 1990; Solo albums: Space Cadet, Wayne Casey/KC, 1981; KC Ten, 1984; US No. 1 hit singles: Get Down Tonight, 1975; That's The Way (I Like It), 1975; Shake Shake Shake, 1976; I'm Your Boogie Man, 1977; UK No. 1 hit single: Give It Up, 1983; Other hits include: Queen of Clubs; Boogie Shoes; Please Don't Go; Yes I'm Ready, duet with Teri De Sario (No. 2, USA). *Current Management:* Saquier Management. *Address:* 4770 Biscayne Blvd, Suite 900, Miami, FL 33137, USA.

CASEY, Howie (Howard William); b. Liverpool, England. Musician (saxophones). m. Sheila, 19 Sept. 1980, 1 d. *Education:* Army Band Kings Regiment. *Career:* Recording, live concerts with: Paul McCartney; Wings (Over The World), 1975–76, 1980; The Who; ABC; Chuck Berry; Jimmy Ruffin; Cliff Richard; Lee Dorsey; PAL (Paice, Ashton, Lord); Roy Young Band; Mark Bolan; Les Humphries Singers. *Recordings:* with Wings: Band On The Run; Wings At The Speed of Sound; Back To The Egg; Wings Over America; Rockestra; Albums with: ABC; Marc Bolan; PAL; Gilbert O'Sullivan; Cliff Richard; Elkie Brooks; Ashton, Gardner, Dyke; The Who. *Membership:* PRS; Musicians' Union. *Address:* 36 R L Stevenson Ave, Bournemouth, Dorset BH4 8EG, England.

CASEY, Karan; b. 5 April 1968, Waterford, Ireland. Vocalist. *Career:* Began performing in Waterford; Moved to Dublin, 1987; Relocated to New York, 1993; Joined Solas; Solo artist, 1997–; Involved with Africans in America TV documentary; Currently touring. *Recordings:* with Solas: Solas, 1996; Sunny Spells and Scattered Showers, 1997; The Words That Remain, 1998; solo: Songlines, 1997; Fused (with Mike McGoldrick), 2000; The Seal Maiden, 2000; The Winds Begin To Sing, 2001. *Honours:* Won 3 NAIRD/AFIM indie awards with Solas; Grammy Award, Best New Age Album, Celtic Solstice, Paul Winter and Friends, 2000. *Current Management:* Tom Sherlock Management, Carysfort Ave, Blackrock, County Dublin, Ireland. *E-mail:* sherlock@altan.ie. *Website:* www.karancasey.com.

CASH, Johnny (John R.); b. 26 Feb. 1932, Kingsland, Arkansas, USA. Country Vocalist; Musician (guitar); Songwriter; Entertainer; Actor. m. June Carter, 1968, 1 s., 4 d. (by previous marriage). *Education:* HHD, Gardner Webb College, 1971; National University, San Diego, 1975. *Career:* Composer, solo recording artist, 1955–; Also member of occasional side-project The Highwaymen (with Kris Kristofferson, Waylon Jennings, Willie Nelson), 1985–; Television includes: Johnny Cash Show, 1969–71; Subject of documentaries including: Johnny Cash, The Man, His World, His Music; Johnny Cash At San Quentin; Actor, films: A Gunfight; North and South; Stagecoach; Television films: The Baron and The Kid; The Last Days of Frank and Jesse; Other television appearances: Columbo; Dr Quinn – Medicine Woman; President, House of Cash Inc; Songs of Cash Inc; Vice-President, Family of Man Music Inc; Collaborations: Ray Charles; Rodney Crowell; Bob Dylan; Emmylou Harris; Kris Kristofferson; Mark O'Connor; Marty Stuart; U2. *Compositions include:* The True West (documentary record); The Gospel Road (co-writer, producer, narrator); Movie soundtracks: I Walk The Line; Little Fauss and Big Halsy. *Recordings:* Over 150 albums, live recordings and compilations, 1957–; Albums include: The Fabulous Johnny Cash, 1959; Ride This Train, 1960; Ring of Fire, 1963; Orange Blossom Special, 1965; Johnny Cash At Folsom Prison, 1968; Johnny Cash At San Quentin (No. 1, USA), 1969; Hello, I'm Johnny Cash, 1970; Man In Black, 1971; One Piece At A Time, 1976; Water From The Wells of Home, 1988; The Mystery of Life, 1991; American Recordings, 1994; Unchained, 1996; Just As I Am, 1999; American III – Solitary Man, 2000; with The Highwaymen: The Highwayman, 1985; Highwaymen 2, 1990; Man In Black: The Very Best Of Johnny Cash, 2002; The Man Comes Around, 2002. Hit singles include: I Walk The Line, 1956; There You Go, 1957; Ballad of a Teenage Queen, 1958; Guess Things Happen That Way, 1958; Ring of Fire, 1963; A Boy Named Sue, 1969; If I Were A Carpenter (duet with June Carter Cash), 1970; A Thing Called Love, 1972. *Publications:* Man In Black, 1975; Man In White (novel), 1986. *Honours:* CMA Award, Best Album, 1968; Grammy Awards: Best Country Duet (with June Carter Cash), 1968, 1971; Best Country Vocal Performance, 1969, 1970; Best Country Song, 1970, 1986; Best Album Notes, 1969, 1970; Best Spoken Word Recording, 1987; Living Legend Award, 1990; 4 UK Country Music Awards, 1970; Special Award of Merit, American Music Awards, 1977; LHD (Hon), National University San Diego, 1976; Inducted into Country Music Hall of Fame, 1980; Aggie Award, Songwriters Guild of America, 1989; Inducted into Rock 'n' Roll Hall of Fame, 1992. *Membership:* Country Music Asscn. *Address:* Suite 118, 5743 Corsa Ave, Westlake Vill, CA 91362, USA.

CASH, June Carter; b. 23 June 1929, Maces Springs, Virginia, USA. Vocalist; Actress. m. Johnny Cash, 1 March 1968, 1 s., 6 d. *Education:* Actor's Studio, New York. *Career:* Singer, Carter family, 1939–43; Carter Sisters, 1943–; Solo artiste; Duo with Johnny Cash, 1963–; Television includes: Johnny Cash Show; Grand Ole Opry; Tennessee Ernie Show; Television films: Stagecoach; The Baron; Gospel Road; Road To Nashville; Television special: The Best of The Carter Family; Television series: Dr Quinn – Medicine Woman (played Dr Ruth); Entertains as singer, actress, musician (guitar, banjo, auto-harp), comedienne. *Recordings:* Songs include: Baby It's Cold Outside; Music Music Music; Love Oh Crazy Love; Let Me Go Lover;

Contributions to recordings by Johnny Cash including: Jackson Duo; If I Were A Carpenter; with Carter family: Wabash Cannon; May The Circle Be Unbroken; Solo album: Press On, 1999. *Publications:* Author: Among My Kledaments, 1979; From The Heart, 1987; Wildwood Flower, screenplay, 1990; Mother Maybelle's Cookbook, 1992; Co-author, Ring of Fire. *Honours:* HHD (Hon), National University, San Diego, 1977; Civic Award, Nashville Women Executives, 1980; Grammy Awards: Best Country Duo Performance (with Johnny Cash), 1968, 1971; CMA Duet Artists of the Year, with Johnny Cash; Virginian of Year, 1989. *Membership:* ASCAP; Grand Ole Opry; Country Music Asscn. *Current Management:* Lou Robin, Artist Consultants Productions, Suite 670, 11777 San Vicente Blvd, Los Angeles, CA 90049, USA.

CASH, Roseanne; b. 24 May 1955, Memphis, Tennessee, USA. Vocalist. m. Rodney Crowell, 1979, divorced. *Education:* Drama, Vanderbilt University; Method acting, Lee Strasberg's Institute, Los Angeles. *Career:* Worked 3 years with (father) Johnny Cash's road show; Worked with Rodney Crowell, Nashville; Recording artiste, 1979–; Collaborations include: Mary Chapin Carpenter; Marc Cohn; Vince Gill; John Hiatt; Lyle Lovett; Carly Simon. *Recordings:* Hit singles include: No Memories Hangin' Round (with Bobby Bare); Couldn't Do Nothin' Right; Take Me Take Me; Never Be You; I Don't Know Why You Don't Want Me (co-written with Rodney Crowell); The Way We Make A Broken Heart; Tennessee Flat Top Box; If You Change Your Mind; Rainway Train; Albums include: Roseanne Cash, 1978; Right Or Wrong, 1979; Seven Year Ache, 1981; Somewhere In The Stars, 1982; Rhythm and Romance, 1985; King's Record Shop, 1988; Hits 1979–89, 1989; Interiors, 1990; The Wheel, 1993; Retrospective, 1995; 10 Song Demo, 1996; What Kinda Girl (live), 1999. *Honours:* Grammy, Best Country Vocal Performance Female, 1985; Top Single Artist Award, Billboard, 1988. *Current Management:* Side One Management, 1026A Third Ave, New York, NY 10021, USA.

CASH, Tommy; b. 5 April 1940, Dyess, Arkansas, USA. Professional Entertainer; Musician (rhythm guitar). m. (1) Barbara Wisenbaker, 18 Aug. 1961, 1 s., 1 d.; (2) Pamela Dyer, 12 March 1978. *Education:* Radio Broadcast School; Real estate school (Realtor); College courses: Tennessee Tech. *Career:* All major country music television shows, many network television programmes; Radio announcer, 1959–64, including: American Forces Network, Germany, 1959–62; Music publisher, 1965–; Professional entertainer, 1965–; Songwriter, songs recorded by: Conway Twitty; Kitty Wells; Faron Young; Jean Sheppard; Johnny Cash; Loretta Lynn; Music published by Tomcat Music, BMI. *Recordings:* More than 20 albums, approximately 65 singles, 1965–; Hits include: Six White Horses, 1970; Rise and Shine; That Certain One; So This Is Love; Gypsy Woman; Gospel album: This Happy Heart of Mine, 1995. *Honours:* Two BMI Awards for Songwriting, 1965, 1975; Music City News Most Promising Vocalist, 1970. *Membership:* AFofM, Nashville; AFTRA, Nashville; National Asscn of Realtors; ROPE Inc. *Current Management:* Joe Taylor, AGN Nashville; Billy Deaton Talent Nashville. *Address:* Hendersonville, Tennessee, USA.

CASSIDY, David; b. 12 April 1950, New York, NY, USA. Actor; Vocalist. *Career:* Actor, The Partridge Family television series; Lead vocalist, Partridge Family recordings; Solo artiste, 1971–; Actor, Joseph and The Amazing Technicolour Dreamcoat; Lead role, musical, Time, 1987. *Recordings:* Albums: Cherish, 1972; Could It Be Forever, 1972; Rock Me Baby, 1972; Dreams Are Nothin' More, 1973; Cassidy Live, 1974; The Higher They Climb, 1975; Greatest Hits, 1977; Romance, 1985; His Greatest Hits, Live, 1986; Didn't You Used To Be…, 1992; Old Trick, New Dog, 1998; Then and Now, 2001; Singles include: with The Partridge Family: I Think I Love You (No. 1, USA), 1970; Solo: Cherish (No. 1, USA), 1971; Could It Be Forever, 1972; How Can I Be Sure? (No. 1, UK), 1972; I Am A Clown, 1973; Daydreamer/The Puppy Song (No. 1, UK), 1973; The Last Kiss, 1985. *Current Management:* c/o Larry Lerner, 20501 Ventura Blvd, Suite 392, Woodland Hills, CA 91364, USA.

CASSWELL, Michael; b. 18 June 1966, Romford, Essex, England. Musician (guitar). *Education:* Art College. *Career:* Signed to RCA America, album, 1986; MCA Records, 2 albums, 1989; Toured in Brian May Band, Back to the Light tour, 1992. *Recordings:* Heroes, 1986; Walk On Fire, 1989. *Membership:* PRS; Musicians' Union. *Current Management:* Agent: Session Connection, Brenda Brooker, RAK Records. *Address:* Angel Cottage, Manor Rd, Lambourne End, Romford, Essex RM4 1NH, England.

CASTLE, Pete; b. 25 Feb. 1947, Ashford, Kent, England. Folk Vocalist; Musician (guitar); Writer. m. Sue Brown, 27 April 1967, 1 s., 1 d. *Education:* Maidstone Technical High School; Bretton Hall College of Education. *Career:* Organizer of Luton Folk Festival, 1976–78; Solo artist, working at clubs, festivals, in schools and on community projects, 1978–; Presenter, Chiltern Radio Folk Show, 1981–87; Collaboration with Aroti Biswas, 1987; Mountsorrel Community Play, 1993; Launched the occasional band Popeluc, 1994; Ed., Facts & Fiction Storytelling Magazine 1999–. *Recordings include:* Bedfordshire Folk Songs, 1981; Rambling Robin, 1982; Punk's Delight, 1985; One Morning By Chance, 1989; Cottage By the Shore, 1992; Two Tongues One Voice, 1994; Keys of Canterbury, 1994; Maramures Et Cetera, 1994; Falsewaters, 1995; Blue Dor, 1996; Mearcstapa, 1999; The Jenny & the Frame & the Mule, 2000. *Membership:* Musicians' Union; PRS; MCPS;

Society for Storytelling. *Address:* 190 Burton Rd, Derby DE1 1TQ, England. *Website:* www.folkmusic.net/petecastle.

CASTLE-HOTEA, Lucy Katherine; b. 15 Feb. 1970, Lincolnshire, England. Musician (fiddle); Ethnomusicologist. m. Ioan Castle-Hotea, 1 d. *Education:* BSc, City University, London. *Career:* Founded, Trio Popeluc with Father Pete Casre and Romanian Musician Ioan Pop, Toured Britain, Romania; Teacher of Violin; Performs with her Husband. *Recordings:* The Broken Pledge; Maramures Et Cetera; Popeuic Live; Blue Dor. *Membership:* ESTA. *Current Management:* Steel Carpet Music, 190 Burton Rd, Derby DE1 1TQ, England. *Address:* 6A Darley St, Darley Abbey, Derby, DE22 1DX.

CATER, Pete; b. 8 Feb. 1963, Lichfield, Staffordshire, England. Musician (drums); Bandleader; Teacher. *Career:* Tour world-wide, with Elaine Delmar in Thank You Mr Gershwin; Played with Arturo Sandoval Quintet; Pete Cater Big Band; Sheena Davis Group; Spike Robinson Group; Rickey Woodard Quartet; Charlie Byrd Trio; Gene Bertoncinni Trio; Freelance session player with: BBC; ITV; Channel 4; BBC Big Band; NYJO; A Ross; Val Doonican; Dave Willetts; S Maughan; Herb Miller Orchestra. *Recordings:* Upswing, with Pete Carter Big Band; Playing With Fire, with Pete Carter Big Band. *Honours:* Outstanding drummer, BBC Radio 2 National Big Band Competition, 1980, 1991; Best Big Band, British Jazz Awards, 2000. *Membership:* Faculty mem., Musicians' Institute, London. *Address:* PO Box 123, Borehamwood, Herts WD6 3ZG, England.

CATLEY, Bob; Vocalist. *Career:* Founder member, lead vocalist, UK rock group Magnum, 1972–; Support tours with: Judas Priest; Whitesnake; Blue Öyster Cult; Def Leppard; Own headline tours world-wide. *Recordings:* Albums: Kingdom of Madness, 1978; Magnum II, 1979; Marauder, 1980; Chase The Dragon, 1982; The Eleventh Hour, 1983; On A Storyteller's Night, 1985; Vigilante, 1986; Wings of Heaven, 1988; Goodnight LA, 1990; The Spirit, 1991; Rock Art, 1994; Stronghold, 1997; Archive, 2000; Numerous compilation albums; Singles include: Kingdom of Madness, 1978; Just Like An Arrow, 1985; On A Storyteller's Night, 1985; Midnight, 1986; Days of No Trust; 1988; Start Talking Love, 1988; It Must Have Been Love, 1988; Rocking Chair, 1990.

CATLEY, Marc; b. 3 Nov. 1959, Birmingham, England. Vocalist; Songwriter; Musician (guitar); Satirist. *Education:* Liverpool University; London Bible College. *Career:* First solo progressive rock album Classical Acoustic Rock, 1986; Numerous radio interviews and airplay in Europe and USA; 4 albums, religious satire with band The Flaming Methodists, 1991–; Television and radio appearances include: Granada TV and Radio 4; Formed progressive rock band Paley's Watch, 1993. *Compositions:* Char, 1996. *Recordings:* Progressive rock albums: with Geoff Mann: The Off The End of The Pier Show, 1991; Fine Difference, 1992; with Paley's Watch: November, 1994; Satirical albums: Peel of Hope, 1991; Make The Tea, 1992; Hot Air For Jesus, 1993; No Tomorrow, 1994. *Membership:* MCPS; PRS; BAC&S; Musicians' Union. *Current Management:* Plankton Records; Sandcastle Productions. *Address:* 236 Sebert Rd, Forest Gate, London E7 0NP, England.

CATO, Pauline; b. 14 Dec. 1968, Ashington, Northumberland, England. Musician (Northumbrian pipes, keyboards). *Education:* BA, Modern Languages, Sheffield University, 1991; PGCE 1992, Sheffield University; Grade 8 piano; Taught Northumbrian Pipes by Richard Butler, piper to the Duke of Northumberland. *Career:* Member, Border Spirit, 1988–90; Solo artiste, 1990–94; Cullercoats Tommy (opera), with Northern Sinfonia Orchestra, 1993; Became full-time musician, 1993; Also working in duo with fiddler Tom McConville; Television and radio appearances: Small Folk, YTV/ Channel 4, 1989; Several Radio 2/3 features; Performed on BBC drama series soundtrack, Badger; AHRB Research Fellow in Creative and Performing Arts, Sheffield University, 2002–. *Recordings:* Hindley Steel, Border Spirit, 1988; Solo albums: The Wansbeck Piper, 1992; Changing Tides, 1994; Various recordings as session musician; By Land and Sea, with Tom McConville, 1996; The Surprise, with Tom McConville, Chris Newman and Maggie Boyle, 1999. *Publications:* Pauline Cato's Northumbrian Choice, with recordings, 1997. *Honours:* Appointed Piper to Mayor of Gateshead, 1989; Hon. Mem., Northumbrian Pipers Society, for Services to Piping; Young Tradition Award Finalist, BBC, 1990; Daily Telegraph Folk Album of the Year, 1996, 1999. *Address:* Tomcat Music, PO Box 2100, Sheffield S36 9BW, England. *Website:* www.tomcatmusic.com.

CATTERMOLE, Paul; b. 7 March 1977, St Albans, England. Vocalist; Actor. *Education:* Mountview Drama School; National Youth Music Theatre. *Career:* Former mem., rock band, Skua; Acted in numerous stage productions; Mem., S Club 7, 1998–2002; Group quickly achieved international success, following sales of TV series Miami 7, 1999, LA 7, 2000, and Hollywood 7, 2001, featuring the band's music, to nearly 100 countries; Also made nature TV series S Club 7 Go Wild, 2000, and various TV specials; First British tour with S Club 7, 2001; Band renamed S Club, 2001; Solo artiste, 2002–. *Recordings:* Albums: S Club, 1999; 7 (No. 1, UK), 2000; Sunshine, 2001. Singles: Bring It All Back (No. 1, UK), 1999; S Club Party, 1999; Two In A Million/You're My Number One, 1999; Reach, 2000; Natural, 2000; Never Had A Dream Come True (No. 1, UK), 2000; Don't Stop Movin' (No. 1, UK), 2001;

Have You Ever (No. 1, UK), 2001. *Honours:* BRIT Award, Best British Newcomer, 2000. *Current Management:* 19 Management, Unit 32, Ransomes Dock, 35–37 Parkgate Rd, London SW11 4NP, England.

CATTINI, Clem; b. 28 Aug. 1939, London, England. Musician (drums). m. Anna, 17 May 1958, 3 d. *Career:* Member, Johnny Kidd and the Pirates; Tornados; Top of the Pops Orchestra (12 years); Toured with: Sir Cliff Richard; Kids From Fame; Lulu; Grace Kennedy; The Drifters; Liza Minnelli; Sandie Shaw; Tom Jones; Engelbert Humperdinck; Television: Michael Barrymore; Lulu; Michael Jackson; Stevie Wonder; Gladys Knight. *Recordings:* Johnny Kidd and the Pirates: Please Don't Touch, 1960; Shakin' All Over, 1971; Tornados: Sound Of; Telstar; More Sounds From; Tornado Rock; Away From It All, 1962–64; Everlasting Love; Devil Woman; Musician on: Roy Harper: Folkjokeopus, 1969; Joe Cocker: With A Little Help From My Friends, 1969; P J Proby: 3 Week Hero, 1969; Bee Gees: To Whom It May Concern, 1972; Lou Reed: Lou Reed, 1972; Phil Everly: Phil's Diner, 1974; Recorded with: Kinks; Dusty Springfield; Lulu; Tom Jones; Engelbert Humperdinck; Gene Pitney; Other albums by: Cliff Richard; Hank Marvin; Justin Hayward; Brian Auger; Claire Hamill; Jimmy Page; Albert Lee; John Paul Jones; Alan Price; Played on 42 No. 1s. *Honours:* Gold Disc, Gold Globe (Telstar); Cup NME Poll Winners (Tornados). *Membership:* Musicians' Union; PRS; MCPS. *Address:* 15 Blenheim Close, London N21 2HQ, England.

CAUDEL, Stephen; b. 29 June 1955, Sheffield, South Yorkshire, England. Composer; Musician (guitar). m. Shelagh Quinn, 17 Dec. 1983, 1 s. *Education:* Classical, Jazz, Light Music, City of Leeds College of Music. *Career:* Numerous television and radio appearances; Concert tours: UK including Royal Albert Hall; Overseas tours including Japan. *Compositions:* Wine Dark Sea (rock symphony, world premiere, London, 1983); Edel Rhapsody, for Wagner Tuba and Orchestra, (world premiere, Carlisle, 1993); The Earth In Turquoise. *Recordings:* Albums: Wine Dark Sea; Bow of Burning Gold; Impromptu Romance; The Earth In Turquoise; Featured guitarist on Hooked On Classics II, with Royal Philharmonic Orchestra. *Membership:* PRS; MCPS; Musicians' Union. *Current Management:* Mr Laurie Mansfield. *Address:* PO Box 2, Brampton CA8 2GB, England. *Website:* www.progressive-rock.com.

CAUSTIC WINDOW. See: **APHEX TWIN.**

CAUTY, Jimi; b. 1954. Musician (guitar). *Career:* Member, Brilliant, 1983–86; Co-founder, KLF Communications, with Bill Drummond, 1987–92; Organized music projects under names: JAMs; Disco 2000; The Justified Ancients of Mu Mu; The Timelords; KLF; Founder, own recording studio, Trancentral, 1988; Appearances include DMC European Convention, Amsterdam, 1990; Film: The White Room, 1988. *Recordings:* Albums: with Brilliant: Kiss The Lips of Life, 1985; as JAMs: 1987, 1987; Shag Times (compilation), 1989; as KLF: The What Time Is Love Story, 1989; Chill Out, 1990; The White Room, 1991; Solo album (as Space): Space, 1990; Singles include: with Brilliant: It's A Man's Man's Man's World, 1985; Love Is War, 1986; Somebody, 1986; as JAMs: All You Need Is Love, 1987; Whitney Joins The Jams, 1987; Downtown, 1987; Who Killed The JAMs, 1988; as Disco 2000: I Gotta CD, 1987; Uptight, 1989; as The Timelords: Doctorin' The Tardis (No. 1, UK), 1988; as KLF: Burn The Beat, 1988; Kylie Said To Jason, 1989; What Time Is Love, 1990; 3AM Eternal (No. 1, UK), 1991; Last Train To Trancentral, 1991; as The Justified Ancients of Mu Mu: It's Grim Up North, 1991; Justified and Ancient, with Tammy Wynette, 1992; as 2K: Fuck The Millennium, 1997; Other collaborations: The Orb, 1989–91; The Black Dog, 1999. *Publications:* The Manual (How To Have A Number One Hit The Easy Way), 1988. *Honours:* BRIT Award, Best British Group (shared with Simply Red), 1992.

CAVALERA, Max; b. 4 Aug. 1969, Belo Horizonte, Brazil. Rock Musician (guitar, percussion); Vocalist. m. Gloria Cavalera, 6 June 1993, 4 s., 1 d. *Career:* Member, Brazilian heavy rock group Sepultura, 1984–97; World-wide tours including USA, Brazil, Russia, Indonesia; Support tours with The Ramones, Ministry, Ozzy Osbourne; Concerts include: Rock in Rio, Brazil; Hollywood Rock, Brazil; Monsters of Rock Festival, Castle Donington, UK; Dynamo Open Air Festival, Netherlands; Roskilde Festival, Denmark; Television appearances: The Word (UK); MTV Most Wanted (UK); Side project, Nailbomb 1994–95; Formed new band, Soulfly, 1997–. *Compositions:* Bleed; Tribe; Eye for an Eye. *Recordings:* Albums: with Sepultura: Morbid Visions, 1985; Schizophrenia, 1988; Beneath The Remains, 1989; Arise, 1991; Chaos AD, 1993; Roots, 1996; Nativity In Black (Black Sabbath tribute); Virus 100 (Dead Kennedys tribute); Tales From The Crypt (soundtrack); Under the Sun, for Nativity in Black II; Nailbomb albums: Point Blank, 1994; Proud To Commit Commercial Suicide, 1995; with Soulfly: Soulfly, 1998; Primitive, 2000. *Honours:* 2 MTV South America Awards; Best Album, Kerrang! magazine, UK, 1994; Best New Band, France. *Membership:* ASCAP; National Wildlife Organization; Co-Founder, Iggy Diabetes Fund. *Current Management:* Gloria Cavalera, Oasis Management, 3010 E Bloomfield, Phoenix, AZ 85032, USA.

CAVALERI, Nathan Michael; b. 18 June 1982, Camden, NSW, Australia. Musician (guitar). *Education:* St Gregory's College, Campbelltown, NSW, Australia. *Career:* San Francisco Blues Festival, with Albert Collins, 1992;

Toured with B. B. King, special guest, 1995; 25th Birthday for Guitar Player magazine; Kennedy Lifetime Achievement Awards, honouring B. B. King, 1995; Out In The Green Festival, Zurich, 1995; Tours, with Jimmy Barnes of Diesel, Australia; Appeared on: Arsenio Hall; Inside Edition; Good Morning America; Conan O'Brian; CNN; Hey Hey It's Saturday Australia; Midday Australia; MMM Network; Radio Australia; Camp Nowhere The Film; Baywatch Nights; Australia Music Awards; Entertainment Network Australia; Commercial for MacDonalds with B. B. King, 1995. *Compositions include:* Song, Lou's Blues, used in Free Willy 2 film soundtrack. *Recordings:* Albums: Jammin' With The Cats (5 co-written songs), 1994; Nathan (6 co-written songs). *Honours:* Variety Club, Australia, Young Variety award, 1993; BMW Jazz and Blues Best New Talent, 1993; Young Australian Achiever, 1994. *Membership:* SAG. *Current Management:* CAA Agency, Linchpin-Russell Hayward, Los Angeles, California. *Address:* 2512 Zorada Dr., Los Angeles, CA 90046, USA.

CAVANAUGH, Page; b. 26 Jan. 1922, Cherokee, Kansas, USA. Musician (piano); Vocalist; Entertainer. *Education:* Private teachers. *Career:* Performed as pianist, vocalist, in films: Record Party, 1947; Romance On The High Seas (2 songs on screen with Doris Day), 1947; A Song Is Born (1 song with Virginia Mayo), 1947; Big City (2 songs with Betty Garret), 1947; Lullaby of Broadway (Song with: Gene Nelson: Zing Went The Strings of My Heart; with Doris Day and Gene: You're Getting to Be A Habit With Me), 1950. *Recordings:* Albums: with Michael Feinstein: Crazy Rhythm; Pure Imagination; with Page Cavanaugh Trio: Digital Page; Page One; Page Two, 1993; The Three Bears; All of Me; Walking My Baby Back Home; Page Cavanaugh Plays For The Cocktail Hour; Something's Happening At Page Cavanaugh's. *Membership:* NAOL; Society of Singers. *Address:* 5442 Woodman Ave, Sherman Oaks, CA 91401, USA.

CAVE, Nick; b. 22 Sept. 1957, Australia. Vocalist; Songwriter; Actor. *Career:* Member, Birthday Party (formerly Boys Next Door), early 1980s; Founder, Nick Cave and The Bad Seeds; Actor, films include: Wings of Desire, 1987; Ghosts of The Civil Dead, 1989. *Recordings:* Albums: with Birthday Party: Prayers On Fire, 1981; Junkyard, 1982; The Bad Seed/Mutiny, 1989; Hee-Haw, 1989; with The Bad Seeds: From Here To Eternity, 1984; The First Born Is Dead, 1985; Kicking Against The Pricks, 1986; Your Funeral, My Trial, 1986; Tender Prey, 1988; Ghost of The Civil Dead, 1989; The Good Son, 1990; Henry's Dream, 1992; Live Seeds, 1993; Let Love In, 1994; Murder Ballads, 1996; The Boatman's Call, 1997; The Very Best of Nick Cave and The Bad Seeds, 1998; No More Shall We Part, 2001; Albums of poetry: The Secret Life of The Love Song/The Flesh Made Word, 1998; And The Ass Saw The Angel; Singles: with Birthday Party: Fiend Catcher; Release The Collaborations, with Lydia Lunch and Einsturzende Neubaten; with the Bad Seeds: In The Ghetto, 1984; Tupelo, 1985; The Singer, 1985; The Mercy Seat, 1988; Oh Deanna, 1988; The Ship Song, 1990; The Weeping Song, 1990; Straight To You, 1992; I Had A Dream Joe, 1992; What A Wonderful World, duet with Shane MacGowan, 1992; Do You Love Me?, 1994; Loverman, 1994; Red Right Hand, 1994; Where The Wild Roses Grow, duet with Kylie Minogue, 1995; Henry Lee, duet with PJ Harvey, 1996; Into My Arms, 1997; Are You The One That I've Been Waiting For?, 1997; As I Sat Sadly By Her Side, 2001; Fifteen Feet of Pure White Snow, 2001; Contributor, film soundtrack, Batman Forever, 1995. *Publications:* And The Ass Saw The Angel (novel), 1989; King Ink (collection of lyrics and verse); King Ink II. *Current Management:* Rayner Jesson at Tender Prey, Studio 4, Ivebury Court, 325 Latimer Rd, London W10 6RA, England.

CAZES, Henrique; b. 2 Feb. 1959, Rio de Janeiro, Brazil. Musician (cavaquinho, acoustic guitar, banjo); Prod; Arranger. m. Maria A C L Fernandes, 2 s. *Education:* Classes in harmony and arrangement with Ian Guest. *Career:* Worked with Radames Gnatelli, 7 years; Tours as cavaquinho soloist: Japan, 1985–90; USA, 1988, 1990; Europe, 1993; Founder member, Orchestra Brazilian Strings; Creator, director, Brasília Orchestra; Carrefour Mondial de la Guitare, Martinique. *Recordings include:* Henrique Cazes, 1988; Henrique Cazes – Tocando Waldir Azevedo, 1990; Henrique Cazes – Waldir Azevedo, Pixinguinha, Hermeto and Cia, 1992; Cristina Buarque e Henrique Cazes Sem Tostao, 1994; Henrique Cazes and The Guitar Family – Since The Choro Is Choro, 1995; Also appears on: Deixa Clarear, 1996; Rhythm and Romance, 1998. *Publications:* Text book Escola Moderna de Cavaquinho. *Honours:* Sharp Awards: 1991, 1992, 1995; Number One Cavaquinho of The World, Japan, 1990. *Membership:* AMAR (Brazilian Asscn of Arrangers and Conductors). *Current Management:* C Fernandes. *Address:* Paulo Barreto, No. 25/802 Botafogo, 22280–010 Rio de Janeiro, RJ, Brazil.

CECA, (Svetlana Raznatovic née Velickovic); b. Serbia. Vocalist. m. Zeljko Raznatovic, 1995, deceased 2000, 2 c. *Career:* Solo artiste, singing modern Serbian folk music; First record deal at 14 years old; Concert, Red Star Stadium, Belgrade, 2002. *Recordings:* Albums: Cvetak Zanovetak, 1988; Ludo Srce, 1989; To Miki, 1990; Babaroga, 1991; Sta Je To U Tvojim Venama, 1993; Ja Još Spavam U Tvojoj Majici, 1994; Fatalna Ljubav, 1995; Emotivna Luda, 1996; Maskarada, 1998; Album 2000, 2000; Decenija, 2001; Jedna Je..., 2001.

CECCARELLI, Andre; b. 5 Jan. 1946, Nice, France. Musician (drums). m. Marcelle Ritling, 8 April 1968, 1 s. *Education:* Music Academy of France. *Career:* Member, Les Chats Suavages, 1961; Worked with Aime Barelli, Monte Carlo, 1964; Played with Rocky Roberts and the Piranas, 1966–68; Freelance musician, 1968–; Worked with artists including: Brian Auger; Tania Maria; Tina Turner; Michel Legrand; Bireli Lagrene; Mike Stern; Tom Harle. *Recordings:* with Ceccarelli Trio: Hat Snatcher; Three Around The Floor; with Dee Dee Bridgewater: Keeping Traditions; Love and Peace; with Tina Turner: Love Explosion; with Tania Maria: Live In Copenhagen; with M Portal: Turbulence; Also recorded with: Michel Legrand and Stéphane Grappelli; Aretha Franklin; Tom Harrell and Bob Berg; Paul Mauriat; Bireli Lagrene and NHOP; Enrico Pieranunzi and H Van De Glyn; Brian Auger; Johnny Mercer; Richard Galliano. *Honours:* Django D'Or, Best Jazz Group, 1993; Victoire de la Musique, Best Jazz Album, 1993; Aigle D'Argent, Nice. *Membership:* SACEM; ADAMI; SPEDIDAM. *Current Management:* Isoard Christiane and Sola Thierry. *Address:* 22 rue Ernest Revillon, 77630 Barbizon, France.

CECH, Christoph; b. 29 June 1960, Vienna, Austria. Composer; Arranger; Musician (keyboards, orchestral percussion). m. Ursula, 5 March 1988, 3 s. *Education:* Matriculation/studies in Architecture, Technical University, Vienna; Studies in piano, rhythmic, orchestral percussion, jazz theory, composition, Vienna Conservatory. *Career:* Jazz fairy tale, F F Company and Co (co-composer with Christian Mühlbacher), 1987; TV production, (ORF), 1993; Concert number 1 for piano and orchestra, radio production (ORF), 1994; Suite for doublebass, bass clarinet and 15 players, The Musikvereinshall, Vienna; Many tours with different ensembles; Teacher, Harmonics and Counterpoint, University of Music, Vienna, 1998–; Leader, Jazz and popular music, Bruckner Conservatory, Linz, 1999–. *Compositions:* Chamber opera, Die Befreiung Des Modulors, State Theatre Schwerin, Germany, 1988; Protophantasm, Concerto Grosso for big band and orchestra; Opera, Aus Allen Blüten Bitternis, Chamber Opera, Vienna, 1996; B.A.C.H. Kantate, Dom St Pölten, 1997; Requiem, 1998; Bruckner Festival, Linz, 1998; Cantata das lied der lieder, 1999; Music Actual; Triple Concerto, Musikvereins Hall, Vienna. *Recordings:* with Nouvelle Cuisine Big Band: Flambée, 1988, 1989; Elephant Terrine, 1990; Phrygian Flight, 1994; Ultimate Sentences, 1997; with Striped Roses: Bonsai Beat, 1990; Insection, 1994; Tulpen, 1997; Solo: Mondautos, 1993; with Jubilo Elf: Missing Link, 1991; with Camerata Obscura, Batpulse, 1997; in duo with Bertl Mütter, Lohgesang, 1997; Requiem, 1998. *Publications:* Keyboard 1–4, 1991. *Honours:* Stipendium for Composition, City of Vienna, 1987, 1995; First Prize, Kunstpreis Leibnitz, Austria, 1994; State Stipendium, Austrian Republic, 1995; Austro Mechana Publicity Prize, 1997. *Address:* Schottenfeldgasse 61/16, 1070 Vienna, Austria.

CECH, Vladimir; b. 22 March 1944, Brno. m. Alena Benesová, 29 Aug. 1975, 1 s. *Education:* Diploma Engineer, Technical University, Brno, 1970; Graduated, Faculty of Musicology and Theatrology, Brno, Masaryka University. *Career:* Regular programmes on Musical and Theatre Life, Radio Brno; Author, Speaker, public playbacks of classical and pop music; Contributions: Regularly to Brno, Prague, Vienna newspapers, especially Slovo, BT – Rovnist, Opus Musicum. *Publications:* Regular reports on music life in Czech Republic, Vienna. *Honours:* Prize, Czech Music Foundation, 1984–90. *Address:* Drobného 16, 602 00 Brno, Czech Republic.

CELLIER, Marcel; b. 29 Oct. 1925, Zurich, Switzerland. Musical Editor. m. Catherine, 15 May 1953, 3 s. *Education:* Studied cello and Ethnomusicology about Eastern Europe. *Career:* Producer, Radio Suisse Romande, 1961–95; ORTF/Radio France, BR Munich, RDRS Zurich-Berne, WDR Cologne; Producer of 4 sound carriers with Gheorghe Zamfir as well as 4 with Mystère des Voix Bulgares. *Recordings:* Albanian, Hungarian, Romanian and Bulgarian folk music and vocal art. *Honours:* Grand Prix et Disque d'or de l'Academie Ch Cros, Paris; Critics Prize, Music Critics of Germany; Grand Prix Audiovisuel de l'Academie Française du Disque; Grammy Award, 1990. *Membership:* Rotary; ICTM; Vice-President, GVS Gesellschaft für Volksmusik in der Schweiz. *Address:* Rue du Bourg-de-Plait, 1605 Chexbres, Switzerland.

CERMAK, Zappa (Johann Leopold); b. 7 July 1949, Heidenreichstein, Austria. Musician (guitar, drums, percussion, harmonica); Vocalist. m. Erika. *Education:* VSA; HSA; Forestry technician. *Career:* Began as: Blues Zappa, 1974–76; Original member, Bluespumpm, 1975; Parallel project with Fritz Glatzl as Blues Zappa and Pumpm Fritz (also with Johannes Müller); Major tours, most European countries; Radio, television: Austria; Slovakia; Slovenia; Hungary; Czech Republic. *Recordings:* with Bluespumpm: Albums: Bluespumpm, 1979; Edlau, 1980; Village, 1981; Live With Friends, 1985; The 5th Ten Years Jubilee, 1987; Live At Utopia, 1988; Live With Friends, 1991; Birthday, 1991; Live In Vienna, 1992; The 5th, 1992; Living Loving Riding, 1994; Singles: Wolfgang Session and Song, 1980; Train and Quick Shoes, 1985; Men From Milwaukee, 1993; with Blues Zappa: Albums: Gitarrero, 1985; Blue Balance, 1987; Glaskar, 1987; Andy Bartosh and Radio 1, 1994; Single: Der Letzte Zug, 1987. *Honours:* Silbenes Ehrenzeichen, 1992; Third Best Blues Album, Rot-Weis-Role Critics Poll, Live In Vienna, 1992. *Membership:* AKM; AUME; LSG. *Current Management:* Peter Steinbach, RGG Management. *Address:* Favoritenstr 53/2/6/18, 1100 Vienna, Austria.

CERVENKOVA, Helena; b. 3 March 1937, Slavicin, Czech Republic. Musician (Cimbal). m. Jaroslav Cervenka, 1958, 1 s., 1 d. *Career:* BROLN, radio broadcasting orchestra, Brno, Soloist, Folk Music, 35 years; Presentation of contemporary Czech music – radio, tv. *Recordings:* Vychodoslovenská Karicka; Romo Slavonica; Jak Kukacka Kuká; Fantasie; Ked sa Janko na Vojnu Bral. *Honours:* Festival of Folk Music in Wales, Third Prize as Soloist, 1958; Best Soloist of Radio, Czech Repub, 1967. *Membership:* Cimbal World Asscn. *Address:* Lerchova 26, 602 00 Brno, Czech Republic.

CETERA, Peter; b. 13 Sept. 1944, Chicago, Illinois, USA. Vocalist; Musician (bass). *Career:* Bassist, The Exceptions; Member, Chicago (formerly Big Thing, Chicago Transit Authority), 1967–85; Solo artiste, 1985–; Regular world-wide tours; Concerts include: Support to Janis Joplin, Jimi Hendrix, 1969; Atlantic Pop Festival, 1969; Isle of Wight Festival, 1970; First rock group to play Carnegie Hall, New York, 1971; Madison Square Garden, New York, 1977. *Compositions include:* Wishin' You Were Here; Baby What A Big Surprise; Hard To Say I'm Sorry (co-writer with David Foster); You're The Inspiration (co-writer with David Foster). *Recordings:* Albums: with Chicago: Chicago Transit Authority, 1969; Chicago II, 1970; Chicago III, 1971; Chicago At Carnegie Hall, 1971; Chicago V, 1972; Chicago VI, 1973; Chicago VII, 1974; Chicago VIII, 1975; Chicago X, 1976; Chicago XI, 1980; Hot Streets, 1978; Chicago 13, 1979; Chicago XIV, 1980; Chicago 16, 1982; Chicago 17, 1984; Chicago 18, 1987; Chicago 19, 1988; Chicago 21, 1991; Various compilations and greatest hits collections; Solo albums: Peter Cetera, 1981; Solitude/Solitaire, 1986; One More Story, 1988; World Falling Down, 1992; One Clear Voice, 1995; Another Perfect World, 2001; Singles: with Chicago: Does Anybody Really Know What Time It Is; Beginnings; Colour My World; If You Leave Me Now (No. 1, USA and UK), 1976; Hard To Say I'm Sorry (No. 1, USA), 1982; Solo singles: Glory of Love (No. 1, USA), 1986; The Next Time I Fall (duet with Amy Grant)(No. 1, USA), 1986; I Wasn't The One Who Said Goodbye (duet with Agnetha Fältskog); One Good Woman; After All (duet with Cher, 1989; Restless Heart; Feels Like Heaven (duet with Chaka Khan); Even A Fool Can See; Forever Tonight; Faithfully; You're The Inspiration; Contributor, Voices That Care, Gulf Crisis Fund benefit record, 1991. *Honours:* Grammy Award, 1977; American Music Award, 1977; Gold Ticket, Madison Square Garden, 1977. *Address:* c/o Agency for the Performing Arts, 9000 Sunset Blvd 12th Floor, Los Angeles, CA 90069, USA.

CETINIC, Meri; b. 15 June 1953, Split, Croatia. Vocalist; Musician (piano); Composer. 1 d. *Career:* 20 years of singing world-wide, including: USA; Canada; Former USSR; Australia; TV, radio shows; humanitarian concerts; State awards for different ways in music. *Recordings:* Albums: The Sea; Meri; I'm A Woman; By The Way; Road Dust; Ace; Golden Dreams; Meri (6); Why Do I Love You; Look For Me. *Honours:* Singer of the Year, 1981–82; 5 Gold albums. *Membership:* Croatian Composer's Society. *Current Management:* ZG Zoe Cetinic, Rendiceva 28, 10000 Zagreb, Croatia. *Address:* Meri Cetinic, Getaldiceva 27, 58000 Split, Croatia.

CHABRIER, Jean-Claude; b. 10 Nov. 1931, Neuilly-sur-Seine, France. Musicologist. 1 s., 1 d. *Education:* Studied sciences and Medicine, 1950; Plastic Surgery training, 1956; HIMT, Electrology, 1959; Dr of Medicine, 1959; Erotology and Sexology, 1999; Studied Oriental Languages, Middle Eastern Civilization and Turkish, Paris; Doctorate in Musicology and Islamic Studies, Sorbonne, 1976; Doctorate in History of Music, Sorbonne, 1995. *Career:* Researcher, CNRS, Paris; Teacher, New University of the Sorbonne, Paris-Sorbonne. *Compositions:* Ten Arabesques. *Recordings:* Ten Arabesques recital album; Anthology of oriental recitals; 10 albums, 1974–84. *Publications:* Analysis of Traditional Music: Identification, Representation, Paris Arabesques, 2 Vols; Over 200 analyses. *Honours:* Five Times Winner, Grand Prix, Academie du disque français, Paris, 1975, and Academie Charles Cros, Paris, 1980. *Membership:* Société française d'Analyse musicale; International Musicology Society; Society for Music Theory; International Council for Traditional Musics; Society for Ethnomusicology; Euro-Seminar for Ethnomusicology. *Address:* 213 Ave de Versailles, 75016 Paris, France.

CHAD, Dominic; b. 5 June 1974, Cheltenham, Gloucestershire, England. Musician (guitar). *Career:* Formed Grey Lantern with Paul Draper and Stove King; Changed name to Mansun; Joined by Andy Rathbone on drums; Numerous live tours and TV appearances. *Recordings:* Singles: Take It Easy Chicken, 1996; Egg Shaped Fred, 1996; Stripper Vicar, 1996; Wide Open Space, 1997; Legacy, 1998; Six, 1999; I Can Only Disappoint You, 2000; Electric Man, 2000; Fool, 2001; Albums: Attack of the Grey Lantern (No. 1, UK), 1997; Six, 1999; Little Kix, 2000.

CHADIMA, Mikolas; b. 9 Sept. 1952, Cheb, Czech Republic. Composer; Musician (saxophone, guitar); Vocalist. m. Marta Zelinkova. *Education:* Karel Velebnr's Jazz School, 1974–78. *Career:* Elektrobus, 1974–76; Extempore Band, 1976–81; MCH Band, 1982–; Kilhets Improvising Group, 1979–80; Prague Jazz Days, 1977, 1979; Concert for Armenia, 1989; Karot, Festival, Budapest, 1990; Alternativa, Prague, 1993, 1996. *Compositions:* The City; We Are Well and We Feel Fine; Es Reut Mich F. . . ; Exodus. *Recordings:* Kilhets, 1979; Extempore, The City, 1980–81; We Are Well and We Feel Fine, 1983; Es Reut Mich F. . ., 1988; Pseudemokritos, 1996; Transparent People, 1998. *Honours:* First Place, Extempore Band, Jazz Bulletin, 1981. *Membership:*

OSA; SAI; Svaz Hudebniku. *Address:* Mikolas Chadima, Cechova 24, 170 00 Prague 7, Czech Republic.

CHADWICK, James Manfred; b. 16 Oct. 1966, Lusaka, Zimbabwe. Jazz Musician (guitar). m. 31 March 1995. *Education:* Shiplake College, Henley-on-Thames; Welsh College of Music and Drama. *Career:* Appeared on live TV programme Heno in 1993; Member of Enrico Quartet performing at 3 venues in Italy in 1994; Various appearances throughout Britain; Tour of Northern England in 1995. *Recordings:* In The Bag, with James Chadwick Quartet, 1992. *Membership:* Musicians' Union. *Address:* 91 Moy Rd, Roath, Cardiff CF2 4TE, Wales.

CHADWICK, Mark; Vocalist; Musician (guitar); Songwriter. *Career:* Singer, guitarist, The Levellers, 1990–; Concerts include: Glastonbury Festival, 1992; Regular UK and European concerts; Support to REM, Eastern Europe. *Recordings:* Singles: 15 Years, 1992; One Way, 1992; Far From Home, 1992; This Garden, 1993; Just The One, 1995; Exodus (Live), 1996; What A Beautiful Day, 1997; Celebrate, 1997; Dog Train, 1997; Too Real, 1998; Bozos, 1998; Happy Birthday Revolution, 2000; Albums: A Weapon Called The Word, 1990; Levelling The Land, 1992; Levellers, 1993; Zeitgeist (No. 1, UK), 1995; Mouth to Mouth, 1997; One Way of Life (Best of compilation), 1998; Special Brew, 2000; Hello Pig, 2000; Green Blade Rising, 2002. *Publications:* The White Book (directory of action groups). *Address:* Levellers, 55 Canning St, Brighton BN2 2EF, England.

CHAKROBARTY, Mridul Kanti; b. Sunamganj. *Education:* Bachelor of Music; Master of Music; PhD. *Career:* Enlisted Artist, Radio Bangladesh, Dhaka; Regular Artist, Bangladesh television. *Compositions:* Sources of Rabindranath Tagore Songs in Western Folk Music; Modifier and Developer, Folk Instrumental Dotara: Surasree. *Recordings:* Tagore Songs: Odhora Madhura; Songs of Hason Raja; Surasree, Folk Instrumental. *Publications:* Hason Raja: His Mystic Songs, 1992; Evolution and Development of Bengali Music, 1993; Ganer Jhorna Tolay, research articles on Tagore songs and folk songs, 1997; Folk Music, 1999. *Honours:* Yuv '77, India; Loknath Award, 1998. *Membership:* Life Mem., National Academy (Bangla Academy); International Council for Traditional Music. *Address:* Department of Theatre and Music, University of Dhaka, Dhaka 1000, Bangladesh.

CHALMERS, Thomas; b. 4 Dec. 1930, Glasgow, Scotland. Musician (saxophone, clarinet, flute). m. Jeanette D McGhee, 21 Dec. 1950, 3 s., 1 d. *Education:* Tutored by member of BBC S V Orchestra. *Career:* Played with Military Band, 1949–54, Ken Stevens Orchestra, 1960–66, Tommy Sampson Orchestra, 1970–86; Member of Fat Sam's Band, Edinburgh, 1986–96; Freelance musician with Bobby Wishart groups and Strathclyde Youth Jazz Orchestra. *Recordings:* with Fat Sam's Band: Boogie On Down; Jive On Down; Ring Dem Bells; Fat Sam's Band Live At. *Membership:* Musicians' Union. *Address:* 5 Beauly Dr., Craigshill, Livingston, West Lothian EH54 5LG, Scotland.

CHAMBERLIN, Jimmy; b. 10 June 1964, Joliet, IL, USA. Musician (drums). *Career:* Jazz Drummer; Mem., Smashing Pumpkins, 1988–95, 1998–2000; Numerous headlining tours, television and radio appearances; Mem., The Last Hard Men. *Recordings:* Albums: with Smashing Pumpkins: Gish, 1991; The Peel Sessions, 1992; Siamese Dream, 1993; Pisces Iscariot, 1994; Mellon Collie And The Infinite Sadness (No. 1, USA), 1995; MACHINA/The Machines Of God, 2000; Machina II: The Friends And Enemies Of Modern Music, 2000; Greatest Hits, 2001; Earphoria, 2002; Vieuphoria (DVD), 2002; with The Last Hard Men: The Last Hard Men, 1998. Singles: with Smashing Pumpkins: Lull (EP), 1992; Today, 1994; Cherub Rock (EP), 1994; Disarm, 1994; I Am One (EP), 1994; Bullet With Butterfly Wings, 1995; Perfect, 1998; Stand Inside Your Love, 2000; Try Try Try, 2000.

CHAMBERS, Guy; Prod; Songwriter; Musician (keyboards). *Career:* Member: The Waterboys; World Party, 1986–91; The Lemon Trees; Co-writer and producer for Robbie Williams, 1997–; Various tours with Williams; Collaborations: Jimmy Nail; Cathy Dennis; Frances Ruffelle; Tom Jones; Holly Johnson, Blast; Julian Cope, Fried. *Compositions:* Co-writer of hits for Robbie Williams: Singles: Lazy Days, 1996; South of The Border, 1997; Angels, 1997; Let Me Entertain You, 1998; Millennium (No. 1, UK), 1998; No Regrets, 1998; Strong, 1999; She's The One (No. 1, UK), 1999; Rock DJ (No. 1, UK), 2000; Kids (duet with Kylie Minogue), 2000; Supreme, 2000; Let Love Be Your Energy, 2001; Eternity/The Road To Mandalay (No. 1, UK), 2001; Albums: Life Thru A Lens, 1997; I've Been Expecting You (No. 1, UK), 1998; Sing When You're Winning (No. 1, UK), 2000; Your Disco Needs You, Kylie Minogue, 2000. *Recordings:* Albums: with World Party: Private Revolution, 1986; Goodbye Jumbo, 1990; with Lemon Trees: Open Book, 1993; Singles: with Lemon Trees: The Way I Feel, 1992; Love Is In Your Eyes, 1992; Child of Love, 1993; I Can't Face The World, 1993; Let It Loose, 1993. *Honours:* BRIT Awards: Best Single, Angels (co-writer), 1999; Rock DJ (co-writer), 2001. *Membership:* Musicians' Union; PRS. *Current Management:* One Management, 43 St Alban's Ave, London W4 5JS, England.

CHAMBERS, Jackie; Musician (guitar). *Career:* Mem., Girlschool, mid-1990s–. *Recordings:* Albums: Live, 1995; Race With The Devil (Live), 1998;

Live On The King Biscuit Flower Hour, 1998; Can't Keep A Good Girl Down, 1999; Very Best Of Remastered, 2002; 21st Anniversary: Not That Innocent, 2002. *Address:* c/o PO Box 33446, London SW18 3XN, England. *Website:* www.girlschool.co.uk.

CHAMBERS, Martin Dale; b. 4 Sept. 1951, Herford, England. Musician (drums). 1 s., 1 d. *Education:* Hereford College of Art. *Career:* Drummer, Pretenders, 1979–85; 1994–; Linda McCartney Tribute, Royal Albert Hall, London; Doug Stewart Spiritual Cowboys; Miss World. *Recordings:* Singles: Kid, 1979; Brass In Pocket (No. 1, UK), 1980; Talk of The Town, 1980; I Go To Sleep, 1981; Back On The Chain Gang, 1982; 2000 Miles, 1983; I'll Stand By You, 1994; Popstar, 1999; Albums include: Pretenders (No. 1, UK), 1980; Pretenders II (No. 1, UK), 1981; Learning To Crawl, 1984; The Singles, 1987; Last of The Independents, 1994; The Isle of View, 1995; Viva El Amor, 1999; Greatest Hits, 2000; Other work includes: Paul McCartney; Pete Townsend; Roger Daltrey. *Current Management:* Gailforce Management, 24 Ives St, London SW3 2ND, England.

CHAMBERS, Wendy Mae; b. 24 Jan. 1953. Composer; Musician. m. Rajesh Karki. *Education:* BA, Barnard College; MA, SUNY. *Career:* CNN; BBC Television; NPR; WWL Television, New Orleans; WWOZ Radio, New Orleans. *Compositions:* 4 CDs; Symphony of The Universe; A Mass For Mass Trombones. *Honours:* NEA Grant, 1983, 1986; American Composers Forum Commission, 1998; CAPS Grant. *Membership:* American Music Center; American Composer Forum. *Address:* 13 E Seventh St, Harvey Ledars, NJ 08008, USA.

CHAMPION, Will; b. 21 July 1977, Southampton, England. Musician (drums); Songwriter. *Education:* University College, London. *Career:* Mem., Coldplay, 1998–. *Recordings:* Albums: Parachutes, 2000; A Rush Of Blood To The Head, 2002. Singles: The Safety EP, 1998; Brothers and Sisters, The Blue Room EP, 1999; Shiver, 2000; Yellow, 2000; Trouble, 2000; Don't Panic, 2001; In My Place, 2002; A Rush Of Blood To The Head, 2002; The Scientist, 2002. *Honours:* BRIT Awards, Best Album, 2001, Best British Group, Best British Album, 2003; Grammy Award, Best Alternative Album, for Parachutes, 2001; MTV Award, Best UK and Ireland Act, 2002; Billboard Group of the Year, 2002; NME Award, Best Album, 2003. *Current Management:* Phil Harvey. *Address:* c/o Parlophone Records, 43 Brook Green, London W6 7EF, England. *Website:* www.coldplay.com.

CHANA, Shan; b. 4 March 1969, Plymouth, Devon, England. Musician (drums, percussion, latin, timpani). *Education:* London College of Music, England; GLCM (Hons). *Career:* West End shows: Crazy For You, Prince Edward Theatre; Grease, Dominion Theatre; Sunset Boulevard, Adelphi Theatre; She Loves Me, Savoy Theatre; Fame, Cambridge Theatre. *Recordings:* Fame, original cast album, Maison Rouge Studios, London; Major sessions at Snake Ranch Studios, London; CTS Studios, London; Sawmills Studios, Cornwall; ICC Studios, Eastbourne. *Honours:* Henry Bromley Derry Music Performance Prize, 1990. *Membership:* Musicians' Union. *Address:* 8 Juniper Court, 71 Mulgrove Rd, Sutton, Surrey SM2 6LY, England.

CHANDLER, Gene, (Eugene Dixon); b. 6 July 1937, Chicago, Illinois, USA. Vocalist. *Career:* Lead singer, Gene Chandler and The Dukays; Solo artiste. *Recordings:* Singles include: Duke of Earl (No. 1, USA), 1962; Rainbow, 1963; Man's Temptation, 1963; Just To Be True, 1964; Nothing Can Stop Me, 1965; Groovy Situation, 1970; Solo single: Get Down, 1990; Albums: The Duke of Earl, 1962; Just Be True, 1964; The Girl Don't Care, 1967; There Was A Time, 1968; The Two Sides of Gene Chandler, 1969; The Gene Chandler Situation, 1970; Get Down, 1978; When You're Number One, 1979; 80, 1980; Live At The Regal, 1965; Soul Master, 1995; The Soul Of, 1996; Numerous compilations and live albums, most recently: The Best of The Duke of Earl, 2000. *Address:* 8829 S Bishop, Chicago, IL 60620, USA.

CHANDLER, Kerri, (Gate-Ah, Paper Mache, Kerri 'Kaoz 6.23' Chandler); b. East Orange, New Jersey, USA. Prod; Remixer; DJ. *Career:* Started DJ career aged 13; Started producing in the late '80s; Set up own label, Express Records; Debut single Superlover/Get It Off released by Atlantic Records, 1991; Founder: Madhouse; Sfere Records; Collaborations: Jerome Sydenham; Dee Dee Brave; Dennis Ferrer; Arnold Jarvis; Byron Stingily; Remixed: Femi Kuti; Shawn Christopher; Ultra Nate; Ce Ce Rogers. *Recordings:* Albums: Hemisphere, 1996; Singles: Superlover/Get It Off, 1991; The Shelter (as Gate-Ah), 1992; Inspiration (with Arnold Jarvis), 1994; Ionosphere EP, 1995; See Line Woman (with The Songstress), 1998; My Old Friend, 1999. *Address:* c/o Champion Records, 181 High St, Harlesden, London NW10 4TE, England.

CHAO, Manu, (Oscar Tramor); b. 26 June 1961, Paris, France. Vocalist; Songwriter. 1 s. *Career:* As teenager played in various bands including Les Hot Pants; Formed Mano Negra, late 1980s, band split, 1995; First single earned group contract with Virgin; Toured Latin America; Moved to Spain, 1995; Formed 10-mem. Radio Bemba Sound System; Spent next few years recording in South and Central America; King of Bongo recording featured on soundtrack to Madonna's The Next Big Thing film; British tour, 2002. *Recordings:* with Mano Negra: Patchanka, 1988; Puta's Fever, 1989; King of

The Bongo, 1991; Hell of Patchinko, 1992; Casa Babylon, 1994; solo: Clandestino, 1998; Próxima Estación: Esperanza, 2001. *Honours:* BBC Radio 3 Award for World Music, Innovator award, 2002. *Website:* www.manuchao.net.

CHAOS AD. See: JENKINSON, Tom.

CHAPIN, Tom, (Thomas Forbes); b. 13 March 1945, Charlotte, North Carolina, USA. Vocalist; Songwriter; Musician (guitar, banjo, autoharp); Actor. m. Bonnie Chapin, 5 June 1976, 2 d., 1 step-s., 1 step-d. *Education:* College graduate, State University of New York, Plattsburgh. *Career:* Host, Make A Wish, ABC TV (award-winning children's show), 1971–76; Broadway: Pump Boys and Dinettes, 1983; Host, National Geographic Explorer, TV TBS, 1986–89; Thousands of concerts (mainly in North America) over last 30 years. *Recordings:* Children's recordings: Family Tree; Moonboat; Mother Earth; Billy The Squid; Zag Zig; Just For Kids; In My Hometown; Great Big Fun For The Very Little One, 2001; Adult's recordings: Life Is Like That; In The City of Mercy; Let Me Back Into Your Life; So Nice To Come Home; Join The Jubilee; Other collaborations include: Cherish The Ladies, John McCutcheon. *Publications:* Book/cassette: Sing A Whale Song, storybook for children. *Honours:* Peabody Award, Make A Wish, 1972, Emmy, Make A Wish, 1975; Harry Chapin Award for Contributions to Humanity, NACA, 1990. *Membership:* AFofM; SAG; AFTRA; NARAS; NAS. *Current Management:* Sundance Music. *Address:* Sundance Music, 100 Cedar St, Suite B-19, Dobbs Ferry, NY 10522, USA.

CHAPMAN, Mike; b. 15 April 1947, Queensland, Australia. Songwriter. *Career:* Member, Tangerine Peel; Songwriting partnership with Nicky Chinn; Producer for Blondie hits; Founder, Dreamland label (with Nicky Chinn), 1979–81. *Compositions:* Hits include: Kiss You All Over, Exile (No. 1, USA), 1978; Hot Child In The City, Nick Gilder (No. 1, USA), 1979; Mickey, Toni Basil (No. 1, USA), 1982; Other hits for: Sweet; Gary Glitter; Mud; Suzi Quatro; Smokie; Patti Smith; Lita Ford. *Recordings:* as producer: with Blondie: Heart of Glass (No. 1, UK and USA), 1979; Sunday Girl (No. 1, UK), 1979; Atomic (No. 1, UK), 1980; The Tide Is High (No. 1, UK), 1980; Rapture (No. 1, USA), 1981; with The Knack: My Sharona (No. 1, USA), 1979; Also for Patti Smith; Lita Ford; Blondie; Pat Benatar.

CHAPMAN, Tracy; b. 30 March 1964, Cleveland, OH, USA. Vocalist; Songwriter. *Education:* BA, Anthropology and African Studies, Tufts University. *Career:* Performer on Boston Folk circuit, 1986; Recording artiste, 1987–; Major concerts include: Nelson Mandela 70th Birthday Tribute, Wembley Stadium, 1988; Human Rights Now world tour, with Peter Gabriel, Bruce Springsteen, Sting, Youssou N'Dour, 1988; AIDS benefit concert, Oakland, California, 1989; Nelson Mandela International Tribute, Wembley Stadium, 1990; Martin Luther King Celebration, Minneapolis, 1991; Bill Graham Memorial concert, San Francisco, 1991; Bob Dylan 30th Anniversary celebration, Madison Square Garden, 1992; Farm Aid V with Living Colour's Vernon Reid, 1992; Regular US and British tours; Television: Motown 30–What's Goin' On (CBS), 1990; True Stories–Too White For Me (Channel 4), 1992; The Tonight Show (NBC), 1992; In Concert (ABC), 1992. *Recordings:* Albums: Tracy Chapman (No. 1, UK and USA), 1988; Crossroads (No. 1, UK), 1989; Matters of The Heart, 1992; New Beginning, 1995; Telling Stories, 2000; Collection (compilation), 2001; Let It Rain, 2002. Singles include: Fast Car, 1988; Talkin' 'Bout A Revolution, 1988; Baby Can I Hold You, 1988 (covered by Boyzone, 1996); Crossroads, 1989; New Beginning, 1995; Smoke and Ashes, 1995; Give Me One Reason, 1996. *Honours:* American Music Award, Favourite New Pop/Rock Artist, 1989; BRIT Awards, Best International Artist Female, Best International Newcomer, 1989; Grammy Awards include: Best Female Pop Vocal Performance, Best Contemporary Folk Recording, Best New Artist, 1989; Boston Music Awards include: Best Female Vocalist, Top Song, Rock Album, 1989. *Current Management:* Gold Mountain Entertainment, Suite 450, 3575 Cahuenga Blvd W, Los Angeles, CA 90068, USA.

CHARLES, Debbie; b. 9 Aug. 1966, London, England. Vocalist; Songwriter. *Career:* Backing vocalist with Fine Young Cannibals; Al Green; Bob Geldof; Gabrielle; Alison Moyet; Lighthouse Family; Member, accapella sextet Mint Juleps. *Membership:* PRS. *Address:* 10 Pemell House, Pemell Close, London E1 4JY, England.

CHARLES, Ray, (Ray Charles Robinson); b. 23 Sept. 1930, Albany, Georgia, USA. Vocalist; Musician (piano); Composer. *Education:* Piano and clarinet, St Augustine's School for Deaf and Blind, Orlando. *Career:* Blind since age 7 (glaucoma); Member, various groups, Florida; Founder, McSon Trio, 1948; Musical director, Lowell Fulson, 1949–51; Bandleader, own group, 1953–; Concerts include: Newport Jazz Festival, 1958; New York Jazz Festival, 1967; Soul Bowl '69, Houston Astrodome, 1969; Royal Festival Hall, London, 1970; Ann Arbor Jazz and Blues Festival, 1973; Kool Jazz Festival, New York, 1983; John Lennon Tribute Concert, Liverpool, 1990; Playboy Jazz Festival, 1991; Television special, Ray Charles – 50 Years In Music, Fox TV, 1991; Film appearances: Ballad In Blue, 1964; The Blues Brothers, 1980; Other cameo roles, US television shows: Moonlighting; St Elsewhere; Who's The Boss. *Recordings:* Singles include: It Should Have Been Me, 1954; Don't You Know, I Got A Woman, 1954; This Little Girl of Mine, 1954; What'd I

Say, 1959; Georgia On My Mind (No. 1, USA), 1960; One Mint Julep, 1961; Hit The Road Jack (No. 1, USA), 1961; Unchain My Heart, 1962; I Can't Stop Loving You (No. 1, USA), 1962; You Don't Know Me, 1962; Take These Chains From My Heart, 1963; Busted, 1963; Cryin' Time, 1966; Seven Spanish Angels, duet with Willie Nelson (US Country No. 1), 1985; I'll Be Good To You, duet with Chaka Khan, 1990; I'll Take Care Of, 1990; Fresh Out of Tears, 1991; Living Without You, 1991; I'll Be There, 1993; Numerous albums include: Ray Charles, 1957; Ray Charles At Newport, 1958; Soul Brothers (with Milt Jackson), 1959; The Genius of Ray Charles, 1960; In Person, 1960; The Genius Hits The Road, 1960; Dedicated To You, 1961; Genius + Soul = Jazz, 1961; What'd I Say, 1961; The Genius After Hours, 1961; Ray Charles and Betty Carter, 1961; The Genius Sings The Blues, 1961; Do The Twist, 1962; Modern Sounds In Country and Western Music Vols 1 and 2, 1962; The Ray Charles Story, 1962; Ingredients In A Recipe For Soul, 1963; Sweet and Sour Tears, 1964; Live In Concert, 1965; Rays Moods, 1966; A Man and His Soul, 1967; Ray Charles Invites You To Listen, 1967; A Portrait of Ray, 1968; Volcanic Action of My Soul, 1971; A Message From The People, 1972; Renaissance, 1975; Porgy and Bess (with Cleo Laine), 1976; Heart To Heart, 1980; Friendship, 1985; Back On The Block, 1990; Ray Charles – The Living Legend, 1993; My World, 1993; Strong Love Affair, 1996; Hit The Road, Ray, 1996; In Concert, 1998; Dedicated To You, 1998; Blues Is My Middle Name, 2001; Several greatest hits collections; Contributor, We Are The World, USA For Africa (No. 1, UK and USA), 1985. *Honours:* Numerous Grammy Awards, 1961–; Inducted into Rock 'n' Roll Hall of Fame, 1986; NARAS Lifetime Achievement Grammy Award, 1988; Legend Award, Rhythm and Blues Foundation, 1991; Atlanta Celebrity Walk, 1991; Los Angeles Distinguished Service Medal, 1992; Black History Honoree Award, Los Angeles, 1992; Songwriters Hall of Fame Lifetime Award, 1993. *Membership:* Rhythm and Blues Foundation, Washington. *Address:* Ray Charles Enterprises, 2107 Washington Blvd, Los Angeles, CA 90018, USA.

CHARLESON, William (Bill); b. 20 June 1940, Oldham, Lancashire, England. Educator; Composer; Arranger; Musician (saxophone). m. Diane Margaret Fox, 18 Aug. 1965, 1 s., 1 d. *Education:* Royal Manchester College of Music; University of York; Director of Studies, Leeds College of Music. *Career:* Appearances with: Ken Mackintosh and Orchestra; BBC Northern Dance Orchestra; BBC Northern Symphony Orchestra; Hallé Orchestra; Royal Liverpool Philharmonic Orchestra; Theatre and cabaret accompanying major British and American artistes; Radio appearances and television sessions for: Granada TV; Yorkshire TV; BBC TV; Consultancy, Open University. *Compositions:* Jazz compositions for National Youth Jazz Orchestra; Brass Band arrangements, compositions recorded by all major bands. *Recordings:* with Joe Jackson; Tucker–A Man and His Dream soundtrack. *Publications:* Jazz Sax 1 (Co-author with J R Brown); Articles for: Crescendo International; British Education Music Journal. *Honours:* YTV/MU Peter Knight Award, 1989; BBC Rehearsal Band Competition: Arranging Prize, 1989. *Membership:* PRS. *Address:* 144 Sunnybank Rd, Mirfield, West Yorkshire WF14 0JQ, England.

CHARLTON, Michael Anthony, (Mad Dog Santini); b. 27 Feb. 1964, South Shields, Tyne and Wear, England. Musician (drums, percussion, keyboards). 1 d. *Education:* BA Hons, Music, University of Northumbria, Newcastle. *Career:* Television, radio and live appearances include: The Tube; TX45; Mainline; Live 95; Worday Open Air Concert; Gypsies Green Stadium; Metro FM; Wear FM; 7FM; Radio Newcastle; The Riverside; Temple Park Leisure Centre. *Recordings:* No More War; Is That It; Smooth Funk; Scratch It; Addicted; Devils In Heaven. *Membership:* PRS; Musicians' Union; Equity. *Current Management:* Hardy Ismail, Axis Promotions. *Address:* 55 Marsden Lane, South Shields, Tyne and Wear, England.

CHARMASSON, Rémi; b. 3 May 1961, Avignon, France. Musician (guitar). *Education:* Baccalaureate, Philosophy; Gold Medal in Jazz, Avignon Conservatory. *Career:* Began with André Jaume, Jimmy Giuffre; Worked with: Charlie Mariano, Charles Tyler, Buddy Colette, Dennis Charles, Tony Coe, Freddie Studer, Jean François Canape, Jenny Clarke, Larry Schneider, Randy Kaye, Barry Altschul, Riccardo Del Fra. *Recordings:* Cinoche, with André Jaume, Rémi Charmasson, Claude Tchamitchian, 1989; Piazza Di Luna, with André Jaume, Rémi Charmasson, Jean-Marc Montera, Fredy Studer, Claude Tchamitchian, Tavagna singers, 1989; FollyFun Music Magic, with Charles Tyler, Rémi Charmasson, Jean Pierre Jullian, Bernard Santacruz, Christian Zagaria, 1990; Caminanado, duo with Claude Tchamitchian, 1990; A Scream For Charles Tyler, with Rémi Charmasson, Dennis Charles, Bernard Santacruz; Casa Blu, with Thierry Maucci; Nemo, trio with F Sugon, Jenny Clarke; 10 records in 5 years, 1993; Current recordings with: André Jaume, Charlie Mariano Quintet; A Jaume and Groupes de Gamelans Indonésiens; A Soler and Larry Schneider. *Honours:* Diapason D'Or, from music newspaper: Diapason. *Current Management:* Asscn pour le Jazz et la Musique Improvisée (AJMI), La Manutention 4, rue escaliers, Ste Anne, 84000 Avignon, France. *Telephone:* (04) 90-31-84-89. *Fax:* (04) 90-86-40-87. *E-mail:* remi-charmasson@wanadoo.fr. *Website:* charmasson.ifrance.com.

CHASE, Katharine Ann; b. 29 April 1963, Ridgecrest, CA, USA. Vocalist; Songwriter; Musician (bass and rhythm guitars). *Education:* BA, Classical

Voice, University of California, Los Angeles. *Career:* Solo appearances with Hootie and the Blowfish; Mary Lou Lord; Exene Cervankova, Elliot Smith; Co-Founder Spanking Violets, 1992; Founder, Katharine Chase Band, 1994; Co-founder, Kindness, 1999. *Compositions:* Cake; The Blasters; Southern Culture On The Skids; Tripping Daisy. *Recordings:* Albums: solo: Loverman, 1994; Band albums: Spanking Violets, 1994; The Truth, 1995; The Truth, 1997; with Kindness: Welcome To Planet Excellent; Contributor, albums: Bigger Better Faster More, 1992; Trinket, 1996; Starene, 1997. *Publications:* Reviews and Interviews, 1995; San Francisco Chronicle, 1997; Bay Magazine, 1996. *Honours:* 12 Gold Medals, Regional Texas State Flute Competitions, 1980–86. *Membership:* BMI; NARAS. *Current Management:* Midnight Sun, 382c Union Ave, Campbell, CA 95008, USA.

CHASEZ, J. C. (Joshua Scott); b. 8 Aug. 1976, Washington, DC, USA. Vocalist; Songwriter. *Career:* Former presenter, The Mickey Mouse Club (television); Honed vocal/songwriting talents working for free in LA and Nashville; Mem., *NSYNC vocal quintet, 1995–; Signed to BMG Ariola Munich, 1997; First headline US tour, 1998. *Recordings:* Albums: *NSYNC, 1998; Home For Christmas, 1998; No Strings Attached, 2000; Celebrity, 2001. Singles include: I Want You Back, 1997; Tearin' Up My Heart, 1997; Let The Music Heal Your Soul (various artists charity single credited to Bravo All Stars), 1999; Music Of My Heart (with Gloria Estefan), 1999; Bye, Bye, Bye, 2000; I'll Never Stop, 2000; It's Gonna Be Me, 2000; This I Promise You, 2000; Pop, 2001; Gone, 2001. *Honours:* Presented with keys to City of Orlando, 2000; American Music Award, Favorite Pop/Rock Band, Duo or Group, 2002. *Address:* c/o Wright Entertainment Group, PO Box 590009, Orlando, FL 32859–0009, USA. *Website:* www.nsync.com.

CHASSAGNITE, François; b. 21 June 1955, Ussel, Correze, France. Musician (trumpet, flugelhorn). *Education:* Ex-veterinary doctor. *Career:* Member, Antoine Hervé Big Band; Gerard Badini Big Band; Jean Loup Lognon Big Band; François Jeanneau's Pandemonium; Orchestre National de Jazz; Laurent Cugny Big Band (2 records and a tour in Europe under Gil Evans direction); Festivals Nice, Juan les Pins; Mariac; Paris. *Recordings:* 2 records with Antoine Hervé; 3 with Frantois Jeanneau; 2 with Laurent Cugny; 1 with G Badini; 1 with Jean Loup Longnon; Several with small combos; 2 with own band Samya Cynthia, 1989; Chazzeology, 1996; With Sorgho: Savane, 1996; Kess-Kess, 1998. *Membership:* SACEM; SPEDIDAM; ADAM. *Address:* 143 Chemin de la Sine, 06140 VENCE, France.

CHAUDAGNE, Remy; b. 26 Aug. 1959, Melun, France. Composer; Musician (electric bass). m. Cora, 13 Jan. 1994, 1 s. *Education:* Piano, saxophone, double bass, electric bass. *Career:* Tour, France, India, Indonesia, Viet Nam, Philippines, Cambodia, Sudan; Performances with: David Liebman; Scott Henderson; F Corneloup; Claude Barthelemy; Andy Sheppard. *Compositions:* Music for short films; theatre, saxophone quartet, Creation with jazz orchestra (24 musicians) or classical (13 musicians). *Recordings:* 7 albums as leader, including last in trio with Peter Erskine and Andy Sheppard: 3 Colors. *Honours:* First Prize, Villembourne Festival, music for film Sem Cor with Katie Adler. *Current Management:* Benoit Lebon. *Address:* 4B rue de la Convention, 94270 Kremlin Bicêtre, France.

CHAULK, (Lloyd) Wayne; b. 10 June 1950, Corner Brook, Newfoundland, Canada. Composer; Arranger; Musician; Prod. m. Denise, 29 March 1975, 1 d. *Education:* Bachelor of Commerce degree; Engineering technician; Real Estate license. *Career:* Canadian Broadcasting Corporation television features, 1993; Over 20 radio interviews, 1992–93; Music featured on international airlines, world-wide; Music played on over 4,000 US premises and on over 400 radio stations; Over 200 original compositions and 18 CDs produced. *Recordings:* Albums: Dreamer's Themes, 1991; New Directions and Christmas Keyboards, 1992; No Regrets, 1993; The Christmas to Remember, 1996; Nature's Splendour, 1996; Journey Home, 1997. *Honours:* Billboard Certificate of Achievement: Your Love Is My Song, 1992; Best Light Rock (Pop) Artist On Record, Aria, 1994, 1995; Albums rated among best instrumentals, Adult Contemporary Music Research Group, USA, 1993–94. *Membership:* SOCAN. *Current Management:* Distributor, Holborne Distribution Inc, Canada. *Address:* c/o Ambassador Music, Deer Valley, PO #43029, Calgary, AB T2J 7A7, Canada.

CHAUTEMPS, Jean-Louis; b. 6 Aug. 1931, Paris, France. Musician (saxophone); Composer. Divorced, 1 s., 1 d. *Education:* Philosophy; Musicology. *Career:* Member, Claude Bolling Orchestra, 1952; Also played with Sydney Bechet; Django Reinhardt; Zoot Sims; Lester Young; Bobby Jaspar; Albert Ayler; Roy Eldridge; Don Byas; European tour with Chet Baker; 3 years as saxophone player, musical arranger, Kurt Edelhagen Orchestra, Cologne, Germany; Played Paris jazz clubs, early 1960s; Played with Kenny Clarke; Martial Solal; Slide Hampton; Eddy Louiss; René Urtreger; Johnny Griffin; Dexter Gordon; Daniel Humair; Composer for films; Teacher, improvisation; Worked with the Ensemble InterContemporain, extensive tours USA with Musique Vivante, early 1970s; Leader, jazz workshop, The Sorbonne, 1975; Founder, Rhizome, 1976; Concerts, tours include Dizzy Gillespie; World premier, Périples For Solo Saxophone by Paul Méfano; Soloist, leader, Albert Mangelsdorff band, 2 years; Member, Martial Solal Big Band; Works for classical and avant garde orchestras; Works with computers and synthesizers; Played at the Guggenheim Museum, New York, with Quatuor de Saxophones, 1987; 3 jazz concerts, Opéra-Bastille, 1992; Also with Ensemble Contrechamps, 1994; Musical director, The Threepenny Opera, Théâtre National de Chaillot, 1995. *Compositions:* Film music includes Les Coeurs Verts; L'Ombre de la Pomme; Music for theatre, television and films. *Recordings:* Album: Chautemps, 1988. *Honours:* Chevalier des Arts et Lettres, Ordre National du Mérite; Prix du Jazz SACEM. *Membership:* Vice-President de l'Assafra. *Current Management:* Agnès Lupovici.

CHAYANNE, (Elmer Figueroa Alce); b. 28 June 1968, Puerto Rico. Vocalist; Actor; Dancer. *Career:* First group: Los Chicos; Moved to Mexico to start a solo career, aged 17; Solo recording debut, 1986; Appeared in first Spanish language commercial on American network TV for Pepsi, 1989; Film appearances include: Dance With Me, 1998; Linda Sara, 1994; Los Chicos En Conexion Caribe; Las Divorciadas (mini series). *Recordings:* Albums include: Chayanne, 1989; Tempo De Vals, 1990; Provocame, 1992; Influencas, 1994; Volver A Nacer, 1996; Atado A To Amor, 1998; Simplemente, 2000. *Honours:* 49 gold and platinum sales awards; MTV Award, Best Internaional Video, Este Ritmo Se Baila Asi, 1989.

CHEB FAUDEL, (Faudel Bellula); b. 6 June 1978, Mantes la Jolie, France. Vocalist; Songwriter. *Career:* Formed the Rai Stars (Les Étoiles du Ra), aged 12; Performed at local parties and weddings; Within three years was opening for MC Solaar and Cheb Khaled; Featured in two French TV shows: Saga Cities; Les Enfants du Ra, 1995; Selected to participate in Festival du Printemps de Bourges, 1996; Sold more than 300,000 copies of Baida; Tours internationally. *Recordings:* Baida, 1998; Samra, 2001; 1 2 3 Soleils (with Khaled and Rachid Taha), 2001. *Honours:* Victoires de la Musique award, 1999. *Website:* www.faudel.com.fr.

CHEB KHALED. See: **KHALED.**

CHEB MAMI, (Mohamed Khélifati); b. 11 July 1966, Graba-el-Oved, Sada, Algeria. Rai Vocalist; Songwriter. *Career:* Signed to Disco Maghreb, after winning second prize in Ihan wa chabab contest on the radio in 1982; Performed, Premier Festival of Rai, Oran, 1985; Tour of Paris, 1985; Performed, Rai Festivals, Villete and Bobigny, 1986; Performed, Olympia Theater, Paris, 1986; Military service, Algeria, 1987–89; Toured the USA, the Netherlands, Germany, Switzerland, Spain, Scandinavia and England; Collaborations: Sting; K-Mel; Gordon Cyrus; Simon Law. *Recordings:* Albums: Douni El Bladi, 1986; Prince Of Rai, 1989; Let Me Rai, 1990; Fatma Fatma; Saida, 1994; Let Me Cry, 1995; Douni El Bladi, 1996; 100% ARABICA (with Cheb Khaled); Meli Meli, 1999; Dellali, 2001. *Honours:* Gold disc, France; World Music Award, Best Selling Arabic Artist, 2001. *Current Management:* Michel Levy. *Address:* c/o Mad Minute Music, 5/7 rue Paul Bert, 93400 St-Ouen, France. *Website:* www.chebmami.net.

CHECKER, Chubby, (Ernest Evans); b. 3 Oct. 1941, South Carolina, USA. Vocalist. *Career:* Television appearances: The Dick Clark Saturday Night Show, ABC TV, 1960; Ed Sullivan Show, 1961; Ready Steady Go, 1965; Featured in films: Twist Around The Clock, 1961; Don't Knock The Twist, 1962; Numerous world-wide tours; Featured artist, Dick Clark's Caravan of Stars, 1961; Performed at Nelson Mandela's 70th Birthday Tribute, Wembley, 1988. *Recordings:* Singles include: The Twist (No. 1, USA), 1960, 1962 (only song ever to reach US No. 1 on two occasions); The Hucklebuck, 1960; Pony Time (No. 1, USA), 1961; Dance The Mess Around, 1961; Let's Twist Again, 1961; The Fly, 1961; Jingle Bell Rock, duet with Bobby Rydell, 1961; Twistin' USA, 1961; Slow Twistin', 1962; Teach Me To Twist, duet with Bobby Rydell, 1962; Dancin' Party, 1962; Limbo Rock, 1962; Birdland, 1963; Loddy Lo, 1963; Let's Limbo Some More, 1963; Hooka Tooka, 1964; The Twist (Yo' Twist), with the Fat Boys, 1988; Doin The Zombie, 1997; Albums: Twist With Chubby Checker, 1960; It's Pony Time, 1961; For Twisters Only, 1962; Your Twist Party, 1962; Bobby Rydell/Chubby Checker, 1962; For Teen Twisters Only, 1962; Twistin' Round The World, 1962; Don't Knock The Twist (film soundtrack), 1962; All The Hits (For Your Dancin' Party), 1961; Limbo Party, 1963; Chubby Checker's Biggest Hits, 1963; Let's Limbo Some More, 1963; Beach Party, 1963; Chubby Checker In Person, 1963; Chubby Checker's Greatest Hits, 1973; The Change Has Come, 1982; Still Twistin', 1986; In Deutschland, 1988; Mister Twist, 2000. *Honours:* Grammy Award, Best Rock and Roll Recording, Let's Twist Again, 1961. *Current Management:* Twisted Entertainment, 320 Fayette St, 2nd Floor, Conshohocken, PA 19428, USA.

CHEN, Tania; Musician (piano). *Education:* Royal College of Music; Studied with Stephen Coombs, Artur Pizarro, John Tilbury; MMus, Goldsmiths College, University of London. *Career:* Performances in England, Europe and Japan; Composed music for piano, electronic sounds and voice. *Recordings:* Cornelius Cardew with Apartment House; Earle Brown Graphic Compositions with Dal Niente, 2002; Cornelius Cardew Piano Sonatas 1, 2, 3; Michael Parsons Piano Music; Alan Hovhaness, Terry Riley, Lou Harrison—Piano Music. *Honours:* Shelley Scholarship in Performing Arts; Masterclasses with Mtslav Rostropovich. *Address:* c/o Goldsmiths College, University of London, New Cross, London SE14 6NW, England. *E-mail:* tania@minuet.freeserve.co.uk. *Website:* www.taniapiano.com.

CHENEOUR, (Ian) Paul; b. 19 April 1952, Southsea, Hampshire, England. Musician (flute). *Education:* Guildhall School of Music and Drama, with Professor Rainer Schielein. *Career:* Member, Dutch Jazz Quintet, France; Leader, own 7 piece group The Cornish Connection; Leader, jazz fusion quartet, Cheneour, 1983–; Leader, The Aeona Flute Quartet, 1991–; Leader, Impromptu, 1993; Freelance musician for films, radios and documentaries; Numerous tours, UK; Europe; Middle East; North America; Canada; Greece, Turkey, 1997; Masterclasses in Improvisation and Composition, and flute playing; New Duo, Paul Cheneour and Dilly Meah, flutes and tabla, 1997. *Recordings:* Solo albums: Chenour Live I, 1987; The Time Has Come, 1995; with Impromptu: Sweet Kafka, 1994; Ocean of Dreams, 1996; Reiki Healing Symbols in Sound, 1997; This Being Human, 1998; Dance in the Fire, 1998; Between Silence, 1998; Feng Shui Soundworld. *Membership:* Musicians' Union; PRS; MCPS; PPL. *Current Management:* Red Gold Music Ltd. *Address:* 87A Queens Rd, East Grinstead, West Sussex RH19 1BG, England.

CHENEVIER, Guigou; b. 21 Nov. 1955, La Tronche, France. Musician (percussion); Composer. 2 s. *Education:* BA, Literature; Piano and drum lessons. *Career:* More than 400 concerts world-wide, include 3 US tours, with Etron Fou Leloublan, 1973–86; Drummer, composer, with Les Batteries; Octavo; Encore Plus Grande; Volapék, 1986–95; Les Figures, collaboration with Maguy Marin, 1996. *Recordings:* Demesure Révolutionnaire, Les Batteries; Reedition, Etron Fou LeLoublan, 1991; Des Pieds et Des Mains, Octavo, 1992; Le Diapason Du Père Ubu, 1993; Le Feu Du Tigre, Volapék, 1995; Slang, 1997; Les Rumeurs de la Ville, 1998. *Current Management:* Inou Productions. *Address:* 3A Maison IV De Chiffre, 26 rue des Teinturiers, 84000 Avignon, France.

CHENG, Sammi, (Cheng Sau Man, Twinnie Cheng); b. 19 Aug. 1972, Hong Kong. Vocalist. *Education:* Tang Shui Kin Victoria Technical School. *Career:* Honoured at seventh Hong Kong Amateur Singing Contest, 1998; Initially signed to local Capital Artists label; Career blossomed following move to Warner Music, 1995; Many film appearances including: Needing You, 2000; Fighting For Love, 2001. *Recordings:* Albums: Sammi, 1990; Holiday, 1991; Never Too Late, 1992; Happy Maze, Big Revenge, 1993; Ten Commandments, Time Place People, Sammi, 1994; After, It's About Time, Can't Let You Go, 1995; Never Want To Let You Go, Worth It, Passion, Sammi X Live, 1996; Waiting For You, Our Theme Song, Life's Language, Sammi Star Show 97, Feel So Good, 1998; Listen To Sammi, I Deserved, Really Love You, Arigatou, Loving Deeply, Love Stories, ¡Concert, 1999; To Love, Ladies First, Mei Fei Seik Mo, Love Is..., Taipei Concert 2000, 2001; Complete, Shocking Pink, 2001. *Honours:* Asian CCTV-MTV Music Award, Best Female Artist, 2000; Singapore Golden Hits Award, Most Popular Female Artist, 2001. *Address:* c/o Warner Music (HK) Ltd, 12/F Peninsula Office Tower, 18 Middle Rd, TST, Kowloon, Hong Kong. *E-mail:* sammi@warnermusic.com.tw.

CHÉNIER, Jacques Jake Pierre Roger; b. 31 July 1961, St Boniface, Winnipeg, Manitoba, Canada. *Education:* 1 year, University of Winnipeg; Graphic Arts Degree, Red River Community College, 1986. *Career:* Winnipeg International Children's Festival, 1988–99; Winnipeg Folk Festival; Stan Rogers Memorial Folk Festival; Ottawa Children's Festival, 1994, 1997; Over 600 school performances; Fred Penner's Place, CBC TV; Dancing With the Dinosaurs, Multimedia planetarium show. *Compositions:* Buzz Buzzity Buzz; Dinosaurs; Ghost in the House; Pizza Paradise; Lobster Twist. *Recordings:* Dancing with the Dinosaurs, 1989; Pizza Paradise, 1992; Content d'être moi, 1994; Walking in the Sun, 1996. *Honours:* John Lennon Songwriting Contest, Grand Prize Winner, 1997. *Membership:* SOCAN; Manitoba Audio Recording Industry Asscn. *Current Management:* Sandcastle Music. *Address:* PO Box 47025, RPO Marion, Winnipeg, Manitoba R2H 3G9, Canada.

CHER, (Cherilyn Sarkisian LaPierre); b. 20 May 1946,, El Centro, California, USA. Vocalist; Actor; Entertainer. m. (1) Sonny Bono, 1964, divorced, deceased, 1 d., (2) Gregg Allman, 1975, divorced, 1 s. *Career:* Worked with Sonny Bono in duo Sonny and Cher, 1964–74; Also solo artiste, 1964–; Performances include: Hollywood Bowl, 1966; Newport Pop Festival, 1968; Television includes: Sonny and Cher Comedy Hour, CBS, 1971; Cher, CBS, 1975–76; Sonny and Cher Show, CBS, 1976–77; Vocalist with rock group Black Rose, including US tour supporting Hall and Oates, 1980; Actress, films: Good Times, 1967; Chastity, 1969; Come Back To The Five and Dime, Jimmy Dean Jimmy Dean, 1982; Silkwood, 1984; Mask, 1985; The Witches of Eastwick, 1987; Moonstruck, 1987; Suspect, 1987; Mermaids, 1989. *Recordings include:* Singles: with Sonny and Cher: I Got You Babe (No. 1, UK and USA), 1975; Baby Don't Go, 1965; Just You, 1965; But You're Mine, 1965; What Now My Love, 1966; Little Man, 1966; The Beat Goes On, 1967; All I Ever Need Is You, 1971; A Cowboy's Work Is Never Done, 1972; Solo hit singles include: All I Really Want To Do, 1965; Bang Bang, 1966; Gypsies Tramps and Thieves (No. 1, USA), 1971; The Way of Love, 1972; Half Breed (No. 1, USA), 1973; Dark Lady (No. 1, USA), 1974; Take Me Home, 1979; Dead Ringer For Love, duet with Meatloaf, 1982; I Found Someone, 1987; We All Sleep Alone, 1988; After All, duet with Peter Cetera (for film soundtrack Chances Are), 1989; If I Could Turn Back Time, 1989; Jesse James, 1989; Heart of Stone, 1990; The Shoop Shoop Song (from film soundtrack Mermaids) (No. 1, UK), 1991; Love and Understanding, 1991; Oh No Not My

Baby, 1992; Love Can Build A Bridge (with Neneh Cherry and Chrissie Hynde; No. 1, UK), 1995; Walking In Memphis, 1995; One By One, 1996; Paradise Is Here, 1996; Believe (No. 1, UK and USA), 1998; Strong Enough, 1999; The Music's No Good Without You, 2001; Albums: with Sonny and Cher: Look At Us, 1965; All I Really Want To Do, 1965; The Wondrous World of Sonny and Cher, 1966; Sonny and Cher Live, 1972; Solo albums include: All I Really Want To Do, 1965; The Sonny Side of Cher, 1966; With Love, 1967; Backstage, 1968; Jackson Highway, 1969; Gypsies Tramps and Thieves, 1972; Foxy Lady, 1972; Greatest Hits, 1974; Stars, 1975; I'd Rather Believe In You, 1976; Take Me Home, 1979; I Paralyze, 1984; Cher, 1988; Heart of Stone, 1989; Love Hurts, 1991; Cher's Greatest Hits 1965–92, 1992; It's A Man's World, 1995; Believe, 1999; Black Rose, 1999; The Greatest Hits, 1999; Living Proof, 2001. Honours: Academy Award, Best Actress, Moonstruck, 1988; Grammy Award, Best Dance Recording (Believe), 2000. Current Management: Bill Sammeth Organisation, PO Box 960, Beverly Hills, CA 90213, USA.

CHERNEY, Ed; Prod; Music Engineer. Career: Apprentice engineer, Chicago, 1976; 5.1 surround sound mixer; Co-Music Dir, DH1 Studios, 2002; Worked with: Jan Arden, B-52's, Eric Clapton, Sonia Dada, Bob Dylan, Goo Goo Dolls, Hootie & the Blowfish, Billy Joel, Keb Mo, Roy Orbison, Bonnie Raitt, Leon Russell, Bob Seger, Steely Dan, The Rolling Stones. Honours: Three Grammy Awards. Address: c/o DH1 Studios, Woolworth Center, 233 Broadway, 22nd Floor, Suite 2200, New York, NY 10279, USA. E-mail: ed@dh1.tv. Website: www.dh1.com.

CHERONE, Gary; b. 24 July 1961, Malden, Massachusetts, USA. Vocalist; Songwriter. Career: Member, Dream; Singer, funk/rock group Extreme, 1985–; Played club circuit, Boston, 1985–88; World-wide appearances include: Regular US tours; American Dream concerts, London, 1992; Concert For Life, Tribute to Freddie Mercury, Wembley, 1992; Support to Bryan Adams, European tour, 1992; Lead singer, Van Halen, 1998–. Recordings: with Extreme: Singles: More Than Words (No. 1, USA), 1991; Get The Funk Out, 1991; Decadence Dance, 1991; Hole-Hearted, 1991; Song For Love, 1992; Rest In Peace, 1992; Stop The World, 1992; Tragic Comic, 1993; There Is No God, 1994; More Than Words, 1995; Albums: Extreme, 1989; Extreme II – Pornograffiti, 1991; III Sides To Every Story, 1992; Waiting For The Punchline, 1994; Running Gag, 1998; Accidental Collision, 1998; Best of Extreme, 2000; with Van Halen: 3, 1998. Honours: Winners, MTV Video contest, 1987; Boston Music Awards: Act of Year; Outstanding Rock Single, Hole-Hearted; Outstanding Pop Single; Outstanding Singer/Songwriter, More Than Words, 1992. Current Management: SRO Management, 189 Carlton St, Toronto, ON M5A 2K7, Canada.

CHERRY, Eagle Eye; b. 1970, Skåne, Sweden. Musician; Vocalist; Songwriter. Education: New York School of the Performing Arts. Career: Played drums in band for his father, Don Cherry; Worked as model and acted in several US TV shows; Wrote and performed debut album including duet with half-sister Titiyo and remixed by Cameron McVey. Recordings: Singles: Save Tonight, 1998; Falling in Love Again, 1998; Are You Still Having Fun, 2000; Long Way Around, 2001; Promises Made, 2001; Albums: Desireless, 1998; Living In The Present Future, 2000.

CHERRY, Neneh, (Neneh Mariana Karlsson); b. 10 March 1964, Stockholm, Sweden. Vocalist. Career: Moved to London; Early band, The Cherries; Joined Rip, Rig and Panic until band broke up; Began solo work and signed record deal; Worked with Cameron McVey and Tim Simenon; Contributed one track, I've Got You Under My Skin for AIDS Benefit Red Hot + Blue, 1990; Worked on second album with Michael Stipe, Gang Starr and Geoff Barrow. Recordings: Singles: Buffalo Stance, 1988; Manchild, 1989; Kisses On The Wind, 1989; I've Got You Under My Skin, 1990; Money Love, 1992; 7 Seconds, with Youssou N'Dour, 1994; Trouble Man, 1995; Love Can Build A Bridge, with Chrissie Hynde and Cher (No. 1, UK), 1995; Woman, 1996; Buddy X (with Dreem Team) 1999; Albums: With Rip Rig and Panic: God, 1981; I Am Cold, 1982; Attidue, 1983; Solo: Raw Like Sushi, 1989; Homebrew, 1992; Man, 1997; Also appeared on The The's Infected, 1986; Eagle Eye Cherry's Living In The Present Future, 2000.

CHESCOE, Laurie; b. 18 April 1933, London, England. Musician (drums). m. Sylviane Yanou Chescoe, 5 Aug. 1960, 1 s., 1 d. Career: Teddy Layton Band, 1957; Monty Sunshine, 1960; Dick Charlesworth, 1964; Bruce Turner, 1965; Bob Wallis, 1966; Alan Elsdon, 1976 (14 years); Midnite Follies Orchestra, 1978; Alex Welsh Band, 1979; Formed own band, Laurie Chescoe's Good Time Jazz, 1990; Performed at all major festivals, television and radio. Recordings: Albums: Two with Midnite Follies; Three with Keith Nicholls; 78s with Eric Allendale New Orleans Knights; Teddy Layton Band; Albums with own band; Six albums with Benny Walters, Ralph Sutton. Membership: Musicians' Union. Current Management: John Boddy Agency. Address: 10 Southfield Gardens, Twickenham TW1 4SZ, England.

CHESLIN, Mat; b. 28 Nov. 1970, Wordsley, West Midlands, England. Musician (bass). Career: Founder member, Neds Atomic Dustbin, 1987–95. Recordings: Albums: Grey Cell Green, 1991; God Fodder, 1991; Are You Normal?, 1993; Brainbloodvolume, 1995; The Best of Ned's Atomic Dustbin,

2000. Membership: Musicians' Union. Current Management: Paul Bolton, Chris 'Tank' Gilks. Address: Stourbridge, West Midlands, England.

CHESNUTT, Mark Nelson; b. 6 Sept. 1963, Beaumont, Texas, USA. Country vocalist; Musician (guitar, drums). Career: Played with father Bob Chesnutt's band around Beaumont region before pursuing solo career, aged 15; Landed a residency at Cutter's Bar, where the house band included Tracy Byrd; Recorded locally successful singles for several independent labels, notably Axbar, mid 1980s; Tape sent to regional promotions director of MCA Records in Houston, who passed it to MCA chief executive Tony Brown in Nashville; Brown flew to Beaumont to see live performance, resulting in record deal, 1990; Supported country legend Geoge Jones live and appeared on his Live In Tennessee video, 1994; Jones was a guest on second album; Continued to chart regularly throughout 1990s; Regularly tours with own New South Band. Compositions include: It's A Little Too Late; Let It Rain. Recordings include: Brother Jukebox, Too Cold At Home, 1990; Almost Goodbye, It Sure Is Monday, 1993; I Don't Want To Miss A Thing, 1998; Albums include: Longnecks and Short Stories, 1992; Almost Goodbye, 1993; Greatest Hits, 1996. Honours: CMA, Horizon Award, 1993; Amusement and Music Operators Asscn, Rising Star of the Year. Address: c/o The BDM Co, 1106 16th Ave S, Nashville, TN 37212, USA. E-mail: nutthouse1@aol.com. Website: www.markchesnutt.com.

CHESTER, Johnny; b. 26 Dec. 1941, Melbourne, Victoria, Australia. m. Larraine, 29 Sept. 1964, 3 d. Career: TV Host, Teen Scene, ABC TV, 1964–65; TV Host, Country Road, ABC TV, 1977–78; DJ, Radio 3U2, Melbourne, 1966–69; Presenter, Radio Australia, 1989–91; Toured Australia and New Zealand with The Beatles, 1964; Australia with Kenny Rogers, 1984; Tammy Wynette, 1992; Performed in Viet Nam, 1968; with own show, Australia Wide, 1961–. Compositions: World Greatest Mum; My Kind of Woman; Highway 31; I Love You So Rebecca; Lord I'd Forgotten. Recordings: Over 200 song titles released, 1961–. Honours: Male Vocalist of the Year, 1981, 1982, 1983; Australia CM Awards. Membership: APRA; TSA; CMAA; CMA (USA). Current Management: Ian B Allen, Dynamic Management, PO Box 101, Seaford, Victoria 3198, Australia.

CHESTERS, Eds; b. 24 Oct. 1971, Darlington, England. Musician (drums); Songwriter. Career: Founding mem., The Bluetones, 1994–; Release records on own label, Superior Quality Recordings, sell through Superior Quality Record Shop; Numerous tours, festivals, television and radio appearances. Recordings: Albums: Expecting To Fly, 1996; Return To The Last Chance Saloon, 1998; Science And Nature, 2000; The Singles 1995–2002, 2002. Singles: Return To Splendour, 1994; Nings Of Desire (EP), 1994; Are You Blue Or Are You Blind?, 1995; Bluetonic, 1996; Slight Return, 1996; Cut Some Rug, 1996; Marblehead Johnson, 1996; Solomon Bites The Worm, 1998; Sleazy Bed Track, 1998; 4-Day Weekend, 1998; If..., 1998; Mudslide, 2000; Keep The Home Fires Burning, 2000; Autophilia Or How I Learned To Stop Worrying And Love My Car, 2000. Honours: Gold disc for Return To The Last Chance Saloon. Address: c/o Mercury Records, Chancellors House, 72 Chancellors Rd, London W6 9QB, England. Website: www.bluetones.co.uk.

CHEVALLIER, D; b. 13 Jan. 1969, Ris Orangis, France. Musician (electric and acoustic guitar); Composer. Education: Classical guitar, Conservatoire National De Région de Paris. Career: Concerts, Rome; Berlin; New York; Rochester; Hartford; Richmond; Prague (EBU big band); Paris Jazz Festival; Nord Jazz Festival (Germany); Festival of Montpellier; Festival of Assier; Souillac; Ramatuelle and Montréal Jazz Festival, July 1996. Recordings: Migration, with Daniel Humoir, Yves Robert; Nilxa: State of Grace; Terre Nova: Danses. Membership: SACEM; SPEDIDAM. Current Management: Celia Productions. Address: 2 Pl. Beaumarchais, 91600 Savigny, S/Orge, France.

CHIARELLI, Robert C; b. 13 Jan. 1963. Mixer; Remix Prod. Education: University of Miami, Florida. Recordings: Producer and/or Mixer for numerous recordings including: Will Smith, The Temptations, Madonna, Janet Jackson, K-Ci and JoJo, Christina Aguilera, Jennifer Paige, The Corrs, Boyz II Men. Honours: 60 Platinum and Gold discs. Membership: American Federation of Musicians; National Academy of Recording Arts and Sciences. Address: 2219 W Olive Ave #102, Burbank, CA 91506, USA.

CHIASSON, Warren; b. 17 April 1934, Cheticamp, Nova Scotia, Canada. Jazz Musician (vibraphone, piano) Composer. Education: St Francis Xavier University, Antigonish, Nova Scotia; Jazz with Lenny Tristano; George Russell; Classical violin lessons for 6 years. Career: George Shearing Quintet, 1959–61, 1972–74; Clubs, concerts, tours with Chet Baker, Tal Farlow, Roberta Flack, 1975–82; Broadway show, Hair (composed the percussion), 1968–72. Compositions: Ultramarine; Bossa Nova Scotia; Bedouin; Hazel Eyes; Bravel; Festival. Recordings: Good Vibes For Kurt Weill; Point Counterpoint; Quartessence; Blues and Jazz, B. B. King. Publications: The Contemporary Vibraphonist. Honours: One of the Top Six Outstanding Jazz Vibraphonists over the last half-century, NY Times, 1989. Membership: ASCAP; Recording Musicians of America; NARAS. Current Management: Abby Hoffer Enterprises. Address: 223 E 48th St, New York, NY 10017, USA.

CHIAVOLA, Kathy; b. 7 March 1952, Chicago, Illinois, USA. Artist; Vocalist; Musician (guitar). *Education:* Oberlin Conservatory, BM, MM; Indiana Conservatory, postgraduate work. *Career:* Sang opera professionally; Moved to Nashville, 1980; Toured with The Doug Dillard Band, Vassar Clements, The Country Gazette; Formed The Lucky Dogs; Toured Eastern Europe with Douglas and Mark O'Connor, USIA tour: The Nashville Masters; UK debut tour, 1993; Voice of State Farm Insurance, television commercial; McDonalds commercial on radio. *Recordings:* Albums: Labor of Love, 1990; The Harvest, 1995; Appeared on Emmylou Harris video, Thanks To You; Recorded with: Garth Brooks; Emmylou Harris; Vince Gill; Kathy Mattea; Ricky Skaggs. *Honours:* Nammie Award, Backup Vocalist of the Year, 1995. *Membership:* IBMA; AFofM; AFTRA; NARAS.

CHILD, Desmond; b. 28 Oct. 1953, Miami, Florida, USA. Songwriter; Prod; Musician (keyboards). *Career:* Formed Desmond Child and Rouge, 1975; Concentrated on songwriting, 1980s. *Compositions:* Hit songs include: You Give Love A Bad Name, Bon Jovi, 1986; Livin' On A Prayer, Bon Jovi, 1986; I Was Made For Loving You, Kiss, 1979; Livin' La Vida Loca, Ricky Martin, 1999; Who Let The Dogs Out, Baha Men, 2001; Other songs for: Cher; Michael Bolton; Alice Cooper; Jimmy Barnes. *Recordings:* Albums: Desmond Child and Rouge, 1978; Runners In The Night, 1979; Desmond Child Discipline, 1991; Singles: You're The Story of My Life, 1991; Love On A Rooftop, 1991; Obsession, 1992. *Current Management:* C Winston Simone Management, 1790 Broadway, 10th Floor, New York, NY 10019, USA.

CHILDERS, Elsie T; b. 26 Sept. 1924, Henderson, Kentucky, USA. Studio Owner; Songwriter. 2 s. *Education:* Business, Midway College, 1941–42; Studied: Snare drum, Piano, Choral, Orchestra, Band, Marching band, Composition. *Career:* Owner, Manager: Trusty Tuneshop Recording Studio; Pianist and soloist for Johnson Island Baptist church 1950–; various radio and cable TV performances. *Compositions:* 380 songs published, over 100 recorded, artists include: Jennifer Nelson, 1991; Barry Russell, 1998; Jeremy Scott Busby, 2000. *Publications:* Instant Knowhow, 1971; Newsletter, 1978–98. *Honours:* Country Music Organizations of America, Song of the Year; Record Label Promoter of the Year; Artist Promoter of the Year; CD of the Year; Record Label of the Year, 2000. *Membership:* CMA; CMOA; Rotary Club. *Current Management:* Trusty International. *Address:* 8771 Rose Creek Rd, Nebo, KY 42441, USA. *E-mail:* trusty@wko.com.

CHILDISH, Billy; b. 1 Dec. 1959, Chatham, Kent. Vocalist; Songwriter; Author. *Career:* The Pop Rivets Live At Detling Village Hall, 1977; The Headcoats Live At Royal Festival Hall, 1999; Band, The Buff Medways. *Compositions:* The Cheeky Cheese; Plump Prizes and Little Gems; Hendrix Was Not The Only Musician. *Recordings:* The Pop Rivets Greatest Hits; Talkin' Bout Milkshakes; Acropolis Now; Ypres 1917 Overture; Which Dead Donky Daddy; In Tweed We Trust; Steady The Buffs, 2002. *Publications:* My Fault, Novel, 1996; Notebooks of a Naked Youth, Novel, 1997; I'd Rather You'd Lied, Poetry, 1999; Chatham Town Welcomes Desperate Men, Novel, 2001. *Membership:* Worshipful Order of Ancient Headcoats. *Address:* 11 Boundary Rd, Chatham, Kent ME4 6TS, England.

CHILDS, Robert Alexander; b. 23 April 1961, London, England. Musician (guitar, steel guitar); Vocalist; Songwriter; Music Journalist. *Career:* Member, country band Greta and The Stray Shots; Major concerts: Johnny Cash Show; Americana Fest; Morecombe International Festival; Television: Country By The Sea, BBC; Radio: Live In Concert, BBC Essex. *Recordings:* Greta and The Stray Shots: EP: Your Foolish Heart, 1988; Albums: Live, 1987; Above and Beyond, 1990; Livewire, 1991; Playtime, 1993; Inclusion of track: I Didn't Mean To Do It, on Declaration of Independence, The Best of British Country, 1994. *Publications:* Articles for: Making Music; Country Music Gazette; International Country Music News. *Membership:* Performing Rights Society. *Current Management:* New Cut Records. *Address:* 40 Fielding Way, Hutton, Essex, England.

CHILDS, William Edward; b. 8 March 1957, Los Angeles, California, USA. Composer; Musician (piano). m. Holly Hamilton, 30 June, 1991, 1 s. *Education:* BM, Composition, University of Southern California. *Career:* Six years with Freddie Hubbard, 1978–84; Played with J J Johnson, 1977; Played with: Allan Holdsworth; Dianne Reeves; Branford Marsalis; Bobby Hutcherson; Played twice as leader, North Sea Jazz Festival; Twice, Monterey Jazz Festival. *Compositions:* Two performed by Los Angeles Philharmonic; One for Akron Symphony Orchestra; One (strings, bass, rhythm section), performed at Monterey Jazz Festival, part of commission series; One at Grenoble Jazz Festival. *Recordings:* Albums: Take For Example This; Twilight Is Upon Us; His April Touch; Portrait of a Player; I've Known Rivers; Child Within, 1996; Skim Coat; Sideman with: Freddie Hubbard; Dianne Reeves; Allan Holdsworth; Eddie Daniels; Kevyn Lettau; Various selections in: New Real Book. *Honours:* Composition Department Award (USC). *Current Management:* Open Door Management, 865 Via de la Paz, Suite 365, Pacific Palisades, CA 90272–3618, USA.

CHILTON, John; b. 16 July 1932, London, England. Musician (trumpet); Arranger; Bandleader; Writer. *Career:* Leader, own band, mid 1950s; Member, arranger, Bruce Turner Jump Band, 1958–63; Played with Alex Welsh and Mike Daniels, early 1960s; Co-leader, the Feetwarmers, late 1960s; Sole bandleader, 1974–; Musical director, George Melly, 1974–; Tours, recordings, broadcasts, as George Melly and John Chilton's Feetwarmers, 1974–2003; Writer and researcher into jazz history. *Publications:* Who's Who of Jazz: Storyville To Swing Street; Louis – The Louis Armstrong Story; Jazz; Billie's Blues, partial biography of Billie Holiday; Historical accounts of: the Jenkins Orphanage bands; McKinney's Cotton Pickers; The Bob Crosby Bobcats; Biographies of: Sidney Bechet; Coleman Hawkins; Louis Jordan; Henry 'Red' Allen; Roy Eldridge; Who's Who of Jazz (Storyville to Swing Street); Who's Who of British Jazz.

CHISHOLM, Melanie Jayne, (Melanie C., Sporty Spice); b. 12 Jan. 1976, Liverpool, England. Vocalist. *Career:* Mem., Touch, later renamed Spice Girls, 1993–; Numerous tours, concerts, television and radio appearances; Film, Spiceworld: The Movie, 1997; World tour incl. UK, Europe, India, USA; Royal Command performances; Solo artiste, 1999–; Solo world tour incl. festival performances. *Recordings:* Albums: Spice (No. 1, UK), 1996; Spiceworld (No. 1, UK), 1997; Forever, 2000. Solo: Northern Star, 1999. Singles: with Spice Girls: Wannabe (No. 1, UK and USA), 1996; Say You'll Be There (No. 1, UK), 1996; 2 Become 1 (No. 1, UK), 1996; Mama/Who Do You Think You Are (No. 1, UK), 1997; Step To Me, 1997; Spice Up Your Life (No. 1, UK), 1997; Too Much (No. 1, UK),1997; Stop, 1998; (How Does It Feel To Be) On Top of the World, with England United, 1998; Move Over/Generation Next, 1998; Viva Forever (No. 1, UK), 1998; Goodbye (No. 1, UK), 1998; Holler/Let Love Lead The Way (No. 1, UK), 2000; Solo: When You're Gone, Bryan Adams featuring Melanie C, 1998; Going Down, 1999; Northern Star, 1999; Never Be The Same Again, with Lisa 'Left-Eye' Lopes (Number 1, UK), 2000; I Turn To You (Number 1, UK), 2000; If That Were Me, 2000. *Honours:* BRIT Awards, Best British Single, Wannabe, 1997, Bestselling British Album Act, 1998, Outstanding Contribution, 2000. *Address:* c/o Virgin Records Ltd, 553–79 Harrow Rd, London W10 4RH, England. *Website:* c3.vmg.co.uk/ spicegirls.

CHIWESHE, Stella Rambisai; b. 8 July 1946, Harare, Zimbabwe. m. (1) 2 d., (2) Peter Reich, 27 Jan. 1988. *Career:* Member, National Dance Company of Zimbabwe, Mbira Soloist, Actress and Dancer, 1981–84; Solotours in Germany, Great Britain and Italy, 1984; Tour through Germany, 1985; Introduction of marimbas for mbira music, 1986; Recording and publication of Ambuya?; Triumphant concert at Hackney Empire, London at Beat Apartheid Road Festival, 1987; European Tour, 1988; Tour in Europe with concerts in Slovenia, Switzerland, Austria, Great Britain, Italy, Poland and Germany, with trio and the Earthquake Band, 1995; Tour in Europe with concerts in the Netherlands, Belgium, Germany, Austria, Hungary, Great Britain and Ireland, 1996; Tour of USA, Netherlands, Germany and Italy, 1998; Appeared at Global Interchange Conference, New York, 1999; Directed music theatre performance of Chiedza – Light, in Cologne, 1999; Forthcoming workshop session for Dimensions Theatre Oakland, USA, 2000. *Compositions:* Kasahwa; Chaa!; Nsuzu Chamakuwende; Mapere. *Recordings:* CD, Tapera, 1999. *Honours:* Billboard Music Award, 1993. *Membership:* GEMA. *Current Management:* Alba Kultur-Aktionen, Birgit Ellinghaus. *Address:* Alba Kulturaktionen, Justinianstr 16, 50679, Koeln, Germany.

CHOLET, Jean-Christophe; b. 11 May 1962, Böhl, Germany. Musician (piano); Composer; Arranger. Divorced, 1 s., 1 d. *Education:* University diploma, piano (schola cantorum), harmony, counterpoint and fugue. *Career:* Concerts, festivals: Radio France (Paris); Coutances; Couches; Sorgues; Toutplellier; Vienna (Austria); Tous le Savnièr; Worms; Mainz; Bonn; Trier, Germany; Le Havre; Avignon. *Recordings:* with Odéjy: Osti Natologie; Suite Alpestre; with Mathias Rüegg and Michel Portal: Third Dream. *Honours:* First Prize, Soloist, Composition and Orchestra, International Festival of Jazz, La Défense, Paris. *Membership:* Union of Jazz Musicians. *Current Management:* Odéjy, Route de St Georges, 8900 Perigny, France. *Address:* 295 Chemin de la Motte, 45200 Paulcourt, France.

CHOLEWA, Tom Mike Werner; b. 4 June 1958, Copenhagen, Denmark. Conductor; Musician (French horn). m. Ellen, 1983, 2 d. *Education:* Degree in Classical Music, Royal Danish Music Academy; French Horn and Musicology, University of Copenhagen. *Career:* Bandmaster of Zealand Life Regiment, 1989–96; Freelance conductor and musician; Music Educator. *Recordings:* Conductor, television production Dagen vi aldrig glemmer, with the Danish vocal group Swing Sisters and Band of Zealand Life Regiment. *Honours:* Second Prize, march competition for Prince Joachim, Denmark. *Membership:* Danish Conductors Asscn. *Address:* Folkevej 19, 2820 Gentofte, Denmark.

CHRIS, Jo; b. 12 Nov. 1960, Balengou, Cameroon. Musician (Piano). m. Ngandjeu Iavre, 6 Aug. 1984, 1 s., 3 d. *Education:* Professor of Music, Lycee de Newbell; Music studies with Billy Mussango. *Compositions:* 17 published songs, arranged by Billy Mussango. *Membership:* Socimada. *Address:* c/o Billy Mussango, PO Box 8363 Yaounde, Cameroon.

CHRISSY BOY, (Chris Foreman); b. 8 Aug. 1958, London, England. Musician (guitar, keyboards). m. (1) 1976, 1 s., (2) 1992, 1 s. *Career:* Founder member, group Madness; Numerous appearances on television programmes including Top of the Pops; Band split in 1987; Became The Madness until

1989; Formed group The Nutty Boys, releasing album Crunch!, 1990; Madness re-formed sporadically, 1992–. *Recordings:* with Madness: Albums include: One Step Beyond, 1979; Absolutely, 1980; 7, 1981; Complete Madness (No. 1, UK), 1982; The Rise and Fall, 1982; Madness, 1983; Keep Moving, 1984; Mad Not Mad, 1985; Peel Sessions, 1986; Utter Madness, 1986; The Madness, 1988; Divine Madness (compilation; No. 1, UK), 1992; Madstock (live), 1993; Wonderful, 1999; Singles include: One Step Beyond, 1979; My Girl, 1980; Baggy Trousers, 1980; Embarrassment, 1980; The Return of The Los Palmas 7, 1981; Grey Day, 1981; Shut Up, 1981; It Must Be Love, 1981; House of Fun (No. 1, UK), 1982; Driving In My Car, 1982; Our House, 1982; Tomorrow's Just Another Day, 1983; Wings of a Dove, 1983; The Sun and The Rain, 1983; Michael Caine, 1984; One Better Day, 1984; Yesterdays Men, 1985; Uncle Sam, 1985; Waiting For The Ghost Train, 1986; Lovestruck, 1999; Drip Fed Fred (with Ian Dury), 2000; with The Nutty Boys: Album: Crunch!, 1990; Singles: Magic Carpet; It's OK I'm A Policeman; Pop My Top. *Honours:* Gold discs; Ivor Novello Award, as songwriter, Our House. *Membership:* PRS; VPL; Musicians' Union. *Address:* c/o PO Box 3087, London NW5 3DZ, England.

CHRISTENSEN, Nikolaj; b. 19 Feb. 1966, Copenhagen, Denmark. Vocalist; Actor. *Career:* Major films: Christian, director, Gabrial Axel; Hjerter I Slor, Jesper W Nielsen. *Recordings:* Piloter, 1990; Jimmy and Vicky, 1991; Hen Over Jorden, 1994; Vi Er På Vej, 1996. *Honours:* Grammy, Best New Artist, 1990. *Membership:* DJBFA. *Address:* Kick Musik, Energivej 42B, 2750 Ballerup, Denmark.

CHRISTENSEN, Soren; b. 6 June 1963, Copenhagen, Denmark. Musician (drums). *Education:* Public Music School, Percussion, 1979; Berklee School of Music, 1980; Numerous trips to New York; Private tuition in Copenhagen. *Career:* Appearances in major festivals throughout Scandinavia; Many appearances on national TV and radio; Appearance in film The Naked Trees. *Recordings:* With EV's Youth Big Band, 1984, 1985; Hens Winther, The Planets; Claus Waidtlow, Claustrophobia; CD of own band, Drumscapes, forthcoming. *Honours:* The Planets, Grammy Award Winner, 1995. *Current Management:* Native Music, Denmark. *Address:* Nyelandsvej 7, U T H, 2000 Frederiksburg, Denmark.

CHRISTENSEN, Thomas Hass; b. 15 March 1961, Frederiksberg, Denmark. Musician (saxophone); Composer. *Career:* Played: 2 weeks, Ronnie Scott's, 1989; Montréal Jazz Festival, with Page One, 1989; Toured with soloists as a sideman. *Recordings:* with Page One: Beating Bop; Live At Ronnie Scott's; Notes In Time, Thomas Hass; A Matter of Fact, The End. *Honours:* The European Jazz Federation Prize, 1977. *Membership:* DMF; DJBFA. *Address:* Sollerod Park, bl 13 no 20, 2840 Holte, Denmark.

CHRISTI, Ellen; b. 7 March 1958, Chicago, Illinois, USA. Vocalist; Composer; Arranger; Prod. *Education:* BA, Music and Arts Management; Studied Composition, Technique and Arranging with Jaki Byard, bello canto technique with Virginia Davidson and Galli Campi. *Career:* Radio appearances in New York, Boston, Chicago, Los Angeles, San Francisco, Washington DC, North and South Carolina, Switzerland, Italy, France, Senegal, Germany, England, Austria, Japan, Australia; TV appearances in Senegal, Milan, Zurich, Munich, Hamburg, Nice. *Compositions:* I'm A Fan (of Every Man); Japanese Twilight; Midnight Moon; Senza Parole; Open Your Eyes; Anna Speaks. *Recordings:* I'm A Fan; Aliens' Talk; Instant Reality; Reconstruction of Sound; Vocal Desires; Piece of the Rock. *Current Management:* Bliss Corporation, Italy. *Address:* 320 W 83rd St 6H, New York, NY 10024, USA.

CHRISTIAN, Garry; b. 27 Feb. 1955, Liverpool, England. Vocalist. *Career:* Member, The Christians, 1984–95, re-formed 2000; Appearances include: Liver Aid Ethiopian Famine benefit, Liverpool, 1985; Support to Fleetwood Mac, British tour, 1988; John Lennon Tribute Concert, Merseyside, 1990; Regular UK and European tours. *Recordings:* Albums: The Christians (No. 2, UK), 1987; Colour (No. 1, UK), 1990; Happy In Hell, 1992; The Best of The Christians, 1993; Singles include: Forgotten Town, 1987; Hooverville (They Promised Us The World), 1987; When The Fingers Point, 1987; Ideal World, 1988; Born Again, 1988; Harvest For The World, 1988; Words, 1989; What's In A Word, 1992; The Bottle, 1993; Contributor, Ferry 'Cross The Mersey, Hillsborough football disaster benefit record (No. 1, UK), 1989; solo: Your Cool Mystery, 1997. *Current Management:* Eternal Management, 55 Lark Lane, Liverpool, Merseyside L17 8UW, England.

CHRISTIAN, James John; b. Milford, Connecticut, USA. Vocalist; Songwriter; Musician (guitar, drums, keyboards); Record Prod. *Career:* Lead singer, LA Rocks; Lead singer, House of Lords; World tours, opened for acts including: Ozzy Osbourne; Queensryche; Cheap Trick; Scorpions; Tesla; Producer, writer, solo musician; Lead singer, Tour of Japan with Pata (lead guitarist with Japanese band X), 1993; Opened own recording studio, Bodeo Rodeo Records. *Compositions include:* Les Ideos Noires, platinum hit single for Julie Masse; Songs for group, Alias. *Recordings:* 3 albums with House of Lords include: House of Lords; Sahara; Solo album: Rude Awakening; Singles include: Can't Find My Way Home; As producer: Album: A Contre Jour, Julie

Masse. *Current Management:* John Dubuque, Dublen Entertainment Group, 330 Merwin Ave, Unit #F1, Milford, CT 06460, USA.

CHRISTIAN, Rick; b. 22 Sept. 1951, Romford, Essex, England. Vocalist; Songwriter; Musician (6 and 12 string guitars). m. Gillian Mary Moore, 11 April 1981. *Career:* Professional musician since 1987; Many radio appearances include: Capital; LBC; BBC and independent local radio stations including Essex, Suffolk, Kent, Bedford, Shropshire; Festivals include: South Downs, Broadstairs; Walton; Co-presenter, Essex Folk, BBC Essex, 1986–94; Organizer, Maldon Folk Club and Maldon Folk Festival; Supported artists including: Jim Couza; Fred Wedlock; Harvey Andrews; Played charity event alongside Griff Rhys Jones, 1990; Tours, Denmark, 1994, 1995; Arizona USA, 1999, 2000, 2001; Folk column writer, Maldon & Burnham Standard; Reviewer, EFN Magazine, Tradition Magazine. *Recordings:* Albums: Reason Enough, 1983; Looking For Signs, 1990; The Open Road, 1996; These Things Happen, 1996; Looking For Signs, 2002. *Publications:* Major contributor: Guinness Who's Who of Folk Music; Guinness Encyclopedia of Popular Music. *Membership:* Musicians' Union; PRS; PPL; Essex Folk Asscn; MCPS. *Address:* PO Box 4099, Maldon, Essex CM9 4YQ, England. *Website:* www.rickchristian.co.uk.

CHRISTIAN, Roger; b. 13 Feb. 1950, Liverpool, Merseyside, England. Vocalist. *Career:* Member, The Christians, 1984–87; Solo artiste, 1989–; Appearances include: Liver Aid Ethiopian Famine benefit, Liverpool, 1985; British tour, 1986. *Recordings:* with The Christians: The Christians (No. 2, UK), 1987; Solo album: Checkmate, 1989; Singles: with The Christians: Forgotten Town, 1987; Hooverville (They Promised Us The World), 1987; When The Fingers Point, 1987; Solo: Take It From Home, 1989. *Current Management:* Eternal Management, 55 Lark Lane, Liverpool, Merseyside L17 8UW, England.

CHRISTIAN, Russell; b. 8 July 1956, Liverpool, Merseyside, England. Vocalist. *Career:* Member, The Christians, 1984–95; Appearances include: Liver Aid Ethiopian Famine benefit, Liverpool, 1985; Regular UK and European tours; Support to Fleetwood Mac, British tour, 1988; John Lennon Tribute Concert, Merseyside, 1990. *Recordings:* Albums: The Christians (No. 2, UK), 1987; Colour (No. 1, UK), 1990; Happy In Hell, 1992; The Best of The Christians, 1993; Singles include: Forgotten Town, 1987; Hooverville (They Promised Us The World), 1987; When The Fingers Point, 1987; Ideal World, 1988; Born Again, 1988; Harvest For The World, 1988; Words, 1989; What's In A Word, 1992; The Bottle, 1992; Contributor, Ferry 'Cross The Mersey, Hillsborough football disaster benefit (No. 1, UK), 1989. *Current Management:* Eternal Management, 55 Lark Lane, Liverpool, Merseyside L17 8UW, England.

CHRISTIANE, Kelvin; b. 16 March 1958, Watford, Hertfordshire, England. Jazz Musician (saxophones, flute, clarinet, keyboards, percussion); Composer. Divorced, 1 s. *Education:* Watford School of Music; City of Leeds College of Music. *Career:* Television appearances, Blue Mercedes, Afrique; Toured Europe and India with: Afrique, 1980; The Flyers, 1981–84; Frequent radio broadcasts promoting albums with Kelvin Christiane band; Toured with Tess Garraway in the Bernard 'Pretty' Purdie band, 1998. *Recordings:* Albums: with Kelvin Christiane Band: Awakening, 1992; Soho, 1993; Great Spirit, 1994; Salute the Sun, 1997; Tribute to Roland Kirk, 1998; Peggy's Back, a toast to Peggy Lee with Tess Garraway, 1999. *Honours:* GDLM. *Membership:* Musicians' Union. *Address:* 43a Grove Rd, Eastbourne, East Sussex BN21 4TX, England.

CHRISTIDES, Konstantinos; b. 30 April 1973, Thessaloniki, Greece. Composer; Musician (piano). *Education:* Studied Harmony, Counterpoint, Fugue, Macedonian Conservatoire, Thessaloniki, Greece, 1984–93; Bachelor in Piano and Composition, London College of Music, 1993–96; Postgraduate Diploma in Scoring for Film and TV, London College of Music, 1997; Graduate Diploma in Scoring for Film and TV, University of Southern California, 1998. *Career:* Scoring for Puzzle Box, short film; The Footsteps of Apostle John, short film; Scoring Assistant to Christopher Young including films Playing by Heart, 1998; Entrapment, 1999; The Big Kahuna, 1999; In Too Deep, 1999; Bless the Child, Wonderboys, The Hurricane, all forthcoming. *Compositions:* Measure for Measure, 1997; Olympic Fanfare, 1998; Out of the Ruins, 1998. *Honours:* Henry Purcell Prize for Composers, 1996; Wilfred Joseph's Prize for Composers, 1997; Sir Malcolm Arnols President's Award, 1997; University of Southern California International Students' Award, 1998. *Membership:* Society of Composers and Lyricists, USA; American Musicians' Union, Los Angeles. *Address:* 1007 S Stanley Ave 104, Los Angeles, CA 90019, USA.

CHRISTIE, Lou, (Lugee Alfredo Giovanni Sacco); b. 19 Feb. 1943, Glenwillard, Pennsylvania, USA. Vocalist; Songwriter; Prod. m. Francesca Winfield, Nov. 1971, 1 s., 1 d. *Education:* Studied voice and classical music, with Miss Joliann Williams, 1957–58; Voice, music arranging/production, with Lennie Martin, 1961–62. *Career:* Leader, The Crewnecks, 1957–58; The Classics, 1959–60; Lugee and the Lions, 1961–62; Sang backgrounds, Marcy Jo, 1961; Solo artist, 1962–; Concerts: Dick Clark Caravan of Stars, 1963–66; First British tour, 1966; Tour, UK, Germany, Netherlands, 1969; Record Star Show, Wembley, 1970; Cabaret tour, UK, 1970; NME Poll Winners Concert,

Wembley, 1970; Club tour, UK, 1972; Tours, USA, 1981–; Television: American Bandstand, 1963–66; Where The Action Is, 1966; Joey Bishop, 1969; Mike Douglas, 1969; The Dating Game, 1969; Top of the Pops, 1970; Midnight Special, 1974; Entertainment Tonight, 1985; Church Street Station, 1986; Nashville Now, 1989. *Recordings:* The Gypsy Cried, 1962; Two Faces Have I, 1963; Have I Sinned, 1964; Lightnin' Strikes, 1965; Rhapsody In The Rain, 1966; Painter, 1966; Wild Life's In Season, 1966; Don't Stop Me, 1967; Genesis and The Third Verse, 1968; I'm Gonna Make You Mine, 1969; Beyond The Blue Horizon, 1973; Guardian Angels, 1981; Enlightnin'ment, 1988; Glory River: The Buddah Years, 1968–72, 1992; Beyond The Blue Horizon: More of the Best of Lou Christie, 1994; Pledging My Love, 1997; The Complete Co and Ce/Roulette Recordings, 1998; Beyond the Blue Horizon/Hey You Cajun, 1998; Lou Christie Strikes Again, 1998; Egyptian Shumba (compilation), 2001; Film soundtracks include: Mondo Trasho, 1969; Rain Man, 1988; Dutch, 1990; A Home of Our Own, 1993; Barcelona, 1994; Before Sunrise, 1995; Burnzy's Last Call, 1995; Waiting for Guffman, 1996; Nick and Jane, 1997; The Last Days of Disco, 1998. *Honours:* 4 Gold records (USA); BMI Citation, 1966; 1 Gold (Japan), 1971; BMI Award, 1994. *Current Management:* Dick Fox Management, 1650 Broadway, New York, NY 10019, USA.

CHUCK D, (Carlton Ridenhour); b. 1 Aug. 1960, Long Island, New York, USA. Rap Artiste. *Education:* Graphic Design, Adelphi University. *Career:* Super Special Mix Show, radio WBAU, 1982; Own mobile DJ and concert promotion company, Spectrum City; Founder mem., US rap group, Public Enemy, 1984–; Concerts include: Support to the Beastie Boys, USA, 1987; Support to LL Cool J, European tour, 1987; Tour of a Black Planet, 1990; British tour, 1990; Apocalypse '91 US tour, with Anthrax, 1991; Headliners, The World's Greatest Rap Show, 1992; Madison Square Garden, 1992; Greenpeace Stop Sellafield concert with U2, Manchester, England, 1992; Reading Festival, England, 1992; Support to U2, Zooropa tour, 1992; Manager, promoter, The Entourage (hip hop venue), Long Island, New York, 1986; Founder, Offda Books, Under the Radar Publishing, 2003. *Recordings:* Albums: Yo! Bum Rush The Show, 1987; It Takes A Nation of Millions To Hold Us Back, 1988; Fear of a Black Planet, 1990; Apocalypse '91 – The Enemy Strikes Back, 1991; Greatest Misses, 1992; Muse Sick 'n' Hour Mess Age, 1994; There's A Poison Goin' On, 1999; Revolverlution, 2002; Solo releases include: No, 1996; Autobiography of Mistachuck, 1996. Singles include: Rebel Without A Pause, 1987; Bring The Noise, 1988; Don't Believe The Hype, 1988; Night of The Living Baseheads, 1988; Fight The Power, theme for film Do The Right Thing, 1989; Welcome To The Terrordome, 1990; 911 Is A Joke, 1990; Brothers Gonna Work It Out, 1990; Can't Do Nuttin For Ya Man, 1990; Bring The Noise (with Anthrax), 1991; Can't Truss It, 1991; Shut 'Em Down, 1992; Nighttrain, 1992; Give It Up, 1994; So Whatcha Gonna Do Now, 1995; He Got Game, 1998. *Honours:* Platinum discs; Best Rap Group, Rolling Stone Readers Picks awards, 1991; Best Rap Album, Soul Train Music Awards, 1992. *Current Management:* Malik Entertainment, 3 Third Pl., Roosevelt, NY 11575, USA.

CHURCH, Charlotte; b. 21 Feb. 1986, Llandaff, Cardiff, Wales. Vocalist (soprano). *Career:* Singer of opera, musical hits, folk songs and contemporary songs; Numerous live concerts, television and radio appearances. *Recordings:* Albums: Voice Of An Angel, 1998; Charlotte Church, 1999; Dream A Dream, 2000; Enchantment, 2001; Prelude... The Best Of Charlotte Church, 2002. *Honours:* Platinum discs, USA. *Address:* c/o Sony Classical, 550 Madison Ave, New York, NY 10022-3211, USA. *Website:* www.charlottechurch.com.

CHURCH, Joseph; b. 25 Nov. 1957, New York, USA. Music Dir; Conductor; Composer; Prof; Arranger; Musician. 1 d. *Education:* BA, Swarthmore College, 1978; MM, University of Illinois, 1980; DA, New York University, 1996. *Career:* Music Director, Conductor, Include National Tour, Little Shop of Horros, 1984–86; Radio City Music Halls Christmas Special, 1988–89; Promenade Theatre, Catch Me If I Fall, 1990; Giuseppe Verdi Society Chorus and Orchestra, Italy, 1991; St James Theatre, Broadway, The Who's Tommy, 1992–95; La Jolla Playhouse, California, 1995–97; Music Director, Conductor, The Lion King, New Amsterdam Theatre; Music Supervisor, The Lion King, London, Japan, Toronto; Adjunct Professor of Music, New York University School of Education, 1998–; Television appearances include The Late Show with David Letterman, The Today Show, Theatre Talk. *Compositions:* Les Fables; Sonata For Two Pianos; Vibrachrome; Mock Opera; Soggiorno; Duo For Violin And Viola. *Honours:* Drama Logue Award; ASCAP Composition Award. *Membership:* ASCAP; American Music Center; College Music Society. *Address:* 305 W 98th St, Apt 3E N, New York, NY 10025, USA.

CHURCHLEY, Richard Allen; b. 13 Nov. 1952, Birmingham, England. Songwriter; Vocalist; Musician (accordion, guitar, mandolin). m. Prue Dobell, 18 Jan. 1975, 2 s. *Education:* BA Hons, German, Reading University, England. *Career:* Appearances with various bands on Folk and acoustic music circuits including: Harry-Ca-Nab; Peaky Blinders; Barker's Knee; Mind Your Own Business; Oh-Cajunal Playboys; Also radio appearances on local radio and BBC Radio 2. *Compositions:* Various Folk songs. *Recordings include:* Mega-Maggot, Harry-Ca-Nab, 1990. *Membership:* Musicians' Union. *Current Management:* Ashtree Agency. *Address:* 1293 Evesham Rd, Astwood Bank, Redditch, Worcestershire B96 6AY, England.

CIARAN, Cian; b. 16 June 1976, Bangor, Wales. Musician (keyboards). *Career:* Member, Super Furry Animals; Early releases on small indie label, then obtained major indie label deal; Numerous British and international tours; Many festival appearances. *Recordings:* Singles: Llanfairpwllgwyngyllgogerychwyndrobwl... EP, 1995; Moog Droog EP, 1995; God! Show Me Magic, 1996; If You Don't Want Me To Destroy You, 1996; The Man Don't Give A Fuck, 1996; Hometown Unicorn, 1996; Something 4 The Weekend, 1996 The International Language of Screaming, 1997; Hermann Loves Pauline, 1997; Demons, 1997; Play It Cool, 1997; Ice Hockey Hair, 1998; Northern Lights, 1999; Fire In My Heart, 1999; Do Or Die, 2000; Juxtaposed With You, 2001; Albums: Fuzzy Logic, 1996; Radiator, 1997; Outspaced (compilation), 1998; Guerrilla, 1999; Mwng, 2000; Rings Around The World, 2001.

CINGL, Pavel; b. 1962, Teplice, Czech Republic. Musician (violin). m. Katerina, 15 July 1989, 2 s. *Education:* Conservatory of Jaroslav Jezek, Prague. *Career:* Support to Alan Stivell in Prague; Tours in Germany, Austria, France, Netherlands, Belgium, Denmark; Regular Czech television and radio appearances. *Recordings:* 16 records with Czech bands. *Current Management:* EXUPERY Art Agency, Krizeneckeho nam 322, 15250 Prague 5, Czech Republic. *Address:* Podlipneho 7, 180 00 Prague 8, Czech Republic.

CISAR, Miroslav; b. 2 Dec. 1929, Prague, Czech Republic. Composer; Conductor. 2 s. *Career:* Mem., Symphonic Orchestra; Conductor, Brass Bands and folk groups; Composer; Arranger; Numerous performances on Radio Prague. *Compositions:* 36 albums. *Publications:* Compositions published. *Honours:* Winner in Radio Competition; Winner, Compositions for Children and Sportsmen. *Membership:* Co of Brass Music; Group Composers, Czech Republic. *Address:* Hronovská 205, 542 33 Rtyne v Podkrkonosi, Czech Republic.

CISAR, Zbynek; b. 6 March 1954, Prague, Czech Republic. Music School Dir. m. Alena Cisarova. *Education:* Music College of Jaroslav Jezek, Masaryk University, Brno; Yamaha Music School. *Career:* Songs; Orchestra Pieces; Songs for Children; Amateur Theatre. *Compositions:* April School, Radio and Theatre Musical for Children. *Recordings:* April School; Children's Note. *Publications:* Text Books; Collection of Songs for Children. *Honours:* Children's Note, first, second and third places. *Membership:* Copyright Organization of Musicians. *Current Management:* Music School. *Address:* Vobcanskem Domove 1, Prague 4 14000, Czech Republic.

CISSOKHO, Malang; b. 27 May 1962, Thies, Senegal. Musician (kora, guitar, bass guitar, percussion); Vocalist; Songwriter. m. Pirjo Saastamoinen, 24 Nov. 1989, 1 s. *Education:* Traditional Musicial Education of Mandinko Griot. *Career:* Kaustinen Folk Music Festival, 1988, 1989, 1995; Jyvaskyla Summer Festival, 1989; Pori Jazz Festival, 1989, 1996; Joensuu Festival, 1994, 1996; Ruisrock, 1996. *Compositions:* Mun-Mun, 1982; Warale, 1985; Yendi, 1985; Touba, 1985; Foroya, 1997; Kano, 1997; Alimaton Salia, 1990. *Recordings:* Solo albums: Lotus, 1990; Foroya, 1997; Dialia, 1997; Contributor: Super Etoile II de Dakar: Náteel Weerwi, Piirpanke: Tuku Tuku; Kristian Blak: Addeq; Rinne Radio: Rok; The Cool Sheiks: Serve Cool, Trance Planet Vol. 3; J Karjalainen and Electric Sauna: Electric Sauna; Piirpauke: Metamorphosis. *Honours:* Emma Award, 1996. *Membership:* Finnish Musician Asscn. *Address:* Haapalahdenkatu 5 G44, 00300 Helsinki, Finland.

CLACKETT, Matthew James; b. 24 Aug. 1972, Dover, Kent, England. Musician (alto, tenor, soprano saxophone). *Education:* Double music A levels, classical training to age 16. *Career:* Numerous session appearances and live concerts include: Roachford; Philip Bent; Peter Maas (Freeez); Worked in: USA; Canada; Japan. *Recordings:* Album: Take One, 1989; Second album due release 1995. *Membership:* Musicians' Union. *Address:* 2 Kew Green, Richmond, Surrey TW9 3BH, England.

CLAIR, Mark, (Mark Mac, Cold Mission); b. London, England. Prod; Remixer; DJ. *Career:* Member: 4 Hero; Manix; Jacob's Optical Stairway; Co-founder, Reinforced Records, 1990; Collaborations: Jill Scott; Ursula Rucker; Terry Callier. *Recordings:* Albums: with 4 Hero: In Rough Territory, 1991; Parallel Universe, 1995; Jacob's Optical Stairway (with Jacob's Optical Stairway), 1996; Two Pages, 1998; Creating Patterns, 2001; Singles: Mr Kirk's Nightmare, 1991; Earth Pioneers, 1997; Escape That, 1999; Les Fleurs, 2001. *Address:* c/o Reinforced Records, 387–389 Chapter Rd, London NW2 5NG, England.

CLAPTON, Eric, (Eric Patrick Clapp); b. 30 March 1945, Ripley, Surrey, England. Musician (guitar); Vocalist; Songwriter. m. Patti Boyd, 1979, divorced, 1 s., deceased. *Career:* Guitarist with groups: The Roosters, 1963; The Yardbirds, 1963–65; John Mayall's Bluebreakers, 1965–66; Cream, 1966–68; Blind Faith, 1969; Derek and the Dominoes, 1970; Delaney and Bonnie, 1970–72; Solo artiste, 1972–; Concerts include: Concert for Bangla Desh, 1971; Last Waltz concert, The Band's farewell concert, 1976; Live Aid, 1985; Record series of 24 concerts, Royal Albert Hall, 1991; Japanese tour with George Harrison, 1991; Film appearance: Tommy, 1974. *Compositions include:* Presence of The Lord; Layla; Badge (with George Harrison). *Recordings include:* Albums: Disraeli Gears, 1967; Wheels of Fire, 1968;

Goodbye Cream, 1969; Layla, 1970; Blind Faith, 1971; Concert For Bangladesh, 1971; Eric Clapton's Rainbow Concert, 1973; 461 Ocean Boulevard, 1974; E C Was Here, 1975; No Reason To Cry, 1976; Slowhand, 1977; Backless, 1978; Just One Night, 1980; Money and Cigarettes, 1983; Behind The Sun, 1985; August, 1986; Journeyman, 1989; 24 Nights, 1992; MTV Unplugged, 1992; From The Cradle, 1994; Rainbow Concert, 1995; Crossroads 2, 1996; Live In Montreux, 1997; Pilgrim, 1998; One More Car, One More Rider, 2002; with Jimmy Page and Jeff Beck, 1999; Riding With The King, 2000; Reptile, 2001; Soundtracks include: Tommy; The Color of Money; Lethal Weapon; Rush; Hit singles include: I Shot The Sheriff; Layla; Lay Down Sally; Wonderful Tonight; Cocaine; Behind The Mask; Tears In Heaven; Contributed to numerous albums by artists including: Phil Collins; Bob Dylan; Aretha Franklin; Joe Cocker; Roger Daltrey; Dr John; Rick Danko; Ringo Starr; Roger Waters; Christine McVie; Howlin' Wolf; Sonny Boy Williamson; The Beatles: The White Album (listed as L'Angelo Mysterioso). *Honours:* numerous including: Grammy Awards, Six in 1993, Best Rock Performance By Duo Or Group, The Calling (with Santana), 2000, Traditional Blues Album, Riding With The King (with B. B. King), 2001, Pop Instrumental Performance, for Reptile, 2002; Q Magazine Merit Award, 1995. *Address:* c/o Michael Eaton, 22 Blades Ct, Deodar Rd, London SW15 2NU, England.

CLARIN, Bjorn A. F; b. 15 Dec. 1936. Songwriter; Composer; CD Prod; Television Scriptwriter. m. Marianne, 26 April 1958, 2 s., 2 d. *Education:* Piano, Flute, Guitar. *Career:* Over 500 appearances, mostly in children's programmes. *Compositions:* Over Sixty Songs with Lyrics by Harry Martinson. *Recordings:* Twenty Five LP and CD Productions of Popular Swedish Music. *Honours:* Fred Winter Scholarship; Swedish Scholarship of Music. *Address:* Hampakersvagen 14, 55 339 Lerum, Sweden.

CLARK, Anne; b. 14 May 1960, London, England. Poet; Songwriter; Performer. *Education:* Piano, violin, viola. *Career:* 10 albums; Major tours, Europe, North America, 1980–; Co-editor, Paul Weller's Riot Stories. *Recordings:* 10 albums; Live album: Psychometry, 2000; Singles: Our Darkness; Sleeper In Metropolis; Abuse. *Publications:* Hard Lines; Notes Taken, Traces Left. *Membership:* PRS; MCPS; GVL. *Address:* 55 Fulham High St, London SW6 3JJ, England.

CLARK, Colin; b. 6 June 1953, Hurstpierpoint, England. Vocalist. m. Solveig Clark. *Career:* Apperances on Meridian Television Pier Programme BBC Radio Sussex; Radio Kent; Radio BBC World Service; Radio Huset, Denmark; Mercury; Radio West Point, Denmark, Belgium; Performed at Copenhagen Country Music Club, 1997; Appearances in Denmark including Scandinavian Country Music Club Festival, Silkeborg, 1998; Numerous radio interviews in Denmark; Guest with Bendix Band, Leif Kerstein and Winchesters and Tomboola Band, 1998; Appearance with The Nashvilles in Denmark, Jan. 2000. *Compositions:* Black Train; Trail of Tears; You Hold The Key To My Heart; Those City Lights Called Your Name. *Recordings:* Songs on forthcoming album: Standing On The Edge of Lonely; That Number's Been Changed; You Haunt The Shadows of My Mind; This Old Honky Tonk; I'm Outta Here; Black Train; Special Kind of Lady; The Price For Loving You; Boogie Woogie Thang; It's Time I Settled Down; Isom Dart, 1998; Those City Lights Called Your Name, 1999. *Address:* Valhijs Allé 91, 7 tv, 2610 Rídovre, Denmark.

CLARK, Graeme; b. 15 April 1966, Glasgow, Scotland. Musician (bass). *Career:* Member, Wet Wet Wet, 1982–; Performances include: Greenpeace charity concert, Royal Albert Hall, 1986; Support to Lionel Richie, British tour, 1987; Prince's Trust Rock Gala, Royal Albert Hall, 1988–90; John Lennon Tribute Concert, Merseyside, 1990; Edinburgh Castle, 1992; Live At The Royal Albert Hall 1992, 1993. *Recordings:* Albums: Popped In Souled Out, 1987; Sgt Pepper Knew My Father, 1988; The Memphis Sessions, 1988; High On The Happy Side, 1992; Wet Wet Wet Live At The Royal Albert Hall, 1993; End of Part One (Their Greatest Hits), 1993; Picture This, 1995; 10, 1997; Singles include: Wishing I Was Lucky, 1987; Sweet Little Mystery, 1987; Angel Eyes (Home and Away), 1988; With A Little Help From My Friends (No. 1, UK), 1988; Temptation, 1988; Sweet Surrender, 1989; Hold Back The River, 1990; Stay With Me Heartache, 1990; Goodnight Girl (No. 1, UK), 1992; More Than Love, 1992; Lip Service, 1992; Shed A Tear, 1993; Cold Cold Heart, 1993; Love Is All Around (No. 1, UK), 1994; She's All On My Mind, 1995; Julia Says, 1995; Don't Want To Forgive Me Now, 1995; Somewhere Somehow, 1995; Morning, 1996; If I Never See You Again, 1997; Strange, 1997; Yesterday, 1997. *Honours:* BRIT Award, Best British Newcomer, 1988. *Current Management:* The Precious Organisation, The Townhouse, 1 Park Gate, Glasgow G3 6DL, Scotland.

CLARK, Guy; b. 6 Nov. 1941, Rockport, Texas, USA. Vocalist; Songwriter. *Career:* Former photographer; Guest singer, artists including: Emmylou Harris; Rodney Crowell; Steve Earle; Jerry Jeff Walker; Hoyt Axton; Waylon Jennings; Don Everly; Gordon Payne; KT Oslin; Rosanne Cash; Vince Gill; Recent concerts include Cambridge Folk Festival, 1995. *Compositions include:* LA Freeway; Jerry Jeff Walker; Desperados Waiting For A Train; Tom Rush; Texas 1947; Johnny Cash; The Last Gunfighter Ballad; Virginia's Real; Heartbroke, Ricky Skaggs; Co-writer with Rodney Crowell: The Partner

Nobody Chose; She's Crazy For Leavin'. *Recordings:* Old No 1, 1975; Texas Cookin', 1976; Guy Clark, 1978; The South Coast of Texas, 1981; Better Days, 1983; Old Friends, 1989; Boats to Build, 1992; Dublin Blues, 1995; Craftsmen, 1995; Keepers, 1997; Cold Dog Soup, 1999. *Current Management:* Side One Management, 1026a Third Ave, New York, NY 10021, USA.

CLARK, Lenny, (Lenny Preacher); b. 3 March 1958, Blackmoor, Hampshire, England. Country Vocalist; Musician (guitar). *Career:* Appeared with many of Britain's country bands; Guest on several albums; Backed many visiting artistes from USA; Toured Europe and Far East; Featured on CMR and radio stations nationwide; Currently fronting his 5-piece band, Preacher. *Recordings include:* Dyin' Ain't Much of a Living; Preacher. *Membership:* Equity. *Address:* Seminole, The St, Preston, Canterbury, Kent CT3 1EB, England.

CLARK, Nicholas; b. 13 April 1963, Gillingham, Kent, England. Musician (guitar). *Education:* OND, HND, Business Studies; Guitar Institute, Intermediate. *Career:* Bands, including sessions: Konstructivitis; Talkies; Elliot Lewis Band; Bazooka Joe. *Recordings:* Session: Black December, Konstructivitis. *Membership:* Musicians' Union. *Address:* 45 Hazelwood Dr., Maidstone, Kent ME16 0EA, England.

CLARK, Petula, (Sally Olwen); b. 15 Nov. 1934, Epsom, Surrey, England. Vocalist; Actress. m. Claude Wolff, 1961, 1 s., 2 d. *Career:* Stage and screen actress, aged 7; Own radio programme, 1943; Numerous film appearances, 1944–; Films include: Medal For The General, 1944; Here Come The Huggetts, 1948; Finian's Rainbow, 1968; Goodbye Mr Chips, 1969; Stage appearances include: Sound of Music, 1981; Someone Like You (also writer), 1989; Blood Brothers, Broadway, 1993–; Host, own BBC television series; US television special Petula, NBC, 1968; Solo singing career, 1964–; Sold over 30m. records to date. *Recordings:* Hit singles include: Ya-Ya Twist, 1960; Downtown (No. 1, USA) and throughout Europe), 1964; The Other Man's Grass; My Love; I Know A Place; Oxygen; Albums: Petula Clark Sings, 1956; A Date With Pet, 1956; You Are My Lucky Star, 1957; Pet Clark, 1959; Petula Clark In Hollywood, 1959; In Other Words, 1962; Petula, 1962; Les James Dean, 1962; Downtown, 1964; I Know A Place, 1965; The New Petula Clark Album, 1965; Uptown With Petula Clark, 1965; In Love, 1966; Hello Paris, Vols I and II, 1966; I Couldn't Live Without Your Love, 1966; Hit Parade, 1967; The Other Man's Grass Is Always Greener, 1968; Petula, 1968; Portrait of Petula, 1969; Just Pet, 1969; Memphis, 1970; The Song of My Life, 1971; Warm and Tender, 1971; Live At The Royal Albert Hall, 1972; Now, 1972; Live In London, 1974; Come On Home, 1974; I'm the Woman You Need, 1975; Don't Sleep in the Subway, 1995; Wind of Change, 1998; With All My Heart, 2001; Spirit of Today, 2001; The Ultimate Collection, 2002. *Honours:* 2 Grammy Awards; Grand Prix Du Disque, 1960; More Gold discs than any other UK female artist; C.B.E., 1998. *Address:* c/o John Ashby, PO Box 288, Woking, Surrey GU22 0YN, England.

CLARK, Roy Linwood; b. 15 April 1933, Meherrin, Virginia, USA. Vocalist; Songwriter; Musician (guitar, banjo, mandolin). *Career:* Winner, National Banjo Championship, aged 16; Former professional boxer; Radio appearances include: Ozark Jubilee; Town and Country Time; Television: Guest, Country Style (Washington TV show), 1955; Host of show, early 60s; Actor, The Beverly Hillbillies; Host, television series Swingin' Country; Co-host, Hee Haw, CBS, 1969–; Lead guitarist, Wanda Jackson; Concerts include: Russia, 1976; Concert with Boston Pops Orchestra, 1976; Carnegie Hall, 1977; Film appearances include: Uphill All The Way, 1986; Member, Grand Ole Opry, 1987–; Later involvement in ranching, publishing, advertising, property. *Recordings:* Albums include: The Lightning Fingers of Roy Clark, 1962; The Tip of My Fingers, 1963; Happy To Be Unhappy, 1964; Guitar Spectacular, 1965; Sings Lonesome Love Ballads, 1966; Stingin' Along With The Blues, 1966; Roy Clark, 1966; Live, 1967; Do You Believe This Roy Clark, 1968; In The Mood, 1968; Urban, Suburban, 1968; Yesterday When I Was Young, 1969; The Everlovin' Soul of Roy Clark, 1969; The Other Side of Roy Clark, 1970; I Never Picked Cotton, 1970; The Magnificent Sanctuary Band, 1971; The Incredible Roy Clark, 1971; Roy Clark Country!, 1972; Family Album, 1973; Superpicker, 1973; Come Live With Me, 1973; Family and Friends, 1974; The Entertainer, 1974; Roy Clark, 1974; So Much To Remember, 1975; Heart To Heart, 1975; In Concert, 1976; Hookin' It, 1977; My Music and Me, 1977; Labour of Love, 1978. *Honours:* CMA Awards: Instrumentalist of the Year, 1977, 1978, 1980. *Address:* Roy Clark Productions, 3225 South Norwood, Tulsa, OK 74135, USA.

CLARK, Terri; b. 5 Aug. 1968, Montréal, Québec, Canada. Vocalist; Songwriter; Musician. *Career:* Tour with George Strait, played dates with Clay Walker and Aaron Tippin, 1994; Performed on Prime Time Country; Recorded At The Ryman; Played on the Grand Ole Opry, 1994; Tour with George Strait, 1996; Tours played to over 1.5m. people, 1996; Appearing in Primestar Presents Clay Walker's Four Star Blowout Tour, 1997; Featured Artist, Calgary Stampede; Tours throughout Canada, 1997. *Recordings:* Better Things To Do; When Boy Meets Girl; If I Were You; Suddenly Single; Poor Poor Pitiful Me; Emotional Girl; Just the Same; Now That I Found You; Albums: Terri Clark; Just the Same; How I Feel; Ugly Duckling. *Honours:* Numerous including: Billboard Music Award, Top New Female Artist, 1995;

Best Female Vocalist, Big Country Awards, 1997; Three Awards, Canadian Country Music Asscn Awards, 1997. *Membership:* AFofM; Broadcast Music Inc; Country Music Asscn; Academy of Country Music. *Current Management:* Woody Bowles, Woody Bowles Management, 1114 17th Ave S, Nashville, TN 37212, USA. *Address:* 5420 Camelot Rd, Brentwood, TN 37027, USA.

CLARK, W. C; b. 16 Nov. 1939, Austin, Texas, USA. Vocalist; Songwriter; Musician (guitar). 1 s., 1 d. *Career:* Toured with Joe Tex Band, 1960s; Member, Southern Feeling with Angela Strehli, Denny Freeman; Worked on Triple Threat Revue, with Stevie Ray Vaughan, Lou Ann Barton, Mike Kindred; Support tours to B. B. King; Bobby Bland; Also performed with Albert Collins; Buddy Guy; Johnny Taylor; Lowell Fulsom; Joe Turner; Lou Rawls; Brooks Benton; Freddie King; Alvin Bishop; George Thorogood; James Brown; Matt Murphy; Jimmy Vaughan; Clarence Holliman; Carol Fran; Appeared on Austin City Limits, 1990. *Compositions:* Cold Shot, co-author; Standing Here at the Crossroads. *Recordings include:* Something For Everybody, 1987; Heart of Gold, 1994; Texas Soul, 1996; Lover's Plea, 1998. *Honours:* Austin Chronicle Music Awards: Best Blues Band, Best Soul Band; Inducted into Texas Music Hall of Fame, 1990; W C Handy Award, Best Blues/Soul Album, 1997; W C Handy Award for first time cotaegory: Artist Most Deserving Wider Recognition, 1999. *Membership:* BMI. *Current Management:* Vicky Gay Moerbe, Crossfire Productions, 304 Braeswood Rd, Austin, TX 78704–7200, USA. *E-mail:* vicky@wcclark.com.

CLARKE, Dave, (Pig City, Directional Force); b. 1968, Brighton, England. Prod; Remixer; Sound Engineer; Radio Presenter; DJ. *Career:* Co-founder, Magnetic North; Recorded for: Bush/Deconstruction; Skint Records; XL; R&S; Strangefruit; K7; News; Icrunch; React; World-wide DJ; Remixes include: DJ Hell; DJ Rush; Chemical Brothers; Gary Numan; New Order; Felix da Housecat; Mirwais; Leftfield; Death in Vegas; Adam Clayton & Larry Mullen (Mission Impossible); Underworld; Depeche Mode; Moby; Laurent Garnier; Green Velvet; Fatboy Slim; Fischerspooner. *Recordings:* Albums: Archive 1, 1995. Singles include: I Like John, 1989; Parameter, 1990; Red 1, 1993; Red 2, 1994; Red 3, Southside, 1995; No One's Driving, 1996; Shake Your Booty, 1997; The Compass, 2001; The Wolf, 2002; Compilations: Electro Boogie, 1997; Electro Boogie, 1998; Fuse Presents, 1999; World Service, 2001. *Honours:* Best Remix, Q Magazine, 1997; Muzik Award, Best Essential Mix, 2000; Best Int. DJ, Outsoon Magazine, Belgium/France, 2001, 2002; Best Album, BBM, 2001; Best Compilation, Danceclub, Portugal, 2001. *Membership:* PRS. *Address:* c/o Paul Benney, Daddy Management, 15 Holywell Row, London EC2A 4JB, England. *Telephone:* (20) 7684-5219. *Website:* www.daveclarke.com.

CLARKE, David Roger; b. 28 Jan. 1948, Essex, England. Musician (guitar, keyboards); Songwriter; Record Co Owner. m. Patricia, 16 Dec. 1966, 1 s., 1 d. *Education:* BSc, MSc, Mathematics; Piano tuition. *Career:* Joined Sapphires aged 13, 1961; Band renamed Blue Angels, 1963; Major USA, European tours, television appearances, 1975–78; Joined Royal Navy, active service Falkland Islands war, HMS Fearless, retired as Commander, 1979–92; Formed Mouse Records, 1993; Tours: Scandinavia; Germany; New Zealand, 1993–94; Lead vocalist, guitarist, keyboards, principal songwriter, producer on majority of recordings. *Recordings:* 2 singles as Danny Clyve and the Blue Angels, 1964; Album as Dave Carlsen: Pale Horse, 1974; Lead vocals, as Chester Baynes, hit single, 1972; Producer, Gaylords single: Hit Me With Music, 1974; with Noel Redding Band: 2 singles, 2 albums, 1975–76; Album, 1994; with Jimmy McCulloch and White Line, 2 singles, 1976, album, 1994; Album as Frigate, 1981; 4 releases as Shut Up Frank, with members of: The Kinks; The Animals; Jimi Hendrix Experience, 1993–97; Dream Machine album, 1995; As Kast off Kinks, with Mick Avory, John Dalton, John Gosling, 2001. *Membership:* PRS; MCPS; PPL; PAMRA; Institute of Management. *Current Management:* Mouse Records. *Address:* 28 Breamore Rd, Seven Kings, Essex IG3 9NB, England.

CLARKE, 'Fast' Eddie; b. 5 Oct. 1950, Isleworth, Middlesex, England. Rock Musician (guitar). *Career:* Guitarist, Continuous Performance; Guitarist, blues band, Curtis Knight; Guitarist, UK heavy rock group Motörhead, 1976–82; Support to Hawkwind, UK 1977; British tours, 1978–80; Heavy Metal Barn Dance, Stafford, UK, 1980; Co-founder, Fastway (with Pete Way), 1982–. *Recordings:* Albums: with Motörhead: Motörhead, 1977; Overkill, 1979; Bomber, 1979; Ace of Spades, 1980; No Sleep 'Til Hammersmith (No. 1 UK), 1981; Iron Fist, 1982; No Class, 2001; with Fastway: Fastway, 1983; All Fired Up, 1984; Waiting For The Roar, 1986; The World Waits For You, 1986; Trick Or Treat, 1987; On Target, 1988; Bad Bad Girls, 1989; Solo album: It Ain't Over Till It's Over, 1994; Singles: with Motörhead include: Louie Louie; Bomber; No Class; Motörhead; Overkill; Ace of Spades; Iron Fist; The Golden Years EP; Beer Drinkers and Hell Raisers EP; St Valentine's Day Massacre EP (with Girlschool).

CLARKE, Kim Annette; b. 14 Nov. 1954, New York, USA. Musician (bass). *Education:* BA, Communications, CUNY, 1978; BA, Music, Long Island University, 1990. *Career:* Freelance musician, 1978–; Bass player, Yusef Lateef Quartet; Defunkt; Lester Bowie's Brass Fantasy; George Gruntz; Joe Henderson Quartet; Kit McLure; Also played with: Billy Taylor; Art Blakey;

Lionel Hampton; Sarah Vaughan; Branford Marsalis; Betty Carter; Mike Manieri; Robert Palmer; Napoleon Revels-Bey.

CLARKE, Kory; b. USA. Rock Vocalist; Songwriter. *Career:* Vocalist, lyricist, US heavy rock group Warrior Soul, 1988–95; subsequently member, Space Age Playboys; Tours and concerts include: Support to Metallica, European tour, 1990; Support to Queensryche, Empire tour, 1991; European tour, 1993; UK and European tours, 1995; European festivals, 1995. *Recordings:* Albums: Last Decade, Dead Century, 1989; Drugs God and The New Republic, 1991; Salutations From A Ghetto Nation, 1992; Chill Pill, 1994; Space Age Playboys, 1995; Odds and Ends, 1996; New Age Underground, 1998; Live In London, 1999. *Current Management:* Q-Prime Inc, 729 Seventh Ave, 14th Floor, New York, NY 10019, USA.

CLARKE, Paul Frazer; b. 25 Sept. 1962, Leicester, England. Songwriter; Prod; Musician (keyboards, drums, guitar). *Education:* Wyggeston Queen Elizabeth I College, Leicester. *Career:* Recording artist (Epic), British tours, 1987; with November One, London's Burning (LWT film/series), 1988; Writer, Warner Chappell, 1987–91; Co-writes with/for Glenn Nightingale; Angie Brown; Rick Astley; Other television appearances include: Rock Goes To College, BBC TV; Wide Awake Club, ITV; Hit Man and Her, LWT; Director, Fast Floor Multimedia Ltd; Writer, MCA, 1996–98; Film/TV Writer, 1998–. *Recordings:* Albums: Deja Vu, Magna Charta; Quest For Intelligence, Fast Floor; Purveyors of the New Groove, Earl Grey; The Eternal Dream, Fast Floor. *Membership:* PRS; MCPS. *Current Management:* c/o Christian Ulf-Hansen, BMI. *Address:* 79 Harley House, Marylebone Rd, London, England.

CLARKE, Sharon D; b. 28 May 1965, London, England. Actress; Vocalist. *Career:* Performances: First British actress to play The Voice of Audrey II in The Little Shop of Horrors, London Bubble Theatre, Leicester Haymarket; The Singing Detective, Dennis Potter, BBC TV; 6 appearances, Top of the Pops, with Nomad; Guest presenter DJ, Saturday Morning Mayhem; Sunset Radio, Manchester; Princess of Wales Birthright Charity Trust; Lead vocalist, Royal Albert Hall; Lead vocalist, Stonewall Concert, Royal Albert Hall, 1995; Played opposite Chaka Khan, Mama I Want To Sing, Mama Winter, Cambridge Theatre, London. *Recordings:* I Wanna Give You (Devotion), Nomad (No. 2, UK charts; World-wide No. 1 club hit); Happiness, Serious Rope (No. 1 club hit, UK). *Honours:* Laurence Olivier Awards, Best Supporting Performer in a Musical, Once On This Island, 1995. *Membership:* Equity. *Address:* 102 Ranelagh Rd, Tottenham, London, England.

CLARKE, Simon C; b. 9 May 1955, Sheffield, South Yorkshire, England. Arranger; Musician (baritone, tenor, alto, flute, piccolo saxophones). m. Helen Sykes, 20 Aug. 1988. *Education:* BA, York University; Played flute to age 21, switched to saxophone. *Career:* Tours with Pete Townshend's Deep End, 1985; The Who, 1989–90; The Waterboys, 1990; Eric Clapton, 1993–95. *Recordings:* session work includes: Blur; China Crisis; Communards; Deacon Blue; Dubstar; Terence Trent D'Arby; Geri Halliwell; Tom Jones; Rolling Stones; Suede; Spiritualized.

CLARKE, Stanley; b. 21 July 1951, Philadelphia, Pennsylvania, USA. Musician (bass). *Education:* Philadelphia Musical Academy. *Career:* Member, various funk groups; Played jazz with Horace Silver; Joe Henderson; Pharoah Sanders; Chick Corea and Return To Forever Band; Partnership with George Duke. *Recordings:* Albums: Stanley Clarke, 1974; Journey To Love, 1975; School Days, 1976; Modern Man, 1978; I Wanna Play For You, 1979; Rocks Pebbles and Sand, 1980; Time Exposure, 1984; Find Out, 1985; Hideaway, 1986; Shieldstone, 1987; If This Bass Could Only Talk, 1988; with Pharoah Sanders: Black Unity, 1972; with George Duke: The Clarke/Duke Project, 1981; The Clarke/Duke Project II, 1983; 3, 1990; with Return To Forever: Return To Forever, 1972; with Aziza Mustafa Zadeh: Dance of Fire, 1995; with Al DiMeola, Jean-Luc Ponty: The Rite of Strings, 1996; Portrait Stanley Clarke, 2000. *Address:* c/o Baker, Winokur, Ryder Public Relations, 405 S Beverly Dr., Fifth Floor, Beverly Hills, CA 90212, USA.

CLARKE, Vince; b. 3 July 1960, Basildon, Essex, England. Musician (keyboards, synthesizers); Songwriter. *Career:* Mem., No Romance In China; Depeche Mode, 1980–81; Yazoo, with Alison Moyet, 1982–83; Erasure, with Andy Bell, 1985–; Numerous UK and international tours, television appearances. *Recordings:* Albums: with Depeche Mode: Speak And Spell, 1981; with Yazoo: Upstairs At Eric's, 1982; You And Me Both (No. 1, UK), 1983; with Erasure: Wonderland, 1986; The Circus, 1987; The Two-Ring Circus, 1987; The Innocents (No. 1, UK), 1988; Wild! (No. 1, UK), 1989; Chorus (No. 1, UK), 1991; Pop!—The First 20 Hits (No. 1, UK), 1992; I Say I Say I Say (No. 1, UK), 1994; Erasure, 1995; Cowboy, 1997; Loveboat, 2000; Other People's Songs, 2003; with Martyn Ware: The Clarke And Ware Experiment, 2000; Pretentious, 2000. Singles: with Depeche Mode: New Life, 1981; Just Can't Get Enough, 1981; with Yazoo: Only You, 1982; Don't Go, 1982; The Other Side Of Love, 1983; Nobody's Diary, 1983; with The Assembly: Never Never, 1983; with Erasure: Who Needs Love..., 1985; Heavenly Action, 1985; Oh L'amour, 1986; Sometimes, 1986; It Doesn't Have..., 1987; Victim Of Love, 1987; The Circus, 1987; Ship Of Fools, 1988; Chains Of Love, 1988; A Little Respect, 1988; Crackers... (EP), 1988; Drama!, 1989; You Surround Me, 1989; Blue Savannah, 1990; Star, 1990; Chorus,

1991; Love To Hate You, 1991; Am I Right? (EP), 1991; Breath Of Life, 1992; Abba-Esque (EP, No. 1, UK), 1992; Who Needs Love..., 1992; Always, 1994; Run To The Sun, 1994; I Love Saturday (EP), 1994; Stay With Me, 1995; Fingers & Thumbs..., 1995; Rock Me Gently, 1996; In My Arms, 1997; Don't Say Your..., 1997; Rain, 1997; Freedom, 2000; Moon & The Sky, 2000; Solsbury Hill, 2003; Contributor to: Red Hot and Blue (AIDS benefit record); Tame Yourself (animal rights benefit record). *Honours:* BRIT Awards, Best British Newcomer, Yazoo, 1983, Best British Group, Erasure, 1989; Ivor Novello Award, Most Performed Work of 1990, Blue Savannah, 1991. *Address:* c/o Mute Records, 429 Harrow Rd, London W10 4RE, England. *Website:* www.erasureinfo.com.

CLARKIN, Tony; Musician (guitar); Songwriter. *Career:* Founder member, guitarist, UK rock group Magnum, 1972–; Regular tours include support tours with Judas Priest; Whitesnake; Blue Oyster Cult; Def Leppard; Own headline tours world-wide. *Recordings:* Albums: Kingdom of Madness, 1978; Magnum II, 1979; Maurauder, 1980; Chase The Dragon, 1982; The Eleventh Hour, 1983; On A Storyteller's Night, 1985; Vigilante, 1986; Wings of Heaven, 1988; Goodnight LA, 1990; The Spirit, 1991; Rock Art, 1994; Stronghold, 1997; Archive, 2000; Numerous compilation albums; Singles include: Kingdom of Madness, 1978; Just Like An Arrow, 1985; On A Storyteller's Night, 1985; Midnight, 1986; Days of No Trust, 1988; Start Talking Love, 1988; It Must Have Been Love, 1988; Rocking Chair, 1990.

CLARKSON, Alison Moira. See: **BOO, Betty.**

CLARKSON, Ian Christopher; b. 7 May 1964, Ormskirk, England. Musician (trumpet); Vocalist. m. Grazia Bevilacqua, 29 Dec. 1993. *Career:* Front man, vocalist and trumpet, with the Jive Aces; Prior to That, Aces of Rhythm, The Emperors of Rhythm; Television: Opportunity Knocks, BBC; Monte Carlo TV; Kenny Live RTE (Dublin); Concerts: Royal Albert Hall; Theatre Royal; Many many European tours, at least 250 gigs per year; Apollo Theatre, Harlem, with Doug E Fresh; Appeared with John Travolta, Lisa Marie Presley and Isaac Hayes, Church of Scientology event, and also Hollywood Palladium, Cotton Club and The Derby, Los Angeles; 25 city tour of US swing clubs and tribute to Louis Prima guest starring trombone player James 'Little Red' Blount. *Compositions:* Blues 4 U; Still; Planet Jive; Imagination or Something Else; Junky Joe. *Recordings:* Albums: Jumping With The Aces; Bolt from the Blue; Planet Jive; Single: Blues 4 U/ Heybarberebop. *Current Management:* Jive Aces. *Address:* St Hill Manor, East Grinstead, West Sussex, England.

CLASTRIER, Valentin; b. 14 Feb. 1947, Nice, France. Musician. *Education:* Classical guitar; Singing. *Career:* Guitar player with Jacques Brel, 1968–69; Guitar, Ricet Barrier, 1975–82; Composer for Hurdy Gurdy (acoustic, electro-acoustic), 1970–; Hurdy Gurdy teacher in training course, Master class, France and abroad. *Recordings:* Vielle à Roue de l'Imaginaire, 1984; Esprit de la Nuit, 1986; Grands Maîtres de la Vielle à Roue, 1988; Hérésie, 1992; Le Bûcher des Silences, 1994; Palude, 1995; Hurdy-Gurdy from Land of Cathars, 1997. *Publications:* Anthology For Hurdy Gurdy, 1985. *Honours:* Chevalier dans L'Ordre des Arts et des Lettres; Grand Prix de l'Académie Charles Cros; Grand Prix Audiovisuel de l'Europe. *Address:* Gué de la Pierre, 18380 Ennordres, France.

CLAUSELL, Deborah Deloris; b. 16 July 1951, Mobile, Alabama, USA. Musician (guitar). *Education:* University of South Alabama, 1984. *Career:* CBS, Afternoon School; Special Emmy Hit; Tuesday Night At The Movies. *Compositions:* The Fewest Words I Need To Say; Major John Pelham; Willing Willie; He Is. *Recordings:* Strong Feeling of Love; Success In Christ; Angels; The Happier I Am In Thee The Greater I Am; Life. *Publications:* The Encyclopedia of Living Artist; Contemporary Art. *Membership:* VFM; US Naval Institute; National Trust For Historic Preservation. *Address:* 5859 N Reams Dr., Mobile, AL 36608, USA.

CLAUSEN, Thomas; b. 5 Oct. 1949, Copenhagen, Denmark. Composer; Musician (piano, keyboards). m. (1) Pi Sveistrup, divorced, 2 d., (2) Tove Bornhift, 1999. *Education:* Private lessons; 3 years, Royal Conservatory, Copenhagen. *Career:* Musician for Dexter Gordon; Palle Mikkelborg; Ben Webster; Jan Garbarek; Leader, own groups 1978–, including Mirror, quartet; Own trio, with NHOP, 1980–83; Trio with Mads Vinding and Alex Riel 1987–. *Compositions:* Prism, 1975; Sonata for Oboe, Cello, Harp, 1989; Woods and Lakes, 1993; Danish Weather, 1996. *Recordings:* Mirror, 1979; Rain, 1980; The Shadow of Bill Evans, 1983; She Touched Me, 1988; Piano Music, 1989; Café Noir, 1990; Flowers and Trees, 1991; Psalm, 1995. *Honours:* Radio Jazz Prize, 1988; Ben Webster Prize, 1989; JASA Prize, 1990; Danish Grammy, 1991; Fanfare Prize, 1992. *Membership:* KODA; NCB; DJFBA; Danish Arts Foundation, 1998. *Address:* Rastestedet 5, 3500 Vaerlose, Denmark.

CLAXTON, Andrew; b. 22 Jan. 1950, London, England. Composer; Musician. Divorced; 2 s. *Education:* National Youth Orchestra of Great Britain; Royal Academy of Music; Bretton Hall College; University of Reading. *Career:* Freelance Composer, Instrumentalist, 1966–; Recorded, Toured With Dead Can Dance, 1987–93; Director, Peacock Epoch, 1985–;

Recorded, Toured With Meltdown, 1998–2001; Musical Director, Gintare, 1999. *Compositions:* Elements, 1988; Fall of The House of Usher, 1992; Six, 1996; Spires and Spirits, 1997; Silent Spaces, 2001. *Recordings:* Liar, 1995; The Big Sleazy, 1996; Drug Raped, 1998; Silent Spaces, 1998; Inside Polygamy, 1999; The Forbidden Journey, 1999; Cobwebs and Cogwheels, 2003; Collaborations: Dead Can Dance Albums, Within The Realm of a Dying Sin, 1987; Toward The Within, 1994; The Mirror Pool, 1995; Dead Can Dance 1981–98 (compilation), 2001. *Honours:* Winner, Oxford Town Hall Centenary Composers Competition, 1997; Finalist, Best Re-Recorded Music Category, British Television Advertising Craft Awards, 1998. *Membership:* BACS; PRS. *Current Management:* Ms Joan Gardner, Ivony, Cumnor Hill, Oxford, Oxfordshire OX2 9JA, England.

CLAYDERMAN, Richard (Philippe Pages); b. 1954, Paris, France. Musician (piano); Composer. *Education:* Paris Conservatory. *Career:* Former bank clerk; Became successful performer and recording artist; Played with French pop stars including Johnny Halliday; Michel Sardou; Top album seller, France, South Africa, Japan, early 1980s; Sellout UK concerts, 1982; Numerous television appearances; Concerts include: Japan; Brazil; Australia. *Recordings:* Albums: Ballade Pour Adeline (The Love Song), 1981; Dreaming (Traumereien), 1981; Dreaming (Traumereien), 3, 1981; Richard Clayderman, 1982; A Comme Amour, 1982; Lettre A Ma Mere, 1982; Musiques De L'Amour, 1982; The Music of Richard Clayderman, 1983; A Pleyel, 1983; Marriage of Love, 1984; The Music of Love, 1984; Christmas, 1984; The Classic Touch (with The Royal Philharmonic), 1985; Hollywood and Broadway, 1986; Songs of Love, 1987; A Little Night Music, 1988; Eleana, 1988; The Love Songs of Andrew Lloyd Webber, 1989; Together At Last, 1991; A Little Romance, 1994; Romance of..., 1995; Christmas Album, 1998; Con Amor, 2000; Amor Latino, 2000; Lettre A Ma Mere, 2001; Concerto For You, 2001. *Current Management:* Gurtman and Mutha Associates, 450 Seventh Ave, #603, New York, NY 10123–10101, USA.

CLAYSON, Alan; b. 3 May 1951, Dover, Kent, England. Composer; Author; Musician (keyboards, guitar); Vocalist. m. Inese Pommers, 31 July 1979, 2 s., 1 d. *Education:* Farnborough Technical College; University of Reading. *Career:* Member, Turnpike, 1971–74; Average Joe and the Men in the Street, 1974–75; Billy and The Conquerors, 1972–75; Portsmouth Sinfonia, viola, 1975; Clayson and The Argonauts, 1975–86; Toured UK, Europe, BBC Radio In Concert show, 1977; Solo performer, 1985–; USA debut, 1992; Worked with: Wreckless Eric; Twinkle; Screaming Lord Sutch; Dave Berry's Cruisers; Dick Taylor (Rolling Stone/Pretty Things); Writer and Presenter, Death Discs, BBC Radio 2, 1996. *Compositions include:* Moonlight Skater with Jim McCarty for Dave Berry and Stairway's Raindreaming album; Sol Nova, 1985; The Landlocked Sailor, for Poacher's Pocket, 1992; Man of the Moment, 1995; Angelette, 1997; The Last Show on Earth, 2002. *Recordings:* Albums: with The Argonauts: What A Difference A Decade Made, 1985; Solo: Soiree, 1997. Singles: with The Argonauts: The Taster, 1978; Last Respects (EP), 1982; Solo: The Moonlight Skater, 2002; Producer, main songwriter, Hostage To The Beat, Dave Berry, 1986; Contributions to compilation albums: Beat Merchants, 1995; Ne Me Quitte Pas, 1998; Nine Times Two: Contemporary English Chanson, 2002. *Publications:* Books: Call Up The Groups! The Golden Age of British Beat, 1985; Back In The High Life – A Biography of Steve Winwood, 1988; Only The Lonely – The Life and Artistic Legacy of Roy Orbison, 1989; The Quiet One – A Life of George Harrison, 1990; Ringo Starr – Straight Man Or Joker, 1991; Death Discs, 1992; Backbeat, with Pauline Sutcliffe, 1994; Aspects of Elvis (edit) with Spencer Leigh, 1994; Beat Merchants, 1995; Jacques Brel, 1996; Hamburg: The Cradle of British Rock, 1997; Serge Gainsbourg: View from the Exterior, 1998; The Troggs File: The Official Story of Rock's Wild Things, 2000; Over Under Sideways Down: The Flight of the Yardbirds, 2000; George Harrison (paperback), 2001; Ringo Starr (paperback), 2001; Edgard Vareae, 2002; The Yardbirds, 2002; Articles for: Record Collector; The Times; Goldmine; Medieval World; The Independent; Folk Roots; Country Music People; Mojo; The Beat Goes On; Gold; The 'Schoolkids' Oz; Erotic Review; Guitar; Hello; Daily Mail; Ugly Things; Discoveries. *Membership:* PRS. *Website:* www.alanclayson.com.

CLAYTON, Adam; b. 13 March 1960, Chinnor, Oxfordshire, England. Musician (bass). *Career:* Founder member, bass player, rock group U2, 1978–; Regular national and world-wide tours; Major concerts include: US Festival, 1983; The Longest Day, Milton Keynes, 1985; Live Aid, Wembley, 1985; Self Aid, Dublin, 1986; A Conspiracy of Hope (Amnesty International Tour), 1986; Smile Jamaica, 1988; Very Special Arts Festival, Washington, 1988; New Year's Eve concert, Dublin (broadcast live to Europe), 1989; Yankee Stadium, New York (second-ever concert there), 1992. *Recordings:* Albums: Boy, 1980; October, 1981; War (No. 1, UK), 1983; Under A Blood Red Sky, 1983; The Unforgettable Fire (No. 1, UK), 1984; Wide Awake In America, 1985; The Joshua Tree (No. 1, USA and UK), 1987; Rattle and Hum, also film (No. 1, USA), 1988; Achtung Baby (No. 1, USA), 1991; Zooropa (No. 1, UK and USA), 1993; Passengers film soundtrack (with Brian Eno), 1995; Pop, 1997; The Best Of 1980–90 (compilation), 1998; All That You Can't Leave Behind, 2001; The Best Of 1990–2000 (compilation), 2002. Hit singles include: Out of Control (No. 1, Ireland), 1979; Another Day (No. 1, Ireland), 1980; New Year's Day, 1983; Two Hearts Beat As One, 1983; Pride (In The Name of Love), 1984; The Unforgettable Fire, 1985; With Or Without You (No. 1, USA), 1987; I Still

Haven't Found What I'm Looking For (No. 1, USA), 1987; Where The Streets Have No Name, 1987; Desire (No. 1, UK), 1988; Angel of Harlem, 1988; When Love Comes To Town, with B. B. King, 1989; The Fly (No. 1, UK), 1991; Mysterious Ways, 1992; Even Better Than The Real Thing, 1992; Who's Gonna Ride Your Wild Horses, 1992; Hold Me, Thrill Me, Kiss Me (from film Batman Forever), 1995; Discotheque (No. 1, UK), 1997; Staring At The Sun, 1997; If God Will Send His Angels, 1997; The Sweetest Thing, 1998; Beautiful Day (No. 1, UK), 2000; Stuck In A Moment That You Can't Get Out Of, 2001; Walk On, 2001; Electrical Storm, 2002; Guest appearances on recordings by: Nanci Griffith, Daniel Lanois, Little Steven, Robbie Robertson, Sharon Shannon. *Honours:* Grammy Awards, Album of the Year, for The Joshua Tree, 1987, Best Rock Album, for All That You Can't Leave Behind, 2001, Best Alternative Music Album, for Zooropa, 1993, Song of the Year, for Beautiful Day, 2000, Record of the Year, for Beautiful Day, 2000, for Walk On, 2001, Best Rock Performance By A Duo Or Group With Vocal, for The Joshua Tree, 1987, for Desire, 1988, for Achtung Baby, 1992, for Beautiful Day, 2000, for Elevation, 2001, Best Pop Performance By A Duo Or Group With Vocal, for Stuck In A Moment You Can't Get Out Of, 2001, Best Music Video, Long Form, for Zoo TV–Live From Sydney, 1994, Best Performance Music Video, for Where The Streets Have No Name, 1988; BRIT Awards: Best International Act, 1988–90, 1992, 1998, 2001; Best Live Album, 1993; Outstanding Contribution To The British Music Industry, 2001; World Music Award, 1993; Q Awards: Best Act In The World, 1990, 1992, 1993; Merit Award, 1994; Juno Award, 1993; American Music Award, Favorite Internet Artist of the Year, 2002; Ivor Novello Award, Best Song Musically and Lyrically, for Walk On, 2002; Golden Globe, Best Original Song, for The Hands That Built America (from film Gangs of New York), 2003; Gold and Platinum discs. *Current Management:* Principle Management, 30–32 Sir John Rogersons Quay, Dublin 2, Ireland. *Website:* www.u2.com.

CLAYTON, Eddy; b. 6 May 1931, Watford, Hertfordshire, England. Musician (drums); Bandleader. m. Margaret Clayton, 20 March 1953, 1 s. *Education:* Studied with Charles Botterill (drummer with Mantovani). *Career:* Formed own band at age 14; Member, RAF Skyliners Dance Band, 1949–51; Leader of own Big Band, 1950s–60s; Currently leader of own quartet performing mainly dance music and jazz. *Membership:* Branch Secretary, Jazz Committee Delegate, Vice-Chair of District Council, Musicians' Union; ABJM; Film Artists Asscn, Equity. *Current Management:* Margaret Clayton. *Address:* Rainbow House, 3 Goodwood Ave, Watford, Hertfordshire WD2 5LA, England.

CLAYTON-THOMAS, David (Thomsett); b. 13 Sept. 1941, Surrey, England. Vocalist. *Career:* Vocalist, Blood Sweat and Tears, 1969–; Performances include: Newport Jazz Festival, 1969; Atlanta Pop Festival, 1969; US State Department sponsored tour, Eastern Europe, 1970; US tour, 1992; Le Festival Les Heros Sont Immortals, Calais, France; 2 reunion concerts, New York. *Recordings:* Albums include: with Blood Sweat and Tears: Blood, Sweat and Tears (No. 1, USA), 1969; Blood, Sweat and Tears 3 (No. 1, USA), 1970; B, S and T – 4, 1971; Mirror Image, 1974; Brand New Day, 1977; Nuclear Blues, 1980; Live and Improvised, 1991; You've Made Me So Very Happy (compilation), 2001; Solo albums: David Clayton-Thomas, 1972; Tequila Sunrise, 1972; Harmony Junction, 1973; Clayton, 1977; Blue Plate Special, 1998; Singles include: You've Made Me So Very Happy, 1969; Spinning Wheel, 1969; And When I Die, 1969; Hi-De-Ho, 1970; Music for film The Owl and The Pussycat, 1971. *Honours:* Grammy Awards: Best Album, Best Contemporary Instrumental Performance, 1970.

CLEGG, Johnny; b. 13 July 1953, Rochdale, Lancashire, England. Vocalist; Composer. *Education:* Social Anthropology, Wits University, South Africa. *Career:* Moved to South Africa, 1959; Duo, Johnny and Sipho (with Sipho Mchunu), 1972; Founder, sextet Juluka, 1976–85; Tours, UK, Europe and USA; Leader, Savuka, 1986; Tours, South Africa and overseas. *Recordings:* Albums: with Juluka: Universal Men, 1979; African Litany, 1981; Ulshule Bemvelo, 1982; Scatterlings of Africa, 1982; Work For All, 1983; Musa Ukungilandela, 1984; The Hope Concerts, 1985; Solo: Johnny Clegg Third World Child, 1986; with Savuka: Savuka, 1987; Freedom, 1989; Heat Dust and Dreams, 1993; In My African Dreams, 1994; Anthology, 2000. Singles: with Juluka: Woza Friday, 1978; Cruel Crazy Beautiful World, 1990; Life Is A Magic Thing, 1992; I Can Never Be, 1993. *Current Management:* HR Music, 6430 Sunset Blvd, Los Angeles, CA 90028, USA.

CLEMENTINE. See: SLATER, Luke.

CLEMONS, Clarence; b. 1 Nov. 1942, Norfolk, Virginia, USA. Musician (saxophone); Entertainer. 3 s. *Education:* Music minor, University of Maryland. *Career:* Member, groups including Bruce Springsteen and E Street Band; Television: Numerous talk shows including David Letterman; Concerts include: Amnesty International tour; Leader, own group West Coast Red Bank Rockers; Films: New York New York; Bill and Ted's Excellent Adventure. *Recordings:* Solo albums: Rescue, 1981; Night With Mr C, 1983; Hero, 1985; Adventure; Peacemaker, 1995; Get It On, 1995; Peace makers, 1995; Albums with Bruce Springsteen: Greetings From Astbury Park, 1973; The Wild, The Willing and The E-Street Shuffle, 1973; Born To Run, 1975; Darkness On The Edge of Town, 1978; The River, 1980; Born In The

USA, 1984; Tunnel of Love, 1987; Live In New York City, 2001; Recent session work: Bad and Blue, Jimmy Dillon, 2000; Ringo Starr's All Starr Band, 2001. *Honours:* Bay Area Music Awards: Outstanding Reed Player, 6 times winner. *Membership:* Musicians' Union. *Current Management:* Alan Niven.

CLEVELAND, Ashley Alexander; b. 2 Feb. 1957, Knoxville, Tennessee, USA. Vocalist; Musician (guitar); Songwriter. m. Kenny Greenberg, 27 April 1991, 1 s., 2 d. *Education:* University of Tennessee, Knoxville, 2 years. *Career:* Featured on US television series The Road; Performed on televised Dove Awards, 1993; Member of John Hiatt's band, 1990–; Performed on Saturday Night Live, David Letterman and Arsenio Hall shows; Appearances in clubs, theatres and festivals. *Recordings:* Albums: Big Town, 1991; Bus Named Desire, 1993; Lesson of Love, 1995. *Honours:* Nashville Area Music Award, Best Contemporary Christian Album, 1995; Grammy Award, Best Contemporary Rock Album, Lesson of Love, 1996. *Membership:* NARAS; GMA; CMA. *Current Management:* Blanton and Harrell Entertainment. *Address:* 2910 Poston Ave, Nashville, TN 37203, USA.

CLIFF, Jimmy (James Chambers); b. 1948, Jamaica. Reggae Vocalist; Composer. 1 s. *Career:* Singer, songwriter, 1960s–; Backing vocalist, London, 1963; Tours world-wide, especially USA, Europe, South America, Africa; Concerts include: Montreux Jazz Festival, 1980; World Music Festival, Jamaica, 1982; Rock In Rio II, Brazil, 1991; Worlds Beat Reggae Festival, Portand, USA, 1992; Actor, films: The Harder They Come (also on film soundtrack), 1972; Bongo Man, 1980; Club Paradise (also on film soundtrack), 1986; Formed own record label, Cliff Records, 1989; Own production company, Cliff Sounds and Films, 1990. *Compositions include:* You Can Get It If You Really Want, Desmond Dekker; Let Your Yeah Be Yeah, The Pioneers; Trapped, Bruce Springsteen, for USA For Africa album. *Recordings:* Singles include: Dearest Beverley, 1962; Hurricane Hattie, 1962; Waterfall, 1968; Wonderful World Beautiful People, 1969; Many Rivers To Cross, 1969; Vietnam, 1969; Wild World, 1970; I Can See Clearly Now (featured on film soundtrack Cool Runnings), 1993; Higher and Higher, 1994; Hakuna Matata, 1995; Breakout, 1997; Albums: Hard Road, 1967; Jimmy Cliff, 1969; Can't Get Enough, 1969; Wonderful World, 1970; Another Cycle, 1971; The Harder They Come, 1972; Struggling Man, 1974; Follow My Mind, 1975; Give Thanx, 1978; I Am The Living, 1980; Give The People What They Want, 1981; Special, 1982; The Power and The Glory, 1983; Cliff Hanger, 1985; Hanging Fire, 1988; Images, 1990; Breakout, 1992; 100% Pure Reggae, 1997; Shout for Freedom, 1999; Humanitarian, 1999; Live and In The Studio, 2000; Wanted (compilation), 2000; Best of Jimmy Cliff, 2001; Fantastic Plastic People, 2002; Contributor, Sun City, Artists Against Apartheid, 1985. *Honours:* Grammy Award, Best Reggae Recording, 1985; MOBO Award, Contribution to Urban Music, 2002. *Address:* c/o DAS Communications, 83 Riverside Dr., New York, NY 10024, USA.

CLIFFORD, (Brisley) Grieg; b. 31 Aug. 1971, Gillingham, Kent, England. Musician (drums). *Education:* Diploma, Photography. *Career:* Drummer with Hit 'n' Run, hard rock band, 1989–94; Tours Britain, Europe; Sessions, airplay, most countries; College radio, USA; Album, 1992; Member, If 6 Was 9 (3 piece rock band), first EP released 1995; Many sessions, studio and live work, for many Rock/Funk bands, notably Suicide Ride; Sessions by singer Mark Lehman, include 2 videos for MTV and National TV; Live sessions for Suicide Ride offshoot band: Creed. *Recordings:* with Hit 'n' Run: Hit 'n' Run, 1992; Suicide Ride session recordings, 1994; with If 6 Was 9: Out of The Fire; Silent Nights; Your Heart Somebody, 1995; Grieg Clifford: Funky Rock Drum Loops. *Membership:* Musicians' Union. *Current Management:* Groovytime Promotions. *Address:* 23 Harsfold Rd, Rustington, West Sussex BN16 2QE, England.

CLIFTON, Bill (William August Marburg); b. 5 April 1931, Riderwood, Maryland, USA. Performing Artiste; Vocalist; Musician (guitar, autoharp). m. Trijntje B Labrie, 31 Oct. 1978, 4 s., 6 d. *Education:* Graduate degree, Business Administration, University of Virginia. *Career:* Extensive work in radio late 1940s to mid 1950s; Recordings 1953–; Organized first all-bluegrass festival, Luray, Virginia, July 4 1961; Founding director, Newport Folk Festival; Compere, weekly BBC Show, Cellar Full of Folk; First bluegrass performer to earn living entirely in Europe, Asia, Africa, Australia, New Zealand. *Compositions:* Little White-Washed Chimney; Mary Dear; Where The Rainbow Finds Its End; Happy Days (instrumental); Recent albums include: Bill Clifton: The Early Years; Autoharp Centennial Celebration; Where The Rainbow Finds Its End; River of Memories. *Publications:* Bill Clifton's 150 Old-time Folk and Gospel Songs; Video: Grassroots to Bluegrass, recorded in Nashville, 1999. *Honours:* Award of Merit, International Bluegrass Music Asscn, 1992; Preservation Hall of Greats, SPBGMA, 1993. *Membership:* International Bluegrass Music Asscn; Birthplace of Country Music Alliance. *Address:* PO Box 69, Mendota, VA 24270, USA.

CLINTON, George; b. 22 July 1940, Kannapolis, North Carolina, USA. Vocalist; Bandleader. 1 s. *Career:* Founder, leader, The Parliaments, 1950s–; Changed name to Funkadelic, 1969; Parliament/Funkadelic, 1970–; Solo artiste, 1982–; Owner, Bridgeport Music; Regular world-wide concerts and tours; Featured in Graffiti Bridge, Prince, 1990. *Recordings:* Albums:

Funkadelic, 1969; Osmium, 1970; America Eats Its Young, 1972; Cosmic Stop, 1973; Standing On The Verge of Getting It On, 1974; Chocolate City, 1975; Mothership Connection, 1976; The Clones of Dr Funkenstein, 1976; Parliament Live/P Funk Earth Tour, 1977; Funkentelechy v. The Placebo, 1977; One Nation Under A Groove, 1978; Motor Booty Affair, 1978; Brides of Funkenstein, 1978; Underjam, 1979; Gloryhallastoopid (Pin The Tale On The Funky), 1979; The Electric Spanking of War Babies, 1981; Computer Games, 1982; You Shouldn't Nuf Bit, Fish!, 1984; Some of My Best Friends Are Jokes, 1985; R&B Skeletons In The Closet, 1986; The Cinderella Theory, 1989; Hey Man... Smell My Finger, 1993; Dope Dogs, 1994; The Music of Red Shoe Diaries, 1995; A Fifth of Funk, 1995; Mortal Kombat (film soundtrack), 1996; TAPOAFOM, 1996; Testing Positive, 1996; Live and Kickin', 1997; Funkadelic – Funk Gets Stronger, 2000; Singles include: One Nation Under A Groove; (Not Just) Knee Deep; Atomic Dog; Walk The Dinosaur, used in film soundtrack Super Mario Brothers. *Address:* c/o Ciccel Enterprises, Suite 102, 1830 S Robertson Blvd, Los Angeles, CA 90035, USA.

CLIVILLES, Robert; b. 1964, New York, USA. DJ; Prod. *Education:* Business management at college. *Career:* DJ, member of production team, C and C Music Factory (with the late David Cole); Club DJ, performances world-wide; Collaborations: Mariah Carey, Aretha Franklin, Ultra Nate. *Recordings:* Numerous C and C recordings including: Gonna Make You Sweat (Everybody Dance Now) (No. 1, USA), 1991; Things That Make You Go Hmmm..., 1991; Pride In The Name of Love, 1992; A Deeper Love, 1992; Do You Wanna Get Funky, 1994.

CLOUT, Tony; b. 25 Feb. 1945, Danbury Palace, Chelmsford, England. Arranger; Copyist; Composer; Musician (bass guitar, guitar). m. Julia Anne Lamprell, 15 Aug. 1977, 4 s., 2 d. *Career:* Guitar with Paul Raven (Gary Glitter), 1960; with The Transatlantics, 1965–69; Recorded 6 singles; Television appearances include: 5 o'Clock Club; Thank Your Lucky Stars; BBC Light Programme, Easy Beat; Saturday Club; Bank Holiday Specials with The Beatles; with The Ross Mitchell Band, 1972; with The Ray McVay Band, 1975–83; Television, radio, records, touring, society functions include Prince Charles' 30th Birthday at Buckingham Palace; Musical Director, Circus Tavern cabaret club, Essex, 1983–93; British tour with Michael Barrymore, Stutz Bear Cats, Roly Polys, 1985; Arranger, copyist, West End Shows: Blood Brothers; Only The Lonely; Good Rockin' Tonite; Provincial Shows: Harry's Web; Thank You For The Music; Shows for BBC Radio 2, artists including: Charles Augins; Warren Mitchell; Chas 'n' Dave; Marti Caine; Bobby Crush; John Inman; Marty Webb and Elaine Paige tours. *Compositions:* La Concordia; Paso Doble De Cadiz; Spring's the Time, 1996. *Recordings:* Singles: Many Things From Your Window; Don't Fight It; Run For Your Life; Albums: Ray McVay dance albums; Pan Pipe Moods; Chas 'n' Dave's Street Party albums. *Membership:* British Music Writers' Council; PaMRA. *Address:* 36 Shirley Gardens, Hornchurch, Essex RM12 4NH, England.

CLOVER, Val, (Valerie Ann Cope); b. 17 Sept. 1952, Liverpool, England. Vocalist; Songwriter; Model; Actress. *Career:* Joined Girl Trio, The Cherolees, 1968; Lead Singer, The Wheels of Fortune, 1969–70; Mem., Justine, 1970; Concerts include: Earls Court Olympia and Buxton Festival; Appearances on Disco 2 (BBC TV) and Sounds of the Seventies (BBC Radio); Solo career, 1976; Sessions; Voice-overs and numerous TV, film and pop videos as Actress; Rock/pop reviewer for Disability Times. *Compositions:* As Co-writer: Don't Make My White Christmas Blue, Iris Williams, 1982; Oikotie Sydameen; Tahtikaaren Taa, Aikakone, 1995; Children of the Sea (English lyricist, Estonian entry in Eurovision Song Contest), 1998. *Recordings:* Album: Justine, 1970. Single: She Brings The Morning With Her, 1970. *Membership:* PRS; MCPS; N©B; BAC&S; Equity. *Current Management:* Mouse Records. *Address:* 28 Breamore Rd, Seven Kings, Essex IG3 9NB, England.

CMIRAL, Elia; b. Czechoslovakia. Composer; *Compositions:* For television: Macklean, 1984; Rosenholm, 1991; Kopplingen, 1992; Nash Bridges, 1996; The Colony, 2002; For computer game: The Last Express, 1997; For film: På liv och död, 1986; Apartment Zero, 1988; Sökarna, 1993; Somebody is Waiting, 1996; Sunsets by Candlelight, 1997; Babies for Babies, 1997; Visions of America, 1998; Ronin, 1998; Prophecies, 1998; The Decadent Visitor, 1998; Stigmata, 1999; Six Pack, 2000; Battlefield Earth, 2000; Bones, 2001; They, 2002. *Membership:* ASCAP. *Current Management:* Gorfaine/Schwartz Agency Inc, 13245 Riverside Dr., Suite 450, Sherman Oaks, CA 91423, USA.

COATES, Bruce Brian Gilbert; b. 3 July 1972, Birmingham, England. Musician (saxophone – BA Hons, Performing Arts (Music); MA, De Monfort University, 1998. *Career:* Music for Island, dance piece by Jo Walker (with Zo Sosinka and Craig Vear), Phoenix Theatre, Leicester, 1992; Contributed improvisations and ambient sound environment for Modal Spaces – A Sound/Architecture Project, (large-scale musical performance by Andrew Hugill), Queens Building, Leicester, 1994; Performance of Burdocks by Christian Wolff (with Zo Sosinka, Christian Wolff, Dave Smith), 25th Anniversary Concert of the Scratch Orchestra, ICA, 1994; Formed Lusus Naturae, trio with Jamie Smith and Zo Sosinka, 1996. *Compositions:* Solos and Accompaniments, with Lusus Naturae, for improvisers, commission, 1996. *Recordings:* Sound Score/Tape Collage for She Ain't Jumping Off That Bridge

(touring physical theatre piece), Conscious Opera Association, premiered Birmingham Dance Centre, 1994; Lusus Naturae-View, 1999. *Publications:* Lol Coxhill, Transcending Boundaries, in Rubberneck, 1995; Liner Notes, Dunmall/Sanders/Adams, Ghostly Thoughts, 1997. *Contributions to:* Rubberneck; Jazz on CD; Avant, 1995–. *Address:* The Octagon, 16 Beeches Farm Dr., Northfield, Birmingham B31 4SD, England.

COATES, Donald Denison; b. 23 March 1935, Orange, New Jersey, USA. Jazz Musician (piano); Composer. m. (1) Jacqueline Dorsey, divorced, (2) Dorothy Hering, 26 June 1988, 1 d. *Education:* Williams College, 1953–57. *Career:* Freelance jazz pianist, 1960–82; Played for: Jack Teagarden; Wild Bill Davison; Newport Jazz Festival All-Stars; Eddie Condon; Roy Eldridge; Solo pianist at: Windows On The World, Waldorf Astoria; Musician with vocalists including Maxine Sullivan, 1980–; Music Advisor, Entertainment Development Network, 1987. *Compositions:* Numerous songs, music for radio and television commercials. *Publications:* Contributor, articles of jazz instruction and history. *Membership:* AFofM. *Address:* 442 W 57th St, New York, NY 10019, USA.

COBAIN, Garry; b. Bedford, England. Musician. *Career:* Projects: Semi Real, Yage, Metropolis, Art Science Technology, Mental Cube, Candese, Intelligent Communication and Smart Systems; Mem., Future Sound of London, Amorphous Androgynous. *Recordings:* under various guises: Albums: Lifeforms, 1994; Urbmix: Flammable Liquid, 1994; Far-Out Son Of Lung And The Ramblings Of A Madman, 1995; ISDN, 1995; Dead Cities, 1996; Accelerator, 1996; Tales Of Ephidrina, 2001; Papua New Guinea: Translations, 2002; The Isness, 2002. Singles: Cascade, 1993; Paths 1–7: Lifeforms (EP), 1994; Papua New Guinea, 1996; My Kingdom, 1996; We Have Explosive, 1997. *Address:* c/o Astralwerks Records, 104 W 29th St, Fourth Floor, New York, NY 10001, USA. *Website:* www.astralwerks.com/fsl/.

COBBI, Daniel; b. 3 May 1953, Paris, France. Musician (piano); Jazz Composer. 1 d. *Education:* Architecture; Boulogne Conservatory, classical piano studies. *Career:* Tours, Italy; Spain; Belgium; Switzerland; Television concert, 1988; Many concerts, Radio France; France Musique; France Culture; Free radio's special solo piano; Played in USA, 1978; Many festivals, Europe. *Recordings:* Music For The Blue Bar, 1980; Eighteen Surprises For Christmas, 1981; Ayanamsa, 1982; Dilation, 1985; For Camille, 1995. *Honours:* First Command in France of the Culture Ministère, 1982. *Address:* 27 Ave d'Italie, 75013 Paris, France.

COBHAM, Billy (William Emmanuel), Jr; b. 16 May 1944, Panama. Musician (drums). m. Marcia Ann McCarthy, 1 s., 1 d. *Education:* High School of Music and Arts, New York, 1962. *Career:* Musician with: Billy Taylor's New York Jazz Sextet, 1967; Dreams, with Michael and Randy Brecker, 1969; Miles Davis, 1971; John McLaughlin's Mahavishnu Orchestra, 1972; Founder member, Spectrum, 1975–; Prolific recording artist and regular guest musician; Taught at numerous drum clinics; Own television series, Billy Cobham's World of Rhythm. *Recordings:* Albums: Spectrum, 1973; Total Eclipse, 1974; Crosswinds, 1974; Shabazz, 1975; A Funky Thide of Sings, 1975; Life and Times, 1976; Live In Europe, 1976; Magic, 1977; Inner Conflicts, 1978; Simplicity of Expression, 1978; BC, 1979; The Best Of, 1980; Flight Time, 1982; Observatory, 1982; Smokin', 1983; Warning, 1985; Powerplay, 1986; Picture This, 1987; Best Of, 1986; Stratus, 1988; Billy's Best Hits, 1988; By Design, 1992; Rudiments – The Billy Cobham Anthology, 2001; Drum 'N' Voice, 2002; with Horace Silver: Serenade To A Soul Sister; with Miles Davis: Directions; Big Fun; Live Evil; Tribute To Jack Johnson; Circle In The Round; On The Cover; with John McLaughlin and Mahavishnu Orchestra: My Goals Beyond; The Inner Mounting Flame; Birds of Fire; Love Devotion and Surrender; Between Nothingness and Surrender; Electric Guitarist; with Ron Carter: Blues Farm; All Blues; Spanish Blue; Yellow and Green; Also featured on albums by: George Benson; Stanley Clarke; McCoy Tyner; Grover Washington; Larry Coryell; Milt Jackson. *Current Management:* The Cameron Organization, 2001 W Magnolia Blvd, Burbank, CA 91506, USA.

COBRIN, Spencer James; b. 31 Jan. 1969, Paddington, London, England. Musician (drums, piano). *Education:* Private lessons, trumpet, drums, piano. *Career:* Played London club circuit, 1986–91; International tours as drummer with Morrissey, 1991–; Television performances include: Tonight Show with Johnny Carson; Saturday Night Live; MTV; Tonight Show with Jay Leno; Later With Jools Holland. *Recordings:* Albums with Morrissey: Your Arsenal, 1992; Southpaw Grammar, 1995; Maladjusted, 1997; Videos: Live In Dallas; Malady Lingers On (compilation). *Publications:* Featured in: Morrissey Shot, by Linder Sterling. *Membership:* Musicians' Union.

COCCIANTE, Richard (Riccardo); b. Saigon, Viet Nam. Composer; Vocalist; Musician (piano); Arranger. m. Catherine Boutet, 1 s. *Career:* Composer, solo artist, 1972–; World-wide television, radio appearances; Tour venues include: Gran Teatro La Fenice, Venice, 1988; Sporting Club, Monaco, 1988, 1990, 1995; Teatro dell'opera Caracalla, Rome, 1991; Vina del Mar Festival, Chile, 1994; Olympia, Paris, 1994, 1996; Zenith, Paris, 1994; Taj Mahal, Atlantic City, 1995; Teatro Sistina, Rome, 1988, 1993, 1995, 1997; Théâtre St Denis, Montréal, 1994, 1996; Stadsschouwberg, Amsterdam, 1995;

Vienna Rathaus, 1997; Collaborated with producers including: Paul Buckmaster; Humberto Gatica, Ennio Morricone, James Newton-Howard; Vangelis; Participated in album World War II, interpreting Michelle with London Symphony Orchestra; soundtrack of Patrice Leconte's film, Tandem, France, 1987; Album, Sand et les Romantiques, interpreting the role of Chopin; Soundtrack of Franco Zeffirelli's film, Storia di una capinera (Sparrow), international release, 1994; soundtrack of Walt Disney's film, Toy Story, Italy, 1996; concert, Christmas In Vienna, with Placido Domingo, Sarah Brightman and Helmut Lotti, 1997; soundtrack of Claude Berri's film, Astérix and Obélix contre César, Italy, 1999; 2000 (Hymne pour la ville de Lyon) commissioned by Raymonde Barre, Mayor of Lyon to celebrate the new millennium. *Compositions:* Notre Dame de Paris, the musical, 1998–99; Solo albums: 16 Italian including: Mu, 1972, Poesia, 1973; Anima, 1974; L'alba, 1975; Concerto per Margherita, 1976; Riccardo Cicciante, A Mano A Mano, 1978;... E Io Canto, 1979; Cervo a Primavera, 1981; Cocciante, (Celeste Nostalgia), 1982; Sincerità, 1983; Il Mare dei Papaveri, 1985; La Grande Avventura, 1987; Se Stiamo Insieme, 1991; Eventi e Mutamenti, 1993; Un Uomo Felice, 1994; Innamorato, 1997; 10 French including: Atlanti, 1973; Quand un Amour, 1974; Concerto pour Marguerite, 1978; Je Chante, 1979; Au Clair de tes Silences, 1980; Vieille, 1982; Sincérité, 1983; L'Homme qui vole, 1986; Empreinte, 1993; L'Instant Présent, 1995; 10 Spanish; 3 English; Some albums common to all four languages. *Recordings:* International hits: Bella Senz' Anima (Italy)/Bella Sin Alma (Spain, Spanish South America), 1973; Quand un Amour (France, Belgium, Canada), 1974; Margherita (Italy)/Marguerite (France, Belgium, Canada)/Margarita (Spain, Spanish South America), 1976–78; Coup de Soleil (France, Belgium), 1980; Cervo a Primavera (Italy)/Yo Renascere (Spain, Spanish South America), 1980; Sincéritié (France)/Sincerità (Italy, Holland)/Sinceridad (Spain, Spanish South America)/Sincerity (USA), 1983; Questione di Feeling – duet with Mina (Italy)/Question de Feeling – duet with Fabienne Thiebeault (France, Belgium, Canada)/Cuestion de Feeling – duet with Melissa (Spain, Spanish South America), 1985–86; Se Stiamo Insieme (Italy, Belgium, Holland, Brazil), 1991; Pour Elle (France)/Per Lei (Italy, Brazil)/I'd Fly (Italy, France, Belgium, Holland)/Por Ella (Spanish South America)/Voorbij (Holland), 1993–95; Il ricordo di un istante (Italy, France, Belgium, Canada, Holland); Belle, Le Temps des Cathédrales, Vivre – excerpts from musical Notre Dame de Paris (France, Belgium, Canada), 1998–99. *Honours:* Rose d'Or Award (Greece), 1981; Rino Gaetana Award (Italy), 1982; Winner, Sanremo Festival (Italy), 1991; Telegatto (Italy), 1991; Notre Dame de Paris – the musical: Felix 98 Award (Canada) for Album of the Year, 1998; Medaille de la Ville de Paris (France), 1998; Victoire de la Musique Award (France) for Song of the Year, 1999; Victoire de la Musique Award (France) for Show of the Year, 1999; Grande ufficiale della Repubblica Italiana (Italy), 1999; World Music Award (Monaco) for Best-selling French Artists/Group, 1999; Rolf Marbot Award (France) for Song of the Year, 1999; Felix 1999 Award (Canada) for Song of the Year, Felix 99 Award (Canada for Show of the Year, 1999; Felix 99 Award (Canada) for Best-selling Album, 1999; Felix 99 Award (Canada) for Album of the Year, 1999. *Current Management:* Boventoon BV. *Address:* Blue Toon/ Boventoon B.V. Information Office, 4 rue Chauveau Lagarde, 75008 Paris, France.

COCHRAN, Hank; b. 2 Aug. 1935, Isola, Mississippi, USA. Songwriter. m. (1) Shirley Kay Foster, 24 July 1954, divorced, 3 s.; (2) Marilyn Jean Seely, 15 June 1969, divorced, 1981; (3) Susan Booth Calder, 18 Aug. 1982, 1 step-d. *Career:* Co-owner, song plugger, writer, Pamper Music Inc, 1950–67; Writer, professional consultant, Tree International, 1967–89; Co-owner, writer, professional consultant, Co-Heart Music Group, 1989–. *Compositions include:* A Little Bitty Tear, 1961; He's Got You, 1962; Funny Way of Laughing, 1962; Tears Break Out On Me, 1962; Make The World Go Away, 1963; You Comb Her Hair, 1963; Make The World Go Away, 1963; Don't Touch Me, 1966; It's Not Love But It's Not Bad, 1973; Can I Sleep In Your Arms, 1973; Why Can't He Be You, 1978; Make the World Go Away (sung by Willie Nelson in the film Honeysuckle Rose, 1979); That's All That Matters To Me, 1980; I Fall To Pieces, 1982; What Would Your Memories Do, 1984; The Chair, 1985; Ocean Front Property, 1988; Set 'Em Up Joe, 1989; Who You Gonna Blame It On This Time, 1989; Don't You Ever Get Tired of Hurting Me, 1989; Right In The Wrong Direction, 1990; Is It Raining At Your House, 1991; I Want To Go With You. *Honours:* Country Music Asscn Walkway of Stars, 1967; Nashville Songwriters Asscn Hall of Fame, 1974; Betty Clooney Foundation, Singer's Salute to Country Songwriter Award, 1993.

COCKBURN, Bruce; b. 1945, Canada. Vocalist; Songwriter. 1 d. *Career:* Singer, songwriter, reflecting Christian beliefs and environmental issues. *Recordings:* Albums include: Bruce Cockburn, 1970; High Winds White Sky, 1971; Sunwheel Dance, 1972; Night Vision, 1973; Hand Dancing, 1974; Salt, Sun and Time, 1974; Joy Will Find A Way, 1975; Further Adventures, 1976; In The Falling Dark, 1976; Circles In The Stream, 1977; Dancing In The Dragon's Jaws, 1979; Humans, 1980; Resume, 1981; Inner City Front, 1981; Stealing Fire, 1984; World of Wonders, 1984; Trouble With Normal, 1985; Rumours of Glory, 1986; Waiting For A Miracle, 1987; Big Circumstance, 1989; Live, 1990; Nothing But A Burning Light, 1991; Christmas, 1993; Dart to the Heart, 1994; Charity of Night, 1997; Breakfast In New Orleans, 1999; Anything Anytime Anywhere, 2002. *Honours:* Officer of the Order of Canada,

2002. *Current Management:* Finkelstein Management Co, 260 Richmond St W, Suite 501, Toronto, ON M5V 1W5, Canada.

COCKER, Jarvis Branson; b. Sept. 1962, Sheffield, South Yorkshire, England. Vocalist; Songwriter. *Education:* BA, Film studies, St Martin's College of Art, London, 1991. *Career:* Lead singer, Pulp, 1980–; Numerous tours, television appearances and festival dates; Contribution to film soundtrack, Mission Impossible, 1996. *Recordings:* Albums: It, 1983; Freaks, 1987; Separations, 1992; His 'N' Hers, 1994; Different Class (No. 1, UK) 1995; This Is Hardcore (No. 1, UK), 1998; We Love Life, 2001; Hits, 2002. Singles: My Lighthouse/Looking For Life, 1983; Everybody's Problem/There Was, 1983; Little Girl (With Blue Eyes), 1985; Dogs Are Everywhere (EP), 1986; They Suffocate At Night, 1986; Master Of The Universe, 1987; My Legendary Girlfriend, 1990; Countdown, 1991; OU, 1992; Babies, 1992; Razzmatazz, 1993; Lipgloss, 1993; Do You Remember The First Time?, 1994; The Sisters (EP), 1994; Common People (No. 2, UK), 1995; Sorted For E's and Whizz/ Misshapes (No. 2, UK), 1995; Disco 2000, 1995; Something Changed, 1996; Help The Aged, 1997; This Is Hardcore, 1998; A Little Soul, 1998; Party Hard, 1998; The Trees/Sunrise, 2001; Bad Cover Version, 2002; Other collaborations: Barry Adamson, All Seeing I. *Honours:* Mercury Music Prize, 1995; BRIT Award, 1996. *Current Management:* Rough Trade Management, 66 Golborne Rd, London W10 5PF, England. *Address:* c/o Island Records, 825 Eighth Ave, New York, NY 10019, USA *Website:* www.pulponline.com.

COCKER, Joe; b. 20 May 1944, Sheffield, South Yorkshire, England. Vocalist; Songwriter. *Career:* Singer, Northern club circuit with group The Grease Band, 1965–69; Solo artiste, 1968–; Regular world-wide tours; Major concert appearances include: National Jazz and Blues Festival, 1968; Denver Pop Festival, 1969; Newport '69 Festival, 1969; Woodstock Festival (filmed), 1969; Isle of Wight Festival, 1969; Co-headliner with Beach Boys, Crystal Palace Garden Party, 1972; Prince's Trust Rock Gala, 1988; Nelson Mandela's 70th Birthday Tribute, Wembley Stadium, 1988; Rock In Rio II Festival, 1991; Guitar Legends, Seville, Spain, 1991; Montreux Jazz Festival, filmed for MTV's Unplugged series, 1992; Blues Music Festival, with B. B. King, 1992; Numerous television and radio broadcasts world-wide. *Recordings:* Hit singles include: With A Little Help From My Friends (No. 1, UK), 1968; Delta Lady, 1969; The Letter, 1970; Cry Me A River, 1970; You Are So Beautiful, 1975; Unchain My Heart, 1987; When The Night Comes, 1990; Night Calls, 1993; Simple Things, 1994; Could You Be Loved, 1998; with Jennifer Warnes: Up Where We Belong (No. 1, USA), theme to film An Officer and A Gentleman, 1982; Contributions to film soundtracks include: Edge of a Dream, for film Teachers, 1984; You Can Leave Your Hat On, for film 9 1/2 Weeks, 1986; Love Lives On, for film Bigfoot and The Hendersons, 1987; (All I Know) Feels Like Forever, for film The Cutting Edge, 1992; Trust In Me, duet with Sass Jordan, for film The Bodyguard, 1992; Albums include: With A Little Help From My Friends, 1969; Joe Cocker, 1970; Mad Dogs and Englishmen, 1970; Cocker Happy, 1971; Something To Say, 1972; I Can Stand A Little Rain, 1974; Jamaica Say You Will, 1975; Live In Los Angeles, 1976; Stingray, 1976; Joe Cocker's Greatest Hits, 1977; Luxury You Can Afford, 1978; Sheffield Steel, 1982; Civilized Man, 1984; Cocker, 1986; Unchain My Heart, 1987; Nightriding, 1988; One Night of Sin, 1989; Joe Cocker Live, 1990; Night Calls, 1992; The Legend – The Essential Collection, 1992; Have A Little Faith, 1994; Organic, 1996; Across from Midnight, 1997; No Ordinary World, 1999; Respect Yourself, 2002; Contributor, Two Rooms (tribute album to Elton John and Bernie Taupin), 1991. *Honours:* Grammy, Best Pop Vocal Performance, Up Where We Belong, 1983; Academy Award, Best Film Song, Up Where We Belong, 1983. *Current Management:* Roger Davies Management, 15030 Ventura Blvd #772, Sherman Oaks, CA 91403, USA.

CODLING, Neil John; b. 5 Dec. 1973, Stratford-Upon-Avon, England. Musician (keyboards, synthesizers). *Career:* Mem., Suede, 1996–2001; Numerous tours and television appearances; Festival dates in UK and Europe; Retired from music, 2001. *Recordings:* Albums: Coming Up (No. 1, UK), 1996; Sci-Fi Lullabies, 1997; Head Music, 1999. Singles: Trash, 1996; Filmstar, 1996; Lazy, 1996; Beautiful Ones, 1996; Electricity, 1999; She's In Fashion, 1999; Everything Will Flow, 1999; Can't Get Enough, 1999.

COE, Tony (Anthony George); b. 29 Nov. 1934, Musician (clarinet, alto and tenor saxophone); Composer. *Career:* Jazz saxophonist and clarinettist; Worked with many ensembles led by musicians including: Joe Daniels; Humphrey Lyttelton; John Dankworth; Clarke-Boland Big Band; John Picard; Derek Bailey; Mike Gibbs; Stan Getz; Dizzy Gillespie; Bob Brookmeyer; Stan Tracey; Leader of many groups including: Axel and Coe; Wheeler and Co (with Kenny Wheeler); Toured Europe with United Jazz and Rock Ensemble; Recorded with Bob Moses and Norma Winstone; Collaborated with Henry Mancini as the soloist on early Pink Panther film soundtracks, 1970s; Other appearances on soundtracks: Superman II; Victor Victoria; Performed under Pierre Boulez and worked with Matrix (small ensemble formed by clarinettist Alan Hacker); Appearances on pop and rock albums by artists including: CCS; Caravan; Spencer Davis Group; Georgie Fame; The Hollies; Joe Jackson. *Compositions:* Film scores: Mer De Chine; Camomile; Peau de Pêche; Works recorded by: Matrix; Danish Radio Big Band; Metropole Orchestra; Skymasters; Wrote Zeitgeist, an orchestral work fusing jazz and rock elements with techniques from European Art Music, 1975. *Recordings:* Albums include: Swingin' Til The Girls Come Home, 1962; Tony Coe With The Brian Lemon Trio, 1971; Zeitgeist, 1976; Nutty On Willisau (with Tony Oxley), 1983; Le Chat Se Retourne, 1984; Canterbury Song, 1989; Captain Coe's Famous Racearound, 1996. *Honours:* Danish Jazzpar Prize, Hon. D Mus, 1995; BT British Jazz Award, Clarinet, 1997.

COFFEY, Cath(erine Muthomi); b. 1965, Kenya. Vocalist. *Career:* Member, Stereo MCs; Numerous gigs and TV appearances. *Recordings:* Singles: Elevate My Mind, 1990; Lost In Music, 1991; Connected, 1992; Step It Up, 1993; Ground Level, 1993; Creation, 1993; Deep Down and Dirty, 2001; We Belong In This World Together, 2001; Albums: 33–45–78, 1989; Supernatural, 1990; Connected, 1992; Deep Down and Dirty, 2001; Solo Single: Wild World, 1997; Tell Me, 1997; Solo Album: Mind The Gap, 1997; Also appeared on: Tricky, Nearly God, 1996. *Honours:* BRIT Awards: Best British Album; Best British Group, 1993.

COGHILL, Jon; b. 26 Aug. 1971. Musician (drums). *Education:* University of Queensland, Botany student. *Career:* Joined Brisbane-based rock group Powderfinger, 1992; Steadily built reputation on many Australian tours/ festival appearances; International breakthrough with Odyssey Number Five album; Constant world-wide touring throughout 2000–01 ending with New Suburban Fables 2001 Australian shows. *Recordings:* Albums: Parables For Wooden Ears, 1994; Double Allergic, 1996; Internationalist, 1998; Odyssey Number Five, 2000; Singles: Powderfinger Blue (EP), Transfusion (EP), 1993; Tail, Grave Concern, 1994; Save Your Skin, Mr Kneebone (EP), 1995; Pick You Up, D.A.F., Living Type, 1996; Take Me In, 1997; The Day You Come, Don't Wanna Be Left Out/Good-Day Ray, 1998; Already Gone, Passenger, 1999; My Happiness, 2000; Like A Dog, The Metre, 2001. *Honours:* ARIA Awards: Album of the Year; Song of the Year; Best Rock Album; Best Cover Artwork, 1999; six times platinum fourth album on Australian chart for 67 weeks by end of 2001; Only home-grown act ever to play more than 3 consecutive nights at Festival Hall, Australia. *Address:* c/o Republic Records, Australia. *Website:* www.powderfinger.com.

COHEN, Leonard (Norman); b. 21 Sept. 1934, Montréal, QC, Canada. Poet; Author; Vocalist; Songwriter. *Education:* BA, English, McGill University, 1955. *Career:* Founder, Country and Western group, The Buckskin Boys, 1951; Novelist; Poet; Solo singer; Subject of BBC documentary. *Compositions include:* Suzanne; Priests (both recorded by Judy Collins); Sisters of Mercy; Hey, That's No Way To Say Goodbye; Story of Isaac; Bird On A Wire. *Recordings:* Albums: The Songs of Leonard Cohen, 1968; Songs From A Room, 1969; Songs of Love and Hate, 1971; Live Songs, 1973; New Skin For The Old Ceremony, 1974; Greatest Hits, 1975; The Best of Leonard Cohen, 1976; Death of a Ladies Man, 1977; Recent Songs, 1979; Various Positions, 1985; I'm Your Man, 1988; The Future, 1992; More Best Of, 1997; Live Songs, 1998; Ten New Songs, 2001. *Publications:* Let Us Compare Mythologies, 1956; The Spice-Box of Earth, 1961; The Favourite Game, 1963; Flowers for Hitler, 1964; Beautiful Losers, 1966; Parasites of Heaven, 1966; Selected Poems 1956–1968, 1968; The Energy of Slaves, 1972; Death of a Lady's Man, 1978; Book of Mercy, 1984; Stranger Music: Selected Poems and Songs, 1993. *Honours:* McGill Literary Award for Let Us Compare Mythologies; William Harold Moon Award, Recording Rights Organization of Canada Ltd, 1984; Juno Hall of Fame, 1991. *Current Management:* Stranger Music. *Address:* c/o Suite 91, 419 N Larchmont Blvd, Suite 91, Los Angeles, CA 90004, USA.

COHEN, Lyor; b. New York, NY, USA. Music Co Exec. *Education:* Marketing and International Finance, University of Miami. *Career:* Worked, Bank Leumi; Hip hop performance promoter, Mix Club, Los Angeles; Worked, Rush Entertainment, 1985, partner in co; Pres. and CEO, Island Def Jam Records. *Address:* c/o Def Jam Records, 2220 Colorado Ave, Santa Monica, CA 90404, USA. *Website:* www.islanddefjam.com.

COHEN SOLAL, Philippe; b. France. Prod; Musician; Composer; DJ. *Career:* Musical supervisor, collaborations with film dirs; Owner, Ya Basta! Records, with Christoph H. Muller; mem. Boyz From Brazil, with Christoph H. Muller; Founder-mem., Gotan Project, 1999–; World-wide Gotan Project tour, 2002, mixing video, pre-recorded and live performances; Collaborations with many tango musicians. *Recordings:* Album: La Revancha Del Tango, 2001. Singles: El Capitalismo Foraneo (EP), 2000; Triptico (EP), 2000; Santa Maria (EP), 2001. *Address:* c/o XL-Recordings, 17–19 Alma Rd, London SW18 1AA, England. *E-mail:* yabastarecords@noos.fr. *Website:* www.gotanproject.com.

COKE, Charles M; b. 15 March 1943, San Jose, California, USA. Record Prod. 2 s., 1 d. *Career:* Toured USA for 20 years; Local television and radio shows. *Recordings:* Producer for: Tiggi Clay; Fizzy Quick; Derrick Hughes; Workforce; II Big; Bedroom Cowboys; John Payne; CP Salt; NVS; Baby Fat with Big Mitch. *Membership:* Musicians' Union (local, San Francisco). *Current Management:* Up Front Management. *Address:* 1906 Seward Dr., Pittsburg, CA 94565, USA.

COLBERT, Laurence John; b. 27 June 1970, Kingston, Surrey, England. Musician (drums). *Career:* Member: Ride 1988–96; Animal House, 1999–;

Concerts include: Royal Albert Hall; Reading Festival; Glastonbury; Television includes: The Word; Top of the Pops; BBC Radio 1 sessions: John Peel; Mark Goodier. *Recordings:* Albums: with Ride: Nowhere, 1990; Going Blank Again, 1992; Carnival of Light, 1994; Live Light, 1995; Tarantula, 1996; with Animal House: The Animal House EP, 1999; Ready To Receive, 2000. *Honours:* Silver discs: Nowhere, 1990; Going Blank Again, 1992. *Membership:* PRS. *Current Management:* Dave Newton. *Address:* PO Box 479, Headington, Oxford OX3 7QW, England.

COLBURN, Richard; b. 25 July 1970. Musician (drums, percussion). *Career:* Member, Belle and Sebastian, 1996–; Collaborations: Snow Patrol; Hefner; Curated Bowlie Weekend Festival with other band members, 1999. *Recordings:* Albums: Tigermilk, If You're Feeling Sinister, 1996; The Boy With The Arab Strap 1998; Fold Your Hands Child – You Walk Like A Peasant, 2000; Storytelling, 2002. Singles: Dog On Wheels EP, Lazy Line Painter Jane EP, 3–6–9 Seconds of Light EP, 1997; This Is Just A Modern Rock Song EP, 1998; Legal Man, 2000; Jonathan David, I'm Waking Up To Us, 2001. *Honours:* BRIT Award, Best Newcomer, 1999. *Current Management:* Banchory Management, PO Box 25074, Glasgow G2 6YL, Scotland. *Website:* www.belleandsebastian.co.uk.

COLBY, Mark Steven; b. 18 March 1949, Brooklyn, New York, USA. Musician (saxophone). m. (1) Janet McIntyre, divorced 1970; (2) Mary Deacon, 21 April 1977, 1 s., 3 d. *Education:* MusB, University of Miami, 1972; MusM, 1975. *Career:* Musician with: Maynard Ferguson, 1975–77; Bob James, 1977–83; Freelance musician, 1980–; Teacher, jazz saxophone, De Paul University, Chicago, 1980–; Clinic musician for Selmer musical instruments, 1987–. *Recordings:* Solo albums: Serpentine Fire, 1978; One Good Turn, 1979; Mango Tango, 1990; Playground, 1991; Reunion with Vince Maggio, 1999; Other. *Recordings include:* with Bill Wyman: Monkey Grip, 1974; Stone Alone, 1976; Destively Bonaroo, Doctor John, 1974; Real Life Ain't This Way, Jay Ferguson, 1979; Cat In The Hat, Bobby Caldwell, 1980; Marbles, Software, 1981.

COLD MISSION. See: CLAIR, Mark.

COLDWELL, Terry (Terence Mark); b. 21 July 1974, Islington, London, England. Vocalist. *Career:* Member, East 17; Numerous television and live appearances. *Recordings:* Singles: House of Love, 1992; Deep, 1993; West End Girls, 1993; It's Alright, 1993; Around The World, 1994; Steam, 1994; Stay Another Day (No. 1, UK), 1994; Let It Rain, 1995; Thunder, 1995; Do U Still, 1996; If You Ever, with Gabrielle, 1996; Hey Child, 1997; Each Time, 1998; Betcha Can't Wait, 1999; Albums: Walthamstow, 1993; Steam, 1994; Up All Night, 1996; Around the World – The Journey So Far, 1996; Resurrection, 1998.

COLE, B. J. (Brian John); b. 17 June 1946, North London, England. Musician (pedal steel guitar); Prod. *Career:* Musician, Country Music circuit, London, 1964–; Pedal steel guitar player, Cochise; Founder member, producer, Hank Wangford Band; Leading exponent of instrument in UK; Currently prolific session musician and solo artiste; Leader, own group Transparent Music Ensemble; Replacement guitarist for the Verve, 1998–. *Recordings:* Solo albums: New Hovering Dog, 1972; Transparent Music, 1989; The Heart of The Moment, 1995; Stop The Panic (with Luke Vibert), 2000; As session musician: Tiny Dancer, Elton John, 1970; Wide Eyed and Legless, Andy Fairweather-Low, 1975; No Regrets, Walker Brothers, 1976; City To City, Gerry Rafferty, 1978; Everything Must Change, Paul Young, 1984; Silver Moon, David Sylvian, 1986; Diet of Strange Places, k d lang, 1987; Montagne D'Or, The Orb, 1995; Possibly Maybe, Björk, 1995; with Hank Wangford: Hank Wangford, 1980; Live, 1982; Other recordings with: Johnny Nash; Deacon Blue; Level 42; Danny Thompson; Alan Parsons Project; Shakin' Stevens; Beautiful South; John Cale; Echobelly; Dot Allison; Richard Ashcroft; Pet Shop Boys; Eliza Carthy; REM; David McAlmont; Robbie Williams; Spiritualized.

COLE, Freddy (Lionel F. Cole); b. 1931, Chicago, Illinois, USA. Musician (piano); Vocalist. *Education:* Roosevelt Institute; Juilliard School of Music; New England Conservatory. *Career:* Younger brother of Nat 'King' Cole; Performed with numerous jazz musicians, New York, 1950s; Festival performances, USA, Japan, Europe; Toured with own quartet, 1997–98; Appearances at Carnegie Hall; Voiceovers for numerous TV commercials. *Recordings include:* Latest albums: Always, 1995; Circle of Love, 1996; To the Ends of the Earth, 1997; Love Makes the Changes, 1998; Le Grand Freddy Sings The Music of Michel Legrand, 2000; Merry Go Round, 2000; Rio De Janeiro Blue, 2001; Contributor, All My Tomorrows, Grover Washington Jr, 1994. *Current Management:* Maxine S Harvard Unlimited, 7942 W Bell Rd, #C5–501, Glendale, AZ 85308, USA.

COLE, Gardner; b. 7 Feb. 1962, Flint, Michigan, USA. Vocalist; Musician (keyboards, drums, guitar). *Education:* 1 year, Berklee College of Music, Boston. *Career:* Two solo albums, 1988, 1991; Drummer with ABC; Keyboard player with A-Ha! on Grammy Awards; Toured as opening act for Toni Tony Tone, 1991. *Compositions:* 60 songs recorded by various artists including Amy Grant, Al Jarreau, Tom Jones, Madonna, Michael McDonald, Brenda Russell,

Vonda Shepard, 3T, Jody Watley, Jane Wiedlin. *Recordings include:* Open Your Heart (No. 1, USA), Madonna, 1987; Most of All and Everything, Jody Watley, 1991; Barrier, Tina Turner; Tear It Up, Michael McDonald. *Honours:* BMI Million-Air Award; 3 BMI Pop Awards; 18 Gold and Platinum records. *Membership:* AFTRA; SAG. *Current Management:* Bennett Freed, One Love Management. *Address:* 5410 Wilshire Blvd, Suite #806, Los Angeles, CA 90036, USA.

COLE, Holly; b. 1963, Halifax, Nova Scotia, Canada. Vocalist. *Education:* Studied classical piano as a child. *Career:* Started singing jazz at 15 after hearing Sarah Vaughan; Moved to Toronto and sang in a big band, early 1980s; Formed own trio, 1985; Debut album released Alert Records (Manhattan label outside Canada), 1990; Continues to record and regularly tours Canada, USA, Japan and Europe. *Recordings:* Girl Talk, 1990; Blame It On My Youth, 1991; Don't Smoke In Bed, 1993; Temptation, 1995; It Happened One Night, 1996; Dark Dear Heart, 1997; Romantically Helpless, 2000; Baby It's Cold Outside, 2001. *Current Management:* W Tom Berry, Alert Music Inc, 41 Britain St, Suite 305, Toronto, ON, M5A 1R7, Canada. *Website:* www.hollycole.com.

COLE, Lloyd; b. 31 Jan. 1961, Buxton, Derbyshire, England. Vocalist; Songwriter. *Career:* Leader, Lloyd Cole and The Commotions, 1984–88; Solo artiste, 1989–. *Recordings:* Albums: with the Commotions: Rattlesnakes, 1984; Easy Pieces, 1985; Mainstream, 1987; Solo albums: Lloyd Cole, 1989; Don't Get Weird On Me Babe, 1991; Bad Vibes, 1993; Love Story, 1995; Singles: Perfect Skin, 1984; Brand New Friend, 1985; Lost Weekend, 1985; Like Lovers Do, 1995; features on: Naked Self, The The, 2000. *Current Management:* John Reid Enterprises Ltd, Singers House, 32 Galena Rd, London W6 0LT, England.

COLE, M. J, (Matthew James Colman); b. 24 Sept. 1973, London, England. Prod; Musician (keyboards); Remixer. *Education:* Classically trained at Royal College of Music. *Career:* Competitor in BBC Young Musician of the Year; Became engineer at SOUR studios in London; Set up Prolific Records, 1998; Collaborations: Elisabeth Troy; Jason Kaye; Remixed: Incognito; Jill Scott; Nitin Sawhney; Masters At Work. *Recordings:* Albums: Sincere, 2000; Back To Mine (compilation), 2002. Singles: Sincere, 1998; Crazy Love, 2000; Hold On To Me, 2000. *Address:* c/o Talkin' Loud Records, Chancellor's House, 72 Chancellor's Rd, London W6 9QB, England.

COLE, Natalie Maria; b. 6 Feb. 1950, Los Angeles, California, USA. Vocalist. m. (1) Marvin J Yancy, 30 July 1976, divorced, (2) Andre Fischer, 17 Sept. 1989, divorced. *Education:* BA, Child Psychology, University of Massachusetts, 1972. *Career:* Stage debut, 1962; Solo recording artist, 1975–; Major concerts world-wide include: Tokyo Music Festival, 1979; Nelson Mandela 70th Birthday Concert, Wembley, 1988; Nelson Mandela tribute, Wembley, 1990; John Lennon Tribute Concert, Liverpool, 1990; Homeless benefit concert with Quincy Jones, Pasadena, 1992; Rainforest benefit concert, Carnegie Hall, 1992; Commitment To Life VI (AIDS benefit concert), Los Angeles, 1992; Television appearances include: Sinatra and Friends, 1977; Host, Big Break, 1990; Motown 30, 1990; Tonight Show, 1991; Entertainers '91, 1991. *Recordings:* Hit singles: This Will Be, 1975; Sophisticated Lady, 1976; I've Got Love On My Mind, 1977; Our Love (No. 1, USA R&B chart), 1977; Gimme Some Time (duet with Peabo Bryson), 1980; What You Won't Do For Love (duet with Peabo Bryson), 1980; Jump Start, 1987; I Live For Your Love, 1988; Pink Cadillac, 1988; Miss You Like Crazy (No. 1, USA R&B charts), 1989; Wild Women Do, from film Pretty Woman, 1990; Unforgettable (duet with father Nat 'King' Cole), 1991; Smile Like Yours, 1997; Albums: Inseparable, 1975; Natalie, 1976; Unpredictable, 1977; Thankful, 1978; Natalie... Live!, 1978; I Love You So, 1979; Don't Look Back, 1980; Happy Love, 1981; Natalie Cole Collection, 1981; I'm Ready, 1982; Dangerous, 1985; Everlasting, 1987; Good To Be Back, 1989; Unforgettable... With Love (No. 1, USA), 1991; The Soul of Natalie Cole, 1991; Take A Look, 1993; Holly and Ivy, 1994; Stardust, 1996; This Will Be, 1997; Snowfall on the Sahara, 1999; Love Songs (compilation), 2000; with Peabo Bryson: We're The Best of Friends, 1980. *Honours:* Numerous Grammy Awards include: Best New Artist, 1976; Best Female R&B Vocal Performance, 1976, 1977; 5 Grammy Awards for Unforgettable, including Best Song, Best Album, 1992; 5 NAACP Image Awards, 1976, 1988, 1992; American Music Awards: Favourite Female R&B Artist, 1978; Favourite Artist, Favourite Album, 1992; Soul Train Award, Best Single, 1988; Various Gold discs. *Membership:* AFTRA; NARAS. *Current Management:* Dan Cleary Management Associates, Suite 1101, 1801 Ave of The Stars, Los Angeles, CA 90067, USA.

COLE, Pamela; b. 1 Jan. 1959, Edmonton, Alberta, Canada. Musician (bass guitar, acoustic guitar). 1 s., 1 d. *Education:* BA, Criminology. *Career:* Member, Country band Quickdraw; Performances include: Calgary Stampede, televised on Calgary Cable 10, 1994; Interviewed live, CKUA Radio, Edmonton, Alberta; Third place, fourth Annual Country Hootenanny, Claresholm, Alberta; International Country Music Grand Prix, Norway, 1 of 10 finalists with: Next To Nothing, 1995. *Recordings:* Change of Heart; Just A Guess; Winning Was The Only Thing; Weekend Cowboy; Next To Nothing; An Angel Told Me So. *Publications:* 2 chapbooks of poetry: In A Corner of My Room; Between Friends. *Honours:* Hon. mention from Billboard Magazine for

Eye On Me; Alberta Music Project Award, 1992; Winner, 960 CFAC Country Showdown, with band Headin' West. *Membership:* SOCAN; ASCAP; ARIA; NCMO 1994. *Address:* 5610 Trelle Dr. NE, Calgary, AB T2K 3V4, Canada.

COLE, Paula; b. 1970, USA. Vocalist; Songwriter. *Education:* Berklee College of Music. *Career:* Singer, Peter Gabriel's Secret World Tour, 1995; Solo Artiste, 1996–. *Recordings:* Albums: Harbinger, 1996; This Fire, 1997; Amen, 1999; Hit Single: Where Have All The Cowboys Gone? (EP), 1997; I Don't Want to Wait, 1999; I Believe in Love, 1999. *Address:* c/o Monterey Peninsula Artists, 509 Hartnell St, Monterey, CA 93940, USA.

COLEMAN, Cy; b. New York, USA. Composer; Prod; Musician (piano); Songwriter. *Career:* Began performing on piano aged 6; Played New York clubs, 1950s; Composed songs before writing for musical theatre; Began as producer with Barnum, 1980; President, Notable Music Co. *Compositions include:* Contributions to revues: John Murray Anderson's Almanac; Ziegfeld Follies; Broadway musicals: Wildcat, 1960; Little Me, 1962; Sweet Charity, re-run on Broadway, 1986; Seesaw; On The Twentieth Century; I Love My Wife; Barnum; City of Angels, 1990; The Will Rogers Follies, 1992; The Life, 1997; Television specials for Shirley MacLaine: If My Friends Could See Me Now; Gypsy In My Soul; Film scores: Father Goose; Power; Garbo Talks; Family Business; Sweet Charity; Songs include: Witchcraft; The Best Is Yet To Come; Hey Look Me Over (from Wildcat); I've Got Your Number (from Wildcat); Real Live Girl (from Little Me); Big Spender (from Sweet Charity); If My Friends Could See Me Now (from Sweet Charity). *Recordings:* Albums include: Cy Coleman, 1955; Flower Drum Song, 1959; Comin' Home, 1963; Barnum, 1980; The Life, 1996; It Started With A Dream, 2002. *Honours:* 3 Emmys, Shirley MacLaine's Television specials; 2 Grammys: Record Producer, Composer, 1992; Numerous Tony awards, including 6 Tonys, City of Angels, 1990; 6 Tonys, Will Rogers Follies, 1992; Johnny Mercer Award, Songwriters Hall of Fame; Doctorate, Music, Long Island University, 1994; Irvin Field Humanitarian Award, National Conference, Christians and Jews; Tribute, Avery Fisher Hall. *Membership:* Vice-President, mem., Board of Directors, ASCAP. *Address:* c/o Notable Music Co Inc, 441 E 57th St, New York, NY 10022, USA.

COLEMAN, George Edward; b. 8 March 1935, Memphis, Tennessee, USA. Musician (tenor, alto, soprano saxophones). m. (1) Gloria Bell, 3 Aug. 1959, divorced, 1 s., 1 d., (2) Carol Hollister, 7 Sept. 1985. *Education:* Private music lessons from older Memphis musicians. *Career:* Played with: B. B. King Blues Band, 1952–53; Max Roach Quintet, 1958–59; Miles Davis Quintet, 1963–64; Lionel Hampton 1965–66; Lee Morgan Quintet, 1969; Elvin Jones Quartet, 1970; George Coleman Quartet and Octet, 1971–; NYU, 1984; New School, 1987; LI University, 1987; Consultant, Lenox Jazz School, Massachusetts, 1988. *Compositions:* 5/4 Thing; You Mean So Much To Me; Blondies Waltz; Amsterdam After Dark; Music in Free Jack. *Recordings:* My Horns of Plenty; Live At Yoshi's; Manhattan Panorama; Duo, with Tete Montelui; with Cedar Walton: Eastern Rebellion; with Miles Davis: My Funny Valentine; My Horns of Plenty; I Could Write a Book. *Honours:* International Jazz Critics Poll, 1958; Artist of the Year, Record World Magazine, 1969; Knight of Mark Twain, 1972; AWD Contribution to Music, Beale Street Asscn, 1977; Tip of the Derby Awards, 1978, 1979; Jazz Audience Award, 1979; Good Note Jazz Award, 1985; Key to City of Memphis, 1991; Grantee, National Endowment for the Arts, 1975, 1985; Lifetime Achievement Award, Jazz Foundation of America, 1996. *Current Management:* Abby Hoffer Enterprises. *Address:* 63 E Ninth St, New York, NY 10003, USA.

COLEMAN, Jaz (Jeremy); b. Cheltenham, Gloucestershire, England. Vocalist; Musician (keyboards). *Education:* Piano lessons; Grade 8 violin; Cathedral choir. *Career:* Lead singer, keyboard player, UK rock band Killing Joke, 1980–; Numerous tours world-wide, television and radio appearances; Arranged Nigel Kennedy's Riders On The Storm, The Doors Concerto, 2000; Collaboration with Hinewehi Mohu on Oceania, 2000. *Compositions include:* 1 symphony. *Recordings:* Albums with Killing Joke: Killing Joke, 1980; What's This For?, 1981; Revelations, 1982; Fire Dances, 1983; Night Time, 1985; Brighter Than A Thousand Suns, 1986; Extremities, Dirt and Various Repressed Emotions, 1990; Pandemonium, 1994; Solo: with Anne Dudley, Outside the Gate, 1988; Songs from the Victorious City, 1998.

COLEMAN, Lisa Annette; b. 17 Aug. 1960, Los Angeles, California, USA. Musician (piano, keyboards); Composer; Prod. *Career:* Appeared on numerous US and European TV shows and Merv Griffin Show with Waldorf Salad at the age of 12; Joined Prince's band at 19 years of age as keyboard player, 1980; Toured and recorded extensively; Featured in film Purple Rain; Part of recording Duo Wendy and Lisa with Wendy Melvoin; Numerous TV appearances in Europe and the USA; Collaborations include: Seal; Joni Mitchell; kd lang; MeShell NdegeOcello; Victoria Williams; Neil Finn. *Compositions:* Scores for films including Dangerous Minds, Soul Food, Hav Plenty. *Recordings:* Albums: Wendy and Lisa, 1987; Fruit At The Bottom, 1988; Eroica, 1990; Girl Bros, 1998; Appears on Prince albums: Dirty Mind, 1980; Controversy, 1981; 1999, 1982; Purple Rain (No. 1, USA), 1984; Around The World In A Day (No. 1, USA), 1985; Parade, 1986; Sign O' The Times, 1987. *Current Management:* Gold Mountain Entertainment. *Address:* Renata Kanclerz, 3575 Cahuenga Blvd W, Suite 450, Los Angeles, CA 90068, USA.

COLEMAN, Ornette; b. 19 March 1930, Fort Worth, Texas, USA. Jazz Musician (saxophone, trumpet, violin); Composer. *Education:* Lennox School of Jazz, Trumpet and violin studies; Studied theory. *Career:* Member, bands with Red Connors, 1946; Pee Wee Clayton, 1949; Own Coleman Quartet (Don Cherry, Charlie Haden, Billy Higgins); Residency at Five Spot Café, New York, 1958–63; Trio with David Izenzon and Charles Moffett, 1965; Created own group, Prime Time, mid 1970s–. *Recordings:* Albums include: Something Else!, 1958; Tomorrow Is The Question, 1959; The Shape of Jazz To Come, 1959; Change of The Century, 1960; This Is Our Music, 1960; Free Jazz, 1961; Ornette!, 1961; Ornette On Tenor, 1961; The Town Hall Concert, 1962, 1963; Chappaqua Suite, 1965; The Great London Concert (aka An Evening With Ornette Coleman), 1966; At The Golden Circle, Vols 1 and 2, 1966; The Empty Foxhole, 1966; Music of Ornette Coleman (aka Saints and Soldiers), 1967; New York Is Now, 1968; Love Call, 1968; Ornette At 12, 1969; Crisis, 1969; Friends and Neighbours, 1970; The Art of Improvisation, 1970; Science Fiction, 1972; Skies of America, 1972; Twins, 1972; Dancing In Your Head, 1976, 1976; Body Meta, 1976; Paris Concert, 1977; Coleman Classics, Vol. One, 1977; Soapsuds (with Charlie Haden), 1977; Broken Shadows, 1982; Opening The Caravan of Dreams, 1985; Prime Time/Time Design, 1985; Song X (with Pat Metheny), Song X, 1986; In All Languages, 1987; Virgin Beauty, 1988; Live In Milano, 1968, 1989; Jazzbuhne Berlin 88, 1990; Naked Lunch, 1992; Tone Dialing, 1995; Colors: Live from Leipzig, 1996; Complete Science Fiction Sessions, 2000; Guest musician: Old and New Gospel, Jackie McLean; Tale of Captain Black, James Blood Ulmer. *Address:* c/o Monterey International Inc, 200 W Superior, Suite 202, Chicago, IL 60610, USA.

COLEMAN, Steve; b. Chicago, Illinois, USA. Jazz Musician (saxophone). *Education:* Music performance at: Wesleyan University; Chicago Music College. *Career:* Moved to New York, 1978; Toured USA, Europe with: Slide Hampton; Sam Rivers; Cecil Taylor; Doug Hammond; Formed Steve Coleman and Five Elements, 1982; Formed M-Base. *Recordings:* Albums: Solo: Motherland Pulse; Five Elements: Black Science; Rhythm People; On The Edge of Tommorrow; World Expansion; Sine Die; Rhythm in Mind; The Tao of Mad Phat Fringe Zones; Curves of Life; The Sonic Language of Myth; Resistance Is Futile, 2002; Played on recordings by: Dave Holland; Branford Marsalis; Geri Allen; Cassandra Wilson; Greg Osby. *Honours:* Regular winner, Downbeat polls. *Current Management:* SESAC. *Address:* 55 Music Sq. E, Nashville, TN 37203, USA.

COLINET, Paul Marie Marcel; b. 27 Jan. 1954, Elisabethville, Belgian Congo. Composer (Classic and Folk); Pianotuner; Musician (violin, viola, cello, mandola, esraj, lyra, diatonic accordion). m. Segers Yvonna, 14 Aug. 1982. *Education:* Private lessons, violin and harmony. *Career:* Piano Tuner; Orchestra, viola; Chamber Music; Member, Trio Michel Terlinck. *Compositions:* 2 mandolin concerts; 1 violin concerto; 4 suites, mandolin, solo; 48 diatonic dances for diatonic accordion; Some compositions for folk instruments including bagpipes, hurdy-gurdy and lyra. *Publications:* 37 own editions of own compositions. *Honours:* First Prize, Instrument Building, Viola d'amore, 1995. *Membership:* SABAM. *Address:* Blvd E Bockstael 294, 1020 Brussels, Belgium.

COLLAZO, Steven André; b. 24 Jan. 1960, Brooklyn, NY, USA. Recording Engineer; Arranger; Composer; Artist; Prod; Keyboardist. m. Linda Susan Dodson, 22 Aug. 1995. *Career:* Nine piece band, formed in High School, appeared throughout New York City; Joined Warner Recording Act, Undisputed Truth; Toured USA with Natalie Cole, The Isleys, Smokey Robinson; Toured UK and Europe with Odyssey, 1981; Appeared on TOTP, 1981. *Compositions:* I've Got to Wonder, 1982; Keep You Comin' Back, 1990s; Do You Right, 1990s; Paradise, 1990s; Waverly Radio, 1997. *Recordings:* Back to My Roots, classic remake of 80s hit, appeared on CH5 Fives Company, 1997; Producer, several Odyssey classics and new material due for release. *Publications:* Sound on Sound, 1997; Mentions in SOS; The Mix and Future, demos and progs, 1996, 1997. *Honours:* Demo Reviews, Sound on Sound, Top Tape, 1997. *Membership:* American Society of Composers, Authors and Publishers. *Address:* 60 Russell Rd, Salisbury, Wiltshire, SP2 7LR, England.

COLLEN, Phil; b. 8 Dec. 1957, Hackney, London, England. Rock Musician (guitar); Vocalist. *Career:* Guitarist, Girl, 1979–82; Guitarist, Def Leppard, 1982–; Concerts include: World tour, 1983; Monsters of Rock Festival, Castle Donington, 1986; BRIT Awards, Royal Albert Hall, 1989; Freddie Mercury Tribute Concert, Wembley Stadium, 1992. *Recordings:* Albums: with Girl: Sheer Greed, 1980; Wasted Youth, 1982; Live At The Marquee, 2001; with Def Leppard: Pyromania, 1983; High and Dry, 1984; Hysteria (No. 1, USA), 1987; Adrenalize (No. 1, UK and USA), 1992; Retroactive, 1993; Vault 1980–95, 1995; Slang, 1996; X, 2002. Singles include: with Def Leppard: Photograph, 1983; Rock of Ages, 1983; Foolin', 1983; Animal, 1987; Pour Some Sugar On Me, 1987; Armageddon II, 1987; Love Bites (No. 1, USA), 1988; Rocket, 1989; Let's Get Rocked, 1992; Make Love Like A Man, 1992; Heaven Is, 1992; Two Steps Behind, featured in film soundtrack The Last Action Hero, 1993; When Love and Hate Collide, 1995; Now, 2002. *Honours:* American Music Awards, Favourite Heavy Metal Album, Favourite Heavy Metal Artists, 1989. *Current Management:* Q-Prime Inc, 729 Seventh Ave, 14th Floor, New York, NY 10019, USA. *Website:* www.defleppard.com.

COLLIE, John Maxwell; b. 21 Feb. 1931, Melbourne, Australia. Musician (trombone). Divorced, 3 s., 2 d. *Career:* Band Leader in Melbourne Max Collie Jazz Bandits, 1948, then Max Collie Jazz Kings, 1952; Came to England, Joined Melbourne New Orleans Jazz Band, 1962; Joined London City Stompers, 1963; Founder, Max Collie Rhythm Aces, 1966; Played at Festivals, Concerts and Theatres in England, Scotland, Wales, Ireland, Germany, France, Spain, Denmark, Belgium, Holland, Switzerland, Austria, Norway, Sweden, Poland, Yugoslavia, USA, Canada, Finland, Japan; Several radio and television appearances. *Recordings include:* Battle of Trafalgar, 1973; World Champions of Jazz, 1976; New Orleans Mardi Gras, 1984; Latest and Greatest, 1993; On tour in the USA; Live in Stuttgart, 1998. *Honours:* Winner, World Championship of Jazz, 1975. *Membership:* Musicians' Union; MCPS; PRS; PPL. *Address:* 26 Wendover Rd, Bromley, Kent BR2 9JX, England.

COLLIER, Pat; b. 20 Oct. 1951, London, England. Record Prod. m. Jill, 1 s., 2 d. *Recordings:* Wonderstuff, 3 albums; Kingmaker, 2 albums; Soft Boys, several albums; Robyn Hitchcock; House of Love, Primal Scream; Katrina and the Waves; New Model Army; The Senators; Voice of The Beehive; Sultans of Ping FC; The Wonder Stuff; The Men They Couldn't Hang; The Wildhearts; The Oyster Band. *Current Management:* Graham Carpenter, Pachuco Management. *Address:* Priestlands, Letchmore Heath, Herts, WD2 8EW, England.

COLLIER, Tom W; b. 30 June 1948, Puyallup, Washington, USA. Musician (drums, vibraphone); Bandleader. m. Cheryl Zilbert, 31 May 1970, 2 d. *Education:* BA, MusB, University of Washington, 1971. *Career:* Northwest Jazz Quintet, 1972–80; Freelance musician, various artists including: Bud Shank; Barbra Streisand; Ry Cooder; Sammy Davis Jr; Olivia Newton-John; Paul Williams; Johnny Mathis; Diane Schuur; Earl Hines; The Beach Boys; Jermaine Jackson; Jazz vibraphonist, duo Collier/Dean, 1977–; Director, N W Percussion Institute, Seattle University, 1989–. *Recordings:* Whistling Midgets, 1981; Illusion, 1987; Pacific Aire, 1991. *Publications:* Jazz Improvistion and Ear Training, 1983. *Honours:* Outstanding Service Award, National Asscn of Jazz Educators, 1980. *Membership:* ASCAP; Percussive Arts Society; National Asscn of Jazz Educators. *Address:* University of Washington School of Music, Seattle, Washington, USA.

COLLING, Jonathon; b. 28 May 1968, England. Programmer; Engineer; Record Prod. *Education:* College; Polytechnic. *Career:* Record producer, Rumour Records/X-Clusive; All types of dance music, including: house, Euro, jungle; Also jingles for radio/television and radio idents for BBC and local radio. *Recordings:* Rhythm Nation, 1993; Inner State, 1993; Prohibition Groove, 1994; Music Is My Life; Remixes for X-clusive Records, under name of Proof. *Membership:* Musicians' Union; PRS. *Address:* 9 Egerton Rd, Hale, Cheshire WA15 8EE, England.

COLLINS, Bootsy (William); b. 26 Oct. 1951, Cincinnati, OH, USA. Musician (bass). *Career:* Musician with James Brown's backing group, The JBs, 1969–71; Mem., George Clinton's Parliament/Funkadelic, 1972–; Also leader, own groups, Bootsy's Rubber Band, Bootzilla Orchestra. *Recordings:* Albums: with Parliament/Funkadelic: America Eats Its Young, 1972; Cosmic Slop, 1973; Up For The Down Stroke, 1974; Standing On The Verge Of Getting It On, 1974; Chocolate City, 1975; Let's Take It To The Stage, 1975; Mothership Connection, 1976; The Clones Of Dr Funkenstein, 1976; Parliament Live, 1977; Funkentelechy v. The Placebo Syndrome, 1977; One Nation Under A Groove, 1978; Motor Booty Affair, 1978; Underjam, 1979; Gloryhallastoopid (Pin The Tale On The Funky), 1979; Trombipulation, 1980; The Electric Spanking of War Babies, 1981; Computer Games, 1982; Dope Dogs, 1994; Solo: Stretchin' Out, 1976; Ahh... The Name Is Bootsy Baby, 1977; Player Of The Year, 1978; Keepin' Dah Funk Alive 4 1995, 1995; Glory B—Da Funk's On Me, 2001; Play With Bootsy, 2002; Collaborations with: Sly & Robbie, Rhythm Killer, 1987; Manu Dibango, Afrijazz, 1987; Keith Richards, Talk Is Cheap, 1988; Herbie Hancock, Perfect Machine, 1988; Cyndie Lauper, Night To Remember, 1989; Dee Lite World Clique, 1990; Ryuichi Sakamoto, Neo Geo, 1991; Praxis Transmutation, 1992; The Last Poets, Holy Terror, 1994; Buckethead Giant Robot, 1994; The Soup Dragons, Hydrophonic, 1995; Randy Crawford, Naked & True, 1995; Dave Stewart, Greetings From The Gutter, 1995; Simply Red, Life, 1995; Lucky Peterson, Lifetime, 1996; Fresh Outta P University, 1997; Sammy Hagar, Marching To Mars, 1997; Victor Wooten, Live In America, 2001. Singles include: Tear The Roof Off The Sucker (Give Up The Funk); Flash Light; One Nation Under A Groove; I'm Leaving; Party Lick-A-Ble's; Back To Good. *Honours:* Inducted, Rock & Roll Hall of Fame, 1997; Grammy Award (with Fatboy Slim), for Weapon of Choice, 2002. *Address:* c/o Bootzilla Productions, PO Box 44158, Cincinnati, OH 45244, USA.

COLLINS, Charlie; b. 26 Sept. 1952, Sheffield, South Yorkshire, England. Musician (saxophone, clarinet, flute, synthesizer); Composer; Prod. *Career:* Member, jazz, improvised and mixed media groups, 1969–; Clock DVA, 1979–81; The Box, 1981–85; The Bone Orchestra, 1985–88; Company Week, 1988; Arts Council Tours, 1988, 1990, 1992; Left Hand Right Hand, 1992–; Solo and production work. *Recordings:* with Clock DVA: Thirst; White Souls In Black Suits; All recordings with The Box; with Hornweb: Sixteen; with

Martin Archer: Wild Pathway Favourites; Telecottage; Left Hand Right Hand; Shockheaded Peters; Ideals of Freedom, Arts Council Funded Composer, 1990. *Address:* c/o The Sound Kitchen, 13 Headland Dr., Sheffield S10 5FX, England.

COLLINS, Edwyn; b. 1959, Edinburgh, Scotland. Vocalist; Musician (guitar); Prod. 1 s. *Career:* Founder, lead singer, Orange Juice (formerly the Nu-Sonics), 1977–84; Solo artiste, 1985–; International tours, including Europe, Japan, Australia; Phoenix Festival, 1995; Owner, recording studio. *Recordings:* Albums: with Orange Juice: You Can't Hide Your Love Forever, 1982; Rip It Up, 1982; Texas Fever, 1984; Orange Juice, 1984; The Esteemed Orange Juice, 1992; Ostrich Churchyard, 1992; The Heather's On Fire, 1993; Best of collections; Solo: Hope and Despair, 1989; Hell Bent On Compromise, 1990; Gorgeous George, 1995; I'm Not Following You, 1997; Doctor Syntax, 2002. Hit singles with Orange Juice: Rip It Up, 1982; Solo singles: A Girl Like You (No. 1, several countries), 1995; If You Could Love Me, 1995; The Magic Piper (of Love), 1997; Producer for: Astrid, Terrorvision. *Address:* c/o The Agency Group, 370 City Rd, London EC1V 2QA, England.

COLLINS, Glenn; b. 7 Feb. 1968, Emsworth, Hampshire, England. Musician (drums). *Career:* First drummer, The Auteurs, 18 months; Tour, America, France; Played at: Glastonbury Festival, 1993; Roskilde Festival, Denmark, 1993; Toured UK twice, including support to Suede; Television: Late Show; 2 times, Chart Show; The Beat with Gary Crowley; Radio: Mark Goodier session, Radio 1, 1993; Sheffield Sound City, 1993; Live Broadcast, Radio 1. *Address:* 83 Coleridge Rd, Crouch End, London N8 8EG, England.

COLLINS, John; b. April 1970. Musician (bass guitar). *Career:* Worked as book salesman; Joined Brisbane-based rock group Powderfinger, 1992; Steadily built reputation on many Australian tours/festival appearances; International breakthrough with Odyssey Number Five album; Constant world-wide touring throughout 2000–01 ending with New Suburban Fables 2001 Australian shows. *Recordings:* Albums: Parables For Wooden Ears, 1994; Double Allergic, 1996; Internationalist, 1998; Odyssey Number Five, 2000; Singles: Powderfinger Blue (EP), Transfusion (EP), 1993; Tail, Grave Concern, 1994; Save Your Skin, Mr Kneebone (EP), 1995; Pick You Up, D.A.F., Living Type, 1996; Take Me In, 1997; The Day You Come, Don't Wanna Be Left Out/Good-Day Ray, 1998; Already Gone, Passenger, 1999; My Happiness, 2000; Like A Dog, The Metre, 2001. *Honours:* ARIA Awards: Album of the Year; Song of the Year; Best Rock Album; Best Cover Artwork, 1999; six times platinum fourth album on Australian chart for 67 weeks by end of 2001; Only home-grown act ever to play more than 3 consecutive nights at Festival Hall, Australia. *Address:* c/o Republic Records, Australia. *Website:* www.powderfinger.com.

COLLINS, Judy Marjorie; b. 1 May 1939, Seattle, Washington, USA. Folk Vocalist; Songwriter. m. Peter A Taylor, divorced, 1 s. *Education:* Private piano study with Dr Antonia Brico, 1953–56. *Career:* Debut as professional folk singer, 1959; Appearances, numerous clubs, USA and world-wide; Concerts include: Newport Folk Festival; Worked with: Joni Mitchell; Joshua Rifkin; Stephen Stills; Radio and television include: Judy Collins: From The Heart, HBO special, 1989; Actress, Peer Gynt, New York Shakespeare Festival, 1969; Producer, director, documentary Antonia – A Portrait of The Woman, 1974. *Compositions include:* Albatross; Since You've Asked; My Father; Secret Gardens; Born To The Breed; Suite – Judy Blue Eyes. *Recordings:* Singles include: Both Sides Now, 1968; Amazing Grace, 1971; Send In The Clowns, from musical A Little Night Music, 1975; Albums: A Maid of Constant Sorrow, 1961; The Golden Apples of The Sun, 1962; Judy Collins #3, 1964; The Judy Collins Concert, 1964; Judy Collins' 5th Album, 1965; In My Life, 1966; Wildflowers, 1967; Who Knows Where The Time Goes, 1968; Recollections, 1969; Whales and Nightingales, 1970; Living, 1971; Colours of The Day, 1972; True Stories and Other Dreams, 1973; Judith, 1975; Bread and Roses, 1976; So Early In The Spring (The First Fifteen Years), 1977; Hard Times For Lovers, 1979; The Most Beautiful Songs of Judy Collins, 1979; Running For My Life, 1980; Time of Our Lives, 1982; Home Again, 1984; Amazing Grace, 1985; Trust Your Heart, 1987; Trust Your Heart, 1987; Sanity and Grace, 1989; Fires of Eden, 1991; Just Like A Woman, 1993; Live at Newport, 1994; Forever: An Anthology, 1997; Both Sides Now, 1998; Very Best of Judy Collins, 2001. *Publications:* Trust Your Heart (autobiography), 1987; Shameless (novel), 1994. *Honours:* Grammy, Best Folk Performance, 1968; Six Gold albums; Silver Medal, Atlanta Film Festival; Blue Ribbon Award, American Film Festival, New York City; Christopher Award; BMI Performance Award, Both Sides Now, 1990. *Current Management:* Gurtman and Murtha Associates, 450 Seventh Ave, Suite 603, New York, NY 10123–0101, USA.

COLLINS, Mark; b. Aug. 1965. Musician (guitar). *Career:* Mem., The Charlatans, 1992–; Signed to Beggars Banquet Records, later Universal Records; Numerous tours, festivals, television and radio appearances. *Recordings:* Albums: Some Friendly (No. 1, UK), 1990; Between 10th And 11th, 1992; Up To Our Hips, 1995; The Charlatans (No. 1, UK), 1995; Tellin' Stories (No. 1, UK), 1997; Melting Pot: The Best Of The Charlatans, 1998; Us And Us Only, 1999; Songs From The Other Side, 2000; Wonderland, 2001; Live It Like You Love It, 2002. Singles: Indian Rope, 1990; The Only One I

Know, 1990; Then, 1990; Me In Time, 1991; Over Rising, 1991; Weirdo, 1992; Tremelo Song, 1992; Can't Get Out Of Bed, 1994; Autograph, 1994; I Never Want An Easy Life If Me And He Were Ever To Get There, 1994; Jesus Hairdo, 1994; Crashin' In, 1994; Just Lookin', 1995; Just When You're Thinkin' Things Over, 1995; One To Another, 1996; North Country Boy, 1997; How High, 1997; Tellin' Stories, 1997; My Beautiful Friend, 1999; Forever, 1999; Impossible, 2000; Love Is The Key, 2001; A Man Needs To Be Told, 2001; You're So Pretty–We're So Pretty, 2002. *Honours:* Gold, Silver and Platinum discs. *Address:* The Charlatans, PO Box 134, Sandbach, Cheshire CW11 1YS, England. *E-mail:* cat@thecharlatans.net. *Website:* www.thecharlatans.net.

COLLINS, Mike (Michael Edmond); b. 25 July 1949, Manchester, England. MIDI Programmer. *Education:* MSc (with Distinction), Music Information Technology; BSc Electro-Acoustics with Music; Private tuition by Oliver Hunt, guitar, keyboards. *Career:* Guitarist, songwriter with jazz-funk band Light of The World; Top 40 success, Ride The Love Train, 1981; Songwriter, producer, Chappell Music, 1982–83; Dick James Music, 1984–85; Session musician, Top of the Pops, and other music television shows, 1985–86; MIDI programmer for records and films, 1987–. *Recordings:* Album: Loops, Music For Multi Media, 1993. *Contributions to:* Sound On Sound; Audio Media; Future Music; PCW; Mac World. *Membership:* Re-Pro; AES; PRS. *Address:* Flat 1c, 28 Pellatt Grove, Wood Green, London N22 5PL, England.

COLLINS, Phil(ip); b. 30 Jan. 1951, Chiswick, London, England. Vocalist; Songwriter; Musician (drums); Prod; Actor; Composer. m. (1) 1976, divorced, 1 s., 1 d., (2) Jill Tavelman, 1984, divorced, 1 d. *Education:* Barbara Speake Stage School. *Career:* Mem., various groups incl. The Real Thing, The Freehold, Hickory, Flaming Youth, 1967–70; Drummer, 1970–96, singer, 1975–96, Genesis; Mem., Brand X, 1975–; Solo recording artiste, 1981–; Numerous world-wide tours, Genesis and solo; Major concerts for charities include Prince's Trust and Live Aid; Record prod. for various artistes; Film appearances include: Buster, 1988; Frauds, 1993. *Recordings:* Albums: with Genesis: From Genesis To Revelation, 1969; Trespass, 1970; Nursery Cryme, 1971; Foxtrot, 1972; Genesis Live, 1973; Selling England By The Pound, 1973; The Lamb Lies Down On Broadway, 1974; A Trick of The Tail, 1976; Seconds Out, 1977; Wind and Wuthering, 1977; And Then There Were Three, 1978; Duke, 1980; Abacab, 1981; Three Sides Live, 1982; Genesis, 1983; Invisible Touch, 1986; We Can't Dance, 1991; The Way We Walk: The Shorts, 1992; The Way We Walk: The Longs, 1993; Calling All Stations, 1997; Turn It On Again, 1999; Archive 1967–75, 1999; Archive 1976–92, 2001; The Way We Walk (DVD), 2002; with Brand X: Unorthodox Behaviour; Moroccan Roll, 1977; Livestock, 1977; Product, 1979; Do They Hurt?, 1980; Is There Anything About?, 1982; Xtrax, 1986; The Plot Thins, 1992; Brand X Featuring Phil Collins, 1996; Live at the Roxy, 1996; Missing Period, 1997; A History 1976–80, 1997; The X-Files, 1999; Solo: Face Value, 1981; Hello, I Must Be Going!, 1982; No Jacket Required, 1985; 12'ers, 1987; …But Seriously, 1989; Serious Hits…Live!, 1990; Both Sides, 1993; Dance Into The Light, 1996; …Hits!, 1998; A Hot Night In Paris, 1999; Tarzan, 1999; Testify, 2002. *Honours:* LVO, 1994; Seven Grammy Awards; Six Ivor Novello Awards; Four BRIT Awards; Two Silver Clef Awards; Two Variety Club of Great Britain Awards; American Music Award, Favourite Adult Contemporary Artist, 2000. *Membership:* Trustee, Prince's Trust. *Current Management:* Hit and Run Music, 30 Ives St, London SW3 2ND, England. *Website:* www.philcollins.co.uk; www.genesis-music.com.

COLMAN, Stuart; b. 19 Dec. 1944, Harrowgate, West Yorkshire, England. Prod; Presenter. m. Janet, 22 Sept. 1973, 1 s., 2 d. *Career:* Producer for: Jeff Beck; The Big Town Playboys; Billy Swan; Cliff Richard; Phil Everly; Duane Eddy; Shakin' Stevens; Little Richard; The Shadows; Gary Glitter; Billy Fury; Kim Wilde; The Hank Wangford Band; Rich Sharp; Presenter, London American, BBC Radio 2, 1999. *Publications:* They Kept On Rockin'. *Honours:* Music Week Award, Top Singles Producer, 1981. *Membership:* Musicians' Union; Country Music Asscn; Nashville. *Current Management:* Dennis Muirhead, Muirhead Management, 202 Fulham Rd, London SW10 9PJ, England.

COLQUHOUN, Tom; b. 24 Oct. 1968, Linwood, Scotland. Musician (guitar). *Career:* Guitarist, specialising in solo and small group projects; composer and arranger; performances include playing two guitars simultaneously. *Compositions:* Wrote and performed theme music for BBC short film, When I'm 21. *Membership:* Musicians' Union; SPNM. *Address:* 14 Barshaw Pl., Paisley PA1 3HJ, Scotland.

COLTART, Robert Alexander Hendry; b. 20 Dec. 1956, West Molesey, Surrey, England. Vocalist; Musician (guitar, bass guitar); Songwriter. m. Angela Gausden, 20 Aug. 1983, 1 d. *Career:* Member, Badge, 1972–75; Bass guitar for Peter Noone (Herman's Hermits), 1975; Whispering Wind, 1976–78; Solo artiste, 1978–80; Life 'N' Soul, 1979; Arthur Kay and The Originals, 1980; Vocalist, guitarist, Maroondogs, 1981; Chuck Berry European Tour, 1988; GLR Nina Myskow Show, with Maroondogs, 1989; Mort Shuman Memorial Concert, 1991; Berlin SKA Festival with Arthur Kay, 1995; Backing Chris Andrews, recording with him, 1992–95; Recording and writing with George Williams, 1997. *Recordings:* Various television and radio commercials; Dark Nights Falling, 1984; Volcanoes, Skatoon Time, 1989; No-One But You; The Chozen I, 1994. *Membership:* PRS; MCPS; Musicians' Union. *Address:* 1 Foord Rd, Folkstone, Kent CT20 1HH, England.

COLTER, Jessi (Miriam Johnson); b. 25 May 1943, Phoenix, Arizona, USA. Vocalist; Musician (piano); Songwriter. m. (1) Duane Eddy, divorced 1968, (2) Waylon Jennings, 26 Oct. 1969, 1 d. *Career:* Church pianist, aged 11; Solo artiste, also with Waylon Jennings, late 1960s–. *Compositions include:* No Sign of The Living (recorded by Dottie West); You Hung The Moon; Storms Never Last; Jennifer; Co-writer (with Waylon Jennings), I'm Not Lisa. *Recordings:* Singles include: Lonesome Road; Guitar On My Mind, with Duane Eddy; I'm Not Lisa; Suspicious Minds; Storms Never Last; The Union Mare and The Confederate Grey; Solo albums: A Country Star Is Born, 1970; I'm Jessi Colter, 1975; Jessi, 1976; Diamond In The Rough, 1976; Mirriam, 1977; That's The Way A Cowboy Rock 'n' Rolls, 1978; Ridin' Shotgun, 1982; Rock 'n' Roll Lullaby, 1984; Albums with Waylon Jennings: Wanted – The Outlaws (with Waylon Jennings and Willie Nelson), 1975; White Mansions, 1978; Leather and Lace, 1981; Right for the Time, 1996; Closing in on the Fire, 1998; Film soundtrack, The Pursuit of D B Cooper, 1982. *Address:* c/o Buddy Lee Attractions, 38 Music Sq. E, Suite 300, Nashville, TN 37203, USA.

COLTRANE, Chi; b. 16 Nov. 1952, Racine, Wisconsin, USA. Vocalist; Songwriter; Prod; Musician (multi-instrumentalist). *Education:* Vocal instruction; Choir and Musical Notation. *Career:* Las Vegas; Tours throughout USA; Special guest star representing USA at International Song Festival, Rio De Janeiro; Many television appearances USA and Europe including: Tonight Show; Johnny Carson; Merv Griffin; Superstars of Rock; Numerous television specials, including Chi Coltrane in Concert with the Edmonton Symphony, 1995; Multiple tours of Europe, approximately 300 concerts in one year; Raised money for South American rain forest project; Worked with: Gary Brooker (Procol Harum); Barry McGuire; Jennifer Rush; Nina; Future tours include: USA and Russia. *Compositions:* Thunder and Lightning; Go Like Elijah; You Were My Friend; Wheel of Life; Who Ever Told You; Ooh Baby; I'm Gonna Make You Love Me. *Recordings:* Chi Coltrane, 1972; Let It Ride, 1973; Special Chi Coltrane, 1975; Best of Chi Coltrane, 1975; Road To Tomorrow, 1977; Silk and Steel, 1981; Ready To Roll, 1983; Chi Coltrane Live, 1982; The Message, 1986; Golden Classics, 1996; Recording featured in film Beaches. *Honours:* Gold Hammer, Silver Hammer, Best Female Artist: Germany; Switzerland; Austria; Netherlands. *Membership:* AFTRA; AFM; ASCAP; SUISA. *Current Management:* Nick Joseph, Stellar Artists Management, 505 S Beverly Dr., Suite 166, Beverly Hills, CA 90212, USA.

COLVILLE, (Creighton) Randolph (Victor); b. 23 May 1942, Glasgow, Scotland. Musician (clarinet, saxophone); Composer; Arranger; Musical Dir; Teacher. m. Joan Winifred Pym, 23 May 1970, 1 s., 1 d. *Education:* Northern School of Music, 1962–66, appointed to teaching staff, 1966. *Career:* Teaching and Freelancing, 1966–75; Permanent Teacher and Conductor, Kent Music School, 1975; Numerous television appearances at home and abroad, including television film Buddy Bolden's Children; Many radio broadcasts for BBC Jazz Club, Jazz Parade, Sounds of Jazz; Frequent engagements as featured soloist at South Bank; Played the Mozart and Brahms Clarinet Quintets at Kenwood House, 1991. *Compositions:* Mantovani Mix-Up; S'Okay; Fuss Pot. *Recordings:* Jungle Nights In Harlem, Midnite Follies Orchestra, 1981; Echoes of The Duke, Humphrey Lyttelton and Helen Shapiro, 1984; The World of Buddy Bolden, Humphrey Lyttelton, 1986; Hot and Cool, Colville Collection, 1992; Hotter Than That, A Elsdon, 1986; Keepers of The Flame, A Elsdon, 1994; Various other recordings including with Keith Nichols Groups. *Honours:* British Jazz Award, Best Clarinettist, 1988. *Membership:* Musicians' Union; Performing Rights Society; The British Music Writers' Council; The British Jazz Musicians Society. *Current Management:* Shirley Walker. *Address:* 28 Childscroft Rd, Rainham, Gillingham, Kent ME8 7SS, England.

COLVIN, Shawn; b. 1956, Vermillion, South Dakota, USA. Vocalist; Songwriter; Musician (guitar). *Education:* Guitar lessons from age 10. *Career:* 15 years as bar musician. *Recordings:* Albums: Steady On, 1989; Fat City, 1992; Cover Girl, 1994; A Few Small Repairs, 1996; Holiday Songs and Lullabies, 1998; Whole New You, 2001. *Honours:* Grammy Awards, Steady On, 1990, Song of the Year, Record of the Year, for Sunny Came Home, 1997. *Current Management:* AGF Entertainment, 30 W 21st St, Seventh Floor, New York, NY 10010–6905, USA.

COMBELLE, Philippe Alix François; b. 14 July 1939, Paris, France. Musician (drums). m. Françoise Ruiz, 4 May 1964, 1 s., 1 d. *Education:* Postgraduate studies; Musical studies with father Alix Combelle (Alix Combelle Big Band), piano, saxophone, drums, tabla. *Career:* Jazz concerts and clubs: Europe; USA; UK; Japan; Africa; Russia; Turkey; Thailand; India; Viet Nam; Israel; Martinique; Guadaloupe; Syria; Jordan; Yemen; Oman; Teacher, Marly Conservatory of Music; International Music School, Paris. *Recordings:* Recorded with: Don Byas; Sonny Criss; Memphis Slim; Willie Dixon; Christian Escoudé; Toots Thielemans; Cat Anderson; Barclay; Buck Clayton; Buddy De Franco; Jimmy Gourley; Marc Johnson; Lavelle; OMD with Ray Brown; Eddie Harris; Guy Lafitte; Alix Combelle; Jimmy Gourley;

Rene Mailhes; Bernard Maury Trio; Pierre Michelot; Daniel Colin. *Membership:* SACEM. *Address:* 36 rue Sibuet, 75012 Paris, France.

COMBS, Sean, (Puff Daddy, P. Diddy); b. 4 November 1969, Harlem, New York, USA. Rap Performer; Prod; Remixer. *Career:* Began work at R&B label Uptown; Talent spotter for artistes such as Jodeci and Mary J. Blige; Produced many top acts including Ma$e, Sting, MC Lyte, Faith Evans, The Lox, Mariah Carey; Launched Bad Boy Entertainment label, 1994; Produced records for Notorious BIG before his death; Remixed and reworked songs by many artists including Sting and The Police; Worked with Jimmy Page for the soundtrack to the film Godzilla; Remixes include the Jackson 5, Goldie, Trent Reznor; Changed performing name to P. Diddy, 2001. *Recordings:* I'll Be Missing You, with Faith Evans (No. 1, UK and USA), 1997; Been Around the World, 1997; Roxanne; Can't Nobody Hold Me Down, featuring Mase (No. 1, USA), 1997; Victory, 19998; Come With Me, 1998; It's All About the Benjamins, 1998; P.E., 2000, 1999; Albums: No Way Out, 1997; Forever, 1999; The Saga Continues, 2001; As Producer: Life After Death, by Notorious BIG, 1997; Cold Rock A Party, MC Lyte; Cupid; 112; Mo Money Mo Problems, Notorious BIG; Honey, Mariah Carey; Feel So Good, Ma$e. *Honours:* Grammy Awards, Best Rap Album and Best Rap Performance by a Duo or Group, 1998. *Address:* c/o Bad Boy Entertainment, 1540 Broadway, 30th Floor, New York, NY 10036, USA. *Website:* www.p-diddy.com.

COMMERFORD, Tim, (Tim C., Tim Bob); Musician (bass guitar). *Career:* Mem., Rage Against the Machine, 1991–2000; Obtained major label deal; Support causes such as Fairness and Accuracy in Reporting, Rock for Choice and Refuse and Resist; Numerous tours incl. Lollapalooza; Tour with Wu Tang Clan; Contribution to soundtrack for Godzilla, 1998; Founder mem., Audioslave, 2002–. *Recordings:* Albums: with Rage Against the Machine: Rage Against The Machine, 1992; Evil Empire, 1996; The Battle Of Los Angeles, 1998; Renegades, 2000; Live And Rare, 2002; with Audioslave: Audioslave, 2002. Singles: with Rage Against the Machine: Killing In The Name, 1993; Bullet In The Head, 1993; Bombtrack, 1993; Freedom, 1994; Bombtrack Plus Live, 1994; Bulls On Parade, 1996; People Of The Sun (EP), 1997; Guerilla Radio, 1999; Sleep Now In The Fire, 2000; with Audioslave: Cochise, 2003. *Address:* c/o Epic Records, 550 Madison Ave, New York, NY 10022-3211, USA. *Website:* www.audioslave.com.

COMMON, (Lonnie Lynn), (Common Sense); b. Chicago, Illinois, USA. Rap Artiste. *Career:* Started recording as Common Sense, releasing debut album Can I Borrow A Dollar, 1992; Involved in court case resulting in name change to simply Common; Recorded second album for Sony; Third for MCA, 2000; Collaborations: Bilal; Slum Village; D'Angelo; Chantay Savage. *Recordings:* Albums: Can I Borrow A Dollar, 1992; One Day It'll All Make Sense, 1997; Like Water For Chocolate, 2000; Singles: Resurrection, 1995; Reminding Me (of Sef), 1997; The Sixth Sense, 2000; The Light, 2000. *Address:* c/o MCA Records, 60 Music Sq. E, Nashville, Tennessee, USA.

COMPAGNO, Tony; b. 16 Nov. 1966, Cork City, Ireland. Vocalist; Songwriter. *Career:* Appearances: RTE Cúrsaí; RTE 89FM; Tours, 1989, 1992, 1994; Cork multichannel, video, 1992. *Recordings:* Debut album: Tony Compagno, 1994; Guest artist to: Jimmy MacCarthy; Hazel O'Connor; Luka Bloom; Cutting Crew; Maura O'Connell; Mary Coughlan; Davy Spillane. *Current Management:* Denis Desmond Promotions. *Address:* Thompson House, MacCurtain St, Cork City, Ireland.

CONLEE, John; b. 11 Aug. 1946, Versailles, Kentucky, USA. Country Vocalist; Songwriter. *Career:* Played guitar on radio, aged 10; Singer, Versailles barbershop group; DJ, Nashville, mid-1970s; Recording artiste, 1978–; Also licensed embalmer, farm owner. *Compositions include:* Rose-Coloured Glasses; Backside of Thirty. *Recordings:* US Country No. 1 hits: Lady Lay Down; Backside of Thirty; Common Man; I'm Only In It For The Love; In My Eyes; As Long As I'm Rockin' With You; Got My Heart Set On You; Conley Country; Songs for the Working Man; Fellow Travelers; Live at Billy Bob's. *Current Management:* John Conlee Enterprises Inc, 38 Music Sq. E 117, Nashville, TN 37203, USA.

CONLEY, Earl Thomas; b. 17 Oct. 1941, Portsmouth, Ohio, USA. Country Vocalist; Songwriter; Musician. *Career:* First artist to have 4 hits from 1 album, 1984; Recorded 18 US Country No. 1 hits. *Compositions include:* Smokey Mountain Memories, Mel Street; This Time I've Hurt Her More, Conway Twitty. *Recordings:* US Country No. 1 hits include: Fire and Smoke; Somewhere Between Right and Wrong; Don't Make It Easy For Me, Your Love's On The Line; Angel In Disguise; Holding Her and Loving You; Duets include: Too Many Times, with Anita Pointer; We Believe In Happy Endings, with Emmylou Harris; Albums: Blue Pearl, 1980; Fire and Smoke, 1981; Somewhere Between Right and Wrong, 1982; Don't Make It Easy For Me, 1983; Treadin' Water, 1984; Greatest Hits, 1985; Too Many Times, 1986; The Heart of It All, 1988; Yours Truly, 1991. *Current Management:* Artists International Management Inc, 9850 Sandalfoot Blvd, Suite 458, Boca Raton, FL 33428, USA.

CONNEFF, Kevin; b. 8 Jan. 1945, Dublin, Ireland. Musician. *Career:* Mem., The Chieftains, 1978–. *Recordings:* Albums: Chieftains 9, 1979; Boil The

Breakfast Early, 1980; Chieftains 10, 1981; The Chieftains In China, 1984; Ballad Of The Irish Horse, 1985; Celtic Wedding, 1987; The Chieftains In Ireland (with James Galway), 1987; Year Of The French, 1988; Irish Heartbeat (with Van Morrison), 1988; A Chieftains Celebration, 1989; Chieftains Collection, 1989; The Celtic Connection – James Galway And The Chieftains, 1990; Bells Of Dublin, 1991; An Irish Evening, 1992; Another Country, 1992; The Celtic Harp (with Belfast Harp Orchestra), 1993; Water From The Well; The Long Black Veil, 1995; Santiago, 1996; Tears Of Stone, 1999; Down The Old Plank Road: The Nashville Sessions, 2002; The Wide World Over: A 40 Year Celebration, 2002. *Address:* c/o RCA Victor Group, 1540 Roadway, New York, NY 10036, USA. *Website:* www.irish.com.

CONNELLY, Chris(topher John); b. 11 Nov. 1964, Edinburgh, Scotland. Vocalist; Musician (guitar). *Education:* Choir, George Heriots School. *Career:* World tours with Ministry; Revolting Cocks; Solo tours, USA. *Recordings:* with Ministry: Mind Is A Terrible Thing To Taste; Psalm 69; Ministry Greatest Fits, 2001; with Revolting Cocks: Beers, Steers and Queers; Solo: Shipwreck; Ultimate Seaside Companion. *Membership:* BMI; PRS. *Address:* PO Box 472, 1573 N Milwaukee Ave, Chicago, IL 60622, USA.

CONNICK, Harry, Jr; b. 11 Sept. 1967, New Orleans, Louisiana, USA. Jazz Musician (piano); Vocalist; Actor. *Education:* New Orleans Center For the Creative Arts; Studied with Ellis Marsalis; Student, Hunter College, Manhattan School of Music. *Recordings:* Albums: Harry Connick Jr, 1987; 20, 1988; When Harry Met Sally (film soundtrack), 1989; We Are In Love, 1990; Blue Light, Red Light, 1991; Lofty's Roach Souffle, 1990; 25, 1992; When My Heart Finds Christmas, 1993; She, 1994; Imagination, 1994; Whisper Your Name, 1995; Star Turtle, 1995; All of Me, 1996; To See You, 1997; Come by Me, 1999; When My Heart Finds Christmas, 2000; 30, 2001; Songs I Heard, 2001; Contributions to other film soundtracks: Memphis Belle (also actor in film), 1990; Little Man Tate, 1991. *Honours:* Grammy Award, Male Jazz Vocal Performance, When Harry Met Sally, 1990. *Current Management:* Wilkins Management, 323 Broadway, Cambridge, MA 02139, USA.

CONROY, Patricia; b. 30 Jan. 1957, Montréal, Québec, Canada. Songwriter; Vocalist. *Career:* Television specials, Canadian networks, TNN; CMT; NCN; CBC. *Recordings:* Albums: Blue Angel, 1990; Bad Day For Trains, 1992; You Can't Resist, 1994. *Honours:* CCMA Album of the Year, 1993; CCMA Female Vocalist of the Year, 1994. *Membership:* AFM. *Current Management:* Tim Rathert, Tony Gottlieb, Morning Star Management. *Address:* PO Box 1770, Hendersonville, TN 37075, USA.

CONSTANTIN, François; b. 2 Dec. 1961, Paris, France. Musician (percussion, drums). m. 10 May 1986, 2 d. *Education:* Normal School of Music of Paris. *Career:* In Jazz and others: Lavel; Arturo Sandoval; Francis Lockwood; Veronique Sanson; France Gall; Elsa; Louis Chedid; Johnny Hallyday; Patrick Bruel; Jean-Patrick Capdeviel; Michel Sardoux; Fabian. *Recordings:* Live records with the above artists; Sessions with Jannick Top; Florent Pagny; Jean Marc Jafet; Own group Latin Jazz. *Address:* 53 rue du Petit Bois, 77200 Torcy, France.

CONSTANTINOU, Chris, (Chris De Niro); b. 20 July 1957, London, England. Musician (bass guitar, guitar, flute); Vocalist; Actor. *Education:* Flute, bass at school; Mainly learned playing live. *Career:* First record with Punk band The Drill and Hollywood Exiles, produced by Chas Chandler, 1976; Joined Adam Ant, as Chris De Niro, 1981–86; Several world tours, playing all major venues; Television appearances include: Saturday Night Live, USA; Solid Gold, USA; American Bandstand; Top of the Pops; Wogan; Russell Harty; Live Aid; Dick Clarke Show; Formed S.F.Go; Formed band and songwriting partnership with Annebella Lwin, ex-Bow Wow Wow singer, with record deal; Currently singer/writer, own band, Jackie On Assid; Film appearances: Lead actor, Touch, BBC2; Play Dead, by Danny Cannon; Shopping, by Paul Anderson. *Recordings:* Drill; Vive Le Rock, Apollo 9, Adam Ant; Do What You Do, with Annabella Lwin; Other hit singles and videos. *Membership:* PRS; MCPS; Equity; Musicians' Union; AFTRA; PAMRA. *Current Management:* Jackie Management. *Address:* PO Box 18106, London, England.

CONTE, Paolo; b. 6 Jan. 1937. Vocalist; Musician (piano, guitar, vibraphone); Composer; Songwriter. *Education:* University of Parma, Law Degree. *Career:* Began career as Jazz musician in various bands; Recorded The Italian Way to Swing with the Paolo Conte Quartet, 1962; Began composing songs, 1960s; Had a number one hit when Adriano Celentano recorded La Coppia piu' Bella Del Mondo, 1967; Songs recorded by artists including: Patty Pravo; Enzo Jannacci; Johnny Hallyday; Shirley Bassey; Solo career, 1974–. *Compositions:* La Coppia piu' Bella Del Mondo. *Recordings:* The Italian Way To Swing, 1962; Paolo Conte, 1974; Gelato Al Limon, 1979; Paris Milonga, 1981; Appunti Di Viaggio, 1982; Concerti, 1985; Aguaplano, 1987; Live, 1988; A Macchina, 1990; 900, Tournée, 1993; Una Faccia In Prestito, 1995; Tournée 2, 1998; Razmataz, 2000.

CONWAY, Tony (James Anthony); b. Bardstown, Kentucky, USA. Entertainment Co Exec. m. Nancy Schaefer, 1976, 1 s., 1 d. *Education:* Graduate, Northwood College, Southern Indiana. *Career:* Opened first talent agency, Lexington, Kentucky; Moved to Nashville; Agent for Buddy Lee Attractions, Inc, 1975; President, Buddy Lee Attractions, Inc, 1987–; Over 30 clients include: Willie Nelson; Emmylou Harris; Ricky Van Shelton; Clay Walker; Mark Chestnutt; Waylon Jennings; Lorrie Morgan; Handles special event department in offices in Nashville, Kansas City, Los Angeles; Director Services of Main Stage Production Enterprises Inc, producing major events, festivals, state fairs, North America; First agent in Nashville to develop new breed of country acts; Artists signed include: George Strait; Mary Chapin Carpenter; Patty Loveless; Garth Brooks; John Anderson; Sawyer Brown; Talent Co-ordinator, FarmAid Concerts, Illinois, Texas; Co-ordinated, booked, Highwayman I and II tours, with: Willie Nelson; Waylon Jennings; Johnny Cash; Kris Kristofferson; Handles international tours for all clients. *Honours:* CMA Agent of the Year, SRO Convention, 1990, 1991; Country Agent of the Year, Performance Magazine Readers Poll, 1992, 1993. *Address:* 38 Music Sq. E, Suite 300, Nashville, TN 37203, USA.

COODER, Ry (Ryland Peter); b. 15 March 1947, Los Angeles, California, USA. Musician (guitar, slide guitar); Composer. *Career:* Member, Jackie DeShannon's backing group, aged 17; Member: The Rising Sons, 1966; Captain Beefheart's Magic Band, 1967; Session guitar work included: Everly Brothers; Paul Revere and The Raiders; Randy Newman; Rolling Stones; Solo recording artist, 1970–; Formed Little Village with Nick Lowe, John Hiatt, Jim Keltner, 1991; Film music writer, 1980s–. *Recordings include:* Solo albums: Ry Cooder, 1971; Into The Purple Valley, 1972; Boomer's Story, 1972; Paradise and Lunch, 1974; Chicken Skin Music, 1976; Live Show Time, 1977; Bop Till You Drop, 1979; Why Don't You Try Me Tonight?, 1986; Get Rhythm, 1987; Pecos Bill, with Robin Williams, 1988; Music By Ry Cooder, 1995; with Little Village: Little Village, 1992; with The Gabby Pahinui Hawaiian Band: The Gabby Pahinui Hawaiian Band and Ry Cooder Vol. 1, 2000; Film soundtracks include: Performance Candy; Blue Collar (with Captain Beefheart); Film scores as composer: The Long Riders, 1980; The Border, 1982; Paris Texas, 1985; Alamo Bay, 1985; Crossroads, 1986; Blue City, 1986; Johnny Handsome, 1989; Geronimo, 1993; Music by, 1995; Buena Vista Social Club, 1997. *Honours:* Grammy Award, Best Recording For Children, 1989. *Address:* c/o Warner Bros Records, 129 Park St, London W1Y 3FA, England.

COOK, David Lynn; b. 11 Nov. 1965, Pascagula, Mississippi, USA. Vocalist; Charity Spokesman; Model. *Education:* Masters, Business; Doctorate, Child Psychology, Divinity; Masters, Music; Doctorate, Musical Composition. *Career:* Member, The Cook Family Singers; David L Cook and the Trinidetts; Performs religious songs; Performed at White House for Ronald Reagan, 1986; Appearances in: Japan; Israel; England; Russia; Netherlands; People's Republic of China; Australia; Television appearances include: 700 Club; Host of The Prestigious Manitoba Awards, 1987, 1988, 1995; Sesame Street; Jerry Lewis Telethon; Night of 100 Stars; Walt Disney World's 35th Anniversary; White House Celebration, 1986. *Recordings include:* Album: Come Follow Me; Singles: My Song; Lift Him Up. *Honours:* 3 Prestigious Manitoba Awards; AMAAA Male Vocalist of Year, 1986–87; AMAAA Composer of Year, 1987–90; ABG Rising Star Award, 1989; Numerous Robi Awards, 1986–90; Gospel Music Humanitarian Award, ARAMA, 1995; 4 Gold Albums; Sacred Music USA Award, Contemporary Christian Artist of the Year, 1996. *Membership:* GMA; NARAS; CMA; AMARA; SAG; SESAC. *Current Management:* Daylyn Ware, American Musical Academy of Arts Assembly. *Address:* 1336 Cheshire Ave, Charlotte, NC 28208, USA.

COOK, Eddie; b. 18 April 1928, Billericay, Essex, England. Publisher; Writer; Musician (saxophone). m. Patricia Mary Beale (deceased), 26 March 1955, 1 s., 1 d.; m. (2) Janet Eva Job, 5 Dec. 1986. *Education:* Taught by mother; Later studied tenor saxophone with Les Evans. *Career:* Amateur and semi-professional musical work, music industry (buying, selling, repairing musical instruments); Publisher, 1960–; Publisher, Jazz Journal, 1979–; Editor, 1983–. *Publications:* Jazz Journal International (also numerous earlier non-music publications). *Address:* Jazz Journal Ltd, 3 and 3A Forest Rd, Loughton, Essex IG10 1DR, England.

COOK, Jeff; b. 27 Aug. 1949, Fort Payne, Alabama, USA. Vocalist; Musician (guitar, keyboards, fiddle, bass guitar, banjo, mandolin). m. Lisa Williams, 1995. *Education:* Electronic Technology, Gadsden State Community College. *Career:* Founder mem., country music group, Young Country, 1969, renamed Wild Country, 1972, renamed Alabama, 1977–; Owner, Cook Sound Studio. *Recordings:* Albums: Alabama, 1980; My Home's In Alabama, 1980; Feels So Right, 1981; Stars, 1982; Mountain Music, 1982; The Closer You Get, 1983; Roll On, 1984; 40 Hour Week, 1985; Alabama Christmas, 1985; The Touch, 1986; Greatest Hits, 1986; Just Us, 1987; Live, 1988; Tennessee Christmas, 1989; Southern Star, 1989; Pass It On Down, 1990; Greatest Hits Vol. 2, 1991; American Pride, 1992; Gonna Have A Party... Live, 1993; Cheap Seats, 1993; In The Beginning, 1994; In Pictures, 1995; From The Archives Vol. 1, 1996; Christmas Vol. 2, 1996; Live at Ebbets Field, 1997; Dancin' On The Boulevard, 1997; Twentieth Century, 1999; Alabama For The Record, 2000; When It All Goes South, 2001; Christmas, 2002. Singles include: I Want To Be With You; Tennessee River; Feels So Right; Love In The First Degree; Pass It On Down. *Honours:* Numerous Country Music Ascn Awards, 1981–84; Numerous Acad. of Country Music Awards, incl. Artist of the Decade, 1989; Numerous American Music Awards, incl. Award of Merit, 2003; Grammy

Awards, for Mountain Music, 1983, for The Closer You Get, 1984; BMI President's Award, 2000; Numerous Billboard Awards. *Current Management:* Dale Morris and Assocs, 818 19th Ave S, Nashville, TN 37203, USA. *Website:* www.wildcountry.com.

COOK, Norman, (Quentin Cook), (Fatboy Slim); b. 31 July 1963, Brighton, England. Musician (guitar); Record Prod; DJ. m. Zoë Ball, 20 Aug. 1999, 1 s. *Career:* Joined The Housemartins, 1985; Numerous television appearances and tours including Red Wedge concerts; Band split, 1988; Worked with Billy Bragg, 1989; Formed Beats International, 1990–92; Formed Freakpower, 1994–98, hit Turn On Tune In Cop Out used for Levi's advertisement; Released records under guises of Pizzaman, 1995, and Mighty Dub Katz, 1997; As Fatboy Slim, 1997–; Remix of Cornershop's No 1 Brimful of Asha and Wildchild's Renegade Master; Numerous DJ sets including appearances at Millennium gigs for Radio 1; Big Beach Boutique concert, Brighton, 2002; Producer for band Blur. *Recordings:* With The Housemartins: Singles: Sheep, 1986; Happy Hour, 1986; Think for a Minute, 1986; Caravan of Love (No. 1, UK), 1986; Five Get Over Excited, 1987; Me and the Farmer, 1987; Build, 1987; There is Always Something There to Remind Me, 1988; Albums: London 0 Hull 4, 1986; The People Who Grinned Themselves to Death, 1987; Now That's What I Call Quite Good, double album, 1988; Solo Single: For Spacious Lies, 1989; With Beats International: Single: Dub Be Good to Me (No. 1, UK), 1990; Album: Excursion on the Version; With Freakpower: Single: Turn On Tune In Cop Out, 1994; Album: Drive Thru Booty, 1994; As Pizzaman: Singles: Happiness, 1995; Trippin' on Sunshine, 1996; Hello Honky Tonks, 1996; Gottaman, 1997; As Might Dub Katz: Magic Carpet Ride, 1997: As Fatboy Slim: Singles: Everybody Needs a 303, 1993; Punk to Funk, 1996; Going Out of My Head, 1997; The Rockefeller Skank, 1998; Gangster Trippin', 1998; Praise You (No. 1, UK), 1999; Right Here, Right Now, 1999; Sunset (Bird of Prey), 2000; Demons, with Macy Gray, 2000; Star 69, 2001; Ya Mama, 2001; Albums: Better Living Through Chemistry, 1996; Let's Hear It, 1998; You've Come A Long Way Baby (No. 1, UK), 1998; Halfway Between The Gutter and The Stars, 2000; A Break From The Norm (mix album), 2001. *Honours:* BRIT Awards, Best British Dance Act, 1999, 2001; Grammy Award, Best Short Form Music Video, for Weapon of Choice, 2002. *Address:* Skint Records, PO Box 174, Brighton BN1 4BA, England. *E-mail:* mail@skint.net. *Website:* www.guttersandstars.com.

COOK, Paul; b. 20 July 1956, London, England. Musician (drums). *Career:* Drummer, UK punk group, The Sex Pistols, 1975–78; Performances include: First gig, St Martin's School of Art, London, 1975; Screen On The Green Special, London, 1976; 100 Club punk rock festival, 1976; Anarchy In The UK Tour, 1976; Tours, Europe, 1977; USA, 1978; Plays dates with Johnny Thunders, 1978; Member band, The Professionals, 1979; Sex Pistols reunion concert, 1996; Collaborations: Edwyn Collins, 1992–97. *Recordings:* Albums: Never Mind The Bollocks – Here's The Sex Pistols, 1977; The Great Rock 'n' Roll Swindle, 1979; Some Product – Carry On Sex Pistols, 1979; Flogging A Dead Horse, 1980; Kiss This, 1992; Jubilee, 2002. Singles: God Save The Queen, 1977; Pretty Vacant, 1977; Holidays In The Sun, 1977; Something Else, 1979; Silly Thing, 1979; C'mon Everybody, 1979; The Great Rock 'n' Roll Swindle, 1979; with Steve Jones and Ronnie Biggs: No One Is Innocent (A Punk Prayer By Ronnie Biggs), 1978.

COOK, Sean; b. 16 April 1969, England. Musician (bass, harmonica). *Career:* Joined Spiritualized, 1993; Formed Lupine Howl, 1999; Numerous live dates including world tour; Concerts at Royal Albert Hall and CN Tower in Toronto. *Recordings:* Singles: Let It Flow, 1995; Electricity, 1997; I Think I'm In Love, 1998; Come Together, 1998; Abbey Road EP, 1998; with Lupine Howl: 125, 2000; Albums: Lazer Guided Melodies, 1992; Pure Phase, 1995; Ladies and Gentlemen We Are Floating In Space, 1997; Royal Albert Hall October 10 1997 (live), 1998; with Lupine Howl: The Carnivorous Lunar Activities Of. . ., 2001; The Bar At The End Of The World, 2002.

COOKE, Mick; b. 15 Dec. 1973. Musician (trumpet, guitar). *Career:* Member: Hardbody, mid 1990s; Belle and Sebastian, 1996–; Amphetameanies; Collaborations: Mojave 3; Ex-Cathedra; Curated Bowlie Weekend Festival with other Belle and Sebastian band members, 1999. *Recordings:* Albums: Tigermilk, If You're Feeling Sinister, 1996; The Boy With The Arab Strap 1998; Fold Your Hands Child – You Walk Like A Peasant, 2000; Singles: Dog On Wheels EP, Lazy Line Painter Jane EP, 3–6–9 Seconds of Light EP, 1997; This Is Just A Modern Rock Song EP, 1998; Legal Man, 2000; Jonathan David, I'm Waking Up To Us, 2001. *Honours:* BRIT Award, Best Newcomer, 1999. *Current Management:* Banchory Management, PO Box 25074, Glasgow G2 6YL, Scotland. *Website:* www.belleandsebastian.co.uk.

COOKE, Paul Anthony; b. 18 Dec. 1961, Hull, England. Musician (drums, piano); Vocalist; Songwriter; Man; Prod. m. Susan Lesley Jarvis, 9 Sept. 1991, 2 s., 1 d. *Education:* BA, Hull University, 2000. *Career:* Drummer, Pride, 1981–82; Founder member, drummer, Sade, 1982–84; Tours: Danceteria, New York City, East Coast, Philadelphia, 1982; U4, Vienna, 1983; Television and radio appearances include: Switch, 1983; Loose Talk, 1983; Top of the Pops, 1984; Radio 1, Peter Powell Sessions, 1983; Singer, Songwriter, Man., Esposito, 1985–86; Papa Divine, 1987–88; Songwriter, Producer, MBDK, 1989–90; Solo artist, 1991–93; Singer, Songwriter, Prod., P Eye Eye, 1994;

Major concerts include: Esposito, Royal Albert Hall, 1986; Papa Divine, Brighton Pavillion, 1987; Business Ventures: P R Clarke Management; PSP Productions; IVI Records Ltd; IVI Management; 88interactive.com; Cybertech Support Services Ltd; IAPC (Int. Asscn of Professional Creators); DigitalDomain.org; PCM (PaulCookeMusic.co.uk); Artist Man. for Esposito; Papa Divine; MBDK; Buff Meaba; Proud; P Eye Eye; Brave; MMJ; TY. *Compositions:* Singles: Co-writer, Smooth Operator and Your Love Is King, Sade, 1984. *Recordings:* Smooth Operator, Sade, 1984; Your Love is King, Sade, 1984; Snakebite, Sade, 1984; Message In A Melody, Esposito, 1986; You Don't Have To Say You Love Me, Paul Cooke, 1991; Love, Paul Cooke, 1991; Emma, Paul Cooke, 1991; Lost At Sea, P Eye Eye, 1994; Rivers, TY, 2002; Album: Diamond Life, Sade, 1984; EMIT2295, P Eye Eye, 1994; Pop Life, Bananarama, 1991; Best of Sade, 1994. *Honours:* BPI Award; Triple Platinum record, Diamond Life, 1984. *Membership:* PRS; MCPS; MU; PAMRA; PPL. *Current Management:* IVI Management. *Address:* 6 Cheyne Walk, Hornsea, North Humberside HU18 1BX, England.

COOL, Tre, (Frank Edwin Wright III); b. 9 Dec. 1972, Willits, CA, USA. Musician (drums, percussion). m. (1) Lisea, divorced, 1 d., (2) Claudia, 2000. *Career:* Mem., Green Day, 1992–; Numerous tours and TV appearances; Obtained major label deal, 1994; Side projects, Pinhead Gunpowder and Screeching Weasel; Provided track for film soundtrack Godzilla; Appeared in cartoon King of the Hill as The Stubborn Stains. *Recordings:* Albums: Dookie, 1994; Insomniac, 1994; Nimrod, 1997; Foot in Mouth, 1998; Warning, 2000; International Superhits (compilation), 2001; Shenanigans, 2002. Singles: Live Tracks (EP), 1994; Welcome To Paradise, 1994; Longview, 1994; Basket Case, 1994; When I Come Around, 1994; Geek Stink Breath, 1995; Stuck With Me, 1995; Bowling Bowling Bowling Parking Parking (EP), 1996; Foot In Mouth (EP), 1996; Brain Stew/Jaded, 1996; Hitchin' A Ride, 1997; Time Of Your Life, 1997; Redundant #1, #2, 1998; Minority, 2000; Warning, 2001; Waiting, 2001. *Address:* c/o Reprise Records, Warner Bros Records Inc, 3300 Warner Blvd, Burbank, CA 91505, USA. *Website:* www.greenday.com.

COOLIDGE, Rita; b. 1 May 1944, Nashville, TN, USA. Vocalist. m. Kris Kristofferson, 1973, divorced 1979. *Career:* Radio commercials with sister, Memphis, Tennessee; Session singer with artistes incl. Eric Clapton, Stephen Stills, mid-1960s; Tours with Delaney and Bonnie; Leon Russell; Solo artiste, 1970–; British tour with Kristofferson, including Royal Albert Hall, 1978; Music for UNICEF Concert, New York, 1979. *Recordings:* Hit singles: Higher and Higher; We're All Alone; The Way You Do The Things You Do; All Time High (theme to film James Bond: Octopussy); Duets with Kris Kristofferson include: Lovin' Arms; A Song I'd Like To Sing; From The Bottle To The Bottom; Albums: Rita Coolidge, 1971; Nice Feelin', 1971; Lady's Not For Sale, 1972; Fall Into Spring, 1974; It's Only Love, 1975; Anytime Anywhere, 1977; Love Me Again, 1978; Satisfied, 1979; Heartbreak Radio, 1981; Never Let You Go, 1983; Inside The Fire, 1988; Cherokee, 1995; Out of the Blues, 1996; Walela, native American recording, 1997; with Kris Kristofferson: Full Moon, 1974; Breakaway, 1975; Natural Act, 1979; Thinkin' About You, 1998. *Honours:* Grammy Awards: Best Country Duo/Group Vocal Performance, with Kristofferson, 1974, 1975. *Current Management:* Axis Artist Management Inc, 6105 Goodland Ave, Valley Glen, CA 91606, USA. *E-mail:* staff@axismanagement.com. *Website:* www.ritacoolidge.com.

COOLIO, (Artis Ivey Jr); b. 1 Aug. 1963, Compton, California, USA. Rap Artiste; Vocalist; Prod. 5 c. *Career:* Rapper from age 15; Former fireman; Joined briefly WC and The Maad Circle; Began Solo rap career, 1994; Collaborations include 40 Thevz; Began own record label, Crowbar, 1997. *Recordings:* Singles: County Line EP, 1993; Fantastic Voyage, 1994; I Remember, 1994; Gangsta's Paradise, used in film soundtrack Dangerous Minds (No. 1, UK and USA), 1995; Too Hot, 1995; It's All The Way Live (Now), 1996; 1, 2, 3, 4 (Sumpin' New), 1996; C U When U Get There, 1997; Ooh La La, 1997; Tuff Jam Uvm Dub, 1997; Winner, 1997; Albums: It Takes A Thief, 1994; Gangsta's Paradise, 1995; My Soul, 1997; Fantastic Voyage – Greatest Hits, 2001; Guest Appearances: WC and The Maad Circle: Ain't A Damn Thang Changed (vocalist), 1991; Quincy Jones: Q's Jook Joint, 1994; Clueless, 1995; Phat Beach, 1996; George Clinton: Greatest Funkin' Hits (vocals), 1996; Forty Thevz: Honor Among Thevz, 1997; 17 Reasons (producer), 1998; Coolio's Crowbar Records Presents, 1999. *Honours:* International Dance Music Award, Best Rap 12 Single, 1996. *Current Management:* Powermove, 8489 W Third St, Suite 1007, Los Angeles, CA 90048, USA.

COOMBES, Bob; b. 27 April 1972, Oxford, England. Musician (keyboards). *Career:* Member, Supergrass, 1995–; Numerous tours, festival dates and TV appearances. *Recordings:* Singles: Lenny, 1996; Richard III, 1997; Sun Hits the Sky, 1997; Late in the Day, 1997; Pumping on Your Stereo, 1999; Albums: In It For The Money, 1997; Supergrass, 1999.

COOMBES, Gaz (Gareth); b. 8 March 1976, England. Vocalist; Musician (guitar). *Career:* Member, The Jennifers; Lead singer, guitarist, Supergrass, 1994–; Major concerts include: Support to Blur, Alexandra Palace, 1994; British tour with Shed Seven, 1994; T In The Park Festival, Glasgow, 1995. *Recordings:* Albums: I Should Coco (No. 1, UK), 1995; In It For The Money, 1997; Supergrass, 1999; Life On Other Planets, 2002. Singles: Caught By The

Fuzz, 1994; Mansize Rooster, 1995; Lenny, 1995; Alright, 1995; Going Out, 1996; Richard III, 1997; Sun Hits the Sky, 1997; Late In The Day, 1997; Pumping On Your Stereo, 1999; Moving, 1999; Mary, 1999; Grace, 2002. *Honours:* Q Award, Best New Act, 1995; BRIT Award, Best British Newcomer, 1996. *Current Management:* Courtyard Management, 22 The Nursery, Sutton Courtenay, Abingdon, Oxon OX14 4UA, England. *Website:* www.supergrass.com.

COONEY, Steve; b. Melbourne, Australia. Musician (guitar, bass, didgeridoo), Songwriter. *Career:* Started playing music, aged 17; Member of Australian bands: Bushwackers; Red Gum; Fruitcake; Moved to Ireland, 1981; Joined Stockton's Wing; Long-term musical partnership with Seamus Begley; Other collaborations include: Sharon Shannon; Altan; Martin Hayes; Mary Black; Kirsty MacColl; Recently established FACE with Laoise Kelly. *Recordings:* Albums include: Meiteal (with Seamus Begley), 1997; Rabhlai Rabhlai, 1998; features on The Chieftains Albums: Long Black Veil, 1995; Santiago, 1996; on Mary Black Albums: Speaking With The Angel, 2000; The Best of Mary Black, 2001; Under the Moon, Martin Hayes, 1995; Way Out Yonder, Andy Irvine, 2001; on Altan Albums: Island Angel, 1993; Blackwater, 1996; Runaway Sunday, 1997; Another Sky, 2000; Lemonade and Buns, Kila, 2000; The Best of Donal Lunny, 2000; on Sharon Shannon Albums: Sharon Shannon, 1991; Each Little Thing, 1997; Spellbound, 1998; The Diamond Mountain Sessions, 2000. *Honours:* Ireland National Entertainment Awards, Most Popular Traditional Act (with Seamus Begley), 1997.

COOPER, Alice, (Vincent Furnier); b. 4 Feb. 1948, Detroit, Michigan, USA. Vocalist. m. Sheryl Goddard, 1 s., 2 d. *Career:* First to stage theatrical rock concert tours; Among first to film conceptual rock promotional videos (pre-MTV); Considered among originators and greatest hard rock artists; Known as King of Shock Rock; Many film, television appearances. *Recordings:* Singles include: I'm Eighteen; Poison; No More Mr Nice Guy; I Never Cry; Only Women Bleed; You and Me; Under My Wheels; Bed of Nails; Albums include: School's Out, 1972; Billion Dollar Babies, 1973; Welcome To My Nightmare, 1976; From The Inside, 1978; Constrictor, 1986; Raise Your Fist and Yell, 1987; Trash, 1988; Hey Stoopid, 1991; Last Temptation, 1994; He's Back, 1997; The Definitive Alice Cooper, 2001; Dragontown, 2001. *Publications:* Wrote foreword to short story book: Shock Rock. *Honours:* Foundations Forum, Lifetime Achievement Award, 1994. *Membership:* BMI; NARAS; SAG; AFTRA; AFofM. *Current Management:* Alive Enterprises. *Address:* PO Box 5542, Beverly Hills, CA 90211, USA.

COOPER, Douglas; b. 3 Sept. 1929, Weymouth, Dorset, England. Musician (drums). m. Blanche, 23 April 1977, 1 s., 1 d. *Education:* London School of Music. *Career:* Worked with: Geraldo; Joe Loss; Tito Burns; Eric Winstone; Edmundo Ross; Paul Fenoulhet; Also worked in USA with Al Grey, Jimmy Forest, Count Basie musicians; Decca sessions for Ray Martin, Norrie Paramor, 1950s; Accompanied many top artists including: Frankie Vaughan; Peter Knight Singers; Matt Monro; Current member, Bournemouth Big Band; Southampton Allstars; Also with own group at local jazz club. *Membership:* Musicians' Union. *Address:* 2 Gloucester St, Weymouth, Dorset DT4 7AP, England.

COOPER, Geoffrey Richard; b. 19 March 1955, Stoke Newington, London, England. Composer; Musician (drums). 2 d. *Education:* Various private tutors; Hailybury College, Hertfordshire. *Career:* with Mothers Ruin; Session work includes many radio and television sessions; with Voyeur (unsigned); Sessions for: Kenny Ball; Michael Schenker; Three Degrees; Tim Rice; Mike Berry; Broken English; Member, The Counterfeit Stones, now left to resume session career. *Membership:* Musicians' Union; PRS; MCPS. *Address:* 15 Lilac Rd, Hoddesdon, Herts EN11 0PG, England.

COOPER, Giles Richard; b. 6 Oct. 1968, Amersham, Buckinghamshire, England. Vocalist; Songwriter; Musician (guitar, bass, keyboards). *Career:* Live concerts throughout London, include Marquee/100 Club; Various bands include Kindred Spirit; Misbeat; Splinter. *Recordings:* Painted Sun; That Was The Year That Was; Fly Away; Don't Play Those Games; Minds Eye. *Membership:* Musicians' Union; International Songwriters Assoc; Guild of International Songwriters and Composers. *Current Management:* A J Promotions. *Address:* Ground Floor, 108 Inderwick Rd, Hornsey, London N8 9JY, England.

COOPER, Paul Joseph; b. 27 Dec. 1959, Liverpool, Merseyside, England. Musician (bass guitar, guitar). m. Jacqueline Ann Iveson, 5 Aug. 1989, 1 s., 1 d. *Career:* Glastonbury Festival; Royal Albert Hall; Wembley Stadium; London Palladium; Budokan Stadium, Tokyo, Japan; Television and radio: Blue Peter; Kaleidoscope; Radio 4; Newsnight. *Recordings:* (own composition) All of The Time, 1983. *Current Management:* Bootleg Beatles.

COOTE, Anthony William John; b. 29 March 1961, Hilderborough, Kent, England. Musician (guitar, bass guitar); Vocalist. *Education:* Canterbury College. *Education:* Kent Music School, guitar, tenor horn. *Career:* with Ruby Blue: major tours, UK; Television: Rock Steady (Channel 4); James Whale Show (ITV); Daytime Live (BBC1); Garden Party (BBC1); Festivals: Glastonbury; Reading; WOMAD; Rebecca Pidgeon: Recording and touring in USA; Animals That Swim: Recording, touring UK, Europe; Tours with Bjorn Again. *Compositions:* Down From Above; The Raven. *Recordings:* Ruby Blue: Down From Above; Virginia Astley: All Shall Be Well; Rebecca Pidgeon: The Raven; Animals That Swim: Workshy; Singles: Ruby Blue: So Unlike Me; Because; Bloomsbury Blue; Stand Together; The Quiet Mind; Primitive Man; Can It Be; John Martyn: Deny This Love; Animals That Swim: Madame Yevonde; Pink Carnations; Animals that Swim: I Was the King, I Really Was the King; Rebecca Didgeon: New York Girls Club; Cinerama: Va Va Voom; Bjorn Again Live at the Albert Hall; Holiday Suite; Cinerama: Disco Volante, 2000; This Is Cinerama, 2000; Videos: Ruby Blue: The Quiet Mind; Primitive Man; Animals That Swim: Madame Yevonde. *Membership:* Musicians' Union. *Current Management:* c/o Elemental Records. *Address:* 64 Mount Grove Rd, London N5 2CT, England.

COPANI, Ignacio Anibal; b. 25 Oct. 1959, Buenos Aires, Argentina. Musician (guitar, piano); Composer; Vocalist. m. Nora Krichmar, 10 March 1981, 3 d. *Career:* Major concerts at main theatres throughout Argentina including: Opera Theatre; Luna Park; Excursionistas Football Stadium; Tours: Argentina; Uruguay; Chile; Colombia; Numerous radio, TV programmes; Own 2 hour daily radio programme. *Recordings:* Ignacio Copani, 1988; Ya Vendram Temps Mejores, 1989; Copani, 1994; Copani Completo, 1992; Afectos Especiales, 1993; Puerto, 1994; Salvese Quien Pued'a, 1995; Compromiso, 1995. *Honours:* Ace, 1994; Winner, Previsario, 1993; Konex, 1995. *Membership:* SADAIC (composers); SADEM (musicians). *Current Management:* Nuevo Canto Producciones. *Address:* 1605 Lavalle St, 4, 8, Buenos Aires, Capital Federal, Argentina.

COPE, Julian; b. 21 Oct. 1957, Bargoed, Wales. Vocalist; Musician (guitar, bass); Songwriter. m. Dorian, 2 d. *Career:* Member, The Crucial Three; Lead singer, musician, The Teardrop Explodes, 1978–82; *Concerts include:* Futurama Festival, Leeds, 1979; Opening of Club Zoo, Liverpool, 1980; Solo artiste, 1983–; Performances include: British tours, 1987–; Glastonbury Festival, 1987; Phoenix Festival, 1993. *Recordings:* Albums: with The Teardrop Explodes: Kilimanjaro, 1980; Wilder, 1981; Everybody Wants To Shag The Teardrop Explodes, 1990; The Greatest Hit (compilation), 2001; Singles: with The Teardrop Explodes: Treason, 1980; Reward, 1981; Passionate Friend, 1981; Solo albums include: World Shut Your Mouth, 1984; Fried, 1984; St Julian, 1987; My Nation Underground, 1988; Skellington, 1990; Peggy Suicide, 1991; Jehovah Kill, 1992; Floored Genius, 1992; 20 Mothers, 1995; Ritey, 1997; Leper Skin, 1999; Solo singles: World Shut Your Mouth, 1986; Beautiful Love, 1991. *Publications:* Head On (Vol. 1 of autobiography), 1991; Kraut Rock Sampler (Guide to German Music 1968–), 1995; The Modern Antiquarian, 1996); Repossessed (Vol. 2 of autobiography), 1999. *Current Management:* Seb Shelton Management, 13 Lynton Rd, London N8 8SR, England.

COPELAND, Stewart; b. 16 July 1952, Alexandria, Egypt. Musician (drums, percussion); Vocalist; Composer. *Career:* Drummer, Curved Air; Drummer, The Police, 1977–86; Numerous world-wide tours, television and radio appearances with The Police; Founder, Animal Logic with Deborah Holland, Stanley Clarke, 1989. *Compositions:* Score for films: Rumble Fish; Wall Steet; Talk Radio; Hidden Agenda; First Power; Men At Work; Ballet: King Lear (for San Francisco Ballet), 1982; Opera: Holy Blood and Crescent Moon, for Cleveland Opera, 1989. *Recordings:* Hit singles include: With The Police: Can't Stand Losing You, 1978; Roxanne, 1979; Message In A Bottle (No. 1, UK), 1979; Walking On The Moon (No. 1, UK), 1979; So Lonely, 1980; Don't Stand So Close To Me (No. 1, UK), 1980; De Do Do Do De Da Da Da, 1980; Invisible Sun, 1981; Every Little Thing She Does (No. 1, UK), 1981; Spirits In The Material World, 1981; Every Breath You Take (No. 1, UK and USA), 1983; Wrapped Around Your Finger, 1983; Synchronicity II, 1983; King of Pain, 1983; Albums: with the Police: Outlandos D'Amour, 1978; Regatta De Blanc (No. 1, UK), 1979; Zenyatta Mondatta (No. 1, UK), 1980; Ghost In The Machine (No. 1, UK), 1981; Synchronicity (No. 1, UK and USA), 1983; Solo album: The Equalizer and Other Cliff Hangers, 1988; Noah's Ark, 1990; Leopard Son, 1996; Four Days In September, 1998; Simpatico, 2000. *Current Management:* Blue Focus Management, 15233 Ventura Blvd, Suite 200, Sherman Oakes, CA 91403, USA.

COPLAND, Clive Rowan; b. 6 June 1956, Hampton Court, England. Musician (guitar). m. Linda Copland, 2 s. *Education:* Grade 3 classical, studied with Andre Edmonds, Kevin Stacey, John Mizarli. *Career:* First band, London soul band The Strutters, 1974; Later worked with Ray Shields Orchestra; Herb Miller Orchestra (brother of Glen Miller); Now freelance musician. *Recordings:* Played on film soundtrack to Yanks; Recording sessions with: Hurricane Smith; John Miller; 4 records with Herb Miller. *Membership:* Asociation of Motion Picture Sound. *Address:* 116 Mortlake Rd, Kew, Richmond, Surrey TW9 4AR, England.

COPPEL, Michael Henry; b. 1 Oct. 1949, Melbourne, Australia. Concert Promoter. m. Michelle Coppel, 15 Feb. 1981, 1 s., 3 d. *Education:* Bachelor of Laws (honour), Bachelor of Commerce, Melbourne University. *Career:* Concerts promoted in last 15 years include: AC/DC, 1981; Narara '83, 3 day Music Festival, Old Sydney Town, 1983; Narara '84, 1984; Whitney Houston tour, 1986; Eurythmics, Revenge Tour, 1987; U2 and B. B. King, Love Comes

To Town Tour, 1989; Tina Turner's Simply The Best Tour, 1993; U2, Zoo TV Tour, 1993; Garth Brooks, 1994; Other tours include: Michael Bolton; UB40; Salt 'n' Pepa; Pet Shop Boys; Pantera; Tori Amos, 1994; Janet Jackson Tour, 1995; Alternative Nation, international and Australian alternative music groups, 1995; Tours for The Cranberries; Violent Femmes; Slayer with Biohazard; Jamiroquai; M People; Sheryl Crow, 1995; Tours for Green Day, Björk, Céline Dion, Smashing Pumpkins, Alanis Morissette, Emmylou Harris, Simply Red, Herbie Hancock, The Fugees; The Corrs, Tina Turner, LeAnn Rimes, Marilyn Manson, Cardigans, Ben Elton, Korn, Sheryl Crow, Victoria Wood, 1997; Joe Cocker, Oasis, Natalie Imbruglia, Metallica, Massive Attack, Public Enemy, 1998; Apollo '98 Dance Festival featuring Fluke, Daft Punk, Ultra Nate, Basement Jaxx, Jimmy Somerville, 1998; Hole, Elvis Costello, Catatonia, UB40, Placebo, Garbage, Reba McEntire, 1999. *Honours:* Australian Concert Promoter of the Year, 1993, 1994. *Membership:* EIEA, Executive Councillor. *Address:* 716–718 High St, Armadale, Victoria 3143, Australia.

COPPIN, Johnny; b. 5 April 1946, South Woodford, London, England. Vocalist; Songwriter; Musician (guitar, piano); Anthologist. m. Gillian Mary Wall, 2 June 1990, 1 s. *Education:* Diploma in Architecture, Gloucester College of Art and Design, 1971; School choirs; Semi-professional and college rock bands. *Career:* Lead singer, songwriter with Decameron, 1969–76; Solo performer, 1976–; Support to Jasper Carrott and Gerry Rafferty; Many European festivals and concert tours; Television appearances: Song of Gloucestershire, BBC2, 1986; Stars In A Dark Night (Channel 4), 1990; Songwriters, HTV, 1995; Radio appearances: Kid Jensen Show, BBC Radio 1, 1981; Kaleidoscope Special, BBC Radio 4, 1989; West Country Christmas, BBC Radio 2, 1993. *Recordings:* 4 albums with Decameron; Solo albums: Roll On Dreamer, 1978; No Going Back, 1979; Get Lucky, 1982; Forest and Vale and High Blue Hill, 1983; Line of Blue, 1985; English Morning, 1987; Edge of Day, with Laurie Lee, 1989; West Country Christmas, 1990; Force of The River, 1993; A Country Christmas, 1995; The Shakespeare Songs, 1997; A Journey, 1999. *Publications:* Forest and Vale and High Blue Hill, 1991; Between The Severn and The Wye, 1993; A Country Christmas, 1996. *Honours:* Hon. Fellow, Cheltenham and Gloucester College of Higher Education, 1997. *Membership:* BAC&S; Equity; PRS; MCPS. *Current Management:* CTM. *Address:* c/o Red Sky Records, PO Box 27, Stroud, Gloucestershire GL6 0YQ, England. *Fax:* (1453) 836877. *E-mail:* Johnny@johnnycoppin.co.uk. *Website:* www.johnnycoppin.co.uk.

CORBI, Rafel; b. 30 July 1966, Palafrugell, Costa Brava, Spain. Radio Personality. m. Mariona Viella, 20 June 1987, 1 s., 1 d. *Career:* Worked in radio since age of 16; Worked for numerous prestigious Spanish newspapers; Featured in all major country music magazines world-wide; Managing Director for RPEM.FM; President, European Country Music Association; President, Spanish Academy of Country Music; Host, WCMN Radio syndicated show. *Honours:* Radio Personality of the Year, 1994, 1997, 1998; Nashville Award, Country Music's European Man of the Year, Airplay Internatinal, 1998; American Eagle Awards, Country Music Asscn of America. *Membership:* CMA, Nashville; European CMA. *Address:* c/o Ample 35, Palafrugell 17200, Costa Brava, Spain.

CORDA, Mike; b. 8 July 1921, New York, NY, USA. Record Co Exec; Composer. m. Helen Marie Wheeler, 7 Dec. 1952, 3 d. *Education:* New York College of Music. *Career:* Bassist, Honolulu Symphony Orchestra, 1945–46; Bassist, original company, Kiss Me Kate, Broadway, 1948–51; Songwriter, various US record companies, 1952–; President, New Horizon Productions, Las Vegas; Record producer, Bluebirds Over The Mountain, Ersel Hickey, 1958; Composer, producer for Mickey Rooney; Robert Goulet; Bill Haley and The Comets; Gloria Lynne; Joe Williams; Writer, prod., Let's Make the Most of a Beautiful Thing, recorded by Nancy Wilson, Sammy Davis Jr., Della Reese, Al Hibbler, Joe Williams, Frank Chacksfield, John Gary and others. *Compositions:* America, I Love You So, 1995; Theatrical Musicals: Vegas on the Rocks; The Devil, The Damsel and Demon Rum. *Membership:* ASCAP. *Address:* Corda Music Inc, 3398 Nahatan Way, Las Vegas, NV 89109, USA.

CORDERO, Jorge Luis; b. 12 May 1952, Holguin, Cuba. Vocalist; Composer; Bandleader. m. Anne Nielsen Cordero, 21 Aug. 1976, 1 s., 1 d. *Education:* Technical College; Percussion ISA and AMI. *Career:* Bandleader, Los Gran Daneses; Concerts, tours include: Germany; Cuba; Poland; Sweden; Norway; Spain; Calle 8 Festival (Miami), 1992; Television and radio, USA, 1993–. *Recordings:* Que Vida, 1975; Salsa Na'ma, 1981; Diferente, 1988; Rompiendo el Hielo, 1994; Del Morte y Tropical, 1996; Al Tiempo, 1999. *Honours:* Representing Denmark in Berlin, 1994. *Membership:* DMF; DJBFA. *Current Management:* Rock On. *Address:* Mondrupsvej 8, 8260 Viby, Denmark.

CORDIER, Thierry; b. 29 May 1963, Mont Saint Martin, France. Writer; Composer; Jazz Musician (guitar, keyboards). m. Joëlle Cordier, 9 Sept. 1989, 2 d. *Career:* One album with Charles Baudelaire, 1986; 200 concerts in France, Luxembourg, Belgium; 2 hits on compilation Coup de Pauce '95; Television includes: FR3: L'Heure du Ci; Radio includes: France Culture, Fun, Nostalgia. *Recordings:* Albums: Correspondances, 9 hits; Tableau Noir, Charles Baudelaire (dedicated to Les Fleurs Du Mal), 1986; Human; Garcon

d'Café; Compilat; Coup d'Pauce '95; Noirs et Couleurs; 1./kri/; Selected Recordings, 2002. Single: Aéroport, 1995. *Membership:* SACEM; ADAMI. *Current Management:* Un Poisson Dans L'Desert. *Address:* 7, rue de la Chappelle, 54400 Longwy, France.

COREA, Chick, (Armando Corea); b. 12 June 1941, Chelsea, Massachusetts, USA. Musician (piano); Composer. m. Gayle Moran, 1 s., 1 d. *Education:* Juilliard School of Music, 1961. *Career:* Pianist with artistes including: Mongo Santamaria, 1962; Blue Mitchell, 1965; Stan Getz, 1966–68; Miles Davis, 1969–71; Sarah Vaughan, 1970; Founder member, leader, pianist with group, Return To Forever, 1971–; Founder, The Elektric Band, 1986. *Recordings:* Piano Improvisations 1 and 2; Leprechaun; My Spanish Heart; Mad Hatter; Delphi 1, 2 and 3; Light As A Feather; Romantic Warrior; Hymn of The Seventh Galaxy; Music Magic; Voyage (with Steve Kujala), 1984; The Chick Corea Akoustic Band, 1989; Elektric Band Inside Out, 1990; Chick Corea Akoustic Band Alive!, 1991; Elektric Band Beneath The Mask, 1991; Time Warp, 1995; Remembering Bud Powell, 1997; Native Sense, 1997; Solo Piano: Standards, 2000; Past Present and Futures, 2001; Numerous appearances on albums with other groups. *Honours:* 9 Grammy Awards; Numerous magazine awards from Downbeat, Keyboard Magazine; Jazz Life Musician of World, Jazz Forum Music Poll, 1974; Best Electric Jazz group, 1990; Best Acoustic Pianist, 1990; Top Jazz Pianist, 1990. *Current Management:* Ron Moss Management, 2635 Griffith Park Blvd, Los Angeles, CA 90039, USA.

CORGAN, Billy; b. 17 March 1967. Vocalist; Musician (multi-instrumentalist). *Career:* Lead singer, Smashing Pumpkins, 1989–2000; Numerous concerts, television and radio appearances; Joined New Order as additional guitarist, 2001; Founding mem., Zwan, 2001–. *Recordings:* Albums: with Smashing Pumpkins: Gish, 1991; The Peel Sessions, 1992; Siamese Dream, 1993; Pisces Iscariot, 1994; Mellon Collie And The Infinite Sadness (No. 1, USA), 1995; The Aeroplane Flies High, 1996; Adore, 1998; MACHINA/ The Machines Of God, 2000; Machina II: The Friends And Enemies Of Modern Music, 2000; Greatest Hits, 2001; Earphoria, 2002; Vieuphoria (DVD), 2002; with Zwan: Mary Star Of The Sea, 2003. Singles: with Smashing Pumpkins: Lull (EP), 1992; Today, 1994; Cherub Rock (EP), 1994; Disarm, 1994; I Am One (EP), 1994; Bullet With Butterfly Wings, 1995; Thirty Three, 1996; Zero, 1996; End Is The Beginning Is The End, 1997; Perfect, 1998; Stand Inside Your Love, 2000; Try Try Try, 2000; Featured on film soundtrack, Singles, 1992. *Current Management:* Coffer/Gershon Management, 26 Park Rd, Bushey, Herts WD2 3EQ, England. *Website:* www.zwan.com.

CORKETT, Paul Alexander; b. 31 Oct. 1964, Hammersmith, London, England. Sound Engineer; Prod. m. Rachel, 19 May 1990. *Education:* Shiplake College. *Career:* Worked at Jacobs Studio and Trident Studio; Now freelance engineer, producer. *Recordings:* Albums: As producer: Smart, Sleeper; Time For The Rest of Your Life, Strangelove; As engineer: Jehovakill, Julian Cope; Violently Happy, Björk; Also worked with: Terrorvision, The Cure, Placebo, Nick Cave, Juliet Roberts. *Current Management:* 140dB Management. *Address:* 1 McCrone Mews, Belsize Village, London NW3 5BG, England.

CORMIER, John Paul; b. 23 Jan. 1969, London, Ontario, Canada. Musician (fiddle, guitar, banjo, mandolin, dobro, bass, piano); Vocalist; Songwriter. m. Hilda Chiasson, 1994. *Career:* Regular Guest, Up Home Tonight, ATV; Studio, stage and session work with Travis Tritt, Waylon Jennings, Marty Stuart, Carl Perkins and Steve Warner; Major Folk and Celtic Festivals including: Tonder Festival, Denmark; Celtic Connections, Scotland; Celtic Colours, CB-NS; Touring extensively in Canada and USA. *Compositions:* Another Morning; Highland Dream; The Island; Gone; Kelly's Mountain; Long for the Sea. *Recordings:* Out of the Blue, 1986; North Wind, 1989; The Fiddle Album, 1990; The Gift, 1992; When January Comes, 1993; Lord of the Dance, 1993; Return to the Cape, 1995; Another Morning, 1997. *Honours:* Canadian Open Guitar Champion, 1986; Maritime Fiddle Champion, 1995; East Coast Music Award Winner, Roots/Traditional Vocal Artist of the Year, 1998. *Membership:* AFofM; SOCAN; CMRRA. *Current Management:* Max McDonald. *Address:* Rave Entertainment Inc, 363 Charlotte St, Sydney, Nova Scotia, B1P 1EI, Canada.

CORNELIUS, Claes; b. 14 May 1949, Copenhagen, Denmark. A&R Man; Publisher; Musician (guitar, keyboards). 1 s. *Education:* Art Academy, Venice, Italy; Piano lessons, various seminars. *Career:* Professional musician, late 1960s, Italy; Studio session musician; Music publishing, Denmark, early 1970s; With Mega Scandinavia, 1983–; Managing Director of Megasong Publishing A/S, 1999. *Recordings:* Countless studio sessions in Italy including Finardi; Claudio Rocchi; Caterina Caselli; Fausto Leali; Also member of Art Class LP. *Honours:* Shared Critics Prize for production in Italy. *Address:* Gronnegade 3, 1107, Copenhagen K, Denmark.

CORNELIUS, Helen Lorene; b. 6 Dec. 1941, Hannibal, Missouri, USA. Vocalist; Songwriter. m. Jerry Garren, 22 June 1981, 2 s., 1 d. *Career:* Songwriter, 1970–; Recording artist, 1975–80; Television appearances include: Nashville On The Road; Host, Helen Cornelius Show, 1976–; Stage performances: Annie Get Your Gun, US touring production, 1984. *Recordings:* Hit single: Lying In Love With You, with Jim Ed Brown; Albums include: Helen Cornelius; Born Believer; I Don't Want To Have To Marry You. *Honours:* CMA Vocal Duo of the Year, 1977. *Membership:* Broadcast Music Inc; AFTRA; CMA; National Assen of Songwriters; West Coast Academy of Country Music. *Address:* c/o Morningstar Pubic Relations, PO Box 83, Brentwood, TN 32027, USA.

CORNELL, Chris; b. 20 July 1964, USA. Vocalist; Songwriter; Musician (guitar). m. Susan Silver. *Career:* Vocalist, US heavy rock group, Soundgarden, 1984–97; Numerous concerts, tours, incl. Lollapalooza II tour, 1992; Reading Festival, 1995; Lollapalooza VI, 1996; Mem., tribute group, Temple of the Dog, 1991; Solo artiste, 1997–2002; Founder mem., Audioslave, 2002–. *Recordings:* Albums: with Soundgarden: Ultramega OK, 1989; Louder Than Love, 1989; Badmotorfinger, 1991; Superunknown (No. 1, USA), 1994; Down On The Upside, 1996; with Temple of the Dog: Temple Of The Dog, 1991; Solo: Euphoria Morning, 1999; with Audioslave: Audioslave, 2002. Singles: with Soundgarden: Flower; Loud Love; Jesus Christ Pose; Outshined; Black Hole Sun, 1994; Spoonman, 1994; Burden In My Hand, 1996; Sunshower, 1998; Solo: Can't Change Me, 1999; with Audioslave: Cochise, 2003. *Honours:* Two Grammy Awards, with Soundgarden, 1995. *Membership:* NARAS. *Current Management:* Jim Guerinot, Rebel Waltz Management, 31652 Second Ave, Laguna Beach, CA 92651, USA. *Address:* c/o Epic Records, 550 Madison Ave, New York, NY 10022-3211, USA. *Website:* www.audioslave.com.

CORNER, Chris; b. 23 Jan. Vocalist; Musician (guitar); Songwriter; Prod. *Career:* Various musical projects, with Liam Howe: first band, 1990, F.R.I.S.K., 1992, Line Of Flight, 1993; Founding mem., Sneaker Pimps, 1995–; Numerous festivals and concerts; Band founded Splinter Recordings, 1999. *Recordings:* Albums: with Sneaker Pimps: Becoming X, 1996; Splinter, 1999; Bloodsport, 2002. Singles: with Line Of Flight: World As A Cone (EP), 1993; with Sneaker Pimps: 6 Underground (EP), 1996; Roll On, 1996; Tesko Suicide, 1996; Spin Spin Sugar, 1997; Post Modern Sleaze, 1997; 6 Underground, 1998; Low Five, 1999; Ten To Twenty, 1999; Sick, 2002. *Address:* c/o Tommy Boy Music, 902 Broadway, New York, NY 10010, USA. *E-mail:* parmesanchic@aol.com. *Website:* www.sneakerpimps.com.

CORNWELL, Hugh; b. 28 Aug. 1949, London, England. Vocalist; Musician (guitar). *Education:* Chemistry graduate. *Career:* Former science teacher; Founder member, UK rock group The Stranglers, 1976–90; Headline tours, Europe; UK; Canada; USA; International concerts include: Supports to Patti Smith, 1976; Climax Blues Band, 1977; Loch Lomond Festival, 1979; Reading Rock Festival, 1983, 1987; Alexandra Palace, 1990; Solo artiste, 1991–; Also worked with Roger Cook and Andy West, 1992. *Recordings:* Albums: Rattus Norvegicus, 1977; No More Heroes, 1978; Black and White, 1978; Live (X Cert), 1979; The Raven, 1979; Themeninblack, 1981; La Folie, 1982; The Collection, 1982; Feline, 1983; Aural Sculpture, 1984; Dreamtime, 1986; All Live and All of The Night, 1988; 10, 1990; Solo albums: Nosferatu, 1979; Wolf, 1988; Wired, 1993; Black Hair, Black Eyes, Black Suit, 1999; First Bus to Babylon, 1999; Hi-Fi, 2000; with Cornwell, Cook and West: C C W, 1992; Singles: with The Stranglers: Get A Grip On Yourself, 1977; Peaches, 1977; Something Better Change, 1977; No More Heroes, 1977; Five Minutes, 1978; Nice 'n' Sleazy, 1978; Walk On By, 1978; Duchess, 1979; Golden Brown (No. 2, UK), 1982; Strange Little Girl, 1982; European Female, 1983; Skin Deep, 1984; Always The Sun, 1986; All Day and All of The Night, 1987; Solo: One In A Million, 1985; Another Kind of Love, 1988. *Publications:* Inside Information. *Honours:* Ivor Novello Award, Most Performed Work of 1982, Golden Brown, 1983.

CORONADO, Gilles; b. 26 Oct. 1966, Avignon, France. Musician (guitar); Composer. *Education:* Superior Technical Brevet of technical drawing; Different School, Banff Jazz Workshop, Canada. *Career:* Various bands (jazz, funk, rock), South of France; Moved to Paris, 1991; Active member, HASK collective (musicians association, Paris); Founder, leader, quartet Urban Mood; Played various festivals: Germany; Belgium; Portugal; France; Collaborator with Dance Performances, 1993–; Teacher. *Recordings:* Urban Mood record due 1996. *Membership:* SACEM. *Address:* Cité Internationale des Arts, 18 rue de l'Hotel de Ville, 75004 Paris, France.

CORR, Andrea Jane; b. 17 May 1974, Dundalk, Co Louth, Ireland. Vocalist; Musician (tin whistle). *Career:* Member, The Corrs; Performed at Boston World Cup for Irish Ambassador, 1994; Signed recording deal; Numerous TV appearances and live shows; Several festival appearances; Film appearances: The Commitments; Evita; The Great Ceili War, 2003. *Recordings:* Singles: Forgiven Not Forgotten, 1996; Right Time, 1996; So Young, 1998; What Can I Do, 1998; Dreams, 1998; Runaway, 1999; Only When I Sleep, 1999; Radio, 1999; Breathless (No. 1, UK), 2000; Irresistible, 2000; Give Me The Reason, 2001; Would You Be Happier, 2001; Albums: Forgiven, Not Forgotten, 1996; Talk On Corners (No. 1, UK), 1998; Corrs Live, 1998; MTV Unplugged, 1999; In Blue (No. 1, UK), 2000; Best of The Corrs (compilation), 2001. *Honours:* BRIT Award, Best International Group, 1999. *Address:* Atlantic Records, 75 Rockefeller Plaza, New York, NY 10019-6907, USA. *Website:* www.thecorrswebsite.com.

CORR, Caroline; b. 17 March 1973, Dundalk, Co Louth, Ireland. Musician (Drums, Bodhran). *Career:* Member, The Corrs; Performed at 1994 World Cup in Boston for Irish Ambassador; Signed recording contract; Numerous TV appearances and live shows; Many festival appearances. *Recordings:* Singles: Forgiven Not Forgotten, 1996; Right Time, 1996; So Young, 1998; What Can I Do, 1998; Dreams, 1998; Runaway, 1999; Only When I Sleep, 1999; Radio, 1999; Breathless (No. 1, UK), 2000; Irresistible, 2000; Give Me The Reason, 2001; Would You Be Happier, 2001; Albums: Forgiven, Not Forgotten, 1996; Talk On Corners (No. 1, UK), 1998; Corrs Live, 1998; MTV Unplugged, 1999; In Blue (No. 1, UK), 2000; Best of The Corrs (compilation), 2001. *Honours:* BRIT Award, Best International Group, 1999. *Address:* Atlantic Records, 75 Rockefeller Plaza, New York, NY 10019-6907, USA. Website: www.thecorrswebsite.com.

CORR, James Steven (Jim); b. 31 July 1968, Dundalk, Co Louth, Ireland. Musician (Guitar, Keyboards). *Career:* Member, The Corrs; Performed for the Irish Ambassador at the 1994 World Cup in Boston; Secured major label recording contract; Numerous TV and live appearances; Many festival dates in Britain and Europe. *Recordings:* Singles: Forgiven Not Forgotten, 1996; Right Time, 1996; So Young, 1998; What Can I Do, 1998; Dreams, 1998; Runaway, 1998; Only When I Sleep, 1999; Radio, 1999; Breathless (No. 1, UK), 2000; Irresistible, 2000; Give Me The Reason, 2001; Would You Be Happier, 2001; Albums: Forgiven, Not Forgotten, 1996; Talk On Corners (No. 1, UK), 1998; Corrs Live, 1998; MTV Unplugged, 1999; In Blue (No. 1, UK), 2000; Best of The Corrs (compilation), 2001. *Honours:* BRIT Award, Best International Group, 1999. *Address:* Atlantic Records, 75 Rockefeller Plaza, New York, NY 10019-6907, USA. *Website:* www.thecorrswebsite.com.

CORR, Sharon; b. 24 March 1970, Dundalk, Co Louth, Ireland. Musician (Violin). *Career:* Member, The Corrs; Performed at 1994 World Cup in Boston for the Irish Ambassador; Secured record contract; Numerous TV appearances and live shows; Many festival dates. *Recordings:* Singles: Forgiven Not Forgotten, 1996; Right Time, 1996; So Young, 1998; What Can I Do, 1998; Dreams, 1998; Runaway, 1999; Only When I Sleep, 1999; Radio, 1999; Breathless (No. 1, UK), 2000; Irresistible, 2000; Give Me The Reason, 2001; Would You Be Happier, 2001; Albums: Forgiven, Not Forgotten, 1996; Talk On Corners (No. 1, UK), 1998; Corrs Live, 1998; MTV Unplugged, 1999; In Blue (No. 1, UK), 2000; Best of The Corrs (compilation), 2001. *Honours:* BRIT Award, Best International Group, 1999. *Address:* Atlantic Records, 75 Rockefeller Plaza, New York, NY 10019-6907, USA. *Website:* www.thecorrswebsite.com.

CORRIGAN, Briana; *Career:* Member, The Beautiful South, 1989–93; Left to pursue solo career. *Recordings:* Singles: with Beautiful South: You Keep It All In, 1989; A Little Time (No. 1, UK), 1990; My Book, 1990; Bell Bottomed Tear, 1992; solo: Love Me Now, 1996; Albums: with Beautiful South: Welcome To The Beautiful South, 1989; Choke, 1990; 0898, 1992; Carry On Up The Charts (compilation; No. 1, UK), 1994; Solid Bronze – Great Hits (compilation), 2001; solo: When Your Arms Wrap Around Me, 1996.

CORSBY, Dave; b. 29 June 1938, Hounslow, Middlesex, England. Composer; Arranger; Musician (saxophones, flute, clarinet, keyboards). m. Jill Corsby, 16 July 1992. *Career:* Founder mem., Cave Jazz Club, Ramsgate, Kent, 1955; Co-organizer, Thanet Jazz Festival, 1982, 1983; Baritone saxophonist, John Burch Octet, 1986–; Radio, television, film and record sessions; Appeared at Dunkirk Jazzopale, 1994; Hot Club of Lyons, 1995; Arts Council tour with John Burch Octet, 1994–95; Ramsgate Spring Festival, 1999; Bandleader, Doctor Crotchet's Good Time Jazz (band for functions); Dave Corsby Quartet (modern jazz group); Mission Impossible Big Band; Business ventures: Carpe Diem Arts; Carpe Diem Music; Lincoln Studios; Played Canterbury Festival, 1998. *Compositions:* The Subterraneans; Rajans Banquet; Samuel Pepys Jazz Suite; Tale of Two Cities Jazz Suite (Arts Council Commission); Seven Deadly Sins, jazz musical; The Endeavour Experience, film score, 1994; Cinque Ports Jazz Suite, Sandwich Festival commission, 1997. *Recordings:* Tale of Two Cities Jazz Suite; Samuel Pepys Jazz Suite; The Seven Deadly Sins; Roll Call. *Membership:* Musicians' Union; Performing Rights Society; Art Pepper Society; Assen of British Jazz Musicians. *Current Management:* Carpe Diem Arts. *Address:* Lincoln Studios, 8 Lincoln Gardens, Birchington-on-Sea, Kent CT7 9SW, England. *Telephone:* (1843) 841501. *Website:* www.jazznotescorsby.com.

CORSO, Terry (Terence); b. 28 Nov. 1971, Riverside, California, USA. Musician (guitar). *Education:* Learned drums and guitar at band workshop programme sponsored by local music store. *Career:* Played with local bands Sinister Fiend, Brother Vibe, Wallop; Member: Alien Ant Farm, 1996–; Self-financed independent LP released to acclaim, 1999; Signed to Papa Roach's New Noize label; Second album released in conjunction with DreamWorks label, leading to major international breakthrough, 2000–01. *Recordings:* Albums: Greatest Hits, 1999; ANThology, 2001; Singles: $100 EP, 1996; Love Songs EP, 1998; Movies, Smooth Criminal, 2001. *Honours:* L.A. Music Award, Best Independent Album, 1999. *Address:* c/o New Noize, 2022 Cliff Dr #123, Santa Barbara, CA 93109, USA. *E-mail:* info@newnoize.com. *Website:* www.alienantfarm.com.

CORTEZ, Alberto, (Jose Alberto Garcia Gallo); b. 11 March 1940, Rancul, Argentina. Vocalist; Composer. m. Renee Govaerts, 2 June 1964. *Education:* Chopin Conservatory, Mendoza, Argentina. *Career:* Performances include: Teatro de la Zarzuela, Madrid, 1967; Lincoln Center, New York, 1990; Teatro Colon, Buenos Aires, 1992. *Compositions:* Over 250 songs include: Distancia; Callajero; En Un Rincon Del Alama; El Abuelo; Cuando Un Amigo Se Va; Mi Arbol y Yo; Castillos En El Aire; Eran Tres; Equipaje; A Partir De Mañana. *Recordings:* Albums: Mr Sucu Sucu, 1960; Welcome To The Latin Club, 1961; Boleros, 1965; Poemas y Canciones, Vol. 1, 1967, Vol. 2, 1968; El Compositor, El Cantante, 1969; Distancia, 1970; No Soy De Aqui, 1971; Ni Poco... Ni Demasiado, 1973; Como El Ave Solitaria, 1974; A Mis Amigos, 1975; Soy Un Charlatan De Feria, 1976; Pensares y Sentires, 1977; En Vivo Desde Madrid, 1978; A Partir De Mañana, 1979; Castillos En El Aire, 1980; Como El Primer Dia, 1983; Gardel... Como Yo Te Siento, 1984; En Vivo, 1985; Sueños y Quimeras, 1986; Como La Marea, 1987; Almafuerte, 1989; Coincidencias, 1990; Si Vieras Que Facil, 1991; Aromas, 1993; Lo Cortez No Quita Lo Cabral, 1994; Lo Cortez No Quita Lo Cabral Vol. II, 1988; A Todo Corazon, 1996. *Publications:* 4 books: Equipaje; Soy Un Ser Humano; Almacen De Almas; Desde Un Rincon Del Alma, 1996. *Membership:* SGAE (Spain). *Current Management:* Raul Arribas. *Address:* c/o Pedro Teixeira 10, 28020 Madrid, Spain.

CORYELL, Larry; b. 12 April 1943, Galveston, Texas, USA. Musician (guitar); Composer. m. Molly Shueler, 3 Sept. 1987, 2 s., 1 d. *Education:* University of Washington; Studied with Jerry Gray, Leon Bolotine, New York City, 1965. *Career:* Jazz guitarist, 1966–; Musician with: Chico Hamilton, 1966; Gary Burton, 1967; Founder, fusion band, Free Spirits; Leader, Eleventh House, 1969; Touring solo guitarist, also in duos with: Philip Catherine; Alphonse Mouzon; Steve Kahn; Emily Remier. *Recordings:* Albums include: Out of Sight and Sound, 1967; Lady Coryell, 1968; Spaces, 1969; Introducing The 11th House, 1974; The Restful Mind, 1975; Aspects, 1976; Basics, 1976; The Lion and The Ram, 1977; Standing Ovation, 1978; Bolero, 1981; Comin' Home, 1984; A Quiet Day In Spring, 1984; Equipoise, 1986; The Dragon Gate, 1989; Twelve Frets To The Octave, 1991; Fallen Angel, 1993; Dynamics, 1994; I'll Be Over You, 1994; Sketches of Coryell, 1996; Spaces Revisited, 1997; Major Jazz Minor Blues, 1998; Cause and Effect, 1998; Monk, Trane, Miles and Me, 1999; Private Concert (live), 1999; At Montreux (with The 11th House), 2000; Barefoot Boy, 2000; Inner Urge, 2001; Also recordings with Michael Urbaniak, Chet Baker, Gary Burton, Sonny Rollins and Laurindo Almeida. *Current Management:* Ted Kurland. *Address:* c/o Ted Kurland Associates, 173 Brighton Ave, Boston, MA 02167, USA.

COSGROVE, Mike; b. 7 Nov. 1975, Long Beach, California, USA. Musician (drums). *Career:* Played with local bands Out of Order, Wallop, Brother Vibe, Tyemus; Member: Alien Ant Farm, 1996–; Self-financed independent LP released to acclaim, 1999; Signed to Papa Roach's New Noize label; Second album released in conjunction with DreamWorks label, leading to major international breakthrough, 2000–01. *Recordings:* Albums: Greatest Hits, 1999; ANThology, 2001; Singles: $100 EP, 1996; Love Songs EP, 1998; Movies, Smooth Criminal, 2001. *Honours:* L.A. Music Award, Best Independent Album, 1999. *Address:* c/o New Noize, 2022 Cliff Dr #123, Santa Barbara, CA 93109, USA. *E-mail:* info@newnoize.com. *Website:* www.alienantfarm.com.

COSMOS. See: MIDDLETON, Tom.

COSTA, Antony Daniel; b. 23 June 1981, Edgware, Middlesex, England. Vocalist. *Career:* Mem., UK band, Blue, 2001–; UK tour, 2002. *Recordings:* Albums: All Rise, 2001; One Love, 2002. Singles: All Rise, 2001; Too Close (No. 1, UK), 2001; If You Come Back (No. 1, UK), 2001; Fly By II, 2002; Sorry Seems To Be The Hardest Word, 2002. *Honours:* Multi-Platinum discs, for All Rise, 2001; Smash Hits Awards, Best Newcomer, 2001, Best Live Act, Best UK Band, 2002; Interactive Music Award, Artist of the Year, 2002; BRIT Award, Best British Newcomer, 2002. *Address:* c/o Virgin Records Ltd, 553–579 Harrow Rd, London W10 4RH, England. *Website:* www.officialblue.com.

COSTA, Gal, (Maria da Graça Costa Pena Burgos); b. 1945, Salvador, Bahia, Brazil. Vocalist. *Career:* Part of Tropicália movement; Remained in Brazil whilst Gilberto Gil and Caetano Veloso were in exile, recording their songs; Has toured internationally and made many TV appearances. *Recordings include:* Albums: Domingo (with Caetano Veloso), 1967; Gal Costa, 1969; Gal, 1969; Gal A Todo Vapor, 1971; India, 1973; Gal Canta Caymmi, 1975; Caras E Bocas, 1977; Gal Tropical, 1979; Aquarel Do Brasil, 1980; Gal Costa, 1981; Fantasia, 1981; Plural, 1983; Baby Gal, 1983; Lua De Mel Como O Diabo Gosta, 1984; Bem Bom, 1985; Gal Canta Tom Jobim, 1999; Bem Bom, 2001. *Honours:* Shell Prize, 1984. *Address:* c/o BMG, Bedford House, 69–79 Fulham High St, London SW6 3JW, England.

COSTEA, Constantin; b. 1 Nov. 1931, Bucharest, Romania. Writer; Dance, Folklore Researcher; Record Prod. *Education:* Liceul Teoretic; Liceul Coregrfie; Special Master of Ballet Courses (3 years). *Career:* Numerous radio and television appearances; Tours, shows: Hungary; Czechoslovakia; Austria; Finland; Germany; France; Netherlands; UK; Sweden; Denmark; Iran.

Recordings: As producer, series of 6 albums: Romanian Folk Dances, 1978–82. *Publications:* Numerous research studies. *Membership:* ICTM. *Address:* Bucaresti, 78468 Str, Moldovei, Nr 40, Sect 1, Romania.

COSTELLO, Elvis, (Declan Patrick McManus); b. 25 Aug. 1955, London, England. Vocalist; Songwriter; Musician; Prod. m. Cait O'Riordan, 1 c. (from previous marriage). *Career:* Mem., Flip City; Lead singer, Elvis Costello and The Attractions, 1977–; Appearances include: British tour, 1977; US tour, 1978; Grand Ole Opry, 1981; Royal Albert Hall, with Royal Philharmonic, 1982; Cambridge Folk Festival, 1995; Television includes: Appearance in Scully, ITV drama, 1985; Also worked with The Specials; Paul McCartney; Aimee Mann; George Jones; Roy Orbison; Wendy James; Robert Wyatt; Jimmy Cliff; Co-organizer, annual Meltdown festival, South Bank Centre, London. *Compositions include:* Alison, 1977; Watching The Detectives, 1977; (I Don't Want To Go To) Chelsea, 1979; Crawling To The USA, 1978; Radio Radio, 1978; Stranger In The House, 1978; Girls Talk, 1979; Oliver's Army, 1979; Boy With A Problem, 1982; Every Day I Write The Book, 1983; Music for television series (with Richard Harvey): G.B.H., 1991; Jake's Progress, 1995; Other songs for artists including Johnny Cash; June Tabor. *Recordings:* Albums include: My Aim Is True, 1978; This Year's Model, 1978; Armed Forces, 1979; Get Happy, 1980; Trust, 1980; Almost Blue, 1981; Taking Liberties, 1982; Imperial Bedroom, 1982; Goodbye Cruel World, 1984; Punch The Clock, 1983; The Best Of, 1985; Blood and Chocolate, 1986; King of America, 1986; Spike, 1989; Mighty Like A Rose, 1991; The Juliet Letters (with the Brodsky Quartet), 1993; Brutal Youth, 1994; The Very Best of Elvis Costello and The Attractions, 1995; Kojak Variety, 1995; Deep Dead Blue, Live At Meltdown (with Bill Frisell), 1995; All The Useless Beauty, 1996; Terror and Magnificence, 1997; Painted From Memory, 1998; The Sweetest Punch: The Songs of Costello, 1999; Best of Elvis Costello, 1999; For The Stars (with Anne Sofie von Otter), 2001; When I Was Cruel, 2002. *Honours:* BAFTA Award, Best Original Television Music, G.B.H., 1992; MTV Video, Best Male Video, 1989; Rolling Stone Award, Best Songwriter, 1990. *Current Management:* Jill Taylor, By Eleven Management, 12 Tideway Yard, 125 Mortlake High St, London SW14 8SN, England. *Website:* www.elviscostello.com.

COTTLE, Laurence; b. 16 Dec. 1961, Swansea, Wales. Musician (bass guitar). m. Alison Hooper, 16 April 1994. *Career:* Currently touring with Jim Mullen (GTR); Played most jazz festivals with Jim Mullen; Tours with Laurence Cottle Quintet include: America; Cuba; Germany; France; Spain; Italy; Collaborations include: Eric Clapton; Labi Siffre; James Taylor Quartet; Jason Rebello; Hue and Cry; Seal; Tom Jones; Rhythm and Blues (with Mark Feltham). *Recordings:* Solo album: Five Seasons; with Laurence Cottle Quintet: Live At 33, 1995. *Membership:* Musicians' Union. *Address:* 52 Highfield Way, Rickmansworth, Hertfordshire WD3 7PR, England.

COULAM, Roger Keith; b. 21 Aug. 1940, Blackburn, Lancashire, England. Musician (piano, organ, keyboards). m. Susan Chadwick, 19 Sept. 1961, 1 s., 2 d. *Education:* Piano, harmony, London Guildhall School of Music and Drama, LGSM. *Career:* Backing Helen Shapiro, 1963; Duane Eddy, 1979; Johnny Howard's Band, Radio 1, Easybeat, 1966; Founder member, Blue Mink, 1969–73; Albert Hall Concert; Tour with Booker T and the MG's; Star Cabaret; Talk of The Town; Television includes: Top of the Pops; Prominent record, radio, television and film musician, 1966–; Sessions include: Tina Turner; Sammy Davis Jr; The Italian Job; Organist on Je T'Aime. *Compositions:* Co-writer several Blue Mink album tracks and B sides including chart single Sunday; Library music 1970, used for various radio, film, television series, including: Budgie; Vision On. *Recordings:* Solo albums: Organ In Orbit, 1966; Blow Hot, Blow Cool, 1969; All Blue Mink recordings, 1969–73; Blue Mink Greatest Hits, 2000. *Honours:* Silver disc, Melting Pot, Blue Mink. *Membership:* Musicians' Union; BMWC; PRS; MCPS; BAC&S.

COULOMBE, Daniel; b. 11 May 1960, Québec City, Canada. Music Prod. *Education:* University Communication. *Career:* Recording Producer; Remix Engineer; Radio Producer. *Recordings:* B-52's, Party Mix, 1981, Best of the B-52's: Dance This Mess, 1990, Party Mix/Mesopotamia, 1991; Icehouse; Indochine; Mitsou.

COUPLAND, Gary; b. 27 March 1964, Dumfries, Scotland. Musician (accordion, keyboards). m. Karen Chaisson, 18 Sept. 1987, 3 d. *Education:* Dumfries Academy; Napier College, Edinburgh, Scotland. *Career:* Musical Director with The Singing Kettle, Scotland's Theatre Box Office Record Breakers, London Palladium and Sadler's Wells; 4 series for Children's BBC TV; Folk musician at Cambridge Folk Festival, Stage 1, 1992. *Recordings:* Appears on Ian Hardie, Ecosse: A Breath of Scotland, 1994; Brian McNeill, No Gods, 1996; Holding Up Half the Sky, Holding Up Half the Sky, 1997. *Publications:* 6 videos. *Honours:* BAFTA, Scotland, Best Children's TV Show. *Membership:* Musicians' Union; Equity. *Address:* 12 Stanley St, Edinburgh EH15 1JJ, Scotland.

COURTOIS, Vincent; b. 21 March 1968, Paris, France. Musician. m. Muriel, 1990, 1 s. *Career:* Played with: Michel Petrucciani; Niels Lan Doky; Tour with Michel Petrucciani, 1994–95. *Recordings:* Cello News; Pleine Lune; Pendulum Quartet; appears on Cheb Khaled, N'ssi N'ssi, 1993, Sahra, 1996; Philippe

Eidel, Mammas, 1997, Imuhar, 1999. *Current Management:* Laurence Voiturier, Artalent. *Address:* 15 Passage de la Main d'Or, 75011 Paris, France.

COUSENS, Peter William Light; b. 2 Nov. 1955, Tamworth, NSW, Australia. Vocalist; Actor. m. Suzanne Roylance, 9 Dec. 1984, 3 d. *Education:* National Institute of Dramatic Art Graduate, 1978. *Career:* Musicals: Camelot (Mordred), with Richard Harris, 1983; Blood Brothers (Eddie), 1987; The Mikado, The Australia Opera, 1986; Les Miserables (Marius), 1989–91; Aspects of Love (Alex), Phantom of the Opera, 1992; Sydney (Raoul), 1993–94; Miss Saigon (Chris), 1995–96; West Side Story (Tony), 1996; London (The Phantom), 1997; Australia Showboat, Ravenal, 1998. *Recordings:* First Album, Corner of the Sky, 1994; Second, From a Distance, 1996; International Symphonic Recording Miss Saigon (Chris), 1996; Are We Nearly There Yet, MBF Children's with Noni Hazelhurst. *Honours:* Variety Club of Australia Heart Award, 1996. *Current Management:* International Casting Service, 147A King St, Sydney. *Address:* c/o ICS, 147A King St, Sydney, 2000, Australia.

COUSIN, Andy; b. 28 June 1963, Lincoln, England. Musician (bass guitar); Vocalist. *Career:* Musician with: All About Eve; The Mission. *Recordings:* All About Eve: All About Eve, 1988; Scarlet and Other Stories, 1989; Touched By Jesus, 1991; Ultraviolet; Winter Words; Live At Glastonbury; Fairy Night Lights Vol. 1, 2000; Live and Electric At The Union Chapel, 2001; The Mission: Neverland. *Address:* 65 Vale Rd, Finsbury Park, London N4 1PP, England.

COVACI, Nicu (Nicolae); b. 19 April 1947, Timisoara, Romania. Musician (6 and 12 string guitar); Vocalist. m. (1) 1976–78; (2) 1980–89. *Education:* High School of Arts; Academy of Arts; 4 years piano and guitar. *Career:* National Student Festival, Iasi, 1968; National Student Festival, Bucharest, 1969–71; Sopot Festival Poland, 1973; Romanian television: Tops of The Week; Romanian radio: Vremuri (EP), 1968; Floarea Stincilor (EP), 1969; Cei Ce Ne-Au Dat Nume, 1971; Mesteroul Manole (EP), 1973; Mugur De Fluier, 1974; Cantafabule, 1975; Transsylvania, 1980; Symphoenix, 1992; Phoenix-Evergreens, 1995. *Honours:* First prize, National Student Festival, Iasi, 1968; Awards for: Composition and Creativity, Bucharest, 1969–71; Originality, Bratislawskalyra, Czechoslovakia, 1973. *Membership:* GEMA; OCMR. *Address:* Im Dütetal 2, 49078 Osnabrück, Germany.

COVERDALE, David; b. 22 Sept. 1949, Saltburn-By-The-Sea, Cleveland, England. Vocalist; Songwriter. m. Tawny Kitaen, 17 Feb., 1989. *Career:* Vocalist, Government; Lead singer, UK rock group Deep Purple, 1973–76; Founder, lead singer, UK heavy rock group Whitesnake, 1977–91; Solo artiste, 1991–; Member, Coverdale/Page, with Jimmy Page, 1993; Regular international tours; Concerts include: Reading Festival, 1979, 1980; Monsters of Rock, Castle Donington, 1981, 1983, 1990; Texas World Music Festival, 1987; Super Rock '90 Festival, Germany, 1990. *Recordings:* Albums: with Deep Purple: Burn, 1974; Stormbringer, 1974; 24 Carat Purple, 1975; Come Taste The Band, 1975; Live At The California Jam, 1996; King Biscuit Flower Hour, 1996; California Jam '74, 1996; with Whitesnake: Whitesnake, 1977; Northwinds, 1978; Trouble, 1979; Ready An' Willing, 1980; Live In The Heart of The City, 1980; Come An' Get It, 1981; Saints 'n' Sinners, 1982; Slide It In, 1984; Whitesnake 1987, 1987; Slip of The Tongue, 1989; Whitesnake's Greatest Hits, 1994; with Coverdale/Page: Coverdale/Page, 1993; solo: Into The Light, 2000; Hit singles: with Whitesnake: Fool For Your Loving, 1980 (re-recorded, 1989); Don't Break My Heart Again, 1981; Here I Go Again, 1982 (re-recorded, No. 1, USA, 1987); Give Me More Time, 1984; Still of The Night, 1987; Is This Love, 1987; Give Me All Your Love, 1987; The Deeper The Love, 1990; with Coverdale/Page: Take Me For A Little While, 1993. *Current Management:* H. K. Management, 8900 Wilshire Blvd #300, Beverly Hills, CA 90211, USA.

COWELL, Sir Harry Edmund; b. 4 Sept. 1960, Dorking, Surrey, England. Artist Man. m. Anita Harriet, 25 Feb. 1995, 1 d. *Career:* Management partner of Simon Napier-Bell; Clients include: Yardbirds; Japan; Marc Bolan; Wham!; Recent success with bands: Asia; Ultravox. *Recordings include:* Hokey Cokey, Captain Sensible, 1994, (for Great Ormond Street Hospital Children's Fund). *Address:* 66 Prince Georges Ave, West Wimbledon, London SW20 8BH, England.

COWELL, Simon; b. 7 Oct. 1959, England. Broadcaster; Television and Record Co Exec; A&R Consultant. *Education:* Dover College; St Columba's College, St Albans. *Career:* Worked, EMI Music Publishing, 1977–82; Founder, Fanfare Records, with Iain Burton, 1982–89; A&R Consultant, BMG Records, 1989–; Founder, co-owner, S Records, 2001–; Judge, Pop Idol (ITV1), 2001–02, American Idol–The Search for a Superstar (Fox TV), 2002; Worked with: Curiosity Killed the Cat, Five, Gareth Gates, Robson and Jerome, Sonia, Westlife, Will Young. *Honours:* Record Exec. of the Year, 1998, 1999; A&R Man. of the Year, 1999. *Address:* S Records, Bedford House, 69–79 Fulham High St, London SW6 3JW, England. *E-mail:* simon.cowell@bmg.com.

COWEN, Jeanine M; b. 4 April 1965, Bettendorf, Iowa, USA. Composer; Musician (percussion). m. Sara Whitman, 2 March 1991, 3 c. *Education:* Northwestern University; Berklee College of Music. *Career:* Film work as

Composer: Home Before Dark, 1997; My Father's Love, 1998; Killing the Badge, 1999; A Far Distant Place, 2000; Killing Cinderella, 2000; Sandy 'Spin' Slade: Beyond Basketball, 2001. *Membership:* IAWM; ASCAP; SCL; WIFVNE. *Address:* PO Box 66297, Auburndale, MA 02466, USA.

COWX, Timothy; b. 23 Sept. 1975, Chester, England. Folk Vocalist; Musician (guitar); Songwriter. *Career:* Acting in various local productions, lead roles in Bugsy Malone, Importance of Being Earnest; Formed Dicey Riler, 1996; Became Solo Artist, playing folk venues; Appeared at International Eisteddfod Fringe, Llangollen. *Recordings:* Fabian Folk, 1997; Sanity EP, 1999; Dictonic, 1999. *Membership:* Musicians' Union. *Current Management:* M.G.E. *Address:* Glan Llyn, Glan Llyn Rd, Bradley, Wrexham, LL11 4BB, Wales.

COX, Carl; b. 29 July 1962, Manchester, England. DJ; Prod; Remixer; Label Owner. m. Rachel Turner, 19 March 1994. *Career:* DJ, 1980–; Sunrise Rave, 1989; Afterward known as '3 Deck Wizard'; One of top DJs on Rave scene, 1989–93; Signed album deal with Perfecto/BMG, 1991; Presently resident, top UK House/Techno clubs including Cream, Liverpool; Final Frontier, London; Also DJ in Germany; Tours: Australia; USA; Japan; France; Switzerland; Austria; Ibiza; Started Ultimate Music Management (managing DJs from around the world), 1993; Started own MMR record label, 1994; Appeared in film Human Traffic, 1998. *Recordings:* Own albums: I Want You Forever, 1991; Does It Feel Good To You, 1992; At The End of the Cliché, 1996; Phuture 2000, 1999; Own record label releases include (own compositions): with Stone Circle: Deep In You; Tonight; with Conquer: Self Destruction; War Path; Solo: Anthemia; Motorway; Det 29–62; Remixed tracks by: Art of Noise; Sunscreen; Cuba Gooding; Yello; Stone Roses; Robert Owens; Patti Day; Jam and Spoon. *Honours:* DJ Magazine, No. 1 Rave DJ, 1992; Stepping Out, Top UK DJ, 1992, 1993; International Dance Awards: DJ of the Year, 1994, 1995; Frontpage Magazine, Top Overseas DJ, Germany, 1994. *Membership:* Musicians' Union. *Address:* 49 Highlands Rd, Horsham, West Sussex RH13 5LS, England.

COX, Deborah; b. 1974, Canada. Vocalist; Songwriter. *Education:* Performing Arts School. *Career:* Singer, commercials and local club circuit, Toronto, age 12; R&B singer, and songwriting partnership with Lascelles Stephens; Tour with Céline Dion; Concerts in Europe; Japan; Asia. *Recordings:* Debut album, 1995; One Wish, 1998; Singles: Sentimental, 1995; The Sound of My Tears, 1996; Nobody's Supposed To Be Here, 1998; It's Over Now, 1999; Appears on: Dan Hill, Greatest Hits and More, 1994; BeBe Winans, 1998; Trina and Tamara, Trina and Tamara, 1999; duet with Whitney Houston, Same Script Different Cast, 2000. *Current Management:* c/o Stiletto Entertainment, 5443 Beethoven St, Los Angeles, CA 90066, USA.

COX, Doc, (Robert Cox); b. 1 July 1946, Sheffield, Yorkshire, England. Vocalist; Songwriter; Musician (ukelele). *Education:* Trained as teacher; 8 cello lessons; 3 guitar lessons; Several years with Bert Weedon book. *Career:* Semi-pro rock 'n' roll bands, 1960s, 70s; Top Twenty record, under name of Ivor Biggun (No. 1, Indie-Punk charts), 1978; 2 top 50 placings; Regular on That's Life, BBC TV, lots of BBC Radio. *Compositions include:* Ketchup Bottle Blues, sung by Marion Montgomery on BBC TV, Radio. *Recordings include:* The Winker's Song, banned by BBC, 1978; The Majorca Song, 1987; Compilation: The Fruity Bits, 1999. *Publications:* Rock Talk; Newspaper, magazine articles. *Honours:* Worthing Tourism Promotions Award. *Membership:* Musicians' Union. *Current Management:* Wendy Downes, 96 Broadway, Bexleyheath, Kent DA6 7DE, England.

COX, Graham Kenneth; b. 24 Nov. 1965, Hammersmith, London, England. Journalist; Vocalist; Songwriter; Prod; Man. *Education:* Sound Engineer, Detla Akustik and Vibration, Copenhagen. *Career:* Support for Depeche Mode, 1980s; A Void Citadel Tour, 1980s; Zenon Tour, Denmark, Infinity Tour, Denmark, late 1980s; Man., Suspected Hippies in Transit, Mushroom Season '94 Tour; Singer, Prod., Low Flying Object, Plant More Trees; Owner, Dir, Navajo Records, 1998–. *Compositions:* Plant More Trees; Low Flying Object; Crazy Horse. *Recordings:* Albums: Dragons; Folklore, Low Flying Object; Maxi CD, Plant More Trees; Northern Lights, Low Flying Object, 2002. *Publications:* Several articles in professional magazines. *Address:* Damhusvej 27 st tv, 5000 Odense C, Denmark. *Website:* www.navajorecords.com.

COX, Peter; b. 17 Nov. 1955. Vocalist; Songwriter; Musician (guitar, keyboards). *Career:* Songwriting partnership with Richard Drummie, ATV Music; Founder member, duo Go West, 1982–; Solo career, 1997–. *Compositions include:* One Way Street (for film soundtrack Rocky IV). *Recordings:* Albums: Go West, 1985; Bangs and Crashes, 1986; Dancing On The Couch, 1987; Indian Summer, 1992; Best of Go West, 2000; Solo album, Peter Cox, 1997 Singles: We Close Our Eyes, 1985; Call Me, 1985; Don't Look Down, 1985; The King of Wishful Thinking, 1990; Solo single, Ain't Gonna Cry Again, 1997. *Current Management:* Blueprint Management, 134 Lots Rd, London SW12 0RJ, England.

COX, Rachel Elizabeth; b. 15 April 1972, British Columbia, Canada. Co Dir. m. Carl Cox, 19 March 1994. *Career:* Director of Flying Records UK Ltd,

1990–92; Founder and Director of Ultimate Music Management, 1993–. *Address:* 49 Highlands Rd, Horsham, West Sussex RH13 5LS, England.

COXON, Graham Leslie; b. 12 March 1969, Rinteln, Germany. Musician (guitar, saxophone). *Education:* Art and Design Diploma; N Essex School of Art; Goldsmiths College; Saxophone lessons at school. *Career:* Member, Blur, –2002; Television, radio appearances include: Top of the Pops; Later With Jools Holland; Extensive tours include: Alexandra Palace; Reading Festival, 1993; Glastobury Festival, 1994; Mile End, 1995; V97, 1997; UK Arena tour, 1997; Glastonbury, 1998; T in the Park, 1999; Reading/Leeds Festival, 1999; Solo artiste, 1998–. *Recordings:* Albums: with Blur: Leisure, 1991; Modern Life Is Rubbish, 1993; Parklife (No. 1, UK) 1994; The Great Escape (No. 1, UK), 1995; Blur (No. 1, UK) 1997; 13 (No. 1, UK), 1999; The Best Of Blur, 2000; Solo: The Sky Is Too High, 1998; The Golden DJ, 2000; Crow Sit On Blood Tree, 2001; The Kiss Of Morning, 2002. Singles: with Blur: She's So High, 1990; There's No Other Way, 1991; Bang, 1991; Popscene, 1992; For Tomorrow, 1993; Chemical World, 1993; Sunday, Sunday, 1993; Girls and Boys, 1994; To The End, 1994; Parklife, 1994; End of a Century, 1994; Country House (No. 1, UK), 1995; The Universal, 1995; Stereotypes, 1996; Charmless Man, 1996; Beetlebum (No. 1, UK), 1997; Song 2, 1997; On Your Own, 1997; MOR, 1997; Tender, 1999; Coffee and TV, 1999; No Distance Left To Run, 1999; Music Is My Radar, 2000. *Honours:* Platinum discs for Parklife, Blur, 13; BRIT Awards, Best Single, Album, Video, Band, 1995; Q Awards, Best Album, 1994, 1995. *Current Management:* CMO Management, Unit 32, Ransome Dock, 35–37 Parkgate Rd, London SW11 4NP, England.

COZENS, Chris; b. 3 June 1959, England. Programmer. m. Mel, 5 Nov. 1988, 1 d. *Education:* City of Leeds College of Music. *Career:* Keyboard player; Composed and performed music for new production: The Rise and Fall of The City of Mahogany, by Brecht; Spent year in Canada, with own band, Long Distanz; Returned to UK, joined Johnny Mars Band; Worked as arranger, orchestrator, session keyboard player, for: John Parr; Cozy Powell; Jan Akkerman; Barry Humphries; Graham Bonnett; Harry Nilsson; Francis Rossi; Demis Roussos; Jon English; producer Terry Britten; Programmer, musician, recording of Paris, rock opera by Jon English and Dave Mackay, with London Symphony Orchestra, Royal Philharmonic Orchestra, 1989; Toured Australia, MD for Jon English; Co-writer, 2 Australian television series, including All Together Now; Collaborated with Alan Parker, Dave Mackay, on incidental music for scores; Writer, portfolio of library music; Working with Alan Attfield on Facades (musical); Produced, recorded series of albums for Telstar Records under name Project D; Credits include: Films and television: What's Eating Gilbert Grape?; Wild Justice; To Be The Best; Voice of The Heart; Red Fox; Van Der Valk; Minder, by Alan Parker; 99 To 1, by Mike Gibbs; Coasting, West Beach, Making Out, by Dave Mackay; Bullseye, John Du Prez; Composer, incidental music, Children's Ward, 1994; Bridge To The Past, 1994; Music for documentary, Burning Rubber. *Recordings include:* Album: Synthesiser Greats, 1994; Lights Camera Action, 2001. *Membership:* PRS; MCPS. *Current Management:* Soundtrack Music Management. *Address:* 22 Ives St, Chelsea, London SW3 2ND, England.

COZENS, Spencer James; b. 11 Feb. 1965, Weston-Super-Mare, England. Musician (piano, keyboards); Composer. *Education:* East Notts Music School; Newark Technical College; Goldsmiths College, 1987–91; B Mus degree. *Career:* Tours with Julia Fordham; Joan Armatrading, 2001–; Producing, touring with John Martyn, 1990–; Writer, producer, albums with Miles Bould (percussion) as Peoplespeak; Also with Jacqui McShee (vocals) Gerry Conway (drums), album: About Thyme; Writer, musician with Carol Decker; Toured with Jacqui McShee's Pentangle. *Recordings:* Albums: with John Martyn: Cooltide (prod., musician); And (prod., musician); No Little Boy (co-prod., musician); Couldn't Love You More (musician); The Church with One Bell (musician); with Steps Ahead: Yin Yang; with Jacqui McShee's Pentangle: Passé Avant (writer, prod., musician); Albums by: Peoplespeak and About Thyme (as prod., writer, musician); Miten; David Hughes: 50 Yards of David Hughes (musician). *Membership:* PRS; MCPS; PAMRA. *Address:* 72 Nottingham Rd, Bingham, Nottinghamshire NG13 8AW, England.

CRACKNELL, Sarah; b. 12 April 1967, Chelmsford, Essex, England. Vocalist. *Education:* Italia Conti Stage School; Drama Studio; Tona De Brett. *Career:* Mem., lead singer, Saint Etienne, 1991–; Mem., LoveCut dB, with Douglas Benford; Numerous television appearances, concerts, tours. *Recordings:* Albums: with Saint Etienne: Foxbase Alpha, 1991; So Tough, 1993; You Need A Mess Of Help To Stand Alone (compilation), 1993; Tiger Bay, 1994; I Love To Paint (compilation), 1995; Fairytales From Saint Etienne (compilation), 1995; Too Young To Die (compilation), 1995; Casino Classics (compilation), 1996; Continental (compilation), 1997; Good Humor, 1998; The Misadventures Of Saint Etienne (soundtrack), 1999; Built On Sand (compilation), 1999; Sound Of Water, 2000; Interlude (compilation), 2001; Smash The System (compilation), 2001; Finisterre, 2002; Solo: Lipslide, 1997. Singles: with Saint Etienne: Nothing Can Stop Us, 1991; Join Our Club, 1992; Avenue, 1992; You're In A Bad Way, 1993; Hobart Paving/Who Do You Think You Are?, 1993; I Was Born On Christmas Day (with Tim Burgess), 1993; Pale Movie, 1994; Like A Motorway, 1994; Hug My Soul, 1994; Reserection (with Etienne Daho), 1995; He's On The Phone, 1995; Xmas '95 (EP), 1995;

Angel/Burnt Out Car, 1996; Valentines Day '97 (EP), 1997; Sylvie, 1998; The Bad Photographer, 1998; Bronx Dogs Mixes, 1998; Lose That Girl, 1998; Xmas '98 (EP), 1998; Lover Plays The Bass, 1999; Places To Visit (EP), 2000; Saturday, 1999; How We Used To Live, 2000; Heart Failed (In The Back Of A Taxi), 2000; Boy Is Crying, 2001; Asleep At The Wheels Of Steel (EP), 2002; Action, 2002; with LoveCut dB: as LoveCut dB: Fingertips, 1991; Heartspin, 1991; Journey To The Centre Of Love, 1991; Solo: Love Is All You Need, 1987; Anymore, 1996; Goldie, 1997; Kelly's Locker (EP), 2000; as Cola Boy: Seven Ways To Love, 1991; He Is Cola, 1991; contribution to Gone, David Holmes, 1996; Tell Me Why, Paul Van Dyk, 2000. *Membership:* Equity. *Current Management:* Martin Kelly, Heavenly Management, 72 Wardour St, London W1, England. *Address:* c/o Mantra Recordings, 17–19 Alma Rd, London SW18 1AA, England. *Website:* www.saint.etienne.net.

CRADDOCK, Billy 'Crash' (William Wayne); b. 16 June 1939, Greensboro, North Carolina, USA. Vocalist. *Career:* Talent shows from age 10; Rock/country recording artiste, 1957–. *Recordings:* US Country No. 1 hits: Rub It In; Ruby Baby; Broken Down In Tiny Pieces; Other hit singles include: Boom Boom Baby; Knock Three Times; Dream Lover; You Better Move On; Ain't Nothin' Shakin'; I'm Gonna Knock On Your Door; I Cheated On A Good Woman's Love; Sea Cruise; Love Busted; Numerous albums include: I'm Tore Up, 1964; Knock Three Times, 1971; You Better Move On, 1972; Still Thinkin' About You, 1975; Crash, with Janie Frickie, 1976; Changes, 1980; Back On Track, 1989; Boom Boom Baby, 1992; Numerous greatest hits compilations including: Crash's Smashes: The Hits of Billy Crash, 1996. *Honours:* Cashbox Award, New Find of Year, 1972. *Address:* c/o Ace Productions, PO Box 292725, Nashville, TN 37229–2725, USA.

CRADOCK, Steve; b. 22 Aug. 1969, Birmingham, England. Musician (guitar, keyboards). *Career:* Member, The Boys; Joined The Fanatics with Simon Fowler and Damon Minchella; Later joined Ocean Colour Scene; Joined Paul Weller's tour, 1993, and subsequent backing band, while still in Ocean Colour Scene; Played on Paul Weller's album Wild Wood; Band had support slot to Oasis 1994 tour; Numerous TV appearances and much radio airplay; Riverboat Song used as theme to TV Show TFI Friday; Several headlining tours. *Recordings:* Singles: with The Boys, Happy Days EP; Sway, 1990; with OCS: Yesterday Today, 1990; Giving It All Away, 1992; Do Yourself A Favour, 1992; Riverboat Song, 1996; The Day We Caught The Train, 1996; You've Got It Bad, 1996; The Circle, 1996; 100 Mile High City, 1997; Travellers Tune, 1997; Better Day, 1997; It's A Beautiful Thing, 1998; July/I Am The News, 2000; Albums: Ocean Colour Scene, 1992; Moseley Shoals, 1996; B-Sides, Seasides and Freerides, 1997; Marchin' Already (No. 1, UK), 1997; One From The Modern, 1999; Mechanical Wonder, 2001; Songs For The Front Row (compilation), 2001.

CRAIG, Carl, (Paperclip People, 69, BFC, Psyche, Innerzone Orchestra); b. 1969, Detroit, Michigan, USA. Prod; Remixer; DJ. *Career:* Protégé of Derrick May; Founder: Retroactive, Planet-E Recordings; Organizer: 2001 Detroit Electronic Music Festival; Remixed: Maurizio, Tori Amos, Gus Gus, Incognito; Collaborations: Derrick May. *Recordings:* Albums: Landcruising, 1995; More Songs About Food and Revolutionary Art, 1997 ; The Secret Tapes of Dr Eich (as Paperclip People), 1997; Programmed (with Innerzone Orchestra), 2000; Singles: Crackdown (as Psyche), 1990; Bug In The Bassbin (as Innerzone Orchestra), 1992; Throw (as Paperclip People), 1994; The Climax (as Paperclip People), 1995; 4 Jazz Funk Classics (as 69), 1994; People Make The World Go Round (as Innerzone Orchestra), 2000. *Current Management:* c/o Talkin' Loud Records, Chancellor's House, 72 Chancellor's Rd, London W6 9QB, England.

CRAIG, David Mark; b. 4 April 1969, Leeds, West Yorkshire, England. Musician (guitar); Songwriter. *Education:* BA Hons Historical Studies (undergraduate). *Career:* Guitarist with Drill, 1990–91; Television: Elements, Channel 4/Tyne Tees, 1990–91; Skin Down, voted album of the wwek on BBC Network, 1991; Recently formed The Sojourners, 1994. *Compositions:* Currently writing material with The Sojourners. *Recordings:* Drill: Skin Down, 1991. *Membership:* Musicians' Union. *Address:* 13 St Joseph's Court, Heburn, Tyne and Wear NE31 2EN, England.

CRAIG, Jay; b. 15 Oct. 1958, Bellshill, Scotland. Musician (baritone saxophone). *Education:* Napier College, Edinburgh; Berklee College of Music, Boston, USA. *Career:* Member, National Youth Jazz Orchestra, 1976–81; Tommy Sampson Orchestra, Glasgow, 1979–82; Buddy Rich Band, 1984–87; BBC Big Band, 1992–; Performances with: Frank Sinatra; Tony Bennett; Sarah Vaughan; Jack Jones; Natalie Cole; Shirley Bassey; Vic Damone; Buddy Greco; Al Martino; Anita O'Day; Syd Lawrence Orchestra; BBC Scottish Radio Orchestra; Various West End shows. *Recordings:* 4 NYJO albums; with Buddy Rich: Live on King Street, San Francisco, 1985; Live In Leonberg, 1986; session work with: Terrorvision; Wet Wet Wet; George Martin. *Address:* 3 Park Way, Ruislip, Middlesex HA4 8PJ, England.

CRAIG, Mikey; b. 15 Feb. 1960, London, England. Musician (bass). *Career:* Member, with Boy George, In Praise of Lemmings; Became Sex Gang Children, then Culture Club; Numerous TV appearances and live dates; Band split, 1987; Worked as Record Producer; Band re-formed, 1998. *Recordings:*

Singles: Do You Really Want To Hurt Me (No. 1, UK), 1982; Time (Clock of the Heart), 1982; Church of the Poisoned Mind, 1983; Karma Chameleon (No. 1, UK and USA), 1983; Victims, 1983; It's A Miracle, 1983; The War Song, 1984; The Medal Song, 1984; Move Away, 1986; God Thank You Woman, 1986; I Just Wanna Be Loved, 1998; Your Kisses Are Charity, 1999; Albums: Kissing to be Clever, 1982; Colour By Numbers (No. 1, UK), 1983; Waking Up With the House on Fire, 1984; From Luxury To Heartache, 1986; Greatest Moments (Live), 1998; Don't Mind If I Do, 1999; Culture Club Box Set, 2002. Honours: BRIT Awards: Best British Newcomer, 1983; Best British Group, 1984; Best-Selling British Single, Karma Chameleon, 1984.

CRANITCH, Matt; b. 27 March 1948, Cork, Ireland. Traditional Musician (fiddle); Lecturer; Ethnomusicologist. m. Liz MacNamara, 17 July 1973, 2 s. Education: BE (Electrical Engineering), University College, Cork, Ireland; Cork School of Music, Ireland; BMus, University College, Cork. Career: Numerous concert performances as soloist, with Na Fili, with Any Old Time, with Sliabh Notes; Festival appearances include: Armagh; Belfast; Brest; Cambridge; Clifden; Cologne; Copenhagen; Cork; Cornwall; Dallas; Derry; Dingle; Dublin; Exeter; Killarney; Kilkenny; Galway; Inverness; Lenzburg; London; Loughborough; Milwaukee; New York; Norwich; Nyon; Orkney; Paris; Penzance; Quimper; Rome; Rotterdam; Shetland; Sligo; Swansea; Turin; Vienna; Radio and television shows include: Bring Down The Lamp; Cúrsaí; The Humours of Donnybrook; The Late Late Show; Live From The Cork Opera House; The Pure Drop; As I Roved Out; Bringing It All Back Home; Sult; Geantraí; Lectures, workshops, master-classes in Ireland and abroad; Research work, ongoing, Irish World Music Centre, University of Limerick; Sr Research Scholar, Government of Ireland, 2002–03; Director, Chairman, Cork Arts Fest, 1993–98. Recordings include: with Dave Hennessy and Mick Daly: Any Old Time, 1982; Phoenix, 1987; Crossing, 1995; Solo: Éistigh Seal, 1984; Take A Bow, 1992; Give It Stick, 1996; with Dónal Murphy and Tommy O'Sullivan: Sliabh Notes, 1995; Gleanntán, 1999; Along Blackwater's Banks, 2002. Publications: The Irish Fiddle Book, 1988, third edition, 1996; contributions to several books on Irish Traditional Music. Membership: Folk Music Society of Ireland; Irish Traditional Music Archive; Irish Music Rights Organisation. Address: Kerry Pike, Co Cork, Ireland.

CRAVEN, Beverly; b. 28 June 1963, Sri Lanka. Vocalist; Songwriter; Musician (piano). Education: Piano lessons. Career: Solo artiste, 1990–; British tour, 1993. Recordings include: Albums: Promise Me, 1990; Love Scenes, 1993; Mixed Emotions, 1999; Single: Promise Me, 1990. Honours: BRIT Award, Best British Newcomer, 1992. Address: c/o Sony Music Europe, A&R, Ricardo Fernandez, 10 Great Marlborough St, London W1V 2LP, England.

CRAWFORD, Randy (Randall Hugh); b. 16 Jan. 1953, Grand Rapids, Michigan, USA. Publisher; Cartoonist; Musician (Guitar). Education: Private instruction, guitar. Career: Wrote and acted in stage play Time Capsule; Wrote play Good Old Spot, performed at Grand Rapids Arts Fair; Interviews on TV to promote film Comic Book Confidential. Compositions: Autumn; Bothered; Sick; Black Velvet Elvis; Children of the Night. Recordings: Produced cassette box cover art, Acid Orangutan; CD cover art, Bloodsucking Mosquitos; Producer, Crooked Foot Live; Assembled compilations, Glove Box Sampler, Bad Exampler Sampler, Black Paper Packages. Publications: Issues on numerous magazines; Comic strip artist, The Three Pals. Honours: Student Award, Haiku, 1971. Membership: BMG Music Service, 1986–. Current Management: Nice Day. Address: 911 Park St SW, Grand Rapids, MI 49504, USA.

CRAWFORD, Randy (Veronica); b. 18 Feb. 1952, Macon, Georgia, USA. Vocalist. Career: Singer, 1967–; Appearances include: World Jazz Association tribute concert to Cannonball Adderley, 1968; Montreux Jazz Festival, 1982; 2 concerts with London Symphony Orchestra, Barbican Centre, London, 1988. Recordings: Singles include: Street Life (with The Crusaders), 1979; One Day I'll Fly Away, 1980; You Might Need Somebody, 1981; Rainy Night In Georgia, 1981; Almaz (own composition), 1987; Knockin' On Heaven's Door, used in film soundtrack Lethal Weapon 2, 1989; Guest vocalist, Diamante, Zucchero, 1992; Albums: Everything Must Change, 1976; Miss Randy Crawford, 1977; Raw Silk, 1979; Now We May Begin, 1980; Secret Combination, 1981; Windsong, 1982; Nightline, 1983; Casino Nights (with Al Jarreau), 1983; Miss Randy Crawford – The Greatest Hits, 1984; Abstract Emotions, 1986; The Love Songs, 1987; Rich and Poor, 1989; The Very Best Of, 1993; Don't Say It's Over, 1993; Naked and True, 1995; Every Kind of Mood – Randy Randi Randee 1998; Play Mode, 2001; Permanent, 2001; Guest vocalist on albums: Please Don't Touch, Steve Hackett, 1977; Marching In The Streets, Harvey Mason, 1978; Street Life, The Crusaders, 1979; Hard To Hold, Rick Springfield, 1984; Lethal Weapon 2, 1989; Best of Smooth Jazz, 1997; Jackie Brown, Music from the Motion Picture Soundtrack, 1997; Funky Jazz Party, 1998; Crusaders, Priceless Jazz, 1998; Classic Gold Vol. 2: The Love Song, 1999; Barry Williams, Return of Johnny Bravo, 1999. Honours: BRIT Award, Best Female Artist, 1982. Current Management: Gross Management Organisation, 930 Third St, Suite 102, Santa Monica, CA 90403, USA.

CRAWFORD, Stephanie; b. 30 Aug. 1942, Detroit, Michigan, USA. Vocalist; Artist; Educator. Education: BA, Fine Arts, Wayne State University, Detroit,

Michigan, USA; Music lessons with Barry Harris, Frank Foster, New York City. Career: Plays clubs and festivals including: Crest Jazz Festival; Aix-En-Provence Jazz Festival; Film appearance, La Vie En Rouge, 1995; Voice teacher, Centre d'Informations Musicales; Institut d'Art, Culture et Perception, Paris. Recordings: The Art of Romance, 1990; A Time For Love, 1991; The Gift, 1992. Honours: Django D'Or, Best Jazz Vocal, 1993. Address: 47 rue Piat, 75020 Paris, France.

CRAY, Robert William; b. 1 Aug. 1953, Columbus, Georgia, USA. Blues Musician (guitar); Vocalist; Songwriter. Career: Began playing guitar aged 12; Member, Albert Collins' band, 1973–75; Formed Robert Cray Band, 1975–; Appearances include: Chuck Berry's 60th Birthday Concert, 1986; US tour as Bad Influence, 1987; Support to Tina Turner, European tour, 1987; Support to Eric Clapton, Royal Albert Hall, London, 1990; Concert with Eric Clapton and Stevie Ray Vaughan (his last), East Troy, Wisconsin, 1990; Guitar Legends, Seville, Expo '92, 1991; Tour with B. B. King, 1992; Festival appearances include: Glastonbury Festival; North Sea Jazz Festival; Newport Jazz Festival; Monterey Jazz Festival; Montreux Jazz Festival; San Francisco Blues Festival; New Orleans Jazz and Heritage Festival; Other concert performances with: The Rolling Stones; Muddy Waters; John Lee Hooker; Willie Dixon; Bonnie Raitt; The Grateful Dead; Film appearances: Animal House; Hail! Hail! Rock and Roll. Compositions: Songs covered by other artists include: Bad Influence, Eric Clapton; Old Love (co-writer with Eric Clapton); Phone Booth, Albert King; Playin' With My Friends, B. B. King. Recordings: Albums: Who's Been Talking, 1980; Bad Influence, 1983; False Accusations, 1985; Strong Persuader, 1986; Don't Be Afraid of The Dark, 1988; Midnight Stroll, 1990; I Was Warned, 1992; Shame and A Sin, 1993; Some Rainy Morning, 1995; Sweet Potato Pie, 1997; In Concert (Live), 1999; Take Your Shoes Off, 1999; Shoulda Been Home, 2001; Singles include: Smoking Gun, 1987; Right Next Door (Because of Me), 1987; Forecast, 1990; Contributor, recordings by artists including: Albert Collins; Eric Clapton; Tina Turner; B. B. King; John Lee Hooker; Chuck Berry; Johnny Copeland; The Memphis Horns; Katie Webster. Honours: National Blues Awards, 1983, 1986; NAIRD Award, Best Blues Album, 1985; Grammy Awards, 1985, 1986, 1988; Numerous W. C. Handy Awards, 1984–, including 6 (Best Male Blues Artist, Vocalist of the Year, Single of the Year, Band of the Year, Song of the Year, Best Contemporary Blues Album), 1987; Numerous magazine awards, from Billboard; Downbeat; Rolling Stone; Esquire; Living Blues. Current Management: Eric Hanson, The Rosebud Agency, PO Box 170429, San Francisco, CA 94117, USA.

CREASEY, Jason M; b. 23 July 1969, Andover, Hampshire, England. Record Prod; Remixer; Composer; Arranger; Musician. Education: GCE A Level Music and Practical Music; Piano, Grade 8 (Trinity College of Music); Trumpet, Grade 8 (AB). Career: Extensive work in areas of writing, arranging, producing for various artists; Music to film; Keyboards and drum programming; Most recent productions in partnership with Hamish Hutchison (also known as remix duo Hiss and Hum for Absolute Basic Productions). Recordings: Producer (including arranging) for: Chesney Hawkes; Big Fun; Glen Goldsmith; Think 2wice (including writing); Deni Lew (additional production only); Remixer for: PJ and Duncan; Love City Groove; Jack 'n' Chill; Chesney Hawkes. Membership: PRS; MCPS; Musicians' Union. Address: 7 St John's St, Aylesbury, Buckinghamshire HP20 1BS, England.

CRÈME, Lol; b. 19 Sept. 1947, Manchester, Lancashire, England. Musician (guitar); Vocalist; Songwriter; Prod; Video and Film Dir. Education: Graphic design, art college. Career: Founder member, guitarist, songwriter, Hotlegs, 1970–71; 10cc, 1972–76; Appearances include: Reading Festival, 1974; Knebworth Festival, 1976; Tours of UK, USA; Producer, songwriter, member, duo Godley and Creme (with Kevin Godley), 1976–; Debut feature film, Howling At The Moon, 1988; Film director, The Lunatic, 1992; Joined Art of Noise, 1998–. Recordings: Albums: with Hotlegs: Thinks: School Stinks, 1970; with 10cc: 10cc, 1973; Sheet Music, 1974; The Original Soundtrack, 1975; How Dare You?, 1976; with Godley and Creme (mostly self-written and produced): Consequences, 1977; L, 1978; Music From Consequences, 1979; Freeze Frame, 1979; Ismism, 1981; Birds of Prey, 1983; The History Mix Vol 1, 1985; The Changing Faces of 10cc and Godley and Creme, 1987; Goodbye Blue Sky, 1988; Images, 1994; Hit singles: with Hotlegs: Neanderthal Man (No. 2, UK), 1970; with 10cc: Donna, 1972; Rubber Bullets (No. 1, UK), 1973; The Dean and I, 1973; Wall Street Shuffle, 1974; Life Is A Minestrone, 1975; I'm Not In Love (No. 1, UK, No. 2, USA), 1976; I'm Mandy Fly Me, 1976; Singles: Under Your Thumb, 1981; Wedding Bells, 1981; Cry, 1985; with Art of Noise: Album: The Seduction of Claude Debussy, 1999; Other session work includes: Tina Turner, Rod Stewart, Producer, Long Distant Romancer, Mickey Jupp, 1981; Director, videos including: Every Breath You Take, The Police; Rockit, Herbie Hancock; Feel The Love, 10cc; Relax, Frankie Goes To Hollywood; Two Tribes, Frankie Goes To Hollywood. Honours: Ivor Novello Awards: Best Beat Song, Rubber Bullets, 1974; Most Performed British Work, Best Pop Song, International Hit of the Year, I'm Not In Love, 1976; 5 MTV Music Video Awards, Rockit, 1984; MTV Video Vanguard Award (shared), 1985.

CRESSWELL, Guy; b. 17 May 1963, Bournemouth, England. Musical Entrepeneur; Musician (bass guitar, flute); Vocalist. m. Kate Snoswell.

Education: 4 year Engineering diploma. *Career:* Six-month tour Europe, R&B band, 1983; Move to London, joined Innocent Party, 1984; Nationwide tours with TSB Rockschool teaching Hi tech, 1985–86; Worked as music demonstrator, Roland UK Ltd, 1986–95; Television appearances with: The Sweet; Jools Holland; Midge Ure; Ton of Joy, 1991–94. *Recordings:* with Playing For Time: With My Heart, 1990; Six Weeks In July; with Ton of Joy: Revealed Part 1. *Membership:* PRS; Musicians' Union. *Current Management:* Promus Productions. *Address:* The Barley Mow Centre, 10 Barley Mow Passage, Chiswick, London W4 4PH, England.

CRETU, Michael; b. 18 May 1957, Bucharest, Romania. Musician (keyboards); Arranger; Prod; Composer. m. Sandra Lauer, 1988. *Education:* Piano Lyzeum No 2, Bucharest, 1966; Academy of Music, Frankfurt, 1975. *Career:* Studio musician, 1978–; Writer, producer, musician, Moti Special; Mike Oldfield; Sylvie Vartan; Sandra; 1983–; Founder member, Enigma, 1990–. *Recordings:* Albums: Solo album: Legionare, 1983; with Enigma: MCMXC AD, 1990; The Cross of Changes, 1993; Le Roi Est Mort, Vive Le Roi!, 1996; Screen Behind The Mirror, 2000; Love, Sensuality and Devotion (compilation), 2001; 6 albums with Sandra; Singles include: with Enigma: Sadeness (No. 1 across Europe), 1990; Return To Innocence, 1994; Maria Magdelena, Sandra (No. 1 in 30 countries); C'est Fatale, Sylvie Vartan; Writer, arranger, tracks for film soundtrack Sliver. *Honours:* Numerous Platinum and Gold discs as producer. *Current Management:* Nizzari Artist Management, 410 W 25th St, Suite 5A, New York, NY 10001, USA.

CRISS, Peter, (Peter Crisscoula); b. 27 Dec. 1947, Brooklyn, New York, USA. Musician (drums); Vocalist; Songwriter. *Career:* Founder member, US rock group Kiss, 1973–80, rejoined 1995; Debut, Academy of Music, New York, with Blue Öyster Cult; Iggy Pop; Teenage Lust; Tours include UK, 1976; Solo artiste, 1980–82; Member, Balls of Fire. *Recordings:* Albums with Kiss: Kiss, 1974; Hotter Than Hell, 1974; Dressed To Kill, 1975; Alive, 1975; Destroyer, 1976; The Originals, 1976; Rock and Roll Over, 1976; Kiss Alive II, 1977; Love Gun, 1977; Double Platinum, 1978; Dynasty, 1979; MTV Unplugged, 1996; Psycho Circus, 1998; Solo albums: Peter Criss, 1978; Out of Control, 1980; Let Me Rock You, 1982; Criss Cat #1, 1994. *Publications:* The Kiss Comic Book, Marvel Comics. *Honours:* Platinum albums; Footprints outside Grauman's Chinese Theatre, Hollywood, 1976; Gold Ticket, Madison Square Garden, New York. *Current Management:* GHR Entertainment Co, Suite 506, 16601 Ventura Blvd, Encino, CA 91436, USA.

CROISILLE, Nicole; b. 9 Oct. 1936, Neuilly-Sur-Seine, France. Vocalist; Actress. *Career:* Tour with mime artist, Marcel Marceau; Lead role, musical, L'Apprenti Fakir; First record, 1961; Worked in USA with Lester Wilson, Lalo Schifrin; Un Homme Et Une Femme (A Man and A Woman), 1966; Olympia, Paris, 1976, 1978; Theatre des Champs-Elysées, Paris, 1981; Bataclan, Paris, 1988; Casino de Paris, 1991; Lead role, Hello Dolly, Thèatre du Chatelet, Paris, 1992–93; Actress, Les Miserables du XXe Siècle, 1995; Appearances: Canada; Latin America; Poland; Morocco; New show at Espace Pierre Cardin Theatre, Paris, 1997. *Recordings include:* Un Homme Et Une Femme; Parlez-Moi De Lui; Femme Avec Toi; T'arrai Voulu Etre Un Artiste; Albums: Croiselle Jazzille; Croiselle Black Et Blanche. *Honours:* Chevalier des Arts et des Lettres. *Membership:* SACEM. *Current Management:* Bertrand Tallec, Showstop Management. *Address:* 64 Château Trompette, 78950 Gambais, France.

CROKER, Brendan; b. 15 Aug. 1953, Bradford, Yorkshire, England. Musician (guitar). *Education:* Studied sculpture, art school. *Career:* Formed duo, Nev and Norris, with fellow guitarist Steve Phillips; Formed own band, the 5 O'Clock Shadows, early 1980s; Member, Notting Hillbillies (with Mark Knopfler, Guy Fletcher, Steve Phillips), 1990; British tour, 1990. *Recordings:* Albums: Close Shave, 1986; Brendan Croker and The 5 O'Clock Shadows, 1989; The Great Indoors, 1992; The Kershaw Sessions, 1996; Not Just A Hillbilly, 2000; with the Notting Hillbillies: Missing... Presumed Having, 1990; Guest musician, Ancient Heart, Tanita Tikaram; Singles: That's The Way All My Money Goes, 1986. *Current Management:* Paul Crockford Management, 56–60 Islington Park St, London N1 1PX, England.

CROMPHOUT, Francis; b. 24 Oct. 1947, Antwerp, Belgium. Vocalist; Songwriter; Musician (saxophone, clarinet, flute). m. Alejandra Anfossi, 20 Jan. 1994, 2 d. *Education:* University Degree in Roman Languages, Ghent State University. *Career:* Several performances in Jazz, Blues and Latin music; Creator and Performer, En Avian La Zizique, song programme around Boris Vian; Founder, Band Leader, Cuisine Cajun and Café con Leche; Songwriter, Cuisine Cajun, Café con Leche and Catherine Delasalle; Concerts in Holland, Germany, Belgium, France; Emmissions in VRT Radio and the RTBF Television. *Compositions include:* Allons au Fais-Do-Do; Le Grand Dérangement, Cofé Bon Dieu, Démarche, (Pigalle). *Recordings:* Le Grand Dérangement, 1996. *Publications:* Als un pas vernielde stad, poetry, 1978. *Honours:* Chevalier dans l'Ordre des Palmes Académiques. *Membership:* SABAM, Belgian Asscn of Authors and Composers; Country and Western Asscn of Belgium. *Current Management:* Berkenhof 7, 9050 Ghent, Belgium. *Address:* Berkenhof 7, 9050 Ghent, Belgium.

CRONIN, Kevin; b. 6 Oct. 1951, Evanston, Illinois, USA. Vocalist; Songwriter. *Career:* Lead vocalist, US rock group REO Speedwagon, 1972; 1976–; Solo artiste, 1973–76; Regular US and international concerts include: Anti-drug Users Are Losers concert, Miami, 1990. *Compositions include:* Keep On Loving You; Can't Fight This Feeling; Hard To Believe, for Home Front Trust (for families of Gulf War casualties). *Recordings:* Albums: with REO Speedwagon: R.E.O. T.W.O., 1972; R.E.O., 1976; REO Speedwagon Live/You Get What You Play For, 1977; You Can Tune A Piano But You Can't Tuna Fish, 1978; Nine Lives, 1979; A Decade of Rock 'N' Roll 1970–80, 1980; Hi Infidelity (No. 1, USA), 1981; Good Trouble, 1982; Wheels Are Turning, 1984; Best Foot Forward, 1985; Life As We Know It, 1987; The Hits, 1988; The Earth, A Small Man, His Dog and A Chicken, 1990; A Second Decade of Rock 'N' Roll, 1981–91, 1991; Building the Bridge, 1996; Ballads, 1999; Live Plus, 2001; Hit singles include: Time For Me To Fly, 1978; Keep On Loving You (No. 1, USA), 1981; Take It On The Run, 1981; Don't Let Him Go, 1981; Keep The Fire Burnin', 1982; I Can't Fight This Feeling (No. 1, USA), 1985; One Lonely Night, 1985; That Ain't Love, 1987; In My Dreams, 1987. *Honours:* Platinum and Gold discs. *Current Management:* Baruck-Consolo Management, 15003 Greenleaf St, Sherman Oaks, CA 91403, USA.

CRONK, William Henry; b. 28 Aug. 1928, Fort Lee, New Jersey, USA. Musician (bass violin, electric bass); Arranger. m. Mary Reisinger, 10 Dec. 1947, divorced, 1 s., 1 d. *Education:* Bass, with M. Hinton, G Duvivier, Robert Brennand; Arranging, with Sy Oliver, Hugo Winterhalter. *Career:* 52nd Street, NYC, with Don Byas, 1945; Tony Pastor, Ray Anthony, Ralph Flanagan, 1946; Joined Tommy Dorsey, 1950; United with Jimmy Dorsey to form The Fabulous Dorseys, 1952; Became associated with Jackie Gleason Show, 1950s; Recorded with: Tommy Dorsey; Jimmy Dorsey; Ray Anthony; Ralph Flanagan; Ray McKinley; Bobby Hackett; Joined Louis Armstrong, early 1960s; Playboy Resort Hotel, New Jersey, 1970s; Playboy In Atlantic City, 1980s; Formed own band for the Meyer Davis Off. *Membership:* AFofM (New York and New Jersey). *Current Management:* Own company, Bel-Cron Music. *Address:* William H Cronk Sr, 400 W 43rd St, Apt 44R, New York, NY 10036, USA.

CROOK, Jenny; b. 16 Jan. 1971, Bath, Avon, England. Musician (non-pedal harp); Vocalist. *Education:* BA Hons, Performance Arts, Middlesex University. *Career:* Folk clubs and Festivals; Television appearances include: Pebble Mill; Summer In The City; Radio appearances in sessions for Folk On 2; Kaleidoscope; Played incidental music, David Attenborough's television series, The Private Life of Plants, BBC; Played at Barbican Festival; Current band, Madigan; Composed theme tume for S4C Club Gweryn series; Session musician and recording artist; Member of Duo, Jenny Crook and Henry Sears; Cythara, duo with Maclaine Colston (hammered dulcimer, vocals), 1991–95. *Recordings:* Evolving Tradition; Cythara, 1992; Pluckin' Hammered, 1995; Uncorked, 1997. *Honours:* Young Tradition Award Finalist, BBC Radio 2, 1993. *Membership:* Musicians' Union; PRS; PAMRA; Clarsach Society. *Address:* 8 Walcot Terrace, London Rd, Bath BA1 6AB, England.

CROSBY, David, (David Van Cortland); b. 14 Aug. 1941, Los Angeles, California, USA. Vocalist; Musician (guitar). m. Jan Dance, 15 May 1987. *Career:* Member, Les Baxter's Balladeers; The Byrds, 1964–67; Crosby Stills and Nash, 1968–; Also, Crosby Stills Nash and Young; Performances include: with the Byrds: Monterey Pop Festival, 1967; with Crosby Stills and Nash: Woodstock Festival, 1969; Altamont Speedway, with the Rolling Stones, 1969; Royal Albert Hall, 1970; Wembley Stadium, 1974; Anti-nuclear concert, Madison Square Garden, New York, 1979; Peace Sunday concert, Rose Bowl, Pasadena, 1982; Live Aid, Philadelphia, 1985; Madison Square Garden, 1988; Amnesty International benefit, Chile, 1990; Farm Aid IV, 1990; Royal Albert Hall, 1992; Film, No Nukes, 1980; Television: guest, Roseanne, ABC TV, 1992; The Simpsons, Fox TV, 1993; Collaborations include: Jeff Bridges; Jackson Browne; Phil Collins; Bob Dylan; Art Garfunkel; Carole King; Joni Mitchell; Stevie Nicks; Neil Young. *Recordings:* Albums include: with the Byrds: Mr Tambourine Man, 1965; Turn! Turn! Turn!, 1965; Fifth Dimension, 1966; Younger Than Yesterday, 1967; with Crosby Stills and Nash include: Crosby Stills and Nash, 1969; Déja Vu, 1970; 4-Way Street, 1971; So Far, 1974; Daylight Again, 1982; ; Looking Forward, 1999; with Graham Nash: Graham Nash/David Crosby, 1972; Wind On The Water, 1975; Whistling Down The Wire, 1976; Crosby/Nash Live, 1977; The Best Of, 1978; Another Stoney Evening, 1998; Solo albums: If Only I Could Remember My Name, 1971; Oh Yes I Can, 1989; Now It's All Coming Back To Me, 1995; King Biscuit Flower Hour, 1996; Live, 2000; Singles include: with the Byrds: Mr Tambourine Man (No. 1, UK and USA), 1965; All I Really Want To Do, 1965; Eight Miles High, 1966; 5D (Fifth Dimension), 1966; Mr Spaceman, 1966; So You Want To Be A Rock 'n' Roll Star, 1967; with Crosby Stills and Nash: Woodstock, 1970; Teach Your Children, 1970; Ohio, 1970; Just A Song Before You Go, 1977; Wasted On The Way, 1982; Southern Cross, 1982. *Publications include:* Stand Up and Be Counted, 2000. *Honours:* Grammy, Best New Artists, Crosby Stills and Nash, 1970; Best International Group, Melody Maker Poll, 1971; MusiCares Man of the Year, NARAS, 1991. *Current Management:* Management Network Inc, 14930 Ventura Blvd #205, Sherman Oaks, CA 91403, USA.

CROSS, Christopher, (Christopher Geppert); b. 3 May 1951, San Antonio, Texas, USA. Musician (guitar); Vocalist; Songwriter. *Career:*

Member, rock group Flash; Support for acts including Led Zeppelin, Jefferson Airplane, Deep Purple; Formed band for own compositions, 1975; Recording artist, 1978; Own publishing company, Pop 'n' Roll, 1978. *Compositions include:* Co-writer (with Burt Bacharach, Carole Bayer Sager, Peter Allen): Arthur's Theme (Best That You Can Do), for film Arthur, 1981. *Recordings:* Albums include: Christopher Cross, 1980; Another Page, 1983; Every Turn of The World, 1985; Back of My Mind, 1988; Rendezvous, 1992; Window, 1995; Walking in Avalon, 1998; Greatest Hits Live, 1999; Red Room, 2000; Singles include: Ride Like The Wind, 1980; Sailing (No. 1, USA), 1980; Never Be The Same, 1980; Say You'll Be Mine, 1981; Arthur's Theme (No. 1, USA), 1981; All Right, 1983; No Time To Talk, 1983; Think of Laura, 1983; A Chance For Heaven (used as swimming theme for Los Angeles Olympics), 1984; Contributor, Pearls – Songs of Goffin and King, Carole King, 1980; Film soundtrack, Nothing In Common, 1986; As co-producer: Long Time Friends, Alessi Brothers, 1982. *Honours:* Grammy Awards: Album of the Year, Christopher Cross; Best New Artist; Record of the Year, Sailing; Song of the Year, Sailing; Best Arrangement, Sailing, (all) 1981; Academy Award, Best Song From A Film, Arthur's Theme, 1982. *Current Management:* Baruck/Consolo, 15003 Greenleaf St, Sherman Oaks, CA 91043, USA.

CROSSLEY, Syd; b. 10 Aug. 1961, Ilford, East London, England. Musician (saxophones, flute, keyboards, guitars); Vocalist; Programmer. 1 s. *Career:* Songwriter, saxophone, Bastard Bros Band, 1986; Songwriter, saxophone, lead vocalist, The Never Again With Rob Barham Band, 1987; Vocalist, co-songwriter, saxophone, Trip Cadets, 1988–91; Co-songwriter, saxophone, The Rubber Club, 1991; Co-songwriter, saxophone, Fat Cat Band, 1992–93; Co-songwriter, artist, programmer, Boom Devils, 1994–95; Co-songwriter, programmer, artist, King Kooba Triptet, 1995, appearances on various King Kooba tracks; Remixes for Senser; Co-songwriter and programmer in geko and itones. *Recordings:* Life's A Bummer EP, Trip Cadets, 1991; Albums: Saxophonist, Seven, James (No. 1, UK), 1992; Currently completing albums: One Minute Away From Perfection, and Metamorphosis, Boom Devils; The Dub Commander Lands On The Kooba Twins, King Kooba Triptet; Roof Top Dub, Itones; King Kooba Triptet EP; Single remix, Utah Saints. *Membership:* Musicians' Union; Founder mem., The Rubber Club. *Current Management:* Boom Devil Productions. *Address:* 236 Canbury Park Rd, Kingston upon Thames, Surrey, England.

CROUCHER, Piers; b. 1 Nov. 1969, Minehead, Somerset, England. Musician (drums, percussion, guitar). Partner, Sadie Doyle. *Education:* Music lessons with Tommy Cuncliffe, Jersey. *Career:* Member, Zapf The Band; Air Stream Stream Trailer; The Bar Flies; Summer seasons, Jersey; Lucy and Freud. *Recordings:* 2 EPs: Lucy and Freud; Field Day. *Membership:* Equity; Musicians' Union. *Current Management:* Robert Smith, Bristol. *Address:* 16 Poundfield Rd, Minehead, Somerset TA24 5EP, England.

CROW, Bill; b. 27 Dec. 1927, Othello, Washington, USA. Musician (bass). m. Aileen Armstrong, 1965, 1 s. *Career:* Bassist, various artists including: Stan Getz; Claude Thorhill; Marian McPartland; Gerry Mulligan; Zoot Sims; Bob Brookmeyer; Clark Terry; Benny Goodman; Walter Norris; Peter Duchin; Musician, Broadway shows, 1975–89. *Publications:* Contributor, The Jazz Review; Jazz Letter; Author: Jazz Anecdotes, 1990. *Membership:* AFofM. *Address:* c/o American Federation of Musicians, New York, USA.

CROW, Sheryl; b. 11 Feb. 1962, Kennett, Missouri, USA. Vocalist; Songwriter; Musician (guitar). *Education:* Classical Music degree, Missouri State University; Organ and piano lessons. *Career:* Backing singer, Michael Jackson tour, 18 months; Also backing singer for Joe Cocker; Rod Stewart; Don Henley; Songwriter, solo performer, mid 1980s–; International concerts and tours with John Hiatt; Crowded House; Big Head Todd; Support tours to Bob Dylan; Eagles, 1994; Joe Cocker, Wembley Arena, 1994; Performed at Woodstock II, 1994. *Recordings:* Albums: Tuesday Night Music Club, 1993; Sheryl Crow, 1996; The Globe Sessions, 1998; Sheryl Crow and Friends: Live in Central Park, 1999; C'mon C'mon, 2002. Singles include: All I Wanna Do, 1994; Leaving Las Vegas, 1994; Strong Enough, 1994; Can't Cry Anymore, 1995; If It Makes You Happy, 1996; Everyday Is A Winding Road, 1996; My Favorite Mistake, 1998; There Goes The Neighbourhood, 1998; Anything But Down, 1999; Sweet Child O' Mine, 1999; Soak Up The Sun, 2002; Contributor, albums: The End of Innocence, Don Henley, 1989; Late Night, Neal Schon, 1989; Other recordings by Eric Clapton; Wynnona Judd; Contributor, film soundtracks: Kalifornia, 1994; Leaving Las Vegas, 1995. *Honours:* 3 Grammy Awards, Tuesday Night Music Club, 1995; BRIT Award, Best International Female Artist, 1997; American Music Award, Best Female Pop/Rock Artist, 2003. *Address:* c/o A & M Records Inc, 595 Madison Ave, New York, NY 10022, USA. *Website:* www.sherylcrow.com.

CROWE, Mark Robert; b. 22 May 1958, Wolverhampton, England. Musician (Saxophone, Clarinet, Flute, Oboe); Arranger. m. Dolores Petrovich, 26 April 1986, divorced, Dec. 1995. *Education:* Wulfrun College, Wolverhampton; GDLM, City of Leeds College of Music; LGSM, Guildhall School of Music; LTCL, Trinity College; PGCE, University of Central England; MA, Monash University, Melbourne, Australia. *Career:* Summer Seasons, 1978–79; P & O Cruising, 1980; QE2 Orchestra, 1983–85; Freelance, London, 1985–89; Theatre Musician and Teacher, Melbourne, 1989–95,

including Cats, La Cage aux Folles, Aspects of Love; QE2 Orchestra, 1996–98; P & O Arcadia, 1998. *Compositions:* Same Time Same Place, 1980; Chaser 1, 1982; Smallbrook Queensway, 1982; Spyro Tap, 1994. *Recordings:* Midland Youth Jazz Orchestra, 1975; Mick Urry Orchestra, 1985; Australia Cotton Club Orchestra, Rhapsody in Red, 1993. *Membership:* Musicians' Union. *Address:* 10 Trentham Close, Paignton, Devon TQ3 3GF, England.

CROWELL, Rodney; b. 7 Aug. 1950, Houston, Texas, USA. Country Vocalist; Songwriter; Musician (guitar). Prod. 4 d. *Career:* Member, songwriter, Emmylou Harris' Hot Band, 1974–79; Worked with Willie Nelson; Ry Cooder; Jim Keltner; Solo artiste, and with own band, 1978–. *Compositions:* 10 US Country No. 1 hits; Songs for Emmylou Harris include: Bluebird Wine, 1974; Till I Gain Control Again, 1975; I Ain't Living Long Like This, 1979; Leaving Louisiana In The Broad Daylight, 1979; 250 versions of own compositions recorded by artists including: Willie Nelson; Foghat; Bob Seger; The Dirt Band; Waylon Jennings; George Jones. *Recordings:* US Country No. 1 hits include: It's Such A Small World, with Roseanne Cash; I Couldn't Leave You If I Tried; She's Crazy For Leaving; Albums: Ain't Living Long Like This, 1978; But What Will The Neighbours Think, 1980; Rodney Crowell, 1981; Street Language, 1986; Diamonds and Dirt, 1988; The Rodney Crowell Collection, 1989; Keys To The Highway, 1989; Life Is Messy, 1992; Jewel of The South, 1995; Soul Searchin, 1995; The Houston Kid, 2001; As producer: recordings for: Guy Clark; Albert Lee; Carl Perkins; Jerry Lee Lewis; Bobby Bare; Roseanne Cash; Lari White; Brady Seals; Beth Nielsen Chapman. *Honours:* Grammy Award, Best Country Song, After All This Time, 1990. *Membership:* CMA; Nashville Songwriters' Assocn; NARAS. *Current Management:* Gold Mountain Entertainment, Suite 450, 3575 Cahuenga Blvd W, Los Angeles, CA 90068, USA. *Address:* c/o Beth Torrell, RC One, PO Box 120576, Nashville, TN 37212, USA.

CRUCIAL BANKIE, (Ian Veira); b. 23 Nov. 1965, St Kitts. Musician (guitar, keyboard); Vocalist. 1 s. *Career:* Bunny Wailer First Antigua Show; Numerous radio broadcasts; Reggae Sunsplash, with Sagittarius Band, 1986, Stud Band, 1988; Performed with: Leroy Horsemouth Wallace; Jose Whale; Brigadier Jerry; Buju Banton; Legendary Bunny Wailer. *Recordings:* Just A Sting, 1978; Sweet Reggae Muzik, 1994; Film: Uptown, soundtrack. *Publications:* The New Music of Reviews. *Membership:* ASCAP. *Current Management:* African Shrine Management. *Address:* 196 Fourth Ave, Suite 2L, Brooklyn, NY 11217, USA.

CRUST, Geoffrey Leonard; b. 30 March 1945, Boston, Lincolnshire, England. Songwriter; Publisher; Musician (guitars, keyboards). m. 5 Oct. 1984, 2 d. *Education:* Privately taught, plus cadet musician, as drummer. *Career:* Songs on Songwriter Round Up albums, 1–4, featuring Ray Jones; Albums: Modern Country Melodies; USA/UK album; Country Headaches. *Compositions:* 67 published songs, both in UK, USA; Songs on 4 American albums with Music Room Records; Sollie Sunshine Records, USA. *Publications:* 15A Magazines, Brum Country Magazine, Spain, Denmark. *Membership:* PRS; MCPS; TMA; ISA; BCMA; PPL Umbrella. *Current Management:* Thatch Records (own publishing company and record label). *Address:* 31 Tower St, Boston, Lincolnshire, England.

CRUZ, Celia; b. 21 Oct. 1924, Havana, Cuba. Vocalist. m. Pedro Knight, 14 July 1962. *Education:* Teacher training; Classes at National Conservatory of Music, Havana. *Career:* First prize, Cuban radio talent show; Member, group Gloria Mantecera; Tours, Mexico, Venezuela, with Roderico Neyra's dance troupe, Las Mulatas de Fuego; Lead vocalist, Sonora Matancera, Radio Progreso, 1950; Recording artiste, 1951–; Collaborations with Tito Puente; Johnny Pacheco; Album debut with Fania All Stars, 1975; UK debut, 1976; Tours with Fania All Stars, Africa; Europe; Regular UK appearances with Tito Puente, 1984–; Subject, television documentary My Name Is Celia Cruz, Arena, BBC TV, 1988; Film appearances: Salsa, 1976; The Mambo Kings Play Songs of Love, 1991. *Recordings:* Albums: Solo: La Excitante Celia Cruz!, 1968; Etc Etc Etc, 1970; Tremendo Caché, 1975; Azuca Negra, 1993; with Tito Puente: Cuba y Puerto Rico Son, 1966; Son Con Guaguanco, 1966; Quimbo Quimbumbia, 1969; Alma Con Alma, 1971; Algo Especial Para Recordar, 1972; Homenaje A Beny Moré Vol. III, 1985; Siempre Viviré, 2000; La Negra Tiene Tumbao, 2002; with Willie Colón: Only They Could Have Made This Album, 1977; Celia y Willie, 1981; The Winners, 1987; with Memo Salamanca: Bravo, 1967; A Ti Mexico, 1968; Serenata Guajira, 1968; Nuevos Exitos de Celia Cruz, 1971; with Johnny Pacheco: Celia and Johnny, 1974; Recordando El Ayer, 1976; Eternos, 1978; De Nuevo, 1985; with Ray Barretto: Tremendo Trio!, 1983; Ritmo En El Corazón, 1988; with Sonora Matancera: Feliz Encuentro, 1982; Live! From Carnegie Hall – 65th Anniversary Celebration, 1989; Azucar Negra, 1993; Homenaje A Los Santos, 1994; Double Dynamite, 1995; Fieston Tropical, 1998. *Honours:* Hon. doctorate, Yale University, 1989; Grammy Award, 1990; Star on Hollywood Walk of Fame, 1990; Latin Grammy Award, Best Salsa Album, for La Negra Tiene Tumbao, 2002. *Current Management:* Ralph Mercado Management, 568 Broadway, Suite 806, New York, NY 10012, USA.

CUBER, Ronnie; b. 25 Dec. 1941, Brooklyn, New York, USA. Musician (Baritone Saxophone). m. Roberta Arnold, 2 s. *Education:* Brooklyn Conservatory of Music. *Career:* Film: Borgia Stick; TV appearances, Saturday

Night Live, 1979–85; Appearances on BBC Radio, National public radio; Played at every major jazz festival in Europe, USA and Japan; Masterclasses and clinics. *Compositions:* Airplay; Passion Fruit; Waltz Furgeralous. *Recordings:* Cuber Libre, 1976; The Eleventh Day of Aquarius, 1978; New York Jazz, 1981; Passion Fruit, 1985; Two Brothers King, 1985; Pin Point, 1985; Best of Ronnie Cuber, 1985; Live At Blue Note, 1986; Scean is Clean, 1993; Three Baritone Saxophone Band, 1998. *Honours:* Talent Deserving Greater Recognition, 1964. *Membership:* DARAS; AFM. *Current Management:* Roberta Arnold. *Address:* 5219 N 24 St, Phoenix, AZ 85016, USA.

CUBIC U. See: **UTADA, Hikaru.**

CUGNY, Laurent; b. 14 April 1955, La Garenne-Colombes, France. Bandleader; Arranger; Musician (piano). m. Philippe Joëlle, 8 Feb. 1992, 1 s., 1 d. *Education:* BA, Economics, Cinema; Piano lessons, aged 10–14. *Career:* Founder, Lumière Big Band, 1979; European tour, Lumière and Gil Evans, 1987; Director, Orchestre National de Jazz (ONJ), 1994–97; European tour, ONJ and Lucky Peterson, 1995. *Recordings:* with Lumière and Gil Evans: Rhythm-A-Ning, 1988; Golden Hair, 1989; with Lumière: Santander, 1991; Dromesko, 1993; with ONJ: Yesternow, 1994; with Abbey Lincoln: A Turtle's Dream, 1995; With Orchestra National de Jazz: Reminiscing, 1995; In Tempo, 1995; Merci, Merci, Merci, 1996. *Publications:* Las Vegas Tango – Une Vie De Gil Evans, 1989; Electrique Miles Davis, 1993. *Honours:* Django Reinhardt Award, Jazz Academy, 1991; Charles-Cros Academy Award, 1991. *Current Management:* Memo, 17 rue de l'Abbé Carton, 75014 Paris, France. *Address:* 5 rue Leon Giraud, 75019 Paris, France.

CUILLERIER, Philippe 'Doudou'; b. 5 Sept. 1961, Versailles, France. Musician (guitar); Lyricist. *Education:* Saxophone from age 7; Guitar from age 17; Lessons with Eric Boell, Frederic Sylvestre. *Career:* Guitar teacher, 1983–; Backing guitarist with: Angelo Debarre; Romane Quintet; Lead guitarist, vocalist with: Fernando Jazz Gang; Little Big Man (blues). *Recordings:* with Fernando Jazz Gang: Gipsy Violin, Swing Guitars; Gipsy Songs; with Romane Quartet: Quintet. *Address:* 2 Ruelle des Poulies, 78490 Montfort-l'Amaury, France.

CULLAZ, Alby; b. 25 June 1941, Paris, France. Musician (double bass). 1 s., 1 d. *Education:* Classical professors for piano and bass. *Career:* Backing for soloists: J Griffin; D Gordon; K Drew; Kenny Clark; H Mobley; Slide Hampton; Philly Joe Jones; Steve Grossman; René Urtreger; Chet Baker; Dee Dee Bridgewater; Alain Jean Marie; Art Farmer; Eric Lelann; Christian Escoude; Jean Luc Pouty; Michel Graillier; Art Taylor. *Recordings:* The Flip, with H Mobley, 1969; Reflections, with Steve Grosman and Simon Goubert, 1990; Duo with Christian Escoude; Jeff Gilson Big Band; Michel Grailler Trio; Christian Escoude Octet; Tac Tic, J. P. Foughet; Recidive, René Urtreger; Pure Be-Bop, 1998. *Honours:* Django Reinhardt Prize, 1973. *Address:* 52 rue du General Delestraint, 75016 Paris, France.

CULLAZ, Pierre Maurice Louis; b. 21 July 1935, Paris, France. Musician (guitar); Teacher. m. Rita Castellano, 24 Feb. 1964. *Education:* Classical, Jazz music, guitar. *Career:* Studio work; Jazz clubs; Tours with many singers; Contemporary classical music; Currently, extensive teaching, mainly jazz guitar. *Publications:* A Guitar Method, edited by Alphonse Leduc. *Address:* 1 rue Charlot, 75003 Paris, France.

CULLIMORE, Stan; b. 6 April 1962, Hull, England. Musician (bass). *Career:* Member, The Housemartins; Obtained recording contract; Numerous television appearances; Live dates including Red Wedge tour; Band split, 1988; Latterly author of children's books. *Recordings:* Singles: Flag Day, 1985; Sheep, 1986; Happy Hour, 1986; Think for a Minute, 1986; Caravan of Love (No. 1, UK) 1986; Five Get Over Excited, 1987; Me and the Farmer, 1987; Build, 1987; There is Always Something There to Remind Me, 1988; Albums: London 0 Hull 4, 1986; The People Who Grinned Themselves to Death, 1987; Now That's What I Call Quite Good, 1988. *Publications include:* The Turtle Who Danced With A Crane; Spider Boy; Long Live The Boy King; Where's Blinky?.

CUMMINGS, Daniel; Musician (percussion); Musical Dir. 1 s. *Career:* Colaborations: Dire Straits, On Every Street, Tour, 1991–92; Tina Turner; George Michael; Simply Red, Life, album; Bon Jovi, Sophie B Hawkins; Brian Kennedy; Incognito; A1; Bryan Adams; Associates; Clannad; Depeche Mode; Tim Finn; Elton John; Lighthouse Family; John Martyn; Pet Shop Boys; Pulp; David Sylvian; The The. *Recordings:* Albums: Dire Straits, On Every Street, UK No 1; Tina Turner, Foreign Affair, UK No 1; George Michael: Without Prejudice, UK No 1; Careless Whisper, UK No 1; Wham, Make It Big!, UK No 1; Holly Johnson, Blast, UK No 1. *Membership:* Musicians' Union. *Current Management:* One Management, 43 St Alban's Ave, London W4 5JS, England.

CUMMINS, Paul; b. 13 Oct. 1953, Portsmouth, Hampshire, England. Artist Man. m. Janice Bellamy, 25 June 1988. *Career:* Tour manager, 1975–79; Artists: Talking Heads; Andy Fairweather-Low; Jesse Winchester; XTC; Gallagher and Lyle; Manager, tour manager, Dire Straits, 1979–. *Current Management:* Damage Management, 16 Lambton Pl., London W11 4LQ, England.

CUNNAH, Peter; b. 30 Aug. 1966, Belfast, Northern Ireland. Vocalist; Songwriter; Performer; Musician (guitar). *Education:* York St Art College, University of Ulster. *Career:* Singer, songwriter with D:ream; songwriter for A1, 2000; Tours and concerts: Support tour with Take That, UK and Europe; UK, 1993, 1994; Australia, 1994; Gay Pride, London; T In The Park, Glasgow; Fri Rock Festival, Copenhagen; Stonewall, Royal Albert Hall, London; Fleadh Festival, London; Gay Games, New York. *Recordings:* Albums: D:ream On Vol. 1, 1993; World, 1995; The Best of D:ream, 2000; Singles include: U R The Best Thing, 1992 (re-released 1993, 1994); Things Can Only Get Better, (No. 1, UK), 1993 (re-released 1997); Unforgiven, 1993; Star/I Like It, 1993; Take Me Away, 1994; Shoot With Me Your Love, 1995; Party Up The World, 1995; The Power (of All The Love In The World), 1995; Remixes for: Deborah Harry; Duran Duran; EMF. *Honours:* IDA Best Dance Act, 1993. *Current Management:* Mark Beder, FXU Records, 97A Scrubs Lane, London NW10 6QU, England.

CUNNINGHAM, Christopher John; b. 7 June 1970, Droylsden, Manchester, England. Musician (acoustic guitar, electric guitar, electronic guitar). *Education:* Tameside College of Technology. *Career:* Toured Ireland and Ulster with Indie guitar band, Poors of Reign; Guitarist for Gavin Friday, 1992–95; Several appearances, mostly musical and some theatrical, on local and national television including Juice, for Granada TV. *Compositions:* Over 200 songs written for guitar, bass and drums. *Membership:* Musicians' Union. *Current Management:* James Joseph Cunningham. *Address:* 37 Wordsworth Ave, Droylsden, Greater Manchester M43 6GA, England.

CUNNINGHAM, Déirdre Mary Gerradine; b. 31 May 1956, Sutton, Surrey, England. Vocalist; Songwriter; Musician (acoustic guitar). m. Liam Cunningham, July 1977, 1 s. *Education:* Secretarial. *Career:* Tours: France; Germany; Netherlands; Ireland; Switzerland; Sweden; Denmark; Finland; Norway; England; Wales; Radio broadcasts: RTE Radio; BBC Radio; First single playlisted on national and local radio; Current album play-listed; Regular appearances on Irish national television, Welsh national television; Tour of Japan, Singapore and Philippines, 1998. *Recordings:* Albums: City of Tribes, 1996; Sunny Days; Cry From the Heart, 1998; Singles: Take Me For A Fool; Hurry Make Love. *Publications:* City of Tribes; Sunny Days; Irish Contemporary Songs; In progress, new album Song of the River. *Membership:* IASC; ISA; IMRO; MCPS. *Current Management:* Lake Records, Cootehall, Boyle, Co Roscommon, Ireland.

CUNNINGHAM, Philip Martin; b. 27 Jan. 1960, Edinburgh, Scotland. Composer; Accordionist; Music Dir; Prod. m. Donna Macrae, 24 Dec. 1982, 1 d. *Education:* Private music tuition from age 3. *Career:* Tours of UK, Europe and USA; Music Director of four series, over 4 years, of Talla A' Bhaile, for BBC Scotland; Music Director, Presenter, Hogmanay Live, for BBC, 1991–94; Co-presenter of weekly radio series, Live From The Lemon Tree, for BBC. *Compositions:* Music for Bill Bryden theatre productions, The Ship and The Big Picnic; Orchestral Suite, premiered 1996; Compositions used for film soundtrack Last of The Mohicans. *Honours:* Hon. Citizen, Reading, Pennsylvania, USA; M.B.E., 2002. *Membership:* Musicians' Union. *Current Management:* Donna Cunningham. *Address:* Cunningham Audio Productions Ltd, Crask of Aigas, By Beauly, Inverness IV4 7AD, Scotland.

CUNNINGHAM, Tom; b. 22 June 1965, Glasgow, Scotland. Musician (drums). *Career:* Member, Wet Wet Wet, 1982–97; Formed The Sleeping Giants, 1999; Performances include: Greenpeace charity concert, Royal Albert Hall, London, 1986; Support to Lionel Richie, British tour, 1987; Prince's Trust Rock Gala, Royal Albert Hall, 1988–90; John Lennon Tribute Concert, Merseyside, 1990; Children In Need, BBC, 1991; Edinburgh Castle, 1992; Live At The Royal Albert Hall (Channel 4), 1993. *Recordings:* Albums: Popped In Souled Out, 1987; Sgt Pepper Knew My Father, 1988; The Memphis Sessions, 1988; Holding Back The River, 1989; High On The Happy Side, 1992; Wet Wet Wet Live At The Royal Albert Hall, 1993; End of Part One (Their Greatest Hits), 1993; Picture This, 1995; 10, 1997; Singles include: Wishing I Was Lucky, 1987; Sweet Little Mystery, 1987; Angel Eyes (Home and Away), 1987; Temptation, 1988; With A Little Help From My Friends (No. 1, UK), 1988; Sweet Surrender, 1989; Broke Away, 1989; Hold Back The River, 1990; Make It Tonight, 1991; Goodnight Girl (No. 1, UK), 1992; Lip Service, 1992; More Than Love, 1992; Shed A Tear, 1993; Cold Cold Heart, 1994; Love Is All Around (No. 1, UK), 1994; She's All On My Mind, 1995; Julia Said, 1995; Don't Want To Forgive Me Now, 1995; Somewhere Somehow, 1995; Morning, 1996. *Honours:* BRIT Award, Best British Newcomer, 1988. *Current Management:* The Precious Organisation, The Townhouse, 1 Park Gate, Glasgow G3 6DL, Scotland.

CUOMO, Rivers; b. USA. Vocalist; Songwriter; Musician (guitar). *Career:* Singer, songwriter, Weezer. *Recordings:* Albums: Weezer—The Album, 1994; Pinkerton, 1996; Meet The Deedles, 1998; Maladroit, 2002. Hit single: Undone. *Current Management:* Third Rail Entertainment, 9169 Sunset Blvd, Los Angeles, CA 90069, USA.

CURNIN, Cy; b. 12 Dec. 1957, Wimbledon, England. Vocalist. m. Peri, 7 Nov. 1985, 2 d. *Education:* Wimbledon College, London. *Career:* Vocalist with Fixx;

US tours throughout 1980s; Tour with The Police, 1983; Appearances on: Saturday Night Live; Old Grey Whistle Test; In Concert (BBC); MTV; VH1. *Recordings:* Shuttered Room, 1981; Reach The Beach, 1983; Hits include: Stand Or Fall, 1982; Red Skids, 1982; One Thing Leads To Another, 1983; Further albums: Phantoms, 1984; Walkabout, 1986; Calm Animals, 1988; Ink, 1990; King Biscuit Flower Hour, 1996; Real Time Stood Still, 1997; Elemental, 1998; 1011 Woodland, 1999; with Tina Turner: What's Love Got To Do With It, 1993. *Honours:* ASCAP; 2m. plays, 1983, 1984. *Membership:* PRS; ASCAP. *Current Management:* Jeff Nebin, USA.

CURRIE, Justin; b. 11 Dec. 1964, Glasgow, Scotland. Vocalist; Songwriter; Musician (bass guitar, piano). *Career:* Founding mem., lead singer, Del Amitri, 1981–; Concerts, UK and international tours; Appearance at Woodstock Festival, 1994. *Recordings:* Albums: Del Amitri, 1985; Waking Hours, 1989; Change Everything, 1992; Twisted, 1995; Some Other Sucker's Parade, 1997; Hatful Of Rain/Lousy With Love, 1998; Can You Do Me Good?, 2002. Singles: Kiss This Thing Goodbye, 1989; Nothing Ever Happens, 1990; Move Away Jimmy Blue, 1990; Spit In The Rain, 1990; Always The Last To Know, 1992; Be My Downfall, 1992; Just Like A Man, 1992; When You Were Wrong, 1993; Here and Now, 1995; Driving With The Brakes On, 1995; Roll To Me, 1995; Tell Her This, 1996; Not Where It's At, 1997; Don't Come Home Too Soon, 1998; Cry To Be Found, 1998; Just Before You Leave, 2002. *Current Management:* JPR Management, The Power House, 70 Chiswick High Rd, London W4 1SY, England. *Address:* c/o A & M Records Inc, 595 Madison Ave, New York, NY 10022, USA. *Website:* www.delamitri.com.

CURSON, Theodore; b. 3 June 1935, Philadelphia, Pennsylvania, USA. Musician (trumpet). m. Marjorie Goltry, 1 April 1967, 1 s., 1 d. *Education:* Granoff Music Conservatory, Philadelphia, 1952–53. *Career:* Trumpeter with Charlie Mingus; Max Roach; Philly Joe Jones; Cecil Taylor; Eric Dolphy, 1960–63; Concerts and jazz festivals include: North Sea; Nice; Antibes; Monterey; Newport; Concerts: Europe; USA; India; Middle East; North Africa; Director, Blue Note Open Jam, 1984–; President, Nosruc Publishing Company, 1961–. *Recordings include:* Plenty of Horn, 1961; Fire Down Below, 1963; New Thing and Blue Thing, 1965; The Urge, 1966; Ode To Booker Ervin, 1970; Pop Wine, 1972; Quicksand, 1975; Jubilant Power, 1976; Tears For Dolphy, 1976; Blue Piccolo, 1976; Flip Top, 1977; Typical Ted, 1977; The Trio, 1979; I Heard Mingus, 1980; Snake Johnson, 1981; 'Round Midnight, 1990; Several film scores. *Honours:* New Star, Monterey Jazz Festival, 1962; Downbeat Critics Poll Winner, 1966; Readers Poll Winner, 1978; Long Island Musicians Society Award, 1970; Pori City Standard, Finland, 1978. *Membership:* AFofM.

CURTIS, Catie; b. 22 May 1965, Biddeford, Maine, USA. Vocalist; Songwriter. *Education:* BA, Brown University. *Career:* Soundtrack work for TV, Dawson's Creek, Chicago Hope; Film, Annie O, A Slipping Down Life; Performances at clubs in the USA, Lilith Fair and other festivals; Theatre tour with Mary Chapin Carpenter, 1998–99. *Recordings:* Truth From Lies, 1996; Catie Curtis, 1997; A Crash Coursse in Roses, 1999; My Shirt Looks Good On You, 2001. *Honours:* GLAMA Album of the Year, 1998. *Membership:* AFTRA. *Current Management:* Gold Mountain. *Address:* Gold Mountain Entertainment, 3575 Cahuenga Blvd W, Suite 450, Los Angeles, CA 90068, USA.

CURTIS, Mac; b. 16 Jan. 1939, Fort Worth, Texas, USA. Vocalist; Musician (guitar); Songwriter. m. Peggy, 3 March 1967, 3 s. *Education:* Graduated, Army Information and Broadcasting School, 1958; Graduated, Anthony School of Real Estate, 1975; Moorpark Community College Real Estates Course, Moorpark, California, USA, 1975–76; Licensed Real Estate Associate California, 1975–80. *Career:* Recorded for King records, 1956; Guest, Big D Jambouree and National Radio Show, 1956; Co-star, Alan Freed Rock 'n' Roll Revue, New York, 1956; Toured as Rock 'n' Roll Rockabilly, until 1960; Country Music DJ, Dallas Radio Station; Recorded Country for Epic and GRT Dj Atlanta, Nashville, LA, 1971. *Compositions:* I'd Run a Mile for Lynn Anderson; Give Us One More Chance. *Recordings:* The King Original Rockabilly Masters; Blue Jean Heart, CD; The Rollin' Rock series, 3 albums; Rollin' Rock Singles CD, Rollin' Rock Switzerland; Rockabilly Ready, with The Rimshots. *Publications:* Goldmine Magazine, Vol. 9, Issue 10, 1983; We Wanna Boogie, 1988. *Honours:* Golden Ear Awards, Country Survey News, 1969; ASCAP Chartbuster Award, 1972. *Membership:* American Society of Composers, Authors and Publishers, 1970–. *Current Management:* Rock 'n' Roll Enterprises, 16 Grove Pl., Penarth, Vale of Glamorgan, CF64 2ND, South Wales.

CURTIS, Sonny; b. 9 May 1937, Meadow, TX, USA. Songwriter; Musician (guitar). *Education:* Music and classical guitar, Valley Conservatory of Music, Los Angeles, 1966; Sherman School of Music, Los Angeles, 1970–71. *Career:* Mem., Buddy Holly and The Three Tunes, 1956, left band, rejoined (now called The Crickets), 1958; Toured as guitarist for Slim Whitman, 1957; Mem., The Everly Brothers, 1959; Solo artiste and songwriter, 1965–; Numerous solo tours; Songs recorded by: Eddy Arnold, Chet Atkins, Bobby Fuller Four, Rosanne Cash, Glen Campbell, The Clash, Perry Como, Rita Coolidge, Bing Crosby, Sammy Davis Jr, Val Doonican, Everly Brothers, Bobby Goldsboro, Waylon Jennings, Buddy Knox, Kris Kristofferson, Gary

Lewis and The Playboys, Matchbox, Anne Murray, Sam Neely, Lou Reed, Johnny Rodriguez, Leo Sayer, Bobby Vee, Keith Whitley, Andy Williams, Hank Williams Jr. *Recordings:* Albums: Beatle Hits, Flamenco Style, 1964; The First Of Sonny Curtis, 1968; The Sonny Curtis Style, 1969; Sonny Curtis, 1979; Love Is All Around, 1980; Rollin', 1981; Spectrum, 1987; Ready, Able And Willing, 1988; No Stranger To The Rain, 1990. *Compositions include:* A Fool Never Learns; Destiny's Child; Gypsy Man; I Fought The Law; I'm No Stranger To The Rain; Love Is All Around (theme song to The Mary Tyler Moore Show), 1970; More Than I Can Say; Rock Around With Ollie Vee; The Real Buddy Holly Story; The Straight Life; Walk Right Back; When You Ask About Love; Where Will The Words Come From. *Honours:* BMI Pop Awards, for Walk Right Back, 1961, for I Fought The Law, 1964, for The Straight Life, 1968, for More Than I Can Say, 1980, for I'm No Stranger To The Rain, 1989; CMA Single of the Year, for I'm No Stranger To The Rain, 1989; Inducted, Nashville Songwriters' Asscn, Songwriters Hall of Fame, 1991; BMI Motion Picture and Television Award, for Evening Shade, 1992.

CURTOLA, (Robert Allen) Bobby; b. 14 April 1943, Thunder Bay, Ontario, Canada. Vocalist; Songwriter. m. Ava, 21 Sept. 1975, 2 s. *Career:* Singer, Rock 'n Roll; Co-Host, After Four, TV series, Canada, 1965–66; Own TV series on CTV, Shake, Rock and Roll; Own Christmas Special in Canada; Performer on Bob Hope Show; Guest, numerous national and regional talk and variety specials in Canada and USA; Headlined in Las Vegas for many years; Rock 'n' Roll Blast, 1999. *Compositions:* The Real Thing, 1966. *Recordings include:* Fortune Teller; Aladdin; 3 Rows Over; Corrina. *Honours:* Winner, Jingle Award for North America, Things Go Better with Coke; Canada's First RPM Top Male Vocalist Juno Award, 1965; Inducted into Canadian Music Industry Hall of Fame, 1996; Order of Canada, 1998; Gold record status for 22 singles and 13 albums. *Membership:* ACTRA; ARIA; AFofM; CARAS; SOCAN. *Current Management:* Mr Robert Hubbard. *Address:* PO Box 5359, Edmonton, AB T5P 4C5, Canada.

CUSSON, Michel; b. 22 Jan. 1957, Drummondville. Musician (guitar); Composer. m. Michelle Alie, 2 d. *Education:* College Degree in Pop Music; CEGEP, Drumondville, one session, McGill University Montréal; 4 months at Boston's Berklee College of Music. *Career:* Composed soundtrack for Omertà, La loi du silence, television series, 1996, 1997, 1998; Composed soundtrack for films: La Comtesse de Baton Rouge (Amdré Forcier), 1997, and L'Automne Sauvage (Gabriel Pelletier), 1992; Numerous themes for Canadian television shows; Music themes for advertising campaigns; Created jazz-world beat group Michel Cusson and the Wild Unit in 1991 and jazz-fusion group UZEB in 1976. *Recordings:* 2 albums with Michel Cusson and the Wild Unit; 10 albums with UZEB. *Honours:* Felix Awards, 1983, twice 1984, 1987, 1990, twice 1992; Gemeaux Awards, 1989, 1996; Socan Awards, 1990, 1993, 1995, 1996; Music Plus Award, 1991; Oscar Peterson Trophy, 1991. *Address:* c/o Productions Flash Rose, 3867 rue Saint Denis, Montréal, QC H2W 2M4, Canada.

CUSTER, Beth; b. 25 Feb. 1958, South Bend, Indiana, USA. Composer; Musician (clarinet, piano, trumpet, percussion); Vocalist. *Education:* Bachelor Degree, Music Performance, SUNY, Potsdam, 1980; Masters Degree, Performance, Michigan and San Francisco State Universities, 1981–85; Clarinet Teachers, Rosario Mazzeo, Suzanne Stephens, Else Ludewig-Verdeht, Don Carroll, James Pyne, Frank Wanger. *Career:* Composer for TV, film, dance and theatre; Member, numerous new music, jazz and trip-hop groups; Collaborated, MacCarthur Fellow; Created soundtracks for independent films; Resident Composer, Joe Goode Performance Group, 1992–96. *Compositions include:* Film and TV: The Twisted Tales of Felix the Cat; Sherlock Jr; Oranges are Not the Only Fruit; Dance: The Maverick Strain; This is Where I Am Now; Stark Night; Theatre: Kingfish; Hamlet; 12 Angry Men; Flathead Flamenco; Buckets of Blood Slash/Play; Commissions: Arranger with Kronos Quartet, The Penguin; Earplay Suite. *Recordings:* with Eighty Mile Beach: Inclement Weather; Arboleda de Manzanitas; There Are No Right Angles Found In Nature; Solo: The Shirt I Slept In; Trance Mission: Head Light; Meanwhile... ; Trance Mission; Club Foot Orchestra: Buster Keaton's Sherlock Jr; Metropolis; Nosferatu; The Cabinet of Dr Caligari; Kidnapped; Wild Beasts; Connie Champagne: La Strada; Dona Luz 30 Besos (with City of Tribes), 2000; Vinculum Symphony, 2000. *Honours:* Isadora Duncan Award; First Place, Berlin Film Festival; WAMMIE Music Awards; GOLDIE Award, Bay Guardian Award for composition; NEA Interarts Grant; Arts International Grant. *Address:* 88 Lundy's Lane, San Francisco, CA 94110, USA.

CYPORYN, Dennis; b. 1 Feb. 1942, Detroit, Michigan, USA. Musician (banjo); Composer. 1 s., 1 d. *Education:* Music Composition, Oakland University; Private theory lessons. *Career:* Dennis Cyporyn Band; Composes own music for band; Showcased at Detroit Music Awards, Motor City Music Awards; Won Best Instrumentalist 2 years, also Group Deserving Wider Recognition and Best Folk Group; Currently with Lonesome and Blue, bluegrass band. *Recordings:* Nashville Alley, 1991; I Must Be Dreaming, 1992; Deja Vu Debut, 1994; Duet to Quintet, 1997; Out of the Blue, 1998. *Publications:* The Bluegrass Song Book, 1972. *Honours:* 5 Awards. *Membership:* IBMA; MCMA. *Address:* Krypton Records, PO Box 372, Highland, MI 48356, USA.

CYRKA, Jan Josef; b. 31 Oct. 1963, Halifax, West Yorkshire, England. Musician (guitar); Composer. *Career:* Member, Max and the Broadway Metal Choir, 1984; Recording engineer, E-Zee Studios, 1985; Member, Zodiac Mindwarp and the Love Reaction, 1986–89; Tours, USA and Canada, supporting Guns N' Roses; Solo artist, 1989–; Session musician, television commercials; Partner, Take It For Granted PR Company; Producer and contributor, cover-mount CD for Guitarist magazine. *Compositions:* Three library albums: Rock Guitar Album, Rock Attitude, Boom; Wrote most of music for BBC Horizon, Great Balloon Race, 1997. *Recordings:* Max and The Metal Choir, 1985; Tattooed Beat Messiah, Zodiac Mindwarp, 1987; Solo albums: Beyond The Common Ground, 1992; Spirit, 1993; Prickly Pear, 1997; Session guitarist, At This Moment, Tom Jones; Co-producer, All Day Long I Shouted, Carmel. *Membership:* Musicians' Union; PRS; MCPS; BMI. *Current Management:* Andrew Farrow, Northern Music Company. *Address:* Cheapside Chambers, 43 Cheapside, Bradford, West Yorkshire BD1 4HP, England.

CYRUS, Billy Ray; b. 25 Aug. 1961, Flatwoods, Kentucky, USA. Country Vocalist. *Career:* Formed own group, Sly Dog, 1983; Worked as car salesman; Solo recording artiste, 1992–. *Recordings:* Singles: Achy Breaky Heart, 1992; Could've Been Me, 1992; In the Heart of a Woman, 1993; Words by Heart, 1994; Trail of Tears, 1996; Time for Letting Go, 1998; Albums: Some Gave All (No. 1, USA), 1992; It Won't Be The Last, 1993; Storm in the Heartland, 1994; Trail of Tears, 1996; Shot Full of Love, 1998; Southern Rain, 2000. *Current Management:* McFadden Artist Corp. *Address:* 818 18th Ave S, Nashville, TN 37203, USA.

CZ; b. 25 June 1969, Charleroi, Belgium. Vocalist; Musician (guitar); Composer. *Career:* Many concerts in Belgium and France under name of Candy Stripe, 1989–92, and Bloodminded, 1992–. *Recordings:* Albums: as Candy Stripe: As Above So Below, 1990; as Bloodminded: Hypocrisy, 1993; Demons for Tea, 1996; Bloodyminded, 1998; other: Rock in Belgium, Vol. 1, 1996; Rock in Belgium, Vol. 2, 1997. *Membership:* SABAM, Brussels, Belgium; Ciney Music Session, Arts Agency, Belgium. *Current Management:* PED Records, rue Vertevoie 13A, 5590 Ciney, Belgium. *Address:* Bloodminded, rue Jean Friot 91, 6180 Courcelles, Belgium.

D

D, Brenda, (Brenda D. Boyd); b. 30 Dec. 1936, Surrey, England. Vocalist; Actress. m. Jerry Haymes, 1 Aug. 1961, 1 s., 1 d. *Education:* Finishing school; Schools of Modelling. *Career:* Film and television actress; Appearances include original Robin Hood series; Opened in England with Fess Parker as Davy Crockett; Toured USA and Europe; First British female singer to perform Country music on BBC; First British female Country singer to perform at Grand Ole Opry. *Recordings:* Major songs: Will You Still Love Me Tomorrow; Little Bitty Tear; Love You More Than I Can Say; Just Enough To Keep Me Hanging On. *Honours:* CMA International Award; Female Vocalist, Art and Entertainment Council; A & E Film Actress Award. *Membership:* Screen Actors Guild; Arts and Entertainments Council. *Current Management:* Umpire Entertainment Enterprises, J Haymes. *Address:* 1507 Scenis Dr., Longview, TX 75604, USA.

DA ONE WAY. See: **IG CULTURE.**

DA SILVA, Rui, (Doctor J, 4 Elements, Teimoso); b. 25 April 1968, Lisbon, Portugal. Prod; Remixer; DJ. *Career:* Began DJ career in Lisbon as member of Underground Sound of Lisbon; Signed to Tribal Records; Relocated to London, 2000; Collaborations: Terry Farley; Chris Coco; DJ Vibe. *Recordings:* with Underground Sound of Lisbon: Albums: Etno City, 2001; Singles: So Get Up, 1994; Are You Looking For Me, 1998; solo: Touch Me (with Cassandra Fox), 2000. *Honours:* Muzik Award, Best Single, Touch Me, 2001. *Membership:* MCPS/PRS. *Address:* c/o Arista Records, Cavendish House, 423 New Kings Rd, London SW6 4RN, England.

DADAWA, (Zhe Zheq); b. 1974, Guangzhou, People's Republic of China. Vocalist. *Career:* Solo artist, New Age music; Debut concerts: Midem Asia, Hong Kong, 1995; London Showcase, 1995. *Recordings:* Albums with He Xuntian: Yellow Child, 1991; Sister Drum, 1995; Voices from the Sky, 1998. *Address:* c/o Warner Records.

DADDY ASH. See: **BEEDLE, Ashley.**

DADDY FREDDY, (Samuel Small); b. Kingston, Jamaica. Rap Artiste. *Career:* Television appearances include: Blue Peter; Record Breakers; BBC Summer TV; Big Breakfast; Radio includes: Tim Westwood, BBC Radio 1. *Recordings:* Albums: Ragamuffin Hip Hop; Ragga House; Pain Killa; Stress; Raggamuffin Soldier; Singles: Crown, 1991; Daddy Freddy's in Town, 1991; Haul and Pull, 1992; Respect Due, 1993; Old School New School. *Honours:* Guinness Book of Records, World's Fastest Rapper. *Membership:* PRS. *Address:* c/o 20 Hanway St, London W1P 9DD, England.

DADDY-G, (Grant Marshall); b. 18 Dec. 1959, Bristol, England. Vocalist. *Career:* Member, Massive Attack; Started with collective The Wild Bunch, featuring Tricky, Goldie, Neneh Cherry and Nellee Hooper; Formed Massive Attack with 3-D and Mushroom, 1986; Collaborations: Shara Nelson; Tricky; Horace Andy; Madonna; Tracey Thorn, Everything But The Girl; Liz Fraser, Cocteau Twins; Numerous gigs in clubs and parties. *Recordings:* Albums: Blue Lines, 1991; Protection, 1994; No Protection: Massive Attack vs Mad Professor, 1995; Mezzanine (No. 1, UK), 1998; DVD compilation of singles promos, 2001; 100th Window, 2003. Singles: Daydreaming, with Shara Nelson; Unfinished Sympathy, with Shara Nelson, 1991; Safe From Harm EP, 1991; Sly, 1994; Protection, 1995; Karmacoma, 1995; Risingson, 1997; Teardrop, with Liz Fraser, 1998; Inertia Creeps, 1998; Angel/Group Four, 1998; 1 Against 1, 2002. *Honours:* BRIT Award, Best British Dance Act, 1996. *Website:* www.massiveattack.co.uk.

DADSWELL, Melvyn John; b. 8 Jan. 1946, Uckfield, Sussex, England. Musician (saxophone); Lecturer; Teacher. m. He Feng Qin, 26 Sept. 1990, 2 s., 2 d. *Education:* BA Hons, Exeter University. *Career:* Began playing jazz, 1959; Teacher, jazz harmony, rhythm to undergraduate music students (privately); Many club concerts and British tours, with band Anthropology; 3 recordings Devon Air Jazz; Occasional session work; Bath Festival, 1988; Moscow, 1990; Schooled Red Army Orchestra in jazz, 1990–91. *Membership:* Musicians' Union. *Current Management:* Phil-Seong Huh. *Address:* Five Poplars, Ford Farm, Chudleigh-Knighton, Newton Abbot, South Devon TQ13 0ET, England.

DAGARA, Hamouka; Musician. *Career:* Appearances on television in Nigeria, 1987; 8 years successful run in show, West Africa. *Compositions include:* Bori-Badossa; Yellerou; Dawa; Boujé Baka Baka; Malta Panther; Zicika la... Soyaya. *Recordings:* Bori Badossa; Yellerow; Boujé Baka Baka; Malta Panther; Album: Bakandarnia. *Honours:* First Prize, Music Competition, Niger, 1990; Third Prize, competition in Niger, 1992; 20th Place, Africa Palmaress, 1997. *Membership:* Gominak; Somair; Sonichar; Societies of Air Mines; Palais Congrés. *Address:* Orchestre Carnayal, De Maradi, DDTSC, Republic of Niger.

DAGLEY, Christopher; b. 23 June 1971, Solihull, West Midlands, England. Musician (drums). *Education:* Grade 8 drumming. *Career:* National Youth Orchestra; BBC Big Band; Various theatre shows; Gemini; Paz; Brian Dee; Various groups. *Recordings:* 10 albums, NYJO; Dancing In The Park, Paz. *Membership:* Musicians' Union. *Address:* 439A Alexandra Ave, Rayners Lane, Harrow, Middlesex HA2 9SE, England.

DAGNELL, John Richard; b. 2 Aug. 1956, Oxford, England. Music, Entertainment Promoter; Record Co Exec; Music Publisher. m. Nicola, 30 July 1983, 1 s., 1 d. *Career:* Promoted various concert tours by: Maddy Prior; The Carnival Band; Gilbert O'Sullivan; Steeleye Span; Pentangle. *Recordings:* Albums: Maddy Prior; Steeleye Span; Gilbert O'Sullivan; Guitar Orchestra; Wild Willy Barrett; New recordings by Kathryn Tickell, Pentangle; New recordings by Lindisfarne and Keltic Fusion. *Membership:* PRS; ILA; PPL. *Address:* Park Records, PO Box 651, Oxford OX2 9RB, England.

DALE, Chris; b. 4 Sept. 1967, London, England. Musician (bass guitar); Vocalist. *Education:* Musicians' Academy, Wapping, London, 1989–90. *Career:* Bassist with funk/rock band Atomseed, 1989–93; Extensive tours in United Kingdom and Europe; Several recordings; Bassist for Bruce Dickinson, tours of UK, Europe, USA, South America and Japan, 1994–96; Bassist and singer, Sack Trick, 1997–. *Compositions:* Co-writer, singles for Atomseed, Rebel; Get in Line; Dead Happy; Co-writer for Bruce Dickinson, various B-sides and album tracks; Music and lyrics for Sack Trick album Mystery Rabbits. *Recordings:* With Atomseed: Get in Line, 1990; Hard Sell Paranoia, 1992; With Bruce Dickinson: Alive in Studio A, 1995; Skunkworks, 1996; With Sack Trick: Mystery Rabbits, 1999; Penguins on the Moon, 2000; track on compilation Any Colour As Long As It's Black, 2000. *Address:* PO Box 16432, London W6 08Q, England.

DALE, Colin; b. 14 April 1963, London, England. Prod; Remixer; DJ. *Career:* Started as a soul/disco DJ on London pirate station Kiss in the '80s; Stayed with licensed Kiss FM presenting weekly Abstrakt Dance show until 2000; Moved to internet station Groovetech, 2001; Founder: Abstrakt Dance Records; Collaborations: Gareth Oxby; Haris Custovic; Access 58; Affie Yusseff. *Recordings:* Singles: Upstate Feeling (with Civil Attack), 1996; Make You High (with Kleer), 2001. *Address:* c/o Abstrakt Dance Records, 78 Mount Nod Rd, Streatham Hill, London SW16 2lJ, England. *E-mail:* colindale@groovetech.com. *Website:* www.abstraktdance.co.uk.

DALE, Micky; b. 22 March 1968. Musician (keyboards, percussion). *Career:* Member, Embrace; Obtained major label deals in UK and USA; Released debut single independently; Support slot on Manic Street Preachers, 1997; Headline tours and TV appearances. *Recordings:* Singles: Fireworks EP, 1997; One Big Family EP, 1997; All You Good Good People, 1997; Come Back To What You Know, 1998; My Weakness Is None of Your Business, 1998; The Good Will Out, 1999; Hooligan, 1999; You're Not Alone, 2000; Save Me, 2000; I Wouldn't Wanna Happen To You, 2000; Make It Last, 2001; Wonder, 2001; Album: The Good Will Out, 1998; Drawn From Memory, 2000; If You've Never Been, 2001. *Address:* c/o PO Box 7, Brighouse, HD6 4UR, England. *Website:* www.embrace.co.uk.

DALEY, Paul; b. 23 Dec. 1962, Margate, Kent, England. Prod; Musician (percussion); Remixer; DJ. *Career:* Co-founder Hard Hands Records with Neil Barnes; World-wide DJ; Member of Leftfield, split 2002; Collaborations: A Man Called Adam, Afrika Bambaataa, Roots Manuva, John Lydon. *Recordings:* Albums: Leftism, 1995; Rhythm and Stealth, 1999; Singles: Not Forgotten, 1990; Release The Pressure, 1992; Song of Life, 1992; Open Up (with John Lydon), 1993; Original, 1995; Afrika Shox (with Afrika Bambaataa), 1999. *Current Management:* c/o Hard Hands Recordings, The Courtyard, Saga Centre, 326 Kensal Rd, London W10 5BZ, England.

DALGLEISH, Lou (Louise); b. 19 Oct. 1967, Birmingham, England. Vocalist; Songwriter; Musician (piano). *Education:* BA, Arts Practice and Cultural Policy; Grade 8 classical piano and theory. *Career:* Professional dancer, theatre, film, including Steven Spielberg's Indiana Jones and the Temple of Doom; Singer-Songwriter, including headline residencies at Ronnie Scott's, Birmingham; Support act to Wet Wet Wet, NEC, Birmingham; Bryan Ferry, Dutch tour; Guestings, Brian Kennedy; National television performances include: BBC and ITV (UK); Belgium; Festival appearances: SXSW Austin, Texas, USA; Lowlands, Waterpop, Valkos, Netherlands; Phoenix, England; National radio sessions include BBC Radio 2 and 5; Netherlands; Belgium. *Recordings:* Singles: Orange Plane, 1995; Sold Out, 1995; Charlie Girl, 1996; EP: Loud Music, 1998; Album: Lou Dalgleish, 1995; Live Album, solo acoustic at Ronnie Scott's, 1997; Calmer, 1999; backing vocals on: The Good Sons, Happiness, 2001. *Membership:* Equity; Musicians'

Union. *Current Management:* c/o Ronnie Scott's Club. *Address:* c/o Ronnie Scott's, Broad St, Birmingham B1 2HF, England.

DALLIN, Sarah Elizabeth; b. 17 Dec. 1961, Bristol, Somerset, England. Vocalist. *Education:* London School of Fashion. *Career:* Singer, all-female group, Bananarama, 1981–; Numerous concerts, television and radio performances. *Recordings:* Albums: Deep Sea Skiving, 1983; Bananarama, 1984; True Confessions, 1986; Wow!, 1987; Greatest Hits Collection, 1988; Pop Life, 1991; Please Yourself, 1993; Ultraviolet, 1996; The Very Best Of, 2001; Exotica, 2001; I Found Love, 2002. Singles: Aie A Mwana, 1981; It Ain't What You Do (with Fun Boy Three), 1982; Really Sayin' Somethin', 1982; Shy Boy, 1982; Na Na Hey Hey Kiss Him Goodbye, 1983; Robert De Niro's Waiting, 1984; Cruel Summer (featured in film The Karate Kid), 1984; Venus (No. 1, USA), 1986; I Heard A Rumour, 1987; Love In The First Degree, 1987; I Want You Back, 1988; Nathan Jones, 1988; Help! (with comedy duo French and Saunders, for Comic Relief charity), 1989; Only Your Love, 1990; Long Train Running, 1991; Preacher Man, 1991; Tripping On Your Love, 1991; Movin' On, 1992; Venus, 1993; More More More, 1993; Please Yourself (EP), 1993; Every Shade Of Blue, 1995; Take Me To Your Heart, 1996; Waterloo, 1998; Contributions to various benefit albums. *Compositions:* Co-writer, Last Thing On My Mind, Steps, 1998. *Address:* c/o Mission Control Artists Agency, Unit 50 City Business Centre, St Olav's Ct, Lower Rd, London SE16 2XB, England.

DALLIO, Patricia; b. 3 Nov. 1958, Chaumont, France. Musician (piano); Composer. *Career:* Tours throughout Europe with Art Zoyd. Concerts include: Berlin; Milan; New York; London, Hong Kong, Adelaide, Mexico, Stockholm, and Yokohama Festivals; Live shows and films include: Nosferatu; Faust; Häxan Composer, Dance theatre, videos. *Recordings:* Procession; Champs de Mars; La Ronce N'est Pas Le Pire; D'où vient l'eau des puits; Barbe Bleue; Que personne ne bouge; Ubique, 2001. *Membership:* Soundtrack (Composer Asscn). *Address:* 11 rue de la Liberté, 52000 Chaumont, France. *E-mail:* dallio.patricia@libertysurf.fr.

DALSETH, Laila; b. 6 Nov. 1940, Bergen, Norway. Jazz Vocalist. m. Totti Bergh, 1 June 1963, 2 d. *Career:* Solo Jazz artist; Television and radio appearances: Scandinavia; Germany; Yugoslavia; England; Scotland; Concerts include: Playboy Jazz Festival; Nice Jazz Festival; Sacramento Jazz Festival; Caribbean Jazz Cruises; Copenhagen Jazz Festival; Molde Jazz Festival; Jakarta Jazz Festival; Currently fronting own group with saxophonist (husband) Totti Bergh. *Recordings include:* Laila Dalseth/Wild Bill Davidson, 1974; with Bengt Hallberg, Arne Domnerus: Glad There Is You, 1978; with Louis Stewart: Daydreams, 1984; with Red Mitchell Quartet: Time For Love, 1986; with Al Cohn: Travelin' Light, 1987; Woman's Intuition, 1995; with Milt Hinton, Derek Smith, B Rosengarden, B Pizarelli: The Judge and I, 1992; with Joe Cohn, Totti Bergh: Remember, 1995; with Philip Catherine, Egil Kapstad: A Woman's Intuition, 1995; One of a Kind, 2000. *Honours:* 3 times Spellemannspris (Norwegian Grammy).

DALTON, Lacy J. (Jill Byrem); b. 13 Oct. 1948, Bloomsburg, Pennsylvania, USA. Country Vocalist. *Career:* Club singer, California, 12 years; Singer, psychedelic group Office, under name Jill Croston; Solo artiste, 1979–; Worked with Earl Scruggs, George Jones and Bobby Bare. *Recordings:* Hit singles: Crazy Blue Eyes; Tennessee Waltz; Hard Times; 16th Avenue; Working Class Man; Albums: As Jill Croston: Jill Croston, 1978; As Lacy J Dalton: Lacy J Dalton, 1979; Hard Times, 1980; Takin' It Easy, 1981; 16th Avenue, 1982; Dream Baby, 1983; Greatest Hits, 1983; Can't Run Away From Your Heart, 1985; Highway Diner, 1986; Blue Eyed Blues, 1987; Survivor, 1989; Lacy J, 1990; Crazy Love, 1991; Chains On The Wind, 1992; Somethin Special, 1995. *Current Management:* c/o Aaron Anderson, Lacy J Dalton Enterprises, PO Box 1109, Mount Juliet, TN 37122, USA.

DALTREY, David Joseph; b. 30 Dec. 1951, London, England. Session Musician (guitar, piano); Tutor (guitar, piano); Composer; Prod. *Education:* Mid Hertfordshire College; Guildhall School of Music and Drama; London College of Music; Studied with Rogers Covey-Crump; Private studies with Ike Isaacs and Jimmy Page. *Career:* Recording artiste; Worked for BBC; Numerous compositions and recordings for various artistes; Session musician, tutor, composer and prod. *Recordings:* Lead vocalist and guitarist, Joseph And The Amazing Technicolour Dreamcoat, 1969, 1971; Tales Of Justine, Albert/Monday Morning, 1967; Petals From A Sunflower, 1998; The Wayfarer, 2003. *Membership:* Musicians' Union; ISM; AES; Institute of Acoustics. *Address:* Flat 3, Hugheson House, 122–123 Northgate St, Bury St Edmunds, Suffolk IP33 1HG, England. *Telephone:* (1284) 762076.

DALTREY, Roger Harry; b. 1 March 1944, Hammersmith, London, England. Vocalist; Actor. m. Heather Daltrey, 2 d., 1 s., 1 s. by previous marriage. *Career:* Mem., UK rock group, The Who, 1964–84; Appearances incl.: National Jazz and Blues Festivals, 1965, 1966, 1969; Monterey Pop Festival, 1967; Rock At The Oval, 1972; Farewell tour, 1982–83; Live Aid, Wembley, 1985; 25th Anniversary Reunion tour, 1989; Solo artiste, 1984–; Actor in films, including Tommy, 1974; Lisztomania, 1975; The Legacy, 1979; McVicar, 1980; Threepenny Opera, 1989. *Recordings:* Albums: with The Who: My Generation, 1965; A Quick One, 1966; The Who Sell Out, 1968; Direct

Hits, 1968; Tommy (rock opera), 1969; Live At Leeds, 1970; Who's Next, 1971; Meaty Beefy Big And Bouncy, 1971; Quadrophenia, 1973; Odds And Sods, 1974; The Who By Numbers, 1975; The Story Of The Who, 1976; Who Are You, 1978; The Kids Are Alright (film soundtrack), 1979; Face Dances, 1981; Hooligans, 1982; It's Hard, 1982; Rarities Vols 1 and 2, 1983; Once Upon A Time, 1983; The Singles, 1984; Who's Last, 1984; Who's Missing, 1985; Two's Missing, 1987; Who's Better Who's Best, 1988; Joined Together, 1990; 30 Years Of Maximum R&B, 1994; My Generation: The Very Best Of The Who, 1996; The BBC Sessions, 2000; Solo: Daltrey, 1973; Ride A Rock Horse, 1975; One Of The Boys, 1977; Best Bits, 1982; If Parting Should Be Painless, 1984; Under A Raging Moon, 1985; I Can't Wait To See The Movie, 1987; Rocks In The Head, 1992; McVicar, 1996; Martyrs And Madmen, 1997; Anthology, 2002. Singles include: with The Who: I Can't Explain, 1965; Anyway Anyhow Anywhere, 1965; My Generation (No. 2, UK), 1965; Substitute, 1966; I'm A Boy (No. 2, UK), 1966; Happy Jack, 1967; Pictures Of Lily, 1967; I Can See For Miles, 1967; Pinball Wizard, 1969; See Me Feel Me, 1970; Won't Get Fooled Again, 1971; Join Together, 1972; Who Are You, 1978; You Better You Bet, 1981; Contributor, Rock and Roll, Rock Aid Armenia, 1991. *Honours:* Gold Ticket, Madison Square Garden, 1982; Ivor Novello Award, Outstanding Contribution To British Music, 1982; BRIT Award, Outstanding Contribution to British Music, 1988; Group inducted into Rock 'n' Roll Hall of Fame, 1990. *Address:* c/o Repertoire Records, Alderhost 17, 22459 Hamburg, Germany.

DALY, Stan; b. 27 Nov. 1929, Grays Inn Road, London. Jazz Musician (drums); Band leader. m. 3 Aug. 1957, 1 s., 3 d. *Education:* Royal Air Force. *Career:* Played in top dance orchestras of Lou Preager, Frank Weir, Jack Nathan, 1950s–60s; Drummer, Harry Gold's Pieces of Eight, for 15 years; Broadcasting, television, concerts; Own band Sonny Dee All-Stars playing Chicago/mainstream jazz; Worked on West Coast America with Wild Bill Davison, Dick Cathcart, Eddie Miller, Bob Enevoldson; Played with: Harry Parry's Radio Sextet; Freddy Randall; Pasadena Roof Orchestra; Sandy Brown; Played almost every top international jazz festival world-wide. *Recordings:* Drummer, many albums. *Address:* 92 Greenway, Totteridge, London N20 8EJ, England.

DAMBRY, Stephane; b. 7 March 1959, Barentin, France. Vocalist. *Education:* Teacher. *Career:* Lead singer, Little Big Band, 1987–97; Solo artist, 1991–. *Recordings:* Talk To The Mirror, 1991; The Fatal Glass of Beer, 1994; The Welsh Rare Beat, 1994; with Little Big Band: Hey! Doc, 1994. *Current Management:* L'Echo du Kazoo Management. *Address:* 1 rue C Nicole, 76800 St Etienne du Rouvray, France.

DAMEN, Paul; b. 26 Jan. , Netherlands. Musician (Drums). *Career:* Mid 80s Leading Dutch Top 40 Band accompanying major Dutch Artists, 1989; Toured in Holland, The Trammps; Jimmy Bo Horne; Dutch Group, Haitai; Numerous jingles and commercials (studio) for : Mercedes; SAAB; General Motors; L'Oreal Cosmetics; TV appearances with Gloria Estefan; Toured with popular Dutch Artist Rob Janszen; Toured with International Artist, CB Milton, 1995; National Studio/Session Drummer, currently. *Recordings:* Promo; Endorser for Remo, Drums and Drumheads. *Current Management:* De Otter and De Vries, Entertainment Productions BC, Hertogin Juliana Singel 34 055, Netherlands. *Address:* Hogehofstraat 26, 5366 CC Megen, Holland.

DAMINESCU, Adrian; b. 2 Oct. 1956, Timisoara, Romania. Musician (cello, piano, guitar, bass guitar); Vocalist. m. Francis Susan Walker, 30 June 1990, divorced. *Education:* Department of voice music and composition, Academy of Music. *Career:* Concerts, tours and recitals throughout Romania; Israel; USSR; Germany; People's Republic of China; Japan; Canada; USA; Czechoslovakia; Television and radio appearances: National Romanian television station; The Stars Duel; 10 weeks in Top 3–2–1; Hit Studio, London 1990; Cable TV; Gloria Hunniford, BBC1; Voice of America; National Radio Station. *Compositions:* Romania; You're Still Beautiful; Looking In My Teacup; Stop; Pleading For Michael Jackson; I Miss My Home; Final Day; Praying For Mercy; Midnight. *Recordings:* I Will Love You (Eu Te Voi Iubi); Pieces of Me (Bucati Din Mine). *Publications:* Currently writing memoirs: Music and My Life. *Honours:* Great Prize, Bucharest Festival, 1986; Most Beautiful Voice of the Festival, Bratislava, 1986; 3 times Great Prize winner as singer, Mamaia National Festival 1986–88; Second Prize, Golden Orpheus Festival, Bulgaria, 1988; 3 Mamaia National Festival Awards as composer: First, 1989; Third, 1991; Second, 1992. *Address:* Constanta 8700, 45 Gen Manu St, Romania.

DAMMERS, Jerry (Gerald Dankin); b. 22 May 1954, Coventry, Warwickshire, England. Musician (keyboards). *Career:* Founder member, Coventry Automatics, 1977; Name changed to Coventry Specials, then Special AKA, then the Specials, 1979–; Support to the Clash, British tour, 1978; Designer, record label 2-Tone, marketed by Chrysalis Records, 1979; Kampuchea benefit concert, with The Who, the Pretenders, London, 1979; Film, Dance Craze, 1981; Formed Artists Against Apartheid, 1986; Organizer, Nelson Mandela 70th Birthday Tribute, Wembley, 1990. *Recordings:* Singles include: Gangsters, 1979; A Message To You, Rudy, 1979; Too Much Too Young EP (No. 1, UK), 1980; Rat Race, 1980; Stereotype, 1980; Do Nothing, 1981; Ghost Town (No. 1, UK), 1981; Nelson Mandela, 1984; Albums: Specials, 1979; More Specials, 1980; Dance Craze, 1981; In The Studio, 1984; The

Specials Singles, 1991; Live – Too Much Young, 1992; Live At The Moonlight Club, 1992; Two Tone Compilation, 1993; Rebirth of Cool Vol. 2, 1994; Fearless, 1998; Stereotypical – As Bs and Rarities (box set), 2000; More Specials, 2002.

DAMONE, Vic, (Vito Farinola); b. 12 June 1928, Brooklyn, New York, USA. Vocalist; Actor. m. (4) Diahann Carroll, 1 s., 3 d. *Education:* Singing lessons. *Career:* Winner, Arthur Godfrey's Talent Scouts, CBS, 1946; Singer, La Martinique nightclub, New York; Recording artiste, 1947–; Own CBS radio show, Saturday Night Serenade, late 1940s; Film apperances include: Rich Young and Pretty, 1951; The Strip (featuring Mickey Rooney, Jack Teagarden, Louis Armstrong), 1951; Hell To Eternity; Athena, 1954; Deep In My Heart, 1954; Hit The Deck, 1955; Kismet, 1955; Crash Boat; Own television series, 1956–57; Regular concert tours, UK, USA and Australia, 1980s–. *Recordings:* Albums: Athena (soundtrack), 1954; Rich Young and Pretty (soundtrack), 1955; The Voice of Vic Damone, 1956; That Towering Feeling, 1956; The Stingiest Man In The World (soundtrack), 1956; The Gift of Love (soundtrack), 1958; Closer Than A Kiss, 1959; Angela Mia, 1959; This Game of Love, 1959; On The Swingin' Side, 1961; Linger Awhile With Vic Damone, 1962; Strange Enchantment, 1962; The Lively Ones, 1962; My Baby Loves To Swing, 1963; The Liveliest, 1963; On The Street Where You Live, 1964; You Were Only Fooling, 1965; Stay With Me, 1976; Damone's Feeling 1978, 1979; Now, 1981; Make Somone Happy, 1981; Now and Forever, 1982; Vic Damone Sings The Great Songs, 1983; The Damone Type of Thing, 1984; Christmas With Vic Damone, 1984; The Best of Vic Damone, Live, 1989; The Glory of Love, 1984; Tender Is the Night, 1995; Best of The Mercury Years, 2001; Various compilations; Hit singles (sold 1m.): Again; You're Breaking My Heart; On The Street Where You Live (No. 1, UK), 1958; Other hits include: I Have But One Heart; You Do; Tzena Tzena Tzena; Cincinnati Dancing Pig; My Heart Cries For You; My Truly Truly Fair; Here In My Heart; April In Portugal; Eternally; Ebb Tide; An Affair To Remember; You Were Only Fooling (While I Was Falling In Love). *Publications:* Recipes For Lovers cookbook. *Current Management:* c/o Stan Scottland, JKE Services Inc, 404 Park Ave S, 10th Floor, New York, NY 10016, USA.

DAMRON, Dick; *Career:* Starday Studios, Recording Country Rockabilly Records with Tommy Hill, 1961; Teamed up with Producer Joe Bob Barnhill, Soldier of Fortune Album, 1971. *Recordings:* Include, Countrified, 1971; Susan Flowers; Jesus It's Me Again; Still Countrified; Dick Damron: The Anthology. *Honours:* 4 Times Top Canadian Country Singer; Best Country Record of 1977; Top Canadian Songwriter; Artist of the Year; Country Gospel Album of the Year, 1996; 7 Times Winner, Outstanding Contribution to Canadian Music; 2 Times Winner, Province of Alberta Award; Country Music Man of the Year; 5 Texas Proud Awards. *Address:* PO Box 270, Bentley, AB T0C 0J0, Canada.

DANA, (Rosemary Brown); b. 30 Aug. 1951, Belfast, Northern Ireland. Vocalist. *Career:* Winner, Eurovision Song Contest, with All Kinds of Everything (No. 1, UK, South Africa, Ireland, Australia), 1970; Over 1m. sales world-wide; Actress, television and pantomime. *Recordings:* Hit singles: All Kinds of Everything, 1970; Who Put The Lights Out, 1971; It's Gonna Be A Cold Christmas, 1975; Please Tell Him That I Said Hello, 1975; Fairy Tale, 1976; Albums: All Kinds of Everything, 1970; World of Dana, 1975; Have A Nice Day, 1977; Love Songs and Fairy Tales, 1977; The Girl Is Back, 1979; Totally Yours, 1982; Everything Is Beautiful, 1980; Let There Be Love, 1985; No Greater Love, 1988; Dana's Ireland, 1991; Lady of Knock, 1992; Say Yes, 1993; Gift of Love, 1996; Best Travelin' Tunes, 1997; Heavenly Portrait, 1999. *Current Management:* The Brokaw Company, 9255 Sunset Blvd, Suite 804, Los Angeles, CA 90069, USA.

DANCE, Stanley (Frank); b. 15 Sept. 1910, Braintree, England. Writer. m. Helen Oakley, 30 Jan. 1947, 2 s., 2 d. *Education:* Framlingham College, 1925–28. *Career:* Reviewer, Jazz Journal, London, 1948–96; Saturday Review, New York City, 1967–72; Music Journal, New York City, 1962–79; Jazz Times, Silver Spring, Maryland, 1980–98. *Publications:* Editor, Jazz Era, 1961; The World of Duke Ellington, 1970; The Night People, with Dicky Wells, 1971; The World of Swing, 1974; The World of Earl Hines, 1977; Duke Ellington in Person, with Mercer Ellington, 1978; The World of Count Basie, 1980; Those Swinging Years, with Charlie Barnet, 1984; Jazz Talking, with Max Jones, 2000. *Honours:* Deems Taylor Award, American Society of Composers, Authors and Publishers, 1979. *Address:* 1745 Bittersweet Hill, Vista, CA 92084–7621, USA.

DANDO, Evan; b. 4 March 1967, USA. Vocalist; Musician (guitar); Songwriter. *Career:* Founder member, The Lemonheads, 1986–97; Numerous world-wide concerts include: Solo tour, Australia, 1992; Solo acoustic concert, Ronnie Scott's, London, 1992; Reading Festival, 1994; Collaborations include: The Blake Babies; Kirsty MacColl; Juliana Hatfield; Godstar. *Recordings:* Albums: Hate Your Friends, 1987; Creator, 1988; Lick, 1989; Lovey, 1990; It's A Shame About Ray, 1992; Come On Feel The Lemonheads, 1993; Car Button Cloth, 1996; Best of the Lemonheads, 1998; Singles include: It's A Shame About Ray; Mrs Robinson (from film soundtrack, 25th Anniversary wide-screen release of The Graduate, 1993); Confetti; Into Your Arms; It's About Time; Contributor, Sweet Relief (Victoria Williams benefit album), 1993.

Honours: Boston Music Awards, Outstanding Modern Rock Act, Single of the Year, 1993. *Current Management:* Gold Mountain Entertainment. *Address:* 3575 Cahuenga Blvd W, Suite 450, Los Angeles, CA 90068, USA.

DANE, Phil; b. 31 Oct. 1961, Leeds, Yorkshire, England. Prod; Engineer; Songwriter. *Education:* City of Leeds, College of Music. *Career:* Mixes and/or productions of: Back To The Planet; Bomb The Bass; Boy George; B T: Darkman; D:ream; East 17; Julia Fordham; Innocence; James; Mike Oldfield; Robert Palmer; Diana Ross; Rozalla; Salt 'n' Pepa; Sasha; Utah Saints; Worlds Apart; Yazz; Aswad; Madonna; Paul Oakenfold; Robbie Williams; Lighthouse Family; Republica; Matt Bianco. *Membership:* Musicians' Union; PRS. *Current Management:* 750 cc. *Address:* 152 Vaughan Rd, Harrow HA1 4EB, England.

DANGAIN, Guy; b. 12 July 1935, Sains-en-Gohelle, France. 1 d. *Education:* First Prize, Conservatoire National Superieur de Musique, Paris, studied clarinet with Professor Ulysse Deleclute; First Prize, Chamber Music, with Professor Ferrand Oubradous. *Career:* Soloist, clarinet, with National Orchestra of France, 1963–93; Professor, Ecole Normale, Paris; Professor, Conservatoire National Superieur du Musique, Paris; Director, International Festival, Haut Bugey. *Compositions:* Over 50 collections of compositions. *Recordings:* Brahms Sonata; Debussy, Rhapsody; Rhapsody with National Orchestra of Martinon; Repertoire from young clarinettist H Mundi; Creation du Monde, du Bernstein; Hommage à Louis Ca Huzoc; Guisganolerie: Hommage à Guisganol; Quinette and Two Songs. *Publications:* Prestige de la clarinette, 1987; A propos de la clarinette, 1991. *Honours:* Chevalier des Arts et des Lettres. *Address:* 14 Ruelle à Potier, Nerville la forêt, 95590 France.

D'ANGELO, (Michael Archer); b. 11 Feb. 1974, Richmond, Virginia, USA. Vocalist; Songwriter; Musician (multi-instrumentalist); Prod. *Career:* Recording artiste, 1992–. *Compositions:* Co-writer, producer, U Will Know, Black Men United. *Recordings:* Albums: Brown Sugar, 1995; Live at the Jazz Cafe, 1998; Voodoo, 1999. Singles: Brown Sugar, 1995; Cruisin', 1996; Lady, 1996; Me and Those Dreaming Eyes of Mine, 1996; Left and Right, 1999. *Honours:* Harlem Apollo Talent Contest Winner, 3 times; Grammy Awards: Best R&B Male Vocal Performance, Untitled – How Does It Feel?; Best R&B Album, Voodoo, 2001. *Address:* c/o William Morris Agency, 1325 Avenue of the Americas, New York, NY 10019, USA.

DANGEROUS, Chris; b. 1978. Musician (drums). *Career:* Mem., Swedish band, The Hives, 1993–; Signed to Universal Music, 2001. *Recordings:* Albums: Barely Legal, 1997; Veni Vidi Vicious, 2000; Your New Favourite Band (compilation, UK only), 2001. Singles: Oh, Lord! When? How? (EP), 1996; aka I.D.I.O.T. (EP), 1998; Hate To Say I Told You So; Main Offender; Supply & Demand. *Honours:* NME Award, Best International Band, 2003. *Address:* The Hives, c/o Pelle Almqvist, Regnbågsvägen 46, 737 43 Fagersta, Sweden. *E-mail:* hives@innocent.com. *Website:* www.hives.nu.

DANIELS, Bob (Robert T. Hahn); b. 2 March 1959, Milwaukee, Wisconsin, USA. Musician (banjo). m. Denise Blank, 1 s., 2 d. *Education:* College; Various private music teachers. *Career:* Professional musician for 20 years; Played in bands: The Nashville Cats; The Nashtown Ramblers; Backroads; Johnny Rodriguez Backup Band; Played with artists including: Charley Collins; Bashful Brother Oswald; Earl Scruggs; Jethro Burns; Duane Stuermer; Jack Grassel; Warren Wiegratz; Infamous Ramblin' Rick Trudell; Grand Old Opry, Opry Land, 1976; Broadway production, 1979; Live radio music appearances, WMIL FM 106, late 1980s; Associate songwriter for BMI; Composes for other singers, commercials, theatre. *Recordings:* Single: Back Home To Yesterday, 1988; Albums: Bob Daniels and A Milwaukee All-Star Pot Pourri, 1990; Bob Daniels, Rick Trudell, Best Banjo, 1995; Bob Daniels, Rick Trudell, Rough Cuts, 1995; Best Banjo, 1995. *Honours:* Rated by HFR as one of best 5 improvisational 5-string banjo players, USA. *Membership:* AFofM. *Current Management:* D J Blank. *Address:* 606 W Wisconsin Ave, Suite 1100, Milwaukee, WI 53203, USA.

DANIELS, Charlie; b. 28 Oct. 1937, Wilmington, North Carolina, USA. Country Vocalist; Songwriter; Musician (multi-instrumentalist). *Career:* Played guitar from age 15; Founder, bluegrass band The Misty Mountain Boys; Changed name to The Jaguars, 1959; Regular session work, Nashville, 1968–; Partnership with Earl Scruggs; Formed Charlie Daniels Band, 1970–; Started Volunteer Jam (became annual event), 1974; Featured on film soundtrack Urban Cowboy; Recorded film theme for Stroker Ace. *Compositions include:* It Hurts Me, Elvis Presley, 1964. *Recordings:* Hit singles include: Uneasy Rider, 1973; The South's Gonna Do It, 1973; The Devil Went Down To Georgia, 1979; Albums: To John, Grease and Wolfman, 1970; Charlie Daniels, 1970; Honey In The Rock, 1973; Way Down Yonder, 1974; Fire On The Mountain, 1975; Nightrider, 1975; Teach Yourself Rock Guitar, 1976; Saddletramp, 1976; High Lonesome, 1976; Volunteer Jam, 1976; Midnight Wind, 1977; Volunteer Jam 3 and 4, 1978; Million Miles Reflections, 1979; Volunteer Jam VI, 1980; Full Moon, 1980; Volunteer Jam VII, 1981; Windows, 1982; A Decade of Hits, 1983; Me and The Boys, 1985; Powder Keg, 1987; Renegade, 1991; Same Ol Me, 1995; By the Light of the Moon, 1997; Tailgate Party, 1999; Road Dogs, 2000; with Bob Dylan: Nashville Skyline, 1969; Self Portrait, 1970; New Morning, 1970; Other recordings with Ringo Starr; Marty Robbins; Hank Williams Jr. *Publications:*

Book of short stories, 1986. *Current Management:* High Lonesome Management Inc, 17060 Central Pike, Lebanon, TN 37087, USA.

DANIELS, Luke; b. 18 Nov. 1973, Reading, England. Musician (button accordion). *Career:* Accordion player with Scarp, formerly with De Danann; Major concerts include: St Chartier Festival, 1993; Philadelphia Festival of Folk Music, 1993; Pebble Mill TV, 1994; Theatre de Ville, Paris, 1995; Accordionist with Riverdance; Composer for English National Opera. *Compositions include:* Musette À Térésa; The Snoring Barber; Wednesday's Tune; Gallowstree Sonata; The King of Prussia; This Love; Breath Without a Sigh. *Recordings:* Tarantella, 1994; Scarp, 1995; Across The Waters; Reeltime (compilation); features on: Kissing Fishes, Broderick, 2000; Broad Street Ballads, Ray Hearne, 2001; Cara Dillon, Cara Dillon, 2001. *Honours:* Young Tradition Award, Folk Musician of the Year, BBC Radio 2, 1992. *Membership:* MU. *Current Management:* Acoustics. *Address:* 4 Lea Rd, Sonning Common, Reading, Berkshire RG4 9LJ, England.

DANIELZ; b. 25 Nov. 1957, Hong Kong. Vocalist; Musician (guitar). *Career:* Lead guitarist with T Rextasy, T Rex tribute group; Tours include: UK arena tour as support to Gary Glitter; Tour with Sweet and Slade, Germany, 1995; Japan, 1995; British tour with Sweet, 1997; VH1 shows T Rextasy concert footage from Cambridge Corn Exchange Bolan birthday show, 1997; major British theatre music tour with Slade, 1999; Television appearances: Unplugged, MTV/VH1, 1995; Glam-Doc documentary, Ch4, 1995. *Recordings:* with T Rextasy: Baby Factory, 1994; Trip and Glide In The Ballrooms of T Rextasy, 1995 (UK and Japan); Album: Savage Beethoven, 1997; Major record deal in Japan. *Publications:* Wilderness of the Mind, biography of Marc Bolan, 1992; Marc Bolan – T Rex, published in Japan, 1999. *Membership:* Musicians' Union; PRS. *Current Management:* Mark Lundquist, 2 The Woodlands, Woking, Surrey GU22 7RU, England. *Address:* 8 Moriatry Close, Holloway, London N7 0EF, England.

DANKO, Harold; b. 13 June 1947, Sharon, Pennsylvania, USA. Musician (piano); Composer; Educator. *Education:* Dana School of Music, 1965–69; BME, Youngstown State University, Ohio, 1969; Additional studies, Juilliard School of Music, 1970. *Career:* Tours, concerts and recordings, 1972–; Pianist with various artistes including: Woody Herman; Chet Baker; Thad Jones and Mel Lewis; Lee Konitz; Gerry Mulligan; Leader, Harold Danko Trio, 1980–; Leader, Harold Danko Quartet, 1990–; Festival appearances include: JVC, New Haven and Clearwater (USA); Montréal (Canada); Metz, TBB and Fort Napoleon (France); Marca and Riva (Italy); Gouvy (Belgium) and North Sea Jazz Festival (Netherlands); Featured artist, Meet The Artist series, Lincoln Center, and Performing Arts Society series, JFK Center; Concert series, Manhattan School of Music, New York funded by NEA fellowship; President, Aaychdee Music; Founder, Jazz Haven (Jazz society); Current music educator, Manhattan School of Music, New York, Hartt School of Music, Hartford, Connecticut and Neighborhood Music School, New Haven. *Compositions include:* Tidal Breeze; Alone But Not Forgotten; Ink and Water Suite; Chasin' The Bad Guys; Shorter By Two; Music for theatre and television. *Recordings:* Coincidence, 1979; Mirth Song, 1982; Shorter By Two, 1983; Alone But Not Forgotten, 1985; The First Love Song, 1988; Next Age, 1991; After The Rain, 1994; New Autumn, 1995; The Feeling of Jazz, 1996; Tidal Breeze, 1997; This Isn't Maybe, 1999; Stable Mates, 2000. *Publications:* Author, The Illustrated Keyboard Series, 1982; Video: Jazz Concepts for Keyboard (Brazil). *Honours:* Awards from ASCAP and National Asscn of Concert and Cabaret Acts (NACCA); Outstanding Service to Jazz Education award, International Asscn of Jazz Educators; Distinguished Alumni award, Youngstown State University; Fellowship, National Endowment for the Arts, 1995. *Membership:* AFofM; ASCAP. *Address:* 172 Alden Ave, New Haven, CT 06515, USA.

DANKWORTH, Alec (Alexander William); b. 14 May 1960, London England. Musician (double bass, acoustic bass guitar). *Education:* Berklee School of Music, Boston, USA. *Career:* Son of John Dankworth and Cleo Laine, brother of singer Jacqui; Played clarinet before taking up double bass; Worked and toured internationally with parents, 1981–91; During this period also worked with: Tommy Chase; Dave O'Higgins; Tommy Smith; Jean Toussaint; Buddy De Franco; Nigel Kennedy; Stephane Grappelli; Michael Garrick; Began long associations with Clark Tracey and Pizza Express Modern Jazz Sextet, late 1980s; Accompanied many visiting American jazz musicians; Toured Europe and South Africa with Abdullah Ibrahim, 1993; Played in the Dankworth Generation Band; Toured and recorded with Van Morrison and Georgie Fame, mid 1990s, and Dave Brubeck, 1999; Collaborations: Julian Joseph; Martin Taylor; Pete King; Pat Crumley; Tommy Smith; Guy Barker. *Recordings:* Albums: We've Been Expecting You (Clark Tracey Quintet), 1992; Nebuchadnezzar (with John Dankworth), 1994; Rhythm Changes (with John Dankworth), 1995; features on: Bartók – Solo Violin Sonata/Ellington – Mainly Black, Nigel Kennedy, 1986; What Goes Around, Jean Toussaint, 1992; Spirit of Django, Martin Taylor, 1994; How Long Has This Been Going On, Van Morrison and Georgie Fame, 1995; Into The Blue, Guy Barker, 1995; Beasts of Scotland, Tommy Smith, 1996; The Healing Game, Van Morrison, 1997; Gold, Martin Taylor, 1997; Brubeck's Back, Dave Brubeck, 1999; Deep Water Drop Off, Sin É, 1999.

DANKWORTH, Jacqui (Jaqueline Caryl); b. 5 Feb. 1963, UK. Vocalist; Actress. *Career:* Daughter of John Dankworth and Cleo Laine, sister of Alec; Acted with the RSC; Stage appearances in London's West End include: Sophisticated Ladies (Ellington revue); Into The Woods (Stephen Sondheim); Les Liaisons Dangereuses; Formed Alec and Jacqui Dankworth Quartet, 1993; First solo album, First Cry, released, 1994; Current ensemble named after second release, Field of Blue. *Recordings:* Albums: First Cry, 1994; Field of Blue, 1996; Still (with Field of Blue), 2000.

DANKWORTH, John Philip William; b. 20 Sept. 1927, Walthamstow, London, England. Composer; Musician (saxophone, clarinet). m. Cleo Laine, 18 March 1958, 2 s., 1 d. *Education:* Royal Academy of Music. *Career:* Involved in post-war development of British Jazz, 1947–60; Formed Jazz orchestra, 1953; Pops Music Dir, London Symphony Orchestra, 1985–90; Principal Guest Pops Conductor, San Francisco Symphony Orchestra, 1987–89; Numerous film scores and albums; With Cleo Laine, founded performing arts centre, Wavendon Stables, 1970–. *Compositions:* Improvisations (with Matyas Seiber), 1959; Escapade, 1967; Tom Sawyer's Saturday, 1967; String Quartet, 1971; Piano Concerto, 1972; Grace Abounding, 1980; Dialogue And Songs For Colette, Cleo Laine, 1980; The Diamond And The Goose, 1981; Reconciliation (for Silver Jubilee of Coventry Cathedral), 1987; Woolwich Concerto (clarinet concerto for Emma Johnson), 1995; Dreams '42 (string quartet, for 1997 Kidderminster Festival); Double Vision (world premiere by BBC Big Band at BBC Proms), 1997; Objective 2000 (for the combined orchestras of the Harpur Trust Schools), 2000; Mariposas (for Peter Fisher, piano and violin), 2001; orchestrated for London Chamber Ensemble, 2002. *Recordings:* Albums include: 5 Steps T Dankworth, 1958; England's Ambassador Of Jazz, 1960; Jazz From Abroad, 1963; Echoes Of Harlem, 1988; Generation Big Band, 1995. *Publications:* Sax from the Start, 1996; Jazz in Revolution, 1998. *Honours:* C.B.E., 1974; Hon. MA, Open University, 1975; Hon. DMus, Berklee College of Music, 1982; Hon. DMus, York University, 1993; Hon. Fellow, Leeds College of Music, 1999; Variety Club of Great Britain Show Business Personality Award (with Cleo Laine), 1977; ISPA Distinguished Artists Award, 1999; Bob Harrington Lifetime Achievement Award (with Cleo Laine), 2001; BBC Radio Jazz Lifetime Achievement Award (with Cleo Laine), 2002. *Membership:* Fellow, Royal Academy of Music. *Current Management:* Dankworth Management. *Address:* The Old Rectory, Wavendon, Milton Keynes MK17 8LT, England. *Website:* www.quarternotes.com.

DANNENBERG, Roger; b. 9 March 1955, Houston, Texas, USA. Composer; Musician (Trumpet). m. Frances Dannenberg, 1 s. *Education:* BSEE, 1977, MSCE, 1979, Rice University; PhD, Carnegie Mellon University, 1982; Studied Trumpet With Nelson Hatt, Frank Tripani, Anthony Pasquarelli; Composition With Paul Cooper. *Career:* Trumpet With George Gee Orchestra, Apollo Theatre, 1986; Greenwich Village Jazz Festival, 1988; Stuck With Each Other, NBC Television Movie, 1989; Trumpet, Composer, Nitely News, World Affairs Conference, 1996; In Transit, Guanajuato, 1997. *Compositions:* Ritual of The Science Makers, 1990; Nitely News, 1992; The Words Are Simple, 1994; Aura, 1998. *Publications:* Combining Instrument and Performance Models For High Quality Music Synthesis, 1998. *Honours:* ICMA Board of Directors; Pittsburgh New Music Ensemble Board of Directors. *Membership:* International Computer Music Asscn. *Address:* 6529 Aylesboro Ave, Pittburgh, PA 15217, USA.

DANTER, John; b. 3 Sept. 1946, Birmingham. Musician; Composer. 1 s. *Education:* MA, Reading University. *Career:* Toured as guitarist with various groups, Germany, Turkey, Greece, USA, 1960s and 70s; Session work on 'Jingles', 1970s; Writing songs, 1980s–90s; Commissioned music for production companies and songwriting for the American country market. *Compositions include:* Have You Ever Been In Love; Making Your Mind up; The Perfect Kiss; Started So Well; Another Beautiful Guy; Daddy Said. *Recordings:* About 1500 Television and Radio Jingles. *Publications:* Sound As Inspiration-Study In Improvisation. *Honours:* Ivor Novello Award, Best Song, musically and lyrically, 1983; Eurovision Song Contest Winner, 1981. *Membership:* PRS; The Lute Society; West Bromwich Albion Supporters Club.

DANTZLER, Russ; b. 5 Dec. 1951, Ainsworth, Nebraska, USA. Agent; Artist Man; Record Prod. *Education:* Business, University of Nebraska. *Career:* Began Hot Jazz Management and Production as hobby, to preserve the Swing tradition, 1974; Hot Jazz became full-time career, New York City, 1989; Clients include: Claude 'Fiddler' Williams; Earl May; Red Richards; Benny Waters; Al Grey; The Duke's Men with Arthur Baron; Carrie Smith; Bross Townsend; Norris Turney; Ken Peplowski; Bill 'Mr Honkey Tonk' Doggett; Contracting work for the Smithsonian Jazz Oral History Department, and Jazz Foundation of America. *Recordings:* Produced: Claude Williams, Live At J's, Vols 1 and 2, 1993; Swingtime In New York, with Claude Williams, Sir Roland Hanna, Bill Easley, Earl May, Joe Ascione, 1995. *Publications:* Columnist, Jam/Jazz Ambassadors Magazine (Kansas City); Scrapple From The Apple, 1993–. *Honours:* Produced recording placing on critic's polls; Asked to write remembrance of Haywood Henry for the Alabama Jazz Hall of Fame archives. *Membership:* Jazz Journalists Asscn; Kansas City Jazz Ambassadors; American Federation of Jazz Societies; Duke Ellington Society; New York Chapter, National Jazz Service Organization. *Address:* Hot Jazz, 328 W 43rd St, Suite 4F, New York, NY 10036, USA.

DANZIG, Glenn (Glen Anzalone); b. 23 June 1955, Lodi, New Jersey, USA. Rock vocalist. *Career:* Vocalist, US punk groups, The Misfits; Samhain; Founder, vocalist, Danzig, 1987–. *Recordings include:* Albums: with the Misfits: Beware, 1979; Walk Among Us, 1982; Static Age, 1995; Collection II, 1995; Box Set, 1996; with Danzig: Danzig, 1988; Danzig II – Lucifage, 1990; Danzig III – How The Gods Kill, 1992; Danzig 4, 1994; Blackacidevil, 1996; Satan's Child, 1999; Live On The Black Hand Side, 2001. *Current Management:* Big FD Management, 10801 National Blvd, Suite 530, Los Angeles, CA 90064, USA.

DAPOGNY, James; b. 3 Sept. 1940, Illinois, USA. Prof. of Music; Jazz Musician (piano); Bandleader. *Education:* University of Illinois. *Career:* Professor of Music, University of Michigan, 1966–; Jazz Pianist, Leader, James Dapogny's Chicago Jazz Band, 1975–; Touring; Recording; Radio and television. *Compositions:* West of The Mississippi; Santa Passed My House By This Christmas; Shortstory; Lobogo; Miles From Home. *Recordings:* Laughing At Life; Original Jelly Blues; Hot Club Stomp; On The Road; Whatcha Gonna Swing Tonight. *Current Management:* Zajonc/Valenti Management. *Address:* 1154 Olden Rd, Ann Arbor, MI 48103, USA.

D'ARBY, Terence Trent; b. 15 March 1962, New York, USA. Vocalist; Songwriter; Prod. 1 d. *Education:* Journalism, University of Central Florida. *Career:* Singer, Touch, Germany, 1982; Solo artiste, 1986–; Concerts include: British tour, support to Simply Red, 1987; Artists Against Apartheid, Royal Albert Hall, 1987; Hardline Introduction, British tour, 1987; British tour, support to David Bowie, 1987; US tour, 1988; Nelson Mandela tribute, Wembley, 1990; John Lennon tribute, Liverpool, 1990; Concerts with Bruce Springsteen, New York, 1993; Concerts with Duran Duran, Mexico, 1993; Television includes: Motown 30 – What's Goin' On, CBS, 1990. *Recordings:* Singles include: If You Let Me Stay, 1987; Wishing Well (No. 1, USA), 1987; Dance Little Sister, 1987; Sign Your Name, 1988; Do You Love Me Like You Say, 1993; Delicate (with Des'ree), 1993; She Kissed Me, 1993; Let Her Down Easy, 1993; Holding On To You, 1995; O Divina, 2001; Albums: Introducing The Hardline According To... (No. 1, UK), 1987; Neither Fish Nor Flesh, 1989; Symphony Or Damn – The Tension Inside The Sweetness, 1993; Vibrator, 1995; Wildcard, 2001; Contributor track to: Music of Quality and Distinction Vol. 2, British Electric Foundation, 1991. *Honours:* BRIT Award, Best International Newcomer, 1988; Platinum disc, Introducing The Hardline, 1988; Grammy Award, Best R&B Vocal Performance, Introducing, 1989; Best Vocal Performance by Duo or Group, with Booker T and the MG's, 1995. *Current Management:* Lippman Entertainment, 8900 Wilshire Blvd, Suite 340, Beverly Hills, CA 90211–1906, USA.

D'ARCY, Doug; b. 23 Feb. 1946, Hull, England. Record Co Exec. m. Catherine Williams, May 1974, 1 s., 1 d. *Education:* Manchester University. *Career:* Chrysalis Records, 1968–89; Managing Director, Dedicated Records, 1990–95. *Current Management:* Songlings Ltd. *Address:* c/o PO Box 20206, London NW1 7FF, England.

DARLING, Helen; b. 5 May, Baton Rouge, Louisiana, USA. Vocalist; Songwriter. m. Dennis Darling. *Education:* Bachelor Degree, Organizational Communication, University of Texas, Austin, Texas. *Career:* Jingle singer, Chicago; Demo singer, Nashville; Female vocalist on Garth Brooks' The Red Strokes; Co-writer with: Bob DiPiero; John Scott Sherill; Karen Staley; Chuck Jones; Michael Omartian. *Compositions include:* Track for own album, co-written with Tena Clark, Gary Prim: When The Butterflies Have Flown Away. *Recordings:* Song: It's So Easy, College Vocal Group Album: Ensemble 109; Single: Jenny Come Back, 1995; Album: Helen Darling, 1995. *Current Management:* Chip Peay, PBH Entertainment.

DARLINGTON, Jay; b. 3 May 1969, Sidcup, England. Musician (keyboards). *Career:* Mem., The Kays, renamed Kula Shaker, 1995–99; Numerous live tours and TV appearances; Many festival appearances. *Recordings:* Albums: K (No. 1, UK), 1996; Peasants Pigs and Astronauts, 1999. Singles: Tattva, 1996; Hey Dude, 1996; Govinda, 1996; Hush, 1997; Sound of Drums, 1998. *Honours:* BRIT Award, Best British Newcomer, 1997.

DARYA, Farhad; b. 22 Sept. 1962, Gozargaah, Kabul, Afghanistan. Vocalist; Songwriter; Composer; Musician (rubab). m. Sultana Emam, 1 s. *Education:* Polytechnic Institute, Kabul, 1982; Faculty of Literature, University of Kabul, 1987. *Career:* Formed band, Goroh-e-Baran, 1983; Goroh-e-Baran becomes the official orchestra for Afghan Radio and Television; Songwriter and composer under the pseudonym Abr; Adjunct prof. of Classical Music, Faculty of Fine Art, University of Kabul, 1985; Exiled, left Afghanistan for the Czech Republic, Germany, France, USA; Solo artiste, singing in many regional Afghan languages and playing traditional Afghan instruments; Concerts world-wide. *Recordings:* Albums: Rahe Rafta, 1981; Afghan Folk Music, 1982; Zaro jane, 1982; Baran, 1983; Ghazal, 1985; Bolbole Awara, 1986; Mazdeegar, 1988; Bazme Ghazal, 1988; Mehrbaani, 1989; Begum Jan, 1991–92; Afghanistan, 1995; Shakar, 1997; In Foreign Land, 1999; Qabila-e-Ashiq, 2000; Golom Golom, 2001; Gularoos, 2001. *Honours:* Youth Magazine & Radio Afghanistan, Best Singer, 1990; International Musical Enterprises, Inc, Best Performer of the Year, 1995; Afghan Radio, Star of the Contemporary Music of Afghanistan, 1996; BBC World Service, Favourite Singer, 1998; A.Y.C

British Columbia & Aina-e-Afghan TV, Best Singer, 1999; Nedaa-e-Watan TV & Radio, Best Singer of Afghanistan, 2000, 2001. *E-mail:* contact@ farhaddarya.info. *Website:* www.farhaddarya.info.

DAURAT, Jean-Sebastien; b. 11 Feb. 1961, Neuilly Sur Seine, France. Musician (guitar). 2 s. *Education:* 3 years art school; Private music lessons. *Career:* Television: Sideman for H Leonard; Corine Marchand; Maria Glen; Marion Montgomery; Erchy Lawson; Own group, Jazz Oil Quintet; Plays in numerous clubs, Paris (international pop, rock, funk, jazz, Latin jazz); 150 more dates in 1998; Bass player on stage for Amarande Story, theatre production; On tour each year in South of France. *Compositions:* St Emilion, 1997; Fête de l'Humanité, 1999. *Recordings:* On Ne Discute Pas, 1997; On ne Panique pas, 1998; Jazz Oil Spirit, 1999; Un Jour, le lendemain, 1999. *Publications:* Jazz Hot Magazine, 1997; La Teste de Buche, 1999. *Membership:* SACEM. *Current Management:* Jules Music, Night and Day Records. *Address:* 86 Ave de Gournay, 94800 Villejuif, France.

DAVENPORT, Bob; b. 31 May 1932, Newcastle upon Tyne, England. Vocalist. *Education:* 4 years, St Martins College of Art, London (sculpture). *Career:* Member, Bob Davenport and The Rakes; Solo folk artiste; Appeared at Newport Folk Festival, with Joan Baez, Phil Ochs, Bob Dylan, Tom Paxton, 1963; Guest on Pete Seeger's Central Park and Tanglewood concerts, 1967. *Recordings:* Wor Geordie, 1962; The Iron Muse, 1963; Farewell Nancy, 1964; Northumbrian Minstrelcy, 1964; Bob Davenport and The Rakes, 1965; Bob Davenport, 1971; Bob Davenport and The Marsden Rattlers, 1971; Pal of My Cradle Days, 1974; Down The Long Road, 1975; Postcards Home, 1977; With The Rakes, 1977; The Good Old Way – British Folk Music Today, 1980; Will's Barn, 1990; From The Humber To The Tweed, 1991; with the Rakes: The Rakes, 1976; The Red-Haired Lad; with Roger Digby: Send Your Best Men Forward, 2001; Wait Till The Work Comes Round, 2002; Guest on albums by David Essex; Mike Harding; Watersons; Flowers and Frolics (on Reformed Characters album), 2000. *Publications:* Cvitanovich's Road To Wigan Pier documentary (Thames TV). *Membership:* Equity. *Address:* 14 Calthorpe St, London WC1X 0JS, England. *E-mail:* bob.davenport@lineone.net.

DAVERNE, Gary Michiel; b. 26 Jan. 1939, Auckland, New Zealand. Musical Dir; Composer; Educator. *Education:* Auckland University; Auckland Teachers' College, Diploma Teaching, 1959; Trinity College of Music, London, FTCL (Composition), 1969; LRSM, 1965. *Career:* Self-employed, international conductor, composer, arranger, record producer, over 40 albums, including 1 Platinum, 2 Gold discs; Conductor and arranger of music for television, film, radio; Formerly teacher, economics, accountancy, 1962–77; Composer in Schools, 1978–79; President, Composers' Association, New Zealand, 1979; Musical director, Auckland Symphony Orchestra, 1975–; Director of Music, Waitangi Day celebrations (before Queen Elizabeth II); Musical Director, Military Searchlight Tattoo, New Plymouth, 1997; Musical Director, premiere of Jewish oratorio Hear! O Israel by Cormac O'Duffy to celebrate Israel's 50th National birthday; Produced record for Sir Howard Morrison; Arranger/ Producer, Kylie Harris's Country Album of the Year, 1998. *Compositions include:* Over 100 pop songs; Operettas; Songs for children; 3 rock operas; Concert accordion music; Many symphonic works for orchestra (recorded by NZSO) include: Rhapsody For Accordion and Orchestra; Over 600 television and radio jingles, film soundtracks. *Honours:* Officer of the New Zealand Order of Merit (ONZM), 1996.

DAVEY, Rick; b. 11 Jan. 1952, Devon, England. Music Publisher; Record Label Owner; Prod. *Education:* BA, Philosophy, London University; ABRSM Grade VIII (Theory). *Career:* Jazz/blues musician, saxophone and keyboards, since age 15; Music consultant, Tomorrows World, BBC; Artist management for Silver Bullet; Tour manager for Big Youth/Alton Ellis; Studio manager, Machelle Alexander; Acts and labels controlled include: Custers Last Stand Records (Kissing The Pink); Black Cat Records (Jungle/Reggae); Flowsound Ltd publish Zion Train; Terence McKenna (Shamen); KOTOT, Dennis Alcapone; Tour manager, Black Uhuru, Mindlink, Justin Hinds, Jonny Osbourne. *Recordings:* New Era, on Face film with Damon Albarn (Blur); Bible and the Gun, Devon Russell; UTE; Black Cat; Tassoulla. *Membership:* PRS; MCPS. *Current Management:* Flowsound Ltd; Black Cat RPM. *Address:* Unit C, Imperial Works, Perren St, London NW5 7EE, England.

DAVID, Craig (Ashley); b. 5 May 1981, Southampton, England. Vocalist; Songwriter. *Education:* Southampton City College, NVQ Electronics student. *Career:* Worked as club DJ and pirate radio presenter before meeting with local musician (and Artful Dodger member) Mark Hill; Provided vocals for Artful Dodger duo, scoring massive UK hit single; Signed solo contract, 1999; Sell-out British tour, 2000; Developed international fanbase 2001. *Recordings:* Albums: Born To Do It, 2000; Slicker Than Your Average, 2002. Singles: Re-Rewind (with Artful Dodger), 1999; Fill Me In (No. 1, UK), Woman Trouble (with Artful Dodger), 7 Days (No. 1, UK), Walking Away, 2000; Rendezvous, 2001. *Honours:* MOBO Awards: Best Newcomer, Best R&B Act, Best UK Single, 2001; Debut album multi-certified by record industries world-wide. *Current Management:* Colin Lester, Wildstar Management. *Website:* www.craigdavid.co.uk.

DAVID, Hal; b. 25 May 1921, Brooklyn, New York, USA. Lyricist. m. Eunice Bernstein, 2 s. *Career:* Songwriter, collaborations with Burt Bacharach; Henry Mancini; Joe Rapaso; Record producer for Dionne Warwick. *Compositions include:* Raindrops Keep Fallin' On My Head; The Look of Love; What's New Pussycat?; Alfie; Wives and Lovers; It Was Almost Like A Song; What The World Needs Now Is Love; To Love A Child; To All The Girls I've Ever Loved Before (recorded by Julio Iglesias, Willie Nelson); Broadway show, Promises Promises; Films include: April Fools. *Honours:* Academy Award, Raindrops Keep Fallin' On My Head; Grammy Award, Promises Promises; Inducted into Songwriters Hall of Fame; Nashville Songwriters Hall of Fame International; NARM Presidential Award; Creative Achievement Award, B'Nai B'rith. *Membership:* ASCAP; Songwriters Guild of America; Lyricists Guild of America; Dramatists Guild; Authors League.

DAVID, Joel; b. 22 Dec. 1948, Blackburn, Lancashire, England. Musician; Vocalist; Actor. m. Maureen Seaberg, 10 July 1984. *Career:* Actor: Brideshead Revisited, GTV, 1981; Strangers, Granada, 1983; Coronation Street, 1981; 3-4-7-9, GTV; Prime Suspect, GTV, 1989; Nature of The Beast, British Screen, CH4, 1987; Singer: Victoria Wood Show, GTV; Radio: Live At Golders Green Hippodrome, BBC Radio Two, Live With The BBC Big Band, 1990; Nightride, BBC Radio 2, 1988–91; We'll Meet Again, BBC Radio 2, 1994; The David Jacobs Show, BBC Radio 2; The Charlie Chester Show, BBC Radio Two, 1994–95. *Recordings:* Old Bones, 1987; Be My Valentine Tonight, 1988; Dance To The End of Love, 1990; Paws For Love, 1995. *Membership:* British Actors Equity Asscn. *Current Management:* Maureen Seaberg. *Address:* Old Records, 17 Moor Close, Darwen, Lancashire BB3 3LG, England.

DAVIDS, Brent Michael; b. 4 June 1959, Madison, Wisconsin, USA. Musician (quartz crystal flutes). *Education:* Master of Music Degree, Composition. *Career:* Appearance on Sunday Morning with the Kronos Quartet, CBS, feature on Sunday Morning, 1997; Performed with Kronos Quartet at Brooklyn Academy of Music, Lincoln Center Out-of-Doors, 1996, 1999; Performed with Joffrey Ballet, 1998–99; Performed with New Mexico Symphony Orchestra, 1999. *Compositions:* Pauwau, for New Mexico Symphony Orchestra; Moon of the Falling Leaves for Joffrey Ballet; Singing Woods; Turtle People, and Native American National Anthem, for Kronos Quartet; Night Chant, for Chanticleer. *Recordings:* Ni-Tcang, CD; Brent Michael Davids; Joe and the Blue Butterfly, forthcoming. *Honours:* ASCAP, 1989; International Music Festival, 1990; National Endowments for the Arts Grant, 1994; Rockefeller Fellowship, 1998; Sundance Institute Composer Fellowship, 1998. *Membership:* American Composers Forum; American Music Center; Society of Composers Inc; ATLATL. *Current Management:* Blue Butterfly Group. *Address:* 3049 10th Ave S, Minneapolis, MN 55407, USA.

DAVIES, Bruce William; b. 25 Nov. 1955, Kirkcaldy, Fife, Scotland. Musician; Vocalist; Songwriter; Entertainer; Radio Presenter. m. (1), 3 s., (2) Anne, 18 Sept. 1993. *Education:* Briefly at Royal Scottish Academy of Music and Drama. *Career:* With folk duo Beggars Mantle, 1983–90; Solo artist, 1990–; Television appearances: BBC Network; Scottish; Border; Grampian; Ulster; numerous US channels; Performances mainly in Scotland, also: UK; Europe; Africa; USA; Canada; Taking accessible but unique style of folk music to audiences both in and out of the folk field. *Recordings:* Numerous; 5 albums currently available; Numerous recordings as session musician; Arranger and producer for other artists. *Current Management:* Rothes Recordings. *Address:* PO Box 7, Glenrothes, Fife KY6 2TA, Scotland.

DAVIES, Gail Patricia; b. 5 June 1948, Broken Bow, Oklahoma, USA. Country Vocalist; Musician. m. (3) Robert Victor Price, 1 s. *Career:* Own touring band featuring husband and son; Appearances on TV including CBS Morning News Show, The Today Show; Featured in TV Special, The Women of Country; Tours with Neil Young, Willie Nelson, Carl Perkins, Glen Campbell, Don Williams; Toured with Roger Miller; Appearance on Merv Griffin Show; Formed Country-Rock band, Wild Choir; Staff Producer, Liberty Records, 1991, developed new acts; Founder, Little Chickadee Records, 1995; Writer and producer of albums. *Compositions:* Bucket to the South, for Ava Barber, 1977; single and album tracks. *Recordings:* Singles include: No Love Have I; Someone Is Looking For Someone Like You; It's A Lovely Lovely World, with Emmylou Harris; Round the Clock Lovin'; Grandma's Song; Singing the Blues; You Turn Me On I'm a Radio; You're A Hard Dog To Keep Under The Porch; Boys Like You; Break Away; Jagged Edge of a Broken Heart; Unwed Fathers, featured Dolly Parton; Albums: Gail Davies, 1978; The Game, 1980; Blue Heartache; I'll Be There, 1980; Giving Herself Away, 1982; Where Is A Woman To Go, 1984; Pretty Words, 1989; The Other Side of Love, 1990; The Best of Gail Davies, 1991; Gail Davies' Greatest Hits, 1998; Live and Unplugged At The Station Inn, 2001. *Honours:* Best New Female Vocalist, DJ's of America; Nominee, Academy of Country Music. *Address:* PO Box 120545, Nashville, TN 37212, USA.

DAVIES, Mark John; b. 19 Nov. 1969, Ampthill, Bedfordshire, England. Musician (keyboards); Vocalist; Record Prod; Remixer. *Education:* BA, German, University of East Anglia, 1988–92; Violin/viola, to Grade 6, Theory, Grade 4. *Career:* Keyboards, vocals with Messiah, 1990–; Album released, worked with Ian Astbury (of the Cult) and Precious Wilson; Television includes: 2 appearances Top of the Pops, 1992; O-Zone; 5 times on Radio One

Roadshow; Major concerts include: Los Angeles, 1992; Scotland; Guernsey, 1993; London. *Recordings:* Album: 21st Century Jesus, 1994; Singles include: There Is No Law (No. 1, USA College Chart), 1991; Temple of Dreams, 1992; I Feel Love, 1992; Thunderdome, 1994; Creator, with Ian Astbury, Peace and Tranquility; 20,000 Hardcore Members (No. 4, UK Dance Charts), 1990; Law of The Night, Marc Almond. *Membership:* Musicians' Union. *Current Management:* Stevo Pearce, Some Bizarre. *Address:* 124 New Bond St, London W19 9AE, England.

DAVIES, Neol Edward; b. 26 April 1952, Coventry, England. Songwriter; Musician (guitar); Teacher (guitar). *Career:* Founded 2 Tone Records with The Specials; Founder member, The Selecter; Tours included: The 2 Tone Tour, 1979; Tours of USA, Europe, Japan, supporting Talking Heads, Blondie, Elvis Costello, The Skatalites, and Prince Buster; Current member, Selecter Instrumental (8-piece instrumental ska band); Television and radio appearances: Top of the Pops; Old Grey Whistle Test; BBC Radio 1. *Recordings:* The Selecter, 1979; On My Radio, 1979; Three Minute Hero, 1980; Too Much Pressure, 1980; Missing Words, 1980; The Whisper, 1980; Celebrate The Bullet, 1981; Selecter Greatest Hits, 1996; Cruel Britannia, 2000. *Membership:* MU. *Current Management:* Roger Lomas Productions and Management. *Address:* 35 Dillotford Ave, Coventry CV3 5DR, England.

DAVIES, Peter Max Crofts; b. 30 Nov. 1950, Salisbury, Wiltshire, England. Luthier; Instrument Designer; Musician (guitar). m. Patricia Anne, 28 Feb. 1981, 1 s., 1 d. *Education:* Learned piano as a child. *Career:* R and D consultant to: Goodfellow Guitars; Patrick Eggle Guitars, to 1993; Guitar technician to major artists, 1987–; Consultant for care and preservation of Jimi Hendrix' Black Stratocaster guitar; Currently involved in design of new MIDI musical interface, Tonepool; Built guitars for Queen video The Miracle, 1989; Invented Melodic Table and Tonepool instrument, and associated new ways to play and learn music; Currently researching playing techniques for Tonepool and preparing for the manufacture of the instrument. *Current Management:* C-thru Music Ltd. *Address:* 6 Pleasant Row, Woodford, Kettering, Northamptonshire NN14 4HP, England.

DAVIES, Ray; b. 21 June 1944, Muswell Hill, London, England. Vocalist; Songwriter; Musician (guitar); Prod. m. 1) Rasa Didztpetris, 12 Dec. 1964, 2 d., 2) Yvonne, 1 d. with Chrissie Hynde. *Education:* Hornsey Art College; Theatre Design, Croydon College of Art. *Career:* Founder, Ray Davies Quartet, aged 16, later named The Ravens; Group became The Kinks, 1963–; UK debut, London, 1963; US debut, Academy of Music, New York, 1965; Concerts and tours world-wide include: Madison Square Garden, New York, 1981; US Festival, San Bernardino, 1981; Earth Day Concert, Foxborough, 1992; Glastonbury Festival, 1993; Royal Albert Hall, 1993. *Recordings:* Numerous albums include: Kinks, 1964; Kinda Kinks, 1965; Face to Face, 1966; Something Else, 1967; Sleepwalker, 1977; Misfits, 1978; Low Budget, 1979; One for the Road, 1980; Glamour, 1981; Give the People What They Want, 1981; State of Confusion, 1983; Think Visual, 1987; Phobia, 1993; To the Bone, 1994; BBC Sessions 1964–77, 2001; Numerous compilations, live albums and greatest hits collections; Solo albums: Return to Waterloo, 1985; The Storyteller, 1998; Hit Singles: Long Tall Sally, 1964; You Really Got Me, (No. 1, UK), 1964; All Day and All of the Night, 1964; Tired of Waiting For You (No. 1, UK), 1965; Everybody's Gonna Be Happy, 1965; Set Me Free, 1965; See My Friend, 1965; Till the End of the Day, 1966; A Well-Respected Man, 1966; Dedicated Follower of Fashion, 1966; Sunny Afternoon (No. 1, UK), 1966; Dead End Street, 1966; Waterloo Sunset, 1967; Autumn Almanac, 1967; Days, 1968; Lola, 1980; Apeman, 1971; Supersonic Rocket Ship, 1972; Come Dancing, 1983; Contributions as songwriter to: The Virgin Soldiers, film soundtrack, 1969; Chorus Girls, play, 1981; Actor, Absolute Beginners, film, 1986. *Honours:* Inducted into Rock 'n' Roll Hall of Fame, 1990; Ivor Novello Award for Special Contribution to Music, 1990. *Address:* c/o Asgard, 125 Parkway, London NW1 7PS, England.

DAVIES, Rhodri John; b. 19 Dec. 1971, Aberystwyth, Wales. Musician (Harp); Improviser; Composer. *Education:* BMus (Hons), University of Sheffield; Postgraduate Certificate in Performance, Trinity College of Music, London; Masters in Music, University of Huddersfield. *Career:* Freelance Harpist, London, 1995–; Worked with Derek Bailey, Evan Parker, Chris Burn, John Butcher, Phil Durrant, John Russell, Orphy Robinson, Pat Thomas, Simon Fell, Mark Wastell, Charlotte Church; John Zorn; Fontella Bass; Peter Kowald; Billy Bang; Cinematic Orchestra. *Compositions:* Lle y bwriaf Angor, 1996; Wstrws, 1998; Eleanor's Song, Mrs Bradley Mystery, BBC Drama, 1998; Still Point, 2001; Decalogue (Es I Wacan Gyda'r Jesu), 2001. *Recordings:* Anagrams to Avoid, 1997; Navigations, Chris Burn's Ensemble, 1997; Ghost Notes, 1998; Assumed Possibilities, 1998; Simon H Fell Composition No 30, 1998; Chris Burn's Ensemble, Navigations, 1998; Strings, with Evan Parker, 2001; Vortices and Angels, 2001; Company in Marseille, 2001. *Membership:* London Musicians Collective. *Address:* 40 Stanley Rd, Bounds Green, London N11 2LE, England. *Telephone:* (20) 8361-5821. *Fax:* (20) 8361-5821. *E-mail:* rhodrid@yahoo.co.uk. *Website:* www.rhodridavies.com.

DAVIES, Saul; b. 28 June 1965, England. Musician (guitar, violin, percussion); Vocalist. *Career:* Mem., James, 1990–2001; Numerous tours, festivals dates and television appearances; Farewell 'Getting Away With It' concert, Manchester Evening News Arena, Dec. 2001. *Recordings:* Albums: Gold Mother, 1990; Seven, 1992; Laid, 1993; Wah Wah, 1994; Whiplash, 1997; The Best Of James, 1998; Millionaires, 1999; B-Sides Ultra, 2001; Pleased To Meet You, 2001; Getting Away With It, 2002. Singles incl.: How Was It For You, 1990; Come Home, 1990; Lose Control, 1990; Sit Down, 1991; Sound, 1991; Born Of Frustration, 1992; Ring The Bells, 1992; Seven, 1992; Sometimes, 1993; Laid, 1993; Say Something/Jam J, 1994; She's A Star, 1997; Tomorrow, 1997; Waltzing Along, 1997; Destiny Calling, 1998; Runaground, 1998; Sit Down (remix), 1998; I Know What I'm Here For, 1999; Fred Astaire, 1999; We're Gonna Miss You, 1999; Getting Away With It (All Messed Up), 2001. *Current Management:* Rudge Management, 1 Star St, London W2 1QD, England.

DAVIS, Chip; Songwriter; Composer. *Career:* New Age Music composer; Formed Mannheim Steamroller; Created American Gramaphone record label; Compositions used extensively on television and radio, including: The Today Show; The Rush Limbaugh Show. *Compositions:* Wrote hit single: Convoy, under pen-name, C W McCall; Series of New Age albums: Fresh Aire 1–8; Music for television documentary: Saving The Wildlife; Six Christmas albums; Ambience Series. *Current Management:* SESAC. *Address:* 55 Music Sq. E, Nashville, TN 37203, USA.

DAVIS, Clive; b. New York, NY, USA. Music Co Exec; Prod. *Career:* Lawyer, 1960, Vice-Pres. and Gen. Man., 1966, CBS; Columbia Records, –1973; Bell Records, later Arista Records, 1974, Pres., until retirement age of 65; Founder, owner, J Records, 2000–; Chair., RCA Music Group; Prod.: Dido, Aretha Franklin, Sarah McLachlan, Whitney Houston, Billy Joel, Janis Joplin, Alicia Keys, Santana, Carlos Santana, Patti Smith, Bruce Springsteen. *Publications:* Clive: Inside the Record Business (autobiography), 1974. *Address:* RCA Records, 1540 Broadway, New York, NY 10036, USA. *E-mail:* info@rcarecords.com. *Website:* www.jrecords.com.

DAVIS, Copeland; b. 16 Aug. 1950, Orlando, Florida, USA. Pop and Jazz Musician (piano); Entertainer. m. Mary Birt Norman, 23 Aug. 1987. *Education:* BFA, Florida Atlantic University; Degree in Composition, Arranging, BFA. *Career:* Arranger for The Fifth Dimension; Conductor for Barbara McNair; Arranger, guest artist, Florida Symphonic Pops Orchestra; Television: Tonight Show; Good Morning America; Three Copeland Davis TV Specials; Newly signed with Atlantic Records. *Membership:* BMI. *Current Management:* Herbert Moon. *Address:* Bowen Agency, 504 W 168th St, New York, NY 10032, USA.

DAVIS, Don; b. 4 Feb. 1957, Anaheim, CA, USA. Composer. *Education:* Music Theory and Composition, UCLA; Composition with Henri Lazarof; Orchestration with Albert Harris. *Compositions:* For television: Hart to Hart, 1979; Sledge Hammer!, 1986; Matlock, 1986; Beauty and the Beast, 1987; Star Trek: The Next Generation, 1987; Bluegrass, 1988; A Stoning in Fulham County, 1988; Quiet Victory: The Charlie Wedemeyer Story, 1988; Home Fires Burning, 1989; Tiny Toon Adventures, 1990; Running Against Time, 1990; Lies Before Kisses, 1991; My Life and Times, 1991; A Little Piece of Heaven, 1991; Notorious, 1992; Capitol Critters, 1992; Woman with a Past, 1992; Murder of Innocence, 1993; SeaQuest DSV, 1993; Leave of Absence, 1994; In the Best of Families: Marriage, Pride & Madness, 1994; Sleep, Baby, Sleep, 1995; Pandora's Clock, 1996; For Love Alone: The Ivana Trump Story, 1996; The Perfect Daughter, 1996; The Beast, 1996; In the Lake of the Woods, 1996; The Third Twin, 1997; House of Frankenstein, 1997; Invasion, 1997; A Match Made in Heaven, 1997; The Alibi, 1997; Not In This Town, 1997; Life of the Party: The Pamela Harriman Story, 1998; The Lake, 1998; In the Company of Spies, 1999; Race for Time, 2000; MK Ultra, 2000; Personally Yours, 2001; For film: Hyperspace, 1985; Blackout, 1988; Spud, 1991; Session Man, 1993; When a Man Loves a Woman (additional music), 1994; Bound, 1995; Warriors of Virtue, 1996; The Lesser Evil, 1997; Weapons of Mass Distraction, 1997; Route 9, 1998; Universal Soldier: The Return, 1999; The Matrix, 1999; House on Haunted Hill, 1999; Turbulence II: Fear of Flying, 1999; Antitrust, 2001; Long Time Dead, 2001; Valentine, 2001; The Unsaid, 2001; Jurassic Park III, 2001; Behind Enemy Lines, 2001. *Honours:* Emmy Awards, Beauty and the Beast, SeaQuest DSV. *Membership:* BMI. *Current Management:* Gorfaine/Schwartz Agency Inc, 13245 Riverside Dr., Suite 450, Sherman Oaks, CA 91423, USA. *Website:* dondavis.filmmusic.com.

DAVIS, Eddy Ray; b. 26 Sept. 1940, Greenhill, Indiana, USA. Composer; Conductor; Musician. *Education:* Purdue University; Chicago University; Cosmopolitan Conservatory; Chicago School of Music. *Career:* Appearances include: Mike Douglas Show; Tonight Show; Carnegie Hall; Jazz and Heritage festivals throughout the world including: Japan; Europe; Australia; Russia; Brazil; Records and tours with Woody Allen; Tours with (film star) George Segal; Tours, recordings with Leon Redbone and Tom Waits; Musical Director, Best of Spike Jones; Makin Whoppee; Warren G; Jazz Leggs. *Compositions include:* Penny Candy; Play For Me A Love Song; Now I'm Blue. *Recordings:* Soundtracks: Radio Days; Fried Green Tomatoes (with Patti Labelle); Sophie's Choice. *Publications:* The Theory Behind Chord Symbols. *Honours:* First place, Fretts Magazine Poll for Four String Banjo; Award from Berliner Theatretaler. *Membership:* The New York Society for the Preservation of

Illegitimate Music; The Bunk Project; The New York Banjo Ensemble. *Current Management:* New York Jazz Productions; Sky King Productions. *Address:* 260 Fifth Ave, New York, NY, USA.

DAVIS, Jean Michel; b. 2 March 1956, Suresnes, Paris, France. Musician (drums, vibraphone, percussion). m. Cynthia Stone, March 1985, 1 s., 1 d. *Education:* Conservatoire de Montreux, Paris; Berklee College of Music, Boston, USA. *Career:* Drummer, vibraphone player, in clubs: New Morning; Hot Brass; Freelance percussionist playing with: Modulations, (contemporary music ensemble of composer Philippe Durville); Les Primitifs Du Futur; Big bands; Paris opera: Die Soldaten de Zimmerman; Television appearances: Stravinsky's Histoire du Soldat, with the Campagnol theatre troupe (FR3); (France 2); Played with rock group Au Bonheur des Dames, 1997; Studio sessions with various artists; Advertising jingles and cartoon theme tunes; Plays with the Broadway Musical Company, tour of Japan, 1998. *Recordings:* Albums with: Les Primitifs Du Futur; The François Fichu Jazz Gang; Cordes Et Lames: Accordion Madness; Paris Scat; Au Bonheur des Dames, Paris Musette 3. *Publications:* 10 ètudes De Vibraphone Jazz (Salabert); Association Française de Percussion. *Address:* 172 Ave de Choisy, 75013 Paris, France.

DAVIS, Jonathan; b. 1971. Vocalist; Musician (guitar, percussion, bagpipes). *Career:* Mem., Korn; Numerous tours and radio appearances; Contributions to film soundtracks, The Crow: City of Angels, Queen of the Damned; Founder, Elementree label. *Recordings:* Albums: Korn, 1995; Life is Peachy, 1996; Quorn Box, 1998; Follow the Leader, 1998; French Remixes, 1999; Freak on a Leash, 1999; Issues, 1999. Singles: No Place to Hide; Good God; A.D.I.D.A.S., 1997; Got the Life, 1998; Freak on a Leash, 1999.

DAVIS, Keith; b. 28 Dec. 1946, Bristol, England. Musician (guitar, dobro, banjo). m. Susan Carole Wilson, 14 Dec. 1984, 1 s. *Education:* Reading University. *Career:* Played on national and local radio; Concerts include: Various clubs; Sidmouth International Festival; Burnley National Blues Festival; Warwick Festival; Tutor at London College of Music. *Recordings:* On The Streets, 1987; Wireless, 1992; Smoke and Mirrors, 1995; Snake Root, 1999. *Publications:* Swagbag Folk Magazine. *Membership:* Musicians' Union; Royal Institution of Chartered Surveyors. *Current Management:* Susie Davis, Ferndale Management. *Address:* 6 North St, Downend, Bristol BS16 5SY, England.

DAVIS, Lena; b. 8 March 1938, London, England. Personal Man; Songwriter; Publicist. 1 s. *Career:* Discovered Ricky Valance, had hit with Tell Laura I Love Her, aged 22; Joined Noel Gay Agency as Personal Manager; Later, freelance artist manager. *Compositions:* Hits for Joe Brown; Kathy Kirby; Polly Perkins; Theme music for BBC TV. *Recordings include:* Tell Laura I Love Her. *Publications:* Currently contributes to 5 magazines. *Address:* Cotton's Farmhouse, Whiston Rd, Cogenhoe, Northants NN7 1NL, England.

DAVIS, Linda Kaye; b. 26 Nov. 1962, Carthage, Texas, USA. Vocalist; Entertainer. m. Lang Jeffrey Scott, 24 Aug. 1984, 2 d. *Career:* Opened shows for superstars including: Garth Brooks; George Strait; Currently touring with Reba McEntire's show; Dream Catcher Recording Artist. *Recordings:* Duet with Reba McEntire: Does He Love You; Album: In a Different Light, 1991; Linda Davis, 1992; Shoot For The Moon, 1994; Some Things Are Meant to Be, 1996; I'm Yours, 1998. *Honours:* CMA Award, 1993; Music City News/TNN Award, 1993; Grammy, 1993. *Membership:* ASCAP; CMA; ACM; AFTRA. *Current Management:* Dream Catcher Entertainment, PO Box 767, Hermitage, TN 37076, USA.

DAVIS, Mac; b. 21 Jan. 1942, Lubbock, Texas, USA. Vocalist; Songwriter. m. Lisë Kristen Gerard, 1983, 3 s. *Education:* Emory University; Georgia State College. *Career:* Manager, Metric Music, 1966–68; Solo singer, 1969–; Television and film performer, 1978–; Screen performances include: North Dallas Forty, 1979; Cheaper To Keep Her, 1980; The Sting II, 1983. *Compositions:* numerous. *Recordings:* Albums include: Mac Davis, 1973; Baby Don't Get Hooked On Me, 1973; Forever Lovers, 1978; Thunder In The Afternoon, 1978; Midnight Crazy, 1981; Texas In My Rear View Window, 1981; Soft Talk, 1984; 20 Golden Greats, 1984; Till I Made It With You, 1986; I Sing the Hits, 1995; The Best of Mac Davis, 2000. *Address:* c/o Gallin Morey Associates, 8730 Sunset Blvd W, Los Angeles, CA 90069, USA.

DAVIS, Paul; b. 7 March 1966. Musician (keyboards). *Career:* Mem., Happy Mondays, 1985–93; Tours, UK, Europe, USA; Support tours to: New Order, UK, 1987; Jane's Addiction, US, 1990; Concerts include: Glastonbury Festival, 1990; Great British Music Weekend, Wembley, 1990; Feile Festival, Tipperary, 1990; Cities In The Park Festival, Prestwich, 1990. *Recordings:* Albums: Squirrel And G-Man Twenty-Four Hour Party People Plastic Face Carnt Smile (White Out), 1986; Bummed, 1988; Pills 'N' Thrills And Bellyaches (No. 1, UK), 1990; Live, 1991; …Yes Please!, 1992; Happy Mondays Greatest Hits, 1999. Singles: Madchester Rave On (EP); Step On, 1990; Kinky Afro, 1990; Judge Fudge, 1991. *Honours:* Best Indie Act, DMC World DJ Awards, 1991. *Address:* c/o London Records, PO Box 1422,

Chancellors House, Chancellors Rd, London W6 9SG, England. *Website:* www.londonrecords.co.uk.

DAVIS, Paul; b. 21 April 1944, Cumberland, England. Record Prod; Music Publisher; Author; Journalist. m. Hazel, 20 March 1965, 1 s., 2 d. *Career:* Presenter/producer, BBC Radio and local radio; Chairman, RTM Radio; Commercial Manager, Word Records; Owner, New Music Enterprises. *Recordings:* Producer for George Hamilton IV; Wes Davis; Jerry Arhelger; Pat Boone; Cliff Barrows; Burl Ives; George Beverly Shea. *Publications:* New Life In Country Music (book); Editor, Publisher, New Music Magazine; Books: The Blackwood Brothers, authorised biography of James and Cecil Blackwood; International Ambassador, authorised biography of George Hamilton IV; Pat Boone's authorised biography; Articles, various music and Christian journals. *Membership:* MCPS; PRS; European Director, Gospel Music Asscn. *Address:* Meredale, Reach Lane, Heath and Reach, Bedfordshire LU7 0AL, England.

DAVIS, Richard; b. 15 April 1930, Chicago, IL, USA. Musician (bass guitar); Teacher; Composer. 3 c. *Education:* MusB, Vanderbrook College of Music, 1952; Postgraduate, Manhattan School of Music, 1966. *Career:* Bandleader, own quartet, 1980–; Performed at: Berkeley Jazz Festival; New Orleans Jazz Heritage Festival; Fletcher Henderson Memorial Concert; International tours with: Elvin Jones; Lalo Schifrin; McCoy Tyner; Sun Ra; Archie Shepp; Don Cherry; Assoc. Prof., Full Tenured Prof. of Music, University of Wisconsin, 1976–; Owner, Sympatico Music Publications Inc; Founder, Richard Davis Foundation for Young Bassists, 1993–. *Recordings:* Albums: with Richard Davis Quartet: With Understanding, 1975; Epistrophy, 1981; Way Out West, 1981; Harvest, 1988; As One; One for Frederick, 1989; Live at Sweet Basil, 1990; The Bassist – Homage To Diversity, 2001; Other recordings with numerous artistes incl.: Janis Ian, Herbie Mann, Van Morrison, Freddie Hubbard, Bo Diddley, Laura Nyro, Melissa Manchester, George Benson, Quincy Jones, Judy Collins, Elvin Jones, Charlie Mingus, Bonnie Raitt, Jimmy Smith, Bruce Springsteen, Loudon Wainwright III, Paul Simon, Carly Simon, Manhattan Transfer. *Publications:* Author, The Bass Tradition, with M.C. Gridley, 1984; Jazz Styles, 1985; Contributor to numerous journals. *Honours:* Downbeat International Critics Poll, Best Bassist, 1967–74; Manfred E. Swarsensky Humanitarian Award, Rotary Club of Madison, 2000; Wisconsin Governor's Award in Support of the Arts, 2001; Urban League of Greater Madison Whitney M. Young Jr Award, 2002; Madison Magazine Best of Madison Diversity Award, 2002; Hon. doctorates in Musical Arts and Humane Letters. *Membership:* International Composers Society; International Society of Bassists; ASCAP; NARAS; National String Artists; American Jazz Foundation; Screen Actors Guild; National Asscn of Jazz Educators. *Address:* 902 West Shore Dr., Madison, WI 53715, USA. *Website:* www.globaldialog.com/~rdavis/.

DAVIS, Rob; Musician (guitar); Songwriter. *Career:* Mem., Mud, 1966–late 1970s; Mem., Darts, late 1970s–early 1980s; Songwriter; Collaborations with Paul Oakenfold, 1988; Songs recorded by: Sonique, Samantha Mumba, Shaznay Lewis, Fragma, Spiller, Kylie Minogue, Grace, Silicone Soul. *Compositions include:* Can't Get You Out Of My Head (co-writer), Kylie Minogue (No. 1, UK), 2001; Toca's Miracle, Fragma (No. 1, UK), 2001; Groovejet (If This Ain't Love), Spiller (No. 1, UK), 2001. *Honours:* Ivor Novello Awards, Most Performed Work, Dance Award, International Hit of the Year, for Can't Get You Out Of My Head, 2002. *Address:* c/o Universal Music Publishing Group, 2440 Sepulveda Blvd, Suite 100, Los Angeles, CA 90064-1712, USA.

DAVIS, Skeeter (Mary Frances Penick); b. 30 Dec. 1931, Dry Ridge, Kentucky, USA. Vocalist. *Career:* Duo, The Davis Sisters, with Betty Jack Davis, on radio, television and recordings, 1949–53; Solo career, 1955–; Worked with Eddy Arnold; Elvis Presley; Regular member, Grand Ole Opry, 1959; Toured extensively, USA, Canada, Europe, Far East; Regular performances with Duke Ellington. *Recordings:* Hit singles include: I Forgot More Than You'll Ever Know, with Betty Jack Davis; Set Him Free; Can't Help You, I'm Falling Too; My Last Date; The End of The World; A Dear John Letter, with Bobby Bare; For Loving You, with Don Bowman; Let's Get Together, with George Hamilton IV; Albums include: with The Davis Sisters: Hits, 1952; Jealous Love, 1952; Solo: I'll Sing You A Song..., 1961; Here's The Answer, 1961; The End of The World, 1961; Cloudy With Occasional Tears, 1963; I Forgot More Than You'll Ever Know, 1964; Written By The Stars, 1965; Sings Buddy Holly, 1967; What Does It Take, 1967; Why So Lonely, 1968; Mary Frances, 1969; Skeeter, 1971; Love Takes A Lot of My Time, 1971; Foggy Mountain Top, 1971; Sings Dolly, 1972; Bring It On Home, 1972; I Can't Believe That It's All Over, 1973; The Hillbilly Singer, 1973; He Wakes Me With A Kiss Every Morning, 1974; Heartstrings, 1984; She Sings They Play, 1985; Stars 3, 1994; The Essential Skeeter Davis, 1996; Other albums with: Porter Wagoner; Bobby Bare; Don Bowman; George Hamilton IV; NRBQ. *Address:* c/o Joe Taylor Artist Agency, 2802 Columbine Pl., Nashville, TN 37204, USA.

DAVIS, Spencer; b. 17 July 1941, Swansea, Wales. Musician (guitar). *Education:* Birmingham University. *Career:* Founder, Spencer Davis Group, 1963–69; Solo artist and duo with Peter Jameson, 1971; Record company executive, Island Records; Played in Blues Reunion, 1988; Re-formed Spencer Davis Group, 1990; Film appearances: The Ghost Goes Gear, 1966; Here We Go Round The Mulberry Bush, 1967; Collaborations include: Keith Moon; Todd Rundgren; Paul Williams; Country Joe McDonald. *Recordings:* Albums: with The Spencer Davis Group: Their First LP, 1965; The Second Album, 1966; Autumn 66, 1966; Gimme Some Lovin', 1967; I'm A Man, 1967; Solo albums: It's Been So Long; Mousetrap; Crossfire, 1984; Singles include: with the Spencer Davis Group: I Can't Stand It, 1964; Strong Love, 1965; Keep On Running (No. 1, UK), 1966; Somebody Help Me (No. 1, UK), 1966; When I Come Home, 1966; Gimme Some Lovin', 1966; I'm A Man, 1967; Mr Second Class, 1968. *Honours:* Carl Alan Award, Most Outstanding Group, 1966. *Current Management:* Richard Martin Management, Agency House, 6 The Steyne, Worthing, West Sussex BN11 3DS, England.

DAVIS, T(eresa) J(ane); b. Leeds, West Yorkshire, England. Vocalist; Musician. *Education:* Diploma, Wakefield Performing Arts College; Jazz and Light Music, Leeds College of Music. *Career:* Lead vocalist, Shiva, album and live concerts incl. Phoenix, 1996, Tribal Gathering, 1996, Northern Exposure, 1996; Featured artiste on single, Brilliant Feeling, Full Monty All Stars; Backing vocalist, D:ream, album, World, featured artiste on single, Power, two UK headlining tours, one Australian headlining tour, various television appearances, incl. EastEnders (BBC1), The Bill (ITV1), 1991; Backing singer for Gary Numan, two tours, 1993; Backing vocalist for Lisa Stansfield, ABC; Played Frida in Bjorn Again, international tours, 1997–98. *Recordings:* Lead and backing vocals for Sonic R (Sega game), 1997; Blur, P. J. Proby/Marc Almond, album Sigue Sigue Sputnik; Bjorn Again Live At The Royal Albert Hall, 1998. *Membership:* Equity; Musicians' Union; PAMRA.

DAVISON, Peter; b. 26 Oct. 1948, Los Angeles, California, USA. Composer; Orchestrator; Conductor; Arranger. m. Iris Pell, 21 Sept. 1984, 1 d. *Education:* BA, MA, Music Composition, California State University, Northridge; Film Scoring Workshops, Earle Hagan, BMI; Fred Karlin, ASCAP; Travel to Bali to study Gamelan music. *Career:* Composed/arranged television series and documentaries, including: Seaquest; Batman – The Animated Series; John Denver Tour Special; Films; Interactive media; Commercials including: Hilton Hotels; India; videos. *Recordings:* As composer, arranger, producer, artist: Winds of Space, 1987; Glide – Star Gazer, 1987; Forest – Mountain, 1994; Traces – Music On The Way, 1994; Adagio For Yoga (soundtrack), 2000; Adagio: Music For Relaxation, 2000. *Membership:* SCL (Society of Composers and Lyricists); ASMA (American Society Music Arrangers); IFP/West; IDA (International Documentary Asscn).

DAWNE, Cliff; b. 13 March 1950, Saskatchewan, Canada. Songwriter; Vocalist; Musician (guitar, keyboard, drums). *Career:* Entertainment Showcase, Baton Broadcasting, Shamrock Profile, Broadcasting Ltd; You Can Be A Star Contest, Nashville. *Compositions:* Ever Been Lonely; Before She Said Goodbye. *Recordings:* Boomerang; Heaven; Physical Attraction; The Strength of My Weakness; Ever Been Lonely. *Publications:* The Voice of Country Music In Canada. *Honours:* Finalist, You Can Be A Star Contest, 1987. *Membership:* Socan Canada; Broadcast Music Inc; American Musicians Asscn. *Current Management:* Little Big Productions, #3 W Broadway Mall, 504 Broadway St, West Yorkton, Sask, Canada.

DAWSON, Dana; b. 1975, New York, USA. Vocalist. *Career:* Performed on Broadway, aged 8; Solo artiste, 1993–; Early success in France; Concerts include: Radio 1's Massive Music tour, 1995. *Recordings:* Albums: Black Butterfly, 1995; Got to Give Me Love, 1995; Singles: Tell Me Bonita, 1991; 3 Is Family, 1995; How I Wanna Be Loved, 1996. *Current Management:* First Avenue Management, The Courtyard, 42 Colwith Rd, London W6 9EY, England.

DAWSON, Mary A; b. 6 April 1944, Chicago, Illinois, USA. Songwriter; Music Publisher; Radio Talk Show Host. m. David L Dawson, 15 April 1966, 2 s., 2 d. *Education:* BS, Education; 14 years of piano study. *Career:* Published songwriter; Music Publisher, President, CQK Music; Host, nationally syndicated radio programme, I Write the Songs, also available on Internet; Songs broadcast on numerous television shows. *Compositions:* Lifelong Friend; The Serenity Prayer; Long Distance Christmas. *Recordings:* The Serenity Songs Project: Twelve Steps to Freedom. *Publications:* How to Get Somewhere in the Music Business from Nowhere with Nothing, 1997; Columnist for 4 online magazines on songwriting. *Membership:* Music Women International. *Address:* CQK Music/ I Write the Songs, PMB 208, 2250 Justin Rd, Suite 108, Highland Village, TX 75077, USA.

DAY, Doris, (Doris Mary Anne von Kappelhoff); b. 3 April 1924, Cincinnati, Ohio, USA. Vocalist; Actress. m. (1) Al Jorden, March 1941, divorced 1943, 1 s., (2) George Weilder, 1946, divorced 1949, (3) Marty Melcher, 3 April 1951, deceased 1968, (4) Barry Comden, 1976, divorced 1981. *Career:* Former dancer, Cincinnati, Doherty and Kappelhoff, Glendale, CA; Singer, shows including: Karlin's Karnival, WCPO-Radio; Bob Hope NBC Radio Show, 1948–50; Singer, bands, Barney Rapp, Bob Crosby, Fred Waring, Les Brown; Doris Day Show (CBS), 1952–53; Solo recording artist, Columbia Records, 1950–; Actress, films including: Romance on the High Seas, 1948; My Dream is Yours, 1949; Young Man With a Horn, 1950; Tea For Two, 1950; West Point Story, 1950; Lullaby of Broadway, 1951; On Moonlight Bay, 1951;

I'll See You in My Dreams, 1951; April In Paris, 1952; By the Light of the Silvery Moon, 1953; Calamity Jane, 1953; Lucky Me, 1954; Yankee Doodle Girl, 1954; Love Me or Leave Me, 1955; Pajama Game, 1957; Teacher's Pet, 1958; The Tunnel of Love, 1958; It Happened to Jane, 1959; Pillow Talk, 1959; Please Don't Eat the Daisies, 1960; Midnight Lace, 1960; Lover Come Back, 1962; Jumbo, 1962; That Touch of Mink, 1962; The Thrill of It All, 1963; Send Me No Flowers, 1964; Do Not Disturb, 1965; The Glass Bottom Boat, 1966; Caprice, 1967; The Ballad of Josie, 1968; Where Were You When The Lights Went Out?, 1968; With Six You Get Egg Roll, 1968; Sleeping Dogs, Hearts and Souls, 1993; That's Entertainment III, 1994; Television: The Doris Day Show, 1970–73; Doris Day and Friends, 1985–86; Doris Day's Best, 1985–86; TV special, The Pet Set, 1972. *Recordings:* Albums: You're My Thrill, 1949; Tea For Two, 1950; Lullaby Of Broadway, 1951; On Moonlight Bay, 1951; I'll See You In My Dreams, 1951; By The Light Of The Silvery Moon, 1953; Young Man With A Horn, 1954; Day Dreams, 1955; Day In Hollywood, 1955; Young At Heart, 1955; Love Me Or Leave Me, 1955; Most Happy Fella, 1956; Day By Day, 1957; Hooray For Hollywood, Vols I and II, 1959; Cuttin' Capers, 1959; Day By Night, 1959; Boys And Girls Together, 1959; Hot Canaries, 1959; Lights, Cameras, Action, 1959; Listen To Day, 1960; Show Time, 1960; What Every Girl Should Know, 1960; I Have Dreamed, 1961; Bright And Shiny, 1961; You'll Never Walk Alone, 1962; Duet, 1962; The Best Of Doris Day, 2002; Singles: Day By Day, 1949; Sugarbush, 1952; Secret Love (No. 1, UK and USA), 1954; The Black Hills of Dakota, 1954; If I Give My Heart To You, 1954; Ready Willing and Able, 1955; Whatever Will Be Will Be (Que Sera Sera) (No. 1, UK), 1956; Move Over Darling, 1964. *Honours:* Winner (with Jerry Doherty), Best Dance Team, Cincinnati; Laurel Award, Leading New Female Personality In Motion Picture Industry, 1950; Top audience attractor, 1962; American Comedy Lifetime Achievement Award, 1991. *Address:* c/o Columbia Records, 550 Madison Ave, New York, NY 10022, USA.

DAY, Mark; b. 29 Dec. 1961. Musician (guitar). *Career:* Mem., Happy Mondays, 1985–93; Tours, UK, Europe, USA; Support tours to: New Order, UK, 1987; Jane's Addiction, US, 1990; Concerts include: Glastonbury Festival, 1990; Great British Music Weekend, Wembley, 1990; Feile Festival, Tipperary, 1990; Cities In The Park Festival, Prestwich, 1990. *Recordings:* Albums: Squirrel And G-Man Twenty-Four Hour Party People Plastic Face Carnt Smile (White Out), 1986; Bummed, 1988; Pills 'N' Thrills And Bellyaches (No. 1, UK), 1990; Live, 1991; ...Yes Please!, 1992; Happy Mondays Greatest Hits, 1999. Singles: Madchester Rave On (EP); Step On, 1990; Kinky Afro, 1990; Judge Fudge, 1991. *Honours:* Best Indie Act, DMC World DJ Awards, 1991. *Address:* c/o London Records, PO Box 1422, Chancellors House, Chancellors Rd, London W6 9SG, England. *Website:* www.londonrecords.co.uk.

DE BETHMANN, Pierre; b. 21 April 1965, Boulogne Billancourt, France. Musician (piano). m. Christel Hua, 22 Sept. 1990, 2 c. *Education:* Baccalauréat C (Science), 1982; ESCP (Paris Graduate School of Management), 1987; Classical piano, 1971–87; Private lessons, jazz piano, 1975–; Some self-training; Berklee College of Music, 1989. *Career:* Management consultant, 1990–94; Professional musician, 1994–; Member, 4 regular groups, including PRYSM, trio with Christophe Wallemme and Benjamin Henocq, 1994; Numerous gigs in most Parisian clubs, various international festivals; Numerous radio and television appearances with PRYSM; Occasionally played with: Vincent Herring; Rick Margitza; Willie Williams; Vanessa Rubin; Sylvain Beuf; Philip Catherine; George Brown; Jean-Loup Longnon; François Jeauneau; François Théberge; Aldo Romano. *Recordings:* PRYSM, PRYSM, 1995; Quoi de Neuf Docteur, Big Band; La Femme Du Bouc èmissaire; 51 Below, 1996. *Honours:* First Prize, La Defense National Jazz Contest, 1994. *Membership:* SACEM; UMJ (Union des Musiciens de Jazz). *Current Management:* Renaud di Matteo, Paris. *Address:* 16 Cité de Trévise, 75009 Paris, France.

DE BURGH, Chris, (Christopher Davison); b. 15 Oct. 1948, Argentina. Vocalist; Songwriter. *Education:* Trinity College, Dublin. *Career:* Irish tour with Horslips, 1973; Solo artiste, 1974–; Album sales, 40m.; Sell-out concerts world-wide; Performances include: Carol Aid, London, 1985; The Simple Truth, benefit concert for Kurdish refugees, Wembley, 1991; Royal Albert Hall, London. *Recordings:* Albums: Far Beyond These Castle Walls, 1975; Spanish Train And Other Stories, 1975; At The End Of A Perfect Day, 1977; Crusader, 1979; Eastern Wind, 1980; Best Moves, 1981; The Getaway, 1982; Man On The Line, 1984; The Very Best Of Chris De Burgh, 1985; Into The Light, 1986; Flying Colours, 1988; From A Spark To A Flame – The Very Best Of Chris De Burgh, 1989; High On Emotion – Live From Dublin, 1990; Power Of Ten, 1992; This Way Up, 1994; Beautiful Dreams, 1995; The Love Songs, 1997; Quiet Revolution, 1999; Notes From Planet Earth, 2001; Timing Is Everything, 2002. Singles: Flying, 1975; Patricia The Stripper, 1976; A Spaceman Came Travelling, 1976; Don't Pay The Ferryman, 1982; High On Emotion, 1984; Lady In Red (No. 1, UK), 1986; Love Is My Decision (theme from film Arthur 2), 1988; Missing You, 1988; So Beautiful, 1997; When I Think Of You, 1999; Guilty Secret, 2002. *Honours:* ASCAP Awards, The Lady In Red, 1985, 1987, 1988, 1990, 1991, 1997; IRMA Awards, Ireland, 1985–90; Beroliner Award, Germany; BAMBI Award, Germany; Midem Trophy,

France. *Current Management:* Kenny Thomson Management, 754 Fulham Rd, London SW6 5SH, England. *Website:* www.cdeb.com.

DE DAVRICHEWY, Irakli; b. 1 Feb. 1940, Paris, France. Bandleader; Musician (trumpet). 1 s., 2 d. *Education:* Early studies, violin, piano. *Career:* Formed first orchestra, 1958; Leader, own groups: The Swing Orchestra; French All-Stars; Jazz Four; Also soloist; Worked as accompanist to: Barney Bigard; Cozy Cole; Arvell Shaw; Claude Hopkins; Wallace Davenport; Christian Morin; Moustache; Numerous television broadcasts for J. C. Averty, with Victoria Spivey; Edith Wilson; Claude Bolling; Also with the Orchestra of Marc Lafferière; with Moustache et les Petits Français: accompanied Buddy Tate; Harry Edison; Al Grey; Cat Anderson; Jimmy Forrest; Eddie Vinson; Jimmy Witherspoon; Dorothy Donnegan; Played with Lionel Hampton; Dizzy Gillespie; Joe Newman; JJ Jones; Sam Woodyard; Joe Muranyi; *Tours:* Sweden; Netherlands; Germany; Switzerland; Jazz festivals include: Antibes; Coulombs; Breda; Nice; Andernos; Montauban; Hamburg; Concerts include: First part, Louis Armstrong concert, Palais des Sports, Paris, 1965; Numerous concerts for the Hot Club de France, 1984. *Recordings:* Abide With Me, Irakli Quartet, 1971; Les Petits Français with G Brassens, 1979; Le Vieux Truc, Raymond Fonsèque, 1984; Mack The Knife, Irakli Swiss All-Stars, 1985; Chicago Southside Sound, Irakli Jazz Four, 1994; Irakli At The Hot Club de Rouen, 1995. *Publications:* Producer, record and booklets for Media 7: Masters of Jazz, Louis Armstrong complete and chronological. *Honours:* Jazz Hot Award, 1959, 1962; Academie du Jazz, 1972. *Membership:* President of the Louis Armstrong Asscn, France; Creation, Paris, Louis Armstrong Square, with City of Paris. *Address:* 10 Ave Fleury, 92700 Colombes, France.

DE GROOTE, Geeraard Albert; b. 3 Sept. 1958, Blankenberge, Belgium. Songwriter; Musician (saxes, guitar, bass); Vocalist. *Education:* School of Economics, Accounting and Modern Languages; Academy of Music, Bruges; Jazz Studio, Antwerp; Jazz Academy, Knokke-Heist. *Career:* Studio recordings and TV appearances with various Belgian artists and bands; TV appearances with Tom Robinson; Belgian concerts with Tom Robinson and Tony O'Malley. *Recordings:* with Hideaway, Soul Spirit, Billy Goat Riders, Cly-An, Blond, Rhythm Deep, various Belgian artistes. *Address:* Westmoere 50, B-8490 Snellegem, Belgium. *Telephone and Fax:* 508-12-03.

DE JOHNETTE, Jack; b. 4 Aug. 1942, Chicago, Illinois, USA. Jazz Musician, (piano, drums); Bandleader; Composer. m. Lydia, 8 Sept. 1968, 2 d. *Education:* Chicago Conservatory of Music. *Career:* Performed and recorded with John Coltrane, Thelonious Monk, Miles Davis, Stan Getz, Bill Evans, Herbie Hancock, Betty Carter; currently with Keith Jarrett Trio; Pat Metheny; Gateway Trio with Dave Holland and John Abercrombie; Also leads own group. *Compositions:* Silver Hollow. *Recordings:* Albums: New Directions Live; Parallel Realities; Earth Walk; Music For The Fifth World; Special Edition; Untitled; Pictures; New Rags; Tin Can Alley; Inflation Blues; Album Album. *Honours:* Grand Prix Du Disque, Academy of Jazz, Paris, 1978; Best Jazz Album of Year, Album Album; NEA Fellow, 1978; CAPS Composers Grantee, 1980; Winner, Downbeat Readers Poll, 13 consecutive years; Numerous drum magazine awards; Swing Journal Video Award; Hon. Doctorate of Music, Berklee College of Music, 1990. *Current Management:* Alison Loerke, 1245 N E 88 St, Seattle, WA 98115, USA.

DE LA ROCHA, Zack; b. 12 Jan. 1970, Long Beach, CA, USA. Vocalist. *Career:* Former member of early bands Headstance, Farside and Inside Out; Mem., Rage Against the Machine, 1991–2000; Obtained major recording deal; Involved in various causes such as Fairness and Accuracy in Reporting, Rock for Choice and Refuse and Resist; Numerous tours including Lollapalooza; Tour with Wu Tang Clan; Contributed to soundtrack of film Godzilla, 1998. *Recordings:* Albums: Rage Against The Machine, 1992; Evil Empire, 1996; The Battle Of Los Angeles, 1998; Renegades, 2000; Live And Rare, 2002. Singles: Killing In The Name, 1993; Bullet In The Head, 1993; Bombtrack, 1993; Freedom, 1994; Bombtrack Plus Live, 1994; Bulls On Parade, 1996; People Of The Sun (EP), 1997; Guerilla Radio, 1999; Sleep Now In The Fire, 2000. *Honours:* Grammy Award, Hard Rock Performance, Guerrilla Radio, 2001. *Website:* www.ratm.com.

DE LONGE, Tom (Thomas Matthew); b. 15 Dec. 1975, San Diego, California, USA. Vocalist; Musician (guitar). m. Jennifer Jenkins, May 2001. *Career:* Co-founder: Blink-182, 1993; Built popularity with string of popular independent 7 singles; Signed to MCA through Cargo Music/MCA joint venture deal, 1997; Numerous TV appearances and concerts world-wide including: The Enema Strikes Back '99 tour, released on CD as The Mark Tom and Travis Show; 11-week US summer tour, 2001; Cameo appearance with group in American Pie film, 1999. *Recordings:* Albums: Fly Swatter (mini album), 1993; Cheshire Cat, 1994; Buddah, 1995; Dude Ranch, 1997; Enema of The State, 1999; The Mark Tom and Travis Show (live), 2000; Take Off Your Pants and Jacket, 2001; Singles: Short Bus (split 7 with The Iconoclasts), 1996; They Came To Conquer Uranus (7 EP), Lemmings (split 7 with Swindle), Dick Lips, Dammit (Growing Up), I Won't Be Home For Christmas, 1997; Josie, 1998; What's My Age Again, All The Small Things, 1999; Adam's Song, Man Overboard, 2000; The Rock Show, Stay Together For

The Kids, 2001. *Honours:* World-wide sales of 1999 album in excess of 7m. *E-mail:* tom@loserkids.com. *Website:* www.blink182.com.

DE LUCIA, Paco, (Francisco Sanchez Gomez); b. 21 Dec. 1947, Algeciras, Spain. Musician (flamenco guitar); Composer. *Career:* Debut on Radio Algeciras, 1958; Member: Paco de Lucia Sextet with brothers (including flamenco guitarist Ramon de Algeciras and vocalist Pepe de Lucia); Accompanied many flamenco singers in the 1960s before long-term association with Camaron de le Isla, 1968–; Worked with dancer Jose Greco and flamenco troupe Festival Flamenco Gitano; Live debut at Carnegie Hall, 1970; Experimented with mixing musical elements in the 1970s, laying the foundations of Nuevo Flamenco; Collaborations with jazz musicians: Chick Corea; John McLaughlin; Larry Coryell; Al DiMeola; Has also performed Spanish classical guitar repertoire. *Compositions:* Soundtracks for films: La Sabina; The Hit; Carmen; Montoyas y Tarantos; Sevillanas. *Recordings include:* Los Chiquitos de Algeciras, 1961; Dos Guitarras Flamencas, Doce Canciones de Garcia Lorca (both with Ricardo Mondrego), 1965; Dos Guitarras Flamencas En America (with Ramon de Algerciras), La Fabulosa guitarra de Paco de Lucia, 1967; Hispanoamerica, Fantasia Flamenca, 1969; Recital de Guitarra, 1971; Fantasia Flamenca de Paco de Lucia, El Duende Flamenco, 1972; En Vivo – Desde El Teatro Real, Fuente Y Caudel, 1975; Almoraima, 1976; Paco de Lucia performs Manuel de Falla with Dolores, 1978; Castro Marin, Friday Night In San Francisco (with John McLaughlin and Al DiMeola), Solo Quiero Caminar, 1981; Passion Grace and Fire (with Al DiMeola and John McLaughlin), 1983; Live... One Summer Night, 1984; Siroco, 1987; Zyryab, 1990; Concierto de Aranjuez, 1991; Live in America, 1993; The Guitar Trio (with Al DiMeola and John McLaughlin), 1996; Luzia 1998. *Honours:* Jerez Flamenco Competition, Special Prize, 1958. *Address:* International Music Network, Fourth Floor, 2 Main St, Gloucester, MA 01930, USA. *Website:* www.pacodelucia.org.

DE MAEYER, Marc; b. 23 April 1966, Willebroek, Belgium. 1 d. *Education:* Academy of Music, Mechelen, Belgium. *Career:* Keyboards and backings in Hardrockband, Rubicon, keyboards and vocals in Flemish Pop Band, Van Gogh; Producer of Demotapes, Prime Mover and Herve and Anton Menke; Writing for Petra, Yasmine and Barbara Dex; Television appointments: Tien omtezien; BRT, Man. b t Lond; Radio appointments: BRT; RSJ. *Compositions:* Elsje; Jij Bent Voor Mij; Icecubes and Diamonds; Shadow King; Moonlite; Een Nachtje Slapen. *Recordings:* Alles Draait Om Haar; Vers Bloed, demotape; Prime Mover, demotape. *Publications:* Alles Draait om Haar, 1994. *Honours:* Semi-final, Rock in Flanders, 1990. *Address:* De Maeyer Marc, Heufstraat 49, BE 3350 Overhespen, Belgium.

DE MARCOS GONZÁLEZ (CÁRDENAS), Juan; b. 1954, Havana, Cuba. Musician (Tres, Guitar); Vocalist; Composer; Arranger; Bandleader. *Education:* Studied Russian and Hydraulic Engineering at university; Agronomic Science Institute, Doctorate, 1989. *Career:* Formed Sierra Maestra, styled on the traditional Cuban septeto group, 1978; Director, arranger and conductor for Afro-Cuban All-Stars; Consultant, co-ordinator, conductor and musician on the sessions for the Buena Vista Social Club series of recordings which featured: Afro-Cuban All-Stars; Rubén Gonzalez; Ibrahim Ferrer; Compay Segundo; Omara Portuonda; Eliades Ochoa; Barbarito Torres; Guajiro Mirabel; Ry Cooder; Appeared in Wim Wenders' documentary film Buena Vista Social Club; Formed Ahora (own production company in Cuba). *Recordings:* Albums: with Sierra Maestra: ¡Dundunbanza!, 1994; Tibiri Tabara; Rumbero Soy, 2002; with Afro Cuban All-Stars: Buena Vista Social Club, A Toda Cuba Le Gusta, 1997; Buena Vista Social Club Presents Ibrahim Ferrer, Distinto Diferente, 1999. *Current Management:* SASA Music, 309 Aberdeen House, 22–24 Highbury Grove, London N5 2EA, England. *Address:* c/o World Circuit Ltd, First Floor, Shoreditch Stables, 138 Kingsland Rd, London E2 8DY, England.

DE MASURE, Geoffrey; b. 16 May 1969, Tourcoing, France. Musician (trombone). *Education:* Musical study in Avignon, 1984–89, with André Jaume in Paris, 1989, in New York and at Banff, Canada, with Steve Coleman, Robin and Kevin Eubanks, Marvin Smith, Kenny Wheeler and Rufus Reid. *Career:* Founder, Tribu; Appearances at La Défense, Concours de jazz d'Etrécchy, 1996, Orchestre National de Jazz, 1997; Appearances with Tribu at Centre Culturel Jean Cocteau, Etréchy, Centre Culturel de Marines, théâtre de Vanves, festival de Radio France de Montpellier, Jazz Club d'Auxerre, Cave Dimière à Argentueil. *Recordings:* Orchestre National de Jazz: A plus tard, 1992; Monk, Mingus, Ellington, 1993; Bouquet final, 1994; Quoi De Neuf Docteur: A l'envers, 1995; 51 degrees below, 1996; Compilation Nato, Les films de ma ville, 1995; Ronan Robert Réunion, 1996; Odejy, Suite alpestre, 1997; Hubert Dupond, Dans le décor, 1997; Malo Vallois Quartet, Complix-cités, 1997; Aka Moon, Elohim, 1997; Jean Marc Padovani: Jazz Angkor, 1998; Minotaure Jazz Orchestra, 1998. *Honours:* First prize Composition, second prize group, Tribu, Concours de Jazz d'Etrechy, 1996; First prize, soloist, third prize for group, with Tribu, third prize composition, Concours National de La Défense, 1997. *Membership:* Union Musiciens Jazz (UMJ). *Address:* Les Denizets, 02540 Vendieres, France.

DE MESMAY, Benoit; b. 10 Oct. 1961, Algeria. Composer; Musician (piano). *Education:* Licence de Droit; State diploma, professor of jazz. *Career:*

European jazz festivals with Gil Evans; Orchestre National de Jazz; Elizabeth Caumont; John Scofield; Lucky Peterson. *Recordings:* 2 albums with Elizabeth Caumont; 3 albums with Laurent Cugny, Gil Evans. *Address:* 9 rue des Mortes Fontaines, 92370 Chaville, France.

DE RYCKE, Herman; b. 20 Aug. 1960, Oudenaarde, Belgium. Musician (Double Bass). m. Maes Riet, 7 Jan. 1989, 2 s. *Education:* Solfège, Double Bass. *Career:* Mem., pop groups, Klepper, 1976–77, Penthouse, 1979–83, Allan Fawn and The State of the Art, 1984, Kandahar, 1983–86, The Peter Band Band; 1986; Mem., contemporary jazz group, Work 4, 1987–89; Mem., gipsy music groups, Kalinka Zigeunertrio, 1991, Kallai, 2001; Television appearance, Villatempo (BAT), 1986. *Compositions:* Blue Ballad, jazz. *Recordings:* Albums: with Penthouse: Neighbour Fool; with Kalinka: Kalinka; with Kallai: Komm Tzigane. Singles: with Penthouse: Neighbour Fool; with Peter Pan Band: Light My Fire. *Honours:* Winner, Humo's Rock Rally, 1986; The Peter Band Band, 1986; Winner, Knack Rhythm 'n Youth Trophy, 1989. *Membership:* SABAM. *Address:* Hoogmeers 9, 9031 Gent, Belgium.

DE SCHOOLMEESTER, Beverley; b. 4 May 1962, Britain. Songwriter; Poet; Musician (bass guitar, piano); Vocalist. *Education:* National Diploma Business Studies; Student of Scientology; Pianoforte to Teaching Standard. *Career:* Solo artist as jazz fusion singer, 1991–; Currently, bass player, backing vocalist for The Dolls, major deal pending; UK nationwide television, radio appearances also in Europe, Indonesia, Singapore, Japan, 1995; Tours: UK; France; Germany; Netherlands; Sweden; Italy; Turkey; Singapore; Indonesia; Ireland. *Recordings:* 3 EPs; Album: The Dolls: No Shame; Solo material: over 30 tracks written and demoed. *Publications:* Various poetry in magazines and local press. *Membership:* Musicians' Union; London Academy of Music. *Address:* 16 Battle St, Reading, Berkshire RG1 7NU, England.

DE SMET, Francis; b. 3 Dec. 1962, Bruges, Belgium. Musical Supervisor; Musician (Keyboards). *Education:* Harmony and Piano, Conservatory of Bruges; Electronic Music Composition, Royal Conservatory of Brussels, Academia Chigichiana, 1992. *Career:* Musical Supervision, Transatlantic Films, Brussels, 1992–; Developing patented sound enhancer. *Compositions:* Filmtrack of The Sexual Life of the Belgians, 1993. *Membership:* AES. *Current Management:* BVBA INTERNETV, Generaal Lemanlaan 151, 8310, Bruges, Belgium.

DE SOUTEIRO, Arnaldo; b. 23 June 1963, Rio de Janeiro, Brazil. Record Prod; Journalist; Publicist; Educator. m. Ithamara Koorax, 15 April 1990. *Education:* Classical Piano, Harmony, privately with mother Pianist and Conductor Delza Agricola. *Career:* Founder and President, Jazz Station Records, 1991–; Jazz Critic, Tribune da Imprensa, 1979–; Brazilian Correspondent, Keyboard Magazine, 1986–95; Produced TV Specials for Globo and Manchete networks including Joao Gilberto and Antonio Carlos Jobim, Dizzy Gillespie, Tony Bennett, Airto, Flora Purim and Chuck Mangione. *Recordings:* As Producer, albums for Luiz Bonfá, The Bonfá Magic; Dom um Romao, Rhythm Traveller; Ithamara Koorax, Serenade in Blue; Joao Gilberto, Ao Vivo/Live in Rio; Thiago de Mello, Amazon; Deodato, Inútil Paisagem; Also produced acclaimed compilation series for Brazilian Horizons and A Trip To Brazil; Produced sessions featuring Herbie Hancock, Yana Purim, Steve Swallow, Antonio Carlos Jobim, Ron Carter, Sadao Watanabe, Larry Coryell and Gonzalo Rubalcaba. *Membership:* Hon. Mem., International Academy of Music, 1985–; Associate Mem., International Asscn of Jazz Educators, 1991–. *Address:* Rua Miguel Lemos 99, Suite 801, 22071–000 Rio de Janeiro, RJ, Brazil.

DE VIS, Alain; b. 6 Sept. 1953, Brussels, Belgium. Musician (Trumpet; Flugelhorn); Composer; Arranger. m. Nanga Marie-Jeanne, 30 June 1984, 4 s. *Education:* Mathematics and Physics; Classical, School in Nivelles, Belgium, 1971. *Career:* Small commercial bands, 1975; Jazz bands and big bands, 1979; Salsa and Brazilian bands, 1979/80–; Concerts with: Fania All Stars, 1981; Brasil Tropical, shows, in Europe; Salsa De Hoy; Dynamita Salsa. *Recordings:* Act Big Band, second album; Many studio sessions for Singers in 1980s. *Membership:* SABAM, Composer. *Current Management:* Dynamic Sounds Productions, rue G Wincqz 24, 7060 Soignies, Belgium. *Address:* Rue G Wincqz 24, 7060 Soignies, Belgium.

DE VORE, David; b. 27 March 1943, Hilo, Hawaii, USA. Prod; Engineer. m. Janine, 3 July 1976, 1 d. *Education:* 2 years college, Engineering/Architecture. *Career:* Producer, Engineer for Fleetwood Mac; Grateful Dead; Santana; Elton John; REO Speedwagon; Ringo Starr; Russ Ballard. *Recordings include:* (as producer) Don't Let The Sun Go Down On Me; Hot Blooded; Can't Fight This Feeling.

DE VRIES, Marius; b. 21 Oct. 1961, London, England. Prod; Remixer; Songwriter; Musician (keyboards); Programmer; Arranger. m. Felicity, 1 April 1989, 1 s., 1 d. *Education:* Peterhouse College, Cambridge; Music Scholarship, St Paul's Cathedral Choir School; Music Scholarship at Bedford School. *Career:* Two world tours with Blow Monkeys; Musical Director for Rick Astley's tour, 1989; Musical Director for Neneh Cherry, 1991; Television appearances include: South Banks Arts Review; Jonathan Ross; Top of the Pops; The Word; The Tube; In studio, 1991–; Music Supervisor for Warner

Bros The Avengers, 1997–98. *Compositions:* Co-composer and Co-producer of score for Baz Luhrman's Romeo and Juliet, 1996. *Recordings:* Albums: with Madonna: Bedtime Stories, 1994; Ray of Light, 1998; with Björk: Debut, 1993; Post, 1995; Homogenic, 1997; Vespertine, 2001; with Massive Attack: Protection, 1994; with Annie Lennox: Diva, 1992; Medusa, 1995; with U2: Hold Me Thrill Me Kiss Me Kill Me, 1995, Pop, 1997; with Robbie Robertson, Contact from the Underground of Red Boy, 1998; with Neil Finn, Try Whistling This, 1998; with Melanie C, Northern Star, 1999. *Publications:* Various magazine articles. *Membership:* PRS; Musicians' Union.

DEACON, John; b. 19 Aug. 1951, Leicester, England. Musician (bass). *Education:* First class (hons) degree, Electronics. *Career:* Bass player, UK rock group, Queen, 1971–; Numerous tours include: UK; USA; Australia; Japan; South America; Major concerts include: Rock In Rio Festival, Brazil, 1985; Live Aid, Wembley, 1985; Knebworth Festival, 1986; A Concert For Life, Wembley, 1992. *Recordings:* Albums include: Queen, 1973; Queen 2, 1974; Sheer Heart Attack, 1974; A Night At The Opera (No. 1, UK), 1975; A Day At The Races (No. 1, UK), 1976; Jazz, 1978; Live Killers, 1979; The Game (No. 1, UK and USA), 1980; Flash Gordon (film soundtrack), 1980; Greatest Hits (No. 1, UK), 1981; Hot Space, 1982; The Works, 1984; The Complete Works, 1985; A Kind of Magic (No. 1, UK), 1986; Live Magic, 1986; The Miracle (No. 1, UK), 1989; Innuendo (No. 1, UK), 1991; Greatest Hits II (No. 1, UK) 1991; Live At Wembley '86, 1992; Made In Heaven (No. 1, UK), 1995; Queen Greatest Hits III, 1998; Small Soldiers, 1998; Surfin' Senorita, 1999; Singles include: Seven Seas of Rhye, 1974; Killer Queen, 1974; Now I'm Here, 1975; Bohemian Rhapsody (No. 1, UK), 1975; You're My Best Friend, 1976; Somebody To Love, 1977; We Are The Champions, 1977; Bicycle Race, 1978; Don't Stop Me Now, 1979; Love of My Life, 1979; Crazy Little Thing Called Love (No. 1, USA), 1979; Save Me, 1980; Play The Game, 1980; Another One Bites The Dust (No. 1, USA), 1980; Flash, 1981; Under Pressure, with David Bowie (No. 1, UK), 1981; Radio Ga Ga, 1984; I Want To Break Free, 1984; It's A Hard Life, 1984; Hammer To Fall, 1984; One Vision, 1985; A Kind of Magic, 1986; I Want It All, 1989; Breakthru, 1989; The Invisible Man, 1989; Innuendo (No. 1, UK), 1991; Headlong, 1991; The Show Must Go On, 1991; These Are The Days of Our Lives/Bohemian Rhapsody (No. 1, UK), 1991; Five Live (live EP with George Michael and Lisa Stansfield) (No. 1, UK), 1993; Heaven For Everyone, 1995; Too Much Love Will Kill You, 1995; Also contributed to recordings by: Elton John, Mick Ronson. *Honours:* Britannia Award, 1977; Gold Ticket, Madison Square Gardens, 1978; Ivor Novello Awards: Best Selling British Record, 1976; Outstanding Contribution to British Music, 1987; Silver Clef Award, Nordoff-Robbins Music Therapy Centre, 1984; BRIT Awards: Outstanding Contribution to British Music, 1990; Best British Single, 1991. *Current Management:* c/o Jim Beach, Queen Productions, 46 Pembridge Rd, London W11 3HN, England. *Website:* www.queen-fip.com.

DEAL, Kim; b. 10 June 1961, Dayton, Ohio, USA. Musician (bass, guitar); Songwriter; Vocalist. m. John Murphy, divorced 1988. *Career:* Joined The Pixies; Early support slots to Throwing Muses; Numerous tours and festival dates; Some television appearances; Band split, 1993; Formed The Breeders; Tours and record releases; Formed The Amps, 1995. *Recordings:* Albums with The Pixies: Come On Pilgrim, 1987; Surfer Rosa, 1988; Doolittle, 1989; Bossanova, 1990; Trompe Le Monde, 1991; Death To The Pixies (compilation), 1997; Live At The BBC (radio sessions), 1998; Complete B-Sides, 2001; with The Breeders: Pod, 1990; Last Splash, 1993; Title TK, 2002; with The Amps: Pacer, 1995. Singles: with The Pixies: Gigantic, 1988; Monkey Gone To Heaven, 1989; Here Comes Your Man, 1989; Velouria, 1990; Dig For Fire, 1990; Planet Of Sound, 1991; Alec Eiffel, 1991; Head On, 1991; Debaser, 1989; with The Breeders: Safari (EP), 1992; Cannonball, 1993; Divine Hammer, 1993; Head To Toe, 1994; with The Amps: Tipp City, 1995. *Address:* c/o 4AD Records, 17–19 Alma Rd, London SW18 1AA, England. *Website:* www.4AD.com.

DEAN, Elton; b. 28 Oct. 1945. Musician (saxello, alto saxophone). m. Marie-Noelle Sala, 16 Jan. 1988, 1 d. *Career:* Worked with: Keith Tippett Sextet; Soft Machine, Proms concert, 1970; Brotherhood of Breath; London Jazz Composer's Orchestra; Carla Bley; Just Us; EDQ; Own nine-piece group Ninesense, 1975; Elton Dean Quintet, tour of Brazil, British Council, 1986; Leader, various groups including: Unlimited Saxophone Company; In Cahoots; Equip Out; Formed quartet with Howard Riley. *Recordings:* with Julie Driscoll: Julie Driscoll; with Julie Tippetts: Sunset Glow; with Soft Machine: Third; Fourth; Fifth; with Robert Wyatt: End of An Ear; with Keith Tippett: I Am There... You Are Here; Dedicated To You... But You Weren't Listening; with Keith Tippett's Centipede: Septober Energy; with Ninesense: Oh! For The Edge; Happy Daze; with Elton Dean Quintet: Boundaries; with Elton Dean and Alan Skidmore: El Skid; with Carla Bley: European tour; with Dean, Gallivan, Wheeler: The Cheque Is In The Mail; Elton Dean's Newsense, 1998; Elton Dean Trio, Into the Nierika, 1998; Elton Dean Headless Qt, 1998; Other. *Recordings include:* Elton Dean Duos, Trios, Quartet; Elton Dean's Unlimited Saxophone Company; Elton Dean/Howard Riley Quartet; Elton Dean: The Vortex Tapes; If Dubois Only Knew, with Paul Dunmall duo, 1996; Silent Knowledge, Elton Dean Quintet, 1996; Rumours of an Incident, Quintet with Roswell Rudd, 1997; Bladik, with Mujician and Roswell Rudd, 1997; Virtually, Soft Machine, 1998; Noisette,

Soft Machine, 1999; One to One, with Howard Riley, 1999; Moorsong, with Fred T Baker, 2000. *Address:* 7 Farleigh Rd, London N16 7TB, England.

DEAN, Johnny; b. 12 Dec. 1971. Vocalist; Songwriter. *Career:* Singer, songwriter, Menswear, 1994–; Television includes: Later With... Britpop Now, 1995; Support tours with: The Charlatans, USA; Pulp, Europe; Several headline British tours; Major concerts include: Heineken Festival, Leeds, 1995. *Recordings:* Albums: Nuisance, 1995; We Love You, 1996; Hay Tiempo, 1998; Singles: I'll Manage Somehow, 1995; Daydreamer, 1995; Being Brave, 1995; Sleeping In, 1995. *Address:* c/o Laurel Records, PO Box 1422, Chancellors House, Chancellors Rd, London W6 9SG, England.

DEARIE, Blossom; b. 28 April 1928, East Durham, New York, USA. Vocalist; Songwriter; Musician (piano). *Education:* Piano lessons from age 5; Studied classical music. *Career:* Joined the Blue Flames, vocal group within the Woody Herman Big Band; Member, The Blue Reys, in the Alvino Rey Band; Moved to Paris, founder member, vocal group, the Blue Stars, 1952; Returned to New York, solo artiste, New York nightclubs; Annual appearances, Ronnie Scott's Club, London, 1966–; Formed own record company, Daffodil Records, 1971; Played Carnegie Hall with Joe Williams, and jazz vocalist Anita O'Day in show the Jazz Singers, 1970s; 6 months a year, The Ballroom, Manhattan, 1983–; Appeared The Pizza on the Park, late 80s/early 90s. *Compositions include:* I Like You You're Nice; I'm Shadowing You; Hey John. *Recordings:* Albums include: My Gentleman Friend, 1961; May I Come In?, 1966; The Special Magic of Blossom Dearie, 1975; My New Celebrity Is You, 1979; Blossom Dearie Sings 1973, 1979; Blossom Dearie Sings 1975, 1979; Winchester In Apple Blossom Time, 1979; May I Come In?, 1981; Blossom Dearie, 1983; Needlepoint Magic, 1988; Featuring Bobby Jasper, 1988; Songs of Chelsea, 1988; Et Tu Bruce, 1989; Tweedledum and Tweedledee, 1991; Once Upon A Summertime, 1993; I'm Hip, 1998. *Honours:* First recipient, Mabel Mercer Foundation Award, 1985. *Current Management:* F Sharp Productions, Penthouse B, 157 W 57th St, New York, NY 10019, USA.

DEARNLEY, Mark; b. 12 Aug. 1957, Barnet, England. Prod; Engineer; Musician (keyboards). *Education:* Southampton University; Piano, Organ. *Career:* Engineer credits include: AC/DC, 3 albums; Circus of Power; The English Beat, 3 albums; Joan Armatrading; Def Leppard, remix; Paul McCartney; Producer credits include: The Dog's D'Amour, 3 albums; Steve Jones; Mother Love Bone; The Quireboys; Loudness; Bang Tango; Die Cheerleader; Owen Paul; The Wild Family; Scream 2; South Park; American Pie. *Honours:* Numerous Platinum, Gold and Silver records. *Current Management:* Worlds End (America) Inc. *Address:* 183 N Martel Ave, Suite 270, Los Angeles, CA 90036, USA.

DEBNEY, John; b. 18 Aug. 1956, Burbank, CA, USA. Composer. *Education:* Music, Loyola University. *Compositions:* For television: Star Trek: The Next Generation, 1987; A Pup Named Scooby-Doo, 1988; Trenchcoat in Paradise, 1989; The Young Riders, 1989; The Face of Fear, 1990; Still Not Quite Human, 1992; Sunstroke, 1992; Praying Mantis, 1993; SeaQuest DSV, 1993; Class of '61, 1993; For Love and Glory, 1993; Kansas, 1995; Doctor Who, 1996; The Pretender, 1996; The Cape, 1996; Running Mates, 2000; For film: The Wild Pair, 1987; Seven Hours to Judgment, 1988; Not Since Casanova, 1988; The Further Adventures of Tennessee Buck, 1988; Jetsons: The Movie, 1990; The Halloween Tree, 1993; Hocus Pocus, 1993; White Fang II: Myth of the White Wolf, 1994; Gunmen, 1994; Little Giants, 1994; Sudden Death, 1995; Runaway Brain, 1995; Chameleon, 1995; Houseguest, 1995; Cutthroat Island, 1995; Getting Away with Murder, 1996; Carpool, 1996; The Relic, 1997; Liar Liar, 1997; I Know What You Did Last Summer, 1997; Paulie, 1998; I'll Be Home for Christmas, 1998; My Favourite Martian, 1999; Lost & Found, 1999; Inspector Gadget, 1999; Dick, 1999; The Adventures of Elmo in Grouchland, 1999; End of Days, 1999; Komodo, 1999; Michael Jordan to the Max, 2000; Relative Values, 2000; The Replacements, 2000; The Emperor's New Groove, 2000; See Spot Run, 2001; Spy Kids, 2001; Heartbreakers, 2001; Cats and Dogs, 2001; The Princess Diaries, 2001; Jimmy Neutron: Boy Genius, 2002; The Scorpion King, 2002. *Honours:* Emmy Awards, The Young Riders, SeaQuest DSV. *Membership:* ASCAP. *Current Management:* Blue Focus Management, 15233 Ventura Blvd, Suite 200, Sherman Oaks, CA 91403, USA. *Website:* www.johndebney.com.

DEBORG, Jerry Simon; b. 30 Oct. 1963, London, England. Musician (guitar); Songwriter; Vocalist. *Education:* Harrow College of Art. *Career:* Member of Jesus Jones, 1986–; Numerous appearances on radio and TV; Several chart hits. *Recordings:* Numerous including: Singles: Info Freako, 1989; Never Enough, 1989; Bring it On Down, 1989; Real Real Real, 1990; Right Here Right Now (No. 2, USA), 1991; International Bright Young Thing, 1991; Who Where Why, 1991; The Devil You Know, 1993; The Right Decision, 1993; Zeroes and Ones, 1993; The Next Big Thing, 1997; Albums: Liquidizer, 1989; Doubt (No. 1, UK), 1991; Perverse, 1993; Already, 1997; London, 2001. *Honours:* Best New Band, MTV, 1991. *Current Management:* Gailforce. *Address:* c/o 30 Ives St, London SW3 2ND, England.

DEDIC, Srdan; b. 13 July 1965, Zagreb, Croatia. Composer; Arranger; Musician (piano). *Education:* Degree in Composition, Zagreb Academy of

Music; Specialization at l'Universitè des Sciences Humaines de Strasbourg; Sweelinck Conservatorium, Amsterdam. *Career:* Participated at Gaudeamus Festival (Amsterdam); International Rostum of Composers (Paris); Music Biennale, Zagreb; Performed solo from own. *Compositions:* Mouvement Concertante, with Zagreb Philharmonic; 9 orchestral performances; Over 50 performances in Europe, America, Australia; Writing music for television, theatres, films. *Compositions:* Snake Charmer, bass clarinet solo, 1986; Beat On, for orchestra, 1988; Canzona, cello, guitar, 1988; Calix, symphonic poem, 1990; At The Party, 1990; Concerto for cello and chamber orchestra; 12 compositions recorded for Croatian Radio; Supercussion album includes composition: At The Party. *Publications:* Composing Using Music Software (brochure). *Honours:* First Prize, UNESCO – International Rostrum of Composers, Paris, 1987; Award, student orchestral works, Music Biennale Zagreb, 1989; Winner, Composition Contest, 29th annual Contemporary Music Festival, Indiana State University, 1995. *Membership:* Croatian Composers Society. *Current Management:* Dr Peter Höhn, Schanze 13, D 57392 Schmallenberg, Germany. *Address:* Srdan Dedic, Hugo de Grootplein 12, 1052 KW Amsterdam, Netherlands.

DEE, Brian; b. 21 March 1936, London, England. Musician (piano); Songwriter. m. 28 Dec. 1966, divorced 1982, 1 s., 1 d. *Career:* Jazz pianist, late 1950s–; Session musician and accompanist; Extensive BBC radio with trio and many bands; Pianist with: Ted Heath Orchestra; Kenny Baker Dozen; Laurie Johnson; Performed at numerous concerts and festivals. *Compositions:* Background music. *Recordings:* Featured on approximately 25 albums in three years, including own albums. *Membership:* PRS; Musicians' Union; BACSA; MCPS; PAMRA. *Address:* 130 Sheering Mill Lane, Sawbridgeworth, Hertfordshire CM21 9ND, England.

DEE, Kiki, (Pauline Matthews); b. 6 March 1947, Bradford, England. Vocalist. *Career:* Leader, Kiki Dee band; Recording artist, 1964–; First white artist signed to Tamla-Motown; Cabaret singer, Europe and South Africa; Appearances, London musicals: Pump Boys and Dinettes, 1984; Blood Brothers, 1989; Solo acoustic tour with guitarist Carmelo Uggeri, support to Jools Holland, UK, 1995. *Recordings:* Albums: I'm Kiki Dee, 1968; Great Expectations, 1971; Loving and Free, 1973; I've Got The Music In Me, 1974; Kiki Dee, 1977; Stay With Me, 1979; Perfect Timing, 1982; Angel Eyes, 1987; Almost Naked, 1995; Singles include: I'm Gonna Run Away From You; Running Out of Fools; Amoureuse, 1973; I've Got The Music In Me, 1974; How Glad I Am, 1975; Don't Go Breaking My Heart, duet with Elton John (No. 1, UK and USA), 1976; Star, 1981; True Love, duet with Elton John (No. 2, UK), 1993.

DEFRANCO, Buddy (Boniface Ferdinand Leonard); b. 17 Feb. 1923, Camden, New Jersey, USA. Musician (clarinet); Bandleader. m. Joyce Yount, 1 s. *Education:* Mastbaum Music School, Philadelphia. *Career:* Clarinet/saxophone player with: Johnny Davis Band, 1939; Gene Krupa Orchestra, 1941–42; Tommy Dorsey Orchestra, 1944–48; Count Basie Septet, 1950; Bandleader, Buddy DeFranco Orchestra, 1951; Clarinettist, Jazz At The Philharmonic All-Star Tours, 1952–54; Conductor, Glenn Miller Orchestra, 1966–74; Bandleader, Buddy DeFranco Group, 1974–; Collaborations include: Fats Navarro; Charlie Barnet. *Compositions:* You Must Believe in Swing, 1997; Finegan's Walk, 1998; Skinnin' Rabbits, 1998. *Recordings:* Albums: Flying Fingers of Art Tatum and Buddy DeFranco; Cross-Country Suite (with Nelson Riddle); Mr Lucky; Mood Indigo; Chicago Fire (with Terry Gibbs); George Gershwin Song Book (with Oscar Peterson); Hark, with Oscar Peterson, 1985; Five Notes of Blues, 1992; Born To Swing, 1993; Buenos Aires Concert, 1995; You Must Believe in Swing, with Dave McKenna, 1997; Do Nothing Till You Hear From Us, with Dave McKenna, 1999; Chip Off the Old Bop. *Publications:* Buddy DeFranco on Jazz Improvisation, 1973; Modern Jazz Studies, 1973; Studies For Clarinet, 1973; Hand in Hand with Hanon. *Honours:* Voted Best Jazz Clarinettist, numerous magazine polls; Grammy Award, Cross-Country Suite, 1956. *Membership:* Fellow, National Assccn Jazz Educators; ASCAP; Board of Directors, ClariNetwork, 1980–. *Address:* PO Box 252, Sunnyside, FL 32461, USA.

DEGAS, Jorge; b. 5 July 1953, Rio De Janeiro, Brasil. Musician (Bass). m. Stenia Degas, 4 s., 1 d. *Education:* Autodidact. *Career:* Festival of Art and Black Culture, Nigeria, 1977; Festival of Cascais, Portugal, 1978; Show, Celebration of Independance, Angola, 1979; Festival in Montreaux, Nyon, 1982; Rock in Rio, 1983; Festival in Avante, Portugal, 1984; Festival Free Jazz, Brazil, 1985; Show, Pao De Acuca, Rio, 1986; Show, Olympia de Paris, 1988; Festival, Jazz in the Garden, Berlin, 1989; Festival, Jazz in July, Berlin, 1990; Copenhagen Jazzhouse Feat, 1991; Midtfyns Festival, Denmark, 1993; Copenhagen Jazz Festival, 1994; Baixo Brasil, Bass Festival, 1996. *Compositions:* Music to Film, Paraiba Mulher Macho; Bom Burges; Dona Beija. *Recordings:* Include, M Resende and Index; Uniao; Muxima; Quarteto Negro; Ready for Changes; Violeiro; Xiame; Shadow of My Soul; Cantar a Vida. *Membership:* The Danish Music Asscn. *Current Management:* Degas Skolevej 9, 5620 Glamsbjerg, Denmark.

DEGIORGIO, Kirk, (As One, Future Past, Esoterik); b. 1967, London, England. Prod; Remixer; DJ. *Career:* Worked in Reckless Records shop in London; Travelled to Detroit: Became inspired by Derrick May and Juan Atkins to make music; On return to London started producing; Founder: A.R.T.; Op-Art Records; Released tracks by artists including: Carl Craig; Black Dog; Also recorded albums for Mo' Wax and Ubiquity Records; Collaborations: Jamie Odell; Ian O'Brien; Dan Keeling; Remixed: Alien; Newcleus; 4 Hero. *Membership:* PRS. *E-mail:* opart@dircon.co.uk. *Website:* www.kirkdegiorgio.com.

DEGO. See: **MACFARLANE, Denis.**

DEGRYSE, Fabien; b. 6 Nov. 1960, Brussels, Belgium. Musician (guitar); Composer; Teacher. m. Guns Colette, 1985, 2 s., 2 d. *Education:* Certificate, Berklee College of Music, Boston, USA, 2 years. *Career:* Played with Zar, 1985–87, including tour in Canada and Belgium; Played with Quadruplex, 1985–92; Concerts with PH Catherine and Toots Thielemans; Played with Panta Rhei including recording of 3 CDs and numerous concerts and festivals between 1994 and 1997, in Europe and Africa; Still plays with L'Ame Des Poetes including Recording of 2 CDs and numerous concerts and festivals and broadcasting in Europe, Africa and Canada, 1994; Tchr, Jazz Guitar, Conservatory of Brussels, Belgium. *Recordings:* Quadruplex, CD, 1990; Medor Sadness, CD, 1992; Hommage á René Thomas, CD, 1997. *Publications:* L'Improvisation Jazz par les arpèges, 1999. *Current Management:* Rue E Laurent 100, 1420 Braine L'Alleud, Belgium.

DEHAVEN, Penny (Charlotte); b. 17 May 1948, Winchester, Virginia, USA. Vocalist; Actress. *Career:* As Penny Starr: Singer on Jamboree USA; Name changed to Penny Dehaven; One of first female singers to entertain US troops in Viet Nam; Film appearances include: Country Music Story; Travelling Light; Honky Tonk Man. *Recordings:* Singles: Grain of Salt; I Feel Fine; Land Mark Tavern (with Del Reeves); We Made Memories (with Boxcar Willie); Albums: Penny DeHaven, 1972; Penny DeHaven, 1984; Film soundtrack, Bronco Billy. *Current Management:* Morningstar Public Relations, PO Box 83, Brentwood, TN 37027, USA.

DEKKER, Desmond, (Desmond Dacres); b. 16 July 1941, Kingston, Jamaica. Vocalist. *Career:* Solo artiste, also with own group, The Aces, 1963–; Concerts and tours include: Caribbean Music Festivals, Wembley, 1969, 1970; Ethiopian Benefit Concert, London (with Smiley Culture, Lee Perry, Dennis Brown), 1985; Regular international tours. *Recordings include:* Albums: This Is Desmond Dekker, 1969; Israelites, 1969; Black and Dekker, 1980; Compass Point, 1981; King of Ska, 1991; Action!, 1994; King of Kings, 1995; Moving Out, 1996; Intensified, 1997; Writing on the Wall, 1998; Halfway To Paradise, 2000; Hit singles: 20 No. 1 recordings in Jamaica; Also: 007 (Shanty Town), 1967; The Israelites (No. 1, UK), 1969; You Can Get It If You Really Want (No. 2, UK), 1970. *Honours:* First Jamaican artiste to have UK No. 1 record, 1969. *Address:* c/o Barry Collings Entertainments, 21a Clifftown Rd, Southend-on-Sea, Essex SS1 1AB, England.

DEL FRA, Riccardo; b. 20 Feb. 1956, Rome, Italy. Musician (double bass); Composer. *Education:* 3 years university, studying Sociology; Double bass, Conservatorio di Frosinone; Private music studies. *Career:* Member, RAI TV Orchestra, Rome; Played with pianist Enrico Pieranunzi; Freelance backing musician, touring with artists in Italy including: Slide Hampton; Art Farmer; Kai Winding; Played with Chet Baker, trio and quartet (9 years partnership, 12 albums, radio, television and films, tours of Europe and Japan); Freelance work with Johnny Griffin; Toots Thielemans (tours of USA and Japan); Bob Brookmeyer; Also played with Art Blakey and the Jazz Messengers; Kenny Wheeler; Paul Motian; Sonny Stitt; James Moody; Clifford Jordan; Joe Diorio (tours of Italy). *Compositions:* Silent Call (for jazz quartet and string orchestra); Inner Galaxy (for tenor sax, double bass and four cellos); Aux Fontaines Du Temple (for jazz septet, flutes, harp and string orchestra); Volo sul Lago, for symphonic orchestra and jazz septet, 1996; Many pieces for different jazz ensembles; Film soundtracks, trilogy of films dir by Lucas Belvaux, Un Couple Épasant, Cavale, Aprés la Vie. *Recordings:* A Sip Of Your Touch; 12 with Chet Baker include: Chet Sings Again; Mr B; At The Capolinea; Paris Suite, with Bob Brookmeyer; Voulouz Loar, duet with Annie Ebrel; Also recorded with Dominique Pifarely, Jacques Pellen. *Honours:* Grand Prix FNAC '89, A Sip of Your Touch, 1989; 'Choc' du Monde de la Musique; Diapason d'Or, 1999. *Address:* 7 Quai de la Garonne, 75019 Paris, France. *E-mail:* r.delfra@free.fr.

DEL NAJA, Robert. See: **3-D.**

DELAGAYE, Freddy; b. 6 June 1944, Eeklo, Belgium. Musician (trumpet); Prod; Impressario. m. Veronica Ng, 7 March 1977, 1 s. *Education:* Economics; Dutch; French; German; English; Music Academy, piano, trumpet. *Career:* Tour with various bands: Gerry Hayes Orchestra; Bob Azzam Band, from early 60s; With own band the Freddy Delagaye Clan, late 70s–; Numerous concerts and television appearances in most European countries, Middle East, South East Asia, 1980–; MSP (Music and Show Productions), own company in Belgium for television, concerts and special events; Represents: Wall Street Crash; Helen Shapiro; Pasadena Roof Orchestra; Les Bubb. *Recordings:* Bob Azzam Band: Mustapha; C'est Ecrit Dans Le Ciel; Luna Capresse; Various studio sessions in: Benelux; Scandinavia; France; Germany; Switzerland. *Honours:* Twice winner: Euro Star Festival, representative of UK Artists:

Cantabile, 1987; Fairer Sax, 1988; Award for organizing 100th day festivities, Ghent, Belgium. *Membership:* BVI (Professional Asscn Impressarios), Belgium. *Address:* Galgestraat 1, 9970 Kaprijke, Belgium. *Telephone:* (9) 3370673. *Fax:* (9) 3372900. *E-mail:* freddy@delagaye.com. *Website:* www.delagaye.com.

DELAKIAN, Michel Horen; b. 6 Nov. 1957, Saint Etienne, France. Musician (trumpet); Composer. m. Isabelle, 20 Feb. 1982, 1 s., 1 d. *Education:* Ecole Nationale de Musique, St Etienne. *Career:* Member, Claude Bolling Big Band, 1982–; Also played with: Martial Solal, 1983–85; Orchestre National de Jazz, 1986–89; Michel Legrand, 1994–95; Sacha Distel et les Collegiens, 1994–95; Leads own quartet; Television: Musiques Au Coeur, France 2, 1992; Jazz A Juan, 1986; Jazz 6, 1988; Tours include: Africa, 1986; Canada, 1987; USA, 1988, 1989, 1991; Thailand; People's Republic of China, 1994; Mexico, 1995; Turkey, 1995. *Recordings:* Solo: Biarritz; with Orchestre National De Jazz: 1986; 1987; with Claude Bolling Big Band: Plays Ellington (Vols 1 and 2); Also recorded with Stephane Grappelli. *Publications:* Nina, 2 compositions, included in Le Livre Du Jazz En France. *Honours:* Prix Sidney Bechet, Académie Du Jazz, 1987. *Membership:* SACEM; ADAMI; SPEDIDAM. *Current Management:* Mathilde Creixams Co-ordination Musicale. *Address:* 14 rue Giradon, 75018 Paris, France.

DELANEY, Larry (Lawrence); b. 30 Aug. 1942, Eastview, Ontario, Canada. Newspaper Editor; Publisher. m. Joanne Bonell, 1 Aug. 1964, 1 s., 1 d. *Education:* College. *Career:* Co-founder, current Editor, Publisher, Country Music News, Canada's national music newspaper, established 1980, providing international exposure and profile for Canadian country music artists and industry. *Publications:* Country Music News. *Honours:* 8 times recipient, Canadian Country Music Asscn: Country Music Person of the Year; Inducted into Builders Category, Canadian Music Hall of Fame, 1989; Inducted into Canadian Country Music Hall of Honour, 1996. *Membership:* CCMA; CMA; CPPA. *Address:* PO Box 7323 Vanier Term, Ottawa, Ont K1L 8E4, Canada.

DELANO, Darlene; b. 27 Sept. 1955, Hartford, Connecticut, USA. PR Exec; Artist Man. m. 23 June 1976 to 28 Oct. 1983, 1 d. *Education:* BA, University of Connecticut. *Career:* Publicist for: Carmine Appice; Yngwie Malmsteen; Coma; Management for: The Itch; Naked Rhythm; John Goodwin. *Honours:* Women In Business Award, 1993. *Membership:* Licensed Talent Agent, State of Florida. *Current Management:* Long Distance Entertainment. *Address:* PO Box 223907, Hollywood, FL 33023, USA.

DELGADO, Junior, (Oscar Hibbert); b. 1958, Kingston, Jamaica. Reggae Vocalist. *Career:* School concerts and local talent contests; Singer with Time Unlimited; Solo artist, 1975–; Owner, Incredible Jux record label, Jamaica; Collaborations: Augustus Pablo; Sinead O'Connor; Yami Bolo. *Recordings:* Singles: with Time Unlimited: Reaction; The Twenty Third Psalm; Numerous solo. *Recordings include:* Rasta Dreadlocks; Skanga; Run Baldhead; Thinking; Every Natty; Tition; Devil's Throne; Love Won't Come Easy; Trickster; Armed Robbery; Away With Your Fussing and Fighting; Fisherman Row; Jah Stay; Nine Fence; Poverty; Illegal Gun; Bus I Skull; Raggamuffin Year; Forward Revolution; Hanging Tree; Riot Inna Juvenile Prison; Dubschool; We A Blood; Another Place in Time; Fearless. *Address:* c/o Rick Davey, Unit C, Imperial Works, Perren St, London NW5 7EE, England.

DELIA, (Sparrow McShade); b. 14 Nov. 1969, London, England. Musician (guitar, flute, drums); Vocalist. *Education:* Grade 3 flute; GCSE Music; Islington Sixth Form Centre. *Career:* Member, Mambo Taxi, 1991–95; Extensive English tours; 1 album, 3 singles; Television and radio appearances include: Chart Show, ITV; Local television; BBC Radio 1; GLR; Member, Phantom Pregnancies, 1995–; Scott Bond Commandos, 1995–; Low Down No Goods, 1995–. *Recordings:* Various split singles and compilation tracks; Latest album: Assassination City, 1995. *Publications:* But That's Downbeat and Ridiculous Shawn. *Honours:* Too Pure Awards, 1994. *Membership:* PRS; Musicians' Union. *Address:* c/o Rough Trade Shop, 130 Talbot Rd, London W11 1JA, England.

DELP, Brad; b. 12 June 1951, Boston, Massachusetts, USA. Musician (guitar); Vocalist. *Career:* Founder member, US rock group Boston, 1976–; One of most successful debut albums ever (17m. album sales in USA alone), 1978; British tour, 1979; US tour, 1987; Guest with Ringo Starr, 1989; Formed RTZ, 1991; Guest with Nelson, 1991. *Recordings:* Albums: Boston (No. 1, USA), 1976; Don't Look Back (No. 1, USA), 1978; Third Stage (No. 1, USA), 1986; with RTZ: Return To Zero, 1991; Hit singles with Boston: More Than A Feeling, 1976; Long Time, 1977; Peace of Mind, 1977; Don't Look Back, 1978; Amanda (No. 1, USA), 1986; We're Ready, 1987; Cantcha Say, 1987; Also worked with: Sammy Hagar. *Current Management:* Boston, PO Box 6191, Lincoln Center, MA 01773, USA. *Address:* c/o PGE, 244 Pleasant St, Franklin, MA 02038, USA.

DELS, Anita; b. 28 Dec. 1971, Amsterdam, Netherlands. Vocalist. *Career:* Singer, 2 Unlimited, 1990–. *Recordings:* Albums: Get Ready, 1992; No Limits, 1993; Real Things, 1994; Hits Unlimited, 1995; Singles: Twilight Zone, 1992; Workaholic, 1992; The Magic Friend, 1992; No Limits (No. 1, UK), 1993; Tribal Dance, 1993; Faces, 1993; Maximum Overdrive, 1993; Let The Beat

Control Your Body, 1994; The Real Thing, 1994; No One, 1994; Here I Go, 1995; Do What's Good For Me, 1995. *Current Management:* Michel Maartens, CBA Artists, PO Box 1495, 1200 BL Hilversum, Netherlands.

DELSON, Brad; b. 1 Dec. 1977, Agoura, CA, USA. Musician (guitar). *Education:* Communications, University of California at Los Angeles; Former trumpet, guitar student. *Career:* Mem., The Pricks, Relative Degree; Founding mem., Xero; Renamed Hybrid Theory and signed to Warner Bros, Spring 2000; Further name change to Linkin Park prior to first record releases; Numerous international appearances; Live shows include: Family Values, Ozzfest tours, KROQ Acoustic Christmas Concert 2001; TV specials include: Live At The Fillmore; Reverb. *Recordings:* Albums: Hybrid Theory, 2000; Reanimation, 2002. Singles: Hybrid Theory (EP), 2000; One Step Closer, 2001; Crawling, 2001; Papercut, 2001; In The End, 2001; Pts.Of.Athrty, 2002. *Honours:* Billboard Award, Best Modern Rock Artist, 2001; Rock Bear Awards, Best International Band, Best International Album, 2001; Kerrang! Award, Best International Newcomer, 2001; Rolling Stone Award, Best Hard Rock/Metal Band, 2001; MTV Awards, Best Group, Best Hard Rock, 2002. *Current Management:* Andy Gould Management, 8484 Wilshire Blvd #425, Beverly Hills, CA 90211, USA. *Website:* www.linkinpark.com.

DELTA HOUSE OF FUNK. See: **BEEDLE, Ashley.**

DELVAUX, Floch; b. 26 Jan. 1968, Bruxelles, Belgium. Vocalist; Musician (guitar); Songwriter. *Education:* Classical music lessons, Brussels. *Career:* Guitarist and Songwriter, Brain Damage and Depth, 1986–89; Singer and songwriter, Brain Damage and Death, 1989–92; Singer, guitarist and songwriter, Goyasnada, 1990–97; Singer, guitarist and songwriter, K-0z Office, 1994–. *Compositions:* Several songs with Goyasnada, some released on several compilations CD; Dreamland, 1992. *Recordings:* LP with Brain Damage and Death, 1993, titled, 1986–92; CD album with K-0z Office, Rage Rage Rage, 1996; Death 2000, 1999. *Address:* 52 rue Emile Claus, Boite 1, 1050 Brussels, Belgium. *E-mail:* kozoffice@cardmail.com. *Website:* www.geocities.com/totalfmr/totalfmrhomepage.html.

DEML, Markus; b. 9 Aug. 1967, Prague, Czechoslovakia. Musician (guitar); Prod; Songwriter. *Education:* Musikhochschule, Hamburg (Music University); Guitar Institute of Technologie, Los Angeles. *Career:* World-wide and European tours with Saga, John Wetton, Kingdom Come, Rödelheimhartreim – project appearances on MTV's Most Wanted Hangin Out; Rock and Ring, Montreaux Jazz Festival. *Compositions:* Earth Nation (Thoughts in Past Future); Errorhead, solo project; The Other Side, album. *Recordings:* Errorhead (The Other Side); Kingdom Come (Twilight Cruiser); Bobby Kimball (Rise Up); Earth Nation (Thoughts in Past Future); Rödelheim HP (Direkt aus Rödelheim); SNAP (Welcome to Tomorrow). *Publications:* Errorhead, The Other Side, 1998. *Membership:* GEMA; GVL. *Address:* Alex Merch Music, Trajamstr 18, 50678, Koeln.

DEMPSEY, Gaylene Katharan; b. 1 Aug. 1960, Winnipeg, Manitoba, Canada. Exec. Dir.. m. David Sherman, 10 April 1993. *Education:* Creative Communications (Journalism Major); Managing and Leading in non-profit Sector Certificate, 1995. *Career:* Editor, Circuit, monthly entertainment paper, 1989–; Editor in Chief, The Insider, monthly entertainment paper, 1990–; Editor, Jazz Winnipeg Festival Programme, 1990–; Volunteer, Winnipeg Folk Festival, 1990–; Executive Director, Manitoba Audio Recording Industry Association (MARIA), 1991–; Represent the Manitoba Music Industry from songwriters to labels; Freelance work. *Publications:* SOCAN Words and Music, several articles; Grafitti Magazine, several articles. *Membership:* FACTOR National Advisory Board; Artspace, Executive Member. *Address:* #1–242 Spence St, Winnipeg, Manitoba, R3C 1Y4, Canada.

DEMPSEY, Paul; b. 25 May 1976. Vocalist; Musician (guitar); Songwriter. *Career:* Sister is vocalist/guitarist in Melbourne group John Smith; Resides in Melbourne, Australia; Founder member: Fish of The Day group, 1994; Developed local following through pub/club gigs; Group became Something For Kate; Signed to Australian label Murmur; Instigated Scared of Horses solo side project during SFK hiatus, 1997–8; Re-formed Something For Kate; Band gradually broke nationally, then internationally with first USA/Japan tour, 2000; Big sell-out Australian shows including Mythology and Echo-la-lalia tours plus Powderfinger support slots, 2001; Occasional solo shows including Lack of Rhythm tour, 2000. *Recordings:* Albums: Elsewhere For Eight Minutes, 1997; An Empty Flight (solo as Scared of Horses), 1998; Beautiful Sharks, 1999; QandA With Dean Martin (compilation), 2000; Echolalia, 2001; Singles: The Answer To Both Your Questions (EP), Dean Martin, 1996; Intermission (EP), Captain (Million Miles An Hour), Prick, 1997; Working Against Me, Roll Credit, Harpoon/Clint, 1998; Electricity, Hallways, Whatever You Want, 1999; The Astronaut, 2000; Monsters, Three Dimensions, Twenty Years, 2001. *Honours:* Australian Music Industry Critics Awards, Album of the Year, 2000; Australian Live Music Awards, Best Live Act, 2000; JJJ Listeners' Poll, Best Album, 2001. *Current Management:* Carlene Albronda, Catapult Management, Sydney, Australia. *E-mail:* carlene@presto.net.au. *Website:* www.somethingforkate.com.

DEMUS, Chaka, (John Taylor); b. 1965, West Kingston, Jamaica. Rap Artiste. *Career:* Rapper, billed as Nicodemus Jr, on various sound systems including Supreme and Jammy's; Changed name to Chaka Demus, 1985; Solo artiste, 1985–91; Rapper, in duo Chaka Demus and Pliers, 1991–. *Recordings:* Singles: as Chaka Demus: Increase Your Knowledge; One Scotch, One Bourbon, One Beer; 2 Foot Walk; Chaka On the Move; with Chaka Demus and Pliers: Tease Me, 1993; She Don't Let Nobody, 1993; Twist and Shout (No. 1, UK), 1993; Murder She Wrote, 1994; I Wanna Be Your Man, 1994; Gal Wine, 1994; Rough this Year; Love Up the Gal; Without Love; Winning Machine; Worl' A Girls; Albums: Solo: Everybody Loves the Chaka, 1988; The Original Chaka, 1989; Unstoppable, 1996; Ruff and Tuff, 1997; with Chaka Demus and Pliers: Gal Wine, 1992; Ruff This Year, 1992; Chaka Demus and Pliers, 1992; Tease Me, 1993; Help Them Lord, 2001; with Shabba Ranks: Rough and Rugged, 1987. *Address:* c/o Free World Music Inc, 230 12th St, Suite 117, Miami Beach, FL 33139–4603, USA.

DENCH, Ian; b. 7 Aug. 1964. Musician (guitar); Songwriter. *Career:* Member, EMF, 1989–96. *Recordings:* Albums: Schubert Dip, 1991; Stigma, 1992; Cha Cha Cha, 1995; Best of EMF, 2001; Singles: Unbelieveable (No. 1, USA), 1990; I Believe, 1991; Children, 1991; Lies, 1991; Unexplained (EP), 1992; They're Here, 1992; It's You, 1992; Perfect Day, 1995; I'm A Believer (with Vic Reeves and Bob Mortimer), 1995; Afro Kung, 1995; Guitarist on Dido, Here With Me, 2000. *Current Management:* Bedlam Management, PO Box 3074, London W4 4ZN, England.

DENIO, Amy Eliott; b. 9 June 1961, Boston, MA, USA. Composer; Vocalist; Musician (saxophones, bass guitar, acoustic and electric guitars, accordion, clarinet). *Education:* BA, Music Composition, Performance and Improvisation, Hampshire College, Amherst, MA, 1983; Jazz India Vocal Institute, Mumbai, 1997. *Career:* Solo concerts in USA, East and Central Europe, Japan, India, Argentina, 1977–; Co-founder, The Entropics, performances in Canada and the USA, 1985–87; Co-founder, Tone Dogs, tours in USA and Europe, 1987–91; Played bass on soundtrack and acted in film, Shredder Orpheus, 1988; Co-founder, Billy Tipton Memorial Saxophone Quartet, tours in USA and Europe, 1988–96; Founder, publishing co and record label, Spoot Music, 1990; Singer with Curlew, tours in USA, 1990–93; Co-founder, Sonic Renegades, tours in Europe, 1992–93; Music Dir for Sit Still, 1992–3; Included in John Cage Exhibit, Venice Biennale, 1993; Co-founder, Nudes/Pale Nudes, tours in USA, Canada, Brazil and Europe, 1994–99, Swiss TV performance 1999; Co-founder, FoMoFlo, tours in USA and Japan, 1995–97; Played accordion and sang with The Four Accordionists of the Apocalypse tour, Europe, 1998; Music Dir for David Dorfman Dances Skydown, 1997, To Lie Tenderly, 2000; Composed and sang for Die Knodel, tours in Seattle and Europe, 1998; Music Dir for clown, Lorenzo Pickle, 1998–; Played saxophone and sang with Kultur Shock, tours in Spain and USA, 1999–; Played accordion, alto saxophone and sang with Zu, tours in Italy, 2000–; Co-founder, Quintetto alla Busara, tours in Europe 2001–; Music Dir for UMO Ensemble, 2001; Played bass and sang with Danny Barnes, tours in USA, 2002–; Radio performances in Europe and USA, 1995–. *Compositions include:* For Jeff Bickford Dance: I & I, 1990, Twilight & the Grove, 1997, Into the Tumbling Ocean, 1997; For Pat Graney Dance: Sax House, 1991, Tattoo, 2000; Bus Horn Concerto, 1992; For Run/Remain Ensemble: Sit Still, 1992, The Sherman Preludes, 1994; Windows, music for Peter Vogt film, 1993; Tempesta: An Urban RAPsody, with poet Luis Rodriguez, 1994; The Seattle Sound, commissioned by RAI 3, Italian National Radio, 1994; Green Fish Symphonette, for Berkley Symphony, 1995; For David Dorfman Dance: Approaching No Calm, 1995, Skydown, 1997, To Lie Tenderly, 2000; Le Serve (The Maids), soundtrack for Jean Genet play, 1997; False Prophets or Just Dang Good Guessers, for Shaking Ray Levi Society, 1997; Non Lo So, Polo, music for Austrian chamber octet, Die Knodel, 1998; five compositions for Relache Ensemble, 1999–2000; Brother Fox, Commissioned by New York Festival of Song, 2001; TASOGARE (Twilight), for Yoko Murao Dance, 2001; AcchorDREAM, for Henry Art Gallery installation, 2001; Synchrony in Estrus, soundtrack for Thomas Edward film, 2001; White Girls, for KT Niehoff/D9 Dance, 2002; Surveillance, for Victor Hugo House installation, 2002; Against Ending, for Victoria Marks Dance, 2002; The Other One, for Aiko Kinoshita Dance, 2002. *Recordings include:* with Tone Dogs: Ankety Low Day, 1989, Early Middle Years, 1991; Birthing Chair Blues, 1991; Tongues, 1993; Curlew with Amy Denio: A Beautiful Western Saddle, 1993; Billy Tipton Memorial Saxophone Quartet: Saxhouse, 1993, Make It Funky God, 1994, Box, 1996; Pale Nudes: Wise to the Heat, 1996, Vanishing Point, 1994, Soul Come Home, 1998; FoMoFlo: Slug and Firearms, 1997, No 11, 1997; Amy Denio: More Spoot, 1997; with The Science Group: …a mere coincidence…, 1999; Die Knoedel: Non Lo So, Polo, 1999; Greatest Hits, 1999; Tattoo, with the Pat Graney Dance Co, 2000; The Memphis Years, with George Cartwright, 2000; Danubians, 2000; Belle Confusion, with Francisco Lopez, 2000; Les Voix Vulgaires, 2001; Quintetto alla Busara, 2002; To Lie Tenderly, with Petunia, 2002. *Honours:* Seattle Arts Commission Individual Artist Award for Composition, 1990; Artist Trust Artist Fellowship, 1996; Best Animated Film Award, New York Underground Film Festival, 1997; Bessie Award for Composition, New York Dance and Performance Award, 1997; ASCAP Special Awards 1996–2001; Civitella Ranieri Artist Fellowship, Italy, 2003. *Membership:* ASCAP; Board Mem., Madrona Arts Centre; Artist Trust; Washington State Arts Alliance; Washington Composers Forum. *Address:*

Spoot Music, PO Box 85154, Seattle, WA 98145, USA. *Website:* www.amydenio.com.

DENNARD, David Brooks; b. 5 July 1950, Dallas, Texas, USA. Record Co Exec; Musician (bass guitar, guitar, dobro, harmonica). m. Mary Anna Austin, 4 Oct. 1980, 2 d. *Education:* Colorado College, Stanford; University of Texas-Austin. *Career:* CBS/Epic Records recording artist with: Gary Myrick and The Figures; President, Owner, Dragon Street Records Inc, 1989–; Director of A&R, Crystal Clear Sound; Director, Steve Records, Dallas. *Recordings:* with Gary Myrick and the Figures: two albums, two singles, seven videos; Recent releases by Ronnie Dawson, Gene Summers, Scott Whitaker, Buck Jones, Centromatic, Meredith Louise Miller and Pump'n Ethyl; Gene Vincent and His Blue Caps, The Lost Dallas Sessions, 1957–58; Johnny Dollar, Mr Action Packed; Groovey Joe Poovey—Greatest Grooves; various artists: The Big 'O' Jamboree Live!; The Gals of the Big 'O' Jamboree; The Guys of the Big 'O' Jamboree. *Honours:* Award of Excellence, Dallas Society of Visual Communications, 1987; 2 Silver Microphone Awards, 1987; Crystal Award, 1988; Topaz Award, Best Record Company, Steve Records, 1997. *Membership:* NARAS; Texas Music Asscn, Dallas; Cable Access of Dallas Inc; Board Mem., Documentary Arts. *Address:* Dragon Street Records Inc, PO Box 670714, Dallas, TX 75367–0714, USA.

DENNEHY, Timothy Christopher; b. 29 Dec. 1952, Cahersiveen, Co Kerry, Ireland. Teacher; Broadcaster; Vocalist. m. Máirín, 19 March 1976, 2 s. *Education:* From oral tradition. *Career:* Numerous radio appearances, local, national, including own programme on Clare FM: Cuaird An Domhnaigh (Keep in Touch); Television programmes dealing with Irish traditional music; Regular performer at workshops, recitals, concerts throughout Ireland; Founded the Góilin Traditional singers club, with Donall De Barra, Dublin, 1979. *Compositions:* Many original songs. *Recordings:* A Thimbleful of Song; A Winter's Tear – Traditional and Original Songs; Farewell to Miltown Malbay, 1997; The Blue Green Door, 2002. *Publications:* Working on biography of writer Sigerson Clifford. *Membership:* IMRO; Cumann Cheoltíre Eireann. *Address:* Markham's Cross, Mullagh, Co Clare, Ireland. *E-mail:* tim@sceilig.com. *Website:* www.sceilig.com.

DENNERLEIN, Barbara; b. 25 Sept. 1964, Munich, Germany. Jazz Musician; Composer; Prod. m. Andre Baldi. *Education:* Study of Music Science, Ludwig Maximilian University, Munich. *Career:* Film Music, (title music), Die Partner; WDR/ARD Concerts at all Important Jazz Festivals, Den Haag, New Zealand, Montréal, Vancouver, Toronto, Edmonton, Victoria, Norway, Berlin, Frankfurt; Concerts world-wide: London, Ronnie Scott's; Tokyo, Blue Note; New York, Blue Note; Paris, Sweet Basil. *Compositions:* 100 pieces on 15 records and CDs. *Recordings:* Jazz Live, 1983; Orgelspiele, 1984; Bebab, 1985; Tribute to Charlie, 1986; Straight Ahead, 1988; B D Plays Classics, 1988; Live on Tour, 1989; B D Due, 1990; Hot Stuff, 1990; Solo, 1992; That's Me, 1992; Take Off, 1996; Junkanovo, 1997; Outhipped, 2000. *Honours:* Jazz Award for Take Off, 1995, 1997; No 1, DWR Downbeat Critics Poll, 1996; Jazz Award for Junkanoo, 1997; 3 times, Preis der Deutschen Schallplattenkritik; Outhipped, 1999. *Current Management:* Newtone Management, Tsingtauer Str 66, 81827 Munchen, Germany. *Address:* c/o Behab Records, Andreas Wagner Str. 39a, 85640 Putzbrunn, Germany. *Telephone:* (89) 95820305. *Fax:* (89) 9582307. *E-mail:* BarbaraDennerlein@behab.com. *Website:* www.barbaradennerlein.com.

DENNIS, Cathy; b. 25 March 1970, Norfolk, England. Vocalist; Songwriter; Prod. *Career:* Featured singer, D-Mob, 1989; British tour; Television appearance: Beverly Hills 90210; Solo artiste, songwriter, prod., 1990–; Songs recorded by: Hear' Say, Ronan Keating, Spice Girls, S Club 7. *Compositions include:* Natural, S Club 7, 1999; Reach, S Club 7, 2000; Never Had A Dream Come True, S Club 7 (No. 1, UK), 2000; Can't Get You Out of My Head (co-writer), Kylie Minogue (No. 1, UK), 2001; Have You Ever, S Club 7 (No. 1, UK), 2001; Anything Is Possible, Will Young (No. 1, UK), 2002. *Recordings:* Albums: Move To This, 1991; Into The Skyline, 1992; Am I The Kinda Girl?, 1996. Singles: C'Mon and Get My Love, with D Mob, 1989; Touch Me (All Night Long), 1991; Just Another Dream, 1991; Too Many Walls, 1991; Irresistible, 1992; Falling, 1993; Why, 1994; West End Pad, 1996; Waterloo Sunset, 1996; Also featured on: A Little Bit of This A Little Bit of That, D-Mob, 1989; Looking Through Patient Eyes, PM Dawn; Songs on numerous film soundtracks. *Honours:* Billboard Award, Best New Female Artist; World Music Award, Best International Newcomer; Capital Radio Award, Best Female Artist; SOS Top Woman Award; SE Asia Awards, Top New Artist and Best Song of Year; Five ASCAP Awards; Ivor Novello Awards, Most Performed Work, Dance Award, International Hit of the Year, for Can't Get You Out Of My Head, 2002. *Membership:* ASCAP. *Current Management:* Simon Fuller, 19 Management Ltd, Unit 32, Ransomes Dock, 35–37 Parkgate Rd, London SW11 4NP, England.

DENNIS, Jon; b. 27 May 1965, Lewisham, London, England. Vocalist; Musician (guitar); Songwriter. *Education:* Leicester University. *Career:* Lead singer and guitarist with Blab Happy, 1987–93; Slinky, 1994–; Tours with Blab Happy: 'Boat' tour, UK, 1991; Support to Kingmaker, 'Eat Yourself Whole' British tour, 1992; Support to Radiohead, 'Pablo Honey' British tour, 1993; with Slinky: 'Shoot Me Down' tour, 1995. *Recordings:* with Blab Happy:

EPs: It's Turned Out Nice Again, 1987; Fruits of Your Labour, 1988; Mad Surge, 1991; Albums: Boat, 1991; Smothered, 1993; Singles: with Blab Happy: Down, 1991; Inside Out, 1992; Tender Hooks, 1993; with Slinky: Shoot Me Down, 1995; Producer, General MIDI, 2001. *Membership:* Musicians' Union. *Address:* 39 Nottingham Rd, Leicester LE5 3TT, England.

DENSMORE, John; b. 1 Dec. 1944, Santa Monica, CA, USA. Musician (drums); Writer; Theatre Prod. *Education:* Santa Monica City College; Cal State Northridge. *Career:* Mem., Psychedelic Rangers, 1965; Mem., The Doors, 1966–72; Performances include: Northern California Folk-Rock Festival, 1968; Hollywood Bowl, later released as video, 1968; Toronto Rock 'n' Roll Revival Show, 1969; Isle of Wight Festival, 1970; Film documentaries: The Doors Are Open, 1968; Feast of Friends, 1969; With surviving mems of The Doors played, Rock and Roll Hall of Fame, Cleveland, 1993; The Doors VH1 appearance, 2001; The Doors reunion tour, 2002–03; Founded The Doors Music Co, Bright Midnight Records, 1997; Mem., The Butts Band, 1972–; Session, solo work, 1972; Mem., Bess Snyder and Co, touring USA; Wrote and appeared in play, Skins, 1984; Appeared in play, Band Dreams and Bebop, 1988; Adapted and appeared in play, The King of Jazz, 1989; Numerous television appearances; Film appearances: Get Crazy, Dudes, The Doors. *Recordings:* Albums: The Doors (No. 1, USA), 1967; Strange Days, 1967; Waiting For The Sun (No. 1, USA), 1968; Morrison Hotel, 1970; Absolutely Live, 1970; L A Woman, 1971; Other Voices, 1971; Weird Scenes Inside the Gold Mine, 1972; Full Circle, 1972; Live At The Hollywood Bowl, 1987; Greatest Hits, 1996; The Doors Box Set, 1997. Singles include: Light My Fire (No. 1, USA), 1967; Love Me Two Times, 1968; Hello I Love You (No. 1, USA), 1968; Touch Me, 1969; Love Her Madly, 1971; Riders On The Storm, 1971. *Publications:* Riders On The Storm – My Life With Jim Morrison and The Doors. *Honours:* LA Weekly Theater Award for Music, for Methusalem; Inducted, Rock and Roll Hall of Fame, 2001. *Address:* c/o Bright Midnight Records, Rhino Handmade, PO Box 30620, Tampa, FL 33630-0620, USA. *E-mail:* BMR@thedoors.com. *Website:* www.thedoors.com.

DENZLER, Bertrand; b. 27 Oct. 1963, Geneva, Switzerland. *Education:* Studied at Zurich Conservatory, Switzerland. *Career:* Concerts, tours and recordings in Europe and South America with musicians including Barry Guy, Mark Sanders, Benoit Delbecq, Hélène Labarrière, Norbert Pfammatter, Christophe Marguet, Hasse Poulsen, Ninh Le Quan, Sophie Agnel; Festival appearances in Willisau, Cologne, Le Mans, Paris, Grenoble, Zurich, Berne, Lausanne, Neuchatel, Fribourg; Appearances at Swiss New Jazz Festival, 1998; Leader, own ensemble, Bertrand Denzler Cluster; Live or studio recordings for national broadcasting corporations throughout Europe. *Compositions:* Around 80 compositions played or recorded with various ensembles; Numerous compositions for film or theatre and for documentaries. *Recordings:* 49 Nord: Animal Language; Chamaeleo Vulgaris: Ouverture Facile; Bertrand Denzler Cluster: Y?; Denzler-Dürst-Pfammatter: Now; Denzler-Haerter Quartet: Minor Works; Burhan Öcal Group: Dervis Mustafa; Denzler-Wiesendanger: Folies. *Membership:* Swiss Musicians' Syndicate. *Address:* 18 rue Littré, 75006 Paris, France.

DEPASS, Michele Karina; b. 5 Jan. 1965, Germany. Vocalist; Songwriter. *Education:* 1 year MSc course, Composition, General Theory, Voice. *Career:* Lead vocals, Saxmachine, 1986–88; Lead vocals, The Happy End, 1986–87; Television, radio, British tour, with Denise Black and The Kray Sisters, 1987; Lead, backing vocals, Luddy Sams and The Deliveries, 1987–88; Lead vocals, Benjamin Zephaniah and The Union Dance Company, 1988; Soundtrack vocals, The Kitchen Child, 1988; Vocals, Haji Ackbar, Pee Wee Ellis, Maceo Parker, 1988; Vocals in Welsh, Sinaid Jones, Si Yn Y Gwnt, 1990; Soundtrack vocals, Prime Suspect, Granada TV, 1992; Backing vocals, 7 Elvis Presley tracks for karaoke, 1994; lead duet vocals, Leo sayer, 1994; Working with T-Rextasy, BV's tribute band to Marc Bolan, 1995; Television include: The Glam Rock Show, Ch4, 1995; Punt and Dennis, BBC1, 1995. *Recordings include:* Co-writer, vocals, single: Pitter Patter Biscuit, 1989. *Membership:* Musicians' Union. *Address:* 13 Tabley Rd, Holloway, London N7 0NA, England.

DEPOLO, Ozren; b. 13 March 1930, Zagreb, Croatia. Musician (saxophones, clarinet, flute); Composer. m. 29 Jan. 1959, Ljerka Polak, 2 s., 1 d. *Education:* Medical Faculty, Zagreb, 1956; Clarinet, Conservatory of Music, Zagreb, graduated 1952. *Career:* Saxophone soloist, jazz and classical music; Lead alto saxophone, Zagreb Radio-TV big band, 1952–91; Jazz Small Combos: Zagreb Jazz Quintet, Zagreb Jazz Sextet; Non Convertible International All Styars; International Festival Big Bands: Slide Hampton, Prague, 1978; Clark Terry, 1979; Jerry Mulligan, 1970; Oliver Nelson, Montreux, 1971; EBU (European RTV Union) Big Bands in Copenhagen; Barcelona; Sarajevo; Oslo; Classical Music: First performances, 3 saxophone concertos, Alto Saxophone and Symphony Orchestra: Despalji, 1964; Glazunov, 1968; Odak, 1980; Avantgarde music: Member, Acezantez group, modern music, 1966–80; Appearances on many Jazz festivals, tours, concerts. *Compositions:* Music for 53 animated (cartoon) films; 4 films; 3 short documentary films; Music, songs, 5 theatre plays; 2 TV serials; many jazz compositions; songs; Music for children; Arrangements; Orchestrations for popular music. *Recordings:* Albums: Saxophone concertos; Mistery of Blues. *Honours:* Josip Slavenski, Musical Achievement. *Membership:* Croatian Composers Society; Croatian Musicians' Union. *Address:* Ljudevita Posavskog 2, 41000 Zagreb, Croatia.

DEQUIDT, Loc; b. 1 May 1973, Arras, France. Jazz Musician (piano, tabla). *Education:* Diploma, Conservatoire National Supérieur de Musique de Paris; Music studies in Italy, with E. Rava, F. D'Andrea; Mathematics, University of Lille, two years. *Career:* Played with Tommy Smith, Claus Stötter, Bruno Tommaso, Riccardo del Fra, Bill Goodwin, Jacques Mahieux, Albert Mangelsdorff; Played in France, Sweden, Denmark, Italy, Scotland, Norway, Belgium, Germany, Holland; Plays with Loc Dequidt Trio, Deco, Colours, Seb Jarrousse Sextet; Radio appearances: France-Musiques, France-Inter. *Address:* 110 rue Lepic, 75018 Paris, France. *E-mail:* mail@loicdequidt.com. *Website:* www.loicdequidt.com.

DERRINGER, Rick, (Richard Zehringer); b. 5 Aug. 1947, Fort Recovery, Ohio, USA. Musician (guitar); Prod. *Career:* Member, The McCoys, late 1960s; Member, Johnny Winter and Edgar Winter groups; Solo artiste, 1974–; Also leader, own group Derringer; Prolific session musician. *Recordings:* Solo albums: All American Boy, 1974; Spring fever, 1975; Derringer, 1976; Sweet Evil, 1977; If You Weren't So Romantic, 1978; Guitars and Women, 1979; Face To Face, 1980; Rick Derringer, 1981; Good Dirty Fun, 1983; Back to the Blues, 1993; Electra Blues, 1994; Required Rocking, 1996; Blues Deluxe, 1998; Jackhammer Blues, 2000; with Edgar Winter: White Trash, 1971; Road Work, 1972; They Only Come Out At Night, 1973; Shock Treatment, 1974; Jasmine Nightdream, 1975; With Rick Derringer, 1975; with Johnny Winter: Johnny Winter and Rick Derringer, 1971; Johnny Winter Live, 1971; Still Alive and Well, 1973; Saints and Sinners, 1974; John Dawson Winter III, 1974; The Johnny Winter Story, 1980; Lead guitar solo, Eat It, Weird Al Yankovic (parody of Michael Jackson's Beat It), 1984; Also featured on albums by: Air Supply; Donald Fagen; Dan Hartman; Cyndi Lauper; Bette Midler; Meat Loaf; Mason Ruffner; Todd Rundgren; Steely Dan; Bonnie Tyler; Rosie Vela. *Current Management:* Slatus Management, 208 E 51st St, New York, NY 10022, USA.

DERUDDER, Peter; Musician. *Education:* Classical, Flute, Uillean, Pipes, Bodhran, Whistles. *Career:* Group Member, The Swigshift; Dranouter Festival, 1995; Labadoux Festival, 1997; Den Ekster, 1996–97; Paulus Festival, 1997; Sloanthe Festival, 1997; De Brakke Grond, Amsterdam, 1997; National Radio, Radio 1 De Groote Boodschap, and several regional radio and television appearances. *Compositions:* Jumpin The Fences; Dirty Wally; Friend's Sadness; Something to Fear; Shut the Pub; A Whistler's Wedding. *Recordings:* 1 CD, Tales From the Great Whiskey Book, 1996. *Honours:* Government Medal for Flute, 1986; Second place, Youth Soloist Festival, 1986; Finale, Westtalent, 1995. *Membership:* Volksmuziekfederatie, Belgium. *Current Management:* KAFT Producties, Akkerwindelaan 20, 8791 Beveren-Leie, Belgium. *Address:* Barrierestraat 49, 8940 Wervik, Belgium.

DESANDRE-NAVARRE, Lavier; b. 11 Oct. 1961, Paris, France. Musician (Drums, percussion); Composer. m. Susan Mouget, 5 Sept. 1992, 1 d. *Education:* Licence in Economics. *Career:* Worked with Gil Evans, Tania Maria, Niels Lan Doky, Cheb Mami, Orchestre National de Jazz, Les Rita Mitsouko, Michel Portal. *Compositions:* Zoom. *Recordings:* Gil Evans, The Complete Recordings; Niels Lan Doky, Asian Sessions; Caccilie Norry, Queen of Bad Excuses; Solo, Zoom. *Address:* 95 Ave Jean Lolive, 93500 Pantin, France.

DESEO, Csaba; b. 15 Feb. 1939, Budapest, Hungary. Musician (Violin). m. Katalin Szony, 1 s. *Education:* Violin Teacher Diploma, Bartók Conservatory, Budapest, 1961. *Career:* Member, Hungarian National Philharmonic Orchestra, 1966–; Jazz Soloist, Combo Leader, 4 own LPs, 3 CDs, 1964–. *Publications:* Monthly jazz-broadcasts in Hungarian Radio; Jazz articles in Hungarian newspapers. *Membership:* Hungarian Jazz Federation; Hungarian Composers' Union. *Address:* Bercsenyi U 36, 1117 Budapest, Hungary.

DESMARAIS, Lorraine; b. 15 Aug. 1956, Montréal, Canada. Jazz Musician (Piano). *Education:* Master's Degree in Classical Piano, 1979; Jazz education in New York and Boston with Kenny Barron and Charlie Banacos. *Career:* Toured across Canada (jazz festivals) and USA, in Switzerland, France, Belgium, Denmark, London, Scotland, Asia (Indonesia, Philippines); Appeared with Tiger Okoshi, Oliver Jones, Sherrie Maricle and the Diva Big Band, Five Play, Hugh Fraser Band, Johanne Brackeen, Marian McPartland, Paquito D'Riviera, Kenny Wheeler, Michel Donato, Alain Caron, Michel Cusson, François Bourassa, Vic Vogel; One Woman show, The History of Piano Jazz; Host, Lorraine Desmarais reçoit... (Radio Canada's cultural network), 2000; Prof. of Jazz Piano, St Laurent College. *Compositions:* Film scores for National Filmboard of Canada; Sonata for flute and piano. *Recordings:* Trio Lorraine: Desmarais, 1985; Andiamo, 1986; Pianissimo, 1987; Vision, 1991; Lorraine Desmarais, 1995; Video: Lorraine Desmarais Quartette with Tiger Okoshi, 1996; I Believe in You, with Diva, 1999; Bleu Silence, 1999; Five Play: On the Brink, 1999; Love, 2002. *Publications:* Sonata for Flute and Piano. *Honours:* Winner, Great American Jazz Piano Competition, Jacksonville, Jazz Festival, Florida, 1986; Winner, Montréal Jazz Festival, 1984; Canada Québec Arts Council Grants; Composer's Award for Socan: Best Jazz Album: Vision, 1991; Oscar Peterson Award, Montréal International Jazz Festival, 2002. *Membership:* SOCAN; Guilde des Musiciens du Québec. *Current Management:* Pierre Bertrand. *Telephone:* (450) 583-3126 (agent); (450) 693-1339. *Fax:* (450) 583-3099 (agent); (450) 963-9123. *E-mail:*

consultartpbertrand@videotron.ca (agent); lorrainedesmarais@videotron.ca. *Website:* www.lorrainedesmarais.com.

DESMOND, Denis Anthony; b. 4 July 1950, Cork, Ireland. Promoter; Band and Artist Man; Musician (piano, keyboards). *Career:* Performer, RTE Radio and TV; Cork Opera House; Many other theatres and venues. *Membership:* IFMandAP. *Address:* Top House, Clontarf St, Cork 1, Ireland.

DES'REE, (Des'ree Weekes); b. 30 Nov. 1968, London, England. Vocalist; Songwriter. *Career:* Solo artiste, 1992–; Contributed music to films: Clockers, Set It Off, Romeo & Juliet; Numerous television appearances and live shows; Toured with Seal, USA, 1995. *Recordings:* Albums: Mind Adventures, 1992; I Ain't Movin', 1994; Supernatural, 1998; Endangered Species, 2000; Dream Soldier, 2003. Singles: Feel So High, 1992; Mind Adventures, 1992; Why Should I Love You, 1992; You Gotta Be, 1994; I Ain't Movin', 1994; Little Child, 1994; Life, 1998; What's Your Sign, 1998; It's OK, 2003; contributed to: Delicate, Terence Trent D'Arby, 1993; Ain't No Sunshine, Ladysmith Black Mambazo, 1993; Plenty Lovin', Steve Winwood; Fire, Babyface. *Honours:* BMI Award; Ivor Novello Songwriting Award; World Music Award. *Address:* c/o Sony Soho Square (S²): 10 Great Marlborough St, London W1V 2LP, England. *Website:* www.desree.co.uk.

DESTAGNOL, Yann; b. 14 July 1978, Paris, France. Musician (drums, keyboards); Prod; Vocalist. *Education:* Mastered flute and clarinet as a child; Studied at the American School of Modern Music, Paris. *Career:* Drummer in several rock bands prior to co-founding group Modjo and record label Modjo Music (with Romain Tranchart). *Recordings:* Album: Modjo, 2001; Singles: Lady (Hear Me Tonight), 2000; Chillin', 2001; What I Mean, 2001. *Honours:* Modjo first French group to score UK number 1 hit. *Current Management:* Modjo Music. *E-mail:* matt@modjo.com.

DESTRUCTION, Dr (Matt); b. 1978. Musician (bass guitar). *Career:* Mem., Swedish band, The Hives, 1993–; Signed to Universal Music, 2001. *Recordings:* Albums: Barely Legal, 1997; Veni Vidi Vicious, 2000; Your New Favourite Band (compilation, UK only), 2001. Singles: Oh, Lord! When? How? (EP), 1996; aka I.D.I.O.T. (EP), 1998; Hate To Say I Told You So; Main Offender; Supply & Demand. *Honours:* NME Award, Best International Band, 2003. *Address:* The Hives, c/o Pelle Almqvist, Regnbågsvägen 46, 737 43 Fagersta, Sweden. *E-mail:* hives@innocent.com. *Website:* www.hives.nu.

DETROIT, Marcella, (Marcy Levy); b. 21 June 1959, Detroit, Michigan, USA. Vocalist; Songwriter; Musician (keyboards, guitar, harmonica). *Career:* Mem., Shakespears Sister, with Siobhan Fahey, 1988–93; Solo artiste, 1993–; Numerous concerts, television and radio performances; Collaborations: Elton John; Hall and Oates. *Recordings:* Albums: with Shakespears Sister: Sacred Heart, 1989; Hormonally Yours, 1992; Solo: Jewel, 1994; Feeler, 1996; Abfab Songs, 1999; Dancing Madly Sideways, 2000. Singles: with Shakespears Sister: You're History, 1989; Break My Heart, 1990; Goodbye Cruel World, 1991; Hello (Turn Your Radio On), 1992; Stay (No. 1, UK), 1992; I Don't Care, 1992; My 16th Apology (EP), 1993; I Can Drive, 1996; Solo: Ain't Nothing Like The Real, 1994; I'm No Angel, 1994; I Believe, 1994; Perfect World, 1995; I Hate You, 1996; Flower, 1997. *Compositions:* Co-writer, Lay Down Sally, Eric Clapton, 1977; with Siobhan Fahey: all tracks on album, Hormonally Yours, 1992. *Honours:* BRIT Award, Best Video, Stay, 1993; Ivor Novello Award, Outstanding Contemporary Song Collection, Hormonally Yours, 1993. *Address:* c/o John Campbell, 55 Chiswick High Rd, London W4 2LT, England.

DEVEREUX, Pete; b. 1972, Southampton, Hampshire, England. Prod; Remixer; DJ. *Education:* Brunel University, music student. *Career:* Played violin in Southampton Youth Orchestra; Formed the Artful Dodger with partner Mark Hill, 1996; Released debut album, 2001; Duo split amicably, 2001; Co-founder: Centric Records (with Hill); Solo production career, 2001–; Collaborations: Craig David; Dreem Teem; Romina Johnson; Liberty; Remixed: Sisqo; Gabrielle. *Recordings:* Albums: It's All About The Stragglers, 2001; Singles: Re-Rewind The Crowd Say Bo Selecta (with Craig David), Movin' Too Fast (with Romina Johnson), 1999; Woman Trouble (with Robbie Craig and Craig David), 2000; It Ain't Enough (with Dreem Teem), 2001. *Honours:* Ivor Novello Awards: Dance Award: Re-Rewind, 2000; Woman Trouble, 2001. *Address:* c/o London Records, Waldron House, 57–63 Old Church St, London SW3 5BS, England.

DEVIC, Lino; b. 10 May 1954, Zagreb, Croatia. Musician (fretless bass, piano). Divorced, 2 s., 1 d. *Career:* Many jazz festivals in former Yugoslavia and Germany; Studio works in France, 1976; Touring Germany with Trini Lopez; Plays with fusion trio, recorded 2 albums, 1994–. *Compositions:* 25 include: Boulevard Barbes; Blue Duck. *Recordings:* Drazen Boic Trio: Mirno Itiho (Peaceful and Quiet); LD Experience: LD Experience. *Honours:* At jazz festivals: Ingolstadt, Germany; Ljubljana; Zagreb; Maribor. *Current Management:* A Zaie 39, Panton, Zagreb, Croatia. *Address:* N Grskovica 58, Zagreb, Croatia.

DEVINE, Frank Thomas; b. 24 Nov. 1946, Dundee, Scotland. Songwriter; Musician (drums, guitar, mandolin). m. Jacqueline Harper, 12 Jan. 1968, 1 s., 1 d. *Education:* Moseley School of Art, Birmingham; Birmingham College of

Art; Private drum tuition with Charles Burlison. *Career:* Tour of England with Jimmy Cliff; Weekly appearances at the Marquee, London; Played with Blues Hounds and Mike Burney; Television appearance: Ready Steady Go (with the Alpines); Currently songwriter and plays guitar and mandolin. *Recordings:* Limited edition album with Steve Winwood and Dave Mason (prior to formation of Traffic). *Membership:* Musicians' Union. *Address:* Milford Hall Cottage, Main Rd, Milford, Staffordshire ST17 0UL, England.

DEVLIN, Adam; b. 17 Sept. 1969, Hounslow, Middlesex, England. Musician (guitar); Songwriter. *Career:* Founding mem., The Bluetones, 1994–; Release records on own label, Superior Quality Recordings, sell through Superior Quality Record Shop; Numerous tours, festivals, television and radio appearances. *Recordings:* Albums: Expecting To Fly, 1996; Return To The Last Chance Saloon, 1998; Science And Nature, 2000; The Singles 1995–2002, 2002. Singles: Return To Splendour, 1994; Nings Of Desire (EP), 1994; Are You Blue Or Are You Blind?, 1995; Bluetonic, 1996; Slight Return, 1996; Cut Some Rug, 1996; Marblehead Johnson, 1996; Solomon Bites The Worm, 1998; Sleazy Bed Track, 1998; 4-Day Weekend, 1998; If. .., 1998; Mudslide, 2000; Keep The Home Fires Burning, 2000; Autophilia Or How I Learned To Stop Worrying And Love My Car, 2000. *Honours:* Gold disc for Return To The Last Chance Saloon. *Address:* c/o Mercury Records, Chancellors House, 72 Chancellors Rd, London W6 9QB, England. *Website:* www.bluetones.co.uk.

DEXTEXTER, Even; b. 7 April 1971, Ellorio, Vizcaya, Spain. Musician (keyboards, bass, drums); Programmer. *Education:* Two years of Psychology, University; 5 years, music and piano studies, Conservatoire of Logrono, La Rioja, Spain, 1982–87. *Career:* Member, Dextexter, Nov. 1994–; Tours include 2 club tours over London; 3 appearances on Basque, Spanish TV; Currently recording auto-produced and released first single. *Membership:* Musicians' Union. *Current Management:* DDT Management. *Address:* 70 Princes Sq., London WL 4NY, England.

DI LEVA, Thomas; b. 23 Oct. 1963, Gavle. Vocalist; Songwriter; Musician (guitar, keyboards). *Career:* 11 major tours 1986–97; Theatre: The City of Mahagonny, by Bertolt Brecht, Gavle Folktheatre, 1987; Hamlet in Hamlet, Gavle Folktheatre, 1990; Films: Tomorrow, Tomorrow, Tomorrow, 1989; Kenny Starfighter, 1997; Several major northern television and radio programmes. *Compositions:* All work self-penned. *Recordings:* Marginal Cirkus, 1982; På Ett Fat, 1985; Pussel, 1986; Flashback #2, 1986; Vem Ska Jag Tro På?, 1987; Rymdblomma, 1989; Noll, 1991; Naked Number One, 1993; Love Is The Heart, 1995; Jag Är Du, 1997; I Am You, 1997; För Sverige I Rymden, 1999; Älska, 2000. *Honours:* Swedish Grammy, Best Artist of 1988; Gold Microphone, Best Live Artist, voted by Swedish listeners, 1997. *Address:* United Stage Artist AB, PO Box 110 29, 100 61 Stockholm, Sweden.

DI MATTEO, Luis; b. 10 May 1934, Bandonfeol. Composer. m. 1 s., 1 d. *Education:* Studied composition and Bandoneon. *Career:* Bandoneon player in orchestras in Montevideo, Uruguay; and in Buenos Aires, Argentina; Astor Piazzolla's orchestra; Composer and Arranger, Bandoneonista; Regular TV appearances; First European concerts, 1983, and regular concert tours, 1983–; Cooperation with Uljanowsk Chamber Orchestra, Russia, 1990; European concert tour with string quartet, 1997–98. *Compositions:* A Sugerencia Club, 1965; A Sugerencia del Club, 1969; Estudio Para Tres, 1971; Tango en Blue Jeans, 1975; Proceso, 1976; Monologando, 1979; Rumbo al Cenit, 1981; Latitud 55, 1983; Tango Contemporáneo, 1984; Le Dernier Tango, 1985; Tango, 1987; Mil Clores, 1987; Por Dentro De Mi, 1988; Del Nuevo Ciclo, 1991; Escribo Para Los Angeles, 1996; Um dia de mi vida, 1997; Concierto para contrabajo y orchestra, 1989. *Recordings:* Tango Contemporaneo, 1984; Le Dernier Tango, 1985; Por Dentro De Mi, 1988; Del Nuevo Ciclo, 1991; Escribo Para Los Angeles, 1997; Um Dia De Mi Vida, 1998. *Publications:* First edition of compositions published with Tonos in Germany, 1998. *Membership:* AGADU, Uruguay. *Address:* Jaro Medien, Bismarckstrasse 43, 28203 Bremen, Germany.

DI MEOLA, Al; b. 22 July 1954, Jersey City, New Jersey, USA. Jazz Musician (guitar); Composer. *Education:* Studied with Robert Aslanian; Berklee College of Music, Boston, 1971, 1974. *Career:* Musician with Barry Miles; Member, Chick Corea's Return To Forever, 1974–76; Solo guitarist, composer, 1976–; Tours as solo artiste; Also toured with acoustic trio (with John McLaughlin and Paco de Lucia); Leader, Al DiMeola Project (musicians include Airto Moreiro), 1985–. *Recordings:* Albums include: with Return To Forever: Where Have I Known You Before, 1974; No Mystery, 1975; Romantic Warrior, 1976; Best Of, 1980; Solo albums: Land of Midnight Sun, 1976; Elegant Gypsy, 1977; Casino, 1978; Splendido Hotel, 1979; Electric Rendevous, 1982; Tour de Force Live, 1982; Scenario, 1983; Cielo e Terra, 1983; Soaring Through A Dream, 1985; Tiramu Su, 1988; World Sinfonia, 1990; Heart of The Immigrants, 1993; Kiss My Axe, 1993; Orange and Blue, 1994; The Essence of Al DiMeola, 1994; The Infinite Desire, 1998; Christmas Winter Nights, 1999; Anthology, 2000; with John McLaughlin and Paco de Lucia: Friday Night In San Francisco, 1980; Passion, Grace and Fire, 1983; with Aziza Mustafa Zadeh: Dance of Fire, 1995; with Jean-Luc Ponty, Stanley Clarke: The Rite of Strings, 1996. *Current Management:* Don't Worry Inc, 111 W 57th St, Suite 1120, New York, NY 11019, USA.

DIAB, Amr; b. Port Said, Egypt. Vocalist. m. Sherin Rida, divorced, 1 d. *Education:* Music, Cairo Academy of Art, 1986. *Career:* Sang national anthem, Biladi, Biladi, on Egyptian Radio when six years old; Amr recorded his first song, El Zamn, 1983; Tours world-wide; Represented Egypt at the Fifth Olympic African Tournament concert, 1990; Collaborations with: Khaled, Angela Dimitriou; Film appearances: El Saginatean, 1988; El Aafareet, 1990; Ice Cream Fi Gleem, 1992; Dhahk We La'ab, 1993. *Recordings:* Albums: Ya Tareeq, 1986; Gany Men Albak, 1986; Asef La Yougad Hal Akhar, 1987; Hala Hala, 1988; Habibe, 1991; Matkhafesh, 1991; Ice Cream Fi Gleem (soundtrack), 1992; Ayamna, 1992; Ya Omrena, 1993; We Yloumouny, 1994; Nour El Ain, 1996; Awedony, 1998; The Best of Amr Diab, 1999; Amarain, 1999; Tamaly Maak, 2000; Aktar Wahed Beyhebak, 2001. *Honours:* Nine awards for album We Yloumouny, 1995; Arabic Festival Awards, Best Video, Best Song, Artist of the Year, 1997, Artist of the Year, 2002; World Music Awards, Best Selling Middle Eastern Artist, 1998, 2002; Platinum discs for Mathkafesh, 1991, Habibe, 1992, Ayamna, 1993, Ya Omrena, 1994, Nour El Ain, 1998. *Address:* EMI Recorded Music Middle East, Corporate Communications Dept, EMI Group PLC, 4 Tenterden St, Hanover Sq., London W1A 2AY, England.

DIABATE, Toumani; b. 10 Aug. 1965, Bamako, Mali. Musician (kora); Composer. *Career:* Son of Sidiki Diabate; Recorded first ever solo kora album, Kaira; Collaborations: Kandia Kouyate; Ketama; Danny Thompson; Ballake Sissoko; Taj Mahal; Damon Albarn; Habib Koite; Keletigui Diabate; Toured Europe and USA. *Recordings:* Albums include: Kaira, 1988; Songhai (with Ketama), 1989; Shake the World (including Habib Koite), 1991; Songhai 2, 1995; Djelika (with Danny Thompson and Keletigui Diabate), 1995; New Ancient Strings (with Ballake Sissoko), Kulanjan (with Taj Mahal), 1999. *Honours:* Froots, Best Album, Kulanjan, 1999.

DIAMOND, Jim; b. 28 Sept. 1951, Glasgow, Scotland. Vocalist. *Career:* Member, bands including Jade; Bandit; PhD; Solo artiste, 1983–. *Recordings:* Solo albums: Double Crossed, 1985; Desire For Freedom, 1986; Jim Diamond, 1993; Singles include: I Won't Let You Down, PhD, 1982; Solo: I Should Have Known Better (No. 1, UK), 1984; Hi Ho Silver, theme song, UK television series Boon, 1986; Session work with: Steve Hackett; Alexis Korner; Tony Banks. *Address:* c/o LJE, 32 Willesden Lane, London NW6 7ST, England.

DIAMOND, Neil Leslie; b. 24 Jan. 1941, Brooklyn, New York, USA. Vocalist; Composer. m. Marcia Murphey, 1975, 4 c. *Education:* Pre-med student, New York University. *Career:* Songwriter for publishing company; Formerly with Bang and MCA Records, 1973–, with Columbia; Record 20 show run at Winter Garden Theatre, 1972; Tours world-wide, include: 2 year, Love In The Round, world tour; Television and radio specials, numerous including: Christmas specials, 1992, 1993; Acted with Sir Laurence Olivier in The Jazz Singer, 1980; Set major box office records world-wide; 92m. albums sold. *Compositions include:* I'm A Believer (number 1 for Monkees); Film scores: Jonathan Livingston Seagull, 1973; Every Which Way But Loose, 1978; The Jazz Singer, 1980. *Recordings:* Albums include: The Feel of Neil Diamond, 1966; Just For You, 1967; Shilo, 1970; Velvet Gloves and Spit, 1968; Touching You Touching Me; Stones, 1971; Hot August Nights; Moods, 1972; Jonathan Livingston Seagull, 1973; Serenade, 1974; Beautiful Noise, 1976; Live At The Greek, 1977; I'm Glad You're Here Tonight, 1977; You Don't Bring Me Flowers, 1978; September Morn, 1980; Jazz Singer, 1980; Song Sung Blue, 1982; Headed For The Future, 1986; Hot August Night II, 1987; The Best Years of Our Lives, 1989; Christmas Album, 1992; Greatest Hits 1966–92, 1992; Up On the Roof – Songs From The Brill Building, 1993; Live In America, 1994; Christmas Album, Vol. II, 1994; Tennessee Moon, 1996; Live in Concert, 1997; The Movie Album, 1998; Three Chord Opera, 2001; Singles include: Sweet Caroline, 1969; Cracklin' Rosie (No. 1, USA), 1970; I Am... I Said, 1971; Song Sung Blue (No. 1, USA), 1972; Beautiful Noise, 1976; You Don't Bring Me Flowers, with Barbra Streisand (No. 1, USA), 1978; Forever In Blue Jeans, 1979; Love on the Rocks, 1980; Hello Again, 1981; Heartlight, 1982; Morning Has Broken, 1992; As Time Goes By, 1998. *Honours:* Platinum, Gold Records; Globe Awards; Grammy, 1973 for: Jonathan Livingston Seagull. *Membership:* SESAC. *Address:* c/o Columbia Records, Media Department, 550 Madison Ave, New York, NY 1002–3211, USA.

DIBANGO, Manu; b. 12 Dec. 1934, Douala, Cameroon. Musician (saxophone, piano). *Education:* Classical piano. *Career:* Moved to Paris, 1949; Then Brussels, Belgium, 1956; Residency at Black Angels Club, Brussels; Joined band led by Joseph Kabsele, African Jazz, 1960; Played with African Jazz in Zaire to 1963; Returned to Cameroon, formed own band, 1963–65; Studio musician, Paris, 1965; Backed musicians including: Peter Gabriel; Sinead O'Connor; Angélique Kidjo; Geoffroy Oryema; Ray Lema; Touré Kunda; Recording artiste, 1968–. *Compositions:* Commissioned by President Ahidjo to write patriotic song for Africa Cup football match, 1971. *Recordings:* Albums: O Boso, 1971; Soma Loba, 1972; Soul Makossa, 1973; Super Kumba, 1974; Manu 76, 1976; Afrovision, 1976; Big Blow, 1976; A L'Olympia, 1977; Ceddo, 1978; Gone Clear, 1980; Ambassador, 1980; Waka Juju, 1982; Deliverance, 1983; Sweet and Soft, 1983; Melodies Africaines Vols 1 and 2, 1983; Deadline, 1984; Electric Africa, 1985; Afrijazzy, 1986; Negropolitains Vol. 2, 1993; Wakafrika, 1994; Bao Bao, 1996; Hit singles: Soul Makossa (hit in USA,

Europe, Africa); Wakafika; Big Blow; Sun Explosion; Abele Dance. *Publications:* Autobiography: Trois Kilos de Café, 1990. *Honours:* Gold disc, Soul Makossa; Grammy Award, Best R&B Instrumental Performance of the Year, 1973. *Membership:* President, Francophone Diffusion. *Current Management:* IPS Management, 11–13 rue Mont-Louis, 75011 Paris, France. *Address:* c/o Francophone Diffusion, 33 rue du Fbg St Antoine, 75011 Paris, France.

DICK, Arthur; b. 4 Aug. 1954, Dundee, Scotland. Musician (guitar); Writer; Arranger. *Education:* BSc Hons, Liverpool University; Performing Diploma (guitar). *Career:* Numerous sessions as guitarist; Television appearances: Granada; Yorkshire; Thames; BBC; Central; Radio broadcasts: BBC; Capital; Picadilly, 1980–; MD for: Berni Flint, 1988; Susan Maughan; Recorded sessions for numerous artistes including: Cliff Richard; Paul McCartney; Cilla Black; Barbara Dickson; Formed Tracks Music for production of television and radio soundtracks, 1986; Lecturer, Goldsmith's College (London University); Guitar studies, recording, 1985–. *Publications:* Numerous for Music Sales Ltd; Works for Eric Clapton; Bon Jovi; Blues and Jazz compilations; Original guitar chord study; Guitar transcriptions of Santana; John Martyn; Robben Ford. *Membership:* PRS; Musicians' Union.

DICKINSON, (Paul) Bruce; b. 7 Aug. 1958, Worksop, Nottinghamshire, England. Vocalist; Author; Air Pilot. *Education:* Degree, History, Queen Mary College, London University, 1979. *Career:* Member: Speed; Shots; Samson, 1980; Lead vocalist, UK heavy rock group Iron Maiden, 1981–93, rejoined 1999; Regular tours world-wide; Concerts include: Reading Festival, 1982; Monsters of Rock Festivals, Castle Donington, 1988, 1992; Monsters of Rock, Germany, 1988; Monsters of Rock Festival, France, 1992; Super Rock '92, Germany, 1992; Pilot for various charter airline companies, incl. Astraeus; Host, music programmes for 6Music (BBC Digital radio station). *Recordings:* Albums: with Samson: Head On, 1980; Shock Tactics, 1981; with Iron Maiden: The Number of The Beast (No. 1, UK), 1982; Piece of Mind, 1983; Powerslave, 1984; Live After Death, 1985; Somewhere In Time, 1986; Seventh Son of a Seventh Son (No. 1, UK), 1988; No Prayer For The Dying, 1990; Fear of The Dark (No. 1, UK), 1992; A Real Live One, 1993; A Real Dead One, 1993; Brave New World, 2000; Solo albums: Tattooed Millionaire, 1990; Balls To Picasso, 1994; Alive In Studio A, 1995; Skunkworks, 1996; Accident of Birth, 1997; Chemical Wedding, 1998; Scream for Me Brazil, 1999; Rock In Rio, 2002. Singles include: with Iron Maiden: Run To The Hills, 1982; The Number of The Beast, 1982; Flight of Icarus, 1983; The Trooper, 1983; 2 Minutes To Midnight, 1984; Aces High, 1984; Wasted Years, 1986; Stranger In A Strange Land, 1986; Can I Play With Madness, 1988; Evil That Men Do, 1988; The Clairvoyant, 1988; Infinite Dreams, 1989; Holy Smoke, 1990; Bring Your Daughter To The Slaughter (from film A Nightmare On Elm Street 5) (No. 1, UK), 1991; Be Quick Or Be Dead, 1992; From Here To Eternity, 1992; Solo singles: Tattooed Millionaire, 1990; All The Young Dudes, 1990; Dive! Dive! Dive!, 1990; Elected (charity single for Comic Relief), 1992; Tears of The Dragon, 1994; Road to Hell. *Publications:* Novels: The Adventures of Lord Iffy Boatrace, 1990; The Missionary Position, 1992. *Current Management:* Sanctuary Music Management Ltd, First Floor Suite, The Colonnades, 82 Bishops Bridge Rd, London W2 6BB, England.

DICKSON, Barbara (Ruth); b. 27 Sept. 1947, Dunfermline, Scotland. Vocalist; Songwriter; Musician (guitar, piano); Actress. m. Oliver Cookson, 25 Aug. 1984, 3 s. *Career:* Television appearances include: Two Ronnies; Taggart; Band of Gold; Own documentaries and most light entertainment shows; UK concert tours, 1977–; Stage performances: John Paul George Ringo and Bert, 1974–75; Blood Brothers, 1982–83, 1993; The 7 Ages of Woman, 1997–98; Friends Like This, 1998; A Slice of Saturday Night, 1999; Spend, Spend, Spend, 1999. *Recordings:* Hit singles: Answer Me, 1976; Another Suitcase, 1977; Caravans, 1980; January, February, 1980; I Know Him So Well (with Elaine Paige) (No. 1, UK), 1985; Albums include: Barbara Dickson Album, 1980; All For A Song, 1982; Tell Me It's Not True, 1983; Heartbeats, 1984; Barbara Dickson Song Book, 1985; Gold, 1985; The Right Moment, 1986; Coming Alive Again, 1989; Don't Think Twice It's Alright, 1992; Parcel of Rogues, 1994; Dark End of The Street, 1996; The 7 Ages of Woman, 1998; Greatest Hits, 2002. *Honours:* SWET Award, Blood Brothers; Platinum and Gold albums; Best Actress in Theatre, Liverpool Echo Arts and Entertainment Awards, 1997; Best Actress In A Musical, Variety Club Showbusiness Awards, 1999; Best Actress In A Musical, Laurence Olivier Awards, 2000; O.B.E., 2002. *Membership:* PRS. *Current Management:* Bernard Theobald. *Address:* The Coach House, Swinhope Hall, Swinhope, Lincolnshire LN8 6HT, England.

DICKSON, Sean; b. 21 March 1967, Bellshill, Scotland. Vocalist; Songwriter; Prod; Musician (guitar, omnichord). *Career:* Singer, songwriter, guitarist, producer for The Soup Dragons, 1986–94, The High Fidelity, 1995–; World-wide tours; Released 3 albums, 18 singles and 15 videos for The Soup Dragons; Member, The High Fidelity; Runs own record label, Plastique Recordings. *Recordings:* Singles: Hang-Ten!, 1987; The Majestic Head, 1988; I'm Free, 1990; Divine Thing, 1990; Mother Universe, 1990; Backwards Dog, 1990; Pleasure, 1992; Can't Take No More; with The High Fidelity; Addicted to a TV, 1998; Luv Dup, 1998; I Thank U, 2000; Unsorry, 2000; 2 Up 2 Down, 2000; Albums: with The Soup Dragons: This Is Our Art, 1988; Lovegod, 1990;

Hotwired, 1992; Hydrophonic, 1994; with The High Fidelity: Demonstration, 2000. *Honours:* 2 Gold records, 1 Silver record. *Membership:* PRS; Musicians' Union. *Current Management:* Rick Rogers. *Address:* 132 Royal College St, Camden, London NW1 0TA, England.

DIDDLEY, Bo, (Otha Bates); b. 28 Dec. 1928, McComb, Mississippi, USA. Musician (guitar); Vocalist. *Career:* Numerous world-wide tours with artists including Ben E King; Ron Wood (as the Gunslingers); Lightnin' Hopkins; The Clash; Major concerts include: Rock 'n' Revival, with Jerry Lee Lewis, Little Richard, John Lennon, Toronto, 1969; Hampden Scene '70, with Chuck Berry, Glasgow, 1970; Regular 1950s Rock 'n' Roll Revivals concerts, USA and UK, 1971–; Jazz and Heritage Festival, New Orleans, 1990; Celebrate The Soul of American Music Festival, Los Angeles, 1991; Guitar Legends, Expo '92, Seville, Spain, 1991; Hopefest, annual charity concert for the homeless, Chicago, 1992; Television commercial for Nike, with Bo Jackson, 1989; Films: Sweet Toronto, 1969 (renamed Keep On Rockin', 1972); Let The Good Times Roll, 1973; Trading Places, 1983. *Recordings:* Albums: Bo Diddley, 1962; Bo Diddley Is A Gunslinger, 1963; Bo Diddley Rides Again, 1963; Bo Diddley's Beach Party, 1964; Two Great Guitars, with Chuck Berry, 1964; Super Blues Band, with Muddy Waters and Little Walter, 1968; Another Dimension, 1971; The London Bo Diddley Sessions, 1973; 20th Anniversary of Rock 'n' Roll, 1976; Hey Bo Diddley, 1986; Live At The Ritz, 1987; Breakin' Through The BS, 1989; Rare and Well Done, 1991; Bo's Blues, 1993; Let Me Pass, 1994; Bo Knows Bo, 1995; A Man Amongst Men, 1996; His Best, 1997; The Essential Collection, 2001; Featured on film soundtracks: La Bamba (No. 1, USA), 1987; Book of Love, with Ben E. King, 1991; Singles include: Bo Diddley (R&B No. 2, USA); Who Do You Love; Say Man; Road Runner; You Can't Judge A Book By It's Over; Mona; Hey Good Lookin'; Ooh Baby. *Honours:* Inducted, Rock and Roll Hall of Fame, 1987; Handprints in Sunset Boulevard's Rock Walk, Los Angeles, 1989. *Current Management:* Margo Lewis, Talent Source, 1560 Broadway, Suite 1308, New York, NY 10036, USA.

DIDDY, (Richard Dearlove); b. 22 Sept. 1966, Marston Green, Birmingham, England. Songwriter; Record Prod; Musician (keyboards, guitar); Vocalist; Artist. *Career:* Pop, dance, singles and remixes. *Compositions:* Small World; Give Me Love, singles released as Diddy. *Recordings:* As Remixer, Producer: Blondie: Atomic, 1994; Heart of Glass, 1995; Rio and Mars: Boy I Gotta Have You; How Deep Is Love; The Tyrell Corporation: Better Days; Retro Dance Club; Now That's What I Call Music. *Membership:* Musicians' Union.

DIDO, (Dido Florian Cloud de Bounevialle Armstrong); b. 25 Dec. 1971, London, England. Vocalist; Musician (piano, violin); Songwriter. *Education:* Guildhall School of Music, London. *Career:* Toured UK with classical music ensemble before joining pop groups aged 16; Toured as backing vocalist with brother Rollo's band, Faithless; Solo artiste; Signed to Arista Records, New York; Track, Thank You, from album incorporated into Eminem's hit single Stan caused world-wide interest; Live promotion of album, 2000–01. *Recordings:* Album: No Angel, 1999. Singles: The Highbury Fields (EP), 1999; Here With Me, 2001; Thank You, 2001; Hunter, 2001; All You Want, 2002. *Honours:* BRIT Awards, Best British Album, for No Angel, Best British Female Solo Artist, 2002; Ivor Novello Songwriter of the Year Award, 2002. *Address:* c/o Cheeky Records, 181 High St, London NW10 4TE, England. *Website:* www.didomusic.com.

DIESEL, (Darren House), (Yellow Sox); b. 8 Feb. 1966, Hayes, London, England. Prod; Remixer; DJ. *Career:* Started DJ career with partner Rocky; Formed X-Press 2 with Ashley Beedle and Rocky, 1993; Signed to Junior Boy's Own label; Member: Ballistic Brothers; Remixed: Fatboy Slim; River Ocean. *Recordings:* Albums: Ballistic Brothers vs The Eccentric Afros, 1995; London Hooligan Soul (with Ballistic Brothers), 1995; My First Acid House (with Problem Kids), 2001; Muzikizum, 2002. Singles: Muzik X-Press, London X-Press, Say What, 1993; Rock 2 House, 1994; The Sound, 1995; Tranz Euro Express, 1996; Flim Flam (as Yellow Sox), 1996; Blacker (with Ballistic Brothers), 1997; AC/DC, 2000; Smoke Machine, Muzikizum, 2001; Lazy (featuring David Byrne), 2002. *Honours:* Muzik Awards, Best Producers, X-Press 2, 2001. *Membership:* MCPS/PRS. *Address:* c/o Skint Records, 73A Middle St, Brighton, Sussex BN1 4BA, England.

DIF, René; b. 17 October 1967, Fredriksberg, Denmark. Vocalist. *Career:* Formed Joyspeed; Changed name to Aqua; Obtained record deal in Denmark; Numerous TV and live appearances. *Recordings:* Singles: Itsy Blitzy, as Joyspeed; Roses Are Red; My Oh My; Barbie Girl; Doctor Jones; Lollipop; Turn Back Time; Good Morning Sunshine; Albums: Aquarium, 1997; Bubble Mix, 1998.

DIFFIE, Joe Logan; b. 28 Dec. 1958, Tulsa, Oklahoma, USA. Country vocalist; Songwriter; Musician (guitar, bass guitar, drums). *Career:* Member of high school gospel group Genesis II and rock group Blitz; Later joined gospel group Higher Purpose and local bluegrass outfit Special Edition; Initial country gigs with aunt Dawn Anita and sister Monica; Earliest recorded song: Love On The Rocks by Hank Thompson; Moved to Nashville and worked for Gibson Guitars; Continued songwriting as staff writer at Forest Hills Music with occasional backing vocals and demo work for publishers; Signed by

Columbia Records after vice-president Bob Montgomery heard demos; Debut Billboard chart entry, 1990; Continued to chart throughout decade; Debut Opry appearance, 1990. *Compositions include:* Honky Tonk Attitude; If You Want Me To; Is It Cold In Here; New Way To Light Up An Old Flame; There Goes My Heart Again. *Recordings include:* Pick Up Man, 1994; Bigger Than The Beatles, 1995; Third Rock From The Sun, 1994; If The Devil Danced (In Empty Pockets), 1991; Home, 1990; Albums include: Regular Joe, 1992; Honky Tonk Attitude, 1993; Third Rock From The Sun, 1994. *Honours:* Billboard Award, Top Singles Artist, 1991; Cash Box, Male Artist of the Year, 1991; BMI award, There Goes My Heart Again, 1990. *Membership:* Grand Ole Opry, 1993. *Address:* c/o Buddy Lee Attractions, 38 Music Sq. E, Suite 300, Nashville, TN 37203, USA. *Website:* www.joediffie.com.

DIFFORD, Chris; b. 4 Nov. 1954, Greenwich, London, England. Vocalist; Musician (guitar); Songwriter. *Career:* Founder member, Squeeze, 1974–; Longstanding writing partnership with Glenn Tilbrook; Performances include: Reading Festival, 1978; Dalymount Festival, Dublin, 1980; US tours, 1978–; Jamaica World Music Festival, 1982; Support to Fleetwood Mac, US tour, 1990; Crystal Palace Bowl, London, 1991; Support to Bryan Adams, British tour, 1992. *Compositions include:* Songs for Labelled With Love, musical, 1983; Worked with Helen Shapiro; Paul Young; Jools Holland; Aimee Mann; Joe Cocker; Mark Knopfler; Lyricist for Marti Pellow album, Smile, 2001. *Recordings:* Albums: Squeeze, 1978; Cool For Cats, 1979; Argy Bargy, 1980; East Side Story, 1981; Sweets From A Stranger, 1982; Singles 45 and Under, 1982; Cosi Fan Tutti Frutti, 1985; Babylon and On, 1987; Frank, 1989; A Round and A Bout, 1990; Greatest Hits, 1992; Some Fantastic Piece, 1993; Ridiculous, 1995; Piccadilly Collection, 1996; Excess Moderation, 1996; Six of One, 1997; Domino, 1998; I Didn't Get Where I Am, 2002; with Glenn Tilbrook: Difford and Tilbrook, 1984; Singles include: Take Me I'm Yours, 1978; Cool For Cats (No. 2, UK), 1979; Up The Junction (No. 2, UK), 1979; Slap and Tickle, 1979; Another Nail In My Heart, 1980; Pulling Mussels From A Shell, 1980; Tempted, 1981; Labelled With Love, 1981; Hourglass, 1987; This Summer, 1995; Heaven Knows, 1996. *Current Management:* Firstars, 3520 Hayden Ave, Culver City, CA 90232, USA.

DIGBY, Roger; b. 19 April 1949, Colchester, Essex, England. Teacher; Musician (concertina). m. Sian Chatterton. 30 Nov. 1985, 2 s. *Education:* BA Hons, Bristol University; MA, Carlton University, Ottawa, Canada. *Career:* Leader, Anglo concertina player, Flowers and Frolics, 10 years; Venues include The Albert Hall, South Bank, Italian Alps; 7 years as co-organizer, acoustic music venue The Empress of Russia, Islington. *Recordings:* Albums: Bees On Horseback; Sold Out; Wait Till The Work Comes Round (with Bob Davenport). *Publications:* Numerous reviews. *Membership:* Musicians' Union; EFDSS; International Concertina Asscn. *Address:* 3 Wolsey Rd, London N1 4QH, England.

DIGITAL, Didge; b. 18 May 1955, Shipley, West Yorkshire, England. Musician (keyboard); Programmer. 1 s. *Education:* Piano lessons from age 6. *Career:* Keyboard player: FM; Tours with: Meat Loaf; Tina Turner; Bon Jovi; Gary Moore; Gerry and the Pacemakers; Status Quo; Television appearances: Pebble Mill; James Whale Show; Chart Show; Garden Party. *Recordings:* Albums: FM: Indiscreet; Tough It Out; Takin' It To The Streets; Chris Norman: Jealous Heart. *Honours:* Second Best Keyboard Player, Metal Hammer, 1987; Fourth Best Keyboard Player, International, 1987. *Current Management:* Flair Management and Agency. *Address:* 28 Cornmill Lane, Liversedge, Heckmondwike, Yorkshire, England.

DIGWEED, John; b. 3 April, 1967, Hastings, East Sussex, England. Prod; Remixer; DJ. *Career:* Began DJ career in Hastings at his own Bedrock events, early '90s; Formed highly successful DJ partnership with Sasha leading to a residency at Twilo in New York; Released several successful mix compilations with Sasha including: Renaissance; Northern Exposure; Founder: Bedrock Records; Member: Bedrock with production partner Nick Muir; Runs Bedrock event at London's Heaven club every month; Remixed: Sasha; Danny Tenaglia; Farley and Heller; The Orb; New Order. *Recordings:* Singles: For What You Dream Of, 1993; Set In Stone, 1997; Heaven Scent, 1999; Voices, 2000; Beautiful Strange, 2001. *Honours:* DJ Magazine, Top 100 DJs in the World, No. 1, 2001. *Membership:* MCPS/PRS. *Address:* c/o Bedrock Records, PO Box 4185, London W1A 6XH, England.

DILLARD, Doug; b. 6 March 1937, East St Louis, Illinois, USA. *Career:* Formed bluegrass group, The Dillards, with brother Rodney, 1962; Left to form Dillard and Clark with Gene Clark, 1968; Occasional sideline, Dillard-Hartford-Dillard, with brother Rodney and John Hartford. *Recordings:* Albums: With The Dillards: Back Porch Bluegrass, 1963; The Dillards Live! Almost, 1964; Pickin' and Fiddlin', 1965; with Dillard and Clark: The Fantastic Expedition of Dillard and Clark, 1968; Through The Morning, Through The Night, 1969; Solo: Dueling Banjos, 1973; You Don't Need a Reason, 1974; Heaven, 1976; with Doug Dillard Band: Jackrabbit, 1997; What's That, 1986; Heartbreak Hotel, 1989; There Is a Time, 1991.

DILLARD, Rodney; b. 18 May 1942, East St Louis, Illinois, USA. Vocalist; Musician (guitar). *Career:* Formed bluegrass group, The Dillards, with brother Doug, 1962–; Various line-up changes, but Dillard remained leader of group;

Occasional sideline, Dillard-Hartford-Dillard, with brother Doug and John Hartford. *Recordings:* Albums: Back Porch Bluegrass, 1963; The Dillards Live! Almost!, 1964; Pickin' and Fiddlin', 1965; Wheatstraw Suite, 1969; Copperfields, 1970; Roots and Branches, 1972; Tribute To The American Duck, 1973; The Dillards Versus The Incredible LA Time Machine, 1977; Mountain Rock, 1978; Decade Waltz, 1979; Homecoming and Family Reunion, 1979; I'll Fly Away, 1988; Let It Fly, 1991; Roots and Branches, 1996; First Time Live, 1999. *Current Management:* Keith Case and Associates, 59 Music Sq. W, Nashville, TN 37203, USA.

DILLON, Cara; b. 1975, Dungiven, County Derry, Northern Ireland. Vocalist; Songwriter. *Career:* Member: Oige; Equation, 1995; Formed writing partnership with Sam Lakeman; Now work as a duo. *Recordings:* Live (with Oige), 1994; Interview With The Angel (with Ghostland), Cara Dillon, 2001. *Honours:* All-Ireland Traditional Singing trophy, 1989; BBC Radio 2 Folk Awards: Best Traditional Track, Black is the Colour; Horizon Award, 2002. *Address:* c/o Glass Ceiling PR. *E-mail:* promo@glassceilingpr.com.

DIMOND, David; b. 23 Nov. 1964, Barking, Essex, England. Freelance Musician (saxophone, clarinet, flute); Music Teacher. *Education:* BSc Hons, Microbiology, University of Surrey; Clarinet, flute Grade 8, Royal Schools of Music; 1 year post-diploma, saxophone (Guildhall School of Music and Drama). *Career:* Mainly jazz-based, duos including Duojazz; Quartets, quintets include Jim Mullen quintet; Octets include Caliban; Big bands include: Superjazz, NYJO; Played Ronnie Scott's; Bass Clef; 606 Club; Royal Albert Hall; Festival Hall; Festivals include: Soho Jazz Festival; Edinburgh Festival; Tour with Bondera. *Compositions:* Over 50. *Recordings:* Recorded with numerous jazz set-ups as well as for library music, jingles on tenor saxophone. *Publications:* Article for international journal on acoustics. *Address:* 18 Osborne Rd, Dagenham, Essex RM9 5BB, England.

DIO, Ronnie James, (Ronald Padavona); b. 10 July 1949, New Hampshire, USA. Rock Vocalist; Musician (bass, piano, trumpet); Songwriter; Prod. m. Wendy Dio. *Career:* Member, various bands including: The Vegas Kings; Ronnie and The Rumblers; Ronnie and The Redcaps, late 1950s; Singer, musician, Ronnie Dio and The Prophets, 1961–67; Founder, Elf (formerly The Electric Elves), 1967–75; Member, Rainbow, 1975–79; Member, Black Sabbath, 1980–82; Founder member, Dio, 1983–91; Member, Black Sabbath, 1992–93; Also organizer of Hear 'N' Aid project (famine relief in Ethiopia), 1986. *Recordings:* Albums: with Ronnie Dio and The Prophets: Dio At Dominos, 1963; with Elf: Elf, 1972; Carolina County Ball, 1974; Trying To Burn The Sun, 1975; Live, 1976; with Rainbow: Ritchie Blackmore's Rainbow, 1975; Rainbow Rising, 1976; Live On Stage, 1977; Long Live Rock 'n' Roll, 1978; with Black Sabbath: Heaven and Hell, 1980; Mob Rules, 1981; Live Evil, 1982; with Dio: Holy Diver, 1983; The Last In Line, 1984; Sacred Heart, 1985; Intermission, 1986; Dream Evil, 1987; Lock Up The Wolves, 1990; Strange Highways, 1994; Angry Machines, 1996; Inferno, 1998; Magica, 2000; Other recordings: The Butterfly Ball, Roger Glover, 1975; Hear 'N' Aid, 1986; Northwinds, David Coverdale, 1978. *Current Management:* c/o Wendy Dio, Niji Management, 12334 Ventura Blvd, Studio City, CA 91604, USA.

DION, Céline; b. 30 March 1968, Charlemagne, QC, Canada. Vocalist. m. Rene Angelil, 17 Dec. 1994, 1 c. *Career:* Began singing in father's restaurant; Recording artiste, 1979–; Winner, Eurovision Song Contest for Switzerland, 1988; Recorded in French until 1990; Las Vegas show, A New Day, opened 2003 (200 shows a year for three years planned). *Recordings:* Albums: Tellement J'ai D'Amour; Dion Chante Plamondon; Incognito; Unison, 1990; Céline Dion, 1991; The Colour of My Love, 1994; D'Eux, 1995; Falling Into You, 1996; Live à Paris, 1996; Let's Talk About Love, 1997; A l'Olympia, 1998; Chansons en Or, 1998; These Are Special Times, 1998; Let's Talk About Love, 1999; All The Way – A Decade of Song, 1999; S'il Suffisait D'Aimer, 2001; A New Day Has Come, 2002. Singles: Les Chemins De Ma Maison, 1984; Melanie, 1985; Une Colombe, 1985; Incognito, 1988; Where Does My Heart Beat Now, 1991; Beauty and The Beast, duet with Peabo Bryson, 1992; When I Feel (Fall) In Love, from film soundtrack Sleepless In Seattle, 1993; The Power of Love (No. 1, USA), 1994; Think Twice (No. 1, UK), 1995; Pour Que Tu M'Aimes Encore, 1995; Misled, 1995; Only One Road, 1995; Falling Into You, 1996; Because You Loved Me, from film Up Close and Personal (No. 1, USA), 1996; It's All Coming Back To Me Now, 1996; All By Myself, 1996; Call The Man, 1997; Tell Him, duet with Barbra Streisand, 1997; The Reason, 1997; My Heart Will Go On, from film soundtrack of Titanic (No. 1, UK and USA), 1998; Immortality, collaboration with The Bee Gees, 1998; I'm Your Angel, duet with R. Kelly (No. 1, USA), 1998; Treat Her Like a Lady, 1999; That's The Way It Is, 1999. *Honours:* Gala de L'Adisq Awards: Pop Album of the Year, 1983; Best Selling Record, 1984, 1985; Best Selling Single, 1985; Pop Song of the Year, 1985, 1988; Female Artist of Year, 1983–85, 1988; Discovery of the Year, 1983; Best Québec Artist Outside Québec, 1983, 1988; JUNO Awards: Album of the Year, 1991; Single of the Year, 1993; Female Vocalist of the Year, 1991–93; Journal de Québec Trophy, 1985; Spectrel Video Award, Best Stage Performance, 1988; American Music Award, Best Adult Contemporary Artist, 2003. *Current Management:* c/o Rene Angelil, Feeling Productions Inc, 755-2540 Daniel-Johnson, Laval, QC H7T 2S3, Canada.

DIOP, Wasis; b. 1950, Dakar, Senegal. Composer; Vocalist; Musician (guitar). *Career:* Toured France with jazz band, West African Cosmos, late 1980s; Worked with record producer Lee Perry in Jamaica, 1989; Worked with Amina Annabi, France, 1990; His song for her, C'est Le Dernier Qui A Raison, won the Eurovision Song Contest, 1991; Toured Japan with saxophonist, Tasuaki Shimizu; Solo career began with his composition of the soundtrack for film, Hyenes, directed by his brother, Djibril Diop Mambety. *Recordings:* Albums: Hyenes, 1992; No Sant, 1995; Toxu, 1998. Single: African Dream. *Address:* c/o Nicolas Gautier, Mercury Records, 20 rue des fossés St Jacques, 75005 Paris, France.

DIRECTIONAL FORCE. See: CLARKE, Dave.

DIRNT, Mike, (Michael Pritchard); b. 4 May 1972, Berkeley, CA, USA. Musician (bass); Backing singer. m. Anastasia, divorced, 1 d. *Career:* Founding mem., Sweet Children, renamed Green Day, 1989–; Numerous tours and TV appearance; Side projects, Pinhead Gunpowder and Screeching Weasel; Obtained major label recording contract; Provided track for film soundtrack Godzilla; Appeared in cartoon King of the Hill as The Stubborn Stains. *Recordings:* Albums: 39/Smooth, 1990; Kerplunk, 1991; Dookie, 1994; Insomniac, 1994; Nimrod, 1997; Foot in Mouth, 1998; Warning, 2000; International Superhits (compilation), 2001; Shenanigans, 2002. Singles: Sweet Children (EP), 1987; 1,000 Hours (EP), 1989; Slappy (EP), 1990; Live Tracks (EP), 1994; Welcome To Paradise, 1994; Longview, 1994; Basket Case, 1994; When I Come Around, 1994; Geek Stink Breath, 1995; Stuck With Me, 1995; Bowling Bowling Bowling Parking Parking (EP), 1996; Foot In Mouth (EP), 1996; Brain Stew/Jaded, 1996; Hitchin' A Ride, 1997; Time Of Your Life, 1997; Redundant #1, #2, 1998; Minority, 2000; Warning, 2001; Waiting, 2001. *Address:* c/o Reprise Records, Warner Bros Records Inc, 3300 Warner Blvd, Burbank, CA 91505, USA. *Website:* www.greenday.com.

DIRTY PIK; b. 1 Sept. 1961, Tielt, Belgium. Vocalist; Musician (guitar). 2 d., 1 s. *Career:* Mem., The Dirty Scums, 1981–; Game Over, 1998–2001. *Recordings:* Albums: Dirty Songs, 1985; Full Speed Ahead!, 1987; Fifth Anniversary Gig, 1988; The Booze And The Chicks, 1989; The Early Years, 1990; If The Barkeepers Are United, The Scums Will Never Be Divided, 1992; The Pils Sessions And Setting New Standards To Stupidity, 1996; Santa Clauz Has Come!, 1997; Proud to be a Punk and Something Else, 1999; Dirtier Than You'll Ever Be, 2000; Insert New Coin, 2000. Singles: Martens, 1986; 'Rit 'n Zatte Skit 'N, 1988; Really High, 1993; R.A.M.O.N.E.S., 2002. *Address:* The Dirty Scums, Kapelleweg 10, 8700 Tielt, Belgium. *Website:* www.thedirtyscums.com.

DISCLEZ, Yves; b. 22 April 1956, Brussels, Belgium. Writer; Composer; Artist. m. Carine Mairesse, 28 April 1990, 1 s., 1 d. *Education:* Music Academy, Ciney, Belgium; Up With People, Tucson, Arizona, as guitar player. *Career:* 839 shows, USA, 1975–76; Up With People programme; Up With People on tour: Intermission of the Super Bowl, Miami 1976 (Television audience 250,000); Chicago Theatre, 3 days; Civic Center, Long Beach; National Television, USA, 1975–76; Belgian television: Palmares, 1983; 4 tours, Belgium, 1982–90; Appearances: RTL/TV1, 19 in 1990, 21 in 1991; All national radio. *Recordings:* Nostalgie, 1983; Compteur A Zero, 1984; J' M'en Fou, 1986; Dazibao, 1989; Conquiatador, 1990; Le Môme de la Bas, 1991; Romanc, 1994. *Publications:* Nostalgie; J'M'en Fou; Romanc. *Honours:* Prize of Belgium Artistic Promotion (PAB), 1986; First prize, French Song, Walcourt, Belgium, 1989. *Membership:* SABAM (Belgium); Copy Right (Washington, USA). *Current Management:* Mr Patrick Decam, Sony Music (Belgium). *Address:* 27, Ave de la Restauration, 5500 Falmagne (Dinant), Belgium.

DISTEL, Sacha; b. 29 Jan. 1933, Paris, France. Vocalist; Songwriter; Musician (guitar). m. Francine Breaud, 1963, 2 s. *Career:* Professional jazz guitarist, age 16; World-wide cabaret star; Films: Les Mordus, 1960; Nous Irons A Deauville, 1962; La Bonne Soupe, 1964; Le Voyou, 1970; Sans Mobile Apparent, 1971; Television presenter, France, England, Germany; Co-star, Golden Songs of The Silver Screen tour; Producer of shows: Sacha Show; Top à Sacha Distel, 1973; Sacha's In Town, 1972; Producer, performer, La Belle Vie, 1984–85. *Recordings:* Hit singles include: Scoubidou, 1959; Raindrops Keep Falling On My Head, 1970; Albums include: Sacha Distel, 1970; Love Is All, 1976; Forever and Ever, 1978; Golden Hour of Sacha Distel, 1978; 20 Favourite Love Songs, 1979; From Sacha With Love, 1979; The Sacha Distel Collection, 1980; Move Closer, 1985; More Than More, 1987; Dedications, 1992; Ecoute Mes Yeux, 1998; Very Best of Sacha Distel, 1998; Collaborated with UK band Dubstar on recording of Poupee De Cire Poupee De Son for TV Eurovision tribute, A Song For Eurotrash, 1998. *Honours:* Best Guitarist, Jazz Hot Magazine, Critics Poll, 1957–59; Chevalier des Arts et des Lettres, 1987; Chevalier de la Legion D'Honneur, 1997. *Address:* c/o Prosadis, 83 rue Michel-Ange, 75016 Paris, France.

DISTLER, Jed (John Edward); b. 8 Dec. 1956, Newark, New Jersey, USA. Composer; Musician (Piano); Artistic Dir of Composers Collaborative. m. Célia Cooke, 24 July 1984. *Education:* BA, Sarah Lawrence College; Composition lessons with Andrew Thomas; Piano with Stanley Lock and William Komaiko. *Career:* Artistic Director, ComposersCollaborative Inc, a non-profit presenting organization for new music; Numerous live appearances on National Public Radio and alternative music stations; Faculty Member, Sarah Lawrence College. *Compositions:* The Death of Lottie Shapiro; Calypso for Piano; Diva Demento; Landscapes for Peter Wyer; Sonata for Violin and Piano and Toy Piano; Assault on Pepper; String Quartet No 1 (Mr Softee Variations). *Recordings:* Three Landscapes for Peter Wyer; Margaret Leng Tan; Arrangements and transcriptions for Conversations with Bill Evans, Reflections on Duke Ellington, with Jean-Yves Thibaudet, pianist; Eleven Art Tatum Transcripts, with Steven Mayer, piano. *Publications:* Transcription books: Art Tatum: Jazz Master; Bill Evans 4; Contributing writer for Gramophone magazine. *Honours:* With ComposersCollaborative: Grants and Awards, Meet the Composer, The Virgil Thomson Foundation, The Aaron Copland Fund for Music, Foundation for Hellenic Culture. *Membership:* American Federation of Musicians (Local 802); American Music Center; American Composers Forum; ASCAP. *Current Management:* Célia Cooke, personal representative.

DITCHAM, Martin Russell; b. 22 Feb. 1951, Ilford, Essex, England. Musician (percussion, drums). *Education:* Studied trumpet, violin, recorder, percussion, at school. *Career:* World tours with Sade; Chris Rea; Live Aid; Everything But The Girl, US tour; British tours with The Beautiful South. *Recordings:* All four Sade albums; Last eight Chris Rea albums; Undercover, Rolling Stones; Ross, Diana Ross; Duets, Elton John; 3 albums with Talk Talk; Nik Kershaw; Mike and The Mechanics; Jimmy Nail; The Sundays; Heather Small; Tanita Tikaram; The Waterboys; International recordings with: Patricia Kaas (France); Westernhagen (Germany); Takanaka (Japan); Presuntas Implicados (Spain). *Honours:* BPI, ASCAP Awards for Sade, Sweetest Taboo (one of most played songs of year). *Membership:* Musicians' Union; PRS. *Current Management:* Real Life Ltd. *Address:* 10 Glyn Mansions, Hammersmith Rd, London W14 8XH, England.

DIVLJAN, Vladimir; b. 10 May 1958, Belgrade, Yugoslavia. Songwriter; Musician (guitar); Vocalist; Film Composer; Sound Designer. *Education:* BSc, Geology, University of Belgrade, 1983; Specialist, Extension Course in Sound Design, AFTRS, Sydney, 1997; programming. *Career:* Songwriter, guitarist and singer, Belgrade based New Wave Band, Idoli (The Idols), 1980–84, National (Yugoslav) Tours, 1981, 1982, 1983; Songwriter, solo performer, film and TV composer, Yugoslavia and Australia, 1985–. *Compositions:* Composed music for features: Six Days in June, 1984; The Rise and Fall of Rock 'N' Roll, 1989; Documentaries: Across Australia, 1993; Heart of the Matter, 1995; You Might as Well Live, 1995. *Recordings:* Realised 13 albums including: Paket Aranzman, 1981; Odbrana I Poslednji Dani, 1982; Tajni Zivot A P Sandorova, 1988; Odbrana I Zastita, 1996. *Honours:* Idoli, ranked Fourth Most Promising Group by 8 leading European magazines, 1988; LP, Odbrana I Poslednji Dani, voted Best Yugoslav Rock Record of All Times, 1988; Quantegy Award for Audio Excellence, AFTRS, 1997. *Membership:* Australian Performers Rights Asscn; Australian Guild of Screen Composers. *Current Management:* Radio B92, Makedonska 22/V, 11000 Beograd, Yugoslavia.

DIXON, Alesha; b. England. Vocalist; Songwriter; MC. *Career:* Mem., Mis-Teeq, 2001–, with Su-Elise Nash and Sabrina Washington; Appeared, Party at the Palace, for Golden Jubilee celebrations, 2002. *Recordings:* Album: Lickin' On Both Sides, 2001. Singles: Why?, 2001; All I Want, 2001; One Night Stand, 2001; B With Me, 2002; Roll On, 2002. *Honours:* Platinum disc, for Lickin' On Both Sides; UK Garage Award, Best Artist, 2001; MOBO Award, Best Garage Act, 2002. *Address:* c/o Telstar Records, 107 Mortlake High St, London SW14 8HQ, England. *Website:* www.mis-teeq.co.uk.

DIXON, Jolyon Keith; b. 6 Dec. 1973, Salisbury, Wiltshire, England. Musician (guitar); Vocalist; Songwriter. *Education:* Music A-Level. *Career:* Tours: Two British tours backing Toyah Willcox; Central American tour with Toyah; 2 support tours as: Friday Forever; 2 Heineken Music Festivals; Support to Bryan Ferry, with Scarlet, UK, 1995; Joined as guitarist in Mark Owen's band, and has toured extensively with them; Sold 1m. albums world-wide with Mark Owen; First band to perform in Abbey Road studios since the Beatles; Numerous radio appearances with: Scarlet; Toyah; Television: 3 times, Top of the Pops; What's Up Doc?; Richard and Judy; Pebble Mill; Parallel Nine. *Recordings:* Toyah: Take The Leap, 1993; Scarlet: Naked, 1995; Green Man with Mark Owen, 1996; Hit single: Independent Love Song; follow-up singles; Unreleased albums: Voice of The Beehive: East/West; Judie Tzuke: Duck. *Publications:* with Mark Owen's band: Child, 1996; Clementine, 1997; I Am What I Am, 1997. *Membership:* Musicians' Union. *Current Management:* Friday's Productions. *Address:* 51A Estcourt Rd, Salisbury, Wiltshire, England.

DIYICI, Senem; b. 30 March 1953, Istanbul, Turkey. Vocalist. m. Alain Blesing, 1989, 2 d. *Education:* Istanbul Music Academy, from age of 6. *Career:* Joined children's choir in Istanbul; 3 albums in Turkey, moved to Germany; Formed several groups, produced 1 album; Arrived in France, in quest for new harmonies and musical crossover; Performs about 100 shows throughout world annually. *Recordings:* Nar Haniti, 1970; Hatimeyva, 1976; Casino No 1, 1979; Anatoliv, 1986; Takalar, 1989; Geste, 1993; Divan, 1995; Jell me Trabizan. *Membership:* SACEM; ADATI; SPEDIDAM. *Current Management:*

Equator Produkties, Netherlands. *Address:* Essenburg Singel 198B, 3022 E N Rotterdam, Netherlands.

DJ HOMICIDE, (Craig Anthony Bullock); b. 17 Dec. 1970. Musician (drum programming; effects); DJ. *Career:* Formerly radio presenter on Los Angeles hip hop stations, K-DAY and The Beat; Worked in studio on Sugar Ray's Lemonade and Brownies album; Joined group for live shows then became full-time member; Act built up world-wide fanbase through touring and TV appearances; Cameo in Fathers Day film, 1997. *Recordings:* Albums: Lemonade and Brownies, 1995; Floored, 1997; 14–59, 1999; Sugar Ray, 2001; Singles: Mean Machine, Iron Mic, 1995; Fly, RPM, 1997; Every Morning, Someday, 1999; Falls Apart, 2000; When It's Over, Answer The Phone, 2001. *Honours:* Second/third albums certified double/triple platinum by RIAA respectively. *Address:* c/o PO Box 12018, Costa Mesa, CA 92627, USA. *E-mail:* management@sugarray.com. *Website:* www.sugarray.com.

DJ JAZZY JEFF, (Jeffrey Townes); b. 22 Jan. 1965, Philadelphia, PA, USA. *Career:* Started as DJ, 1970s; Formed duo with Will Smith, as DJ Jazzy Jeff and the Fresh Prince; Collaborated with Will Smith on Smith's solo album, Big Willie Style, 1997; guest on I Don't Know, Slum Village, 2000; Formed A Touch of Jazz Inc, collective of producers working on rap and R&B projects. *Recordings:* Singles: Girls Ain't Nothing But Trouble, 1986; Just One of Those Days; Parents Just Don't Understand; A Nightmare on Elm Street; Brand New Funk; The Groove; I Think I Can Beat Mike Tyson; Summertime; Ring My Bell; The Things That U Do; Boom! Shake the Room; I'm Looking for the One (To Be With Me); Albums: Rock the House, 1987; He's the DJ, I'm the Rapper, 1988; An In This Corner, 1989; Homebase, 1991; Code Red, 1993; The Magnificent, 2002. *Honours:* Grammy Awards, as DJ Jazzy Jeff and the Fresh Prince, Best Rap Performance, 1988, 1991.

DJ KILMORE, (Chris Kilmore); b. 21 Jan. 1973, Pittsburgh, Pennsylvania, USA. DJ. *Career:* Shortly after relocation to LA, replaced DJ Lyfe in Immortal/Epic-signed group Incubus, 1998; Built US and European following from support slots on tours with: Sugar Ray; Black Sabbath; Korn; Drive reached #1 on US Modern Rock Chart, 2001; First Japanese and Australian live dates, 2001. *Recordings:* Albums: Make Yourself, 1999; Morning View, 2001; Singles: Pardon Me, 1999; Stellar, When Incubus Attacks Vol. 1 EP, 2000; Drive, Wish You Were Here, 2001. *Honours:* Make Yourself album certified double platinum by RIAA; Billboard Award, Modern Rock Single of the Year, 2001. *Current Management:* Steve Rennie, REN Management, California, USA. *Website:* www.enjoyincubus.com.

DJ KRUST. See: **KRUST.**

DJ KUTMASTER LAVSKI. See: **LAVELLE, James.**

DJ LETHAL, (Leor DiMant); b. 18 Dec. 1972, Latvia. DJ; Musician (rhythm/sound effects). *Career:* Member: House of Pain, 1992–96; Limp Bizkit, 1996–; Striking live shows at concerts and festivals; Group spearheaded 'nu-metal' breakthrough in Europe, 2001; Various remixes and executive production for other artists including: Sugar Ray; Rob Zombie. *Recordings:* Albums: with House of Pain: House of Pain, 1992; Same As It Ever Was, 1994; Truth Crushed To Earth Shall Rise Again, 1996; with Limp Bizkit: Three Dollar Bill, Y'All $, 1997; Significant Other, 1999; Chocolate Starfish and The Hot Dog Flavored Water, 2000; New Old Songs (remix album), 2001; Singles: with House of Pain: Jump Around, Shamrocks and Shenanigans, 1992; Top O' The Morning To Ya, Who's The Man, 1993; On Point, It Ain't A Crime, 1994; Fed Up, 1996; with Limp Bizkit: Faith, 1997; Nookie, Rearranged, 1999; Break Stuff, Take A Look Around (from Mission Impossible 2 OST), My Generation, 2000; Rollin', My Way, Boiler, 2001. *Honours:* Second and third Limp Bizkit albums both debuted at #1 on US chart; Significant Other sales in excess of 6m.; American Music Award, Favourite Alternative Artist, 2002. *Current Management:* The Firm (Management), 9100 Wilshire Blvd, Suite 400W, Beverly Hills, CA 90212, USA. *Website:* www.limpbizkit.com.

DJ MUGGS, (Lawrence Muggerud); b. 28 Jan. 1968, New York, USA. DJ; Prod. *Career:* Member, Cypress Hill; Numerous tours including Lollapalooza; Collaboration with Pearl Jam on the film soundtrack Judgement Night, 1993; Solo project, Muggs Presents... The Soul Assassins, 1997; Refused further touring with the band. *Recordings:* Singles: Phuncky Feel One, 1991; Hand on the Pump, 1991; Latin Lingo, 1991; Insane the Brain, 1993; We Ain't Goin' Out Like That, 1994; Throw Your Set in the Air, 1995; Boom Biddy Bye Bye, 1996; Unreleased and Revamped, 1996; Illusions, 1996; Tequila Sunrise, 1998; Rap Superstar, 2000; Albums: Cypress Hill, 1991; Black Sunday, 1993; Cypress Hill III – Temples of Boom, 1995; IV, 1998; Stoned Raiders, 2001.

DJ ÖTZI, (Gernot Friedle); b. 7 Jan. 1971, St Johann, Tyrol, Austria. Vocalist; DJ. m. Sonja Kein, 8 Aug. 2001. *Education:* Stams boarding school; Imst Agricultural College. *Career:* Became DJ with assistance of professional DJ father. *Recordings:* Albums: Anton – Das Album, 2000; Never Stop The Alpenpop, 2001; Love Peace and Vollgas, 2001; Singles: Anton Aus Tirol, 1999; Gemma Bier Trinken, 2000; Hey Baby (Uhh, Ahh), 2000; Do Wah Diddy, 2001; X-mas Time, 2001. *Honours:* German Echo Music Award, Best

International Rock/Pop Single, Anton Aus Tirol, 2001. *Address:* c/o Herbert Fechter, Sieveringerstrasse 194, 1190 Vienna, Austria. *E-mail:* office@fechter-management.com.

DJ PREMIER, (Chris Martin), (Primo); b. Houston, Texas, USA. Prod; DJ. *Career:* Formed Gang Starr with rapping partner Guru, 1989; Debut album No More Mr Nice Guy released on Wild Pitch Records; In-demand producer for acts including: Common; Black Eyed Peas; Collaborations: Rakim; Jay-Z; Mos Def; Jeru The Damaja. *Recordings:* Albums: No More Mr Nice Guy, 1989; Step In The Arena, 1990; Daily Operation, 1992; Hard To Earn, 1994; Moment of Truth, 1998; Singles: Jazz Thing, 1990; Lovesick, 1991; Code To The Street EP, 1994; You Know My Steez, 1997. *Address:* c/o Chrysalis Records, EMI House, 43 Brook Green, London W6 7EF, England.

DJ SHADOW, (Josh Davis); b. 1973, USA. DJ; Prod. *Career:* One of the first Hip Hop DJ's; Joined artists' collective Sole Sides; Remixed Zimbabwe Legit; Obtained record deal; Worked with Paris, DJ Krush, Depeche Mode and Massive Attack; Support slot live to Radiohead; Work on collective U.N.K.L.E. with James Lavelle and Thom Yorke of Radiohead; Provided film soundtrack to Wim Wenders's The End of Violence, 1997. *Recordings:* Singles: Asia Born, 1993; Chief Xcel; DJ Shadow and the Groove Robbers: In/Flux/Hindsight; Lost and Found, with DJ Krush; What Does Your Soul Look Like, 1996; A Whim, with DJ Krush; Midnight In a Perfect World, 1995; Stem, 1996; High Noon, 1997; Camel Bobsled Race, live mix, with Q-Bert, 1997; The Number Song; Dark Days, 2000; Albums: Endtroducing, 1996; Preemptive Strike, 1998; The Private Press, 2002.

DJAVAN, (Djavan Caetano Viana); b. 1949, Maceio, Alagoas, Brazil. Vocalist; Musician (guitar); Songwriter. *Career:* Started own band, LSD, playing Beatles covers in local venues, aged 16; Moved to Rio de Janeiro, 1973; Hired to sing TV soap opera themes between regular night club appearance; Composition Abertura placed second in TV Globo's festival of same name, 1975; First album released, 1976; Eponymous album brought national success, 1979; Signed to CBS and began recording in USA, 1982; Returned to roots and Rio, 1986; Regular album releases ever since. *Recordings:* Albums include: A Voz E O Violao, 1976; Djavan, 1979; Alumbramento, 1980; Seduzir, 1981; Luz, 1982; Lilas, 1984; Meu Lado, 1986; Nao E Azul Mas E Mar, 1987; Oceano, 1989; Coisa De Acendar, 1992; Novena, 1994; Malasia, 1996; O Bicho Solto, 1998; Ao Vivo, 1999; Malageiro, 2001; Para Siempre, 2002. *Honours:* Latin Grammy, Best Brazilian Song, Acelerou, 2000. *Current Management:* Sony Music Brazil. *Website:* www.djavan.com.br.

DJINDI, Dilon, (Venancio de Conceicao Dilone Jinge); b. 14 Aug. 1927, Marracuene, Mozambique. Vocalist; Musician (guitar); Songwriter. *Career:* Started playing home-made guitar, 1939; Formed first group Estrela de Marracuene (Star of Marracuene), 1960; First recording for local radio broadcast, 1964; Member: Mabulu, 1998; First international appearance with Mabulu, 2001. *Recordings:* with Mabulu: Karimbo, 2000; Soul Marrabenta, 2001. *E-mail:* promusic@teledata.mz.

DMX, (Earl Simmons), (DMX The Great, Dark Man X); b. 18 Dec. 1970, Baltimore, Maryland, USA. Rap Artiste; Prod. *Career:* Became a DJ in the local projects; Released debut single on Columbia Records after winning Source magazine's Unsigned Hype Award, 1991; Signed to Ruff Ryders/Def Jam label, 1998; Debut album entered the Billboard chart at #1; Collaborations: Ja Rule; Jayo Felony; Ice Cube; Jay-Z; Eve; Limp Bizkit. *Recordings:* Albums: It's Dark and Hell Is Hot, Flesh of My Flesh – Blood of My Blood, 1998; And Then There Was X, 1999; The Great Depression, 2001; Singles: Get At Me Dog, I Can Feel It, 1998; Slippin', 1999; Party Up, 2000; What's My Name, 2001; Who We Be, 2002. *Honours:* Source Award, Artist of the Year, 1999; American Music Award, Favourite Rap/Hip Hop Artist, 2000. *Address:* c/o Def Jam, 825 Eighth Ave, New York, USA.

DOBES, Pavel; b. 22 March 1949, Frydek-Mistek. Songwriter; Vocalist; Musician (guitar). m. Ing Dana Hostinska, 3 s., 2 d. *Education:* Traditional School of Art. *Career:* Songs regularly transmitted on private and National Radio; About 100 concerts a year, at home and outside Czech Republic. *Compositions:* Jarmila; Blazek; Zapomenuty Trumf; Vite Vono Holky; Neco O Lasce; Zpatky do Trenek; Lisa z NYC. *Publications:* Still Life In A Company with Worms, Panton Records; Back To The Shorts, Monitor Records; Something About America, Monitor EMI Records; Pilot Voyage, Monitor EMI. *Membership:* OSA; Intergram. *Current Management:* Monitor EMI, Kovarova 39, CZ 155 00 Prague 5; Pear Agency, Sekaninova 416, CZ 500 11 Hradec Kralove. *Address:* Pavel Dobes, Sekaninova 416, CZ 500 11 Hradec Kralove.

DOBRE, Liudmila; b. 12 Sept. 1941, Chisinau, Moldavia. Agent; Impressario. m. Victor Dobre, 3 Feb. 1979, 1 s. *Education:* 3 years supplementary music school, canto. *Career:* Worked for the state before the Revolution; Now Managing Director of own agency, with rock, folk, pop and easy listening artistes; Also worked as solo singer and in theatre in Arad, Romania. *Address:* West Artistic Agency, Str Grigorescu 7, 2900 Arad, Romania.

DOCTOR J. See: **DA SILVA, Rui.**

DOKKEN, Don; b. 29 June 1953, USA. Rock Vocalist. *Career:* Backing vocalist, Scorpions (recordings unreleased), 1982; Founder, lead singer, rock group Dokken, 1982–88; Solo artiste, 1989–; World-wide concerts. *Recordings:* Albums: with Dokken: Breaking The Chains, 1982; Tooth and Nail, 1984; Under Lock and Key, 1985; Back For The Attack, 1987; Beast From The East, 1988; Back On The Streets, 1989; Dysfunctional, 1995; One Live Night, 1995; Shadowlife, 1997; Very Best of Dokken, 1999; Erase The Slate, 1999; Live From The Sun, 2000; solo: Up From The Ashes, 1990. *Honours:* Multi-platinum discs.

DOKY, Christian Minh; b. 7 Feb. 1969, Glostrup, Denmark. Musician; Composer; Prod. *Career:* Classical piano, age 5–14; Electric bass, age 15 (acoustic bass, age 17); Working professionally, age 16, Copenhagen; Moved to New York, 1988; Alumni, Michael Brecker, Randy Brecker, Trilok Gurtu, David Sanborn, Mike Stern, Ryuichi Sahamod; Signed with Blue Note Records, 1995. *Recordings:* Solo: Appreciation, 1988; The Sequel, 1989; Letters, 1990; Doky Bros, 1996; Doky Bros 2, 1997; Minh, 1998; Listen Up, 2000; Cinematique, 2002. *Publications:* On Bass, 1998; JazzKitchen, 2001. *Honours:* Simon Spies Award for Artist of the Year, 1991; Ad Lib magazine Top Ten Bassists readers poll, 2000, 2001. *Current Management:* J. Rotsbol, Balthazar Brtist Management, NY, USA. *Address:* c/o Capitol Music, Dronningstværgade 7, Copenhagen 1302 K, Denmark. *E-mail:* mail@balthazarmanagement.com.

DOKY, Niels Lan; b. 3 Oct. 1963, Copenhagen, Denmark. Composer; Prod; Jazz Musician (piano). m. Valentine Farlot, 3 June 1989, 1 s., 1 d. *Education:* Degree, Berklee College of Music. *Career:* Solo artist; Co-leader of Doky Brothers Band (with brother Chris); Tours, concerts, television and radio appearances world-wide with: Randy Brecker; Joe Henderson; Charlie Haden; Jack DeJohnette; John Scofield; Producer for Verve. *Recordings:* 20 albums as Niels Lan Doky on jazz labels. *Publications:* Jazz Transcription; Compositions and Improvisations, 1996. *Honours:* Oscar Peterson Award, 1984; Simon Spies Musik Prize, 1993. *Membership:* DJBFA; NCB; KODA. *Current Management:* Healy Entertainment Inc, Copenhagen. *Address:* 18 Ave De Chavoe, 78124 Mareil, Sur Mauldre, France. *E-mail:* mail@nielslandoky.com. *Website:* www.nielslandoky.com.

DOLBY, Ray M; Engineer; b. 1933, Portland, OR, USA. Inventor. m. Dagmar. *Education:* BS, Stanford University, 1957; Marshall Scholarship and National Science Foundation graduate fellowship, PhD, Physics, 1961, University of Cambridge. *Career:* Worked at Ampex Corpn, 1949–57; Consultant to the United Kingdom Atomic Energy Authority, 1961; United Nations advisor in India, 1963–65; Founder and Chair., Dolby Laboratories Inc, London, 1965–; Established further offices and laboratories in San Francisco, 1976; Inventor, Dolby noise-reduction units; Dolby 'A' system sold to recordings studios; Work on noise-reduction for tape cassette and 8-track cartridge led to Dolby 'B' system, 1971; Now adopted world-wide; Adapted for cinema, 1978; Film soundtrack, Star Wars, first to be enhanced by Dolby noise reduction; Dolby systems upgraded for digital recordings, 1991; Holds more than 50 US patents. *Contributions to:* Papers on video tape recording, long wavelength X-ray analysis, and noise reduction. *Honours:* Audio Engineering Society, Silver and Gold Medals; Society of Motion Picture and Television Engineers, Samuel L. Warner Memorial Award, Alexander M. Poniatoff Gold Medal, Progress Medal; Academy of Motion Picture Arts and Sciences, Scientific and Engineering Award, 1979; Hon. Fellow of Pembroke College, Cambridge, 1983; Hon. O.B.E., 1986; Academy Award, 1989; Emmy Award, National Academy of Television Arts and Sciences, 1989; US National Medal of Technology, 1997; IEEE Masaru Ibuka Consumer Electronics Award, 1997; American Electronic Association Medal of Achievement, 1997; Hon. Doctor of Science, University of Cambridge; Hon. Doctorate, University of York, 1999. *Membership:* Fellow, Audio Engineering Society; Fellow, British Kinematograph, Sound and Television Society; Hon. Mem., Society of Motion Picture and Television Engineers. *Address:* c/o Dolby Laboratories, Wootton Bassett, Wiltshire SN4 8QJ, England. *Website:* www.dolby.com.

DOLBY, Thomas, (Thomas Morgan Robertson); b. 14 Oct. 1958, Cairo, Egypt. Musician (synthesizers); Vocalist; Songwriter; Programmer; Prod. m. Kathleen Beller. *Education:* Meteorology. *Career:* Built own synthesizers and PA system; Sound engineer, various groups; Co-founder, Camera Club, 1979; Musician with Lene Lovich, 1980; Solo recording artiste, 1981–; Musician with David Bowie, Live Aid, Wembley, 1985. *Compositions include:* New Toy, Lene Lovich; Film scores include: Howard – A New Breed of Hero. *Recordings:* Albums: The Golden Age of Wireless, 1982; The Flat Earth, 1985; Aliens Ate My Buick, 1988; Astronauts and Heretics, 1992; Gate to the Mind's Eye, 1994; Hyperactive, 1999; Singles: Urges; Europa and The Pirate Twins, 1981; Windpower, 1982; She Blinded Me With Science, 1983; Hyperactive, 1984; Close But No Cigar, 1992; Contributor, recordings by: Foreigner; Joan Armatrading; M; Stevie Wonder; Grace Jones; Howard Jones; Herbie Hancock; Ofra Haza, Robyn Hitchcock, Belinda Carlisle, Dusty Springfield; Record producer for artists including: Joni Mitchell; Prefab Sprout. *Current Management:* Mary Coller Management. *Address:* 11288 Ventura Blvd, Suite 304B, Studio City, CA 91604, USA.

DOLENZ, Mickey (George Michael Jr); b. 8 March 1945, Tarzana, Los Angeles, California, USA. Musician (drums); Vocalist; Actor; Prod; Author. m. (1) Samantha Juste, 1968, divorced, (2) Trina Dow, 1977. *Education:* Architectural Design at Valley College and Los Angeles Technical Institute. *Career:* Child actor, television series, Circus Boy, 1956–58; Other acting roles in Peyton Place; Route 66; Mr Novak; As musician: Member, The One Nighters; The Missing Links; Member, The Monkees, 1966–70; 1985–91; Actor, Monkees TV series, 1966–68; Other television includes: 33 1/3 Revolutions Per Monkee TV Special, NBC; Film appearance, Head; Stage performances: Remains To Be Seen, 1970; The Point, 1978; Solo artiste, 1971–72; Broadway production of Grease, 1994; Member, Dolenz Jones Boyce and Hart, 1975–76; Also television director, producer, 1977–85; Voiceovers for: My 3 Sons; Scooby Doo; Adam 12; Devlin; Solo artiste, Rockin' Back To The 60s Tour, 1992; Monkees reunion concert, 1997. *Recordings:* Albums: The Monkees (No. 1, USA and UK), 1966; More of The Monkees (No. 1, USA and UK), 1967; Headquarters (No. 1, USA), 1967; Pisces, Aquarius, Capricorn and Jones (No. 1, UK); The Birds, The Bees and The Monkees, 1968; Head (soundtrack), 1969; The Monkees Greatest Hits, 1969; The Monkees Present, 1969; Instant Replay, 1969; Changes, 1970; Then and Now, 1986; Pool It!, 1987; Listen to the Band, 1991; Greatest Hits, 1995; Music Box, 2001; Hit singles: Last Train To Clarksville (No. 1, USA), 1966; I'm A Believer (No. 1, UK and USA), 1966; I'm Not Your Steppin' Stone, 1967; A Little Bit Me, A Little Bit You, 1967; Alternate Title, 1967; Daydream Believer (No. 1, USA), 1967; Valleri, 1968; Tear Drop City, 1969. *Publications:* I'm A Beliver: My Life of Monkees, Music and Madness (autobiography), with Mark Bego. *Honours:* NARM Awards, Best Selling Group and Album, 1967; Emmy, Outstanding Comedy Series, 1967; 3 BMI Awards, 1968; Monkees Day, Atlanta, 1986; Star on Hollywood Walk of Fame, 1989. *Address:* c/o Nationwide Entertainment Services, 2756 N Green Valley Parkway, Suite 449, Las Vegas, NV 89014–2100, USA.

DOLLIMORE, Chris; Musician (guitars); Prod. *Career:* Mem., Del Amitri, 1997–. *Recordings:* Albums: Hatful Of Rain/Lousy With Love, 1998; Can You Do Me Good?, 2002. Singles: Don't Come Home Too Soon, 1998; Cry To Be Found, 1998; Just Before You Leave, 2002. *Address:* c/o A & M Records Inc, 595 Madison Ave, New York, NY 10022, USA. *Website:* www.delamitri.com.

DOMAY, Michael; b. 23 Oct. 1945, Newcastle upon Tyne, England. Medical Laboratory Scientist; Music teacher (guitar, bass, piano); Musician (guitar, bass). m. Stephanie Dennant, 18 April 1970, 2 s., 1 d. *Education:* Salisbury College; Bristol Polytechnic; Vocal training, church choir, 1955–59; Head soloist, 1957–59; Piano and theory training, 1955–60. *Career:* Established rock bands: The Falcons, with Jim Cregan (Rod Stewart); Unit 4, with Greg Lake (Emerson Lake and Palmer) and John Wetton (Asia, King Crimson), 1960–69; Freelance bass guitar, guitar, in dance bands, pit orchestras, cabaret bands, 1970–; Private teacher, guitar, bass guitar, keyboards, piano; Many exam successes to date (students include Lydia Cascarino of Dear John; Richard Oakes of Suede); Examiner, Registry of Guitar Tutors. *Honours:* John-Louis Riccardi Finalist, Young Guitarist of the Year, 1998. *Membership:* Musicians' Union; Registered teacher with Associated Board, Guild Hall, Rock School, RGT; Fellow, Institute of Biomedical Scientists; British Andrology Society; British Electrophoresis Society. *Current Management:* MD Music, Dorset. *Address:* 20 Argyll Rd, Parkstone, Dorset BH12 2DR, England.

DOMINIQUE, Carl-Axel Martinelli; b. 1 Sept. 1939. m. Monica Dominique, 3 s. *Education:* Royal Academy of Music, Stockholm; Studied with Martin Canin, Juilliard School of Music, NY, 1965; Swedish Film School, 1969–70. *Career:* Concert Pianist, 1965; Soloist, All Swedish Symphony Orchestras, 1968; led jazz fusion group, Solar Plexus; Composer, Theatre Productions, Television Shows. *Compositions:* 31 Songs from Aniara; Music for Television, Film, Theatre; Songs and Orchestral Works. *Recordings:* Blinded; D Messiaen; Vingt Regards Sur L'Enfant Jesus; Complete Bird Music for Piano Solo (BIS). *Publications:* We Play Together, Co Written with Monica Dominique. *Honours:* Expressen Musical Prize, 1984. *Membership:* Swedish Composers of Popular Music. *Current Management:* The Music Production Company, Dominique Musik AB. *Website:* www.dominiquemusik.se.

DOMINIQUE, Monica; b. 20 July 1940, Sweden. m. Carl-Axel Dominique, 3 s. *Education:* Royal Academy of Music, Stockholm. *Career:* Solo Piano Program, Swedish Radio; Played with Best Swedish Singers, Theatres, Concert Halls, Radio, Television; Joined Vocalgroup Gals and Pals, 1967; Cabaret Artist, Solo Singer and Actress, 1970–75; Led Jazz Fusion Group, Solar Plexus. *Compositions:* Swedish Love in Southern Bronx; Inside The Rainbow; No Man Is An Island; Oh, What a Wonderful World; ODA; Tillagnan. *Recordings:* Monica-Monica; Tillagnan; Inside the Rainbow. *Publications:* We Play Together, Co Written with C A Dominique. *Honours:* Expressen Musical Prize, 1994; The Evert Taube Award, 1994. *Membership:* Swedish Composers of Popular Music; Swedish Jazz Academy; Swedish Jazz Musicians. *Current Management:* Music Production Company, Dominique Musik AB. *Website:* www.dominiquemusik.se.

DOMINO, Fats (Antoine); b. 26 Feb. 1928, New Orleans, USA. Musician (piano); Vocalist; Songwriter. *Education:* Piano lessons with Harrison Verrett. *Career:* Legendary R&B performer, 1949–; Regular US R&B tours, 1954–;

Debut UK performance, 1967; Long-standing partnership with bandleader, arranger, writer Dave Bartholomew; Film appearances: Shake, Rattle and Roll; Jamboree; The Big Beat; The Girl Can't Help It; Any Which Way You Can; Television special, Fats Domino and Friends, 1987. *Recordings:* Numerous hit singles include: The Fat Man; Every Night About This Time; Goin' Home; Don't You Know; Goin' To The River; Please Don't Leave Me; Ain't That A Shame; You Done Me Wrong; Walking To New Orleans; I'm In Love Again; Blueberry Hill; My Girl Josephine; Valley of Tears; Blue Monday; Whole Lotta Loving; I Want To Walk You Home; Be My Guest; Albums: Carry On Rockin', 1955; Fats Domino – Rock and Rollin', 1956; This Is Fats Domino!, 1957; Here Stands Fats Domino, 1958; Let's Play Fats Domino, 1959; Fabulous Mr D, 1958; Fats Domino Sings, 1960; I Miss You So, 1961; Twistin' The Stomp, 1962; Just Domino, 1963; Here Comes Fats Domino, 1963; Fats On Fire, 1964; Fats Domino '65, 1965; Getaway With Fats Domino, 1966; Fats Domino, 1966; Stompin' Fats Domino, 1967; Trouble In Mind, Fats Is Back, 1968; Very Best Of, 1970; Sleeping On The Job, 1979; My Blue Heaven, 1990; They Call Me The Fat Man, 1991; Whole Lotta Loving, 1992; Greatest Hits: Live, 1992; Out of New Orleans, 1993; Concert Collection: Blueberry Hill, 1993; Christmas is a Special Day, 1993; The Fats Man, 1995; Fat Man Sings, 1996; You Can Call Me Fats, 1997; Gold Collection, 1998; Live at Gilley's 1999; Domino Effect, 1999; Blast From The Past, 2001. *Honours:* Inducted, Rock and Roll Hall of Fame, 1986; Grammy, Lifetime Achievement Award, 1987. *Current Management:* Al Embry International. *Address:* PO Box 23162, Nashville, TN 37202, USA.

DONAGHY, Siobhan; b. London, England. Vocalist. *Career:* Founding mem., Sugababes, 1998–2001; Signed to London Records, 2000. *Recordings:* Album: One Touch, 2000. Singles: Overload, 2000; New Year, 2000; Run For Cover, 2001; Soul Sound, 2001. *Address:* c/o Island Records, 825 Eighth Ave, New York, NY 10019, USA. *Website:* www.sugababes.com.

DONALD, Howard; b. 28 April 1968, Droylsden, Manchester, England. Vocalist. *Career:* Mem. UK all-male vocal group, Take That, 1990–96; Television includes Take That and Party (Channel 4), 1993; Take That Away documentary (BBC2), 1993; Take That In Berlin, 1994; Solo artiste, 1996–. *Recordings:* Albums: Take That And Party, 1992; Everything Changes (No. 1, UK), 1993; Nobody Else (No. 1, UK), 1995; Greatest Hits (No. 1, UK), 1996. Singles: Promises, 1991; It Only Takes A Minute, 1992; I Found Heaven, 1992; A Million Love Songs, 1992; Could It Be Magic, 1992; Why Can't I Wake Up With You, 1993; Pray (No. 1, UK), 1993; Relight My Fire (with Lulu) (No. 1, UK), 1993; Babe (No. 1, UK), 1993; Everything Changes (No. 1, UK), 1994; Love Ain't Here Anymore, 1994; Sure (No. 1, UK), 1994; Back For Good (No. 1, UK), 1995; Never Forget (No. 1, UK), 1995; How Deep Is Your Love (No. 1, UK), 1996. *Honours:* Seven Smash Hits Awards, 1992; BRIT Award, Best British Single, 1994.

DONALDSON, John; b. 29 June 1954, London. Composer; Musician (Piano). m. Agotha Coffey, 2 s., 1 d. *Education:* Anglia University. *Career:* US Broadcasts With Eddie Henderson, Richie Cole; BBC With Septpiece, Dick Pearce Quartet; Film, Painted Lady With Helen Mirren; Festivals Include, San Francisco, San Sebastian, Bath, London, Appleby, Malta. *Compositions:* Cakes and Wine; Medjugorje; Carneo; Django's Dilemma; Mirror Image; HRD; Plain Song; Balance. *Recordings:* Septpiece; Sing The Line; Meeting In Brooklyn. *Honours:* Best Soloist, 1980; Cambridge University Press Prize for Performance, 1982. *Membership:* PRS; Musicians' Union. *Current Management:* Clever Dick Management. *Address:* 22 Albany Rd, St Leonards On Sea, East Sussex TN38 0LN, England.

DONALDSON, Louis (Lou); b. 1 Nov. 1926, Badin, North Carolina, USA. Jazz Musician (alto saxophone). m. Maker, 1950, 2 d. *Education:* Political Science, North Carolina A & T University; Began clarinet at age 9. *Career:* Played in Navy band, 1945; Moved to New York, 1950; Played with numerous notable musicians including: Charlie Parker; Sonny Stitt; Bud Powell; Milt Jackson; Philly Joe Jones; Horace Silver; Clifford Brown; Member, Art Blakey's Jazz Messengers; Toured extensively in Europe and Japan. *Recordings:* Albums: Blues Walk, No 1 album; Alligator Boogaloo; New Faces, New Sounds; A Night at Birdland; Her 'Tis Midnight Creeper; Hot Dog; Sassy Soul Strut; Forgotten Man; Birdseed; Caracas; Sweet Papa Lou; Sentimental Journey; with Jimmy Smith: The Sermon. *Honours:* Charlie Parker Memorial Medal; Baseball field named in his honour, Badin, North Carolina; Scholarship established in his name, North Caroline AandT University. *Current Management:* Maxine S Harvard Unlimited. *Address:* c/o Maxine S Harvard Unlimited, 7942 W Bell Rd, Suite C-5, Glendale, AZ 85308, USA.

DONELIAN, Armen; b. 1 Dec. 1950, New York, NY, USA. Musician (Piano); Composer; Bandleader; Author. *Education:* Artists' Certificate, Westchester Conservatory of Music; Bachelor of Music, Columbia University; Private study with Carl Bamberger (conducting), Ludmila Ulehla (harmonic analysis), Richard Beirach (jazz piano), Harold Seletsky (Schoenberg harmony and counterpoint). *Career:* Performed with Sonny Rollins, Chet Baker, Mongo Santamaria, Billy Harper, Lionel Hampton, Paquito D'Rivera, Joe Williams and other jazz musicians in festivals, concerts, clubs, TV and radio, world-wide, 1975–. *Compositions:* Over 40 recorded by various artists; Several published arrangements including Metropolitan Madness, Harem Girl,

Stargazer. *Recordings:* Stargazer; A Reverie; Secrets; The Wayfarer; Trio '87; Wave; Mystic Heights. *Publications:* Training the Ear, 1992; Rutgers Annual Review of Jazz Studies, 1994–95; Downbeat, 1997–98; Keyboard, 1997. *Honours:* 6 Jazz Performance Fellowships, National Endowment for the Arts, 1984, 1987, 1990, 1992, 1994, 1996; Fulbright Scholarship Award, 2002. *Current Management:* Donelian Music, New Jersey. *Address:* 37 Overlook Ave, West Orange, NJ 07052, USA.

DONELLY, Tanya; b. 14 July 1966, Newport, RI, USA. Vocalist; Songwriter; Musician (guitar). m. Dean Fisher, 22 Sept. 1996. *Career:* Founding Member, Throwing Muses, 1985–91; Member, The Breeders, 1989–92; Member, Belly, 1992–96; Solo career, 1996–; Appearances on David Letterman (USA); The Tonight Show (USA); Conan O'Brien (USA); The Word (England); The Later Show (England); Mark Radcliffe (England); The Black Sessions (France); Support tour to REM. *Recordings:* with Throwing Muses: Singles: Chains Changed, 1987; Dizzy, 1989; Counting Backwards, 1991; Not Too Soon, 1991; Albums: Throwing Muses, 1986; The Fat Skier, 1987; House Tornado, 1988, Hunkpapa, 1989; The Real Ramona, 1991; with The Breeders: Pod, 1990, Safari EP, 1992; With Belly: Singles: Slowdust, 1992; Gepetto, 1992; Feed The Tree, 1993; Now They'll Sleep, 1995; Seal My Fate, 1995; Albums: Star (No. 2, UK), 1993; King, 1995; Solo career: Singles: Sliding and Driving, 1996; Pretty Deep, 1997; The Bright Light, 1997; Sleepwalk, 2001; Albums: Lovesongs for Underdogs, 1997; Beauty Sleep, 2002. *Current Management:* Gary Smith. *Address:* Fort Apache, One Camp St, Suite 2, Cambridge, MA 02140, USA.

DONNELLY, Johnny; b. 14 Feb. 1972, Dublin, Ireland. Musician (drums). *Career:* Member, The Saw Doctors; Tours: Ireland; UK; Europe; USA; Canada; Australia; Television and radio appearances include: BBC Late Show; Documentary, Saw Doctors, RTE; Channel 4; BBC Radio 1. *Recordings:* Albums: If This Is Rock and Roll I Want My Old Job Back; All The Way From Tuam. *Honours:* Best Band; Best Live Band; Biggest selling single ever in Ireland. *Membership:* PRS; Musicians' Union. *Current Management:* Ollie Jennings. *Address:* 13 St Mary's Terrace, Taylors Hill, Galway City, Ireland.

DONNELLY, Kerr; b. 1 May 1964, Lanarkshire, Scotland. Vocalist; Songwriter; Entertainer; Musician (guitar). m. Lynn Fullwood, 1 s., 2 d. *Career:* Mem., Legend, 1978, Tennessee Flash Cats 1982, Crazy Wolf, 1982, Kerr Donnelly Band, 1987–; Numerous radio interviews; Concerts: Americana—Country in the Park (biggest UK open-air country music festival); Established KDML record label. *Compositions:* Over 300 songs incl.: Country Boy; One Burger One Coke; That's Life; Sneakin 'n' Cheatin; Rattlesnake Rock; As The Curtain Falls, 1999; A Little Unfair, 2000; If I Knew Then What I Know Now, 2000; Homewrecker, 2000; Heartache Heartache, 2001; Reckless And Lonely, 2001; A Haunted House On Broken Hearted Hill, 2001. *Recordings:* Albums: No Help Needed, 1987; EPs and Early Days, 1992; Haunted Heart, 1992; Rough Cuts, 1995; Country Rocker, 1995; The Singles And Album Picks, 1997; Guess Who?, 1998; As The Curtain Falls 20/21, 1999; That's Right, 2001; Kerr Thru' The Years, 2002; The Day The Clown Cried, 2003. *Membership:* International Songwriters Asscn; Performing Rights Society; Songlink International. *Current Management:* KDML Records and Publishing, 36 Sankey Rd, Blackfords Estate, Cannock, Staffordshire WS11 2DT, England. *Website:* www.kerr-donnelly.countrymusic.co.uk.

DONNER, Otto; b. 16 Nov. 1939, Tampere, Finland. Composer; Musician (trumpet). *Education:* Sibelius Academy, Helsinki; Studied with Ligeti. *Career:* Began jazz career, Tampere, late 1950s; Worked at Siemens electronic music studios, Germany; Co-leader, jazz quintet with Christian Schwindt; Worked with American composer Terry Riley; Founder, record label Love Records, 1966–79; Director, Finnish Radio's entertainment section, 1970–74; Leader, The Otto Donner Treatment; Performing new material with own band. *Compositions include:* Music for numerous Finnish films; Dalens Ande (The Spirit of The Valley) suite; Pieces for UMO (New Music Orchestra). *Recordings:* Album: Quintet with Christian Schwindt: Friends and Relatives; with The Otto Donner Treatment: En Soisi Sen Päättyvän, 1970; Kuinka Myohään Valvoo Blues?, 1980. *Address:* Jomalvik, 10600 Tammisaari, Finland.

DONOHOE, David; b. 22 May 1940, Ashton-Under-Lyme, Lancashire, England. Musician (trombone); Bandleader. m. Victoria Hancock, 8 Sept. 1962, 2 s., 2 d. *Education:* Regional College of Art, Manchester (part time); Private music tuition, 1 year; Brass Band, 1 year. *Career:* Concert with Woody Allen (actor, clarinet player), New Orleans Festival, 1971; 6 times guest, radio chat shows; 6 television appearances; Tour of USA with International Band including: Butch Thompson, Sammy Rimmington, 1977; 10 appearances, Ascona Festa, New Orleans Music; Switzerland; 3 tours with bands from New Orleans, Switzerland. *Recordings:* 10 albums, 6 in own name. *Honours:* Ambassador of Ninove, Belgium, for services to music, 1989. *Membership:* Musicians' Union. *Current Management:* Terry Dash Management, Herts. *Address:* 5 Saddleworth Fold, Uppermill, Oldham OL3 6EQ, England.

DONOVAN, (Donovan Leitch); b. 10 May 1946, Maryhill, Glasgow, Scotland. Folk Vocalist; Songwriter. m. Linda Lawrence, Oct. 1970, 1 s., 2 d.

Career: Appearances include: NME Poll Winners Concert, Wembley, 1965; Newport Folk Festival, with Bob Dylan, 1965; World-wide concerts, tours include: Royal Albert Hall, 1967; National Blues Festival, Windsor, 1967; International Film Festival, Cannes, France, 1968; Woburn Music Festival, 1968; Carnegie Hall, New York, 1968; Bath Festival, 1970; Isle of Wight Festival, 1970; Tour, Australia and New Zealand, 1975; Edinburgh Festival, 1980; Support to Happy Mondays, Wembley Arena, 1990; British tour, 1992. *Compositions include:* Own recorded songs; Songs for film: If It's Tuesday It Must Be Belgium, 1969; The Pied Piper, 1971; Film score, Brother Sun, Sister Moon, 1972. *Recordings:* Singles include: Catch The Wind, 1965; Colours, 1965; Universal Soldier, 1965; Sunshine Superman, 1966; Mellow Yellow, 1966; There Is A Mountain, 1967; Jennifer Juniper, 1968; Hurdy Gurdy Man, 1968; Atlantis, 1969; Barabajagal (Love Is Hot), with the Jeff Beck Group, 1969; Albums include: What's Bin Did and What's Bin Hid, 1965; Catch The Wind, 1965; Fairy Tale, 1965; Sunshine Superman, 1966; The Real Donovan, 1966; Mellow Yellow, 1967; Universal Soldier, 1967; A Gift From A Flower To A Garden, 1968; Like It Is, Was and Evermore Shall Be, 1968; Donovan In Concert, 1968; Barabajagal, 1969; The Best of Donovan, 1969; Open Road, 1970; Donovan P Leitch, 1970; HMS Donovan, 1971; Cosmic Wheels, 1973; Essence To Essence, 1974; 7-Tease, 1974; Slow Down World, 1976; Donovan, 1977; Neutronica, 1980; Love Is The Only Feeling, 1980; Lady of The Stars, 1983; Rising, 1990; Troubadour – The Definitive Collection 1964–76, 1993; Island of Circles, 1991; Live in Concert, 1992; Originals, 1995; Sutras, 1996. *Current Management:* Monarch Productions, 8803 Mayne Street, Bellflower, CA 90706, USA.

DONOVAN, Ida M; b. 6 Sept. 1948, Canada. Song Writer; Musician. m. Edwin Donovan, 1 s., 4 d. *Career:* Country Gospel Group. *Membership:* Canadian County Music Asscn. *Address:* 211 Macintyre Lane, Glace Bay, NS B1A 4S1, Canada.

DONOVAN, Jason Sean; b. 1 June 1968, Melbourne, Australia. Vocalist; Actor. *Career:* Actor, Australian television series: Skyways, 1979; I Can Jump Puddles, 1979; Neighbours, 1985–89; Heroes, 1988; Shadows of The Heart, 1988; Stage appearances: Lead role, Joseph and The Amazing Technicolour Dreamcoat, London Palladium, 1991–92; Appeared in Rocky Horror Picture Show, West End; Concert tours, Australia; Far East; Europe. *Recordings:* Albums include: Ten Good Reasons, 1989; Between The Lines, 1990; Joseph and The Amazing Technicolour Dreamcoat, 1991; Greatest Hits, 1991 (reissued 1999); Hit singles include: Nothing Can Divide Us, 1988; Especially For You (duet with Kylie Minogue) (No. 1, UK), 1988; Too Many Broken Hearts (No. 1, UK), 1989; Sealed With A Kiss (No. 1, UK), 1989; Everyday, 1989; Hang On To Your Love, 1990; Another Night, 1990; Rhythm of The Rain, 1990; Doing Fine, 1990; Any Dream Will Do (No. 1, UK), 1991; Happy Together, 1991; Dream, 1991; RSVP, 1991; Rough Diamonds, 1994. *Honours:* Numerous show business awards. *Address:* Richard East Productions Pty Ltd, Toorak Rd, South Yarra, VIC 3141, Australia.

DONY; Vocalist; Musician (bass); Songwriter; Arranger. *Career:* Member, Atlas, Bulgaria, 1987–93; Formed Dony and Momchil, 1993–; Numerous tours, Bulgaria, include Sofia National Theatre (unplugged with National Philharmony), 1995. *Recordings:* with Atlas: Doll; with Dony and Momchil: CD Albums: The Album!, 1993; The Second One, 1994. *Honours:* Best Band, Atlas, 1991; Orpheus: Best Single: The Little Prince; Best Video For Duo Or A Group.

DOONICAN, Val (Michael Valentine); b. 3 Feb. 1927, Waterford, Ireland. Vocalist; Musician (guitar, mandolin); Presenter. *Education:* Guitar, mandolin. *Career:* Member, various Irish bands; Member, vocal group The Four Ramblers; Group had radio series over 2 years, Riders of The Range, BBC, 1951; Solo artiste, late 1950s–; Television appearances: Beauty Box; Sunday Night At The London Palladium, 1964; Own show, 1964–88; Radio includes: Dreamy Afternoon; A Date With Val; Videos, Songs from My Sketchbook – Memories are Made of This; Thank You For The Music, 1993. *Recordings:* 30 albums include: Val Doonican Rocks But Gently, 1967; Song Sung Blue, 1974; Some of My Best Friends Are Songs, 1977; By Request, 1987; Love Songs, 1999; Singles include: Walk Tall, 1964; The Special Years, 1965; Elusive Butterfly, 1966; What Would I Be (No. 2, UK), 1966; Memories Are Made of This, 1967; If The Whole World Stopped Loving, 1967; If I Knew Then What I Know Now, 1968; Morning, 1971. *Publications:* Walking Tall The Special Years. *Honours:* TV Personality of the Year (3 times). *Current Management:* Bernard Lee Management.

DORAN, Brian John; b. 2 March 1965, Croydon, Surrey, England. Vocalist; Songwriter; Musician (guitar, flute). m. Jane Kendrick, 19 Aug. 1994. *Education:* Diploma in dispensing optics; Grade 8 theory, singing, flute. *Career:* Lead singer, Orchid Waltz, 1983–86; Played all over England; Acoustic duo Richard III's with Lee Collinson (now popular folk artist); Solo acoustic world tour, 1990–91; Currently solo and session work. *Compositions:* Song: Lady of The 80s, written for Edinburgh Festival. *Recordings:* Orchid Waltz; Trident (album not released); Solo album: Acoustics, 1991; Backing vocals, Compassion, Keith Hancock, 1993. *Membership:* Branch committee mem., Musicians' Union. *Current Management:* 124 Lisbon Ave, Twickenham, Middlesex TW2 5HN, England.

DORE, Michael; b. Cleethorpes, Lincolnshire, England. Vocalist; Musician (piano). *Education:* GGSM, Guildhall School of Music and Drama, London; PGCE. *Career:* Mem., Swingle Singers, Synergy Vocals, Singcircle, Electric Phoenix, Chameleon; Concert soloist with: BBC Radio 2, Royal Philharmonic Orchestra, BBC Concert Orchestra, Berlin Philharmonic Orchestra, Chicago Symphony, Orchestre Nationale de Lyons, Philharmonique de Monte Carlo, Canadian Brass, London Symphony Orchestra, Los Angeles Philharmonic, Swedish National Radio, Royal Variety Performances, Music of Andrew Lloyd Webber, Jesus Christ Superstar (Peter), Magic of the Musicals, Rogers and Hammerstein at the Barbican; Worked for: Royal National Theatre, RSC, Nederlands Dans Theater; West End credits incl.: Cats, Starlight Express, Grease; Debuts: Carnegie Hall (New York); Royal Albert Hall Proms, 1994. *Recordings:* Albums: Solo: Simply... Michael Dore; with Royal Philharmonic Orchestra: Here Come The Classics, Vol. 5: Christmas; Here Come The Classics: Musicals; with BBC Concert Orchestra: West Side Story, 1993; Crazy For Gershwin; Let's Face The Music (tribute to Fred Astaire); Hits Of Broadway; Love And Romance; Passion (original London cast); Wonderful Town (with Simon Rattle); Every Song Has Its Play (with Gilbert O'Sullivan, manager); with Berio: Sinfonia, Canticum. *Membership:* British Actors Equity; Musicians' Union. *Current Management:* World Showcase Promotions, 48 Shadeland Ct, Cambridge, ON N1T 1V2, Canada. *Telephone:* (519) 624-9176. *Fax:* (519) 624-5334. *E-mail:* cheryl-wspromotions@rogers.com. *Address:* c/o Brett Records, PO Box 36210, London SE19 1YR, England. *Telephone:* (20) 8761-0843. *E-mail:* brettrecords@aol.com. *Website:* www.michaeldore.com.

DORGE, Pierre; b. 28 Feb. 1946, Frederiksberg, Denmark. Composer; Conductor; Musician (guitar). m. Irene Becker, 24 Aug. 1985. *Education:* Music, KDAS, College of Copenhagen. *Career:* Formed own group, Copenhagen Jazz Quintet, 1960; Formed New Jungle Orchestra, 1980; Recorded with: Niels-Henning Orsted Petersen; John Tchicai; Svend Asmussen; Marilyn Mazur; Johnny Dyani; Tours: Europe; USA; Canada; Indonesia; Ghana; USSR; Australasia. *Compositions:* Symphony in C, 1994. *Recordings include:* with New Jungle Orchestra: Pierre Dorge and New Jungle Orchestra, 1982; Brikama, 1984; Even The Moon Is Dancing, 1985; Johnny Lives, 1987; Different Places – Different Bananas, 1989; Peer Gynt, 1989; Live in Chicago, 1991; David Murray and the Jazzpar Prize, 1992; Karawane, 1993; Polar Jungle Orchestra, 1994; Absurd Bird, 1995; Music from the Danish Jungle, 1996; China Jungle, 1997; Giraf, 1999; Swinging Europe, 1999. *Honours:* Grants, Danish Arts Council; JASA prize, 1985. *Current Management:* Copenhagen Concerts.

DORNEY, Tim; b. 30 March 1965, Ascot, Berkshire, England. Musician (Keyboards). *Career:* Former member, Flowered Up; Formed Republica; Numerous TV appearances and festival dates; Contributed track Are Friends Electric for Gary Numan tribute album, 1997. *Recordings:* with Flowered Up: Singles: It's On, 1990; Phobia, 1990; Take It, 1991; Weekender, 1992; Albums: A Life With Brian, 1991; with Republica: Singles: Out of This World, 1994; Bloke, 1994; Ready to Go, 1996; Drop Dead Gorgeous, 1996; From the Rush Hour With Love, 1998; Albums: Republica, 1996; Speed Ballads, 1998.

DORONJGA, Sinisa; b. 15 March 1942, Zagreb, Croatia. Musician; Vocalist; Entertainer; Actor. m. Bosiljka Kello, 22 March 1969, 1 s., 1 d. *Education:* Secondary music school. *Career:* Singer, musician, Bijele Strijele, 1961; World tour, 1968–69; Producer, composer, songwriter, arranger, Suzy record label; Television entertainer. *Recordings:* Hit album: Domestic songs, Platinum, 1979; 7 Gold albums, 1979–95; Main songs from albums: Hrvatska Mati; Boze Dragi Sacuvaj Hrvate; Hrvatski Sinovi. *Publications:* Book, video, Dosel Je Sv Martin (St Martin) traditional ceremony in Croatia. *Honours:* Croatian Government and Croatan Music AID Awards, Order for a lifetime of music work. *Membership:* General secretary, Croatian Musicians' Union. *Current Management:* Simpy and Friends Production and Management. *Address:* Sinisa Doronjga, Siget 18 b/v, 10020 Zagreb, Croatia.

DOROUGH, Howard Dwaine, (Howie D.); b. 22 Aug. 1973, Orlando, FL, USA. Vocalist. *Career:* Film appearances: Cop, Parenthood; Community Theatre; Mem., Backstreet Boys, 1993–; Numerous tours and television appearances. *Recordings:* Albums: Backstreet Boys, 1996; Live in Concert, 1998; Backstreet's Back, 1998; Millennium, 1999; Black And Blue, 2000; Greatest Hits Chapter 1, 2001. Singles: We've Got It Goin' On, 1995; Quit Playing Games, 1998; I'll Never Break Your Heart, 1998; Everybody, 1998; As Long As You Love Me, 1998; Anywhere for You, 1998; All I Have to Give, 1998; I Want It That Way (No. 1, UK), 1999; Larger Than Life, 1999; Show Me The Meaning of Being Lonely, 2000; The One, 2000; Shape of My Heart, 2000; Drowning, 2001; The Call, 2001. *Honours:* MTV European Music Award, Best Pop Act, 1997, Best Group, 1999; Billboard Music Awards, Best Group, Best Adult Contemporary Group, 1998, Album of the Year, Artist of the Year, 1999; MTV Music Video Awards, Best Group Video, 1998, Viewer's Choice, for I Want It That Way, 1999; World Music Awards, Best-Selling Pop Group, 1999, 2000, Best-Selling R&B Group, 1999, 2000, Best-Selling Dance Group, 1999, 2000, Best American Group, 2000; American Music Awards, Favorite Pop/Rock Band, Duo or Group, 2000, 2001. *Website:* www.backstreetboys.com.

DORSET, Ray; b. 21 March 1946, Ashford, Kent, England. Musician (guitar); Vocalist. *Career:* Member, Mungo Jerry, 1970–; Appearances include: Hollywood Pop Festival, Staffordshire, 1970; Briefly member, Katmandu, with Peter Green, 1986. *Compositions include:* Feels Like I'm In Love, Kelly Marie (No. 1, UK), 1980. *Recordings:* Albums: Mungo Jerry, 1970; Electronically Tested, 1971; You Don't Have To Be In The Army To Fight In The War, 1971; Boot Power, 1972; Greatest Hits, 1973; Golden Hour, 1974; Long Legged Woman, 1974; Impala Saga, 1976; Lovin' In The Alleys, Fightin' In The Streets, 1977; File, 1977; Ray Dorset and Mungo Jerry, 1978; Six Aside, 1979; Together Again, 1981; The Early Years, 1992; Best of Mungo Jerry, 1998; Solo album: Cold Blue Excursion, 1972; with Katmandu: A Case For The Blues, 1986; Singles include: In The Summertime (No. 1, UK), 1970; Baby Jump (No. 1, UK), 1971; Lady Rose, 1971; You Don't Have To Be In The Army To Fight In The War, 1971; Alright Alright Alright, 1973; Longlegged Woman Dressed In Black, 1974. *Address:* c/o Hal Carter Organisation, 101 Hazelwood Lane, London N13 5HQ, England.

DORUZKA, David; b. 25 Jan. 1980, Prague, Czech Republic. *Education:* BMus, Berklee College of Music, 2002; Participant in the Thelonious Monk Institute Jazz Colony, Aspen, Colorado, 2000. *Career:* Band leader, Eye of the Hurricane; Mem., Jaromir Honzak Trio; Performances with Christian McBride, Django Bates, Tiger Okoshi, Rodney Green, Orrin Evans, Kenwood Dennard; Performances and tours in USA, Czech Republic, Slovakia, Poland, Sweden, Denmark, Germany, Switzerland, France, Netherlands, Spain, Portugal; Appearances at Montréal Jazz Festival, Canada, 1996, Monterey Jazz Festival, USA, 2000, IAJE Conference, Long Beach, USA, 2002, Vienne Jazz Festival, France, 2002; Several radio and television broadcasts. *Compositions:* Forgotten Time, on You Know What I Mean, 1997; Was This The Last Time, on Czech Radio, 1996; 12 + 3/4, Ups and Downs, Sincerely, Czech Radio, 1998. *Recordings:* with Jorge Rossy, Phil Wilson, Greg Hopkins, Don Grusin; with Karel Ruzicka Jr: You Know What I Mean, 1997; with Jaromir Honzak: Earth Life, 1998. *Honours:* Best Talent of the Year, Czech Jazz Society, 1994; Jimi Hendrix Awards, 2000, 2001, Wayne Shorter Award, 2000, John LaPorta Award, 2000, Herb Pomeroy Award, 2001, Berklee College of Music. *Membership:* Czech Jazz Society. *Address:* Zeleny pruh 14, 14700 Prague 4, Czech Republic. *Telephone:* (2) 4446-4205. *Fax:* (2) 4446-4449. *E-mail:* ddoruzka@yahoo.com.

DORUZKA, Lubomir; b. 18 March 1924, Prague. Jazz Writer. m. Blazena Doruzkova, 1 s. *Education:* Charles University, Prague. *Career:* Editor of Music Journals; International Copyright Manager, Supraphon Prague; Lecturer, Prague Conservatoire. *Publications:* Karel Vacek Biography; Popular Music Industry, Business, Art; Panorama of Memoirs; Czech Jazz 1968–89. *Honours:* Personality of the Year, 1998; F. X. Šalda Prize for Art Criticism, 1999. *Membership:* International Jazz Federation. *Address:* 14 Zeleny Pruh, 147 00 Prague 4, Czech Republic.

DOSS, Buster (Colonel); b. 4 Feb. 1925, Jefferson, Texas, USA. Entertainer; Prod; Writer. m. Barbara Ann Solomon, 14 April 1967, 1 s., 1 d. *Education:* College; Began playing mandolin age 4, guitar, age 5, bass, age 6. *Career:* Writer, over 500 songs recorded by artists including: Billy Walker; Billy Grammer; Tex Ritter; Marty Robbins; Producer, 1949–, over 2,000 albums; Manager, Grand Ole Opry acts; Owned 7 radio stations; 7 newspapers; Owner, record labels; Owner, 3 publishing companies; Co-owner, 7 publishing companies; Owner, Theme Parks: Codyland, Missouri; Six Shooter Junction, Texas; Television shows: Star of The Cactus Kid; Magic on Ed Sullivan Show, Tonight Show; Owned Country Music theatres: Missouri; Harlingen, Texas; Ashdown, Arkansas; Mt Pleasant, Athens; Georgetown, Texas; Winchester (Tennessee); Moved to Shreveport, for Louisiana Hayride, 1948, included Kitty Wells, Elvis Presley, Jim Reeves as an announcer; Numerous appearances, 1949–, Grand Ole Opry. *Publications:* Owner The Country Gazette. *Honours:* Over 1000 awards for excellence in show business, including: Pioneer Award and Living Legend, CMA of America. *Membership:* BMI. *Current Management:* Colonel Buster Doss Presents. *Address:* 341 Billy Goat Hill Rd, Winchester, TN 37398, USA.

DOUCET, Michael Louis; b. 14 Feb. 1951, LaFayette, Louisiana, USA. Cajun Musician (fiddle, guitar, bass, mandolin, piano). m. Sharon Lee Arms, 14 Feb. 1951, 2 s., 1 d. *Education:* BS, English Major, Louisiana State University, 1973. *Career:* First band Coteau dissolved 1977; Formed Beausoleil, 1975; Projects with Savoy-Doucet band and solo work; Performed at Jimmy Carter's inaugural gala, 1977; World-wide tours with Beausoleil, including Carnegie Hall, New York, 1982; Great American Music Hall, San Francisco, 1988; Numerous television and radio appearances: Austin City Limits; Today Show; Conan O'Brien; Good Morning; Prairie Home Companion. *Compositions:* Danse De La Vie; Zydeco Gris Gris; L'Ouragon; Music for films: Belizaire The Cajun, 1985; The Big Easy, 1987. *Recordings:* Solo albums: Beau Solo; Cajun Fiddle; Beausoleil albums include: Bayou Boogie, 1985; Cajun Conja, 1991; Danse De La Vie, 1993; L'Echo, 1994; Mad Reel, 1994; 3 albums with Savoy-Doucet. *Honours:* Master Folk Musician, Louisiana; National Endowment for the Arts Grant, 1975; First Clifton Chenier Award, 1990. *Current Management:* The Rosebud Agency. *Address:* PO Box 170429, San Francisco, CA 94117, USA.

DOUDELLE, Jacques; b. 4 July 1949, Paris, France. Musician (soprano and tenor saxophones); Bandleader. *Career:* Formed Jacques Doudelle Orchestra,

Festival du Marais, Paris, 1975; Numerous appearances across France include: Casino de Paris; Marciac Jazz Festival (3 times); Sidney Bechet Night, 1993, 1994; Festivals in Italy; Belgium; Switzerland; Germany; Greece; Turkey; Television: Accords Parfaits, with Pierre Petit; Jazz 6, with Philippe Adler; Sacrée Soirée, with Jean-Pierre Foucault. *Compositions include:* T'Exagères; Moulin à Légumes; Détournement de Mineur; Coeur de Perles; Film music: Des Enfants Gâtés; Félicité. *Recordings:* 5 albums, 1978–95; Recordings with Roger Guerin; Jean Lou Longnon; Fabrice Eulry; Sidney Bechet Jr. *Honours:* Laureate, Concours National de Jazz de la Défense, 1986. *Membership:* President, Sidney Bechet Academy. *Address:* Jacques Doudelle Jazz Orchestra, 58 Ave Philippe de Girard, 93420 Villepinte, France.

DOUGANS, Brian; b. Glasgow, Scotland. Musician. *Career:* Solo artiste, as Humanoid, releasing Stakker Humanoid, 1988; Projects: Semi Real, Yage, Metropolis, Art Science Technology, Mental Cube, Candese, Intelligent Communication and Smart Systems; Mem., Future Sound of London, Amorphous Androgynous. *Recordings:* under various guises: Albums: Lifeforms, 1994; Urbmix: Flammable Liquid, 1994; Far-Out Son Of Lung And The Ramblings Of A Madman, 1995; ISDN, 1995; Dead Cities, 1996; Accelerator, 1996; Tales Of Ephidrina, 2001; Papua New Guinea: Translations, 2002; The Isness, 2002. Singles: Cascade, 1993; Paths 1–7: Lifeforms (EP), 1994; Papua New Guinea, 1996; My Kingdom, 1996; We Have Explosive, 1997. *Address:* c/o Astralwerks Records, 104 W 29th St, Fourth Floor, New York, NY 10001, USA. *Website:* www.astralwerks.com/fsl/.

DOUGLAS, Jack; b. New York, USA. Prod; Recording Engineer; Songwriter. *Education:* Studio of Audio Engineering, New York. *Career:* Janitor, Asst Engineer, Engineer, Prod., Record Plant Studio; Independent Prod.; Prod., The Sopranos (television series); Instructor, Sound Arts Dept, Studio Etiquette and Psychology, Expression Center for New Media; Worked with: Aerosmith, Blue Oyster Cult, David Bowie, Cheap Trick, Alice Cooper, Bob Dylan, Gypsy Queen, Mick Jagger, The Knack, John Lennon, New York Dolls, Yoko Ono, Lou Reed, Slash, Patti Smith, The Who. *Honours:* Grammy Award, Album of the Year, for John Lennon and Yoko Ono's, Double Fantasy, 1981. *Address:* c/o Sound Arts Department, Expression Center for New Media, 6601 Shellmound St, Emeryville, CA 94608, USA.

DOUGLAS, John Henry; b. 19 June 1920. Composer; Arranger; Conductor. m. (1) Babs, deceased, 1 s., 1 d, (2) Marion. *Career:* Pianist, Neville Hughes Sextet, 1939; Formed own RAF dance band; Arranging for many dance bands including: Bert Ambrose, Ted Heath and Edmundo Ros; Staff Arranger to George Elrick; Pianist, Arranger with the Cyril Stapleton Band; Staff Arranger, music publishers, 1948; Scoring and conducting vocal backings for Decca, 1952, first hit was Tex Ritter's High Noon; 1960: Scored and conducted 80 LPs for RCA; Composing and scoring for films; Own BBC Radio programme, Swing Song, ran for 2 years; Composed and arranged the wall-to-wall music for the American TV animation series Spiderman and His Amazing Friends, Dungeons and Dragons, The Incredible Hulk, The Transformers; Arranging, TV shows for international stars including Shirley Jones, Howard Keel, Vera Lynn, Shirley Bassey. *Compositions:* Johnny Douglas in Concert. *Recordings include:* Seven albums. *Honours:* Melody Maker Jazz Jamboree Award; Gold Disc. *Address:* 39 Tadorne Rd, Tadworth, Surrey KT20 5TF, England. *Website:* www.dulcimarecords.com.

DOUGLAS, Leslie; b. 1 May 1914, London, England. Vocalist; Bandleader; Songwriter. m. Marian Cherry, 29 March 1969, 4 s., 2 d. *Education:* Composition, Charles Prentice, Music Bac Percussion, Wag Abbey. *Career:* Featured singer, radio, and recording bands including: Henry Hall; Carrol Gibbons; Ambrose; Charlie Kunz; Teddy Joyce; Phil Green; Fred Hartley; Joined RAF, 1940; Organizer, director, Bomber Command Dance Band; Tours include: India, Malaysia, Germany; Later bandleader, Leslie Douglas and his Orchestra; Numerous radio broadcasts, variety concerts and ballroom functions. *Compositions:* Swing Serenade; Oh Miss Muffet; Lead; Little Miss Valentine; Le Touquet; Swinging Inbetween; Old Country; New Boots; One Man Went To Blow; Boys and Girls; Nursery Rhythm. *Recordings:* As bandleader, and with Carrol Gibbons; Ambrose; Henry Hall. *Membership:* PRS; British Academy of Songwriters; Musicians' Union. *Current Management:* Able Artistes and Associates. *Address:* 32 Manor Rd, Wallington, Surrey SM6 0AA, England.

DOUGLAS, Robert James Elliot; b. 13 May 1942, Gifford, East Lothian, Scotland. Musician (Guitar, Banjo). m. Margaret, 18 March 1983, 1 s. *Career:* Clyde Valley Stompers, 1960–61; It's All Happening, with Tommy Steele and On the Beat, Norman Wisdom; Aley Welsh Band, 1963–82; Newport Jazz Festival, 1966; Freelance, 1982–; Working with Keith Smith, Dave Shepherd, Digby Fairweather. *Recordings:* Complete Discography with Pamra; All Aley Welsh LPs; 2 CDs with Great British Jazz Band; 2 CDs recorded in Namburg with Vaché, Brother/Bob Haggart; Various LPs accompanying American Stars. *Honours:* British Jazz Award (Guitar), 1992. *Membership:* Musicians' Union Pamra. *Address:* 20 Gillan Way, Houghton Regis, Dunstable, Beds, LU5 5RD, England.

DOWDING, Andrew Maurice; b. 23 July 1961, Lowestoft, Suffolk, England. Musician (drums, percussion); Teacher. *Career:* Toured with Linda Lewis, Ben

E King and extensive international tours with Suzi Quatro. *Recordings:* Played on albums for Wayland and Suzi Quatro. *Membership:* Musicians' Union. *Address:* 9A Ellis Rd, Clacton-on-Sea, Essex CO15 1EX, England.

DOWNES, David; b. 9 June 1975, Dublin, Ireland. *Education:* Music degree, Trinity College, Dublin. *Career:* Live and television shows for Phil Coulter (including US tour); Eleanor McEvoy and Alan Stivell. *Compositions:* Numerous soundtracks for RTE TV; Many orchestral works and arrangements. *Recordings:* Solo albums: Saltwater, 1994; Pavilion, 1995; Rusted Wheel of Things, 1995; Also collaborated with: Maire Brennan, Clannad, Fir Na Keol, James Galway. *Membership:* Irish Musicians' Rights Organisation. *Current Management:* Real Good Management Ltd. *Address:* 17 Dame Court, Dublin 2, Ireland.

DOWNES, Geoffrey; b. 25 Aug. 1952, Stockport, Manchester, England. Musician (keyboards); Songwriter; Prod. m. Suzanne Baker, 25 Sept. 1999, 1 step-s., 2 d. *Education:* City of Leeds College, graduated in Modern Music Studies. *Career:* Session musician; Jingles composer; Record producer; Best known as artist with: The Buggles; Yes; Asia; First band to sell out 16 consecutive concerts at Madison Square Gardens, with Yes, 1980; First video shown MTV: Buggles, Video Killed The Radio Star, 1981; First live MTV global satellite broadcast with Asia, from Budokan, Tokyo to 25m. people, 1983; First band to play Moscow Olympic Stadium, 1990; Solo artist, with New Dance Orchestra. *Recordings:* with Buggles: Singles: Video Killed The Radio Star (No. 1, UK), 1979; The Plastic Age, 1980; Clean Clean, 1980; Elstree, 1980; Albums: Age of Plastic, 1979; Adventures In Modern Recording, 1981; with Yes: Drama, 1980; with Asia: Asia, 1982; Alpha, 1983; Astra, 1985; Then and Now, 1990; Live In Moscow, 1991; Aqua, 1992; Aria, 1994; Arena, 1995; Archiva, 1996; Anthology, 1998; Aura, 2001; with GTR: GTR, 1986; Geoff Downes with NDO: The Light Program, 1987; Vox Humana, 1993; Evolution, 1995; The World Service, 2000; Various artists: Earthquake, 1989; Kate Bush; Mike Oldfield; Thompson Twins. *Honours:* Over 40 Silver, Gold, Platinum discs; with Buggles: NME Award, 1980; Deutsche Gramaphon Award, 1980; with Asia: Billboard, Cashbox and Circus Magazine awards, 1982; FM Magazine Award, 1983; Ampex Gold Reel, 1979, 1980, 1986; Keyboard Magazine Awards, 1980, 1982, 1983; ASCAP Best Rock Song, 1982, 1983. *Membership:* PRS; Musicians' Union; ASCAP; PAMRA; MCPS. *Current Management:* Asia Management, Plas Llecha, Llanhennock, Newport, Monmouthshire NP18 1LU, Wales.

DOWNEY, Brian; b. 27 Jan. 1951, Dublin, Ireland. Musician (drums). *Career:* Founder member, drummer, rock group Thin Lizzy, 1969–83; Member, Grand Slam (with Thin Lizzy's Phil Lynott), 1984; Regular UK and international appearances with Thin Lizzy include: Reading Festival, 1974, 1975, 1983; Great British Music Festival, London, 1975; World Series of Rock, Cleveland, 1983; Monsters of Rock European tour, 1983. *Recordings:* with Thin Lizzy: Hit singles: Whiskey In The Jar, 1973; Wild One, 1975; The Boys Are Back In Town, 1976; Don't Believe A Word, 1977; Dancin' In The Moonlight, 1977; Rosalie, 1978; Waiting For An Alibi, 1979; Sarah, 1979; Killer On The Loose, 1980; Killers Live EP, 1981; Cold Sweat, 1982; Albums: Thin Lizzy, 1971; Shades of a Blue Orphanage, 1972; Vagabonds of The Western World, 1972; Nightlife, 1974; Fighting, 1975; Jailbreak, 1976; Johnny The Fox, 1976; Bad Reputation, 1977; Live and Dangerous, 1978; Black Rose (A Rock Legend), 1979; Chinatown, 1980; The Adventures of Thin Lizzy, 1981; Renegade, 1981; Thunder and Lightning, 1983; Dedication – The Very Best of Thin Lizzy, 1991; Wild One, 1996.

DOWNING, Paul Scott; b. 4 March 1966, London, England. Composer; Musician (Bass Guitar). *Education:* Leeds College of Music; Guildhall School of Music and Drama. *Career:* Worked With Martha Reeves, Mark Murphy, Jimmy Ruffin, Cayenne, Coup D'Etat, Anne Clark, John Etheridge, Vile Bodies, Evalution, Victoria Newton, Eva Abraham, Peter Byrne. *Compositions:* Flight Through Sunlit Clouds; Elegy For A Lost Summer; So Quiet Here; Come In; At Midnight; Summer Night In Paris; Beetles Party. *Recordings:* The Law Is An Anagram of Wealth; Elegy For A Lost Summer; Flight Through Cloudless Skies; Live 'n' Hot At Ronnie Scott's. *Honours:* Licentiate of The Guildhall School of Music and Drama. *Membership:* Musicians' Union; PRS; MCPS; PAMRA.

DOWNING, Will; b. 29 Nov. 1963, Brooklyn, New York, USA. Vocalist. 1 s., d. *Education:* Virginia Union University. *Compositions:* That Good Morning Love; Don't Wait For Love; I Can't Make You Love Me; Just A Game. *Recordings:* Albums: Will Downing, 1988; Come Together as One, 1989; A Dream Fulfilled, 1991; Love's the Place to Be, 1993; Moods, 1995; Invitation Only, 1997; Pleasures of the Night, 1998; All The Man You Need, 2000; Singles: Just A Game, early 1980s; Where Is the Love, Top 20, Duet with Mica Paris, 1990; Wishing on a Star, 1990; Don't Make Me Wait, 1991; I Go Crazy, 1991; I Try, 1991; There's No Living Without You, 1993; Do You Still Love Me, 1993; Break Up To Make Up, 1994; Sorry I, 1995; Pleasures of the Night, 1998; I Can't Make You Love Me, 1999.

DOWNS, Jeanne; b. 6 Jan. 1967, Rustington, Sussex, England. Vocalist; Songwriter; Television Presenter; Actress; Prod. m. Aron Friedman, 15 May 1993. *Education:* Arts Education School (Stage School). *Career:* Continually writing, recording, producing; Developing own music for Manuka, with album deal; Television appearances include: Presenter, Children's ITV, 1989–91; Disney Club; TV Weekly; Ghost Train; MotorMouth; Television commercial voiceovers: Kelloggs Honey Nut Loops; Coco Pops; Ultimate Dance; Kiss FM radio jingles. *Recordings:* as Jeanne Dee: Simple Solution, 1992; No Life Without Love, 1993. *Membership:* Musicians' Union; Pact; PRS; Equity. *Current Management:* Billy Budis, Kudos Management, Crown Studios, 16–18 Crown Rd, Twickenham, Middlesex TW1 3EE, England.

DOWSETT, Ian David; b. 30 Sept. 1963, Chesterfield, England. Musician (fingerstyle jazz guitar). *Education:* Classical guitar evening classes, De Bovoir Institute; Jazz and Pop course, Goldsmith's College. *Career:* Began in Rock and Blues bands, occasional solo gigs, Spanish guitar; Recently playing in duos: saxophone and guitar, 2 guitars; Performances: Union Chapel; Festival Hall Foyer; Conway Hall; Recording for EMI Bachology project, Abbey Road Studio. *Address:* 28 Westpoint, Avondale Sq., Old Kent Rd, London SE1 5NY, England.

DOY, Carl William; b. 6 May 1947, Camberley, Surrey, England. Musician (piano); Arranger; Composer; Prod. m. Kathleen Mary, 1973, 2 s. *Education:* Royal College of Music (Herbert Howells, Eric Harisson). *Career:* Staff arranger at TVNZ for 15 years; Resident Pianist New Zealand Today and Saturday Live; Arranged, recorded with Dame Kiri Te Kanawa; Played for Gladys Knight and The Pips; Bob Hope; B. B. King; Shirley Bassey. *Recordings:* Double album: Piano By Candlelight (Platinum), 1995; Moonlight Piano, USA, Australian release, 1995. *Honours:* Artistic Award World Song Festival, Los Angeles, 1984; Grand Prix, Pacific Song Contest, 1979; Winner, American Song Festival, 1981. *Membership:* APRA. *Current Management:* Murray Thom. *Address:* PO Box 35–767, Browns Bay, Auckland 10, New Zealand.

DOYLE, Candida; b. 25 Aug. 1963, Belfast, Northern Ireland. Musician (keyboards). *Career:* Mem., Pulp, 1984–; Numerous tours, television appearances and festival dates; Contribution to film soundtrack, Mission Impossible, 1996. *Recordings:* Albums: Freaks, 1987; Separations, 1992; His 'N' Hers, 1994; Different Class (No. 1, UK) 1995; This Is Hardcore (No. 1, UK), 1998; We Love Life, 2001; Hits, 2002. Singles: Little Girl (With Blue Eyes), 1985; Dogs Are Everywhere (EP), 1986; They Suffocate At Night, 1986; Master Of The Universe, 1987; My Legendary Girlfriend, 1990; Countdown, 1991; OU, 1992; Babies, 1992; Razzmatazz, 1993; Lipgloss, 1993; Do You Remember The First Time?, 1994; The Sisters (EP), 1994; Common People (No. 2, UK), 1995; Sorted For E's and Whizz/Misshapes (No. 2, UK), 1995; Disco 2000, 1995; Something Changed, 1996; Help The Aged, 1997; This Is Hardcore, 1998; A Little Soul, 1998; Party Hard, 1998; The Trees/Sunrise, 2001; Bad Cover Version, 2002. *Honours:* Mercury Music Prize, 1995; BRIT Award, 1996. *Address:* c/o Island Records, 825 Eighth Ave, New York, NY 10019, USA. *Website:* www.pulponline.com.

DOYLE, Patrick; b. 6 April 1953, Uddington, Scotland. Composer; Musician; Actor. *Education:* Royal Scottish Academy of Music and Drama. *Compositions:* For film: Look Back in Anger (TV), 1989; Henry V, 1989; Shipwrecked, 1990; Dead Again, 1991; Into the West, 1992; Indochine, 1992; Needful Things, 1993; Carlito's Way, 1993; Much Ado About Nothing, 1993; Exit to Eden, 1994; Mary Shelley's Frankenstein, 1994; Une femme française, 1995; A Little Princess, 1995; Sense and Sensibility, 1995; Mrs Winterbourne, 1996; Hamlet, 1996; Donnie Brasco, 1997; Great Expectations, 1998; Quest for Camelot, 1998; Love's Labour's Lost, 1999; East West, 2000; Bridget Jones' Diary, 2001; Gosford Park, 2002. *Membership:* ASCAP. *Current Management:* Air-Edel, 1416 N La Brea Ave, Los Angeles, CA 90028, USA.

DOYLE, Teresa; b. 26 Jan. 1951, Prince Edward Island, Canada. Vocalist. m. Brett Bunston, 1 s. *Education:* BA, University of Prince Edward Island, Canada; McGill Conservatory of Music. *Career:* Performed at festivals and concerts in Japan, Canada, the USA and UK; Performed with Chieftains. *Recordings:* Prince Edward Isle, Adieu; Forerunner; Stowaway; Songs for Lute and Voice; Dance to Your Daddy; If Fish Could Sing. *Honours:* East Coast Music Award, Children's Album of the Year. *Membership:* American Federation of Musicians. *Current Management:* Jensen Productions, Box 3445, Charlottetown, C1A 8W5 Canada. *Address:* RR #3, Belfast, Prince Edward Island C0A 1A0, Canada.

DOZIER, Lamont; b. 16 June 1941, Detroit, Michigan, USA. Composer; Record Prod. *Career:* Motown artist, 1950s–67; Member, songwriting and production team Holland/Dozier/Holland (with Eddie and Brian Holland), 1963–73; Co-founder, Invictus and Hot Wax Records, 1967; Resumed solo recording career, 1972–; Founder, own Megaphone label, 1983. *Recordings:* Solo albums: Out Here On My Own, 1973; Black Bach, 1974; Love and Beauty, 1975; Right There, 1976; Peddlin' Music On The Side, 1977; Bittersweet, 1979; Working On You, 1981; Lamont, 1982; Bigger Than Life, 1983; Inside Seduction, 1991; Going Back To My Roots, 2000; Solo singles include: Let's Talk It Over, 1960; Why Can't We Be Lovers, 1972; Tryin' To Hold On To My Woman, 1974; Fish Ain't Bitin', 1974; Let Me Start Tonite, 1974; Love in the Rain, 1991; As co-writer/producer: with Marvin Gaye: Can I Get A Witness?; Little Darling; How Sweet It Is; You're A Wonderful One;

with Martha and The Vandellas: Heatwave; Quicksand; Nowhere To Run; Jimmy Mack; with the Supremes: You Can't Hurry Love; You Keep Me Hanging On; Love Is Here and Now You've Gone; Where Did Our Love Go?; Baby Love; Come See About Me; Stop! In The Name of Love; Back In My Arms Again; with the Isley Brothers: This Old Heart of Mine; Put Yourself In My Place; I Guess I'll Always Love; with the Four Tops: Baby I Need Your Loving; I Can't Help Myself; (It's The) Same Old Song; Reach Out and I'll Be There; Bernadette; Standing In The Shadows of Love; Other recordings for artistes including: The Miracles; Kim Weston; Aretha Franklin; Al Wilson; Freda Payne. *Address:* c/o McMullen and Co, 9744 Wilshire Blvd #301, Beverly Hills, CA 90212–1828, USA.

DR BANJO. See: WERNICK, Peter.

DR DRE, (Andre Young); b. 18 Feb. 1965, Los Angeles, CA, USA. Rap Artiste; Hip Hop Prod. *Career:* Mem., World Class Wreckin' Cru; Mem., NWA, 1980s; Worked with Snoop Doggy Dogg, Warren G; Co-founder, Death Row Records, 1992–96; Prod., numerous acts incl. Blackstreet and Foxy Brown; Founder, Prod., Aftermath label, 1996–, sold to Interscope Records, 2001; Worked with Eminem on The Slim Shady LP, 1999; The Marshall Mathers LP, 2000; Film appearance, Training Day, 2002. *Recordings:* Albums: The Chronic, 1992; Concrete Roots, 1994; Back N Tha Day, 1996; Dr Dre Presents the Aftermath, 1996; Chronic 2001, 1999; Dre, 2001. Singles: Deep Cover, 1992; Nuthin' But a 'G' Thang, 1993; 2, 1993; House Calls, 1993; Dre Day, 1994; Juice, 1995; Dre's Beats, 1995; Hit Hip-Hop on Hot Vinyl, 1995; Keep Their Heads Ringin', 1995; Zoom, 1998; Lil' Ghetto Boy, 1999. *Honours:* Grammy Award, Best Rap Solo Performance, Let Me Ride. *Address:* c/o Interscope Records, 2220 Colorado Ave, Santa Monica, CA 90404, USA.

DR ROBERT, (Bruce Robert Howard); b. 2 May 1961, Norfolk, England. Vocalist. *Career:* Former footballer, Norwich City Football Club; Former pop music journalist; Member, The Blow Monkeys, 1984–. *Recordings:* Albums: Limping For A Generation, 1984; Animal Magic, 1986; She Was Only A Grocer's Daughter, 1987; Whoops There Goes The Neighbourhood, 1989; Choices, 1989; Atomic Lullabies (compilation), 2001; Singles include: Digging Your Scene, 1986; It Doesn't Have To Be This Way, 1987; (Celebrate) The Day After You (featuring Curtis Mayfield), 1987; Choice?, 1989; Slaves No More (featuring Sylvia Tella), 1989; Springtime For The World, 1990; The Coming of Grace; Contributor, You Don't Own Me, to soundtrack for film Dirty Dancing; as Dr Robert: Duet with Kym Mazelle: Wait, 1989; Solo albums: Realms of Gold, 1996; Bird's Gotta Fly, 2001; Also recorded with: Paul Weller, Beth Orton. *Address:* c/o Primary Talent, London, England.

DR TREVIS. See: REDMAN.

DRAGON, Daryl; b. 27 Aug. 1942, Los Angeles, California, USA. Musician (keyboards); Songwriter. m. Toni Tennille, 14 Feb. 1974. *Career:* Keyboard player, co-writer, The Beach Boys stage band; Member, Natalie Cole's Malibu Music Men; Member, duo Captain and Tennille (with Toni Tennille), 1972–80; Tour with The Beach Boys, 1972; White House Dinner, in honour of Queen Elizabeth II, 1976; The Captain and Tennille, premiere, ABC TV, 1976; Runs Rambo Rec studio, 1979–. *Recordings:* Albums: with The Captain and Tennille: Love Will Keep Us Together (No. 2, USA), 1975; Song of Joy, 1976; Come In From The Rain, 1977; Captain and Tennille's Greatest Hits, 1978; Dream, 1978; Make Your Move, 1980; Twenty Years of Romance, 1995; Casablanca Records' Greatest Hits, 1996; Size 14, 1997; Tennille Sings Big Band, 1998; Incurably Romantic, 2001; Hit singles include: The Way I Want To Touch You, 1975; Love Will Keep Us Together (No. 1, USA), 1975; Lonely Night (Angel Face), 1976; Muskrat Love, 1976; Shop Around, 1976; Can't Stop Dancin', 1977; You Never Done It Like That, 1979; Do That To Me One More Time (No. 1, USA), 1980. *Honours:* Grammy Award, Record of the Year, Love Will Keep Us Together, 1976; JUNO Award, Best International Single, Love Will Keep Us Together, 1976. *Current Management:* c/o Cheri Ingram Enterprises, 2225 E Flamingo Rd, Suite 303, Las Vegas, NV 89119, USA.

DRAMINSKY HOJMARK, Jakob; b. 18 Nov. 1959, Copenhagen, Denmark. Composer; Musician (Bass Clarinet; Sopranino Saxophone). *Education:* Instrumental and composition studies with Pierre Dorge, Copenhagen, Wolfgang Fuchs, Berlin and Gabriel Brncic, Barcelona; Electroacoustic workshops in DIEM, IRCAM and PHONOS. *Career:* Car-Horn Concert, concrete music event for cars and trucks in Copenhagen; Münchausen in Århus, with Tzarina Q Cut, 25th anniversary of National Danish Arts Foundation; Stairways performed by Frith, Cora and Fuchs; Margrethe Fjorden, Intermedia event, curated by Eric Andersen, Roskilde, Denmark; Slip 'n' Slide sonata for construction equipment; Collaborated with French toy pianist Pascal Comelade with recordings, tours, festivals in France, Spain and Germany. *Compositions:* Turandot, cabaret-like opera, 1993; Memory: song cycle for choir and piano, 1997; En Landsoldats dagbog electroacoustic, pocket opera, 64928, electroacoustic chamber opera for 3 voices, cello and electronics, 1998. *Recordings:* At the Gallery, 9 collected chamber works; Memory; En landsoldats dagbog, Dreamjingles. *Honours:* Grants from the National Danish Art Foundation. *Membership:* DJBFA. *Current Management:* Multisounds. *Address:* H C Orstedsvej 17 III, 1879 Frb C, Denmark.

DRAPER, Paul; b. Chester, Cheshire, England. Vocalist. *Education:* Wrexham Art College. *Career:* Lead singer/songwriter, Mansun. *Recordings include:* Debut album, Attack of The Grey Lantern, 1997; Singles: Egg Shaped Fred (EP), 1996; Take It Easy Chicken (EP), 1996; Stripper Vicar (EP), 1996; Wide Open Space (EP), 1996; Taxloss, EP, 1997; Closed for Business, EP, 1998; Legacy, EP, 1998; Being A Girl, EP, 1998; Negative, EP, 1998; I Can Only Disappoint You, 2000; Electric Man, 2000; Fool, 2001; Albums: Attack of the Grey Lantern (No. 1, UK), 1997; Six, 1998; Little Kix, 2000. *Current Management:* Rock 'n' Roll Management, Studio 2, 108 Prospect Quay, Point Pleasant, London SW18 1PR, England.

DRE, (Andre Benjamin); b. 27 May 1975, Georgia, USA. Rap Artiste. *Education:* Tri-City High School, Atlanta. *Career:* Mem., Outkast, with Big Boi; Signed to LaFace Records; Designed Outkast Clothing line. *Recordings:* Albums: Southernplayalisticadillacmuzik, 1994; ATLiens, 1996; Aquemini, 1998; Stankonia, 2000; Dungeon Family... Even In The Darkness, 2001; Big Boi And Dre Present..., 2002. Singles: Player's Ball (No. 1, USA), 1994; Elevators (Me & You), 1996; Ms Jackson (No. 1, USA). *Honours:* Platinum disc; American Music Award, Best Hip Hop/R&B Group, 2003. *Address:* LaFace Records, A&R Dept, 1 Capital City Plaza, 3350 Peachtree Rd, Suite 1500, Atlanta, GA 30326, USA. *Website:* www.outkast.com.

DREES, Michèle Marie; b. Carshalton, Surrey, England. Musician (drums, percussion). *Education:* GSMD post graduate, advanced jazz course. *Career:* Marc Almond tour video, television, 1993; Member of houseband, Jonathan Ross TV Show, backing k d lang; Suzanne Vega; Mica Paris; Candy Dulfer; Hair, musical, Old Vic, 1993; Freak Power, 1993, 1994; Many jazz concerts, played with: Jean Toussaint; Dill Katz; Tim Whitehead; salsa band Candela; Seal; Eurovision Song Contest; Crystal Aquarium film, CH4, 1995; Marie-Clare D'Ubaldo. *Membership:* Musicians' Union; Equity. *Current Management:* Simon Harrison. *Address:* Lavender Cottage, Love Lane, Kings Langley, Hertfordshire WD4 9HN, England.

DREVER, Ivan Cursiter; b. 10 June 1956, Orkney. Vocalist; Songwriter; Musician (guitar). 2 s., 2 d. *Career:* Solo/duo work, 6 years; Joined Wolfstone, 1991; Toured America, Canada, Spain, Denmark, Germany and Far East; Networked in appearances with band. *Compositions:* Many compositions recorded. *Recordings:* with Wolfstone: Unleashed, 1991; Chase, 1992; Year of the Dog, 1994; Half Tail, 1996; Pick of the Litter, 1997; This Strange Place, 1998; 3 solo albums; 3 duo albums with Knowe O'Deil. *Honours:* 2 Gold Discs for albums, Unleashed and The Chase. *Membership:* MCPS; PRS. *Address:* 10B View Pl., Inverness IV2 4SA, Scotland.

DREW, Martin; b. 11 Feb. 1944, Northampton, England. Musician (drums). m. Tessa Denise Rose, 5 Sept. 1965, 1 s., 2 d. *Education:* Taught by George Fierstone. *Career:* Worked with Oscar Peterson, 1974–; Ronnie Scott, 1975–; Played world-wide with many major artists including television, radio, album appearances; Played with: George Coleman; Niels H O Pedersen; James Moody; Dizzie Gillespie; Zoot Sims; Michael Brecker. *Recordings:* Featured with: Oscar Peterson; Ronnie Scott; Arturo Sandoval; Chucho Valdes; Bill Watrous; Joe Pass; Warren Vache; Dick Morrissey; John Critchinson; Joe Temperley; Tony Lee; Freddy Hubbard; Harry Edison. *Honours:* 3 times winner, British Jazz Awards (Drums). *Membership:* Musicians' Union; Jazz Umbrella.

DREWETT, Steve; b. 29 Oct. 1954, Islington, London, England. Vocalist; Songwriter; Musician (guitar). *Career:* John Peel Sessions, BBC Radio 1; Old Grey Whistle Test, BBC 2; Support tour with Billy Bragg. *Recordings:* Albums: Beggars Can Be Choosers, 1983; Repercussions, 1985; Kickstarting A Backfiring Nation, 1986; Is Your Washroom Breeding Bolsheviks, 1988; 45 Revolutions Per Minute, 1990. *Membership:* Musicians' Union. *Current Management:* No Wonder Management. *Address:* 154 Bishopsfield, Harlow, Essex, England.

D'RIVERA, Paquito; b. 4 June 1948, Havana, Cuba. Musician (saxophone, clarinet); Bandleader; Composer; Arranger. *Career:* Performs with Paquito D'Rivera Ensemble and the Caribbean Jazz Project; Conducts Dizzy Gillespie's UN Orchestra; Guest soloist, jazz, classical, Latin/Caribbean music concerts; Television appearances include: CBS Sunday Morning; The David Letterman Show. *Compositions:* The New York Suite, for saxophone quartet, 1987; Aires Tropicales, for woodwind quintet, 1994; 5 Pieces for brass quintet, 1997. *Recordings:* Over 20 solo albums, bebop, classical, Latin/Caribbean music. *Publications:* Music Minus Me instructional tapes, albums; Lessons With the Greats; Jamey Aebersold, Play-along, Vol. 77; My Saxual Life, 1999. *Honours:* Lifetime Achievement Award, Contribution to Latin music, Carnegie Hall; Grammy Award, for Portraits of Cuba, 1997; Diploma h.c., Universidad de Alcalá de Henares, Spain. *Membership:* Artistic Director, New Jersey Chamber Music Society; Board of Directors, Chamber Music America. *Current Management:* Havana-NY Music Co. *Address:* PO Box 4899, Weehawken, NJ 07087, USA.

DROGE, Peter; b. 11 March 1969, Eugene, Oregon, USA. Vocalist; Songwriter. *Career:* Tours supporting Tom Petty; Melissa Etheridge; Sheryl Crowe; Appearance, Late Night With David Letterman; Included on

soundtracks for films: Beautiful Girls; Dumb and Dumber; Tour supporting Neil Young. *Recordings:* Albums: Necktie Second, 1994; Find a Door, 1996; Spacey and Shakin', 1998; Singles: If You Don't Love Me, 1995. *Honours:* Find a Door voted Most Overlooked Album of the Year, The Rocket, 1996. *Membership:* ASCAP. *Current Management:* Curtis Management. *Address:* 417 Denny Way, Suite 200, Seattle, WA 98109, USA.

DROSSOS, Petros; b. 11 June 1966, Athens, Greece. Sound Engineer; Prod. *Career:* Tape Operator, several Parisian studios, 1986; Assistant Engineer, Polysound Studios, Athens, Greece, 1987; In-house Engineer, Davout Studios, Paris, France, 1988–91; Freelance engineer, music, television, post-production, 1991–. *Recordings:* Engineer, producer: Single: with Mano Negra: King Kong Five; Albums: Raggabuzzin (French Reggae Compilation); with Rosemary's Babies: Lutte De Classe; Engineer: Mano Negra: Live à la Cigale (TV programme tracks); with Hector Zazou and Les Polyphonies Corses, Ghetto Youth Progress (French Ragga Hip Hop Compilation); IAM: Red, Black and Green (maxi-single). *Address:* 213 Blvd Davout, 75020 Paris, France.

DRU NASTY. See: **SISQÓ**.

DRUMMIE, Richard; Vocalist; Musician (guitar, keyboards); Songwriter. *Career:* Songwriting partnership with Peter Cox, ATV Music; Founder member, duo Go West, 1982–. *Compositions include:* One Way Street (for film soundtrack Rocky IV). *Recordings:* Singles: We Close Our Eyes, 1985; Call Me, 1985; Don't Look Down, 1985; The King of Wishful Thinking, 1990; What You Won't Do For Love, 1993; Albums: Go West, 1985; Bangs and Crashes, 1986; Dancing On The Couch, 1987; Cries and Whispers, 1989; Indian Summer, 1992; Session work: White Men Can't Jump, 1992; Deborah, for Deborah Gibson, 1997; Growing Pains, for Billie Myers, 1997; Moonchild, for Deborah Gibson, 2000. *Current Management:* Blueprint Management, 134 Lots Rd, London SW12 0RJ, England.

DRUMMOND, Bill (William Butterworth); b. 29 April 1953, South Africa. Prod.; Label Man; Musician. *Career:* Former fisherman, set designer, carpenter, Scotland; Mem., Big In Japan, 1977; Founder, Zoo Records and Zoo Publishing, with David Balfe; Man., prod., Teardrop Explodes; Echo and The Bunnymen; A&R consultant, WEA Records, 1985; Formed KLF Communications, with Jimmy Cauty; Various recordings as: JAMS, 1987–88; Disco 200, 1987–89; Timelords, 1988; KLF, 1989–92; Justified Ancients of Mu Mu, 1991–92; 2K, 1997; DMC European Convention, Amsterdam, 1990; Own studios, Transcentral 1988; Announced departure from music business, 1992. *Recordings:* Albums: Solo: Bill Drummond–The Man, 1986; Time For A Change, 1989; as the KLF: The White Room, 1989; Chill Out, 1990. Hit singles: as The Timelords: Doctorin' The Tardis (No. 1, UK), 1988; as The KLF: What Time Is Love, 1990; 3am Eternal (No. 1, UK), 1991; Last Train To Transcentral, 1991; Justified and Ancient (with Tammy Wynette), 1992; America – What Time Is Love?, 1992; as Justified Ancients of Mu Mu: It's Grim Up North, 1991; as 2K: Fuck The Millennium, 1997. *Publications:* The Manual: How to Have a Number One the Easy Way, 1988; Bad Wisdom (with Mark Manning), 1996; 45, 2000; How To Be An Artist, 2002. *Honours:* Gold discs: The White Room, 1991; 3am Eternal, 1991; BRIT Award, Best British Group, KLF (co-winners with Simply Red), 1992. *Address:* c/o Bar/None Records, PO Box 1704, Hoboken, NJ 07030, USA.

DRUSKY, Roy Frank; b. 22 June 1930, Atlanta, Georgia, USA. DJ; Country Vocalist; Songwriter; Television Host. *Education:* Veterinary medicine, Emory University. *Career:* Formed Southern Ranch Boys; Radio DJ, television announcer, 1950s; Member, Grand Ole Opry, 1958–; Concerts include: Regular British tours; Wembley Festival; Film appearances: Forty Acre Feud; The Golden Guitar; White Lightning Express; Now involved in production and publishing; Hosts own television programme. *Compositions include:* Alone With You, Faron Young (US Country No. 1), 1958. *Recordings:* Hits include: Three Hearts In A Tangle; Second Hand Rose; Yes Mr Peters, duet with Priscilla Mitchell; If The Whole World Stopped Loving; Numerous albums include: Anymore With Roy Drusky, 1961; It's My Way, 1962; Yesterday's Gone, 1964; Country Song Express, 1966; All My Hard Times, 1970; Peaceful Easy Feeling, 1974; This Life of Mine, 1976; Roy, 1981; Night Flying, 1976; English Cold, 1980; Songs of Love and Life, 1995; with Priscilla Mitchell: Love's Eternal Triangle, 1965; Together Again, 1966; We Belong Together, 1968.

DUBE, Lucky; b. 3 Aug. 1964, Ermelo, Eastern Transvaal, South Africa. Vocalist; Songwriter. *Career:* Formed The Skyway Band in school; Recorded first album Mbaqanga (with The Love Brothers), 1982; First solo album Lengane Ngeyetha went gold; Recorded first ever South African reggae album, 1985; Third reggae release Slave was first ever album to sell more than 300,000 copies in South Africa; Performed at Reggae Sunsplash in 1991; Starred in and composed score for the film Getting Lucky; Also appeared in film Voice in the Dark. *Recordings:* Albums include: Slave, 1987; Prisoner, 1989; House of Exile, 1991; Victims, 1993; Trinity, 1995; Serious Reggae Business, 1996; Taxman, 1997; The Way It Is, 1999; Soul Taker, The Rough Guide to Lucky Dube, 2001. *Honours:* OKTV Award, Best Male Vocalist; Kora

Award, Best African Video, The Way It Is, 2000. *Address:* c/o Gallo, PO Box 2897, Parklands 2121, South Africa. *Website:* www.luckydube.net.

DUBFIRE, (Ali Shirazinia); b. 19 April 1971, Iran. Prod; Remixer; DJ. *Career:* Relocated to Washington DC, USA; Formed Deep Dish and founded Deep Dish/Yoshitoshi Records with partner Sharam, 1992; Released BT's A Moment of Truth, 1993; Signed to Tribal Records, 1993; Moved to Deconstruction, 1996; Collaborations: Danny Tenaglia; John Selway; Everything But The Girl; Remixed: Madonna; De'Lacy; Billie Ray Martin; Joi Cardwell; Dusted; Sven Vath; The Shamen; Eddie Amador. *Recordings:* Albums: Junk Science, 1998; Singles: A Feeling (as Moods), 1992; Sexy Dancer (as Quench), 1993; The Dream, 1994; Love Songs (as Chocolate City), Stay Gold, 1996; The Future of The Future, 1998. *Honours:* Grammy Award, Remixer of the Year, 2001. *Address:* c/o Deconstruction, Bedford House, 69–79 Fulham High St, London SW6 3JW, England.

DUBOWSKY, Jack Curtis; b. 16 Aug. 1965, Connecticut, USA. Composer; Arranger; Record Prod; Musician (guitar, bass, piano); Vocalist. *Education:* Graduate, University of California. *Career:* Radio appearance on German radio, 1990; Recording Technician with Metallica, Live Shit box set, 1994; Actor with Sick and Twisted Players, San Francisco; Currently playing with Snopea Chamber Ensemble; Produced Glen Meadmore, Hot Horny and Born-Again, 1998, and Virgin Whore Complex, Succumb, 1998. *Compositions:* The Silver Whistle, chamber opera, 1995; Slave, chamber opera, 1997. *Recordings:* Diazepam Nights, 1989; Helot Revolt, 1992; Fallout, 1990; Duchampians, 1991; Produced Glen Meadmore's songs for film Hustler White, 1996; Voyagers, chamber opera, At The Mercy. *Honours:* Zellerbach Family Fund Grant, 1998; Friends of the San Francisco Library grant, 1997; Meet the Composer grant, 1998. *Membership:* BMI. *Current Management:* De Stijl Records. *Address:* PO Box 170206, San Francisco, CA 94117–0206, USA.

DUCAS, George; b. 1 Aug. 1966, Texas City, Texas, USA. Artist; Vocalist; Songwriter; Musician (guitar). *Education:* BA Economics, Vanderbilt University, Nashville, Tennessee. *Career:* Moved to Nashville, 1991; Began songwriting and playing local clubs; Signed with Capitol Records, 1994; Television appearances include: CBS This Morning; CNN Showbiz Today; Entertainment Tonight; Good Day New York; Sound FX; FX Breakfast Time; Live From Queens; At The Ryman. *Recordings:* Singles, videos: Teardrops; Lipstick Promises (Top 10); Hello Cruel World, 1995; Kisses Don't Lie, 1995; Every Time She Passes By, 1996; Albums: George Ducas, 1995; Where I Stand, 1997. *Membership:* ASCAP; County Music Asscn. *Current Management:* Coast to Coast.

DUCHARME, Annette Marie-Jeanne Thérèse; b. 23 Feb. , Windsor, Ontario, Canada. Recording Artiste; Vocalist; Songwriter; Musician (guitar, bass, piano, keyboards). *Education:* BA, Drama, English. *Career:* Appeared: Peter Czowski show modelling for Evelyn Roth, 1977; Sang, played keyboards, Grade 8 Concert, St Mary's Academy; As lead singer, writer, bass player, toured with Bowers/Ducharme Trio, 1980–81; Keyboards, tour with John Lee Hooker, 1982–83; Opened for Richard Marx with own band, cross-Canada tour, 1989; Own band, opening tour for Larry Gowan, 1994; Sang at Kumbaya Benefits, 1993, 1994; Sang at: Grey Cup Half-time Show, with Tom Cochrane, 1994. *Compositions:* Sinking Like A Sunset, recorded by Tom Cochrane. *Recordings:* Bowers/Ducharme, 1981; Blue Girl, 1988–89; Mad Mad World, 1992; Sanctuary, 1994; Ragged Ass Road, 1995; Flowers In The Concrete, 1995; Don't Argue with Her, 1996; Mythos, 1998. *Honours:* (West Coast) Caras Award for Most Promising New Artist, 1995; CMPA Award for number 1 Rock Song of the Year, 1993; SOCAN Award for Pop Song of the Year, 1993; Last two for: Sinking Like A Sunset. *Membership:* SOCAN. *Current Management:* TKO Management. *Address:* 1669 E 13th Ave, Vancouver, BC V5N 2B7 Canada.

DUCHEMIN, Philippe; b. 2 Jan. 1957, Toulouse, France. Jazz Musician (piano). *Career:* Played with Kenny Clarke; Lionel Hampton; Ray Brown; Joe Newman; Benny Powell; Wild Bill Davis; Frank Wess; Toured Europe with many French and American musicians, 1985–; Performed at Jazz Festivals with own trio throughout Europe, North Africa, 1990–. *Recordings:* Middle Jazz Quartet, 1980; Hommage à Count Basie, 1985; François Guin Et Les Four Bones, 1987; with Philippe Duchemin Trio: Alizés, 1990; Live!, 1992; Three Pieces, 1994; Trio with Dominque Vernhes, 1995; with Paris Barcelona: Swing Connection, 1990; Hard Swing, 1991; Wild Cat, 1992; Frank Wess Meets The Paris Barcelona, 1992; Three Colours, 1998. *Address:* 42 rue de la Madeleine, 72000 Le Mans, France. *Telephone:* (2) 43-77-11-36. *Fax:* (2) 43-87-06-80. *E-mail:* duchemin@noos.fr. *Website:* mapage.noos.fr/duchemin.

DUDLEY, Anne; Musician (keyboards); Arranger; Prod; Composer; Songwriter. *Career:* Pianist, Playschool, BBC TV; Founder member, Art of Noise, 1984–90, 1999–; Solo artiste, composer, producer, arranger, 1990–. *Compositions include:* Television commercials: Volvo; Vauxhall Astra; Reebok; Television scores: Jeeves and Wooster; Anna Lee, Crime Traveller, Kavanagh QC. *Recordings:* Early session work includes: The Lexicon of Love, ABC, 1982; Duck Rock, Malcolm McLaren, 1983; Two Tribes, Frankie Goes To Hollywood, 1984; Albums: with The Art of Noise: Albums: (Who's Afraid Of) The Art of Noise, 1984; In Visible Silence, 1986; Daft, 1987; In No Sense? Nonsense!,

1987; The Best of The Art of Noise, 1988; The Ambient Collection, 1990; The Seduction of Claude Debussy, 1999; Solo albums: Songs From The Victorious City, with Jaz Coleman, 1990; Ancient and Modern, 1999; A Different Light, 2001; Singles: with The Art of Noise: Into Battle, 1983; Beat Box, 1984; Close To The Edit, 1985; Peter Gunn, with Duane Eddy, 1986; Paranoimia, 1986; Kiss, with Tom Jones, 1988; Art of Love, 1990; Minarets and Memories, 1990; Ziggarats of Cinnamon, 1991; Film themes and scores: include: Buster; Wilt; Say Anything; Mighty Quinn; The Crying Game; The Grotesque (with Sting); Hollow Reed; The Full Monty; Monkeybone; Also worked as arranger with: Lloyd Cole; A-Ha; Phil Collins; Rush; Boyzone; Spice Girls, Elton John, Paul McCartney, Pet Shop Boys, Pulp, The The, S Club 7. *Honours:* Grammy, Best Rock Instrumental Performance, Peter Gunn, 1987; Academy Award, Best Original Comedy Score, for The Full Monty, 1998. *Current Management:* Air Edel, 18 Rodmarton St, London W1H 3FW, England.

DUDLEY, Dave, (David Darwin Pedruska); b. 3 May 1928, Spencer, Wisconsin, USA. Country vocalist; Songwriter; Musician (guitar). *Career:* Played semi-pro baseball in Wisconsin and for the Gainsville Owls in Texas until injury stopped career; DJ and singer at radio stations: WTWT Wausau, Wisconsin; KBOK, Waterloo, Iowa; KCHA, Charles City, Minnesota; Formed Dave Dudley Trio and worked throughout Midwest, 1953–60; First country chart single, Maybe I Do, on Vee Records, 1961; Signed to Mercury Records, 1963; Became especially known for records with a trucking theme including Six Days On The Road; Awarded a solid gold security card by the Truckers Union in appreciation of musical services on behalf of truckers. *Compositions include:* Comin' Down; Fly Away Again. *Recordings include:* The Pool Shark, 1970; Six Days On The Road, 1963; Truck Drivin' Son-Of-A-Gun, 1965; Cowboy Boots, 1963; What We're Fighting For, 1965; Albums: Truck Drivin' Son-Of-A-Gun, 1965; Lonelyville, 1966; Travelin' With Dave Dudley, 1964. *Address:* c/o Country Music Asscn, 1 Music Circle S, Nashville, TN 37203, USA.

DUFEK, Milan; b. 6 May 1944, Prague, Czech Republic. m. Dr Stana Dufkova, 2 s. *Education:* Konzervator Jaroslava Jezka, 1984–88. *Career:* Member of Group Rangers, Plavci, 1965–98; 20 Television Shows. *Compositions:* 100 Songs Including, Memories of Home; Gettin' Married; Let Say I Do; Left Hand. *Recordings:* 14 CDs; 21 Records Including, Country Our Way; On The Country Road; Country Grass Band. *Publications:* Rangers I; Rangers II; Ranger On The Road. *Honours:* Porta Festival Prize, 1968, 1969; Country Festival Prague Prize, 1970; Country Radio Prague Award, 1997, 1998. *Address:* Pod Stadiony 5, 150 00 Prague 5, Czech Republic.

DUFFIN, Graeme Ian; b. 28 Feb. 1956, Glasgow, Scotland. Musician (guitar). m. Pamela, 15 April 1978, 1 s., 1 d. *Education:* HNC, Medical Laboratory Science (Biochemistry); Piano training. *Career:* Member, folk group New Celeste, 1977–80; Member, Wet Wet Wet, 1985–; Major tours in UK, Europe, USA, Far East and Australia; Live video recorded at Glasgow Green, Edinburgh Castle and Royal Albert Hall. *Recordings:* Albums: Popped In Souled Out 1987; The Memphis Sessions, 1988; Holding Back The River, 1989; High On The Happy Side, 1991; End of Part One (Greatest Hits), 1993; Picture This, 1995; 10, 1997; Best of British Folk Rock; Hit singles include: Wishing I Was Lucky, 1987; Sweet Little Mystery, 1987; Angel Eyes, 1987; With A Little Help From My Friends (No. 1, UK), 1988; Sweet Surrender, 1989; Goodnight Girl (No. 1, UK), 1992; Love Is All Around (No. 1, 15 weeks, UK charts); Julia Says, 1995. *Honours:* BRIT Awards, Best Newcomers, 1987; Award for co-production of Love Is All Around. *Current Management:* The Precious Organisation, 14/16 Spiers Wharf, Port Dundas, Glasgow, Scotland.

DUFFY, Billy; b. 12 May 1959, Manchester, England. Musician (guitar). *Career:* Guitarist, Theatre of Hate; The Cult (formerly Southern Death Cult and Death Cult), 1983–; World-wide tours; Concerts with: Bauhaus; Billy Idol; Big Country; Metallica; Guns N' Roses; Lenny Kravitz; Concerts include: Futurama Festival, Leeds, 1983; A Gathering of The Tribes, USA, 1990; Cult In The Park '92 Festival, Finsbury Park, London, 1992; Guns N' Roses concert, Milton Keynes, 1993. *Recordings:* Albums: Southern Death Cult, 1983; Dreamtime, 1984; Love, 1985; Electric, 1987; Sonic Temple, 1989; Ceremony, 1991; Pure Cult, 1993; The Cult, 1994; Ghost Dance, 1996; High Octane Cult, 1996; Forever Mod, 1998; Ten Years After, 1998; Rare Cult, 2000; Beyond Good and Evil, 2001; Singles include: Fat Man, 1983; Spiritwalker, 1984; She Sells Sanctuary, 1985; Rain, 1985; Love Removal Machine, 1987; Lil' Devil, 1987; Wild Flower, 1987; Fire Woman, 1989; Edie (Ciao Baby), 1989; Sweet Soul Sister, 1990; Wild Hearted Son, 1991.

DUFFY, Keith Peter Thomas John; b. 1 Oct. 1974, Dublin, Ireland. Vocalist; Man. m. Lisa Smith, 1 s. *Career:* Mem., Boyzone, 1993–2001; Television appearances: Presenter, FBi (BBC), 2000; Presenter, The Race (ITV2), 2001; Celebrity Big Brother (Channel 4), 2001; Coronation Street (ITV1), 2002; Film appearance: The Gift, 2001; Co-man., band Broken Hill, 2002–. *Recordings:* Albums: Said And Done, 1995; A Different Beat, 1996; Where We Belong, 1998; By Request, 1999. Singles: Working My Way Back To You, 1994; Key To My Life, 1995; Love Me For A Reason, 1995; So Good, 1995; Father and Son, 1995; Coming Home Now, 1995; Words (No. 1, UK), 1996; A Different Beat (No. 1, UK), 1996; Isn't It A Wonder, 1997; Baby Can I Hold You Tonight, 1997; Musical Experience, 1997; Picture of You,

1997; All That I Need (No. 1, UK), 1998; I Love The Way You Love Me, 1998; When The Going Gets Tough (No. 1, UK), 1999; You Needed Me (No. 1, UK), 1999; Every Day I Love You, 1999; Girl You Know It's True (with Shane Lynch), 2000. *Address:* c/o John Noel Management, 10a Belmont St, Second Floor, London NW1 8HH, England.

DUFFY, Martin; Musician (keyboards). *Career:* Member, Primal Scream; Obtained record deal with Creation; Work remixed by DJ Andrew Weatherall, and collaborations with Jah Wobble, Denise Johnston and Alex Paterson of The Orb; Other session work includes: Felt; Beth Orton; Dr John; Charlatans; Shack; Numerous tours and festival appearances; Contributed track, The Scream Team meets the Barmy Army Uptown for the Irvine Welsh film Trainspotting, 1996. *Recordings:* Singles: Loaded EP, 1990; Come Together EP, 1990; Higher Than The Sun, 1991; Don't Fight It, Feel It, 1991; Movin' On Up, 1991; (I'm Gonna) Cry Myself Blind, 1994; Jailbird, 1994; Rocks/ Funky Jam, 1994; The Big Man and the Scream Team Meet the Barmy Army Uptown, 1996; Star, 1997; Burning Wheel, 1997; Kowalski, 1997; If They Move, Kill 'Em, 1998; Swastikka Eyes, 1999; Kill All Hippies, 2000; Accelerator, 2000; Miss Lucifer, 2002. Albums: Sonic Flower Groove, 1987; Primal Scream, 1989; Screamadelica, 1991; Give Out But Don't Give Up, 1994; Echo Dek, 1997; Vanishing Point, 1997; XTRMNTR, 2000; Evil Heat, 2002. *Honours:* Mercury Music Prize Winners, 1992. *Website:* www.primalscream.net.

DUFFY, Stephen Anthony James; b. 30 May 1960, Birmingham, England. Vocalist; Songwriter. *Education:* Birmingham Polytechnic. *Career:* Founder mem., Duran Duran, 1978–79; Solo artiste, under own name and as Dr Calculus, 1982–; Leader, own group Duffy, 1994–; Founder mem., The Lilac Time, 1987–91; Founder mem., The Devils, with Nick Rhodes, 1999–. *Recordings:* Albums: Solo: The Ups and Downs, 1985; Because We Love You, 1986; Designer Beatnik (as Dr Calculus), 1986; Music In Colours, with Nigel Kennedy, 1993; with The Lilac Time: The Lilac Time, 1987; Paradise Circus, 1989; And Love For All, 1990; Astronauts, 1991; Duffy, 1995; Kiss Me, 1995; I Love My Friends, 1998; Looking for a Day in the Night, 1999; Lilac 6, 2001; with The Devils: Dark Circles, 2002. Singles: Solo: Kiss Me, 1982; Hold It, 1982; Kiss Me (re-release), 1985; Icing On The Cake, 1985; London Girls, 1995; Sugar High, 1995; with The Lilac Time: Return To Yesterday, 1988; Needle Mythology; 17+3; with Me Me Me: Hanging Around, 1996; Other collaborations include: Donovan, Saint Etienne. *Address:* PO Box 2, Bromyard, Herefordshire HR7 4UU, England.

DUFORT, Denise; Musician (drums). *Career:* Mem., heavy metal band Girlschool, 1978–89; Introduced to management deal with Bronze label by Lemmy from Motörhead, 1980; Supported Motörhead on their Overkill tour; Numerous tours, television performances and hit singles; Further collaborations with Motörhead; Tours in Canada and the USA; Tour of Russia, supporting Black Sabbath; Formed band Strangegirls, with Toyah, Kim McAuliffe and Enid Williams; Girlschool re-formed, 1992. *Recordings:* Albums: Demolition, 1980; Hit 'N' Run, 1981; Screaming Blue Murder, 1982; Play Dirty, 1983; Running Wild, 1995; Nightmare At Maple Cross, 1986; Take A Bite, 1988; Girlschool, 1992; Live, 1995; Race With The Devil (Live), 1998; Live On The King Biscuit Flower Hour, 1998; Can't Keep A Good Girl Down, 1999; Very Best Of Remastered, 2002; 21st Anniversary: Not That Innocent, 2002. Singles: Take It All Away; Race With The Devil; St Valentine's Day Massacre (EP with Motörhead, as Headgirl); Please Don't Touch, 1981; Hit And Run, 1981; C'mon Let's Go, 1981; I'm The Leader Of The Gang (I Am) (with Gary Glitter). *Address:* c/o PO Box 33446, London SW18 3XN, England. *Website:* www.girlschool.co.uk.

DUGMORE, Geoff; Musician (drums); Songwriter; Prod. 1 s. *Compositions:* The Europeans, Vocabulary LP, Live LP and Recurring Dreams LP; Wildlife, Wildlife LP. *Recordings:* Played on records for: Deborah Harry; Stevie Nicks, US No. 1; Killing Joke; Tina Turner, UK No. 1 Foreign Affair; Jeff Beck; Gabrielle, both albums; Art of Noise; Gypsy Kings; Zoe; Rod Stewart; Joan Armatrading; Underworld; Tim Finn; Bob Geldof; Dido, Natalie Imbruglia; Heather Nova, Robbie Williams, Russell Watson; Produced records for: Wildlife; Deborah Harry; Belouis Some; Boss Beat; Sonny Roche; Jason Feddy. *Current Management:* One Management, 43 St Alban's Ave, London W4 5JS, England.

DUJMIC, Ratko; b. 7 Aug. 1954, Zagreb, Croatia. Musician (piano, violin, electronic keyboards). m. Snjezana Simek-Dujmic, 2 Dec. 1990, 1 s. *Education:* Music Academy, Theory of Music and Pedagogy. *Career:* Fourth and sixth places, Eurovision Song Contests, 1987, 1988; Winner, Eurovision song contest, 1989; Sold 38m. recordings; 4 solo television shows; 1 film score, much theatre music; Large number world tours include Opera House, Sydney, Australia. *Compositions:* About 800 works, many compositions for children and TV Series. *Recordings:* Around 90, audio and video, world-wide. *Honours:* All Festivals in former Yugoslavia. *Membership:* Union Professional Musicians; Society of Composers, Croatia (DHS). *Current Management:* Croatia Records; Avet Publishing Company. *Address:* LL Maksimirsko Naselje I/V, 41000 Zagreb, Croatia.

DUKE, George; b. 12 Jan. 1946, San Rafael, California, USA. Jazz Musician (keyboards); Composer. *Education:* Piano lessons at school; BMus, San Francisco Conservatory, 1967. *Career:* Keyboardist, recording artist, 1966–; Accompanist, Dizzy Gillespie, 1965–67; Jean Luc Ponty, 1969; Member, Frank Zappa's Mothers of Invention, 1970–75; Formed jazz-fusion duos with Billy Cobham and Stanley Clarke; Also played with Cannonball Adderley; Bobby Hutcherson; Airto and Flora Purim; John Scofield; Lee Ritenour; Paulinho Da Costa; Major concerts include Nelson Mandela Tribute, Wembley. *Recordings:* Albums include: Save The Country, 1969; George Duke, 1969; The Inner Source, 1971; Inner Source, 1973; Feel, 1974; Faces In Reflection, 1975; I Love The Blues She Heard Me Cry, 1975; The Aura Will Prevail, 1975; Liberated Fantasies, 1976; Live In Europe, 1976; Solo Keyboard Album, 1976; From Me To You, 1977; Reach For It, 1977; Don't Let Go, 1978; Follow The Rainbow, 1979; Master of The Game, 1979; A Brazilian Love Affair, 1980; Dream On, 1982; Guardian of The Light, 1983; Secret Rendezvous, 1984; Thief In The Night, 1988; Night After Night, 1989; George Duke Collection, 1991; Snapshot, 1992; Muir Woods Suite, 1996; Three Originals, 1994; Illusions, 1995; Rendezvous, 1995; Is Love Enough, 1997; After Hours, 1998; Cool, 2000; Numerous albums with Stanley Clarke include: Clarke Duke Project, 1981; Clarke Duke Project 2, 1982; 3, 1990; with Jean Luc Ponty: Live In LA, 1971; with Frank Zappa: Apostrophe, 1972; Roxy and Elsewhere, 1975; with Billy Cobham: Crosswinds, 1974; Live In Europe, 1976; BC, 1979; with Miles Davis: Tutu, 1986; Also recordings by: Airto; George Benson; Billy Cobham; Aretha Franklin; Freddie Hubbard; Michael Jackson; Al Jarreau; Shalamar. *Current Management:* Herb Cohen Management. *Address:* 740 N LaBrea Ave, Los Angeles, CA 90038, USA.

DUKES, Rebecca W. (Becky); b. 21 Nov. 1934, Durham, North Carolina, USA. Vocalist; Musician (Piano); Songwriter. m. Charles A Dukes Jr, 20 Dec. 1955, 2 s., 1 d. *Education:* BA, Duke University; Vocal student with Todd Duncan. *Career:* Numerous stage performances including The Kennedy Center, Normandie Farm Lounge, Dulles Holiday Inn, The Castle, Thompson's Restaurant, Ocean City, Capitol Hill Club, Post Office Pavilion; Most recent stage show as feature artist for Philharmonic sponsored concert; Performed with US Navy Band commemorating 200 years of balloon flight in America; 2 cable specials, 1990s. *Compositions:* 47 individual compositions recorded. *Recordings include:* Alive, 1992; Rainbow, 1994; Borrow the Sun, 1995; Almost Country, 1999. *Publications:* Poetry published in several editions, 1992–94. *Honours:* 5 ASCAP Awards for Pop Writing, 1994–98; Numerous Awards, Mid-Atlantic Song Contest, 1984–92; American Women Composers' Song Contest Award; Billboard Award, For the Children of the World, 1996. *Membership:* ASCAP; NARAS; SAI; SAW; NSAI; FMMC. *Address:* 7111 Pony Trail, Hyattsville, MD 20782, USA.

DULFER, Candy; b. 19 Sept. 1969, Amsterdam, Netherlands. Musician (saxophone). *Education:* Soprano saxophone from age 7. *Career:* First recording with father Hans Dulfer, aged 11; Founder, jazz-funk group Funky Stuff, aged 15; Support to Madonna, Dutch tour, 1987; Prince, Dutch tour, 1988; Also played with: Van Morrison; Aretha Franklin; Pink Floyd; Dave Stewart. *Recordings:* Albums with Funky Stuff; Solo albums include: Saxuality, 1991; Sax-A-Go-Go, 1994; Big Girl, 1996; For the Love of You, 1997; What Does it Take, 1999; Girls Night Out, 2001; Also featured on We Too Are One, Eurythmics, 1989; Film soundtrack, De Kassiere, with Dave Stewart, 1990; Singles: with Prince: Party Man; with Dave Stewart: Lily Was Here (No. 1, Netherlands), 1990; 2 Funky, 1993; Gititon, 1997; Saxy Mood, 1998. *Address:* c/o Inge Dulfer, PC Hoofstraat 154, 1071 CG Amsterdam, Netherlands.

DUMBRECK, Allan M; b. 11 March 1961, Edinburgh, Scotland. Music Lecturer; Musician (keyboards). *Education:* BSc, Electrical Engineering, Edinburgh University. *Career:* Keyboard player, Big Dish, 1986–87; Horse, 1988–89; Lecturer, Jewel and Esk Valley College, 1986–91; North Glasgow College, 1991–98; University of Westminster, 1998–99; James Watt College, 1999–2001; University of Paisley, 2001–; Ariadne Publications, 1998–; Established HND Music, Performance and Promotion; NGM Records, 1993; NGM Publishing, 1994. *Recordings:* The Same Sky, Horse, 1990; Rifferama, Thrum, 1994. *Publications:* Music Education Directory, editor and compiler, 1996–. *Membership:* PRS. *Address:* c/o Ariadne Publications, 20 Kensington Gate, Glasgow G12 9LQ, Scotland.

DUMONT, Tom; b. 11 Jan. 1968, Los Angeles, CA, USA. Musician (guitar). *Career:* Mem., US group, No Doubt, 1988–. *Recordings:* Albums: No Doubt, 1992; Beacon Street Collection, 1994; Tragic Kingdom, 1995; Return Of Saturn, 2000; Rock Steady, 2001. Singles: Just A Girl, 1995; Don't Speak (No. 1, UK), 1997; New, 1999; Ex-Girlfriend, 2000; Simple Kind Of Life, 2000; Bathwater, 2000; Hey Baby, 2001; Hella Good, 2002; Tour (EP), 2002; Underneath It All, 2002. *Address:* c/o Interscope Records, 2220 Colorado Ave, Santa Monica, CA 90404, USA. *Website:* www.nodoubt.com.

DUNBAR, Sly (Noel Charles); b. 10 May 1952, Kingston, Jamaica. Reggae Musician (drums); Prod. *Career:* Played with: The Upsetter; Skin Flesh and Bones; The Revolutionaries; Member, houseband, Channel One label; Member, US rhythm partnership, Sly and Robbie, with Robbie Shakespeare, 1975–; Formed own record label Taxi; Prolific session musician with numerous artistes including: Peter Tosh; Bunny Wailer; Black Uhuru; Grace Jones; Bob Dylan; Ian Dury; Joan Armatrading; Buju Banton; Beenie Man; Dennis Brown; Jimmy Cliff; Mikey Dread; Gregory Isaacs; King Tubby; The Mighty Diamonds; Sugar Minott; U-Roy; Tours with Black Uhuru. *Recordings:* Solo albums: Simple Sly Man, 1978; Sly Wicked and Slick, 1979; Sly-Go-Ville, 1982; with Sly and Robbie: Sly and Robbie Present Taxi, 1981; A Dub Extravaganza, 1984; Language Barrier, 1985; Sly and Robbie Meet King Tubby, 1985; Reggae Greats, 1985; The Sound of Taxi, Vol. 1, Vol. 2, 1986; Rhythm Killers, 1987; Taxi Fare, 1987; Uhuru In Dub, 1987; The Summit, 1988; Hardcore Dub, 1989; Silent Assassin, 1990; Remember Precious Times, 1993; Mambo Taxi, 1997; Fatigue Chic, 1999; Dub Fire, 2000; In Good Company, 2001. *Current Management:* Starline Entertainment, 1045 Pomme de Pin Lane, New Port Richey, FL 34655, USA.

DUNCAN, Johnny (John Richard); b. 5 Oct. 1938, Dublin, Texas, USA. Country vocalist; Songwriter; Musician (guitar). *Education:* Texas Christian University, studied English. *Career:* Cousin of country singers Dan Seals and Jim Seals from pop duo Seals and Crofts; Moved from Dublin, Texas, to Clovis, New Mexico, 1959; Recorded demos with Norman Petty; Unsuccessfully promoted by Petty as pop singer, visiting England to have string section added to recordings; DJ on WAGG-Franklin radio station, Tennessee, 1964; Appeared on Nashville local TV shows with Ralph Emery; Spotted and signed by Columbia Records producer Don Law, 1967; Initial recordings produced by Frank Jones; Debut country chart entry, 1967; Minor hits until run of 9 consecutive country top ten hits (including 3 #1s), 1976–79; Collaborations: June Stearns; Janie Frickie (aka Janie Fricke). *Compositions include:* I'd Rather Love You; Summer Sunday; Fools; I Ain't All Bad; She's Too Good To Be True. *Recordings include:* Thinkin' of a Rendezvous, 1976; It Couldn't Have Been Any Better, Come A Little Bit Closer (with Janie Fricke), 1977; She Can Put Her Shoes Under My Bed (Anytime), Hello Mexico (and Adios Baby To You), 1978; Albums include: The Best of Johnny Duncan, 1976; Greatest Hits, 1978; In My Dreams, Nice 'N' Easy (with Janie Fricke), 1980. *Address:* c/o Country Music Asscn, 1 Music Circle S, Nashville, TN 37203, USA.

DUNCAN, Torey Atkins; b. 5 Aug. 1961, Summerfield, North Carolina, USA. *Career:* Regular Member, father's band, Bobby Atkins and the Countrymen; Recorded with father on Old Homestead Records, 10 years; Guest Starred, The Country Side of Bobby Atkins, album. *Recordings:* Enough to Keep Me Dreaming On; Lost Below Heaven. *Address:* c/o Bobby Atkins, PO Box 251, Summerfield, NC 27358–0251, USA.

DUNCKEL, Jean Benoit; b. Versailles, France. Prod; Keyboards. *Education:* Studied at the Conservatoire, Paris. *Career:* Formed Orange with Alex Gopher; Band joined by fellow Conservatoire student Nicolas Godin; After departure of Gopher from band, formed duo Air, 1995; Released debut single, 1996; Signed to Virgin and released their debut album, 1997; Collaborations: Jean Jacques Perrey; Francoise Hardy; Alex Gopher; Gordon Tracks; Remixed: Depeche Mode; Neneh Cherry. *Recordings:* Albums: Moon Safari, 1997; The Virgin Suicides, Premieres Symptoms, 1999; 10000 Hz Legend, 2001; Singles: Modulor, Casanova 70, 1996; Sexy Boy, 1997; Kelly Watch The Stars, 1998; Playground Love, 2000; Radio No. 1, 2001. *Address:* c/o Source Records, 113–117 Farringdon Rd, London EC1R 3BX, England.

DUNHAM, Aubrey; b. Houston, Texas, USA. Vocalist; Blues Musician (saxophone); Writer; Arranger; Prod. *Education:* BA, Musical Education, Texas Southern University. *Career:* Tours, performances with artists including: Wilton Felder; Johnny Clyde Copeland; The O'Jays; The Temptations; Roy Head; Hank Crawford; Leader, own band, Aubrey Dunham and The Party Machine; Writer, arranger, producer. *Recordings:* Album: Now I'm Singing The Blues, songs include: I Used To Be A Dog (hit single); Shot Gun; I'm Glad About My Good Time. *Membership:* Houston Blues Society. *Current Management:* Sirron Kyles, Samuel Rogers and Associates. *Address:* PO Box 8305, Houston, TX 77288, USA.

DUNKELMAN, Stephan; b. 7 May 1956, Brussels. Composer. m. 1 s., 1 d. *Compositions:* Signallures; Rituellipses; Metharcana; Thru, Above and Between, 1998; Dreamlike Shudder In An Airstream, 1999. *Recordings:* Acousnatica; Signallures; Aquaeray; Rituellipses. *Honours:* Stockholm Electronic Arts Award, mention, 1993; Stockholm Electronic Arts Award, for Metharcana, 1998; Ars Electronica, Special Mention. *Membership:* SACEM; SACD; ACSR; CEC. *Address:* Loutrier St 42, B 1170 Brussels, Belgium.

DUNKLEY, Craig Anthony Spencer; b. 25 March 1964, Leicester, England. Musician (percussion). *Education:* Artist in Education Course at Polytechnic. *Career:* Two week tour of Russia; Interview on Russian TV; 3 Week tour of Germany; 5 Day tour of Ireland; Local Radio sessions and interviews; Video shown on Channel 4 TV programme, D-Energy. *Recordings:* Album with TYD. *Honours:* Endorsed by Premier Percussion. *Membership:* Musicians' Union. *Current Management:* Access to Music; Big Wheel. *Address:* 86 Hopefield Rd, Leicester LE3 2BL, England.

DUNLOP, Andy; b. 16 March 1972, Scotland. Musician (guitar). *Career:* Mem., Travis, 1997–; Numerous tours, festivals and television appearances.

Recordings: Albums: Good Feeling, 1997; The Man Who (No. 1, UK), 1999; The Invisible Band (No. 1, UK), 2001. Singles: U16 Girls, 1997; All I Want To Do Is Rock, 1997; Tied To The Nineties, 1997; Happy, 1997; More Than Us, 1997; Writing To Reach You, 1999; Driftwood, 1999; Why Does It Always Rain on Me?, 1999; Turn, 1999; Coming Around, 2000; Sing, 2001; Side, 2001. *Honours:* Q Magazine Award, Best Single, 1999; Select Magazine, Album of the Year, 1999; BRIT Awards, Best British Group, Best British Album, 2000, Best British Group, 2002. *Address:* c/o Independiente Ltd, The Drill Hall, 3 Heathfield Terrace, London W4 4JE, England. *Website:* www.travisonline.com.

DUNMALL, Paul Norman; b. 6 May 1953, London, England. Musician (saxophones, woodwind, bagpipes). *Education:* Clarinet, Blackheath Conservatoire. *Career:* Tours, Europe with Marsupilami, 1970–71; USA with Blue Aquarius, 1972–74; USA/Europe tour with Johnny Guitar Watson; Tours of Europe in 1980s with: Spirit Level; Tenor Tonic; London Jazz Composers Orchestra; Danny Thompson; Mujician in Russia, 1991. *Recordings:* Ain't That A Bitch; Johnny Guitar Watson; Mice In The Wallet; Killer Bunnies; Spirit Level; Andy Sheppard; Journey; Poem About the Hero; Birdman; Industry; Bladek; Colours Fulfilled; Solo albums: Soliloquy, 1986; Bebop Starburst, 1999; East West North South, 2001. *Honours:* Best Soloist, Dunkirk Jazz Festival, 1979. *Membership:* PRS; MCPS. *Current Management:* Nod Knowles. *Address:* Linley House, 1 Pierre Pl., Bath, Avon BA1 1JY, England.

DUNN, Alan R; b. 19 Oct. 1955, Boothstown, Lancashire, England. Musician (accordion, keyboards, tinwhistles). m. Wendy Elizabeth, 6 Jan. 1984. *Career:* Musician for various projects with artistes include: Richard Thompson; Loudon Wainwright III; Bob Geldof; Rolf Harris; Vladimir Asriev; Tour with Toy Dolls, 1997–98. *Recordings:* Albums: Clannad: Magical Ring, 1983; Lyle McGuiness Band, 1983; Richard Thompson: Across a Crowded Room, 1985; Watching the Dark, 1993; Doom and Gloom, 1994; Toy Dolls, One More Megabyte; Alison Moyet, Essex, 1994; Rolf Harris, Can You Tell What It Is Yet?, 1997; John Tams, Unity, 2000. *Address:* 10 Holden House, Deptford Church St, London SE8 45Q, England.

DUNN, Gary Michael; b. 7 March 1960, Sunderland, England. Musician (guitar). *Career:* Tours, Europe and USA, including Glastonbury Festival (Pyramid stage); Reading Festival; Appearances at major concert halls including Dominion Theatre; Sadlers Wells; Town and Country Club; Television and radio appearances include: Whistle Test; Jools Holland. *Recordings:* Albums with: Martin Stephenson and the Dainties: Boat To Bolivia; Gladsome Humour and Blue; Salutation Road and The Boys Heart. *Membership:* Musicians' Union; PRS; MCPS. *Address:* 280 Fulwell Rd, Sunderland SR6 9AP, England.

DUNN, Holly S; b. 22 Aug. 1957, San Antonio, Texas, USA. Vocalist; Songwriter. *Education:* Bs, Abilene Christian University, 1979. *Career:* Today Show; Prime Time Country; Crook and Chase; Vicki Lawrence Show; Maury Povich; Hosted morning radio show; Host of Opry Backstage on TNN; Appeared on numerous country music specials and award shows. *Compositions:* Daddy's Hands; You Really Had Me Going; Love Someone Like Me; Are You Ever Gonna Love Me; Only When I Love; Strangers Again. *Recordings:* Albums, Holly Dunn; Cornerstone; Across The Rio Grande; The Blue Rose of Texas; Heart Full of Love; Getting It Done; Milestones-Greatest Hits; Life and Love and All The Stages; Leave One Bridge Standing; Maybe; A Face In The Crowd. *Honours:* Academy of Country Music, New Female Country Singer, 1986; Country Music Foundation, Horizon Award; BMI Songwriter of the Year, 1988. *Membership:* AFTRA; AFM; NARAS. *Current Management:* Refugee International Management. *Address:* 209 10th Ave S, Suite 347, Nashville, Tennessee 37203, USA.

DUNN, Ronnie Gene; b. 1 June 1953, Coleman, Texas, USA. Country vocalist; Prod; Songwriter. *Career:* Lead vocalist, country duo Brooks and Dunn (with Kix Brooks). *Compositions include:* Boot Scootin' Boogie; Brand New Man; Darned If I Don't – Danged If I Do; Hard Workin' Man; He's Got You; Honky Tonk Truth; I Can't Get Over You; I'll Never Forgive My Heart; A Man This Lonely; Little Miss Honky Tonk; My Next Broken Heart; Neon Moon; You'll Always Be Loved By Me; She's Not The Cheatin' Kind; She Used To Be Mine; That Ain't No Way To Go; We'll Burn That Bridge; Whiskey Under The Bridge; You're Gonna Miss Me When I'm Gone. *Recordings:* solo: It's Written All Over Your Face, 1983; She Put The Sad In All His Songs, 1984; as Brooks and Dunn: Brand New Man, 1991; My Next Broken Heart, 1991; Neon Moon, 1992; Boot Scootin' Boogie, 1992; Hard Workin' Man, 1993; We'll Burn That Bridge, 1993; She Used To Be Mine, 1993; Rock My World (Little Country Girl), 1993; That Ain't No Way To Go, 1994; She's Not The Cheatin' Kind, 1994; Little Miss Honky Tonk, 1995; You're Gonna Miss Me When I'm Gone, 1995; Whiskey Under The Bridge, 1995; My Maria, 1996; I Am That Man, 1996; A Man This Lonely, 1996; He's Got You, 1997; Honky Tonk Truth, 1997; How Long Gone, 1998; Husbands and Wives, 1998; I Can't Get Over You, 1999; You'll Always Be Loved By Me, 2000; Ain't Nothing 'Bout You, 2001; Only In America, 2001; The Long Goodbye, 2002; Albums include: Brand New Man, 1991; Hard Workin' Man, 1993; Waitin' On Sundown, 1994; Borderline, 1996; The Greatest Hits Collection, 1997; If You See Her, 1998; Tight Rope, 1999; Steers and Stripes, 2001. *Honours:* various including: CMA, Vocal Duo of the Year, 1993–98. *Website:* www.brooks-dunn.com.

DUPONT, Hubert; b. 5 May 1959, Versailles, France. Jazz Musician (contrebass); Composer. m. 13 Oct. 1990, 1 s. *Education:* Engineering diploma, INSA (Lyon); Master classes. *Career:* Played with: Steve Lacy; Glenn Ferris; Mathieu Michel; Harold Land; Robin Eubanks; Stefano Di Battista; Noël Akchoté; George Brown; Tommy Smith; Steve Potts; Laurent De Wilde; Le Marmite Infernale (ARFI); Mathias Rüegg; Paolo Fresu; Benoit Delbecq; Guillaume Orti. *Recordings:* Altissimo, Hubert Dupont; Pression, Kartet; A L'Envers, Quoi De Neuf Docteur. *Membership:* Collectif HASK; UMJ (Union des Musiciens de Jazz). *Address:* 9 Ave Pasteur, 93100 Montreuil, France.

DUPREE, Cornell; b. 19 Dec. 1942, Fort Worth, Texas, USA. Musician (guitar). m. Erma, 23 June 1959, 2 s., 1 d. *Education:* 1 year college; High School saxophone lessons. *Career:* Joined King Curtis Band, New York City, 1962, appeared with Jimi Hendrix, Chuck Rainey; Session player, more than 2500 records with artists including: Sam Cooke; Wilson Pickett; Miles Davis; Joe Cocker; Michael Bolton; Mariah Carey; Bonnie Raitt; Toured and recorded with Aretha Franklin, 1967–76; Tours with: Roberta Flack; Joe Cocker; Grover Washington Jr; Currently tours with Herbie Mann and The Deep Pocket Band; Early 70s, teamed with Richard Tee, Steve Gadd to form STUFF, house band for Saturday Night Live. *Recordings:* Albums: Teasin', 1973; Shadow Dancing, 1978; Guitar Groove, 1987; Coast to Coast, 1988; Can't Get Through, 1991; Child's Play, 1993; Bop 'n' Blues, 1994; Uncle Funky, 1998; Unstuffed, 1998; Double Clutch, 1998; Also appeared on: King Curtis: Soul Seranade; Brook Benton: Rainy Night In Georgia; Aretha Franklin: Live At Fillmore West; Joe Cocker: Sting Ray; Barbra Streisand: Guilty; Donny Hathaway: Live At the Bitter Inn; Stuff: Stuff. *Publications:* Coast To Coast; Happy Farms; Southern Comfort. *Membership:* NARA; ASCAP. *Current Management:* Fred Hirsch.

DURAL, Stanley 'Buckwheat', Jr; b. 14 Nov. 1947, Lafayette, Louisiana, USA. Musician (zydeco, accordion). m. Bernite Dural. *Career:* Professional musician from age 9; Formed Buckwheat and the Hitchikers, 1970s; Joined 'father of zydeco' Clifton Chenier, 1978–80; Formed Buckwheat Zydeco, 1979; Signed to Island Records, 1987 (first zydeco artist on major record label). *Recordings include:* Ma 'Tit Fille; What You Gonna Do; Also recorded with artists including: Eric Clapton; Willie Nelson; Dwight Yoakam; Keith Richards. *Current Management:* Ted Fox. *Address:* c/o Ted Fox, PO Box 561, Rhinebeck, NY 12572, USA.

DURHAM, Judith; b. 3 July 1943, Melbourne, Australia. Vocalist; Songwriter; Musician (piano, tambourine). m. Ron Edgeworth, 21 Nov. 1969, deceased 1994. *Education:* Secretarial course, Royal Melbourne Institute of Technology; AMusA, Piano, with Ronald Farren Price, Melbourne University, 1961. *Career:* First international female chart-topping recording artiste, 1965; Lead vocalist, folk pop group, The Seekers; Success following concert, Palladium, England, 1964; Royal Command Performance, 1966; Guinness Book of Records, for largest crowd in southern hemisphere; Highest ever rating, Australian TV show Seekers Down Under, 1967; The World of the Seekers (film), 1968; Group split, 1968; Solo artiste, 1967–. *Compositions:* Australia Land Of Today; Gotta Be Rainbows (musical); Colours Of My Life; One World Love; Calling Me Home; It's Hard To Leave; Songs on solo album, Let Me Find Love. *Recordings:* With The Seekers: I'll Never Find Another You (No. 1, UK), 1965; A World Of Our Own, 1965; The Carnival Is Over (No. 1, UK), 1965; Someday One Day, 1966; Walk With Me, 1966; Morningtown Ride, 1966; Georgy Girl, 1967; When Will The Good Apples Fall, 1967; Seven albums including Future Road, 1997; Solo albums include: Mona Lisas, 1996; Hot Jazz Duo, 2001; Onto Your Dream, 2001; Three solo jazz albums with husband. *Honours:* Australian of the Year (with The Seekers), 1967; Aria Hall of Fame, 1997; Medal of the Order of Australia. *Membership:* Patron, Motor Neurone Disease Asscn. *Address:* c/o Shelley Bovey, 90 Above Town, Glastonbury, Somerset BA6 8JG, England.

DURITZ, Adam; b. 1 Aug. 1964, Baltimore, Maryland, USA. Vocalist; Musician (piano). *Career:* Formed acoustic duo with David Bryson, later joined with Matt Malley, Charlie Gillingham and Steve Bowman to record a demo; Joined by Dan Vickrey and began recording as Counting Crows; Numerous live tours and TV appearances including several on MTV; Bowman left, replaced by Ben Mize. *Recordings:* Singles: Round Here, 1994; Mr Jones, 1994; Rain King, 1994; Angels of the Silence (live), 1996; Albums: August and Everything After, 1993; Recovering the Satellites, 1996; Across a Wire: Live in New York, 1998; Long December, 1999; Daylight Fading, 1999; Hard Candy, 2002; Appearances on: Sweet Relief: Benefit for Victoria, 1993; Nanci Griffith: Flyer, 1994; Wallflowers: Bringing Down the Horse, 1996; Dog's Eye View: Daisy, 1997; Ryan Adams: Gold, 2001.

DURRANT, Bertie (Brian); b. 25 July 1945, Gloucester, England. Jazz Musician (clarinet, soprano, tenor and baritone saxophones, blues harmonica). m. (1) Janice Newman, 1966; m. (2) Diane Thompson, 1976, 2 s., 1 d. *Education:* Mid-Essex Technical College; University of East London. *Career:* Industrial and advertising photographer; Professional musician, 1983–; Founder member, City Vagabonds (prize-winning Essex trad band); Numerous other bands including Tom Collins (4 years); Currently running own name line-up; tours, Europe; North America; Played jazz

festivals throughout UK. *Membership:* Asscn of British Jazz Musicians. *Address:* 23 Upper Moors, Great Waltham, Essex CM3 1RB, England.

DURRANT, Clare Joanne Mary; b. 2 Dec. 1962, Southport, England. Musician (keyboards, percussion, violin, guitar); Vocalist. *Education:* Lancaster University; Salford University College; Music lessons with John Hammond, Tommy Odueso, Wadada, Clare Hogan-Taylor, Salford University College. *Career:* Keyboard player for Suns of Arqa as Ireti, 1987–; Major concerts include: Womad Festival; Phoenix Festival; Hit The North, BBC Radio session; Set up Ireti Percussion workshops; Formed Otherworld, 1992. *Recordings:* Album: with Otherworld: Messages; Also tracks licensed for Compilations; with Suns of Arqa as Ireti: Hey Jagunath; Bhoopali (track part of BBC Radio 5 session Hit The North). *Address:* 52 Riverbank Tower, Salford M3 7JY, England.

DURRANT, Richard; b. 2 Nov. 1962, Brighton, England. Musician (Guitar, Mandolin, Banjo, Double Bass, Bodhran). m. Louise, 2 d., 1 s. *Education:* Royal College of Music. *Career:* Debut, Purcell Room, London, 1986; Prolific concert guitarist and recording artiste; Busy Multi Instrumentalist; Composer of Concert and Television Music. *Compositions:* Acoustic Rain; A Lowland Cinderella; The Rucenitsa Quartet; Exploring the Deep; The Early Learning Sonata. *Recordings:* Guitar Latina; The Music of Mario Castelnuovo-Tedesco; The Summer EP; Pandora. *Membership:* PRS; MCPS; MU. *Current Management:* LongMan. *Address:* West House, Forthaven, Shoreham By Sea, West Sussex BN43 5HY, England.

DURST, Fred (William Frederick); b. 20 Aug. 1970, Gastonia, North Carolina, USA. Vocalist; Record Co Exec; Prod; Music Video Dir. m. 1990, divorced, 1 s. *Career:* Senior Vice-Pres. of A&R, Interscope Records; Founder and owner, Flawless Records; Founding mem., Limp Bizkit, 1994–; Signed to Flip/Interscope on strength of demo tape; Live shows at concerts and festivals; Group spearheaded 'nu-metal' breakthrough in Europe, 2001; Solo artiste, 2001–. *Recordings:* Albums: Three Dollar Bill, Y'All $, 1997; Significant Other, 1999; Chocolate Starfish and The Hot Dog Flavored Water, 2000; New Old Songs (remix album), 2001; Singles: Faith, 1997; Nookie, Rearranged, 1999; Break Stuff, Take A Look Around (from Mission Impossible 2 OST), My Generation, 2000; Rollin', My Way, Boiler, 2001. *Honours:* Second and third albums both debuted at #1 on US chart; Significant Other sales in excess of 6m.; American Music Award, Favourite Alternative Artist, 2002. *Current Management:* The Firm (Management), 9100 Wilshire Blvd, Suite 400W, Beverly Hills, CA 90212, USA. *Website:* www.limpbizkit.com.

DUTIRO, Chartwell; b. 26 Dec. 1957, Bindura, Zimbabwe. Vocalist; Musician (mbira, saxophone, hosho); Songwriter. *Education:* Learned mbira from family; Later saxophone; SOAS, University of London, MMus in Ethnomusicology, 1998. *Career:* Played mbira in traditional ceremonies from early teens; Member: Rhodesia Prison Band; Thomas Mapfumo's Blacks Unlimited, 1988–94; Relocated to UK; Formed Spirit Talk Mbira; Teaches mbira, singing and percussion at School of Oriental and African Studies. *Recordings:* Albums include: with Thomas Mapfumo: Zimbabwe – Mozambique, 1988; Chamunorwa, 1990; with Spirit Talk Mbira: Ndonga Mahwe – Return As Spirit, 1997; Nhimbe, 1998; Dzoro, 1999; Voices of Ancestors, 2000. *Address:* c/o Rachel Levay, Ingoma, 52 Picton St, Bristol, BS6 5QA, England. *E-mail:* rachel@ingoma.co.uk. *Website:* www.dham.net/soe/stm.

DUTOT, Pierre; b. 11 June 1946, Caen, France. Musician (trumpet); Trumpet teacher. m. Catherine Groult, 21 June 1975, 1 s., 2 d. *Education:* CAPEPS in EPS; DUEL in Psychology; Premier Prix Conservatoire National Supérieur de Musique, Paris, 1971. *Career:* Solo trumpeter, National Orchestra of Lyon; Professor CNSM Lyon and CNR Bordeaux ; Solo concert artiste; Tutor, international Master Classes; Member, numerous ensembles: Hexagone; Trompolis; Polygone; Jericho. *Recordings:* 10 albums as solo artiste; Recordings with: Hexagone; Trompolis; Polygone. *Current Management:* Concept Music BPZ, 69126 Brindas-Lyon, France. *Address:* Domaine des Cerisiers, 105 Chemin du Soyard, 69126 Brindas-Lyon, France.

DUVIVIER, Jérôme; b. 9 Oct. 1965, St Cloud, France. Jazz Vocalist. *Education:* Little Singers of Paris; Lessons with Stephanie Crawford, Michelle Hendricks. *Career:* Concerts in jazz clubs, France: Le Sunset; Le Petit Journal Montparnasse. *Recordings:* Un Effet Boeuf; L'Ennui; Courtoisies; Epilogue. *Honours:* Prix de la SACEM, Crest Festival. *Membership:* Jazz on the Blocks (French Jazz Singers Asscn). *Address:* 29 rue Basfroi, 75011 Paris, France.

DVORAK, Jim; b. 16 Dec. 1948, New York, NY, USA. Musician (trumpet); Composer; Teacher. *Education:* Eastman School of Music. *Career:* Regular international jazz festivals and concert tours; Connected with South African musicians, including Brotherhood of Breath, District Six, Zila, 1970s–80s; Also played with: Dreamtime; In Cahoots; Leader, own band Bardo State Orchestra; Workshop leader with Community Music, London; Major tour of Netherlands with Bardo State Orchestra and with Tibetan Gyuto Monks, 1998. *Compositions include:* Score for jazz drama Animal Farm, 1979; Co-writer, score for Kosh Theatre Company's production, The Jago, 1983. *Recordings:* with District Six: Aguzwakale; Ingoma Yabantwana; Leave My Name At The Door; To Be Free; with Annabel Lamb: Once Bitten; The Flame; When Angels Travel; Brides; Justice; with In Cahoots: Live In Japan; Recent Discoveries; Parellel; with Research: Laws of Motion; Social Systems; with Harry Moscoe: Country Boy; Sexy Dancer; Bunny Up, Dreamtime; Innocence, Joe Gallivan; Mama, Mama Quartetto; Gland, Fonolite; Joy, Joy; Thunder In Our Hearts, Jabula; Stanislav Sojka, Stanislav Sojka; Gasoline Band, Gasoline Band; Hat Music, Katie Perks; This Isn't Sex, Eric Mingus; Newsense, Elton Dean; The Covenant, Wally Brill; Zenfish, Dreamtime. *Honours:* Young Jazz Musicians Award, Greater London Arts, 1976; Bachelor of Music. *Membership:* Performing Right Society; Composers Guild. *Address:* 43B Mulkern Rd, London N19 3HQ, England.

DVORSKY, Petr; b. 29 June 1966, Czech Republic. Musician (double bass). *Education:* Conservatory of Jaroslav Jezek. *Career:* Brecon Jazz Festival, 1996; Festival Pragues Spring, 1994; Festival Liege, Belgium, 1998; Mem., Radio Prague Bigband, 2002–. *Recordings:* The Four: Space and Rhythm; Stever Houben, Buhemia After Dark; Roman Pokorny, Jazz Perception. *Membership:* Czech Society Jazz Society. *Address:* Veleslavinska 43, 162 00 Prague 6, Czech Republic.

DVORZAK, Zlatko; b. 5 March 1939, Zagreb, Croatia. Musician (piano); Composer; Conductor; Arranger; Teacher. m. Gordana Dvorzak, Oct. 1970, 1 s., 1 d. *Education:* Zagreb Musical Academy, graduated 1970. *Career:* Tours of Poland; Bulgaria; Russia; Hungary; Austria; Germany, 1961–76; Played and recorded with: Ernie Wilkins; Clark Terry; Art Farmer; Albert Mangelsdorff; Kai Winding; John Lewis; Bosco Petrovic; Stan Getz; Bud Shank; Al Porcino; Lee Harper; Sal Nistico; Gianni Basso; Ozren Depolo; Dusko Gojkovic; Johnny Griffin; Also performed music for radio and television. *Compositions include:* Revue; Amoroso; Clarinetorama; Black Street; All That Swing; Discopathia; Fender Express; Mr Hammond; Trumpet Swing; Jazz Concertino for String Quartet and Jazz Sextet; Croatian Folk Motives. *Recordings:* with BP Convention Big Band: Blue Sunset, 1975; Green Lobster Dream, 1978; Josipa Lisac and BP Convention, 1975; Croatian Big Band, 1977. *Honours:* First Prize, Contest for Young Pianists, Croatia, 1958; Best Arrangement, Belgrade Pop Festival, 1971. *Membership:* Croatian Composers' Society; Orchestras Society; Jazz Club, Zagreb. *Address:* Buconjiceva 26, 10000 Zagreb, Croatia.

DWECK, Sydney Stevan; b. 28 Dec. 1926, New York, NY, USA. Musician. Divorced, 2 s. *Education:* AA, honours, Los Angeles Valley College, 1966; BA, honours, California State University at Northridge, 1968; PhD, University of Southern California, 1977. *Career:* Freelance drummer and percussionist, Broadway shows including Hello Dolly, fiddler on the Roof, Kismet, Pajama Game; Film soundtracks include: Double Trouble, The Swinger, Made in Paris; Percussionist, TV Specials including Bob Hope, Lucille Ball, Perry Como, Fred Astaire, Perry Mason, Liberace; Albums include Stan Kenton, Freddy Martin, Jack Jones; Musical Director, artists including Debbie Reynolds, Carol Channing, Liza Minelli, Jane Russell; Command performances for Royal Family of Monaco, England, Presidents Kennedy, Johnson, Nixon, Bush, Reagan. *Compositions:* Scores, Altoon's Dance, 1965; Danny Thomas Show. *Membership:* American Federation of Musicians; Masonic lodge. *Address:* 1507 Seacrest Dr., Corona Del Mar, CA 92625, USA.

DYENS, Roland; b. 19 Oct. 1955, Tunis, Tunisia. Musician (guitar); Composer (classic-fusion style). m. Claire Fischbein, 7 Sept. 1986, 1 s., 1 d. *Education:* Concert degree, Ecole Normale de Musique de Paris. *Career:* Concert artist playing throughout world; Guitar festivals include: Nice; Cannes; Paris; Festival du Marais (Paris); Aix En Provence; Radio France Festival, Montpellier; Midem; Printemps de Bourges; Musicora; Carrefour Mondial De La Guitare (Martinique); Liège (Belgium); Arvika (Sweden); Tichy (Poland); Estergom (Hungary); Marktoberdorf (Germany); Classical Guitar Festival of Great Britain; Tours: Middle East; Indonesia; Scandinavia; Poland; Brazil; Numerous television and radio shows; Composer and arranger; Teacher; Member of juries of international contests including Montélimar; Geneva; Fort de France; Bari. *Compositions include:* Works for guitar solo; 2 octets; Concerto Métis (for guitar and string orchestra); Concerto En Si (for guitar and ensemble of 21 guitars). *Recordings:* Heitor Villa-Lobos Preludes and Roland Dyens works; Hommage à Brassens with the Enesco Quartet and Roland Dyens works; Ao Vivo (jazz trio); Suite Populaire Brésilienne, Heitor Villa-Lobos (concerto for guitar and string orchestra); French Songs Vols 1 and 2; Concerto En Si (for guitar and ensemble of 21 guitars). *Honours:* Grand Prix du Disque, Academie Charles-Cros. *Membership:* SACEM; ADAMI.

DYLAN, Bob, (Robert Allen Zimmerman); b. 24 May 1941, Duluth, Minnesota, USA. Vocalist; Musician (guitar, piano, harmonica, autoharp); Poet; Composer. *Career:* Solo folk/rock artist, also performed with The Band;

The Traveling Wilburys; Grateful Dead; Songs recorded by estimated 3000 artists, including U2, Bruce Springsteen, Rod Stewart, Jimi Hendrix, Eric Clapton, Neil Young; Numerous tours: USA, Europe, Australia, 1961–; Film appearances include: Pat Garrett and Billy The Kid; Concert For Bangladesh; Hearts of Fire. *Compositions include:* Blowin' In The Wind; Like A Rolling Stone; Mr Tambourine Man; Lay Lady Lay; Forever Young; Tangled Up In Blue; Gotta Serve Somebody; Don't Think Twice; It's Alright; A Hard Rain's Gonna Fall; The Times They Are A-Changin'; Just Like A Woman; I'll Be Your Baby Tonight; I Shall Be Released; Simple Twist of Fate; Paths of Victory; Dignity. *Recordings:* Over 40 albums include: The Freewheelin' Bob Dylan, 1964; Bringing It All Back Home, 1965; Highway 61 Revisited, 1965; Blonde On Blonde, 1966; John Wesley Harding, 1968; Nashville Skyline, 1969; Self Portrait, 1970; New Morning, 1970; Before The Flood, 1974; Hard Rain, 1976; Desire, 1976; Street Legal, 1978; Slow Train Coming, 1979; Infidels, 1983; Empire Burlesque, 1985; Knocked Out Loaded, 1986; Down In The Groove, 1988; Biograph (5 record set), 1988; Oh Mercy, 1989; Under The Red Sky, 1990; MTV Unplugged, 1995; Time Out of Mind, 1997; Love and Theft, 2001; with The Band: Planet Waves, 1974; Blood On The Tracks, 1975; with Traveling Wilburys: Traveling Wilburys, 1988; Vol. 3, 1990; with Grateful Dead, Dylan and The Dead, 1989; Singles include: One Too Many Mornings, 1965; Mr Tambourine Man, 1966; Love Sick, 1997. *Publications:* Tarantula, 1966; Writings and Drawings, 1973; The Songs of Bob Dylan 1966–75, 1976; Lyrics 1962–85, 1986. *Honours:* Hon. D Mus, Princeton University, 1970; Inducted, Rock and Roll Hall of Fame, 1988; Grammy, 1990. *Current Management:* Jeff Rosen, PO Box 870, Cooper Station, New York, NY 10276, USA.

DYNNESEN, Lise Kruuse; b. 24 Dec. 1956, Copenhagen, Denmark. Musician (piano, keyboards); Composer (church organ, piano). *Education:* University studies: Danish Literature; Music; Student, organ, Royal Danish Academy of Music, 1991–. *Career:* Freelance musician, composer, experimental, rhythmic music scene, Copenhagen, 1978–; Bands include: Primi Band with Marilyn Mazur, 1982–85; Salsanama, 1988–91. *Compositions:* Sleigh Song – Or Minea's Tale, for organ, 1994. *Honours:* Scholarships from: The Art Foundation of The Danish State; The Royal Danish Academy of Music; The Society of Danish Jazz Beat Folk Authors (DJBFA). *Membership:* DJBFA. *Address:* Bregnegangen 5, 2300 Copenhagen S, Denmark.

DYRASON, Orri Päll; b. Iceland. Musician (drums). *Career:* Mem., Icelandic band, Sigur Rös; Signed to MCA/Universal, USA, FatCat Records, UK; Music featured in film, Vanilla Sky, 2001; North American tour, 2001; European tour, 2002. *Recordings:* Albums: Von; Agœtis Byrjun, 2000; ( ), 2002. Singles: Ny Batteri, 2000; Svefn-G-Englar, 2001; Contributed to: Angels of the Universe (soundtrack), 2001. *Honours:* Shortlist Music Prize, 2001. *Address:* c/o FatCat Records, PO Box 3400, Brighton BN1 4WG, England. *Website:* www.sigur-ros.com.

DYSON, John; b. 11 March 1948, Sheffield, England. Musician (keyboards, guitar); Music Prod; Analytical Chemist. *Education:* Technical college. *Career:* Formed Wavestar (electronic music), with Dave Ward-Hunt, 1983; Concerts include: UK Electronica '85, Sheffield; Concerts throughout UK; Festivals in France; Record label folded, band split 1988; Formed UK Label Surreal to Real with current partner/director Anthony Thrasher; Played major Dutch Festival, 1990–92; Now established as UK's leading independent label for contemporary instrumental/synthesizer music. *Recordings:* with Wavestar: Mind Journey; Zenith; Moonwind; Solo: Evolution; Aquarelle; Different Values; Various others for compilation; Wavestar albums re-released on own label. *Honours:* Voted Best Newcomer, National German Radio E M Show, 1991. *Membership:* PRS; MU. *Current Management:* Surreal To Real. *Address:* PO Box 33 Evesham, Worcestershire WR11 6UX, England.

DZIERZANDWSKI, Udo; b. 23 June 1964. Musician (Guitar). *Education:* Guitar Craft, 1987. *Career:* International Touring, Europa String Choir; CD, The Starving Moon; Appearance on John Schaeffa's New Sounds Programme, New York; Local and National Radio, England, Italy and Germany. *Recordings:* The Starving Moon, 1995; Real Promo Demo, 1998. *Address:* 95 Albert Rd, Parkstone, Poole, Dorset BH12 2BX, England.

DZIUBINSKI, Tomasz; b. 14 Sept. 1961, Katowice, Poland. Artist Man; Promoter. m. Mariola Bractawik, 27 Dec. 1990, 2 s. *Education:* Building Engineer, Technical University. *Career:* Promoter for: Deep Purple; AC/DC; Metallica; Black Sabbath; Fish; Chris Rea; Europe; Slayer; Paradise Lost; Sepultura; Faith No More; Dr Alban; Biohazard. *Recordings:* Produced over 20 albums of best Polish heavy metal bands including: Acid Drinkers; Kat; Turbo; Flapjack; Dynamind. *Membership:* IFPI; ILMC. *Address:* ul Szeligiewicza 8/21, 40–044 Katowice, Poland.

E

EARL SIXTEEN, (Earl Daley); b. 9 May 1958, Kingston, Jamaica. Songwriter; Vocalist; Record Prod. Seperated, 2 s. *Career:* Producer for L. Perry; Mikey Dread; Derrick Harriott; Neil Frazer; Douglas; Soundtrack of Judge Dredd with Leftfield; Currently touring with Dreadzone Band; Major Concert, Glastonbury, 1995. *Compositions include:* Love Is A Feeling, Studio One; Release The Pressure. *Recordings:* Solo albums include: Reggae Sound, 1981; Babylon Walls, 1992; Also appears on: World War Three, Mikey Dread, 1980; Holding Back The Years (single), Simply Red, 1985; Leftism, Leftfield, 1995; Second Light, Dreadzone, 2001. *Honours:* Silver disc, Leftfield album. *Membership:* PRS; Musicians' Union; MCPS. *Current Management:* Martin Poole. *Address:* 30 Jackson Rd, Holloway, London N7, England.

EARLE, Steve; b. 17 Jan. 1955, Fort Monroe, VA, USA. Vocalist; Songwriter; Musician (guitar). m. Lou Anne. *Career:* Bar room musician, Nashville; Solo artiste, with own band The Dukes, 1986–. *Compositions include:* My Old Friend The Blues, recorded by Janie Frickie; The Devil's Right Hand, recorded by Waylon Jennings; The Rain Came Down, for Farm Aid II benefit concert. *Recordings:* Albums: Guitar Town, 1986; Early Tracks, 1987; Exit O, 1987; Copperhead Road, 1988; The Hard Way, 1990; Shut Up And Die Like An Aviator, 1991; Essential Steve Earle, 1993; Train A Comin', 1995; I Feel Alright, 1996; El Corazón, 1997; The Mountain, 1999; Transcendental Blues, 2000; Together At The Bluebird Cafe, 2001; Sidetracks, 2002; Jerusalem, 2002. *Current Management:* Asgard Management, London, England; Four Twenty Two Management, Nashville, USA. *Address:* Dan Gillis Management, 1815 Division St, Suite 205, Nashville, TN 37203, USA.

EARLY, David; b. 6 April 1956, Lewisham, London, England. Musician (drums, ethnic hand, atmospheric, percussion). *Career:* Recording, performance with Mud; Dollar; National Youth Jazz Orchestra; The Nolans; Spitting Image; Sade; Andy White; Maura O'Connell; The Chieftains; Chris Rea; Van Morrison; Mary Black; Kieran Goss and Francis Black; Brian Kennedy; Carmena; Tamalin. *Recordings:* with Sade: Diamond Life; Promise; with Van Morrison: Avalon Sunset; Enlightenment; Greatest Hits Vol. 1; Hymns To The Silence; Live From The Beacon Theatre; Carrying A Torch; Tom Jones/Van Morrison; Francis Black and Kieran Goss; with Tom Moore: Gorgeous and Bright; with Mary Black: The Holy Ground; The Circus. *Membership:* The Legendary Unknowns. *Address:* Belfast, Northern Ireland.

EASTON, Sheena, (Sheena Shirley Orr); b. 27 April 1959, Bellshill, Glasgow, Scotland. Vocalist; Actress. m. Rob Light, 15 Jan. 1985. *Education:* Speech and Drama, Royal Scottish Academy of Music and Drama. *Career:* Singer, Glasgow club circuit, 1979; Featured in television series The Big Time, BBC1, 1980; Solo recording artiste, 1980–; Concerts and tours world-wide, including: Royal Variety Show, 1980; The Big Day festival, Glasgow, 1990; Television appearances include: TV special, Sheena Easton... Act 1, NBC, 1983; Actress, Miami Vice, NBC, 1987; Stage debut, Man of La Mancha, Chicago, then Broadway, 1991–92; Launched own Seven Minute Flat Stomach fitness video. *Recordings:* Albums: Sheena Easton, 1981; You Could Have Been With Me, 1981; Madness Money and Music, 1982; Best Kept Secret, 1983; A Private Heaven, 1985; Do You, 1985; The Lover In Me, 1989; For Your Eyes Only – The Best of Sheena Easton, 1989; The Collection, 1989; What Comes Naturally, 1991; No Strings, 1993; My Cherie, 1995; Body and Soul, 1997; Freedom, 2000; Fabulous, 2000; Hit singles include: Modern Girl, 1980; Morning Train (9 To 5) (No. 1, USA), 1981; One Man Woman, 1981; When He Shines, 1981; For Your Eyes Only, theme music to James Bond film, 1981; We've Got Tonight, duet with Kenny Rogers, 1983; Telefone, 1983; Strut, 1984; Sugar Walls, 1985; U Got The Look, duet with Prince, 1987; The Lover In Me (No. 2, USA), 1989; What Comes Naturally, 1991; You Can Swing It, 1991; To Anyone, 1991; Contributor, Voices That Care charity record, 1991; Givin' Up Givin' In, 2001; Contributor, film soundtracks: Santa Claus – The Movie, 1985; About Last Night, 1986; Ferngully... The Last Rainforest, 1992. *Honours:* Grammy Awards: Best New Artist, 1982; Best Mexican/American Performance, with Luis Miguel, 1985; First artist in history to have Top 5 hits in all major US charts (Pop, R&B, Country, Dance, Adult Contemporary), 1985; Emmy Award, Sheena Easton... Act 1, 1983. *Current Management:* Harriet Wasserman Management, 15250 Ventura Blvd, Suite 1215, Sherman Oaks, CA 91403–3201, USA.

EASTWOOD, Al 'Bama'; b. 26 Oct. 1943, Birmingham, England. Musician (guitar, flute, drums, harmonica); Vocalist. *Career:* Played drums, rock and roll bands; Member, backing group for Gene Vincent; Television, radio include: Thank Your Lucky Stars; Beat Club, BBC; Jazz FM; John Cirl Show; Paul Jones Show; American radio. *Recordings:* Album: Seeds; Album and single (own compositions). *Membership:* Musicians' Union. *Address:* 104 Maughn Court, Palmerston Rd, Acton, London W3, England.

EASY MO'T'. See: **MOTEN, Frank, Jr.**

EATON, Christopher; b. 16 Sept. 1958, Dudley, West Midlands, England. Vocalist; Songwriter; Musician (keyboards). *Education:* Grade 6 Piano. *Career:* Songwriter for: Cliff Richard; Janet Jackson; Amy Grant; Sheena Easton; Patti Austin; Michael Ball; CeCe Winans; Sheila Walsh; Tours with Amy Grant and Cliff Richard; Performed at Grammy Awards, New York, 1992; Solo recording career, contemporary Christian and pop music. *Compositions include:* songs for Heat In Motion, Amy Grant (5m. copies sold); Saviours Day, Cliff Richard, (No. 1, UK), 1990. *Recordings:* Solo albums: Vision, 1986; Wonderful World, 1995; What Kind of Love, 1998. *Honours:* Christian Song of the Year, Breath of Heaven, 1993, USA. *Membership:* Musicians' Union; Equity. *Current Management:* Stuart Ongley, SGO Music. *Address:* The Old Brewery, Church St, Tisbury, Wilts, England.

EATON, Nigel; b. 3 Jan. 1966, Southampton, Hampshire, England. Musician (hurdy-gurdy). *Education:* Guildhall School of Music. *Career:* Member, Blowzabella, 1985–90; Ancient Beatbox, 1990; Whirling Pope Joan, 1993–; Robert Plant and Jimmy Page, 1995–; Also with Howard Skempton: Hurdy-gurdy Concerto; Bournemouth Sinfonietta, 1994; BBC Welsh Symphony, 1992; Aldeburgh Festival with Scottish Chamber Orchestra; Films: Aliens; Friends; Harnessing Peacocks; Mansfield Park, 1999; The Hunchback of Notre Dame, 1999; Video: Snub TV, 1989, VHI, 1995. *Recordings:* 5 albums, Blowzabella; Album: Ancient Beatbox; Spin, Whirling Pope Joan, 1994; Unledded, MTV; No Quarter, Plant and Page, 1995; Sessions for: Marc Almond, 1987; Loreena McKennitt, 1994; Scott Walker, 1995; Gary Kemp, 1995; Peter Gabriel, 1999; Loreena McKennitt, 1999; Afro-Celt Sound System, 1999; Solo: Music Of The Hurdy-Gurdy, 1987. *Address:* 15 Becondale Rd, Upper Norwood, London SE19 1QJ, England.

EAVIS, Michael; Farmer; Glastonbury Festival Organizer and Host. *Career:* Founder, Pilton Festival, 1970, renamed Glastonbury Fayre, 1971, later renamed Glastonbury Festival. *Address:* Worthy Farm, Pilton, Shepton Mallett, Somerset BA4 4BY, England. *E-mail:* worthy@glastonburyfestivals.co.uk. *Website:* www.glastonburyfestivals.co.uk.

EBB, Fred; b. 4 Aug. 1936, New York, NY, USA. Songwriter; Lyricist. *Education:* NYU graduate; Columbia University Masters. *Career:* Lyrics for: Cabaret; Flora; The Red Menace; Zorba; Happy Time; 70, Girls, 70; Woman of the Year; The Rink; Kiss of the Spider Woman; Chicago; The Act; And the World Goes Round. *Compositions:* Steel Pier, 1997. *Honours:* 3 Tonys; 4 Emmys; 1 Grammy; Songwriters Hall of Fame; Peabody and Ace Awards; Kennedy Center Award, 1998. *Membership:* BMI Dramatics Guild; AFTRA; Equity. *Current Management:* Sam Cohn, ICM, 40 W 57 St, New York, USA. *Address:* 146 Central Park W, New York City, New York, USA.

EBBAGE, Leonard Charles; b. 21 Aug. 1931, Gorleston-on-Sea, England. Bandleader; Musician (keyboards, accordion). m. (1) Hazel Brown 13 June 1953, 3 s.; m (2) Gwen Leach, 1 July 1981, 1 d. *Education:* Piano lessons, 5 years; 20 years working in holiday camps. *Career:* Broadcast with Hughie Green and Opportunity Knocks; Over 20 full summer seasons for Pontins; Ladbrooks; Holimarine; Warners; Walk-on, BBC and ITV; Now one of the top sequence dance bands in the country, playing short break dance holidays and sequence festivals all over England. *Recordings:* Albums: Goody-Goody; 50 Years of Dancing; Dancing Time; Sequence and Party Dances; Say It With Music. *Honours:* Played for Carl Alan Awards, 1994. *Membership:* Musicians' Union; Equity. *Address:* Rosanne, Dyers End, Stambourne, nr Halstead, Essex CO9 4NE, England. *Website:* www.danceholidays.org.

ECCLES, Albert; b. 25 June 1940, Aston, Birmingham. Musician (Bass Guitar). 3 s. *Career:* Ready Steady Go; Top of the Pops; 1966 Beatle Tour. *Compositions:* Decca. *Recordings:* Go Now; Easy Child; Bottom of My Heart; Everyday; This Is My House; Magnificent Moodies. *Honours:* Gold Discs. *Membership:* Musicians' Union.

ECKERT, John Wallace; b. 13 March 1939, New York, USA. Musician (trumpet, horns). *Education:* BA, Music, University of Rochester, 1961. *Career:* Musician with Stan Kenton; Si Zentner; American Brass Quintet; Buddy Morrow; Maynard Ferguson; Ten Wheel Drive; Deodato; Simon and Garfunkel; Benny Goodman; Gerry Mulligan; Toshiko Akiyoshi Jazz Orchestra, 1984–; American Jazz Orchestra, 1988–; Buck Clayton, 1989–. *Recordings:* Albums include: Brief Replies, Ten Wheel Drive, 1970; Chris Williamson, Chris Williamson, 1971; Whirlwinds, Deodato, 1974; Concert In Central Park, Simon and Garfunkel, 1981.

ECKERT, Vojtech; b. 27 Jan. 1956, Prague, Czechoslovakia. m. Iva Hanusova, 7 March 1997. *Education:* Faculty of Medicine, Charles University; Private Student of famous Czech Jazzman Karel Velebny. *Career:* Played piano, from age 4; Multi-instrumentalist, since age 15; Leader of many groups, since age 15; Established top Czech Jazz Trio in Prague, 1983.

Compositions: CD Blues; A First Piece; Humoresque From Phillips' Hill; Hammond Intermezzo; Blues for Unknown Queen. *Recordings:* CD with CSABA DESEO, Magic Violin, 1995; LP Eva Olmerova, 1986; Radio records, 1986–; Svatopluk Kosvanec, CD, 1998. *Publications:* Regular articles from sphere of jazz criticism and education in monthly periodical, Muzikus, 1992–95. *Membership:* Czech Jazz Society. *Address:* MUDr Vojtech Eckert, Balbinova 5, 120 00 Prague 2, Czech Republic.

E-DANCER. See: **SAUNDERSON, Kevin.**

EDDIE, (Jon Edwards); b. 1 April 1951, Hampstead, London, England. Musician (drums, percussion). m. Dee Dee, 3 Nov. 1989, 1 s., 1 d. *Education:* Studies with Joel Rothman. *Career:* Member, The Vibrators; Member, The Inmates; Numerous television and radio appearances world-wide, including Top of the Pops. *Recordings:* Albums: 14 albums with The Vibrators include: Pure Mania; V2 (UK Top 30); Hunting For You; 25 Years of Pure Mania (compilation), 2001; 10 albums with The Inmates include: First Offence (US Top 30); Five; Fast Forward; Singles include: Dirty Water; The Walk; Also recorded with: Chris Spedding; PIL; Christophe J; Garrie Lammin. *Membership:* Musicians' Union. *Address:* 16 Crouch Hill, London N4 4AU, England.

EDDY, Duane; b. 26 April 1938, Corning, New York, USA. Musician (guitar); Songwriter; Prod. m. Miriam Johnson, Aug. 1961. *Career:* Bandleader, The Rebels, 1958; Appearances include: British tour, with Bobby Darin, Clyde McPhatter, Emile Ford, 1960; British tour, 1967; First Rock 'n' Roll Show, London, 1968; US tour, with band including Ry Cooder, 1983; Film appearances; Because They're Young, 1960; The Savage Seven, 1967; Kona Coast, 1967. *Recordings:* Albums: Have Twangy Guitar Will Travel, 1959; Especially For You, 1959; The Twang's The Thang, 1960; Songs of Our Heritage, 1960; A Million Dollar's Worth of Twang, 1961; Girls Girls Girls, 1961; Twistin' and Twangin', 1962; Twangy Guitar – Silky Strings, 1962; Dance With The Guitar Man, 1963; Twanging Up A Storm, 1963; Lonely Guitar, 1963; Duane Eddy, 1986; Twang Twang, 1993; As producer: Star Spangled Springer, Phil Everly, 1973; Singles include: Moving 'n' Groovin', 1958; Rebel Rouser, 1958; Ramrod, 1958; Cannonball, 1959; The Lonely One, 1959; Yep!, 1959; Peter Gunn Theme, 1959; Forty Miles of Bad Road, 1959; Some Kinda Earthquake, 1959; Kommotion, 1960; Because They're Young (No. 2, UK), 1960; Bonnie Come Back, 1960; Pepe, 1961; Theme From Dixie, 1961; Ring of Fire, 1961; Caravan, 1961; The Ballad of Paladin (theme for television series Have Gun Will Travel), 1962; Dance With The Guitar Man, 1962; Boss Guitar, 1963; Play Me Like You Play Your Guitar, 1975; Peter Gunn, with Art of Noise, 1986; Other recordings include session work with: Phil Everly, Foreigner, Waylon Jennings, Kenny Rogers, Marty Stuart. *Honours:* NME Top Readers Poll Winner, World Musical Personality, 1960; Grammy, Best Rock Instrumental Performance, 1986. *Current Management:* Fat City Artists and Management, 1906 Chet Atkins Plaza, Suite 502, Nashville, TN 37205, USA.

EDE, Terence Frederick (Terry); b. 4 Aug. 1935, London, England. Musician (saxophones, clarinets, flute, oboe). m. Brenda Bonner, 14 March 1959, 1 s., 1 d. *Education:* Private, first tuition on piano. *Career:* Professional freelance player, 1962–; Tours include: Englebert Humperdinck; Jimmy Witherspoon; Larry Williams; Johnny Ray; Well-known teacher both at various schools and privately. *Membership:* Musicians' Union; Asscn of British Jazz Musicians. *Address:* 7 Church Farm Lane, Cheam, Surrey SM3 8PT, England.

EDELMAN, Randy; b. 10 June 1947, Patterson, NJ, USA. Composer. *Education:* University of Cincinnati. *Career:* Orchestrator for James Brown; Staff writer, CBS; Singer-songwriter. *Compositions:* For television: Blood Sport, 1973; Snatched, 1973; Ryan's Four, 1983; A Doctor's Story, 1984; MacGyver, 1985; Dennis the Menace, 1987; The Adventures of Brisco County Jr, 1993; Citizen X, 1995; For film: Outside In, 1972; Executive Action, 1973; The Chipmunk Adventure, 1987; Feds, 1988; Twins, 1988; Troop Beverly Hills, 1989; Ghostbusters II, 1989; Quick Change, 1990; Come See the Paradise, 1990; Kindergarten Cop, 1990; V. I. Warshawski, 1991; Drop Dead Fred, 1991; Eyes of an Angel, 1991; The Distinguished Gentleman, 1992; My Cousin Vinny, 1992; Beethoven, 1992; The Last of the Mohicans, 1992; Gettysburg, 1993; Dragon: The Bruce Lee Story, 1993; Beethoven's 2nd, 1993; Pontiac Moon, 1994; Greedy, 1994; Angels in the Outfield, 1994; The Mask, 1994; Billy Madison, 1995; Tall Tale, 1995; While You Were Sleeping, 1995; The Indian in the Cupboard, 1995; The Big Green, 1995; Down Periscope, 1996; Diabolique, 1996; The Quest, 1996; Dragonheart, 1996; Daylight, 1996; Anaconda, 1997; Gone Fishin', 1997; Leave It to Beaver, 1997; For Richer or Poorer, 1997; Six Days Seven Nights, 1998; Edtv, 1999; The Hunley, 1999; The Skulls, 2000; The Whole Nine Yards, 2000; Shanghai Noon, 2000; Passion of Mind, 2000; Head Over Heels, 2001; XXX, 2002. *Membership:* BMI. *Current Management:* Gorfaine/Schwartz Agency Inc, 13245 Riverside Dr., Suite 450, Sherman Oaks, CA 91423, USA.

EDER, Linda; b. 3 Feb. 1961, Tucson, Arizona, USA. Vocalist. m. Frank Wildhorn. *Career:* Duo Paul and Linda, 1980–87; Work with Pianist Jeremy Roberts; Winner on TV talent show Star Search, 1987–88; Appeared in

musical Jekyll and Hyde, 1990–, Svengali, 1991–. *Recordings:* Albums: Linda Eder, 1990; Highlights from Jekyll and Hyde, 1990; The Complete Work Jekyll and Hyde: The Gothic Music Thriller, 1994; And So Much More, 1994; The Scarlet Pimpernel, 1995; It's Time, 1997; It's No Secret Anymore, 1999; Christmas Stays The Same, 2000. *Address:* c/o Kragen and Co, 1112 N Sherbourne Dr., Los Angeles, CA 90069, USA.

EDGE, (THE), (David Evans); b. 8 Aug. 1961, Wales. Musician (guitar); Songwriter. m. Morleigh Steinberg, 22 June 2002. *Career:* Founder member, guitarist, rock group U2, 1978–; Regular national and world-wide tours; Major concerts include: US Festival, 1983; The Longest Day, Milton Keynes, 1985; Live Aid, Wembley, 1985; Self Aid, Dublin, 1986; A Conspiracy of Hope (Amnesty International tour), 1986; Smile Jamaica (hurricane relief fundraiser), 1988; Very Special Arts Festival, White House, Washington, 1988; New Year's Eve Concert, Dublin (broadcast live Europe), 1989; Yankee Stadium, New York (second ever concert there). *Compositions include:* Music to A Clockwork Orange 2004, RSC, 1990. *Recordings:* Albums: Boy, 1980; October, 1981; War (No. 1, UK), 1983; Under A Blood Red Sky, 1983; The Unforgettable Fire (No. 1, UK), 1984; Wide Awake In America, 1985; The Joshua Tree (No. 1, UK and USA), 1987; Rattle and Hum, also film (No. 1, UK and USA), 1988; Achtung Baby (No. 1, USA), 1991; Zooropa (No. 1, USA and UK), 1993; Passengers, film soundtrack (with Brian Eno), 1995; Pop, 1997; The Best Of 1980–90 (compilation), 1998; All That You Can't Leave Behind, 2001; The Best Of 1990–2000 (compilation), 2002. Hit singles include: Out of Control (No. 1, Ireland), 1979; Another Day (No. 1, Ireland), 1980; New Year's Day, 1983; Two Hearts Beat As One, 1983; Pride (In The Name of Love), 1984; With Or Without You (No. 1, USA), 1987; I Still Haven't Found What I'm Looking For (No. 1, USA), 1987; Where The Streets Have No Name, 1987; Desire (No. 1, UK), 1988; Angel of Harlem, 1988; When Love Comes To Town, with B. B. King, 1989; All I Want Is You, 1989; The Fly (No. 1, UK), 1991; Mysterious Ways, 1992; Even Better Than The Real Thing, 1992; Who's Gonna Ride Your Wild Horses, 1992; Stay, 1993; Hold Me, Thrill Me, Kiss Me (from film Batman Forever), 1995; Discotheque (No. 1, UK), 1997; Staring At The Sun, 1997; If God Will Send His Angels, 1997; The Sweetest Thing, 1998; Beautiful Day (No. 1, UK), 2000; Stuck In A Moment That You Can't Get Out Of, 2001; Walk On, 2001; Electrical Storm, 2002; Contributor, Mystery Girl, Roy Orbison, 1988; Red Hot + Blue, 1990; Pavarotti and Friends, 1996. *Honours:* Grammy Awards, Album of the Year, for The Joshua Tree, 1987, Best Rock Album, for All That You Can't Leave Behind, 2001, Best Alternative Music Album, for Zooropa, 1993, Song of the Year, for Beautiful Day, 2000, Record of the Year, for Beautiful Day, 2000, for Walk On, 2001, Best Rock Performance By A Duo Or Group With Vocal, for The Joshua Tree, 1987, for Desire, 1988, for Achtung Baby, 1992, for Beautiful Day, 2000, for Elevation, 2001, Best Pop Performance By A Duo Or Group With Vocal, for Stuck In A Moment You Can't Get Out Of, 2001, Best Music Video, Long Form, for Zoo TV–Live From Sydney, 1994, Best Performance Music Video, for Where The Streets Have No Name, 1988; BRIT Awards: Best International Act, 1988–90, 1992, 1998, 2001; Best Live Act, 1993; Outstanding Contribution To The British Music Industry, 2001; JUNO Award, 1993; World Music Award, 1993; Q Magazine Awards: Best Producer (with Flood, Brian Eno), 1993; Best Act In The World, 1990, 1992, 1993; Merit Award, 1994; American Music Award, Favorite Internet Artist of the Year, 2002; Ivor Novello Award, Best Song Musically and Lyrically, for Walk On, 2002; Golden Globe, Best Original Song, for The Hands That Built America (from film Gangs of New York), 2003; Numerous magazine poll wins and awards; Gold and Platinum discs. *Current Management:* Principle Management. *Address:* 30–32 Sir John Rogersons Quay, Dublin 2, Ireland. *Website:* www.u2.com.

EDMUNDS, Dave; b. 15 April 1944, Cardiff, Wales. Vocalist; Musician (guitar); Record Prod. *Career:* Member, bands including 99ers; The Raiders; The Image; Member, Love Sculpture, 1968–69; Solo artiste, 1969–77; Founder, Rockpile, 1977–81; Solo artiste, 1981–; Record producer, 1969–; Built own Rockfield Recording Studios, 1969; Numerous tours include: with Bad Company, USA, 1977; with Nick Lowe, 1977, 1978; Elvis Costello, Mink DeVille, USA, 1978; Rock 'n' Roll Revue, US tour, 1990; Concerts include: Knebworth Festival, 1978; Concert For Kampuchea, with Wings, Elvis Costello, 1979; Reading Festival, 1982; US Festival, 1982; Prince's Trust Rock Gala, Wembley Arena, 1987; John Lennon Tribute Concert, Merseyside, 1990; Television includes: South Bank Show; Blue Suede Shoes, Carl Perkins special (Channel 4); Film appearance: Stardust, 1974. *Recordings:* Albums: with Love Sculpture: Blues Helping, 1968; Forms and Feeling, 1969; with Rockpile: Tracks On Wax, 1978; Repeat When Necessary, 1979; Seconds of Pleasure, 1980; Solo: Rockpile, 1972; Subtle As A Flying Mallet, 1975; Get It, 1977; Tracks On Wax, 1978; Twangin', 1981; The Best of Dave Edmunds, 1982; DE7, 1982; Information, 1983; Riff Raff, 1984; Closer To The Flame, 1990; I Hear You Rockin', 1993; Plugged In, 1994; Musical Fantasies, 1999; A Pile of Rock (live), 2001; Singles include: with Love Sculpture: Sabre Dance, 1968; Solo: I Hear You Knocking (No. 1, UK), 1970; Baby I Love You, 1973; Born To Be With You, 1973; I Knew The Bride, 1977; Girls Talk, 1979; Queen of Hearts, 1979; Singin' The Blues, 1980; The Race Is On, 1981; Contributor, I Fell In Love, Carlene Carter, 1990; Producer for artistes including: Brinsley Schwartz; The Flamin' Groovies; Shakin' Stevens; Stray Cats; Nick Lowe, Fabulous Thunderbirds; Everly Brothers; Status Quo; k d lang; Music for film soundtracks: Porky's Revenge; Planes, Trains and Automobiles. *Current Management:* Gold Mountain Entertainment, 3575 Cahuenga Blvd W, Suite 450, Los Angeles, CA 90068, USA.

EDRISSI, Tahir El; b. Morocco. Vocalist; Musician (sintir, percussion). *Career:* Left Morocco for London, 1980s; Founder member of band MoMo (Music of Moroccan Origin); Act's fusion of North African Gnawa music with western-style drum kit, samples and contemporary dance styles (including house and garage) described as 'Dar'; Popular live band; Released first album, 2001. *Recordings:* Album: The Birth of Dar, 2001.

EDWARDS, Bloater B; b. 2 Dec. 1971, Aldershot, Hampshire, England. Vocalist; Musician (guitar, drums, bass guitar, piano). m. Lisa Janine, 29 April 1995. *Career:* Band: Big Boy Bloater and His Southside Stompers; Appearances include: Lyon Jazz Festival; Birmingham Jazz Festival; London's Forum; Hammersmith Palais; Hemsby Rock 'n' Roll Festival; Classic Cars, Channel 4 TV; Actor: Let Him Have It; Lipstick On Your Collar; Shine On Harvey Moon. *Recordings:* Album: (1 track) Haunted Highway; Jump For Joy With The Big Boy (EP), Big Boy Bloater and His Southside Stompers. *Membership:* Musicians' Union. *Address:* Aldershot, Hampshire, England.

EDWARDS, Dave; b. 9 Aug. 1948, Shrewsbury, England. Music Teacher; Musician (steel pan, guitar). m. Andrea, 28 Dec. 1978, 1 s. *Education:* Shoreditch College of Education, Surrey; Graduate Courses, Wolverhampton Polytechnic and Northumbria University; Qualified Special Needs Teacher. *Career:* Scandinavian tour with Razzle Dazzle Gatemouth Spasm String Band, 1973; Member and Musical Director, Pan L Beaters Steel Band, 1992–96; Member, Steel Spirit Steel Band, 1999–; Television: with North Tyneside Steelband: Boom, 1991; Local news, 1994, 1996; Numerous local radio broadcasts; Freelance Tutor and Workshop Leader, Musical Director for Steel Bands; Teacher, GCSE Music and Music Appreciation; Helped organize 3 national steelband festivals, 1994–96. *Compositions:* Steelband: Sunshine; Geordie Calypso; Several other steelband compositions and arrangements. *Recordings:* Some self-promoted recordings. *Publications:* Steelpan booklet, 1991. *Honours:* Blood donor (silver); Certificate of Merit, North Tyneside Steel Band, National Steelband Festival, 1991. *Membership:* Musicians' Union; NUT. *Address:* Aynuck's Lodge, 20 Glendale Ave, Whitley Bay, Tyne and Wear NE26 1RX, England.

EDWARDS, Don; b. 20 March 1939, Boonton, New Jersey, USA. Vocalist; Songwriter; Musician (acoustic guitar, banjo, mandolin). m. Kathy Jean Davis, 7 Jan. 1978, 2 d. *Career:* Started as actor, singer, stuntman, Six Flags Over Texas, 1961; First record, 1964; Part owner, White Elephant Saloon, Fort Worth, Texas; Recognition through Cowboy Poetry Gathering, Elko; Tours USA; Canada; Britain; New Zealand; Europe; Performs solo, with cowboy band, with horse, with cowboy poet Waddie Mitchell as The Bard and The Balladeer; As The Cowboy Jubilee; Musicologist, author on Western and traditional cowboy music; Educational services to universities; Appeared with Fort Worth, Las Vegas and Colorado Springs symphony orchestras. *Recordings:* Happy Cowboy; America's Singing Cowboy; Songs of The Cowboy; Guitars and Saddle Songs; Desert Nights and Cowtown Blues; Songs of The Trail; Goin' Back to Texas; West of Yesterday; Saddle Songs; My Hero, Gene Autry; The Bard and The Balladeer (with Waddie Mitchell); Prairie Portrait, 2000; Kin To The Wind, 2001; Also recorded on: Other Voices, Other Rooms, Nanci Griffith; The Wild West (soundtrack); How The West Was Swung, Tom Morrell; Ridin' West, Vols I and II; with Buckaroo: Visions and Voices of The American Cowboy; A Christmas Tradition; with Michael Martin Murphey: Cowboy Songs; Cowboy Christmas. *Publications:* Classic Cowboy Songs; Book/tape anthologies: Songs of The Cowboy; Guitars and Saddle Songs. *Honours:* Western Heritage Wrangler Award, Outstanding Traditional Music, Cowboy Hall of Fame, 1992; Western Heritage Wrangler Awards, 1992, 1996. *Membership:* AFTRA. *Current Management:* Scott O'Malley and Associates. *Address:* PO Box 9188, Colorado Springs, CO 80932, USA.

EDWARDS, Janet; b. Huddersfield, Yorkshire, England. Vocalist; Musician (piano). m (1), 2 s.; m (2). *Education:* College of Technology, Huddersfield; Studied piano with Dr Michael Kruszynski. *Career:* Piano and song recitals, 1974–; Performed with artists including those from Royal Opera House, ENO soloists; Performances: Italy; France; Germany; United Kingdom including South Bank, Wigmore Hall; Devised, performed own shows: Sounds Entertaining; I Say I Play; Munich, London, other British halls; Solo work, classical, popular, theatre, jazz music, in: Europe; Scandinavia; Middle East; Accompanist, assistant musical director, Royal Gala Performance of works by Stephen Sondheim, Theatre Royal Drury Lane; Work as voice coach began Royal Academy of Music, early 1980s; Master class group sessions working with professionals and non-professionals, 1989–; Played: Anna in Girls Were Made To Love and Kiss, West End, 1994; Also runs professional seminar in auditioning techniques, workshops and seminars for the general public; Began one-woman show, 'S' Wonderful, 'S' Marvellous, in theatres and venues in the UK, 1997–; London shows including Pizza on the Park, performing own songs and recording, 1999–. *Honours:* Diploma with distinction, Huddersfield College of Technology; ARCM; LTCL Dip Ed.

EDWARDS, Terry David; b. 10 Aug. 1960, Hornchurch, Essex, England. Musician (saxophones, trumpet, guitar, piano). *Education:* BA (Hons), University of East Anglia, 1979–82. *Career:* Founder member, The Higsons, 1980–86; Co-founder, with Mark Bedford, Butterfield 8, 1988–; Solo artist with and without The Scapegoats, 1991–; Session player with: Madness; Jimi Tenor; Lydia Lunch; PJ Harvey; Spleen; Jesus and Mary Chain; Lush; Julian Cope; Gallon Drunk; JJ Stone; Nick Cave; The Brood; Drugstore; Frank and Walters; Tindersticks; Billy Bragg; Robyn Hitchcock; Keziah Jones; Dopesmugglaz; Delakota; Boo Radleys; 18 Wheeler; The Creatures; Spiritualized; Scott 4; Strangelove; Anthony Moore; David Holmes; Jack; Serious Drinking; Dept S; Test Department; Moonshake; Farmers Boys; Bikini Beach; Wire; Snuff; Repair Man; Sarah-Jane Morris; Glen Matlock; Anjali. *Compositions:* Pump, for symphony orchestra, 1998; Slow Bossa/Wallflower, for cello and piano, 1997. *Recordings:* Blow, with Butterfield 8, 1988; Plays, Salutes, and Executes, 1993; No Fish is Too Weird for Her Aquarium, 1994; I Was Dora Suarez, with Derek Raymond and James Johnston, 1994; My Wife Doesn't Understand Me, 1995; I Didn't Get Where I Am Today, 1997; Large Door, 1998; Birth of The Scapegoats, 1998; Yesterday's Zeitgeist, 1999; Ontogeny (No Fish Is Too Weird For Her Aquarium, Vol. II), 2000; 681 At The Southbank/Plays, Salutes & Executes, 2002; Butterfield 8, 2003. *Membership:* Associate mem., PRS; MCPS; SPNM; Musicians' Union. *Address:* c/o PO Box 30608, London E1 1TS, England. *Website:* www.terryedwards.co.uk.

EDWINS, Myron; b. 4 Jan. 1958, Washington, PA, USA. Vocalist; Musician (bass guitar, keyboards); Entertainer; Prod. *Career:* Solo artist from 1989–; Tours with The Edwards Generation in Switzerland, Norway, Germany, Japan and Canada; Appeared on TV specials: Mike Douglas in San Francisco, Evening Magazine and Zoom; Business Ventures: MEP; EPB Management, Music publishing; Currently lead singer and keyboardist for R&B group, Movin'. *Recordings:* Do You Love Me, 1990; Do You Like The Way I Do It, 1991; Love Is, 1993; Let Me Entertain You, 1994; The Best Thing To Do, 1994; I'll See You Again, Myron Edwins, 1995. *Current Management:* Entertainment Agency; MEP. *Address:* Myron Edwins Productions, Box 8442, Pittsburg, CA 94565–8442, USA.

EGAN, Kian John Francis; b. 29 April 1980, Sligo, Ireland. Vocalist. *Career:* Mem., Westlife, 1999–; Numerous tours, festivals and television appearances. *Recordings:* Albums: Westlife, 1999; Coast To Coast (No. 1, UK), 2000; World of Our Own (No. 1, UK), 2001; Where Dreams Come True, 2001; Unbreakable: The Greatest Hits, 2002. Singles: Swear It Again (No. 1, UK), 1999; If I Let You Go, 1999; Flying Without Wings (No. 1, UK), 1999; I Have A Dream (No. 1, UK), 1999; Fool Again (No. 1, UK), 2000; Against All Odds (with Mariah Carey, No. 1, UK), 2000; My Love (No. 1, UK), 2000; What Makes A Man, 2000; Uptown Girl (for Comic Relief charity, No. 1, UK), 2001; Queen Of My Heart (No. 1, UK), 2001; World Of Our Own (No. 1, UK), 2002; Bop Bop Baby, 2002; Westlife Unbreakable, 2002. *Honours:* BRIT Awards, Best Pop Act, 2001, 2002. *Address:* c/o RCA Records, 1540 Broadway, New York, NY 10036, USA. *Website:* www.westlife.co.uk.

EINARSDOTTER, Elise; b. 11 July 1955. Musician (piano). m. Olle Steinholtz, 1 d. *Education:* Diploma of Arranging and Composition, Berklee College of Music, USA, 2 years; Royal Academy of Music, Stockholm, 2 years. *Career:* Leads, Elise Einarsdotter Ensemble, 1984–; Composes music to lyrics; Writes for choir and orchestra; Tours in Scandinavia, Italy, USA, Sweden, Norway, France, Belgium, Holland, England, Ethiopia and India. *Compositions:* My Heart; Alexandrinen; Sphinx Acre; Ljus, Dagg, Grönska; I Live in Music. *Recordings:* CDs: Sacred Hearts; Secrets of Living; Senses; Rosenäng; Sketches of Roses; Green Walk, Slow Talk, 1998. *Publications:* Rosenäng. *Honours:* Numerous grants and awards; Lo-Kulturpris, 1993; Stockholm City Award of Honor, 1998. *Membership:* Swedish Academy of Jazz; NYA IDUN. *Current Management:* Mistral Music. *Address:* Bandyvägen 47, 129 49 Hagersten, Sweden.

EINZIGER, Mike (Michael Aaron); b. 21 June 1976, Los Angeles, California, USA. Musician (guitar). *Career:* Formed group Incubus with school friends in Calabasas, California, 1991; Initially played small parties, graduating to support slots in Hollywood, California; Circulated demo tapes of Closet Cultivation and Incubus before independent album release, 1995; Group signed by Immortal/Epic; Built US and European following on support slots on tours with: Sugar Ray; Black Sabbath; Korn; Drive reached #1 on US Modern Rock Chart, 2001; First Japanese and Australian live dates, 2001. *Recordings:* Albums: Fungus Amongus, 1995; S.C.I.E.N.C.E., 1997; Make Yourself, 1999; Morning View, 2001; Singles: Enjoy Incubus EP, 1997; Pardon Me, 1999; Stellar, When Incubus Attacks Vol. 1 EP, 2000; Drive, Wish You Were Here, 2001. *Honours:* Make Yourself album certified double platinum by RIAA; Billboard Award, Modern Rock Single of the Year, 2001. *Current Management:* Steve Rennie, REN Management, California, USA. *Website:* www.enjoyincubus.com.

EISLER, Fil; Musician (bass, guitar); Prod; *Recordings:* Robbie Williams; Machine; Imogen Head; Jason Feddy; Ali Thompson and Yazz; Messiah; Galliano; Denzil; Crazy Little Trees. *Current Management:* One Management Ltd, 43 St Alban's Ave, London W4 5JS, England.

EKBERG, Ulf 'Buddha'; b. 6 Dec. 1970, Sweden. Prod; Songwriter; Vocalist. *Career:* Member, Ace of Base, 1990–. *Recordings:* Albums: Happy Nation, 1993; The Bridge, 1995; Singles of The 90s (compilation), 1999; Singles: All That She Wants (No. 1, UK), 1993; Wheel of Fortune, 1993; The Sign (No. 1, USA), 1994; Don't Turn Around, 1994; Lucky Love, 1995; Life Is A Flower, 1998; Cruel Summer, 1998; Always Have Always Will, 1998; No. 1 records in UK; USA; Canada; Across Europe; Australia; New Zealand; Israel; Argentina. *Honours:* Highest-ever world-wide sales for a debut album (Happy Nation, 19m.); Platinum discs world-wide. *Current Management:* Siljemark Production AB, Gårdsvägen 4, 171 52 Solna, Sweden.

ELASTIC CHAKRA. See: BT.

ELDRITCH, Andrew, (Andrew Taylor); b. 15 May 1959, England. Vocalist. *Education:* Oxford University. *Career:* Founder member, Sisters of Mercy, 1980–85; Regular international tours; Concerts include: York Rock Festival, 1984; Royal Albert Hall, London, 1985; Performed as the Sisterhood, 1986; Reforms Sisters of Mercy, 1987–; European tour, 1990; Tune In Turn On Burn Out tour, with Public Enemy, Gang of Four, Warrior Soul, 1991; Reading Festival, 1991; Support to Depeche Mode, Crystal Palace, 1993. *Recordings:* Albums: First and Last and Always, 1985; Gift (as the Sisterhood), 1986; Floodland, 1988; Vision Thing, 1990; Some Girls Wander By Mistake, 1992; Greatest Hits, Vol. 1, 1993; Slight Case of Overbombing, 1993; Go Figure, with SSV, 1997; Singles include: Temple of Love, 1983; Body and Soul, 1984; Walk Away, 1984; This Corrosion, 1987; Dominion, 1988; Lucretia My Reflection, 1988; More, 1990; Temple of Love (1992), 1992; Under The Gun, 1993. *Current Management:* Hard To Handle Management, 1133 Broadway Suite 1301, New York, NY 10010, USA.

ELEPHANT MAN, (O'Neil Bryan); b. 11 Sept. 1975, Seaview Gardens, Jamaica. Vocalist. *Career:* Mem., Scare Dem Crew, 1995–2000; Solo artiste, 2000–; Collaboration with Mr Vegas on songs, Jump Jump, What's Up, Ain't No Way, Dainty; Collaboration with Harry Toddler for song, War War War. *Recordings:* Albums: with Scare Dem Crew: Scare Dem Crew The Album, 1999; Scared From The Crypt, 1999; Solo: Comin' 4 You!, 2000; Log On, 2001; Higher Level, 2002. Singles: Solo: Watchi Pum, Replacement Killer, You Slacker You, Pum Pum; Bombing, 2001. *Address:* Greensleeves Records Ltd, Unit 14, Metro Centre, St Johns Rd, Isleworth, Middlesex TW7 6NJ, England.

ELFMAN, Danny; b. 29 May 1954, USA. Composer; Musician (guitar); Vocalist. *Career:* Lead singer, songwriter, guitarist, band Oingo Boingo; Film and television score composer. *Recordings:* Albums: with Oingo Boingo: Only A Lad, 1981; Nothing To Fear, 1982; Good For Your Soul, 1983; Dead Man's Party, 1985; Boingo, 1986; Skeletons In The Closet, 1989; Dark At The End of The Tunnel, 1990; Article 99, 1992. *Compositions:* For television: Amazing Stories, 1985; Pee-wee's Playhouse, 1986; Fast Times, 1986; Sledge Hammer!, 1986; Tales from the Crypt, 1989; Beetlejuice, 1989; The Simpsons, 1989; The Flash, 1990; For film: Forbidden Zone, 1980; Pee-Wee's Big Adventure, 1985; Wisdom, 1986; Back to School, 1986; Summer School, 1987; Hot to Trot, 1988; Big Top Pee-Wee, 1988; Beetlejuice, 1988; Midnight Run, 1988; Scrooged, 1988; Batman, 1989; Dick Tracy, 1990; Nightbreed, 1990; Darkman, 1990; Edward Scissorhands, 1990; Pure Luck (theme), 1991; Batman Returns, 1992; Article 99, 1992; Army of Darkness (theme), 1993; Sommersby, 1993; The Nightmare Before Christmas, 1993; Shrunken Heads (theme), 1994; Black Beauty, 1994; Dolores Claiborne, 1995; To Die For, 1995; Dead Presidents, 1995; Mission: Impossible, 1996; The Frighteners, 1996; Freeway, 1996; Extreme Measures, 1996; Mars Attacks!, 1996; Men in Black, 1997; Flubber, 1997; Good Will Hunting, 1997; Scream 2 (additional music), 1997; Psycho (adaptation), 1998; A Simple Plan, 1998; A Civil Action, 1998; Instinct, 1999; Anywhere But Here, 1999; Sleepy Hollow, 1999; The Family Man, 2000; Proof of Life, 2000; Planet of the Apes, 2001; Spider-Man, 2002; Men In Black II, 2002; Red Dragon, 2002. *Current Management:* Blue Focus Management, 15233 Ventura Blvd, Suite 200, Sherman Oakes, CA 91403, USA.

ELIS, Hefin; b. 4 June 1950, Port Talbot, Wales. Composer; Arranger; Musician (piano, guitar, bass guitar). m. Marian Thomas, 25 July 1981, 2 d. *Education:* University College of Wales, Aberystwyth. *Career:* Founder member, Welsh language rock band, Edward H Dafis; Recording Engineer, Producer for Sain Records. *Compositions:* I'r Gad. *Recordings:* Ysbryd Y Nos. *Membership:* PRS; Musicians' Union. *Address:* Bryn Gellyg, 22 Lon Ddewi, Caernarfon, Gwynedd, Wales.

ELLIOT, Sean Andrew; b. 24 Jan. 1970, London, England. Musician (guitar); Programmer. *Education:* Private guitar tuition; Part time musicianship, Goldsmiths College. *Career:* UK circuit tour with: Out of My Hair; TV Sky Star Search with Earthworks, 1991; Many regional radio appearances and live radio 1, GLR, 1994–95. *Recordings:* Guitar on: Out of My Hair; Debut album, 2 singles, 1994–95; Sessions for alternative mixes of Seal's Crazy. *Membership:* Musicians' Union. *Current Management:* Space Band Management. *Address:* 32B Weinster Sq. London W2 4NQ, England.

ELLIOTT, Anthony (Tony); b. 18 Dec. 1963, Liverpool, Merseyside, England. Songwriter; Musician (bass guitar, guitar, piano/keyboard). *Education:* Qualifications in Sound Engineering. *Career:* Member: Sebastian's

Men, 1982–85; Various appearances on UK regional and national radio including Radio 1 John Peel session; 16 Tambourines, 1986–90; Signed to BMG Publishing; Various British tours supporting Wet Wet Wet, Hue and Cry and Squeeze; Numerous appearances on regional/national TV and radio (including Radio 1 sessions); The Tambourines, 1990–93; Various European dates including Barcelona Olympic Festival; Numerous headlining tours, shared billing with Echo and the Bunnymen, River City People and The Real People; Catapult, 1996–99; British tour and various appearances; Partner in writing/production projects: The Elliott Davis Project, 1999–; Alto Music Productions (TV and radio advertisements), 1999–2001; Catapult Enterprises, 2001–; working on Patches Flemmings Loons and Spoons, The Somnambulists and further music for advertisements. *Recordings:* with Sebastians Men: Horizon, 1984; with 16 Tambourines: Singles: If I Should Stay; How Green Is Your Valley, 1990; Album: How Green Is Your Valley; with The Tambourines: She Blows My Mind EP; You're So Beautiful, 1992; 5 Miles Wide, featured track on Unearthed compilation, 2001; with Catapult: Everybody Gets There In The End, featured track on Transpotting compilation, 1998. *Membership:* Musicians' Union. *Address:* 210 Mather Ave, Allerton, Liverpool, Merseyside, L18 9TG, England.

ELLIOTT, Chris; b. 5 Aug. 1966, Lidlington, England. Musician (piano, keyboards); Songwriter, Arranger. m. Kerry, 24 June 1995, 1 d., Georgette. *Education:* Dartington College of Arts; Goldsmiths College, London. *Career:* Played piano and keyboards with Anne Clark 1993–96; Performer, writer and arranger with Bruce Woolley and the Radio Science Orchestra, 1994–; performed with Paul McCartney, George Michael, Elvis Costello, Sinead O'Connor, Marianne Faithful, The Pretenders, Tom Jones, Neil Finn, Johnny Marr, 1999; Anne Clark, 2000; played piano for The Pretenders, TFI Friday and Later with Jools Holland, 1999. *Recordings:* Ambient Orchestral, Chappell, 1996; Memories of the Future, Radio Science Orchestra, 1997; Storm (from the film 'The Avengers') for Grace Jones and the Radio Science Orchestra, 1999; Reverb, Radio Science Orchestra, 1999; Different Roads, Joe Cocker, Piano, 1999; Orchestral Arrangements: I Wish You Love, (from the film 'Eye of the Beholder'); Chrissie Hynde, 1998; Storm, Grace Jones and Radio Science Orchestra, 1998; Live and Let Die, Geri Halliwell, 1999; Film and TV: Century, Nagano Olympic Theme, 1998; The Second World War in Colour, 1999; Churchill's Secret Army, 1999; Moulin Rouge (Orchestration) 2000. *Honours:* Ivor Novello Scholarship, Dartington International Summer School, 1992. *Membership:* Musicians' Union; Performing Right Society. *Current Management:* Richard Kirstien, Zomba Music.

ELLIOTT, Joe; b. 1 Aug. 1959, Sheffield, England. Vocalist. *Career:* Vocalist, UK rock group Def Leppard, 1977–; Concerts include: Tours supporting Sammy Hagar; AC/DC; Ted Nugent; Reading Rock Festival, 1980; World tour, 1983; Monsters of Rock Festival, Castle Donington; BRIT Awards, Royal Albert Hall; Freddie Mercury Tribute Concert, Wembley, 1992; Radio includes: Stand-in DJ for Simon Bates, BBC Radio 1, 1992. *Recordings:* Albums: On Through The Night, 1980; High 'n' Dry, 1981; Pyromania, 1983; Hysteria, 1987; Adrenalize, 1992; Retroactive, 1993; Vault 1980–95, 1995; Slang, 1996; Euphoria, 1999; X, 2002. Singles include: Hello America, 1980; Photograph, 1983; Rock of Ages, 1983; Foolin', 1983; Animal, 1987; Pour Some Sugar On Me, 1987; Hysteria, 1987; Armageddon It, 1988; Love Bites (No. 1, USA), 1988; Rocket, 1989; Let's Get Rocked (No. 2, UK), 1992; Make Love Like a Man, 1992; Have You Ever Never Needed Someone So Bad, 1992; Stand Up (Kick Love Into Motion); Heaven Is, 1993; Tonight, 1993; Two Steps Behind, featured in film The Last Action Hero, 1993; When Love and Hate Collide (No. 2, UK), 1995; All I Want Is Everything, 1996; Promises, 1999; Now, 2002. *Honours:* American Music Awards: Favourite Heavy Metal Album, Favourite Heavy Metal Artists, 1989; RIAA Diamond Award, 10 Million copies of Hysteria sold. *Current Management:* Q-Prime Inc, 729 Seventh Ave, 14th Floor, New York, NY 10019, USA. *Website:* www.defleppard.com.

ELLIOTT, Missy 'Misdemeanour'; b. 1971, Portsmouth, VA, USA. Rap Artiste; Prod; Vocalist. *Career:* Joined vocal group, Sista, obtained record deal; Began collaborating with Tim Mosley on singles with Aaliyah; Guest rapper on various releases; Obtained solo record deal; Founded own company, The Gold Mind, 1996; Began releasing solo records as vocalist and rapper; Numerous successful acts signed to own company; Supervised and guest on soundtrack of film, Why Do Fools Fall in Love, 1998; Live appearances include Lilith Fair travelling festival, 1998; Started own lipstick line with Iman Bowie's cosmetics line. *Recordings:* Albums: Supa Dupa Fly, 1997; Da Real World, 1999; So Addictive, 2001; Under Construction, 2002. Singles: Sock it 2 Me, 1997; Rain, 1998; Hit 'Em Wit Da Hee, 1998; Beep Me 911, 1998; She's a Bitch; I Want You Back, featuring Melanie G (No. 1, UK), 1998; All 'N My Grill, with MC Solaar, 1999; Hot Boyz, 2000; Get Ur Freak On, 2001; One Minute Man, 2001. *Address:* c/o Elektra Records, 75 Rockefeller Plaza, New York, NY 10019, USA. *Website:* www.missyelliott.tv.

ELLIS, Bobby (Robert); b. 2 July 1932, Kingston, Jamaica. Musician (trumpet). 4 s., 3 d. *Education:* At Alpha Boys School, tutor, Raymond Harper, Rueben Delgado. *Career:* Played with Tony Brown Band; Val Bennett; Luther Williams; Joined The Mighty Vikings, 1962; Played with The Soul Brothers; Lyn Taitt and The Jetts; Billy Vernon; Lance Helwell; The Wailers; Bob Marley and The Wailers (Peace Concert, Jackson 5, Stevie Wonder); Jimmy

Cliff (BBC Concert); Toots and The Maytals; Brent Dowe; John Holt; Dennis Brown; The Two Ton Machine; Burning Spear (including Sunsplash Tour); Bunny Wailer (Music City Hall, Madison Square Garden). *Compositions:* Wrote with Cyrus; Sweet Meat; Up Park Camp; Stormy Weather; Rhythm for reggae hit: Diseases, Michigan and Smiley, 1983–84; Songs: Shaka; Pep-Up; Jiheje Chant; Cutlass; Sounds of Reggae; Three Finger Jack; Doreth. *Recordings:* Early records with Burning Spear include: Shaka; All records by Burning Spear; Other recordings by: Herbie Mann; Blazing Horns; Bobby Ellis Meets The Aggravators; Tommy McCook; Numerous singles. *Membership:* JFM. *Address:* 13 Savannah Rd, Independence City, Gregory Park PO, Saint Catherine, Jamaica.

ELLIS, John Stewart Maxwell; b. 22 Feb. 1945, Lower Slaughter, Gloucestershire, England. Teacher. *Education:* RMSM Kneller Hall, Bretton Hall College. *Career:* Armed Forces, 1960–72; Brass Teacher, 1972–77; Founder, Director of Music, Doncaster Youth Jazz Association, 1973–, (priority, preparing young musicians for modern profession); Performance tours: Russia; Germany; Poland; Sweden; France; USA; Doncaster Jazz Orchestra first UK band to appear jazz festivals: Montreux, 1979; Nice, 1981; Royal Performance invitations to Buckingham Palace and Windsor Castle, 1991; Numerous television and radio appearances; Currently, band masterclasses and workshops; Jazz panel adjudicator (home and abroad); Head of Music Department, Northcliffe School. *Recordings:* 6 jazz albums, 1979–: Live From Montreux; France... Here Again; A Celebration; A Concert For Friends; You're Nobody Till Somebody Loves You (Second, Jazz Journal International Record of the Year, 1988); Just For Phil. *Honours:* MBE, for Services to Education, 1995; European Curriculum Award, 1992; BBC Big Band of the Year, 1994; 7 NFMY Outstanding Performance Awards, 1977–87. *Membership:* International Asscn of Jazz Educators (IAJE); Musicians' Union; NUT. *Address:* High-Holme, 25 Sandcliffe Rd, Wheatley Hills, Doncaster DN2 5NP, England.

ELLIS, Katherine Jane Margaret; b. 21 June 1965, Bromley, Kent, England. Vocalist; Songwriter. m. Aug. 1998. *Education:* Private classical singing lessons. *Career:* Don't Dream It's Over – Less Stress featuring Katherine Wood for Boys Own, Substance, 1990–91; Regular demos for PWL Ltd (Pete Waterman) include: Loveland demos; 6 single releases, 1994–95; Hundreds of jazz, soul, R&B concerts, 1984–; Supported Rod Stewart, Elton John, Stevie Wonder; Backing singer, Belinda Carlisle, European Tour, 1995–; Album, 1995; Lawnmower Man II session on soundtrack, plays Radio 1, Sussex, Kiss, GLR, BSBF, Choice, 1995; Single, Whole Lotta Love with Goldbug, appeared live on Top of the Pops, 1996; In choir for entire Evita soundtrack; Backing vocals for Chaka Khan on National Lottery Show; 4 tracks on Speaker album, 1997; With '70s cover band, Fret Monkey, played at Peter Phillips' 21st birthday party, Windsor Castle, 1998. *Compositions:* Co-wrote Dreaming, Ruff Driverz and Arrolla, 1998. *Recordings:* Single: with Voice of Public Demand: Celebrate The World, 1995; Out of The Blue, Wood, Henshall, Phillips; Wrote and sung theme tune for International television series Dolphin Stories; With Ruff Driverz: Don't Stop; Deeper Love; Dreaming. *Membership:* PRS; MCPS; Musicians' Union; British Music Writers' Council; PAMRA; Equity.

ELLIS, Paul David; b. 27 April 1956, Manchester, England. Composer; Arranger; Prod; Musician (keyboards); Programmer. m. Yasuko Fukuoka, 12 March 1993. *Education:* BA Hons, Fine Art, Sunderland. *Career:* Tours with Hot Chocolate: Germany, UK, 1983; Middle East, 1984, 1985; Australia, 1986; British tour with Alison Moyet, 1984; Tours with Billy Ocean: UK, USA, 1986, 1988; Japan, 1986; Japanese tour with Epo, 1988; Software Consultant, Yamaha R & D Centre, London, 1990–. *Recordings:* Player, arranger, 2 Top 10 albums with Koji Tamaki (Japanese artist); Producer, tours, album, Epo, 1988; Many UK sessions, 1981–90. *Membership:* Musicians' Union. *Current Management:* The Music Network Ltd (own company). *Address:* 55D Stapleton Hall Rd, London N4 3QF, England.

ELLIS, Ron; b. 12 Sept. 1947, Southport, England. DJ; Broadcaster; Writer. m. Sue Hargreaves, 5 Aug. 1978, 2 d. *Education:* John Moores University, Liverpool. *Career:* Radio presenter, Dune FM; Promotions Manager, WEA Records; Music Historian and Biographer. *Compositions:* Hot California Nights, recorded by P J Proby. *Recordings:* Boys On The Dole (Top 10, New Wave Charts), 1979; New CD from The Johnny Ace Show, forthcoming. *Publications:* Journal of a Coffin Dodger; Murder First Glass; Snort of Kings; Playground Pets, 2000; Diary of a Discotheque; Ears of the City, Headline, 1998; Mean Streets, 1998; Framed, 1999; The Singing Dead, 2000; Last of the Lake Poets; Grave Mistake, 2001; Single Shot, 2002. *Honours:* Most Jobs In Britain: Daily Mail, 1976, Sun, 1989. *Membership:* Crime Writers' Asscn. *Address:* 5 Mayfield Court, Freshfield, Liverpool L37 7JL, England.

ELLIS-BEXTOR, Sophie; b. May 1979. Vocalist. *Education:* Godolphin and Latimer School, Hammersmith, London. *Career:* Daughter of TV director Robin Bextor and presenter Janet Ellis; Fronted group theaudience, scoring 3 UK hit singles, 1998; Teamed up with Italian DJ Cristiano Spiller for international hit, 2000; Solo career 2001–. *Recordings:* Albums: theaudience, 1998; solo: Read My Lips, 2001; Singles: with theaudience: If You Can't Do It When You're Young When Can You Do It?, A Pessimist Is Never

Disappointed, I Know Enough (I Don't Get Enough), 1998; with Spiller: Groovejet (If This Ain't Love), UK #1, 2000; solo: Take Me Home, 2001; Murder On The Dancefloor, 2001. *Address:* c/o Polydor UK, 72–80 Black Lion Lane, London W6 9BE, England.

ELMS, Gerald; b. 18 June 1961, London, England. Prod. *Career:* Began with various up and coming bands; Became session musician (keyboards); Currently record producer. *Recordings:* Right Said Fred album; First Contact, Roger Sanchez, 2001; Singles: G-Club, 1997; The Way To Find Love, 1998. *Address:* 57 Devereux Rd, London SW11 6JR, England.

ELSDON, Alan Robert; b. 15 Oct. 1934, Chiswick, London, England. Musician; Trumpet Player; Band Leader; Jazz Vocals; BBC Panelist; Record Reviews. m. June Patricia Elsdon, 21 May 1960, 2 s. *Education:* Private tuition with Tommy McQuater; Freddie Staff and Phil Parker. *Career:* Joined CY Laurie's Band, aged 19 and Graham Stewart 7; Recorded with both groups; Moved to Terry Lightfoot's Band, 1959–61; Formed own group, 1961; Backed many visiting US Musicians including Edmond Hall, Albert Nicholas, Bud Freeman, Wingy Mannone, Warren Vache, Kenny Daverne and Marti Grosz; Broadcasts include Easy Beat Saturday Club; Jazz Club. *Recordings:* Keepers of the Flame; Hotter Than That, CD; The Alan Elsdon All Star Jazz Band; Played guest slots over Europe and Middle East, including Germany, Belgium, Holland, Hong Kong. *Honours:* Played in Westminster Abbey at Philip Larkin's Funeral. *Address:* 29 Dorchester Rd, Northolt, Middlesex UB5 4PA, England.

ELSNER, Jürgen; b. 22 April 1932, Finsterwalde. Musicologist. *Education:* Music Theory, Musicology. *Career:* Assistant, Senior Assistant, Humboldt University, Berlin, Marx University, Leipzig, 1958–70; Lecturer, Ethnomusicology, Humboldt University, 1970; Chair Ethnomusicology, Humboldt University, 1975–96. *Publications:* Nordafrika, 1983. *Honours:* Hanns Eisler Prize, 1971. *Membership:* ICTM; SEM. *Address:* Heinerstr 97, D16341 Zepernick, Germany.

ELY, Joe; b. 9 Feb. 1947, Amarillo, Texas, USA. Vocalist; Songwriter; Musician (guitar). m. Sharon Thompson, 17 April 1983, 1 d. *Career:* Concerts include: 8 European tours; David Letterman TV show; Appearances on: Country Music Awards TV; The Road ABC TV Show; 3 Austin City Limits TV; Radio City Music Hall Madison Square Gardens. *Recordings:* Albums: Joe Ely, 1977; Honky Tonk Masquerade, 1978; Down On The Drag, 1979; Live Shots, 1980; Musta Notta Gotta Lotta, 1981; Hi Res, 1983; Lord Of The Highway, 1987; Dig All Night, 1988; Live At Liberty Lunch, 1989; Love And Danger, 1992; Letter To Laredo, 1995; Twistin' In The Wind, 1999; Live At Antone's, 2000; From Lubbock To Laredo: Best Of, 2002. *Honours:* Rolling Stone Top 10 of 70s. *Membership:* ASCAP; BMI; NARAS. *Current Management:* Fitzgerald-Hartley Co. *Address:* 34 N Palm Ave, Suite 100, Ventura, CA 93001, USA.

EMERICK, Geoff; b. 1946. Engineer; Prod. *Career:* Second Engineer, Engineer, 1966, Abbey Road Studios, EMI; Engineer, Apple Records; Worked with: America, Badfinger, The Beatles, Jeff Beck, Cilla Black, Elvis Costello, Tim Hardin, Paul McCartney, Manfred Mann, Matt Monro, Nazareth, Split Enz, Supertramp, Robin Trower, Wings, The Zombies. *Honours:* Insect Award, Distinguished Engineers Audio Federation Awards, 1978; Inductee, Technical Excellence & Creativity Hall of Fame, 2002. *Address:* EMI Group PLC, 4 Tenterden St, Hanover Sq., London W1A 2AY, England.

EMERSON, Darren; b. 30 April 1971, Hornchurch, Essex, England. Prod; Remixer; DJ. *Career:* Started as DJ around London, early 1990s; Became major figure in London's progressive house scene; Formed Underworld group with Rick Smith and Karl Hyde, 1990; Act signed to Boy's Own label; Released debut album, 1993; Left Underworld to concentrate on DJ career, 2000; Founder: Underwater Records; Remixed: Bjork; Shakespears Sister; Slam; Massive Attack. *Recordings:* Albums: Dubnobasswithmyheadman, 1993; Second Toughest In The Infants, 1996; Beaucoup Fish, 1998; Everything Everything, 2000; Episode 1 (mix album with Tim Deluxe), 2002. Singles: Mmm Skyscraper I Love You, Rez, 1993; Dark and Long, 1994; Born Slippy, 1995; Jumbo, 1999; King of Snake, 1999; Scorchio (with Sasha), 2000; H2O, 2002. *Membership:* PRS. *Address:* c/o Underwater Records, Fulham Palace, Bishop's Ave, London SW6 6EA, England.

EMERSON, Keith; b. 2 Nov. 1944, Todmorden, West Yorkshire, England. Musician (keyboards); Composer. *Career:* Member, The T-Bones; Emerson Lake and Palmer (ELP), 1970–; Solo artiste; Also recorded as: Emerson Lake and Powell (with Cozy Powell), 1985–86; 3, 1988; Performances include: Isle of Wight Festival, 1970; Mar-Y-Sol Festival, Puerto Rico, 1972; Film, Pictures At An Exhibition, 1973. *Recordings:* Albums: Emerson Lake and Palmer, 1970; Tarkus (No. 1, UK), 1971; Pictures At An Exhibition, 1971; Trilogy, 1972; Brain Salad Surgery, 1974; Welcome Back My Friends..., 1974; Works, 1977; Works Vol. Two, 1977; Love Beach, 1978; Emerson Lake and Palmer In Concert, 1979; The Best of Emerson Lake and Palmer, 1979; Emerson Lake and Powell, 1986; To The Power of Three, 1988; Black Moon, 1992; The Atlantic Years, 1992; Live At The Royal Albert Hall, 1992; Return of The Manticore, 1993; ELP Live In Poland, 2001; Solo albums: Inferno;

Nighthawks; Best Revenge; Muderock; Harmageddon, 1987; The Christmas Album, 1988; Changing States, 1995; Singles include: Fanfare For The Common Man, 1977; Solo: Honky Tonk Train Blues, 1976. *Address:* c/o Premier Talent, L3 E 54th St, 14th Floor, New York, NY 10022, USA.

EMILIO, (Navaira); b. 23 Aug. 1962, San Antonio, Texas, USA. Tejano and Country Music Vocalist. m. Cindy Casias, 29 Nov. 1986, 2 s. *Education:* Voice Scholarship, Southwest Texas State University, San Marcos. *Career:* Toured with David Lee Garza, 1985–88; Founder, own group Rio, 1989; Currently solo artiste; Major peformances include: CMA Awards show, 1995; San Antonio Livestock Show and Rodeo, 1994, 1995; Texas State Fair, Cotton Bowl, Dallas, 1995; Houston Livestock Show and Rodeo, with Selena, Houston Astrodome (set concert attendance record for the year), 1995; National Anthem at NBA All-Star Game, 1996; Suuport to Alan Jackson, US tour, 1996; Shared billing with: George Strait; Ricky Van Shelton; Pam Tillis; Vince Gill; Also performed with Dallas and San Antonio Symphony Orchestras. *Recordings:* Albums: Emilio y Rio, 1989; Sensaciones, 1990; Shoot It, 1991; Unsung Highways, 1992; Emilio Live, 1992; Southern Exposure, 1993; Sound Life, 1994; Life Is Good, 1995; Quedate, 1996; It's on the House, 1997; A Mi Gente, 1997; 10 Anniversario, 1999. *Honours:* Numerous Tejano Music Awards including: Male Vocalist of the Year, 4 times; Album of the Year, 6 times; Male Entertainer of the Year, 7 times; Listed in top 10 New Stars of 1996, County America magazine, 1996. *Membership:* Tejanos For Children Foundation. *Current Management:* Stuart Dill, Refugee Management International. *Address:* 209 10th Ave S, Suite 347, Nashville, TN 37203, USA.

EMINEM, (Marshall Bruce Mathers III), (Slim Shady); b. 17 Oct. 1972, St Joseph, MO, USA. Rap Artiste. m. Kim Mathers, 1999, divorced, 2001, 1 d. *Career:* Moved to Detroit, aged 12; Dropped out of high school to join local rap groups, Basement Productions, D12; Released debut album, The Infinite, on independent label FBT; After releasing Slim Shady EP, made guest appearances with Kid Rock and Shabbam Shadeeq, leading to deal with Dr Dre's Aftermath Records; Collaborations: Dr Dre; Kid Rock; D12; Missy Elliott; Dido; Founder, owner, Shady Records, 1999–; Appeared in semi-autobiographical film, 8 Mile, 2002. *Recordings:* Albums: The Infinite, 1997; The Slim Shady LP, 1999; The Marshall Mathers LP, 2000; The Eminem Show (No. 1, USA), 2002. Singles: The Slim Shady EP, 1998; Just Don't Give A F***, 1999; My Name Is, 1999; Guilty Conscience, 1999; The Real Slim Shady, 2000; The Way I Am, 2000; Stan, 2000; Without Me, 2002. *Honours:* MTV Awards, Best Album, The Marshall Mathers LP, Best Hip Hop Artist, 2000, Best Male Artist, Best Album, for The Eminem Show, Best Hip Hop Act, 2002; American Music Awards, Best Male Pop/Rock Artist, Best Pop/Rock Album, for The Eminem Show, Best Male Hip Hop/R&B Artist, Best Hip Hop/ R&B Album, for The Eminem Show, 2003; BRIT Awards, Best International Male Artist, Best International Album, 2003. *Address:* c/o Interscope Records, 2220 Colorado Ave, Santa Monica, CA 90404, USA. *Website:* www.eminem.com.

EMMETT, Rik; b. Canada. Musician (guitar); Vocalist. *Career:* Founder member, Canadian rock group Triumph, 1975–88; Later worked with Lee Aaron. *Recordings:* Albums: Triumph, 1976; Rock 'n' Roll Machine, 1977; Just A Game, 1979; Progressions of Power, 1980; Allied Forces, 1981; Never Surrender, 1982; Thunder Seven, 1984; Stages, 1985; The Sport of Kings, 1985; Surveillance, 1987; Classics, 1989; Absolutely, 1990; Spiral Notebook, 1996; Raw Quartet, 1999; Live At Berklee, 2000. *Honours:* Toronto Music Award, 1987. *Current Management:* Randon Entertainment Group, 121 Logan Ave, Toronto, ON M4M 2M9, Canada.

ENDRESEN, Sidsel Margrethe; b. 19 June 1952, Trondheim, Norway. Vocalist; Composer; Lyricist. *Education:* University Degrees in English and Social Anthropology, University of Oslo, 1975–79; Various private music teachers. *Career:* Singer, poet, composer, 1981–; Toured Scandinavia and Europe; Various radio and TV programmes in Scandinavia, Europe and USA; Composed music for various theatre and dance productions, Norway; Worked with many Norwegian and international jazz musicians; Fronted numerous groups. *Compositions:* Pagan Pilgrimage, commission for Molde Jazz Festival, 1993; Exile, 1994; also compositions and lyrics on all recordings. *Recordings:* Jivetalking, 1981; Polarities, 1982; City Visions, 1984; Stories, 1985; Pigs And Poetry, 1987; So I Write, 1990; Exile, 1994; Nightsong, 1994; Duplex Ride, 1998; Out Here: In There (with Bugge Wesseltoft), 2002. *Honours:* Norwegian Grammy, 1981, 1985, 1998; Radka Toneff Memorial Prize, 1993; State Cultural Scholarship, 1995–98. *Membership:* Norwegian Jazz Federation; Norwegian Popular Composers. *Current Management:* ACT Music and Vision, Germany.

ENEVOLD, Per; b. 4 Aug. 1943, Copenhagen, Denmark. Choir Conductor. m. Margrete Enevold, 3 d. *Education:* Masters Degree, Music, University of Copenhagen; Diploma for Nationally Approved Music Teachers' Certificate in Singing, Royal Danish Conservatoire of Music; Studied under Conductors Eric Ericson, Stockholm and Arvid Jansons, Leningrad. *Career:* Artistic Director, Chamber Choir Trinitatis Kantori, 1993–; Founder and Conductor, Copenhagen Chamber Choir, Camerata, 1965–85; Cantor, Copenhagen Cathedral, Vor Frue Kirke, 1983–90; Conductor, Copenhagen Boys' Choir,

1984–91; Conductor, Danish National Radio Choir, 1985–88; Visiting Professor, Music Department, St Olaf College, Northfield, Minnesota, USA, 1991; Cantor, Trinitatis Kirke, Copenhagen, 1997–. *Recordings:* Trinitatis Kantori; Camerata; Copenhagen Boys' Choir; Radio Choir. *Honours:* The Gladsaxe Award, 1976; First Prize, Bela Bartok Competition, Debrecen, Hungary, 1978; The Mogens Wöldlike Award, 1982. *Membership:* Danish Conductors Asscn. *Address:* Strandvejen 61, 2th, 2100 Copenhagen, Denmark.

ENGDAHL, Elisabeth; b. 17 Dec. 1956, Karlskrona, Sweden. Musician; Composer. m. Thomas Gustafsson, 7 April 1985, 2 d. *Education:* Degree, Afro-American Arrangement, Swedish Academy of Music, 4 years. *Career:* Orchestral Leader and Performing Musician in a small big band and lady band, 1987–93; Orchestral Leader, Performing House Band Pianist, television show, Good Morning Sweden, 1989–90; Performing Saxophonist, in charge of musical arrangement of a Swedish Talk Show, 1993–95; Concert Performances in Shanghai, People's Republic of China, 1994. *Compositions:* Musical Score, Kurt Olsson – The Movie About My Life As Myself, 1989; The Love Project Jazz Opera, 1996. *Recordings:* Musical Arrangements of three records with Kurt Olsson's Lady Band, 1987, 1988, 1990. *Membership:* Swedish Popular Music Composers; Swedens Media Composers. *Address:* Landalagangen 5, 411 30 Goteborg, Sweden.

ENGEL, Soren Peter Bjarne; b. 6 April 1947, Copenhagen, Denmark. Musician (guitar, bass guitar). m. Anne Grethe, 9 May 1991, 1 s. *Career:* Television appearances in France; Germany; Sweden; Finland; Norway; Denmark; European tours with Bo Diddley; Link Wray; Sonny Terry; Brownie McGee; Delta Cross Band. *Recordings:* with Delta Cross Band: No Overdubs, 1979; Rave On, 1980; Up Front, 1981; Slide, 1984; Through Times, 1991; with C V Jorgensen: Tidens Tein, 1980; Vinden Vender, 1982. *Honours:* Several Silver, Gold and Platinum records. *Membership:* Danish Artists' Union. *Current Management:* Århus Musik Kontor.

ENGLAND, Ty; b. 5 Dec. 1963, Oklahoma City, USA. Vocalist; Musician (guitar). m. Shanna Burns England, 3 s., 1 d. *Education:* Oklahoma State University, USA, 2 years; Graduate, Central State University. *Career:* Harmony Vocalist and Acoustic Guitarist for former college room-mate Garth Brooks, 6 years; Started solo career, released 2 albums, Ty England, 1995; Two Ways to Fall, 1996. *Recordings:* Singles: Should've Asked Her Faster; Smoke In Her Eyes; Irresistible You; Too Many Highways, 1998; Albums: Ty England, 1995; Two Ways to Fall, 1996; Highways and Dancehalls, forthcoming. *Honours:* National Spokesperson for the Future Farmers, American Alumni Asscn, 1996–97. *Current Management:* Mike Palmer, Nashville. *Address:* 1111 17th Ave S, Nashville, TN 37212, USA.

ENGLISH, Michael; Vocalist. *Career:* Toured with The Singing Americans; Joined, The Goodmans; Joined Gospel Group with Legend Bill Gaither; Solo Artist; Signed Record Contract with Curb Records, 1994; Member, The Gaither Vocal Band, 1995; Appeared On Trinity Broadcasting Networks, Praise The Lord, 1997. *Recordings:* In Christ Alone; Michael English; Hope; Healing; Freedom; Your Love Amazes Me; I Bowed On My Knees; Heaven To Earth, 2000. *Honours:* 6 Trophies Including Artist of the Year and Best Male Vocalist, 1994 Dove Awards; Dove Award for Best Southern Gospel Recorded Song of the Year. *Address:* c/o Trifecta Ent, 209 10th Ave S, Suite 302, Nashville, TN 37203, USA.

ENGLUND, Sverker; b. 26 Nov. 1968, Stockholm, Sweden. Ethnomusicologist. *Education:* BA, Major in Ethnology, Minor in Musicology; PhD Student, Department of Ethnology, Stockholm University. *Publications:* De sista ljuva åren: upptäcktsresor i oldranders musikaliska landshap, 1996; Srigfinnare i pensionarsland, 1998; Det Gemensamma Minners Melodier, in Pigga pensionärer och populärkultur, 1998. *Membership:* International Council for Traditional Music. *Address:* c/o M Eklund, Torkel Knutssonsg 33 IV, 11849 Stockholm, Sweden.

ENO, Brian Peter George; b. 15 May 1948, Melton, Suffolk, England. Prod; Musician (keyboards); *Recordings:* Albums as producer include: with John Cale: Fear, 1974; with Robert Calvert, Lucky Lief and The Longships, 1975; with Michael Nyman: Decay Music, 1976; with Penguin Café Orchestra: Music From The Penguin Café, 1976; with Ultravox: Ultravox, 1977; with Talking Heads: More Songs About Buildings and Food, 1978; Remain In Light, 1980; with Devo: Q- Are We Not Men? A- We Are Devo, 1978; with U2: The Unforgettable Fire, 1984; The Joshua Tree, 1987; Achtung Baby, 1991; Zooropa, 1993; Passengers (film soundtrack), 1995; All That You Can't Leave Behind, 2000; with Carmel: The Falling, 1986; with Geoffrey Oryema: Exile, 1990; with James: Laid, 1993; Wah Wah, 1994; Whiplash, 1997; Millionaires, 1999; Pleased To Meet You, 2001; with Laurie Anderson: Bright Red, 1994; Collaborations include: with Roxy Music: Virginia Plain, 1972; Roxy Music, 1972; For Your Pleasure, 1973; Pyjamarama, 1973; with David Bowie: Low, 1977; Heroes, 1977; Lodger, 1979; As guest musician: Captain Lockheed and The Starfighters, Robert Calvert, 1974; The End, Nico, 1974; The Lamb Lies Down On Broadway, Genesis, 1974; with Phil Mazanera: Diamond Head, 1975; Listen Now, 1977; with John Cale: Slow Dazzle, 1975; Helen of Troy, 1975; Rain Dances, Camel, 1977; Exposure, Robert Fripp, 1979; Yellow Rain, The Neville Brothers, 1989; Rattle and Hum, U2, 1989; Mamouna, Bryan

Ferry, 1994; with Jah Wobble: Spinner, 1995; Solo albums include: Here Come The Warm Jets, 1974; Taking Tiger Mountain, 1974; Another Green World, 1975; Before and After Science, 1977; Music For Films, 1978; Ambient 1: Music For Airports, 1978; Apollo: Atmospheres and Soundtracks, 1983; Thursday Afternoon, 1987; Nerve Net, 1992; The Drop, 1997; I Dormienti, 1999; Drawn From Life, 2001; Remix productions include: Unbelieveable, EMF, 1992; I Feel You, Depeche Mode, 1993; The River, Geoffrey Oryema, 1993; I'm Only Looking, INXS, 1993; In Your Room, Depeche Mode, 1993; Brian Eno: Box I and Box II, 1993; Introducing The Band, Suede, 1994; 39 Steps, Bryan Ferry, 1994; Protection, Massive Attack, 1994. *Honours:* Dr, Technology, University of Plymouth; Ivor Novello Award; 2 Grammy Awards; BRIT Awards: Best Producer, 1994, 1996; Q Magazine Awards: Best Producer (with Flood, The Edge), 1993; Inspiration Award (with David Bowie), 1995. *Membership:* PRS; BAC&S. *Current Management:* Anthea Norman-Taylor, Opal Ltd. *Address:* 3 Pembridge Mews, London W11 3EQ, England.

ENTHOVEN, David John; b. 5 July 1944, Windsor, Berkshire, England. Co Dir; Artist Man. Twice married, 1 s., 1 step-s., 1 d., 1 step-d. *Career:* Founded EG Group of Companies, 1969; Signed: King Crimson; T Rex; Emerson Lake and Palmer; Roxy Music; Brian Ferry; Founded IE Music Ltd, 1988; Artist Manager for Robbie Williams, Horace Andy, Archive, Jamie Catto. *Address:* IE Music Ltd, 111 Frithville Gardens, London W12 7JG, England.

ENYA, (Eithne Casado); b. 17 May 1961, Gweedore, Co Donegal, Ireland. Vocalist; Musician (piano, keyboards); Composer. m. Sergio Casado, 2002. *Education:* Classical piano. *Career:* Mem., folk group Clannad, 1980–82; Solo artiste, 1988–. *Recordings:* Albums: with Clannad: Crann Ull, 1980; Fuaim, 1982; Solo: Enya, 1987; Watermark, 1988; Shepherd Moons, 1991; The Celts, 1992; The Memory Of Trees, 1995; Paint The Sky With Stars, 1997; A Day Without Rain, 2000; Wild Child, 2001; Only Time, 2002. Singles include: Orinoco Flow (No. 1, UK), 1988; Evening Falls, 1988; Storms In Africa (Part II), 1989; Caribbean Blue, 1991; How Can I Keep From Singing, 1991; Book Of Days, 1992; Anywhere Is, 1995; Only If, 1997; Oiche Chiun, 1998. *Compositions:* Music for film and television scores: The Frog Prince, 1985; The Celts, BBC, 1987; LA Story, 1990; Green Card, 1990; Lord of the Rings: The Fellowship of the Ring, 2001. *Honours:* Three Grammy Awards; Six World Music Awards; IRMA Award, Best Irish Female Artist, 1993; Ivor Novello International Achievement Award, 1998. *Current Management:* Aigle Music, 6 Danieli Dr., Artane, Dublin 5, Ireland. *Address:* Manderley, Victoria Rd, Killiney, Co Dublin, Ireland. *Website:* www.enya.com.

EPPLE, Kat; b. 21 Aug. 1952, Ohio, USA. Musician (Flute); Composer. *Education:* BA, Electronic Music and Anthropology, University of South Florida; Synclavier technique, 1996. *Career:* Concerts at: Guggenheim Museum, New York City, 1997, National Gallery, Washington DC, Hollywood Palace, Guggenheim Museum, Bilbao, Spain; Concerts in Russia, People's Republic of China, Africa, Europe, Japan, Columbia, Brazil and Peru; Live performances with Parson's Dance Company. *Compositions:* Television soundtracks for National Geographic, PBS-Nova, Carl Sagen, Guiding Light, Another World, CNN; Musical Director, feature film Captiva Island, 1996. *Recordings:* Dragon Wings, 1978; Whispered Visions, 1979; Sound Trek, 1980; Aqua Regia, 1981; Valley of the Birds, 1982; Nocturne, 1983; Lights of the Ivory Plains, 1985; Catspaw, 1986; Dreamspun, 1988; Manatee Dreams, 1990; White Crow, 1997. *Honours:* 6 Emmy Awards for Music, 1978, 1982, 1983, 1985, 1989, 1998. *Membership:* BMI; Board Mem., Alliance of the Arts of Lee County; Board Mem., New Arts Festival. *Address:* PO Box 3156, North Fort Myers, FL 33918, USA.

ERGUNER, Kudsi; b. 4 Feb. 1952, Diyarbakir, Turkey. Musician (ney); Composer; Musicologist; Teacher. *Career:* Learned to play the ney (reed flute) from his father, Ulvi Erguner; Brother of Süleyman Erguner; Mem., Istanbul Radio Orchestra, 1969; Concert and festival appearances world-wide; Researched for Peter Brook's film Meetings With Remarkable Men, 1967, film Mahabharata, 1988; Moved to France to study architecture and musicology, 1975; Founded Mevlana institute of Sufi music, 1981; Concert at Royal Albert Hall, London, 1987; Founded Fasl group, later renamed Kudsi Erguner Ensemble, 1988; Worked with Peter Gabriel on soundtrack to film The Last Temptation of Christ, 1988; Composed music for ballet, Neva by Carolyn Carlson, 1991; Composed music for ballet, Le Voyage Nocturne by Maurice Béjart, 1997; Performed at Royal Festival Hall, London, 1999. *Recordings:* Albums: The Mystic Flutes Of Sufi, 1988; The Mahabharata, 1990; Sufi Music Of Turkey (with Suleyman Erguner), 1991; Turquie Musique Soufi, 1991; Oriental Dreams (with Mahmoud Tébrizizadeh); Gazel (with others); L'orient De L'occident, 1994; Kudsi Erguner, 1995; Psaumes De Yunus Emre, 1996; Tatyos Efendi; Chemins (with Derya Turkan); Le Concert De Nanterre (with others), 1998; Ottomania (with others), 1999; Ottomania Kudsi Erguner Sufi-Jazz-Project; Kudsi Erguner: Islam Blues.

ERGUNER, Süleyman; b. Turkey. Musician (ney); Conductor; Teacher. *Education:* PhD, Faculty of Social Sciences, Marmara University, 1999. *Career:* Father and grandfather were leading ney (reed instrument) players; Brother of Kudsi Erguner; Founder, with brothers, of Erguner School of music; Taught ney at Istanbul University Conservatory, 1980–81; Ney player, Itanbul State Radio and Television, 1981; Leader, Istanbul Mevlana Ensemble,

1995; Faculty member, Istanbul University Turkish Music Conservatory; Conductor, Classical Turkish Music Chorus and the Mystic Music Ensemble, Istanbul State Radio and Television; Has given many solo concerts, 1975–; Artistic dir, Women's Ensemble of Istanbul; Founder, Erguner Ensemble Instrumental-Choeur Musique Turque, Erguner Dervishes Tourneurs, Erguner Musique Ottoman, Harem Ensemble of Istanbul Women. *Recordings:* Albums: Erguner Bruders: Süleyman-Kudsi Erguner, 1987; Mevlana Dervishes Music, 1987; Mevlana Beyati Ayini ve Acemaéiran Ayini; Mevlana Beste-i Kadim Pencügah Mevlevi Ayini, 1988; Mevlana Instrumantal Mevlevi Music: Hicaz Mevlevi, 1988; Sufi Music of Turkey, 1990; Fasl Musique De L'Empire Ottoman, 1990; Ilahiler Sufi Music Istanbul Sema Grubu Mutrip Heyeti, 1990; Sharki, 1991; Gazel, 1991; Ottoman Music Chants du Harem, 1994; Süleyman Erguner Ney Improvisations, 1994; Süleyman Erguner, Lawrence Butch Morris: Conduction 25–26, 1995; Tatyos Efendi, 1996; Les Dervishes de Turquie: Musique Sufi; Áárá Daáá Efsanesi & Tayfun, 1997; Mevlana Whirling Dervishes III Selamlar, 1999; Mevlana Whirling Dervishes: Peérev, 1999; Ney Ile Tasavvuftan Seçmeler, 1999; Rumi: Süleyman Erguner, 2000. *Publications:* Book about the ney. *Honours:* Numerous awards world-wide; Best Artist, Turkish Writers' Committee, 1997.

ERICSON, Peter R; b. 2 July 1950, Uppsala, Sweden. Composer; Prod; Musician (guitar); Vocalist. m. Nina, 1975, 2 s., 1 d. *Education:* Journalism School; English, University; 1 year, St Martins College, Lancaster, England; 1 year, guitar; 4 years, piano. *Career:* Four albums with group, Mobben, 1970s; 6 solo albums, 1980s, 1990; Television, radio appearances and regular tours; Currently writing music for major film. *Compositions:* Music for major Swedish artists including: Monica Zetterlund; Cornelis Vreeswijk. *Recordings:* 6 solo albums; Many albums as producer. *Current Management:* Hawk Records; Taby, Stockholm, Sweden. *Address:* Hawk Records, Scandinavian Songs Music Group, Box 109, 18212 Danderyd, Sweden.

ERIKSON, Duke (Doug); b. USA. Musician (guitar, bass guitar, keyboards). *Career:* Guitarist and singer, Spooner, Firetown; Worked with Nine Inch Nails, L7, U2; Mem., Garbage, 1994–; Numerous tours, festivals, television and radio appearances. *Recordings:* Albums: Garbage, 1995; Version 2.0, 1998; Beautifulgarbage, 2001. Singles: Vow, 1994; Subhuman, 1995; Queer, 1995; Only Happy When It Rains, 1995; Stupid Girl, 1995; Milk, 1996; #1 Crush, 1997; Push It, 1998; I Think I'm Paranoid, 1998; Special, 1998; When I Grow Up, 1999; The Trick Is To, 1999; You Look So Fine, 1999; The World Is Not Enough (theme from James Bond: The World is Not Enough), 1999; Androgyny, 2001; Breaking Up The Girl, 2001; Shut Your Mouth, 2002. *Address:* c/o Mushroom Records, 1 Shorrolds Rd, London SW6 7TR, England. *Website:* www.garbage.com.

ERNA, Sully (Salvatore Paul); b. 7 Feb. 1968, Lawrence, Massachusetts, USA. Vocalist. *Career:* Ex-drummer of Sire/Reprise act Stripmind; Joined Godsmack group as vocalist, 1995; Recorded independent debut album for $2500 over 3 days with money borrowed from friend, 1996; Heavy local airplay on Boston-based WAAF radio station led to deal with Republic/Universal, 1998; Debut LP remixed/repackaged with eponymous title; Album banned by US Wal-Mart and K-Mart stores for profane content; US and European gigs in 1999 and 2000 including: Woodstock '99; Ozzfest; MTV's Return of The Rock tour; Second album recorded in warehouse in Massachusetts, 2000; First major amphitheatre tour, 2001. *Recordings:* Albums: All Wound Up, 1997; Godsmack, 1998; Awake, 2000; Singles: Whatever, Keep Away, 1998; Voodoo, Bad Religion, 1999; Awake, 2000; Greed, Bad Magick, 2001. *Honours:* Whatever single spent record total of 33 weeks on Billboard Top 10; Boston Music Awards, Act of the Year, 2000 and 2001; Billboard Award, Rock Artist of the Year, 2001. *Address:* c/o Paul Geary, PGM, PO Box 9134, Boston, MA 02205, USA. *E-mail:* godsmack@pgmglobal.com. *Website:* www.godsmack.com.

ESCALLE, Jean-Louis; b. 3 March 1954, Aurimont, Gers, France. Jazz Musician (drums). m. Marie-Jeanne, 24 May 1982, 1 s., 2 d. *Education:* Toulouse Conservatory, 6 years. *Career:* Jazz sideman, with regional and national jazz musicians, South of France. *Recordings:* 4 records with regional musicians: J M Pilc; R Calleja; Ch Brun. *Address:* Orbessan, 32260 Sissan, France.

ESCOVEDO, Alejandro; b. 1951, San Antonio, TX, USA. Vocalist; Songwriter; Musician (guitar); Arranger. m. (1), deceased, (2). *Career:* Mem., the Nuns, 1977–79; Mem. of bands, Rank and File, True Believers, –1987; Solo artiste, 1992; Tours with his band, Buick MacKane, and Alejandro Escovedo Orchestra. *Recordings:* Albums: Solo: Gravity, 1992; With These Hands, 1998; Thirteen Years, 1993; Bourbonitis Blues, 1999; A Man Under The Influence, 2001; More Miles Than Money: Live 1994–96, 2001; By The Hand Of The Father, 2002; with the Nuns: The Nuns, 1980. *Honours:* Austin Music Awards, Musician of the Year, 1993, Best Album, 2001. *Address:* c/o Blue Rose Records, Rauheckstr. 10, 74232 Abstatt, Germany.

ESOTERIK. See: **DEGIORGIO, Kirk.**

ESSEX, David, (David Albert Cook); b. 23 July 1947, Plaistow, East London, England. Vocalist; Musician (drums); Actor. *Career:* 20 British tours;

Many world tours; Television appearances include: Top of the Pops; David Essex Specials; Cher; Johnny Carson; Grammy Awards; Subject, This Is Your Life, 1995; Stage performances: Jesus, Godspell, 1971–73; Che, Evita, 1978; Lord Byron, Childe Byron, at Young Vic; Fletcher Christian, Mutiny; Films: That'll Be The Day; Stardust; Silver Dream Racer; Wrote most of own recordings. *Recordings:* 23 UK hit singles, (2 at No. 1), including: Gonna Make You A Star; Hold Me Close; Rock On (No. 1, USA); Silver Dream Machine; Winter's Tale; Numerous albums include: Rock On, 1973; David Essex, 1974; All The Fun of The Fair, 1975; Out On The Street, 1976; Imperial Wizard, 1979; Collection, 1980; Stagestruck, 1982; The Whisper, 1983; Centre Stage, 1986; Touching The Ghost, 1989; Spotlight, 1991; Cover Shot, 1993; Back To Back, 1994; Living in England, 1995; Missing You, 1996; Here We Are All Together, 1998; Everlasting Love, 2000; Also appeared on Jeff Wayne's War of The Worlds (with Richard Burton, Justin Hayward, Phil Lynott), 1978. *Honours:* Variety Club of Great Britain, Best Newcomer, 1971; Best Performer, Evita, 1978; Ambassador, Voluntary Service Overseas. *Membership:* American Federation Television; American Screen Actors Guild; Equity UK. *Current Management:* Derek Bowman, Lamplight Music Ltd; Mel Bush Organisation. *Address:* 109 Eastbourne Mews, London W2 6LQ, England.

ESSIET, Chief Udoh; b. 21 Nov. 1959, Ikot Ekpene, Nigeria. Musician (African percussion); Vocalist; Composer; Bandleader. m. Sherry Margolin, 1 s. *Career:* In Nigeria until 1983; Performed traditional native music, Highlife music, with Dr Victor Olaiya; Rex Williams; Rex Lawson; Juju (Sunny Ade); Performed Afrobeat music with Fela Anikulapo Kuti, 1978–83; Based in Paris, 1983–; Founded Ghetto Blaster, first part for Fela, James Brown, 1984; Mory Kante; Salif Keita; Formed Afrobeat Blaster, tours in Europe, 1989–. *Recordings:* with Ghetto Blaster: Preacher Man, 1984; People, 1986; with Salif Keita: Soro; with Sixun, Fela Anikulapo Kuti: ITT; Unknown Soldier; Coffin For Head of State; Authority Stealing; 2000 Black (with Roy Ayers); with Afrobeat Blaster: No Condition Is Permanent, 1991. *Publications:* Film: Ghetto Blaster, 1983. *Honours:* Chief of African Feeling, Amsterdam, 1986. *Membership:* SACEM; SPEDIDAM; ADAMI.

ESSING, John Leo Thomas; b. 15 Aug. 1964, Stockholm. Musician (guitar, synthesizer, percussion). *Career:* Member, bob hund, 1991; More than 300 gigs around Scandinavia; Played at famous Roskilde, Lollipop, Ruisrock, Quartfestivalen and Hultsfred. *Compositions:* I Stället för Musik, 1996; Düsseldorf, 1996. *Recordings:* bob hund – bob hund, 1993; bob hund – Edvin Medvind, 1994; bob hund – Omslag: Martin Kann, 1996; Düsseldorf, 1996; Ett fall and en lösning, 1997; Nu är det väl revolution på gång?, 1998; Jag rear ut min själ! Allt skall bort!!!, 1998; Helgen V, 1999; Sover aldrig, 1999. *Honours:* Grammy, best live act, 1994; Grammy, best lyrics, 1996. *Membership:* STIM; SAMI. *Address:* c/o bob hunds förlag, Råsundavägen 150, 169 36 Solna, Sweden.

ESTEFAN, Gloria Maria, (Gloria Fajado); b. 1 Sept. 1957, Havana, Cuba. Vocalist; Songwriter. m. Emilio Estefan, 1 Sept. 1978. *Education:* BA, Psychology, Univeristy of Miami, 1978. *Career:* Singer, backed by Miami Sound Machine, 1974–; Billed as Gloria Estefan, 1989–; Appearances include: Tokyo Music Festival, Japan, 1985; World tour, 1991; The Simple Truth, benefit concert for Kurdish refugees, Wembley, 1991; White House State Dinner, for President of Brazil, 1991; South American tour, 1992; Royal Variety Performance, London, before Prince and Princess of Wales, 1992; Co-organizer, benefit concert for victims of Hurricane Andrew, Florida, 1992; 45m. albums sold to date. *Compositions include:* Anything For You; Don't Wanna Lose You; Oye Mi Canto (co-written with Jorge Casas and Clay Ostwald); Cuts Both Ways; Coming Out of The Dark (co-written with Emilio Estefan and Jon Secada); Always Tomorrow; Christmas Through Their Eyes (co-written with Dianne Warren). *Recordings:* Albums: Renacer, 1976; Eyes of Innocence, 1984; Primitive Love, 1986; Let It Loose, 1988; Anything For You (No. 1, UK), 1989; Cuts Both Ways, 1989; Exitos De Gloria Estefan, 1990; Into The Light, 1991; Greatest Hits, 1992; Mi Tierra, 1993; Christmas Through Your Eyes, 1993; Hold Me, Thrill Me, Kiss Me, 1994; Abriendo Puertas, 1995; Destiny, 1996; Gloria!, 1998; Alma Caribena, 2000; Greatest Hits Vol. 2, 2001; Also featured on: Jon Secada, Jon Secada (also co-producer), 1991; Til Their Eyes Shine (The Lullaby Album), 1992; Hit singles include: Dr Beat, 1984; Conga, 1986; Hot Summer Nights, used in film soundtrack Top Gun, 1986; Bad Boy, 1986; Words Get In The Way, 1986; Rhythm Is Gonna Get You, 1987; Can't Stay Away From You, 1988; Anything For You (No. 1, USA), 1988; 1–2–3, 1988; Oye Mi Canto (Hear My Voice), 1989; Here We Are, 1989; Don't Wanna Lose You, 1989; Get On Your Feet, 1989; Coming Out of The Dark (No. 1, USA), 1991; Remember Me With Love, 1991; Always Tomorrow, 1992; Cuts Both Ways, 1993; Go Away, 1993; Mi Tierra, 1993; Turn the Beat Around, 1994; Abrienda Puertos; Tres Deseos; Mas Alla. *Honours:* Grand Prize, Tokyo Music Festival, 1985; Numerous Billboard awards, 1986–; American Music Award, Favourite Pop/Rock Duo or Group, 1989; Crystal Globe Award, 21 Club, New York, 1990; Latin Music Award, Crossover Artist of Year, 1990; Humanitarian Award, B'Nai B'rith, 1992; Desi Entertainment Awards, Performer of Year, Song of Year, 1992; Humanitarian Award, National Music Foundation (for helping victims of Hurricane Andrew), 1993; American Music Award, Special Award of Merit, 2000. *Address:* c/o Estefan Enterprises, 555 Jefferson Ave, Miami Beach, FL 33139, USA.

ESTER, Pauline; b. 18 Dec. 1963, Toulouse, France. Vocalist. *Education:* Private lessons; Different vocal coaches. *Career:* Tours: France; Belgium; Bulgaria; Canada; Canada, Québec; Opening act, Patrick Bruel tour, 1991; Appearances on all major television and radio shows, France, Canada, Québec. *Recordings:* Albums: Le Monde Est Fou, 1990; Je L'Autre Côté, 1992; Singles: Il Fait Chaud; Oui, Je T'Adore; Le Monde Est Fou; Une Fenêtre Ouverte. *Honours:* France Internationonal, 1991; Trophy Radio, SACEM: Best Song of Year, 1991; Best New Artist, 1992. *Membership:* SACEM, 1989. *Current Management:* Jean-Claude Camus Production. *Address:* 6 rue Daubigny, 75017 Paris, France.

ESTRIN, Mitchell Stewart; b. 23 Dec. 1956, New York, USA. Performer; Educator. m. Jane Estrin, 1 s. *Education:* BA, MMus, Juilliard School. *Career:* Clarinetist, New York Philharmonic, 1979–99; Professor of Clarinet, University of Florida, 1999–; Television Appearances, Phil Donahue Show; Live From Lincoln Center; Late Show With David Letterman. *Recordings:* The Shadows of October; New York Philharmonic; Amadeus Ensemble; Motion Picture Sountracks. *Honours:* Naumburg Scholarship; Sudler Foundation Award; Outstanding Young Men In America. *Membership:* American Federation of Musicians; Recording Musicians of America; College Music Society. *Address:* University of Florida, College of Fine Arts, School of Music, PO Box 117900, Gainesville, FL 32611, USA.

ETHERIDGE, John M. G; b. 12 Jan. 1948, London, England. Musician (guitar). 1 s., 1 d. *Education:* BA, History of Art, University of Essex. *Career:* Soft Machine, 1975–79; Stephane Grappelli, 1976–81; Solo tours: Australia; USA; England; 1982–84; MD, Bertice Reading, 1985–90; European tour with Birelli Lagrene, Vic Juris, 1989; European tours with Dick Hextall-Smith (saxophone); Danny Thompson's Whatever, 1989–93; Own Quartet, 1990–; Andy Summers Duo, 1993–; Nigel Kennedy Group, 1993–. *Recordings:* with Soft Machine: Soft; Alive and Well; Triple Echo; with Stephane Grappelli: At The Winery; Live At Carnegie Hall; with Stephane Grappelli and Yehudi Menuhin: Tea For Two; Strictly For The Birds; with Nigel Kennedy, Kafka, 1996; Kennedy Experience, 1999; with own quartet: Second Vision, 1981; Sweet Chorus: Tribute to Stephane Grappelli, 1999; with Vic Juris: Bohemia, 1989; with Dick Heckstall-Smith: Obsession Fees, 1990; with Danny Thompson: Elemental, 1991; with Andy Summers: Invisible Threads, 1993; with Wolf: Saturation Point, 2001; Solo albums: Ash, 1994; Sweet Chorus dedicated to Grappelli, 1998. *Publications:* The Guitar, OUP, editor, Michael Stimpson; Numerous articles for guitar magazines. *Current Management:* Andy Morley. *Address:* Exeter and Devon Arts Centre.

ETHERIDGE, Melissa Lou; b. 29 May 1961, Leavenworth, Kansas, USA. Vocalist; Songwriter; Musician (guitar). *Education:* Berklee College of Music, Boston. *Career:* Musician, Los Angeles bars, 5 years; Recording artiste, 1988–. *Recordings:* Albums: Melissa Etheridge, 1988; Brave and Crazy, 1989; Never Enough, 1992; Yes I Am, 1993; Your Little Secret, 1995; Breakdown, 1999; Skin, 2001; Singles: I'm the Only One, 1994; Come to My Window, 1994; If I Wanted To, 1995; Nowhere to Go, 1996; Angels Would Fall, 1999. *Current Management:* Bill Leopold, W F Leopold Management.

EUBANKS, Robin; b. 25 May 1955, Philadelphia, Pennsylvania, USA. Jazz Musician (trombone). *Career:* Played in bands on Broadway; Appeared in film: Cotton Club; Member, Duke Ellington and Cab Calloway bands; Played on Motown Television special; Played with: Art Blakey; Abdullah Ibrahim; Marvin 'Smitty' Smith; Geri Allen; Dave Holland; Wynford and Branford Marsalis; Steve Coleman; Regular tours: USA; Europe; Japan. *Recordings:* Different Perspectives, 1988; Dedications, 1989; Karma, 1990; Mental Images, 1994; Wake Up Call, 1997; 4:JJ/Slide/Curtis and Al, 1998; Get 2 It, 2001; Musician on: Art Blakey: Live At Montreux and Northsea; Not Yet; Kevin Eubanks: Guitarist; Steve Coleman: World Expansion; Sine Die; Marvin 'Smitty' Smith: Keeper of The Drums; Geri Allen: Open On All Sides; Mark Helias: The Current Set; Herb Robertson: Shades of Bud Powell; Dave Holland: The Razor's Edge; Branford Marsalis: Scenes In The City. *Address:* SESAC, 55 Music Sq. E, Nashville, TN 37203, USA.

EURIPIDES, Georganopoulos; b. 12 Dec. 1961, Thessaloniki, Greece. Composer; Prod; Musician (keyboards). m. Dr Agnes Leotsakos, 22 Feb. 1992, 1 s. *Education:* ARCM, Dip, Royal College of Music. *Career:* Writing music for television and video productions; Director, Optimus International Ltd (music production company); Composition, production work in UK, France, Germany, Malta, Greece, Poland. *Recordings:* Arranger, producer, Hits of The War Years (No. 4, UK Music Video Charts), 1995. *Membership:* BAC&S; Musicians' Union; PRS; MCPS. *Address:* 35 Elm Rd, London SW14 7JL, England.

EVANS, Dan (David Rhys); b. 26 May 1956, Middlesbrough, Cleveland, England. Folk Musician (dulcimer, guitar). m. Mary Collins, 12 May 1995. *Education:* BSc, Dunelm. *Career:* Performer in folk clubs, art centres, theatres in UK; frequent radio appearances; frequent performances in USA. *Recordings:* Sampler, 1988; Guardian Spirit, 1993; Spirit Dancing, 1997; Autumn Dance, 2002. *Contributions to:* Dulcimer Players News, USA); Nonsuch Dulcimer Newsletter, UK. *Membership:* PRS; MCPS; PPL; MU. *Current Management:* DanSing Music. *Address:* 61 Sillswood, Olney, Bucks MK46 5PN, England.

EVANS, David. See: EDGE, (THE).

EVANS, Faith; b. 10 June 1973, Lakeland, FL, USA. Vocalist; Songwriter; Arranger. m. (1) Christopher Wallace (Notorious BIG), 4 Aug. 1994, deceased 1997, 1 s., 1 d. (by previous relationship), (2) Todd Russaw, 1 c. *Career:* Started as backing singer for Mary J Blige and Color Me Badd; Released debut solo single You Used To Love Me, 1995; Performed on tribute single to murdered rapper husband, I'll Be Missing You, 1997; *Collaborations:* Puff Daddy; Whitney Houston; Eric Benet; DMX. *Recordings:* Albums: Faith, 1995; Keep The Faith, 1998, Faithfully, 2002. Singles: You Used To Love Me, 1995; I'll Be Missing You (with Puff Daddy and 112), 1997; Love Like This, 1998; All Night Long, 1999; You Gets No Love, 2002. *Honours:* First single to debut at No. 1 on US and UK singles charts. *Address:* c/o Bad Boy Records, 1540 Broadway 33rd Floor, New York, USA.

EVANS, Frank; b. 1 Oct. 1936, England. Jazz Musician (guitar); Arranger. m. Mary, 23 May 1954, 2 s. *Career:* Tours with bands; Television: Parkinson (solo); BBC Jazz Club, World Service; Strictly Instrumental, Composed for more than 60 television dramas, documentary films. *Recordings:* Jazz Tete-á-Tete Tubby Hayes, Tony Coe; Mark Twain Suite (77 records); Noctuary; Soiree; Ballade; Frank Evans For Little Girls; Stretching Forth. *Publications:* The Jazz Standard, 1998. *Honours:* Inclusion in The Great Jazz Guitarists. *Membership:* PRS; MCPS; PRC. *Current Management:* Don Percival, Artists Promotion. *Address:* 9 Holbrook House, Paul's Cray Rd, Chislehurst, Kent BR7 60E, England.

EVANS, Lee; b. 7 Jan. 1933, New York, USA. Composer; Musician (piano). *Education:* BA, NYU, 1957; MA, Columbia University, 1958; EdD, 1978. *Career:* Worked with various artists include: Tom Jones; Cat Stevens; Engelbert Humperdinck; Gilbert O'Sullivan; Professor, Five Towns College, Seaford, 1977–78; President, Piano Plus Inc, 1973–; Leader, Lee Evans Trio, 1966–73; Featured pianist, television specials, The Gershwin Years; Ed Sullivan; Merv Griffin; Performed at 2 White House Command Performances for President Lyndon B Johnson. *Publications:* Author, series of jazz keyboard books; Contributor to journals. *Membership:* ASCAP; AFofM; National Asscn of Jazz Educators. *Address:* Piano Plus Inc, New York, USA.

EVANS, Sara; b. 2 May 1971, Booneville, Missouri, USA. Country vocalist. m. Craig Schelske. *Career:* First performed on mandolin aged 4 as part of a family act, The Evans Family Band, started by mother Pat and including seven year old Matt on banjo and nine year old Jay; Group played local PTA meetings and bluegrass festivals; Group became the Sara Evans Band; Switched to country music and played in various groups; First regular gig at the Country Stampede, Columbia, Missouri; Worked as waitress and wrote songs on first trip to Nashville, 1991; Met future husband Craig Schelske, joined a band with his two brothers and returned to Oregon; Played country club venues for next three years as Sara Evans and North Santiam; Returned to Nashville, singing demos for Tree Publishing, 1995; Introduced by RCA to Dwight Yoakam's producer Pete Anderson who eventually produced moderately successful debut album Three Chords and The Truth; Popularity increased significantly with second album and stature has grown subsequently; Hosted the British Country Music Awards, 1997; Teamed up with Martina McBride and Reba McEntire for first all-female country music tour, Country Divas, 2001. *Compositions include:* Born To Fly; No Place That Far; Three Chords and The Truth. *Recordings include:* Not That Far, 1999; Born To Fly, 2000; I Couldn't Ask For More, 2001; Albums include: Three Chords and The Truth, 1997; No Place That Far, 1998; Born To Fly, 2000. *Address:* c/o Country Music Asscn, 1 Music Circle S, Nashville, TN 37203, USA. *Website:* www.saraevans.net.

EVANS, Tania; Vocalist. *Career:* Singer, German dance act Culture Beat, 1990–. *Recordings:* Singles: Erdbeermund, 1990; I Like You, 1993; Mr Vain (No. 1 throughout Europe, including UK, Germany), 1993; Anything, 1994; World In Your Hands, 1994; Prisoner of Love, 1998; Insanity, 2001. *Current Management:* Pyramid Entertainment Group, Los Angeles, USA. *Address:* c/o Epic Records, 10 Great Marlborough St, London W1V 2LP, England.

EVE, (Eve Jihan Jeffers), (Eve of Destruction); b. 10 Nov. 1978, Philadelphia, PA, USA. Rap Artiste; MC. *Career:* Signed to Aftermath, signed to Ruff Ryders label; Guest vocalist; Solo artiste; Film appearances: XXX, 2002; Barbershop, 2002; Television appearances incl. Third Watch, 1999. *Recordings:* Albums: Ruff Ryders' First Lady (No. 1, USA), 1999; Scorpion, 2001; Eve-olution, 2002; Contribution to film soundtrack, Barbershop, 2002. *Honours:* MTV Video Music Award, Best Female Video, for Let Me Blow Ya Mind, 2001. *Address:* c/o Interscope Records, 2220 Colorado Ave, Santa Monica, CA 90404, USA. *Website:* www.evefansonly.com.

EVELYN, George; b. 15 Jan. 1970, England. *Education:* Drums at High School. *Career:* Promoter, Funky Mule and The Headz Club, Leeds; DJ, under name of E A S E (Experimental Sample Expert), Leeds; Founder mem., Nightmares on Wax, with Kevin Harper, 1988–. *Recordings:* Albums: A Word Of Science, 1991; Smoker's Delight, 1996; Car Boot Soul, 1999; DJ Kicks, 2000; Mind Elevation, 2002. Singles: Dextrous; Stating A Fact; Aftermath; A Case of Funk (EP); Set Me Free; Happiness; Alive; Finer, 1999. *Membership:*

PRS. *Current Management:* Timebomb, Concorde. *Address:* 2 Authorpe Rd, Leeds LS6 4JB, England. *Website:* www.nightmaresonwax.com.

EVENTHAL, Avril; b. 21 May 1947, Liverpool, Merseyside, England. Entertainer; Prod. (Honky Tonk piano). m. Philip Howard Eventhal, 12 Aug. 1975. *Education:* Salford Technical College, Sound Engineer. *Career:* Television appearances: The Gong Show with Frankie Howerd, CH4; My Kind of People, Michael Barrymore; Support to 3 Degrees, Hippodrome Club, London; Prepared Bad Taste Tour of England, BBC Radio, 1988. *Recordings:* Paris Is For Lovers; The Man In My Life; You're A Man (No. 10 in Buzzcharts); Yesterday's Lovers; 2 commercial videos: Sex Slaves of New Orleans. *Membership:* PRS; BAC&S; Equity; MCPS; PPL. *Address:* 26 Dovedale Ave, Prestwich, Manchester M25 0BU, England.

EVERARD, Christopher; b. 26 May 1964, Widnes, England. Vocalist; Songwriter; Musician (guitar, piano). Partner, Karen Halliburton, 2 s., 2 d. *Career:* Hundreds of small venue gigs include Mean Fiddler; Appearance, Granada TV Arts Festival, 1990; Several sessions on local radio. *Compositions:* Tracks: Just To Survive; The Hunger; Far Over The Fields; Goodnight Angel; Fat Cats. *Recordings:* Debut album released 1995. *Publications:* Widnes Weekly News; Weekly World. *Membership:* Musicians' Union.

EVERHART, Robert; b. 16 June 1936, Nebraska, USA. Musician (12 String Guitar, Harmonica). m. Sheila Dawn Armstrong, 1 d. *Education:* College University of Nebraska, 1959–62; Iowa West BVN College, 1971; University of Oklahoma, 1990. *Career:* Associate Producer, Host, PBS National Program, Old Time Country Music; Producer, Host of Nationally Syndicated Radio Show, Old Time Music Hour; DJ, Various Stations; Curator, Owner, Pioneer Music Museum. *Compositions:* Songwriter, BMI Royal Flair Music Pub, 1964; Lets Go; Dream Angel; She Sings Sad Songs; Bad Woman Blues; Fish Pole John; Time After Time; Street Sleepers; No One Comes Near; Berlin Folksinger; I Like It Raw; Desparados Ride Again. *Recordings:* 1 Waitin For A Train; Time After Time; Everhart International; Everhart Takes The Fifth; Everhart Alive At Avoca; Keepin' It Country; Headed West; Paid Our Dues. *Publications:* Tradition Magazines; Clara Bell; Hartsbluff; Listen To The Mocking Bird; Silver Bullets; Prairie Sunrise; Snoopy Goes to Mexico; Life of Jimmie Rodgers. *Honours:* National Traditional Music Performer Award; PMECI Hall of Fame; Country Music Showcase International Hall of Fame; First Place, Old Time Country Music contests over 10 years; Lifetime Achievement Award from World Music Events; Kentucky Col. *Membership:* PMECI; SPBGMA; World Music Events; NTCMA; Great Plains Old Time Music Asscn. *Current Management:* Prairie Music, PO 492, Anita, IA 50020, USA.

EVERLY, Don (Isaac Donald); b. 1 Feb. 1937, Brownie, Kentucky, USA. Vocalist; Musician (guitar); Songwriter. m. Adela Everly, 22 March 1997. *Career:* Member, the Everly Brothers (with brother Phil), 1955–73; 1983–; Solo artiste, 1973–83; Performances include: Debut, Grand Ole Opry, 1957; British tour, supported by Bo Diddley, Rolling Stones, 1963; Represented USA, Grand Gala Du Disque, Holland, 1965; Reunion Concert, Royal Albert Hall, 1983; British tour, 1991; US tour, 1992; Royal Albert Hall, 1993; Televison includes: Everly Brothers Show, ABC TV, 1970. *Recordings:* Albums include: The Everly Brothers – They're Off and Running!, 1958; Songs Our Daddy Taught Us, 1958; It's Everly Time!, 1960; The Fabulous Style of The Everly Brothers, 1960; A Date With The Everly Brothers, 1961; Instant Party, 1962; The Golden Hits Of, 1962; The Very Best of The Everly Brothers, 1964; Gone Gone Gone, 1965; Rock 'n' Soul, 1965; In Our Image, 1966; Two Yanks In England, 1966; The Hit Sound of The Everly Brothers, 1967; The Everly Brothers Sing, 1967; The Everly Brothers Show, 1970; The Everly Brothers Original Greatest Hits, 1970; Stories We Could Tell, 1972; Pass The Chicken and Listen, 1973; The Very Best Of, 1974; Walk Right Back With..., 1975; Living Legends, 1977; Love Hurts, 1983; The Reunion Concert, 1984; Born Yesterday, 1986; Some Hearts, 1989; Classic Everly Brothers, 1992; Heartaches and Harmonies, 1994; Craftsmen, 1995; Heroes of Country Music, 1996; Brothers in Rhythm, 1998; Devoted To You, 2000; Solo albums: Don Everly, 1971; Sunset Towers, 1974; Brother Jukebox, 1977; Singles include: Bye Bye Love; Wake Up Little Susie; All I Have To Do Is Dream (No. 1, USA), 1958; Bird Dog; Problems; (Til) I Kissed You; Let It Be Me; Cathy's Clown (No. 1, USA), 1960; When Will I Be Loved; So Sad (To Watch Good Love Go Bad); Like Strangers; Walk Right Back (No. 1, UK), 1961; Temptation (No. 1, UK), 1961; Crying In The Rain. *Honours:* Star on Hollywood Walk of Fame, 1986; Inducted into Rock 'n' Roll Hall of Fame, 1986; Inducted into Jukebox Legends Hall of Fame, 1990; Lifetime Achievement Grammy, 1997. *Current Management:* International Creative Management, 8942 Wilshire Blvd, Beverly Hills, CA 90211, USA.

EVERLY, Phil; b. 19 Jan. 1939, Chicago, Illinois, USA. Vocalist; Musician (guitar); Songwriter. *Career:* Member, The Everly Brothers (with brother Don), 1955–73; 1983–; Solo artiste, 1973–83; Performances include: Debut, Grand Ole Opry, 1957; British tour, supported by Rolling Stones, 1963; Represented USA, Grand Gala Du Disque, Holland, 1965; The Reunion Concert, Royal Albert Hall, 1983; British tour, 1991; US tour, 1992; Royal Albert Hall, 1993; Television includes: The Everly Brothers Show, ABC TV,

1970. *Recordings:* Albums include: The Everly Brothers – They're Off and Running!, 1958; Songs Our Daddy Taught Us, 1958; It's Everly Time, 1960; The Fabulous Style Of, 1960; A Date With The Everly Brothers, 1961; Instant Party, 1962; Everly Brothers Sing Great Country Hits, 1963; The Very Best Of, 1964; Gone Gone Gone, 1965; Rock 'n' Soul, 1965; In Our Image, 1966; Two Yanks In England, 1966; The Everly Brothers Show, 1970; Stories We Could Tell, 1972; Pass The Chicken and Listen, 1973; Living Legends, 1977; The New Album, 1977; The Reunion Concert, 1984; EB 84, 1984; Some Hearts, 1989; Classic Everly Brothers, 1992; Heartaches and Harmonies, 1994; Heroes of Country Music, 1996; Brothers in Rhythm, 1998; Devoted To You, 2000; Solo albums: Star Spangled Springer, 1973; There's Nothing Too Good For My Baby, 1975; Mystic Line, 1975; Living Alone, 1982; Phil Everly, 1983; Louise, 1987; Singles include: Bye Bye Love, 1957; Wake Up Little Susie (No. 1, USA), 1957; All I Have To Do Is Dream (No. 1, USA), 1958; Bird Dog; (Til) I Kissed You; Let It Be Me; Cathy's Clown (No. 1, USA); When Will I Be Loved; So Sad (To Watch Good Love Go Bad); Like Strangers; Temptation (No. 1, USA); Crying In The Rain; Duets with: Cliff Richard, She Means Nothing To Me, 1983; Nanci Griffith, You Made This Love A Teardrop, 1989. *Honours:* Star on Hollywood Walk of Fame, 1986; Inducted into Rock 'n' Roll Hall of Fame, 1986; Inducted into Jukebox Legends Hall of Fame, 1990. *Current Management:* International Creative Management, 8942 Wilshire Blvd, Beverly Hills, CA 90211, USA.

EVERS, Jörg; b. 21 June 1950, Bayreuth, Germany. Composer; Prod; Arranger; Musician (guitar). m. Anna Maria, 18 March 1981, 1 s., 1 d. *Education:* Musical Science (Uni München); Richard Strauss Konservatorium München. *Career:* Tours in Europe with: Embryo; Amon Düül II; Peter Maffay; Pack. *Recordings:* Claudja Barry: Boogie Woogie Dancin' Shoes; Sylvie Vartan: Disco Queen; Claudja Barry: Down and Counting; Television: Herzblatt; Advertising: McDonalds; Odol; Maggi; Burger King; Löwenbräu; Wrigley's; Reebok; Esso. *Honours:* Best Composer's Award, Ninth Tokyo Music Festival, 1980; NY Clio Award, 1991; Div Platinum, Gold Records. *Membership:* GEMA. *Address:* PO Box 1122, 85765 Unterföhring, Munich, Germany.

EVORA, Cesaria, (La Diva aux Pieds Nus); b. 27 Aug. 1941, Mindelo, Sao Vincento, Cape Verde. Vocalist; Songwriter. *Career:* Niece of composer B Leza; Sang in bars in Mindelo from late teens; Left the island for the first time in her forties; Travelled to Lisbon to record two tracks for a compilation of Cape Verdean singers; Later went to Paris to record first solo album; Critical acclaim for Miss Perfumado; First large-scale US tour, 1995; Continues to tour internationally. *Recordings:* Albums include: Miss Perfumado, 1992; Cesaria, 1995; Mar Azul, 1999; Café Atlantico, 1999; Sao Vincente di Longe (featuring Caetano Vaeloso, Chucho Valdes and Bonnie Raitt), 2001. *Address:* c/o Lusafrica, 13 rue Auger, 93500 Pantin, France. *Website:* www.lusafrica.com.

EWANJE, Charles; b. 19 Dec. 1937, Douala, Cameroon. Musician (guitar). m. Michelle Lissandre, 12 July 1973, 3 s., 5 d. *Education:* Bachelor's Degree, Economics, French Baccalaureat. *Career:* Dance Band Musician, Guitar, Flute and Arrangements, 1960–72; Classical Guitar Teacher, 1972–76; Artist, African Classical Guitar, 1977–; Participation in Cameroon and French Televisions. *Compositions:* Makala Ma Mbasi; African Strings for Luther King; Munenge Mwe o Mboa; Earth Paradise; Esok'am; Longe Lasu. *Recordings:* Munenge and Esok'am; Ewanje; Longe Lasu. *Honours:* First Prize of Composition, Guitar Word Thoroughfare, 1982; Arranger Diploma, 1991. *Address:* 35 rue Savier, 92240 Malakoff, France.

EWING, Thomas D; b. 1 Sept. 1946, Columbus, Ohio, USA. Musician (guitar); Vocalist. m. (1) Margaret Avren, 10 June 1967; (2) Pamela Gwen

McReynolds, 12 June 1994, 2 s., 1 d., 1 step-s., 1 step-d. *Education:* BA, Journalism, BS, Education, The Ohio State University. *Career:* Earl Taylor and the Stoney Mountain Boys, 1974–77; Bill Monroe and His Blue Grass Boys, 1986–96; David Davis and the Warrior River Boys, 1996–97; 1999–2001; Jim and Jesse and the Virginia Boys, 1998; Tours: USA; Europe; Japan; Carnegie Hall, 1988; WSM Grand Ole Opry; The Nashville Network, television; Appeared in film: High Lonesome. *Recordings:* Albums: with Earl Taylor: Body and Soul, 1976; with Bill Monroe: Bluegrass '87, 1987; Southern Flavour, 1988; 50 Years at Grand Ole Opry, 1989; Cryin' Holy Unto The Lord, 1991; Solo albums: Take Me Home, 1989; Lookin' Out A Window, 1990; It's Good To Be Home, 1993. *Publications:* 30 Years Ago This Month, Bluegrass Unlimited Magazine; Editor, The Bill Monroe Reader, 2000. *Membership:* AFofM. *Address:* 564 Ziegler's Fort Rd, Gallatin, TN 37066, USA.

EYDMANN, Stuart Anthony; b. 1 May 1953, Dunfermline, Fife, Scotland. Musician (fiddle, concertina); Ethnomusicologist. m. Mairin Downes, 27 July 1991, 1 s., 1 d. *Education:* Diploma, Glasgow School of Art, 1975; PhD, The Open University, 1995. *Career:* Performer, various Scottish traditional music groups, 1972–79; Member, Whistlebinkies, 1980–; Composer, Scottish Circus, including collaborations with John Cage; Worked with: Scottish Chamber Orchestra; Scottish Ballet; Royal Scottish National Orchestra; Yehudi Menuhin, in works by Edward McGuire; Various film scores; Edinburgh International Festival and Festival Fringe; Sessions with The Cutting Crew; Tours: Sweden; France; People's Republic of China; Hong Kong; Holland; Engaged in ethnomusicological research, 1985–. *Recordings:* As performer, co-writer, co-producer: The Whistlebinkies 3, 1980; The Whistlebinkies 4, 1982; The Whistlebinkies, 1985; The Whistlebinkies Anniversary, 1991; The Whistlebinkies Inner Sound, 1991; Wanton Fling, 1996; As guest: The Music of Midlothian, 1990. *Honours:* The Glenfiddich Living Scotland Award, 1984. *Membership:* Fellow, Society of Antiquarians of Scotland; Musicians' Union; Traditional Music and Song Asscn of Scotland. *Current Management:* Jester Management. *Address:* 41 Hamilton Dr., Glasgow G12 8DW, Scotland.

EYRE, Simon James; b. 30 Nov. 1964, Sheffield, England. Musician (Guitar, Bass, Vocals). *Career:* Concert tours with Elaine Paige, The Style Council, Womack and Womack, Jimmy Ruffin; TV appearances with Randy Crawford, Jim Diamond, Sister Sledge, Second Image and Lenny Henry. *Recordings:* With Robert Palmer, Shara Nelson, and Errol Brown; Also with The Lighthouse Family, Ocean Drive album and singles Ocean Drive and Lifted. *Honours:* Quadruple Platinum Award, for Ocean Drive. *Membership:* Musicians' Union; Associate Mem., PRS. *Address:* 4 Luffman Rd, London SE12 9SX, England.

EZEKE, (Ezekel Gray); b. 26 Oct. 1943, Jamaica. Vocalist; Broadcaster; Entertainer; Composer; Caterer. m. Linda Lewis, 11 Oct. 1974, 1 s., 1 d. *Education:* Catering, Clarendon College of Further Education, Nottingham; Royal School of Church Music. *Career:* Television appearances include Opportunity Knocks; Search For A Star; Nationwide; Pebble Mill At One; Arena; Resident performer, Monte Carlo Sporting Club, 1979–84; Extensive Tours: Europe; Asia; Middle East; Radio Broadcaster, Radio ERI (Cork City, Eire); BBC Radio 3 Counties, 1986; BBC Radio One (Sunshine Show), 1990–93; BBC Radio One (Ones On One), 1993. *Recordings:* Sitting In The Moonlight, 1961; Righteous Festival, 1972; Rastaman A Come, 1972; Who's Grovelling Now? (with Tony Greig, England Cricket Captain), 1978; Ragga Ragga 1994; Oh Diana, 1994; Soon You'll Be Gone. *Publications:* Jakmandora (children's stories). *Honours:* Voted Jamaica's Top Entertainer, 1970–75; Sony Awards Certificate; Stanford St Martin Religious Broadcasting, third prize, 1992, first prize, 1994. *Membership:* Musicians' Union. *Current Management:* Habana Productions Ltd.

F

FABBRI, Franco; b. 7 Sept. 1949, Sao Paulo, Brazil. Musician; Musicologist. m. Monica Silvestris, 31 May 1980, 1 d. *Education:* Chemistry, State University of Milan; Composition, Conservatory Giuseppe Verdi, Milan; Musicology, University of Gothenburg, Sweden. *Career:* Member, experimental rock group, Stormy Six/Macchina Maccheronica, 1965–82; Freelance writer and lecturer, 1983–85; Consultant to musical institutions in Milan: Musica Nel Nostro Tempo; G Ricordi and Co, (publishers). *Recordings:* 9 albums with group La Chitarra Rotta; Domestic Flights, 1983; Tempo Rubato, 1983; La Casa Parlante, 1984; Various soundtracks and stage music. *Publications:* La Musica In Mano, 1978; Elettronica e Musica, 1984; La Musica Che Si Consuma, 1985; What Is Popular Music? (ed.), 1985; Compositore, 1986. *Address:* Strada Ave, Torre 1, San Felice, 20090 Segrate, Italy.

FABER, Shane; b. 23 Dec. 1953, Gainesville, FL, USA. Prod; Songwriter; Midi Expert; Musician (guitar, keyboards). m. Elizabeth Burkland, 22 May 1994. *Education:* Bachelor Music/Jazz Guitar, University of Miami, Florida, 1977. *Career:* Member, Bad Sneakers, 1979–86; Video, Caught in the Act; Moved to New York, 1986; Engineer for: De La Soul; A Tribe Called Quest; Queen Latifah; Brand Nubians; Biz Markie; Omar; China Black; Musical Supervisor, film Double Platinum, 1999. *Compositions:* Shine On; Ladies First. *Recordings:* Producer/mixer of albums: Reachin', Digable Planets; Debut album, Bass Is Base; Singles: Cool Like Dat; Turtle Power, from Teenage Mutant Ninja Turtles soundtrack; Digital Flavor on the Sonic Frontier, by JeepJazz Project. *Honours:* Numerous Golden Reel Awards; 2 Gold albums; 1 Platinum album; 2 Gold singles. *Current Management:* Steven Scharf Entertainment, New York. *Address:* c/o JeepJazz Music, 1 Riverdale Ave No. 3, Riverdale, NY 10463, USA.

FABIANO, Roberta Mary; b. 25 June 1952, New York, USA. Musician (guitar); Vocalist; Composer. *Education:* BA, Composition and Arrangement, Berklee College of Music, Boston, 1975. *Career:* Guitarist, composer, Lester Lanin and Peter Duchin Orchestras, 1983–84; Doc Pomus, 1984–; Songwriter for Count Basie Band; Performed for HRH Queen Elizabeth, 1985, 1986; Also performed with: Cleo Laine; Melissa Manchester; Al B Sure!; Debbie Gibson; Carol Channing; Gloria Loring; Julia Budd. *Recordings include:* Working Girl (film soundtrack). *Honours:* American Song Festival Award, 1982; New York Songwriters Showcase Award, 1984; New York State Senate Achievement Award, 1984. *Membership:* AFofM; Songwriters Guild; AFTRA.

FABRY, Anne; b. 13 Aug. 1950, Uccle, Belgium. Musician (drums, piano, keyboards). Divorced, 2 s. *Recordings:* Drava; Vent; Deux; Trio. *Address:* 163 Ave Brugmann, Boite 4, 1190 Brussels, Belgium.

FAGAN, James; b. 27 Jan. 1972, Australia. Vocalist; Musician (bouzouki, mandolin, tin whistle, clarinet, guitar, piano); Composer. *Career:* Son of Bob and Margaret Fagan, prominent participators of Sydney folk scene; Half of a duo with Nancy Kerr and also recorded and toured as part of trio with Nancy and Sandra Kerr. *Recordings:* Albums: with Nancy Kerr: Starry Gazy Pie, 1997; Steely Water, 1999; Between The Dark and The Light, 2002; features on Scalene, Sandra and Nancy Kerr, 1999; Yellow Red and Gold, Sandra Kerr, 2000. *Honours:* BBC Horizon Award, Best New Act, Nancy Kerr and James Fagan, 2000.

FAGEN, Donald; b. 10 Jan. 1948, Passaic, New Jersey, USA. Vocalist; Musician (keyboards). *Career:* Member, Steely Dan, 1972–81, reunited 1990s; Solo artiste, 1981–; Tours world-wide; Organized New York Rock and Soul Revue, New York, USA, 1990, 1991; Music Editor, US film magazine Premiere, 1988. *Recordings:* Albums: with Steely Dan: Can't Buy A Thrill, 1973; Countdown To Ecstacy, 1973; Pretzel Logic, 1974; Katy Lied, 1975; The Royal Scam, 1977; Aja, 1977; Greatest Hits, 1979; Metal Leg, 1980; Gaucho, 1981; Steely Dan Gold, 1982; Reelin' In The Years, 1985; Do It Again, 1987; Remastered – The Very Best of Steely Dan, 1993; Citizen Steely Dan – 1972–80, 1993; Alive In America, 1995; Two Against Nature, 2000; Solo albums: The Nightfly, 1982; Kamakiriad, 1993; Singles include: Do It Again, 1972; Reelin' In The Years, 1973; Show Biz Kids, 1973; My Old School, 1973; Rikki Don't Lose That Number, 1974; Black Friday, 1975; Haitian Divorce, 1976; Deacon Blues, 1977; Peg, 1977; FM (No Static At All), 1978; Hey Nineteen, 1980; Time Out of Mind, 1981; Solo singles: True Companion; Century's End, used in film Bright Lights Big City, 1988; I G Y (What A Beautiful World), 1982; Tomorrow's Girls, 1993; Contributor, Zazu, Rosie Vela, 1987; The New York Rock and Soul Revue – Live At The Beacon, 1992. *Honours:* Grammy Award, Best-Engineered Non-Classical Recording, Aja, 1978; Q Inspiration Award, 1993; Inducted into Hollywood's Rock Walk, 1993; 4 Grammy Awards, including Album of the Year, for Two Against Nature, 2001. *Current Management:* HK Management, 8900 Wilshire Blvd, Suite 300, Beverly Hills, CA 90211, USA. *Website:* www.steelydan.com.

FAHEY, Siobhan; b. 10 Sept. 1957, London, England. Vocalist; Songwriter. m. Dave Stewart, 1 Aug. 1987. *Career:* Press officer, Decca Records; Singer, all-female group, Bananarama, 1981–88, reunion recording, 1998; Mem., Shakespears Sister, with Marcella Detroit, 1988–93; Solo artiste 1993–; Numerous concerts, television and radio performances. *Recordings:* Albums: with Bananarama: Deep Sea Skiving, 1983; Bananarama, 1984; True Confessions, 1986; Wow!, 1987; with Shakespears Sister: Sacred Heart, 1989; Hormonally Yours, 1992; Also appeared on: Aerial No. 5: A Journey In Sound, 1992; Greetings From The Gutter, 1995; Divas Of Pop, 1996. Singles: with Bananarama: Aie A Mwana, 1981; It Ain't What You Do (with Fun Boy Three), 1982; Really Sayin' Somethin', 1982; Shy Boy, 1982; Na Na Hey Hey Kiss Him Goodbye, 1983; Robert De Niro's Waiting, 1984; Cruel Summer (featured in film The Karate Kid), 1984; Venus (No. 1, USA), 1986; I Heard A Rumour, 1987; Love In The First Degree, 1987; Waterloo, 1998; with Shakespears Sister: You're History, 1989; Break My Heart, 1990; Goodbye Cruel World, 1991; Hello (Turn Your Radio On), 1992; Stay (No. 1, UK), 1992; I Don't Care, 1992; My 16th Apology (EP), 1993; Solo: Waiting (for film Shopping), 1994; Prehistoric Daze (for film The Flintstones); I Can Drive, 1996; Bitter Pill, 2002; Contributor, Do They Know It's Christmas?, Band Aid (No. 1, UK), 1984; Let It Be, Ferry Aid (Zeebrugge ferry disaster relief, No. 1, UK), 1987. *Compositions:* Co-writer, Young At Heart, The Bluebells, 1984 (No. 1, UK, 1993); with Marcella Detroit: all tracks on album, Hormonally Yours, 1992. *Honours:* BRIT Award, Best Video, Stay, 1993; Ivor Novello Award, Outstanding Contemporary Song Collection, Hormonally Yours, 1993. *Address:* c/o God Made Me Hardcore Ltd, Studio 200, Cable St Studios, 566 Cable St, London E1W 3HB, England. *Website:* www.siobhanfahey.com.

FAIRBAIRN, Keith; b. 14 Jan. 1963, Horsham, Surrey, England. Musician (percussion). *Education:* Guildhall School of Music. *Career:* Worked with: Shirley Bassey; Mike Oldfield; Lulu; Judie Tzuke; Madelaine Bell; Vic Damone; Dionne Warwick; Joe Longthorne; Madonna; Tom Jones; Numerous television shows for BBC; LWT; Granada. *Recordings:* Andrew Lloyd Webber; Jim Steinman; Nick Heyward; Shirley Bassey; Madelaine Bell; Joe Longthorne; Evita; Cats; Whistle Down the Wind; Numerous films, shows, library music. *Honours:* AGSM. *Membership:* Musicians' Union. *Address:* 11 Craydon Rd, Amptuill, Bedfordshire MK45 2CE, England.

FAIRLEY, Colin; Prod; Engineer; Musician (drums). *Career:* Former drummer; Engineer, Air Studios; Freelance record producer, engineer, 1981–. *Recordings:* As producer/engineer, albums include: with Nick Lowe: Cowboy Outfit; The Rose of England; Pinker Than Proud; for Elvis Costello: Punch The Clock; Goodbye Cruel World; Blood and Chocolate; for The Teardrop Explodes: Wilder; Everybody Wants To Shag The Teardrop Explodes; also T-Bird Rhythm, Fabulous Thunderbirds; Sisters, The Bluebells; Gentlemen Take Polaroids, Japan; Welcome To The Cruise, Judie Tzuke; Stop, Sam Brown; Titles, Mick Karn; Porcupine, Echo and The Bunnymen; Singles include; with Madness: It Must Be Love; Grey Day; Driving In My Car; also Pills and Soap, Elvis Costello; Young At Heart, The Bluebells; Quiet Life, Japan; Reward, Teardrop Explodes; Stay With Me 'Til Dawn, Judie Tzuke. *Current Management:* c/o Stephen Budd Management. *Address:* 109B Regents Park Rd, London NW1 8UR, England.

FAIRWEATHER-LOW, Andy; b. 8 Aug. 1950, Ystrad Mynach, Hengoed, Wales. Vocalist; Musician (guitar). *Career:* Member, The Taffbeats; The Sect Maniacs; Founder member, Amen Corner, 1966–69; Performances include: Headline act, Pop Proms, Royal Albert Hall, 1969; Solo artiste; Session musician for artists including: Pink Floyd; Roger Waters; Sang with All-Star ARMS band (benefit for research into multiple sclerosis), 1987; Tour with Chris Rea, 1990; Tour with George Harrison, Eric Clapton, Japan, 1991; Member, Eric Clapton's backing band, 1990s; Film appearance, Scream and Scream Again, 1969. *Recordings:* Albums: with Amen Corner: Round Amen Corner, 1968; Explosive Company, 1969; Solo albums: Beginning From An End, 1971; Spider Jivin', 1974; La Booga Rooga, 1975; Be Bop 'N' Holla, 1976; Mega-Shebang, 1980; with Eric Clapton: Unplugged, 1992; From The Cradle, 1994; Pilgrim, 1996; Reptile, 2001; Singles include: Gin House Blues, 1967; World of Broken Hearts, 1967; Bend Me Shape Me, 1968; High In The Sky, 1968; (If Paradise Is) Half As Nice (No. 1, UK), 1969; Solo: Natural Sinner, 1970; Reggae Tune, 1974; Wide Eyed and Legless, 1975.

FAITHFULL, Marianne; b. 29 Dec. 1946, Hampstead, London, England. Vocalist. 1 s. *Career:* Recording artist, 1964–; Tours, appearances include: British tour with Roy Orbison, 1965; US tour with Gene Pitney, 1965; Uxbridge Blues and Folk Festival, 1965; Montreux, Golden Rose Festival, 1966; Roger Water's The Wall, Berlin, 1990; Chieftains' Music Festival, London, 1991; Acting roles include: I'll Never Forget Whatisname, 1967; Three Sisters, Chekkov, London, 1967; Hamlet, 1970; Kurt Weill's Seven Deadly Sins, St Ann's Cathedral, New York, 1990; Film appearance, Girl On A Motorcycle, 1968. *Recordings:* Singles include: As Tears Go By; Come and

Stay With Me; This Little Bird; Summer Nights; Something Better/Sister Morphine; The Ballad of Lucy Jordan; Dreaming My Dreams; Electra, 1999; Albums: Come My Way, 1965; Marianne Faithfull, 1965; Go Away From My World, 1966; Faithfull Forever, 1966; Marianne Faithfull's Greatest Hits, 1969; Faithless, with the Grease Band, 1978; Broken English, 1979; Dangerous Acquaintances, 1981; A Child's Adventure, 1983; Strange Weather, 1987; Blazing Away, 1990; A Secret Life, 1995; 20th Century Blues, 1997; The Seven Deadly Sins, 1998; Vagabond Ways, 1999; Stranger On Earth (compilation), 2001; Contributor, Lost In The Stars – The Music of Kurt Weill, 1984; The Bells of Dublin, The Chieftains, 1992. *Publications:* Faithfull (ghost written by David Dalton). *Current Management:* Art Collins Management, PO Box 561, Pine Bush, NY 12566, USA.

FAKANAS, Viorgos; b. 18 July 1961, Athens, Greece. Composer; Arranger; Musician (bass); Author. m. Nicoletta Pitsikali, 12 June 1992, 1 s. *Education:* Diploma, Economics, University of Athens; Classical guitar; Classical piano. *Career:* Only Greek correspondant as bass player, Europe, (European Community Youth Jazz Orchestra), 1981–84; Founder, ISKRA (major Greek jazz group), 1984–88; Numerous concerts, Greece and abroad, include: Locabettus Theatre; Herodio, Athens Concert Hall, performed own composition: Topazi, A Composition For Large Strings and Jazz Ensemble; Founder, tutor, Contemporary Music School of Athens; Numerous TV, radio appearances; Currently leader of own jazz group. *Recordings:* A New Day, 1986; Horizon, 1989; Parastasis, 1990; Amorosa, 1992; Stand-Art, 1995; Session musician, more than 200 recordings with major Greek artists. *Publications:* Educational books: For The Bass (Vol. I, II); Scales of Modern Music, Jazz Harmony, Modern Counterpoint. *Honours:* Hon. Mem., Greek Radio and TV's Jazz Orchestra. *Membership:* Mem., Hellenic Musicians' Union. *Current Management:* Nicoletta Pitsivalli. *Address:* 3 L Possidonas St, 18344 Moshato – Athens, Greece.

FALLON, Peter Sean; b. 3 June 1968, Reigate, Surrey, England. Record Prod; Songwriter. *Education:* Piano from age 6. *Career:* Signed to Big One Records aged 18, 1986; UK Club Promo Tour, signed to Swanyard Records, 1990; Performed at Cesmé 91 Festival in Turkey; Top of the Pops; Pebble Mill; This Morning, ITV, 1993; BBC Radio 1 Session, 1994. *Recordings:* with Twin Beat: Let's Pick Up The Pieces, 1988; with Fallon: Get On The Move, 1990; with Technotronic: Get Up Remix, 1991; with Stevie Wonder: You Never Lose Remix, 1991; As writer, producer: with David Hasselhoff: If I Could Only Say Goodbye, 1993; Tighter and Tighter, 1993; with Dannii Minogue: Love and Affection; As writer: with Céline Dion: Don't Turn Away From Me; with Groove U: Step By Step. *Membership:* PRS; BAC&S; ASCAP. *Current Management:* EMI Music Publishing London. *Address:* c/o Broadhill Recording Studios, Ockley Lane, Keymer, Hassocks, West Sussex BN6 8PA, England.

FÄLTSKOG, Agnetha Åse; b. 5 April 1950, Jönköping, Sweden. Vocalist; Actress. m. (1) Björn Ulvæus, 1971, divorced, (2) Tomas Sonnenfeld. *Career:* Solo recording artiste, aged 17; Actress, Jesus Christ Superstar, Sweden; Mem., Swedish pop group, Abba, 1973–82; Winner, Eurovision Song Contest, 1974; World-wide tours; Concerts include: Royal Performance, Stockholm, 1976; Royal Albert Hall, London, 1977; UNICEF concert, New York, 1979; Wembley Arena, six sell-out performances, 1979; Reunion with Abba, Swedish TV's This Is Your Life, 1986; The Story of Abba (Channel 4), 1991; Solo artiste, 1982–90; Films: Abba: The Movie, 1977; As actress: Rakenstam, 1983. *Recordings:* Albums: with Abba: Waterloo, 1974; Abba, 1976; Greatest Hits, 1976; Arrival, 1977; The Album, 1978; Voulez-Vous, 1979; Greatest Hits Vol. 2, 1979; Super Trouper, 1980; The Visitors, 1981; The Singles: The First Ten Years, 1982; Thank You For The Music, 1983; Absolute Abba, 1988; Abba Gold, 1992; More Abba Gold, 1993; Forever Gold, 1998; The Definitive Collection, 2001; Solo: Eleven Women In One Building, 1975; Wrap Your Arms Around Me, 1983; Eyes of a Woman, 1985; I Stand Alone, 1988; My Love My Life, 1998. Singles include: with Abba: Ring Ring, 1973; Waterloo (No. 1, UK), 1974; Mamma Mia (No. 1, UK), 1975; Dancing Queen (No. 1, UK and USA), 1976; Fernando (No. 1, UK), 1976; Money Money Money, 1976; Knowing Me Knowing You (No. 1, UK), 1977; The Name Of The Game (No. 1, UK), 1977; Take A Chance On Me (No. 1, UK), 1978; Summer Night City, 1978; Chiquitita, 1979; Does Your Mother Know?, 1979; Angel Eyes/Voulez-Vous, 1979; Gimme Gimme Gimme (A Man After Midnight), 1979; I Have A Dream, 1979; The Winner Takes It All (No. 1, UK), 1980; Super Trouper (No. 1, UK), 1980; On and On and On, 1981; Lay All Your Love On Me, 1981; One Of Us, 1981; When All Is Said and Done, 1982; Head Over Heels, 1982; The Day Before You Came, 1982; Under Attack, 1982; Thank You For The Music, 1983; Solo: I Was So In Love (No. 1, Sweden); The Heat Is On; Can't Shake You Loose; I Wasn't The One (Who Said Goodbye). *Honours:* with Abba: Gold discs; Best-selling group in history of popular music, Guinness Book of Records, 1979; World Music Award, Best Selling Swedish Artist, 1993. *Website:* www.abbasite.com.

FAME, Georgie, (Clive Powell); b. 26 Sept. 1943, Leigh, Lancashire, England. Vocalist; Musician (keyboards). *Career:* Member, Billy Fury's backing group, The Blue Flames, 1961; Band replaced with the Tornados; London residencies, Georgie Fame and the Blue Flames, 1961–63; Tours, concerts television include: UK Tamla Motown Package Tour, 1965; National

Jazz and Blues Festival, 1965, 1966; Pop From Britain concert, Royal Albert Hall, 1965; Grand Gala Du Disque, Amsterdam, 1966; Founder, Georgie Fame Band, 1966; Concerts include: International Popular Music Festival, Brazil, 1967; Royal Albert Hall, 1967, 1969; Television series with Alan Price, 1971; Concerts as leader of various groups and ensmebles; Television variety shows and commercials, 1971–; Keyboard player, Van Morrison tour, 1989; International Jazz Festival, Blackpool, 1992; Continues to play on jazz circuit. *Recordings:* Hit singles: Yeh Yeh (No. 1, UK), 1965; In The Meantime, 1965; Get Away (No. 1, UK), 1966; Sweet Things, 1966; Sunny, 1966; Sitting In The Park, 1967; Because I Love You (own composition), 1967; The Ballad of Bonnie and Clyde (No. 1, UK), 1968; Peaceful, 1969; Rosetta, with Alan Price, 1971; Albums: Rhythm and Blues At The Flamingo, 1963; Fame At Last, 1964; Sound Venture, 1966; Hall of Fame, 1967; Two Faces of Fame, 1967; The Third Face of Fame, 1968; Seventh Son, 1969; Fame and Price, Price and Fame Together, 1971; All Me Own Work, 1972; Georgie Fame, 1974; That's What Friends Are For, 1978; Georgie Fame Right Now, 1979; Closing The Gap, 1980; Hoagland, with Annie Ross, 1981; In Goodman's Land, 1983; My Favourite Songs, 1984; No Worries, 1988; Georgie Fame – The First 30 Years, 1989; Cool Cat Blues, 1991; Three Line Whip, 1995; Blues and Me, 1996; Walking Wounded, 1999; Name Droppin', 1999; Poet In New York, 2001; How Long Has This Been Going On, with Van Morrison, 1996; Contributor, Avalon Sunset, Van Morrison, 1989; Contributor, film soundtrack Glengarry Glen Ross, 1992. *Address:* The Leighton Pope Organisation, 8 Glenthorpe Mews, 115a Glenthorne Rd, Hammersmith, London W6 0LJ, England.

FANFANT, Thierry; b. 27 March 1964, Paris, France. Musician (Bass Guitar). *Education:* Diploma of Audiovisual Technician. *Education:* Private music lessons, 1986–87; Course in musical centre, 1 year. *Career:* Olympia, with Michel Pugain, 1993; Casino de Paris, 1995; France Follies, La Rochelle, 1994, 1995, 1996; France Follies, Montréal; Pantemps de Bourges, 1990, 1991, 1995; Festival Jazz, Nice, 1994; Petit Journal, 1997. *Compositions:* Don d'organe; Ernest et firmin; Pausove Muen. *Recordings:* With: Enzo-Enzo; Michel Fugain; Maria Glen; Tuluo De Piscopo; Hajime Mizoguehi; Shukichi Kina; Beethova Obas; Mario Canonge; Taratata; Tery Boise. *Honours:* Success Prize of the Year, 1994. *Address:* 3 Allée, Claude Bernard, 93440 Dugny, France.

FANNING, Bernard; b. 15 Aug. 1969. Vocalist; Musician (guitar, keyboards). *Education:* University of Queensland, Journalism student. *Career:* Joined Brisbane-based rock group Powderfinger, 1992; Steadily built reputation on many Australian tours/festival appearances; International breakthrough with Odyssey Number Five album; Constant world-wide touring throughout 2000–01 ending with New Suburban Fables 2001 Australian shows. *Recordings:* Albums: Parables For Wooden Ears, 1994; Double Allergic, 1996; Internationalist, 1998; Odyssey Number Five, 2000; Singles: Powderfinger Blue (EP), Transfusion (EP), 1993; Tail, Grave Concern, 1994; Save Your Skin, Mr Kneebone (EP), 1995; Pick You Up, D.A.F., Living Type, 1996; Take Me In, 1997; The Day You Come, Don't Wanna Be Left Out/Good-Day Ray, 1998; Already Gone, Passenger, 1999; My Happiness, 2000; Like A Dog, The Metre, 2001. *Honours:* ARIA Awards: Album of the Year; Song of the Year; Best Rock Album; Best Cover Artwork, 1999; six times platinum fourth album on Australian chart for 67 weeks by end of 2001; Only home-grown act ever to play more than 3 consecutive nights at Festival Hall, Australia. *Address:* c/o Republic Records, Australia. *Website:* www.powderfinger.com.

FARGO, Donna (Yvonne Vaughn); b. 10 Nov. 1945, Mount Airy, North Carolina, USA. Country Vocalist; Songwriter. m. Stan Silver. *Career:* Solo recording artist, 1969–; Numerous television and stage appearances include Country Music Festival, Wembley, 1978. *Compositions include:* Funny Face, 1972; The Happiest Girl In The Whole USA, 1972; Superman, 1973; You Were Always There, 1973; You Can't Be A Beacon (If Your Light Don't Shine), 1974; That Was Yesterday; Soldier Boy (all US Country No. 1 hits); Members Only (duet with Billy Joe Royal), 1988; Albums include: The Happiest Girl in the Whole USA, 1972; My Second Album, 1973; Shame on Me, 1977; Dark-Eyed Lady, 1978; Brotherly Love, 1981, Winners, 1986; Country Sweethearts, 1996. *Publications:* Trust in Yourself, 1997; To the Love of My Life, 2001. *Honours:* Billboard, Best New Female Country Artist, 1972; NARM Best Selling Country Artist, 1972–73; ACM Top Female Vocalist, 1972–73; Robert J Burton Award, Most performed country Song, 1972–73; C & W Record of Year on Jukeboxes, 1973; Grammy, Best Female Country Performer, for Funny Face, 1973; Gold discs world-wide. *Current Management:* c/o Stan Silver, Prima-Donna Entertainment Corpn, PO Box 150527, Nashville, TN 37215, USA. *Website:* www.donnafargo.com.

FARLEY, Terry; b. 13 June 1959, London, England. Prod; Remixer; DJ. *Career:* Co-founder: Boy's Own fanzine (with Andrew Weatherall and Cymon Eccles), Boy's Own Records (later Junior Boy's Own, now Junior Recordings); Promoter/DJ at Boy's Own events; Remixed (with Pete Heller): Ultra Nate, Primal Scream, Janet Jackson, Happy Mondays; Member: Bocca Juniors, Fire Island, Roach Motel; Collaborations: Pete Heller, Andrew Weatherall, Rui Da Silva. *Recordings:* Singles: Raise (with Bocca Juniors), 1990; In Your Bones (with Fire Island), 1992; There But For The Grace of God (with Fire Island), 1994; Ultra Flava (with Pete Heller), 1995; The Rising Sun (with Pete Heller),

1999. *Current Management:* c/o Junior Recordings, The Saga Centre, 326 Kensal Rd, London W10 5BZ, England.

FARNELL, Thomas; b. 24 Aug. 1947, Birmingham, England. Musician (drums). m. 22 Sept. 1968, 1 s., 2 d. *Career:* Toured USA extensively with Savoy Brown; Worked with Fairport Convention; Worked with Raymond Frogatt (Top British Country singer). *Recordings:* Recorded with: Savoy Brown; Fairport Convention; Raymond Froggatt. *Honours:* Diploma Ed, Percussion. *Membership:* Musicians' Union. *Address:* 94 Leasow Dr., Edgbaston, Birmingham B15 2SW, England.

FARNHAM, John Peter; b. 1 July 1949. Vocalist. m. April 1973, 2 s. *Career:* Singer; Entertainer; TV Host; Ld Singer, Little River Band, 1982–85; Launched Greenpeace album, Rainbow Warriors, Moscow, 1989. *Recordings include:* Uncovered, 1980; Whispering Jack, album, 1986; Age of Reason, 1988; Chain Reaction, 1990; Full House Album, 1991; Played Jesus in Jesus Christ Superstar, Jesus Christ Superstar – The Album, 1992; Romeo's Heart, album, 1996; 33 1/3, 2000; Highlights of the Main Event, live recording of concert with Olivia Newton-John and Anthony Warlow. *Honours:* Whispering Jack, biggest selling album in Australia by Australian Artist; Australian of Year, 1988; Talk of the Town Tour largest grossing Australian tour, 1994; AO, 1996; Most Broadcast Australian Artist, Phonographic Performance Company of Australia, 1997. *Address:* c/o Talentworks Pty Ltd, Suite 1, 633 Victoria St, Abbotsford, Victoria 3067, Australia.

FARRELL, Perry, (Perry Bernstein); b. 29 March 1959, New York, USA. Vocalist. *Career:* Member, Jane's Addiction, 1980s; Originator, Lollapalooza rock festival; Jane's Addiction split; Formed Porno for Pyros, 1993; Collaboration with Steven Perkins, and David Navarro and Flea from Red Hot Chili Peppers on soundtrack for Howard Stern film Private Parts, 1997; Set up Insect World record label; Contributed track Tonight (from West Side Story) for MOM2 charity album; Band split, 1998. *Recordings:* Singles with Jane's Addiction: Been Caught Stealing, 1990; Stop, 1990; Classic Girl, 1991; Then She Did, 1991; Albums: Jane's Addiction, 1987; Nothing's Shocking, 1988; Ritual do lo Habitual, 1990; Singles with Porno for Pyros: Pets, 1993; Sadness, 1994; Albums: Porno for Pyros, 1993; Good God's Urge, 1996; Solo albums: Rev, 1999; Song Yet To Be Sung, 2001.

FARRENDEN, Shaun; b. 17 April 1962, Bishopstoke, England. Musician (didjeridu). *Career:* Concerts include: Glastonbury Festival; Glastonbury Assembly Rooms. *Recordings:* Albums: Earth Songs, 1992; Double Spiral, 1994; Yidaki, 1996; With Global: Shamanka; Gig na Gig; Guest musician, Welcome To The Cali, Ron Kavana and the Bucks; Television music for Channel 4. *Publications:* Earth Vibrations, An Introduction To The Didjeridu. *Membership:* Musicians' Union. *Address:* 125 Ashmore Rd, London W9 3DA, England.

FARRER, Rob; b. 20 March 1974, Leicester. Musician (percussion). *Education:* Charles Keene College; Guildhall School of Music and Drama, 1992–96; GSMD Post Diploma Orchestral Training Course, 1996–97. *Career:* TFI Friday; Top of the Pops; Saturday Live with Lee Hurst; Glastonbury, 1998; Radio 1 Sessions. *Recordings:* Casanova; Short Album About Love; Fin De Siecle. *Current Management:* Divine Management, Top Floor, 1 Crowcross St, London EC1M. *Address:* The Grange, 50 Main St, Hoby, Leicester LE14 3DT, England.

FARRINGTON, Clive; b. 25 Sept. 1957, Altrincham, South Manchester, England. Vocalist; Musician (bass guitar, keyboards, programming, drums, percussion). *Education:* Civil Engineering City and Guilds; A Level Music Theory, Technology. *Career:* Vocalist, bass guitarist, When In Rome, 2 major US tours, 1985, 1986; Tours: Europe, Brazil, 1992; Remix for Diesel track Man Alive, Australia, 1994; Remix, Chill Factor track One Touch, Australia; Writer, producer, Underground Circus on tracks: Wrapped Around Your Finger; Crazy; Tree Without A Shadow; Remix for Bing Abrahams track One Touch; Currently working with John McGeoch on project Blue, as vocalist, programmer, producer. *Recordings:* Writer, producer, lead vocalist, album: When In Rome (hit in USA, Europe, South America); Single: The Promise (No. 1, USA Dance chart). *Membership:* Musicians' Union; PRS (Associate mem.). *Current Management:* William Hunt. *Address:* 68 Neal St, Covent Garden, London WC2, England.

FARROW, Andrew McGregor; b. 24 July 1964, Hamilton, Bermuda. Music Man; A&R Consultant. *Education:* Sheffield Polytechnic. *Career:* Vocalist, Living Dead, 1980–82; Established AMF Music, 1987; Partner, Far North Music, 1988; Proprietor, (renamed) Northern Music Company. *Honours:* BA (Hons). *Address:* Northern Music Company, Cheapside Chambers, 43 Cheapside, Bradford BD1 4HP, England.

FASSIE, Brenda; b. 1964, Cape Town, South Africa. Vocalist; Songwriter. *Career:* Singing for tourists by age 5; Went to Johannesburg and joined vocal trio Joy, aged 15; Moved on to group Family and recorded international hit Weekend Special; Group renamed Brenda and The Big Dudes; Welcomed Mandela at his home on release and recorded Black President in his honour; Has toured Africa and Europe. *Recordings:* Albums include: Brenda Fassie,

1990; Too Late For Mama; 1991; Amagents, 1993; Now Is The Time, Umuntu Uyashitsha, 1996; Paparazzi, 1997; Memeza, 1998; Nomakanjani, 1999; Aamadlozi, 2000; Mina Nawe, 2001. *Honours:* Memeza (Shout) album was first South African recording to go platinum on its first day of release, selling more than 500,000 units; Kora All Africa Music Award, Best Female Artist, 1999; South African Music Award, Best Selling Recording Artist, 2001.

FAST, (Brian Leiser); b. 29 March, USA. Musician (keyboards, bass, trumpet, harmonica, programming). *Career:* Founding mem., Fun Lovin' Criminals, 1993–; Numerous tours, festivals and television appearances. *Recordings:* Albums: Come Find Yourself, 1996; 100% Colombian, 1998; Mimosa—The Lounge Album, 1999; Loco, 2001; Bag Of Hits, 2002. Singles: The Grave And The Constant (EP), 1996; The Fun Lovin' Criminal, 1996; Scooby Snacks, 1996; King Of New York, 1997; I'm Not In Love, 1997; Love Unlimited, 1998; Big Night Out, 1998; Korean Bodega, 1999; Loco, 2001; Bump/Run Daddy Run, 2001. *Address:* c/o Chrysalis Group plc, The Chrysalis Bldg, Bramley Rd, London W10 6SP, England. *Website:* www.fun-lovin-criminals.co.uk.

FATBOY SLIM. See: **COOK, Norman**.

FATONE, Joey (Joseph Anthony, Jr); b. 28 Jan. 1977, Brooklyn, NY, USA. Vocalist. *Career:* Father sang in New York dco-wop group The Orions; Relocated to Orlando aged 12; Mem., *NSYNC vocal quintet, 1995–; Signed to BMG Ariola Munich, 1997; First headline US tour, 1998. *Recordings:* Albums: *NSYNC, 1998; Home For Christmas, 1998; No Strings Attached, 2000; Celebrity, 2001. Singles include: I Want You Back, 1997; Tearin' Up My Heart, 1997; Let The Music Heal Your Soul (various artists charity single credited to Bravo All Stars), 1999; Music Of My Heart (with Gloria Estefan), 1999; Bye, Bye, Bye, 2000; I'll Never Stop, 2000; It's Gonna Be Me, 2000; This I Promise You, 2000; Pop, 2001; Gone, 2001. *Honours:* Presented with keys to City of Orlando, 2000; American Music Award, Favorite Pop/Rock Band, Duo or Group, 2002. *Address:* c/o Wright Entertainment Group, PO Box 590009, Orlando, FL 32859–0009, USA. *Website:* www.nsync.com.

FAWCETT, David Everington; b. 27 March 1938, Watford, Hertfordshire, England. Commercial Man; Musician (banjo). m. Gloria Ann (née Jeffrey), 1 s., 1 d. *Career:* Television: Winner, with Main Avenue Jazz band, Opportunity Knocks, 1978; Radio broadcasts, with TJ4, Sounds of Jazz, BBC Radio, 1982–85. *Recordings:* with TJS: Richard Leach's Northside Jazzband. *Membership:* Musicians' Union. *Address:* 31 Langley Rd, Watford, Herts WD1 3PR, England.

FEEHAN, David; b. 9 Oct. 1948, Wellington, New Zealand. Vocalist; Songwriter; Prod; Vocal Tutor. m. Shelley Catherine Melody, 3 s. *Education:* UE Accountancy Units; Classical to Grade 8, 3 years New Zealand Opera Company. *Career:* EMI Session vocalist, 1964–70; Lead singer, top New Zealand band Tapestry, 1970–78; Lead singer, Rodger Fox Big Band, 1976–88; Concerts at Ronnie Scott's, London; Montreux Jazz Festival, Switzerland; Hong Kong; Singapore; New York; Poland; Los Angeles; Sydney; Vancouver; Leader of David Feehan Band, 1988–; Appearances on all major New Zealand television shows and concerts; Played Jesus in Jesus Christ Superstar, 1983. *Recordings:* with Tapestry: It's Wrong, number 3 hit, 1973; Vocalist on Rodger Fox Big Band albums including: Montreux Live, 1980–; Montreux II Live, 1981; New York Tapes, 1980; Runner-up, Songwriters Contest, San Diego with: Still The One, 1989; 2 solo albums: Ballade, 1986; DF, 1993; Appearances on over 20 other albums. *Publications:* Two children's books due for publication; Writing a vocal technique book. *Honours:* Finalist, APRA and Best New Artist Awards (Composition); Best Jazz Album Award. *Membership:* Music tutor at Massey University, Wellington, New Zealand. *Current Management:* Tapestry Music Ltd. *Address:* PO Box 575 Wellington, New Zealand.

FEEHILY, Mark Michael Patrick; b. 28 May 1980, Sligo, Ireland. Vocalist. *Career:* Mem., Westlife, 1999–; Numerous tours, festivals and television appearances. *Recordings:* Albums: Westlife, 1999; Coast To Coast (No. 1, UK), 2000; World of Our Own (No. 1, UK), 2001; Where Dreams Come True, 2001; Unbreakable: The Greatest Hits, 2002. Singles: Swear It Again (No. 1, UK), 1999; If I Let You Go, 1999; Flying Without Wings (No. 1, UK), 1999; I Have A Dream (No. 1, UK), 1999; Fool Again (No. 1, UK), 2000; Against All Odds (with Mariah Carey, No. 1, UK), 2000; My Love (No. 1, UK), 2000; What Makes A Man, 2000; Uptown Girl (for Comic Relief charity, No. 1, UK), 2001; Queen Of My Heart (No. 1, UK), 2001; World Of Our Own (No. 1, UK), 2002; Bop Bop Baby, 2002; Westlife Unbreakable, 2002. *Honours:* BRIT Awards, Best Pop Act, 2001, 2002. *Address:* c/o RCA Records, 1540 Broadway, New York, NY 10036, USA. *Website:* www.westlife.co.uk.

FEHLING, Annika; b. 25 Oct. 1962, Gothenburg, Sweden. Vocalist; Songwriter; Musician (guitar, piano). *Education:* University of Lund, Sweden, 1981–82; Theatre Art School of Skara, 1982–83; State School of Theatre, Malmo, 1988; Singing and Piano lessons; Course in arranging and composing, Stockholm, 1993. *Career:* Mére Ubu in King Ubu, musical; Solo-singer, Duke Ellingtons Sacred Concert; Participated in films, Women on the Roof, Petri Tears; Participating in the Sweden Song Contest, televised, 1998; Concerts with Visby Big Band in Norway, Poland, Rhodes. *Compositions:* A Woman's Jazz. *Recordings:* Singles: Oktoberbarn (October Child), 1993; Naren Stjarna Faller (When a Star Falls), 1998; Solo Albums: Jazz Fehlings, 1996; Alskar Du? (Do You Love), 1997. *Publications:* The Real Swede, 1997. *Honours:* STIM, Swedens ASCAP Prize, 1992, 1996, 1999; State Art Prize, Art Cncl, 1993, 1994, 1999; SKAP Prize, 1997. *Membership:* STIM; SKAP. *Current Management:* Musicano Records, c/o Arne Söderquist, Strandg 22 II, 62156 Visby, Sweden.

FEIGIN, Leo; b. 1 Feb. 1938, Leningrad, USSR. m. Lora Feigin Denisenko, 1 s. *Education:* Institute of Physical Culture and Sports, Leningrad; Pedagogical Institute. *Career:* Master of Sports, USSR, 1959; Broadcaster, World Service, BBC, 1974–92; Producer, Presenter, Weekly New Music Programme, 1974–98; Proprietor, Leo Records, 1979–. *Recordings:* Over 400 LPs and CDs. *Publications:* Russian Jazz, 1985; New Music From Russia, Documentary. *Membership:* PRS; MCPS. *Address:* Leo Records, The Cottage, 6 Anerley Hill, London SE19 2AA, England.

FEINSTEIN, Michael Jay; b. 7 Sept. 1956, Columbus, OH, USA. Vocalist; Musician (piano); Actor; Musicologist. *Career:* Archivist, Ira Gershwin, 1977–83; Assistant to Harry Warren, 1979–81; Hotel residencies in USA, 1984–89; Accompanist, artistes including Liza Minnelli; Estelle Reiner; Rose Marie; Jessie Matthews; Rosemary Clooney, 1991–; Numerous concerts include: George Gershwin 50th Anniversary celebration, Los Angeles, 1987; Irving Berlin 100th Anniversary celebration, Los Angeles, 1988; Royal Command Performance, London, 1988; Cole Porter 100th Birthday Concert, Carnegie Hall, New York, 1991; Michael Feinstein in Concert–Isn't It Romantic, Broadway/US tour, 1988–89; Stage: Ira Gershwin Centennial, Carnegie Hall, 1996; Television appearances include: Broadway Sings – The Music of Jule Styne, 1987; George Gershwin Remembered, 1987; Thirtysomething, 1987; Omnibus, 1989; Sing a Song of Hollywood, 1995. *Compositions:* Film score and songs for Get Bruce, 1997. *Recordings:* Numerous albums include: Pure Gershwin, 1985; Live At The Algonquin, 1986; Michael Feinstein Sings Irving Berlin, 1987; Isn't It Romantic, 1987; Over There–Songs of War and Peace, 1989; The Mem Album, 1989; Burton Lane Song Book, Vol. I, 1990; Jule Styne Song Book, 1991; Pure Imagination, 1991; Jerry Herman Song Book, 1994; Hugh Martin Song Book, 1995; Such Sweet Sorrow, 1995; Nice Work If You Can Get It, 1996; Nobody But You, 1998; Big City Rhythms, 1999; Michael Feinstein With The Israel Philharmonic Orchestra, 2001. *Publications:* Editor, Ira Gershwin Song Book; Contributor, Washington Post and New York Times; Autobiography, Nice Work If You Can Get It, 1995. *Honours:* 3 Golden Laurel Awards; San Francisco Council For Entertainment; NYC Seal of Approval, 1987; Drama Desk Award, 1988; Outer Critics Circle Award, 1988; Doctorate of Fine Arts, California State University at Los Angeles, 1997; Scholarships in his honour established in New York colleges. *Membership:* ASCAP. *Address:* 648 N Robertson Blvd, Los Angeles, CA 90069, USA.

FELDMAN, Samuel Leon; b. 14 March 1949, Shanghai, People's Republic of China. Entertainment Co Exec. 1 s., 2 d. *Career:* President, S L Feldman and Associates, a Division of A & F Music Ltd, fully-integrated entertainment company, co-owned with partner Bruce Allen; Management clients include: Bryan Adams, Joni Mitchell, The Chieftains and Sissel; Partner, TMP, largest independent publisher in Canada. *Address:* #200–1505 W Second Ave, Vancouver, British Columbia V6H 3Y4, Canada.

FELICIANO, José; b. 10 Sept. 1945, Lares, Puerto Rico. Vocalist; Musician (guitar, bass, drums, piano, percussion). *Career:* Moved to New York as child; Performer, English and Latin music, becoming one of most popular artists in Spanish-speaking world and English pop music world; Chosen to sing The Star Spangled Banner, World series baseball, first one to ever stylise it, 1968; Recorded albums in Argentina, Mexico, Venezuela, Italy, USA, Austria; Television show throughout South America; Sang and composed theme music to TV series Chico and The Man; Recording artiste, classical guitar music, English pop, Spanish-language and jazz recordings. *Recordings include:* The Voice and Guitar of José Feliciano, 1964; A Bag Full of Soul, 1965; Feliciano!, 1967; Feliciano 10 To 23, 1969; Alive Alive-O, 1969; Souled, 1969; Fireworks, 1970; That The Spirit Needs, 1971; José Feliciano Sings, 1972; Compartments, 1973; And The Feeling's Good, 1974; Just Wanna Rock 'N' Roll, 1974; Sweet Soul Music, 1976; José Feliciano, 1980; Escenas De Amor, 1982; Romance In The Night, 1983; Los Exitos De José Feliciano, 1984; The Best of José Feliciano, 1985; Portrait, 1985; Tu Immenso Amor, 1987; I'm Never Gonna Change, 1989; Steppin' Out, 1990; Latin Street '92, 1992; A Tribute To The Beatles, 1993; Americano, 1996; On Second Thought, 1997; Senor Bolero, 1998; Noches De Bohemia, 2000; Singles: Light My Fire; Hi Heel Sneakers; The Sun Will Shine. *Honours:* Six Grammy Awards; Billboard Lifetime Achievement Award; ASCAP Golden Note Award. *Current Management:* John Regna, 297–101 Kinderkamack Rd, Oradell, NJ 07649, USA.

FELIX DA HOUSECAT, (Felix Stallings), (Sharkimaxx, Thee Maddkatt Courtship, Aphrohead, Thee Maddkatt Chronicles); b. 1971, Detroit, Michigan, USA. Prod; Remixer; DJ. *Career:* Based in Chicago; Started producing house tracks with DJ Pierre; Pierre's Phantasy Club classic

Phantasy Girl released, 1986; Founder: Radikal Fear; Clashbackk; Thee Black Label; Recorded tracks for numerous labels including: Strictly Rhythm; Soma; Guerilla; FFRR; Collaborations: DJ Pierre; Miss Kittin; Mark Bell; Harrison Crump; K Alexi. *Recordings:* Albums: By Dawn's Early Light, 1994; Metropolis Present Day?; Thee Album, 1995; I Know Electrikboy, 1999; Kittins and Thee Glitz, 2001; Singles: Thee Dawn, In The Dark We Live (Thee Lite), 1993; Clashback (as Sharkimaxx), 1994; Dirty Motha (with Qwilo), 1996; My Life Muzik, 1999; Crybaby, Silver Screen/Shower Scene, 2001. *Honours:* Muzik Award, Best Album, Kittins and Thee Glitz, 2001. *Address:* c/o London Records, Waldron House, 57–63 Old Church St, London SW3 5BS, England.

FELL, Simon Howard; b. 13 Jan. 1959, Dewsbury, West Yorkshire, England. Musician (Double Bass); Composer. m. Jo Fell, 2 Oct. 1982. *Education:* Fitzwilliam College, University of Cambridge; Double Bass with Peter Leah, 1974–78. *Compositions:* Compilation I, 1985; Compilation II, 1990; Four slices of Zappa, 1992; Music for 10(0), 1993; LeoSuite, 1996; Icons, 1997; Cubism, 1998; Composition N 30, 1998; Papers, 1998; Three Mondrians, 1999. *Recordings:* Compilation I, 1985; Compilation II, 1990; Music for 10(0), 1995; Composition No 30, 1998; Registered Firm, 1998; Pure Water Construction, 1998; Ghost Notes, 1998; Frankenstein, 1998. *Publications:* Report on the Composition of Improvised Music Nos 1–4, 1993, 1994, 1997, 1998. *Membership:* PRS; MCPS; Musicians' Union. *Current Management:* Bruce's Fingers. *Address:* c/o PO Box 57, Haverhill, Suffolk CB9 8RD, England.

FELLOUÉ, Guillermo; b. 10 Feb. 1932, Havana, Cuba. Musician (bugle, trumpet). m. Rosana Felloué, 15 July 1969. *Education:* Conservatory; Private teachers. *Career:* Professional from age 13; First trumpet and soloist with leading Cuban singers: Arsenio Rodriguez; Benny More; Soloist with Perez Prado, South America; Tours, Europe, Japan with Havana Cuban Boys of Armando Orefiche; First trumpet and soloist, with the Rosana and Guil Afro-Cuban jazz show, 2 tours Japan; Arrived in Paris aged 19; Played at Moulin Rouge; Casino de Cannes; Palm Beach; First trumpet soloist, Big Band from Bourdeaux-Aquitane for radio; Casino, Sporting Club, Monte-Carlo, for 7 years; First trumpet, soloist, Bekummernis of Luc Le Masne; Television concerts, tours with singer Ellie Medeiros: Japan; New York; Canada; Co-director, Los Salseros. *Recordings:* with Arseño Rodriguez Conjunto Colonial, Cuba; 3 albums with Bekumernis de Luc Le Masne; Album and single with: Ellie Medeiros; Album: Los Salseros; Single with Pierre Vassiliu. *Address:* 20 rue de Rungis, 75013 Paris, France.

FELTHAM, Mark; b. 20 Oct. 1955, London, England. Musician (harmonica); Composer. m. Susan, 25 June 1994, 1 s. *Education:* South East London Technical School, Greenwich. *Career:* Founder member, Nine Below Zero, 1977–82; Harmonica player with Rory Gallagher for last 11 years; Varied studio work including: Georgie Fame, 1984; Godley and Creme (harmonica album), 1986; New Model Army; Deacon Blue, 1988; Texas, 1988; The The, 1989–91; Talk Talk, 1989–92; Joan Armatrading, 1992; Annie Lennox, 1995. *Recordings include:* Albums: with Nine Below Zero: Packed Fair and Square, 1979; Live At The Marquee, 1980; Don't Point Your Finger, 1981; with Godley and Creme: Goodbye Blue Sky, 1986; Other recordings include albums by: Rory Gallagher; Roger Daltrey; Roy Harper; Talk Talk; Paul Young; Lightning Seeds; Oasis; Annie Lennox; Joe Cocker; Michael Ball; Robbie Williams; Ocean Colour Scene; Television documentary scores, live guest appearances. *Membership:* Musicians' Union. *Current Management:* Session Connection, London SW9, England.

FELTS, Narvel; b. 11 Nov. 1938, Keiser, Arkansas, USA. Country/Rockabilly Vocalist; Musician (guitar). m. Loretta Stanfield Felts, 30 April 1962, 1 s., deceased, 1 d. *Career:* High School talent contest aged 17, Bernie, Missouri; One of original rockabillies, career lasting over 43 years; One of the major country artists of the '70s. *Compositions:* Three Thousand Miles; Lonely Hours; Red Hair and Green Eyes; Four Seasons of Life; Foggy Misty Morning; When We Were Together; Away. *Recordings:* Reconsider Me; Lonely Teardrops; Drift Away; Somebody Hold Me (Until She Passes By); Funny How Time Slips Away; When Your Good Love Was Mine; Everlasting Love; My Prayer; All in the Name of Love; Honey Love. *Honours:* Single of the Year, Billboard and Cashbox, 1975; 10 ASCAP Awards, 1973, 1974, 1977, 1979; ASCAP Artist of the Year, 1977; Rockabilly Hall of Fame, 1997. *Membership:* American Federation of Musicians; Reunion of Professional Entertainers. *Current Management:* Joe Taylor Artist Agency. *Address:* 2802 Columbine Pl., Nashville, TN 37204, USA.

FENDER, Freddy, (Baldemar G. Huerta); b. 4 June 1937, San Benito, Texas, USA. Vocalist; Musician (guitar). m. Evangelina Muniz, 10 Aug. 1957, 2 s., 1 d. *Education:* Sociology degree. *Career:* Solo Country music singer; Founder member, Texas Tornados, 1990; Film appearance: The Milagro Beanfield War, 1987. *Recordings:* Singles: Don't Be Cruel; Wasted Days Wasted Nights; Before The Next Teardrop Falls (No. 1, USA); Secret Love; Vaya Con Dios; You'll Lose A Good Thing; Albums include: Before The Next Teardrop Falls, 1975; Since I Met You Baby, 1975; Are You Ready For Freddy?, 1975; If You're Ever In Texas, 1976; Rock 'n' Country, 1976; Don't You Love Me, 1977; Swamp Gold, 1978; The Texas Balladeer, 1979; Tem-Mex,

1979; Together We Drifted Apart, 1980; El Mejor De Freddy Fender, 1986; Crazy Baby, 1987; 16 Greatest Hits, 1993; with Texas Tornados: Texas Tornados, 1990; Zone of Your Own, 1991; The Freddy Fender Collection, 1991; Canciones de Mi Barrio, 1993; Wasted Days and Wasted Nights, 1995; In His Prime, 1997; Crazy Cajun Recordings, 1999; Tell It Like It Is, 1999. *Honours:* Grammy, Outstanding Mexican-American award, 1977. *Membership:* CMA; AFTRA; Broadcast Music Inc; AFofM. *Current Management:* Jim Halsey Co. *Address:* 3225 South Norwood, Tulsa, OK 74135, USA.

FENGER, Sos; b. 2 Dec. 1961, Copenhagen, Denmark. Vocalist; Songwriter. 1 s. *Education:* Piano, guitar and singing lessons. *Career:* Touring with Pop Band, News, early 1980s; Soulband with brother, Love Construction, 1986–89; Solo Career, 1989–; Tour with Doky Brothers and Adam Nussbaum; Recording with Toots Thielemanns and Randy Brecker; Contributor on several Scandinavian Albums. *Recordings:* Vinterdage, 1989; Sos Fenger on Holiday, 1992; Et Kys Herfra, 1994; Camouflage, 1996; Greatest Hits, 1998. *Honours:* Female Singer of the Year, 1986, 1990; Grammy Awards; Spies Fondet's Music Award, 1993. *Current Management:* Annetta Elmo, Holbergsgade 16, Copenhagen K, Denmark. *Address:* Kanslergade 7, 2100 Copenhagen, Denmark.

FENTON, George; b. 19 Oct. 1950, London, England. Composer; Musician (guitar); *Compositions:* For television: Hitting Town, 1974; Out, 1978; Rain on the Roof, 1980; The History Man, 1981; Bergerac (theme), 1981; Fox, 1981; A Woman of No Importance, 1982; Saigon: Year of the Cat, 1983; An Englishman Abroad, 1983; East of Ipswich, 1987; Talking Heads, 1987; 102 Boulevard Haussmann, 1991; China: Beyond the Clouds, 1994; Talking Heads 2, 1998; For film: Private Road, 1971; Bloody Kids, 1979; Hussy, 1980; Gandhi, 1982; Runners, 1983; The Company of Wolves, 1984; Billy the Kid and the Green Baize Vampire, 1985; Clockwise, 1986; Walter and June, 1986; 84 Charing Cross Road, 1986; Cry Freedom, 1987; White Mischief, 1987; High Spirits, 1988; A Handful of Dust, 1988; The Dressmaker, 1988; Dangerous Liasions, 1988; We're No Angels, 1989; Memphis Belle, 1990; White Palace, 1990; The Long Walk Home, 1990; The Fisher King, 1991; Hero, 1992; Final Analysis, 1992; Groundhog Day, 1993; Shadowlands, 1993; Born Yesterday, 1993; China Moon, 1994; Ladybird Ladybird, 1994; The Madness of King George (adaptations), 1994; Mixed Nuts, 1994; Land and Freedom, 1995; The Viking Sagas, 1995; Mary Reilly, 1996; Heaven's Prisoners, 1996; Multiplicity, 1996; Carla's Song, 1996; The Crucible, 1996; In Love and War, 1996; The Woodlanders, 1998; Dangerous Beauty, 1998; The Object of My Affection, 1998; My Name is Joe, 1998; Ever After, 1998; Living Out Loud, 1998; You've Got Mail, 1998; Entropy, 1999; Grey Owl, 1999; Anna and the King, 1999; Bread and Roses, 2000; Center Stage, 2000; Lucky Numbers, 2000. *Current Management:* The Ryan Co. *Address:* c/o Debonair Records, Eaton House, 39 Lower Richmond Rd, Putney, London SW15 1ET, England.

FENTON, Graham; b. 28 May 1949, West London, England. Vocalist. m. Caroline, 25 May 1991. *Career:* Various bands, 1970s; Matchbox, 1979–86; Television and radio includes over 12 appearances Top of the Pops; Hits, tours, Germany, Holland, Switzerland, Spain, Austria, Belgium, Yugoslavia; Television commercial, Japan; Tour with Gene Vincent's Blue Caps, UK and Europe, 1993; Solo tour, television and radio, Australia, 1994; Buddy Holly tribute, Clear Lake, Iowa, USA, 1994; Occasional work with original hit line-up of Matchbox as well as solo work. *Recordings:* Rockabilly Rebel, (No. 1 hit in many countries); Buzz Buzz A Diddle It; Midnite Dynamoes; When You Ask About Love (No. 4, UK charts); Over The Rainbow; Babes In The Wood; Recent compilations: Matchbox Live, 2000; Rockabilly Rebel, 2000; Films: Blue Suede Shoes; Born Too Late (biography). *Honours:* Gold, Silver, UK, Australia, Finland, Yugoslavia. *Membership:* Musicians' Union. *Current Management:* Paul Barrett, Rock 'n' Roll Enterprises. *Address:* 16 Grove Pl., Penarth, South Glamorgan CF6 2LD, South Wales.

FENWICK, Raymond John; b. 18 July 1946, Romford, Essex, England. Musician (guitar); Prod. *Education:* Guitar lessons. *Career:* Member, The Sydicats, 1965; Marty Wilde, 1965; The Tee Set, 1966; After Tea, 1968; The Spencer Davis Group, 1968–72; Fancy, 1974; The Ian Gillan Band, 1977; Forcefield, 1984–92; Johnny Mars Band, 1990; Concerts include: US tours with The Spencer Davis Group, 1968–72; Fancy, 1974; Butterfly Ball, 1974; Ian Gillan Band, 1977; Japanese tour, 1978; Wizzard's Convention, 1995. *Recordings:* After Tea, 1968; Magpie, television theme music, 1970s; Bo Diddley sessions, London, 1972; with Fancy: 2 US Top 20 singles: Wild Thing, 1974; Touch Me, 1974; with The Ian Gillan Band: Albums: Live At The Budokan, 1978; Child In Time, 1976; Clear Air Turbulence, 1977; Scarubs, 1977; What I Did on My Vacation, 1986; Rockfield Mines, 1997; Live at the Rainbow, 1998; Solo album: Keep America Beautiful – Get A Haircut, 1997; Riding The Rock Machine (compilation), 1997. *Membership:* PRS; MCPS; Repro. *Current Management:* Fenwick Productions. *Address:* 4 Cassons Close, Weston Hills, Lincolnshire PE12 6DX, England.

FERAL. See: BRANN, Chris.

FERGUSON, David; b. 24 May 1953, London, England. Composer. m., 1 s. *Education:* BA Hons, School of Slavonic and East European Studies, 1971–74.

Career: Keyboards, composer with Random Hold, 1978–83; Touring Europe and USA with Peter Gabriel; XTC; Orchestral Manouevres In The Dark. *Compositions:* TV series include: Cracker; The Gambling Man; American Visions; Black Box; Barbara Vine Trilogy; Inspector Rebus Quartet; TV films: Disaster At Valdez; Coded Hostile; Hostile Waters; The Woman in White; The Ice House; Jekyll and Hyde, 2003. *Membership:* Chair., British Academy of Composers and Songwriters; Chair., Creators' Rights Alliance. *Current Management:* Music For Films. *Address:* 34 Batchelor St, London N1 0EG, England. *Website:* www.davidferguson.com.

FERGUSON, James Warner; b. 10 Dec. 1950, Missouri, USA. Musician (Bass); Vocalist. m. Antonia F Ferguson, 1 d. *Education:* MM, Jazz Performance, University of South Carolina, 1981. *Career:* Staff Bassist, The American Popular Singer, NPR; Staff Bassist, Main St Jazz Festival, PBS; Staff Singer, Country Music Association Awards. *Compositions:* Not Just Another Pretty Bass. *Recordings:* The Messiah – A Soulful Celebration; Together At Last; Great Hits of the Past; Shadowlands; Three Good Reasons; Cheek to Cheek; River of Love; First Christmas; Our Love Is Here To Stay; Not Just Another Pretty Bass. *Honours:* Music Department Aluminus of the Year, 1997. *Membership:* Screen Actors Guild; American Federation of Television and Radio Artists; American Federation of Musicians. *Current Management:* Jim Ferguson Music, 210 Mayfair Rd, Nashville, TN 37205, USA.

FERGUSON, Maynard; b. 4 May 1928, Montréal, QC, Canada. Musician (trumpet); Bandleader. *Career:* Trumpet player with Boyd Raeburn, Jimmy Dorsey, Charlie Barnet, 1940s; Trumpeter, Stan Kenton Orchestra, 1950–53; Freelance musician, 1953–56; Leader, own 13 piece orchestra, 1957–65; Leader, own sextet, 1965–; Worked with Slide Hampton; Don Sebesky; Bill Chase; Don Ellis; Bill Berry, 1950s–60s. *Recordings:* Numerous albums include: Sketches On Standards, with Stan Kenton, 1953–55; Dimensions, 1954; Maynard Ferguson Octet, 1955; Around The Horn With Maynard Ferguson, 1955; Maynard Ferguson Conducts The Birdland Dream Band, 1956; Boy With A Lot of Brass, 1957; A Message From Newport, 1958; Swingin' My Way Through College, 1958; A Message From Birdland, 1959; Plays Jazz For Dancing, 1959; Newport Suite, 1960; Let's Face The Music and Dance, 1960; Straightaway Jazz Themes, 1961; Si! Si!, M F, 1962; Message From Maynard, 1963; The New Sound Of..., 1964; Come Blow Your Horn, 1964; Color Him Wild, 1964; The Blues Roar, 1964; Sis By Sis, 1965; Ridin' High, 1966; Live At Expo '67 Montréal, 1967; M F Horn, 1970; Alive and Well In London, 1971; Magnitude, 1971; M F Horn 2, 1972; M F Horn 3, 1973; M F Horn 4 + 5, Live At Jimmy's, 1973; Chameleon, 1974; Primal Scream, 1975; New Vintage, 1977; Hot, 1977; Carnival, 1978; Uncle Joe Shannon, 1978; Conquistador, 1978; It's My Time, 1980; Hollywood, 1982; Storm, 1982; Live From San Francisco, 1983; High Voltage, 1988; Big Bop Nouveau, 1989; Footpath Cafe, 1993; Live from London, 1993; These Cats Can Swing, 1994; One More Trip to Birdland, 1996; Brass Attitude, 1998. *Address:* c/o Rogers and Cowan PR, 1888 Century Park E, Suite 500, Los Angeles, CA 90067–1709, USA.

FERGUSON, Neil; b. 6 Dec. 1954, Castleford, Yorkshire, England. Prod; Engineer; Musician (guitar, keyboards). m. Helen Mary Ferguson, 11 Dec. 1976, 1 s., 1 d. *Career:* Records produced, engineered for: Black Lace; Chumbawamba; Smokie; Credit To The Nation; Chris Norman; Nick Berry; Current member, Chumbawamba. *Recordings:* Agadoo; Teenage Sensation; Heartbeat (television theme music); Tubthumping, by Chumbawamba (No. 2, UK), 1997; Amnesia, by Chumbawamba, 1997; Tacky Love Song, by Credit To The Nation, 1998; Top of The World, by Chumbawamba, 1998; Uneasy Listening album, by Chumbawamba, 1999; backing vocals on This Is The Voice, by The Oyster Band, 1999; Readymades album, by Chumbawamba, 2002. *Membership:* Musicians' Union; PRS. *Address:* 185 Highgate, Bradford BD9 5PU, England. *E-mail:* fergieneil@aol.com.

FERGUSON, Sheila Diana; b. 8 Oct. 1947, Philadelphia, Pennsylvania, USA. Vocalist; Actress; Author; Presenter. m. Christopher L Robinson, 8 March 1980, two d. (twins). *Career:* Lead singer, Three Degrees, 1965–86; Solo artist; Star of Thames sitcom: Land of Hope and Gloria, 1990; Cameo roles: French Connection; Sandford and Son; Desmonds; Brookside; Presenter GMTV; BBC, LWT variety shows; Major world tours; West End debut, Always: The Musical, 1997; Grande Theatre, Blackpool, 1996; Ronnie Scott's, 1997; Performed for the armed forces in Bosnia, Germany, Falklands, Cyprus, N Ireland. *Recordings:* 28 Gold records include: Dirty Old Man; When Will I See You Again (No. 1, UK), 1974; Take Good of Yourself; T S O P; The Runner; Givin' Up Givin' In; Toast of Love; Golden Lady Movie; Also appears on: Best of the Three Degrees, 1996; Great R&B Female Groups, 1998. *Publications:* Soul food: Classic Cuisine of The American South, 1990. *Honours:* Tokyo Music Festival; 28 Gold Records. *Membership:* Equity Councilor; Musicians' Union; SAG; AFTRA; Founder Director, PAMRA. *Current Management:* Brian Marshall (Variety); Jean Diamond, London Management (Acting). *Address:* PO Box 1400, Maidenhead Berkshire, SL6 8LX, England.

FERRER (PLANAS), Ibrahim; b. 1927, Santiago, Cuba. Vocalist. *Career:* Sang with local bands from age 13 including: Los Jóvenes del Son; Conjunto

Sorpresa; Conjunto Wilson; Pacho Alonso's Maravilla de Beltran; Hit record El Platanar de Bartolo with Orquesta Chepin-Chóven, 1955; Worked with Orquesta Ritmo Oriental and Beny Moré; Toured internationally with Los Bocucos, 1962; Retired, 1991; Made a comeback on the Buena Vista Social Club recordings; Appeared in Wim Wenders' documentary film Buena Vista Social Club; London Jazz Festival, 2001; Collaborations: Ruben González; Omara Portuonda; Ry Cooder; Afro-Cuban All-Stars; Sings various Cuban song styles including: Guaracha; Son; Bolero. *Recordings:* recent Albums: Buena Vista Social Club, 1997; Buena Vista Social Club Presents Ibrahim Ferrer, 1999; appears on: Toda Cuba Le Gusta (with Afro Cuban All-Stars), 1997; Distinto Diferente (with Afro Cuban All-Stars), 1999; Chanchullo (with Ruben González), 2000; Latin Simone, Qué Pasa Contigo (with Gorillaz), 2001. *Honours:* Grammy, Best New Artist, 2000. *Address:* c/o World Circuit Ltd, First Floor, Shoreditch Stables, 138 Kingsland Rd, London E2 8DY, England.

FERRERA, Stephen; b. 26 Dec. 1959, Boston, Massachusetts, USA. Prod; Songwriter; Musician; Record Exec. *Education:* BM, New England Conservatory of Music; MM, Juilliard School of Music. *Career:* As producer, songwriter, arranger, musical director, musician, worked with: Bob Dylan; Billy Joel; Chaka Khan; Eurythmics; Suzanne Vega; Julian Cope; Shakespears Sister; Holly Cole; Shawn Colvin; Tom Jones; Mica Paris; Womack and Womack; Dave Stewart; Currently Head of A&R, The Echo Label. *Honours:* Platinum and Gold records. *Membership:* Musicians' Union; NARAS; ASCAP. *Address:* The Echo Label, The Chrysalis Building, 13 Bramley Rd, London W10 6SP, England.

FERRIS, Jim; b. 29 March 1955, Coventry, England. Musician (drums); Drum Tutor. m. Janice, 1990. *Education:* Coventry School of Music. *Career:* Member, Coventry Corps of Drums, age 11–16; Appeared Albert Hall aged 15; Supported many major television artists in cabaret; Several BBC radio broadcasts, German television, West Country television; Worked in cabaret bands, theatre orchestra, rock bands. *Recordings:* 2 albums released by AJ's Big Band; Session recording work at studios in London and the Midlands. *Publications:* Mere Mortals Guide To Drumming, Levels 1–4, 1994–99. *Honours:* Described as 'a fantastic drummer', Stage and TV Today. *Membership:* Musicians' Union. *Current Management:* Jim Ferris. *Address:* Brodick House, 31 Hereford Close, Exmouth, Devon EX8 5QT, England.

FERRONE, Stephen; b. 25 April 1950, Brighton, West Sussex, England. Musician (drums). 1 s., 1 d. *Education:* Nice Conservatory of Music, France. *Career:* Played with: Brian Auger; Average White Band; Eric Clapton; Duran Duran; Tom Petty and The Heartbreakers; Chaka Khan; Jeffery Osbourn; George Benson; Anita Baker; Chris Botti; David Bowie; Sophie B Hawkins; Al Jarreau; Scritti Politti; Steve Winwood; Paul Young; Tribute To Buddy Rich. *Recordings:* with Average White Band: Cut The Cake; Soul Searching; Person To Person; Journey Man-Unplugged, Eric Clapton; I Feel For You, Chaka Khan; Secret Story, Pat Metheny; Wildflowers, Tom Petty; Stay With Me Tonight, Jeffery Osborne; I'm Your Baby Tonight, Whitney Houston. *Membership:* ASCAP. *Current Management:* Steve White (Cavaricci and White). *Address:* 120 E 56th St, Suite 1150, New York City, NY 10022, USA.

FERRY, Bryan; b. 26 Sept. 1945, Washington, County Durham, England. Vocalist; Songwriter; Musician. 4 s. *Education:* Fine Art, Newcastle University. *Career:* Formed Roxy Music, 1971–83, re-formed for concert tour 2001; Solo artiste, 1973–; Worked with: Brian Eno; Phil Manzanera; Andy Mackay; Steve Ferrone; David Williams; Robin Trower; Pino Palladino; Nile Rodgers; Carleen Anderson; Shara Nelson; Jhelisa; Numerous world-wide tours; Major concerts include: Crystal Palace, 1972; Live Aid, Wembley, 1985; Radio City, New York, 1988; Wembley, 1989; Support tours, Alice Cooper, David Bowie; Television appearances include: Subject of Without Walls documentary, 1992; Videos: New Town (live), 1990; Total Recall (documentary), 1990. *Recordings:* Albums: Solo: These Foolish Things, 1973; Another Time Another Place, 1974; Let's Stick Together, 1976; In Your Mind, 1977; The Bride Stripped Bare, 1978; Boys and Girls (No. 1, UK), 1985; Bete Noire, 1987; The Ultimate Collection, 1988; Taxi, 1993; Mamounia, 1994; As Time Goes By, 1999; Frantic, 2002; with Roxy Music: Roxy Music, 1972; For Your Pleasure, 1973; Stranded, 1973; Country Life, 1974; Siren, 1975; Viva Roxy Music, 1976; Manifesto, 1979; Flesh and Blood (No. 1, UK), 1980; Avalon, (No. 1, UK), 1982; The High Road (live mini album), 1983; The Atlantic Years, 1983; Street Life, 1987; Compilations include: The Thrill of It All, 1995; More Than This – The Best of Roxy Music and Bryan Ferry, 1995; Slave To Love – Best of The Ballads, 2000; The Very Best of Roxy Music, 2001. Singles include: Love Is The Drug, 1975; Dance Away, 1979; Angel Eyes, 1979; Over You, 1980; Jealous Guy (No. 1, UK), 1981; Slave To Love, 1985; The Right Stuff, 1987; I Put A Spell On You, 1993. *Honours:* Grand Prix Du Disque, Best Album, Montreux Golden Rose Festival, 1973. *Current Management:* IE Management, 59a Chesson Rd, London W14 9QS, England.

FEW, Bobby (Robert); b. 21 Oct. 1935, Cleveland, Ohio, USA. Musician (piano); Composer. m. 7 July 1972, 1 s., 2 d. *Education:* Cleveland Institute of Music; 2 private teachers. *Career:* Played vibraphone with Bob Cunningham (cousin); Played with Hyawatha Edmonson; Dick Shelton; Member, Bill Dixon's Free Jazz Workshop, 1958; Worked with Frank Wright; Booker Ervin;

Formed own trio; Pianist, musical director, 3 major tours with, Brook Benton; Accompanist, Frank Foster; Roland Kirk; Formed group Center of The World; Collaboration with Alan Silva's Celestial Communication Orchestra; Member of Steve Lacy's Sextet, tours USA, 1980–; Several solo piano television appearances, Paris; Live concerts, television and radio, France, Japan, Italy, Spain, Morocco. *Recordings:* Solo albums: Few Coming Thru; More Or Less Few; Continental Jazz Express; Mysteries; With own trio: Bobby Few Trio; with Steve Lacy: The Owl; The Flame; Dreams; Prospectus; Songs; Ballets; Momentum; Brion Gysin Songs; Condor; Live At The Sweet Basil In New York; with Center of The World Group: Center of The World; Last Polka In Nancy; Solo and Duets; Uhuru Na Umoja (with Art Taylor); with Albert Ayler: Reevaluations; Music Is The Healing Force; Last album; with Archie Shepp: Coral Rock; Peachin' Can; The In-Between, Booker Erwin; Traffic, Noah Howard; Egyptian Oasis, Talib Kibwe; Indians, Sunny Murray; El Saxofon, Hans Dulfer; What Else Is New, Mike Ellis; Secrets From The Sun, Joe Lee Wilson; Diom Futa, Jo Maka; Flowers Around Cleveland, David Murray 1995; Also appears on: Vespers, 1993; Critics Picks Vol. 2, 1997. *Membership:* SACEM. *Address:* 42 rue Deuingand, 92300 Levallois, France. *E-mail:* boobyfew@minitel.net.

FIALA, Vît; b. 13 June 1943, Mladà, Boleslav. Musician (Double Bass); Composer; Arranger. m. Lidmila Hlusková 1 s., 1 d. *Education:* Charles University, Prague. *Career:* Hana Hegerová Ensemble; Eva Pilarová Ensemble; Jazzee-Czech; Jazz Festivals, Europe. *Compositions:* Mene Tekel Blues; More Note Samba; I Remember Jobim; I Remember Rogers; Super Blue Note Blues. *Recordings:* The Famous Jazz Tunes, Tea For Two; Eva Emingerová; Blue Soul; Irena Budweiserová. *Membership:* Czech Jazz Society. *Address:* Judr Vît Fiala Spanelská 8, 120 00 Prague 2, Czech Republic.

FIDRI, Ladislav; b. 30 May 1940, Osijek, Croatia. Musician (trumpet); Arranger; Conductor. m. Mia Fidri, 11 March 1961, 1 s. *Education:* Pedagogue Teacher's College of Music. *Career:* Soloist, Radio-television Big Band, Zagreb, Croatia; Played most jazz festivals, Europe; Member, Gerry Mulligan's International Big Band, Europe; Also played with Clark Terry Big Band; Several times member, EBU Big Bands in Europe; Played, recorded with: Lucky Thompson; Stan Getz; Johnny Griffin; Sou Nistico; Leo Wright; Art Farmer; Albert Mangelsdorf; Kai Winding; Buddy DeFranco; Maynard Ferguson. *Publications:* Jazz Greetings From The East; Blue Sunset; Nuages. *Membership:* HRT Big Band; Croatian Musician Union. *Current Management:* Raimund Frick. *Address:* Kreuzacker 5, 85049 Ingoldstadt, Germany.

FIELD, Lauren Danielle; b. 15 July 1962, London, England. Vocalist. m. 7 June 1990, Charles Foskett, 1 s. *Education:* Drama School Diploma; Grade 5 Music Theory; Grade 6 Piano; Voice Theory; Singing. *Career:* Musical Theatre: Duke of York's; New End, Hampstead; Recording sessions for many top artists; Television appearances: Top of the Pops; Pebble Mill; Radio sessions for BBC Radio 2 and local stations; Leader, own 7-piece band; Currently playing London showcases; Opened own school and workshops for vocal coaching and tuition, 1997; Co-writer, co-producer, Joe Cocker, 1997. *Membership:* PRS; Equity. *Current Management:* Veracruz Music International. *Address:* 43 Capron Rd, Dunstable, Bedfordshire LU5 5AL, England.

FIGES, Kevin John; b. 29 Aug. 1964, Portsmouth, England. Jazz, Classical Musician (saxophone); Composer. *Education:* Hons Degree, Masters Degree, Electrical and Electronic Engineering; Diploma, Classical Saxophone (Guildhall School Music). *Career:* Performed in own jazz quartet, all major venues, West Country, across UK; Appeared on Radio 2 Jazz Parade and on Radio 4; Writes own material for quartet; Performed with contemporary jazz orchestra Ultrasound. *Compositions:* Bacon Madras, 1997; HP Source, 1997. *Recordings:* Dishy; Critical Moment, with Ultrasound. *Honours:* South West touring awards, 1994; Lottery Funding for CD, 1997; Jazz Services Touring Award, 1997. *Membership:* Musicians' Union. *Address:* 64 Robertson Rd, Eastville, Bristol BS56 6JT, England.

FILAN, Shane Steven; b. 5 July 1979, Sligo, Ireland. Vocalist. *Career:* Mem., Westlife, 1999–; Numerous tours, festivals and television appearances. *Recordings:* Albums: Westlife, 1999; Coast To Coast (No. 1, UK), 2000; World of Our Own (No. 1, UK), 2001; Where Dreams Come True, 2001; Unbreakable: The Greatest Hits, 2002. Singles: Swear It Again (No. 1, UK), 1999; If I Let You Go, 1999; Flying Without Wings (No. 1, UK), 1999; I Have A Dream (No. 1, UK), 1999; Fool Again (No. 1, UK), 2000; Against All Odds (with Mariah Carey, No. 1, UK), 2000; My Love (No. 1, UK), 2000; What Makes A Man, 2000; Uptown Girl (for Comic Relief charity, No. 1, UK), 2001; Queen Of My Heart (No. 1, UK), 2001; World Of Our Own (No. 1, UK), 2002; Bop Bop Baby, 2002; Westlife Unbreakable, 2002. *Honours:* BRIT Awards, Best Pop Act, 2001, 2002. *Address:* c/o RCA Records, 1540 Broadway, New York, NY 10036, USA. *Website:* www.westlife.co.uk.

FILEK, Michal; b. 22 April 1964, Pardubice, Czech Republic. Musician (double bass); Jazz/Blues Vocalist. m. Marie Kurova, 1985, 1 d. *Education:* Jaroslav Jezek's Conservatory, Prague; Summer courses in Frydland; General Double Bass Teachers, Frantisek Uhlir, Jaromir Honzák. *Career:* Jazz

Entertainer, Bass Player, Singer, Twin Q, Prague, Metropolitan Jazz Band; Jazz-Blues Singer, Twin Q Group; Teacher, state school bass and improvisation; Accompaniment of many prominent soloists and groups. *Compositions:* Berny Blues; Everywhere is It Good, At Home is My Wife. *Recordings:* Twin Q and Elena, 1995; Metropolitan Jazz Band, 1996; Everybody's Looking for Wonders; Lenka Filipova, 1998. *Membership:* Jazz Club Sydney. *Current Management:* Volf Music Centre, Str Mechenická 2556/10, 141 00 Prague 4, Czech Republic. *Address:* Nevanova 1054, 16300 Prague 6, Czech Republic.

FILT, Anni Martensen; b. 23 Nov. 1955, Thorsted, Denmark. Vocalist; Songwriter. m. Klaus Filt, 25 June 1977. *Career:* Lead singer, Anni and the Countrysun, 1989–92; Savannah Rose Band, 1992–; Television host, 1991–93. *Recordings:* Show Me The Way To Nashville, 1989; Tall Dark Stranger, 1991; Giving It All, 1993; Savannah Rose Band, 1995; Dream Catcher, 1997; Clovo Walker, 1999. *Membership:* Danish Artists Union. *Address:* Smedevaenget 12, 8464 Galten, Denmark.

FINER, Jem; b. Stoke on Trent. Musician. m. Marcia Farquhar, 12 March 1983, 2 d. *Education:* BA, Computer Science, Keele University. *Career:* Films: Straight to Hell; French Connection IV; Member, Pogues, 1981–96, played Banjo, Saxophone, Hurdy Gurdy; Experimental electronic music, film music, sound art, industrial country and western, 1994–. *Compositions:* Wall of Sound; Tilt; Longplayer; Fiesta; Fairytale of New York; Misty Morning Albert Bridge; Numerous other Pogues songs; Film and installation music. *Recordings:* Wall of Sound; Tilt; The Library; 8 Pogues albums including: Red Roses For Me, 1984; Rum, Sodomy and The Lash, 1985; If I Should Fall From Grace With God, 1988; Peace and Love, 1989; Hell's Ditch, 1990; Best of The Pogues, 1991; Rest of The Pogues, 1992; Waiting For Herb, 1993; Pogue Mahone, 1995; numerous singles including: A Pair of Brown Eyes, 1985; Sally Maclennane, 1985; Dirty Old Town, 1985; Poguetry In Motion (EP), 1986; Haunted, 1986; The Irish Rover, with the Dubliners, 1987; Fairytale of New York, with Kirsty MacColl (No. 2, UK), 1987; Fiesta, 1988; Tuesday Morning, 1993. *Publications:* 3 Essays on Autodestruction, 1998–99; Plot, 1999. *Honours:* J F Sloane Golden Academy Award, Long Duration Music, 1990–99. *Membership:* PRS.

FINLAY, Neil M; b. 25 Dec. 1955, Hamilton, New Zealand. Musician (electric and acoustic guitar, harmonica). Separated, 2 d. *Education:* Bursary photography. *Career:* Harmonica player with Brownie McGhee, tours throughout New Zealand; Special guest appearances at folk festivals throughout New Zealand; Appeared with Champion Jack Dupree, Billy Joe Shaver. *Recordings:* Solo album: Jumping The Tracks; Session work with The Topp Twins; Al Hunter; Patsy Rigger. *Membership:* Penonport Folk Club. *Current Management:* Sun Pacific Records. *Address:* 271 Henderson Valley Rd, Auckland, New Zealand.

FINLAYSON, Rhonda, (Maria Valery Finlayson); b. 28 Aug. 1954, Kingston, Jamaica. Vocalist; Actress; Lyricist; Songwriter. *Education:* BA Hons, Creative Arts; Diploma in Careers Guidance and Recreational Arts for Community. *Career:* Backing singer with Little Douglas Band, 1984; Lead vocalist, Rhonda, 1985–89; Velvet Palm, 1989–. *Recordings:* Bugs On The Wire, compilation album; 1 track for Radio Lancashire; Black and Strange, Bop cassette tape with Rhonda band. *Membership:* Musicians' Union. *Address:* Flat 87, Lowton Court, Teddington Rd, Moston, Manchester M40 0DW, England.

FINN, Neil; b. 27 May 1958, Te Awamutu, New Zealand. Vocalist; Musician (guitar); Songwriter. *Career:* Member, Split Enz, 1977–85; Founder member, Crowded House, 1985–96; Duo with brother Tim, 1995; International concerts include: A Concert For Life, Centennial Park, Sydney, 1992; WOMAD Festival, 1993; Television appearances include: Late Night With David Letterman, NBC; The Tonight Show, NBC; In Concert '91, ABC; Return To The Dome, Ch4; MTV Unplugged; Top of the Pops, BBC1. *Recordings:* Albums: with Split Enz: Frenzy, 1978; True Colours, 1979; Beginning of The Enz, 1980; Waita, 1981; Time and Tide, 1982; Conflicting Emotions, 1984; See Ya Round, 1985; History Never Repeats Itself – The Best of Split Enz, 1993; Oddz and Endz, 1993; Rear Enz, 1993; with Crowded House: Crowded House, 1986; Temple of Low Men, 1988; Woodface, 1991; Together Alone, 1993; Seductive and Emotional, 1994; Unplugged in the Byrdhouse, 1995; Recurring Dream (No. 1, UK), 1996; Originals, 1998; with Tim Finn: Finn, 1995; Solo Albums: Try Whistling This, 1998; Encore!, 1999; One Nil, 2001; Singles: with Split Enz include: I See Red, 1979; I Got You, 1980; History Never Repeats, 1981; Six Months In A Leaky Boat, 1982; with Crowded House include: Don't Dream It's Over (No. 2, USA), 1987; Something So Strong, 1987; Better Be Home Soon, 1988; Chocolate Cake, 1991; Fall At Your Feet, 1991; Weather With You, 1992; Four Seasons In One Day, 1992; Distant Sun, 1993; Nails In My Feet, 1993; Instinct, 1996; Solo Singles: Sinner, 1998; She Will Have Her Way, 1998; Last One Standing, 1999; Can You Hear Us, 1999. *Honours:* Q Awards: Best Live Act (with Crowded House), 1992; Best Songwriter, 1993; O.B.E., for services to New Zealand, 1993. *Current Management:* Grant Thomas Management, 3 Mitchell Rd, Rose Bay, NSW 2029, Australia.

FINN, Tim; b. 25 June 1952, Te Awamutu, New Zealand. Vocalist; Musician (piano, guitar, drums); Songwriter. *Education:* Auckland University. *Career:* Founder member, Split Enz, 1972–85; Solo artiste, 1983–86; Member, Crowded House, 1991; Solo artiste, 1992–; Member, ALT (with Andy White and Liam O'Maonlai), 1994; Duo with brother Neil, 1995; Appearances include: Tours, UK Australia, New Zealand, USA; Television include: Late Night With David Letterman, NBC; The Tonight Show, NBC; In Concert '91, ABC. *Recordings:* Solo albums: Escapade, 1983; Big Canoe, 1985; Tim Finn, 1989; Before and After, 1993; Say It Is So, 2000; Feeding The Gods, 2001; Albums: with Crowded House: Woodface, 1991; with ALT: Altitude, 1994; with Neil Finn: Finn, 1995; Solo singles: Not Even Close, 1989; Hit The Ground Running, 1993; Persuasion, 1993; How'm I Gonna Sleep, 1993; Runs in the Family, 1994; Magnificent Nose and Other Stories, 1996; Singles: with Split Enz include: I See Red, 1979; I Hope I Never, 1981; Dirty Creature, 1982; Six Months In A Leaky Boat, 1982; with Crowded House: Chocolate Cake, 1991; Weather With You, 1992; Fall At Your Feet, 1991. *Honours:* O.B.E., Services to New Zealand, 1993. *Current Management:* Grant Thomas Management, 3 Mitchell Rd, Rose Bay, NSW 2029, Australia.

FINNEY, David Steven; b. 3 June 1963, Stoke Newington, London, England. Writer; Musician; Tutor. m. Anne Catherine, 18 Sept. 1988, 1 s., 1 d. *Career:* Five years, pop/indie band The Company She Keeps; Wide television and radio coverage of first single includes video starring Rick Mayall; Second single became jingle on Garry Davies Show, BBC Radio 1; Solo venture backed by Gerry Cott (formerly Boomtown Rats). *Recordings:* with The Company She Keeps: What A Girl Wants; The Men Responsible. *Publications:* Flesh. *Honours:* Single of The Week, Smash Hits/Record Mirror. *Membership:* Musicians' Union; PRS. *Address:* 15 River Way, Loughton, Essex IG10 3LJ, England.

FIRESTAR; b. 18 Oct. 1958, Iserlohn, Germany. Musician (Harp; Flute). 1 s. *Education:* Degree in Business and Artist Management, Marketing and Public Relations; Grade 12, Royal Conservatory Diploma for Additional Theory, Composition, Copyright and Legal Graduate Courses in Canada. *Career:* Composer; Musician; 28 years of performance live on television in Canada; Various programmes, CBC composing soundtracks for film and television; Performing live on radio. *Compositions:* 2 albums published, recorded: Heavenly Angels; Crescent Moon. *Recordings:* Heavenly Angels, album; Crescent Moon, album. *Honours:* Many local performance honours, cash money won towards recordings on albums. *Membership:* Pacific Music Industry Asscn; Society of Composers, Authors and Music Publishers of Canada. *Current Management:* Eachdraidh Productions Inc. *Address:* 5241 S Santa Fe Dr., Littleton, CO 80120, USA. *E-mail:* music.daviefirestar.com@att.net.

FIRTH, Steve; b. 1 Feb. 1968. Musician (bass). *Career:* Member, Embrace; Obtained major label deals in UK and USA, 1996; Released debut single independently; Support slot to Manic Street Preachers, 1997; Headline tours and TV appearances. *Recordings:* Singles: Fireworks, 1997; One Big Family, 1997; All You Good Good People, 1997; Come Back To What You Know, 1998; My Weakness Is None of Your Business, 1998; The Good Will Out, 1998; Hooligan, 1999; Save Me, 2000; Wonder, 2001; Albums: The Good Will Out, 1998; Drawn From Memory, 2000; If You've Never Been, 2001; Fireworks (Singles 1997–2002), 2002. *Address:* c/o PO Box 7, Brighouse HD6 4UR, England. *Website:* www.embrace.co.uk.

FISH, (Derek William Dick); b. 25 April 1958, Edinburgh, Dalkeith, Scotland. Vocalist; Lyricist. *Career:* Member, Stone Dome; Lead singer, lyricist, UK progressive rock group, Marillion, 1981–88; Regular tours, UK; Europe; USA; Concerts include: Theakston Festival, 1982; Reading Festival, 1982, 1983; Nostell Priory Festival, 1982, 1984; Support to Rush, New York City Music Hall, 1983; Milton Keynes Bowl, 1984; Monsters of Rock Festival, Castle Donington, 1985; Colombian Volcano Appeal Concert, Royal Albert Hall, 1986; Solo artiste, 1988–. *Recordings:* Albums: with Marillion: Script For A Jester's Tear, 1983; Fugazi, 1984; Real To Reel, 1985; Misplaced Childhood (No. 1, UK), 1985; Brief Encounter, 1986; Clutching At Straws, 1987; B-Sides Themselves, 1988; Anorak In The UK Live, 2002; Solo: Vigil In A Wilderness Of Mirrors, 1990; Internal Exile, 1991; Songs From The Mirror, 1993; Yin, 1995; Yang, 1995; Sunsets On Empire, 1997; Raingods With Zippos, 1999; Fellini Days, 2001. Singles: with Marillion: Market Square Heroes, 1982; He Knows You Know, 1983; Garden Party, 1983; Punch and Judy, 1984; Kayleigh (No. 2, UK), 1985; Lavender, 1985; Heart of Lothian, 1985; Incommunicado, 1987; Sugar Mice, 1987; Warm Wet Circles, 1987; Solo: Shortcut To Somewhere (with Tony Banks), 1986; State of Mind, 1989; Big Wedge, 1990; A Gentleman's Excuse Me, 1990; Internal Exile, 1991; Credo, 1991; Just Good Friends (with Sam Brown), 1995; Incomplete, 1999.

FISHER, Damian Robert; b. 21 Jan. 1971, Dartford, Kent, England. Musician (drums). *Education:* Masterclass Studios, Bob Armstrong. *Career:* Hank Wangford tour; Only The Lonely (West End Show); The Sound of Fury (stage show); Bobby Davro Show; Concerts with: The Bert Kaempfert Orchestra; Stutz Bear Cats; Johnny Howard Band; Gerrard Kenny. *Membership:* Musicians' Union. *Address:* Flat 5, Duncombe Court, Wingrove Dr., Purfleet, Essex RM19 INF, England.

FISHER, Morgan; b. 1 Jan. 1950, London, England. Musician (keyboards). m. Aki Kuniyasu, 26 May 1987. *Education:* Hendon County Grammar School, 1968. *Career:* Keyboard player, rock/soul band Love Affair, 1968–70; Leader, progressive rock band Morgan, 1971–2; Keyboard player, rock band Mott The Hoople, 1973–6; Solo recording artist, producer, founder, experimental music label Pipe Records, 1977–81; Keyboard player, rock band Queen, 1982; Solo musician, composer, producer, 1984–. *Compositions include:* Electronic Music for Institute of Contemporary Art, London, 1971; Numerous film and television soundtracks. *Recordings include:* Single: Everlasting Love, Love Affair, 1968; Albums: The Hoople, Mott The Hoople, 1972; As producer: Miniatures (concept album) featuring 51 contemporary artists such as Robert Fripp, Michael Nyman, Penguin Cafe Orchestra, The Pretenders, The Damned, XTC, Gavin Bryars, Pete Seeger, George Melly, 1980; Slow Music, 1980; Echoes of Lennon, ambient versions of John Lennon songs, with guest Yoko Ono, 1990. *Publications:* Far East Tour Diary (account of a tour with a Japanese rock band), 1995. *Honours:* Two Gold discs and one Silver disc for record sales, Mott The Hoople. *Membership:* Phonographic Performance Limited; Performing Rights Society; National Academy of Recording Arts and Sciences; Performing Artists Media Rights Asscn. *Address:* 2–9–7 Narita-Higashi, Suginami-ku, Tokyo 167, Japan.

FISHER, Reuben (Ruby); b. 20 Aug. 1923, New York, USA. Composer; Lyricist; Record Prod. m. Sheila Ratner, 11 June 1950, 2 s. *Education:* City University of New York; Manhattan School of Music. *Career:* Producer, Live at the Blazer!, for Big Band Jump, syndicated radio programme, 1997. *Compositions:* Shame, Shame, Shame (Baby Doll); Last Bicycle to Brussels; This One Day (General Hospital); Thai Silk (with Lionel Hampton); The Dolphin (with Luis Eça). *Recordings:* Bill Kenny, Star Sapphire; Ink Spots, Command Me; Dolores Gray, Tattered and Torn; Bobby Scott, Johnny River; Steve Clayton CD, At His Very Best; 3 Lew Anderson CDs: Feelin' Good, Yeah…, Fired Up, Live at the Blazer!; Swingin' for Hamp, Concord Jazz. *Honours:* US Bicentennial Composition Award, 1976; ASCAP Pop Music Award, 1998. *Membership:* ASCAP; Songwriters Guild of America; National Academy of Recording Arts and Sciences. *Address:* Aloft Music Enterprises Inc, 1501 Broadway, Suite 1310, New York, NY 10036, USA.

FISHER, Sharon Mary; b. 29 Sept. 1944, Orange, New Jersey, USA. Vocalist; Musician (Harp). m. Andrew Fisher IVth, 16 Aug. 1969. *Education:* BMusEd, Westminster Choir College, 1966; Academy of Vocal Arts, Philadelphia, Opera Scholarship, 1967; Temple University, Philadelphia. *Career:* Member, Westminster Choir, 1964–66; Vocal Music Teacher, Philadelphia Public School, 1967–69; Section Leader, Philadelphia Boys' Choir, 1969; Manhattan Light Opera, 1969–70; Soprano Soloist, St Peter's Episcopal Church, Manhattan, 1975–79; Organist, Church of the Saviour, Denville, New Jersey, 1981–84; Harpist/Singer and Lecturer in USA, Scotland Ireland, 1986–. *Recordings:* Solo recordings: Voice and Harp Concert Memories, 1991; Ireland, Land of Harp and Song, 1998. *Honours:* Harp/Voice Trophy, O'Carolan Harp Festival Competition, Keadue, Ireland, 1988; Scots Awards, 1988, 1989; Marietta MacLeod Award, 1989. *Membership:* American Harp Society; Clarsach Society; National Asscn of Teachers of Singing; Comhaltas Ceoltoiri Eireann. *Address:* 46 W Shore Rd, Denville, NJ 07834, USA.

FISHKIN, Paul E; b. 29 April 1943, Philadelphia, Pennsylvania, USA. Record Co Exec. m. Janis Beckerman, 3 July 1982, 1 s., 1 d. *Education:* BSc Pharmacy (Phila College, Pharmacy and Science). *Career:* Co-owner, Bearsville Records, with Albert Grossman, 1971–79; Established careers of Todd Rundgren; Foghat; Paul Butterfield; Jesse Winchester; Founder, Modern Records with Danny Goldberg, 1979; Signed and established solo careers of Stevie Nicks and Natalie Cole. *Membership:* RIAA. *Address:* 8295 Sunset Blvd, Los Angeles, CA 90046, USA.

FISK, Zebadi, (Thomas William Fisk); b. 24 June 1968, Little Thorpe, County Durham, England. Performer (guitar, mandolin); Vocalist; Composer; Teacher. m. Traci Ann Firby, 4 March 1989. *Career:* Lead guitarist, The Rye until 1994; Lead guitarist, Voodoo Guru, 1994–. *Recordings:* with The Rye: Songs of Innocence and Experience, 1991; Twist, 1992; Burst, 1993; Flying High, 1994; Even As We Speak, 1994; with Voodoo Guru: Do. *Membership:* Musicians' Union; Registry of Music Teachers. *Current Management:* Tony Davies. *Address:* PO Box 181, Darlington DL3 6YX, England.

FITZGERALD, Cathleen Bernadette Maureen (Cathy); b. 1 April 1964, Kitchener, Ontario, Canada. Entertainer; Vocalist; Artist. *Education:* Fourth year, BA in Psychology. *Career:* Performing, 1986–; Involved, several variety/charity events; Prime time country since 1990; Won 3 consecutive championships, Canadian Open Country Singing Competition, Simcoe, Ontario; Several firsts at Ontario Open Singing Competition: Toronto; Ottawa; Many local radio and television programmes; Released 2 singles, Canada and Europe, 1992–; Currently working with producer Gary Buck out of Nashville, on first 10 song album to be released, USA, 1995; Single to be released in: USA; Canada; Europe. *Honours:* Many trophies Canadian singing competitions, nine first place victories since 1989. *Membership:* Canadian Country Music Asscn, 1991–. *Current Management:* Howard Scales, Target

Entertainment Group. *Address:* 100 Denlow St, Kitchener, ON N2B 3T7, Canada.

FITZGERALD, Dandan; b. 14 Dec. 1955, Cork, Ireland. Recording Engineer; Prod; Live Engineer. *Education:* Electronic Technical College. *Recordings:* No Frontiers, by Mary Black; A Different Shore, by Nightnoise; Horse with a Heart, by Altan; Celts Rise Again, 1990; Good People All, 1993; Best of Altan, 1997; Winter's Tale, 1998; Bastard Complex, 1999. *Membership:* AES. *Current Management:* Dennis Muirhead, Chelsea, London. *Address:* 2 Ivy Cres., Riverway, S Douglas Rd, Cork, Ireland.

FITZGERALD, Greg; Prod; Songwriter. *Career:* Worked with: Atomic Kitten, Sophie Ellis-Bextor, Girls @ Play, Lulu, Martine McCutcheon, Kylie Minogue, Nightcrawlers, Reel. *Address:* c/o Stephen Budd Management Ltd, 109b Regents Park Rd, Primrose Hill, London NW1 8UR, England. *Website:* www.record-producers.com.

FITZGIBBON, Martin William; b. 11 May 1950, West Drayton, Middlesex, England. Musician (drums); Vocalist. m. Frances Trussell, 20 June 1981. *Education:* National Youth Jazz Association, private tuition. *Career:* Appearances: Original production, The Rocky Horror Show, London, 1973; BBC radio and television; Major concerts, tours, throughout UK. *Recordings:* The Rocky Horror Show, original London cast; Moondog Man; The Dockery Boys; Zydcajun Cowboy; Do You Feel Like Dancing. *Membership:* Musicians' Union. *Current Management:* Mike Batt Management. *Address:* c/o Nibley House, Blakeney, Gloucestershire GL15 4AR, England.

FITZSIMMONS, Keven Robert Mario; b. Glasgow, Scotland. Musician (keyboards, guitar) Conductor; Composer; Screenwriter; Actor; Dir. *Education:* Royal Scottish Academy of Music and Drama, 1972–78; Graduated, London Royal Academy of Music, 1979. *Career:* Theatre includes: Andrew Lloyd Webber's Jesus Christ Superstar, Evita, Cats, Song and Dance; Anthony Phillips' Alice (founder member/ex of Genesis); Television includes: LWT, The South Bank Show; Own groups: The Little Concert; The 13th Guest; The Trio of Doom; Film appearances include: Indiana Jones and the Temple of Doom; Deva, 1994; Wasted Youth (also composer), 1994; The Stated Dose (co-writer, composer, actor, director), 1994; Latter three premiered, Edinburgh Film Festival, 1995; Film scores include: Hoppla (Special Commendation, Channel 4 Young Film Maker of the Year Award), 1994; Wasted Youth; The Stated Dose; Co-writer, The Enlightening One – The Life of Ho Chi Minh (forthcoming). *Recordings:* Marti Webb: Gershwin/Performance albums, 1994; Jesus Christ Superstar, 20th Anniversary Album; K Fz – Film Music (1 and 2). *Current Management:* TDS Media/Tutti Sruti Music. *Address:* 5 E London St, Edinburgh EH7 4BN, Scotland.

FIX, Michael; b. 23 Sept. 1959, Wollongong, NSW, Australia. Musician (guitar); Composer; Performer. m. Susan Jarvis, 4 s. *Education:* Diploma of Teaching. *Career:* Leading Acoustic Guitarist; Sydney Band Hat Trick, 1984–90; Working with award-winning singer/songwriter Graeme Connors, touring Australia as Lead Guitarist with Connor's Prodigal Sons band, 1991–95. *Recordings:* Tantalise, 1992; Fingerpaintings, 1993; The Heart Has Reasons, 1996; Single: Falling, 1996; Video: No Secrets!, 1997; Single: Breakup Breakdown, 1997; Promise, 1998; Walkin' the Walk, 1999; Gershwin Country, 1999. *Honours:* Winner Instrumental of the Year Category, 1999, 2000, CMAA Awards; Instrumental of the Year Finalist, 1994–2000. *Membership:* APRA; AMCOS. *Address:* PO Box 1194, Sunnybank Hills, Qld 4109, Australia.

FIXX-IT, (Guam Elmzoom); b. 1 July 1970, Paramaribo, Suriname. Rap Artiste; Dancer; Dressman; Composer. 1 s. *Education:* Private dance training and show education. *Career:* Founder, Twenty 4 Seven, 1988; 3 European major hits; Solo career, 1990–; Male Rapper on Cappella and Anti-Capella songs, 1994–95; Member, Anti-Cappella. *Recordings:* with Twenty 4 Seven: I Can't Stand It, 1990; with Cappella: Move On Baby (co-writer); U and Me (co-writer); Anti-Cappella: Move Your Body. *Honours:* 3 Golden singles. *Membership:* FNV Kunstenbond. *Current Management:* Hans Van Pol Management. *Address:* PO Box 9010, 1006 AA Amsterdam, Netherlands.

FLACK, Roberta; b. 10 Feb. 1937, Black Mountain, North Carolina, USA. Vocalist. m. Stephen Novosel, 1966, divorced 1972. *Education:* BA, Music Education. *Career:* Teacher, music and English literature, 1959–67; Recording artist, 1968–; Appearances include: Star, ABC TV Special, The First Time Ever, 1973. *Compositions:* (with Jesse Jackson, Joel Dorn) Go Up Moses; Television theme song Valerie. *Recordings:* Singles include: The First Time Ever I Saw Your Face, used in film Play Misty For Me, 1972; Where Is The Love, 1973; Killing Me Softly With His Song, 1973; The Closer I Get To You, 1978; Back Together Again, with Donny Hathaway, 1980; Making Love, 1982; Tonight I Celebrate My Love, with Peabo Bryson, 1983; Set The Night To Music, with Maxi Priest, 1991; Albums include: First Take, 1970; Chapter Two, 1970; Quiet Fire, 1972; Killing Me Softly, 1973; Feel Like Makin' Love, 1974; Blue Lights In The Basement, 1978; Roberta Flack, 1978; Roberta Flack Featuring Donny Hathaway, 1980; Live and More, 1981; The Best of Roberta Flack, 1981; I'm The One, 1982; Born To Love, 1983; Hits and History, 1984; Roberta Flack's Greatest Hits, 1984; Roberta Flack, 1985; Oasis, 1989;

Roberta, 1995; Christmas Album, 1997; Collaborated with Quincy Jones on When You're Smiling, for film $ (sometimes called The Heist), 1971; Also contributed to albums including: Coming Around Again, Carly Simon, 1986; Les Is More, Les McCann, 1990; Peculiar Situation, Earl Klugh, 1999; Unconditional Love, Peabo Bryson, 1999. *Honours:* Gold record, First Time Ever I Saw Your Face, 1972; Grammy Awards: Best Record, 1972, 1973; Best Pop Vocal Duo, 1972; Best Female Pop Vocal, 1973; Roberta Flack Human Kindness Day, Washington DC, 1972. *Current Management:* Magic Lady, 234 Fifth Ave, Suite 504, New York, NY 10001, USA.

FLAHANT, Richard; b. 12 April 1968, Ipswich, Suffolk, England. Musician (keyboards); Vocalist. *Education:* Jazz studies, Chichester College of Technology, 1989–90. *Career:* The Addicts, 1985–; Venues include: 100 Club and The Marquee, 1989–90; Function bands include: Caribbean Cruise; Appearances, Big Breakfast Show, 1986–94; Recording with co-writer Matt Gray on various projects, 1993–; Signed to Albinus Records, 1994. *Recordings:* Singles: After The Fall, 1994; Meaning of Our Life, 1995. *Membership:* Musicians' Union; PRS. *Address:* 62 Dover Rd, Walmer, Deal, Kent CT14 7JN, England.

FLAHERTY, Nicholas Simon; b. 18 Feb. 1967, Brewood, Staffordshire, England. Vocalist; Songwriter. *Career:* Singer, Voodoo Sioux, 1991–; Support tours with Little Angels; Terrorvision; Rockhead; Headline concert, Milton Keynes Day of Rock, 1994; Radio appearances: Radio One session, 1993; Won Radio One Rock War, 1993; Television appearances: Noisy Mothers (interview and video), ITV, 1994; European, UK, Japanese tours, June 1995–. *Recordings:* Debut album: Skrape, Voodoo Sioux, 1995. *Membership:* Musicians' Union; PRS; MCPS. *Current Management:* c/o Bill Sneyd, White Buffalo, 2 Chillington Close, Cheslyn Hay. *Address:* 1 Victoria Court, Victoria Rd, Shifnal, Shropshire TF11 8AF, England.

FLANAGAN, Kevin Edward; b. 25 Feb. 1954, Lowell, Massachusetts, USA. Musician (tenor saxophone, alto saxophone, flute, clarinet); Composer. *Education:* Goldsmiths, London, England, Music degree; Anglia Polytechnic University, Cambridge, England, MA in Composition. *Career:* Worked as jazz musician around New England, USA before moving to UK with British Wife, mid 1980s; Played in London Jazz scene and did session work, late 1980s and early 1990s; Currently teaches saxophone and lectures in Jazz at Anglia Polytechnic University, Cambridge, UK; Recorded two albums with vocalist and pianist Chris Ingham, double bassist Andy Brown and drummer Russ Morgan under the name Flanagan-Ingham quartet; Band play gigs and tour regularly; An album of jazz settings of Beat poets currently under production; Recently began composing pieces that explore the cross-fertilization between contemporary composition and jazz. *Recordings:* with Flanagan/Ingham Quartet: Zanzibar, 1995; Textile Lunch, 1999; features on: Walking On Sunshine, Katrina and The Waves, 1983; The Pros and Cons of Hitch Hiking, Roger Waters, 1984; Live At Heartbreak Hotel, The Pretty Things, 1984; Eureka, The Bible, 1988; Groove Merchant, Tommy Chase, 1991. *E-mail:* kflanagan@btinternet.com. *Website:* www.flanaganingham.f9.co.uk.

FLANAGAN, Larry; b. 5 Dec. 1953, Detroit, Michigan, USA. Musician (viola, violin). *Career:* Violist with several orchestras in: Michigan; South Carolina; Ontario, Canada; Violinist/violist for various artists including Natalie Cole; Gladys Knight and the Pips; Melissa Manchester; Barry White; Geri Allen; Isaac Hayes; Sylvia Moy; Concerts include: Montreux Jazz Festival; Detroit Jazz Festival; Film appearance, as fiddler, Disney's Perfect Harmony, 1991; Lecturer, music consultant for schools in Decatur, Georgia.

FLANAGAN, Mark 'Sonny'; b. 27 Oct. 1957, Liverpool, England. Musician. *Career:* Resident musician on BSkyB satellite television; 26 shows, Happening; Don't Forget Your Toothbrush (Channel 4); Occasionally on Later With Jools Holland, BBC2; Recorded songs for film: Roadrunner, with George Harrison; Twice played live on Wogan; Numerous other television, radio, tours. *Honours:* (as band mem.) Don't Forget Your Toothbrush, Golden Rose Montreux, 1995. *Membership:* Musicians' Union; PAMRA; PRS. *Current Management:* Paul Loasby, One Fifteen, Greenwich, London. *Address:* Helicon Mountain, Halstow Rd, Greenwich, London SE3 7LP, England.

FLANZER, Richard; b. 30 Feb. 1951, New York, USA. Personal Man; Television Prod; Concert Promoter. m. Janice Rothman, 9 Feb. 1990, 2 s., 1 d. *Education:* Boston University. *Career:* Clients have included: Roger Daltrey; Manhattan Transfer; Jackson Browne; Dr John; Producer, largest two-day gross and fastest sell-out in history at Carnegie Hall, Roger Daltrey and Friends, 1994; Producer, largest festival in Florida history (115,000 audience), Florida Sunfest, 1977; Producer, A Day In The Country (first festival ever at Rose Bowl), Pasadena, California; Consultant to Jimi Hendrix Estate; Producer, National Music Critics Awards. *Membership:* ASCAP; Chairman, National Critics Awards, 1995. *Address:* 152 W 57th St, 40th Floor, New York, NY 10019, USA.

FLASKETT, Peter; b. 9 July 1950, Woking, Surrey, England. Guitar Teacher; Musician (guitar, bass guitar). m. Patsy Poley, 24 June 1983. *Education:* London College of Furniture and Music, 1968–70. *Career:* Worked with: Long John Baldry; Screaming Lord Sutch; Tex Withers; Savoy Brown;

Jim McCarty (of the Yardbirds); Recorded and toured extensively with: Emile Ford and The Checkmates; The Ramrods; The Flying Tigers; 30 years teaching guitar; 20 years repairing guitars. *Recordings:* Numerous recordings with Emile Ford; Extensive session work on guitar and bass guitar. *Membership:* Institute of Musical Instrument Technology; Musicians' Union. *Current Management:* Kernow Entertainments, Falmouth, Cornwall. *Address:* 23 Bridge, St Columb Major, Cornwall, England.

FLAVELL, Roger Barry; b. 10 Feb. 1946, Ruislip, England. Musician (bass guitar); Vocalist. m. Annie Conlon, 31 July 1971, 2 d. *Career:* Magic Roundabout, 1966–68; Sessions, 1969; Geno Washington's Ram Jam Band, 1970; Tommy Hunt Band, 1971–72; Christie, 1973–74; Tommy Hunt Band, 1975; Lonnie Donegan Band, Johnny Wakelin and The Kinshasha Band, 1976; Sessions, 1977–78; Band leader, top cabaret venue, 1978–88; The Byron Band, 1982; Sessions, 1989–95. *Compositions include:* Music for television: The Animates, co-written with Vic Elmes; 2 songs for From Out of The East album, 1999. *Recordings:* Albums: Judd, Kris Ife; Live At Wigan Casino, Tommy Hunt; A Sign of The Times, Tommy Hunt; On The Rocks, Byron Band; Only One, Joe Longthorne; Hold Fast, Roger Flavell; Christie: singles and album. *Membership:* PRS; BACS. *Address:* Marlow, Buckinghamshire, England.

FLAVOR FLAV, (William Drayton); b. 16 March 1959, Roosevelt, Long Island, USA. Rap Artiste. 3 c. *Career:* Founder member, US rap group Public Enemy, 1984–; Concerts include: Support to the Beastie Boys, US tour, 1987; Support to LL Cool J, European tour, 1987; British tour, 1990; Tour of a Black Planet, 1990; Apocalypse '91 US tour, with Anthrax, 1991; The World's Best Rap Show Ever, 1992; Greenpeace Stop Sellafield concert, with U2, Manchester, 1992; Reading Festival, 1992; Support to U2, Zooropa tour, 1992; MC, The Entourage (hip hop venue), Long Island, New York, 1986; Solo recording artist, 1993–. *Recordings:* Yo! Bum Rush The Show, 1987; It Takes A Nation of Millions To Hold Us Back, 1988; Fear of a Black Planet, 1990; Apocalypse '91... The Enemy Strikes Back, 1991; Greatest Misses, 1992; Muse Sick 'n' Hour Mess Age, 1994; He Got Game, OST, 1998; There's A Poison Goin' On, 1999; Revolverlution, 2002; Solo album: Flavor Flav, 1993; Singles include: Rebel Without A Pause, 1987; Bring The Noise, 1988; Don't Believe The Hype, 1988; Night of The Living Baseheads, 1988; Black Steel In The Hour of Chaos, 1988; Fight The Power, theme for film Do The Right Thing, 1989; Welcome To The Terrordome, 1990; 911 Is A Joke, 1990; Brothers Gonna Work It Out, 1990; Can't Do Nuttin' For Ya Man, 1991; Can't Truss It, 1992; Shut 'Em Down, 1992; Nighttrain, 1992; Give It Up, 1994; Do You Wanna Go Our Way?, 2000; Also guest on: Amerikka's Most Wanted, Ice Cube, 1990; Bring The Noise, Anthrax, 1991; Burning, Material, 1999. *Honours:* Platinum discs; Rolling Stone Readers Poll, Best Rap Group, 1991; Best Rap Album, Soul Train Music Awards, 1992. *Current Management:* Malik Entertainment Management, 3 Third Pl., Roosevelt, NY 11575, USA.

FLEA, (Michael Balzary); b. 16 Oct. 1962, Melbourne, Australia. Musician (bass guitar). *Career:* First trumpet, Los Angeles Jr Philharmonic; Founding mem., Anthem, later renamed Red Hot Chili Peppers, 1983–; Trumpet player, Trulio Disgracias, 1988; Founder, punk band Hate, playing Hollywood clubs, 1988; Numerous tours, festivals and television appearances; Guest host, The Ben Stiller Show, Fox TV, 1992; Film appearances: The Decline of Western Civilization, 1991; Suburbia, 1991; Motorama, 1992. *Recordings:* Albums: The Red Hot Chili Peppers, 1984; Freaky Styley, 1985; Uplift Mofo Party Plan, 1987; Mother's Milk, 1989; Mother's Milk Gold, 1989; Blood Sugar Sex Magik, 1991; What Hits!?, 1992; One Hot Minute, 1995; Under The Covers, 1998; Californication, 1999; By The Way, 2002. Singles: Abbey Road (EP), 1988; Higher Ground, 1989; Taste the Pain, 1989; Give It Away, 1991; Under The Bridge, 1992; Suck My Kiss, 1992; Breaking the Girl, 1993; If You Have to Ask, 1993; Soul 2 Squeeze (EP), 1994; My Friends, 1995; Aeroplane, 1996; Love Rollercoaster, 1997; Warped, 1998; Scar Tissue, 1999; Behind the Sun, 1999; Around The World, 1999; Otherside, 1999; Californication, 2000; Road Trippin', 2001; The Zephyr Song, 2002; Contributor, Peace Choir, 1991; Beavis and Butthead Experience, 1993. *Honours:* MTV Music Video Awards, 1992; Rolling Stone Readers' Poll Winner, Best Bassist, 1993; Grammy Awards, Best Hard Rock Song, for Give It Away, 1993, Best Rock Song, for Scar Tissue, 2000; American Music Award, Favorite Alternative Artist, 2000; MTV Awards, Best Live Act, Best Rock, 2002. *Current Management:* Lindy Goetz Management, 11116 Aqua Vista, Suite 39, Studio City, CA 91602, USA. *Address:* c/o Rockinfreakapotamus, The Red Hot Chili Peppers Official Fan Club, PO Box 801, Rockford, MI 49341, USA. *Website:* www.redhotchilipeppers.com.

FLECK, Bela; b. New York, NY, USA. Musician (banjo); Vocalist; Composer. *Education:* Graduate, New York High School of Music and Art, 1976; Studied banjo with Tony Trishka, Erik Darling, Mark Horowitz. *Career:* Banjo player, composer, 1976–; Played with: Tasty Licks, 1976–79; Spectrum, 1979–81; New Grass Revival, 1982–91; Formed Bela Fleck and the Flecktones, 1989–; Concerts include support to Bonnie Raitt, British tour, 1992; Also recorded solo albums; Studio work, Nashville, with Loretta Lynn; The Statler Brothers; Randy Travis; Television appearances: Hee Haw; Nashville Now; Lonesome Pine Specials. *Recordings include:* Crossing The Tracks, 1980; Natural Bridge, 1982; Deviation, 1984; Daybreak, 1987; Inroads (with Jerry Douglas, Mark

O'Connor), 1987; Places, 1988; Bela Fleck and The Flecktones, 1990; Flight of The Cosmic Hippo, 1992; UFO TOFU, 1993; Tales From The Acoustic Planet, 1994; Outbound, 2000; Perpetual Motion, 2001; Live At The Quick, 2002; Contributor, Hot House, Bruce Hornsby, 1995. *Honours:* Frets Readers Poll Winner, Top Banjo Player, more than 6 times, 1981–. *Current Management:* Firstars, 3520 Hayden Ave, Culver City, CA 90232, USA.

FLEDELIUS, Soren; b. 7 Feb. 1969, Vejle, Denmark. Vocalist; Songwriter; Musician. *Education:* Higher Business Degree, Horsens Business School, Denmark, 1989. *Career:* 'Voldvo', Denmark Tour 1991; Touring with Stonejuice, 1992–94; Studio Musician for Hege Tokle, Norway, 1995; Touring Denmark with Oktoberdrengene, 1995; Ich Bin So Geil Tour 96, with Halla Da; Halla Da USA Tour, 1996; Appeared in Starship Troopers, Live Concert, Danish National Radio, 1997; Halla Da Denmark Tour, 1997; All Major Festivals. *Compositions:* Hvorfor Fa'en Skal vi Vare Sa Brune; Von Hinten Fritz; Theme From Shotgunfire Blues. *Recordings:* Halla Da Albums: Ich Bin So Geil, 1995, Hvorfor Fa'en Skal vi Vare Sa Brune, 1996; Ultra-Brun Edition 2, 1997. *Honours:* Danish Champion of Rock, 1997. *Current Management:* Louis Fontaine, World Records. *Address:* Off-Beat Productions, West End 15, 1661 Copenhagen V, Denmark.

FLEEMAN, Jim; b. 21 June 1966, Chesterfield, England. Musician (drums, percussion). m. 11 Feb. 2001. *Education:* City of Leeds College of Music; Guildhall School of Music and Drama. *Career:* Tour, concerts, with Omar; Dana Bryant; Tour, concerts with Guildhall Jazz Band; Kenny Wheeler, London concerts; Various theatrical productions; Instrumental tuition and workshops; Senior Percussion Tutor, Brunel University College; Various network and cable television and radio broadcasts; Music Consultant, various corporate clients. *Recordings:* Featured soloist, Essence, Guildhall Jazz Band, 1989; Various commercial, theatrical recordings. *Address:* 95 Belgrave Rd, London SW1V 2BQ, England.

FLEETWOOD, Mick; b. 24 June 1942, London, England. Musician (drums). m. (1) Jenny Boyd, (2) Sara Recor, 1988, 2 d. *Career:* Drummer, John Mayall, 1967; Drummer, Fleetwood Mac, 1967–; Appearances and tours include: USA; Scandinavia; Europe; Concerts; Fillmore East; Miami Pop Festival Fillmore West, San Francisco; Reading Festival; Tampa Stadium, Florida, with the Eagles; Madison Square Garden; Hollywood Bowl, Los Angeles; US Festival, with Jackson Browne, The Cars, The Grateful Dead, Eddie Money; The Police; Santana; Talking Heads, 1982; Forms new band, Zoo, signs to Capricorn Records, 1992; Fleetwood Mac reunion, Presidential Inauguration concert, 1993; Film appearance: The Running Man, 1987; Owner, Fleetwoods club, Los Angeles, 1991. *Recordings:* Albums: Fleetwood Mac, 1968; English Rose, 1969; Pious Bird of Good Omen, 1969; Then Play On, 1969; Blue Jams At Chess, 1969; Kiln House, 1970; Fleetwood Mac In Chicago, 1971; Black Magic Woman, 1971; Future Games, 1971; Bare Trees, 1972; Penguin, 1973; Mystery To Me, 1973; Heroes Are Hard To Find, 1974; Rumours, 1977; Tusk, 1979; Tango In The Night, 1987; Behind The Mask, 1990; Time, 1995; The Dance, 1997; The Blues Years, 2000; Also appears on: I'll Sleep When I'm Dead, 1996; Susanna Hoffs, 1996; As It All Began, 1998; Solo: The Visitor, 1981; I'm Not Me, 1983; Singles include: Black Magic Woman; Need Your Love So Bad; Albatross; Man of The World; Over My Head; Rhiannon (Will You Ever Win); Go Your Own Way; Don't Stop; Tusk; Sara; Think About Me; Hold Me; Love In Store; Big Love; Everywhere; As Long As You Follow. *Publications:* My Life and Times In Fleetwood Mac, 1990. *Honours:* Favorite Band, Duo or Group, Pop/Rock, American Music Awards, 1978; Grammy: Album of the Year, Rumours, 1978; Gold Ticket, Madison Square Garden, 1990; Platinum, Gold discs. *Current Management:* Courage Management, 2899 Agoura Blvd, Suite 562, Westlake, CA 91361, USA.

FLEMING, Kye; b. 9 Oct. 1951, Pennsacola, Florida, USA. Songwriter; Publisher. *Education:* 2 years college. *Career:* President, Publishing Companies: Dream Catcher Music; Gila Monster Music; Painted Pony Music. *Compositions:* Co-wrote: Smokey Mountain Rain; Give Me Wings; I Was Country When Country Wasn't Cool; Nobody; Some People's Lives; Years; Sleeping Single In A Double Bed; Roll On Mississippi; Walk The Line (album), Kennedy-Rose. *Recordings:* with James Galway, Wayward Wind, 1982; with Marti Jones, Used Guitars, 1988. *Honours:* 43 BMI Awards; Three-time BMI Songwriter of the Year; NSAI Songwriter of the Year; CMA Triple Play Award. *Membership:* NSAI; CMA; BMI. *Current Management:* Dream Catcher; Gila Monster Music. *Address:* 1109 16th Ave S, Nashville, TN 37212, USA.

FLEMING, Mark; b. 6 Jan. 1962, Montréal, Canada. Music Publisher; Artist Man; Film and Television Composer Agent. *Education:* BA in Political Science and Communications; Legal and Practical Aspects of Recording and Music Publishing, University of California, Los Angeles; Basic Theory, Piano. *Career:* Manager, Eddie Murphy for Transition Music; Developed Crash Test Dummies, BMG Music Publishing Canada Inc; Own business, MERS Music, publisher, film and television composer agent; Manager for Ian Halperin; Mandela Benefit Concert at Wembley; DJ Ray. *Recordings:* As producer: Giving You The Best That I Got, Anita Baker; As administrator for: The Bee Gees; Annie Lennox; Dave Stewart; Film soundtrack, Beverly Hills Cop.

Membership: AIMP; SOCAN; BMI. *Address:* 1396 Ste Catherine St W, Suite 424, Montréal, QC H3G 1P8, Canada.

FLETCHER, Andrew John; b. 8 July 1961, Nottingham, England. Musician (keyboards). m. Grainne Mullan, 16 Jan. 1993, 1 s., 1 d. *Career:* Founder Member, Depeche Mode, 1980–. *Recordings:* 11 Top Ten Singles including: Just Can't Get Enough, 1981; See You, 1982; Everything Counts, 1983; People Are People, 1984; Master and Servant, 1984; Enjoy the Silence, 1990; I Feel You, 1993; Condemnation, 1993; In Your Room, 1994; Barrel of a Gun, 1997; It's No Good, 1997; Dream On, 2001; 12 Top Ten Albums including: Speak and Spell, 1982; A Broken Frame, 1982; Construction Time Again, 1983; Some Great Reward, 1984; The Singles 81–85, 1985; Black Celebration, 1986; Music For the Masses, 1987; 101, 1989; Violator, 1990; Songs of Faith and Devotion, 1993; Ultra, 1997; The Singles: 86>98, 1998; Exciter, 2001; One Night In Paris, 2002. *Honours:* BPI BRIT Award, Enjoy the Silence, 1991. *Current Management:* Jonathan Kessler, Baron Inc, 41 River Terrace, #3308 New York, NY 10282, USA. *Address:* First Floor, Regent House, 106 Marylebone High St, London W1M 3DB, England. *Website:* www.depechemode.com.

FLETCHER, Christopher Jeffrey; b. 1 July 1952, Berlin, Germany. Musician (percussion, drums); Vocalist. m. Kate Cochrane, 1 s., 1 d. *Career:* Percussion and backing vocals for many artists 1969–, including: Chris Rea, Road To Hell Tour, 1989–90; Christians, Couler Tour, 1990–91; Beautiful South, 0891 Tour, 1991–92; Judie Tzuke, Wonderland Tour, 1992; Marc Almond, Jacques Tour; Live appearances with: Fergal Sharkey; Roger Chapman; Dusty Springfield; Steve Williams; Cayenne; Paz; Stretch; Morrissey Mullen; The Montellas; Neucleus; Limmie and The Family Cooking; Currently running a 16 piece band of top session players. *Recordings:* Albums by: Beautiful South; Manfred Mann; Roger Chapman; Cayenne, 2 albums; Paz, 4 albums; Stretch; Morrissey Mullen, 5 albums; John Critchinson; Martin Drew; Peter Green; Molly Duncan; The Montellas; Neucleus; Alan Price. *Current Management:* Chance Management. *Address:* 106 Cleveland Gardens, London SW13 0AH, England.

FLETCHER, Matt James Harry; b. 27 Feb. 1968, Lambeth, London, England. Musician (keyboards); Programmer; Engineer; Prod. *Education:* Goldsmiths College, University of London, BSc Psychology. *Career:* Keyboards for Bros' TV appearances; Numerous remixes including Shine, by Aswad; Numerous TV commercials and themes; Regular freelance work; Technical advisor to Youth; Signed as Rampage, 1994; Currently writing and producing Betty Boo's third album. *Recordings:* Top of the Pops theme, 1991–95; One Foot In The Grave, theme remixes; For Rampage: Monkees; Why; Godfather; Album: Priority One; Betty Boo's singles, 1995. *Publications:* Tuning Your Breakbeat, article, Sound On Sound, May 1993. *Honours:* D & AD Silver Award, Best TV Soundtrack, Glad, Miller-Lite, 1991. *Membership:* Musicians' Union. *Current Management:* Jazz Summers, Big Life Management. *Address:* 15a Little Portland St, London W1N 5DE, England.

FLICK, Vic; b. 14 May 1937, Worcester Park, Surrey, England. Musician (guitar); Composer. m. Judith Mary, 19 May 1960, 1 s., 1 d. *Education:* Graduate diploma; Piano and theory LRAM, guitar. *Career:* Recorded with most major recordings artistes including: Tom Jones; Nancy Sinatra; Henry Mancini; Engelbert Humperdinck; John Barry; Cilla Black; The Walker Brothers; Shirley Bassey; Sandie Shaw; Bee Gees. *Compositions:* Themes and background music for television, radio and film includes: Music scores for The Europeans; Conquest of Light, Irish Tourist Board; Commercials: Cheseboro-Ponds; Palitoy. *Honours:* Two Royal Command Performances. *Membership:* PRS; ASCAP. *Address:* 2021 Ocean Ave No. 225, Santa Monica, CA 90495, USA.

FLINT, Keith; b. 17 Sept. 1969. Vocalist. *Career:* Member, The Prodigy, 1990–; Festival appearances include: Glastonbury, 1995, 1997; V97, 1997; Lollapalooza, 1997. *Recordings:* Albums: Experience, 1992; Music for the Jilted Generation (No. 1, UK), 1994; The Fat of the Land (No. 1, UK and USA), 1997; Evolution, 1998; Star Profiles, 1998; Interview, 1999; The Dirtchamber Sessions, 1999; Hit Singles: Charly, 1991; Everybody In the Place, 1991; Fire, 1992; Out of Space, 1992; Wind It Up, 1993; One Love, 1993; No Good (Start the Dance), 1994; Voodoo People, 1994; Poison, 1995; Firestarter (No. 1, UK), 1996; Breathe (No. 1, UK), 1996; Smack My Bitch Up, 1997. *Address:* c/o XL Recordings, 17–19 Alma Rd, London SW18 1AA, England.

FLOREK, Jaki; b. Bradford, Yorkshire, England. Vocalist; Lyricist. 2 s., 1 d. *Education:* Cardiff College of Art. *Career:* Tours with Shattered Dolls and Adam's Family; Editor, Feedback Music magazine. *Recordings:* Singles: with Shattered Dolls: Lipstick Killer (EP); with Adam's Family: Sometimes I Wonder (EP), 1987; Frustration, 1994; Album: with Adam's Family: Disease, 1995, CD, 1997. *Publications:* Adam's Family: The Scouse Phenomenon, Vols 1 and 2; Stories in anthologies. *Membership:* PRS; Musicians' Union. *Current Management:* Loose Records. *Address:* PO Box 67, Runcorn, Cheshire WA7 4NL, England.

FLORES, Remedios, (Alendrina De Los Remedios Flores); b. 30 Jan. 1952, Ronda, Malaga, Spain. Flamenco Vocalist. m. Rodrigo Flores, 7 July 1973, 2 s., 1 d. *Education:* Learned from family. *Career:* Toured for 20 years with famous guitarist Rodrigo; Under contract to Los Angeles City Schools, presenter, flamenco music; State grants to present Flamenco Song in concert atmosphere; Principle vocalist, El Cid, tablao flamenco, Hollywood (most prestigious flamenco nightclub in world). *Compositions:* music to National Geographic Special, The Soul of Spain. *Recordings:* Albums: Flamenco Caravan; Remedios Flores-Gipsy Flamenco Singer; The Gipsy 4; Rumba Festival; Trio Flamenco; Passionate Flamenco Dances; La Familia Flores; Inpiraciones; Flamenco Fantastico (Live); Video: Flamenco Sounds. *Honours:* Winner, Billboard Magazine Song Contest (Latin Category): Nos Volvemos A Querer. *Membership:* National Asscn Female Executives. *Current Management:* Sounds-Vision Music. *Address:* PO Box 3691, La Mesa, CA 91944, USA.

FLOWERS, Herbie; b. 19 May 1938, London, England. Musician (bass guitar, double bass, tuba). m. Ann, 1 Aug. 1959, 1 s., 1 d. *Education:* RAF School of Music. *Career:* Played tuba in Royal Air Force, 1955–63; Played double bass, Fender bass, London theatre, club, studio circuit; Joined Blue Mink, 1970; Worked for David Bowie, tour of USA, 1974; Member, T-Rex, 2 years; Played on recordings with: Elton John; David Essex; Paul McCartney; Al Kooper; Nilsson; Tom Jones; Tiny Tim; Dusty Springfield; Henry Mancini; George Harrison; Ringo Starr; Formed Sky with John Williams; Is now in demand as a jazz double bass player; Gary Potter; David Jones; Tina May; Lectures, Fun With Music, East Sussex County Council; Residential free week-long music courses, RockShops, on University campuses. *Recordings:* Albums: Transformer, Lou Reed; Diamond Dogs, David Bowie; Burn Down The Mission, Elton John; Rock On, David Essex; Broad Street, Paul McCartney; 10 albums by Sky; Recent albums include: The Business, with Mike Hatchard, 1998. *Address:* 15 High St, Ditchling, East Sussex BN6 8SY, England.

FLOYD, Eddie; b. 25 June 1937, Montgomery, Alabama, USA. Vocalist; Prod; Composer. 6 s, 2 d. *Education:* Wayne School of Music, Detroit. *Career:* Founder member, The Falcons, 1954–62; Solo artist, 1962–; Guest singer, The Original Blues Brothers Band, Booker T and the MG's; World-wide tours with the above; President, Floyd Entertainment Group Inc. *Compositions:* Songs for Otis Redding, Wilson Pickett, and Sam and Dave, including 634–5789; Ninety-Nine and A Half (Just Won't Do); You Don't Know What You Mean To Me; Knock On Wood. *Recordings:* With The Falcons: You're So Fine; I Found A Love; Solo albums: Knock On Wood; I've Never Found A Girl; Rare Stamps; You've Got To Have Eddie; California Girl; Down To Earth; Baby Lay Your Head Down; Soul Street; Experience; Try Me; Flashback; Back To The Roots; All The Hits Plus More, 2001; with the Blues Brothers Band: Live In Montreux; The Red White and Blues; California Girl. *Honours:* Governors Award/Memphis Blues Foundation Inductee, Tennessee; Honourary Lieut Col, Alabama; President Bush Performance Award; Alabama Hall of Fame Inductee; NAACP BMI 1 Million Performances Award, Knock On Wood; BMI Award. *Membership:* BMI. *Current Management:* Andy Nazer, Performance Representation. *Address:* 39 Hopton Rd, London SW16 2EH, England.

FOAD, Paul; b. 26 Sept. 1957, Liverpool, England. Musician (guitar); Songwriter; Guitar Teacher. m. Kim Hamilton (singer), 7 May 1994, 1 s., 4 d. *Education:* Birmingham Guitar School, 3 years; Barney Kessel Workshop summer School. *Career:* With group Au Pairs: BBC TV, Old Grey Whistle Test; BBC Radio 1: 3 John Peel sessions; Janice Long; Kid Jensen session; Local radio; 3 tours, USA; 5 tours, Europe, including Pink Pop, Netherlands; Session guitar for jazz artist Andy Hamilton; Session for local artists; Solo guitar, Birmingham International Film Festival; Member, Andy Hamilton's band, Blue Notes. *Recordings:* Au Pairs: (studio albums) Playing With A Different Sex; Sense and Sensibility; (live album) Live In Berlin; 1 radio compilation CD: Equal But Different. *Publications:* One chapter on Au Pairs in: In The Fascist Bathroom, by Greil Marcus; Author, The Caged Guitarist, guitar tutor book. *Honours:* Songwriters Award, New York's Village Voice, 1980. *Membership:* MCPS; PRS; Musicians' Union. *Current Management:* EMI Publishing; RPM Records. *Address:* 41 Garfield Rd, North Chingford, London E4 7DG, England.

FOGELBERG, Dan; b. 13 Aug. 1951, Peoria, Illinois, USA. Musician (guitar, piano); Songwriter. *Education:* University of Illinois; Piano from age 14. *Career:* Musician, California folk circuit, including tours with Van Morrison, 1971; Recording artiste, 1974–; Support to the Eagles, 1975. *Recordings:* Singles include: Longer, (No. 2, USA), 1980; Same Auld Lang Syne, 1981; Leader of The Band, 1981; Rhythm of the Rain, 1990; Albums: Home Free, 1973; Souvenirs, 1975; Captured Angel, 1975; Netherlands, 1977; Twin Sons of Different Mothers, with Tim Weisberg, 1977; Phoenix, 1980; The Innocent Age, 1981; Windows and Walls, 1984; Greatest Hits, 1985; High Country Snows, 1985; Exiles, 1987; The Wild Places, 1990; Dan Fogelberg Live – Greetings From The West, 1991; River of Souls, 1993; No Resemblance Whatsoever, 1995; Love Songs, 1995; First Christmas Morning, 1999; Live – Something Old New Borrowed and Some Blues, 2000. *Current Management:* HK Management, 8900 Wilshire Blvd, Suite 300, Beverly Hills, CA 90211, USA.

FOGERTY, John; b. 28 May 1945, Berkeley, California, USA. Vocalist; Composer; Songwriter; Musician (guitar). *Career:* Member, Blue Velvets, (later known as the Golliwogs), 1959–67; Group became Creedence Clearwater Revival, 1967–71; Solo artiste, 1972–. *Compositions include:* Almost Saturday Night, recorded by Dave Edmunds; Rockin' All Over The World, recorded by Status Quo. *Recordings:* Albums: with Creedence Clearwater Revival: Creedence Clearwater Revival, 1968; Bayou Country, 1969; Green River, 1969; Willie and The Poor Boys, 1969; Cosmo's Factory, 1970; Pendulum, 1970; Mardi Gras, 1972; Live In Europe, 1973; Live At The Royal Albert Hall, 1980; Creedence Clearwater Revival (box set), 2001; Solo albums: The Blue Ridge Rangers, 1973; John Fogerty, 1975; Centerfield, 1985; Eye of a Zombie, 1986; Blue Moon Swamp, 1997; Premonition, 1998; Singles: with the Golliwogs: Don't Tell Me No More Lies; Fight Fire; Walk Upon The Water; with Creedence Clearwater Revival: Suzie Q; I Put A Spell On You; Proud Mary; Green River; Bad Moon Rising; Down On The Corner; Travellin' Band; Up Around The Bend; Looking Out My Back Door; Have You Ever Seen The Rain; Solo: Bayou, 1973; Hearts of Stone, 1975; Comin' Down The Road, 1975; The Old Man Down The Road, 1985; Blueboy, 1997. *Current Management:* 15030 Ventura Blvd, Suite 777, Sherman Oaks, CA 91403, USA.

FOLEY, Thomas Henry; b. 1 April 1961, London, England. Dir, React Music Ltd. *Career:* Ed., Songplugger, 1986–87; Publisher and Ed., Bandit, 1988–90; Personal Asst to Dave Pearce, Reachin Records, –1991; Fmr Dir, React Music Ltd. *Address:* 138B West Hill, Putney, London SW15 2UE, England.

FOLLETT, Marie-Claire; b. 11 May 1975, Cardiff, Wales. Vocalist; Songwriter; Actress; Dancer. *Education:* Brooklands College; Academy of Live and Recorded Arts. *Career:* Radio broadcasts include: Radio Warsaw, Poland; Thicker Than Water, BBC Radio 2; The Hardcore Show, Kiss FM, 1998; Television appearances include: Regis and Kathy Lee Show, ABC TV, USA; Legionnaires, 1999; Concerts include: Marquee; The Orange; Earls Court; Birmingham NEC; Finalist in Yamaha Music Quest; Bands include Subway; Nemesis; Abba Vision; The Fortune Cookies; Antisocial; Tina Turner support, 1999. *Recordings:* Spreadeagle, Sky TV; A Guide For The Divorced Child, Jann Turner (film soundtrack); Singles: Cry; Indestructable; Get Into Love, with Antisocial, 1999. *Membership:* Musicians' Union; Equity. *Current Management:* Richard Gillinson. *Address:* 1.3 The Alaska Works, 61 Grange Rd, London SE1 3BA, England.

FONTANA, Wayne (Glyn Ellis); b. 28 Oct. 1940, Manchester, Lancashire, England. *Career:* Founder member, The Jets; The Mindbenders, 1963–65; Solo artiste, 1965–; Tours include: UK, with Brenda Lee, 1964; UK, supporting Del Shannon, 1965; British Song Festival, Brighton, 1965; Tour, with Herman's Hermits, The Fortunes, Billy Fury, 1965; Swinging '66 Tour, with the Small Faces, 1966; Resident songwriter, Chappell music publishers, 1970–; English Invasion Revival US tour, 1973; Resumed recording career, 1976; Revival tour, 1979; Festival of The 10th Summer, Manchester, 1986. *Recordings:* Albums include: Wayne Fontana and The Mindbenders, 1965; Eric, Rick, Wayne and Bob, 1966; The Mindbenders, 1966; Hit singles: with The Mindbenders: Um Um Um Um Um Um, 1964; The Game of Love (No. 2, UK), 1965; Just A Little Bit Too Late; She Needs Love; Solo: Come On Home; Goodbye Bluebird; Pamela Pamela. *Address:* c/o Barry Collings Entertainments, 21a Clifftown Rd, Southend-on-Sea, Essex SS1 1AB, England.

FONTENOT, Glenn Dale; b. 23 Aug. 1951, Jennings, Louisiana, USA. Vocalist; Musician (Guitar). m. Jenny Fontenot, 14 Feb. 1997, 2 d. *Education:* McNeese State University, Louisiana. *Career:* Singer and Leader of the Renegades, performing night clubs, fairs, festivals and private parties. *Compositions:* 10 songs for album, Memories, 1990. *Recordings:* Memories. *Membership:* Chamber of Commerce, Picayune; Louisiana Fair and Festival Asscn. *Address:* 303 Hwy 43 S No. 10, Picayune, MS 39466, USA.

FORBERT, Steve; b. 15 Dec. 1954, Meridian, MS, USA. Vocalist; Songwriter; Musician (guitar, harmonica). *Career:* Solo artiste, 1978–; Signed to Nemperor Records, 1977–82; Songwriter, Nashville, 1980s–90s; Signed to Geffen, 1988, Giant Records, 1995, Paladin Records, 1998, Koch Records, 2000. *Recordings:* Albums: Solo: Alive On Arrival, 1978; Jackrabbit Slim, 1979; Little Stevie Orbit, 1980; Steve Forbert, 1982; Streets Of This Town, 1988; The American In Me, 1992; Be Here Now: Solo Live, 1994; Mission Of The Crossroad Palms, 1995; In Concert 1982, 1995; Rocking Horse Head, 1996; Be Here Again Live Solo 1998, 1998; Evergreen Boy, 2000; Acoustic Live: The WFUV Concert, 2000; Young Guitar Days, 2001; More Young Guitar Days, 2002; Any Old Time, 2002; with the Rough Squirrels: Here's Your Pizza, 1998; Live At The Bottom Line, 2001. *Current Management:* Mongrel Music. *E-mail:* info@mongrelm.com. *Website:* www.steveforbert.com.

FORCE, (THE). See: **KING BRITT.**

FORCIONE, Antonio; b. 2 May 1960, Italy. Musician (guitar); Composer. 1 d. *Education:* Visual Arts, 5 years; Private Jazz and Folk tuition in Italy. *Career:* World-wide tours as solo artist and with bands, Antonio Forcione

Acoustic Band and Acoustic Mania, in theatres and major festivals; Numerous radio and television appearances; Performed with Barney Kessel, Martin Taylor, Birelli Lagrene, Claudio Roditi and others; Double bills with John McLaughlin, opened for Phil Collins, Barclay James Harvest, Zucchero, Jools Holland, Pino Daniele, Bobby McFerrin; Masterclasses world-wide; Composed music for TV, radio and documentaries. *Recordings:* Albums: Light and Shade, 1984; Eurotour, 1986; Celebration, 1987; Poema, 1992; Acoustic Revenge, 1993; Live Edinburgh Festival, 1993; Dedicato, 1996 Talking Hands, 1997; Meet Me in London, 1998; Ghetto Paradise, 1998. *Membership:* Musicians' Union; PRS. *Current Management:* Kunst Music Promotions. *Address:* 28a Devonshire Rd, London W4 2HD, England.

FORD, Baby (Peter Ford), (Twig Bud, Solcyc); b. 1960, England. Prod; Remixer; DJ. *Career:* Started recording career as part of the Acid House explosion, late 1980s; Co-founder of Trelik and Ifach Records, two of England's most respected techno labels; Collaborations: Eon; Mark Broom. *Recordings:* Albums: Fordtrax, 1988; Ooo The World of Baby Ford, 1989; BFord 9, 1992; Headphone Easyrider, 1997; Singles: Oochy Koochy, Chikki Chikki Ahh Ahh, 1988; Children of The Revolution, 1989; Beach Bump, 1990; Fetish, 1992; Treatment Feel (with Minimal Man), 1994; Normal, 1998. *Address:* c/o Ifach Records, PO Box 1797, London, England.

FORD, Gerry; b. 25 May 1943, Athlone, Eire. Country Music Entertainer; DJ; Journalist; Vocalist; Songwriter. m. Joan, 4 April 1964, 1 s. *Career:* Qualified Baker, Confectioner; Served in Edinburgh City Police until 1976; Became professional entertainer, while broadcasting 2 country music programmes for Radio Forth, Edinburgh and performing in clubs; Joined BBC Radio Scotland, Country music presenter, 1978–93; Own series, BBC Radio 2, 1988–89. *Recordings:* 15 albums, 1977–; 7 duets with Jean Shepard. *Honours:* 3 Albums of the Year, BCMA, 1986; BCM Radio Play Album of the Year, 1991; Presenters Award, 1993; Hon. Citizen, Nashville, Tennessee; 21 appearances, Grand Ole Opry, Nashville; 33 Awards, Male Vocalist, Recording Artiste, various country music clubs and magazines. *Address:* 4 Inchview, Seafield Towers, Kirkcaldy, Fife KY1 1SS, Scotland. *Telephone:* (1592) 641219. *E-mail:* gerryford@madasafish.com. *Website:* www.gerryford.co.uk.

FORD, Lita; b. 23 Sept. 1959, London, England. Vocalist; Musician (guitar). m. Chris Holmes, divorced. *Career:* Original member, all-girl group, The Runaways, 1976–79; Solo artiste, 1980–. *Recordings:* Albums: with the Runaways: The Runaways, 1976; Queens of Night, 1977; And Now The Runaways, 1979; Flamin' Schoolgirls, 1980; Solo albums: Out For Blood, 1983; Dancin' On The Edge, 1984; Lita, 1988; Stiletto, 1990; Dangerous Curves, 1991; Black, 1995; Singles: Hungry, 1990; Lisa, 1990; Shot of Poison, 1991; Playin' with Fire, 1992; Killin' Kind, 1995; Greatest Hits Live, 2000; Hit singles include: Kiss Me Deadly; Close My Eyes Forever (duet with Ozzy Osbourne).

FORD, Vince; b. 9 April 1962, Newark, Nottinghamshire, England. Vocalist; Songwriter; Prod; Record Co Exec. m. Julie, 14 Sept. 1991, 1 s. *Career:* Formed Capital Queue, 1979; Formed Temper, Temper, 1987; Formed Sheer Bravado Records, 1989. *Membership:* PRS. *Address:* 7 Backs Close, Waddington, Lincoln LN5 9SG, England.

FORDE, Brinsley; Vocalist; Musician (guitar). *Career:* Child actor, Here Come The Double Deckers, BBC TV, 1971; Founder member, UK reggae group Aswad, 1975–; Performances include: Cliff Richard – The Event, Wembley Stadium, 1989; Nelson Mandela International Tribute concert, Wembley, 1990; Glastonbury Festival, 1990; Reggae Sunsplash US tour, 1991; Heineken Festival, Leeds, 1995; Musician, actor, film Babylon, 1980; Please Sir, Diamonds are Forever, Leo The Last; Also featured in Bob Marley Tribute, Rapido, BBC2 TV, 1991; Presenter, Soul Vibration, VH-1. *Recordings:* Singles include: Back To Africa, 1976; Don't Turn Around (No. 1, UK), 1988; Give A Little Love, 1988; Set Them Free, 1988; Beauty's Only Skin Deep, 1989; On and On, 1989; Next To You, 1990; Smile, 1990; How Long (with Yazz), 1993; Dance Hall Mood, 1993; Shine, UK No 5; Albums: Aswad, 1976; Hulet, 1979; New Chapter, 1980; Not Satisfied, 1982; Live and Direct, 1983; Rebel Soul, 1984; To The Top, 1986; Distant Thunder, 1988; Renaissance, 1989; Too Wicked, 1990; Live, 1991; Roots Rocking, 1997; Big Up, 1997; Roots Revival, 1999. *Honours:* Reggae Industry Award, Best Group, 1995. *Current Management:* Hit and Run Music, 30 Ives St, London SW3 2ND, England.

FORDHAM, Julia; b. 10 Aug. 1962, Hampshire, England. Vocalist; Songwriter; Musician (guitar). *Career:* Began performances own material, folk music clubs, age 14–15; 5 years as backing vocalist; Signed solo record deal, 1987. *Recordings include:* Albums: Julia Fordham, 1988; Porcelain, 1989; Swept, 1991; Falling Forward, 1994; East West, 1997; Julia Fordham Collection, 1998; Concrete Love, 2002. Singles include: Happy Ever After, 1988; Love Moves In Mysterious Ways, 1992. *Honours:* Silver Prize, Tokyo Music Festival, 1989; 4 Gold records, Japan. *Membership:* Musicians' Union; Equity. *Current Management:* JFD Management. *Address:* Unit 9, Acklam Workshops, 10 Acklam Rd, London W10 5QZ, England.

FORRESTER, John; b. 16 March 1969, Pembury, Kent, England. Musician (bouzouki, bass, acoustic guitar); Vocalist. *Career:* Vocals, bass, Killing The

Rose, 1986–87; Vocals, bass, The Colour Mary, 1988–92; Vocals, bass, bouzouki, Pressgang, 1992–94; Solo artiste, vocals, bouzouki, acoustic guitar, 1993–; Vocals, bass, WOB, 1993–94; Vocals, bouzouki, bass, Sunspeak, 1995; Bass, vocals, Nozzle, 2000–; Bass, vocals, Silverlead, 2002–; Tours: with Pressgang: England, France, Germany; with WOB: England, France, Germany, Austria, Holland; Solo: England, France, Germany; with Nozzle: Germany, Switzerland; with Silverleaf: England, Wales, Scotland; Radio: The Colour Mary Live From The Marquee, BBC Radio 1, 1990. *Recordings:* EPs: with The Colour Mary: Trash and Treasure, 1988; The World Don't Spin, 1989; Black and White, 1990; Sunspeak, 1991; Mindfield, 1992; with Pressgang: Donkey, 1993; Albums: with Pressgang: Burning Boats, 1994; with WOB: Can't Stay Long, 1995; Straight On Til Morning, 1998; Solo: Scars and Memories, 1993; Tales of Nothing, 1997; Lanterns, EP, 1998; All The Wrong Things, 2000; Ne Me Quitte Pas, songs by Brel, 1998; with Nozzle: Twisted Vision, 2003. *Membership:* Musicians' Union. *Current Management:* Seaview Music. *Address:* Seaview Music, 46 Florence Rd, Maidstone, Kent ME16 8EL, England. *Website:* www.forrester.uk.com.

FORRÓ, Daniel; b. 19 Feb. 1958, Jihlava, Czech Republic. Composer; Musician; Musicologist; Product Specialist; Teacher; Writer; Consultant. *Education:* Brno State Conservatory; MA, 1986, PhD, 1999, Janaceks Academy of Music (JAMU), Brno. *Career:* Keyboards in Rock Groups, 1978–84; Own Project of EA and Computer Music, Forrotronics, 1983–; Plays with Drum Group Dama Dama; Founder and owner, Museum of EMI, 1989–; Teacher, JAMU, 1991–, Head of Computer and Electronic Music Dept; Editor, Writer, Music Magazine Muzikus, 1991–2002; Product Specialist, Yamaha Europe Export Division, Hamburg, 1991–2002; Product Specialist, Czech and Slovak Korg Distributor MusicPark, 2002–; Writer, Series of Expert Books on Musitronics, 1993–; Founder and Chair., Society for Microintervallic Music, 1995; International Master Summer Classes, JAMU, 1996–; National Rock/Pop/Jazz Music Academy, 1998–; Founder and Chair., Society for Creative Improvisation, 2001. *Compositions:* Over 1,100 of all Styles. *Publications:* MIDI—Communication In Music; Computers and Music; Home Recording; World of MIDI; Samplers; Analog and Analog-Digital Synthesizers; Historical EMI; Other EMI; Creative Improvisation, Microintervallic Music. *Membership:* Society for EA Music; Society for Microintervallic Music; Society for Creative Improvisation; Society Q. *Current Management:* D F, Lucni 60, 616 00 Brno, Czech Republic. *Telephone:* (5) 41243076. *Fax:* (5) 41243076. *E-mail:* danfor@jamu.cz. *Website:* www.forrotronics.cz.

FORSMAN, Ingela 'Pling'; b. 26 Aug. 1950, Stockholm, Sweden. Lyricist; Record Prod; Recording Artist. m. Lars, 1990, 1 s. *Education:* English, University of Stockholm. *Career:* Former recording artist with girl group Bambis; Tours: Sweden; Germany; Lyricist, 1971–; 12 years in record business, some as producer; Translated musicals into Swedish: Cats; Grease; Fame; Hair; Also translated songs in films, including: The Little Mermaid; Beauty and The Beast; Hymn for Swedish Hymnbook; Written over 1000 lyrics, most of them recorded. *Honours:* Swedish Song Contest (Two first places, many in Top 3); SKAP Award. *Membership:* STIM; NCB; SKAP.

FORWARD, Fast; b. 24 March 1954, Whitley Bay, England. Composer. m. Lucienne Vidah, 9 Nov. 1993. *Education:* Ashington Technical College; Jacob Kramer Art College, Leeds, 1972; BFA, Fine Arts, Newcastle upon Tyne Polytechnic, 1976; MFA, Centre for Contemporary Music, Mills College, Oakland, California, USA, 1978. *Career:* Performances and concerts include Whitney Museum of American Art, New York; National Gallery, Hamburger Bahnhof, Berlin; Museum of Modern Art, Montréal, Canada; Merkin Concert Hall, New York; Walker Art Center, Minneapolis; Shaffy Theatre, Amsterdam; Tenjin Barca Festival, Osaka, Japan; Studio 200, Tokyo; Time of Music Festival, Finland; New Music America Festival, Philadelphia; Guest Musician, Merce Cunningham Dance Company, 1994–97; Producer of his own music and also musical events; Curated The Accident, 9 evenings of performance, with Wooster Group; Composed and performed music for dance companies and theatre performances. *Compositions include:* Red Raw Steel Drum, 1985; The Dream State, 1988; Machine Guns, 1988; Rollerball, 1990; Waterball, 1990; Flip Flop, 1990; Simultaneous Music, 1995; Feeding Frenzy, 1995; 186, 1998; Questionnaire, 1999; Raw Footage, 1999; No Fly Zone, 1999. *Recordings:* Same Same; Panhandling; The Caffeine Effect; %; Rotorblade. *Honours:* New York State Council on the Arts Commissions, 1986, 1992; DAAD Fellowship, Berlin, 1988, 1998; Meet the Composer, Fellowship, New York Foundation for the Arts, 1989; Asian Cultural Council Fellowship, New York, 1997. *Membership:* ASCAP. *Current Management:* Bent out of Shape Productions. *Address:* 224 E Seventh St No. 17, New York, NY 10009, USA.

FOSKETT, Charles A; b. 27 March 1949, Newcastle upon Tyne, England. Musician (guitar, bass); Composer; Prod. m. Lauren Daniele Field, 7 June 1990, 1 s. *Career:* Major tours, television and radio sessions including Andy Peebles, BBC; Tyne Tees, Chat Show; Started in Newcastle, played alongside The Animals, 1960s; Put together The Anti Heroin Project, EMI, 1985, 1986, 1987; Wrote, produced double album: It's A Live In World, featuring and bringing together hundreds of big name artists; Worked with: Kim Wilde; Ringo Starr; Precious Wilson; John Cleese; Bonnie Tyler; Elkie Brooks; Daryl Pandy; Cliff Richard; Holly Johnson; Sheila Ferguson; Robin Gibb; Nik Kershaw; Hazel O'Connor; Founder, Veracruz Music International, record production company. *Compositions:* Theme music, Strike Command, TV advertisement, 1996; Theme music, ITV six-part series, 1997; Theme music, High 5, Channel 4, 1997; New Age Jazz, ambient music for Midnight Music, film for TV, Los Angeles; Compositions for: Sarah Jory, Joe Cocker; I Wanna Be There, Prudential Mexico '97. *Recordings:* Writer/producer for artists including: Bonnie Tyler; Kim Wlde; Elkie Brooks; Ringo Starr; Holly Johnson; Cliff Richard; Jim Diamond; Sheila Ferguson; Robin Gibb; Nik Kershaw; Hazell Dean; Zak Starkey; Hazel O'Connor; Catherine Zeta-Jones; Produced: Sinitta; Edwin Star; Phil Fearon; John Parr; Mike Peters/Eddie McDonald (The Alarm); Steve Harley; Suggs (Madness); Bucks Fizz; Chas and Dave; Brinsley Forde/Drummie Zeb (Aswad); Nick Heywood; The Icicle Works; Elvis Costello; Thompson Twins; Sarah Jory; Joe Cocker. *Honours:* Royal Academy Artist. *Membership:* PRS; Equity. *Current Management:* Veracruz Music International. *Address:* 43 Capron Rd, Dunstable, Bedfordshire LU5 5AL, England.

FOSSATI, Ramon; b. 14 Sept. 1965, Barcelona, Spain. Musician (guitar, trombone); Composer; Prod. *Career:* Creator, co-leader, Paris-Barcelona Swing Connection; Played with Frank Wess; Teddy Edwards; Wild Bill Davis; Performed at Jazz Vienne (France), 1993; Jazz Festival, Birmingham, 1992–94; Terrassa, Spain, 1993–95; Frankfurt, 1995; More than 500 concerts around Europe. *Recordings:* with the Paris-Barcelona Swing Connection: Hard Swing; Live In Barcelona; with Frank Wess: Frank Wess Meets The Paris-Barcelona Swing Connection; with Wild Bill Davis: Wild Cat. *Current Management:* Foscar Society. *Address:* 41 Ave Saint Saëns, 91600 Savigny Sur Orge, France.

FOSSEN, Sverre; b. 4 Oct. 1973, Trondheim, Norway. Musician (guitar). *Education:* College. *Career:* Joined Hedge Hog, 1990; Several tours, Norway; Toured Europe, 1994, 1995. *Recordings:* Erase, 1992; Surprise, 1992; Primal Gutter, 1993; Mercury Red, 1994; Mindless, 1994; The Healing EP, 1995; Thorn Cord Wonder, 1995. *Publications:* Sverre – A Voice From the Gutter, 1994. *Membership:* Norwegian Asscn of Musicians.

FOSTER, Geoff; b. 5 May 1965, Wimbledon, London, England. Recording Engineer. Partner: Dawn Tait, 2 d. *Education:* Marlborough College; Brunel University; Electronics Degree. *Career:* Worked for Stones Mobile, 1985; Cold Storage Studios, 1986; Air Studios, 1987; Chief Engineer, 1994. *Recordings:* Film scores: Stargate; Restoration; Romeo and Juliet; Mighty Ducks 3; Don Juan de Marco; Last of the Dogmen; Meet Wally Sparks; Smilla's Sense of Snow; Photographing Fairies; Alien Love Triangle; Amy Foster; B. Monkey; Black Beauty; City of Angels; Cousin Bette; Dreaming of Joseph Lees; Entrapment; Great Expectations; Jack and Sarah; James and the Giant Peach; Les Visiteurs; Loss of Sexual Innocence; Lost Souls; Mickey Blue Eyes; Midsummers Night Dream; Peacemaker; Plunkett and Macleane; Pola X; Prince of Egypt; Purdita Durango; Ride with the Devil; Robinson Crusoe; Shadows of the Empire; Summer of Sam; The Avengers; The Beach; The Bone Collector; The Gold Diggers; The Last September; The Matchmaker; The Other Conquest; The Place of Lions; The Visitor; The War Zone; Tobacco Project; Tomorrow Never Dies; The World Is Not Enough; Tropical Island Hum; Une Femme Francaise; What Dreams May Come True; Wing Commander; Wings of a Dove; When A Man Loves A Woman; Albums: George Martin; Martin Okasili; John Martyn; Crowded House; Debbie Harry; Hothouse Flowers; Jethro Tull; Grace Jones; Pulp; Roachford; Robert Palmer; Sting; The Pretenders; Paul Carrack; Radiohead; The The; Kula Shaker; David Essex; José Carreras; Vanessa-Mae; John Williams; Akin; Akira; Alisha's Attic; All Saints; Baby Bird; Bjork; Blur; Bone Muffin; Cast; Cilla Black; Dario G; David Cassidy; Petula Clarke; David McCalmont; Debbie Gibson; Eliza Carthy; Elkie Brooks; Elton John; Fine Young Cannibals; Fredrick; Garbage; Gary Barlow; Gilbert O'Sullivan; Hombres G; Irene Barnes; Jimmy Nail; Joni Mitchell; Jo Hisaishi; Phil Collins; Leftfield; Lisa Stone; Madonna; Maestro Hattori; Mel C; Michael Ball; Michael Jackson; Michael Crawford; Mike Oldfield; Ofra Haza; Outfield; Paul Brady; Peter Cox; Phil Campbell; Rolph Harris; Rory McLeod; Sisters of Mercy; Stephen Duffy; Nigel Kennedy; Sugar Ray; The Pet Shop Boys; The Trash Can Sinatras; Tyrell Corporation; Virginia McNaughton; Yell; Eliza Carthy; Ute Lemper; Pulp; Sir Neville Marriner; Placido Domingo; Giselle Bendor; Jose Carreras; Kiri Te Kawana; John Adams. *Membership:* AMIEE. *Current Management:* Air Management, Lyndhurst Hall, Lyndhurst Road, London NW3 5NG, England.

FOUNTAIN, Peter; b. 3 July 1930, New Orleans, LA, USA. Clarinettist. m. Beverly, 27 Oct. 1951, 2 s., 1 d. *Career:* Operator night club Pete Fountain's New Orleans; Member, Basin Street Six, 1949–54, Lawrence Walk Orchestra, 1957–60; Leader, own group; Appeared in (films), Pete Fountain Sextet, 1962, Pete's Place, 1966, The New Orleans Jazz Museum, 1967; Featured in: PBS spl, Dukes of Dixieland and Friends, 1980; Featured Guest with major orchestras throughout world; Co-author: A Closer Walk: The Pete Fountain Story, 1972; Appeared on Johnny Carson Show, 59 times; Performed for Papal visit, White House for Presidents Eisenhower, Nixon, Ford and Reagan, 1987. *Recordings:* 85 albums including: The Blues; Down on Rampart Street; Swingin' Blues, 1991; High Society, 1992; Cheek to Cheek, 1993. *Honours:* 3 Gold Albums; 1 Gold Single (A Closer Walk). *Address:* 2 Poydras St, New Orleans, LA 70130–1656, USA.

4 ELEMENTS. See: **DA SILVA, Rui.**

FOWLER, Simon; b. 25 April 1965, Birmingham, England. Vocalist; Musician (guitar). *Career:* Formed The Fanatics with Damon Minchella; Formed Ocean Colour Scene; Gained recording deal with indie label !Phffft, taken over by Fontana; Many support slots on tours including Paul Weller's 1993 tour; Joined Paul Weller as backing vocalist, 1993; Support to Oasis tour, 1994; Major record deal, 1995; Numerous TV and radio appearances; Riverboat Song used as theme tune for TV show TFI Friday; Several headlining tours. *Recordings:* Singles: With Fanatics, Suburban Love Songs EP; Riverboat Song, 1996; The Day We Caught The Train, 1996; You've Got It Bad, 1996; The Circle, 1996; 100 Mile High City, 1997; Travellers Tune, 1997; Better Day, 1997; It's A Beautiful Thing, 1998; July/I Am The News, 2000; Up On The Downside, 2001; Albums: Ocean Colour Scene, 1992; Moseley Shoals, 1996; B-Sides, Seasides and Freerides, 1997; Marchin' Already (No. 1, UK), 1997; One From The Modern, 1999; Mechanical Wonder, 2001; Songs For The Front Row (compilation), 2001. *Website:* www.oceancolourscene.com.

FOX, Angela; b. 31 July 1960, Birkenhead, Cheshire, England. Musician (guitar, dulcimer); Vocalist. *Career:* Appearances most folk clubs, festivals, New Zealand; Several radio appearances includes National radio interview, during tour, 1991; Television, 1995. *Recordings:* Two solo albums: Takin' A Chance, 1990; Deceptive Love, 1992; Worked on over 50 recording projects as session vocalist, guitarist, arranger, second engineer, producer. *Address:* 193 Scenic Dr., Titirangi, Auckland, New Zealand.

FOX, Donal L; b. 17 July 1952, Boston, Massachusetts, USA. Composer; Musician (Piano); Improviser, Jazz and Classical. *Education:* New England Conservatory of Music, 1962–64; Berklee College of Music, 1968; Berkshire Music Center, Tanglewood, 1969; Studied Theory and Counterpoint with Avram David, 1972–74, Composition and Harmony with T J Anderson, 1975–76, Composition and Orchestration with Gunther Schuller, 1977–82. *Career:* TV Show, Donal Fox and David Murray in Session, 1993; The Fox/Troupe Project, TV show, 1993; World premiere of Oliver Lake's Movements Turns and Switches for violin and piano, Library of Congress, Washington, piano and improviser, with Regina Carter, violin, 1993; World premiere, The Demon, International Ottawa Jazz Festival, National Gallery of Canada, 1995; World premiere of Anthony Kelley's Africamerica, for piano and orchestra, piano and improviser, 1999. *Compositions:* Dialectics for Two Grand Pianos, 1988; Variants on a Theme by Monk, for alto saxophone and piano, 1990; Jazz Sets and Tone Rows, for alto saxophone and piano, 1990; Vamping with T.T., for bass clarinet and piano, 1993; T-Cell Countdown, for voice, piano and double bass, 1993; River Town Packin House Blues, The Old People Speak of Death, Following the North Star Boogaloo, for piano and poet, 1993; Gone City, ballet in three movements, for clarinet, piano and double bass, 1994. *Recordings:* Boston Duets, 1992; Videmus, 1992; Ugly Beauty, 1995; Donal Fox: Mellow Mood, 1996; Donal Fox: Gone City, 1997. *Honours:* Meet the Composer/Rockefeller Foundation/National Endowment for the Arts Grant, 1991; Guggenheim Fellowship in Music Composition, 1997; Bogliasco Fellowship in Music Composition, 1998; Djerassi Foundation Fellowship in Music Composition, 1999. *Membership:* Massachusetts Cultural Council, 1984–; BMI, 1993–. *Current Management:* Leonellis Music. *Address:* 14 Highland Park Ave, Roxbury, MA 02119, USA.

FOX, George William; b. 23 March 1960, Cochrane, Alberta, Canada. Vocalist; Songwriter. *Career:* Over 75 TV appearances include: George Fox's New Country, CBC, 1990; Nashville Now, 1991; Newsworld, CBC, 1992; Tommy Hunter Show, 1992; All About Country, 1992; Country Gold, 1992; Canada Day – Seville, Spain, 1992; New Year's Eve Niagara, Baton Broadcasting, 1993; Crook and Chase, TNN, 1993; Sang National Anthem, World Series, Toronto, 1993; Juno Awards, 1989–94, 1996; Rita and Friends, CBC, 1994, 1995; George Fox – Time of My Life, CBC Special, 1995; Terri Clark – Coming Home, 1998; A George Fox Christmas, CBC Special, 1999. *Compositions:* Angelina, 1993; Mustang Heart, 1993; Breakfast Alone, 1993; Honest Man, 1993; No Hasta La Vista Tonight; 1994; Wear and Tear On My Heart, 1994; What's Holding Me, 1995; First Comes Love, 1995; I Give You My Word, 1997; Survivor, 1998; How Do I Get There From Her, 1999. *Recordings:* George Fox (Gold), 1988; With All My Might (Gold), 1989; Spice of Life, 1991; Mustang Heart (Gold), 1993; Time of My Life (Gold), 1995; Greatest Hits 1987–97, 1997 (Gold); Survivor, 1998; A George Fox Christmas, 1999. *Honours:* Canadian Country Music Asscn, Vista Rising Star, 1989; Country Male Vocalist, 1989–93; Juno Awards, Country Male Vocalist of Year, 1990, 1991, 1992; SOCAN Song of Year, Clearly Canadian, 1993. *Membership:* CARAS; NARAS; CMA; CCMA; ACTRA; AFofM. *Address:* c/o Balmur Inc, 1105 17th Ave, Nashville, TN 37212, USA.

FOX, John, (David Bell, Peter Balding); b. 30 April 1926, Sutton, Surrey, England. Composer; Arranger; Conductor; Musician (piano). m. Joy Devon, 17 May 1980, 2 s., 1 d. *Education:* Royal College of Music (ARCM); Composition scholarship, Fitznells College of Music. *Career:* Pianist, arranger, numerous groups; Arranger, conductor, BBC Radio Orchestra, 1960s; Conducted Krakow Radio Symphony Orchestra, recordings, Poland; Broadcasts with John Fox Orchestra and voices; Recorded in London, Customs easy listening music for USA networks; Over 200 easy listening arrangements on the internet;

Concerts: John Fox Concerts, BBC, Pebble Mill, Musical World of John Fox, Magic of John Fox (London), Numerous String Sound and Romantic Strings, broadcast sessions, 1980s; Also acapella broadcasts with John Fox Singers, Friday Night Is Music Night, BBC Radio; Conductor, arranger, for concerts with vocalist (wife) Joy Devon, Philharmonie Concert Hall, Cologne, Germany; Performed Earth and Space Suite, Huntingdon, England; Owner, publishing company, Coniston Music Publishing; The Musical World of John Fox Talks with musical illustrations at different venues throughout the UK and USA. *Compositions:* Over 1,500 published works with Sonoton Music, Amphonic Music and Sound Stage, EMI; *Arrangements:* well over 1,000 in BBC Music Library. *Recordings:* Memory; Unforgettable Melodies, Nos 1 and 2; Love Is A Many-Splendoured Thing; Whispers of Love; Pomp and Glory; Heartstrings; Earth and Space; Sailing By; Two's Company; Instrumental Pops (series); John Fox Presents, Vols 1–18; with J F Orchestra and Voices: Gershwin; Here There and Everywhere; with J F Singers: Fairest Isle; Animal Lovers; Listen Easy (1) 60s; Listen Easy (2) 70s (BBC World-wide); Produced (with Joy Devon) albums own material (with large symphony orchestras), Munich, Berlin, Leipzig, London, Yugoslavia, Budapest, Poland. *Honours:* STEMRA Music Award, Netherlands, for Best Film, 1993. *Membership:* PRS; MCPS; MU; APC; BAC&S. *Current Management:* Coniston Music Publishing Co, 26 Garratts Lane, Banstead, Surrey SM7 2EA, England.

FRAITURE, Nikolai; b. 13 Nov. 1979, New York, NY, USA. Musician (bass guitar). *Career:* Mem., The Strokes, 1998–. *Recordings:* Albums: Is This It, 2001. Singles: The Modern Age, 2001; Hard To Explain/New York City Cops, 2001; Last Nite/When It Started, 2001. *Honours:* NME Awards, Band of the Year, Best New Act, Album of the Year, 2001; BRIT Award, Best International Newcomer, 2002. *Current Management:* Ryan Gentles, Wiz Kid Management. *Address:* c/o RCA Records, 1540 Broadway, New York, NY 10036, USA. *Website:* www.thestrokes.com.

FRAME, Roddy; b. 29 Jan. 1964, East Kilbride, Scotland. Vocalist; Songwriter; Musician (guitar). *Career:* Founder member, Aztec Camera, 1980–; International appearances include: Support to Elvis Costello, USA, 1983; The Ritz, New York, 1985; Royal Albert Hall, 1988; Cambridge Folk Festival, 1991; Edinburgh Festival, 1991; Support to Bob Dylan, 1993; Phoenix Festival, 1995. *Compositions include:* Composed all songs on albums. *Recordings:* Singles include: Oblivious, 1983; Walk Out To Winter, 1983; How Men Are, 1988; Somewhere In My Heart, 1988; Working In A Goldmine, 1988; Good Morning Britain, 1990; Spanish Horses, 1992; Sun, 1995; Reasons for Living, 1998; Albums: High Land, Hard Rain, 1983; Knife, 1984; Love, 1987; Stray, 1990; Dreamland, 1993; Frestonia, 1995; North Star, 1998; The Best of Aztec Camera (compilation), 1999; Surf, 2002; Contributor to: Red Hot + Blue, 1990; Ruby Trax (duet with Andy Fairweather-Low), 1992. *Honours:* Gold Discs: High Land Hard Rain, 1983; Knife, 1985; Platinum disc, Love, 1988. *Current Management:* Southside Management, 20 Cromwell Mews, London SW7 2JY, England.

FRAMPTON, Peter; b. 22 April 1950, Beckenham, Kent, England. Musician (guitar); Vocalist. *Career:* Member, The Herd; Session musician, Johnny Hallyday; Member, Humble Pie, 1969–71; Solo artiste, 1971–; Performances include: Support to J Geils Band, New York, 1972; Don Kirshner's Second Annual Rock Music Awards, CBS, 1976; Madison Square Garden, New York, 1979; Guitarist, Glass Spider tour, David Bowie, 1987; Tour with Stevie Nicks, 1987; Formed new backing band, Escape, 1990; Appearance, Lynyrd Skynyrd and Friends 20th Anniversary concert, 1993; Film appearance, Sgt Pepper's Lonely Hearts Club Band, 1978. *Recordings:* Albums with Humble Pie: As Safe As Yesterday Is, 1969; Town and Country, 1969; Humble Pie, 1971; Rock On, 1971; Performance – Rockin' The Fillmore, 1972; Solo albums: Wind of Change, 1972; Frampton's Camel, 1973; Somethin's Happening, 1974; Frampton, 1974; Frampton Comes Alive, 1976; I'm In You, 1977; Where Should I Be, 1979; Breaking All The Rules, 1981; The Art of Control, 1982; Premonition, 1983; Peter Frampton Classics, 1987; New World, 1988; When All The Pieces Fit, 1989; Shine On – A Collection, 1992; Peter Frampton, 1994; Peter Frampton Comes Alive II, 1995; Love Taker, 1995; Winds of Change, 1998; A Day in the Sun, 1999; Beat the Bootleggers, 1999; Live In Detroit, 2000; Solo singles include: Show Me The Way, 1976; Baby I Love Your Way, 1976; Signed, Sealed Delivered (I'm Yours), 1977; I Can't Stand No More, 1979; The Bigger They Come, featured in film Harley Davidson and The Marlboro Man, 1991. *Honours:* Gold Ticket, Madison Square Gardens, 1979. *Address:* Firstars, 3520 Hayden Ave, Culver City, CA 90232, USA.

FRANCE, Martin Perry; b. 29 Feb. 1964, Rainham, Kent, England. Musician (drums, percussion). *Education:* Music O Level; 10 year's private study. *Career:* To date Performed in 36 countries, all usually recorded for television/radio; Featured in various newspapers, music magazines; Performed with many leading jazz musicians; 1994–, working in new quartet led by Kenny Wheeler with John Taylor, Dave Holland. *Recordings:* First House: Erendira; Cantilena; Iain Ballamy: Balloon Man; All Men Amen; Cleveland Watkiss: Green Chimneys; Julian Argnelles: Phaedrus; Django Bates: Music For The Third Policeman; Summer Fruits and Unrest; Winter Truce and Homes Blaze; Django Bates: Loose Tubes: Loose Tubes Live; Human Chain: Pyrotechnics; Mark Lockheart: Clec; Perfect Houseplants; New Folk Songs, 2001; Billy Jenkins: Aural Art; Sounds Like Bromley;

Summer Fest; Eddie Parker: Eddie Parker; Buckley/Batchelor: Whole and The Half; Arguelles, Swallow, Walker and France. *Current Management:* P Partnerships, 5 Dryden St, London WC2 9NW. *Address:* 2 Dewhurst Lane, Wadhurst, E Sussex, England.

FRANCE, Nicolas Michael; b. 30 March 1956, Standon, Hertfordshire, England. Musician (percussion, drums, piano). m. Billie (Susan Mary) Preston, 21 Oct. 1983, 1 s., 2 d. *Education:* Chorister, Ely Cathedral; G Mus Diploma (Music), CCAT, Cambridge. *Career:* Professional musician, 1980–; Worked with: Tanita Tikaram; Bill Withers; Jackie Graham; Working Week; Mose Allison; Recorded with Pete Townshend; Thomas Dolby; L Shankar; Session player with artists including: Phil Todd; Robbie Macintosh; Snake Davies; Laurence and Richard Cottle; Danny Cummings; Martin Ditcham; Played with jazz artists including: Loose Tubes; Ronnie Scott Quintet; John Taylor; Alan Holdsworth; Jim Mullen; Concerts and tours include: Tours with Loose Tubes, 1983–86; 3 European tours, 3 festivals with Working Week, 1984–87; 2 tours, UK, Europe, 1988–89; Tour, including Montreux and Nice festivals, with Heitor; 3 world tours with Tanita Tikaram, 1990–95. *Recordings:* with Loose Tubes: Loose Tubes; Delightful Precipice, 1983–85; The Way Through The Woods, Bronte Brothers, 1993; Johnson, The Fat Lady Sings, 1993; with The Working Week: Working Nights; Companeros; Fire In The Mountain; Rodrigo Bay from Absolute Beginners; Fire In The Mountain; Supergrass; Comic Strip Movie (film soundtrack), 1984–87; with Tanita Tikaram: Everybody's Angel; Eleven Kinds of Loneliness; Lovers In The City, 1990–95. *Honours:* G Mus, Music diploma. *Membership:* PRS.

FRANCES, Andrew; b. 17 March 1950, New York, NY, USA. Record Co Exec; Prod; Man. *Education:* Graduated New York City High School of the performing Arts; Bachelor degree, Northwestern University. *Career:* Worked for labels: MCA; RCA; Millennium; RSO; Founded own labels: Chameleon/Elektra; North South/Atlantic; Grammy Award-winning recordings on own labels; Own management company Adwater and Stir; Artists handled include: David Bowie; Wang Chung; Ruth McCartney; Benny Mardones. *Membership:* NARAS; CMA. *Address:* 1303 16th Ave S, Nashville, TN 37212, USA.

FRANCIS, Chris; b. 11 Aug. 1948, London, England. Bandleader; Jazz Musician (alto/soprano saxophone, G flute). m. Penny, 1976, 1 s. *Education:* Manchester and Chelsea Art Schools; Studied music privately. *Career:* Founded Naima, band ranging from trio to fifteen piece, toured Europe, Britain; Founder member, Joy quintet; Recorded with many pop stars, toured with rock bands and folk groups. *Recordings:* Herm Island Suite, BBC Radio; (session man) Adam Ant: Goody Two Shoes; Numerous broadcasts of own compositions. *Honours:* Joint winner, GLAA: Young Jazz Musicans Award, 1976. *Membership:* Musicians' Union; PRS; MCPS. *Current Management:* Art Services. *Address:* 10a Putney High St, London SW15 1SL, England.

FRANCIS, Connie, (Concetta Rosa Maria Franconero); b. 12 Dec. 1938, Newark, New Jersey, USA. Vocalist. *Education:* Began playing accordion age 4. *Career:* Professional musician, 1949–; Winner, Arthur Godfrey Talent Show; Recording artiste, 1955–; Charity work for organizations including UNICEF; Entertained US troops, Viet Nam, 1960s; Retired from public performance, 1970s; Resumed performances, 1981–; London Palladium, 1989; Las Vegas, 1989. *Recordings:* Albums include: Who's Sorry Now?, 1958; The Exciting Connie Francis, 1959; My Thanks To You, 1959; Italian Favourites, 1960; Rock 'n' Roll Million Sellers, 1960; Country and Western Golden Hits, 1960; Sings Great Jewish Favorites, 1960; Songs To A Swinging Band, 1961; Never On Sunday, 1961; Folk Song Favorites, 1961; Do The Twist, 1962; Second Hand Love and Other Hits, 1962; Country Music Connie Style, 1962; Modern Italian Hits, 1963; In The Summer of His Years, 1964; Great Country Favourites, with Hank Williams Jr, 1964; A New Kind of Connie, 1964; Connie Francis Sings For Mama, 1965; Love Italian Style, 1967; Happiness, 1967; My Heart Cries For You, 1967; Hawaii Connie, 1968; Connie and Clyde, 1968; The Wedding Cake, 1969; Connie Francis Sings Great Country Hits, Vol. 2, 1973; Sings The Big Band Hits, 1977; I'm Me Again – Silver Anniversary Album, 1981; Connie Francis and Peter Kraus, Vols 1 and 2, 1984; Country Store, 1988; Various compilations including: Star Power, 2001; Ultimate EP Collection, 2002. Singles: Who's Sorry Now (No. 1, UK); Stupid Cupid (No. 1, UK); Everybody's Somebody's Fool (No. 1, USA); My Mind Has A Heart of Its Own (No. 1, USA); Don't Break The Heart That Loves You (No. 1, USA). *Current Management:* Stan Scottland c/o JKES Services Inc. *Address:* 404 Park Ave S, 10th Floor, New York, NY 10016, USA.

FRANCIS, Eddie; b. Ontario, Canada. Country Vocalist; Writer; Musician (guitar). *Education:* BA; BEd. *Career:* Various Radio Appearances; Singer, Musician In Countless Shows; Actor, Singer In Various Amateur Theatres. *Compositions:* Peterson Road. *Recordings:* CD Album, Hills and Valleys. *Membership:* CCMA; OSSTF. *Current Management:* Independent Associate In Commonlight Music Canada. *Address:* PO Box 186 Mill St, Combermere, ON K0J 1L0, Canada.

FRANCIS, Terry, (Love Panda); b. 1966, Leatherhead, Surrey, England. Prod; Remixer; DJ. *Career:* Began DJ career at the legendary Stern's Club; Co-founder: Wiggle Records and underground house night in London with Nathan Coles; Compiler and mixer of Architecture series for Pagan Records;

Resident DJ at Fabric club in London; Member: 2 Smokin' Barrels; The Delinquents; Collaborations: Nathan Coles; Housey Doingz. *Recordings:* Albums: Architecture Vols 1 and 2 (DJ-mixed compilations); Singles: Dub Town, 1997; Took From Me, 1998; Breaking The Law EP (with The Delinquents), 1998; Smokey Rooms EP, 1999; Strong Woman EP, 2001. *Honours:* Muzik Awards, Best New DJ, 1997. *Address:* c/o Wiggle Records, 2 Vanbrugh Park Rd W, Blackheath, London SE3 7QD, England.

FRANCOMBE, Mark; b. 4 Dec. 1963, Ongar, Essex, England. Musician (guitar, bass, keyboards). *Education:* Portsmouth Art College. *Career:* Numerous tours of Europe and USA with the Cranes; Also support tour with The Cure, USA and Europe, 1992; Various radio and television appearances include: 2 sessions on John Peel show, BBC Radio 1; MTV; Snub TV, BBC. *Recordings:* with The Cranes: Self Non Self; Wings of Joy; Forever Loved; Radio Oddyssey, 1996; Population 4, 1997. *Current Management:* Adrian Maddox; Agent: AMPI.

FRANKLIN, Aretha; b. 25 March 1942, Memphis, Tennessee, USA. Vocalist; Songwriter. m. Glynn Turman, 1978. *Career:* Recording artist, 1960–; European tour, 1968; Appearances include: Inaugural Eve Gala, Jimmy Carter, Washington DC; Jamaica World Music Festival, 1982; Budweiser Superfest, 1982; Actress, film The Blues Brothers, 1980; Subject, TV specials: Aretha Franklin – The Queen of Soul, 1988; Aretha Franklin – Duets, 1993. *Recordings:* Albums include: The Great Aretha Franklin, 1960; The Electrifying Aretha Franklin, 1962; The Tender, The Moving, The Swinging, 1962; Unforgettable – A Tribute To Dinah Washington, 1964; Runnin' Out of Fools, 1965; Yeah!!!, 1965; Soul Sister, 1966; I Never Loved A Man (The Way I Loved You), 1967; Aretha Arrives, 1967; Aretha: Lady Soul, 1968; Aretha In Paris, 1968; This Girl's In Love With You, 1969; Spirit In The Dark, 1970; Aretha Live At Fillmore West, 1971; Amazing Grace, 1972; Hey Now Hey (The Other Side of The Sky), 1973; Let Me In Your Life, 1974; With Everything I Feel In Me, 1975; You, 1975; Sweet Passion, 1977; Almighty Fire, 1978; La Diva, 1979; Aretha, 1980; Love All The Hurt Away, 1981; Jump To It, 1982; Get It Right, 1983; Who's Zoomin' Who?, 1985; The First Lady of Soul, 1986; Aretha, 1987; One Lord, One Faith, One Baptism, 1988; Through The Storm, 1989; What You See Is What You Sweat, 1991; Queen of Soul, 1993; Greatest Hits 1980–94, 1994; A Rose Is Still A Rose, 1998; You Grow Closer, 1998; Love Songs, 2001; Hit singles include: I Never Loved A Man (The Way I Loved You), 1967; Respect (No. 1, USA), 1967; Baby I Love You, 1967; (You Make Me Feel Like A) Natural Woman, 1967; Chain of Fools, 1968; (Sweet Sweet Baby) Since You've Been Gone, 1968; Think, 1968; I Say A Little Prayer, 1968; Call Me, 1970; Don't Play That Song, 1970; You're All I Need To Get By, 1971; Rock Steady, 1972; Young Gifted and Black, 1972; Day Dreaming, 1972; Until You Come Back To Me, 1974; Sisters Are Doin' It For Themselves, duet with Annie Lennox, 1985; I Knew You Were Waiting For Me, duet with George Michael (No. 1, UK and USA), 1987; Through The Storm, duet with Elton John, 1989; Contributor, film soundtracks including: Sparkle, 1976; Jumpin' Jack Flash, 1986; White Men Can't Jump, 1992. *Honours:* Aretha Franklin Day, Detroit, 1967; Numerous Grammy Awards, 1968–; American Music Awards; Inducted into Rock 'n' Roll Hall of Fame, 1987; Living Legend Award, NARAS, 1990; Rhythm and Blues Foundation Lifetime Achievement Award, 1992. *Current Management:* Aretha Franklin Management, 30150 Telegraph Rd, Suite 444, Birmingham, MI 48025, USA.

FRANKLIN, Kirk, (Kirk Smith); b. 26 Jan. 1970, Fort Worth, TX, USA. Vocalist; Songwriter; Record Co Exec. m., 1 s. *Career:* Choir Dir., Greater Strangers Rest Baptist Church, Fort Worth, 1988; Worked with Dallas-Fort Worth Mass Choir on various albums; Formed choir group, the Family; Founded record co., Fo Yo Soul. *Recordings:* Albums: with the Family: I Will Not Let Nothing Separate Me, 1991; Kirk Franklin and the Family, 1992; Another Chance, 1993; Christmas, 1995; Watcha Lookin' 4, 1996; Kirk Franklin's Nu Nation, 1997; The Nu Nation Project, 1998. Singles: Stomp, 1997. Contribution to film soundtracks: My Life Is In Your Hands (for Get on the Bus), 1996; Joy (for The Preacher' Wife), 1996. *Publications:* Church Boy: My Music and My Life (autobiography), 1998. *Honours:* Grammy Awards, Best Contemporary Soul Gospel Album, for Watcha Lookin' 4, 1997, Best Gospel Album by a choir or chorus, for God's Property from Kirk Franklin's Nu Nation, 1998, Best Contemporary Soul Gospel Album, for The Nu Nation Project, 1999. *Address:* c/o Gerald Wright, Wright Group, 5609 S Archbridge Ct, Arlington, TX 76017, USA.

FRANOLIC, Drazen; b. 4 July 1961, Biograd, Croatia. Musician (Arabian lute); Composer. m. Vesna Gorse, 20 June 1992. *Career:* Member, Franolic-Gorse Duo; Gorse-Franolic Trio; Tao; Concerts: Zagreb; Belgrade; Ljubljana; Sarajevo; Rijeka; Dubrovnik; Italy; Czechoslovakia; Live album recordings, Lisinsui Concert Hall, 1992, 1995. *Recordings:* with Vesna Gorse: Waterfalls, 1986; New Era of Instrumental Music, 1990; Wonderland, 1990; Asgard Live, 1993; Just A Music, 1995. *Membership:* Croatian Composers' Society; Croatian Music Union; Amnesty International. *Current Management:* Vesna Gorse. *Address:* Vankina 3/4, 41020 Zagreb, Croatia.

FRANZÉN, K. B. V. Hawkey; b. 29 March 1946, Böda, Kalmarlän, Sweden. Composer; Vocalist; Songwriter; Artist; Actor; Musician (guitar, keyboard, accordion, tenor saxophone). *Career:* Lea Riders Group, 1962–68; Jason's

Fleece, 1970–71; Solo Performer, Theatremusic-composer and for radio and TV; Filmmusic, Dom Kallar Oss Mods (They Call Us Misfits). *Compositions:* LP: Visa Från Djupvik, 1969; Visa Från Gungor och Sand, 1970; Visa Från och Till, 1971; Jason's Fleece, 1970; Visa Av och Med, 1972; Smulvisor and Bitlåtar, 1981; Det Blåser På Månen, 1985; Plötsligt Skulle Vi Skiljas, 1988. *Recordings:* Lea Riders Group, 1989; Många Varv Kring Solen, CD, 1996. *Honours:* Stockholm City; Prize for Best Private Theatre Play, 1969; Konstnärsnämnden, Arts Grants Cttee Schlsps, 1971, 1975, 1985, 1986, 1989, 1990, 1992, 1993, 1996, 1997, 1998; STIM, Swedish Performing Rights Society, 1995, 1997. *Membership:* Swedish Performing Rights Society; Swedish Society of Popular Music Composers; Swedish Artists and Musicians Interest Organisation; Svenska Teaterförbundet, Swedish Actors Equity Asscn. *Current Management:* Linnéa Musik Produktion. *Address:* Nygatan 5 nb, 599 31 Ödeshög, Sweden.

FRASER, Elizabeth; b. 29 Aug. 1963, Grangemouth, Scotland. Vocalist. 1 d. *Career:* Member, Cocteau Twins; Sang on collective projects with This Mortal Coil; Collaboration with pianist Harold Budd; Guest appearances with Ian McCullough on Candleland album, with Future Sound of London on Lifeforms, with Massive Attack on Teardrop single and tracks on their Mezzanine album. *Recordings:* Singles: Lullabies, 1982; Peppermint Pig, 1983; Sunburst and Snowblind, 1983; Pearly Dewdrops' Drops, 1984; Aikea-Guinea, 1985; Tiny Dynamine, 1985; Echoes in a Shallow Bay, 1985; Love's Easy Tears, 1986; Iceblink Luck, 1990; Evangeline, 1993; Frosty the Snowman, 1993; Bluebeard, 1994; Twinlights, 1995; Otherness, 1995 Tishbite, 1996; Violaine, 1996; with This Mortal Coil, Song to the Siren, 1983; Teardrop, with Massive Attack, 1998; Albums: Garlands, 1982; Head Over Heals, 1983; Treasure, 1984; The Pink Opaque, 1985; Victorialand, 1986; The Moon and the Melodies, with Harold Budd, 1986; Blue Bell Knoll, 1988; Heaven or Las Vegas, 1990; Four Calendar Café, 1993; Milk and Kisses, 1996; The BBC Sessions, 1999; Stars and Topsoil (compilation), 2000.

FRATER, Josephine; b. 16 May 1963, Glasgow, Scotland. Vocalist; Composer; Musician (percussion). m. Stephen D Taylor, 6 Sept. 1991. *Education:* Goldsmiths University; Guildhall School of Music and Drama. *Career:* Joint owner, i.2.i Records with Steve Taylor; Co-run The Runners with Steve Taylor; Appeared on cable TV; Concerts include: Ronnie Scott's; The Jazz Cafe; British tour; International tour, 1996. *Compositions:* Hours; Crooked Man; Be Yourself Tonight; Secret World; Journeying. *Recordings:* Album: Phonetic. *Honours:* Advanced Certificate Jazz and Pop Music; Postgraduate diploma, Jazz and Studio Music. *Membership:* PRS; Musicians' Union. *Address:* PO Box 7038, London N3 2HF, England.

FRAZIER, Stan (Charles Stanton); b. 23 April 1968. Musician (drums). *Career:* Played colleges and parties with local group The Tories; Group became The Shrinky Dinx; Signed to Atlantic Records following circulation of self-made demo video; Act renamed Sugar Ray owing to threat of legal action prior to record releases; Built up world-wide fanbase through touring and TV appearances; Cameo in Fathers Day film, 1997. *Recordings:* Albums: Lemonade and Brownies, 1995; Floored, 1997; 14–59, 1999; Sugar Ray, 2001; Singles: Mean Machine, Iron Mic, 1995; Fly, RPM, 1997; Every Morning, Someday, 1999; Falls Apart, 2000; When It's Over, Answer The Phone, 2001. *Honours:* Second/third albums certified double/triple platinum by RIAA respectively. *Address:* c/o PO Box 12018, Costa Mesa, CA 92627, USA. *E-mail:* management@sugarray.com. *Website:* www.sugarray.com.

FREDERICKX, Jan; b. 30 Sept. 1971, Mol, Belgium. Vocalist; Songwriter; Musician (bass guitar, guitar). *Education:* Ancient Latin and Greek Languages; Psychology; Socio-Cultural Sciences; Classical Guitar, Music Academy, Geel, Belgium, two years. *Career:* Played in bands including: Hellsaw; MSD; Extreem; Acoustic Grinder; Concerts with: Napalm Death; Extreme Noise Terror; The Varukers; Death; The Gathering; Doom; John Peel-Session, BRTN Session; 3 official live videos, BRTN TV. *Compositions:* Agathocles: Riek Boois, 1988; Cabbalic Gnosticism, 1988; Disgorge, 1989; Fascination of Mutilation, 1989; If This is Cruel, 1989; Violent Noise Attack, 1990; Blood, 1990; Putrid Offal, 1990; Morbid Organs Mutilation, 1990; Nasum, 1990; Agarchy, 1991; Psycho, 1991; Violent Headache, 1992; Kompost, 1993; Distrust and Abuse, 1993; Nyctophobic, 1993; Man is the Bastard, 1993; Patareni, 1993; Audiorrea, 1993; Social Genocide, 1993; No Use (Hatred), 1993; Punisher, 1994; Carcass Grinder, 1994; Plastic Grave, 1994; Back to 1987, 1994; Mincemongers in Barna, 1994; Unholy Grave, 1996; Praparation H, 1996; Krush, 1996; Excruciating Terror, 1997; Shikabane, 1997; Theatric Symbolisation of Life, 1991; Black Clouds of Determinate, 1994; Black Sharp Daggers, 1995; Thanks for Your Hostility, 1996; Humarrogance, 1997; Agathocles Tribute CD, South Africa; X-piration, 1997; Deadmocracy, 1998; Bloodsuckers, 1998; Skitliv, 1998; Unholy Grave, 1999; Grind Buto, 1999. *Honours:* BRTN, Session, 1996; John Peel, Session, 1997; Kill Your Idols, CD, Tribute to Agathocles CD. *Current Management:* Agathocles, Asberg 8, 2400 Mol, Belgium.

FREDERIKSEN, Lars; b. 1972. Musician (guitar); Vocalist. m. Megan, 1998. *Career:* Member, UK Subs; Joined Cajones; Formed Slip, 1992, gigged with Rancid; Joined Rancid; Numerous live shows. *Recordings:* Singles: Radio, Radio, Radio, 1994; Roots Radicals, 1995; Time Bomb, 1995; Ruby Soho, 1996;

Bloodclot, 1998; Hooligans, 1998; Brad Logan, 1998; Albums: Let's Go, 1994; And Out Come the Wolves, 1995; Life Won't Wait, 1998; Rancid, 2000.

FREDRICKSSON, Marie; b. 29 May 1958, Sweden. Vocalist. 1 d. *Career:* Solo recording artiste, 1980s; Founding mem., Roxette, with Per Gessle, 1984–; Numerous television, radio and live appearances world-wide. *Recordings:* Albums: Pearls Of Passion, 1986; Look Sharp!, 1988; Joyride, 1991; Tourism, 1992; Den Sjunde Vagen, 1993; Den Standiga Resa, 1993; Efter Stormen, 1993; Mammas Barn 1993; Crash! Boom! Bang!, 1994; Het Vind, 1995; Don't Bore Us, Get To The Chorus—Roxette's Greatest Hits, 1995; Balades En Español, 1996; Have A Nice Day, 1999; Room Service, 2001. Singles include: The Look (No. 1, 23 countries), 1989; Listen To Your Heart (No. 1, USA), 1989; Dangerous, 1989; Dressed For Success, 1989; It Must Have Been Love (from film Pretty Woman, No. 1, USA), 1990; Joyride (No. 1, 19 countries), 1991; Fading Like A Flower (No. 2, USA), 1991; The Big L, 1991; Spending My Time, 1991; Church Of Your Heart, 1992; How Do You Do!, 1992; Queen Of Rain, 1992; Almost Unreal (from film Super Mario Brothers), 1993; Sleeping In My Car, 1995; You Don't Understand Me, 1996; Wish I Could Fly, 1999; Anyone, 1999; Stars, 1999. *Honours:* Platinum and Gold discs; Grammy Awards; MTV Awards; Achievement medals from King Carl XVI Gustaf of Sweden, 2003. *Current Management:* Rascoff/Zysbalt Organization, 110 W 57th St, New York, NY 10019, USA.

FREELAND, Adam; b. 1974 London, England. Prod; Remixer; DJ. *Career:* Founder: Marine Parade Records, Friction club night (pioneering the Nu-Skool Breakbeat sound); World-wide DJ; Remixed: Pressure Drop, Aquasky, BT; Member: Tsunami One; Collaborations: Kevin Beber. *Recordings:* Albums (DJ-mixed compilations): Coastal Breaks #1, 1997; Coastal Breaks #2, 1998; Tectonics, 2000; On Tour, 2001; Singles: No 43 With Steamed Rice Please (with Tsunami One), 1997; Hip Hop Phenomenon (with Tsunami One), 1999. *Current Management:* c/o Marine Parade Recordings, 29 Kensington Gardens, Brighton, BN1 4AL, England.

FREEMAN, John David; b. 2 Jan. 1955, Jarrow, Tyne and Wear, England. Musician (Bass Guitar); Vocalist; Songwriter; School Teacher. m. Alison Freeman, 11 Aug. 1979, 2 s. *Education:* Loughborough College of Education. *Career:* Bass Player, Vocalist and Co-writer of material for band, Havana Fireflies, playing at Glastonbury Festival, 1993 and 1994; Radio appearances include: Johnny Walker Show, and as unsigned band of the week on Steve Wright Show, BBC Radio 1; also airplay of album on GWR Radio; Various television appearances on HTV West shows, Spotlight and First Cut. *Recordings:* Barbed Wire Prophets, by The Havana Fireflies. *Membership:* Musicians' Union. *Address:* 40 High St, Dilton Marsh, Wiltshire, England.

FREEMAN, Matt; b. 1966, Albany, New York, USA. Musician (bass); Vocalist. *Career:* Formed Operation Ivy with Tim Armstrong, 1987; Joined MDC, 1990; Formed Rancid with Tim Armstrong. *Recordings:* Singles: Rancid, 1993; Radio, Radio, Radio, 1994; Roots Radicals, 1994; Time Bomb, 1995; Ruby Soho, 1996; Bloodclot, 1998; Hooligans, 1998; Brad Logan, 1999; Albums: Rancid, 1993; Let's Go, 1994; And Out Come the Wolves, 1995; Life Won't Wait, 1998.

FREHLEY, Ace (Paul); b. 22 April 1951, Bronx, New York, USA. Musician (guitar). *Career:* Member, US rock group Kiss, 1973–82; Numerous US, UK, European and world-wide tours; Left Kiss following serious car accident, 1982; Founder, guitarist, Frehley's Comet, 1987–. *Recordings:* Albums: with Kiss: Kiss, 1974; Dressed To Kill, 1975; Alive!, 1975; Destroyer, 1976; The Originals, 1976; Rock and Roll Over, 1976; Kiss Alive II, 1977; Love Gun, 1977; Double Platinum, 1978; Dynasty, 1979; Kiss Unmasked, 1980; Music From The Elder, 1981; Killers, 1982; Creatures of The Night, 1982; Solo albums: Ace Frehley, 1978; Trouble Walking, 1989; with Frehley's Comet: Frehley's Comet, 1987; Live + 1, 1988; Second Sighting, 1989; 12 Picks, 1998; Loaded Deck, 1998; Singles include: Rock 'N' Roll All Nite; Beth; Detroit Rock City; Hard Luck Woman; Calling Dr Love; I Was Made For Lovin' You; Also features on: Post Orgasmic Chill, Skunk Anansie, 1999. *Honours:* Footprints at Grauman's Chinese Theatre, Hollywood, 1976; Gold Ticket, Madison Square Garden, 1979; Gold and Platinum discs. *Current Management:* The Sewitt Group, 17 Ash Court, Highland Mills, NY 10930, USA.

FRENCH, Frank; b. 19 Aug. 1952, Oakland, California, USA. Musician (piano); Composer. m. Carolyn Massonneau French, 19 Jan. 1991. *Education:* 4 years college; San Francisco Conservatory of Music; San Francisco State University; Bachelor of Music. *Career:* Performances in United States, Canada, Europe, Australia; Public radio, television appearances; American and foreign music festival appearances. *Compositions:* Original compositions featured on La Bambula, Frontiers; Lacumbia, 1992; Womba Bomba, 1995; Toca con Clave, suite for piano, 1997. *Recordings:* The Well Tempered Clavier, 48 preludes and fugues, by Bach; Tangos of Ernesto Nazareth; La Bambula; More American Souvenirs; Frontiers; (with David Thomas Roberts, Scott Kirby); Terra Verde, new music for piano solo with Scott Kirby and David Thomas Roberts; Creole Music, Piano duets with Scott Kirby; American Originals, music of Louis Moreau Gottschalk, for solo piano. *Membership:* BMI; Piano Technicians Guild. *Current Management:* Artia Concerts,

Sumner, Washington. *Address:* Frank French, PO Box 4034, Boulder, CO 80306, USA.

FRENGEL, Mike; b. 20 Jan. 1972, Mountain View, California, USA. Composer; Musician (guitar). *Education:* BA, Music Composition, San Jose State University; MA, Electro-Acoustic Music Composition, Dartmouth College; PhD, Music Composition, City University, London, England. *Career:* Participant as composer/performer in international contemporary music festivals, 1990–; Early internet broadcast of electro-acoustic music at ArtNet Concert, San Jose State University, 1995; Completed Polyrhythmic Modulation Studies for Masters Thesis, 1999. *Compositions:* Three Short Stories; Long Slender Heels; Rock Music; Variations on an Already Complex Theme No 1; Dropped On My Head, Upside Down; And Then, Romina..., 1999; The 3 Faces of Karen Black, 2000. *Recordings:* ICMC'97 Hong Kong; CDCM Vol. 26; Sonic Circuits VII; Luigi Russolo, 2000. *Honours:* Luigi Russolo Prize, 2000. *Membership:* American Composer's Forum (ACF); International Computer Music Asscn (ICMA); Society for Electro-Acoustic Music in the United States (SEAMUS); Broadcast Music Inc (BMI); Electronic Arts Focus, London, founder and board mem.

FRESTON, Thomas; b. 22 Nov. 1945, New York, NY, USA. Media Exec. m. Margaret Badali, 1980, 1 s. *Education:* MBA. *Career:* Dir. of Marketing MTV, MTV Networks, New York, 1980–81; Dir. of Marketing, The Movie Channel, 1982–83; Vice-Pres. Marketing MTV, MTV Networks, 1983–84; Vice-Pres. Marketing, 1984–85, Sr Vice-Pres. and Gen. Man. Affiliate Sales, Marketing, 1985, Sr Vice-Pres. and Gen. Man. MTV, VH-1, 1985–86, Pres. Entertainment, 1986–87, Pres. and CEO, 1987–89, Chair. and CEO, 1989–, MTV Networks; Mem., Board Dirs, Cable Advertising Bureau, 1987–, MTV Europe, London, 1986–, Rock and Roll Hall of Fame, 1986–; Mem., Smithsonian Comm. Music in America, 1987–; Cable TV Administration and Marketing Asscn, National Acad. of Cable Programming. *Address:* c/o MTV Networks, 1515 Broadway, 14th Floor, New York, NY 10036, USA.

FRESU, Paolo; b. 10 Feb. 1961, Berchidda, Sardinia, Italy. Musician (Trumpet, Flugelhorn, Arr, Comp). *Education:* Electronics Expert, Certificate, University/DAMS, Bologna, Italy; Conservatory of Music, Cagliari, Sardinia; March Band, 1972–80; Pop Music, 1976–80; Conservatory of Music, Certificate, 1982. *Career:* Professor, Siena Jazz National Seminars, 1985–; Jazz University courses at Terni, 1987–; Winter courses, Siena and sems in Nuoro, 1989–; Guest Soloist, many innovative jazz recording projects; Artistic Director, Time in Jazz Festival in Berchidda, 1988–; Eurojazz Concorso Internazionale per Giovani Musicisti Europei' in Oristano, 1994 and Jazz Seminary in Nuoro, 1989–. *Recordings:* Ostinato, 1984; Inner Voices, 1986; Live in Montpellier, 1980; Ensalada Mistica, 1994; Mythscapes, 1995; Night on the City, 1995; Wanderlust, 1997; Angel, 1998; Metamorfosi, 1999. *Publications:* The first 63 jazz compositions, 1989; 49 compositions, 1996. *Honours:* Best Italian Musician, 1990; First Italian Young Musician, 1994; Best European Musician, 1996. *Current Management:* Pannonica, Albani Vittorio, Bolzano, Italy. *Address:* PO Box 6, 40047, Riola, Italy.

FREY, Glenn; b. 6 Nov. 1948, Detroit, Michigan, USA. Musician (guitar); Vocalist. *Career:* Member, Longbranch Pennywhistle (duo with J D Souther), 1968–71; Founder member, The Eagles, 1971–. *Recordings:* with Longbranch Pennywhistle: Longbranch Pennywhistle, 1969; with The Eagles: The Eagles, 1972; Desperado, 1973; On The Border, 1974; One of These Nights (No. 1, USA), 1975; Their Greatest Hits 1971–75 (No. 1, USA), 1976; Hotel California (No. 1, USA), 1978; The Long Run, 1979; Eagles Greatest Hits, Vol. 2, 1982; The Best of The Eagles, 1985; Hell Freezes Over, 1994; Selected Works 1972–99, 2000; Solo albums: No Fun Aloud, 1982; The Allnighter, 1984; Soul Searchin', 1992; Strange Weather, 1993; Singles include: Witchy Woman, 1972; Peaceful Easy Feeling, 1973; The Best of My Love (No. 1, USA), 1975; One of These Nights (No. 1, USA), 1975; Lyin' Eyes, 1975; Take It To The Limit, 1976; Hotel California (No. 1, USA), 1977; Heartache Tonight (No. 1, USA), 1979; The Long Run, 1980; I Can't Tell You Why, 1980; Seven Bridges Road, 1981; Solo hits: The Heat Is On (from film Beverly Hills Cop), 1985; You Belong To The City, 1986; Also contributed to recordings by: Jackson Browne; Dan Fogelberg; Don Henley; Elton John; Joni Mitchell; Randy Newman; Linda Ronstadt; Bob Seger; Carly Simon; Joe Walsh; Warren Zevon. *Honours:* Grammy Awards: Best Vocal Performance, 1976; Record of the Year, Hotel California, Best Arrangement For Voices, 1978; American Music Awards, Favourite Album, 1977. *Current Management:* Peter M Lopez, 2049 Century Park E, Suite 3180, Los Angeles, CA 90067, USA.

FRICK, Bob Scott; b. 19 April 1940, Indiana, Pennsylvania, USA. Musician (guitar); Vocalist; Prod; Publisher; Minister. m. Ruth Cornman, 13 May 1961, 2 s. *Career:* Play guitar, singer, throughout USA, Canada; Produce recordings for many artists; Publisher of hundreds of songs; Also duplicate tapes for many artists; Personal appearances are at churches, fairs; Appearances at Jerry Lewis Telethon; Grand Ole Opry (gospel); Videos on ACTS TV; Jerry Falwell and others. *Recordings:* Release Me (gospel); I Found Jesus In Nashville (tape and video); The King and I; You and Me Jesus. *Publications:* Message In Song (song book). *Membership:* ASCAP; BMI. *Current Management:* S & S Talent Agency. *Address:* 404 Bluegrass Ave, Madison, TN 37115, USA.

FRICKIE, Janie, (Jane Fricke); b. 19 Dec. 1947, South Whitley, Indiana, USA. Country Vocalist. m. Randy Jackson. *Education:* University. *Career:* Session singer, Los Angeles; Member, Lea Jane Singers, Nashville; Uncredited backing voice to Johnny Duncan; Solo recording artiste; Tours with Alabama; Regular session singer; Vocalist with own group Heartache. *Recordings:* US Country No. 1 hits: Don't Worry 'Bout Me, Baby; He's A Heartache (Looking For A Place To Happen); It Ain't Easy Bein' Easy; Tell Me A Lie; Other singles include: What're You Doing Tonight? Please Help Me I'm Falling; Albums: Singer of Songs, 1978; Love Notes, 1979; From The Heart, 1980; I'll Need Someone To Hold Me When I Cry, 1981; Nice 'n' Easy, with Johnny Duncan, 1980; Sleeping With Your Memory, 1981; It Ain't Easy, 1982; Love Lines, 1983; The First Word In Memory Is Me, 1984; Someone Else's Fire, 1985; Black and White, 1986; After Midnight, 1987; Saddle The Wind, 1988; Labor of Love, 1989; Janie Fricke, 1991; Crossroads, 1992; Now and Then, 1993; Bouncin' Back, 2000; Numerous recording sessions as backing vocalist include: with Johnny Duncan: Jo and The Cowboy; Stranger; Thinkin' of a Rendevous; It Couldn't Have Been Any Better; I'll Get Over You, Crystal Gayle; My Way, Elvis Presley; (I'm A) Stand By My Woman Man, Ronnie Milsap; Here's Some Love, Tanya Tucker; I'd Love To Lay You Down, Conway Twitty; Duets include: Till The End, with Vern Gosdin; On My Knees, with Charlie Rich (US Country No. 1); A Place To Fall Apart, with Merle Haggard (US Country No. 1); All I want To Do In Life, with George Jones; The Cowboy and the Lady, Tommy Cash; From Time To Time, with Larry Gatlin; Who Cares?, with Ray Charles. *Address:* c/o Janie Frickie Concerts, PO Box 798, Lancaster, TX 75146, USA.

FRIDAY, Gavin, (Fionan Hanvey); b. 1959, Dublin, Ireland. Vocalist; Songwriter. *Career:* Member, The Virgin Prunes; Solo artiste, 1990–. *Compositions:* Co-writer, film score: In The Name of The Father; In production: Passion of Darkly Noon; Angel Baby. *Recordings:* Virgin Prunes albums: If I Die I Die, 1982; The Hidden Lie, 1986; Sons Find Devils, 1998; Solo albums: Each Man Kills The Thing He Loves, 1990; Adam and Eve, 1992; Shag Tobacco, 1995; Film soundtrack: The Boxer (with Maurice Seezer), 1998. *Address:* c/o Island Records, 22 St Peters Sq., London W6 9NW, England.

FRIED, Gerald; b. 13 Feb. 1928, New York, NY, USA. Composer; Conductor; Musician (Oboe). 3 s., 1 d. *Education:* BS, Juilliard School, 1948. *Career:* Jazz Saxophonist, New York, 1945–51; Principal Oboe, English Horn, Dallas Symphony, Pittsburgh Symphony, New York Little Orchestra, Los Angeles Philharmonic, 1948–59; Composer, Conductor, Arranger, numerous motion pictures, TV and mini series, theatre works, operas and albums. *Compositions:* Scores for motion pictures include: Birds Do It, Bees Do It; Whatever Happened to Aunt Alice; One Spy Too Many; One of Our Spies Is Missing; The Cabinet of Dr Caligari; A Cold Wind in August; Cast A Long Shadow; Machine Gun Kelly; Paths of Glory; The Killing; Blood Money; Fear and Desire; Animation: The Great Rights; Scores for numerous mini series and TV pilots and series including Flamingo Road; Roots; Police Woman; Star Trek; The Man from UNCLE; The Mouse That Roared; Gunsmoke; Rawhide; Symphonic suites for Roots; The Bell Jar; The Mystic Warrior; Time Travel for Oboe and Orchestra. *Recordings:* Vampire Circus; Return of Dracula; The five early Stanley Kubrick films; Star Trek Vol. 1; Roots; More Music from The Man from UNCLE; The Cabinet of Dr Caligari; The Mystic Warrior; Sounds of the Night, with Johnny Mercer. *Honours:* Emmy Award, 1977; Teacher of the Year Award, UCLA, 1992. *Membership:* AMPAS; ASCAP; ATAS; SGA. *Current Management:* Soundtrack Music Asscn. *Address:* 6585 Portshead Rd, Malibu, CA 90265, USA.

FRIED, Joshua; b. 8 July 1959, Los Angeles, California, USA. Composer; Performance Artist. *Education:* BA, Cornell University, 1981. *Career:* Pioneer of headphone-driven performance, and musical shoes, activated by electronics; Remixed works by They Might Be Giants, Chaka Khan and Ofra Haza; Work presented at New Music America, Israel Festival, ICC Tokyo, Café de la Danse, Lincoln Centre, Dutch Royal Palace, Knitting Factory, The Kitchen, Limelight, Irving Plaza, La MaMa Experimental Theatre; Group Sound Art Exhibition, Constriction, New York, 1996; Visiting Composer, Yale University, Bucknell University, 1997. *Recordings:* New Live Dub, 1985; Jimmy Because (My Name Is), single, 1987; Hello The Band, 1993; Insane, single, 1996. *Honours:* NEA Composers Fellowship, 1994; New York Foundation for the Arts Fellowship, 1995; American Composers Forum Commission, 1996; Rockefeller Foundation Residency, 1997; Grand prize, Danish Radio's Competition in Sound, 1997; MacDowell Colony Fellowship, 1997; Yaddo Residency, 1998. *Address:* 277 N Seventh St, Apt 4R, Brooklyn, NY 11211, USA. *Website:* composer.home.acedsl.com.

FRIPP, Robert; b. 16 May 1946, Wimborne, Dorset, England. Musician (guitar); Composer; Prod. m. Toyah Willcox, 16 May 1986. *Career:* Member, Ravens; The League of Gentlemen; Founder member, Giles, Giles and Fripp, which became King Crimson, 1969–84; Regular UK, Europe, US and Far East tours; Collaborations with Brian Eno; The League of Gentlemen, 1980–81; Solo recording artiste, 1979–; Founder, Guitar Craft guitar school, 1985; Re-formed King Crimson, 1994–. *Recordings:* Albums: with Giles, Giles and Fripp: The Cheerful Insanity of Giles, Giles and Fripp, 1968; with King Crimson: In The Court of The Crimson King, 1969; In The Wake of Poseidon, 1970; Lizard, 1971; Earthbound, 1972; Larks' Tongues In Aspic, 1973;

Starless and Bible Black, 1974; Red, 1974; USA, 1975; Discipline, 1981; Beat, 1982; Three of a Perfect Pair, 1984; Vrooom, 1995; Thrak, 1995; B'Boom, 1995; THRaKaTTak, 1996; Epitaph, 1997; The Nightwatch, 1997; Absent Lovers, 1998; Live at the Marquee, 1969, 1998; Live at Jacksonville 1972, 1998; The Beat Club Bremen 1972, 1999; Cirkus, 1999; Live at Cap D'Adge 1982, 1999; On Broadway, 1999; Live in Mexico City, 1999; No Construkction, 2000; Vrooom Vrooom, 2001; with Brian Eno: No Pussyfooting, 1975; Evening Star, 1976; with The League of Gentlemen: The League of Gentlemen, 1981; God Save The King, 1985; Solo albums: Exposure, 1979; God Save The Queen/ Under Heavy Manners, 1980; Let The Power Fall, 1981; Robert Fripp and The League of Crafty Guitarists, 1986; Network, 1987; Live II, 1990; Show of Hands, 1991; The Bridge Between, 1995; Soundscapes – Live In Argentina, 1995; A Blessing of Tears, 1995; Radiophonics, 1996; That Which Passes, 1996; November Suite, 1997; The Gates of Paradise, 1997; with FFWD (Fripp, Fehlman, Weston, Dr Alex): FFWD, 1994; with Andy Summers: I Advance Masked, 1982; Bewitched, 1984; with Toyah: Kneeling At The Shrine, 1991; The Lady and The Tiger, 1987; with David Sylvian: The First Day, 1993; Damage, 1994; Contributor, albums by David Bowie; Peter Gabriel; Daryl Hall; Producer: Gabriel; Hall; Roches; several experimental jazz releases.

FRISCH, Al(bert T.); b. 27 March 1927, New York, USA. Composer; Musician (piano, saxophone). m. Celia Hirschorn Frisch, 1 d. *Career:* Saxophonist in nightclubs, on ocean liners and summer resorts; also entertainer, pianist and singer; Writer, weekly column, Music in print, Billboard magazine; Wrote words and music, songs, instrumentals, albums, shows and TV special material; Chief Collaborators, Roy Alfred, Buddy Bernier, Johnny Burke, Sylvia Dee, Buddy Kaye, Larry Kusick, Julian More, Allan Roberts, Al Neiburg, Bernard Spiro, Charles Tobias, Sid Wayne, Fred Wise. *Compositions:* This Is No Laughing Matter; Two Different Worlds; I Won't Cry Anymore; Roses in the Rain; All Over the World; That's What They Meant By the Good Old Summertime; Monte Carlo Melody; Congratulations to Someone; Flowers Mean Forgiveness; The Show Must Go On; Winner Take All; Broadway at Basin Street; What Lies Over the Hill; The Language of Love; Just Married Today; Sipping Cider By the Zuyder Zee; Let It Rain; The Best President We Ever Had (pancho Maximillian Hernandez); The Cool School; The Wonderful World of Christmas; Come On, Come In; Late in December; Starry-Eyed and Breathless; Little Miss Irish; My Mother's Lullaby; She Never Left the Table; April and You; Something for Nothing; Let's Harmonize; Go You Where Go; Tears to Burn; The Same Old Moon; Here Comes That Heartache Again; The Melancholy Minstrel; Now; Palermo; Lovin' Up a Storm The Moment of Truth; Have Have to Believe in Someone; Weep for the Boy; Winter in Miami; Music From Out of Space; If I'm Elected; Gregory's Chant; It Must Be Emily; Come Back to Rome; Idle Conversation; Always Love Me; I've Got Some Cryin' to Do; All I Get From You are Heartaches; A Chocolate Sundae on a Saturday Night; In Time; Not So Long Ago; My Need For You; He Came on a Long Long Journey; Wherefore Art Thou Romeo; Sweet Brown-Eyed Baby; What More Is There to Say; Give Me the Right; Unafraid; Four Walls, Two Windows, and One Broken Heart; He Cha Cha'd In; After the Fall; No Hard Feelings; Really O, Truly O; Mama, Teach Me to Do the Charleston; Io Canto; You Pass This Way Only Once; People, Places and Things; Fiddle Rock; The Hornet's Nest; Tunes for Muzak; TV Shows: My Love Song to You; Song of the Racoons; Bordello, Show-Queen's Theatre, London; A Place Like This; Yourself; A Country Bride; Morality; Business Tango; Simple Pleasures; Art Should Be Art; Family Life; If You Should Leave Me; Madame Misia; All the Time in the World; I Love Me; The Way I See It; The Girl in Cabin 54; What Does It Take; Can-Can Ballet; Hallucination Ballet; Show Christy; When the Penny Poets Sing; A Somewhere Rainbow; Where's My Rainbow; To Please the Woman in Me; Grain of the Salt of the Earth; Until the Lives of You; Come Out Wherever You Are; Picture Me; The Morning After; It's a Lonesome Thing; All's Fair in Love and War; Great Company; With One Fell Swoop; Beach Ballet; The Heart's Wonder; Down the Hatch; Gallant Little Swearers' Be a Hero. *Address:* Myra Music Co, 33F, 177 White Plains Rd, Tarrytown, NY 10591, USA.

FRISCHMANN, Justine Elinor; b. 16 Sept. 1969, Twickenham, London, England. Vocalist; Musician (guitar); Songwriter. *Career:* Rhythm guitarist for band, Suede, late 1980s–91; Formed own band, Elastica, 1993–2001; Toured extensively world-wide; Television appearances include Top of the Pops. *Recordings:* Albums: Elastica (No. 1, UK), 1995; The Menace, 2000; The Radio 1 Sessions, 2001. Singles: with Suede: Be My God/Art; with Elastica: Stutter, 1993; Line-Up, 1994; Connection, 1994; Waking Up, 1995; Elastica EP, 1999. *Honours:* NME Readers' Award for Best New Band. *Current Management:* CMO Management International Ltd, Unit 32, Ransomes Dock, 35–37 Parkgate Rd, London SW11 4NP, England.

FRISELL, Bill; b. 18 March 1951, Baltimore, Maryland, USA. Jazz Musician (guitar, banjo, ukulele, bass). *Education:* North Colorado University, 1969–71; Diploma, arranging, composition, Berklee College of Music, Boston, 1977. *Career:* Played with artists including: Eberhard Weber; Mike Gibbs; Jan Garbarek; Charlie Haden; Carla Bley; John Scofield; Member, Power Tools (with Ronald Shannon Jackson, Melvin Gibbs); John Zorn's Naked City; The Paul Bley Quintet (with Paul Bley, Paul Motian, John Surman); Paul Motian Trio (with Paul Motian, Joe Lovano); David Sylvian; Bono; Marianne

Faithfull; Robin Holcomb; Gavin Bryars; Brian Eno; Daniel Lanois. *Recordings:* Albums: In Line, 1983; Rambler, 1985; Lookout For Hope, 1988; Before We Were Born, 1989; Is This You?, 1990; Where In The World?, 1991; Have A Little Faith, 1993; Music From The Films of Buster Keaton (comprising The High Sign/One Week and Go West), 1995; Quartet, 1996; Nashville, 1997; Gone, Just Like a Train, 1998; Songs We Know, 1998; Good Dog, Happy Man, 1999; Ghost Town, 2000; Blues Dream, 2001; Bill Frisell With Dave Holland and Elvin Jones, 2001; Selected Recordings, 2002; The Willies, 2002; with Tim Berne: Theoretically, 1984; with John Zorn, George Lewis: News For Lulu, 1987; More News For Lulu, 1992; with Power Tools: Strange Meeting, 1987; with John Scofield: Grace Under Pressure, 1992; with Elvis Costello: Deep Dead Blue, Live At Meltdown, 1995; The Sweetest Punch 1999; with Ginger Baker Trio: Going Home Again, 1995. *Honours:* Harris Stanton Guitar Award; Guitarist of the Year, Downbeat Critics' Poll, 1998; Deutsche Schallplatten Preis, 1998; Critics Award, Best Guitarist, Industry Award, Best Guitarist, Annual Jazz Awards, 1998. *Current Management:* Songline/Tone Field Productions, 1649 Hopkins St, Berkeley, CA 94707, USA.

FRISTORP, Göran; b. 26 May 1948, Skara, Sweden. m. 1 July 1975, 1 d. *Education:* Conservatory of Gothenburg and Framnäs in Ojebyn. *Career:* Winner, European Song Contest, Sweden, 1973; Many television and radio appearances; 20 LPs and CDs. *Compositions:* I Belong; Lyrics: Hal David; Music: Göran Fristorp. *Recordings:* Sings Nils Ferlin; Atersken; Riktning; Psalmer; Evert Taube; Flickan Från Fjärran. *Publications:* Nils Perlin, 1975; Egna Ltar, 1974; Psalmer, 1989; Flickan Prån Fiärran, 1996. *Honours:* Evert Taube Prize, 1997; Nils Ferlin Troubadour Prizedeolith, 1998; Several Artists Prizes. *Membership:* STIM; SKAP; GRAMO (Norway); SAMI. *Current Management:* Stageway, Bergen Norway.

FRIZZELL, John; b. 1966, New York, NY, USA. Composer. *Education:* Manhattan School of Music. *Compositions:* For television: VR.5, 1995; It Was Him or Us, 1995; Whose Daughter Is She?, 1995; Crime of the Century, 1996; Deadly Pursuits, 1996; Possessed, 2000; James Dean: An Invented Life, 2001; For film: Red Ribbon Blues, 1995; Opposite Corners, 1995; The Rich Man's Wife, 1996; Beavis and Butt-head Do America, 1996; Undertow, 1996; Dante's Peak, 1997; The Empty Mirror, 1997; Alien: Resurrection, 1997; Jane Austen's Mafia!, 1998; I Still Know What You Did Last Summer, 1998; Office Space, 1999; Teaching Mrs Tingle, 1999; Turkey. Cake., 1999; Beautiful, 2000; Lockdown, 2001; 13 Ghosts, 2002. *Membership:* ASCAP. *Current Management:* Gorfaine/Schwartz Agency Inc, 13245 Riverside Dr., Suite 450, Sherman Oaks, CA 91423, USA.

FROSCH, Wolfgang; b. 2 July 1960, Knittelfeld, Austria. Musician (bass); Backing Vocalist. m. Maria, 31 March 1989, 1 s., 2 d. *Education:* Carpenter. *Career:* Member, Blues Pumpm, 1978–; Member, Giant Blonder, 1988–94; Tours, television and radio appearances throughout Europe. *Recordings:* Albums: with Giant Blonder: Colours of Rock; with Blues Pumpm: Albums: Bluespumpm, 1979; Edlau, 1980; Village, 1981; Live With Friends, 1985; The 5th Ten Years Jubilee, 1987; Live At Utopia, 1988; Live With Friends, 1991; Birthday, 1991; Live In Vienna, 1992; The 5th, 1992; Living Loving Riding, 1994; Singles: Wolfgang Session and Song, 1980; Men From Milwaukee, 1993. *Honours:* Silbernes Ehrenzeicher, 1992; Third Best Blues Album Ö3 Rot-Weiss-Rote Critics Poll, Live In Vienna, 1992. *Membership:* AKM; AUME; LSG. *Current Management:* Peter Steinbach, RGG Management.

FROST, Jenny; b. 22 Feb. 1978, Liverpool, England. Vocalist. *Career:* Represented UK in Eurovision Song Contest, 1999, as part of female vocal quintet Precious; Mem., Atomic Kitten (to replace Kerry Katona), 2001–; Appearance, Party at the Palace, Buckingham Palace Jubilee celebrations, 2002. *Recordings:* Albums: with Precious: Precious, 2000; with Atomic Kitten: Right Now (reissue), 2001; Feels So Good, 2002. Singles: with Precious: Say It Again, 1999; Rewind, 2000; It's Gonna Be My Way, 2000; New Beginning, 2000; with Atomic Kitten: Eternal Flame, 2001; It's OK, 2002; Tide Is High, 2002; Last Goodbye/Be With You, 2002. *Current Management:* Integral Management, 51–55 Highfield St, Liverpool L3 6AA, England. *Address:* c/o Innocent Records, Kensal House, 553–579 Harrow Rd, London W10 4RH, England. *Website:* www.atomickitten.com.

FROST, Per Christian; b. 30 Oct. 1954, Århus, Denmark. Musician (guitar, bass guitar); Vocalist. m. Dorthe Th. Holtet, 25 July 1987, 2 s. *Education:* 1 year, Art Academy. *Career:* Member, Gnags, 1974–; Tours: Europe; Africa; India; Cuba; Nicaragua; Numerous television appearances; Also solo artist, guest musician. *Recordings:* with Gnags, 17 albums; Solo albums: Ned Ad Gaden, 1979; Old Friend's Back, 1990; Breakin' Ice, 1995. *Honours:* Award of Honour, Danish Musicians' Union, 1988; IFPI Prize, (Danish Grammy), 1990. *Membership:* DMF; DJBFA; KODA. *Current Management:* Rock On International, Copenhagen, Denmark.

FROST, Soren; b. 5 Feb. 1965, Århus, Denmark. Musician (drums, percussion). *Education:* Drummer Collective, 10 Week Certificate Program, New York City, 1988. *Career:* Played Pop Rock, Jazz and Chorus Line, Sweet Charity Jesus Christ Superstar; Worked with Lillian Boutte, Dr John, Bob Berg, Eliane Elias, Lee Konitz, Bob Brookmeyer, Thad Jones, Slide Hampton, Dee Dee Bridgewater; Many TV and radio shows and tours of Japan, 1990,

USSR, 1988, Thailand, 1991, USA, 1997. *Recordings:* Lillian Boutte: The Jazz Book; The Danish Radio Orchestra: Fusion Symphony; Nikolaj Bentzon: Brotherhood; Jazzgroup 1990 with Bob Berg: Live in Denmark, My Sisters Garden. *Honours:* Grants from Danish Companies to Go to New York. *Current Management:* Blegdamsvej 84 5th, 2100 Copenhagen O, Denmark.

FRUITBAT, (Leslie Carter); b. 12 Feb. 1958, *Career:* Founder member (with Jimbob), duo, Carter The Unstoppable Sex Machine (later billed as Carter USM), 1988–; International concerts, including USA, Japan. *Recordings:* Albums: 101 Damnations, 1990; 30 Something, 1991; 1992 – The Love Album (No. 1, UK), 1992; Post Historic Monsters, 1994; Worry Bomb, 1995; Straw Donkey, 1996; A World Without Dave, 1997; I Blame The Government, 1998; Live, 1999; Singles: Sheltered Life, 1988; Sherriff Fatman, 1989; Rubbish, 1990; Anytime, Anyplace, Anywhere, 1990; Bloodsports For All, 1991; After The Watershed, 1991; Only Living Boy In New Cross, 1992; Lean On Me I Won't Fall Over, 1993; Glam Rock Cops, 1994; Let's Get Tattoos, 1994; Young Offenders Mum, 1995; Born On Fifth November, 1995. *Current Management:* Adrian Boss Promotions. *Address:* c/o 3 Gunstor Rd, London N16 8HF, England.

FRUSCIANTE, John; b. 5 March 1970, New York, NY, USA. Musician (guitar). *Career:* Mem., Red Hot Chili Peppers, 1988–92, 1998–; Numerous tours, festivals and television appearances. *Recordings:* Albums: with Red Hot Chili Peppers: The Red Hot Chili Peppers, 1984; Freaky Styley, 1985; Uplift Mofo Party Plan, 1987; Mother's Milk, 1989; Mother's Milk Gold, 1989; Blood Sugar Sex Magik, 1991; What Hits!?, 1992; Under The Covers, 1998; Californication, 1999; By The Way, 2002; Solo: Niandra Ladies And Usually Just A T-Shirt, 1995; Smile From The Streets You Hold, 1997; To Record Only Water For Ten Days, 2001. Singles: Abbey Road (EP), 1988; Higher Ground, 1989; Taste the Pain, 1989; Give It Away, 1991; Under The Bridge, 1992; Suck My Kiss, 1992; Warped, 1998; Scar Tissue, 1999; Behind the Sun, 1999; Around The World, 1999; Otherside, 1999; Californication, 2000; Road Trippin', 2001; The Zephyr Song, 2002; Other session work includes: Perry Farrell; Tricky. *Honours:* MTV Music Video Awards, 1992; Grammy Award, Best Rock Song, for Scar Tissue, 2000; American Music Award, Favorite Alternative Artist, 2000; MTV Awards, Best Live Act, Best Rock, 2002. *Address:* c/o Rockinfreakapotamus, The Red Hot Chili Peppers Official Fan Club, PO Box 801, Rockford, MI 49341, USA. *Website:* www.redhotchilipeppers.com.

FRY, Martin; b. 9 March 1958, Manchester, Lancashire, England. Vocalist; Prod. *Education:* English Literature, Sheffield University. *Career:* Launched fanzine, Modern Drugs, 1979; Lead singer, ABC, 1980–; UK and world tour, 1982; Featured in Julien Temple's film Man Trap, 1983; Subject, BBC documentary, That Was Then, This Is Now, 1990. *Recordings:* Albums with ABC: The Lexicon of Love (No. 1, UK), 1982; Beauty Stab, 1983; How To Be A Zillionaire, 1985; Alphabet City, 1987; Up, 1989; Absolutely, 1990; Abracadabra, 1991; Skyscraping, 1997; Hello – An Introduction To ABC, 2001; The Look of Love (The Very Best of ABC), 2001; Singles include: Tears Are Not Enough, 1981; Poison Arrow (No. 6, UK), 1982; The Look of Love (No. 4, UK), 1982; All of My Heart (No. 5, UK), 1982; That Was Then But This Is Now, 1983; Be Near Me, 1985; When Smokey Sings, 1987; The Night You Murdered Love, 1987; One Better World, 1989.

FRY, Tristan Frederick Allan; b. 25 Oct. 1946, London, England. m. Dorothy E Garland, 25 Oct. 1993. *Education:* Taught by Peter Allen, Royal Academy of Music and many amateur orchestras and groups, London. *Career:* Concerts with Sky in Europe; Australia; Asia; First group to play Westminster Abbey (televised concert); Concerts with Academy of St Martin In The Fields Orchestra around world. *Compositions include:* Connecting Rooms; Then and Now. *Recordings:* All Sky singles and albums; 3 recordings, Bartôk's 2 piano and percussion concerto; Academy albums include award winning Amadeus; Film score albums include: James Bond, Pink Panther; Also recorded with many artists world-wide including: Kevin Ayers; Nick Drake; Keith Emerson; John Martyn. *Membership:* Royal Society of Musicians.

FUGLER, Jon; Vocalist; Musician; Sound Engineer. *Career:* Founder member, Fluke, 1983–; Concerts include: British tour, 1994; Glastonbury Festival; Appearances include: Smash Hits Poll Winners Party, with Björk; MTV Awards, with Björk. *Recordings:* Albums: The Techno Rose of Blighty, 1991; Out (mini album); Six Wheels On My Wagon; Oto, 1995; Singles: Thumper; Joni; Slid; Electric Guitar; Groovy Feeling; Bubble; Bullet; Remix, Big Time Sensuality, Björk. *Address:* c/o Circa Records, Kensal House, 553–579 Harrow Rd, London W10 4RH, England.

FUJII, Naoki; b. 1 July 1960, Japan. Lutenist. *Education:* Royal Conservatory, The Hague, Netherlands, 1979–84. *Career:* Amsterdam Concertgebouw; Radio France; NHK FM Japan; University of Coimbra, Portugal. *Recordings:* Haru No Umi. *Address:* Stuyvesantstraat 9–1, 1058 AJ Amsterdam, Netherlands.

FULKS, Robbie; b. 25 March 1963, Pennsylvania, USA. Vocalist; Songwriter; Musician. m. Donna, 3 s. *Education:* Columbia College, New York. *Career:* Two Mountain Stage appearances, 1997, 1998; 1 Fresh Air

NPR, 1998; 3 World Cafe and 2 Acoustic Cafe Appearances, 1996–99; 1 Austin City Limits, 1998; Cast Member, Woody Guthrie's American Song, 1990–93; Staff Instructor, Old Town School of Folk Music, Chicago; Films Featuring Performances of Original Songs. *Recordings:* Country Love Songs, 1996; South Mouth, 1997; Let's Kill Saturday Night, 1998; The Very Best of Robbie Fulks, 2000; Couples In Trouble, 2000; 13 Hillbilly Giants, 2001. *Address:* PO Box 1512, Lake Villa, Illinois 60076, USA.

FULLER, Parmer; b. 15 July 1949, San Francisco, California, USA. Composer; Conductor; Music Dir; Musician (Piano). m. Narcissa C Vanderlip, 14 March 1982, 1 d. *Education:* BA, cum laude, Music, Harvard University; MM, Music Composition, Indiana University; PhD, Music Composition, University of California at Los Angeles. *Career:* Composer, music for feature films including Daddy's Girl, Reflections on a Crime, Mortal Passions, Time Trackers, Spirit of the Eagle, Ulterior Motives; music for TV shows: The Morton Downey Jr Show, Distant Cousins, Easy Street, Dynasty, Family, Ronn Lucas Show, Monsters; Miscellaneous compositions for educational films, interactive CDs; Solo performances as Pianist including shows for President Reagan, George Bush, Gerald Ford and Richard Nixon; Conductor, Young Musicians' Foundation Orchestra concerts; Coached actor James Caan in conducting skills; Appeared as self in Easy Street. *Compositions include:* Concert works: Spirit of the Eagle; Twice Upon a Time; A Child's Christmas in Wales; Alpine Wanderings; Music Comedy: Director and Conductor: The Sound of Music; Singin' in the Rain; Oklahoma; Little Shop of Horrors; Guys and Dolls; Crazy For You; Into The Woods; My Fair Lady; Camelot; Opera: Composer, Solferino; Numerous arrangements, including works for Pavarotti and Jack Lemmon. *Honours:* Frank Sinatra Prizes; Henry Mancini Award. *Membership:* ASCAP; BMI; SCL; AFM. *Current Management:* None. *Address:* 10374 Cheviot Dr., Los Angeles, CA 90064, USA.

FULLER, Simon; Promoter; Artiste Manager; Business Exec. *Career:* Man., Paul Hardcastle, 1985; Artiste man., Annie Lennox, Emma Bunton, Will Young, Gareth Gates, Kelly Clarkson; Former man., Madonna, Paul Hardcastle, Cathy Dennis, Spice Girls, –1997, S Club 7 (later S Club, including television series and S Club Juniors), 21st Century Girls; Creator, Popstars (ITV1), Pop Idol (ITV1), American Idol–The Search for a Superstar (Fox TV); Popstars–The Rivals (ITV1); Founder, Dir, 1985, 19 Group, comprising 19 Brands, 19 Entertainment, 19 International Sports Management, 19 Management, 19 Merchandising, 19 Productions, 19 Recordings, 19 Songs, 19 Touring, 19 TV, Brilliant 19; Dir, many other companies. *Address:* c/o 19 Management, Unit 32, Ransomes Dock, 35–37 Parkgate Rd, London SW11 4NP, England. *Website:* www.19.co.uk.

FUMAROLA, Martin Alejandro; b. 22 Nov. 1966, Argentina. Composer; Music Researcher; Computer Specialist. *Education:* Composition Studies with Cesar Franchisena and Ariel Martinez, National University of Cordoba. *Career:* Associate Composer, Electroacoustic Music Studio, National University of Cordoba; Concert Curator, in many International Festivals of Electroacoustic Music, pieces performed world-wide. *Compositions:* Estatismo; In Movile; Set In; Peregrinar de la Arana; Callejuelas; Shaguir; Omen. *Honours:* Scholarship, Argeninian National Endowment for the arts; Grant of the Spanish Ministry of Culture. *Membership:* ICMA; SEAMUS; CEC; FARME. *Address:* Casilla de Correo 1145, Correo Central, Cordoba RA 5000, Argentina.

FUNK DOCTA SPOCK. See: REDMAN.

FUNK JUNKEEZ. See: SANCHEZ, Roger.

FUNKEY; b. 20 July 1961, Sint-Niklaas, Belgium. Musician (synthesizer); Vocalist. *Career:* Gigs: debut, Keyboard player and singer, The Soap, 1992; Oortcloud, 1993; Radio: Several times on Bassta, 1995–96; TV: Prettig Gestoord, 1996. *Publications:* Oortcloud: Raindances, 1995; Colour Dot: Floating Atmospheres, 1997. *Honours:* Studio Brussels' Candidate for Debut Rock Contest. *Membership:* SABAM; ZAMU. *Current Management:* Higher Grow Productions, Damstraat 2, B9100 Sint-Niklaas, Belgium.

FUREY, Eddie; b. 23 Dec. 1944, Tipperary, Ireland. Musician (guitar, mandola, mandolin, harmonica, fiddle, bodhran); Vocalist. m. Bibi, 5 c. *Career:* Member, duo, with brother Finbar, 1960s; Joined Clancy Brothers, US tour, 1969; Member, Tam Linn, with Davey Arthur, Paul Furey; Apperances include: Cambridge Folk Festival; Member, The Fureys and Davey Arthur, 1980. *Recordings:* Albums: The Sound of The Fureys and Davey Arthur, 1981; When You Were Sweet Sixteen, 1982; Steal Away, 1983; In Concert, 1984; Golden Days, 1984; At The End of The Perfect Day, 1985; The First Leaves of Autumn, 1986; The Fureys Finest, 1987; The Fureys Collection, 1989; The Scattering, 1989; The Very Best Of, 1991; The Winds of Change, 1992; Irish Folk Favourites, 1994; Best of Irish Folk, 1998; Essential Fureys, 2001; with Finbar Furey: The Dawning of The Day, 1970; Traditional Irish Pipe Music, 1998; Singles include: When You Were Sweet Sixteen, 1981; Green Fields of France; Red Rose Café. *Membership:* IMRO. *Current Management:* Joe McCadden Promotions, Dublin. *Address:* 19 Stockton Green, Castleknock, Dublin 15, Ireland.

FUREY, Finbar; b. 28 Sept. 1946, Dublin, Ireland. Musician (uillean pipes, banjo, whistles, flute); Vocalist. *Career:* Member, duo with Eddie Furey, 1960s; Played clubs, radio work; Joined Clancy Brothers, US tour, 1969; European tours, 1972; Joined Tam Linn, with Eddie and Paul Furey, Davey Arthur; Appeared at Cambridge Folk Festival; Later became The Fureys and Davey Arthur, 1980–. *Recordings:* Albums: The Cisco Special, 1960; Songs of Woody Guthrie, 1961; I Ain't Got No Home, 1962; The Sound of The Fureys and Davey Arthur, 1981; When You Were Sweet Sixteen, 1982; Steal Away, 1983; In Concert, 1984; Golden Days, 1984; At The End of a Perfect Day, 1985; The First Leaves of Autumn, 1986; The Fureys Finest, 1987; The Fureys Collection, 1989; The Scattering, 1989; The Very Best Of, 1991; The Winds of Change, 1992; Wind and the Rain, 1997; Traditional Irish Pipe Music, 1998; ; Essential Fureys, 2001; with Eddie Furey: The Dawning of The Day, 1972; Solo album: Love Letters, 1990; Singles include: When You Were Sweet Sixteen, 1981. *Address:* c/o Joe McCadden Promotions, 19 Stockton Green, Castleknock, Dublin 15, Ireland.

FUREY, George; b. 11 June 1951, Dublin, Ireland. Vocalist; Musician (guitar, accordion, mandola, autoharp, whistles); Songwriter. m. Mary, 1971, 3 s., 3 d. *Career:* Member, The Buskers, 1972; Later became The Furey Brothers; TV appearances in the UK and Ireland. *Compositions include:* Evening Falls, 1979; Green Fields of France. *Recordings:* Albums: The Cisco Special, 1960; Songs of Woody Guthrie, 1961; I Ain't Got No Home, 1962; The Sound of The Fureys and Davey Arthur, 1981; When You Were Sweet Sixteen, 1982; Steal Away, 1983; In Concert, 1984; Golden Days, 1984; At The End of Perfect Day, 1985; The First Leaves of Autumn, 1986; The Fureys Finest, 1987; The Fureys Collection, 1989; The Scattering, 1989; The Very Best of The Fureys and Davey Arthur, 1991; The Winds of Change, 1992; Through the Eyes of an Irishman, 1997; The Fureys: 21 Years On This Year, 1999; Essential Fureys, 2001; Singles include: When You Were Sweet Sixteen; I Will Love You (Every Time When We Are Gone); Green Fields of France; Red Rose Café. *Honours:* Playing for the Pope in Ireland, 1979; Gold Albums in Australia, South Africa, Canada, UK, USA, New Zealand and Germany. *Membership:* IMRO; Phonographic Performance Ltd. *Current Management:* Joe McCadden Promotions, Dublin. *Address:* 19 Stockton Green, Castleknock, Dublin 15, Ireland.

FUREY, Paul; b. 6 May 1948, Dublin, Ireland. Musician (accordion, melodeon, concertina, whistles); Vocalist. m. Catherine, 1977, 3 s. *Career:* Member, The Buskers (with George Furey, Davey Arthur), 1972; Member, Tam Linn; Appeared at Cambridge Folk Festival; Member, The Fureys and Davey Arthur, 1980–; Mbr, The Furey Brothers; TV appearances in the UK and Ireland. *Recordings:* Albums: The Cisco Special, 1960; Songs of Woody Guthrie, 1961; I Ain't Got No Home, 1962; When You Were Sweet Sixteen, 1982; Steal Away, 1983; In Concert, 1984; Golden Days, 1984; At The End of a Perfect Day, 1985; The First Leaves of Autumn, 1986; The Scattering, 1989; Winds of Change, 1993; Traditional Irish Pipe Music, 1998; Various compilations including: Essential Fureys, 2001; Singles include: When You Were Sweet Sixteen, 1981; Green Fields of France; Red Rose Café. *Membership:* IMRO. *Current Management:* Joe McCadden Promotions, Dublin. *Address:* 19 Stockton Green, Castleknock, Dublin 15, Ireland.

FURIC, Stephane; b. 15 July 1965, Paris, France. Composer. 2 s. *Education:* Diploma, Professional Music, Berklee College of Music, Boston, USA; Private studies with William H. Curtis, David Liebman. *Career:* Concerts including international jazz festivals, tours, radio shows, with Stephane Furic Project (also featuring Chris Cheek, Patrick Goraguer, Jim Black); Hiroshi Minami; Philippe Le Baraillec; Antonio Hart; Guillaume Orti (Europe, USA, Japan); Television shows. *Compositions:* Kishinev, 1990; Gorag' Rag, 1991; Suite Of Dances, 1994; Song Of The Open Road, 1994; Song Of The Universal, 1994; Words, 1997; The Nightingale And Me, 2001; Penelope, 2002. *Recordings:* Kishinev, 1991; The Twitter-Machine, 1993; Crossing Brooklyn Ferry, 1995. *Membership:* BMI; SACEM (as writer and publisher). *Address:* Fressanges, 87260 Vicq s/ Breuilh, France.

FURTADO, Nelly Kim; b. 2 Dec. 1978, Victoria, BC, Canada. Vocalist; Musician (guitar, ukelele, trombone); Songwriter. *Career:* Trombonist in various jazz/marching/concert bands while at school; Performed and recorded with trip-hop outfit, Nelstar, aged 18; Discovered by current manager at Toronto talent contest; Relocated to Toronto to forge songwriting partnership with Gerald Eaton and Brian West of successful Canadian group, The Philosopher Kings; Solo artiste. *Recordings:* Albums: Whoa Nelly!, 2000. Singles: I'm Like A Bird, 2000; Turn Off The Light, 2001. *Honours:* Grammy Award, Best Female Pop Vocal, for I'm Like A Bird, 2002. *Current Management:* Chris Smith Management Inc, 21 Camden St, Toronto, ON, Canada. *Website:* www.chrissmithmanagement.com.

FURUHOLMEN, Mags, (Magne); b. 1 Nov. 1962, Manglerud, Oslo, Norway. Musician (keyboards); Vocalist. *Career:* Mem., A-Ha, 1983–94; Mem., Timbersound; Band re-formed, 1999–; Numerous tours world-wide, television and radio appearances. *Recordings:* Albums: Hunting High And Low, 1985; Scoundrel Days, 1986; Stay On These Roads, 1988; East Of The Sun West Of The Moon, 1990; Deadlines: The Hits Of A-Ha, 1991; Memorial Beach, 1993; Minor Earth Major Sky, 2000; Lifelines, 2002. Singles: Take On Me (No. 1,

USA), 1985; The Sun Always Shines On TV (No. 1, UK), 1985; Train Of Thought, 1986; Hunting High And Low, 1986; I've Been Losing You, 1986; Cry Wolf, 1986; Manhattan Skyline, 1987; The Living Daylights (theme music for James Bond film), 1987; Stay On These Roads, 1988; The Blood That Moves The Body, 1988; Touchy!, 1988; You Are The One, 1988; Crying In The Rain, 1990; I Call Your Name; Dark Is The Night; Can't Take My Eyes Off You (for film soundtrack Coneheads); Angel. *Honours:* Eight MTV Music Video Awards, for Take On Me and The Sun Always Shines On TV, 1986; BMI Award, One Million Broadcast Performances, for Take On Me, 1991; World Music Award, Best Selling Norwegian Artist of the Year, 1993. *Current Management:* Bandana Management, London, England. *Address:* c/o WEA Germany, Warner Music Germany Group, Oberbaumbrücke 1, 20457 Hamburg, Germany. *Website:* www.a-ha.com.

FUSE. See: **HAWTIN, Richie.**

FUTURE PAST. See: **DEGIORGIO, Kirk.**

FYFFE, William John Angus; b. 18 Sept. 1927, Margate, Kent, England. Musician (piano); Musical Dir. m. (1) Michelle Franks, 1951, 1 s., 1 d.; (2) Sue Addams, 1968, 1 s., 1 d.; Present partner, Anthea Askey. *Education:* George Watson's College, Edinburgh. *Career:* Son of Will Fyffe, comedian, writer of song I Belong To Glasgow; Joined Rank Organisation film studios, 1948; Moved to Chappells as song plugger; A&R, Decca Records; Personal accompanist to artists including: Allan Jones, Josef Locke, Evelyn Laye, Frankie Vaughan, Petula Clark, Ronnie Hilton, 1950s–70s; Senior MD, Triumph Productions; In Concert act with Anthea Askey; Numerous appearances, television, radio and stage. *Compositions:* Music score for Glasgow Belongs To Me (working title); Songs include: My September; With A Love Like Ours. *Membership:* PRS; BAC&S. *Address:* Appletree Lodge, Golden Acre, Angmering On Sea, West Sussex BN16 1QP, England.

G

G, Kenny, (Kenneth Gorelick); b. 1959, Seattle, WA, USA. Musician (saxophone); Composer. *Education:* Accounting, University of Washington. *Career:* European tour with Franklin High School Band, 1974; Musician with Barry White's Love Unlimited Orchestra, 1976; Backing musician, numerous artistes including: Whitney Houston; Natalie Cole; Aretha Franklin; Toni Braxton; Peabo Bryson; Member, Cold, Bold and Together; Member, jazz fusion group Jeff Lorber Fusion; Solo artiste, 1981–; Regular collaborations with Michael Bolton, including US tour, 1990. *Recordings:* Solo albums: Kenny G, 1982; G Force, 1983; Gravity, 1985; Duotones, 1986; Silhouette, 1988; Kenny G Live, 1989; Breathless, 1992; Miracles, 1994; The Moment, 1996; Classics in the Key of G, 1999; Faith, 1999; with Michael Bolton: Soul Provider, 1989; Time, Love and Tenderness, 1991. *Honours:* Multi-platinum records. *Current Management:* Turner Management Group, 3500 W Olive Ave, Suite 690, Burbank, CA 91505, USA.

GABRIEL, (Gabriel J. Maciocia); b. 8 Oct. 1948, Providence, RI, USA. Record Prod; Songwriter; Playwright. *Education:* Masters Degree, RIC, 1972; Masters in arranging and composition of music. *Career:* Producer: Budweiser Girls Band (Single of Week, Cashbox Magazine); Produced 18 albums; Produced for Joey Welz of Caprice Records; Also, Four Tops, for Arista, Warner, Slack Records; Writer of play, Christmas Holiday on the Moon; Writer of music score and screen play for film, Hearts of Bounty; currently filming film on location abroad. *Compositions:* Elvis is Smiling, 1989; You Don't Own Me, 1989. *Recordings:* Sexy Lady, The Four Tops; Crying Shame, Gloria Gaynor; Elvis Is Smiling; Ice Cream, Soda Pop and Wine, Joey Welz; Wild Weekend. *Publications:* Whisper Pines (novel). *Honours:* Single of Week, Nov. 1988, Cashbox Magazine. *Membership:* BMI; ASCAP. *Current Management:* Caprice Records, Lititz PA, Joey Welz. *Address:* 108 Humbert St, North Providence, RI 02911, USA.

GABRIEL, Gilles (Blacky); b. 1 Nov. 1946, Clermont Ferrand, France. Musician (drums). Divorced, 1 s., 1 d. *Education:* Percussion, double bass, Music High School, Nancy, 1968–69. *Career:* First professional appearance, cabaret, Nancy, 1967; Member, Dance Orchestra, 1967–; Appearances include: World Circus Festival, Nancy, 1968; Casinos include: Vichy; Châtel Guyon; Cruise Ships: Massalia; Mermoz (with Isabelle Aubret, Nicole Croisille); Azur; Meridien Hotels: Dakar (with Francis Lemarque); Abu Dhabi; Accompanied Pierre Douglas, Michel Lebb, Monte Carlo (sporting), 1978; Concerts with US musicians: Hal Singer; Benny Waters; John Littleton; Mickey Backer; Stars of Faith; French musicians: Michel Hausser; Dany Doriz; Laurent Gianez; Françoise Pujol; Eddy Gaddum (Surinam); Member, big bands including Swing Orchestra; Packard Blues: First sets: Toots Thielemans (Belgium); Mint Julep (UK); Jimmy Johnson (USA); Big Wheeler (USA); Many concerts in France, Germany, Luxembourg, Belgium; Jazz festivals include: Nancy; Strasbourg; Many concerts with jazzmen in John's Place, Saarbrücken, Germany; with Eddy Gaddum (Jazz Combo) concerts in Luxemburg, Germany, Belgium; Jazz Festival, Luxemburg, 1995; Teacher, music school, private lessons; Leader, Myster Black (jazz), 1989–; Jaguars, 1995; Pat and the Blue Wizards, 1999–. *Membership:* SLAM. *Address:* 6 rue du Maréchal Oudinot, 54000 Nancy, France.

GABRIEL, Juan (Alberto Aguilera Valadéz); b. 7 Jan. 1950, Parácuaro, Michoacán, Mexico. Vocalist; Songwriter; *Recordings:* Singles include: Perdoname (Forgive Me); Lagrimas Y LLuvia (Tears and Rain); La Costumbre (The Habit); Amor Eterno (Eternal Love); Pero Que Necesitad (But The Need); Over 50 albums including: Juan Gabriel En El Palacio De Bellas Artes; Debo Hoceria; Gracias Por Esperar; Celebrando, 25 años de Juan Gabriel, 1998. *Current Management:* Hauser Entertainment Inc. *Address:* PO Box 978, 11003 Rooks Rd, Pico Rivera, CA 90660, USA.

GABRIEL, Peter; b. 13 Feb. 1950, Cobham, Surrey, England. Vocalist; Songwriter. *Career:* Founder member, Genesis, 1969–75; Appearances include: with Genesis: Reading Festival, 1971, 1972, 1973; UK and US tours; Solo artiste, 1975–; Solo appearances include: World-wide tours; Knebworth II, 1978; Reading Festival, 1979; Inaugurator, WOMAD Festival Bath, 1982–; Amnesty International benefit tour, 1987; Hurricane Irene Benefit, Japan, 1987; Prince's Trust Rock Gala, 1988; Nelson Mandela tribute concerts, Wembley, 1988, 1990; Senegal (with Youssou N'Dour), 1991; The Simple Truth concert for Kurdish refugees, Wembley, 1991. *Compositions include:* Co-writer: Bully For You, Tom Robinson; Listen To The Radio, Tom Robinson; Animals Have More Fun, Jimmy Pursey; Film scores: Birdy, 1985; Last Temptation of Christ, 1989; Original music for Millennium Dome show, Greenwich, London, 2000. *Recordings:* Albums: with Genesis: From Genesis To Revelation, 1969; Foxtrot, 1972; Genesis Live, 1973; Selling England By The Pound, 1973; Nursery Crime, 1974; The Lamb Lies Down On Broadway, 1974; Solo: 4 albums all entitled Peter Gabriel, 1977–82 (third album No. 1, UK, 1980); Peter Gabriel Plays Live, 1983; So (No. 1, UK), 1986; Passion, 1989; Shaking The Tree – Sixteen Golden Greats, 1990; Us, 1992; Revisited,

1992; Secret World, 1995; Come Home to Me Snow, 1998; Ovo, 2000; Long Walk Home (from film Rabbit-Proof Fence), 2002; Up, 2002; Featured on: All This and World War II, 1975; Exposure, Robert Fripp, 1979; Conspiracy of Hope (Amnesty International), 1986; Set, Youssou N'Dour, 1989; Exile, Geoffrey Oryema, 1990; It's About Time, Manu Katche, 1992; Until The End of The World, (soundtrack), 1992; Tower of Song (Leonard Cohen tribute), 1995; Compiler, Plus From Us, 1993; Singles include: Solsbury Hill, 1977; Games Without Frontiers, 1980; Biko, 1980 (live version, 1987); Shock The Monkey, 1982; Sledgehammer (No. 1, USA), 1986; In Your Eyes, 1986; Don't Give Up (duet with Kate Bush), 1986; Big Time, 1987; Red Rain, 1987; Digging In The Dirt, 1992; Steam, 1993; Blood of Eden, 1993; Kiss That Frog, 1993; Come Talk to Me, 1993; Lovetown, 1994; Snow Flake, 1994; The Barry Williams Show, 2002; Contributor, Sun City, Artists United Against Apartheid, 1985; Rainbow Warriors, 1989; Until The End of The World (soundtrack), 1991; Give Peace A Chance, the Peace Choir, 1991. *Honours:* Ivor Novello Awards: Outstanding Contribution To British Music, 1983; Best Song, 1987; BRIT Awards: Best British Male Artist, Best British Music Video, Sledgehammer, 1987; Best Producer, 1993; 9 Music Video Awards for Sledgehammer, and Video Vanguard Trophy, 1987; Grammy Awards: Best New Age Performance, 1990; Best Short Form Video, 1993. *Address:* c/o Real World Inc, Real World Studios, Box, Wiltshire SN13 8PL, England. *Website:* www.petergabriel.com.

GABRIELLE, (Louisa Gabrielle Bobb); b. 16 May 1970, Hackney, London, England. Vocalist; Songwriter. *Career:* Solo recording artiste, 1993–; US tour, 1994; British tour, 1996; Performed with Paul Weller. *Recordings:* Albums: Find Your Way, 1993; Gabrielle, 1996; Rise (No. 1, UK), 2000; Dreams Can Come True: Greatest Hits Vol. 1, 2001; Hit singles: Dreams (No. 1, UK), 1993; Going Nowhere, 1993; I Wish, 1994; Because of You, 1994; Give Me A Little More Time, 1996; Forget About The World, 1996; If You Really Cared, 1996; If You Ever, with East 17, 1996; Walk On By, 1997; Sunshine, 1999; Rise (No. 1, UK), 2000; When A Woman, 2000; Should I Stay, 2000; Out of Reach, featured in film Bridget Jones' Diary, 2001; Don't Need The Sun To Shine (To Make Me Smile), 2001. *Honours:* BRIT Awards: Best Newcomer, 1994; Best British Female Solo Artist, 1997. *Address:* c/o Go Beat Records, Fulham Palace, Bishops Ave, London SW6 6EA, England.

GAGE, Peter; b. 31 Aug. 1954, London, England. Musician (Guitar, Keyboards); Prod; Arranger; Programmer; Engineer. m. 1) Elkie Brooks, 2) Ruby James, 15 Aug. 1996. *Education:* Eltham College, London, England; BSc, Computing, University of Westminster, London. *Education:* O Level Music; Grade 5 Classical Piano. *Career:* Formed and Lead, Geno Washington and the Ram Jam Band; Formed Dada and Vinegar Joe; Featuring Robert Palmer and Elkie Brooks; 1973: Musical Director for Elkie Brooks; Commenced Production, Engineering career with Debut LP for Joan Armatrading, 1974; TVs including Best of the Old Grey Whistle Test. *Compositions:* She's Lost You, for film, Less Than Zero; Hazy Shade of Winter, Bangles; Black Smoke, Calumet, UK Top 20, 1972. *Recordings:* Back To The Night, Joan Armatrading, album, 1974; Wrecking Crew, album; Johnny Remember Me, The Meteors, 1985; Live at the Klubfoot, 1985–87. *Current Management:* c/o Stamina Management. *Address:* 47 Prout Grove, London NW10 1PU, England.

GAHAN, David; b. 9 May 1962, Epping, England. Vocalist. m. 1) Joanne Fox, 4 Aug. 1985, 1 s., 2) Theresa Conroy, 11 April 1992, 3) Jennifer Skilas, 14 Feb. 1999, 1 d. *Career:* Founder Member, Depeche Mode, 1980–. *Recordings:* 12 Top Ten Singles include: Just Can't Get Enough, 1981; See You, 1982; Everything Counts, 1983; People Are People, 1984; Master and Servant, 1984; Enjoy the Silence, 1990; I Feel You, 1993; Condemnation, 1993; In Your Room, 1994; Barrel of a Gun, 1997; It's No Good, 1997; Dream On, 2001; 13 Top Ten Albums include: Speak and Spell, 1981; A Broken Frame, 1982; Construction Time Again, 1983; Some Great Reward, 1984; The Singles 81–85, 1985; Black Celebration, 1986; Music For the Masses, 1987; 101, 1989; Violator, 1990; Songs of Faith and Devotion, 1993; Ultra, 1997; The Singles 86–98, 1998; Dream On, 2001; One Night In Paris (DVD), 2002. *Honours:* BRIT Award, Enjoy the Silence, 1991. *Current Management:* Jonathan Kessler, Baron Inc, 41 River Terrace, #3308 New York, NY 10282, USA. *Address:* First Floor, Regent House, 106 Marylebone High St, London W1M 3DB, England. *Website:* www.depechemode.com.

GALANIN, Sergey; b. 16 Nov. 1961, Moscow, Russia. Vocalist; Songwriter; Musician (guitar, bass guitar). m. Olga Galanina, 5 Feb. 1982, 1 s. *Education:* Railroad College; Music School. *Career:* Member of various bands including: Redkaya Ptitsa, Gulliver, Brigada S, Brigadiry Ser'ga; Regular tours in Russia, and appearances at festivals; Concerts in Finland, 1987; Tours of Germany and USA, 1989; Concerts in Poland and Czechoslovakia; Played at Moscow Musik Peace Festival in 1989 with Bon Jovi, Scorpions, Ozzy and others. *Recordings:* All This Is Rock 'N' Roll, by Brigada S; Rivers, by Brigada

S; I Adore Jazz, by Brigada S; Dog's Waltz, by Ser'ga, 1994; Ser'ga, 1995. *Current Management:* Dmitri Griosman. *Address:* 121309 Moscow, Novozavodskaya St 27, Russia.

GALLAGHER, Benny; b. Largs, Ayrshire, Scotland. Vocalist; Songwriter; Musician (guitar). *Career:* Songwriting partnership with Graham Lyle, 1960s–; Member, McGuinness Flint, 1969–71; Folk duo, Gallagher and Lyle, 1972–79; Solo artiste, 1980–. *Compositions:* Co-writer with Graham Lyle: Mr Heartbreak's Here Instead, Dean Ford; International, Mary Hopkin; for McGuinness Flint: When I'm Dead and Gone; Malt and Barley Blues; for Gallagher and Lyle: Heart On My Sleeve; I Wanna Stay With You. *Recordings:* Albums: with Gallagher and Lyle: Gallagher and Lyle, 1972; Willie and The Lap Dog, 1973; Seeds, 1973; The Last Cowboy, 1974; Breakaway, 1976; Love On The Airways, 1977; Showdown, 1978; Gone Crazy, 1979; Lonesome No More, 1979; The Best Of, 1980; Breakaway, 1981; Live In Concert, 1999; Singles: I Wanna Stay With You, 1976; Heart On My Sleeve, 1976; Also contributed to albums by: Sandy Denny, Slim Chance, Jim Diamond, Isla St Clair.

GALLAGHER, Eve; b. 12 Feb. 1956, Sunderland, England. Vocalist. *Education:* Drama at College; Language Schools; Swiss Schools; Opera lessons. *Career:* Actress, singer, various West End musicals include: Hair; Oh Calcutta; Signed by, and co-writer with Boy George, More Protein Records. *Recordings:* Hit Dance single: Love Come Down, 1991; Love Is a Master of Disguise, 1995; The Dubs EP, 1996; Heartbreak, 1996; Album: Woman Can Have It, 1995; features on: The Unrecoupable One Man Bandit, Boy George, 1999. *Honours:* Best Actress in Shakespeare aged 18: Queen Margaret in Richard III. *Current Management:* Action Artist Management, Förrlibuckstrasse 66, 8005 Zurich, Switzerland. *Address:* 7 Pepys Court, 84 The Chase, London SW4, England.

GALLAGHER, Liam (William John Paul); b. 21 Sept. 1972, Burnage, Manchester, England. Vocalist; Musician (guitar, keyboards); Prod. m. Patsy Kensit, 7 April 1997, divorced 2000, 1 s., 1 d. (with Lisa Moorish) Nicole Appleton, 1 s. *Education:* St Mark's High School, Didsbury, Manchester. *Career:* Founder mem., Oasis, 1991–; Signed to Creation Records, 1993; Support tours with Verve; Concerts include: Glastonbury Festival, 1994; US debut, Wetlands, New York; Earls Court, London (UK's largest-ever indoor concert), 1995; Glastonbury, headlining, 1995; Knebworth (largest-ever outdoor concert), 1996; Finsbury Park, London, 2002; Regular tours, UK, Europe, USA; Left Creation Records to set up Big Brother label, 2000. *Recordings:* Albums: Definitely Maybe (No. 1, UK), 1994; What's The Story (Morning Glory)? (No. 1, UK), 1995; Be Here Now (No. 1, UK), 1997; The Masterplan, 1998; Standing On The Shoulder Of Giants (No. 1, UK), 2000; Familiar To Millions (Live), 2001; Heathen Chemistry, 2002. Singles include: Supersonic, 1994; Shakermaker, 1994; Cigarettes and Alcohol, 1994; Live Forever, 1994; Whatever, 1994; Some Might Say (No. 1, UK), 1995; Wonderwall (No. 2, UK), 1995; Roll With It (No. 2, UK), 1995; Don't Look Back In Anger (No. 1, UK), 1996; D'You Know What I Mean, (No. 1, UK), 1997; Stand By Me (No. 2, UK), 1997; All Around the World (No. 1, UK), 1998; Go Let It Out (No. 1, UK), 2000; Who Feels Love?, 2000; Sunday Morning Call, 2000; Stop Crying Your Heart Out, 2002; Little By Little/She Is Love, 2002; The Hindu Times, 2002. *Honours:* BRIT Awards: Best Newcomers, 1995; Best Album, Best Single, Best Video, Best British Group, 1996; Q Awards: Best New Act, 1994; Best Live Act, 1995; 2 Multi-Platinum albums; NME Awards, Best UK Band, Artist of the Year, 2003. *Current Management:* Ignition Management, 54 Linhope St, London NW1 6HL, England. *Website:* www.oasisnet.com.

GALLAGHER, Noel David Thomas; b. 29 May 1967, Burnage, Manchester, England. Vocalist; Songwriter; Musician (guitar); Prod. m. Meg Matthews, 6 June 1997, divorced 2001, 1 d. *Career:* Roadie, guitar technician, Inspiral Carpets, 1990–93; Mem., Oasis, 1991–; Full-time mem., 1993–; Debut performance, Boardwalk, Manchester, 1991; Signed to Creation Records, 1993; Support tours with Verve; Concerts include: Glastonbury Festival, 1994; US debut, Wetlands, New York, 1994; Earl's Court, London (UK's largest ever indoor concert), 1995; Glastonbury, headlining, 1995; Knebworth, largest ever outdoor concert, 1996; Finsbury Park, London, 2002; Regular tours, UK; Europe; USA; Left Creation Records to set up Big Brother label, 2000; Set up own Sour Mash record label, 2001; Also mem., Tailgunner. *Recordings:* Albums: Definitely Maybe (No. 1, UK), 1994; What's The Story (Morning Glory)? (No. 1, UK), 1995; Be Here Now (No. 1, UK), 1997; The Masterplan, 1998; Standing On The Shoulder Of Giants (No. 1, UK), 2000; Familiar To Millions (Live), 2001; Heathen Chemistry, 2002. Singles include: Supersonic, 1994; Shakermaker, 1994; Cigarettes and Alcohol, 1994; Live Forever, 1994; Whatever, (No. 3, UK), 1994; Some Might Say (No. 1, UK), 1995; Wonderwall (No. 2, UK), 1995; Roll With It (No. 2, UK), 1995; Don't Look Back In Anger (No. 1, UK), 1996; D'You Know What I Mean, (No. 1, UK), 1997; Stand By Me (No. 2, UK), 1997; All Around the World (No. 1, UK), 1998; Go Let It Out (No. 1, UK), 2000; Who Feels Love?, 2000; Sunday Morning Call, 2000; Stop Crying Your Heart Out, 2002; Little By Little/She Is Love, 2002; The Hindu Times, 2002; Also contributed vocals to Chemical Brothers' singles: Setting Sun (No. 1, UK), 1996; Let Forever Be, 1999. *Honours:* BRIT Awards: Best Newcomers, 1995; Best British Group, Best

Album, Best Single, Best Video, 1996; Q Awards: Best New Act, 1994; Best Live Act, Ivor Novello Award 1995; 2 Multi-Platinum albums; Music Week Award, Top Songwriter, 1996; NME Awards, Best UK Band, Artist of the Year, 2003. *Current Management:* Ignition Management, 54 Linhope St, London NW1 6HL, England. *Website:* www.oasisnet.com.

GALLAGHER, Rob, (Rob Galliano, Earl Zinger); b. 18 Oct. 1964, London, England. Vocalist; Prod. *Career:* Founder and member of Galliano, 1988–96; Group signed to Gilles Peterson's Talkin' Loud label; Solo career, recording as Earl Zinger; Collaborations: Mick Talbot; Valerie Etienne; Ski Oakenfull. *Recordings:* Albums: In Pursuit of The 13th Note, 1991; A Joyful Noise Unto The Creator, 1992; The Plot Thickens, 1994; 4our, 1996; Put Your Phazers On Stun and Throw Your Health Food Skyward (as Earl Zinger), 2001; Singles: Frederick Lies Still, 1989; Prince of Peace, Skunk Funk, 1992; Roofing Tiles, 1996; Song 2 (as Earl Zinger), 2000. *Membership:* PRS. *Address:* c/o Red Egyptian Records, 15 Allen Rd, Stoke Newington, London N16 8SB, England.

GAMBLE, Patsy; b. 13 Sept. 1963, Stroud, Gloucestershire. Saxophonist; Teacher. *Career:* Teacher, Schools and Improvisation Workshops, 1990–; Toured with British Blues Circuit with The Little Big Horns; Worked With 90 Proof, Ray Sharpe, Eddie Martin, Steve Winwood, Gary Baldwin, Dick Heckstall-Smith. *Recordings:* Albums, Life On The Plains; Blue To The Bone; Fires and Floods. *Membership:* Musicians' Union; PAMRA. *Current Management:* P Gamble, Hendy, Butterrow Lane, Stroud, Gloucester GL5 2LX, England.

GANC, David; b. 24 May 1958, Rio De Janeiro, Brazil. Musician (flute and saxophone); Arranger. m. Monique C Aragao, 1 s. *Education:* Graduate, Music, Federal University of Rio de Janeiro; BA Professor of Music, Berklee College of Music; Flute pro-art Semibars (Odette Ernest Dia), Norton Morozonicz, Federal University of Rio with C Noltzenlogel, Berklee College with Joe Viola, Gary Burton; Harmony with John Neschling. *Career:* Side musician, recording and playing with artists including: Stevie Wonder (Free Jazz Festival '95); Gal Costa; Simone; Paulo Moura; Luiz Melodia; Nivaldo Ornelas; Elba Ramalho; Geraldo Azevedo; Monique Aragao; Emilio Santiago; Recording musician at Globo TV; Special radio programme with David Ganc Quartet at Radio Mec; Played as guest saxophonist, Brazilian Symphony Orchestra; Also from Brasilia. *Recordings:* Solo album: Brazilian Ballads, 1996; Solo track at Contemporary Woodwind Brazilian Players, 1994; More than 60 CDs and records, as musician; Appears on: Visom Brazil, 1993; Antonio Carlos Sings the Music of Jorge Amado, 1997; Recorded for films, theatre, ballet soundtracks. *Current Management:* Zillion Prod Art LTDA. *Address:* R Miguel Couto 134–404 Rio de Janeiro RJ, Brazil.

GANE, Tim; b. 12 July 1964, Barking, Essex, England. Musician (guitar, keyboards, percussion, programming); Songwriter. *Career:* Member: Unkommuniti, early 1980s; McCarthy, c. 1985–90; Stereolab, 1991–; Blip; Turn-On; Son Alex with band member Laetitia Sadier; Collaborations: Ui; Brigitte Fontaine; Nurse With Wound; Herbie Mann. *Recordings:* Albums include: Peng!, 1992; Transient Random Noise Bursts With Announcements, 1993; Mars Audiac Quintet, 1994; Music For The Amorphous Body Study Center, 1995; Emperor Tomato Ketchup, 1996; Dots and Loops, 1997; Cobra and Phases Group Play Voltage In The Milky Night, 1999; The First of The Microbe Hunters, 2000; Sound-Dust, 2001. *Current Management:* Martin Pike c/o Duophonic Ultra High Frequency Disks. *Website:* www.stereolab.co.uk.

GANG RELATED. See: **KRUST.**

GANLEY, Allan; b. 11 March 1931, Tolworth, Surrey, England. Musician (drums); Arranger; Composer. m. June, 15 Aug. 1970, 1 d. *Education:* Composing, arranging, Berklee School of Music, Boston, USA, 1970. *Career:* Started 1953, with big bands of Jack Parnell; Ambrose; Geraldo; John Dankworth; Own small band, later joined The Tubby Hayes Quintet; Accompanied many American artistes, including: Jim Hall, Stan Getz; Ronnie Scott; Clark Terry; Performed with: Al Haig; Dizzy Gillespie; Bobby Brookmeyer; George Shearing; Peggy Lee; Blossom Dearie; The Pizza Express All-Star Band; Dave Shepherd Quintet; Stephane Grappelli; Carol Kidd; Cleo Laine and John Dankworth; 10 years in Bermuda; Invited to Florida to appear in March of Jazz programme. *Compositions:* Composed, arranged and conducted for BBC Radio Orchestra; BBC Radio Big Band; Jack Sharpe Orchestra; Arrangements for Marion Montgomery; Carol Kidd; Elaine Delmar; Georgie Fame. *Recordings:* with: Henry Mancini; Robert Farnon; George Shearing; Yehudi Menuhin; Stephane Grappelli; Nelson Riddle; two albums with Scott Hamilton; series of albums with Warren Vache and Tony Coe; Recorded in New York with Jim Hall. *Honours:* Melody Maker Poll winner, several times, 1950s–60s; British Jazz Awards, 1980s, 1990s; Best Arranger/Composer, British Jazz Awards, 1998, 2001. *Address:* 5 Asher Dr., Ascot, Berkshire SL5 8LJ, England.

GANNON, Oliver; b. 23 March 1943, Dublin, Ireland. Jazz Musician (guitar). m. Patty Hervey, 14 Feb. 1979, 1 s., 1 d. *Education:* 2 years, Engineering, University of Manitoba; BMus, Berklee College of Music, Boston, USA. *Career:* Lives and performs in Vancouver area; Played at major jazz festivals world-wide including Montreux, Switzerland; Concord, USA;

North Sea, Netherlands; Toronto; Québec; Montréal; Winnipeg; Vancouver; 3 Russian tours with Fraser MacPherson Quartet. *Recordings:* with Fraser MacPherson: Live At The Planetarium; Live From Montreux; I Didn't Know About You; Indian Summer; Honey and Spice; Encore; In The Tradition; with Ian MacDougall Quartet: Rio; Three; The Warmth of the Horn; also albums with George Robert Quintet; Pacific Salt; Fred Stride; Kenny Colman; Wynton Marsalis and Pearl Brown; Gary Guthman; Charles Mountford. *Honours:* JUNO Award, Best Jazz Album, I Didn't Know About You, 1982. *Membership:* SOCAN; Musicians' Asscn. *Address:* 2781 McKenzie Ave, White Rock, BC V4A 3H5, Canada.

GARBAREK, Jan; b. 4 March 1947, Norway. Musician (saxophone); Songwriter; Prod. *Career:* Group with Jon Christensen, Arild Andersen, Terje Rypdal, 1960s; Played with: Keith Jarrett's Belonging, Ralph Towner, 1970s; Leader, own groups, featuring Bill Frisell, Eberhard Weber, Nana Vasconcelos, 1980s–; Also played with: Don Cherry; George Russell. *Recordings:* Albums: Esoteric Circle, 1969; Afric Pepperbird, 1971; Triptykon, 1972; Sart, 1972; Dis, 1977; Places, 1978; Photo With, 1979; Eventyr, 1980; Paths, Prints, 1982; Wayfarer, 1983; Works, 1984; It's OK To Listen To The Gray Voice, 1985; All Those Born With Wings, 1986; Legend of The Seven Dreams, 1988; I Took Up The Runes, 1990; Twelve Moons, 1993; Visible World, 1996; Rites, 1999; Mnemosyne, 1999; Rosensfole, 2000; Selected Recordings, 2002; with Keith Jarrett: Belonging; My Song; Luminesence; Arbour Zena; with Ralph Towner: Solstice; Sounds and Shadows; with George Russell: Othello Ballet Suite; Trip To Prillarguri; Electronic Sonata For Souls Loved By Nature; with L Shankar: Song For Everyone; Art Lande: Red Lanta, 1974; with Bobo Stenson: Witchi-Tai-To, 1974; Dansere, 1976; with Charlie Haden and Egberto Gismonti: Magico, 1980; Folk-songs, 1981; with Kjell Johnsen: Aftenland, 1980; with Agnes Buen Garnås: Rosensfole, 1991; with Ustad Fateh Ali Khan: Ragas and Sagas, 1993; with The Hilliard Ensemble: Officium, 1994; with Anouar Brahem, Madar, 1994. *Address:* c/o ECM Records, 1540 Broadway, New York, NY 10036-4098, USA.

GARBUTT, Vin; b. South Bank, Middlesbrough, England. Folk Musician (guitar, tin-whistle); Vocalist; Songwriter; Humorist. *Career:* Professional musician, songwriter, 1969–; Appearances include: USA; Canada; Australia; Hong Kong; Indonesia; Europe; New Zealand; Bermuda; Festivals world-wide including: Cambridge; Edinburgh; Wath; Auckland; Fylde; Television show, Small Folk, Yorkshire TV (proceeds to Save The Children Fund). *Recordings:* Albums include: The Valley of Tees, 1972; Young Tin Whistle Pest, 1974; King Gooden, 1976; Eston California, 1978; Tossin' A Wobbler, 1978; Little Innocents, 1983; Shy Tot Pommy, 1986; When The Tide Turns, 1989; The South Banker Show, 1991; The Bypass Syndrome, 1992; Bandalised, 1994; Plugged, 1995; When The Tide Turns Again, 1998; Word of Mouth, 2001; Video: The South Banker Show, 1991; Appeared on: Street Cries, Ashley Hutchings, 2001.

GARCIA, Dean; b. 3 May 1958, London, England. m. J P Fletcher, 1 s., 1 d. *Career:* World tours: Eurythmics; Sinead O'Connor; Tours: Bryan Ferry; Curve (own band), radio, television, world touring; Television: Ian Dury; Japan; Established multimedia internet company. *Compositions include:* Chinese Burn, for Sony Minidisc advertisement, 1998. *Recordings:* Albums: Curve: Doppleganger, 1992; Cuckoo, 1993; Public Fruit; Come Clean, 1998; Open Day At The Hate Fest, 2001; Gift, 2001; Eurythmics: Touch, 1983; Be Yourself Tonight, 1985; Mick Jagger: Primitive Cool, 1987; Lethal Weapon 1, film soundtrack; Gang of Four: Tattoo; Ultrasound: Flying Saucer; Last of England soundtrack (Derek Jarman); Recoil: Liquid, 2000; Strange Hours, 2000. *Membership:* PRS; Musicians' Union; PAMRA. *Current Management:* Scott Rodger Quest Management. *Address:* c/o mushimushi, PO Box 26332, London N8 9WZ, England. *Website:* www.mushimushi.net.

GARDEUR, Jacques; b. 9 Nov. 1953, Paris, France. Musician (guitar); Composer. m. 7 July 1990, 2 s. *Education:* University; Study, Music department, Paris 8 University; Master class with: Barre Philips, Charlie Haden; Jose Barrense-Dias. *Career:* Began career, 1965; Album recorded with choir school; Session man with several blues, jazz and funk music groups, 1975–; Currently plays with Gwendoline Sampe, jazz singer. *Compositions:* TV film music for Antenne 2 (France TV). *Membership:* Union des Musiciens de Jazz (UMJ). *Current Management:* Mezza-voce. *Address:* 1 rue de L'Emaillerie, 93200 St Denis, France.

GARDINER, Bobby; b. 1939, Aughdarra, County Clare, Ireland. Musician (accordion); Teacher. *Career:* Member: Kilfenora Ceili Band; Malachy Sweeney band, 1950s; Moved to New York, 1961; Made recordings and joined US Army; Returned to Ireland, 1970s; Member: Bru Boru; Teaches at University College, Cork. *Recordings:* Albums: Memories of Clare, 1962; Bobby Gardiner At Home, 1979; The Best of Bobby Gardiner, 1982; The Master's Choice, 1989; The Clare Shout, 1998. *Address:* c/o Bobby Gardiner, Burncourt, Cahir, County Tipperray, Ireland.

GARDINER, Boris Oliver Patrick; b. 13 Jan. 1943, Kingston, Jamaica. Vocalist; Musician (bass, piano, guitar). Divorced, 2 s., 2 d. *Career:* Lead singer, singing group, The Rhythm Aces, 1960; Kes Chin and Souvenirs Band, 1962; Bassist, vocalist, Carlos Malcolm Afro Jamaican Rhythm Band, 1964;

Formed own band, The Boris Gardiner Happening, 1968–82; Performances: USA; Canada; Central America; Caribbean Islands; Bahamas; Guyana; major concerts: Dupon Plaza, Miami; New York Hilton; Playboy Hotel, Jamaica; Sun Splash, Jamaica; The Cat and Fiddle, Nassau, Bahamas; Oslo, Norway; UK; Shared stages with: Jackie Wilson; Brook Benton; Roy Hamilton; The Stylistics; Nina Simone; The Blue Notes; Bob Marley; Radio, TV include: Top of the Pops, BBC1 TV; France; Spain; Netherlands. *Recordings:* Elizabethan Reggae, 1970; I Wanna Wake Up With You (No. 1, UK), 1986; You Are Everything To Me, 1986; Next to You, 1992; Reggae Happening, 1968; Melting Pot, 1999; Solo albums include: Is What's Happening, 1995; Studio musician, bass guitar,. *Recordings include:* Punky Reggae Party, Bob Marley; Young Gifted and Black, Bob and Marcia; Police and Thieves, Junior Marvin and The Upsetter – Lee Perry. *Honours:* Best Vocalist, Swing Magazine Awards, 1972; Canadian Reggae Music International Awards, Top Reggae Single, I Wanna Wake Up With You, 1986; Annual Hall of Fame Award, Excellence In The Arts, Jamaica. *Membership:* MCPS; PRS. *Address:* 2 Solo Way, Queensborough, Kingston 19, Jamaica.

GARDNER, Colin David; b. 16 Jan. 1952, Quernmore. Vocalist; Musician (rhythm guitar). m. Caroline Gardner, 2 s., 2 d. *Career:* Lead singer; Air play on major radio stations; Interview on Louth Meath FM. *Compositions:* Thoughts of Yesterday; Mother Natures Miracle Anew; Hands of Time; Brand New Dawn; Reasons; Honky Tonking; Missing You; Boomers Bar Blues; My Wife; Mr Blues. *Recordings:* Brand New Dawn; In The Stillness of The Night. *Membership:* PRS. *Current Management:* Mike Croft, Monster Music. *Address:* 28 Glen View Cres., Heysham, Morecambe, Lancashire LA3 2QW, England.

GARDNER, Jeff; b. 23 Oct. 1953, New York, USA. Musician (piano); Composer; Educator. *Education:* 2 years Harvard University; Music study with Hall Overton; Nadia Boulanger; John Lewis; Jaki Byard; Don Friedman; Ivan Tcherepnin. *Career:* Played in Brazil with Wayne Shorter; Hermeto Pascoal; Pat Metheny; Helen Merrill; Helio Delmiro; Monterey Jazz Festival, with Victor Assis Brasil, Clark Terry, Slide Hampton, 1980; European tours with Steve Lacy and Eddie Harris; Concerts with Gary Peacock; Freddie Hubbard; Solo concerts for French television and radio; Piano Quartet with Martial Solal, Paul Bley, Jaki Byard, 1985; Solo concert tour, Brazil, 1992; Tour, France with Rick Margitza, 1995; Also played with Kenny Wheeler; André Ceccarelli; Paulo Moura; Charlie Mariano; Etta Cameron; Duo with Andrew Schloss, performed IRCAM, Paris; Germany; USA; Worked with soprano S'Ange Susan Belling; Concerts include: October Jazz Festival, Saint Lucia; CMAC, Martinique; Paris Jazz Festival; Madajazzcar Festival, Antananarivo; Tour of Japan, with Lisa Ono, 1996. *Recordings:* Continuum, trio with Eddie Gomez, Billy Hart; Alchemy, duo with Gary Peacock; Spirit Call; Sky Dance, with Gilberto Gil; Second Home, with Rick Margitza; California Daydream, Kenny Wheeler. *Publications:* Jazz Piano – Creative Concepts and Techniques; Co-author, Jazz Transcription, with Niels Lan Doky. *Membership:* SACEM. *Current Management:* Lena Michals, 1802 Laurel Canyon Blvd, Los Angeles, CA 90046, USA. *Address:* 44 rue Sarrette, 75014 Paris, France.

GARFUNKEL, Art (Arthur); b. 5 Nov. 1941, Forest Hills, New York, USA. Vocalist; Actor. m. Kim Cermak, 18 Sept. 1988, 1 s. *Education:* BA, Columbia, 1965; MA, 1967. *Career:* Member of duo Simon and Garfunkel (with Paul Simon), 1966–70; Appearances with Paul Simon include: Royal Albert Hall, 1967, 1968; Monterey Pop Festival, 1967; Madison Square Garden, 1972; Central Park, New York, 400,000 audience, 1981; Several other reunion tours and benefit concerts; Solo artiste, 1972–; Concerts include: Carnegie Hall, New York, 1981; Sofia, Bulgaria, for 1.4m. people, 1990; Film appearances include: Catch 22, 1970; Carnal Knowledge, 1971; Bad Timing... A Sensual Obsession, 1980; Good To Go, 1986. *Recordings:* Albums include: with Simon and Garfunkel: Wednesday Morning 3AM, 1966; Sounds of Silence, 1966; Parsley Sage Rosemary and Thyme, 1967; Bookends (No. 1, UK and USA), 1968; The Graduate (soundtrack) (No. 1, UK and USA), 1968; Bridge Over Troubled Water (No. 1, UK and USA), 1970; Greatest Hits, 1972; Concert in Central Park, 1982; Old Friends, 1997; Tales From New York (compilation), 2000; Solo: Angel Clare, 1973; Breakaway, 1975; Watermark, 1978; Fate For Breakfast, 1979; Scissors Cut, 1981; The Art Garfunkel Album, 1984; The Animals Christmas, 1986; Lefty, 1988; Garfunkel, 1991; Up 'Til Now, 1993; Across America, 1997; Songs from a Parent to a Child, 1997; Numerous hit singles include: with Simon and Garfunkel: The Sound of Silence (No. 1, USA), 1965; Homeward Bound, 1966; I Am A Rock, 1966; Hazy Shade of Winter, 1966; At The Zoo/59th Street Bridge Song (Feelin' Groovy), 1967; Scarborough Fair, 1968; Mrs Robinson (No. 1, USA), 1968; The Boxer, 1969; Bridge Over Troubled Water (No. 1, UK and USA), 1970; Cecilia, 1970; El Condor Pasa (If I Could), 1970; America, 1972; My Little Town, 1975; Solo: All I Know, 1973; I Only Have Eyes For You (No. 1, UK), 1975; Crying In My Sleep, 1977; Bright Eyes (film theme for Watership Down) (No. 1, UK), 1979; Contributed vocals to: Grateful, John Bucchino, 2000. *Honours:* Numerous Grammy Awards, for Mrs Robinson, 1969; Bridge Over Troubled Water, 1971; Britannia Award, 1977; Inducted into Rock and Roll Hall of Fame, 1990. *Current Management:* Metropolitan Entertainment, PO Box 1566, 7 N Mountain Ave, Montclair, NJ 07042, USA.

GARIEPY, Kevin; b. 7 March 1958, Montréal. Residential Counsellor. 1 d. *Education:* BA, McGill University, Psychology; Classical Guitar with Mike Nipoliano and Juan Tomas. *Career:* Part Time Musician, Multi Instrumentalist; Composer and Publisher with Ursa Major Music. *Compositions:* Drums of Change; The Rhythm King; Wonderous World. *Address:* 15713 Thrift Ave, White Rock, BC V4B 2M3, Canada.

GARLAND, Hank 'Sugarfoot' (Walter Louis); b. 11 Nov. 1930, Cowpens, South Carolina, USA. Jazz and Country Musician (guitar); Songwriter. *Career:* Session guitarist, Nashville; Played numerous sessions with Elvis Presley, 1958–61; Concerts with Elvis include: Benefit Show, Honolulu, 1961; Moved into country-jazz; Television and radio shows include New York City and Chicago; Car accident affected playing ability, 1961. *Recordings include:* Solo albums: The Velvet Guitar of Hank Garland; Jazz Winds From A New Direction, 1961; Unforgettable Guitar; And His Sugar Footers, 1992; with Elvis Presley: Original 50 Gold Award Hits; Something For Everybody; Elvis Is Back; Elvis Aron Presley; His Hand In Mine; Other. *Recordings include:* A Legendary Performer, Jim Reeves; Original Golden Hits, Jerry Lee Lewis; Lonely Weekends, Charlie Rich; Gibson, Guitars, and Girls, Don Gibson; Country Hall of Fame, Patsy Cline; with Webb Pierce: The Best Of; Western Express; Boogie With A Bullet, Dutch Redita; The Red Foley Story, Red Foley; Also recorded with: Justin Tubb; Patti Page; Grady Martin; Owen Bradley; Autry Inman; Tommy Jackson; Hank Williams Sr; Johnny Horton; Bobby Darrin; The Nashville All-Stars; Various anthologies. *Honours:* Rock and Roll Hall of Fame; Gibson Hall of Fame; Country Music Hall of Fame. *Membership:* BMI; ASCAP. *Current Management:* Brother Billy. *Address:* Jacksonville, Florida, USA.

GARLAND, Tim, (Tim Garland-Waggett); b. 19 Oct. 1966, Ilford, Essex, England. Musician (saxophone); Composer. m. Amanda Phillipa Cooper, 28 July 1995. *Education:* West Kent College; Guildhall School of Music. *Career:* Joined Ronnie Scott's Band, aged 23; Started jazz/folk fusion band Lammas; Several British tours; Radio appearances include: Radio 3, Lammas with strings; Circle Suite, South Bank; Dankworth Generation Band, Jason Rebello, London Jazz Orchestra; Full time member of Chick Corea's Origin sextet, 1999; CD recorded for Stretch Records, spring 2000. *Compositions include:* Dance For Human Folk, for big band (recorded by BBC Big Band). *Recordings:* Lammas: Lammas; Lammas: This Morning; The Broken Road, 1995; Source Book, 1997; Sea Changes, 1999; Dankworth Generation Band: Nebucadnezzar; Live At Ronnies; Solo: Enter the Fire, 1996. *Honours:* BBC Soloist Award, 1988; British Jazz Awards: Best Ensemble, 1993; BBC Composition Award, 1995. *Membership:* PRS; MCPS. *Address:* Lammas, Flat 7, 75 West Hill, London SW15 2UL, England.

GARNIER, Laurent; b. 1 Feb. 1966, Boulogne Sur Seine, France. Prod; Remixer; DJ. *Career:* Trained as a chef; Moved to London to work in French embassy; Relocated to Manchester; DJ at the world famous Hacienda club; Co-founder: F Communications record label; Resident DJ at the Rex Club, Paris; Remixed: Reese Project; System 7. *Recordings:* Albums: A Shot In The Dark, 1994; 30, 1996; Unreasonable Behaviour, 2000; Singles: Acid Eiffel, Astral Dreams, 1994; Club Traxx EP, 1995; Crispy Bacon, Flashback, 1997; The Man With The Red Face, Greed, 2000. *Honours:* Victoire De La Musique Award, 30 (album), 1996. *Address:* c/o F Communications, 20–22 rue Richer 75009 Paris, France. *E-mail:* info@fcom.fr.

GARRETT, Kenny; b. 1960, Detroit, Michigan, USA. Musician. *Career:* Joined The Duke Ellington Orchestra, 1978; Musician, The Mel Lewis Orchestra and the Dannie Richmond's Quintet, 1982; Numerous concerts world-wide; Extensive Tours. *Recordings:* Black Hope; Triology; Pursuance: The Music of John Coltrane; Song book; Amandla Dingo; Live Around The World; Miles Davis and Quincy Jones: Live at Montreux; Introducing Kenny Garrett; Prisoner of Love; African Exchange Student; Simply Said, 1999; Old Folks, 2001; Happy People, 2002; Also guests on recordings by: Cindy Blackman; Art Blakey; Donald Byrd; Herbie Hancock; Jon Hassell; Freddie Hubbard; Branford Marsalis; Marcus Miller; Jon Scofield. *Honours:* Named Hot Jazz Artist, Rolling Stone, 1996; Named Alto Saxist of the Year, Down Beat Readers Poll, 1996. *Current Management:* Burgess Management, 3225 Prytania St, New Orleans, LA 70115, USA.

GARRETT, Peter Robert; b. 16 April 1953, Wahroonga, NSW, Australia. Vocalist. m., 3 d. *Education:* BA, Australian National University; BLLB, University of New South Wales, 1977. *Career:* Member, Rock Island Line; Lead singer, Midnight Oil, 1976–2002; Regular tours world-wide including: Earthquake benefit concert, New South Wales (with Crowded House), 1990; Solo performance, Earth Day Sound Action benefit, Foxboro, Massachusetts (with Joan Baez, Steve Miller, The Kinks), 1992; Earth Day Sound Action Benefit, Columbia, 1993; Strong links with ecological groups; Benefit concerts for: Aboriginal Rights Association; Tibet Council; Song proceeds for Deadicated to Rainforest Action Network and Cultural Survival; Protest concert, Exxon Building (Exxon Valdez oil spill), 1990; Ran for Australian Senate, Nuclear Disarmament Party, 1984; Pres., Australian Conservation Foundation, 1989–91, 1998–; Mem. of board, Greenpeace International, 1991–93. *Recordings:* Albums: with Midnight Oil: Head Injuries, 1979; Bird Noises, 1980; Place Without A Postcard, 1981; Red Sails In The Sunset, 1982;

10 9 8 7 6 5 4 3 2 1, 1983; Diesel and Dust, 1987; Blue Sky Mining, 1990; Scream In Blue – Live Earth, Sun and Moon, 1992, 1993; Breathe, 1996; 20,000 Watt RSL – The Midnight Oil Collection, 1997; Redneck Wonderland, 1998; The Real Thing (live), 2000; Hit single: Beds Are Burning, 1989; Contributor, Artists United Against Apartheid album, 1985; Deadicated (Grateful Dead tribute album), 1991. *Publications:* Political Blues, 1987. *Honours:* Four Australian Record Industry Asscn Awards, 1991; Crystal Globe Award, Sony Music, 1991; Hon. DLitt, University of NSW; Australia's Living Treasures Award, National Trust of Australia, 1999; Gold and Platinum discs. *Membership:* Past President, Australian Conservation Foundation, 1987; Board mem., Greenpeace International. *Current Management:* Gary Morris Management, 63 Glebe Point Rd, Glebe, NSW 2037, Australia. *Telephone:* (2) 9517-9776. *Fax:* (2) 9517-1072. *E-mail:* oils@ozemail.com.au. *Website:* www.petergarrett.com.au.

GARRETT, Siedah; b. 1963, Los Angeles, California, USA. Vocalist; Songwriter. *Career:* Backing Singer for Quincy Jones and Michael Jackson; Joined Brand New Heavies, 1997–98; Solo career. *Recordings:* Don't Look Any Further, duet with Dennis Edwards, 1984; I Just Can't Stop Lovin' You (duet with Michael Jackson) (No. 1, UK), 1987; co-wrote Man In The Mirror, Michael Jackson (No. 1, USA), 1988; Solo: Kiss of Life, 1991; K.I.S.S.I.N.G., 1991; Refuse to Be Loose, 1991; Backing vocals: Madonna, True Blue, 1986; Michael Jackson, Bad, 1987; Sarah Vaughan, Brazilian Romance, 1987; Barbra Streisand, Till I Loved You, 1988; Aretha Franklin, Through the Storm, 1989; Curtis Stigers, Curtis Stigers, 1991; Michael Jackson, Dangerous, 1992; Mica Paris, Whisper a Prayer, 1993; Quincy Jones, Q's Jook Joint, 1994; Michael Jackson, History: Past, Present and Future, 1995; Dionne Warwick, Aquarela Do Brazil, 1995; Dumb and Dumber, film soundtrack, 1995; Brand New Heavies, Shelter, lead vocals and arrangements, 1997; Ray Charles, Ultimate Hits Collection, 1999; Quincy Jones, I'm Yours, single, 1999; Scorpions, Eye II Eye, 1999; Enrique Iglesias, Escape, 2001.

GARRICK, Michael; b. Enfield, England. Composer; Bandleader; Musician (piano, organ); Teacher; Lyricist. *Education:* BA Hons, London; Postgraduate Certificate in Education; Open Fellowship to Berklee College of Music, Boston, Massachusetts, USA. *Career:* BBC broadcasts, 1960–; Director, Poetry and Jazz in Concert, 1961–69; Director of Travelling Jazz Faculty, Founder, Wavendon Jazz Course; Director, Jazz Academy vacation courses and record label; Group Leader of Trio, Sextet, Big Band, ensembles; First jazz musician to give concerts on pipe organs at St Paul's Cathedral, 1969; Royal Festival Hall, 1969; Coventry Cathedral, 1973; Guest Conductor, European Community Youth Jazz Orchestra; Faculty, RAM 1985–98, Trinity College of Music, Guildhall summer school. *Compositions include:* Jazz Praises, 1967: Mr Smith's Apocalypse, 1969; Judas Kiss, 1971; The Hobbit Suite, 1973; Heavenly Bodies, 1977; Underground Streams, 1979; Faces of Love, 1980; Catechism, 1981; Zodiac of Angels, 1988 (symphony orchestra); Carioca Celebration, 1983; New Flower of Europe, 1981; The Stirring, 1982; Romance of the Rose, 1986 (Rhapsody for jazz violinist and orchestra); Hardy Country, 1990; Garrick's Jazz Characters, 1960–; The Royal Box, 1993; Bovingdon Poppies, 1993; A Diana Sonata, 1997; Asha's Ear, 1999; For Children: All God's Children; Tree of Dreams; What is Melody?; Norman Gnome and the Rhinoceros; Jazz Curries. *Recordings:* Poetry and Jazz in Concert (4 Vols); October Woman; Promises; Black Marigolds; Heart is a Lotus; Home Stretch Blues; Troppo; You've Changed; Kronos; Cold Mountain; Anthem; Jazz Praises at St Paul's, 1968; A Lady in Waiting, 1993; Meteors Close at Hand, 1994; Parting is Such, 1996; For Love of Duke… and Ronnie, 1998; Down on Your Knees, 1999. *Contributions to:* Jazz Now; Times Educational Supplement; The Stage; Piano Magazine. *Honours:* Hon. ARAM; Whittingham Award, 1997. *Membership:* Royal Society of Musicians; Asscn of British Jazz Musicians; President, Berkhamsted Jazz Society. *Current Management:* Jazz Academy Resources, 12 Castle St, Berkhamsted, Hertfordshire HP4 2BQ, England.

GARRITY, Freddy; b. 14 Nov. 1936, Manchester, England. Vocalist. *Career:* Member, groups The Red Sox; The John Norman Four; The Kingfishers, later changed to Freddy and The Dreamers; Performances include: Cavern Club, with the Beatles, 1962; Royal Albert Hall, 1963; British tour with Roy Orbison, 1964; Beatles Christmas Show, Hammersmith Odeon, London, 1964; Regular television appearances include: Let's Go; Beat Show; Sunday Night At The London Palladium; Shindig; Hullaballoo; Film appearances: What A Crazy World, 1963; Every Day's A Holiday, 1964; Regular club and cabaret performances with the New Dreamers, 1968–; Concerts include: The Biggest '60s Party In Town, Olympia Hall, London, 1992; Actor, stage performance, The Tempest, 1988. *Recordings:* Hit singles: If You Gotta Make A Fool of Somebody, 1963; I'm Telling You Now (No. 1, USA), 1963; You Were Made For Me, 1963; I Understand, 1964; Albums: Greatest Hits, 1998. *Address:* c/o Jason West Agency, Gables House, Saddlebow, Kings Lynn, Norfolk PE34 3AR, England.

GARTSIDE, Green, (Green Strohmeyer-Gartside); b. 22 June 1956, Cardiff, Wales. Vocalist; Songwriter. *Education:* Leeds Art School. *Career:* Founder member, Scritti Politti, 1977–; Concerts include: British tour, support to Joy Division, 1979; Futurma Festival, Leeds, 1979; Montreux Pop

Festival, 1988. *Compositions:* The Sweetest Girl, 1981 (also recorded by Madness); The Perfect Way, 1985 (also recorded by Miles Davis); Love of a Lifetime, Chaka Khan, 1986; L Is For Lover (co-written with David Gamson), Al Jarreau, 1986. *Recordings:* Albums: with Scritti Politti: Songs To Remember, 1982; Cupid and Psyche 85, 1985; Provision, 1988; Anomie and Bonhomie, 1999; Singles: The Sweetest Girl, 1981; Faithless, 1982; Asylums In Jerusalem/Jacques Derrida, 1982; Wood Beez (Pray Like Aretha Franklin), 1984; Absolute, 1984; Hypnotize, 1984; The Word Girl, 1985; The Perfect Way, 1985; Oh Patti, 1988; She's A Woman (with Shabba Ranks), 1991; Take Me In Your Arms and Love Me, 1991; Tinseltown To The Boogiedown, 1999; Contributor: Sweet Dreams (Are Made of This) album, Eurythmics, 1982; film soundtrack Who's That Girl?, 1987; Music of Quality and Distinction Vol. II, British Electric Foundation compilation album, 1991. *Current Management:* c/o Simon Hicks, PO Box 2950, London W11 3ZX, England.

GARVEY, Phil; b. 14 Jan. 1965, Reading, Berkshire, England. Vocalist; Musician (guitar, percussion). *Career:* Random Music, 1985–86; Plumbers, 1986–87; Solo folk clubs to 1990; Daisy Telethon Band, 1990; Free Spirits, 1991–94; Misfits Menagerie, 1994–. *Compositions:* 93 titles include: Would She Dance For Me; Step Out Your Frame; Nobody Fights Time; Here Comes The Twist. *Recordings:* Dance With Me Daisy (comedey record), 1990; Free Spirits album: Spirited Approach, 1993. *Publications:* A Good Day To Run Away, short novel, 1994. *Membership:* Musicians' Union. *Current Management:* J Cooper. *Address:* J Cooper, 44 Springhill Rd, Goring, Berkshire RG8 0DA, England.

GARZON, Albert; b. 26 Feb. 1960, Newburgh, New York, USA. Record Prod; Ragtime Musician (piano); Co Pres. *Education:* BS, Fredonia State College, New York.; Studied piano; Music composition; Sound recording. *Career:* Produced over 50 albums for artists including: 10,000 Maniacs; Brenda Kahn; Hypnolovewheel; Arson Garden; Antietam; Solo Piano Rags of James Scott; President, Com Four Distribution, import/exporter of CDs and LPs. *Recordings:* Music of James Scott. *Address:* 7 Dunham Pl., Brooklyn, New York, NY 11211, USA.

GATE-AH. See: **CHANDLER, Kerri.**

GATELY, Stephen Patrick David; b. 17 March 1976, Dublin, Ireland. Vocalist. *Career:* Mem., Boyzone, 1993–2001; Solo artiste, 2000–. *Recordings:* Albums: with Boyzone: Said And Done, 1995; A Different Beat, 1996; Where We Belong, 1998; By Request (No. 1, UK), 1999; Solo: A New Beginning, 2000. Singles: with Boyzone: Working My Way Back To You, 1994; Key To My Life, 1995; Love Me For A Reason, 1995; So Good, 1995; Father and Son, 1995; Coming Home Now, 1995; Words (No. 1, UK), 1996; A Different Beat (No. 1, UK), 1996; Isn't It A Wonder, 1997; Baby Can I Hold You Tonight, 1997; Musical Experience, 1997; Picture of You, 1997; All That I Need (No. 1, UK), 1998; I Love The Way You Love Me, 1998; When The Going Gets Tough (No. 1, UK), 1999; You Needed Me (No. 1, UK), 1999; Every Day I Love You, 1999; Solo: New Beginning, 2000; I Believe, 2000; Stay, 2001. *Address:* c/o Concorde International Artistes, Concorde House, 101 Shepherd's Bush Rd, London W6 7LP, England.

GATICA, Humberto; b. Rancagua, Chile. Prod. *Career:* Owner with David Foster, 143 Records, Miami; Worked with: Chicago, Andrés de León, Céline Dion, Myriam Hernández, Michael Jackson, La Ley. *Honours:* Three Grammy Awards. *Address:* c/o WEA Latina, 5201 Blue Lagoon Dr., Suite 200, Miami, FL 33126, USA.

GATLIN, Larry Wayne; b. 2 May 1948, Seminole, Texas, USA. Vocalist; Songwriter. m. Janis Gail Moss, 9 Aug. 1969, 1 s., 1 d. *Career:* Country singer, songwriter, 1971–; Member, Gatlin Brothers. *Recordings:* Albums: with Gatlin Brothers: Partners; Living In The Land of Dreams; Cooking Up A Storm; Live At 8pm; Pure 'n' Simple; Solo albums include: Houston To Denver, 1984; Straight Ahead; Adiois, 1992; Moments to Remember, 1993; In My Life, 1998; 16 Biggest Hits, 2000. *Honours:* 2 BMI Songwriter Awards for Delta Dirt, 1975; Broken Lady, 1976; 3 ACM Awards, Best Album, Single, Male Vocalist, 1980. *Membership:* CMA. *Address:* c/o Gatlin Enterprises, 7003 Chadwick Dr., Suite 360, Brentwood, TN 37027, USA.

GATTO, Olivier; b. 22 Jan. 1963, Manosque, France. Musician (double bass); Arranger; Composer. m. Lydia Filipovic, 11 Sept. 1993. *Education:* University of Sciences, Bordeaux, France; Berklee College of Music, Boston, USA. *Career:* Concerts with Joe Henderson Quartet; Billy Cobham Quartet; Ravi Coltrane Quartet; Roy Hargrove and Antonio Hart; Julian Joseph; Ernie Watts; Bill Evans; Benny Golson Quartet; Vincent Herring Quartet; Mark Turner; Jerry Bergonzi; European tour with John Stubblefield, George Cables and Billy Hart; French television shows, Radio France, Voice of America. *Recordings:* Album: Here and There (featuring Billy Cobham, George Cables, John Stubblefield), 1996; Craig Bailey, Brooklyn, featuring Rufus Reid. *Current Management:* Danielle Gatto. *Address:* 2 Ave Jules Valles, 77176 Savigny le Temple, France.

GAUDETTE, Claude; b. 15 Oct. 1959, Montréal, Québec, Canada. Composer; Prod; Musician (keyboards). *Education:* Montréal Conservatory of

Music; Dick Grove School of Music, Los Angeles; New York Recording Workshop. *Career:* Musical Director, France Joli, Yamaha International Song Festival, 1985; Keyboards, David Foster's Super Producer '94 Tour, Japan. *Recordings:* Producer, writer, musician on albums: The Colour of My Love, Céline Dion; Belinda, Belinda Carlisle; Everlasting, Good To Be Back, Natalie Cole; Slip of The Tongue, Whitesnake; also albums by Fiona; Michael Bolton; Peter Cetera; Earth Wind and Fire; Roberta Flack; Sergio Mendes; Eddie Money; Dionne Warwick; Kenny Loggins; Five Star; Little River Band; Smokey Robinson; Martika; Barry Manilow; George Benson; The Commodores; Céline Dion; Ricky Martin; Singles: Mad About You, Belinda Carlisle; Wind Beneath My Wings, Bette Midler; Time of My Life, Bill Medley and Jennifer Warnes; Make Me Lose Control, Eric Carmen; I Live For Your Love, Pink Cadillac, Natalie Cole; Walk Away, Dionne Warwick; also singles by Sheena Easton; Kenny Loggins; Melissa Morgan; Ziggy Marley; Film soundtracks include: Pretty Woman; Three Men and A Little Lady; Raw Deal; Dirty Dancing; Beaches. *Membership:* BMI; NARAS; SCL. *Address:* 4912 Stern Ave, Sherman Oaks, CA 91423, USA.

GAUDRY, Michel-Marie-Marcel; b. 23 Sept. 1928, Eu, France. Divorced, 2 d. *Education:* Piano from ages 5 to 8; Clarinet from 8 to 23, then bass. *Career:* Jazz music, singers; TV shows; Accompanied Billie Holiday; Carmen McRae; Blues singers; T Flanagan; Sweden; Madagascar; La Reunion; Les Autilles; European Jazz Orchestra (London); Europe; Russia; Japan; Africa; South America; USA; Canada; England. *Recordings:* With Duke Ellington; Louis Armstrong; Billy (Strayhorn); Barney Kessel; Bud Powell Trio; Double-Six of Paris; Records with Barbera; G Moustaki; C H Dumont. *Honours:* Representing France, Big-Band Jazz Europe, London.

GAUL, Sven H; b. 11 April 1953, Flensburg, Germany. Musician (drums); Television Personality. *Education:* Degree, German, University of Århus. *Career:* Member, rockband, Taurus, 1974–80; Member, Pop/rockband, TV-2, 1980–; Host, television show, Lul, Lul, Rocken Gaar, 1989; Member, Danish Music Council, 1991–. *Recordings:* 1 live recording and numerous other releases. *Honours:* Danish Grammy, 1985. *Membership:* Danish Musician Union. *Address:* Arhus Musikkontor, Mindegadelo, 8000 Århus, Denmark.

GAUSDEN, Guy; b. 8 Aug. 1965, Bromley, Kent, England. *Career:* Member of The Beloved, until 1987; Drummed with various artists; Director, 13 Artists Agency; Manager, Element and Fanzine. *Address:* 13 Artists, 36 Langham St, London W1N 5RH, England.

GAUTHIER, Marcel; b. 7 Nov. 1963, Iberville, Québec, Canada. Arranger; Publisher. 1 s., 1 d. *Education:* BAC, Musique Generale; DEC, Musique Professionel; Classical Guitar, 1977–; Jazz Piano, 1985. *Career:* Arranger and Copyist, Samedi de Rire, Demons du Midi, Country Centre-Ville, Double Etoiles, La Fureur, La Boite à Chansons, ADiSQ. *Compositions:* Il fait toujours beau quelque part, Radio theme, Radio Canada; Un pitbull chez les moules (big band); Desert (recorded by Robin Grenon); Stimulus (Robin Grenon). *Recordings:* Stimulus (with Robin Grenon, harp); Dionne (with Jean-Marie Dionne); Carmen Bonifacio (keyboards); Claude Olivier (keyboards); Secret Lake (with Christian Vanderre). *Membership:* SOCAN. *Current Management:* Notason. *Address:* 440 de L'Église, Verdun, QC H4G 2M4, Canada.

GAUTHIER, Mary Veronica; b. Thibodaux, LA, USA. Vocalist; Musician (guitar); Songwriter. *Education:* Louisiana State University, studied Philosophy. *Career:* Surname pronounced 'go-shay'; Sometimes bracketed as a country artist but is more in the singer-songwriter or alternative country area; After a troubled few years as an adolescent and young adult involving crime, drugs and alcohol, went to University and opened an award-winning restaurant; Now concentrates on music career and plays many of the top USA folk festivals including: Kerrville; Philadelphia; Newport. *Recordings:* Dixie Kitchen, 1997; Drag Queens In Limousines, 1999; Filth And Fire, 2002. *Honours:* GLAMA (Gay and Lesbian American Music Awards), Country Artist of the Year, 2000. *Website:* www.marygauthier.com.

GAVIN, Frankie; b. 1956, Corrandulla, County Galway, Ireland. Musician (fiddle, whistle, flute); Composer. m. Tracey Harris. *Education:* Learned music from parents. *Career:* Founder: De Danann, 1973; Performed for: President Kennedy; Prince Charles; Francois Mitterand; Collaborations: Rolling Stones; Yehudi Menuhin; Stephane Grappelli; Appeared in TV series Bringing It All Back Home, 1992; Wrote soundtrack for TV series The Irish Rhm. *Recordings:* Albums include: Anthem (with De Danann), 1985; Omos Do Joe Cooley (with Paul Brock), 1986; Jigs and Jazz (with Stephane Grappelli), 1993; Welcome To The Hotel Connemara (with De Danann), 2000; solo: Croch Suas E, 1983; Frankie Goes To Town, 1991; Fierce Traditional, 2001. *Honours:* Winner: All Ireland Fiddle; All Ireland Flute competitions, 1973; Gold disc, How The West Was Won, 2000; AIB, Traditional Music Award, 1996. *Website:* home.att.net/~FrankieGavin/.

GAY, Albert; b. 25 Feb. 1928, London, England. Clarinet; Soprano Sax; Tenor Sax. m. Doreen Gay, 1 Sept. 1983, 1 d. *Education:* Guildhall School of Music. *Career:* Many broadcasts with Freddy Randall, Alex Welsh, Al Gay Quartet (BBC Jazz Club); Background Music in films: Two Left Feet; L-

Shaped Room; TV: Alex Welsh; Bob Wallis; Keith Smith; Harry and Laurie Gold; Jo Daniels Bands. *Compositions:* South Track for South Bank Show; Band Leader, Queen Mary, 1961. *Recordings:* CDs; Paul Jones-Elaine Delmar; Ruby Braff, Alex Welsh and Freddy Randall; The World's Greatest Jazz Band, Stockholm. *Membership:* Musicians' Union. *Current Management:* Freelance. *Address:* Lanterns, North St, Winkfield, Berks, SL4 4SY, England.

GAYLE, Crystal, (Brenda Gail Webb); b. 9 Jan. 1951, Paintsville, Kentucky, USA. Country Vocalist. m. Vassilios (Bill) Gatzimos, 1 s., 1 d. *Career:* Recording artiste with Decca Records, late 1960s; Regular appearances, Jim Ed Brown's television show, The Country Place; Played UK concerts with Kenny Rogers; Loretta Lynn (sister); Appeared at Wembley Country Music Festivals, 1971, 1977, 1979; First US country artist to perform in People's Republic of China, 1979; Contributor, film soundtrack, One From The Heart, 1982. *Recordings:* Hit singles include: Wrong Road Again; Beyond You; I'll Get Over You; Don't It Make My Brown Eyes Blue; Talking In Your Sleep; Your Kisses Will; Your Own Cold Shoulder; Half The Way; Cry; You and I, with Eddie Rabbitt; Making Up For Lost Time, with Gary Morris; Albums include: Crystal Gayle, 1974; Somebody Loves You, 1975; Crystal, 1976; We Must Believe In Magic, 1977; When I Dream, 1978; I've Cried The Blues Right Out of My Eyes, 1978; We Should Be Together, 1979; Miss The Mississippi, 1979; A Woman's Heart, 1980; These Days, 1980; Hollywood/Tennessee, 1981; True Love, 1982; One From The Heart, with Tom Waits, 1982; Cage The Songbird, 1983; Nobody Wants To Be Alone, 1985; Crystal Gayle, 1986; Straight To The Heart, 1986; What If We Fall In Love, 1987; Nobody's Angel, 1988; Ain't Gonna Worry, 1990; Three Good Reasons, 1992; Someday, 1995; Walk with Me, 1996; Mountain Christmas, 1996; Sings the Heart and Soul of Hoagy Carmichael, 1999; In My Arms, 2000. *Honours:* Female Vocalist of the Year, Academy of Country Music, 1976; Grammy Awards: Beat Female Country Vocal Performance, Best Country Song; Female Vocalist of the Year, CMA. *Current Management:* Gayle Enterprises Inc, 51 Music Sq. E, Nashville, TN 37203, USA.

GAYLE, Michelle; b. 2 Feb. 1971, London, England. Vocalist; Songwriter; Actress. m. Mark Bright. *Career:* Actress, UK television series: Grange Hill; EastEnders; Solo singer, 1993–; Concerts include: Radio 1's Massive Music British tour, 1995; Starred in Beauty and the Beast, West End show, London. *Recordings:* Albums: Michelle Gayle, 1995; Sensational, 1997; Hit singles: Looking Up, 1993; Sweetness, 1994; I'll Find You, 1994; Freedom, 1995; Happy Just To Be With You, 1995; Sensational, 1997; Do You Know, 1997; Contributor, The Gift of Christmas, Child Liners, 1995; Guest vocals on In My Room, Me One, 2000. *Honours:* Smash Hits Awards; Gold Disc, Michelle Gayle. *Current Management:* Denis Ingoldsby, First Avenue Management, The Courtyard, 42 Colwith Rd, London SW6 1RU, England.

GAYNOR, Gloria; b. 7 Sept. 1947, Newark, New Jersey, USA. Vocalist. *Career:* Singer with the Soul Satisfiers, 1960s; Solo disco music artiste, 1970s–. *Recordings:* Albums: Never Can Say Goodbye, 1975; Experience Gloria Gaynor, 1976; I've Got You, 1976; Glorious, 1977; Love Tracks, 1979; I Have A Right, 1979; Stories, 1980; I Kinda Like Me, 1981; Gloria Gaynor, 1983; I Am Gloria Gaynor, 1984; The Power of Gloria Gaynor, 1986; Best Of, 2000; The Album, 2002; Hit singles: Never Can Say Goodbye, 1974; Reach Out I'll Be There, 1975; I Will Survive (No. 1, USA and UK), 1979; I Am What I Am, 1983; Can't Take My Eyes Off of You, 1991; Love Is Just a Heartbeat Away, 1995; Mighty High, 1997; Set Me Free, 1998. *Current Management:* Cliffside Music Inc, PO Box 374, Fairview, NJ 07022, USA.

GEDDES, Chris; b. 2 Oct. 1975. Musician (piano, keyboards). *Career:* Member: Belle and Sebastian, 1996–; V Twin 1999–; Golden Rodeo; Collaborations: Arab Strap; Salako; Curated Bowlie Weekend Festival with other Belle and Sebastian band members, 1999. *Recordings:* Albums: Tigermilk, If You're Feeling Sinister, 1996; The Boy With The Arab Strap 1998; Fold Your Hands Child – You Walk Like A Peasant, 2000; Storytelling, 2002. Singles: Dog On Wheels EP, Lazy Line Painter Jane EP, 3–6–9 Seconds of Light EP, 1997; This Is Just A Modern Rock Song EP, 1998; Legal Man, 2000; Jonathan David, I'm Waking Up To Us, 2001. *Honours:* BRIT Award, Best Newcomer, 1999. *Current Management:* Banchory Management, PO Box 25074, Glasgow G2 6YL, Scotland. *Website:* www.belleandsebastian.co.uk.

GEERS, Didier; b. 9 Sept. 1954, Ghent, Belgium. Musician (drums, percussion); Vocalist. m. Naima Barbro Johansson, 10 Aug. 1986, 2 s., 1 d. *Education:* Ghent Music Conservatoir; Drums and percussion lessons; Vocal coaching by Richard Boone. *Career:* 32 albums as Contributor: Sammy Rimington Band, Waso Quintet, George Probert, Al Casey, Bill Dillard Earl Warren; 3 Solo Albums: Didier Geers Jazz and Blues Band, 1986–89; Touring with Eddie Burns Guitar (blues); Member of Papa Bue's Viking Jazz Band, Copenhagen-DK, 7 years; Actual, with own trio The DNA Band. *Honours:* Golden Mermaid Award, Oostende, 1971. *Current Management:* Wim Wigt Productions, Roghorst 303, PO Box 201, 6700 AE, Wageningen, Holland. *Address:* Didier Geers, Karl Nils väg 15–17, 290 11 Linderöd, Sweden.

GEFFEN, David; b. 21 Feb. 1943, Brooklyn, NY, USA. Film, Recording and Theatre Exec. *Education:* New Utrecht High School, Brooklyn. *Career:* Worked at William Morris talent agency as mail clerk, 1964, promoted to junior agent; Co-founder (with Laura Nyro), Tunafish Music Publishing; Joined Ashley Famous Agency, appointed Exec. Vice-Pres., Creative Man., 1968, later International Creative Man.; Co-founder (with Elliot Roberts), Asylum Records and Geffen-Roberts Man. Co, 1970; Sold Asylum to Warner Communications, but remained Pres., 1971, merged it with Elektra, signed up Bob Dylan, Joni Mitchell and The Eagles; Vice-Chair., Warner Brothers Pictures, 1975–76; Founder, and Pres. 1980–, Geffen Records, signed up Elton John, John Lennon, Yoko Ono, Nirvana and Guns N' Roses, sold label to Music Corpn of America Inc, 1990; Founder, Geffen Film Co, prod. Little Shop of Horrors, Beetlejuice, 1988, Men Don't Leave, Defending Your Life, Risky Business; Co-prod., musicals: Dreamgirls, 1981–85; Little Shop of Horrors; Cats, 1982; Madame Butterfly, 1986; Social Security; Chess, 1990; Miss Saigon; Launched new film studio, DreamWorks SKG, with Steven Spielberg and Jeffrey Katzenberg, 1996; Founder, DGC record label. *Address:* c/o DreamWorks SKG, 100 Universal City Plaza, Bldg 477, Universal City, CA 91608, USA.

GEILS, Jerome; b. 20 Feb. 1946, New York, USA. Musician (guitar). *Education:* Worcester Technical College. *Career:* Member, The Hallucinations; Founder member, guitarist, The J Geils Blues Band, 1968–85; Appearances include: Fillmore East, New York, with the Allman Brothers, Beach Boys and Mountain, 1971; Mar Y Sol Festival, Puerto Rico, 1972; Pink Pop Festival, Netherlands, 1980; Regular tours, Europe, USA, UK; Group disbands, 1985; Concert as Magic Dick/J Geils Blue Time, Paradise Club, Boston, 1992; Television includes: In Concert, ABC TV, 1973; Runs vintage and sports car shop, 1992–. *Recordings:* Albums: J Geils Band, 1971; The Morning After, 1971; Live, 1971; Bloodshot, 1973; Nightmares..., 1974; Hotline, 1975; Blow Your Face Out, 1975; Monkey Island, 1977; Sanctuary, 1979; Love Stinks, 1980; Freeze Frame (No. 1, USA; No. 3, UK), 1982; Showtime!, 1983; You're Getting Even While I'm Getting Odd, 1984; Flashback, 1987; The J Geils Band Anthology: A Houseparty, 1993; The Best of The J Geils Band, 1998; Singles include: Looking For Love; Give It To Me; Must've Got Lost; Centrefold (US No. 1, 6 weeks); Angel In Blue; Freeze Frame; I Do; Fright Night, title track for film Fright Night. *Honours:* Rolling Stone magazine, Most Promising New Band, 1971; Various Gold discs; Platinum disc for Freeze Frame, 1982.

GELDOF, Bob; b. 5 Oct. 1954, Dublin, Ireland. Vocalist; Songwriter; Charity Promoter. m. Paula Yates, deceased, 3 d. *Education:* Black Rock College. *Career:* Journalist, New Musical Express, Melody Maker; Founder member, Boomtown Rats, 1975–84; Organizer, Band Aid Trust (incorporating Live Aid, Band Aid, Sport Aid), for Ethiopian famine relief, 1984–92; Solo artiste, 1986–; International tours, including UK, Europe, USA, Japan, Australia; Major concerts include: California Music Festival, 1979; Live Aid, Wembley Stadium, 1985; Freddie Mercury Tribute, Wembley Stadium, 1992; Gosport Festival, 1992; Green Belt Festival, 1992; WOMAD's 10th Birthday, 1992; Film appearances: The Wall, 1982; Number One, 1985; Organizer, Do They Know It's Christmas?, Band Aid, (No. 1, UK), 1984; Participator, We Are The World, USA For Africa, 1984; Organizer, Live Aid concerts, Wembley and Philadelphia (estimated television audience of 2 billion, raising $70m.), 1985; Total of $144m. raised by 1992; Owner, television production company, Planet 24, creators of The Word (Channel 4 UK, 1990–95), The Big Breakfast (Channel 4 UK, 1992–), Survivor (ITV UK, 2001). *Recordings:* Albums with Boomtown Rats: The Boomtown Rats, 1977; A Tonic For The Troops, 1978; The Fine Art of Surfacing, 1979; Mondo Bongo, 1981; V Deep, 1982; Solo: Deep In The Heart of Nowhere, 1986; The Vegetarians of Love, 1990; The Happy Club, 1993; Sex Age And Death, 2001; Singles include: Looking After No 1, 1977; She's So Modern, 1978; Like Clockwork, 1978; Rat Trap (No. 1, UK), 1978; I Don't Like Mondays (No. 1, UK), 1979; Diamond Smiles, 1979; Someone's Looking At You, 1980; Banana Republic, 1980; House On Fire, 1982; Solo: This Is The World Calling, 1987; Love Like a Rocket, 1987; The Great Song of Indifference, 1990; Love or Something, 1990. *Publications:* Autobiography, Is That It?, 1987. *Honours:* KBE (Hon), 1986; 4 Ivor Novello Awards; Order of Two Niles, Sudan; Order of Leopold II, Belgium; Irish Peace Prize; UN World Hunger Award; EEC Gold Medal; MTV Video Award, Special Recognition Trophy, 1985; American Music Award, Special Award of Appreciation, 1986; Gold and Platinum discs; Hon. degrees, Kent, London, Ghent Universities. *Current Management:* Jukes Productions, 330 Harrow Rd, London W9 2HP, England.

GENEST, Francis; b. 31 Dec. 1960, Paris, France. Musician (percussion). *Education:* Translator, Interpreter, Mastership in English; Worked with Giovanni Hidalgo, Farafina. *Career:* Performed at many festivals throughout Europe (France, Spain, Belgium, Italy), USA; Several concerts for Radio France and the French Speaking Public Radios Community; Founder, El Tu Yo and La Comparsita street orchestra. *Recordings:* Albums with the Cache-Cache Trio: L'Océane; Tandems. *Honours:* First prize, National Jazz Contest with Cache-Cache trio. *Membership:* Union des Musiciens de Jazz, Paris. *Address:* La Guéraudière, 37380 Nouzilly, France.

GENTELET, Hugues; b. France. Tour Man; Co-Dir. *Career:* French tour manager for: Whigfield; Reel 2 Reel; Adeva; Rozalla; Dr Alban; Imagination; Boney M; Pasadenas; Kool and The Gang; Numerous other dance acts; Commercial director, Nuits Magiques Production. *Address:* Nuits Magiques

Production, 50 Ave Du President Wilson, BT 104, 93214 La Plaine St Denis CDX, France.

GENTRY, Bobbie, (Roberta Lee Streeter); b. 27 July 1944, Chicasaw County, Mississippi, USA. Vocalist; Songwriter; Musician (guitar). m. (1) Bill Harrah, (2) Jim Stafford. *Education:* Philosophy, Music. *Career:* Recording artiste, 1967–; UK television series, The Bobbie Gentry Show, 1969; Retired from performing to look after business interests. *Recordings:* Hit singles: Ode To Billie Joe (No. 1, USA), 1967; Let It Be Me, with Glen Campbell; All I Have To Do Is Dream, with Glen Campbell; I'll Never Fall In Love Again (No. 1, UK), 1969; Albums: Bobbie Gentry and Glen Campbell, 1968; Local Gentry, 1968; Touch 'Em With Love, 1969; I'll Never Fall In Love Again, 1970; Fancy, 1970; Patchwork, 1971; Sittin' Pretty/Tobacco Road, 1971; Greatest Hits, 1990; The Golden Classics, 1998; Ode To Bobbie Gentry, 2000.

GENTRY, Teddy Wayne; b. 22 Jan. 1952, Fort Payne, Alabama, USA. Musician (bass guitar); Vocalist; Songwriter. m., 1 d., 1 s. *Career:* Founder mem., country music group, Young Country, 1969, renamed Wild Country, 1972, renamed Alabama, 1977–. *Recordings:* Albums: Alabama, 1980; My Home's In Alabama, 1980; Feels So Right, 1981; Stars, 1982; Mountain Music, 1982; The Closer You Get, 1983; Roll On, 1984; 40 Hour Week, 1985; Alabama Christmas, 1985; The Touch, 1986; Greatest Hits, 1986; Just Us, 1987; Live, 1988; Tennessee Christmas, 1989; Southern Star, 1989; Pass It On Down, 1990; Greatest Hits Vol. 2, 1991; American Pride, 1992; Gonna Have A Party... Live, 1993; Cheap Seats, 1993; In The Beginning, 1994; In Pictures, 1995; From The Archives Vol. 1, 1996; Christmas Vol. 2, 1996; Live at Ebbets Field, 1997; Dancin' On The Boulevard, 1997; Twentieth Century, 1999; Alabama For The Record, 2000; When It All Goes South, 2001; Christmas, 2002. Singles include: I Want To Be With You; Tennessee River; Feels So Right; Love In The First Degree; Pass It On Down. *Honours:* Numerous Country Music Asscn Awards, 1981–84; Numerous Acad. of Country Music Awards, incl. Artist of the Decade, 1989; Numerous American Music Awards, incl. Award of Merit, 2003; Grammy Awards, for Mountain Music, 1983, for The Closer You Get, 1984; BMI President's Award, 2000; Numerous Billboard Awards. *Current Management:* Dale Morris and Assocs, 818 19th Ave S, Nashville, TN 37203, USA. *Website:* www.wildcountry.com.

GEORGE, Jimmy; Composer; Prod; Record Label Owner; Publisher. *Career:* Studio guitarist, played on many No 1 hits; Produced many top recording artists; Owner, recording studio; Two vocal hits while at University; Produced Mary Kaye Trio; Performed, Night clubs in Los Angeles; Toured US with the Beach Boys; Wrote and recorded with Jackie DeShannon, Dr John; Played guitar on hits for Michael Jackson, the Jackson Five, Diana Ross, Marvin Gaye, Thelma Houston; Performer, recording producer and musician for Etta James, Little Richard, Leon Russell, Chuck Berry, Ike and Tina Turner and Kenny Rogers; Songs recorded by Carl Anderson, Nancy Sinatra, Bobby Womack, the Commodores, Smokey Robinson, Taylor Dayne, The Temptations and George Benson; Performed in many major venues world-wide with Jimi Hendrix, Sly and the Family Stone, Crosby, Stills, Nash and Young, Janis Joplin; Performed on TV commercials and programmes; Toured as guitarist/bass player with Shaun Cassidy, Leif Garrett, Gary Lewis and the Playboys. *Compositions:* Numerous including: Magic Man; Just To See Her; I Wonder Who She's Seeing Now, The Temptations; I'll Always Love You, Taylor Dayne; Real Thing; Love Remembers, George Benson; Everything Reminds Me of You, Commodores; A Night To Remember. *Honours:* Numerous Grammy Awards. *Membership:* Musicians' Union, Los Angeles; American Federation of Television and Radio Artists; National Academy of Recording Arts and Sciences; Los Angeles World Affairs Council.

GEORGE, Siwsann; b. 2 April 1956, Treherbert, Rhondda, Wales. Musician (harp, concertina, guitar, spoons); Teacher; Broadcaster. m. Roger Plater, 29 June 1991, 1 s. *Education:* Graduate, Aberystwyth University; Welsh College, Music and Drama. *Career:* Lead singer, Mabsant (Welsh roots band), 1980–2002; Tours: USA; Far East; Western Europe; Latvia; Hungary; British Council; As soloist: British tour with Ray Fisher and Jo Freya, 1995; Purcell Room, London, 1995; With Robin Williamson, 1996; Founder, Siwsann George Welsh Road Show (SGWRS), 1997–. *Recordings:* With Mabsant: over a dozen recordings; Solo: Traditional Songs of Wales, with various musicians accompanying, 1994; Several television and film scores. *Publications:* Mabsant – Book of 54 Welsh Folk Songs. *Honours:* 3 times Pan Celtic Singing Winner, 1980–90. *Membership:* Musicians' Union; Equity; Welsh Folk Song Society. *Address:* 26 Bassett St, Abercynon CF45 4SP, Wales. *E-mail:* siwsann.george@getreal.co.uk.

GERALDO, Neil; b. 29 Dec. 1955. Musician (guitar); Record Prod. m. Pat Benatar, 20 Feb. 1982. *Career:* Guitarist, Derringer; John Waite; Guitarist, record producer, Pat Benatar, 1977–. *Compositions:* many for Pat Benatar. *Recordings:* with Pat Benatar: Albums: Crimes of Passion, 1980; Precious Time, 1981; Get Nervous, 1982; Get Nervous (producer), 1982; Live From Earth, 1983; Tropico, 1984; In The Heat of The Night, 1985; Seven The Hard Way, 1985; Best Shots, 1987; True Love (producer), 1991; Gravity's Rainbow (co-producer), 1993; Also appears on: Best of Steve Forbert, 1993; Rock and Roll Hoochie Coo, 1996; Yesterday Today Tomorrow, 1997; Best of Rick Springfield, 1999; Singles include: Heartbreaker; All Fired Up; Treat Me

Right; Love Is A Battlefield; Hell Is For Children; Invincible; Hit Me With Your Best Shot; Sex As A Weapon; We Belong. *Current Management:* Gold Mountain Management, 3575 Cahuenga Blvd W, Suite 450, Los Angeles, CA 90068, USA.

GERIMON, Paul; b. 14 Oct. 1954, Dinant, Belgium. Vocalist (Deep Bass). *Education:* Classic Humanities, St Paul's College and Dinant's Royal Athenee; Superior Diplomas Violin and Voice; Opera Studio Brussels; Centre de Musique Baroque, Paris. *Career:* First appearance on Belgian Television singing Spirituals, 1972; Sings Opera, Standards, Original Songs, Musicals, Baroque and Contemporary, 1974–; First part of Kid Creole, with Allez Allez, 1982; Bass Soloist, Opera Royal Wallonie, 1983–86; TV-Radio appearances on Rai, O Globo, Radio France, RTB, WDR, FR3; Regularly invited at Festival D'Aix, TRM of Brussels, Berlin Philharmonie, Barbican Centre, Brooklyn Academy, Amsterdam, Lisbon, Rome, Paris, New York; Played part of Don Juan at Theatre, 1990; Tricentenary of La Monnaie, 1995; International tour with R. Jacobs and Trisha Brown Company, 1998–99; The Phantom of the Opera, 2000. *Recordings:* M. Kolbe, 1989; DuMont, 1992; WOMA, 1992; Sodoma, 1993; L'Orfeo, 1995; Intra Muros, 1996; Allez Allez, 1997; Euridice, 1998; Don Giovanni, 1999; TV-Films: La Vida Breve, 1985; M. Kolbe, 1989; L'Orfeo, 1998; Le Dernier Chant d'Orphée, 1998. *Honours:* Orphée D'or, 1991, De L'Académie du Disque, Paris. *Membership:* Union Des Artistes, Brussels. *Address:* Concertbureau Arien, De Boeystraat 6, 2018 Antwerpen, Belgium.

GERRITSEN, Rinus; b. 9 Aug. 1946, The Hague, Netherlands. Vocalist; Musician (bass). *Career:* Founder member, Dutch rock group, Golden Earring, 1961–; Tours, Europe; Canada; USA; Support to The Who, European tour, 1972; Support to Rush, 1982. *Recordings:* Albums: with Golden Earring: Just Earrings, 1965; Winter Harvest, 1966; Miracle Mirror, 1968; On The Double, 1969; Eight Miles High, 1969; Golden Earring, 1970; Seven Tears, 1971; Together, 1972; Moontan, 1973; Switch, 1975; To The Hilt, 1976; Contraband, 1976; Golden Earring Live, 1977; Grab It For A Second, 1978; No Promises, No Debts, 1979; Prisoner Of The Night, 1980; 2nd Live, 1981; Cut, 1982; N.E.W.S., 1984; Something Heavy Goin' Down, 1984; The Hole, 1986; Keeper Of The Flame, 1989; The Complete Singles Collection 1975–91, 1991; Bloody Buccaneers, 1991; The Naked Truth, 1992; Face It, 1995; Lovesweat, 1995; Naked II, 1997; The Complete Naked Truth, 1998; Paradise In Distress, 1999; Last Blast Of The Century, 2000; The Devil Made Us Do It, 2000; Numerous compilation albums; with Michel Van Dijk: Gerritsen & Van Dijk, 1979. *Current Management:* Rob Gerritsen, Wingerd 38, 2496 VC Den Haag, Netherlands. *Telephone:* (15) 380-55-88. *Fax:* (15) 380-55-91.

GERUP, Martin; b. 24 Feb. 1960, Himmelev Sogn, Denmark. Vocalist; Composer, Musician (keyboards). m. Dorte Schou, 13 May 1995, 1 d. *Education:* Danish Conservatory of Jazz, Rock and Latin Music. *Career:* Roskilde Festival, with Dieters Lieder, 1988; Roskilde Festival, with Flying Fish, 1993; Several radio and television shows. *Recordings:* with Dieters Lieder: Jeg Ka' Lieder, 1983; Hvorflink Ka' Man Blive?, 1986; with Flying Fish: It's Almost Fairytime, 1993. *Membership:* Danish Artists Society; Danish Jazz, Rock and Folk Authors. *Address:* Danish Artist Society, Vendersgade 24, 1363, Copenhagen K, Denmark.

GESSLE, Per; b. 12 Jan. 1959, Halmstad, Sweden. Musician (guitar); Vocalist: Songwriter. *Career:* Mem., Gyllene Tider; Solo artiste and songwriter; Founding mem., Roxette, with Marie Fredricksson, 1984–; Numerous television, radio and live appearances world-wide; Founder and owner, music publishers, Jimmy Fun Music, Hip Happy, Tom Bone Music; Co-owner, Gessle Music, Happy Accident Music. *Recordings:* Albums: Pearls Of Passion, 1986; Look Sharp!, 1988; Joyride, 1991; Tourism, 1992; Den Sjunde Vagen, 1993; Den Standiga Resa, 1993; Efter Stormen, 1993; Mammas Barn 1993; Crash! Boom! Bang!, 1994; Het Vind, 1995; Don't Bore Us, Get To The Chorus—Roxette's Greatest Hits, 1995; Balades En Español, 1996; Have A Nice Day, 1999; Room Service, 2001. Singles include: The Look (No. 1, 23 countries), 1989; Listen To Your Heart (No. 1, USA), 1989; Dangerous, 1989; Dressed For Success, 1989; It Must Have Been Love (from film Pretty Woman, No. 1, USA), 1990; Joyride (No. 1, 19 countries), 1991; Fading Like A Flower (No. 2, USA), 1991; The Big L, 1991; Spending My Time, 1991; Church Of Your Heart, 1992; How Do You Do!, 1992; Queen Of Rain, 1992; Almost Unreal (from film Super Mario Brothers), 1993; Sleeping In My Car, 1995; You Don't Understand Me, 1996; Wish I Could Fly, 1999; Anyone, 1999; Stars, 1999. *Honours:* Platinum and Gold discs; Grammy Awards; MTV Awards; Achievement medals from King Carl XVI Gustaf of Sweden, 2003. *Current Management:* D & D Management, Lilla nygatan 19, 111 28 Stockholm, Sweden.

GHIGLIONE, Bill Barita Daniel; b. 5 July 1947, Nice, France. Composer; Arranger; Musical Dir; Musician (keyboards). *Education:* University Literature Diploma (second cycle); Classical piano studies. *Career:* Tours include: Eddy Mitchell, 1976–77; Claude Nougaro, 1977; Johnny Halliday, 1978–79; Michel Polnareff, Japan (musical director), 1979; Maxime Le Forestier, Europe, 1982–83; Member, Dallas; Performer, theme music, television series Dallas; Producer, composer, Lasya Victory. *Recordings:* Dallas album, 1981; with Lasya Victory: L'Age D'or, 1989; Tout Ça Nous Fait Mal, 1990; Messie Est De Retour, 1991; Tout S'Arrange, 1992; Mona, 1993;

Sound Design, television series Inventions of Life 3, 1995; Léa Ivanne, A Prendre ou à Laisser, 1999; Song of the Universal Exposition 2000 (Hanovre) Pavillion de France, To Enlighten The World, by Léa Ivanne (WEA). *Honours:* Double Gold Record Award, Dallas theme, 1982; Best French Record of Year, Tout Ça Nous Fait Mal, 1990. *Membership:* SACEM; SCPP. *Address:* 15 bis rue J J Rousseau, 94200 Ivry/Seine, France.

GIANEZ, Laurent, (Laurent Gilbert Gianesini); b. 13 May 1942, Moyeuvre-Grande, France. Musician (flute). *Education:* Diploma, flute, Conservatory, Metz. *Career:* Member various jazz groups including Duo J M Albertucci-Gianez; Ecaroh (style of Art Blakey); Quartet Gianez (own compositions, Samba music); Annual concert with Archie Shepp and Ted Curson. *Recordings:* Album with Duo Denis Moog-Gianez: Car La Rouille N'Aura Pas Raison Du Jazz (saxophone, guitar, trumpet); Currently recording own quartet. *Membership:* SACEM (Paris). *Address:* 26 rue de l'Eglise, 57140 Saulny, France.

GIBB, Barry Alan Crompton; b. 1 Sept. 1946, Douglas, Isle of Man, England. Vocalist; Songwriter. m. Linda Gray, 1 Sept. 1970, 4 s., 1 d. *Career:* Formed The Bee Gees, with brothers Robin and Maurice, 1958–69; Re-formed group, 1971; Appeared on own weekly television show, Australia; Returned to England; Signed with NEMS Enterprises, 1967; Performed live with Barbra Streisand, One Voice Concert/Video, 1987. *Compositions:* Co-writer (with brothers), Saturday Night Fever soundtrack, 1977 (40m. copies sold); Producer, co-writer, albums for: Andy Gibb; Barbra Streisand: Guilty; Dionne Warwick: Heartbreaker; Diana Ross: Eaten Alive; Kenny Rogers: Eyes That See In The Dark; Second most Top Ten hits written (after Lennon and McCartney); 5 simultaneous US Top Ten hits written by the Gibb brothers, 1978; Only artists to write and produce 6 consecutive No. 1 singles, 1979; Producer, writer, Grease, for Frankie Valli; Bee Gees songs recorded by artists including: Boyzone, Take That, Steps, 911, Tina Turner, Céline Dion, Elton John, Eric Clapton, Elvis Presley, Janis Joplin, Andy Williams, Glen Campbell, Rod Stewart, Roberta Flack, Frankie Valli, Michael Bolton; Saturday Night Fever musical stage show at London Palladium, Broadway and Sydney, as well as Cologne, Germany and Japan; Sell-out stadium concerts in Dublin, Wembley Stadium, London, Buenos Aires, South Africa, 1998; Stadium concerts, New Zealand, new Olympic stadium in Sydney, 1999; Millennium Eve concert, South Florida, 1999; 6 shows in Europe planned for 2000. *Recordings:* Albums include: Bee Gees 1st, 1967; Horizontal and Idea, 1968; Odessa, 1969; Cucumber Castle, 1971; Two Years On, 1971; Trafalgar, 1972; Life In A Tin Can, 1973; Mr Natural, 1974; Main Course, 1975; Children of The World, 1976; Here At Last... Live, 1976; Saturday Night Fever, 1977; Spirits Having Flown, 1978; Greatest Hits, 1979; Living Eyes, 1980; ESP, 1988; One, 1989; The Very Best of The Bee Gees, 1990; Tales From The Brothers Gibb (A History In Song 1967–90), 1990; High Civilisation, 1991; You Wouldn't Know, 1992; Size Isn't Everything, 1993; Solo: Now Voyager, 1984; Hawks, 1988; Still Waters, 1997; One Night Only (live), 1998; This Is Where I Came In, 2000; Their Greatest Hits – The Record, 2001; Singles include: To Love Somebody, 1967; Massachusetts (No. 1, UK), 1967; World, 1967; Words, 1968; I Gotta Get A Message To You (No. 1, UK), 1968; Don't Forget To Remember, 1969; Run To Me, 1972; Jive Talkin' (No. 1, USA), 1975; You Should Be Dancing (No. 1, USA), 1976; How Deep Is Your Love (No. 1, USA), 1977; Stayin' Alive (No. 1, USA), 1978; Night Fever (No. 1, UK and USA), 1978; Too Much Heaven (No. 1, USA), 1978; Tragedy (No. 1, UK and USA), 1979; Love You Inside Out (No. 1, USA), 1979; Spirits Having Flown, 1979; You Win Again (No. 1, UK), 1987; Secret Love, 1991; For Whom The Bell Tolls, 1993; Alone, 1997; Immortality, with Céline Dion, 1998; This Is Where I Came In, 2001. *Honours:* 7 Grammy Awards; Inducted into Songwriters Hall of Fame; Inducted in Rock and Roll Hall of Fame, Cleveland; Lifetime Achievement Award, BRIT Awards, London; International Artist Award, American Music Awards, Los Angeles; C.B.E., 2002. *Membership:* Musicians' Union; Equity. *Current Management:* Left Bank Organization, 9255 Sunset Blvd, Second Floor, Los Angeles, CA 90069, USA. *Address:* c/o 1801 Bay Rd, Miami Beach, FL 33139, USA.

GIBB, Robin Hugh; b. 22 Dec. 1949, Douglas, Isle of Man, England. Vocalist; Songwriter. m. Dwina Murphy, 31 July 1985, 2 s., 1 d. *Career:* Formed the Bee Gees with brothers Maurice and Barry, 1958; First single, 1963; Own weekly television show, Australia, 1960s; Moved to England, 1967; First US TV appearance, American Bandstand, 1967; Saturday Night Fever musical stage show opens at London Palladium 1998, Cologne, Germany and Broadway, 1999; Sydney and Japan, 2000; Sell-out stadium concerts in Dublin, Wembley Stadium, London, Buenos Aires, South Africa, 1998; Stadium concerts in New Zealand and at new Olympic stadium in Sydney, 1999; Millennium Eve concert, South Florida, 1999; 6 shows planned in Europe during 2000. *Compositions:* Co-writer, Saturday Night Fever soundtrack, 1977 (40m. copies sold); Co-writer, albums: Guilty, Barbra Streisand; Heartbreaker, Dionne Warwick; Eaten Alive, Diana Ross; Eyes That See In The Dark, Kenny Rogers; Second only to Lennon and McCartney for most Top 10 hits written; Five simultaneous US Top 10 hits, 1978; Six consecutive No. 1 singles, 1979; Bee Gees songs recorded by: Boyzone; Take That; Steps; 911; Tina Turner; Eric Clapton; Elton John; Céline Dion; Al Green; Elvis Presley; Janis Joplin; Sarah Vaughan; Johnny Mathis; Andy Williams; Glen Campbell; Richie Havens; Jose Feliciano; Rod Stewart; Eric

Burdon; Roberta Flack; Nina Simone; Frankie Valli; Michael Bolton. Most covered songs: Massachusetts; Stayin' Alive; To Love Somebody; How Do You Mend A Broken Heart. *Recordings:* Albums: Bee Gees 1st, 1967; Horizontal and Idea, 1968; Odessa, 1969; Cucumber Castle, 1971; Two Years On, 1971; Trafalgar, 1972; To Whom It May Concern, 1972; Life In A Tin Can, 1973; Mr Natural, 1974; Main Course, 1975; Children of The World, 1976; Here At Last. Live, 1976; Saturday Night Fever, 1977; Spirits Having Flown, 1978; Greatest Hits, 1979; Living Eyes, 1980; ESP, 1988; One, 1989; The Very Best of The Bee Gees, 1990; Tales From The Brothers Gibb (A History In Song 1967–90), 1990; High Civilisation, 1991; You Wouldn't Know, 1992; Size Isn't Everything, 1993; Still Waters, 1997; One Night Only (live), 1998; This Is Where I Came In, 2000; Their Greatest Hits – The Record, 2001; Singles include: To Love Somebody, 1967; Massachusetts (No. 1, UK), 1967; World, 1967; Words, 1968; I Gotta Get A Message To You (No. 1, UK), 1968; Don't Forget To Remember, 1969; Run To Me, 1972; Jive Talkin' (No. 1, USA), 1975; You Should Be Dancing (No. 1, USA), 1976; How Deep Is Your Love (No. 1, USA), 1977; Stayin' Alive (No. 1, USA), 1978; Night Fever (No. 1, UK and USA), 1978; Too Much Heaven (No. 1, USA), 1978; Tragedy (No. 1, UK and USA), 1979; Love You Inside Out (No. 1, USA), 1979; Spirits Having Flown, 1979; You Win Again (No. 1, UK), 1987; Secret Love, 1991; For Whom The Bell Tolls, 1993; Alone, 1997; Immortality, with Céline Dion, 1998; This Is Where I Came In, 2001; Solo singles: Saved By The Bell, 1969; Juliet (No. 1, many European countries), 1983. Solo albums: Robin's Reign, 1970; How Old Are You, 1982; Secret Agent, 1984; Walls Have Eyes, 1986 Singles include: Alone; Solo albums: Robin's Reign, 1970; How Old Are You, 1982; Secret Agent, 1984; Walls Have Eyes, 1986. *Honours:* 6 Grammy Awards; Inducted into Songwriters Hall of Fame; Inducted into Rock and Roll Hall of Fame, Cleveland; Lifetime Achievement Award, BRIT Awards, London; International Artist Award, American Music Awards, Los Angeles; C.B.E., 2002. *Membership:* Musicians' Union; Equity. *Current Management:* Left Bank Organization, 9255 Sunset Blvd, Second Floor, West Hollywood, CA 90069, USA. *Address:* c/o 1801 Bay Rd, Miami Beach, Florida 33139, USA.

GIBBONS, Beth; b. 4 Jan. 1965, Devon, England. Vocalist; Songwriter. *Career:* Advertising agency in Bristol; Mem., lead singer, Portishead, 1991–; Worked with Paul Webb, 2001–; *Recordings:* Albums: with Portishead: Dummy, 1994; Herd of Instinct, 1995; Portishead, 1997; PNYC, 1998, Glory Times, 1998; Roseland, New York (DVD), 2002; with Paul Webb: Out Of Season, 2001. Singles: Numb (EP), 1994; Sour Times, 1994; Glory Box, 1995; All Mine, 1997; Cowboys (EP), 1997; Over, 1997; Only You, 1998; Motherless Child (duet with Tom Jones, on his album Reload), 1999. *Honours:* Mercury Music Prize, Best Album, 1995; NME Brat Award, 1995. *Current Management:* Fruit Management, Unit 104, Saga Centre, 326 Kensal Rd, London W10 5BZ, England. *Address:* c/o Go Beat Records, The Fulham Palace, Bishops Ave, London SW6 6EA, England. *Website:* www.portishead.co.uk; www.bethgibbons.com.

GIBBONS, Ian Ronald; b. 18 July 1952, Rochford, Essex, England. Musician (keyboards, accordion). m. Amanda Gaskin, 8 June 1985. *Education:* Grade 6 Piano accordion. *Career:* Worked with: The Kinks; Sweet; Roger Chapman; The Crystals; The Shirelles; Dr Feelgood; Eddie and the Hotrods; Chris Farlowe; Kursaal Flyers; The Inmates; Television includes: Top of the Pops; Saturday Night Live. *Recordings:* All Kinks albums, 1979–, also single: Come Dancing; Recent Albums with Dr Feelgood (Chess Masters, 2000) and Roger Chapman (In My Own Time, 1999). *Honours:* Rock and Roll Hall of Fame, as mem. of The Kinks. *Membership:* PRS. *Current Management:* Pete Scarbrow, Pro Active Management. *Address:* Mushroom Studios, Lubards Farm, Hullbridge Rd, Rayleigh, Essex SS6 9QG, England.

GIBBONS, Steve; Vocalist; Songwriter; Musician (guitar). *Career:* Founder, own R&B band The Steve Gibbons Band, 1971; Tours with The Who, Europe, USA; First foreign act to play in German Democratic Republic. *Compositions:* Numerous songs recorded by other artists. *Recordings:* Tulane, 1977; Other singles include: Sweetheart; Take Me Home; Eddy Vortex; Get Up and Dance; Loving Me, Loving You; Personal Problem; Albums include: Short Stories, 1971; Any Road Up, 1976; Rolling On, 1977; Caught In The Act, 1977; Down In The Bunker, 1978; Street Parade, 1980; Saints and Sinners, 1981; On The Loose, 1986; From Birmingham to Memphis, 1995; The Dylan Project, 1998; On The Loose, 2000. *Current Management:* Jim McPhee, Acorn Entertainments. *Address:* Winterfold House, 46 Woodfield Rd, Kings Heath, Birmingham B13 9UJ, England.

GIBBS, Terri; b. 15 June 1954, Augusta, Georgia, USA. Vocalist; Musician (piano). *Career:* Gospel singer as teenager; Formed own group, Sound Dimension; Residency in Augusta restaurant, 1975; Recording artist, 1981–. *Recordings:* Singles: Somebody's Knockin'; Rich Man; Mis'ry River; Somedays It Rains All Day Long; Anybody Else's Heart But Mine; Slow Burning Fire (duet with George Jones); Albums: Somebody's Knockin', 1981; I'm A Lady, 1981; Somedays It Rains All Night, 1982; Over Easy, 1983; Hiding From Love, 1984; Old Friends, 1985; Comfort the People, 1991; The Best of Terri Gibbs, 1996; Turn Around. *Address:* c/o Richard A Barz and Associates, 25 Cobble Creek Dr., RD 1, Box 91, Tannersville, PA 18372, USA.

GIBERT, Alain; b. 1 Jan. 1947, Langogne, France. Musician (trombone); Composer; Arranger. m. Nadine Faure, 26 April 1970, 3 s. *Education:* Mathematics. *Career:* Co-founder, ARFI (Association à la Recherche d'un Folklore Imaginaire); Member, various bands: Marvelous Band; Marmite Infernale; Apollo; Bomonstre. *Compositions:* Music for Louis Sclavis; Steve Waring. *Recordings:* L'Age Du Cuivre, Apollo; Trombonist, singer, Chariot D'Or; Pticado; As composer, arranger: Le Roi Demonte; L'Art De La Retraite Sonne. *Membership:* SACEM; ARFI. *Current Management:* ARFI, 13 rue de l'Arbre Sec, 69001 Lyon, France. *Address:* Montmorin, 63160 Billom, France.

GIBSON, Deborah; b. 31 Aug. 1970, Brooklyn, New York, USA. Vocalist; Songwriter; Musician (piano); Actress. *Education:* Private piano and voice lessons. *Career:* Youngest performer to have written, performed and produced a number 1 song; Sold over 9m. records world-wide; Starred in Grease, London, West End, 1994. *Recordings:* Only In My Dreams; Shake Your Love; Out of The Blue, 1987; Foolish Beat (No. 1, USA), 1988; Lost In Your Eyes (No. 1, USA), 1989; Electric Youth, 1989; No More Rhyme; Anything Is Possible, 1990; Losin' Myself; Body Mind Soul, 1993; Think With Your Heart, 1995; Deborah, 1997; What You Want, 2000; MYOB, 2001. *Honours:* ASCAP, Writer of the Year. *Current Management:* Gibson Management, 300 Main St #201, Huntington, NY 11743, USA.

GIBSON, Don; b. 3 April 1928, Shelby, North Carolina, USA. Musician (guitar); Songwriter. *Career:* Recording artist, 1949–. *Compositions include:* Sweet Dreams, recorded by Faron Young, Patsy Cline, Emmylou Harris, Roy Buchanan, Reba McIntyre, Elvis Costello; I Can't Stop Loving You, also recorded by Kitty Wells, Ray Charles, Van Morrison; (I'd Be) A Legend In My Time, recorded by Ronnie Milsap; Album of own songs, Roy Orbison Sings Don Gibson, Roy Orbison, 1967; Oh Lonesome Me; Woman (Sensuous Woman). *Recordings:* Albums include: The King of Country Soul, 1968; Dottie and Don, with Dottie West, 1969; A Perfect Mountain, 1970; Country Green, 1972; Woman (Sensuous Woman), 1972; Sample Kisses, 1972; Am I That Easy To Forget, 1973; The Two of Us Together, with Sue Thompson, 1973; Touch The Morning, 1973; Warm Love, with Sue Thompson, 1973; Just Call Me Lonesome, 1973; Snap Your Fingers, 1974; Bring Back Your Love To Me, 1974; Just One Time, 1974; Oh How Love Changes, with Sue Thompson, 1975; Don't Stop Loving Me, 1975; Starting All Over Again, 1978; Look Who's Blue, 1978; Rockin' Rollin' Gibson, Vol. 1, 1982; Vol. 2, 1982; Don Gibson and Los Indios Tabajaras, 1986; Currents, 1992; Country Spotlight, 1992; Sings Hank Williams Sr, 1992; Oh Lonesome Me, 1998; Greatest Hits, 1999; RCA Country Legends, 2001.

GIBSON, Lee; b. 5 March 1950, Watford, Hertfordshire, England. Vocalist. m. Gerry Boyce (musician), 1 Aug. 1973, 1 d. *Education:* BA Hons, Humanities. *Career:* Worked all over Europe with: UMO Danish Orchestra, Helsinki; Danish Radio Band, Copenhagen; Skymasters, Metropol Orchestra, Netherlands; Television appearances in France, Belgium, Italy; Album of television concert with Sarah Vaughan and Francy Boland Band, Dusseldorf; WDR Band, Cologne; Montreux Festival; Over 1,000 BBC solo broadcasts, UK; Film, television includes: The Great Muppet Movie; Privates On Parade; Victor Victoria; Yentl; An American Tale; Willow; Benny Hill Show; Only Fools and Horses; Morecambe and Wise Show; Barrymore, 3 Royal Variety Shows; Concerts include: tours with Syd Lawrence Orchestra; Don Lusher Band; Big Band Specials, BBC Radio Band; Guest appearances with Glen Miller UK Orchestra; Herb Miller Band; Singer, The Music of Andrew Lloyd Webber, concert for Prince and Princess of Wales at Expo '92, Seville; Singer, UK jazz circuit, including: Barbican; Queen Elizabeth Hall; Festival Hall; Rotherham Arts Centre; Brecon, Southampton Jazz Festivals; Ronnie Scott's; Ruislip Jazz Club; Pizza On The Park. *Recordings:* Chorale; One World One Peace; You Can See Forever; Never Let Me Go; Also appears on: Music of Andrew Lloyd Webber, 1988; Broadway Musicals, 1991; Jesus Christ Superstar, 1992; Swing Boogie, 1999. *Publications:* Music reviews for The Musician. *Honours:* Singers Prize, Knikke Festival. *Membership:* Musicians' Union; Equity.

GIFFORD, Alex; b. 1965. Musician (saxophone, keyboards); Recording Engineer. *Career:* Musician, brass section with The Stranglers; Sound engineer for The Grid; Member of Propellerheads, with Will White. *Recordings:* Albums: with Propellerheads: Drumsanddecksandrockandroll, 1998; Extended Play, 1999; Singles: On Her Majesty's Secret Service (with David Arnold), 1997; Dive, 1997; Take California (EP), 1997; Spybreak (EP), 1997; History Repeating (with Shirley Bassey), 1997; Guest musician on Enlightenment, Van Morrison; Producer of album VIP, Jungle Brothers, 1999. *Address:* c/o Wall of Sound, Office 3, 9 Thorpe Close, London W10 5XL, England.

GIFT, Roland; b. 28 May 1962, Birmingham, England. Vocalist; Musician (saxophone); Actor. *Career:* Musician and actor, Hull, 1980s; Singer, Fine Young Cannibals, 1984–; Regular UK and US tours; Film appearances: Group featured in Tin Men, 1987; Actor, films: Sammy and Rosie Get Laid, 1987; Scandal, 1989; Theatre: Romeo, in Romeo and Juliet, UK rep tour, 1990; Solo artiste. *Recordings:* Albums: with Fine Young Cannibals: Fine Young Cannibals, 1985; The Raw and The Cooked (No. 1, UK and USA), 1989; Beautiful Girls, 1996; Finest, 1996; Solo: Roland Gift, 2002. Singles include:

with Fine Young Cannibals: Johnny Come Home, 1985; Suspicious Minds, 1986; Ever Fallen In Love, 1987; She Drives Me Crazy (No. 1, USA), 1989; Good Thing (No. 1, USA), 1989; Don't Look Back, 1989; Contributions to film soundtracks: Something Wild, 1986; Tin Men, 1987; Contribution, Red Hot + Blue, 1990. *Honours:* BRIT Awards, Best British Group, Best British Album, 1990. *Address:* c/o Universal Music Group, Universal Studios, 100 Universal City Plaza, Universal City, CA 91608, USA.

GIGOT, Raquel; b. 9 Nov. 1965, Ottignies, Belgium. Chromatic and Diatonic Accordions; Composer. *Career:* Professional Musician, 1990–; Numerous Radio and TV performances in different countries; Studio musician recording with different artists. *Compositions:* Bully Wully Jig; Blue Room; Road to Bally Heighue; Rue Des Dunes; Lesidren; Mouse in the Kitchen. *Recordings:* 1990; Blue Room; Restless Home; Leaving the World Behind; Histoires de Rue; Oceanides; About to Go. *Current Management:* VZW Worm Productions, 136 Chaussee De Wemmel, 1090 Brussels, Belgium.

GIL, Gilberto, (Gilberto Passos Gil Moreira); b. 3 March 1942, Salvador, Brazil. Vocalist; Musician (guitar, accordion); Songwriter. *Education:* Federal University, Bahia, Business Administration. *Career:* Began playing accordion aged 8; Played with Os Desafina Dos whilst studying; Composed songs for Television advertisements in early 1960s; Appeared in Nos Por Exemplo, a show directed by Caetano Veloso, 1964; After moving to Sao Paulo in 1965, had first hit when Elis Regina recorded Louvação; Sang protest songs, which proved controversial with the military dictatorship, and was part of the Tropicalia movement; After imprisonment in 1968 relocated to UK; Worked with groups such as Pink Floyd, Yes, Incredible String Band and Rod Stewart's band in London Clubs; Returned to Brazil, 1972; Toured with Caetano Veloso, Gal Costa and Maria Bethania; Became involved in politics in early 1990s and was elected to office in Salvador; Appointed, Minister of Culture, Brazil, 2003–. *Recordings include:* Albums: Louvação, 1967; Gilberto Gil, 1968; Tropicália ou Panis et Circensis, 1968; Gilberto Gil, 1969; Expresso 2222, 1972; Barra 69, 1972; Temporada de Verão, 1974; Gilberto Gil ao Vivo, 1974; Gil Jorge Ogum Zangô, 1975; Refazenda, 1975; Doces Bárbaros, 1976; Refavela, 1977; Refestança, 1978; Antologia do Samba-Choro: Gilberto Gil e Germano Mathias, 1978; Gilberto Gil ao Vivo em Montreux, 1978; Nightingale, 1978; Realce, 1979; A Gente Precisa Ver o Luar, 1981; Brasil: João Gilberto Gil, Caetano e Bethânia, 1981; Um Banda Um, 1982; Extra, 1983; Quilombo, 1984; Vamos Fugir (with The Wailers), 1984; Raça Humana, 1984; Dia Dorim Noite Neon, 1985; Gilberto Gil em Concerto, 1987; Ao Vivo Em Tóquio, 1987; Soy Loco por Ti, América, 1987; O Eterno Deus Mu Dança, 1989; Parabolicamará, 1992; Tropicália 2, 1993; Gilberto Gil Unplugged, 1994; Quanta, 1997; O sol de Oslo, 1998; Ensaio Geral, 1999; Cidade do Salvador, 1999; O Viramundo, 1999; Gilberto Gil - Satisfação, 1999; Gil & Milton, 2000; São João Vivo, 2001; Kaya N'Gan Daya, 2002; contributions to various film soundtracks. *Honours:* Shell Prize, 1990. *Address:* c/o Ministry of Culture, Esplanada dos Ministérios, Bloco B, 3° andar, 70068-900 Brasília, DF, Brazil. *Website:* www.gilbertogil.com.br.

GILBERT, Gillian; b. 27 Jan. 1961, Manchester, England. Musician (keyboards, guitar). *Education:* Stockport Technical College, Stockport. *Career:* Musician, all-girl punk group, The Inadequates; Member, New Order, 1980–; The Other Two, 1991–; Tours: UK; Europe; USA; Far East; South America; Australia; New Zealand; Concerts include: Futurama Festival, Leeds, 1982; Glastonbury Festival, 1981, 1987; San Remo Festival, 1988; Reading Festival, 1989; Television includes: Documentary, Celebration, BBC, 1982; Rock Around The Clock, BBC, 1985. *Compositions:* (with Stephen Morris) numerous tracks for New Order; Television soundtracks: Making Out; Shooting Stars; Reportage. *Recordings:* Albums with New Order: Movement, 1981; Power Corruption and Lies, 1983; Peel Sessions, 1984, 1986; Brotherhood, 1986; Substance, 1987; Technique (No. 1, UK), 1989; BBC Radio 1 Live In Concert, 1992; Republic (No. 1, UK), 1993; Best of New Order, 1994; Rest of New Order, 1995; Blue Monday 95, 1995; Get Ready, 2001; Back To Mine (compilation), 2002; with The Other Two: The Other Two and You, 1994; Superhighways, 1999; also appears on: Technology Alert, 1996; Singles include: with New Order: Temptation, 1982; Blue Monday, 1983; Confusion, 1983; Thieves Like Us, 1984; The Perfect Kiss, 1985; Subculture, 1985; Shellshock, 1986; Bizarre Love Triangle, 1986; True Faith, 1987; Touched By The Hand of God, 1987; Fine Time, 1988; Round and Round, 1989; World In Motion (with England World Cup Football Squad) (No. 1, UK), 1990; How Does It Feel?, 1992; Regret, 1993; Ruined In A Day, 1993; World, 1993; Spooky, 1963, 1995; Crystal, 2001; 60 Miles An Hour, 2001; Here To Stay, 2002; with The Other Two: Tasty Fish, 1991; Selfish, 1993. *Website:* www.neworderweb.com.

GILBERT, Grant Mitchell; b. 11 Aug. 1957, London, England. Music Prod; Artistic Dir; Creative Prod; and Co-ordinator. 1 s, 2 d. *Education:* Implosion at The Roundhouse, Camden Town, 1970–72. *Career:* Co-founded Torch Song and Guerilla (Productions), with William Orbit and Laurie Mayer, 1983; Founded The Crucial Chemystry Corporation (CCC), 1988; Launched E Zee Possee and Jeremy Healy's DJ career; Set up CCC in Japan introducing British graphic designer Neville Brody and numerous House/Techno artists and DJ's; Co-producer of Glastonbury Festival Green Futures Field, 1993–. *Recordings:* Torch Song, with William Orbit and Laurie Maye; EZ Posse:

Everything Starts with An E; Producer, solar-powered CD, Deep Green: Music to Wake Up, featuring Solar Quest. *Honours:* Artistic Director of Green Futures Field Gaiasphere Stage, Glastonbury, 1995. *Current Management:* CCC. *Address:* CCC, PO Box 10, London N1 3RJ, England.

GILBERT, Paul; b. 6 Nov. 1966, Carbondale, Illinois, USA. Musician (guitar). *Career:* Guitarist, rock groups: Racer X, 1986–88; Mr Big, 1989–96. *Recordings:* Albums: with Racer X: Street Lethal, 1986; Second Heat, 1987; Extreme Volume... Live, 1988; with Mr Big: Mr Big, 1989; Lean Into It, 1991; Bump Ahead, 1993; Hey Man, 1996; Solo: King of Clubs, 1998; Flying Dog, 1999; Beehive Live, 1999; Alligator Farm, 2001; Singles include: Green-Tinted Sixties Mind; To Be With You. *Current Management:* Herbie Herbert Management, 2501 Third St, San Francisco, CA 94107, USA.

GILBERT, Simon; b. 23 May 1965, Stratford-Upon-Avon, England. Musician (drums). *Career:* Member, Suede, 1991–; Concerts include: Glastonbury Festival, 1993; Tours, UK; Europe; America; Japan; Television appearances include: Top of the Pops, BBC1; 12th BRIT Awards, Alexandra Palace; The Beat, ITV; Later With Jools Holland, BBC2; The Tonight Show, NBC. *Recordings:* Albums: Suede (No. 1, UK), 1993; Dog Man Star, 1994; Coming Up, 1996; Sci-Fi Lullabies, 1997; Head Music, 1999; A New Morning, 2002. Singles: The Drowners, 1992; Metal Mickey, 1992; Animal Nitrate, 1993; So Young, 1993; Stay Together, 1994; We Are The Pigs, 1994; The Wild Ones, 1994; New Generation, 1995; Trash, 1996; Beautiful Ones, 1996; Saturday Night, 1997; Lazy, 1997; Filmstar, 1997; Electricity, 1999; She's In Fashion, 1999; Everything Will Flow, 1999; Can't Get Enough, 1999; Positivity, 2002; Obsessions, 2002. *Honours:* Mercury Music Prize, 1993. *Current Management:* Interceptor Enterprises, The Greenhouse, 34–38 Provost St, London N1 7NG, England. *Address:* c/o Sony Music Entertainment, European Regional Office, 10 Great Marlborough St, London W1F 7LP, England. *Website:* www.suede.net.

GILBERTO, Astrud; b. 30 March 1940, Bahia, Brazil. Vocalist. m. Joao Gilberto. *Career:* Singer with husband Joao Gilberto (guitar) and Stan Getz (saxophone); Tours with Stan Getz. *Recordings:* Albums: The Astrud Gilberto Album, 1965; The Shadow of Your Smile, 1965; Once Upon A Summertime, 1971; Haven't Got Anything Better To Do, 1968; The Girl From Ipanema, 1977; Best Of, 1982; The Essential Astrud Gilberto, 1984; Look To The Rainbow, 1986; So and So, 1988; with James Last: Plus, 1986; Astrud Gilberto, 1996; Live in New York, 1999; Astrud Gilberto's Finest Hour, 2001; Hit single: The Girl From Ipanema, 1964. *Address:* c/o Subrena Artist Corpn, 330 W 56th St, Suite 18-M, New York, NY 10019, USA.

GILBERTO, Bebel; b. 1966, New York, NY, USA. Vocalist; Songwriter. *Career:* Daughter of Joao Gilberto and Miucha, niece of Chico Buarque; Made first appearance with mother and Stan Getz at Carnegie Hall, 1975; Appeared on children's TV in Brazil, late 1970s; Recorded vocals for various soundtracks, 1980s; Released solo EP, 1989; Returned to New York City, 1991; Became influenced by the dance club scene and started performing on the club circuit; Worked with musicians including: David Byrne; Arto Lindsay; Romero Lubambo; Co-wrote club hit Technova (with Towa Tei), 1995; Moved to London, 1997; Contributed vocals to Kenny G's recording of The Girl From Ipanema, 1999; Signed to Ziriguiboom and released first solo album, 2000. *Compositions:* Technova; Preciso Dize Que Te Amo; Tanto Tempo; August Day Song; Sem Contencao; Mais Feliz; Alguem; Lonely; Close Your Eyes. *Recordings:* Bebel Gilberto EP, 1986; Tanto Tempo, 2000; features on: Next Stop Wonderland OST; Classics In The Key of G, Kenny G. *Honours:* Primio Sharp Award, Best Single, Preciso Dize Que Te Amo, 1989. *Address:* c/o Ziriguiboom, Crammed Discs, 43 rue General Patton, Brussels, Belgium. *E-mail:* crammed@crammed.be. *Website:* www.bebelgilberto.com.

GILBERTO, João; b. 10 June 1931, Juazeiro, Bahia, Brazil. Vocalist; Musician (guitar), Songwriter. m. (1) Astrud Gilberto, (2) Miucha. *Career:* father of Bebel Gilberto; Started playing guitar, aged 14; On radio in Salvador by age 18; Joined the station's band Garotos Da Lua and moved with them to Rio de Janeiro; Left band to do live solo gigs in Porto Alegre; Signed record deal with Odeon and released Chega De Saudade, 1959; Upon success of this and 2 follow-up LPs, relocated to USA, 1961–80; Made classic bossa nova records with Stan Getz during this period; Still performing and making records, but prefers to life away from public glare. *Compositions include:* Bim Bom; Ho-Ba La La; Minha Saudade; Abraco No Bonfa. *Recordings:* Albums include: Chega De Saudade, 1959; O Amor O Sorriso E A Flor, 1960; João Gilberto, 1961; Getz/Gilberto, 1963; Getz/Gilberto #2, 1966; João Gilberto En Mexico, 1970; João Gilberto, 1973; Best of Two Worlds, 1976; Amoroso, 1977; João Gilberto Prado Pereira De Oliveira, 1980; Brasil, 1981; João Gilberto Live In Montreux, 1986; João, 1991; Eu Sei Que Vou Te Amar, 1994; João – Voz E Violao, 2000. *Address:* Universal Brasil, Rio de Janeiro, RJ, Brazil.

GILKYSON, Eliza; b. 24 Aug. 1950, Hollywood, California. Vocalist; Musician (piano, guitar); Songwriter. m. Reavis Moore, 23 Aug. 1981, 1 s., 1 d. *Career:* Tours with Ladysmith Black Mambazo; Dan Fogelberg; Arlo Guthrie; Andreas Vollenweider; Mary Chapin Carpenter; Television appearances: Austin City Limits; Showtime Concert Special; Film appearances: Two Lane Blacktop; Eight Minutes To Midnight. *Compositions:* Rosie Strike Back,

recorded by Roseanne Cash. *Recordings:* Albums: Pilgrims; Legends of Rainmaker; Through The Looking Glass; Eolian Minstrel, with Andreas Vollenweider; Undressed, 1994; Redemption Road, 1997; Misfits, 2000; Hard Times In Babylon, 2000; Lost And Found, 2002; Also appeared on albums by: Tom Paxton; Tom Russell. *Current Management:* Open Door Management. *Address:* PO Box 9858, Santa Fe, NM 87504, USA.

GILL, Andy; b. 1 Jan. 1957, Manchester, England. Musician (guitar); Composer. *Education:* BA Hons, Fine Art, Leeds University. *Career:* Formed Gang of Four, 1977. *Compositions include:* 8 Gang of Four albums; Solo album: Dispossession; Other recordings with: Anthony More; Louise Goffin; The Red Hot Chili Peppers; Almighty Hi Fi; Hugh Cornwell; Terri Nun, Berlin; Television includes: Zero Option, BBC1 (also arranger, producer, recording engineer); Pandora's Box, BBC1, 1992; The Westminster Programme, BBC2, 1992; Westminster Daily, BBC2, 1992; Westminster Live, BBC2, 1993; Scrutiny, BBC, 1993; Films: Karate Kid; Dogs In Space; The Last of England; Pump Up The Volume; Urgh! A Music War; Requiem Apache; Delinquent (composer, performed as Gang of Four). *Recordings:* As performer and producer: with Gang of Four: Entertainment, 1979; Solid Gold, 1981; Songs of The Free, 1982; Hard, 1983; Mall, 1991; Shrinkwrapped, 1995; At The Palace (live); Entertainment, 1995; 100 Flowers Bloom, 1998; Compilation: A Brief History of The 20th Century; As producer: with Red Hot Chili Peppers (Gold disc); What Hits!? (Platinum disc); with Busta Jones: Hands Are Shaking; with The Balancing Act: Curtains; Tracks for: The Most Beautiful Girl; Downey Mildew; Addie Brik; Miracle Legion, for film A Matter of Degrees; with MCD: Tantric Sex Disco, 1995; with Inastella: What Y'Gonna Do, 1995; with The Morgans: Tell Me What You Taste EP; for Michael Hutchence: Michael Hutchence, 1999; Diversity album in production. *Membership:* PRS. *Current Management:* Polar Union; Sanctuary Group. *Address:* The Colonnades, 82 Bishops Bridge Rd, London W2 6BB, England.

GILL, Janis; b. 1 March 1955, Torrance, California, USA. Vocalist; Musician (guitar). m. Vince Gill, 1 d. *Education:* Studied Music Theory. *Career:* Member, duo Sweethearts of The Rodeo with sister Kristine Arnold; Signed to Columbia Records; Sugar Hill Records; Winners, Wrangler Country Showcase, 1985. *Recordings:* Sweethearts of The Rodeo, 1986; Anthology, 2000; Top 20 hits include: Since I Found You; Midnight Girl/Sunset Town; Satisfy You; Chains of Gold, 1987; Rodeo Waltz, 1993; Video: Things Will Grow. *Honours:* CMA's Vocal Duo, 9 consecutive years; Music City News, Best Vocal Duo; TNN Viewers Choice Award, Favourite Group; NAIRD Award, Best Country Album, 1994. *Current Management:* M Hitchcock Management. *Address:* PO Box 159007, Nashville, TN 37214, USA.

GILL, Vince (Vincent Grant); b. 5 April 1957, Norman, Oklahoma, USA. Country Vocalist; Musician (guitar); Songwriter. m. Janis Oliver. *Career:* Member, Mountain Smoke (as a schoolboy); Member, Bluegrass Alliance, 1975–79; Member, Pure Prairie League, 1979–81; Member, Rodney Crowell's band, The Cherry Bombs, 1982; Solo artiste, 1983–. *Compositions include:* Never Knew Lonely; Look At Us (co-written with Max Barnes). *Recordings:* Hit singles: When I Call Your Name, duet with Patti Loveless; Pocket Full of Gold; Liza Jane; Look At Us; I Still Believe In You (US Country No. 1); Take Your Memory With You); A Little More Love; Albums: with Pure Prairie League: Can't Hold Back, 1979; Firin' Up, 1980; Something In The Night, 1981; Solo album: Turn Me Loose, 1983; The Things That Matter, 1984; Vince Gill, 1985; The Way Back Home, 1987; When I Call Your Name, 1989; Pocket Full of Gold, 1991; I Never Knew Lonely, 1992; I Still Believe In You, 1992; Let There Be Peace on Earth, 1993; When Love Finds You, 1994; The Essential, 1996; The Key, 1998; Let's Make Sure We Say Goodbye, 2000; Contributor: Patti Loveless albums; On Every Street, Dire Straits; recordings by Alison Brown; George Jones; Lyle Lovett; Reba McEntire; Mark O'Connor; Faith Hill; Trisha Yearwood. *Honours:* CMA Single of the Year, with Patti Loveless; CMA Male Vocalist of Year, 1991, 1992; Song of the Year, Look At Us, 1992. *Current Management:* Fitzgerald Hartley Co, 1212 16th Ave S, Nashville, TN 37203, USA.

GILLAN, Ian; b. 19 Aug. 1945, Hounslow, London, England. Vocalist. m. Bronwen, 21 July 1984, 1 d. *Career:* Lead singer, rock bands: Episode Six; Deep Purple; Gillan; Black Sabbath; Gillan and Glover (with Roger Glover); Singer on over 20 albums, selling in excess of 100m. copies; Numerous world-wide tours, television and radio appearances; Singer, Jesus Christ Superstar. *Compositions include:* Woman From Tokyo; Smoke On The Water; Black Night; Child In Time. *Recordings:* Albums include: with Episode Six: Here There and Everywhere, 1966; with Deep Purple: In Rock, 1969; Best Of, 1970; Machine Head, 1972; Who Do We Think We Are, 1973; 24 Carat Purple, 1975; Perfect Strangers, 1984; Purpendicular, 1996; with Gillan: Child In Time, 1976; Gillan, 1978; Mr Universe, 1979; Glory Road, 1980; Future Shock, 1981; Double Trouble, 1981; Magic, 1982; with Black Sabbath: Born Again, 1983; with Gillan and Glover: Accidentally On Purpose, 1988; with Ritchie Blackmore: Rainbow; No Smoke Without Fire, 2000; with The Javelins: Sole Agency and Representations, 2001. *Current Management:* Phil Banfield, Performing Artistes Network. *Address:* No. 1 Water Lane, Camden Town, London NW1 8NZ, England.

GILLESPIE, Bobby; b. 22 June 1964, Scotland. Vocalist. *Career:* Drummer, Jesus and Mary Chain, 1984; Singer, Primal Scream, 1984–; Performances include: Miners Benefit Trust Concert, Sheffield Arena, 1992. *Recordings:* Singles include: All Fall Down, 1985; Crystal Crescent, 1986; Ivy Ivy Ivy, 1989; Loaded, 1990; Come Together, 1990; Higher Than The Sun, 1991; Don't Fight It Feel It, 1991; Dixie-Narco (EP), 1992; Rocks/Funky Jam, 1994; Jailbird, 1994; Cry Myself Blind, 1994; Kowalski, 1997; Star, 1997; Burning Wheel, 1997; Swastikka Eyes, 1999; Kill All Hippies, 2000; Accelerator, 2000; Miss Lucifer, 2002. Albums: Psychocandy, 1985; Sonic Flower Groove, 1987; Primal Scream, 1989; Screamadelica, 1991; Give Out But Don't Give Up, 1994; Let Your Dim Lights Shine, 1995; Vanishing Point, 1997; Echo Dek, 1997; XTRMNTR, 2000; Evil Heat, 2002; Contributor, Dope Dogs, Parliament/Funkadelic, 1994; Surrender, The Chemical Brothers, 1999; The Contino Sessions, Death In Vegas, 1999; Bow Down To The Exit Sign, David Holmes, 2000; Get Ready, New Order, 2001. *Honours:* Mercury Music Prize, Screamadelica, 1992. *Current Management:* Scream Heights Management. *Website:* www.primalscream.net.

GILLESPIE, Dana; b. 30 March 1949, England. Vocalist; Songwriter; *Recordings:* 30 albums released; Foolish Seasons, 1967; Box of Surprises, 1968; Jesus Christ Superstar, 1972; Weren't Born a Man, 1973; Ain't Gonna Play No Fiddle, Mojo Blues Band, 1974; Blue Job, 1982; Solid Romance, 1984; Below The Belt, 1984; It Belongs To Me, 1985; Move Your Body Close To Me, 1986; I'm a Woman, 1986; Hot News', 1987; Amor, 1990; Blues It Up, 1990; Where Blue Begins, 1991; Boogie Woogie Nights, 1991; Big Boy, with Joachim Palden, 1992; Methods of Release, 1993; Andy Warhol, 1994; Blue One, 1994; One to One, 1995; Hot Stuff, 1995; Have I Got Blues for You, 1996; Mustique Blues Festivals, 1996; Inner View, 1996; Cherry Pie, with Big Jay McNeeley, 1997; Jan Mustique Bluesfest, 1997; Back to the Blues, 1999; Experienced, 2000. *Honours:* Voted Top British Female Blues Vocalist, 1993, 1994, 1995, 1996.

GILLEY, Mickey Leroy; b. 9 March 1936, Natchez, Mississippi; Country vocalist, Musician (piano, guitar); Songwriter; Actor. *Career:* Local record success, 1960s; Country hits on labels: Playboy; Epic; Airborne Records, 1974–89; Owner of Gilley's night club, Pasadena, Texas with Sherwood Cryer, 1971–89; Club featured in film Urban Cowboy with Gilley in cameo role; Opened own theatre Branson, Missouri, early 1990s; TV appearances include: Murder She Wrote; Dukes of Hazzard; Fantasy Island; Cousin of country vocalist Jerry Lee Lewis and evangelist Rev Jimmy Swaggart. *Recordings include:* I Overlooked An Orchid, 1974; Window Up Above, 1975; She's Pulling Me Back Again, 1977; Lonely Nights, 1981; Paradise Tonight (with Charly McClain), 1983; Albums: Room Full of Roses, City Lights, 1974; Overnight Sensation, 1975; Gilley's Smokin', Gilley's Greatest Hits Vol. 1, 1976. *Address:* c/o The Mickey Gilley Theater, 3455 W Hwy 76, Branson, MO 65616, USA.

GILLINGHAM, Charlie; b. 12 Jan. 1960, Torrance, CA, USA. Musician (keyboards). *Career:* Member, Counting Crows; Numerous headlining tours and TV appearances including MTV. *Recordings:* Singles: Round Here, 1994; Mr Jones, 1994; Rain King, 1994; Angels of the Silence (live), 1996; Albums: August and Everything After, 1993; Recovering the Satellites, 1996; Across a Wire: Live In New York, 1998; Long December, 1999; Daylight Fading, 1999; Hard Candy, 2002.

GILLIS, Verna; b. 14 June 1942, New York, USA. Artist Man; Record Prod. m. Brad Graves, 1 May 1965. *Education:* PhD, Ethnomusicology. *Career:* Host, Radio Programme, WBAI, 1975–83; Founder, Director, Soundscape Performance Space, New York City, 1979–85; Record Producer; Artist Manager for: Youssou N'dour, Yomo Toro, Salif Keita, Malouma Mint Maideh, Habib Faye, Ivan Rubenstein-Gillis. *Publications:* DIW, Live From Soundscape. *Honours:* Woman of the Year, 1975. *Current Management:* Roswell Rudd/Raquel Hithet. *Address:* 799 Greenwich St, New York, NY 10014–1843, USA.

GILMOUR, David; b. 6 March 1946, Cambridge, England. Vocalist; Musician (guitar); Composer. m. Polly Samson, 1994, 8 c. *Career:* Member, Pink Floyd, 1968–; Performances include: Rome International Pop Festival, 1968; Hyde Park, London, 1968; Bath Festival, 1970; Montreux Festival, Switzerland, 1971; Pink Floyd Live At Pompeii (recorded for film release), 1972; Knebworth Festival, 1975; Guitarist with Bryan Ferry, Live Aid, Wembley, 1985; Played at Colombian Volcano Appeal, Royal Albert Hall, 1986; Discovered Kate Bush, Executive Producer for her album The Kick Inside; Solo show, Royal Festival Hall, 2001. *Recordings:* Albums: with Pink Floyd: A Saucerful Of Secrets, 1968; More (film soundtrack), 1969; Ummagumma, 1969; Atom Heart Mother (No. 1, UK), 1970; Relics, 1971; Meddle, 1971; Obscured By Clouds, 1972; The Dark Side Of The Moon (No. 1, USA), 1973; Wish You Were Here, (No. 1, UK and USA) 1975; Animals, 1977; The Wall (No. 1, USA), 1979; The Final Cut (No. 1, UK), 1983; A Momentary Lapse Of Reason, 1987; The Delicate Sound Of Thunder, 1988; Shine On (box set), 1992; The Division Bell (No. 1, UK and USA), 1994; Pulse (No. 1, UK and USA), 1995; Echoes: The Very Best of Pink Floyd, 2001; Solo: David Gilmour, 1978; About Face, 1984; Live In Concert, 2002; Appears on: I'll Sleep When I'm Dead, 1996; Very Best of John Martyn, 1998; Madcap Laughs, 1999; Bête

Noire, Bryan Ferry; Slave To The Rhythm, Grace Jones; So Red The Rose, Arcadia; Tribute To Muddy Waters. Singles include: Another Brick In The Wall (No. 1, UK and USA), 1979; When The Tigers Break Free, 1982; Not Now John, 1983; Learning To Fly, 1987; On The Turning Away, 1987; 1 Slip, 1988; Take It Back, 1994; High Hopes, 1994; Contributor, film soundtrack of Zabriskie Point, 1970. *Honours:* Silver Clef Award, Nordoff-Robbins Music Therapy, 1980; MTV Music Video Award, 1988; Ivor Novello Award, Outstanding Contribution To British Music, 1992; Q Award, Best Live Act, 1994; Inducted into Rock and Roll Hall of Fame, 1996; Grammy Award, Producer in Best Instrumental Performance for Marooned. *Current Management:* Steve O'Rourke, EMKA Productions Ltd, 43 Portland Rd, Holland Park, London W11 4LJ, England.

GILTRAP, Gordon; b. 6 April 1948, East Peckham, Tonbridge, Kent, England. Musician (guitar). *Career:* Played college, folk club and university circuit; Regular tours, with Ric Sanders; Solo work; Duets with John Renbourn and Juan Martin; Collaborations with Martin Taylor. *Compositions include:* Heartsong, theme to Holiday programme, BBC TV, 1980s; Other television music for: Wish You Were Here; The Open University; Hold The Back Page, 1985. *Recordings:* Albums: Early Days, 1968; Gordon Giltrap, 1968; Portrait, 1969; Testament of Time, 1971; Giltrap, 1973; Visionary, 1976; Perilous Journey, 1977; Fear of The Dark, 1978; Performance, 1980; The Peacock Party, 1981; Live, 1981; Airwaves, 1982; Elegy, 1987; A Midnight Clear, 1988; Gordon Giltrap – Guitarist, 1988; Mastercraftsman, 1989; One To One, with Ric Sanders, 1989; A Matter of Time, with Martin Taylor, 1991; Live at the BBC, 1995; Music for the Small Screen, 1995; Live At Oxford, 2000; Compilations: The Very Best of Gordon Giltrap, 1988; The Best of Gordon Giltrap – All The Hits Plus More, 1991; Giltrap And Taylor, 2002. *Publications:* Contributor, Guitarist magazine. *Current Management:* NE Music Management, Priory House, 55 Lawe Rd, South Shields, Tyne and Wear NE33 2AL, England.

GIMENES, Raymond François; b. 12 Dec. 1939, Fes, Morocco. Arranger; Conductor; Prod; Musician (guitar); Composer. m. Beatrice Belthoise, 11 Sept. 1987, 2 s., 1 d. *Education:* Sciences at University; First Prize for Violin; Studied harmony, counterpoint, fuga and composition. *Career:* Backing guitarist for Petula Clark, Dean Martin, Shirley Bassey; Musical Director for Sacha Distel, Henri Salvador, Charles Aznavour; Solo guitarist for Paul Mauriat Orchestra, including US tour, 1971; Japanese tours, 1971, 1986, 1988, 1990. *Recordings:* 4 albums as leader of Guitars Unlimited; As guitarist: Wings, Michael Colombier; Slide Hampton with Jazz Big Band; Hajime Mizoguchi; Dionne Warwick In Paris. *Publications:* Orchestration for Paganini's Sonata for Viola and Symphonic Orchestra. *Honours:* Award for commercial, Radio Spot, 1989. *Membership:* SACEM; SPEDIDAM; ADAMI. *Current Management:* Charley Marouani, 37 rue Marbeuf, 75008 Paris, France. *Address:* 185 bis rue Paul Doumer, 78510 Triel sur Seine, France.

GINAPÉ, Viviane; b. 30 April 1955, Paris, France. Vocalist. m. Lionel Bouton, 12 Nov. 1988. *Education:* CNRBB, Supérieur. *Career:* Singer with: Urban/Sax; Claude Bolling; Denis Badault; Yochk 'O Seffer; François Mechali. *Recordings:* Fraction Sur Le Temps, Urban Sax, 1989; Opéra Jazz François Mechali, L'Archipel, 1995; Café, Viviane Ginapé Quartet, 1999. *Current Management:* Charlotte Productions. *Address:* 1 rue de la Dhuis, 75020 Paris, France.

GINGER, (David Walls); b. 1964, South Shields, Tyne and Wear, England. Rock Vocalist; Songwriter; Musician (guitar). *Career:* Member, rock groups, The Quireboys; The Throbs; Founder, The Wildhearts, 1991–; Numerous tours, UK; Europe; Ireland; Support tours with Pantera; Manic Street Preachers; The Almighty; Suicidal Tendencies; Performances include: Monsters of Rock Festival, Castle Donington, 1994; Reading Festival, 1994. *Recordings:* Albums: with The Quireboys: A Bit of What You Fancy, 1989; with The Wildhearts: Earth Vs The Wildhearts, 1993; Fishing For Luckies, 1994; P H U Q, 1995; The Best of The Wildhearts, 1996; Endless, Nameless, 1997; Singles with The Wildhearts: Mondo Akimbo A-Go-Go (EP), 1992; Don't Be Happy... Just Worry (EP), 1992; TV (EP), 1993; Suckerpunch, 1994; Caffeine Bomb, 1994; I Wanna Go Where The People Go, 1995; Geordie In Wonderland; Just In Lust, 1995; Sick of Drugs, 1996; Red Light Green Light EP, 1996; Anthem, 1997; Urge, 1997; with Clam Abuse: Stop Thinking, 1999; with Supershit 666: Supershit 666, 2000; Solo single: I'm A Lover, Not A Fighter, 2001; Solo album: Grevious Acoustic Behaviour: Live At The 12 Bar, 2001. *Current Management:* Tribal Management, 7 Vicarage Rd, Wednesbury, West Midlands WS10 9BA, England.

GINGER SPICE. See: HALLIWELL, Geri.

GINMAN, Lennart Vidar; b. 2 March 1960, Copenhagen, Denmark. Composer; Musician (double bass). m. Lisbeth Maria Hansen, 31 Dec. 1987, 2 d. *Education:* Private studies, Copenhagen, New York. *Career:* Began professional career around 1985; Now one of most sought after bassists in Denmark; Tours with: Kenny Werner; Harry 'Sweet' Edison; Al Foster; Lee Konitz; Cæcilie Norby. *Recordings:* 1991, Lennart Ginman/Kirk Lightsey; Blachman Introduces Standard Jazz and Rap, Thomas Blachman; Cæcilie Norby: Cæcilie Norby, 1994; My Corner of the Sky, 1997; Beatin' Bop, Page

One; Jens Winther, Scorpio Dance, 1994. *Honours:* Composers Honour Award, 1992, DJBFA. *Address:* C F Richsvej 80, 2000 Frederiksberg, Denmark.

GIROT, Pierre; b. 11 May 1936, Neuilly, France. Jazz Musician (guitar). m. 30 June 1960, 2 d. *Education:* Académie de Guitare de Paris; Student of Henri Salavador. *Career:* Accompanied Josephine Baker, Charles Trenet, Worked with jazz artists: Trio Arvanitas; Guy Lafitte; Lou Bennett; Bill Coleman; Hal Singer; International Festivals include: Antibes Juan-les-Pins; Zurich; San Sebastian; Souillac; Marciac; Montpellier; Clermont-Ferrand; French radio and television. *Compositions:* Flamenco Blues, 1996; Melancoliquement Vôtre, Mister JC, 1996; Birdy, 1996. *Recordings:* Album: Jazz and Brazilian guitar with Quatuor Galilé. *Publications:* Festival 92; Birdy; Clin d'Oeil, 1998. *Honours:* Third prize, Festival of Juan-les-Pins, 1960. *Membership:* SACEM; SPEDIDAM. *Address:* Chemin de Fadat, 19100 Brive, France.

GIUFFRE, James P. (Jimmy); b. 26 April 1921, Dallas, Texas, USA. Musician (saxophones, flutes, clarinet); Composer. m. Juanita Odjenar Giuffre, 22 June 1961. *Education:* BA, North Texas State; Private Studies with Dr Wesley La Violette. *Career:* Lincoln Center; Carnegie Hall; Numerous European tours; Television and filmscores (art films, 1 feature). *Compositions:* Four Brothers; Train; The River. *Recordings:* Free Fall; The Jimmy Giuffre 3. *Publications:* Jazz Phrasing and Interpretation. *Honours:* Guggenheim Fellowship, National Endowment of The Arts. *Membership:* Broadcast Music Inc. *Current Management:* Thomas Stowsand, Soudades Tourneen, Austria.

GIUSSANI, Claudio D. C; b. 19 Sept. 1969, London, England. Musician (keyboards, percussion, djembe); Programmer; Engineer; Remixer. *Education:* BEng, University of Warwick, Coventry. *Career:* Formed band Urban Shakedown (making new breakbeat music), 1990; Formed Union Jack (trance music), 1992, 93; Regular tours, USA; Canada; Russia; Europe; PA in clubs. *Recordings:* With Urban Shakedown: Some Justice (Top 20 hit); Bass Shake; With Union Jack: Album: There Will Be No Armageddon, 2001; Single: Two Full Moons and A Trout; Productions include: Speed Limit 140 BPM, 1994; All Mixed Up, 1995; Dimensions in Ambience, 1996; Platipus Records Ultimate Dream, 1996; Journey into Ambient Groove, 1996; Quando Un Musicista, 1999. *Membership:* PRS; MCPS; PPL. *Current Management:* Platipus Records.

GJERSTAD, Frode; b. 24 March 1948, Stavanger, Norway. Musician (saxophone). m. Judith Sorvik, 24 March 1983, 1 s., 1 d. *Career:* Worked with: John Stevens; Johnny Dyani; Kent Carter; Billy Bang; Bobby Bradford; Borah Bergman; Derrek Bailey; Paul Rutherford; Terje Isungset; Audun Kleive; Pierre Dorge; Bjorn Kjellemyr; Peter Brötzmann; William Parker; Rashid Baker; Harold Drake. *Recordings:* Backwards and Forwards, 1983; Okhela, 1984; Ness, 1987; Way It Goes, 1988; Accent, 1989; In Time Was, 1991; Less More, 1992; Enten Eller, 1993; Sunshine, 1996; Seeing New York from the Ear, 1996; Last Detail, 1996; Remember to Forget, 1998; Borcalis, 1998; Ikosa Mure, 1998; ISM, 1998; Invisible Touch, 1999; Ultima, 1999. *Honours:* Jazz Musician of the Year, Norway, 1997. *Current Management:* Circulasione Totale. *Address:* Gansveien 15, 4017 Stavanger, Norway.

GLADWELL, Robert; b. 16 June 1950, Colchester, England. Musician (guitar, bass); Journalist. Married, divorced, twice; 4 s., 1 d. *Education:* Martin Lukins School of Music (studied guitar). *Career:* Session guitarist, clinician, worked for Gibson Guitars for 10 years; Own guitar workshop, building, customising guitars; Toured extensively with Steve Harley and Cockney Rebel; Currently touring, recording with Suzi Quatro, 1990s–. *Recordings:* with Twink: Mr Rainbow, 1990; with Steve Harley: Yes You Can, 1992; Christmas All Stars Album, 1994; with Suzi Quatro: Free The Butterfly, 1995; What Goes Around, 1996. *Publications:* Dr Robert column, guitarist magazine, 11 years; Guitar Electronics and Customising, book, 1995. *Membership:* Musicians' Union. *Current Management:* Jive Music Management.

GLADWIN, Tom; b. 1973, England. Musician (bass). *Career:* Member, Shed Seven; Obtained major label record deal; Numerous live and television appearances. *Recordings:* Singles: Mark, 1994; Dolphin, 1994; Speakeasy, 1994; Ocean Pie, 1994; Where Have You Been Tonight?, 1995; Getting Better, 1996; Going For Gold, 1996; Bully Boy, 1996; On Standby, 1996; Chasing Rainbows, 1996; She Left Me On Friday, 1998; The Heroes, 1998; The Devil in Your Shoes, 1998; Disco Down, 1999; Cry For Help, 2001; Albums: Change Giver, 1996; A Maximum High, 1996; Let It Ride, 1998; Going for Gold: The Best of Shed Seven, 1999; Truth Be Told, 2001. *Website:* www.shedseven.com.

GLAMOUR GOLD. See: KRUST.

GLASSER, Adam; b. 20 Sept. 1955, Cambridge, England. Musician (keyboards, chromatic harmonica). m. Vivien Roberts, 21 May 1994, 1 d. *Education:* BA (Hons) English and European Literature, Warwick University. *Career:* MD, The Manhattan Brothers (SA Township legends); Toured, recorded with DuDu Pukwana; Tour and television with Martha Reeves and The Vandellas; Concerts with Jimmy Witherspoon; Appeared in Musicians In Exile, Ch4; SA Blues, BBC2; Performed with Joe Zawinul Syndicate; Harmonica with Eurythmics, Sting, BBC Concert Orchestra. *Recordings:*

August One on Zila '86 album; Title music for Battle of The Bikes, Ch4, 1994; Talking Woods, with Thebe Lipere; Pedalmarch (for Jazz Sextet) features on continental bike racing in Cycle Sport; Filmscore, Hard Rain, played harmonica with Toots Thielemans; Film scores with London Philharmonic Orchestra: Harmonica on Chinese Coffee, 1998; EXistenZ, 1998; with Dominic Alldis: If Love Were All, 2000; with Dominic Miller: Second Nature, 2000. *Honours:* Winner, Peter Whittingham Award, Musicians' Benevolent Society, 1997. *Membership:* Musicians' Union; Asscn Internat des Journalistes du Cyclisme.

GLATZL, Friedrich; b. 17 March 1956, Gmünd, Austria. Musician (guitar); Backing Vocalist. m. Marianne, 3 Dec. 1982, 1 s., 1 d. *Education:* VSA; HSA; Sales Manager. *Career:* Founder member, Giant Blonder, 1972–83; Guest musician on: Blues Pumpm Live With Friends Tour, 1982; Member: Blues Pumpm, 1983–; Television, radio tours, most of Eastern Europe. *Recordings:* Albums: with Giant Blonder: Giant Blonder; Rock and Blues 2; Single: with Johannes Müller Blues Zappa and Pumpm Fritz: Der Letzte Zug; with Blues Pumpm: Albums: Live With Friends, 1985; The 5th Ten Years Jubilee, 1987; Live At Utopia, 1988; Birthday, 1991; Live In Vienna, 1992; The 5th, 1992; Living Loving Riding, 1994; Singles: Train and Quick Shoes, 1985; Men From Milwaukee, 1993. *Honours:* Silbernes Ehrenzeichen, 1992; Third Best Blues Album Ö3, Rot-Weiss-Rote Critics Poll, Live In Vienna, 1992. *Membership:* ALM; AUME; LSG. *Current Management:* RGG Management, Peter Steinbach.

GLAZER, Tom (Thomas Zacariah); b. 2 Sept. 1914, Philadelphia, Pennsylvania, USA. Folk Vocalist; Writer; Composer. m. Miriam Reed Eisenberg, 25 June 1944, divorced, 2 s. *Education:* City College of New York, 1938–41. *Career:* Recording artist, 1946–; Folk singer. *Compositions:* Melody of Love, 1956; Till We Two Are One; A Worried Man; Skokiaan; On Top of Spaghetti; Songs and Score, Film, A Face in the Crowd. *Recordings:* First artist to record Greensleeves and Twelve Days of Christmas. *Publications:* Tom Glazer's Treasury of Songs for Children, 1963; America The Beautiful, 1987; Limited edition selections of poems. *Honours:* Several Peabody Awards for Radio and TV Shows. *Membership:* ASCAP; AFTRA; American Federation of Musicians; Screen Actors' Guild; Songwriters' Guild of America. *Address:* PO Box 165, Scarborough, NY 10510, USA.

GLEESON, David Sean; b. 3 June 1968, Newcastle, Australia. Vocalist. *Education:* Music, Higher School Certificate. *Career:* Played with local rock band Aspect, 1985; Played with The Screaming Jets, 1989–; 3 British tours, 2 US tours, 2 European tours; Toured with the Quireboys and Thunder. *Recordings:* Albums with The Screaming Jets: All For One; Tear of Thought; The Screaming Jets; Engineer on albums by: Mariah Carey; Kenny G; Michael Bolton; Céline Dion; Jennifer Lopez; Linda Ronstadt; Savage Garden; Destiny's Child, Jessica Simpson. *Current Management:* c/o Aaron Chugg, Grant Thomas Management, PO Box 176, Potts Point, NSW 2011, Australia.

GLEN, Alan; b. Wupperthal, Germany. Musician (harmonica, guitar). m. Jacqueline Lewis, 31 May 1975, 3 s. *Career:* with Nine Below Zero: Sting, tour of Spain, Scandinavia, 1993; Toured with and supported Eric Clapton, Scandinavia, 1993, Royal Albert Hall, 1994; ZZ Top; Joe Cocker, 1994; Alvin Lee, 1994; Played and recorded with: Alannah Myles, Canadian tour, 1994; Alvin Lee, US tour, 1994; Television, radio appearances: USA; Canada; Italy; Sweden; Switzerland; France; Hungary; Austria; Germany; Britain; Member, Little Axe, 1996–97; Member, Yardbirds, 1998–. *Compositions:* Bad Town Blues, film soundtrack for Circuitry Man II; Another Kind of Love; It's Nothing New; Crazy Life; A Little Bit More; Tell Me The Truth. *Recordings:* Albums: with Nine Below Zero: Off The Hook, 1993; Best of Nine Below Zero, 1994; Hot Music For A Cold Night, 1994; Ice Station Zebro, 1995; Singles: with Nine Below Zero: Soft Touch, 1993; Workshy, 1993; with Alannah Myles: Never Loved A Man, 1994; Down By The River, 1995; with Little Axe: Slow Fuse, 1996; Hard Grind, 2002; with Dr Feelgood, On the Road Again, 1996; with Junior Delgado, Reasons, 1999; with Dub Syndicate: Acres of Space, 2001; with The Yardbirds: Birdland, 2003. *Membership:* BAC&S; Musicians' Union. *Current Management:* Mickey Modern, Arctic King Management. *Address:* 72 Woods Rd, London SE15 2SW, England. *E-mail:* glenalan9@aol.com. *Website:* www.hants.org.uk/barcodes.

GLENNIE, James (Jim); b. 10 Oct. 1963, Manchester, England. Musician (bass guitar); Songwriter. *Career:* Founder mem., James, 1982–2001; Numerous tours, festival dates and television appearances; Farewell 'Getting Away With It' concert, Manchester Evening News Arena, Dec. 2001. *Recordings:* Albums: Stutter, 1986; Strip Mine, 1988; One Man Clapping, 1989; Gold Mother, 1990; Seven, 1992; Laid, 1993; Wah Wah, 1994; Whiplash, 1997; The Best Of James, 1998; Millionaires, 1999; B-Sides Ultra, 2001; Pleased To Meet You, 2001; Getting Away With It, 2002. Singles incl.: Jimone (EP), 1983; Jim 2 (EP), 1985; How Was It For You, 1990; Come Home, 1990; Lose Control, 1990; Sit Down, 1991; Sound, 1991; Born Of Frustration, 1992; Ring The Bells, 1992; Seven, 1992; Sometimes, 1993; Laid, 1993; Say Something/Jam J, 1994; She's A Star, 1997; Tomorrow, 1997; Waltzing Along, 1997; Destiny Calling, 1998; Runaground, 1998; Sit Down (remix), 1998; I Know What I'm Here For, 1999; Fred Astaire, 1999; We're Gonna Miss You,

1999; Getting Away With It (All Messed Up), 2001. *Current Management:* Rudge Management, 1 Star St, London W2 1QD, England.

GLENNIE-SMITH, Nicholas Hugh; b. 3 Oct. 1951, Kingston-On-Thames, England. Composer; Musician (keyboards); Engineer. m. Janet, 21 Dec. 1974, 2 s., 2 d. *Education:* Chorister, New College Oxford; Trinity College, London. *Career:* Tours with: David Essex; Randy Edelman; Glen Campbell; Classic Rock; Roger Waters, The Wall, Berlin. *Compositions:* Two if by Sea, 1995; The Rock, 1996; The Preacher's Wife, 1996; Fire Down Below, 1997; Home Alone 3, 1997; The Man in the Iron Mask, 1998; Lion King II: Simba's Pride, 1998; The Secret Adventures of Jules Verne, 1999. *Recordings:* Albums: with Cliff Richard: I'm No Hero, 1980; Wired For Sound, 1981; Silver, 1983; with Leo Sayer: Living In A Fantasy, 1980; Strange Day In Berlin, 1983; with Nik Kershaw: Human Racing, 1984; with Tina Turner: Private Dancer, 1984; Break Every Rule, 1986; Foreign Affair, 1989; with The Adventures: Theodore and Friends, 1985; Sea of Love, 1988; with Beltane Fire: Different Breed, 1986; Also appeared on albums by: Phil Collins; Paul McCartney; Roger Waters; Roger Daltrey; Katrina and The Waves; Five Star; Barbara Dickson; Film soundtracks: The Lion King; K2; Point of No Return; Calendar Girl; Con Air; Cool Runnings; House of The Spirits; I'll Do Anything; Monkey Trouble; Renaissance Man; Beyond Rangoon; Bad Boys; Crimson Tide; 9 Months. *Honours:* Grammy, as Musician, What's Love Got To Do With It. *Membership:* ASCAP; PRS. *Current Management:* Kraft Benjamin Engel Management, California. *Address:* Belle Haven 275, James River Rd, Scottsville, VA 24590, USA.

GLITTER, Gary, (Paul Gadd); b. 8 May 1944, Banbury, Oxfordshire, England. Singer; Entertainer; Songwriter. *Career:* Leader, skiffle group, Paul Russell and the Rebels; Worked in Germany as Paul Raven; Relaunched career as glam rock singer, Gary Glitter, 1971–; Numerous concerts, television appearances; Presenter, Night Network, 1988; Toured USA in Quadrophenia with The Who, 1996. *Compositions:* Numerous hits co-written with Mike Leander. *Recordings:* Albums: Glitter, 1972; Touch Me, 1973; Remember Me This Way, 1974; Always Yours, 1975; GG, 1975; I Love You Love, 1977; Silver Star, 1978; The Leader, 1980; Boys Will Be Boys, 1984; Leader II, 1991; Numerous compilations. Singles include: Rock 'N' Roll Part 2, 1972; I Didn't Know I Loved You (Till I Saw You Rock 'N' Roll), 1972; Do You Wanna Touch Me, 1973; Hello Hello I'm Back Again, 1973; I'm The Leader Of The Gang, (No. 1, UK), 1973; I Love You Love Me Love, (No. 1, UK), 1973; Always Yours (No. 1, UK), 1974; Remember Me This Way, 1974; Oh Yes You're Beautiful, 1974; Love Like You And Me, 1975; Doin' Alright With The Boys, 1975; Another Rock 'N' Roll Christmas, 1984. *Publications:* Leader–The Autobiography of Gary Glitter, 1991. *Honours:* Nordoff Robins Lifetime Achievement Award, 1997; BASCA Gold Badge Award, 1997. *Current Management:* Jef Hanlon Management Ltd. *Address:* 1 York St, London W1H 1PZ, England.

GLOCKLER, Nigel Ian; b. 24 Jan. 1953, Hove, Sussex, England. Musician (drums, percussion). *Education:* Brighton College. *Career:* Member: The Associates, 1980–82; Toyah, 1980–81; Saxon, 1981–87; GTR, 1987–88; Saxon, 1989–; Tours with Toyah, Saxon; Television and radio appearances. *Recordings:* Albums include: with Associates: The Affectionate Punch; Sulk; with Toyah: Anthem; with Saxon: The Eagle Has Landed; Power and The Glory; Crusader; Solid Ball of Rock; Dogs of War; Forever Free; Rock The Nations; Innocence Is No Excuse; Unleash the Beast; with Asia: Aqua; Japanese film soundtrack album; Archiva; with Steve Howe: Turbulenz; Guitar Speak; with Tony Martin: Back Where I Belong; with Fastway: Bad Bad Girls. *Membership:* PRS; MCPS; Musicians' Union. *Current Management:* Blackmail Management. *Address:* 60 Cleveland Rd, New Malden, Surrey KT3 3QJ, England.

GLOJNARIC, Silvestar; b. 2 Dec. 1936, Ladislavec, Croatia. m. Ana Jurisic, 7 July 1962, 1 s., 1 d. *Education:* Zagreb Music Academy, Composition and Theory Department. *Career:* Tours, concerts, Zagreb Jazz Quartet, Europe; Tours with Zagreb Radio Big Band, Europe including Russia; Television, radio appearances with various orchestras as composer, arranger, conductor; Most European Jazz Festivals. *Recordings:* Zagreb Big Band with: Art Farmer; Slide Hampton; Stan Getz; J Griffin; SFB Big Band, Berlin; NDR Big Band, Hamburg; Ljubljana Big Band; John Lewis, A Mangelsdorf: Animal Dance; Buck Clayton, BJ Turner: Feel So Fine; Georgie Fame. *Membership:* Croatian Composers' Asscn. *Current Management:* Silverstar Glojnaric. *Address:* Cujetno Naseltje 3, 41430 Samobar, Croatia.

GLOSSOP, Mick; b. Nottinghamshire, England. Prod; Engineer; Mixer. m. Elva Williamson, 1 d. *Career:* Recording Engineer, various studios, UK and Canada, until 1979; Freelance record prod. and engineer, 1980–; Prod. for: Camel, Lloyd Cole, Pino Daniele, Ian Gillan, Van Morrison, No Guru..., Revolver, The Ruts, The Skids, Suede, UFO, The Waterboys, The Wonder Stuff, Frank Zappa. *Honours:* Certificate of work with John Lee Hooker, National Academy of Recording Arts and Sciences. *Membership:* Music Producers Guild. *Address:* c/o Stephen Budd Management Ltd, 109b Regents Park Rd, London NW1 8UR, England. *E-mail:* mickg@bigfoot.com.

GLOVER, Corey; b. 6 Nov. 1964. Vocalist; Actor. *Career:* Actor, film: Platoon, 1985; Reunion, 2001; Singer, funk rock group Living Colour, 1985–95; Tours include: Support to Cheap Trick; Robert Palmer; Anthrax; Billy Bragg; Rolling Stones, Steel Wheels North American Tour, 1989; Miracle Biscuit tour, 1990; Lollapalooza tour, 1991; Stained In The UK tour, 1993; Concerts include: Earth Day concert, Central Park; Reading Festival, 1990; Phoenix Festival, 1993. *Recordings:* Albums: Vivid, 1988; Time's Up, 1990; Biscuits, 1991; Stain, 1993; Also appears on: In from the Storm, 1995; Rhythm of the Games, 1996; Black Night, 1997; Guest on Primitive Cool, Mick Jagger, 1986; Singles include: Cult of Personality, 1989; Glamour Boys, 1989; Love Rears Its Ugly Head, 1991; Solace of You, 1991; Leave It Alone, 1993; Solo album: Hymns. *Honours:* Elvis Award, Best New Band, International Rock Awards, 1989; MTV Awards: Best New Artist, Best Group Video, Best Stage Performance, 1989; Grammy Award, Best Hard Rock Performance, Time's Up, 1991; Rolling Stone Critics Poll Winners, Best Band, 1991. *Membership:* Black Rock Coalition. *Address:* c/o Jim Grant, Suite 1C, 39A Gramercy Park N, New York, NY 10010, USA.

GLOVER, Roger; b. 30 Nov. 1945, Brecon, Powys, Wales. Musician (bass); Composer; Record Prod. *Career:* Founder, The Madisons; Member, Episode Six, including 9 singles, 1966–69; Member, Deep Purple, 1970–73; Record producer, albums for: Nazareth; Status Quo; Judas Priest; Rory Gallagher; Rainbow; Elf; David Coverdale; Pretty Maids; Spencer Davis; Ian Gillan; Rupert Hine; Barbi Benton; Young and Moody; Solo recording artiste; Member, Rainbow, 1979–84; Concerts include: Monsters of Rock Festival, UK, 1980; Member, Deep Purple, 1984–; Also worked with Ian Gillan; Numerous world-wide tours with the above. *Compositions include:* The Butterfly Ball (led to book and film), 1974; Co-writer, with Ritchie Blackmore; All Night Long; Can't Happen Here. *Recordings:* Albums: with Deep Purple: Concerto For Group and Orchestra, 1970; In Rock, 1970; Fireball, 1971; Machine Head, 1972; Made In Japan, 1973; Who Do We Think We Are?, 1973; Perfect Strangers, 1984; House of Blue Light, 1987; Nobody's Perfect, 1988; Slaves and Masters, 1990; The Battle Rages On, 1993; Purpendicular, 1996; Abandon, 1998; Solo: Elements, 1978; Mask, 1984; with Gillan/Glover: Accidentally On Purpose, 1988; with Rainbow: Down To Earth, 1979; Difficult To Cure, 1981; Straight Between The Eyes, 1982; Bent Out of Shape, 1983; Finyl Vinyl, 1986; Hit singles: with Deep Purple: Black Night, 1970; Strange Kind of Woman, 1971; Smoke On The Water, 1973; Knocking At Your Back Door, 1985; with Rainbow: Since You've Been Gone, 1979; All Night Long, 1980; I Surrender, 1981; Can't Happen Here, 1981; Also performed with: Dave Cousins; Andy Mackay; Dan McCafferty. *Current Management:* Thames Talent, 45 E Putnam St, Greenwich, CT 06850, USA.

GNATYUK, Mikola; b. 14 Sept. 1952, Ukraine. Vocalist. 1 s. *Education:* Music Institut, Rovno, Ukraine. *Career:* Numerous television and radio appearances: Moscow; Ukraine; Germany, including: Aein Kessel, Rund; Concerts: Prague; Warsaw; Tours: Russia; Ukraine; Germany. *Recordings:* Songs: Bazaban; Molinovoi Zvon; Belii Stavni (number 1, Ukraine), 1994; Shas Rikog Pluve; Starenki. *Honours:* First prize, Sopot Festival, Poland; Grand Prix Festival, Dresden. *Membership:* SVIATO. *Current Management:* Mother in Kiev. *Address:* Vasilkovski 2A/126, 252040 Kiev, Ukraine.

GOBAC, Davor; b. Karlovac, Croatia. Vocalist; Composer; Entertainer; Actor; Text-writer. m. Deana Pavic, 5 Feb. 1994, 1 s. *Career:* Netherlands tour, 1989; Support to Ramones, Zagreb, Ljubgjana, 1990; Russian tour, 60 concerts, 1991; Toronto, 1993; Germany, Italy, Austria; 3 clips, MTV; Marcel Vanhilt Show; Many television and radio shows, Croatia. *Recordings:* Godina Zmaja (Year of Dragon), 1988; Live In Amsterdam, 1989; Sexy Magazin, 1990; Tko Je Ubio Mickey Mousea (Who Killed Mickey Mouse), 1991; Skrebrne Svinje (Silver Pigs), 1993, 1994; Video: Brkiant Video Pop, 1989. *Honours:* Croatian Film and Video Award, Oktavijan Miletic, 1995. *Membership:* Hrvatska Glalbena Vnija (Croatian Musicians' Union). *Address:* Sljemeuska 27, 41211 Zapresic, Croatia.

GODFREY, Mary; b. 10 Sept. 1960, Chicago, Illinois, USA. Vocalist; Songwriter; Musician (bass, guitar). *Education:* Organ and bass guitar lessons. *Career:* Has performed for past four years at South by Southwest Music Conference, Austin, Texas. *Compositions:* Temperature Change, 1990; Hit and Run, 1991; Mine Tonight and Send Me An Angel, 1994; The Edge in the Night, 1995. *Recordings:* Faces of Emotion: Hot Love, 1987; Back to the Light, 1988; TOC Album, 1989; Solo Recordings: Mary Godfrey, 1991; Contributor: Down O'Keele, backing vocal, 1993. *Honours:* Chicago Talent Search Winner, 1990; Second Place Lead Vocalist, Chicago Rocker Awards, 1990; Second Place Mem., Dunce Category, Chicago Rocker Awards, 1990. *Membership:* NARAS, Vice-President for WIM (Chicago Outreach Committee, 1989–91); ASCAP; National Academy of Songwriters. *Current Management:* English Cathy, Transatlantic Management, Box 2831, Tucson, AZ 85702, USA.

GODIN, Nicolas; b. Versailles, France. Prod; Musician (keyboards). *Education:* Studied at the Conservatoire, Paris. *Career:* Met Jean Benoit Dunckel at Conservatoire, Paris; Joined Dunckel's band Orange; After departure of Alex Gopher from band, formed duo Air, 1995; Released debut single, 1996; Signed to Virgin and released their debut album, 1997;

Collaborations: Jean Jacques Perrey; Francoise Hardy; Alex Gopher; Gordon Tracks; Remixed: Depeche Mode; Neneh Cherry. *Recordings:* Albums: Moon Safari, 1997; The Virgin Suicides, Premieres Symptoms, 1999; 10000 Hz Legend, 2001; Singles: Modulor, Casanova 70, 1996; Sexy Boy, 1997; Kelly Watch The Stars, 1998; Playground Love, 2000; Radio No. 1, 2001. *Address:* c/o Source Records, 113–117 Farringdon Rd, London EC1R 3BX, England.

GODINHO, Sergio; b. 31 Aug. 1945, Portugal. Vocalist; Songwriter. *Career:* 17 CDs of original songs; Hundreds of live shows; Film score writer; Actor; Occasional script writer; Director. *Compositions:* O Primeiro Dia, Lisboa Que Amanhece. *Recordings:* Noites Passadas; Rivolitz. *Publications:* Book For Children; Play. *Honours:* Record of the Year; Artist of the Year. *Membership:* SPA. *Current Management:* Praça Das Flores, R Da Imprensa Nacional 36, 1250 Lisboa, Portugal.

GODLEMAN, Martin John; b. 6 Jan. 1958, Hammersmith, London, England. Vocalist; Writer; Musician (drums). *Education:* BA Hons, Hatfield Polytechnic, 1979; MA, University of Surrey, 1991. *Career:* Bands: Faut Parler, 5 piece (Serge Gainsbourg jazz band), Mean Fiddler, 1993; Adventures of Parsley, 5 piece (vocals, percussion), Radio One, Mark Radcliffe Show, 1995; Mark Lamarr Show, GLR, 1995; Comedy Cafe Anniversary Show, London, 1995; Adventures of Parsley, Leadline 5 piece (vocals); Big Breakfast TV Show, (Comedy Cafe gig highlights), Ch4, 1995; Edinburgh Fringe (Gilded Balloon), (Adventures of Parsley), 1997. *Recordings:* Singles: Magpie, Adventures of Parsley, 1995; Intoxicated Man, Faut Parler, 1996; Minder (Adventures of Parsley), 1997; Albums: Top TV Themes (Adventures of Parsley), 1997. *Publications:* Chapter in The Power of The Page, 1993. *Membership:* FRA (Royal Academy); Collingwood Athletic Club. *Current Management:* Norbert J Hetherington Management. *Address:* 6 Roxburgh Court, 69 Melrose Rd, London SW18 1PG, England.

GODLEY, Kevin; b. 7 Oct. 1945, Manchester, Lancashire, England. Vocalist; Musician (drums); Songwriter; Prod; Video Dir. *Career:* Founder member, drummer, 10cc, 1972–76; Appearances include: Reading Festival, 1974; Knebworth Festival, 1976; US and British tours; Producer, songwriter, duo Godley and Creme (with Lol Creme), 1976–; Television includes: One World One Voice, series of programmes, with contributions from artists including: Sting, Peter Gabriel, Lou Reed, Chrissie Hynde, Stewart Copeland; Feature film, Howling At The Moon, 1988. *Recordings:* Albums: with 10cc: Sheet Music, 1974; Original Soundtrack, 1975; Greatest Hits, 1975; How Dare You?, 1976; Meanwhile, 1992; Mirror Mirror, 1995; Greatest Hits, 1998; with Godley and Creme (mostly self-written and produced): Consequences, 1977; L, 1978; Music From Consequences, 1979; Freeze Frame, 1979; Long Distant Romancer, 1981; Ismism, 1981; Birds of Prey, 1983; The History Mix, Vol. 1, 1985; The Changing Faces of 10cc and Godley and Creme, 1987; Goodbye Blue Sky, 1988; Singles include: with 10cc: Donna, 1972; Rubber Bullets (No. 1, UK), 1973; The Dean and I, 1973; Wall Street Shuffle, 1974; Silly Love, 1974; Life Is A Minestrone, 1975; I'm Not In Love (UK No. 1, USA No. 2), 1975; Art For Art's Sake, 1975; I'm Mandy Fly Me, 1976; with Godley and Creme: Under Your Thumb, 1981; Wedding Bells, 1981; Cry, 1985; Producer, albums including Long Distant Romancer, Mickey Jupp, 1981; One World One Voice, 1989; Director, videos including: Every Breath You Take, The Police; Rockit, Herbie Hancock; Feel The Love, 10cc; Relax, Frankie Goes To Hollywood; Two Tribes, Frankie Goes To Hollywood; Kele Le Roc; Duran Duran; Black Crowes; Sting; Charlatans; Director, TV commercials, including: Seafrance, PSEG. *Honours:* Ivor Novello Awards: Best Beat Song, Rubber Bullets, 1974; Most Performed British Song, Best Pop Song, International Hit of the Year, I'm Not In Love, 1976; 5 MTV Video Awards, Rockit, 1984; MTV Video Vanguard Award, 1985. *Membership:* Co-founder, environmental organization, ARK.

GOETHE-MCGINN, Lisa; b. 31 Jan. 1965, St Louis, Missouri, USA. Musician (Flute). m. Gregg McGinn, 10 Aug. 1996. *Education:* BM, Millikin University, Decatur, Illinois, 1987; MM, University of Illinois at Urbana, 1993. *Career:* Performer and Interpreter of contemporary music and free improvisation; Performed at many festivals and music series in the USA and abroad; Committed to performing music by contemporary composers; Active member, numerous new music ensembles in Chicago; Has worked with composers including Helmut Lachenmann, Salvatore Martirano and Herbert Brün; Performed at Museum of Contemporary Art, The Arts Club of Chicago Renaissance Society and others. *Honours:* Participator, Fishoff Chamber Music Competition, 1993, Gaudeamus International Interpreters Competition, 1995, 1999. *Membership:* American Composers Forum; National Flute Asscn; Chicago Flute Club. *Address:* 142 Harrison St No. 2, Oak Park, IL 60304, USA.

GOFFEY, Danny; b. 7 Feb. 1974, Oxford, England. Musician (drums). *Career:* Member, The Jennifers; Drummer, Supergrass, 1994–; Concerts include: Support to Blur, Alexandra Palace, 1994; British tour with Shed Seven, 1994; T In The Park Festival, Glasgow, 1995. *Recordings:* Albums: I Should Coco (No. 1, UK), 1995; In it for the Money (No. 2, UK); Supergrass, 1999; Life On Other Planets, 2002. Singles: Caught by the Fuzz, 1994; Mansize Rooster, 1995; Lenny, 1995; Alright (No. 2, UK), 1995; Going Out, 1996; Richard III (No. 2, UK), 1997; Sun Hits the Sky, 1997; Late In The Day,

1997; Pumping On Your Stereo, 1999; Moving, 1999; Mary, 1999; Grace, 2002. *Honours:* Q Award, Best New Act, 1995. *Current Management:* Courtyard Management, 22 The Nursery, Sutton Courtenay, Abingdon, Oxon OX14 4UA, England. *Website:* www.supergrass.com.

GOHIL, Jitesh; b. 3 April 1967, Kenya. Record Exec. *Education:* First Class Degree, Economics, Accounting, Bristol University. *Career:* Joined Multitone Records, 1988; Multitone developed into largest Asian record label in world, pioneered Bhangra genre; Multitone Records joined BMG Group, 1992; Now Managing Director, Multitone. *Address:* 1274 Uxbridge Rd, Hayes End, Middlesex UB4 8JF, England.

GOLBEY, Brian James; b. 5 Feb. 1939, Pycombe, Sussex, England. Musician (guitar, fiddle); Vocalist; Journalist. m. (1) 20 Sept. 1969, divorced, 2 s.; (2) Sandi Stubbs, 3 May 1980, 1 s. *Career:* Television with Pete Stanley (partner, 27 years) includes: 3 times Blue Peter; George Hamilton IV shows, BBC2; Many local television appearances; Old Grey Whistle Test; Cajun Moon, 1975; Magpie, ITV, 1969–; Concerts, most theatres include: Wembley Festival of Country Music, several times; London Palladium; Royal Albert Hall; Recordings for Pye, 1970; Emerald/Decca, 1973–74; Chrysalis, 1975; Waterfront Records, 1979–80s. *Publications:* Regular columnist, Country Music People, 1989–; Essay for Aspects of Elvis, 1994. *Honours:* Billboard; Record Mirror Award, Top UK artist, 1972; CMA Award, Top UK Soloist, 1972; BCMA Committee Award for long and continuing service to Country music in Britain, 1993. *Membership:* PRS. *Address:* 7 Hallcroft Beeston, Nottingham NG9 1E2, England.

GOLD, Harry; b. 26 Feb. 1907, Dublin, Ireland. Musician (clarinet, all saxophones including bass). m. Margaret (Peggy), 4 Oct. 1936, deceased 2 July 1995, 4 s. *Education:* London College of Music, Bachelor of Music. *Career:* Professional, 1923–; Composer, arranger, orchestrator, musical director; Founder, leader, Pieces of Eight Jazz Band; Rhapsody In Green, Radio Telefis Concert Orchestra; Television: Lowest of The Low. *Compositions:* Very numerous, about 50 compositions and arrangements published. *Publications:* Autobiography published, February 2000. *Honours:* BBC Special Award; Freeman of City of Londonderry, Northern Ireland; Blarney, Co Cork; Patron, Cork Jazz Festival. *Membership:* Musicians' Union; British Academy of Songwriters, Composers and Authors; PRS. *Address:* Flat 126, 53 Foxham Rd, London N19 4RR, England.

GOLDBERG, Barry; b. 25 Dec. 1942, Chicago, Illinois, USA. Musician (piano); Songwriter. m. Gail, 15 May 1971, 1 s. *Career:* Appeared at Newport Folk Festival with Bob Dylan, 1965; Played at Woodstock and Monterey pop festivals; Has written the score or contributed songs for films: Forrest Gump; Ruby; Flashback; Pow-Wow Highway; Dirty Dancing; Nobody's Fool; Adventures In Babysitting; Studio sessions with: Leonard Cohen; The Byrds; Mitch Ryder; The Ramones; Charlie Musselwhite; Additional associations with: Electric Flag; Bob Crewe; Jimi Hendrix; Gerry Goffin; Neil Young; Solomon Burke; Merry Clayton; Percy Sledge. *Recordings:* I've Got To Use My Imagination, recorded by Gladys Knight, Joe Cocker and Bobby Blue Bland; It's Not The Spotlight, recorded by Rod Stewart; Sittin' In Circles, recorded by Steve Miller; Additional songs recorded by artists including: Tom Jones; B J Thomas; Manhattan Transfer; Ben E King; The Neville Brothers; Jeff Healey; The Persuasions; Carole King; Junior Walker; Sam Moore. *Honours:* Pioneer Award, BMI, USA. *Membership:* BMI; NARAS; AFofM. *Current Management:* Christopher Nassif Agency, Joe Schneider, CNA, Century City, Los Angeles, California, USA.

GOLDENTHAL, Elliot; b. 2 May 1954, New York, NY, USA. Composer. *Education:* Manhattan School of Music. *Compositions:* For television: Criminal Justice, 1990; Roswell, 1994; For film: Cocaine Cowboys, 1979; Blank Generation, 1980; Drugstore Cowboy, 1989; Pet Cemetery, 1989; Grand Isle, 1991; Alien 3, 1992; Demolition Man, 1993; Interview with the Vampire, 1994; Golden Gate, 1994; Cobb, 1994; Voices, 1995; Batman Forever, 1995; Heat, 1995; Michael Collins, 1996; A Time to Kill, 1996; Batman & Robin, 1997; The Butcher Boy, 1998; Sphere, 1998; In Dreams, 1998; Titus, 1999; Final Fantasy: The Spirits Within, 2001; Frida, 2002. *Honours:* Golden Globe, Best Score, for Frida, 2003. *Membership:* ASCAP. *Current Management:* Gorfaine/Schwartz Agency Inc, 13245 Riverside Dr., Suite 450, Sherman Oaks, CA 91423, USA.

GOLDFRAPP, Allison; b. Enfield, Middlesex, England. Vocalist; Musician (keyboards); Composer. *Education:* Fine Arts, Middlesex University. *Career:* Vocalist on Tricky's album, Maxinquaye, 1995; Worked with: Add N to (X), Howie B, Pete Briquette, Kelli Dayton, Bryan Ferry, Robert Fowler, Grant Fulton, Steve Musters, Rowen Oliver, Orbital, Kevin Petrie, Alice Retif, Patti Russo, Troy Stanton, Paul Anthony Taylor, Keith G. Thompson, Martin Wheatley, David E. Williams; Solo artiste; Formed Goldfrapp with Will Gregory, late 1990s; Signed to Mute Records, 1999. *Recordings:* with Goldfrapp: Album: Felt Mountain, 2000. Singles: Utopia, 2000; Pilots, 2002; Appearances on: Howie B's Another Late Night, 2001; Bryan Ferry's Frantic, 2002; Orbital's Snivilisation, 1994, Are We Here?, 1995, The Box, Work 1989–2002, 2002; Tricky's Maxinquaye, 1995, Ruff Guide, 2002. *Address:* c/o Mute Records, 429 Harrow Rd, London W10 4RE, England.

GOLDIE, (Clifford Price); b. 1966, Wolverhampton, England. Prod; Actor. *Career:* Producer, Drum 'n' bass/jungle music; Acting roles include EastEnders (BBC1), 2000; Appeared on Celebrity Big Brother (Channel 4), 2002. *Recordings:* Albums: Goldie Presents Metalheadz: Timeless, 1995; Saturnz Return, 1998; Incredible Sound of Drum N Bass, 2000; Singles: Inner City Life, 1995; Kemistry, 1997; Digital, 1997; Temper Temper, 1998; Ring of Saturn, 1998; Believe, 1998. *Current Management:* NUR Entertainment, Canalot Studios, Unit 218A, 222 Kensal Rd, London W10 5BN, England.

GOLDING, Lynval; b. 24 July 1951, Coventry, England. Vocalist. *Career:* Member, The Specials; Early tours supporting The Clash; Established own record label, 2-Tone; Debut album produced by Elvis Costello; Numerous tours and television appearances; Left band, formed Fun Boy Three with Terry Hall and Neville Staples, split 1983. *Recordings:* with The Specials: Singles: Gangsters, 1979; A Message to You, Rudi, 1979; Too Much Too Young (Live EP) (No. 1, UK), 1980; Rat Race, 1980; Stereotype, 1980; Do Nothing, 1980; Ghost Town (No. 1, UK), 1981; Albums: The Specials, 1979; More Specials, 1980; Singles, 1991; Stereotypes (As, Bs and Rarities), 2000; With Fun Boy Three: The Lunatics Have Taken Over the Asylum, 1981; It Ain't What You Do, with Bananarama, 1982; Really Saying Something, with Bananarama, 1982; The Telephone Always Rings, 1982; Tunnel of Love, 1983; Our Lips Are Sealed, 1983; Albums: Fun Boy Three, 1982; Waiting, 1983; More Specials, 2002.

GOLDSBORO, Bobby; b. 18 Jan. 1941, Marianna, Florida, USA. Musician (guitar); Vocalist; Songwriter. *Career:* Guitarist, Roy Orbison, 1960; Solo artiste, 1964–; Later, country artiste, 1980s. *Recordings:* Hit singles include: See The Funny Little Clown, 1964; Whenever He Holds You; Little Things; Voodoo Woman; It's Too Late; Blue Autumn; Honey (No. 1, USA; No. 2, UK), 1968; Watching Scotty Grow; Summer (The First Time); Albums include: Honey, 1968; Today, 1969; Muddy Mississippi Line, 1970; We Gotta Start Lovin', 1971; Come Back Home, 1971; Goldsboro, 1977; Roundup Saloon, 1982; Also numerous compilations; Albums: The Bobby Goldsboro Album, 1964; Honey, 1968; Easter Egg Mornin', 1993; The Best of Bobby Goldsboro, 1996; The Greatest Hits, 1999; Hello Summertime, 2001. *Current Management:* Jim Stephany Management, 1021 Preston Dr., Nashville, TN 37206, USA.

GOLDSMITH, Harvey; b. 4 March 1946, London, England. CEO; Impresario. m. Diana Gorman, 1971, 1 s. *Education:* Christ's College; Brighton College of Technology. *Career:* Partner, Big O Posters, 1966–67; Organized first free open-air concert in Parliament Hill Fields with Michael Alfandary, 1968; Opened Round House, Camden Town, 1968, Crystal Palace Garden Party series of concerts, 1969–72; Merged with John Smith Entertainments, 1970; Formed Harvey Goldsmith Entertainments (rock tours promotion company), 1976; Acquired Allied Entertainments Group (rock concert promotions company), 1984; Formed Classical Productions with Mark McCormack, 1986; Promoter and Producer of pop, rock and classical musical events including: Concerts: Bruce Springsteen; The Rolling Stones; Elton John; The Who; Pink Floyd; Opera: Ada, 1988, Carmen, 1989, Tosca, 1991, Earls Court; Pavarotti at Wembley, 1986; Pavarotti in the Park, 1991; The Three Tenors, 1996; Lord of the Dance, 1996–97; Cirque du Soleil, 1996–97; Mastercard Masters of Music, 1996; Music for Montserrat at the Royal Albert Hall, 1997; The Bee Gees, 1998; Ozzfest, 1998; Paul Weller, 1998. *Honours:* CBE, 1996. *Membership:* Chairman, Concert Promoters Asscn, 1986; Chairman, National Music Festival, 1991; Co-Chairman, President's Club, 1994; Vice-Chairman, Prince's Trust Action Management Board, 1993; Vice-President, REACT, 1989; Vice-President, Music Users Council, 1994; Trustee, Band Aid, 1985; Trustee, Life Aid Foundation, 1985; Trustee, Royal Opera House, 1995; Trustee, CST, 1995; British Red Cross Communications Panel, 1992; Prague Heritage Fund, 1994; London Tourist Board, 1994. *Address:* Greenland Pl., 115–123 Bayham St, London NW1 0AG, England.

GOLDSMITH, Jerry; b. 10 Feb. 1929, Los Angeles. Film Music Composer; Conductor. m. Carol Sheinkopf. *Education:* Los Angeles City College; MusD, Berklee College of Music; University of Southern California, studied with Jakob Gimpel, Mario Castelnuevo-Tedesco; Studied film composition with Miklós Rózsa. *Career:* Guest conductor with many American and European symphony orchestras; Tours world-wide. *Compositions:* Numerous scores for ballet, radio and television; For film: Black Patch, 1956; City of Fear, 1959; Face of a Fugitive, 1959; Studs Lonigan, 1960; The Crimebusters, 1961; The General with the Cockeyed Id, 1961; Lonely Are The Brave, 1961; Freud, 1962; The Stripper, 1962; The Spiral Road, 1962; The List of Adrian Messenger, 1963; A Gathering of Eagles, 1963; Take Her, She's Mine, 1963; Lilies of the Field, 1963; The Prize, 1963; Seven Days in May, 1963; In Harm's Way, 1964; Fate Is the Hunter, 1964; Rio Conchos, 1964; Shock Treatment, 1964; Morituri, 1965; The Satan Bug, 1965; Von Ryan's Express, 1965; A Patch of Blue, 1965; The Blue Max, 1965; Our Man Flint, 1965; Seconds, 1965; Stagecoach, 1966; The Sand Pebbles, 1966; One of Our Spies Is Missing, 1966; To Trap a Spy, 1966; The Trouble with Angels, 1966; The Flim Flam Man, 1967; Warning Shot, 1967; Hour of the Gun, 1967; In Like Flint, 1967; Planet of the Apes, 1968; The Detective, 1968; Bandolero!, 1968; Sebastian, 1968; Justine, 1969; The Chairman, 1969; The Illustrated Man, 1969; 100 Rifles, 1969; The Ballad of Cable Hogue, 1969; Tora! Tora! Tora!,

1970; Patton, 1970; Rio Lobo, 1970; The Traveling Executioner, 1970; Escape from the Planet of the Apes, 1971; The Last Run, 1971; The Mephisto Waltz, 1971; Wild Rovers, 1971; The Other, 1972; The Man, 1972; Shamus, 1973; Ace Eli and Rodger of the Skies, 1973; The Don Is Dead, 1973; One Little Indian, 1973; Papillon, 1973; Chinatown, 1974; The Reincarnation of Peter Proud, 1974; S*P*Y*S, 1974; Take a Hard Ride, 1975; The Terrorists, 1975; Breakout, 1975; Logan's Run, 1975; The Wind and the Lion, 1976; The Omen, 1976; Islands in the Stream, 1976; The Cassandra Crossing, 1976; Breakheart Pass, 1976; Twilight's Last Gleaming, 1977; Damnation Alley, 1977; High Velocity, 1977; MacArthur, 1977; Coma, 1977; Capricorn One, 1978; The Swarm, 1978; Magic, 1978; The Boys from Brazil, 1978; Damien – Omen II, 1978; Alien, 1979; Star Trek: The Motion Picture, 1979; The First Great Train Robbery, 1979; Players, 1979; Caboblanco, 1980; Night Crossing, 1981; The Salamander, 1981; The Final Conflict, 1981; Outland, 1981; Raggedy Man, 1981; Mrs. Brisby: The Secret of NIMH, 1982; Poltergeist, 1982; First Blood, 1982; The Challenge, 1982; Inchon, 1982; Twilight Zone: The Movie, 1983; Psycho II, 1983; Under Fire, 1983; Gremlins, 1984; Runaway, 1984; Supergirl, 1984; The Lonely Guy, 1984; Baby... Secret of the Lost Legend, 1985; King Solomon's Mines, 1985; Legend (European version), 1985; Explorers, 1985; Rambo: First Blood II, 1985; Poltergeist II: The Other Side, 1986; Hoosiers, 1986; Link, 1986; Lionheart, 1987; Innerspace, 1987; Extreme Prejudice, 1987; Rent-a-Cop, 1988; Rambo III, 1988; Warlock, 1989; Criminal Law, 1989; The 'Burbs, 1989; Leviathan, 1989; Star Trek V: The Final Frontier, 1989; Total Recall, 1990; Gremlins 2: The New Batch, 1990; The Russia House, 1990; Not Without My Daughter, 1991; Sleeping With the Enemy, 1991; Medicine Man, 1991; Love Field, 1992; Mom and Dad Save the World, 1992; Basic Instinct, 1992; Mr Baseball, 1992; Forever Young, 1992; Matinee, 1992; The Vanishing, 1993; Dennis the Menace, 1993; Malice, 1993; Rudy, 1993; Six Degrees of Separation, 1993; Angie, 1994; Bad Girls, 1994; The Shadow, 1994; I.Q., 1994; The River Wild, 1994; First Knight, 1995; Congo, 1995; Powder, 1995; City Hall, 1995; Executive Decision, 1996; Chain Reaction, 1996; The Ghost and the Darkness, 1996; Star Trek: First Contact, 1996; Fierce Creatures, 1996; L.A. Confidential, 1997; Air Force One, 1997; The Edge, 1997; Deep Rising, 1997; U.S. Marshals, 1998; Small Soldiers, 1998; Mulan, 1998; Star Trek: Insurrection, 1998; The Mummy, 1999; The 13th Warrior, 1999; The Haunting, 1999; Hollow Man, 2000; Along Came a Spider, 2001; The Last Castle, 2001; The Sum of All Fears, 2002; Star Trek X: Nemesis, 2002; Timeline, 2003. *Recordings:* Numerous soundtrack recordings; Goldsmith Conducts Goldsmith, 2002. *Honours:* Max Steiner Award, National Film Society, 1982; Edgar Allan Poe Award, 1982; Saturn Award, 1984; first annual Richard Kirk Award, BMI, 1987; Golden Score Award, American Society of Music Arrangers, 1990; Career Achievement Award, Society for Preservation of Film Music, 1993; first American Music Legend Award, Variety, 1995; Academy Award, for The Omen; Emmy Awards, for QB VII, Babe, Masada, Star Trek: Voyager. *Membership:* BMI. *Current Management:* Blue Focus Management, 15233 Ventura Blvd, Suite 200, Sherman Oaks, CA 91403, USA.

GOLDSMITH, Timothy Simon; b. 1 Dec. 1962, West London, England. Musician (drums). *Career:* Tours with: Paul Brady; Tanita Tikaram; Nik Kershaw; Joan Armatrading; Jaki Graham; Television appearances include: Top of the Pops; Old Grey Whistle Test; Live radio, videos. *Recordings include:* Albums: Alf, Alison Moyet; Go West, Go West; Track Record, Joan Armatrading. *Membership:* Musicians' Union. *Address:* 343a Upper Richmond Rd W, East Sheen, London SW14, England.

GOLT, Debbie; b. 2 April 1952, London, England. Consultant; Music and Arts Management. 2 d. *Education:* BA, History, York University; PG Diploma, Applied Youth and Community Work, Manchester Polytechnic. *Career:* Diverse career on alternative/independent circuit; Parallel career in youth work and Arts Management; Ran sound system battles and concerts with Rock Against Racism, 1977–80; Managed major UK-based African Band, Taxi Pata Pata (first UK-based African band on BBC RI and Arts Council support); Dir, Nyrangongo record label, 1985–90; Co-dir, Half The Sky, first promotions group promoting female world music; Introduced Oumau Sangare to UK and top television/press coverage; Panelist for RI Sound City, In The City, Umbrella, 1991–93; Set up Eleventh Hour Arts; Co-Dir, Portobello Jazz Festival; Co-Man., Frank Chickens, 1994–96; Man., MoMo (Music Of Moroccan Origin), 1997–; Advisor to Frank Chickens, Gifty Naa DK, Sandira, Rose Dede Tetteh, TaxiPata Pata; Co-ordinator, World Music Portobello Festival; Consultant for festivals, global music, women's music; Established Outerglobe, 2000–; Host, Year of the Artist residency, Gaialive, 2000; Man., Weird MC, 2002–; Consultant Assoc, Helen Denniston Assocs. *Contributions to:* Worldbeat; World Music Magazine; Guardian; Froots; Straight No Chaser; Black Film Maker Magazine; Women in Music Now; Topical, 1991–93; Bubble Jam; Radio programmes on Radio 1, Radio 5, GLR and local radio; DJ and Presenter on gaialive internet radio; Modal FM. *Membership:* Women In Music, fmr chair.; Sound Sense; IMF; Advisory Board of Modal. *Address:* Outerglobe, 113 Cheesemans Terrace, London W14 9XH, England. *E-mail:* outerglobe@yahoo.com.

GONZALEZ, Celina; b. Jovellanos, Cuba. Vocalist. m. Rentilio Dominguez, Dec. 1971, 1 s. *Career:* Country singer, formerly duo with husband, now with own band Campo Alegre; Daily radio show, Radio Taino, Havana; Regular television appearances include: Palmas y Canas, Cuba; Tours throughout Cuba, Dominican Republic, Columbia; Concerts in New York, and Cali Fest, 1984. *Recordings:* Singles: Santa Barbara, 1994; La Rica Cosecha, 1997; Salsa, 1998; Celina Gonzalez, 2000. *Honours:* Distinction of National Culture; Egrem Silver disc; 6 Premios Girasoles; Most popular artist in Cuba. *Address:* c/o World Circuit Records, 106 Cleveland St, London W1P 5DP, England.

GONZALEZ, Kenny, (Kenny Dope, The Bucketheads, Untouchables, Powerhouse, Swing Kids); b. 7 June 1970, Brooklyn, New York, USA. Prod; Remixer; DJ. *Career:* Started producing for New York labels: Strictly Rhythm; Nu Groove; Formed Masters At Work with Louie Vega; Duo also recorded as Nu Yorican Soul; Co-founder: MAW Records; Collaborations: India; Marc Anthony; Jocelyn Brown; James Ingram; Stephanie Mills; Remixed: Shanice; Tito Puente; Barbara Tucker; Jamiroquai; Atmosfear; Incognito; Luther Vandross; Ce Ce Peniston; Martha Wash; Ballistic Brothers; Alex Gopher; Melanie B. *Recordings:* Albums: Nu Yorican Soul, 1997; Our Time Is Coming (as Masters At Work), 2002. Singles: Makin' A Livin (as Powerhouse), 1991; I Can't Get No Sleep (as Masters At Work), 1992; Deep Inside (as Hardrive), 1993; Love and Happiness (as River Ocean), 1994; The Nervous Track (as Nu-Yorican Soul), 1994; The Bomb (as The Bucketheads), 1995; I Am The Black Gold of The Sun (as Nu-Yorican Soul), 1996; What A Sensation (as Kenlou), 1996; To Be In Love, 1997; Brasilian Beat, 1998; Brazilica, 2001. *Address:* c/o Strictly Rhythm, 920 Broadway 1403, New York, USA.

GONZÁLEZ, Rubén; b. April, 1919, Santa Clara, Cuba. Musician (piano). *Career:* Played with La Orquesta Paulina, Conjunto Canayo, Los Hermanos, Raúl Planas, Mongo Santamaría and Arsenio Rodríguez, 1940s; Toured Panama and South America; Back in Havana played with various bands including Conjunto Kubavana de Alberto Ruiz and Conjunto de Senen Suárez; Played with Enrique Jorrín in 1980s and took over as bandleader on Jorrín's death; Retired, late 1980s; Made comeback with the Buena Vista Social Club series of recordings; Appeared in Wim Wenders' documentary film Buena Vista Social Club. *Recordings:* recent Albums: Buena Vista Social Club, Introducing Rubén González, A Toda Cuba Le Gusta (Afro Cuban All-Stars), 1997; Buena Vista Social Club Presents Ibrahim Ferrer, 1999; Buena Vista Social Club Presents Omara Portuonda, Chanchullo, 2000; features on Distinto Diferente (with Afro Cuban All-Stars), 1999. *Address:* c/o World Circuit Ltd, First Floor, Shoreditch Stables, 138 Kingsland Rd, London E2 8DY, England.

GOOD, Larry J; Entertainer; Musician (guitar). m. (1), 1 d., (2) Jennifer, 22 Feb. 1985. *Education:* Playing with Grand Ole Opry stars. *Career:* Shows with major artists including: Charley Pride; Waylon Jennings; Marty Robbins; Roy Acuff; Ray Price; Ernest Tubb; Television appearances: Regular on several local television shows; Ernest Tubb Midnight Jamboree. *Recordings:* Albums include: Some Old Some New; As Good As It Gets; Moving Country; Jesus is My Hero (gospel); The Best of Larry Good; Singles include: Raise Your Glass; Long Way To Kansas City. *Honours:* Nebraska Country Music Hall of Fame. *Current Management:* Lari-Jon Promotions. *Address:* PO Box 216, 325 W Walnut, Rising City, NE 68658, USA.

GOODACRE, Tony; b. 3 Feb. 1938, Leeds, England. Vocalist; Entertainer; Musician (guitar). m. (1) Cherry, 18 June 1960, 1 s., 2 d.; (2) Sylvia, 29 July 1974. *Career:* First professional engagement, 1956; First recording, 1957; Radio debut, 1958; Formed band Goodacre Country, 1969; Guest, The Arthur Smith Show, USA television, 1973; First appearance, Grand Ole Opry, Nashville, 1977; Wembley Festival, 1982, 1983; Started own Music Publishing Company: Sylvantone Music, 1983; Promoted career of Stu Page, 1984–86; Sarah Jory, 1987–88. *Recordings:* Albums: Roamin' Round In Nashville, 1974; Grandma's Feather Bed, 1975; Thanks To The Hanks, 1976; Written In Britain, 1977; The Best of Tony Goodacre, 1978; Mr Country Music, 1978; You've Made My Life Complete, 1979; Recorded Live In Ilkley, 1980; 25th Anniversary, 1981; Red Roses, 1983; Sylvantone Song Book, Vols 1 and 2, 1984–85; The Tony Goodacre Collection, 1986; Country Favourites, 1988; Something Special, 1989; Livin' On Livin', 1992; 40th Anniversary Album, 1996; The Millennium Project, 2000. *Honours:* Record Mirror Award, 1973; 3 British Country Music Asscn Awards, 1982–84; Favourite Male Vocalist in Europe, Country Gazette (Dutch Magazine), 1986; 18 Country Music Club Awards, Top Solo Artist; 3 Country Music Club Awards, Top Duo, with Sarah Jory, 1987. *Current Management:* Sylvantone Promotions. *Address:* 17 Allerton Grange Way, Leeds LS17 6LP, England.

GOODIER, David Charles Gray; b. 11 July 1954, Salisbury, England. Musician (bass guitar fretted/fretless, double bass). Partner, Lynn Thompson, 1 s., 2 d. *Education:* BEd Hons, St Luke's College, Exeter University; Studied music briefly with Peter Ind and Rufus Reid. *Career:* Interests Funk, Fusion, Salsa, Mainstream, Modern and contemporary jazz; Worked in theatre pit bands made radio broadcasts (R3, R2); Television and radio sessions; Many festival appearances: Brecon; Glastonbury; Worked with jazz musicians, including: Guy Barker; Dave De Fries; Tal Farlow; Art Farmer; Slim Gaillard; Dick Morrissey; Gerard Presencer; Don Rendell; Andy Sheppard; Norma Winstone; Often as part of the Dave Gordon Trio with Tony Orrell; Musical Director, Bristol Jazz Workshop, 1991–. *Recordings:* John Parricelli, Mark

Lockheart: Matheran; The Korgis: This World's For Everyone; Brass Reality: For Real. *Current Management:* LDT Management.

GOODMAN, Clare; b. 19 May 1966, Frimley, Surrey, England. Vocalist; Dancer. *Education:* West Street School of Performing Arts. *Career:* Live: Joseph and The Amazing Technicolour Dreamcoat, British tour, 1994–95; Appearance with Just Music (for anti-racist alliance) Arafest '94; *Films:* Frankenstein (Mary Shelley's); The Muppet Christmas Carol; *Video:* Give Me Just A Little More Time, Kylie Minogue; I've Got A Spell On You, Bryan Ferry; *Commercials:* Kool-aid; Red Stripe. *Membership:* Musicians' Union. *Current Management:* Pineapple Agency. *Address:* 29 Womersley Rd, Crouch End, Hornsey, London N8 9AP, England.

GOODRICK, Mick; Jazz Musician (guitar). *Education:* BM Berklee College of Music. *Career:* Former faculty member, Berklee College of Music; Faculty member, Jazz Studies, New England Conservatory of Music; Performed and recorded with: Jack DeJohnette; Gary Burton; Paul Motian; Steve Gadd; Pat Metheny; Michael Brecker; Charlie Haden. *Recordings:* In Passing, 1978; Biorhythms, 1990; Cities, 1992; Rare Birds, 1993; Sunscreams, 1993; 2 albums with Jack DeJohnette's Special Edition. *Publications:* Author, The Advancing Guitarist. *Address:* New England Conservatory of Music, 290 Huntington Ave, Boston, MA 02115, USA.

GOODRIDGE, Robin; b. 10 Sept. 1966, Crawley, West Sussex, England. Musician (drums). *Career:* Former Member, Future Primitive, became Bush; Obtained major US record deal; Heavy radio airplay in USA and numerous headlining tours; UK gigs and festival appearances. *Recordings:* Singles: Little Things, 1995; Comedown, 1995; Swallowed, 1997; Greedy Fly, 1997; Cold Contagious, 1999; Chemicals Between Us, 2001; Albums: Sixteen Stone, 1994; Razorblade Suitcase, 1996; Deconstructed, 1997; The Science of Things, 1999; Golden State, 2001. *Website:* www.bush-music.com.

GOODWIN, Christopher Neil; b. 10 Aug. 1962, Oldham, England. Musician (drums). *Education:* Graduated from Tameside College. *Career:* Various TV appearances including a Granada TV special, High and Dry; 2 British tours and a European tour; Appeared in Leeds supporting Happy Mondays; Radio sessions on the Mark Goodier and Mark Radcliffe shows. *Recordings:* Albums: Somewhere Soon, with The High, and Hype, with The High; Singles: Tomorrow's Sunset, with Buzzcocks, and Exiles, with Buzzcocks. *Membership:* PRS; Musicians' Union. *Current Management:* Stuart Windsor Inc. *Address:* 27 Lausanne Rd, Withington, Manchester, England.

GOODWIN, Jimi; Vocalist. *Career:* Mem., UK band, Sub Sub, late 1980s; Changed band name to Doves, 1998; Tours in UK and USA; Signed to Heavenly Recording, 2000. *Recordings:* Albums: with Doves: Lost Souls, 2000; The Last Broadcast, 2002. Singles: with Sub Sub: Ain't No Love (Ain't No Use); Firesuite; with Doves: Cedar (EP), 1998; Sea Song (EP), 1999; Here It Comes (EP), 1999; The Cedar Room, 2000; Catch The Sun; The Man Who Told Everything; There Goes The Fear, 2002. *Address:* c/o Heavenly Recording, PO Box 607, London SW6 4YY, England. *Website:* www.doves.net.

GOODWIN, Len; b. 24 Aug. 1940, Sheffield, England. Songwriter; Author. m. Lynne Abbott, 18 Sept. 1982, 1 s., 2 d. *Career:* Own songs performed by various artists on Crackerjack, BBC TV; Video Entertainers, Granada Network; Starburst, Granada Network; This Morning, Granada Network; Granada Reports, Granada TV; BBC Radio 1 and 2, local and independent radio. *Compositions:* Writing credits on recordings: Good Old Coronation Street; Special Train; This Is A Record of My Love (Happy Birthday Darling); Here We Are, (England Football Song); Football Anthem; Ain't This A Funny World, If Only Women Cry; Handle Me With Care. *Publications:* The Money Making Secrets of Successful Songwriting, 1997, new edition as So You Wannabe a Songwriter, 1998. *Membership:* PRS; MCPS; PPL. *Current Management:* Tram Promotions/Gable Records. *Address:* 16 Pendle Court, Astley Bridge, Bolton, Lancashire BL1 6PY, England.

GORCE, Partrick; b. 23 May 1962, Alger, Algeria. m. Odile, 24 April, 1 s., 1 d. *Education:* Baccalauréat, Music with Mention, 1981; First Prize, L'Ecole Superiour de Batterie, Dante Agostini, Paris. *Career:* Tours, USA; Europe; Performed Paris clubs, Zénith, Olympia, New Morning; Played with: Ghetto Blaster; Luis Antonio; Jean-Claude Borrelli; Richard Clayderman; TV series; Teacher, Drumming and Traditional Percussion. *Compositions:* Tambours De La Paix (50 participants). *Recordings:* African Vibration, Samy Samiamam; Clypso O'Samba, Ile Axe; Percussions of Latin America; Travel and See, Nomadic Activities. *Honours:* Titulaire de la Bourse 'Lavoisier', Ministry of Foreign Affairs. *Membership:* SPEDIMAM. *Address:* 21 bis rue Solferino, 94100 St Maur, France.

GORDON, Kim; b. 28 April 1953, Rochester, NY, USA. Artist; Vocalist; Musician (bass guitar). m. Thurston Moore, 1 d. *Career:* Founding mem., Sonic Youth, 1981–; Founding mem., Ciccone Youth, 1986–. *Recordings:* Albums: with Sonic Youth: Sonic Youth, 1981; Confusion Is Sex; Sonic Death–Early Sonic Youth 1981–83; Kill Yr Idols; Bad Moon Rising; E.V.O.L., 1986; Sister, 1987; Hold That Tiger, 1987; Daydream Nation, 1988; Goo, 1990; Dirty, 1992; A Thousand Leaves, 1998; NYC Ghosts & Flowers, 2000; Condo

Painting: Life From A Different Angle, 2002; Murray Street, 2002; with Ciccone Youth: The Whitey Album, 1989; Other releases with Sonic Youth: Anagrama (syr1); Slaapkamers met Slagroom (syr2); Invito al Cielo (syr3); Goodbye 20th Century (syr4); Kim Gordon/Ikue Mori/DJ Olive (syr5); Contributed to film and television soundtracks: Pump Up The Volume, 1990; My So-Called Life, 1995; End Of Days, 1999. *Address:* c/o Smells Like Records, PO Box 6179, Hoboken, NJ 07030, USA. *Website:* www.sonicyouth.com.

GORDON, Noah Adrian; b. 19 Sept. 1971, Pinckneyville, Illinois, USA. Vocalist; Writer; Musician (guitar, drums). *Education:* 14 years; Degree in Electrical Engineering Technology. *Career:* Charlie Daniels' Volunteer Jam, 1992; Nashville Now; Music City Tonight; Country Music Television; The Nashville Network; Nascar Country; Wal-Mart Country Music Across America Tour; TNN Wildhorse Saloon, 1994–95. *Recordings:* I Need A Break, 1995; Christmas Time In Dixie, Charlie Daniels, 1994–95. *Membership:* AFTRA; AFofM. *Current Management:* Entertainment Artist Inc, 819 18th Ave S, Nashville, TN 37203, USA.

GORDON, Robert; b. 4 Oct. 1966, Sheffield, England. Music Programmer. 2 d. *Career:* Recording Engineer, Producer. *Compositions:* Track With No Name, The Forgemasters. *Recordings:* House Arrest, Krush, 1987; Wanted, album, Yazz, 1988; Track With No Name, The Forgemasters; Rob Gordon Projects, album, 1996; Ozooma, 1996; Produced Lost In Music and Why Are People Grudgeful (singles) and Shiftwork (album), The Fall, 1993; Remixed Pop Will Eat Itself, Art of Noise, Yellow Magic Orchestra. *Honours:* Silver Disc, Krush, 1988; Double Platinum Disc, Yazz, 1988. *Membership:* PRS; MCPS; PEMRA; PPL; Musicians' Union. *Address:* 18 Talbot Gardens, Sheffield, S2 2TE, England.

GORDON, Rod; b. 6 Feb. 1934, Flatbush, Alberta, Canada. Songwriter; Recording Artist; Musician (guitar). m. Jennette Richardson, 9 May 1964, 2 s., 2 d. *Career:* Appeared on GERN-TV, Edmonton, Alberta and CHLT-TV, Sherbrooke, Québec; Personal radio shows across Canada; Club bookings across Canada. *Compositions:* 200 compositions including Little Girl. *Recordings:* 2 singles released. *Honours:* Certificate of Merit for Outstanding Efforts in Advancement of Country Music. *Membership:* Canadian Country Music Assocn; Country Music Assocn of Nashville. *Current Management:* 21st Century Records. *Address:* 530 Third Ave S No. 2, Nashville, TN 37210, USA.

GORDON, William 'Flash'; b. 16 March 1947, Miami, Florida, USA. Vocalist; Songwriter; Musician (bass, guitar); Actor. m. Mary Ellen Jesse. *Education:* United States Army Engineering School; Miami Dade Jr College. *Career:* Played at Willie Nelson's Fourth of July Picnic, 1974, 1976; Member: David Allan Coe band; Toured with: Charlie Walker; Justin Tubb; Jan Howard; Bobby Lewis; various Grand Ole Opry stars. *Compositions:* All You Ever Have To Do Is Touch Me, Charlie Rich; My Woman's Honky Tonkin' Me To Death, Mel Tillis; As Far As This Feeling Will Take Us, David Allan Coe; In The Arms of Cocaine, Hank Williams Jr (on gold-selling album); (She Won't Have A Thing To Do With) Nobody But Me, Alabama (on triple platinum-selling album). *Recordings:* Albums: Alternative Country, 1992; Flash II, 1995; Confessions of a Cowboy Singer, 1999. *Membership:* BMI; Nashville Publishers Network. *Current Management:* Georgia Boy Management, Box 265, Springfield, Tennessee 37172, USA. *Address:* 4545 Mount Sharon Rd, Greenbrier, TN 37073, USA. *E-mail:* wgordon327@aol.com.

GORDY, Berry, Jr; b. 28 Nov. 1929, Detroit, Michigan, USA. Record Co Exec; Songwriter. m. Grace Eaton, 17 July 1990, 6 c. *Career:* Owner, record store, Detroit, 1955; Composer and independent producer, late 1950s; Founder, Jobete Music, 1958; Tamla Records, 1959; Motown Record Corporation, 1961–88; Chairman, The Gordy Co; Executive Producer, film Lady Sings The Blues, 1972. *Recordings:* As composer / producer: Reet Petite, Jackie Wilson; Shop Around, The Miracles; Do You Love Me, The Contours; Try It Baby, Marvin Gaye; Shotgun, Junior Walker and The All-Stars; I Want You Back and ABC, The Jackson 5; Compilation: The Music, The Magic, The Memories of Motown, 1995. *Honours:* American Music Award, Outstanding Contribution to Music Industry, 1975; Inducted into Rock and Roll Hall of Fame, 1988; NARAS Trustees Award, 1991. *Address:* Gordy Co, 6255 Sunset Blvd, Los Angeles, CA 90028, USA.

GORE, Lesley; b. 2 May 1946, New York, USA. Vocalist; Actress. *Education:* BA, English and American literature, Sarah Lawrence College, Bronxville, New York. *Career:* Appearances include: Greatest Record Show of 1963; TAMI Show (released as film Gather No Moss), with Beach Boys, Chuck Berry, Rolling Stones, 1964; Richard Nader's Rock 'n' Roll Revival, Madison Square Garden, 1975; Acting debut, The Donna Reed Show, 1966; Also appeared in Batman; Theatrical debut, Half A Sixpence, 1967; Nightclub and stage work, 1970s. *Recordings:* Albums: I'll Cry If I Want To, 1963; Lesley Gore Sings of Mixed-Up Hearts, 1964; Boys Boys Boys, 1964; Girl Talk, 1964; The Golden Hits of Lesley Gore, 1965; My Town, My Guy and Me, 1965; California Nights, 1967; Someplace Else Now, 1972; Love Me By Name, 1975; Back to Back, 1992; Lesley Gore, 1992; The Essential Collection, 2001; Singles include: It's My Party (debut sold 1m.; No. 1, UK), 1963; Judy's Turn To Cry; She's A Fool; You Don't Own Me; That's The Way The Boys Are; Maybe I

Know; Sunshine Lollipops and Rainbows; My Town My Guy and Me; California Nights. *Current Management:* c/o Stan Scottland, JKE Services Inc, 404 Park Ave S, 10th Floor, New York, NY 10016, USA.

GORE, Martin Lee; b. 23 June 1961, London, England. Musician (keyboards, guitar); Vocalist; Songwriter. m. Suzanne (Boisvert), 27 Aug. 1994, 2 d. *Career:* Founder Member, Depeche Mode, 1980–. *Compositions:* As Depeche Mode's Principal Songwriter since 1982, has written vast majority of songs recorded by the band. *Recordings:* 12 Top Ten Singles including: Just Can't Get Enough, 1981; See You, 1982; Everything Counts, 1983; People Are People, 1984; Master and Servant, 1984; Enjoy the Silence, 1990; I Feel You, 1993; Condemnation, 1993; In Your Room, 1994; Barrel of a Gun, 1994; It's No Good, 1997; Dream On, 2001; 13 Top Ten Albums including: Speak and Spell, 1981; A Broken Frame, 1982; Construction Time Again, 1983; Some Great Reward, 1984; The Singles 81–85, 1985; Black Celebration, 1986; Music For the Masses, 1987; 101, 1989; Violator, 1990; Songs of Faith and Devotion (No. 1, UK and USA), 1993; Ultra (No. 1, UK), 1997; The Singles 86–98, 1998; Exciter, 2001; One Night In Paris (DVD), 2002; Solo album: Counterfeit, 1989. *Honours:* BPI BRIT Award, Enjoy the Silence, 1991; Ivor Novello Award – International Achievement, 1999. *Current Management:* Jonathan Kessler, Baron Inc, 41 River Terrace, #3308 New York, NY 10282, USA. *Address:* First Floor, Regent House, 106 Marylebone High St, London W1M 3DB, England. *Website:* www.depechemode.com.

GORE, Simon Anthony; b. 14 Nov. 1962, Bristol, England. Musician (drums). *Education:* Technical College. *Career:* Television debut at age 14 on BBC 1; Touring and recording with Andy Sheppard including many television and radio appearances, 1986–91; Currently teaching at several schools in Bristol and The Welsh College of Music and Drama in Cardiff. *Recordings:* Andy Sheppard, 1987; Introductions In The Dark, 1988; Soft On The Inside, also on video, 1990. *Membership:* Musicians' Union; PAMRA. *Address:* 133 British Rd, Bedminster, Bristol BS3 3BY, England.

GORHAM, Scott; b. 17 March 1951, Santa Monica, California, USA. Rock Musician (guitar). *Career:* Guitarist, pub circuit, with Fast Buck, early 1970s; Guitarist, UK rock group Thin Lizzy, 1974–83; Founder member, 21 Guns, 1992; Appearances with Thin Lizzy include: Reading Festival, 1974, 1975, 1983; Great British Music Festival, London, 1975; World Series of Rock, Cleveland, 1979; Monsters of Rock, European tour, 1983; Reunion tribute to Phil Lynott, Self Aid concert, Dublin (with Bob Geldof), 1991. *Recordings:* with Thin Lizzy: Singles: The Boys Are Back In Town, 1976; Dancin' In The Moonlight, 1977; Rosalie, 1978; Sarah, 1979; Waiting For An Alibi, 1979; Chinatown, 1980; Killer On The Loose, 1980; Killers Live (EP), 1981; Cold Sweat, 1982; Thunder and Lightning, 1983; Albums with Thin Lizzy: Nightlife, 1974; Fighting, 1975; Jailbreak, 1976; Johnny The Fox, 1976; Bad Reputation, 1977; Live and Dangerous, 1978; Black Rose (A Rock Legend), 1979; Chinatown, 1980; Adventures of Thin Lizzy, 1981; Renegade, 1981; Thunder and Lightning, 1983; Dedication – The Very Best of Thin Lizzy, 1991; Thin Lizzy Live, 1992; Wild One, 1996; One Night Only, 2000; with 21 Guns: Salute, 1992. *Address:* 49 Oakhill Rd, Putney, London SW15, England.

GORMAN, Steve; b. 17 Aug. 1965, Muskegon, MI, USA. Musician (drums). *Education:* Western Kentucky University. *Career:* Mem., Mary My Hope; Mem., Black Crowes, 1987–; Major concerts include: Support tours to Heart, 1990; Robert Plant, 1990; ZZ Top, 1991; Memphis In May Festival, 1991; Monsters of Rock Festival, Castle Donington, 1991; Glastonbury Festival, 1993; Phoenix Festival, 1993. *Recordings:* Albums: Shake Your Money Maker, 1990; The Southern Harmony and Musical Companion, 1992; Amorica, 1994; Three Snakes and One Charm, 1996; Sho Nuff: The Complete Black Crowes, 1998; By Your Side, 1999; Live At The Greek, 2000; Tribute To A Work In Progress: Greatest Hits 1990–1999, 2001; Lions, 2001; Live, 2002. *Honours:* Rolling Stone magazine, Best New American Band, Best Male New Singer, 1991. *Address:* c/o V2 Records, 14 E Fourth St, New York, NY 10012, USA. *E-mail:* info@theblackcrowes.com. *Website:* www.blackcrowes.com.

GORME, Eydie (Edith); b. 16 Aug. 1931, New York, USA. Vocalist. m. Steve Lawrence, 29 Dec. 1957. *Career:* Toured with Tommy Tucker; Tex Beneke; Night club singer; Recording artiste, 1952–; Own radio show, Cita Con Eydie; Regular shows and recordings with husband Steve Lawrence, 1953–; Member, Steve Allen's Troupe, Tonight Show, 1954; Stage performances: Jerry Lewis Stage Show, Broadway, 1967; Golden Rainbow, Broadway, 1968; Numerous other US stage performances and television specials, including tributes to George Gershwin, Cole Porter, Irving Berlin; Television adaptation, Alice In Wonderland, 1987; Support to Frank Sinatra, Diamond Jubilee world tour, 1991. *Recordings:* Singles: I've Gotta Crow; Tea For Two; Fini; Too Close For Comfort; Mama Teach Me To Dance; Love Me Forever; You Need Hands; with Steve Lawrence: I Want To Stay Here; I Can't Stop Talking About You; Numerous albums include: Eydie Gorme, 1957; Eydie Swings The Blues, 1957; Eydie In Love, 1958; On Stage, 1959; Eydie Sings Showstoppers, 1959; Eydie In Dixieland, 1960; Come Sing With Me, 1961; I Feel So Spanish, 1962; Blame It On The Bossa Nova, 1963; Let The Good Times Roll, 1963; Amor, 1964; More Amor, 1965; Don't Go To Strangers, 1966; Tonight I'll Say A Prayer, 1970; Toname O Dejame, 1985; Come In From The Rain, 1985; Canta, 1987; Blanca Navidad, 1990; Muy Amigos,

1993; Personalidad, 1996; Corazon, 1998; Eres Tu, 1999; with Steve Lawrence: We Got Us, 1960; Cozy, 1961; On Broadway, 1967; What It Was, Was Love, 1969; Real True Lovin', 1969; We Can Make It Together, 1975; Our Best To You, 1977; Alone Together, 1989; Black Hole Sun, recorded for Loungeapalooza compilation, 1998. *Honours:* Grammy Awards: We Got Us, 1960; Female Vocalist of the Year, 1967; 7 Emmy Awards, Steve and Eydie Celebrate Irving Berlin. *Address:* c/o Premier Artists Services, 1401 University Dr. #305, Coral Springs, FL 33071, USA.

GORNA, Jarmila Xymena; b. 26 April 1967, Lodz, Poland. Musician (Piano, Vocalist); Composer. *Education:* MA, Karol Szymanowski Academy of Music. *Career:* Sovay (television documentary), 1989; OKF Concert, 1990; Trolley Stop, 1995–97; Radio 3FM Interview, 1996; Union Chapel, 1997; Jerusalem, Bird of Paradise Cafe, 1997; Music to Bram Stoker's Dracula, Bruntion Theatre Co, 1997; London ICA, 1998; The Singularity Show, Albany Theatre, London, 1998; Trojan Women, Cambridge Arts Theatre, 1998; Jazz Cafe, 1999; Broadcast of music and interview by BBC World Service and TV Polonia, 1999; Elektra, Cambridge Arts Theatre, 2001; Composed and performed music to TV documentary, Hidden Children, 2001; Sang on soundtrack to Italian film, Luna Rossa, 2001. *Compositions:* Numerous including, Which Way?; Swansong; Always?; Dark Spell; The Swallow's Flight Dream; Tatra; Pebbles and Seagulls; Fairy Tale World; It's OK; Love Search; Until We Find It!; A Seal Upon Thy Heart; Approaching Your Insanity; My Hope; From There To Here; Closing. *Recordings:* Hashgachah; Furmanka. *Membership:* Musicians' Union. *Address:* Flat 3, 51 Clapton Common, London E5 9AA, England.

GORR, Jon Carl; b. 26 Sept. 1958, Fredericksburg, Virginia, USA. Composer; Musician (keyboards). *Education:* Jazz Composition, Chatauqua Institute, 1975; BM, Jazz Composition, Berklee College of Music, 1980. *Career:* President, Massmedia, 1983–; Songwriter, Cortlem Production, 1983–88; Castle Music, 1984–87; Keyboard player for: I-Tones; Eek-A-Mouse; Mighty Diamonds; Horace Andy, 1980–88; Steve Recker, 1986–87; Bo Diddley, 1987–88; Keyboard player, Gladiators (Europe), 1988–89; Composer, television and film music; Film appearance: Day of The Dead, 1976; Television appearance: Spenser For Hire, 1987. *Recordings:* Albums: It's No Lie, 1985; Walk On By, 1985; On The Right Track, 1988. *Honours:* Boston Music Award, Best Reggae Band, 1987; Beat Magazine Readers Poll, Best Keyboard Player, 1987.

GORRIE, Alan; b. 19 July 1946, Perth, Scotland. Vocalist; Musician (bass). *Career:* Member, The Vikings, Scotland, 1964–67; Member, Scots of St James, London, 1967–68; Member, Forever More, 1969–71; Founder, The Average White Band, 1972–83; Renaissance, 1989; Member, Daryl Hall and Hall and Oates, 1993–94; Currently with Average White Band; International performances include: Lincoln Festival, 1972; Support to Eric Clapton, London, 1973; US tours, 1973; The Summer of 80 Garden Party, Crystal Palace, London, with Bob Marley, Joe Jackson, 1980; Group re-formed, 1989. *Compositions include:* Pick Up the Pieces, 1974; Cut the Cake, 1972, 1975; When Will You Be Mine, 1978; Lets Go Round Again, 1980; Sleepless Nights, 1984; Every Beat of My Heart, 1995. *Recordings:* Singles include: Pick Up The Pieces (No. 1, USA), 1975; Cut The Cake, 1975; Let's Go Round Again, 1980; Albums: Show Your Hand, 1973; Average White Band, 1974; Cut The Cake, 1975; Soul Searching, 1976; Person To Person, 1977; Benny and Us, 1977; Warmer Communications, 1977; Atlantic Family Live at Montreux, 1977; Feel No Fret, 1979; Shine, 1980; Vol. VIII, 1980; Cupid's In Fashion, 1982; Sleepless Nights, solo, 1985; Aftershock, 1989; Soul Alone, with Daryl Hall, 1993; Soul Tattoo, 1996; Very Best of, 1998; Played on Tommi Mischell, Tommi Mischell, 2001. *Honours:* ASCAP R&B Awards, 1993, 1996; 14 Platinum, Gold and Silver Discs world-wide, 1975, 1976, 1977, 1978, 1980, 1992, 1993. *Membership:* PRS; ASCAP. *Current Management:* Wm Morris Agency, 151 El Camino Dr, Beverly Hills, CA 90212, USA; Miracle Artists, 1 York St, London W1H 1PZ, England.

GORSE, Vesna; b. 30 Sept. 1961, Skopje, Macedonia. Musician (alto saxophone); Composer; Writer. m. Drazen Franolic, 20 June 1992. *Career:* Gorse-Franolic duo; Gorse-Franolic trio; Group: Tao; Concerts: Vatroslav Lisinski Concert Hall, Zagreb; Ljubljana; Belgrade; Sarajevo; Dubrovnik; Rijeka; Maribor, Italy; Multimedia festival, Czechoslovakia; Live album recordings at Lisinski. *Recordings:* with Drazen Franolic: Waterfalls, 1986; New Era of Instrumental Music, 1990; Wonderland, 1990; Asgard Live, 1993; Just A Music…, 1995. *Membership:* Croatian Composers' Society; Croatian Music Union; Amnesty International; World SF. *Current Management:* Vesna Gorse. *Address:* Vankina 3, Zagreb, Croatia.

GOSDIN, Vern; b. 5 Aug. 1934, Woodland, Alabama, USA. Country Vocalist; Songwriter; Musician (guitars, banjo, mandolin). *Career:* Member, Gosdin Family (with brothers), radio station, Birmingham, Alabama; Nightclub owner, Chicago, 1956; Member, Golden State Boys, early 1950s; The Hillmen, with Chris Hillman; Session musician, includes Gene Clark, 1966; Owner, glass shop, Atlanta, 1967–76; Solo artiste, and as Gosdin Brothers, 1977–. *Compositions include:* Someone To Turn To, The Byrds. *Recordings:* US Country No. 1 hits: I Can Tell By The Way You Dance; Set 'Em Up Joe; Other hits: Hangin' On; Yesterday's Gone; Till The End; Albums: with The Hillmen:

The Hillmen, 1969; with The Gosdin Brothers: Gene Clark With The Gosdin Brothers, 1966; Sounds of Goodbye, 1968; Solo albums: Till The End, 1977; Never My Love, 1978; You've Got Somebody, 1979; Passion, 1981; If You're Gonna Do Me Wrong, Do It Right, 1983; Today My World Slipped Away, 1983; Dream Lady, 1984; There Is A Season, 1984; If Jesus Comes Tomorrow, 1984; Time Stood Still, 1985; Chiseled In Stone, 1988; Alone, 1989; Out of My Heart, 1991; Nickels and Dimes and Love, 1993; The Gospel Album, 1995; Set 'Em Up, 1995; If You're Gonna Do Me Wrong, 1996; 24 Karat Heartache, 1997; Silver Eagle Cross Country, 1997; Time Stood Still, 1998. *Address:* c/o Kathy Gangwisch and Associates Inc, 5100 Harris Ave, Kansas City, MO 64133–2331, USA.

GOSS, Kieran John; b. 18 May 1962, Newry, Northern Ireland. Songwriter; Vocalist. *Education:* LLB, Queen's University, Belfast. *Career:* Various TV appearances, Ireland; UK; Australia include: Late Late Show; Wogan; Kenny Live; Tours in Ireland; UK; Australia; New Zealand; USA. *Recordings:* Brand New Star; Frances Black and Kieran Goss; New Day, 1995; Worse Than Pride, 1998; Red Letter Day, 2000. *Honours:* Platinum record, Folk Album of Year In Scotland, for New Day, 1995. *Membership:* Musicians' Union. *Current Management:* George McCann, SMA Management. *Address:* 77 Castle St, Belfast BT1, Northern Ireland.

GOSSARD, Stone; b. 20 July 1966, Seattle, WA, USA. Rock Musician (guitar). *Career:* Member, Green River, 1987–89; Guitarist, Mother Love Bone, 1989; Member, Pearl Jam, 1990–; Member, tribute group Temple of The Dog, 1991; Formed Shame (renamed Brad), 1993–; Concerts with Pearl Jam: Support to Alice In Chains, 1991; Lollapalooza Festival tour, 1992; Group appeared in film Singles, 1992; Drop In The Park concert, Seattle, 1992; Neil Young's Bridge School Benefit, with Elton John, Sammy Hagar, James Taylor, 1992; Concert appearances with Keith Richards; Neil Young. *Recordings:* with Mother Love Bone: Shine (EP), 1989; Apple, 1990; Albums with Pearl Jam: Ten (No. 2, USA), 1992; Vs. (No. 1, USA), 1993; Vitalogy, 1994; No Code, 1996; Yield, 1998; Live on Two Legs, 1998; Binaural, 2000; Live, 2000; Riot Act, 2002; with Temple of The Dog: Temple of The Dog, 1992; with Brad: Shame, 1993; Interiors, 1997; Welcome To Discovery Park, 2002. Singles with Pearl Jam: Alive, 1992; Even Flow, 1992; Jeremy, 1992. *Honours:* Platinum discs; American Music Awards, Favourite New Artist, Pop/Rock and Hard Rock categories, 1993; Rolling Stone Readers' Awards: Best New American Band, Best Video, 1993; 4 MTV Awards, 1993; Highest 1-week album sales total in history, Vs., 1993. *Current Management:* Curtis Management, 417 Denny Way, Suite 200, Seattle, WA 98109, USA.

GOTT, Karel; b. 14 July 1939, Plzen, Czech Republic. Vocalist. 2 d. *Education:* Studied under Professor Karenin, Prague Conservatory. *Career:* Member, Semafor Theatre, Prague, 1963–65; Member, Apollo Theatre, Prague, 1965–67; Freelance artiste, 1967–; Numerous foreign tours; Co-operation with record companies; Founder, chairman, Interpo Foundation, 1993–. *Honours:* Numerous Golden Nightingale Trophies, annual pop singer poll, 1963–; MIDEM Prize, Cannes, 1967; Music Week, Star of the Year, 1974, 1975; Artist of Merit, 1982; Gold Aerial, BRT radio station, Belgium, 1984; National Artist, 1985; Polydor Golden Pin, Germany, 1986; Gold discs. *Address:* Nad Bertramkou 18, 15000 Prague 5, Czech Republic.

GOTT, Larry; b. 24 July 1957, England. Musician (guitar). *Career:* Mem., James, 1985–95; Numerous tours, festival dates and television appearances; Returned for farewell 'Getting Away With It' concert, Manchester Evening News Arena, Dec. 2001. *Recordings:* Albums: Stutter, 1986; Strip Mine, 1988; One Man Clapping, 1989; Gold Mother, 1990; Seven, 1992; Laid, 1993; Wah Wah, 1994; Getting Away With It, 2002. Singles incl.: Jim 2 (EP), 1985; How Was It For You, 1990; Come Home, 1990; Lose Control, 1990; Sit Down, 1991; Sound, 1991; Born Of Frustration, 1992; Ring The Bells, 1992; Seven, 1992; Sometimes, 1993; Laid, 1993; Say Something/Jam J, 1994.

GOTT, Susan (Susi); b. 4 Sept. 1962, Asheville, NC, USA. Musician (fiddle); Vocalist; Songwriter. m. Christian Séguret, 30 Sept. 1990, 1 s., 1 d. *Education:* BA, Environmental Science. *Career:* Performing, including The Smithsonian National Institute, 1977; The Kennedy Center, with Masters of Bluegrass, 1986; NPR's All Things Considered, 1982; Nashville Networks' Fire on the Mountain; The Knoxville World's Fair, 1982; Sacrée Soirée, Paris, with Hugues Aufray. *Compositions:* Bound for New Orleans; Dancing Man; Hole in the Deep Blue Sea, with Christian Séguret. *Recordings:* CMH with Eddie Adcock and Talk of the Town; Cowbell Hollow; A Video Postcard of the Blue Ridge, with David Holt; Talking Feet, with Mike Seeger; Guitars, with Christian Séguret and Thierry Massoulore. *Honours:* Champion Fiddler, Fiddler's Grove, 1978, 1984; First Place Songwriter, Chris Austin Songwriting Contest, 1996. *Membership:* International Bluegrass Music Asscn; Women in Bluegrass; SACEM. *Current Management:* Co-Prod Music. *Address:* 1 rue du Pourtour, 45340 Auxy, France.

GOTTI, Irv, (Irv Lorenzo); b. Hollis, Queens, New York, USA. Music Co Exec.; Prod. m. Debbie. *Career:* DJ Irv; Prod. at Island Def Jam, artistes such as Ashanti, Charli Baltimore, Toni Braxton, DMX, Ja Rule, Jay-Z; CEO, Murder Inc Records. *Recordings:* Irv Gotti Presents… series of albums.

Address: c/o Murder Inc Records, 2220 Colorado Ave, Santa Monica, CA 90404, USA. *Website:* www.murderincrecords.com.

GOTTLIEB, Gordon; b. 23 Oct. 1948, Brooklyn, New York, USA. Musician (percussion). *Education:* BM, 1970, MS, 1971, Juilliard School of Music. *Career:* Performed with Stevie Wonder, Ray Charles, Patti LaBelle, Tony Bennett, Paula Abdul, Michael Bolton, Bette Midler, Sarah Vaughan, Quincy Jones, Al Jarreau, Paul Winter. *Compositions:* The River Speaker; Improvisations with Jay Gottlieb; Ritual Dancer; Fanfare, with Paul Winter; Various jingles. *Recordings:* History, Michael Jackson; Kingdom of the Sun, film with Sting; Bulletproof Heart, with Grace Jones; A Secret Life, with Marianne Faithfull; Romulus Hunt, My Romance, with Carly Simon; Sostice Live!, Prayer for the Wild Things, with Paul Winter; Pete, Pete Seeger; Many films and jingles; Currently recording latest album with Steely Dan. *Publications:* The Percussion of Carnival, for Modern Percussionist magazine, 1984; World Influences: Africa and South India, 1985; 3 articles on studio playing, 1985. *Honours:* Grammy Awards, Paul Winters, Prayer for the Wild Things, 1994, Pete Seeger, Pete; NARAS Most Valuable Player Award, New York Studios, 1989; Grants: Martha Baird Rockefeller Grant, 1980, Meet the Composer Grant, 1989. *Membership:* Percussive Arts Society; NARAS; Recording Musicians Asscn. *Address:* 29 W 17th St Fl 8, New York, NY 10011, USA.

GOUGH, Damon. See: **BADLY DRAWN BOY.**

GOUGH, Orlando; b. 24 Aug. 1953, Brighton, England. Composer. m. Joanna Osborne, 2 Dec. 1989, 2 s. *Career:* Member of Bands: The Lost Jockey, 1978–82; Man Jumping, 1983–87; Founded the choir The Shout, 1998. *Compositions:* Hoovering the Beach, 1979; Buzz Buzz Buzz Went the Honeybee, 1980; Secret Gardens, 1981; New Tactics, 1982; Further and Further into the Night, 1984; Mozart At Palm Springs, 1983–84; Bosendorfer Waltzes, 1985; Weighing The Heart, 1986–87; Goes Without Saying, 1988; Mathematics of a Kiss, 1989; Savage Water, 1989; Currulao, 1989; Late, 1991; Lives of the Great Poisoners, 1991; Slow Walk, Fast Talk, 1992; The Air Shouts, 1992; Earth Bound, 1993; Saeta, 1993; The Empress, 1992–93; Escape at Sea, 1994; On the Rim of the World, 1994–97; Badenheim, 1995; People's Century, 1995–97; Sleeping with Audrey, 1996; Hotel, 1996–97; Room of Cooks, 1996–97; Room of Cooks, 1997; Axaxaxas Mlo, 1997; When We Stop Talking, 1998; The Shouting Fence, 1998; Why Do You Sing?, 1998; Corona, 1999; Pierrot: A Biography, 1999; Fortune Cookies, 1999. *Recordings:* Message From the Border, 1996; The Dancing Lawn, 1999. *Publications:* The Complete A Level Maths, 1987. *Current Management:* Soundtrack, 25 Ives St, London SW3 2ND, England. *Address:* 12 Spencer Rise, London NW5 1AP, England.

GOUIRAND, Doudou (Gérard); b. 28 April 1940, Menton, France. Musician (alto and soprano saxophones). m. Monica Adrian, 28 Oct. 1966, 2 s., 1 d. *Education:* University degree. *Career:* Various European festivals; Most French jazz festivals; Tours and festivals, Canada; Africa; Scandinavia; Lithuania; Algeria; Middle East; UK (including Pan-Africa Festival, London, 1984); Poland. *Recordings:* Albums: Islands, with Chris McGregor, 1981; Mouvements Naturels, with J. Dyaui/Pierre Dorge, 1982; Chanting and Dancing, with World Music Company, 1985; Forgotten Tales, with Don Cherry, 1986; Space, with Mal Waldron, 1987; La Nuit De Wounded Knee, 1990; Le Matin D'Un Fauve, with Mal Waldron, 1994; Nino Rota Fellini, W. G. Pansanel, 1995. *Current Management:* Opus Productions, Montpellier, France.

GOULD, Tony; b. 21 Feb. 1940, Melbourne, Australia. Musician (piano); Composer; Educator. *Education:* BMus, Melbourne University; MA, Monash University; PhD, LaTrobe University. *Career:* Lecturer, University of Melbourne, 1973–83, Head, Postgraduate Department and Improvisation Department, School of Music, Victorian College of Arts, Melbourne; Chief Music Critic, Herald Sun. *Compositions:* Concerto for Percussion, Violin, Viola Piano and Saxophone; Music for Narration of Dylan Thomas's Under Milk Wood; Music for various jazz ensembles. *Recordings:* Gould Plus Gould; Best of Friends; Tony Gould Quartet; Chronicle; Lirill; Tin Roof For The Rain. *Publications:* Contributor, New Grove Dictionary of Jazz, 1988, 1999, Oxford Companion to Australian Music, 1997. *Membership:* Australia Council Music Fund. *Current Management:* Ruben Zylbenspic, St Kilda, Victoria. *Address:* PO Box 605, Woodend, Vic 3442, Australia.

GOULDMAN, Graham Keith; b. 10 May 1946, Manchester, England. Songwriter; Musician (guitar, bass). m. Gill, 7 Oct. 1988, 2 s., 2 d. (1 s., 1 d., by previous marriage). *Career:* Many concert tours, television and radio appearances as member of 10cc. *Compositions:* for The Yardbirds: For Your Love; Heart Full of Soul; for The Hollies: Bus Stop; Look Thru Any Window; for Herman's Hermits: No Milk Today; Co-wrote for 10cc: Rubber Bullets; Wall Street Shuffle; I'm Mandy Fly Me; Good Morning Judge; I'm Not In Love; Things We Do For Love; Dreadlock Holiday; Co-wrote for Wax: Bridge To Your Heart; Co-wrote Straight To Video, with Kirsty MacColl, for her album Tropical Brainstorm, 1999. *Recordings include:* 10cc hit singles: Donna, 1972; Rubber Bullets (No. 1, UK), 1973; The Dean and I, 1973; Wall Street Shuffle, 1974; Silly Love, 1974; Life Is A Minestrone, 1975; I'm Not In Love (No. 1, UK; No. 2, USA), 1975; Art For Art's Sake, 1975; I'm Mandy Fly

Me, 1976; The Things We Do For Love, 1976; Good Morning Judge, 1977; Dreadlock Holiday (No. 1, UK), 1978; solo: Graham Gouldman Thing, 1968; Animalolympics, 1980. *Honours:* Ivor Novello Awards for: Rubber Bullets; I'm Not In Love; BMI citations for most of the above songs. *Membership:* Musicians' Union; PRS; SODS (Society of Distinguished Songwriters). *Current Management:* Harvey Lisberg. *Address:* Harvey Lisberg Associates, 6 Highgate, St Margarets Rd, Altrincham, Cheshire WA14 2AP, England.

GOUPY, Christian; b. 21 June 1962, Evreux, France. Composer; Musician (piano). *Education:* Brevet de Technician Superieur Mechanique et Automatisme; American School of Modern Music; Conservatoire International, Paris. *Career:* Concerts in France with The Footprints Quintet and The Croco Jazz Big Band; Pianist, Dagorno Restaurant, Paris; Now working with the marching band, Les Pieds Mobiles (piano, sax and drums) playing jazz, funk and groove music. *Recordings:* Escale, Footprints Quintet; Oh Happy Day, Voce Vita Gospel Group; Next To, Croco Jazz Big Band. *Publications:* Editions Combre, Paris; Quatuors de Saxs. *Current Management:* Christian Goupy Asscn Evasion. *Address:* 18 Impasse St Sébastien, 75011 Paris, France.

GOURDIKIAN, Herve; b. 31 Dec. 1966, Lyon, France. Musician (saxophones, piano). m. Olga Kroutolapova, 23 April 1992, 1 d. *Education:* Two years at Berklee College of Music, Boston; French Conservatory, Lyon. *Career:* Tour, Rêve Orange (Liane Foly); Tour, Les Petites Notes (Liane Foly); Concert Place de la Concorde for Liberation of Paris (audience 500,000); TV show: Taratata; Nulle Part Ailleurs with Andoine de Camaes. *Recordings:* With Liane Foly: Reve Orange; Cameleon; Lumières; Sweet Misery; Also with: Nilda Fernandez; HMF; Mellow Man; Brigitte Fontaine; Mario Stanchen. *Honours:* Gold record, Lumières, Liane Foly. *Address:* 258 Ave Georges Clemenceau, 92000 Nanterre, France.

GOURLEY, Jimmy (James Pasco, Jr); b. 9 June 1926, St Louis, Missouri, USA. Musician (guitar); Vocalist; Composer. *Career:* Began in Chicago, 1944; Member, Jay Burkhart Orchestra with Sonny Stitt, Gene Ammons, Lou Levy; Member, Jackie Cain, Roy Kral Quintet; Played in Chicago with Chubby Jackson, Anita O'Day, 1951, 1954–57; Worked in Paris with Lester Young, Kenny Clarke, Stan Getz, Stéphane Grappelli, 1957–96. *Recordings:* (with) Clifford Brown; Zoot Sims; Bob Brookmeyer; Kenny Clarke; Eddy Louiss; Lou Bennett; Henri Renaud; Lee Konitz; Chubby Jackson; Lester Young; Duke Ellington; Guy Lafitte; Richard Galliano; (Own recordings) Jimmy Gourley and the Paris Heavyweights, 1972; Graffitti, 1976; Repetition, 1981; Feeling Jazzy, 1983; The Jazz Trio, 1983; The Left Bank of NY, 1986; Flying The Coop (with Richard Galliano Four), 1991; The Jazz Trio, 1995; Jazz Guitar – Essential Jazz, 1995; Our Delight, 1995; Highlights, 1995; with Stan Getz: Stan Getz, 1958; Live In Europe, 1958; with Stéphane Grappelli: Satin Doll, 1972; Plays Gershwin, 1973; Plays Cole Porter, 1973. *Membership:* SACEM. *Address:* 114 Ave Anatole France, 94190 Villeneuve St Georges, France. *Telephone:* (1) 43-82-38-32. *Fax:* (1) 43-82-38-32.

GOURLEY, Sean; b. 12 Dec. 1963, Paris, France. Jazz Musician (guitar); Vocalist. *Education:* Classical guitar, age 6–14; Jazz harmony, USA, 1983–84; Jazz harmony, with father, Jimmy Gourley and personal coaches. *Career:* Player, singer, arranger, own band, playing bebop jazz, concerts, clubs; Plays with father Jimmy Gourley in Family Affair Band; Festivals include: Calvi, Corsica; Madagascar (US Embassy); Guitar Masters of Pau, France; Played with: Barney Wilen; Stephanie Crawford; Kim Parker; Also with arrangers Onzy Mathews; Mundell Lowe; Various French musicians. *Address:* 6 rue Sauffroy, 75017 Paris, France.

GOVERT, Eddy (Van Mouffaert); b. 15 Jan. 1949, Bruges, Belgium. Accordionist; Songwriter; Prod. m. Anneke Van Thorre, 12 Aug. 1991, 2 d. *Education:* Muziek Conservatorium, Bruges. *Career:* Many appearances, band player, 1964–70; Singer, songwriter, as Eddy Govert, 1970–; Solo as international accordion act Le Grand Julot, 1973–; Founded Jump Records and Music, 1975; Professional singer, 1980s. *Recordings:* with Paul Severs: Ik Ben Verliefd Op Jou, 1971; Love, 1972; with Ronald and Donald: Couac Couac, 1974; with Ricky Gordon: Such A Night; with Margriet Hermans: Don Bosco; Many top 10 hits, 1975–81; as Eddy Govert: Te Kort Van Duur, 1988; Albums: International 1, 1991; International 2, 1993; Belgian Accordion Championship, 1965. *Honours:* Golden Lion Joepie, 1974; Gold Record, 1974; Cultuurprys Erpe-Mere, 1996. *Membership:* SABAM; URADEX, Brussels; ZAMU, Brussels. *Current Management:* Happy Melody VZW. *Address:* Langemunt 71, G420 Aaigem, Belgium.

GRABOWSKI, Stephan A; b. 18 Dec. 1964, Copenhagen, Denmark. Musician; Vocalist; Composer; Prod; Arranger. 1 d. *Education:* Private Lessons by Hans Fagt, Hanne Bekow. *Career:* Played with Lars H.U.G., 1987–93; Several national tours; Several television and radio appearances and gigs in France, Russia, Greenland; With Love Shop, Janes Rejoice, Goldfinger and special appearances with Peter Bell, Caroline Henderson, Thomas Di Leva, Elisabeth, Shirtsville, Nina Forsberg. *Compositions:* Girl in the Ghetto, 1993; Crazy Restless Summer, Who Are You?, 1996; Verden Folo Af Frugt, Gaderne Huisker, 1997. *Recordings:* Glitter Angels, 1993; Songs For Night Clubs, 1996; Underligere End Kaerlighed, 1997. *Honours:* Reward,

National Arts Trust, 1994, 1996; Numerous Grammy Awards with Lars H.U.G., 1990–92. *Membership:* Artisten; Danish Artist Union; DPA. *Address:* c/o Skriver, Guldbergsgade 12 St Tv, 22000 Copenhagen N, Denmark.

GRACE, Whyte; b. England. Composer; Musician (electronic keyboards, guitar); Vocalist; Poet. m. twice, single 1986–, 3 s., 1 d. *Career:* Toured schools, clubs libraries, playing acoustic guitar solos, reading poetry, singing folk songs in Bedfordshire, 1970s–80s; Performer, keyboards at dinners, matinees, festivals, London, 1990s–; Show, Life's a Gas with Grace; Fundraiser for ChildLine. *Compositions:* Over 100 instrumentals and ballads; Over 100 poems for adults and children; Programme for children of music, singing, stories, poems, dancing, games, puppets; Currently compiling album of musical stories for children. *Publications:* 18 anthologies of poetry; The Londonium Bug, book of verse and cartoons, 1997. *Honours:* Poetry competition winner, 1970; Pictures exhibited; Inducted into the International Poetry Hall of Fame. *Membership:* Musicians' Union; Designers and Artists Copyright Society (DACS); ABI; IBC. *Address:* 56 Warltersville Mansions, Warltersville Rd, London N19 3AS, England.

GRACIE, Charlie (Charles); b. 14 May 1936, Philadelphia, PA, USA. Vocalist; Musician (guitar). m. Joan D'Amato, 15 Feb. 1958, 1 s., 1 d. *Education:* Tutored by father, Sam Gracie; Studied guitar under professional teacher. *Career:* Youthful Guitar Prodigy, Paul Whiteman TV Teen Show; Played on radio commercials for the Sealtest, Big Top, CBS Program; Headlined, The Alan Freed Show, Brooklyn Paramount, 1957; Ed Sullivan Show; Numerous appearances on American Bandstand TV; Headlined the London Hippodrome and Palladium, 1957; Headlined Yarmouth Rock Festival, England, 1980s; Continues to tour Europe, Italy, Germany, England; Starred in Warner Brothers Rock Movie, Jamboree, 1958; Opened major US shows for, and recording with, Van Morrison, 2000. *Compositions:* Fabulous, incl. on album, Run Devil Run, Paul McCartney, 1999. *Recordings:* Albums: Charlie Gracie—The Cameo Parkway Sessions, 1979; Amazing Gracie, 1982; Charlie Gracie—Live At The Stockton Globe 1957, 1996; It's Fabulous—It's Charlie Gracie (compilation), 1996; I'm All Right, 2001. Singles incl.: Butterfly; Fabulous; I Love You So Much. *Honours:* Gold disc, Butterfly, 1957. *Membership:* ASCAP. *Current Management:* Paul Barrett, R & R Enterprises, 16 Grove Pl., Penarth CF64 2ND, Wales. *Address:* 820 Edmonds Ave, Drexel Hill, PA 19026, USA. *Website:* www.charliegracie.com.

GRAESSER, Johann Peter, (Hanno); b. 26 Dec. 1961, Wehrda, Germany. Violin Teacher; Publisher; Music Scientist. *Education:* State Exam for Violin Teachers, Music College, Dortmund, 1989; MA, Music Education, Music and Theatre Science, University of Munich, 1993; Dr Phil, Jazz Research, University of Giessen, 1995. *Publications:* Jazz Violin, 1991; Stéphane Grappelli's Violintechnik, 1994; Der Jazzgeiger Stéphane Grappelli, 1996; Stéphane Grappelli und die Musik des Quintette du Hot Club de France, 1997; Electric Violins, 1998. *Membership:* International Society for Jazz Research, 1992–. *Address:* Lenzhalde 88, 73732 Esslingen, Germany.

GRAHAM, Bruce Hebenton; b. 9 Nov. 1941, Dundee, Scotland. Musician (multi-instrumentalist); Composer; Author; Entertainer. m. (1) Phyllis Elizabeth McFarlane, 18 Sept. 1963, 1 (adopted) d., (2) Sharon Belinda Maxim, 7 April 1988. *Education:* Private tuition; Schillinger Course of Composition; Pupil, Henry Nelmes Forbes, ABCA. *Career:* Session musician; Musical Director, London recording, television and film studios, West End Theatres; Founder, Jingles Records and Jingles Music, 1985; Featured in cabaret, Old Tyme Music Halls, one-man keyboard concerts, 1988; Worked with: Andy Williams; Rock Hudson; Juliet Prowse; Lulu; The Three Degrees; Sacha Distel; Bob Hope; Sir Harry Secombe; Faith Brown; Tommy Steele; Paul Daniels; Cleo Laine and John Dankworth; Matt Monro; Bruce Forsyth; Marti Webb; Richard Chamberlain; Vince Hill; Jimmy Shand; Jeff Wayne; Des O'Connor; Rolf Harris; Val Doonican; Anthony Newley; Helen Reddy; Wayne Sleep; David Hemmings; Michael Crawford; Lionel Blair; Gemma Craven; Tony Basil; Miss World TV Orchestra; Andrew Lloyd Webber; Phil Tate; Ray McVay; Johnny Howard; Ike Isaacs; Geoff Love; Orchestras include: Sydney Thompson's Old Tyme; National Philharmonic; London Concert; BBC Radio; Scottish Radio; Northern Dance; London Palladium; Own small groups. *Compositions include:* Two Symphonies; A Divertimenti For Strings; Reverie For Brass Band; 10 Suites for Large Jazz Orchestra; One-act Ballet; A Musical; Over 300 songs and shorter pieces. *Publications:* Magazine articles; Music and The Synthesizer, 1969. *Membership:* Musicians' Union; Equity; British Music Writers' Council. *Address:* 25 Milton Rd, Wallington, Surrey SM6 9RP, England.

GRAHAM, Irvin; b. 18 Sept. 1909, Philadelphia, Pennsylvania, USA. Composer; Lyricist. m. Lillian Gologter, 2 Sept. 1943. *Career:* Composer of numerous popular tunes; Wrote Walt Disney's The Whale Who Wanted to Sing at the Met; TV appearances: Your Show of Shows; Fred Waring; Jane Freman. *Compositions:* I Believe; You Better Go Now; With a Twist of the Wrist; In Love with a Married Man. *Recordings:* I Believe, recorded by Barbra Streisand, Elvis Presley; You Better Go Now, recorded by Billie Holliday, Chet Baker, Ben Webster, Johnny Mathis, Jeri Southern. *Honours:* Fellow of the Arts, Yaddo, Banff, Virginia, The MacDowell Colony. *Membership:*

ASCAP; WGA; SAG; AFTRA; Dramatists Guild. *Address:* 366 E 55th, New York, NY 10022, USA.

GRAHAM, Mikey (Michael Charles Christopher); b. 15 Aug. 1972, Dublin, Ireland. Vocalist; Record Prod. 1 d. *Career:* Mem., Boyzone, 1993–2001; Solo artiste, 2001–; Formed Mikey Graham Network. *Recordings:* Albums: with Boyzone: Said And Done, 1995; A Different Beat, 1996; Where We Belong, 1998; By Request (No. 1, UK), 1999; Solo: Meet Me Half Way, 2001. Singles: with Boyzone: Working My Way Back To You, 1994; Key To My Life, 1995; Love Me For A Reason, 1995; So Good, 1995; Father and Son, 1995; Coming Home Now, 1995; Words (No. 1, UK), 1996; A Different Beat (No. 1, UK), 1996; Isn't It A Wonder, 1997; Baby Can I Hold You Tonight, 1997; Musical Experience, 1997; Picture of You, 1997; All That I Need (No. 1, UK), 1998; I Love The Way You Love Me, 1998; When The Going Gets Tough (No. 1, UK), 1999; You Needed Me (No. 1, UK), 1999; Every Day I Love You, 1999; Solo: You're My Angel, 2000; If You'd Only, 2000; You Could Be My Everything, 2001. *Website:* www.mikeygraham.co.uk.

GRAHAME, Alan; b. Cornwall, England. Musician (percussion). m. Dulcie Sawyer, 1 s., 2 d. *Career:* Ralph Sharon Sextet, London Jazz Club groups; Jerry Allen Trio: Variety; Music Hall; Freelance studio percussionist; Major tours, UK and Europe with Tom Jones; Shirley Bassey; Perry Como; Englebert Humperdinck; Howard Keel; Radio broadcasts: BBC Radio Orchestra; London Studio Players; Ken Moule Strings; Played with orchestras of: Alec Gould; Ronnie Aldrich; Frank Chacksfield; Cy Payne; Colin Sell; Television appearances include: Jerry Allen Trio; Lunch Box, ATV (8 years); BBC Top of the Pops Orchestra; Benny Hill; Come Dancing; Two Ronnies; Morecambe and Wise; Wogan; Parkinson; Pebble Mill; Miss World; Basil Brush; Crackerjack; Torvil and Dean; Last of The Summer Wine; Tomorrow's World; Playschool; Record Breakers; With artistes: Tom Jones; Shirley Bassey; Roy Castle; Dionne Warwick; Neil Diamond; Buddy Greco; Richard Clayderman; Demis Roussos; Stylistics; Trini Lopez; Vic Damone. *Recordings:* With: Tom Jones; Shirley Bassey; Englebert Humperdinck; Matt Monro; Love Affair; White Plains; Brotherhood of Man; Casuals; 101 Strings; Dana; Lena Zavaroni; Rolf Harris; Frank Pourcell; Jack Emblow; David Essex; Mike Batt; Les Reed; Jeff Wayne; Bee Gees; Peters and Lee; Lena Martell; contributed to albums: Festivals Blues and Saunters, 2000; Rumba, 2001. *Publications:* Articles in Percussion Press (drums, percussion). *Membership:* ISM; Musicians' Union.

GRAILLIER, Michel François; b. 18 Oct. 1946, Lens, France. Musician (piano, synthesizer). m. Micheline Pelzer, 9 July 1982. *Education:* Electronic Engineering; Private teacher for 10 years. *Career:* Tours with group Magma, 1972–73; Juan-les-Pins Festival, 1977–84; Japan with Chet Baker, 1986; Videos: Candy and Live At Ronnie Scott's with Chet Baker; Liege Jazz Festival, 1992; Radio: MG's trio in 1991–94. *Recordings:* Albums: Ad Lib, 1976; Portrait In Black & White, 1995; Fairly, 2002; As leader with: Ad Lib; Fairly; Dream Drops; Others with: Chet Baker; M & B; Al Capolinea; Candy; Chet Sings Again; At Ronnie Scott's; French Ballad; Barney Wilen: Moshi; S Glossman: Born At The Same Time. *Honours:* Django Reinhardt Prize, France, 1978. *Membership:* SACEM; SPEDIDAM; ADAMI. *Current Management:* Micheline Pelzer. *Address:* 1 Passage Cottin, 75018 Paris, France.

GRAINGE, Lucian Charles; b. Afghanistan. Music Co Exec. *Career:* Dir and Gen. Man., RCA Publishing; Established PolyGram Publishing's UK office, 1986; Chair., Britannia Music Co Ltd; Chair. and CEO, Universal Music UK Ltd, following merger of Universal and PolyGram. *Address:* Universal Music UK Ltd, 1 Sussex Pl., London W6 9XS, England.

GRAMM, Lou, (Louis Grammatico); b. 2 May 1950, Rochester, New York, USA. Vocalist; Songwriter. *Career:* Lead singer, Black Sheep, 1975; Foreigner, 1976–90, 1992–; Regular world-wide tours; Major concerts include: California Jam II, 1978; Reading Festival, 1979; New York State Fair, 1994; Also founder member, Shadow King, 1990–91; Also solo artiste. *Recordings:* Albums: with Black Sheep, Black Sheep, 1975; Encouraging Words, 1975; with Foreigner: Foreigner, 1977; Double Vision, 1978; Head Games, 1979; 4 (No. 1, USA), 1981; Records, 1983; Agent Provocateur (No. 1, UK), 1984; Inside Information, 1987; The Very Best Of, 1992; The Very Best... and Beyond, 1992; Mr Moonlight, 1994; Solo albums: Ready Or Not, 1987; Foreigner in a Strange Land, 1988; Long Hard Look, 1989; Hit singles: with Foreigner: Feels Like The First Time, 1977; Cold As Ice, 1977; Long Way From Home, 1978; Hot Blooded, 1978; Double Vision, 1978; Blue Morning Blue Day, 1979; Head Games, 1980; Urgent, 1981; Juke Box Hero, 1981; Waiting For A Girl Like You, 1981; I Want To Know What Love Is (No. 1, USA), 1985; That Was Yesterday, 1985; I Don't Want To Live Without You, 1988; Solo: Midnight Blue, 1987; Just Between You and Me, 1990; Provided backing vocals for: Drivers Eyes, Ian McDonald, 1999. *Address:* c/o Dennis Katz, 845 Third Ave, New York, NY 10022, USA.

GRANAT, Endre; b. 3 Aug. 1937, Hungary. Musician (violin). m. Mimi, 21 Aug. 1993, 1 s. *Education:* University; Pupil, Joseph Gingold, Jascha Heifetz. *Career:* Tours: Europe; USA; South America; Asia; Concert master, soloist, major Hollywood films. *Honours:* Ysaye Award; Grand Prix du Disque. *Membership:* AFofM. *Current Management:* CAMS.

GRANDE, Johnny; b. Philadelphia, USA. Musician (piano). *Career:* Original member, Bill Haley's Comets, 1952–62; Leading innovator of rock 'n' roll music; First rock band to headline a film. *Recordings:* Rock Around The Clock (No. 1, UK and USA), 1955; See You Later Alligator, 1956; Crazy Man Crazy; Shake Rattle and Roll, 1954; Rock The Joint, 1957; Mambo Rock, 1955; Rudy's Rock, 1956; Florida Twist; Skinny Minnie; On The Air (compilation), 2001. *Publications:* Rock Around The Clock; We're Gonna Party; Never Too Old To Rock. *Honours:* Best Vocal Group, 1954; Best Instrumental Group, 1956; Rock and Roll Hall of Fame; Gold Records. *Address:* Rock It Concerts, Bruno-Hofer Platz 1, 80937 Munich, Germany.

GRANDMASTER FLASH, (Joseph Saddler); b. 1 Jan. 1958, Barbados. DJ; Rap Artiste. *Career:* Mobile DJ, The Bronx, New York; Formed Grandmaster Flash and the 3 MCs, the Furious Five, 1977–83; Solo artiste, 1985–; Performed, UK Fresh, Capital Music Festival, Wembley, 1986; European tour, 2002. *Recordings:* Albums: with the Furious Five: The Message, 1982; Greatest Messages, 1984; Solo: They Said It Couldn't Be Done, 1985; The Source, 1986; Ba Dop Boom Bang, 1987; On the Strength, 1988; Greatest Hits, 1992; Adventures On The Wheels of Steel (compilation), 1999; The Official Adventures of Grandmaster Flash, 2002. Singles: with the Furious Five: Freedom, 1980; The Adventures of Grandmaster Flash On The Wheels of Steel, 1981; The Message, 1982; White Lines (Don't Do It), 1983; Dance to the Beat, 1998; Solo: Sign of The Times, 1985; U Know What Time It Is?, 1987. *Address:* c/o Richard Walters Entertainment Inc, 421 S Beverly Dr., Eighth Floor, Beverly Hills, CA 90212, USA.

GRANFELT, Ben Edward; b. 16 June 1963, Helsinki, Finland. Musician (guitar); Songwriter. m. Nanna Granfelt, 14 Jan. 1997. *Career:* Films: Leningrad Cowboys Meet Moses; Tours in Europe, Scandinavia, England, USA, Australia, Japan, with Leningrad Cowboys, Europe, USA, England; Support to Status Quo, with Gringos Locos; Leningrad Cowboys Meet the Alexandrow Red Army, chorus and ensemble, Live. *Recordings:* Ben Granfelt: The Truth; Radio Friendly Live; Guitar Slingers: I; Song and Dance; That Little Something; Leningrad Cowboys: We Cum From Brooklyn; Leningrad Cowboys Go Space; Let's Work Together; Russian Red Army Ensemble; Live in Prowinzz; Gringos Locos: Raw Deal; Punch Rock; Gringos Locos, Ego, 2000. *Honours:* Pro Musica Award, Gymnasiet Grankulla Samskola. *Current Management:* Sprucefield Oy Ltd, Viipurinkatu 8 B 65, 00510 Helsinki, Finland.

GRANT, Amy Lee; b. 25 Nov. 1960, Augusta, Georgia, USA. Vocalist; Songwriter. m. Gary W Chapman, 19 June 1982, 1 s., 2 d. *Education:* Furman University; Vanderbilt University. *Career:* Contemporary Christian (later also pop) singer, songwriter; Began recording career, 1978–; Has sold 18m. records world-wide; First full tour, 1981; Longest tour, Unguarded Tour, 18 months 1985–86; Star of TV Christmas Special: Headin' Home For The Holidays, with Dennis Weaver, Art Garfunkel, Jimmy Webb, 1986. *Compositions include:* Tender Tennessee Christmas (co-writer). *Recordings include:* Amy Grant In Concert Vols I and II; Age To Age, 1982; A Christmas Album, 1983; Unguarded, 1985; Lead Me On, 1988; Heart in Motion, 1991; Home for Christmas, 1992; House of Love, 1994; Behind the Eyes, 1997; A Christmas to Remember, 1999; A Special Wish, 2001. *Publications:* Amy Grant's Heart To Heart Bible Stories, book and cassette. *Honours:* 5 Grammy Awards; 17 Dove Awards including Artist of the Year (4 times); Pax Christi, St John's University (First entertainer, third woman to receive this), 1994. *Current Management:* Blanton/Harrell Entertainment. *Address:* 2910 Poston Ave, Nashville, TN 37203, USA.

GRANT, Eddy, (Edmond Montague Grant); b. 5 March 1948, Plaisance, Guyana. Vocalist; Prod; Musician (multi-instrumentalist). *Career:* Member, The Equals; Founder, own production company; Solo artiste, 1977–; Founder, record label Ice Records; Own studio, The Coach House. *Recordings:* Albums: Message Man, 1977; Walking On Sunshine, 1979; Love In Exile, 1980; Can't Get Enough, 1981; Killer On The Rampage, 1982; Going For Broke, 1984; All The Hits, 1984; File Under Rock, 1988; The Best of Eddy Grant, 1989; Barefoot Soldier, 1990; Paintings of the Soul, 1992; Soca Baptism, 1993; I Don't Wanna Dance, 1997; Eddy Grant's Greatest Hits, 2001; Singles: with The Equals: Baby Come Back (No. 1, UK), 1968; Viva Bobbie Joe, 1969; Black Skin Blue Eyed Boys, 1970; Solo: Living On The Front Line, 1979; Do You Feel My Love, 1980, Can't Get Enough of You, 1981; I Don't Wanna Dance (No. 1, UK), 1982; Electric Avenue (No. 2, UK and USA), 1983; Gimme Hope Joanna, 1988; Electric Avenue (remix), 2001; Walking On Sunshine (remix), 2001. *Current Management:* Metro Management, 24–7 Coda Centre, 189 Munster Rd, London SW6 6AW, England.

GRANT, Ian Fraser; b. 17 Dec. 1950, Lancing, Surrey, England. Artist Management. m. 6 Nov. 1975, 1 s., 1 d. *Education:* GCE and Royal Schools of Music, pianoforte. *Career:* Manager, acts include: The Stranglers, 1975–80; The Skids, 1980–81; Big Country, 1982–; The Cult, 1985–88; Hazel O'Connor, 1980–81; The Members, 1980–81; Maxi Priest, 1987–88. *Current*

Management: Ian Grant Management, PO Box 107, South Godstone, Redhill, Surrey RH9 8JL, England.

GRANT, Manson; b. 9 April 1951, John O'Groats, Scotland. Vocalist; Musician (keyboards, trumpet, accordion). *Education:* HNC, Business studies; Studied piano. *Career:* Television appearances include: Grampian TV; Channel 4; Holiday Programme, BBC2; Concerts include: CMA Fan Fair, Nashville, Tennessee (representing Scotland); Wembley Country Music Festival, London; Joined Dynamos Band, 1970. *Recordings:* 15 albums/cassettes; 3 CDs; 2 videos. *Honours:* More than 60 club and theatre awards. *Membership:* Musicians' Union. *Current Management:* R Cameron. *Address:* Achnaclyth, Tannach, Wick, Caithness KW1 5SF, Scotland.

GRANT, Wanda L; b. 6 May 1965, Antigonish, Nova Scotia, Canada. Songwriter. *Education:* BA, Religious Education; Grade 7, Royal Conservatory. *Compositions:* Christmas Musicals: I've Been Searchin', 1993; Miracle Morn, 1994; The Fisherman's Trade, Breakin' Tradition, 1996. *Membership:* Gospel Music Asscn. *Current Management:* W L Grant. *Address:* PO Box 305, Port Hawkesbury, Nova Scotia B0E 2V0, Canada.

GRAY, Catherine; b. 28 Feb. 1946, Glasgow. Musician. 2 s. *Education:* BA, University of Edinburgh; London College of Music; The Royal Academy of Music. *Publications:* Guide To The Collection, 1987; The Guinness Encyclopedia, Music From Around The World, 1990; Women's Rights in Uganda, 1992; Patterns of Textual Recurrence in Kiganda Song, 1992; The Endongo, A Ugandan Lyre and Its Music, 1993; Compositional Techniques in Roman Catholic Church Music in Uganda, 1996; Temporalistes: Temps, Rhythmes et Musiques, 1996; Static and Dynamic Codes in Kiganda Lyre Song, 1998; Temporal Heterogeneities in Kiganda Music, 1998. *Membership:* Society of Ethnomusicology; British Forum of Ethnomusicology; International Council for Traditional Music. *Address:* 15 Jocks Hill Cresent, Linlithgow, West Lothian EH48 7BJ, Scotland.

GRAY, David; b. 1970 Manchester, England. Vocalist; Musician (multi-instrumentalist); Songwriter. m. Olivia Rooney. *Education:* Ysgol Dewi Sant, St Davids, Pembrokeshire; University of Liverpool, studied art. *Career:* Relocated to Wales with family, aged 9; Experimented in various punk bands prior to residence in London; Signed to Hut/Virgin then EMI for first 3 albums; Built up reputation through live performances; Recorded and released acclaimed fourth album on self-owned IHT label; Contributed tracks to and appeared in film This Year's Love, 1998; Major concert, festival appearances and US tour, 2000–01. *Recordings:* Albums: A Century Ends, 1993; Flesh, 1994; Sell, Sell, Sell, 1996; White Ladder, 1999; Lost Songs 95–98, 2000; A New Day At Midnight, 2002. Singles: Birds Without Wings, 1992; Shine, 1993; Wisdom, 1993; Babylon, 1998; This Year's Love, 1999; Please Forgive Me, 1999; Sail Away, Say Hello–Wave Goodbye, 2001. *Honours:* Ivor Novello Award, Best Song Lyrically and Musically, Babylon, 2001. *Current Management:* c/o East-West Records, United Kingdom. *Website:* www.davidgray.com.

GRAY, Howard; Record Engineer; Prod; Musician. *Career:* Engineer to Steve Lillywhite; Independent Producer mid 1980s; Recording artiste with Apollo 440; Numerous remixes/production credits. *Recordings:* Producer, Mixer, Recording Engineer: Terence Trent D'Arby: Introducing The Hardline; Danny Wilson: Danny Wilson; The Cure: Head On The Door; UB40: Labour of Love; OMD: Sugar Tax; Scritti Politti: Cupid and Psyche '85; Tom Verlaine: Cover; Blue Pearl: Naked; Other recordings by: Yazz; Mori Kante; Geoffrey Williams; Kirsty MacColl; Genesis; U2; Duran Duran; Youssou n'Dour; Manic Street Preachers; Skunk Anansie; Siegman; Dust Junkys; Apollo 440 Singles include: Astral America, 1994; Liquid Cool, 1994; Don't Fear The Reaper, 1995; Krupa, 1996; Ain't Talkin' Bout Dub, 1997; Raw Power, 1997; Rendezvous 98, 1998; Lost In Space, 1998; Stop The Rock, 1999; Heart Go Boom, 1999; Charlie's Angels, 2000. *Current Management:* XL. *Address:* Studio 7, 27A Pembridge Villas, London W11 3EP, England.

GRAY, Les; b. 9 April 1946, Carshalton, Surrey, England. Vocalist. m. Carol, 16 April 1980. *Career:* Member, skiffle and trad jazz bands; Lead singer, Mud, 1967–; Concerts include: Search For Sound, Song Contest Winners, 1967; British tour supporting Tom Jones, 1973; British tours, 1974, 1978; Second Hemsby 70s and Glam Rock Weekender (with Glitter Band, Alvin Stardust, ShowaddyWaddy, Sweet, Rubettes, Mungo Jerry), 1991. *Recordings:* Hit singles with Mud include: Dyna-Mite, 1974; Tiger Feet, (No. 1, UK), 1974; The Cat Crept In, (No. 2, UK), 1974; Rocket, 1974; Lonely This Christmas, (No. 1, UK), 1974; The Secrets That You Keep, (No. 3, UK), 1975; Oh Boy, (No. 1, UK), 1975; L-L-Lucy, 1975; Show Me You're A Woman, 1975; Lean On Me, 1976; Albums: Mud Rock, 1974; Mud Rock Vol. 2, 1975; Mud's Greatest Hits, 1975; Use Your Imagination, 1975; Mudpack, 1978; Rock On, 1979; As You Like It, 1979; Mud, 1983; Let's Have A Party, 1991; Greatest Hits, 2000. *Membership:* Musicians' Union; Equity; PRS; PPL; PRC. *Current Management:* Sharon Sly. *Address:* 99 Wood Vale, London N10 3DL, England.

GRAY, Macy, (Natalie McIntyre); b. 1969, Canton, Ohio, USA. Vocalist; Songwriter. Divorced, 3 d. *Education:* Seven years' classical piano training; Studied, Screenwriting Programme, USC Film School. *Career:* Began as lyricist for musician friends; Began to fill in as singer; Worked as session jazz singer; Signed recording contract, 1998, released first single and album. *Recordings:* Singles: Do Something, 1999; I Try, 1999; Still, 2000; Why Didn't You Call Me, 2000; Demons, with Fatboy Slim, 2000; Sweet Baby, with Erykah Badu, 2001; Sexual Revolution, 2001; Albums: On How Life Is, 1999; The Id, 2001. *Honours:* BRIT Awards: Best International Newcomer, Best International Female Artist, 2000; Grammy Award, Female Pop Vocal Performance, I Try, 2001. *Address:* c/o Sony Music Entertainment (UK) Head Office, 10 Great Marlborough St, London W1F 7LP, England. *Website:* www.macygray.com.

GRAY, Tom; b. 1976, Southport, England. Musician (guitar, bass, keyboards, percussion); Vocalist. *Career:* Founding mem., Gomez, 1996–; Numerous concerts, festival, radio and television appearances. *Recordings:* Albums: Bring It On, 1998; Liquid Skin, 1999; Abandoned Shopping Trolley Hotline, 2000; In Our Gun, 2002. Singles: 78 Stone Wobble, 1998; Whippin' Piccadilly, 1998; Get Myself Arrested (EP), 1998; Bring It On, 1999; Rhythm And Blues Alibi, 1999; We Haven't Turned Around (in soundtrack to film, American Beauty), 1999; Machismo (EP), 2000. *Honours:* Mercury Music Prize, 1998. *Address:* c/o Hut Records, Kensal House, 553–579 Harrow Rd, London W10 4RH, England. *Website:* www.gomez.co.uk.

GREBENSHCHIKOV, Boris Borisovitch; b. 27 Nov. 1953, Leningrad, Russia. Musician (guitar); Vocalist; Poet; Composer. m. Irina Grebenshchiova, 29 May 1992, 1 s., 2 d. *Education:* Applied Mathematics, Leningrad University. *Career:* Computer programmer, 1977–80; Formed Aquarium, 1972; Started recordings (not government approved), 1980; Tapes widely circulated throughout Russia to great success; After Peristroika, toured extensively in Russia and abroad; Solo album, produced by Dave Stewart, 1988–89; Subject of film: Long Way Home (Granada TV); Painter, exhibitions throughout Russia and abroad. *Recordings:* 10 albums, 1980–86; Aquarium, 1887; Radio Africa, 1987; Assa (soundtrack), 1988; Equinox, 1988; Radio Silence, 1989; Black Rose (soundtrack), 1990; Russian Album, 1992; Rameses The IV Favourite Songs, 1992; Sands of St Petersburg (soundtrack), 1993; Kostroma Mon Amour, 1994; Navigator, 1995; Snow Lion (soundtrack), 1996; Hyperborea, 1997; Lilith, 1997; Refuge, 1998; Psi, 1999. *Publications:* Ivan and Danilo (poetry and song lyrics), 1989; Master Bo's Business, 1991; 14 song books, 1992; Prose, 1993; Complete Works, Vols I–II, 1997. *Honours:* Triumph Prize, for major addition to Russian culture, 1998. *Membership:* Russian Cinematographer's Union; PEN, 1997. *Current Management:* Aquarium Management. *Address:* Flat 3, 2 Marata St, St Petersburg 191025, Russia. *Telephone:* (812) 311-04-58. *Fax:* (812) 272-05-41. *E-mail:* bg@aquarium.ru. *Website:* www.aquarium.ru.

GREEN, Barnaby; b. 4 Oct. 1967, Farnborough, Kent, England. *Education:* Centre for Young Musicians, Pimlico, London; BA, Music, Cambridge College of Arts and Technology; PGCE, Music, Open University. *Career:* Glastonbury Festival, Avalon Stage, with Junction, 1995; WOMAD One, World Stage, with Roots Progress, 1996; Gigs at Ronnie Scott's, the Jazz Cafe, Royal Albert Hall, Festival Hall and St Paul's Cathedral; Principal Percussionist, working with Stockhausen, British Premiere of Sternklang, Huddersfield Contemporary Music Festival; Musical Director, Composer, Viva O Carnival, Lillian Bayliss Theatre, Sadlers Wells, London; Wrote music for 2 short films, Seeing Things and Open and Shut Case; Percussion Tutor, Morley College, London. *Compositions:* I'm On My Way, with Green Pig; Spin Out, with Blunt. *Recordings:* Random Groove Movement (band); When Love Gives You Up, CD single. *Membership:* Musicians' Union; Asscn of Teachers and Lecturers; Professional Asscn of Teachers. *Address:* 36 Middleton Rd, London E8 4BS, England.

GREEN, Earl Oliver; b. 11 Feb. 1945, Kingston, Jamaica. Vocalist. m. Valerie Jean, 3 Oct. 1973, 1 s., 1 d. *Career:* Most major blues festivals in Europe including: Belgium Rhythm and Blues Festival; Nyon Festival; Lugano Festival, Switzerland; Diamond Awards, Antwerp; Radio broadcasts include: Paul Jones Show, BBC Radio 2; GLR; Mary Costello Show; Radio in Netherlands; Television appearances: Spain; Netherlands; Belgium; Switzerland; France; UK, McKewans The Concert, James Whale Show. *Recordings:* Always Hot, Otis Grand and The Dance Kings; Special Delivery, He Knows The Blues, Otis Grand. *Membership:* PRS; Musicians' Union. *Current Management:* George McFall. *Address:* 213 Staines Rd, Laleham, Middlesex TW18 2R8, England.

GREEN, Edward; b. 11 Nov. 1951, Queens, NY, USA. Composer; Musician (keyboards). *Education:* BA, Oberlin College, 1973; MA, New York University, 2003; Studied Aesthetic Realism with philosopher Eli Siegel, 1974–78. *Career:* Staff Composer, Imagery Films, 1980–, working with dir, Ken Kimmelman: film scores incl. What Does a Person Deserve?; Musical Dir, Aesthetic Realism Foundation, 1978–: productions incl. The Melody Persists, Ethics is a Force; Faculty, Manhattan School of Music: classes incl. Songwriting, Film Composition, Non-Western Music; Faculty, Aesthetic Realism Foundation; Performs duet with flautist Barbara Allen (played keyboards). *Compositions:* Piano Concertino; Chamber Symphony For Guitars And Flutes; Brass Quintet; Quartet For Guitars; Shakespeare Songs; Constitutional Amendment; Overture To Aesthetic Realism Autobiographies; Trumpet

Concerto. *Publications:* The Press Boycott of Aesthetic Realism, 1978. *Contributions to:* Over 200 articles published world-wide on music, social issues, Aesthetic Realism; Editorial Columnist, US African Eye, 1998–; Smithsonian Institute sponsored lecture on the music of Duke Ellington. *Honours:* Delius Award for Musical Composition, 1985; First Prize, Julius Albert Composers' Competition, 1996; First Prize, Zoltan Kodaly Composers' Competition, 1996; African Music Hall of Fame, 2002. *Membership:* ASCAP. *Address:* 208 E Broadway, J1007, New York, NY 10002, USA.

GREEN, Ian; b. 8 Oct. 1969. Prod; Writer; Mixer; Musician (keyboards, bass, drums, guitar). *Career:* Various television appearances including Wogan and Pebble Mill. *Recordings:* Voices, Kenny Thomas; Wait For Me, Kenny Thomas; True Spirit, Carleen Anderson; Closer To You, Brand New Heavies; Midnight At The Oasis, Brand New Heavies; Also recordings for Nu Colours; Misty Oldman; Monie Love. *Membership:* Musicians' Union; Performing Rights Society. *Current Management:* BAMN Management. *Address:* c/o A&M Records, 136–144, New Kings Rd, London SW6 4LZ, England.

GREEN, Ian Michael; b. 19 Nov. 1957, London, England. Musician (percussion, drums). m. Carolyn Margaret Morris, 7 May 1994. *Education:* Kingsdale, 1968–74. *Career:* Musician with: Mike Oldfield, 1972–73; Druid, 1977–78; Catherine Howe; Randy Edelman; Lindsey De Paul; Sally Oldfield (Germany), 1978–79; Matt Monroe (London), 1980–81; Michael Crawford, Barnum, TV and radio; Tony Britten; Sammy Davis Jr (Monte Carlo), 1988; Jerry Lee Lewis (Monte Carlo), 1991–92. *Recordings:* with artistes including: Michael Crawford; Mike Oldfield; Anthony Newley, produced single: What Kind of Fool Am I?; Film and television: Lace 1 and 2; Lennon The Movie; Casualty; Head Over Heels; Shows: Barnum, 1981; Guys and Dolls, 1987; She Loves Me, 1994; The Snow Queen, 1995; Fame, 1995; Singing In The Rain; Stop The World. *Membership:* Musicians' Union; ISM. *Address:* 223 Hayes Lane, Kenley, Surrey CR8 5HN, England.

GREEN, John R; b. 8 May 1971, London, England. Musician (keyboards, guitars); String Arranger; Composer. *Career:* Left college, 1989; Session artist; Co-Producer, album for Ruby Blue; Recorded with J. B. Horns; Sessioned, Power of Dreams; Co-wrote and toured world-wide with Marc Almond on various albums; Joined Sleeper as keyboard player, 1996; Played keyboards and wrote string arrangements for Manic Street Preachers on Everything Must Go, toured with band, 1998; Pete Wylie and the Mighty Wah; Music Director, Liz Horsman's recording, Heavy High, and tour; Recorded with Feeder; Muse (live TV), 2000; Arielle, also string arrangement, 2001; Toured with JJ72 as keyboard player, 2001; Toured with Bluetones as keyboard player, guitarist; Musical Dir for Ruby Tyler, 2002, 2003; Musical Dir For Tom Jones. *Current Management:* Titled Management. *Address:* 62 Ashleigh Rd, Mortlake, London SW14 8PX, England. *Website:* www.81x.com/thegreener/JGWB1.

GREEN, Sam; b. 2 Jan. 1960, Melbourne, Australia. Vocalist; Songwriter (guitar, keyboard). *Education:* Diploma in Horological Studies. *Career:* Played live to air with Greenmoss, group, 1979; Played in streets of Europe, 1980; Played with Tome the Poet and street poets, 1982–86; Players All Are We: Live to air Southern FM, 1995; Appeared on Asylum channel 31, 1995; Host of Local and Live (7 months), 1995; Appeared New Year's Eve, channel 31; Made video played on Rage channel 2, 1996. *Compositions:* For the Ocean, 1986; Angel of the Morning, 1994. *Recordings:* Live But For Love, 1986; Players All Are We, 1994; I Think It's About Time, 1997. *Membership:* APRA; ASA, full mem.; AMCOS affiliated. *Current Management:* B. Green Management. *Address:* 242 Swan St, Richmond, Victoria 3121, Australia. *E-mail:* samgreen@bigpond.com. *Website:* www.mrmusicman.com.

GREEN(E), Al; b. 13 April 1946, Forrest City, Arkansas, USA. Soul Vocalist; Songwriter. *Career:* Founder, The Creations, 1964; Singer, Al Greene and The Soul Mates; Founder, own record label, Hot Line Music Journal, 1967; Performances include: Tokyo Music Festival, Japan, 1978; Nelson Mandela's 70th Birthday Tribute, Wembley, 1988; New Orleans Jazz and Heritage Festivals, 1992; Ann Arbor Blues and Jazz Festival, 1992. *Recordings:* Albums: Al Green Gets Next To You, 1971; Let's Stay Together, 1972; I'm Still In Love With You, 1972; Green Is Blues, 1973; Call Me, 1973; Livin' For You, 1974; Al Green Explores Your Mind, 1975; Greatest Hits, 1975; Al Green Is Love, 1975; Full of Fire, 1976; Have A Good Time, 1977; Greatest Hits Vol. II, 1977; Truth 'n' Time, 1978; The Belle Album, 1978; Cream of Al Green, 1980; The Lord Will Make A Way, 1980; Higher Plane, 1982; Precious Lord, 1983; I'll Rise Again, 1983; White Christmas, 1983 Going Away, 1986; Soul Survivor, 1987; Hi-Life – The Best of Al Green, 1988; I Get Joy, 1989; Greatest Hits, 1991; Al, 1992; Love and Happiness (box set), 2001; Hit singles include: Tired of Being Alone, 1971; Let's Stay Together (No. 1, USA), 1972; Look What You've Done For Me, 1972; I'm Still In Love With You, 1972; You Ought To Be With Me, 1972; Call Me (Come Back Home), 1973; Here I Am (Come and Take Me), 1973; Sha-La-La (Make Me Happy), 1974; L-O-V-E (Love), 1974; Sailin' On The Sea of Love, duet with Shirley Caesar, 1985; Going Away, 1986; Everything's Gonna Be Alright, 1987; Put A Little Love In Your Heart, duet with Annie Lennox, (used in film Scrooged), 1988; As Long As We're Together, 1989. *Honours:* American Music Award, Favourite Soul/

R&B Album, 1974; Grand Prize, Tokyo Music Festival, 1978; Al Green Day, Los Angeles, 1978; Soul Train, Best Gospel Recording, 1987; Numerous Grammy awards include: Best Soul Gospel Performances, 1982–85, 1988, 1990; Best Male Soul Performance, 1987. *Address:* c/o Al Green Music, 3208 Winchester, Memphis, TN 38118, USA.

GREENE, Jack Henry; b. 7 Jan. 1930, Maryville, Tennessee, USA. Country vocalist; Songwriter; Musician (guitar, drums). *Career:* Known as The Jolly Green Giant; Vocalist and guitarist with the Cherokee Trio, Atlanta, 1940s; On WGAP radio, Maryville with Clyde Grubbs; Member: Clyde Grubbs and the Tennessee Valley Boys; Drummer with the Rhythm Ranch Boys, 1950; Played with Peachtree Cowboys, mid-1950s; Drummer, later vocalist, with Ernest Tubb, 1962; Formed the Jolly Green Giants, later renamed the Renegades, 1965; Signed to Decca, 1965; Debut single Ever Since My Baby Went Away; Billboard country single chart hits including duets with Jeannie Seeley until 1984; Hits included There Goes My Everything, later a pop hit for Engelbert Humperdinck, 1967. *Recordings include:* There Goes My Everything, 1966; All The Time, 1967; Statue of a Fool, 1969; Until My Dreams Come True, 1968; You Are My Treasure, 1968; Albums: There Goes My Everything, 1967; All The Time, 1967; What Locks The Door, 1967. *Honours:* various including: CMA: Single of the Year; Song of the Year; Album of the Year, There Goes My Everything; Male Vocalist of the Year, 1967; Cash Box, Most Promising Male Vocalist of the Year, 1967; Record World, Most Promising Male Vocalist of the Year, 1967; Cash Box, Most Programmed Song, All The Time, 1968. *Membership:* Grand Ole Opry, 1967. *Address:* c/o Fat City Artists, 1226 17th Ave S, Suite 2, Nashville, TN 37212, USA.

GREENSLADE, Dave; b. 18 Jan. 1943, Woking, Surrey, England. Composer; Musician (keyboards). m. Jan Greenslade, 2 d. *Career:* Keyboard player with Chris Farlowe's The Thunderbirds; Worked with Geno Washington in the Ram Jam Band; Formed Colosseum, with Jon Hiseman; Wrote and co-wrote hit album: Valentyne Suite; Colosseum disbanded 1971; Founder, Greenslade, 1972; Colosseum re-formed, reunion tour of Europe and album, 1994; Wrote hit albums, also solo project: Cactus Choir; Wrote television score for BBC series: Gangsters, success led to full time composition; Reforming Greenslade with original line-up. *Compositions:* Worked on more than 35 drama series, single plays, films, stage plays; Credits include: Kinsey, BBC TV; A Very Peculiar Practice, BBC TV; Wipe Out, Granada TV; Tales of The Unexpected, Anglia TV; The Detective, BBC TV; Bratt Farrer, BBC TV; Bird of Prey, BBC TV; The Houseman's Tale, BBC TV; A Family Man, BBC TV; Films: Artemis, BBC Films; Jekyll and Hyde, BBC films; Worked with novelist Terry Pratchett on recording project based on the DiscWorld fantasy novel series; Storms Behind the Breeze; The Playground; No Pleasin'; Wherever I Go; The Other Side of the Sky. *Recordings include:* Colosseum: Daughter of Time; Live; Valentyne Suite; Albums with Greenslade (now re-issued on CD); Cactus Choir; Pentateuch, double album based on illustrations of Patrick Woodroffe; DiscWorld project, 1995; Large Afternoon, 2000; Live 1973–75, 2000. *Honours:* Premio Ondas TV Award at Barcelona Film Festival; Won Prix Italia at Palermo; Toyama Prize, Japan. *Membership:* Musicians' Union; PRS; MCPS. *Current Management:* Soundtrack Music Management. *Address:* 16 Queens Rd, Berdhamsted, Hertfordshire HP4 3HU, England.

GREENWICH, Ellie; b. 23 Oct. 1940, Brooklyn, New York, USA. Songwriter; Record Prod; Vocalist. *Education:* BA, Holfstra University, 1962. *Career:* Singer, 1958–; Songwriting partnership with Jeff Barry, 1960–67; Founder member, The Raindrops, 1963; Solo artist and songwriter; Performed in revue Leader of The Pack. *Compositions:* Hit songs include: Hanky Panky, Tommy James and The Shondells; Da Doo Ron Ron, The Crystals; And Then He Kissed Me, The Crystals; Do Wah Diddy Diddy, The Exciters; Leader of The Pack, The Shangri-Las; River Deep Mountain High, Ike and Tina Turner; Baby I Love You, The Ronettes; Be My Baby, The Ronettes; Writer, producer, songs recorded by Neil Diamond; Cyndi Lauper; Bette Midler; Nona Hendryx. *Recordings:* Albums: Ellie Greenwich Composes Produces and Sings, 1968; Let It Be Written, Let It Be Sung, 1973; I Can Hear Music, 1999; Backing vocals on: Dreaming, Blondie, 1979; Girls Just Wanna Have Fun, Cyndi Lauper, 1983. *Honours:* 19 BMI Awards; Inducted into Songwriters Hall of Fame; National Academy of Popular Music Award, 1984. *Membership:* Songwriters Guild.

GREENWOOD, Bernard Paul; b. 21 April 1940, Bath, England. Dr; Musician (saxophone, keyboards). *Education:* Medicine, London, Oxford; Social Anthropology, Cambridge. *Career:* Saxophone player, Chris Farlowe and the Thunderbirds; The Glands; Doctor Kitch; Alkasalsa; Joey The Lips; Jazz Posse; Dicky Pride and the Original Topics; King Cobra and the Rattlesnakes; Tour with Lindsay Kemp. *Recordings:* Buzz With The Fuzz; Treat Her Right; The Fool; Mr Pitiful (with Chris Farlowe). *Publications:* Buzz With The Fuzz. *Address:* Woodcote, Chagford, Devon TQ13 8JF, England.

GREENWOOD, Colin Charles; b. 26 June 1969, Oxford, England. Musician (bass). *Education:* English Literature, University of Cambridge. *Career:* Mem. and lead singer, On A Friday, 1987, renamed Radiohead, 1991–; Numerous

tours, festivals and television appearances. *Recordings:* Albums: Pablo Honey, 1993; The Bends, 1995; OK Computer, 1997; Kid A, 2000; Amnesiac, 2001; I Might Be Wrong, 2001. Singles: Drill (EP), 1992; Creep, 1993; Anyone Can Play Guitar, 1993; Pop Is Dead, 1993; Stop Whispering, 1993; Itch (EP), 1994; My Iron Lung (EP), 1994; Live Au Forum (EP), 1995; High and Dry, 1995; Fake Plastic Trees, 1995; Just, 1995; Street Spirit (Fade Out), 1996; The Bends, 1996; Paranoid Android, 1997; Karma Police, 1997; No Surprises, 1997; Climbing Up The Walls, 1997; Airbag/How Am I Driving? (EP), 1998; Pyramid Song, 2001; Knives Out, 2001; I Might Be Wrong, 2001. *Honours:* Grammy Award, Best Alternative Rock Performance, 1998; Q Award, Best Act in the World Today, 2002. *Address:* c/o Parlophone Records, 43 Brook Green, London W6 7EF, England. *Website:* www.radiohead.com.

GREENWOOD, Jonny (Jonathan Richard Guy); b. 5 Nov. 1971, Oxford, England. Musician (guitar, piano, keyboards, synthesizer). m. *Career:* Mem. and lead singer, On A Friday, 1987, renamed Radiohead, 1991–; Numerous tours, festivals and television appearances. *Recordings:* Albums: Pablo Honey, 1993; The Bends, 1995; OK Computer, 1997; Kid A, 2000; Amnesiac, 2001; I Might Be Wrong, 2001. Singles: Drill (EP), 1992; Creep, 1993; Anyone Can Play Guitar, 1993; Pop Is Dead, 1993; Stop Whispering, 1993; Itch (EP), 1994; My Iron Lung (EP), 1994; Live Au Forum (EP), 1995; High and Dry, 1995; Fake Plastic Trees, 1995; Just, 1995; Street Spirit (Fade Out), 1996; The Bends, 1996; Paranoid Android, 1997; Karma Police, 1997; No Surprises, 1997; Climbing Up The Walls, 1997; Airbag/How Am I Driving? (EP), 1998; Pyramid Song, 2001; Knives Out, 2001; I Might Be Wrong, 2001. *Honours:* Grammy Award, Best Alternative Rock Performance, 1998; Q Award, Best Act in the World Today, 2002. *Address:* c/o Parlophone Records, 43 Brook Green, London W6 7EF, England. *Website:* www.radiohead.com.

GREENWOOD, Lee Melvin; b. 27 Oct. 1942, Southgate, California, USA. Country Vocalist. m. Melanie Cronk. *Recordings:* Singles: It Turns Me Inside Out; IOU; Ring On Her Finger, Time On Her Hands; Ain't No Trick; She's Lyin'; Going Going Gone; Fools Gold; with Barbara Mandrell: To Me; It Should Have Been Love By Now; Albums: Inside and Out, 1982; If There's Any Justice, 1983; Somebody's Gonna Love You, 1983; The Wind Beneath My Wings, 1984; You've Got a Good Love Comin', 1985; Christmas is Christmas, 1987; God Bless The USA, 1990; Holdin' a Good Hand, 1991; American Patriot, 1992; Back to Back, 1996; Wounded Heart, 1998; Same River Different Bridge, 2000; Have Yourself A Merry Little Christmas, 2001; with Barbara Mandrell: Meant For Each Other. *Honours:* CMA Male Vocalist of Year, 1983, 1984; ACM Male Vocalist of Year, 1984; Cash Box Choice Award, 1984; Music City Awards, Best Male Vocalist, 1984, 1985. *Address:* Lee Greenwood Inc, PO Box 6537, Seiverville, TN 37864, USA.

GREGORY, Colin; b. 30 Dec. 1961, Radcliffe, Manchester, England. Musician; Songwriter. *Education:* Lancaster University. *Career:* Tours of USA, Europe and Japan, 1992; TV and Radio appearances in USA, 1994; UK television appearances include: Snub; The Beat; Northern Routes; The Chart Show; John Craven's Newsround; Look North; Many radio sessions on John Peel, Mark Radcliffe, Janice Long, Mark Goodier and Johnny Walker shows. *Recordings:* 3 albums in the UK, 2 albums in USA and 2 albums in Japan; 10 UK singles and 8 singles internationally; Albums with One Thousand Violins: One Thousand Violins, 2001. *Membership:* Musicians' Union; PRS. *Current Management:* Rockmasters Management. *Address:* Brunswick Studios, 7 Westbourne Grove Mews, London W11 2RU, England.

GREGORY, Will; Composer; Songwriter; Musician (saxophones, oboe, fiddle); Arranger. *Career:* Worked with: Jim Barr, Marc Bessant, John Cornick, Stephen Cottrell, Jenny Crook, The Cure, Clive Deamer, Peter Gabriel, Chloë Goodchild, Stuart Gordon, William Gregory, Johnny Kalsi, Rowen Oliver, John Parish, Portishead, Hossam Ramzy, David Rhodes, Adrian Utley, B. Waghorn, Tim Wheater; Formed Goldfrapp with Allison Goldfrapp, late 1990s; Signed to Mute Records, 1999. *Recordings:* with Goldfrapp: Album: Felt Mountain, 2000. Singles: Utopia, 2000; Pilots, 2002; Appearances on: Tori Amos' Little Earthquakes, 1992; Jim Eanes' Classic Bluegrass, 1992; Apollo Saxophone Quartet's First and Foremost, 1994; David Ferguson's View From Now, 1998; Cecelia's Voice of Violet 1999. *Address:* c/o Mute Records, 429 Harrow Rd, London W10 4RE, England.

GREGSON, Clive James; b. 4 Jan. 1955, Ashton-Under-Lyne, Lancashire, England. Musician; Vocalist; Songwriter; Record Prod. m. Nancy Ann Kirkland, 6 Nov. 1993. *Education:* Crewe and Alsager College of Education. *Career:* Founder, leader, Any Trouble, 1976–84; Member, duo, Clive Gregson and Christine Collister, 1985–92; Member, Richard Thompson Band, 1987–92; Solo artist, 1992–. *Recordings:* with Any Trouble: Where Are All The Nice Girls, 1980; Live At The Venue, 1980; Wheels In Motion, 1981; Any Trouble, 1983; Wrong End of The Race, 1984; Solo: Strange Persuasions, 1985; Welcome To The Workhouse, 1990; Carousel of Noise, 1994; People and Places, 1995; I Love this Town, 1996; Happy Hour, 1999; Comfort and Joy, 2001; With Gregson and Collister: Home and Away, 1986; Mischief, 1987; A Change In The Weather, 1989; Love Is A Strange Hotel, 1990; The Last Word, 1992; with Eddi Reader and Boo Hewerdine: Wonderful Lie/Last Night I Dreamt That Somebody Loved Me/Who's Your Jailer Now?, 1993. *Membership:* PRS; BAC&S; EFDSS; Musicians' Union. *Current Management:*

John Martin. *Address:* Gregsongs, 50 Stroud Green Rd, London N4 3EF, England.

GREINKE, Arthur Joseph; b. 19 March 1963, Milwaukee, USA. PR Exec. *Education:* BA Mass Communications, Journalism, University of Wisconsin, Milwaukee. *Career:* Freelance entertainment journalist, Milwaukee, 1981–89; Program co-ordinator, The Great Circus Parade, Milwaukee, 1985–; Principal Partner, Greinke, Eiers and Associates, Milwaukee, 1985–; Director, Public relations and advertising, Eastside Compact Disc, 1988–; Cooler Music Promotions, USA, Inc, 1990–; Executive Producer (music group), Project Mix, 1985–87. *Publications:* Articles on national, regional recording industry news to college newspapers, local trades, Rolling Stone magazine; Advertising copy; Rock news scripts for Milwaukee television video show. *Membership:* PRSA; IABC, Treasurer, 1989, President, 1990; SPJ; NARAS. *Address:* 2557C N Terrace Ave, Milwaukee, WI 53211–3822, USA.

GRESSWELL, Steve; b. 20 Jan. 1955, Reading, Berkshire, England. Composer; Prod; Musician (keyboards); Programmer. m. Jacqui, 1 Oct. 1993, 1 s., 1 d. *Career:* Justin Canns, 1971–76; Scorpio, 1977–81; Steve Gresswell Band, 1981–82; Dream, 1982–84; Poiema, 1984–85; After Dark, 1985; Guardian Angel, 1985–86; Formed own label, Sumo Records, with recording studio, 1988; Video with SG Band: Just For You, 1989; Robin Wilson Productions, 1990; Coalition, 1992–. *Compositions:* Story of The Gods, Rock Oratorio. *Recordings:* with Scorpio: Taking England By Storm, 1977; with Oddjob: Express Yourself, 1977; with Dream: Just For You, 1982; with Poiema: 2 singles from play: Cross Purposes, 1984; with After Dark: Call of The Wild, 1985; Album: Masked By Midnight, 1985; with SG Band: Just For You (Official Record for Lockerbie Air Disaster Fund), 1989; Producer, single for duo, Vincent, 1989; Composer, musician, engineer, producer, album for Czech rock guitarist Karel Espandr, 1990; Producer, composer, Robin Wilson Project single (fundraising for child with Cerebral Palsy), 1990; Steve Gresswell: Spirit of Freedom, 1994; Coalition: Rise of the Coalition, 1996, 1997; Steve Gresswell: Visions, 1997; Produced and arranged Brent Morley, Burn, 1997. *Membership:* Musicians' Union; PRS; PPL; MCPS; BAC&S; BSWC; PAMRA. *Current Management:* Sumo Records. *Address:* Searles, The Chapel, 26a Munster Rd, London SW6 4EN, England.

GREY, Carola; b. 5 Aug. 1968, Munich, Germany. Musician (drums); Composer; Prod. *Education:* Classical Piano, for 12 years; Master degree, Music and Music Education (Jazzdrums). *Career:* Performed and/or recorded with: Mike Stern, Ravi Coltrane, Benny Green, Craig Handy and other jazz artistes; Drummer for New York based all female gothic rock band, Maria Excommunikata Bandleader, 1989–; Clubs and festivals in Europe, US and Asia (Thailand International Jazz Festival, 1996; Jakarta Jazz Festival, 1995–96; Indian Music Festival, Chennai, 1996); TV features include: Deutsche Welle, Berlin (Germany); Star TV, (India) WDR, Cologne (Germany), Polish TV. *Recordings:* Carola Grey, Noisy Mama, 1992; Carola Grey, The Age of Illusion, 1994; Carola Grey, Girls Can't Hit, 1996; Composer, all music for band; Music for minor films and dance theatres: Vox, international cable; MC for the Zildjian Day Berlin, Germany, 1997. *Honours:* Govt Grant, for extraordinary artists, 1995. *Membership:* International Drum Organisation. *Current Management:* Noisy Mama Productions, Rattenbergerstr 22, 81373, München, Germany.

GRIDLEY, Andrew David; b. 3 May 1960, Maldon, Essex, England. Musician (6- and 12-string guitars, keyboards); Vocalist; Songwriter. *Education:* Performing Arts at college. *Career:* Appearances include: Production, London Lights, Ingatestone; Chelmsford Youth Spectacular, Civic Theatre; England Entertains, Clacton, Essex; First EP released Essex Radio, Witham; Live Elvis performance, Southend-On Sea, Cliffs Pavilion; Played guitar for Dr Barnardo's Charity; Accompanied Helen Shapiro on 12 string guitar. *Compositions:* Forever, 1997; I Want You, 1997; You're Sexy, 1997; Smile on My Pinstripe, 1997. *Recordings:* Day Through To Night; Leading Lady; Green; Love and Affection; From Me To You; Lonely As A Cloud; Love Can Be; Summer Sun; Take Me; Beautiful; Wild Wild Women; Taking a Chance on Love; I'm a Fool in Love; Lost in Time (Reflections). *Publications:* Total Guitar, 1997. *Contributions to:* Times Education Supplement. *Honours:* Recommended, One of best guitar and music teachers, Times Educational Supplement. *Membership:* PRS; BAC&S; MCPS. *Address:* 17 Coopers Ave, Heybridge, Maldon, Essex, England.

GRIFF, Ray; b. 22 April 1940, Vancouver BC, Canada. Artist; Writer; Musician (Piano, Guitar). m. Trudy Griff. *Career:* Own Television Series, Host, Goodtime Country; Ray Griff Show; Sun Parlour Country; Guest, Includes Rollin' On The River, Dean Martin Show, Kenny Rogers, Grand Ole Opry, Porter Wagoner Show, Calgary Stampede. *Compositions:* Written Over 2000 Songs, Including Baby; Step Aside; The Morning After Baby Let Me Down; Darlin'; It Couldn't Have Been Any Better; Canadian Pacific; Where Love Begins; After The Laughter; Who's Gonna Play This Old Piano; Better Move It On Home. *Recordings:* Over 550 Including, Baby; Better Move It On Home; Hold Me; Getting Back To Norma; You're Wearin' Me Down; After The Laughter; Where Love Begins; Step Aside; It Couldn't Have Been Any Better; Between This Time and The Next. *Honours:* 7 BMI Citations for Song Writing and Publishing; 87 ASCAP hit song Awards for Artist, Producer, Song Writer

and Publisher; Hall of Fame Walkway, Nashville; Calgary White Hat Honour. *Membership:* ASCAP; NSA; BMI; CMA; CCMA. *Address:* Suite 193, 132–250 Shawville Blvd SE, Calgary, AB T2Y 2Z7, Canada.

GRIFFIN, Richard. See: **PROFESSOR GRIFF.**

GRIFFIN, Sid (Albert Sidney); b. 18 Sept. 1955, Louisville, Kentucky, USA. Musician; Journalist; DJ; Record Co Exec. m. Kate St John, 5 May 1993. *Education:* BA, Journalism, University of South Carolina, 1977. *Career:* Played with The Frosties, 1973–77; The Unclaimed, 1979–82; The Long Ryders, 1982–87; Soloist and Leader with The Coal Porters; Released various singles, EPs and albums with these bands; Owner, Prima Records Ltd; DJ, Mean Country 1035AM, London. *Recordings:* With the Long Ryders: 10–5–60 (EP), 1983; Native Sons, album, 1984; State of Our Union, 1985; Two-Fisted Tales, 1987; Metallic BO, 1988; Anthology, 1998; Others: Danny and Dusty, The Lost Weekend, 1986; Rebels Without Applause, The Coal Porters, 1992; Land of Hope and Crosby, The Coal Porters, 1994; Los London, The Coal Porters, 1995; Solo: Little Victories, 1997; Roulette (EP), 1998; The Gram Parsons Tribute Concert, 1999; The Chris Hillman Tribute Concert, The Coal Porters, 2001. *Publications:* Contributor to Q, Mojo, BAM, and Country Music International magazines. *Honours:* Hon. Mem. of Athenaeum Literary Asscn; Lifetime Achievement Plaque, Premio Piero Ciampi Festival, Italy, 2002. *Membership:* AFofM; The Paisley Underground. *Current Management:* Prima International, London, England. *Address:* PO Box 2539, London NW3 6DF, England.

GRIFFITH, Nanci; b. 6 July 1953, Seguin, Texas, USA. Vocalist; Songwriter; Musician (guitar). *Education:* Studied Education, University of Texas. *Career:* Professional musician, 1977–; Formed backing band, The Blue Moon Orchestra, 1986; Formed own publishing company. *Compositions include:* Love At The Five and Dime; The Wing and The Wheel; Ford Econoline; Outbound Plane (co-written with Tom Russell). *Recordings:* There's A Light Beyond These Woods, 1978; Poet In My Window, 1982; Once In A Very Blue Moon, 1984; Last of The True Believers, 1986; Lone Star State of Mind, 1987; Little Love Affairs, 1988; One Fair Summer Evening, 1988; Storms, 1989; Late Night Grand Hotel, 1991; Flyer, 1994; Blue Roses from the Moons, 1997; Revisited, 1999; The Dust Bowl Symphony, 1999; Clock Without Hands, 2001. *Current Management:* Vector Management, PO Box 128037, Nashville, TN 37212, USA.

GRIFFITHS, Franny; b. 1970. Musician (keyboards); Songwriter. *Career:* Member, Space; Numerous tours and television appearances. *Recordings:* Singles: If It's Real, 1993; Money, 1995; Neighbourhood, 1996; Female of the Species, 1997; Me and You vs the World, 1997; Dark Clouds, 1997; Avenging Angels, 1997; The Ballad of Tom Jones, with Cerys Matthews, 1998; Begin Again, 1998; Bad Days, 1998; Albums: Spiders, 1996; Remixes and B-Sides, 1997; Tin Planet, 1998; Greatest Hits, 2001; Also collaborated with Tom Jones, Sunny Afternoon (on Reload album), 1999.

GRIFFITHS, Marcia; b. 1954, Kingston, Jamaica. Reggae Vocalist. *Career:* Singer with Byron Lee and the Dragonaires, 1964–; Studio singer for Studio One; First Jamaican No. 1 hit, Feel Like Jumping, 1968; Mem., Bob and Marcia, with Bob Andy, 1969–74; Mem., I-Threes, with Rita Marley and Judy Mowatt; Worked with the Wailers, and Bob Marley, –1981; Signed to VP Records, 1988; Worked with artistes including: Owen Boyce, Free-I, Tony Gregory, Bob Marley, Judy Mowatt, Max Romeo, Sanchez, Martha Velez, Bunny Wailer. *Recordings:* Albums: The Original–At Studio One, 1973; Sweet Bitter Love, 1974; Young, Gifted And Black, 1976; Naturally, 1978; Steppin', 1979; Rock My Soul, 1986; I Love Music, 1986; Marcia, 1988; Carousel, 1990; Indomitable, 1993; Put A Little Love In Your Heart: The Best Of... 1969–1974, 1993; Truly, 1998; Certified, 1999; with the I-Threes, include: Many Are Called, 1983; Beginning, 1986; Appearances on Bob Marley albums: Live, 1975; Rasta Man Vibration, 1976; Exodus, 1977; Kaya, 1978; Babylon By Bus, 1978; Survival, 1979. *Address:* c/o VP Records Inc, 89-05 138th St, Jamaica, NY 11435, USA.

GRIFFITHS, Matthew David; b. 6 March 1968, Cardiff, Wales. Musician (percussion); Composer. m. Sarah Fisher, 18 Sept. 1993. *Education:* BA, First Class Honours in Performing Arts, specialising in Music, Leicester Polytechnic, 1989. *Career:* Solo percussion recitals, 1989–; Concerts include: St David's Hall, Cardiff; Cheltenham Town Hall; Bradford Alhambra; Phoenix Arts, Leicester; Bath Festival; Warwick Festival; Swansea Festival; Chichester Festival; Sounds Like Birmingham; Percussion '90 Festival; Television appearances include: The Clothes Show, BBC1; Heno, Channel 4/S4C; Midlands Today; Radio appearances include: Radio Wales; Radio Leicester; Radio WM; Worked with dance companies in the theatre and for various contemporary music ensembles; Gives workshops, and composer in residence projects in schools, hospitals, prisons and day centres. *Compositions:* Concerto for Percussion and Embroidery Machine, premiere at Warwick Festival, 1991; Miles Around, with Warwick Festival premiere, 1992; World of Hospitality, commissioned by Rubbermaid, premiered at Earls Court, 1994. *Publications:* The North Indian Tabla and Its Use in Modern, Western Music (dissertation), 1989. *Honours:* ABSA Award, Concerto for Percussion and Embroidery Machine. *Membership:* Musicians' Union;

Advisor, Arts Council. *Address:* 15 Bartletts Rd, Bedminster, Bristol BS3 3PL, England.

GRIFFITHS, Ryan; b. 1978. Musician (acoustic guitar). *Career:* Mem., The Vines, 2002–; Short UK, US and Canadian tours, incl. Glastonbury Festival, England; Carling Weekend Festival, Reading, Leeds; Coachella Festival, Los Angeles; Troubadour, Los Angeles; Mercury Lounge, New York; WHFS Festival, Washington, 2002; Sign to EMI Australia, 2002; Television appearances: Top Of The Pops, Later With Jools Holland, The Late Show with David Letterman, 2002; Australian tour, late 2002; Performed, MTV Video Music Awards, 2002. *Recordings:* Albums: Highly Evolved, 2002. Singles: Factory, 2001; Sun Child/Hot Leather, 2002; Heavenly, 2002; Get Free, 2002; Highly Evolved, 2002. *Honours:* NME Award, Best Single, for Get Free, 2003. *Current Management:* Winterman and Goldstein Management, PO Box 545, Newtown, NSW 2042, Australia. *Address:* c/o Capitol Records, 1750 N Vine St, Hollywood, CA 90028, USA. *Website:* www.thevines.com.

GRIGOROV, Robert (Robo); b. 25 Sept. 1964, Bratislava. Vocalist; Composer; Prod. 1 d. *Career:* Film: Fontana Pre Zuzanu 1, actor and singer, 1986; Music for Theatre: Eunuch, 1985; Music for Films: Obyeany Den, 1985; Most, 1993; Touring with own group, Midi, 1982–. *Compositions:* Robo and Midi, 1985; Mohy, LP, 1986; Olohy, 1984; Cierny Kon, 1989; Chcemja Najst, 1985; Espresso Orient, 1987; Unplugged, 1994; Udychni Reggae, 1995; The Best of Chodci Sveta, 1997. *Recordings:* About 13 LPs and CDs. *Publications:* Zuvacka za uchom, 1983; EDO, 1984; Monika, 1985; Dvaja, 1984; Ona Je Madona, 1993. *Honours:* Bratislavska Lira, 1984, 1985, 1986; Cena Hulobne'ho Fontu, 1985; Diskosla'vik, 1984. *Membership:* SOZA; Slovenskyhudobny Fond; Lita. *Address:* Stredna 26, 82104 Bratislava, Slovakia.

GRILLO, Alex; b. 7 March 1956, Fiume-Veneto, Italy. Musician (vibraphone). *Education:* Conservatory: Percussion, Harmony and Orchestration. *Career:* Jazz concert, Radio France, 1982; Nîmes Jazz Festival, 1985; Duo with Steve Lacy, 1987–88; Orchestra De Nove, Paris, New Morning, Angoulême, 1988; First underwater musician with Michel Redolfi, 1989; Nice, 1989; Brisbane, 1991; Lisbon, 1993; Duo with Terry Riley by satellite, 1993; Duo with Barre Philips, 1994. *Recordings:* A Table!, 1985; Neuf Pour Neuf, 1988; Mass For Choir and Organ; Music for theatre and ballet, 1990, 1991; Album: Vibraphone Alone, 1993; Sweet Desdemone (rock jazz oratorio), 1995. *Publications:* C'est Tout Droit (suite for xylophone). *Membership:* SACEM; SACD; UMJ. *Address:* 182 rue de Charenton, 75012 Paris, France.

GRIM, Joy Marie Goodman; b. 19 Oct. 1948, Sharon, PA, USA. Country Gospel Vocalist; Musician (woodwind). m. Harold L Grim Jr, 1 s., 1 d. *Education:* BA from Bob Jones University (Early Childhood Education); Piano, aged 9; Flute, aged 11; Clarinet, aged 12; Oboe, aged 14; Saxophone, aged 20; Melodica, aged 35. *Career:* Appearances at Govenor's Palace Theatre, Pigeon Forge, TN; Video with James Blackwood and numerous appearances with Blackwood Quartet; Bruce, Community TV broadcast in Bruce, MS. Happy; I Stood Alone; For God So Loved; Mama; Soldiers III, Home From Kosovo. *Recordings:* Ashes To Gold; Praise His Dear Name; Album: Ashes To Gold, 2000. *Honours:* Country Gospel Music Guild Golden Harp Award, Female Horizon Artist, 2001. *Membership:* Christian Country Music Asscn; Country Gospel Music Guild. *Current Management:* Blackwood Management, 1106 Tramel Rd, Sevierville, TN, 37862, USA. *Website:* www.joygrim.com.

GRIMBLE, Ian; Prod; Mixer; Music Engineer. *Career:* Worked with as Prod.: Aslan, Dark Star, Beth Orton, Puressence, The Screaming Orphans, Travis, The Wannadies; Worked with as Engineer/Mixer: The Beautiful South, The Clash, The La's, Lightning Seeds, Manic Street Preachers, Mansun, Morcheeba, Texas. *Address:* c/o Stephen Budd Management Ltd, 109b Regents Park Rd, Primrose Hill, London NW1 8UR, England. *Website:* www.record-producers.com.

GRIMES, Ged; b. 28 March 1962, Dundee, Scotland. Musician (bass guitar, upright bass, percussion, keyboards, drum programming); Writer. m. Patricia Colette Boyle, 13 July 1991. *Education:* Duncan of Jordanstone College of Art. *Career:* Founder member, Danny Wilson, 1983–90; Tours: USA, UK, Japan; Toured with Eddi Reader, 1994–95; Television and radio appearances: Montreux Rock Festival; Top of the Pops; Chart Show; The Late Show; Jools Holland Show; Radio 1 sessions. *Compositions:* Soundtrack for computer game Earthworm Jim 3D, 1999. *Recordings:* Hit single: Mary's Prayer, 1987; Albums: with Danny Wilson: Meet Danny Wilson, 1987; Be-Bop Mop-Top, 1988; Sweet Danny Wilson, 1991; with Gary Clark: Ten Short Songs About Love, 1993; contributed to: White Lillies Island, Natalie Imbruglia, 2001. *Membership:* Musicians' Union; PRS; PPL; PAMRA. *Address:* c/o Jack's Hoose Recording Studios, The Radio Tay Building, 6 N Isla St, Dundee DD3 7JQ, Scotland.

GRIP, Erik; b. 2 July 1947, Nykobing, Denmark. Vocalist; Songwriter; Composer; Musician (guitar, piano). m. Joan Riboe, 2 s., 1 d. *Education:* Cand Arch. *Career:* Danish folk singer; General Secretary, Danish Society for Jazz,

Rock and Folk Composers (DJBFA), 1976–86. *Recordings:* 15 albums released. *Address:* Stationsvej 23, 4320 Lejre, Denmark.

GRISOLIA, Bill (William Francisco); Vocalist; Songwriter; Musician (piano); Bandleader; Prod. m. Yolanda Vincenza Foley, 1 s., 1 d. *Education:* University of Valencia, Spain; University of San Francisco, California; University of Michigan at Ann Arbor; Kansas State University, Manhattan, Kansas. *Career:* Live performances include Opening for Johnny Mathis, 1994, Dionne Warwick, 1996, Burt Bacharach, 1996; Performances in Europe, North America and Mexico, 1976–; Television work includes interviews and performances in Los Angeles; Satellite broadcast on Spanish National television, Un paso por el Tiempo, 1994; Capicua, Valencia, 2000; Radio interviews and performances in USA. *Compositions:* Rosarita. *Recordings:* Blue Café, 1999; Wish Upon a Song, 2000. *Membership:* National Academy of Recording Arts and Sciences; California Lawyers for the Arts.

GROBER, Jacques; b. 11 Feb. 1951, Paris, France. Writer; Composer; Vocalist. 2 d. *Education:* Baccalaureat, Licence et Maitrise de Russe; Private music lessons with Sarah Gorby. *Career:* Singer, traditional Yiddish and Russian songs, and own compositions; Appearances in Paris: Theatre 18, Centre Mandapa, TN Chaillot, 1989; Theatre du Tourtour, 1991–92, 1997–98; Bobigny, 1994; Maison de Radio-France, 1995; Théâtre des Songes, 1999; Other appearances include: Strasbourg, Nancy, Grenoble, Orleáns, Toulouse, Rennes (Festival Tombées de la Nuit); Out of France: Zurich; Brussels; Amsterdam; Germany; Romania. *Recordings:* Le Paon Doré; Autres Chants Yiddish; Voix du Ghetto (collection); Il faut crier toujours jusqu'a la fin du monde, collection. *Membership:* Animateur Chorale Yiddish. *Address:* 58 rue de L'Egalité, Le Verseau 31, 92130 Issy Les Moulineaux, France.

GROCOTT, Stephen; b. 21 Feb. 1953, London, England. Composer; Musician (guitar, mandolin, harmonium, flowerpots); Vocalist; Teacher. *Education:* BA Hons, Literature, Kent University; Traditional music, Ireland; Carl Orff Society, England. *Career:* Television and radio appearances with: The Wise Monkeys, 1990; The Drones, BBC1, 1991; Ch4, Radio 4 and 5, 1995; The Toy Symphony premiered by The Drones at the Purcell Rooms and Norwich Festival. *Compositions:* Playing With Fire (music for bonfire, pyrotechnics, quartet), 1991; The Toy Symphony (music for toys and instruments) 1992. *Recordings:* Albums: with The Drones: The Drones, 1992; Giant Bonsai, 1994; with Rory McLeod: Angry Love, 1996; Footsteps and Heartbeats, 1996. *Membership:* PRS (associate); Musicians' Union; Carl Orff Society. *Current Management:* The Shed Studios.

GROHL, Dave; b. 14 Jan. 1969. Musician (drums). *Career:* Mem., Dave Bramage Band; Scream; Nirvana, 1990–94; World-wide appearances include: European tour with Sonic Youth, 1991; Reading Festivals, 1991, 1992; Transmusicales Festival, Rennes, France, 1991; Benefit concert, Washington State Music Coalition, 1992; Benefit concert, Bosnian Women's group, San Francisco, 1993; Mem., Foo Fighters, 1994–; Concerts include Reading Festival, 1995. *Recordings:* Albums: with Nirvana: Nevermind (No. 1, USA), 1991; Incesticide, 1993; In Utero (No. 1, UK and USA), 1993; Unplugged In New York, 1994; From the Muddy Banks, 1996; Hormoaning, 1999; with Foo Fighters: Foo Fighters, 1995; Colour and Shape, 1997; There Is Nothing Left to Lose, 1999; One By One, 2002. Singles: with Nirvana: Smells Like Teen Spirit, 1991; Come As You Are, 1992; Lithium, 1992; In Bloom, 1992; Oh, The Guilt, 1993; Heart-Shaped Box, 1993; All Apologies, 1993; Contribution to The Beavis and Butthead Experience album, 1993; with Foo Fighters: This Is A Call, 1995; I'll Stick Around, 1995; For All the Cows, 1996; Big Me, 1996; Monkey Wrench, 1997; Everlong, 1998; My Hero, 1998; Learn to Fly, 1999; Breakout, 2000; Next Year, 2000; The One, 2002. *Honours:* 2 MTV Music Video Awards, Smells Like Teen Spirit, 1992; BRIT Award, Best International Newcomer, with Nirvana, 1993; Grammy Award, Rock Album, 2001. *Address:* c/o Gold Mountain Entertainment, Suite 450, 3575 Cahunega Blvd W, Los Angeles, CA 90068, USA. *Website:* www.foofighters.com.

GROOM, Don; b. 10 Nov. 1939, Walthamstow, London, England. Session Musician (drums). m. Lorna Heather, 16 Nov. 1963, 1 s., 2 d. *Education:* Music theory, Royal Academy of Music; Drum tuition, Max Abrams, Frank King; Arranging, Berklee School of Music, Boston. *Career:* Professional musician, 1960–; Tours in Germany including Hamburg's Top Ten Club and Kaiser Keller; Drummer with: Mike Berry and the Outlaws, 1962; John Leyton; The Crickets, including tours with Bobby Vee, 1962; The Beatles, 2 tours, 1963–64; Rolling Stones tours, 1963–64; Backed Frankie Valli and Four Seasons, English tour, 1964; Backed Jet Harris, NME Poll Winners Concert, Wembley. *Recordings:* with Mike Berry: Don't You Think It's Time; with John Leyton: Son This Is She; Two Sides of John Leyton (album), 1962; with Pinkerton's Assorted Colours: Mirror Mirror.

GROOVEBOX. See: **VEGA, Louie.**

GROSZ, Martin Oliver; b. 28 Feb. 1930, Berlin, Germany. Musician (guitar). m. Rachel Whelan, 1956, 2 s. *Education:* 2 years at college. *Career:* Professional musician, 1948–; Recorded under own name in 1950s; Lived in Chicago, 1954–75; Performed with: Village Stompers; Dukes of Dixieland; Bandleader, Sounds of Swing, for National public television; New York Jazz repertory group, Soprano Summit, 1975–76. *Recordings:* Hooray For Bix, Riverside '57, 1975; Let Your Fingers Do The Walking (Guitar Duets), 1978; Swing It; Unsaturated Fats. *Publications:* Writer on Jazz Guitars and Frank Teschemacher for Time/Life magazines. *Honours:* Winner, Jazzology Guitar Poll, 1986. *Membership:* Musicians' Union, New York. *Current Management:* Popinjay Productions, 46 Upper Ritie St, Piermont, NY 10968, USA.

GRUNTZ, George; b. 24 June 1932, Basel, Switzerland. Musician; Composer; Bandleader. *Education:* Studies, Basel, Zurich. *Career:* Member, European All-Star Band, Newport International Band, 1958; Appearances at Most Major Jazz Festivals, including: Newport/Kool/JVC, 1958, 1969, 1982, 1984, 1989, 1994, Berlin, Warsaw, Monterey, 1967, 1977, Antibes, Montreux, Pori, Northsea; Several radio and television productions; Accompanied Many US Top Jazz Artists on European Tours; Chief Musical Director, Zurich State Theatre (Schauspielhaus), 1971–87; Program Director, Producer, Berlin Jazz Festival, 1972–94. *Compositions include:* Spanish Castles; Capricci Cavallereschi; Spring Song; Perambulation I and II; Concerto Sequenzes; Steppenwolf Concorde Suite; Thundermove, for large orchestra; Cosmopolitan Greetings, jazz opera commissioned by Hamburg State Opera, 1988. *Honours:* Several First Prizes in Many Jazz Festivals; First Prize, Best Performance Award, Japanese Music Critics Asscn, 1988; German Legion of Honour (Bundessverkienstkreut, klasse 1), 1997. *Current Management:* Euromusic, Therwil, Switzerland. *Address:* Weiherweg 1, 4123 Allschwil, Switzerland. *Website:* www.eurojazz.ch.

GRUSIN, Dave; b. 26 June 1934, Littleton, Colorado, USA. Composer; Record Prod; Musician (piano, keyboards). *Education:* University of Colorado. *Career:* Director of Music, Andy Williams Show, 1959–66; As pianist, played with Art Pepper; Spike Robinson; Terry Gibbs; Benny Goodman; Thad Jones; Carmen McRae; Sarah Vaughan; Arranger for: Phoebe Snow; Peggy Lee; Barbra Streisand; Patti Austin; The Byrds; Grover Washington Jr; Al Jarreau; Donna Summer; Co-founder, owner, GRP Records, with Larry Rosen, 1976–; Client roster includes: Grover Washington Jr, Dizzy Gillespie, Lee Ritenour; Chick Corea; Dianne Schuur; Dave Valentin; Gary Burton; Michael Brecker; Steve Gadd; David Benoit; Don Grusin; Solo pianist, also performs with brother Don Grusin, and jazz-fusion septet NY-LA Dream Band. *Compositions:* For numerous films including: Three Days of The Condor; The Graduate; Heaven Can Wait; On Golden Pond; Tootsie; Reds; The Little Drummer Girl; The Goonies; The Milago Beanfield War; The Fabulous Baker Boys; Also television themes: St Elsewhere; Roots; Numerous television films. *Recordings:* Solo albums: Candy, 1961; The Many Moods of Dave Grusin, 1962; Kaleidoscope, 1964; Discovered Again, 1976; One of a Kind, 1977; Dave Grusin and the GRP All-Stars, 1980; Out of The Shadows, 1982; Mountain Dance, 1983; The NY-LA Dream Band, 1988; Cinemagic, 1987; One of a Kind, 1988; Migration, 1989; Havana, 1990; The Dave Grusin Collection, 1991; The Gershwin Collection, 1992; Homage To Duke, 1993; The Orchestral Album, 1994; Two for the Road, 1996; Presents West Side Story, 1997; Two Worlds, 2000; with Lee Ritenour: Harlequin, 1984; with Don Grusin: Sticks and Stones, 1988; Also recorded with Billy Joel; Paul Simon; Gerry Mulligan. *Honours:* Academy Award, Original Score, The Milagro Beanfield War, 1988. *Current Management:* Gorfaine/Schwartz Agency Inc, 13245 Riverside Dr., Suite 450, Sherman Oakes, CA 91423, USA. *Address:* c/o GRP Records, 555 W 57th St, New York, NY 10019, USA.

GRUZ, Sergio; b. 17 Feb. 1968, Buenos Aires, Argentina. Musician (piano); Composer. *Education:* University of Buenos Aires; Jazz music and classical. *Career:* Festival Des Allumées, 1992; Festivals in France; European Jazz Competition with Sergio Gruz Trio, Germany; Concours National de Jazz à la Défense, Paris; Belgian Jazz Festival. *Recordings:* Bernardo Baraj Quintet, Argentina, 1992; Tierra del Fuego, France, 1994; Sergio Gruz Trio, France, 1995; Misanthrope, France, 1997; Point de vue, Sergio Gruz Quintet, 1998. *Address:* 12 rue du Plateau, 75019 Paris, France.

GRYTT, Kajsa; b. 20 June 1961, Stockholm, Sweden. Vocalist; Songwriter; Musician (guitar). 1 s. *Career:* Leader, Tant Strul, punk group. *Compositions:* Amason, Dunkar varmt, Sucka Migren, Igen, Vand Digbort, Han Sager, Om Du Kunde Semig, Som Om Himlen; Revolution; Visa Horman Alskar. *Recordings:* Tant Strul; Amason; Ojag Onskar Dig; Historier Fran En Vag; Den Andra Varuden, Kajsa Grytt, Revolution. *Publications:* Amason, 1983; Dunkar Varmt, 1983; Historier Fran En Vag, 1986; Revolution, 1994. *Honours:* Skap Stipendie, 1981. *Membership:* SKAP; Svenska Musiker Föbundet. *Current Management:* Warner Chappell.

GUBAIDULINA, Sofia Asgatovna; b. 24 Oct. 1931, Chistopol, Russia. Composer. m. Peter Meschaninov, 1 d. *Education:* Kazan and Moscow Conservatories, composition with Nikolai Peiko and Vissarion Shebalin, piano with Grigori Kogan. *Career:* First noticed abroad, Paris, 1979; British debut, 1987 (Symphony in 12 Movements); Lives in Germany, 1991–. *Compositions include:* Orchestral pieces: The Steps, 1971; The Hour Of Soul, 1976; Offertorium, 1980; Stimmen… verstummen (symphony), 1986; Zeitgestalten (symphony), 1994; 2nd cello concerto, 1994; Viola concerto, 1998; concertos for solo instruments with chamber orchestra; Cantatas: The Night In Memphis, 1968; Rubaiyat, 1969; Perception, 1983; Dedication To Marina Tsvetaeva, 1984; Johannes Passion, 2000; Instrumental music for non-traditional groups.

Honours: Polar Music Prize, Royal Swedish Acad. of Music, 2002. *Current Management:* 2d Pugachevskaya 8, Korp. 5, Apt 130, 107061 Moscow, Russia. *Telephone:* (095) 161-80-61. *Address:* Ziegeleiweg 12, 25482 Appen, Germany.

GUÉRAULT, Stéphane; b. 19 Dec. 1936, Reims, France. Musician (clarinet, saxophone); Bandleader. m. Isabelle Escoffier, 19 July 1985, 2 d. *Education:* University graduate, Law; Studies with Madame Dussequier. *Career:* Bandleader; Sideman with: Bill Coleman; Wild Bill Davis; Numerous concerts throughout France; Festival appearances include: Lille; Nice; Marciac. *Recordings:* with Wild Bill Davis; Bill Coleman; Marc Fosset. *Honours:* Sidney Bechet Award, French Musical Academy, 1993. *Membership:* SACEM. *Address:* 20 rue Murillo, 75008 Paris, France.

GULBRANDSSEN, Arve; b. 25 Sept. 1972, Namsois, Norway. Musician (drums). *Education:* University, 3 years; 2 years, University of Trondheim. *Career:* Played in various jazz bands like: Fotveita; Smaagnagerne; Joined Hedge Hog, 1993; Toured Europe, 1994, 1995. *Recordings:* Primal Gutter, 1993; Mercury Red, 1994; Mindless, 1994; The Healing EP; Thorn Cord Wonder, 1995; Party Terror Vol. 2, 1996. *Membership:* Norwegian Asscn of Musicians.

GULLEY, J. K. (John Kenneth); b. 11 Oct. 1954, Toronto, Ontario, Canada. Vocalist; Songwriter; Prod; Musician (guitar). m. Wilma Schmidt, 1 May 1987, 2 s., 3 d. *Career:* 15 charted singles; Tours across Canada; USA; Europe; Scandinavia; with Glen Campbell; Billie Jo Spears; Freddie Hart; Michelle Wright; Television appearances: Ronnie Prophet Show, CTV; John Cameron, CBC; Global Easy Country, NCN; CMT Video and Songwriters Café Special; Producer for John Cowan, Tami Haskell, John Landry, Jamie Warren. *Recordings:* Over 100 songs recorded and released, including, Dusty Road, 1978; Under Cover, 1987; Blue Jeans Boy, 1990; If She Only Knew Me, 1995. *Honours:* RPM Big Country Awards; Vista Rising Star Award, CCMA, 1986; SOCAN Song of the Year Award, Blue Jeans Boy, 1990. *Membership:* CCMA; AFofM; CARAS. *Current Management:* Steve Thompson, Backstage Productions. *Address:* PO Box 21086, Barrie, ON L4M 3CO, Canada.

GULLIN, Peter; b. 12 April 1959, Milani, Italy. Composer; Musician (Saxophone). *Education:* Music Conservatory of Stockholm. *Career:* Debut as Saxophonist and Composer; Written Classical Music and Big Band Stuff; Television Program, Sologram; Played In Festival Classic; Own Music With String Quartet, New Trio Forms. *Compositions:* Unital, 1986; Suite Per Chitarra e Quintetto a Fiati, 1986; Tokdárarnas Paradis, 1988; Tresma Midsummer Sagor, 1988. *Recordings:* CDs, Unita With Jazz Composers Orchestra; Ved Profetens Shaegg; Tenderness; Transformed Evergreen; Untold Story. *Publications:* Sunnanvind i Andevärlden, Collection of Short Fantasy Tales. *Honours:* Golden Record Award, 1992. *Address:* Jenny Linds Vag 24, 75650 Uppsala, Sweden.

GUMBLEY, Christopher James; b. 22 May 1958. Musician (clarinet, saxophones, piano). 1 s. *Education:* Huddersfield School of Music, 1976–79. *Career:* Classical and jazz music; Work includes television, radio, session work, classical recitals, theatre work, international exhibitions; Tours of Europe, Caribbean; Member, Saxtet, resident ensemble at Birmingham Conservatoire; Appeared at Edinburgh Festival; Television and radio: BBC Children In Need; Pebble Mill; Loose Ends, BBC Radio 4; Founded Gumbles Jazz Club, Stafford; Established annual jazz course, Stoke-on-Trent; Music workshops nationwide; Recently worked with the Pasadena Roof Orchestra in Britain, Germany and Abu Dhabi and on the touring Joseph and His Amazing Technicolour Dreamcoat show; Professor of Saxophone, Birmingham Conservatoire. *Recordings:* with Saxtet: Safer Sax. *Publications:* Cops Caps and Cadillacs (5 Jazz-rock pieces for clarinet or saxophone and piano); Game Show Addicts, duets. *Honours:* BA Hons, Music; LTCL (Clarinet Performers). *Membership:* Musicians' Union. *Address:* 53 Peel Terrace, Stafford ST16 3HE, England.

GUNDECHA, Ramakant; b. 24 Nov. 1962, Ujjain, Madhya Pradesh, India. Musician. m. Renu Ramakant, 1 s. *Education:* MMus; MCom; Madhya Pradesh government scholarship. *Career:* Performed Dhrupad Music (vocal) with brother, Umakant, all major festivals in India and in Germany, Switzerland, England, France, USA, Norway, Singapore and Hong Kong; Television and radio appearances. *Honours:* National Fellowship, 1987–89; Ustad Allauddin Khan Fellowship, 1993; Sanskriti Award, 1994; Kumar Gandharva Award, 1998. *Membership:* Multi Arts Complex, Bharat Bhavan, Bhopal, MP, India. *Address:* Sundaram, 15 Professor Colony Bhopal 462002, Madhya Pradesh, India.

GUNDECHA, Umakant; b. 8 May 1959, Ujjain, Madhya Pradesh, India. Musician. m. Aruna Umakant, 1 s., 1 d. *Education:* MMus; MA, Economics; Madhya Pradesh government scholarship. *Career:* Performed Dhrupad Music (vocal) with brother, Ramakant, all major festivals in India and in Germany, Switzerland, England, France, USA, Norway, Singapore and Hong Kong; Television and radio appearances. *Honours:* National Fellowship, 1987–89; Ustad Allauddin Khan Fellowship, 1993; Sanskriti Award, 1994; Kumar Gandharva Award, 1998. *Membership:* Multi Arts Complex, Bharat, Bhavan,

Bhopal, MP, India. *Address:* Sundaram, 15 Professor Colony Bhopal, 462002, Madhya Pradesh, India.

GUNN, Andrew David; b. 13 Dec. 1974, Paisley, Scotland. Musician (guitar); Songwriter. *Education:* Charleston Academy, Inverness. *Career:* Appeared at Pointblank Blues Festival, The Borderline Club, London, 1992; Eddi Reader's Musicality TV show, No Stilletoes, on BBC Radio 1, 2 and 4, Clyde and Forth Radio; Numerous concerts in Scotland. *Compositions:* Wrote and recorded album, Shades of Blue, Jumpin' The Gunn, 1992; Many blues-based songs. *Membership:* PRS; MCPS; Musicians' Union. *Address:* 16A Pict Ave, Inverness IV3 6LX, Scotland.

GUO, Wenjing; b. 1 Feb. 1956, Chongqing, People's Republic of China. Composer. 1 d. *Education:* Chongqing Song and Dance Ensemble, 1970–77; Graduated, Composition, Central Conservatory of Music, 1983. *Career:* Dean and Professor, Composition Department, Central Conservatory of Music, Beijing; Works performed at major festivals in Europe; Works performed by London Sinfonietta, New York Music Consort, Lincoln Center Chamber Music Society, Hong Kong Chinese Orchestra; Visiting Scholar, Asian Cultural Council, USA; Lectured at Swedish Royal Institute of Music, University of Cincinnati, Manhattan School of Music; Appeared in film Broked Silence; Numerous appearances on TV talk shows. *Compositions:* Wolf Cub Village, chamber opera, 1994; Night Bouquet, chamber opera, 1998. *Address:* Central Conservatory of Music, 43 Baojia St, Beijing 100031, People's Republic of China.

GURD, Geoffrey Robert; b. 24 Feb. 1951, Nottingham, England. Composer; Songwriter; Musician (guitar, keyboards). *Education:* Manchester University; Film-scoring classes, UCLA. *Career:* Guitarist, singer with Crystal, The Sadista Sisters, 1975–79; Musical Director, acts including: The Flirtations, Ritz, Love Bandit; Member, The Twentieth Century Saints, 1979–81; Member, The Flying Fratellinis, 1981–82; Chief Sound Engineer, Red Shop Studios, London, 1982–85; Member, Design For Living, 1985–86; Started own production company, 1986; Formed own publishing company, De Mix Music, 1989; Lived in Los Angeles, 1991–93; Started own record label, DiscoVery, 1994. *Compositions:* As producer: Hold On, Claudia, 1985; Library music album, music for Corporate videos, commercials including: British Airways; Legal and General; Export Financing, 1986; Writer, producer for artists including: Freddie McGregor, Lisa Stansfield, June Montana, 1986–89; Love Is A House, Force MDs, 1987; Better Be Good Tonight, Nick Kamen, 1988; Music for APV Films, Artworks, ITV; Music for Eye To Eye, BBC TV; Songs for Gina Foster, Chyna, 1989–91; Don't Be A Stranger, Dina Carroll, for So Close album, 1993. *Recordings include:* Travels Within, Richmond Gurd (duo), 1994. *Honours:* Quadruple Platinum disc, Don't Be A Stranger. *Membership:* BAC&S; PRS; Musicians' Union; BMI. *Current Management:* De Mix Music Ltd. *Address:* De Mix Music Ltd, PO Box 5705, London W10 6WG, England.

GURTU, Trilok; b. 30 Oct. 1951, Mumbai, India. Vocalist; Musician (percussion); Composer; Prod. *Career:* Son of Indian classical singer, Shobha Gurtu; Father also well-known as sitar player; Played with prominent jazz musicians for many years including: John McLaughlin; Ralph Towner; Pat Metheny; Larry Coryell; Jan Garbarek; Bill Evans; Nana Vasconcelos; Joe Zawinul; Member, Don Cherry's band, 1976–78; Oregon (acoustic jazz-fusion group), 1984–88; Began making solo albums, late 1980s; More recently moved towards a fusion between Indian and African music with African Fantasy and the Beat of Love in collaboration with musicians such as: Oumou Sangare; Angelique Kidjo; Salif Keita; Zap Mama's Sabine Kabongo. *Recordings:* Albums include: Usfret, 1987; Living Magic, Similado, 1990; Crazy Saints, 1993; Believe, Bad Habits Die Hard, 1995; Glimpse, 1997; Kathak, 1998; African Fantasy, 2000; The Beat of Love, 2001; Remembrance, 2002; with Oregon: Ecotopia, 1987; 45th Parallel, 1988; features on: End of August, Philip Catherine, 1982; Song For Everyone, Lakshminarayana Shankar, 1984; Song For Everyone, Jan Garbarek 1985; My People, Joe Zawinul, 1992; Somethin' Else, Jack Bruce, 1993; Promise, John McLaughlin, 1995; Visible World, Jan Garbarek, 1995; Rythmagick, Ayib Dieng/Bill Laswell, 1997; O Sol De Oslo, Gilberto Gil, 1998; Tala Matrix, Tabla Beat Science, 2000; Crossing Borders, Larry Coryell, 2001.

GURU, (Keith Elam), (Bald Head Slick); b. Boston, Massachusetts, USA. Rap Artiste; Prod. *Career:* Name stands for Gifted Unlimited Rhymes Universal; Formed Gang Starr with production partner DJ Premier, 1989; Debut album No More Mr Nice Guy released on Wild Pitch Records; Started Jazzmatazz, solo project with guest vocalists and musicians, 1993; Collaborations include: Ronny Jordan; Dee C Lee; Bilal; Craig David; Bahamadia; N'Dea Davenport; Angie Stone; Chaka Khan; Macy Gray. *Recordings:* Albums: with Gang Starr: No More Mr Nice Guy, 1989; Step In The Arena, 1990; Daily Operation, 1992; Hard To Earn, 1994; Moment of Truth, 1998; solo: Jazzmatazz Vol. 1, 1993; Jazzmatazz Vol. 2, 1995; Streetsoul – Jazzmatazz Vol. 3, 2001; Singles: with Gang Starr: Jazz Thing, 1990; Lovesick, 1991; Code To The Street EP, 1994; You Know My Steez, 1997; solo: Trust Me (with N'Dea Davenport), No Time To Play (with Dee C Lee), 1993; Watch What You Say (with Chaka Khan), Feel The Music, 1995; Livin' In This World/Lifesaver, 1996; Keep Your Worries (with Angie Stone),

2000; Supa Love (with Kelis)/Certified (with Bilal), 2001. *Address:* c/o Virgin Records, 304 Park Ave S, New York, USA.

GUSEV, Nickolai; b. 12 May 1957, St Petersburg, Russia. Composer; Songwriter; Lyrics Author; Musician (Keyboards). m. Marina Guseva, 31 May 1987, 2 d. *Education:* St Petersburg Electrical Engineering Institute; History of Philosophy, St Petersburg University; Jazz Piano, Music College; Composition, St Petersburg, ongoing. *Career:* Founder and Member, alternative bands, Strannye Igry and Avia; Russian tours, international tours, with Avia; Toured UK, Germany, Netherlands, Italy, France, Belgium, Finland, 1988–93; Author, Promotional spots for FM Radio and for TV; Music for films. *Compositions:* I Don't Like You, with Avia; St Petersburg region anthem, 1997. *Recordings:* Albums with Strannye Igry: Red Wine, 1984; Keep Your Eyes Open, 1986; With Avia: Zudov, 1987; Avia for Everybody, 1989; Horray!, 1991; The Songs About Love and Nature, 1994; Solo: Zdanov, soundtrack, 1995; No Mistakes!, 1997. *Honours:* Best Keyboard Player, St Petersburg Open Rock Festivals, 1985, 1987, 1988, 1990, 1992. *Membership:* Russian Authors Asscn; Russian Journalists Society. *Address:* Moskovsky Prospekt 204, F2, 196135 St Petesburg, Russia.

GUTHRIE, Arlo; b. 10 July 1947, Coney Island, New York, USA. Folk Vocalist; Songwriter. *Career:* Appearances on folk circuit include Newport Folk Festival, 1967. *Compositions:* Alice's Restaurant Massacre; Highway In The Wind; Presidential Rag; Children of Abraham. *Recordings:* Albums: Alice's Restaurant, 1967; Arlo, 1968; Running Down The Road, 1969; Alice's Restaurant (soundtrack), 1969; Washington County, 1970; Hobo's Lullaby, 1972; Last of The Brooklyn Cowboys, 1973; Arlo Guthrie, 1974; Together In Concert (with Pete Seeger), 1975; Amigo, 1976; Outlasting The Blues, 1979; Power of Love, 1981; Someday, 1986; Son of the Wind, 1992; Arlo Guthrie/ Pete Seeger, More Together Again, 1994; Alice's Restaurant The Massacre Revisited, 1995; Mystic Journey, 1996; Appears on: The Girls Won't Leave The Boys Alone, Cherish The Ladies, 2001. *Address:* c/o Rising Son Records, PO Box 657, Housatonic, MA 01236, USA.

GUTHRIE, Robin; b. 4 Jan. 1962, Grangemouth, Scotland. Musician (guitar, keyboards); Prod. m. 1 d. (with Elizabeth Fraser). *Career:* Member, Cocteau Twins, 1980–97; Member, Violet Indiana, 1999–; Worked with 4AD collective This Mortal Coil; Collaboration with pianist Harold Budd; Producer for numerous indie acts including Lush, Ian McCulloch, Felt, Guy Chadwick; Established own label Bella Union; Contributed with band to Found Sound by Spooky, 1996. *Recordings:* with Cocteau Twins: Singles: Lullabies, 1982; Peppermint Pig, 1983; Sunburst and Snowblind, 1983; Pearly Dewdrops' Drops, 1984; Aikea-Guinea, 1985; Tiny Dynamine, 1985; Echoes in a Shallow Bay, 1985; Love's Easy Tears, 1986; Iceblink Luck, 1990; Evangeline, 1993; Frosty the Snowman, 1993; Bluebeard, 1994; Twinlights, 1995; Otherness, 1995; Tishbite, 1996; Violaine, 1996; Song to the Siren, with This Mortal Coil, 1983; Albums: Garlands, 1982; Head Over Heels, 1983; Treasure, 1984; The Pink Opaque, 1985; Victorialand, 1986; The Moon and the Melodies, with Harold Budd, 1986; Blue Bell Knoll, 1988; Heaven or Las Vegas, 1990; Four Calendar Café, 1993; Milk and Kisses, 1996; The BBC Sessions, 1999; Stars and Topsoil (compilation), 2000; Solo album: Drifting, 1999; with Violet Indiana: Singles: Choke EP, 2000; Special EP, 2001; Killer Eyes, 2001; Album: Roulette, 2001.

GUTIERREZ, Ivan; b. 17 May 1967, New York, USA. Songwriter; Vocalist; Musician (guitar). *Education:* BA, Mathematics, BA, Philosophy, SUNY, Binghamton; MA, Philosophy, University of Wisconsin, Madison; 4 semesters of music theory, SUNY, Binghamton. *Career:* Extensive stage performances; TV and radio appearances in Czech Republic and Slovakia, 1993–; Sporadic stage performances in New York, Wisconsin, Minnesota, USA. *Compositions:* America; Jaruska; La Violencia; Siendo fuego. *Recordings:* Tres; Vera Bila and Kale, Guest Guitar. *Address:* Zuzana Hanousková, Jugoslavskych Partyzanu 36, 160 00 Prague 6, Czech Republic.

GUTJAHR, Michael; b. Mühlacker, Germany. Man; Vocalist; Songwriter. m. Andrea Gutjahr, 27 April 1990, 1 s. *Education:* Management, CaroCord Gimbtt Music Company; Music lessons with Stromberger (music group); Composing and Text. *Career:* ZDF Volkstumliche Hitparade; ARD Schlagerparade der Volksmusik; MDR, SWF television shows and radio interviews. *Compositions include:* As lyricist and composer: Jeden Tag Nur Sonnenschein; Das Ist Unser Land; Menschen Helfen Menschen; Frage Nicht; Flieg Vogel Flieg. *Recordings:* Mitdem Glück Per Du, Stromberger; 5 albums with Stromberger and others. *Honours:* SDR Golden 7, 1993. *Membership:* GEMA; IFPI; GVL. *Current Management:* CaroCord Gmbh, Music Company. *Address:* CaroCord Gmbh, Aischbühlstr 28, 75443 Ötisheim, Germany.

GUY, Athol; b. 5 Jan. 1940, Victoria, Australia. Vocalist; Musician (bass guitar). *Career:* Founder mem., folk/pop group The Seekers, with Keith Portger and Bruce Woodley, later joined by Judith Durham; Success following concert, Palladium, England, 1964; Group split, 1968. *Address:* c/o Shelley Bovey, 90 Above Town, Glastonbury, Somerset BA6 8JG, England.

GUY, Buddy (George); b. 30 July 1936, Lettsworth, Louisiana, USA. Blues Musician (guitar). *Career:* Played with artists including Slim Harpo; Lightnin'

Slim; Member, Rufus Foreman Band; Solo artiste; Member, houseband, Chess Records, including sessions with Muddy Waters; Howlin' Wolf; Musical partnership with Junior Wells; Performances include: Support to Rolling Stones, tour, 1970; Guest, Eric Clapton's Blues Night, Royal Albert Hall, London, 1990. *Recordings:* Albums: Blues From Big Bill's Copa Cobana, 1963; A Man and The Blues, 1968; This Is Buddy Guy, 1968; Hold That Plane!, 1972; I Was Walking Through The Woods, 1974; Hot and Cool, 1978; Got To Use Your House, 1979; Dollar Done Fell, 1980; DJ Play My Blues, 1982; The Original Blues Brothers – Live, 1983; Ten Blue Fingers, 1985; Live At The Checkerboard, Chicago, 1979, 1988; Breaking Out, 1988; Damn Right I Got The Blues (with Eric Clapton, Jeff Beck, Mark Knopfler), 1991; My Time After Awhile, 1992; Feels Like Rain, 1993; American Bandstand, Vol. 2, 1993; Slippin' In, 1994; I Cry, 1995; Live! The Real Deal, 1996; As Good As It Gets, 1998; Heavy Love, 1998; Last Time Around, 1998; The Real Blues, 1999; 20th Century Masters – The Millennium Collection, 2000; with Junior Wells: Buddy and The Juniors, 1970; Buddy Guy and Junior Wells Play The Blues, 1972; Drinkin' TNT and Smokin' Dynamite, 1982; Alone and Acoustic, 1991; Alive In Montreux, 1992; Various compilations; Singles include: First Time I Met The Blues; Stone Crazy; Contributions to Junior Wells: Hoodoo Man Blues; It's My Life Baby. *Current Management:* The Cameron Organisation Inc, 2001 W Magnolia Blvd, Suite E, Burbank, CA 91506–1704, USA.

GYPSYMEN. See: **TERRY, Todd**.

H

HACKETT, Eric Dexter; b. 13 April 1956, Los Angeles, USA. Musician (keyboards). *Education:* BMus, University of South California, 1977. *Career:* Keyboard player with: Diana Ross and the Supremes; Talk Back, Forward Motion; Scheme Payne; The Temptations; The Four Tops; Musical Dir, Curtis Mayfield, 1977–83; Pres., Can't Hack It Music, 1978–. *Membership:* NARAS; AFofM.

HACKETT, Steve; b. 12 Feb. 1950, London, England. Musician (guitar). *Career:* Member, Quiet World; Genesis, 1971–77; Concerts include: Reading Festivals, 1971–73; Regular UK and US tours, 1973–; Lamb World tour, 1974; Film premiere, Genesis In Concert (attended by Princess Anne), 1977; Solo artiste, 1975–; Member, GTR, 1986. *Recordings:* Albums: with Genesis: Nursery Cryme, 1971; Foxtrot, 1972; Genesis Live, 1973; Selling England By The Pound, 1973; The Lamb Lies Down On Broadway, 1974; A Trick of The Tail, 1976; Wind and Wuthering, 1977; Seconds Out, 1977; Archive Vol. 1: 1967–75, 1999; Archive Vol. 2 1976–92, 2001; Solo albums: Voyage of The Acolyte; Please Don't Touch; Spectral Mornings; Defector; Cured; Highly Strung; Bay of Kings; Till We Have Faces; Blues With A Feeling; Momentum, 1988; Time Lapse, 1992; Guitar Noir, 1993; There are Many Sides to the Night, 1995; Genesis Revisited, 1996; A Midsummer Nights Dream, 1997; Tokyo Tapes, 1999; Darktown, 1999; Sketches of Satie, 2000; Feedback 86, 2001; Live Archive, 2001; with GTR: GTR, 1986. *Honours:* Ivor Novello Award, 1979. *Current Management:* Kudos Music, Crown Studios, 16–18 Crown Rd, Twickenham, Middlesex TW1 3EE, England.

HADDAWAY, Nester Alexander; b. Tobago. Vocalist; Dancer. *Career:* Founder, group Elegato, Germany; Solo singer, dance music, 1992–. *Recordings:* Albums: Haddaway – The Album, 1993; The Drive, 1995; Let's Do It Now, 1999; Singles: What Is Love?, 1993; I Miss You, 1994; Rock My Heart, 1994; Stir It Up, 1994; What Is Love?, 1999; All The Best (compilation), 2001. *Address:* c/o Coconut Records, Nachtigalenweg 34, 53758 Hennef, Germany.

HADJINEOPHYTOU, George Constantinou; b. 28 Oct. 1965, London, England. Composer; Musician (bouzouki, saz, lyra). m. Eleni, 23 Oct. 1994. *Education:* GCE O Level, Grade 5 Theory. *Career:* International Eisteddfod (Wales); BBC World Service, London Greek Radio; Mad About Music, BBC TV. *Recordings:* Psyche and Eros (animation), Channel 4; Grandmother's Hands (short film for television). *Honours:* Drama Film Festival (Greece). *Membership:* PRS; Musicians' Union; MCPS; PRC. *Address:* 41 Burlington Rise, East Barnet, Hertfordshire EN4 8NH, England.

HADJOPOULOS, Sue; b. 26 June 1953, New York, USA. Musician (percussion); Vocalist. *Education:* BA, Anthropology, Columbia University, 1975; Mannes College of Music. *Career:* Professional percussionist, 1970–; Founder member, female salsa group Latin Fever; Tours include: World tours with Joe Jackson, 1982–83, 1991–; World tour with Simple Minds, 1985–86; True Colors tour with Cyndi Lauper; Support tours with The Who; The Rolling Stones; Performed and recorded as freelance musician with: Laurie Anderson; Mick Jones; Michael Monroe; Laura Nyro; Teena Marie; Percussionist for numerous commercials. *Recordings:* with Joe Jackson: Night and Day, 1982; Mike's Murder (soundtrack), 1983; Live 1980–86, 1988; Blaze of Glory, 1989; Laughter and Lust, 1991; Heaven and Hell, 1997; Night and Day II, 2000; with Simple Minds: Once Upon A Time, 1985; Live In The City of Light, 1987; also appears on: Strange Angels, Laurie Anderson, 1989; David Byrne, David Byrne, 1994; Factory Showroom, They Might Be Giants, 1996. *Publications:* One of Top Latin Percussionists, Modern Drummer Magazine Poll, 1984; Platinum discs with Joe Jackson, Simple Minds. *Membership:* AFTRA; ASCAP; NARAS; AFofM; Percussive Arts Society; Recording Musicians Asscn.

HADLEY, Tony (Anthony); b. 2 June 1960, Islington, London, England. Vocalist. *Career:* Member, Spandau Ballet, 1979–90; Performances include: Royal Albert Hall, 1983; Royal Festival Hall, 1983; Wembley Arena, 1984; Live Aid, Wembley, 1985. *Recordings:* Singles include: To Cut A Long Story Short, 1980; The Freeze, 1981; Musclebound, 1981; Chant No. 1 (I Don't Need This Pressure On), 1981; Instinction, 1982; Lifeline, 1982; Communication, 1983; True (No. 1, UK), 1983; Gold, 1984; Only When You Leave, 1984; I'll Fly For You, 1984; Highly Strung, 1984; Round and Round, 1984; Solo: Lost In Your Love, 1992; For Your Blue Eyes Only, 1992; The Game of Love, 1992; Absolution, 1993; Build Me Up, from the film When Saturday Comes, 1996; Save a Prayer, 1998; Dance with Me, 1998; Obsession (Live), 2000; Dance With Me, 2001; with Erikah Karst, Separate Lies, 1997; with Tin Tin Out, Dance with me, 1997; Albums: Journey To Glory, 1981; Diamond, 1982; True, 1983; Parade, 1984; The Singles Collection, 1985; Through The Barricades, 1986; Heart Like A Sky, 1989; The Best of Spandau Ballet, 1991; Solo album: Tony Hadley, 1997; Contributor, Do They Know It's Christmas?, Band Aid, 1984. *Honours:* BRIT Awards, Sony Trophy For Technical Excellence, 1984.

HADWEN, Julie; b. 4 Jan. 1965, Reading, Berkshire, England. Vocalist; Songwriter; Musician (piano, guitar). *Education:* Private studies, piano, guitar, classical, blues, jazz. *Career:* Supported Kane Gang on tour, 1984; Montreux Jazz Festival, 1985; British Big Sound Authority tour, 1985; Televison appearances include: The Tube; Old Grey Whistle Test; Top of the Pops; Wogan; Oxford Road Show; Live radio sessions for Bruno Brookes, Janice Long. *Recordings:* Albums: An Inward Revolution; Sanctuary; Singles: This House Is Where Your Love Stands; Bad Town; Moving Heaven and Earth; Don't Let Our Love Start A War. *Membership:* Musicians' Union. *Address:* 72 Makepeace Ave, Highgate, London N6 6HB, England.

HADZO, (Davor Kodzoman); b. 27 Jan. 1967, Zagreb, Croatia. Musician (guitar, bass guitar); Songwriter; Music Writer; Vocalist. *Education:* Electrical Engineer. *Career:* Underground out of Yugoslavia, TV documentary, 1986; J Peel Show, Radio 1, played Stop the War, Bring the Noiz 7, 1992; Fiju Briju 1, 1993, 3, 1995, 4, 1996, Fiju Briju, 1997; Biggest festivals in Croatia and Salata, 1997; Ecstazy, Berlin, 1990; Zoro, Leipzig, Germany, 1993. *Compositions:* Obrij me Majko Motornom Pilom; Fuck You All, 1993; Pataren; Sank; Nema Vise; MTV. *Publications:* Croatian Pop/Rock Encyclopedia, 1994; Patareni Tribute, 1996; Patareni Buka, We Can't Be Banned From Here, 1991. *Honours:* Porin, Best Alternative Album, 1993, Hladno Pivo Dzinovski, 1994. *Membership:* Croatian Musicians' Union. *Current Management:* Jabukaton, B Trenka 9, 10000 Zagreb, Croatia. *Address:* Mandroviceva 5, 10000 Zagreb, Croatia. *E-mail:* patareni@hgu.hr.

HAFER, John Richard (Dick); b. 29 May 1927, Wyomissing, Pennsylvania, USA. Musician (Tenor Saxophone, Clarinet, Flute, Oboe, English Horn). m. 1 s., 1 d. *Education:* Studied Theory and Harmony privately; Studied Saxophone, Clarinet, Flute and Oboe privately, and Oboe with Albert Golter of the New York Philharmonic. *Career:* Played with: Charlie Barnet Orchestra; Claude Thornhillock; Woody Herman Orchestra; Charles Mingod Orchestra; Bobby Hackett band; Appeared on Merv Griffin TV Show for 12 years; Appeared in Broadway shows No No Nanette, How to Succeed in Business, Fade On, Fade Out, Molly, Golden Boy Morne, They're Playing Our Song; Played with Benny Goodman Orchestra, Ruby Broff. *Recordings:* Road Band, Woody Herman; Classic Jazz, Charlie Barnet; The Black Saint and the Sinner Lady and Mingus, Mingus, Mingus, with Charlie Mingus; Prez Impressions, Dick Hafer Quartet; In A Sentimental Mood: Dick Hafer. *Membership:* AFM Life Member. *Address:* 10500 Reseda Blvd, Northridge, CA 91326, USA.

HAGAR, Sammy; b. 13 Oct. 1947, Monterey, California, USA. Rock Vocalist; Musician (guitar); Songwriter. *Career:* Singer, bands: Fabulous Castillas; Skinny; Justice Brothers; Dust Cloud; Lead singer, Montrose, 1973–75; Support to The Who, London; Solo artiste, 1975–87; Support to Kiss; Boston; Kansas; One-off project, HSAS (with Neal Schon, Kenny Aaronson and Michael Shrieve), 1984; Lead singer, US rock group Van Halen, 1987–97; Regular US and international tours including Monsters of Rock US tour, 1988; Co-host, Westwood One radio show with Michael Anthony, 1992. *Recordings:* with Montrose: Montrose, 1973; Paper Money, 1974; Solo albums: Nine On A Scale of Ten, 1976; Sammy Hagar Two, 1977; Musical Chairs, 1978; All Night Long-Live, 1978; Street Machine, 1979; Danger Zone, 1979; Loud and Clear, 1980; Standing Hampton, 1982; Rematch, 1982; Three Lock Box, 1983; Live From London To Long Beach, 1983; VOA, 1983; Voice of America, 1984; Looking Back, 1987; Sammy Hagar, 1987; Red, 1993; Unboxed, 1994; Marching to Mars, 1997; Red Voodoo, 1999; Ten Thirteen, 2000; with HSAS: Through The Fire, 1984; with Van Halen: 5150 (No. 1, USA), 1986; OU812 (No. 1, USA), 1988; For Unlawful Carnal Knowledge (No. 1, USA), 1991; Balance, 1995; Singles include: Solo: Your Love Is Driving Me Crazy; I Can't Drive 55; Heavy Metal, film theme from film Heavy Metal; Winner Takes All, from film Over The Top; Give To Live; Eagles Fly; with Van Halen: Why Can't This Be Love, 1986; Love Walks In, 1986; Dreams, 1986; When It's Love; Finish What Ya Started, 1988; Feels So Good, 1989; Poundcake, 1991; Top of The World, 1991; Right Now, 1992. *Honours:* Numerous Platinum discs; Grammy Award, Best Hard Rock Performance, 1992; American Music Award, Favorite Album, 1992; Bay Area Music Awards, Outstanding Male Vocalist, 1992, 1993; MTV Music Video Award, 1992. *Current Management:* KP Management, 24608 Varese Court, Valencia, CA 91355, USA.

HAGGARD, Merle; b. 6 April 1937, Bakersfield, California, USA. Vocalist; Songwriter. *Career:* Accompanied Wynn Stewart, 1960; Founder, The Strangers; Successful songwriting and recording career, including 40 US Country No. 1 records. *Recordings:* Hit singles (own compositions) include: I'm A Lonesome Fugitive, 1966; Okie From Muskogee, 1969; I Take A Lot of Pride In What I Am; Silver Wings; Today I Started Loving You Again; If We Make It Through December; Poncho and Lefty, with Willie Nelson; Albums include: Just Between The Two of Us, with Bonnie Owens, 1966; Same Train

A Different Time, 1969; The Land of Many Churches, with Bonnie Owens, Carter Family, 1971; My Love Affair With Trains, 1976; A Taste of Yesterday's Wine, with George Jones, 1982; Poncho and Lefty, with Willie Nelson, 1983; Heart To Heart, with Leona Williams, 1983; That's The Way Love Goes, 1983; The Epic Collection – Live, 1983; It's All In The Game, 1984; Kern River, 1985; Amber Waves of Grain, 1985; Out Among The Stars, 1986; A Friend In California, 1986; Seashores of Old Mexico, 1987; Chill Factor, 1988; 5:01 Blues, 1989; Blue Jungle, 1990; Super Hits, Vol. 2, 1994; Super Hits, Vol. 3, 1995; If I Could Only Fly, 2000; New Light Through Old Windows, 2000; Cabin In The Hills, 2001. *Publications:* Autobiography, Sing Me Back Home, with Peggy Russell. *Current Management:* Hag Inc, PO Box 536, Palo Cedro, CA 96073, USA.

HÄGGMAN, Ann-Mari (Solveig); b. 19 Sept. 1941, Vasa, Finland. Music Organization Exec. m. Lars-Eric Häggman, 11 April 1964, 1 s., 1 d. *Education:* PhD in Ethnomusicology. *Career:* Researcher and Head of Svenska litteratursällskapets Folkkulturarkiv; Assistant Professor, Department for Folklore, Helsinki University, 1993–95; Head of the Institute of Finland-Swedish Traditional Music, 1985–. *Publications:* Magdalena på källebro (The Ballad of Mary Magdalene's Conversion), dissertation, 1992; Numerous articles, CDs and films about folk music in Finland. *Membership:* Word of Honour of the Finlands svenska spelmansförbund (League of Traditional Musicians); Board Mem., Swedish Literature Society; Pres., SFV Foundation for Adult Education and Culture, 1998–; Numerous folk music organizations. *Address:* c/o Finlands svenska folkmusikinstitut, Handelsesplanaden 23A, 65100 Vasa, Finland.

HAGUE, Mel (Melvyn Ian); b. 20 Jan. 1943, Whiston, South Yorkshire, England. Vocalist; Entertainer; Songwriter; Musician (guitar); Novelist. m. Ivy Walton, 6 Aug. 1966, 1 s., 1 d. *Career:* Grew up in Canada, 1951–61; Played most UK concert venues, including Wembley Conference Centre; All UK Country music festivals; Several European tours; *Appearances:* Regional television stations: Country Club, BBC2; Nightride; WSM Nashville radio, television; Much regional radio, TV; Own record label, OGB Records. *Recordings:* 17 albums (11 on own label), 1974–2002. *Contributions to:* Music, book reviewer, Doncaster Entertainer; Traditional Music Maker; Country Music Round-Up; Country Music & Dance; South Yorkshire Times; Goole & Thorne Courier; Brum Country; The Storyman. *Honours:* Aria Guitars/Daily Mirror Golden Guitar Award, Top Country Entertainer, 1981. *Membership:* Performing Rights Society; British Country Music Asscn. *Address:* 37 Wroot Rd, Finningley Village, Doncaster DN9 3DR, England. *E-mail:* melhague@lineone.net. *Website:* www.melhaguecountry-western.com.

HAGUE, Stephen; Prod. *Career:* Worked with: Ace of Base, Dicte, Dink, Dubstar, Extra Very, Gregory Grey, Jaguar, James, Tom Jones, Manbreak, Manic Street Preachers, Maren Ord, New Order, Robert Palmer, Planet Claire, The Pogues, Pretenders, Robbie Williams. *Address:* c/o Worlds End Records, 183 N Martel Ave, Suite 270, Los Angeles, CA 90036, USA. *Website:* www.worldsend.com.

HAHN, Joe (Joseph); b. 15 March 1977, Glendale, CA, USA. DJ. *Education:* Painting, Pasadena Art College of Design. *Career:* Joined Xero; Renamed Hybrid Theory and signed to Warner Bros, Spring 2000; Further name change to Linkin Park prior to first record releases; Numerous international appearances; Live shows include: Family Values, Ozzfest tours, KROQ Acoustic Christmas Concert 2001; TV specials include: Live At The Fillmore; Reverb. *Recordings:* Albums: Hybrid Theory, 2000; Reanimation, 2002. Singles: Hybrid Theory (EP), 2000; One Step Closer, 2001; Crawling, 2001; Papercut, 2001; In The End, 2001; Pts.Of.Athrty, 2002. *Honours:* Billboard Award, Best Modern Rock Artist, 2001; Rock Bear Awards, Best International Band, Best International Album, 2001; Kerrang! Award, Best International Newcomer, 2001; Rolling Stone Award, Best Hard Rock/Metal Band, 2001; MTV Awards, Best Group, Best Hard Rock, 2002. *Current Management:* Andy Gould Management, 8484 Wilshire Blvd #425, Beverly Hills, CA 90211, USA. *Website:* www.linkinpark.com.

HAIMOVICI, Fabien-David; b. 22 April 1968, Bordeaux, France. Musician (drums). *Education:* College; 4 years in France, drum school; 1 year in Los Angeles, Musicians Institute. *Career:* Played with Bireli Lagrene; Tours all over USA, Europe, Japan; Tour with French artistes Jacques Higelin; Nicole Croisille; Tours in Japan, France; Played with international artists in France including Lucky Peterson; Currently plays and records with Coke Tale (comprised of top Paris studio musicians). *Recordings:* Solo rock album. *Honours:* Diploma: Outstanding Student of the Year, Musicians Institute, Los Angeles. *Address:* 16 rue des cascades, 75020 Paris, France.

HAINES, Luke; b. 7 Oct. 1967, Walton-on-Thames, Surrey, England. Vocalist; Songwriter. *Career:* Member: UK groups: The Auteurs; Black Box Recorder. *Recordings:* with The Auteurs: Singles: Showgirl, 1992; Lenny Valentino, 1993; How Could I Be Wrong, 1993; Chinese Bakery, 1994; Back With The Killer, 1995; Light Aircraft On Fire, 1996; The Rubettes, 1999; Albums: New Wave, 1993; Now I'm A Cowboy, 1994; After Murder Park, 1996; How I Learned To Love The Bootboys, 1999; with Black Box Recorder: Singles: Child Psychology, 1998; England Made Me, 1998; The Facts of Life,

2000; The Art of Driving, 2000; Albums: England Made Me, 1998; The Facts of Life, 2000; Solo albums: The Oliver Twist Manifesto, 2001; Christie Malry's Own Double-Entry (soundtrack), 2001; Also appears on: Baader Meinhof, 1997. *Current Management:* Tony Beard, PROD.

HAINES, Margaret Ewart Blackwood; b. 28 April 1941, Detroit, MI, USA. m. Peter E. Haines, 28 Aug. 1965, 1 s., 1 d. *Education:* BA, Elementary Education, Minor in Music, Albion College, Albion, MI, USA; Independent study in composition, theory, harmony, orchestration. *Career:* Marge and Friends, TV programme, 1980–83, 1984–85; Featured interviews with leading Christian national and local people, 1980–83. *Compositions:* Love Song: You Are The Love Of My Life; Songs Of Jesus; Cantos de Jesus (six Spanish scripture/Worship songs); Cantata to Revelation; Revelation of Jesus Christ, 1999; Orchestration, 2003. *Recordings:* Songs Of Jesus; Are You Ready: 20 Gospel Favorites; The Revelation Of Jesus Christ!; Elaine O'Neill: Favorite Hymns. *Publications:* Revelation of Jesus Christ (song book), 1997; Orchestration, 2003; Songs of Jesus (song book and cassette), 1996; Children's Scripture Song Book. *Honours:* Senior Piano Recital: Albion College, 1963; Music study grant, 1970–71. *Membership:* National Religious Broadcasters; Christian Copyright Licensing International; ASCAP; American Music Center. *Address:* PO Box 66, 85 Crease Rd, Budd Lake, NJ 07828, USA. *Fax:* (973) 691-0885. *E-mail:* pehmah1@aol.com.

HAJDOVSKA-TLUSTA, Katerina; b. 27 Feb. 1953, Prague, Czech Republic. Vocalist; Musician (percussion); Songwriter. m. Martin Tlusty, 30 Jan. 1982, 2 step-d. *Education:* Special Pedagogy, Prague Charles' University. *Career:* FOK, folk-rock; Foersters Choir; J Vycpálek Folklore Music; Ukrainian Folklore Music, Ignis; Prague Madrigals, Chesed, Jewish music; Ester, Jewish music; Music and Musicotherapy Teacher; Czech Radio broadcasts. *Recordings:* Albums: with Ester: To You, Jerusalem; with Alexander Hajdovsky, Ester: Shalom, Chaverim, 1998; with Chesed: Jewish Feasts in Songs; Jewish Songs Live. *Current Management:* K Hajdovská-Tlustá, Michnova 1626, 149 00 Prague 4, Czech Republic.

HAJDOVSKY-POTAPOVIC, Alexandr 'Lesik'; b. 27 Feb. 1953, Prague, Czech Republic. m. Miroslava Hajdovska-Vlková, 7 Dec. 1973, 2 s. *Career:* Documentary film music; Advertisement music; Member of Czech television and radio broadcasting groups: FOK, folk rock; Svehlik, rock; Mazelé, rap; Extempore, rock/humour; Ester, Jewish traditional songs. *Recordings:* Albums: Jizák; Lesik Hajdovsky: Uz horisvíce; Lesik Hajdovsky: Manzelé; Prague: Zizkov Kuplets; Svehlík: There's No Time; Ester: Shalom Chaverim, with Katerina Hajdovska-Tlusta, 1998. *Honours:* Mlady svet – Bílá Vrána; Melodie magazine award, 1991. *Membership:* OSA. *Current Management:* Katerina Hajdovská-Tlustá, Michnova 1626, 149 00 Prague 4, Czech Republic. *Address:* Brodského 1672, 149 00 Prague 4, Czech Republic.

HALE, Alan Spencer; b. 31 May 1965, Morristown, Tennessee, USA. m. Michelle, 2 d. *Career:* Opened Shows, Concerts for Exile, Mel McDaniel, Marty Stuart, Confederate Railroad, Western Flyer, Highway 101, Ricochet; Opened Third Annual Forks of the River Jam; Featured Performer and Master of Ceremonies, First Night in Kingsport; Closed The Season for Bonnie Lou and Buster Smoky Mountain Hayride Show; Featured Performer for Las Vegas Producer, John Stuarts Country Music Show; FOA Network Aired 2 Television Specials; Performed at Pegeon Forge, The Music Mountain Amphia Theater, The Rainbow Theater, Tennessee Music Theater, 1993–. *Compositions:* I'll Be True; The Weight; The Band; Once In A Lifetime. *Recordings:* Ain't Man Enough; Come On In; Happiness; Forever Gone; Can't Get There; Better Or Worse; Slippin' Away; Lady Lied; Once In A Lifetime; The Weight; I'll Be True. *Honours:* Kingsport Key To City. *Address:* Alan Spencer Hale Fan Club, St Paul Rd, Morristown 5476 TN 37813, USA.

HALE, Keith; b. 6 Nov. 1950, Hull, East Yorkshire, England. Songwriter; Musician (keyboards); Record Prod. 1 d. *Education:* Dartington College of Arts, Devon. *Career:* Formed Blood Donor, 1977; Support to J J Burnel on Euroman Tour; Member, Hawkwind, 1980; Left with Ginger Baker, formed Ginger's Nutters, toured Europe, 1981; Member, Toyah's band for Warrior Rock tour, 1982. *Compositions:* It's A Mystery, 1981. *Recordings:* Producer, Toyah's first album Sheep-Farming In Barnet; Other albums include: Zones/Stonehenge, Hawkwind; Toyah On Tour, 1983; Ginger Baker In Concert, 1985; Toyah – Live and More, 1998. *Membership:* PRS; MCPS; Musicians' Union. *Current Management:* Gems. *Address:* Firs Cottage, 5 Firs Close, London SE23 1BB, England.

HALE, Simon B; b. 23 April 1964, Birmingham, England. Composer; Arranger; Prod; Musician (keyboards). m. Claire Moore, 15 Oct. 1994, 1 s., 1 d. *Education:* A Level Music, Grade VIII piano, violin; Bachelor of Music, Goldsmiths College, University of London, 1985. *Career:* Keyboards with Seal: World tour; US Grammy Awards, 1992; Top of the Pops; Wogan; Live videos; Keyboards with: Howard New; Wendy and Lisa; Tri; Gail Ann Dorsey; Geoffrey Williams; Arranger for: Incognito; George Benson; Yo Yo Honey; Shawn Lee; Maysa Leak; Conductor, MD, concert with Incognito, Royal Festival Hall, 1995; Producer for: 2 albums, Kumiko Yamashita. *Compositions:* George Benson; British Film Institute; Nescafé; Solo album, 1992; String arranger: 100° and Rising, Incognito; String arranger, composer,

George Benson; Composer, orchestrator, Tomoyasu Hotei; Solo album: East Fifteen, 1994; Seal, single, EP; BBC TV theme tune The Vote Race, 1992. *Recordings:* with Jamiroquai: Travelling without Moving, 1996; Canned Heat, 1999; Synkronized, 1999; with Duncan Sheik: Duncan Sheik, 1996; Humming, 1998; M People, 1997; Rat Bat Blue, 1997; with Incognito: No Time Like The Future, 1999; with Steps, Buzz, 2000; with Becky Taylor, A Dream Come True, 2001. *Membership:* Musicians' Union; PRS; MCPS; Asscn of Professional Composers. *Current Management:* c/o IRc2 (London) Ltd. *Address:* 1 Star St, London W2 1QD, England.

HALEY, Mark Jonathan; b. 2 Feb. 1961, Portsmouth, Hampshire, England. Musician (keyboards, guitar). *Education:* Classical training in piano, guitar, trumpet. *Career:* Began Haley Brothers, 1976; Television appearance, Rund Pop show, East Germany, 1984; Toured with Billy Fury, 1982; Joined The Monkees comeback tours, 1986–89; Member, The Kinks, 1989–93; The Chaps, 1994–96; Current member, The Rubettes, joined January 2000; Formed Gorge, 1997; Album: On This. *Compositions:* Don't Answer, on The Other Side of Hank Marvin, 1998. *Recordings:* with Haley Brothers: One Way Love Affair, 1978; with The Monkees: That Was Then, This Is Now, 1986; with The Kinks: Down All The Days, 1991; with The Chaps: The Collector, 1995; Programmer, This Is Hardcore, Pulp album, 1998. *Publications:* Journeyman, autobiography on internet, 1999. *Honours:* Ivor Novello Award Services To Music (The Kinks). *Membership:* PRS; Executive Committee Mem., Musicians' Union; MCPS; BRIT Awards Voting Academy. *Current Management:* Via Management.

HALFORD, Rob; b. 25 Aug. 1951, Birmingham, England. Vocalist. *Career:* Lead singer, UK heavy rock group Judas Priest, 1974–90; Tours include: Support to Led Zeppelin, USA, 1977; Support to Kiss, 1979; Turbo – Fuel For Life tour, 1986; Painkiller tour, USA, 1990; US tour, with Alice Cooper, Motörhead, 1991; Concerts, festivals include: Reading Festival, 1976; Monsters of Rock Festival, Castle Donington, 1980; Heavy Metal Sunday, San Bernadino, California, 1983; Live Aid, Philadelphia, 1985; Founder, lead singer, heavy rock group Fight, 1991–; Appearance as stand-in singer for Black Sabbath, Pacific Amphitheatre, California, 1992. *Recordings:* Albums: with Judas Priest: Rocka Rolla, 1974; Sad Wings of Destiny, 1976; Sin After Sin, 1977; Stained Class, 1978; Killing Machine, 1978; Unleashed In The East, 1979; British Steel, 1980; Point of Entry, 1981; Screaming For Vengeance, 1982; Defenders of The Faith, 1984; Turbo, 1986; Priest Live, 1987; Ram It Down, 1988; Painkiller, 1990; A Touch of Evil, 1991; Metal Works 1973–93, 1993; Best of Judas Priest, 1998; with Fight: War of Words, 1994; Mutations, 1994; A Small Deadly Space, 1995; Solo album: Resurrection, 2000; Singles include: with Judas Priest: Take On The World; Living After Midnight; Breaking The Law; You've Got Another Thing Coming. *Contributions to:* : Stars, Hear 'n' Aid (charity record for Ethiopian famine relief), 1986; Singer, with Pantera, for film soundtrack Buffy The Vampire Slayer, 1992. *Current Management:* c/o John Baxter, EMAS, PO Box 55810, Phoenix, AZ 85078, USA.

HALL, Chris; Musician (accordion, drums); Vocalist; Agent; Record Co Exec; Journalist; Radio Presenter; Festival Organizer. *Career:* Accordion player, vocalist with R Cajun and The Zydeco Brothers; The Bearcats; Accordion Player with Zydecomotion; Tour organizer, US and UK agent, for Cajun and Zydeco; Writer, co-partner, Cajun Users Manual; Radio presenter, BBC Radio 2; Club organizer, The Swamp Club; Manager, Bearcat Records; Recorded and appeared on TV with Paul McCartney; featured accordion player on McCartney's Run Devil Run album recorded at Abbey Road and also featuring Dave Gilmour (Pink Floyd), Ian Paice (Deep Purple), Mick Green (The Pirates) and Pete Wingfield. *Address:* Swamp, PO Box 94, Derby DE22 1XA, England.

HALL, Daryl, (Daryl Franklin Hohl); b. 11 Oct. 1948, Pottstown, Pennsylvania, USA. Vocalist; Musician (guitar); Songwriter. *Education:* Temple University. *Career:* Member, Kenny Gamble and The Romeos; Gulliver; Session singer, Sigma Sounds Studios; Backing singer, The Stylistics; The Delfonics; Member, duo Hall and Oates, with John Oates, 1969–; Concerts world-wide include: Live Aid, Philadelphia, 1985; Rainforest benefit concert, Madison Square Garden, with The Grateful Dead, 1988; Earth Day, Central Park, New York, 1990; USA Harvest National Hunger Relief concert, 1991; The Simple Truth, benefit concert for Kurdish refugees, Wembley, 1991. *Compositions:* Many hit songs co-written with John Oates; Other songs include: Sara Smile; Wait For Me; Kiss On My List (co-written with Janna Allen); One On One; Did It In A Minute (co-written with Sara and Janna Allen); Foolish Pride; Everything Your Heart Desires; Swept Away, for Diana Ross; Film theme, Ruthless People (co-written with Mick Jagger and Dave Stewart). *Recordings:* Albums: with Hall and Oates: Whole Oats, 1972; Abandoned Luncheonette, 1974; War Babies, 1974; Daryl Hall and John Oates, 1975; Bigger Than Both of Us, 1976; No Goodbyes, 1977; Beauty On A Back Street, 1977; Livetime, 1978; Along The Red Edge, 1978; X-Static, 1979; Private Eyes, 1981; H2O, 1982; Big Bam Boom, 1984; Live At The Apollo With David Ruffin and Eddie Kendricks, 1985; Ooh Yeah, 1988; Change of Season, 1990; The Best Of..., 1991; Solo albums: Sacred Songs, 1980; Three Hearts In The Happy Ending Machine, 1986; Soul Alone, 1993; Can't Stop Dreaming, 1999; Best of The Ballads, 2000; US No. 1 singles with Hall and

Oates: Rich Girl, 1977; Kiss On My List, 1981; Private Eyes, 1981; I Can't Go For That (No Can Do), 1982; Maneater, 1982; Out of Touch, 1984; Numerous other hit singles include: She's Gone, 1976; Every Time You Go Away, 1980; You've Lost That Lovin' Feelin', 1980; Family Man, 1983; Say It Ain't So, 1983; Method of Modern Love, 1985; Solo hits: Dreamtime, 1986; Stop Loving Me, Stop Loving You, 1993; Featured on: Journeyman, Eric Clapton, 1989. *Contributions to:* : We Are The World, USA For Africa, 1985; Sun City, Artists Against Apartheid, 1985; The Last Temptation of Elvis, 1990; Two Rooms – Celebrating The Songs of Elton John and Bernie Taubin, 1991. *Honours:* American Music Awards: Favourite Pop/Rock Duo or Band, 1983–85; 19 US Gold and Platinum discs (most successful duo in US recording history). *Current Management:* All Access Entertainment. *Address:* 53 W 23rd St, 11th Floor, New York, NY 10010, USA.

HALL, Gary Martin; b. 29 Nov. 1964, Ormskirk, Lancashire, England. Vocalist; Songwriter; Musician (guitar). *Career:* Member, The Stormtroopers, 1986–92; Television appearances: Granada TV, three times; Italian TV; Numerous appearances on radio; Tours of Europe. *Recordings:* Writer, all songs on albums: Garage Heart, 1989; Wide Open To The World, 1991; What Goes Around, 1993; Twelve Strings and Tall Stories, 1996; Return to the Flame, 1998; Also collaborated with: Townes Van Zandt; John Prine; Guy Clark. *Honours:* Rising Star Award, BCMA, 1995. *Membership:* PRS; MCPS. *Address:* 10 Rose Terrace, Ashton, Preston, Lancashire PR2 1EB, England.

HALL, G(raham) P(eter); b. 15 July 1943, Hampton Hill, England. Artist; Composer; Ambient Sound Sculptures; Musician (saxophone, bass, flamenco guitar, synthesizer, electric guitar). m. Päivi Annikki Vilkman, 26 June 1987, 4 s., 2 d. *Education:* Studied flamenco guitar. *Career:* Member, blues bands, 1960s; Toured Europe, 1962–68; Video: The Estates, 1977; Tour: Estates, 1977; Festivals: France; Germany; Spain; Holland, 1982; North Africa, 1983; Southwest England, 1992; Docklands The Space performance, 1998; Radio includes: Radio Bristol; Radio Sussex; Radio Mercury; Radio Surrey; Radio Lotus, Denmark; Radio Lux, Ukraine; Television: Wire TV; Germany; Netherlands; Queen Elizabeth Hall, London, 1996; Western Isles tour, 1997. *Compositions:* Commissioned, Sea Sorrow (Isle of Lewis), 1997. *Recordings:* New Town Suite; The Estates, 1977; Manifestations; Full Moon Over Madrid, 1979; Harbinger, Colours, 1986; Imaginary Seasons, 1992; Slipstreams, Glow, 1994; Shooting Stars, 1995; Eclectic Guitars, 1996; Figments of Imagination, 1996; Mar-Del-Plata, 1997; Steel Storm and Tender Spirits, double CD, 1998; Marks on the Air, live at The Spitz, London and Phantom Theatre, Wilshire, 1998; Recorded 143 titles, all instrumental; Video: Paths of The Lonely, 1995. *Publications:* River Flow; Off The Shell; Filmtrax; Prototype; Countdown Productions. *Membership:* PRS; Musicians' Union; MCPS; PAMRA. *Current Management:* Imaginary Music.

HALL, Jim (James S.); b. 4 Dec. 1930, Buffalo, New York, USA. Musician (guitar). m. Jane Herbert, 9 Sept. 1965, 1 d. *Education:* Cleveland Institute of Music. *Career:* Musician with Chico Hamilton, Jimmy Guiffre Trio, 1957–59; Ella Fitzgerald, 1959–60; Sonny Rollins, 1961–62; Formed Quartet with Art Farmer, 1962–64; Leader, own trio/quartet, 1962–; Concerts include: The White House; Carnegie Hall; Duke Ellington's Birthday Party; Jazz Festivals include: Berlin; Concord; Monterey; Newport; Umbria; Many club appearances in USA, Canada, England, France, Japan; Television appearances world-wide including The Sound of Jazz, CBS; The Tonight Show; Film appearance: Jazz On A Summer's Day, 1958. *Recordings:* Albums include: with Bobby Brookmeyer and Jimmy Raney: Street Swingers; with Bill Evans: Undercurrent; Intermodulation; with Sonny Rollins: The Bridge; with Art Farmer: Big Blues; with Paul Desmond: Paul Desmond and Friends; Easy Living; with Ron Carter: Alone Together; Live At The Village West; Telephone; with Michel Petrucciani's Power of Three (featuring Jim Hall and Wayne Shorter): Three; Solo, own ensembles: All Across the City; Live At Town Hall, Vols 1 and 2; Subsequently: Youkali; Something Special; Dedications and Inspirations; Other recordings with Red Mitchell; George Shearing; Tom Harrell. *Publications:* Jazz Improvisation, Transcriptions of Jim Hall Solos, 1980; Exploring Jazz Guitar, 1991; Master Sessions with Jim Hall, (instructional video), 1993; Jim Hall-Jazz Guitar Environments, 1994. *Honours:* Downbeat Critics Poll Awards, 1963–; Downbeat Reader's Poll Winner, 1965–66; Playboy All-Star Poll Winner, 1968–71; Jazz Magazine Award, Best Performer, 1965–66. *Current Management:* Mary Ann Topper, Jazz Tree Agency. *Address:* 648 B'way Suite 703, New York, NY 10012, USA.

HALL, Keith Robert; b. 24 April 1951, Edgware, Middlesex, England. Musician (drums). *Education:* Studied with Joe Hodson; Frank King; Joe Morello. *Career:* Professional musician, 1966–; Founder member, Pickettywitch, 1969–72; Member, Gerry and The Pacemakers, 1973–77; Terry Lightfoot, 1978–84; Musicals: Hair National Tour; 1980; Godspell, 1980; Joseph and The Amazing Technicolour Dreamcoat, 1981; Freelance musician, played with: Kenny Ball; Maxine Daniels; Bertice Redding; Fiona Duncan; Jay McShan; Ellen Rucker; Ritchie Cole, 1984–; Formed jazz-rock fusion band Storm Warning, with Jill Jarman, 1987; Concerts include: Festivals throughout Europe; Toured with Engelbert Humperdinck; with June Harris, 1987–89; Also toured Scandinavia; Worked with: Tom Whittle; Januz Carmello; Al Gray; Spike Robinson; Dick Hestall-Smith, 1990; Moved to Helsinki, 1990; Regular drummer with Antti Sarpila Swing Band; Also worked with: UMO; Espoo Big Band; Pentti Lasanen; Severi Pyysalo; Karita Mattila; Appearances at most Finnish music festivals, including the Pori International Jazz Festival 1992–95, 1997–99 and on Finnish television and radio; Republic of Finland's President's Independence Day gala party in Helsinki, with the Antti Sarpila swing band, 1999. *Recordings:* with Pickettywitch: That Same Old Feeling, 1970; Sad Old Kinda Movie, 1970; Baby I Won't Let You Down, 1970; with Gerry and The Pacemakers: Lovely Lady, 1974; Albums: with Pickettywitch: Pickettywitch, 1970; Spirit Level albums include: Storm Warning, 1988; Killer Bunnies; Mice In The Wallet, On The Level; Proud Owners; with Antti Sarpila: Father, Son and Holy Swing, 1993; Chrisse Schwindt Memorial Concert, 1993; Live At Storyville, 1994; with Claus Anderson: Chrisse Schwindt Memorial Concert, 1993; with Swing Gentlemen: Swing Gentlemen's Ball, 1995. *Membership:* Musicians' Union; Finnish Drummers Asscn; Finnish Musicians' Union; PAMRA; GAMEX. *Address:* Rakuunantie 17 A12, 00330 Helsinki, Finland.

HALL, Martin; b. 26 April 1963, Copenhagen, Denmark. Vocalist; Composer; Musician (multi-instrumentalist). *Education:* Academy of Piano and Music, Copenhagen; Royal Academy of Fine Arts, Copenhagen. *Career:* Singer, composer, Ballet Mécanique; Ritual, The World Music Days, Århus Musikhus, 1983; Requiem, The Taksigelses Church, Copenhagen, 1989; Inskription, The Danish National Radio, 1983; Gud Og Grammatik, Danish Academy of Fine Arts, 1984; Current Works, Danish Natonal Radio, 1995. *Recordings:* Avenues of Oblivion, 1980; The Icecold Waters of The Egocentric Calculation, 1981; For, 1982; Ritual, 1983; Apparently All The Same, 1984; Free Force Structure, 1984; Fusion, 1985; Relief, 1985; Warfare, 1985; Treatment, 1985; Cutting Through, 1986; Beat of The Drum, 1988; Presence, 1988; Surreal Thing, 1989; The Martin Hall Document, 1989; Crush: The Point of No Return Soundtrack, 1989; Prime Material, 1990; Imperfect, 1990; Dreamworld, 1990; Palladium, 1990; The Rainbow Theatre, 1990; Read Only Memory, 1991; Sweet Mystery, 1993; All The Way Down, 1993; Strange Delight, 1993; A Touch of Excellence, 1993; Angel of The Night, 1994; Phantasmagoria, 1994; Random Hold, 1996; Testcards 1989–95, 1997; Performance, 1997. *Publications:* 4 books; 5 anthologies; 28 albums, magazines, works; The World Days, 1996. *Honours:* Hon. Award, Danish Asscn of Composers, 1995; The 3 Year Major Grant, National Fund For The Endowment of the Arts, 1995; Asscn of Danish Composers (DJBFA); KODA; GRAMEX; NCB. *Current Management:* Motor Danmark. *Address:* Motor Danmark, Linnésgade 14, 1361 Copenhagen K, Denmark.

HALL, Terry; b. 19 March 1959, Coventry, Warwickshire, England. Vocalist. *Career:* Singer, The Special AKA (later as The Specials), 1977–81; International concerts and tours include: Concert for People of Kampuchea, London, 1979; Founder member, Fun Boy Three, 1981–83; Founder, Colourfield, 1983–88; Member, Terry, Blair and Anouchka, 1989–90; Member, Vegas (with Dave Stewart), 1992; Also solo artiste. *Recordings:* with The Specials: Singles: Gangsters, 1979; A Message To You Rudy, 1979; Too Much Too Young (No. 1, UK), 1980; Rat Race, 1980; Stereotype, 1980; Do Nothing, 1981; Ghost Town (No. 1, UK), 1981; Albums: Specials, 1979; More Specials, 1980; Dance Craze (film soundtrack), 1981; More Specials, 2002; Singles Collection, 1991; Stereotypes (compilation), 2000; with Fun Boy Three: Singles: The Lunatics Have Taken Over The Asylum, 1981; It Ain't What You Do (with Bananarama), 1981; Summertime, 1982; The Telephone Always Rings Twice, 1982; The Tunnel of Love, 1983; The More I See, 1983; Our Lips Are Sealed, 1983; Albums: Fun Boy Three, 1982; Waiting, 1983; Best Of..., 1984; with The Colour Field: Singles: Thinking of You, 1985; Castles In The Air, 1985; with Terry Blair and Anouchka: Albums: Ultra-Modern Nursery Rhymes, 1990; with Vegas: Album: Vegas, 1992; Solo: Singles: Forever J, 1994; Rainbows, 1995; Albums: Terry Hall – The Collection, 1993; Home, 1995; Laugh, 1997; Co-writer, Sense, The Lightning Seeds, 1992; Jollification, The Lightning Seeds, 1994; Guest vocals: Poems, Nearly God (collaboration with Tricky), 1996. *Current Management:* Asgard Management, 125 Parkway, London NW1 7PS, England.

HALL, Thomas James; b. 19 May 1957, Longview, Washington, USA. Record Prod; Sound Engineer. *Education:* BA, radio and television production, East Washington University, 1980. *Career:* Producer, sound engineer, Viacom Studios; Logic West Studios; London Bridge Studios; Triad Studios, 1982–. *Recordings:* As producer/sound engineer: with Queensryche: Queensryche, 1983; Mindcrime Live, 1991; with Kenny G: Kenny G Live, 1990. *Address:* Triad Studios, 4572 150th Ave NE, Redmond, WA 98052, USA.

HALL, Tom T; b. 25 May 1936, Olive Hill, Kentucky, USA. Songwriter; Vocalist; Author. *Career:* Broadcaster, musician, WMOR radio station, Kentucky, with Kentucky Travellers, 1950s–60s; Leader, own touring band The Storytellers; Currently concentrating on novel-writing and composing children's songs. *Compositions include:* DJ For A Day, Jimmy C Newman; Goodbye Sweetheart, Hello Viet Nam, Johnny Wright; Mama Tell 'Em What We're Fighting For, Dave Dudley; Harper Valley PTA, Jeannie C Riley; I Can't Dance, Gram Parsons and Emmylou Harris; Margie's At The Lincoln Park Inn, Bobby Bare; A Week In The County Jail; Pinto The Wonder Horse Is Dead; I Miss A Lot of Trains; Old Dogs, Children and Watermelon Wine. *Recordings:* Albums include: The Storyteller, 1972; The Rhymer and Other Five and Dimers, 1973; For The People In The Last Hard Town, 1973;

Country Is, 1974; Songs of Fox Hollow, 1974; Faster Horses, 1976; The Magnificent Music Machine, 1976; About Love, 1977; New Train Same Rider, 1978; Places I've Done Time, 1978; Saturday Morning Songs, 1979; Ol' T's In Town, 1979; Soldier of Fortune, 1980; The Storyteller and The Banjoman (with Earl Scruggs), 1982; In Concert, 1983; World Class Country, 1983; Everything From Jesus To Jack Daniels, 1983; Natural Dreams, 1984; Songs In A Seashell, 1985; Country Songs For Kids, 1988; Loves Lost and Found, 1995; Songs from Sopchoppy, 1996; Homegrown, 1997; A Soldier of Fortune, 1997; The Ultimate Collection, 2000; features on: Write Your Story, Scott Burnett, 2001. *Publications:* The Songwriter's Handbook; The Storyteller's Nashville; The Laughing Man of Woodmont Cove; Spring Hill (novel). *Honours:* Grammy Award, Tom T Hall's Greatest Hits. *Address:* c/o Tom T. Hall Enterprises, PO Box 1246, Franklin, TN 37065, USA.

HALLAM, Nick (The Head); b. 11 June 1960, Nottingham, England. Prod; DJ. *Career:* Founder, Gee Street Studio and Record Label; Founder Member, Stereo MCs; Remixed artists including Jungle Brothers, U2, PM Dawn, Queen Latifah, Disposable Heroes of Hiphoprisy, Monie Love, Electronic, Madonna (Frozen); Established music publisher, Spirit Songs; Numerous gigs and TV appearances with Stereo MCs. *Recordings:* Elevate My Mind, 1990; Lost in Music, 1991; Connected, 1992; Step It Up, 1993; Ground Level, 1993; Creation, 1993; Deep Down and Dirty, 2001; We Belong In This World Together, 2001; Albums: 33–45–78, 1989; Supernatural, 1990; Connected, 1992; Stereo MCs, 1993; Deep Down and Dirty, 2001. *Honours:* BRIT Awards: Best British Album; Best British Group, 1993.

HALLDORSSON, Bjorgvin Helgi; b. 16 April 1951, Hafnarfjordur, Iceland. Vocalist. m. Ragnheidur B Reynisdottir, 9 Dec. 1977, 2 s., 1 d. *Education:* Piano with private tutor, Brauner. *Career:* Appearances, Little Shop of Horrors, 1985; Evita, 1997; Köldum klaka, 1991; Eurovision Song Contest, 1996. *Compositions:* Skyiö; Riddari Gotunnar; Vertu ekki aö plata mig I útvarpinu heyröi ég lag; Ennpá thessi asni; Undi blaum mana. *Recordings:* Bjorgvin, 1982; Kristján Johannson, 3 albums; Diddú, 3 albums; Iceland Symphony Orchestra, 3 albums. *Honours:* 28 Gold Records, 1974–98. *Membership:* APRS; STEF of Iceland; FTT, Iceland. *Current Management:* Skifan HF, Iceland. *Address:* PO Box 520, 220 Hafnarfjordur, Iceland.

HALLIWELL, Geri Estelle; b. 7 Aug. 1972, Watford, England. Vocalist. *Career:* Mem., Touch, later renamed Spice Girls, 1993–98; Numerous tours, concerts, television and radio appearances; Film: Spiceworld: The Movie, 1997; World tour incl. UK, Europe, India, USA; Nominated UN Goodwill Ambassador, 1998–; Solo artiste, 1998–; Signed to Chrysalis Records, 1999; Judge, Popstars–The Rivals (ITV1), 2002. *Recordings:* Albums: With Spice Girls: Spice Girls (No. 1, UK), 1996; Spiceworld (No. 1, UK), 1997; Solo: Schizophonic, 1999; Scream If You Wanna Go Faster, 2001. Singles: With Spice Girls: Wannabe (No. 1, UK and USA), 1996; Say You'll Be There (No. 1, UK), 1996; 2 Become 1 (No. 1, UK), 1996; Mama/Who Do You Think You Are (No. 1, UK), 1997; Spice Up Your Life (No. 1, UK), 1997; Too Much (No. 1, UK), 1997; Stop, 1998; (How Does It Feel to Be) On Top of the World, as part of England United, 1998; Move Over/Generation Next, 1998; Viva Forever, 1998; Solo: Look At Me, 1999; Mi Chico Latino (No. 1, UK), 1999; Lift Me Up (No. 1, UK), 1999; Bag It Up (No. 1, UK), 2000; It's Raining Men, (No. 1, UK), 2001; Scream If You Wanna Go Faster, 2001. *Publications:* If Only (autobiography), 1999; Just for the Record (autobiography), 2002. *Honours:* with Spice Girls: BRIT Awards, Best Single, for Wannabe, Best Video, for Say You'll Be There, 1997; Two Ivor Novello songwriting awards, 1997; Smash Hits Award, Best British Band, 1997; Three American Music Awards, 1998; Special BRIT Award for International Sales, 1998. *Address:* c/o A&R Dept, Chrysalis Records, 43 Brook Green, London W6 7EF, England. *Website:* www.geri-halliwell.com.

HALLYDAY, Johnny, (Jean-Philippe Smet); b. 15 June 1943, Paris, France. Vocalist; Musician (guitar). m. Sylvie Vartan. *Education:* Violin lessons. *Career:* Radio debut, 1960; Film appearance: Les Parisiennes, 1961. *Recordings:* Numerous albums include: Johnny Hallyday Sings America's Rockin' Hits, 1962; Flagrant Delit, 1975; Drole De Metier, 1986; Trift De Rattles, 1986; Les Grandssuccess De Johnny Hallyday, 1988; La Peur, 1988; La Nuit Johnny, 1993; Parc De Princes, 1993; Tes Tendres Annees, 1994; Destination Vegas, 1996; Rough Town, 1996; Aimer Vivre, 1997; Retiens La Nuit, 1997; Ce Que Je Sais, 1998; Insolitudes, 1999; Derriere l'Amour, 1999; Sang Pour Sang, 2000; A La Vie, A La Mort!, 2002. Singles include: T'Ai Mer Follement; Let's Twist Again (bilingual version), 1961; If I Were A Carpenter (duet with Emmylou Harris), 1985. *Address:* c/o 6 rue Daubigny, 75017 Paris, France.

HALSALL, Jennie; b. 23 Jan. 1954, London, England. Media Exec; Man; Dir. *Education:* Kilburn Polytechnic, London. *Career:* Jacksons Advertising Agency; Cue Films Ltd; EMI Records, UK; David Geffen and Elliot Roberts Management, USA; Elektra Asylum Records, USA; Independent PR; Formed own business, Jennie Halsall Consultants (media consultants in Europe and the world outside USA), 1980–. *Honours:* PR of the Year, 1980. *Address:* 208A King St, London W6 0RA, England.

HAMAHANG, Abdul; b. Afghanistan. Vocalist; Musician; *Recordings:* Albums: Gul-e Naz; Zolf-e Sya. *Honours:* Afghanistan's cultural award of Ustad, 2002.

HAMASAKI, Ayumi; b. 2 Oct. 1978, Fukuoka, Kyushu, Japan. Vocalist; Musician (piano); Songwriter. *Career:* Moved to Tokyo to act and model; Released moderately successful rap record; Relocated to New York for vocal lessons, 1997; Combines music with advertising/modelling career; Concert tours of Japan, 2000–01; Launched own range of cellphones, 2001. *Recordings:* Albums: Nothing From Nothing (as Ayumi featuring Dohzi-T and DJ Bass), 1995; A Song For XX, Love Appears, 1999; Duty, 2000; A Best, 2001; Singles: Nothing From Nothing (as Ayumi featuring Dohzi-T and DJ Bass), 1995; Poker Face, You, Trust, For My Dear…, Depend On You, 1998; Whatever, Love – Destiny, To Be, Boys and Girls, Monochrome, Appears, Kanariya, 1999; Fly High, Vogue, Far Away, Seasons, Surreal, Audience, M, 2000; Evolution, Never Ever, Endless Sorrow, Unite!, Dearest, A Song Is Born (with Keiko), 2001. *Honours:* Japan Music Award, Grandprix Award, 2001; Japan Gold Disc Award, Artist of the Year (for record sales in excess of 11m. in one year), 2001; World Music Award, Best Selling Japanese Artist, 2001. *Address:* c/o Rhythm Republic/Axex, Japan. *Website:* www.avexnet.or.jp/ayu.

HAMBE, Alf; b. 24 Jan. 1931, Sweden. Composer; Song Writer; Author; Poet; Artist; Musician. m. Ulla, 1 s., 1 d. *Education:* Private Studies in Composition, Piano, Accordion and Guitar. *Career:* Debut, First Song Collection, Astronaut on Horseback, 1962; Full-time writer, composer, 1962–; Stage, television and radio appearances. *Compositions:* 15 collections of songs and poems. *Recordings:* Alf Hambe in Molom; 20 Recordings with Songs From My Collections; Song in Molom; Scandinavian Songs with Alice and Svend. *Publications:* Song in Molom; Another Song About The Forest of the Green Mist. *Honours:* Prize to the Memory of Ulf Peder Olrog, 1975; Nils Ferlin Prize, 1988; 2 Evert Taube Prizes, 1990. *Membership:* Swedish Composers of Popular Music; Swedish Composers International Association; Swedish Authors Association. *Address:* Alf Hambe, Steninge, 31042 Haverdal, Sweden.

HAMILL, Andy; b. 25 March 1972, Glasgow, Scotland. Session Musician (double bass, bass guitars). *Career:* Session player, many jazz, pop and drum 'n' bass bands, incl.: 4 Hero, Nitin Sawhney, Chris Bowden; Co-prod., musician, June Babies, debut album of Rebecca Hollweg. *Recordings:* Album: Solo: Bee For Bass. *Membership:* Musicians' Union. *Address:* 14A Emu Rd, London SW8 3PR, England. *Website:* www.andyhamill.com.

HAMILTON, Andy, (Raphael Thomas Hamilton); b. 26 March 1918, Port Maria, Jamaica. Jazz Musician (tenor saxophone). m. Mary, 4 s., 6 d. *Career:* Moved to Birmingham, 1949; Worked with Jean Toussaint; Mick Hucknall; David Murray; Steve Williamson; Andy Sheppard; Jason Rebello; Bernardo Sassetti; Son, Graeme (trumpet player); Concerts: St Lucia Jazz Festival; Co-producer with Jean Toussaint. *Recordings:* Albums: Silvershine, 1991; Jamaica By Night, 1993; with Steve Byrd: Late and Live, 1997. *Current Management:* Alan Cross, 120 Lightwoods Rd, Bearwood, Birmingham B67 5BE. *Address:* c/o World Circuit Records, 106 Cleveland St, London W1P 5DP, England.

HAMILTON, Chico; b. 21 Sept. 1921, Los Angeles, California, USA. Jazz Musician (drums); Bandleader. *Career:* Drummer with: Dexter Gordon, Charles Mingus, Buddy Collette, whilst at school; Lionel Hampton, Slim Gaillard, 1940; Count Basie, Lester Young, late 1940s; Lena Horne, 1948–55; Founder, own quartet, 1955; Own bands (trio, quartet, quintet, octet) featured musicians including: Buddy Collette; Fred Katz; Ron Carter; Jim Hall; Eric Dolphy; Gabor Szabo; Larry Coryell; Eric Gayle; John Abercrombie; Film appearances: Sweet Smell of Success, 1957; Jazz On A Summer's Day, 1958; Leader, own group Euphoria, 1980s. *Recordings:* Numerous albums include: Spectacular, 1955; Sweet Smell of Success, 1957; Newport Jazz, 1958; The Three Faces of Chico, 1959; That Hamilton Man, 1959; Passin' Thru, 1962; Man From Two Worlds, 1963; Chic Chic Chico, 1965; The Dealer, 1966; The Further Adventures of El Chico, 1966; The Gamut, 1967; El Exigente, 1970; Head Hunters, 1974; Peregrinations, 1975; Chico Hamilton and The Players, 1976; Reaching For The Top, 1978; Nomad, 1979; Euphoria, 1986; Reunion, 1989; Chico The Master, 1992; Trio, 1992; My Panamanian Friend, 1992; Dancing to a Different Drummer, 1993; Timely, 1999; The Original Ellington Suite, 2000; Foreststorm, 2001. *Address:* Chico Hamilton Productions Inc, 321 E 45th St Penthouse A, New York, NY 10017, USA.

HAMILTON, Frank; b. 3 Aug. 1934, New York, NY, USA. Musician; Vocalist. m. Mary Hamilton, 15 Jan. 1983. *Education:* Los Angeles City College, 1952, 1955, 1966; Roosevelt University, Chicago, 1960–61; Los Angeles Valley College, Van Nuys, 1963–64; Santa Monica City College, 1964–69; California University, Los Angeles, 1970, 1978; Santa Barbara City College, 1974; California University, Northridge, 1978; Georgia State University, 1984–87. *Career:* Co-Founder of The Old Town School of Folk Music, Chicago, 1957; House Musician, Gate of Horn, Chicago, 1958–62; Newport Folk Music Festival, 1959; With Folk Music Group, The Weavers, Carnegie Hall, Lincoln Center, Forest Hills Stadium, 1963; Concert with Pete Seeger, Abbott Hall, Marblehead, MA, 1984; Meridian Folk Trio, 1986–2000. *Compositions:* We Shall Overcome, 1956; Survival, 1965; The Surfers, 1964;

Baby, What I Mean, 1965; I Feel It, 1967. *Recordings:* A Folksinger's Folksongs; Frank Hamilton Sings Folksongs; Nonsuch, with Pete Seeger; The World of Frank and Valucha; Weavers Reunion at Vanguard Carnegie Hall; Folk Festival at Newport; Long Lonesome Home, 1999; Goodnight Irene (Weavers compilation), 2000. *Publications:* Choosing a Guitar Teacher, 1981. *Honours:* Composition Award, Los Angeles Valley College, 1963. *Membership:* Chicago Historical Society; Irish Arts of Atlanta; Founder, Hot Club of Atlanta. *Current Management:* Frank Hamilton Productions. *Address:* 852 Cinderella Court, Decatur, GA 30033, USA.

HAMILTON, George, IV; b. 19 July 1937, Winston-Salem, North Carolina, USA. Vocalist; Musician; Songwriter. m. Adelaide Peyton, 1958. *Education:* University of North Carolina. *Career:* Recording artist, 1956–; Tours with Buddy Holly; Eddie Cochran; Gene Vincent; Broadway appearance with Louis Armstrong; Regular UK appearances include: Wembley Country Music Festival; First country artist to perform in USSR; Occasionally works with son, George Hamilton V. *Recordings:* Hit singles include: A Rose and A Baby Ruth; If You Don't Know I Ain't Gonna Tell You; Why Don't They Understand; Only One Love; Now and For Always; The Teen Commandments of Love (with Paul Anka and Johnny Nash); I Know Where I'm Going; Abilene; Break My Mind; Fort Worth, Dallas Or Houston; She's A Little Bit Country; Albums include: On Campus, 1958; Mister Sincerity, 1965; By George, 1966; Canadian Pacific, 1969; Down Home In The Country (with Skeeter Davis), 1971; Heritage (with The Hillsiders), 1971; Down East Country, 1972; Bluegrass Gospel, 1974; Fine Lace and Homespun Cloth, 1977; Feel Like A Million, 1978; Forever Young, 1979; Cuttin' Across The Country, 1981; One Day At A Time, 1982; Songs For A Winter's Night, 1982; Music Man's Dream, 1984; Hymns Country Style, 1985; A Country Christmas, 1989; American Country Gothic (with the Moody Brothers), 1989; Country Classics (with George Hege Hamilton V), 1992; County Boy, 1996; George Hamilton IV, 1999; Beyond The River, 2001. *Honours:* International Ambassador of Country Music, Country Music People magazine, 1974; Trendsetter Award, Billboard magazine, 1975. *Current Management:* Blade Productions, PO Box 1556, Gainesville, FL 32602, USA.

HAMILTON, Mark; b. 21 March 1977, Lisburn, Northern Ireland. Musician (bass guitar). *Career:* Founding Mem., Ash; Early releases on indie label; Numerous headline tours, UK festivals and television appearances; Record deal and tour of USA; Contributed track to film, A Life Less Ordinary, 1997. *Recordings:* Albums: Trailer, 1994; 1977, 1996; Live At The Wireless, 1997; Nu-Clear Sounds, 1998; Free All Angels, 2001; Intergalactic Sonic 7's: The Best Of Ash, 2002; Envy, 2002. Singles: Jack Names the Planets, 1994; Petrol, 1994; Uncle Pat, 1994; Kung Fu, 1995; Girl From Mars, 1995; Angel Interceptor, 1995; Goldfinger, 1995; Oh Yeah, 1996; A Life Less Ordinary, 1997; Jesus Says, 1998; Numbskull (EP), 1999; Wild Surf, 2001; Burn Baby Burn, 2001; Shining Light, 2001; Sometimes, 2001; Candy, 2001; Tokyo Blitz, 2002; There's A Star, 2002. *Honours:* Ivor Novello Award, Best Contemporary Song, for Shining Light, 2002. *Address:* Infectious Records, 1 Shorrolds Rd, London SW6 7TR, England. *E-mail:* mark@ash-official.com. *Website:* www.ash-official.com.

HAMILTON, Natasha Maria; b. 17 July 1982, Kensington, Liverpool, England. Vocalist. *Career:* Mem., Atomic Kitten, 1999–; UK Support tours 1999–2000; Co-spearheaded MTV Asia Awards, 2000; Pan-European breakthrough with Whole Again single; Guest at Celebrate South Africa Freedom Concert, London, 2001; Appearance, Party at the Palace, Buckingham Palace Jubilee celebrations, 2002. *Recordings:* Albums: Right Now, 2000 (reissue 2001); Feels So Good, 2002. Singles: Right Now, 1999; See Ya, 2000; I Want Your Love, 2000; Follow Me, 2000; Whole Again, 2001; Eternal Flame, 2001; It's OK, 2002; Tide Is High, 2002; Last Goodbye/Be With You, 2002. *Current Management:* Integral Management, 51–55 Highfield St, Liverpool L3 6AA, England. *Address:* c/o Innocent Records, Kensal House, 553–579 Harrow Rd, London W10 4RH, England. *Website:* www.atomickitten.com.

HAMILTON, Page; b. Eugene, Oregon, USA. Musician (guitar). *Education:* MA, Jazz Guitar, Manhattan School of Music, New York. *Career:* Played in Glenn Branca's Guitar Orchestra; Member, Band of Susans; Formed Helmet, 1989; Numerous live dates; Appears on: Opening Credits, Laptop, 2000. *Recordings:* Singles: Born Annoying; In the Meantime; Unsung; Primitive; Just Another Victim; Biscuits for Smut; Wolma's Rainbow, EP; Exactly What You Wanted; Albums: Strap It On, 1990; Meantime, 1992; Betty, 1994; Aftertaste, 1997.

HAMILTON, Patrick; b. 16 March 1963, Bruges, Belgium. Prod; Musician (Keyboards); Songwriter. *Education:* Classical Music Degree. *Career:* Played with several well known bands in Belgium; Owner, The Globe, recording studio. *Compositions:* Composed for Sandra Kim, Eurovision contest winner mid 1980s; 2 Lips; Partyzone; Monday Justice; Marisa; Kabouter Plop; Q-Bric. *Address:* Hoekweg 3, 8020 Hertsberge, Belgium. *Telephone:* (477) 603105. *E-mail:* info@the-globe.be. *Website:* www.the-globe.be.

HAMLISCH, Marvin; b. 2 June 1944, New York, USA. Composer; Conductor; Musician (piano); Entertainer. m. Terre Blair, 29 May 1989.

Education: Professional Children's School; Queen's College, New York; Juilliard School, New York. *Career:* Debut as pianist, Minnesota Orchestra, 1975; Solo concert tours; Conductor of various orchestras throughout USA; Principal Pops conductor for: Pittsburgh Symphony Orchestra; National Symphony Orchestra, 2000–; Musical director and conductor, Barbra Streisand tours: The Concert, 1994; And Timeless, 1999. *Compositions include:* Film scores: Frankie and Johnny, 1966; The Swimmer, 1968; Take The Money and Run, 1969; Bananas, 1971; The Way We Were, 1974; The Sting (adaptation), 1974; Same Time Next Year, 1979; Starting Over, 1979; Ordinary People, 1980; Seems Like Old Times, 1980; Sophie's Choice, 1982; Film themes for: The January Man; Three Men and A Baby; Little Nikita; The Experts; Popular songs: Sunshine Lollipops and Rainbows; Good Morning America; Nobody Does It Better; Broadway musicals: A Chorus Line, 1975; They're Playing Our Song, 1979; The Goodbye Girl, 1993; Other works: Anatomy of Peace, Symphony In One Movement, 1991; One Song, for Barcelona Olympics, 1992. *Publications:* The Way I Was (autobiography), 1992. *Honours:* Three Academy Awards; Four Grammy Awards; Three Emmy Awards; Tony Award; Three Golden Globes; Pulitzer Prize, for show A Chorus Line. *Membership:* ASCAP. *Address:* c/o Nancy Shear Arts Services, 180 West End Ave, Suite 28N-P, New York, NY 10023, USA.

HAMMARLUND, Jan; b. 17 July 1951, Stockholm, Sweden. Vocalist; Songwriter; Musician (guitar); Translator. *Education:* Private singing lessons, 1981–92. *Career:* Festivals: Gärdet, Stockholm; Västervik; Roskilde; Midtfyn; Hultsfred; Mariposa; Chile Crea; Tour of England, 1978; California, 1979; Denmark, 1978–86; Chile, 1991; Swedish TV Portrait, 1990. *Compositions:* Songs: Ville, 1979; Translations of Violeta Parra; Dag Vill Leva I Europa, 1981; Malvina Reynolds. *Recordings:* 12 LPs, 1972–86; Tusentals Swarnor Over Chile, 1974; Karlek Olh Sang, 1981; Among 6 CDs: Jan Hammarlund, 1972–92; Tvars Over Garn, French cabaret songs, 1995; Om Trädgärdsbevattning, songs by Brecht, 1996. *Honours:* Awards with Grants: SKAP, 1978; STIM, 1989; Konstnärsnämnden (Artists committee), 1992–96; José Martí Award, 1994. *Membership:* STIM; Svenska Teateförbundet, SKAP; Musikcentrum. *Address:* Skördemane AB, c/o Hammarlund, Vapengatan 22, 12652 Hagersten, Sweden.

HAMMEL, Joan; b. 11 Aug. , Lake Forest, Illinois, USA. Vocalist. *Education:* Columbia College. *Career:* Professional Singer, performing primarily in the USA; toured the Caribbean; hosted the Midday Show, on radio; numerous commercials, television and film work. *Compositions:* Learn To Fly; Love Prevails; Run Like The Wind; The Gift; Give It To Me Straight; Timeless; See Ya. *Recordings:* Oh Lady Di, Tribute To Princess Diana. *Honours:* Emmy, Best Children's Special, 1987; ITVA Award, Best Health Care Video, 1986, 1987; National and International Vocal Competition Medals. *Membership:* NARAS; NATAS; ACCOP. *Current Management:* Paxton Productions, PO Box 486, Grayslake, IL 60030, USA.

HAMMER, Jan; b. 17 April 1948, Prague, Czechoslovakia. Musician (keyboards); Composer. *Education:* Prague Academy of Music and Arts, 1966–68; Berklee College of Music, Boston, USA, 1968. *Career:* Moved to USA, 1968; Jazz musician, 1968–71; Member, John McLaughlin's Mahavishnu Orchestra, 1971–73; Freelance musician and bandleader, 1973–. *Compositions:* Film scores: A Night In Heaven, 1983; Secret Admirer, 1985; Television series soundtrack: Miami Vice, 1984–. *Recordings:* Singles: Theme From Miami Vice (No. 1, USA), 1985; Crockett's Theme (No. 2, UK), 1987; Too Much to Lose, 1989; Solo albums: Like Children, 1974; First Seven Days, 1975; Timeless, 1975; Make Love, 1976; Oh Yeah, 1976; Melodies, 1979; Black Sheep, 1979; Escape From TV, 1987; Snapshots, 1989; Behind The Mind's Eye, 1993; Country and Eastern Music, 1993; Drive, 1994; Snapshots 1.2, 2000; with John McLaughlin: Inner Mounting Flame, 1971; Birds of Fire, 1973; Love Devotion and Surrender, 1973; with Jeff Beck: Wired, 1976; Live With The Jan Hammer Group, 1977; There and Back, 1980; Flash, 1985; with Al Di Meola: Elegant Gypsy, 1977; Splendido Hotel, 1979; Electric Rendezvous, 1982; Tour de Force, 1982; Scenario, 1983; with John Abercombie: Timeless, 1975; Five Years Later, 1982; Other recordings with: Tommy Bolin; Stanley Clarke; Billy Cobham; Steve Lukather; Santana; Jerry Goodman; Neal Schon.

HAMMER, Joseph; b. 7 June 1954, San Antonio, Texas, USA. Musician (drums, Fairlight); Composer. m. Jacqueline Henry, 28 Feb. 1983, 1 s. *Education:* Drum Instruction, Berklee School of Music; Boston School of Electronic Music. *Career:* Studio production, 1975–85; Co-production for Daniel Balavoine; Tours, concerts, with Daniel Balavoine, France Gall, Jean-Michel Jarre. *Compositions:* Summer Dreaming; Love of a Woman. *Recordings:* Daniel Balavoine; Jean-Michel Jarre; Jon Anderson; Mick Jagger; Peter Gabriel. *Publications:* Trophee Sonor, 6–10 Drums. *Membership:* Institut de Percussions Modernes. *Current Management:* La Fretite Studios. *Address:* La Fretite Studios, 10 rue Jean Lefevbre, 95530 La Frette, Paris, France.

HAMMER, (Stanley Kirk Burrell); b. 30 March 1962, Oakland, California, USA. Rap Artiste; Dancer. *Career:* Former baseball player; Member, rap duo Holy Ghost Boys; Founder, Bustin Records; Solo artiste (originally as MC Hammer), 1987–; Concerts include: Please Hammer, Don't Hurt 'Em US tour,

1990; US tour, with Vanilla Ice and En Vogue, 1990; UK and Japan tours, 1991; The Simple Truth (benefit concert for Kurdish refugees), Wembley, 1991; Too Legit To Quit tour, with Boyz II Men, 1992; USA Harvest Hunger Relief Concert, 1992; Kiel Summer Jam, largest rap festival ever, 1992; Television includes: Lou Rawls Parade of Stars, 1990; Ray Charles, 50 Years In Music Uh-Huh, 1991; Hammer's MTV Birthday Bash, 1992; Hammer From The Heart, CBS, 1992; Hammerman Cartoon series, ABC, 1992; Founder, management, production and video company, Roll-Wit-It Entertainment, 1992. *Recordings:* Hit singles include: U Can't Touch This, 1990; Have You Seen Her?, 1990; Pray, (No. 2, USA), 1990; Here Comes The Hammer, from Rocky V film soundtrack, 1991; Yo! Sweetness, 1991; Addams Groove, from Addams Family film soundtrack, 1992; 2 Legit 2 Quit, 1992; Do Not Pass Me By, 1992; It's All Too Good, 1994; Pumps and A Bump, 1994; Don't Stop, 1994; Going Up Yonder, 1995; Sultry Funk 1995; Albums: Feel My Power, 1987; Please Hammer Don't Hurt 'Em (No. 1, USA, 10m. copies sold), 1990; Too Legit To Quit, 1991; The Funky Headhunter, 1994; Inside Out, 1995; Family Affair, 1998; Active Duty, 2001. *Honours:* Several American Music Awards, 1990–91; 3 Grammy Awards, 1991; People's Choice Award, 1991; BRIT Award, Best International Newcomer, 1991; MC Hammer Day declared, Fremont, California, 1991; 2 Bammy Awards, 1991; JUNO Award, International Artist of the Year, 1991; 3 Rolling Stone Readers Poll Wins, 1991; 4 Soul Train Awards, including Sammy Davis Jr Award, 1991–92; 4 NARM Awards, 1991. *Current Management:* Superstar Management, 7633 Sunkist Dr., Oakland, CA 94605, USA.

HAMMETT, Barry James; b. 31 Oct. 1944, Swansea, Wales. Musician (guitar); Guitar Teacher. m. 16 March 1968 to 19 March 1978, 2 d. *Education:* Swansea Technical College. *Career:* Lead guitar, Johnny Kidd and Pirates, 7 years; Swansea Top Rank (resident band), 7 years; P&O Cruises, 14 months with Kiki Dee, Blood Brothers tour. *Recordings:* Numerous radio and TV sessions as featured band, backing musician. *Membership:* Musicians' Union. *Address:* 52, Ael-y-Bryn, Fforestfarch, Swansea, West Glamorgan, SA5 8JB, Wales.

HAMMETT, Kirk; b. 18 Nov. 1962, USA. Musician (guitar). *Career:* Guitarist, Exodus; Joe Satriani; Member, US heavy rock group Metallica, 1983–; World-wide tours include: Masters of Puppet world tour, 1986–87; US tour, 1988; Damaged Justice British tour, 1989; World tour, 1991–; Also tours with Raven; Ozzy Osbourne; Twisted Sister; Motörhead; Major concerts include: Monsters of Rock Festival, Castle Donington, 1985, 1987, 1991; German Monster Rock festivals, 1987; Monsters of Rock, Europe and US tours, 1988, 1991; Day On The Green, Oakland, 1991. *Recordings:* Albums: Kill 'Em All, 1983; Ride The Lightning, 1984; Master of Puppets, 1986;... and Justice For All, 1988; Metallica (No. 1, USA and UK), 1991; Live Shit, 1993; Load, 1996; Reload, 1997; Mama Said, 1998; SandM, 1999; Singles: Garage Days Revisited (EP), 1987; Harvester of Sorrow, 1988; One, 1989; Enter Sandman, 1991; The Unforgiven, 1991; Nothing Else Matters, 1992; Wherever I May Roam, 1992; Sad But True, 1992; Until It Sleeps, 1996; Hero of the Day, 1996; Memory Remains, 1997; The Unforgiven, 1998; Whisky in the Jar, 1999; Die Die My Darling, 1999; I Disappear, 2000; Stone Cold Crazy, track featured on Rubáiyát (Elektra's 40th Anniversary compilation). *Honours:* Platinum and Gold discs; Grammy Awards: Best Heavy Metal Performance: One, 1989; Stone Cold Crazy, 1991; The Unforgiven 1992; Best Hard Rock Performance: Whiskey In The Jar, 2000; Rock Instrumental Performance, Call of The Ktulu, 2001; American Music Award, Favourite Heavy Metal Artist, 1993; Bay Area Music Awards: Outstanding Album, 1992; Outstanding Heavy Metal Album, Outstanding Group, Outstanding Guitarist, 1993; Rolling Stone Readers Poll Winners, Best Heavy Metal Band, 1993. *Current Management:* Q-Prime Inc. *Address:* 729 Seventh Ave, 14th Floor, New York, NY 10019, USA.

HAMMILL, Peter; b. 5 Nov. 1948, London, England. Vocalist; Musician (guitar, piano). *Career:* Founder member, Van Der Graaf Generator, 1968–72, 1975–78; Also recording artiste. *Recordings:* Albums with Van Der Graaf Generator: Aerosol Grey Machine, 1968; The Least We Can Do Is Wave To Each Other, 1969; H To He Who Is The Only One, 1970; Pawn Hearts, 1971; Godbluff, 1975; Still Life, 1976; World Record, 1976; The Quiet Zone; The Pleasure Dome, 1977; Box Set 1968–78, 2001; Solo albums include: Fool's Mate, 1971; Chameleon In The Shadow of Night, 1972; The Silent Corner and The Empty Stage, 1974; In Camera, 1974; Nadir's Big Chance, 1975; Over, 1977; The Future Now, 1978; PH7, 1979; A Black Box, 1980; Sitting Targets, 1981; Enter K, 1982; Patience, 1983; The Love Songs, 1984; Skin, 1986; And Close as This, 1986; In a Foreign Town, 1986; Out of Water, 1990; The Fall of The House of Usher, 1991; Fireships, 1992; The Noise, 1993; Roaring Forties, 1994; X My Heart, 1996; Everyone You Hold, 1997; This, 1998; None of The Above, 2000; What Now, 2001. *Current Management:* Gailforce Management, 24 Ives St, London SW3 2ND, England.

HAMMOND, Albert, Jr; b. April 1980, Los Angeles, CA, USA. Musician (guitar). *Career:* Son of Albert Hammond; Mem., The Strokes, 1998–. *Recordings:* Albums: Is This It, 2001. Singles: The Modern Age, 2001; Hard To Explain/New York City Cops, 2001; Last Nite/When It Started, 2001. *Honours:* NME Awards, Band of the Year, Best New Act, Album of the Year, 2001; BRIT Award, Best International Newcomer, 2002. *Current*

Management: Ryan Gentles, Wiz Kid Management. *Address:* c/o RCA Records, 1540 Broadway, New York, NY 10036, USA. *Website:* www.thestrokes.com.

HAMMOND, John Paul; b. 13 Nov. 1942, New York, NY, USA. Blues Musician (guitar); Vocalist. *Career:* Began playing guitar aged 17; Recording artist, 1962–; British tours, 1960s; Worked with artistes including Duane Allman; JJ Cale; John Lee Hooker; Robbie Robertson; Bill Wyman; Charles Brown; Charlie Musselwhite; Duke Robillard; Bob Dylan; Michelle Shocked; Host, performer, television documentary The Search For Robert Johnson, 1992. *Recordings:* Albums: John Hammond; Big City Blues; Country Blues; So Many Roads; Mirrors; I Can Tell; Sooner Or Later; Southern Fried; Source Point; I'm Satisfied; Triumvirate; Can't Beat The Kid; John Hammond Solo; Footwork; Hot Tracks; Mileage; Frogs For Snakes; John Hammond Live; John Hammond Live In Greece; Nobody But You; Got Love If You Want It; Trouble No More; Found True Love; Wicked Grin, 2001; Featured on film soundtracks: Little Big Man, 1971; Matewan, 1987; Long as I Have You. *Honours:* Grammy Award, Blues Explosion (with Stevie Ray Vaughan, Koko Taylor), 1985. *Current Management:* Tri Tone Management, 331 Carrera Dr., Mill Valley, CA 94941, USA.

HAMPTON, Andy; b. 8 May 1958, Sheffield, England. Composer. m. Jennifer Stirling, 22 July 1994, 1 s., 1 d. *Education:* York University, BA Hons; MA, Open University; Guildhall, London; LTCL Trinity College, London. *Career:* Appearance as actor/musician, Lennon, London's West End 1985. *Compositions:* Themes for: BBC Radio 1; BBC Radio 2; Granada TV; Sky Network; Screensport. *Publications:* Jazzworks for Clarinet, Saxophone students; Unbeaten Tracks; Saxophone Basics. *Honours:* Best Music, National Student Drama Festival, 1979. *Membership:* PRS; MCPS. *Address:* 28 Harold Rd, London N8 7DE, England.

HAMZA, Kawkab; b. 1 July 1944, Babylon, Iraq. Composer. Divorced, 1 s., 2 d. *Education:* Fine Art Institute, Baghdad; 5 years, USSR High Institute. *Career:* Composed first song, 1966, Moved to Syria, 1983, wrote 4 theatre plays, 2 television series; Moved to Detroit, composed for theatre; Now refugee in Denmark, Composing for theatre; Takes part in international musical festivals. *Compositions:* 6 theatre plays; 4 documentary films; 2 television, music classes; more than 70 songs including: Songs for: Husein Naamah; Fuaad Salim; Saadun Jaber; Anwar Abd Alwahab; Albums: Nehebbkum Wallah Nehebkum; New Babylon Music; Sar Alumur Mahetat. *Membership:* Danish Society for Jazz, Rock, Folk Composers. *Address:* Tårnvej 209–2, 2610 Rodovre, Denmark.

HANCOCK, Herbie; b. 12 April 1940, Chicago, IL, USA. Composer; Jazz Musician (piano, synthesizer). m. Gudrun Meixner, 31 Aug. 1968, 1 d. *Education:* BA, Grinnell College, Iowa; Manhattan School of Music, New York, 1 year. *Career:* Chicago Symphony Orchestra, 1952; Miles Davis Quartet, 1963–68; Television: Coast To Coast (Showtime), Host; Television Scores: Hey, Hey, Hey, It's Fat Albert – Bill Cosby Special; Film Scores: Blow Up, 1966; Death Wish, 1974; A Soldier's Story, 1974; Round Midnight, 1986; Jo Jo Dancer, Your Life Is Calling, 1986; Colors, 1988. *Recordings:* Taking Off, 1962; Maiden Voyage, 1965; Speak Like A Child, 1967; Headhunters, 1973; Thrust, 1974; Manchild, 1975; VSOP, 1977; Sunlight, 1979; Feets Don't Fail Me Now, 1979; Future Shock, 1983; Sound System, 1984; Perfect Machine, 1988; Tribute To Miles, 1994; Dis Is Da Drum, 1995; The New Standard, 1996; Night Walker, 2000; Future 2 Future, 2001; Directions In Music (with Michael Brecker, Roy Hargrove), 2002; with Miles Davis Quartet: Miles In The Sky; Nefertiti; Sorcerer; ESP; Miles Davis In Concert (My Funny Valentine); In A Silent Way; Jack Johnson; Seven Steps To Heaven; Contributor, Colour and Light – Jazz Sketches On Sondheim, 1995. *Publications:* A Tribute to Miles, 1994; Dis is Da Drum, 1994; The New Standard, 1996; I H with Wayne Shorter, 1997; Gershwin's World, 1998. *Honours:* Jay Award, Jazz Magazine, 1963; Downbeat Award, 1967; Several Awards, Black Music Magazine, 1967–71; 5 MTV Awards, including Best Concept Video, Rock It, 1983; 3 Grammy Awards, including Best R&B Instrumental Performance, Rock It, 1983; Academy Award, Best Original Score, Round Midnight, 1986. *Membership:* AFofM; NARAS; AFTRA; SAG; AMPAS. *Current Management:* DPE. *Address:* c/o 3 E 28th St, Sixth Floor, New York, NY 10016, USA.

HANCOCK, Keith; b. 28 Oct. 1953, Manchester, England. Vocalist; Songwriter; Musician (diatonic accordion). m. Janet Karen Wood, 29 Sept. 1979, 2 s. *Career:* Progressed through English Country dance bands; Began writing, 1984; Toured: Europe; Canada; New Zealand; Hong Kong; Australia; TV Ballads (BBC2), 1995; New Band, Keith Hancock's Famous Last Words, 1996. *Compositions include:* Chase The Dragon; Absent Friends. *Recordings:* This World We Live In, 1985; Madhouse, 1988; Compassion, 1993; Born Blue, 1997. *Membership:* Musicians' Union; Equity. *Current Management:* Lighthouse Music Agency. *E-mail:* info@lighthouse-music.co.uk. *Website:* www.lighthouse-music.co.uk.

HANCOCK, Robin Jonathon Coventry; b. Croydon, Surrey, England. Record Prod; Musician (guitar). *Education:* BSc Electric Engineering, Reading University; Grade 6, Classical guitar. *Recordings:* Erotica, Madonna; Cyberpunk, Billy Idol; Seal, Seal; Other recordings by Tina Turner; Simple

Minds; Robert Miles. *Current Management:* Sarm Productions. *Address:* 38 Turneville Rd, West Kensington, London W14 9PS, England.

HAND, Richard; b. 27 Nov. 1960, Marsden, Yorkshire, England. Musician (guitar). *Education:* Open Scholarship to Royal Academy of Music. *Career:* Member, English Guitar Quartet: Tours of Israel; Member, flute and guitar duo: The Lightfingered Gentry; Tours include: Germany; Holland; Gulf States; Egypt; Member, Hand/Dupré Guitar Duo tours: Norway; Poland; India; Bangladesh; Sri Lanka; Philippines; Malaysia; Indonesia; Singapore; Hong Kong; Television, radio appearances world-wide include: BBC Radio 2, 3, 4; Premieres of new works by: Peter Dickinson; Tim Souster; Jonathon Lloyd; David Bedford; Roger Steptoe; Michael Ball; Brian May; Judith Bingham; Wilfred Josephs. *Honours:* Julian Bream Prize; Associate of Royal Academy of Music. *Membership:* ISM; Musicians' Union. *Address:* 61 Balcombe St, Marylebone, London NW1 6HD, England. *E-mail:* info@richardhand.net. *Website:* www.richardhand.net.

HANLEY, Ged, (Ray Kershwin); b. 22 March 1960, Scotland. Musician (guitar, piano); Vocalist. m. Donna Marie Archibald, 25 Nov. 1994, 2 s., 1 d. *Career:* Tours (backing vocals) with Runrig; Wreck On The Highway; BBC appearances and recording. *Membership:* Musicians' Union. *Address:* 114 Carnethie St, Rosewall, Midlothian EH24 9AL, Scotland.

HANLON, Jef; b. 5 July 1943, Blackpool, England. Artist Man; Concert Promoter; Agent. m. Alice Welsh, 8 Dec. 1973. *Career:* Guitarist, England and Germany, 1958–64; Personal/tour manager: Wayne Fontana; Herman's Hermits; Extensive world tours, 1964–69; Partner, Billings-Hanlon Management, 1969–73; Clients: Jimmy Ruffin, Kiki Dee, The Hermits; Director, Rock Artist Management Group of Companies, 1973–76; Clients included: Gary Glitter; The Glitter Band; Bay City Rollers; Barry Blue; Hello; New Seekers; The Damned; Springfield Revival; Director, Derek Block Artists Agency and Derek Block Concert Promotions, 1976–89; Clients included: Duran Duran; UB40; The Police; Tears For Fears; Gary Glitter; The Clash; Ian Dury; Agent for William Morris Agency Inc, (USA), 1977–84; Clients included: Diana Ross; Stevie Wonder; Barry Manilow; Rod Stewart; Concert promotions include: Rod Stewart; Chuck Berry; David Brubeck; Simon and Garfunkel; Stevie Wonder; Bob Hope; Bing Crosby; Duran Duran; Gary Glitter; B. B. King; Johnny Mathis; The Everly Brothers; Neil Sedaka; The Temptations; Don McLean; Also major tours: Australasia; Japan; Europe; UK; Formed Jef Hanlon Management Ltd, 1990–; Major client: Gary Glitter; Also managed The Wild Swans; Promoted tours: Bob Hope; Don McLean; Juan Martin's Flamenco Dance Company (Seville); Village People; Bootleg Beatles; Joaquin Cortes; Recently promoted Dave Brubeck Quartet, Culture Club, and co-promoted B. B. King. *Membership:* President, Agents' Asscn of Great Britain, 1995–97; Chairman, International Managers' Forum, 1998–; Mem., Concert Promoters' Asscn. *Address:* 1 York St, London W1H 1PZ, England.

HANNAN, Neil; b. 12 Aug. 1952, Christchurch, New Zealand. Musician (bass). m. Jacqui Fitzgerald, 16 Dec. 1993, 1 d. *Education:* Two years Victoria University, Wellington, New Zealand; Various private tutors from age seven, piano, guitar. *Career:* Professional musician since age 19; Performed in New Zealand with Randy Crawford, Renee Geyer; Member, popular New Zealand bands: Hello Sailor; Coup d'Etat; Midge Marsden's Country Flyers; Numerous radio programmes and recordings; Professional work in Australia, UK, USA. *Recordings:* Solo albums: Scoop This Loop; 24 Hour Oasis. *Publications:* Working on Bass Teaching book. *Honours:* Single of Year (with Coup d'Etat), 1981. *Membership:* Australasian Peforming Right Asscn (APRA); Recording Industry Asscn of New Zealand (RIANZ). *Address:* 19 Wynyard Rd, Mt Eden, Auckland, New Zealand.

HANNAN, Patrick Edward Dean; b. 4 March 1966, Lymington, Hampshire, England. Musician (drums). 1 d. *Career:* Two major world tours with the Sundays. *Recordings:* Albums: with the Sundays: Reading Writing Arithmetic, 1990; Blind, 1992; Static and Silence, 1997; with Perry Rose: Bright Ring of The Day, 1995; with Arnold, Windsor Park, 1997; Hillside, 1998; with Tim Keegan, Long Distance Information, 1998; with theaudience, theaudience, 1998; with Robyn Hitchcock, Jewels for Sophia, 1999; Singles: with Star 69: Mama Don't Let, 1995; You Are Here, 1995. *Honours:* Gold and Silver Discs; Gold US Disc. *Membership:* Musicians' Union.

HANNIBAL, Lars; b. 15 July 1951, Risskov, Denmark. Musician (lute, guitar). m. Michala Petri, 2 d. *Education:* Guitar, Royal Danish Conservatory, Århus; Lute, with Toyohiko Satoy, The Hague. *Career:* Jazz/Rock Musician; Toured as Chamber Musician, throughout Europe, USA, Japan, 1980–; Worked with musicians such as Michala Petri, Kim Sjøgren, Palle Mikkalborg, Niels Henning, Orsted Pedersen, Svend Asmussen; Formed duo with baritone singer Lars Thodberg Bertelsew. *Compositions:* Du Drømmer; Vesterled, both for lute and violin. *Recordings:* Albums: with Duo Concertante: 10 albums (violin and guitar, including music by Giuliani, Paçanini, Sarasate and Lalo and contemporary music); Solo: Romance (album); with recorder player Michala Petri: Air; Souvenir; Kreisler Inspirations; with trumpeter Michael Brydenfelt: Memory, 1999. *Honours:* FiF Cultural Prize, 1991; Danish Soloist Union, Anniversary Grant, 1993; Deutschen Schallplattenpreis, 2002. *Membership:* DMF; Danish Soloist

Union; Solistforeninen. *Address:* Nordskrænten 3, DK-2980 Kokkedal, Denmark. *Telephone:* 45-86-25-77. *Fax:* 45-86-56-77. *E-mail:* mail@michapetri.com. *Website:* www.michapetri.com.

HANNON, (Edward) Neil (Anthony); b. 7 Nov. 1970, Londonderry, Northern Ireland. Songwriter; Vocalist; Musician (guitar). *Career:* Member, The Divine Comedy; Released five albums and two mini albums; 10 top forty singles; Numerous live and TV appearances including Top of the Pops, TFI Friday, Later, with Jools Holland. *Compositions:* Something for the Weekend; Songs of Love (theme to TV comedy series Father Ted); In Pursuit (Theme from Tomorrow's World). *Recordings:* Singles: Something For The Weekend, 1996; Becoming More Like Alfie, 1996; The Frog Princess, 1996; Everybody Knows, 1997; I've Been To A Marvellous Party, 1998; Generation Sex, 1998; The Certainty of Chance, 1998; National Express, 1999; The Pop Singer's Fear of The Pollen Count, 1999; Gin Soaked Boy, 1999; Love What You Do, 2001; Bad Ambassador, 2001; Perfect Lovesong, 2001; Albums: Liberation, 1993; Promenade, 1994; Casanova, 1996; Fin de Siecle, 1998; Secret History (compilation), 1999; Regeneration, 2001; Vocals on: No Regrets (single), Robbie Williams, 1998; Reload, Tom Jones, 1999; Punishing Kiss, Ute Lemper, 2000. *Current Management:* Divine Management, Top Floor, 1 Cowcross St, London EC1M 6DR, England.

HANOT, Pierre; b. 25 March 1952, Metz, France. Vocalist; Writer; Composer; Artist. m. Martine Bonici, 28 Feb. 1992, 2 d. *Education:* Modern and classical French; Guitar. *Career:* More than 700 concerts, in clubs, festivals, pubs, cultural centres, 1975–; Dates in: France; Germany; Luxemboug; Belgium; Spain. *Recordings:* Rock Derivé, 1985; En Un Instant Damnés, 1995. *Membership:* SACEM. *Current Management:* Martine Bonici. *Address:* 8A Pl. du Temple, 57530 Courcelles Chaussy, France.

HANRAHAN, Michael; b. 19 Sept. 1958, Ennis, County Clare, Ireland. Songwriter; Musician (guitar); Vocalist. m. Donna Barnes, 3 Sept. 1994. *Career:* Tours world-wide with Stockton's Wing, 1974–94; Performed with Sammy Davis Jr, Dublin; Numerous television, radio shows; Solo artiste. *Compositions:* Most successful songs: Beautiful Affair; Walk Away. *Recordings:* Seven albums with Stockton's Wing. *Membership:* Irish Music Rights Organisation (Board mem.). *Current Management:* Kara Hanahoe. *Address:* 29, St Fintans Villas, Deansgrange, Co Dublin, Ireland.

HANSARD, Glen; b. 21 April 1970, Dublin, Ireland. Vocalist; Musician (guitar); Songwriter. *Career:* Busker on the streets of Dublin; Founder member: The Frames, late 1980s; Set up own label Plateau Records; Tours of USA and Europe with The Frames and solo; Appeared as Outspan in The Commitments film. *Recordings:* Another Love Song, 1992; Fitzcarraldo, 1994; Dance the Devil, 1999; For the Birds (produced by Steve Albini), 2001. *Honours:* For the Birds album reached Irish Top 10. *E-mail:* cleadbitter@framesoffice.freeserve.co.uk.

HANSEN, Jacob; b. 9 Nov. 1970, Denmark. Musician (guitar); Vocalist. *Career:* Touring and Recording with Heavy Metal Band, Invocator, 1986–94; Released 4 Albums; Appeared three times on National Television; 2 European Tours; Freelance Producer, Engineer, 1993–. *Recordings:* Excursion Demise, 1991; Weave The Apocalypse, 1993; Early Years, 1994; Dying To Live, 1994. *Membership:* KODA; GRAMEX. *Address:* Kongensgade 84, 6700 Esbjerg, Denmark.

HANSEN, Kai; b. Germany. Vocalist; Rock Musician (guitar). *Career:* Founder member, German rock band, Helloween, 1984; Numerous tours across Europe; Appearances include: Monsters of Rock Festival, Castle Donington, 1988; Founder, Gamma Ray, 1989; Extensive tours in Europe and Japan. *Recordings:* Albums: with Helloween: Helloween (mini album), 1985; Walls of Jericho, 1986; Keeper of The Seven Keys, Part I, 1987; Part II, 1988; Live In The UK, 1989; with Gamma Ray: Heading For Tomorrow, 1990; Sigh No More, 1991; Insanity and Genius, 1993; Land of the Free, 1995; Somewhere out in Space, 1998; Alive '95, 1998; Power Plant, 1999; Blast From The Past, 2000; No World Order, 2001; Features on Dark Assault, Iron Saviour, 2001; Also tracks featured on: Death Metal, compilation album, 1984. *Current Management:* Sanctuary Music (Overseas). *Address:* First Floor Suite, The Colonnades, 82 Bishops Bridge Rd, London W2 6BB, England.

HANSON, Lloyd A; b. 1 Nov. 1964, Fredericton, New Brunswick, Canada. Musician (bass); Record Prod; Recording Engineer. *Education:* Berklee College of Music, Boston, USA, 1986. *Career:* Recording career from 1988; Played bass in many jazz, folk, experimental ensembles at major festivals including: Mama's and Papa's, 1987; Harvest Jazz and Blues Festival, with Long John Baldry, 1992; Formed Thrash Peninsula, 1993; Producer, engineer, composer, arranger. *Recordings:* with Thrash Peninsula: A Different Drummer; A D Shade Café; Thunder God's Wife; with Brent Mason: Down To Heaven; with Ned Landry: Fiddling Champ. *Honours:* New Brunswick Arts Branch Creation Grant, 1992. *Membership:* AFofM; Musicians' Union; SOCAN. *Address:* 741 McEvoy St, Fredericton, New Brunswick E3A 3B8, Canada.

HANSON, Simon; b. 3 Feb. 1964, Grantham, Lincolnshire, England. Musician (drums). m. Kath Hanson, 3 Aug. 1994. *Education:* Lincolnshire

Youth Orchestra, 1977–80. *Career:* Drummer/programmer for Radio Science Orchestra; European Tour: Energy Orchard; Full time member, The Blessing; UK, European tours. *Recordings:* The Blessing: Locust and Wild Honey; Radio Science Orchestra: Arcitec; Film Soundtrack: Tall Story. *Publications:* Regular columnist, UK Rhythm Magazine, 1994–. *Membership:* Musicians' Union. *Current Management:* Paul Crockford Management; Agent: Simon Harrison. *Address:* c/o 8 Kingston Rd, Ewell Village, Surrey KT17 2AA, England.

HANZICK, Helene Hommel Brincker; b. 18 June 1958, Copenhagen, Denmark. Musician (bass guitar); Songwriter; Vocalist. m. Poul F Hanzick, 15 Aug. 1987. *Career:* Singer, Mayflowers band, 1980; Solo Musician, 1981–82; Formed country duo, Twins, with husband; Twins have played all over Denmark and in Norway, Sweden, Holland and Canary Islands; Moved to Sweden, 1994. *Compositions:* From Alaska to LA, 1989; No Good Full-Time-Cheating, Good-For-Nothing Son-Of-A-Gun, 1991, 1996; Ten Days Together, 1991; She'll Come Again, 1991. *Recordings:* Champagne and Bourbon, CD, 1989; Days Together, CD, 1991; I Love You/Blue Moon of Kentucky, single, 1986. *Honours:* Danish Championship in Country Music, 1989. *Membership:* Danish Musicians' Union. *Address:* PO Box 35, 28221 Tyringe, Sweden.

HANZICK, Poul Fynbo; b. 22 May 1954, Mariager, Denmark. Musician (guitar); Vocalist. m. Helene H B Hanzick, 15 Aug. 1987. *Career:* Played in several dance and rock bands, 1969–82; Formed the country duo, Twins, with wife Helene; Twins have played all over Denmark and in Norway, Sweden, Holland and Canary Islands; Moved to Sweden, 1994. *Recordings:* I Love You, Blue Moon of Kentucky, single, 1986; Days Together, CD, 1991; Champagne and Bourbon, CD, 1989. *Honours:* Won Danish Championship in Country Music, 1989. *Membership:* Danish Musicians' Union. *Current Management:* Freelance. *Address:* PO Box 35, 28221 Tyringe, Sweden.

HAQUE, Asadul; b. 1 March 1930, Pabna, Bangladesh. Retired. m. Firoza Asad, 3 June 1955, 1 s., 1 d. *Education:* Studies of Classical, Semi Classical and Folk Songs. *Career:* Researcher, National Poet Kazi Nazrul Islam and Classical Music of the Sub-Continent; Music Producer, Radio Pakistan, Karachi, 1963–65, Rawalpindi, 1969–71; Performer, Vocal Songs on Radio and Television. *Publications include:* Nazrul Sangiter Rupaker, 1990; Nazrul Saralipi, Vol. 4, 1990; Antaranga Aloke Nazrul O Pramila, 1994; Chalachitrey Nazrul, 1994; Nasruler Hindi Gan, 1995; Amar Surer Jadukar, 1996. *Contributions to:* Leading newspapers of Bangladesh and Kolkata. *Honours:* Sanad E Khidmat, First Class, Pakistan Government, 1970; Nazrul award, Churulia Nazrul Academy, West Bengal, 1997. *Membership:* Bangla Academy, Dhaka. *Address:* 12/D Eastern Housing, Sidheswari, Dhaka 1217, Bangladesh.

HARBO, Nils; b. 12 May 1956, Nyborg, Denmark. Musician; Record Prod. m. Ulla Rasmussen, 3 s. *Career:* Rock Musician, Guitar Player, 1978–90; Record Producer, var artists, 1990–; Own Projects, Jimi Bikini, Jox, Palle Pirat, A.O.; Editor, Danish Music Yearbook. *Compositions:* Fidt På Fyn, 1991; Palle Pirat, 1996; Out of Control, 1997; Cant Let Go, 1997. *Recordings:* Palle Pirat. *Publications:* Improvisation, 1981; Danish Music Yearbook, 1992–2003. *Membership:* KODA; NCB; DMF; DJBFA. *Current Management:* Techpoint. *Address:* Birkebakken 8, 2500 Valby, Denmark.

HARCOURT, Stephen David; b. 30 Nov. 1973, Harlow, Essex, England. Musician (guitar); Sequencing. *Career:* Formed Collapsed Lung, 1992; Several tours, UK and Ireland; Reading Festival; Minor stage, Phoenix Festival; Radio: In Session (Mark Goodier's), Radio 1; Television: Raw Soup, MTV; The Beat; Song, Eat my Goal, used for Coca-Cola advertising campaign; Collapsed Lung split, 1997; Now working as solo and in partnership under names Jack Slack (solo), Spoiler (with Lee Edwards), Aerobic Christians (with Donald Cummings) and Slackwagon (solo). *Compositions:* with Slackwagon, Dirty Monkeys; Italian Jobbers; Short film scores, 1998. *Recordings:* Albums: Jackpot Goalie, 1995; with Collapsed Lung, Cooler, 1996; Singles: Thundersley Ivacar, 1993; Chainsaw Wedgie, 1993; Down With The Plaid Fad, 1994; Dis-MX, 1994; As G L Stealers, Interactive, 1995; Eat My Goal/London Tonight, 1996; Board Games, 1996. *Membership:* Musicians' Union; PRS. *Current Management:* Bell Management. *Address:* Slackwagon Productions, 139 Pennymead, Harlow, Essex CM20 3JB, England.

HARDAKER, Sam; b. 1971, London, England. Prod; Remixer. *Career:* Started as studio engineer; Began remixing with partner, Henry Binns, under the name Zero 7; Produced own material as Zero 7; Collaborations: Sia Furler; Sophie Barker; Mozez; Remixed: Terry Callier; Radiohead; Lenny Kravitz; Lambchop; NERD. *Recordings:* Albums: Simple Things, 2001. Singles: EP 1, 1999; EP 2, 2000; Destiny (featuring Sia and Sophie), 2001; I Have Seen (featuring Mozez), 2001; In the Waiting Line (featuring Sophie) 2001; Distractions (featuring Sia), 2002. *Honours:* Muzik Award, Best New Artist, 2001. *Membership:* PRS. *Address:* c/o Solar Management Ltd, 42–48 Charlbert St, London NW8 7BU, England. *Telephone:* (20) 7722-4175. *Fax:* (20) 7722-4072. *E-mail:* info@solarmanagment.co.uk. *Website:* www.solarmanagement.co.uk.

HARDCASTLE, Paul; b. 10 Dec. 1957, London, England. Musician (keyboards); Composer; Mixer; Record Prod; *Compositions:* The Wizard (used as Top of the Pops theme, BBC), 1986–91; Songwriter, composer for television, including: Themes to BBC series, Supersense and Lifesense; Founder, own record label Fast Forward. *Recordings:* Singles: 19 (No. 1, UK), 1985; Just For Money, 1985; Don't Waste My Time, with Carol Kenyon, 1986; The Wizard, 1986; Rainforest 90, 1991; Can't Stop Now, 1994; Other recordings under pseudonym: Def Boys; Beeps International; Jazzmasters; Kiss The Sky (with Jaki Graham); Albums: Hardcastle, 1996; Cover to Cover, 1997; First Light, 1997; Jazzmasters III, 1999; Jazzmasters: The Greatest Hits, 2000; P.H., 2001; Producer for: LW5; Phil Lynott; Carol Kenyon; Remixed: Third World; Ian Dury.

HARDING, Mike (Michael); b. 23 Oct. 1944, UK. Vocalist; Musician (english concertina, banjo guitar); Comedian; Writer; Broadcaster; Actor. *Education:* Degree in Education. *Career:* Played in skiffle and rock bands, 1960s; After a variety of jobs, took a degree in education whilst working in folk clubs; Began telling jokes to fill pauses as band tuned up during a gig with the Edison Spasm Band at Leeds University, 1967; Jokes and real-life storytelling became part of act; National exposure with UK hit single The Rochdale Cowboy, 1975; In addition to folk music, has diversified into areas including: travel writing; comedy writing; poetry; playwriting; short stories; photography; First acting role as Valdimir in Beckett's Waiting For Godot, Octagon Theatre, Bolton; Presents radio programme Folk on 2. *Recordings:* Singles: The Rochdale Cowboy, 1975; Albums: A Lancashire Lad, 1972; Mrs 'Ardin's Kid, 1975; The Rochdale Cowboy Rides Again, One Man Show, 1976; Mike Harding's Back, Old Four Eyes Is Back, 1977; Captain Paralytic and The Brown Ale Cowboys, 1978; On The Touchline, Komic Kutz, 1979; The Red Specs Album, 1981; Take Your Finger Off It, 1982; Rooted!, 1983; Bombers' Moon, 1984; Roll Over Cecil Sharp, 1985; Foo Foo Shufflewick and Her Exotic Banana, 1986. *Website:* www.mikeharding.co.uk.

HARDING, Stan (Walter Stanley); b. 11 March 1930, Islington, London, England. Musician (drums); Vocalist; Songwriter; Actor. m. Joyce Matthews, 5 June 1954, 2 s., 1 d. *Career:* Toured American Air Force Bases with Bill Kenyon Combo, 1958–62; Shared billing with Cliff Richard, 1959; Short residency at Royal Garden Hotel; Concert appearances with Jack Emblow; Singer with Billy Smart's Circus; Starred in cabaret at Pizza On The Park; Appearance on Late Night BBC; Regular supporting actor, EastEnders (BBC1). *Compositions:* Costa Brava, samba for The Polka Dots, 1963, and broadcast by Billy Cotton and Edmundo Ros. *Recordings:* Flying High, with Jack Emblow and Tony Compton. *Publications:* Costa Brava. *Membership:* Musicians' Union; Equity. *Address:* 9 Lilford Rd, Billericay, Essex CM11 1BS, England. *Telephone:* (1277) 655850. *E-mail:* stanharding@fsnet.co.uk.

HARDY, Françoise; b. 17 Jan. 1944, Paris, France. Vocalist; Author; Lyricist; Actress; Songwriter; Astrologer. m. Jacques Dutronc, 1981, 1 s. *Education:* Le Bruyère College. *Career:* Recording artiste, 1962–; Lyricist for artistes including: Julien Clerc; Diane Tell; Alaine Lubrano; Khalil Chanine; Also worked as model and actress. *Recordings:* Numerous since 1962–; Recent albums include: Clair Obscur, 2000; En Resume, 2000; Singles include: Tous Les Garçons Et Les Filles, 1962; All Over The World, 1965. *Publications:* Le Grande Livre De La Vierge, with B Guenin; Entre Les Lignes Entre Les Signes, with Anne-Marie Simond, 1991; Notes Secrètes, W E Dumont, 1991; Françoise Hardy Présente L'Astrologie Universelle, 1986. *Address:* 13 rue Hallé, 75014 Paris, France.

HARJO, Joy; b. 9 May 1951, Tulsa, OK, USA. 1 s., 1 d. *Education:* Institute of American-Indian Arts; University of New Mexico; University of Iowa. *Career:* Indigo Girls, Tour, 1995; Bumbleshoot Festival, 1995; Cultural Olympica, 1996; European Tour; A Map of The Next World; Reggee In The River, 1999. *Compositions:* Letter From The End of The 20th Century; the Musician Who Became A Bear. *Recordings:* Letter From The End of The 20th Century; Eagle Song (video), 2002. *Publications:* She Had Some Horses; In Mad Love and War; The Woman Who Fell From The Sky; A Map To The Next World; How We Became Human. *Honours:* Outstanding Musical Achievement; NM Gov.'s Award; Eagle Spirit Award. *Membership:* National Council On The Arts. *Current Management:* Mekko Rabbit Productions Inc, 1140 D Alewa Dr., Honolulu, HI 26817, USA.

HARKET, Morten; b. 14 Sept. 1959, Konigsberg, Norway. Vocalist; Songwriter. *Career:* Singer with various groups including: Mercy; Laelia Anceps; Soldier Blue; Mem., A-Ha, 1983–94; Solo artiste, 1994–; Band re-formed, 1999–; Numerous tours world-wide, television and radio appearances; Starred in film Kamilla Og Tyven, 1989; Host, Eurovision Song Contest, 1996. *Recordings:* Albums: with A-Ha: Hunting High And Low, 1985; Scoundrel Days, 1986; Stay On These Roads, 1988; East Of The Sun West Of The Moon, 1990; Deadlines: The Hits Of A-Ha, 1991; Memorial Beach, 1993; Minor Earth Major Sky, 2000; Lifelines, 2002; Solo: Wild Seed, 1995. Singles: with A-Ha: Take On Me (No. 1, USA), 1985; The Sun Always Shines On TV (No. 1, UK), 1985; Train Of Thought, 1986; Hunting High And Low, 1986; I've Been Losing You, 1986; Cry Wolf, 1986; Manhattan Skyline, 1987; The Living Daylights (theme music for James Bond film), 1987; Stay On These Roads, 1988; The Blood That Moves The Body, 1988; Touchy!, 1988; You Are The One, 1988; Crying In The Rain, 1990; I Call Your Name; Dark Is The Night; Can't Take My Eyes Off You (for film soundtrack Coneheads); Angel; Solo: A Kind of Christmas Card (No. 1, Norway), 1995. *Honours:* Eight MTV Music Video

Awards, for Take On Me and The Sun Always Shines On TV, 1986; BMI Award, One Million Broadcast Performances, for Take On Me, 1991; World Music Award, Best Selling Norwegian Artist of the Year, 1993. *Current Management:* Bandana Management, London, England. *Address:* c/o WEA Germany, Warner Music Germany Group, Oberbaumbrücke 1, 20457 Hamburg, Germany. *Website:* www.a-ha.com.

HARLEY, Steve; b. 27 Feb. 1951, London, England. Vocalist. *Career:* Former journalist; Founder member, Cockney Rebel, 1973–77; 1989–; Solo artiste, 1978–88; Appearances include: Reading Festival, 1974; Support to The Kinks, USA, 1975; All Is Forgiven reunion tour, UK, 1989; Heineken Music Big Top, Portsmouth, 1992; Presenter, Sounds of The 70s, BBC Radio 2, 1999–. *Recordings:* Albums: Human Menagerie, 1973; The Best Years of Lives, 1975; Timeless Flight, 1976; Love's A Prima Donna, 1976; Face To Face – A Live Recording, 1977; Hobo with a Grin, 1978; Candidate, 1979; Greatest Hits, 1988; The Best of Steve Harley and Cockney Rebel, 1992; Make Me Smile, 1996; Stripped to Bare Bones, 1999; Yes You Can, 2000; In Pursuit of Illusion, 2000; Singles: with Cockney Rebel: July Teen, 1974; Mr Soft, 1974; Make Me Smile (Come Up and See Me), 1975; Mr Raffles (Man It Was Mean), 1975; Here Comes The Sun, 1976; Solo: The Phantom of The Opera (duet with Sarah Brightman), 1986. *Contributions to:* Whatever You Believe, UK TV telethon charity single, 1988. *Address:* c/o Arctic King Music, Cambridge House, Card Hill, Forest Row RH18 5BA, England.

HARMACEK, Václav; b. 6 Nov. 1952, Prague, Czech Republic. Musician (clarinet, saxes, viola); Recording Dir; Teacher. Divorced, 2 d. *Education:* Philosophical Faculty, Charles University, Prague, 1977. *Career:* Appearance in numerous jazz festivals as Member of various bands and orchestras (notably Prague Big Band, Original Prague Syncopated Orchestra, Causa Bibendi); Several TV and radio appearances in various types of programmes (notably Causa Bibendi or the Reason for a Drink, Czech TV, 1994). *Contributions to:* albums of the orchestras: Prague Big Band, 1974–78; Original Prague Syncopated Orchestra, 1979–84; Causa Bibendi – Czech Swingharmonic Orchestra, 1992; Blue World, 1996; Prague Folklore Cymbalon Orchestra, 1975–91. *Publications:* Editor and Contributor, Small Encyclopaedia of Music, 1983. *Address:* Studentská 2, 160 00 Prague 6, Czech Republic.

HARMAN, Buddy; b. 23 Dec. 1928, Nashville, Tennessee, USA. Musician (drums). *Career:* Studio musician, Nashville, 1952–; Thousands of recording sessions with Elvis Presley, records and films. *Recordings:* Hits with Elvis Presley: A Fool Such As I, 1958; A Big Hunk O'Love, 1958; Stuck On You, 1960; The Girl of My Best Friend, 1960; It's Now Or Never, 1960; Are You Lonesome Tonight, 1961; Surrender, 1961; His Latest Flame, 1961; Suspicion, 1961; Good Luck Charm, 1962; Devil In Disguise, 1963; Crying In The Chapel, 1965; Love Letters, 1966; Also worked with: Jerry Lee Lewis, Connie Francis, Doc Watson, Charlie Rich, Brenda Lee. *Honours:* NARAS Superpicker Awards, 1965–70. *Membership:* AFofM (executive board of directors, 1981).

HARMAN, James Gary; b. 8 June 1946, Anniston, Alabama, USA. Bandleader; Vocalist; Songwriter; Prod; Musician (harmonica). m. Ella Caroline Harman, 2 s. *Education:* Gulf Coast College, University of Florida. *Career:* Bandleader, Southern dance circuit, 1962–; Recording artist, 1964–; Bandleader, house band Ash Grove Club, Los Angeles, 1970s; International tours; Numerous appearances, television, radio, festivals world-wide; Songs for films; Several songs used in TV shows; Plays in every major blues festival world-wide; Played harmonica on ZZ Top single, What's Up With That; Appeared on David Letterman Show, 1997. *Recordings:* Recent albums include: Do Not Disturb, 1991; Two Sides To Every Story, 1993; Cards On The Table, 1994; Back and White, 1995; Extra Napkins, 1997; Takin' Chances, 1998; Extra Napkins Vol. II, 1999; Mo'Na'Kins, 2000; Other. *Recordings include:* So Many Women, Invasion; Kiss of Fire, The Accused; Jump My Baby (in 3 films). *Honours:* Alabama Music Hall of Fame. *Current Management:* Icepick Productions. *Address:* 718 Schwarz Rd, Lawrence, KS 66049, USA.

HARNICK, Sheldon Mayer; b. 30 April 1924, Chicago, Illinois, USA. Lyricist. m. (1) Mary Boatner, 1950, (2) Elaine May, 1962, (3) Margery Gray, 1965, 1 s., 1 d. *Education:* Northwestern University. *Career:* Contributor to revues: New Faces of 1952; Two's Company, 1953; John Murray Anderson's Almanac, 1954; The Shoestring Revue, 1955; The Littlest Revue, 1956; Shoestring 1957, 1957; with composer Jerry Bock: Body Beautiful, 1958; Fiorello, 1959; Tenderloin, 1960; Smiling The Boy Fell Dead (with David Baker), 1961; She Loves Me, 1963; Fiddler On The Roof, 1964; The Apple Tree, 1966; The Rothschilds, 1970; Captain Jinks of The Horse Marines (opera with Jack Beeson), 1975; Rex (with Richard Rodgers), 1976; Dr Heidegger's Fountain of Youth (opera with Jack Beeson), 1978; Gold (cantata with Joe Raposo), 1980; Translations: The Merry Widow, 1977; The Umbrellas of Cherbourg, 1979; Carmen, 1981; A Christmas Carol, 1981; Songs of The Auvergne (musical; book; lyrics), 1982; The Appeasement of Aeolus, 1990. *Contributions to:* ABC: A Tribute To Adler, Bock and Coleman, 2000. *Address:* Kraft, Haiken and Bell, 551 Fifth Ave, Ninth Floor, New York, NY 10176, USA.

HARPER, Phillip Melbourne; b. 16 Nov. 1970, Islington, London, England. Musician (drums, percussion). *Education:* GCSE Music, Certificate in music workshop skills. *Career:* Drummer for Pete Brown (songwriter with Cream); Phil Ryan (ex-keyboard player, Man); The Interceptors British tour, 1995; Percussionist, Ronnie Laws band, featured guest Jean Carne, Shepherd's Bush Empire; Percussionist, Akwaaba People; Live performance, GLR Radio, 1995; Performances: Ronnie Scott's, 1995; Jazz Café, 1995; Festivals: Hackney Show; Phoenix; Jazz Izz, Highbury Fields, 1995; Live TV (cable channel), 1995; Teacher, drums, percussion, Secondary schools: Highbury Grove; Parliament Hill; Acland Burghley; Islington Sixth form centre; Young Musicmakers (Independent). *Membership:* Musicians' Union. *Address:* 27 Approach Close, Spencer Grove, London N16 8UG, England.

HARPER, Ray; b. 6 Jan. 1961, Copperhill, Tennessee, USA. Vocalist; Entertainer; Musician (guitar, fiddle, banjo). *Education:* 4 quarter management course; Other technical courses. *Career:* Hamby Mt Music Park, Baldwin, Georgia; Many guest appearances, Carl Story Radio Program, WESC, Greenville, South Carolina; Former member, Carl Story's Rambling Mountaineers; Also worked with Bill Monroe, Larry Sparks and others; Played shows, festivals across USA with audiences up to 10,000; Guest appearances on Rambling Mountain Bluegrass Radio Show WESC in Greenville; Now performs as Ray Harper and Friends. *Recordings:* Ray Harper and Friends with Special Guest Carl Story, 1992; Solo: What A Wonderful Saviour Is He, 1994. *Membership:* International Bluegrass Music Asscn; Bluegrass Music Asscn of Georgia, South Carolina, North Carolina. *Address:* 1131 Farrs Bridge Rd, Pickens, SC 29671, USA.

HARPER, Roy; b. 12 June 1941, Manchester, England. Vocalist; Songwriter. *Career:* Busker, played across Europe; Residency, Les Cousins club, London; Solo recording artiste, 1966–. *Compositions include:* McGoohan's Blues; The White Man; Tom Tiddler's Ground; Hell's Angels; When An Old Cricketer Leaves The Crease; One of Those Days In England; Watford Gap. *Recordings:* Albums: The Sophisticated Beggar, 1966; Come Out Fighting Genghis Smith, 1967; Folkjokeopus, 1969; Flat Baroque and Berserk, 1970; Stormcock, 1971; Lifemask, 1973; Valentine, 1974; Flashes From The Archives of Oblivion, 1974; HQ (aka When An Old Cricketer Leaves The Crease), 1975; Bullinamingvase, 1977; Harper 1970–75, 1978; The Unknown Soldier, 1980; Work of Heart, 1981; Whatever Happened To Jugula, 1985; Born In Captivity, 1985; In Between Every Line, 1986; Descendents of Smith, 1988; Loony On The Bus, 1988; Once, 1990; Death Or Glory?, 1992; Return of the Sophisticated Beggar, 1997; Dream Society, 1998; The Green Man, 2001; Hats Off! (compilation), 2001; Guest vocalist, Have A Cigar, on album Wish You Were Here, Pink Floyd.

HARRELL, Bill (George William); b. 14 Sept. 1934, Marion, Virginia, USA. Vocalist; Musician (guitar, mandolin); Songwriter. m. 8 Dec. 1959, deceased 14 Dec. 1982, 2 s., 1 d. *Education:* University of Maryland. *Career:* Television and radio appearances: Monthly, Jimmy Dean Show, ABC Network, 1961–63; Numerous guest spots, Grande Ole Opry, Nashville, Tennessee; 6 months regularly wheeling West Virginia Jamboree; WWVA Radio; The Today Show, NBC, 1985. *Recordings:* After the Sunrise, 1994; and Friends, 1995; Blue Virginia Blue, 1997; Song for Everyone, 1997; The Cat Came Back, 1998; Ballads and Bluegrass. *Honours:* Spigma Bluegrass Singer of Year, 1985; Virginia Music Hall of Fame. *Membership:* BMI. *Current Management:* Attoway Music. *Address:* 938 St George Barber Rd, Davidsonville, MD 21035, USA.

HARRIGAN, Katie; b. 17 Sept. 1963, Irvine, Scotland. Musician (Celtic harp). *Education:* BA Hons, French and Spanish, Heriot Watt University, UK; Diploma in European Politics, College of Europe, Bruges, Belgium; Studied Clarsach (Celtic harp) with Sanchia Pielou and studied piano. *Career:* Celtic harpist with: Flumgummery, 1981–83; Hamish Moore, including US tour, 1985–86; Ceolbeg, 1988–91; Toured Canada and USA with Vale of Atholl Pipe Band, 1988; Periodically has worked with Billy Ross; Currently, solo harpist. *Recordings:* Flumgummery One, with Flumgummery, 1982; Highland Mandolin, with Dagger Gordon, 1988; Not The Bunny Hop, with Ceolbeg, 1990; Celtic Connection, with KPM, 1994. *Honours:* Solo Clarsach Champion, National MOD, 1980 and 1982; Solo Clarsach Champion, Edinburgh Music Festival, 1981. *Membership:* Life mem. of Clarsach Society. *Address:* 9 Coleherne Rd, London SW10 9BS, England.

HARRIS, Dale G; b. 25 July 1968. Musician (guitar). *Education:* Brooklands College, Weybridge, Surrey; West London Institute, Brunel University, Isleworth, Middlesex, England. *Career:* Guitarist and arranger with Pretty Blue Gun; UK radio airplay on Virgin Radio, BBC Radio 1, and GLR, 1990–93; Guitarist with The Lorne Gibson Trio, 1993–. *Recordings:* with Pretty Blue Gun: The Only Girl; Big Blue World. *Current Management:* Standfast Music. *Address:* 48 Atney Rd, Putney, London SW15 2PS, England.

HARRIS, Emmylou; b. 2 April 1947, Birmingham, Alabama, USA. Vocalist. 2 d. *Education:* UNC, Greensboro. *Career:* Toured with Fallen Angel Band; Performed across Europe, USA; Recording artiste; Appeared in rock documentary, The Last Waltz. *Compositions:* Songs; Co-writer, co-producer, Ballad of Sally Rose with Paul Kennerley, 1985. *Recordings:* Singles include:

Together Again, 1975; Two More Bottles of Wine, 1978; Beneath Still Waters, 1979; (Lost His Love) On Our Last date, 1982; To Know Him is to Love Him (Trio), 1987; We believe in Happy Endings (duet with Earl Thomas Conley), 1988; Wheels of Love, 1990; Never Be Anyone, 1990; High Powered Love, 1993; Albums include: Gliding Bird, 1969; Pieces of The Sky, 1975; Elite Hotel, 1976; Luxury Liner, 1977; Quarter Moon In A Ten-Cent Town, 1978; Blue Kentucky Girl, 1979; Roses in the Snow, 1980; Evangeline, 1981; Cimarron, 1981; Last Date, 1982; White Shoes, 1983; Profile: Best of Emmylou Harris, 1984; The Ballad of Sally Rose, 1985; Thirteen, 1986; Trio (with Dolly Parton, Linda Ronstadt), 1987; Angel Band, 1987; Bluebird, 1989; Brand New Dance, 1990; Duets (with Nash Ramblers), 1990; At The Ryman, 1992; Cowgirls Prayer, 1993; Wrecking Ball, 1995; Portraits, 1996; Nashville, 1996; Spyboy, 1998; Light of the Stable, 1999; Red Dirt Girl, 2000; Singing With Emmylou Vol. 1, 2000; Anthology, 2001; Assisted Gram Parsons on album GP, Grievous Angel, 1973. *Honours:* 7 Grammy Awards, 1976–95; Female Vocalist of the Year, Country Music Asscn, 1980; Academy Country Music Award, Album of the Year, 1987. *Membership:* President, Country Music Foundation, 1983. *Current Management:* Monty Hitchcock Management, PO Box 159007, Nashville, TN 37215, USA. *Address:* c/o WEA Records, Time Warner, 75 Rockefeller Plaza, New York, NY 10019, USA.

HARRIS, Kenneth Philip (Kenny); b. 21 May 1927, London, England. Musician (drums); Author. *Education:* Brooklyn School of Modern Music, USA. *Career:* Musician on Queen Mary and Mauretania, 1950–53; Played for shows in France and Germany, 1953; Jazz Clubs in London, 1953–56; Emigrated to USA, 1956; Played in Clubs; To Bermuda, 1960; Played in Hotels and worked as Producer, Bermuda Broadcasting Company; To Canada, 1970; Worked for Capitol Records, own Record Company and Producer at Radio Stations, CKNW, CFMI, C-JAZ; Bermuda, 1983; Bermuda Broadcasting Company; Defontes Broadcasting, 1991; To UK, 1992. *Recordings:* Ralph Sharon Sextet, 1953; Joe Wylie Trio, 1964; Gene Harris Trio, 1958; Gene Harris Trio, 1959; British Jazz Trio, 1959. *Publications:* Author, First Call Drummer Don Lamond, 1997; Geraldo's Navy, 1998. *Honours:* Juno Award, Canadian Academy of Arts and Sciences, 1981. *Membership:* Society of Composers, Authors and Publishers of Canada. *Address:* 36, The Maltings, Riverside Way, Brandon, Suffolk, IP27 0BL, England.

HARRIS, Paul; b. 9 June 1964, London, England. Vocalist; Musician (piano); Composer. m. Alison Harris, née Dodd, 3 s. *Education:* Kingston Art College; Private music tuition from age 7–16. *Career:* Appearances: Top of the Pops, 1995; BBC1 Song For Europe, with co-written entry, Spinning Away; Live radio: Radio 1, Radio 2, London Talkback, Radio Coventry; Live gigs with own band; BFBS Radio (world-wide); County Sound Radio; Eclipse Radio; Tours: UK; Portugal. *Compositions:* Spinning Away, with M Smith; I Don't Care, with M Smith; It Never Rains, with S Root; The Great Divide, with M Smith, S Root, S Emney. *Recordings:* Singles: Spinning Away, with Paul Harris Band, 1995; The Warning, 1996; Dream EP, 1996; Also appears on numerous other recordings by other artists, 1966–99. *Membership:* Musicians' Union. *Current Management:* Music Business PHD. *Address:* 21 Walton St, Walton-On-The-Hill, Tadworth, Surrey KT20 7RR, England.

HARRIS, Roland Oliver; b. 6 April 1962, Havant, England. Record Prod; Music Recording Engineer. *Education:* Queen Mary College, University of London. *Career:* PRT Studios, recording and maintenance engineer; Nova Studios, chief engineer, eight years; Various freelance recording, arranging, prod. work with an emphasis on sound synchronised to picture; Live sound/production includes: Rata Blanca; Spain, Mexico (Monsters of Rock, Mexico), Rupert Parker, UK and Europe. *Recordings:* Several albums with Rupert Parker; Various television, theatre recordings with Michael Nyman; Two albums with Rata Blanca. *Membership:* Musicians' Union. *Current Management:* Mabley Street Productions Ltd, PO Box 5834, Wellingborough, Northamptonshire NN8 2ZS, England.

HARRIS, Rolf; b. 30 March 1930, Perth, Australia. Entertainer; Vocalist; Musician (piano, accordion, digeridoo, wobbleboard); Artist. m. Alwen Myfanwy Wiseman Hughes, 1 March 1958, 1 d. *Education:* University of Western Australia; Piano Grade 1, AMEB. *Career:* Represented Australia at seven World Fairs, 1969–85; International television entertainer, artist and host: The Rolf Harris Show (BBC TV), 1967–71; Cartoon Time; Animal Hospital (BBC TV), 1994–; Rolf's Amazing Animals, 1997–; Bligh of the Bounty–World Navigator (host and narrator), 1998–99; Played, Glastonbury Festival, 2002; Rolf On Art, 2002. *Recordings:* Albums include: King Rolf, 2001. Singles include: Tie Me Kangaroo Down Sport, 1960; Sun Arise, 1962; Jake The Peg; Two Little Boys (No. 1, UK), 1969; Stairway To Heaven, 1993; The Court of King Caractacus; Can You Tell What It Is Yet?. *Publications:* Write Your Own Pop Song, 1973; Rolf Harris Picture Book of Cats, 1978; Your Cartoon Time, 1986; Win or Die, 1989; Your Animation Time, 1991; Personality Cats, 1992; Me and You and Poems Too, 1993; Tall Animal Tales, 2000; Can You Tell What It Is Yet (autobiography), 2001; Rolf on Art, 2002. *Honours:* O.B.E.; Hon. mem., Royal Society of British Artists. *Membership:* Equity. *Current Management:* Jan Kennedy, Billy Marsh Associates Ltd. *Address:* c/o Billy Marsh and Assocs, 174–178 N Gower St, London NW1 2NB, England. *Website:* www.rolfharris.com.

HARRIS, Sam; b. 4 June 1961, Cushing, Oklahoma, USA. Actor; Vocalist; Writer. *Education:* UCLA. *Career:* Concerts and shows include: Carnegie Hall; Universal Amphitheatre, Los Angeles; London's West End; Grease, Broadway; Joseph and The Amazing Technicolour Dreamcoat, National tour; The Life, Broadway; Television includes: Star Search; Oprah Winfrey Show; Rosie O'Donnell Show; Tonight Show; Numerous television specials and talk shows. *Compositions:* Musicals: Hurry! Hurry! Hollywood!; Hard Copy; Television sitcom, Down To Earth. *Recordings:* Sam Harris; Sam-I-Am; Standard Time; Different Stages; The Life, cast album; Grease, cast album; A Hollywood Christmas; A Gershwin Tribute; Best of the Motown Sessions; Revival, 1999; On This Night, 2000; Film: In The Weeds. *Honours:* Dramalogue Awards for Hard Copy and Different Hats; RIAA Gold Album status for Sam Harris and Sam-I-Am. *Current Management:* Mark Sendroff, 1500 Broadway #2001, New York, NY 10036 USA. *Address:* 250 W 57th St, Suite 703, New York, NY 10107, USA.

HARRIS, Sean; Vocalist; Songwriter. *Career:* Founder member, UK rock group Diamond Head, 1977–85; One of leading groups in New Wave of British Heavy Metal (NWOBHM), UK, 1980s; British tours, 1980, 1982; Monsters of Rock Festival, Castle Donington, 1983; Member, Notorious, with Robin George, 1990; Re-formed Diamond Head, 1991–; Tours include support to Metallica. *Compositions include:* In The Heat of The Night; Am I Evil; Helpless; It's Electric. *Recordings include:* Albums with Diamond Head: Lightning To The Nations, 1980; (remixed as Behold The Beginning, 1986); Canterbury, 1983; Death and Progress, 1993; with Robin George: Notorious, 1990; Rising Up (mini album), 1992; To Heaven from Hell, 1997; Diamond Nights, 2000; Compilation: Am I Evil, 1987.

HARRIS, Simon Kenneth; b. 10 Sept. 1962, London, England. DJ; Prod. *Career:* Record Producer and Remixer with 2 Top 40 Hits; Production Credits include: Derek B, Ambassadors of Funk, Daddy Freddy; Remix Credits include: Stone Roses; James Brown; Tony Toni Tone; Real Thing; DMB; Prince; Steve Silk Hurley; Joyce Simms; Appeared on Top of the Pops, Good Morning, Big Breakfast. *Recordings:* Solo singles include: Bad On The Mike, 1987; Bass (How Low Can You Go), 1988; Here Comes That Sound, 1988; Another Monsterjam 1989; Don't Stop The Music, 1990. *Honours:* NME Rap Label of the Year, 1988–89. *Membership:* PRS; BMI. *Current Management:* Chris France, Music of Life. *Address:* Liscombe Park, Soulbury, LU7 0JL, England.

HARRIS, Steve; b. 12 March 1957, Leytonstone, London, England. Rock Musician (bass). *Career:* Member, pub band, Smiler; Founder member, UK heavy rock group Iron Maiden, 1976–; Regular tours world-wide; Concerts include: Reading Festival, 1980, 1982; Monsters of Rock Festival, Castle Donington, 1988, 1992; Monsters of Rock, Germany, 1988; Monsters of Rock, France, 1992; Super Rock '92, Germany, 1992. *Recordings:* Albums: Iron Maiden, 1980; Killers, 1981; The Number of The Beast (No. 1, UK), 1982; Piece of Mind, 1983; Powerslave, 1984; Live After Death, 1985; Somewhere In Time, 1986; Seventh Son of a Seventh Son (No. 1, UK), 1988; No Prayer For The Dying, 1990; Fear of The Dark, 1992; A Real Live One, 1993; A Real Dead One, 1993; The X-Factor, 1995; Best of the Beast, 1996; Virtual XI, 1998; Ed Hunter, 1999; Brave New World, 2000; Rock In Rio, 2002. Hit singles include: Running Free, 1980; Run To The Hills, 1982; The Number of The Beast, 1982; Flight of Icarus, 1983; The Trooper, 1983; 2 Minutes To Midnight, 1984; Aces High, 1984; Wasted Years, 1986; Can I Play With Madness, 1988; Evil That Men Do, 1988; The Clairvoyant, 1988; Infinite Dreams, 1989; Holy Smoke, 1990; Bring Your Daughter To The Slaughter (No. 1, UK), 1991; Be Quick Or Be Dead, 1992; From Here To Eternity, 1992; Fear of The Dark, 1993; Hallowed Be Thy Name, 1993; Man On The Edge, 1995; Virus, 1996. *Address:* c/o Sanctuary Music (Overseas), First Floor Suite, The Colonnades, 82 Bishops Bridge Rd, London W2 6BB, England.

HARRISON, Gavin; b. 28 May 1963, Harrow, London, England. Musician (drums, bass, keyboards); Composer. *Career:* Founder member, Dizrhythmia; Worked with: Level 42; Paul Young; Iggy Pop; Eros Ramazotti; Claudio Baglioni; Incognito. *Recordings:* Albums include: with Sam Brown: Stop, 1988; with Incognito: Inside Life; Always There; Also recorded with: Tom Robinson; Kevin Ayers; Black; Dave Stewart; Paul Young; Iggy Pop. *Publications:* Rhythmic Illusions Book; Columns for: Rhythm, Modern Drummer magazines. *Current Management:* B and H Management. *Address:* Lavender Cottage, Love Lane, Kings Langley, Hertfordshire WD4 8EW, England.

HARRISON, Oscar; b. 15 April 1965, Birmingham, England. Musician (drums, keyboards). *Career:* Member, jazz rock reggae band Echo Base; Joined The Fanatics; Band split, joined Ocean Colour Scene; Support slot on 1994 Oasis tour; Numerous TV appearances and much radio play; Riverboat Song used as theme tune to TV series TFI Friday; Several headlining tours. *Recordings:* Singles include: Riverboat Song, 1996; The Day We Caught The Train, 1996; You've Got It Bad, 1996; The Circle, 1996; 100 Mile High City, 1997; Travellers Tune, 1997; Better Day, 1997; It's A Beautiful Thing, 1998; July/I Am The News, 2000; Up On The Downside, 2001; Albums: Ocean Colour Scene, 1992; Moseley Shoals, 1996; B-Sides, Seasides and Freerides, 1997; Marchin' Already (No. 1, UK), 1997; One From The Modern, 1999;

Mechanical Wonder, 2001; Songs For The Front Row (compilation), 2001. *Website:* www.oceancolourscene.com.

HARRY, Debbie (Deborah Ann); b. 1 July 1945, Miami, Florida, USA. Vocalist; Songwriter; Actress. *Career:* Former Playboy bunny waitress; Singer, groups: Wind In The Willows; The Stilettos; Founder, Blondie, 1974–83, re-formed 1998; Appearances include: New York punk club, CBGBs, 1974; Support to Iggy Pop, USA, 1977; Solo recording career, 1981–; Actress, films including: Blank Generation, 1978; The Foreigner, 1978; Union City, 1979; Roadie, 1980; Videodrome; Hairspray; The Killbillies; Intimate Stranger, 1991. *Recordings:* Hit singles: with Blondie: Denis (Denee), 1978; (I'm Always Touched By Your) Presence Dear, 1978; Picture This, 1978; Hanging On The Telephone, 1978; Heart of Glass (No. 1, UK), 1979; Sunday Girl (No. 1, UK), 1979; Dreaming, 1979; Union City Blue, 1979; Call Me (No. 1, USA and UK), 1980; Atomic (No. 1, UK), 1980; The Tide Is High (No. 1, UK), 1980; Rapture (No. 1, USA), 1981; Island of Lost Souls, 1982; Maria (No. 1, UK), 1999; Solo: Backfired, 1981; French Kissin' (In The USA), 1986; I Want That Man, 1989; I Can See Clearly, 1993; Albums with Blondie: Blondie, 1976; Plastic Letters, 1978; Parallel Lines (No. 1, USA), 1978; Eat To The Beat (No. 1, UK), 1979; Autoamerican, 1980; The Best of Blondie (No. 1, UK), 1981; The Hunter, 1982; No Exit, 1999; Livid, 2000; Solo albums: Koo Koo, 1981; Rockbird, 1986; Def, Dumb and Blonde, 1989; Debravation, 1993; Compilations: Once More Into The Bleach, 1988; The Complete Picture, 1991; Blonde and Beyond, 1993. *Contributions to:* film soundtracks: American Gigolo, 1980; Roadie, 1980; Scarface; Krush Groove, 1984. *Publications:* Making Tracks – The Rise of Blondie (co-written with Chris Stein), 1982. *Membership:* ASCAP; AFTRA; Equity; Screen Actors Guild. *Current Management:* Overland Productions, 156 W 56th St, Fifth Floor, New York, NY 10019, USA.

HARSCH, Eddie; b. 27 May, Toronto, Canada. Musician (keyboards). *Career:* Joined James Cotton's band, 1981–86; Played with Albert Collins, 1989–90; Mem., The Black Crowes, 1991–. *Recordings:* Albums: Amorica, 1994; Three Snakes and One Charm, 1996; Sho Nuff: The Complete Black Crowes, 1998; By Your Side, 1999; Live At The Greek, 2000; Tribute To A Work In Progress: Greatest Hits 1990–1999, 2001; Lions, 2001; Live, 2002. *Address:* c/o V2 Records, 14 E Fourth St, New York, NY 10012, USA. *E-mail:* info@theblackcrowes.com. *Website:* www.blackcrowes.com.

HART, Angela Ruth; b. 8 March 1972, Adelaide, Australia. Vocalist; Musician. *Career:* Solo artiste; Also singer with Frente; Australian tour, 1992–93; US tour, 1994; Support to Beautiful South; Crowded House; Counting Crows; They Might Be Giants. *Recordings:* Albums: Marvin The Album, 1993; Ruby's Arm, Tom Waits Tribute, 1995; Shape, 1996; Singles: Whirled, 1991; Clunk, 1992; Accidentally Kelly Street, 1992; No Time EP, 1993; Ordinary Angels, 1994; Lonely, 1994; Labour of Love, 1994; Bizarre Love Triangle, 1994; What's Come Over Me, 1996. *Honours:* DBL Platinum album, Australia; Gold album, Canada, Indonesia, Phillipines, Malaysia, Thailand.

HART, Freddy, (Frederick Segrest); b. 21 Dec. 1926, Loachapoka, Alabama, USA. Country vocalist; Songwriter; Musician (guitar). *Career:* Left school, aged 12; Joined marines at 15 by lying about age; Saw action in Guam and Iwo Jima; Returning to Nashville, became roadie for Hank Williams Sr, 1949; First song cut Every Little Thing Rolled Into One, George Morgan, 1949; Toured with Lefty Frizzell, 1950–53; Regular on Home Town Jubilee TV Show in Hollywood; Composition, Loose Talk, a country chart hit for Carl Smith, 1954; Song subsequently recorded by others including Patsy Cline; Signed to Columbia Records, 1959; Label debut, The Wall, was first of many Billboard chart entries until 1987; Most successful in early 1970s; Easy Loving made US Top 20 pop chart, 1971; Semi-retired, concentrating on business interests, running school for handicapped children. *Compositions include:* Bless Your Heart; Easy Loving; Got The All Overs For You; Hang In There Girl; Hank Williams' Guitar; If You Can't Feel It (It Ain't There); Loose Talk; My Hang-Up Is You; Trip To Heaven. *Recordings include:* Easy Loving, 1971; My Hang Up Is You, Got The All Overs For You (All Over Me), Bless Your Heart, 1972; Super Kind of Woman, Trip To Heaven, 1973; Albums: Easy Loving, 1971; Got The All Overs For You, My Hang-Up Is You, Bless Your Heart, 1972; Super Kind of Woman, 1973; Greatest Hits, 1975. *Honours:* Numerous including: CMA, Song of the Year, Easy Loving, 1971 and 1972; ACM: Entertainer of the Year; Top Male Vocalist; Single of the Year, Easy Loving; Album of the Year, Easy Loving, 1971. *Membership:* Grand Ole Opry, early 1960s. *Current Management:* Richard Davis Management, 1030 North Woodland, Kansas City, MO 64118, USA.

HARTNOLL, Paul; b. 19 May 1968, Dartford, Kent, England. Musician (keyboards). *Career:* Mem., Noddy and the Satellites; Mem., Orbital, with brother Phil, 1987–; Signed to ffrr Records, 1989; Numerous live appearances at clubs and raves; Glastonbury Festival, Tribal Gathering, V Festival, Phoenix Festival; Royal Albert Hall Concert; Collaborations with Metallica's Kirk Hammett and composer Michael Kamen; Contributions to film soundtracks: Shopping, 1994; The Saint, 1996; Spawn, 1997; Event Horizon, 1997; xXx, 2002. *Recordings:* Albums: Untitled ('the green album'), 1991; Untitled ('the brown album'), 1992; Snivilisation, 1994; Peel Session, 1994; In

Sides, 1996; Middle Of Nowhere, 1999; The Altogether, 2001; Back To Mine (compilation), 2002; Work 1989–2002, 2002. Singles: Chime, 1990; Omen, 1990; Diversions (EP), 1992; Impact, 1993; Lush, 1993; Halcyon, 1993; Times Fly, 1995; Are We Here?, 1995; The Box, 1996; Satan Live, 1996; The Saint, 1997; Style, 1999; Beached (with Angelo Badalamenti), 2000; Funny Break (One Is Enough), 2001; Rest And Play (EP), 2002. *Honours:* NME Award, Best Dance Act, 1993, BRAT Award, 1995; Dance Star Tiscali World Dance Music Award, Dance Star of the Year, 2002. *Address:* c/o London Records, PO Box 1422, Chancellors House, Chancellors Rd, London W6 9SG, England. *Website:* www.loopz.co.uk/orbital.

HARTNOLL, Phil; b. 9 Jan. 1964, Dartford, Kent, England. Musician (keyboards). *Career:* Mem., Orbital, with brother Paul, 1987–; Signed to ffrr Records, 1989; Numerous live appearances at clubs and raves; Glastonbury Festival, Tribal Gathering, V Festival, Phoenix Festival; Royal Albert Hall Concert; Collaborations with Metallica's Kirk Hammett and composer Michael Kamen; Contributions to film soundtracks: Shopping, 1994; The Saint, 1996, Spawn, 1997; Event Horizon, 1997; xXx, 2002. *Recordings:* Albums: Untitled ('the green album'), 1991; Untitled ('the brown album'), 1992; Snivilisation, 1994; Peel Session, 1994; In Sides, 1996; Middle Of Nowhere, 1999; The Altogether, 2001; Back To Mine (compilation), 2002; Work 1989–2002, 2002. Singles: Chime, 1990; Omen, 1990; Diversions (EP), 1992; Impact, 1993; Lush, 1993; Halcyon, 1993; Times Fly, 1995; Are We Here?, 1995; The Box, 1996; Satan Live, 1996; The Saint, 1997; Style, 1999; Beached (with Angelo Badalamenti), 2000; Funny Break (One Is Enough), 2001; Rest And Play (EP), 2002. *Honours:* NME Award, Best Dance Act, 1993, BRAT Award, 1995; Dance Star Tiscali World Dance Music Award, Dance Star of the Year, 2002. *Address:* c/o London Records, PO Box 1422, Chancellors House, Chancellors Rd, London W6 9SG, England. *Website:* www.loopz.co.uk/orbital.

HARVEY, Brian (Lee); b. 8 Aug. 1974, Edmonton, London, England. Vocalist. *Career:* Member, East 17; Numerous television and live appearances. *Recordings:* Singles include: House of Love, 1992; Deep, 1993; West End Girls, 1993; It's Alright, 1993; Around The World, 1994; Stay Another Day (No. 1, UK), 1994; Steam, 1994; Thunder, 1995; If You Ever, with Gabrielle, 1996; Hey Child, 1997; Each Time, 1998; Betcha Can't Wait, 1999; Albums: Walthamstow, 1993; Steam, 1994; Up All Night, 1996; Around the World – The Journey So Far, 1996; Resurrection, 1998; Solo: Singles: True Step Tonight, with the True Steppers and Donell Jones, 2000; Straight Up (No Bends), 2001; Loving You, with The Refugee Crew, 2002.

HARVEY, Mick (Michael John); b. 29 Aug. 1958, Rochester, Australia. Musician (guitar, drums); Arranger; Prod; *Compositions:* The Mercy Seat; Red Right Hand. *Recordings:* The Birthday Party, entire catalogue; Nick Cave and the Bad Seeds, entire catalogue; Intoxicated Man, 1995; Pink Elephants, 1997; Co-Prod., Stories from the City, Stories from the Sea, P. J. Harvey; Film scores: Chopper, 2000; Australian Rules, 2002. *Honours:* Aria Award, Best Soundtrack, To Have and To Hold, 1997. *Membership:* APRA; PPCA; PAMRA. *Address:* c/o Mute Records, 429 Harrow Rd, London W10 4RE, England.

HARVEY, P(olly) J(ean); b. 9 Oct. 1969, England. Vocalist; Songwriter; Musician (guitar, percussion, keyboards). *Career:* Formed P. J. Harvey trio, 1991; Signed to Island Records, 1993; Solo artiste, 1993–; Television appearances include: MTV's Most Wanted; 120 Minutes; David Letterman Show; Jay Leno Show; Conan O'Brien Show; Top of the Pops; The White Room; Later With Jools Holland; Concerts include Glastonbury Festival, 1995; Tours, USA, Europe, Japan, 1995; Film appearance: The Book of Life, 1998; Collaborations include: John Parish, Eric Drew Feldman, Joe Gore, Pascal Comelade, Tricky, Nick Cave, Mick Harvey; Exhibited sculpture in galleries in the USA. *Recordings:* Albums: with P. J. Harvey trio: Dry, 1992; Rid of Me, 1993; Solo: 4-Track Demos, 1993; To Bring You My Love, 1995; Is This Desire?, 1998; Stories From The City, Stories From The Sea, 2000. Singles: with P. J. Harvey trio: Dress, 1991; Sheela-Na-Gig, 1992; Solo: 50ft Queenie, 1993; Man-Size, 1993; Down by the Water, 1995; C'Mon Billy, 1995; Perfect Day Elise, 1998; Wind, 1999; Good Fortune, 2000; This Is Love, 2001; A Place Called Love, 2001; Contributed to film soundtracks, including Basquiat, Cradle Will Rock, Stella Does Tricks. *Publications:* Poetry. *Honours:* Rolling Stone Awards, Best Songwriter, Best New Female Singer, 1992, Artist of the Year, 1995; Mercury Music Prize, Best Album, 2001. *Current Management:* Principle Management, 30–32 Sir John Rogersons Quay, Dublin 2, Ireland. *Website:* www.pjharvey.net.

HARVEY, Tim; b. 1 Nov. 1973, Leeds, England. Musician (bass); Songwriter. *Education:* BEng, Leeds Met University. *Career:* Played violin in North Yorkshire Youth Orchestra, 1980–87; Took up bass guitar playing throughout North East England with various jazz and pop bands, 1990–; Studio session work leading to the formation of The Saints, indie pop band. *Recordings:* Composition and session work for A Dark Affair, 1993; Someone, Toytown, 1994; If I Was Your Father Christmas, Toytown, 1995; I Can Save You (EP), The Saints, 1995. *Address:* 1 Malpas Rd, Northallerton, North Yorkshire DL7 8TJ, England.

HARVIE, Ian; b. 19 May 1962, Glasgow, Scotland. Musician (guitar, mandolin, dobro); Vocalist; Prod. m. Madeline, 1 s. *Education:* Architecture, Glasgow School of Arts. *Career:* Founding mem., Del Amitri, 1981–; Numerous tours; Session recorded for the BBC with DJ John Peel. *Recordings:* Albums: Del Amitri, 1985; Waking Hours, 1989; Change Everything, 1992; Twisted, 1995; Some Other Sucker's Parade, 1997; Hatful Of Rain/Lousy With Love, 1998; Can You Do Me Good?, 2002. Singles: Kiss This Thing Goodbye, 1989; Nothing Ever Happens, 1990; Move Away Jimmy Blue, 1990; Spit In The Rain, 1990; Always The Last To Know, 1992; Be My Downfall, 1992; Just Like A Man, 1992; When You Were Wrong, 1993; Here and Now, 1995; Driving With The Brakes On, 1995; Roll To Me, 1995; Tell Her This, 1996; Not Where It's At, 1997; Don't Come Home Too Soon, 1998; Cry To Be Found, 1998; Just Before You Leave, 2002. *Address:* c/o A & M Records Inc, 595 Madison Ave, New York, NY 10022, USA. *Website:* www.delamitri.com.

HASLAM, Annie; b. Bolton, England. Vocalist; Songwriter. m. Marc I Hoffman, 8 June 1991, divorced. *Education:* Art College; 9 months' opera training with Sybil Knight, London. *Career:* 65 tours, USA with rock band Renaissance; Tours: Canada; UK; Europe; Middle East; Performances include: Carnegie Hall (New York Philharmonic and Renaissance), 1975; Royal Albert Hall (Royal Philharmonic Orchestra and Renaissance), 1978; Tour of Japan (Annie Haslam Band), 1991; Solo guest with New York Philharmonia Virtuosi, 1986. *Recordings:* with Renaissance: Prologue, 1972; Ashes Are Burning, 1973; Turn of The Cards, 1974; Scheherazade and Other Stories, 1975; Live At Carnegie Hall, 1976; Novella, 1977; In The Beginning, 1978; Song For All Seasons, 1978; Azure d'Or, 1979; Camera, Camera, 1981; Timeline, 1983; Tales of 1001 Nights, Vols 1–2, 1990; Solo: Annie In Wonderland, 1977; Still Life (with Royal Philharmonic Orchestra), 1985; Annie Haslam, 1989; with Annie Haslam's Renaissance: Blessing In Disguise, 1994; Annie Haslam Live in Brazil, 1997; Novella, 1998; Azure d'Or, 1998; Live Under Brazilian Skies, 1998; The Dawn of Ananda, 2000; It Snows In Heaven Too, 2001; Guest on: Intergalactic Touring Band, 1977; with Mike Read: Betjeman, 1990; with Akio Dobashi: Fox, 1990; with Raphael Rudd: Skydancer, 1991; Guest on: Tales from Yesterday (Yes tribute), 1995; Suppers Ready (Genesis tribute), 1995; with Raphael Rudd, Awakenings, 1996; Renaissance Live at the Royal Albert Hall, with the Royal Philharmonic Orchestra, Vols 1 and 2; Songs from Renaissance Days: Rarities, recorded 1977, 1984. *Honours:* Silver disc for: Single Northern Lights, 1978; Fifth Top Female Singer, Melody Maker, 1978; Silver album, Song For All Seasons. *Membership:* Equity. *Current Management:* The White Dove Organisation Inc, PO Box 1157, Doylestown, PA 18901, USA.

HASLAM, George; b. 22 Feb. 1939, Preston, Lancashire, England. Jazz Musician (baritone saxophone, tarogato). m. Beryl Murphy, 7 Dec. 1960, 4 s., 1 d. *Education:* Manchester University; Glasgow University; Some private music tuition. *Career:* Two albums on Spotlite, early 1980s; Extensive work in Eastern Europe; Tour of Mexico; Cervantino Festival, led first British jazz group to play in Cuba, 1986; Founded record label, SLAM, 1989; First British Jazz musician to play in Argentina, 1990; Founder, Oxford Jazz Festival, 1990; Featured in Impressions of George Haslam, BBC Radio 3, 1993; Working in Ukraine, Russia and Finland, 1996–, including first jazz concert in Odessa Opera House and first CD of improvised music released in Ukraine; Regular tours include: Argentina, Cuba, Hong Kong, Europe; Leads blues and improvisation workshops; Worked with Mal Waldron 1994–2002. *Recordings:* Live In Hungary, 1984; The Healing, 1986. *Membership:* Musicians' Union; PRS; MCPS. *Address:* 3 Thesiger Rd, Abingdon, Oxfordshire OX14 2DX, England. *Telephone:* (1235) 529012. *Fax:* (1235) 529012. *E-mail:* georgehaslam@aol.com. *Website:* members.aol.com/GeorgeHaslam.

HASSELL, David; b. 26 Nov. 1947, Manchester, England. Musician (drums, percussion). m. Valerie, 29 April 1967, 1 s., 2 d. *Education:* Private tuition; Studies with Geoff Riley; Jim Blackley; Manik Popatkar; Tony Oxley. *Career:* Performer, almost every style of music: Jazz; Funk; Rock; Folk; Latin; Show; Cabaret; Symphonic; Session musician for television including: Coronation Street; Brideshead Revisited; Old Grey Whistle Test; Jim'll Fix It; Sunday Night At The London Palladium; Emmerdale Farm; Musician for radio, jingles, records and films; Performed numerous sessions with top artistes including: ABBA; The Three Degrees; The Drifters; Cliff Richard; Barbara Dickson; Vince Hill; The Ramones; The Platters; Harold Melvin and The Blue Notes; Les Miserables; Lilly Savage; Maddy Prior; Shirley Bassey; Gloria Gaynor; Bertice Redding; Alan Price; Kiki Dee; Happy Mondays; Sad Cafe; Lisa Stansfield; Roger Whittaker; George Hamilton IV; Mary O'Hara; Moira Anderson; Ute Lemper; Conductors include: Ronnie Hazelhurst; Michel Legrand; Alan Aynsworth; Leader, Apitos, one of UK's foremost Latin American ensembles; Lecturer, Drums and Percussion, Royal Northern College of Music; Royal Academy of Music, London; Salford College of Technology; Chetham's School of Music; Royal Scottish Academy of Music and Drama; Trinity College. *Recordings:* Both Hands Free, 1976; with Stan Barker: The Gentle Touch, 1990; Also appears on: Changing Winds, Maddy Prior; Snap Crackle Bop, John Cooper-Clarke; Pauline Murray and the Invisible Girl, Pauline Murray; Morning Like This, Sandi Patti; Bummed, Happy Mondays. *Publications:* Graded Course For Drum Kit 1–2 (book and tape); Latin Grooves (book and tape), 1994. *Membership:* Musicians' Union;

NAPT; PAS. *Address:* 22 Park Rd, Timperley, Altrincham, Cheshire WA14 5AU, England.

HASSELQUIST, Eric; b. 15 Sept. 1965, Stockholm, Sweden. Record Co Exec. *Education:* Master Degree in Business Economics. *Career:* Music Manager for Readers Digest Scandinavia, 1990–91; General Manager, Stockholm Records, 1991–. *Recordings:* Impact (EP), Rimshot Party, 1991. *Address:* PO Box 20504, 16102 Bromma, Sweden.

HASTINGS, Deborah; b. 11 May 1959, Evansville, Indiana, USA. Musician (bass guitar); Photographer. *Education:* Music, University of Wisconsin. *Career:* Freelance bass player, 1975–; Photographer, 1976–81; Performed with: Ron Wood; Bo Diddley; Chuck Berry; Jerry Lee Lewis; Ben E King; Little Anthony; Performed at President George Bush Inauguration, with Billy Preston, Dr John, Carla Thomas, Sam Moore, 1979; Founder, A-Prompt Computer Teleprompting Services Inc, 1995; Performed with Johnnie Johnson; Played at President Clinton's inauguration, 1997. *Recordings:* Bo Diddley, A Man Amongst Men. *Publications:* Author, Photographers Market, 1981. *Address:* c/o Talent Source, 1560 Broadway, Suite 1308, New York, NY 10036, USA.

HATCH, Tony; b. 30 June 1939, England. Composer; Arranger; Musical Dir; Songwriter. *Education:* London Choir School. *Career:* Band Coldstream Guards, 1959–61; Record Producer, Pye Records, 1961–71; Producer for Petula Clark; Jackie Trent; The Searchers; Musical Director, Carols In The Domain, (Australia) 1984–94; Television: Regular Panelist, New Faces, 1973–78; Films: Travels With My Aunt; Sweeney II. *Recordings:* Singles: Downtown; Call Me; I Know A Place; Where Are You Now; Joanna; Don't Sleep In The Subway; I Couldn't Live Without Your Love; Television theme music for Neighbours; Crossroads; Emmerdale; Musical: The Card; Compilation: Hatchback, 2001. *Publications:* So You Want To Be In The Music Business, 1975. *Honours:* Several Ivor Novello Awards; ASCAP Awards; BMI Awards. *Current Management:* Billy Marsh Associates. *Address:* c/o Lyric Productions Ltd, 3 Warwick Way, London SW1V 1QU, England.

HATFIELD, Bobby; b. 10 Aug. 1940, Beaver Dam, Wisconsin, USA. Vocalist. *Career:* Member, The Variations; Formed The Righteous Brothers with Bill Medley, 1962–67; Support to the Beatles, US tour, 1964; Duo continued with Jimmy Walker, 1967–73; Reforms Righteous Brothers with Bill Medley, 1974–; Solo recording artiste, 1968–; Appearance on Cheers, 1991. *Recordings:* Singles include: You've Lost That Lovin' Feelin' (No. 1, UK and USA), 1964; Just Once In My Life, 1965; You Can Have Her, 1965; Justine, 1965; Unchained Melody, 1965; Ebb Tide, 1966; You're My Soul and Inspiration, 1966; Solo: Nothing Is Too Good For You, 1969; Rock 'n' Roll Heaven, 1974; Albums: You've Lost That Lovin' Feelin', 1965; Some Blue-Eyed Soul, 1965; This Is New!, 1965; Just Once In My Life, 1965; Back To Back, 1966; Soul and Inspiration, 1966; The Best of The Righteous Brothers, 1966; Go Ahead and Cry, 1966; Sayin' Somethin', 1967; Greatest Hits, 1967; One For The Road, 1968; Re-Birth, 1969; Greatest Hits, Vol. 2, 1969; Righteous Brothers Greatest Hits, 1990; The Best Of..., 1990; The Very Best Of..., 1990; Anthology (1962–74), 1990; Out of Our Souls, 2001. *Address:* c/o William Morris Agency.

HATFIELD, Juliana; b. 27 July 1967, Wiscasset, Maine, USA. Vocalist; Songwriter. *Education:* Berklee School of Music. *Career:* Member: Blake Babies, 1986–92; Juliana Hatfield Three, 1993–95; Solo career, 1995–; Recent concerts include: Reading Festival, 1995. *Recordings:* Albums: with The Blake Babies: Nicely Nicely, 1987; Slow Learner, 1989; Earwig, 1990; Sunburn, 1992; Innocence and Experience (compilation), 1993; with The Lemonheads: It's A Shame About Ray, 1992; with The Juliana Hatfield Three: Become What You Are, 1993; Only Everything, 1995; Solo albums include: Hey Babe, 1992; Forever Baby; Bed; Juliana's Pony – Total System Failure, 2000; Beautiful Creature, 2000; Singles include: Universal Heartbeat, 1995; Please Do Not Disturb. *Publications:* The Music of Juliana Hatfield. *Membership:* AFofM. *Current Management:* c/o Gary Smith, One Camp St, Suite 2, Cambridge, MA 02140, USA.

HATHERLEY, Charlotte Franklin; b. 20 June 1979, London, England. Musician (guitar, keyboards). *Career:* Former Mem., Night Nurse; Mem., Ash, 1997–; Contributed track to film, A Life Less Ordinary, 1997; Headlining tours and TV appearances. *Recordings:* Albums: Trailer, 1994; 1977, 1996; Live At The Wireless, 1997; Nu-Clear Sounds, 1998; Free All Angels, 2001; Intergalactic Sonic 7's: The Best Of Ash, 2002; Envy, 2002. Singles: Jack Names the Planets, 1994; Petrol, 1994; Uncle Pat, 1994; Kung Fu, 1995; Girl From Mars, 1995; Angel Interceptor, 1995; Goldfinger, 1995; Oh Yeah, 1996; A Life Less Ordinary, 1997; Jesus Says, 1998; Numbskull (EP), 1999; Wild Surf, 2001; Burn Baby Burn, 2001; Shining Light, 2001; Sometimes, 2001; Candy, 2001; Tokyo Blitz, 2002; There's A Star, 2002. *Honours:* Ivor Novello Award, Best Contemporary Song, for Shining Light, 2002. *Address:* Infectious Records, 1 Shorrolds Rd, London SW6 7TR, England. *E-mail:* charlotte@ash-official.com. *Website:* www.ash-official.com.

HAUG, Ian; b. 21 Feb. 1970, Tasmania, South Australia. Musician (guitar). *Education:* Brisbane University, Architecture student. *Career:* Joined Brisbane-based rock group Powderfinger, 1992; Steadily built reputation on many Australian tours/festival appearances; International breakthrough with Odyssey Number Five album; Constant world-wide touring throughout 2000–01 ending with New Suburban Fables 2001 Australian shows; Also member of side-project group F.O.C. *Recordings:* Albums: Parables For Wooden Ears, 1994; Double Allergic, 1996; Internationalist, 1998; Odyssey Number Five, 2000; Singles: Powderfinger Blue (EP), Transfusion (EP), 1993; Tail, Grave Concern, 1994; Save Your Skin, Mr Kneebone (EP), 1995; Pick You Up, D.A.F., Living Type, 1996; Take Me In, 1997; The Day You Come, Don't Wanna Be Left Out/Good-Day Ray, 1998; Already Gone, Passenger, 1999; My Happiness, 2000; Like A Dog, The Metre, 2001. *Honours:* ARIA Awards: Album of the Year; Song of the Year; Best Rock Album; Best Cover Artwork, 1999; Six times Platinum. *Address:* c/o Republic Records, Australia. *Website:* www.powderfinger.com.

HAUGEN, Tom Jackie; b. 29 Sept. 1961, Telemark, Norway. Songwriter; Folk Vocalist; Musician (Guitar). 1 d. *Career:* Television NRK, Reisen Til Sputnikland Miote Med Prestestranna Vel Vel Vel; Television 2, Go Ettermiooag Norge; Television 3, Pa Tide and Los Pa Traden; Television Norge, Sommatkveld; Radio, Norsktoppen, 10 I Skuooet, Nitimen, Sonoagsposten. *Compositions:* Gunnaer Gt; Bestefars Hevn; Veivesenet Farrsvant Me Potetakern; Terror I Dobbeltseng. *Recordings:* Haeimomkring, 1992; Bestefars Hevn, 1993; Ingrid Bergman, 1994; Rosmala Neger, 1998. *Honours:* This Years Artist, 1994; Language Prize, 1995. *Current Management:* M and P, Greveveien 9A, 3257 Larvik, Norway. *Address:* Tordalsun 52, 3750 Drangedal, Norway.

HAURAND, Ali; b. 15 Nov. 1943, Viersen, Germany. Musician (double bass); Teacher. 1 d. *Education:* Studied classical music, Folkwangschool, Essen, Germany. *Career:* Member, leader, founder, George Maycock Trio, 1967–79; Quintet with Philly Joe Jones, 1968–69; International Jazz Quintet with Jon Eardly, 1969–70; Third Eye, 1970; European Jazz Quintet, 1977; SOH Trio, 1978–84; The Quartet, 1982; European Jazz Ensemble, 1984; Numerous tours and festivals in Europe, USA, Canada and Australia with these and other ensembles featuring: Bobby Jones; Don Byas; Ben Webster; John Handy; Jan Akkerman; John Surman; Gerd Dudek; Joachim Kühn; Enrico Rava; Numerous television and radio appearances including: Jazz at Midnight, German television, 1991; Talking Jazz, Superchannel, 1993; Over 50 recordings with: The Quartet, European Jazz Ensemble; European Jazz Quintet, 1970–; Played at Celebration, 20th Anniversary with European Jazz Ensemble, 1996, 25th Anniversary tour, 2001; Presenter, German TV WDR for Jazz Series Round Midnight and Fullhouse, 1991–; Played with Charlie Mariano and Daniel Humair as Mariano-Haurand-Humair, played festivals in Paris, Barcelona, Amsterdam, Geneva, 1999; Played pantomime and Jazz with Milan Sládek; Art Dir, 11th International Jazz Rally, Dusseldorf, 2003; Art Dir, 17th International Jazzfestival, Viersen Germany, 2003. *Compositions:* Pulque; Television music on three CDs. *Honours:* European Jazz Poll, Jazz Forum, 7 times. *Membership:* Jazz Union, Germany. *Current Management:* Connexion Agency, Konrad Adenauer Ring 10, D-41747 Viersen, Germany. *Telephone:* (2162) 18408. *Fax:* (2162) 15373. *E-mail:* Connexion@jazzbox.com. *Website:* www.jazzbox.com.

HAUSER, Tim; b. 1942, New Jersey, USA. Vocalist; Songwriter. *Career:* Founder member, singer, Manhattan Transfer, 1971–; Television includes: Mary Tyler Moore Television Special, 1975; Own television show, 1975; Star Parade, Germany; Regular US and European tours; Performed at MIDEM, Cannes, France, 1977. *Recordings:* Hit singles: Tuxedo Junction; Chanson D'Amour; Birdland; Boy From New York City; Albums include: Junkin' (Unofficial), 1971; Manhattan Transfer, 1975; Coming Out, 1976; Pastiche, 1978; Live, 1978; Extensions, 1979; Mecca For Moderns, 1981; Best of Manhattan Transfer, 1981; Bodies and Souls, 1983; Bop Doo-Wop, 1985; Vocalese, 1985; Live, 1987; Brasil, 1988; The Off-Beat of Avenues, 1991; Contributor, film soundtrack A League of Their Own, 1992. *Honours:* German Grammy, Best New Group, 1975; Numerous Grammy Awards (Best Vocal Arrangement, Best Jazz Fusion Performance, Best Jazz Vocal Performance, Best Pop Vocal Performance, Best Contemporary Jazz Performance), 1980–, including 3 Grammy Awards, for Vocalese album, 1985. *Address:* c/o Columbia Records, 10 Great Marlborough St, London W1V 2LP, England.

HAUTA-AHO, Teppo; b. 27 May 1941, Finland. Composer; Musician (bass). *Education:* Diploma, Sibelius Academy, 1970; Studied with Professor Frantisek Posta. *Career:* Bassist, Helsinki Philharmonic, 1965–72; Finnish National Opera, 1975–; Played with numerous artists including: Seppo Paakkunainen, early 1960s; Juhani Vilkki; Kaj Backlund Big Band; Pekka Pöyry quartet; Tuohi Quartet; Leader, own group Kalmisto-Klang; Member, Quintet Moderne, 1980s–; Also classical and chamber musician; Performed at annual festivals, Kuhmo; Currently concentrating on composing; Duos with: singer/pianist Carita Holmström; pianist/composer Eero Ojanen; Member, Cecil Taylor European quintet. *Compositions include:* Fantasy, for trumpet and orchestra; Kadenza, for contrabass, used as set piece in international bass competitions, 1990–99. *Honours:* Composer's Prize, Royal Academy, Stockholm; First prize, Reine Marie José competition, Geneva, 1986; Winner with Tuohi Quartet, EBU competition for jazz groups, Montreux, 1971. *Address:* Mechelininkatu 27 B, 00100 Helsinki, Finland.

HAVENS, Richie; b. 21 Jan. 1941, Brooklyn, NY, USA. Vocalist. *Career:* Performances include: Tribute concert to Woody Guthrie, Carnegie Hall, New York, 1968; Miami Pop Festival, 1968; Woodstock Music and Art Fair, Bethel, New York, 1969; Isle of Wight Festival, 1970; Crystal Palace Garden Party, London, 1972; Stage debut, rock opera, Tommy, 1972; Stonehenge Free Festival, 1977; The Gold Medal Celebration, Carnegie Hall, 1987; Freedom Festival '90, 1990; Troubadours of Folk Festival, Los Angeles, 1993; Actor, Othello, in Jack Good's Catch My Soul, 1974; Film appearances: Greased Lightning, 1977; Hearts of Fire, 1987. *Recordings:* Albums include: Mixed Bag, 1967; Stonehenge, 1970; Alarm Clock, 1971; The Great Blind Degree, 1971; Richard P. Havens, 1983; Sings Beatles and Dylan, 1990; Best Of—The Millennium Collection, 2000; Wishing Well, 2002. *Current Management:* ELD Productions, 123 W 44th St, Suite 11F, New York, NY 10036, USA.

HAVER, Greg; Prod. *Career:* Worked with: John Cale, Catatonia, Cosmic Rough Riders, Gorky's Zygotic Mynci, Manic Street Preachers, Super Furry Animals. *Address:* c/o Stephen Budd Management Ltd, 109b Regents Park Rd, Primrose Hill, London NW1 8UR, England. *Website:* www.record-producers.com.

HAVET, Didier; b. 9 March 1964, Lille, France. Musician (tuba, bass trombone). m. 12 March 1994, 1 d. *Education:* Lille Conservatory; Paris Conservatory. *Career:* Member, National Jazz Orchestra, France (ONJ), 1986–94; Worked with orchestras of: Martial Solal; Jean Loup Longnon; Ivan Jullien; Laurent Cugny; Jean Jacques Ruhlman; Luc Le Masne; Marc Steckar; Jean Marc Padovani; Bertrand Reaudin; Gerard Badini; Bass trombone player with Belmondo Big Band; Tour, Europe, with Mingus Big Band of New York, 1994; Paris and Nice Jazz Festival, 1995; Tours, Netherlands; Norway; Finland; Member, Bloc-notes Quintet, Peru and Columbia, 1995; Regular work in traditional jazz and dixieland. *Recordings:* 5 records with National Orchestra of Jazz, France; Other recordings with: Michel Legrand; Claude Bolling; Julien Clerc; Jacques Higelin; Georges Moustaki; William Sheller; Also appears on: Santander, with Laurent Cugny; Golden Hair, with Gil Evans; Danses, with Terra Nova; Cyclades, with Jean-Loup Longnon; 20 Ans de Jazz en France; Mingus Cuernavaca, with Padovani/Cormann; Montgolfiere, with Gianmaria Testa. *Address:* 3 rue Robert Lavergne, 92600 Asnières, France.

HAWKEN, Dominic; b. 19 April 1967, Welwyn Garden City, Hertfordshire, England. Musician (keyboards); Songwriter; Prod; Remixer; Multimedia and Internet Consultant. *Education:* Piano, classically trained to Grade VIII. *Career:* Session keyboard player, performed with Joy Polloi, Kid Deluxe, Eric and the Good Good Feeling, late '80s–early '90s; Writer and prod., various leading artistes, 1994–; Keyboard/remix credits incl.: Shamen; Donna Summer; Malcolm McLaren; A Tribe Called Quest; Errol Brown; Kym Mazelle; Hammer; Mike Oldfield; Black Duck; Writing/production credits incl.: North and South; Alphaville; Shiona; Right Said Fred; Babe Instinct; Rey; David Fernandez; Prod.: Adam Masterson; Directorships: AL Digital Ltd (multimedia and internet technology); Volume Records Ltd; Federation Records Ltd; Proprietor, WhiteHouse recording studios, London. *Compositions:* Co-writer, East 17 tracks: Stay Another Day (Christmas No. 1, UK), 1994; Be There, 1994; Let It All Go, 1994; I Remember, 1995; Don't You Feel So Good, 1995; Someone To Love, 1995; Ant and Dec tracks: Cloud 9, 1997; Bound, 1997. *Recordings:* Albums: on keyboards: Steam, East 17; as writer/keyboard player: Up All Night, East 17, 1995; All Around the World, East 17, 1996–97; as writer/prod.: The Cult of Ant and Dec, 1997. Singles: as additional prod./remixer/keyboards: Don't Call Me Baby (No. 1, UK), Madison Avenue, 2000; Prickly Heat (theme music, Sky TV), 2001; Double A side incl. Stay Another Day (No. 1, UK), Girls Aloud, 2002; Mixer and prod. for various artistes incl. Part 3, Katia, Lamja, Machines, Hussey; Writing for various projects incl. Atlantis. *Membership:* BAC&S; PRS; Musicians' Union. *Current Management:* The Deluxe Corpn, 13 Charnhill Cres., Bristol BS16 9JU, England. *Website:* www.aldigital.co.uk.

HAWLEY, Richard; Musician (guitar). *Career:* Mem., The Longpigs, 1994–; Mem., Pulp, 2001–02; Session work for various artistes; Solo artiste, 2001–. *Recordings:* Albums: with The Longpigs: The Sun Is Often Out, 1996; Mobile Home, 1999; Solo: Richard Hawley, 2001; Late Night Final, 2002; Lowedges, 2003. Singles: with The Longpigs: Happy Again, 1995; She Said, 1995; Jesus Christ, 1995; Far, 1996; On and On, 1996; Lost Myself, 1996; Blue Skies, 1999; The Frank Sonata, 1999; Solo: Coming Home, 2001. *Address:* c/o Setanta Records, 94 E Seventh St, New York, NY 10009, USA.

HAWORTH, Bryn; b. 29 July 1948, Blackburn, Lancashire, England. Musician (guitars, especially slide, mandolin); Vocalist. m. Sally, 22 Jan. 1973. *Career:* Joined Fleur De Lys, Motown/soul band, house band for Atlantic Records, late 1960s; Went to California, toured USA in bands including: Jackie Lomax Band; Wolfgang; Returned to England, 1973; Signed to Island Records; Numerous radio and television appearances include: 2 Old Grey Whistle Test; Tours, England, Europe, supporting artistes including: Traffic; Bad Company; Gallagher and Lyle; Fairport Convention; Worked with musicians including: Chris De Burgh; Marianne Faithfull; John Cale; Ian Matthews; Joan Armatrading; Gerry Rafferty; Cliff Richard (toured with as member of band); Currently leader, The Bryn Haworth Band, extensive tours, UK; Notable exponent slide guitar. *Recordings:* Albums include: Let The Days Go By, 1974; Sunny Side of The Street, 1975; Grand Arrival, 1978; Keep The Ball Rolling, 1979; The Bryn Haworth Band Live; 6 Gospel albums include: Gap; Pass It On; Wings of The Morning; 12 Classics; Mountain Mover; with Gerry Rafferty: On A Wing and A Prayer; Over My Head, 1995; Slide Don't Fret, 1996; The Finer Things in Life, 1997. *Publications:* Bryn Haworth Song Book, Vol. One. *Address:* PO Box 28, Teddington, Middlesex TW11 0QU, England.

HAWTIN, Richie, (Plastikman, Fuse); b. 1970 Banbury, Oxfordshire, England. Prod; DJ. *Career:* Co-founder Plus 8 Records (with John Aquaviva); World-wide DJ; Collaborations: Eddie Richards, Joey Beltram. *Recordings:* Albums: Dimension Intrusion (as Fuse), 1993; Sheet One (as Plastikman), 1993; Musik (as Plastikman), 1994; Consumed (as Plastikman), 1998; Decks, EFX and 909 (DJ mix album), 1999; DE9 – Closer To The Edit (DJ mix album), 2001; Singles: F.U. (as Fuse), 1991; Substance Abuse (as Fuse), 1991; Krakpot (as Plastikman), 1993; Spastik (as Plastikman), 1993; Do Da Doo (as Robotman), 1994; Sickness (as Plastikman), 1997; Minus Orange, 1999. *Current Management:* c/o Mute Records, 429 Harrow Rd, London W10 4RE, England.

HAY, Barry; b. 16 Aug. 1948, Saizabad, Netherlands. Vocalist; Musician (guitar, flute, saxophone). *Career:* Member, Dutch group, Golden Earring, 1966–; Tours, Europe; Canada; USA; Support to The Who, European tour, 1972; Support to Rush, 1982. *Recordings:* Albums: with Golden Earring: Just Earrings, 1965; Winter Harvest, 1966; Miracle Mirror, 1968; On The Double, 1969; Eight Miles High, 1969; Golden Earring, 1970; Seven Tears, 1971; Together, 1972; Moontan, 1973; Switch, 1975; To The Hilt, 1976; Contraband, 1976; Golden Earring Live, 1977; Grab It For A Second, 1978; No Promises, No Debts, 1979; Prisoner Of The Night, 1980; 2nd Live, 1981; Cut, 1982; N.E.W.S., 1984; Something Heavy Goin' Down, 1984; The Hole, 1986; Keeper Of The Flame, 1989; The Complete Singles Collection 1975–91, 1991; Bloody Buccaneers, 1991; The Naked Truth, 1992; Face It, 1995; Lovesweat, 1995; Naked II, 1997; The Complete Naked Truth, 1998; Paradise In Distress, 1999; Last Blast Of The Century, 2000; The Devil Made Us Do It, 2000; Numerous compilation albums; Solo: Only Parrots, Frogs And Angels, 1972; Victory Of Bad Taste, 1987. *Current Management:* Rob Gerritsen, Wingerd 38, 2496 VC Den Haag, Netherlands. *Telephone:* (15) 380-55-88. *Fax:* (15) 380-55-91.

HAY, Deborah Leigh; b. 30 May 1970, Middlesex, England. Musician (guitar); Vocalist; Composer; Teacher. m. Wayne Wiggins, 1 d. *Education:* BA, Visual and Performing Arts, Brighton, 1988–91; Jr student, Trinity College of Music, London, 1982–88; MBT, The Playground, London, 1991. *Career:* Guitarist, Divas Dance Co; Arranger, El Punal Entra En El Corazón, 1991–93; Performed throughout Europe; Concerts include Queen Elizabeth Hall, 1991; Classic FM broadcast, 1993; Mute Opera, 1992–95; Composer, guitarist, Gaudette; Concerts include British tours. *Compositions include:* Gaudette, 1992. *Recordings:* Nothing But Love, 1988; El Punal Entra En El Corazón, 1992; Gaudette, 1993. *Honours:* Alliance and Leicester Award, El Punal Entra En El Corazón, 1992; Billy Mayerl Award, 1987; Cornelius Cardew Composition Award, Gaudette, shortlisted 1993; South East Arts Award, Mute Opera. *Membership:* Musicians' Union; Brighton New Music; Brighton Guitar Orchestra.

HAY, Roy; b. 12 Aug. 1961, Southend-on-Sea, Essex, England. Musician (guitar, keyboards). *Career:* Member, Russian Bouquet; Joined Culture Club, 1981–87, re-formed 1998–; Landed major recording contract, 1982; Numerous TV appearances and live tours; Various solo projects; Composer for television including: Fitz, ABC, 1996–97. *Recordings:* Singles: Do You Really Want to Hurt Me (No. 1, UK), 1982 (re-released 1998); Church of the Poisoned Mind, 1983; Victims, 1983; It's a Miracle, 1983; Karma Chameleon (No. 1, UK and USA), 1983; The War Song, 1984; The Medal Song, 1986; I Just Wanna Be Loved, 1998; Your Kisses Are Charity, 1999; Albums: Kissing to be Clever, 1982; Colour By Numbers, 1983; Waking Up With The House On Fire, 1984; From Luxury to Heartache, 1986; Greatest Moments (Live), 1998; Don't Mind If I Do, 1999; Culture Club Box Set, 2002; Also recorded with: Paul Young, Jaki Graham, The Beach Boys.

HAYDEN, Joe; b. 25 Dec. 1972, Louisville, Kentucky, USA. Recording Engineer; Prod. *Education:* Conservatory of Recording Arts and Sciences, Phoenix, Arizona, USA. *Career:* Produced many acts in Nashville, Tennessee; Engineer, numerous recording sessions, music of all types including rock, country, jazz, bluegrass, latin, orchestral. *Recordings:* Engineer, Heaven'z Movie by Bizzy Bone, and for Bruce Robison, Victor Wooten, Members of Phish, Robbie Fulks; Jimmy Buffett. *Address:* 1720 Timber Ridge Rd 164, Austin, TX 78741, USA.

HAYES, Darren Stanley; b. 8 May 1972, Brisbane, Australia. Vocalist; Songwriter. m. Colby Taylor, divorced. *Education:* Kelvin Grove University, Australia. *Career:* Played in Red Edge until breaking away with fellow group mem., Daniel Jones, to form Savage Garden, 1996; Successful world-wide; Live performances include closing ceremony of Olympic Games, Sydney, 2000; Savage Garden split, 2001; Solo career, 2001–. *Recordings:* Albums: with Savage Garden: Savage Garden, 1997; Affirmation, 1999; Solo: Spin, 2002.

Singles: with Savage Garden: I Want You, 1996; To The Moon and Back, 1996; Truly Madly Deeply (No. 1, UK), 1997; Break Me Shake Me, 1997; Universe, 1997; The Animal Song, 1999; I Knew I Loved You (No. 1, UK), 1999; Affirmation, 2000; Crash and Burn, 2000; Chained To You, 2000; Hold Me, 2001; Solo: Insatiable, 2001. *Honours:* First LP sales of over 11m.; ARIA Awards, won a record 10 awards, 1997; APRA Award, Songwriters of the Year, 2000; Truly Madly Deeply set new record for longest stay on Billboard Adult Contemporary Airplay Chart (106 weeks), 2000. *Current Management:* Leonie Messer. *Address:* c/o Roadshow Music, Australia. *Website:* www.darrenhayes.com.

HAYES, Isaac; b. 20 Aug. 1942, Covington, Tennessee, USA. Vocalist; Arranger; Musician (keyboards, organ). 11 c. *Career:* Leader, various groups; In-house keyboard player, staff songwriter (with David Porter) for Sam and Dave, Stax Records, 1964; Leader, arranger, Isaac Hayes Movement; Television actor, including Soul Survivors, BBC, 1995; Rockford Files; Voice featured on South Park animation, Comedy Central, 1997–. *Compositions include:* Film scores: Shaft; Truck Turner; Tough Guys; As co-writer with David Porter: Hold On I'm Coming, Sam and Dave; Soul Man, Sam and Dave; B.A.B.Y., Carla Thomas; I Had A Dream, Johnnie Taylor. *Recordings:* Presenting Isaac Hayes, 1967; Hot Buttered Soul, 1969; The Isaac Hayes Movement, 1970; To Be Continued, 1971; Shaft, 1971; Black Moses, 1971; Joy, 1973; Live At The Sahara Tahoe, 1973; Tough Guys, 1974; Truck Turner, 1974; Chocolate Chip, 1975; Use Me, 1975; Disco Connection, 1976; Groove-A-Thon, 1976; Juicy Fruit, 1976; New Horizon, 1977; Man and A Woman, with Dionne Warwick, 1977; New Horizon, 1977; Memphis Movement, 1977; For The Sake of Love, 1978; Don't Let Go, 1978; Royal Rappin', with Millie Jackson, 1980; And Once Again, 1980; Light My Fire, 1980; A Lifetime Thing, 1981; U Turn, 1986; Isaacs Moods, 1988; Love Attack, 1988; Branded, 1995; Raw and Refined, 1995; Thanks to the Fool, 1995; Fragile, 1995; Simultaneous, 1999; The Man (compilation), 2001; Hit singles include: Walk On By, 1969; By The Time I Get To Phoenix, 1969; I Stand Accused, 1970; The Look of Love, 1971; Never Can Say Goodbye, 1971; Theme From Shaft (No. 1, USA), 1971; Do Your Thing, 1972; Theme From The Men, 1972; Joy, 1973; Wonderful, 1974; Disco Connection, 1976; Don't Let Go, 1979; Chocolate Salty Balls (No. 1, UK), 1998. *Honours:* Academy Award, Best Original Score, Shaft, 1972; Platinum disc, Hot Buttered Soul. *Current Management:* Ron Moss Management, 2635 Griffith Park Blvd, Los Angeles, CA 980039, USA.

HAYES, (Tony) Wade; b. 20 April 1969, Bethel Acres, Oklahoma, USA. Country vocalist. *Career:* Began playing music, initially on mandolin but switching to guitar, age 11; Sang backing vocals in father's band Country Heritage; Dropped out of school to pursue music career, returning to Nashville; Played guitar on demos and wrote songs with producer Chick Rains, who organized audition with Columbia's A&R director Don Cook Hayes; Signed to Columbia Records and Tree publishing; Made progress throughout 1990s and into 2000s, charting regularly and touring extensively with own road band Wheel Hoss. *Compositions include:* I'm Still Dancin' With You; Old Enough To Know Better. *Recordings include:* Old Enough To Know Better, 1994; I'm Still Dancin' With You, Don't Stop, What I Meant To Say, 1995; On A Good Night, 1996; The Day That She Left Tulsa (In A Chevy), 1997; Albums: Old Enough To Know Better, 1995; On A Good Night, 1996; When The Wrong One Loves You Right, 1998; Highways and Heartaches, 2000. *Honours:* various including: ACM, Top New Male Vocalist, 1995; TNN/Music City News, Male Star of Tomorrow, 1997. *Current Management:* Mike Robertson Management, 1227 17th Ave S, Second Floor, Nashville, TN 37212, USA.

HAYMES, Jerry; b. 30 Aug. 1940, Vernon, Texas, USA. Musician (drums, guitar); Vocalist; Actor; Speaker. m. (1) Brenda D, 1 Aug. 1961, 1 s., 1 d.; (2) Joan New, 1 Jan. 1987. *Education:* BSc, Abilene Christian University; Kilgore College Police Academy; Associate Music, Southern Methodist University. *Career:* World tours; Performed with Hometown USA Show, World Trade Fair, Berlin, 1961 (first Country show to do so); Performed in Russia at Russian Embassy's request; Armed Forces Radio; Television personality, newsman; Original member, Sun Records Legends Group; Session musician, many hits, various labels. *Recordings:* Major hits: Rose Marie; Smile of a Clown; Big Big World; Marry Me; So Fine (Caroline); Let's Have A Party; Party Doll; What Then (gospel hit for Mahalia Jackson). *Publications:* Southwest Conference Baseball Umpire. *Honours:* Male vocalist, Bandleader, Video commercial, Gospel Music Asscn Songwriter Awards. *Membership:* AFofM; President, Texas Art and Entertainment Council. *Current Management:* Umpire Entertainment Enterprises.

HAYNE, Michael (Shane); b. 22 Nov. 1937, Plymouth, England. Vocalist. m. Heather Anne Tarry, 26 June 1971, 1 s., 1 d. *Education:* Warren's College, Plymouth. *Career:* Lead vocalist, R&B band The Betterdays, 1963–66; Television appearances: Westward TV; TSW; Radio: BBC Plymouth; BBC Radio Devon; Plymouth Sound; Tours throughout UK, 1991–. *Recordings:* Here Tis; Cracking Up; Aw Shucks; Hush Your Mouth; Don't Want That; Honey What's Wrong; (all 1964–65); EPs: Howl of The Streets, 1991; Down On The Waterfront, 1992; Here Tis, 1992; No Concessions, 1993; Also featured on compilation albums, Australia, France, USA. *Current Management:* Mike

Weston. *Address:* 4 Ashburnham Rd, West Park, Plymouth PL5 2LR, England.

HAYNES, Kevin; b. 5 Feb. 1965, Paddington, London, England. Musician (saxophone, percussion). 1 s. *Education:* North London College of Performing Arts, 1984–85; Theory, Kingsway College, 1986–87. *Career:* Concerts: Tours, Oshmare Brazilian Theatre and Dance Companies; Tours with: Steve Williamson, UK; Courtney Pine, UK, Israel, 1990; Own group, British tour, 1994; Radio: BBC Radio 3 and 4 (Kaleidoscope). *Recordings:* Albums: Ed Jones: The Home Coming, 1988; Steve Williamson: Waltz For Grace, 1989; with Courtney Pine: Bath Jazz Festival, 1993; Kevin Haynes Group: Eleggra, 1994; Recording track for Bachology, 1995. *Membership:* Musicians' Union. *Current Management:* Fish Krish.

HAYNES, Warren Dale; b. 6 April 1960, Ashville, North Carolina, USA. Vocalist; Songwriter; Musician (guitar, slide guitar); Prod. *Career:* David Allan Coe, 1980–84; Studio musician, 1984–87; Dickey Betts Band, 1987–89; Allman Bros Band, 1989–; Currently solo artist, member of Government Mule, 1994–; World-wide tours: Johnny Carson; Jay Lane; Conan O'Brian; David Letterman. *Compositions:* (co-writer), Two of a Kind (Workin' On A Full House) for Garth Brooks; True Gravity; A Kind of a Bird. *Recordings:* Allman Bros Band albums: Seven Turns; Shades of Two Worlds; An Evening With... ; Where It All Begins; Second Set; Solo album: Tales of Ordinary Madness; Also appears on: Language, with Richard Leo Johnson, 2000. *Honours:* Allman Bros Band inducted into R&R Hall of Fame, 1995. *Membership:* AFTRA; AFofM; BMI. *Current Management:* Doc Field, Creative Action Music. *Address:* 865 Bellevue Rd, Suite E-12, Nashville, TN 37221, USA.

HAYWARD, (David) Justin; b. 14 Oct. 1946, Swindon, Wiltshire, England. Vocalist; Musician (guitar). *Career:* Member, The Offbeats; Marty Wilde trio; Singer, The Moody Blues, 1967–74; 1978–; Appearances include: Isle of Wight Festival, 1969; Royal Albert Hall, 1969; Royal Festival Hall, London, 1970; Carnegie Hall, New York, 1970; Opened own recording studio, London, 1974; Solo recording career, 1974–. *Recordings:* Singles include; (own composition) Nights In White Satin, 1968; Question (No. 2, UK), 1970; Isn't Life Strange, 1972; I'm Just A Singer (In A Rock 'n' Roll Band), 1973; Gemini Dream, 1981; The Voice, 1981; Your Wildest Dreams, 1986; Solo: Forever Autumn, 1978; It Won't Be Easy, 1987; Albums: with the Moody Blues: Days of Future Passed, 1967; In Search of The Lost Chord, 1968; On The Threshold of a Dream (No. 1, UK), 1969; To Our Children's Children's Children, 1969; Caught Live + 5, 1969; A Question of Balance (No. 1, UK), 1970; Every Good Boy Deserves Favour (No. 1, UK), 1971; Seventh Sojourn (No. 1, USA), 1972; This Is The Moody Blues, 1974; Octave, 1978; Out of This World, 1979; Long Distance Voyager (No. 1, USA), 1981; The Present, 1983; Voices In The Sky, 1985; The Other Side of Life, 1986; Sur La Mer, 1988; Keys of The Kingdom, 1991; Live At Red Rock, 1993; Strange Times, 1999; Live At The Royal Albert Hall, 2000; Journey Into Amazing Caves, 2001; Solo albums: Blue Jays, with John Lodge, 1975; Songwriter, 1977; Night Flight, 1980; Moving Mountains, 1985; Classic Blue, 1989; View from the Hill, 1996; Contributor, War of The Worlds, Jeff Wayne, 1978. *Honours:* Ivor Novello Award, Outstanding Contribution to British Music (with the Moody Blues), 1985. *Address:* c/o Bright Music Ltd, 2 Harwood Terrace, London SW6 2AB, England.

HAZELL, Patrick James; b. 23 Sept. 1945, Burlington, Iowa, USA. Musician (piano, organ, harmonica, drums); Vocalist; Songwriter. m. Pamela Ann Cummings, 28 Oct. 1967, 3 s., 1 d. *Education:* College Degree; College classes, recording techniques. *Career:* Professional musician, 1960–; Founder, Mother Blues Band, 1968–70; Founder, Sound Pool, 1972; Member, Rocket 88's; Re-formed Mother Blues Band, 1973–83, 1997–; Solo performer, 1983–; Music instructor, Washington High School, 1987–95; Numerous tours, Midwest USA, Europe, Paraguay; Concerts supporting: Led Zeppelin; Jefferson Airplane; John Mayall; Robert Cray; Muddy Waters; John Lee Hooker; George Thorogood; Suzy Bogguss; Luther Allison; Asleep At The Wheel; Junior Walker. *Recordings:* Albums include Band Music, Vol. 1, 1975; Vol. 2, 1978; Vol. 3, 1980; Vicksburg Vol. 1, 1981; Vol. 2, 1981; Christmas Visions, 1982; Studios Solos, 1985; The New Cool, 1986; Solo Improvisations, 1986; Patrick Hazell-Live!, 1987; Blues Jam, 1988; East of Midnight, 1989; Nemo's Island, 1989; Mystery Winds, 1989; Santa Was Eating The Christmas Tree/Nicci and The Project, 1989; Tuba and Piano Jam Session, 1990; Blues on the Run, 1995; Patrick Hazell and the Mother Blues Band, 1975–80, 1996; In The Prairieland, 1996; Dreamcatcher, 1996; Blue Blood, 1997; Soundtracks, 1997; Cityscape Precipice, 1997. *Honours:* 4 Prairie Sun Awards, Best Rhythm and Blues Band. *Membership:* Arts Midwest; Iowa Arts Council; Touring Arts Team of Iowa; Official endorsee, Hohner Harmonicas. *Address:* 220 E 17th St, Washington, IA 52353, USA. *Website:* www.patrickhazell.com.

HEALEY, Jeff; b. 25 March 1966, Toronto, Ontario, Canada. Blues/Rock Musician (guitar, multi-instrumentalist); Vocalist; Songwriter; Actor. *Career:* Blind since age 1; Founder, Blue Direction aged 15, Toronto; Played with Albert Collins; Stevie Ray Vaughan; Founder, Jeff Healey Band, 1985; Own record label, Forte, 1985–88; World tour, 1990; Actor, singer, film Roadhouse, 1989. *Recordings:* Singles: Confidence Man, 1988; Angel Eyes, 1989; Full

Circle, 1990; Cruel Little Number, 1992; Stuck In The Middle With You, 1995; Albums: See The Light, 1989; Hell To Pay, 1990; Feel This, 1992; Cover To Cover, 1995; The Very Best of Jeff Healey, 1998; The Master Hits, 1999; Featured on film soundtrack, Roadhouse, 1989. *Address:* c/o Forte Records and Productions, 320 Spadina Rd, Toronto, ON M5R 2V6, Canada.

HEALY, Francis; b. 23 July 1973, Scotland. Vocalist; Musician (guitar). *Career:* Mem., Travis, 1997–; Numerous tours, festivals and television appearances. *Recordings:* Albums: Good Feeling, 1997; The Man Who (No. 1, UK), 1999; The Invisible Band (No. 1, UK), 2001. Singles: U16 Girls, 1997; All I Want To Do Is Rock, 1997; Tied To The Nineties, 1997; Happy, 1997; More Than Us, 1997; Writing To Reach You, 1999; Driftwood, 1999; Why Does It Always Rain on Me?, 1999; Turn, 1999; Coming Around, 2000; Sing, 2001; Side, 2001. *Honours:* Q Magazine Award, Best Single, 1999; Select Magazine, Album of the Year, 1999; BRIT Awards, Best British Group, Best British Album, 2000, Best British Group, 2002. *Address:* Independiente Ltd, The Drill Hall, 3 Heathfield Terrace, London W4 4JE, England. *Website:* www.travisonline.com.

HEALY, Jeremy; b. 18 Jan. 1962, Woolwich, London, England. DJ; Prod. *Career:* Formed band Haysi Fantayzee with Kate Garner; 2 hits world-wide; Became scratching-mixing DJ. *Recordings:* Albums: Mixmag Live, 1995; House Collection Vol. 4, 1996; British Anthems, 1998; Ibiza The Closing Party, 1999; Singles: Stamp, 1996; Argentina, 1997; Other recordings: with Haysi Fantayzee: John Wayne Is Big Leggy, 1982, Shiny Shiny, 1983; Sabres of Paradise; Everything Starts With An 'E', E-Zee Possee, 1989. *Honours:* Gold album, Haysi Fantayzee; Silver single, John Wayne Is Big Leggy; DJ of the Year, Mixmag, 1995; Most Popular Face, 1995. *Membership:* PRS. *Current Management:* Francesca Cutler, Selective Management. *Address:* 6 Brewer St, London W1R 3FR, England.

HEARD, Paul; b. 5 Oct. 1960, London, England. Musician (keyboards, programming). *Career:* Former Member, Orange Juice; Joined M People, 1990; Numerous live dates and television appearances; Song, Search for the Hero used in TV advertisement. *Recordings:* Singles: How Can I Love You More, 1991; Colour My Life, 1991; Padlock, 1992; Excited, 1992; One Night in Heaven, 1993; Moving on Up (No. 2, UK), 1993; Don't Look Any Further, 1993; Renaissance, 1994; Sight For Sore Eyes, 1994; Open Your Heart, 1995; Search for the Hero, 1995; Love Rendezvous, 1995; Itchycoo Park, 1995; Just for You, 1997; Fantasy Island, 1997; Angel St, 1998; Testify, 1998; Dreaming, 1999; Albums: Northern Soul, 1992; Elegant Slumming, 1993; Love Rendezvous, 1995; Bizarre Fruit, 1994; Fresco, 1997. *Honours:* BRIT Award, Best Dance Band, 1992; Mercury Music Prize, 1993.

HEARN, Martin Peter; b. 3 Dec. 1955, London, England. Musician (drum, percussion); Teacher. m. Noelle Loyd, 16 Aug. 1986, 4 s. *Education:* National Youth Jazz Association. *Career:* Worked with: The Drifters; David Soul; Joe Longthorne; Ben E King; Tommy Cooper; Cilla Black; Michael Barrymore; Bob Monkhouse; Joe Longthorne; John Paul James; National Youth Jazz Orchestra; London West End Shows: Cats; Evita; Me and My Girl; Rocky Horror Show; NYSO; North Sea Festival; Montrose Jazz Festival; Pebble Mill; Sunday Sunday; Founder of STIX School of Rhythm, Music school for the rhythm section of modern music, working bands, 1994. *Honours:* Rock and Roll Hall of Fame, with the Drifters, 1985. *Membership:* National Youth Jazz Assocn; NYSO; Musicians' Union; Chamber of Commerce and Trade. *Current Management:* STIX School of Rhythm, Noëlle Hearn. *Address:* STIX School of Rhythm, Kings Arm Yard, Church St, Ampthill, Bedfordshire MK45 2PJ, England.

HEATH, Martin; b. 12 March 1961, Sussex, England. Record Co Exec. *Education:* BA Hons. *Career:* Managing Director, UK-based indie record label, Rhythm King Records, co-founded with Adele Nozedar, 1986; Founder, Renegade Software and Perfect World Programmes. *Address:* c/o Rhythm King Records, 121 Salisbury Rd, London NW6 6RG, England.

HEATH, Rohan Vernon; b. 19 July 1964, Wembley, London, England. Songwriter; Musician (keyboards). *Education:* BSc, Biology; MSc, Entomology; Grade IX Piano, Victoria College of Music. *Career:* Keyboards, A Guy Called Gerald, 1990–91; Keyboards, Together, 1991–92; Keyboards, Eek A Mouse, 1992–93; Leader, Urban Cookie Collective, 1993–; Tours include: USA, Canada, Australia, Japan, Singapore, UK, Europe, Israel, Lithuania, Turkey. *Compositions:* co-wrote: Automatik, A Guy Called Gerald. *Recordings:* Urban Cookie Collective singles: The Key The Secret (No. 2, UK), 1993; Spend the Day; Feels Like Heaven; Sail Away; High On A Happy Vibe; Tales from the Magic Fountain; Bring It On Home; Reggae Summer Splash; Compilation: Very Best of The Urban Cookie Collective, 2000. *Publications:* The Phylogenetic Significance of The Ventral Nervous Chord In Carabid Beetles, Journal of Entomology. *Honours:* Platinum and Gold discs; Music Week Independent Single, 1994; Perfect 10 Award, Best Live Act, Singapore, 1994. *Address:* c/o Blitz, Edgwarebury Farm, Edgwarebury Lane, Edgware HA8 8QX, England.

HEATLIE, Bob; b. 20 July 1946, Edinburgh, Scotland. Musician (keyboards, saxophone, flute). m. Mary Jane Davie, 3 March 1967, 3 s. *Education:* Taught by father, Thomas Heatlie. *Recordings:* Aneka: Japanese Boy, No. 1; Merry Christmas Everyone, No. 1; Cry Just A Little Bit; Many television theme tunes. *Honours:* 8 Gold discs (singles); 1 Silver and 1 Platinum (albums); 2 ASCAP Awards. *Membership:* MCPS; PRS; BAC&S. *Address:* 3 Victoria St, Edinburgh EH1 2HE, Scotland.

HEATON, Mike; b. 18 Sept. 1968, *Career:* Member, Embrace; Obtained major label deals in UK and USA, 1996; Released debut single independently; Support slot in tour with Manic Street Preachers, 1997; Headline tours and TV appearances. *Recordings:* Albums: The Good Will Out, 1998; Drawn From Memory, 2000; If You've Never Been, 2001; Fireworks (Singles 1997–2002), 2002. Singles: Fireworks, 1997; One Big Family, 1997; All You Good Good People, 1997; Come Back To What You Know, 1998; My Weakness Is None of Your Business, 1998; Hooligan, 1999; You're Not Alone, 2000; Save Me, 2000; I Wouldn't Wanna Happen To You, 2000; Wonder, 2001.

HEATON, Paul David, (Biscuit Boy); b. 9 May 1962, Birkenhead, Merseyside, England. Vocalist; Songwriter; Musician. *Career:* Lead singer, The Housemartins, 1983–88; Had six Top 20 hits; Founder mem., The Beautiful South, 1988–; 11 Top 40 singles; Five Top 5 albums; Concerts include: T In The Park Festival, Glasgow, 1995; McAlpine Stadium, Crystal Palace Stadium, 1997. *Recordings:* Albums: with the Housemartins: London 0 Hull 4, 1986; The People Who Grinned Themselves To Death, 1987; Now That's What I Call Quite Good, 1988; with The Beautiful South: Welcome To The Beautiful South, 1989; Choke, 1990; 0898, 1992; Miaow, 1994; Carry On Up The Charts (No. 1, UK), 1994; Blue Is The Colour, (No 1, UK), 1996; Quench, 1998; Painting It Red, 2000; Solid Bronze (compilation), 2001; Solo, as Biscuit Boy: Fat Chance, 2001. Singles: with the Housemartins: Flag Day, 1985; Sheep, 1986; Happy Hour, 1986; Think For A Minute, 1986; Caravan of Love (No. 1, UK), 1986; Five Get Over Excited, 1987; Me And The Farmer, 1987; Build, 1987; There's Always Something There To Remind Me, 1988; with The Beautiful South: Song For Whoever, 1989; I'll Sail This Ship Alone, 1989; You Keep It All In, 1989; A Little Time (No. 1, UK), 1990; My Book, 1990; Let Love Speak Up Itself, 1991; Old Red Eyes Is Back, 1992; We Are Each Other, 1992; Bell-Bottomed Tear, 1992 Good As Gold, 1994; Everybody's Talkin', 1994; Prettiest Eyes, 1994; One Last Love Song, 1994; Pretenders To The Throne, 1995; Rotterdam, 1996; Don't Marry Her, 1996; Blackbird on the Wire, 1997; Liars Bar, 1997; Perfect 10, 1998; Dumb, 1998; How Long's A Tear Take to Dry?, 1999; The River, 2000; Solo, as Biscuit Boy: Mitch, 2001. *Contributions to:* Introduction to Blades Business Crew, by Steve Cowans. *Honours:* BPI Awards: Best Newcomers, the Housemartins, 1987; Best Video, A Little Time, The Beautiful South, 1991. *Address:* The Beautiful South, PO Box 87, Hull, East Yorkshire HU5 2NR, England. *Website:* www.beautifulsouth.co.uk; www.biscuitboy.co.uk.

HECKARD, Gary Davis; b. 15 March 1974, Los Angeles, USA. Composer; Improvisor. *Education:* EdM, Teachers' College Columbia University; Manhattan School of Music, BM, Berklee College of Music. *Career:* Composer in Residence, the Greenwich Village Orchestra; Member, Grussner Band, Toured World-wide, Radio Broadcasts on National Radios. *Compositions include:* Triple Concerto for Jazz Orchestra, 1995; Three Months in Rotterdam, 1996; Two Pages in the New City, 1997; Continuation, 1 997;... Fore, 1998; Untitled, 1998; Recollection, 1999. *Recordings:* Gary Davis Heckar – Improvisations. *Membership:* Compose NY; The American Music Center; BMI; BMI Classical.

HECTOR, Kevin Jon; b. 17 Jan. 1967, Nantwich, Cheshire, England. Prod; Musician (guitar); Electronic artiste. *Education:* Fashion, St Martins; Classical singing; Jazz/classical guitar. *Career:* Session guitarist, 1983–87; London Club DJ, 1988–; Dance producer, 1990–; Autocreation world tour, 1993; Including live broadcast on Japan TV. *Compositions:* Miscellaneous dance compositions. *Recordings:* Mettle, Autocreation. *Address:* PO Box 3605, London NW8 0DD, England.

HEDEGAARD, Svend; b. 19 Dec. 1959, Sonderborg, Denmark. Musician; Composer. *Education:* Private studies and several seminars in composition; Guitar and piano lessons. *Career:* Guitarist, numerous rock, fusion and jazz bands, 1979–98; Composer, 15 theatre plays, 6 television productions, several major works for different classical ensembles and orchestras in Denmark, 1986–98; Wind O Four, jazz fusion quartet, 1991–. *Compositions:* Maximal/Minimal, 1991; Some Colours Remain, Some Remind, 1991; Twins Turn, 1996; Efter regnen sas..., 1996; Sangenes Sang, 1997; Via, 1998. *Recordings:* With Wind O Four, Jazz Quartet, 1995, Voices, 1997. *Honours:* Laurens Bogtman Fondens Haederslegat, 1996; DJBFA, Arbejdslegat, 1997. *Membership:* Danish Musicians' Union; Danish Jazz, Beat and Folk Music Composers; KODA. *Address:* Romersgade 23 2 tv, 1362 Copenhagen K, Denmark.

HEDGES, Mike; Record Prod. *Career:* Engineer, Morgan Studios, late 1970s–80s; Founder, Playground Studio, 1980s; Converted Chateau Rouge Motte, Normandy, into full residential studio, 1990; Moved to Wessex Studio, London, 2002. *Recordings:* Producer, albums include: with Siouxie and The Banshees: Kiss In A Dreamhouse; Hyena; Peep Show; Nocturne; Through The Looking Glass; with Marc Almond: Vermine In Ermine; Stories of Johnny; A

Woman's Story; Mother Fist; Virgin's Tale No. 2; with The Beautiful South: Welcome To The Beautiful South; Choke; with The Cure: Three Imaginary Boys; Seventeen Seconds; Faith; Split; Lush; with McAlmont and Butler: Yes; Sound of McAlmont and Butler; with Manic Street Preachers: Everything Must Go, 1996; This is My Truth, 1999; Know Your Enemy, 2001; Also: Baby The Stars Shine Bright, Everything But The Girl; Drop, The Shamen; Mask, Bauhaus; Songs of Strength and Heartbreak, Mighty Wah!, 2000; with U2: Best of 1990–2000, 2000; Lene Martin, 2003; Also singles with Wah!; Bauhaus; The Cure; Siouxie and The Banshees; The Creatures; Marc Almond; Everything But The Girl; The Beautiful South; U2; Cooper Temple Clause; a1; Darius. *Current Management:* Jessica Norbury, 3Khz Management, 54 Pentney Rd, London SW12 0NY, England. *E-mail:* threekhz@hotmail.com.

HEIL, Gail A; b. 20 Aug. 1945, St Louis, MO, USA. Musician (fiddle, banjo, guitar, autoharp); Vocalist. m. Bob Bovee. *Education:* University of Missouri. *Career:* Regular Tours of USA, 1981–; Iowa Public Television; River City Folk; Rural Route 3; Other Syndicated Radio Shows; Festival of American Fiddle Tunes. *Recordings:* For Old Times Sake, 1985; Behind The Times, 1986; Come All You Waddies, 1988; Come Over and See Me, 1991; Rural Route 2, 1996; Master Fiddler For Iowa State Folk Arts Apprenticeship Program and Minnesota State Folk Arts Apprenticeship Program. *Address:* Rt 2 Box 25, Spring Grove, MN 55974, USA.

HEINILA, Kari Juhani; b. 31 Oct. 1966, Kiukainen, Finland. m. Arja Mäkelä, 2 s., 1 d. *Education:* Classical Piano and Flute in Music School, Saxophone and Improvisation in Sibelius Academy's Jazz Department, 1984–88; Private composing studies, 1993–95. *Career:* Saxophonist, Umo Jazz Orchestra, 1987–93; Jazz Groups under own name, 1987–; Recordings and concerts with the top names in Finnish Jazz; Performing with such internationally respected Jazz artistes as Billy Hart, Tim Hagans, Vince Mendoza, Anders Jormin and Wayne Krantz; Active Composer in contemporary jazz scene; Regular Teacher, Sibelius Academy's Jazz Department, 1993–. *Compositions:* Frozen Petals; Blue in the Distance; Crossings; Wavestar. *Recordings:* Espoo Big Band: Grand Mystery; Jarmo Savolainen: Blue Dreams, True Image; Edward Vesala: Lumi; Umo Jazz Orchestra: Selected Standards; Pekka Luukka, Splash of Colors; Jukka Linkola, The Tentet; Sonny Heinla, Tribus. *Honours:* BAT-Finland Composition Prize, 1992; Pori Jazz Festival's Artist of the Year Prize, 1995. *Address:* Hannuksenkuja 4A3, 02270 Espoo, Finland.

HELFER, Erwin; b. 20 Jan. 1936, Chicago, Illinois, USA. Blues and Jazz Musician (piano); Piano teacher. *Education:* Mus B American Conservatory of Music; Mus M, Northeastern Illinois University. *Career:* Annual performances at Chicago Blues Festival; Annual concert tours, Europe, Rolf Schubert Concertburo, Cologne, Germany; Plays in local jazz and blues clubs, Chicago; College tours, USA; Recording artiste for Flying Fish; Steeple Chase; Red Beans; CMA. *Recordings:* Erwin Helfer and Friends On The Sunny Side of The Street, 1979; Erwin Helfer Plays Chicago Piano, 1986; Appears on: Voice of Blues, Angela Brown, 2000. *Honours:* Critics Choice Award, Maybe I'll Cry, Downbeat Magazine, 1983; Illinois Arts Council Grant, 1986. *Current Management:* Erwin Helfer, 2240 N Magnolia, Chicago, IL 60614, USA.

HELLER, Jana Louise Greenberg; b. 18 July 1948, California, USA. Vocalist; Songwriter; Musician (guitar, dulcimer, piano, celestaphone). m. A Gilhooley, 1999. *Education:* Stephens College, Missouri, University of Southern California, USA; UCLA, Santa Monica City College; 8 years piano. *Career:* Solo work; Bands: AAAHS; The Phantoms; Concerts; folk music festivals: UK; USA; Poland; Radio: KPFK's Folkscene, Los Angeles, USA; Kroc, USA; Radio Poznan, Poland; BBC Radio II (We Stayed In With Jungr and Parker); GLR Radio; London Talkback Radio; BBC Radio Essex Folkscene; Kazu Radio, USA; Brian Willoughby's All Stars. *Recordings:* Mad Waltzing, 1986; Twist and Turn, 1990; Laughing In Crime, 1995. *Honours:* American Song Festival, winner lyric division. *Membership:* Musicians' Union; PRS. *Current Management:* Mr Squashy Agency. *Address:* 2 Friars Close, Wilmslow, Cheshire SK9 5PP, England. *E-mail:* info@janaheller.com. *Website:* www.janaheller.com.

HELLER, Pete, (Stylus Trouble); b. 1965, London, England. Prod; Remixer; DJ. *Career:* Part of Boy's Own collective; Remixed (with Terry Farley): Ultra Nate, Primal Scream, Janet Jackson, Happy Mondays; Member: Bocca Juniors, Fire Island, Roach Motel; Collaborations: Terry Farley, Andrew Weatherall, Rui Da Silva. *Recordings:* Singles: Raise (with Bocca Juniors), 1990; In Your Bones (with Fire Island), 1992; There But For The Grace of God (with Fire Island), 1994; Ultra Flava, 1995; The Rising Sun (with Terry Farley), 1999; Big Love, 1999; Sputnik One (as Stylus Trouble), 2001. *Current Management:* c/o Junior Recordings, The Saga Centre, 326 Kensal Rd, London W10 5BZ, England.

HELLQUIST, Mats; b. 15 May 1964, Stockholm, Sweden. Musician (bass, guitar). 1 s., 2 d. *Career:* Member, bob hund, 1991; More than 300 gigs around Scandinavia; Played at famous Roskilde, Lollipop, Ruisrock Quartfestivalen and Hultsfred. *Compositions:* I Stället för Musik: Förvirring, 1996, Düsseldorf, 1996. *Recordings:* bob hund, 1993; Edvin medvind, 1994; I stället för musik: Förvirring, 1996; Omslag: Martin Kann, 1996; Düsseldorf, 1996; Ett fall and

en lösning, 1997; Nu är det väl revolution på gång, 1998; Jag rear ut min själ Allt skall bort!!!, 1998; Helgen V, 1999; Sover aldrig, 1999. *Honours:* Grammy, best live act, 1994; Grammy, best lyrics, 1996. *Membership:* STIM; SAMI. *Address:* c/o bob hunds förlag, Råsundavägen 150, 169 36 Solna, Sweden.

HELLRIEGEL, Jan; b. 2 Sept. 1967, Auckland, New Zealand. Musician (piano, guitar); Vocalist; Songwriter; Actor. *Education:* BA, University of Otago; Classical singing and piano; Rock guitar; University papers. *Career:* Four national solo tours, eight with band; TVNZ Music Awards Television and Film Awards, New Zealand, 1993; Big Day Out Concert, supporting David Byrne, The Cure. *Recordings:* Singles: The Way I Feel; Manic Is A State of Mind; Solo albums: It's My Sin, 1993; Tremble, 1995; with Cassandras Ears Band: Private Wasteland (EP), 1990; Your Estimation, 1992 (EP); with Working With Walt: 5 Sides (EP), 1990. *Honours:* Songwriter of the Year, 1993; Most Promising Female Vocalist, 1993. *Current Management:* MGM Management, 9 Dundas Lane, Albert Park, Victoria 3206, Australia.

HELMIS, Dimitrios; b. 11 Jan. 1962, Pireaus, Greece. Promoter; Agent. 1 s. *Career:* Owner, Neo Revma International Ltd, 10 years promoting and booking international and local acts in Greece and Balkan area; Hundreds of shows include: Pink Floyd; Michael Jackson; The Scorpions; Stevie Wonder; Guns N' Roses; Metallica; Philip Glass; Goran Bregovic; Michael Nyman; Neville Brothers. *Address:* Neo Revma International Ltd, 8 Ainanos Str 104–34, Athens, Greece.

HELMS, Mickey; b. 4 Sept. 1972, California, USA. Composer. *Education:* AA, De Anza College, 1992; BM, San Jose State University, 1997. *Career:* Composer. *Compositions:* Whispering Modulations, 1996; Variations On A Theme By Chris Mann, 1996; Music For Tuba and Piano, 1998. *Recordings:* Frog Peak Collaborations Project, 1998; Music From Cream, 1998. *Membership:* BMI; International Computer Music Association; Society of Electro-Acoustic Music in the United States; Society of Composers. *Current Management:* Mickey Helms. *Address:* 244 Corral Ave, Sunnyvale, CA 94086, USA.

HELSON, Robert (Bob); b. 20 Aug. 1949, Bristol, England. Music (drums, percussion). *Education:* Drum lessons with Geoff Smith, 1966–69. *Career:* Drummer with: Plasma, early 1970s; Bullit, 1974–90; Appearances with Bullit include: Bracknell Festival, 1986; Le Mans Jazz Festival, 1987; Will Menter's Wind and Fingers, appearing at Bristol Arnolfini and Dunkirk Jazz Festival, 1976; Both Hands Free, 1976–82; Community, appearing at Palais de Beaux Arts, Brussels and Arnolfini, 1980–81; Out Loud, 1984–87; Keith Tippett's Canoe, 1984–85; Dance and percussion duet with dancer Beppie Blankert, Bristol Arnolfini, 1981; Broadcasts on BBC Radio 3, Jazz In Britain, with: Both Hands Free, 1979; Steve Mulligan Quartet, 1983, 1984; Out Loud, 1986; Bullit, 1987. *Recordings:* with Both Hands Free: Use From The Pocket, 1978; Solo percussion improvisations: Noise Reduction, 1979; Will Menter's Community, 1981. *Address:* Basement Flat, 34 Cornwallis Cres., Clifton, Bristol BS8 4PH, England.

HEMINGWAY, Dave; b. 20 Sept. 1960, Hull, England. Vocalist. *Career:* Former Member, The Housemartins, 1987–88; Founder member, The Beautiful South, 1988; Numerous TV appearances and tours; Festival appearances. *Recordings:* with The Housemartins: Singles: Five Get Over Excited, 1987; Me and The Farmer, 1987; Build, 1987; There's Always Something There To Remind Me, 1988; Albums: The People Who Grinned Themselves To Death, 1987; Now That's What I Call Quite Good, 1988; with The Beautiful South: Singles: Song For Whoever, 1989; You Keep It All In, 1989; My Book EP, 1991; One Last Love Song, 1992; Prettiest Eyes, 1994; Everybody's Talking, 1994; Rotterdam (Or Anywhere); Don't Marry Her, 1996; Liar's Bar, 1997; Perfect 10, 1998; Dumb, 1999; The River, 2000; Albums: Welcome To the Beautiful South, 1989; Choke, 1990; 0898, 1992; Miaow, 1994; Carry On Up The Charts, 1994; Blue is The Colour, 1996; Quench, 1998; Painting It Red, 2000; Solid Bronze (compilation), 2001. *Address:* The Beautiful South, PO Box 87, Hull, East Yorkshire HU5 2NR, England. *Website:* www.beautifulsouth.co.uk.

HEMMINGS, Paul; b. 24 May 1963, Liverpool, England. Musician (guitar, lap steel, mandolin). *Education:* BA, History and Politics, North Staffs Polytechnic. *Career:* Guitarist with the La's, 1986–87; Guitarist with The Onset, The Australians, Sensurround, 1988–93; Guitarist, Lightning Seeds, 1994–; Tours: UK; Europe; USA; Various radio sessions; Television appearances include: Danny Baker Show; Music Box; What's Up Doc; Top of the Pops; German TV. *Compositions:* Co-writer, Saddest Song; Shake, Shake, Shake. *Recordings:* Albums: Pool of Life, The Onset, 1988; Timeless Melody, The La's, 1990; Electric Mothers of Invention, Neuro # Project, 1993; Pool of Life Revisited, The Onset, 1994; Other recordings: Way Out (EP), The La's, 1987; What You Say (EP), The Onset, 1990; When I Get To Heaven (single), Sensurround, 1993; Lucky You (live single), Lightning Seeds, 1994; With Lightning Seeds, What If; Here Today (live version); Three Lions 98, with Lightning Seeds, with Skinner and Baddiel; Hillsborough Justice Concert, 3 live tracks with Lightning Seeds and Holly Johnson. *Honours:* BRIT Awards, 2 consecutive years. *Membership:* Musicians' Union; PRS. *Address:* Woodcroft, Beaconsfield Rd, Liverpool L25 6EJ, England.

HENDERSON, Hamish Scott; b. 11 Nov. 1919, Blairgowrie, Perthshire, Scotland. Poet; Songwriter. m. Felicity Schmidt, 16 May 1959, 2 d. *Education:* Downing College, Cambridge; Musical tuition with traditional singers, Perthshire and Aberdeenshire. *Career:* Collection of soldiers songs in WWII, published in Ballads of World War II, 1947; Collection of North-East Scottish folk songs with Alan Lomax, 1951; Joined School of Scottish Studies, Edinburgh University, 1952; Collection of Gaelic and Lowland Scottish Songs and Tales. *Compositions:* Numerous songs popular with Scottish folk revival include: The Freedom Come-All-Ye; The 51st Highland Division's Farewell To Sicily; The Gillie More; The Men of Knoydart. *Recordings:* Album: Freedom Come-All-Ye. *Publications:* Elegies For The Dead In Cyrenaica, 1948; Alias MacAlias, essays on folklore, 1992; The Armstrong Nose, selected letters, 1996; Gramsci's Prison Letters, 1996. *Honours:* Somerset Maugham Award, 1949. *Membership:* Hon. Mem., Saltire Society, Edinburgh; Hon. Mem., Folklore Fellows, Helsinki; Hon. Fellow, School of Scottish Studies.

HENDERSON, Scott; b. 26 Aug. 1954, West Palm Beach, Florida, USA. Composer; Musician (guitar). *Education:* Florida Atlantic University, 1 year Musicians Institute. *Career:* Touring, recording, 1981–; 3 years with Jean-Luc Ponty; 1 year, Chick Corea; 4 years, Joe Zawinul; 10 years, Tribal Tech (co-led, Gary Willis). *Recordings:* Albums: with Tribal Tech: Spears; Dr Hee; Nomad; Tribal Tech; Illicit; Face First; Reality Check; Dog Party; Primal Tracks; Giddy Up Go; Tore Down House; Vital Tech Tones; Thick; with Joe Zawinul: The Immigrants; Black Water; with Chick Corea: Elektrik Band; Solo: Thick, 1999. *Publications:* The Scott Henderson Guitar Book. *Honours:* Best Jazz Guitarist, Guitar World magazine, 1990; Guitar Player magazine, 1991; Best Blues Album, Dog Party, Guitar Player magazine, 1994. *Address:* 6044 Buena Vista, Los Angeles, CA 90042, USA.

HENDRICKS, Jon; b. 16 Sept. 1921, Newark, Ohio, USA. Vocalist; Lyricist. *Education:* Studied Law. *Career:* Sang on local radio in Toledo; After serving in military during WWII, switching to jazz playing drums and writing songs; Composition I Want You To Be My Baby recorded by Louis Jordan, 1952; Made own first recordings in 1957 with the Dave Lambert Singers on self-penned lyric versions of classic jazz instrumentals including Four Brothers; Cloudburst; Later same year, teamed up with Lambert and Annie Ross forming vocal trio Lambert Hendricks and Ross; Toured and recorded together (Ross replaced by Yolande Bevan, 1962) until 1964; Moved to Europe, 1965; Returned as jazz critic for the San Francisco Chronicle, early 1970s; Began teaching jazz; Formed The Hendricks Family (with wife and 2 children) which continues to perform and tour. *Compositions:* Transformed instrumental solo parts of bebop jazz instrumentals by writing lyrics for classic works including: I Remember Clifford; Airgin; Centrepiece; Little Pony; Sing Joy Spring; Birdland. *Recordings:* with Lambert Hendricks and Ross: Sing A Song of Basie, 1957; The Swingers, Sing Along With Basie, 1958; The Hottest New Group In Jazz, 1959; Lambert Hendricks and Ross Sing Ellington, 1960; The Way-Out Voices of Lambert Hendricks and Ross, 1961; with Lambert Hendricks and Bevan: Live At Basin Street, At Newport '63, Havin' A Ball At The Village Gate, 1963; solo: A Good Git-Together, New York New York, 1959; Evolution of The Blues Song, 1960; Fast Livin' Blues, 1961; In Person At The Trident, Salute To Joao Gilberto, 1963; Cloudburst, 1972; Tell Me The Truth, 1975; September Songs, 1976; Love, 1981; Freddie Freeloader, 1990; In Person, 1991; Boppin' At The Blue Note, 1993; Birdmen and Birdsongs, 2000. *Current Management:* B H Hopper Management. *Website:* www.hopper-management.com.

HENDRICKS, Michele; b. 27 Sept. 1953, New York, USA. Vocalist. m. Pierre Bornard, 28 July 1992. *Education:* 2 years college; Music major at college. *Career:* Appearances at: North Sea Festival; Monterey Festival; Montréal Festival; Vienna; Pori; Marciac; Juan Les Pins; Nice; Crest; Mt Fuji; Television: Johnny Carson; Mike Douglas; various local television in Europe, Japan, USA; Has sung with: Jon Hendricks; Buddy Rich; Stan Getz; Count Basie; Bennie Golson; Slide Hampton; George Benson; Al Jarreau; Bobby McFerrin; Roland Hannah; Herbie Hancock; Freddie Hubbard. *Recordings:* Me and My Shadow; Keepin' Me Satisfied; Carryin' On; Live At Ronnie Scott's With Buddy Rich; Live with Jon Hendricks and Company; The Peacocks with Stan Getz and Jimmy Rowles; Vocal Summit; Santa's Bag; Second Impression; Boppin' At The Blue Note. *Membership:* ASCAP; Shellrose Music (ASCAP). *Current Management:* Pee Bee Jazz, Pierre Bornard. *Address:* 182 rue Nationale, 75013 Paris, France.

HENDY, John (Jonathan Darren); b. 26 March 1971, Barking, Essex, England. Vocalist. *Career:* Member, East 17; Numerous television and live appearances. *Recordings:* Singles include: House of Love, 1992; Deep, 1993; West End Girls, 1993; It's Alright, 1993; Around The World, 1994; Stay Another Day (No. 1, UK), 1994; Steam, 1994; Thunder, 1995; If You Ever, with Gabrielle, 1996; Hey Child, 1997; Each Time, 1998; Betcha Can't Wait, 1999; Albums: Walthamstow, 1993; Steam, 1994; Up All Night, 1996; Around the World – The Journey So Far, 1996; Resurrection, 1998.

HENLEY, Don; b. 22 July 1947, Linden, Texas, USA. Musician (drums); Vocalist. *Career:* Member, The Four Speeds, 1963; Member, Shiloh, 1970; Founder member, The Eagles, 1971–; Solo artiste, 1982–; Performances include: California Jam Festival, 1974; Solo appearances: Guest drummer

with Guns N' Roses, American Music Awards, 1989; Indian River Festival, 1991; Madison Square Garden, 1991. *Recordings:* Albums: with the Eagles: The Eagles, 1972; Desperado, 1973; On The Border, 1974; One of These Nights (No. 1, USA), 1975; Their Greatest Hits 1971–75 (No. 1, USA), 1976; Hotel California (No. 1, USA), 1977; The Long Run (No. 1, USA), 1979; Live, 1980; Eagles' Greatest Hits, Vol. 2, 1982; The Best of The Eagles, 1985; Solo albums: I Can't Stand Still, 1982; Building The Perfect Beast, 1984; The End of Innocence, 1989; Inside Job, 2000; Featured on Leap of Faith (film soundtrack), 1992; Contributor, Amused To Death, Rogers Waters, 1992; Actual Miles, 1995; Producer, title track, Tell Me The Truth, Timothy B Schmit, 1990; Singles include: The Best of My Love (No. 1, USA), 1975; One of These Nights (No. 1, USA), 1975; Lyin' Eyes, 1975; Take It To The Limit, 1976; New Kid In Town (No. 1, USA), 1977; Hotel California (No. 1, USA), 1977; Heartache Tonight (No. 1, USA), 1979; Duet with Stevie Nicks: Leather and Lace, 1982; Solo hits: Dirty Laundry, 1983; The Boys of Summer, 1985, 1999. *Honours:* Grammy Awards: Best Pop Vocal, 1976; Record of the Year, 1978; Best Rock Vocal, 1986; American Music Awards, 1977, 1981; MTV Music Video Awards, 1985, 1990; People For The American Way's Spirit of Liberty Award, 1990; Boston Music Awards, Special Recognition Award, 1992. *Current Management:* c/o Irving Azoff, Revolution, 8900 Wilshire Blvd, Suite 200, Beverly Hills, CA 90211, USA.

HENNES, Peter Michael; b. 25 Feb. 1954, Great Lakes, Illinois, USA. Musician (guitar, bass); Educator. *Education:* Wayne State University, 1972; University of Michigan, 1973–74; Professional diploma, Berklee College of Music, Boston, 1978. *Career:* Musician with numerous artistes including: Frank Sinatra; Liza Minnelli; Perry Como; Anthony Newley; Marvin Hamlisch; Musician, touring stage productions including: Grease; Evita; A Chorus Line; 42nd Street; La Cage Aux Folles; Instructor, Jazz Studies, Georgia State University School of Music, 1982–88. *Membership:* AFofM.

HENNING, Ann-Marie Elisabeth; b. 2 Dec. 1952, Stockholm, Sweden. Jazz Musician; Composer; Arranger. *Education:* Royal Academy of Music, Stockholm, 5 years; Berkelee College of Music, Boston, USA, 2 years. *Career:* Tours in Sweden and Europe with Rockband NQB, 1973–74; Member, Jazzrock Group, Wave Play, 1978; Own Jazz Group, Blue Cluster, 1987; Jazz Festivals, Radio Concerts; Out of Blue Cluster, Formed Red Cluster, 1992; Pianist, Big Band Jatin Dolls, Television, Saturday Night Live Show, Theatre Shows; Accompanist to Musical Artists. *Compositions:* April Light, for Big Band; The Trees Are Listening; Waltz for Evert; The Rubber Jolly Boat. *Recordings:* Blue Cluster, 1989; Tidal Dreams, 1997. *Publications:* Co-author, The Real Swede. *Honours:* Swedish Composers Organization Grant, 1987, 1996; Swedish Composers of Popular Music Grant, 1993. *Membership:* Swedish Composers Organization; Swedish Composers of Popular Music; Swedish Jazz Musicians Organization. *Address:* Finnbodav 9B, 131 31 Nacka, Sweden.

HENOCQ, Benjamin; b. 1969. Musician (drums). *Education:* Private lessons, 1976–83; Conservatoire du Centre de Paris, 1983–85; Ecole Agostini, IACP, 1985–87; Private lessons with Daniel Humair; Paul Motian; Keith Copeland. *Career:* Member, PRYSM, Jean-Christophe Beney Quartet; Jean-Christophe Cholet Quartet; David Patrois Quintet; Philippe Sellam Quintet; Les Standardistes (Funk Octet); Phantastique Orchestre Modulaire; Quoi de Neuf Docteur Big Band; Numerous clubs, Paris; Festivals, France; Played with: Eric Le Lann; Stéphane Belmondo; Robin Eubanks; Glenn Ferris; Tommy Smith; Red Holloway; Rick Margitza; François Janneau; Lionel Belmondo; Sylvain Beuf; Geoffroy de Mazure; Peter Osborne; Olivier Ker-Ourio; Philip Catherine; Louis Winsberg; Harold Land; Laurent de Wilde; Franck Amsallem; Andy Emler; Denis Badault; Wayne Dockery; Henri Texier; Michel Benita; Patrice Caratini; Paul Breslin; Jean-Marc Thorès; KARTET; Teacher, IACP, 1986–88. *Recordings:* Le Retour, Quoi de Neuf Docteur Big Band, 1991; Hask, KARTET, 1992; En Attendent La Pluie, Quoi de Neuf Docteur Big Band, 1993; AL'Envers, Quoi de Neuf Docteur Big Band, 1994; Pression, KARTET, 1995; La Compil, Instant Charirés, 1995; PRYSM, PRYSM, 1995. *Honours:* First Prize, La Défense National Jazz Contest, 1994; Soloist Award, La Défense National Jazz Contest, 1994. *Address:* 55 rue Navier, 75017 Paris, France.

HENRIK, Wellejus; b. 15 Dec. 1954, Frederiksberg, Copenhagen, Denmark. Composer; Musician. *Education:* Private music lessons. *Career:* Theatre Music Appearances: En Rede i Traeet, 1983; Det Umuligste Af Alt, 1986; Fra Bord Til Bord, 1987; Hvor Godtfolk Er, 1988; Orla Frösnapper, 1990; Otto Er Et Naesehorn, 1993. *Honours:* Winner, Music Contest, Young Music Magazine. *Membership:* Danish Songwriters Guild. *Current Management:* Radiophelia, 928 MHZ, Box 6, 3100 Hornbaek, Denmark. *Address:* Sauntevaenget 14B, 3100 Hornbaek, Denmark. *Website:* www.henrikwellejus.dk.

HENRIKSON, Richard Ralph; b. 27 Nov. 1948, Portland, Oregon, USA. Composer; Lyricist; Musician (violin). *Education:* BS, Juilliard School of Music, 1972; MusM, 1973. *Career:* Violinist, various orchestras and chamber ensembles, 1970–; Violinist, Barnum, Broadway, 1980–82; Musical director, numerous stage productions include: Singing In The Rain; Sweet Charity; Me and My Girl; Fiddler On The Roof; Les Miserables, 1991–; Musical director, violinist, numerous artistes including: Tom Jones; Billy Ocean; George

Benson; Freddie Jackson; Jeffrey Osborne; Stephanie Mills; Gregg Allman; Rick Wakeman; Paul Anka. *Recordings:* Albums with: Music Minus One; The Tango Project; Hampton String Quartet; Violinist, film soundtracks: The Wiz; Silkwood; The Cotton Club; When Harry Met Sally; Do The Right Thing; Recordings by numerous artists including: Diana Ross; Sheena Easton; Paul Simon; Billy Cobham; John Sebastian. *Membership:* ASCAP; AFofM; NARAS; Recording Musicians of USA and Canada. *Address:* Hampton String Quartet, 344 W 72nd St, New York, NY 10023, USA.

HENRY, Jay Edward; b. 17 Feb. 1950, Brooklyn, New York, USA. Record Prod.; Sound Engineer. *Education:* Broadcasting Engineering, Cabrillo College; San Francisco State University. *Career:* Producer, engineer, Visual Music, 1983–; Secret Society Records, 1986–. *Recordings:* Albums include: with LL Cool J: Bigger and Deffer, 1987; Walking With A Panther, 1989; with Heavy D: Livin' Large, 1987; with Public Enemy: It Takes A Nation of Millions, 1987; with Run DMC: Tougher Than Leather, 1988; with Defunkt: Defunkt In America, 1988; with Living Colour: Vivid, 1989; with Pet Shop Boys: Behavior, 1990; with George Michael: Five Live, 1993; with Elton John: Duets, 1993; with Deniece Williams: Love Solves It All, 1996. *Honours:* 5 Gold Reel Awards, Ampex, 1986–89; Numerous Platinum and Gold records; International Producer Award, 1990. *Membership:* NARAS; Audio Engineering Society.

HENRY, Michael Anthony; b. 10 March 1963, London, England. Vocalist; Composer; Musician (saxophone, clarinet); Arranger; Songwriter. *Education:* Centre for Young Musicians, 1977–81; Royal College of Music, 1981–85. *Career:* Singer, writer with Buddy Curtess and The Grasshoppers, 1985–89; Singer and Songwriter with The Flying Pickets, 1991–95; Singer, songwriter, co-producer with Cut 2 Taste, 1994–; Tours include: support to Roy Orbison, 1985; Backing vocalist, Pet Shop Boys, 1989; Flying Pickets, 1991–95; Concerts: Support concerts to: Beach Boys, Wembley, 1986; Bo Diddley, Hammersmith Odeon, 1987; Dr Feelgood, 1987; Glastonbury, main stage, 1987; Television and radio appearances include: The Tube, 1987; Saturday Live, 1987; Ruby Wax, 1988; Meltdown, 1988; BBC1 and Channel 4 Schools workshops, 1991–93; Opera performances, 1991–93; Presenter, Young Musician of the Year, 1992; Judge, Choir of the Year, 1993; Concert support, Ray Charles, 1993; Cue The Music, 1995; Support to Michael Jackson, tour, 1997. *Compositions:* Wind Quartet No. 1; Say Ave For Me, for saxophone and piano, performed on BBC Radio 3. *Recordings:* with Buddy Curtess and the Grasshoppers: Shoobey Baby; Shout; Hello Suzie; Bridge Over Troubled Water; Design For Me; Forever Young, Pretenders, 1992; Sugar Daddy, Billy Bragg, 1996; Other. *Recordings include:* Caravan, John Harle, all vocals, 1990; Rain Song, Moodswings, 1990; Real Love, Driza Bone, 1991; The Warning, Flying Pickets, 1993. *Publications:* 3 Interludes for saxophone and piano; Birdwatching, for clarinet quartet, 1998. *Honours:* Dip RCM, ARCM; Winner of composition prizes: Joseph Horowitz; Stanford; Cornelius Cardew; Time Out Magazine Best Live Act, 1986, 1987. *Membership:* Musicians' Union; PRS; Equity; Society For Promotion of New Music (SPNM) ISM. *Address:* 83 Lucien Rd, London SW17 8HS, England.

HENSHALL, Ruthie; b. 1967, Bromley, Kent, England. Vocalist; Actor. *Education:* Studied musical theatre at Laine Theatre Arts, Surrey, England. *Career:* Joined British tour of a Chorus Line followed by appearances in: Cats; Miss Saigon; Children of Eden; Spent a summer at the Chichester Festival Theatre; Returned to West End, subsequent appearances include: Les Miserables; Crazy For You; She Loves Me; Peggy Sue Got Married; Chicago; Joined New York cast of Chicago, leading to other Broadway roles including: Putting It Together; Ziegfeld Follies of 1939; The Vagina Monologues; US and UK TV credits include: Law and Order; Deadline; Mysteries of 71st Street; Get Back; Currently pursuing recording career. *Recordings:* Albums: cast recordings: Children of Eden, 1991; Crazy For You, 1993; Godspell, 1993 (studio cast); She Loves Me, 1994; Divorce Me Darling, 1997; Chicago, 1998; solo: Love Is Here To Stay, 1994; Pilgrim, 2001. *Honours:* Olivier Award, Best Actress In A Musical, She Loves Me, 1994. *Website:* www.ruthiehenshall.co.uk.

HENSLEY, Ken; b. 24 Aug. 1945, London, England. Musician (guitar, keyboards); Vocalist; Record Prod. *Career:* Musician, singer, Kit and The Saracens; Jimmy Brown Sound; The Gods; Musician, singer, producer, UK rock group Uriah Heep, 1969–80; US rock group Blackfoot, 1981–84; Director, artistic relations, St Louis Music Inc, 1987–. *Recordings:* Albums: with Uriah Heep: Very 'Umble, Very 'Eavy, 1970; Salisbury, 1971; Look At Yourself, 1971; Demons and Wizards, 1972; Magician's Birthday, 1972; Live, 1973; Sweet Freedom, 1973; Wonderworld, 1974; Return To Fantasy, 1975; Best Of, 1975; High and Mighty, 1976; Firefly, 1977; Innocent Victim, 1978; Fallen Angel, 1978; Conquest, 1980; Time of Revelation, 1996; Classic Heep, 1998; Rarities, 2000; Ballads, 2000; Blood On Stone, 2001; with Blackfoot: Siogo, 1983; Vertical Smile, 1984. *Honours:* Gold and Platinum discs. *Address:* St Louis Music Inc, 1400 Ferguson Ave, St Louis, MO 63133, USA.

HERMAND, Charles; b. 23 June 1960, Namur, Belgium. *Career:* Brasov Festival in Romania with Boy George and James Brown, 1994; Support to Dave at Cirque Royal in Brussels, 1997. *Recordings:* Save Me Now, 1992; Les Petits Pains seventies, 1993; Vague d'Amour, 1993; Les Yeux vers le Ciel,

1994; Trop Fatigué, 1995; Rien ne nous sépare, 1999; Album: A tescôtés, 1999. *Membership:* SABAM, Belgium. *Current Management:* Up Way Music. *Address:* Rue de Vrière 67–69, 1020 Brussels, Belgium.

HERMANS, Jozef Eduard; b. 1 March 1948, Antwerp, Belgium. Psychologist; Vocalist; Songwriter. m. Faes Monique, 31 Jan. 1998, 1 s., 1 d. *Career:* Psychologist, City of Antwerp; Member, Flemish Folkgroup, Katastroof; Radio and TV appearances, occasionally. *Compositions:* More than 100 songs on 13 albums of Katastroof; Met De Wijven Niks As Last; Het Geloof; Paterkesdans; Johnny. *Recordings:* 12 CDs with Katastroof; 3 CDs with Jos Smos: Jos Smos in het Blote Beestenbus, 1996; Smarten en Andere Lappen, 1997; Over Het Geloof, 1998. *Membership:* Sabam, Belgium. *Address:* Tweelingenstraat 15, 2018 Antwerp, Belgium.

HERMITAGE, Richard; b. 20 Oct. 1955, London. Agent; Man; Record Co Exec. *Career:* Agent, artistes included: The Human League; Steel Pulse; ABC; INXS; UB40; Psychedelic Furs; Aswad; Daf; The Art of Noise; The Residents; Agencies worked at: March Artists; TKA; Asgard; ITB; Fair Warning, 1974–85; Management, artistes included: The Human League; Pale Saints; The Darling Buds; Slowdive; The Boo Radleys; Teenage Fanclub; Denim, 1986–93; Currently Manager, management company War Zones; General Manager, record company 4AD, 1994–95. *Current Management:* War Zones (management). *Address:* 33 Kersley Rd, London N16 0NT, England.

HERNDON, Mark Joel; b. 11 May 1955, Springfield, MA, USA. Musician (drums). m., 1 d. *Career:* Mem., country music group, Alabama, 1979–. *Recordings:* Albums: Alabama, 1980; My Home's In Alabama, 1980; Feels So Right, 1981; Stars, 1982; Mountain Music, 1982; The Closer You Get, 1983; Roll On, 1984; 40 Hour Week, 1985; Alabama Christmas, 1985; The Touch, 1986; Greatest Hits, 1986; Just Us, 1987; Live, 1988; Tennessee Christmas, 1989; Southern Star, 1989; Pass It On Down, 1990; Greatest Hits Vol. 2, 1991; American Pride, 1992; Gonna Have A Party... Live, 1993; Cheap Seats, 1993; In The Beginning, 1994; In Pictures, 1995; From The Archives Vol. 1, 1996; Christmas Vol. 2, 1996; Live at Ebbets Field, 1997; Dancin' On The Boulevard, 1997; Twentieth Century, 1999; Alabama For The Record, 2000; When It All Goes South, 2001; Christmas, 2002. *Honours:* Numerous Country Music Asscn Awards, 1981–84; Numerous Acad. of Country Music Awards, incl. Artist of the Decade, 1989; Numerous American Music Awards, incl. Award of Merit, 2003; Grammy Awards, for Mountain Music, 1983, for The Closer You Get, 1984; BMI President's Award, 2000; Numerous Billboard Awards. *Current Management:* Dale Morris and Assocs, 818 19th Ave S, Nashville, TN 37203, USA. *Website:* www.wildcountry.com.

HERRING-LEIGH, Judy; b. 3 Oct. 1945, Cape Girardeau, Missouri, USA. Concert Artist; Recording Artist; Songwriter; Vocal Music Teacher; Minister of Music; Children's Choir Co-ordinator. m. Jim Leigh, 1 Oct. 1994, 1 s., 1 d. *Education:* Bachelor Music Performance; Master Early Childhood Education; Private voice training, 13 years; 4 year Voice Major, Oklahoma Baptist University; Life Vocal Music Certification grades K-12; Music courses in Master's Program. *Career:* 26 years in Music Ministry; Five concert tours, England, also crusades; 6–10 US tours over past 20 years; Recorded 3 albums, 1 live performance tape, 1 gospel songs tape; Musical evangelist, public relations representative for Virginia Baptists; Morningstar album No. 16 on gospel music charts of Christian Broadcasting Network, April, 1977; Appeared, PTL, CBN, BBC networks, 1978–79; Sang for Governor's Prayer Breakfast, President's Prayer Breakfast, 1980; Minister of Music, 9 churches over 26 years; Music teacher; 10 concert tour, England, Scotland, 1997; Soloist, Good News Mission Trip, Odessa, Ukraine, 1997. *Compositions:* Morningstar; God's Rose; Suffer The Little Children; The Woman; Brand New Start; Arrangements: Take My Life and Let It Be; Victory In Jesus; I've Been Redeemed. *Recordings:* Albums: Morningstar; Christmas Means Thinking of Jesus; God's Rose; Tapes: Old Gospel Hymns; Live in Concert; Cherished Moments, 1997; Tribute to Fanny Crosby and George Beverly Shea. *Publications:* Reflections On God's Rose, article, New Music Magazine, 1979; Experiencing Loss With A Youth Ministry, Equipping Youth Magazine, 1985. *Honours:* Dimitri Mitropolis Award; Personalities of The South, 1979; Stylemaker of the Year, 1979. *Membership:* SESAC; Southern Baptist Convention's Music Evangelists, USA; Gospel Music Asscn, Nashville, Tennessee.

HERSH, Kristin; b. 7 Aug. 1966, Atlanta, Georgia, USA. Musician (guitar); Vocalist. 3 s. *Career:* Singer, Musician, Throwing Muses, 1986–97; Solo Singer/Songwriter, 1994–. *Recordings:* Albums: Hips and Makers, 1994; Strings, 1994; Strange Angels, 1998; Sky Motel, 1999; Sunny Border Blue, 2001; Singles: The Holy Single, 1995; Like You, 1998; Echo, 1999; Also appears: with Throwing Muses: Throwing Muses, 1986; Chains Changed, 1987; House Tornado, 1988; The Fat Skier, 1987; Hunkpapa, 1989; The Real Ramona, 1991; Red Heaven, 1992; University, 1995; Limbo, 1996. *Membership:* AFofM. *Current Management:* Throwing Music Ltd, 520 Southview Dr., Athens, GA 30605, USA.

HERZHAFT, Gerard; b. 8 Nov. 1943, Meyzieu, France. m. Lise Briere de L'Isle, 27 Sept. 1967, 1 s., 1 d. *Education:* Licence of History, Sorbonne, Paris. *Career:* Numerous radio broadcasts and TV shows; Musician (blues); Concerts:

Blues Passion, Cognac; Thullins Festival; Café Campus (Montréal); Parthenay Blues; Doua De Jazz; Sathonay Blues Festival. *Compositions:* It It Wasn't For Muddy Waters; Rhone River is Rising; Old Bluesman From Texas; Redneck Blues; My Blues Will; Write, Gerard, Write, 1998; A Full Bank Account, 1998. *Recordings:* Albums: with Herzhaft Blues: Never Been Plugged; Two Brothers And A Pick; Herzhaft Special, 2000. *Publications include:* Encyclopedia of the Blues; A Long Blues in a Minor; Le Blues; La Country Music; Catfish Blues; John Lee Hooker; Le dernier chant de l'Inca, 1999; Guide de la Country Music et du Folk, 1999. *Honours:* Grand Prix Littéraire de la Ville de Lyon, 1986; Prix Des Auteurs et Ecrivains Lyonnais, 1987; Prix Societe des Gens De Lettres, 1995; Prix Des Lyceens D'Ile De France, 1997. *Address:* 57 rue Florian, 69100 Villeurbanne, France.

HESSION, Paul; b. 19 Sept. 1956, Leeds, England. Musician (drums). m. Cecilia Jane Charnley, 23 May 1987, 1 s., 1 d. *Education:* Studied instrument technology. *Career:* Toured Mexico and Cuba with The Siger Band, 1986; Played in Derek Bailey's Company week in London (twice); Duos with Alan Wilkinson on BBC Radio 3, Mixing It; Music for radio play, BBC Radio 4 with Keith Jafrate; Sound symposium, St Johns, Newfoundland, Canada, with Hession, Wilkinson, Fell. *Recordings:* Album: The Real Case, with Hans-Peter Hiby; Albums with Hession/Wilkinson/Fell: Foom Foom; The Horrors of Darmstadt; with Mick Beck: Start Moving Earbuds; Solo: St Johns, 2000. *Honours:* Jazz bursaries from ACGB, 1986, 1991. *Membership:* Musicians' Union. *Address:* 41 Hanover Sq., Leeds L53 1BQ, England.

HESTER, Paul; b. 8 Jan. 1959, Melbourne, Australia. Musician (Drums). *Career:* Member, Crowded House; Early acoustic gigs in restaurants and clubs; Numerous headlining tours, festival dates and TV and radio appearances; Left band, 1994; Rejoined for Sydney Harbour Bridge and Opera House Farewell Concert, 1996 and for new tracks on Best of compilation album; Band split. *Recordings:* Singles include: World Where You Live, 1986; Crowded House EP, 1986; Something So Strong, 1987; Don't Dream It's Over, 1987; Sister Madly, 1988; I Feel Possessed, 1989; Four Seasons In One Day, 1991; Fall at Your Feet, 1991; Weather With You, 1991; It's Only Natural, 1992; Pineapple Head, 1993; Locked Out, 1993; World Where We Live, 1993; Distant Sun, 1993; Nails in My Feet, 1994; Not the Girl You Think You Are, 1996; Everything Is Good For You, 1996; Albums: Crowded House, 1986; Temple of Low Men, 1988; Woodface, 1991; Together Alone, 1993; Recurring Dream: The Best of Crowded House, 1996.

HETFIELD, James Alan; b. 3 Aug. 1963, Los Angeles, California, USA. Musician (guitar); Vocalist. *Career:* Member, Obsession; Leather Charm; Member, US heavy rock group Metallica, 1981–; World-wide tours include: Master of Puppets world tour, 1986–87; US tour, 1988; Damaged Justice tour, UK, 1989; World tour, 1991–; Also tours with Raven; Twisted Sister; Ozzy Osbourne; Motörhead; Major concerts include: Monsters of Rock Festival, Castle Donington, 1985, 1987, 1991; German Monster Rock festival, 1987; Monsters of Rock Europe, US tours, 1988, 1991; Day On The Green, Oakland, 1991; Freddie Mercury tribute, Wembley, 1991. *Recordings:* Albums: Kill 'Em All, 1983; Ride The Lightning, 1984; Master of Puppets, 1986;... and Justice For All, 1988; Metallica (No. 1, UK and USA), 1991; Live Shit, 1993; Garage Inc, 1998; SandM, 1999; Singles: Garage Days Revisited (EP), 1987; Harvester of Sorrow, 1988; One, 1989; Enter Sandman, 1991; The Unforgiven, 1991; Nothing Else Matters, 1992; Wherever I May Roam, 1992; Sad But True, 1992; Stone Cold Crazy, track featured on Rubáiyát (Elektra's 40th anniversary compilation); I Disappear, 2000. *Honours:* Platinum and Gold discs; Grammy Awards: Best Heavy Metal Performance: One, 1989; Stone Cold Crazy, 1991; The Unforgiven, 1992; Best Hard Rock Performance: Whiskey In The Jar, 2000; Rock Instrumental Performance, Call of The Ktulu, 2001; American Music Award, Favourite Heavy Metal Artist, 1993; Bay Area Music Awards: Outstanding Album, 1992; Outstanding Metal Album, Outstanding Group, 1993; Rolling Stone Readers Poll Winners, Best Heavy Metal Band, 1993. *Current Management:* Q-Prime Inc. *Address:* 729 Seventh Ave, 14th Floor, New York, NY 10019, USA.

HEURLIN, Martin; b. 20 Nov. 1963, Frederiksberg, Denmark. Musician (guitar, bass, keyboards); Vocalist; Prod. 3 s. *Career:* Founder, rock band Sy-Daff; Member, KB Hallen, 1980; Support act to Sweet, 1982; Played at Roskilde Festival, 1983; Played club circuit in Los Angeles, 1986–88; Guitarist on Danish television for Michael Penn, John Farnham, Anders Glenmark and Tomas Ledin, 1990; Pupil Live, television and radio broadcasts, 1998. *Compositions include:* TV show theme, Set and Swet; Pupil, Frederik Jorgensen, major hit in Denmark, 1997. *Recordings:* Soundtracks for many Danish television documentary programmes, 1990–; Albums with: Sy-Daff, 1982; Mr Man, 1987; James Thomas, 1991; Pupil, 1997; Solo album, 1995. *Publications:* Pupil: Superglasojne, 1997. *Membership:* DJFBA. *Current Management:* TBA, Strulasgade 14, 2300 Copenhagen S, Denmark. *Address:* Ryesgade 108B Kld, 2100 Copenhagen O, Denmark.

HEWAT, Corrina Dawn; b. 21 Dec. 1970, Edinburgh, Scotland. Vocalist; Musician (harp, clarsach); Composer. *Education:* BA, one year, Performance, Royal Scottish Academy of Music and Drama; Hons Degree, Jazz, Contemporary and Popular Music, City of Leeds College of Music. *Career:* Band, Bachué, formed with David Milligan, 1995; Band, Chantan, formed

1996; Appeared on Taile A Bhaile, BBC 2, Channel 4, Radio 3 and Demo TV; Writing music for audio books, Saltire Society; Teaching, Visiting Tutor, Balnain House, Home of Highland Music, Inverness and Fettes College, Edinburgh; Working with Lammas, Carol Kidd, Eric Bibb, Seannachie; Commissions: Songs of Redshank, The Highland Festival, 1997; Making the Connection, Celtic Connections Festival 1998; Photons In Vapour, 2000; Many compositions of a traditional nature recorded. *Recordings:* Bachué Café, 1996, 1998; Primary Colours, 1997; A Certain Smile, 1999; Contributor: Something Blew, 1995; Northlins, 1995; Vol. 4 of Burns' Complete Works, 1998. *Honours:* Finalist, Young Traditional Musician of the Year, 1995. *Membership:* Musicians' Union; Clarsach Society; UKHA; PRS; MCPS; PAMRA. *Current Management:* The Balnain Agency, 40 Huntly St, Inverness IV3 5HR, Scotland.

HEWERDINE, Boo; Songwriter; Prod. *Career:* Worked with as Prod. and Songwriter: The Corrs, Rosalie Deighton, Nicky Love, Eddi Reader, Scarlet; Worked with as Songwriter: Melanie C, Fever Pitch, Hepburn, Natalie Imbruglia, Brian Kennedy, Heather Small, Suggs, James Taylor, Twenty Four Seven. *Address:* c/o Stephen Budd Management Ltd, 109b Regents Park Rd, Primrose Hill, London NW1 8UR, England. *Website:* www.record-producers.com.

HEWINS, Mark Jesson; b. 24 March 1955, Hertfordshire, England. Musician (guitar); Composer. m. Yvonne, 23 Sept. 1989, 1 d. *Career:* Started as professional guitarist aged 15; Tours, Europe and USA; Played with musicians including: Phil Collins; Julie Felix; Joe Lee Wilson; Long association with Casio as Midi guitarist, leading to compiled sample libraries, supplied accompaniment patterns, demonstration tunes for their keyboards; Introduced Lou Reed to Midi guitar; Midi consultant. *Compositions include:* music for guitar, strings, orchestra. *Recordings:* Featured on many albums; Solo album: The Electric Guitar; Veritable Centaur, Soft Heap. *Publications:* Markie's Little Fake Books 1 and 2; Canterbury Tales (relating to Canterbury music scene), published extensively in various journals. *Membership:* Musicians' Union; PRS; MCPS; British Music Writers' Council. *Current Management:* Y A Ledley, Musart Services. *Address:* c/o Musart Services, 81 Knollys Rd, London SW16 2JW, England.

HEWITT, Steve; b. 22 March 1971, England. Musician (drums, percussion). *Career:* Played in early bands The Electric Crayons, with Tim Burgess of The Charlatans, Mystic Deckchairs; Joined Breed, toured Germany; Joined the Boo Radleys, worked on their debut album, and played numerous gigs; Played with K-Klass, dance outfit; Numerous contracts with session work and provided music for advertisements; Returned to tour with Breed, including tour with Nick Cave and the Bad Seeds; Joined Placebo as drummer. *Recordings:* Singles: Come Home, 1996; 36 Degrees, 1996; Teenage Angst, 1996; Nancy Boy, 1997; Bruise Pristine, 1997; Pure Morning, 1998; You Don't Care About Us, 1998; Every You Every Me, 1999; Without You I'm Nothing, featuring David Bowie, 1999; Taste In Men, 2000; Slave To The Wage, 2000; Albums: Without You I'm Nothing, 1998; Black Market Music, 2000.

HEWSON, Paul. See: BONO.

HEX, Andrew (Andy) Joe; b. 25 June 1966, Houston, Texas, USA. Musician (piano); Vocalist. *Education:* Banner University, Kingwood, Texas (Evangelical Ministries; Praise and Worship Music Ministerial Studies). *Career:* Scored and produced music for Taking The Turf, 2000. *Compositions:* She Knows, 1999. *Recordings:* She Knows, 1999; God's Amazing Grace, 2001. *Membership:* BMI; CMA; Gospel Music Asscn; Texas Accountants and Lawyers for the Arts. *Address:* 8723 Meadowview, Houston, TX 77037, USA.

HEYWARD, Nick; b. 20 May 1961, South London, England. Vocalist; Musician (guitar); Songwriter. *Career:* Founder, Haircut 100, 1981–82; Solo artiste, 1983–; Major concerts include: Support to Wham!, The Final farewell concert, Wembley, 1986. *Compositions:* Most recordings self-written. *Recordings:* Albums: with Haircut 100: Pelican West (No. 2, UK) 1982; Solo albums: North of a Miracle, 1983; Postcards From Home, 1986; I Love You Avenue, 1989; The Best of Nick Heyward and Haircut 100, 1989; From Monday To Sunday, 1993; Tangled, 1995; The Apple Bed, 1996; Pizza Tears; Hit singles with Haircut 100: Favourite Shirts (Boy Meets Girl), 1981; Love Plus One, 1982; Fantastic Day, 1982; Nobody's Fool, 1982; Solo singles: Whistle Down the Wind, 1983; Take That Situation, 1983; Blue Hat For Blue Day, 1983; Rollerbalde, 1996; The Man You Used to Be, 1997; Today, 1997; Stars in Her Eyes, 1998.

HIATT, John; b. 20 Aug. 1952, Indiana, USA. Vocalist; Songwriter; Musician (guitar). *Career:* Member, bands: Four Fifths; The White Ducks; Joe Lynch and The Hangmen; Songwriter, Tree Publishing, Nashville, early 1970s; Solo artiste, 1974–; Also musician for Sonny Terry and Brownie McGhee; Leon Redbone; Tom Waits; Tours with: Leo Kottke; Southside Johnny and the Astbury Jukes; Edie Brickell; Joined Ry Cooder's backing band, 1981; Concerts include: A Black and White Night, with Roy Orbison, Los Angeles, 1987; Reading Festival, 1988; Roy Orbison Concert Tribute, Universal City, California, 1990; Formed Little Village, with Ry Cooder, Nick Lowe, Jim Keltner, 1992. *Compositions include:* Thinking of You, Tracy Nelson; As Sure

As I'm Sitting Here, Three Dog Night; Bring Back Your Love To Me, Earl Thomas Conley. *Recordings:* Albums: Hangin' Round The Observatory, 1974; Overcoats, 1974; Slug Line, 1979; Two Bit Monsters, 1980; All of a Sudden, 1982; Riding With The King, 1983; Warming Up To The Ice Age, 1985; Bring The Family, 1987; Slow Turning, 1988; Stolen Moments, 1990; Love Gets Strange, 1993; Perfectly Good Guitar, 1993; Walk On, 1995; Litle Head, 1997; The Best of John Hiatt, 1998; Crossing Muddy Waters, 2000; The Tiki Bar Is Open, 2001; with Little Village: Little Village, 1992; Featured on: Borderline, Ry Cooder, 1981. *Honours:* As songwriter: BMI Country Music Award, Bring Back Your Love To Me, Earl Thomas Conley, 1991. *Current Management:* Metropolitan Entertainment Group, 2 Penn Plaza 26th Fl, New York, NY 10121, USA.

HIBBERT, Frederick (Toots); Vocalist. *Career:* Lead singer, reggae group The Maytals, later billed as Toots and the Maytals; Leading vocal group in Jamaica, 1960s and 1970s; Film appearance, The Harder They Come. *Recordings include:* The Sensational; Never Grow Old; Sweet and Dandy; From The Roots; Monkey Man; Funky Kingston; In The Dark; Slatyam Stoot; Reggae Got Soul; Toots Live; Life Could Be A Dream; Toots in Memphis; with Otis Reading: Otis! The Definitive Otis Redding, 1993; Appears on: The Good The Bad and The Funky, Tom Tom Club, 2000; Hits include: Daddy/It's You (No. 1, Jamaican charts), 1965; 54–46 That's My Number; Do The Reggay; Monkey Man. *Honours:* Winners (with the Maytals), Jamaican Festival Song Competition, 1966, 1969 and 1972. *Address:* c/o Zoe Productions, 450 Broome St, Eighth Floor, New York, NY 10013, USA.

HICKLING, Anna Jo; b. 5 Sept. 1966, Stockport, Cheshire, England. Vocalist; Songwriter; Prod; Record Label Owner. *Education:* University of Bath; O-Level Music; Singing, piano, trumpet tuition; Recording studio engineering course. *Career:* Backing vocalist for various Manchester bands: Victor Brox; The Glee Company, 1983; Local clubs include Band On The Wall; Writer, lead vocalist Inside Out, 1984; Concerts at The Boardwalk, Manchester; Lead vocalist, Touch of Spice, 1987; Played Moles Club, Bath; Womad Festival; Various universities, HTV appearance; Invited to play and record at Real World Studios; Backing vocalist, Tammy Payne, British tour; Also played at Southport Soul Weekender; The Thekla, Bristol; The Underworld, London; Ashton Court Festival. *Recordings:* Session vocals for: Smith and Mighty; Banderas remix; Startled Insects; Toop (EP); Lead vocals, band member, writing and production work on EPs with: Tommorowland; (Currently) Transport; Remix for single: I Am Free, Morgan King. *Membership:* Musicians' Union; PRS; PAMRA. *Address:* Revelstoke Rd, Wimbledon Park, London, England.

HICKS, Hinda; b. 1977, Tunisia. Vocalist. *Career:* Basketball Player and Coach; Member, The Fabulous Fug Band; Began solo career; Numerous live dates including tours with Boyzone and 911; Television appearances; Collaborations: Lynden David Hall; A+. *Recordings:* I Wanna Be Your Lady, 1997; If You Want Me, 1998; You Think You Own Me, 1998; Truly, 1998; My Remedy, 2000; Albums: Hinda, 1998; Everything To Me, 2000.

HICKS, Ivan; b. 6 July 1940, Upper Sackville, New Brunswick, Canada. Musician (fiddle, guitar, mandolin). m. Vivian Paulette Webb, 4 July 1970. *Education:* BA; BEd; MEd. *Career:* As teenager, formed: The Golden Valley Boys; 1964, began teaching, Salisbury, New Brunswick; Formed danceband Marshwinds, 1969–89; Formed old time and bluegrass band: Ivan Hicks and Maritime Express, 1979–; Workshops; Teacher fiddling; Television appearances include: Up Home Tonight (ATV), 1980s, 8 years; Host, weekly radio show, CFQM Moncton, 1982–95; MC of Maritime Old-Time Fiddling Contest (CBC), 1985–; Concerts: Canada, USA; Entertainer, special occasions; Organizer, promoter, concerts, tours; Retired from entertaining, 1996. *Compositions include:* Apohaqui; Gram Lee's Waltz; Jim, The Fiddle Maker; Marshwinds Waltz; Purple Violet Waltz; Riverview Jig; Maritime 40; Forever Friends; Memories of Father James Smith; Fiddler's Roast; The MacDonalds of Highfield; The Fiddler From Douro; Sussex Avenue Fiddlers Two Step. *Recordings:* The Life and Music of Ivan and Vivian Hicks (video); For You; Shingle The Roof; Old Time Christmas; Fiddlingly Yours; Swinging Fiddles; Purple Violet Fiddling; Friendly Fiddling The Maritime Way; Fiddling For Fun and Friends; The Strength of God's Hand, 1997. *Publications:* Ivan Hicks Fiddle Tunes and Souvenirs; Ivan Hicks: Fifty Years of Fabulous Fiddle Music by Allison Mitcham, 1996. *Honours:* Two-time winner, Maritime Fiddling Contest, 1979–80; Finalist: Canadian Fiddling Contest; 1985, Inducted into New Brunswick Country Music Hall of Fame; Inducted into North American Fiddlers Hall of Fame, 1990; Recipient, Governor General's Caring Canadian Award, 1999. *Membership:* Canadian Country Music Asscn; Director, Maritime Fiddlers Asscn; Director, National Oldtime Fiddlers Asscn; East Coast Music Asscn; President, Fiddles of the World Society; Director, New Brunswick Country Music Hall of Fame; Director, Music New Brunswick. *Address:* 157 Sussex Ave, Riverview, New Brunswick E1B 3A8, Canada.

HICKS, Jacqueline (Jacqui); b. 7 July 1966, Pontefract, West Yorkshire, England. Vocalist; Musician (saxophone, flute, clarinet); Songwriter. m. Patrick Hartley. *Education:* Wakefield District College; City of Leeds College of Music, 1984–87; Guildhall School of Music and Drama, 1987–88. *Career:*

Four years with National Youth Jazz Orchestra; Matt Bianco; Tours: Japan; Indonesia; Europe; Tour with Shakatak, South East Asia; South Africa; Japan; Also with: John Dankworth; Dick Morrisey; Harry Becket; Don Lusher; Supported George Benson, 1993; Own jazz/funk band, Jacqui Hicks Band; Tours with Shakatak in Moscow, Georgia and Lithuania. *Recordings:* Own album: Looking Forward, Looking Back, 1990; Spellbound, 1999; with Macfarlane Group: Bright Lights Big City; with NYJO: Cooking With Gas; with Matt Bianco: Another Time Another Place; Gran Via; with Matt Bianco: A Collection; with Shakatak: Let the Piano Play; View from the City; Live at Ronnie Scott's; Latin Trip, with CPD, 2001.

HIGHAM, Darrel; b. 5 Jan. 1970, Bedford, England. Musician (lead guitar, double bass); Vocalist; Songwriter; Prod. *Career:* Solo career, Singer, Guitarist with backing band, The Enforcers; Supported Chuck Berry, 1995; Played Lead Guitar for Rocky Burnette, Glen Glenn, Johnny Carroll, Vernon Taylor, Merrill E Moore, Don and Dewey; Toured USA, 1992 fronting Eddie Cochran's original backing band, The Kelly Four; Worked in London's West End, Lead guitar and Singing, Elvis The Musical, 8 months, 1996; TV work includes appearances on Blue Peter, Theatreland; Many radio appearances; Currently tours in UK, throughout Europe and USA. *Compositions:* Prolific Songwriter with over 30 compositions released world-wide. *Recordings:* 5 solo albums: Mobile Corrosion (Nervous), 1995; Let's Rock Tonight (Fury), 1995; Rockin' At the Coconut Top (Crazy Love), 1996; The Cochran Connection (Rockstar), 1997; Darrel Higham and the Barnshakers (Gaofin'), 1998; How To Dance The Bop, 2000; 2 solo EPs; 3 Albums with Bob and the Bearcats; 2 with Johnny Bach and the Moonshine Boozers; 1 with Dave Phillips; 1 with the Blue Devils as Lead Guitarist. *Membership:* Musicians' Union. *Address:* 18 Biggleswade Rd, Upper Caldecote, Beds SG18 9BL, England.

HIGHAM, Mike; Programmer. *Career:* Worked with Seal on Spacejam, film soundtrack, Fly Like An Eagle; Completed work for Tina Turner, Barry White and Boyzone; Other projects include: The Art of Noise, Public Demand, Gary Barlow, Eric Clapton; Clients include: Seal: MTV Unplugged, album; Seal II, album; A Prayer For the Dying 12 remix; Bobby Brown, Every Little Step I Take 12 remix; Tina Turner, Wildest Dreams, album; Ministry of Sound, 6 albums; Whitney Houston, I'm Your Baby Tonight; Rod Stewart: Spanner in the Works; Spice Girls: Spiceworld; Eric Clapton: Pilgrim; Geri Halliwell, Scream If You Wanna Go Faster. *Address:* SARM Productions, SP2 Holdings Ltd, The Blue Building, 42/46 St Luke's Mews, London W11 1DG, England.

HILBORNE, Phil; b. 20 Jan. 1959, Poole, Dorset, England. Musician (guitar); Prod; Teacher; Journalist. m. 17 Feb. 1977, divorced, 2 s., 1 d. *Education:* Classical guitar studied with Professor W Grandison, Harpsichordist D Galbraith, Trinity College. *Career:* UK, Europe and USA tours with Phil Hilborne Band and Nicko McBrain (Iron Maiden); Live demonstrations for companies including: Gibson; Ampeg; Vigier; Paiste; Sonor; Zildjian, Fender; Kitty Hawk; Marshall; PRS; Music Editor, Guitarist magazine (Playing Rock Guitar/Solo Analysis articles plus various features and interviews), 1985–95; Music/CD Editor, Guitar Techniques magazine, 1994–; Felsted Music School, Head of Guitar, 1993–99; Guitar tutorials throughout Europe including the Bath International Guitar Festival, 1999–2002; Owns and runs Essex-based WM Studios. *Recordings include:* Are You Serious?, 1992; 'Bout Time, 1993; featured solo tracks on compilations: Bath International Guitar Festival CD, 2000; Fret-King CD, 2001; 15th Anniversary Album, 2001; featured peformances include: John McEnroe and Pat Cash with the Full Metal Rackets, Rock and Roll (single), 1991; Angel Easy, Lightning Strikes, 1990; Geoff Whitehorn, Big In Gravesend, 1994; Drome, Overload, 1996; Memphis Roots, Things Can Change, 1998; Blaze Bayley, Silicon Messiah, 2000; Greg Fitch, This Is Greg Fitch, 2000; Eric Roche, Spin, 2001; various tracks for specialist guitar magazine CDs, 1994–; Collaborations include: Maria Kern; Mark Cherrie; Tony Muschamp; Frank Gambale; Productions include: Dave Kilminster and Fraser T Smith, Playing With Fire, 1996; Genelab, Anorak Lou (unplugged), 1999; numerous demos, radio/TV sessions. *Publications:* Solo, 1987; Led Zeppelin Off The Record, 1988; Editor: Reijo Hittunen's Guitar Chord Method, 1993. *Contributions to:* Jimi Hendrix Electric Gypsy, 1990; Elton John Rockscore, 1991; Instructional Video: Phil Hilborne Rock Basics, 1992. *Membership:* Musicians' Union. *Current Management:* Phil Hilborne Band Management. *Address:* Phil Hilborne Band/Widdle Music, PO Box, 1001, Basildon, Essex, SS13 1SR, England.

HILL, Beau; b. 25 Sept. 1952, Dallas, Texas, USA. Record Prod; Musician (keyboards, guitar). *Education:* BA, Music and Western European History; Classical training 1958–; Music Major, University of Colorado. *Career:* Signed as recording artist, Columbia Records, 1978; Chrysalis Records, 1981; BMI writer, 1981–; Producer for Bob Dylan: Down in the Groove; Alice Cooper: Constrictor; Ratt: Dancin' Undercover; Warrant: Cherry Pie; Winger, Winger; Europe: Prisoners in Paradise; Chaka Khan; Fiona; Roger Daltrey; John Miles; Gary Moore; Steve Stevens; Bad Brains. *Recordings:* Compilations: Europe 1982–2000, Europe, 2000; Greatest and Latest, Warrant, 2000. *Membership:* NARAS; AES. *Address:* c/o Stuart Silfell, 488 Madison Ave, New York, NY 10023, USA.

HILL, Dave; b. 4 April 1946, Fleet Castle, Devon, England. Musician (guitar). *Career:* Member, The Vendors, Wolverhampton, 1965; Member, UK rock group Slade (formerly N'Betweens, Ambrose Slade), 1966–; Currently billed as Slade II; Concerts include: First British tour, 1972; Fanfare For Europe festival, London Palladium, 1973; Great British Music Festival, 1978; Reading Festival, 1980; Film: Flame, 1974. *Recordings:* Albums: Beginnings (as Ambrose Slade), 1969; Play It Loud, 1970; Slade Alive, 1972; Slayed, 1973; Sladest, 1973; Old New Borrowed Blue, 1974; Slade In Flame (soundtrack), 1974; Nobody's Fool, 1976; Slade Alive Vol. 2, 1978; Return To Base, 1979; Slade Smashes, 1980; Till Deaf Do Us Part, 1981; We'll Bring The House Down, 1981; Slade On Stage, 1982; The Amazing Kamikaze Syndrome, 1983; Slade's Greats, 1984; Rogue's Gallery, 1985; Crackers, 1985; You Boyz Make Big Noize, 1987; Wall of Hits, 1991; Keep On Rockin', 1996; Slade II, 2001; UK No. 1 hit singles: Coz I Luv You, 1971; Take Me Bak 'Ome, 1972; Mama Weer All Crazee Now (later recorded by Mama's Boys, Quiet Riot), 1972; Cum On Feel The Noize, 1973; Skweeze Me Pleeze Me, 1973; Merry Christmas Everybody, 1973; Other hits: Look Wot You Dun, 1972; Gudbuy T'Jane, 1972; My Friend Stan, 1973; Everyday, 1974; Bangin' Man, 1974; Far Far Away, 1974; Thanks For The Memory, 1975; In For A Penny, 1975; We'll Bring The House Down, 1981; My Oh My, 1983; Run Run Away, 1984; All Join Hands, 1984. *Publications:* Life story. *Honours:* Hon. Fellow, University of Wolverhampton, 2002. *Current Management:* Len Tuckey. *Address:* c/o Hal Carter Organisation, London, England.

HILL, Dusty (Joe Michael); b. 19 May 1949, Dallas, Texas, USA. Musician (bass); Vocalist. *Career:* Formed The Warlocks, with brother, Rocky, 1967; Renamed American Blues, 1968; Formed ZZ Top, 1970; Regular tours, 1970–; Tours include: Eliminator tour, 1984; Afterburner tour, 1985–87; Recycler tour, 1990; Rock The Bowl '91, Milton Keynes, 1991. *Recordings include:* Albums: 2 with The American Blues, 1968; with ZZ Top: ZZ Top's First Album 1970; Rio Grande Mud, 1972; Tres Hombres, 1973; Fandango, 1975; Best Of, 1978; Deguello, 1979; El Loco, 1981; Eliminator, 1983; Afterburner, 1985; Recycler, 1990; Greatest Hits, 1992; Antenna, 1994; Rhythmeen, 1996; XXX, 1999; Singles include: La Grange, 1974; Tush, 1975; Gimme All Your Lovin', 1983; Sharp Dressed Man, 1983; Legs, 1984; Sleeping Bag, 1985; Velcro Fly, 1986; Stages, 1986; Rough Boy, 1986; Doubleback, from film Back To The Future Part III, 1990; Viva Las Vegas, 1992. *Honours:* Several MTV Video Awards; ZZ Top Day, Texas, 1991; Silver Clef Award, Nordoff-Robbins Music Therapy Foundation, 1992. *Current Management:* Lone Wolf Management, PO Box 163690, Austin, TX 78716, USA.

HILL, Faith, (Audrey Faith Perry); b. 21 Sept. 1967, Jackson, MS, USA. Country Vocalist. m. Tim McGraw, 1996, 2 c. *Career:* Moved to Nashville, 1989; Signed to Warner Bros Records, 1992. *Recordings:* Albums: Take Me As I Am, 1993; It Matters To Me, 1995; Faith (aka Love Will Always Win), 1998; Breathe, 1999; Cry, 2002. Singles include: Wild One, 1993; Piece Of My Heart, 1994; Take Me As I Am, 1994; Let's Go To Vegas, 1995; Someone Else's Dream, 1996; A Man's Home Is His Castle; Keep Walkin' On (with Shelby Lynne); I Can't Do That Anymore; It Matters To Me, 1996; It's Your Love (with Tim McGraw), 1997; This Kiss, 1998. *Honours:* Platinum disc, Take Me As I Am; Country Music Asscn Award, for It's Your Love, 1997; American Music Award, Favourite Country Female Artist, 2002. *Address:* c/o Warner Bros Records Inc, 3300 Warner Blvd, Burbank, CA 91505, USA. *Website:* www.faithhill.com.

HILL, Jason; b. 28 Aug. 1948, Portsmouth, Hampshire, England. Barn Dance Caller; Musician (guitar, melodeon, autoharp). m. Gwyneth Mair Bound, 22 Feb. 1986. *Education:* University of Keele, 1967–71; Birmingham University, 1990–91. *Career:* Caller and musician with Oatcake Billy's Ideal Band, 1977–90; Alf Alfa and The Wild Oats, 1991–; Radio broadcast: Shropshire Folk Programme, 1993; Festivals: Potteries Folk Festival 1991; Crewe and Nantwich Folk Festival, 1992. *Recordings:* with Alf Alfa: Climbing The Walls, 1995. *Membership:* Musicians' Union; English Folk Dance and Song Society. *Current Management:* Barn Dance Agency Ltd. *Address:* 62 Beechwood Rd, South Croydon, Surrey CR2 0AA, England.

HILL, Lauryn; b. 26 May 1975, South Orange, NJ, USA. Vocalist; Actor. 1 s. *Education:* Columbia University. *Career:* Joined Tranzlator Crew, with Wyclef Jean and Pras Michel; Renamed as The Fugees; Numerous television and live appearances; Minor acting roles including As The World Turns on television and in film in Sister Act II; Solo artiste–; Wrote, Rose is Still a Rose for Aretha Franklin. *Recordings:* Albums: with The Fugees: Blunted on Reality, 1994; The Score (No. 1, USA), 1996; Solo: The Miseducation of Lauryn Hill, 1998; Lauryn Hill Story, 2000; MTV Unplugged No. 2.0, 2002. Singles: with The Fugees: Boof Baf, 1993; Nappy Heads, 1994; Vocab, EP, 1994; Ready or Not (No. 1, UK), 1996; The Score, 1996; Fu-Gee-La, 1996; Killing Me Softly (No. 1, UK), 1996; Rumble in the Jungle, 1997; Solo: Doo Wop (That Thing), 1998; Ex-Factor, 1998; Everything is Everything, 1999; Also contributed to recordings by: Whitney Houston; Mary J. Blige. *Honours:* BRIT Award, Best International Group, 1997; Five Grammy Awards, Album of the Year, Best New Artist, Best Female R&B Vocal Performance, Best R&B Song, Best R&B Album, 1999; American Music Awards, Favorite Soul/R&B Female Artist, 2000; Favourite Album, for The Miseducation of Lauryn Hill, 2000.

HILL, Mark; b. 1972, Wales, England. Prod; Remixer; DJ. *Education:* Southampton University, music student. *Career:* Played violin in Southampton Youth Orchestra; Formed the Artful Dodger with partner Pete Devereux, 1996; Released debut album, 2001; Co-founder: Centric Records (with Devereux); Duo split amicably, 2001; Continues to record and produce under Artful Dodger name; Collaborations: Craig David; Dreem Teem; Romina Johnson; Melanie Blatt; Remixed: Sisqo; Gabrielle. *Recordings:* Albums: It's All About The Stragglers, 2001; Singles: Re-Rewind The Crowd Say Bo Selecta (with Craig David), Movin' Too Fast (with Romina Johnson), 1999; Woman Trouble (with Robbie Craig and Craig David), Please Don't Turn Me On (with Lifford), 2000; It Ain't Enough (with Dreem Teem), Twentyfourseven (with Melanie Blatt), 2001. *Honours:* Ivor Novello Awards: Dance Award: Re-Rewind, 2000; Woman Trouble, 2001; Songwriters of the Year (with Craig David); Best Contemporary Song, 7 Days (co-writer), 2001. *Address:* c/o London Records, Waldron House, 57–63 Old Church St, London SW3 5BS, England.

HILL, Warren; b. Canada. Musician (alto, soprano saxophone). *Education:* Berklee College of Music, Boston. *Career:* Television appearances including: Tonight Show; Arsenio Hall Show; Unforgettable tour supporting Natalie Cole; Also supported: Ray Charles; Air Supply; Four Play; Worked with: Mitch Malloy; Sheila E; Alex Acuna; Lenny Castro; Jeff Pocaro; Ricardo Silveira. *Recordings:* Albums: Kiss Under The Moon, 1982; Devotion, 1993; Truth, 1994; Shelter, 1997; Life Thru Rose Coloured Glasses, 1998; Performed on: Restless Heart: Tell Me What You Dream (No. 1 Billboard charts); Also The Passion Theme, from Body of Evidence soundtrack; Can't Get You Out of my mind, with Aswad and General Levy; Jazz at Midnight; Hot Summer Swing. *Current Management:* SESAC. *Address:* 55 Music Sq. E, Nashville, TN 37203, USA.

HILLERED, Eva Karin Maria; b. 4 April 1958, Stockholm, Sweden. Vocalist; Songwriter; Singing Teacher. m. Peter Ostman, 1 d. *Education:* Drama, music and psychology, University; Choir leader tuition, 1 year; Studied singing, 1 year. *Career:* Backing Singer, Bob Manning, Py Backman, Eva Dahigren, Anne-Grete Preus, Rolf Wikstrom, Marie Bergman; Toured with Rock Runt Riket, Py Backman, Anne-Grete Preus, Eva Dahlgren, Rolf Wikstrom, Riksteaterns Cornelis-show; Own shows in Stockholm. *Recordings:* Inte Varfor Utan Hur, 1988; Straets langd, 1990; Jag Vet, 1995; Oppningsskedet, 1996. *Membership:* STIM; SKAP. *Current Management:* Diva Records, Sweden. *Address:* Tureholms Gard, 619 92 Trosa, Sweden.

HILLMAN, Chris; b. 4 Dec. 1944, Los Angeles, California, USA. Musician (bass, guitar); Songwriter; Vocalist. *Career:* Musician, groups: Scottsville Squirrel Barkers; Golden State Boys; The Hillmen; The Byrds, 1964–68; Performances include: Beach Boys Summer Spectacular, 1966; Monterey Festival, 1967; Grand Ole Opry, 1968; Newport Pop Festival, 1968; McGuinn Clark and Hillman (with Gene Clark and Roger McGuinn); The Flying Burrito Brothers; Manassas; Souther Hillman Furay Band; Desert Rose Band. *Recordings:* Albums with the Byrds: Mr Tambourine Man, 1965; Turn! Turn! Turn!, 1965; Fifth Dimension, 1966; Younger Than Yesterday, 1967; The Notorious Byrd Brothers, 1968; Sweetheart of The Rodeo, 1968; History of The Byrds, 1973; The Byrds, 1990; with The Flying Burrito Brothers: The Gilded Palace of Sin, 1969; Burrito Deluxe, 1970; The Flying Burrito Brothers, 1971; The Last of The Red Hot Burrito Brothers, 1972; Flying Again, 1976; Airborne, 1976; Close Encounters On The West Coast, 1978; Live In Tokyo, Japan, 1978; Flying High, 1980; Back To The Sweethearts of The Rodeo, 1988; Southern Tracks, 1990; with Manassas: Manassas, 1972; Down The Road, 1973; with Souther Hillman Furay Band: Souther Hillman Furay, 1974; Trouble In Paradise, 1974; with Desert Rose Band: The Desert Rose Band, 1987; Running, 1988; Pages of Life, 1990; True Love, 1991; A Dozen Roses, 1991; Life Goes On, 1994; Solo: Slippin' Away, 1976; Sixteen Roses: Greatest Hits, 1995; Bakersfield Bound, 1996; Like a Hurricane, 1998; with Rice, Rice, Hillman and Pederson: Running Wild, 2001; Singles with the Byrds include: Mr Tambourine Man (No. 1, USA), 1965; All I Really Want To Do, 1965; Eight Miles High, 1966; So You Want To Be A Rock 'n' Roll Star, 1967. *Honours:* Inducted into Rock and Roll Hall of Fame, 1991.

HINCHLIFFE, Keith Phillip; b. 4 Jan. 1951, Glossop, Derbyshire, England. Musician (guitar); Vocalist. *Education:* BA, English, Leicester University; Doctorate in English, Hull University. *Career:* Several years, Folk and Blues club and concert circuit; Member, Albion Band, 1991–92; Extensive tuition and workshop experience; Several appearances, BBC Radio, ITV. *Recordings:* Albums: Carolan's Dream, 1994; The Albion Band: Captured, 1994; Islands, 1999. *Publications:* Carolan's Dream, 1995; Original guitar music in Guitar International; O'Carolan for Everyone, 1999. *Membership:* PRS; Musicians' Union; PAMRA. *Address:* 23A Spring Hill, Sheffield S10 1ET, England.

HINCHLIFFE, Roger Redman; b. 27 Dec. 1944, Springfield, Vermont, USA. Vocalist; Composer; Translator. m. Karen Soderberg, 30 Sept. 1995, 2 d. *Education:* BA, Bowdoin College, 1966; MBA, Cornell University, 1968; Swedish, Stockholm University, 1974; Voice and Theoretical Studies, Glee Club. *Career:* Ten Tours of USA as solo vocalist, including 80 Concerts in 20 States, 1988–; Guest appearances on Television and Radio in the USA and Sweden. *Compositions:* Over 30 English Translations and Solo Recordings of

Sweden's Greatest Popular Songs; 12 Original Compositions. *Recordings:* Cantalucha, 1979; Festival Theme, 1980; Swedens Greatest, 1988; Swedes on Love, 1992; Master Olofs Choir, 1994. *Publications:* Over 100 including: Films Translated from Swedish to English: Three Loves, 1990; Greta Garbo, 1994; Who Killed Olof Palme?, 1995; Jerusalem, 1996; Tattooed Widow, 1997. *Honours:* 10 Festival Awards for Translations, Cannes, Montreux, 1986–98. *Membership:* American Asscn of Sweden; Compact Disc Asscn. *Current Management:* c/o RogeRecords, PO Box 414, Cedar Mt, NC 28718, USA.

HINDLEY, Guy Niall; b. 5 July 1956, Manchester, England. Musician (Accordion, bass trombone). m. Aileen, 6 July 1996. *Education:* BA, Geography; MSc, Transport Technology; Piano lessons. *Career:* Second accordion with Carousel Ceilidh Band, 1997; Playing bass trombone. *Membership:* Musicians' Union. *Address:* 32 Tuxford Rd, Ansdell, Lytham St Annes, Lancashire FY8 4BH, England.

HINDS, David; Vocalist; Songwriter; Musician (guitar). *Education:* Handsworth School, Birmingham. *Career:* Founding mem. and lead singer, Steel Pulse, 1975–, with Basil Gabbidon, Ronald McQueen; Supported Burning Spear; Signed to Island Records, Elektra Records, MCA Records, Tuff Gong International; Television appearances include: Arsenio Hall, The Tonight Show with Jay Leno, Late Night with Conan O'Brien, The Keenan Ivory Wayans Show; Performed at the inauguration of President Bill Clinton, Washington, DC, 1993; Extensive world-wide tours; Band mems vary, currently nine-piece band; Performances with: Bob Dylan, Herbie Hancock, INXS, Bob Marley & the Wailers, Robert Palmer, Santana, Sting, The Stranglers, Peter Tosh, Stevie Wonder. *Recordings:* Albums: Handsworth Revolution, 1978; Tribute To The Martyrs, 1979; Caught You (aka Reggae Fever), 1980; True Democracy, 1982; Earth Crisis, 1984; Reggae Refreshers, 1985; Babylon The Bandit, 1985; State of Emergency, 1988; Victims, 1991; Rastafari Centennial, 1992; Smash Hits, 1993; Vex, 1994; Rastanthology, 1996; Rage & Fury, 1997; Sound System: The Island Anthology, 1996; Living Legacy, 1999. *Honours:* Grammy Award, for Babylon The Bandit. *Address:* Steel Pulse, 42 Upper Dean St, Digbeth, Birmingham, West Midlands B5 4SG, England. *E-mail:* info@steel-pulse.com. *Website:* www.steel-pulse.com.

HINE, Rupert Neville; b. 21 Sept. 1947, Wimbledon, England. Record Prod; Musician (multi-instrumentalist). m. Natasha, 1 s. *Career:* Songwriter for: Tina Turner; Stevie Nicks; Wilson Phillips; Robert Palmer; Dusty Springfield. *Recordings:* Albums include: with Quantum Jump: Quantum Jump, 1976; Barracuda, 1977; Solo albums: Pick up a Bone, 1971; Unfinished Picture, 1973; Immunity, 1981; Waving Not Drowning, 1982; Wildest Wish to Fly, 1983; Deep End, 1995; Producer of over 100 albums for artists including Tina Turner; Bob Geldof; Rush; The Fixx; Howard Jones; Chris De Burgh; Stevie Nicks; Duncan Sheik; Numerous film scores and television projects, including One World One Voice featuring: Peter Gabriel; Chrissie Hynde; Suzanne Vega; Lou Reed; Laurie Anderson; Dave Stewart; Sting; Also 300 other musicians from 6 continents. *Honours:* Producer, Grammy award-winning tracks; Numerous Gold discs. *Current Management:* Jukes Productions Ltd. *Address:* c/o Jukes Productions Ltd, 63 Sutherland Ave, London W9 2HF, England.

HINKLER, Simon Thomas; b. 13 Nov. 1959, Sheffield, England. Musician (guitar, keyboards); Prod; Programmer. *Career:* Multi-instrumentalist with Artery, Pulp, 1980–85; Guitarist, The Mission, 1986–90; World-wide tours (first western band to play Paraguay), numerous television appearances; Programmer, prod., freelance, 1994–. *Recordings:* Albums: with Artery: Oceans, 1982; Pulp-it, 1983; Artery Live In Amsterdam, 1985; The Flight Commander, 1985; God's Own Medicine, 1986; The First Chapter, 1987; Children, 1988; Carved In Sand, 1990; Room Full of This, 1993; with Pulp: Pulpintro–The Gift Recordings, 1993; Pulped (compilation), 2001; with The Mission: Salad Daze, 1994. *Publications:* Names Are For Tombstones Baby, 1993. *Honours:* Gold Discs, all Mission albums. *Membership:* Musicians' Union; PRS; PPL. *Current Management:* Curveball Management. *Address:* PO Box 899, Walkley, Sheffield S6 2YY, England.

HIRABAYASHI, Makiko; b. 17 Sept. 1966, Tokyo, Japan. Musician. m. Morten Kargaard Nielsen, 24 Sept. 1990. *Education:* Music Degree, Berklee College of Music; Major, Piano, Rhythmic Conservatory, Denmark. *Career:* Performed with Morten Kargaard Group and Sisters, Copenhagen Jazz Festival, 1991–97; Japan Tour with Third Floor Jazz Quartet, 1992, 1993, 1994; Performed, Yokohama Jazz Promenade, 1993, 1994; Performed with Sisters, Stockholm Water Festival, 1996, 1997; Performed with Maravilla, Roskilde Festival, 1997. *Recordings:* Later Still, 1993; Colour of a Moment, 1996; Elk Dance, 1996; Sa Ka La Musika, 1997; A Story of Multiplicity, 1998; BIMWO Swing, 1998. *Honours:* Third Prize, Best Arrangement, Public Award, Europe Jazz Contest, Belgium, 1995. *Address:* Linnesgade 33 3tv, 1361 Copenhagen K, Denmark.

HIRD, Colin; b. 21 April 1964, Sunderland, England. Musician (Bass, Chapman Stick, Keys); Prod. m. Jane Hird, 24 April 1991. *Education:* HND in Music Technology; Studied Bass under Nick Beggs. *Career:* It's Crucial tour, 1985; McCallum, Left Handed Tour, 1988; TV appearance on BBC 2's Out of Our Heads, 1988, and ITV's Comedy Bites, 1995 with Morgan Le Fay.

Recordings: Left Handed, with McCallum, 1988; Growing Up In Public, with The Flair, 1994. *Membership:* Musicians' Union. *Current Management:* Major Management, Blyth, Northumberland, England. *Address:* 2 Cowpen Rd, Blyth, Northumberland NE24 5BS, England.

HIRST, Clare; b. 13 Aug. 1959, Alston, Cumbria, England. Musician (saxophone); Vocalist; Composer. m. Alan Barnes, 31 July 1995, 1 s. *Education:* Some private tuition. *Career:* Member, pop band The Bellestars, 1981–86; Played on Live Aid with David Bowie; Toured with The Communards; Sandie Shaw; Iggy Pop; Hazel O'Connor; Maxi Priest; Amazulu; Quireboys; Television appearances include: Jazz 606, BBC2. *Recordings:* All Belle Stars recordings; with The Communards: Don't Leave Me This Way (No. 1, UK), 1986; with Luxuria: Unanswerable Lust, 1988; with Clare Hirst Quartet: Tough and Tender, 1995; Singles with The Belle Stars include: Iko Iko, 1982; The Clapping Song, 1982; Sign of The Times, 1982; Sweet Memory, 1983; The Entertainer, 1983. *Current Management:* c/o 33 Records, 33 Guildford St, Luton, Bedfordshire, England.

HIRST, Willie; b. 2 May 1941, Barnsley, South Yorkshire, England. Bandleader; Musical Dir; Arranger; Musician (saxophone, clarinet, flute, recorder). m. Hazel Irene Rainbow, 4 April 1966, 2 s. *Education:* Huddersfield College of Music; Bretton Hall College. *Career:* Musical director, Wakefield Theatre Club, for 15 years; Tours: Bobby Vee; Tony Christie; Marti Caine; Lionel Blair; Concerts: Johnny Mathis; Tony Bennett; Buddy Greco; Victor Borge; Sacha Distel; Tommy Steele; Bruce Forsyth; Matt Monro; Drifters; Des O'Connor; Bob Monkhouse; Gladys Knight and the Pips; Television appearances: Les Dawson; Three Two One; Play Guitar; Radio: Jimmy Young Show; Late Night Show; Early Breakfast Show. *Honours:* LRAM (saxophone); ARCM (clarinet); LTCL (recorder); Certificate of Education; Lecturer in Instrumental Music at Bretton Hall College and Leeds College of Music. *Membership:* Musicians' Union. *Current Management:* Partner with Hazel Hirst, Maestro Music and Entertainment Agency. *Address:* Belmont House, 32 Bell Lane, Ackworth, Pontefract, West Yorkshire WF7 7JH, England.

HITZ, Michael; b. 12 Oct. 1968, Baden, Switzerland. Jazz/Pop Vocalist; Musician. *Education:* Private Instructions, Acting, Singing, Phonetics. *Career:* Church Singing, Nightclubs, 1986; Stage Cariete Polygon, Zuerich, 1989; Radio Show, Risiko, Seeperle, DRS Kultur, 1992; Tour Switzerland and Germany, Worked with The Platters, Sina, Maja Brunner, Musical Remember Me, 1994; Talk Show, Bernard Theatre Zurich, 1997–98. *Recordings:* CDs, Polygon, Clowns, Remember Me, Like A River Flows. *Membership:* Freunde Des Leedes, SUISA. *Current Management:* Daisy Entertainment. *Address:* Thurwiesenstrasse 15, 8037 Zurich, Switzerland.

HNILICKA, Jaromir; b. 11 Feb. 1932, Bratislava. Composer; Musician. Divorced, 2 d. *Education:* Graduate, State Conservatory for Music. *Career:* Trumpet Soloist, Gustav Brom Big Band; Composer, Arranger, 1953–. *Compositions:* Missa Jazz, 1968, 1989. *Recordings:* Missa Jazz, 1968, 1989. *Honours:* Prize, Josef Blaha; Prize, Ludek Hulan; Prize, Composers Asscn. *Membership:* OSA. *Address:* Kupkova 22, 63800 Brno, Czech Republic.

HO, Fred Wei-Han Houn; b. 10 Aug. 1957, Palo Alto, California, USA. Composer; Musician (Baritone Saxophone); Writer; Prod. *Education:* BA, Sociology, Harvard University. *Career:* Next Wave Festival, Brooklyn Academy of Music, 1997; San Francisco Jazz Festival, Herbst Theatre, 1998. *Compositions:* Warrior Sisters, opera; Night Vision, opera; Journey Beyond the West: The New Adventure of Monkey; A Chinaman's Chance, opera. *Recordings:* Warrior Sisters; Monkey: Part One and Part Two; Underground Railroad to My Heart; Tomorrow Is Now!; Turn Pain Into Power!. *Publications:* Sounding Off!, Music as Subversion, 1996; Womyn Warriors Calendar. *Honours:* Duke Ellington Distinguished Artist Lifetime Achievement Award, 1988; National Endowment for the Arts Jazz Competition Fellowship, 1992. *Membership:* ASCAP; American Composers Forum; American Music Center. *Current Management:* Big Red Media. *Address:* 443 12th St, Brooklyn, NY 11215, USA.

HOBBS, Paul Ernest Leonard; b. 28 Dec. 1948, Burnt Oak, Edgware, Hendon, Middlesex, England. Musician (drums). m. (1) Jane Pitkin, 26 July 1975, (2) Sylvia Picton, 25 July 1987, 2 d. *Education:* Tuition from Buddy Rich, Phil Seaman, James Blades, Sylvia Hobbs, Diana Clement. *Career:* Mem., 'Twas Brillig, 1964–65; Dr John and the Blues Preachers, 1965–67; Dream Machine, 1967–68; Support to John Mayall's Blues Breakers, 1967; Mahogany, 1968–72; Support to Peter Green's Fleetwood Mac/Status Quo, 1968; Utrecht Railway Museum performances for Jam (Dutch TV), 1970, 1971; Late Night Line-up, with Marty Wilde (BBC), 1970–71; BBC Radio One Club. *Recordings:* Albums: Mahogany, 1969; Mahogany With Marty Wilde, 1970; Bring Back Rock 'N' Roll; Roy Powell Combo, 1971–72; Old Nick's Trainset, 1972; Good Rockin' Now And Then, Marty Wilde, 1973; Kirsch, 1973; Graunch, 1973–74; Pale Lights, 1973–76; Resident drummer, Gatsby's Nightclub, Chesham, England; Cochise, 1980–82; T-Bone Boogie Band, 1983–84; Pink 'N' Black, 1984; The Anxious Brothers, 1987–89; W. Arts And All, 1990–99; Robert Bee Blues Corporation 1992–93; Danny White And The Shadds, 1995–98; Ray Cave And Paul Hobbs (Sounds And Colour), 1998–99;

Tigger And Paul, 2001–. *Membership:* Musicians' Union. *Address:* 82 Bourne Cres., Kingsheath, Northampton, Northamptonshire NN5 7JA, England.

HOBBS, Rebecca Ann (Becky); b. 24 Jan. 1950, Bartlesville, Oklahoma, USA. Vocalist; Songwriter. *Education:* 1 year college, Tulsa University; 6 years piano lessons. *Career:* Performed in more than 40 countries; Performed on: Hee Haw; Academy of Country Music Awards Show; Nashville Now; Prime Time Country; Pop! Goes The Country; Staler Bros Show. *Compositions:* co-wrote Angels Among Us, recorded by Alabama; Co-wrote I Want To Know You Before We Make Love, number 1 country hit for Conway Twitty; Co-wrote, recorded, Jones On The Jukebox; Other songs recorded by: George Jones; Loretta Lynn; Glen Campbell; Emmylou Harris; Helen Reddy; Shirley Bassey. *Recordings:* Albums include: From Oklahoma With Love, 1998. *Honours:* Most Promising International Act, In Country Music Round-Up, 1989; Top Female On Independent Label, 1994. *Membership:* NSAI; AFofM; AFTRA; CMA. *Address:* Becky Hobbs, c/o Beckaroo Music, PO Box 150272, Nashville, TN 37215, USA. *E-mail:* beckaroomusic@lycos.com. *Website:* www.beckyhobbs.com.

HOBROUGH, Mark; b. 11 Sept. 1965, Cheshire, England. Record Co Exec; Artiste Man. *Education:* BA Hons in Archaeology, Dunelm. *Career:* Spin Promotions Ltd, 1989; Managing Director, Revolution Promotions and Lemon Records, 1991; Managing Director, Revolution Promotions and Jealous Records; Manager of Sack and Darling Sugar Honey (Revolution Management), 1995. *Address:* 172A Arlington Rd, Camden, London NW1 7HL, England.

HOCHMAN, Larry; b. 21 Nov. 1953, New Jersey, USA. Composer; Orchestrator. m. Diane Hochman, 1 step-s., 1 step-d., 1 d. *Education:* Manhattan School of Music, 1972–75. *Career:* Co-Founder, with Larry Gates, Newfound Music Productions. *Compositions include:* Stephen Spielberg's Amazing Stories, 1986; Views of a Vanishing Frontier, 1987; Phantom of the Opera, 1990; In Memoriam, 1993; Dear America, 1993; American Portraits, 1996; The Very Last Butterfly, 1997; Music for the Movies, 1998; Hot Klezmer, 1998; Orchestrated: How Glory Goes, Audra McDonald, 2000. *Recordings:* One Man Band; In Memoriam. *Honours:* New Jersey Theatre Group Applause Award; Various CLIO Awards; ASCAP Award; Bistro Cabaret Award. *Membership:* American Federation of Musicians; Pushcart Players. *Address:* 10 Kershner Pl., Fair Lawn, NJ 07410, USA.

HODES, Paul William; b. 21 March 1951, New York, NY, USA. Attorney; Record Co Pres; Musician. Prod. m. Margaret A Horstmann, 29 June 1979, 1 s., 1 d. *Education:* BA cum laude, Dartmouth College, 1972; JD cum laude, Boston College Law School, 1978. *Career:* Founder, Town Meeting Theatre Workshop, Vermont; Worked as Actor, Director, Producer, Film Maker, Playwright; Assistant Attorney General; Trial and Entertainment Attorney, Shaheen and Gordon PA, Concord, New Hampshire; Founding Member, Peggosus, rock group; President, Big Round Records Inc. *Recordings:* Peggosus Jubilee!, 1986; Peggosus Diggin' in the Dirt, 1991; Peggot Paul Patchwork Quilt, 1996; Peggo and Paul's Winter's Light, 2000. *Honours:* ASCAP Awards; Parents Choice Honours, 1987, 1996. *Membership:* ASCAP; Chairman, Capitol Center for the Arts, 1990–96; Board Mem., Concord Community Music School, Children's Entertainment Asscn, New Hampshire Children's Alliance. *Current Management:* CandM Management Group, Brentwood, Tennessee. *Address:* Shaheen and Gordon PA, Box 2703, Two Capital Plaza, Concord, NH 03302, USA.

HODGE, Andrew; b. 17 Aug. 1966, Ickenham, Middlesex, England. Freelance Musician (bass guitar). m. Susan Louise Jinks (Madeleine Harvey), 27 Sept. 1992. *Education:* Colin Spencer, Classical Guitar Studio, Torquay. *Career:* Lorna Luft, Dave Willetts Magical World of The Musicals Tour; Jerry Playle, album promotional tour Beyond Silence; Brotherhood of Man, British tour, 1994–95; Home and Away, National Tour; That'll Be The Day, British tour, 1999–2000. *Recordings:* Albums: L and A, acoustic; Foreverly Yours; with Dangerously Big: Dangerously Big; with Innocence Lost: Love Is In. *Membership:* Musicians' Union. *Address:* 26 The Reddings, Borehamwood, Herts WD6 4ST, England.

HODGE, Philip Norman; b. 11 Sept. 1953, Aylesbury, Buckinghamshire, England. Musician (keyboards); Computer Engineer. m. Lisa Mary Jane Stacey, 18 June 1994. *Education:* Piano Grade 6. *Career:* Semi-pro band: Synthesis, 1970–75; Steve Hillage Band (Virgin), British tour, 1976; American tour, support to ELO, 1977; Hyde Park concert with Queen, 1976; TV: Old Grey Whistle Test, 1976; European TV shows, concerts; Semi-pro bands: Six; As Above So Below; Radio 1, Friday Rock Show; Concert with Dave Stewart, Barbara Gaskin, as keyboard player. *Publications:* Articles, keyboard reviews, Organ Player Magazine. *Address:* 50 Corbet Ride, Linslade, Leighton Buzzard, Bedfordshire LU7 75J, England.

HODGES, Chas (Charles Nicholas); b. 28 Dec. 1943, Edmonton, London, England. Musician (piano, guitar, bass); Entertainer; Songwriter. m. Joan Adeline Findley, 6 Oct. 1966, 2 d., 1 s. *Career:* Turned professional, 1960; Member of bands: Mike Berry and the Outlaws; Cliff Bennett and the Rebel Rousers; Heads, Hands and Feet; Cockney duo Chas and Dave (with Dave

Peacock); World-wide tours; Numerous radio and television appearances; Collaborations: Billy Fury; Oliver Nelson; Bobby Graham; Gene Vincent; Albert Lee; Labi Siffre. *Compositions:* Over 300 songs; Biggest hit single Ain't No Pleasin' You, Chas and Dave, co-written with Dave Peacock (No. 2, UK), 1982; Biggest Hit Album/Video: Chas and Dave's Street Party (No. 3, UK), 1995. *Recordings include:* with Chas and Dave: Gertcha, 1979; Rabbit, 1980; Stars Over 45, 1981; Margate, 1982; Snooker Loopy, with The Matchroom Mob, 1986; Hit records with all the above artists. *Publications:* Chas Before Dave, autobiography. *Honours:* Bass Player of Year, 1962; Over 20 Gold albums and singles. *Membership:* PRS; MCPS; Musicians' Union. *Current Management:* Bob England, Hurricane Entertainments.

HODGSON, Lee James; b. 18 May 1961, Chelmsford, England. Musician (guitar, midi); Vocalist; Educator. m. Gloria Maria Ricardo, 20 Aug. 1984, 2 s. *Career:* Club concerts from age 16; Professional, age 18; Tours with Odyssey, 1980–81; Bobby Thurston, 1980; Television and radio commercial sessions, mid-1980s; Several years with comedy showband Barley; Formed country band Memphis Roots, 1987; Concerts include: Wembley Arena; Royal Albert Hall; Festivals; Instructor, Guitar Institute, 1990s. *Recordings:* Best of Memphis Roots; Good Noise: The Best of Western Line Dancing. *Publications:* Grade pieces for Rockschool Ltd; Hot Country, guitar tutorial, 1997; Columnist, Guitar Techniques magazine, Guitarist magazine. *Membership:* Musicians' Union; PRS. *Address:* 2 The Poplars, Pitsea, Basildon, Essex SS13 2ER, England.

HØEG, Thorsten Sehested, (Dane T. S. Hawk); b. 6 Jan. 1957, Copenhagen, Denmark. Musician (saxophone); Bandleader; Composer; Writer; Entertainer. *Education:* Studied with saxophonist and composer, John Tchicai, 1973–78, composer and arranger, Bob Brookmeyer, 1997–99. *Career:* Mem., John Tchicai and his Festival Band, 1975–78, Sods/Sort Sol, 1980–83; Formed trio, Cockpit Music, 1978–, numerous concerts and tours, Denmark, Finland, Sweden, Switzerland, former Czechoslovakia, Yugoslavia; National and international tours, solo, 1980–; Bandleader, 1981–85, Somesax, 1985–90; Formed 12-piece big band, Dane T. S. Hawk and his Great Mongo Dilmuns, 1990–; Concerts incl. Copenhagen Jazz Festival, Venue Festival, Roskilde Festival, Århus Festuge, jazz-, rock- and technoclub circuit, also Slovenia, Croatia and Expo 2000; Formed Dane T. S. Hawk & the Locomotion Starsemble, 2002–. *Compositions:* Pieces for many groups; Scores to Danish and French dance companies, 1980s; The Royal Danish Theatre, Billedstofteatret, Denmarks Radio; The Sweet Devil On The Loose / I am 3, 1994; SOAP (opera score, with libretti by Morti Vizki), 1995; Listen, No Heavy Breathing, Just Knock It Off (percussion), 1997; I've Been Chopping Wood, That Makes Me A Hungry Man (piano concerto), 1998; Mista BB, You Pushed My Wall, 1999; Tromfoniske Maskineter, 1999; 3 Betingelser For Liv, 1999; Millenniature, 2000. *Recordings:* as musician: Transworlds Of Sounds, 1981; Snow Lake City, 1982; Salute For General Wasteland, 1983; Stop/Go, 1985; Hands Up, 1989; The Great Dividing Range, 1996; Tales From The North, 1999; as bandleader: Flapper, 1990; Don't Hesitate (To Get Out There), 1996; Bøh—Music To An Imaginary Nordic Horror Tale, 1997; Death Disco, 1998; Dreamblues, 2002; Det Talte Ord & Raske Råberemser, 2000. *Publications:* Books: Træer vinkler vandstråle i en kort forvintret sommer, 1981; Amokoma,1982; Landskab ruller zone, 1983; ½ så gammel som tiden, 1987; Hotel Kontinental i likvidation, 1990; Gutboy, 1996; Ramt af jordens midte, 1998; Radio plays: Tilbud, 1989; Som Det Er Her I Landet, 1992; Damian Dagligdags Byrdefulde Brydningsår, 1994; Dengang Der Var Fremtid Til, 2000; Theatre plays: Alt Op Fra Grunden, 1987; De Syv Dødssynder, 1992; Saxo Vender Tilbage II, 1997. *Honours:* Several awards and grants for literature and music. *Membership:* PEN; DJBFA; DSF. *Address:* Frederiksberg Allé 7, 1621 Copenhagen V, Denmark. *E-mail:* DaneT.S.Hawk@tshoeg.dk. *Website:* www.t.s.hoeg.dk.

HOFF, Jan Gunnar; b. 22 Oct. 1958, Bodo, Norway. Musician (piano); Composer. *Education:* 3 year jazz study, Trondelag Music Conservatory, 1986–89; Private classes with Harold Danko, 1987, Django Bates, 1994, Andy Laverne, 2000. *Career:* Debut concert, Harstad Music Festival as solo artiste, 1992; Concerts with Jan Gunnar Hoff Group: Vossajazz, Norway, 1995; Molde International Jazzfestival, 1996, (with Pat Metheny), 2001; Oris London Jazz Festival, Barbican, 1996; Bergen Festival, 1996, 1998; Stavanger International Jazz Festival, 1998; Collaborations with drummers, Kenwood Dennard, 1999, Martin France, 2000; Norwegian House concert, Paris, 2000; La Maroquenerie club, Paris, 2000. *Recordings:* Syklus, 1993; Moving, 1995; Crosslands, 1998. *Honours:* The Stubö Prize, 1997; Government Grant, 2000–01. *Membership:* NOPA (popular composers); Gramart (recording artistes). *Address:* Harald Langhellesvei. 16B, 8003 Bodø, Norway. *Website:* www.jangunnarhoff.no.

HOFFS, Susannah; b. 17 Jan. 1959, Los Angeles, California, USA. Vocalist; Musician (guitar). *Education:* Graduate, University of California, Berkeley. *Career:* Founder member, all-female group The Bangles (originally Supersonic Bangs, then The Bangs), 1981–89; Tours and concerts include: Support to The Beat, 1982; Debut British tour, 1984; World tour, 1986; Support to Simple Minds, Milton Keynes Bowl Pop Festival, 1986; Support to Queen, Ireland, 1986; US tour, 1986; Solo recording career, 1989–; US tour, support to Don Henley, 1991; Actress, The Allnighter, 1986. *Recordings:* Albums: with The

Bangles: The Bangles, 1982; All Over The Place, 1984; Different Light, 1986; Everything, 1988; Bangles' Greatest Hits, 1989; All Over the Place/Different Light, 1997; with Tom Petty: Playback, 1995; featured on Poptopia 80s Power Pop Classics, 1997; Solo albums: When You're A Boy, 1991; Susannah Hoffs, 1996; Hit singles: Manic Monday, 1986; If She Knew What She Wants, 1986; Going Down To Liverpool, 1986; Walk Like An Egyptian, (No. 1, USA), 1986; Hazy Shade of Winter (used in film soundtrack Less Than Zero), 1988; In Your Room, 1988; Eternal Flame (No. 1, UK), 1989; Be With You, 1989; Solo singles: My Side of The Bed, 1991; All I Want, 1996. *Current Management:* c/o Gold Mountain Entertainment, Suite 450, 3575 Cahuenga Blvd W, Los Angeles, CA 90068, USA.

HOFSTEIN, Francis; b. 9 Oct. 1937, France. Psychoanalyst; Critic; Writer. m. Nicole Cerf, 3 s. *Education:* Docteur En Medecine; Conservatoire de Musique. *Publications:* Au Miroir Du Jazz; Oakland Blues; James Pichette Et Le Jazz; Le Rhythm and Blues; Jazz-Suite Pour Sacha; Blue Moon; Muddy Waters (biography); Le Poison de la Dépendence. *Contributions to:* Books: Dictionnaire du Jazz; Blues; Les Incontournables; Guide du Jazz; Journals: Jazz Magazine; Soul Bag; Essaim; Le Bloc-notes de la Psychanalyse; Chief Ed., L'Art du Jazz. *Membership:* Academie du Jazz; École Freudienne de Paris. *Address:* 5 rue Ernest et Henri Rousselle, 75013 Paris, France.

HOGAN, Michael Gerard; b. 29 April 1973, Limerick, Ireland. Musician (bass guitar). *Career:* Founding mem., The Cranberry Saw Us, renamed The Cranberries, 1990–; Numerous headlining tours, festivals, radio and television appearances. *Recordings:* Albums: Everybody Else Is Doing It, So Why Can't We? (No. 1, UK), 1993; No Need To Argue, 1994; To The Faithful Departed, 1996; Bury The Hatchet, 1999; Bury The Hatchet: The Complete Sessions, 2000; Wake Up And Smell The Coffee, 2001; Treasure Box, 2002; Stars: The Best Of 1992–2002, 2002. Singles: Dreams, 1993; Linger, 1993; Zombie, 1994; Ode To My Family, 1994; I Can't Be With You, 1995; Ridiculous Thoughts, 1995; Salvation, 1996; Free To Decide, 1996; Promises, 1999; Animal Instinct, 1999; Just My Imagination, 1999; You And Me, 2000; Analyse, 2001; Time Is Ticking Out, 2002; This Is The Day, 2002; Stars, 2002. *Current Management:* Timeless Music Ltd. *Address:* The Cranberries, PO Box 180, Limerick, Ireland. *Website:* www.cranberries.com.

HOGAN, Noel Anthony; b. 25 Dec. 1971, Limerick, Ireland. Musician (guitar). *Career:* Founding mem., The Cranberry Saw Us, renamed The Cranberries, 1990–; Numerous headlining tours, festivals, radio and television appearances. *Recordings:* Albums: Everybody Else Is Doing It, So Why Can't We? (No. 1, UK), 1993; No Need To Argue, 1994; To The Faithful Departed, 1996; Bury The Hatchet, 1999; Bury The Hatchet: The Complete Sessions, 2000; Wake Up And Smell The Coffee, 2001; Treasure Box, 2002; Stars: The Best Of 1992–2002, 2002. Singles: Dreams, 1993; Linger, 1993; Zombie, 1994; Ode To My Family, 1994; I Can't Be With You, 1995; Ridiculous Thoughts, 1995; Salvation, 1996; Free To Decide, 1996; Promises, 1999; Animal Instinct, 1999; Just My Imagination, 1999; You And Me, 2000; Analyse, 2001; Time Is Ticking Out, 2002; This Is The Day, 2002; Stars, 2002. *Current Management:* Timeless Music Ltd. *Address:* The Cranberries, PO Box 180, Limerick, Ireland. *Website:* www.cranberries.com.

HOGARTH, Steve; b. 14 May 1959, Kendal, Cumbria, England. Musician; Vocalist; Songwriter. m. 16 Aug. 1980, 1 s., 1 d. *Career:* Singer, groups The Europeans; How We Live; Lead singer, UK progressive rock group, Marillion, 1989–; Tours include: UK, 1991; North America, 1992; South America, 1992; Colaborations with The The, Julian Cope and Toni Childs; World tours with the Europeans; 5 world tours with Marillion. *Recordings:* Albums: with The Europeans: Vocabulary, 1982; Recurring Dreams, 1984; with Marillion: Season's End, 1989; Holidays In Eden, 1991; A Singles Collection 1982–92, 1992; Brave, 1994; Afraid of Sunlight, 1995; Made Again, 1996; This Strange Engine, 1997; Radiation, 1998; Afraid of Sunlight, 1999; Anorak In The UK Live, 2002; Solo as H: Ice Cream Genius; Singles: Hooks In You, 1989; Uninvited Guest, 1989; Easter, 1990; Cover My Eyes (Pain and Heaven), 1991; No One Can, 1991; Dry Land, 1991; Sympathy, 1992. *Current Management:* Hit and Run Music Ltd. *Address:* 30 Ives St, London SW3 2ND, England.

HÖGLUND, Kjell; b. 8 Dec. 1945, Östersund, Sweden. Songwriter; Artist; Musician (guitar). Partner, Margaretha Granström. *Education:* Bachelor of Arts. *Career:* 12 albums with own songs; Pioneer of making own records; Legend, Swedish underground music. *Compositions include:* Songs: Witch-Trial; Smooth Water; Sea of Gennesaret; One Big Strong; One Gets Accustomed; The Last Battle. *Recordings:* Albums: Wonder, 1971; Flower Season, 1972; Witch-Trial, 1973; Baskervilles Hound, 1974; The Heart Is To The Left, 1975; Dr Jekyll's Will, 1979; The Road Towards Shangri-La, 1980; Signs of The Times, 1984; Secret Love, 1986; Year of The Serpent, 1989; Höglund Forever, 1992; Incognito, 1995. *Publications:* Song book: Burnt Ships, 1987; Novels: Magnum Opus, 1991; The Sicilian Seal, 1997. *Honours:* Numerous scholarships. *Current Management:* RMP Management, Stockholm. *Address:* Atlantis Records, Karlbergsvägen 57, 113 35 Stockholm, Sweden.

HÖH, Volker; b. 24 April 1959, Altenkirchen, Pfalz, Germany. Musician (guitar). m. Jutta Maria Höh, 20 June 1980, 2 d. *Education:* University

Rheinland-Pfalz, Koblenz; Staatliche Hochschule für Musik, Westfalen-Lippe, Münster. *Career:* Recitalist and soloist with orchestras; Radio and TV engagements; Performed in most major cities and festivals; Teacher, guitar, University of Koblenz; Masterclasses and workshops. *Recordings:* Solo: Cantos de Cuba; Danzas Fantásticas; Triops-Botschaft; Matthias Drude: Kammermusik; Duets: Calliope-Calls (with Christina Ascher); Annette Schlünz: Kammermusik; 7. und 8. Dresdner Tage der zeitgenössischen Musik; Played on: The Straits of Magellan, Turfan Ensemble; Fünf Stücke op. 10, RSO Frankfurt; Zwei Suiten für Jazzorchester, RSO Frankfurt; Von Heute Auf Morgen, RSO Frankfurt; Die Jakobsleiter, RSO Frankfurt; Cristoforo Colombo, RSO Frankfurt. *Publications:* Editor, Pedagogic and Chamber Music guitar literature; Author of articles on guitar in music periodicals. *Honours:* Stipends and Scholarships from Kultusministerium Rheinland-Pfalz, Darmstädter Ferienkurse, Richard Wagner Verband, Deutscher Musikrat. *Membership:* EGTA; BDZ. *Address:* Am Nörrenpfad 30 A, 56337 Eitelborn, Germany. *Website:* www.volker-hoeh.de.

HOIER, Svein; b. 18 Nov. 1970, Oslo, Norway. Musician (guitar, keyboard, drums). *Education:* 4 years, Trondheim University. *Career:* Started as drummer: Closet Queens; Joined Hedge Hog, playing guitar, keyboard, sampler, 1994; Toured Europe, 1994, 1995. *Recordings:* Closet Queens: Closet Queens, 1993; Hedge Hog: Mindless, 1994; The Healing EP, 1995; Thorn Cord Wonder, 1995. *Publications:* 2 short films released: Smoking; Svein. *Honours:* Svein, Best Film, Trondheim Film Festival, 1995.

HOLDER, Noddy (Neville); b. 15 June 1950, Walsall, Warwickshire, England. Vocalist; Songwriter; Musician (guitar). *Career:* Guitarist, backing vocalist, Steve Brett and The Mavericks; Vocalist, guitarist, UK rock group, Slade (formerly N'Betweens, Ambrose Slade), 1966–91; Concerts include: First British tour, 1972; Fanfare For Europe festival, London Palladium, 1973; Great British Music Festival, 1978; Reading Festival, 1980; Radio presenter, Piccadilly Radio, Manchester; Capital Gold, London; Numerous TV appearances, including: The Grimleys (ITV1), 1997–2001; I Love 1973 (BBC2), 2000; Film: Flame, 1974; Host, Noddy Holder's Party Crazee (105.4 Century FM), 2002–. *Compositions:* Co-writer, all Slade's Top 20 hits, with Jimmy Lea. *Recordings:* Albums: Beginnings (as Ambrose Slade), 1969; Play It Loud, 1970; Slade Alive, 1972; Slayed, 1973; Sladest, 1973; Old New Borrowed Blue, 1974; Slade In Flame (soundtrack), 1974; Nobody's Fool, 1976; Slade Alive Vol. 2, 1978; Return To Base, 1979; Slade Smashes, 1980; Till Deaf Do Us Part, 1981; We'll Bring The House Down, 1981; Slade On Stage, 1982; The Amazing Kamikaze Syndrome, 1983; Slade's Greats, 1984; Rogue's Gallery, 1985; Crackers, 1985; You Boyz Make Big Noize, 1987; Wall of Hits, 1991; UK No. 1 hit singles: Coz I Luv You, 1971; Take Me Bak 'Ome, 1972; Mama Weer All Crazee Now (later recorded by Mama's Boys, Quiet Riot), 1972; Cum On Feel The Noize, 1973; Skweeze Me Pleeze Me, 1973; Merry Christmas Everybody, 1973; Other hits: Look Wot You Dun, 1972; Gudbuy T'Jane, 1972; My Friend Stan, 1973; Everyday, 1974; Bangin' Man, 1974; Far Far Away, 1974; Thanks For The Memory, 1975; In For A Penny, 1975; We'll Bring The House Down, 1981; My Oh My, 1983; Run Run Away, 1984; All Join Hands, 1984. *Honours:* Hon. Fellow, University of Wolverhampton, 2002. *Address:* c/o 105.4 Century FM, Laser House, Waterfront Quay, Salford Quays, Manchester M5 2XW, England.

HOLDSWORTH, Allan; b. 6 Aug. 1948, Bradford, West Yorkshire, England. Jazz/Rock Musician (guitar). 1 s., 1 d. *Career:* Mem., Level 42, 1991–94; Tours, television appearances world-wide. *Recordings:* Solo albums: The Sixteen Men of Tain, 2000; 'Igginbottom's Wrench, 2000; Flat Tire, 2001; Recordings with: Tempest; Soft Machine; Gordon Beck; Allan Holdsworth Band: Sand; Atavachron; Secrets; IOU; Wardenclyffe Tower; Hard Hat Area; Tony Williams; Bill Bruford; Donovan. *Honours:* Guitar Hall of Fame. *Current Management:* Marco Polo. *Address:* 3 The Lilacs, 50 Elm Grove, Hayling Island, Hampshire PO11 9EF, England.

HOLGATE, David Edward; b. 19 April 1939, Romford, Essex, England. Musician (double bass, bass guitar). m. Anne Malmström, 1 April 1962, 1 s., 1 d. *Education:* Private lessons pianoforte to higher grade RSM. *Career:* Anglia TV session work for many years include: Crescendo; Miss Anglia; About Anglia; The Mid-day Show; Music Match; BBC Radio One Club; Mr and Mrs; The Seeds of Love; Beach Boys support group: The Rainbow People. *Recordings:* Singles include: The Walk'll Do You Good; Dreamtime; The Sailing Song; Rainbows. *Membership:* Musicians' Union. *Address:* 18 Cow Hill, Norwich NR2 1HD, England.

HOLIDAY, Doc, (Edward Wohanka); b. 29 Jan. 1943, New Jersey, USA. Record Prod; Recording Artist; Record Co Exec. 1 s., 2 d. *Education:* Degrees in Music from Juilliard School of Music; Berkeley University; University of Miami. *Career:* Television appearances include: The Tonight Show; American Bandstand; Merv Griffin Show; Joe Franklin Show; Grammy Awards Show; 76 US Country No. 1 hits as a record producer. *Recordings include:* As recording artist: Expressway To Your Heart; Just My Imagination; Walkin' In Memphis; As producer: Cajun Baby, Hank Williams Jr; Louisiana Man, Doug Kershaw; Mr Jones, Big Al Downing. *Honours:* 36 Music Awards; 2 Grammy Awards; ICMA Producer of the Year, 1993–95. *Membership:* BMI; ASCAP;

SESAC. *Address:* c/o Doc Holiday Productions, 10 Luanita Lane, Newport News, VA 23606, USA.

HOLLAND, Annie (Annabel); b. 26 Aug. 1965. Musician (bass guitar). *Career:* Member of Elastica, 1992–95; Toured extensively world-wide. *Recordings:* Albums: Elastica (No. 1, UK), 1995; The Menace, 2000; The BBC Sessions, 2001; Singles: Stutter, 1993; Line Up, 1994; Connection, 1994; Waking Up, 1995; Elastica, EP. *Honours:* NME Readers Award for Best New Band. *Current Management:* CMO Management International Ltd, Ransomes Dock, 35–37 Parkgate Rd, London SW11 4NP, England.

HOLLAND, Brian; b. 15 Feb. 1941, Detroit, Michigan, USA. Composer; Record Prod. *Career:* Lead singer, the Satintones, 1950s; Member, composition and production team Holland/Dozier/Holland (with brother Eddie Holland and Lamont Dozier), 1963; Joined Motown label, 1960s; Co-founder, Invictus and Hot Wax record labels, 1967–75. *Recordings:* As co-writer, producer: with Marvin Gaye: Can I Get A Witness?, 1963; You're A Wonderful One, 1964; How Sweet It Is (To Be Loved By You), 1964; Little Darling, 1966; with Martha and The Vandellas: Heatwave; Quicksand; Nowhere To Run; Jimmy Mack; with Diana Ross and the Supremes: Where Did Our Love Go (No. 1, USA), 1964; Baby Love (No. 1, UK and USA), 1964; Come See About Me (No. 1, USA), 1965; Stop! In The Name of Love (No. 1, USA), 1965; Back In My Arms Again (No. 1, USA), 1965; You Can't Hurry Love (No. 1, USA), 1966; You Keep Me Hanging On (No. 1, USA), 1966; Love Is Here and Now You're Gone (No. 1, USA), 1967; The Happening (No. 1, USA), 1967; with the Four Tops: Baby I Need Your Loving, 1965; I Can't Help Myself (No. 1, USA), 1965; (It's The) Same Old Song, 1965; Reach Out I'll Be There (No. 1, UK and USA), 1966; Bernadette, 1967; Standing In The Shadows of Love, 1967; with the Miracles: Mickey's Monkey; I'm The One You Need; with the Isley Brothers: This Old Heart of Mine, 1966; Put Yourself In My Place, 1969; I Guess I'll Always Love You, 1966; Other recordings with Aretha Franklin; Kim Weston; Freda Payne; Chairmen of The Board.

HOLLAND, David; b. 5 April 1948, Northampton, England. Musician (drums). *Career:* Member, Pinkerton's Assorted Colours, 1966–69; Trapeze, 1969–79; Judas Priest, 1979–88; Over 20 North American and European tours; Numerous radio and television appearances with the above. *Recordings:* Albums: with Trapeze, 1970–78: Trapeze, 1970; Medusa, 1970; You Are The Music We're Just The Band, 1972; The Final Swing, 1974; Hot Wire, 1974; Trapeze, 1975; Hold On, 1978; Running, 1978; with Judas Priest 1980–88: British Steel, 1980; Point of Entry, 1980; Screaming For Vengeance; Defenders of The Faith, 1984; Turbo, 1986; Priest-Live, 1987; Ram It Down, 1998; Also featured on: Play Me Out, Glenn Hughes, 1977; Songwriter, Justin Hayward, 1977; Nightflight, Justin Hayward, 1980; Dangerous Music, Robin George, 1985. *Honours:* Over 20 Platinum, Gold, Silver albums with Judas Priest; Crystal Globe Award.

HOLLAND, Dexter, (Bryan Keith Holland); b. 29 Dec. 1966, Orange County, California, USA. Vocalist; Musician (guitar). m. Kristinia Luna, 1 d. *Education:* University of Southern California, PhD graduate in molecular biology. *Career:* Former drummer; Formed group Manic Subsidal with fellow school cross-country team members, 1984; Group metamorphosised into The Offspring, 1985; Privately pressed single took over 2 years to sell 1000 copies, 1987; Signed to independent labels, Nemesis and Epitaph, for 1988–95 releases; Major US breakthrough following heavy MTV/radio play rotation, 1994; Accused of betraying punk roots when signing to Columbia after dispute with former label, 1996; Consolidated world-wide success by scoring UK no. 1 hit single, 1999; Live shows include: Woodstock festival, 1999; KROQ Weenie Roast, 2000; European tour, 2001; Band gave lucky fan $1m. in Offspring prize draw, 2000; Co-owner: Nitro label with Offspring manager Jim Guerinot, releasing records by Guttermouth and The Vandals. *Recordings:* Albums: The Offspring, 1989; Ignition, 1992; Smash!, 1994; Ixnay On The Hombre, 1997; Americana, 1998; Conspiracy of One, 2000; Singles: I'll Be Waiting, 1987; Baghdad EP, 1988; Come Out and Play (Keep 'Em Separated), Self-Esteem, 1994; Gotta Get Away, 1995; All I Want, Gone Away, 1997; Pretty Fly (For A White Guy), 1998; Why Don't You Get A Job?, The Kids Aren't Alright, She's Got Issues, 1999; Original Prankster, 2000; Want You Bad, Million Miles Away, 2001. *Honours:* Over 9m. copies of Smash album sold world-wide, best selling independent record of all time. *Current Management:* Jim Guerinot, Rebel Waltz Management, 31652 Second Ave, Laguna Beach, CA 92651, USA. *Website:* www.offspring.com.

HOLLAND, Eddie; b. 30 Oct. 1939, Detroit, Michigan, USA. Composer; Record Prod. *Career:* Member, the Fideltones; Member, songwriting and production team Holland/Dozier/Holland (with Brian Holland and Lamont Dozier); Co-writer, producer, numerous records by major Motown artists, including a dozen US number 1 hits, 1963–68; Split from Motown, 1967; Co-founder, Invictus and Hot Wax record labels, 1967–75. *Recordings:* As co-producer, writer: with Marvin Gaye: Can I Get A Witness?, 1963; You're A Wonderful One, 1964; How Sweet It Is (To Be Loved By You), 1964; Little Darling, 1966; with Martha and The Vandellas: Heatwave; Quicksand; Nowhere To Run; Jimmy Mack; with Diana Ross and the Supremes: Where Did Our Love Go (No. 1, USA), 1964; Baby Love (No. 1, UK and USA), 1964; Come See About Me (No. 1, USA), 1965; Stop! In The Name of Love (No. 1,

USA), 1965; Back In My Arms Again (No. 1, USA), 1965; You Can't Hurry Love (No. 1, USA), 1966; You Keep Me Hanging On (No. 1, USA), 1966; Love Is Here and Now You're Gone (No. 1, USA), 1967; The Happening (No. 1, USA), 1967; with the Four Tops: Baby I Need Your Loving, 1965; I Can't Help Myself (No. 1, USA), 1965; (It's The) Same Old Song, 1965; Reach Out I'll Be There (No. 1, UK and USA), 1966; Bernadette, 1967; Standing In The Shadows of Love, 1967; with the Miracles: Mickey's Monkey; I'm The One You Need; with the Isley Brothers: This Old Heart of Mine, 1966; Put Yourself In My Place, 1969; I Guess I'll Always Love You, 1966; Other recordings with Aretha Franklin; Kim Weston; Freda Payne; Chairmen of The Board.

HOLLAND, Jools (Julian); b. 24 Jan. 1958, London, England. Musician (keyboards); Broadcaster; Bandleader. 1 s., 2 d. *Career:* Founder member, pianist, Squeeze, 1974–81, 1985–90; Solo artiste and bandleader: Jools Holland and his Big Band, 1982–84; Jools Holland and his Rhythm and Blues Orchestra, 1991–; Radio presenter, BBC Radio 2, 1997–; Television presenter, music shows: The Tube (Channel 4), 1982–87; Later With Jools Holland, BBC2, 1993–; Various other television specials, including Sunday Night, NBC, 1989; The Groovy Fellers, Channel 4, 1989; Juke Box Jury, BBC2, 1989–90; The Happening, BSB, 1990; Beat Route, BBC 2, 1998–99. *Recordings:* Albums: with Squeeze: Squeeze, 1978; Cool For Cats, 1979; Argy Bargy, 1980; Cosi Fan Tutti Frutti, 1985; Babylon and On, 1987; Frank, 1989; Solo albums: A World of His Own, 1990; The Full Complement, 1991; A To Z of The Piano, 1992; Live Performance, 1994; Solo Piano, 1994; Sex and Jazz and Rock and Roll, 1996; Lift the Lid, 1997; The Best of Jools Holland, 1998; Sunset Over London, 1999; Hop The Wag, 2000; Small World, Big Band Vol. I, 2001; Small World, Big Band Vol. II: More Friends, 2002. Hit singles include: with Squeeze: Take Me I'm Yours, 1978; Cool For Cats, 1979; Up The Junction, 1979; Slap and Tickle, 1979; Another Nail In My Heart, 1980; Pulling Mussels From A Shell, 1980; Hourglass, 1987; 853 5937, 1988; Also contributed to numerous albums including: Soul Mining, The The, 1983; The Raw and The Cooked, Fine Young Cannibals, 1989; Sam Brown; Dr John. *Membership:* Musicians' Union; Equity; Writer's Guild. *Current Management:* c/o Paul Loasby, One Fifteen, The Gallery, 28–30 Wood Wharf, Horseferry Pl., London SE10 9BT, England.

HOLLINGWORTH, Roy; b. 12 April 1949, Derby, England. Vocalist; Songwriter; Musician (guitar); Poet; Writer. *Education:* Nottingham University. *Career:* Feature writer, critic with Melody maker, London, 1970–74; Editor, Melody Maker, American Bureau, New York, 1973; Session musician, New York, 1973–78; Performance poet, singer, Greenwich Village, New York, 1973–80; American, Canadian tours, Germany, 1995; European Tour, 1997. *Recordings:* Albums: Guitarist, Electric Shocks, Roger Ruskin Spear, 1973; Solo album: Roy Hollingworth – In The Flesh, 1994; with Barclay James Harvest: Barclay James Harvest, 1994. *Honours:* BBC Radio One, London, Rock Writer of the Year, 1972. *Membership:* GEMA, Germany (artists and composers). *Address:* 10 Genoa Ave, London SW15 6DY, England.

HOLLOWAY, Laurence; b. 31 March 1938, Oldham, Lancashire. Musician (Piano); Composer; Musical Dir. m. Marion Montgomery, 16 June 1965, 2 d. *Career:* Touring Dance Band Pianist, 1950s; Cyril Stapleton Showband; Joe Daniels Hotshots, 1950s; Cunard Line, 1956–57; London Weekend Television, regular pianist, 1967–80; Musical Director, Engelbert Humperdinck, 1970–75; Played at studios in London, 1975–85; Musical Director for many top artistes such as Judy Garland. *Compositions:* Numerous TV signature tunes including Blind Date, Beadle's About. *Recordings:* Solo albums: Blue Skies; Showtime; Cumulus; About Time; Also recorded with many artists including Kiri Te Kanawa, Marion Montgomery, Robert Farnon, Rolf Harris. *Honours:* Gold Badge of Merit, BAC&S. *Current Management:* Ann Zahl. *Address:* Elgin, Fishery Rd, Bray, Berkshire SL6 1UP, England.

HOLLWEG, Rebecca; b. 30 June 1964, London, England. Vocalist; Songwriter. *Education:* BA, French, German, University of Oxford; Guildhall School of Music and Drama, Jazz Course. *Career:* Venues include: South Bank Centre; Borderline, London; arts centres and theatres around the UK; Numerous radio appearances around the UK; Support artiste to Roger McGuinn of The Byrds, 2001–02; Founder, Emu Records, with Andy Hamill. *Recordings:* Albums: The Demos, 1999; June Babies, 2001. *Membership:* PRS; Musicians' Union; Equity. *Address:* c/o EMU Records, 14A Emu Rd, London SW8 3PR, England.

HOLM, Georg (Goggi); b. Iceland. Musician (bass guitar). *Career:* Founding mem., Icelandic band, Sigur Rös, 1994–; Signed to MCA/Universal, USA, FatCat Records, UK; Music featured in film, Vanilla Sky, 2001; North American tour, 2001; European tour, 2002. *Recordings:* Albums: Von; Agœtis Byrjun, 2000; ( ), 2002. Singles: Ny Batteri, 2000; Svefn-G-Englar, 2001; Contributed to: Angels of the Universe (soundtrack), 2001. *Honours:* Shortlist Music Prize, 2001. *Address:* c/o FatCat Records, PO Box 3400, Brighton BN1 4WG, England. *Website:* www.sigur-ros.com.

HOLMBERG, Patricia; b. 21 Oct. 1934, Montana, USA. Musician; Composer; Piano Teacher. m. Russell Holmberg, 1 s., 3 d. *Education:* BMus, University of Colorado, 1955; MM, University of Colorado, 1958. *Compositions:* Various Choral Anthems, Art Songs and Piano Pieces, 1973–;

Songs For Seniors; Concerto For Jazz Piano and Concert Band. *Recordings:* Boulder Rags; Songs For Seniors; Christmas In The Rockies; Mountain Images; Hymns We All Remember. *Honours:* Grant, City of Boulder. *Membership:* BMI; American Federation of Musicians; American Music Center; Music Teachers' National Asscn. *Address:* 2244 Kincaid Pl., Boulder, Colorado 80304, USA.

HOLMES, David; b. 1969, Belfast, Northern Ireland. Prod; Remixer; DJ. *Career:* Started as concert promoter in Belfast; Began to DJ at own club night, Sugar Sweet, early 1990s; First recorded with Ashley Beedle as the Disco Evangelists, 1992; Remix work followed; Signed to Go! Discs as solo artiste; Produces music for film soundtracks; Collaborations: Ashley Beedle; Bobby Gillespie; Remixed: Saint Etienne; U2; Monkey Mafia; Manic Street Preachers. *Recordings:* Albums: This Film's Crap—Let's Slash The Seats, 1995; Resurrection Game (OST), Let's Get Killed, 1997; Out Of Sight (OST), 1998; Bow Down To The Exit Sign, 2000; Come Get It I Got It, 2002; Ocean's Eleven (OST), 2002; David Holmes Presents The Free Association, 2002. Singles: De Niro (with Disco Evangelists), 1992; Gone, My Mate Paul, 1996; Don't Die Just Yet, Gritty Shaker, 1997. *Membership:* PRS. *Address:* c/o Go! Discs, 72 Black Lion Lane, Hammersmith, London W6 9BE, England. *Website:* www.davidholmes.tv.

HOLMES, Ian Johnstone; b. 11 March 1935, Dumfries, Scotland. m. Margaret Bell, 6 Nov. 1958, 2 d. *Education:* Accordion lessons with Alex Carter. *Career:* Appeared on TV in White Heather Club; Recorded TV shows in Germany; Broadcast on BBC Radio Scotland, 1958–, as Soloist and Bandleader, 1962–. *Compositions:* Around 275 tunes in various styles, especially Scottish dance music, and also accordion tunes in French, Norwegian, Swedish and Swiss styles. *Recordings:* 16 albums, mostly of Scottish dance music; Recordings of music by the Beatles and Scandinavian and Swiss accordion music. *Publications:* The Dumfries Collection of Music by Ian Holmes, Vols 1, 2 and 3. *Honours:* All-Scotland Champion of Traditional Music, 1957; Honourary mem. of the Bromolla Accordion Orchestra (Sweden) in 1987. *Membership:* MCPS; PRS; Phonographic Performance; PAMRA. *Address:* 11 Averill Cres., Rotchell, Dumfries DG2 7RY, Scotland.

HOLSKE, Robin M; b. 24 July 1941. Piano Teacher; Jazz Musician (piano). 2 d. *Education:* Friends Academy, NY, 1959; Antioch College, OH, 1965. *Career:* Played Piano, Salsa Bands, New York; Led Numerous Jazz Groups, New Hampshire, 1974–. *Compositions:* David, Saul and Jonathan; Eleanor; Cassanova. *Recordings:* Rey Davila-Ya Era Tiempo. *Honours:* Billboard International Award. *Membership:* AFM. *Address:* 296 Corn Hill Rd, Boscawen, NH 03303, USA.

HOLSTEIN, Christina Staël von; b. 13 Aug. 1969, Lausanne, Switzerland. Vocalist; Musician (guitar); Lyricist; Composer. *Education:* Guildhall Singing Grade 5 – Honours. *Career:* Member, bands The New Quartet; Vers La Flammes; Here Lies A Crime; Paper Fish; Guest vocalist, Wax Club; Jaded Halo; Musicals: West Side Story; Sweeney Todd, The Demon Barber of Fleet Street; The Boyfriend. *Membership:* Musicians' Union; Montessori School, Balderton Street; British School of Complementary Therapists, Harley Street; The Place To Be (charity for children with learning and emotional difficulties). *Address:* 44 Palace Gardens Terrace, London W8 4RR, England.

HOLYFIELD, Wayland D; b. 15 March 1942, Mallettown, AR, USA. Songwriter. *Education:* Hendrix College, 1960–61; BA, Marketing, University of Arkansas, 1961–65. *Career:* Moved to Nashville, 1972; Signed publishing contract with Jack Clement, as songwriter, 1973; Signed publishing contract with Bill Hall, 1974; Sang, Arkansas, You Run Deep In Me, President Bill Clinton's inauguration, 1993; Songs recorded by: Rex Allen Jr, American Brothers, John Anderson, Rayburn Anthony, Eddie Arnold, Baillie and the Boys, Ava Barber, Bobby Bare, Jessica Bouche, Brentwood, T. Graham Brown, Ed Bruce, The Capitols, Tom Cash, Carol Chase, Mark Chestnut, Roy Clark, John Conlee, Gail Davies, Mac Davis, Billy Dean, Johnny Duncan, Stoney Edwards, Janie Fricke, Crystal Gayle, Terri Gibbs, Mickey Gilley, Tom Grant, Lee Greenwood, Gus Hardin, Wayland Holyfield, Con Hunley, Julio Iglesias, Lois Johnson, The Judds, Nicolette Larson, Dickey Lee, Johnny Lee, Zella Lehr, Lincoln City Sound, Bob Luman, Charlie McClain, Reba McEntire, Bill Medley, Ronnie Milsap, Lorrie Morgan, Michael Martin Murphy, Anne Murray, Juice Newton, Nitty Gritty Dirt Band, The Oak Ridge Boys, Merrill Osmond, Pirates of the Mississippi, Charley Pride, Jeannie Pruett, Rex Nelson Singers, Johnny Russell, Jack Ruth, Telly Savalas, Shenandoah, T. G. Sheppard, Joel Sonnier, The Statler Brothers, Keith Stegall, Gary Stewart, Mel Street, Terry Sumsion, Joe Sun, The Tams, Verlon Thompson, Randy Travis, Conway Twitty, Jacky Ward, Shelly West, Keith Whitley, Don Williams, Danny Wood, Tammy Wynette. *Compositions include:* Arkansas, You Run Deep In Me; Could I Have This Dance (with Bob House); Don't Count The Rainy Days; Down In Tennessee; I'll Do It All Over Again; Nobody Likes Sad Songs (with Bob McDill); Only Here For A Little While (with Richard Leigh); Rednecks, White Socks And Blue Ribbon Beer (with Bob McDill and Chuck Neese); She Reminded Me Of You; Some Broken Hearts Never Mend; Till The Rivers All Run Dry; (Wish I Had A) Heart Of Stone; You're My Best Friend. *Honours:* NSAI Presidential Award, 1979; ASCAP, Country Writer of the Year (joint winner), 1983; Inducted, Nashville Songwriters Hall of Fame, 1992; 14 BMI Performance Awards; 16 ASCAP Performance Awards. *Membership:* ASCAP, board mem., 1990.

HOLZHAUER, Rudy; b. 14 Dec. 1951, Hamburg, Germany. Music Publisher; Man. *Career:* Live engineer; Studio engineer; Music publisher; Artiste manager; Owner, Musikverlag Progressive GmbH. *Membership:* GEMA; DMV; DKV. *Address:* Bramfelder Chaussee 238c, 22177 Hamburg, Germany.

HONK, J. (Herbert Gebetsroither); b. 5 Oct. 1957, Linz a. d. Donau, Austria. Musician (guitar, piano); Songwriter; Performing Artist; Music Publisher; Instrumental Music Teacher. *Education:* Guitar, piano, voice, theory (jazz), Franz Schubert Conservatory, Vienna. *Career:* Member, US salsa and latin band Obote; Tours of Germany and Netherlands; Founder, Jivi Honk and band, 1983–; 500 live concerts in and around Austria, 1985–; Various own projects include Jivi Honk and the Funkplanet; The Honk Rock Project, Honk Instrumental Project, 1990; Concerts include: U4, Vienna; Vienna State Opera; Budapest Town Hall; Italian tour, 1989; Velden; Zürs; Television appearances include: ORF FS1; radio includes: Over 1000 appearances on German and Austrian public radio and various European stations, 1988–; Tokyo FM, 1990–. *Recordings:* Instrumentals: Lovedancer; Space Me To The Stars, 1988; Sunrider; Vienna Skyline; Moonrider; Highway of Fame; Golden Days, 1993, 1994; Albums: as Jivi Honk: Got My Style, 1990; Sunrider, 1993; Moonrider, 1993; Golden Days, 1994; Live At The Garage, 1995; Stardance, 1999. *Membership:* AKM; Austro Mechana; LSG/Östig. *Current Management:* Honk Music, Warner Chappel Group, Austria. *Address:* Hormayrgasse 3/25, 1170 Vienna, Austria.

HOOK, Peter; b. 13 Feb. 1956, Salford, Lancashire, England. Musician (bass). *Career:* Member, Joy Division, 1977–80; New Order, 1980–; Revenge, 1989–96; Monaco, 1996–; Tours: UK; Europe; Australia; New Zealand; Far East; USA; South America; Concerts include: Glastonbury Festival, 1981, 1987; Futurama Festival, Leeds, 1982; San Remo Festival, 1988; Reading Festival, 1989; Leader, house band, The Mrs Merton Show, Granada/BBC, 1994–95. *Recordings:* Albums: with Joy Division: Unknown Pleasures, 1979; Closer, 1980; Still, 1981; The Peel Sessions, 1988; Also featured on: Short Circuit – Live At The Electric Circus, 1978; with New Order: Movement, 1981; Power Corruption and Lies, 1983; Low Life, 1985; Brotherhood, 1986; Substance, 1987; Technique (No. 1, UK), 1989; Republic (No. 1, UK), 1993; The Best of New Order, 1994; The Rest of New Order, 1995; Get Ready, 2001; Back To Mine (compilation), 2002; with Revenge: One True Passion, 1990; with Monaco: Music For Pleasure, 1997; Singles include: with Joy Division: An Ideal For Living EP, 1978; Transmission, 1979; Atmosphere, 1980; Love Will Tear Us Apart, 1980; with New Order: Ceremony, 1981; Procession/Everything's Gone Green, 1981; Temptation, 1982; Blue Monday, 1983, remixed 1988, 1995; Confusion, 1983; Thieves Like Us, 1984; The Perfect Kiss, 1985; Subculture, 1985; Shellshock, 1986; State of The Nation, 1986; Bizarre Love Triangle, 1986; True Faith, 1987; Touched By The Hand of God, 1987; Fine Time, 1988; Round and Round, 1989; World In Motion (with England World Cup Football Squad) (No. 1, UK), 1990; How Does It Feel?, 1992; Regret, 1993; Ruined In A Day, 1993; World, 1993; Spooky, 1993; 1963, 1995; Crystal, 2001; 60 Miles An Hour, 2001; Here To Stay, 2002; with Revenge: Reasons, 1989; Pineapple Face, 1990; Slave, 1990; Gun World Porn, 1991; with Monaco: What Do You Want From Me?, 1997; Sweet Lips, 1997; Shine, 1997. *Address:* c/o London Records, PO Box 1422, Chancellors House, Chancellors Rd, London W6 9SG, England. *Website:* www.neworderweb.com.

HOOKER, Jake; b. 5 March 1951, New York, USA. Songwriter; Record Prod; Musician (guitar). m. 7 Sept. 1994, 1 s., 2 d. *Career:* Wrote No. 1 international hit I Love Rock and Roll; Formed UK group The Arrows, 1974. *Recordings:* I Love Rock and Roll; Destination Unknown (from film soundtrack Top Gun); Sweetest Victory (from film soundtrack Rocky IV); Iron Eagle (from film soundtrack Iron Eagle); with Edgar Winter, Not a Kid Anymore, 1994; Real Deal, 1996; with Justin Trevino, Loud Music and Strong Wine, 2000. *Publications:* The Arrows Biography. *Honours:* Several Platinum and Gold records. *Membership:* NARAS; BMI; AFofM. *Current Management:* HEI.

HOOKER, Steve; b. 19 May 1953, Rochford, Essex, England. Musician (guitar) Vocalist; Songwriter; Prod. m. (1) 1 s., (2) Elaine, 11 Aug. 1992. *Education:* Southend Art College, Cordwainers, London. *Career:* The Heat, 1977; Shakers, 1982–87; Jeremy Gluck, 1987; Steve Hooker and Wilko Johnson, (recording project) 1988; Boz and the Bozmen, 1988; Steve Hooker Band, 1989–91; Rumble, 1994; Steve Hooker and the ST's, 1999; Television includes: Marquee series (Anglia TV); FR3 (France); Several radio appearances; Musical contributor to soundtrack, Burnin' Love, film noir. *Compositions include:* Elmore Stroll, on Hell for Leather, Rumble, 1996; The Raid, Captain Drugbuster, 1997. *Recordings:* with The Shakers: Temptation Walk, Catch On; Solo album: Boogie-Chal; Also featured on: Really Gone, 1984; Wild Heroine, Boz and the Bozmen, 1988; Dress In Deadmens Suits, 1988; Rockin' Ace of Spades, on Locorumble, 1998. *Publications:* Sleeve notes with journalist John Tobler. *Honours:* Diploma in design of shoe and footwear. *Membership:* Musicians' Union.

HOOPER, Nellee; Record Prod; Arranger. *Career:* Member, The Wild Bunch Crew; Member, mixing crew Massive Attack; Joined Soul II Soul, offering sound systems services to UK dance clubs, 1985; Residency, Africa Centre, Covent Garden, London; Relocated to Fridge Club, Brixton, 1988; Opened 2 shops, London, 1988; Developed video and film company, fan club, talent agency, record company, 1990–. *Recordings include:* Albums: with Soul II Soul: Club Classics Vol. I, 1989; Vol. II, A New Decade, 1990; Vol. III – Just Right, 1992; Singles include: Keep On Movin', 1989; Back To Life (However Do You Want Me), 1989; A Dream's A Dream, 1990; Missing You, with Kym Mazelle, 1990; Joy, 1992; Just Right, 1992; Move Me No Mountain, 1992; Wish, 1993; As producer: with Massive Attack: Unfinished Sympathy; Protection; with Madonna: Bedtime Stories; with Björk: Debut; Post; Universal James, James Brown, 1993; with Madonna: Something to Remember, 1995; Special Brew: Special Brew, 1996; with All Saints, All Saints, 1997; Best of Bond... James Bond, 1999; As arranger (with Jazzie B): Nothing Compares To U, Sinead O'Connor, 1990 Contributor, Mad About The Mouse (Disney compilation), 1991. *Honours:* Platinum discs; Top Dance Sales Artists, Billboard, 1989; 3 American Music Awards, 1990; 4 British DMC Dance Awards, 1990; Grammy Award, Best R&B Instrumental Performance, 1990; 3 Soul Train Awards, 1990; BMI College Radio Award, Back To Life, 1991; ASCAP Award, Back To Life, 1991; BRIT Award, Best Producer, 1995.

HOPE-EVANS, Peter John; b. 28 Sept. 1947, Brecon, Wales. Composer; Performer; Musician (mouth organ, mouth bow, Jews harp). m. Christine Frances Rich, 26 Oct. 1973. *Education:* MA, Romanticism and Modernism, 1991–92; Lessons with Texas Slim, Maurice Blanchot, Edgar Fünf. *Career:* Played with: Medicine Head; Pete Townshend; Deep End; Ronnie Lane; The Ravishing Beauties; Films: White City, 1986; Mourning; Radio: Strange Navigations (Pirate Radio), 1993–; Embers/descendres/eschenglet, 1994; Classical: 4'33 uncaged (Fünf), 1981, 1985, 1989; Multimedia: sigh code: airilicked, 1993; Theatre: La Folie Du Jour, 1989; Manslaughter/Woman's Laughter, 1992. *Recordings:* New Bottles Old Medicine, 1970; with Pete Townshend: Pete Townshend Live, 1999; with Tears for Fears: Seeds of Love, 1999; with Robbie McIntosh, Wide Screen, 2001; Cassette only series: Elgin Moveme(a)nts; Closer Than Breath (Itself); In The Sacred Cedars; Shadow of The Object; Theatre: Up Your Ass Solanas, 1992; The Tempest (RSC), 1995. *Publications:* Harmonica Yoga, 1990; Philosophising With A Harmonica (Back To Nietzsche), 1992. *Honours:* Prix Italia (music and arts): Strangefish (DV8) 1994. *Address:* 14 Eastbank Rd, Hampton Hill, Middlesex TW12 1RP, England.

HOPKIN, Mary; b. 3 May 1950, Pontardawe, Wales. Vocalist. *Career:* Winner, talent show, Opportunity Knocks, 1968; Debut hit, Those Were The Days, also recorded in Spanish, French, German, Italian, Hebrew (sales exceeded 8m.); British tour, 1969; Backing vocals for various artistes, 1970s; Member, harmony trio, Sundance, 1980; Lead vocalist with Oasis (with Peter Skellern, Julian Lloyd Webber), 1984; Performances include: The Chieftains' Music Festival 1991, London Palladium, 1991. *Recordings:* Albums: Post Card, 1969; Earth Song – Ocean Song, 1971; Those Were The Days, 1972; Spirit, 1991; with Oasis: Oasis, 1984; with Dave Cousins: Bridge, 1994; with Ralph McTell: Sand in your Shoes, 1996; with Future Sound of London: My Kingdom; Dead Cities, 1996; with Brian Willoughby: Black and White, 1999; Singles include: Those Were The Days (No. 1, UK), 1968; Goodbye, 1969; Temma Harbour, 1970; Knock Knock Who's There, UK Eurovision entry, (No. 2, UK), 1970; Think About Your Children; If You Love Me. *Contributions to:* The King of Elfland's Daughter, 1977; Dylan Thomas' Under Milk Wood, 1988.

HOPKINS, Philip Nicholas; b. 5 Feb. 1962, Surrey, England. Musician (percussion, chromatic harmonica). m. Barbara Mason, 17 July 1993. *Education:* MA, Oxford University; Music scholarship, King's School, Canterbury. *Career:* Sweeney Todd, National Theatre, UK/Europe Tours, 1993–94; London theatre work includes A Little Night Music, National Theatre, 1995; Concert tours, USA with: Phil Coulter; Maura O'Connell; Liam Clancy including Carnegie Hall, New York; Played harmonica for film Fanny and Elvis, and TV series Roger Roger, 1998. *Recordings:* Television, album work with: Leon Redbone; Phil Coulter; Billy Connolly; The Dubliners; Rory Gallagher; Val Doonican; Television, radio sessions include: Next of Kin; Men of The World, BBC1, 1995; Appeared on CD of Royal National Theatre's production A Little Night Music, 1996, Lady in the Dark, 1997, Oklahoma!, 1998. *Publications:* Articles in Modern Drummer, USA. *Membership:* Musicians' Union. *Address:* 5 Claygate Rd, Dorking, Surrey, England.

HOPKINSON, Rusty (Russell Keith); b. May 1964, Perth, WA, Australia. Musician (guitar, drums, percussion); Vocalist. *Career:* Mem., Vicious Circle, Nursery Crimes; Mem., Australian rock band, You Am I, 1993–; Numerous world-wide tours; Mem., Sneeze, 1999; Owner, Illustrious Artists label. *Recordings:* Albums: Sound As Ever, 1994; Hi Fi Way (No. 1, Australia), 1995; Hourly, Daily (No. 1, Australia), 1996; # 4 Record (No. 1, Australia), 1998; Saturday Night, 'Round Ten, 1999; Dress Me Slowly, 2001; Deliverance, 2002. Singles: Adam's Ribs; Berlin Chair; Someone Else's Crowd (limited edition EP); Jaimmes Got A Gal; When You Got Dry; Cathy's Clown; Jewels And Bullets; Purple Sneakers, 1995; Mr Milk, 1995; Soldiers, 1996; Good Mornin', Tuesday; Trike; What I Don't Know 'Bout You, 1998; Rumble, 1998; Heavy

Heart, 1998; Damage; Get Up; Kick Hole In The Sky; Dirty Deeds Done Dirt Cheap; Trouble. *Honours:* Gold discs; ARIA Awards, incl. Best Alternative Release, 1995; Six Industry Awards, 1996. *Address:* c/o BMG Australia Ltd, 194 Miller St, North Sydney, NSW 2060, Australia. *Website:* www.youami.com.au.

HOPPER, Hugh; b. 29 April 1945, Whitstable, Kent, England. Musician (bass guitar); Composer. 2 d. *Career:* Wilde Flowers; Soft Machine; Isotope; Carla Bley; Robert Wyatt; Own bands. *Compositions:* Memories, Robert Wyatt and Whitney Houston; Facelift, Soft Machine; Was A Friend, Shleep, Robert Wyatt. *Recordings:* Soft Machine 2–6; Hoppertunity Box; 1984; Caveman Hughscore; Delta Flora; Cryptids, 2000; The Swimmer, 2001. *Publications:* Rock Bass Manual. *Membership:* Musicians' Union; MCPS; PRS; PAMRA. *Address:* 29 Castle Rd, Whitstable, Kent CT5 2DZ, England. *E-mail:* hhopp@ukonline.co.uk.

HOPPUS, Mark (Markus Allen); b. 15 March 1972, Ridgecrest, California, USA. Musician (bass guitar). m. Skye Everly, 2001. *Career:* Co-founder: Blink-182, 1993; Built popularity with string of popular independent 7 singles; Signed to MCA through Cargo Music/MCA joint venture deal, 1997; Numerous TV appearances and concerts world-wide including: The Enema Strikes Back '99 tour, released on CD as The Mark Tom and Travis Show; 11-week US Summer tour, 2001; Cameo appearance with group in American Pie film, 1999. *Recordings:* Albums: Fly Swatter (mini album), 1993; Cheshire Cat, 1994; Buddah, 1995; Dude Ranch, 1997; Enema of The State, 1999; The Mark Tom and Travis Show (live), 2000; Take Off Your Pants and Jacket, 2001; Singles: Short Bus (split 7 with The Iconoclasts), 1996; They Came To Conquer Uranus (7 EP), Lemmings (split 7 with Swindle), Dick Lips, Dammit (Growing Up), I Won't Be Home For Christmas, 1997; Josie, 1998; What's My Age Again, All The Small Things, 1999; Adam's Song, Man Overboard, 2000; The Rock Show, Stay Together For The Kids, 2001. *Honours:* World-wide sales of 1999 album in excess of 7m. *E-mail:* mark@loserkids.com. *Website:* www.blink182.com.

HOPWOOD, Freddy; b. 22 Dec. 1948, Lichfield, England. Musician (drums, penny whistle, concertina). m. Beryl Agnes Nutt, 17 May 1974, 2 s. *Education:* Uttoxeter and Burton Technical College. *Career:* Member, Dr Strangely Strange, 1970–71; Television appearances, John Peel session, BBC Radio 1; Member, Sutherland Brothers Band, 1972; Support tours, Free, Mott The Hoople; David Bowie; Performance at Montreux Golden Rose Festival; Television appearances: Switzerland; Denmark; France; Numerous television and radio appearances, 1987–2002; Member, R Cajun and Zydeco Bros, 1984–; Zydeco Hot Rods, 1993–; Formed Vice Bishop's Blues Band, 1997; Session work for Paul McCartney, 1998. *Recordings:* Albums/singles with Sutherland Brothers Band, 1971; Leonard and Squires, 1976; R Cajun and the Zydeco Brothers, 1984–2000; Yeah Jazz, 1992; Vice-Bishops of Uttoxeter, 1995; Big Red Kite, 1996; House of Cards, with Vice-Bishops' Blues Band, 2000. *Membership:* PRS; MCPS; PAMRA. *Current Management:* Smalltown Records. *Address:* 17 Colne Mount, Uttoxeter, Staffs ST14 7QR, England.

HORABIN, Gren; b. 15 May 1939, Rainhill, Liverpool, England. Senior Lecturer (director of studies); Musician (alto and tenor saxophones, clarinet). m. Catherine Rawlinson, 28 Dec. 1968, 1 s. *Education:* Technical Teachers' Certificate; Private tuition, pianoforte, saxophone clarinet; Bandsman in Royal Air Force. *Career:* Bands include: Leader, alto clarinet, Gren Horabin Combo; Alto saxophone, Band of The Royal Air Force, Bridgnorth; Leader, saxophones, clarinet, Crescendo; Currently tenor clarinet, John Shepherd Combo; Alto, tenor clarinet, Leader, 42nd Street Swing; Jazz, dance gigs, various venues in Midlands with Pete King, Mick Large, Ricky Allan; Allan Billings; various small mainstream groups; Productions include: Lady Audley's Secret; Dirty Work At The Crossroads; Hits From The Blitz; Concert Style In Jazz (with Duncan Swift, Geraint Ellis); Creator, author, original Jazz Studies Units, BTEC National Diploma Level, Kidderminster College, Worcestershire; Senior Lecturer, Director of Studies, Creative Arts and Community Studies, Kidderminster College, retired; Currently leading own band, 42nd Street Swing; Alto, Tenor and Clarinet with John Shepherd Band. *Compositions include:* Jingle, Calypso Lipstick commercial for Prides Ltd; Classical, modern, theatre and dance. *Honours:* Skills Assessors and Verifiers Awards. *Membership:* Musicians' Union; Asscn of British Jazz Musicians. *Address:* 9 Waterlaide Rd, Hartlebury, Worcestershire DY11 7TP, England.

HORN, Shirley; b. 1 May 1934, Washington DC, USA. Vocalist; Musician (piano). 1 d. *Education:* Havard University. *Career:* Concerts include: Lincoln Center, New York, 1989; Blue Note, Tokyo, 1989. *Recordings:* Albums: Cat On A Hot Fiddle, 1959; Embers and Ashes, 1960; Live At The Village Vanguard, 1961; Loads of Love, 1963; Shirley Horn With Strings, 1963; Travelin' Light, 1965; For Love of Ivy, 1968; A Dandy In Aspic, 1968; Where Are You Going?, 1972; A Lazy Afternoon, 1979; All Night Long, 1982; Violets For Your Ears, 1983; The Sentimental Touch, 1985; I Thought About You, 1987; Softly, 1988; Close Enough For Love, 1988; Tune In Tomorrow, 1990; You Won't Forget Me, 1991; Dedicated To You – Tribute To Sarah Vaughan (with Carmen McRae), 1991; I Love You, Paris, 1992; Light Out of Darkness, 1993; The Main Ingredient, 1995; Loving You, 1997; I Remember Miles, 1998; You're My

Thrill, 2001. *Current Management:* Sheila Mathis Enterprises, 200 Haven Ave, Suite 5P, New York, NY 10033, USA.

HORN, Trevor; b. 15 July 1949. Record Prod; Record Co Exec; Vocalist; Musician (guitar). m. Jill Sinclair. *Career:* Session musician, 1970s; Founder, Buggles, 1977–80; Member, Yes, 1980–81; Member, Art of Noise, 1983–85, 1998–; Independent record producer, 1982–; Founder, ZTT Records. *Compositions include:* Theme music, television series The Tube. *Recordings:* Albums: with Buggles: The Plastic Age, 1980; with Yes: Drama, 1980; with Art of Noise: Who's Afraid of The Art of Noise, 1984; Daft, 1986; The Seduction of Claude Debussy, 1999; Singles with Buggles: Video Killed The Radio Star (No. 1, UK), 1979; The Plastic Age, 1980; Clean Clean, 1980; Elstree, 1980; I Am A Camera, 1981; Singles with Art of Noise include: Into Battle EP, 1983; Beatbox, 1983; Close (To The Edit), 1984; Moments In Love, 1985; As producer: Albums include: The Lexicon of Love, ABC, 1982; Duck Rock, Malcolm McLaren, 1983; 90125, Yes, 1983; Welcome To The Pleasure Dome, Frankie Goes To Hollywood, 1984; Seal, Seal, 1991; Tubular Bells II, Mike Oldfield, 1992; Singles include: with Dollar: Hand Held In Black and White, 1981; Mirror Mirror, 1981; Give Me Back My Heart, 1982; Videotheque, 1982; with ABC: Poison Arrow, 1982; The Look of Love, 1982; All of My Heart, 1982; with Spandau Ballet: Instinction, 1982; with Malcolm McLaren: Buffalo Gals, 1982; Double Dutch, 1983; with Yes: Owner of a Lonely Heart (No. 1, USA); with Frankie Goes To Hollywood: Relax (No. 1, UK), 1983; Two Tribes (No. 1, UK), 1984; The Power of Love (No. 1, UK), 1984; Rage Hard, 1986; with Propaganda: Dr Mabuse, 1984; with Grace Jones: Slave To The Rhythm, 1985; with Pet Shop Boys: Left To My Own Devices, 1988; It's Alright, 1989; with Simple Minds: Belfast Child (No. 1, UK), 1989; This Is Your Land, 1989; with Seal: Crazy, 1990; Killer, 1991; Kiss From A Rose, 1994; with Rod Stewart: Downtown Train, 1990; Rhythm of My Heart, 1991; with Marc Almond: Jacky, 1991; The Days of Pearly Spencer, 1992; with Tom Jones: If I Only Could, 1994; Other recordings with Tina Charles; Hans Zimmer; Tina Turner; Genesis; LeAnn Rimes; Cher. *Honours:* BRIT Awards: Best British Producer, 1985, 1992; Q Award, Best Producer, 1991. *Current Management:* Sarm Productions, The Blue Building, 42–46 St Lukes Mews, London W11 1DG, England.

HORNE, Lena; b. 30 June 1917, Brooklyn, New York, USA. Vocalist; Actress. m. Lennie Hayton, 1947 (deceased 1971). *Career:* Chorus singer, Cotton Club, Harlem, 1934; Singer with Noble Sissle's Society Orchestra, 1935–36; Charlie Barnet, 1940–41; Film appearances: Panama Hattie, 1942; Cabin In The Sky, 1943; Stormy Weather, 1943; Thousands Cheers; I Dood It; Swing Fever; Broadway Rhythm; Two Girls and A Sailor; Ziegfeld Follies; Till The Clouds Roll By; Words and Music; Duchess of Idaho; Meet Me In Las Vegas; Death of a Gunfighter; The Wiz; Television appearances include: Harry and Lena, 1970; Cosby Show; Sanford and Son; Stage appearances: Dance With Your Gods, Broadway, 1934; Blackbirds of 1939; Jamaica, Broadway, 1957; The Lady and Her Music, Broadway, 1981; Recent appearances include: JVC Jazz Festival, 1993. *Recordings:* Hits include: Stormy Weather; Deed I Do; As Long As I Live; Love Me Or Leave Me; Albums include: The Men In My Life, 1989; We'll Be Together Again, 1994; An Evening with Lena Horne, 1994; Lena Horne Christmas, 1995; Being Myself, 1998; Once in a Lifetime, 1999; Best of The War Years, 2000; Also recorded with: Cab Calloway; Artie Shaw; Teddy Wilson. *Publications:* Lena (with Richard Schickel); In Person. *Honours:* Tony Award, Distinguished Achievement In The Theatre; Drama Desk Award; New York Drama Critics' Special Award; Handel Medallion, New York City; Emergence Award, Dance Theatre of Harlem; 2 Grammy Awards; NAACP Springarn Award; Honour For Lifetime Contributions To The Arts, 1984; Paul Robeson Award, Actor's Equity, 1985; Hon. doctorate, Harvard University, 1979. *Address:* c/o Casterbridge Ltd, 1204 Third Ave, Suite 162, New York, NY 10021, USA.

HORNER, James; b. 14 Aug. 1953, Los Angeles, CA, USA. Film Music Composer. *Education:* Royal College of Music, London; BMus, University of South Carolina; MMus and PhD, Music Composition and Theory, University of California at Los Angeles. *Compositions:* For television: A Few Days in Weasel Creek, 1981; Angel Dusted, 1981; Rascals and Robbers: The Secret Adventures of Tom Sawyer and Huck Finn, 1982; A Piano for Mrs Cimino, 1982; Between Friends, 1983; In Crisis, 1985; Surviving, 1985; Amazing Stories, 1985; Tales from the Crypt, 1989; Extreme Close-Up, 1990; Fish Police, 1992; Freedom Song, 1999; For film: The Watcher, 1978; Up from the Depths, 1979; The Lady in Red, 1980; Battle Beyond the Stars, 1980; Humanoids from the Deep, 1980; Deadly Blessing, 1981; The Hand, 1981; Wolfen, 1981; The Pursuit of D. B. Cooper, 1981; 48 Hours, 1982; P.K. and the Kid, 1982; Star Trek II: The Wrath of Khan, 1982; Something Wicked This Way Comes, 1983; Krull, 1983; Brainstorm, 1983; Testament, 1983; Gorky Park, 1983; The Dresser, 1983; Uncommon Valor, 1983; The Stone Boy, 1984; Star Trek III: The Search for Spock, 1984; Let's Go, 1985; Heaven Help Us, 1985; Cocoon, 1985; In Her Own Time, 1985; Volunteers, 1985; Journey of Natty Gann, 1985; Commando, 1985; Off Beat, 1986; Captain Eo, 1986; Aliens, 1986; Where the River Runs Black, 1986; The Name of the Rose, 1986; An American Tail, 1986; Project X, 1987; Batteries Not Included, 1987; Willow, 1988; Red Heat, 1988; Vibes, 1988; Cocoon: The Return, 1988; The Land Before Time, 1988; Tummy Trouble, 1989; In Country, 1989; Field of Dreams, 1989; Honey, I Shrunk the Kids, 1989; Dad, 1989; Glory, 1989; I Love

You to Death, 1990; Another 48 Hours, 1990; Once Around, 1991; Norman and the Killer, 1991; My Heroes Have Always Been Cowboys, 1991; Class Action, 1991; The Rocketeer, 1991; An American Tail: Fievel Goes West, 1991; Thunderheart, 1992; Patriot Games, 1992; Unlawful Entry, 1992; Sneakers, 1992; We're Back! A Dinosaur's Story, 1993; Swing Kids, 1993; A Far Off Place, 1993; House of Cards, 1993; Jack the Bear, 1993; Once Upon a Forest, 1993; Searching for Bobby Fischer, 1993; The Man Without a Face, 1993; Bopha!, 1993; The Pelican Brief, 1993; The Pagemaster, 1994; Clear and Present Danger, 1994; Legends of the Fall, 1994; Braveheart, 1995; Casper, 1995; Apollo 13, 1995; Jumanji, 1995; Jade, 1995; Balto, 1995; The Spitfire Grill, 1996; Courage Under Fire, 1996; Ransom, 1996; To Gillian on Her 37th Birthday, 1996; The Devil's Own, 1997; Titanic, 1997; Mighty Joe Young, 1998; The Mask of Zorro, 1998; Deep Impact, 1998; The Perfect Storm, 2000; How the Grinch Stole Christmas, 2000; Enemy at the Gates, 2001; A Beautiful Mind, 2001; Iris, 2001; Windtalkers, 2002; The Four Feathers, 2002. *Honours:* Academy Award, Titanic; Golden Globe, Titanic; Grammy Awards, Glory, Titanic. *Membership:* ASCAP. *Current Management:* Gorfaine/Schwartz Agency Inc, 13245 Riverside Dr., Suite 450, Sherman Oaks, CA 91423, USA. *Website:* www.james-horner.com.

HORNSBY, Bruce Randall; b. 23 Nov. 1954, Richmond, Virginia, USA. Musician (piano); Songwriter. m. Kathy Lynn Yankovich, 31 Dec. 1983, 2 s. *Education:* BA, Music, University of Miami, 1977. *Career:* Played on over 100 albums for other artists including: Bob Dylan; Grateful Dead; Bonnie Raitt; Don Henley; Bob Seger; Willie Nelson; Branford Marsalis; Chaka Khan; Squeeze; Robbie Robertson; 10 US top 40 hits (six as an artiste, four as a songwriter); Written songs with: Don Henley; Robbie Robertson; Leon Russell; Chaka Khan; Tupac Shakur; Lennie Meat. *Recordings:* Albums: The Way It Is, 1986; Scenes From the Southside, 1988; A Night On The Town, 1990; Harbour Lights, 1993; Hot House, 1995; Spirit Trail, 1998; Here Come The Noise Makers, 2000; Big Swing Face, 2002. *Honours:* 3 Grammys; 8 times winner, Keyboard Magazine Readers Poll; Daytime Emmy Award, Outstanding Achievement in Music, 1987–88; ASCAP Song of the Year: The Way It Is, 1987; Elvis Award, International Rock Awards, 1991; Album of the Year: Downbeat Readers Poll: Harbour Lights, 1994; Platinum, Gold albums, world-wide. *Membership:* ASCAP; AFofM. *Current Management:* Marmaluke Inc, VA, USA. *Address:* PO Box 3545, Williamsburg, VA 23187, USA.

HOROWITZ, Adam; b. 31 Oct. 1966, New York, USA. Rap Artiste; Musician. *Career:* Founder member, US rap/rock group The Beastie Boys, 1983–; Appearances include: Support to Madonna, Virgin Tour, 1985; Supports to Run DMC, Raisin' Hell Tour, 1986, Co-headliners with Run DMC, Together Forever Tour, 1987; Reading Festival, 1992; Made horror film, Scared Stupid; Film appearances: Krush Groove; Run-DMC film, Tougher Than Leather. *Recordings:* Albums include: Licensed To Ill, 1986; Paul's Boutique, 1989; Check Your Head, 1992; Ill Communication, 1994; Root Down, 1995; The In Sound From Way Out, 1996; Hello Nasty, 1998; Sounds of Science (compilation), 1999; Singles include: Fight For Your Right To Party, 1987; No Sleep Till Brooklyn, 1987; She's On It, 1987; Hey Ladies, 1989; Pass the Mic, 1992; Jimmy James, 1992; Get It Together/Sabotage, 1994; Sure Shot, 1994; Intergalactic, 1998; Body Movin', 1998; Remote Control, 1999; Alive, 1999. *Current Management:* Gold Mountain Entertainment, 3575 Cahuenga Blvd W, Suite 450, Los Angeles, CA 90068, USA.

HORSLEY, Richard; b. 5 Jan. 1970, Chelmsford, Essex, England. Record Co Exec; Musician (drums); Recording Artist; Prod. *Education:* 10 years drum tuition. *Career:* Underground producer, recording artist under name of Timeslip; Numerous remixes; Private commissioned work; Owner, record label, R H Records. *Recordings:* Kinky and Hypnotiq, 1996. *Membership:* PPL; PRS; BAC&S. *Address:* R H Records, Greatworth House, Greatworth, Banbury, Oxon OX17 2DR, England.

HOTATSU, Nami; b. 3 Sept. 1969, Tokyo, Japan. Vocalist; Songwriter; Musician (piano, keyboards, synthesizer, Irish harp). *Education:* Graduated, Kunitachi College of Music, Tokyo, Japan, 1992; Classical Piano, 4 years old; Musicology, Kunitachi College of Music; Vocal lesson, Japanese Traditional Style and Pop Style. *Career:* Shu Uemura Make Up Installation, 1992; Eden in the Sky, Yellow, 1993–94; Partheno-Jenesis, Ambient Opera, Tokyo, 1995; Earth Festival, Fili Festival, 1996; Haruomi Hosono and Japanese Sea's Mongoloid, 1996; WaterScape, Nagoya, 1996; Earth Sonic, Tokyo, 1996; The World of Shakespeare, Dramatic Reading, Shakespeare Country Park, Chiba, Japan, 1997. *Compositions:* Making Sense of Jewel, 1993; Hotatsu-Nami, 1994; Luna Drifting On the Glittering Waves, 1995; Stranger Than Movies, 1997. *Recordings:* Happy Birthday to Me Itaka, 1996. *Membership:* Japan Soundscape Asscn. *Current Management:* Macaroni Tone, #201, 1–5–4 Sakuradai, Nerima-ku, Tokyo 176, Japan. *Address:* #201, 1–5–4 Sakuradai Nerima-ku, Tokyo 176, Japan.

HOTT NIKKELS. See: **METHOD MAN.**

HOTTE, Kevin Richard; b. 16 Nov. 1959, Port Colbourne, Ontario, Canada. Composer; Prod. m. 16 Oct. 1982. *Education:* Graphic Arts, Photography, Niagara College; Privately trained: drums, percussion, keyboards. *Career:* Owner, Musicom Music Productions; The Sound Kitchen Recording Studio;

Creative Images Media; Creative Images, sydicated radio show about photography technique. *Compositions:* Various radio jingles, corporate video scores. *Recordings:* Windows (14 song debut album). *Membership:* SOCAN; ASCAP. *Address:* St Catharines, Ontario, Canada.

HOUSTON, Cissy, (Emily Drinkard); b. 1933, Newark, New Jersey, USA. Vocalist. 1 d. *Career:* Member, family gospel group Drinkard Singers; Backing singers for numerous artists including: Wilson Pickett; Solomon Burke; Vocalist, Sweet Inspirations, 1967–70; Prolific session singer. *Recordings:* Albums: Cissy Houston, 1977; Warning Danger, 1979; Step Aside For A Lady, 1980; Mama's Cooking, 1987; I'll Take Care of You, 1992; Face to Face, 1996; He Leadeth Me, 1997; Singles: I'll Be There, 1970; Be My Baby, 1971; Think It Over, 1978; Other albums: with Whitney Houston (her daughter): Whitney Houston, 1985; Whitney, 1987; with Aretha Franklin: Let Me Into Your Life, 1974; Love All The Hurt Away, 1981; Jump To It, 1982; with Van Morrison: Moondance, 1970; No Sheets, 1974; with Diana Ross: Diana's Duets, 1982; Silk Electric, 1982; The Wiz (soundtrack), 1978; with Paul Simon: Paul Simon, 1972; Greatest Hits etc, 1977; with Luther Vandross: Never Too Much, 1981; Forever, For Always, For Love, 1982; Busy Body, 1987; The Night I Fell In Love, 1985; Give Me The Reason, 1987; Other recordings with numerous artists including: Joe Cocker; Judy Collins; Kiki Dee; Jackie DeShannon; Gregg Allman; The Drifters; J Geils Band; Chaka Khan; Don McLean; John Prine; Linda Ronstadt.

HOUSTON, Thelma; b. 7 May 1943, Leland, Mississippi, USA. Vocalist; Actress. *Career:* Singer, gospel group the Art Reynolds Singers, late 1960s; Solo artiste, 1969–; Also recorded with Jerry Butler; Actress, films: Death Scream; Norman... Is That You?; The Seventh Dwarf. *Recordings:* Albums: Sunshower, 1969; Thelma Houston, 1973; Anyway You Like It, 1977; The Devil In Me, 1978; Ready To Roll, 1978; Ride To The Rainbow, 1979; Breakwater Cat, 1980; Never Gonna Be Another One, 1981; I've Got The Music In Me, 1981; Qualifying Heats, 1987; Throw You Down, 1990; The Best of Thelma Houston, 1991; With Jerry Butler: Thelma and Jerry, 1977; Two To One, 1978; Hit singles: Don't Leave Me This Way (No. 1, USA), 1976; If You Feel It, 1981; You Used To Hold Me So Tight, 1984. *Current Management:* Gross Management Organization, 930 Third St, Suite 102, Santa Monica, CA 90403, USA.

HOUSTON, Whitney; b. 9 Aug. 1963, Newark, NJ, USA. Vocalist. m. Bobby Brown, 18 July 1992, 1 d. *Education:* Singing lessons with mother, Cissy Houston. *Career:* New Hope Baptist Jr Choir, age 8; Nightclub performances with mother, 1978; Backing vocalist, Chaka Khan and Lou Rawls, 1978; Model, Glamour and Seventeen magazines; Actress, television shows, USA; Solo artiste, 1985–; First US and European tours, 1986; Montreux Rock Festival, 1987; Nelson Mandela Tribute concert, Wembley, 1988; National anthem, Super Bowl XXV, Miami, 1991; Speaker, HIV/AIDs rally, London, 1991; Television specials include: Welcome Home Heroes (return of Gulf troops), 1991; Whitney Houston – This Is My Life (ABC), 1992; Actress, films: The Bodyguard, 1992; Waiting to Exhale, 1995; The Preacher's Wife, 1996. *Recordings:* Albums: Whitney Houston, 1985; Whitney, 1987; I'm Your Baby Tonight, 1990; My Love Is Your Love, 1998; Greatest Hits, 2000; Love, Whitney, 2001; Just Whitney..., 2002; Film soundtracks: The Bodyguard (No. 1 in 20 countries), 1992; Waiting To Exhale, 1995; The Preacher's Wife, 1996; Singles include: You Give Good Love, 1985; Saving All My Love For You (No. 1, UK and USA), 1985; How Will I Know (No. 1, USA), 1986; Greatest Love of All (No. 1, USA), 1986; I Wanna Dance With Somebody (No. 1, UK and USA), 1987; Didn't We Almost Have It All (No. 1, USA), 1987; So Emotional (No. 1, USA), 1987; Where Do Broken Hearts Go (No. 1, USA), 1988; Love Will Save The Day, 1988; One Moment In Time (No. 1, UK), 1988; I'm Your Baby Tonight (No. 1, USA), 1990; All The Man That I Need (No. 1, USA), 1991; Miracle, 1991; My Name Is Not Susan, 1991; I Will Always Love You (No. 1 in 11 countries), 1992; I'm Every Woman, 1993; I Have Nothing, 1993; Run To You, 1993; Queen Of The Night, 1994; Something In Common (with Bobby Brown), 1994; Exhale (Shoop Shoop), 1995; Count On Me (with CeCe Winans), 1996; Why Does It Hurt So Bad, 1996; Step By Step, 1997; I Believe In You And Me, 1997; When You Believe (with Mariah Carey), 1998; It's Not Right But It's Okay, 1999; My Love Is Your Love, 1999; I Learned From The Best, 1999; If I Told You That (with George Michael), 2000; Could I Have This Kiss Forever (with Enrique Iglesias), 2000; Heartbreak Hotel (with Faith Evans and Kelly Price), 2000; Whatchulookinat, 2002; One Of Those Days, 2002. *Honours:* Three Grammy Awards, incl. Female R&B Vocal Performance, It's Not Right But It's Okay, 2000; Seven American Music Awards; Emmy, 1986; Songwriter's Hall of Fame, 1990; Numerous Gold and Platinum discs. *Address:* c/o Arista Records, 6 W 57th St, New York, USA. *Website:* www.whitneyhouston.com.

HOVMAN, Klavs; b. 27 Oct. 1957, Århus, Denmark. Musician (double bass, bass). 1 d., 1 s. *Career:* Member, Savage Rose, 1991–92; Played with numerous jazz/rock bands; Toured with: Ernie Wilkins Almost Big Band; Horace Parlan; Toots Thielemans; Lee Konitz; Svend Asmussen; Bassist with Etta Cameron's jazz and world groups, 1980–; Gospel concerts, Europe, 1990s; Member, Marilyn Mazur's groups Future Song and Pulse Unit. *Compositions:* Music for New Music Orchestra, Copenhagen Jazz Festival Event. *Recordings:* Album: Baraban, Peter Danemo, 1991; Månebarn, Savage Rose, 1992; Marilyn

Mazur's Future Song, 1992; Echoez Of..., Harry Beckett and Pierre Dorge, 1992; Being, Lotte Anker/Mette Peterson Quintet, 1993; Savage Rose 25, Savage Rose, 1993; Gospel Concert, Etta Cameron, 1995; Circular Chant, Marilyn Mazur/Pulse Unit, 1995.

HOWARD, Dominic James; b. 12 July 1977. Musician (drums). *Career:* Spent pre-teen years in Rotherham, England; Formed group Gothic Plague in adopted hometown of Teignmouth, aged 13; Group became Fixed Penalty then Rocket Baby Dolls before finally settling on name Muse; Released two 1,000-copy EPs on UK independent label Dangerous; Signed to Madonna's US label Maverick following lauded UK In The City '98 and New York CMJ festival appearances; Rapid rise to fame followed; Live shows include: Ill-fated Woodstock '99 US festival; Headline slots at UK's Leeds, Reading and T In The Park festivals, 2000; European tours, 2001. *Recordings:* Albums: Showbiz, 1999; Origin of Symmetry, 2001; Hullabaloo, 2002. Singles: Muse EP, 1998; Muscle Museum EP, Uno, Cave, 1999; Sunburn, Unintended, 2000; Plug In Baby, New Born, Bliss, Hyper Music/Feeling Good, 2001; Dead Star In Your World, 2002. *Honours:* NME Award, Best Newcomer, 2000; Kerrang! Award, Best British Band, 2001. *Current Management:* Taste Media/SJP Management, 263 Putney Bridge Rd, London SW15 2PU, England. *Website:* www.muse-official.com.

HOWARD, James Newton; b. 9 June 1951, Los Angeles, CA, USA. Composer. *Education:* University of Southern California; Music Acad. of the West. *Compositions:* For television: Go to the Light, 1988; The Image, 1990; Revealing Evidence: Stalking the Honolulu Strangler, 1990; Somebody Has to Shoot the Picture, 1990; Descending Angel, 1990; A Private Matter, 1992; ER, 1994; From the Earth to the Moon, 1998; For film: Tough Guys, 1986; Nobody's Fool, 1986; Head Office, 1986; Wildcats, 1986; 8 Million Ways to Die, 1986; Russkies, 1987; Campus Man, 1987; Five Corners, 1987; Promised Land, 1988; Off Limits, 1988; Tap, 1989; Some Girls, 1989; Major League, 1989; The Package, 1989; Marked for Death, 1990; Pretty Woman, 1990; Coupe de Ville, 1990; Flatliners, 1990; Three Men and a Little Lady, 1990; The Prince of Tides, 1991; My Girl, 1991; Grand Canyon, 1991; Guilty by Suspicion, 1991; King Ralph, 1991; Dying Young, 1991; The Man in the Moon, 1991; Night and the City, 1992; Glengarry Glen Ross, 1992; American Heart, 1992; Diggstown, 1992; The Saint of Fort Washington, 1993; Alive, 1993; Falling Down, 1993; Dave, 1993; The Fugitive, 1993; Intersection, 1994; Wyatt Earp, 1994; Junior, 1994; Restoration, 1995; Just Cause, 1995; Outbreak, 1995; French Kiss, 1995; Waterworld, 1995; Eye for an Eye, 1996; The Juror, 1996; Primal Fear, 1996; The Trigger Effect, 1996; The Rich Man's Wife (theme), 1996; Space Jam, 1996; One Fine Day, 1996; Dante's Peak (theme), 1997; Liar Liar (theme), 1997; Fathers' Day, 1997; My Best Friend's Wedding, 1997; The Devil's Advocate, 1997; The Postman, 1997; A Perfect Murder, 1998; Snow Falling on Cedars, 1999; Mumford, 1999; Stir of Echoes, 1999; Dinosaur, 2000; Unbreakable, 2000; Vertical Limit, 2000; Signs, 2002. *Membership:* ASCAP. *Current Management:* Gorfaine/Schwartz Agency Inc, 13245 Riverside Dr., Suite 450, Sherman Oaks, CA 91423, USA.

HOWARD, John; b. 9 April 1953, Bury, Lancashire, England. Record Co Exec; Musician (keyboards). *Education:* Art College; Private piano tuition, age 7–16. *Career:* Songwriter; Singer; Signed to CBS Records, 1973; Moved to Ariola Records with Trevor Horn, 1977; Returned to CBS with Nicky Graham, 1980; Member of Quiz, with Steve Levine and Graham Broad, 1981–83; Label Manager, Conifer Records, 1985; A&R Manager, Pickwick Records, 1986; Strategic Marketing Manager, MCA Records, 1993; A&R Director, Carlton Records, 1995. *Recordings:* Albums: Kid In A Big World, 1975; On Reflection, 1993; Singles: with Quiz: It's You I Want; And The World; Solo: Nothing More To Say; Songs: Casting Shadows, for film Open Season; with Dave Willetts: Stages of Love; with Stephanie Lawrence: Footlights; with Des O'Connor: Blue Days; International Music Development, Reader's Digest, 1997. *Address:* Reader's Digest, 11 Westferry Circus, Canary Wharf, London E14 4HE, England.

HOWARD, Johnny; b. 5 Feb. 1931, Croydon, Surrey, England. Bandleader; Musician (saxophone). m. 28 Sept. 1970, 1 s., 1 d. *Education:* Private tuition. *Career:* Professional big band leader, 1959–; Worked Mecca Dancehall circuit until 1967; Radio broadcasts, including 5 years on Easybeat, own lunchtime show, One O'Clock Jump; Television includes: Come Dancing, 1960s–70s; Played corporate and conference engagements, 1980s–90s. *Recordings:* More than a dozen albums and singles, 1960s–70s; Hit single: Rinky Dink (used by Radio Caroline as theme tune). *Honours:* Carl Alan Award, Britain's Best Band, 1967. *Current Management:* Fanfare 3000. *Address:* The Folly, Pinner Hill Rd, Pinner, Middlesex HA5 3YQ, England.

HOWARD, (Kevin) Robert; b. 31 Oct. 1962, Huddersfield, England. Engineering Technician; Semi-Professional Musician (drums). m. Nicola Jane, 24 June 1989, 2 s. *Education:* HNC, Industrial Measurement and Control; Studied privately with Geoff Myers, Leeds, from age 13, drums. *Career:* Les Howard's Northern Dance Orchestra (NDO), 1988–94; Currently with Herb Miller Orchestra, touring Great Britain and Europe, 1996–; Radio appearances: Several on BBC Radio 2, Jazz Parade; Radio 2 Arts Programme; Appearances at many jazz festivals around Britain. *Recordings:* with Rod Mason's Concept, 1984–88; Alan Skidmore, 1993; Memphis Bell Orchestra,

1995; New Squadronaires Orchestra, 1998; played with many bands, eg Syd Lawrence Orchestra, Andy Prior Orchestra, Andy Ross Orchestra. *Membership:* Musicians' Union. *Address:* 9 Golcar Brow Rd, Meltham, Huddersfield, West Yorkshire HD7 3LD, England.

HOWARD, Rex; b. 23 July 1930, Thunder Bay, Ontario, Canada. Vocalist; Musician (pedal steel guitar, dobro). m. Candice James, 12 May 1990, 1 s., 2 d. *Education:* 1 year university. *Career:* Member, Bootleg, support tour with John Anderson; Toured USA, as opening act and steel player and sideman with: Hank Williams Sr; Ernest Tubb; Dave Dudley; Performed in Western Canada with the band Saddlestone. *Recordings:* Little Peg and The Blind Man; A Heartache As Big As Texas; Roadside Ride; If Heaven's Missin' An Angel; An Old Dusty Heartache. *Honours:* Instrumentalist of the Year, SCCMA; Male Vocalist of Year, 1993. *Membership:* SOCAN; AFofM; CIRPA. *Current Management:* Silver Bow Management. *Address:* 6260–130 St, Surrey, British Columbia V3X 1R6, Canada.

HOWE, Bob; b. 22 Dec. 1956. Musician (guitars, harmonica); Vocalist; Composer. m. Karen Versace, 21 Nov. 1992. *Career:* Australian Cabaret Artist and Session Musician; Musical Director for Frank Ifield, 1984–88; Guy Mitchell, 1991; Portrayed Paul McCartney, Australian Production of Lennon – The Musical, 1986–87; Toured with many Australian artistes, Lucky Starr, Slim Dusty. *Compositions:* White Man's Blues; Some People Change. *Recordings:* Contributor to: John Chester Love in the Meantime; Waltzing Matilda, Diana Trask; Cross Country, Sarah Jory; The Fire Still Burns, Frank Ifield. *Publications:* Cowboys in Cyberspace, 1997. *Honours:* Most Popular Guitarist, Musician and Newcomer, Southern Hemisphere Country Music Awards, 1982. *Membership:* Music Arrangers' Guild of Australia. *Address:* PO Box 7341, Bondi Beach, NSW 2026, Australia.

HOWE, Brian; b. 22 July 1957, Portsmouth, Hampshire, England. Vocalist. 1 s., 1 d. *Career:* Member, Ted Nugent Band; Lead singer, rock group Bad Company, 1986–93; US Holy Water tour with Damn Yankees, 1990–91; Last Rebel Here Comes Trouble US Tour, supporting Lynyrd Skynyrd, 1993; Solo Artiste, 1993–; Numerous television appearances including: MTV, VH1, Tonight Show, Letterman. *Compositions:* Co-writer and performer as lead singer on How About That, the no. 11 Song of All Time in 100 year Billboard Chart Edition in Album Rock. *Recordings:* Albums: Penetrator, Ted Nugent, 1984; Fame and Fortune, 1986; Dangerous Age, 1988; Holy Water, 1990; Here Comes Trouble, 1992; Best of Bad Company Live, 1993; Solo album: Tangled in Blue, 1997; Hit Singles include: Shake It Up, 1986; Holy Water, 1990; If You Needed Somebody, 1991; Walk Through Fire, 1991; How About That, 1992; This Could Be The One, 1992. *Membership:* NARAS, Grammy Voting Member. *Current Management:* TopNotch Entertainment Corp, Box 1515, Sanibel Island, FL 33957–1515, USA.

HOWE, Liam; b. 29 Sept. Musician (keyboards); Songwriter; Prod. *Career:* Various musical projects, with Chris Corner: first band, 1990, F.R.I.S.K., 1992, Line Of Flight, 1993; Founding mem., Sneaker Pimps, 1995–; Numerous festivals and concerts; Band founded Splinter Recordings, 1999. *Recordings:* Albums: with Sneaker Pimps: Becoming X, 1996; Splinter, 1999; Bloodsport, 2002. Singles: with Line Of Flight: World As A Cone (EP), 1993; with Sneaker Pimps: 6 Underground (EP), 1996; Roll On, 1996; Tesko Suicide, 1996; Spin Spin Sugar, 1997; Post Modern Sleaze, 1997; 6 Underground, 1998; Low Five, 1999; Ten To Twenty, 1999; Sick, 2002. *Address:* c/o Tommy Boy Music, 902 Broadway, New York, NY 10010, USA. *E-mail:* parmesanchic@aol.com. *Website:* www.sneakerpimps.com.

HOWE, Ronald; b. 7 Dec. 1957, Leatherhead, Surrey, England. Musician (tenor saxophone). m. Carolanne Edge, 6 July 1989, 1 d. *Education:* Private tuition, adult education, Goldsmith's, London. *Career:* Concerts, tours with many bands; Large amount of studio work and recording; Toured and recorded with: Fools Can Dance; Worked on Cure album; Worked live with Damned; Currently with The Bucket Band; Videos; Major venues include: Hammersmith Palais; Teaching saxophone (theory, performance, improvisation); Brass/horns arrangement; Music transcription. *Recordings:* A Night Like This; The Cure; Box Office Poison; Beyond The Twilight Zone; Checkmate; Numerous others. *Membership:* Musicians' Union; PAMRA. *Address:* 7 Wentworth, Aurum Close, Horley, Surrey RH6 9BE, England.

HOWE, Steve; b. 8 April 1947, London, England. Musician (guitar). *Career:* Member, The Syndicats; The In Crowd; Tomorrow; Bodast; UK progressive rock group Yes, 1970–81; Concerts included: Queen Elizabeth Hall, London; Reading Festival; Madison Square Garden; Asia, 1981–90; World-wide tours, including Asia In Asia concert, Tokyo, Japan (broadcast by MTV to audience of 20m.), 1983; Member, GTR, 1986–91; Rejoined Yes, 1991–; Concerts include: Yesshows '91 – Round The World In 80 Dates Tour, 1991. *Recordings:* Albums: with Yes: Time and A Word, 1970; The Yes Album, 1971; Fragile, 1971; Close To The Edge, 1972; Yessongs, 1973; Tales From The Topographic Ocean, 1973; Relayer, 1974; Yesterdays, 1975; Going For The One, 1977; Tormato, 1978; Yesshows, 1981; Union, 1991; Yesstory, 1991; Symphonic Music of Yes, 1993; History of The Future, 1993; Open Your Eyes, 1998; Ladder, 1999; with Asia: Asia, 1982; Alpha, 1983; Astra, 1985; Aqua, 1992; Archiva Vol. 1, 1996; Anthology, 1999; with GTR: GTR, 1986: Solo

albums: Beginnings, 1975; Steve Howe Album, 1979; Turbulence, 1991; The Grand Scheme of Things, 1993; Mothballs, 1994; Not Necessarily Acoustic, 1994; Seraphim, 1995; Voyagers, 1995; Homebrew, 1996; Quantum Guitar, 1998; Pulling Strings, 1999; Portraits of Bob Dylan, 1999; With Anderson Bruford Wakeman Howe: Anderson Bruford Wakeman Howe, 1989; Singles include: Yes: Roundabout; Wondrous Stories; Going For The One; Brother of Mine; Lift Me Up; with Asia: Heat of The Moment; Only Time Will Tell; Don't Cry; with GTR: When The Heart Rules The Mind; The Hunter; Solo albums include: Homebrew 2, 2000; Natural Timbre, 2001. *Contributions to:* Welcome To The Pleasuredome, Frankie Goes To Hollywood, 1984; A Secret Wish, Propaganda, 1985. *Honours:* Gold Ticket, Madison Square Garden, with Yes, 1978; Top New Artist, Top Album, with Asia, Billboard magazine, 1982. *Current Management:* Tiz Hay Management, 44 Oswald Close, Leatherhead, Surrey KT22 9UG, England.

HOWELL, Mark; b. 11 July 1952, USA. Composer; Performer; Musician (Guitar, Trumpet). m. Stephanie Artz. *Education:* BA, University of Southern Mississippi; MA, SUNY, Stony Brook, NY. *Career:* Stop at Nothing, The Kitchen, 1987; Zero Pop, 1986–96; In Memory, 1989; Gt Schubertide, 1997. *Compositions:* History of Magic, 1990; For A Birthday, 1996; To The Heart, 1997. *Recordings:* Include, Swimman, Better Than Death Twin Tone, 1987; North America, Moers, 1986; Glows in the Dark, Zero Pop, 1992; Parts and Labour, Rough Trade, 1992; Quartets, 1994. *Publications:* Locronets: An Automatic Sketching Technique, The Improviser, 1989. *Membership:* BMI; Society for Ethnomusicology. *Address:* 344 E Sixth St, Apt #2D, New York, NY 10003, USA.

HOWELL-JONES, Richard Mark; b. 18 April 1960, Altrincham, Cheshire, England. Actor; Musician (drums, percussion); Vocalist. *Education:* Manchester Polytechnic. *Career:* Drummer, vocalist, with R&B band Flat Hedgehog, 1981–83; Theatre performance band Celebration of Joe, 1984–85; Roy Woodward Big Band, 1985–87; R&B band The Shades, 1990–91; Television: King Lear (Channel 4), 1983; Dear Ladies, BBC TV, 1984; Films: The Last Meeting, 1996; Currently touring Dusty Pens by Derek Martin. *Recordings:* Celebration of Joe, with Brian Roberts, 1984. *Membership:* Musicians' Union; Equity. *Address:* 18 Wardle Rd, Sale, Cheshire M33 3DB, England.

HOWLETT, Liam; b. 21 Aug. 1971. Songwriter; Musician (keyboards); DJ. *Career:* Member, The Prodigy, 1990–; Festival appearances include: Glastonbury, 1995, 1997; V97, 1997; Lollapalooza, 1997. *Recordings:* Albums: Experience, 1992; Music for the Jilted Generation (No. 1, UK), 1994; The Fat of the Land (No. 1, UK), 1997; The Dirtchamber Sessions, 1999; Hit Singles: Charly, 1991; Everybody In the Place, 1991; Fire, 1992; Out of Space, 1992; Wind It Up, 1993; One Love, 1993; No Good (Start the Dance), 1994; Voodoo People, 1994; Poison, 1995; Firestarter (No. 1, UK), 1996; Breathe (No. 1, UK), 1996; Smack My Bitch Up, 1997; Poison, 1997. *Honours:* BRIT Awards, Best British Dance Act, 1997, 1998. *Current Management:* Midi Management Ltd. *Address:* The Old Barn, Jenkins Lane, Great Hallingbury, Essex CM22 7QL, England.

HOYDAL, Annika; b. Tórshaun, The Faroe Islands. m. Klavs Lockwood, 25 June 1994. *Education:* Graduated, Actress, Statens Teaterskole, Copenhagen, Denmark, 1973. *Career:* The Faroe Islands, 1966; Freelance Actress and Singer, throughout Scandinavia. *Compositions include:* Mit Eget Land; Min Krop; Hjemme; Drimmen; Bekendelse; Mírket; Lammet; Aldan, Dråben; Kasper; Til Dans; Tjipp; Munnur; Á Palli; Á Havi; Morgun; Snigil; Alt; Dulcinea; Hvalspýggja; Taraloppa; Ljós; Kópagenta; Dreymahav; Inn Móti Landi; Marmennil; Farin; Sjólátin; Nú Sigla...; Tid; Find en Sten. *Recordings include:* Til Børn og Vaksin, 1975; Annika og Jógvan, 1979; Spor í Sjónum, 1983; Dulcinea, 1991; Havid/The Ocean, 1997. *Honours:* Melodi Grand Prix for Faroe Islands, Denmark, 1979. *Membership:* Dansk Artist Forbund; Danish Jazz Beat and Folk Music Composers Organization; Dansk Solist-Forbund. *Current Management:* Arte Booking, Copenhagen. *Address:* Admiralgade 22 2 tv, 1066 Copenhagen K, Denmark. *E-mail:* hoydal@image.dk.

HRADECKY, Emil; b. 25 Feb. 1953, Prague, Czech Republic. Teacher; Composer. m. Alexandra Hradecká, 10 Nov. 1978. *Education:* Prague Conservatory. *Compositions:* (classical) Love Songs, song cycle for tenor and piano; String Quartet; Meditace per flauto solo; Melancolic danza a rondo, flute quartet; Nine variations and fugue on a theme by Mozart, piano; Suite for flute and violin. *Recordings:* Omnis sermo Dei ignitus; Ne glorieris in crastinum ignorans; Principium sapientiae timor Domini, for mixed boys and male voice choir. *Publications:* Little Jazz Album; Little Jazz Pieces for 20 Fingers; Dances For The Guitar; Jazz Flute and MC; Jazz Trumpet and MC; Jazz Trombone and MC; Von Blues Bis Disco and MC; Jazz Etudes; Der Kinderkarneval; Kleine Jazz-Stücke Für 20 Finger; Zwei-Seiten Stücke; Klienes Jazz-Album; Tanz-Kompositionen Für Vier Hände; Tänze für Gitarre; Fox-Polka; Swing-Polka; Der Sonnige Rag; We Play The Piano According To The Chord Marks. *Honours:* Musical Prize, Children's Choirs, Prague, 1995, 1997. *Address:* Konselská 11, 180 00 Prague 8, Czech Republic.

HUCKNALL, Mick (Michael James); b. 8 June 1960, Manchester, England. Vocalist; Songwriter. *Education:* BA, Manchester Polytechnic. *Career:* Formed early band, Frantic Elevators, 1979; Formed Simply Red, 1984–, essentially a solo career with changing band members; Numerous hit singles, television appearances; Numerous tours and festival dates worldwide; Founder, Blood and Fire label, dedicated to vintage reggae tracks; Mem., Government Task Force on the Music Industry, 1997–. *Recordings:* Albums: Picture Book, 1985; Early Years, 1987; Men and Women, 1987; A New Flame (No. 1, UK), 1989; Stars (No. 1, UK), 1991; 12ers, 1995; Life (No. 1, UK), 1995; Greatest Hits (No. 1, UK), 1996; Blue, 1998; Love And The Russian Winter, 1999; It's Only Love, 2001; Home, 2003. Singles: Money's Too Tight to Mention, 1985; Holding Back the Years (No. 1, USA), 1986; Ev'ry Time We Say Goodbye, 1987; The Right Thing, 1987; It's Only Love, 1989; If You Don't Know Me By Now (No. 1, USA), 1989; A New Flame, 1989; Something Got Me Started, 1991; Stars, 1991; For Your Babies, 1992; Thrill Me, 1992; Your Mirror, 1992; Fairground (No. 1, UK), 1995; Remembering The First Time, 1995; Never Never Love, 1996; We're In This Together, 1996; Angel, 1996; To Be Free; Night Nurse, with Sly and Robbie, 1997; Say You Love Me, 1998; The Air That I Breathe, 1998; Ghetto Girl, 1998; Ain't That A Lot of Love, 1999; Your Eyes, 2000. *Honours:* Hon. MSc, UMIST, 1997; BRIT Awards, Best British Band, 1991, 1992, Best Male Solo Artist, 1992; Ivor Novello Awards, Songwriter of the Year, 1992, Outstanding Song Collection, 2002; MOBO Award for Outstanding Achievement, 1997; Manchester Making It Happen Award, 1998. *Address:* c/o Silentway Ltd, Unit 61b, Pall Mall Deposit, 124–128 Barlby Rd, London W10 6BL, England. *Website:* www.simplyred.com.

HUDSON, Colin, (Colin Hudd); b. 8 Dec. 1950, Tilbury. DJ; Prod. 1 d. *Education:* Private. *Career:* Audio De Luxe, 1984–92; Colin Hudson, DJ; Talis Mantra, New Band. *Compositions:* 60 Seconds; We Are Not Alone; The Damn Thing Keeps Kickin; Stones. *Recordings:* 60 Seconds; We Are Not Alone; The Damn Thing Keep Kickin; Stones. *Honours:* Blackechoes Club DJ, 1983, 1984; Blues and Soul Club DJ, 1985, 1986. *Membership:* Musicians' Union. *Current Management:* Midi Management Ltd. *Address:* The Old Barn, Kenkins Lane, Gt Hallingbury, Essex CM22 7QL, England. *E-mail:* colin@colinhudd.com. *Website:* www.colinhudd.com.

HUEY. See: **MORGAN, Huey.**

HUGGETT, Mark J; b. 3 July 1961, Birmingham, England. Musician (drums). *Education:* BA Fine Art, Reading University. *Career:* Concerts: Italia '90 (official Irish rock promotion with Pepe jeans); Reading Festival, 1992; Fleadh Festival, 1992; Television and radio includes: BBC2 Taking Liberties; MTV, RTE, Ireland; Dave Fanning, Irish radio; RTI, Italy; Italian radio; Simon Mayo, BBC Radio One. *Recordings:* Albums: Red Harvest: Strange; Saved; Singles: World Won't Listen; Dr Millar and The Cute Hoors: Romance In A Flat (number 12, Irish charts); Currently recording with Chant. *Current Management:* Johnny Rogan. *Address:* 101/103 Devonport Rd, Shepherds Bush, London W12 8PB, England.

HUGHES, Christoper Merrick; b. 3 March 1953. Record Prod; Musician (drums). m. Elizabeth, 2 s., 1 d. *Career:* Drummer, Adam and the Ants. *Compositions:* Co-Work, Everybody Wants To Rule The World. *Recordings:* Kings of The Wild Frontier; Songs From The Big Chair; Everybody Wants To Rule The World. *Honours:* Record Producer of the Year Award, 1981. *Current Management:* Isisglow Ltd, The Wool Hall, Castle Corner, Beckington, Somerset BA3 6TA, England.

HUGHES, David Alan; b. 25 April 1960, Birkenhead, England. Composer; Musician (keyboards); Prod. m. 25 April 1984, 1 s., 1 d. *Career:* World-wide tours, OMD and Thomas Lang; Founder member, electronic duo, Dalek 1; Composer, film scores with composer John Murphy; Television appearances include: The Tube; Wired; Top of the Pops; Old Grey Whistle Test. *Compositions:* Film scores: Il Paladini; CHUD; Hearts and Armour; Film scores with John Murphy: Leon The Pig Farmer; Feast At Midnight; Solitaire For Two; Welcome To The Terrordrome; Beyond Bedlam; Body Memories; Dinner In Purgatory; Destroying Angels; Proteus; Giving Tongue; Clockwork Mice; For television: White Men Are Cracking Up; All The President's Women. *Recordings:* As composer, producer: 4 albums with Thomas Lang. *Membership:* Musicians' Union; PRS; BAC&S. *Current Management:* Soundtrack Music Management. *Address:* 22 Ives St, Chelsea, London SW3 2ND, England.

HUGHES, David James; b. 1 June 1950, Rotherham, Yorkshire, England. Musician (guitar, cello); Composer; Arranger. *Education:* Art School, Fine Art, Sir John Cass, Goldsmiths; Cello study with Alfia Bekova. *Career:* Channel 9 (band); Roy Hill Band; Television, radio, tours: EMI Outbar, TV Pebble Mill At One; 73 children's shows; Radio One Live. *Compositions:* Disco Eddy; Away From The Heat; When The Bad Men Come; The Lion Within; Radio One Chart Show (intro music and chart read-out underlay). *Honours:* Arts Council GLAA Award, Jazz Musician of the Year, 1980. *Address:* 7A Cleveland Rd, London N1 3ES, England.

HUGHES, Garry; Prod; Programmer. *Career:* Currently working with Trevor Horn; Recent production work includes: Tina Turner, Unfinished Sympathy (Wildest Dreams), album; Suggs: Cecilia; Camden Town; Selected programming and playing credits: Bjork, Debut Album; Gabrielle, Forget About the World; Charles and Eddie: Would I Lie To You; Duophonic (first album); Chocolate Milk (2nd album); D Mob: It's Time to Get Funky; Put Your Hands Together; The Way of the World; Come On and get My Love; Bayete and Jabu Khanyil: Africa Unite; Vitamin C: Vitamin C; Genesis: Turn It On Again; Pokemon: The First Movie. *Address:* SARM Productions, SP2 Holdings Ltd, The Blue Building, 42/46 St Luke's Mews, London W11 1DG, England.

HUGHES, James William; b. 18 May 1960, Liverpool, England. Musician (drums, percussion); Backing Vocalist. 1 d. *Education:* Studied with Red Carter, Liverpool. *Career:* Member, Black; Tours of Europe and Japan; Member, The Darling Buds; Tour of USA; Television appearances: Top of the Pops; Wogan; Jim'll Fix It; The Chart Show; The Roxy; The Tube; Various children's programmes; Played drums for Isaac Hayes' band in film, Soul Survivors; Numerous gigs and tours with Pete Wylie's Mighty WAH; Sessions with The Fourmost and Ian McNab. *Recordings:* Albums: Wonderful Life, Black; with The Darling Buds: Crawdaddy; Erotica. *Honours:* Gold disc, for Wonderful Life. *Membership:* Musicians' Union. *Address:* 247 Fernhill Rd, Bootle, Merseyside L20 0AQ, England. *Telephone:* (151) 476-2567.

HUGO, Chad (Chase); b. Virginia, USA. Prod; Remixer; Musician. *Career:* Formed The Neptunes production duo, with Pharrell Williams, 2000–; Formed recording act, N.E.R.D. (Nobody Ever Really Dies), 2001–; Co-founder, Star Trak Entertainment label; Worked with: Air, Mary J. Blige, Foxy Brown, Jay-Z, Kelis, Ludacris, Mystikal, Nelly, No Doubt, *NSYNC, Ol' Dirty Bastard, Britney Spears, Justin Timberlake, Usher. *Recordings:* with N.E.R.D.: Albums: In Search Of..., 2001. Singles: Lapdance, 2001. *Honours:* Source Award, Producer of the Year, The Neptunes, 2001; MOBO Award, Best Producer, The Neptunes, 2002. *Address:* c/o Virgin, 304 Park Ave S, Fifth Floor, New York, USA. *Website:* www.n-e-r-d.com.

HULAN, Miroslav; b. 23 April 1959, Brno, Czech Republic. Guitar, Mandolin Player. m. Drahomira Spidlikova, 4 July 1981, 2 s. *Career:* With Group Poutnici, 1980; Member, Group Poutnici, 1980–; Duo with Michal Hromcik, 1995–. *Compositions:* Pocta Davidovi. *Recordings:* Supraphon: Poutnici, 1987; Wayfaring Strangers, 1989; Chromi kone, 1990; The Days of Auld Lang Syne, 1991; Poutnici Live, 1991; GZ: Je to v nas, 1992; UMG: Pisne brnenskych kovboju, 1994; GZ: Co uz je pryc, 1997. *Publications:* Guitar School for Beginners, 1993; Guitar School for Advanced, 1997. *Honours:* Best Non-American Bluegrass Recordings, 1989, 1990. *Membership:* Czech Bluegrass Music Asscn. *Address:* Blatnicka 3, 628 00 Brno, Czech Republic.

HULJIC, Tonci; b. 29 Oct. 1961, Split, Croatia. Composer; Prod. m. Vjekosava Huljic, 5 Sept. 1987, 1 s., 1 d. *Education:* High School of Music, piano; Law. *Career:* Leader, composer, most popular group in Croatia: Magazin; 15 albums (9m. copies sold); 7 major tours; Many television shows; Tours: Russia: USA; Canada; 20 Gold, Platinum, Diamond records with Magazin and other popular Croatian singers; Eurovision Song Contest, sixth place with song Nostalgia, 1995; Many Grand prix in music festivals, Croatia, 1995–96; European promotion of trilogy; Songs published in Benelux countries, Scandinavia; USA; South Africa. *Honours:* Composer of the Year, 1988, 1989, 1994; Special Prize for Record Sales. *Membership:* Croatian Music Society; President, Croatian Music Union; Croatian Composers Asscn; Rotary Club. *Current Management:* Skalind Production, Croatia; Bim, Slavia Publishing, Asse, Belgium.

HUME, Alastair Martin Roderick; b. 1 Aug. 1958, London, England. Musician (flute, saxophone, keyboards); Arranger; Teacher. m. Vanessa V A Cowlard, 22 July 1989, 1 d. *Education:* Guildhall School of Music and Drama; Homerton College, Cambridge. *Career:* Cambridge Footlights, 1979; De Blahdeblah Jazz Orchestra, 1979; MD, Littlehampton Community School Big Band, 1982–86; Royal Oman Symphony Orchestra Instructor, 1986–88; Backed Penny Lane and Gordon Scott; Taverners Big Band, German tour, 1983, 1996; MD, Swing Bin and The Liners, 1990–; Tours: Canada, 1991; Lake Geneva, 1994; Lake Garda/Venice, 1996; Brass Roots; Choral conductor, Gli Amici Della Musica, 1977–83; Poole Arts Centre, 10th anniversary concert, 1979. *Honours:* GGSM Hons; Cert Ed Cantab. *Membership:* Musicians' Union. *Address:* 3 Donnelly Rd, Tuckton, Bournemouth, Dorset BH6 5NW, England.

HUMPERDINCK, Engelbert, (Arnold George Dorsey); b. 3 May 1936, Chennai, India. Vocalist. m. Patricia Healey, 1963, 2 s., 1 d. *Career:* Originally billed as Gerry Dorsey; Television includes: Oh Boy, 1950s; Changed name, late 1960s; Own series, The Engelbert Humperdinck Show, 1970; Regular concerts, USA and UK. *Recordings:* Hit singles: Release Me (No. 1, UK), 1967; There Goes My Everything (No. 2, UK), 1967; The Last Waltz, 1967; Other hits include: Am I That Easy To Forget; The Way It Used To Be; Les Bicyclettes De Belsize; A Man Without Love; Winter World of Love; Albums include: Release Me, 1967; The Last Waltz, 1967; A Man Without Love, 1968; Engelbert, 1969; Engelbert Humperdinck, 1969; We Made It Happen, 1970; Another Time Another Place, 1971; Live At The

Riviera, 1972; Greatest Hits, 1974; Getting Sentimental, 1975; Remember I Love You, 1987; The Engelbert Humperdinck Collection, 1987; Hello Out There, 1992; Golden Love; Ultimate; King of Hearts; Last of The Romantics; Back To Back (with Tom Jones), 1993; Love Unchained, 1995; Lovely Way to Spend an Evening, 1997; In the Still of the Night, 1999; The Ultimate Collection, 2000. *Honours:* Georgie Award, American Guild of Variety Artists, Best Singer, 1978; Over 50 Gold and 15 Platinum discs. *Current Management:* 3D Management, PO Box 16817, Beverly Hills, CA 90209–2817, USA.

HUNT, Bill; b. 23 May 1947, Birmingham, England. Music Educator; Musician. *Education:* Birmingham School of Music. *Career:* Original member, ELO; First ELO tour, Italy; Original member, Wizzard; Video and live performances with Raymond Froggatt. *Compositions:* Co-wrote songs for Slade (with Dave Hill). *Recordings:* First album and single, ELO; First album and hit singles, Wizzard; Various tracks, Slade and Slade II; Miles Hunt; Featured on ELO compilation, Flashback, 2000. *Honours:* Hon. Treasurer, Don Arden Veterans Appreciation Society. *Address:* Bromsgrove, Worcestershire, England.

HUNT, Brian George Edward; b. 7 June 1937. Vocalist; Musician. 1 s. *Education:* Clavissimo Music School, Antwerp, Belgium. *Career:* Guitarist, Group, The Blue Tones, 1960s'; International Country, Folk, Soft Rock, Ballad Music; Television and Radio in Belgium; Support Act to Steeleye Span and Frank Ifield. *Recordings:* Louisa From Louisiana; Sing This Song With Me Tonight. *Honours:* Award, Assistant in the Promotion of Country Music World-wide, 1981. *Membership:* Country Music Asscn. *Address:* Karel De Preterlei 212, 2140 Borgerhout, Belgium.

HUNT, Crispin; b. London, England. Musician (Guitar); Vocalist. *Career:* Member, Longpigs. *Recordings:* Singles: Happy Again; She Said; Jesus Christ; Far; On and On; Lost Myself; Blue Skies; The Frank Sonata; Albums: The Sun is Often Out; Mobile Home.

HUNT, Kevin Tony; b. 17 Dec. 1962, Great Yarmouth, Norfolk, England. Musician (drums). *Career:* Member, group Runestaff, 1981–86; Released self-titled album and 2 singles; Extensive radio, television and live appearances; Member, Thieving Gypsies, 1991–; Recently changed name to Sliver; Debut single/album, 1996; Extensive work with Prince's Trust charity, including work with Phil Collins. *Recordings:* with Runestaff: Album: Runestaff; Singles: Road To Ruin; Do-It!. *Membership:* PRS; MCPS. *Current Management:* John Giacobbi, Entertainment Law Associates, 9 Carnaby St, London W1V 1PG, England.

HUNTER, Ian; b. 3 June 1946, Shrewsbury, Shropshire, England. Vocalist. *Career:* Singer, Mott The Hoople, 1969–74; Solo artiste, 1975–; Performances include: Royal Albert Hall, London, 1971; Woodstock of The West Festival, Los Angeles, 1972. *Recordings:* Hit singles include: with Mott The Hoople: All The Young Dudes, 1972; All The Way From Memphis, 1973; Roll Away The Stone, 1973; Solo: Once Bitten Twice Shy, 1975; Albums: with Mott The Hoople: Mott The Hoople, 1969; Mad Shadows, 1970; Wild Life, 1971; Brain Capers, 1971; All The Young Dudes, 1972; Rock 'n' Roll Queen, 1972; The Hoople, 1974; Mott The Hoople – Live, 1974; Solo albums: Ian Hunter, 1975; All American Alien Boy, 1976; Overnight Angels, 1977; You're Never Alone With A Schizophrenic, 1979; Shades of Ian Hunter, 1979; Ian Hunter Live/Welcome To The Club, 1980; Short Back and Sides, 1981; All The Good Ones Are Taken, 1983; YUIOrta, 1990; Dirty Laundry, 1995; Artful Dodger, 1997; Welcome to the Club, 1998; Missing In Action, 2000; Rant, 2001. *Publications:* Diary of a Rock 'n' Roll Star, Ian Hunter.

HUNTER, James; b. 2 Oct. 1962, Colchester, Essex, England. Vocalist; Musician (guitar, harmonica); Actor. *Career:* Formerly performed as, Howlin' Wilf; Television appearances: The Tube, 01 For London, and Wide Angle; Radio guest on Andy Kershaw and Paul Jones shows; Theatre appearance in Buddy; Toured UK, Europe and USA as guest with Van Morrison R&B Revue. *Recordings:* Albums: Cry Wilf, Howlin' Wilf and The Vee-Jays; A Night In San Francisco, Van Morrison; Believe What I Say featuring Van Morrison and Doris Troy, 1996; Kick It Around, 2001; EPs and mini albums include: Blue Men Sing The Whites; Shake Your Hips; Six By Six; Days Like This; Duet with Van Morrison. *Membership:* Musicians' Union; PRS; Equity. *Current Management:* Frank Warren, Matters Musical. *Address:* The Loft, Rear of 8 West St, Dorking, Surrey RH4 1BL, England.

HUNTER, Mark; b. 5 Nov. 1968, England. Musician (keyboards). *Career:* Mem., James, 1990–2001; Numerous tours, festival dates and television appearances; Farewell 'Getting Away With It' concert, Manchester Evening News Arena, Dec. 2001. *Recordings:* Albums: Gold Mother, 1990; Seven, 1992; Laid, 1993; Wah Wah, 1994; Whiplash, 1997; The Best Of James, 1998; Millionaires, 1999; B-Sides Ultra, 2001; Pleased To Meet You, 2001; Getting Away With It, 2002. Singles incl.: How Was It For You, 1990; Come Home, 1990; Lose Control, 1990; Sit Down, 1991; Sound, 1991; Born Of Frustration, 1992; Ring The Bells, 1992; Seven, 1992; Sometimes, 1993; Laid, 1993; Say Something/Jam J, 1994; She's A Star, 1997; Tomorrow, 1997; Waltzing Along, 1997; Destiny Calling, 1998; Runaground, 1998; Sit Down (remix), 1998; I Know What I'm Here For, 1999; Fred Astaire, 1999; We're Gonna Miss You,

1999; Getting Away With It (All Messed Up), 2001. *Current Management:* Rudge Management, 1 Star St, London W2 1QD, England.

HUNTER, Robert (Bob); b. 30 Oct. 1936, Corbridge, Northumberland, England. Vocalist; Musician (violin). m. Margaret, 13 Aug. 1960, 1 s., 1 d. *Education:* Violin from early age; Studied voice in Royal Engineers Band. *Career:* Appeared every televised show, The Black and White Minstrels, 1959–; Also radio series with George Mitchell Singers; Now freelance, worked with many groups, radio and television including: The Two Ronnies, various Command Performances; Summer seasons in major resorts with The Black and White Minstrel Show; More recently with The Minstrel Stars; Concerts, cabaret with Original Blend and The Square Pegs, including radio programmes: Friday Night Is Music Night; Round Midnight; Among Your Souvenirs, BBC Radio 2. *Recordings:* Albums: The Black and White Minstrel Show; Around The World In Song; The Minstrel Stars; Original Blend Entertains. *Membership:* Equity; Musicians' Union. *Address:* 15 Lynwood Rd, Ealing, London W5 1JQ, England.

HUNT-TAYLOR, Amanda; Songwriter. *Career:* Songwriter with Warner Chappell Music, 1991; Songwriter with Bluewater Music, Nashville, 1996; Co-writer credits with: Rick Giles; Steve Bogard; John Scott Sherrill; Gene Nelson; Kent Robbins; Janis Ian; Rory Bourke; Director, AmandaRick Records, 1999–. *Compositions:* Your Love Amazes Me, recorded by John Berry; Tanya Tucker; Andy Childs; Joel Nova; All She Wants, recorded by Rena Gaile; No One Else Like You, recorded by Janis Ian; Able, recorded by Happy Goodmans; Wish I Could Wish On A Star, recorded by Mandy Barnett; A Fire In The Rain, recorded by Doug Supernaw; I Really Do Love You Lovin' Me, recorded by Lori Morgan; Wishing It All Away, recorded by Tania Tucker. *Recordings:* Backup vocalist on Janis Ian's Revenge album; vocals on Jay Turner, Celebration Day, 2001; Debut CD: Only When I Breathe, 1999. *Honours:* For Your Love Amazes Me: SESAC Songwriter of the Year, 1994, SESAC Song of the Year, 1994; NSAI Achievement Award, 1995; Music City News Country Songwriters Award, Song of the Year, 1995; Song of the Year, 2nd Annual Country Radio Music Award Show, 1995; 2 NSAI Awards. *Address:* PO Box 140494, Nashville, TN 37214, USA.

HURLEY, Luke; b. 31 Aug. 1957, Nyeri, Kenya. Songwriter; Musician (guitar); Performer. m. Jann, 16 May 1992, 1 s., 2 d. *Education:* 1 year university. *Career:* Major shows since early 1982 specialising in Houseconcerts; Support act for Michelle Shocked, Marianne Faithfull, New Zealand; Only performer to play live, Radio With Pictures television show; Touring Europe, 1998–99; Invented product for the CD industry. *Compositions:* Mona Lisa; Fait Accompli; Japanese Overdrive; Greenfields; Precious Time; Missing You; Hungry Gun Song; Information Station. *Recordings:* Albums: Policestate; Japanese Overdrive; Make Room; First Civilian; Alone in Her Field; Reha; Videos: Japanese Overdrive; Make Room; Mona Lisa.

HURLEY, Steve 'Silk', (J. M. Silk, Jack Master Silk); b. 9 Nov. 1962, Chicago, Illinois, USA. Prod; Remixer; DJ. *Career:* Started as a DJ in Chicago, c. 1979; Own show on local radio station WBMX; First release Music Is The Key (as JM Silk), 1985; Set up Silk Entertainment, 1997; Remixer and songwriter; Collaborations: Chantay Savage; Jamie Principle; Maurice Joshua; Keith Nunnally; Remixed: Michael Jackson; Kym Sims; Ce Ce Peniston; Melanie B; Rahsaan Patterson; Madonna. *Recordings:* Albums: Hold Onto Your Dreams, 1987; Singles: Music Is The Key, Jack Your Body, 1985; Let The Music Take Control, 1987. *Address:* c/o Silk Entertainment Inc, 3011 W 183rd St #302, Homewood, Illinois, USA. *E-mail:* silkentertainment@msn.com.

HUSBAND, Gary; b. 14 June 1960, Leeds, Yorkshire, England. Musician (drums, piano, keyboards). *Education:* Classical piano. *Career:* Mem., Allan Holdsworth; Jack Bruce Trio; Billy Cobham Band; Gary Moore; Level 42, –1994; Gary Husband Group; Solo artiste. *Compositions:* Written for albums by Allan Holdsworth and Level 42; Diary of a Plastic Box; From The Heart, The New Gary Husband Trio; Skin Fever, album, 1998. *Recordings:* Albums: with Allan Holdsworth: Metal Fatigue, 1985; with Level 42: Staring At The Sun, Steve Topping: Time and Distance, 1988; Focused, 1988; Solo: The Things I See, 2001; also with Lemon D, Dick Heckstall-Smith, Jimmy Nail, Dillinger, Geoff Keezer, Billy Cobham, Randy Brecker Group; Video: Interplay and Improvisation, 1998. *Membership:* Musicians' Union; PRS.

HUSBANDS, Simon Patrick; b. 2 Feb. 1957, Nottingham, England. Musician (keyboards, guitar, bass guitar); Songwriter; Programmer; Vocalist. m. Janet Johnson, 9 July 1994. *Education:* Newark-Sherwood College. *Career:* Keyboard player, bass player, singer with band Blue Train; Single All I Need Is You, used in Baywatch television show, 1991; Current solo projects include DIN and UXB. *Recordings:* Co-producer, album The Business of Dreams; Singles: All I Need Is You (13 weeks, US charts); The Hardest Thing; The Business of Dreams. *Membership:* PRS; Musicians' Union; BMI, USA. *Current Management:* GOSH! Productions, UK; Gary Heller Management, 11692 Chenault St #202, Los Angeles, CA 91411, USA. *Address:* 40 Millicent Rd, West Bridgford, Nottingham NG2 7PZ, England.

HUSEIN, Hasanefesic; b. 30 Jan. 1954, Banja Luka, Croatia. Musician (guitar); Songwriter. m. Viki Peric, 22 March 1980, 1 s., 1 d. *Education:* 8 years music school, Zagreb. *Career:* 20 years on top with own band, Parni Valjek (Steam Roller). *Recordings:* 15 albums (most of them Platinum). *Honours:* 7 Porins (Croatian equivalent of Grammy), 1995. *Membership:* HGU; HDS. *Current Management:* HGU, HDS, Nenas Drobnjak. *Address:* Zelengaj 67, 10000 Zagreb, Croatia.

HUSKY, Ferlin, (Simon Crum, Terry Preston); b. 3 Dec. 1927, Cantwell, Missouri, USA. Country vocalist; Songwriter; Musician (guitar, bass); Actor; Comedian. *Career:* DJ in Bakersfield, California, 1940s; Played bass with Big Jim DeNoone and fiddler Fred McMurray; Later with Smiley Burnette and Gene Autry in Salinas, California; Recorded guitar instrumentals as Tex Terry; Later as Terry Preston on 4 Star Records, 1949; Worked with Tennessee Ernie Ford; Signed to Capitol Records, 1951; Over 50 Billboard country chart entries, 1953–75; Early records miscredited to Ferlin Huskey; Recorded as Ferlin Husky, 1957–; Occasional releases as comedy alter ego Simon Crum; Hosted Arthur Godfrey TV and radio show, 1950s; Appearances in Kraft Television Theatre show, 1957; Toured with group The Hushpuppies, 1960s to mid-1970s; Appearances in films include: Mister Rock and Roll, 1957; Country Music Holiday, 1958; Las Vegas Hillbillys (aka Country Music USA), 1966; Hillbillys In A Haunted House, 1967; Forty Acre Feud, 1968; Swamp Girl, 1971; That's Country, 1977; Appeared at Christy Lane's Theater, Branson, Missouri. *Compositions include:* Country Music Is Here To Stay; Timber I'm Fallin'. *Recordings include:* Dear John Letter (with Jean Shepard), 1953; Gone, Just For You, 1957; Country Music Is Here To Stay, 1958; Wings of a Dove, 1960; Albums: By Request, 1964; I Could Sing All Night, 1966; Just For You, 1968. *Honours:* Volunteer Gunner Citation, WWII. *Membership:* Grand Ole Opry; The Order of Police; National Sherrifs Asscn. *Current Management:* Richard Davis Management, 1030 North Woodland, Kansas City, MO 64118, USA.

HUSSAIN, Zakir, (Zakir Hussain Allarakha Qureshi); b. 9 March 1951, Mumbai, India. Musician (tabla); Prod; Actor; Composer. *Career:* Tabla player, son of Ustad Alla Rakha; Plays with: Ali Akbar Khan, Birju Maharaj, Ravi Shankar, Shivkumar Sharma; Formed Shakti, Remember Shakti with John McLaughlin; Formed percussion group, Rhythm Experience; Founder, Moment! Records, 1992–; Composed music for opening ceremony, Olympic Games, Atlanta, USA, 1996; Contributed to film soundtracks: In Custody, The Mystic Masseur, Little Buddha; Film appearance: Heat and Dust, 1982; Tours and appearances world-wide. *Recordings:* Albums: Making Music, 1987; Tabla Duet (with Ustad Alla Rakha), 1988; Zakir Hussain And The Rhythm Experience, 1991; Venu 1972, 1991; Essence Of Rhythm, 1998. *Honours:* Grammy Award, for Planet Drum. *Address:* c/o Polygram, Universal Music Group, Universal Studios, 100 Universal City Plaza, Universal City, CA 91608, USA.

HUSSENOT, Emmanuel; b. 29 Sept. 1951, Saint Cloud, France. Variety Artiste; Jazz Musician (cornet, trumpet, saxophone, recorder). 1 d. *Career:* Cornet player, French traditional band, Sharkey and Co; Composer, singer, trumpet, saxophone and recorder player, Orpheon Celesta, 1980–. *Recordings:* with Sharkey and Co, 1972–78; with Orpheon Celesta: Siphonnée Symphonie; La Prehistoire du Jazz; Best Of; La vocalise en carton. *Honours:* Prix Sydney Bechet de l'Academie du Jazz, 1990; Grand Prix du Festival d'Humour de Saint Gervais, 1994; La Vocalise en carton, 1998. *Current Management:* Blue Line, Paris. *Address:* 74 rue Alexandre Guilmant, 92190 Meudon, France. *E-mail:* ehussenot@gree.fr.

HUSSEY, Wayne; b. 26 May 1959. Musician (guitar); Vocalist. *Career:* Member, groups Dead Or Alive; The Walkie Talkies; Member, Sisters of Mercy, 1983–85; Concerts include York Festival, 1984; The Mission, 1986–; Regular UK, European and world-wide tours, including concerts with The Cult and U2; Appearances include: Reading Festival, 1986, 1987, 1989; Lockerbie Air Disaster Fund benefit concert, 1989; Hillsborough football disaster benefit concert, 1989; Finsbury Park, London, 1991; Off The Street benefit concert, London, 1993. *Recordings:* Albums: with Sisters of Mercy: First and Last and Always, 1985; Possession, 1991; Slight Case of Overbombing, 1993; with The Mission: God's Own Medicine, 1986; The First Chapter, 1987; Children (No. 2, UK), 1988; Carved In Sand, 1990; Masque, 1992; Neverland, 1995; Resurrection, 1999; Singles: with Sisters of Mercy: Temple of Love, 1983; Body and Soul, 1984; Walk Away, 1984; with The Mission: Stay With Me, 1986; Wasteland, 1987; Severina, 1987; Tower of Strength, 1988; Beyond The Pale, 1988; Butterfly On A Wheel, 1989; Deliverance, 1990; Hands Across The Ocean, 1990; Like A Child Again, 1992.

HUTCHINGS, Ashley Stephen; b. 26 Jan. 1945, Southgate, Middlesex, England. Musician (bass guitar); Songwriter; Prod; Dancer; Scriptwriter. m. 6 Aug. 1971, to 1978, 1 s. *Career:* Founding mem., folk-rock groups, Fairport Convention, 1967; Steeleye Span, 1970–; Albion Band, 1972–; Music Dir, National Theatre, London, 1977–81. *Recordings include:* Albums: with Fairport Convention: Fairport Convention, 1968; What We Did In Our Holidays, 1969; Unhalfbricking, 1969; Liege And Leaf, 1970; with Steeleye Span: Hark The Village Wait, 1970; Please To See The King, 1971; Ten Man Mop, 1971; with The Albion Band: Battle of The Field, 1976; Prospect Before

Us, 1977; Rise Up Like The Sun, 1978; Albion River Hymns March, 1979; Light Shining Albino, 1984; The Wild Side of Town, 1987; I Got New Shoes, 1987; Give Me A Saddle I'll Trade You A Car, 1989; 1990, 1990; Acousticity, 1993; Albion Heart, 1995; Solo: By Gloucester Docks I Sat Down and Wept, 1987; Twangin' N' A-Traddin', 1993; Crab Wars Remembered, 1994; Sway With Me, 1996; The Guv'nor, 1999; Along The Downs, 2000; Street Cries, 2001. *Publications:* A Little Music (collection of folk songs, tunes and dances). *Membership:* PRS; MCPS. *Current Management:* c/o 994 Burnage Lane, Manchester M19 1TD, England.

HUTCHINSON, Steff; b. 11 May 1964, Halton, England. Vocalist, Musician (guitar). *Education:* BA, Portsmouth Polytechnic; PGCE, City of Birmingham Polytechnic. *Career:* Solo Singer, Guitarist, 1978; Various bands, 1981–90; Member of Dead After Dark, 1991–99; Current member of Firedaze; Appeared on BBC in the Midlands Radio; Live At The Y, Leicester Cable Television; Soundwaves, Colt Television. *Compositions:* Co Writer, of all Dead After Dark and Firedaze songs. *Recordings:* Album, No Time To Waste, 1996; EP, See, 1998; EP, Firedaze, 1999. *Honours:* Finalist, Radio One Battle of The Bands, 1989; Finalist, Live Television Battle of The Bands, 1996. *Membership:* Musicians' Union. *Address:* DeAD Music, PO Box 213, Leamington Spa, Warwickshire, CV31 1ZP, England.

HUTCHISON, Hamish; b. 22 July 1968, Beckenham, Kent. Record Prod; Remixer; Mixing Engineer; *Recordings:* Producer, numerous acts including: Chesney Hawkes; Big Fun; Glen Goldsmith; Booker Newbury III; Remixer for: PJ and Duncan; China Crisis; Lucianna; Jack 'N' Chill; Chesney Hawkes. *Membership:* Musicians' Union. *Address:* c/o Time and Space, PO Box 306, Berkhamsted, Herts HP4 3EP, England.

HUTMAN, Olivier; b. 12 Nov. 1954, Boulogne, France. Musician (piano); Arranger; Composer. *Education:* PhD, Ethnology on Urban Music in Ghana; 10 years study, piano, National Conservatory of Music, St Maur. *Career:* Jazz performer, accompanist for pop singers; Founder, Moravigne, 1975; Member, Chute Libre, 1975–77; Founds own trio, 1983–84; Member Eric Lelann Quartet, 1984–88; Tours, festivals include: Singapore; Mumbai; Montréal; Prague; Tokyo, 1991, 1993; Newport, USA, 1993; Tahiti, 1995; Martinique, 1994, USA (Boston, San Fransisco, Los Angeles), 1995; Antibes; Nimes; La Reunion; Montreux. *Compositions:* Composer, arranger in jazz, theatre, films: jingles, music for industrial films, TV documentaries, Long Range Films include: Mon Oncle, 1985; High Speed, 1987; Printemps Perdu, 1990; Ma Soeur Chinoise, 1994; Commissioned by International Musik Fetsival, Davos, to write suite performed by members of New York Philharmonia, 1993. *Recordings:* with: Moravagine; Chute Libre; J P Debarbat; G Ferris; Eric Lelann; Christian Escoude; Toots Thielemans; C Bellonzi; C Barthelemy; P Delletrz; J P L Labador; S Marc; G Acogny; Abus; Barney Wilen, 1992; A Brunet; M Barrot Quartet; R Galliano; Stephane Grappelli; Luigi Trussardi; Solo: Six Songs, 1984; The Man With The Broken Tooth, trio with Marc Bertaux, Tony Rabeson, 1987; Creole and African music recordings. *Honours:* Prix Boris Vian, French Academy of Jazz, for Best Record of the Year, 1983; 2nd European Keyboardist in Jazz, Hot Magazine, 1987; Awards for music for films: Mon Oncle, 1986; Printemps Perdu, 1990. *Current Management:* A21 Muth Productions, 14 rue Bleue, 75009 Paris. *Address:* 36 rue de Fontanay, 94300 Vincennes, France.

HUTTON, Mick; b. 5 June 1956, Chester, England. Jazz Musician (double bass, piano, cuatro, steel drums, bass guitar, guitar, tuba drums, synthesizer, trumpet); Teacher. Separated, 1 s. *Education:* Studied piano, organ and cello at school. *Career:* Professional musician, 1981–; Toured and recorded extensively with numerous artistes; Fmr mem., Gordon Beck's Band, Bill Bruford's Earthworks, Jim Mullen's Quartet; Mem., Humphrey Lyttelton Band; Formed the Boat Rockers; Appeared on over 40 jazz albums and over 200 radio broadcasts; Work in film, TV and with West End, London, shows; Played on the soundtrack of films, Absolute Beginners, Whore; Taught jazz double-bass, Guildhall School of Music and Drama, Glamorgan Jazz Summer School; Visiting examiner, Royal Northern College, Royal College of Music, Trinity College; Prof., Trinity College; Teaches in schools and runs numerous workshops in steel drums, trumpet. *Compositions include:* See You PB; Souvenir; Arcadia; Ken Blake; Lister; Turing; HPT; Looga Barooga; Nowhere. *Recordings include:* Blue Glass, with John Taylor Trio; Busy Listening, with Steve Arguelles Band; Time Will Tell, with Tina May; Cantelina, with First House; Earthworks and Heavenly Bodies, with Bill Bruford's Earthworks; This Old Gang of Ours, with Humphrey Lyttelton; Morning Sunrise, with Barry Nathan Trio; 1 2 3, with Nick Purnell Group; Blues in the Night, with The Cast; Amazing Grace, with Martin Speake; Chris Biscoe Sextet; PyroTechnics, various artistes; Triple Exposure, with Mark Edwards; From the Heart, with Gary Husband Trio; Alternative Therapy, with Estelle Kokot; Trouble in Mind, with Humphrey Lyttelton and Elkie Brooks; Somewhere in the Hills, with Jim Mullen Quartet. *Membership:* Musicians' Union; PRS. *Address:* 16 Birch St, Birch, Essex CO2 0NF, England.

HVASS, Claus; b. 4 Feb. 1959. Composer; Prod; Musician (guitar). m. Birgitte Rode, 14 June 1992, 1 s. *Career:* Roskilde Festival; Toured England; Concerts: California; France; Norway; Germany; Sweden; Denmark; Grand Prix, Slovenia; National and international television and radio. *Compositions:*

Medea. *Recordings:* with Johnny and The Cold Demons: Paraneuropa; with Walk The Walk: Walk The Walk; Feet On the Ground; Frog Dance. *Publications:* The International Discography of New Wave, Dansk Rock. *Honours:* 5 National Music Awards, 1991–95. *Membership:* DJBFA. *Current Management:* Zing Zing Musicproduction and Management. *Address:* Kirkegaardsgade 3, 9000 Alborg, Denmark.

HYDE, Maria Jane; b. 23 Jan. 1969, London, England. Vocalist; Actress. m. Dr Uwe Bodzian, 21 July 1995. *Career:* Acted: Peppee, in Annie, Victoria Palace, 1980; Ovaltines singing group, 1982; Various TV shows, Children's Royal Variety Performance, London Palladium; Acted: Pearl, Starlight Express, London, 1985–88; Pearl, Starlight Express, Bochum, West Germany, 1989–91, 1994–95; Assistant Dance and Skate Coach, 1995. *Recordings:* Albums: Ovaltine Group Album, 1982; Heaven Sent (No. 5, German charts), 1995; Single: Heaven Sent, UK, 1994. *Membership:* Equity. *Current Management:* Edward Hyde. *Address:* Morland House, 11 Woodside Green, London SE25 5EY, England.

HYDE, Roger Erik; b. 3 June 1951, Hollywood, USA. Composer; Record Prod; Theorist. *Education:* AB in Music Theory and Composition, UCLA, 1975, with special endorsements in electronic music and composition for film; Studied history of jazz with Paul Tanner (Glen Miller Band), Composition with Gerald Strang, Film scoring with David Raksin, Production with Nik Venet. *Career:* Folk Scene radio concert, 1970; Series of Los Angeles salon concerts and readings, 1975–76; Director of Washoe Records, producer for Scatman Crothers, 1980–81; Director and Producer, Blue Planet Records, 1985–. *Compositions:* Our Hearts and Our Hands, song cycle, 1979; Pittsburg; 2811; Symphony à Trois. *Recordings:* As producer, Scatman Crothers and the Hollywood Radio Hooligans. *Publications:* Novels: Famous Death, and Weighing of Secret Burdens. *Contributions to:* The Whole Earth Catalogues. *Membership:* AES. *Address:* PO Box 91922, Los Angeles, CA 90009, USA.

HYDER, Ken; b. 29 June 1946, Dundee, Scotland. Musician (drums); Vocalist. *Education:* Harris Academy, Dundee; Studied with John Stevens. *Career:* Moved to London 1970; Formed Celtic-Jazz band, Talisker; Played and recorded with Celtic musicians including Dick Gaughan, then with Tibetan monks, Russian musicians, duo with Tim Hodgkinson, South African musicians, Siberian shamans. *Recordings:* with Talisker: Dreaming of Glenisla; Land of Stone; The Last Battle; The White Light; Humanity; Under The Influence; The Big Team; Fanfare For Tomorrow, with Dick Gaughan; Shams, with Tim Hodgkinson; The Goose, with Hodgkinson, Ponomareva; Piping Hot, with Dave Brooks; The Crux of The Catalogue, with Tomas Lynch; Hot Sounds From The Arctic, with Vladimir Rezitsky; The Ultimate Gift, Bardo State Orchestra; Urban Ritual, Ntshuks Bonga's Tshisa; Stillness in the Solouki, Northern Lights; In the Stone, Ken Hyder with Maggie Nichols and Dave Brooks. *Honours:* Order of The Red Banner, Angarsk. *Membership:* London Musician Collective. *Current Management:* Oor Wullie Presentations. *Address:* 69 Ravenslea Rd, Balham, London SW12 8SL, England.

HYLAND, Brian; b. 12 Nov. 1943, New York, NY, USA. Vocalist; Musician (guitar, keyboards, bass, harmonica). m. Rosmari Dickey, July 1970, 1 s. *Education:* Church Choir. *Career:* Television and radio appearances: Host, American Bandstand, 1960–70; Murray The K Show, with Jackie Wilson, 1961; Television special, Japan, 1961; Thank Your Lucky Stars; Jukebox Jury; Saturday Club, UK Radio, 1963; Top of the Pops, 1975; RandR Palace, Nashville Now, 1988; Numerous tours include: Japan, South America, USA, UK, South East Asia. *Recordings:* Itsy Bitsy. . . Polka Dot Bikini, 1960; Let Me Belong To You, 1961; Ginny Come Lately, 1962; Sealed With a Kiss, 1962; Warmed Over Kisses, 1962; The Joker Went Wild, Run Run Look and See, 1966; Tragedy, 1968; Gypsy Woman, 1970; Greatest Hits, 1994; Very Best of Brian Hyland, 1998. *Honours:* 3 Gold records; Gee Gee Award, Star of Tomorrow, 16 Magazine, 1961–62. *Membership:* AFofM; AGVA; AFTRA; ASCAP. *Current Management:* Stone Buffalo. *Address:* PO Box 101, Silver Lakes, CA 92342–0101, USA.

HYLAND, Vic; b. 7 June 1959, Wilmington, Kent, England. Musician (guitar); Vocalist; Educator. m. Jane Parker, 28 May 1993, 4 d. *Education:* Studies in classical guitar, Indian music under Helen Lohmueller, Kessel and Lobb. *Career:* Guitarist, various musical styles from rock and jazz to Indian music; Brief spell playing classical concerts; Worked with Geoff Moore Project, mid-1980s; Established as leading guitar educator in Kent area; Formed Red Touch, late 1980s; Currently with record deal, sponsorship, radio support.

Recordings: Grahams Garden; I Don't Care; Before I Made You Cry; Album: Walk On, forthcoming. *Publications:* Advanced Techniques and Creative Guitar; Self Improvement For Musicians. *Membership:* Musicians' Union; Registry of Electric Guitar Tutors. *Current Management:* RTI. *Address:* 5 Pleasant Villas, Kent St, Mereworth, Kent ME18 5QN, England.

HYND, Richard; b. 17 June 1965, Aberdeen, Scotland. Musician (Drums). *Career:* Member, Texas; Numerous tours and festivals; TV appearances. *Recordings:* Singles include: I Don't Want a Lover, 1989; Tired of Being Alone, 1993; Say What You Want, 1997; Halo, 1997; Put Your Arms Around Me, 1997; Black Eyed Boy, 1997; In Our Lifetime, 1999; Summer Son, 1999; When We Are Together, 1999; In Demand, 2000; Inner Smile, 2001; Albums: Southside, 1989; Mother's Heaven, 1991; Rick's Road, 1993; White on Blonde, 1997; The Hush, 1999; Greatest Hits, 2000.

HYNDE, Chrissie; b. 7 Sept. 1951, Akron, Ohio, USA. Vocalist; Musician (guitar); Songwriter. *Education:* Kent State University. *Career:* Model, St Martin's School of Art; Writer, New Musical Express, 1973; Member of groups The Frenchies; Jack Rabbit; Berk Brothers; Founder member, singer, guitarist, The Pretenders, 1978–; World tours made include UK, USA, Far East, Australia; Concerts include: Concert For Kampuchea, London, 1979; Heatwave Festival, Toronto, Canada, 1980; Concerts in Japan, Hong Kong, Australia, 1982; US Festival, San Bernardino, California, 1983; Radio City Music Hall, 1984; Live Aid, Philadelphia, 1985; Nelson Mandela Tribute, Wembley Stadium, 1990; Bob Dylan 30th Anniversary Tribute, Madison Square Garden (USA), 1992; Rock and Roll Hall of Fame; Cleveland Municipal Stadium, 1995; Burt Bacharach Tribute, Hammerstein Ballroom, New York, 1998; Here, There and Everywhere – Tribute to Linda McCartney, London, 1999. *Recordings:* Albums: Pretenders, 1980; Extended Play, 1981; Pretenders II, 1981; Learning to Crawl, 1984; Get Close, 1986; The Singles, 1987; Packed!, 1990; Last of the Independents, 1994; The Isle of View, 1995; Viva El Amor, 1999; Singles include: Stop Your Sobbing, 1979; Kid, 1979; Brass In Pocket (No. 1, UK), 1979; Talk of The Town, 1980; Message of Love, 1981; I Go To Sleep, 1981; Back On the Chain Gang, 1983; 2000 Miles, 1983; Middle of the Road, 1984; Thin Line Between Love and Hate, 1984; Don't Get Me Wrong, 1986; Hymn to Her, 1987; Night in My Veins, 1994; I'll Stand by You, 1994; Human, 1999. *Contributions to:* Tame Yourself, animal rights album, 1991; Stone Free – A Tribute To Jimi Hendrix, 1993; The Concert for the Rock and Roll Hall of Fame, 1996; The Bridge School Concerts Vol. I, 1997; Film Soundtracks: King of Comedy (Back on the Chaingang, 1983); The Living Daylights (Where Has Everybody Gone and If there was a Man, 1987); Indecent Proposal (I'm Not in Love, 1993); With Honours (Forever Young, 1994); 1969 (Windows of the World, 1988); Boys on the Side (Everyday is Like Sunday, 1995); G I Jane (Goodbye and The Homecoming, 1997); The Other Sister (Loving You is All I Know, 1999); Musical collaborations: UB40 (I Got You Babe No 1 UK, 1985 and Breakfast in Bed, 1988); Moodswings (Spiritual High, 1992); Frank Sinatra (Luck be a Lady, 1994); Emmylou Harris (She – Tribute to Gram Parsons, 1999). *Honours:* Honoured at the People For The Ethical Treatment of Animals (PETA) 10th Anniversary Humanitarian Awards Gala, 1988; International Rock Awards MUP Lead Female Singer, ASCAP pop Award, 1995, 1996; Gibson Guitar award for Best Female Rock Guitarist, 1996; Ivor Novello Award for Outstanding Contribution to British Music, 1999. *Address:* 24 Ives St, London SW3 2ND, England.

HYNDMAN, Clint; Musician (drums). *Career:* Resides in Australia; Joined Fish of The Day group, 1994; Developed local following through pub/club gigs; Group became Something For Kate; Signed to Australian label Murmur; Temporary hiatus to recruit new bassist, 1997–8; Band re-formed and gradually broke nationally, then internationally with first USA/Japan tour, 2000; Big sell-out Australian shows including Mythology and Echo-la-la-lalia tours plus Powderfinger support slots, 2001; Group subject of JJJ radio station special, 2001. *Recordings:* Albums: Elsewhere For Eight Minutes, 1997; Beautiful Sharks, 1999; QandA With Dean Martin (compilation), 2000; Echolalia, 2001; Singles: The Answer To Both Your Questions (EP), Dean Martin, 1996; Intermission (EP), Captain (Million Miles An Hour), Prick, 1997; Working Against Me, Roll Credit, Harpoon/Clint, 1998; Electricity, Hallways, Whatever You Want, 1999; The Astronaut, 2000; Monsters, Three Dimensions, Twenty Years, 2001. *Honours:* Australian Music Industry Critics Awards, Album of the Year, 2000; Australian Live Music Awards, Best Live Act, 2000; JJJ Listeners' Poll, Best Album, 2001. *Current Management:* Carlene Albronda, Catapult Management, Sydney, Australia. *E-mail:* carlene@presto.net.au. *Website:* www.somethingforkate.com.

I

IAN, Janis, (Janis Fink); b. 7 April 1951, New Jersey, USA. Vocalist; Songwriter; Musician (guitar, piano, French horn); Columnist; Lecturer. Partner: Patricia Snyder. *Career:* Solo artiste, 1965–; Debut hit single, Society's Child, featured in Leonard Bernstein's television special, Inside Pop – The Rock Revolution, 1966; Performances include: Royal Festival Hall and Royal Albert Hall, London; Carnegie Hall and Philharmonic Hall, New York; Sydney Opera House; Carre, Amsterdam; Appearances on most major television shows, including 8 times on Tonight Show. *Compositions include:* Society's Child, 1966; Jesse, recorded by Roberta Flack; At Seventeen, 1976; Fly Too High (co-writer with Giorgio Moroder) for film soundtrack Foxes, 1979; Tattoo; When Angels Cry; Some People's Lives, recorded by Bette Midler; Other compositions recorded by artistes including: Mel Tormé; Dianne Schuur; Chet Atkins; Stan Getz; John Mellencamp; Hugh Masekela. *Recordings:* Albums: Janis Ian, 1967; A Song for All the Seasons of Your Mind, 1968; The Secret Life of J Eddy Fink, 1969; Who Really Cares, 1969; Present Company, 1971; Stars, 1974; Between The Lines, (No. 1, USA), 1975; Aftertones, 1976; Miracle Row, 1997; Janis Ian, 1978; Night Rains, 1979; Restless Eyes, 1981; Breaking Silence, 1993; Revenge, 1995; Hunger, 1997; The Bottom Line Encore, 1999; God and The FBI, 2000. *Publications:* Monthly columnist, The Advocate; Regular columnist, Performing Songwriter Magazine; Book of poetry, 1968, 2002. *Honours:* 2 Grammy Awards; GLCCLA Award for Creative Integrity, 1993; Fisk University Award for Creative Excellence, 1994; Multiple Platinum records world-wide, including Japan, Australia and USA. *Address:* PO Box 121797, Nashville, TN 37212, USA. *Website:* www.janisian.com.

IANORA, Stéphane; b. 16 Jan. 1960, Paris, France. Musician (drums). m. Motomi Ryu, 17 March 1989, 2 d. *Education:* University (Japanese Ursus); Graduated (Dev6). *Career:* Drummer, Bird X funk band, featuring Wally Badatov, 1979; Concerts with William Sheller, 1981–84; Concerts, tours, with: David Koven; Kurim Kalel; Rachid Bahri; Elli Medeiros; Jeanne Mas; World tours with Richard Clayderman, 1989–; Television shows with Vanessa Paradis. *Recordings:* with William Sheller: J'suis Pas Bien; Live Olympia, 89; Karim Kalel: P'tite Soeur; David Koven: David Koven; Etè Torride; Marvin; Elli Medeiros: Elli; Jeanne Mas: En Concert; Sheila: Live Olympia 89; Richard Clayderman: English Pop Songs. *Address:* 4 Allée des Tilleuls, 94220 Charenton, France.

IBOLD, Mark; b. 1967, Cincinnati, Ohio, USA. Musician (Bass). *Career:* Member, Pavement; Joined band, 1992; Numerous headlining tours; Appearance on cartoon Space Ghost Coast to Coast, 1997. *Recordings:* Singles: Trigger Cut, 1992; Cut Your Hair, 1994; Gold Soundz, 1994; Range Life, 1995; Rattled by La Rush, 1995; Father to a Sister of Thought, 1995; Pacific Trim EP, 1996; Stereo, 1997; Shady Lane EP, 1997; Spit on a Stranger, 1999; Carrot Rope, 1999; Albums: Slanted and Enchanted, 1992; Crooked Rain, Crooked Rain, 1994; Wowee Zowee, 1995; Brighten the Corners, 1997; Terror Twilight, 1999.

IBRAHIM, Abdullah, (Adolphe 'Dollar' Brand); b. 9 Oct. 1934, Capetown, South Africa. Jazz Musician (piano); Composer. m. Sathima Bea Benjamin, 1965. *Education:* Studied piano from age 7. *Career:* Became professional musician, 1949; Member: The Jazz Epistles (with Hugh Masekela and Kippi Moeketsi); Met Duke Ellington in the Africana Club, Zurich and recorded album together, 1963; Appeared at the Newport Jazz Festival, 1965; Several appearances as Ellington's substitute with the Ellington Orchestra; Collaborations: Elvin Jones; Don Cherry; Gato Barbieri; Max Roach; Munich Radio Philharmonic Orchestra toured with arrangements of his work, 1998; 1988 album Mindif used as soundtrack for film Chocolat. *Recordings:* Albums include: Duke Ellington Presents The Dollar Brand Trio, 1963; Mindif, African Sun, Tintinyana, Blues for a Hip King, African Horns, Voice of Africa, 1988; African River, 1989; Mantra Mode, 1991; Yarona, 1995.

ICE CUBE, (O'Shea Jackson); b. 15 June 1969, Los Angeles, California, USA. Rap Artiste. *Education:* Architectural Degree, University of Phoenix, 1988. *Career:* Worked with Public Enemy; Began rapping with CIA with partner Sir Jinx; Formed N.W.A. with Dr Dre; Formed new rap posse Da Lench Mob; Began own corporation, including work by protegée YoYo, which he wrote and produced; Numerous tours including Lollapalooza; Converted to Islam, 1992; Film appearances: Boyz N The Hood, 1991; Trespass, 1992; CB4, 1993; The Glass Shield, 1994; Higher Learning, 1995; Friday (also wrote, directed and produced), 1995; Dangerous Ground, 1997; Anaconda, 1997; The Player's Club (also wrote, directed and produced), 1997; Three Kings, 1999; Next Friday (also wrote, directed and produced), 2000; Ghosts of Mars, 2001; All About the Benjamins, 2001. *Recordings:* Singles: AmeriKKKa's Most Wanted, 1990; Kill At Will EP, 1990; It Was A Good Day, 1993; Check Yo Self, 1993; Really Doe EP, 1994; You Know How We Do It EP, 1994; Bop Gun (One Nation) EP, 1994; My Posse, 1995; World Is Mine, 1997; Pushin' Weight, 1998; Albums: AmeriKKKa's Most Wanted, 1990; Death Certificate, 1991; The

Predator, 1992; Wicked, 1992; Lethal Injection, 1993; Bootlegs and B Sides, 1994; War and Peace, 1998; War and Peace 2 – The Peace Disc, 2000; Greatest Hits, 2001.

ICE-T, (Tracey Marrow); b. 14 Feb. 1959, Newark, New Jersey, USA. Rap Artiste; Actor. *Career:* Innovator of LA Gangsta Rap; Recording artiste, 1987–; Rapper, rock group Body Count, 1992; Tours: UK; Europe; USA; Canada; South America; Asia; Australia; Middle East; Actor, films include New Jack City; Trespass; Breakin'; Tank Girl; Television includes: Players; Baadasss TV; Owner, Rhyme Syndicate Records; Lecturer and spokesman, major US universities; Also involved in Hands Across Watts and South Central Love, 2 youth intervention programmes. *Recordings:* Singles include: Lifestyles of Rich and Infamous, 1991; New Jack Hustler, 1991; What Really Goes On, 1998; Valuable Game, 1999; Albums: Rhyme Pays; Power; The Iceberg... ; Freedom of Speech – Just Watch What You Say; O. G.–Original Gangster; Home Invasion; Ice VI–Return Of The Real; with Body Count: Body Count; Born Dead; Cold as Ever; Seventh Deadly Sin; Also featured on film soundtracks: Colors; Dick Tracy. *Publications:* The Ice Opinion, 1994. *Honours:* Best Male Rapper, Rolling Stone Readers Poll, 1992; Grammy Award, Best Rap Song for Back on the Block. *Current Management:* Rhyme Syndicate Management, 4902 Coldwater Canyon Ave, Sherman Oaks, CA 91423, USA.

IDIR, (Hamid Cheriet); b. 1955, At Lahcêne, Kabylia, Algeria. Vocalist; Songwriter; Poet. *Career:* Sang on Radio Algiers, 1973; Army, 1973–75; Moved to France, 1975, signed to Pathé-Marconi; Organized and appeared in aid concert, Algerie, La Vie (Algeria, Life), 1995; Collaborations with artistes including: Dan Ar Braz, Manu Chao, Frederic Galliano, Khaled, Orchestre National de Barbes, Geoffrey Oryema. *Recordings:* Album: A Vava Inouva, 1976; (second album), 1979; Identités, 1999; Deux Rives Un Rêve, 2002. *Address:* c/o Sony Music France, 131 ave de Wagram, 75017 Paris, France.

IDOL, Billy, (Willem Wolfe Broad); b. 30 Nov. 1955, Stanmore, Middlesex, England. Vocalist; Musician (guitar); Composer. *Career:* Lead singer, guitarist, UK punk group Generation X, 1977–81; Solo artiste, 1981–; World-wide concerts include: Charmed Life Tour, 1990; Rock In Rio II Festival, 1991; Roskilde Festival, Denmark, 1991; Supported Bon Jovi, Milton Keynes Bowl, 1993. *Recordings:* Albums: with Generation X: Generation X, 1978; Valley of The Dolls, 1979; Kiss Me Deadly, 1981; Solo albums: Don't Stop, 1981; Billy Idol, 1982; Rebel Yell, 1984; Vital Idol, 1985; Whiplash Smile, 1986; Idol Songs, 1988; Charmed Life, 1990; Cyberpunk, 1993; L A Woman, 1993; All Summer Single, 1993; Don't Need a Gun, 1993; featured on: Punk Lost and Found, 1996; Retro 80s Vol. 1, 1998; Solo singles include: Hot In The City, 1982; White Wedding, 1983; Rebel Yell, 1984 (both re-released 1985); Eyes Without A Face, 1984; Flesh For Fantasy, 1984; Catch My Fall, 1984; To Be A Lover, 1986; Don't Need A Gun, 1987; Sweet Sixteen, 1987; Mony Mony (No. 1, USA), 1987; Cradle of Love (No. 2, USA), featured in film Adventures of Ford Fairlane, 1990; LA Woman, 1990; Shock To The System, 1993. *Honours:* Double Platinum disc, Rebel Yell, 1984. *Current Management:* East End Management, 8209 Melrose Ave, 2nd Floor, Los Angeles, CA 90046, USA.

IEUAN, Dafydd; b. 1 March 1969, Bangor, Wales. Musician (drums). *Career:* Mem., Catatonia, 1993–96; Joined Super Furry Animals, 1996–; Early releases on small indie label, then obtained major indie label deal; Numerous tours in the UK and abroad; Many festival appearances. *Recordings:* Albums: with Catatonia: Way Beyond Blue, 1996; Greatest Catatonia Hits, 2002; with Super Furry Animals: Fuzzy Logic, 1996; Radiator, 1997; Outspaced, 1998; Guerrilla, 1999; Mwng, 2000; Rings Around The World, 2001. Singles: with Catatonia: Hooked (EP), 1994; with Super Furry Animals: Llanfairpwllgwyngyllgogerychwyndrobwl... (EP), 1995; Moog Droog (EP), 1995; God! Show Me Magic, 1996; If You Don't Want Me To Destroy You, 1996; The Man Don't Give A Fuck, 1996; Hometown Unicorn, 1996; Something 4 The Weekend, 1996; The International Language of Screaming, 1997; Hermann Loves Pauline, 1997; Demons, 1997; Play It Cool, 1997; Ice Hockey Hair, 1998; Northern Lights, 1999; Fire In My Heart, 1999; Do Or Die, 2000.

IF, Owen, (Ian Frederick Rossiter); b. 20 March 1959, Newport, Wales. Musician (Drums). *Career:* Member, Stereo MCs; Numerous club and live appearances, TV appearances and radio sessions. *Recordings:* Singles: Elevate My Mind, 1990; Lost In Music, 1991; Connected, 1992; Step It Up, 1993; Creation, 1993; Albums: Supernatural, 1990; Connected, 1992; Stereo MCs, 1993.

IG CULTURE, (Ian George Grant), (Son of Scientist, Da One Way, Likwid Biskit); b. 17 June 1965, London, England. Prod; Remixer; DJ. *Career:* Started production career as part of Dodge City Productions, 1990; Founder: Main Squeeze label, late '90s; Co-promoter: The Co-Op club night in

London with 4 Hero and Phil Asher; Formed the New Sector Movements collective, debut album released 2001; Collaborations: 4 Hero; Kaidi Tatham; Frank McComb; Julie Dexter; Dodge; Ronny Jordan; Remixed: 4 Hero; Noel McKoy; Luniz. *Recordings:* Albums: Steppin' Up and Out (with Dodge City Productions), 1993; Download This (with New Sector Movements), 2001; Singles: As Long As We're Around (with Dodge City Productions), 1992; Unleash Your Love (with Dodge City Productions), Tings A Gwan, 1993; My History (with New Sector Movements), 1997; No Tricks EP (with New Sector Movements), The Sun (with New Sector Movements), 2001. *Membership:* MCPS/PRS. *Address:* c/o Main Squeeze Records, Adela St, 326 Kensal Rd, London W10 5BZ, England.

IGLAUER, Bruce; b. 10 July 1947, Ann Arbor, Michigan, USA. Record Co Exec. m. Jo Kolanda, 5 Aug. 1995. *Education:* BA, Lawrence University, Appleton, Wisconsin. *Career:* Founder, Alligator Records, 1971; President, Alligator Records; Released over 150 contemporary blues recordings. *Recordings:* Produced almost 100 blues albums including artistes: Albert Collins; Koko Taylor; Johnny Winter; Ray Buchanan; Saffire; Bob Margolin. *Publications:* Co-founder: Living Blues Magazine. *Membership:* Founder, Senior Board of Trustees mem., National Asscn of Independent Record Distributors and Manufacturers. *Address:* PO Box 60234, Chicago, IL 60660, USA.

IGLESIAS, Enrique; b. 8 May 1975, Madrid, Spain. Vocalist; Songwriter. *Career:* Son of Julio Iglesias; Numerous tours; Sings in English and Spanish. *Recordings:* Albums: Enrique Iglesias, 1996; Vivir, 1997; Cosas Del Amor, 1998; Enrique, 1999; Escape, 2001; Quizás, 2002. Singles: Experiencia Religiosa; No Llores Por Mi; Bailamos (No. 1, USA), 1999; Be With You (No. 1, USA), 2000; Hero (No. 1, UK), 2002. *Honours:* Grammy Award, 1997; Eight Premios Los Nuestro; Billboard Awards, Artist of the Year, Album of the Year, 1997; ASCAP Award, Songwriter of the Year, 1998; American Music Awards, Favourite Latin Artist, 2002, 2003; Platinum and Gold discs. *Address:* Interscope Records, 2220 Colorado Ave, Santa Monica, CA 90404, USA. *Website:* www.enriqueiglesias.com.

IGLESIAS, Julio, (Julio Jose Iglesias de la Cueva); b. 23 Sept. 1943, Madrid, Spain. Vocalist; Songwriter. m. Isabel Preisler, 20 Jan. 1971, divorced, 3 s. *Education:* Law student, Cambridge University. *Career:* Goalkeeper, Real Madrid junior team; Winner, Spanish Song Festival, Benidorm, 1968; Professional singer, songwriter, 1968–; Winner, Eurovision Song Contest, Netherlands, 1970; Major success in Latin America, 1970s; English Language releases, 1981–; Concerts and television appearances world-wide; In excess of 100m. records sold to date. *Compositions include:* La Vida Sigue Igual; Mi Amor; Yo Canto; Alguien El Alamo Al Camino; No Ilores. *Recordings:* Over 70 albums include: Soy, 1973; El Amor, 1975; A Mis 33 Anos, 1977; De Nina A Mujer, 1981; 1100 Bel Air Lace, 1984; Un Hombre Solo, 1987; Starry Night, 1990; La Carretera, 1995; Tango, 1996; Corazon Latino, 1998; Noche De Cuatro Lunas, 2000; Una Donna Puo Cambiar La Vita, 2000; Ao Meu Brasil, 2000; Also on: Duets (with Frank Sinatra), 1993; Hit singles include: Manuela, 1975; Hey, 1979; Begin The Beguine, 1981; To All The Girls I've Loved Before, duet with Willie Nelson, 1983; My Love, duet with Stevie Wonder, 1988. *Publications:* Autobiography: Entre El Cielo y El Infernierno, 1981. *Honours:* Grammy, Best Latin Pop Performance, 1987; Diamond Disc Award, Guinness Book of Records (most records in most languages), 1983; Medaille de Vermeil de la Ville de Paris, 1983; Eurovision Song Contest Winner, 1970. *Membership:* Hon. Mem., Spanish Foreign Legion. *Address:* c/o Anchor Marketing, 1177 Kane Concourse PH, Bay Harbour Island, FL 33154, USA.

IGREC, Mario; b. 24 May 1959, Zagreb, Croatia. Musician (guitar); Composer; Arranger; Guitar Teacher; Backing Vocalist. m. Snjezana Drkulec Igrec, 22 Nov. 1986, 3 s. *Education:* Professor of Philosophy; Conservatory; Degree, jazz guitar. *Career:* Member, various groups including Zagreb Jazz Portrait; Hot Club Zagreb; Steve Klink Quartet; Mario Igrec Quintet; Pentagon; Good Day; Ritmo Loco; Jazz Big Band HGZ; Big Festival Orchestra; Live concerts and programmes for state television in Slovenia, Austria, Croatia; International jazz festivals include: Croatia; Slovenia; Germany; Hungary. *Compositions:* Vanova; A Better Tomorrow; Brimbi; Daimonion; Blues No 4; Balrog. *Recordings:* Moment Notice; Zagreb Jazz Portrait, 1984; with Ritmo Loco: Baila Como Yo, 1992; For A Love of One Woman, 1995. *Honours:* Heineken Award for Jazz Band, Croatia, 1995. *Membership:* Croatian Music Union (HGU); Jazz Club, Zagreb. *Current Management:* Vesna Vrandecic, Zitnak 1, 41000 Zagreb, Croatia. *Address:* Mario Igrec, Ozaljska 93, 41000 Zagreb, Croatia.

IHA, James; b. 26 March 1968, Elk Grove, IL, USA. Musician (guitar). *Career:* Mem., Smashing Pumpkins, 1989–2000; Numerous headlining tours, television and radio appearances; Launched Stratchie Records with D'Arcy Wretzky, 1997; Contributed two tracks to soundtrack of film, Batman and Robin. *Recordings:* Albums: Gish, 1991; The Peel Sessions, 1992; Siamese Dream, 1993; Pisces Iscariot, 1994; Mellon Collie And The Infinite Sadness (No. 1, USA), 1995; The Aeroplane Flies High, 1996; Adore, 1998; MACHINA/ The Machines Of God, 2000; Machina II: The Friends And Enemies Of Modern Music, 2000; Greatest Hits, 2001; Earphoria, 2002; Vieuphoria

(DVD), 2002. Singles: Lull (EP), 1992; Today, 1994; Cherub Rock (EP), 1994; Disarm, 1994; I Am One (EP), 1994; Bullet With Butterfly Wings, 1995; Thirty Three, 1996; Zero, 1996; End Is The Beginning Is The End, 1997; Perfect, 1998; Stand Inside Your Love, 2000; Try Try Try, 2000.

ILLESLEY, John; b. 24 June 1949, Leicester, England. Musician (Bass). *Career:* Member, Dire Straits; Obtained major label deal and subsequent management contract; Support slot on Talking Heads 1978 European tour; Numerous headlining tours and TV appearances; Prince's Trust Concert and Nelson Mandela 70th Birthday tribute concert, 1988. *Recordings:* Singles: Sultans of Swing, 1978; Romeo and Juliet, 1981; Private Investigations (No. 2, UK), 1982; Twisting By the Pool, 1983; So Far Away, 1985; Walk of Life (No. 2, UK), 1985; Money for Nothing, featuring Sting (No. 1, USA), 1985; Brothers In Arms, 1985; Your Latest Trick, 1986; Calling Elvis, 1991; Albums: Dire Straits, 1978; Communiqué, 1979; Making Movies, 1980; Love Over Gold (No. 1, UK), 1982; Alchemy, 1984; Brothers in Arms (No. 1, UK and USA), 1985; Money For Nothing (No. 1, UK), 1988; On Every Street (No. 1, UK), 1991; On the Night, 1993; Live At the BBC, 1995; Sultans of Swing – The Very Best Of, 1998.

IMBRUGLIA, Natalie; b. 4 Feb. 1975, New South Wales, Australia. Vocalist; Songwriter; Actress. *Career:* Actress, TV series Neighbours, Australia; Moved to London, 1995; Solo recording artiste, 1997–. *Recordings:* Albums: Left of The Middle, 1997; White Lillies Island, 2001. Singles: Torn, 1997; Wishing I Was There, 1998; Big Mistake, 1998; Smoke, 1998. *Honours:* BRIT Award, Best International Female, Best International Newcomer, 1999. *Address:* c/o RCA Records, Bedford House, 69–79 Fulham High St, London SW6 3JW, England.

INABA, Kazuhiro; b. 12 June 1960, Osaka, Japan. Musician (5-string banjo, guitar, fiddle). m. Tomoe Mori, 4 June, 1994, 1 s. *Education:* BA, Kansai University for Foreign Studies. *Career:* Played with many artistes from USA including: Butch Robbins; Larry Stephenson; The Lonesome River Band; Bill Clifton; Producer, Bluegrass concerts; Interpreter, Leon Russell, Japan Tour, 1995. *Recordings:* Albums: Shore To Shore, 1986; Hard Times Come Again No More, 1989; Goin' Across The Sea, 1993. *Publications:* Featured articles, Moonshiner magazine, Japan (Bluegrass Journal). *Honours:* Second place, Bluegrass Banjo, Galax Fiddlers Convention, 1983. *Membership:* Musicians' Union, Japan; IBMA (International Bluegrass Music Asscn), Owensboro, Kentucky. *Current Management:* Office White Oak. *Address:* 4–2–16, Nishi-Tezukayama, Sumiyoshi, Osaka 558, Japan.

INAMDAR, Jayshree S; b. 20 Sept. 1974, Kalyan, India. Tabla Player; Actor. *Education:* Diploma in Computer Management, Datapro Institute, India; Diploma in Hindustani Vocal Light Music, Mumbai University. *Career:* TV Programme of Marathi songs, Gudi Padva festival; Radio programme, Sangli Radio Centre, Yuva Vani; Professional stage drama in Marathi, 1999; Acting in Hindi TV serial, Marathi. *Address:* A/6, Bldg No. 2, First Floor, Neelkanth jyot Co-op Housing Society, Near Tilak Nagar High School, Tilak Nagar, Dombivli (E), India.

INDERBERG, John Pål; b. 6 Aug. 1950, Steinkjer, Norway. Musician (saxophone); Music Prof. m. Kirsten Oxaal, 23 July 1976. *Education:* University of Trondheim. *Career:* Played with J Eks; Bob Brookmeyer; Lee Konitz; Warne Marsh; Many albums and tours; EBU Musician, soloist with Symphony Orchestra; Duos with Henning Sommerro; Professor of Music, Music Conservatory, Trondheim, Norway. *Recordings:* Albums: with Warne Marsh: Sax of a Kind, 1987; For The Time Being, 1988; with Siri's Svale Band: Blackbird, 1990; with Lee Konitz: Steps Towards A Dream, 1995; Baritone Landscape, 2001. *Honours:* Buddy Award, Norwegian Jazz Federation. *Membership:* Norwegian Musicians' Federation. *Address:* Kjøpmannsgt ,12, 7013 Trondheim, Norway. *Telephone:* 90834640. *Fax:* 73597301. *E-mail:* john.pal.inderberg@hf.ntnu.no. *Website:* www.inderberg.com.

INEZ, Mike; b. 14 May 1966, San Fernando, California, USA. Musician (Bass). *Career:* Joined Alice in Chains; Numerous tours and TV appearances including MTV Unplugged. *Recordings include:* Singles: Heaven Beside You, 1998; Albums: Facelift, 1990; Dirt, 1992; Sap, 1992; Jar of Flies, 1994; Alice in Chains, 1995; I Stay Away, 1995; Unplugged, 1996; Music Bank, 1999; Live, 2000.

INFINITI. See: **ATKINS, Juan.**

INGEBRIGTSEN, Christian; b. 25 Jan. 1977, Oslo, Norway. Vocalist; Musician (piano, guitar); Songwriter. *Education:* Liverpool Institute for Performing Arts, England. *Career:* Son of Norwegian '70s pop star Stein Ingebrigtsen; Grandfather spent 17 years as violinist in the Chicago Symphony Orchestra; Joined A1 pop group; Signed recording contract, 1999; Sell-out theatre tours of South-East Asia and UK, 2000–01. *Recordings:* Albums: Here We Come, 1999; The A List, 2000; Make It Good, 2002. Singles: Be The First To Believe, Summertime of Our Lives, Ready Or Not/Everytime, 1999; Like A Rose, Take On Me, Same Old Brand New You, 2000; No More, 2001; Caught In The Middle, 2002. *Honours:* BRIT Award, Best Newcomer,

2001; Also honoured at MTV Mandarin Music Awards. *Current Management:* c/o Byrne Blood Ltd. *Website:* www.a1-online.com.

INGMAR; b. 31 Dec. 1970, Antwerp, Belgium. Composer; Musician (keyboards); Vocalist; Writer; Translator. *Education:* Modern Languages; Basics in Jazz, Jazz Studio, Antwerp. *Career:* Secretary/Translator, until 1998; Freelance; Several national radio appearances; Several major stage live gigs (including one for His Majesty The Former King of Belgium). *Compositions:* The Quest for Beauty and Truth Continues, 1996; Ramifying Parallels on USA Import Music, 1997. *Recordings:* Insanity; Sister Sun; Amour Fatale; Exceptional; Solitude; The Quest; Beyond the Stars; The Dream. *Publications:* The Quest on Club Excentrique, 1996; Waiting... In These Skies, poem trilogy, 1997; Ramifying Parallels and Humanity, 1997; Solitude (No. 1 album), 1999; 18 Poems and a Song, an introduction, poetry book, 1999. *Honours:* Requested to write composition in honour of King of Belgium, 1991; Laureate in national New Song Contest, SABAM, 1993. *Membership:* SABAM, International Copyright Institute; International Writers and Artists Asscn.

INGRAM, Charlie Alexander; b. 24 Oct. 1972, Cheltenham, England. Musician (guitar, mandolin); Vocalist. *Education:* Studying for BA Hons Music Technology, Rose Bruford College. *Career:* with Eden Burning, touring extensively throughout UK and Europe, 1993–. *Recordings:* Mirth and Matter, 1994; You Could Be The Meadow (EP), 1994; Be An Angel, 1995; Brink, 1995. *Membership:* Musicians' Union. *Address:* 9 Wildmoor Lane, Catshill, Bromsgrove B61 0NT, England.

INNERSOUND. See: **MCBEAN, Colin.**

INNERZONE ORCHESTRA. See: **CRAIG, Carl.**

INNES, Andrew; Musician (guitar). *Career:* Member, Primal Scream; Numerous tours and festival appearances; Collaborations with DJ Andrew Weatherall, vocalist Denise Johnson, Jah Wobble and Alex Paterson from The Orb. Contributions to: One Dove, Morning Dove White, 1993; title track to the film Trainspotting, co-written with Irvine Welsh, 1996. *Recordings:* Singles: Loaded EP, 1990; Come Together EP, 1990; Higher Than The Sun, 1991; Don't Fight It, Feel It, 1991; Movin' On Up, 1991; (I'm Gonna) Cry Myself Blind, 1994; Jailbird, 1994; Rocks/Funky Jam, 1994; The Big Man and the Scream Team Meet the Barmy Army Uptown, 1996; Star, 1997; Burning Wheel, 1997; Kowalski, 1997; If They Move, Kill 'Em, 1998; Swastika Eyes, 1999; Kill All Hippies, 2000; Accelerator, 2000; Miss Lucifer, 2002. Albums: Sonic Flower Groove, 1987; Primal Scream, 1989; Screamadelica, 1991; Give Out But Don't Give Up, 1994; Echo Dek, 1997; Vanishing Point, 1997; XTRMNTR, 2000; Evil Heat, 2002. *Honours:* Mercury Music Prize Winner, 1992. *Website:* www.primalscream.net.

IOMMI, Tony; b. 19 Feb. 1948, Birmingham, England. Rock Musician (guitar); Composer. *Career:* Guitarist, UK heavy rock group Black Sabbath, 1967–; Major appearances include: Madison Square Gardens, New York, 1975; Live Aid, Philadelphia, 1985. *Recordings:* Singles include: Paranoid; Iron Man; War Pigs; Never Say Die; Albums: Black Sabbath, 1969; Paranoid, 1970; Master of Reality, 1971; Vol. 4, 1972; Sabbath Bloody Sabbath, 1973; Sabotage, 1975; Technical Ecstasy, 1976; Never Say Die, 1978; Heaven and Hell, 1980; Mob Rules, 1981; Live Evil, 1983; Born Again, 1983; Seventh Star, 1983; The Eternal Idol, 1987; Headless Cross, 1990; Tyr, 1990; Dehumanizer, 1992; Forbidden, 1995; Under Wheels of Confusion, 1996; Reunion, 1998; Numerous compilations; Solo album: Iommi, 2000. *Current Management:* Gloria Butler Management, PO Box 2686, Knowle, Birmingham B94 5NQ, England.

IOVINE, Jimmy; Record Co Exec; Prod. *Career:* Engineer, worked with John Lennon, Bruce Springsteen; Prod., worked with Dr Dre, Marilyn Manson, Stevie Nicks, Nine Inch Nails, No Doubt, 2Pac, Tom Petty, Pretenders, Brian Setzer Orchestra, Patti Smith, U2; Co-founder, Interscope Records, 1989; Co-Chair., Interscope Geffen A&M; Founder, with Doug Morris, Chair. and CEO, Jimmy and Doug's Farm Club (project incorporating a record label, website and cable television show), 1999–. *Honours:* Rolling Stone magazine, Prod. of the Year, two times. *Address:* Interscope Records, 2220 Colorado Ave, Santa Monica, CA 90404, USA. *Website:* www.interscope.com; www.farmclub.com.

IREDALE, Simon James; b. 21 Nov. 1970, Bradford, West Yorkshire, England. Songwriter; Performer; Musician (guitar, keyboards). *Education:* Grade V, Music and Theory at age 9. *Career:* Mem., various bands, incl. Terrorize and The Love Generation, Hothead; UK tours with these bands; Radio appearances on Pennine Radio, BBC Radio 1, and BBC GLR programme, Unplugged with Janice Long. *Recordings:* Numerous recordings, with Hothead. *Membership:* Musicians' Union; National Band Register. *Current Management:* Calderbank and Clarke Management. *Address:* 22 Devonshire Rd, Chorley, Lancashire, England.

IRELAND, Michael E; b. 10 Feb. 1962, Kansas City, Missouri, USA. Country Vocalist; Songwriter; Musician (bass). Divorced. *Education:* BA, Music Education; MA, English, University of Missouri at Columbia. *Career:*

Appearance, Prime Time Country, TNN, 1998, World Cafe, WXPN radio, 1998, Acoustic Cafe, national syndicated radio, 1998. *Recordings:* Learning How to Live, 1998. *Membership:* BMI. *Current Management:* Joyce Linehan Management, Boston. *Address:* 10 A Burt St, Boston, MA 02124, USA.

IRON LUNG. See: **METHOD MAN.**

IRONS, Jack; b. 18 July 1962, Los Angeles, CA, USA. Musician (drums). *Career:* Founding mem., Anthem, later renamed Red Hot Chili Peppers, 1983–88; Joined Pearl Jam, 1994; Numerous tours and TV appearances. *Recordings:* Albums: with Red Hot Chili Peppers: Freaky Styley, 1985; The Uplift Mofo Party Plan, 1987; with Pearl Jam: Vitalogy, 1994; No Code, 1996; Live on Two Legs, 1998; Yield, 1998; Riot Act, 2002. Singles: with Red Hot Chili Peppers: Abbey Road EP, 1988; with Pearl Jam: Animal, 1994; Spin the Black Circle, 1994; Merkin Ball, 1995; Not for You, 1995; Immortality, 1995; I Got Id EP, 1995; Who You Are, 1996.

ISAACS, Gregory; b. 1951, Kingston, Jamaica. Reggae Vocalist. *Career:* Solo singer, 1970s–; Established own African Museum Shop and label, with Errol Dunkley, 1973; Extensive international tours. *Recordings:* Numerous albums include: Mr Isaacs; Extra Classic; The Early Years; Sly and Robbie Present; The Best Of, Vols 1 and 2; Cool Ruler; Soon Forward; Lonely Lover; My Number One; Red Roses for Gregory; Taxi Show Case; Night Nurse; Out Deh; Warning; Can't Stay Away, 1992; No Luck, 1993; Private Lesson, 1995; Mr Love, 1995; Memories, 1995; Mr Cool, 1996; Live at Maritime Hall, 1998; Cool Ruler, 1999; Turn Down the Lights, 1999; The Best of Gregory Isaacs Vol. 1 and 2, 1999; Private and Confidential, 2000; Dancing Floor, 2000; Reasoning With The Almighty, 2001. *Address:* c/o Fantasma Tours International, 2000 S Dixie Hwy, West Palm Beach, FL 33401, USA.

ISAACS, Jason; b. 30 April 1968, England. Vocalist; Songwriter; Musician (guitar). m. Marion. *Career:* Dance Macabre, 1985; The Promise, 1994; Triggerfish, 1996; Solo artiste, 1996–, various radio apps; Various sessions as Backing Vocalist. *Compositions:* A Girl Called Jesus; Sigh; C-Life; Bike; Funky Chuny; Gun; Only A Northern Band; News; Hold It Down; Who Says I Can; Cornucopia. *Recordings:* Debut single, 1997, A Girl Called Jesus, 1998. *Current Management:* Sound Judgement Partnership, 42 Brent Moor Rd, Bramhan, Stockport, Cheshire SK7 3PT, England.

ISAAK, Chris; b. 26 June 1956, Stockton, CA, USA. Vocalist; Songwriter; Actor. *Education:* Degree, English and Communication Arts. *Career:* Singer, 1984–; Extensive international tours include: Turku Festival, Finland, 1993; Support to Tina Turner, US tour, 1993; Television appearances include: The Last Resort; The Tonight Show; Saturday Night Live; Late Show With David Letterman; Actor, films: Married To The Mob, 1988; Wild At Heart, 1989; The Silence of The Lambs, 1990; Twin Peaks – Fire Walk With Me, 1993; Little Buddha, 1993. *Compositions:* Music for films: Blue Velvet; Wild At Heart; Music for television: Days of Our Lives; The Preppie Murder; Private Eye. *Recordings:* Albums: Silvertone, 1985; Chris Isaak, 1987; Heart Shaped World, 1989; Wicked Game, 1991; San Francisco Days, 1993; Forever Blue, 1995; Baja Sessions, 1996; Speak Of The Devil, 1998; Wicked Ways Anthology, 1998; Always Got Tonight, 2002. Singles include: Blue Hotel, 1987; Wicked Game, 1989; Blue Spanish Sky, 1991; Don't Make Me Dream About You, 1991; Two Hearts, 1993; Can't Do A Thing (To Stop Me), 1993; Dark Moon, 1993; Solitary Man, 1993; Go Walking Down There, 1995; Somebody's Crying, 1995; Please, 1998; Bad Thing, 1999. *Honours:* International Rock Award, Best Male Vocalist of the Year, 1991; 3 MTV Music Video Awards, Wicked Game, 1991. *Current Management:* Howard Kaufman, H. K. Management, 8900 Wilshire Blvd, Suite 300, Beverly Hills, CA 90211, USA.

ISHAM, Mark; b. 7 Sept. 1951, New York, NY, USA. Composer; Prod; Sound Engineer; Jazz Musician (trumpet). m. Donna Linson, 24 Feb. 1990. *Career:* Mem., jazz ensemble, Group 87, The Rubisa Patrol, Sons of Champlin. Film scores include: Never Cry Wolf, 1983; Mrs Soffel, 1984; The Times of Harvey Milk, 1984; Country, 1984; Trouble in Mind, 1985; The Hitcher, 1986; Made in Heaven, 1987; Tibet, 1988; The Moderns, 1988; The Beast, 1988; Everybody Wins, 1990; Love at Large, 1990; Reversal of Fortune, 1990; Mortal Thoughts, 1991; Crooked Hearts, 1991; Point Break, 1991; A Midnight Clear, 1991; Little Man Tate, 1991; Billy Bathgate, 1991; Cool World, 1992; Of Mice and Men, 1992; The Public Eye, 1992; A River Runs Through It, 1992; Hidden Hawaii, 1993; Nowhere to Run, 1993; Fire in the Sky, 1993; Made in America, 1993; Short Cuts, 1993; Romeo is Bleeding, 1993; The Browning Version, 1994; Timecop, 1994; Thumbelina, 1994; Safe Passage, 1994; The Getaway, 1994; Quiz Show, 1994; Mrs Parker and the Vicious Circle, 1994; Nell, 1994; Miami Rhapsody, 1995; Losing Isiah, 1995; The Net, 1995; Home for the Holidays, 1995; Waterworld (additional music), 1995; Last Dance, 1996; Fly Away Home, 1996; Night Falls on Manhattan, 1997; Afterglow, 1997; The Education of Little Tree, 1997; Kiss the Girls, 1997; The Gingerbread Man, 1998; Blade, 1998; Free Money, 1998; At First Sight, 1999; Varsity Blues, 1999; Breakfast of Champions, 1999; October Sky, 1999; Body Shots, 1999; Galapagos: The Enchanted Voyage, 1999; Rules of Engagement, 2000; Where the Money Is, 2000; Men of Honor, 2000; Save the Last Dance, 2001; Don't Say a Word, 2001; Hardball, 2002; Life as a House, 2002; The Majestic, 2002;

For television: Sketch Artist, 1992; Chicago Hope, 1994; Gotti, 1996; EZ Streets, 1996; Michael Hayes (theme), 1997; Nothing Sacred (theme), 1997; The Defenders: The Payback, 1997; The Defenders: Choice of Evils, 1998; From the Earth to the Moon, 1998; The Defenders: Taking the First, 1998; Family Law, 1999. *Recordings:* Solo: Vapor Drawings, 1983; Castalia, 1988; Mark Isham, 1991; Miles Remembered: The Silent Way Project, 1999; Blue Sun (with Charles Jankel), 1995; Deal It Out (with America); View From the Ground (with Van Morrison); Live at the Belfast Opera House; Into the Music; Inarticulate Speech of the Heart; Common One; Beautiful Vision (with Art Lande); Story of Baku; Eccentricities of Earl Dant; Rubisa Patrol; Desert Marauders; We Begin (with Group 87); Group 87; A Career In Dada Processing (with the Rolling Stones); Voodoo Lounge (with Bruce Springsteen); Human Touch (with Willie Nelson); Across the Borderline (with Toots Thielmans); Toots. *Honours:* Emmy Award, EZ Streets; American Music Award, Favourite Soundtrack, for Save the Last Dance, 2002. *Membership:* ASCAP. *Current Management:* Ron Moss Management.

ISLAM, Yusuf, (Steven Demetre Georgiou, Cat Stevens); b. 21 July 1948, London, England. Writer; Dir of Production Co. m. Fawzia Mubarik Ali, 7 Sept. 1979, 2 s., 1 deceased, 4 d. *Career:* Commenced with release of I Love My Dog, Oct. 1966; Achieved international status with multi-platinum sales of albums Tea For The Tillerman, 1970; Teaser and The Firecat, 1971; Following extensive tours, including: Bamboozle, 1974; Majikat, 1976; Numerous television appearances; Decided to retire at summit of popularity in 1978 after embracing Islam. *Recordings include:* Hit singles: I Love My Dog, 1966; Matthew and Son (No. 2, UK), 1967; I'm Gonna Get Me A Gun, 1967; A Bad Night, 1967; Lady D'Arbanville, 1970; Moonshadow, 1971; Morning Has Broken, 1971; Can't Keep It In, 1972; Another Saturday Night, 1974; Remember The Days of The Old School Yard, 1977; Albums include: Matthew and Son, 1967; New Masters, 1968; World of Cat Stevens, 1970; Mona Bone Jakon, 1970; Tea For The Tillerman, 1971; Teaser and The Firecat, 1971; Very Young and Early Songs, USA, 1971; Catch Bull At Four, 1972; Foreigner, 1973; Buddha and The Chocolate Box, 1974; View From The Top, 1974; Numbers, 1975; Greatest Hits, 1975; Iztso, 1977; Back To Earth, 1978; Cat's Cradle, 1978; Footsteps In The Dark (Comp), 1984; Classics Vol. 24 – Cat Stevens, 1989; Very Best of Cat Stevens, 1990; As Yusuf Islam: The Life of The Last Prophet(s), 1995; A Is For Allah, 2000. *Publications:* Cat Stevens-Definitive Career, Chris Charlesworth; The Boy Who Looked At The Moon, David Evans, 1995. *Membership:* Musicians' Union; Mem., exclusive club of artistes whose composition has been performed more than 2m. times, in US alone (with Morning Has Broken). *Address:* c/o Cat Music, 3 Furlong Rd, London N7 8LA, England.

ISLEIFSSON, Arni; b. 18 Sept. 1927, Reykjavík, Iceland. Musician. m. Kristin Axelsdottir, 1 s., 3 d. *Education:* Music School. *Career:* Television and radio appearances. *Compositions:* Children's songs, 3 records, 1960, 1961; Record, 1984. *Honours:* Invited as Jazz Music Director, Trip to New Orleans by Atlanta Airlines and Channel 2 and Travelbureou Samvinnuferdir Landsyn. *Membership:* Jazzclub Egilsstadir; Egilsstadir Jazz Festival. *Current Management:* Egilsstadir Jazz Festival. *Address:* Hraunbar 122 110 Reykjavík, Iceland.

ISLEY, Ernie; b. 7 March 1952, Cincinnati, OH, USA. Musician (guitar, drums). *Career:* Mem., The Isley Brothers, with brothers Rudolph, Ronald, O'Kelly, Marvin and cousin Chris Jasper, 1969–84; Group billed as The Isley Brothers Featuring Ronald Isley, 1989–; Mem., Isley, Jasper, Isley (with Marvin and Chris), 1984–. *Recordings:* Albums: with The Isley Brothers: The Brothers Isley, 1969; Live At Yankee Stadium, 1969; Givin' It Back, 1971; Brother Brother Brother, 1972; The Isleys Live, 1973; The Isleys' Greatest Hits, 1973; Live It Up, 1974; The Heat Is On (No. 1, USA), 1975; Harvest For The World, 1976; Go For Your Guns, 1977; Forever Gold, 1977; Showdown, 1978; Winner Takes All, 1979; Go All The Way, 1980; Grand Slam, 1981; Inside You; 1981; The Real Deal, 1982; Between The Sheets, 1983; Eternal, 2001; Greatest Hits, Vol. I, 2002; with Isley Jasper Isley: Broadway's Closer To Sunset Boulevard, 1985; Caravan of Love, 1985; Masterpiece, 1985; Different Drummer, 1987; Solo album: High Wire, 1990; Tracks of Life (with Marvin and Ronald), 1992; Beautiful Ballads, 1994; Funky Family, 1995; Mission to Please, 1996; It's Your Thing: The Story of the Isley Brothers, 1999; Love Songs, 2001; Eternal, 2001; Singles include: with the Isley Brothers: Love The One You're With, 1971; Spill The Wine, 1971; That Lady, 1973; Summer Breeze, 1974; Fight The Power, 1975; For The Love of You (Part 1 and 2), 1975; Who Loves You Better, 1976; Harvest For The World, 1976; It's Disco Night (Rock Don't Stop), 1979; with Isley, Jasper, Isley: Caravan of Love, 1985. *Honours:* Gold Ticket, Madison Square Garden, 1980; Inducted into Rock and Roll Hall of Fame, 1992. *Current Management:* Ron Weisner Management, 9200 Sunset Blvd, Penthouse 15, Los Angeles, CA 90069, USA. *Website:* www.theisleybrothers.com.

ISLEY, Marvin; b. 18 Aug. 1953, Cincinnati, OH, USA. Musician (bass, percussion). *Career:* Mem., The Isley Brothers, with brothers Rudolph, Ronald, O'Kelly, Ernie and cousin Chris Jasper, 1969–84; Group billed as The Isley Brothers Featuring Ronald Isley, 1989–; Mem., Isley, Jasper, Isley (with Ernie and Chris), 1984–. *Recordings:* Albums with the Isley Brothers include: The Brothers Isley, 1969; Brother Brother Brother, 1972; The Isleys Live,

1973; The Isleys' Greatest Hits, 1973; Live It Up, 1974; The Heat Is On (No. 1, USA), 1975; Harvest For The World, 1976; Go For Your Guns, 1977; Showdown, 1978; Winner Takes All, 1979; Go All The Way, 1980; Grand Slam, 1981; Inside You, 1981; The Real Deal, 1982; Between The Sheets, 1983; Eternal, 2001; Greatest Hits, Vol. I, 2002; with Isley Jasper Isley: Broadway's Closer To Sunset Boulevard, 1985; Caravan of Love, 1985; Different Drummer, 1987; Tracks of Life, (with Ernie and Ronald), 1992; Beautiful Ballads, 1994; Funky Family, 1995; Mission to Please, 1996; It's Your Thing: The Story of the Isley Brothers, 1999; Love Songs, 2000; Eternal, 2001; Singles include: It's Your Thing, 1969; Love The One You're With, 1971; Spill The Wine, 1971; Lay-Away, 1972; Pop That Thang, 1972; That Lady, 1973; Summer Breeze, 1974; Highway of My Life, 1974; Fight The Power, 1975; For The Love of You, 1975; Harvest For The World, 1976; It's A Disco Night, 1979; Goodnight (It's Time For Love), 1980. *Honours:* Gold Ticket, Madison Square Garden, 1980; Inducted into Rock and Roll Hall of Fame, 1992. *Current Management:* Ron Weisner Management, 9200 Sunset Blvd, Penthouse 15, Los Angeles, CA 90069, USA. *Website:* www.theisleybrothers.com.

ISLEY, Ronald, (Mr Biggs); b. 21 May 1941, Cincinnati, OH, USA. Vocalist. m. Angela Winbush. *Career:* Mem., gospel group, Isley Brothers, early 1950s; Formed trio with Rudolph and O'Kelly, 1955; First British tour, 1964; Formed T-Note record label, as prod. and writer, 1969; Group joined by brothers Ernie, Marvin, and cousin Chris Jasper, 1969–84; Group billed as The Isley Brothers Featuring Ronald Isley, 1989–; Collaborations with: Quincy Jones, Nas, Lil' Kim, 112, Angela Winbush, Steve Harvey; Man. for The Johnson Sisters, 2001–. *Recordings:* Albums: Twist and Shout, 1959; This Old Heart of Mine, 1966; It's Your Thing, 1969; Givin' It Back, 1971; Brother Brother Brother, 1972; The Isleys Live, 1973; The Isleys' Greatest Hits, 1973; Live It Up, 1974; The Heat Is On (No. 1, USA), 1975; Harvest For The World, 1976; Go For Your Guns, 1977; Forever Gold, 1977; Showdown, 1978; Winner Takes All, 1978; Go All The Way, 1978; Grand Slam, 1978; Inside You, 1978; The Real Deal, 1978; Between The Sheets, 1978; Masterpiece, 1985; Smooth Sailin', 1987; Spend The Night, 1989; Tracks of Life (with Ernie and Marvin), 1983; Live, 1993; Beautiful Ballads, 1994; Funky Family, 1995; Mission to Please, 1996; It's Your Thing: The Story of the Isley Brothers, 1999; Love Songs, 2000; Eternal, 2001; Greatest Hits, Vol. I, 2002. Singles include: Shout, 1959; Twist and Shout, 1962; Testify, 1964; This Old Heart of Mine, 1966; I Guess I'll Always Love You, 1966; Behind A Painted Smile, 1968; It's Your Thing, 1969; I Turned You On, 1969; Put Yourself In My Place, 1969; Love The One You're With, 1971; Spill The Wine, 1971; Pop That Thang, 1972; Work To Do, 1972; That Lady, 1973; Summer Breeze, 1974; The Highway of My Life, 1974; Fight The Power, 1975; For The Love of You, 1975; Who Loves You Better, 1976; Harvest For The World, 1976; Livin' In My Life, 1978; Goodnight (It's Time For Love), 1980; Spend The Night, 1989. *Honours:* Grammy Award, Best R&B Vocal Performance, It's Your Thing, 1969; Inducted into Rock and Roll Hall of Fame, 1992; Soul Train Awards, Quincy Jones Award, 2001. *Current Management:* Ron Weisner Entertainment, 9200 Sunset Blvd, Penthouse 15, Los Angeles, CA 90069, USA. *Website:* www.theisleybrothers.com.

ISLEY, Rudolph; b. 1 April 1939, Cincinnati, OH, USA. Vocalist. *Career:* Member, Isley Brothers, gospel group, early 1950s; Formed trio with brothers Ronald and O'Kelly, 1955; Formed T-Neck record label, writing, producing, became vice-pres., 1969; Group joined by brothers Ernie, Marvin, and cousin Chris Jasper, 1969–84; Group billed as The Isley Brothers Featuring Ronald Isley, 1989–. *Recordings:* Albums: Shout, 1959; Twist and Shout, 1962; This Old Heart of Mine, 1966; It's Your Thing, 1969; The Brothers, 1969; Live At Yankee Stadium, 1969; Brother Brother Brother, 1972; The Isleys Live, 1973; The Isleys' Greatest Hits, 1973; Live It Up, 1974; The Heat Is On (No. 1, USA), 1975; Harvest For The World, 1976; Go For Your Guns, 1977; Showdown, 1978; Winner Takes All, 1978; Go All The Way, 1978; Grand Slam, 1981; Inside You, 1981; The Real Deal, 1982; Between The Sheets, 1983; Smooth Sailin', 1987; The Isley Brothers Greatest Hits, 1988; Spend The Night, 1989; Love Songs, 2000; Eternal, 2001; Greatest Hits, Vol. I, 2002. Singles include: This Old Heart of Mine, 1966; I Guess I'll Always Love You, 1966; Behind A Painted Smile, 1968; It's Your Thing, 1969; I Turned You On, 1969; Put Yourself In My Place, 1969; Spill The Wine, 1971; Love The One You're With, 1971; That Lady, 1973; Summer Breeze, 1974; What It Comes Down To, 1974; Highway of My Life, 1974; For The Love of You (Part 1 and 2), 1975; Harvest For The World, 1976; It's Disco Night (Rock Don't Stop), 1979; Goodnight (It's Time For Love), 1980. *Honours:* Grammy Award, Best R&B Vocal Performance, 1970; Gold Ticket, Madison Square Garden, New York, 1980; Inducted into Rock and Roll Hall of Fame, 1992. *Current Management:* Ron Weisner Entertainment, 9200 Sunset Blvd, Penthouse 15, Los Angeles, CA 90069, USA. *Website:* www.theisleybrothers.com.

ITAMARACÁ, Lia De, (Maria Madalena Correio do Nascimento); b. 1944, Itamaracá, Brazil. Vocalist; Songwriter. *Career:* Singing cirandas (dance song set to distinctive percussive rhythm with mostly rurally-themed lyrics) since aged 11; Composed Esta Ciranda Quem Me Deu Foi Lia with Teca Calazans, aged 18; Song became well known all over Brazil; Recorded her first LP, 1977, but subsequently faded from the limelight; Continued to perform cirandas in Itamaracá and recent national interest in this folk form has revived career; Performed shows all over Brazil and recorded second album Eu Sou Lia. *Compositions:* Esta Ciranda Quem Me Deu Foi Lia. *Recordings:* Eu Sou Lia, 2000.

IVEY, Lee (Carole Lee); b. Kentucky, North Carolina, USA. *Career:* Performed with Bobby Atkins; Screenwriter; The Legend of Broken Heart Creek, screenplay, 6 months, 1993; Songwriter; Currently working on script for Come Back to Broken Heart Creek. *Recordings:* Bunnie Mills and Friends, CD; It's Your Lie, 1998; Just for Old Times Sake, 1998. *Address:* 4100 N Ohenry Blvd, Lot#158 Greensboro, NC 27405, USA.

IWAN, Dafydd; b. 24 Aug. 1943, Glanaman, Wales. Vocalist; Songwriter; Record Co Dir; Politician. m. (1), 2 s., 1 d., (2) Bethan Jones, 24 Sept. 1988, 2 s. *Education:* Brynaman, Rhydaman, Bala, University of Wales. *Career:* Regular stage performances (as solo artiste, with folk group, and with own band), 1962–; Regular television appearances, 1965–; Tours: North America; Europe; Celtic countries. *Recordings:* 11 albums; Songs include: Yma O Hyd; Carlo; Pam Fod Eira'n Wyn; Ai Am Fod Haul; Hawl I Fyw; Cynnar; Caneuon Gwerin; Dal i Gredu; Can Celt. *Publications:* Several song books including: Holl Ganeuon (151 songs). *Honours:* Hon. mem., Gorsedd of Bards; Gold Disc for Services to Welsh Recording Industry, 1990; Hon. Fellow, University of Wales (Bangor and Aberystwyth), for Services to Welsh Music and Language, 1998. *Membership:* Vice-Pres., Plaid Cymru; Llys Eisteddfod Genedlaethol Cymru. *Current Management:* Sain. *Address:* Canolfan Sain, Llandwrog, Caernarfon, Gwynedd LL54 5TG, Wales. *E-mail:* dafydd@sain.wales.com; dafyddiwan@cymru1.net.

J

JA RULE, (Jeffrey Atkins); b. 29 Feb. 1977, Queens, New York, NY, USA. Rap Artiste. *Career:* Began rapping at 16; First appeared on Mic Geronimo's Time To Build, 1995; Collaborations: Jay-Z; Blackstreet; So Plush; DJ Clue; Dru Hill; Jennifer Lopez; Film appearances: Turn it Up, 2000; Backstage, 2000; Da Hip Hop Witch, 2000; The Fast and the Furious, 2001; Crime Partners 2000, 2001. *Recordings:* Albums: Venni Vetti Vecci, 1999; Rule 3.36, 2001; Pain Is Love, 2001; The Last Temptation, 2003. Singles: Murdergram, 1998; Holla Holla, 1999; Put It On Me, Between Me And You, 2001. *Honours:* MOBO Awards, Best Hip Hop Artist, 2002. *Address:* c/o Def Jam, 825 Eighth Ave, New York, 10019-7472, USA. *Website:* www.defjam.com/jarule/.

JACKSON, Alan Eugene; b. 17 Oct. 1958, Newnan, Georgia, USA. Vocalist; Songwriter. m. Denise Jackson, 12 Dec. 1979, 3 d. *Education:* 2 years college. *Career:* Multi-platinum album sales, over 24m.; Performed before over 3m. fans; Appeared on numerous award shows; Television includes: The Late Show with David Letterman; The Tonight Show; Regis and Kathie Lee. *Compositions include:* Chattahoochee (No. 1, USA). *Recordings:* Albums: Here In The Real World, 1990; Don't Rock The Jukebox, 1991; A Lot About Livin', 1992; Who I Am, 1994; Greatest Hits Collection, 1995; Everything I Love, 1996; High Mileage, 1998; Under the Influence, 1999; Super Hits, 1999; When Somebody Loves You, 2000; Drive, 2002. *Honours:* Academy of Country Music Male Artist of the Year, 1995; Country Music Asscn Entertainer of the Year, 1995. *Membership:* ASCAP; NARAS; ACM; CMA. *Current Management:* Chip Peay Entertainment. *Address:* Alan Jackson Fanclub, PO Box 121945, Nashville, TN 37212-1945, USA.

JACKSON, Bob; b. 6 Jan. 1949, Coventry, England. Musician (keyboards, guitar); Vocalist; Songwriter. m. Christine, 18 Oct. 1980, 2 s., 1 d. *Career:* Bands: Indian Summer; with Ross: 2 US tours, 1 supporting Eric Clapton, 1974; with Badfinger: British tour with Man, 1974; 4 US tours, 1982–85; BBC television documentary, 1986; with Dodgers: Television and radio include: In Concert, Crackerjack, Supersonic; Scene; David Byron Band; Fortunes. *Compositions:* Various songwriting deals with Essex, Island, 16 song releases. *Recordings:* Album/single releases with all the above bands. *Membership:* PRS; MCPS; Musicians' Union. *Current Management:* Brian Yeats. *Address:* Home Farm House, Canwell, West Midlands B75 5SH, England.

JACKSON, Carl Eugene; b. 18 Sept. 1953, Louisville, Mississippi, USA. Songwriter; Musician (banjo). *Career:* Musician, Jim and Jesse; The Sullivan Family; Glen Campbell, 1972–84; Songwriter, Glen Campbell Publishing, 1984–87; Ricky Skaggs/Polygram Music Publishing, 1987–90; Famous Music Publishing, 1990–93; McSpadden Smith Music, 1993–96; Colonel Rebel Music, 1996–. *Compositions:* Letter To Home; Little Mountain Church House; Put Yourself In My Place; Breaking New Ground; Against The Grain; No Future In The Past; Fit For A King; Lonesome Dove. *Recordings:* Albums: Roll On, Alabama, 1984; 13, Emmylou Harris, 1987; Angel Band, Emmylou Harris; Trio III, Linda Ronstadt, Dolly Parton, Emmylou Harris; Sevens, Garth Brooks; Ropin' The Wind, Garth Brooks; This Time, Dwight Yoakam; Gone, Dwight Yoakam. *Honours:* IBMA Song of the Year, Little Mountain Church House, 1990; Grammy for Best Bluegrass album, Spring Training, 1991; Dove Award for Best Southern Gospel Song, Where Shadows Never Fall, 1991. *Membership:* CMA; ACM, NARAS.

JACKSON, Clarence; b. 28 Dec. 1923, Green Sea, South Carolina, USA. Recording Artist; Prod; Musician (steel guitar, dobro). m. Carolyn W Jackson, 5 June 1949, 1 s. *Education:* Clemson College; Coyne Electrical School; Elkin's Radio School. *Career:* Radio and television personality; Tent, theatre, school and park Country shows; Toured with Western film stars: Al 'Lash' Larue; Cowboy Tex Ritter; Shows on US armed forces radio, World War II; Recorded 500 pure dobro guitar tunes (world record for dobroist); PBS radio broadcasting; Traditional music dobro man, comedian. *Recordings include:* with Sister Foye Turner: Country Gospel; Old Time Country Songs; with Roger Hopkins: Smokey Mountain Favourites; with Billie and Gordon Hamrick: Gospel Time; with Bernard Sturkie: Gene Autrey Favourites; with Mutt Poston: Favourite Waltzes; James Wall Sings 20 Carter Family Songs; Hoedowns; Hawaiian and Country; Country Get Together; Red White and Country Gospel; with Roy Rea: Dobro Honky-Tonking; with Maggie Country Singers: Country Favourites; Heart Warming Recitations, with C Band; Big John Demarcus: Jimmie Rogers Favourites; The Carolina Boys; 23 guitar instructional videos: How To Play By Ear The Clarence Jackson Way. *Publications:* Autobiography. *Honours:* US Air Force; US National Guard; US Army; Country Music Asscns. *Address:* 308 Starbright Lane, Moncks Corner, SC 29461, USA.

JACKSON, David Nicholas George; b. 15 April 1947, Stamford. Musician; Teacher; Consultant. m. Susan Elizabeth Jackson, 1 s., 1 d. *Education:* MA, St Andrews University; PGCE, Surrey University. *Career:* Van Der Graaf Generator, 1969–77; Teacher, 1978–89; Musician, Soundbeam Consultant, David Jackson's Tonewall, an interactive performance with Soundbeams, Echo-Mirrors and Jelly-bean Tree suitable for all abilities and disabilities, 1990; Radio 1 Newsbeat, Radio 3 and 4, Soundbeam Specials; Television, Tomorrows World. *Compositions:* The House That Cried; Beam Machine, Star Messenger. *Recordings:* Van Der Graff Generator; Long Hello Series; Fractal Bridge; Peter Hamill. *Publications:* Special Children; Soundbeam Artistry. *Membership:* PRS; MCPS; Sound Sense. *Address:* 37 Carey Rd, Wokingham, Berkshire, RG40 2NP, England.

JACKSON, Elizabeth Lilian Mary, (Elizabeth Hoey); b. 4 Dec. 1946, Hendon, London, England. Vocalist (Mezzo Soprano). m. Peter W Jackson, 16 Aug. 1969, 1 s. *Education:* Watford College of Further Education, Hertfordshire; Watford School of Music, 1965–66; Royal College of Music, 1966–69; Birmingham School of Music (pt-time), 1969–72. *Career:* Singer, Coombe Abbey Medieval Banquets; Formed Welsh Road Warblers, 3 singers and acoustic guitar, 1987; Appearances in voluntary clubs and societies in the West Midlands; Interview, CWR, 1996; Local charity rock and light entertainment, concerts, 1998; Light-hearted music, poetry and comedy sketches. *Recordings:* Folk Seasons; Sam Richard's Evening Love Song, 1996; A Bird in the Hand; Eliz: The Drummer and Cookie, 1997. *Membership:* Music for Disabled. *Current Management:* Jo Tucker, Leamington Spa. *Address:* Holly Tree House, School Lane, Priors Marston, Southam CV47 7RR, England.

JACKSON, Janet; b. 16 May 1966, Los Angeles, USA. Vocalist; Actress. m. El DeBarge, 1984, divorced 1986. *Career:* First appearance with family singing group The Jacksons, aged 7; Television actress, 1977–81; Appeared in US television series: Good Times, CBS; Diff'rent Strokes; Fame; A New Kind of Family; Solo recording artiste, 1982–; Concerts and tours include: Rhythm Nation World Tour (USA, Europe, Far East), 1990; Film debut, Poetic Justice, 1993. *Recordings:* Albums: Janet Jackson, 1982; Dream Street, 1984; Control, 1986; Janet Jackson's Rhythm Nation (No. 1, USA), 1989; Janet (No. 1, UK and USA), 1993; Design of a Decade 1986–96, 1995; The Velvet Rope, 1997; All For You, 2001; Hit singles include: What Have You Done For Me Lately, 1986; Nasty, 1986; When I Think of You (No. 1, USA), 1986; Control, 1987; Let's Wait Awhile, 1987; The Pleasure Principle, 1987; Miss You Much (No. 1, USA), 1989; Rhythm Nation, 1989; Come Back To Me, 1990; Escapade (No. 1, USA), 1990; Alright, 1990; Black Cat (No. 1, USA), 1990; Love Will Never Do (Without You), 1990 (No. 1, USA), 1991; The Best Things In Life Are Free, duet with Luther Vandross, from film Mo' Money, 1992; That's The Way Love Goes (No. 1, USA), 1993; If, 1993; Again (No. 1, USA), 1993; Because of Love, 1994; Any Time Any Place, 1994; You Want This, 1994; Whoops Now, 1995; Scream, with Michael Jackson, 1995; Runaway, 1995; Twenty Foreplay, 1996; When I Think of You, 1996; Got Til It's Gone, 1997; Together Again, 1997; Go Deep, 1998; Every Time, 1998; I Get Lonely, 1998; Girlfriend, 1999; What's It Gonna Be, with Busta Rhymes, 1999; Doesn't Really Matter (No. 1, USA), 2000. *Honours:* American Music Award, Favourite Pop/Rock Female Artist, 2002. *Current Management:* Roger Davies Management, 15030 Ventura Blvd #772, Sherman Oaks, CA 91403, USA.

JACKSON, Jermaine Lajuan; b. 11 Dec. 1954, Gary, Indiana, USA. Vocalist; Musician (bass); Record Prod. m. Hazel Gordy, 15 Dec. 1973. *Career:* Member, Jackson Five (later The Jacksons), US family singing group, 1969–75; Solo recording artiste, 1972–; Career development of artistes including Devo; Michael Lovesmith; Syreeta; Formed own production company, and record label, WORK Records; Producer, US television series The Jacksons – An American Dream, ABC, 1992. *Recordings include:* Albums: with The Jacksons: Diana Ross Presents The Jackson 5, 1970; ABC, 1970; Third Album, 1970; Christmas Album, 1970; Maybe Tomorrow, 1971; Looking Through The Windows, 1972; Skywriter, 1973; Get It Together, 1973; Anthology, 1976; Victory, 1984; Motown Legends, 1993; Ultimate Collection, 1995; Solo albums: Jermaine, 1972; Come Into My Life, 1973; My Name Is Jermaine, 1976; Feel The Fire, 1977; Let's Get Serious, 1980; Jermaine, 1981; I Like Your Style, 1981; Let Me Tickle Your Fancy, 1982; Jermaine Jackson, 1984; Precious Moments; Don't Take It Personal, 1990; You Said, 1992; The Heritage Collection, 2000; Singles include: Daddy's Home, 1973; Let's Get Serious, 1980; Let Me Tickle Your Fancy, with Devo, 1982; What Do You Do, 1985; I Think It's Love, 1985; Do What You Do, 1993. *Contributions to:* film soundtracks: Voyage of The Rock Aliens, 1985; Perfect, 1985; As record producer: Tracks for Whitney Houston debut album, 1986.

JACKSON, Joe; b. 11 Aug. 1954, Burton-Upon-Trent, Staffordshire, England. Vocalist; Songwriter. *Education:* Violin and piano lessons; S Level, Music; Composition, orchestration, piano and percussion, Royal College of Music, London. *Career:* Played with Johnny Dankworth; Member, National Youth Jazz Orchestra; Musical director, Coffee and Cream, 1977; Singer, 1978–; Regular UK and international tours, 1978–; Concerts include: The Summer of '80 Garden Party, with Bob Marley, Average White Band, Crystal

Palace, 1980. *Compositions include:* Film scores: Mike's Murder, 1983; Shijin No Ie (House of The Poet), 1985; Tucker, 1988. *Recordings:* Albums: Look Sharp!, 1979; I'm The Man, 1979; Beat Crazy, 1980; Joe Jackson's Jumpin' Jive, 1981; Night and Day, 1982; Big World, 1986; Will Power, 1987; Live 1980/86, 1988; Blaze of Glory, 1988; Laughter and Lust, 1990; Steppin' Out – The Best of Joe Jackson, 1990; Night Music, 1994; Heaven and Hell, 1997; Symphony 1, 1999; Summer In The City, 2000; Night and Day II, 2001; Hit singles include: Is She Really Going Out With Him?, 1978; It's Different For Girls, 1980; Steppin' Out, 1982, 1996, 1998. *Honours:* Grammy Award, Pop Instrumental Album, Symphony 1, 2001. *Current Management:* C Winston Simone Management, 1790 Broadway, 10th Floor, New York, NY 10019, USA.

JACKSON, LaToya; b. 29 May 1956, Gary, Indiana, USA. Vocalist. *Career:* Began as backing vocalist for Jackson family; Turned solo artist, 1979; Backing vocals on Michael Jackson's Thriller album; Numerous TV appearances. *Recordings:* Singles: Bet'cha Gonna Need My Lovin'; Heart Don't Lie; Sexual Feel; Albums: LaToya Jackson, 1980; My Special Love, 1981; Heart Don't Lie, 1984; Imagination, 1986; LaToya, 1988; From Nashville to You, 1994; Be My Lover, 1995; Bad Girl, 1995; You're Gonna Get Rocked, 1995; Moulin Rouge, 2001.

JACKSON, Michael (Joseph); b. 29 Aug. 1958, Gary, IN, USA. m. (1) Lisa Marie Presley, divorced, (2) Debbie Rowe, divorced, 1 s., 1 d. *Career:* Lead singer, family singing group Jackson Five (later the Jacksons), 1969–75; Solo artiste, 1971–; Lengthy world tours, including Bad Tour, 1987; Dangerous World Tour, 1992; Film appearances: The Wiz, 1978; Captain Eo, 1986; Moonwalker, 1988; TV: The Jacksons, 1976; Guest voice, The Simpsons (as John Jay Smith), 1991; Founder, Heal The World Foundation (children's charity); Owner, ATV Music Company (including rights for John Lennon and Paul McCartney songs); Owner, MJJ record label; Hon. Dir, Exeter City Football Club, 2002–; Living With Michael Jackson (documentary, ITV1), 2003. *Compositions include:* Co-writer with Lionel Richie, We Are The World, USA For Africa famine relief single, 1985. *Recordings:* Albums: with Jackson Five/Jacksons include: Diana Ross Presents The Jackson Five, 1969; ABC, 1970; Third Album, 1970; Goin' Back To Indiana, 1971; Maybe Tomorrow, 1971; Looking Through The Windows, 1972; Farewell My Summer, 1973; Get It Together, 1973; Skywriter, 1973; Dancing Machine, 1974; Moving Violation, 1975; Joyful Jukebox, Music, 1976; The Jacksons, 1976; Goin' Places, 1977; Destiny, 1978; Triumph, 1980; Boogie, 1980; Live, 1981; Victory, 1984; Solo albums: Got To Be There, 1971; Ben, 1972; Music and Me, 1973; Forever Michael, 1975; The Best Of, 1975; The Wiz (film soundtrack), 1978; Off The Wall, 1979; ET – The Extra Terrestrial (film soundtrack), 1982; Thriller (No. 1 in every Western country), 1982; Bad (No. 1, UK and USA), 1987; Dangerous (No. 1, USA and UK), 1991; HIStory – Past, Present and Future Book I, 1995; Invincible, 2001; Hit singles with Jackson Five/Jacksons include: I Want You Back (No. 1, USA), 1969; ABC (No. 1, USA), 1970; The Love You Save (No. 1, USA), 1970; I'll Be There (No. 1, USA), 1970; Never Can Say Goodbye, 1971; Maybe Tomorrow, 1971; Looking Through The Windows, 1972; Doctor My Eyes, 1973; Dancing Machine, 1973; Enjoy Yourself, 1976; Show You The Way To Go, 1977; Blame It On The Boogie, 1978; Shake Your Body Down To The Ground, 1979; Lovely One, 1980; Can You Feel It?, 1981; Walk Right Now, 1981; State of Shock, 1984; Numerous solo hit singles include: Got To Be There, 1971; Rockin' Robin, 1972; Ain't No Sunshine, 1972; Ben (No. 1, USA), 1972; Don't Stop Till You Get Enough (No. 1, USA), 1979; Off The Wall, 1979; Rock With You (No. 1, USA), 1980; One Day In Your Life (No. 1, UK), 1981; She's Out of My Life, 1980; The Girl Is Mine, duet with Paul McCartney (No. 1, UK), 1982; Billie Jean (No. 1, USA and UK), 1983; Beat It (No. 1, USA), 1983; Wanna Be Startin' Somethin', 1983; Human Nature, 1983; Say Say Say, duet with Paul McCartney (No. 1, USA), 1983; Thriller, 1983; PYT, 1984; Farewell My Summer Love (recorded 1973), 1984; I Can't Stop Loving You, with Siedah Garrett (No. 1, UK and USA), 1987; Bad (No. 1, USA), 1987; The Way You Make Me Feel (No. 1, USA), 1988; The Man In the Mirror (No. 1, USA), 1988; Dirty Diana (No. 1, USA), 1988; Another Part of Me, 1988; Smooth Criminal, 1988; Leave Me Alone, 1989; Liberian Girl, 1989; Black and White (No. 1, UK and USA), 1991; Remember The Time, 1992; In The Closet, 1992; Jam, 1992; Heal The World, 1992; Give In To Me, 1992; Scream (with Janet Jackson), 1995; You Are Not Alone (No. 1, UK), 1995; Earth Song (No. 1, UK), 1995; They Don't Care About Us, 1996; Ghosts, 1997; Stranger in Moscow, 1997; Blood on the Dance Floor 1997 (No. 1, UK); You Rock My World, 2001; Cry, 2001. *Contributions to:* recordings by Minnie Ripperton; Carol Bayer Sager; Donna Summer; Paul McCartney. *Publications:* Moonwalk (autobiography), 1988; Dancing The Dream (poems and reflections), 1992. *Honours:* Numerous Grammy Awards, 1980– (including seven awards, 1984; Song of the Year, Legend Award, 1993); Numerous American Music Awards, 1980– (including 11 awards, 1984; Special Award of Achievement, 1989; Artist of the Century, 2002); BRIT Awards: Best International Artist, 1984, 1988, 1989; Artist of a Generation, 1996; Soul Train Awards, 1988–; MTV Video Vanguard Award, 1988; 2 NAACP Image Awards, 1988; Entertainer of the Decade, American Cinema Awards Foundation, 1990; First recipient, BMI Michael Jackson Award, 1990; 3 World Music Awards, 1993; Most successful album ever, Thriller (50m. copies sold world-wide); Star on Hollywood Walk of Fame, 1984; Numerous magazine poll wins and awards; Gold and Platinum records; won Artist of the

Century award at American Music Awards, 2002. *Current Management:* MJJ Productions, 10960 Wilshire Blvd, 2204 Los Angeles, CA 90024, USA.

JACKSON, Millie; b. 15 July 1944, Thompson, Georgia, USA. Vocalist. *Career:* Professional singer, 1964–; R&B singer, then Country singer; Collaborations with Isaac Hayes. *Recordings:* Ask Me What You Want; Hurts So Good, from film Cleopatra Jones; My Man A Sweet Man; Act of War, duet with Elton John; Albums: Millie Jackson, 1972; It Hurts So Good, 1973; Caught Up, 1974; Soul Believer, 1974; Still Caught Up, 1975; Best of Millie Jackson, 1976; Free and In Love, 1976; Lovingly Yours, 1977; Get It Out 'Cha System, 1978; A Moment's Pleasure, 1979; Live and Uncensored, 1980; For Men Only, 1980; Just A Lil' Bit Country, 1981; Live and Outrageous, 1982; Hard Times, 1982; ESP (Extra Sexual Persuasion), 1984; An Imitation of Love, 1986; The Tide Is Turning, 1988; Will You Love Me Tom, 1989; Back to the Shit, 1989; Young Man Older Woman, 1991; Check in the Mail, 1994; Love Quake, 1994; Rock N' Soul, 1994; It's Over, 1995; Breaking Up Somebody's Home, 1996; Did You Think I Wouldn't Cry, 1997; Not For Church Folk, 2001. *Current Management:* Keishval Enterprises, 133 Cedar Lane, Suite 208, Teaneck, NJ 07666, USA.

JACKSON, Ronald Shannon; b. 12 Jan. 1940, Fort Worth, Texas, USA. Jazz Musician; Bandleader. *Career:* Musician, Charles Mingus; Betty Carter; Albert Ayler; Ornette Coleman; Cecil Taylor; Bandleader, RSJ and The Decoding Society, 1979–; Musician with Bill Laswell, Bill Frisell, 1980–. *Recordings:* 12 albums with RSJ and The Decoding Society; Over 40 albums with other artistes. *Current Management:* World-wide Jazz, 1128 Broadway, Suite 425, New York, NY 10001, USA.

JACKSON, Steve; Sound Engineer; Mixer; *Recordings:* Dire Straits: Brothers in Arms; Money For Nothing; Wet Wet Wet, Holding Back the River; Bryan Adams, So Far So Good; Paul Young, Simply Red, Roachford, James Taylor Quartet, Tori Amos, Sting, Deacon Blue, Capercaillie, Cast, Whipping Boy, Mark Knopfler. *Honours:* Studio Master Award for Excellence for Homelands by Steve Booker, 1990. *Address:* 43 St Alban's Ave, London W4 5JS, England.

JACKSON, Stevie; b. 16 Jan. 1969. Vocalist; Musician (guitar); Songwriter. *Career:* Member: Belle and Sebastian, 1996–; Curated Bowlie Weekend Festival with other band members, 1999. *Recordings:* Albums: Tigermilk, If You're Feeling Sinister, 1996; The Boy With The Arab Strap 1998; Fold Your Hands Child – You Walk Like A Peasant, 2000; Storytelling, 2002. Singles: Dog On Wheels EP, Lazy Line Painter Jane EP, 3–6–9 Seconds of Light EP, 1997; This Is Just A Modern Rock Song EP, 1998; Legal Man, 2000; Jonathan David, I'm Waking Up To Us, 2001. *Honours:* BRIT Award, Best Newcomer, 1999. *Current Management:* Banchory Management, PO Box 25074, Glasgow G2 6YL, Scotland. *Website:* www.belleandsebastian.co.uk.

JACKSON, Stonewall; b. 6 Nov. 1932, Tabor City, North Carolina, USA. Country Vocalist; Musician (guitar). *Career:* Member of Grand Ole Opry, 1956; Worked with Ernest Tubb; Recording artiste, 1957–. *Compositions include:* Don't Be Angry, recorded by Daniel O'Donnell; I Washed My Face In Muddy Water; Stamp Out Loneliness. *Recordings:* Hit singles include: Life To Go, 1958; Waterloo (US Country No. 1), 1959; BJ The DJ (US Country No. 1), 1963; Me and You and A Dog Named Boo, 1971; Numerous albums include: The Dynamic Stonewall Jackson, 1959; Sadness In A Song, 1962; I Love A Song, 1963; Trouble and Me, 1965; The Exciting Stonewall Jackson, 1966; All's Fair In Love 'N' War, 1966; Help Stamp Out Loneliness, 1967; Stonewall Jackson Country, 1967; The Great Old Songs, 1968; Thoughts of a Lonely Man, 1968; Nothing Takes The Place of Loving You, 1968; I Pawned My Past Today, 1969; The Old Country Church, 1969; A Tribute To Hank Williams, 1969; The Real Thing, 1970; The Lonesome In Me, 1970; Stonewall Jackson Recorded Live At The Grand Ole Opry, 1971; Waterloo, 1971; Me and You and A Dog Named Boo, 1971; World of Stonewall Jackson, 1972; Nashville, 1974; Stonewall, 1979; My Favorite Sin, 1980; Stonewall Jackson, 1982; Solid Stonewall, 1982; Greatest Hits, 1982; Alive, 1984; Up Against The Wall, 1984; 20 Greatest Hits, 1994; All the Best, 1995; Classic Country, 1998; Stonewall Jackson, 1999. *Address:* c/o Ace Productions, PO Box 292725, Nashville, TN 37229–2725, USA.

JACKSON, Tito; b. 15 Oct. 1953, Gary, Indiana, USA. Vocalist. *Career:* Member, The Jackson 5; Signed to Motown Records, 1969; Numerous television appearances and concerts; Later became The Jacksons. *Recordings include:* Singles: I Want You Back (No. 1, USA), 1969; ABC (No. 1, USA), 1970; The Love You Save (No. 1, USA), 1970; I'll Be There (No. 1, USA), 1970; Rockin' Robin, 1972; Mama's Pearl, 1972; Never Can Say Goodbye, 1971; Looking Through The Windows, 1972; Doctor My Eyes, 1973; Dancing Machine, 1973; Enjoy Yourself, 1976; Show You The Way To Go (No. 1, UK), 1977; Blame It On The Boogie, 1978; Shake Your Body (Down to the Ground), 1979; Who's Lovin' You?; Heartbreak Hotel, 1980; Walk Right Now, 1981; Can You Feel It?, 1981; Nothin' That Compares 2 U, 1989; Albums: I Want You Back; Diana Ross Presents the Jackson 5; ABC; Goin' Back to Indiana; Maybe Tomorrow; Looking Through the Windows; Skywriter; Get It Together; Dancing Machine; Stand; Moving Violation; Joyful Jukebox Music; Motown

Special; Goin' Places; Destiny; Zip a Dee Doo Dah; Boogie; Live; Fliphits; Victory; 2300 Jackson Street; Children of the Light; Never Can Say Goodbye.

JACKSON, Trevor, (The Underdog); b. London, England. Prod; Remixer. *Career:* Producer: The Brotherhood; Remixed: Massive Attack, Sabres of Paradise, The Pharcyde; Member: Playgroup. *Recordings:* Albums: Elementalz (with The Brotherhood), 1996; Playgroup (with Playgroup), 2001; Singles: Alphabetical Response (with The Brotherhood), 1995; One Shot (with The Brotherhood), 1996; Punk Funk (with The Brotherhood), 1996; Make It Happen (with Playgroup), 2000; Number One (with Playgroup), 2001. *Current Management:* c/o Source Records, 113–117 Farringdon Rd, London EC1R 3BX, England.

JACKSON, Wanda Lavonne; b. 20 Oct. 1937, Maud, Oklahoma, USA. Vocalist; Songwriter. *Career:* Toured with Hank Thompson Band; Red Foley; Recording artiste, 1956–; Began recording Christian music, 1970s. *Compositions include:* Right Or Wrong (hit for Ronnie Dove, George Strait). *Recordings:* Albums include: Wanda Jackson, 1958; Rockin' With Wanda, 1960; There's A Party Goin' On, 1961; Right Or Wrong, 1961; Lovin' Country Style, 1962; Wonderful Wanda, 1962; Love Me Forever, 1963; Two Sides of Wanda Jackson, 1964; Blues in My Heart, 1964; Sings Country Songs, 1966; Reckless Love Affair, 1967; You'll Always Have My Love, 1967; The Best Of, 1967; Cream of The Crop, 1968; The Happy Side Of, 1969; Many Moods Of, 1969; Country!, 1970; Woman Lives For Love, 1970; I've Gotta Sing, 1971; I Wouldn't Want You Any Other Way, 1972; Praise The Lord, 1972; When It's Time To Fall In Love Again, 1973; Country Keepsakes, 1973; Now I Have Everything, 1974; Rock 'N' Roll Away Your Blues, 1984; Greatest Country Hits, 1985; Early Wanda Jackson, 1986; Rockin' In The Country, 1990; Ultimate Compilation, 1996; Tears Will Be the Chaser for Your Wine, 1997; Queen of Rockabilly, 2000; Singles include: I Gotta Know; Let's Have A Party; In The Middle of a Heartache. *Address:* c/o Wanda Jackson Enterprises, PO Box 891498, Oklahoma City, OK 73189–1498, USA.

JACOBI, Gina; b. 12 Dec. 1962, Hammerdal, Sweden. Composer; Vocalist; Musician (keyboards). 3 d. *Education:* Preschool Teacher, University, 2.5 years. *Career:* Director, 5 projects including music, singing, theatre, choirs with young people; Composed music for theatres, commercial videos; 3 bigger tours after release of albums; 5 videoclips to songs; Appearances in Swedish TV, 20 times; Appearances in Kurdish Satelite. *Recordings:* Bagateller, Trifles, album, 1985; Tid and Rum, Time and Space, album, 1986; Pa jakt efter solen, Haunting, album, 1988; Ga som pa natar, Walking as Upon, album, 1989; Gare Seretaye, The Kurdish Cassette, album, 1996; Alla ar, Everybody In, album, 1996. *Honours:* Best Female Artist, Swedish Grammis Galan. *Address:* Gränsz 28, 852 38 Sundsvall, Sweden.

JACOBS, Jon; Engineer; Mixer; *Recordings:* Engineered, Mixed, Produced: Tom Ribiero, album, 1990; The Slow Club, World of Wonders, album, 1990; Graham Parker, Burning Questions, album, 1992; Mary McLaughlin, Daughter of Lir, 1993; The Pretenders, 1992/93; Wendy James, singles, 1993; The Ya Ya's, See No Rain, single, 1993; Kenji Jammer, album mixed, 1993; Psychedelix, Psychadelix II, album mixed, 1993; Raw, 1993; Planet Claire, After the Fire, album mixed, 1993; Rynten Okazaki, album, 1994; Pacifists, album, 1994; Gota, album, 1995; Rynten Okazaki, album, soundtrack film, 1994; Psychedelix, 1995; Yuki Saito, album, 1995; Elio, Eat the Phikus, 1996; The Beatles, new singles, 1995–96; Elvis Costello, All This Useless Beauty, 1996; Paul McCartney: Flaming Pie, 1996; World Tonight, 1997; The Divine Comedy: Short Album about Love, 1997; Fin de Siecle, 1998; Certainty of chance, 1999; Secret History: Best of Divine Comedy, 1999. *Current Management:* Muirhead Management, 202 Fulham Rd, Chelsea, London SW10 9PJ, England.

JACOBS, Judith (Judy) Kaye; b. 27 Sept. 1957, Lumberton, North Carolina, USA. Vocalist. m. James Eric Tuttle, 24 July 1993. *Education:* BA, Christian Education, Minor in Music; Production and Arrangement, with Lari Goss, Lee College, Cleveland, Tennessee. *Career:* Trinity Broadcasting, PTL; Recording artiste for New Vision Records with radio airplay all over USA; Performed with Larnelle Harris; Carmen; Brooklyn Tabernacle Choir; Four Him; Major annual tours world-wide. *Recordings:* For Times Like These, 1993; Once and For All, 1995. *Honours:* Awarded Distinguished Music Performer, as special guest with Brooklyn Tabernacle Choir. *Current Management:* Jamie Tuttle, His Song Ministries. *Address:* His Song Ministries, Inc, 233 Broad St NW, PO Box 0891, Cleveland, TN 37364, USA.

JACOBS, Laurie; b. 16 April 1950, London, England. Jazz Promoter; Musician (saxophone). m. Ann Cummings, 12 Sept. 1974, 3 s. *Education:* Medical Graduate, Edinburgh University, 1974; Clarinet, saxophone, Leslie Evans. *Career:* Founded Peterborough Jazz Club, 1992; Monthly presentations, best in British and American Jazz; As musician, played Dean Street; Pizza Express; Pizza-On-The-Park; Appeared at Soho Jazz Festival. *Honours:* Peterborough City Leisure Award for Jazz Club, 1996. *Membership:* Musicians' Union. *Address:* 38 Church St, Werrington, Peterborough, Cambridgeshire PE4 6QE, England.

JACOBSEN, Bo; b. 13 March 1945, Copenhagen, Denmark. Musician (drums, alto saxophone); Vocalist. 1 s., 1 d. *Education:* Architecture studies, 1966–70. *Career:* Member, Blue Sun, 1969–75; Osiris (with Lone Kellermann); Nada, 1977–83; Paul Ehlers Quartet, 1985–88; Crescent, 1988–89; Dream City, 1991–98; Support tours with Jimi Hendrix; Procol Harum; Dollar Brand; Memphis Slim; Numerous festivals include: Roskilde Festival; Århus International Jazz Festival; Midtfyn Festival; Langeland Festival; Djurs Blues Festival; Started teaching in music schools, 1996; Playing with Flower Pot Party at major concerts and festivals across Denmark, 1996–98; Chairman of Musicians' Union, Grenaa Dep, 1998; Founded own band, Bo Jacobsen World Jazz Orchestra, 1999; Mem., blues soul band, Soulshape, 2002; Mem., orchestra, Dancing Moon, 2002; Founder, management co and record label, Beejaymusic, 2002. *Compositions:* Sagarmantha Suite, electro-acoustic music CD, 1994–97. *Recordings:* with Blue Sun: Peace Be Unto You, 1970; Festival, 1970; Blue Sun, 1971; Blue Sun 73, 1973; with Nada: Nada 1, 1978; Nada 2, 1979; African Flower, 1982; with Dream City: Do The Blues, 1993; Syre, with Dream City, CD, 1996; with Bo Jacobsen's World Jazz Conspiracy: Thank You For Your Tips, 2001. *Membership:* Danish Musicians' Union; DJFBA; KODA; Gramex; NCB; Chairman of Musicians' Union, 1998. *Current Management:* Beejaymusic. *Address:* Emmelev Kaervej 3, 8500 Grenaa, Denmark. *Telephone:* 86387515. *Fax:* 86387887. *E-mail:* beejay@vip.cybercity.dk. *Website:* www.beejaymusic.dk.

JACOBSEN, Sonia Michelle; b. 5 Feb. 1967, Camden, Australia. *Education:* Jazz Degree, The New School, Mannes, New York; Musicology Degree, Grenoble and Lyon University, France; Jazz Degree, Chambery Conservatory, France. *Career:* Co-Leader, Composer, Conductor, Mosaic Orchestra; Composer, Musical Director, No Strings Attached; Leader, Melting Pot. *Compositions:* Tryzone Suite; Melting Pot. *Recordings:* Avalanche, 1995; No Strings Attached, 1997. *Membership:* American Music Center. *Current Management:* Sun Sounds, PO Box 60, Cold Spring Harbor, NY 11724, USA. *Address:* 183 Harbor Rd, Colo Spring, Harbor, NY 11724, USA.

JACOBSSON, (Ruth) Ewa (Maria); b. 8 Dec. 1956, Uppsala, Sweden. Composer; Vocalist; Musician (piano). 2 s. *Education:* Konstfack, School of Arts and Handicraft (painting); Stockholm, Sweden; The Royal Academy of Fine Arts (Painting; Mixed Media, Performance); Copenhagen, Denmark; Classical piano, pianist Kerstin Åberg, Uppsala, Sweden; Classical song education, Uppsala, Sweden, Copenhagen, Denmark. *Career:* Emerald Song, 1985, Concert and television appearances, Stockholm, Sweden; Found Language, 1987, in collaboration with choreographer Jody Oberfelder-Riehm, New York, USA; Die Menschmaschine, in collaboration with composer Morten Carlsen and theatre group Exment, Copenhagen; Voix concert, 1989, Copenhagen; Delta concert and radio appearance, 1991–92, Copenhagen; Lingua concert, 1993, Copenhagen; Guldbukar concert, 1994, Copenhagen; Interferens, Danish Radio, 1997; Ways of Red, concert, 1998; Xfelt, exhibition, Museum of Contemporary Art, Roskilde, Denmark, 1998; Contemporary Lies I, exhibition, Eindhoven, Netherlands, 1998. *Compositions:* Voix, 1989 (tape, vocal, poem); Détour, 1990 (solo performance, vocal, tape, 8mm film, poem); Delta, choir, words by Martin Sondergaard, 1991–92; Lingua, 1993, (solo performance, tape, vocal, poem, photographic movement); Guldbukar (Golden Belly), 1994, (tape, colour-slides); Anonymous (solo performance, vocal, tape, photo and objects), 1996; LOGR (solo performance, vocal, tape, objects, waterfountain Gefjon), 1996; Kongehoved (choir, tape, photo, words by Jens Bjorneboe), 1996; Cold Dews (tape, poem), 1996; No Title (installation with tape, poem, objects, twin pictures), 1998; Ways of Red (solo performance, vocal, tape, objects), 1998; Contemporary Lies I (soundbook, tape, text, photo), 1998. *Membership:* DJBFA; DICEM (Danish section, International Confederation for Electroacoustic Music); SKRAEP, Experimental Music Forum for Composers. *Address:* Evens Gate 7, 0655 Oslo, Norway.

JACQUEMIN, André; b. 16 Jan. 1952, Hampstead, London, England. Composer; Sound Designer; Prod; Musician (bass player); Music Programmer. m. 24 Jan. 1988, 1 d. *Education:* Guitar course; APRS engineering course. *Career:* Joined recording industry aged 17 as studio runner and started engineering after 9 months to present date; Record producer for Monty Python and produced every Python project, 1972–; Live performances include: Tis-Was; Top of the Pops; Various venues in UK and live interviews for national TV. *Compositions include:* Co-writer: Every Sperm Is Sacred (Monty Python's Meaning of Life); The Brian Song (Monty Python's Life of Brian); Six songs for Wind In The Willows, feature film; Six songs for Mumbo Jumbo, feature film; Score for The Big Freeze, Eric Sykes feature film; Score for The Hound of the Baskervilles, feature film; A Christmas Adventure; Love Potion No. 9; Ezekiel; Rubbish King of the Jumble, network cartoon series; One Foot in the Grave; Plus many commercials and incidental music compositions. *Recordings:* include: Girlschool; Classix Nouveaux; Powerhouse; Geordie; Mungo Jerry. *Publications:* Future Music; Sound On Sound; Home Studio Recording; Pro Sound News; Sound Engineer and Producer; Sound International; Radio Month; Professional; International Musician. *Honours:* Over 80 awards for sound productions in film and television. *Membership:* Re-Pro Producers Guild of Great Britain. *Current Management:* Old Man Jobson's.

JAFET, Jean Marc; b. 8 May 1956, Nice, France. Musician (bass). *Education:* Conservatoire de Musique de Nice. *Career:* Played with: Didier Lockwood; Toots Thielmans; Christian Escoude; Christian Vander (Magma); Trio Ceccarelli; Richard Galliano; Own band Agora. *Recordings:* Dolores, Agora; 3 albums with Trio Ceccarelli; 3 albums with Kalil Chahine; Brazilian Witch, Christian Escoude. *Publications:* Dolores; Hat's Snatcher; L'Arcange. *Honours:* For Hat's Snatchers, Trio Ceccarelli, Victoires Music 1994. *Membership:* SACEM. *Current Management:* Marie Poindront. *Address:* 12 rue Seuignet, 94370 Sucy Enbrie, France.

JAFFE, Jerry; b. 12 Sept. 1946, New York, NY, USA. Artist Man. m. Celeste Kringer, 9 Oct. 1983. *Education:* PhD, Columbia University, New York, 1972. *Career:* Man.: Joey McIntyre; King Size; Ann Marie Montade; Jesus and Mary Chain; Catherine; Course of Empire; Nancy Boy; Saint Etienne; Co-man. with Chris Morrison: Dead Or Alive; Midge Ure; John Moore; US Head, Creation Records, 1992–94; Former Senior Vice-Pres. (Rock Division) and Vice-Pres. Promotion and A&R, Polygram Records, USA; Promotion; Press; Artiste development. *Address:* Management By Jaffe, 1560 Broadway, New York, NY 10036, USA.

JAGGER, Sir Mick (Michael Philip); b. 26 July 1943, Dartford, Kent, England. Vocalist; Songwriter. m. Bianca Pérez Morena de Macias, 1971 (divorced 1979), 1 d., (2) Jerry Hall, 2 s., 2 d.; 1 d. by Marsha Hunt. *Education:* London School of Economics. *Career:* Member, Rolling Stones, 1962–; Numerous tours, concerts include: National Jazz and Blues Festival, Richmond, 1963; Debut British tour, 1963; Debut US tour, 1964; Free concert, Hyde Park, 1969; Free concert, Altamont Speedway, 1969; Knebworth Festival, 1976; Live Aid, Philadelphia, 1985; Solo tour including Japan, 1988; Steel Wheels North American tour, 1989; National Music Day Celebration of The Blues, with Gary Moore, 1992; Voodoo Lounge World Tour, 1994–95; Bridges to Babylon Tour, 1997–98; Final world tour, 2002–03; Films include: Ned Kelly, 1970; Performance, 1970; Freejack, 1992; Bent, 1996. *Compositions:* Co-writer for the Rolling Stones, with Keith Richards (under the psuedonym The Glimmer Twins). *Recordings:* Albums: with The Rolling Stones: The Rolling Stones (No. 1, UK), 1964; The Rolling Stones No 2 (No. 1, UK), 1965; Out of Our Heads (No. 1, USA), 1965; Aftermath (No. 1, UK), 1966; Between The Buttons, 1967; Their Satanic Majesties Request, 1967; Beggar's Banquet, 1968; Let It Bleed (No. 1, UK), 1969; Get Yer Ya-Ya's Out (No. 1, UK), 1969; Sticky Fingers (No. 1, UK and USA), 1971; Exile On Main Street (No. 1, UK and USA), 1972; Goat's Head Soup (No. 1, UK and USA), 1973; It's Only Rock and Roll (No. 1, USA), 1974; Black and Blue (No. 1, USA), 1976; Some Girls (No. 1, USA), 1978; Emotional Rescue (No. 1, UK and USA), 1980; Tattoo You (No. 1, USA), 1981; Still Life, 1982; Undercover, 1983; Dirty Work, 1986; Steel Wheels, 1989; Flashpoint, 1991; Voodoo Lounge (No. 1, UK), 1994; Stripped, 1995; Bridges to Babylon, 1997; Forty Licks, 2002; Solo: She's The Boss, 1985; Primitive Cool, 1987; Wandering Spirit, 1993; Goddess In The Doorway, 2001. Singles include: with The Rolling Stones: Come On, 1963; I Wanna Be Your Man, 1963; Not Fade Away, 1964; It's All Over Now (No. 1, UK), 1964; Little Red Rooster (No. 1, UK), 1964; The Last Time (No. 1, UK), 1965; (I Can't Get No) Satisfaction (No. 1, UK and USA), 1965; Get Off of My Cloud (No. 1, UK and USA), 1965; 19th Nervous Breakdown, 1966; Paint It Black (No. 1, UK), 1966; Have You Seen Your Mother Baby, Standing In The Shadow, 1966; Let's Spend The Night Together/Ruby Tuesday (No. 1, USA), 1967; We Love You, 1967; Jumping Jack Flash (No. 1, UK), 1968; Honky Tonk Women (No. 1, UK and USA), 1969; Brown Sugar (No. 1, USA), 1971; Tumbling Dice, 1972; Angie (No. 1, USA), 1973; It's Only Rock N Roll, 1974; Fool To Cry, 1976; Miss You (No. 1, USA), 1978; Emotional Rescue, 1980; Start Me Up, 1981; Waiting On A Friend, 1981; Undercover of The Night, 1983; Harlem Shuffle, 1986; Mixed Emotions, 1989; Rock and A Hard Place, 1989; Highwire, 1991; Love Is Strong, 1994; Out of Tears, 1994; I Go Wild, 1995; Like A Rolling Stone, 1995; Solo: Memo From Turner, 1970; State of Shock, with The Jacksons, 1984; Just Another Night, 1985; Dancing In The Street, with David Bowie (No. 1, UK), 1985; Ruthless People, 1986; Let's Work, 1987; Sweet Thing, 1993. *Honours:* with Rolling Stones include: Grammy Lifetime Achievement Award, 1986; Inducted into Rock and Roll Hall of Fame, 1989; Q Award, Best Live Act, 1990; Ivor Novello Award, Outstanding Contribution To British Music, 1991; K.B.E., 2002. *Current Management:* Rupert Loewenstein, 2 King St, London SW1Y 6QL, England. *Website:* www.rollingstones.com.

JAKATTA. See: LEE, Dave.

JAM, Jimmy (James Harris); b. USA. Prod. *Career:* Joined Terry Lewis' band Flyte Tyme, 1972; Rejoined Flyte Tyme, renamed The Time, 1981–83; Formed (with Terry Lewis) Flyte Tyme Productions, 1982–; Built Flyte Tyme Studios, Minneapolis, 1984; Launched own label (with Terry Lewis), Perspective Records, 1991–; Helped launch new acts including Sounds of Blackness; Involved with International Association of African American Music (IAAAM), 1990–. *Recordings:* Producer (with Terry Lewis): Wild Girls, Klymaxx, 1983; Just Be Good To Me, SOS Band, 1983; Heat of The Heart, Patti Austin; Encore, Cheryl Lynn; I Didn't Mean To Turn You On, Cherelle; Saturday Love, Cherelle and Alexander O'Neal; Runaway, Janet Jackson; The Best Things In Life Are Free, Janet Jackson and Luther Vandross; Albums with Janet Jackson: Control; Rhythm Nation; Janet (all No. 1, USA); Other

recordings with: Mint Condition; Low Key; George Michael; Karyn White; Boyz II Men; Johnny Gill; Fine Young Cannibals; New Edition; Mariah Carey; Shaggy; Yolanda Adams; Chante Moore; Mary J Blige; The Human League; The Isley Brothers; Film soundtrack, Mo' Money. *Honours:* R&B Songwriting Awards, American Society of Composers and Publishers, 1989–94.

JAMAL, Ahmad; b. 2 July 1930, Pittsburg, Pennsylvania, USA. Musician (piano). Divorced, 1 d. *Education:* Private master classes with Mary Caldwell Dawson and James Miller. *Career:* George Hudson Orchestra, national tour, 1949; First group, The Four Strings, 1949; Accompanist to The Caldwells, 1950; Trio, The Three Strings, 1950–; Television: The Sound of Jazz, 1962; Many concert tours (including Philip Morris); Exclusive Steinway artiste, 1960s–; Appeared on film soundtracks: Mash, 1970; Bridges of Madison County, 1995. *Compositions:* Comissions: 6 works for Asai Quartet, Yale University, 1994; New Rhumba; Ahmad's Blues; Night Mist Blues; Extensions; The Awakening; Excerpts From The Blues; Tranquility; Manhattan Reflections. *Recordings:* Over 50 albums include: Poinciana; But Not For Me, (including Bridges of Madison County), 1995; Olympia, 2000. *Honours:* Man of the Year, Pittsburgh Jay Cee's, 1958; NEA American Jazz Master; Duke Ellington Fellow, Yale University; Pittsburgh Mellon Jazz Festival dedication, 1994; Django D'Or Award, Paris for Essence Part 1, 1996. *Current Management:* Ellora Management. *Address:* PO Box 295, Ashley Falls, MA 01222, USA.

JAMES, Alex (Stephen Alexander); b. 21 Nov. 1968, Bournemouth, Dorset, England. Musician (bass guitar). *Education:* Goldsmith's College; Violin lessons at school. *Career:* member, Blur; Television, radio, includes: Top of the Pops; Later With Jools Holland; Extensive tours include: Alexandra Palace; Reading Festival, 1993, 1999; Glastonbury Festival, 1994, 1998; Mile End, 1995; V97, 1997; All UK Arena's, 1997; Glastonbury, 1998; T In The Park, 1999; Reading/Leeds Festival, 1999. *Recordings:* Blur: Albums: Leisure, 1991; Modern Life Is Rubbish, 1993; Parklife, 1994; The Great Escape, 1995; Blur, 1997; 13, 1999; The Best of Blur, 2000; Singles: She's So High, 1990; There's No Other Way, 1991; Bang, 1991; Popscene, 1992; For Tomorrow, 1993; Chemical World, 1993; Sunday Sunday, 1993; Girls and Boys, 1994; To The End, 1994; Parklife, 1994; End of a Century, 1994; Country House (No. 1, UK), 1995; The Universal, 1995; Stereotypes, 1996; Charmless Man, 1996; Beetlebum (No. 1, UK), 1997; Song 2, 1997; On Your Own, 1997; MOR, 1997; Tender, 1999; Coffee and TV, 1999; No Distance Left To Run, 1999; Music Is My Radar, 2000; Solo recordings: Hanging Around, Me Me Me, 1996; Vindaloo, Fat Les, 1998; Naughty Christmas, Fat Les, 1998; Jerusalem, Fat Les, 2000. *Honours:* Platinum disc, for Parklife; BRIT Awards, Best Single, Video, Album, Band, 1995; Q Awards, Best Album, 1994, 1995; Q Awards, Best Band, 1999; Blur, Platinum, 1999; 13, Platinum, 1999. *Current Management:* CMO Management, Unit 32, Ransome Dock, 35–37 Parkgate Rd, London SW11 4NP, England.

JAMES, Duncan Mathew; b. 7 April 1979, Salisbury, Wiltshire, England. Vocalist. *Career:* Mem., UK band, Blue, 2001–; UK tour, 2002. *Recordings:* Albums: All Rise, 2001; One Love, 2002. Singles: All Rise, 2001; Too Close (No. 1, UK), 2001; If You Come Back (No. 1, UK), 2001; Fly By II, 2002; Sorry Seems To Be The Hardest Word, 2002. *Honours:* Multi-Platinum discs, for All Rise, 2001; Smash Hits Awards, Best Newcomer, 2001, Best Live Act, Best UK Band, 2002; Interactive Music Award, Artist of the Year, 2002; BRIT Award, Best British Newcomer, 2002. *Address:* c/o Virgin Records Ltd, 553–579 Harrow Rd, London W10 4RH, England. *Website:* www.officialblue.com.

JAMES, Etta, (Jamesetta Hawkins); b. 25 Jan. 1938, Los Angeles, USA. Vocalist. *Career:* Performed and recorded with Harvey Fuqua; Muscle Shoals (Chess Records houseband); Solo soul/R&B singer, 1961; Sang at opening ceremony, Los Angeles Olympics, 1988. *Recordings:* Albums: At Last!, 1961; Second Time Around, 1961; Etta James, 1962; Etta James Sings For Lovers, 1962; Etta James Top Ten, 1963; Etta James Rocks The House, 1964; Queen of Soul, 1965; Tell Mama, 1968; Etta James Sings Funk, 1970; Losers Weepers, 1971; Etta James, 1973; Peaches, 1973; Come A Little Closer, 1974; Etta Is Betta Than Evah!, 1978; Deep In The Night, 1978; Changes, 1980; Good Rockin' Mama, 1981; Chess Masters, 1981; Tuff Lover, 1983; R&B Queen, 1986; Blues In The Night, 1986; Late Show, 1986; Her Greatest Sides, Vol. I, 1987; R&B Dynamite, 1987; Chicago Golden Years, 1988; On Chess, 1988; Seven Year Itch, 1989; Stickin' To My Guns, 1990; The Right Time, 1992; Time After Time, 1995; Mystery Lady, 1995; I Just Wanna Make Love To You – The Best Of, 1996; Love's Been Rough on Me, 1997; Hickory Dickory Dock, 1998; The Heart of a Woman, 1999; Burnin' Down The House, 2002; Hit singles: All I Could Do Was Cry, 1960; At Last, 1961; I Just Wanna Make Love To You, 1961 (re-released in 1996); Stop The Wedding, 1962; Pushover, 1963; Security, 1967; Tell Mama/I'd Rather Go Blind, 1967; Good Rocking Daddy, 1981. *Current Management:* De Leon Artists, 4031 Panama Court, Piedmont, CA 94611, USA.

JAMES, Jessica; b. 1 Dec. 1981, Los Gatos, California, USA. Vocalist; Songwriter. *Career:* Signed to A&M Records, aged 13; Stage performances: Wizard of Oz; Annie; A Winter's Tale; Sang with local bands, performing with

Smokey Robinson, Rodney Dangerfield; Singer, own band, America's Most Wanted Band; Television appearances: Up All Night; Channel 11 Morning News; Arsenio Hall; Subject of documentary, BBC, England; Singer, National Anthem, major US sporting events and Democratic State Convention; Numerous charity functions; Featured soloist, Gospel Choir, First African Methodist Episcopalian Church, Los Angeles. *Membership:* Screen Actors' Guild. *Current Management:* Rick Frio. *Address:* 3050 N Chandelle Rd, Los Angeles, CA 90046, USA.

JAMES, Mo; b. 16 March 1951, Darlington, England. Vocalist; Musician (piano); Radio Prod; Presenter. m. Mike Jowett, 23 July 1983, 1 s., 1 d. *Education:* Northumbria Studio of Music. *Career:* Lead Singer: White Rabbit, 1968–70; Solo artiste; Numerous concert appearances, including Greenbelt Festival, Knebworth; Royal Gospel Gala, Albert Hall; Television appearances: Pebble Mill; TVAM; Rock Gospel Show; Leader, No James Soul Band, 1984–90; Solo artiste, 1990–; Producer, presenter, regular talk shows on BBC Radio (North). *Recordings:* Debut album: More Love, 1982, (with Joe English). *Publications:* Music reviewer, Crossrhythms magazine. *Membership:* Musicians' Union; Asscn of Christians in Local Broadcasting. *Current Management:* Stanley Joseph, ATS Ltd. *Address:* 26 St Michael's Rd, Headingley, Leeds LS6 3AW, England.

JAMES, Rick; b. 1 Feb. 1948, Buffalo, New York, USA. Performer; Prod. *Career:* Formed The Mynah Birds, with Neil Young, Bruce Palmer (Buffalo Springfield) and Goldy McJohn (Steppenwolf); Worked as Writer and Producer for Motown, with artistes including The Detroit Spinners and The Marvelettes; Protegés, The Mary Jane Girls. *Recordings:* Singles: Give It To Me Baby; Super Freak (sampled by MC Hammer for U Can't Touch This); Fire and Desire (with Teena Marie); Dance Wit' Me; Cold Blooded; 17; Glow; Albums: Come and Get It; Bustin' Out of L Seven; Fire It Up; Wild and Peaceful; Garden of Love; Street Songs; Reflections of Rick; You; Glow; Rick and Friends; Urban Rhapsody; 20th Century Masters, 2000.

JAMES, Ruby; b. 23 May 1957, Manchester, Jamaica. Vocalist. *Career:* Lead Singer, Stax; Recorded with Micky Most, Dick Lehy and other producers; Session singer – George Michael, Boy George, Erasure, Spandau Ballet, Blancmange, James Last Orchestra; Cabaret and Sessions; TV Concert; Live Aid with Spandau Ballet. *Recordings:* Locomotion with Ritz. *Membership:* Musicians' Union and Equity. *Current Management:* Stamina Management, 47 Prout Grove, London NW10 1PU, England.

JAMES, Sian; b. 24 Dec. 1961, Wales. Folk Vocalist; Songwriter. m. Gwyn Jones, 2 s. *Education:* BMus, Bangor University; Harp lessons, 11 years old; Piano lessons, 6 years old; Violin lessons, 8 years old. *Career:* Various tours around folk festivals in Brittany, Galicia, Spain, Italy, America, Canada, Japan, Ireland, Wales, England, Scotland, 1980–97; Appearances in stage shows for various theatre companies in Wales, 1987–94; Leading role in major film for S4C: Tylluan Wen (White Owl); Own series on S4C. *Recordings:* Cysgodion Karma (Shadows of Karma), 1990; Distaw (Silent), 1993; Gweini Tymor (Traditional album), 1996; Di-Gwsg (Sleepless), 1997; Birdman, BBC World-wide. *Membership:* Equity; PRS; MCPS; PAMRA. *Current Management:* Sain Records, Llandwrog, Caernarfon, Gwynedd, Wales.

JAMES, Sonny, (James Loden); b. 1 May 1929, Hackleburg, Alabama, USA. Country Musician (guitar, fiddle). *Career:* Recording artiste, 1953–; Film appearances: Second Fiddle To An Old Guitar; Nashville Rebel; Las Vegas Hillbillies; Hillbilly In A Haunted House. *Recordings:* 72 US Country chart hits; 23 US Country No. 1's include: You're The Only World I Know; Behind The Tear; Take Good Care of Her; The Minute You're Gone; A World of Our Own; I'll Never Find Another You; That's Why I Love You Like I Do; Only The Lonely; It's Just A Matter of Time; Running Bear; When The Snow Is On The Roses; Is It Wrong (For Loving You)?; Other hit singles include: That's Me Without You; She Done Give Her Heart To Me; For Rent; The Cat Came Back; Young Love; First Date, First Kiss, First Love; Numerous albums, 1957– include Young Love, 1962; Only the Lonely, 1969; Empty Arms, 1971; American Originals, 1989; Young Love: The Classic Hits, 1997; Sonny 1957, 2000; As producer: Paper Roses, Marie Osmond.

JAMES, Stafford Louis; b. 24 April 1946, Evanston, Illinois, USA. Musician (double bass, piano); Composer. m. Claudine Decouttère, 17 April 1992, 1 d. *Education:* Loop College, Chicago; Chicago Conservatory College; Mannes College of Music, New York. *Career:* Member, Ukrainian National Orchestra, Limberg, 1991; International Congress of Viola D'amore, Europansches Musik Festival, Stuttgart, 1988; WDR Radio, Köln, Germany, 1989, 1992, 1994–97; European tours with Stafford James Project (trio) and Stafford James Special Project (quartet), Netherlands; France; Luxembourg; Germany; Italy; Austria; Sicily; Spain; Switzerland; European tour with Stafford James Project, Autumn 2001, France, Austria, Belgium, Germany; Television: The Days and Nights of Molly Dodd, 1987; USIA tours: India, Syria, Sudan, Egypt, Morocco, 1984; Argentina, Peru, Chile, Uruguay, Mexico, 1986; Played with: Art Blakey and The Jazz Messengers; Betty Carter; Jimmy Heath; Pharoah Sanders; Woody Shaw; Dexter Gordon; Joe Williams; Mingus Dynasty; Randy Weston; The Gounawas (from Morocco); Teacher, double bass, UN International

School, New York, 5 years; New School of Social Research, New York, 2 years; Privately in Paris, France. *Compositions:* More than 150 pieces (many written for double bass as lead melodic voice) including: Les Pyrénées à la Mer; Sonatina (duet for viola d'Amore/contrabass); That's What Dreams Are Made Of; Ethiopia Suite; Bertha Baptist; Game; Teotiuacan; Sashianova; Nighthawk; Blues in The Pockets; Des Alpes aux Carpates; Conspectus; Changing World; Muguet; Rejuvenation; Sixth Sense; Kaleidoscope; Horizon; Us Together; Conscience, Mujiza; Meissa; Morning Dew; Metamorphosis; Bouncybernaughty. *Recordings:* Music Is The Healing Force of The Universe, Albert Ayler, 1969; Homecoming, Dexter Gordon, 1976; with Woody Shaw: Little Red's Fantasy Muse, 1975; For Sure, 1980; Night Music, 1980; United, 1980; Stafford James Ensemble. *Honours:* Grants from NEA, NYSCA; Gold Medal, Music, Karlstad, Sweden; Civitella Ranieri Foundation Fellowship, 1998. *Membership:* SACEM; BMI; BIMC; Thomastik-Infeld Sponsoree, 2000. *Current Management:* STAJA Music. *Address:* 6 Quai des Célestins, 75004 Paris, France. *E-mail:* staja.music@wanadoo.fr.

JAMES, Stephen; b. 6 Feb. 1956, New York, NY, USA. Composer; Musician (sarod, violin). m. Judith Papp, 11 April 1986. *Education:* North Indian Classical Music, 1973–83; Shri Vasant Rai, Pandit Ravi Shankar, 1983. *Career:* Boston MIT; Zakir Hussain and Sitara Devi; New York, Festival of India, Empire State Building; Asia Society and Columbia University; Shri Ram Center, North Delhi India; Franz Liszt Academy, Budapest; Zurich Hallenstadion; Frankfurt Messe Halle; Milan Pallazzrussardi; Appeared at festivals in: Hungary; Italy; France; Switzerland; Germany; Mumbai; Delhi Doordashan; Radio and television. *Recordings:* with Annindo Chatterjee: Raga; Tala; Makam; with Bill Laswell and Nicky Skopelitis: Axiom; with Bebo Baldan and David Torn: Earth Beat; Diving Into the World; Solo: Waiting For The Dawn, 2000. *Honours:* Bhartiya Vidya Bhavan, New York. *Membership:* Founder mem., Central Europe RIMPA (Ravi Shankar Institute For Music and Performing Arts). *Current Management:* Stress Management. *Address:* Sabrak ul. 3, 1141 Budapest, Hungary.

JAMES, Steve; b. 19 Feb. 1954, London, England. Record Prod. 3 s., 1 d. *Career:* Record Producer and engineer, various projects, several years; Early production work includes albums with Toyah; Later credits include soundtrack, The Rutles; Monty Python's The Life of Brian, featuring the single Always Look On The Bright Side of Life; Worked with Angel City, Mental As Anything, The Screaming Jets in Australia, 1988–93; Returned to UK, worked with: Paul Young; Kiki Dee; Peter Skellern; Way of Thorns. *Recordings include:* Numerous as producer, co-producer, engineer including: Albums: with Toyah: Sheep Farming In Barnet, 1979; Toyah Toyah Toyah, 1982; with Peter Skellern: Astaire, 1980; The Continental, 1981; Stardust Memories, 1994; with Neil Innes: Off The Record, 1981; with Ginger Baker: Nutters, 1983; with Mental As Anything: Cyclone Raymonde, 1989; with The Screaming Jets: All For One, 1990; Tear of Thought, 1991; with The Angels: Redback Fever, 1992; with Kiki Dee: Best of Kiki Dee, 1994; with Paul Young: Acoustic tracks, 1994; Live tracks, 1995; 2 tracks, animated version of Wind In The Willows, Kirsty MacColl and Tim Finn, 1995; Singles include: In The City, The Jam, 1979; Something Else, The Sex Pistols, 1979; Rock and Roll Music, Mental As Anything, 1988; Other recordings with: Shirley Bassey, 1976; Thin Lizzy, 1977; Pat Travers, 1977; Golden Earring, 1978; Ryan Douglas, 1993; Way of Thorns, 1995; The Rutles, LP, 1996; The Screaming Jets, album, 1997; The Teletubbies, LP, 1997; Oblivia and Cold Chisel, 1998; Weta and H-Block, 2000. *Membership:* Producers' Guild. *Current Management:* Clive Banks. *Address:* c/o Clive Banks Ltd, 1 Glenthorne Mews, 115a Glenthorne Rd, London W6 0LJ, England.

JAMES, (Walter) Kevin (Earl); b. 19 Aug. 1967, Greenville, Texas, USA. Country Vocalist; Songwriter. *Education:* Commerce, Texas A&M University; Private study. *Career:* Best Little Whorehouse in Texas, stage appearance; Ernest Tubb's Midnight Jamboree, Nashville, Tennessee; Mesquite Opry, stage; Oklahoma Opry, stage; Good Morning Texas, TV Show; Airplay US coast to coast and in parts of Europe; TNN appearances. *Compositions:* Late to Breakfast; Generation Tex; First Sight, Second Look; Jealous; Don't Answer That. *Recordings:* Wrapped in Hope, album; True Americans, single; Generations, album. *Membership:* BMI; Press Club of Dallas, IFCO. *Current Management:* CQK Records, Dallas, and Dick McVey Ent, Nashville. *Address:* 2402 Beverly Dr., Greenville, TX 75402, USA.

JAMISON, Jimi; b. 23 Aug. 1951, Durant, Mississippi, USA. Vocalist; Songwriter; Musician (guitar, piano). m. Deborah Teal, 1 May 1985, 1 s., 2 d. *Education:* University of Memphis, two years; High School Choir. *Career:* Lead singer, major tours with: Target, 1976; Cobra, 1979–82; Survivor, 1983–; Solo artiste, 1990–; Numerous television appearances include Solid Gold; MTV guest VJ; American Video Awards, 1986; Empires, 1999. *Compositions:* I'm A Fighter; Vital Signs; High On You; I Can't Hold Back; Is This Love; Burning Heart (Rocky IV soundtrack); Moment of Truth (Karate Kid soundtrack); In Good Faith; When Seconds Count; Rebel Son; The Search Is Over; Too Hot To Sleep; Man Against The World; Rock Hard; When Love Comes Down; Co-writer, I'm Always Here (Baywatch TV theme). *Recordings:* with Target (2 albums); with Cobra (1 album); with Survivor (6 albums) including: Vital Signs, 1984; When Seconds Count, 1986; Too Hot To Sleep, 1988; Lead singer on all tracks; Hit. *Recordings include:* Burning Heart, 1988; Lead singer on all tracks; Hit. *Recordings include:* Burning Heart,

Survivor, 1985; Solo albums: When Love Comes Down, 1991; Empires, 2000; Backing vocals for: ZZ Top; Jeff Healey; Fabulous Thunderbirds; George Thorogood; Colin James; Point Blank; Johnny Diesel; Krokus; De Garmo and Key; Joe Walsh; Gary Chapman; Ten Years After; Rick Vito; Michael Anderson; Empires, 1999. *Publications:* Burn Magazine, 1999; Metal Hammer, 1999. *Honours:* Voted in Top 10 Male Vocalists in World, Kasey Kasem Countdown; St Jude Special Olympics Award; Arkansas Governor's Award; Ohio Governor's Award; Tennessee Governor's Award; Numerous Gold and Platinum albums for Survivor, Rocky IV, ZZ Top, and Krokus. *Membership:* AFTRA; SAG; NARAS; Grammy Award Committee, 1992.

JAN, Hajnal; b. 11 Dec. 1943, Kojice, Slovakia. m. Maria Hajnalova, 14 Dec. 1968, 1 d. *Education:* Piano, Classical Music Degree, Elementary Music School, 10 years; Konzervatorium in Kojice, Piano and Double Bass; Some lessons from best Slovak Composers. *Career:* Several own TV programmes as a Pianist; Numerous recordings in Slovak Radio as a Pianist, Composer, Arranger, Leader, Jazz and higher popular music; Participant of jazz festivals in Europe; Solo performance and small groups – jazz music; Piano Entertainer performance in America, Asia, Europe; Solo piano and 2 pianos perfomances (jazz) on classic music festival in Kojice, 1995. *Compositions:* Monk's Tatran Dream, 1994; Mosebacke, Early Morning, Geneiro, Home made Blues, many others. *Recordings:* Slovak Jazz Mainstream, CD, 1994; Samplers from Slovak Jazz Days with Slovak Jazz Quintet. *Publications:* Recorded in main Czechoslovak Lexikon of Popular Music, 1982–. *Honours:* First Prize, Frame of the Year, Slovak Music 1996 Competition for Composition: Monk Tatran Dream. *Membership:* Slovak Jazz Society; Slovak Music Fond. *Current Management:* Slovak Music Fond Bratislava.

JANDA, Dalibor; b. 21 March 1953, Hranice Na Morave, Czech Republic. Vocalist; Songwriter; Musician. m. Jirina Jandova, 3 April 1981, 1 s., 1 d. *Education:* Classical Music Degree, 4 year Guitar Studium. *Career:* Singer in various rock bands, 1969–79; First recording in radio, 1979; Professional Singer, 1981; First single, 1983; First LP, named Hurricane, 1985; Second LP, MC KDE JSI (Where Are You?), 1987; Third album, 1988. *Compositions:* Ten Fingers for Living; Take Them to Mars, 1988; Dalbiro Janda and Prototype, 1989. *Recordings:* Jen Ty Samotna A Ja (Only You and Me), 1989; Povidant Spisnickami (Talking with Singing), 1990; Cose Ma'stat (What Was Happened), 1992. *Publications:* Zlaty Vyber, Gold Best, 1994; Vlasce Nejsou Maty (There is no Maps in Cove), 1995; Krasne Silena (Pretty Crazy), 1996. *Honours:* Gold Decin Pop Festival, 1985; Gold Nightingale, 1986, 1987, 1988; Six gold albums, one platinum album. *Current Management:* Hurricane Records. *Address:* c/o Hurricane Records, Kamenicka 39/303, 170 00 Prague 7, Czech Republic.

JANDA, Petr; b. 2 May 1942, Prague, Czech Republic. Composer; Musician (guitar); Vocalist. m. (1) Jana, 7 Sept. 1966; (2) Martina, 7 March 1992, 1 s., 2 d. *Education:* University degree; Conservatory Jaroslava Jezka, Prague; Conservatory Jaroslava, Jezka, Prague (composition). *Career:* Leader, famous rock group, Olympic, 32 years, 6 Gold Records. *Recordings:* Albums: Zelva; Ptak Rosom'k; Prazdniny Na Zemi; Ulice; Jasna Zprava; Okno Me Lasky. *Publications:* Encyklpedie Ceske Hydby. *Honours:* Grammy (Olympic), 1993. *Membership:* OSA. *Current Management:* Best IA, Pristavni 31, 17000 Prague 7, Czech Republic.

JANIS, Conrad; b. 11 Feb. 1938, New York, NY, USA. Jazz Musician (trombone); Actor; Film Dir. m. Maria Grimm, 30 Nov. 1987. *Education:* Private tuition, trombone, piano, violin. *Career:* As actor: Film credits include: Airport '75; Buddy Holly Story, 1977; The Duchess and The Dirtwater Fox, 1976; Mr Saturday Night, 1992; The Feminine Touch, 1995; Television series include: Mork and Mindy; Quark; St Elsewhere; I Bonino; Over 350 starring roles include: Murder She Wrote; Golden Girls; Kojak; Happy Days; Laverne and Shirley; Talk show appearances include: 25 Tonight Shows, with Johnny Carson; 12 times, Mike Douglas; Dinah Shore; Several TV specials; As Jazz musician: Bandleader, Beverly Hills Unlisted Jazz Band; Tailgate Jazz Band; TV Specials: Jerry Lee Lewis Telethon; Bert Convey Special; American Jukebox Special; This Joint Is Jumping; That's A Plenty; Don Lane Show; Concerts include: New York Town Hall, 1962; Phil Academy of Music, 1955; Carnegie Hall, 1981; Monterey Festival, 1983–87; Victoria BC Terrivic Festival, 1989–93; LA Classic Jazz Festival, 1984–95; Worked with: Roy Eldridge; Henry Red Allen; Wild Bill Davison; Yank Lawson; Claude Hopkins; Coleman Hawkins; Panama Francis; Hot Lips Page; Herbie Hancock; Jimmy McPartland. *Recordings:* CJ and The Talegate Jazz Band, 1950–58; Jammin' At Rudi's, 1953; with Tony Parenti: A Night At Jimmy Ryan's, 1972; with Conrad Janis and The Beverly Hills Unlisted Jazz Band: Way Down Yonder In Beverly Hills, 1986; America, 1987; This Joint Is Jumpin', with Jack Lemmon, Bea Arthur, Dudley Moore, 1989; with Tom Kubis: At Last, 1992. *Current Management:* Maria Janis. *Address:* 1920 S Beverly Glen, Suite 306, Los Angeles, CA 90025, USA.

JANKE, Daniel Jacob; b. 8 Sept. 1957, Edmonton, Alberta, Canada. Composer; Piano; Kora. m. Susan Alton, 31 Aug. 1993, 2 s., 1 d. *Education:* MA, Ethnomusicology. *Career:* CBC Radio, Two New Hours; BBC, Kaleidoscope and Mixing It; Radio France, La Muse En Circuit. *Compositions:* Commission, Music Canada 2000, 1999. *Recordings:* Debut, 1984; Big Dance,

1989; In A Room, 1997; Not Too Dark, Longest Night Orchestra, 1999. *Honours:* Canada Council B Grant. *Membership:* Canadian Music Centre, Associate Composer. *Current Management:* David Petkovich. *Address:* PO Box 5381, Whitehorse, Yukon Y1A 4Z2, Canada.

JANNAH, Denise; b. 11 May 1956, Paramaribo, Suriname. Vocalist; Songwriter; Voice Teacher. *Education:* Law Studies, University of Utrecht, Netherlands; Degree, Jazz Dept, Conservatory of Hilversum, Netherlands; Teaching degree. *Career:* Performed with Carnegie Hall Jazz Orchestra, Dutch Jazz Orchestra, The Rosenberg Trio, Jon Hendricks, Willem Brekker Collective, Dutch Metropole Orchestra; Own Band: Denise Jannah Quintet; Musicals: A Night at the Cotton Club, 1989–90; Joe, The Musical, 1997–98; Musical Show: Ain't Misbehaving, 1998–99; Vocal Director, Theatre Plays, 1987–99; International TV: EBU Jazz Night (16 European Countries, 1994); Bet on Jazz (USA, 1996); Opening Act for Wynton Marsalis (Barbados, January 2000); Perfomance for Queen Beatrix of Holland and the President of USA, Bill Clinton and his First Lady, Hilary Clinton; Top of European Union, International Concerts, Festivals and Tours; Teacher at conservatories of Rotterdam and Utrecht, Netherlands. *Compositions:* Alone, Never Lonely, 1995; I'll Always be Here, 1996; Your Eyes, 1996; Never Meant to Be, 1996; Different Colours, One Rainbow, 1997; If Only, 1999; Wide Awake, 1999; The Madness of Our Love, 1999. *Recordings:* All Solo Albums: Take It From the Top, 1991; A Heart Full of Music, 1993; I Was Born in Love With You, 1995; Different Colours, 1996; The Madness of Our Love, 1999; International TV: Hallo 2000, (50 countries world-wide), 1999. *Publications:* Film Documentary: Jannah, New Lady in Jazz, 1996. *Honours:* DDR: Lieder Festival, Menschen und Meer, 1989; Third Prize, International Golden Orpheus Festival, Bulgaria 1992; First Prize, Dutch Edison Award for Album, A Heart Full of Music. *Current Management:* Management for Europe, International Music Holland, Sloterweg 1254, 1066 CW Amsterdam, Netherlands. *Address:* I B Bakker-Laan 29, 3582 VE Utrecht, Netherlands.

JANOW, Steven; b. 12 July 1973, Rhinebeck, New York, USA. Composer; Musician (Saxophone). *Education:* Liberal Arts, State University of New York; Studies at North Carolina School of the Arts; Bachelor of Music, University of Hartford. *Career:* Performances in New York City, upstate New York. *Compositions:* Piano Sonata; New Blues or Ojan; Symphony; Symphony No. 2, for Saxophone Orchestra; Manifesto on Music; Untitled music for brass and saxophone band; Flight of the Dragon, Jazz/metal fusion; Various jazz and serious compositions. *Honours:* ASCAP Awards, 1998, 1999, 2000, 2001, 2002, 2003; Hon. mem., CRS Artists. *Membership:* ASCAP. *Address:* 69 Chestnut St, Rhinebeck, NY 12572, USA.

JANS-BROWN, Andrew Michael; b. 8 May 1970, Victoria, Australia. Vocalist; Musician (guitar); Songwriter; Poet. *Education:* Studied acting at National Institute of Dramatic Arts; Studied opera with Maggie Norman; Jazz theory at Sydney Conservatorium of Music; Musical theatre with Andrew Ross and Terrence Clark whilst at NIDA. *Career:* Vocalist with band Iris; Various minor roles in film, TV and theatre. *Compositions:* Seek Beauty; Autumn; This Is Eden. *Recordings:* Distance 'Till Empty (EP), 2000; You Got Me Thinking, 2001. *Address:* PO Box 3/41, Gould St, Bondi Beach, Sydney 2026, Australia. *E-mail:* kofad@hotmail.com. *Website:* www.irisdaband.com.

JANSCH, Bert; b. 3 Nov. 1943, Glasgow, Scotland. Vocalist; Musician. *Career:* Folk musician; Founder member, folk group, Pentangle, 1967–72; 1982–; Also solo artiste. *Recordings:* Solo albums: Bert Jansch, 1965; It Don't Bother Me, 1965; Jack Orion, 1966; Bert and John (with John Renbourn), 1966; Nicola, 1967; Birthday Blues, 1968; Lucky Thirteen, 1969; Stepping Stones (with John Renbourn), 1969; Rosemary Lane, 1971; Moonshine, 1973; LA Turnaround, 1974; Santa Barbara Honeymoon, 1975; A Rare Conundrum, 1978; Avocet, 1979; Thirteen Down, 1980; Heartbreak, 1982; From The Outside, 1985; Leather Laundrette, 1988; Bert Jansch and Jack Orion, 1993; When The Circus Comes To Town, 1995; Crimson Moon, 2000; Live In Australia, 2001; Edge Of A Dream, 2002; Various compilations; with Pentangle: The Pentangle, 1968; Sweet Child, 1968; Basket of Light, 1969; Cruel Sister, 1970; Reflections, 1971; History Book, 1971; Solomon's Seal, 1972; Open The Door, 1982; Pentangling, 1973; The Pentangle Collection, 1975; Anthology, 1978; The Essential Pentangle Vol. 1, 1987; The Essential Pentangle Vol. 2, 1987; In The Round, 1988; So Early In The Spring, 1989; One More Road, 1993; People On The Highway 1968–71, 1993. *Current Management:* Folklore Inc, 1671 Appian Way, Santa Monica, CA 90401, USA.

JANSEN, Steve, (Stephen Batt); b. 1 Dec. 1959. Musician (drums). *Career:* Member, Japan, 1977–83; The Dolphin Brothers (with Richard Barbieri), 1987; Rain Tree Crow (with 3 members of Japan), 1991; Tours include: British tour supporting Blue Oyster Cult, 1978; Backing musician to No-Man, British tour, 1991; Abstract Day tour of Japan with Jansen, Barbieri and Karn, 1997; Mick Karn Bestial Cluster Tour, Europe, 1994; Yukhiro Takahashi tours of Japan, 1985, 1986, 1998. *Recordings:* Albums with Japan: Adolescent Sex, 1978; Obscure Alternatives, 1978; Life In Tokyo, 1979; Quiet Life, 1980; Gentlemen Take Polaroids, 1980; Assemblage, 1981; Tin Drum, 1982; Japan, 1982; Oil On Canvas, 1983; Exorcising Ghosts, 1984; with David Sylvian: Brilliant Trees, 1984; Gone to Earth, 1986; Secrets of the Beehive, 1987; Dead Bees on a Cake, 1999; with The Dolphin Brothers: Catch The Fall,

1987; with Rain Tree Crow: Rain Tree Crow, 1991; with Richard Barbieri: Stories Across Borders, 1991; Stone To Flesh, 1995; Other Worlds in a Small Room, 1996; with Richard Barbieri and Mick Karn: Beginning to Melt, 1994; Seal, 1994; with Richard Barbieri and N Takemura: Changing Hands, 1997; with Yukikieu Takahashi: Pulse, 1997; Ism, 1999; Kinoapparatom, 2001; Singles: with Japan: The Art of Parties, 1981; Quiet Life, 1981; Visions of China, 1981; Ghosts, 1982; Cantonese Boy, 1982; Life In Tokyo, 1982; Night Porter, 1982; Canton, 1983. *Address:* c/o Medium Productions, 74 St Lawrence Rd, Upminster, Essex RM14 2UW, England.

JARDINE, Al; b. 3 Sept. 1942, Lima, Ohio, USA. Musician (guitar); Vocalist. *Career:* Member, the Beach Boys, 1961–62; 1963–; Numerous tours and concerts include: Beach Boys Summer Spectacular, Hollywood Bowl, 1966; London Palladium, 1968; Big Sur Folk Festival, Monterey, 1970; Carnegie Hall, 1971; Royal Festival Hall, London, 1972; Wembley Stadium, 1975, 1980; Knebworth Festival, 1990; Independence Day concert, Washington DC, 1980; Live Aid, Philadelphia, 1985. *Recordings:* Albums: Surfer Girl, 1963; Little Deuce Coupe, 1963; Shut Down Vol. 2, 1964; All Summer Long, 1964; The Beach Boys Concert, 1964; The Beach Boys Christmas Album, 1964; The Beach Boys Today, 1965; Summer Days (and Summer Nights), 1965; Surfin' USA, 1965; Beach Boys Party, 1966; Pet Sounds, 1966; The Beach Boys Today, 1966; Smiley Smile, 1967; Wild Honey, 1968; Friends, 1968; Close-Up, 1969; Greatest Hits, 1970; Surf's Up, 1971; Carl and The Passions/So Tough, 1972; Holland, 1973; The Beach Boys In Concert, 1974; Endless Summer (No. 1, USA), 1974; Spirit of America, 1975; Good Vibrations – Best Of..., 1975; 15 Big Ones, 1976; The Beach Boys Love You, 1977; LA (Light Album), 1979; Ten Years of Harmony (1970–80), 1982; The Very Best Of..., 1983; The Beach Boys (with Stevie Wonder), 1985; Made In The USA, 1986; Still Cruisin', 1989; Summer Dreams, 1990; Summer In Paradise, 1992; Good Vibrations, 1993; Stars and Stripes Vol. 1, 1996; Ultimate Christmas, 1998; Greatest Hits, Vol. 2, 1999; Singles include: Surfin' USA, 1963; Surfer Girl, 1963; Little Deuce Coupe, 1963; Fun Fun Fun, 1964; I Get Around (No. 1, USA), 1964; When I Grow Up (To Be A Man), 1964; Dance Dance Dance, 1965; Help Me Rhonda (No. 1, USA), 1965; California Girls, 1965; The Little Girl I Once Knew, 1965; Barbara Ann, 1965; Sloop John B, 1966; God Only Knows/ Wouldn't It Be Nice, 1966; Good Vibrations (No. 1, UK and USA), 1966; Heroes and Villains, 1967; Wild Honey, 1967; Darlin', 1968; Do It Again (No. 1, UK), 1968; I Can Hear Music, 1969; Breakaway, 1969; Cottonfields, 1970; Sail On Sailor, 1973; Rock and Roll Music, 1976; Here Comes The Night, 1979; Lady Lynda, 1979; Getcha Back, 1985; Kokomo (No. 1, USA), 1988; Fun Fun Fun, collaboration with Status Quo, 1996. *Honours:* Inducted into Rock and Roll Hall of Fame, 1988; Special Award of Merit, American Music Awards, 1988. *Current Management:* Elliott Lott, 4860 San Jacinto Circle W, Fallbrook, CA 92026, USA.

JARLETT, Dee; b. 28 Oct. 1951, Manchester, England. Vocalist; Voice Arranger. m. (1) John Jarlett, 9 Oct. 1977, divorced 1997, 2 s., 1 d., (2) Scott Wood, 1997. *Education:* DipEd, Teaching Music; RSA Diploma, Teaching Adults. *Career:* Member, folk duo Orion, 1983–98; British tours of folk clubs; Numerous local radio appearances; Played film music for Rosie The Great, HTV; Member, Sweet Soul Sisters, 1987–99; Radio appearances: Start The Week, BBC Radio 4; Woman's Hour, BBC Radio 4; BBC Radio 2 arts programme, local radio and HTV; Member, Naked Voices, Edinburgh Fringe, 1997, 2001, 2002. *Recordings:* with Orion: Jack Orion, 1987; Chicken Soup, 1989; with Sweet Soul Sisters: Live and Lovin' It, 1990; Freshly Squeezed, 1995; Chemistry; with Naked Voices: Uncovered; Chambers St Gasworks Choir 1–7. *Honours:* Pick of the Fringe, Edinburgh Fringe Festival; Gilded Balloon. *Address:* 27 Narroways Rd, St Werburghs, Bristol BS2 9XB, England. *Telephone:* (117) 941-1440. *Fax:* (117) 902-5680. *E-mail:* deejarlett@blueyonder.co.uk. *Website:* www.naked-voices.co.uk; www.gasworkschoir.freeuk.com.

JARRE, Jean-Michel; b. 24 Aug. 1948, Lyons, France. Musician (synthesizers, keyboards); Composer; Record Prod. m. Charlotte Rampling, 1977. *Education:* Piano and guitar from age 5; Conservatoire de Paris, with Jeanine Reuff. *Career:* Solo debut, Paris Opera, 1971; Youngest composer to appear, Palais Garnier, 1971; Major concerts, often including lasers and fireworks, filmed for video releases include: Beijing, People's Republic of China, 1981; Bastille Day, Place De La Concorde, 1979; Houston, Texas (1.3m. audience), 1986; London Docklands, 1988; La Defense, Paris (2.5m. audience), 1990; Sun City, Johannesburg, South Africa, 1993; Member of jury, First International Visual Music Awards, Midem, France, 1992. *Compositions* include: Oxygène Part IV, used for several television themes; Ballet and film scores include: Des Garçons Et Des Filles, 1968; Deserted Palace, 1972; Les Granges Brûlées, 1973; La Maladie De Hambourg, 1978; Gallipoli, 1979. *Recordings:* Albums (all self-composed and produced): Deserted Palace, 1971; Oxygène, 1977; Magnetic Fields, 1981; The Concerts In China, 1982; The Essential Jean-Michel Jarre, 1983; Zoolook, 1984; Rendez-Vous, 1986; In Concert Lyons/Houston, 1987; Revelations (No. 2, UK), 1988; Jarre Live, 1989; Waiting For Cousteau, 1990; Images – The Best of Jean-Michel Jarre, 1991; Chronologie, 1993; Jarre Hong Kong, 1994; Cities in Concert, 1997; China Concert, 1999; Metamorphoses, 2000. *Honours:* Grand Prix, Academie Du Disque, Zoolook, 1985; First Western artiste to play in People's Republic of

China, 1981; Numerous Platinum and Gold discs world-wide. *Address:* c/o Dreyfus Records, 26 Ave Kléber, 75116 Paris, France.

JARRE, Maurice Alexis; b. 13 Sept. 1924, Lyons, France. Composer. m. (1) France Pejot, 1946, 1 s., (2) Dany Saval, 1965, 1 d., (3) Laura Devon, 1967, (4) Khong Fui Fong, 1984. *Education:* Conservatoire National Supéreur de Musique. *Career:* Musician, Radiodiffusion Française, 1946–50; Director of Music, Théâtre National Populaire (TNP), 1950–63. *Compositions:* Symphonic music; Music for theatre and ballet include: Roland Petit's Notre-Dame de Paris (Paris Opera), 1966; Numerous film scores include: Lawrence of Arabia, 1963; Dr Zhivago, 1965; Ryan's Daughter, 1970; Shogun, 1980; Doctors In Love, 1982; A Passage To India, 1985; The Mosquito Coast, 1987; Tai-Pan, 1987; Gaby, 1988; Gorillas In The Mist, 1989; Ghost; Dead Poets Society, 1990; Fatal Attraction, 2002. *Honours:* Officer, Légion d'Honneur, Commander des Arts et Lettres; Prix Italia, 1955, 1962; Grand Prix du Disque, Academy Charles Cros, 1962; Hollywood Golden Globe, 1965, 1984; People's Choice Award, 1988. *Current Management:* Blue Focus Management, 15233 Ventura Blvd, Suite 200, Sherman Oakes, CA 91403, USA. *Address:* c/o Paul Kohner Inc, 9169 Sunset Blvd, Los Angeles, CA 90069, USA.

JARREAU, Al; b. 12 March 1940, Milwaukee, USA. Vocalist. *Education:* BS Psychology, Ripon College, 1962; MS Psychology, University of Iowa, 1964. *Career:* Solo artiste, 1975–. *Recordings:* Solo albums: We Got By, 1975; Glow, 1976; Look To The Rainbow Live, 1977; All Fly Home, 1978; This Time, 1980; Breaking Away, 1981; Jarreau, 1983; High Crime, 1984; Al Jarreau Live in London, 1985; L Is For Lover, 1986; Heart's Horizon, 1988; Heaven and Earth, 1992; Tenderness, 1994; Best of Al Jarreau, 1996; Tomorrow Today, 2000; Also appeared on: I Heard That!, Quincy Jones, 1976; The Love Connection, Freddie Hubbard, 1980; Friends, Larry Carlton, 1983; Two Eyes, Brenda Russell, 1983; Back On The Block, Quincy Jones, 1989. *Honours:* Grammy Awards: Best Jazz Vocal, Look To The Rainbow, 1977; All Fly Home, 1978; Best Pop Vocal, Breakin' Away, 1981; Best Jazz Vocal, Breakin' Away, 1981; Best R&B Vocal, Male, Heaven and Earth, 1992; Downbeat Reader's Poll Winner, 1977–79. *Current Management:* Bill Darlington, 1103 11th St, Santa Monica, CA 90403, USA.

JARRETT, Anita; b. 8 Aug. 1964, London, England. Vocalist; Songwriter. 1 s., 1 d. *Career:* Television and radio performances Europe; Yo Yo Honey, 1990–92; Solo mini tour, Jamaica, 1993. *Recordings:* with Yo Yo Honey: Voodoo soul album; Angel; Ghetto Blues; Rolling Stones remix: You Got Me Rocking, 1994; with Pressure Drop: Elusive, 1997; Vocal, Oakenfold Project. *Publications:* Still Waiting and Persevering to Achieve and Reach the So Called Perfection of Expression Via the Medium of Music. *Membership:* Musicians' Union. *Current Management:* Trenton, NUR Entertainment. *Address:* Camelot Studios, Unit 218A, 222 Kensal Rd, London W10 5N, England.

JARRETT, Keith; b. 8 May 1945, Allentown, PA, USA. Musician (piano); Composer. *Career:* First solo concert, age 7, followed by professional appearances; Solo concert, own compositions, 1962; Led own trio, Boston; Worked with: Roland Kirk, Tony Scott; Joined Art Blakey, 1965; Tours, Europe, with Charles Lloyd, 1966; with Miles Davis, 1970–71; Soloist, leader, own groups, 1969–. *Recordings:* Albums: Personal Mountains, 1974; Luminessence, 1974; Mysteries, 1975; Changeless, 1987; At The Blue Note— The Complete Recordings, 1994; La Scala (live), 1995; Tokyo '96 (live), 1998; The Melody At Night With You, 1999; Whisper Not, 2000; Inside Out, 2001; Always Let Me Go, 2002; Selected Recordings, 2002. *Honours:* Polar Music Prize, Royal Swedish Acad. of Music, 2003. *Address:* c/o Don Lucoff, D. L. Media, 270 Park Ave S, Suite 5C, New York, NY 10010, USA.

JARVIS, Jane; b. 31 Oct. 1915, Vincennes, Indiana, USA. Musician (piano, organ); Composer; Lyricist. 1 s., 2 d. *Education:* Bachelor Pace University, New York City, New York; Scholarships to Bush Conservatory; Chicago Conservatory; De Paul School of Music. *Career:* Staff Pianist, WJKS; Featured in High School musicals with Karl Maldin and Red Skelton; Staff musician, WJMJ, Milwaukee and WOC Davenport; Rehearsal Pianist, NBC, New York; Vice-President, Muzak Corporation; Lecturer, Yale University; Performed with Clark Terry; Lionel Hampton; Chosen by Smithsonian Institute for Jazz Archives. *Compositions:* Over 300 original compositions. *Recordings:* Organ Magic; Cut Glass; LA Jazz Quartet; To Duke; Back To Basics; Statesmen of Jazz; Two-Time (musical). *Publications:* Various profiles of fellow musicians. *Honours:* Governor Kentucky for song; Governor Indiana; Made Sagamare Indian Chief; Jane Jarvis Jazz Festival, Tampa, Florida, in her honour. *Membership:* ASCAP; NARAS, former Governor.

JARVIS, Toby J; b. 8 May 1965, London, England. Composer; Musician (piano, percussion, samplers, guitar, synthesizers). *Career:* Arranger, music for films and television; Composed music for television themes and shows, UK, USA; Composed music for over 4000 television commercials world-wide; Wrote, recorded songs for: Maxine Harvey; Hunter (The Gladiators); Georgia Lewis. *Compositions:* Numerous dance and club hits including Twink Goes Disco and Goin' Outa My Head. *Recordings:* Loved Up, BBC TV; Schofield's Quest, LWT; Outlaws, BSkyB; Beat That, Channel 4; Super Champs,

Thames; British Comedy Awards, LWT; Comedy Club, LWT; Hot House People, BBC. *Honours:* EDLE Prix De Jeunesse, for Beat That. *Membership:* SPAM; Musicians' Union; PRS; Stonewall. *Current Management:* Mcasso Music Production. *Address:* 9 Carnaby St, London W1V 1PG, England.

JAY, David (Dave) John; b. 13 Nov. 1971, Brentwood, Essex, England. Vocalist; Songwriter; Musician (guitar, keyboard). *Education:* BA, Politics. *Career:* Remix work with Vibe Alive Production for London Records and Atlantic Records, USA; Solo and session work for Mr Exe, Wubble-U, Acorn Arts and various independent labels. *Recordings:* After The Dance, Austin; Ain't It Rough, The Dave Jay Project; Dedicated To Love, The Journeyman (5 track EP); House of Love, East 17; Love Is Blind, Echora; Spring Box EP, Dilemma; Change the Style/Windows…, Mighty Alliance; Spring Box Remix, Matrix vs Dilemma; Taking It Back, Stone Players featuring Soul Hooligan. *Membership:* Musicians' Union. *Address:* 8 The Meads, Cherry Trees, Ingatestone, Essex CM13 1LX, England.

JAY DEE, (James Yancey); b. Detroit, MI, USA. Prod; Musician. *Career:* Started as part of a Tribe Called Quest's production team, The Ummah; Founding mem., Slum Village, 1990s; Prod. for artistes incl.: Common; D'Angelo; Erykah Badu; Bilal; Remixed: Spacek; Busta Rhymes. *Recordings:* Albums: Solo: Welcome To Detroit, 2001; with Slum Village: Fantastic Vol. 2, 2000; Trinity (Past, Present and Future), 2002. Singles: with Slum Village: Climax, 1998; I Don't Know, 2000; Raise It Up, 2001; Tainted, 2002. *Address:* c/o Source Records, 113–117 Farringdon Rd, London EC1R 3BX, England.

JAY, Martin; b. 27 July 1949, London, England. Vocalist; Musician (guitar); Writer; Prod. m. Lorraine Jay, 6 Nov. 1985, 1 s. *Career:* Television appearances on Top of the Pops with 5,000 Volts and Enigma; with Cockney Rebel: Yamaha Song Festival, In Concert, LWT; Chile Song Festival. *Recordings:* with 5,000 Volts: I'm On Fire; Dr Kiss Kiss; Medleys with Enigma: Ain't No Stoppin'; I Love Music; Back To The 60s, Tight Fit; Saturday Night Fever 'Megamix'. *Membership:* Musicians' Union; Equity. *Address:* 17 Brook Way, Chigwell, Essex IG7 6AW, England.

JAY, Michael, (Michael Jay Margules) b. 17 Dec. 1959, Chicago, Illinois, USA. Songwriter; Record Prod. *Education:* Lincoln College, Illinois; Illinois State University. *Career:* A&R for Curtis Mayfield, Curtom Records, Chicago, 1980; Discovered Martika, 1988. *Compositions:* Declaration of Love, 1996; Bridge of Hope, 1996. *Recordings:* Producer, Toy Soldiers, Martika; Cross My Heart, Patsy Kensit and Eighth Wonder; Hot Summer Nights, Gloria Estefan (Top Gun soundtrack); The World Still Turns, Kylie Minogue; I Wish The Phone Would Ring, Exposé; The Slightest Touch and If I Say Yes, Five Star; Writer and producer, Shining Through, recorded by Nancy Kerrigan, Olympic Silver Medallist ice-skater; Declaration of Love, Céline Dion; Bridge of Hope, Lara Fabian. *Honours:* AMPEX Golden Reel Awards, Silk and Steel and Martika; Grammy Award Album of the Year, Falling For You, Céline Dion, 1996. *Membership:* NARAS; BAFTA; BMI. *Current Management:* Alan Melina. *Address:* Shankman DeBlasio Melina, 740 La Brea Ave, Hollywood, CA 90038, USA.

JAY, Norman; b. London, England. DJ; Prod; Remixer. *Career:* Co-founder: Good Times sound system (with brother Joey); Played at Notting Hill Carnival; Set up pirate radio station Kiss FM with Gordon Mac; Presented The Original Rare Groove Show; Put on some of London's first warehouse parties with partner Judge Jules as Shake and Fingerpop, mid 1980s; Resident DJ and promoter of High On Hope club, early '90s; Presents weekly Giant 45 radio show on London Live; Remixed: Azzido Da Bass; Montano vs Trumpetman. *Honours:* Blues and Soul Magazine, Club DJ of the Year, 1996–97. *Current Management:* c/o Slice PR. *E-mail:* slice@slice.co.uk.

JAY, Robert; b. 15 Nov. 1967, Dieren, Netherlands. Musician (guitar); Artist; Vocalist. *Education:* Higher Business Economics and Trade; Conservatory. *Career:* Schüttorf Open Air Concert; 4 television (national) shows; De 5 Uur show; Glamourland; Actor, television series; Tour manager, clients include: Emmylou Harris; Freddy Fender; Chris Beckers; Ernie Watts; Randy Bernsen; Performed in USA; Canada; Germany; Israel; Egypt; Spain; France; Artistes performed with: Hans Dulfer; Candy Dulfer; Jan Akkerman; Adje Vanderberg; Jasper Van't Hof; Joe Sample; Writer for several pop journals; Organizer, music festivals. *Membership:* EMI Music/Publishing. *Current Management:* Frisbee Management, PO Box 658, 7500 AR Enschade, Netherlands.

JAY-Z, (Shawn Carter); b. 4 Dec. 1969, Brooklyn, NY, USA. Rap Artiste. *Career:* Co-founder, Roc-A-Fella Records, 1995–, now incl. Roc-A-Wear clothing line and film co; Writer and dir, semi-autobiographical film, Streets Is Watching, 1998; Collaborations: Puff Daddy; Lil' Kim; Foxy Brown; Notorious BIG; Mary J. Blige; Mariah Carey; Timbaland. *Recordings:* Albums: Reasonable Doubt, 1996; In My Lifetime Vol. 1, 1997; Vol. 2, Hard Knock Life, 1999; Vol. 3, Life And Times Of S. Carter, 1999; The Dynasty—Roc La Familia, 2000; The Blueprint, 2001; The Best Of Both Worlds (with R. Kelly), 2002; The Blueprint 2: The Gift And The Curse, 2002. Singles: Ain't No Nigga, 1996; Can I Get A…, 1998; Hard Knock Life (Ghetto Anthem), 1998; Anything, 2000; Big Pimpin', 2000; Izzo (H.O.V.A.), 2001; Girls Girls Girls,

2002; Bonnie & Clyde, 2003. *Honours:* MOBO Award, Best International Hip Hop Act, 1999. *Address:* c/o Roc-A-Fella Records, 825 Eighth Ave, New York, NY 10019-7472, USA. *Website:* www.rocafella.com.

JAZZIE B, (Beresford Romeo); b. 16 Jan. 1963, London, England. Musician; Prod; Songwriter. *Career:* Founder Member, Soul II Soul, collective with Philip Daddae Harvey and producer Nellee Hooper; Joined by vocalists Do'reen and later Caron Wheeler; Launched fashion label and clothes shops; Remixer/arranger for many artists including Sinéad O'Connor, Fine Young Cannibals and The Family Stand; Caron Wheeler left, 1990; Nellee Hooper left to become independent producer, 1993; Wheeler returned, 1993; Numerous club appearances and appearances on TV and radio. *Recordings:* Singles: Fairplay, 1988; Feel Free, 1988; Keep On Moving, 1989; Back To Life (However Do You Want Me) (No. 1, UK), 1989; Get A Life, 1989; A Dream's A Dream/Jazzie's Groove, 1990; Missing You, 1990; People, 1990; Joy, 1992; Move Me No Mountain, 1992; Just Right, 1992; Wish, 1993; Love Enuff, 1995; I Care, 1995; Pleasuredome, 1997; Represent, 1997; Albums: Club Classics Vol. I, 1989; Keep On Moving, 1989; Vol. II 1990 – A New Decade, 1990; Vol. III Just Right, 1992; I Care, 1995; Vol. V Believe, 1995; Time for Change, 1997.

JAZZY M, (Michael Schiniou); b. 5 Jan. 1962, Edmonton, London, England. Prod; Remixer; DJ. *Career:* Started as a mobile DJ in London; Worked in Spin Off Records; Landed job as a DJ on LWR Radio; Presented The Jacking Zone, responsible for introducing house music to London on the airwaves; Opened Vinyl Zone record shop on the King's Road, London; Founder: Oh Zone Records, original label of Orbital's club hit Chime; Resident DJ at Ministry of Sound club; Collaborations: Julian Jonah; Mr Fingers; Remixed: Infinity and Duane Harden; Ramsey and Fen; Double 99. *Recordings:* Singles: Soft To Hard/Boom Ah! (as Klubzone 1), 1992; Forever On (as Zoogie), 1992; Be Yourself Be Free (as Sao Paulo), 1998; Jazzin' The Way You Know, 2000. *Address:* c/o Ministry of Sound, 103 Gaunt St, London SE1 6DP, England.

JEAN, Wyclef (Jeannel); b. 17 Oct. 1972, Haiti. Vocalist; Rap Artiste. *Career:* Formed Tranzlator Crew with Lauryn Hill and Pras Michel; Renamed The Fugees; Numerous television and live appearances; Producer, Destiny's Child; Collaboration with Bono for Drop the Debt campaign. *Recordings:* Albums: with The Fugees: Blunted on Reality, 1994; The Score, 1996; Solo: The Carnival, 1997; Ecleftic: Two Sides II A Book, 2001; Masquerade, 2002. Singles: with The Fugees: Boof Baf, 1993; Nappy Heads (EP), 1994; Vocab (EP), 1994; Ready Or Not (No. 1, UK), 1996; The Score, 1996; Fu-Gee-La, 1996; Killing Me Softly (No. 1, UK), 1996; Rumble In The Jungle, 1997; Solo: We Trying to Stay Alive, 1997; The Sweetest Thing (with Lauryn Hill), 1997; Guantanamera, 1997; Gone Till November (with Bono), 1998; Cheated, 1998; New Day, 1999; 911 (with Mary J. Blige), 2000; Perfect Gentleman, 2001. *Honours:* BRIT Award, Best International Group, 1997.

JEANES, Alan Lloyd; b. 22 May 1923, Penarth, South Wales. Composer; Arranger. *Education:* Jazz Musicianship, Goldsmiths College, London. *Career:* Founder, former director, University of Greenwich Big Band; Tutor, Jazz Musicianship for various authorities, England and Wales; Arranger for jazz groups. *Address:* 4 Oldfield Rd, Bickley, Bromley, Kent BR1 2LF, England.

JEAN-MARIE, Alain (Judes); b. 29 Oct. 1945, Pointe-A-Pitre, Guadaloupe. Musician (piano). *Career:* Prix Django Reinhardt, 1979; Concerts with: Chet Baker; Art Farmer; Johnny Griffin; Hal Singer; Slide Hampton; Clark Terry; Records with: Abbey Lincoln; Charles Tolliver. *Recordings:* Latin Alley, with Niels Henning Orsted Pedersen, 1987; The Scene Is Clean, with Aldo Romano, Henri Texier, 1996; Biguines Reflections, 1997; Serenade, 1998; Firoliu with Teca Calazan, 1999. *Honours:* Prix Django Reinhardt, Academie du Jazz, 1979. *Current Management:* Martine Palmé, 33 bis rue Doudeauville, 75018 Paris, France. *Address:* Chemin Des Cotillons, 95130 Franconville, France.

JECZALIK, Jonathan Edward Stephen; b. 11 May 1955, Banbury, Oxfordshire, England. Musical Dir. m. Joanna Louise Hill, 2 d. *Education:* Hons degree, Geography. *Career:* Programmer, Fairlight CMI; Producer for Pet Shop Boys; Artiste with Art of Noise and Art of Silence (current). *Recordings:* Singles include: with Art of Noise: Into Battle EP, 1983; Beatbox, 1983; Close To The Edit, 1984; Moments In Love, 1985; Peter Gunn (Grammy Award winner), 1986; Paranoimia, 1986; Dragnet, 1988; Kiss, collaboration with Tom Jones, 1988; Albums include: Who's Afraid of The Art of Noise, 1984; In Visible Silence, 1986; In No Sense Nonsense, 1987; Best of The Art of Noise, 1988; Below The Waste, 1989; The Ambient Collection, 1990; Producer of: Kiss Me, Stephen Tin Tin Duffy, 1985; Opportunities, Pet Shop Boys, 1985. *Honours:* Grammy Award, Best Rock Instrumental, 1986. *Membership:* Musicians' Union.

JEFFERSON, Marshall; b. 19 Sept. 1959, Chicago, Illinois, USA. Prod; Remixer; DJ. *Career:* Inspired by listening to Ron Hardy DJ at the legendary Music Box club, Chicago, started producing own tracks with other Chicago house producers including Adonis, mid 1980s; Recorded for Chicago's Trax Records; Formed group Virgo (with Vince Lawrence and Adonis); Produced Ten City's debut album; Remixed: The Pasadenas; Tom Jones; System 7; Kym

Mazelle. *Recordings:* Albums: Virgo (with Virgo), 1989; Singles: I've Lost Control (with Sleazy D), Move Your Body (The House Music Anthem), 1986; Open Our Eyes (with The Truth), 1988; Do You Know Who You Are (with Virgo), 1989; Mushrooms (with Noosa Heads), 1998; Everybody Dance (Clap Your Hands) (with DJ Pierre), 2001. *Address:* c/o Milk and 2 Sugars, Broadway Studios, 28 Tooting High St, London SW17 ORG, England.

JEFFRIES, Peter John Martin; b. 1 March 1928, London, England. Composer; Arranger; Musician (piano); Musical Dir. m. Pauline Lander, 7 April 1955, 1 s., 1 d. *Education:* Eastman School of Music; Private lessons. *Career:* Pianist, arranger, Phil Tate Orchestra; Arranger, musical director, Philips Records, Pye Records, Decca Records; Radio appearances include: Own broadcasting orchestra, Breakfast special, Radio 2, 1967–72; Accompanist for: Kenny Lynch; Jimmy Tarbuck; Morecambe and Wise; Anne Shelton; Vera Lynn. *Compositions:* Composer, conductor, 21 film scores, 1966–80; Co-arranger, If My Friends Could See Me Now, Cy Coleman. *Membership:* PRS; MCPS; BAC&S. *Address:* 15 Collins Court, Lea Close, Bushey, Hertfordshire WD23 3PY, England.

JELAVIC, Matko; b. 29 March 1958, Split, Croatia. Vocalist; Composer; Musician (drums). m. 31 July 1982, 2 s. *Education:* Dipl OECC; Music School (guitar). *Career:* Drummer, rock band Metak; Drummer in studios; More than 50 albums of different singers and groups; Singer, composer, 1988–; Very successful in Croatia and among Croatians abroad; Biggest concert in Sydney, Australia, audience 10,000 people. *Recordings:* Album: Dobra Vecer Prijatelji, 1988; (Biggest hit) Majko Stara, 1988; Ljube Ljubavi, 1989; Sretno Ti Bilo Andele, 1990; Matko Jelavic Mix, 1992; Moja Ljubavi, 1993; Pianino, 1995. *Honours:* 3 Gold albums, rest Silver; Winner, Split Festival, 1988; Most Popular Song Award In Croatia, 1988. *Membership:* HGU (Croatian Music Union); DSH (Union of Composers). *Current Management:* Mr Branko Paic, CBS Zagreb. *Address:* Dubrovacka 25, Split, Croatia.

JENKINS, Delyth, (Delyth Evans); b. 28 May 1955, Oswestry, Shropshire, England. Musician (celtic harp). m. Nigel Jenkins, 29 June 1982, 2 d. *Education:* Hons Degree, English and French. *Career:* Welsh Folk band Cromlech, 1978–82; Aberjaber, 1982–; Solo work; Tours: UK; Europe. *Recordings:* Gwlith Y Bore, 1980; Igam Ogam, 1982; Aberjaber, 1985; Aber-Dau-Jaber, 1988; Delta, 1991; Aberjaber – The Perfect Bucket, 1997; Ar Y Ffin, 1998. *Publications:* Del Y Delyn, 1994. *Current Management:* Elizabeth Jones Entertainments, 3 Conifer Heights, Sunningdale, Knightwick, Worcestershire WR6 5TP, England. *Address:* 124 Overland Rd, Mumbles, Swansea SA3 4EU, Wales.

JENKINSON, Tom, (Squarepusher, Chaos AD); b. 1977. Musician; DJ. *Career:* Solo artiste and DJ; Signed to Warp Records, 1996; Performances incl.: Glastonbury Festival, UK; Mount Fuji Rock Festival, Japan; Ten Days of Techno, Belgium; Video collaboration with Chris Cunningham. *Recordings:* Albums: as Chaos AD: Buzz Caner; Remixes; as Squarepusher: Feed Me Weird Things, 1996; Hard Normal Daddy, 1997; Big Loada (mini album), 1997; Burningn'n Tree', 1997; Music Is Rotten One Note, 1998; Selection Sixteen, 1999; Budakhan Mindphone, 1999; Go Plastic, 2001; Do You Know Squarepusher, 2002. Singles: as Squarepusher: Squarepusher Theme, 1996; Port Rhombus (EP), 1996; Conumber, 1997; Vic Acid, 1997; Big Loada, 1997; My Sound/Don't Go Plastic, 1998; Maximum Priest (EP), 1999; I Am Carnal, 1999; My Red Hot Car, 2001; Untitled, 2001; Other: Alroy Road Tracks featuring the Duke of Harringay; Dragon Disc 2: Dunderhead/Tom Jenkinson. *Address:* c/o Warp Records Ltd Spectrum House, 32–34 Gordon House Rd, London NW5 1LP, England. *Website:* www.warprecords.com.

JENSEN, Mark Russell; b. 20 Nov. 1959, Eastbourne, England. Composer; Arranger; Conductor; Prod; Recording Artiste. *Education:* Eastbourne College; Private lessons with Rodney Sadler, John Walker, MA. *Career:* Arranger, conductor, record prod., 1978–; Recording artiste, 1985–; Composer, arranger, conductor for film, television, theatre, 1992–; Recorded as Spritzo Scaramanga, –1993, as Mark Jensen, 1994–. *Compositions:* Film and Television: The Papermen, 1993; Angleterre Underground, 1994; Caravan To Arcadia, 1995; Monk Dawson (pilot), 1995; Famine, 1998; Theatre: Romeo and Juliet, 1993; The Changeling, 1994; The Tempest, 1994; Hamlet, 1995; The Way of Danger (ballet score), 1996; Monk Dawson (feature), 1997; Maestro, 1999–2000. *Recordings:* Albums: Monk Dawson (original soundtrack), 1998; as Mark Jensen: Zoom In... The Zest Zone, 1999. Singles: as Spritzo Scaramanga: single, 1993; as Mark Jensen: The Naidax EP. *Membership:* Performing Rights Society; British Music Writers' Council; Musicians' Union. *Address:* c/o Zest Zone, 44 Carew Rd, Eastbourne, East Sussex BN21 2JN, England.

JENSEN, Soren Kjær; b. 1 Dec. 1961, Århus, Denmark. Musician (bass); Composer; Prod. m. Turid N Christensen, 22 July 1995. *Education:* University of Århus; Studied jazz at the New School for Social Science, New York, USA. *Career:* Teacher, Royal Conservatory of Music, Ålborg; Musik Projekt Århus; Space invaders production for Multimedia; Lecturer, Anthropology of Music, University of Århus; Musical Director and Producer; Numerous television appearances. *Compositions:* Numerous works for television, video, film, Planetaria, theme parks, CD-Roms and CD-I; Producer and co-producer:

Waaberi, New Dawn, 1997; Maryam Mursal, 1998. *Recordings:* Appeared on recordings by many artistes including: Maryam Mursal (The Journey), Jacob Haugaard, Evald Krog, Holger Laumanns Orkester, Extrem Normal, Nikos Veropoulos and Bonehead. *Honours:* Scholarships from: Danish Music Council; Danish Arts Council; Danish Rock Council; Queen Margrethe and Prince Henriks Foundation; European Commission, Innovation Programme; Ministry for the Interior; Danish Cultural Foundation; Awards: Best CD-ROM in Scandinavia, 1997; Industrial Design Award, 1998. *Membership:* KODA; NCB; Danish Musicians' Union. *Current Management:* Target Music. *Address:* Mejlgade 50, 1 tv, 8000 Århus C, Denmark.

JENSEN, Theis Eigil; b. 5 Aug. 1938, Copenhagen, Denmark. Vocalist; Musician (trumpet); Graphic Designer. m. Lesley Celina Geen, 3 June 1961, divorced 1976. *Education:* Graduate, Graphic Design, Art School, 1959. *Career:* Member: Louisiana Jazzband, 1952–55; Henrik Johansen's Jazzband, 1955–56; Adrian Bentzon's Jazzband, 1956–63; Co-leader, Theis/Nyegaard Jazzband, 1963–98; Theis' Jazzband, 1998–; Tours and festivals: Europe; USA; Argentina; Brazil; Uruguay; Australia; Television and radio appearances: Scandinavia; South America. *Recordings:* Traditional Jazz, 1964; Theis/Nyegaard Concert At Gothenburg, 1969; Theis/Nyegaard Live At Montmartre, 1972; Papa Bue's Viking Jazz Band Live At Vingården, 1976; Jazztage Hanover, 1977; Jazz For Hatz-Lovers, 1979; Theis Jensen 1956–72, 1980; Mand Mand, 1980; Los Estudiantes Daneses En El Hot Club De Buenos Aires, 1980; Gamle Er Unge, Der Er Blevet Aeldre, 1981; The First 25 Years, 1988; Jorgen Svare Meets Theis Jensen, 1991; Jazz Event, 1992; Theis-Nyegaard Jazzband, Tonight Live, 1996. *Publications:* Historier Om Theis, 1992; Love and Jazz, 2002. *Honours:* Jazz Musician of the Year, 1965. *Membership:* DJBFA. *Address:* Lovenborg Alle 11, 4420 Regstrup, Denmark.

JERBIC, Zeljko; b. 10 Oct. 1954, Koprivnica, Croatia. Record Prod; Teacher. *Education:* Academy of Pedagogics; High School of Music. *Recordings:* As Music and Executive Producer: Damned Die Hard, Phonebox Vandals, 1990; Foxxin, Messerschmitt, 1990; Ikona, Lola V Stain, 1990; 4 x 12, Borghesia, 1991; Mansarda, Lola V Stain, 1992; Asgard Live, Vesna Gorse and Drazen Franolic, 1993; So Shine, Don't, 1995; Ulje Je Na Vodi, Haustor, 1995; KC Rock 98, 1998. *Membership:* Croatian Musicians' Union. *Address:* Attn Mr Zeljko Jerbic, Blind Dog Records, Svilarska 34, 480 00 Koprivnica, Croatia.

JERROLF, Mats; b. 28 Aug. 1951, Stockholm, Sweden. Composer; Musician. *Education:* Archaeology, Ethnology, University, 1977. *Career:* Touring in Sweden; Appearances in various Folk music programmes in radio. *Compositions:* Bekannelsen I Logen, 1991; Adjo Till Stockholms Stad, 1993; Krakemala Namdemanlard, 1993; Förskingrarvisan, 1995. *Recordings:* Skanska Lasses Visor, 1987; Flickan Fran Bellmansro, 1988; Collage, 1990; Haveri, 1993; Namdemans Blandning, 1995. *Publications:* Birka, 1981; Historisk Malarresa, 1981. *Honours:* STIM Award, 1991, 1995, 1997; Folk Music Foundation Award, 1992; SKAP Award, 1995. *Membership:* SKAP; SAMI. *Address:* Reimersholmsi 8, 117 40 Stockholm, Sweden.

JERVIER, Paul Joseph; b. 21 Nov. 1966, London, England. Musician (drums); Music Prod; *Recordings:* 4 UK No. 1 singles with Take That; Other recordings for artistes include: Yazz; Eternal; Kaos; Gabrielle; R Kelly; Danny Rampling. *Membership:* Musicians' Union. *Address:* 108 Perry Rise, London SE23 2QU, England.

JESSE, Graham; b. 19 Oct. 1955, Sydney, Australia. m. Peta, 24 May 1986, 1 s., 1 d. *Education:* Sydney Conservatorium of Music to Study Flute; Conservatorium Jazz Course; Studied Saxophone with Dave Liebman and Musical Composition with Ludmilla Uhlehla, New York, 1981–82. *Career:* Member, Midday Show, live daily TV entertainment programme, 15 years; Toured with Daly Wilson Big Band, Peter Allen, David Atkins; Performed with Sydney Dance Company, James Morrison, Marcia Hines. *Compositions:* Reflections, CD; In the Company of Women, Sydney Dance Company. *Recordings:* Leader: Reflections, CD, 1996; In the Flow, CD, 2000; Featured Soloist: Tommy Emmanuel: Dare to Be Different; Up From Down Under; Gondwanaland; Featured soloist and composer: Pamela Knowles, Boites De Jazz; The Sydney All Star Big Band, Doin' Our Thing, 2001. *Honours:* Bicentennial Music Week Award, Most Outstanding Studio Musician, 1988. *Membership:* Australian Musicians' Union; ARRA. *Address:* 50 Sugarloaf Cres., Castlecrag, NSW 2068, Australia. *E-mail:* grahamjesse@netscape.net.

JETT, Joan; b. 22 Sept. 1960, Philadelphia, USA. Vocalist; Musician (guitar). *Career:* Member, US all-female group, The Runaways, 1976–79; Solo artiste, with own backing band, The Blackhearts, 1979–. *Recordings:* Albums: with The Runaways: The Runaways, 1976; Queens of Noise, 1977; Live In Japan, 1977; Solo/with The Blackhearts: Bad Reputation, 1980; I Love Rock 'N' Roll, 1981; Album, 1983; Glorious Results of a Misspent Youth, 1984; Up Your Alley, 1988; Good Music, 1989; Hit List, 1990; Notorious, 1991; Pure and Simple, 1994; Fetish, 1999; Fit To Be Tied, 2001; Singles: I Love Rock 'n' Roll (No. 1, USA), 1981; Don't Surrender, 1991; As I Am, 1994; Love Is All Around, 1996. *Address:* c/o Blackheart Records Group, Suite 6H, 155 E 55th St, New York, NY 10022, USA.

JEWELL, Jimmy; b. 18 Feb. 1945, Brierfield, Lancashire, England. Musician (saxophones); Composer; Arranger. m. Mary-Kay Lombardo, 9 Oct. 1983, 2 d. *Career:* Keef Hartley Band: Woodstock Festival; 4 years touring, recording with Gallagher and Lyle; Original member, Ronnie Lane's Slim Chance; McGuiness-Flint recorded with Joan Armatrading (Love and Affection solo). *Recordings:* 2 solo albums, jazz fusion, 1977, 1978; Several privately produced tapes, jazz featuring original compositions; Recently released First Phase, 2000; Almost Straight Ahead, 2001. *Membership:* Musicians' Union; PRS; MCPS. *Address:* 105 Britton St, Gillingham, Kent ME7 5ES, England.

JIA-ZI, Zhao; b. 30 Aug. 1934, Jiang-Su, People's Republic of China. Musicology. m. Xu Si-Jie, 1 s., 1 d. *Education:* Shanghai Conservatory of Music, 1956–61. *Career:* Research Scholar, Music University of New Dheli, The Indian Art Centre, Chennai Ethonomusicology Research Institute, 1986–88; Head of Institute Music Research of Shanghai Conservatory of Music; Full Time Supervisor, Shanghai Conservatory of Music; Deputy Director, World Ethnomusicological Association, Oriental Music Association. *Publications:* Collection of Writings on the Music of Shen Zhi-Bai; Indian Music Around The Period of Sui and Tang Dynasty; Rabindranath Tagore and his Music; Gamelan Music in Java and Bali; A Comparative Study of Wu Dan-Qi Shen and Qi Tiao Bei. *Membership:* Indian Musicological Society; Singapore Asscn for Asian Studies; Chinese Writers' Asscn; Chinese Musicians' Asscn. *Address:* 6 Garden Court, The Ave, Sunny Bank Hills 4109, Brisbane, Australia.

JIMBOB, (James Morrison); b. 22 Nov. 1960. Musician. *Career:* Founder member (with Fruitbat), duo Carter The Unstoppable Sex Machine (later known as Carter USM); Founder member, Jim's Super Stereoworld, 1998; International tours, USA, Japan; Extensive British tour, 1999. *Recordings:* 101 Damnations, 1990; 30 Something, 1991; 1992 – The Love Album, 1992 (No. 1, UK); Post Historic Monsters, 1994; Worry Bomb, 1995; Straw Donkey, 1996; A World Without Dave, 1997; I Blame The Government, 1998; Live, 1999; Singles: Sheltered Life, 1988; Sherriff Fatman, 1989; Rubbish, 1990; Anytime, Anyplace, Anywhere, 1990; Bloodsports For All, 1991; After The Watershed, 1991; Only Living Boy In New Cross, 1992; Lean On Me I Won't Fall Over, 1993; Glam Rock Cops, 1994; Let's Get Tattoos, 1994; Young Offenders Mum, 1995; Born On 5th November, 1995; Bonkers In The Nut; Could UB The One I Waited 4; Solo album: JR. *Current Management:* Adrian Boss Promotions, 3 Gunstor Rd, London N16 8HF, England.

JIMENEZ-OLARIAGA, Marcos Andres; b. 25 April 1960, Madrid, Spain. Jazz Musician (piano). 1 d. *Education:* Classical studies, Geneva CPM, with S Risler. *Career:* Various concerts with saxophonist M Magnoni; Television and radio shows with own band: Chris Cross; Cully Jazz Festival with singer, C Python. *Recordings:* Albums: Chris Cross; Allastor; Outland Souvenirs; Nirohda. *Publications:* Helas Moulino, edited in Le Livre du Jazz en France. *Honours:* Piano certificate with jury congratulations. *Membership:* AMR, Geneva. *Address:* 801 Chemin des Broues, 01220 Divonne, France.

JIRUCHA, Jan; b. 24 June 1945, Novy Bydzov, Czech Republic. Musician (Trombone and Vocal). m. 15 Sept. 1973, 1 s., 1 d. *Education:* Private elementary music school. *Career:* Numerous concert appearances. *Recordings:* Studio, traditional jazz, 1984; Echoes and Confessions, traditional jazz, 1987; Classic Jazz Collegium, 1988; Big Fat Mammah, 1991; TJS, 1994; Revival Swing, 1995; J J Jazzmen, Sunday Swing, 1997. *Current Management:* J J Jazzmen Band Agency. *Address:* Cestmirova 8, 140 00 Prague 4, Czech Republic.

JOAN, Marianne; b. 12 March 1973, Jamestown, ND, USA. Vocalist. *Education:* MFA in voice, California Institute of the Arts; BA in voice, Peabody Conservatory; Studied with Sopranos Phyllis Bryn-Julson, Jacqueline Bobak and Irene Gubrud. *Career:* Voice for Brigantia, recorded score by Clay Chaplin, Canadian Choreographer Anik Bouvrette; Created new multimedia works with trio, Three Lanes Over, Los Angeles, 1999, and the Digital Improvisation Ensemble, Los Angeles, 1998; Soloist with Schola Antiqua, a medieval music ensemble. *Membership:* AES; ICMA.

JOBE, Badou; b. Gambia. Musician (bass guitar). *Career:* Started career with Foyer band, late 1950s; Joined African Jazz; Founder member: Super Eagles, 1968; Name change to Ifang Bondi, 1973; Based in Holland, 1984–. *Recordings:* with The Super Eagles: Viva Super Eagles, 1969; Senegambian Sensation; with Ifang Bondi: Saraba, 1976; Mantra, 1983; Sanjo, 1989; Daraj, 1994; Gis Gis, 1998; Ifang Bondi Live, 2001. *Honours:* EverGreen Award, Gambia, 1997; Kora Award, 1999. *E-mail:* mail@ifanbondi.demon.nl.

JOE, (Joseph Thomas); b. 1972, Cuthbert, Georgia, USA. Vocalist; Prod. *Career:* Started singing in the choir of parents' Pentecostal Church, Alabama; Moved to New Jersey; Worked in a gospel music store; Played guitar at a local church; Introduced to Vincent Herbert and recorded a 3-song demo together; Signed to Jive Records as solo artiste, 1997; Recordings have featured on soundtracks including: Don't Be A Menace; Booty Call; Rush Hour; Collaborations: Brandy; Jay-Z; SWV; Big Punisher; Case; Mariah Carey. *Recordings:* Albums: Everything, 1993; All That I Am, 1997; My Name Is Joe,

2000; Better Days, 2001; Singles: I'm In Luv, 1993; The One For Me, All Or Nothing, 1994; All The Things (Your Man Won't Do), 1996; Don't Wanna Be A Player, The Love Scene, 1997; No-One Else Comes Close, Still Not A Player, Faded Pictures, All That I Am, 1998; I Wanna Know 1999; Thank God I Found You (with Mariah Carey and 98°), Treat Her Like A Lady, 2000; Stutter, 2001. *Address:* c/o Jive Records, 137–139 W 25th St, New York, USA.

JOEL, Billy (William Martin); b. 9 May 1949, Bronx, New York, USA. Musician (piano); Vocalist; Songwriter. m. Christie Brinkley, 23 March 1989, divorced 1994, 1 d. *Education:* LHD (hon), Fairfield Univesity, 1991; HMD (hon), Berklee College Music, 1993. *Career:* Popular solo recording artiste, 1972–. *Compositions include:* Just The Way You Are, 1978; Honesty, 1979; We Didn't Start The Fire, 1989; The River of Dreams, 1994. *Recordings:* Hit singles include: Piano Man, 1973; The Entertainer, 1974; Just The Way You Are, 1978; Movin' Out (Anthony's Song), 1978; My Life, 1978; All For Leyna, 1980; It's Still Rock 'n' Roll To Me (No. 1, USA), 1980; Allentown, 1982; Tell Her About It (No. 1, USA), 1983; Uptown Girl (No. 1, UK), 1983; An Innocent Man, 1984; The Longest Time, 1984; We Didn't Start The Fire (No. 1, USA), 1989; River of Dreams, 1993; All About Soul, 1993; Albums include: Cold Spring Harbor, 1972; Piano Man, 1973; Streetlife Serenade, 1974; Turnstiles, 1976; The Stranger, 1978; 52nd Street (No. 1, USA), 1978; Glass Houses (No. 1, USA), 1980; Songs In The Attic, 1981; Nylon Curtain, 1982; An Innocent Man, 1983; Greatest Hits, Vols I and II, 1985; The Bridge, 1986; KOHUEPT-Live In Leningrad, 1987; Storm Front (No. 1, USA), 1989; River of Dreams (No. 1, USA), 1993; Greatest Hits, 1997; 2000 Years – The Millennium Concert, 2000. *Honours:* 6 Grammy Awards include: Record of Year, Song of Year, Best Male Vocal Performance, 1978; Best Album, 1979; American Music Award, Best Album, 1980; Grammy Legend Award, 1990; Inducted into Songwriters Hall of Fame, 1992; ASCAP Founders Award, 1997; Hon. DHL, Hofstra University, 1997. *Address:* c/o Maritime Music Inc, 200 W 57th St, Suite 308, New York, NY 10019, USA.

JOHANSEN, Per Oddvar Eide; b. 1 March 1968, Oslo, Norway. Musician (drums). *Education:* Music Gymnasium, Rud High School, three years; Studied Jazz at Trondelag Music Conservatory of Music, Trondheim, three years. *Career:* Freelance drummer, mostly Jazz and improvised music; Has toured in Norway and Europe with numerous groups including: Airamero; Kenny Weeler; John Surman; Karin Krog; Nils Petter Molvaer; Jon Christensen; Tore Brunborg; Vigleik Storaas; The Source; Close Erase. *Recordings:* include: Airamero, Airamero; Olemanns Kornett, The Source; This Is You, Jacob Young; Close Erase; No. 2. *Honours:* Spellemannsprisen for Vigleile Storans trio, Bilder, 1995; Spellemannsprisen for Vigleile Storans trio, Andre Bilder, 1997. *Membership:* Norwegian Jazz Federation; Norwegian Musical Union. *Address:* Gamleveien 122E, 1350 Lommedalen, Norway.

JOHANSSON, Lasse (Lars-Olof); b. 23 Feb. 1973, Huskvarna, Sweden. Musician (keyboards, guitar). *Career:* Mem., The Cardigans, 1993–; Contributed tracks to films Romeo and Juliet and A Life Less Ordinary; Numerous concert tours, festivals, television and radio appearances. *Recordings:* Albums: Emmerdale, 1994; Life, 1995; First Band On The Moon, 1996; Other Side Of The Moon, 1998; Gran Turismo, 1998. Singles: Rise And Shine; Black Letter Day; Sick And Tired, 1995; Carnival, 1995; Hey! Get Out Of My Way; Lovefool (No. 2, UK), 1996; Been It, 1997; Your New Cuckoo, 1997; My Favorite Game, 1998; Erase/Rewind, 1999; Hanging Around, 1999; Gran Turismo Overdrive, 2000; with David Arnold: Theme From 'Randall & Hopkirk Deceased' (BBC1), 2000. *Honours:* Slitz Magazine, Best Band, 1994; BMI Best Song, 1997, Best Album, 1998, Best Group, 1996, 1998. *Current Management:* Motor, PO Box 53045, 400 14 Gothenburg, Sweden. *Address:* c/o Stockholm Records, Positionen 146, 115 74 Stockholm, Sweden. *Website:* www.cardigans.net.

JOHANSSON, Markku; b. 22 March 1949, Lahti, Finland. Conductor; Arranger; Composer; Musician (trumpet, flugelhorn). m. Riita Kvitunen, June 1971, 1 s., 1 d. *Education:* Music conservatory in Lahti; Sibelius Academy in Helsinki; Jazz studies in New York, with Thad Jones, Lew Soloff. *Career:* Radio, television, recording artiste, as conductor, arranger, trumpet player; Conductor, UMO Jazz Orchestra, 1992–93; Conductor, Vantaa Pops Orchestra, 1988–. *Recordings:* Blue Echoes; Tenderly; Exorbitant; Vantaa Pops Orchestra; Umo Jazz Orchestra; with Nils Lindberg: Saxes Galore, Brass Galore, 1994; with Lena Jansson: Lena Jansson, 1995; with Thad Jones: Thad Jones, Mel Lewis and Umo, 1995. *Honours:* Yrjö Award 1993 (Musician of the Year). *Current Management:* MJ-Music Oy. *Address:* Aalto 6 B 18, 02320 Espoo, Finland.

JOHN, Sir Elton, (Reginald Kenneth Dwight); b. 25 March 1947, Pinner, Middlesex, England. Vocalist; Songwriter; Musician (piano). m. Renate Blauer, 14 Feb. 1984, divorced 1988. *Education:* Piano lessons aged 4; Royal Academy of Music, 1958. *Career:* Member, Bluesology, 1961–67; Worked at Mills Music Publishers; Solo artiste, 1968–; Long-term writing partnership with Bernie Taupin, 1967–; Partnership wrote for Dick James Music; Founder, Rocket Records, 1973; Own publishing company, Big Pig Music, 1974; Performances include: Wembley Stadium, 1975; First Western star to perform in Israel and USSR, 1979; Live Aid, Wembley, 1985; Wham's farewell concert, Wembley, 1985; Prince's Trust concerts, London, 1986, 1988; Farm

Aid IV, 1990; AIDS Project Los Angeles – Commitment To Life VI, 1992; Appeared in Jubilee concert, Buckingham Palace, 2002; Film appearance, Tommy, 1975. *Recordings:* Albums: Elton John, 1970; Tumbleweed Connection, 1971; Friends, 1971; 17–11–70, 1971; Madman Across The Water, 1972; Honky Chateau (No. 1, USA), 1972; Don't Shoot Me, I'm Only The Piano Player (No. 1, UK and USA), 1973; Goodbye Yellow Brick Road (No. 1, UK and USA), 1973; Caribou (No. 1, UK and USA), 1974; Captain Fantastic and The Brown Dirt Cowboy (No. 1, USA), 1975; Rock of The Westies (No. 1, USA), 1975; Here and There, 1976; Blue Moves, 1976; A Single Man, 1978; Lady Samantha, 1980; 21 At 33, 1980; Jump Up!, 1982; Too Low For Zero, 1983; Breaking Hearts, 1984; Ice On Fire, 1985; Leather Jackets, 1986; Live In Australia, 1987; Reg Strikes Back, 1988; Sleeping With The Past (No. 1, UK), 1989; The Very Best of (No. 1, UK), 1990; The One, 1992; Made In England, 1995; Big Picture, 1997; Love Songs, 1998; Live in Australia, 1999; Songs From The West Coast, 2001; Greatest Hits 1970–2002, 2002. Singles include: Your Song, 1971; Rocket Man, 1972; Crocodile Rock (No. 1, USA), 1973; Daniel, 1973; Saturday Night's Alright For Fighting, 1973; Goodbye Yellow Brick Road, 1973; Candle In The Wind, 1974; Don't Let The Sun Go Down On Me, 1974 (live version with George Michael, No. 1, UK and USA), 1991); Philadelphia Freedom (No. 1, USA), 1975; Lucy In The Sky With Diamonds (No. 1, USA), 1975; Island Girl (No. 1, USA), 1975; Pinball Wizard, from film Tommy, 1976; Don't Go Breaking My Heart, duet with Kiki Dee (No. 1, UK and USA), 1976; Sorry Seems To Be The Hardest Word, 1976; Bennie and The Jets (No. 1, USA), 1976; Song For Guy, 1979; Blue Eyes, 1982; I Guess That's Why They Call It The Blues, 1983; I'm Still Standing, 1983; Kiss The Bride, 1983; Sad Songs (Say So Much), 1984; Passengers, 1984; Nikita, 1985; Sacrifice (No. 1, UK), 1989; The One, 1992; True Love (with Kiki Dee), 1993; Don't Go Breaking My Heart, with RuPaul, 1994; Ain't Nothing Like The Real Thing, with Marcella Detroit, 1994; Can You Feel The Love Tonight, 1994; Circle of Life, 1994; Made In England, 1995; Blessed, 1995; Believe, 1995; You Can Make History, 1996; Live Like Horses, 1996; Candle In The Wind 97/Something About The Way You Look Tonight (No. 1, World-wide, over 33m. copies sold), 1997; If The River Can Bend, 1998; Written in the Stars, 1999; I Want Love, 2001; This Train Don't Stop There Anymore, 2001; Contributor, That's What Friends Are For, Dionne Warwick and Friends (charity record), 1986. *Honours:* First album to go straight to No. 1 in US charts, Captain Fantastic…, 1975; Numerous Ivor Novello Awards for: Daniel, 1974; Don't Go Breaking My Heart, 1977; Song For Guy, 1979; Nikita, 1986; Sacrifice, 1991; Star on Hollywood Walk of Fame, 1975; Madison Square Gardens; Hall of Fame, 1977; Walk of Fame (first non-athlete), 1992; American Music Awards: Favorite Male Artist, Favourite Single, 1977; Silver Clef Award, Nordoff-Robbins Music Therapy, 1979; BRIT Awards: Outstanding Contribution To British Music, 1986; Best British Male Artist, 1991; Grammy, Best Vocal Performance By A Group, 1987; MTV Special Recognition Trophy, 1987; Hitmaker Award, National Academy of Popular Music, 1989; Hon. Life President, Watford Football Club, 1989; Inducted into Songwriters Hall of Fame (with Bernie Taupin), 1992; Q Magazine Merit Award, 1993; Officer of Arts and Letters, Paris, 1993; K.B.E., 1998. *Current Management:* c/o Simon Prytherch, Elton John Management, 7 King St Cloisters, Clifton Walk, London W6 0GY, England. *Website:* www.eltonjohn.com.

JOHN, Lee; b. 23 June 1967, Hackney, London, England. Vocalist; Songwriter; Musician (keyboards); Record Prod; Arranger. *Education:* Hewanoma Strolling Players; Anna Sher Stage School; World-wide Productions, New York. *Career:* Lead singer, Imagination; Backing vocalist, major artists; Concerts include: Prince's Trust Concert (played to Prince and Princess of Wales), Royal Albert Hall; Concerts for: Mandela family; President of Algeria; Princess Caroline, Prince Albert of Monaco; Sellout tours with Imagination, 1982–83. *Recordings:* with Imagination: Body Talk, 1981; Flashback, 1981; In and Out of Love, 1981; Just An Illusion (No. 2, UK), 1982; Music and Lights, 1982; In The Heat of The Night, 1982; Changes, 1982; Looking At Midnight, 1983; Thank You My Love, 1984; Instinctual, 1988; Albums include: Body Talk, 1981; Scandalous, 2000; Solo: Let There Be Love (featured with Arthur Baker); The Mighty Power of Love; Your Mind Your Body Your Soul, 2000. *Honours:* Diamond Award; Gold and Platinum discs world-wide; Blues and Soul Award. *Membership:* Musicians' Union; BAC&S; PRS; PPL. *Current Management:* Johnny X Productions, c/o Gina Smith Management. *Address:* 22 Croftside, Vigo Village, Kent DA13 0SH, England.

JOHNNY BLAZE. See: **METHOD MAN**.

JOHNSON, Alastair; b. 1 July 1966, Oxford, England. Recording Engineer; Record Prod; Programmer; Writer. *Career:* Initially live sound engineer, then house engineer, various UK studios including: Red Bus, Jacobs, Wool Hall, late 1980s; Artiste manager, 2 years; Returned to studio as freelance engineer, producer. *Recordings:* Engineer, albums: First of a Million Kisses, Fairground Attraction; Extricate, The Fall; Infinity, Donovan. *Current Management:* Strongroom Management. *Address:* Strongroom Studios, 120 Curtain Rd, London EC2A 3PJ, England.

JOHNSON, Brian; b. 5 Oct. 1947, Newcastle. Vocalist; Lyricist. *Career:* Lead singer, UK rock band Geordie; Lead singer, heavy rock group AC/DC,

1980–; Appearances include: Monsters of Rock Festival, Castle Donington, 1981, 1984; European rock festivals, Switzerland, Hungary, Belgium, Germany, 1991; Concert, Moscow, 1991. *Recordings:* with Geordie: Hope You Like It, 1973; Don't Be Fooled By the Name, 1974; Brian Johnson and Geordie, 1981; with AC/DC: Singles include: Back In Black, 1981; You Shook Me All Night Long, 1981; Rock 'n' Roll Ain't Noise Pollution, 1981; Let's Get It Up, 1982; For Those About To Rock (We Salute You), 1982; Guns For Hire, 1983; Nervous Shakedown, 1984; Shake Your Foundations, 1985; Who Made Who, 1985; That's The Way I Wanna Rock 'n' Roll, 1988; Heatseeker, 1988; Thunderstruck, 1990; Moneytalks, 1991; Are You Ready, 1991; Big Gun (used in film The Last Action Hero), 1993; Hard As A Rock, 1995; Stiff Upper Lip, 2000; Albums: Back In Black (No. 1, UK), 1980; For Those About To Rock (We Salute You) (No. 1, USA), 1981; Flick of The Switch, 1983; Fly On The Wall, 1985; Who Made Who, 1986; Blow Up Your Video, 1988; The Razor's Edge, 1990; Live, 1992; Ballbreaker, 1995; Bonfire, 1997; Stiff Upper Lip, 2000; Also appears on: Zappa The Yellow Shark, 1993; Adventures of the OC Supertones, 1996; Chase the Sun, 1999. *Current Management:* Hard To Handle Management, 640 Lee Rd, Suite 106, Wayne, PA 19087, USA.

JOHNSON, David Paul; b. 8 Oct. 1957, WA, USA. Composer; Musician; Educator. 1 s., 2 d. *Education:* BA, Whitman College, 1979; MA, Music University of Oregon, 1992; PhD, Music University of Oregon, 1997. *Career:* Blue Buddha Performance at the International Computer Music Conference, 1996; Informatique Musicale, 1996; These Sins Will Not Be Forgiven. *Compositions:* Blue Buddha; These Sins Will Not Be Forgiven; Ozone; Warwords; Empathy Atrophied. *Recordings:* David Paul Johnson 5 x 5. *Honours:* Composer in Residence, 1992. *Membership:* Music Educators National Conference; International Computer Music Asscn. *Address:* 445 W 19th, Eugene, OR 97401, USA.

JOHNSON, Derick; b. 7 June 1963, Manchester, England. Musician (bass guitar). 2 s. *Career:* Started 52nd Street, 1983–86; Played with Swing Out Sister, 1989–; 4 tours: Italy; Phillipines; Spain; UK; Japan; America; Radio One sessions, Top of the Pops, Tube, The Word, Pebble Mill. *Compositions:* That's The Way It Goes; Low Down Dirty Business; Cool As Ice. *Recordings:* Live album: Swing Out Sister; Get In Touch With Yourself; The Living Return. *Membership:* Musicians' Union. *Address:* 66 Avebury Rd, Boguley, Wytheshowe, Manchester M23 2QE, England.

JOHNSON, Henry Joseph, Jr; b. 28 Jan. 1954, Chicago, Illinois, USA. Jazz Musician (guitar); Vocalist. *Education:* Indiana University. *Career:* Guitarist, for organist Jack McDuff, 1976; Singer, Donny Hathaway, 1977; Pianist, Ramsey Lewis, 1979–82; 1985–; Singer, Joe Williams, 1986–; Saxophonist, Stanley Turrentine, 1995–; Solo artiste, 1987–; Performances include: All jazz festivals including Playboy Jazz Festival; JVC Jazz Festival; North Seas Jazz Festival. *Recordings:* 5 as solo artiste, include: You're The One; Future Excursions; New Beginnings; 3 with jazz vocalist, Joe Williams; 6 with pianist, Ramsey Lewis. *Honours:* Downbeat: CD: You're The One, awarded 5 stars; Billboard Top 100 List, 1986, 1987, 1988. *Membership:* Musicians' Union; AFTRA; NARAS. *Current Management:* John Levy Enterprises. *Address:* 2810 W Charleston Blvd G-72, Las Vegas, NE 89102, USA.

JOHNSON, Holly (William); b. 9 Feb. 1960, Liverpool, England. Vocalist; Songwriter; Author; Artist; Actor. *Career:* Member, Big In Japan; Founder Member, Frankie Goes to Hollywood, 1980–87; Appearances include: World tours; Montreux Rock Festival, MTV, in the Motion Picture Body Double, 1995, Band Aid single, Hillsborough Justice Concert, 1997; Solo Artiste, 1987–; Exhibition of paintings and sculptures, The House of Holly, Cork Street Gallery, London, 1996; Owner, Pleasuredome record label. *Recordings:* Albums: with Frankie Goes to Hollywood: Welcome to the Pleasuredome, (No. 1, UK), 1984; Liverpool, 1986; Blast (No. 1, UK), 1989; Hollelujah, 1989; Dreams That Money Can't Buy, 1991; Bang! – Greatest Hits of Frankie Goes to Hollywood, 1993; Reload, 1994; Maximum Joy, 2000; Solo album: Soulstream, 1999; Singles include: Relax, (No. 1, UK), 1984; Two Tribes (No. 1, UK), 1984; The Power of Love (No. 1, UK), 1984; Welcome to the Pleasuredome, 1985; Rage Hard, 1986; Warriors of the Wasteland, 1986; Watching the Wildlife, 1986; Solo singles: Love Train, 1989; Americanos, 1989; Atomic City, 1989; The Power of Love, 1999; Soulstream, 1999. *Contributions to:* Ferry Cross The Mersey, charity single with The Christians, Paul McCartney and Gerry Marsden (No. 1, UK), 1989; Last Temptation of Elvis, compilation album, 1990. *Publications:* A Bone in My Flute, autobiography, 1994. *Honours:* Only group to have 2 Platinum singles with first 2 releases, first three singles went to No. 1, UK, 1984; Two BRIT Awards, Best British Single, Best British Newcomer, 1985; Ivor Novello Award, Best Contemporary Song, Two Tribes, 1985. *Address:* Pleasuredome, PO Box 425, London SW6 3TX, England.

JOHNSON, John (J. J.); b. 27 Oct. 1951. Newark, Nottinghamshire, England. Musician (drums, keyboards); Vocalist; Prod. Partner, Christine Robertson, 2 s. *Career:* Drummer, Wayne County and The Electric Chairs, 1976–80; with Mystere Five; Drums, vocals, Flying Lizards, Thomas Dolby; Skids; Nico; GBM, drums, vocals. *Recordings:* with The Electric Chairs: The Electric Chairs (EP), 1977; Blatently Offensive (EP), 1978; Albums: The Electric Chairs, 1977; Storm The Gates of Heaven, 1978; Things Your Mother

Never Told You, 1979; 8 singles include: Thunder When She Walks, 1977; Trying To Get On The Radio, 1978; Eddie and Sheena, 1978; Waiting For The Marines, 1979; Berlin, 1979; So Many Ways, 1979; with Mystere 5 singles include: Heart Rules The Head and No Message, 1980; with The Flying Lizards; album: Fourth Wall, 1981; Single: Lovers and Other Strangers; Jungle Line (EP), Thomas Dolby, 1981; Albums: Drama of Exile, Nico; Joy, The Skids, 1981; Ten Thirty On A Summer's Night, Richard Jobson, 1983; with GBM, album: Method In The Madness; with Neil Finn: One Nil, 2001; Singles: Strange News; Diction and Fiction; Whistling In The Dark, 1983–84. *Membership:* Musicians' Union. *Address:* GBM Productions, 41B Kingsgate Rd, London NW6 4TD, England.

JOHNSON, Kelly; Musician (guitar); Vocalist. *Career:* Joined Girlschool, 1978; Introduced to management deal with Bronze label by Lemmy from Motörhead, 1980; Supported Motörhead on their Overkill tour; Numerous tours, television performances and hit singles; Further collaborations with Motörhead; Tours in Canada and the USA; Left band, 1984; Unsuccessful solo career; Briefly rejoined re-formed group, 1995, for European tour; Contributed to albums, 2000–. *Recordings:* Albums: Demolition, 1980; Hit 'N' Run, 1981; Screaming Blue Murder, 1982; Play Dirty, 1983; Running Wild, 1995; Can't Keep A Good Girl Down, 1999; Very Best Of Remastered, 2002; 21st Anniversary: Not That Innocent, 2002. Singles: Take It All Away; Race With The Devil; St Valentine's Day Massacre (EP with Motörhead, as Headgirl); Please Don't Touch, 1981; Hit And Run, 1981; C'mon Let's Go, 1981. *Address:* c/o PO Box 33446, London SW18 3XN, England.

JOHNSON, Kenny; b. 11 Dec. 1939, Halewood, Merseyside, England. Country Vocalist; Songwriter; Musician (guitar). 1 s., 1 d. *Education:* Rock 'n' Roll clubs around Liverpool. *Career:* Leader of group Northwind; 40 years professional; Television appearances throughout UK, Europe and USA; Major tours with: Marty Robbins; Billie Jo Spears; Johnny Cash; Major concerts: Rhyman Auditorium, original Grand Ole Opry tour, USA; Grand Ole Opry, Tennessee; Falklands, 3 times; Belize, twice; Euromasters Festival, Holland; Presenter, weekly radio shows, BBC Radio Merseyside, BBC Northwest; Owner, Stocks Records. *Recordings:* 16 albums include: Today: City Lights; Today; Summer Nights; Blue Rendezvous. *Honours:* 2 British Country Music Radio Awards, 1992; CMRU International Publishers Award, 1993; BCMA Award, Best British Male Performer, 1993; Gold Star Award, Netherlands; Best Male Vocalist, Variety Club of Great Britain; 2 MCM Awards. *Membership:* Musicians' Union; PRS. *Address:* 54 Edward Rd, Whiston, Merseyside L35 5AJ, England.

JOHNSON, Laurie; b. 1927, London, England. Composer. m., 1 d. *Education:* Royal College of Music. *Career:* Taught at Royal College of Music; Orchestral pieces broadcast by age 20; Composer, arranger, Ted Heath Band and all major bands and orchestras of 1950s; Entered film industry, 1955; Co-owner, film production companies including Gainsborough Pictures, 1979–; Founder, The London Big Band (25 British jazz and orchestral musicians), for concerts and recordings with international star guests, 1994. *Compositions include:* Lock Up Your Daughters, musical; Pieces of Eight, revue; The Four Musketeers, musical; Scores for over 400 cinema and television films including: Dr Strangelove; First Men In The Moon; The Avengers; The Professionals; The New Avengers; Television themes include: This Is Your Life; World In Action; Whicker's World. *Recordings:* Synthesis, symphony; The Wind In The Willows, tone poem; Suite for symphonic band (RAF commission for 50th anniversary of Battle of Britain); The Conquistadors, music for Royal occasions; Numerous albums with own studio orchestra. *Honours:* Various awards for music scores and record or film productions. *Address:* The Laurie Johnson Organisation Ltd, 10 College Rd, Harrow, Middlesex HA1 1DA, England.

JOHNSON, Matt; b. 15 Aug. 1961, East London, England. Vocalist; Songwriter; Musician (guitar); Record Prod. *Career:* Member, first band Road Star, aged 11; Recording engineer, London, aged 15, 1976; Formed The The, aged 17, 1979; The The, general music collective, over 300 artistes (including Sinead O'Connor, Jools Holland, Johnny Marr, Neneh Cherry, Zeke Manyika, Warne Livesey), 1979–; Concerts and tours include: Residency at Marquee, London (with Marc Almond, Zeke Manyika), 1983; World tours, 1989–90, 1992–93; Royal Albert Hall, 1990; Headliners, Reading Festival, 1993; Films: Infected (long-form video to accompany album), 1987; The The Versus The World, 1991; From Dusk 'Til Dawn, 1994. *Recordings:* Albums: Burning Blue Soul, 1981; Soul Mining, 1983; Infected (also film and book), 1986; Mind Bomb, 1989; Dusk, 1993; Solitude, 1994; Hanky Panky, 1995; Naked Self, 2000; with Orang: Herd of Instinct, 1995; with Shudder to Think: First Love Last Rites, 1998; Singles include: Controversial Subject, 1981; Uncertain Smile, 1982; Perfect, 1983; This Is The Day, 1983; Sweet Bird of Truth, 1986; Heartland, 1986; Infected, 1986; Slow Train To Dawn, 1987; Armageddon Days, 1989; The Beat(en) Generation, 1989; Gravitate To Me, 1989; Shades of Blue, EP, 1991; Dogs of Lust, 1993; Slow Emotion Replay, 1993; Love Is Stronger Than Death, 1993; Dis-Infected EP, 1994; I Saw The Light, 1995. *Publications:* Infected (lyrics and paintings), 1987. *Honours:* Best Long Form Video, Montreux Film and Music Festival, Infected, 1988; Platinum, Gold or Silver records for all albums. *Current Management:* c/o Fran Musso, REN Management, 1125 Coldwater Canyon, Beverly Hills, CA 90210, USA.

JOHNSON, Mike; b. 27 Aug. 1965, Grant Pass, Oregon, USA. Musician (guitar, bass); Songwriter; Vocalist. m. Leslie, 21 Nov. 1994. *Education:* AA. *Career:* Solo artiste; Bassist, Dinosaur Jr, 1992–; Cameo; Appearances in Grace of My Heart. *Recordings:* Where Am I, 1994; Year of Mondays, 1996; I Feel Alright, 1998; with Dinosaur Jr: Whatever's Cool with Me, 1991; Where You Been?, 1993; Without a Sound, 1994; Hand It Over, 1997; The BBC Sessions, 2000; Ear-Bleeding Country (compilation), 2001. *Membership:* BMI. *Current Management:* BYD Management. *Address:* c/o BYD, 501 N 36th #196, Seattle, WA 98103, USA.

JOHNSON, Robb Jenner; b. 25 Dec. 1955, London, England. Vocalist; Songwriter; Musician (guitar). m. Meeta Kanabar, 22 Aug. 1992. *Education:* BA Hons, MA, English Literature. *Career:* Folk clubs, 1975–80; Band, Grubstreet, 1980–84; Agit-prop trio, Ministry of Humour, 1984–86; Solo, then duo with Pip Collings, 1989–94; Solo: Nicaragua TV, Managua Concert for the 10th anniversary of the Revolution, 1989; CH4 documentary, Beyond The Maypole, 1991; Tour of Belgium, 1995; 25th Anniversary, Glastonbury Festival, 1995. *Recordings:* Albums: Skewed Stewed and Awkward, 1987; Small Town World, 1989; Overnight, 1991; Heart's Desire, 1993; Lack of Jolly Ploughboy, 1994; This Is The UK Talking, 1994. *Publications:* Rosa's Lovely Daughters; I Close My Eyes; Boxing Day; Herald of Free Enterprise. *Honours:* 1980 Northwest Songwriters Competition. *Membership:* Musicians' Union; PRS. *Address:* c/o Rhiannon Records, Freepost LON 6347, London E8 2BR, England.

JOHNSON, Stanley Glen; b. 1 Sept. 1953, Hillsdale, Michigan, USA. Recording Artiste; Artiste Man. m. Jacalyn Joy Ware, 29 Aug. 1970, 1 s., 2 d. *Education:* Jackson Community College. *Career:* Radio in USA; Local church concerts and special fair programmes. *Compositions:* As songwriter: Hold On; There'll Be Hell To Pay; Not Guilty. *Publications:* The Singing News; The Gospel Voice; Gospel Music News. *Honours:* Editors Choice Awards; National Library of Poetry. *Membership:* BMI. *Current Management:* CER Records, USA.

JOHNSON, Wilko; b. 12 July 1947, Canvey Island, Essex, England. Vocalist; Musician (guitar). m. Irene Knight, 6 April 1968, 2 s. *Education:* BA Hons, English. *Career:* Guitarist, songwriter, founder member of Dr Feelgood; Played with Ian Dury and The Blockheads, 1980–82; Extensive tours with own band, 1985–. *Compositions include:* Back in the Night; She Does It Right; Roxette. *Recordings:* Albums include: Down By the Jetty, 1975 and Stupidity, 1976 (with Dr Feelgood); Barbed Wire Blues; Don't Let Your Daddy Know; with Mick Farren: Vampires Stole My Lunch Money, 1978; with Ian Dury: Laughter, 1980; with Stranglers: Live in Concert, 1995; Solo Albums: Solid Senders, 1978; Ice on the Motorway, 1981; Bottle Up and Go, 1983; Pull the Cover, 1995; Going Back Home, 1998; Dr Feelgood compilations include: Live At The BBC 1974–75, 1999; The BBC Sessions 1973–78, 2001; Singled Out (As Bs and Rarities), 2001. *Membership:* MCPS; PRS. *Current Management:* Irene Knight.

JOHNSON, Yana; b. 23 Sept. 1969, England. Vocalist; Songwriter. *Education:* BSc Environmental Control; Grade 1 Classical. *Career:* Writer, scripts and song material for theatrical productions; Backing vocalist, 291 Talent Show; Worked with Total Contrast; Session work with artistes including: Massive Attack; Neneh Cherry; Raw Stylus; Cold Cut; British tour with Drizabone. *Recordings:* Songs: I Do, Total Contrast (on compilation album Full Swing); Believe, Cold Cut; Writer, producer, demo material, I've Found You, Troi; also written with Shola Ama on second album: That Thing; Surrender; Album: Bring It On. *Membership:* Musicians' Union. *Current Management:* Urban Management, c/o Nick Sellars.

JOHNSTON, Jim; b. 20 Dec. 1954, Dundalk, Ireland. Vocalist; Songwriter; Dancer. m. Patricia, 19 June 1981, 1 s., 2 d. *Education:* Teaching Diploma, St Patrick's Training College, Drumcondra, Dublin; Tuition in Drums, CCÉ, Dundalk; Studied Traditional Fiddle with Rose O'Connor; Matthews School of Irish Dance. *Career:* Songwriter and Dancer; Toured Czechoslovakia with Dún Dealgan Cabaret, 1978; Comhaltas Tour of Britain, 1980; Toured Austria with Lá Lugh (traditional band), 1995; Irish Music Festival, Copenhagen, 1996; Appeared on RTÉ Live at 3, 1997; Síbín Tna G, 1998; Played support to: Mary Coughlan, 1994, Mick Hanly, 1994, Sonny Condell, 1995, Don Baker, 1995, Freddie White, 1996; Something Happens, Drogheda, 1998. *Compositions:* Victory or Defeat; Squeeze Gut Alley Blues; Fairhill – Time Stood Still; It's The Same Sun; The Paragon Seven. *Recordings:* The Factories – They're All Closing Down, 1986; Rian An Uaignis, 1993, CD version, 1996; Guested on Orla – The Blue Note, 1998; Album, Politics of The Heart, 1999. *Publications:* Pléaráca Dhún Dealgan (The Humours of Dundalk: Collection of Folk Songs), 1985. *Honours:* Men's World Irish Dancing Champion, 1975, 1977, 1979. *Membership:* Irish Music Rights Organization. *Current Management:* Uaigneas Music.

JOHNSTON, Timothy John; b. 12 Nov. 1963, Newcastle upon Tyne, England. Musician (drums). *Education:* 1 year light music course, Newcastle College. *Career:* Toured extensively with Pauline Murray and The Storm, including full tour supporting The Mission, 1985–; Television and radio appearances with The Light Programme and Swing Palace, 1987–94; Regular appearances at national jazz festivals; Toured with Deacon Jones and the Sinners, 1994; Performing in resident band, Bourbon Street, at Hilton, Park Lane, London, 1995. *Recordings:* 2 albums with The Light Programme, 1987, 1989; Album Storm Clouds, 1989, and 2 singles, This Thing Called Love and New Age, with Pauline Murray; 2 albums with Swing Palace, 1991, 1993. *Membership:* Musicians' Union. *Address:* 20 Highbury, Monkseaton, Whitley Bay, Tyne and Wear NE25 8EF, England.

JOLLY ROGER. See: **RICHARDS, Eddie.**

JONASSON, Jonas; b. 28 Aug. 1967, Angelholm, Sweden. Musician (synthesizer, vocoder, melodica). m. Malin Jonasson-Sahlstedt, 16 May 1992, 2 d. *Career:* Member, bob hund, formed in 1991; More than 300 gigs around Scandinavia; Played at famous Roskilde, Lollipop, Ruisrock, Quartfestivalen and Hultsfred. *Compositions:* I Stället för Musik: Förvirring, 1996; Düsseldorf, 1996. *Recordings:* bob hund – bob hund, 1993; bob hund – Edvin Medvind, 1994; bob hund – Omslag: Martin Kann, 1996; bob hund – Omslag: Martin Kann, 1996; bob hund, Stenaldern Kan Borja, 2001. *Honours:* Grammy, best live act, 1994; Grammy, best lyrics, 1996. *Membership:* STIM; SAMI. *Address:* c/o Bob Hunds Förlag, Råsundavägen 150, 169 36 Solna, Sweden.

JONES, Alan John; b. 2 April 1947, Rotherham, Yorkshire, England. Musician (Bass Guitar). 2 c. *Education:* Eric Guilder School of Music, London. *Career:* Appearances at London Palladium, Royal Albert Hall, Caesar's Palace, Las Vegas; Musician, film music for Live and Let Die, with George Martin and Paul McCartney, theme music for Taggart, STV, theme tune for quiz show Blockbusters; music for advertisement, Milk Tray. *Compositions:* A Shadow in Time, for Bucks Fizz; Puttin' On the Style, for Lonnie Donegan; Somewhere in England, for George Harrison; Gone Troppo, for Julio Iglesias; Libra, for Hank Marvin. *Recordings:* Appearances on The Best of Hank Marvin and the Shadows; The Freddie Mercury Album; Gilbert O'Sullivan Himself; Back to Front; I'm a Writer Not a Fighter; Greatest Hits; 20 Golden Greats, for Cliff Richard; I'm Nearly Famous. *Publications:* A Shadow in Time, 1986. *Honours:* Appearance on Royal Variety Performance with Cliff Richard and The Shadows, 1984. *Membership:* Musicians' Union; POAMRA. *Address:* 4A Mercury Close, Bampton, Oxon OX18 2AH, England.

JONES, Bill (Belinda Helen); b. 17 Aug. 1973, Codsall, Wolverhampton, England, UK. Vocalist; Musician (accordion, piano, flute, whistle); Composer. *Education:* London City University. *Career:* Folk musician; worked with Scots accordionist Phil Cunningham; BBC radio sessions for Folk on 2 and Andy Kershaw. *Recordings:* Singles: Bits and Pieces, 2001; Albums: Turn To Me, 2000; Panchpuran, 2001. *Honours:* BBC Horizon Award for New Talent, 2001. *Current Management:* Felicity Jones, 10 Meadowbank Ave, Weston, Stafford, ST18 OHE, England. *Website:* www.brickwallmusic.com.

JONES, Bobby Louis; b. 1939, Hindreas, TN, USA. Gospel Vocalist; Television broadcaster; Teacher. m. Ethel Williams Jones. *Education:* BEd, Elementary Education, MEd, Elementary Education, Tennessee State University; PhD, Reading and Special Education, Vanderbilt University, 1980. *Career:* Teacher, elementary schools in Tennessee and Missouri; Textbook consultant; Instructor in reading and study skills, Tennessee State University, 1972–85; Gospel singer, early 1970s–; Presenter, Fun City 5 (WTBF); Formed gospel group, New Life, 1975; Appearance, Sister Sister (television film), 1982; Presenter, Bobby Jones World, 1978–84, The Bobby Jones Gospel Hour (Black Entertainment Television), 1980–, Video Gospel, 1989–; Founder, touring show Bobby Jones Gospel Explosion, 1989–; Presenter, The Bobby Jones Gospel Countdown (radio); Other programmes include: Bobby Jones Presents... Gospel on Stage, 2001–; Bobby Jones Presents... Gospel Classics, 2001–. *Recordings:* with New Life: Sooner Or Later, 1976; There Is Hope In This World, 1978; Caught Up, 1979; Tin Gladje, 1981; Soul Set Free, 1982; Come Together, 1984; I'll Never Forget, 1990; Bring It To Jesus, 1993; Another Time, 1996; with Nashville Superchoir: Just Churchin', 1998. *Compositions:* Make A Joyful Noise (gospel opera), 1980. *Publications:* Make A Joyful Noise: My 25 Years in Gospel Music (autobiography, with Lesley Sussman), 2000. *Honours:* Gabriel Award, 1980; International Film Festival Award, for Make A Joyful Noise, 1980; Gospel Music Association, Dove Award for Black Contemporary Album of the Year, 1984; Grammy Award, Best Vocal Duo for a Soul/Gospel Performance, for I'm So Glad I'm Standing Here Today, 1984; NAACP Image Award, 1984; Gospel Music Asscn, Commonwealth Award for Outstanding Contribution to Gospel Music, 1990; Hon. doctorate, Theology, Payne Theological Seminary, Wilberforce, OH, 1991. *Address:* Millennium Entertainment, 1314 Fifth Ave N, Nashville, TN 37208, USA. *Website:* www.bobbyjonesgospel.com.

JONES, Booker T; b. 12 Nov. 1944, Memphis, Tennessee, USA. Musician (keyboards); Songwriter; Record Prod. m. Priscilla Coolidge. *Career:* Session musician, Memphis; Leader, Booker T and The MGs (Memphis Group), 1962–71; Concerts include: Soul Sensation British tour, 1967; Monterey Pop Festival, 1967; Solo songwriter and vocalist, 1971–; Reunions with the MGs: Album, 1977; Tours of Europe, USA, 1990; Backing band for Neil Young's US tour, 1993. *Compositions include:* Film score, Up Tight, 1969; Songwriter, musician with Sam and Dave; Wilson Pickett; Otis Redding; Rufus Thomas. *Recordings:* Albums: Up Tight, 1969; Booker T and Priscilla, 1971; The

Runaway, 1972; Try and Love Again, 1978; with the MGs: Green Onions, 1964; Hip Hug-Her, 1967; Back To Back, 1967; Doin' Our Thing, 1968; Soul Limbo, 1968; Best Of..., 1968; The Booker T Set, 1969; McLemore Avenue, 1970; Greatest Hits, 1970; Melting Pot, 1971; Union Extended, 1976; Universal Language, 1977; As producer: Stardust, Willie Nelson, 1978; Singles include: Green Onions, 1962 (included in film soundtrack Quadrophenia); Boot-Leg, 1965; Hip Hug-Her, 1967; Groovin', 1967; Soul Limbo, 1968; Hang 'Em High, used as film theme, 1969; Time Is Tight, from film Up Tight, 1969; Melting Pot, 1971. *Honours:* Rock and Roll Hall of Fame, Booker T and the MGs, 1992. *Address:* c/o Concerted Efforts, PO Box 99, Newtonville, MA 02169, USA.

JONES, Chris; b. 10 Jan. 1963, Paris, France. Author; Composer; Writer; Prod. m. Anne Nbole, Salome Mga, Helene Betala, 4 d. *Education:* Composition; Musicology; Copyright Law Business. *Career:* Concentrated On Studio Work and Writing. *Compositions:* Include, Silent Over; Till The Middle of The Night; Call Me; Hold On Me; Boys Come and Go; Lovin' Livin' Givin'; Stay Around; Boogie Dancin' Shoes. *Recordings:* Silent Lover; Till The Middle Of The Night; Call Me; Lovin' Livin' Givin'. *Publications:* Surviving For Your Love. *Membership:* SACEM; ASCAP. *Address:* PO Box 6101, Yaounde, Cameroon, Africa.

JONES, Chris Alan; b. 18 Dec. 1966, Reading, England. Musician (drums, percussion). *Education:* Drum lessons, 1993–. *Career:* Drummer, Mega City Four, 1987–; 6 albums; Major world tours with each release; Appeared on: Chart Show; The Word; MTV 120 Minutes; Recorded 2 sessions, John Peel Show. *Recordings:* with Mega City Four: Tranzophobia, 1989; Who Cares Wins, 1990; Terribly Sorry Bob, 1991; Sebastopol Road, 1992; Magic Bullets, 1993; 2 sessions, John Peel Show, album, 1994. *Publications:* Tall Stories and Creepy Crawlies, by Martin Roach. *Membership:* Musicians' Union. *Current Management:* Paul Bolton, ICM/Fair Warning. *Address:* 5 Rother Rd, Cove, Farnborough, Hampshire GU14 9LP, England.

JONES, Daniel; b. 22 July 1973, Essex, England. Musician (multi-instrumentalist). *Education:* Shailer Park High, Logan City, Australia. *Career:* Relocated to Brisbane, Australia, as a child; Worked as a printer and in a supermarket; Played in Red Edge until breaking away with fellow group mem., Darren Hayes, to form Savage Garden, 1996; Hugely successful world-wide; Live performances include closing ceremony of Olympic Games, Sydney, 2000; Savage Garden split, 2001; Move into production work, 2001–. *Recordings:* Albums: Savage Garden, 1997; Affirmation, 1999. Singles: I Want You, 1996; To The Moon and Back, 1996; Truly Madly Deeply (No. 1, UK), 1997; Break Me Shake Me, 1997; Universe, 1997; The Animal Song, 1999; I Knew I Loved You (No. 1, UK), 1999; Affirmation, 2000; Crash and Burn, 2000; Chained To You, 2000; Hold Me, 2001. *Honours:* First LP sales of over 11m.; ARIA Awards, won a record 10 awards, 1997; APRA Award, Songwriters of the Year, 2000; Truly Madly Deeply set new record for longest stay on Billboard Adult Contemporary Airplay Chart (106 weeks), 2000. *Address:* c/o Larry Tollin Entertainment, 9255 Sunset Blvd, Suite 411, Los Angeles, CA 90069, USA. *E-mail:* savage@village.com.au. *Website:* www.savagegarden.com.

JONES, Davy; b. 30 Dec. 1945, Manchester, Lancashire, England. Vocalist; Actor; Musician (guitar). *Career:* Member, The Monkees, 1966–70; 1986–89; Actor, The Monkees comedy television series, 1966–68; 33 1/3 Revolutions Per Monkee, TV Special, NBC; Television actor in: June Evening; Coronation Street; Z-Cars; Ben Casey; Farmers Daughter; Trainer; Stage performances include: Oliver; Pickwick; The Point; Founder, Davy Jones Presents record label, 1967; Owner, Zilch Boutique, 1967; Member, Dolenz, Jones, Boyce and Hart, 1975–76. *Recordings:* Albums: The Monkees (No. 1, USA and UK), 1966; More of The Monkees (No. 1, USA and UK), 1967; Headquarters, (No. 1, USA), 1967; Pisces, Aquarius, Capricorn and Jones Ltd, 1967; The Birds, The Bees and The Monkees, 1968; Head (soundtrack), 1969; The Monkees Greatest Hits, 1969; The Monkees Present, 1969; Instant Replay, 1969; Then and Now, 1986; Pool It, 1987; Monkees Greatest Hits, 1999; Music Box, 2001; The Definitive Monkees, 2001; with Big Foot Chester: Devil in Me, 1998; Tabernacalin', 1998; Singles: Last Train To Clarksville (No. 1, USA), 1966; I'm A Believer (No. 1, USA), 1966; (I'm Not Your) Steppin' Stone, 1967; A Little Bit Me, A Little Bit You, 1967; Alternate Title, 1967; Pleasant Valley Sunday, 1967; Daydream Believer (No. 1, USA), 1967; Valleri, 1968; Tear Drop City, 1969. *Honours:* NARM Awards, Best Selling Group, Best Album, 1967; Emmy Award, Outstanding Comedy Series, 1967; 3 BMI Awards, 1968; Monkees Day, Atlanta, 1986; Star on Hollywood Walk of Fame, 1989. *Address:* c/o Nationwide Entertainment Services, 2756 N Green Valley Parkway, Suite 449, Las Vegas, NV 89014–2100, USA.

JONES, Donell; b. Chicago, IL, USA. Vocalist. *Career:* Influenced by gospel singer father; Noticed by Eddie F of Untouchables Entertainment at Black Radio Exclusive conference; Signed within a month to Untouchable/LaFace Records; Debut album My Heart released, 1996; Written and produced tracks for Silk, Brownstone and Usher; Contributed vocal arrangements to Madonna's Bedtime Stories album; Collaborations: Guru; True Steppers; Lisa 'Left Eye' Lopes. *Recordings:* Albums: My Heart, 1996; Where You Wanna Be, 1999; Life Goes On, 2002. Singles: Knocks Me Off My Feet, 1997; U Know

What's Up, 1999; Shorty, 2000. *Honours:* American Music Award, Favorite New Artist, 2001. *Address:* c/o LaFace Records, 3350 Peachtree Rd 1500, Atlanta, Georgia, USA.

JONES, Ed (Edgar Francis); b. 8 July 1961, Amersham, Buckinghamshire, England. Musician (saxophone); Composer. *Education:* BA Music, Middlesex University. *Career:* World-wide tours, television and radio with US3; Incognito; Ed Jones Quartet/Quintet; Television appearances include: MTV; CNN; Stations in USA; Europe; Japan; Far East. *Recordings:* Solo: The Home Coming, 1989; Pipers Tales, 1995; Seven Moments, 2002; Featured on compilations: Mellow Mahem, 1988; Talkin' Land II, 1993; Bachology, 1995; Other. *Recordings include:* Hand On The Torch, US3, 1993; Where One Is, Dick Heckstall-Smith, 1989; New Cool, John Stevens, 1994; Sound Advice, Ron Wallen, 1993; Siren Song, Jessica Lauron, 1994; 100% and Rising, Incognito. *Membership:* PRS; MCPS; Musicians' Union. *Address:* Flat C, University House, 16 Victoria Park Sq., London E2 9PE, England.

JONES, George Glenn; b. 12 Sept. 1931, Saratoga, Texas, USA. Country Vocalist; Musician (guitar). m. (1) Tammy Wynette, 1969, divorced 1975, (2) Nancy Sepulveda, 1983. *Career:* Recording artiste, 1953–; Worked under names of Johnny Williams, Hank Davis, Glen Patterson; Worked with The Big Bopper; Johnny Preston; Johnny Paycheck; Recorded duets with Gene Pitney; Melba Montgomery; Tammy Wynette; Elvis Costello; James Taylor; Willie Nelson. *Compositions include:* The Window Up Above, Mickey Gilley; Seasons of My Heart, Johnny Cash, Jerry Lee Lewis. *Recordings:* 150 Country hits include: Why Baby Why; White Lightning; Tender Years; She Still Thinks I Care; You Comb Her Hair; Who Shot Sam?; The Grand Tour; He Stopped Loving Her Today; Recorded over 450 albums; Recent albums include: First Time Live, 1985; Who's Gonna Fill Them Shoes, 1985; Wine Coloured Roses, 1986; Super Hits, 1987; Too Wild Too Long, 1987; One Woman Man, 1989; Hallelujah Weekend, 1990; You Oughta Be Here With Me, 1990; And Along Came Jones, 1991; Friends In High Places, 1991; Salutes Bob Wills and Hank Williams, 1992; Live At Dancetown USA, 1992; Walls Can Fall, 1992; One, 1995; I Lived to Tell It All, 1996; In a Gospel Way, 1997; It Don't Get Any Better Than This, 1998; The Cold Hard Truth, 1999; Live with the Possum, 1999; The Rock Stone Cold Country, 2001; with Tammy Wynette: We Can Go Together, 1971; Me and The First Lady, 1972; Golden Ring, 1976; Together Again, 1980. *Honours:* Grammy Award, Male Country Vocal Performance, Choices, 2000. *Address:* c/o Nancy Jones, Jones Country, 48 Music Sq. E, Nashville, TN 37203, USA.

JONES, Gordon Thomas; b. 21 Nov. 1947, Birkenhead, Merseyside, England. Musician (guitar); Record Co Exec. m. Jackie Jones, 26 May 1984, 1 s. *Education:* Art College, Edinburgh, Scotland. *Career:* Founder, Scottish folk band Silly Wizard, recording 9 albums; Founder, partner, Harbourtown Records, producing 36 albums to date including 2 MRA award winners; Toured Europe and USA over 17 years. *Recordings:* All Silly Wizard albums; Produced most Harbourtown Productions. *Honours:* 2 MRS Awards as producer; Naird Award as musician, 1986. *Membership:* MCPS; PRS; PPC. *Address:* PO Box 25, Ulverston, Cumbria LA12 7UN, England.

JONES, Grace; b. 19 May 1952. Vocalist; Composer; Actor; Model. *Career:* Film appearances include: Gordon's War; A View To Kill. *Recordings:* Albums: Portfolio, 1977; Fame, 1978; Muse, 1979; Warm Leatherette, 1980; Night Clubbing, 1981; Living My Life, 1982; Island Life, 1985; Slave To The Rhythm, 1985; Inside Story, 1986; Bulletproof Heart, 1990; Private Life: The Compass Point Sessions, 1998; The Dance Collection, 2000; Singles include: Private Life, 1980; Pull Up To The Bumper, 1981; The Apple Stretching/ Nipple To The Bottle, 1982; My Jamaican Guy, 1983; Slave To The Rhythm, 1985; La Vie En Rose, 1986; Love Is The Drug, 1986; I'm Not Perfect, 1986; Pull Up To The Bumper, with Funkstar DeLuxe, 2000; Appearance on: The Notorious K.I.M., Lil' Kim, 2000. *Current Management:* Pyramid Entertainment Group (USA), 89 Fifth Ave, Seventh Floor, New York, NY 10003, USA.

JONES, Jack (John Allen); b. 14 Jan. 1938, Los Angeles, California, USA. Vocalist; Actor. *Education:* Studied singing at high school. *Career:* Club singer, 1957; Recording artiste, 1962–; Appearances with Jerry Lewis; Bob Hope; Actor, television: The Palace; Funny Face; Love Boat; Condominium; The Comeback; Film appearance: Juke Box Rhythm; Stage performance, Guys and Dolls, USA, 1991; Regular concert tours, USA and UK. *Recordings:* Albums include: Call Me Irresponsible, 1963; Wives and Lovers, 1963; Bewitched, 1964; Dear Heart, 1965; My Kind of Town, 1965; There's Love and There's Love and There's Love, 1965; For The In Crowd, 1966; The Impossible Dream, 1966; Jack Jones Sings, 1966; Lady, 1967; Our Song, 1967; Without Her, 1967; If You Ever Leave Me, 1968; Where Is Love, 1968; A Time For Us, 1969; A Song For You, 1972; Breadwinners, 1972; Together, 1973; Write Me A Love Song Charlie, 1974; Harbour, 1974; The Full Life, 1977; All To Yourself, 1977; I've Been Here All The Time, 1980; I Am a Singer, 1987; Sings Michel Legrand, 1993; Live at the Sands, 1993; New Jack Swing, 1997; Numerous compilations; Hit songs include: Lollipops and Roses, 1961; Wives and Lovers, 1963; Call Me Irresponsible, 1963; The Impossible Dream, 1966; Film music includes: A Ticklish Affair, 1963; Where Love Has Gone, 1964; Love With A Proper Stranger, 1964; Kotch, 1967. *Honours:* Grammy Awards: Lollipops and

Roses, 1962; Wives and Lovers, 1964; Cash Box Award, Most Promising Vocalist, 1962, 1963; Golden Globe Award, film theme for Kotch, 1967. *Current Management:* Roy Gerber and Associates, 515 N Rexford Dr., Beverly Hills, CA 90210, USA.

JONES, (John) Howard; b. 23 Feb. 1955, Southampton, Hampshire, England. Songwriter; Vocalist; Musician (keyboards, computer); Record Prod. m. Janet Lesley Smith, 25 Oct. 1978. *Education:* Royal Northern College of Music, Manchester. *Career:* Piano teacher; Solo recording artiste, 1983–; Tours include: US tour, support to Eurythmics, 1984; British tour, 1984; Live Aid, Wembley Stadium, 1985; Tour, North America, 1992. *Recordings:* Albums: Human's Lib, 1984; The Twelve Inch Album, 1984; Dream Into Action, 1985; Action Replay, 1986; One To One, 1986; Cross That Line, 1989; The Best of Howard Jones, 1993; In The Running, 1998; Greatest Hits; Working In The Backroom, 1997; Live Acoustic America, 1996; Angels and Lovers, 1997; People, 1998; Pefawm, 2000; Singles include: New Song (No. 3, UK), 1983; What Is Love (No. 2, UK), 1984; Hide and Seek, 1984; Pearl In The Shell, 1984; Like To Get To Know You Well, 1984; Things Can Only Get Better, 1985; Look Mama, 1985; Life In One Day, 1985; No One Is To Blame, 1986; All I Want, 1986; You Know I Love You… Don't You?, 1986; Everlasting Love, 1987; The Prisoner, 1989; Lift Me Up, 1992; What Is Love, 1993; IGY, 1993; Tomorrow Is Now, 1998; Let the People Have Their Say, 1999. *Contributions to:* Live-in World (Anti-Heroin Project charity album), 1986; Rubáiyát (Elektra's 40th Anniversary album), 1990. *Membership:* ASCAP; PRS. *Current Management:* David Stopps, Friars Management. *Address:* 33 Alexander Rd, Aylesbury, Bucks HP20 2NR, England.

JONES, John Paul (John Baldwin); b. 3 June 1946, Sidcup, Kent, England. Musician (bass); Prod; Arranger; Composer. *Career:* Member, UK rock group Led Zeppelin, 1968–80; Also reunion concerts, Live Aid, Philadelphia, 1985; Atlantic's 40th Anniversary concert, Madison Square Gardens, 1988; Producer; Arranger; Session musician; Film score composer; Performances include: Bath Festival, 1969, 1970; Newport Jazz and Blues Festival, 1969; Montreux Jazz Festival, Switzerland, 1970; Madison Square Garden, 1970; Earls Court, 1975; Knebworth Fair, 1979; UNICEF Rock For Kampuchea, 1979; Film appearance, The Song Remains The Same, 1976; Producer for acts including: Butthole Surfers; Stefan Grossman; Ben E King; The Mission; John Renbourn; Arranger for artists including: REM; Raging Slab. *Recordings:* Albums: with Led Zeppelin: Led Zeppelin, 1969; Led Zeppelin II (No. 1, USA), 1969; Led Zeppelin III (No. 1, USA), 1970; Four Symbols (No. 1, UK), 1971; Houses of The Holy (No. 1, UK), 1973; Physical Graffitti (No. 1, USA), 1975; Presence (No. 1, USA), 1976; The Song Remains The Same (No. 1, UK), 1976; In Through The Out Door (No. 1, UK) 1979; Coda, 1982; Kingdom of Zep, 1991; Remasters, 1992; Complete Studio Recordings, 1993; Pleeease!, 1994; Solo albums: Zooma, 1999; Lovin' Up A Storm, 2000; The Thunderthief, 2001; Contributor to Comin' Atcha, Madeleine Bell, 1973; Also appears on recordings by: Jimmy Page; Paul McCartney; Brian Eno; Jeff Beck; Butthole Surfers; Singles include: Whole Lotta Love, 1970; Immigrant Song, 1971; Black Dog, 1972; Rock and Roll, 1972. *Honours:* Ivor Novello, Outstanding Contribution To British Music, 1977. *Current Management:* c/o Hip Music Group, 326 N Western Ave, Suite 150, Los Angeles, CA 90004, USA.

JONES, Kelly; b. 3 June 1974, Aberdare, Wales. Musician (guitar); Vocalist; Songwriter. *Career:* Ex-market trader and aspiring boxer; Founder member: Tragic Love Company, 1991; Name change to Stereophonics prior to joining Richard Branson's newly-formed V2 records, 1996; Toured UK, Europe and USA supporting acts including: Manic Street Preachers; Ocean Colour Scene; The Who; Aerosmith; Headlined various UK gigs and festivals including: Hillsborough Benefit Concert, 1997; Cardiff Castle, 1998; Reading Leeds and Glasgow Festivals, 2000; Donington, Chepstow, T In The Park, 2001; Undertook solo tour to promote group album release, 2001. *Recordings:* Singles: Looks Like Chaplin, 1996; Local Boy In The Photograph, More Life In A Tramp's Vest, A Thousand Trees, Traffic, 1997; The Bartender and The Thief, 1998; Just Looking, Pick A Part That's New, I Wouldn't Believe Your Radio, Hurry Up and Wait, 1999; Mama Told Me Not To Come (with Tom Jones), 2000; Mr Writer, Have A Nice Day, Step On My Old Size Nines, Handbags and Gladrags, 2001; Albums: Word Gets Around, 1997; Performance and Cocktails, 1999; Just Enough Education To Perform, 2001; Vegas Two Times, 2002. *Honours:* BRIT Award, Best Newcomer, 1998; Kerrang: Best New Band, 1998; Best Band, Best Album, 1999; Q Awards, Best Live Act, 1999; BAFTA Cymru, Best Music Programme, Stereophonics – Live At Morfa, 1999. *Current Management:* Marsupial Management Ltd, Unit 3, Home Farm, Welford, nr Newbury, Berkshire RG20 8HR, England. *E-mail:* marsupial@btinternet.com. *Website:* www.stereophonics.com.

JONES, Mick; b. 27 Dec. 1944, London, England. Musician (guitar); Songwriter; Record Prod. m. Ann. *Career:* Musician with: Nero and The Gladiators; Johnny Hallyday; Spooky Tooth; Leslie West; Also worked with Otis Redding; Jimi Hendrix; Jimmy Page; Founder member, rock group Foreigner, 1976–; World-wide appearances include: California Jam II, 1978; Headliners, Reading Festival, 1979; North American tour, 1982; American tour, 1991; New York State Fair, 1994; World Tour, 1994–95; American Tour, 1996. *Compositions:* Bad Love, recorded by Eric Clapton; Street Thunder,

1984 Olympic Marathon Theme; Numerous tracks for Foreigner, including: Feels Like The First Time; I Want to Know What Love Is; I Don't Want to Live Without You; As co-writer (with Lou Gramm): Dirty White Boy; Waiting For A Girl Like You; That Was Yesterday. *Recordings:* Albums: with Foreigner: Foreigner, 1977; Head Games, 1979; 4 (No. 1, USA), 1981; Records, 1982; Agent Provocateur (No. 1, UK), 1985; Inside Information, 1988; Unusual Heat, 1991; The Very Best Of, 1992; The Very Best... and Beyond, 1992; Mr Moonlight, 1994; Solo album: Mick Jones, 1989; As producer: 5150, Van Halen, 1986; Fame and Fortune, Bad Company, 1986; Stormfront, Billy Joel, 1989; In Deep, Tina Arena, 1997; Singles with Foreigner include: Feels Like The First Time, 1977; Cold As Ice, 1977; Long Long Way From Home, 1978; Hot Blooded, 1978; Double Vision, 1978; Blue Morning Blue Day, 1979; Dirty White Boy, 1979; Head Games, 1979; Urgent, 1981; Juke Box Hero, 1981; Waiting For A Girl Like You, 1982; I Want To Know What Love Is (No. 1, UK), 1985; That Was Yesterday, 1985; I Don't Want To Live Without You, 1988. *Honours:* Grammy Award, Bad Love, 1989. *Current Management:* Somerset Songs Publishing Inc, 214 E 70th St, New York, NY 10021, USA.

JONES, Mickey Wayne; b. 10 June 1941, Houston, Texas, USA. Actor; Musician (drums). m. (1) Sandra Davis, 1976; (2) Phyllis Star, 7 June 1980, 1 s., 1 d. *Education:* North Texas State College, 1959–62. *Career:* Drummer for Trini Lopez, 1957–64; Johnny Rivers, 1964–66; Bob Dylan, 1966–67; Kenny Rogers, 1967–76; Actor, 1976–; Film appearances include: Starman; National Lampoon's Vacation; Stir Crazy; Nadine; The Couch Trip; Television appearances include: V; Mash; The Incredible Hulk; The Colbys; T J Hooker; Numerous other guest roles, commercials, theatre. *Recordings:* Albums include: with Trini Lopez: Live At P J's; with Bob Dylan: Blonde On Blonde; with Johnny Rivers: Last Boogie In Paris; Also for Jan and Dean, Kenny Rogers; Singles include: with Johnny Rivers: Maybelline; Mountain of Love; Secret Agent Man; with Kenny Rogers and The First Edition: Just Dropped In To See What Condition My Condition Was In; Ruby, Don't Take Your Love To Town. *Membership:* AFTRA; Screen Actors Guild; AFofM; AGVA; Screen Extras Guild.

JONES, Nigel Mazlyn; b. 26 June 1950, Dudley, West Midlands, England. Performer; Songwriter; Musician (acoustic guitar, santoor). Divorced, 1 s., 1 d. *Career:* Professional performer, 1975–; Toured folk clubs, colleges; Special guest to Judie Tzuke, Renaissance, national tours; Special guest, Euro Major venue circuit with Barclay James Harvest, 1980; Also, Eurorock circuit, 1984; Glastonbury Festival, 1990; Featured solo on BBC documentary, Festival; Bob Geldof British tour, 1993; Music used on TV landscape films; Two BBC TV commissions. *Recordings:* Albums: Ship To Shore, 1976; Sentinel, 1979; Breaking Cover, 1981; Water From The Well, 1987; Video album: Beyond This Point, 1988; Mazlyn Jones, 1991; Angels Over Water, 1993; CD Album, Mazlyn Jones Live with Guy Evans and Nik Turner, 1997; BBC2 TV feature programme, Planet For Sale, 1998; CD Album, Behind The Stone, 1999. *Membership:* Musicians' Union; PRS; MCPS. *Current Management:* Isle of Light. *Address:* PO Box 1, Polzeath, Cornwall PL27 6YZ, England.

JONES, Norah; b. 30 March 1979, New York, NY, USA. Vocalist; Musician (piano). *Education:* Booker T. Washington High School for the Performing and Visual Arts, Dallas, TX, USA; Jazz Piano, North Texas University. *Career:* Daughter of musician Ravi Shankar; Mem., Wax Poetic; Formed band with Jesse Harris, Lee Alexander and Dan Rieser; Signed to Blue Note Records, 2001; Touring, 2002. *Recordings:* Album: Come Away With Me, 2002. EP: First Sessions, 2001; Appearances on: Wax Poetic, 2000; Charlie Hunter Quartet, 2001; Dirty Dozen Brass Band, 2002. *Honours:* MOBO Award, Best Jazz Act, 2002; BRIT Award, International Breakthrough Artist, 2003. *Current Management:* Macklam Feldman Management, Suite 200, 1505 W Second Ave, Vancouver, BC V6H 3Y4, Canada. *Address:* c/o Blue Note Records, 304 Park Ave S, Third Floor, New York, NY 10010, USA. *Website:* www.norahjones.com.

JONES, Paul; b. 5 Feb, Llanrwst, Wales. Musician (bass guitar). *Career:* Member, Y Cyrff (Welsh-language band), –1991; Member, Catatonia, 1993–2001; Signed to Blanco Y Negro, 1996. *Recordings:* Albums: Way Beyond Blue, 1996; The Sublime Magic of Catatonia, 1996; International Velvet, 1998; Equally Cursed and Blessed, 1999; Paper Scissors Stone, 2001; Greatest Catatonia Hits, 2002. Singles: Hooked, 1994; Bleed/Do You Believe In Me, 1996; Mulder and Scully, 1998; Road Rage, 1998; Strange Glue, 1998; Londinium, 1999.

JONES, Paul; b. 24 Feb. 1942, Portsmouth, Hampshire, England. Vocalist; Musician (harmonica); Composer; Actor; Broadcaster. m. Fiona Hendley, 16 Dec. 1984, 2 s. (previous marriage). *Education:* Edinburgh Academy; Jesus College, Oxford; Cathedral Choir. *Career:* Lead singer, harmonica player with Manfred Mann; Television includes: Thank Your Lucky Stars; Top of the Pops; Ready Steady Go; Solo tours of UK, Australia, New Zealand and Europe, 1966–; Theatre: Conduct Unbecoming, London and New York; The Beggar's Opera; Guys and Dolls, National Theatre; Kiss Me Kate, RSC; Vocalist, harmonica player with Blues Band, 1979–; Actor, films and television; TV presenter; Radio: Radio 2 Rhythm and Blues, 1985–; JFM radio, 1990–. *Compositions include:* 54321 (Theme for Ready Steady Go); Songs recorded by: Brian Poole and The Tremeloes; Helen Shapiro; Eric

Clapton; Ten Years After; TV and film scores: Intimate Reflections; Fighting Back; The Wednesday Play. *Recordings:* All Manfred Mann albums to 1966; Blues Band albums include: Bootleg; Ready; Itchy Feet; Paul Jones Collection Vol. 1–3, 1996–98. *Contributions to:* The Independent on Sunday; Sight and Sound; Tribune. *Honours:* British Blues Connection, Male Singer, 1990, 1991; Scroll of Honour, 1993. *Membership:* Musicians' Union; BACSA; Equity. *Current Management:* Chatto and Linnit.

JONES, Quincy; b. 14 March 1933, Chicago, Illinois, USA. Record Prod; Composer; Arranger; Musician (trumpet); Conductor; 5 c. *Education:* Seattle University; Berklee College of Music; Boston Conservatory. *Career:* Trumpeter, arranger, Lionel Hampton Orchestra, 1950–53; Arranger for various singers, orchestra leaders include: Count Basie; Frank Sinatra; Peggy Lee; Dinah Washington; Sarah Vaughan; Trumpeter, Dizzy Gillespie, 1956; Leader, own orchestra, concerts, television appearances, 1960–; Music Director, Mercury Records, 1961; Vice-President, 1964. *Recordings:* Hit singles include: Soul Bossa Nova, 1962; Stuff Like That, 1978; Ai No Corrida, 1981; Razzmatazz, 1981; I'll Be Good To You, with Ray Charles and Chaka Khan; Solo albums include: You've Got It Bad Girl, 1973; Walking In Space, 1974; Body Heat, 1974; Mellow Madness, 1975; I Heard That!, 1976; Quintessence, 1977; Sounds and Stuff Like That, 1978; The Dude, 1981; Bossa Nova, 1983; The Q, 1984; Back On The Block, 1989; QD III Soundlab, 1991; Q – The Musical Biography of Quincy Jones, 2001; Producer, video Portrait of An Album, 1986; Q's Jook Joint, 1995; Music, television series Fresh Prince of Bel Air, 1990–; Guest musician, albums: with George Benson: Shape of Things To Come, 1976; Give Me The Night, 1980; with James Ingram: It's Your Night, 1983; Never Felt So Good, 1986; with Michael Jackson: Thriller, 1982; Bad, 1987; Singles include: Blues in the Night, 1989; Listen Up, 1991; I'm Yours, 1999; Conductor, film music includes: In The Heat of The Night, 1967; The Slender Thread, 1968; McKenna's Gold, 1968; For The Love of Ivy, 1968; Banning, 1967; The Split, 1968; Bob and Carol and Ted and Alice, 1969; The Out-Of-Towners, 1970; The Anderson Tapes, 1971; The Hot Rock, 1972; The New Centurions, 1972; The Getaway, 1972; The Wiz, 1978; The Color Purple, 1985. *Honours:* Golden Note, ASCAP, 1982; Hon degree, Berklee College, 1983; Over 20 Grammy Awards; Lifetime Achievement, National Academy of Songwriters, 1989; ASMAC Golden Score Award. *Address:* c/o Quincy Jones Productions, 3800 Barham Blvd #503, Los Angeles, CA 90067, USA.

JONES, Richard; b. 23 May 1974, Aberdare, Wales. Musician (bass). *Career:* Ex-electrician, scaffolder and coalman; Founder member: Tragic Love Company, 1991; Name change to Stereophonics prior to joining Richard Branson's newly-formed V2 records, 1996; Toured UK, Europe and USA supporting acts including: Manic Street Preachers; Ocean Colour Scene; The Who; Aerosmith; Headlined various UK gigs and festivals including: Hillsborough Benefit Concert, 1997; Cardiff Castle, 1998; Reading Leeds and Glasgow Festivals, 2000; Donington, Chepstow, T In The Park, 2001. *Recordings:* Singles: Looks Like Chaplin, 1996; Local Boy In The Photograph, More Life In A Tramp's Vest, A Thousand Trees, Traffic, 1997; The Bartender and The Thief, 1998; Just Looking, Pick A Part That's New, I Wouldn't Believe Your Radio, Hurry Up and Wait, 1999; Mama Told Me Not To Come (with Tom Jones), 2000; Mr Writer, Have A Nice Day, Step On My Old Size Nines, Handbags and Gladrags, 2001; Albums: Word Gets Around, 1997; Performance and Cocktails, 1999; Just Enough Education To Perform, 2001; Vegas Two Times, 2002. *Honours:* BRIT Award, Best Newcomer, 1998; Kerrang: Best New Band, 1998; Best Band, Best Album, 1999; Q Awards, Best Live Act, 1999; BAFTA Cymru, Best Music Programme, Stereophonics – Live At Morfa, 1999. *Current Management:* Marsupial Management Ltd, Unit 3, Home Farm, Welford, nr Newbury, Berkshire RG20 8HR, England. *E-mail:* marsupial@btinternet.com. *Website:* www.stereophonics.com.

JONES, Rickie Lee; b. 8 Nov. 1954, Chicago, Illinois, USA. Vocalist; Songwriter. *Career:* Signed to Warner Brothers (after own composition recorded by Lowell George on his album, Thanks I'll Eat Here), 1977; US tour, 1979; Appearance, Saturday Night Live, 1979; Jam session with Bruce Springsteen and Boz Scaggs at Whiskey A Go-Go club, Los Angeles, 1979; Major tour, includes Carnegie Hall, 1979; Singer of ballad for film: King of Comedy, 1983; The Magazine tour, 1984; Tours, Australia, Europe, UK, Eastern bloc concerts, 1985; Saturday Night Live, NBC TV, 1989; 2 US tours, 1990; Bread and Roses benefit, San Francisco, 1991; US tour, 1991; Appearances at Wiltern Theatre, Los Angeles, 1992; Dominion Theatre, Royal Festival Hall, London, 1992; The Tonight Show, 1993. *Compositions include:* Easy Money; The Last Chance; Texaco; Chuck E's In Love (platinum hit record, 1979). *Recordings:* Albums: Rickie Lee Jones, 1979; Pirates, 1981; Girl At Her Volcano, 1983; The Magazine, 1984; Flying Cowboys, 1989; Pop Pop, 1991; Traffic From Paradise, 1993; Naked Song, 1995; Ghostyhead, 1997; It's Like This, 2000; Features on: Duets, Rob Wasserman, 1989; The Bells of Dublin, The Chieftains, 1991; Joshua Judges Ruth, Lyle Lovett, 1992. *Honours:* Grammy: Best New Artist, 1979; Rolling Stone Awards, 1979, 1981; Grammy: Best Jazz Vocal Performance, Duo or Group, 1990. *Current Management:* Gold Mountain Entertainment, Suite 450, 3575 Cahuenga Blvd W, Los Angeles, CA 90068, USA.

JONES, Simeon; b. 10 March 1964, London, England. Musician (saxophone, flute, harmonica). 2 s. *Education:* BSc English. *Career:* Tours, television with various name acts including: Gary Glitter; Take That; Bad Manners; Geno Washington; Otis Grand. *Recordings:* With acts including: Gary Glitter; Take That; Tom Jones; Edwyn Collins; Black; Sam Brown; Shampoo; Blessing. *Membership:* MU. *Address:* 105 Taybridge Rd, London SW11 5PX, England.

JONES, Simon; Musician (bass). *Career:* Founder mem., The Verve, 1990–95, 1997–99; Obtained record deal, 1991; Support slots with The Black Crowes, and live dates on Lollapalooza tour, 1994; Numerous live shows and festival dates; Headline appearance at Reading festival, 1997; Mem., The Shining, 2002–. *Recordings:* Albums: with The Verve: A Storm In Heaven, 1993; No Come Down, 1994; A Northern Soul, 1995; Urban Hymns (No. 1, UK), 1997; with The Shining: True Skies, 2002. Singles: with The Verve: She's A Superstar, 1992; Gravity Grave, 1992; All In The Mind, 1993; Slide Away, 1993; Blue, 1993; This Is Music, 1995; On Your Own, 1995; History, 1995; Bittersweet Symphony (No. 2, UK), 1997; Lucky Man, 1997; Drugs Don't Work (No. 1, UK), 1997; with The Shining: Quicksilver; I Wonder How; Young Again. *Honours:* with The Verve: BRIT Awards, Best British Group, Best British Album, 1998. *Website:* www.theshiningarehere.com.

JONES, Steve; b. 3 May 1955, London, England. Musician (guitar). *Career:* Guitarist, UK punk group, The Sex Pistols, 1975–78; Performances include: First gig, St Martin's School of Art, London, 1975; Screen On The Green Midnight Special, London, 1976; 100 Club punk rock festival, 1976; Anarchy In The UK Tour, 1976; Tours: Europe, 1977; USA, 1978; Winterland Ballroom, San Francisco, 1978; Films: The Great Rock 'n' Roll Swindle, 1979; The Filth and The Fury, 2000; Reunion concert, 1996. *Recordings:* Albums: Never Mind The Bollocks – Here's The Sex Pistols (No. 1, UK), 1977; The Great Rock 'n' Roll Swindle, 1979; Some Product – Carry On Sex Pistols, 1979; Flogging A Dead Horse, 1980; Kiss This, 1992; Jubilee, 2002. Singles: Anarchy In The UK, 1976; God Save The Queen (No. 2, UK), 1977; Pretty Vacant, 1977; Holidays In The Sun, 1977; No One Is Innocent (A Punk Prayer By Ronnie Biggs), 1978; Something Else, 1979; Silly Thing, 1978; C'mon Everybody, 1979; The Great Rock 'n' Roll Swindle, 1979; Solo Albums: Mercy, 1987; Fire and Gasoline, 1989; with Siouxsie and the Banshees: Kaleidoscope, 1980; with Generation X: Perfect Hits 1975–81, 1986; with Si Kahn: I Have Seen Freedom, 1991; with Buckcherry: Buckcherry, 1999. *Address:* c/o Eclipse Entertainment, 100 Wilshire Blvd, Suite 1830, Santa Monica, CA 90028, USA.

JONES, Steven; Vocalist; Songwriter. *Career:* Founder/Main Member, Baby Bird; Member, theatre troupe, Dogs in Honey; Began making recordings at home; Wrote hundreds of pop songs; Obtained music publishing deal; Progressed to record deal; Formed band, numerous television appearances and live dates. *Recordings:* Singles: Goodnight, 1996; You're Gorgeous, 1996; Candy Girl, 1997; Cornershop, 1997; Bad Old Man, 1998; If You'll Be Mine, 1998; Back Together, 1999; The Word, 2000; Out of Sight, 2001; Albums: I Was Born A Man, 1995; Bad Shave, 1995; Fatherhood, 1996; The Happiest Man Alive, 1996; Ugly Beautiful, 1996; Dying Happy, 1997; Something's Going On, 1998; Bugged, 2000; Compilation: 1985–2000, 2001. *Website:* www.babybird.co.uk.

JONES, Tom, (Thomas Jones Woodward); b. 7 June 1940, Pontypridd, Wales. Vocalist; Entertainer. m. Melinda Trenchard, 1956, 1 s. *Career:* Former bricklayer, factory worker, construction worker; Singing debut, aged 3, later sang in clubs, dance halls, with self-formed group, The Playboys; Solo artiste, 1963–; First hit record It's Not Unusual, 1964; Numerous television and radio appearances, continuous tours, 1970s–; Television show, This Is Tom Jones, 1969–71; Many international hit singles, albums in Top 10 charts, Europe, USA; Score, musical play Matador; Concerts for: Amnesty International, Simple Truth, Rainforest Foundation, Shelter; Television series: The Right Time, 1992. *Recordings:* Albums: Along Came Jones, 1965; A-Tom-Ic Jones, 1966; From The Great, 1966; Green, Green Grass Of Home, 1966; Live At The Talk Of The Town, 1967; Delilah, 1968; Help Yourself, 1968; Tom Jones Live In Las Vegas, 1969; This Is Tom Jones, 1969; Tom, 1970; I, Who Have Nothing, 1970; Tom Jones Sings She's A Lady, 1971; Tom Jones Live At Caesar's Palace, Las Vegas, 1971; Close Up, 1972; The Body And Soul Of Tom Jones, 1973; Somethin' 'Bout You Baby I Like, 1974; Memories Don't Leave Like People, 1975; Say You'll Stay Until Tomorrow, 1977; Rescue Me, 1980; Darlin', 1981; Matador: The Musical Life Of El Cordobes, 1987; At This Moment, 1989; After Dark, 1989; Move Closer, 1989; Carrying A Torch, 1991; The Lead And How To Swing It, 1994; Reload, 1999; Mr Jones, 2002; Reload 2, 2002; Many compilation albums. Singles include: It's Not Unusual (No. 1, UK), 1965; What's New Pussycat, 1965; Thunderball, 1966; Green Green Grass of Home (No. 1, UK), 1966; Detroit City, 1967; Funny Familiar Forgotten Feelings, 1967; I'll Never Fall In Love Again, 1967; I'm Coming Home, 1967; Delilah, 1968; Help Yourself, 1968; Love Me Tonight, 1969; Without Love, 1969; Daughter of Darkness, 1970; I Who Have Nothing, 1970; She's A Lady, 1971; Till, 1971; The Young New Mexican Puppeteer, 1972; Can't Stop Loving You; Letter To Lucille, 1973; Something Bout You Baby I Like, 1974; Say You Stay Until Tomorrow, 1976; A Boy From Nowhere, 1987; Kiss, with Art of Noise, 1988; All You Need Is Love, 1993; If I Only Knew, 1994; Burning Down The House, with The Cardigans, 1999; Baby It's Cold Outside, with Cerys Matthews, 1999; Mama Told Me Not To Come, with

Stereophonics, 2000; Sex Bomb, with Mousse T, 2000; You Need Love Like I Do, with Heather Small, 2000; Tom Jones International, 2002. *Honours:* Hon. Fellow, Welsh College of Music and Drama, 1994; BRIT Award, Best British Male Solo Artist, 2000; Nodnoff Robbins Silver Clef Award, 2001; BRIT Lifetime Achievement Award, 2003. *Membership:* SAG; AFTRA; AGVA. *Current Management:* Mark Woodward, William Morris Agency. *Address:* Tom Jones Enterprises, 10100 Santa Monica Blvd, Suite 205, Los Angeles, CA 90067, USA. *Website:* www.tomjones.com.

JONES, Tommy; b. 5 Oct. 1926, Liverpool, England. Musician (drums); Bandleader; Musical Dir. m. Kathy Knight (vocalist), 26 April 1954, 3 s., 1 d. *Education:* Max Abrams (noted drum tutor), Trinity College of Music; London College of Music. *Career:* Played, concerts, clubs, broadcasts with bands incl.: Pete Pitterson Quintet; Cab Quaye Trio; Dill Jones Trio; Jack Butler (USA) Band; Leslie 'Jiver' Hutchinson Band; Bertie King Band; Dave (Jazz FM) Lee Trio; Tubby Hayes Band; Jimmy Deucher All-Stars; Acker Bilk Band; Major Holly and Rose Murphy (USA); Bruce Turner Band; Hutchinson/Henderson Band; Humphrey Lyttleton Band; Mike McKenzie Trio; Joe Harriot Quintet; Shake Keane Quintet; Sliderulers; Tommy Jones Trio; Tommy Eytle Trio; Just Jazz, 1950–; Bernard Hilda Orchestra, Paris and Monte Carlo; Arthur Briggs, Paris and Geneva; Venues incl.: Royal Festival Hall, 1953, 1954, 1956; First National Jazz Federation Jazz Today Concerts, Royal Festival Hall; Edinburgh Festival of Jazz, 1958; Les Ambassadeurs Club, 1960; Residency, Lunchtime Jazz, Bishopsgate, 1961; Bix's Club, San Francisco, 1989; Hollywood Savoy Restaurant, Paris, 1990; La Cigal jazz café, Paris; Films: Blood Orange, 1951; Rough and The Smooth, 1958; Phoelix, 1979; Television incl.: Crane (TV series), 1956; BBC experimental colour transmission at Alexandra Palace, 1957; The Jack Jackson Show; Mike McKenzie Trio; 6.5 Special (BBC TV), 1958; Episode, Danger Man, 1958; Producer, director, Cable Jazz, Cable London TV, 1992; House of Eliot, 1991; Radio incl.: Carribean Carnival series, 1955; Number Please, 1955–56; BBC Jazz Club, 1956, 1958, 1960; Jazz at the Marquee, 1960; Commercial, Smiths Crisps, 1993; Musical Director, Clark Brothers' (USA) Dancers, 1966–68. *Recordings:* Jazz At Club Basie, 1956; In My Condition, Shake Keane Quintet, 1960; With Shake Keane Quintet, 1961. *Current Management:* Tom Jones Jr, Tuff Productions, 2a Middle Lane Mews, Crouch End, London N8 8PN, England. *Address:* 11 Albany Rd, London N4 4RR, England.

JONES, Trevor; b. 23 March 1949, Cape Town, South Africa (British citizen). Composer. *Education:* Royal Academy of Music; MA, Film and Media Music, York University; National Film School. *Compositions:* For television: Joni Jones, 1982; One of Ourselves, 1983; Those Glory, Glory Days, 1983; The Last Days of Pompeii, 1984; Aderyn Papur... and Pigs Might Fly, 1984; This Office Life, 1984; The Last Place on Earth, 1985; Dr Fischer of Geneva, 1985; A Private Life, 1988; Murder by Moonlight, 1989; By Dawn's Early Light, 1990; Chains of Gold, 1990; Guns: A Day in the Death of America, 1991; Death Train, 1993; Gulliver's Travels, 1996; Merlin, 1998; Cleopatra, 1999; Dinotopia, 2002; For film: Brittania: The First of the Last, 1979; Black Angel, 1979; The Dollar Bottom, 1980; Brothers and Sisters, 1980; The Beneficiary, 1980; The Appointment, 1981; Excalibur, 1981; The Sender, 1982; The Dark Crystal, 1982; Nate and Hayes, 1983; Runaway Train, 1985; From an Immigrant's Diary, 1985; Labyrinth, 1986; Angel Heart, 1987; Sweet Lies, 1988; Mississippi Burning, 1988; Just Ask for Diamond, 1988; Dominick and Eugene, 1988; Sea of Love, 1989; Bad Influence, 1990; Arachnophobia, 1990; True Colors, 1991; Criss Cross, 1992; Freejack, 1992; Blame It on the Bellboy, 1992; The Last of the Mohicans, 1992; In the Name of the Father, 1993; Cliffhanger, 1993; De Baby built, 1994; Loch Ness, 1995; Hideaway, 1995; Kiss of Death, 1995; Richard III, 1995; Brassed Off, 1996; Roseanna's Grave, 1997; G.I. Jane, 1997; Lawn Dogs, 1997; The Mighty, 1998; Desperate Measures, 1998; Titanic Town, 1998; Dark City, 1998; Talk of Angels, 1998; Notting Hill, 1999; Thirteen Days, 2000; Molly, 2000; From Hell (with others), 2001; Crossroads, 2002; The Long Run, 2002. *Address:* c/o Varese Sarabande Records, 11846 Ventura Blvd, Suite 130, Studio City, CA 91604, USA.

JONES, Wizz; b. 25 April 1939, Croydon, Surrey, England. Musician (acoustic guitar); Vocalist. m. Sandy, 14 Sept. 1963, 3 s., 1 d. *Career:* Began as itinerant busking skiffle/folk singer, late 1950s; Formed bluegrass duo with banjo-picker Pete Stanley, recorded single, album, played Folk Club and College circuit, 1960s; Solo artiste, 1967–; Collaborated with songwriter Alan Tunbridge, guitarist Peter Berryman; Played in group Lazy Farmer with wife Sandy; Appears festivals, tours of acoustic folk and blues circuit, 1990s. *Recordings:* Albums include: The Grapes of Life, 1988; The Village Thing Tapes, 1993; Late Nights and Long Days (with saxophonist son Simeon); Dazzling Stranger, (first US release) 1995; Lucky the Man, 2001; 2 tracks on Acoustic routes, from BBC TV documentary on Bert Jansch. *Membership:* Musicians' Union; PRS. *Current Management:* Guitar Classics. *Address:* 38 Webbs Rd, London SW11 6SF, England.

JOOLZ; b. 16 April 1966, London, England. Vocalist; Actress; Dancer; Presenter. *Education:* O Level Music. *Career:* Session work with artistes including: Neneh Cherry; Neil Diamond; Danny Red; Soul II Soul; Tours, world-wide with Soul II Soul, including appearances on children's shows; Member, R&B group Just Good Friends; Supported Glen Jones; H. Town; Silk; Brandy; Keith Sweat; Appeared on Count Prince Miller's Jamaican

Independence television special; Cable TV special supporting Don Campbell. *Recordings:* Looking For An Answer, 1993; The More I Try, Just Good Friends. *Membership:* Musicians' Union. *Current Management:* Phat Management. *Address:* 35 Tubbs Rd, Harlesden, London NW10 4RA, England.

JORDAN, Cathy; b. 1 April 1969, Roscommon, Ireland. Vocalist; Musician (bodhran). *Career:* Solo singer for 5 years, mainly based in Ireland; Joined Dervish, 1990; Tours internationally. *Recordings:* Harmony Hill, 1993; Playing With Fire, 1995; At The End of The Day, 1996; Live In Palma, 1997; Midsummer's Night, 1999; Decade, 2001. *Honours:* Hot Press magazine, Traditional Folk Album of the Year, At The End of The Day, 1996; Irish Music magazine Readers' Poll, Best Overall Traditional Folk Band of the Year, 1997; Irish Times, Best Traditional Album, Midsummer's Night, 1999; Irish Music magazine, Best Compilation Album, Decade, 2001. *Address:* c/o Dervish/Whirling Discs Ltd, Business Innovation Centre, Unit G-2001, Institute of Technology Campus, Ballinode, Sligo, Ireland. *E-mail:* whirling@oceanfree.net. *Website:* www.dervish.ie.

JORDAN, Lorraine; b. 22 Nov. 1965, Wales. Vocalist; Songwriter; Musician (guitar, bouzouki). *Education:* Family influences in Irish music. *Career:* Singer, guitarist and bouzouki player, bands Mooncoin and Malin Head; Solo artiste, 1991–; Toured Europe and Scandinavia extensively, performing in numerous major folk festivals; Appearances on television and radio; Leader, own band or solo performer. *Recordings:* Inspiration, 1991, 1993; Crazy Guessing Games, 1994; features on: Sophistry and Illusion, Dalriada, 2001. *Membership:* Musicians' Union. *Address:* c/o Katherine Alexander, Saltire Promotions, Broadwood, Gilkerscleugh, Abington, Lanarkshire ML12 6SQ, Scotland.

JORDAN, Marc Wallace; b. 6 March 1948, New York, USA. Musician (guitar, keyboards); Songwriter; Recording Artiste. m. Amy Sky, 31 Jan. 1989, 1 s., 1 d. *Education:* University; Private guitar and piano lessons. *Compositions include:* Songs recorded by: Diana Ross (2); Manhattan Transfer (6); Rod Stewart (2); Bette Midler (2); Joe Cocker; Chicago; Kansas; Natalie Cole; Fall From Grace, Amanda Marshal; 9 platinum in Canada. *Recordings:* 7 albums include: Blue Desert, 1979; A Hole In The Wall, 1983; Talking Through Pictures, 1987; Reckless Valentine, 1992; Taxi-taxi, Cher, 1998–9; features on: Soul and Inspiration, Barry Mann, 2000. *Honours:* Juno Award, Producer of the Year, 1993. *Membership:* AFTRA; ACTRA; AFofM. *Current Management:* Kathleen Shea, Revolution Man, 343 Danforth Ave #2, Toronto, Canada. *Address:* 9744 Wilshire Blvd, Suite #305, Beverly Hills, CA 90212, USA.

JORDAN, Montell; b. 1968, Los Angeles, California, USA. Recording Artiste; Prod; Songwriter; Musician (piano, saxophone). *Education:* BA in Organizational Communication, Pepperdine University, Malibu. *Career:* Budweiser Superfest tour, with Boyz II Men, TLC, Mary J Blige; Television includes: Ricki Lake Show; Rolanda Show; The Beat Winter Cooldowns; Host, MTV Jams; Film appearance, The Nutty Professor. *Recordings:* Albums: This Is How We Do It, 1995; I Am LV; More to Tell, 1996; Let's Ride, 1998; Singles include: This Is How We Do It (No. 1, USA), 1995; Daddy's Home, 1995; I Like, 1996; What's on Tonight, 1997; I Can Do That, 1998; Get It On... Tonite, 1999; Jungle Groove (used in film soundtrack Pet Detective); Nutty Professor (film soundtrack); Smooth/Ghetto Life; Other recordings include collaborations with: Kelly Price; Gina Thompson; Lil Mo; Peter Andre; Deborah Cox. *Membership:* ASCAP. *Current Management:* Mad Money Management. *Address:* 8726 S Sepulveda Blvd, Suite C-161, Los Angeles, CA 90018, USA.

JORDAN, Stanley; b. 31 July 1959, Chicago, Illinois, USA. Jazz Musician (guitar, piano). *Education:* Theory, electronic music and composition, Princetown University. *Career:* Member, various Chicago groups, 1970s; Regular international jazz festivals, 1976; Musician with Dizzy Gillespie; Benny Carter; Dionne Warwick; Booker T and the MG's; Mark Knopfler; Solo recording artiste, 1982–; Leading exponent of hammering-on technique. *Recordings:* Albums: Touch Sensitive, 1982; Magic Touch, 1985; Standards, 1986; Cornucopia, 1990; Street Talk, 1990; Stolen Moments, 1990, Bolero, 1994; Live in New York, 1998. *Current Management:* c/o Mario Tirado, Agency for the Performing Arts, 888 Seventh Ave, Suite 200, New York, NY 10106, USA. *Website:* www.stanleyjordan.com.

JORGENS, Peter Ole; b. 20 April 1958, Sorgenfri, Denmark. Multi Instrumentalist, mostly percussion including Marimba and Vibe. m. Reneé Paaschburg, 30 May 1992. *Education:* Classical Percussion with Suzanne Ibstrup, 1970–76, Improvisation with John Tchicai, 1975–77, Percussion with Paul Motian, 1978. *Career:* John Tchikai's Festival Band, 1975–78; Tchikai/ Dorge Quartet, 1976–77; Cockpit Music, 1978–; Gronvirke, 1982–83; Global Guaranty Orchestra, 1983–; Clinch, 1987–89; The Wild Mans Band, 1990–; Dog God, 1992–; Sweethearts in a Drugstore, 1996; David Moss/PO Jorgens Duo, 1989–96; Ghost in the Machine, 1989–; Played solo concerts, 1995, Knitting Factory, New York and 1997 at LEM Festival Barcelona; Gefion Calls, 1996, with David Thomas (Pere Ubu), Jorgen Teler and Per Bull Acs, Two Midnight concerts in The Fountain, Gefion, Copenhagen. *Compositions*

include: Soil, 1990; Metal 1–10, 1992; Digital Metal, 1994; Cambodia, 1995; Black Box, 1995; Springtime 1–15, 1996; Somfoni, 1996; The War Kitchen, 1996; The Joy of Feeding Birds, 1997; The Adventure of Hale Bob, 1997. *Recordings include:* Dog God: Dog God, 1993; Global Guaranty Orchestra, Musical Hair-Splitting in a Remote World, 1993; Wiuf/Jorgens/DeRegt: Catchuptime, 1994; Evan Parker/Ghost in the Machine, 1995; Cockpit Music, The Great Dividing Range, 1996; Dog God: God is Love, 1997; PO Jorgens: The Technology of Touch, 1997; Sweethearts in a Drugstore:, 1997. *Honours:* 3 Year Grant for Composing From, The Danish Arts Foundation, 1984; One Year Grants, nearly every year, 1982–. *Membership:* SKREP (Danish Experimental Composers); DJBFA. *Current Management:* Ninth World Music. *Address:* PO Jorgens, Frydenlund, Humlebaekvej 56, 3480 Fredensborg, Denmark.

JORGENSEN, Carsten Valentin; b. 9 May 1950, Lyngby, Denmark. Vocalist; Musician (guitar); Composer; Poet. m. Anne Marie Albrectsen, 27 Jan. 1979. *Education:* Graduate, Art School, 1975. *Career:* Founder, own band, C V Jorgensen, 1974–; Tours: Denmark, Sweden, Norway, Germany, 1976–; Roskilde Festival, 6 appearances; Television appearances: Numerous C V Jorgensen specials, 1980–94; Danish Live Aid, 1985; Dylan and The Danes, 1991; Leonard Cohen Talkshow, 1992; Performed on films: Kloden Rocker, 1978; Som Et Strejf, 1992; Lyricist/vocalist, film soundtracks: Mig and Charly, 1978; Johnny Larsen, 1979. *Recordings:* Storbyens Små Oaser, 1977; Tidens Tern, 1980; Lediggang Agogo, 1982; Vennerne and Vejen, 1985; Indian Summer, 1988; Sjaelland, 1994. *Honours:* Poetens Pris (Poets Award), 1989; 2 Grammy Awards, Songwriter of Year, Rock Album of Year, 1991; Prize of Honour, DJBFA; 2 Danish State Art Foundation Awards, 1993, 1994. *Membership:* Nordic Copyright Bureau; KODA; Gramex; DJBFA. *Current Management:* Rock On.

JORGENSEN, Per; b. 9 Sept. 1952, Bergen, Norway. Musician (trumpet, guitar, percussion); Vocalist). m. Else Vågen, 8 May 1987, 1 d. *Education:* Pre-school teacher. *Career:* Freelance musician, 20 years; All major Scandinavian Jazz Festivals with different groups; Tours, concerts in: India; Japan; USA; Germany; Spain; France; Austria; Numerous concerts recorded for television and radio; Jazz visit, teaching and working with Danish musicians, Copenhagen, 1997. *Recordings:* with Jokleba (trio): On and On; with Jokleba and the Magnetic North Orchestra: Further; with Anders Jormin: Jord; with Marilyn Mazur: Circular Chant; with Tamma (including Don Cherry and Ed Blackwell): Tamma; with David Murray: Jazzpar Prize, 1991; with Jon Balke: Nonsenstration, 1992; with Michael Mantler: School of Understanding, 1997; with Sjogren/Voust: The Thule Spirit, 1997. *Honours:* Vossajazz Prize, 1990; Jazz Musician of the Year in Norway, 1991. *Address:* Lia 17, 5280 Dalekvam, Norway.

JORY, Sarah Elizabeth; b. 20 Nov. 1969, Reading, Berkshire, England. Professional Entertainer; Country Vocalist; Songwriter. *Career:* Television appearances include: Opportunity Knocks; Pebble Mill; The South Bank Show; RTE TV Ireland; Ulster TV; Dutch and Belgian TV; Satellite TV world-wide; CBS News America; Anglia TV; East Midlands TV; Concerts: London Palladium; Toured with: Eric Clapton, Glen Campbell and Charley Pride; Broadcasts on BBC Radio 1, 2, 4 and all local radio. *Compositions:* 4 instrumentals. *Recordings:* 12 solo recordings; Two for record company: Sarah On Steel, 1984; Cross Country, 1985; The Way To Survive, 1987; No Time At All, 1988; Deep In The Heart of Texas, 1988; Dallas City Lights, 1989; Especially For You, 1990; Sarah's Dream, 1990; New Horizons, 1992; Web of Love, 1994; Love With Attitude, 1995; Kiss My Innocence, 1998; Sarah Jory Band Live, 2000. *Honours:* 6 British Country Music Awards; 3 European Awards; Many other regional awards. *Membership:* PRS; Musicians' Union. *Current Management:* Arthur Jory (personal). *Address:* 10 Tennyson Rd, Balderton, Newark, Notts NG24 3QH, England. *Website:* www.sarahjory.co.uk.

JOSEPH, Julian Rapheal Nathaniel; b. 11 May 1966, London, England. Musician (piano); Composer. *Education:* Classical Composition, Berklee College of Music, Boston, USA. *Career:* Julian Joseph Weekend, Barbican Centre; Julian Joseph Series, Wigmore Hall; The Proms, Royal Albert Hall, London, 1995; Montréal Jazz Festival. *Compositions include:* Film score, A Tale of a Vampire; Commissioned work, Winds of Change; Orchestral works. *Recordings:* Albums: The Language of Truth; Reality; Julian Joseph In Concert At The Wigmore Hall; Universal Traveller, due 1996. *Honours:* Award to Study at Berklee College of Music; Southern Comfort Award, Best Jazz Group; John Dankworth Award. *Membership:* PRS; MCPS; BAC&S. *Current Management:* James Joseph Music Management. *Address:* 85 Cicada Rd, London SW18 2PA, England.

JOURGENSEN, Al(len); b. 9 Oct. 1958, Havana, Cuba. Vocalist; Musician (Guitar). *Career:* Member, Ministry; Signed major label contract, 1983; Numerous side projects including Revolting Cocks, Lard, with Jello Biafra of Dead Kennedys, 1000 Homo DJs, with Trent Reznor of Nine Inch Nails, Pigface, with Steve Albini, Jello Biafra, Chris Connelly and Dwayne Goettell; Worked with Butthole Surfers' Gibby Haynes; Numerous tours including Lollapalooza; Contributed track to Neil Young's Bridge School Benefits album, 1998. *Recordings:* Singles: Cold Life, 1981; I Wanted To Tell Her,

1983; Revenge, 1983; Work for Love, 1983; All Day, 1985; Cold Life, 1985; Over the Shoulder, 1985; Halloween Remix, 1987; Stigmata, 1988; Burning Inside, 1989; Jesus Built My Hotrod, 1991; N.W.O., 1992; Just One Fix, 1992; The Fall, 1995; Lay Lady Lay, 1996; Bad Blood, 1995; Albums: With Sympathy, 1983; Twitch, 1985; Twelve Inch Singles 1981–84, 1987; The Land of Rape and Honey, 1988; The Mind is a Terrible Thing to Taste, 1989; In Case You Didn't Feel Like Showing Up (Live), 1990; Psalm 69: The Way To Succeed and the Way To Suck Eggs, 1992; Filth Pig, 1996; Dark Side of the Spoon, 1999; Greatest Hits (compilation), 2001; with Revolting Cocks: Beers, Steers and Queers, 1990; With Lard: Pure Chewing Satisfaction, 1997.

JOYCE, (Joyce Silveiro Palhano de Jesus); b. 31 Jan. 1948, Rio de Janeiro, Brazil. Vocalist; Musician (guitar, violin); Songwriter. *Career:* First recorded as part of vocal group, 1964; Solo debut, 1968; Dropped out of the music business until invitation by Vinicius de Moraes to join him on international tour, 1975; Moved to New York City, 1977; Signed contract with EMI, 1980; Independent releases, 1984–; 1990s brought a new audience when the 'drum 'n' bossa' style rejuventated interest in recordings. *Recordings:* Albums include: Veu De Noiva, 1969; Nelson Angelo E Joyce, 1972; Passarinho Urbano, 1977; Aqua E Luz, 1980; Tardes Cariocas, 1981; Music Inside, 1990; Language and Love, 1991; Sings Antonio Carlos Jobim and Vinicius De Moraes, 1993; Ilha Brasil, 1996; Astronauta – Songs of Elis, 1998; Tudo Bonito, 2000; Gafieira Moderna, 2001. *Address:* c/o Far Out Records. *Website:* www.joyce.com.

JUB; b. Oxfordshire, England. Musician (double bass); Vocalist. *Education:* Guildhall School of Music, London. *Career:* Bass player, Kreisler String Orchestra; English National Opera; London Festival Ballet; London Contemporary Dance Theatre; Member, The Carnival Band, 1985–; Appearances include: Glasgow Cathedral; Birmingham Symphony Hall; Barbican Centre; Arts centres and theatres; Plays material from: Sweden; Croatia; USA; Bolivia; Spain; UK; France. *Recordings:* Album with Maddy Prior: Christmas Carols. *Current Management:* c/o Jim McPhee, Acorn Entertainments. *Address:* Winterfold House, 46 Woodfield Rd, Kings Heath, Birmingham B13 9UJ, England.

JUDD, Naomi Ellen; b. 1 Nov. 1946, Ashland, Kentucky, USA. Vocalist; Songwriter; Author; Speaker. m. Larry Strickland, 6 May 1989; 2 d. *Education:* RN degree. *Career:* Member, country music duo The Judds, with daughter Wynonna, 1984–90; Sold 15m. albums; Most successful duo in country music history. *Recordings include:* Singles: Had A Dream For The Heart, 1983; Mama He's Crazy, 1984; Why Not Me, 1984; Girls Night Out, 1985; Rockin' With The Rhythm of The Rain, 1986; Let Me Tell You About Love, 1989; Albums: The Judds, 1984; Why Not Me?, 1985; Rockin With The Rhythm of The Rain, 1986; Heartland, 1987; Greatest Hits, 1988; River of Time, 1989; Love Can Build A Bridge, 1990; The Judds Collection, 1991; The Essential, 1996; Collection, 1997; Otherside, 1997; New Day Dawning, 2001. *Publications:* Love Can Build A Bridge. *Honours:* 7 Grammy Awards; 4 Academy Country Music Awards, Best Duet; 3 Country Music Asscn Awards, Best Vocal Duo; Undefeated, 3 major Country Music Award shows, 8 consecutive years. *Current Management:* William Morris. *Address:* The Judd House, 325 Bridge St, Franklin, TN 37064, USA.

JULES, Judge, (Julius O'Riordan); b. 26 Oct. 1965, London, England. DJ; Record Prod; Remixer; Radio Presenter; A and R. *Education:* Degree in Law, London School of Economics. *Career:* World-wide appearances in over 30 countries; Remixed and produced over 20 top 30 singles, 1994–. *Recordings include:* I Like To Move It, Reel 2 Real; Doop, Doop; Saturday Night, Tempo; High on a Happy Vibe; I Put a Spell on You; Funky Groove; Down with the Underground; Pulsating Rhythms; Albums include: Clubbed, 2001. *Contributions to:* The Face, ID, Mix Mag, and DJ Mag. *Honours:* Best Club DJ, DJ Mag, 1995; Best DJ, London Club Awards, 1995. *Membership:* Musicians' Union. *Current Management:* Serious Artist Management. *Address:* PO Box 13143, London N6 5BG, England.

JUNGR, Barb; b. 9 May 1954, Rochdale, England. Vocalist; Performer; Songwriter; Musician (mandolin, harmonica); Cabaret Artiste. *Education:* BSc, Leeds; MMus, Goldsmiths College; Doctoral Research, Voice and Emotion. *Career:* Television appearances with Julian Clary in all series of Sticky Moments, Terry and Julian; Radio broadcasts: 5 series, We Stayed In With Jungr and Parker, BBC Radio 2; National tours with Alexei Sayle and Julian Clary. *Compositions:* Television themes, 1990–2000; Theatre, 1990–2000. *Recordings:* 3 Courgettes; Barb; The Stroke; Jungr and Parker; Bare, 1999; Chanson, 2000; Every Grain Of Sand—Barb Jungr Sings Bob Dylan, 2002. *Honours:* Perrier Award, 1987; Swansea Fringe Award, 1988. *Membership:* PRS; PPL; MCPS; British Voice Asscn; Malawian Musicians Asscn; British Forum Ethnomusicology; Centre Performance Research; Musicians' Union; Equity; ICTM; Women In Music; Jazz Singers Network. *Current Management:* Sonia Beldom Brown, London. *Address:* c/o Linn Records, 257 Drakemire Dr., Glasgow G45 9SZ, Scotland.

JUNKERA, Kepa, (Kepa Junquera Urraza); b. 1965, Bilbao, Spain. Musician (trikitixa); Composer. *Career:* Basque folk musician; Plays the trikitixa (Basque diatonic accordion); Performed with band Oskorri and continues to guest on their albums and tours; Collaboration with John Kirkpatrick and Riccardo Tesi (known as the Trans-Europe Diatonic project), with associated album and international tours, brought Junkera to wider European audience; Collaborations with renowned Basque musicians and international artistes including: The Chieftains; Julio Pereira; Carlos Nuñez; Dulce Pontes; Andreas Vollenwaider; As composer, has combined jazz with own folk music and written pieces performed with Bilbao Symphony Orchestra. *Recordings:* Albums: with Kepa Zabaleta eta Motriku: Infernuko Auspoa, 1987; Triki Up, 1990; solo: Trikitixa Zoom, 1991; Trans-Europe Diatonic (with Riccardo Tesi and John Kirkpatrick), 1992; Kalejira Al-Buk, 1994; Lau Eskutara (with Julio Pereira), 1995; Leonen Orroak (with Ibon Koteron), 1996; Bilbao 00–00h, 1996; Maren, 2001. *Honours:* Young Contemporary Folk Musician Prize, 1990. *Website:* www.kepajunkera.com.

JURICIC, Max Wilson; b. 10 June 1958, Zagreb, Croatia. Musician (guitar); Backing Vocalist. m. Vanja Matujec, 11 June 1988, 1 s., 1 d. *Education:* Economist. *Career:* Member, Azra, 1977–78; Film, 1978–86; Le Cinema, 1986–88; Vjestice, 1989–99; Ziu Zao, 1995; So! Mazgoon, 1999. *Recordings:* with Film: Film 1; Live Kulusic; Zona Sumraka; Sva Cuda Svijeta; Signali U Noci; with Le Cinema: Live Kulusic; with Vjestice: Totalno Drukciji Od Drugih; Bez Tisine; Live In Schwarzwald; Djevojke U Ljetnim Haljinama Volim; Kradljivac scra; with So! Mazgoon: So! Mazgoon, 1999. *Honours:* Porin 1987, for best album in alternative music. *Membership:* HGU. *Address:* Auzvinkl Tomisalavov trg 19, Zagreb, Croatia.

K

K, Greg, (Gregory David Kriesel); b. 20 Jan. 1965, Glendale, CA, USA. Musician (bass guitar). m. Jane Costello, 1 s. *Education:* BA, Finance, Long Beach State University, California. *Career:* Member, The Offspring; Privately pressed single took over 2 years to sell 1,000 copies, 1987; Signed to independent labels, Nemesis and Epitaph, for 1988–95 releases; Major US breakthrough following heavy MTV/radio play rotation, 1994; Accused of betraying punk roots when signing to Columbia after dispute with former label, 1996; Consolidated world-wide success by scoring UK No. 1 hit single, 1999; Live shows include: Woodstock festival, 1999; KROQ Weenie Roast, 2000; European tour, 2001; Band gave lucky fan $1m. in Offspring prize draw, 2000. *Recordings:* Albums: The Offspring, 1989; Ignition, 1992; Smash!, 1994; Ixnay On The Hombre, 1997; Americana, 1998; Conspiracy of One, 2000; Singles: I'll Be Waiting, 1987; Baghdad EP, 1988; Come Out and Play (Keep 'Em Separated), Self-Esteem, 1994; Gotta Get Away, 1995; All I Want, Gone Away, 1997; Pretty Fly (For A White Guy), 1998; Why Don't You Get A Job?, The Kids Aren't Alright, She's Got Issues, Original Prankster, 2000; Want You Bad, Million Miles Away, 2001. *Honours:* Over 9m. copies of Smash album sold world-wide, best selling independent record of all time. *Current Management:* Jim Guerinot, Rebel Waltz Management, 31652 Second Ave, Laguna Beach, CA 92651, USA. *Website:* www.offspring.com.

KAAS, Patricia; b. 5 Dec. 1966, Forbach, France. Vocalist. *Career:* Scène de Vie tour, 1990–91 (196 concerts, audience 750,000, 12 countries); Tour de Charme, 1993–94 (145 concerts, audience 600,000, 19 countries). *Recordings:* Mademoiselle Chante, 1988; Scène De Vie, 1990; Carnet De Scène (double live album) 1991; Je Te Dis Vous, 1993; Tour de Charme, (live album) 1994; Dans Ma Chair, 1997; Rendez-Vous, 1998; Le Mot de Passe, 1999; Live, 2000; Longbox, 2001; Les Indispensables, 2001. *Publications:* Patricia Kaas-Tour De Charme, 1994. *Honours:* 6 Victoires de la Musique; 2 World Music Awards. *Current Management:* Cyril Prieur, Richard Walter. *Address:* Talent Sorcier, 3 rue des Petites Écuries, 75010 Paris, France.

KAASINEN, Sari Johanna; b. 15 Sept. 1967, Rääkkylä, Finland. Vocalist; Musician (kanteler); Record Prod. m. Heikki Kemppainen, 21 June 1991, 1 d. *Education:* Master of Music, Sibelius Academy, Helsinki, 1994. *Career:* Leader, Singer, Värttinä, 1983–96; Tours, Festivals throughout Europe and USA include: Kaustingen, Finland, 1985–; WOMAD, UK, 1992; Dranouter, Belgium, 1992; Glastonbury, UK, 1993; Ruisrock, Finland, 1993; Molde Jazz Festival, Norway, 1994; Owner, Producer, Mipu Music; Television appearances: Music From Karelia, Finnish documentary, 1990; Late Late Show, Dublin, 1991; Prize of Europe, 1994; Leading Sirmakka group currently; Persuing solo project; Teacher of Music, Rääkkylä. *Compositions:* Iro, 1996; Pojaton, 1996; Limoni Ennen, 1996. *Recordings:* Albums with Värttinä: Värttinä, 1987; Musta Lindu, 1989; Oi Dai, 1991; Seleniko, 1992; Aitara, 1994; Kokko, 1996; With Sirmakka, Tsihi Tsihi, 1997; with Hector Zazou: Songs From The Cold Seas, 1995. *Honours:* Emma Award, Finland, 1992; State Music Art Prize, 1992; Northern Karelian Music Art Prize, 1992. *Membership:* Finnish State Music Art Committee, 1995–97. *Current Management:* Hoedown. *Address:* Laivurinrinne 2, 00120 Helsinki, Finland.

KAERSAA, Morten; b. 26 Sept. 1957, Copenhagen, Denmark. Musician (piano); Vocalist. 1 s. *Career:* Member of band, Sneakers; Member of Moonjam. *Compositions:* 9 albums for Moonjam; All Sneakers material. *Recordings:* Moonjam: Songs for Saxophone; Saxophone Songs Vol. II; Sarai; Bag De Bla Bjerge; Osten Fur Solen. *Honours:* Platinum album for Songs for Saxophone, 1992; Platinum album for Moonjam's Greatest Hits. *Current Management:* FPH Management, Copenhagen. *Address:* Moonlab Dampfaergevej 2 CD, 2100 Copenhagen, Denmark.

KAERSAA, Rasmus; b. 29 Dec. 1960, Copenhagen, Denmark. Musician (bass). m. Annika Hueg, 25 June 1995, 1 s. *Career:* Member, Danse Orkestret; Member, Moonjam. *Compositions:* Below the Yellow Moons; National hit, Kom Tilbage Nu (Come Back Now), with Jacob Andersen. *Recordings:* Albums with Moonjam: Songs for Saxophone; Saxophone Songs Vol. II; With Danse Orkestret: Danse Orkestret. *Honours:* Platinum album, Danse Orkestret, 1986; Platinum album, Songs for Saxophone, 1992. *Current Management:* FDH Management, Copenhagen. *Address:* Moonlab Damfaergevej 2 CD, 2100 Copenhagen, Denmark.

KAGADEEV, Andrei; b. 9 July 1961, Moscow, Russia. Songwriter; Musician. m. Tatiana Kagadeeva, 2 March 1985, 1 d. *Education:* Humanitarian University Courses, Technical University of St Petersburg; Guitar Lessons. *Career:* Songwriter, Composer for the NOM Band; Appearances on Western European Television Channels; Participation in Big Festivals, Les Allummees, Nantes, 1991, Sziget, Budapest, 1995; Concert Tours in Western Europe. *Compositions:* Films: Masters of the USSR or Ape's Snout, 1994; Made In Europe, (documentary), 1996. *Recordings:* Albums: Brutto, 1989; To Hell With It, 1991; Superdisc, 1992; Senka-Mosgas, 1994; In the Name of

Mind, 1996; Ultracompact, 1996; Live is Game, 1996; Gire, 1997. *Honours:* Grand Prix, Alternative Video Contest, Exotica 95, Moscow; Best Low Budget Video, Ukrblues, Midem 96 Fair, Cannes, France. *Current Management:* Agency of Gerhard Busse, St Petersburg, Russia. *Address:* Bogatyrsky pr 5/1–283, St Petersburg 197348, Russia.

KAJDAN, Jean-Michel; b. 16 July 1954, Paris, France. Musician; Songwriter; Vocalist. *Career:* Sideman, Didier Lockwood, Michel Jonasz, Eddy Mitchell, Lionel Ritchie, Eddy Louiss; The Big Blue (film); Subway (film); Taratata, (television with L Ritchie); Taratata (television with D E Mitchell); Montreux Jazz Festival (with Lassy Carlton), 1997. *Compositions:* The Spy (D Lockwood Album); Spying Taranto; Song for LC. *Recordings:* Blue Scales; Blue Noise; Fasten Seat Belts; La Mouvellevie. *Membership:* SACEM; SPEDIDAM; ADAMI; SACD. *Current Management:* Maurice Suissa, Suissa Despa Productions. *Address:* 1 rue du Général de Gaulle, 27500 Pont Audemer, France.

KALANIEMI, Maria Helena; b. 27 May 1964, Espoo, Finland. Musician; Composer. m. Olli Caris. *Education:* MMus, Sibelius Academy, 1992. *Career:* Leader, Member, Various Ensembles and Side Projects, Including, Niekku, Helsinki Melodeon Ladies, Anna Kaisa Liedes Group, Ramunder, Vesa Matti Loiri Group, 1983–; Teacher, Sibelius Academy Folk Music Department, Leader, Composer of Ensemble Aldargaz, 1992–; Member of Group Accordion Tribe, 1996–. *Compositions:* Hermannin Riili, 1992; Lomasavel, 1995; Iho, 1995; Ahma, 1998; Kaamos, 1998; Kamppi, 1998; Lovina, 1998. *Recordings:* Maria Kalaniemi, 1992; Iho, 1995; Accordion Tribe, 1998; Ahma, 1999. *Honours:* Golden Accordion Competition, 1983; Prize of Finland, 1996; 3 Years Composer Grant, 1997. *Current Management:* Hoedown, Laivurinrinne 2, 00120 Helsinki, Finland. *Address:* Kellonsoittajantie 1B, 02770 Espoo, Finland.

KALASZ, Juraj; b. 14 Nov. 1963, Bratislava, Czechoslovakia. m. Dr Krausova Dagmar, 15 Dec. 1990, 1 s. *Education:* Machine Engineering University, 6 years (Slovak Technological University), Dipl Ing, 1983–89; Studying Double Bass, State Conservatory in Bratislava, 1991–97. *Career:* First Prof Eng, 1987 with local (Bratislava) groups (Exprit, Bratislava Trio), 1991; Just Jazz (tours in Denmark and Czech Republic), 1993; Czechoslovak Quintet (Bratislava Jazz Days Festival); 1995 Tubu (tour in Spain); 1995 Member of Janusz Muniak, Quartet (Cracow, Poland); 1996 Member of Shawn Loescher Trio). *Compositions:* Tribute to Charlie Parker, recorded for Slovak Radio. *Recordings:* Czechoslovak Quintet, for Slovak Radio, 1993; Chamber Jazz Trio, 1996. *Publications:* Walking Double Bass, 1997. *Honours:* Prize for Outstanding Performance, Zilina Jazz Festival, 1989. *Membership:* Slovak Jazz Society. *Address:* Rara Musica (Adrian Raiter), Fand Who 1, 81103 Bratislava, Slovakia.

KALIMOULLIN, Rashid; b. 6 May 1957, Zelenodolsk City, Tatarstan, Russia. Composer. m. Rosa Kalimoullina, 7 July 1979, 1 s., 1 d. *Education:* Degree in Composition, Kazan State Conservatoire; Postgraduate Studies. *Compositions include:* Opera, Cuckoo's Cry, Libretto by I Yuziev, 1989; Symphonic Works: Concert for clarinet with orchestra, 1985; Bulgary, poem, 1986; Silence and Tranquillity, vocal symphonic poem, 1987; Chamber works: Quartet for wooden wind instruments, 1981; About Silence, poem for voice and piano, lyrics by N Arslanov, 1985; Sonata for piano No. 1, 1985; Sonata for cello solo No. 1, 1986; About Happiness, poem for voice and two flutes, lyrics by R Mingalimov, 1989; Forgotten Prayer, fantasy for organ, 1992; Morning in Istanbul, fantasy for piano, 1993; Quartet No. 4, for two violins, viola and cello, 1994; We Are Answerable to God, for choir a capella, 1995; Fantasy for Saxophone, 1997; Head Into the Noose, for violin and percussion (one performer), 1998; Fantasy for oboe solo, 1998. *Recordings:* Rashid Kalimoullin: Chamber Music, 1989; Piano arrangements of songs by the Beatles: Hyper Beatles, 1993; Chamber Works CD, 1994; String Quartet No 4, CD, 1996. *Honours:* First Prize, K M Veber Competition, Germany, 1987; Shostakovich Award, Russia, 1998. *Membership:* Chairman, Union of Composers of Tatarstan. *Address:* 44/6, 49 Dostoevsky Str, 420043 Tatarstan, Russia.

KALLIN, Ivor; b. 28 Sept. 1957, Glasgow, Scotland. Deputy Headteacher; Musician (Violin, Viola, Double Bass, Bass Guitar). m. Jenny Kallin, 26 Aug. 1979, 1 s., 2 d. *Education:* BA, Social Studies; PGCE. *Compositions:* Mainly involved in improvised music. *Recordings:* Kneel Down Like A Saint, with London Electric Guitar Orchestra; Gorilla, CD; 13 Lumps of Theatre, CD; Relay, contribution to CD; Moonbrake, track; Unmen, track. *Membership:* London Musicians' Collective. *Address:* 13 Alconbury Rd, Clapton, London E5 8RG, England.

KALOGJERA, Niko Nikica; b. 19 May 1930, Beograd, Croatia. Conductor; Composer. m. Ljupka Dimitrovska, 2 March 1978, 2 s., 1 d. *Education:*

Medical University; High Music Academy. *Career:* Chief conductor, Croatian Radio-television Orchestra, International Festival Awards, 28 include: Split 1969; MIDEM, 1969; Athens, 1970; Rio, 1971; Malaga, 1971; Vina Del Mar, 1971; Tokyo, 1971; Dresden, 1972; Eurovision Song Contest, 1989. *Compositions:* Over 1000 songs on LP, MC, CD, VC (about 400 in foreign countries); Music for theatre, films; Artistes: Mireille Mathieu; Claudio Villa; Raymond Lefevre; Tony Christie. *Publications:* Columnist in many music publications. *Membership:* Vice-president, Croatian Composers Asscn. *Current Management:* AVET, Zagreb, Croatia. *Address:* 10000 Zagreb, Tuskanac 33, Croatia.

KAMAI, Allen; b. 6 Dec. 1960, Marin County, California, USA. Musician (Bass). *Education:* College of Marin. *Career:* Tours with: Oleta Adams; Sheena Easton; Wendy and Lisa; The Rainbirds; Michael Penn; Jude Cole; Ronnie Montrose; Extensive television and video performances in USA; Europe; Canada; Japan. *Recordings:* Sass Jordan; Curt Smith; Miki Howard; Jeanette Katt; Bronx-Style Bob; Pretty In Pink; The Rainbirds; Chanise Wilson; Wendy and Lisa; Kristian Vigard; Jim Chappell. *Honours:* Yamaha Soundcheck, Outstanding Bassist, 1987. *Current Management:* Doug Buttleman Management. *Address:* 14625 Dickens #207, Sherman Oaks, CA 91403, USA.

KAMEN, Michael; b. 15 April 1948, New York, USA. Composer. *Education:* Oboe, Juilliard School of Music. *Compositions:* For television: Liza's Pioneer Diary, 1976; S*H*E, 1980; Shoot for the Sun, 1986; Amazing Stories, 1985; Edge of Darkness, 1986; Tales from the Crypt, 1989; The Heart Surgeon, 1997; From the Earth to the Moon, 1998; Band of Brothers, 2001; For film: The Next Man, 1976; Stunts, 1977; Between the Lines, 1977; Boardwalk, 1979; Polyester, 1981; Venom, 1982; Pink Floyd: The Wall, 1982; Angelo My Love, 1983; The Dead Zone, 1983; Brazil, 1985; Lifeforce (additional music), 1985; Rita, Sue and Bob Too, 1986; Highlander, 1986; Mona Lisa, 1986; Shanghai Surprise, 1986; Suspect, 1987; Someone to Watch Over Me, 1987; Adventures in Babysitting, 1987; Lethal Weapon, 1987; The Raggedy Rawney, 1988; Crusoe, 1988; Action Jackson, 1988; Homeboy, 1988; Die Hard, 1988; The Adventures of Baron Munchausen, 1988; Rooftops, 1989; For Queen and Country, 1989; Road House, 1989; Licence to Kill, 1989; Dead Bang, 1989; Lethal Weapon 2, 1989; Renegades, 1989; The Krays, 1990; Cold Dog Soup, 1990; Die Hard 2: Die Harder, 1990; Robin Hood: Prince of Thieves, 1991; Nothing but Trouble, 1991; Let Him Have It, 1991; Company Business, 1991; Hudson Hawk, 1991; The Last Boy Scout, 1991; Blue Ice, 1992; Shining Through, 1992; Lethal Weapon 3, 1992; Wilder Napalm, 1993; Splitting Heirs, 1993; Last Action Hero, 1993; The Three Musketeers, 1993; Stonewall, 1995; Mr Holland's Opus, 1995; Circle of Friends, 1995; Don Juan DeMarco, 1995; Die Hard: With a Vengeance, 1995; Jack, 1996; 101 Dalmatians, 1996; The Winter Guest, 1997; Inventing the Abbotts, 1997; Remember Me?, 1997; Event Horizon, 1997; What Dreams May Come, 1998; Fear and Loathing in Las Vegas, 1998; Lethal Weapon 4, 1998; Frequency, 2000; X-Men, 2000. *Honours:* Ivor Novello Award for Best Original Score, X-Men, 2000. *Membership:* BMI. *Current Management:* Gorfaine/Schwartz Agency Inc, 13245 Riverside Dr., Suite 450, Sherman Oaks, CA 91423, USA. *Website:* www.michaelkamen.com.

KANAL, Tony; b. 27 Aug. 1970, Kingsbury, London, England. Musician (bass guitar). *Career:* Mem., US group, No Doubt, 1987–. *Recordings:* Albums: No Doubt, 1992; Beacon Street Collection, 1994; Tragic Kingdom, 1995; Return Of Saturn, 2000; Rock Steady, 2001. Singles: Just A Girl, 1995; Don't Speak (No. 1, UK), 1997; New, 1999; Ex-Girlfriend, 2000; Simple Kind Of Life, 2000; Bathwater, 2000; Hey Baby, 2001; Hella Good, 2002; Tour (EP), 2002; Underneath It All, 2002. *Address:* c/o Interscope Records, 2220 Colorado Ave, Santa Monica, CA 90404, USA. *Website:* www.nodoubt.com.

KANDA BONGO MAN; b. 1955, Inono, Democratic Republic of Congo. Vocalist; Songwriter. *Career:* Started singing in Kinshasa, 1973; Member: Orchestre Bella Mambo, 1976; Moved to Paris, 1979; Performed at WOMAD UK, 1983; International career began; Accredited with birth of kwassa kwassa dance rhythm; Later Minister of Arts and Culture in new Democratic Republic of Congo. *Recordings:* Iyole, 1981; Non Stop Non Stop, 1985; Amour Fou, 1985; Kwassa Kwassa, 1989; Zing Zong, 1991; Soukous in Central Park, 1992; Francophonix, 1995; Welcome to South Africa, 1998; Sweet, 1999; Best of Kanda Bongo Man, 1999; Balobi, 2001; Very Best of Kanda Bongo Man, 2002. *Address:* c/o Gallo Records, PO Box 2897, Parklands 2121, South Africa. *Website:* www.gallo.co.za.

KANE, Gregory; b. 11 Sept. 1966, Coatbridge, Strathclyde, Scotland. Vocalist; Lyricist; Composer. *Education:* Engineering student. *Career:* Formed Hue and Cry with brother Patrick; Concerts include: Royal Albert Hall; Support to Madonna, Wembley Stadium; Composer for television themes and musical scores. *Recordings:* Albums: Seduced and Abandoned, 1987; Ordinary Angel, 1988; Bitter Suite, 1989; Remote, 1989; Stars Crash Down, 1991; Labours of Love, 1993; Showtime!, 1994; Piano and Voice, 1995; Jazz Not Jazz, 1999; Next Move, 2000; Singles: Labour of Love, 1987; Violently, 1989; Looking For Linda, 1989.

KANE, Patrick; b. 10 March 1964, Coatbridge, Strathclyde, Scotland. Vocalist; Musician (piano, keyboards); Songwriter; Journalist. *Education:*

Degree, English and Media Studies. *Career:* Formed Hue and Cry with brother Gregory; Concerts include Royal Albert Hall; Support to Madonna, Wembley Stadium; Also journalist, The Guardian; Radio presenter, Usual Suspects, BBC Radio Scotland; Broadcaster, Radio 4; Rector, Glasgow University. *Recordings:* Albums: Seduced and Abandoned, 1987; Ordinary Angel, 1988; Bitter Suite, 1989; Remote, 1989; Stars Crash Down, 1991; Labours of Love, 1993; Showtime!, 1994; Piano and Voice, 1995; Jazz Not Jazz, 1999; Next Move, 2000; Singles: Labour of Love, 1987; Violently, 1989; Looking For Linda, 1989. *Membership:* Founder, Artists For An Independent Scotland. *Address:* c/o BBC Radio Scotland, Queen Margaret Dr., Glasgow G12 8DG, Scotland.

KANE, Stevie (Stephen); b. 13 April 1961. Musician (fretted and fretless bass, double bass). *Career:* Tours with The Silencers: Dance To The Holyman European tour, 1992; Seconds of Pleasure tour, 1993–94; So Be It, 1995; Other concerts include: Rock-Am-Ring, 1993; London Fleadh, 1993; St Gallen, 1994; Appearances include: Radio 1 Roadshow, 1993; Free Wheels, 1993; Live Aus Dem Nachtwerk, 1993; Summit In The City, 1993. *Recordings:* with The Silencers: Seconds of Pleasure; So Be It. *Current Management:* Tartan Ghost. *Address:* 423 Merry St, Motherwell, Strathclyde ML1 4BP, Scotland.

KANNBERG, Scott; b. 1967, Stockton, California, USA. Musician (Guitar); Vocalist. *Career:* Founder Member, Pavement; Released first EP on own label; Obtained bigger indie label deal; Numerous live gigs; Appearance of group in cartoon Space Ghost Coast to Coast. *Recordings:* Singles: Perfect Sound Forever EP, 1990; Watery, Domestic, EP, 1992; Trigger Cut, 1992; Cut Your Hair, 1994; Gold Soundz, 1994; Range Life, 1995; Rattled by La Rush, 1995; Father to a Sister of Thought, 1995; Pacific Trim EP, 1996; Shady Lane/Slowly Typed, 1997; Stereo, 1997; Spit on a Stranger, 1999; Carrot Rope, 1999; Albums: Slanted and Enchanted, 1992; Crooked Rain, Crooked Rain, 1994; Wowee Zowee, 1995; Brighten the Corners, 1997; Terror Twilight, 1999; features on: Brilliant Career, Film School, 2001.

KANTARDZIJEV-MLINAC, Petko; b. 21 Oct. 1945, Sofia, Bulgaria. Composer; Sound Engineer; Prod; Musician (piano). m. Mirjana, 15 Aug. 1971, 1 d. *Education:* Faculty of Electronics, 1971; High School for Music, department, Composing and Piano, 1964. *Career:* Rock musician, 1961–69; Music editor, TV Zagreb, 1969; Rehearser, music, Comedy Theatre, Zagreb: A Man From La Mancha; Fiddler On The Roof; Promises Promises, 1969–71; Radio-television, Zagreb, 1970–89; Music Producer, Suzy Record Company, 1971–72; Sound engineer, Jugoton Record Company, 1974–76; Director, Multimedia Youth Centre, 1987–88; Pianist, 1990–. *Compositions:* Over 150 compositions and arrangements, pop, easy listening, classical, number recorded for Radio Zagreb and various records. *Recordings:* As sound engineer: More than 200 soundtracks; films; animations; documentaries; Television series; films; 100 albums include: John Luis; Clark Terry; Sal Nistico; Art Farmer. *Honours:* First prizes, Best Soundtracks, Yugoslavia, 1982, 1984, 1985, 1986; First prizes, Festivals in: Opatja, 1968; Zagreb, 1986; Fish Eye animated film, Ottawa, 1981. *Membership:* Croatian Composers' Asscn; Croatian Artistes' Asscn. *Address:* Maksimirska 81, 10000 Zagreb, Croatia.

KANTNER, Paul; b. 12 March 1941, San Francisco, California, USA. Musician (guitar). 1 d. *Education:* University of Santa Clara, 1959–61; San Jose State College, 1961–63. *Career:* Founder member, Jefferson Airplane, 1965–73; Renamed Jefferson Starship, 1974–84; Member, Planet Earth Rock 'n' Roll Orchestra, 1984–85; KBC (Kantner Balin Casady) Band, 1985–88; Rejoined Jefferson Airplane (later as Jefferson Starship: The Next Generation), 1989–; Appearances include: Berkeley Folk Festival, 1966; Monterey Jazz Festival, 1966; Monterey Pop Festival, 1967; Newport Pop Festival, 1968; Isle of Wight Festival, 1968; Atlantic City Festival, 1969; Woodstock Music and Art Fair, 1969; Altamont Speedway, with Rolling Stones, 1969; Bath Festival, 1970; Festival of Hope, 1970; Knebworth, 1978; Free concert, Golden Gate Park, 1989. *Recordings:* Albums: Jefferson Airplane Takes Off, 1966; Surrealistic Pillow, 1967; After Bathing At Baxter's, 1968; Crown of Creation, 1968; Bless Its Pointed Little Head, 1969; Blows Against The Empire, 1970; The Worst of Jefferson Airplane, 1971; Sunfighter, 1972; Long John Silver, 1972; 30 Seconds Over Winterland, 1973; Baron Von Tollbooth and The Chrome Nun, 1973; Dragonfly, 1974; Red Octopus, 1975; Spitfire, 1976; Flight Log (1966–76), 1977; Jefferson Starship Gold, 1979; Freedom At Point Zero, 1980; Modern Times, 1981; Winds of Change, 1983; Nuclear Furniture, 1984; Jefferson Airplane, 1989; Jefferson Airplane Loves You, 1992; A Guide Through the Chaos, 1996; Jefferson Airplane and Beyond, 1997; Windows of Heaven, 1999; Roar of Jefferson Airplane, 2001; Ignition, 2001; with KBC Band: KBC Band, 1986; Solo: The Planet Earth Rock and Roll Orchestra, 1983; Singles include: Miracles, 1975; With Your Love, 1976; Runaway, 1978; Jane, 1980. *Publications:* Author, Nicaraguan Diary, 1988. *Current Management:* Bill Thompson Management, 2051 Third St, San Francisco, CA 94107, USA.

KANTONEN, Seppo; b. 13 Nov. 1963, Kivijärvi. Finland. Musician (piano, keyboards). *Education:* Sibelius Academy, Helsinki, 1979. *Career:* Began career playing with Nono Söderberg and Otto Donner Treatment; Pianist with UMO (New Music Orchestra); Pianist with Eero Koivistoinen, 1980s–;

Jazz soloist, accompanist, Afro-American tradition; Worked with numerous rock bands including Mustat Lasit, 1980s; Recorded as duo with Jarmo Savolainen. *Recordings:* Albums: with Jarmo Savolainen: Phases; with Eero Koivistoinen: Dialog, 1995. *Honours:* Yrjö Award, Finnish Jazz Federation, 1985. *Address:* Ruusankatu 6 A 18, 00250 Helsinki, Finland.

KAPELLE, Frances; b. 21 Aug. 1956, London, England. Vocalist. m. Paul Raymond Oldridge, 26 May 1978, divorced, 1 d. *Education:* College. *Career:* Backing vocalist for singers including: Ian Shaw; Carol Grimes; Brian Kennedy; Mary Coughlan; Preproduction singer, backing vocal arranger, writer with Violet Williams, film soundtrack The Commitments. *Recordings:* Albums: Junk Puppets, An Emotional Fish (backing vocals); Why Don't They Dance, Carol Grimes. *Membership:* Musicians' Union. *Address:* Brockton Farm, Egerton Rd, Charing Heath, Kent TN27 0AX, England.

KAPHAN, Bruce Robert; b. 7 Jan. 1955, San Francisco, California, USA. Musician; Prod; Composer; Engineer. m. Michele White, 12 Dec. 1987. *Career:* Tours with American Music Club, USA, Western Europe; Television appearances with Jewel (Saturday Night Live and MTV Unplugged), 1997; European and USA tours with David Byrne, including television appearances on the Late Show with David Letterman and Sessions at W 54th St on PBS. *Recordings:* with John Lee Hooker: Chill Out; with The Black Crowes: Amorica; with Chris Isaak: Forever Blue; with American Music Club: Everclear; Mercury; San Francisco; Black Crowes, Three Snakes and One Charm, Love and Rockets, Sweet FA; Jellyfish, Spilt Milk; Red House Painters, Songs for a Blue Guitar; Francesco di Gregori, Premiere E Lasciare; Susanna Hoffs, Susanna Hoffs; Tara MacLean, Silence; Suzanne Little, Be Here Now; Mark Eitzel, 60 Watt Silver Lining, West; Up, REM; Legacy, Jewel; Solo album: Slider–Ambient Excursions For Pedal Steel Guitar, 2001. *Honours:* Award Winner, Northern California Film and Video Festival, 2000. *Membership:* AFofM. *Address:* PO Box 2012, Fremont, CA 94536, USA.

KAPILIDIS, Nick; b. 2 Jan. 1955, Zanthi, Greece. Musician (drums). m. 1973–92, 1 s., 1 d. *Education:* Ethnico Conservatory, 4 years piano, 1 year flute, private lessons drums. *Career:* Jazz festivals, Patea, Athens, Thessaloniki; Live performances with J. Stubblefield; D. Hayes; M. Boyd; G. Bailey; K. Rampton; D. Lynch; Y. Fakaqnas; L. Christofis; TV appearances with many famous Greek composers and singers. *Recordings:* Electric Jazz Trio, 1990; Flying To The Unknown, M Alexiou, 1995; Oramata, L. Christofis, 1996. *Publications:* Book: Modern Greek Odd Rhythms. *Membership:* Greek Musicians' Union. *Address:* Markou Botsazi 24, Galatsi 1145, Athens, Greece.

KAPOOR, Steven. See: **APACHE INDIAN.**

KAPSEU, Jean Robert; b. 30 Sept. 1968, Bangoua. Songwriter; Composer; Musician (Guitar). 2 s., 1 d. *Career:* Musical Concerts, 1996–; Appearances, Radioscopy of a Star, 1997. *Compositions:* Let's Fight for Life, The Road Is Not A Mystery; Confirmation. *Recordings:* Union Plus; Luttons Laus La Vie; Que Faire; Travailler, La Vie N'est Pas Facile; Sida, Passera Jariais Pas Moi; L'Hymne Bangoua. *Publications:* The Age of Maturity, 1990; Let's Fight For Life, 1996; Confirmation, 1999. *Membership:* Socinada; AA Mont. *Address:* PO Box 11624, Yaoundé, Cameroon.

KARAKOSTOVA, Rumiana; b. 12 May 1951, Sofia, Bulgaria. Musicologist. m. Lubomir Karakostov, 26 Oct., 1 d. *Education:* Pancho Vladigerov, State Music Academy, Sofia. *Career:* Dramatist, Stefan Makedonsky, State Music Theatre, Sofia; Show scripts with State Musical Theatre; Broadcasts for Bulgarian national radio; Screenplays for biographical films of Bulgarian musicians and actors; Lecturer, National Academy of Theatre and Cinema Art, Plovdiv Fine Arts Academy. *Publications:* Bulgarian Music Theatre; State Music Theatre Stefan Makedonski: Historical Development and Contemporary Problems, in Guide for Operetta Theatres Abroad, 1991; Numerous essays in musicological and music history journals. *Contributions to:* Bulgaria Encyclopaedia Vols IV and VI; History of Bulgarian Music. *Membership:* Union of Bulgarian Composers; Vienna Club, Sofia. *Address:* 136 ap, 8ent, 131 bl, Suhodolska-1 St, Zapaden Park, Krasna Polyana, Sofia 1373, Bulgaria.

KARGES, (Matthew) Murphy; b. 20 June 1967. Musician (bass guitar). *Career:* Toured USA with LA punk group The Weirdos, 1990; Joined The Shrinky Dinx; Group signed to Atlantic Records following circulation of self-made demo video; Act renamed Sugar Ray owing to threat of legal action prior to record releases; Built up world-wide fanbase through touring and TV appearances; Cameo in Fathers Day film, 1997. *Recordings:* Albums: Lemonade and Brownies, 1995; Floored, 1997; 14–59, 1999; Sugar Ray, 2001; Singles: Mean Machine, Iron Mic, 1995; Fly, RPM, 1997; Every Morning, Someday, 1999; Falls Apart, 2000; When It's Over, Answer The Phone, 2001. *Honours:* Second/third albums certified double/triple platinum by RIAA respectively. *Address:* c/o PO Box 12018, Costa Mesa, CA 92627, USA. *E-mail:* management@sugarray.com. *Website:* www.sugarray.com.

KARN, Mick, (Anthony Michaelides); b. 24 July 1958, Nicosia, Cyprus. Musician (Bass Guitar). *Career:* Member, Japan, 1977–82; Member, Dali's Car, 1984; Japan reunion, 1989; Member, Rain Tree Crow (with 3 members of Japan), 1991; Member, Polytown, 1994; Member, Jansen, Barbieri, Karn (with 2 members of Japan), 1995 Sculptor, exhibition of work, London, 1981, 1992, Japan, 1982, Italy, 1985. *Recordings:* Albums: with Japan: Adolescent Sex, 1978; Obscure Alternatives; 1978; Quiet Life, 1980; Gentlemen Take Polaroids, 1980; Assemblage, 1981; Tin Drum, 1981; Oil On Canvas, 1983; Exorcising Ghosts, 1985; Solo albums: Titles, 1982; Dreams of Reason Produce Monsters, 1987; Bestial Cluster, 1994; The Tooth Mother, 1995; with Dali's Car: The Waking Hour, 1984; with Rain Tree Crow: Rain Tree Crow, 1991; Singles include: with Japan: The Art of Parties, 1981; Quiet Life, 1981; Visions of China, 1981; Ghosts, 1982; Cantonese Boy, 1982; Life In Tokyo, 1982; Night Porter, 1982; with Dali's Car: The Judgement is the Mirror, 1984; Solo: Sensitive, Buoy, 1982; 1987; With Polytown: Polytown, 1994; With Jansen, Barbieri, Karn: Beginning to Melt, 1995; Seed, 1996; Liquid Glass, Yoshihiro Hanno, 1998; Ism, 1999; Each Eye A Path, 2001. *Current Management:* Medium Productions, 74 St Lawrence Rd, Upminster, Essex RM14 2UW, England.

KÄRTSY, (Kari Hatakka); b. 17 Dec. 1967, Helsinki, Finland. Musician; Composer; Lyricist; Vocalist. *Career:* European tours, 1993–97; Lead singer, Finnish rock band, Waltari, 1994; Roskilde Festival, Denmark, 1994, 1995; Ethno Meets Metal tour with Angelin Tytöt, 1995; European tours, 1995, 1996, 1997. *Recordings:* Monk Punk, 1991; Torcha!, 1992; So Fine!, 1994; Big Bang, 1995; Yeah! Yeah! Die! Die! Death Metal Symphony in Deep C, 1996; Space Avenue, 1997; Decade, 1998. *Current Management:* East Border/Jone Nuutinen. *Address:* Tallberginkata 1 D, Fifth Floor, 00180 Helsinki, Finland.

KARVONEN, Jartsa; b. 27 June 1955, Finland. Musician (drums). *Education:* Oulunkylä Institute, 1976. *Career:* Began playing, Rovaniemi, Lapland; Played with bands: Blue Train; Jukka Syrenius Band; Tapiola Big Band, including appearance at Detroit Festival; Played with numerous artistes including: Jukka Linkola; Olli Ahvenlahti; Pentti Lahti; Mircea Stan; Regular member, UMO (New Music Orchestra), 1989. *Honours:* Musician of the Year, 1989; Voted Best Drummer, Finnish Jazz Federation's magazine JazzIt Readers Poll, 1989. *Address:* Paraistentie 11 A 6, 00280 Helsinki, Finland.

KASPERSEN, Jan Per Sommerfeldt; b. 22 April 1948, Copenhagen, Denmark. Musician (piano); Composer; Arranger. 1 s. *Career:* Musician, European Jazz scene, 1969–; Bandleader, trios up to quintets, using name Space and Rhythm Jazz. *Recordings:* 23 releases, including Memories of Monk; Live At Sofie's Cellar; Heavy Smoke; Ballads and Cocktails; Special Occasion Band: Live In Copenhagen Jazz-House; Space and Rhythm Jazz; Joining Forces; Jan Kaspersen and the Danish Radio Jazz Orchestra: Live in Copenhagen Jazzhouse; Out of Sight; Katuaq Concert; More Ballads and Cocktails. *Honours:* DJBFA Jazz Composer prize, 1987; JASA prize, 1988. *Membership:* Danish Musicians' Union; Society of Danish Bandleaders. *Current Management:* Space and Rhythm Jazz, Danish Music Agency. *Address:* c/o Space and Rhythm Jazz, Copenhagen, Denmark.

KÄTKÄ, Ismo (Ippe) Paavo Matias; b. 19 March 1948, Seinajoki, Finland. Composer Prod. Musician (Drums, Keyboards). Divorced, 1990, 2 s. *Career:* Local bands, dance, pop, rock, jazz, 1965–; Starboys, Tangopojat, Yahoos, Kari Larne Group, Woodoo, Matthews, Kirka and Islanders, Royals, Pekka Pohjola Group, Veltto and Heru, Ippe Kätkä Band, Tampere Jazz Orchestra, Juice Leskinen, Dave Lindholm, Anssi Tikanmäki Film Orchestra, Krakatau, Ismo Alanko, Galaxy (Senegal); International tours: Pekka Pohjola Group, 1980–82, A T Film Orchestra, 1989–93, Krakatau, 1993–96, Galaxy, 1993–. *Compositions:* For films, TV, radio, theatre, modern dance ranging from classics through Shakespeare to modern poetry. *Recordings:* Royals: Spring 76; Out; Live; Pekka Pohjola Group: Kätkävaaran Lohikäärme; Veltto and Heru: Tahdon; Ippe Kätkä Band: Tre Jazz Orchestra: Makumoka; Juice: Minä; Sinä; Dave: Sissi; Sillalla; A T Film Orchestra: Greed; Krakatau: Matinale; Ismo Alanko: Irti; Taiteilijaelämää; Galaxy: Nobeel. *Honours:* Several state grants, 1982–; Tampere City Creative Musician Award, 1989; Critics' Poll, Best Group and Best Album of Year, 1985, 1994; KOURA Award for the best radio programme, 1997. *Current Management:* Global Music Centre, Mikkolantie 17, Fin 00640 Helsinki, Finland. *Address:* Tallberginkatu 1c/47, 00180 Helsinki, Finland.

KATONA, Kerry (Jane Elizabeth); b. 6 Sept. 1980, Warrington, England. Vocalist. m. Bryan McFadden, Jan. 2002, 1 d. *Career:* Mem., Atomic Kitten, 1999–2001; UK Support tours 1999–2000; Co-spearheaded MTV Asia Awards, 2000. *Recordings:* Albums: Right Now, 2000. Singles: Right Now, 1999; See Ya, 2000; I Want Your Love, 2000; Follow Me, 2000; Whole Again, 2001. *Current Management:* Innocent Records, Kensal House, 553–579 Harrow Rd, London W10 4RH, England.

KATZ, Simon; b. 16 May 1971, Nottingham, England. Musician (Guitar). *Career:* Member, Jamiroquai; Numerous tours and TV appearances. *Recordings:* Singles: When You Gonna Learn, 1992; Too Young To Die, 1993; Blow Your Mind, 1993; Emergency on Planet Earth, 1993; Space Cowboy EP, 1994; Half The Man, 1994; Stillness In Time, 1995; Virtual Insanity, 1996; Cosmic Girl, 1996; Light Years, 1996; Alright, 1997; Deeper Underground (No. 1, UK), 1998; High Times, 1998; Canned Heat, 1999; Supersonic, 1999; King

For A Day, 1999; Little L, 2001; You Give Me Something, 2001; Albums: Emergency on Planet Earth, 1993; Travelling Without Moving, 1996; Synkronized, 1999; A Funk Odyssey, 2001. Honours: Numerous Gold and Platinum Albums; Many MTV Video Music Awards.

KAUKONEN, Jorma; b. 23 Dec. 1940, Washington, DC, USA. Musician (guitar, dobro, steel guitar). Education: BA, Sociology, Santa Clara University; Antioch College; Studied music under Ian Buchanan and Rev Gary Davis. Career: Member, The Triumphs; Member, Jefferson Airplane, 1966–72; Member, side project Hot Tuna, 1968–78, 1992–; Jefferson Airplane Reunion, 1989–90; Appearances include: Berkeley Folk Festival, 1966; Monterey Jazz Festival, 1966; Monterey Pop Festival, 1967; Newport Pop Festival, 1968; Isle of Wight Festival, 1968; Atlantic City Pop Festival, 1969; Woodstock Festival, 1969; Altamont Speedway, with the Rolling Stones, 1969; Bath Festival, 1970. Recordings include: Albums: Jefferson Airplane Takes Off, 1966; After Bathing At Baxter's, 1968; Crown of Creation, 1968; Bless It's Pointed Little Head, 1969; Volunteers, 1969; Blows Against The Empire, 1970; Long John Silver, 1972; Flight Log (1966–76), 1977; Jefferson Airplane, 1989; Jefferson Airplane Loves You, 1992; with Hot Tuna: First Pull Up Then Pull Down, 1971; Burgers, 1972; The Phosphorescent Rat, 1974; America's Choice, 1975; Yellow Fever, 1975; Hoppkorv, 1976; Double Dose, 1978; 2400 Fulton Street, 1987; Quah; Jorma; Barbeque King; Too Hot To Handle; Land of Heroes, 1995; Jorma Kaukonen Christmas, 1996; Too Many Years, 1998; Solo: Blue Country Heart, 2002; Guest musician, If Only I Could Remember My Name, David Crosby, 1972. Current Management: Vanessa Lillian, Gabra Management, 37000 Kingsbury Rd, Pomeroy, OH 45769, USA.

KAVANAGH, Niamh; b. 13 Feb. 1968, Dublin, Ireland. Vocalist; Recording Artiste. Education: Voice training, 4 years, Bel canto school. Career: Appearance on Grammy Awards 1992, with Commitments, 1992; Television and radio throughout Europe, 1993–; Eurovision Song Contest, 1993. Recordings: Tracks on Commitments soundtracks Vols I and II; Eurovision winner: In Your Eyes, 1993; Debut solo album: Flying Blind, 1995. Honours: Yamaha International Award of Excellence; Eurovision Song Contest Winner, In Your Eyes, 1993. Membership: Musicians' Union. Current Management: Mairead Wright. Address: 49 Old Shore Rd, Trooperslane, Carrickfergus, Co Antrim BT38 8PF, Northern Ireland.

KAVANAGH, Ron; b. Fermoy, County Cork, Ireland. Musician; Prod; Arranger; Songwriter; Composer. Career: Former session musician, producer, arranger; Worked with artistes including: Charlie Watts; Richard Thompson; Paddy Moloney; The Pogues; Elvis Costello; Dr John; Clarence Henry; Doug Sahm; Big Jay McNeely; Member, various groups including: Loudest Whisper; Panama Red; Chris Farlowe Band; Identity Kit, with guitarist Ed Deane; Juice On The Loose; In-house bandleader, producer for Ace Records; Member, various bands with Alexis Korner, 1980s; Bees Make Honey; Leader, own band Alias Ron Kavana; 3 support tours with The Pogues; Other projects include: Home Fire; The Bucks; Founder, director, member of LILT (London Irish Live Trust), non-profit making organization committed to peace in Northern Ireland; Appearances, songwriter for films including: Ryan's Daughter; Sid and Nancy; Clash of The Ash, RTE; Hidden Agenda. Compositions include: Co-writer with The Pogues: Young Ned of The Hill; Every Man Is A King. Recordings: Solo albums: Rollin' and Coasting; Home Fire; with Alias Ron Kavana: Think Like A Hero, 1989; Coming Days, 1991; Galway To Graceland, 1995; with Loudest Whisper: The Children of Lire; with Donovan, Liam Og O'Fynn, Philip Donnelly, RTE Chamber Orchestra: The Children of Lire (re-recorded), 1993; with The Bucks: Dancing To The Ceilli Band, 1995; with LILT: For The Children; Guest musician with The Pogues: Sid and Nancy (soundtrack); Fall From Grace. Honours: Best Live Act In The World, Folk Roots Magazine, 1989–91. Current Management: c/o Jim McPhee, Acorn Entertainments. Address: Winterfold House, 46 Woodfield Rd, Kings Heath, Birmingham B13 9UJ, England.

KAY, Jason (Jay); b. 30 Dec. 1969, Manchester, England. Vocalist. Career: Member, Jamiroquai; Numerous tours and TV appearances. Recordings: Singles: When You Gonna Learn, 1992; Too Young To Die, 1993; Blow Your Mind, 1993; Emergency on Planet Earth, 1993; Space Cowboy EP, 1994; Half The Man, 1994; Stillness In Time, 1995; Virtual Insanity, 1996; Cosmic Girl, 1996; Light Years, 1996; Alright, 1997; Deeper Underground (No. 1, UK), 1998; High Times, 1998; Canned Heat, 1999; Supersonic, 1999; King For A Day, 1999; Little L, 2001; You Give Me Something, 2001; Albums: Emergency on Planet Earth, 1993; Travelling Without Moving, 1996; Synkronized, 1999; A Funk Odyssey, 2001. Honours: Several Gold Albums: Numerous MTV Video Music Awards.

KAY, Simon; b. 1 May 1960, London, England. Songwriter; Prod; Musician (keyboards). Career: Keyboard player, Ultramarine; US Tour, Orbital, 1992; Concerts include: Glastonbury Festival; Strawbery Fayre; Radio and television include: Radio 1; Radio 5; 5 Live sessions; MTV Live; Tours with Björk include: USA, Europe, 1993; Britronica; Russian Tour; Glastonbury Festival; Forest Fayre; Megadog, 1994; Formed Exile with partner Tim Ericson; Exile production credits include debut album by Cry. Recordings: with Ultramarine: Album: United Kingdom; Single: Kingdom; Happy Land; Hymn; As producer: Single: with Cry: (It's About) Time For Love. Current

Management: MRM. Address: Panther House, 38 Mount Pleasant, London WC1X 0AP, England.

KAYE, Carol; b. 24 March 1935, Everett, Washington, USA. Musician (Electric Bass, Guitar). 1 s., 2 d. Career: Professor, Guitar, 1949–; Taught Electric Bass, 1969–; On The Road, Big Band, 1954–55; Played Bebop Jazz, Black Night Clubs, 1956–61; Studio Electric Bassist, 1957–66; Studio Electric Bassist, 1963–; Invented 16th Note Bass Recording Styles. Recordings: credits on guitar include: Zippity Doo Dah; Birds and Bees; The Beat Goes On; You've Lost That Lovin Feelin; credits on bass include: Way We Were; Feelin Alright; Good Vibrations; Wouldn't It Be Nice; Heat of Night; I Don't Need No Doctor; Little Green Apples; Baby Love; River Deep Mountain High. Publications: Writer, composer of over 30 tutorials; How to Play the Electric Bass; Jazz Improvisation for Bass; CDs: Carol Kaye: Bass; Thumbs Up; Carol Kaye Guitars '65. Membership: Musicians' Union. Address: PO Box 2122, Canyon Country, CA 91386 2122, USA. E-mail: carolkaye@earthlink.net. Website: www.carolkaye.com.

KAYE, Hereward Hilken Swain; b. 29 June 1953, Middlesbrough, Cleveland, England. Vocalist; Songwriter; Composer. m. Patricia Mary Lord, 6 July 1974, 3 s. Education: Drama College. Career: Member, The Flying Pickets, 4 albums; International tours from Australia to Iceland. Compositions: Moby Dick, Cameron Mackintosh musical, Piccadilly Theatre, 1992; Arranger, musical director, Return To The Forbidden Planet; Composer, lyricist, Hell Can Be Heaven, computer game, musical, opening 1996; with Flying Pickets: Blue Money, 1996; Composer lyricist, Underworld, musical, Seattle, 1998. Honours: Evening Standard Musical of the Year, Are You Lonesome Tonight (as Musical Director). Membership: PRS. Current Management: Sacha Brooks, 55 Greek St, London W1V 5LR, England. Address: 4 Orchard Rd, Linthorpe, Middlesbrough, Cleveland TS5 4PW, England.

KAZAN, Paul; b. 9 April 1956, Taplow, Buckinghamshire, England. Vocalist; Musician (piano, violin); composer; Prod. m. Montserrat Arruga, 21 Oct. 1994, 1 s. Education: 1 year at Bristol University; Grade VIII Piano; Grade VII violin. Career: Classical background; Settled in Spain, 1976; Session musician, arranger until 1990; Solo artiste, 1990–; Presented first solo album in concert at Barcelona Olympic Games, 1992. Recordings: Albums: Stay, 1992; Miracle Street, 1996. Membership: Spanish Society of Authors (SGAE). Current Management: Oniria International, S L. Address: Alzines, 3, Sant Quirze Park, 08192 Sant Quirze Del Valles, Barcelona, Spain.

KAZASSIAN, Hilda; b. 1970, Sofia, Bulgaria. Vocalist; Musician (keyboards, drums, percussion); Composer; Arranger. Education: Graduate, Academy of Popular Music, Sofia, 1993; Studied percussion in the United Kingdom and Italy. Career: Hot Jazz debutant; Guest appearances at several jazz festivals; Winner of percussion competitions in Rome and London; Currently working with Acoustic Version (Bulgaria's leading jazz combo); Writes and arranges own compositions. Recordings: Albums: Cover Girl, 1994; Why Not, 1996. Address: c/o Union Media Ltd, 71 Evlogi Georgiev Blvd, Entr. A, Sofia 1142, Bulgaria.

KAZDA, Jan; b. 3 Oct. 1958, Prague, Czech Republic. Musician (Bass, Guitar); Composer; Prod. m. Karen K, 1988, 1 s. Education: Classical Music Degrees; Artists Maturity Degree. Career: Tours with: Ginger Baker, Randy Brecker, Peter Brötzmann, Sonny Sharrock; with own band: Das Pferd and KAZDA, Frankfurt Jazz Festival, Sibiu Jazz Festival (Rumanian), Ruhr-Jazz Leverkusener Jazz Festival; Rockpalast TV HR/WDR TV. Compositions: Composer, 5 CDs with Das Pferd; 2 CDs with KAZDA, 1994–97; 4 CDs with singer Tom Mega, 1988–92. Recordings: Das Pferd, KAZDA, Tom Mega, 1987–97; Recorded with Ginger Baker, Harry Beckett, Randy Brecker, Marilyn Mazur, Ronnell Bey, Frank Wunsch, Nordwestdeutsche Philharmonique (classical orchestra), Therion. Address: Dörpfeldstr 41, 42369 Wuppertal, Germany.

KEANE, Dolores; b. 1953, Caherlistrane, County Galway, Ireland. Vocalist; Musician (flute). Career: First recording for Radio Eireann, aged 5; Founding member of De Danann; Collaborations: Planxty; The Chieftains; Lead role in Dublin production of Brendan Behan's play The Hostage; Also appeared on stage, again in Dublin, in The Playboy of the Western World; Contributed to the RTE/BBC TV production Bringing It All Back Home, 1992; Continues to record and tour internationally. Recordings: Albums include: There Was A Maid, 1978; Sail Og Rua, 1983; Ballroom (De Danann), 1987; Dolores Keane, 1988; Lion In A Cage, 1989; Solid Ground, 1994; The Best of Dolores Keane, 1997; Night Owl, 1998; How The West Was Won (De Danann), 1999; featured on soundtrack: Dancing At Lughnasa, 1998. Honours: Topped Irish charts with singles, The Rambling Irishman and Lion In A Cage, and The Best of Dolores Keane album; Featured track on Ireland's biggest ever selling album, A Woman's Heart, 1992; Awarded Fiddler's Green Hall of Fame, 1995; Irish Music Magazine: Best Female Folk Performer; Best Folk CD, The Best of Dolores Keane, 1997. Website: www.doloreskeane.com.

KEANE, Seán; b. 24 Aug. 1961, Co. Galway, Ireland. Vocalist. Career: Mem., Shegui, 1970s; Reel Union, 1980s; Arcady; Shaskeen; The Chieftains, 1978–;

Solo artiste, 1994. *Recordings:* Albums: with Shegui: Around The World For Sport; with Reel Union: There Was A Maid; with Shaskeen: Atlantic Breeze, with the Keane family: Muintir Chathain; with The Chieftains: Chieftains 9, 1979; Boil The Breakfast Early, 1980; Chieftains 10, 1981; The Chieftains In China, 1984; Ballad Of The Irish Horse, 1985; Celtic Wedding, 1987; The Chieftains In Ireland (with James Galway), 1987; Year Of The French, 1988; Irish Heartbeat (with Van Morrison), 1988; A Chieftains Celebration, 1989; Chieftains Collection, 1989; The Celtic Connection: James Galway And The Chieftains, 1990; Bells Of Dublin, 1991; An Irish Evening, 1992; Another Country, 1992; The Celtic Harp (with Belfast Harp Orchestra), 1993; Water From The Well; The Long Black Veil, 1995; Santiago, 1996; Tears Of Stone, 1999; Down The Old Plank Road: The Nashville Sessions, 2002; The Wide World Over: A 40 Year Celebration, 2002; Solo: All Heart No Roses, 1994; Turn A Phrase, 1996; No Stranger, 1996; The Man That I Am (featuring Nanci Griffith and an arrangement by Sir George Martin), 2000; The Best Of Seán Keane, 2001; Seánsongs, 2002. *Honours:* Won 13 All-Ireland titles; Irish Music Magazine, Performer of the Year, 1997–98, Best Male Folk Singer, 1997–2001. *Address:* c/o RCA Victor Group, 1540 Roadway, New York, NY 10036, USA. *Website:* www.irish.com; www.seankeane.com.

KEAREY, Ian; b. 14 Oct. 1954, London, England. Vocalist. Musician (guitar, bass guitar, banjo, mandolin). m. Rebekah Zoob, 19 April 1986, 1 s., 1 d. *Education:* University of Kent, Canterbury. *Career:* Member, Oyster Band, 1976–88; Member, Blue Aeroplanes, 1983–; Producer for: Michelle Shocked; Bootfare; Many television appearances include: Top of the Pops; Many radio appearances include: Radio 1, Radio 2 sessions; Freelance sessions, 1986–; Member, Heaven Factory, 1990–. *Recordings include:* with Blue Aeroplanes: Bop Art, 1984; Swagger, 1990; Beatsongs, 1991; Life Model, 1993; Rough Music, 1994; Cavaliers, 2000; with Oyster Band: Liberty Hall, 1985; Step Outside, 1986; Wide Blue Yonder, 1987; Trawler, 1995; Granite Years (compilation), 2000; with Gerard Langley: Siamese Boyfriends, 1987; with Heidi Berry: Love, 1991; with Leon Rosselson: Perspectives, 1998. *Publications:* Contributor, Folk Roots Magazine, 1984–. *Honours:* Freedom of the City of Bangor, 1980; Hon. BSC, Indian Institute of Technology, 1986. *Membership:* Musicians' Union. *Current Management:* E Bunbury, RFM. *Address:* 88 Roundhill Cres., Brighton, East Sussex BN2 3FR, England.

KEATING, Ronan Patrick John; b. 3 March 1977, Dublin, Ireland. Vocalist; Songwriter. m. Yvonne Connelly, 1 s., 1 d. *Career:* Lead Singer, Boyzone, 1993–2001; Co-host, Eurovision Song Contest, Ireland; Solo artiste, 1999–. *Recordings:* Albums: Said And Done, 1995; A Different Beat, 1996; Where We Belong, 1998; By Request (No. 1, UK), 1999; Solo: Ronan, 2000; Destination, 2002. Singles: with Boyzone: Working My Way Back To You, 1994; Key To My Life, 1995; Love Me For A Reason, 1995; So Good, 1995; Father and Son, 1995; Coming Home Now, 1995; Words (No. 1, UK), 1996; A Different Beat (No. 1, UK), 1996; Isn't It A Wonder, 1997; Picture Of You, 1997; Baby Can I Hold You Tonight, 1997; Mystical Experience, 1997; All That I Need (No. 1, UK), 1998; No Matter What (No. 1, UK), 1998; I Love The Way You Love Me, 1998; When The Going Gets Tough (No. 1, UK), 1999; You Needed Me (No. 1, UK), 1999; Every Day I Love You, 1999; Solo: When You Say Nothing At All (No. 1, UK), 1999; Life Is A Rollercoaster (No. 1, UK), 2000; The Way You Make Me Feel, 2000; Lovin' Each Day, 2001; If Tomorrow Never Comes, 2002. *Publications:* No Matter What, 2000; Life is a Rollercoaster, 2000. *Current Management:* The Outside Organization, 180–182 Tottenham Court Rd, London W1P 9LE, England. *Address:* c/o Polydor (UK), 72 Black Lion Lane, London W6 9BE, England. *Website:* www.ronankeating.com.

KEEL, Howard, (Harold C. Leek); b. 13 April 1917, Gillespie, Illinois, USA. Vocalist; Actor. *Career:* In-house entertainer, Douglas aircraft manufacturing company; Appeared in musicals: Carousel, 1945; Oklahoma, London; Film appearances: The Small Voice, 1948; Annie Get Your Gun, 1950; Show Boat, 1951; Kiss Me Kate, 1953; Calamity Jane, 1953; Rose Marie, 1954; Seven Brides For Seven Brothers, 1954; Kismet, 1955; Various western films; US revival tours, 1960s; Regular television appearances, US series Dallas, 1981–; Solo recording artiste, 1984–; Farewell Tour, UK, 1993. *Recordings:* And I Love You So, 1984; Reminiscing, 1985; The Collection, 1989; The Great MGM Stars, 1991; Close To My Heart, 1991; With Love for Yesterday, Today and Tomorrow, 1998; And I Love You So, 2001; Various soundtrack albums. *Address:* c/o Producers Inc, 11806 N 56th St, Suite B, Tampa, FL 33617, USA.

KEEREMAN, Peter; b. 21 Aug. 1968, Brugge, Belgium. Prod; Composer; Musician (piano). *Education:* Degree in Music Education, Ghent, Belgium; Graduate, Berklee, College of Music, Music Production and Engineering. *Career:* Concert tours with Belgian artistes; Performances for BRT—Radio and Television. *Compositions:* Everlasting Love and Revende Hemel (Intersong Primakera); Spaceflight/Snow Flakes; Crazy Comedy Capers (Parsifal). *Membership:* SABAM Author Organisation. *Address:* Doornstraat 47, 8200 Brugge, Belgium.

KEEZER, Geoffrey Graham; b. 20 Nov. 1970, Eau Claire, Wisconsin, USA. Jazz Musician (piano); Composer; Arranger. m. Mayumi Tomokane, 23 April 1995. *Education:* 1 year, Berklee College, Boston. *Career:* Pianist with Art

Blakey and the Jazz Messengers, 1989–90; Pianist with Art Farmer, 1991–95; Leader of Geoff Keezer trio and quartet, 1988; Tours: Japan; England; Europe; Russia; Scandinavia; Canada; Performed: at Lincoln Center; with Carnegie Hall Jazz Orchestra; with Hollywood Bowl Orchestra. *Compositions:* Many large and small ensemble pieces. *Recordings:* As leader: Here and Now, 1991; World Music, 1992; Other Spheres, 1993; All For One, with Art Blakey; The Key Players, with The Contemporary Piano Ensemble; Color and Light—Jazz Sketches On Sondheim; Some of My Best Friends..., with Ray Brown; Turn Up The Quiet, 1998; Zero One, 2000; Live At Starbucks, 2001. *Membership:* BMI; AMRA. *Address:* The Jazz Tree, 648 Broadway, Suite 703, New York, NY 10012, USA.

KEITA, Salif; b. 1949, Djoliba, Mali. Vocalist. *Career:* Japan Tour, 1993; Grande Parade du Jazz de Nice, 1992; WOMAD Festivals: Reading, 1992; Adelaide, 1993; Las Palmas, 1993; Australian tour, 1993; Annual European tour including summer festivals; Montreux Jazz Festivals, 1993, 1995; Canadian tour, 1994; US tour, 1994; African tour, including South Africa, 1994; Parkpop Festival, The Hague, Holland, 1995. *Recordings:* Soro, 1987; Koyan, 1989; Destiny of a Noble Outcast, 1991; Amen, 1991; Mansa of Mali, 1994; Folon, 1995; Rail Band, 1996; Seydou Bathili, 1997; Papa, 1999; Sosie, 2001; Compilation, 1969–80, 2001; Moffou, 2002. *Publications:* Video: Noble of an Outcast. *Honours:* Chevalier of Arts and Letters, France; Chevalier of Order of The Nation, Mali; Grammy Award. *Current Management:* Mad Minute Music, Paris, contact Corinne Serres. *Address:* c/o Mad Minute Music, 5–7 Paul Bert, 93400 St Ouen, France.

KEITH, (John) Larry; b. 1 March 1955, Hendersonville, North Carolina, USA. Musician (guitar, bass); Vocalist. m. Denna O Nix, 23 Dec. 1988, 1 s., 2 d. *Education:* Blue Ridge Community College, Hendersonville, North Carolina. *Career:* WKIT-WHKP Radio Hendersonville, The Charlie Renfro Concerts, 1980–84; Appearances with: Carl Story and The Ramblin' Mountaineers; The Boys From Indiana; Jim and Jesse and the Virginia Boys; Bill Monroe and The Bluegrass Boys; Doyle Lawson and Quicksilver; Mac Wiseman; Dolly Parton's Premiere Bluegrass Band, Pigeon Forge, Tennessee, 1984–88. *Recordings:* Albums: First Time Around; On and On; Head Over Heels; Second Time Around; The Old Country Church. *Publications:* The Bluegrass Newsletter (monthly). *Membership:* IBMA; The Bluegrass Music Asscns of North Carolina, South Carolina, Georgia. *Current Management:* The McMinn Family Band. *Address:* PO Box 384, Tuxedo, NC 28784, USA.

KEITHLEY, Joseph Edward; b. Burnaby, BC, Canada. m. Laura Susan, 2 s., 1 d. *Career:* 20 years in punk rock band, DOA; Solo acoustic folk act; Appeared in cult films, Terminal City; The Widower. *Compositions:* 10 albums with DOA. *Recordings:* Bloodied But Unbound; War on 45; Last Scream of the Missing Neighbours. *Publications:* Spin, 1985; High Times, 1995; Rolling Stone, 1997. *Current Management:* Laurie Mercer Management, PO Box 27070, Collingwood PP, Vancouver, BC, Canada.

KELIS, (Kelis Rogers), (Thunderbitch); b. 1979, Harlem, New York, USA. Vocalist. *Education:* La Guardia High School of Music and Art and the Performing Arts, New York. *Career:* Started singing in Boys and Girls Choir of Harlem; Collaborated with the Gravediggaz before joining girl group B.L.U.; Began solo career working with The Neptunes production team; Collaborations: Ol' Dirty Bastard; Busta Rhymes; Foxy Brown. *Recordings:* Albums: Kaleidoscope, 2000; Wanderland, 2001; Singles: Caught Out There, Good Stuff, Get Along With You, 2000; Young Fresh n' New, 2001. *Honours:* NME Award, Best R&B Artist, 2001. *Address:* c/o Virgin America, 304 Park Ave S, Fifth Floor, New York, USA.

KELLARD, Colin Alan; b. 9 Jan. 1941, Bury St Edmunds, Suffolk, England. Musician (banjo, guitar). m. Pamela Randall, 24 Sept. 1966, 1 s., 1 d. *Career:* Insurance Claims Inspector; Member of Alvin Roy Saratoga Jazz Band, 1959–63; Tours of Germany, 1961 and 1962; Television appearance: Let's Go, BBC, 1961; Member of Rad Newton Jazz Friends, with various appearances at jazz festivals in UK and Holland, 1987–92; Leader, own Jazz band, 1992–. *Recordings:* Many recordings with Alvin Roy Saratoga Jazz Band; Own label recordings with Tad Newton Jazz Friends and Colin Kellard Band. *Honours:* Winner, Soho Fair Jazz Band Contest with Alvin Roy Saratoga Jazz Band, 1960. *Address:* 15 Nathaniel Walk, Tring, Hertfordshire HP23 5DQ, England.

KELLERMANN, Lone; b. 20 March 1943, Copenhagen, Denmark. Vocalist. *Career:* Member of several bands; Numerous film, television, theatre and radio appearances, newspaper interviews. *Recordings:* 5 solo albums; Several other recordings. *Membership:* DJBFA; Danish Artistes' Union. *Current Management:* Danish Artistes' Union. *Address:* Amagengade 11, 1423 Copenhagen, Denmark.

KELLIE, Michael Alexander; b. 24 March 1947, Birmingham, England. Musician (drums). m. (1) April 1969, 1 d., (2) Elizabeth, Sept. 1997, 2 s. *Career:* Original member, Island Records family, 1966–76; Spooky Tooth, 1967 to end; The Only Ones, 1976–81; World tours with above; Recordings with many others; Currently involved in running Spookytooth.com; Writing a book; Working with church musicians to promote Christian music. *Recordings:* Spooky Two, Spooky Tooth; With A Little Help From My Friends,

Joe Cocker; Tommy (film soundtrack), The Who; Cross Purpose, Spooky Tooth, CD, 1999. *Membership:* Musicians' Union; PAMRA. *Current Management:* Alec Sutton, Attic Music. *Address:* GEK, 22 Holly Rd, Edgbaston, Birmingham B16 9NH, England.

KELLNER, Olda; b. 14 March 1948, Prague, Czech Republic. Vocalist; Musician (Guitar, Keyboards); Composer; Record Studio Owner. m. Vera Spalova, 27 March 1971, 1 d. *Education:* Conservatoire. *Career:* Member, Prague Rock Group, Blue Effect, 1981–88. *Publications:* Encyklopedie Jazzu a Moderni Popula'rní Hudby, 1990. *Membership:* OSA Prague; Intergram Prague. *Address:* Konstantinova 10, 14900 Prague 4, Czech Republic.

KELLY, Charles; b. 19 Aug. 1930, Dallas, Texas, USA. Vocalist; Writer; Musician (trombone). m. Bev Kelly, 2 s. *Education:* BA, MA, Sierra University; University of California; Oklahoma University. *Career:* Wrote and Edited Numerous Policies and Procedures, Manuals, Software Manuals, Proposals, Northrop, Boeing, Hughes Aircraft Company; Group Singer; Television Performer; Numerous Commercials, 1959–76; Motion Picture Voice Tracks, 1965–70. *Publications:* Over 500 Articles and Stories; Technical Editor: Pharmacology, Biology and Clinical Applications of Anrogens; The Alchemy of Intelligence; Editor: The Book of Love and Sex; Ghostwriter: Love Making: The Psychology of Making Love; Writer: The Amazing John Holmes; Sammy; Silent Obsession; Work in progress: Memoirs of a Personal Manager: From The Glenn Miller Singers to Johnny Carson. *Membership:* ASCAP; AFTRA; SAG. *Address:* 248 Laverne Ave, Long Beach, CA 90803, USA.

KELLY, Jeff; Songwriter; Musician (multi-instrumentalist). m. Susanne. *Career:* Formed the Green Pajamas, 1984–; Also solo artiste. *Compositions include:* Kim The Waitress, covered by Material Issue and Sister Psychic. *Recordings:* Albums: with The Green Pajamas: Summer of Lust, 1984, 1990; Halloween, 1984; Book of Hours, 1987; November, 1988; Ghosts of Love, 1990; In A Glass Darkly, 2001; Solo: Baroquen Hearts, 1985; Coffee In Nepal, 1987, 1991; Portugal, 1990; Twenty Five, 1991; Private Electrical Storm, 1992; Ash Wednesday Rain, 1995; Melancholy Sun, 1999; Indiscretion, 2001; Featured on compilations: Monkey Business, 1986; Splat Sampler, 1988; Time Will Show The Wiser, 1989; The Fourth Adventure, 1991.

KELLY, Jon; Record Prod. 3 c. *Career:* Prod. for: The Beautiful South, Heather Nova, Tori Amos, Paul McCartney, Roddy Frame, Prefab Sprout, Rosalie Deighton, Paul Heaton, Kate Bush, Chris Rea, Deacon Blue, The Damned, The Levellers, New Model Army, The Bible, Jimmy Nail. *Current Management:* Stephen Budd Management Ltd, 109b Regents Park Rd, Primrose Hill, London NW1 8UR, England. *Website:* www.record-producers.com.

KELLY, Juliet; b. 6 May 1970, London, England. Jazz Vocalist. *Education:* BSc (Hons), Economics; MA, Television Production; Post-graduate Jazz course, Guildhall School of Music and Drama. *Career:* Part of a cappella Group, Darker Than Blue (formerly Jazz Voices); Performed at Purcell Room, South Bank, part of London Jazz Festival, 1994; Festivals in Germany, 1995; Australia, 1996; Touring with Orphy Robinson, Phoenix Dance Company Project, across UK, including Sadlers Wells, 1995. *Membership:* Musicians' Union.

KELLY, Laoise; b. 1973, Westport, County Mayo, Ireland. Musician (harp, fiddle). *Education:* Maynooth; University College, Cork. *Career:* Member: Ciabh Rua, age 15; Bumblebees, 1996; Harp teacher at UCC, 1993; Performed in: Bill Whelan's Seville Suite, 1993; Micheal O'Suilleabhain's Lumen, Eurovision, 1995; Charlie Lennon's Famine Suite; Toured USA and Australia, 1997; Collaborations: Natalie MacMaster; The Chieftains; Tunde Jegede; Co-founder: FACE (with Steve Cooney); Teacher, DIT, Dublin; Appearances in TV series: River of Sound, 1995; Sult, 1996; Sin E E (with Liam O Maonlai); Geantrai (with Matt Molloy), 1996. *Recordings:* with Bumblebees: Bumblebees, 1996; Buzzin', 1999; solo: Just Harp, 1999. *Honours:* All-Ireland titles: 1989; 1991; 1992; Keadue O'Carolan Festival, winner, 1989; Granard harp competitions: 1989; 1990 1992; Belfast Bicentennial Harp Festival, winner, 1992. *E-mail:* laoise.kelly@face.ie.

KELLY, Mark; b. 9 April 1961, Dublin, Ireland. Musician (keyboards). *Career:* Member, Chemical Alice; UK progressive rock group, Marillion, 1981–; Appearances include: Theakston Festival, 1982; Reading Festival, 1982; Nostell Priory Festival, 1982, 1984; Glastonbury Festival, 1983; Support to Rush, Radio City Music Hall, New York, 1983; Milton Keynes Bowl, 1984; Monsters of Rock Festival, Castle Donington, 1985; Nelson Mandela Birthday Party with Midge Ure, Wembley Stadium, 1987; Welcome To The Garden Party, Milton Keynes Bowl, 1986. *Recordings:* Albums: Script For A Jester's Tear, 1983; Fugazi, 1984; Real To Reel, 1984; Misplaced Childhood, 1985; Brief Encounter, 1986; Clutching at Straws, 1987; B-Sides Themselves, 1988; The Thieving Magpie, 1988; Season's End, 1989; Holidays In Eden, 1991; A Singles Collection 1982–92, 1992; Brave, 1994; Afraid of Sunlight, 1995, 1999; This Strange Engine, 1997; Radiation, 1998; Marillion.com, 1999; Anoraknophobia, 2001; Made Again Live, 2001; Anorak In The UK Live, 2002. Singles include: Market Square Heroes, 1982; He Knows You Know, 1983; Garden Party, 1983; Punch and Judy, 1984;

Assassing, 1984; Kayleigh (No. 2, UK), 1985; Lavender, 1985; Heart of Lothian, 1985; Incommunicado, 1987; Sugar Mice, 1987; Warm Wet Circles, 1987; Freaks, 1988; Hooks In You, 1989; Uninvited Guest, 1989; Easter, 1990; Cover My Eyes (Pain and Heaven), 1991; No One Can, 1991; Dry Land, 1991; Sympathy, 1992. *Current Management:* Hit and Run Music Ltd, 30 Ives St, London SW3 2ND, England.

KELLY, Paul; b. 23 July 1962, England. Musician (guitar); Songwriter. *Career:* with groups: East Village; Saint Etienne; British tours, 1988–90 with East Village; Played with Saint Etienne, 1992–; Tours: UK; Europe; Japan; USA; Festivals: Glastonbury; Roskilde; Hultsfred; Television includes: Top of the Pops; The Beat; The Word; Later With Jools Holland, Glastonbury, 1994; BBC Radio 1 session with St Etienne, 1994. *Recordings:* Albums: with East Village: Drop Out; Hot Rod Hotel; with Birdie: Some Dusty, 1999; Triple Echo, 2001.

KELLY, R(obert); b. 8 Jan. 1969, Chicago, IL, USA. Prod; Vocalist; Musician; Songwriter. *Career:* Began work with band Public Announcement; Wrote and produced hits for Aaliyah, Mary J. Blige, Toni Braxton, The Isley Brothers, Kelly Price and Janet Jackson; Wrote You Are Not Alone, recorded by Michael Jackson for HIStory album; Produced soundtrack for film Lifers featuring Eddie Murphy. *Recordings:* Singles include: Why You Wanna Play Me, 1990; She's Got That Vibe, 1991; Sex Me, 1993; Your Body's Callin', 1994; Bump N' Grind (No. 1, USA), 1994; Summer Bunnies, 1994; You Remind Me of Something, 1995; Down Low, 1996; I Can't Sleep, 1996; I Believe I Can Fly (No. 1, USA), 1997; Gotham City, 1997; Half on a Baby, 1998; Home Alone, 1999; I'm Your Angel, with Céline Dion (No. 1, USA), 1998; Did You Ever Think?, 1999; If I Could Turn Back The Hands of Time, 1999; Satisfy You, with Puff Daddy, 2000; Only The Loot Can Make Me Happy, 2000; I Wish, 2000; Albums: Born into the 90s, 1992; 12 Play, 1993; R Kelly, 1995; R, 1998; TP-2.com, 2000; The Best Of Both Worlds (with Jay-Z), 2002. *Honours:* Grammy Awards for Best Male R&B Vocal Performance, Best R&B Song and Best Song Written For a Motion Picture, Television or Other Visual Media; Favourite Soul/R&B Male Artist, 2000.

KELLY, Roger; b. 3 April 1953, Balby, Doncaster, England. Musician (guitar). m. Sabine Kirchner, divorced. *Education:* BA, Business Studies. *Career:* Toured with Streetband (with Paul Young); Appeared Top of the Pops, 1979; Appeared Rock Palast, Germany with Starry-Eyed and Laughing; Session work with Sandy Shaw in 1980s; Teaching and transcription work, also production. *Recordings:* Albums: Streetband: London; Dilemma; Hit single: Toast (B Side of Hold On) 1979; Co-wrote, produced all album, single material with Paul Young and co-member, John Gifford. *Membership:* PRS. *Address:* 1 Salvington Gardens, Worthing, Sussex, England.

KELSEY, Peter R; b. 25 Jan. 1949, Lincoln, England. Recording Engineer; Prod. m. Catherine Deguilly, 22 Oct. 1985, 2 d. *Education:* BSc Hons, Mathematics. *Career:* Started Trident Studios, London, 1972; Chief Engineer, 1976; Freelance Engineer, 1978; Moved to USA, 1979; Freelance engineer and producer, recordings, film and television music. *Recordings:* Goodbye Yellow Brick Road, Elton John; Heat Treatment, Graham Parker; Discreet Music, Brian Eno; Dialects, Zawinul; Sans Regrets, Veronique Sanson; Outside From The Redwoods, Kenny Loggins; with Kitaro: Mandala; Heaven and Earth; 7 albums with Jean-Luc Ponty including Mystical Adventures; No Absolute Time; Television: Thirtysomething; Picket Fences; Tekwar; Films: Color of Night; Best of Best 2; Poison Ivy. *Honours:* NME Engineering Award, Cafe Jacques, 1976; Emmy Award, sound mixing for Ally McBeal, 1998–2000. *Membership:* NARAS; Re-Pro; ATAS. *Address:* 11022 Haskell Ave, Granada Hills, CA 91344, USA. *E-mail:* piquet49@earthlink.net.

KEMANIS, Aina; b. 15 June 1952, Berkeley, California, USA. Folk/Rock Vocalist. *Career:* Contemporary Jazz with Barre Phillips, 1979–82; Sang in Kitka, Eastern European Women's Chorus, 1987–88; Toured Europe and Scandinavia with Marilyn Mazur, 1988–99; Member Alex Cline Ensemble, 1987–99. *Recordings:* Journal Violone II, 1979; The Lamp and The Star, 1989; Future Song, 1993; Montsalvat, 1995; Small Labyrinths, 1997; Sparks Fly Upward, 1999. *Address:* 3 South Trail, Orinda, CA 94563, USA.

KEMP, Gary; b. 16 Oct. 1959, Islington, London, England. Musician (guitar); Songwriter; Actor. *Career:* Founder member, Spandau Ballet (originally the Makers), 1979–90; Performances include: Royal Albert Hall, 1982; Royal Festival Hall, 1982; Wembley Arena, 1984; Live Aid, Wembley, 1985; Solo appearances: Labour Party Red Wedge Tour, 1986; Prince's Trust Rock Gala, 1987; Actor, films: The Krays (with brother Martin), 1988; The Bodyguard, 1992; Killing Zoe, 1994; Dog Eat Dog, 2001. *Compositions:* All hit singles by Spandau Ballet. *Recordings:* Singles include: To Cut A Long Story Short, 1980; The Freeze, 1981; Musclebound, 1981; Chant No. 1 (I Don't Need This Pressure On), 1981; Instinction, 1982; Lifeline, 1982; Communication, 1983; True (No. 1, UK), 1983; Gold, 1983; Only When You Leave, 1984; I'll Fly For You, 1984; Highly Strung, 1984; Round and Round, 1984; Fight For Ourselves, 1986; Through The Barricades, 1986; Be Free With Your Love, 1989; Sample of True used as basis for Set Adrift On Memory Bliss, PM Dawn (No. 1, USA), 1991; Albums: Journeys To Glory, 1981; Diamond, 1982; True, 1983; Parade, 1984; The Singles Collection, 1985; Through The

Barricades, 1986; Heart Like A Sky, 1989; The Best of Spandau Ballet, 1991; Gold, 2001; Solo album: Little Bruises, 1995. *Honours:* BRIT Award, Sony Trophy for Technical Excellence, 1984. *Current Management:* Steve Dagger, Dagger Enterprises, 14 Lambton Pl., London W11 2SH, England.

KEMP, Martin; b. 10 Oct. 1961, Islington, London, England. *Education:* Acting lessons, Anna Scher's Children's Theatre, 1970. *Career:* Member, Spandau Ballet, 1979–90; Concerts include: Royal Albert Hall, Sadlers Wells, Royal Festival Hall, London, 1983; Live Aid, Wembley, 1985; TV special, Ibiza 92, 1987; Actor, films: The Krays (with brother Gary), 1988; Waxwork II: Lost In Time, 1992; Actor, television series: Growing Rich, 1991; EastEnders, 1998–. *Recordings:* Albums: Journeys To Glory, 1981; Diamond, 1982; True, 1983; Parade, 1984; The Singles Collection, 1985; Through The Barricades, 1986; Heart Like A Sky, 1989; The Best of Spandau Ballet, 1991; Gold, 2001; Singles include: To Cut A Long Story Short, 1980; The Freeze, 1981; Musclebound, 1981; Chant No. 1 (I Don't Need This Pressure On), 1981; Paint Me Down, 1981; Instinction, 1982; Lifeline, 1982; Communication, 1983; True (No. 1, UK), 1983; Gold (used for BBC's Olympics coverage, 1984), 1983; Only When You Leave, 1984; Highly Strung, 1984; Round and Round, 1984; Fight For Ourselves, 1986; Through The Barricades, 1986; Be Free With Your Love, 1989; Contributor, Do They Know It's Christmas?, Band Aid, 1984. *Honours:* BRIT Award, Sony Trophy For Technical Excellence, 1984. *Current Management:* AIM, 5 Denmark St, London WC2H 8LP, England.

KENDALL, Tony, (The Essex Man); b. 9 May 1944, Walthamstow, Essex, England. Musician (acoustic bass, guitar, fiddle). m. Carole Anne Bailey, 18 June 1966, 1 d. *Education:* East Ham CAT, London University. *Career:* Collector, writer, performer, traditional and original songs, County of Essex (1,000 songs in repertoire); Regular broadcaster for BBC Essex; Appeared at Royal Festival Hall, London Barbican, folk club, history societies nationwide; Musician, Chingford Morrismen, Barnet Fair Ceilidh Band; Good Easter Molly. *Recordings:* Albums: Rose Of Essex; Closer To The Heartland; An Essex Terret; A Christmas Wassail; A Bicycle Ride With Vaughan Williams; Fairlop Fair, 2000. *Membership:* Musicians' Union; PRS; MCPS. *Current Management:* Stormforce Arts. *Address:* 18 Edward Ave, Chingford, London E4 9DN, England.

KENNEDY, Brian; b. 12 Oct. 1966, Belfast, Northern Ireland. Vocalist; Musician (guitar); Songwriter. *Career:* Toured internationally and recorded with Van Morrison's band; Performed duet with Morrison in Belfast for President Clinton's visit, viewed by TV audience of one billion; Toured with The Corrs and Tina Turner; Appeared on film soundtracks: When A Man Loves A Woman; Moondance; Broadway debut in Riverdance, 2000; Recent collaboration with Juliet Turner. *Recordings:* Albums include: with Van Morrison: One Night In San Francisco, 1993; No Prima Donna, 1994; Days Like This, 1995; The Healing Game, 1997; Back On Top, 1999; featured on: Ronan, Ronan Keating, 2000; solo: The Great War of Words, 1990; A Better Man, 1996; Now That I Know What I Want, 1999; Get On With Your Short Life, 2001. *Honours:* A Better Man gained quadruple platinum status in Ireland; IRMA, Best Irish Male Album; Hot Press/2TV Award, Best Irish Male Artist. *Website:* www.briankennedy.co.uk.

KENNEDY, Peter Douglas; b. 18 Nov. 1922, London, England. Ethno-Musicologist. m. Beryl, 3 s., 1 d. *Education:* Architectural Association School of Architecture, London, 1940–42. *Career:* Sometimes referred to as Mr Folk; Was main catalyst in post-war Folk Revival in England; North East Area Representative, English Folk Dance and Song Society, 1947–48; Joined BBC Staff, Bristol, 1949; Started mobile recording of traditional folk singers and instrumentalists, Britain and Ireland, 1950–; Leader, own Haymakers Folk Dance band, including Village Barn Dance radio broadcasts, 1951; BBC Folk Music and Dialect Recording Scheme, with Seamus Ennis, 1952–58; EFDSS staff, London, 1958–68; Established Performers Booking Agency and first Folk Song Club in London; Co-organizer, first National Folk Festival, Keele University, 1964, and National Folk Federation, 1965; Degree Lecturer, Folk Studies, Dartington College of Arts, Totnes, Devon, 1969–79; Set up International Folk Archive, 1980; Regular radio and television broadcaster, 1950–70; As I Roved Out, 1953–57. *Recordings:* Numerous field recordings of traditional singers and players, customs, dialect and traditions, 1950–; Also recorded many well-known folk performers including Ewan McColl, Bert Lloyd, The Dubliners and the Liverpool Spinners; Recent CDs include: Sea Songs and Shanties; Songs of the Travelling People, 1994; Traditional Songs of Ireland, 1995; Bagpipes of Britain and Ireland, 1996; Traditional Dance Music of Ireland, 1997; English Customs and Traditions, 1997; World Library of Folk and Primitive Music: England and Yugoslavia, 1998. *Publications include:* The Fiddler's Tunebook, 2 Vols, 1951, 1953; Everybody Swing, Square Dance music, 1952; Editor, UNESCO International Folk Film Directory, 1970; Editor, International Folk Directory, 1973; The Folk Songs of Britain and Ireland, 1975; Fiddler's Book of Reels, 1997; Fiddler's Book of Jigs, 1998; Fiddler's Book of Hornpipes, 1999. *Honours:* McColvin Award, Outstanding Reference Book of 1975. *Membership:* The English Folk Dance and Song Society; The Folklore Society; The Society for Folk-Life Studies. *Address:* Folk and Blues International Archive, 16 Brunswick Sq., Gloucester GL1 1UG, England.

KENNELL, Richard W. (Rick); b. 8 Nov. 1952, Fort Wayne, Indiana, USA. Musician (bass guitar); Recording Artiste; Record Prod. m. Leah Marie Waybright, 8 Jan. 1976. *Education:* Indiana University; James Madison University. *Recordings:* 6 albums currently available: Happy The Man: Happy The Man; Crafty Hands; Better Late; Beginnings; Retrospective; Happy The Man Live; Death's Crown; Also: Run Into The Ground. *Membership:* ASCAP; NARAS; AES. *Current Management:* The Inner Circle. *Address:* 77 Tarrytown Rd, Suite 201, White Plains, NY 10607, USA.

KENNY DOPE. See: **GONZALEZ, Kenny.**

KENRICK, Hilgrove; b. 13 Feb. 1977, Birmingham, England. Composer; Vocalist; Musician (piano, clarinet, tenor saxophone). *Education:* ABRSM Grades in Theory, Piano and clarinet. *Career:* Piano Singer, West Midlands, 1994–96; Resident Pianist, Harry Ramsden's, Birmingham, 1995; Scores for Solihull School dramatic production The Right Place, 1995; Macbeth, 1996; Music Director, Handsworth Parish, 1996–97; Choirs: Birmingham Cathedral, Head Chorister, Blue Coat School, Selhell Barbershop Quartet. *Compositions:* Theatrical score, Death Threat, 1997; Film score, Witchcraft, 1998; Music for Methodist Youth Conference, NEC Birmingham, 1999. *Recordings:* Produced album, In Remembrance of Me, R-Men, 1996; Ad-Hoc, One Hot Day, 1999. *Membership:* Musicians' Union. *Address:* 37 Richmond Hill Rd, Edgbaston, Birmingham B15 3RR, England.

KENT, Andy (Andrew Charles); b. 1971, Wellington, New Zealand. Musician (bass guitar). *Career:* Mem., Australian rock band, You Am I, 1991–; Numerous world-wide tours. *Recordings:* Albums: Sound As Ever, 1994; Hi Fi Way (No. 1, Australia), 1995; Hourly, Daily (No. 1, Australia), 1996; # 4 Record (No. 1, Australia), 1998; Saturday Night, 'Round Ten, 1999; Dress Me Slowly, 2001; Deliverance, 2002. Singles: Snake Tide (EP), 1991; Goddamn (EP), 1991; Can't Get Started (EP), 1992; Coprolalia (EP), 1993; Adam's Ribs; Berlin Chair; Someone Else's Crowd (limited edition EP); Jaimmes Got A Gal; When You Got Dry; Cathy's Clown; Jewels And Bullets; Purple Sneakers, 1995; Mr Milk, 1995; Soldiers, 1996; Good Mornin'; Tuesday; Trike; What I Don't Know 'Bout You, 1998; Rumble, 1998; Heavy Heart, 1998; Damage; Get Up; Kick Hole In The Sky; Dirty Deeds Done Dirt Cheap; Trouble. *Honours:* Gold discs; ARIA Awards, incl. Best Alternative Release, 1995; Six Industry Awards, 1996. *Address:* c/o BMG Australia Ltd, 194 Miller St, North Sydney, NSW 2060, Australia. *Website:* www.youami.com.au.

KENT, Jeffrey John William (Jeff); b. 28 July 1951, Stoke-on-Trent, England. Musician (keyboards, percussion); Vocalist[No. /profession]Writer; Lecturer. m. Rosalind Ann Downs, 14 July 1987. *Education:* BSc Econ, Hons, International Relations, University of London, 1973; Postgraduate Teaching Certificate, Crewe College of Higher Education, 1974. *Career:* Freelance Writer, 1972–; Performing Musician, 1975–; Dragon Fair, 1984; Open Air Concert, Chamberlain Square, Birmingham, 1984; Green Party Conference Concert, 1987; Artists for the Planet Concert, 1989; Appearance on BBC Midlands TV, launching new album, 1992. *Compositions:* Butcher's Tale/Annie, with the Dancing Eyes, single, 1981; Tales from the Land of the Afterglow, albums Part 1, Part 2, 1984; Port Vale Forever, album, 1992; Only One World, album, 2000. *Recordings:* all compositions recorded. *Publications:* The Rise and Fall of Rock, 1983; The Last Poet: The Story of Eive Burdon, 1989; Port Vale Forever album song book, 1992. *Address:* Cherry Tree House, 8 Nelson Cres., Cotes Heath, via Stafford ST21 6ST, England.

KENT, Rolfe; b. 18 April 1963, St Albans, Hertfordshire, England. Composer; Film Composer. *Education:* BSc Hons, Psychology, Leeds University. *Career:* Film scores: Final Combination, 1993; Voices From A Locked Room, 1995; Mercy, 1995; Television scores: Big City Metro, 1989; Shalom Joan Collins, CH4, 1989; So Haunt Me, BBC, 1991; Inside Out, 1990; Musicals: Air and Opportunity, 1995. *Honours:* AICP (American Independent Commercial Producers) Award, Best Music, 1993. *Membership:* PRS; AFofM; BMI. *Current Management:* David May, Santa Monica, California, USA.

KENYON, Duncan; b. 10 Dec. 1961, Wembley, Middlesex, England. Rehearsal Studio Owner; Musician (bass guitar, guitar). m. 6 Sept. 1991, divorced 1993. *Career:* With French Impression; Toured with The Cool Notes; Support to Rose Royce; Odyssey; German television Oldie Parade with Hello, performed Tell Him and New York Groove; Currently touring with Hello. *Recordings:* Singles with French Impression: Breaking Love, 1984–5; Get Up and Dance; Currently recording Hello album, and Christmas songs. *Membership:* PRS; Musicians' Union. *Current Management:* David Blaylock. *Address:* 39 Leyton Rd, Harpenden, Herts AL5 2JB, England.

KERNON, Neil Anthony; b. 13 Sept. 1953, London, England. Record Prod; Sound Engineer. m. Kellie O'Neal, 13 July 1991. *Career:* Recording engineer, Trident Studios, UK, 1971–75; Le Chateau d'Herouville, France, 1975; Startling Studios, UK, 1976–79; Independent producer, USA, 1979–. *Recordings:* As engineer, producer: Albums with Hall and Oates: Voices, 1980; Private Eyes, 1981; H2O, 1982; Rock 'n' Soul Part 1, 1983; Sign In Please, with Autograph, 1984; with Dokken: Under Lock and Key, 1985; Back For The Attack, 1987; Singles: with Hall and Oates: Kiss On My List, 1980; Private Eyes, 1981; I Can't Go For That, 1981; Maneater, 1982. *Honours:*

Platinum and Gold discs. *Current Management:* Louis Levin Management, 130 W 57th St, #10B, New York, NY 10019, USA.

KERR, Jim; b. 9 July 1959, Glasgow, Scotland. Vocalist. m. (1) Chrissie Hynde, 1984, divorced, 1 d., (2) Patsy Kensit, 1993, divorced, 1 s. *Career:* Founder, Scottish rock group Simple Minds, 1978–; World-wide tours and concerts include: WOMAD Festival, Somerset, 1982; Phoenix Park, Dublin, 1983; Support to the Pretenders, US tour, 1984; Live Aid, Philadelphia, 1985; Headliners, Milton Keynes Bowl Pop Festival, 1986; Nelson Mandela 70th Birthday Tribute, 1988; Nelson Mandela: An International Tribute concert, Wembley, 1990. *Recordings:* Albums: Life In A Day, 1979; Real To Real Cacophony, 1980; Empires and Dance, 1980; Sons and Fascinations, 1981; Sister Feelings Call, 1981; Celebration, 1982; New Gold Dream, 1982; Sparkle In The Rain (No. 1, UK), 1984; Once Upon A Time (No. 1, UK), 1985; Live In The City of Light (No. 1, UK), 1987; Street Fighting Years (No. 1, UK), 1989; Themes (4 vols), 1990; Real Life, 1991; Glittering Prize 81–92, 1992; Good News From The Next World, 1995; Neapolis, 1998; Neon Lights, 2001; Cry, 2002. Hit singles include: Promised You A Miracle, 1982; Glittering Prize, 1982; Someone Somewhere (In Summertime), 1982; Waterfront, 1983; Speed Your Love To Me, 1984; Up On The Catwalk, 1984; Don't You Forget About Me, used in film Breakfast Club (No. 1, USA), 1985; Alive and Kicking, 1985; Sanctify Yourself, 1986; All The Things She Said, 1986; Ghostdancing, 1986; Promised You A Miracle (Live), 1987; Belfast Child (No. 1, UK), 1989; This Is Your Land, 1989; Kick It In, 1989; The Amsterdam EP, 1989; Let There Be Love, 1991; See The Lights, 1991; Stand By Love, 1991; Love Song, 1992; She's A River, 1995; Hypnotized, 1995; Glitterball, 1998. *Honours:* Q Award, Best Live Act, 1991. *Current Management:* Clive Banks, 1 Glenthorne Mews, 115A Glenthorne Rd, London W6 0LJ, England.

KERR, Nancy; b. 29 July 1975, England. Folk Vocalist; Musician (violin, viola, cello, guitar, mandolin); Composer. *Career:* Plays predominantly traditional material, both instrumentals and songs; Toured and recorded with Eliza Carthy and also made an album with mother, folk singer Sandra Kerr, before forming duo with Australian musician James Fagan. *Recordings:* Eliza Carthy and Nancy Kerr, 1993; Shape of Scrape (with Eliza Carthy), 1995; with Sandra Kerr: Neat and Complete, 1996; Scalene, 1999; with James Fagan: Starry Gazy Pie, 1997; Steely Water, 1999; Between The Dark and The Light, 2002; On Reflection (with Eliza Carthy), 2002; features on: Waterson Carthy, 1994; Yellow Red and Gold, Sandra Kerr, 2000; Mazurka Berserker, John Kirkpatrick, 2001. *Honours:* BBC Horizon Award, Best New Act, Nancy Kerr and James Fagan, 2000. *Address:* c/o Mrs Casey Music, PO Box 296, Matlock, Derbyshire DE4 3XU, England.

KERR, Sandra, (Sandra Joan Faulkner); b. 14 Feb. 1942. Vocalist; Folk Vocalist; Musician (concertina, guitar); Songwriter. *Career:* Recorded music for UK children's TV series Bagpuss with John Faulkner; Member of female vocal group Sisters Unlimited with Janet Russell, Rosie Davis and Peta Webb, performing close harmony renditions of contemporary and traditional songs exploring women's issues; Recently recorded and toured with daughter, Nancy Kerr, and James Fagan. *Recordings:* John and Sandra, 1969; Nuclear Power, 1981; Supermum, 1984; We Were There, 1987; Neat and Complete (with Nancy Kerr), 1996; Scalene (with Nancy Kerr and James Fagan), 1999; Yellow Red and Gold, 2000; with Sisters Unlimited: No Limits, 1991; No Bed of Roses, 1995; features on: Nancy Kerr and James Fagan Albums: Starry Gazy Pie, 1997; Steely Water, 1999.

KERSHAW, Martin John; b. 13 July 1944, Shipley, Yorkshire, England. Musician (guitar, banjo, bouzouki, mandolin, ukelele); Composer. Divorced, 1 d. *Career:* Mem., bands incl. Manfred Mann; Moved to London, 1966; Played with: John Dankworth Big Band; Jack Parnell Orchestra; James Last Orchestra; Session guitarist; Guitarist on all 120 Muppet Shows; Television shows, performances include: Perry Como, Michael Jackson; Randy Crawford; Kate Bush; John Denver; Jack Jones; David Essex; David Bowie; Elton John; Buddy Rich; Johnny Cash; Ray Charles; Tom Jones; Glen Campbell; Bing Crosby; Petula Clark; Crystal Gayle; Diana Ross; Dusty Springfield; Andy Williams; Linda Ronstadt; Dizzy Gillespie; Burt Bacharach; Peggy Lee; Julie Andrews; Englebert Humperdinck; Playing featured in films including: Passage To India; Mad Max Thunderdome; Little Shop of Horrors; Diamonds Are Forever; Ghandi; You Only Live Twice; Live and Let Die; TV series, Riders; Began composing, 1983–; Toured with Sacha Distel. *Compositions include:* Film: Nightmare Weekend; Advertisements: Sainsbury's; Interflora; Persil; Dulux Paint; Unipart; Boots; Television themes: Eurosport coverage Olympic Games, 1992; Russell Harty Show; London Programme; Incidental music: Prisoner Cell Block H; A Bouquet of Barbed Wire; Cagney and Lacey; Within These Walls; Promotional videos; Titles for Production Music Libraries include: Bruton; Music House; Peer; Weinberger. *Recordings:* Album: Acoustic Dreams, 1998. *Membership:* Musicians' Union; PRS. *Address:* BMG Records: 1540 Broadway, Times Sq., New York, NY 10036, USA.

KERSHAW, Nik (Nicholas David); b. 1 March 1958, Bristol, England. Vocalist; Musician (guitar); Songwriter. m. Sheri. *Career:* Member, jazz-funk group Fusion; Solo artiste, with backing band The Krew, 1983–. *Compositions include:* The One and Only, Chesney Hawkes (No. 1, UK), 1991. *Recordings:* Albums: Human Racing, 1984; The Riddle, 1984; Radio Musicola, 1986; The

Works, 1990; The Collection, 1991; Wouldn't It Be Good, 1994; The Best of Nik Kershaw, 1998; 15 Minutes, 1999; The Essential, 2000; To Be Frank, 2001. Singles: I Won't Let The Sun Go Down On Me (No. 2, UK), 1984; Wouldn't It Be Good, 1984; Somebody Loves You, 1999; Wounded, 2002. *Address:* c/o Eagle Records, Eagle House, 22 Armoury Way, Wandsworth, London SW18 1E, England. *Website:* www.nikkershaw.net.

KERSHAW, Sammy, (Samuel Cashat); b. 24 Feb. 1958, Abbeville, Louisiana, USA. Country vocalist; Songwriter; Musician (guitar); Actor. *Career:* Played in local bands, including Blackwater; DJ work; Cut first singles for local labels (later collected on a 1993 MTE Records album entitled Sammy Kershaw); Recording contract with Mercury Records after performing a showcase for Harold Shedd and Buddy Cannon; First Billboard charting single Cadillac Style released, 1991; Hits continued throughout the 1990s; Appeared in the film Fall Time directed by Paul Warner, 1995. *Recordings include:* She Don't Know She's Beautiful, 1993; Love of My Life, 1997; Third Rate Romance, 1994; National Working Woman's Holiday, 1994; Cadillac Style, 1991; Albums include: Don't Go Near The Water, 1991; Haunted Heart, 1993; Feelin' Good Train, 1994; Politics, Religion and Her, 1997; Labor of Love, 1997; Maybe Not Tonight, 1999; The Hits: Chapter One, 1995; Coverin' The Hits, 2000; The Hits: Chapter Two, 2001. *Current Management:* James Dowell Management, 50 Music Sq. W, Suite 207, Nashville 37203, USA. *Website:* www.sammykershaw.com.

KERSHAW, Steve P; b. 17 March 1959, Bradford, Yorkshire, England. Musician (double bass, bass guitar). *Education:* Bristol University, BA Hons, 1978–81; PhD, 1986; Bass Institute of Technology, Hollywood, California. *Career:* Member, British Youth Symphony Orchestra, 1978–82; After Hours; False Idols; Then There Were Six; Claude Bottom and The Lion Tamers; The Honkin' Hep Cats; The Rascals of Rhythm; Stekpanna; The John Hoare 4; The Flat Back Four; Television: Out West, HTV; ITV Telethon; Film: The Clothes In The Wardrobe; Great Moments in Aviation; Radio: The Usual Suspects; Jungr and Parker At The Edinburgh Festival; Loose Ends; Mary Costello Show; Breakfast Breakout; Honkin' With The Hep Cats At The Edinburgh Festival. *Recordings:* with After Hours: All Over Town, 1980; with False Idols: Ten Seconds To Midnight, 1981; Centre of Attention, 1985; Fine Blue Line, 1987; with L'Orange, Si J'Etais Vous, 1991; with The Honkin' Hep Cats: What's The Use?, 1989; Honkin' 'n' Stompin', 1992; Rantin' Ravin' 'n' Misbehavin', 1994; with Stekpanna: Standin' Tall, 1997; with The Steve Tayton Quartet and The Rolls Royce Brass Band, Dark To Light, 1999; with Luis D'Agostino, Otros Caminos, 1999; with The Flat Back Four, Dig-Dig. *Honours:* Outstanding Vocational Honours Award, GHS, 1996, Outstanding Student of the Year Award, Fender, 1996, Musicians Institute. *Membership:* Musicians' Union; International Society of Bassists. *Current Management:* Flat Five Management. *Address:* 5 Cardwell Cres., Headington, Oxford OX3 7QE, England.

KERWIN, Michael Thomas; b. 19 Feb. 1970, Freiburg, Germany. Prod; Engineer. *Education:* Hons in Music, Humber College, 1994. *Career:* Founder, Newmarket Multimedia Recording Studio, 1994; Co-Founder, Limit Records Inc, 1995. *Recordings:* Producer, Engineer: 30 Odd 6, 1996; Beru's Nephew, 1996; Stone Idols, 1997; Co Producer, Engineer: Woodrow, 1997; The Salads, 1997; Engineer: Sarah Sloan, 1997; Al Connelly, 1996. *Current Management:* Last Call Promotions, Unit 5, Newmarket, ON, L3Y 3E3, Canada. *Address:* 312 Maple St, Newmarket, ON L3Y 3K3, Canada.

KEVORKIAN, Francois; b. 10 Jan. 1954, Rodez, France. Prod; Remixer; DJ; Musician (drums). *Career:* Drummer with various French bands before relocation to New York in 1975; Continued to perform in nightclubs until finding work as DJ at New York New York; A&R work for disco label Prelude Records led to remix projects, firstly Musique's In the Bush; Subsequently remixed: D-Train, Yazoo, Depeche Mode, The Cure; Opened Axis Studios in New York; Founder of Wave Records; Resident DJ at Body and Soul club in New York. *Recordings:* Singles: FK EP, 1995; Time and Space, 1998. *Current Management:* c/o Wave Records, King St, New York City, New York USA.

KEYS, Alicia; b. 25 Jan. 1981, Manhattan, USA. Vocalist; Musician (piano); Songwriter. *Education:* Classically trained pianist; Professional Performance Arts School, Manhattan, majored in Choir Studies. *Career:* Signed to Clive Davis' new J Records label, 1999; Appeared at all-star charity telethon in aid of World Trade Center tragedy victims, 2001; Collaborations: Angie Stone; Jimmy Cozier. *Recordings:* Albums: Songs In A Minor, 2001; Singles: Girlfriend, Fallin', A Woman's Worth, 2001. *Honours:* Quadruple-Platinum discs; Grammy Awards, Best R&B Album, for Songs In A Minor, Song of the Year, for Fallin', Best New Artist, Best Female R&B Vocal Performance, for Fallin', Best R&B Song, for Fallin', 2001; American Music Awards, Favourite New Artist, Pop/Rock, Favourite New Artist, Soul/R&B, 2002; MOBO Award, Best Album, for Songs In A Minor, 2002; MTV Award, Best R&B Act, 2002. *Address:* c/o Jeff Robinson, MBK Entertainment Inc, 156 W 56th St, New York, NY 10019, USA. *Website:* www.aliciakeys.net.

KHALADJ, Madjid; b. 11 Nov. 1962, Ghazvin, Iran. Musician (percussion; tombak); Composer. *Education:* Graduate, School of Fine Arts, Paris; Graduate, Traditional Academy of Persian Art Music, Iran. *Career:* Concerts and radio appearances: Grand Palais, Paris, 1991; Barbad Symposium, Tadjikstan, with Master Shadjarian, 1991; Grande Auditorium de Radio France, with Master Alizadeh, 1992, 1994; Opéra de Lille, 1992; Los Angeles Festival, USA, J Paul Getty Museum, 1993; Théâtre de la Ville, Paris, 1993; Théâtre de la Colline and Radio France, with Master Tala'i, 1994. *Recordings:* Persian Classical Music, 1992; Persian Art Music, 1992; Iran-The Art of Tombak, 1993; Music of Iran, Vols 1 and 2, 1993; Iranian Music, Improvisations, 1994; Persian Classical Music, 1994; Los Angeles Festival, 1995; Tombak and Percussion, 1996; Anthology of Iranian Rhythms, Vol. 1, 1997; Vol. 2, 1999. *Membership:* SACEM. *Current Management:* Madjid Khaladj Management, 56, rue de Sèvres, 92100 Boulogne, France.

KHALED, (Khaled Hadj Brahim, Cheb Khaled); b. 29 Feb. 1960, Wahrane, Algeria. Vocalist; musician (keyboard, accordion); Songwriter. *Career:* Member: The Five Stars; First recording, aged 14; First hit Trigue Al Lissi (The Way To School), 1975; Lyrics censored in Algeria until 1983; Relocated to Paris, 1990; First international rai hit Didi (produced by Don Was), 1992; Collaborations: Chaba Zahouania; Rachid Taha and Faudel; over 100 cassettes released. *Recordings:* Albums include: Rai King of Algeria, 1985; Fuir Mais Ou?, 1991; Khaled, 1992; N'ssi N'ssi, 1993; Sahra, 1996; Kenza, 1997; Les Monstres Sacrés du Rai; Ya Taleb (with Chaba Zahouania); Best Of The Early Years, 2002. *Honours:* Crowned King of Rai at the first rai festival in Oran, 1985; Cesar Award, Best Soundtrack, N'ssi N'ssi. *Website:* www.nascente.co.uk.

KHAN, Ali Akbar; b. 14 April 1922, Shivpur, Bangladesh. Musician (sarode); Composer. *Career:* Musician, 1936–; Numerous tours, concerts and major festivals world-wide, 1955–; Founder, Ali Akbar College of Music, Kolkata, India, 1956; San Rafael, California, 1968; Basel, Switzerland, 1982; Collaborations with artistes including: Yehudi Menuhin; Ravi Shankar; Duke Ellington; Lecture recitals, major universities, USA and Canada; Owner, record company Alam Madina Music Productions; Founder, Ali Akbar Khan Foundation, 1994; MacArthur Foundation Fellowship, 1991. *Compositions:* Concerti, orchestral pieces and ragas, including Chandranadan; Gauri Manjari; Alamgiri; Medhavi. *Recordings include:* Legacy, 1996; Passing on the Tradition, 1996. *Honours:* President of India Awards, 1963, 1966; Grand Prix Du Disque, 1968; Hon DLitt Rabindra Bharati University, Kolkata, 1974; Padmabhibhushan Award, 1989; Dr of Arts, California Institute of Arts, 1991; Kalidas Award, 1992; Bill Graham Lifetime Award, BAM, 1993; Meet the Composer Award, 1996; National Heritage Fellowship, National Endowment for the Arts, 1997; Asian Paints Shiromani Award, Hall of Fame, Kolkata, 1997; Governor's Award for Outstanding Achievement, NARAS, 1998; Indira Gandhi Gold Plaque, Asiatic Society, Kolkata, 1998; Swaralaya Puraskaram Award, New Dehli, 1999; Appointed Distinguished Adjunct Professor of Music, University of California at Santa Cruz, 1999. *Current Management:* Gregory Digiovine, Santana Management, 121 Jordan St, San Rafael, CA 94901, USA. *Address:* Ali Akbar College of Music, 215 West End Ave, San Rafael, CA 94901, USA.

KHAN, Amjad Ali; b. 9 Oct. 1945, Gwalior, Madhya Pradesh, India. Musician (sarod); Composer. m. Subhalakshmi Barooah, 1976, 2 s. *Education:* Modern School, New Delhi. *Career:* Sarod player; Numerous concert performances, including Pakistan, 1981, People's Republic of China, 1981, Hong Kong Arts Festival, 1982, Festival of India, London, 1982; Numerous recordings for major recording cos in India and abroad; Recording Raag Bhairav named one of best CDs in world, BBC Music Magazine, 1996; Mem., World Arts Council, Geneva; Founder-Pres., Ustad Hafiz Ali Khan Memorial Society (promotion of Indian classical music and dance); Visiting Prof., University of York, UK, 1995, University of Pennsylvania, University of New Mexico; Radio includes: promenade concert, BBC, 1995. *Compositions include:* Many ragas; Music for Kathak ballets Shan E Mughal, Shahajahan Ka Khwab, Ganesh; Orchestral compositions Ekta Se Shanti, Ekta Ki Shakti, Tribute to Hong Kong (for Hong Kong Philharmonic Orchestra). *Honours:* Hon. DUniv, York, 1997, Delhi, 1998; UNESCO Award, Int. Music Forum, 1970, 1975; Special Honour, Sahitya Kala Parishad, Delhi, 1977; Musician of Musicians, Bhartiya Vidhya Bhavan, Nagpur, 1983; Amjad Ali Khan Day, MA, USA, 1984; Acad. National Award, Tirupathi, 1987; Raja Ram Mohan Roy Teacher's Award, 1988; Sangit Natak Acad. Award, 1989; Tansen Award, National Cultural Organization, New Delhi, 1989; Vijaya Ratna Award, India International Friendship Society, New Delhi, 1990; Crystal Award, World Economic Forum, 1997; Hon. Citizen, Nashville, TN, 1997, Houston, TX, 1997; Padma Shree, 1975; Padma Bhusan, 1991; Sarod Samrat, Gwalior, 1993; Padma Vibhushan, 2001. *Address:* 3 Sadhna Enclave, Panchsheel Park, New Delhi 110 017, India. *Website:* music@sarod.com.

KHAN, Chaka, (Yvette Stevens); b. 23 March 1953, Great Lakes, Illinois, USA. Vocalist. *Career:* Member, Afro-Arts theatre, Chicago; Member, groups Shades of Black; Lock and Chain; Rufus, 1972–79; Renamed Rufus and Chaka Khan, 1978; Appearances include: Support to Elton John, Wembley, 1975; Rock 'n' Bowl, for US Special Olympics, 1977; Solo artiste, 1978–; Concerts and tours include: European tour, 1988; World tour, 1992; A Night On The Town Concert Tour, 1993; Montreux Jazz Festival, 1993; North Sea Jazz Festival, The Hague, 1993; JVC Jazz Festival, Nice, 1993. *Recordings:* Albums: with Rufus: Rufus, 1979; Rags To Rufus, 1974; Rufusized, 1975;

Rufus Featuring Chaka Khan, 1976; Ask Rufus, 1977; Street Player, 1978; Numbers, 1979; Masterjam, 1980; Camouflage, 1981; Party 'Til You're Broke, 1981; Live: Stompin' At The Savoy, 1983; Life Is A Dance: The Remix Project, 1989; Sweet Things: Greatest Hits, 1993; Solo albums: Chaka, 1978; Naughty, 1980; What Cha' Gonna Do For Me, 1981; Chaka Khan, 1983; I Feel For You, 1984; Destiny, 1986; C.K., 1989; The Woman I Am, 1992; Come 2 My House, 1998; I'm Every Woman, 1999; Contributor, Echoes of An Era, Lenny White, 1982; Rock Rhythm and Blues compilation, 1989; Music of Quality and Distinction compilation, 1991; Hallelujah!, Quincy Jones, 1992; Hot House, Bruce Hornsby, 1995; Hit singles: with Rufus: Tell Me Something Good, 1974; You Got The Love, 1974; Once You Get Started, 1975; Sweet Thing, 1976; Solo singles: I'm Every Woman, 1979; Ain't Nobody, 1983; I Feel For You, 1984; This Is My Night, 1985; Eye To Eye, 1985; Own The Night (used in television series Miami Vice), 1986; Love of a Lifetime, 1986; Underground, duet with David Bowie, for film Labyrinth, 1986; Feels Like Heaven, duet with Peter Cetera, 1992; Don't Look at Me That Way, 1993; Miles Blowing, 1995; Love Me Still, 1995; Never Miss the Water, 1996; Contributor, Dreamland, Joni Mitchell, 1978; Stuff Like That, Quincy Jones, 1978; Higher Love, Steve Winwood, 1986; I'll Be Good To You, Quincy Jones, 1990. *Honours:* Grammy Awards: Best R&B Vocal Performance, Chaka Khan, Best R&B Performance, Ain't Nobody, Best Vocal Arrangement, Be Bop Medley, 1984; Best Female R&B Vocal Performance, I Feel For You, 1985; Best R&B Performance, The Woman I Am, 1993; Gold discs; MOBO Lifetime Achievement Award, 2002. *Current Management:* The Brokaw Company, 9255 Sunset Blvd, Suite 804, Los Angeles, CA 90069, USA.

KHAN, Steve Harris; b. 28 April 1947, Los Angeles, California, USA. Musician (guitar); Prod. *Education:* BA, Composition, UCLA. *Career:* Solo guitarist and prolific session musician. *Recordings:* Solo albums: Tightrope, 1977; The Blue Man, 1978; Arrows, 1979; Evidence, Best Of, 1980; 1981; Blades, 1982; Eyewitness, 1983; Casa Loco, 1983; Helping Hand, 1987; Local Colour, 1988; Public Access, 1990; Let's Call This, 1991; Crossing Bridges, 1993; Got My Mental, 1996; You Are Here, 1998; Other recordings with numerous artistes including: Ashford and Simpson; Patti Austin; George Benson; Michael and Randy Brecker; Billy Cobham; Judy Collins; Larry Coryell; Blood, Sweat and Tears; Luther Allison; Donald Fagen; Aretha Franklin; Billy Joel; Chaka Khan; Kenny Loggins; David Sanborn; Phoebe Snow; Steely Dan; Grover Washington; Bob James. *Publications:* Wes Montgomery Guitar Folio, 1978; Pat Martino Guitar Solos, 1991; Steve Khan Song Book, 1991. *Current Management:* Christine Martin Management. *Address:* 688 Hands Creek Rd, East Hampton, NY 11937, USA.

KHAN, Ustad Vilayat; Musician (sitar); Composer. *Career:* Sixth generation in a family of renowned sitar players; Tours world-wide; Compositions include film scores. *Recordings:* Albums: Ustad Vilayat Khan; Uphaar (live); Raga Bhankar; Raga Hameer; Eb Adat; Shahnana & Bageshree; Live at the Royal Festival Hall (live, with Sabir Khan); Raga Sanjh Saravali; Raga Marwa (live); Dawn To Dusk; Raga Shree; Ragas To Riches, Vol. I, Vol. II. *Address:* c/o Kalavant Center for Music and Dance Inc, 326 E 11th St, Suite 2, New York, NY 10003, USA.

KHANYILE, Jabu; b. 1959, Soweto, South Africa. Vocalist; Songwriter. *Career:* Earned living through busking; Member: The Editions; The Movers; Joined Bayete as drummer; Bayete disbanded, 1993; Re-formed under Khanyile. *Recordings:* Albums include: Mbombela, 1987; Hareyeng Haye, 1990; Mmalo-we (world-wide release), 1994; Umkhayalo, 1995; Africa Unite, 1997; Prince Umbele 2001. *Honours:* Mmalo-We certified gold and won various South African Awards; Kora Award, Best Artist or Group from Southern Africa, 2000; SAMA Award, Best Duo or Group, 2001. *Address:* c/o Gallo Records, PO Box 2897, Parklands 2121, South Africa. *Website:* www.gallo.co.za.

KHARISSOV, Ildar; b. 21 Jan. 1972, Yelabuga, Russia. Musicologist; Ethnomusicologist. *Education:* State Conservatoire of Kazan; Free University of Berlin. *Contributions to:* Numerous papers in academic journals. *Membership:* International Council For Traditional Music. *Address:* Erich Weinert Str 21, D-10439 Berlin, Germany. *E-mail:* kharissov@gmx.de.

KHÉLIFATI, Mohamed. See: **CHEB MAMI.**

KHOZA, Valanga; b. 21 Dec. 1959, Tzaneen, South Africa. Vocalist; Songwriter; Musician (kalimba, guitar, marimbas, kora, mouthharp, m'bira, flute). *Education:* University of South Africa, Pietersburg; BA, Business Accounting, Goshen University, Indiana, USA. *Career:* Solo peformance, Hemisphere, 5 piece acapella and percussion; Band Safika, 8 piece; Toured Australia extensively; Support act to Geoffrey Oryema, Lucky Dube, 1996; Lady Smith Black Mambazo, 1995; Soweto String Quartet, 1997; Major festivals all over Australia; Festival of Cultures, Sydney Opera House; Images of Africa, Festival Copenhagen, Denmark, 6 weeks tour, 1996; ABC Music Deli Program (radio); Jaslyn Halls World Music; Live to air, Australian Broadcasting Commission. *Recordings:* Sebe. *Honours:* Finalist, Aria Awards World Music Category, 1996. *Current Management:* KU Promotions, Box 77, Uki, 2484, Australia.

KID COCO, (Marc Diericx); b. 11 Nov. 1964, Ghent, Belgium. Vocalist; Composer; Musician (guitar, keyboards). *Career:* Lead vocalist, The Dinky Toys, 1981–94; Solo artiste, 1995–. *Recordings:* Albums with The Dinky Toys: The Colour of Sex, 1992; Colourblind, 1993; Keep Hope Alive, 1994. *Honours:* Several No. 1 and Top 10 hits; Platinum album; ZAMU Award, Best Live Performer, 1994. *Membership:* SABAM/ZAMU. *Current Management:* Luc Standaert, Tempo Belgium. *Address:* Krijgslaan 61–9000 Gent, Belgium.

KID CREOLE, (August Twelfth Darnell); b. 12 Aug. 1950, Bronx, New York, USA. Entertainer; Vocalist. 4 s., 3 d. *Education:* BA, Hofstra University. *Career:* Leader, Kid Creole and the Coconuts; World-wide tours, 15 years; Member, Dr Buzzard's Original Savannah Band, 3 years; Starred in West End Production of Oh What A Night, London. *Recordings:* Hit singles include: Me No Pop I, with Coati Mundi, 1981; I'm A Wonderful Thing, Baby, 1982; Stool Pigeon, 1982; Annie I'm Not Your Daddy (No. 2, UK), 1982; Dear Addy, 1982; There's Something Wrong In Paradise, 1983; The Lifeboat Party, 1983; The Sex of It, 1990; Albums include: Tropical Gangsters, 1982; Fresh Fruit In Foreign Places, 1982; Doppelganger, 1983; Cre-ole, 1984; Private Waters in the Great Divide, 1990; Kiss Me Before the Light Changes, 1995; To Travel Sideways, 1995; Too Cool To Conga, 2001. *Honours:* BPI Best International Act, Kid Creole, 1982. *Membership:* BMI; AFTRA.

KIDJO, Angélique; b. 14 July 1960, Ouidah, Benin. Vocalist; Songwriter. m. Jean Hebrail. *Career:* Performed with mother's theatre group from age 6; Later in the Kidjo Brothers Band; One of Benin's only professional female singers by age 20; Moved to Holland, then Paris; Mem., Pili Pili; Solo artiste, 1989–; Signed to Island Records, 1989; Collaborations: Carlos Santana; Manu Dibango; Branford Marsalis; Toured USA with Dave Matthews Band, Neville Brothers and Macy Gray, 2001. *Recordings:* Albums: Parakou, 1989; Logozo, 1991; Aye, 1994; Fifa (featuring Carlos Santana), 1996; Oremi (featuring Branford Marsalis, Cassandra Wilson), 1996; Black Ivory Soul, 2002; featured on soundtracks: Ace Ventura 2; Ma Saison Preferee. *Honours:* MOBO Award, Best World Music Act, 2002. *Website:* www.angeliquekidjo.com.

KIEDIS, Anthony, (Antoine the Swan); b. 1 Sept. 1962, Grand Rapids, MI, USA. Vocalist. *Career:* Film appearance as Sylvester Stallone's son, F.I.S.T.; Founding mem., Anthem, later renamed Red Hot Chili Peppers, 1983–; Signed to EMI records; Musical contribution to The Simpsons; Numerous tours, festivals and television appearances. *Recordings:* Albums: The Red Hot Chili Peppers, 1984; Freaky Styley, 1985; Uplift Mofo Party Plan, 1987; Mother's Milk, 1989; Mother's Milk Gold, 1989; Blood Sugar Sex Magik, 1991; What Hits!?, 1992; One Hot Minute, 1995; Under The Covers, 1998; Californication, 1999; By The Way, 2002. Singles: Abbey Road (EP), 1988; Higher Ground, 1989; Taste the Pain, 1989; Give It Away, 1991; Under The Bridge, 1992; Suck My Kiss, 1992; Breaking the Girl, 1993; If You Have to Ask, 1993; Soul 2 Squeeze (EP), 1994; My Friends, 1995; Aeroplane, 1996; Love Rollercoaster, 1997; Warped, 1998; Scar Tissue, 1999; Behind the Sun, 1999; Around The World, 1999; Otherside, 1999; Californication, 2000; Road Trippin', 2001; The Zephyr Song, 2002; Guest vocals, Blowback, Tricky, 2001. *Honours:* MTV Music Video Awards, 1992; Grammy Awards, Best Hard Rock Song, for Give It Away, 1993, Best Rock Song, for Scar Tissue, 2000; American Music Award, Favorite Alternative Artist, 2000; MTV Awards, Best Live Act, Best Rock, 2002. *Address:* c/o Rockinfreakapotamus, The Red Hot Chili Peppers Official Fan Club, PO Box 801, Rockford, MI 49341, USA. *Website:* www.redhotchilipeppers.com.

KIENLEIN, Kevin D; b. 12 July 1960, Vernon, BC, Canada. Vocalist; Entertainer; Songwriter; Musician (guitar, fiddle, violin, bass, organ, piano, tenor banjo). *Career:* First performances were: organ at church, guitar, church coffeehouse; Joined The BC Oldtime Fiddlers, 1980; Joined the Velvet Rodeo Band, 1989; Solo performances; Joined String Loaded Bluegrass, 1995; at Festivals, Special Events, Benefits, Concerts, 1995–; Inspirational Speaking. *Compositions:* 16 original fiddle tunes published in 169 Brand New Oldtime Fiddle Tunes, 12 in Canadian Fiddle Music. *Recordings:* Fiddlers Rag; Heartbeats. *Membership:* SOCAN, BC Oldtime Fiddlers; National Oldtime Fiddlers Asscn; BC Country Music Asscn; Canadian Country Music Asscn; Catgut Acoustical Society. *Current Management:* Krash Productions. *Address:* 3101 18 Ave, Vernon, BC V1T 1C6, Canada.

KIERAN, (Donley); b. 1 Nov. 1970, Manchester, England. DJ; Record Prod; Recording Artiste. *Career:* Promoting Spectrum Oxford; Dance music DJ at Universe and Fantazia among many others; Recording artiste as: Oxide and Hoi Polloi. *Membership:* Musicians' Union. *Current Management:* Adrian Hicks, Equation. *Address:* 9 Cavell Rd, Oxford, England.

KIKABIDZE, Vakhtang Konstantinovich; b. 19 July 1938, Tbilisi, Georgia. Actor; Vocalist. m. Irene Kebadze, 1964, 1 s. *Career:* Soloist and leader of Georgian pop-group Orero, 1966–; Film début, Meeting in the Hills, 1967; Films include: Don't Grieve, 1968; I'm a Detective, 1969; The Stone of the First Water, 1970; Pen-name Lukach; The Melodies of Verikysky Block, 1973; Lost Expedition, 1973; Completely Gone, 1972; Mimino, 1978; TASS is Authorized to Inform; Hi! Friend (TV film), 1981; To Your Health Dear (dir, scriptwriter, actor), 1983; Man and all the Others (scriptwriter, prod., actor), 1985; Fortuna (actor), 2000; Solo music career, 1988–. *Recordings:* Albums:

My Years, My Wealth, 1994; Larisa Ivanovna Please!, 1995; Letter To A Friend, 1996; Tango Of Love, 1999; Greatest Hits, 2000. *Honours:* USSR State Prize, 1978; People's Artist of Georgian S.S.R., 1980; Order of Honour, Georgia, 1994; Order of Konstantine, Russia, 1997; Order of St Nicholaus, 1998; Golden Gramophone Prize, 1998; Leonid Utesov Prize for Achievement in field of Music, 2000. *Address:* S Chikovani St 20, Apt 38, 380015 Tbilisi, Georgia.

KILGORE, Merle; b. 8 Sept. 1934, Chickasha, OK, USA. Artiste Man. m. Judy Kilgore, 1 s., 2 d. *Career:* Louisiana Hayride; Coal Muhers Daughter; Nashville; WW and The Dixie Dance Kings; Roadie; Living Proof; Willa. *Compositions:* Ring of Fire; Wolverhampton MT; More and More; Johnny Reb; Baby Rocked Her Dolly; She Went A Little Bit Farther. *Recordings:* Dear Mama; Love Has Made You Beautiful. *Honours:* SRD Manager of the Year, 1990; Louisiana Hall of Fame, 1993; Byrd High School Hall of Fame, 1993. *Membership:* CMA; NSAI; ROPE; NSF; AFM; SAG. *Current Management:* Merle Kilgore Management. *Address:* 2 Music Circle S, Nashville, TN 37203, USA.

KILKELLY, Frank; b. 17 Sept. 1960, Republic of Ireland. Musician (acoustic guitar). *Education:* BSc, Marketing; Piano, guitar lessons. *Career:* Regular touring in Europe, USA; Television includes: Pebble Mill At One, BBC; Anderson On The Box, BBC, Northern Ireland; Kenny Live, RTE, Ireland; Late Late Show, RTE, Ireland; Radio broadcasts: Digby Fairweather's Jazz Notes, BBC2; Anderson's Fine Tunes; Travelling Folk, BBC Scotland. *Recordings:* Luke Daniels, Tarantella, CD, 1994; Zumzeaux, Blazing Fiddles, CD, 1995; Kimbara Brothers, Now!, cassette, 1995; Kimbara Brothers, Time To Leave, CD, 1995; Power and Kilkelly, Jig Jazz, CD, 1996; Simon Mayor: New Celtic Mandolin, video, 1997; Mandolin Essentials, CD, 1997; Simon Mayor: New Celtic Mandolin, CD, 1998; Maggie Boyle Gweebarra, CD, 1998; Pierre Schryer and Dermot Byrne, CD, 1999; with The Grappelli Trio: Gipsy Swing, 2000. *Publications:* Accompanying Irish Music on Guitar, book and CD, 1999. *Current Management:* Brass Tacks, Orchard House, Gloucester Rd, Hartpury, Gloucestershire GL19 3BG, England.

KILMORE, Chris. See: **DJ KILMORE.**

KIMBALL, Bobby (Robert Toteaux); b. 29 March 1947, Vinton, Louisiana, USA. Vocalist. *Career:* Supported acts including: Jackson Browne; Aretha Franklin; Barbra Streisand; Lead vocalist, Toto, 1978–84; Solo artiste, 1984–; Member, Far Corporation. *Recordings:* Albums: with Toto: Toto, 1979; Hydra, 1979; Turn Back, 1981; Toto IV, 1982; Isolation, 1984; Past to Present, 1990; Toto XX, 1998; Mindfields, 1999; Solo: Rise Up, 1996; Singles: with Toto: Hold The Line, 1979; Georgy Porgy, 1980; 99, 1980; Rosanna, 1982; Make Believe, 1982; Africa (No. 1, USA), 1983; I Won't Hold You Back, 1984; with Far Corporation: Stairway To Heaven, 1986; Woods to Stock, 1995; Backing vocalist, albums by Boz Scaggs: Silk Degrees, 1976; Down Two Then Left, 1977. *Honours:* 6 Grammy Awards with Toto: Best Record, Best Album, Best Producer (Toto), Best Engineered Recording, Best Vocal Arrangement, Best Instrumental Arrangement, 1983. *Current Management:* Artists International Management, 9850 Sandalfoot Blvd, Suite 458, Boca Raton, FL 33428, USA.

KIMSEY, Chris; Prod. *Career:* Worked with: Ash, Bad Company, The Chieftains, Jimmy Cliff, The Cult, Deacon Blue, Duran Duran, ELP, Peter Frampton, Gypsy Kings, INXS, Killing Joke, Marillion, Proclaimers, Psychedelic Furs, The Rolling Stones, Ten Years After, Peter Tosh. *Address:* c/o Stephen Budd Management Ltd, 109b Regents Park Rd, Primrose Hill, London NW1 8UR, England. *Website:* www.record-producers.com.

KINCAID, Jan; b. 17 May 1966, Ealing, London, England. Musician (Drums). *Career:* Founder Member, The Brand New Heavies; Obtained independent label record deal; Worked with several vocalists including Jaye Ella Ruth, N'Dea Davenport, Siedah Garrett and Carleen Anderson; Numerous television appearances and live dates. *Recordings:* Singles: Stay This Way, 1991; Never Stop, 1991; Dream Come True, 1991; Spend Some Time, 1994; Dream on Dreamer, 1994; Mind Trips, 1995; You've Got A Friend, 1997; You Are the Universe, 1997; Sometimes, 1997; Shelter, 1998; Saturday Nite, 1999; Apparently Nothing, 2000; Albums: The Brand New Heavies, 1990; The Brand New Heavies, 1992; Heavy Rhyme Experience, 1992; Brother Sister, 1994; Original Flava, 1994; Excursions, 1995; Shelter, 1997.

KING, B. B. (Riley); b. 16 Sept. 1925, Itta Bena, Mississippi, USA. Vocalist; Musician (guitar). *Career:* Performed with the Elkhorn Singers; Played with Sonny Boy Williamson, 1946; Regular broadcast slot, The Sepia Swing Show, Radio WDIA; Averaged 300 performances a year, 1950s–70s; Numerous world-wide tours with wide variety of R&B and pop artistes; Appearances include: Newport Jazz Festival, 1969, 1989; Atlantic City Pop Festival, 1969; Atlanta Pop Festival, 1970; Mar Y Sol Festival, Puerto Rico, 1972; Kool Jazz Festival, New York, 1983; Live Aid concert, Philadelphia, 1985; Benson and Hedges Blues Festival, Dallas, 1989; JVC Jazz Festival, Newport, 1990; Memphis In May Festival, 1991; Montreux Jazz Festival, 1991; San Francisco Blues Festival, 1991; Guitar Legends, Expo '92, Seville, Spain, 1991; Westbury Music Fair, New York, 1993; Pori Jazz, Finland, 1995; Opened B.

B. King's Memphis Blues Club, Memphis, Tennessee, 1991. *Recordings:* Albums: Completely Well, 1970; The Incredible Soul of B. B. King, 1970; Indianola Mississippi Seeds, 1970; Live In Cook County Jail, 1971; Live At The Regal, 1971; B. B. King In London, 1971; LA Midnight, 1972; Guess Who, 1972; The Best Of.., 1973; To Know You Is To Love You, 1973; Friends, 1974; Lucille Talks Back, 1975; King Size, 1977; Midnight Believer, 1978; Take It Home, 1979; Now Appearing At Ole Miss, 1980; There Must Be A Better World Somewhere, 1982; Love Me Tender, 1982; Blues 'n' Jazz, 1984; Six Silver Strings, 1986; Live At San Quentin, 1991; Blues Summit, 1993; Lucille and Friends, 1995; Live in Japan, 1999; Makin' Love Is Good For You, 2000; A Christmas Celebration of Hope, 2001; Anthology, 2001; with Bobby Bland: Together For The First Time: Live, 1974; Together Again: Live, 1976; Hit singles include: Three O'Clock Blues; You Didn't Want Me; Please Love Me; You Upset Me Baby; Sweet Sixteen; Rock Me Baby; The B. B. Jones (used in film soundtrack For The Love of Ivy); The Thrill Is Gone; Blues Come Over Me; Also featured on: Happy Anniversary, Charlie Brown!, 1989; When Love Comes To Town, U2, 1989; Heroes and Friends, Randy Travis, 1990; The Simpsons Sing The Blues, 1990. *Honours:* Grammy Awards: Best Male R&B Vocal Performance, 1971; Best Ethnic or Traditional Recording, 1982; Best Traditional Blues Recording, 1984, 1986, 1991, 1992; with Dr John: Pop Collaboration With Vocals, 2001; with Eric Clapton: Traditional Blues Album, Riding With The King, 2001; Inducted into Rock and Roll Hall of Fame, 1987; Lifetime Achievement Awards include: NARAS, 1988; Songwriters Hall of Fame, 1990; Gibson Guitars, 1991; Star in Hollywood Walk of Fame, 1990; MTV Video Award, with U2, 1989; Q Inspiration Award, 1992. *Membership:* Co-chairman, Foundation For The Advancement of Inmate Rehabilitation and Recreation. *Current Management:* Sidney A. Seidenberg Inc, 1414 Sixth Ave, New York, NY 10019, USA.

KING, Ben E. (Benjamin Earl Nelson); b. 28 Sept. 1938, Henderson, North Carolina, USA. Vocalist; Songwriter. *Career:* Singer, bands including The Four Bs; The Moonglows; The Crowns; Featured vocalist, The Drifters, 1957–60; Solo artiste, 1960–; Cabaret and club circuit, 1968–73; Member, Soul Clan, 1978; Rejoins The Drifters for tours, 1978–; Appearances include: San Remo Festival, Italy, 1964; Prince's Trust Rock Gala, Wembley Arena, 1987; Glastonbury Festival, 1987; Television: UK television debut, Ready Steady Go!, 1964; David Letterman's Sixth Anniversary Special, 1988. *Compositions include:* Co-writer, There Goes My Baby; Co-writer, Don't Play That Song (also recorded by Aretha Franklin); Stand By Me, later used in: film soundtrack, Stand By Me, 1986; Levi 501 jeans commercial (No. 1, UK) 1987; How Can I Forget. *Recordings:* Albums: Supernatural, 1975; Let Me Live In Your Life, 1978; Music Trance, 1980; Street Tough, 1981; Stand By Me (The Ultimate Collection), 1987; Dancing In The Night, 1987; Save The Last Dance For Me, 1988; Anthology, 1993; Drifters, 1996; Shades of Blue, 1999; Eleven Best, 2001; Hit singles include: with The Drifters: There Goes My Baby, (No. 2, USA); Dance With Me; True True Love; This Magic Moment; Save The Last Dance For Me (No. 1, USA; No. 2, UK); I Count The Tears; Solo: Spanish Harlem; Stand By Me (R&B No. 1, USA); Amor; I Who Have Nothing; Seven Letters; Supernatural Thing (R&B No. 1, USA); Other recordings: with Average White Band: Benny and Us, 1977; Book of Love, with Bo Diddley, featured in film Book of Love, 1991; Guest vocalist, Coast To Coast, Paul Shaffer, 1989. *Honours:* One of BMI's Most Performed Songs 1940–90 (over 3m. plays), Stand By Me, 1990. *Current Management:* Randy Irwin Associates. *Address:* 7231 Radio Rd, Naples, FL 33942, USA.

KING, Bob (Robert); b. 2 July 1955, Kilmarnock, Scotland. Musician (guitar). m. Hazel, 30 March 1974, 2 s. *Education:* Diploma of Higher Education. *Career:* Appearances most major country music festivals include: Americana, British and Irish Country Music Festival, Worthing; The Inverness Festival of Country Music. *Recordings:* Several compositions recorded by artistes in Ireland. *Honours:* Sylvia Saunders Trophy Winner, 1994; Several Act of the Year Awards throughout career. *Membership:* PRS; Equity. *Address:* 10 Hector Rd, Longsight, Manchester M13 0QN, England.

KING, Carole; b. 9 Feb. 1942. Vocalist; Songwriter. *Career:* Songwriter in partnership with Gerry Goffin; Worked with artistes including: Eric Clapton; Crosby and Nash; Branford Marsalis; David Sanborn; Numerous concerts and tours; Actress in theatre including: Starring role, Mrs Johnstone, Broadway production, Blood Brothers, 1994; Environmental activist for natural forest preservation; Studied European traditional music. *Compositions:* Hit songs include: Will You Love Me Tomorrow; Take Good Care of My Baby; Go Away Little Girl; The Locomotion; Up On The Roof; Chains; One Fine Day; Hey Girl; I Feel The Earth Move; Natural Woman; Smackwater Jack; You've Got A Friend; Now and Forever (For film, A League of Their Own); Soundtrack, animated film, Really Rosie. *Recordings include:* Albums: The City, 1968; Writer, 1970; Tapestry, 1971; Rhymes and Reasons, 1972; Music, 1972; Fantasy, 1973; Wrap Around Joy, 1974; Thoroughbred, 1975; Really Rosie, 1975; Simple Things, 1977; Welcome Home, 1978; Greatest Hits, 1978; Touch The Sky, 1979; Pearls, 1980, 1994; One To One, 1982; Speeding Time, 1983; City Streets, 1989; For Our Children, 1991; A League of Their Own, 1992; 'Til Their Eyes Shine, 1992; Colour of Your Dreams, 1993; In Concert, 1994; Time Gone By, 1994 A Natural Woman, 1994; Carnegie Hall Concert, 1996; Goin' Back, 1998; Love Makes The World, 2001; Single: Anyone at All, 1999. *Honours:* Inducted Songwriters' Hall of Fame, 1987; Rock and Roll Hall of

Fame, 1990; National Academy of Songwriters' Lifetime Achievement Award, 1988; Grammy Awards; Multi-Platinum, Platinum and Gold discs. *Membership:* AFTRA; AMPAS: NARAS; NAS; SAG; AFofM. *Current Management:* Lorna Guess. *Address:* 11684, Ventura Blvd, #273, Studio City, CA 91604, USA.

KING, Eileen Maria Goretti; b. 6 Aug. 1959, Bandbridge, Co Down, Northern Ireland. Vocalist. m. Joe Rafferty, 21 July 1987. *Education:* College. *Career:* Television apperances: BBC, UTV, RTE; Concerts include: Wembley Festival; Fanfare Grand Ole Opry, Nashville; Has recorded in Nashville, The Fireside Studios; The Porter Wagoners Studio. *Recordings:* 6 albums. *Honours:* Won numerous music awards. *Membership:* Equity. *Current Management:* JR Promotions. *Address:* 229 Newtownhamilton Rd, Armagh, Co Armagh, Northern Ireland.

KING, Evelyn 'Champagne'; b. 1 July 1960, Bronx, New York, USA. Vocalist. *Career:* Soul/dance music singer, 1977–. *Recordings:* Albums: Smooth Talk, 1977; Music Box, 1979; Call On Me, 1980; I'm In Love, 1981; Get Loose, 1982; Face To Face, 1983; So Romantic, 1984; A Long Time Coming, 1985; Flirt, 1988; The Best Of, 1990; The Essential Works Of, 1992; Singles include: Shame, 1977; I Don't Know If It's Right, 1979; I'm In Love, 1981; Get Loose, 1982; Face To Face, 1983. *Address:* c/o Nationwide Entertainment Services, 2756 N Green Valley Parkway, Suite 449, Las Vegas, NV 89014–2100, USA.

KING, Jonathan; b. 6 Dec. 1944, London, England. Vocalist; Music Journalist; Television Presenter. *Education:* English, Cambridge University. *Career:* Occasional recording artiste, 1965–; Talent spotter for Decca Records (discovered Genesis, produced their first album); Launched UK Records, 1972; Newspaper and magazine columnist, radio and television presenter, including own show Entertainment USA, BBC, 1980s; Organizer, A Song For Europe (UK's Eurovision Song Contest qualification show), 1995–. *Recordings:* Solo albums: Or Then Again, 1965; King Size King, 1982; The Butterfly That Stamped, 1989; The Many Faces of Jonathan King, 1993; Singles include: As Jonathan King: Everyone's Gone To The Moon; Green Is The Grass; It's Let It All Hang Out; Una Paloma Blanca; Wild World; Involved in novelty hits including: Johnny Reggae, The Piglets'; Sugar Sugar, Sakkarin; The Same Old Song, The Weathermen; Leap Up and Down (Wave Your Knickers In The Air), St Cecilia; Producer: Genesis, 4 albums; Rocky Horror Picture Show, 1984; Kylie Minogue; Eric Felton.

KING, Mark; b. 20 Oct. 1958, Cowes, Isle of Wight, England. Vocalist; Musician (bass). 4 c. *Career:* Founder member, Level 42, 1980–94; Regular international tours, 1983–; Concerts include: Prince's Trust Rock Gala, 1986, 1987, 1989; Crystal Palace Bowl, 1991; Midem Festival, Cannes, France, 1992. *Recordings:* Albums with Level 42: Level 42, 1981; The Pursuit of Accidents, 1982; Standing In The Light, 1983; A Physical Presence, 1985; World Machine, 1985; Running In The Family, 1987; Level Best, 1989; Guaranteed, 1991; Solo: Influences, 1984; One Man, 1999; Hit singles: The Chinese Way, 1983; The Sun Goes Down (Living It Up), 1983; Hot Water, 1984; Something About You, 1985; Leaving Me Now, 1985; Lessons In Love (No. 1 in 8 European countries), 1986; Running In The Family, 1987; To Be With You Again, 1987; It's Over, 1987; Heaven In My Hands, 1988; Tracie, 1988; Guaranteed, 1991. *Honours:* Making Music magazine poll, Best Bass Player, 1987; BMI Award, 1m. US performances, Something About You, 1991. *Current Management:* Paul Crockford Management, 56–60 Islington Park St, London N1 1PX, England. *Website:* www.mark-king.com; www.level42.com.

KING, Michael Weston; b. 11 Nov. 1961, Derbyshire, England. Vocalist; Songwriter; Musician (guitar, harmonica). m. (1) Ann Carter, Aug. 1987, divorced 2000, 3 s., 1 d., (2) Lou Dalgleish, Aug. 2002. *Career:* Lead singer, songwriter, Fragile Friends, 1982–87; Solo artiste, 1988, 1999–; Guitarist, Gary Hall and The Stormkeepers, 1989–93; Lead singer, songwriter, The Good Sons, 1993–2002; UK, European and American tours; Television appearances on BBC, ITV, RTE, Ireland and various European and American TV stations; Broadcasts on various radio stations including sessions on BBC Radio 1, Radio 2, Virgin Radio GLR and numerous local stations; Numerous contributions and articles for The Independent newspaper, Country Music International, Maverick, Get Rhythm. *Recordings:* Albums: with Fragile Friends: For Play; with The Stormkeepers: Wide Open To The World; with The Good Sons: Singing The Glory Down, 1995; The King's Highway, 1996; Wines, Lines and Valentines, 1997; Angels In The End, 1998; Happiness, 2001; solo: God Shaped Hole, 1999; Live...In Dinky Town, 2002; A Decent Man, 2003; Singles: with Fragile Friends: Paper Doll; The Novelty Wears Off; with The Stormkeepers: Jesus Christ/Lighten Up Your Load Suzanne; Where The River Meets The Sea (EP); with The Good Sons: The Good Sons (EP), 1994; Various songs recorded by other artistes: Riding The Range, Townes Van Zandt; Watch My Dreamboats Sail, Tower of Strength, Carolyn Hester; In Her Father's Bed, Arthur Brown; From These Hills, Carolyn Hester, 1996; Rear View Mirror, Townes van Zandt, 1997; Out of the Blue Vol. I, 1995, Vol. II, 1996, Vol. III, 1997. *Publications:* Beautiful Lies...The Songs of Michael Weston King. *Current Management:* CMP. *Address:* 34 Market St, Southport, Merseyside PR8 1HJ, England. *Fax:* (121) 499-8455. *E-mail:* info@michaelwestonking.com. *Website:* www.michaelwestonking.com.

KING, Morgana; b. 4 June 1930, Pleasantville, New York, USA; Vocalist; Actor. *Career:* Trained as opera singer but switched to jazz, c. 1955; Recording career began with release of For You For Me Forever More on Mercury Records, 1956; Worked the New York City club circuit, late 1950s–early 1960s; Recorded for many labels including: Mercury; United Artists; Mainstream; Reprise; Verve; Muse; Acting roles include Mama Carmella Corleone in The Godfather trilogy. *Recordings:* Albums include: For You For Me Forever More, 1956; Morgana King Sings The Blues, 1958; A Taste of Honey, 1964; It's A Quiet Thing, 1965; Cuore Di Mama, 1972; Everything Must Change, 1978; Simply Eloquent, 1986; This Is Always, 1992; Tender Moments, 2000.

KING, Peter; b. 1941. Musician (alto saxophone). *Career:* Played opening night, Ronnie Scott's, 1959; Played, recorded with numerous American artistes including: Zoot Sims; Philly Joe Jones; Red Rodney; Nat Adderley; Hampton Hawes; Big bands of Maynard Ferguson, Tubby Hayes; Own quartets, quintets, 1980s; Popular in France, extensive tours; Began with Ben Watt (Everything But The Girl), 1982; Featured soloist, Count Basie Band, 1990; Berlin Jazz Festival with Tete Montoliu, 1990; Partnership with Charlie Watts, appearances include: Ronnie Scott's, London and Birmingham, England; Blue Note, New York; Spiral Hall, Tokyo; Played with Horace Parlan Quartet, 1994; Tour of Spain; Festival, Belgium; Took place of Steve Grussman in quartet at festivals: Molde, Norway; Pori, Finland, 1994; Peter King Quartet, Top of The Bill, Ronnie Scott's, 1994; with Phil Woods, Jackie McLean, Count Basie Orchestra, Berlin Jazz Festival, 1994; with Rene Urtreger, Middleheim Festival, Belgium, 1994; with George Coleman, Ronnie Scott's, 1995; Adviser, Consultant to Christies Auction House, Sale of Charlie Parkers Grafton Saxophone. *Recordings:* New Beginning, 1982; East 34th Street, 1983; Peter King Quintet; Brother Bernard, 1988; Peter King In Paris; High Fly; Crusade; Tete Montoliu featuring Peter King; Speed Trap, 1996; Also featured on four Everything But The Girl albums.

KING, Stove; b. 8 Jan. 1975, Ellesmere Port, Merseyside, England. Musician (Bass). *Career:* Formed Grey Lantern with Paul Draper and Dominic Chad; Changed name to Mansun; Numerous live and TV appearances. *Recordings:* Take It Easy Chicken, 1996; Egg Shaped Fred, 1996; Stripper Vicar; Wide Open Space; Legacy, 1998; Six, 1999; Albums: Attack of the Grey Lantern, 1997; Six, 1999.

KING AD-ROCK, (Adam Horowitz); b. 31 Oct. 1966, Manhattan, New York, USA. Rap Artiste; Musician (guitar). *Career:* Founder member, US rap/rock group Beastie Boys, 1983–; Appearances include: Support to Madonna, Virgin Tour, 1985; Supports to Run DMC, Raisin' Hell Tour, 1986; Coheadliners with Run DMC, Together Forever Tour, 1987; Reading Festival, 1992; Film appearances: Krush Groove; Run DMC film Tougher Than Leather; Scared Stupid; Acting roles: The Equalizer, TV series; Santa Ana Project; Lost Angels; Roadside Prophets. *Recordings:* Singles: She's On It, 1987; Fight For Your Right To Party, 1987; No Sleep Till Brooklyn, 1987; Girls/She's Crafty, 1987; Hey Ladies, 1989; Pass The Mic, 1992; Get It Together/Sabotage, 1994; Sure Shot, 1994; Intergalactic, 1998; Body Movin', 1998; Remote Control, 1999; Alive, 1999; Albums: Licensed To Ill, 1986; Paul's Boutique, 1989; Check Your Head, 1992; Ill Communication, 1994; Root Down, 1995; The In Sound From Way Out, 1996; Hello Nasty (No. 1, UK and USA), 1998; Sounds of Science, 1999. *Current Management:* Gold Mountain Entertainment. *Address:* 3575 Cahuenga Blvd W, Suite 450, Los Angeles, CA 90068, USA.

KING BRITT, , (The Force, Oba Funke); b. Philadelphia, Pennsylvania, USA. Prod; Remixer; DJ. *Career:* Started as on-tour DJ for Philadelphia rap outfit Digable Planets; Co-founder: Ovum Records (with Josh Wink); Formed Sylk 130; Debut album released on Ruffhouse/Columbia, 1998; World-wide DJ; Residency at London's The End club; Collaborations: Josh Wink; Vikter Duplaix; Martin Fry; Alison Moyet; Remixed: 4Hero; Donna Lewis; Tori Amos; Jazzanova; Macy Gray. *Recordings:* Albums: When The Funk Hits The Fan (with Sylk 130), 1998; Re-Members Only (with Sylk 130), 2001; Singles: Tribal Confusion (as E-Culture), 1991; Strong Song (as Just King and Wink), 1992; Supernatural (as Firefly), 1995; Last Night A DJ Saved My Life (with Sylk 130), 1998. *Current Management:* Elite Music Management, PO Box 3261, Brighton, East Sussex, BN2 4WA, England. *Website:* www.kingbritt.net.

KINNAIRD, Alison Margaret; b. 30 April 1949, Edinburgh, Scotland. Musician (scottish harp, clarsach). m. Robin Morton, 23 Feb. 1976, 1 s., 1 d. *Education:* MA, Edinburgh University; Studied Scottish harp with Jean Campbell. *Career:* Freelance musician, 1971–; Concerts: Edinburgh; London; New York; San Francisco; Hawaii; Tokyo; Berlin; Presenter, The Music Show, Channel 4, 1995. *Recordings:* The Harp Key, 1978; The Harper's Gallery, 1980; The Harpers Land, 1983; Music In Trust I and II, 1988; The Quiet Tradition, 1989; Mactalla, 1994; features on: Gun Sireadh Gun Larraidh, Christine Primrose, 2001. *Publications:* The Harp Key; The Small Harp Tutor; Tree of Strings (with Keith Sanger). *Honours:* MTA Music Award, 1983; Living Tradition Award, 1995; MBE for Services to Music and Art, 1997. *Membership:* Life mem., The Clarsach Society. *Current Management:* Robin Morton, Shillinghill, Temple. *Address:* Shillinghill, Temple, Midlothian EH23 4SH, Scotland.

KINNEY, Sean; b. 27 May 1966, Seattle, Washington, USA. Musician (Drums). *Career:* Member, Alice in Chains; Numerous tours and TV appearances including MTV Unplugged. *Recordings:* Singles: Sap EP; Would?, 1993; Them Bones, 1993; Angry Chair, 1993; Down In A Hole, 1993; Grind, 1995; Heaven Beside You, 1996; Albums: Facelift, 1990; Dirt, 1992; Sap, 1992; Jar of Flies, 1994; Alice in Chains, 1995; I Stay Away, 1995; Unplugged, 1996.

KINSEY, Tony; b. 11 Oct. 1927, England. Composer; Musician (drums, piano). m. Patricia, 1 d. *Education:* Studied percussion with Bill West, Cozy Cole, Jazz College, New York; Composition, orchestration, arrangement with Bill Russo, Columbia College, Chicago. *Career:* Professional musician from age 18; Joined John Dankworth, as drummer with Dankworth 7; Preferred drummer in 1960s–70s, for visiting jazz stars including: Oscar Peterson; Ella Fitzgerald; Lena Horne; Sarah Vaughan; Billie Holiday; Ben Webster; Clarke Terry; Musical director, That's Life, BBC TV, 3 years. *Compositions include:* Films: Souvenir; On The Bridge; Televison: That's Life, BBC; Castle of Adventure, TVS; The John Bird Show, BBC; The Londoners, BBC; A Tribute To Her Majesty; Colour; Four Seasons; Life At The Limit; Two's Company; Over 100 commercials including: Lloyds Bank; Kellogg's Rice Krispies; Danish Bacon; Baby Cham; Domecq; Marshall Cavendish; Raleigh Bicycles; Classical. *Compositions:* Pictures; Three Suites For String Quartet; River Thames Suite; Alice Through The Looking Glass. *Recordings include:* (own compositions) Alice Through The Looking Glass; Classical Lines 1, 2; Time Gentlemen Please; How To Succeed In Business; Jazz At The Flamingo; The Tony Kinsey Quintet; Foursome; Lougerhythms; River Thames Suite; Aspects of Jazz; Jazz Scenes; Midnight Sax; It Had To Be You. *Current Management:* Soundtrack Music Management. *Address:* 22 Ives St, Chelsea, London SW3 2ND, England.

KIPPER, (Marc Eldridge); b. 19 March 1962, Frimley, Surrey, England. Prod; Arranger; Writer; Musician (guitar, keyboards). *Education:* Guitar from 9 years old, Jazz and Classical training. *Career:* Member, One Nation; Toured with: Jeff Beck; The Temptations; Ruby Turner; MD with Beijing Spring; Toured with: Curtis Stigers; Richard Marx; 3 major tours as guitarist for Gary Numan. *Recordings:* with One Nation: Strong Enough; Big Life Big Tears; Machine and Soul; with David Essex: Back 2 Back; with Sting: Brand New Day, 2000. *Publications:* The Complete Singer, 1995. *Membership:* PRS. *Address:* East Manor Barn, Manor Yard, Fringford, Bicester, Oxon OX6 9DQ, England.

KIRK, Nicholas Kenneth; b. 27 Dec. 1945, Bradford, West Yorkshire, England. Musician (New Orleans jazz banjo); Electronics Engineer. *Education:* BSc Hons, University of Wales; Postgraduate Diploma in Communications, Southampton University; Postgraduate Diploma in R F and Microwave, Bradford University. *Career:* Appearances on radio and Television Wales with Clive Evans' River City Stompers, 1966–67; Appeared at the Keswick Jazz Festival, Bude Jazz Festival, Marsden Jazz Festival, and at jazz clubs and pubs in Yorkshire, Wales and South of England, with the Dennis Browne Creole Band; Appeared at the 100 Club in London with the New Era Jazzband; Author of British patent for apparatus for recording and replaying music (The Musical Arranger and Sequencer, sold to Waddingtons, now called Compute-a-Tune and Wizard). *Compositions:* Clouds. *Recordings:* Float Me Down The River, with the Dennis Browne Creole Band, cassette; City of a Million Dreams, cassette. *Membership:* Musicians' Union; Fellow, Royal Microscopical Society. *Address:* 36 Kilpin Hill Lane, Staincliffe, Near Dewsbury, West Yorkshire WF13 4BH, England.

KIRKE, Simon Frederick; b. 28 July 1949, London, England. Musician (drums, guitar, piano); Songwriter. m. Lorraine Dellal, 15 Dec. 1982, 1 s., 3 d. *Career:* Member, Black Cat Bones; Founder Member, Free; Founder Member, Bad Company, 1973–83; Performed at 2 Isle of Wight Festivals; Many US tours, 2 world tours; Television: Several Top of the Pops; Radio includes: John Peel. *Compositions:* Bad Company with Paul Rodgers; Several songs on Free and Bad Company albums. *Recordings:* With Champion Jack Dupree: Single: I Haven't Done No One No Harm, 1968; Album: When You Feel the Feelin' You Was Feeling, 1968; With Free: Singles: All Right Now (No. 2, UK), 1970; My Brother Jake, 1971; Little Bit of Love, 1972; Wishing Well, 1973; Albums: Tons of Sobs, 1968; Free, 1969; Fire and Water, 1970; Highway, 1971; Live, 1971; Free At Last, 1972; Heartbreaker, 1973; The Free Story, 1973; Best of Free, 1991; Walk in My Shadow: An Introduction to Free, 1998; With Amazing Blondel: Albums: Blondel, 1973; Mulgrave Street, 1974; With Bad Company: Singles: Can't Get Enough; Feel Like Makin Love; Young Blood; If You Need Somebody; Holy Water; Here Comes Trouble; Hey Hey; Hammer of Love; Albums: Bad Company, 1974; Straight Shooter, 1975; Run With The Pack, 1976; Burning Sky, 1977; Desolation Angels, 1979; Rough Diamonds, 1982; 10 From 6, 1985; Fame and Fortune, 1986; Dangerous Age, 1988; Holy Water, 1990; Here Comes Trouble, 1992; Company of Strangers, 1995; Albums: With John Wetton, Caught in the Crossfire, 1980; With Wildlife, Wildlife, 1983; With Mick Ralphs, Take This, 1983; With Jim Colpody, Let the Thunder Die; Also recorded with Jim Diamond, Snowy White, Bon Jovi, Ringo Starr; John Wetton. *Honours:* Gold Disc, All Right Now; 12 Gold and Platinum Albums with Bad Company. *Membership:* Musicians' Union. *Address:* c/o Gremlin Productions, PO Box 148, Fincham, Norfolk PE33 9EH, England.

KIRKPATRICK, Chris(topher Allan); b. 17 Oct. 1971, Clarion, PA, USA. Vocalist. *Education:* Associate of Arts Degree, Valencia College, Dayton, OH; Dance and vocal training at Rollins College, OH. *Career:* Mem., *NSYNC vocal quintet, 1995–; Signed to BMG Ariola Munich, 1997; First headline US tour, 1998; Appointed spokesman for Child Watch of North America; Owner of FuMan Skeeto clothing firm. *Recordings:* Albums: *NSYNC, 1998; Home For Christmas, 1998; No Strings Attached, 2000; Celebrity, 2001. Singles include: I Want You Back, 1997; Tearin' Up My Heart, 1997; Let The Music Heal Your Soul (various artists charity single credited to Bravo All Stars), 1999; Music Of My Heart (with Gloria Estefan), 1999; Bye, Bye, Bye, 2000; I'll Never Stop, 2000; It's Gonna Be Me, 2000; This I Promise You, 2000; Pop, 2001; Gone, 2001. *Honours:* Presented with keys to City of Orlando, 2000; American Music Award, Favorite Pop/Rock Band, Duo or Group, 2002. *Address:* c/o Wright Entertainment Group, PO Box 590009, Orlando, FL 32859–0009, USA. *Website:* www.nsync.com.

KIRKPATRICK, David Gordon (Slim Dusty); b. 13 June 1927, Kempsey, New South Wales, Australia. Entertainer; Country Vocalist; Recording Artiste. m. Joy McKean, 22 Dec. 1951, 1 s., 1 d. *Career:* Called himself Slim Dusty, 1938; Records first songs: Song for the Aussies; My Final Song, 1942; Record six titles: When the Rain Tumbles Down in July, 1946; Launches Slim Dusty Show, 1954; Showground Partnership with Frankie Foster, 1956–63; The Pub With No Beer, (Australia's first Gold Record Award), 1952; Released first album: Slim Dusty Sings, 1960. *Recordings:* Albums include: Slim Dusty Sings, 1960; Walk a Country Mile, 1979; No 50 Gold Anniversary, 1981; Trucks on the Track, 1985; Beer Drinking Songs of Australia, 1986; Neon City, 1987; G'day, 1989; Coming Home, 1990; Two Singers, One Song, 1991; Live into the Nineties, video, 1992; Country Way of Life, 1995; 91 Over 50, 1996; A Time to Remember, 1997; Makin' a Mile, 1997; Looking Forward Looking Back, 2000; Down The Dusty Road, 2001. *Publications:* Walk a Country Mile (autobiography, with J. Lapsley), 1979; Another Day, Another Town (autobiography, co-author), 1996. *Honours:* MBE, 1970; AO, 1998; Australian Country Music Roll of Reknown; Australian Record Industry Asscn Hall of Fame. *Membership:* Chairman, Country Music Asscn of Aust. *Address:* PO Box 115, St Ives, NSW 2075, Australia.

KIRKPATRICK, John Michael; b. 8 Aug. 1947, Chiswick, London, England. Musician (melodeon, button accordion, anglo concertina). m. Sue Harris, divorced. *Career:* Joined Hammersmith Morris Men in their second week, 1959; Took up the melodeon, button accordion and, finally, the anglo concertina whilst with them; Member: Albion Country Band; Magic Lantern; The Richard Thompson Band; Umps and Dumps; Steeleye Span; Brass Monkey; Trans-Europe Diatonique; Band of Hope; Played with numerous ceilidh bands and made many albums with, then wife, Sue Harris; Collaborations include: Leon Rosselson; Roy Bailey; Martin Carthy; Ashley Hutchings; Sandy Denny; Ralph McTell; Gerry Rafferty; Founder: The Shropshire Bedlams morris team, 1975; Performed with The Albion Band for National Theatre productions of Lark Rise and Candleford; Also worked with: The Victoria Theatre (later The New Victoria Theatre), North Staffordshire; The Orchard Theatre Touring Company, Devon; As songwriter, composer, choreographer and musical director, has contributed to over sixty plays in the theatre and on radio. *Recordings:* Albums include: Jump At The Sun, 1972; The Compleat Dancing Master (with Ashley Hutchings), 1974; Plain Capers, 1976; Going Spare, 1978; Three In A Row (The English Melodeon), 1983; Blue Balloon, 1987; Sheepskins, 1988; Earthling, 1994; Welcome To Hell (John Kirkpatrick Band), 1997; One Man and His Box, 1998, Mazurka Berserker, 2001; with Sue Harris: The Rose of Britain's Isle, 1974; Among The Many Attractions At The Show Will Be A Really High Class Band, 1976; Shreds and Patches, 1977; Facing The Music, 1980; Stolen Ground, 1989; with Junkera, Tesi and Kirkpatrick: Trans-Europe Diatonic, 1993; with Brass Monkey: Brass Monkey, 1983; See How It Runs, 1986; Sound and Rumour, 1998; Going and Staying, 2001; with Steeleye Span: Storm Force Ten, Live At Last, 1978; with Albion Band: No Roses, 1971; Battle of The Field, 1976; Larkrise To Candleford, 1979; BBC Sessions, 1998; with Band of Hope: Rhythm and Reds, 1994; features on: Richard Thompson albums: Henry The Human Fly, 1972; Hand of Kindness, 1983; Amnesia, 1988; Rumour and Sigh, 1991; Sweet Talker, 1991; Mirror Blue, 1994; Richard and Linda Thompson albums: I Want To See The Bright Lights Tonight, 1974; Hokey Pokey, 1974; First Light, 1978; Sunnyvista, 1979; Martin Carthy albums: Because It's There, 1979; Out of The Cut, 1982; Right of Passage, 1988; Leon Rosselson albums: That's Not The Way It's Got To Be (Roy Bailey and Leon Rosselson), 1975; Bringing In News From Nowhere, 1986; I Didn't Mean It, 1988; other featured appearances: Young Hunting, Tony Rose, 1970; Roy Bailey, 1971; Morris On, 1972; Sandy, Sandy Denny, 1972; Rave On, 1974; Amaranth, Shirley Collins, 1976; Julie Covington, 1978; Slide Away The Screen, Ralph McTell, 1979; Night Owl, Gerry Rafferty, 1979; Still Pause, Maggie Holland, 1983; Leaves From A Tree, Roy Bailey, 1988; The Tenement Year, Pere Ubu, 1988; Jali Roll, Dembo Konte and Kausu Kuyateh, 1991; Reve De Siam, Dan Ar Braz, 1992; Fanafody, Tarika Sammy, 1992; Till The Grass O'Grew The Corn, 1997; Wassail!, 1997; The Garden of Love, Frankie Armstrong, 1999. *Website:* johnkirkpatrick.co.uk.

KISSEL, Michael Case; b. New York, USA. Musician; Composer; Lyricist; Record Prod. m. Elena Thorton, 29 June 1985. *Career:* Former bandleader,

Los Amigos de Las Americas, Honduras; Musician, composer, producer, vocalist, various artistes include: The Drifters; The Pointer Sisters; Gloria Gaynor; Elvin Bishop; Jocelyn Brown; Otis Rush; Ernie Isley; Toots and The Maytals. *Recordings:* Albums: Surrender, Robin Clark and David Bowie, 1985; Healing Session, Babatunde Olatunji, 1991; Peace Is The World Smiling, Babatunde Olatunji, Pat Seeger, Taj Mahal, 1989; Film soundtracks: In The Blood, 1990; Best Shots, 1990; Pumping Iron II, 1985. *Membership:* ASCAP; NARAS; Songwriters' Guild; AFofM.

KITCHEN, Elizabeth Jane; b. 1 April 1959, Rochdale, England. Composer; Arranger; Musician (drums). *Education:* Studied with: James Blades; Gilbert Webster RNCM. *Career:* Writes, arranges for television: Playdays; Monster Cafe; Roundabout Stop; Dot Stop; Worked on films/TV: Life and Loves of a She Devil; King of The Ghetto; Played with the Blues Band; Barbara Dickson in Blood Brothers; Works with Chickenshed company. *Recordings:* Freelanced with the Hallé Orchestra; RLPO; Northern Ballet; Opera North; Written many theatre shows: Young Vic; Battersea Arts Centre. *Honours:* Graduate: RNCM; PRNCM. *Membership:* PRS; MCPS. *Address:* 1 Warwick Rd, London N11 2SA, England.

KITT, Eartha Mae; b. 26 Jan. 1928, Columbia, South Carolina, USA. Actress; Vocalist; Entertainer. 1 s. *Education:* High School of Performing Arts, New York. *Career:* Dancer and vocalist, Katherine Dunham Dance Group, 1948; Night club singer, Europe, 1949–; Appearances world-wide; Stage performances: Dr Faust, Paris, 1951; New Faces of 1952, New York, 1952; Mrs Patterson, Broadway, 1954; Shinbone Alley; The Skin of Our Teeth; The Owl and The Pussycat; Bunny; The High Bid; Timbuktu, Broadway, 1978; Blues In The Night, 1985; Follies, London, 1988; A Night At The Cotton Club, UK revue tour; Film appearances: New Faces, 1953; Accused, 1957; St Louis Blues, 1957; Mark of The Hawk, 1958; Anna Lucasta, 1959; Saint of Devil's Island, 1961; Synanon, 1965; Up The Chastity Belt, 1971; Dragonard; Ernest Scared Stupid, 1991; Boomerang, 1992; Fatal Instinct; Numerous television appearances include: I Spy; Mission Impossible; Played the original Catwoman in Batman series; Living Single; New York Undercover; Jack's Place; Matrix; Subject, documentary All By Myself, 1982; Featured, Unzipped, 1995; International concerts in over 100 countries. *Recordings:* Numerous albums include: Down To Eartha, 1955; Thursday's Child, 1956; Revisited, 1961; Bad But Beautiful, 1976; At Her Very Best, 1982; C'est Si Bon, 1983; I Love Men, 1984; The Romantic Eartha Kitt, 1984; That Bad Eartha, 1985; In Person At The Plaza, 1988; My Way, 1988; I'm Still Here, 1989; Best of Eartha Kitt, 1990; Live In London, 1990; Thinking Jazz, 1992; Back In Business, 1994; My Greatest Songs, 1998; The Best of Eartha Kitt, 1999; Purr-Fect: Greatest Hits, 1999; Excellent and Decadent, 2001. *Publications:* Autobiographies: Thursday's Child, 1954; Alone With Me, 1976; Confessions of a Sex Kitten, 1989. *Honours:* NANM Woman of the Year, 1968; Star on Hollywood Walk of Fame. *Current Management:* c/o Stan Scottland, JKE Services Inc, 404 Park Ave S, 10th Floor, New York, NY 10016, USA.

KJAER, Torben Edvard; b. 26 Oct. 1946, Gentofte, Denmark. Jazz Musician (piano); Composer; Arranger; Conductor. m. Marianne Kampmann, 28 Sept. 1968, 1 s. *Education:* Theory, Composition, Conducting, Institute Music and Science, University of Copenhagen, 1966–73; Studied with George Russell, 1971; Piano degree, Copenhagen Music Conservatory, 1973. *Career:* Professional Musician, 1973–; Pianist with: Dexter Gordon; Dizzy Gillespie; Ben Webster; Clark Terry; Al Grey; Roy Eldridge; Red Mitchell; Milton Batiste; Rasheema; Founder, own jazz quartet; Conductor, Danish Radio Jazz Group, 1973–79; Danish Radio Light Orchestra, 1979–88; Danish Radio Big Band; Royal Orchestra; Orchestra Leader, TV Shows, 1986–92; Composer/ Arranger for numerous groups including Tritonius (Danish Gospel Choir) and Copenhagen Music Ensemble; Arrangements include: Chamber Version, Candide; Faust, Royal Theatre, Copenhagen; Arranger, musicals including: Guys and Dolls; My Fair Lady; Chicago; Kiss Me Kate; also music for television, radio, film, theatre, cabaret, commercials. *Compositions include:* Mass of Peace, 1976; Christmas Oratory, 1981; Concerto Grosso, 1983; David and Batseba, 1985. *Recordings include:* Whalesongs, 1983; Jazz In Danish, 1988; Tower At The End of The World, 1988; Stolen Moments, Rasheema, 1995. *Honours:* Awards, Danish State Fund of Art; Best Popular Composer, 1979. *Membership:* Vice-President, Danish Jazz, Beat and Folk Music Authors. *Address:* Skovvej 12, 2820 Gentofte, Denmark.

KJELLEMYR, Bjorn; b. 4 Dec. 1950, Bamble, Norway. Bassist (Accoustic and Electric). m. Mette Havrevold, 2 s. *Education:* Academy of Music, Oslo. *Career:* European tours mainly with Terje Rypdal, appearing at festivals and other concerts, appearing with Joe Henderson, Chet Baker, and Palle Mikkelborg. *Recordings:* Chasers, 1986; Blue, 1988; Singles Collection, 1989; If Mountains Could Sing, 1995; Heat, 1995; Electronique Noire, 1998. *Honours:* Jazz Musician of the Year, Norway, 1991; Buddy Award, 1995. *Current Management:* PJP, 5000 Bergen, Norway.

KKOSHI, Chaz (The Bat); b. 3 Feb. 1962, London, England. Record Prod; Musician (keyboards, drums); Vocalist. m. Maria Capsalis, 23 May 1993, 1 d. *Education:* Tottenham Technical College, A Level Technical Drawing; Trinity Musical College Grade 8, pianoforte. *Career:* Spartacus World Tour, 1982; Hammersmith Odeon, Double Take, Eurovision, 1986; BBC Radio 1

Roadshow, 1992, 1994, 1995; 6 O'Clock Show, LWT, 1991; The Word, 1994; Des O'Connor Show, 1994; Several appearances, Top of the Pops, 1984–. *Recordings:* Party 4 The Word, Steve Walsh; Gypsy Kings remix; Four Seasons remix; Awesome: The Singles; Supernatural Love, Alex Brown; Shadows and Elton John compilation; Culture Club Album, 1999; Numerous dance hits. *Membership:* Musicians' Union. *Current Management:* Pass Go Productions.

KLAKEGG, Rune; b. 19 April 1955, Skien, Norway. Musician (piano); Composer. m. Kathryn Bresee, 14 Aug. 1992, 2 d. *Education:* 2 years study, University of Oslo. *Career:* Freelance jazz musician, composer, since late 1970s; Appeared with groups: Cutting Edge; Out To Lunch; Soyr; Rune Klakegg Trio; All major jazz festivals; Arranger, band leader, Van Morrison, Vossajazz, 1988. *Recordings:* Cutting Edge: CE, 1982; Our Man In Paradise, 1984; Duesenberg, 1986; Out To Lunch: OTL, 1988; Kullboksrytter, 1995; Soyr: Vectors, 1988; Bussene lengter hjem, 1994; Med Kjott og Kjarlighet, 1997; R K Trio: Anaerobics, 1992; Fuzzy Logic: FL, 1996. *Honours:* NOPA Best Composition of the Year for Pamplemousse, 1995. *Membership:* TONO; NOPA. *Address:* Ole Bullsgt 45, 0475 Oslo, Norway.

KLASTERKA, Zeljen; b. 24 Jan. 1958, Zagreb, Croatia. Musician (guitar); Composer; Guitar Teacher. m. Neda Urlicic, 1 July 1995. *Education:* University graduate; 14 years, Faculty of Music University, Zagreb. *Career:* Lead guitarist with Notturno; Ritmo Loco; Patchwork; Studio musician; Classical guitar duet with Milivoj Majdak, Stanko Selak Big Band (orchestra of Music Academy); Music editor, major television show in Croatia: 7 NOC. *Recordings:* Album: Canto Latino, Patchwork video live concert of Zagreb Bienalle, 1994; Nek'ti Bude Ljubav Sva, Eurovision song contest entry, 5 video spots, Croatian Television. *Honours:* First Prize, Croatian Contest, Eurovision Song Contest. *Membership:* HGU; ZAMP. *Current Management:* Neda Urlicic-Klasterka. *Address:* Davor 3, 10000 Zagreb, Croatia.

KLEIN, Harry; b. 25 Dec. 1928, London, England. Musician (baritone saxophone). *Education:* Various music teachers including Harry Hayes. *Career:* Tours with Stan Kenton with groups backing Tony Bennett, Ella Fitzgerald, Aretha Franklin, 1960s–80s; Now semi-retired doing various solo dates. *Recordings:* Played on Lady Madonna (No. 1, UK), Honey Pie, Savoy Truffle, The Beatles, 1968; It's Not Unusual (No. 1, UK), Tom Jones, 1965; Compilation with group The Jazz Five: The Five of Us, 2001; solo: Nemo; Big Ben. *Honours:* Poll Winner, Melody Maker Poll, 1952–58. *Membership:* Musicians' Union. *Address:* 8 Bowling Green House, Chelsea, London SW10, England.

KLEINENBERG, Sander; b. 1972, The Hague, Netherlands. Prod; Remixer; DJ. *Career:* Started to DJ in 1987; Resident DJ at The Roxy in Amsterdam; Remixed: Oliver Lieb, Junkie XL, Destiny's Child. *Recordings:* Albums: Sander Kleinenberg Presents Melk, 1998; Singles: My Lexicon, 2000; Penso Positiva, 2000; 4 Seasons, 2000. *Current Management:* c/o London Records, PO Box 1422, 72 Chancellor's Rd, London W6 9SG, England.

KLEMMER, John; b. 7 July 1956, Chicago, Illinois, USA. Musician (saxophones, flutes, clarinets, kalimba, piano, keyboards, synthesizers, percussion); Vocal composer. *Education:* Interlochen National Music Camp; Private studies, age 5 to mid 20s; Studied, classical saxophone, flute, clarinet; Jazz improvisation with Joseph Daly; Studied composition, arranging, conducting; Private studies, orchestration, film scoring with Albert Harris. *Career:* Tours with: George Benson; Herbie Hancock; Miles Davis; Weather Report; others; With Don Ellis Orchestra, USA, Europe, England; State Department tour of 11 countries of French West Africa with Oliver Nelson Septet, Impulse Artists on tour; Live Performances, concerts, clubs include: Shellys Manne Hole, The Light House, all major jazz and rock clubs, concert venues, USA; Carnegie Hall; Newport Jazz Festival; Antibes Jazz Festival; Montreux Jazz Festival; Television and radio include: Voice of America shows; Midnight Special; Rock Concert; Merv Griffin Show; At One With; Dial M for Music; Live at Tanglewood PBS Special; Kitty Hawk, featuring John Klemmer solo saxophone PBS Special; WWTW presents John Klemmer; Started own record company, Touch Records, 1999. *Compositions include:* Walk In Love, recorded by Manhattan Transfer, Acker Bilk; The Old Man's Tear; Last Summer's Spell, recorded by Don Ellis; Lost In Love, recorded by Freda Payne, 1975; The Beauty of Her Soul; Touch. *Recordings include:* Blow on Gold, 1969; Touch, 1975; Barefoot Ballet, 1976; Cry, solo saxophone, 1980; Hush, solo saxophone, 1981; Life, solo saxophone, 1981; Making Love Vol. 1, 1998. *Publications:* The Jazz Styles of John Klemmer. *Honours:* Down Beat Magazine International Jazz Critics Poll, Talent Deserving Wider Recognition, 1973. *Membership:* BMI; ASCAP; NARAS. *Current Management:* Borman Entertainment, Gary Borman. *Address:* Sally Poppe, 9220 Sunset Blvd, Suite 320, Hollywood, CA 90069, USA.

KLUGH, Earl; b. 16 Sept. 1953, Detroit, Michigan, USA. Musician (guitar). *Career:* Member, George Benson Group; Chick Corea's Return To Forever; Solo recording artiste, 1975–; Performed with numerous artistes including George Shearing; Flora Purim; McCoy Tyner; Bob James; Chet Atkins. *Recordings:* Solo albums include: Earl Klugh, 1976; Living Inside Your Love, 1977; Finger Paintings, 1977; Magic In Your Eyes, 1978; Heart String, 1979;

Dream Come True, 1980; Late Night Guitar, 1980; Crazy For You, 1981; Two of a Kind, 1982; Delta Lady, 1983; Low Ride, 1983; Night Songs, 1984; Wishful Thinking, 1984; Key Notes, 1985; Life Stories; Soda Fountain Shuffle; Whispers and Promises; Solo Guitar; Midnight In San Juan; Best of Earl Klugh, 1991; Sounds and Visions, 1991; Cool, 1992; Move, 1993; Sudden Burst of Energy, 1995; Peculiar Situation, 1999; with George Benson: White Rabbit; Body Talk; with Al Jarreau: This Time; with Jimmy Buffet: One Particular Harbour; with Jennifer Holliday: Say You Love Me; with McCoy Tyner: Inner Voices; with Flora Purim: Stories To Tell; with Bob James: Touchdown; One On One. *Address:* EKI, 24225 W Nine Mile Rd, Southfield, MI 48034, USA.

KNAUER, Wolfram; b. 28 Jan. 1958, Germany. Musicologist; Dir. *Education:* Kiel University, 1980–89. *Career:* Director, Jazz-Institute Darmstadt; Teaching appointments at several major universities in Germany; Speaker at international conferences in Europe, USA. *Publications:* Numerous including, Zwischen Bebop Und Free Jazz; Jazz In Deutschland; Jazz In Europa; Translations from English into German; Scholarly essays; Many articles, interviews, concert, book and record reviews. *Membership:* Hessische Jazzakademie; International Society for Jazz Research. *Address:* Jazz Institute Darmstadt, Bessunger Strase 88d, D 64285 Darmstadt, Germany.

KNEPPER, James Minter (Jimmy); b. 22 Nov. 1927, Los Angeles, California, USA. Jazz Musician (trombone). m. Maxine Fields, May 1954, 1 s., 1 d. *Education:* Harmony, Orchestration, LA City and State Colleges. *Career:* Played with: Charlie Spivak; Charlie Parker; Charley Barnet; Charlie Mingus; Benny Carter; Benny Goodman; Thad Jones; Gil Evans; Toshike; Stan Kenton; Woody Herman; Eric Dolphy; Miles Davis; Al Kooper; Kenny Burrell; Mose Allison; Herbie Mann, State Dept tour in Africa, 1960; Mingus Dynasty; Broadway: Funny Girl; On Your Toes (revival); Me Nobody Knows; National Jazz Ensemble; American Jazz Orchestra; Smithsonian Jazz Orchestra; George Grunz Concert Jazz Band; Tony Scott; Joe Albany; Joe Maini; Dean Benedetti. *Honours:* International Critics Poll; Readers Poll of Down Beat Magazine. *Membership:* AFofM. *Address:* 11 Bayview Pl., Staten Island, NY 10304, USA.

KNIGHT, Emrys Glyn; b. 15 June 1951, South Glamorgan, Wales. Musician (lead guitar). *Career:* Member, Rose Among Thorns; Common Ground; Snatch It Back; Tours, UK and Europe; Numerous television and radio appearances; Concerts and albums with the above; British tours with Ralph McTell; Toured with Stone Free (Jimi Hendrix tribute band) in the UK and Europe. *Membership:* Musicians' Union; PRS; MCPS. *Address:* 187 College Rd, Whitchurch, Cardiff CF14 2NT, Wales.

KNIGHT, Gavin; b. 17 April 1966, Southampton, Hampshire, England. Musician (drums, percussion); Writer; Prod; Programmer; Arranger; Remixer. *Education:* Studied music with Antony Christmas, 2 years and Albert Cooper, 2 years, Southampton. *Career:* Drummer with The Shamen, 1991–95; Extensive world tours including Europe, Scandinavia, USA, Australia and the Far East; Headlined Glastonbury Festival; Numerous TV appearances worldwide; Drummer, Maroontown, 1993–94; European shows and album recording; Urban Hype, live UK shows, 1992; The Good Strawberries, live UK shows and TV, 1994; Played for Marc Almond, major show at the Royal Albert Hall, London, TV appearances and album recording, 1995–98; with Victoria Wilson-James, European shows and TV appearances, 1996–; Russian shows with Jam and Spoon, 1997; Remixed, programmed various projects include: The Shamen; Co-writer and Producer, single release, Urban Hype, 1992; Marc Almond; Rhythm programming for album and single, Angelique Kidjo; Victoria Wilson-James; Assisted the Shamen on theme tune, The Ozone, TV programme, 1995; Worked with P J Proby, Co-Composer, TV programme for Meridian Television, 1996; Co-Member, dance production team, Universal State of Mind, 1996; Rhythm programming for commercial Release, Viva!, 1996. *Recordings:* Syncronous, Inca, 1994; Tunnel Vision, The Ticket Men, 1995; Co-writer, The Feeling, with Urban Hype, 1992 (released in Japan on compilation album); All Because of You, Universal State of Mind, 1997. *Membership:* Musicians' Union; PAMRA. *Address:* c/o The Cottage, 1a Bursledon Rd, Hedge End, Southampton, Hampshire SO30 0BP, England.

KNIGHT, Gladys; b. 28 May 1944, Atlanta, Georgia, USA. Vocalist. *Career:* Singer, Gladys Knight and the Pips, 1957–89; Signed to Motown Records, 1966; Appearances include: Grand Gala Du Disque, Amsterdam, 1969; European tour, 1974; Kool Jazz Festival, San Diego, 1977; London Palladium, 1978; World Music Festival, 1982; Solo artiste, 1989–; Concerts include: Westbury Music Fair, New York, 1992; Television includes: Gladys Knight and The Pips Show, NBC, 1975; Happy New Year America, CBS, 1986; Motown 30: What's Goin' On, 1990; Ray Charles: 50 Years In Music, Uh-Huh!, 1991; Gladys Knight's Holiday Family Reunion, ABC TV, 1991; Actress, film Pipe Dreams, 1976; Actress, US sitcoms: Charlie and Co, 1985–86; Guest star, Out All Night, 1992. *Recordings:* Albums: Everybody Needs Love, 1967; Feelin' Bluesy, 1968; Silk 'n' Soul, 1969; Gladys Knight and The Pips' Greatest Hits, 1970; If I Were Your Woman, 1971; Standing Ovation, 1972; Neither One of Us, 1973; All I Need Is Time, 1973; Imagination, 1974; Anthology, 1974; Knight Time, 1974; Claudine, 1974; A Little Knight Music, 1975; I Feel A Song, 1975; 2nd Anniversary, 1975; The Best of Gladys Knight and The Pips, 1976; Pipe Dreams, 1976; Still Together, 1977; 30 Greatest, 1977; The One and Only, 1978; About Love, 1980; A Touch of Love, 1980; Visions, 1983; The Collection: 20 Greatest Hits, 1984; Solo: Good Woman, 1991; Just for You, 1994; Many Different Roads, 1998; At Last, 2000; Hit singles include: I Heard It Through The Grapevine (No. 2, USA), 1967; If I Were Your Woman, 1971; Help Me Make It Through The Night, 1972; The Look of Love, 1973; Neither One of Us (Wants To Be The First To Say Goodbye) (No. 2, USA), 1973; Midnight Train To Georgia (No. 1, USA), 1973; I've Got To Use My Imagination, 1974; Best Thing That Ever Happened To Me, 1974; On and On, 1974; The Way We Were, 1975; Baby Don't Change Your Mind, 1977; Bourgie Bourgie, 1980; That's What Friends Are For, with Elton John, Stevie Wonder and Dionne Warwick (No. 1, USA), 1985; Licence To Kill, 1989. *Current Management:* Newman Management Inc, 2110 E Flamingo Rd, Suite 300, Las Vegas, NV 89119, USA.

KNIGHT, Holly; b. 24 Sept. 1956, New York, NY, USA. Songwriter; Prod; Musician (keyboards, piano). m. Michael Whitis-Knight, 24 March 1990, 2 s. *Education:* Classical piano, age 4–14 years. *Career:* Member, Spider, 2 albums; Member, Device, album 1989; Have written many hits and film songs. *Compositions include:* for Pat Benatar: Love Is A Battlefield; Invincible; Sometimes The Good Guys Finish First; for Tina Turner: Better Be Good To Me; One of The Living; The Best; Ask Me How I Feel; Love Thing; Be Tender With Me Baby; You Can't Stop Me Loving You; for Heart: Never; All Eyes; There's The Girl; Tall Dark Handsome Stranger; I Love You; Love Touch, Rod Stewart; Ragdoll, Aerosmith; Change, John Waite; The Warrior, Patti Smyth; Stick To Your Guns, Bon Jovi; Space, Cheap Trick; Pleasure and Pain, the Divinyls; Soul Love, Hall and Oates; Baby Me, Chaka Khan; Just Between You and Me, Lou Gramm; Hide Your Heart, Bonnie Tyler; Turn It On, Kim Wilde; Stiletto, Lita Ford; Hide Your Heart, Kiss; Try A Little Harder, Aaron Neville; It's Over When The Phone Stops Ringing, Patsy Kensit; Wrap Your Arms Around Me, Agnetha Falkstog; Time Waits For No-One, Dusty Springfield; Between Two Fires, Jimmy Barnes; Slow Burn, Ozzy Osbourne; Tracks for: solo album; Spider; Device; A Night In Heaven film soundtrack (with Michael Desbarres). *Recordings:* Albums include: with Spider: Spider; Between The Lines; with Device: 22B3; Solo: Holly Knight, 1989; Knightworks, 1997. *Honours:* 3 Grammy Awards, Best Rock Vocal, Better Be Good To Me; Love Is A Battlefield; One of The Living. *Membership:* ASCAP; Songwriters Guild.

KNIGHT, Larry, (Fuzzy); b. 21 Oct. 1950, St Louis, Missouri, USA. Musician (bass); Vocalist; Songwriter. m. Aleda Trabue, 26 Oct. 1974, 1 d. *Education:* 3 years college; One year St Louis Conservatory of Music. *Career:* Played with: Albert King; Chuck Berry; Little Milton; Ike Turner, 1964–69; Tim Rose; Delaney-Bonnie and Friends; Peter Kaukenon, 1969–73; Albert Collins, Spirit, 1971–80; The Urge, 1985; Bandleader, Bassist and Lead Vocalist, Blowin' Smoke, R&B band, 1994–2000; Tours world-wide over 12 years; Appeared on many US rock shows, also Old Grey Whistle Test, England; Rock Palace, Germany; Recorded over 26 albums; 1 live Spirit album produced by Miles Copeland, Rainbow Theatre, London. *Recordings:* Tim Rose; Delaney-Bonnie and Friends; 6 Spirit albums; Peter Kaukenon; Albert Collins; The Urge; Albert Lee; Kaptain Kopter and The Famous Twirlybirds; Randy California; Beyond The Blues Horizon, with The Blowin' Smoke Rhythm and Blues Band, CD, 1999; Deborah Gibson, 2000. *Honours:* Gold disc for Spirit. *Membership:* NAMM; VSDA; Musicians' Union. *Current Management:* Lawrence Weisberg, Blowin' Smoke Management and Bookings. *Address:* 7438 Shoshone Ave, Van Nuys, CA 91406–2340, USA.

KNOPFLER, David; b. 27 Dec. 1952, Glasgow, Scotland. Musician (Guitar). *Career:* Former Social Worker; Member, Dire Straits; Obtained major label record deal and subsequent management contract; Support slot on tour with Talking Heads; Numerous headlining tours and TV appearances; Left band, 1980. *Recordings:* Singles: Sultans of Swing, 1978; Lady Writer, 1979; Romeo and Juliet, 1980; Making Movies, 1980; Albums: Dire Straits, 1978; Communiqué, 1979; Making Movies, 1980; Money For Nothing (compilation) (No. 1, UK), 1988; Sultans of Swing: The Best Of, 1998.

KNOPFLER, Mark; b. 12 Aug. 1949, Glasgow, Scotland. Musician (guitar); Vocalist; Songwriter; Record Prod. m. Lourdes Salomone, Nov. 1983, 2 s. *Education:* English Graduate. *Career:* Former journalist, Yorkshire Evening Post; Mem., Brewer's Droop; Café Racers; Founder mem., Dire Straits, 1977–88, 1991–; World-wide concerts and tours, 1978–; Major concerts include: San Remo Song Festival, Italy, 1981; Live Aid, Wembley, 1985; Prince's Trust Rock Gala, Wembley, 1986; Nelson Mandela 70th Birthday Tribute, 1988; Guitarist and vocalist, Eric Clapton US tour, 1988; Nordoff-Robbins charity concert, Knebworth Park, 1990. *Compositions include:* Private Dancer, Tina Turner, 1985; Setting Me Up, Waylon Jennings, 1984; Money For Nothing (with Sting), 1985; Water of Love, The Judds, 1989; Film music: Local Hero, 1983; Cal, 1984; The Princess Bride, 1987; Last Exit to Brooklyn, 1989; Metroland, 1998; Wag the Dog, 1998; A Shot at Glory, 2001. *Recordings:* Albums: with Dire Straits: Dire Straits, 1978; Communiqué, 1979; Making Movies, 1980; Love Over Gold (No. 1, UK), 1982; Extendedanceplay, 1983; Alchemy: Dire Straits Live, 1984; Brothers In Arms (No. 1, 20 countries), 1985; Money For Nothing (No. 1, UK), 1988; On Every Street (No. 1, UK), 1991; On The Night, 1993; Live at the BBC, 1995; Sultans of Swing,

1998; with Chet Atkins: Neck and Neck, 1990; with Notting Hillbillies: Missing… Presumed Having a Good Time, 1990; Solo: Comfort and Joy, 1984; Golden Heart, 1996; Sailing To Philadelphia, 2001; The Ragpicker's Dream, 2002; Contribution to: Screenplaying, 1993. Hit singles: with Dire Straits: Sultans of Swing, 1979; Romeo and Juliet, 1981; Tunnel of Love, 1981; Private Investigations (No. 2, UK), 1982; Twisting By The Pool, 1983; So Far Away, 1985; Money For Nothing (first video shown on MTV Europe) (No. 1, USA), 1985; Brothers In Arms (first-ever CD single), 1985; Walk of Life (No. 2, UK), 1986; Your Latest Trick, 1986; Calling Elvis, 1991; On Every Street, 1992; Solo: Going Home (theme from film Local Hero), 1983; Darling Pretty, 1996; Why Aye Man, 2002; Guest on albums including: Slow Train Coming, Bob Dylan, 1979; Solo In Soho, Phil Lynott, 1980; Gaucho, Steely Dan, 1980; Beautiful Vision, Van Morrison, 1982; The Phil Lynott Album, 1982; Boys and Girls, Bryan Ferry, 1985; Down In The Groove, Bob Dylan, 1988; The Shouting Stage, Joan Armatrading, 1988; Land of Dreams, Randy Newman, 1988; As producer: Infidels, Bob Dylan, 1984; Knife, Aztec Camera, 1984; Human, Rod Stewart, 2000. *Honours:* Ivor Novello Awards: Outstanding British Lyric, 1983; Best Film Theme, 1984; Outstanding Contribution to British Music, 1989; Nordoff-Robbins Silver Clef Award, Outstanding Services To British Music, 1985; BRIT Awards: Best British Group, 1983, 1986; Best British Album, 1987; Grammy Awards: Best Rock Performance, Money For Nothing, 1986; Best Country Performance, with Chet Atkins, 1986, 1991; Hon. music doctorate, University of Newcastle Upon Tyne, 1993. *Address:* c/o Terry Kilburn, Mark Knopfler News, PO Box 5900, Matlock DE4 2YY, England. *Website:* www.mark-knopfler.com.

KNORR, Marianne; b. 3 Feb. 1949, Copenhagen, Denmark. Folk Vocalist; Musician (guitar); Actress. m. Preben Friis, 13 May 1989, 2 s. *Education:* Danish State Theatre School, 4 years; Studied voice with Jens Chr Schmidt for 12 years. *Career:* Has appeared at Rimfaxe Theatre, Skagen Festival, Roskilde Festival, in Radio concerts and on Television; Concerts in Denmark, Norway, Sweden, Iceland and Greenland. *Recordings:* 4 Solo albums: Valmuer Og Jernbeton, Sa Laenge Fuglene Flyver, Sange Af Brecht, and Sommerregn. *Membership:* Danish Actors' Asscn; Danish Society of Jazz and Beat Authors. *Address:* Strandvejen 138, 5600 Faaborg, Denmark.

KNOWLES, Beyoncé; b. 4 Sept. 1981, Houston, TX, USA. Vocalist; Songwriter; Prod. *Career:* Founding mem., GirlsTyme vocal group, 1989, with Kelly Rowland, later joined by LaTavia Roberson and LeToya Luckett; Group renamed Something Fresh then The Dolls before settling on Destiny's Child; Signed to Columbia Records, 1996; Numerous TV appearances, including Tonight Show, Donnie & Marie, Regis & Kathie Lee, Rosie O'Donnell; Live performances include: Soul Train Awards; Tour with Christina Aguilera, 2000; United We Stand concert, USA, 2001; Lead role in MTV's Hip Hopera, Carmen, 2001; Played Foxy Cleopatra in film Austin Powers in Goldmember, 2002; Appearance, film The Fighting Temptations, 2003; Simultaneous solo career, 2001–. *Recordings:* Albums: with Destiny's Child: Destiny's Child, 1998; The Writing's On The Wall, 1999; Survivor, 2001; Eight Days Of Christmas, 2001; This Is The Remix, 2002; Solo: Soul Survivors, 2002. Singles: No No No (with Wyclef Jean), 1997; With Me (with Timbaland), 1998; She's Gone (with Matthew Marsden), 1998; Get On The Bus (from film Why Do Fools Fall in Love), 1999; Bills Bills Bills (No. 1, USA), 1999; Bug-A-Boo (No. 1, USA), 1999; Say My Name (No. 1, USA), 2000; Jumpin' Jumpin', 2000; Independent Women (from film Charlie's Angels, No. 1, UK, USA), 2000; Survivor, 2001; Bootylicious, 2001; Emotion, 2001; Eight Days Of Christmas, 2001; Contributions to film soundtracks, including Men In Black, Romeo Must Die, Life. *Honours:* Billboard Awards, Artist of the Year, Group of the Year, Hot 100 Singles Artist of the Year, Hot 100 Group of the Year, 2000; American Music Awards, Favorite Soul/R&B Group, 2001, Favorite Pop/Rock Album, for Survivor, Favorite Pop/Rock Band, Duo or Group, 2002; Grammy Awards, Best R&B Song, for Say My Name, Best R&B Performance by a Duo or Group with Vocal, for Say My Name, 2001; NAACP Image Award for Outstanding Duo or Group, for Say My Name, 2001; Best R&B Video MTV Video Award, for Say My Name, 2001; Sammy Davis Jr Award for Entertainer of the Year, Soul Train Awards, 2001; BRIT Award, Best International Group, 2002; 13 Gold, Platinum and multi-Platinum Awards. *Current Management:* Mathew Knowles. *Address:* c/o Mathew Knowles, Music World Entertainment, 9898 Bissonnet, Suite 625, Houston, TX 77036, USA. *Website:* www.destinyschild.com.

KNOX, (Ian Milroy Carnochan); b. 4 Sept. 1945, London, England. Vocalist; Musician (guitar, keyboards). *Career:* Lead singer, songwriter, The Vibrators; Solo artiste, 1983; Singer, songwriter, The Fallen Angels; Member, Urban Dogs. *Recordings:* with The Vibrators: 11 studio albums; Solo album, 1983; with The Fallen Angels: 3 studio albums; with Urban Dogs: 2 studio albums; with Die Toten Hosen: Baby, Baby; Troops of Tomorrow. *Honours:* Gold disc, Baby, Baby (Germany). *Membership:* PRS; MCPS.

KNOX, Keith; b. 1933, Belper, Derbyshire, England. Record Co Exec; Record Prod; Music Journalist. *Education:* Southampton University; Brighton College of Advanced Technology. *Career:* Served with Royal Air Force, 1955–57; Record producer, various recording companies including: Caprice; Storyville; Sonet; WEA; Universal Folk Sounds; Album sleeve note writer; Founder, Executive Producer, own jazz label Silkheart Records, Sweden, 1986–.

Recordings: Artistes on own label include Steve Lacy; Charles Gayle; David S Ware; Dennis Gonzalez; Matthew Shipp; Booker T Williams; Assif Tsahar; Jim Hobbs; Dennis Charles; Joel Futterman; Alvin Fielder; Rob Brown. *Publications:* Author, Jazz Amour Affair (The Lars Gullin Story); Contributor, jazz magazines including: Jazz Monthly; Jazz Forum (International Jazz Federation magazine); Jazznews; Articles include: The Parametric Music of Terry Riley, 1967; Relax and Fully Concentrate: The Music of Terry Riley; Terry Riley: This is Our Period. *Address:* Silkheart Records, Dalagatan 33, 113 23 Stockholm, Sweden.

KNUCKLES, Frankie; b. 18 Jan. 1955, South Bronx, New York City, USA. Prod; Remixer; DJ. *Career:* DJ at The Warehouse in Chicago USA (club associated with the birth of House music); Remixed: Alison Limerick, Lisa Stansfield, Janet Jackson, Luther Vandross, Sounds of Blackness, Michael Jackson, Chaka Khan; Member of Def Mix crew (alongside David Morales and Satoshi Tomiie); Collaborations: Jamie Principle, Satoshi Tomiie. *Recordings:* Albums: Frankie Knuckles Presents, 1989; Beyond The Mix, 1991; Welcome To The Real World, 1995; Singles: Waiting On My Angel (with Jamie Principle), 1985; Your Love/Baby Wants To Ride (with Jamie Principle), 1987; Only The Strong Survive, 1988; Tears (with Satoshi Tomiie), 1989; The Whistle Song, 1991; It's Hard Sometimes, 1991; Too Many Fish (with Adeva), 1995; Keep On Movin', 2001. *Current Management:* c/o Def Mix, 928 Broadway, Suite 400, New York, USA.

KNUDSEN, Hans; b. 7 Sept. 1950, Copenhagen, Denmark. Musician (piano); Vocalist; Songwriter. *Education:* College of Education; Guitar lessons, 1960s. *Career:* Former teacher, Music and Biology, 1975–80; Professional musician, 1980–; Worked and toured with leading Danish jazz and blues artists, 1980–83; Member, New Orleans singer Lillian Boutté's band, 1983–90; Leader, own group Hans Knudsen Jumpband, 1990–. *Compositions include:* Music Is My Life, with Lillian Boutté. *Recordings:* with Lillian Boutté: Music Is My Life, 1984; Let Them Talk, 1986; with Hans Knudsen Jumpband: So Long John, 1995; Jump In Focus, 1997. *Address:* Kildebakkegårds Allé 92, 1 tv, 2860 Soborg, Denmark.

KNUDSEN, Karl Emil; b. 16 June 1929, Copenhagen, Denmark. Record Co Owner. *Career:* Founder and Owner, Storyville Records, Sonet; Represents every genre of jazz music; Series, Masters of Jazz, The Blues Masters, The Sounds of New Orleans and recordings of the JAZZPAR Project, 1991–; Includes work of Hank Jones, Tommy Flanagan, Roy Haynes, Tony Coe, Jim Hall; Release of home videos of artistes such as Louis Armstrong, Duke Ellington, Benny Goodman; TV Documentaries, The Mills Brothers Story, The Spike Jones Story; Established book publishing business, Jazz Media. *Publications:* Jazz Records, 1942–80, compiled by Erik Raben; Discographical works on Miles Davis, Ben Webster, Chet Baker, Duke Ellington. *Address:* Dortheavej 39, Copenhagen, 2700, Denmark.

KNUDSEN, Kenneth; b. 28 Sept. 1946, Copenhagen, Denmark. Composer; Musician (keyboard). m. Christine Heger, 22 March 1987, 1 s. *Education:* Architect, Royal Danish Academy of Fine Arts. *Career:* Member of jazz/fusion groups: Coronarias Dans, 1969; Secret Oyster, 1976; Anima, 1979; Heart To Heart Trio, 1986; Bombay Hotel, 1988; Special project with Jan Akkerman and Jon Hiseman, 1982; Numerous concerts and television in Scandinavia, Europe, UK, Hong Kong and Japan. *Compositions:* Film scores; Ballet music for New Danish Dance Theatre and The Royal Danish Ballet; Works for string quartet, cello, piano, choir and electronics; Prizewinning commercials for Carlsberg Breweries. *Recordings:* I Me Him, 1989; Compacked, 1989; Sounds and Silence, 1994; Appeared on more than 100 records including Garland, Svend Asmussen and L. Subramaniam; It Could Happen To You, Jan Akkerman; Entrance, Heart To Heart, with Palle Mikkelborg; Pictures and Heart To Heart with Niels Henning Orsted Pedersen; Aura, Miles Davis; Anima, Kenneth Knudsen; Music For Eyes, CD, 1998; Light and Metal, CD, 1998; Diamond, Miniatures, 2002. *Honours:* Jazz Musician of the Year, 1973; Niels Matthiasen Memorial Grant, 1987; Danish Art Foundation Grant, 1992–94; Lifelong Grant from the Danish Art Foundation, 1998. *Membership:* Danish Composers Society. *Address:* PO Box 51, 2840 Holte, Denmark.

KNUDSEN, Marius Dahl; b. 30 June 1947, Grinsted, Denmark. Musician (guitars, didgeridoo). m. Lise Jelsbech Knudsen, 14 July 1979, 2 s., 1 d. *Education:* Classical Guitar, Degree in Music Teaching. *Career:* Member, Ostjydsk Musikforsyning, 20 years; Danish show-band with numerous appearances on national TV and radio; Stage: Arhus Teater: Rocky Horror Show; Return to the Forbidden Planet; Vejle Teater: Folk Og Rovere; Dansk Spildtid: Elverhoj. *Recordings:* Det Beskidte Dusin; Århus Syncopaterne. *Honours:* Hon. Mem., Danish Musicians' Union, Arets Revykomponist, 1996. *Membership:* Danish Musicians' Union. *Current Management:* Ostjydsk Musikforsyning, Ved Kirken 2, 8320 Marslet, Denmark. *Address:* Langballeves 44, 8320 Marslet, Denmark.

KNUDSEN, Ole; b. 15 Sept. 1943, Koge, Denmark. Music Teacher; Multi-instrumentalist; Vocalist; Composer. *Education:* Music Teacher, Teacher training school, 1970. *Career:* Jazz drummer, 1965–70; Lead singer, guitarist, pianist, percussionist, Danish jazz-rock group: Fujara, 1970–76; Performances: Roskilde Festival, 1971–75; Leader, Arbejdersanggruppen,

1976–82; Freelance jazz-drummer, teacher, 1982–. *Recordings:* Fujara, 1973; Nattevandring, 1977; Jens Borges Fodselsdag (children's songs), 1979; Hvor Laenge Skal Vi Vente, 1980; Det Handler Om Kaerlighed, (solo) 1992. *Honours:* LO (Danish Organization of Labour) Culture Prize, Arbejdersanggruppen, 1981. *Membership:* Danish Jazz Musicians' Organization; Danish Jazz Beat Folk Music Authors.

KNUTSEN, Cecilie; b. 9 May 1967, Trondheim, Norway. Vocalist. *Education:* Conservatory of Music, Oslo, 3 years; Conservatory of Music, Århus, Denmark, 3 years. *Career:* TV Norway, national, 1982; TV Norway, national, 1984, 1995, 1997; TV Denmark, national, 1993; Toured with Deepak Chopra, Louise Hay, Wayne Dyer and Stuart Wilde. *Recordings:* Voice of the Feminine Spirit, 1994; Violet 19, 1996. *Honours:* Gold Album, England. *Membership:* Gramart. *Current Management:* Eivind Brydoy, Artist Partner as Grini Naering Sparn 17, 1345, Osteraas, Norway.

KOITÉ, Habib; b. 1958, Bamako, Mali. Vocalist; Musician (acoustic guitar, flute); Songwriter. *Education:* National Institute of Arts (INA), Bamako, degree (graduated first in class), 1982. *Career:* Born to a griot family; Music teacher at the INA; Sang and played on Toumani Diabate's Shake the World, 1991; Formed Bamada, 1988; Hit single Cigarette Abana; Recorded first album, 1994; Became a regular on the European festival scene; Toured USA with the Voices of Mali tour, 2000. *Recordings:* Albums; Muso Ko, 1994; Ma Ya, 1998; Baro, 2001. *Honours:* Voxpole Festival in France, first prize, 1991; Radio France International Discoveries Prize, 1994; Kora Award, Best Artist–West Africa, 2002. *Address:* c/o Putumayo World Music, 324 Lafayette St, Seventh Floor, New York, NY 10012, USA. *Website:* www.putumayo.com.

KOIVISTOINEN, Eero; b. 13 Jan. 1946, Finland. Composer; Musician (tenor, soprano saxophone). *Education:* Sibelius Academy, Helsinki, 1968–70, 1973–74; Berklee College of Music, Boston, USA, 1971–73. *Career:* Leader, own quartet; Performed at international jazz competition, Montreux, Switzerland, 1969; Newport Festival, USA; Founder, composer, arranger for UMO (New Music Orchestra), 1975–; Leader, Dialog, 1995–; Established PRO Records Label, 1983; Teaching, 1980s. *Compositions include:* Ballet, Mother Earth, 1979; Suite, Ultima Thule, represented Finland in Nordring radio competition, 1981. *Recordings:* 16 solo albums, Later albums include Pictures In Three Colours (with John Scofield and Jack DeJohnette); Ultima Thule, UMO; Dialog, 1995. *Honours:* First recipient, Yrjö (Georgie) Award, Finnish Jazz Federation, 1967; Best Jazz Ensemble, Montreux Festival, 1969; Best Arranger, Nordring radio competition, Jersey, 1981. *Address:* Lapinlahdenk 21 A 11, 00180 Helsinki, Finland.

KOJIMA, Ian (Koko); b. 28 Dec. 1951, Toronto, Canada. Musician (saxophone, Acoustic, electric guitars, keyboards); Composer (filmscores). m. Anne Peters, 11 Nov. 1977, 1 s. *Education:* 2 years, University of Toronto, Arts; 2 years, Humber College (composition, theory, improvisation. *Career:* Saxophonist for Stampedes, Ken Tobias; Multi-instrumentalist for: Chris De Burgh; Peter Hoffman; David Hasselhoff. *Recordings:* Chris De Burgh: Live In Dublin; Man on the Line; Into the Light; High on Emotion; Filmscore: Circus On The Moon (composer, musician, actor). *Contributions to:* Canadian Music. *Membership:* Toronto MA; British MU. *Current Management:* Ken Thompson Management, Redhead Touring. *Address:* Thornhill, Ontario, Canada.

KOKKAS, Vassilios; b. 30 Sept. 1965, Athens, Greece. Composer. *Education:* Piano, Flute, Harmony, Counterpoint, Orchestration, Composition, The Hochschule Der Kunste, 1990–96. *Publications:* Navigation In Metamorphosis: Navigable Music, 1996. *Membership:* German Society For Musical Rights; DEGEM. *Current Management:* Institute For Research In Music and Acoustics, 105 Adrianou St, Athens. *Address:* Manteuffelstr 68, D 10999 Berlin, Germany.

KOLLOWRAT, Peter; b. 5 March 1967, Vienna, Austria. Musician (guitar). m. Birgit Kollowrat, 29 Oct. 1994. *Education:* Salzburger Musik-Schulwerk; Diploma, MA, Mozarteum, Salzburg, 1996; Studied guitar with J. Clerch and Eliot Fisk; Masterclasses with F. Bungartem, L. Brouwer, A. Pierri and S. Isbin. *Career:* Concerts in Italy, Belgium, Germany and Austria; Soloist with Halleiner Chamber Orchestra. *Recordings:* Jason und die Argonauten!!: Live in Riff-Cafe, 1996; CD with Eliot Fisk and Friends, 1999. *Honours:* Premio di Musica Cesare Grigoletto, 1997; Medal of the President of Italy, 1997. *Address:* Trautmannstr 6A, 5020 Salzburg, Austria.

KOMPPA, Kari; b. 5 Jan. 1939, Helsinki, Finland. Composer; Musician (tenor saxophone). *Career:* Jazz session saxophonist, band leader, television conductor/arranger, YLE/TV2, Tampere; Founder, leader, writer, member, Break Big Band, played Pori Festival, 1970, 1972, 1982, 1984; Writer for Radio (YLE) Jazz Orchestra, the UMO; Founder, leader, composer, member, Tampere Jazz Orchestra, 1981–84; Represented Finnish Broadcasting Company (YLE), throughout Europe, including Nordring Festival, Belgium; Teacher, Big Band leader, Tampere Conservatory of Music; EBU Jazz Concert, Pori; Saxophonist, writer for Ippe Kätkä Band, 1980s; Teacher, Sibelius Academy Jazz Department, Helsinki; Currently (from the end of 1980s) withdrawn from active public performance and teaching; Still occasionally writing for UMO Jazz Orchestra and Radio (YLE); Formed Zone, (an association of forefront Finnish jazz composers), 1991; Jazz and Electronic compositions for Zone. *Compositions include*: Aldebaran, 1977; Tethys, 1981; Free Aspects, 1981; Protoscope, 1991; First Definition, 1994; Tampere Jazz Orchestra; Ippe Kätkä Band; Music for Radio Jazz Orchestra and UMO. *Recordings*: LPs: Makumoka; Ippe Kätkä Band; CDs: Nordjazz Big 5; Umo Jazz Orchestra, 1997; Zone: First Definition, 1999; Also: arranger of John Coltrane's composition, Untitled Original, on Dave Liebman CD, Joy. *Honours*: Winner (with Break Big Band), Finnish Big Band championship, 1973; Winner, EBU orchestral composition contest, Tethys, 1981; Yrjö (Georgie) Award, Finnish Jazz Federation, 1982. *Membership*: Teosto RY; Elvis RY; Zone RY. *Address*: Martinlaaksontie 40 F 39, 01629 Vantaa, Finland.

KONTÉ, Mamadou; b. June 1945, Tambacunda, Senegal. Music Dir, Concert Organizer. 1 s. *Career*: Founder, Director, Africa Fete Festival, Paris, 1979–; USA, 1993–; Dakar, Senegal, West Africa, 1993–. *Honours*: Chevalier des Arts et des Lettres, France. *Membership*: Vice-President, de Zoue Franche. *Address*: Africa Fete, 29 Wagane Diouf, Dakar; 29 rue Gerna'n Pilou 75010, Paris, France.

KOOPER, Al; b. 5 Feb. 1944, Brooklyn, New York, USA. Musician (keyboards); Vocalist; Songwriter; Prod. *Career*: Guitarist, The Royal Teens, 1959; Session musician with artistes including: Tom Rush, Peter Paul and Mary, New York; Member, The Blues Project, 1966–67; Concerts include: Monterey International Pop Festival, 1967; Founder member, Blood Sweat and Tears, 1967–68; Producer at Columbia Records; Solo artiste; Established own record label, Sounds of The Earth (acts included Lynyrd Skynyrd); Founder, Sweet Magnolia, 1970s; Recording artiste, computerised soundtrack music. *Compositions*: with Bobby Brass and Irwin Levine include: This Diamond Ring, Gary Lewis and The Playboys; I Must Be Seeing Things, Gene Pitney; The Water Is Over My Head, The Rocking Berries. *Recordings*: Albums with The Blues Project: Projections, 1966; Live At Town Hall, 1967; with Blood Sweat and Tears: The Child Is Father To The Man, 1968; Solo albums: Super Session (with Mike Bloomfield and Stephen Stills), 1968; The Live Adventures of Al Kooper and Mike Bloomfield, 1969; I Stand Alone, 1969; You Never Know Who Your Friends Are, 1969; Kooper Session, 1970; Easy Does It, 1970; Landlord, 1971; New York City (You're A Woman), 1971; A Possible Projection of the Future, 1972; Naked Songs, 1973; Act Like Nothing's Wrong, 1976; Four on the Floor, 1979; Championship Wrestling, 1982; Rekooperation, 1994; Soul of a Man, 1995; Kooper Sessions, 1999; Guest musician with Bob Dylan: Highway 61 Revisited, 1965; Blonde On Blonde, 1966; New Morning, 1970; Under The Red Sky, 1990; Also featured on: Electric Ladyland, Jimi Hendrix, 1968; Let It Bleed, Rolling Stones, 1969; Producer, recordings by Nils Lofgren; Don Ellis; The Tubes; Green On Red. *Publications*: Backstage Pass, Al Kooper.

KOOYMANS, George; b. 11 March 1948, The Hague, Netherlands. Vocalist; Musician (guitar). *Career*: Founder member, Dutch rock group Golden Earring, 1961–; Tours, Europe; Canada; USA; Support to The Who, European tour, 1972; Support to Rush, 1982. *Recordings*: Albums: with Golden Earring: Just Earrings, 1965; Winter Harvest, 1966; Miracle Mirror, 1968; On The Double, 1969; Eight Miles High, 1969; Golden Earring, 1970; Seven Tears, 1971; Together, 1972; Moontan, 1973; Switch, 1975; To The Hilt, 1976; Contraband, 1976; Golden Earring Live, 1977; Grab It For A Second, 1978; No Promises, No Debts, 1979; Prisoner Of The Night, 1980; 2nd Live, 1981; Cut, 1982; N.E.W.S., 1984; Something Heavy Goin' Down, 1984; The Hole, 1986; Keeper Of The Flame, 1989; The Complete Singles Collection 1975–91, 1991; Bloody Buccaneers, 1991; The Naked Truth, 1992; Face It, 1995; Lovesweat, 1995; Naked II, 1997; The Complete Naked Truth, 1998; Paradise In Distress, 1999; Last Blast Of The Century, 2000; The Devil Made Us Do It, 2000; Numerous compilation albums; Solo: Jojo, 1972; Solo, 1987. *Current Management*: Rob Gerritsen, Wingerd 38, 2496 VC Den Haag, Netherlands. *Telephone*: (15) 380-55-88. *Fax*: (15) 380-55-91.

KOPECKY, Ladislav; b. 8 April 1944, Prague, Czech Republic. Musician (trombone). 2 d. *Education*: Economics, Faculty of International Trade, Charles University, Prague. *Career*: Mem., different bands; Songwriter (lyrics); More than 60 songs broadcast by Czech television and radio; Co-operation with singer and songwriter, Petr Ulrych. *Compositions*: Pojote Dal (Hana Ulrychova); Mec A Preslice; Ententyny; Bylinky; Musical: Nikola Suhaj the robber. *Recordings*: Songs: Javory (Maple Tree); Jizda Kralu (Ride of the Kings); Trava (Grass); Kridla (Wings); Bylinky (Herbs); Kamen (Stone); Ententyny. *Honours*: Silver Prize, 1976, Golden Prize, 1980, Bratislavska Lyra Festival; Bronze Prize, 1977, Bronze Prize, 1979, Decinska Kotva Festival. *Membership*: OSA. *Address*: Ladislav Kopecky, Ujezd 41, 11800 Prague 1, Czech Republic.

KOPPEL, Anders; b. 17 July 1947, Copenhagen, Denmark. Composer; Musician (organ, piano). m. Ulla Lemvigh-Müller, 11 Aug. 1969, 1 s., 2 d. *Education*: Clarinet and piano lessons. *Career*: Child performer, piano and clarinet; Member, Savage Rose, 1967–74; Member, Bazaar, 1975–; Tours: Europe, USA. *Compositions*: Music for 10 ballets; 200 films and plays; 3 musicals; 1 opera; Piano concerto; Percussion concerto; Marimba concerto; Saxophone concerto; Bass trombone concerto; Flute/Harp concerto; Trio for

saxophone, cello, piano; Trio for violin, cello, piano; Toccata for vibes, marimba and orchestra; String Quartet; Partita for chamber ensemble; Concertino for chamber ensemble; Trio for violin, horn, piano; Duo for two guitars; Portrait for sextet; Trio for three clarinets. *Recordings*: 7 solo albums. *Honours*: Wilhelm Hansen Prize; Danish State Art Foundation Lifelong Award. *Membership*: Danish Composers Asscn. *Current Management*: Wilhelm Hansen, Copenhagen. *Address*: Cæciliavej 70, 2500 Valby, Copenhagen, Denmark.

KOPPEL, Annisette; b. 29 Aug. 1948, Copenhagen, Denmark. Vocalist; Songwriter; Writer. m. Thomas Koppel, 1971, 2 d. *Career*: Numerous tours in Europe, USA, etc; Numerous TV and radio appearances internationally; Newport Jazz Festival, 1969; Montreux Festival and numerous other festivals, 1970–97; Lead character in own musical, Bella Vita, 1997, with Thomas Koppel; Lead Singer, Savage Rose, 1968–. *Compositions*: Numerous songs recorded by Savage Rose, 1968–98; Musical Bella Vita, with Thomas Koppel, 1996–97; Lyrics for Symphonic Compositions by Thomas Koppel. *Recordings*: 19 albums with The Savage Rose; Bella Vita, 1995; Black Angel, 1996; Tameless, 1998–99. *Honours*: Award of Honour, Danish Songwriters' Asscn; Grammy, 1996, 1999; Numerous awards from Trade Unions and Organizations. *Membership*: Danish Artists' Union; DJBFA; KODA; Gramex. *Current Management*: South Harbour Productions. *Address*: 2464 Lindsay Lane, Los Angeles, CA 90039, USA.

KOPPEL, Thomas; b. 24 April 1944, Sweden. Musician (piano); Composer; Prod. m. Annisette Hansen, 1971, 2 s., 2 d. *Education*: Soloist Diploma, Royal Danish Conservatory. *Career*: Debut concert as piano soloist, 1967; Numerous concerts and performances of symphonic works since 7 years of age; Started The Savage Rose, 1967; Numerous international tours and TV and radio appearances since 1968; Newport Festival, 1969; Numerous Scandinavian and European festivals. *Compositions*: Phrases, 1964; Visions Fugitives, 1965; Ouverture Solennelle, 1964; Opera, A Mother's Tale, Royal Theatre, 1964; Ballet, Triumph of Death, TV, Royal Theatre, 1970–73; The Moonchild's Dream, 1991; Symphony No 2, 1995; Musical, Bella Vita, 1996; Musical drama, Mass, 1995; Concerto for soprano, strings and celesta, 1999. *Recordings*: 19 albums with The Savage Rose, 1968–98; Recorder concerto, The Moonchild's Dream, 1994; Ballet, Triumph of Death; Musical drama, Mass, 1995; Bella Vita, 1995. *Honours*: Carl Nielsen Prize, 1965; First Prize, International Composers' Competition, City of Copenhagen 800 Years Anniversary, 1966; Numerous awards from trade unions and organizations; H. C. Lumbye Award, Tivoli Gardens, 1992; Keyboard Player of the Year, 1996; Grammy, 1996. *Membership*: Danish Composers' Asscn; Danish Artists' Union; KODA; NCB; Gramex. *Address*: 2464 Lindsay Lane, Los Angeles, CA 90039, USA.

KORB, Ron; b. 7 Sept. 1961, Scarborough, Ontario, Canada. Musician (flute, keyboards); Vocals. *Education*: Music Bachelor in Performance, University of Toronto; Royal Conservatory of Music. *Recordings*: Tear of The Sun, 1990; Japanese Mysteries, 1993; Flute Traveller, 1994; Behind The Mask, 1995; Taming the Dragon, 1999; Titanic Odyssey, 1999; Persian Arabesque, 2000; Celtic Heartland, 2000. *Honours*: RTHK (radio and television, Hong Kong), Best Original Composition, 1993. *Membership*: AFM; SOCAN. *Current Management*: Humble Dragon Entertainment. *Address*: 48 Pine Ave, Toronto, ON M4E 1M1, Canada.

KORJUS, Tapio; b. 18 June 1950, Pieksamaki, Finland. Man.-Dir. m. Eija Savolainen, 7 Dec. 1984, 1 d. *Education*: Tampere University. *Career*: Founder, Rockadillo Management, 1971; Rockadillo Records and Publishing, 1982; Rockadillo Agency, 1983; Zen Master Records and Publishing, 1993; Finnish Music and Media Happening, 1989. *Recordings*: Appears on: Space Waltz, Pekka Pohjola, 1986. *Membership*: The Finnish Rock Booking Agents' Asscn; Finnish Music Publishers Asscn. *Current Management*: Rockadillo. *Address*: Rockadillo, PO Box 35, 33201 Tampere, Finland.

KORN, Daniel, (The Wolf); b. 23 Feb. 1958, Oak Park, Illinois, USA. Musician (Electric Guitar, Keyboards). *Education*: 4 years of private instruction; Some college training. *Career*: Musician and lead singer in numerous bands; Performances include Kessler's Silver Dome Ballroom. *Recordings*: Numerous songs recorded on independent labels including Mary Show Me Again; Sarah; I Bad; A Christmas Song. *Publications*: Books: How to Rock and Roll, Vols 1 and 2; I, Daniel: The Original Story of the Wolf. *Honours*: Winner of numerous talent shows. *Address*: 901 S Farwell St, 130, Eau Claire, WI 54701, USA.

KOS, Lada; b. 12 Nov. 1944, Zagreb, Croatia. Vocalist; Writer; Composer; Arranger; Musician (violin, guitar, piano). *Education*: Musical Academy for Violin. *Career*: Solo concerts in Barcelona, Paris, Milan, Berlin, Frankfurt, Vienna; Tours to Croatia, Russia, France, Italy, Germany, Austria, Slovenia; TV appearances on RAI, Moscow, St Petersburg, Tallin among others, also on various TV series. *Recordings include*: Zbog Ljubavi; Covjek Covjeku; Igracica Vjetrova; Music for the Theatre includes: B M Koltés, Roberto Zucco, S Sembera, Hodanje Prugom, E Kisevic, Macak u Trapericama, B Jelusic, Slava Voli Hranislava, V Parun, U Cast Darkerke Djevice Orleanske. *Honours*: 23 awards for Best Singer, Writer, Composer and Arranger. *Membership*:

Croatian Composers' Society. *Current Management:* Best Music, Zagreb, Croatia. *Address:* Menceticeva 26, 41000 Zagreb, Croatia.

KOSIORKIEWICZ-KSIEZCKA, Jadwiga; b. 16 March 1945, Lublin, Poland. Musician (piano, guitar). m. Adam Ksiezycki (deceased 1987), 1 s. *Education:* Chemist. *Career:* Pop singer; School organist, for play in church; Composer, poetic lyrics, also sacro-poetry (150 songs, songs for children); Sings in own programme, clubs, churches, for Catholic radio, with poets. *Recordings:* (Own compositions) Christmas songs; Sacro-songs (singer). *Membership:* Polish Authors, Composers; ZAKR; ZAJKS.

KOSVANEC, Svatopluk; b. 2 Jan. 1936, Usti nad Labem, Czech Republic. Musician (Trombone). m. Marie Kosvanec, 30 March 1963, 1 s., 1 d. *Education:* Violin, Secondary music school. *Career:* Film by Vera Chutilova, Kalamita; Musical Festivals of Jazz in Denmark, Norway, 1965, Stuttgart, Germany, 1966, Switzerland, 1967, Poland, 1969, Spain, 1991; Trombone Workshop of Jazz, Prague, 1971, Italy, 1983, San Remo, 1987, Eilat, Israel, 1995. *Recordings:* Radio Big Band Prague; Old Men Play Swing; In Ironplate Pack; Jazz Cellula; Kamil Hala's Big Band; Evro Big Band, Ljubljama. *Publications:* Encyclopaedia of Jazz, Czech Republic, 1997. *Honours:* Jazz Festival, Prorov, 1966, 1967. *Membership:* Radio Big Band; Military Band; National Theatre Big Band. *Address:* Nova 36, Strekov, Usti nad, Labem 40003, Czech Republic.

KOTEK, Josef; b. 11 April 1928, Prague, Czech Republic. Musicologist. 2 s. *Education:* Charles University, Prague. *Career:* Editor, Music Journal, Music Horizon, 1957–61; Academy of Sciences, Institute for Musicology, Prague, 1962–97. *Publications:* Kronika Ceske Synkopy I/II; Dejiny Ceske Popularni Hudby a Zpevu I/II. *Honours:* Prize Czech Radio, 1993; Prize Czech Academy of Sciences, 1994. *Membership:* Asscn of Czech Musicians and Musicologists. *Address:* Severni II/3, 141 00 Prague 4, Czech Republic.

KOTRUBENKO, Viktor; b. 27 Nov. 1948. Composer; Saxophonist. 1 d. *Education:* College of Technology, Electrotechnical Faculty; Clarinet, School of Music, Prague. *Compositions:* Radio Productions Music: Mum, Dad, Sore Made; Film Music: Bohemian Ruby, The Light of Hope, Faul; Music for television serials: Rambles Round Bohemia and Moravia; Ecuador. *Recordings:* The Cat Crawls Through a Hole; Shadow; Virgin Eva; Virgin Bozena and a Little Dog Bobbie; Ballad About a Treefrog or When I Went Water A Little Garden; White Show; Attention Pothole; Accelerate. *Publications:* Secret of the Synthesizers. *Honours:* Prize, Saxophonist, International Jazz Festival, Prague, 1971; Silver Tablet, 1977; Appreciation for Composition, 1977; The Golden Pip, from the Asscn of the Czech Advertising Agencies for the Sound Spot Citizen. *Membership:* Asscn of Composers and Scientists; Vice-Pres., Music-ecological Asscn of the Czech Republic. *Address:* Cerchovska 6, 120 00 Prague 2, Czech Republic. *Website:* www.toleration.cz/kotrubeuko.

KOUYATE, Kandia; b. 1958, Kita, Mali. Vocalist; Songwriter. *Education:* Learned music from parents (father balafon player, mother singer). *Career:* Born into a griot family; Member: The Apollos, in Bamako; Moved to Abidjan and recorded first cassette, 1980; Formed own band including Toumani Diabate, early 1980s. *Recordings:* Albums include: Amary Dou presents Kandia Kouyate, 1985: Project Dabia, 1987; Kita Kan (including Ousmane Kouyate), 1999.

KOVERHULT, Tommy; b. 11 Dec. 1945, Stockholm, Sweden. Musician (tenor and soprano saxophone, flute). m. 17 May 1974, divorced, 4 s., 1 d. *Education:* Franz Schartau's Institute of Commerce, Stockholm. *Career:* Played in cellar clubs, Stockholm, 1960s; Member, Eje Thelin's Group, with festival appearances in Belgium, 1967; Played in study group with musicians from the Bernt Rosengren Quartet and Maffy Falay's SEVDA, 1967; Member of Bernt Rosengren Big Band and Octet; Member, Jan Wallgren's Quintet, including tour of Germany, 1973; Founder, The Tommy Koverhult Quintet, 1980–; Freelance musician, 1989–. *Compositions:* Several by the Tommy Koverhult Quintet. *Recordings:* with Jan Wellgren: Steel Band Rock, 1970; Tommy Koverhult With The Jan Wallgren Quintet, 1973; with the Bernt Rosengren Quartet: Improvisations, 1969; Fly Me To The Sun, 1971; Live In Stockholm, Vols One and Two, 1974; with Lasse Werner: Saxofonsymfoni, 1972; with Maffy Falay and SAVDA: Live At Fregattan, 1973; with own Quintet: Jazz in Sweden '83, 1983; Live At Nefertiti, 1985; Various artistes: Notes From Underground, 1973; with Bernt Rosen Octet: Porgy and Bess, 1996; solo: Tommy Koverhult Plays Evert Taube, 1999, Vol. II, 2002; Tommy Koverhult Plays Kurt Weill, 2000. *Honours:* Golden Disc Award, Orkester Journalen magazine, 1970; Winner, Orkester Journalen/Tonfallet Readers' Poll, 1983. *Address:* Tjustgatan 3, 118 27 Stockholm, Sweden.

KOZLOWSKI, James John, (Koz); b. 7 Sept. 1949, Hartford, Connecticut, USA. Dir Artiste Development. m. Lula Shepard, 11 June 1994. *Education:* BSc, Engineering Management, Boston University, 1971; MBA, Human Behaviour, 1973; 5 years lessons, clarinet, alto, tenor saxophones. *Career:* Managed retail outlet; Started nationally syndicated radio programmes, Rock Around The World and Modern Music; Director of Purchasing, import companies, Peters International, Important Record Distributors; Held

position as Label Director, Production Manager, Director Publicity, Director Creative Marketing, Director Artiste Management for Relativity Records, Maze and Viceroy Music. *Recordings:* Project Co-ordinator, Surfing With The Alien, Joe Satriani; Also for all Viceroy Music acts, including Rattlesnake Guitar: The Music of Peter Green. *Publications:* Writer for Creem; Trouser Press; King Biscuit Times; Various freelance publications. *Honours:* RIAA Gold, Platinum records for Surfing With The Alien, Joe Satriani. *Address:* 230 E 44th St #5G, New York, NY 10017, USA.

KRALL, Diana; b. 16 Nov. 1966, Nanaimo, British Columbia, Canada. Vocals; Musician (piano); Composer. *Career:* Began classical piano, aged 4; First gig playing piano in local restaurant, aged 15; Won Vancouver Jazz Festival scholarship to study at Berklee College in Boston; Won Canada Arts Council grant and relocated to Los Angeles to study with Jimmy Rowles; Moved to New York City, playing the night club circuit, 1990; Recorded first album for Montréal label Justin Time Records, 1993; Signed to GRP/Impulse/ Verve, 1994; Regular tours of North America, Britain, Europe and the Far East. *Recordings:* Steppin' Out, 1993; Only Trust Your Heart, 1995; All For You, 1995; Love Scenes, 1997; When I Look In Your Eyes, 1999; The Look Of Love, 2001; features on soundtracks: Midnight In The Garden of Good and Evil; True Crime. *Honours:* Grammy Award, Best Jazz Vocal, When I Look In Your Eyes, 1999; Gold disc, for The Look Of Love. *Current Management:* S L Feldman and Associates, Stephen Macklam and Sam Feldman, 1505 W Second Ave, Suite 200, Vancouver, BC V6H 3Y4, Canada. *Website:* www.dianakrall.com.

KRAMER; b. 30 Nov. 1958, New York, NY, USA. Songwriter; Record Prod; Record Label Owner; Performer. m. Shannon, 30 Aug. 1982, 1 d. *Education:* Classical organ and singer. *Career:* Founded/performed in: Gong, 1979; The Chadbournes, 1980–82; The Fugs, 1982–84; Shockabilly, 1982–85; Butthole Surfers, 1985; Half Japanese, 1986–88; BALL, 1987–90; Bongwater, 1987–91; Ween, 1990; Captain Howdy (with Penn Jillette), 1993–; Founder, 3 record labels: Shimmy-Disc, 1987; Kokopop, 1990; Strangelove, 1994. *Recordings:* Albums: Guilt Trip, 1992; Secret of Comedy, 1994; Let Me Explain, 1998; Songs from the Pink Death, 1998; Producer for: Palace Songs; New Radiant Storm Kings; Galaxie 500; White Zombie; King Missile; GWAR; Low; Urge Overkill, including track Girl You'll Be A Woman Soon, from Pulp Fiction soundtrack; Maureen Tucker; Daniel Johnston; Jon Spenser; Dogbowl; John Zorn. *Current Management:* Steve Moir, Santa Monica, California.

KRAMER, Billy J, (William Howard Ashton); b. 19 Aug. 1943, Bootle, Lancashire, England. Vocalist; Musician (guitar). *Career:* Guitarist, The Phantoms; Singer, The Coasters; Signed by manager Brian Epstein, 1963; Singer with backing group, The Dakotas, 1963–68; Regular British tours; Appearances include: Star Club, Hamburg, Germany; Mersey Beat Showcase concert, with The Beatles, Gerry and The Pacemakers, 1963; The Beatles Christmas Show, London, 1963; NME Poll Winners Concert, Wembley, with The Beatles, Cliff Richard and the Shadows, Rolling Stones, 1964; Played for HRH Queen Mother, 1964; British Song Festival, 1965; Star Scene 65 tour, with the Everlys, Cilla Black, 1965; Solo career, club tours, 1968–; Appearances include: British Re-Invasion US tour, 1973; Solid Silver Sixties Show tour, with the Searchers, Gerry and The Pacemakers, 1993. *Recordings:* Albums: Listen To Billy J Kramer, 1963; Little Children, 1964; Best of Billy J Kramer and the Dakotas, 1993; Singles include: with The Dakotas: Do You Want To Know A Secret? (No. 2, UK), 1963; Bad To Me (No. 1, UK), 1963; I'll Keep You Satisfied, 1963; Little Children (No. 1, UK), 1964; From A Window, 1964; It's Gotta Last Forever, 1965; Trains and Boats and Planes, 1965. *Honours:* Melody Maker Poll Winner, Best Newcomer, 1963. *Current Management:* Barry Collings Entertainments. *Address:* 21a Clifton Rd, Southend-on-Sea, Essex SS1 1AB, England.

KRAMER, Eddie; b. South Africa. Prod; Engineer; Musician (piano, cello, violin). *Education:* South African College of Music. *Career:* Joined Pye Studios, 1964; Established KPS Studios, 1965, later part of Regent Sound; Joined Olympic Sound Studios; Joined Record Plant, New York, 1968; Independent Prod., 1969–70; Recorded Woodstock festival, later many live concerts and festivals; Established Electric Lady Studios, Dir of Engineering, 1970–74; Independent Prod., Prod. for Kiss, 1975–; Numerous press tours; Dir, The Making of Electric Lady Land (documentary film, BBC), 1997; Product development work with numerous companies; Established Kramer Archives with Peter Kavanaugh, company exhibiting and selling limited-edition photographs of artistes; Exhibition, From the Other Side of the Glass, installed at the Rock and Roll Hall of Fame, 2002; Worked with: Ace Frehley, Alcatraz, Angel, Anthrax, Bad Company, The Beatles, Big Sugar, Havana Black, David Bowie, The Chrysalids, Petula Clark, Joe Cocker, Vince Converse, Sammy Davis Jr, Clayton Denwood, Derek and The Dominoes, Fair Verona, Fastway, Peter Frampton, The Gabe Dixon Band, Jimi Hendrix, Lena Horne, The Jewel Thieves, The Kinks, Kiss, Led Zeppelin, Loudness, John Mayall, Curtis Mayfield, Wilson Pickett, Raven, The Rolling Stones, Santana, Seven Sisters, Carly Simon, Traffic, Triumph, Robin Trower, Twisted Sister, Vanilla Fudge, Dionne Warwick, Whitesnake, Johnny Winter. *Publications:* Hendrix: Setting the Record Straight (with John McDermott); Jimi Hendrix Sessions (contributing ed.), 1995; Adventures in Modern Recording (video); From the Other Side of the Glass (photographs). *Membership:* Mem., Advisory

Board of Dirs, Mars Music Stores. *E-mail:* info@kramerarchives.com. *Website:* www.kramerarchives.com.

KRAUSS, Alison; b. 23 July 1971, Champaign, Illinois, USA. Vocalist; Bluegrass Musician (fiddle). *Career:* Singer, musician since age 14; Lead singer with backing band Union Station; 3 British tours. *Recordings:* 6 albums with Union Station; Solo album: Now That I've Found You, 1995; So Long So Wrong, 1997; Forget About It, 1999; New Favorite, 2001; Singles include: Baby Now That I've Found You; When You Say Nothing At All. *Honours:* Grammy Award, 1987; Country Music Television, Rising Star of 1995; 4 CMA Awards: Female Vocalist of the Year; Best New Artist; Vocal Event of the Year; Single of the Year, 1995; Great British Country Music Award: International Female Vocalist of the Year, 1996; Gavin Americana Album of the Year, So Long So Wrong, 1997; Great British Country Music Award: International Bluegrass Band of the Year, 1997–98; Dove Award, 1998; Nashville Music Award, 1998. *Address:* c/o Keith Case and Associates, 1025 17th Ave S, Nashville, TN 37203, USA.

KRAVITZ, Lenny; b. 26 May 1964, New York, USA. Vocalist; Musician (piano, guitar); Songwriter; Record Prod. m. Lisa Bonet, divorced. *Career:* Actor, as teenager; Member, California Boys Choir and Metropolitan Opera; Solo artiste, 1989–; Headline tours, UK, USA and world-wide, 1990–; Concerts include: Support to Bob Dylan, New York, 1990; John Lennon Tribute Shows, Tokyo, 1990; Support to the Cult, Toronto, 1991; On-stage with Prince, New York, 1993; World tour, 1993; Glastonbury Festival, 1993; Torhout and Wechter Festival, 1993; Universal Love Tour, 1993; Television includes: Tonight Show; Arsenio Hall Show; Saturday Zoo; Saturday Night Live; Late Show with David Letterman. *Recordings:* Albums: Let Love Rule, 1989; Mama Said, 1991; Are You Gonna Go My Way (No. 1, UK), 1993; Circus, 1995; 5, 1998; Greatest Hits, 2000; Lenny, 2001; Singles: It Ain't Over Till It's Over (No. 2, USA), 1991; Are You Gonna Go My Way, 1993; Believe, 1993; Heaven Help, 1993; Is There Any Love In Your Heart, 1993; Rock 'n' Roll Is Dead, 1995; Get You Off, 1996; Can't Get You Off My Mind, 1996; I Belong to You, 1998; If You Can't Say No, 1998; Fly Away (No. 1, UK), 1998; American Woman, 1999; Black Velveteen, 1999; Other. *Recordings include:* Use Me, duet with Mick Jagger, Wandering Spirit album, 1993; Film soundtrack, Superfly (with Curtis Mayfield); As producer, songwriter: Be My Baby, Vanessa Paradis, 1992; Justify My Love, Madonna (No. 1, USA); Also as co-writer: Line Up, Aerosmith. *Honours:* BRIT Award, Best International Male, 1994; Grammy Awards, Male Rock Vocal Performance, 2000, 2001; American Music Award, Favourite Pop/Rock Male Artist, 2002. *Address:* c/o Virgin Records America Inc, 338 N Foothill Rd, Beverly Hills, CA 90210, USA. *Website:* www.lennykravitz.com.

KRIEF, Hervé; b. 3 Aug. 1965, Paris, France. Musician (guitar); Vocalist; Composer; Arranger. *Career:* 500 concerts, France and abroad. *Recordings:* Albums: Paris Funk, SAEP, 1988; Comme C'Est Bizarre, SAEP, 1990; Live In Paris, Hervé Krief Big Band, 1991; Barbés Blues, Hervé Krief Blues Trio, 1992; La Dolce Vita, Hervé Krief Big Band, 1994; Paris-Bruxelles, Hervé Krief Blues Trio, 1995; Strong Love Affair, 1996. *Current Management:* Gilles Ouakil, BSM Productions. *Address:* 29 rue Championnet, 75018 Paris, France.

KRIEGER, Robby (Robert Alan); b. 8 Jan. 1946, Los Angeles, CA, USA. Musician (guitar). *Education:* UCLA. *Career:* Mem., The Doors, 1965–72; Mem., The Butts Band, 1972–; Also formed Robbie Krieger and Friends; Versions; Performances include: Northern California Folk-Rock Festival, 1968; Hollywood Bowl, later released as a video, 1968; Toronto Rock 'n' Roll Revival Show, 1969; Isle of Wight Festival, 1970; Annual performances, The Love Ride, benefit for Muscular Dystrophy, 1990; Film documentaries: The Doors Are Open, 1968; Feats of Friends, 1969; Founded, The Doors Music Co, Bright Midnight Records, 1997; With surviving mems of The Doors played, Rock and Roll Hall of Fame, Cleveland, 1993; The Doors VH1 appearance, 2001; The Doors reunion tour, 2002–03. *Recordings:* Albums: The Doors, 1967; Strange Days, 1967; Waiting For The Sun, 1968; Morrison Hotel, 1970; Absolutely Live, 1970; L A Woman, 1971; Other Voices, 1971; Weird Scenes Inside The Gold Mine, 1972; Full Circle, 1972; Best of The Doors, 1973; Live At The Hollywood Bowl, 1987; The Doors Box Set, 1997; Solo: No Habla, 1990; RKO Live, 1995; Versions, 1996. Singles include: Light My Fire (No. 1, USA), 1967; Love Me Two Times, 1968; Hello I Love You (No. 1, USA), 1968; Touch Me, 1969; Love Her Madly, 1971; Riders On The Storm, 1971. *Address:* c/o Bright Midnight Records, Rhino Handmade, PO Box 30620, Tampa, FL 33630-0620, USA. *E-mail:* BMR@thedoors.com. *Website:* www.thedoors.com.

KRISHNAMURTI, Kavita, (Kavita Krishnamurhty Subramaniam); b. Delhi, India. Vocalist. m. L Subramaniam. *Education:* Degree, Economics, St Xaviers College, Mumbai; Began vocal training as a child. *Career:* Indian film playback singer; First recording for a Bengali film song was done with Lata Mangeshkar; First Hindi film under Laxmikant Pyarelal, Maang Bharo Sajna, was followed by Pyar Jhukta Nahin; Other films include: Mr India; Karma; Saudagar; Khuda Gawah; Chaalbaaz; 1942: A Love Story; Yaarana; Mohara; Mumbai; Saaz; Khamoshi; Pardesh; Bhairavi; Agnisakshi; Prem Agan; Kuch Kuch Hota Hai; Bade Miyan Chhote Miyan; Wajood; Has sung more than 1500 songs in Indian films in several languages; Has recorded and performed with internationally famous Indian Classical violinist husband on

several occasions. *Recordings:* soundtracks include: Lovers, 1983; Pyaar Jhukta Nahin, 1984; Chaalbaaz, 1989; Deewana Mujhsa Nahin, Khilaaf, 1990; First Love Letter, Saudagar, 1991; Ek Ladka Ek Ladki, Khiladi, 1992; Aankhen, Boyfriend, Chandramukhi, Dalaal, Darr, Khalnayika, Phool, Sangram, Shreeman Aashique, Waqt Hamara Hai, 1993; 1942: A Love Story, Bombay, Madhosh, Mohra, 1994; Dhanwaan, Kartavya, Milan, Nazar Ke Saamne, Tu Chor Main Sipahi, Vaarana, 1995; Agnisakshi, Chaahat, Dushmani, Jaan, Jeet, Khamoshi The Musical, Papa Kehte Hain, Rajkumar, Tere Mere Sapne, The Great Robbery, 1996; Aar Ya Paar, Betaabi, Ishq, Judwaa, Koyla, Virasat, 1997; Dil Se.., Jeans, Keemat, Kuch Kuch Hota Hai, Prem Aggan, 1998; Dil Kya Kare, Dillagi, Hum Dil De Chuke Sanam, Hum Saath-Saath Hain, Khoobsurat, Mann, Shool, Taal, Vaastav, 1999; Badal, Dil Hi Dil Mein, Hadh Kar Di Aapne, Hera Pheri, Kya Kehna, Mela, Pukar, 2000; Daman, Dil Chahta Hai, Pyaar Ishq Aur Mohabbat, 2001; Solo albums: Koi Akela Kahan; Meera Ka Ram; Pop Time; Devotional Melodies. *Honours:* Film Fare Awards: 1942: A Love Story, 1995; Yaarana, 1996; Khamoshi, 1997; Screen Award: Khamoshi, 1997; Sansui Viewers Choice Award, 1998; Screen Videocon Award, Hum Dil De Chuke Sanam, 1999; Lux Zee Cine Award, Hum Dil De Chuke Sanam, 1999; Stardust Millennium Award, Best Singer, 2000.

KRISTENSEN, Paul; b. 21 June 1965, Oslo, Norway. Songwriter; Musician (bass guitar, drums). *Education:* Graphic Printer. *Career:* Formed Backstreet Girls, 1984; Tours: Norway; Sweden; Denmark; England; USA, 1987–92; Tour, Norway, with Casino Steel and The Crybabys, 1992. *Recordings:* Mental Shakedown, 1986; Boogie Till You Puke, 1988; Party On Elm Street, 1989; Coming Down Hard, 1990; Let's Have It, 1992; Live, 1993; Don't Fake It Too Long, 1995; Nykter, 1996; Hellway To High, 1999; Guest appearances with: Ziggy and The Rhythm Bulldogs; Casino Steel; Comic Messiah; A Technicolour Dream; Also several compilations. *Membership:* TONO; GRAMO; GRAMART. *Current Management:* Gram Art, Arb Samfunnets Plass 1, 0181 Oslo, Norway.

KRISTIANSEN, Morten; b. 4 April 1971, Trondheim, Norway. Musician (guitar); Vocalist. *Education:* 2 years, University. *Career:* Started Hedge Hog, 1989; Several tours Norway; Toured Europe, 1994, 1995. *Recordings:* Erase, 1992; Surprise, 1992; Primal Gutter, 1993; Mercury Red, 1994; Mindless, 1994; The Healing EP, 1995; Thorn Cord Wonder, 1995. *Membership:* Norwegian Asscn of Musicians.

KRISTINA, Sonja; b. 14 April 1949, Brentwood, Essex. Vocalist; Musician (guitar, saxophone, flute, piano). m. Stewart Copeland, 16 July 1982, divorced 1992, 3 s. *Education:* Extensive music performance studies. *Career:* Lead Vocalist, Curved Air, rock group; Chrissy, Original London Cast of Hair; Several Fringe Theatre Projects including Shona, directed Claire Davidson; Pentameters Hampstead, 1989. *Recordings:* Back Street LVV, single, 1971; It Happened Today, single, 1970; 8 albums with Curved Air, 1971–76; Songs From the Acid Folk; Sonja Kristina; Harmonies of Love. *Honours:* Sounds Poll, Voted Top Female Vocalist, 1971. *Membership:* Equity; Musicians' Union; AOTOS. *Current Management:* Mystic Records. *Address:* 226A Haverstock Hill, London NW3 2AE, England.

KRISTOFFERSON, Kris; b. 22 June 1936, Brownsville, Texas, USA. Vocalist; Songwriter; Actor. m. (1), 1 s., 1 d., (2) Rita Coolidge, 19 Aug. 1973, divorced, 1 s.; (3) Lisa Meyers, 19 Feb. 1983, 2 s., 1 d. *Education:* PhD, Pomona College; BA, Oxford University, England. *Career:* Songwriter, 1965–; Solo recording artiste, 1969–; Numerous concerts world-wide, including: Isle of Wight Festival, 1970; Big Sur Folk Festival, 1971; New York Pop Festival, 1977; UNICEF charity concert, New York, 1978; Farm Aid II, 1987; Bob Dylan Tribute, New York, 1992; Also member of side project The Highwaymen (with Willie Nelson, Johnny Cash, Waylon Jennings), 1985–; Appeared at Farm Aid V, 1992; Actor, 1972–; Film appearances include: Cisco Pike, 1972; Pat Garret and Billy The Kid, 1973; Alice Doesn't Live Here Any More, 1974; The Sailor Who Fell From Grace With The Sea, 1976; A Star Is Born, 1976; Semi-Tough, 1977; Convoy, 1978; Heaven's Gate, 1980; Rollover, 1981; Flashpoint, 1984; Songwriter, 1984; Trouble In Mind, 1985; Big Top Pee Wee, 1988; Millennium, 1989; Christmas In Connecticut, 1992; Lone Star, 1996; Blade, 1998; Planet of The Apes, 2001; Numerous appearances, television films and mini-series. *Compositions include:* Help Me Make It Through The Night; Me and Bobby McGee, (also recorded by Janis Joplin); Why Me; For The Good Times. *Recordings:* Albums include: Kristofferson, 1970; The Silver-Tongued Devil and I, 1971; Border Lord, 1972; Jesus Was A Capricorn, 1973; Full Moon, with Rita Coolidge, 1973; Spooky Lady's Sideshow, 1974; Who's To Bless and Who's To Blame, 1975; Breakaway, with Rita Coolidge, 1975; A Star Is Born (soundtrack), 1977; Surreal Thing, 1976; Songs of Kristofferson, 1977; Easter Island, 1978; Natural Act, with Rita Coolidge, 1979; Shake Hands With The Devil, 1979; Help Me Make It Through The Night, 1980; To The Bone, 1981; The Winning Hand, 1983; Music From Songwriter, with Willie Nelson, 1984; Repossessed, 1986; Third World Warrior, 1990; A Moment of Forever, 1995; The Austin Sessions, 1999; with The Highwaymen: Highwayman, 1985; Highwaymen 2, 1992. *Honours:* CMA Song of the Year, Sunday Morning Coming Down, 1970; Grammy Awards: Best Country Song, 1972; Best Country Vocal Performance (with Coolidge), 1973, 1976; Golden Globe, Best Actor, 1976; Inducted into Songwriters Hall of Fame, 1985; with The Highwaymen: ACM Single of the

Year, Highwayman, 1986; 2 American Music Awards, 1986. *Current Management:* Rothbaum and Garner, 36 Mill Plain Rd, Suite 406, Danbury, CT 06811, USA.

KRIZIC, Davor; b. 29 March 1966, Zagreb, Croatia. Musician (trumpet, flugelhorn); Composer. *Education:* Musical High School, Zagreb; 3 years of Jazz Music, University of Graz. *Career:* Played with: Ernie Wilkins; Ed Thighpen; James Woody; David Liebmon; Soloist, Croatian Radio-TV Big Band; Played at Jazz Fair, Zagreb, 1990, 1992–95; Ingolstadt Jazz Festival, 1990; Springtime Jazz Feever, 1995; Many television and radio appearances in Croatia; Greentown Jazz Band German tour. *Compositions:* Beleavin'; Some Blues; Urony. *Recordings:* Albums: with Miro Kadoic: Dry, 1994; with Mia: Ne Ne Ker Se Ne Sme, 1994; with Miljenko Prohaska: Opus 900, 1994; Leader, Boilers Jazz Quartet, Zagreb. *Honours:* Best Young Jazz Musician, Jazz Fair, Zagreb, 1990. *Membership:* Jazz Club, Zagreb; Croatian Music Union; Croatian Artistes' Society (ZUH). *Address:* Palmoticeva 25, 10000 Zagreb, Croatia.

KROEGER, Chad; b. 15 Nov. 1974, Canada. Vocalist; Musician (guitar). *Career:* Mem., lead singer, rock band, Nickelback, 1996–; Brother of band mem., Mike Kroeger; Extensive touring of North America; Signed to EMI Canada and Roadrunner Records; Single, Yanking Out My Heart, used in soundtrack to film The Scorpion King, 2002; Duet with Josey Scott, Hero, used in soundtrack to film Spider-Man, 2002; Collaboration with Santana, 2002; Founder, 604 Records label, overseeing a number of tracks on the Spider-Man film soundtrack by bands on his label. *Recordings:* Albums: with Nickelback: Curb, 1996; The State, 1999; Silver Side Up, 2001. Singles: with Nickelback: Hesher (EP), 1996; Breathe, 2000; Old Enough, 2000; Leader Of Men, 2000; How You Remind Me (No. 1, USA), 2002; Too Bad, 2002; Solo: Hero (with Josey Scott), 2002. *Honours:* Juno Awards, Best New Group, 2001, Best Group, Best Single, for How You Remind Me, Best Rock Album, for Silver Side Up, 2002; MuchMusic Video Awards, Best Video, for Too Bad, Best Rock Video, for How You Remind Me, 2002; MTV Video Music Award, Best Video from a Film, for Hero, 2002; Platinum discs. *Address:* c/o Roadrunner Records Inc, 902 Broadway, Eighth Floor, New York, NY 10010, USA. *Website:* www.nickelback.com.

KROEGER, Mike; b. 25 June 1974, Canada. Musician (bass guitar). *Career:* Mem., rock band, Nickelback, 1996–; Brother of band mem., Chad Kroeger; Extensive touring of North America; Signed to EMI Canada and Roadrunner Records; Single, Yanking Out My Heart, used in soundtrack to film The Scorpion King, 2002. *Recordings:* Albums: Curb, 1996; The State, 1999; Silver Side Up, 2001. Singles: Hesher (EP), 1996; Breathe, 2000; Old Enough, 2000; Leader Of Men, 2000; How You Remind Me (No. 1, USA), 2002; Too Bad, 2002. *Honours:* Juno Awards, Best New Group, 2001, Best Group, Best Single, for How You Remind Me, Best Rock Album, for Silver Side Up, 2002; MuchMusic Video Awards, Best Video, for Too Bad, Best Rock Video, for How You Remind Me, 2002; Platinum discs. *Address:* c/o Roadrunner Records Inc, 902 Broadway, Eighth Floor, New York, NY 10010, USA. *Website:* www.nickelback.com.

KROEGHER, Freddy; b. 23 Sept. 1967, St-Etienne, France. Vocalist; Composer; Musician (lead guitar, bass); Entertainer. 1 d. *Education:* Studied from 17–20 at AIMRA Jazz School, Lyons, France. *Career:* Francofolies of La Rochelle, 1993; Festival of Young Creators, Tignes, 1993; National FNAC Tour, special broadcast interview in France-Inter Radio; TV clip video (Killer) 1993; Concerts; Radio appearances; TV interviews, newspapers. *Recordings:* Albums: Freddy Kroegher: Le Meilleur, 1993; Secoue Ton Seve, 1995; 3 singles; Studio session, backing guitars with: Laoassenko, 1990; Nilda Fernandez, 1991; Jimmy Oihid, 1992; Michel Nouyve, 1993; Gillo Coquard, 1994. *Honours:* Twice Best Rock Artist, Rhone-Alpes region, France, 1990, 1991. *Membership:* RONDOR; SACEM. *Current Management:* Freddy Kroegher Production. *Address:* Route de Parisièves, 42360 Cottance, France.

KROG, Karin; b. 15 May 1937, Oslo, Norway. Jazz Vocalist. m. Johannes Bergh, 21 Sept. 1957, 2 d. *Education:* Business School; Private music study with Anne Brown, 1962–69; Ivo Knecevic, 1969–72. *Career:* Member of Kjell Karlsen Quartet, Frode Thingnaes Quintet and Egil Kapstad Trio; Leader of own groups, 1962–; Worked with Don Ellis; Clare Fischer; Mikkel Flagstad; Einar Iversen; John Surman; Bengt Hallberg; Red Mitchell; Nils Lindberg; Warne Marsh; Richard Rodney Bennett; Founder, First Chairman, Norwegian Jazz Forum, 1965–66; World-wide live, television and radio appearances include jazz festivals in Antibes, France and Norway, 1965; Warsaw and Prague, 1966; Hamburg and Berlin, 1967; Osaka, 1970; Australia, 1985; Hungary, 1989; USSR, 1990; Djakarta, 1992; Bulgaria, 1994; Umbria (Italy), Bath (England), Sardinia, 1994; Concert, Beijing, 1996; Concert, The Purcell Rooms, London, 1999; Formed Meantime Records, 1987. *Compositions include:* ballet music for Carolyn Carlson and Lario Ekson. *Recordings:* By Myself, 1964; Jazz Moments, 1966; Some Other Spring, with Dexter Gordon, 1970; Hi-Fly, with Archie Shepp, 1972; I Remember You, with Red Mitchell and Warne Marsh, 1980; Two of a Kind, with Beng Hallberg, 1981; Nordic Quartet, with John Surman, Terje Rypdal, Vigleik Storaas, 1995; Compilation: Jubilee, 30 years in recorded music, 1994; Bluesand, with John Surman, 1999. *Honours:* Buddy Award, Norwegian Jazz Foundation, 1965;

Down Beat Poll Winner, Talent Deserving Wider Recognition, 1967; Spellemanns Prize, 1974; Grammy, Norway, 1974; Female Singer of the Year, European Jazz Federation, 1975; 2 Swing Journal Awards, Record of the Year, Japan, 1970 and 1978; Oslo Council Artist Award, 1981; Won the Spellemann's Prize, 1999; Awarded The Radka Toneff Memorial Prize, 1999; Several government grants and scholarships. *Membership:* Norwegian Musicians' Federation; NOPA. *Address:* Nobelsgate 35, 0268 Oslo, Norway.

KRUST, (Kirk Thompson), (DJ Krust, Gang Related, Glamour Gold); b. 1968, Bristol, Avon, England. Prod; Remixer; DJ. *Career:* First releases on Ten Records, late 1980s; Began releasing material with Roni Size on V Recordings and on Size's own Full Cycle Records; Co-founder: Reprazent (with Roni Size); Released debut solo album, 2000; Collaborations: Roni Size; DJ Die; Remixed: Bjork; Moloko; DJ Rap; Nicolette. *Recordings:* Albums: New Forms (with Reprazent), 1997; Coded Language, 2000; In The Mode (with Reprazent), 2001; Singles: Deceivers EP, 1993; Jazz Note, 1994; Quiz Show, 1995; Angles, 1996; Genetic Manipulation EP, 1997; Brown Paper Bag (with Reprazent), 1997; True Stories, 1998; Decoded EP, 2000. *Honours:* Mercury Music Prize, winner, New Forms, Roni Size/Reprazent, 1997. *Address:* c/o Talkin' Loud Records, Chancellors House, 72 Chancellors Rd, London W6 9QB, England.

KRZISNIK, Borut; b. 7 Oct. 1961, Zagreb. Composer; Musician (Guitar). *Education:* Graduated, Psychology, Ljubljana University. *Career:* Numerous works performed including Love Song No 1, with Symphonic Orchestra of Slovenian Philharmony; Questions, Enzo Fabiani Quartet; Festival appearances with own band Data Direct: Druga Godba, 1993; Music of 20th Century, Skopje, 1994; Vorax, Vicenza, 1994. *Recordings:* Currents of Time, 1991, with Data Direct: La Dolce Vita, 1995; The Stories from Magatrea, 1999; Permanent collaboration with theatre directors Emil Hrvatin and Julie-Anne Robinson; Music for Theatre: Camillo, at Piccolo Teatro, Milan, 1998; Yard, Bush Theatre, London, 1998; Two Gentlemen of Verona, Royal National Theatre, 1999; The New Organon, Drustvo 51, Cankarjev Dom; Music for Video, Labyrinth, 1993. *Honours:* First Prize, Napoli Danza Festival, Il Coreografo Eletronico, 1994. *Current Management:* Falcata-Galia Recordings. *Address:* Bratov Ucakar 46, 1000 Ljubljana, Slovenia.

KUBES, Stanislav; b. 4 March 1952, Prague, Czech Republic. Musician (Guitar); Songwriter. m. Marcela, 28 Aug. 1973. *Education:* Guitar, Public School of Art. *Career:* The Wizards, 1970; Eminence Group, 1972; Benefit Group, 1973; Respect Group, 1974–75; JIFT Schelinger Group, 1975–81; Tour of Poland with Smokie, 1977; Romance za korunu, Movie, 1975; SLS Group, 1981–85; ETC... Band, 1985–; Support for Rolling Stones, Urban Jungle Tour, Prague, 1990. *Compositions:* Jsem pry blazen jen, 1978; Vanda a Zanda, LP and TV clip, 1985; Za vodou, CD, MC, 1997; 15 titles published. *Recordings:* 35 singles, 1975–81; Hrr na ne!, LP, 1975; Nám se Líbi, 1976; SLS, LP, 1982; Coloured Dreams, LP, 1984; ETC..., 1986; ETC... 4, 1987; 20 deta duse, LP, CD, 1989; Jen se smej, CD, 1994; ETC... Band, Unplugged Live, CD, 1996; Mésto z périn, CD, 1997. *Current Management:* Syrinx, Svornosti 8, 15000 Prague 5, Czech Republic. *Address:* Mladenovova 3231, CZ 14300 Prague 4, Czech Republic.

KUCERA, Josef Simon, (Saxophone Joe); b. 8 July 1943, Prague, Czech Republic. Musician (saxophones, flute). *Career:* Framus Five, soul band, Czechoslovakia, 1967–68; Musical, Hair, 1969–70; Duo: Jesse Ballard and Saxophone Joe, 1972–74; Sessions with Alexis Korner, London; Paradise Island Band, Berlin, 1976; Member, Pete 'Wyoming' Bender Band, 1980–90; Jazz Festival Karlovy Vary, Czech Republic, 1990, 1993; Japan Tour with Marta Kubisova, 1993. *Compositions:* Day Dream; Anyway; 1000 Reasons; Waltz for My Friends; Anotherway. *Recordings:* Control, 1975; Crossroads, 1982; Swindia, 1984; Balance, solo album, 1986; Triangle, Live, 1997. *Membership:* Rock and Pop Musikverband. *Current Management:* Events and Arts, H Degner, Grüntenstr 54, 12 107 Berlin, Germany. *Address:* Koloniestr 28, 13359 Berlin, Germany.

KUJAHN, Lars B; b. 22 June 1958, Denmark. Musician (drums). *Education:* Attended Lectures in Rhythms, Istanbul Conservatory, 1988, Cairo, 1989, Casablanca, 1992, Fanoon, 1997. *Career:* Playing Jazz-Rock in Passengers, Milky Way, 1979–86; Playing Gypsy Music in Svira, 1982–87; Leader of Oriental Mood, 1991; Teacher, Oriental Percussion, 1991–. *Compositions:* Raqsa Maghzebia, 1992; Yallah Mustagbad, 1992; Macera, 1995; Hobb Harr, 1995; Gediid, 1995; Oriental Moods, 1996; Ahman, 1997; Mapsut, 1997; 12 Ok, 1997. *Recordings:* Travels, 1994; Oriental Moods, 1996; Oriental Garden, 1996; Ax Kurdistaan, 1996; Cölbanein, 1998; Expoessive Mahala. *Membership:* Danish Musicians' Union; Danish Rhythmic Composers Organization. *Address:* Oriental Percussion, Hane Tavsons Gade 17 4 tv, 2200 Copenhagen N, Denmark.

KUKKO, (Jyrki) Sakari; b. 8 July 1953, Kajaani, Finland. Bandleader; Composer; Arranger; Musician (flute, saxophone, keyboards). m. Marta Cecilia Renza Villanueva, 1981, divorced 1986. *Education:* Classical music, Sibelius Academy, Helsinki; Jazz with Edward Vesala. *Career:* Founder, Piirpauke, 1974–; Concerts include: Festivals in Tbilisi; Mumbai; Zürich; Paris; Cannes; Barcelona; Concerts, tours with Piirpauke in 30 different countries (4 continents); Also with: Youssou N'Dour; Okay Temiz; Alameda; Aster Aweke; Television and radio appearances world-wide. *Compositions:* for the Espoo Big Band: Moonlight Caravan; Finnish Characters. *Recordings:* 20 albums with Piirpauke; 2 solo albums: Will of The Wisp, 1979; Music For Espoo Big Band, 1989; with Sensation Band Ethiopia '76: Ethiopian Groove; features on: Am Universum, Amorphis, 2001; Music for films, theatre, dance. *Honours:* Yrjö Award, Finnish Jazz Federation, 1976. *Current Management:* Tapio Korjus, Rockadillo. *Address:* Sakari Kukko, Koutaniementie 30 A, 87100 Kajaani, Finland; c/o Rockadillo, Keskustori 7 A 11, 33100 Tampere, Finland.

KULAS, Michael; Musician (guitar, percussion); Backing Vocalist. *Career:* Mem., James, 1997–2001; Numerous tours, festival dates and television appearances; Farewell 'Getting Away With It' concert, Manchester Evening News Arena, Dec. 2001. *Recordings:* Albums: with James: Whiplash, 1997; The Best Of James, 1998; Millionaires, 1999; B-Sides Ultra, 2001; Pleased To Meet You, 2001; Getting Away With It, 2002; solo: Mosquito, 1995; Another Small Machine, 2001. Singles incl.: with James: She's A Star, 1997; Tomorrow, 1997; Waltzing Along, 1997; Destiny Calling, 1998; Runaground, 1998; Sit Down (remix), 1998; I Know What I'm Here For, 1999; Fred Astaire, 1999; We're Gonna Miss You, 1999; Getting Away With It (All Messed Up), 2001. *Current Management:* Rudge Management, 1 Star St, London W2 1QD, England.

KULICK, Bruce; b. 12 Dec. 1953, Brooklyn, New York, USA. Musician (guitar). *Career:* Member, various groups including: Blackjack; Goodrats; Member, US rock group Kiss, 1985–; Appearances include: US tour, with Cheap Trick, 1988; Marquee Club, 1988; US tour, 1990; Revenge '92 Tour, 1992. *Recordings:* with Kiss: Albums: Asylum, 1985; Crazy Nights, 1987; Smashes Thrashes and Hits, 1988; Hot In The Shade, 1989; Revenge, 1992; Kiss Alive III, 1992; Carnival of Souls: The Final Session, 1997; with ESP: ESP, 1999; solo album: Audio Dog, 2001; Contributor, Hear 'N' Aid (Ethiopian famine relief charity album), 1986; Singles include: Tears Are Falling; Crazy Crazy Nights; Reason To Live; Hide Your Heart; Forever; God Gave Rock and Roll To You, featured in film: Bill and Ted's Bogus Journey, 1992. *Honours:* Inducted into Hollywood's Rock Walk, 1993; Kiss Day proclaimed, Los Angeles, 1993. *Current Management:* Entertainment Services Unlimited, Main St Plaza 1000, Suite 303, Voorhees, NJ 08043, USA.

KUPPER, Eric S; b. 10 July 1962, New York, NY, USA. Prod; Remixer; Musician; Songwriter. m. Gianna F Bavido, 1 s., 1 d. *Education:* BA, Music; BA, Theatre and Film, Hunter College, CUNY. *Career:* Top of the Pops with Frankie Knuckles; Arsenio Hall Show with Rupaul. *Compositions include:* The Whistle Song, Frankie Knuckles; Imitation of Life. *Recordings include:* P M Dawn, I'll Be Waiting; Rupaul, Supermodel, album; K-Scope, From the Deep; Instant Music. *Membership:* NARAS; ASCAP; AFM. *Current Management:* Seven PM.

KUSSIN, Al; b. 24 Aug. 1952, Edmonton, Canada. Prod; Musician (keyboards). *Education:* BA; MA, Economics; Grade VII Royal Conservatory, Grade II Theory. *Recordings:* Lorraine Scott: All Talk; Lorraine Scott, 1995; Party Mix: Party Mix '94; Tropirollo Vols II–VI; Céline Dion: Unison; Swing Mix, 1998; Party Mix, 1998; VIP, 1998; Code Five, 1998; Joee, 1999. *Honours:* 4 Platinum discs. *Membership:* SOCAN; CIRPA; AULA; CARAS. *Current Management:* Slak Productions. *Address:* 9 Hector Ave, Toronto, ON M6G 3G2, Canada.

KUTI, Femi Anikulapo; b. 1962, Lagos, Nigeria. Vocalist; Musician (saxophone); Songwriter. m. Funke, 1 s. *Education:* Lagos, Nigeria. *Career:* Substituted for father, Fela Kuti, in The Egypt 80 at the Hollywood Bowl, 1985; Specializes in Afrobeat music; Formed the Positive Force, c. 1987; Signed to Motown, 1995; Later to Barclay/Polygram, 1997; Numerous concerts, television and radio appearances; Established New Shrine open-air nightclub, 2000. *Recordings:* Albums include: No Cause For Alarm (with the Positive Force), 1989; M.Y.O.B., 1991; Femi Kuti, 1995; Wonder Wonder, 1995; Shoki Shoki, 1998; Fight To Win, 2001. *Publications:* AIDS in Africa, essay published by UNICEF in its Progress of Nations report, 2000. *Honours:* Kora Awards: Best Male Artist, Best West African Artist, 1999; World Music Award, Best Selling African Artist, 2000. *Current Management:* Wrasse Records.

KUVEZIN, Albert; b. 27 Nov. 1965, Kyzyl, Tuva, Russia. Vocalist; Musician (Marinkhur: ethnic folk string instrument). m. Natalia Toka, 16 Dec. 1990, 2 d. *Education:* Kyzyl Musical College; Folk Instrument Class. *Career:* As member of Yat-Kha: Voice of Asia Festival (Brian Eno Special Prize), 1990; Sweden, 1991; Siberia Interweek, 1992–94; Berlin Independent Days, 1993; Italy, 1993; WOMAD, 1994; USA, 1995. *Recordings:* Yat-kha, 1993; Huun-Huur-Tu: Go Horses In My Herd. *Publications:* Numerous in Russian, US, Italian, Scandinavian press. *Honours:* Voice of Asia, 1990; Wales Folk Fest, 1992. *Current Management:* Etz/Artemy Troitsky. *Address:* PO Box 107, 125212 Moscow, Russia.

KWATEN, Kwame; Musician (keyboards). *Career:* Mem., jazz funk quartet, D-Influence, 1990–; Support to Prince, Michael Jackson; Tours, television appearances; D-Influence also production team for R&B music; Group owns Freakstreet label. *Recordings:* Albums: Good 4 We, 1992; Prayer 4 Unity, 1995; London, 1997; D-Influence Presents D-Vas, 2002. Singles: I'm The One/The Classic, 1990; Midnite, 1995; Waiting, 1995. *Address:* c/o Dome Records Ltd, 59 Glenthorne Rd, London W6 0LJ, England.

KWATINETZ, Jeffrey; b. Brooklyn, NY, USA. Exec. Prod.; Artiste Management Exec. *Education:* Graduate, Harvard Law School. *Career:* Founder, Q Management; Manager, Gallin-Morey & Assocs; Founder, with Michael Green, CEO and Co-Chair, artiste management company, The Firm, 1997–; Acquired film artists' agency, Artists Management Group, 2002; The Firm represents music clients such as Mary J. Blige, The Dixie Chicks, Korn, Limp Bizkit, Linkin Park, actors and sports people, owns Pony sportswear company, Build-a-Bear Workshop, has departments devoted to clothing, recording, animation, concerts, television and film production. *Address:* The Firm, 9100 Wilshire Blvd, Suite 400, Beverly Hills, CA 91212, USA.

KWOK, Aaron, (Guo Fu Cheng, Kwok Fu Shing); b. 26 Oct. 1965, Hong Kong. Vocalist; Actor. *Career:* Joined Hong Kong TVB company TV show for 3 years as professional dancer, aged 16; Transferred to TVB acting class, aged 21; Several small acting engagements before employing former college director Siu Mei as manager for professional singing/acting career; Major celebrity status in Asia following spectacular live concerts and high profile film roles including ParaPara Sakura, 2001; Records/performs in Cantonese and Mandarin languages. *Recordings:* selected Mandarin Albums: No End Love, 1990; Should I Leave Silently, Who Can Tell Me, 1991; Please Bring My Love Home, Love You, 1992; Aaron Kwok Loves You Deeply, Leave You With All My Love, Hard To Hold Back The Dreams, 1993; End of The Dream, Desire, Lover For Life, 1994; Here Is My Start, Non Stop Wind, 1995; Love Dove, 1996; Sharing Love/Who Will Remember Me, Devoted, 1997; So Afraid, 1999; Journey/Cheer, 2000; Give You All My Love, 2001; selected Cantonese Albums: Hot Beat, 1992; Without Your Love, Merry Christmas, 1993; Starting From Zero, Wild City, A Moment of Romantic II, Iron Attraction, AK-47, 1994; You're Everything, Tale of Purity, Memorandum, 1995; Most Exciting Empire, Song In The Wind, 1996; Love's Calling, Generation Next, 1997; The Best Remix, 1998; Live In Concert '98, 1999; Amazing Dream, 2000; Wu Ji vs Wei Lai (EP), Memorandum, Live On Stage In Concert (includes Mandarin), Xin Tian Di (includes Mandarin), Absolute, 2001. *Address:* c/o Warner Music, 12/F, The Peninsula Office Tower, 18 Middle Rd, TST Kowloon, Hong Kong. *Website:* www.aaronkwokonline.com.

KYRKJEBO, Sissel; b. 24 June 1969, Bergen, Norway. Vocalist. m. Eddie Skoller, 21 Aug. 1993. *Career:* Singer, 1985–; Sold 1.5m. discs, Norway, 1986–; World-wide tours including Scandinavian concerts with Neil Sedaka, 1991; Barcelona Cathedral; Christmas Concert in Vienna with Placido Domingo; Musical Ambassador, singer for Olympic Hymn, Winter Olympic Games, Norway, 1994; Theatre: Maria Von Trapp, Sound of Music; Solveig, Peer Gynt. *Recordings:* Albums: Sissel, 1986; Glade Jul, 1987; Soria Moria, 1989; Gift of Love, 1992; Innerst I Sjelen, 1994; All Good Things, 2001; Hit single: Fire In Your Heart (Olympic Hymn) with Placido Domingo; Vocals on the Titanic score. *Honours:* Norwegian Grammy; Artist of the Year; H C Andersen Award; Platinum disc, Innerst I Sjelen. *Membership:* GRAMO. *Current Management:* c/o Arne Svare, Stageway Impresario A/S, Skuteviksboder 11, 5035 Bergen, Norway.

L

LA PORTE-PITICCO, Laurie Margaret; b. 31 Aug. 1960, Sudbury, ON, Canada. Vocalist; Songwriter; Musician (rhythm guitar). m. Steve Piticco, 1 s., 1 d. *Education:* Played with musical family from age 15. *Career:* Rhythm guitarist, singer, songwriter with South Mountain; Television appearances include: Band hosted own series, 4 years, CHRO TV; Tommy Hunter Show; Canadian Country Music Awards Show; Concerts: Support to Vince Gill, Charlie Pride. *Compositions:* Co-writer: I've Got The Blues, South Mountain (Top 10 hit); Several original songs on South Mountain album: Where There's A Will. *Honours:* Vista Rising Star Award, CCMA, 1991. *Membership:* SOCAN; Canadian Country Music Asscn. *Current Management:* Savannah Music Inc; Catherine Faint, Agent, Stony Plain Records. *Address:* PO Box 64, South Mountain, ON K0E 1W0, Canada.

LA SALLE, Denise; b. 16 July 1941, Mississippi, USA. Vocalist; Songwriter; Publisher. m. James E. Wolfe, 16 July, 1977, 1 s., 1 d. *Career:* Dick Clark; Soul Train; Rhythm and Blues Award; Blues Going On; Toured West Africa, 1972; Europe 1974–78; Co-owner, WFKX Radio Station (KIX96 FM), 1984–; Malaco World Tour, 1989; Soul Blues European Tour: France; Italy; England; Austria; Netherlands; Finland; Norway; Sweden, 1993; 5 nights at Le Meridien Hotel Lounge in Paris, 2001; Owner, Denise La Salle's Chique Boutique and Wigs; Co-owner, The Celebrity Club, Jackson, Tennessee; Formed own record label, Ordena Records, 1999. *Recordings:* Trapped By A Thing Called Love; Down Home Blues; Married But Not To Each Other; The Bitch Is Bad; Lady In The Street; A Mansize Job; Now Run and Tell That; Smokin' In Bed, 1997; God's Got My Back, 1999; Down on Clinton, 1999; This Real Woman, 2000; There's No Separation, 2001; Still the Queen 2002. *Publications:* America's Prodigal Son, 1989; A Short Story About The Blues; How To Be A Successful Songwriter, booklet. *Honours:* Jackie Award, Chicago, 1974; BMI Award. *Membership:* Founder: National Asscn For Preservation of Blues (NAPOB); BMI; NARAS. *Current Management:* Roger Redding and Associates Maconga. *Address:* c/o Denise La Salle, Ordena Entertainment Inc, 17 Henderson Rd, Jackson, TN 38305, USA.

LABARRIERE, Jacques; b. 29 Nov. 1956, Paris, France. Composer; Arranger; Musician (piano). *Education:* Licence de Musicologie; Prize for harmony, counterpoint. *Career:* Shows include: Gospel; Cats; Fantasticks; 42nd Street; Trouble in Tahiti; Radio-France broadcast: ACR de France Culture; Concerts: Jazz with Joe Lee Wilson; Anette Lowman; Eric Barret; Philippe Selam; Jean-Louis Mechali; Singers: C Combe; C Magny; Perone. *Recordings:* Cats; Tie Break, Second Set; Entre 3 and 5. *Membership:* SACEM; SACD; ADAMI; SPEDIDAM; SCAM.

LABELLE, Patti, (Patricia Holt); b. 24 May 1944, Philadelphia, Pennsylvania, USA. Vocalist; Actress. *Career:* Founder member, The Blue Belles, 1961; Appearances include: Ready Steady Go, ITV, Thank Your Lucky Stars, ITV, British tour, 1966; Group name changed to Labelle, 1970–76; Solo artiste, 1976–; Concerts include: Live Aid, JFK Stadium, Philadelphia, 1985; Nelson Mandela International Tribute, Wembley Stadium, England, 1990; Appearance, gospel musical, Your Arm's Too Short To Box With God, Broadway, New York, 1982; Actress, film A Soldier's Story, 1984; Television appearances: Actress, Unnatural Causes, NBC, 1986; Motown 30 – What's Goin' On, CBS, 1990; Arsenio Hall Show special, devoted to Labelle, 1991; Going Home To Gospel with Patti LaBelle, 1991; Own sitcom, Out All Night, NBC, 1992. *Recordings:* Singles: with Blue Belles: I Sold My Heart To The Junkman, 1962; with LaBelle: Lady Marmalade, 1975; On My Own, duet with Michael McDonald (No. 1, USA), 1986; Oh People, 1986; Love Has Finally Come At Last, duet with Bobby Womack; Feels Like Another One, 1991; New Attitude, 1991; Somebody Loves You Baby, 1992; On My Own, 1992; The Right Kinda Love, 1994; When You Talk About Love, 1997; When You've Been Blessed, 1997; Albums: with LaBelle: LaBelle, 1971; Gonna Take A Miracle, 1971; Moonshadow, 1972; Nightbirds, 1974; Phoenix, 1975; Chameleon, 1976; Solo albums: Patti LaBelle, 1977; Tasty, 1978; It's Alright With You, 1979; Released, 1977; The Spirit's In It, 1981; I'm In Love Again, 1984; Winner In You, 1986; Be Yourself, 1989; This Christmas, 1990; Burnin', 1991; Live!, 1992; Gems, 1994; Contributor, The Poet II, Bobby Womack, 1984; Good Woman, Gladys Knight, 1990; Hallelujah!, Quincy Jones, 1991; Am I Cool Or What?, 1992; At the Apollo, 1995; Yo Mister, 1997; Flame, 1997; Live at the Apollo, 1999; The Best of the Early Years, 1999; When A Woman Loves, 2001; Contributor, film soundtracks: Beverly Hills Cop, 1985; Outrageous Fortune, 1987; Dragnet, 1987; Licence To Kill, 1989; Leap of Faith, 1992. *Honours:* Award of Merit, Philadelphia Art Alliance, 1986; Lifetime Achievement Award, CORE (Congress of Racial Equality), 1990; NAACP Entertainer of Year, 1992; American Music Award, Favourite Female R&B/Soul Artist, 1993; Star on Hollywood Walk of Fame, 1993. *Current Management:* PAZ Entertainment Co. *Address:* 2041 Locust St, Philadelphia, PA 19103, USA.

LACK, Andrew; b. 16 May 1947, New York, NY, USA. Business Exec; Music Co Exec. m. Betsy Kenny Lack, 2 s., 1 d. *Education:* Sorbonne, France; BFA, Boston University, 1968. *Career:* Joined CBS News division, 1976, Prod., 60 Minutes, 1977, Exec. Prod., West 57th, 1985–89, Sr Exec. Prod., CBS Reports, 1978–85, prod., various documentaries, left CBS, 1993; Pres., NBC News, 1993–2001; Pres. and Chief Operating Officer, NBC, 2001–; Chair and CEO, Sony Music Entertainment Inc, 2003–. *Address:* Sony Music Entertainment Inc, 550 Madison Ave, New York, NY 10022-3211, USA. *Website:* usa.sonymusic.com.

LACY, Steve, (Steven Lacritz); b. 23 July 1934, New York, USA. Jazz Musician (soprano saxophone); Songwriter. m. Irene Aebi. *Career:* Performed with artistes including: Pee Wee Russell; Buck Clayton; Cecil Taylor; Gil Evans Orchestra, 1957; Leader, own groups; Founder, own quartet with Roswell Rudd, early 1960s; Formed sextet, Paris, 1970; Played duets with Mal Waldron, 1979–. *Recordings include:* Soprano Sax, 1957; Reflections – Steve Lacy Plays Thelonius Monk, 1958; Evidence, with Don Cherry, 1961; Paris Blues, with Gil Evans, Raps, 1977; with Steve Lacy Three: New York Capers, 1979; The Way, 1979; Ballets, 1980; Songs, 1985; Prospectus, 1986; Steve Lacy Two, Five and Six Blinks, 1986; Steve Lacy Nine: Futurities, 1986; Anthem, 1990; with Mal Waldron: Herbe de L'Oubli, 1981; Snake Out, 1981; Let's Call This, 1986; Hot House, 1991; Live at Sweet Basil, 1991; Spirit of Mingus, 1991; Actuality, 1996; Communique, 1997; Scratching the 70s/Dreams, 1997; Sands, 1998; Cry, 1999; The Rent, 1999; Monks Dream, 2000; Snips – Live At Environ, 2000. *Honours:* Downbeat Magazine Poll winner, Best Soprano Saxophonist, several times; MacArthur Foundation Fellowship, 1992; Commandeur des Arts et des Lettres, 2002. *Address:* 57 rue de Temple, 75004 Paris, France.

LADINSKY, Gary; b. 2 May 1947, Los Angeles, California, USA. Recording Engineer. 2 s. *Education:* BA, California State University, Northridge, 1970. *Career:* Recording engineer, Record Plant, Los Angeles, 1971–75; President, Gary Ladinsky Inc/Design FX Audio, 1979–. *Recordings:* Engineer, albums by: Lynyrd Skynyrd; Van Morrison; Moody Blues; Cheap Trick; Donna Summer; George Benson; Manhattan Transfer; Mixer, film scores: Ferris Bueller's Day Off, 1987; Trains, Planes and Automoblies, 1987; Naked Gun, 1988. *Membership:* NARAS; Audio Engineering Society; Society Professional Audio Recording Services, IATSE. *Address:* c/o Design FX Audio, PO Box 491087, Los Angeles, CA 90049, USA.

LADY BO, (Peggy Jones); b. 19 July 1940, New York, NY, USA. Musician (guitar); Vocalist; Dancer; Songwriter; Arranger; Prod; Choreographer. m. Walter Malone, 20 Oct. 1968. *Education:* Complete Performing Arts School, New York. *Career:* First female guitarist in history of Rock and Roll, Rhythm and Blues, Soul, Pop, Jazz, Blues, 1957; First female guitarist hired, major act, 1959; First female member, original Bo Diddley recording and stage act, 1959; Principal player, protegée of Bo Diddley; The Jewels, No. 1 club band, New York, 1961–67; Backing musician: Chuck Berry, 1971; Richard Berry, 1983; Play: Thunder Knocking on the Door, San Jose Repertory Theatre, 1997; Major concerts: HIC Arena, Hawaii; Monterey Jazz Festival, 1973, 1974; Greek Theatre; Circle Star Theatre; Ventura County and Nevada State Fair; Monterey Bay Blues Festival, 1994, 1995, 1999; Tours: USA, Canada, 1965–80s; Europe, 1987; NIKE Endorsement, Bo Knows, 1989; Television: The Jewels, The Mod Mecca TV Special, NYC/BBC, England, 1967; Kenny Rogers, Toronto, 1971; Donnie and Marie, Hollywood, 1976–77; Live Concert, Sweden, 1987; Arts and Entertainment Special, world-wide coverage, 1990; Lady Bo and the BC Horns, South Bay Scene, USA, 1996; Film: The Lost Boys, 1987; Video: Bo Diddley with Lady Bo and The Family Jewel: I Don't Sound Like Nobody, UK, 1992; Flashbacks: Volume One Soul Sensations, 1994; Lady Bo and The BC Horns, Say That You Love Me, 1995. *Recordings:* Albums: with Bo Diddley: Bo Diddley, 1958; Go Bo Diddley, 1959; Have Guitar, Will Travel, 1960; Bo Diddley In The Spotlight, 1961; Bo Diddley Is A Lover, 1961; Bo Diddley Is A Gunslinger, 1962; Road Runner, 1964; Bo Diddley, 16 All-Time Greatest Hits, 1964; The Mighty Bo Diddley, Ain't It Good To Be Free, USA, 1984; France, 1988; Bo Diddley – The Chess Box, 1990; Bo Diddley, The EP Collection, 1992; Bo Diddley, The Chess Years, box set, 1993; The Mighty Bo Diddley, 1994; Bo Knows Bo, 1995; Bo Diddley – His Best, 1997; with Les Cooper: Wiggle Wobble, 1962, 1988; with Fred Waring Orchestra: The Two Worlds of Fred Waring, 1966; Various artistes: Feeling Happy, 1978; The Doo Wop Era: Harlem, New York, 1987; New York R&B, Harlem Holiday, 1988; King Curtis: Soul Twist and Other Golden Classics, 1988; Lady Bo and The BC Horns, Shebo-Shebad, 2000; Singles: 19 with Bo Diddley; 8 as the Jewels; Greg and Peg; Peggy and Bob; The Bob Chords Vocal Group. *Publications:* Listed: The Great Gretsch Guitars Hall of Fame; She's A Rebel: The History of Women In Rock 'n' Roll, 1992; The Complete Bo Diddley Sessions, by George R White, 1993; Bo Diddley – Living Legend Bio, 1995; Doo Wop, The Chicago Scene, 1996; Guitar Player books, 1974, 1987, 1990; Suede News, Lady Bo, cover feature, 1997; Rolling Stone Book of Women in

Rock, 1998. *Honours:* Lifetime Achievement Award, South Bay Blues Awards, 1993. *Membership:* AFM Local No. 153; SheBo Shebad Music Publishing, BMI. *Current Management:* LB-BCH Productions. *Address:* 14680 Bear Creek Rd, Boulder Creek, CA 95006, USA.

LAFFY, Stephen; b. 29 May 1953, London, England. Musician; Songwriter; Prod. m. Lynn Heather, 21 March 1994, 2 d. *Career:* Performed at Glastonbury Festival; WOMAD; Notting Hill Carnival; Overseas tours, television and radio; Formed own band Rhythm Rising. *Recordings:* When 2000 Comes, 1995; Don't Go Breaking Down; Carry On; Everybody Needs Someone. *Membership:* Musicians' Union; PRS; MCPS.

LAGERBERG, Bengt Fredrik Arvid; b. 5 July 1973, Karolinska Sjukhuset, Stockholm, Sweden. Musician (drums, bassoon, guitar, bass guitar, piano, trumpet, harmonica). *Career:* Mem., Diver, Giraffe; Mem., The Cardigans, 1992–; Contributed tracks to films Romeo and Juliet and A Life Less Ordinary; Numerous concert tours, festivals, television and radio appearances. *Recordings:* Albums: Emmerdale, 1994; Life, 1995; First Band On The Moon, 1996; Other Side Of The Moon, 1998; Gran Turismo, 1998. Singles: Rise And Shine; Black Letter Day; Sick And Tired, 1995; Carnival, 1995; Hey! Get Out Of My Way; Lovefool (No. 2, UK), 1996; Been It, 1997; Your New Cuckoo, 1997; My Favorite Game, 1998; Erase/Rewind, 1999; Hanging Around, 1999; Gran Turismo Overdrive, 2000; with David Arnold: Theme From 'Randall & Hopkirk Deceased' (BBC1), 2000. *Honours:* Slitz Magazine, Best Band, 1994; BMI Best Song, 1997, Best Album, 1998, Best Group, 1996, 1998. *Current Management:* Motor, PO Box 53045, 400 14 Gothenburg, Sweden. *Address:* c/o Stockholm Records, Positionen 146, 115 74 Stockholm, Sweden. *Website:* www.cardigans.net.

LAGRÈNE, Bireli; b. 4 Sept. 1966, Saverne, Alsace, France. Vocalist; Musician. *Career:* Solo artiste, 1978–; Extensive European tours. *Recordings:* Albums: Routes To Django: Live At The Krokodil, 1980; Bireli Swing '81, 1981; Concert And Space (with Joseph Bowie), 1981; 15, 1982; Down In Town, 1983; Musique Tzigane/Manouch, 1984; Erster Tango, 1985; Bireli Lagrene Ensemble Live Featuring Vic Juris, 1985; Stuttgart Aria, 1986; Foreign Affairs, 1986; Zum Tratz, 1986; Inferno, 1987; Bireli Lagrene, 1988; Bireli & Jaco (with Jaco Pastorious), 1988; Acoustic Moments 1990; Standards, 1992; Live In Marciac, 1996; Blue Eyes, 1998; The Gypsy Project, 2001. *Honours:* Musicien Français de Jazz, 2001. *Address:* c/o Dreyfus Records Inc, 19 W 44th St, Suite 1716, New York, NY 10036, USA.

LAHBIB, Lahcen; b. Morocco. Vocalist; Musician (percussion). *Career:* Left Morocco for London, 1980s; Founder member of band MoMo (Music of Moroccan Origin); Act's fusion of North African Gnawa music with western-style drum kit, samples and contemporary dance styles (including house and garage) described as 'Dar'; Popular live band; Released first album, 2001. *Recordings:* Album: The Birth of Dar, 2001.

LAHTI, Pentti; b. 15 Aug. 1945, Finland. Musician (reeds, flutes, saxophones). *Career:* Musician with Eero Koivistoinen Octet, and Mircea Stan Quartet, early 1970s; Member, Jukka Linkola Octet; Member, UMO (New Music Orchestra); Finnish Broadcasting Company tours to Oslo, 1973; Laren Festival, Holland, 1977; Annual appearance, Pori Festival; Reed player, Wasama Quartet and Ilkka Niemeläinen's Instinct, 1980s. *Recordings:* Solo album: Ben Bay; Also appears: with Edward Vesala, Nan Madol, Mau-mau; with Umo Jazz Orchestra. *Honours:* Yrjö Award, Finnish Jazz Federation, 1983. *Address:* Kärpänkuja 8, 04230 Kerava, Finland.

LAIDLAW, Raymond Joseph; b. 28 May 1948, Tynemouth, England. Musician (drums). m. Lesley, 9 April 1976, 2 s. *Education:* Newcastle Art College; Club A GoGo, Newcastle. *Career:* Drummer, Lindisfarne, 1969–; Now studio owner, music publisher. *Compositions:* Joint composer: Scotch Mist instrumental (B side of Lindisfarne hit: Meet Me On the Corner). *Recordings:* Hit singles: Meet Me On The Corner, 1972; Lady Eleanor, 1972; Run For Home, 1978; Fog On The Tyne, with Paul 'Gazza' Gascoigne, 1990; Albums include: Nicely Out of Tune, 1970; Fog On The Tyne (No. 1, UK), 1971; Dingly Dell, 1972; Finest Hour, 1975; Back and Fourth, 1978; On Tap, 1994; Buried Treasure Vol. 1, 2000; Complete BBC Recordings 1971–75, 2000. *Membership:* Musicians' Union. *Current Management:* Lindisfarne Musical Productions. *Address:* Hi-level Recording, 18 Victoria Terrace, Whitley Bay, Tyne and Wear, England.

LAIDVEE, Meelis; b. 10 Jan. 1964, Pärnu, Estonia. Musician (keyboards). m. Eve Laidlee (Lublo), 1 March 1985, 2 d. *Education:* Private lessons. *Career:* Concerts, tours, 1978–; Television and radio hitlists with: Provints; Uncle Bella; The Tuberkubited, 1988–. *Recordings:* 3 abums with The Tuberkuloited. *Honours:* Radio Top 10 Award, 1994, 1995. *Address:* PO Box 2225, EE 0035, Tallinn, Estonia.

LAINE, Dame Cleo, (Clementina Dinah Dankworth); b. 28 Oct. 1927, Southall, Middlesex, England. Vocalist; Actress. m. John Dankworth, 18 March 1958, 2 s., 1 d. *Career:* Vocalist, Dankworth Orchestra, 1953–58; Lead role, Seven Deadly Sins, Edinburgh Festival and Sadlers Wells, 1961; Showboat, 1972; Colette, 1980; Also appeared in: A Time To Laugh; Hedda

Gabler; The Women of Troy; The Mystery of Edwin Drood, Broadway, 1986; Into The Woods, US National Tour, 1989; Numerous television appearances; Film: Last of the Blonde Bombshells, 2000. *Recordings include:* Feel The Warm; I Am A Song; Live At Melbourne; Best Friends; Sometimes When We Touch; Jazz, 1993; Blue And Sentimental, 1994; Solitude, 1995; The Very Best Of Cleo Laine, 1997; Live In Manhattan, 2001; Quality Time, 2002. *Publications:* Cleo (autobiography), 1994; You Can Sing If You Want To, 1997. *Honours:* D.B.E., 1997; O.B.E., 1979; Golden Feather Award, Los Angeles Times, 1973; Edison Award, 1974; Hon. MA, Open University, 1975; Singer of the Year, TV Times, 1978; Hon. MusD, Berklee College of Music, 1982; Grammy Award, Best Female Vocalist, 1985; Theatre World Award, 1986; NARM Lifetime Achievement Award, 1990; British Jazz Award, Best Female Vocalist, 1990; Variety Club of Great Britain Show Business Personality of Year, 1977; ISPA Distinguished Artists Award, 1999; Hon. DA, Luton University, 1994; Hon. MusD, York University, 1993; Bob Harrington Lifetime Achievement Award (with John Dankworth), 2001; Freedom of Worshipful Company of Musicians, 2002; BBC Radio Jazz Award, Lifetime Achievement (with John Dankworth), 2002; Numerous Platinum discs, Gold discs. *Current Management:* Dankworth Management. *Address:* The Old Rectory, Wavendon, Milton Keynes MK17 8LT, England. *Website:* www.quarternotes.com.

LAINE, Frankie, (Francesco Paolo Lo Vecchio); b. 30 March 1913, Chicago, IL, USA. Vocalist; Songwriter. m. Nanette Gray, 15 June 1950, deceased 1993, 2 d. *Education:* Studied with Frank Teschemacher. *Career:* Singer, dance teacher, Merry Garden Ballroom, late 1920s; Dancer, numerous dance marathons; Mem., Freddy Carlone band, 1937; First billed as Frankie Laine, 1938; First record deal, 1946; Concerts world-wide include: Royal Variety Performance for Queen Elizabeth II, 1954; Film appearances include: When You're Smiling, 1950; Sunny Side of the Street, 1951; Rainbow Round My Shoulder, 1952; Bring Your Smile Along, 1955; He Laughed Last, 1956; Performed title songs, films: Man With A Star; High Noon; Gunfight At The OK Corral, 1957; Blazing Saddles, 1974; Featured in The Last Picture Show, 1971; Lemon Popsicle, 1978; Raging Bull, 1980; Television includes: Frankie Laine Time; The Frankie Laine Show; Acted in: Rawhide (sang title theme); Perry Mason; Burke's Law. *Compositions:* Co-writer: Put Yourself In My Place Baby (with Hoagy Carmichael); It Ain't Gonna Be Like That, with Mel Tormé; Magnificent Obsession (with Freddie Karger); Torchin' (with Al Lerner; We'll Be Together Again (with Carl Fischer); Recorded by over 100 artistes including Louis Armstrong; Tony Bennett; Ray Charles; Rosemary Clooney; Ella Fitzgerald; Sammy Davis Jr; Jack Jones; Frank Sinatra; Billie Holiday. *Recordings:* 80 albums and EPs, 1947–; Singles include: Jezebel, 1951; High Noon, 1952; I Believe (No. 1, 18 weeks, UK), 1953; Where The Winds Blow, 1953; Hey Joe (No. 1, UK), 1953; Answer Me (No. 1, UK), 1953; Blowing Wild, 1953; Granada, 1954; Kid's Last Fight, 1954; My Friend, 1954; Cool Water, 1955; A Woman In Love (No. 1, UK), 1956; Moonlight Gambler, 1956; Rawhide, 1959; Making Memories, 1971; Lord You Gave Me A Mountain, 1969; Albums: Memories, 1985; Mule Train, 1989; All of Me, 1993; Duets, 1994; Dynamic, 1996; Young Master, 1998; Life is Beautiful, 1998; Cocktail Hour, 2000. *Publications:* That Lucky Old Son (autobiography), co-author with Joseph Laredo. *Address:* PO Box 6910, San Diego, CA 92166, USA. *Website:* www.frankielaine.com.

LAINE, Reino; b. 11 July 1946, Finland. Musician (drums). *Career:* Played drums from age 16; Member, quartet with Pekka Pöyry, Montreux, 1968; Played with Eero Koivistoinen, winning group competition, Montreux, 1969; Also appeared at Newport Jazz Festival; Member, Seppo Paakunainen's Conjunto Baron, 1970s; Percussionist, numerous plays at Helsinki City Theatre; Played with major Finnish musicians, also artistes including: Dexter Gordon; Clifford Jordan; Charlie Mariano; Appeared with Juhani Aaltonen group, The Finnish Middle-Aged All Stars, Pori Festival, 1985. *Honours:* Yrjö Award, Finnish Jazz Federation, 1981. *Membership:* Mem. of board, Finnish Jazz Federation; Pop Musicians' Union; Mem. of government-appointed organizations. *Address:* Hakaniemenranta 26 A 63, 00530 Helsinki, Finland.

LAIZEAU, Francois; b. 19 Nov. 1955, Paris, France. 1 d. *Education:* Agostini School, 1973–76. *Career:* Sideman for: Tania Maria; Magma; Eddy Louiss; Michel Legrand; Toots Thielemans; Louis Sclavis; Michel Portal; Dominique Pifarely; Martial Solal; Kenny Wheeler; Claus Stotter. *Recordings:* Albums with H Kaenzig and K Wheeler; Live At Fat Thursday, Michel Legrand; Eddy Louiss; Nuit Etoilée; 3 recordings with the National Jazz Orchestra; Magma, Retrospective Vol. 3, 1981; Joelle Ursull, Comme Dans Un Film December 1993, 1996; Jean-Loup Longnon, Cyclades, 1996; 20 Ans de Jazz en France, 1996. *Membership:* UMJ. *Address:* 82 rue de Rochechouat, 75009 Paris, France.

LAJOIE-DESAVBIN, May-Cecile; b. 25 May 1972, Victoria Hospital, Mahe, Seychelles. Research Officer; Linguist, Ministry of Education and Culture; Singer, The Waves, band. m. Teddy Desavbin, 6 Jan. 1996, 1 s. *Career:* Music-Wise, performing in hotels every weekend with band, Waves; Performed for Miss Seychelles Beauty Pageant; Performed for Miss World, Seychelles. *Compositions:* Lavi Rezete; Only A Dream; Viktorya; Venges-Moi; Ecris-Moi; Nov Devwar; Lot Kote; Konplent Paran; Fer Mwan Oubliye. *Recordings:* Albums: Lanbeli with the Waves; Victoria, personal album, 1996.

Publications: Lavi Rezete, song, 1995. *Honours:* Media Prizes; Best Singer Award, Radio, 1996; Best Song Award, Radio, 1996; Best Singer Award, People Magazine, 1996; Best Song Award, People Magazine, 1996; Best Band Award, Waves, 1996. *Address:* Anse Aux Pins, Mahé, Republic of Seychelles.

LAKE, Greg; b. 10 Nov. 1948, Bournemouth, Dorset, England. Musician (bass); Vocalist. *Career:* Member, The Gods, 1968; King Crimson, 1969–70; Emerson Lake and Palmer (ELP), 1970–78; Also as Emerson Lake and Powell (with Cozy Powell), 1985–86, 1992–; Asia, 1983; Festival performances include: Isle of Wight Festival, 1970; Mar-Y-Sol Festival, Puerto Rico, 1972. *Recordings:* Albums: with King Crimson: In The Court of The Crimson King, 1969; In The Wake of Poseidon, 1970; A Beginner's Guide To... (compilation), 2000; with ELP: Emerson Lake and Palmer, 1970; Tarkus (No. 1, UK), 1971; Pictures At An Exhibition, 1971; Trilogy, 1972; Brain Salad Surgery, 1974; Welcome Back My Friends To The Show That Never Ends – Ladies and Gentlemen... Emerson Lake and Palmer, 1974; Works, Vol. Two, 1977; Love Beach, 1978; Emerson Lake and Powell, 1986; Black Moon, 1992; Live At The Royal Albert Hall, 1993; Return of The Manticore, 1993; In The Hot Seat, 1994; Isle of Wight, 1997; Live In Poland, 2001; Solo albums: Greg Lake, 1981; Manoeuvres, 1983; In Concert on the King Biscuit Flower Hour, 1996; From the Beginning – The Greg Lake Retrospective, 1997; Singles include: with ELP: Fanfare For The Common Man (No. 2, UK), 1977; Solo: I Believe In Father Christmas (No. 2, UK), 1975. *Current Management:* Booking Agent: Pilato Entertainment, 277 Alexander St, Suite 813, Rochester, NY 14607, USA. *Address:* c/o Premier Talent, 3 E 54th St, 14th Floor, New York, NY 10022, USA.

LAKE, Suzanne; b. 26 June 1929, New Jersey, USA. Vocalist; Actress. m. George A. De Vos. *Education:* Opera, Juilliard; Voice, Queena Mario, Joseph Florestano; Acting, Claudia Franck, Yul Brynner, Larry Blyden; Piano Harmony and Theory, Mayhew L. Lake. *Career:* Broadway and National Tour, Tuptim, The King and I, 1951–54; Broadway and National Tour, Helen Chao, Flower Drum Song, 1961–62; Revival No No, Nanette, 1964; Featured in Leonard Bernstein's History of Musical Comedy, ABC TV, USA; Starring Acts, with Guy Lombardo, Desert Inn, Las Vegas, Tampa, Caribbean, Canada, 1963–72; Blossom Music Festival Concerts, USA and Asia, 1970–92; Teaching, 1980–90. *Recordings:* The Soul of Chanson; Potpurri; Marieke. *Membership:* Agma; Actors Equity; Aftra; Agva. *Address:* 2835 Morley Dr., Oakland, CA 94611, USA.

LALENDLE, Luvuyo; b. 4 April 1964. Music Educationist. m. Nomahlubi Tabitta Zulu, 1 s., 2 d. *Education:* Bachelor of Pedagogics, University of Fort Hare, majored in Music Education and Pedagogics; BEd, University of Venda, South Africa; Master in Music Education, University of Iowa, USA. *Career:* Senior Lecturer, University of Venda, South Africa; Interview with Radio South Africa, Durban, 1989; Appearance on Zimbabwe National Television, 1994. *Publications:* Music In and Out of School, Iowa Music Educators' Journal; Music Programmes in a Post-Apartheid South Africa. *Honours:* Ackerman's Scholarship, 1987; Atlas (USAID) Scholarship, 1998. *Membership:* International Council for Traditional Music, Executive Board mem., 1997–. *Address:* c/o Music Department, University of Venda, P/B X5050, Thohoyandou 0970, South Africa.

LAMB, Andrew John; b. 13 July 1969, North Kensington, London, England. Musician (guitar, bass). *Education:* Currently studying at the Guitar Institute in London. *Career:* Member of band Slander; 2 British tours, 1992–94; Various radio appearances including: Rock Wars, BBC Radio 1; European and American radio. *Recordings:* Composed and recorded own album with Slander; Various demos with other bands as a studio session musician; Live recordings. *Membership:* Musicians' Union. *Address:* 24 Rowsley Rd, St Annes-on-Sea, Lancashire FY8 2NS, England.

LAMB, Paul; b. 9 July 1955, Blyth, Northumberland, England. Musician (harmonica). Divorced, 1 s. *Career:* Festivals, Europe and UK; Television shows include: Spender, UK; Late Late Show, Ireland; Other shows in Germany; Scandinavia; France; UK; Radio programmes: BBC Radio 2; Jazz FM; Greater London Radio; Radio stations around Europe; Concerts with Mark Knopfler; West End Show: A Slice of Saturday Night. *Recordings:* with The Blues Burglars: Breakin In; John Henry Jumps In; The Blue Album; Blues Burglars Whoopin'; with Paul Lamb and The King Snakes: Paul Lamb and the King Snakes; Shifting Into Gear; Fine Condition; She's a Killer; Harmonica Man; Compilation CDs and box sets: Cooking With The Blues; Blues Harp Boogie Music Club International; The Deluxe Blues Band, with Big Joe Louis, Otis Grand; Confessin' The Blues; Recent releases include: Take Your Time and Get It Right, 2000; Paul Lamb and The King Snakes, 2001; Session work includes: Evil, Lucky Lopez Evans. *Publications:* Blues In Britain. *Honours:* First as team in the World Harmonica Championships, Germany; Second as soloist, 1975; Voted Best UK Harmonica Player for 5 years, British and Blues Connection. *Membership:* Musicians' Union; NHL; British Blues Connection; PRS. *Address:* 17 Pollard Rd, Whetstone, London, England.

LAMB, Tracey; Musician (bass guitar). *Career:* Mem., Rock Goddess; Joined Girlschool, 1987; Tour of Russia, supporting Black Sabbath; Band split, 1989;

Band re-formed, 1992; Left band, but contributed to albums, 2000–. *Recordings:* Albums: Take A Bite, 1988; Girlschool, 1992; Live, 1995; Race With The Devil (Live), 1998; Live On The King Biscuit Flower Hour, 1998; Can't Keep A Good Girl Down, 1999; Very Best Of Remastered, 2002; 21st Anniversary: Not That Innocent, 2002. *Address:* c/o PO Box 33446, London SW18 3XN, England.

LAMBE, Rick; b. 4 Aug. 1960, Birmingham, England. Musician (slide guitar, guitars, bass, drums). m. Corinne Croucher, 29 July 1992, 1 s. *Education:* Grade 5, Electric Guitar; Audio technology course, Kidderminster College, 1996–98. *Career:* Concerts include: Telford Blues Festival, 1989–90; Played 25 concerts in 1 night for Children In Need charity for BBC; Coventry Blues Festival, 1991; Appeared on BBC show celebrating 21 years of Pebble Mill programme; Appeared as Band of The Week on John Taynton Show, 1992; Live radio appearances on radio, Children In Need, and Christmas Day radio broadcast; Various sessions for BBC TV; New Year's Eve Concert with Official Receivers Soul Band, Centenary Square, Birmingham performing to over 70,000 people; Recorded an album for local folk hero Gary O'Dea; Played on Love Love, a Charlie Landsborough album; Currently teaching National Diploma in Audio Technology at Kidderminster College. *Recordings:* Two Bhangra recordings for Achanak and Ananki; Two tracks on Hazell Dean's album; Abba tribute song forthcoming; Are You Receiving Us, The Official Receivers, 1996; Loud and Clear, with Curtis Little and the Receivers, live CD, 1998; There's A Storm Comin', album, 1999. *Membership:* Musicians' Union; PAMRA; PRS. *Current Management:* White Lamb. *Address:* 32 Ombersley Close, Woodrow South, Redditch, Worcestershire B98 7UU, England.

LAMBERT, David; b. 3 Dec. 1965, Wye, Kent, England. Label Head, Club and Radio DJ. *Education:* BA Hons, Social Science, University of Westminster. *Career:* Helped launch Touch Magazine; Began as DJ, 1989; Performing throughout UK, Europe and Latin America; Founder (with Nick Halkes) and A&R, Positiva Dance Label at EMI, 1993–98; Label Head of AM:PM Records of Universal Island Records, 1998–; Started Saturday Night radio show on ILR station TFM (Stockton-on-Tees), 1999. *Address:* c/o AM:PM, 22 St Peters Sq., London W6 9NW, England.

LAMBERT, Ronnie (Busker); b. 3 Oct. 1950, Newcastle, England. Vocalist; Musician (guitar, harmonica); Bricklayer. m. Hazel Welsh, 24 Sept. 1974, 1 s., 1 d. *Career:* Rock on the Tyne concert at Gateshead International Stadium, 1981; Appeared as singer on BBC TV four times, and on local ITV 4 times; Many radio appearances and interviews on BBC Radio, 1982–94; Metro Radio; Radio Magpie. *Recordings:* Singles: Home Newcastle, 1981; River Tyne EP, 1982; Goin' Up (Newcastle United official promotional song), 1984; Buildin' Site, 1990; Black and White, 1993, re-recorded 1994; Album: Pure Geordie, 1991. *Honours:* Newcastle United Football Club play his music at their home games. *Membership:* PRS; MCPS; Musicians' Union. *Current Management:* QC Entertainment. *Address:* Newburn Industrial Estate, Newburn, Northumberland, England.

LAMBERTH, Dag (Ebbe Olaf); b. 13 May 1923, Mjölby, Sweden. Musician (Piano); Composer; Author, Teacher. m. (1) Stina Lindblad-Rogers, (2) Marion Brechbilder-Boecher, 1 s., 2 d. *Education:* BA, MA, Musicology, Slavic Languages, Russian, Literary History, Nordic Languages, German, Universities of Stockholm and Uppsala; MA, Musicology and Piano, Conservatory of Stockholm and private masterclasses. *Career:* Early performances with Lamberth Family and also with brother (famous solo trumpeter) Arne Lamberth and Copenhagen; Radio recordings. *Compositions:* Jolly Party, for symphony band and orchestra; Love in Monte Carlo; Christine Swedish Blonde; Adaptation of poem by Per Lägerkvist for soloist and choir; Swedish translation of French waltz Pigalle. *Recordings:* Jolly Party; Love in Monte Carlo; Schwarze Ballade. *Publications:* Critical articles in Swedish newspapers and German musicological journals. *Honours:* Great Award of the Swedish State for Composers, 1968. *Membership:* International Asscn of Swedish Composers (STIM); Swedish Composers of Popular Music (SKAP). *Address:* Bellevuevägen 43 A, 217 72 Malmö, Sweden.

LAMBRECHT, Dimitri; b. 9 April 1967, Aalst, Belgium. Prod; Composer. *Career:* First Band: PLB System, Concerts in Belgium and France, 1988, 1989; Currently on tour with Natural Born Deejays. *Compositions:* Singles: For Fun, 1991; Jump, 1992; A Good Day, 1996; Sonar Contact, 1997; Deejays Mind, 1997; Oxygen, 1998; Airplay, 1998; The Deejays Are Here, 1999. *Recordings:* Artificial Defence, 1989; A Good Day, 1996; Today, 1998. *Current Management:* King International Service, Leuvensesteenweg 120 Diest 3290, Belgium.

LAMMERS MEYER, Hermann; b. 7 Dec. 1952, Aschendorf, Germany. Musician (pedal steel guitar); Vocalist. m. Anke Barenborg, 21 May 1988, 1 s. *Career:* Worked with Clay Baker and the Texas Honky Band; Success of Texas Country Road Show in USA followed by tours of Europe, including British tour, 1981; Writes and records own songs; Tours with own band The Emsland Hillbillies, all over Europe, UK, USA; Solo project: The Honky Tonk Hearts performed for Germany on Euro Country Music Masters TV Show, Netherlands. *Recordings include:* with Emsland Hillbillies: Albums: Texas

Country Road Show, Vols I, 1979; Vol. II, 1981; Texas Lone Star, 1981; Solo: Singles: Moonshine Ladies/Neon Leon, 1987; Southern Comfort/You Ought To Hear Me Cry, 1989; Death of a Clown/A Song For Sarah, 1998; Waltz of The Wind, 1999; Album: Half My Heart's In Texas, 1989; Above All The Starday Session, Nashville; The End of Time; The Last Country Song; Zeitlos, 1998; I'd Like To Live It Again, with David Frizzell, Lois Johnson, Marion Möhring, 2000; Duets with: Norma Jean; Kitty Wells; Willie Nelson; Johnny Bush. *Honours:* Country Album of the Year, GACMA in Germany, 1992; European Country Music Assocn Artist of the Year; Last Country Song, Album of the Year, 1996. *Current Management:* Desert Kid Records/E L Hillbillies Music, Drosselweg 15 26871 Aschendorf, Germany.

LAMOND, George; b. 25 Feb. 1967, Georgetown, Washington DC, USA. Recording Artiste; Vocalist. m. Oct. 1994. *Education:* New York High School of Art and Design; Various keyboards and Midi courses. *Career:* Rick Dee's TV Show; CNN Showbiz Today (profile and interview); Entertainment Tonight (profile and interview); No More Games Tour, opened for New Kids On The Block; TV Show, Showtime At The Apollo Theatre. *Recordings:* Albums: Bad of The Heart; In My Life; (Spanish) Creo Enti (2 Billboard Top 10 Latin singles); Entrega; The Hits and More; Que To Vas Remixes; GL, 2001; Singles: Bad of The Heart, Top 40, Billboard Chart; Look Into My Eyes; No Matter What; Love's Contagious; Baby, I Believe in You; It's Always You (EP); I Want You Back. *Honours:* Winter Music Conference, Best Dance 12 Award. *Membership:* NARAS. *Current Management:* Chris Barbosa Management.

LAMOND, Mary Jane; b. 5 Nov. 1960, Kingston, Ontario, Canada. Gaelic Vocalist. *Education:* Degree in Celtic Studies. *Career:* Fifth Estate, 1997; Lilith Fair, 1997; Capercaillie British tour, 1997; Chieftains Canada Tour, 1997; Hanging Garden Soundtrack, 1997; Chieftains US Tour, 1998; Contributor: albums: Hi How Are You Today?; Ashley MacIsaac, 1995; Chieftains, 1997; Fire In The Kitchen, 1998; Suase!, 1998. *Recordings:* Bho Thir Nan Craobh, Suas e!, 1997, Làn Dùil, 2000. *Honours:* ECMA Song, Sleepy Maggie, 1997; Much Music Global Groove Video Award, Bog a Lochain, 1997. *Membership:* SOCAN; CARAS; ECMA. *Current Management:* Jones and Co. *Address:* 5212 Sackville St, Suite 100, Halifax, NS, B3J 1K6, Canada.

LAMONT, Duncan; b. 4 July 1931, Greenock, Scotland. Musician (tenor saxophone, woodwinds); Composer. m. Bridget, 20 Feb. 1960, 2 s. *Education:* Private music study, Glasgow. *Career:* Started as jazz trumpet player, aged 14; Joined Kenny Graham Afro Cubist Band, age 20; Switched from trumpet to tenor saxophone, played with many Big bands; Studio Jazz player, accompanied major stars including: Frank Sinatra; Bing Crosby; Fred Astaire; Became composer, wrote several suites, success with songs, lyrics, performed by most major singers in England, USA. *Compositions include:* Songs: Tomorrow's Standards; Best of Bossa Novas; Summer Sambas; I Told You So, recorded by Cleo Laine; Not You Again, recorded by Cleo Laine and George Shearing; Suites include: The Young Person's Guide To The Jazz Orchestra; Sherlock Holmes Suite (For City of London); The Carnival of The Animals; Cinderella; Children's television programmes: Mr Benn; King Rollo; Spot (the dog); Towser; Spot's Magical Xmas (for Disney Studios) 1995. *Publications:* Tomorrow's Standards. *Honours:* Tomorrow's Standards, The Music Retailers Asscn Annual Awards For Excellence, 1995; Best Song of Year, ASAC, USA: I Told You So, 1995. *Membership:* PRS; ASCAP. *Current Management:* Bucks Music, 1 Farm Pl., London W8 7SX, England.

LAMPRELL, Adam Charles; b. 14 June 1965, Sutton, Surrey, England. Musician (guitar). m. Penny Britchfield, 11 June 1994, 1 s. *Education:* BA Hons, Graphic Design (specializing in Photography). *Career:* Recording sessions for Michael Prophet and Ricky Tuffy; Recording sessions for Bryan Ferry; TV commercials and theme music, including BBC2 series, Nurse; Joint bandleader, The Scissormen; World-wide recording, tours, television and radio. *Recordings:* with The Scissormen: Albums: Nitwit, 1992; Mumbo Jumbo, 1995; Glee (EP), 1997; Skyscraper album, Shooters, 1998; Bryan Ferry LP, 1999; Joey Tempest, The Final Countdown; Sessions for Michael Prophet, Ricky Tuffy, album: Get Ready; Singles include: Kicks; Recording on remixes include: Chaka Demus and Pliers; Freddie McGregor. *Membership:* Musicians' Union; PRS; MCPS. *Address:* 53 Highclere St, London SE26 4EX, England.

LANCE, Dirk, (Alex Katunich); b. 18 Aug. 1976. Musician (bass guitar). *Career:* Formed group Incubus with school friends in Calabasas, California, 1991; Initially played small parties, graduating to support slots in Hollywood, California; Circulated demo tapes of Closet Cultivation and Incubus before independent album release, 1995; Group signed by Immortal/Epic; Built US and European following support slots on tours with: Sugar Ray; Black Sabbath; Korn; Drive reached No. 1 on US Modern Rock Chart, 2001; First Japanese and Australian live dates, 2001. *Recordings:* Albums: Fungus Amongus, 1995; S.C.I.E.N.C.E., 1997; Make Yourself, 1999; Morning View, 2001; Singles: Enjoy Incubus EP, 1997; Pardon Me, 1999; Stellar, When Incubus Attacks Vol. 1 EP, 2000; Drive, Wish You Were Here, 2001. *Honours:* Make Yourself album certified double platinum by RIAA; Billboard Award, Modern Rock Single of the Year, 2001. *Current Management:* Steve Rennie, REN Management, California, USA. *Website:* www.enjoyincubus.com.

LANDA, Omar; b. 30 Nov. 1970, Morelia, Michoacan, Mexico. Musician (Drums, Keyboards). *Education:* Conservatoria de Las Rosas en Morelia; Drum lessons with Abraham Calleros in Guadalajara. *Career:* Radio appearances in Mexico City, WFM Radio Station; Opening concerts for Caifanes and Maná; TV appearances playing live, Channel 2. *Compositions:* 13, 1992; Llananina, 1994; Musgosa Caja, 1994; Tierra, 1996; BaxLtTrt, 1998. *Recordings:* La Parca, 1994; BaxLtTrt, 1998; Pulso, 1999. *Honours:* Best Rock Group from Province, Nuestro Rock Awards, 1994, 1995, 1996. *Current Management:* Fatal Productions. *Address:* La Privada a Gertrudis Boconegra No. 48, Morelia, Michoacan, Mexico.

LANDER, Judd; b. 1 March 1948, Liverpool, England. Session Musician; Actor; Television Prod; Record Co Exec. m. (1) Janine de Wolfe, 3 July 1987, 2 d., (2) Danielle, (3) Sienna Tuesday. *Career:* Mem., The Hideaways, 1960s; Mem., The Selofane, 1968; Moved to London, 1970s; Session musician, CBS Records, 1974; Session musician for Badfinger; Walker Brothers; Scaffold; Bay City Rollers; Nazareth; Madness; The The; ABC; Maxi Priest; Prefab Sprout; Communards; Mike Oldfield; Dina Caroll; Tina Turner; Kirsty MacColl; Richard Ashcroft; Numerous performances include: The Cavern, Liverpool; Kampuchea charity concert, (with Paul McCartney), 1979; Assoc. prod., St Lucia Jazz Festival, 1991; Floor Dir, BRIT Awards, 1994–2000; Television appearances include: Top of the Pops; The Tube; Old Grey Whistle Test; Wogan; Des O'Connor Show; MTV; Montreux Pop Festival; Later With Jools Holland; Prod., television documentary, Jerry Lee Lewis; Concerts: Wembley Stadium; Wembley Arena; Knebworth House; Reading Festival; London Palladium; Royal Albert Hall; Culture Club Tour, 1998–99. *Compositions:* Resting Rough (film score); Music for The Short Show (LWT). *Recordings:* Albums: Flowers In The Dirt, Paul McCartney, 1989; Medusa, Annie Lennox, 1995; Alone With Everybody, Richard Ashcroft, 2000. Singles: Church Of The Poisoned Mind, Karma Chameleon, Culture Club (lead harmonica lines); Say You'll Be There, Spice Girls, 1996. *Honours:* Gold Award, British Academy of Songwriters, Composers and Authors, 1997. *Membership:* Musicians' Union; Equity; BAC&S. *Current Management:* Noel Gay Artists, 24 Denmark St, London WC2H 8NJ, England.

LANDGREN, Nils Lennart; b. 15 Feb. 1956, Degerfors, Sweden. Musician (trombone); Vocalist; Composer. m. Beatrice Jaras-Landgren, 9 July 1979. *Education:* College degree; Classical Music degree; Soloist diploma, University of Music in Arvika, Sweden. *Career:* Professional Trombone Player, age 19; Freelance work in Stockholm, Sweden; Recording and stage performance with all major Swedish artistes; Star, Skål, musical, Stockholm, running 2 years; Star, Villon, musical, Stockholm. *Compositions:* Red Horn, with Bruce Swedien; Aint Nobody, recorded with Maceo Parker; Cheyenne, with Michael Ruff. *Recordings:* Planet Rock; You're My No. 1; Streetfighter; Miles From Duke, with B A Wallin; Follow You Heart; Ch 2, with Johan Norberg; CH 2 – Two; Ballads; Gotland; Live in Stockholm; Paint It Blue; Swedish Folk Moderne; Contributions (as trombonist) to: Abba, Voulez-vous; Bose Broberg, Regni, 1995; Josefin Nilsson, Shapes, 1996; Bernard Purdie, Soul to Jazz; Norrbotten Big Band, 1996. *Honours:* 2 Swedish Grammy Awards; German Jazz Award, 1997. *Current Management:* Walter Brolund Inc, Kungsv 6, 19040, Rosersberg, Sweden. *Address:* Lillkalmar vägen 100B, 18265 Djurshom, Sweden.

LANE, Davey (David); b. Boronia, WA, Australia. Musician (guitar); Vocalist; Songwriter. *Career:* Mem., Odeon Sound; Mem., Australian rock band, You Am I, 1999–; Mem., The Brides, later renamed The Twin Set. *Recordings:* Albums: with You Am I: Saturday Night, 'Round Ten, 1999; Dress Me Slowly, 2001; Deliverance, 2002; with Tim Rogers and The Twin Set: What Rhymes With Cars and Girls, 1998. Singles: with You Am I: Singles: Damage; Get Up; Kick Hole In The Sky; Dirty Deeds Done Dirt Cheap; Trouble. *Honours:* Gold discs. *Address:* c/o BMG Australia Ltd, 194 Miller St, North Sydney, NSW 2060, Australia. *Website:* www.youami.com.au.

LANE, Jamie; b. 15 Sept. 1951, Kolkata, India. Musician (drums); Record Prod; Engineer; Programmer. m. Katerina Koumi, 8 June 1991, 1 d. *Education:* BA Hons, MA, Magdalene College, Cambridge. *Career:* Member, bands: The Movies, 1976–80; Sniff 'n' The Tears, 1980–82; Session drummer, 1982–; Played with: Tina Turner; Mark Knopfler; 10cc; Joan Armatrading; Agnetha; Van Morrison; Randy Newman; Ben E King; Paul Brady; Chage and Aska; Blancmange; Producer for: Microdisney; Railway Children; Pete Townshend; Paul Brady; Falco; Nick Kamen; Hot House; Jackie Quinn; Microgroove; Do Re Mi. *Compositions:* Deep Water, Jackie Quinn. *Recordings:* As drummer, Living On The Ceiling, Blancmange; As producer: Don't Come To Stay, Hot House; I Promised Myself, Nick Kamen. *Membership:* Musicians' Union. *Current Management:* Stephen Budd Management.

LANE, Rick; b. 22 April 1953, London, England. Composer; Prod; Musician (keyboards, guitar, bass, percussion); Backing Vocalist. *Education:* Guildhall Exhibition Scholar. *Career:* Founder, Rent Boys; Private Lives; 3 tours with The Edgar Broughton Band; Now produces music for film, television, radio, commercials, corporate video, station idents and multimedia. *Recordings:* with Rent Boys: 2 singles, 1 album; with Private Lives: 3 singles, 2 albums; Over 200 television, cinema, radio commercials, documentary and features for BBC, LWT, Granada, Anglia. *Honours:* N London Music Festival, Silver Medal;

Highly Commended, Roland Syn/Sound, 1992; D and AD Gold Pencil, 1993. *Membership:* British Music Writers' Council; Society of Producers of Applied Music; Performing Rights Society; MCPS; BAC&S; Musicians' Union; Alliance of Composer Organisations; Assen of Professional Composers; Composers Guild of Great Britain. *Current Management:* Nim Nim Musik. *Address:* Garden Studio, 19 Venetia Rd, London W5 4JD, England.

LANE, Stevens; b. 7 Nov. 1921, Hammersmith, London, England. Semi professional Musician (cornet); Bandleader. *Education:* Cornet teacher, Phil Parker. *Career:* Leader, own band, The Southern Stompers, 1950–; Re-named Red Hot Peppers, 1985–; Concerts include: Poland; Czechoslovakia; France; Germany; Netherlands; Denmark; Numerous broadcasts, BBC Jazz club. *Compositions:* Songs and instrumental pieces written or arranged for the band. *Recordings:* Albums released on VJM, Major-Minor, Stomp Off and Azure labels. *Membership:* Musicians' Union; MCPS; PRS. *Address:* 32 Kenton Lane, Harrow, Middlesex HA3 8TX, England.

LANG, Andy Lee; b. 26 July 1965, Vienna, Austria. Vocalist; Entertainer; Musician (piano). *Education:* Commercial School; Private studies with grandfather (Music Professor and Conductor). *Career:* Piano-player of Chuck Berry, European tour, 1992–93; Concerts with: Jerry Lee Lewis; Wanda Jackson; Carl Perkins; The Magic Platters; Fats Domino; Concerts, television and radio shows in: USA; Morocco; France; Switzerland; Germany; Austria. *Recordings:* Back To Rock 'n' Roll, 1990; Rockin' Piano Man, 1991; Back In Town, 1993; That's Entertainment Live, 1994; Rockin' Christmas, 1994. *Honours:* Golden Microphone, 1991. *Membership:* Austrian Composer Assen. *Current Management:* Star Box, Angela Kascha. *Address:* Simmerringer Haide 6/543, 1110 Vienna, Austria.

LANG, k. d. (Kathryn Dawn); b. 2 Nov. 1961, Consort, AB, Canada. Vocalist; Composer; Actress. *Career:* Played North American clubs with own band, The Reclines, 1982–87; Performed at closing ceremony, Winter Olympics, Calgary, 1988; Performed with Sting, Bruce Springsteen, Peter Gabriel and Tracy Chapman in Amnesty International tour, 1988; Headlining US tour, 1992; Royal Albert Hall, 1992; Earth Day benefit concert, Hollywood Bowl, 1993; Sang with Andy Bell, BRIT Awards, 1993; Television includes: Late Night With David Letterman; Wogan; The Arsenio Hall Show; The Tonight Show; Top of the Pops; Subject, South Bank Show documentary, ITV, 1995; Film appearances: Salmonberries, 1991, Teresa's Tattoo, 1994; The Last Don, 1997. *Recordings:* Albums: A Truly Western Experience, 1984; Angel With A Lariat, 1986; Shadowland, 1988; Absolute Torch and Twang, 1989; Ingénue, 1992; Even Cowgirls Get The Blues (soundtrack), 1993; All You Can Eat, 1995; Drag, 1997; Australian Tour, 1997; Invincible Summer, 2000; Live By Request, 2001; Features on soundtrack to film Dick Tracy; Singles include: Crying (duet with Roy Orbison), 1992; Constant Craving, 1992; Mind of Love, 1993; Miss Chatelaine, 1993; Just Keep Me Moving, 1993; If I Were You, 1995; Other. *Recordings include:* Duets, with Elton John, 1993; Love Makes The World, Carole King, 2001. *Honours:* Canadian CMA Awards: Entertainer of Year, 1989; Album of Year, 1990; Grammy Awards: Best Female Country Vocal Performance, 1990; Best Pop Vocal, 1993; Album of the Year, Ingénue, 1993; American Music Award: Favourite New Artist, 1993; Songwriter of the Year, with Ben Mink, 1993; BRIT Award, Best International Female, 1995. *Address:* c/o WEA Records, The Warner Building, 28 Kensington Church St, London W8 4SP, England. *Website:* www.kdlang.com.

LANG, Penny; b. 15 July 1942, Montréal, Québec, Canada. Folk Vocalist; Songwriter; Musician (guitar). 1 s. *Education:* 1 year, Sir George Williams University, Montréal. *Career:* National Folk Festival, Australia; Philadelphia Folk Festival; Vancouver, Winnipeg, Mariposa Folk Festivals; The Bitter End and Gerdes Folk City, CBGB's, New York; The Riverboat, Yellow Door, Pornographic Onion Coffeehouses, Canada; Caffe Lena, New York; The Folkway, New Hampshire; The Ark, Michigan; Montréal Jazz Festival; Toronto Soul 'n' Blues Fest (Harborfront); Music for NFB documentary Marilyn Waring – Who's Counting? Sex, Lies and Global Economics; Tour of UK and France, 1998; Tönder Folk Festival, Denmark, 1998; Women's Blues Revue, Toronto, 1998. *Compositions:* Open Up Our Hearts to See; Ain't Life Sweet; Carry On Children; November Blues; Firewater; Senses of Your Leave. *Recordings:* YES!!, 1991; Live (solo), 1992; Carry On Children, 1993; Ain't Life Sweet, 1996; Penny Lang and Friends Live, 1998. *Publications:* Lyrics/music, Open Up Our Hearts To See, Sing Out magazine; Articles, reviews for: Toronto Star; Montréal Gazette; Dirty Linen. *Honours:* Several Canada Council awards for touring, writing, recording; Grant from Québec Ministère des Affaires Culturelles. *Membership:* SOCAN.

LANGBORN, Torbjorn; b. 17 May 1955, Stockholm, Sweden. Musician; Composer. 2 d. *Education:* Adolf Fredrik Music School; Musicology, Stockholm University; Piano, Pedagogic, Royal Academy of Music, Stockholm. *Career:* Live Gigs, Radio and some Television Appearances through Sweden, Finland, Poland, Norway; Freelance Pianist, Salsa, Tango and Jazz; Teacher, Improvisation, Afro American and Jazz Theory. *Compositions:* Sangre nueva; En Estocolmo no pasa nada; Sad Samba; Salsa; Oiga mi Compadre; Canciones del Alma. *Recordings:* Hot Salsa – Maldito Primitivo; Hot Salsa Meets Swedish Jazz; Torbjorn Langborn and his Feel Life

Orchestra. *Membership:* STIM; SAMI; SKAP; Musicians' Union. *Address:* Hjalmar Söderbergs Väg 16 D 2tr, 112 52 Stockholm, Sweden.

LANGE, Barbara Rose; b. 14 Jan. 1955, Casper, New York, USA. Ethnomusicologist. *Education:* PhD, Ethnomusicology, University of Washington, 1993. *Career:* Assistant Professor, Moores School of Music, University of Houston, 1996–. *Publications:* Lakadalmas Rosk and the Rejection of Popular Culture in Post-Socialist Hungary, in Retuning Culture, 1996; Hungarian Romanian (Gypsy) Political Activism and the Development of Folkier Ensemble Music, 1997; What Was the Conquering Magic... : The Power of Discontinuity in Hungarian Gypsy Nota, in Ethnomusicology, 1997. *Honours:* IREX Exchange Fellowship, Hungary, 1990–91; Fulbright Graduate Grant, Hungary, 1990–91; Mellon Postdoctoral Fellow, Cornell University, 1995–96. *Membership:* Society for Ethnomusicology; International Council for Traditional Music. *Address:* Moores School of Music, University of Houston, TX 77204, USA.

LARATTA, David Ottavio; b. 19 April 1970, Saint Denis, France. Musician (bass, drums, trumpet). *Education:* Arts and Letters (A3). *Career:* Guest musician, guest Youssou N'Dour, 1990; Francopholies, La Rochelle, France, 1992; Television show, TF1, 1992; 20th Anniversary, Sony France, 1993; National Concours Jazz in Paris, La Défense, with Used 2b Bop, 1995; Numerous concerts, shows, appearances, throughout France, with various bands; Marcel Sabiani Trio; Lewis Robinson, 1997; Léa loCicero, 1997; Divan du monde, with Cheick Tidiane Seck 'Tribute to Fela', 1997; Gino Williams, 1998; Caravana, Afro Cuban, Mars, 1998. *Membership:* SPEDIDAM; SACEM. *Address:* 4 rue de la République, 93450 L'Ile Saint Denis, France.

LARSEN, Jens Kjaer; b. 30 May 1964, Copenhagen, Denmark. Rap Artiste; Vocalist; Songwriter. m. Camilla Palikaras, 4 Aug. 1997. *Career:* Member, Cut 'n' Move Band, Several Television Shows, Tours of Europe, Australia, USA and Asia. *Compositions:* Get Serious; Spread Love; Give It Up; I'm Alive; 4 Albums. *Recordings:* Get Serious; Peace Love and Harmony; The Sounds of Now; Into The Zone. *Honours:* Silver Lion, Germany; 4 Grammy Awards, Denmark. *Current Management:* TG Management, Denmark. *Address:* 1120 Kobenhavn K, Copenhagen, Denmark.

LARSEN, Jon; b. 7 Jan. 1959, Jar, near Oslo, Norway. Musician (guitar); Composer; Record Prod. m. Barbara Jahn, 2 July 1994, 1 step-d., 2 d. *Education:* High School of Music. *Career:* Full-time professional guitarist/ composer with Hot Club de Norvege, 1979–; World-wide touring since 1990; Established Hot Club de Norvege (quartet), 1979; The Django Festival, Norway, 1980; Hot Club Records, 1982–; Norwegian Music Distribution, 1985–; The Vintage Guitar Series, 1988–; The Music Operators, 1995–; The International Gypsy Jazz Archive, 1998–; The Robert Normann Society, 1999; The Robert Normann Museum, 2000–. *Recordings:* 15 albums with Hot Club de Norvege; Produced nearly 250 albums for Hot Club Records, with Chet Baker, Ph Catherine, Stephane Grappelli, Warne Marsh, The Rosenberg Trio; Guitar on: Gipsy Swing, The Grappelli Trio, 2000. *Honours:* NOPA Composer of the Year, Norway, 1994. *Membership:* Composers' Society of Norway (NOPA); Record Producers' Society of Norway (FONO). *Current Management:* Frost Publishing Ltd, Norway. *Address:* PO Box 5202 Majorstua, 0302 Oslo, Norway.

LARSSON, Anders; b. 13 April 1958, Malmo, Sweden. Man. *Career:* Own management for Scandinavian artistes, 10 years; Currently, 30 artistes in pop, jazz, blues, rock; Name of company: United Stage Production AB. *Membership:* Mem. of Board, Swedish Impressario Assen; Swedish Publishers' Assen. *Current Management:* United Stage Production AB. *Address:* PO Box 9174, 200 39 Malmo, Sweden.

LASCELLES, Jeremy; b. 14 Feb. 1955, London, England. CEO, Chrysalis Music. 1 s., 2 d. *Career:* Artiste Management, 1972–75; Tour Management, 1975–79; A&R Consultant, 1979–80, Dir of Marketing 1980–82, Dir of A&R, 1982–88, Virgin Records; Man. Dir, Ten Records, 1988–92; Offside Productions and Management, 1993–94; Man. Dir, 1994–2001, CEO 2001–, Chrysalis Music; Man. Dir, The Echo Label, 1998–2001. *Address:* 13 Bramley Rd, London W10 6SP, England.

LASSEN, Nils; b. 10 March 1960, Denmark. Composer. m. Sisse Lassen, 1 d. *Career:* Composing for Theatre and Film, Denmark and Danish Television, including The Royal Theatre. *Compositions:* Boy of 1000 Tears, 1997; Riders of Depression, 1997; No Lilacs, No Lillies, No More, 1997. *Recordings:* Lament for Ronni, 1997; Lost in the Woods, 1997; Most of Us Prefer Not To Think, 1997; Inside/Outside, 1997. *Membership:* DJBFA. *Address:* Lille Istedgade 5, 1706 Copenhagen V, Denmark.

LAST, James (Hans); b. 17 April 1929, Bremen, Germany. Bandleader; Arranger. *Career:* Member, Radio Bremen Dance Orchestra, 1946; Bandleader, Becker-Last Ensemble, 1948–55; Arranger, radio stations, Polydor Records, 1955; Bandleader, combination of classics, dance, pop and country music, 1965–; Worked with artistes including: Caterina Valente; Astrud Gilberto; Richard Clayderman; Over 50m. records sold world-wide. *Recordings:* Albums include: Non Stop Dancing, 1965; This Is James Last, 1967; Hammond A Go

Go, 1967; James Last Goes Pop, 1968; Ole, 1973; Country And Square Dance Party, 1974; Ten Years Non Stop Party Album, 1975; Make The Party Last, 1975; Christmas James Last, 1976; In London, 1978; East To West, 1978; Last The Whole Night Long, 1979; Christmas Classics, 1979; Caribbean Nights, 1980; Seduction, 1980; Classics For Dreaming, 1980; Hansimania, 1981; Roses From The South—The Music of Johann Strauss, 1981; Tango, 1983; Christmas Dancing, 1983; Greatest Songs Of The Beatles, 1983; Games That Lovers Play, 1984; Rose Of Tralee And Other Irish Favourites, 1984; All Aboard With Cap'n James, 1984; In Russia, 1984; In Allgau (In The Alps), 1984; In Scotland, 1985; In Holland, 1987; The Berlin Concert, 1987; Dance Dance Dance, 1987; Flute Fiesta, 1988; By Request, 1988; Plays Bach, 1988; Happy Heart, 1989; Classics By Moonlight, 1990; Together At Last, 1991; My Favourites, 1995; In Scandinavia, 1997; Macarena, 1998; Meisterstucke, 1998; Tenderly, 1998; Classics From Russia, 2000; Hammond and Trumpet, 2001; Gentlemen Of Music, 2002. Single: The Seduction, used in film American Gigolo, 1981.

LASWELL, Bill; b. 14 Feb. 1950. Musician (bass, guitar); Record Co Exec; Record Prod. *Career:* Leader, groups: Material; Curlew; Last Exit; Founder, record labels OAO, Celluloid; Record producer for Herbie Hancock. *Recordings:* Solo albums: Baselines, 1984; Best of Bill Laswell, 1985; Point Blank, 1986; Low Life, 1987; Hear No Evil, 1988; Psychonavigation, 1994; Axiom Ambient: Lost in the Translation, 1994; Web, 1995; Cymatic Scan, 1995; Silent Recoil, 1995; Bass Terror, 1995; Dark Massive, 1996; Oscillations, 1996; Dub Meltdown, 1997; City of Light, 1997; Jazzonia, 1998; Divination: Sacrifice, 1998; Invisible Design, 1999; Imaginary Cuba, 1999; Lo Def Pressure, 2000; Radioaxiom, A Dub Transmission, 2000; Filmtracks, 2001; Points of Order, 2001; with Material: Temporary Music, 1980; Third Power; Memory Serves; One Down; with Last Exit: The Noise of Trouble; with Herbie Hancock: Future Shock; Perfect Machine, 1988; with John Zorn and Eugene Chadbourne: The Parachute Years (7-disc set), 1997; Also producer for numerous artistes including: Yoko Ono; Mick Jagger; Gil Scott-Heron; Nona Hendryx; Manu Dibango; PiL; Fela Kuti; Iggy Pop; Motörhead; Laurie Anderson; Afrika Bambaataa; Yellowman. *Current Management:* AGM (UK), 145A Ladbrooke Grove, London W10 6HJ, England.

LATCHFORD-EVANS, Lee; b. 28 Jan. 1975, Chester, England. Vocalist. *Career:* Toured in various theatre productions; Mem., Steps, 1997–2001; Popular with UK teen audience; Numerous television appearances, incl. Steps To The Stars; Tours, incl. Gold–Greatest Hits tour, 2001; Played Teen Angel in West End production of musical, Grease, 2002. *Recordings:* Albums: Step One, 1998; Steptacular, 1999; Buzz, 2000; Gold, 2001; The Last Dance, 2002. *Honours:* BRIT Award, Best Selling Live Act, 2000. *Address:* c/o Zomba Records Ltd, Zomba House, 165–167 Willesden High Rd, London NW10 2SG, England. *Website:* www.stepsofficial.com.

LATHAM, Anthony John Heaton; b. 30 Oct. 1940, Wigan, England. University Lecturer. m. Dawn Catherine Farleigh, 10 Nov. 1990. *Education:* BA, Medieval and Modern History, Birmingham, 1964; PhD African Studies, Birmingham, 1970; Clarinet tuition. *Career:* Debut, Wigan Jazz Club, 1958; Penn-Latham Quintet, University of Birmingham, 1961–63; Harlech Television, 1967; Axiom Jazz Band, Swansea, 1967–68; J. J.'s Rhythm Aces, Swansea University, 1982–84; Speakeasy Jazz Band, Swansea, 1984–; John Latham's Jazztimers, 1995–; Brecon Jazz Festival, 1986–89, 1991, 1996–99; Cork Jazz Festival, 1987; Birmingham Jazz Festival, 1987, 1988; BBC Wales, 1989, 1990, 1992, 1994; Llangollen Jazz Festival, 1995–98; Bude Jazz Festival, 1998; Clubs: Fritzel's; Gazebo; Bonaparte's Retreat; In New Orleans, 1988. *Recordings:* Blanche Finlay with The Speakeasy Jazzband, 1987; John Latham's Jazztimers, Sandy's Bar, Cardiff, 1997; John Latham's Jazztimers, 1998; Sandy and Co, 1998. *Publications:* Al Fairweather Discography, 1994; Eurojazz Discographies, No 34; Stan Greig Discography, 1995; Eurojazz Discography, No 42; Sandy Brown Discography, 1997; Eurojazz Discography, No 5. *Contributions to:* New Orleans Music Vol. 2 No. 1, 1990; Jazz Journal International, Jan, Sept, 1993, June, 1994, May, 1996; British Jazz Times, Sept.–Oct., 1994; The Jazz Rag, March–April, Nov.–Dec., 1998, July–Aug., 1999. *Membership:* Musicians' Union; Secretary, Sandy Brown Society, 1997–.

LATTIKAS, Urmas; b. 17 Aug. 1960, Tapa, Estonia. Composer; Arranger; Conductor; Musician (piano). m. Kaia, 22 Dec. 1993, 2 s. *Education:* Graduated as composer, Estonian Music Academy, 1977–86; Post-graduate studies, jazz composition, piano, Berklee College of Music, Boston, USA, 1990. *Career:* Performing artiste, founder, leader, own jazz group Urmas Lattikas Quintet; Arranger, jazz, pop, classical styles; Accompanist, numerous vocal and instrumental performances; Extensive club, concert appearances, numerous jazz events, Estonia and abroad; Recordings, appearances, radio and television; Urmas Lattikas Quintet represented Estonian jazz in European Jazz Night television programme; Conducted Estonian song, Eurovision Song Contest, 1994. *Compositions:* Symphonic, choral, chamber music, film scores; Music for single and album. *Recordings:* Single: In A Twilight Room; Album: Freedom To Love, Freedom To Lose. *Honours:* First Prize, U Naissoo composition contest, 1983, 1984; Levi Jaagup Award, Keyboard Player of the Year, 1990. *Address:* Nurme 26, Tallinn EE 0016, Estonia.

LAUDET, François; b. 11 Nov. 1958, Paris, France. Musician (drums). *Education:* Baccalaureat. *Career:* Best Big Band Jazz Drummer in France; Band Leader; Appearances at several Festivals and Television Shows; Replacement of Butch Miles in Count Basie Orchestra in European tour, 1997. *Compositions:* Memphis Belle Blues. *Recordings:* With: Saxomania, Ellingtomania Ornicar Big Band, Super Swing Machine, Francois Laudet Big Band. *Honours:* Prix Sydney Bechet, 1994; Academie du Jazz. *Membership:* Union des Musiciens de Jazz. *Current Management:* François Laudet and Corinne Bondu. *Address:* 14 rue des Carrieres, 93230 Romainville, France.

LAUDET, Philippe; b. 11 Dec. 1959, Nanterre, France. Composer; Arranger; Musician (trumpet, piano). m. Catherine Laudet, 19 Dec. 1987, 1 s., 2 d. *Education:* Astrophysics, until age 28; Classical piano from age 6–16; Jazz piano from age 10; Jazz trumpet from age 15. *Career:* Leader, composer, Ornicar Big Band, 1980–95; Played all major jazz festivals in France: Paris; Nice; Salon de Provence; Marciac; Vienne; Trumpet soloist, Tuxedo Big Band, 1992–; Played in Marciac, Coutance, Spain. *Recordings:* with Ornicar Big Band: Mais où est Donc Ornicar?, 1984; Le Retour d'Ornicar, 1986; Jazz Cartoon, 1989; L'Incroyable Huck, 1991; 3 recordings with Tuxedo Big Band: Rhythm is our business, 1994; Siesta at the Fiesta, 1996; For Ella and Chick, 1998; Beautiful Love, Philippe Laudet Quartet, 1996. *Honours:* Winner, Concours National de la Defense, Paris, with Ornicar Big Band, 1982; Prizes from Academy of Jazz and Hot Club of France, with Tuxedo Big Band, 1994; Hot Club de France, for Siesta at the Fiesta, 1996. *Membership:* SACEM; SPEDIDAM; UMJ.

LAUK, Tiit; b. 9 Jan. 1948, Tartu, Estonia. Musician (piano, keyboards). m. Eleonora Lauk, 22 Aug. 1952, 1 s. *Education:* Estonian Academy of Music; Pianist, leader, teacher, Jazz Education at Bob Brookmeyer's. *Career:* Over 35 years as pianist and leader, 15 years, piano and jazz teacher; 3 years as Producer, Musical Programmes, Estonian TV; Director, Estonian Jazz Foundation 1991–; Debut, Gintarine Triuba Festival, Lithuania, 1968; Numerous festivals, solo concerts in former USSR, Europe; Tours with famous Estonian opera singers in Sweden, Finland; Projects with Finnish, Swedish, British, Russian musicians; Numerous recordings, Estonian Radio, Estonian TV, 1972–. *Compositions:* Over 300 instrumental and vocal arrangements for jazz orchestra/band. *Recordings:* Numerous recordings since 1970 for Estonian Radio, Estonian Television; MC KohtumispaiK Jazzkaar, 1995; Pendel, 1997. *Publications:* By The Path of Estonian Light Music, Lithuania, 1987; Jazz Improvisation: Practical Course For Piano (I Bril), translation into Estonian; Several reviews in several publications in Estonia, Finland, France, Lithuania. *Honours:* Order of Nicola Rolin (France); Jazzclub du Vallage (France); Jazzclub of Tartu (Estonia). *Membership:* International Asscn of Schools of Jazz.

LAUPER, Cyndi (Cynthia Anne Stephanie); b. 22 June 1953, Queens, New York, USA. Vocalist; Songwriter; Actress. *Career:* Club singer, Manhattan; Lead singer, Doc West; Member, Flyer, 1974–77; Formed Blue Angel, 1978–79; Solo recording artiste, 1983–; World-wide tours; Participant, Music Speaks Louder Than Words summit, USSR, 1988; American Music Awards concerts, Tokyo, 1991; Actress, films: Vibes, 1988; Mother Goose Rock 'n' Rhyme, Disney Channel, 1990; Paradise Paved, 1990; Off and Running, 1992; Participant, The Wall by Roger Waters, Berlin, 1990. *Recordings:* Albums: with Blue Angel: Blue Angel, 1980; Solo albums: She's So Unusual, 1983; True Colors, 1986; A Night To Remember, 1989; Music Speaks Louder Than Words, 1990; Hat Full of Stars, 1993; Singles include: Girls Just Want To Have Fun, 1984; Time After Time (No. 1, USA), 1984; She Bop, 1984; All Through The Night, 1984; True Colors (No. 1, USA), 1986; Change of Heart, 1987; What's Going On, 1987; I Drove All Night, 1989; The World Is Stone, 1992; That's What I Think, 1993; Hey Now Girls, 1994; Come on Home, 1995; You Don't Know, 1997; Ballad of Cleo and Joe, 1997; Disco Inferno, 1999; Guest vocals, Blowback, Tricky, 2001; Contributor, charity records: We Are The World, USA For Africa, 1984; Give Peace A Chance, The Peace Choir, 1991; Put On Your Green Shoes, 1993. *Honours:* American Video Award, 1984; MTV Music Video Award, 1984; American Music Awards: Favourite Female Artist, Favourite Female Video Artist, 1985; Grammy Award, Best New Artist, 1985. *Current Management:* Hard To Handle Management, 640 Lee Rd, Suite 106, Wayne, PA 19087, USA.

LAURENCE, Graham Richard; b. 1 April 1964, Croydon, Surrey, England. Songwriter; Musician (guitar). *Education:* City of London Polytechnic; Goldsmiths University. *Career:* Guitarist, Danielle Dax, European Tour, 1986; Guitarist/songwriter, Queen B; Appearances: TVAM; Jonathan Ross; Box Office, Radio 1; Radio 1 News; Radio 1 Tour. *Recordings:* Red Top Hot Shot; I Love You; Satellite; Loving You. *Membership:* Musicians' Union; Performing Rights Society. *Current Management:* Important Management. *Address:* Marlow, Bucks, England.

LAURENT, Mark; b. 15 March 1954, Auckland, New Zealand. Vocalist; Songwriter; Musician (electric guitar, acoustic guitar, harmonica, Rowan lute, percussion, bass). m. (1) Adrienne Lovegrove, 5 Feb. 1977, 1 s., (2) Brenda Liddiard, 4 Aug. 1990. *Career:* Band or solo performer, playing throughout England, New Zealand and Australia, 1968–; Studio producer, 1985–; Major tours supporting Larry Norman, 1984; Barry Maguire, 1987; Larbanois

Carrero, 1989; Adrian Plass, 1993; Thom Bresh, 1995; Wishbone Ash, 2000; Major festivals include: Sweetwaters, 1985; Mainstage, 1987; Jackey's Marsh, Tasmania, 1990; Shelterbelt, 1993; Auckland Folk Festival, 1993–99; Parachute, 1994, 1995; Tahora, 1989–2002; Wellington Folk Festival, 1999; New Spirit, 1997–2001. *Recordings:* Mark Laurent, 1982; Kindness In A Strong City, 1986; Songs For Our Friends (collaboration), 1989; Trust, 1992; Heart Attack, 1996; Tahora 21, collaboration, 1997; Millennium Hippies, 1998; Trebox, 2000; Stations Of The Cross, 2001; The Light And The Shadowland, 2001; Waiting For Donald, 2001; Journeys (compilation), 2002; Songwriter, Producer, musician, other artistes' albums. *Publications:* Perhaps (poetry), 1995; Various articles for music magazines. *Membership:* Australasian Performing Rights Ascn. *Current Management:* Distribution: Someone Up There Records; Digital Flower Productions. *Address:* 7b Sylvan Ave W, Mt Eden, Auckland, New Zealand. *E-mail:* hippies@kiwilink.co.nz. *Website:* www.kiwilink.co.nz/~hippies.

LAURITSEN, Joergen; b. 9 Aug. 1966, Svendborg, Denmark. Conductor; Composer; Arranger; Musician. m. Pia Boysen. *Education:* MA, Music Theory, Conducting, Royal Danish Academy of Music, 1990; MA, Piano, Composition, Rhythmic Music Conservatory, Copenhagen, 1992. *Career:* All major musicals in Denmark for the last 5 years; Chess in concert with Elaine Paige, Tommy Korberg, 1997; Solo with Harolyn Blackwell, 1997; Live Symphonic with Lisa Nilsson, 1988. *Compositions:* Sarajevo Butterfly; Dance of the Clogs; Songs in the Wind; Mixed Love; Intonation For The Wizard, Danish Radio Concert Orchestra, 1998. *Recordings:* Mixed Love; Les Miserables. *Honours:* Danish Ministry of Culture, 1991; Denmark-America Foundation, 1992. *Membership:* Danish Society of Jazz, Rock and Folk Composers; Danish Conductors Ascn. *Address:* Kirsten Pilsvej 10, Isal, 2920 Charlottenlund, Denmark.

LAVELLE, Caroline; Musician (cello); Vocalist; Songwriter. *Career:* Leader, all-female trio Electra Strings; Group toured with Nigel Kennedy; As session musician, played with Massive Attack; Peter Gabriel; Ride; The Fall. *Recordings:* Albums: Spirit, 1995; Brilliant Midnight, 2001; Brilliant Midnight 2.0, 2002. Single: Moorlough Shore; Contributor: Kiss in the Dream House, Siouxsie and the Banshees; Waking Hours, Del Amitri; In Ribbons, Pale Saints; Sex and Misery, Voice of the Beehive; Expecting to Fly, Bluetones; Home of The Whale, Massive Attack, 1992; Us, Peter Gabriel, 1992; Dream Harder, The Waterboys, 1993; The Bends, Radiohead, 1995; Kafka, Nigel Kennedy, 1996; The Book of Secrets, Loreena McKennitt, 1997; Origin of Symmetry, Muse, 2001. *Website:* www.carolinelavelle.com.

LAVELLE, James, (DJ Kutmaster Lavski); b. 22 Feb. 1974, Oxford, England. Prod; DJ. *Career:* Worked at Honest Jon's Record Shop, Ladbroke Grove; Set up Mo' Wax Records with a small loan aged 19, 1993; Co-founder: That's How It Is club night (with Gilles Peterson) at London's Bar Rumba; Formed U.N.K.L.E. with production partner DJ Shadow; Resident DJ at Fabric in London; Collaborations: DJ Shadow; Thom Yorke; Ian Brown; Slam; Remixed: The Verve; Radiohead; Breakbeat Era; Howie B. *Recordings:* Psyence Fiction, 1998; Singles: The Time Has Come, 1994; Berry Meditation, 1996; Rock On, 1997; Rabbit In Your Headlights, 1998; Be There, 1999. *Membership:* MCPS. *Address:* c/o Mo' Wax Labels Ltd, 1 Codrington Mews, London W11 2EH, England.

LAVIGNE, Avril R; b. 27 Sept. 1984, Napanee, ON, Canada. Vocalist; Songwriter; Musician (guitar). *Career:* Signed to Arista Records. *Recordings:* Album: Let Go, 2002. Singles: Let Go, 2002; Complicated, 2002. *Current Management:* Nettwerk Management. *Address:* c/o Arista Records, 6 W 57th St, New York, USA. *Website:* www.avril-lavigne.com.

LAVIS, Gilson; b. 27 June 1951, Bedford, England. Musician (drums, percussion); Songwriter. m. Nicola Mercedes Keller, 10 Nov. 1993, 1 s. *Career:* Drummer for: The Bo Weavils; Headline News; Springfield Revival; Chris Rea; Squeeze, 1975–91; Pick up drummer, Chuck Berry, Jerry Lee Lewis; Cabaret drummer for artistes including: Tommy Cooper; Bob Monkhouse; Lulu; Freddie Starr; David Frost; Engelbert Humperdinck; Member, Jools Holland and the Rhythm and Blues Orchestra, 1991–; Concerts, tours with: Chris Rea, Europe; Chuck Berry, 2 tours, UK, Europe; Jerry Lee Lewis, British tour; Squeeze, 20 British tours, 20–25 USA/Canada tours, 1 Australia tour; Jools Holland, 14 UK, 2 Ireland tours; Television includes: with Squeeze: Top of the Pops; Old Grey Whistle Test; with Jools Holland: Don't Forget Your Toothbrush, CH4, as house band drummer, working with: Jimmy Somerville, Robert Palmer, Cher, Neil Sedaka, Chaka Khan, Lulu, Roger Daltrey, Barry White, Lemmy, Vic Reeves and Bob Mortimer, Roy Wood, Kylie Minogue, Suggs, Kim Wilde, Michelle Gayle; The Happening, BSB/Sky, with artistes including: Midge Ure; Mica Paris; Later With Jools Holland, BBC2, with artistes including: Dusty Springfield, Sting, Stevie Winwood, Maria Mckee; All Saints; The Corrs; B. B. King; Tom Jones; Dr John; House band drummer, Name That Tune, Channel 5; Drummer with the Eno and Jools Holland Rhythm and Blues Orchestra at the opening ceremony of the Millennium Dome. *Compositions:* with Jools Holland: Biggy Wiggy; Birdcage Walk. *Recordings:* Hit singles with Squeeze: Take Me I'm Yours, 1978; Cool For Cats (No. 2, UK), 1979; Up The Junction (No. 2, UK), 1979; Another Nail In My Heart, 1980; Pulling Mussels From A Shell, 1980; Labelled With Love, 1981; Tempted, 1981; Hourglass, 1987; Albums with Squeeze: Squeeze, 1978;

Cool For Cats, 1979; Argy Bargy, 1980; East Side Story, 1981; Sweets From A Stranger, 1982; Babylon and On, 1987; Frank, 1989; Play, 1991; Greatest Hits, 1992; with Jools Holland: A World of His Own, 1990; The Full Compliment, 1991; The A to Z of The Piano, 1992; Live Performance, 1994; Sex and Jazz and Rock and Roll, 1996; Lift The Lid, 1997; Jools Holland The Best Of, 1998; Jools Holland's Swing Album, 2001; Small World Big Band, 2001; Solo album: Drumbaba, 1998. *Honours:* Gold, Silver, Platinum discs. *Address:* One Fifteen Ltd, The Gallery, 28–30 Wood Wharf, Horseferry Pl., London SE10, England.

LAW, Michael Charles Ewan; b. 30 March 1960, Dar Es Saalam, Tanzania. Musician (piano); Vocalist; Musical Dir; Composer; Lecturer. *Education:* BA, Gonville and Caius College, Cambridge, 1979–82; Royal College of Music, 1982–86. *Career:* Musical Dir, The Piccadilly Dance Orchestra, 1988–; Numerous television, radio appearances, concerts and tours. *Compositions:* Play Me An Elegant Song; I'm Singin' A Swing Song Now. *Recordings:* Five albums with The Piccadilly Dance Orchestra, 1989, 1993, 1995, 1997, 1999. *Membership:* PRS; MCPS. *Current Management:* Alan Bennett. *Address:* Piccadilly Dance Orchestra, 27 Caesar Ave, Kingsnorth, Ashford, Kent TN23 3PZ, England.

LAWLER, Fergal Patrick; b. 4 March 1971, Limerick, Ireland. Musician (drums, percussion). *Career:* Mem., The Cranberries, renamed The Cranberry Saw Us, 1990–; Numerous headlining tours, festivals, radio and television appearances. *Recordings:* Albums: Everybody Else Is Doing It, So Why Can't We? (No. 1, UK), 1993; No Need To Argue, 1994; To The Faithful Departed, 1996; Bury The Hatchet, 1999; Bury The Hatchet: The Complete Sessions, 2000; Wake Up And Smell The Coffee, 2001; Treasure Box, 2002; Stars: The Best Of 1992–2002, 2002. Singles: Dreams, 1993; Linger, 1993; Zombie, 1994; Ode To My Family, 1994; I Can't Be With You, 1995; Ridiculous Thoughts, 1995; Salvation, 1996; Free To Decide, 1996; Promises, 1999; Animal Instinct, 1999; Just My Imagination, 1999; You And Me, 2000; Analyse, 2001; Time Is Ticking Out, 2002; This Is The Day, 2002; Stars, 2002. *Current Management:* Timeless Music Ltd. *Address:* The Cranberries, PO Box 180, Limerick, Ireland. *Website:* www.cranberries.com.

LAWLESS, Jim (Hugh James); b. 18 Feb. 1935, Woolwich, London, England. Musician (tuned percussion). m. Carole Ann, 6 April 1968, 3 d. *Education:* HNC in Electronics; 3 years piano lessons. *Career:* Became professional, joined The Eric Delaney Band on Ronnie Scott's recommendation, 1960; Worked at Hammersmith Palais, Lyceum Empire, Leicester Square, 1963–65; Freelance session player, records, television, broadcasts, films, 1965; Played jazz, Hollywood Bowl; US tour with George Shearing; US tour with Charlie Watts. *Recordings:* Recorded with: LSO; Royal Philharmonic; Ted Heath; Jack Parnell; Stéphane Grappelli; Bob Parnow; Joe Loss; BBC Big Band; George Shearing; Henry Mancini; Mel Tormé; Peggy Lee; Lena Horne; Nelson Riddle; Kiri Te Kanawa; Nearly all 60s, 70s pop stars including Lulu, The Beatles, Tom Jones. *Membership:* Musicians' Union; PRS. *Current Management:* 1 The Strand, Ferring, West Sussex BN12 5QX, England.

LAWRENCE, Andrew (Andy); b. 2 Nov. 1954, Swindon, Wiltshire, England. Musician (Trumpeter, Arranger/Composer, Vocalist). 3 d. *Education:* Trumpet lessons, age 11; Brass band training. *Career:* Professional on British and US soul music scene, 1972–; 5 years touring continent, 1973–78, with Roy Pellett Jazzband; Settled West Berlin, Germany, 1976–; Freelance Studio work, Arranger, Club work, Concerts, TV (SFB, ARD, RTL) and Radio; Moved to Stuttgart, 1983; Lecturer, Instructor, Baden-Würtenberg Youth Jazz Orchestra, 1984; Numerous concert tours with Peanuts Hucko, Ben Waters, George Kelly; Lead for Joe Schwarz Orchestra (5 years); Led large and small own ensembles; Over 120 original compositions, some recorded; Authority on swing music; Currently, much in demand as arranger, soloist and vocalist. *Recordings:* 15 albums as featured Soloist – one as Leader. *Current Management:* Andy Lawrence, Altenbergstr 32, 70180 Stuttgart, Germany. *Address:* Altenbergstr 32, 70180 Stuttgart, Germany.

LAWRENCE, Denise; b. 15 Feb. 1956, Hayes, Middlesex, England. Jazz Vocalist; Bandleader. m. Tony Lawrence, 16 Aug. 1985, 2 d. *Career:* Vocalist, bandleader, The Denise Lawrence Band; Denise Lawrence and Storeyville Tickle jazz band, 15 years; Also: Denise Lawrence and Her Trio; Tony Lawrence (husband) as pianist and Musicial Director; Most major jazz clubs, festivals, UK, Europe; Compere, co-organizer, residential festivals, various holiday locations; Appears, cabaret and theatres; Particular interest, gospel music, hymns, spirituals; Regularly on radio, and television: ITV, BBC, include: Songs of Praise. *Recordings:* 10 albums, Let It Shine; Can't Help Lovin' These Men of Mine; Hangin' Around, 1997; Ain't That Good News, 1997; I Guess There's An End To Everything, 2000; Music Maestro Please, 2002. *Honours:* Best vocalist, UK Jazz Travel Awards, 1994; Let It Shine, Best New Jazz Recording of Year, Der Jazzfreund, German magazine. *Membership:* Musicians' Union. *Address:* 189 Loddon Bridge Rd, Woodley, Reading, Berkshire RG5 4BP, England. *Telephone:* (118) 969-0625. *E-mail:* tony@jazzbreaks.freeserve.co.uk. *Website:* www.denise lawrence.co.uk; www.jazzbreaks.com.

LAWRENCE, Peter Raymond; b. 29 Oct. 1957, Leamington Spa, England. Prod; Publisher; DJ. 1 s, 1 d. *Career:* Manager, Our Price Records; Sales Manager, Making Waves Distribution; Owner, Cooking Vinyl Records; Owner, Global Headz; Founder, The Big Chill. *Recordings:* Producer: Michelle Shocked, Texas Campfire Tapes. *Address:* PO Box 7378, London N4 3RH, England.

LAWRENCE, Rohn; b. New Haven, Connecticut, USA. Jazz Musician (guitar); Vocalist. *Education:* Began playing guitar aged 2; Building guitars aged 9; Played electric guitars aged 13. *Career:* Played in New Haven funk bands Good News; The Lift; Performed with: Marion Meadows; George Duke; Dianne Reeves; Jonathon Butler; Alex Bugñon; Freddie Jackson; Najee; Moved to Boston, 1993. *Recordings:* Hanging On A String, 1993; See Ya Around, 1998; with Pieces of a Dream: Pieces, 1997; with Will Downing, Invitation Only, 1997; with Jay Rowe: Jay Walking, 1997; Bread and Butter: Adventures of Bread and Butter, 1998; with Boney James, Body Language, 1999. *Current Management:* Kim Ewing, Atlantic Jazz Publicity.

LAWRENCE, Steven; b. 29 Sept. 1961, Glasgow, Scotland. Musician (bouzouki, cittern, mandola, dulcimer, percussion); Prod. *Education:* HNC in Electrical Engineering. *Career:* Appeared at Celtic Connections Festival, Glasgow, 1993, 1994; Member, Iron Horse; Appearances include: Poland; Eygpt; Tours of Netherlands, Germany, Brittany; Appeared at major European Festivals; National television and radio appearances in Scotland, Poland, Egypt and Sweden; Performed live with Tannas, Anna Murray, Ross Kennedy; Producing and arranging for many artists within traditional music; Composer, theme and incidental music for videos and exhibitions; Member of Canterach, 1997–. *Recordings:* Doll's House, with Marylyn Middleton Pollock, 1992; Thro' Water Earth and Stone, with Iron Horse, 1993; Five Hands High, with Iron Horse, 1994; Coineadh, with Heather Innes, 1994; Gossamer Mansion, with Arran Bede, 1994; Celtic Dawn, with Whirligig, 1995; Voice of the Land, with Iron Horse, soundtrack to BBC Documentary The Gamekeeper, 1995; Summer in Skye, with Blair Douglas, 1996; Into Indigo, with Anne Murray, 1996; Border Ballads, various artists, 1998; Fyre and Sworde, 1998; On The West Side, 1999; The White Swan, 1999; Canterach Canterach, 2000; Also appears on: Calluna, Calluna, 2000; John Wright, A Few Short Lines, 2000; Whirligig, First Frost, 2001; Bram Taylor, Fragile Peace, 2001. *Honours:* Music Retailers' Asscn Award, Best Folk Album, for Thro' Water, Earth and Stone. *Membership:* Musicians' Union; Performing Rights Society; PAMRA; PRC. *Current Management:* KRL Records, 9 Watt Rd, Hillington, Glasgow G52, Scotland; Lee Wolfe, Canto Del Rey 28, Faro De Arriba, 33199 Oviedo, Asturias, Spain.

LAWRENCE, Tracy Lee; b. 27 Jan. 1968, Atlanta, Texas, USA. Country vocalist; Songwriter; Musician (guitar); *Compositions include:* How A Cowgirl Says Goodbye; Can't Break It To My Heart; If The World Had A Front Porch; Lessons Learned; My Second Home; Stars Over Texas. *Recordings include:* Sticks and Stones, 1991; Today's Lonely Fool, 1992; Runnin' Behind, 1992; Alibis, 1993; Can't Break It To My Heart, 1993; My Second Home, 1993; If The Good Die Young, 1994; I See It Now, 1994; Any Fool Can See, 1994; Texas Tornado, 1995; If The World Had A Front Porch, 1995; If You Love Me, 1995; Time Marches On, 1996; Stars Over Texas, 1996; Is That A Tear, 1996; Better Man Better Off, 1997; How A Cowgirl Says Goodbye, 1997; The Coast Is Clear, 1997; Lessons Learned, 2000; Albums include: Sticks and Stones, 1991; Alibis, 1993; I See It Now, 1994; Time Marches On, 1996; The Coast Is Clear, 1997; Lessons Learned, 2000, Tracy Lawrence, 2001. *Address:* c/o Country Music Asscn, 1 Music Circle S, Nashville, TN 37203, USA. *Website:* www.tracylawrence.com.

LAYTON, Paul Martin; b. 4 Aug. 1947, Beaconsfield, Buckinghamshire, England. Entertainer; Musician (bass guitar). m. Patricia Peters, 14 June 1981, 1 s., 1 d. *Education:* Hendon Music College. *Career:* Actor, films include: I Could Go On Singing, with Judy Garland; Television includes: Dixon of Dock Green; Emergency Ward 10, 1965–70; Vocalist, bass guitarist, The New Seekers, 1970–; Major world concert tours and television include: The White House for Nixon; Royal Command; Ed Sullivan. *Compositions include:* Ride A Horse; Sweet Louise. *Recordings:* I'd Like To Teach The World To Sing; Never Ending Song of Love; Circles; You Won't Find Another Fool Like Me; I Get A Little Sentimental Over You; Look What They've Done To My Song Ma; Beg, Steal or Borrow (Eurovision 1972). *Honours:* Sun Award, Best Vocal Group. *Membership:* Equity; Musicians' Union. *Current Management:* Hal Carter Organisation.

LAZAREVITCH, Serge; b. 18 Nov. 1957, St Germain En Laye, France. Jazz Musician (guitar); Educator. *Education:* Jazz diploma, Berklee College of Music, Boston, USA. *Career:* Concerts throughout Europe with various jazz bands; Member, Orchestre National de Jazz, 1989–91; Tours, Europe, Asia; Head of Jazz Department, Perpignan Conservatory; Clinics, France, Switzerland; Belgium; Germany; Italy. *Recordings:* CDs: (as leader) Cats Are Welcome, 1987; London Baby, 1989; Walk With A Lion, 1993; Many recordings as sideman. *Honours:* Choc of The Month, Record of the Year, in Jazz Man, for Walk With A Lion. *Membership:* UMJ (Union des Musiciens de Jazz). *Address:* 7 rue Durand, 34000 Montpellier, France.

LAZY HARRY, (Mark Stephens); b. 15 June 1947. Vocalist; Songwriter. m. Wendy, 1 s., 1 d. *Education:* BA, Hons, Melbourne University. *Career:* Wrote and sang Proud to be Australian for Bicentenary, 1988; USA Tours, 1990–94; German Tour, 1995; Tour of Australia, 1998. *Compositions:* Proud to be Australian; Edward Kelly; Riverboats Song; Weary Dunlop; Visiting Australia. *Recordings:* Big Aussie Album; Lazy Harry Vol. II; My Country; Ned Kelly Story; Riverboats of Australia; Bound for Botany Bay. *Publications:* Lazy Harry Song Book, 1988; Video, Songs of Australia, 1998. *Membership:* Australian Performing Rights Asscn.

LE BON, Simon; b. 27 Oct. 1958, Bushey, Hertfordshire, England. Vocalist; Lyricist. m. Yasmin Parveneh, 27 Dec. 1985, 3 d. *Education:* Birmingham University. *Career:* Vocalist, Dog Days; Lead vocalist, Duran Duran, 1980–; Arcadia, 1985–86; Performances include: British tour, supporting Hazel O'Connor, 1980; MENCAP concert, attended by HRH the Prince and Princess of Wales, 1983; Live Aid, Philadelphia, 1985; The Secret Policeman's Third Ball, 1987; An Acoustic Evening With Duran Duran, Birmingham, 1989. *Recordings:* Albums: with Duran Duran: Duran Duran, 1981; Rio, 1982; Carnival, 1982; Seven and The Ragged Tiger (No. 1, UK), 1983; Arena, 1984; Notorious, 1986; Big Thing, 1988; Decade, 1989; Liberty, 1990; Duran Duran (The Wedding Album), 1993; Thank You, 1995; Medazzaland, 1997; Greatest, 1998; Pop Trash, 2000; with Arcadia: So Red The Rose, 1985; Singles include: Planet Earth, 1981; Girls On Film, 1981; My Own Way, 1981; Hungry Like The Wolf, 1982; Save A Prayer, 1982; Rio, 1982; Is There Something I Should Know (No. 1, UK), 1983; Union of The Snake, 1983; New Moon On Monday, 1984; The Reflex (No. 1, UK and USA), 1984; The Wild Boys, 1984; A View To A Kill, film theme tune (No. 1, USA), 1985; Notorious, 1986; Skin Trade, 1987; Meet El Presidente, 1987; I Don't Want Your Love, 1988; All She Wants, 1989; Do You Believe In Shame, used in film Tequila Sunrise, 1989; Liberty, 1990; Violence of Summer, 1990; Serious, 1990; Ordinary World, 1993; Come Undone, 1993; Too Much Information, 1993; White Lines, 1995; Singles with Arcadia: Election Day, 1985; Goodbye Is Forever, 1986; The Flame, 1986; Contributor, Do They Know It's Christmas?, Band Aid, 1984; Pavarotti and Friends (Bosnia charity record), 1996. *Honours:* Grammy Awards: Best Video and Best Album, 1984; BRIT Award, Best British Music Video, Wild Boys, 1985; Ivor Novello Award, International Hit of Year, The Reflex, 1985; Star on Hollywood Walk of Fame, 1993. *Current Management:* The Left Bank Organisation, 6255 Sunset Blvd #1111, Hollywood, CA 90028, USA.

LE GENDRE, Dominique; b. Trinidad. Musician (guitar); Composer. *Education:* Guitar tuition by Ramon de Herrera, Conservatoire Municipal de Paris XVII; Degree, Musicology, Sorbonne University; Conservatoires: Regional d'Orsay, Municipal de Pars VI; Diploma in Advanced Sound Recording; Production Techniques, Media Production Services. *Career:* Television: Body of a Poet, Channel 4; 7 Go Mad in Peru, Channel 4, 1995–96; Radio: The Darkest Eye, Hinterlands, Let Them Call it Jazz, Radio 3, 1996; Film: Sixth Happiness, produced by Waris Hussein. *Compositions:* Music for television: The Healer, BBC1; B D Women (Channel 4); Synchro, ITV; Ragga Gyuls D'Bout, Carlton/Arts Council; Booker Prize '93, BBC2; Disabled Lives, BBC2; Kaiso For July (Channel 4); Films: Aliki Ou La Bague Engloutie; La Petite Valse; I Is A Long Memoried Woman; Theatre music includes: Measure For Measure, London Bubble Theatre; Orinoco, National Theatre Studio; Trapped In Time, Avon Touring Theatre Company; Love At A Loss, Wild Iris Theatre; When The Bough Breaks, Theatre Centre; BBC Radio includes: A Midsummer Night Dream; The Wizard of Oz; Edward II; Dance music for: The Burial of Miss Lady, Irie! Dance Company. *Recordings:* Romeo and Juliet, King John, Twelfth Night, All's Well That Ends Well, The Merchant of Venice, A Midsummer Night's Dream, The Taming of the Shrew; In production: complete plays of Shakespeare. *Honours:* Best Performance Art Video (I Is A Long Memoried Woman), New York, 1991. *Membership:* PRS; Musicians' Union. *Current Management:* Soundtrack Music Management. *Address:* 22 Ives St, Chelsea, London SW3 2ND, England.

LE MESSURIER, James; b. 20 July 1958, Guernsey, Channel Islands. Musician (percussion); Arranger; Bandleader. m. Flavia Chévez De La Cruz, 23 April 1994. *Education:* Bachelor of Music, Major in Professional Music, Berklee College of Music, Boston, USA. *Career:* Leader, percussionist, arranger, London-based Salsa group La Clave, 1986–; Numerous appearances clubs, festivals: UK; Eire; France; Italy; Holland; Germany; Switzerland; Featured on BBC Radio One, Andy Kershaw Show, 1994; Freelance percussionist, El Sonido de Londres, Alfredo Rodriguez, Orlando Watussi, Adalberto Santiago. *Membership:* PRS; Musicians' Union. *Address:* 38 Forestholme Close, Forest Hill, London SE23 3UQ, England.

LE, Nguyên; b. 14 Jan. 1959, Paris, France. Musician (guitar, bass); Synthesizer Programmer; Composer; Arranger. *Education:* Graduate in Visual Arts; Majored in Philosophy. *Career:* Co-creator, multi-ethnic band Ultramarine, 1983; Member, National Jazz Orchestra, 1987; Guest soloist, WDR Big Band, with Vince Mendoza, Bob Brookmeyer, 1993; Concerts and tours throughout Europe; Martinique; Ile de la Réunion; Madagascar; Ivory Coast; USA; Canada; North Africa. *Recordings:* Miracles, 1989; Zanzibar, 1992; Init, 1993; Million Waves, 1995; Tales From Vietnam, 1996; Three Trios, 1997; with Ultramarine: Dé, 1989; Esimala, 1991. *Publications:* Isoar and Question Mark published in Real Book Vol. III. *Honours:* with

Ultramarine: Best World Music Album: 1989; Telerama, 1992; Tales from Vietnam, 1996; Drapson d'Or, choice du monde de la musique; Choice of the Year, 1996 Jazzman second best CD, for Jazzthing. *Current Management:* Siegfried Loch, ACT Publishing. *Address:* Gustav Freytag Strasse 10, 22085 Hamburg, Germany.

LEA, Jimmy; b. 14 June 1952, Wolverhampton, England. Musician (bass, piano, violin); Songwriter; Record Prod. *Career:* Member, UK rock group Slade (formerly N'Betweens, Ambrose Slade), 1966–91; Concerts include: First British tour, 1972; Fanfare For Europe festival, London Palladium, 1973; Great British Music Festival, 1978; Reading Festival, 1980; Film appearance: Flame, 1974; Record prod., UK rock group Chrome Molly. *Compositions:* Co-writer, all Slade's Top 20 singles, with Noddy Holder. *Recordings:* Albums: Beginnings (as Ambrose Slade), 1969; Play It Loud, 1970; Slade Alive, 1972; Slayed, 1973; Sladest, 1973; Old New Borrowed Blue, 1974; Slade In Flame (soundtrack), 1974; Nobody's Fool, 1976; Slade Alive Vol. 2, 1978; Return To Base, 1979; Slade Smashes, 1980; Till Deaf Do Us Part, 1981; We'll Bring The House Down, 1981; Slade On Stage, 1982; The Amazing Kamikaze Syndrome, 1983; Slade's Greats, 1984; Rogue's Gallery, 1985; Crackers, 1985; You Boyz Make Big Noize, 1987; Wall of Hits, 1991; UK No. 1 singles: Coz I Luv You, 1971; Take Me Back 'Ome, 1972; Mama Weer All Crazee Now (later recorded by Mama's Boys, Quiet Riot), 1972; Cum On Feel The Noize, 1973; Skweeze Me Pleeze Me, 1973; Merry Christmas Everybody, 1973; Other hits include: Look Wot You Dun, 1972; Gudbuy T'Jane, 1972; My Friend Stan, 1973; Everyday, 1974; Bangin' Man, 1974; Far Far Away, 1974; Thanks For The Memory, 1975; In For A Penny, 1975; We'll Bring The House Down, 1981; My Oh My, 1983; Run Run Away, 1984; All Join Hands, 1984; Radio Wall of Sound, 1991. *Honours:* Hon. Fellow, University of Wolverhampton, 2002.

LEACH, Alan; b. 1970, England. Musician (Drums). *Career:* Member, Shed Seven; Numerous live dates, tours and television appearances. *Recordings:* Singles: Mark, 1994; Dolphin, 1994; Speakeasy, 1994; Ocean Pie, 1994; Where Have You Been Tonight?, 1995; Getting Better, 1996; Bully Boy, 1996; On Standby, 1996; Chasing Rainbows, 1996; She Left Me on Friday, 1998; The Heroes, 1998; The Devil in Your Shoes, 1998; Disco Down, 1999; Albums: Change Giver, 1996; A Maximum High, 1996; Let It Ride, 1998; Going for Gold: The Best of Shed Seven, 1999; Truth Be Told, 2001. *Website:* www.shedseven.com.

LEBEUGLE, Patricia; b. 19 May 1963, Le Mans, France. Jazz Musician (bass). *Career:* Played with Walter Bishop; Bob Mover; Bobby Porcelli; Peter Ecklund; Mark Murphy; Ted Brown; European tours with many French and American musicians, 1985–; Jazz festivals throughout Europe with Philippe Duchemin Trio, 1990–; Tour, South Africa, with pianist Jack Van Poll. *Recordings:* with Philippe Duchemin Trio: Alizés, 1990; Live!, 1992; Three Pieces, 1994; Philippe Duchemin Trio with Dominique Vernhes, 1995; Three Colors, with Philippe Duchemin, CD, 1998; with Marcel Azzola and Dany Doriz, Jazzola, 1999; Philippe Duchemin with Magali Leon, Magali chante Ella, 1999. *Address:* Le Boulay, 72440 St Mars de Locquenay, France.

LECKIE, John; b. 23 Oct. 1949, London, England. Prod; Engineer. m. Christina, 1 d. *Education:* Quintin School; Ravensbourne College of Art; Rajneesh Neo-Sannyas Commune. *Career:* Tape Operator and Balance Engineer, Abbey Road Studios, 1970; Sessions included: John Lennon; Mott The Hoople; Roy Harper; various classical; Freelance producer 1978–. *Recordings include:* Albums: Sunburst Finish, Be-Bop Deluxe, 1976; White Music, XTC, 1978; Real Life, Magazine, 1978; Empires and Dance, Simple Minds, 1980; The Stone Roses, The Stone Roses, 1989; The Bends, Radiohead, 1995; K, Kula Shaker, 1996; Showbiz, Muse, 1999; Anuthma Zone, Dr John, 2000; Missing You (Mi Yeewnii), Baaba Maal, 2001; Good Morning Aztlan, Los Lobos, 2002. *Honours:* Music Week, Best Producer, 1996; Q Magazine, Best Producer, 1996; BRIT Awards, Best Producer, 1997. *Membership:* Music Producers Guild UK. *Current Management:* Safta Jaffery, SJP, 263 Putney Bridge Rd, London SW15 2PU, England. *Address:* The Well, Wainmill, Chinner, Oxfordshire OX39 4AB, England.

LEDIN, Tomas Jonas Folke; b. 25 Feb. 1952, Östersund, Sweden. Artist; Songwriter; Prod. m. Marie Anderson, 22 May 1982, 2 s. *Education:* Art Major, 1970; Graduate, Swedish Gymnasium, 1972; Musical Science, Uppsala University, 1977. *Career:* First album released, 1972; Tours: Sweden and Scandinvia, 1980–; USA, with ABBA; Canada, Europe, 1979; Japan, 1980; Initiated Rocktrain tour, 1991; Toured with the Rocktrain, 1992–93; Appeared on all major television shows, Sweden. *Recordings:* 18 albums include: Greatest Hits, 1990; Tillfälligheternas Spel, 1990; Du Kan Lita På Mej, 1993. *Honours:* 2 Grammy Awards, 1991; Rockbjörn Award, 1991, 1992; Mozart prize, 1991; World Music Award, 1992; Represented Sweden, Eurovision Song Contest, 1980; Platinum and Gold discs. *Membership:* SKAP (Swedish Composers Society). *Current Management:* Jan Beime, Desert Music.

LEE, Albert; b. 21 Dec. 1943, Leominster, Hertfordshire, England. Musician (guitar). *Career:* Guitarist, Chris Farlowe and The Thunderbirds, 1960s; In-demand session musician; Also member of Country Fever; Member, Poet and The One Man Band (with Chas Hodges of Chas 'n' Dave); Group became Heads Hands and Feet; Member, the Crickets; Emmylou Harris' Hot Band;

Touring bands of Eric Clapton; Jackson Browne; Jerry Lee Lewis; Dave Edmunds; Concerts include: Everly Brothers Reunion, Royal Albert Hall, 1983. *Recordings:* Solo albums: Hiding, 1979; Albert Lee, 1983; Speechless, 1986; Gagged But Not Bound, 1987; Black Claw and Country Fever, 1991; In Full Flight, 1994; Country Legend, 1998; Con Sabor Latino, 2000; Other recordings: Albums with Eric Clapton: Just One Night, 1980; Another Ticket, 1981; Money and Cigarettes, 1983; with Joe Cocker: With A Little Help From My Friends, 1969; Stingray, 1976; with The Crickets: Bubblegum, Pop, Ballads and Boogie, 1973; Remnants, 1973; with Dave Edmunds: Repeat When Necessary, 1979; DE7, 1982; with Chris Farlowe: Chris Farlowe and The Thunderbirds, 1966; Stormy Monday, 1966; Out of The Blue, 1985; with Emmylou Harris: Luxury Liner, 1977; Quarter Moon In A Ten Cent Town, 1978; Blue Kentucky Girl, 1979; Christmas Album, 1979; Roses In The Snow, 1980; Evangeline, 1981; Cimarron, 1981; Ballad of Sally Rose, 1985; with Head Hands and Feet: Head Hands and Feet, 1971; Tracks, 1972; Old Soldiers Never Die, 1973; with Jimmy Page and John Paul Jones: No Introduction Necessary, 1984; Also recorded on albums with: Chas and Dave; Bobby Bare; Gary Brooker; Teresa Brewer; Guy Clark; Rodney Crowell; Bo Diddley; Lonnie Donegan; Don Everly; Everly Brothers; Nancy Griffith; Jerry Lee Lewis; Jon Lord; Steve Morse; Juice Newton; Dolly Parton; Ricky Skaggs; Shakin' Stevens.

LEE, Alex; b. 16 March 1970. Musician (keyboards, guitar). *Career:* Mem., Strangelove; Joined Suede, 2001. *Recordings:* Album: A New Morning, 2002. Singles: Positivity, 2002; Obsessions, 2002. *Address:* c/o Sony Music Entertainment, European Regional Office, 10 Great Marlborough St, London W1F 7LP, England. *Website:* www.suede.net.

LEE, Alvin; b. 19 Dec. 1944, Nottingham, England. Musician (guitar, vox); Songwriter. *Career:* First band: The Jailbreakers, age 13, Became The Jaybirds, then Ten Years After; Moved to London, 1966; Friday residency, Marquee Club, 1968; Fillmore East and West, Woodstock, USA, 1969; Arena dates, 28 tours in 5 years, led to band disbanding, 1976; Solo recordings, collaboration with gospel singer, Mylon Lefevre; Short reunion of Ten Years After, 1988; Returned to solo work. *Recordings include:* Albums: with Ten Years After: Ten Years After, 1967; Undead, 1968; Ssssh, 1969; Cricklewood Green, 1970; Watt, 1971; A Space In Time, 1971; Alvin Lee and Company, 1972; Rock and Roll Music To The World, 1972; Recorded Live, 1973; Positive Vibrations, 1974; Goin' Home, 1975; Hear Them Calling, 1976; The Classic Performances Of, 1977; Greatest Hits, 1979; Profile, 1980; Portfoloio, 1983; Universal, 1988; About Time, 1989; Texas International Pop Festival, 1992; Pure Blues, 1995; with Mylon Lefevre: On The Road To Freedom; Solo: In Flight, 1974; Pump Iron, 1975; Let It Rock, 1978; Rocket Fuel (and Ten Years Later), 1978; Chrysalis Classics, 1978; Ride On (and Ten Years Later), 1979; Free Fall (Alvin Lee Band), 1980; RX5, 1981; Detroit Deisel, 1986; Zoom, 1992; Nineteen-Ninety-Four, 1993; I Hear You Knockin', 1994; Pure Blues, 1995; Live in Vienna, 1996; Solid Rock, 2000; Guest artiste on recordings including: The Session, Jerry Lee Lewis, 1973; Dark Horse, George Harrison, 1974; 20th Anniversary of Rock and Roll, Bo Diddley, 1976; Revue, Vol. 2, Earl Scruggs, 1976; Bull In A Ming Vase, Roy Harper, 1977; Night of The Guitar Live (1988), 1989; Under No Obligation, Roger Chapman, 1991; 38317, Peter Maffay, 1991. *Current Management:* Skarda. *Address:* Bergstrasse 13, 82069 Hohenshäftlarn, Germany.

LEE, Brenda, (Brenda Lee Tarpley); b. 11 Dec. 1944, Lithonia, Georgia, USA. Vocalist. *Career:* Solo recording artiste, 1950s–60s; Actress, film The Two Little Bears. *Recordings:* Hit singles include: Sweet Nothin's, 1960; I'm Sorry (No. 1, USA), 1960; I Want To Be Wanted (No. 1, USA), 1960; Let's Jump The Broomstick, 1961; Speak To Me Pretty, 1962; One Step At A Time; Rockin' Around The Christmas Tree, 1962; Losing You, 1963; I Wonder, 1963; As Usual, 1963; Nobody Wins; Thanks A Lot, 1965; Too Many Rivers, 1965; Albums include: Grandma, What Great Songs You Sang, 1959; Brenda Lee, 1960; This Is Brenda, 1960; Emotions, 1961; All The Way, 1961; Sincerely, 1962; Brenda, That's All, 1962; The Show For Christmas Seals, 1962; All Alone Am I, 1963; Let Me Sing, 1963; By Request, 1964; Merry Christmas From Brenda Lee, 1964; Top Teen Hits, 1965; The Versatile Brenda Lee, 1965; Too Many Rivers, 1965; Bye Bye Blues, 1966; Coming On Strong, 1966; For The First Time (with Pete Fountain), 1968; Johnny One Time, 1969; The Brenda Lee Story, 1974; LA Sessions, 1977; Even Better, 1980; Little Miss Dynamite, 1980; 25th Anniversary, 1984; The Golden Decade, 1985; The Best of Brenda Lee, 1986; Love Songs, 1986; Brenda Lee, 1991; Rockin' Around, 1995; Jingle Bell Rock, 1995; Live Dynamite, 1997; Wiedersehn Ist Wunderschon, 1997; In the Mood for Love, 1998; Miss Dynamite Live, 2000; Guest singer, Shadowland, k d lang, 1988. *Current Management:* Brenda Lee Management, 2174 Carson St, Nashville, TN 37211, USA.

LEE, Christopher James; b. 24 June 1961, Cheltenham, Gloucester. Musician (Trumpet, Steel Pan). m. Lucy, 1 s., 1 d. *Career:* Founder Member, Pigbag, 1979; Toured Europe, America and Japan, 1980–83; Appeared on Top of the Pops, 1982–83; Radio sessions, John Peel, Kid Jensen, 1983–; Involved in Jazz and improvised musics, 1997–. *Compositions:* The Shell Suite; The Arrow of Time; the Magician of Riga; On The Swing of a Prayer; Jakes Dance. *Recordings:* Papas Got A Brand New Pigbag; Pigbag; The Shell Temple At Margate. *Honours:* Lottery award money to make recording with Sweet

Thunder. *Membership:* PRS; Musicians' Union; PAMRA. *Address:* 46 Ferndale Rd, Leytonstone E11 3DN, England.

LEE, Crissy; b. 17 June 1943, Colchester, Essex, England. Musician (drums, percussion); Music Teacher. *Career:* Joined Ivy Benson Dance Band, aged 17, tours world-wide; Appeared with artistes including: Dinah Washington; Frank Sinatra; Fats Domino; Caterina Valente; Tom Jones; Support on The Beatles first Spanish tour; Formed the Crissy Lee Band; Worked alongside: Al Jarreau; Faith Brown; Marion Montgomery; Madeleine Bell; Musical Director for guests including: Roy Castle; Ken Dodd; Bob Monkhouse; Launched and managed Koffee and Kreme duo, winners of New Faces television talent show; Other musical projects include Beauty and the Beat, backing band for acts including The Supremes, Johnny Bristol; Sam Dees; Formed The Crissy Lee and her All Female Orchestra (only 17-piece all-female band in Europe); Television appearances include: Barrymore; Wogan; Cilla Black Show; Russell Harty Show; Jack Parnell Big Band Special; Millicent Martin Show; Lady Be Good; Goldeneye; David Frost Chat Show. *Recordings:* The Beat Chics EP; The Beat Chics: Skinny Mini/Now I Know. *Membership:* Equity; Musicians' Union; ABJM (Asscn of British Jazz Musicians). *Current Management:* Neil Simpson, World-wide Management. *Address:* 3 Alston Rd, Bispham, Blackpool, Lancashire FY2 0TD, England.

LEE, Dave, (Joey Negro, Raven Maize, Doug Willis, Z Factor, Sessomato, Akabu, Jakatta); b. 18 June 1964, Colchester, Essex, England. Prod; Remixer; DJ. *Career:* Founder: Republic Records (one of the first UK House labels), Z Records; First British artiste to record for cult New York label Nu-Groove; Remixed: Sister Sledge, Lisa Stansfield, Pet Shop Boys, Diana Ross, M People; Member: Sunburst Band, Hed Boys; Collaborations: Mark Ryder, Taka Boom, Blaze. *Recordings:* Albums: Universe of Love (as Joey Negro), 1993; Here Come the Sunburst Band, 2000: Can't Get High Without You (Compilation), 2000; Back to the Scene of the Crime, 2001; Singles: Get Acidic (with M-D-EMM), 1988; Forever Together (as Raven Maize), 1989; Do It Believe It (as Joey Negro), 1991; Do What You Feel (as Joey Negro), 1991; One Kiss (with Pacha), 1991; Enter Your Fantasy EP (as Joey Negro), 1992; Girls and Boys (with Hed Boys), 1994; Gotta Keep Pushin' (as Z Factor), 1998; Must Be the Music (with Taka Boom), 1999; Moody (as Sessomatto), 2000; American Dream (as Jakatta), 2001; The Real Life (as Raven Maize), 2001. *Current Management:* c/o Azuli Records, 25 D'Arblay St, London W1V 3FH, England.

LEE, Geddy (Gary); b. 29 July 1953, Willowdale, Canada. Musician (bass); Vocalist. *Career:* Member, Canadian rock group Rush, 1969–; Sell-out tours, USA, Canada; UK; Europe; Played on bills with ZZ Top; Areosmith; Kiss; Uriah Heep. *Recordings:* Albums: Rush, 1973; Fly By Night, 1975; Caress of Steel, 1975; 2112, 1976; All The World's A Stage, 1976; A Farewell To Kings, 1977; Archives, 1978; Hemispheres, 1978; Permanent Waves, 1980; Moving Pictures, 1981; Exit... Stage Left, 1981; Great White North, 1982; Signals, 1982; Grace Under Pressure, 1984; Power Windows, 1985; A Show of Hands, 1989; Presto, 1989; Chronicles, 1990; Roll The Bones, 1991; Counterparts, 1993; Test for Echo, 1996; Retrospective, Vol. 2: 1981–87, 1997; Different Stages, 1998; My Favorite Headache, 2000; Vapor Trails, 2002. Singles include: Spirit of Radio; Tom Sawyer; Vital Signs; New World Man; Closer To The Heart; Countdown; The Big Money; Time Stand Still. *Honours:* Juno Awards: Most Promising Group, 1975; Best Group, 1978, 1979; Group named Official Ambassadors of Music, Canadian Government, 1979; Gold Ticket Award, Madison Square Garden, 1991. *Current Management:* Anthem Entertainment, 189 Carlton St, Toronto, ON M5A 2K7, Canada.

LEE, Jack; b. 30 July 1929, Lakewood, Ohio, USA. Conductor; Voice Coach; Musician (Piano); Musical Dir. Divorced. *Education:* BMus, Voice and Piano, BA Drama, Baldwin-Wallace College Conservatory of Music. *Career:* Off-Broadway show: Valmouth; Broadway shows: Sweet Charity, Funny Girl, Applause, No Strings, Billy, Peter Pan, My One and Only, Grand Hotel, My Fair Lady; Participated in the Music Foundation Noel Coward Evening, Carnegie Hall, Mabel Regina and Carmen Jones Revival; Movies: Postcards from the Edge, Sweet Charity. *Recordings:* My One and Only; Grand Hotel; Sweet Charity. *Membership:* The Players' Club; Tony Nominating Committee; Faculty, New York University Teaching School. *Address:* 37 W 72nd St Apt 10 D, New York, NY 10023, USA.

LEE, Jon; b. 26 April 1982, Croydon, England. Vocalist; Actor. *Education:* Sylvia Young Theatre School. *Career:* Moved to London aged 12 to star in West End production of Oliver!; Various TV acting work, incl. soap opera EastEnders (BBC1); Mem., S Club 7, 1998–; Group quickly achieved international success, following sales of TV series Miami 7, 1999, LA 7, 2000, and Hollywood 7, 2001, featuring the band's music, to nearly 100 countries; Also made nature TV series, S Club 7 Go Wild, 2000, and various TV specials; First British tour with S Club 7, 2001; Band renamed S Club, 2001. *Recordings:* Albums: S Club, 1999; 7 (No. 1, UK), 2000; Sunshine, 2001; Seeing Double, 2002. Singles: Bring It All Back (No. 1, UK), 1999; S Club Party, 1999; Two In A Million/You're My Number One, 1999; Reach, 2000; Natural, 2000; Never Had A Dream Come True (No. 1, UK), 2000; Don't Stop Movin' (No. 1, UK), 2001; Have You Ever (No. 1, UK), 2001; You, 2002. *Honours:* BRIT Awards, Best British Newcomer, 2000, Best British Single, for

Don't Stop Movin', 2002; Record of the Year Award, for Don't Stop Movin', 2001. *Current Management:* 19 Management, Unit 32, Ransomes Dock, 35–37 Parkgate Rd, London SW11 4NP, England. *Website:* www.sclub.com.

LEE, Philip Robert; b. 8 April 1943, London, England. Musician (guitar). m. Doris Anna Zingerli, 31 March 1964. *Career:* First bands: John Williams Big Bands, Graham Collier Septet, 1960s; Henry Lowther, Tony Coe, 1970s; Musician with singers Annie Ross; Marian Montgomery; Sylvia Sims; Norma Winstone; Member, fusion band, Gilgamesh; Played for Americans including Benny Goodman, 1980s; Member, Dardanelle, 1990s; Worked with Jessye Norman in London and Greece, 1999; Appeared in film, Eyes Wide Shut, 1999; Tour dates in London and Dublin with Rosemary Clooney and Michael Feinstein, 2001; Annual tour dates with Jimmy Smith. *Recordings:* Gilgamesh, with Gilgamesh; Another Fine Tune You've Got Me Into, with Gilgamesh; Twice Upon A Time, with Phil Lee and Jeff Clyne; Swingin' In London, with Dardanelle; Meteors Close At Hand, with Michael Garrick; Unity, with John Horler and Phil Lee. *Membership:* PRS; Musicians' Union. *Address:* 7c Thurlow Rd, London NW3 5PJ, England.

LEE, Robert E, (Robert Greehy); b. 30 May 1956, Leeds, England. Vocalist; Musician (drums, guitar, bass, keyboards). *Education:* Roundhay Grammar School, Leeds. *Career:* Session musician, 1975–79; Member, London Cowboys, 1980–85; Tours: Europe; Japan; USA; Scandinavia; UK; including 2 support tours, Johnny Thunders, 1981, 1982; 2 support tours, Hanoi Rocks, 1982, 1983; Producer, session musician, 1986–; World-wide television and radio appearances; Full time member of The Infidels; with The Infidels: produced debut CD, 1998; Toured England, 1998; TV and radio appearances in USA, 1998. *Compositions:* Long Time Lonely, 1998; co-wrote Faithless and Blue. *Recordings:* Albums: Animal Pleasure; Tall In The Saddle; Long Time Coming; Dead Or Alive; Singles: Centrefold; Hook, Line and Sinker; Dance Crazy; Let's Get Crazy; Street Full of Soul; Faithless and Blue, 1998; Infidels, 2000. *Publications:* Country Music International, 1998; Mojo, 1998. *Honours:* Best New British Band, Country Music International, Alternative Rock/Country Crossover. *Membership:* PRC; PRS; MU; MCPS.

LEE, Sara; b. 18 Aug. 1955, Hereford, England. Musician (bass guitar). *Career:* League of Gentlemen, 1980; US and European Tour, 1981–84; Moved to New York, 1984; Toured With Thompson Twins, B 52's, Joan Osborne, 1987–99; Television, Tonight Show, Lonan O'Brian, D Letterman. *Recordings:* League of Gentlemen; Robyn Hitchcock: Gang of Four; Cosmic Thing; Good Stuff; Living In Clip; Little Plastic Castle; Solo album: Make It Beautiful, 2000. *Current Management:* Peter Casperson Invasion Group. *Address:* 113 W 25 St, Fifth Floor, New York, NY 10001, USA.

LEE, Tommy, (Thomas Lee Bass); b. 3 Oct. 1962, Athens, Greece. Musician (drums). m. (1) Heather Locklear, 1986; (2) Pamela Anderson, 1995, 2 s. *Career:* Member, groups Suite 19; Christmas; Founder member, US heavy rock group Mötley Crüe, 1981–; World-wide concerts include: Tours with: Y&T, 1981, 1982; Kiss, 1983; Ozzy Osbourne, 1984; Iron Maiden, 1984; Cheap Trick, 1986; Theatre of Pain World tour, 1985–86; World tours, 1987, 1989; Major festivals: US Festival, 1983; Monsters of Rock Festival, Castle Donington, 1984; Moscow Music Peace Festival, 1989. *Recordings:* Albums: Too Fast For Love, 1981; Shout At The Devil, 1983; Theatre of Pain, 1985; Girls, Girls, Girls (No. 2, USA), 1987; Dr Feelgood (No. 1, USA), 1989; Decade of Decadence (No. 2, USA), 1991; Til Death Do Us Part, 1994; Generation Swine, 1997; Greatest Hits, 1998; Supersonic and Demon Relics, 1999; Solo: Never A Dull Moment, 2002. Singles: Stick To Your Guns, 1981; Looks That Kill, 1984; Too Young To Fall In Love, 1984; Smokin' In The Boys Room, 1985; Home Sweet Home, 1985; You're All I Need, 1987; Dr Feelgood, 1989; Kick Start My Heart, 1990; Without You, 1990; Don't Go Away Mad, 1990; Same Old Situation, 1990; Primal Scream, 1991. *Contributions to:* Nine Inch Nails, Downward Spiral, 1994; Methods of Mayhem, 1999. *Publications:* The Dirt: Confessions of the World's Most Notorious Rock Band (with Mötley Crüe), 2001. *Current Management:* The Left Bank Organisation, 6255 Sunset Blvd, Suite 1111, Hollywood, CA 90028, USA.

LEES, John; b. 13 Jan. 1947, Oldham, Lancashire, England. Vocalist; Musician (guitar). *Career:* Member, Barclay James Harvest (originally the Blues Keepers), 1967–; Regular international tours, UK and Europe, including Free concert, Berlin Wall, 1980. *Recordings include:* Albums: Barclay James Harvest, 1970; Barclay James Harvest Live, 1974; Time Honoured Ghosts, 1975; Gone To Earth, 1977; Harvest XII, 1978; Eyes of The Universe, 1980; Turn of The Tide, 1981; Concert For The People, 1981; Ring of Changes, 1981; Face To Face, 1987; Glasnost, 1988; Welcome To The Show, 1990; Alone We Fly, 1990; The Harvest Years, 1991; The Best of Barclay James Harvest, 1992; Solo album: A Major Fancy, 1977; Barclay James Harvest Through The Eyes of John Lees, featuring Wooly Wolstenhulme, 1999. *Current Management:* Handle Artists Management. *Address:* The Handle Group of Companies, Pinewood Studios, Pinewood Rd, Iver Heath, Buckinghamshire SL0 0NH, England.

LEES, Simon (Buggy); b. 16 May 1970, Wolverhampton, England. Musician (guitar, drums); Vocalist; Songwriter; Entertainer. *Education:* BTEC ONC at Wulfrun College. *Career:* Formed Osprey, 1986; Nitebreed, 1990 (support band for The Mock Turtles); Member, The Red House Snakes, 1990; Formed Plain Jain, 1992; Member, Tantrum, 1994; Radio appearances: The Reaper Rock Show, Freedom FM, Chester; Jenny Wilkes Show, BBC Radio WM, 1999. *Recordings:* Playing Truant, recorded live at London Music Show, Wembley Conference Centre, 1994; My World, solo album, 1998. *Publications:* Guitarist magazine. *Honours:* Guitarist of the Year finalist, 1993–95, winner, 1998. *Membership:* Musicians' Union. *Address:* 34 Strathmore Cres., Wombourne, Wolverhampton, Staffordshire WV5 9AS, England.

LEFTWICH, Bradley Rush; b. 30 June 1953, Stillwater, Oklahoma, USA. Musician (traditional American fiddle, banjo); Vocalist. m. Linda Higginbotham, 1 May 1982, 1 s. *Education:* BA, Anthropology, Oberlin College; MA, Anthropology, University of Chicago. *Career:* Founding Member, Plank Road, 1975–77; Toured with Linda Higginbotham as Leftwich and Higginbotham, 1981–, with the Humdingers, 1990s, and with Tom Sauber and Alice Gerrard as Tom, Brad and Alice, 1997–; Stage appearances include: The White House, Philadelphia and Winnipeg folk festivals, Piccolo Spoleto, Charleston, Bele Chere, Asheville; Radio appearances on Wheeling Jamboree, Renfro Valley Barn Dance, The Flea Market, Our Front Porch and on Danish national TV and radio. *Recordings:* Been There Still; Say, Old Man; Carrying On The Tradition; Learn to Play Old-Time Fiddle, vols 1 and 2; Rounder Fiddle; A Moment in Time; No One To Bring Home Tonight; Banging and Sawing; Buffalo Gal; Southern Clawhammer Banjo; Vocal and Instrumental Blend; Plank Road Stringband. *Publications:* Bowing Workshop, series of columns in Old-Time Herald magazine; Reflections on Southern Appalachian Fiddling, article, 1995; Clawhammer Banjo, Round Peak Style, 1999. *Honours:* Recommended LP, Buffalo Gal, Billboard Magazine, 1983; First Place, Fiddle, First Place, Band, Appalachian String Band Music Festival, 1990. *Membership:* Advisory Board, Old-Time Herald magazine; North American Folk Alliance.

LEGER, Kenny; b. Copenhagen. Vocalist; Composer; Project Man. *Education:* BA, Kingston. *Career:* 10 minor television and film productions; One grand production, The African Evasion Eclipse; Various appearances on national television and radio. *Membership:* KODA. *Current Management:* Snedker. *Address:* 77 Hillfield Rd, Hampstead, London NW6 1QB, England.

LEGGETT, Andy; b. 31 March 1942, Much Wenlock, England. Musician (saxophone, clarinet, guitar); Songwriter; Arranger. m. Teri Penfold, 5 Sept. 1975, 2 s., 1 d. *Education:* BA, French, University of Hull, 1964; School Orchestra. *Career:* Member of Alligator Jug Thumpers, 1968; Pigsty Hill Light Orchestra, 1970; duo with Pete Finch, 1973; Avon Touring Theatre, 1974; Formed Sweet Substitute, 1975; Later became Musical Director, writer and arranger for them; Toured with: Midnite Follies Orchestra, Pasadena Roof Orchestra, Syd Lawrence, Bob Kerr's Whoopee Band, Temperance Seven; Playing clarinet and saxophone, Rod Mason's Hot Five, 1996–. *Compositions:* for Sweet Substitute: Tiger Blues; Dear Mr Berkeley, Sleepy Suzie, A Musical Christmas Card; for Henry's Bootblacks: Everyone's Got Horns, New Orleans Feels Like Home, Sugar Makes Your Teeth Fall Out; Co-wrote songs for the play The Godmother, directed by Mel Smith; Music for film, Betjeman Revisited, HTV, 1995. *Membership:* Associate Mem., PRS, MCPS. *Address:* Orffstrasse 22, KAARST-Büttgen, 41564, Germany.

LEGRAND, Benjamin; b. 16 Oct. 1962, Paris, France. Vocalist; Musician (piano, drums). 1 d. *Education:* Piano, drums, singing lessons, Paris. *Career:* Appearances include: Television shows, Paris; Olympia Hall, Paris; Tours: Japan; Tunisia; Belgium; Switzerland; Bobino Music Hall, Paris; Concerts in Korea; Eurodisney concerts; Cannes Jazz Festival; Calvi Jazz Festival, Corsica; Radio Shows include France Inter. *Recordings:* Album with Michel Legrand Big Band; Chansons De Paris (album of French songs); Record of Jazz Trio; Participating in album of French Songs; Album with Baden Powell and Phillipe Baden Powell. *Publications:* Letemps Qui Passe (poetry); La Pensée Universalle. *Membership:* SPEDIDAM; SACEM. *Address:* 14 Villa Molitor, 75016 Paris, France.

LEGRAND, Michel; b. 24 Feb. 1932, Paris, France. Composer; Musician (piano); Conductor; Vocalist; Arranger. m. Isabelle, 21 Nov. 1994, 2 s., 2 d. *Education:* Paris Conservatoire. *Career:* Conducted, appeared with Pittsburgh Symphony Orchestra, The National Symphony Orchestra, Minnesota Orchestra, Buffalo Philharmonic, Symphony Orchestras of Vancouver, Montréal, Atlanta, Denver, New Orleans; Collaborated with Maurice Chevalier, Miles Davis, Kiri Te Kanawa, Johnny Mathis, Neil Diamond, Sarah Vaughan, Stan Getz, Aretha Franklin, Jack Jones, James Galway, Ray Charles, Lena Horne, Barbra Streisand and numerous others; Films: (with Miles Davis) Dingo, 1990; Directed, Cinq Jours En Juin, 1989; Masque de Lune, 1991; Theatre productions, television appearances and film scores including Prêt-à-Porter, 1994. *Compositions include:* Images; I Was Born In Love With You; I Will Wait For You; Love Makes The Changes; Noelle's Theme; On My Way To You; One At A Time; Once Upon A Summertime; Little Boy Lost; The Summer Knows; Summer Me, Winter Me; Watch What Happens; The Way He Makes Me Feel; What Are You Doing The Rest of Your Life?; The Windmills of Your Mind; You Must Believe In Spring; Scored films include: The Thomas Crown Affair, 1968; Summer of '42, 1971; Yentl, 1982; Never Say Never Again, 1983; Ready To Wear, 1994; Madelaine, 1997.

Recordings include: Erik Satie By Michel Legrand; Four Piano Blues; Michel Plays Legrand; Paris Jazz Piano, 2001. *Publications:* Michel Legrand Song Book. *Honours:* 5 Grammy Awards, 1972–75; 3 Academy Awards, Thomas Crown Affair, 1968; Summer of '42, 1971; Yentl, 1983; Australian Film Institute Award, Dingo, 1991. *Membership:* Songwriters' Guild; Dramatists' Guild; NARAS; Academy of Motion Arts and Sciences. *Current Management:* Jim DiGiovanni.

LEHRER, Thomas Andrew; b. 9 April 1928, New York, NY, USA. Musician (piano); Vocalist; Songwriter; Satirist. *Education:* BA, 1946, MA, 1947, Harvard University. *Career:* Singer and satirical songwriter, 1943–; Part-time teacher, mathematics, Harvard University, 1947–51; Theoretical physicist, Baird-Atomic Inc, Cambridge, MA, 1953–54; Tours of clubs, 1953–55, 1957–60, 1965–67; US Army, 1955–57; Lecturer, Business Administration, Harvard Business School, 1961, Education, Harvard University, 1963–66, Psychology, Wellesley College, 1966, Political Science, MIT, 1962–71, University of California at Santa Cruz, 1972–; Wrote for US edition of That Was The Week That Was (TV series), 1964–65; Signed to Reprise Records, 1965; Wrote for The Electric Company (TV series), 1972; Revue, Tomfoolery, based on his songs, adapted by Robin Ray and Cameron Mackintosh, 1980; An Evening Wasted With Tom Lehrer (BBC Radio 2), 1998. *Recordings:* Songs By Tom Lehrer, 1953; More Of Tom Lehrer, 1959; An Evening Wasted With Tom Lehrer, 1959; Tom Lehrer Revisited, 1960; That Was The Year That Was, 1965; Songs By Tom Lehrer (re-recording of first album), 1966. *Publications:* Tom Lehrer Song Book, 1954; Tom Lehrer's Second Song Book, 1968; Too Many Songs by Tom Lehrer, 1981. *Contributions to:* Annals of Mathematical Statistics; Journal of Societies of Industrial and Applied Maths. *Address:* 11 Sparks St, Cambridge, MA 02138, USA.

LEICK, Vagn; b. 13 April 1939, Lydersholm, Denmark. Composer; Musician (piano). m. Jo Skovsbog, 19 April 1985, 2 s., 1 d. *Education:* PhD, Biochemistry; Private study in Jazz improvisation and composition. *Career:* Television and radio appearances in Denmark; USA; France. *Recordings:* Twilight; Thing; Jazz Digit; Songscapes. *Membership:* Danish Society of Jazz, Beat and Folk Authors. *Current Management:* Orbit Productions. *Address:* Ved Glyptoteket 6 3th, 1575 Copenhagen V, Denmark.

LEIGH, Joy; b. 23 April 1964, Montgomery, West Virginia, USA. Country/ Southern Gospel Vocalist. Divorced. *Education:* Associate degree, Nursing, West Virginia Institute of Technology. *Career:* Performed on stage, Grand Ole Opry, Don Reed Talent Competition; Showcase artiste, King Eagle Awards Show, Nashville, Tennessee; Headlined Fayette County, West Virginia, Fair, 1994, 1995; Performed at Boone County, West Virginia, Fair, 1994, 1995; Summerville, West Virginia's Suumerfest, 1994; Rotary Club of Montgomery, West Virginia, 1994, 1995. *Recordings:* What's In It For Me?; Walk Away. *Honours:* Montgomery Rotary Festival Award; United Community Services Entertainment Award. *Membership:* Gospel Music Asscn, Nashville, Tennessee. *Current Management:* Claudia Johnson, Johnson and Johnson Music Group, PO Box 182 Cannelton, WV 25036, USA. *Address:* Joy Leigh Enterprises, PO Box 182, Cannelton, WV 25036, USA.

LEIGHTON, Brian; b. 30 June 1970, Minneapolis, Minnesota, USA. Vocalist; Musician (acoustic guitar, harmonica). *Career:* G B Leighton Band; Movie, The Marksmen; Woman Thing Music, Phillip Morris. *Recordings:* One Time, One Life; Come Alive; Live from Pickle Park; It's All Good, 2000. *Membership:* ASCAP. *Current Management:* Blue Sky Artists. *Address:* PO BOx 68124, Minneapolis, MN 55418, USA.

LEINER, Boris; b. 28 Jan. 1957, Cakovec, Croatia. Musician (drums, percussion); Vocalist. Divorced, 1 d. *Education:* Study, Art Academy, Zagreb; Art University, Utrecht, Holland, 1983–86. *Career:* Drummer, Singer, Rock Band, Azra, 1977–87; Vjestice, 1987–; Naturalna Mistika, Reggae band, 1983–; Berlin's Band, Love-Sister-Hope, International Tour, 1980–92; European Tour, Vjestice, 1989–90. *Compositions:* Balkan, 1979; Lijepe Zene Prolaze Kroz Grad, 1980; Provedimo Vikend Zajedno, 1981; Uzas Je Moja Furka, 1981; Klincek Stoji Pod Oblokom, 1983; Totalno Drukciji Od Drugih, 1989. *Recordings:* Azra-Azra; Suncana Strana Ulice Azra; Ravno Do Dna-Azra Djevojke U Ljetnim Haljinama Volim, Vjestice; Kradljivci SRCA Vjestice, Totalno Drukciji Od Drugih. *Publications:* Azra I, 1980; Suncana Strana Ulice, 1981; Azra Ravno Do Dna, 1981; Krivo Srastanje, 1984; Totalno Drukciji Od Drugih, 1988; Vjestice, Kradljivci Srca, 1996. *Honours:* 3 Porin Awards, Cro Music, 1996; Kradljivci Srca, Best Alter, CD; Status Award, Best Drummer, 1996. *Membership:* HGU, Croatian Musicians' Union; HZSU, Croatian Union of Independent Artists. *Current Management:* Combat Rock Management, Jurici Tomislavov Trg 19, Zagreb, Croatia. *Address:* Duzice 23, 1000 Zagreb, Croatia.

LEITNER, George; b. 24 Nov. 1959, Vienna, Austria. Agent. Man. m. Dr Brigitte Leitner-Friedrich, 29 Sept. 1991. *Education:* College, South Africa; University, Vienna; Private piano lessons. *Career:* 1977, founded Number One Music (with Andreas Eggar); 1980, founded George Leitner Productions, representing: James Brown; Kool and the Gang; Jimmy Cliff; Blood Sweat and Tears; VSOP; The Commodores; George Clinton; others. *Publications:*

Analysis of The European Music Industry (university thesis). *Honours:* Mag, Rer Soc Ök. *Address:* Hütteldorfstr 259, 1140 Vienna, Austria.

LEJEUNE, Philippe; b. 6 Feb. 1954, Eu, France. Musician (piano). m. Irene, 5 July 1986, 2 s. *Education:* DUT, Tech de Co; Conservatoires, Rouen, Reims. *Career:* Appearances: Detroit Jazz Festival; Festival Radio France; Festival de Jazz de Montauban; Nuits Piano Jazz Lutetia, Paris; Cincinnati Queen City Blues Festival; Monterey Blues Festival. *Recordings:* Piano Duet With Memphis Slim, 1980; Live At Blue Moon, 1990; Chicago Non Stop, 1993; 100% Blues and Boogie Woogie, 1996; Piano Groove, 1999. *Membership:* SACEM; SPEDIDAM; ADAMI. *Current Management:* Asscn Jazz Vivant, PO Box 2065, 31018 Toulouse, Cedex 2, France.

LEMMY, (Ian Kilmister); b. 24 Dec. 1945, Stoke-on-Trent, Staffordshire, England. Musician (bass); Vocalist. *Career:* Member, several groups including: The Rainmakers; The Motown Sect; The Rockin' Vicars; Sam Gopal's Dream; Opal Butterfly; Also road crew member, Jimi Hendrix; Member, UK rock group Hawkwind, 1971–75; Founder, UK heavy rock group Motörhead, 1975–; Regular UK, US and international tours; Major concerts include: Heavy Metal Barn Dance, 1980; Monsters of Rock Festival, Castle Donington, 1986; Film appearance: Eat The Rich, 1987. *Recordings:* Albums: with Hawkwind: In Search of Space, 1971; Doremi Fasol Latido, 1972; Space Ritual, 1973; Hall of The Mountain Grill, 1974; Warrior On The Edge of Time, 1975; with Motörhead: Motörhead, 1977; Overkill, 1979; Bomber, 1979; Ace of Spades, 1980; No Sleep 'Til Hammersmith, 1981; What's Words Worth, 1983; Another Perfect Day, 1983; No Remorse, 1984; Orgasmatron, 1986; Rock 'N' Roll, 1987; No Sleep At All, 1988; 1916, 1991; March Or Die, 1992; Bastards, 1993; Fistful of Aces: Best of Motörhead, 1994; We Are Motörhead, 2000; Hammered, 2002; Solo: Best of Lemmy: Born to Lose Live to Win, 1995; Rock 'n' Roll Forever, 2000; Singles: with Hawkwind: Silver Machine, 1972; Urban Guerilla, 1973; with Motörhead: Motörhead/City Kids, 1977; Louie Louie, 1978; No Class, 1979; Bomber, 1979; The Golden Years (EP), 1980; Beer Drinkers and Hell Raisers, 1980; St Valentine's Day Massacre, with Girlschool, 1981; Iron Fist, 1982; I Got Mine, 1983; Shine, 1983; Killed By Death, 1984; Deaf Forever, 1986; The One To Sing The Blues, 1991; Contributor, Hear 'N' Aid, 1987; Let It Be, Ferry Aid, 1987; The Last Temptation of Elvis, 1990. *Publications:* Lemmy, The Autobiography: White Line Fever, 2002. *Current Management:* Singerman Entertainment, Penthouse West, 8833 Sunset Blvd, Los Angeles, CA 90069, USA. *Website:* www.imotorhead.com.

LEMPER, Ute; b. 4 July 1963, Münster, Germany. Vocalist; Dancer; Actress. 1 s., 1 d. *Education:* Dance Academy, Cologne; Max Reinhardt Seminar on Dramatic Art, Vienna. *Career:* Leading role in Viennese production of Cats, 1983; Appearances: Peter Pan, Berlin; Cabaret, Düsseldorf and Paris; Chicago, London and New York, 1997–99; Life's a Swindle tour, 1999; Punishing Kiss tour, 2000; Film appearances include: L'Autrichienne, 1989; Moscou Parade, 1992; Coupable d'Innocence, 1993; Prêt à Porter, 1995; Bogus, 1996; Combat de Fauves; A River Made to Drown In; Appetite, 1997; Television apearances include: L'Affaire Dreyfus; Tales from the Crypt; Illusions; The Look of Love. *Recordings:* Albums: Ute Lemper Sings Kurt Weill, Vol. 1, 1988, Vol. 2 1993; Threepenny Opera, 1988; Mahagonny Songspiel, 1989; Illusions, 1992; Espace Indécent, 1993; City Of Strangers, 1995; Berlin Cabaret Songs, 1996; All That Jazz/The Best Of Ute Lemper, 1998; Punishing Kiss, 2000. *Honours:* Molière Award, 1987; French Culture Prize, 1993; Laurence Olivier Award, 1997. *Address:* c/o Oliver Gluzman, 40 rue de la Folie Régnault, 75011 Paris, France. *E-mail:* info@visiteursdusoir.com. *Website:* www.visiteursdusoir.com.

LENDING, Kenn; b. 8 Feb. 1955, Copenhagen, Denmark. Musician (guitar); Composer; Songwriter; Vocalist. m. Karina Nevermann, 15 May 1993. *Education:* Private lessons, music-writing, composing; Classical guitar lessons with Jan Ronnow, Royal Danish Academy of Music. *Career:* Member, Himmelexpressen, 1972–79; Member, Survivors, 1976–78; Member, Blues Nite, 1977–79; Formed duo with American blues pianist, singer, Champion Jack Dupree, 1979–92; Played over 1000 concerts; Formed Kenn Lending Blues Band, 1980–; Used as backing band by Jan Harrington; Louisiana Red; Jack Dupree; Luther Allison; Support tours, Fats Domino, Germany, 1987; B. B. King, Netherlands, 1988, Denmark, 1989; Recorded with The Band in Woodstock, 1991; Worked with Lillian Boutté Musicfriends, Spirit of Louisiana Gospel Tour, including Gospel United with Stig Rossen, 1994; Gospel United Tour with Lillian Boutté, 1995. *Recordings include:* with Kenn Lending Blues Band: Live!, 1981; I'm Coming Home, 1983; Blues For People, 1985; Steamin' Hot, 1988; Diggin' The Blues, 1990; Heartache Motel, 1993; Game of Life, 1995; with Champion Jack Dupree: An Evening With Champion Jack Dupree, 1981; Still Fighting The Blues, 1981; I Had That Dream, 1982; Blues Is Freedom To All, 1987; Back Home In New Orleans, 1990; Forever and Ever, 1991; One Last Time, 1992; After All, 1994; Live Gospel United, 1994; Louisiana Spice: 25 Years of Louisiana Music, various artistes, 1995; Gospel United, People Get Ready, 1995; High on the Hog, with The Band, 1996; Portrait of Champion Jack Dupree, 2000; Also recorded with: Memphis Slim; Louisiana Red; Mickey Baker; Aron Burton; Jan Harrington; Lillian Boutté. *Honours:* Danish Blues Musician of the Year, 1995. *Membership:* Danish Musicians' Union; DJBFA; KODA. *Current Management:* Marsk

Music, Farup Kirkevej 27, 6760 Ribe, Denmark. *Address:* Kenn Lending, Vendsysselvej 7, 2720 Copenhagen-Vanlose, Denmark.

LENDORPH, Jorn; b. 14 June 1966, Copenhagen, Denmark. Vocalist; Songwriter; Prod. *Education:* Graduated, Sct Annae Music College; Copenhagen's Boys' Choir; Piano and Singing lessons. *Career:* Played in Danish TV serial, Everyone Loves Debbie, composed background music and sung title song, 1987; Leading role in film An Abyss of Freedom, wrote one song which was released as single, 1989; Composed music for various short films and songs for own album; Has sung in various TV shows, live concerts and on TV commercials; Background singer, various releases including Sound of Seduction and Shirley, Sanne Graulund. *Recordings:* Title song to Danish version of Disney's Beauty and the Beast, 1991; Loosen Up, solo album, 1996; Produced soundtrack for Danish film The Eighteenth, 1997; Produced Sanne Graulund's debut album, Better Get Some Dreams, 1998. *Membership:* Danish Artists' Union. *Current Management:* Scandinavian Records. *Address:* Viktoria Gade 6 2th, 1655 Copenhagen V, Denmark.

LENGSTRAND, Gert O; b. 30 May 1942, Gothenburg, Sweden. Songwriter; Publisher. m. Jeanette, 14 Aug. 1987, 1 s., 4 d. *Career:* Singer, The Streaplers, Swedish pop group, 1957–68; Songwriter, Record Producer, 1969–. *Compositions:* Hasta La Vista, Silvia, 1974; Eloise, Arvingarna, 1993. *Recordings:* Diggity Doggerty, 1963; Rockin' Robin, 1965; Mule Skinner Blues, 1964. *Honours:* Ampex Golden Reel Award, Eloise, 1993. *Current Management:* GL Productions Ltd. *Address:* GL Productions Ltd, PO Box 632, 44217, Kungälv, Sweden.

LENGWINAT, Katrin; b. 10 Dec. 1960, Berlin, Germany. Musicologist. m. Eduardo Briceño, 16 April 1994, 1 s. *Education:* Bachelor degree; Dr phil, Musicology, Polish and German universities; Studied piano, guitar and folkharp. *Career:* Musicologist, Academy of Fine Arts, Berlin; Musicologist, Foundation of Ethnomusicology and Folklore, Caracas, Venezuela; Leader for Musicology, Free University of Berlin and Central University of Venezuela; Researcher of folk and popular music in Germany, Venezuela and Peru. *Publications:* Arpa, Maraca y Buche, 1998; Joropo Central, 1998. *Membership:* International Council for Traditional Music (ICTM). *Address:* PO Box 40.052, 1040 Caracas, Venezuela.

LENGYEL, Peter M; b. 5 June 1946, New York, USA. Musician (Piano); Composer; Arranger. Divorced. *Education:* BA, Glassboro St College; MM, Theory, Indiana University, 1973. *Career:* University Teacher, 1971–85; Full time composer and arranger, 1985–; Clinician and Judge for jazz bands, marching bands, concert bands, throughout the USA; Teacher of jazz and conductor; President, P & D Jazz Publications; Head of Jazz Studies, Eastfield College, Texas, 1971–81; Performances with Don Ellis, Bill Watrous, Clark Terry, Frank Rosolino. *Compositions:* 25 large jazz ensemble pieces including performances at many major events; 4 pieces for symphony band; Jazzamorphosis, commissioned by Army Ground Forces Band. *Honours:* Award for Teaching Excellence, University of Texas at Arlington College of Liberal Arts Music Department, 1983, 1984, 1985. *Membership:* Texas Bandmasters; Patron mem., International Asscn of Jazz Educators. *Address:* 4453 Wesley Way, Austell, GA 30106, USA.

LENINE, (Osvaldo Lenine Macedo Pimentel); b. Pernambuco, Brazil. Vocalist; Musician (guitar); Songwriter. *Career:* Mixes North Eastern-Brazilian grooves with pop music; As Voltas Que O Mundo Dá used in major Brazilian soap opera Ana Raio e Zé Trovão; Collaborations include: Gilberto Gil; Chico César; Djavan; Elba Ramalho; Songs recorded by: Dionne Warwick; Gilberto Gil; Danilo Caymmi; Sergio Mendes. *Recordings include:* Singles: Prova De Fogo, 1981; Baque De Era, 1983; Albums: Baque Solto (with Lula Queiroga), 1983; Olha De Peixe (with Marcos Suzano), 1993; O Dia Em Que Faremos Contato, 1997; Na Pressao, 1999. *Honours:* Sharp Prize, Best Song, A Ponte (with Lula Queiroga), 1998.

LENNEVALD, (John) Dhani; b. 24 July 1984, Stockholm, Sweden. Vocalist. *Education:* Gärdeskolan school, Stockholm. *Career:* Picked to be member of A*Teens group following auditions at Leslie Kühler's dance school, 1998; Continued educational studies whilst pursuing musical career; Prestigious US support tours for *NSYNC and Britney Spears, 2000. *Recordings:* Albums: The Abba Generation, 1999; Teen Spirit, 2001; Singles: Mamma Mia, Super Trouper, Gimme! Gimme! Gimme!, Happy New Year, 1999; Dancing Queen, Upside Down, 2000; Halfway Around The World, Sugar Rush, 2001. *Honours:* Broke Swedish sales records with first album and single; World-wide sales of first album in excess of 3m.; Viva Music Awards, Best International Newcomer, 2000. *Address:* c/o Stockholm Records, Sweden. *Website:* www.stockholmrecords.com.

LENNI; b. 17 April 1941, Stalybridge, Cheshire, England. Musician (saxophone); Vocalist. m. Irene Dale, March 1963, 1 s. *Education:* Theory, Composition, Arrangement. *Career:* Member, Gladiators, 1959; Corvettes, 1964; St Louis Union, 1965; Tony Christie's Band, 1968–70; Sad Cafe, 1979; Norman Beaker Band, 1986; Look Twice, 1987; Supercharge, 1990; Support tours with Carlos Santana; Toto; Otis Redding; Atlantic Star; Chuck Berry; American Bluesmen: Lowell Fulson; Phil Guy; Larry Garner; Louisianna Red;

Johnny Mars; Rockin' Sydney; Also played for: Jack Bruce; Dave Dee; Kiki Dee; Vince Hill; Paul Jones; Lou Rawls; Lisa Stansfield; Alvin Stardust; Herbie Goins; Claire Moore; Gavin Sutherland; Victor Brox; Carl Wayne; When In Rome. *Recordings:* Sad Cafe (8 albums); Paul Jones R&B Show (3 albums); Norman Beaker Band (3 albums); Judy Boucher (2 albums); Also albums by Cannon and Ball; Magna Carta; Gilbert O'Sullivan; Eric Stewart; 10cc; Ruby Turner; Lurrie Bell; Louisiana Red; Featured on television themes and radio commercials. *Honours:* Gold album, Facades; Silver album, Sad Cafe 4. *Membership:* Musicians' Union; PAMRA; MENSA. *Current Management:* Actual Music. *Address:* 14A Moorside Rd, Heaton Moor, Stockport, Cheshire SK4 4DT, England.

LENNON, Julian; b. 8 April 1963, Liverpool, England. Vocalist; Songwriter; Musician; *Recordings:* Albums: Valotte, 1984; The Secret Value of Daydreaming, 1986; Mr Jordan, 1989; Help Yourself, 1991; Photograph Smile, 1998; VH1 – Behind The Music, 2001; Singles include: Valotte; Day After Day; Too Late For Goodbyes; Now You're In Heaven; Salt Water. *Address:* c/o Music From Another Room Ltd, The Penthouse, 20 Bulstrode St, London W1M 5FR, England.

LENNON, Sean; b. 1976. Vocalist; Songwriter; Musician (guitar). *Career:* Numerous live dates and television appearances. *Recordings:* Single: Home, 1998; Albums: Into the Sun, 1998; Half Horse Half Musician, 1999; Also appeared on: Push The Button, Money Mark, 1998; Primitive, Soulfly, 2000; Change Is Coming, Money Mark, 2001; Blueprint For A Sunrise, Yoko Ono, 2001.

LENNOX, Annie; b. 25 Dec. 1954, Aberdeen, Scotland. Vocalist; Lyricist. m. (1) Rahda Raman, March 1984, divorced, (2) Uri Fruchtmann, 1 s., 2 d. *Education:* Royal Academy of Music. *Career:* Member, with Dave Stewart, The Catch, 1977; Re-named The Tourists, 1979–80; Formed Eurythmics with Dave Stewart, 1980–89; World-wide concerts incl Nelson Mandela's 70th Birthday Tribute, Wembley, 1988; Solo artiste, 1988–; Eurythmics re-formed, 1999; TV incls: Documentary, Diva, BBC2, 1992; Unplugged concert, MTV, 1992; Actress, film Revolution, 1985; 10m. albums sold to date. *Recordings:* with the Tourists: The Tourists; Reality Affect; Luminous Basement; with Eurythmics: In The Garden, 1981; Sweet Dreams (Are Made of This), 1982; Touch (No. 1, UK), 1983; 1984 (For The Love of Big Brother), 1984; Be Yourself Tonight, 1985; Revenge, 1986; Savage, 1987; We Too Are One (No. 1, UK), 1989; Eurythmics Greatest Hits (No. 1, UK), 1991; Eurythmics Live 1983–89, 1993; Peace, 1999; Solo: Diva (No. 1, UK), 1992; Medusa (No. 1, UK), 1995. *Contributions to:* Red Hot + Blue, 1990; Rock The World, 1990; Hit singles include: with the Tourists: I Only Want To Be With You, 1979; So Good To Be Back Home, 1979; with Eurythmics: Sweet Dreams (Are Made of This) (No. 1, USA), 1983; Love Is A Stranger, 1983; Who's That Girl?, 1983; Right By Your Side, 1983; Here Comes The Rain Again, 1984; Sex Crime, from film, 1984; Would I Lie To You?, 1985; There Must Be An Angel (Playing With My Heart), (No. 1, UK), 1985; Sisters Are Doing It For Themselves, duet with Aretha Franklin, 1985; It's Alright (Baby's Coming Back), 1986; When Tomorrow Comes, 1986; Thorn In My Side, 1986; Missionary Man, 1986; The Miracle of Love, 1986; Beethoven, 1987; Shame, 1987; I Need A Man, 1988; You Have Placed A Chill In My Heart, 1988; Revival, 1989; Don't Ask Me Why, 1989; The King and Queen of America, 1990; Angel, 1990; I Changed the World Today, 2000; Feels Like I'm Seventeen Again, 2000; Solo: Put A Little Love In Your Heart, with Al Green, from film soundtrack Scrooged, 1988; Why, 1992; Walking On Broken Glass, 1992; Precious, 1992; Cold, 1992; Little Bird/Love Song For A Vampire, from film Bram Stoker's Dracula, 1993; No More I Love You's, 1995; Whiter Shade of Pale, 1995; Waiting In Vain, 1995; Something So Right, 1995; Videos: Eurythmics Live; Sweet Dreams; Savage. *Honours:* Grammy Awards; BRIT Awards, including Outstanding Contribution, 1999; Ivor Novello Awards; Rolling Stone Readers Poll Winner, Best Female Singer, 1993. *Current Management:* 19 Management, Unit 32, Ransomes Dock, 35–37 Parkgate Rd, London SW11 4NP, England.

LEON, Craig; b. 7 Jan. 1952, Miami, Florida, USA. Prod; Arranger; Composer; Recording Artiste. m. Cassell Webb, 10 June, 1984. *Compositions:* Izzy Album, 1998; Elysium Album, 2000. *Recordings:* 3 albums as featured artiste: Nommos, 1981; Visiting, 1982; Klub Anima Theatre score, 1993; Premiered Bristol Old Vic theatre, 1993; 1 album in collaboration with Arthur Brown: Tape From Atoya, 1981; 5 albums in collaboration with Cassell Webb: Llano, 1985; Thief of Sadness, 1987; Songs of a Stranger, 1989; Conversations At Dawn, 1990; House of Dreams, 1992; Producer, Ramones, 1976; Blondie, 1977; Suicide, 1977; Richard Hell, 1977; Rodney Crowell, 1980; Sir Douglas Quintet, 1980; The Bangles, 1983; The Roches, 1983; Dr and the Medics, 1986; The Pogues, 1986; The Primitives, 1986; Adult Net, 1988; The Fall, 1989–92; Jesus Jones, 1990; New FADS, 1992; Front 242, 1993; Eugenius, 1994; Angel Corpus Christi, 1995; Martin Phillips and the Chills, 1996; Mark Owen, 1996; Cobalt 60, 1996; Psyched Up Janis, 1997; Blondie, No Exit, 1998; Izzy, 1998. *Membership:* British Record Producers' Guild; Nominating Committee, BRIT Awards. *Current Management:* Atlas Realisations Music, Trendalls Cottage, Beacons Bottom, Buckinghamshire HP14 3XF, England.

LEOPOLD, Sinisa; b. 16 April 1957, Grubisno Polje, Croatia. Music Prof. m. Ljiljana Leopold (Rogic), 22 June 1985, 2 s. *Education:* Academy of Music.

Career: Chief conductor, HRT Tambura Orchestra, 1985; Lecturer, Academy of Music, University of Zagreb, 1986–; Conductor, Ferdo Livadic Tambura Orchestra, Samobor, 1985. *Recordings:* Many compositions, arrangements for Tambura Orchestras. *Publications:* Tambura School T, 1992; Tambura Among Croatians, 1995. *Honours:* Croatian Discography Award: Porin 95; Many awards at festivals. *Membership:* Croatian Society of Composers; Croatian Folklore Society. *Address:* Rapska 37A, 41000 Zagreb, Croatia.

LEPALLEC, Bernard; b. 20 Dec. 1951, Paris, France. Musician (saxophone). 2 d. *Education:* Doctorate of Philosophy, Sorbonne, Paris. *Career:* Composer, saxophone player, improvised music; Member, jazz band Ar Jazz; Playing improvised concerts in France; Poland; Italy; Greece. *Recordings:* Albums: Band Ar Jazz, Bernard Lepallec; Bissa. *Membership:* SACEM. *Address:* Venelle de Cosquelou, 22470 Plouezec, France. *Telephone:* (2) 96-55-45-31. *Fax:* (2) 96-55-45-31.

LEROY, Christian; b. 23 Nov. 1952. Composer; Musician (piano). m. Nathalie Cuvelier, 2 s. *Education:* General electronic studies; Drum lessons. *Career:* Composed works for RTBF Programme 3; Works for theatre plays including Le Monde est Rond, Le Baiser de la Femme Araignée, Le Roi et le Cadavre, The Merchant of Venice; Works with Sandro Somaré, Bram Bogart, Miguel Berrocal; Lindström and others; Member of Métarythmes de l'Air musical group and Piano Kvartet, group of 4 pianists. *Compositions:* Le 37 Janvier, opera; Music for Dracula, film of Tod Browning; Music for Robert Flaherty's Nanouk the Eskimo; Images du Tarot, recorded. *Recordings:* Métarythmes de l'Air; Piano Duet with Fred Van Hove; Phagocyte; 33 Petits Tours; Le Temps Qui Passe; Les Chemins de Lumière; La Roue des Corps; Le Temps des Sabbats; The Merchant of Venice; Mystères d'un Théâtre et d'une Vie; Dracula et Nanouk l'Esquimau. *Honours:* Prix de Hainaut, 1982; Special Mention for Film Music, Caracas, 1983; Prix de la Presse, SPA Festival; Prix de la Pensée, Wallonne. *Address:* 8 rue des Berceaux, 7061 Casteau, Belgium.

LESKANICH, Katrina; b. 1960, Topeka, Kansas, USA. Vocalist. *Career:* Lead singer, Katrina and the Waves, 1982–; Presenter, BBC Radio 2, 1999–2000. *Recordings:* Albums: Walking On Sunshine, 1983; Katrina and The Waves 2, 1984; Waves, 1985; Katrina and The Waves, 1985; Break of Hearts, 1989; Vol. 2, 1995; Anthology, 1995; Walk on Water, 1997; Hit singles: Walking On Sunshine, 1985; Going Down To Liverpool (later recorded by the Bangles), 1985; Sun Street, 1986; Love Shine A Light, 1997. *Honours:* Eurovision Song Contest, winner, Love Shine A Light, 1997. *Address:* c/o Jason West Agency, Gables House, Saddlebow, Kings Lynn, Norfolk PE34 3AR, England.

LESSARD, Stefan Kahil; b. 4 June 1974, Anaheim, California, USA. Musician (bass guitar). *Education:* Tandem Music School, Charlottesville, USA. *Career:* Former member of Charlottesville-Albermarle Youth Orchestra; Teamed up with Dave Matthews to assist with demo recording on recommendation of music tutor/local jazz guru John D'Earth, 1990; Became member of The Dave Matthews Band, 1991; Rapid growth of fanbase through touring; First album released on group's own Bama Rags label certified gold by RIAA; First national US tour in support of RCA debut album, 1994; Many world-wide concerts and festival appearances since including 2001 album tour; Group permits fans to tape-record shows for personal use; I Did It single officially released through Napster, 2001. *Recordings:* Albums: Remember Two Things (live), 1993; Under The Table and Dreaming, 1994; Crash, 1996; Live At Red Rocks 8–15–95, 1997; Before These Crowded Streets, 1998; Listener Supported (live), 1999; Everyday, Live In Chicago 12–19–98, 2001; Singles: Recently (EP), 1994; What Would You Say, Jimi Thing, Ants Marching, 1995; So Much To Say, Too Much, 1996; Don't Drink The Water, 1997; Satellite, Crash Into Me, Crush, 1998; I Did It, The Space Between, Everyday, 2001. *Honours:* Grammy Awards: Best Rock Performance By A Duo Or Group With Vocal, 1997; US VH-1 Awards: Favourite Group; Must Have Album; Song of the Year, 2001; Top-grossing touring band in USA, 2000. *Address:* c/o Red Light Communications, 3305 Lobban Pl., Charlottesville, VA 22903, USA. *E-mail:* info@rlc.net. *Website:* www.dmband.com.

LESTER, Gregory; b. Brighton, England. Musician (guitar); Songwriter. *Education:* Studied classical guitar. *Career:* Session musician, composer, co-writer on albums by: Shola Ama, Camelle Hinds, Jeb Loy Nichols, Truce, Terminalhead, Lucid Source, Ultimate Kaos, The Collective, Love City Groove; Tours, recordings, radio, television appearances with: Julia Fordham, Des'ree, Danielle Gaha, John O'Kane, Joe Roberts, Sylvia Powell; Concerts incl.: with John O'Kane: support to Sting, Soul Cages tour, UK/European legs; with Des'ree: Summer festivals at Wembley Stadium, Old Trafford, Gateshead International; Tour of Japan; Jeb Loy Nichols, UK and US dates; Maggie Reilly, Polar Star featuring Cara Dillon; Radio and television appearances with: Kindred Spirit, 25th of May, Kim Appleby, Shania Twain. *Recordings:* Numerous sessions incl.: Adam F., Aco, Adeva, Atlantique, Azizi, Barry Adamson, Daniel Beddingfield, Caroline Bonnet, Blade, Cornelius, Danielle Dax, Des'ree, Definition of Sound, E-Type, Ace of Bass, Everything But The Girl, EYC, Dark Flower, Freaky Realistic, Love City Groove, Gangstarr, Camelle Hinds, Rodeo Jones, Karl Keaton, Lush Life, Lindy Layton, Alison Limerick, London Beat, James McMillan, Monie Love, Kylie Minogue, Jeb Loy Nichols, Nightcrawlers, Noriyuki Makahara, Osibisa, Peter Brown,

Tconnection, Pop Will Eat Itself, Joe Roberts, Maria Rowe, Tom Robinson, Stex, Jimmy Somerville, Shola Ama, Shy FX & T Power, Sunscream, Spice Girls, Soundstation, Dave Stewart, Whitney Houston, Workshy, Worlds Apart, Keith Washington, Trumpet Thing, Tyrell Corporation; Live video: Porcelain—Live In Concert, Julia Fordham; Played on various television commercials; Played on film music incl.: My Boy (Channel 4); The Beat (theme music); Painted Lady (Granada TV); Ali G the Movie. *Honours:* BPI Awards: Platinum, three times, Spice Girls; Gold, Kylie Minogue, EBTG; Silver, Des'ree. *Membership:* PRS; MCPS Musicians' Union; Pamra. *Address:* PO Box 34261, London NW5 4YT, England. *Website:* www.greglester.com.

LEURS, Lawrence; b. 9 July 1965, Bree, Belgium. Vocalist; Songwriter; Musician (guitar). m. Peeters Saskia, 11 June 1994. *Education:* Licentiate in History, University of Brussels; Degree, Academy of Word and Music Maaseik, Belgium. *Recordings:* Albums: Ball and Chain, 1989; Trigger Happy, 1990; Major Panic, 1993; Be My Star, 1996; El Diablo, 1998. *Membership:* ZAMU, Union of Musical Artists, Belgium. *Current Management:* Oyster Records, Setsesteenweg 222, 1081 Brussels, Belgium. *Address:* Koningin Astridlaan 37, 3680, Maaseik, Belgium.

LEVAN, Christophe; b. 29 Dec. 1959, Marseilles, France. Musician (contrabass, bass guitar). 1 s. *Education:* Dental studies, Marseilles. *Career:* Concerts with: Michel Legrand; Michel Portal; Chet Baker; Sonny Stitt; Phil Woods; Peter King; Dee Dee Bridgewater; Nicole Croisille; Television and radio broadcasts include: Françaises Variétés et Jazz; Radio France; France Musique. *Compositions:* Minou; Libreto; Swing Gome; Merci Glop; Waltz For Theo. *Recordings:* About 20 records include: Swinging Marilyn, Gerard Badini Swing Machine; Debussy Meets Mister Swing, Gerard Badini Big Band; Chassaguite Quartet; Johnny Griffin et Hervé Sellin' Sextet; Tribute To Jazz Michel Gaucher; Cannon Blues, Hervé Meschinet Quartet. *Honours:* Django D'Or, Hervé Meshinet Quartet, 1998; Victoires de la Musique, 1998. *Membership:* Syndicate des Musiciens; Membre de la Sacem, 1998. *Address:* 30 rue de Musselburgh, 94500 Champigny-sur-Marne, France.

LEVANDER, Jan; b. 29 March 1959, Stockholm. Composer; Musician (Saxophone, Flute, Clarinet). m. Malin Hülphers. 1, 1 d. *Education:* Stockholm Community Music Institute; Stockholm Music Conservatory. *Career:* Led, wrote music for and played in own Jazz groups, Kamel Kombo; Jan Levanders Oktett; Toured, Jazz Clubs; Festivals; Radio; Musician, arranger, conductor in musicals and theatre music. *Compositions:* Gerlögs Runa, Opera; 12 Piece Jazzband, Festivalsvit; Big Band and String Quartet and Percussion, EBU; Jazz compositions; Chamber Music; Theatre Music. *Recordings:* Musaik; Spion För En Främmande Makt; For trio and ten piece band. *Address:* LustigKullavägen 7 5 tr, 117 66 Stockholm, Sweden.

LEVERIDGE, Paul (Kermit); b. 10 Nov. 1969, Manchester, England. Vocalist. *Career:* Member, Ruthless Rap Assassins; Member: Black Grape; Numerous gigs and festival appearances including Tribal Gathering and Reading Festivals, 1997. *Recordings:* Singles: Reverend Black Grape, 1995; In The Name of The Father, 1995; Kelly's Heroes, 1995; England's Irie, 1996; Fat Neck, 1996; Get Higher, 1997; Marbles, 1998; Albums: It's Great When You're Straight... Yeah, 1995; Stupid Stupid Stupid, 1997.

LEVIEV, Milcho; b. 19 Dec. 1937, Plovdiv, Bulgaria. Composer; Musician (piano); Arranger; Conductor. m. Deborah Rothschild, 19 July 1990, 1 d. *Education:* Masters in Composition, Bulgarian State Conservatory, 1960. *Career:* Conductor, Bulgarian Radio and TV Pop Orchestra, 1962–66; Composer, Bulgarian Feature Film Studios, 1963–69; Arranger, Radio Frankfurt, 1970; Pianist, composer, arranger, Don Ellis Orchestra, Billy Cobham Band, Art Pepper Quartet; Music Director, Lanie Kazan Show; Co-leader, Free Flight quartet; Lecturer, University of Southern California. *Compositions:* Concerto For Jazz Combo and Strings; Music For Big Band and Symphony Orchestra; Sympho-Jazz Sketches; Orpheus Rhapsody for Piano and Orchestra; The Green House – Jazz Cantata; Film and Theatre Music. *Recordings:* Over 35 records under own name and over 50 records as a sideman; Blues For The Fisherman; Easter Parade; Live At Vartan Jazz; Anti Waltz. *Publications:* 8 Jazz Pieces, 1968; Milcho Leviev-Fake Book; 2 Songs For Jazz Choir, 1991. *Honours:* Dr h.c., Music Acad., Plovdiv, 1995; Dr h.c., New Bulgarian University, 1999. *Membership:* AFofM; NARAS; BMI; GEMA.

LEVIN, Michael David; b. 29 May 1954, Syracuse, New York, USA. Musician; Composer. *Education:* BA, University of Illinois; AM, University of Chicago; PhD, University of Illinois, Institute of Communications Research. *Career:* Performed and recorded with David Bromberg, Oscar Brown Jr, Barrett Deems, Hamid Drake, The Four Tops, Fireworks Jazz, Jerry Goodman, Charlie Musselwhite, Night on Earth, Jim Post, Bernard Purdie, Claudia Schmidt, Diane Schuur, The Supremes, The Temptations, Clark Terry, The Chicago Jazz Ensemble, The Illinois Philharmonic Orchestra, The Ethos Chamber Orchestra; Appearances at numerous jazz and pop festivals. *Recordings:* Over 50 Albums. *Address:* 1336 1/2 S Austin, Apartment D, Cicero, IL 60804, USA.

LEVINE, Steve; Prod; Songwriter. *Career:* Working on soundtrack to musical, Boy Band (West End, London); Worked with: Alsou, The Beach Boys,

The Beauties, Darren Berry, The Creatures, Culture Club, The Honeyz, Louise, Ziggy Marley, Mis-Teeq, 911, Owen, Rozalla, Denice Williams. *Address:* c/o Stephen Budd Management Ltd, 109b Regents Park Rd, Primrose Hill, London NW1 8UR, England. *Website:* www.record-producers.com.

LEVITIN, Daniel J; b. 27 Dec. 1957, San Francisco, CA, USA. Cognitive Psychologist; Record Prod; Musician; Journalist. m. Caroline A Traube. *Education:* AB, Stanford University; MSc, PhD, University of Oregon; Berklee College of Music. *Career:* Television, Close To You: Remembering The Carpenters; Radio, The Sound of Musique; Music Production Editor, REP Magazine, 1989–92; Staff Writer, Billboard Magazine, 1990–93; Director, A&R; 415/Columbia Records, 1984–89; Assistant Professor of Psychology, McGill University, 2000–. *Compositions:* First Strike; Now That You Are Gone; I Should've Told You. *Recordings:* Heart Shaped World (Chris Isaak); Imaginoos (Blue Oyster Cult); Rockin' and Romance (Jonathan Richmond); Good News About Mental Health (The Afflicted). *Publications:* The John Fogerty Interview; Liner notes for Stevie Wonder; Music, Cognition and Computerized Sounds; The Billboard Encyclopedia of Record Producers. *Honours:* Platinum Records; Gold Medal, Venice Film Festival, Best Soundtrack, 1986. *Membership:* NARAS; AES. *Address:* CCRMA, Deptartment of Music, Stanford University, Stanford, CA 94305, USA.

LEVY, Alain M; b. 19 Dec. 1946, France. Record Co Exec. *Education:* Ecole des Mines, France; MBA, University of Pennsylvania. *Career:* Asst. to the Pres., New York, 1972–73; Vice-Pres. Marketing for Europe, Paris, 1973, CBS International; Vice-Pres. of Creative Operations for Europe, also Man., CBS Italy, 1978; Man. Dir., CBS Disques, France, 1979; CEO, PolyGram France, 1984; Exec. Vice-Pres., PolyGram Group, France and Federal Republic of Germany, 1988; Man. US Operations, PolyGram Group, 1990–98; Pres., CEO, mem. of Board, Man., PolyGram USA, 1991–98; Mem. Group Managerial Committee, Philips Electronics, 1991–98; Majority shareholder, PolyGram USA, 1991–98; Chair. of Board, EMI Group PLC, 2001–; Chair. and CEO, EMI Recorded Music, 2001–. *Address:* c/o EMI Group PLC, 4 Tenterden St, Hanover Sq., London W1A 2AY, England. *Website:* www.emigroup.com.

LEVY, Andrew; b. 20 July 1966, Ealing, London, England. Musician (Bass). *Career:* Founder Member, The Brand New Heavies; Worked with numerous vocalists including Jaye Ella Ruth, N'Dea Davenport, Siedah Garrett and currently Carleen Anderson; Numerous television appearances and live dates, including club dates. *Recordings:* Singles: Stay This Way, 1991; Never Stop, 1991; Dream Come True, 1991; Don't Let It Go To Your Head, 1992; Spend Some Time, 1994; Dream on Dreamer, 1994; Back To Love, 1994; Midnight At The Oasis, 1994; Mind Trips, 1995; Close To You, 1995; You've Got A Friend, 1997; You Are the Universe, 1997; Sometimes, 1997; Shelter, 1998; Albums: The Brand New Heavies, 1990; The Brand New Heavies, 1992; Heavy Rhyme Experience, 1992; Brother Sister, 1994; Original Flava, 1994; Excursions, 1995; Shelter, 1997.

LEVY, Rick; b. 1 Nov. 1949, Allentown, PA, USA. Musician (Guitar); Man; Songwriter; Divorced, 1 s. *Education:* BA, Sociology, University of Pennsylvania, 1971; Education Degree, Moravian College, 1985; Guitar lessons, 5 years; Berklee School of Music, 1 year. *Career:* Tour USA with Jay and The Techniques, 1985–; Manager, Jay and The Techniques; The Box Tops; Performed at Rock 'n' Roll Hall of Fame, September 1996; Pres: Rick Levy Management, Flying Governor Music, Luxury Records. *Compositions:* Rock Roots, History of American Pop Music. *Recordings:* Love's Just Not For Sale; Ricochet Waltz; The Limits, Songs About Girls; The Main Course, Jay and The Techniques. *Honours:* Penna-Broadcasters Asscn, Rock Roots, Best Single, Children's Program, 1992. *Membership:* NARAS. *Current Management:* Rick Levy Management, 4250 A1A S, D-11 St Augustine, FL 32084, USA.

LEWIN, Giles; b. Rayleigh, Essex, England. Musician (fiddle, medieval bagpipes, recorders, shawm); Vocalist. *Education:* Violin, flute, viol, at school; Music, Cambridge University. *Career:* Member, The Dufay Collective; Plays with: The New London Consort; The Chuckerbutty Ocarina Quartet; Lost Jockey; Afterhours; Music director, The Medieval Players, tours world-wide; Student of Egyptian Fiddle styles and culture; Member, The Carnival Band, 1984–; Appearances include: Glasgow Cathedral; Birmingham Symphony Hall; Barbican Centre; Numerous Arts theatres and festivals; Plays material from: Sweden; Croatia; USA; Bolivia; Spain; UK; France.

LEWINSON, Stephen Owen Lloyd; b. 19 Feb. 1966, Coventry, England. Musician (bass). *Career:* Tours with: Phil Bent Quartet, 1989; Reggae Philharmonic Orchestra, 1990–91; Courtney Pine, 1991–92; Steve Williamson, 1992; Bomb The Bass, 1992; Tim Finn, 1992; Tom Browne, 1992; Nelson Rangell, 1992; Rebirth of The Cool, 1993; Juliet Roberts, 1993; Ronny Jordan world tour, 1993–94; Tony Remy, Mica Paris, Boy George, Orphy Robinson, Massive Attack world tour, 1995; Simply Red world tour, 1995–96; Everything But The Girl tour, 1996–97; Lisa Stansfield, 1997; Spice Girls world tour, 1997–98; Eurythmics, 1999. *Recordings:* Spice World, Spice Girls; Greatest Hits, Simply Red; Blue, Simply Red; Invisible, Five; Peace, Eurythmics; Brighter, Ronny Jordan; Tilt, Lightning Seeds; Woman In Me,

Louise; Help, Massive Attack; Courtney Pine; Tony Remy; for Kylie Minogue: Light Years, 2000; Fever, 2001; for Sugababes: One Touch, 2001. *Membership:* PRS; MCPS; PAMRA; Musicians' Union. *Current Management:* Timeless Music Ltd. *Address:* 38 Coolhurst Rd, London N8, England.

LEWIS, Aaron; b. 13 April 1972. Vocalist. m. Vanessa. *Career:* Played with The Geckoes; Formed Staind with Mike Mushok and others; First live gig, 1995; Released self-financed debut album, 1996; Album sold 4,000 copies; Discovered by Fred Durst, 1997; Signed to Flip/Elektra; Presented to rock cognoscenti at Limp Bizkit gold record party for Three Dollar Bill Y'All $, 1998; Major breakthrough with unscheduled smash US No. 1 radio hit Outside; Appeared on bill for Korn-founded Family Values tours, 1999, 2001; Headlined MTV's Return of the Rock tour, 2000. *Recordings:* Albums: Tormented, 1996; Dysfunction, 1999; Break The Cycle, 2001; Singles: Mudshovel, Just Go, 1999; Home, Outside, 2000; It's Been Awhile, Fade, 2001. *Honours:* Break The Cycle certified quadruple platinum by RIAA; It's Been Awhile topped Billboard Modern Rock Singles Chart for record-equalling 16 weeks; VH-1 Award, Your Song Kicked Ass But Was Played Too Damn Much prize, 2001. *Address:* c/o The Firm, Inc, 9100 Whilshire Blvd, Suite 400W, Beverly Hills, CA 90212, USA. *Website:* www.staind.com.

LEWIS, Cass (Richard Keith); b. 1 Sept. 1960, London, England. Musician (bass guitar). *Career:* Founder mem., Skunk Anansie, 1994–2001; Signed to indie label One Little Indian, 1994, Virgin Records, 1996; Numerous headlining tours, festival appearances, television and radio shows. *Recordings:* Albums: Paranoid and Sunburnt, 1995; Stoosh, 1996; Post Orgasmic Chill, 1999. Singles: Little Baby Swastikkka, 1994; Selling Jesus, 1995; I Can Dream, 1995; Charity, 1995; Weak, 1996; All I Want, 1996; Twisted (Everyday Hurts), 1996; Hedonism, 1997; Brazen (Weep), 1997; Charlie Big Potato, 1999; Secretly, 1999; Lately, 1999. *Address:* c/o Virgin Records America Inc, 338 N Foothill Rd, Beverly Hills, CA 90210, USA. *Website:* www.skunkanansie.com.

LEWIS, David A. R; b. 15 Feb. 1964, Morecambe, Lancashire, England. Songwriter; Composer; Musician (guitar). m. Andrea Lewis, 20 Sept. 1992. *Education:* J L Academy. *Career:* Appearances on National and Granada TV; Single of the Week, Red Rose, Lancashire, Capital; Extensive touring throughout UK; Support to Blur at pop club; Support to Youssou N'Dour, Womad Festival, 1992. *Compositions include:* Independence Day; The Other Side; This Is England; Sunday; Revolution. *Recordings:* Jerusalem; Maralyn; Treason. *Membership:* Musicians' Union. *Current Management:* Ice Factory (Management) Co Ltd. *Address:* Ice Factory (Managament) Co Ltd, c/o John Lewis, 253 Marine Rd, Morecambe, Lancashire LA4 4BJ, England.

LEWIS, Huey, (Hugh Cregg III); b. 5 July 1950, New York, USA. Vocalist; Musician; Actor; Songwriter. *Career:* Member, Clover, 1976–79; Founder, Huey Lewis and The News, 1979–; Major concerts include: Over 30 US and Canadian tours; Notable concerts include: Madison Square Gardens, New York, Superdrome, New Orleans, attendance set at numerous venues including: Poplar Creek Amphitheatre, Illinois, Alpine Valley Amphitheatre, Wisconsin, Summerfest, Milwaukee; 7 European tours; 4 Japan Tours; 1 Australia tour; Film appearances: Back to the Future, 1985; Short Cuts, 1993; Sphere, 1998. *Recordings:* Albums: with Clover: Clover, 1977; Love on the Wire, 1977; with Huey Lewis and the News: Huey Lewis and the News, 1980; Picture This, 1982; Sports, 1983; Fore!, 1986; Small World, 1988; Hard at play, 1991; Four Chords and Several Years Ago, 1994; Time Flies (Best of), 1996; If This Is It, 1997; Only One, 1998; Plan B, 2001; Singles include: Do You Believe in Love, 1982; Workin' for a Livin', 1982; Heart and Soul, 1983; I Want a New Drug, 1983; The Heart of Rock 'n' Roll, 1984; If This Is It, 1984; Walking on a Thin Line, 1984; The Power of Love (No 1, USA), 1985; Stuck With You, (No 1 USA), 1986; Hip to be Square, 1986; Jacob's Ladder (No 1 USA), 1987; Doing It All For My Baby, 1987; I Know What I Like, 1987; Perfect World, 1988; Small World Pt 1 and 2 (featuring Sam Getz), 1988; Give Me the Keys, 1988; Couple Days Off, 1991; It hit Me Like a Hammer, 1991; He Don't Know, 1991; It'a Alright (A capella from People Get Ready, tribute album to Curtis Mayfield), 1993; Some Kind of Wonderful, 1994; But It's Alright, 1994; Little Bitty Pretty One, 1994; Contributor to We Are the World, USA for Africa recording, 1985; Numerous film videos. *Honours:* American Music Awards: Favorite Single, 1986, Favorite Band, 1987; British Music Awards, Best International Group, 1986.

LEWIS, Jerry Lee; b. 29 Sept. 1935, Ferriday, Louisiana, USA. Vocalist; Musician (piano); Entertainer. m. 6 times. *Career:* Appeared on Louisiana Hayride, 1954; Film appearances: Jamboree, 1957; High School Confidential, 1958; Be My Guest, 1965; Concerts include: National Jazz and Blues Festival, 1968; Rock 'n' Revival Concert, Toronto, 1969; First appearance, Grand Ole Opry, 1973; Rock 'n' Roll Festival, Wembley, 1974; Numerous appearances with own Greatest Show on Earth; Subject of biographical film, Great Balls of Fire, 1989. *Recordings:* Hit singles include: Whole Lotta Shakin' Goin' On, 1957; Great Balls of Fire, 1958; Breathless, 1958; High School Confidential, 1958; What I'd Say, 1961; Good Golly Miss Molly, 1963; To Make Love Sweeter For You, 1969; There Must Be More To Love Than This, 1970; Would You Take Another Chance On Me?, 1971; Me and Bobby Gee, 1972; Chantilly Lace, 1972; Albums include: Jerry Lee Lewis, 1957; Jerry Lee's Greatest,

1961; Live At The Star Club, 1965; The Greatest Live Show On Earth, 1965; The Return of Rock, 1965; Whole Lotta Shakin' Goin' On, 1965; Country Songs For City Folks, 1965; By Request – More Greatest Live Show On Earth, 1967; Breathless, 1967; Together, with Linda Gail Lewis, 1969; Rockin' Rhythm and Blues, 1971; Sunday Down South, with Johnny Cash, 1972; The Session, with Peter Frampton, Rory Gallagher, 1973; Jerry Lee Lewis, 1979; When Two Worlds Collide, 1980; My Fingers Do The Talking, 1983; I Am What I Am, 1984; Keep Your Hands Off It, 1987; Don't Drop It, 1988; Great Balls of Fire! (film soundtrack), 1989; Rocket, 1990; Young Blood, 1995; Keep Your Eyes Off of It, 2000; By Invitation Only, 2000; Many compilations; Contributor, film soundtracks: Roadie, 1980; Dick Tracy, 1990. *Honours:* Inducted into Rock 'n' Roll Hall of Fame, 1986; Star on Hollywood Walk of Fame, 1989. *Current Management:* Al Embry International, PO Box 23162, Nashville, TN 37202, USA. *Address:* The Lewis Ranch, Box 384, Nesbit, MS 38651, USA.

LEWIS, Laurie; b. 28 Sept. 1950, Long Beach, California, USA. Musician (fiddle, guitar, bass); Vocalist; Vocalist; Songwriter. *Education:* Traditional knowledge, skills passed on within folk/old time music community in oral tradition. *Career:* Performing, touring nationally, internationally since early 1970s; Television appearances: Music City Tonight, TNN; The Grand Ole Opry; The American Music Show; Lonesome Pine Specials, PBS, Later with Jools, BBC; Prairie Home Companion, NPR; Mountain Stage; World Cafe. *Recordings:* Restless Rambling Heart; Love Chooses You; Singing My Troubles Away; Together (with Kathy Kallick); True Stories; The Oak and The Laurel, with Tom Rozum; Earth and Sky: Songs of Laurie Lewis; Seeing Things; Winter's Grace, with Tom Rozum, 1999; Kristin's Story, 2001. *Honours:* NAIRD Award, Best Country Album; IBMA Awards, Female Vocalist of the Year, 1992, 1994; Song of the Year, 1994. *Membership:* ASCAP; International Bluegrass Music Asscn. *Current Management:* Cash Edwards, Under The Hat Productions. *Address:* 1121-B Bluebonnet Lane, Austin, TX 78704, USA. *Website:* www.laurielewis.com.

LEWIS, Linda; b. 27 Sept. 1953, London, England. Vocalist; Songwriter; Musician (guitar, piano). m. Jim Cregan, 18 March 1977, divorced, 1 s. *Education:* Peggy O'Farrels Stage School. *Career:* Toured with Cat Stevens, Elton John and Richie Havens, 1970s; Appeared at first Glastonbury Festival; Television appearances include: In Concert; Old Grey Whistle Test; Supersonic; Top of the Pops; Appearance with Courtney Pine; Jazz Cafe; Ronnie Scott's; numerous others. *Recordings:* Albums: Say No More; Lark; Fathoms Deep; Not A Little Girl Any More (featuring Luther Vandross, Lowell George, Deniece Williams); Woman Overboard; Second Nature, 1995; Whatever, 1998; Kiss of Life, 1999; Also appeared on: Aladdin Sane, David Bowie, 1973; Do You Think I'm Sexy, Rod Stewart, 1978; Emergency On Planet Earth, Jamiroquai, 1993; Standing On The Shoulder of Giants, Oasis, 2000; recordings by Family and Steve Harley. *Honours:* Saturday Scene British Pop Award, 1975. *Membership:* PRS; Equity; PAMRA. *Current Management:* Tenderhook Music. *Address:* c/o Ella McQuery, 175 Stafford Rd, Caterham, Surrey CR3, England.

LEWIS, Luke; Record Co Exec. *Career:* Head of Mercury Nashville, 1992–; Founder, CEO, Lost Highway Records, as part of Universal Music Group, 2001–; Worked with: Ryan Adams, Kim Richey, Shania Twain, Lucinda Williams. *Honours:* Grammy Award (with Bonnie Garner and Mary Martin), Best Country Album, for Timeless: Hank Williams Tribute, 2001. *Address:* Lost Highway Records, 100 Universal City Plaza, Universal City, CA 91608, USA.

LEWIS, Monica; b. 5 May, Chicago, IL, USA. Vocalist. m. Jennings Lang, 1 Jan. 1956. *Education:* Taught by mother (opera singer) and by father (conductor, composer, pianist). *Career:* Radio appearances, recording artiste, personal appearances, TV shows and films. *Recordings include:* I Wish You Love, 1956; Albums: My Favorite Things; Swings Jule Styne. *Honours:* First Grammy Award. *Address:* 1100 Alto Louea Rd, Los Angeles, CA 90069, USA.

LEWIS, Pamela; b. 23 Nov. 1958, Rhinebeck, New York, USA. PR/Marketing Consultant; Media Exec; Event Planning. *Education:* BA, Wells College; Practitioner, Religious Science International; Leadership Music. *Career:* CEO, founder, PLA Media, Los Angeles, Nashville; NBC Specials: This Is Garth Brooks; This Is Garth Brooks Too; 7-year career as manager to Garth Brooks, including International World Tour, 1993–94. *Publications:* Dan Rivers Poetry Anthology; American Poetry Anthology. *Honours:* CMA Manager of Year, 1991; Pollstar Manager of the Year, 1991, 1992; Performance Manager of Year, 1992, 1993. *Membership:* Country Music Asscn; Academy of Country Music; Blair School of Music; Belmont School of Music. *Current Management:* PLA Media. *Address:* 1303 16th Ave So, Nashville, TN 37212, USA.

LEWIS, Ramsey E, Jr; b. 27 May 1935, Chicago, Illinois, USA. Musician (piano). m. Janet Tamillon, 10 June 1990, 5 s., 2 d. (from previous marriage). *Education:* College, 1955–57; Chicago Musical College, 1955–56. *Career:* Performed, nightclubs, concerts, festivals, in USA, Canada, Western Europe, Japan, Mexico, The Caribbean, 1957–; Also with symphony orchestras; Host, weekly syndicated radio programme; Host 1 hour weekly segment, BET's Jazz Central. *Recordings:* Over 60 albums include: The Incrowd, 1965; Sun

Goddess, 1974; Ivory Pyramid, 1992; Sky Islands, 1993; Urban Knights, 1995; Finest Hour, 2000; Meant To Be (with Nancy Wilson), 2002. *Honours:* Hon. doctorates: Depaul University, 1993; University of Illinois, Chicago, 1995; White House State Dinner Performance, 1995; 3 Grammy Awards; 5 Gold records. *Membership:* Ravinia Artistic Director, Jazz Series. *Current Management:* Andi Howard, Gardner Howard Ringe Entertainment.

LEWIS, Ronald Chapman; b. 20 Aug. 1950, Louisville, Kentucky, USA. Musician (Guitar); Songwriter; Music Publisher. m. LaQuetta Wilson, June 1972, 2 s. *Education:* Associate Degree in Music, JCC University, School of Music, Louisville, 1985. *Career:* BMI Songwriter and Publisher; Show Host, Cable TV. *Compositions:* When the Spirit of the Lord; Spraggie. *Recordings:* Spraggie, Hanlon Robinson, Swindell Brothers. *Honours:* Up and Coming Songwriter's Award, Billboard Magazine. *Current Management:* Harry Fox Agency. *Address:* Mr Wonderful Productions, 1730 Kennedy Rd, Louisville, KY 40216, USA.

LEWIS, Shaznay T; b. 14 Oct. 1977, England. Vocalist; Songwriter. *Career:* Founding member, female vocal group All Saints, 1993–2001. *Recordings:* Singles: Silver Shadow, 1994; I Know Where It's At, 1997; Never Ever (No. 1, UK), 1997; Lady Marmalade/Under The Bridge (No. 1, UK), 1998; Bootie Call (No. 1, UK), 1998; War of Nerves, 1998; Pure Shores (No. 1, UK), 2000; Black Coffee (No. 1, UK), 2000; Album: All Saints, 1997; Saints and Sinners, 2000; All Hits, 2001. *Honours:* BRIT Award, Best Single, Never Ever, 1998. *Current Management:* John Benson.

LEWIS, Terry; b. USA. Record Prod. *Career:* Founder member, Flyte Time, 1972–; Joined by Jimmy Jam, become backing band for Morris Day, renamed The Time, 1981–83; Formed Flyte Tyme Productions with Jimmy Jam, 1982–; Built Flyte Tyme Studios, Minneapolis, 1984–85; Founded own label (with Jimmy Jam), Perspective Records, 1991; Helped launch new acts including Sounds of Blackness; Involved with International Association of African American Music (IAAAM), 1990–. *Recordings:* As co-producer with Jimmy Jam: Wild Girls, Klymaxx, 1983; Just Be Good To Me, SOS Band, 1983; Change of Heart, Change, 1984; Heat of The Heart, Patti Austin, 1984; Encore, Cheryl Lynn, 1984; I Didn't Mean To Turn You On, Cherelle, 1984 (covered by Robert Palmer, 1985); Saturday Love, Cherelle and Alexander O'Neal, 1985; The Finest, SOS Band, 1986; Human, The Human League (No. 1, USA), 1987; Keep Your Eye On Me, Herb Alpert, 1987; Criticize, Alexander O'Neal, 1987; Sensitivity, Ralph Tresvant, 1990; Optimistic, Sounds of Blackness, 1991; Co-writers and co-producers, Janet Jackson, 1986–, including: What Have You Done For Me Lately?, 1986; Nasty, 1986; When I Think of You (No. 1, USA), 1986; Let's Wait Awhile, 1987; Miss You Much (No. 1, USA), 1989; Rhythm Nation, 1989; Escapade (No. 1, USA), 1990; Alright (No. 1, USA), 1990; Love Will Never Do Without You (No. 1, USA), 1990; The Best Things In Life Are Free, with Luther Vandross, 1992; That's The Way Love Goes (No. 1, USA), 1993; If, 1993; Runaway, 1995; Doesn't Really Matter, 2001; All For You, 2001; Albums with Janet Jackson: Control, 1986; Rhythm Nation, 1989; Janet, 1993 (all No. 1, USA); Other recordings with: Mint Condition; Low Key; Sounds of Blackness; George Michael; Karyn White; Boyz II Men; Johnny Gill; New Edition; Fine Young Cannibals; Film soundtrack, Mo' Money, 1993. *Honours:* R&B Songwriting Awards, American Society of Composers and Publishers, 1989–94. *Address:* c/o Perspective Records, 1416 N La Brea Ave, Hollywood, CA 90028, USA.

LEYERS, Jan; b. 16 May 1958, Antwerp, Belgium. Vocalist; Musician (guitar, bass keyboards); Composer. *Career:* Soulsister. *Compositions:* Billboard Hot Country Chart, 1995 (No. 1); Soulsister, Repertoire; Changes, Tom Jones; The Way to Your Heart; That's As Close as I'll Get to Loving You. *Recordings:* Soulsister: It Takes Two; Heat; Simple Rule; Live Savings; Swinging Like Big Dogs; The Very Best; My Velma: Exposed. *Honours:* World Music Award, Monaco, 1990; Jozef Platteau, 1991; BMI Country Award, 1996; Golden Eye Award, 1992, 1993. *Membership:* SABAM. *Current Management:* Johan P Berckmans. *Address:* Mereldreef 3, 3140 Keerbergen, Belgium.

LIANA, (Liana C. Di Marco); b. 25 March 1966, Toronto, ON, Canada. Vocalist; Songwriter; Musician (guitar); Multimedia Artiste. *Education:* BA, Social Science; Private instruction with leading vocalists and instrumentalists. *Career:* Played viola in two local orchestras prior to 1986; Solo career as singer, songwriter, 1988–; Business ventures: LCDM Entertainments Productions, music label, and Indie Tips and The Arts, publications. *Recordings include:* Glitters and Tumbles, 1993; Songs published: Degree In Love; Sweep Me Off My Feet; By My Side; Glitters and Tumbles; You'll Never Know; Boom; Non Fa Differenza Dove Vai; Thinking of You; Country Funky. *Publications:* Indie Tips and The Arts. *Honours:* Awards in Music, Journalism, French and Cinematography. *Membership:* CCMA; SAC; Theatre Ontario; UGA. *Current Management:* CAG Consultants; LCDM Entertainment.

LIBRA. See: **BT.**

LIBRETTI, Andrea; b. 9 Nov. 1953, Italy. Musician (Trumpet, Keyboard) Music Teacher; Composer. *Education:* G Verdi Conservatory of Milan. *Career:* Muis Therapist with L M Lorenzetti, Centro di Neurologia, Milan; Member

Board of Directors, Centro di Documentazione e Studio per la Musica Elettronica; Musical Consultant, Italian Commercial Television; Freelance Composer, Producer of Music for Films, Advertisments, Graphic Installations; Teacher of Electronic Music and Analysis and History of Contempoary Music, Conservatory G Verdi. *Compositions:* Anarhmoniosis; Seohento 3; Even Event; Frastagliate; Seghento 4; Frammento Da Ho. *Address:* Via Moncalvo 52/A, 20146 Milano, Italy.

LIDDIARD, Brenda Christine; b. 14 Feb. 1950, Essex, England. Writer; Performer; Musician (guitar, keyboards). m. Mark Clive Laurent, 4 Aug. 1990, 1 step-s., 1 d. *Education:* Piano, to Grade 6. *Career:* Played in bands, duos, solos, 1978–; Major performances: UN Environmental Song Festival, Bangkok, 1988; Concert For The Living Earth, Auckland, 1989; QE II Arts Council, 6-week New Zealand tour, 1990; Shelterbelt Festival, 1993; Parachute Festival, 1994, 1995; Garth Hewitt, UK support, 1995; Auckland Folk Festival, 1993–95, 1999; Session player, recording, concerts. *Recordings:* Land of Plenty, Spangled Drongoes, 1985; Songs For Our Friends, with Mark Laurent, 1989; Songs of Protest and Survival, 1991; For The River, Save The Daintree, featured on award winning documetary, Earth First; Heart Attack, 1996; Millennium Hippies, 1998. *Honours:* Winner, UN Asia Pacific Environmental Song Contest, 1988. *Membership:* NZ Composers' Foundation; APRA (Australian Performing Rights Society). *Current Management:* Digital Flower Productions. *Address:* 21 Parkfield Terrace, Grafton, Auckland, New Zealand.

LIEBMAN, David; b. 4 Sept. 1946, Brooklyn, New York, USA. Musician (Saxophone); Composer; Teacher. m. Caris Visentin, 30 Nov. 1986, 1 d. *Education:* BSc, New York University, USA; Studied with Joseph Allard, Lennie Tristano and Charles Lloyd. *Compositions:* 200 original compositions. *Recordings:* On the Corner, Miles Davis; Live at the Lighthouse, Elvin Jones; Lookout Farm, D Liebman; Homage To Coltrane, D Liebman; Long Distance Runner, D Liebman; West Side Story, D Liebman; New Vista, D Liebman; Water: Giver of Life; Meditation Suite; Recent releases: Time Immemorial, 2001; Liebman Plays Puccini – A Walk In The Clouds, 2001; The Unknown Jobim, 2001. *Publications:* Developing A Personal Saxophone Sound, 1989; A Chromatic Approach to Jazz, 1991; Self Portrait of a Jazz Artist, 1996; Jazz Connections, Miles Davis and David Liebman, 1996. *Honours:* Group Deserving of Wider Recognition Downbeat Magazine, 1976; Hon. Doctorate, Sibelius Academy, Helsinki, 1997; Composer Grant, National Endowment of the Arts. *Membership:* Artistic Director and Founder, International Asscn of School of Jazz; BMI; SPEDIDAM; Gramex; Naras. *Address:* 2206 Brislin Rd, Stroudsburg, PA 18360, USA.

LIEVEMAA, Tommi Tapani; b. 10 Dec. 1966, Uusikaupunki, Finland. Musician (electric, acoustic guitar, mandolin). *Education:* Commercial School, Finland, 1982–86; Jazz, rock guitar, theory studies, Jyvaskyla School of Music, 1986–89; Jazz Course, Guildhall School of Music and Drama, London 1993–94. *Career:* Constant touring, Finland, with Ohilyönti, 1986–93; With Dixie Fred, 1987–92; Tour with Finnish pop star, Katri-Helena, 1992; National Jazz Competition, Finland, with Sale's Promotion, 1986; International Jazz Competition, Spain, Getxo, with John Crawford Group, 1994; Television appearances, Finnish TV, include: Documentary about recording process, Dixie Fried's first album, Channel 1, 1988; Pop Panel, with Dixie Fried, Channel 1, 1988; Nightline, Dixie Fried, Channel 2; Kaikki on Korassa, with Estonian Television, 1990; Haapaves: Folk Festival, Channel 2, 1991; Very many radio appearances. *Recordings:* Dixie Fried albums: Dixie Fried, 1988; Six Dicks of Dynamite, 1990; New Deal, 1991; Ohilyonti: OHOH, 1989; Himmeneuva Q, 1989; Sandels On, 1989; Markan Possu, 1990; Soita Soita, 1990; On Karhut Noussect Juhlimaan, 1992; Ankkapaallikko Anna Liisa, 1993; with R Keskinin and Co: Kapteeni, 1993; Charity album, Valaiskoon (with various Finnish stars), 1993; High Register Orchestra, Jühtü, 1993. *Honours:* First Prize, National Children's Song Contest, Finland, 1990, 1991. *Membership:* Musicians' Union, London. *Address:* Ylinenkatu 44 A 8, 23500 Uusikaupunki, Finland.

LIFESON, Alex; b. 27 Aug. 1953, Fernie, Canada. Musician (guitar). *Career:* Guitarist, founder member, Canadian rock group Rush, 1969–; Concerts include: world-wide tours, 1974–; Sellout concerts include Madison Square Garden, New York; Maple Leaf Gardens, Toronto; Wembley Arena, London; Also member of side-project Victor, 1995–. *Recordings:* Albums: with Rush: Rush, 1969; Fly By Night, 1975; Caress of Steel, 1975; 2112, 1976; All The World's A Stage, 1976; A Farewell To Kings, 1977; Archives, 1978; Hemisphere, 1978; Permanent Waves, 1980; Moving Pictures, 1981; Exit… Stage Left, 1981; Grace Under Pressure, 1984; Power Windows, 1985; Hold Your Fire, 1987; A Show of Hands, 1989; Presto, 1989; Chronicles, 1990; Roll The Bones, 1991; Vapor Trails, 2002; with Victor: Victor, 1996; Counterparts, 1993; Test For Echo, 1996; Different Stages, 1998; Singles include: with Rush: Spirit of Radio; Tom Sawyer; New World Man; Closer To The Heart; Countdown; The Big Money; Time Stand Still; Producer: Lifer Lifer, 2001. *Honours:* JUNO Awards: Most Promising Group, 1975; Best Group, 1978–79; Group named Official Ambassadors of Music, Canadian Government, 1979; Gold Ticket Award, Madison Square Garden, 1991; Officer of The Order of Canada, Canadian Government. *Current Management:* Anthem Entertainment, 189 Carlton St, Toronto, ON M5A 2K7, Canada.

LIGGINS, Len, ('The Legendary' Len Liggins); b. 9 Feb. 1957, London, England. Vocalist; Songwriter; Musician (guitar, violin, bass). *Education:* BA, Russian Studies, University of Leeds. *Career:* Solo artiste, 1984–; Lead singer, guitarist for: The Sinister Cleaners, 1984–87; Lead singer, fiddle, balalaika and sopilka player, Ukrainian line-up of: The Wedding Present, 1987–89; Lead singer, fiddle player for The Ukrainians, 1991–. *Recordings:* Solo: A Remedy For Bad Nerves, 1985; The Sinister Cleaners: Lemon Meringue Bedsit, 1985; The Wedding Present: Ukrainski Vistupi V Johna Peela, 1988; The Ukrainians: Pisni Iz The Smiths, 1993; Vorony, 1994; Kultura, 1994; Music for a Changing World, 1995. *Current Management:* c/o 23 Lushington Rd, London NW10 5UX, England.

LIGHTFOOT, Gordon Meredith; b. 17 Nov. 1938, Orilla, Ontario, Canada. Vocalist; Songwriter. m. Elizabeth Moon. *Education:* Westlake College of Music, Los Angeles, 1958. *Career:* Singer, songwriter, 1959–; Member, Swinging Singing Eight (square-dance ensemble), Canada; Folk duo Two Tones, 1960; Solo artiste, 1961–; Major concerts include: Town Hall, New York, 1967; Royal Festival Hall, 1969; Bob Dylan's Rolling Thunder Review, 1976; Westbury Music Fair, Westbury, New York, 1989; Carnegie Hall, 1991; Television appearances include: Host, BBC series, 1963; Let's Sing Out, CTV, 1963; Film appearance: Harry Tracy, 1982. *Compositions include:* Early Morning Rain (recorded by Peter Paul and Mary); Ribbon of Darkness (No. 1, Country charts, for Marty Robbins); If You Could Read My Mind; Canadian Railroad Trilogy; Sundown; Carefree Highway; Race Among The Ruins; The Wreck of The Edmund Fitzgerald. *Recordings:* Albums: Lightfoot, 1965; The Way I Feel, 1967; Did She Mention My Name; Back Here On Earth; Sunday Concert; If You Could Read My Mind, 1971; Summer Side of Life; Classic Lightfoot, 1971; Don Quixote, 1972; Old Dan's Records, 1972; Sundown, 1974; The Very Best Of. . ., 1974; Cold On The Shoulder, 1975; Gord's Gold, 1976; Summertime Dream, 1976; Endless Wire, 1978; Dream Street Rose, 1980; The Best Of., 1982; Shadows, 1982; Salute, 1985; East of Midnight, 1986; The Original Lightfoot, 1992; Waiting For You, 1993; A Painter Passing Through, 1998; Song book, box set, 1999; Singer Songwriter, 2001. *Honours:* Numerous awards include: Order of Canada, 1970; Juno Hall of Fame, 1986; Juno Gold Leaf Awards; Gold and Platinum discs; Canadian Male Artist of Decade, 1980. *Current Management:* Early Morning Productions, 1365 Yonge St, Suite 207, Toronto, ON M4T 2P7, Canada.

LIKWID BISKIT. See: **IG CULTURE.**

LIL' KIM, (Kimberley Jones), (Queen Bee); b. Brooklyn, New York, USA. Rap Artiste. *Career:* First appeared on Notorious B.I.G.'s Junior M.A.F.I.A. project; Released debut album with production by Puff Daddy, 1996; Most recent material released on Atlantic Records; Collaborations: Missy Elliott; Puff Daddy; Lil' Cease; Jay-Z; Notorious B.I.G.; Too $hort; Sisqo. *Recordings:* Albums: Conspiracy (with Junior M.A.F.I.A.), 1995; Hard Core, 1996; The Notorious KIM, 2000; Singles: Gettin' Money (with Junior M.A.F.I.A.), I Need You Tonight, 1995; No Time, 1996; Crush On You, Not Tonight, 1997; No Matter What They Say, How Many Licks, 2000. *Honours:* MTV Award, Best Female Artist, 1997. *Address:* c/o Atlantic Records, 1290 Avenue of the Americas, New York, USA.

LILLYWHITE, Steve; Record Prod. *Career:* Leading international record producer, 1980–; Currently working with: Bono; Morrissey. *Recordings:* Produced: Ultravox: Ultravox; Ha Ha Ha; Siouxie and The Banshees: The Scream; XTC: Drums and Wires; Black Sea; Peter Gabriel: Peter Gabriel 3; Psychedelic Furs: Psychedelic Furs; Talk Talk Talk; Joan Armatrding: Walk Under Ladders; The Key; Sleight of Hand; Big Country: The Crossing; Steeltown; Simple Minds: Sparkle In The Rain; U2: Boy; October; War; Joshua Tree; Achtung Baby; Talking Heads; Rolling Stones: Dirty Work; Kirsty MacColl: Kite; Electric Landlady; Titanic Days; David Byrne: Rei Momo; The Pogues: If I Should Fall From Grace; Peace and Love; The La's: The La's; Red Hot + Blue (Executive Producer of 1990 AIDS Project including: U2; Annie Lennox; Sinead O'Connor; Neville Bros; Deborah Harry; Iggy Pop; Alison Moyet: Hoodoo; World Party, Bang!; Morrissey: Vauxhall and I; The Dave Matthews Band: Under The Table and Dreaming; Also: Engine; Alley; Marshall Crenshaw; The Smiths; Pretenders; Happy Mondays; David Bowie. *Current Management:* XL Talent. *Address:* Studio 7, 27A Pembridge Villas, London W11 3EP, England.

LIMERICK, Alison; b. 1959, London, England. Vocalist. *Career:* Performer, stage musical Starlight Express; Backing Vocalist, Style Council's Our Favourite Shop, 1985; Appeared on 4AD collective Filigree and Shadow (Acid, Bitter and Sad); Worked with Peter Murphy (ex Bauhaus) on Holy Smoke, 1992; Began solo career. *Recordings:* Singles: Where Love Lives (Come On In), 1991; Come Back For Real Love, 1991; Make It On My Own, 1992; Time of Our Lives, 1994; Put Your Faith In Me, 1997; Albums: Club Classics; With A Twist; Spirit Rising, 1999. *Honours:* Best Dance Record of 1991, for Where Love Lives, Billboard Magazine, USA, 1991.

LIMIC, Marin Kresimir; b. 8 Aug. 1946, Klis, Split, Croatia. Composer; Musician (piano, keyboard). m. Dubravka Zauhar, 6 Feb. 1982, 2 s. *Education:* 4 semesters, Music Academy. *Career:* Over 500 television appearances including: live concerts of group Stijene, 1982–94; Television shows, 1982–83; Live concert, TV Zagreb, 1983; Tonight With You, interview, 1995; Seventh Night, HTV, 1995; Akustkoteka, unplugged concert; Fest Split, 1996, 1998–99; Voice of Asia, 1997; Cro-Turneja, 1998; Big Concert Split, 1999; International Festival, Kiev, 1999. *Compositions:* Songs: Sve Je Neobicno Ako Te Volim; Ima Jedan Svijet; Singing That Rock 'N' Roll; Balkanska Korida; Ja Sam More Ti Si Rijeka; Zaplesimo Kao Nekada; Zbogom Prva Ljubavi; Znaj, Volim Te, 1997; Jos Te Volim Kao Nekada, 1998; Caca Moj, 1998; Dodi Nam Dodi, 1999. *Recordings:* 6 singles, 1974–84; Albums: Cementna Prasina (Silver record), 1980–81; Jedanaest I Petnaest (Gold, Silver record), 1982–83; Balkanska Korida; Stijene IV, 1994; Best of Stijene, 1995; Split, 1996, 1998–99; Stijene Promo, 1997; Voice of Asia, 1997; Obecanje, 1998. *Honours:* Gold, Silver discs; Awards from festivals: Zagreb, 1980; Split, 1981, 1982, 1990; Sarajevo, 1981, 1988; First prize, Split Fest, 1996, 1998–99; Fourth prize, Voice of Asia. *Membership:* HDS (Asscn of Croatian Composers); President, Split Asscn of Musicians; Vice-President, Split Musicians' Sydicate; Artist-Composer, Republic of Croatia (ZUH Zagreb); HGU (Croatian Music Union). *Current Management:* Vladimir Mihaljek, Zagreb; House Rec, Croatia Records, Zagreb.

LINCE, (John) Louis (James); b. 22 July 1941, St Helens, Lancashire, England. Musician (banjo, guitar); Bandleader. m. Gillian Everil Walker, 9 Dec. 1961, 2 d. *Career:* Member, Ken Colyer Allstars, 1976–82; Savoy Jazzmen, 1975–83; Louis Lince's New Orleans Band, 1986–; Founder member, Annie Hawkins' New Orleans Legacy, 1997; Occasional appearances with Jambalaya and Louisiana Joymakers, 1987–; Worked in New Orleans with Tuba Fats' Chosen Few, 1992–95; Lionel Ferbos, 1996, Reginald Koehler, 1996. *Recordings:* Just A Little While To Stay Here, Ken Colyer Allstars, 1978; You've Got the Right Key, 1979; Savoy Rag, 1981; Jubilee, 1983; Algiers Strut, 1985; Hot At The Dot, 1991; Backstairs Session, 1992; Yearning, 1993; Walking With The King, 1994; More Savoy Jazzmen, 1994; Louis Lince's Jelly Roll Kings, 1995; Good Morning to Heaven, 1996; Mardi Gras Parade, 1997. *Current Management:* Hot Jam International. *Address:* 102A E Hill, Wandsworth, London SW18 2HF, England.

LINDEN, Nick; b. 17 Nov. 1962, Woolwich, England. Musician (bass, guitar, keyboards). *Education:* Music O Level. *Career:* Bass guitar, rock band Terraplane; Signed to Epic Records, 1984–89; Reading Festival, 1982; British tour supporting Meatloaf; Foreigner; ZZ Top; Various video and television appearances. *Recordings:* with Terraplane: Black and White, 1985; Moving Target, 1987; with Waterboys: Waterboys, 1983; Pagan Place, 1984; This Is The Sea, 1985; Best of the Waterboys, 1991; Secret Life of the Waterboys, 1994. *Address:* 60 Victoria Way, Charlton, London SE7 7NQ, England.

LINDENMAIER, Heinrich Lukas; b. 5 March 1946, Basel, Switzerland. Musician (drums, percussion, electronics). *Education:* Academy of Arts, Munich, Germany, 1968–72; Private tuition at various workshops. *Career:* Eric Dolphy Memorial Band, 1984; John Tchicai Workshop Orchestra, 1987; Querstand, for Radio WDR and Radio RTSI; F-Orkestra, 1987–; Kxutrio, 1985–; Cecil Taylor Large Ensembles, 1988–92; Die Pilzfreunde, 1985–; Weg ins Freie, film music, 1993; Jazz Swissmade, TV film music. *Compositions:* Stage music for play Orestes, 1992; The Break Broken; Bright Pink, Yellow and Software; Die Feenfalle; Others for small ensembles or jazz orchestra. *Recordings:* Riffifi (Kxutrio); Legba Crossing (C. Taylor); Open (Stauss-Chaine-Lindenmaier); Die Pilzfreunde; En-Passent and Other Duets; Freiburg Loopholes (with F-Orkestra and John Tchicai). *Publications:* 25 Years of Fish Horn Recording, 1982; The Man Who Never Sleeps, 1983. *Address:* Wilhelmstr 32, 79098 Freiburg, Germany.

LINDENS, Traste; b. 6 May 1960, Gävile, Sweden. Vocalist. m. Caroline Zielfelt. *Education:* The Grafic Institut, Stockholm. *Career:* Band: Traste Lindens' Kvintette; Tours: Tågtur, 1987; Never Ending Tour, 1990–93; Festivals: Hultsfred, 1988, 1991; Roskilde, 1992; Storsjeyran, 1992; Television documentary: Traste Lindens' Kvintette. *Recordings:* Traste Lindens' Kvintette: Sportfiskarn, 1987; Bybor, 1989; Jolly Bob Gåriland, 1991; Gud Hjåpe, 1992; Utsålt, 1993; Som På Film, 1994; Also; Traste and Superstarana, 1980; Provins, 1985. *Honours:* Hälsinge Akademins Pris, 1992. *Current Management:* PO Box 171 80, 104 62 Stockholm, Sweden.

LINDES, Hal; b. 30 June 1953, Monterey, California, USA. Composer; Musician (guitar). m. Mary Elizabeth Frampton, 2 Aug. 1979, 2 s., 1 d. *Education:* University of Maryland, USA. *Career:* Replaced David Knopfler in Dire Straits, 1980; Began Making Movies World Tour playing sellouts in small clubs, ended playing sold-out stadiums; Recorded, toured with band to midway through making Brothers In Arms album, 1985; Also made guest appearances with Tina Turner on release of Private Dancer album; Actor in BBC film: Drowning In The Shallow End, 1989; Began career as film and television composer. *Compositions:* Television themes include: Between The Lines, BBC; Band of Gold, Granada; Thieftakers, Carlton; The Guilty, Central; The Trial, BBC; FIA Formula 1 Grand Prix Logo Theme, FIA; Legacy – Great Civilisations of The World, Central; Into the Land of Oz, CH4; Joyriders, Granada; Drowning In The Shallow End, BBC; Born Kicking, BBC; Commercials include: Avon; Ford; Kwik Fit; Kelloggs Special K; Johnson and Johnson. *Recordings:* with Dire Straits: Singles: Private Investigations, 1982; Twisting By The Pool, 1983; Albums: Love Over Gold (No. 1, UK), 1982;

Alchemy, 1984; Money For Nothing, 1988; Live at the BBC, 1995; Sultans of Swing, 1998; with Mark Knopfler: Local Hero; with Tina Turner: Private Dancer/Steel Claw; Simply the Best; with Kiki Dee: Angel Eyes; with Fish: Vigil In A Wilderness of Mirrors; Solo: Between The Lines; Senses; Best of TV Detectives; Best of German TV Themes; Game of Hearts-Rugby World Cup Theme. *Membership:* PRS; ASCAP; British Equity. *Current Management:* Joel Roman, William Morris Agency (USA); Seifert Dench Associates; EMI (Music) Publishing Ltd (World). *Address:* c/o Seifert Dench, 24 D'Arblay St, London W1V 3FH, England.

LINDHOLM, Dave (Ralf Henrik); b. 31 March 1952, Helsinki, Finland. Vocalist; Songwriter; Musician (guitar). m. Kirsi Koivunen, 9 Sept. 1993, 1 s., 2 d. *Career:* Member of bands: Ferris; Orfeus; Rock 'n' Roll Band; Pen Lee and Co; Bluesounds; 12 Bar; Dave Lindholm and Ganpaza Gypsys; Concerts in most of Europe and Texas, USA; Several blues festivals. *Recordings:* 34 albums, own music; Albums include: with Bluesounds: Black, 1980; On, 1981; Native Sons of Far Away Country, 1981; with Jonas Hellborg, 1988; Silverbuilt, 1998; Some studio sessions with various artistes. *Current Management:* Tiina Vuorinen, Well Done. *Address:* c/o Well Done, Sorvaajarskatu 9A, 00810 Helsinki, Finland.

LINDRIDGE, Nigel Paul James; b. 22 March 1950, Croydon, Surrey, England. Vocalist; Songwriter. m. Lynda Cauvain, 1 d., 1 step-d. *Education:* Medway College of Technology. *Career:* Lead Singer, Founder, The Menaces, 1966–68; Country Duo with John Lynott, 1970–72; Solo Act, 1972–76; Country Band, The Taverners, 1977–87; Song Writer, 1994. *Compositions:* Album, Love Is Blind; You Know Me. *Recordings:* Live Is Blind; You Know Me. *Membership:* Musicians' Union; Performing Rights Society. *Address:* 5 Folland Rd, Glanamman, Ammanford, Carms SA18 2BX, Wales.

LINDSEY, Mort; b. 21 March 1923, Newark, New Jersey, USA. Conductor; Composer; Orchestrator; Musician (piano). m. Betty J Bonney, 9 Oct. 1954, 2 s., 1 d. *Education:* BA, MA, EdD, Columbia University, New York City; Private study: Tibor Serly; Paul Creston. *Career:* Staff conductor, NBC; CBS and NBC Networks; Musical Director for: Judy Garland; Barbra Streisand; Merv Griffin; Pat Boone; Musical Director, Merv Griffin Show, 22 years. *Recordings:* 3 orchestra albums under own name; Film soundtrack albums; Conducted, composed, 8 major films. *Publications:* Seven Ages of Man (ballet); Popular songs: Lorna, with Johnny Mercer; Stolen Hours, with Marilyn and Allan Bergmann. *Honours:* Grammy Award: Judy Garland At Carnegie Hall; Emmy Award: Barbra Streisand in Central Park. *Membership:* ASCAP; AFofM; Sinfonia; Composers and Lyricists Guild.

LINDSTROM, Maria; b. 30 Aug. 1953, Stockholm, Sweden. Vocalist; Songwriter; Musician (guitar). m. Kjell Andersson, 24 Aug. 1995. *Education:* Musicology, University of Lund; Music Teacher Exam, 1976. *Career:* Actress, Musician, Fringe Theatre Group, 1977–88; Freelance, 1988–; Cabaret Artiste, TV. *Compositions:* More than 100 songs including lyrics and music for stage. *Recordings:* 1 LP, 1989; 1 CD, 1995; 1 CD, songs by Birger Sjöberg, 1998. *Publications:* Produced about 15 shows. *Honours:* Swedish SKAP Prize, 1997. *Current Management:* Agneta Neumann, Nojesprod AB, Malmo.

LINDUP, Mike; b. 17 March 1959. Musician (keyboards); Vocalist. *Career:* Founder member, Level 42, 1980–94; Appearances include: Support to the Police, 1981; Prince's Rock Gala, Wembley Arena, 1986, 1987, 1989; Crystal Palace Bowl, 1991; Midem Festival, Cannes, France, 1992; Regular British tours. *Recordings:* Albums: with Level 42: Level 42, 1981; The Pursuit of Accidents, 1982; Standing In The Light, 1983; True Colours, 1984; A Physical Presence, 1985; World Machine, 1985; Running In The Family, 1987; Staring At The Sun, 1988; Guaranteed, 1991; Forever Now, 1994; Live at Wembley, 1996; Solo album: Changes, 1990; Hit singles: The Chinese Way, 1983; The Sun Goes Down (Living It Up), 1983; Hot Water, 1984; Something About You, 1985; Leaving Me Now, 1985; Lessons In Love (No. 1 in 8 countries), 1986; Running In The Family, 1987; To Be With You Again, 1987; It's Over, 1987; Heaven In My Hands, 1988; Tracie, 1989; Guaranteed, 1991; Keyboards on: Second Nature, Dominic Miller, 2000. *Honours:* BMI Award, 1m. US performances, Something About You, 1991. *Current Management:* Paul Crockford Management, 56–60 Islington Park St, London N1 1PX, England.

LINKA, Rudy; b. 29 May 1960, Prague, Czech Republic. Musician (Jazz Guitar); Composer. m. Solveig Linka, 26 July 1985, 1 d. *Education:* People's Prague Conservatory, 2 years; Musik Institute, Stockholm; Berklee College of Music, Boston; New School, New York. *Career:* Performed with Red Mitchell, Bob Mintzer, John Abercrombie; Performed with own jazz group, at jazz clubs including Birdland, Blues Alley, Blue Note, Moods, Bimhuis. *Compositions:* Room 428; Waltz for Stephanie; To Be Named Later; The Old and New Orleans; Folk Song. *Recordings:* Rudy Linka, 1990; News from Home, 1991; Mostly Standards, 1992; Live it Up, 1993; Czech It Out, 1995; Always Double Czech, 1997. *Honours:* Jim Hall Fellowship, Berklee College of Music; Jazz Composition Grant, National Endowment for the Arts. *Membership:* BMI; GEMA. *Current Management:* Anna Eksell Management. *Address:* 55 West End Ave 8C, New York, NY 10023, USA.

LINKOLA, Jukka; b. 21 July 1955, Espoo, Finland. Composer; Musician (piano); Conductor. *Education:* Sibelius Academy, Helsinki. *Career:* Has conducted Danish Radio Big Band, Bohuslän Big Band, Oslo Groove Company, UMO Big Band, Prag Radio Big Band, Ljubljana Radio Big Band, Finnish Radio Big Band, Finnish Radio Syphony Orchestra, Helsinki Philharmony, Finnish National Opera Orchestra; Musical Director, Helsinki City Theatre, 1979–90; Currently freelance composer, Jazz, symphony, chamber and theatre music. *Compositions include:* Ronja The Robber's Daughter (ballet) for Finnish National Opera, premiered 1989; Crossings, for symphony orchestra, 1983; Two trumpet concertos, 1988, 1993; Angelika, opera, 1990; Elina, opera, 1992; String Quartet, 1996; Pegasos, for big band. *Recordings:* Albums with own octet: Protofunk; Lady In Green; Scat Suite; Ben Bay; with Eija Ahvo: Kuinka Myöhään Valvoo Blues; Crossings and Trumpet Concerto; The Tentet; EQ; Libau; Ronia the Robber's Daughter; Protofunk; Lady in Green; Sketches from Karelia. *Honours:* Yrjö Award, Finnish Jazz Federation, 1979; Finnish Broadcasting Company, Record of the Year, with singer Eija Ahvo; First Prize, LUSES competition, 1993; First Prize, Paris Opera Screen, 1993; First Prize, Midem Awards, 1994; First Prize, Concours International de Composition de la Ville du Havre, 1994; EQ; Libau, Record of the Year, 1998. *Membership:* Society of Finnish Composers. *Current Management:* Syrene Music. *Address:* c/o Syrene Music, Saarnitie 14 A, 00780 Helsinki, Finland.

LINNET, Anne Kristine; b. 30 July 1953, Århus, Denmark. Composer; Musician; Songwriter; Vocalist. m. Holger Laumann, divorced, 2 s., 1 d. *Education:* Diploma, Conservatory of Music, Jutland, 1985. *Career:* Performed in group Tears, 1970; Formed own band Shit and Chanel in 1974, recording 5 albums until 1979; Formed the Anne Linnet Band with Sanne Salomonsen and Lis Soerenson, 1981, touring Scandinavia and Germany; Formed new band Marquis de Sade in 1983; Composed and recorded the musical Berlin '84, 1984; Formed own record company, Pladecompagniet in 1988; Partnership with poet and priest Johannes Moellehave composing music to his poetry; Premiere of musical Krig og Kaerlighed (War and Love) in 1990; Worked on several major classical compositions; Participating in PaPapegoje, an album of children's songs performed by major Danish rock and pop artistes; Composer of song for 1995 Eurovision Song Contest, performed by Ulla Henningsen. *Recordings:* Anne Linnet Band, 1981; Cha Cha Cha, 1982; Marquis de Sade, 1983; Hvid Magi (White Magic), 1985; En elsker, 1986; Solo: Barndommens Gade, 1986; Jeg er jo lige her (I'm Right Here), 1988; Det' saa dansk, (It is so Typical Danish), 1991; Tal til mig (Talk To Me), 1993; with Johannes Moellehave: Miri Sang (My Song), 1989. *Honours:* Recipient of numerous Gold and Platinum records. *Address:* Linnet Songs, Bohlendachvej 45, Holmen, 1437 Copenhagen K, Denmark.

LINSTEAD, Johannes; b. 6 Aug. 1969, Oakville, Ontario, Canada. Composer; Musician (guitar); Songwriter. *Education:* Private instruction on flamenco and classical guitar. *Career:* Solo performer and band leader of instrumental Latin guitar music; Theme music for television and films; Contemporary pop music written for various solo artistes; Solo recording artiste with Real Music, Sausalito, California. *Recordings:* Sol Luna Tierra; Cleanse; Head is Angry; Alive and Wandering. *Honours:* Jazz Band Musician of the Year, 1989. *Membership:* Society of Composers, Authors and Music Publishers, Canada. *Current Management:* Earthscape Media. *Address:* 1312 Speers Rd, Oakville, ON L6L 2X4, Canada.

LIPA, Peter; b. 30 May 1943, Presov, Slovakia. Vocalist; Songwriter; Bandleader. m. Norina Bobrovská, 7 Feb. 1980, 3 s., 1 d. *Education:* Technical University, Bratislava, Slovakia; Private lessons, violin, vocal. *Career:* Bands: Strings, Blues Five, Revival Jazz Band, Blues Band; Peter Lipa Combo; Peter Lipa and Band; Andrej Seban Band; Hundreds of TV and Radio Performances, in Slovak, Czech, German, Hungarian, Polish Radio, TV. *Recordings:* Moanin'; That's the Way It Is; Naspat Na Stromy; Spirituals; Peter Lipa; (La, La, La) Boogie Up; Cierny Peter. *Honours:* Hon. Citizen of Bratislava, 1995; Martonik Annual Jazz Prize, 1995. *Membership:* President, Slovak Jazz Society; Lions Club International. *Current Management:* East-West Promotion Kuzmanyho 4, 81106, Bratislava, Slovakia. *Address:* Kuzmanyho 4, 81106 Bratislava, Slovakia.

LIPSON, Stephen James; b. 16 March 1954, London, England. Record Prod; *Recordings:* Record producer for: Propaganda, A Secret Wish, 1985; Grace Jones, Slave To The Rhythm, 1985; Frankie Goes To Hollywood, Liverpool, 1986; Pet Shop Boys, Introspective, 1988; Simple Minds, Street Fighting Years (No. 1, UK), 1989; Annie Lennox, Diva, 1992; Prefab Sprout, If You Don't Love Me, 1992; Backstreet Boys, Drowning, 2001; Also: Paul McCartney; Gary Barlow; Boyzone; Cher; Paul Brady; Ronan Keating; S Club 7. *Honours:* Producer of the Year. *Current Management:* Zomba Management. *Address:* 165–167 High Rd, London NW10 2SG, England.

LISAK, Ivan-Vanja; b. 23 Nov. 1941, Zagreb, Croatia. Composer; Musician (piano). m. Ksenija Zivkovic, 27 March 1982, 2 d. *Education:* Music Academy, Teacher of Theory. *Career:* Pop festivals including: Director of oldest festival in Zagreb, 1975–79; Jazz festivals including: Bled 1983; Sofia, 1985; Prague, 1985; Moscow; Kiev; Petrograd, 1986–90; Italy, 1992–94; Tours: Concerts for Croats In Europe, Australia, USSR, USA; Numerous television and radio appearances, 1962–95. *Recordings:* Swing Party I, 1983; II, 1985; III, with Peppino Principe, accordion, 1989; Happy Jazz I, 1991; II, 1994; Cassette: The Tree In The Yard, instrumental. *Honours:* Festival Awards, 1974, 1979, 1981, 1984. *Membership:* Society of Musical Composers; HGU (Croatan Musical Union). *Address:* 35, Marticeva St, Zagreb 41000, Croatia.

LISBERG, Harvey Brian; b. 2 March 1940, Manchester, England. Impressario; Artiste Man. m. Carole Gottlieb, 5 Nov. 1969, 2 s. *Education:* Manchester University. *Career:* First in discovering: Graham Gouldman; Andrew Lloyd Webber; Tim Rice; Herman's Hermits; Tony Christie; Sad Café; Godley and Creme; 10cc; Currently representing: 10cc; Graham Gouldman; Eric Stewart; George Stiles; Anthony Drewe; Cleopatra. *Current Management:* Harvey Lisberg Associates. *Address:* Kennedy House, 31 Stamford St, Altrincham, Cheshire WA14 1ES, England.

LITRELL, Brian Thomas, (B-Rock); b. 20 Feb. 1975, Lexington, KY, USA. Vocalist. m. Leighanne, 1 s. *Career:* Mem., Backstreet Boys, 1993–; Numerous tours and television appearances. *Recordings:* Albums: Backstreet Boys, 1996; Live in Concert, 1998; Backstreet's Back, 1998; Millennium, 1999; Black And Blue, 2000; Greatest Hits Chapter 1, 2001. Singles: We've Got It Goin' On, 1995; Quit Playing Games, 1998; I'll Never Break Your Heart, 1998; Everybody, 1998; As Long As You Love Me, 1998; Anywhere for You, 1998; All I Have to Give, 1998; I Want It That Way (No. 1, UK), 1999; Larger Than Life, 1999; Show Me The Meaning of Being Lonely, 2000; The One, 2000; Shape of My Heart, 2000; Drowning, 2001; The Call, 2001. *Honours:* MTV European Music Award, Best Pop Act, 1997, Best Group, 1999; Billboard Music Awards, Best Group, Best Adult Contemporary Group, 1998, Album of the Year, Artist of the Year, 1999; MTV Music Video Awards, Best Group Video, 1998, Viewer's Choice, for I Want It That Way, 1999; World Music Awards, Best-Selling Pop Group, 1999, 2000, Best-Selling R&B Group, 1999, 2000, Best-Selling Dance Group, 1999, 2000, Best American Group, 2000; American Music Awards, Favorite Pop/Rock Band, Duo or Group, 2000, 2001. *Website:* www.backstreetboys.com.

LITTLE RICHARD, (Richard Wayne Penniman); b. 5 Dec. 1932, Macon, GA, USA. Vocalist; Musician (piano); Songwriter. *Education:* Theological college, 1957. *Career:* R&B singer, various bands; Tours and film work with own band, The Upsetters; Gospel singer, 1960–62; World-wide tours and concerts include: Star Club, Hamburg, Germany, with Beatles, 1962; European tour, with Beatles, Rolling Stones, 1963; British tour with Everly Brothers, 1963; Rock 'n' Revival Concert, Toronto, with Chuck Berry, Fats Domino, Jerry Lee Lewis, Gene Vincent, Bo Diddley, 1969; Toronto Pop Festival, 1970; Randall Island Rock Festival, with Jimi Hendrix, Jethro Tull, 1970; Rock 'N' Roll Spectaculars, Madison Square Garden, 1972–; Muhammad Ali's 50th Birthday; Benefit For Lupus Foundation, Universal City, 1992; Westbury Music Fair, 1992; Giants of Rock 'n' Roll, Wembley Arena, 1992; US tour, 2002, before retirement; Film appearances: Don't Knock The Rock, 1956; Mr Rock 'N' Roll, 1957; The Girl Can't Help It, 1957; Keep On Rockin', 1970; Down and Out In Beverly Hills, 1986; Mother Goose Rock 'n' Rhyme, Disney Channel, 1989. *Recordings:* Albums: Cast A Long Shadow, 1956; Little Richard, Vol. 1, 1957; Little Richard, Vol. 2, 1957; Little Richard, Vol. 3, 1957; Here's Little Richard, 1957; The Fabulous Little Richard, 1959; Clap Your Hands, 1960; Pray Along With Little Richard, Vol. 1, 1960; Pray Along With Little Richard, Vol. 2, 1960; King Of The Gospel Singers, 1962; Sings Spirituals, 1963; Sings the Gospel, 1964; Little Richard Is Back, 1965; The Wild and Frantic Little Richard, 1965; The Explosive Little Richard, 1967; Rock 'N' Roll Forever, 1967; Good Golly Miss Molly, 1969; Little Richard, 1969; Right Now, 1970; Rock Hard Rock Heavy, 1970; Little Richard, 1970; Well Alright!, 1970; Mr Big, 1971; The Rill Thing, 1971; The Second Coming, 1971; Dollars, 1972; The Original, 1972; You Can't Keep A Good Man Down, 1972; Rip It Up, 1973; Talkin' 'Bout Soul, 1974; Recorded Live, 1974; Keep A Knockin', 1975; Sings, 1976; Little Richard Live, 1976; Now, 1977; Lucille, 1988; Shake It All About, 1992; Shag On Down By The Union Hall, 1996. Hit singles include: Tutti Frutti, 1956; Long Tall Sally, 1956; The Girl Can't Help It, 1957; Lucille, 1957; She's Got It, 1957; Jenny Jenny, 1957; Keep A Knockin', 1957; Good Golly Miss Molly, 1958, Baby Face, 1959; Bama Lama Bama Loo, 1964. *Honours:* Inducted, Rock and Roll Hall of Fame, 1986; Star, Hollywood Walk of Fame, 1990; Little Richard Day, Los Angeles, 1990; Penniman Boulevard, Macon, named in his honour; Platinum Star, Lupus Foundation of America, 1992; Grammy Lifetime Achievement Award, 1993. *Address:* c/o Richard de la Font Agency Inc, 4845 S Sheridan Rd, Suite 505, Tulsa, OK 74145-5719, USA.

LITTON, Martin; b. 14 May 1957, Grays, Essex, England. m. Rebekah Morley-Jones, 15 Aug. 1992. *Education:* BA Hons, Music, Colchester Institute, England, 1978. *Career:* Pieces of Eight, with Harry Gold, 1980–82; Kenny Ball and His Jazzmen, 1982–84; Tours of Middle East and Russia; Freelance work with many American Musicians, including Bob Wilber, George Masso, Peanuts Hucko, Joe Muranyi, Al Casey, Scott Hamilton; Recorded with Kenny Davern, Wild Bill Davison, Yank Lawson, Marty Grosz; Work with leading British Musicians includes recordings with Humphrey Lyttleton, Wally Fawkes and Digby Fairweather; Tours include Fabulous Fats, with Keith Smith; Australia, New Zealand and Japan, with the Swedish Jazz Kings; Frequent performer at London's South Bank Arts Centre; Mem., Pizza

Express Allstars, 2002–. *Compositions:* Forever Afternoon; Striding Down 52nd Street; Litton on the Keys; Eight Bars – Eight to the Bar; For Rebekah. *Recordings include:* Martin Litton Jazz Piano; Ring Dem Bells; Falling Castle. *Membership:* PRS. *Address:* 7 Bridge St, Hay-on-Wye, Herefordshire, HR3 5DE, England.

LITWIN, Ralph Henry; b. 11 April 1950, Morristown, New Jersey, USA. Vocalist; Musician (5-string banjo, guitar, harmonica). m. Stephanie Kraft, 29 Oct. 1981, 1 s., 1 d. *Education:* BFA, Rhode Island School of Design; Juris Dr, Rutgers Law School, Newark, New Jersey. *Career:* Host and Producer, Horses Sing None of It!, award-winning series, Manhattan, New York, Philadelphia, and cable stations in New Jersey; Music used in soundtrack for The Black West; Numerous TV and radio guest appearances including: The Today Show, The Howard Stern Show, The Uncle Floyd Show, KTV Show, Anything Goes, Jersey Beat, The Joe Franklin Show. *Compositions:* The Band with a Thousand Names; Love is Like Washing a Potato; I'd Rather Say Goodbye to You than Give Up an Indoor Toilet. *Recordings include:* Makes My Heart Feel Happy, 1990; Wild and Lazy, 1993; Ralph Litwin and the Band with a Thousand Names, 1998. *Honours:* First Place, New Jersey Old Style Banjo Championship, twice; Cash Box Magazine Indie Album Choice; Hon. Mention, Billboard Magazine Song Contest, three times; Winner, Hometown Video Festival, three times; National Old Time Banjo Championship Finalist, 1996; First Place, Freewheelin' Style, 2nd Place, Harmonica, Uncle Dave Macon Days, Tennessee, 1996. *Membership:* North American Folk Alliance; Folk Project. *Address:* 140 Morris St, Morristown, NJ 07960, USA.

LIU HUAN; b. Aug. 1963, Tianjin, People's Republic of China. Vocalist. *Education:* Beijing International Relations Institute. *Career:* Numerous albums; Songs include theme from The Water Margin (TV). *Address:* Dept of French, Beijing International Relations Institute, Beijing, People's Republic of China.

LIVESEY, Warne; b. 12 Feb. 1959, London, England. Record Prod. m. Barbara, 18 May 1983. *Recordings:* Producer, albums: Diesel and Dust, Midnight Oil; Blue Sky Mining, Midnight Oil; Infected, The The; Mind Bomb, The The; When The World Knows Your Name, Deacon Blue; Perverse, Jesus Jones; Suddenly Tammy!; Prick; St Julian, Julian Cope; Babe Rainbow, House of Love; Underdogs, Matthew Good Band; Work, Lovelife, Miscellaneous, by David Devant and his Spirit Wife. *Membership:* Musicians' Union. *Current Management:* John Reid, JPR Management Ltd. *Address:* The Power House, 70 Chiswick High Rd, London W4 1SY, England.

LL COOL J, (James Todd Smith); b. 14 Jan. 1968, St Albans, Queens, New York, USA. Rap Artiste. *Career:* Began rapping aged 9; Concerts include: Support to Run DMC, Raising Hell tour, 1986; Headliner, Def Jam '87 tour, 1987; Performed at Farm Aid IV, 1990; Budweiser Superfest, 1991; European tour, 1993; Film appearances: Krush Groove, 1985; The Hard Way, 1991; Toys, 1992; Founder, Uncle Records, 1992. *Recordings:* Singles include: I Can't Live Without My Radio, 1985; I Need Love, 1987; Goin' Back To Cali, 1988; I'm That Type of Guy, 1989; Around The Way Girl, 1991; How I'm Comin', 1993; Pink Cookies In A Plastic Bag, 1993; Stand By Your Man, 1993; Hey Lover, 1995; Loungin', 1996; Dooin' It, 1996; Ain't Nobody (No. 1, UK), 1996; Phenomenon, 1997; 4321, 1997; Candy, 1998; Father, 1998; Ripper Strikes Back, 1999; Hot Hot Hot, 1999; Say What, 1999; Albums: Radio, 1985; Bigger and Deffer, 1987; Walking With A Panther, 1989; Mama Said Knock You Out, 1990; 14 Shots To The Dome, 1993; Mr Smith, 1996; Phenomenon, 1997; The G.O.A.T. (Greatest of All Time), 2000; 10, 2002; Contributor, King of Rock, Run DMC, 1985; Simply Mad About The Mouse, 1991. *Publications:* I Make My Own Rules, autobiography, 1997. *Honours:* Platinum discs; Soul Train Music Awards: Best Rap Album, Best Rap Single, 1988; MTV Music Video Award, Best Rap Video, 1991; Billboard Top Rap Singles Artist, 1991; Grammy Awards, Best Rap Solo Performance, Mama Said Knock You Out, 1992, Hey Lover, 1996; MTV Video Vanguard Award, 1997. *Current Management:* Rush Artist Management, 160 Varick St, New York, NY 10013, USA. *Address:* LL Cool J. Inc, 186–39 Illian Ave, Jamaica, NY 11412, USA.

LLABADOR, Jean-Pierre; b. 15 Dec. 1952, Nemours, Algeria. Jazz Musician (guitar); Composer. m. Annie Soulet-Pujol, 28 June 1976, 2 d. *Education:* BA, English; Degree Philosophy; Conservatoire, France; Los Angeles GIT graduate (2 special awards). *Career:* Member, various jazz, fusion and rock bands including Coincidence (tours, radio and television shows, recordings), 1975–85; Lead guitarist, composer, with own bands, 1985–; Many tours, Europe and Africa; International festival appearances include: Nîmes, Montpellier-Radio-France, Nancy Jazz Pulsation, Midem, Barcelona, Laseyne sur Mer, Cardiff, Bath; Numerous radio and television appearances: Radio-France, TF1, FR2, FR3, M6; Artistic Director, OJLR (Region Languedoc Jazz Orchestra). *Recordings:* Albums (mostly own compostions): French Guitar Connection, quartet (USA); 5th Edition, quintet (Germany); Friendship, duo/trio (Germany); Dialogues, OJLR (France); Birds Can Fly, quintet/sextet (France); El Bobo, from duo to orchestra (France). *Membership:* Composer, improviser, SACEM; SPEDIDAM. *Current Management:* TRIAD Diffusion. *Address:* 700 Chemin des Mendrous, 34170 Castelnau-Le-Lez, France. *E-mail:* j-p.llabador@caramail.com.

LLACH, Lluís; b. 7 May 1948, Girona, Catalonia, Catalan. Vocalist; Songwriter; Musician (piano, guitar). *Career:* Singer, songwriter since late 1960s; Pioneer, Nova Cançó (Catalan protest-song movement against General Franco); Member, El Setze Jutges, 1967; Major concerts include: Olympia, Paris, 1973, 1988; Stade de Barcelona, 1985; Edinburgh Arts Festival, 1993. *Compositions:* Arranger, songwriter on albums by: Teresa Rebull; Francesc Pi de la Serra; Dolors Lafitte; Marina Rossell; Josep Tero; Maria del Mar Bonet; Joan Americ; Carles Cases. *Recordings:* Over 25 solo albums, 1967–; Albums include: Viatge a Itaca, 1975; Campanades a Morts, 1977; El Meu Amic el Mar, 1978; Maremar, 1986; Astres, 1987; Geografia, 1988; Un Pont de Mar Blava, 1993; Porrera, 1995; Music for three films: Borrasca, 1977; La Forja de un Rebelde, 1990; El Ladrón de Niños, 1992; Numerous solo singles/EPs, including best known anthem, L'Estaca, 1974. *Publications:* Poemes i Cançons, 1979; Lluís Llach, 1979; Lluís Llach – Catalogne Vivre, 1979; Un Trobador per a un Poble, 1982; Història de les Seves Cançons Explicada a Josep Maria Espinàs, 1986; La Dáraison d'Etat, 1987; La Geografia del Cor, 1992; Lluís Llach, 1993. *Membership:* Societat General d'Autors i Editors (SGAE); Associació de Cantants i Intérprets en Llengua Catalana (ACIC). *Current Management:* Andréas Claus. *Address:* Sepúlveda, 147–149 Principal 1a, 08011 Barcelona, Catalonia, Spain.

LLOYD, Andrew Reginald, (Popman); b. 2 June 1960, Halesowen, Birmingham, England. Vocalist; Songwriter; Musician (guitar). Entertainer; Actor; Record Prod. *Career:* Bands: Mickey Mouse Revival, 1972–76; Andy Lloyd and the Wedge, 1978–79; The Bloomsbury Set, 1980–83; Popman and the Raging Bull, 1986–88; Popman and the Disciple, 1989–93; Radio sessions, Peter Powell, Radio 1, 1981–86; Tours: Judie Tzuke, 1981; Duran Duran, 1982; Various support tours, 1986–92; Headline tour, 1993; Solo acoustic US tour, 1994; Television appearances: Get It Together; Pop 77; Oxford Road Show; Track 1; Razzmatazz; TV appearances: lead guitarist for Dolly Parton on The National Lottery, 1998; Des O'Connor Show, 1998. *Recordings:* Back To School, 1978; It's Up To You, 1978; Living In America, 1979; Letters To Eva, 1979; This Year Next Year, 1981; The Other Side of You, 1981; Sweet Europeans, 1982; Hanging Around With The Big Boys, Getting Away From It All, Dress Parade, Serenade, 1983; Just Like A Woman, Casual Acquaintance, 1986; Fields In Motion, Hustling Man, 1987; New Feelings, Friends and Lovers, 1988; Pirate, 1989; Girl of My Best Friend, 1990; Little White Lies, The Same Girl, 1991; Weekend, 1992; Acoustic set, 1994; Plugs Out, 1995; Food, 1996. *Membership:* MU; Equity; Songwriters Guild; PRS; MLPS. *Current Management:* Nick Titchener, Don't Panic Promotions. *Address:* 74 The Archway, Ranelagh Gardens, London SW6 3UH, England.

LLOYD, Gary; b. 29 Jan. 1965, Ottawa, Canada. Composer. *Education:* BA, Mathematics, University of Liverpool Chester College, England, 1986. *Career:* Ran recording studio, 1987–89; Composition and Soundtrack composer since 1989; Scored music for more than 400 productions including works for TV, film, theatre, contemporary dance, son et lumiere, art installations; First commission Neil Gaiman's Violent Cases, stageplay soundtrack, 1988. *Compositions include:* A Return To Love, for TV drama, 1994; Ignition, music for Fireworks, 1994; Land of Many Waters, for A/V show and CD release, 1995; Precis for String Orchestra, performed Cholmondeley Castle, Cheshire, England, 1996; The Ghost Tour, filmscore, 1997; Curiously England, documentary, 1997; Alien Blood, filmscore, 1998. *Recordings:* Albums: The Bridge, with Iain Banks, 1996; Brought to Light, with Alan Moore, 1998. *Current Management:* Music for Films, 34 Batchelor St, Islington, London N1 0EG, England. *Address:* c/o Gallery Productions, PO Box 1363, Chester, CH2 3WN, England.

LLOYD, Richard; b. 17 Jan. 1961, Miami Beach, Florida, USA. m. Linda Westauss, 8 June 1996. *Education:* Music School, Miami Community College; Music Major, studied with the late Cag Thaler and Charles Perry. *Career:* 20 years performing as Drummer and as a Producer; Performed across country with groups such as Stevie Rae Vaughan, The Thunderbirds; ZZ Top. *Compositions:* The Answer, 1985; The Alternatives, 1985; Lady Sabre, 1987; The Sharks, 1989; The Ones, 1981; The Leap, 1983. *Recordings:* As above, plus: The Cover Doesn't Matter, 2001. *Honours:* Battle of the Bands, Houston, Texas, 1981. *Membership:* Department of Professional Regulation. *Address:* 1515 University Dr. 108A, Coral Springs, FL 33071, USA.

LLOYD WEBBER, Andrew, (Baron Lloyd Webber of Sydmonton); b. 22 March 1948, London, England. Composer; Prod. m. Sarah Jane Hugill, 1971, divorced 1983, 1 s., 1 d., (2) Sarah Brightman, 1984, divorced 1990, (3) Madeleine Astrid Gurdon, 1991, 2 s., 1 d. *Education:* Magdalen College, Oxford; Royal College of Music. *Career:* Composer and prod., musicals; Composer, film scores; Deviser, board games, And They're Off, Calamity!; Founder, The Really Useful Group Ltd, 1977–, involved in theatre, film, television, concerts, publishing, recording and merchandising. *Compositions:* Musicals: Joseph and the Amazing Technicolour Dreamcoat (lyrics by Tim Rice), 1968; Jesus Christ Superstar (lyrics by Tim Rice), 1970; Jeeves (lyrics by Alan Ayckbourn), 1975; Evita (lyrics by Tim Rice), 1976; Tell Me On A Sunday (lyrics by Don Black), 1980; Cats (based on poems by T. S. Eliot), 1981; Song and Dance, 1982; Starlight Express (lyrics by Richard Stilgoe), 1984; The Phantom of the Opera (lyrics by Richard Stilgoe and Charles Hart), 1986; Aspects of Love (lyrics by Don Black and Charles Hart), 1989; Sunset

Boulevard (lyrics by Don Black and Christopher Hampton), 1993; By Jeeves (lyrics by Alan Ayckbourn), 1996; Whistle Down the Wind (lyrics by Jim Steinman), 1996; The Beautiful Game (lyrics by Ben Elton), 2000; Bombay Dreams (music by A. R. Rahman, lyrics by Don Black), 2002; Film scores: Gumshoe, 1971; The Odessa File, 1974; Jesus Christ Superstar, 1974; Others: Requiem, 1985; Variations on a Theme of Paganini for orchestra, 1986; Amigos Para Siempre (official theme for 1992 Olympic Games), 1992; When Children Rule The World (official theme for the 1998 Winter Olympics opening ceremony). *Recordings:* Album: Gold: The Definitive Hit Singles Collection, 2002; Hit songs include: Don't Cry For Me Argentina, Julie Covington (No. 1, UK), 1976; Take That Look Off Your Face, Marti Webb, 1980; Memory, Elaine Paige, 1981; The Phantom of The Opera, Sarah Brightman and Steve Harley, 1986; All I Ask of You, Cliff Richard and Sarah Brightman, 1986; The Music of The Night, Michael Crawford, 1987; Love Changes Everything, Michael Ball, 1989; Any Dream Will Do, Jason Donovan (No. 1, UK), 1991; Amigos Para Siempre, Sarah Brightman and Jose Carreras, 1992; No Matter What, Boyzone (No. 1, UK), 1998. *Publications:* Evita (with Tim Rice), 1978; Cats: The Book of the Musical, 1981; Joseph and the Amazing Technicolour Dreamcoat (with Tim Rice), 1982; The Complete Phantom of the Opera, 1987; The Complete Aspects of Love, 1989; Sunset Boulevard: From Movie to Musical, 1993; Restaurant critic, Daily Telegraph, 1996–99. *Honours:* Five Laurence Olivier Awards; Seven Tony Awards; Four Drama Desk Awards; Three Grammy Awards; FRCM, 1988; ASCAP Triple Play Awards, 1988, 1996; K.B.E., 1992; Praemium Imperiale Award, 1995; Richard Rogers Award, 1996; Golden Globe Award; Academy Award, Best Song (with Tim Rice), 1997; Life Peer, 1997; London Critics' Circle Best Musical, 2000. *Address:* c/o The Really Useful Group Ltd, 22 Tower St, London WC2H 9NS, England. *Website:* www.reallyuseful.com.

LO, Cheikh N'Digel; b. 1955, Bobo Dioulasso, Burkina Faso. Vocalist; Musician (guitar); Songwriter. *Career:* Member: Orchestra Volta Jazz, 1976; Moved to Dakar, 1980; Worked as a drummer for five years; Emigrated to Paris, 1985; Continued to work as a session drummer; Met Youssou N'Dour, 1989; N'Dour produced Ne La Thiass album, 1995; Appeared in the USA with Africa Fete, 1998; Played at WOMAD Reading, 2001; Member and follower of the Baye Fall. *Recordings:* Albums: Ne La Thiass, 1996; Bambay Gueej (featuring Juan de Marcos Gonzalez, Oumou Sangare and Bigga Morrison), 1999. *Honours:* Kora Award, Best Newcomer, 1997; Ordre National de Merite de Leon, presented by the president of Senegal, 2001. *Address:* c/o World Circuit, 138 Kingsland Rd, London E2 8DY, England. *Website:* www.worldcircuit.co.uk.

LÔ, Ismaël; b. Aug. 1956, Senegal. Vocalist; Composer; Musician. m. *Education:* Institut des arts de Dakar. *Career:* Singer and composer of African folk songs in Wolof and French. *Recordings:* 21 albums including: Iso, 1995; Jammu Africa, 1996; Dabah, 2001. *Address:* Syllart Productions, c/o Next Music, 52 rue Paul Lescop, 92000 Nanterre, France.

LOBO, Edu, (Eduardo De Goes Lobos); b. 1943, Rio De Janeiro, Brazil. Vocalist; Musician (guitar); Composer; Songwriter. *Career:* Has written songs that combine Brazilian folk music with bossa nova harmonies; Despite being born in Rio, lyrics often object to the injustice and misery of Brazil's Northeast region; Met Carlos Lyra, mid 1960s; Greatly influenced by Lyra's new bossa style, elements of northeastern music and socially conscious lyrics; First album released, 1964; Protest songs not popular with Brazilian military dictatorship in power during late 1960s, so left for the USA, 1969; Supplied four songs and played guitar on saxophonist Paul Desmond's album From The Hot Afternoon; Since return to Brazil in 1971, has mainly written music for plays, films and ballets. *Recordings:* Albums: Musica De Edu Lobo Por Edu Lobo, 1964; Reencontro, Folklore E Bossa Nova Do Brasil, 1966; Edu, 1968; Sergio Mendes Presents Lobo, 1969; Cantiga De Longe, 1971; Nissa Breve, 1973; Limite Das Aguas, 1975; Camaleão, 1978; Tom E Edu, Jogos De Danca, 1981; O Grande Circo Mistico, 1983; Edu E Bethania, 1984; Corrupião, 1993; Meia Noite, 1995; features on: From The Hot Afternoon, Paul Desmond, 1969. *Honours:* First place TV in record festival, Borandá, 1967; Gramado Film Festival, Best Soundtrack, Barra Pesada, 1979.

LOCK, Eddie; b. 10 Feb. 1969, Bury St Edmunds, England. Musician; DJ; Prod. m. Maxine, 20 July 1996. *Career:* DJ, 1987; Member, Carpe Diem and SMC Project. *Compositions:* Calling My Name; Got To Get Up, 1998; La Noche Vista, 1999. *Recordings:* The Buzz; Don't Wanna Be Free; Hypnotic; Music Takes You; Snakecharmer; Space is the Place; Turkish Delight; The Phuture, 2000; Come Close to Me, 2000; Dance to the Music, 2001; Spaced, 2001; Bang to the Beat of the Drum, 2002; Psychology of the Dreamer, 2002. *Membership:* MCPS; BPI; PRS; Music Publishers Asscn. *Current Management:* Worldmaster DJ Management Ltd. *Address:* The Coach House, Mansion Farm, Liverton Hill, Sandway, Maidstone, Kent ME17 2NJ, England.

LOCKETT, Peter Robert; b. 8 April 1963, Portsmouth, Hampshire, England. Musician (percussion). *Education:* Madras Academy, 1991–93. *Career:* Live TV work, recording, touring with Kula Shaker; Live TV work and recording with Vanessa Mae; Duo concerts at Royal Festival Hall with Joji Hirota; Series on drum programming, The Mix, magazine; World percussion sample CDs for The Mix, magazine; Films: City of Angels; Plunkett and Maclean; The World Is Not Enough; The Bone Collector. *Recordings:* with Bjork; Bill Bruford; David Arnold; A R Rahman; 2 albums with top Danish guitarist, Henrik Anderson; with Natacha Atlas, Transglobal Underground; Tomorrow Never Dies, Bond film; with Mel C; Pet Shop Boys; Nitin Sawhney; Junior Delgado; Arts Council CMN tour for Pete Lockett's Network of Sparks, featuring Bill Bruford, 2000; Taiko and Tabla, Joji Hirota/ Pete Lockett. *Publications:* Drum technique articles for Modern Drummer and Rhythm Magazine. *Address:* Flat F, 26 Upper Park Rd, Belsize Park, London NW3 2UT, England.

LOCKHEART, Mark; b. 31 March 1961, Hampshire, England. Musician (saxophones, clarinet, flute); Composer. m. Andrea Margo Tosic, 30 July 1985. *Education:* Trinity College of Music. *Career:* Saxophone, Loose Tubes, Lysis Steve Berry Trio, 1985–91; Leader, own Perfect Houseplant Group; Co-leader, Matheran; Currently member, Django Bates' Delightful Precipice; Also bands with June Tabor, Billy Jenkins; Session work with Jah Wobble; Prefab Sprout; The High Llamas; Stereolab; Radiohead (Kid A, No. 1, UK and USA, 2000). *Recordings:* with Perfect Houseplants: Perfect Houseplants, 1993; Clec, 1995; with Matheran: Mark Lockheart-John Paracelli, 1994; with Django Bates: Summer Fruits and Unrest, 1994; with June Tabor: Some Other Time, 1989; Angel Tiger, 1992; Against The Streams, 1994; Aleyn, 1997. *Honours:* Scottish Arts Commission: Semana Santa, Multicommission, 1991. *Current Management:* Eccentric Management, 29A Connaught St, London W2 2AY, England.

LOCKWOOD, Didier André Paul; b. 11 Feb. 1956, Calais, France. Musician (violin); Jazz Composer. m. Casadesus, 15 Oct. 1993, 3 d. *Education:* College; Conservatoire de Calais (violin, trumpet, piano); École Normale Supérieure de Musique, Paris. *Career:* First Prize, at Conservatory, age 16; Professional musician with French group, Magma, 1973; Worked with Stéphane Grappelli, 1978; Formed own groups, 1980–; Appearances include: Royal Albert Hall, London, 1979; Carnegie Hall, New York, 1981; 1983; Major jazz festivals; Concerts world-wide incl. Théatre des Champs Elysées, 1993; Peking, 1993. *Compositions:* Jazz and contemporary music; Violin concerto: Les Mouettes, (with symphony orchestra). *Recordings:* Recordings: Over 20 include: New World, with Antony Williams (drums), 1981; Live In Montreux, 1982; The Kid; Out of The Blue, 1986; New York Rendevouz, 1994; Storyboard, 1996; Children's Songs, 1997; Tribute To Stephane Grappelli, 2000; Om Kara, 2001. *Publications:* Violin Jazz Method book; 1 song book. *Honours:* Blue Note Award, Newy; 2 Victoires de la Musique; Grand Prix, SACEM; Prix Charles Cross; Chevalier des Arts et des Lettres; Grand Officier, Légion d'honneur, 2002. *Current Management:* Isoard-Sola.

LOCKWOOD, Robert, Jr; b. 27 March 1915, Turkeyscretch, Arkansas, USA. Musician (guitar). m. Annie Roberts, 13 Sept. 1970, 5 s., 2 d. *Career:* Belgian National Radio; Blues Festival, Peer, July 1994; Helen, Arkansas Blues Festival, Oct. 1994; KFFA Radio; WCPN Radio; Lady Luck Casino; Rhythm and Blues, Lula, Mississippi. *Recordings:* Little Boy Blue; Take A Little Walk With Me, 1948; Something To Do, 1990; What's The Score?, 1990; Hanged On; Come Day Go Day, 1993; Majors Minors and Ninths, 1993; I Got To Find Me A Woman, 1999; Complete Trix Recordings, 1999; Just the Blues, 1999; Delta Crossroads, 2000. *Publications:* Vol. I Blues; Who, Who, Living, Blues. *Honours:* W C Handy, 1988; Achievement for Black History, 1994; Blues Hall of Fame, 1998. *Current Management:* Annie Lockwood; Agent: Concentrated Efforts Inc. *Address:* 7203 Lawnview Ave, Cleveland, OH 44103, USA.

LODDER, Steve (Stephen John); b. 1951. Musician (keyboards); Composer. *Education:* Cambridge (Gonville and Caius), Organ scholarship, 1969. *Career:* Before musical freelance career worked as music teacher in a comprehensive school and ran a coffee/wholefood store; Played with many artistes on the London jazz scene including: Paul Nieman; Carol Grimes; Maggie Nichols; Jan Ponsford; John Etheridge; Henry Thomas; Harry Beckett, late 1970s–80s; Toured and recorded with George Russell's Living Time Orchestra, late 1980s; Also played keyboards on three Carol Grimes albums (writer/arranger on Why Don't They Dance?); Member: Brian Abrahams' District Six; Tours in Germany and UK; Musical director for Sarah Jane Morris during a six week tour supporting Simply Red, 1989; Also commenced long musical collaboration, touring and recording, with Andy Sheppard; Worked with John Harle on Duke Ellington tribute, Shadow of the Duke, 1992; Toured with John Harle (performing his Terror and Magnificence and Elvis Costello singing his Twelfth Night Settings), 1995; Worked with Paul McCartney and helped orchestrate his Standing Stones; Collaborations: Mark Ramsden; Monica Vasconcelos; Carla Bley. *Recordings:* Albums: features on: Eyes Wide Open, Carol Grimes, 1987; Why Don't They Dance?, Carol Grimes, 1989; Imgoma Yabantwana, Brian Abraham's District Six, 1989; Introductions In The Dark, Andy Sheppard, 1989; Soft On The Inside, Andy Sheppard, 1989; The London Concert, George Russell's Living Time Orchestra, 1990; In Co-Motion, Andy Sheppard, 1991; Shadow of The Duke, John Harle, 1992; Rhythm Method, Andy Sheppard, 1993; Inclassificable, Andy Sheppard, 1994; Delivery Suite, Andy Sheppard, 1994; Terror and Magnificence, John Harle, 1996; Above The Clouds, Mark Ramsden/Steve Lodder, 1996; Moving Image, Andy Sheppard, 1996; It's About Time, George

Russell's Living Time Orchestra, 1996; Nois, Monica Vasconcelos, 1997; Standing Stones, Paul McCartney, 1997; Learning To Wave, Andy Sheppard, 1998; Nois Dos, Monica Vasconcelos, 1999; Dancing Man and Woman, Andy Sheppard, 2000; The Gathering, Annie Whitehead, 2000; TV soundtracks: Ali Bongo – The Wacky Wizard; TV/radio soundtracks with Andy Sheppard: The Art Wrap; The Postman Always Rings Twice; Arena: Peter Sellers; Joseph Emidy; Syrup (short film). *E-mail:* steve@stevelodder.com. *Website:* www.stevelodder.com.

LODGE, John Charles; b. 20 July 1945, Birmingham, England. Musician (bass guitar); Vocalist. m. Kirsten, 30 Sept. 1968, 1 s., 1 d. *Education:* Birmingham College of Advanced Technology. *Career:* Member, El Riot and The Rebels; The Carpetbaggers; John Bullbreed; Member, Moody Blues, 1966–; Also solo artiste; Numerous tours, concerts include: Royal Albert Hall; Hollywood Bowl; Isle of Wight Festival, 1970; Wembley Arena, 1993. *Recordings:* Albums: In Search of The Lost Chord, 1968; On The Threshold of a Dream, 1969; To Our Children's Children, 1969; A Question of Balance, 1970; Every Good Boy Deserves Favour, 1971; Days of Future Passed, 1972; Seventh Sojurn, 1972; This Is The Moody Blues, 1974; Blue Jays, 1975; Octave, 1978; Long Distance Voyager, 1981; Voices In The Sky/The Best of The Moody Blues, 1985; The Other Side of Life, 1986; Sur La Mer, 1988; Greatest Hits, 1988; Keys of The Kingdom, 1991; Live At Red Rocks, 1993; Time Traveller, 1994; Anthology, 1998; Live At The Royal Albert Hall, 2000; Solo: Natural Avenue, 1977 (re-released 1996); Singles include: Nights In White Satin, 1968; Voices in The Sky, 1968; Tuesday Afternoon, 1968; Ride My See Saw, 1968; Question (No. 2, UK), 1970; Isn't Life Strange, 1972; I'm Just A Singer (In A Rock 'n' Roll Band), 1973; Blue Guitar, duet with Justin Hayward, 1975; Gemini Dream, 1981; The Voice, 1981; Your Wildest Dreams, 1986. *Honours:* ASCAP Awards, Singer In A Rock 'n' Roll Band; Gemini Dream; 2 Ivor Novello Awards; Outstanding Contribution To British Music, Ivor Novello Awards, 1985. *Membership:* PRS; BAC&S; Songwriters Guild of America. *Current Management:* ICM (New York and Los Angeles). *Address:* c/o Threshold Records Ltd, 53 High St, Cobham, Surrey KT11 3DP, England.

LOEB, Lisa; b. USA. Vocalist; Musician (guitar); Songwriter. *Career:* Solo artiste, billed as Lisa Loeb and Nine Stories, 1994–. *Recordings:* Albums: Tails, 1995; Firecracker, 1998; Singles: Stay (I Missed You), from film soundtrack Reality Bites, 1994; Do You Sleep?, 1995; Waiting for Wednesday, 1996; Taffy, 1996; I Do, 1997; Let's Forget About It, 1998. *Honours:* BRIT Award, Best International Newcomer, 1995. *Current Management:* Manage This!. *Address:* c/o Manage This!, 154 w 57th St # 133, New York, NY 10019, USA.

LOEFFLER, Tony; b. 5 April 1947, Paterson, New Jersey, USA. Musician (guitar); Songwriter. m. 27 April 1968, 1 s., 2 d. *Education:* Psychology major. *Career:* Festival appearances include: Bay Shore Arts Festival, Long Island, New York, 1986; Rainbow Bash Festival, Sparta, New Jersey, 1993; Cross Rhythms Festival, Devon, UK, 1995, 1996, 1997; Sur Montreux Anniversary Jazz/Rock Festival, Switzerland, 1996, 1998; Tours throughout USA; Numerous television and radio appearances; Regular tours with Tony Loeffler and The Blue Angels. *Recordings:* 12 albums. *Publications:* Foundation (the Solid Rock Newsletter). *Membership:* Recording Industry Asscn of America (RIAA); Gospel Music Assocn; Broadcast Music Inc. *Current Management:* Lord and Associates Music.

LOFGREN, Nils; b. 21 June 1951, Chicago, Illinois, USA. Musician (guitar); Songwriter; Arranger; Vocalist. *Career:* Member, Grin, 1970s; Solo artiste, 1974–; Appearances with Neil Young and Crazy Horse, including Tonight's The Night tour, 1973; Trans tour, 1983; Joined Bruce Springsteen's E Street Band, 1984–; Continues as solo artiste. *Recordings:* Albums: Nils Lofgren, 1975; Back It Up (official bootleg), 1976; Cry Tough, 1976; I Came To Dance, 1977; Night After Night, 1977; Nils, 1979; Night Fades Away, 1981; Wonderland, 1983; Flip, 1985; Code of The Road, 1986; Silver Lining, 1991; Crooked Lining, 1992; Everybreath, 1994; Damaged Goods, 1995; Acoustic Live, 1997; with Bruce Springsteen and the E-Street Band: Live In New York City, 2001. *Current Management:* Anson Smith Management, 3 Bethesda Metro Center, Suite 505, Bethesda, MD 20814, USA.

LOGGINS, Kenny (Kenneth Clarke); b. 7 Jan. 1947, Everett, Washington, USA. Vocalist; Songwriter; Musician (guitar). m. Eva Ein, 31 Dec. 1976, divorced. *Education:* Music, Pasadena City College. *Career:* Member, Gator Creek; Second Helping; Duo, Loggins and Messina (with Jim Messina), 1971–76; Solo artiste, songwriter, 1977–. *Compositions include:* House At Pooh Corner, recorded by Nitty Gritty Dirt Band, 1971; Your Mama Don't Dance, recorded by Loggins and Messina, Elvis Presley, Poison, 1973; Danny's Song, recorded by Anne Murray; Co-writer with Michael McDonald, What A Fool Believes, recorded by Doobie Brothers (No. 1, USA), 1979; Co-writer with Melissa Manchester, Whenever I Call You Friend, 1979. *Recordings:* Hit singles include: This Is It, 1980; I'm Alright, from film Caddyshack, 1980; Don't Fight It, duet with Steve Perry, 1982; Heart To Heart, 1983; Footloose, from film Footloose (No. 1, USA), 1984; Danger Zone, from film Top Gun (No. 2, USA), 1986; Meet Me Half Way, from film Over The Top, 1987; Nobody's Fool, from film Caddyshack 2, 1988; Solo: Selections from December, 1998; Albums: with Loggins and Messina: Kenny Loggins With Jim Messina Sittin'

In, 1971; Loggins and Messina, 1972; Full Sail, 1973; On Stage, 1974; Mother Lode, 1974; So Fine, 1975; Native Sons, 1976; Finale, 1977; The Best of Friends, 1977; Solo albums: Celebrate Me Home, 1977; Nightwatch, 1978; Keep The Fire, 1979; Kenny Loggins: Alive, 1980; High Adventure, 1982; Footloose, film soundtrack (No. 1, USA) 1984; Vox Humana, 1985; Top Gun, film soundtrack (No. 1, USA) 1986; Back To Avalon, 1987; Kenny Loggins On Broadway, 1988; Leap of Faith, 1991; Outside – From The Redwoods, 1993; Return to Pooh Corner, 1994; The Unimaginable Life, 1997; December, 1998; More Songs From Pooh Corner, 2000; Contributor, We Are The World, USA For Africa, 1985. *Honours:* Grammy, Song of the Year, What A Fool Believes, 1980; Best Pop Vocal Performance, This Is It, 1981; Platinum and Gold discs. *Current Management:* Next Step, 105 Foothill Rd, Ojai, CA 93023, USA.

LOHAN, Sinead; b. 21 June 1971, Cork City, Ireland. Vocalist; Musician. *Education:* Piano lessons. *Career:* Toured with Womans Heart, Support to Paul Brady, 1995, The Blue Nile, 1996, Joan Baez, 1997; Appearance at Newport Folk Festival, 1997. *Compositions include:* Who Do You Think I Am; Sailing By; Everything Around Me is Changing; Out of the Woods. *Recordings:* Albums: Who Do You Think I Am, 1995; No Mermaid, 1998; Also appears on: Womans Heart 2, 1995; Loving Time, 1997. *Honours:* Triple Platinum; Best Newcomer, Irish National Entertainment Awards. *Current Management:* Pat Egan. *Address:* c/o Merchants Court 24, Merchants Quay, Dublin 8, Ireland.

LOHRER, Eric; b. 15 Feb. 1965, Paris, France. Jazz Musician (guitar); Composer. 1 s. *Education:* Philosophy, Lycée Henri IV; La Sorbonne, Paris. *Career:* Bandleader for groups Eric Lohrer Trio, Open Air, 1987–93; Red Whale, 1991–95; Olympic Gramofón, solo programme based on music of Theolonius Monk, 1995–96; Tours, festivals, France; Europe; Africa; Radio appearances: France Inter; France Musique; Europe 1; Television appearances: FR3; A2. *Recordings:* Eric Lohrer Trio, 1989; Queekegg, Red Whale, 1991; Dans Le Bleu, Eric Lohrer Trio, 1992; Attitudes, Open Air, 1992; Big One, Jean-Michel Pilc, 1993; Mozol, Red Whale, 1995. *Publications:* Time and Improvisation In Jazz Music, 1986. *Honours:* First Prize, soloist and band, Vienna International Jazz Contest, 1987; 2 Band Prizes: La Défense National Jazz Contest, 1988, 1989. *Membership:* SACEM; SPEDIDAM. *Current Management:* Supernova. *Address:* 94 rue du Mail, 95310 St Ouen L'Aumône, France.

LOKKE LARSEN, Birgit; b. 11 July 1967, Fr-Vaerk, Denmark. School teacher; Musician (drums, percussion). *Education:* School teacher, Biology, Arts, 1993; Private lessons: Adam Nussbaum; Alex Riel; Participated in several drum clinics; Played at 1991 Jazz Award presentations. *Career:* Toured with: Savage Rose; Embla; The Big Bang with Palle Danielson, Lars Jansson, Han Bennink, Alex Riel; NORDICAE with Niels Petter Molvaer, Eivin Aarset, Veslemoy Solberg, Sven Ohrvik, Rune Arnsen and Edvard Askeland; ONCE with Anders Jormin, Thomas Gustafsson; SOUK with Kim Kristensen and Thomas Agergaard; April Light Orchestra (Nordic all-women big band); Member of The Ship, tour of Denmark, Norway, Sweden and Greenland, where Marilyn Mazur composed the music; Member of trio with Hugo Rasmussen and Arne Forchammer. *Compositions:* Dans Under Broen; Dansen; Ballovira; music for: play, Mac and Beth, Copenhagen, 1997; play, Minotaurus, Copenhagen, 1999. *Recordings:* Moonchild, with Savage Rose, 1992; Strength of The Runes, with Veslemoy Solberg, 1996; Pulse of Time, with Kim Kristensen, 1999; Kjaerestebilder, with Veslemoy Solberg, 1999; Assimilation with Arne Forchhammer, 2000. *Honours:* Highest award, Arts examination.

LOLLIO, Lou; b. 30 Dec. 1949, West Virginia, USA. Vocals; Musician (guitar, piano). Man. m. Jean Lollio, 11 Nov. 1990. *Career:* Film: A Star Is Born, 1978; Up In Smoke, 1979; Blues Brothers Movie, 1980; Fantasy Island, 1981; The Mystery Train, Nashville, 1984; Supporting act for Van Halen, 1985; Opening Act for Little Richard, 1984; Buffalo Springfield Revisited Tour, 1986. *Recordings:* Music producer, Film: LA's Lost Angels, 1969. *Publications:* Andy Warhol interview. *Membership:* Screen Actors Guild (SAG); AFTRA; American Federation of Television and Radio Artistes; ASCAP. *Current Management:* J. Lollio Management. *Address:* 264 So Lacienega Bl #327, Beverly Hills, CA 90211, USA.

LOMAS, Roger David; b. 8 Oct. 1948, Coventry, England. Record Prod. m. Linda Lomas, 21 Dec. 1966, 2 s., 1 d. *Career:* Record producer for: The Specials; Bad Manners; The Selecter; Desmond Dekker; The Bodysnatchers; The Modettes; Special-Beat; Roy Wood. *Recordings:* 17 hit singles, 10 albums include: with Bad Manners: Can Can; Special Brew; My Girl Lollipop; Walking In The Sunshine; Lip Up Fatty; with The Selecter: On My Radio; Missing Words; Roy Wood, I Wish it Could be Christmas Everyday, live version; 18 hit singles altogether; Recent productions: for The Specials: Skinhead Girl, 2000; Conquering Role, 2001. *Honours:* Gold and Silver awards for Bad Manners and Selecter albums and singles. *Membership:* PRS. *Address:* 35 Dillotford Ave, Coventry, West Midlands CV3 5DR, England.

LOMAX, John; b. 20 Aug. 1944. Artiste Management; International Consultant; Journalist. m. Melanie Wells, 1 s., 1 d. *Education:* BA, MSLS, University of Texas, Austin. *Career:* A and R Consultant, Demon Records;

Manage 3 Acts; Freelance Writer, Country Music International; Founder, President, SFL Tapes and Discs, Music City Exporters. *Recordings:* Dulcimer Deluxe; Dulcimer Player; Dulcimer Sessions. *Publications:* Nashville: Music City, USA; The Country Music Book. *Honours:* Leadership Music, 1998. *Membership:* CMA; IMF; NARAS, Board of Governors, Nashville Chapter; NEA; CMAA. *Current Management:* Kasey Chambers, EMI Australia and Asylum (USA/Canada).

LONE RANGER, (THE). See: **Q-TIP.**

LONGNON, Jean-Loup; b. 2 Feb. 1953, Paris, France. Musician (trumpet, piano); Vocalist; Arranger; Composer; Conductor. *Career:* Trumpet player, various bands and big bands; Soloist or bandleader performing in concerts, recording studios, jazz clubs, master classes, festivals, tours, TV, radio, in France; Throughout Europe; Turkey; Israel; Egypt; Tunisia; Morocco; Reunion Island; Mauritius; USA; Cuba (Varandero Festival); Brazil; Played with artistes including: Dizzy Gillespie; Stan Getz; Clark Terry; Arturo Sandoval; Martial Solal; Stéphane Grappelli; Didier Lockwood; Michel Petrucciani; Antoine Hervé; Kenny Clarke; Chet Baker; Winton Marsalis; Michel Legrand. *Compositions:* Torride, Aquarelles, Jazz à Paris, Nathalie… Un Matin; Variations on John Coltrane themes (commissioned by National Jazz Orchestra); Suite for Orchestra on Dizzy Gillespie (commissioned by Michel Legrand for television show Grand Echiquier); Symphonic poem L'Ours (commissioned by Concert Arban brass quintet and Martin Publications); Cyclades suite for jazz soloist and symphonic orchestra (commissioned by Musique Française d'Aujourdhui). *Recordings:* include: Jean-Loup Longnon and His New York Orchestra; Bop Dreamer, CD, 1998. *Honours:* Winner, Festival de la Défense, Paris, 1977; Django Reinhardt Prize; Boris Vian Prize; European Audivisual Grand Prix; Django d'Or, 1995. *Membership:* SACEM. *Address:* 52 Blvd Saint Germain, 75005 Paris, France.

LOOP 7. See: **TOMIIE, Satoshi.**

LOPEZ, Jennifer, (J.Lo); b. 24 July 1970, Bronx, NY, USA. Vocalist; Actor; Dancer; Songwriter; Businesswoman. m. Chris Judd, 2001, divorced. *Career:* Latin singer; Films: My Little Girl, 1986; My Family—Mi Familia, 1995; Money Train, 1995; Jack, 1996; Blood and Wine, 1997; Selena, 1997; Anaconda, 1997; U-Turn, 1997; Antz (voiceover), 1998; Out of Sight, 1998; Thieves, 1999; Pluto Nash, 1999; The Cell, 2000; Angel Eyes, 2000; The Wedding Planner, 2000; Enough, 2002; Maid in Manhattan, 2002; Television appearances: Second Chances, Hotel Malibu, Nurses on the Line: The Crash of Flight 7; Collaborations: Ja Rule; Big Pun; Fat Joe. *Recordings:* Albums: On The 6, 1999; J.Lo, 2001; J To Tha L-O! (remixes), 2002; This Is Me… Then, 2002. Singles: If You Had My Love, Waiting For Tonight, 1999; Feelin' So Good, Love Don't Cost A Thing, 2000; Play, Ain't It Funny, I'm Real, 2001; featured on: All-Star Tribute benefit single What's Going On. *Honours:* Golden Globe, 1998; MTV Movie Award, 1999; Billboard Latin Award, Hot Latin Track of the Year, 2000; FHM Magazine, 100 Sexiest Women In The World, First place; MTV Video Music Award, Best Dance Video, 2000; VH1/ Vogue Fashion Awards, Versace Award, 2000; MTV Europe Music Award, Best Female Act, 2001; MTV Award, Best Female, 2002. *Current Management:* International Creative Management, 8942 Wilshire Blvd, Beverly Hills, CA 90211, USA. *Address:* c/o Sony Music Entertainment Inc, 550 Madison Ave, New York, NY 10022-3211, USA. *Website:* www.jenniferlopez.com.

LOPEZ, Orlando 'Cachaito', (Orlando Lopez Vergara); b. 1933, Havana, Cuba. Musician (double bass). *Career:* Born into a family with a long tradition of double bass virtuosity (son of Orestes López and nephew of Israel 'Cachao' López), his career has spanned popular, classical and jazz genres; Collaborations: Omara Portuondo; Ibrahim Ferrer; Rubén González; César Portillo de la Luz; Los Zafiros; Chucho Valdes; Paquito D'Rivera; Played on most of the Buena Vista Social Club series of recordings and with the Afro-Cuban All-Stars; Appeared in Wim Wenders' documentary Buena Vista Social Club; Solo album released, 2001. *Recordings:* recent Albums: Buena Vista Social Club, 1997; Cachaito, 2001; features on: Introducing Santiago, Chieftains, 1996; Tibiri Tabara, Sierra Maestra, 1997; Rubén González, 1997; Toda Cuba Le Gusta (with Afro-Cuban All-Stars), 1997; Buena Vista Social Club Presents Ibrahim Ferrer, 1999; Distinto Diferente (with Afro-Cuban All-Stars), 1999; Buena Vista Social Club Presents Omara Portuonda, 2000; Chanchullo (with Rubén González), 2000. *Honours:* BBC World Music Album of the Year (Americas), Cachaito, 2002. *Address:* c/o World Circuit Ltd, First Floor, Shoreditch Stables, 138 Kingsland Rd, London E2 8DY, England.

LOPEZ, Ramon; b. 6 Aug. 1961, Alicante, Spain. Musician (drums, tabla). m. Pilar Dominguez, 20 March 1992, 1 s. *Education:* Electronics specialist; Tabla student of Krishna Govinda K C, Lucknow, India. *Career:* Teacher, Indian and modal music, Paris Conservatoire (CNSMDP); Plays with: Claude Tchamitchian; Philippe Deschepper; Enrico Rava; Howard Johnson; Jean-Marc Padovani; Yves Robert; François Cotinaud; Jean-Marie Machado; J F Jenny Clark; Glenn Ferris; Daunik Lazro; Paul Rogers; Sophia Domancich; New groups, Onj 97/2000, National Orchestra of Jazz, conducted by Didier Levallet; Many appearances, Radio France; Television: M6 Jazz 6; Cable Paris Premiere: Capitale Jazz; F3, F3 Region; RTVE (Spain); RTSR

(Switzerland); RTBF (Belgium); TRI (Indonesia); WDR (Germany); Druskininkai TV, Baltic TV (Lithuania); Armenia TV. *Recordings:* Opera (with Frantois Cotinaud), 1993; Princesse, Frantois Cotinaud Quartet, 1990; Face Au Silence, Double Face, 1991; Pyramides (featuring Enrico Rava), 1992; Lousadzak, Claude Tchamitchian Septet, 1994; Portraits, Patrice Thomas Quartet, 1995; With Marc Steckar: Elephant Tuba Horde, 1987; Steckar Trinity, 1988; Tubakoustic, 1989; Jean-Marie Machado; Denis Colin Trio; Recent recordings: Eleven Drums Songs, 1998; Songs of The Spanish Civil War, 2000. *Publications:* La Region Internacional, 17 Aug. 1993; Batteur Magazine, no 44, Mar 1992; Informacion de Alicante, Nov. 1985; Jan. 1986; July 1986; Mar 1990. *Membership:* SACEM; SACD; SPEDIDAM; CNSMDP. *Current Management:* Jazz Bank Ass, Ramon Lopez.

LOPEZ, Trini; b. 15 May 1937, Dallas, TX, USA. Vocalist; Musician (guitar). *Career:* Nightclub performer, debut appearance, 1967; Recorded for Frank Sinatra, 1963–68; World-wide entertainer, 1963–; Film roles include: Marriage on the Rocks; A Poppy is Also a Flower; The Dirty Dozen; Antonio; Television appearances: Adam 12; The Reluctant Heroes; If I Had a Hammer. *Recordings include:* If I Had A Hammer; Trini Lopez Live At PJ's; More Trini Lopez At PJ's By Popular Demand; Trini Lopez In London; Trini Lopez Now; Trini Lopez Live At Basin Street East; Trini Lopez Greatest Hits; Trini—Transformed By Time; The Best Of Trini Lopez; Hit singles include: I'm Coming Home Cindy; Michael; Lemon Tree; Kansas City; If I Had A Hammer; America; La Bamba. *Honours:* Goodwill Ambassador for USA; Honoured by Congress for work in international relations; Gold disc, If I Had A Hammer; Nosotros Living Legend Award; Inducted, Las Vegas Casino Hall of Fame. *Membership:* AFofM; SAG. *Address:* 1139 Abrigo, Palm Springs, CA 92262, USA.

LOPEZ-REAL, Carlos Enrique; b. 25 Oct. 1969, Nairobi, Kenya. Musician (saxophone); Composer. *Education:* Psychology, Philosophy, Oxford University; Guildhall School of Music and Drama, post-graduate jazz and studio. *Career:* Leader, own quartet at festivals including Glastonbury, Oxford; Studied with Jean Toussaint; Played with Django Bates and Norma Winstone; Venues include Barbican Concert Hall; London clubs include Jazz Café, Vortex. *Compositions:* Folk Song; Para Michele; Mtengene; Soundtracks include film In Profile. *Recordings:* Dr Dig; Other sessions. *Membership:* Musicians' Union; Clarinet and Saxophone Society. *Address:* 38 Claverley Grove, Finchley, London N3 2DH, England.

LORD, Jon; b. 9 June 1941, Leicester, England. Musician (keyboards). *Education:* Central School of Speech and Drama, London; London Drama Centre. *Career:* Member, groups including: Artwoods; Flowerpot Men; Founder member, Deep Purple, 1968–76; Member, Paice Ashton Lord, 1976–77; Member, Whitesnake, 1978–84; Also solo recording artiste; Member, Deep Purple, 1984–; World-wide tours with Deep Purple and Whitesnake; Major concerts include: with Deep Purple: USA; Japan; UK; Australia; Europe; Knebworth Festival; with Whitesnake: Reading Festival, 1979, 1980; Tours with AC/DC, Jethro Tull, USA, 1980; Monsters of Rock Festival, 1981, 1983. *Recordings:* All recordings by Deep Purple; Albums: with Ashton and Lord: First of The Big Bands, 1974; with Paice Ashton Lord: Malice In Wonderland, 1977; with Whitesnake: Trouble, 1978; Lovehunter, 1979; Ready An'Willing, 1980; Live In The Heart of The City, 1980; Come and Get It, 1981; Saints 'N' Sinners, 1982; Slide It In, 1984; Solo albums: Gemini Suite, 1970; Windows, 1974; Sarabande, 1976; Before I Forget, 1982; Country Diary of An Edwardian Lady, 1986; Pictured Within, 1997; Abandon, 1998; Anthems, 2000; Also recorded with: Tommy Bolin; Graham Bonnet; Sam Brown; David Gilmour; George Harrison; Alvin Lee; Bernie Marsden; Nazareth; Cozy Powell. *Current Management:* Thames Talent, 45 E Putnam Ave, Greenwich, CT 06830, USA. *Address:* Nr Henley-on-Thames, Oxfordshire, England.

LOREN, Gina, (Gina Bellamy-Loren); b. 23 April 1957, Dallas, TX, USA. Record Co Exec; Record Prod; Vocalist; Songwriter. m. J. F. Kahn, Sept. 1982, divorced 1993, 1 s., deceased. *Education:* Hospital/Surgical Nursing Studies, University of Texas, 1980–82; Geology, University of Texas, Arlington; Classical guitar, voice, music composition. *Career:* Began recording, singing career, aged 13; Duet concerts with some radio and television appearances; Stand-in actor on television series, Dallas; Organized Scootertunes Incorporated, Scooter Records, Scooter Productions and J. B. Quantum Music; Participated in the live radio broadcast of Willie Nelson's Farm Aid, 1994. *Recordings:* True Love Conquers All, Gina Bellamy-Loren, 1994; The Fever, The Fever (contemporary country group), 1995; Feelings of Christmas/Santa's All Star Revue, 1996; Lavender Blue, 1997; Wild Honey, 1999. *Membership:* AFofM; ASCAP; BMI; NARAS. *Current Management:* Scootertunes Inc, PO Box 610166, Dallas, TX 75261, USA. *E-mail:* scootune@gte.net. *Website:* www.scootertunes.com.

LOTZ, Rainer E; b. 27 Aug. 1937, Hamburg, Germany. Discographer; Music Historian; Engineer; Economist. m. Birgit Lotz, 1 s., 3 d. *Education:* Master, Mechanical Engineering, Karlsruhe Technical University; Doctorate in Economics, Tübingen University; Postgraduate Study in Development Policy, Berlin Institute for Development Policy. *Career:* Technical Adviser, IFCT, Bangkok, Thailand; Acting Chief of Operations, East African Development Bank, Kampala, Uganda; Head, Latin America Department, Federal German

Ministry of Economic Cooperation and Development. *Recordings:* Compiler of CDs and LPs including: Harlequin anthology of the history of jazz and dance music. *Publications:* 160 articles in scholarly journals; 50 sleeve notes for CDs and LPs; Acknowledgements in 170 books by other authors; Publisher of 30 books; author of 80 monographs including Grammophonplatten aus der Ragtime-Àra, 1979; German Ragtime and Prehistory of Jazz: Vol. 1: The Sound Documents, 1985; The AFRS Jubilee Show: A Discography Vols 1 and 2, 1985; Mike Danzi: The Story of an American Musician in Berlin 1925–39, 1986; Co-editor, Under the Imperial Carpet: Essays in Black History, 1987; The Banjo on Record: A Bio-Discography, 1993; Hitler's Airwaves: The Inside Story of Nazi Radio Broadcasting and Propaganda Swing, 1997; Black People: Entertainers of African Descent in Europe and Germany, 1997; Vorbei—Beyond Recall: A Record of Jewish Musical Life in Nazi Berlin 1933–1938, 2001; Editor of the German National Discography. *Honours:* ARSC Lifetime Achievement Award, for published recorded sound research, 1998. *Membership:* IASA; IAJRC; ARSC. *Address:* Jean Paul Str 6, 53173 Bonn, Germany. *Website:* www.lotz-verlag.de.

LOUIS, Eric; b. 28 Oct. 1959, Malo Les Bains, France. Musician (trombone); Music Teacher. 1 d. *Education:* Conservatoires de Perpignan, 1978; St Quentin, 1979; Ville De Paris, 1980. *Career:* Played concerts with: Diana Ross; Charles Aznavour; Jerry Lewis; Lambert Wilson; Julia Migenes-Johnson; Member, jazz groups with: Michel Legrand; Patrice Caratini; Luc Lemasne; Yanko Nilovic; Laurent Cuny; 3 tours Japan with Raymond Lefèvre; Numerous revues and shows include: Cats; 42nd Street; Cabaret; Folies Bergères; Numerous appearances on French television include 4 telethons (1988–94); Several other musical and theatrical works; Performed with Orchestre Philharmonique d'Europe, Orchestre du Luxembourg and various other orchestras; Music teacher in Guéret, 1981–82; Lucé, 1988–89; Gentilly, 1989–90; Chatou, 1991–92. *Recordings:* Lisa Minelli; Charles Aznavour; Julia Migenes-Johnson; Pierre Perret; Georges Aperghis; Thomas Fersen; André Hoder. *Address:* 23 Ave Gütenberg, 92800 Puteaux, France.

LOUISE, (Louise Redknapp), (Louise Nurding); b. 1974, London, England. Vocalist. m. Jamie Redknapp. *Education:* Italia Conti Stage School. *Career:* Singer, UK all-female vocal group, Eternal, 1992–95; Solo artiste, 1995–. *Recordings:* Album: with Eternal: Always and Forever, 1993; Solo Albums: Louise, 1996; Woman In Me, 1997; Elbow Beach, 2000; Best Of, 2001; Hit singles: with Eternal: Stay, 1993; Save Your Love, 1994; Just A Step From Heaven, 1994; Oh Baby I, 1994; Solo hits: Light of My Life, 1995; In Walked Love, 1996; Naked, 1996; Undivided Love, 1996; One Kiss From Heaven, 1996; Arms Around The World, 1997; Let's Go Round Again, 1997; All That Matters, 1998; 2 Faced, 2000; Beautiful Inside, 2000; Stuck In The Middle With You, 2001. *Honours:* Smash Hits Award. *Current Management:* First Avenue Management, The Courtyard, 42 Colwith Rd, London W6 4EY, England.

LOURAU, Julien; b. 2 March 1970, Paris, France. Musician (saxophone). 1 d. *Career:* Performed at Marciac Festival; Vienna Festival; Blue Note, New York City; Hot Brass, Paris; Auditorium des Halles, Paris; Festival Banlieues Bleues; Radio-France. *Recordings:* Appears on: Scampi Fritti, 1994; Turtle's Dream, 1994; Who Used to Dance, 1996; Mad Nomad, 1997. *Publications:* A Turtle's Dream; Abbey Lincoln; Bojan Z Quartet; Julien Lourau Groove Gang. *Honours:* First prize, soloist, Concours de la Défense, 1993. *Current Management:* Carine Tedesco, Artalent. *Address:* 15 Passage de la Main D'Or, 75011 Paris, France.

LOUVIN, Charlie; b. 7 July 1927, Alabama, USA. Vocalist. *Career:* Appearances include: Nashville Now; Ralph Emery Show; At The Ryman; Grand Ole Opry Live; Backstage At The Opry. *Recordings:* See The Big Man Cry; Will You Visit Me On Sundays? Cry Myself To Sleep; Albums: And That's The Gospel, 1991; Hoping That You're Hoping, 1992; Live in Holland, 1995; Longest Train, 1996. *Honours:* Alabama Music Hall of Fame; Songwriters Hall of Fame; Grammy Award. *Membership:* AFofM; AFTRA. *Current Management:* Susie Reed, Mountain Magic Talent. *Address:* PO Box 140324, Nashville, TN 37214, USA.

LOVANO, Joe; b. 29 Dec. 1952, Ohio, USA. Musician (tenor saxophone, clarinet, bass clarinet); Composer. m. Judi Silvano, 30 Sept. 1984. *Education:* Berklee College of Music, Boston. *Career:* Toured with: Woody Herman Big Band; Thad Jones-Mel Lewis Orchestra; John Scofield Quartet; Paul Motian Trio (with Bill Frisell); Formed own bands, tours world-wide. *Recordings:* Rush Hour; Tenor Legacy; Universal Language Sextet; Tenor Legacy, 1993; Ten Tales, 1994; Quartets: Live at the Village Vanguard, 1994; Celebrating Sinatra, 1996; Flying Colours, 1997; Trio Fascination, 1998; Friendly Fire, 1999; Unknown Voyage, 2000; 52nd Street Themes, 2000; Flights of Fancy, 2001; Recorded with Joshua Redman. *Honours:* Jazz Artist of the Year, Downbeat Magazine Critics Poll, 1995. *Membership:* AFofM. *Current Management:* The Merlin Company.

LOVE, Courtney; b. 9 July 1964. Vocalist; Musician (guitar); Actor. m. Kurt Cobain, 24 Feb. 1992, deceased, 1 d. *Career:* Member, Faith No More, 1 year; Founder, singer/guitarist, Hole, 1991–; Tours include: Support tour to Nine Inch Nails; Reading Festival, 1994, 1995; Film appearances: Straight To Hell;

Sid and Nancy; Feeling Minnesota; The People vs Larry Flynt; Man on the Moon. *Recordings:* Albums: Pretty On The Inside, 1991; Live Through This, 1994; Celebrity Skin, 1998; Singles: Doll Parts, 1994; Ask for It, 1995; Celebrity Skin, 1998; Malibu, 1998; Awful, 1999. *Current Management:* Q-Prime Inc, 729 Seventh Ave, 14th Floor, New York, NY 10019, USA.

LOVE, Mike; b. 15 March 1941, Baldwin Hills, California, USA. Vocalist. *Career:* Member, Beach Boys, 1961–; Own band, Endless Summer, 1981; Numerous tours, concerts, include: The Beach Boys Summer Spectacular, Hollywood Bowl, 1966; UNICEF concert, Paris, 1967; Carnegie Hall, 1971; Royal Festival Hall, London, 1972; Grand Gala Du Disque, Amsterdam, 1972; Wembley Stadium, 1980; Knebworth Festival, 1980; Independence Day concerts, Washington DC, 1980s; Presidential Inaugural Gala, for President Reagan, 1985; Live Aid, Philadelphia, 1985; Tour with Chicago, 1989; Tour, supported by The Everly Brothers, 1991. *Compositions include:* Co-writer, theme for film: Almost Summer, 1978; Co-writer, song: Rock 'n' Roll To The Rescue, 1986. *Recordings:* Albums Include: Surfin' Safari, 1962; Surfer Girl, 1963; Little Deuce Coupe, 1963; Shut Down Vol. 2; All Summer Long, 1964; Christmas Album, 1964; The Beach Boys Today!, 1965; Summer Days (and Summer Nights), 1965; Beach Boys Party, 1966; Pet Sounds, 1966; Smiley Smile, 1967; Wild Honey, 1968; Friends, 1968; 20/20, 1969; Sunflower, 1970; Carl and The Passions/So Tough, 1972; Holland, 1973; Endless Summer (No. 1, USA), 1974; 15 Big Ones, 1976; The Beach Boys Love You, 1977; MIU, 1978; LA (Light Album), 1980; The Beach Boys, 1985; Still Cruisin', 1989; Two Rooms, 1991; Summer In Paradise, 1992; Good Vibrations (box set), 1993; Stars and Stripes Vol. 1, 1996; Ultimate Christmas, 1998; Greatest Hits, Vol. 2, 1999; Numerous compilations; Solo album: Looking Back With Love, 1981; Singles include: Surfin' USA, 1963; Fun Fun Fun, 1964; I Get Around (No. 1, USA), 1964; When I Grow Up (To Be A Man), 1964; Dance Dance Dance, 1965; Help Me Rhonda (No. 1, USA), 1965; California Girls, 1965; The Little Girl I Once Knew, 1965; Barbara Ann, 1966; Sloop John B, 1966; God Only Knows, 1966; Good Vibrations (No. 1, UK and USA), 1966; Wouldn't It Be Nice, 1966; And Then I Kissed Her, 1967; Heroes and Villains, 1967; Wild Honey, 1967; Darlin', 1967; Friends, 1968; Do It Again (No. 1, UK), 1968; Bluebirds Over The Mountain, 1968; I Can Hear Music, 1969; Break Away, 1969; Cottonfields, 1970; Sail On Sailor, 1973; California Saga, 1973; Rock and Roll Music, 1976; Here Comes The Night, 1979; Lady Lynda, 1979; Good Timin', 1979; Come Go With Me, 1982; Getcha Back, 1985; California Dreaming, 1986; Kokomo (No. 1, UK), 1988. *Honours:* Inducted into Rock and Roll Hall of Fame, 1988: Special Award of Merit, American Music Awards, 1988. *Current Management:* Elliott Lott, 4860 San Jacinto Circle W, Fallbrook, CA 92026, USA.

LOVELESS, Patty; b. 4 Jan. 1957, Pikeville, Kentucky, USA. Country Vocalist; Musician (guitar). m. (1) Terry Lovelace, 1976, (2) Emory Gordy Jr, 1989. *Career:* Summer job singing with the Wilburn Brothers, 1971; Singer, nightclubs and hotels, North Carolina; Moved to Nashville, 1985; Worked with Vince Gill and Emmylou Harris, including CBS' 70th Anniversary of the Grand Ole Opry; Television appearances include: The Tonight Show; Late Night With Conan O'Brian; Good Morning America; ABC In Concert Country; Music City Tonight; The Road; TNN Country News; Grand Ole Opry Live. *Recordings:* Albums: Only What I Feel, 1992; When Fallen Angels Fly, 1995; The Trouble With The Truth, 1996; Long Stretch of Lonesome, 1998; Classics, 1999; Strong Heart, 2000; Mountain Soul, 2001; Singles include: Blame It On Your Heart; Nothin' But The Wheel; You Will; How Can I Help You Can Say Goodbye; You Don't Even Know Who I Am; Halfway Down; You Can Feel Bad; You Don't Seem To Miss Me. *Honours:* Country Music Awards, 1993, 1995; Country Music Television Award, Female Artist of the Year, 1994; Real Country Listener Award, Female Vocalist of the Year, 1995; Academy of Country Music Award, 1997. *Current Management:* Fitzgerald-Hartley Co, 1908 Wedgewood Ave, Nashville, TN 37212, USA.

LOVEMUSCLE, Johnny; b. 3 April 1961, Hounslow, England. Record Prod; Writer; Designer; Actor; Vocalist. *Education:* Design Degree. *Career:* Founder, The Rhythm Men, 1982; Founder, The Adventures of Johnny Lovemuscle, 1984; Formed partnership with Martin Noakes, as producers for: Gene and Jim Are Into Shakes; Afrikadelic; Little Caesar, 1988; Managed by Pete Waterman; Published by Warner Chappell. *Recordings:* Shake! (How About A Sampling Gene?); The Whole of The Moon; Piti Pata; Eez-Zee-Boo-Gie. *Membership:* Musicians' Union; PRS; Equity. *Current Management:* Management To The Stars. *Address:* 28–30 Ecton Rd, Addlestone, Surrey KT15 1UE, England.

LOVERING, David; b. 6 Dec. 1961, Boston, Massachusetts, USA. Musician (Drums). *Career:* Member, The Pixies; Early support slots to Throwing Muses; Numerous tours and festival appearances; Some television appearances; Band split, 1993; Formed The Martinis with Joey Santiago, 1995. *Recordings:* Singles: Gigantic, 1988; Monkey Gone to Heaven, 1989; Here Comes Your Man, 1989; Velouria, 1990; Dig for Fire, 1990; Planet of Sound, 1991; Alec Eiffel, 1991; Head On, 1991; Debaser, 1997; Albums: Come on Pilgrim, 1987; Surfer Rosa, 1988; Doolittle, 1989; Bossanova, 1990; Trompe le Monde, 1991; Death To The Pixies, 1997; Live At The BBC, 2000; Complete B-Sides, 2001.

LOVETT, Lyle; b. 1 Nov. 1957, Klein, Texas, USA. Vocalist; Songwriter; Actor. m. Julia Roberts, 1993, divorced 1995. *Career:* Backing vocalist, Nanci Griffith, 1985; Solo singer, songwriter, 1986–; Television appearances include: Late Night With David Letterman, 1992, 1993; The Tonight Show, NBC TV, 1993; Willie Nelson – The Big Six-O, CBS TV, 1993; Regular US tours; Film appearances: The Player, 1992; Short Cuts, 1993. *Recordings:* Albums: Lyle Lovett, 1986; Pontiac, 1988; Lyle Lovett and His Large Band, 1989; Joshua Judges Ruth, 1992; Leap of Faith (soundtrack), 1992; I Love Everybody, 1994; Road to Ensenada, 1996; Step Inside This House, 1998; Live in Texas, 1999; Can't Resist It, 1999; Dr T and The Women, 2000; Backing vocalist, The Last of The True Believers, Nanci Griffith, 1985; Great Big Boy, Leo Kottke, 1991; Producer, King Tears, Walter Hyatt, 1990; Contributor, Deadicated (collection of Grateful Dead covers), 1991. *Current Management:* Vector Management, PO Box 128037, Nashville, TN 37212, USA.

LOVSIN, Peter; b. 27 June 1955, Ljubljana, Slovenia. Vocalist; Songwriter. m. Darija Lovsin, 21 Dec. 1980, 1 s., 1 d. *Education:* Faculty for Journalism. *Career:* Lead singer, punk bands: Pankrti, 1977–87; Sokoli, 1988–93; Currently solo, with support band Vitezi Om'a (The Divers). *Recordings:* 6 albums with Pankrti; 3 with Sokoli; 2 solo albums. *Publications:* Poetry: In The Service of Rock 'n' Roll. *Honours:* Croatian Youth Organisation Awards, 1980. *Current Management:* Tales, Lovsin in Ostali. *Address:* Zadruzna 1, 61000 Ljubljana, Slovenia.

LOWE, Chris(topher Sean); b. 4 Oct. 1959, Blackpool, Lancashire, England. Prod; Musician. *Education:* Architecture, Liverpool University. *Career:* Founder mem., West End, renamed Pet Shop Boys, 1981–, with Neil Tennant; Film: It Couldn't Happen Here, 1988; Numerous television appearances; Tours: Europe, Hong Kong, Japan, UK, USA, Canada; Host (with Neil Tennant), Simon Bates Show, BBC Radio One, one week, 1991, 1992; Launched record label, Spaghetti, 1991; Prod., songwriter, artistes incl.: Dusty Springfield, Patsy Kensit, Liza Minnelli, Boy George, Electronic; Musical, Closer to Heaven (written with Neil Tennant and Jonathan Harvey), West End, London, 2001. *Recordings:* Albums: Please, 1986; Disco—The Remix Album, 1986; Actually, 1987; Introspective, 1988; In Depth (Japan only), 1989; Behaviour, 1990; Discography, 1991; Very, 1993; Very Relentless, 1993; Disco 2, 1994; Alternative, 1995; Bilingual, 1996; Originals (Please, Actually, Behaviour box set), 1997; Bilingual Special Edition, 1997; Essential Pet Shop Boys, 1998; Nightlife, 1999; Please—Further Listening 1984–1986, 2001; Actually—Further Listening 1987–1988, 2001; Introspective—Further Listening 1988–1989, 2001; Behaviour—Further Listening 1990–1991, 2001; Very—Further Listening 1992–1994, 2001; Bilingual—Further Listening 1995–1997, 2001; Release, 2002; Disco 3, 2003. Singles: West End Girls; Opportunities; Suburbia; Love Comes Quickly; It's A Sin; What Have I Done To Deserve This?; Rent; Heart; Always On My Mind; Domino Dancing; Left To My Own Devices; It's Alright; So Hard; Being Boring; Where The Streets Have No Name (I Can't Take My Eyes Off You)/How Can You Expect To Be Taken Seriously; Jealousy; DJ Culture; DJ Culture Remix; Was It Worth It; Can I Forgive Her; Go West; I Wouldn't Normally Do This Kind Of Thing; Liberation; Yesterday When I Was Mad; Absolutely Fabulous; Before; Se A Vida E; Single Bilingual; A Red Letter Day; Somewhere; I Don't Know What You Want But I Can't Give It Anymore; New York City Boy; You Only Tell Me You Love Me When You're Drunk; Home And Dry; I Get Along. *Publications:* Pet Shop Boys, Annually; Pet Shop Boys Versus America; Pet Shop Boys, Literally, 1990. *Honours:* Ivor Novello Awards, 1987, 1988; BPI Award, Best Single, 1987; Best Group, 1988; Berolina, Germany, 1988. *Address:* Pet Shop Boys Partnership, 8 Pembridge Studios, 27a Pembridge Villas, London W11 3EP, England. *Website:* www.petshopboys.co.uk.

LOWE, Jez; b. 14 July 1955, Sunderland, England. Vocalist; Songwriter; Musician. *Education:* Sunderland Polytechnic. *Career:* Professional on folk circuit, 1980–; Toured, mainly Europe, USA. *Compositions:* for Fairport Convention: London Danny; Back In Durham Jail (10 cover versions); for The Clancy Brothers: Father Mallory's Dance. *Recordings:* over 10 solo albums including: Tou A Roue, 2001; Live At The Davy Lamp, 2001; Honesty Box, 2002; Many others as session musician and with Bad Pennies. *Publications:* Songs of Jez Lowe, 1988; Songs of Jez Lowe Vol. II. *Honours:* PRS Composers In Education Award, 1993. *Membership:* Musicians' Union. *Current Management:* Lowe Life Music (UK); Nancy Carlin Associates (USA). *Address:* c/o Lowe Life Music, PO Box 25, Horden, Peterlee, County Durham SR8 3YZ, England.

LOWE, Mark. See: **M. K. SHINE.**

LOWE, Nick; b. 24 March 1949, Woodchurch, Suffolk, England. Vocalist; Musician (bass); Record Prod. m. Carlene Carter, 15 Aug. 1979. *Career:* Member, Brinsley Schwarz, 1969–75; Rockpile (with Dave Edmunds), 1977–81; Leader, own band Nick Lowe and The Chaps, 1981; Founder, Little Village (with Ry Cooder, John Hiatt, Jim Keltner), 1992; Appearances include: Support to Van Morrison, 1970; Knebworth Festival, 1978; Support to Blondie, USA, 1979; Camridge Folk Festival, 1988, 1995; Film appearance, Stardust, 1974; Documentary, Born Fighters, UK TV, 1979. *Recordings:* Albums: with Brinsley Schwarz: Brinsley Schwarz, 1970; Despite It All, 1970; Silver Pistol, 1972; Please Don't Ever Change, 1973; Original Golden Greats,

1974; The New Favourites of Brinsley Schwartz, 1974; Solo albums: Jesus of Cool, 1978; The Abominable Snowman, 1983; Nick's Knack, 1986; Basher – The Best of Nick Lowe, 1989; Party of One, 1990; The Impossible Bird, 1994; Dig My Mood, 1998; The Convincer, 2001; with Rockpile: Labour of Lust, 1979; Seconds of Pleasure, 1980; with His Cowboy Outfit: Nick Lowe and His Cowboy Outfit, 1984; Rose of England, 1985; with Little Village: Little Village, 1992; Singles include: I Love The Sound of Breaking Glass, 1978; Crackin' Up, 1979; Cruel To Be Kind, 1979; You Inspire Me, 1998; Albums as record producer: with Elvis Costello: My Aim Is True, 1977; This Year's Model, 1978; Armed Forces, 1979; Get Happy, 1980; Blood and Chocolate, 1986; with Carlene Carter: Musical Shapes, 1980; Blue Nun, 1981; Also: Chocs Away, Kursaal Flyers, 1975; Malpractice, Dr Feelgood, 1975; Get It, Dave Edmunds, 1976; Rhythm, Fabulous Thunderbirds, 1982; Riding With The King, John Hiatt, 1984; Katydids, Katydids, 1990; Contributor, film soundtracks: Rock 'n' Roll High School, 1978; Americathon, 1980. *Address:* c/o Riviera Global Record Productions, 20 Cromwell Mews, London SW7 2JY, England.

LU WIN, Annabella, (Myant Myant Aye); b. 1966, Rangoon, Burma. Vocalist. *Career:* Singer, Bow Wow Wow, 1980–83; Solo artiste. *Recordings:* Albums: See Jungle..., 1981; I Want Candy, 1982; When The Going Gets Tough..., 1983; The Best of Bow Wow Wow, 1989; Singles: C30, C60, C90, Go!, 1980; Chihuahua, 1981; Go Wild In The Country, 1982; I Want Candy, 1982; Louis Quatorze, 1982; Solo albums include: Fever, 1986. *Current Management:* ESP Management, 888 Seventh Ave #2904, New York, NY 10106–0001, USA.

LUBIN, Jean-Claude; b. 2 Oct. 1935, Paris, France. Musician (piano); Information Scientist. *Education:* Dr in Science (Geology); Studied classical piano from 8 to 11 years. *Career:* Member, various groups, New Orleans, 1953–56; Musician, Paris, with: F Jeanneau; M Saury; A Nicholas; A Reweliotty; Also played with: B Wilen; G Laffite; L Fuentes; J L Chautemps; S Grapelly; J L Ponty; J F Jenny Clarke; A Romano; H Texier; A Lorenzi; D Humair; M Roques; J Griffin; C Baker; D Byrd; L Konitz; D Gordon; G Coleman; J McLean; D Cherry; G Barbieri. *Recordings:* The Fabulous Pescara Jam Session (with C Baker), 1975. *Address:* Jean-Claude Lubin, 3 rue d'Alembert, 92130 Issy-Les-Moulineaux, France.

LUCAS, David Jonathan; b. 4 Nov. 1963, Brentwood, Essex, England. Musician (electric guitar, acoustic guitar, electric bass, double bass); Vocalist. *Career:* Double bassist with the Rhythm Doctors, 1994–; Tours of: Austria, Holland, Dutch TV, 1996; Holland, Austria, Belgium, 1997; Holland, Germany, 1998; Canada, 1999. *Recordings:* Guitarist, vocalist, The Is, The Is, 1993; Various session work on guitar, bass, vocals and as producer, engineer, arranger, 1996–99; Guitar, vocals, songwriter, co-producer, Poppy, by Field, 2000. *Membership:* Musicians' Union.

LUCKETT, LeToya; b. 11 March 1981, Houston, TX, USA. Vocalist; Songwriter. *Career:* Numerous print and TV commercial appearances prior to professional music career; First international solo vocal performance in Tokyo, Japan, 1990; Joined GirlsTyme vocal group, 1992, with Beyoncé Knowles, LaTavia Roberson and Kelly Rowland; Group renamed Something Fresh then The Dolls before settling on Destiny's Child; Signed to Columbia Records, 1996; Acrimonious split from group, February 2000; Formed new group Anjel with fellow former Destiny's Child mem., LaTavia Roberson. *Recordings:* Albums: with Destiny's Child: Destiny's Child, 1998; The Writing's On The Wall, 1999. Singles: with Destiny's Child: No No No (with Wyclef Jean), 1997; With Me (with Timbaland), 1998; She's Gone (with Matthew Marsden), 1998; Get On The Bus (from Why Do Fools Fall In Love), 1999; Bills Bills Bills (No. 1, USA), 1999; Bug-A-Boo (No. 1, USA), 1999; Say My Name (No. 1, USA), 2000; Jumpin' Jumpin', 2000; Contributions to film soundtracks including, Men In Black, Romeo Must Die, Life; with Anjel: 10 Things I Hate About You, 2001. *Address:* c/o 581 Records/So So Def/Columbia, 550 Madison Ave, New York, NY 10022-3211, USA. *Website:* www.sonymusic.com.

LUKA BLOOM, (Barry Moore); b. 23 May 1955, Newbridge, County Kildare, Ireland. Vocalist; Musician (guitar); Songwriter. *Career:* Younger brother of Christy Moore; Performed in Dublin pubs and folk clubs around Europe, mid 1970s – mid 1980s; Brief stint as leader of rock band Red Square; Relocated to USA and changed name to Luka Bloom, 1987; Toured the country as opening act for the Pogues and Hothouse Flowers; Signed by Reprise and, later, Sony Music. *Recordings:* as Barry Moore: Treaty Stone, 1978; In Groningen, 1980; No Heroes, 1982; as Luka Bloom: Riverside, 1990; Acoustic Motorbike, 1992; Turf, 1994; Salty Heaven, 1998; Keeper of The Flame, 2000; The Barry Moore Years, 2001; Between The Mountain and The Moon, 2002. *Website:* www.lukabloom.com.

LUKATHER, Steve; b. 21 Oct. 1957, Los Angeles, California, USA. Musician (guitar). *Career:* Member, Toto, 1978–. *Compositions include:* Commissioned (with Toto) to write theme for Los Angeles Olympic Games, 1984; Co-writer (with Randy Goodrum), I'll Be Over You, 1986. *Recordings:* Albums: with Toto: Toto, 1979; Hydra, 1979; Turn Back, 1981; Toto IV, 1982; Isolation, 1984; Dune (film soundtrack), 1985; Fahrenheit, 1986; The Seventh One, 1988; Past To Present 1977–90, 1990; Kingdom of Desire, 1992; Luke, 1997; Lukather, 1998; Singles: with Toto include: Hold The Line, 1979; Georgy

Porgy, 1980; 99, 1980; Rosanna, 1982; Make Believe, 1982; Africa (No. 1, USA), 1983; I Won't Hold You Back, 1983; I'll Be Over You, 1986; Without Your Love, 1987; Pamela, 1988; Contributor, We Are The World, US For Africa charity single, 1985. *Honours:* 6 Grammy Awards: Best Record, Best Album, Best Engineered Recording, Best Producer (Toto), Best Vocal Arrangement, Best Instrumental Arrangement, 1983. *Address:* c/o Fitzgerald-Hartley Co, 50 W Main St, Ventura, CA 93001, USA.

LULU, (Marie MacDonald McLaughlin Lawrie); b. 3 Nov. 1948, Lennox Castle, Scotland. Vocalist; Entertainer. m. Maurice Gibb (divorced), (2) John Freda, 1976, 1 s. *Career:* Singer, Lulu and the Luvvers, 1963–66; Solo artiste, 1966–; British tours with: Gene Pitney, Peter and Gordon, Roy Orbison, The Beach Boys, 1965–66; Tour, Poland, with the Hollies, 1966; The Royal Variety Show, 1967, 1981; Host, own variety show, BBC1, 1968; Joint winner for UK (with France, Netherlands and Spain), Boom-Bang-A-Bang, Eurovision Song Contest, 1969; Berlin Disc Gala, 1971; Film appearance: To Sir With Love, 1966; Theatre and television includes: Guys and Dolls; Song and Dance; The Secret Diary of Adrian Mole Aged 13³/₄; New record deal and forthcoming album being recorded; Guest Presenter, Red Alert, National Lottery programme. *Recordings:* Albums: To Sir With Love, 1967; New Routes, 1970; The Most of Lulu, 1971; Take Me To Your Heart Again, 1982; Don't Take Love For Granted, 1978; Lulu, 1981; Independence, 1993; Absolutely, 1997; The Best of Lulu, 1998; Together, 2002. Hit singles include: Shout, 1964; Leave A Little Love, 1965; Try To Understand, 1965; The Boat That I Row, 1967; Let's Pretend, 1967; To Sir With Love, 1967; Me The Peaceful Heart, 1968; I'm A Tiger, 1968; Boom-Bang-A-Bang, 1969; The Man Who Sold The World, 1974; Independence, 1993; I'm Back For More, duet with Bobby Womack, 1993; Guest vocalist, Relight My Fire, Take That (No. 1, UK), 1993; Hurt Me So Bad, 1999. *Current Management:* Running Dog Management Ltd, PO Box 225, Sunbury-on-Thames, Middlesex TW16 5RT, England.

LUMHOLDT, Sara Helena; b. 25 Oct. 1984, Stockholm, Sweden. Vocalist. *Education:* Näsbydals skola, Stockholm. *Career:* Picked to be member of A*Teens group following auditions at Leslie Kühler's dance school, 1998; Continued educational studies whilst pursuing musical career; Prestigious US support tours for *NSYNC and Britney Spears, 2000. *Recordings:* Albums: The Abba Generation, 1999; Teen Spirit, 2001; Singles: Mamma Mia, Super Trouper, Gimme! Gimme! Gimme!, Happy New Year, 1999; Dancing Queen, Upside Down, 2000; Halfway Around The World, Sugar Rush, 2001. *Honours:* Broke Swedish sales records with first album and single; World-wide sales of first album in excess of 3m.; Viva Music Awards, Best International Newcomer, 2000. *Address:* c/o Stockholm Records, Sweden. *Website:* www.stockholmrecords.com.

LUNDEN, Petri H; b. 29 Nov. 1963, Helsinki. Promoter; Booking Agent; Man.-Dir. 1 d. *Career:* Breaking the following acts in Scandinavia: Bjoku; Green Day; Nirvana; Offspring; Stereo MCs; Blue Oasis; Prodigy; Cranberries; Soul Asylum; Weezer; The Orb; Swedish acts worked with, world-wide: Clawfinger; Cardigans; Popsicle; Stanna Bo. *Honours:* Most Interesting Promoter of the Year, 1994. *Membership:* ECPA. *Address:* PO Box 53045, 40014 Goteborg, Sweden.

LUNDSTEN, John; Sound Engineer. *Career:* Assistant, the Film Editor, BBC and Yorkshire TV Productions including Horizon, Omnibus, Whicker's World, 1967–69; Sound Engineer, Radio Gerinomo, Live recordings, freelance film recorder for films including Pulp with Michael Caine and O Lucky Man, recorded Glastonbury festival for album and film directed by Nic Roeg, 1969–70; Assistant Recordist for film with Peter Sellers, Daily Record film contest, 1971–74; 12 concerts for Camden Jazz Festival, Raj in Orchestra, Pakistani/Western music project, started designing and building own mixing studio, 1981; Recorded live punk album for Peter and the Test Tube Babies, Pissed and Proud, 1982; Opera and masterclass recordings of Placido Domingo, Buddy Holly memorial concert with Paul McCartney, began using digital stereo recorder, 1983; Programme of music of Count Basie with Helen Shapiro on vocals, film of band Level 42 including post-production, using digital technology, also post-production for Erasure and Status Quo, 1984; Mincing Machine tour with Julian Clary, Irish Music Festival for RTE Dublin, 2 programmes on African music for S4C, Lecturer for National Film School on Digital Auto and Stereo recording techniques, 1989; Recording and post-production for Alan Price concert, recording and sound supervision for Wet Wet Wet, recordings for numerous TV programmes on world music, started work on a sound FX database, 1990–91; Recording for documentary for Rex: The Grateful and the Dead, recording for documentary on Ute Lempe, plan for building of Alchemea College of audio engineering, 1992; Lecturer, Course Co-ordinator and Curriculum Development at Alchemea, other recording projects, 1993–95; Designed 4 studios in Chipping Norton and 2 Surround-Sound mixing rooms at Alchemea, more teaching at National Film School and other projects. *Address:* Alchemea, The Windsor Centre, Islington, London N1 8QG, England.

LUNDSTEN, Ralph; b. 6 Oct. 1936, Ersnäs, Sweden. Composer; Film maker; Artist; Author; Studio owner. *Career:* Owner of Andromeda Picture and electronic music studio, including the Love Machine and other invented synthesizers, 1959–; More than 600 opus and 91 records, 12 short films, art exhibitions, a book with CD – Lustbarheter; Work for Opera House in Stockholm in Stockholm and Oslo, the Modern Museum and National Museum in Stockholm, the Louvre and the Biennale in Paris, the Triennale in Milano and the Museum of Contemporary Crafts in New York; Subject of a number of Radio and TV portraits, 1971–98; Special portrait-exhibition at the Music Museum in Stockholm, 1991–92, 2000. *Compositions include:* Nordic Nature Symphony No 1, The Water Sprite; Johannes and the Lady of the Woods; A Midwinter Saga; A Summer Saga; Bewitched; Landscape of Dreams; The Seasons; Erik XIV and Gustav III; Cosmic Love; Ourfather, Nightmare; Horrorscope; Shangri-La; Universe; Discophrenia; Alpha Ralpha Boulevard; Paradise Symphony; The New Age; Pop Age; Music for Relaxation and Meditation; Cosmic Phantazy; The Dream Master; The Gate of Time; The Ages of Man; Sea Symphony; Mindscape Music; Nordic Light; The Symphony of Joy; The Symphony of Light; The Symphony of Love; In Time and Space; Andromedian Tales; Happy Earthday; Inspiration; At the Fountain of Youth; A Vagabond of the Soul. *Honours:* Grand Prix Biennale, Paris, France, 1967; Swedish Film Institute Prize, 1964–67; About 40 other awards for music and film making; Schwingungen Preis, Oscar of Electronic Music, 1999; Cultural Ambassador for Luleå. *Membership:* London Diplomatic Acad., 2000. *Address:* Frankenburgs väg 1, SE-132 42 Saltsjö-Boo, Sweden. *E-mail:* ralph.lundsten@andromeda.se. *Website:* www.andromeda.se.

LUNDSTREM, Oleg Leonidovisch; b. 2 April 1916, Chita, Siberia, Russia. Composer; Orchestra Leader. Widower. *Education:* High Technical Centre, Faculty of Architecture, Shanghai, 1944; Graduate, musical college, Harbin, People's Republic of China, 1935; Kazan Conservatory, as composer and symphony conductor, Russia, 1953. *Career:* Leader, professional jazz band, Kharbin, 1934; Leader, Concert Jazz Orchestra, Moscow, 1956; Film, A Song Without End, 1965; Many appearances on radio and television. *Compositions include:* Suite on Tatar Folklore, for Symphony Orchestra; Symphony in C Minor; Melody for Violin and Piano; Pieces for jazz big band: Interlude; Mirage; Impromptu; Together Again; Bokhara Ornament; In The Mountains of Georgia. *Recordings:* Together Again; Tribute to Jazz Masters; In Swing Time; Nowadays; In A Mellow Tone. *Honours:* People's Artist of Russia, 1984; DSc, International Academy of Sciences, San Marino, 1993; Prize of Moscow, for literature and art, 1995; Laureate of the National Musical Prize Ovation, 1996; Order, Services for the Fatherland, III degree, 1996. *Membership:* Union of Composers, Russia; Union of Theatre Workers; International Union of Musical Workers. *Address:* Cherkisovskaya h 3, B J Apt 49, Moscow 107061, Russia.

LUNGHINI, Elsa; b. 20 May 1973, Paris, France. Vocalist; Actress; Author; Composer. 1 s. *Career:* Singer: Solo artiste, 1986–; European tour and Olympia, Paris, 1990; In duets with Glenn Medeiros: diamond awards, Antwerp, 1988; Actress: Festival de Cannes, for film: Le Retour de Casanova, with Alain Delon, 1991. *Recordings:* T'en Va Pas (Please Don't Go), 1986; with Glenn Medeiros: Love Always Finds A Reason, 1988; First album: Elsa, 1988; Rien Que Pour Ça, 1990; Dance Violence, 1992. *Honours:* Gold and Platinum singles and albums; Grand Prix SACEM, 1993. *Current Management:* BMG France/Ariola, 2 rue des quatre Fils, 75003 Paris, France (Music); Artmedia, 10 Ave Georges V, 75008 Paris, France (Films).

LUNN, John Lawrence; b. 13 May 1956, Scotland. Composer; Musician. m. Sara, 1 s. *Education:* Glasgow University; Royal Scottish Academy of Music; Electronic Music, Massachusetts Institute of Technology. *Career:* Formed pop group: Earplay, 1981; Later joined avant garde music group, The Lost Jockey; Developed into: Man Jumping, mid-1980s. *Compositions:* Films: Four Weddings and A Funeral; The Cormorant, BBC2; The Gift, BBC1; After The Dance, BBC; Life of Stuff, 1998; Wisdom of Crocodiles, 1998; Get Real, 1998; Baby Mother, 1998; Other television: Finney, YTV; Hamish Macbeth, BBC; The Last Machine, BBC; Beatrix, BBC; Heart of Shelley, Anglia; The Dance House, BBC2; Focal Point, BBC Scotland; Getting Hurt, 1998; Ballets: Weighing The Heart; Goes Without Saying; In Dream I Loved A Dream; Classical pieces: Le Voyage; Verve; Echoes; Leonce and Elena; Jazz Pointilliste; Strange Fruit; Black and Blue; Operas: Mathematics of a Kiss; Misper, 1998; The Maids, 1998. *Honours:* Scholarship, Scottish Arts Council; Royal Television Society, Best Drama Score for Getting Hurt, 1998. *Membership:* Musicians' Union; PRS. *Current Management:* Sound Track Music Associates Ltd, 22 Ives St, Chelsea, London SW3 2ND, England.

LUNNY, Donal; b. 1947, Newbridge, County Kildare, Ireland. Musician (guitar, bouzouki, bodhran); Prod. *Career:* First musician to introduce bouzouki to Irish music; Member: Rakes of Kildare (with Christy Moore); Emmett Spiceland; Planxty; The Bothy Band; Moving Hearts; Coolfin; Involved with production of first interactive CD-ROM compilation of Irish music; Collaborations: Kate Bush; Mary Black; Van Morrison; Elvis Costello; Sinead O'Connor; Involved with TV programmes: Bringing It All Back Home, 1992; A River of Sound, 1995; Presented music programme Sult, 1996; Involved in over 100 albums. *Recordings:* Albums include: Faoilean, Triona and Maighread Ni Dhomhnaill, 1975; Live Hearts, Moving Hearts, 1983; Ride On, Christy Moore, 1984; No Frontiers, Mary Black, 1989; Bringing It All Back Home, 1991; Seville Suite, Bill Whelan, 1992; Sult, 1996; Coolfin, 1998; Duiseacht, 2000; My Name Is Napoleon Bonaparte, 2001. *Honours:* The Late Late Show Special Tribute to Donal Lunny, 1996.

LUNNY, Manus Bernard; b. 8 Feb. 1962, Dublin, Leinster, Republic of Ireland. Vocalist; Musician (guitar, bouzouki, bodhran). *Career:* Brother of Donal Lunny; Began career as member of The Wild Geese; Toured with Andy M Stewart and Phil Cunningham; Joined Scottish folk band Capercaillie, 1988; Group, along with original material, specialise in fusing traditional Gaelic songs with contemporary arrangements; Act had first UK top 40 single in Gaelic, Coisich A Ruin (from A Prince Among Islands EP), 1992; In-demand session musician and composer; Worked on several TV series with top folk musicians including: Tacsi; Togaidh Sinn Fonn. *Recordings:* Albums: with Capercaillie: Sidewalk, 1989; Delirium, 1991; Get Out, 1992; The Blood Is Strong, Secret People, 1993; Capercaillie, 1995; To The Moon, 1996; Beautiful Wasteland, 1997; Glenfinnan – Songs of The '45 (recorded 1995), 1998; Nàdurra, 2000; group feature on: Rob Roy OST, 1995; features solo on: Fire In The Glenn, Andy Stewart and Phil Cunningham, 1986; Dublin Lady, Andy Stewart, 1987; Donal Lunny, Donal Lunny, 1987; At It Again, Andy Stewart, 1990; Songs of Robert Burns, Andy Stewart, 1990; Somebody, Connie Dover, 1991; The Dreaming Sea, Karen Matheson, 1996; Wishing Well, Connie Dover, 1994; If I Ever Return, Connie Dover, 1997; Identities, Idir, 1999; Fused, Michael McGoldrick, 2000; Tacsi (TV series), 2000.

LUSCOMBE, Stephen Alfred; b. 29 Oct. 1954, Hillingdon, Middlesex, England. Musician (keyboards); Composer; Prod. *Education:* John Steven's Music Workshops, 1971–72. *Career:* Member, Portsmouth Sinfonia, avant garde orchestra, 1972–74; Member, Spontaneous Music Orchestra, 1972–74; Founder, performer, Music Workshop Miru, 1973–77; Founder, with Neil Arthur, electro-pop duo Blancmange, 1979–86; Numerous tours, television and radio broadcasts, recordings; Co-founder, West India Company, with Pandit Dinesh, 1984–; With artistes including: Asha Bhosle; Boy George; Apache Indian; Saeed Jaffrey; La La La Human Steps; Numerous commissions for television, radio, theatre, film productions including National Theatre, 1994; BBC Radio Drama, 1994; Lonely Planet Travel Guide (CH4), 5 programmes, 1995; Music for film Masala, starring Saeed Jaffrey and Zora Seghal, Canada, 1991; Music composition and direction for R National Theatre Production, Wicked Year, 1994. *Recordings:* with Portsmouth Sinfonia: Play The Popular Classics, 1973; Live At The Albert Hall, 1974; with Blancmange: Happy Families, 1982; Mange Tout, 1984; Believe You Me, 1985; Greatest Hits, 1990; Also 8 top 40 singles include: Living On The Ceiling; with West India Company: Ave Maria (EP), 1984; Music From New Demons, 1989; The Art of Love – Readings From The Kama Sutra, Saeed Jaffrey, 1992; Music From The Lonely Planet, with others, 1995. *Membership:* PRS; PPL. *Current Management:* Notting Hill Music Ltd. *Address:* 87 Notting Hill Gate, London W11 3JZ, England.

LUSHER, Don; b. 6 Nov. 1923, Peterborough, England. Musician (trombone); Bandleader. *Career:* Member, Joe Daniels and His Hot Shots; Joined Lou Preager at Hammersmith Palais; Member, Maurice Winnick's Band, The Squadronaires and the Ted Heath Band; Extensive tours with artistes including Frank Sintara, 1960s; Leader, big bands, for television and radio appearances; Educator, USA; Japan; Australia; UK. *Recordings:* Albums include: Lusher and Lusher, 1972; Collection, 1976; Don Lusher Big Band, 1981; Don Lusher Pays Tribute To The Great Bands Vol. 2, 1988; Just Good Friends, 1993; Performance, with Marti Webb, 1994; Trippin' the Light Fantastic, with the London Starlight Orchestra, 1998; Most Beautiful Melodies of the Century, 1999. *Publications:* The Don Lusher Book. *Honours:* O.B.E., 2003. *Current Management:* Derek Boulton Management, 76 Carlisle Mansions, Carlisle Pl., London SW1P 1HZ, England.

LUSSIER, Damien; b. 7 Nov. 1975, St Anne's, Manitoba, Canada. Vocalist; Songwriter; Musician (guitar, piano). 1 d. *Education:* Study in Guitar, Conservatoire du Musique de Montréal. *Career:* CBC TV Production, Télé-Relais; Boîte à Chanson II; Boîte à Chanson III; Short interviews on 2 local TV Stations; Numerous interviews on Radio Canada and local radio stations. *Compositions:* Alice; Les artistes au Rendezvous. *Recordings:* D'ailleurs. *Membership:* SOCAN. *Address:* 1067 Clarence Ave, Winnipeg, Manitoba R3T 1S5, Canada.

LUTHER, Paul James; b. 1 Sept. 1974, Salisbury, England. Musician (guitar). *Education:* 11 years, private tuition, classical guitar. *Career:* Two British tours backing Toyah Willcox; Concerts for British forces, Belize; Heineken festival concerts, Gateshead, Plymouth, 1994; Member, Scarlet supporting Bryan Ferry, British tour, 1995; Further Scarlet tour supporting Wet Wet Wet, 1995; Currently pursuing career with new band, Ebb, 1998; Television: 3 appearances with Scarlet, Top of the Pops; Pebble Mill; Parallel 9; What's Up Doc with singer David Dixon. *Recordings:* with Toyah Willcox: Take The Leap, 1993; with Scarlet: Naked, 1995; The Friday's Duck; Singles: with Scarlet: Independent Love Song (Top 20, UK charts); I Wanna Be Free. *Membership:* Musicians' Union; PAMRA. *Address:* 295 Devizes Rd, Salisbury, Wiltshire SP2 9LU, England.

LYDON, John, (Johnny Rotten); b. 31 Jan. 1956, Finsbury Park, London, England. Vocalist. *Career:* Vocalist, UK punk group the Sex Pistols, 1975–78; Founder, Public Image Ltd, 1978–; Performances include: First gig, St Martin's School of Art, London, 1975; Screen on The Green Midnight Special, Islington, London, 1986; Tour, Anarchy In The UK, 1976; Europe, 1977; USA,

1978; Last live show, Winterland Ballroom, San Francisco, 1978; Sex Pistols reunion concert, Finsbury Park, London, 1996; Phoenix Festival, 1996; Film appearances: The Great Rock 'n' Roll Swindle, 1980; The Filth and The Fury, 2000; Presenter, Billion Dollar Baby: The Alice Cooper Story (BBC Radio 2), 2002. *Recordings:* Albums: Never Mind The Bollocks – Here's The Sex Pistols (No. 1, UK), 1977; The Great Rock 'n' Roll Swindle, 1979; Some Product – Carry On Sex Pistols, 1979; Flogging A Dead Horse, 1980; Kiss This, 1992; With Public Image Ltd: Public Image, 1978; Metal Box, 1979; Paris Au Printemps, 1980; Flowers of Romance, 1981; This Is What You Want, This Is What You Get, 1984; Album, 1986; Happy?, 1987; 9, 1989; Greatest Hits So Far, 1990; That What Is Not, 1992; Plastic Box, 1999; Jubilee, 2002. Singles include: with The Sex Pistols: Anarchy In The UK, 1976; God Save The Queen (No. 2, UK), 1977; Pretty Vacant, 1977; Holidays In The Sun, 1977; with Public Image Ltd: Public Image, 1978; Death Disco, 1979; Flowers of Romance, 1981; This Is Not A Love Song, 1983; Rise, 1986; Seattle, 1987; Disappointed, 1989; Don't Ask Me, 1990; Cruel, 1992. *Contributions to:* Timezone, World Destruction, 1984; Leftfield, Open Up; In the Sun; Album: Leftism, 1995; Solo Album: Psycho's Path, 1997. *Publications:* Rotten: No Irish, No Blacks, No Dogs (autobiography), 1994. *Current Management:* DMA Entertainment, 2029 Century Park E, Suite 600, Los Angeles, CA 90067, USA.

LYLE, Graham; b. Largs, Ayrshire, Scotland. Vocalist; Songwriter; Musician (guitar). *Career:* Songwriting partnership with Benny Gallagher, 1960s; Member, McGuinness Flint, 1969–71; Folk duo, Gallagher and Lyle, 1972–79; Solo artiste, 1980–. *Compositions:* Co-writer with Benny Gallagher: Mr Heartbreak's Here Instead, Dean Ford; International, Mary Hopkin; for McGuinness Flint: When I'm Dead and Gone; Malt and Barley Blues; for Gallagher and Lyle: I Wanna Stay With You; Heart On My Sleeve; Co-writer with Terry Britten: What's Love Got To Do With It, Tina Turner; Just Good Friends, Michael Jackson. *Recordings:* Albums: with Gallagher and Lyle: Gallagher and Lyle, 1972; Willie and The Lap Dog, 1973; Seeds, 1973; The Last Cowboy, 1974; Breakaway, 1976; Love On The Airwaves, 1977; Showdown, 1978; Gone Crazy, 1979; Lonesome No More, 1979; The Best Of, 1980; Heart On My Sleeve, 1991; Singles: I Wanna Stay With You, 1976; Heart On My Sleeve, 1976.

LYNCH, Colm; b. 29 April 1952, Dublin, Ireland. Musician. 1 s., 1 d. *Education:* Social Pedegog, Denmark; Drums, piano, guitar, through school; Private tutor in School of Music, Dublin. *Career:* Successful appearances on RTE (TV, Ireland): Meitheal; Saoire Samhradh; Spin Off; Jimmy Saville show, BBC; Danish radio, television. *Compositions:* Songwriter in Ireland, Singer/songwriter in UK, wrote hit singles. *Recordings:* Album: Early One Morning; Hit singles: Violence Has Many Faces; Devil Among The Tailors. *Honours:* Top Selling Album, 1973; Top Irish Artist, 1973; Best Group. *Membership:* KODA (Danish PRS); DJBFA (Danish Society, Jazz, Rock and Folk Composers). *Address:* Mejlgade 89, 8000 Århus C, Denmark.

LYNCH, Edele Claire Christina Edwina; b. 15 Dec. 1979, Dublin, Ireland. Vocalist. *Career:* Member, B*Witched; Numerous tours and television appearances; Several hit singles. *Recordings:* Singles: C'est La Vie (No. 1, UK), 1998; Rollercoaster (No. 1, UK), 1998; To You I Belong (No. 1, UK), 1998; Blame it on the Weatherman (No. 1, UK), 1998; Jesse Hold On, 1999; I Shall Be There, with Ladysmith Black Mambazo, 1999; Jump Down, 2000; Albums: B*Witched, 1998; Awake and Breathe, 1999. *Website:* www.bwitched.com.

LYNCH, Ged; b. 19 July 1968, Oswaldtwistle, England. Musician (Drums). *Career:* Member, Black Grape; Numerous live gigs and festival appearances including Tribal Gathering and Reading festivals, 1997. *Recordings:* Singles: Reverend Black Grape, 1995; In The Name of The Father, 1995; Kelly's Heroes, 1995; England's Irie, 1996; Fat Neck, 1996; Get Higher, 1997; Marbles, 1998; Albums: It's Great When You're Straight... Yeah, 1995; Stupid Stupid Stupid, 1997; Also percussionist on: Michael Hutchence, Michael Hutchence, 1999; Afterglow, Dot Allison, 1999; Twisted Tenderness, Electronic, 1999; Wonderland, The Charlatans, 2001.

LYNCH, Keavy-Jane Elizabeth Annie; b. 15 Dec. 1979, Dublin, Ireland. Vocalist; Musician (saxophone, drums, guitar). *Career:* Member, B*Witched; Numerous tours and television appearances; Several hit singles. *Recordings:* Singles: C'est La Vie (No. 1, UK), 1998; Rollercoaster (No. 1, UK), 1998; To You I Belong (No. 1, UK), 1998; Blame it on the Weatherman (No. 1, UK), 1998; Jesse Hold On, 1999; I Shall Be There, with Ladysmith Black Mambazo, 1999; Jump Down, 2000; Albums: B*Witched, 1998; Awake and Breathe, 1999. *Website:* www.bwitched.com.

LYNCH, Shane Eamon Mark Stephen; b. 3 July 1976, Donaghmede, Dublin, Ireland. Vocalist. m. Easther Bennett. *Career:* Mem., Boyzone, 1993–2001. *Recordings:* Albums: Said And Done, 1995; A Different Beat, 1996; Where We Belong, 1998; By Request (No. 1, UK), 1999. Singles: Working My Way Back To You, 1994; Key To My Life, 1995; Love Me For A Reason, 1995; So Good, 1995; Father and Son, 1995; Coming Home Now, 1995; Words (No. 1, UK), 1996; A Different Beat (No. 1, UK), 1996; Isn't It A Wonder, 1997; Baby Can I Hold You Tonight, 1997; Musical Experience, 1997;

Picture of You, 1997; All That I Need (No. 1, UK), 1998; I Love The Way You Love Me, 1998; When The Going Gets Tough (No. 1, UK), 1999; You Needed Me (No. 1, UK), 1999; Every Day I Love You, 1999; Girl You Know It's True (with Keith Duffy), 2000.

LYNGSTAD, Frida (Anni-Frid); b. 15 Nov. 1945, Ballangen, Narvik, Norway. Vocalist. m. Benny Andersson, 1978, divorced 1981, 1 s., 1 d. (from previous relationship). *Career:* Leader, own dance band, Anni-Frid Four; Mem., Swedish pop group, Abba, 1973–82; Winner, Eurovision Song Contest, 1974; World-wide tours; Concerts include: Royal Performance, Stockholm, 1976; Royal Albert Hall, London, 1977; UNICEF concert, New York, 1979; Wembley Arena, six sell-out performances, 1979; Reunion with Abba, Swedish TV's This Is Your Life, 1986; The Story of Abba (Channel 4), 1991; Solo artiste, 1983–; Film: Abba: The Movie, 1977. *Recordings:* Albums: with Abba: Waterloo, 1974; Abba, 1976; Greatest Hits, 1976; Arrival, 1977; The Album, 1978; Voulez-Vous, 1979; Greatest Hits Vol. 2, 1979; Super Trouper, 1980; The Visitors, 1981; The Singles: The First Ten Years, 1982; Thank You For The Music, 1983; Absolute Abba, 1988; Abba Gold, 1992; More Abba Gold, 1993; Forever Gold, 1998; The Definitive Collection, 2001; Solo: Frida Alone, 1976; Something's Going On, 1982; Shine, 1983; Djupa Andetag, 1996; Frida 1967–72, 1998; Frida: The Mixes, 1998; Svenska Popfavoriter, 1998. Singles include: with Abba: Ring Ring, 1973; Waterloo (No. 1, UK), 1974; Mamma Mia (No. 1, UK), 1975; Dancing Queen (No. 1, UK and USA), 1976; Fernando (No. 1, UK), 1976; Money Money Money, 1976; Knowing Me Knowing You (No. 1, UK), 1977; The Name Of The Game (No. 1, UK), 1977; Take A Chance On Me (No. 1, UK), 1978; Summer Night City, 1978; Chiquitita, 1979; Does Your Mother Know?, 1979; Angel Eyes/Voulez-Vous, 1979; Gimme Gimme Gimme (A Man After Midnight), 1979; I Have A Dream, 1979; The Winner Takes It All (No. 1, UK), 1980; Super Trouper (No. 1, UK), 1980; On and On and On, 1981; Lay All Your Love On Me, 1981; One Of Us, 1981; When All Is Said and Done, 1982; Head Over Heels, 1982; The Day Before You Came, 1982; Under Attack, 1982; Thank You For The Music, 1983; Solo: Time (duet with B. A. Robertson). *Honours:* with Abba: Gold discs; Best-selling group in history of popular music, Guinness Book of Records, 1979; World Music Award, Best Selling Swedish Artist, 1993. *Website:* www.abbasite.com.

LYNN, Loretta, (Loretta Webb); b. 14 April 1935, Butcher Hollow, Kentucky, USA. Vocalist. m. Oliver Lynn, 1948, 6 c. *Career:* Sang local clubs with group The Trailblazers; Regular appearances, Grand Ole Opry; Weekly television show, with the Wilburn Brothers, Nashville; Regular duets with Ernest Tubb and Conway Twitty. *Recordings include:* 16 No. 1 singles, 60 other hits, 15 number 1 albums; Hit singles include: I'm A Honky Tonk Girl; Success; Before I'm Over You; Blue Kentucky Girl; Don't Come Home A-Drinkin' (With Lovin' On Your Mind); Coal Miner's Daughter; Pregnant Again; Albums include: Loretta Lynn Sings, 1963; Before I'm Over You, 1964; Songs From The Heart, 1965; Blue Kentucky Girl, 1965; Hymns, 1965; I Like 'Em Country, 1966; You Ain't Woman Enough, 1966; Don't Come Home A-Drinkin', 1967; Singin' With Feelin', 1967; Fist City, 1968; Your Squaw Is On The Warpath, 1969; Woman of The World, 1969; Coal Miner's Daughter, 1971; I Want To Be Free, 1971; Alone With You, 1972; Love Is The Foundation, 1973; They Don't Make 'Em Like Our Daddy, 1974; Home, 1975; Somebody Somewhere, 1976; Out of My Head and Back In My Bed, 1978; Loretta, 1980; Lookin' Good, 1980; Makin' Love From Memory, 1982; Just A Woman, 1985; Still Country, 2000; with Ernest Tubb: Mr and Mrs Used To Be, 1965; Singin' Again, 1967; If We Put Our Heads Together, 1969; with Conway Twitty: We Only Make Believe, 1971; Lead Me On, 1971; Lousiana Woman, Mississippi Man, 1973; Country Partners, 1974; Feelin's, 1975; United Talent, 1976; Dynamic Duo, 1977; Country Partners, 1974; Honky Tonk Heroes, 1978; Diamond Duets, 1979; Two's A Party, 1981; Making Believe, 1988; Who was That Stranger, 1989; Hey Good Lookin', 1993; Country's Favorite Daughter, 1994; An Evening with Loretta Lynn, 1995. *Publications:* Coal Miner's Daughter (autobiography). *Honours:* First woman inducted into Nashville Songwriters International Hall of Fame; First woman to be voted Country Music Assoc's Entertainer of the Year, 1972; CMA Vocal Duo of the Year (with Conway Twitty), 1972. *Current Management:* Loretta Lynn Enterprises, PO Box 120369, Nashville, TN 37212, USA.

LYNN, Dame Vera, (Margaret Lewis); b. 20 March 1917. Vocalist. m. Harry Lewis, 1941, 1 d. *Career:* Debut performance, 1924; Appeared with Joe Loss, Charlie Kunz, 1935; Ambrose, 1937–40; Applesauce, Palladium, London, 1941; Became known as the Forces Sweetheart, 1939–45; Radio show Sincerely Yours, 1941–47; Tour of Burma, entertaining troops, 1944; 7 Command performances; Appearances, Europe; Australia; Canada; New Zealand; Performed at 50th Anniversary of VE Day Celebrations, London, 1995; Own television shows: ITV, 1955; BBC1, 1956; BBC2, 1970; First British artiste to top Hit Parade. *Recordings include:* Auf Wiederseh'n (No. 1, USA; over 12m. copies sold), 1952; My Son My Son (No. 1, UK), 1954; Recent albums include: With All My Heart, 2000. *Publications:* Vocal Refrain (autobiography), 1975. *Honours:* Order of St John; LLD; MMus. *Current Management:* Anglo-American Enterprises, 806 Keyes House, Dolphin Sq., London SW1V 3NB, England.

LYNNE, Jeff; b. 30 Dec. 1947, Birmingham, England. Record Prod; Vocalist; Songwriter; Musician (guitar); Arranger. *Career:* Member, Idle Race, 1966–70;

Member, The Move, 1970–72; Founder member, The Electric Light Orchestra (ELO), 1972–85; Regular international tours, 1973–; Record producer, 1983–; Formed the Traveling Wilburys (with Bob Dylan, Roy Orbison, George Harrison, Tom Petty), 1988; Also solo artiste. *Recordings:* Albums include: with ELO (as singer, guitarist, writer and producer): Electric Light Orchestra, 1972; ELO II, 1973; On The Third Day, 1973; Eldorado, 1974; The Night The Light Went On In Long Beach, 1974; Face The Music, 1975; Olé ELO, 1976; A New World Record, 1976; Out of The Blue, 1977; Discovery, 1979; ELO's Greatest Hits, 1979; Xanadu (film soundtrack), 1980; Time (No. 1, UK), 1982; Secret Messages, 1983; Perfect World of Music, 1985; First Movement, 1986; Balance of Power, 1986; Afterglow, 1990; Strange Magic, 1995; Live at Wembley, 1998; Flashback, 2000; Zoom, 2001; with Traveling Wilburys (also co-writer and co-producer): Traveling Wilburys, Vol. 1, 1988; Vol. 3, 1991; Solo: Armchair Theatre, 1990; As producer: Information, Dave Edmunds, 1983; Cloud Nine, George Harrison, 1987; Mystery Girl, Roy Orbison, 1988; Full Moon Fever, Tom Petty, 1988; Singles include: with ELO: 10538 Overture, 1972; Roll Over Beethoven, 1972; Can't Get It Out of My Head, 1974; Evil Woman, 1976; Strange Magic, 1976; Livin' Thing, 1976; Telephone Line, 1977; Mr Blue Sky, 1978; Sweet Talkin' Woman, 1978; Shine A Little Love, 1979; Don't Bring Me Down, 1979; Xanadu, collaboration with Olivia Newton-John (No. 1, UK), 1980; All Over The World, 1980; Hold On Tight, 1981; Rock 'n' Roll Is King, 1983; Calling America, 1986; with the Traveling Wilburys: Handle With Care, 1988; Solo: Doin' That Crazy Thing; As producer / co-producer: You Got It, Roy Orbison, 1988; Into The Great Wide Open, Tom Petty, 1991; Free As A Bird, The Beatles, 1995; Real Love, The Beatles, 1995. *Honours:* Nationwide Music Award, Album of the Year, Out of The Blue, 1978; Ivor Novello Awards: Outstanding Contribution To British Music, 1979; Best Film Song, Xanadu, 1981; Grammy Award, Traveling Wilburys Vol. 1, 1989; Rolling Stone Award, Best Producer, 1989; BMI Songwriters Award, on broadcasts of Evil Woman, USA, 1992. *Membership:* ASCAP; BAC&S. *Current Management:* Craig Fruin. *Address:* PO Box 1428, Ross, CA 94957–1428, USA.

LYNNE, Shelby, (Shelby Lynn Moore); b. 22 Oct. 1968, Quantico, VA, USA. Musician (guitar); Vocalist. *Career:* Appearances on Nashville Now (TNN); Signed to Epic Records, 1988; Debut single, duet with George Jones, If I Could Bottle This Up, 1988; Signed to Morgan Creek Entertainment; Single, Killin' Kind, in film Bridget Jones's Diary, 2001. *Recordings:* Albums: Temptation, 1993; Sunrise, 1989; Tough All Over, 1990; Soft Talk, 1991; Restless, 1995; I Am Shelby Lynne, 1999; Love, Shelby, 2001. *Honours:* Grammy Award, Best Newcomer, 2001. *Address:* c/o Mercury Records, Universal Music Group, 2220 Colorado Ave, Santa Monica, CA 90404, USA. *Website:* www.islandrecords.com/shelbylynne/.

LYON, Steve; Recording Engineer; Prod; Mixer. *Career:* Trained under supervision of producer, Glyn Jones, West Sussex studio; Engineer, prod., Virgin Studio Group; Worked at The Townhouse; The Manor; Chief Engineer, Master Control, Los Angeles; Air Studios, London; Freelance, 1988–; Worked with: Depeche Mode, The Wedding Present, Nitzer Ebb, Suzanne Vega, Tears For Fears, Dave Stewart, Paul McCartney, Berlin, Prefab Sprout, UFO, Labi Siffre, Breathe, The Outfield, The Cure, The Creatures, The Dhamers, Recoil, Paradise Lost, Spooky Ruben, EMF, Reamonn, Thunder, Soul Asylum. *Current Management:* c/o Stephen Budd Management, 109b Regents Park Rd, Primrose Hill, London NW1 8UR, England. *Website:* www.record-producers.com.

LYONS, Ken, (Tigger); b. 11 April 1951, Northallerton, Yorkshire, England. Musician (bass guitar); Songwriter; Composer. m. Linda Fletcher, 19 April, 1 d. *Education:* Hammersmith College of Art and Building. *Career:* with Flesh; Melody Maker Competition Finals, The Roundhouse, 1971; with Hustler: UK Queen Tour, 1974; Status Quo European Tour, 1975; Geordie Scene; Kid Jenson's 45; Radio 1 In Concert; with London club/pub band The Brain Surgeons, 1976–79; with LA band The Shots, 1980–83; KROQ Nick Stavross Show. *Compositions include:* for Hustler: Get Outta Me House (Get Out of My

House); Little People; for Brain Surgeons: Me and My Guitar; for The Shots: Reject; Also appears on: Vineyard Sound Vol. 3, 1997. *Membership:* MCPS; PRS. *Address:* Lion Music, 29 Derby Rd, Uxbridge, Middlesex UB8 2ND, England.

LYSDAL, Jens; b. 12 Jan. 1960, Sweden. Vocalist; Musician (guitar, keyboards); Arranger; Record Prod. *Education:* Royal Danish Music Conservatory, 1981–85. *Career:* Backing musician with Superchancen DR (Denmark's radio/television company), backing artistes including Pointer Sisters; Donna Summer; Sergio Mendes, 1993; Television show, Meyerheim After 8, backing Lill Lindfors, TV2, 1994; European Song Contest as member of DR Pop-orchestra, DR, 1995; As solo singer and guitarist, Meyerheim After 8, TV 2, 1994; Bent Fabricius Bjerre's 50 year Jubilee Show, DR, 1995; Tjek Ind Hos Mygind, TV 3, 1995; Go' Morgen TV, 1998; Arranger for symphony orchestra, for Mikael Wiehe; Tamra Rosanes; Majbritte Ulrikkeholm; Peter Busborg; Kirsten Siggaard; Ulla Henningsen; Producer for Kurt Ravn and Rikke Milgaard. *Recordings:* Music for A Day In October, Kenneth Madsen film, 1990; Solo album: A Matter of Time; Music for film: The Treasure of the Forest by Nicolas Gaster; Mr Who, by Michael Brammer, 1999; Producer/ arranger for Poul Dissing, Alberte, with Denmark Radio Symphony Orchestra, 2000. *Honours:* Arnold, for music to commercial, Kim's Peanuts; Winner, Golden Stag, Romania; CD of the Year, 1997. *Membership:* DJBFA. *Current Management:* Musik and Sang, Wildersgade 56, 1408 Copenhagen, Denmark. *E-mail:* j.lysdal@mobilixnet.dk.

LYTLE, Marshall; b. 1933, Old Fort, North Carolina, USA. Musician (upright bass); Vocalist. Married. *Career:* Original member, Bill Hayley's Comets, 1948–55; Invented rock 'n' roll; First rock band to headline a film; Member, The Jodimans, 1955–58. *Recordings:* Rock Around The Clock; See You Later Alligator; Crazy Man Crazy; Shake Rattle and Roll; Rock The Joint; Mambo Rock; Rudy's Rock; Florida Twist; Skinny Minnie; Let's All Rock Together; Now Dig This; From the Original Master Tapes; Decca Years and More. *Publications:* Rock Around The Clock; Stage Clear; We're Gonna Party; Never Too Old To Rock. *Honours:* Rock and Roll Hall of Fame; Gold records; Best vocal group of 1953. *Address:* Rock It Concerts, Bruno Mefer Platz 1, SU937 Munchen, Germany.

LYTTELTON, Humphrey Richard Adeane; b. 23 May 1921, Eton, Buckinghamshire, England. Bandleader; Jazz Musician (trumpet); Journalist; Broadcaster; Author. m. (1) Patricia Braithwaite, 1948, divorced, (2) Elizabeth Richardson, 1952, 2 s., 2 d. *Education:* Camberwell School of Art; Piano lessons. *Career:* Member, George Webb's Dixielanders, 1947; Bandleader, own band, 1948–; Festival appearances include: Nice; Zurich; Montreux; Warsaw; Newcastle; Edinburgh; Glasgow; Recorded and played with artistes including: Sidney Bechet; Buck Clayton; Buddy Tate; Helen Shapiro; Kenny Davern; Jimmy Rushing; Big Joe Turner; Founder, own record label, Calligraph, 1984; Owner, music publishing company Humph Music; Numerous television and radio appearances as musician and presenter; Compère, BBC radio programmes: Jazz Club; Jazz Scene; The Best of Jazz; I'm Sorry I Haven't A Clue; Freelance music journalist and critic. *Compositions:* Numerous original compositions. *Recordings:* Numerous albums include: Delving Back and Forth with Humph, 1948; Jazz at the Royal Festival Hall, 1951; Some Like it Hot, 1955; Echoes of Harlem, 1981; This Old Gang of Ours, 1985; Beano Boogie, 1989; Rock me Gently, 1991; Rent Party, 1991; At Sundown, 1992; features on: Amnesiac, Radiohead, 2001. *Publications:* I Play As I Please, 1954; Second Chorus, 1958; Take It From The Top, 1975; The Best of Jazz: Basin Street To Harlem, 1978; Humphrey Lyttelton's Jazz and Big Band Quiz, 1979; The Best of Jazz 2: Enter The Giants, 1981; Why No Beethoven?, 1984. *Contributions to:* Melody Maker; Harpers and Queen; Punch; High Life. *Honours:* Hon DLitt, Warwick, 1987; Loughborough, 1988; Hon DMus, Durham, 1989; Keele, 1992; Hon. Professor of Music, Keele, 1993; Sony Gold Award, radio awards, 1993; DLitt, University of Hertfordshire, 1995; Waterford Crystal Award, IEAN, 1996; DArts, De Montfort University, 1997. *Current Management:* Susan Da Costa, Bull's Head Row, The Green, Surrey RH9 8DZ, England.

M

M. K. SHINE, (Mark Lowe); b. England. Vocalist; Songwriter; Reggae Club Owner. *Education:* Certificate, Building Construction, College, Jamaica; School of Music, London. *Career:* Lead singer, founder, Destiny, with brother, 1986; Played round islands; Played Tokyo, 1989; Solo artist, using name M K Shine, 1991–; 2 week tour, Mexico, special guest at Rock Y Reggae Festival; Television, radio interviews. *Recordings:* Wild Gilbert, 1988; My Dream, 1994; Simply Magic. *Honours:* Represented Jamaica, Caribbean Broadcasting Union, 1990. *Current Management:* Sirron Kyles, Samuel Rogers and Associates. *Address:* PO Box 8305, Houston, TX 77288, USA.

MAAETOFT, Nils; b. 17 Nov. 1950, Vejle, Denmark. Vocalist; Songwriter; Musician (guitar). *Career:* Singer, guitarist, main songwriter for Danish rock group The Intellectuals; Wrote, performed, under pseudonym M. T. Purse; 1992, formed group M. T. Purse. *Recordings:* with The Intellectuals: Half A-Live, 1986; Health and Happiness, 1987; as M. T. Purse: Cross Talk, 1992; Throwing Rocks At The Moon, 1995. *Membership:* The Danish Society for Jazz Rock Folk Composers. *Current Management:* c/o Warner/Chappell Music, Denmark. *Address:* Anker Heegaardsgade 2, 1572 Copenhagen, Denmark.

MAAL, Baaba; b. 1953, Podor, Senegal. Vocalist; Musician (guitar); Songwriter. *Education:* Dakar Conservatoire; Conservatoire des Beaux Arts, Paris. *Career:* Formed band Daande Lenol; Regular collaborations with Mansour Seck; Representative of United Nations Development Programme speaking out on the issue of HIV/AIDS in Africa; Involved with HIV/AIDS awareness campaign music projects: Red Hot and Gershwin; Fela Kuti tribute Red Hot and Riot. *Recordings:* Albums include: Djam Leelii, 1989; Lam Toro, 1993; Tono, 1994; Sunugal, 1995; Firin' In Fouta, 1995; Nomad Soul, 1998; Missing You—Mi Yeewnii (produced by John Leckie, featuring Mansour Seck, Kante Manfila and Kaouding Cissokho), 2001. *Honours:* Froots Critic Poll, Best New Album, Missing You—Mi Yeewnii, 2001. *Address:* c/o Palm Pictures, 8 Kensington Park Rd, London W11 3BU, England.

MAAS, Timo; b. Germany. Prod; Remixer; DJ. *Career:* Made breakthrough as resident DJ at The Tunnel, Hamburg; Produced Die Herdplatte with fellow resident Gary D, which led to recordings with Bristol's Hope Recordings; In-demand remixer; Holds club residency at New York's Twilo; Remixed: Madonna; Azzido Da Bass; Placebo; Fatboy Slim. *Recordings:* Albums: Loud, Music For The Maases, 2001. Singles: Die Herdplatte, 1995; Mama Konda, 1998; Der Schieber, 1999; Better Make Room, 2000; Island, 2001; Shifter, 2002. *Honours:* German Dance Award, Best National DJ, 2001. *Address:* c/o Perfecto Records, 1 Shorrolds Rd, London SW6 7TR, England.

MABUS, Joel Dwight; b. 13 Sept. 1953, Belleville, Illinois, USA. Vocalist; Songwriter; Musician (guitar, banjo, fiddle, mandolin). *Education:* Michigan State University. *Career:* Vancouver Folk Festival; Philadelphia Folk Festival; Winnipeg Folk Festival; Kerrville Folk Festival; Appearances on: A Prairie Home Companion, American public radio. *Recordings:* 10 solo. *Recordings include:* Promised Land; Flatpick and Clawhammer; Short Stories; Six Of One; Also appears on: Old Time Music on the Air, 1996. *Publications:* Big Words – The Lyrics of Joel Mabus. *Honours:* Detroit Metro Times, Instrumentalist of the Year. *Membership:* AFofM; The Folk Alliance. *Address:* c/o Fossil Records, PO Box 4754, East Lansing, MI 48826, USA. *Website:* www.joelmabus.com.

MABY, Graham Geoffrey; b. 1 Sept. 1952, Gosport, Hampshire, England. Musician (bass guitar, guitar); Vocalist. m. Mary Beth Bernard, 15 Feb. 1987, 2 s., 1 d. *Education:* 1 year technical college. *Career:* Performances, live, television, video, with: Joe Jackson; Marshall Crenshaw; Graham Parker; Jules Shear; Garland Jeffreys; The Silos; Freedy Johnston; Darden Smith; Chris Stamey; Peter Holsapple; Delevantes; They Might Be Giants; Henry Lee Summer; Glen Burtnik; Shania Twain; Film: Peggy Sue Got Married, 1986; Tours mainly with Joe Jackson: Europe; North America; Japan; Australia; Laughter and Lust Tour, now on Virgin Video. *Recordings:* with Joe Jackson: Look Sharp, 1978; I'm The Man, 1979; Beat Crazy, 1980; Jumpin' Jive, 1981; Night and Day, 1982; Mike's Murder, 1983; Body and Soul, 1984; Live '79–84, 1987; Blaze of Glory, 1989; Laughter and Lust, 1991; Night Music, 1994; Summer In The City, 2000; Night And Day II, 2000; with Marshall Crenshaw: Mary Jean and Nine Others, 1987; Good Evening, 1989; My Truck Is My Home, 1994; with Freedy Johnston: Can You Fly, 1991; This Perfect World, 1994; with Chris Stamey: It's Alright, 1987; Fireworks, 1991; with Henry Lee Summer: Henry Lee Summer, 1988; I've Got Everything, 1989; with David Broza: A Time of Trains, 1993; Second Street, 1994; Little Victories, Darden Smith, 1993; with They Might Be Giants: John Henry, 1994; Why Does the Sun Shine, 1994; Factory Showroom, 1996; Severe Tire Damage, 1998; Also with: Patty Smyth; Graham Parker; Jules Shear; Jill Sobule; David Wilcox. *Honours:* Gold records include: Night and Day; Look Sharp; Body and Soul. *Membership:* ASCAP; AFTRA; AFofM.

MAC DONNCHA, Johnny Mháirtín Learaí; b. 9 April 1937, Galway, Ireland. Small Farmer; Craftsman; Vocalist. *Career:* Sean-nós singer, Specializing in traditional Irish songs, many from West Connemara; Travelled throughout Ireland as singer; Collects and teaches songs; Winner in Corn Uí Riada, Oirreachtas, Cork, 1985. *Recordings:* Bruach Na Beirtrí; Cassette, 1988; Album, 1993; Contae Mhuigheo. *Honours:* Corn Uí Riada, Winner, Cork, 1985. *Current Management:* Cló Iar-Chonnachta, Indreabhán, Co Na Gaillimhe, Ireland.

MCALL, Barnaby Jonathon; b. 3 Jan. 1966, Box Hill, Victoria, Australia. Jazz Musician (piano). *Education:* Studied Literature, Melbourne University; Graduated, Victorian College of the Arts, Bachelor of Music; Studied in New York City with Barry Harris, Mulgren Miller, Dave Kikoski, Chucho Valdez. *Career:* Toured Europe, 3 times, playing major festivals including Montreax, North Sea, 1996; Played Blue Note, Tokyo, Japan with the Groove collective; Extensive touring of Italy, Canada; Wrote music for stage show, Solstice, part of Adelaide International Festival. *Compositions:* Hindered on his way to heaven; Exit. *Recordings:* Exit, CD; Widening Circles, CD, featuring Billy Harper; Live At The Jazz Standard NYC, with Gary Bartz Quartet. *Honours:* Best Jazz Composition, APRA, 1993; First Prize, National Jazz Piano Competition. *Current Management:* Martin Jackson, 16 Neave St, Hawthorn 3122, Victoria, Australia. *Address:* 97 Pembroke Rd, Mooroolbark 3138, Victoria, Australia.

MCALMONT, David; Vocalist; Lyricist. *Career:* Singer, duo Thieves (later as McAlmont), 1993; Member, duo McAlmont and Butler (with Bernard Butler), 1994–95; Appearances include: Phoenix '95 Festival, 1995. *Recordings:* Albums: with McAlmont and Butler: The Sound of McAlmont and Butler, 1995; Bring It Back, 2002; Solo: McAlmont, 1994; Working, 2001; With David Arnold, Shaken and Stirred, 1997; Singles: Solo: Either, 1994; Honey, 1998; with McAlmont and Butler: Yes, 1995; You Do, 1995. *Address:* c/o MRM Productions, 9–11 Liverpool Rd, Islington, London N1 0RP, England.

MCALOON, Paddy (Patrick Joseph); b. 7 June 1957, England. Musician; Vocalist; Songwriter. *Education:* BA, English and History, Ushaw College, Co Durham, University of Northumbria. *Career:* Singer, songwriter, Prefab Sprout; Extensive tours: UK; Europe; Japan; Numerous television appearances. *Compositions:* Songs covered by Kylie Minogue; Jimmy Nail; The Zombies; Cher; Contributed songs to television series Crocodile Shoes and Where the Heart Is. *Recordings:* Singles include: Lions In My Own Garden, 1983; Don't Sing, 1984; Couldn't Bear To Be Special, 1984; When Love Breaks Down, 1984; Faron Young, 1985; Appetite, 1985; Johnny Johnny, 1986; Cars And Girls, 1988; The King Of Rock N Roll, 1988; Hey! Manhattan, 1988; Nightingales, 1988; The Golden Calf, 1989; Looking For Atlantis, 1990; We Let The Stars Go, 1990; Carnival 2000, 1990; The Sound of Crying, 1992; If You Don't Love Me, 1992; Life Of Surprises, 1993; All The World Loves Lovers, 1993; A Prisoner Of The Past, 1997; Electirc Guitars, 1997; Albums include: Swoon, 1984; Steve McQueen, 1985; From Langley Park To Memphis, 1988; Protest Songs, 1989; Jordan – The Comeback, 1990; Life of Surprises: Best of Prefab Sprout, 1992; Andromeda Heights, 1997; The Gunman And Other Stories, 2001. *Membership:* BAC&S. *Current Management:* Keith Armstrong, Kitchenware Records. *Address:* St Thomas St Stables, Newcastle Upon Tyne, England.

MACALPINE, Tony; b. USA. Rock Musician (guitar, piano). *Education:* Classical piano. *Career:* Solo artiste, rock guitarist, 1986–90; Formed MARS, short-lived supergroup, 1987; Founder, Squawk record label; Formed won band MacAlpine, 1990–. *Recordings:* Albums: Solo artiste: Edge of Insanity, 1986; Maximum Security, 1987; with MARS: Project Driver, 1987; with MacAlpine: Eyes of The World, 1990; Freedom to Fly, 1992; Madness, 1994; Premonition, 1994; Evolution, 1995; Master of Paradise, 1999; CAB, 2000; CAB2, 2000; Chromaticity, 2001. *Website:* www.tonymacalpine.com.

MCANDREW, Ian; b. 20 Oct. 1966, Sudbury, Suffolk, England. Artist Man. *Career:* Manager of artists and producers; Founded Wildlife Entertainment, 1986; Manager, Tasmin Archer; The Brand New Heavies; Bomb The Bass; Carleen Anderson; Tim Simenon; Travis; Conner Reeves. *Recordings:* 13 hits from 14 releases. *Honours:* 2 Platinum discs; 3 Gold discs; 1 Silver disc. *Membership:* Council Mem., International Managers Forum. *Address:* Wildlife Entertainment Ltd, 21 Heathmans Rd, Parsons Green, London SW6 4TJ, England.

MCATHEY, Brent; b. 4 Aug. 1967, Calgary, Alberta, Canada. Vocalist; Songwriter. *Career:* Performs solo with prerecorded tracks or with 5 piece band in Canada; 7 piece Nashville Band in USA, Europe; Opened for: Joan Kennedy; Dick Damron; Michelle Wright; Prairie Oyster; Television: Capitol Country; Up and Coming; The Breakfast Show; Christmas Special; Radio: Canadian Super Country. *Recordings:* Brent McAthey, 9 songs composed by

McAthey; Waitin' For The Sun, 1994, 3 songs by McAthey, 1 song co-written and duet with Dick Damron, 7 by Nashville Writers; Believe in Me. *Publications:* The Brent McAthey International Fan Club Newsletter. *Honours:* Alberta's Male Recording Artist of the Year, Alberta Recording Industry Asscn, 1994–95. *Membership:* Country Music Asscn of Calgary; Alberta Recording Industry Asscn; Canadian Music Asscn; CMA, Nashville; Texas Country Music Asscn; Arts Touring Alliance of Alberta; Canadian Asscn of Fairs and Exhibitions; Calgary Convention and Visitors Bureau; International Fan Club Organization. *Current Management:* PO Box 831, Black Diamond, AB T0L 0H0, Canada.

MCAULEY, Jackie; b. 14 Dec. 1946, Coleraine, Belfast, Northern Ireland. Musician (guitar); Songwriter. *Career:* Member, Them (with Van Morrison), aged 17; Founder member, Cult; Belfast Gypsies (with brother Pat); Trader Horn; Also solo artiste; Mem., The Poor Mouth. *Compositions:* Dear John, recorded by Status Quo (No. 1, UK charts), 1982; 2 No. 1 recordings with the Heptones; Other. *Recordings include:* Jackie McAuley Plus; Bad Day At Black Rock.

MCAULIFFE, Kim; b. 13 April 1959, England. Vocalist; Musician (guitar). *Career:* Founder mem., heavy metal band Painted Lady, with Enid Williams; Joined by Kelly Johnson and Denise Dufort, 1978, band renamed Girlschool; Introduced to management deal with Bronze label by Lemmy from Motörhead, 1980; Supported Motörhead on their Overkill tour; Numerous tours, television performances and hit singles; Further collaborations with Motörhead; Tours in Canada and the USA; Tour of Russia, supporting Black Sabbath; Band splits, 1989; Worked with Beki Bondage; Presenter, cable show Raw Power; Formed band Strangegirls, with Toyah, Denise Dufort and Enid Williams; Girlschool re-formed, 1992. *Recordings:* Albums: Demolition, 1980; Hit 'N' Run, 1981; Screaming Blue Murder, 1982; Play Dirty, 1983; Running Wild, 1995; Nightmare At Maple Cross, 1986; Take A Bite, 1988; Girlschool, 1992; Live, 1995; Race With The Devil (Live), 1998; Live On The King Biscuit Flower Hour, 1998; Can't Keep A Good Girl Down, 1999; Very Best Of Remastered, 2002; 21st Anniversary: Not That Innocent, 2002. Singles: Take It All Away; Race With The Devil; St Valentine's Day Massacre (EP with Motörhead, as Headgirl); Please Don't Touch, 1981; Hit 'n' Run, 1981; C'mon Let's Go, 1981; I'm The Leader Of The Gang (I Am) (with Gary Glitter). *Address:* c/o PO Box 33446, London SW18 3XN, England. *Website:* www.girlschool.co.uk.

MCBEAN, Colin, (Mr G, Innersound, Mango Boy); b. London, England. Prod; Remixer; DJ. *Career:* Started as DJ with London's KCC crew; Met Cisco Ferreira and started recording together, 1990; Formed The Advent; First release, 1994; The Advent split, 1999; Continued as solo artist, Mr G; Remixed: New Order; Lottie; Roger Sanchez; Hatiras. *Recordings:* Albums: with The Advent: Elements of Life, 1995; A New Beginning, 1997; Singles: solo: Get It Got It Good EP, Moments, Homeward Bound, 2001. *Address:* c/o Duty Free Recordings, Third Floor, 67 Farringdon Rd, London EC1M 3JB, England.

MCBRIDE, Martina; b. 29 July 1966, Medicine Lodge, Kansas, USA. Country Vocalist. m. John McBride, 2 d. *Career:* World-wide concert tours. *Recordings:* Albums: The Time Has Come, 1992; The Way That I Am, 1993; Wild Angels, 1995; Evolution, 1997; White Christmas, 1998; Emotion, 1999; White Christmas, 1999; Greatest Hits, 2001. *Honours:* CMA Video of the Year, 1994–95; CMA Song of the Year, 1995; Music Row Industry Awards Breakthrough Video; Nammy Award, Video of the Year; Nashville Music Awards, 1995–6; CMA Female Vocalist of the Year, 1999; American Music Award, Best Female Country Artist, 2003. *Address:* Bruce Allen Talent, 406–68 Water St, Vancouver, BC V6B 1A4, Canada.

MCBRIDE, Sean David; b. 7 Sept. 1953, San Francisco. Musician (saxophone, flute, clarinet); Vocalist; Writer; Arranger; Instrument Teacher. m. Jean McBride, 1 s., 2 d. *Education:* BA, Essex University. *Career:* Progression of bands covering different styles of Rock Music, Soul, Reggae, Rock 'n' Roll, Blues and Boogie; Permanent tour with That'll Be The Day, 7 years; Sessions and other media work; Public and private music tuition, Bath and NE Somerset; New Deal for Musicians advisor. *Membership:* Musicians' Union; Equity; PRS; NASUWT. *Address:* 9 Tidenham Way, Bristol, BS34 5LA, England. *Telephone:* (117) 969-0565. *E-mail:* seanmcbride@blueyonder.co.uk.

MCBRIDE, Terry; b. Canada. Artiste Management Exec; Prod. *Career:* Founder, CEO, Nettwerk Productions, originally as a record label, later artist management, television, etc.; Clients incl.: Dido, Avril Lavigne, Sarah McLachlan, Sum 41, US representation for Coldplay, Stereophonics. *Address:* Nettwerk Productions, 1650 W Second Ave, Vancouver, BC V6J 4R3, Canada. *E-mail:* info@nettwerk.com. *Website:* www.nettwerk.com.

MCBROOM, Amanda; b. 9 Aug. 1947, Los Angeles, California, USA. Songwriter; Playwright; Vocalist; Actress. m. George Ball, 1 Dec. 1974. *Education:* BA, Drama, University of Texas. *Career:* Television: Mash; Star Trek; Hawaii 5-0; See-Saw, Broadway; Jacques Brel, Off-Broadway; Several appearances on The Tonight Show; Carnegie Hall; Rainbow and Stars; The Russian Tea Room; Greek Theatre; Great American Music Hall; Kennedy Center. *Compositions include:* The Rose. *Recordings:* Growing Up In Hollywood Town; West of Oz; Dreaming; Midnight Matinee; Amanda McBroom Live At Rainbow and Stars; Heartbeats-the cast album; Waiting Heart; Portraits: Best of Amanda McBroom, 1999. *Honours:* Golden Globe Award, Best Film Song, The Rose, 1980. *Membership:* Actors Equity Asscn; Screen Actors Guild; NAS. *Current Management:* Garry George Management.

MCCABE, Nick; Musician (guitar). *Career:* Founder Member, The Verve, 1990; Obtained record deal, 1991; Support slots to The Black Crowes in USA; Numerous live dates including Lollapalooza tour, 1994, and T in the Park festival; Band split; Rejoined, 1997; More live dates including Reading Festival, 1997; Split again, 1999. *Recordings:* Singles: She's A Superstar, 1992; Gravity Grave, 1992; All in the Mind, 1992; Slide Away, 1993; Blue, 1993; This is Music, 1995; On Your Own, 1995; History, 1995; Bittersweet Symphony, 1997; Lucky Man, 1997; The Drugs Don't Work (No. 1, UK), 1997; Albums: A Storm in Heaven, 1993; No Come Down, 1994; A Northern Soul, 1995; Urban Hymns (No. 1, UK), 1997; Guitar on: Prochaine Fois, Neotropic, 2001. *Honours:* BRIT Awards, Best British Group, Best British Album, 1998.

MCCAFFERTY, Dan; Vocalist. *Career:* Founder member, Scottish rock group Nazareth, 1968–; Regular tours, UK, USA, Europe. *Recordings:* Albums: Nazareth, 1971; Exercises, 1972; Razamanaz, 1973; Loud 'N' Proud, 1974; Rampant, 1974; Hair of The Dog, 1975; Greatest Hits, 1975; Hot Tracks, 1976; Close Enough For Rock 'N' Roll, 1976; Playin' The Game, 1976; Expect No Mercy, 1977; No Mean City, 1978; Malice In Wonderland, 1980; The Fool Circle, 1981; 'Snaz, 1981; 2XS, 1982; Sound Elixir, 1983; The Catch, 1984; 20 Greatest Hits, 1985; Play The Game, 1985; Anthology – Nazareth, 1988; The Early Years, 1992; No Jive, 1992; From The Vaults, 1993; Move Me, 1995; Nazareth: Greatest Hits, 1996; Live at the Beeb, 1998; Boogaloo, 1998; Back To The Trenches, 2001; Singles include: Broken Down Angel, 1973; Bad Bad Boy, 1973; This Flight Tonight, 1973; My White Bicycle, 1975; Love Hurts, 1977; May The Sunshine, 1979. *Current Management:* c/o Variety Artists International Inc, 846 Higuera St, Suite 5, San Luis Obispo, CA 93403, USA.

MCCANN, Eamon; b. Creggan, Omagh, Northern Ireland. Vocalist; Musician (guitar). m. Margaret, 28 July 1979, 1 s., 3 d. *Education:* FTC; IRTE. *Career:* Television appearances include: RTE TV: Kenny Live; Live At 3; Its Bibi; Play The Game; Live From The Olympia; Lifelines; The Big Top; Summer Cabaret; Cúrsaí; Country Cool; Winning Streak; A Stretch in the Evening; Southern Nights; The Lyric Board; Anderson On The Box, Breakfast TV, PK to Right, Anderson on the Road, BBC; Kelly, UTV; Scotch 'N' Irish, Grampian Television; Radio appearances: Live on National Music Day, BBC Radio 2, 1994; RTE Radio 1; 2 FM; DTR; BBC Radio Ulster. *Compositions:* Joseph's Dream, 1998. *Recordings:* Everything That I Am; Can't Break It To My Heart; Bunch of Bright Red Roses; Gold In The Mountains; I Give You Music; I've Gone Crazy/Happy Birthday, CD single; Touch Wood, CD album; I Will Love You ('Til This Ring Turns Green); Clear Cut Country, CD Album. *Publications:* Don't Call Me; When You Come To Land; Life After You; Love Is Blind; The Gift of Love; Bunch of Bright Red Roses; Everything That I Am; More Than Two Weeks; The Love From Loneliness; Touch Wood; Exactly What I meant; Do I Really Have to Tell You That I Love You; My Home Ireland; I've Gone Crazy; Happy Birthday. *Honours:* Irish Showcase Award, Best New Male Singer, 1992; Northern Sound Radio, Best Male Singer, 1993; Donegal CMC, Best Male Singer, 1993, 1994; Rehab, Person of the Year, 1992; Ready Penny Inn, Best Male Singer of New Country, 1994, 1995; Personalities Entertainment Magazine Awards: Best Singer/Songwriter, 1995–96, Best Singer of New Country, 1995–96, Favourite Male Entertainer, 1996–97; Doubla K CMC Band of the Year, Dumfries, Scotland, 1996–97; Personalities Entertainment Magazine Awards Best Album, 1997–98; Irish World Awards Best Country Singer, 1997–98. *Membership:* PRS; IMRO. *Current Management:* 21st Century Promotions. *Address:* 8 Forthill Rd, Enniskillen, County Fermanagh BT74 6AW, Northern Ireland.

MCCANN, Les, (Leslie Coleman); b. 23 Sept. 1935, Lexington, Kentucky, USA. Musician (piano, trumpet, keyboards). m. Charlotte Acentia Watkins, 1 s., 3 d. *Education:* LA City College; Westlake College of Music; LA City College. *Career:* White House Concert, with Aretha Franklin, 1994; Soul To Soul; African Tour and Movie; Tonight Show; Arsenio Hall Show; ROC, Fox TV; Ed Sullivan Show, CBS; Sunday Morning, CBS; Jazz Central, BET TV; Hands Across America; All major jazz festivals. *Recordings:* 84 albums; Much Les, 1968; Swiss Movement, 1969; Recent releases include: On the Soul Side, 1994; Listen Up, 1995; Pacifique, 1998; Second Movement, 1998; Pump It Up, 2002; With Lou Rawls: Stormy Monday, 1962; with Yousef Lateef: Anthology, 1994; Featured on Atlantic Jazz Classics, 1998; Jazz for When You're Alone, 1999; Features on: Bill Eavns, Soul Insider, 2001. *Publications:* Musican As Artist (paintings). *Honours:* First person chosen to teach at Harvard University: Artist As Performer. *Membership:* BMI; ASCAP. *Current Management:* Fred Hirsch Management.

MCCANN, Peter; Songwriter; Vocalist. *Education:* Graduate, Fairfield University, Connecticut, 1970. *Career:* Signed to Motown Records, 1971; 20th Century Fox Records, 1977 (bought by CBS, 1978); Moved to Nashville, 1985; Association with EMI music publishing; Songs recorded by: Julio Iglesias; Anne Murray; Crystal Gayle; Kenny Rogers; Oak Ridge Boys; Isaac Hayes; K

T Oslin; Lynn Anderson; Ricky Nelson; Andy Williams; Paul Anka; Karen Carpenter; Whitney Houston; Kathy Mattea; Lectures on songwriting for music organizations. *Recordings:* Do You Wanna Make Love?, Peter McCann, 1977; The Right Time of The Night, Jennifer Warnes, 1977; One on One, 1979; She's Single Again, Janie Fricke (No. 1); Nobody Falls Like A Fool, Earl Thomas Conley (No. 1); Treat Me Like A Stranger, Baillie and the Boys; What Christmas Really Means, 1995. *Membership:* Vice-president, Nashville Songwriters Asscn, Co-chair, Legislative committee. *Current Management:* SESAC. *Address:* 55 Music Sq. E, Nashville, TN 37203, USA.

MCCARROLL, Tony; Musician (drums). *Career:* Founder mem., Rain, with Paul McGuigan and Paul Arthurs; Joined by Liam Gallagher and changed band name to Oasis; Joined by Noel Gallagher; Debut performance, Boardwalk, Manchester, 1991; Numerous support slots to The Milltown Brothers, BMX Bandits, The Verve, Liz Phair, The Real People, Dodgy; Signed to Creation Records, 1993; Numerous tours and television appearances; Festival dates; Left band, 1995. *Recordings:* Album: Definitely Maybe, 1994.

MCCARTNEY, Michelle; b. 5 April 1960, Paris, France. Vocalist; Musician (bass guitar). *Career:* Pop rock/folk singer; Major tour with Jackie Lomax (legendary blues performer); Television appearances, USA; Many radio interviews in America; Performed at major US Theatres, International Trade Shows; Tours, major US college and university circuit. *Recordings:* Singles: Everybody Wants My Man; Rocomotion; Money For Honey; Michelle; Billet-Doux; Till I Get You Back. *Publications:* The Beatles Book, UK fanzine. *Honours:* Best Dee-Jay Pop Pick in USA, for Till I Get You Back, 1993. *Membership:* ASCAP. *Current Management:* Allstar Management Incorporated. *Address:* 189 rue du Temple, 75003 Paris, France.

MCCARTNEY, Sir Paul; b. 18 June 1942, Liverpool, England. Vocalist; Songwriter; Musician (bass, piano, organ, trumpet). m. (1) Linda Eastman, 12 March 1969, deceased April 1998, 1 s., 2 d., 1 step-d.; (2) Heather Mills, 11 June 2002. *Career:* Mem., The Quarrymen, 1956–59; The Beatles, 1960–70; World-wide tours with The Beatles, 1963–66; Attended Transcendental Meditation Course, Maharishi's Academy, India, 1968; Founder, Apple Ltd, after collapse of Apple Corpn Ltd, 1970; Formed MPL Group of Companies, 1970; Solo artiste, 1970–; Founder, group Wings, 1971–81; Released film, album, Give My Regards to Broad Street, 1984; Founder, Liverpool Institute of Performing Arts, 1995; US Solo tour, 2002; Golden Jubilee Concert, Party at the Palace, Buckingham Palace grounds, 2002. *Compositions:* Co-writer, songs with John Lennon include: Love Me Do; Please Please Me; From Me To You; She Loves You; Can't Buy Me Love; I Want To Hold Your Hand; I Saw Her Standing There; Eight Days A Week; All My Loving; Help!; Ticket To Ride; I Feel Fine; A Hard Day's Night; Yesterday; Eleanor Rigby; Yellow Submarine; Penny Lane; All You Need Is Love; Lady Madonna; Hey Jude; We Can Work It Out; Day Tripper; Paperback Writer; When I'm Sixty-Four; A Day In The Life; Back In The USSR; Hello Goodbye; Get Back; Let It Be; Later. *Compositions:* Band On The Run; Mull of Kintyre; Coming Up; Ebony and Ivory; No More Lonely Nights; Pipes Of Peace; Other works include: Give My Regards To Broad Street (film score), 1984; Liverpool Oratorio, conducted by Carl Davis, 1991; Standing Stone (orchestral work), commisioned for EMI Centenary celebrations, debut by LSO at Albert Hall, London, 1997. *Recordings:* Albums: with the Beatles: Please Please Me, 1963; With The Beatles; A Hard Day's Night, 1964; Beatles For Sale, 1964; Help!, 1965; Rubber Soul, 1965; Revolver, 1966; Sgt Pepper's Lonely Hearts Club Band, 1967; Magical Mystery Tour, 1967; The Beatles (White Album), 1968; Yellow Submarine, 1969; Abbey Road, 1969; Let It Be, 1970; 1962–1966 (Red Album), 1973; 1967–1970 (Blue Album), 1973; Past Masters Vol. One, 1988; Past Masters Vol. Two, 1988; The Beatles Anthology: 1, 1995; The Beatles Anthology: 2, 1996; The Beatles Anthology: 3, 1996; 1, 2000; Numerous other anthologies; with Wings: Wild Life, 1971; Red Rose Speedway, 1973; Band On The Run, 1973; Venus and Mars, 1975; Wings At The Speed of Sound, 1976; Wings Over America, 1976; London Town, 1978; Wings Greatest, 1978; Back To The Egg, 1979; Wingspan, 2001; Solo: McCartney, 1970; Ram, 1971; McCartney II, 1980; Tug Of War, 1982; Pipes Of Peace, 1983; Give My Regards To Broad Street, 1984; Press To Play, 1986; All The Best!, 1987; Flowers In The Dirt, 1989; Tripping The Live Fantastic, 1990; Unplugged, 1991; CHOBA B CCCP: The Russian Album, 1991; Paul McCartney's Liverpool Oratorio, 1991; Off The Ground, 1993; Paul Is Live, 1993; Flaming Pie, 1997; Standing Stone, 1997; Run Devil Run, 1999; Working Classical, 1999; A Garland for Linda (with eight other composers), 2000; Driving Rain, 2001; Back In The US: Live, 2002. *Honours:* M.B.E., 1965; Numerous Grammy Awards; Guinness Book of Records Award, most successful composer to date, 1979; Ivor Novello Awards, International Achievement, 1980, International Hit of the Year, for Ebony and Ivory, 1982; Outstanding Contribution to Music, 1989; Freeman, City of Liverpool, 1984; Q Merit Award, 1990; K.B.E., 1997. *Address:* c/o MPL Communications, 1 Soho Sq., London W1V 6BQ, England. *Website:* www.paulmccartney.com.

MCCARY, Michael Shawn 'Bass'; b. 16 Dec. 1971, Philadelphia, PA, USA. *Education:* Philadelphia High School of Creative and Performing Arts. *Career:* Mem., Boyz II Men, 1988–; Established Stonecreek label; Signed to Arista Records. *Recordings:* Albums: Cooleyhighharmony, 1993; II, 1995; Evolución,

1997; Nathan Michael Shawn Wanya, 2000; Full Circle, 2002. Singles: Motownphilly, 1991; I'll Make Love To You; On Bended Knee; One Sweet Day (with Mariah Carey, No. 1, USA). *Address:* c/o Arista Records, 6 W 57th St, New York, USA. *Website:* www.boyziimen.com.

MCCAULEY, John(ny); b. 23 April 1925, Co Derry, Northern Ireland. Songwriter; Vocalist; Musician (guitar). m. Phyllis, 25 June 1949, 1 s. *Education:* Weekly music education class (voluntary), St Eugene's School. *Career:* Over 70 Country and Irish songs recorded by many major artists in Ireland including many No 1 hits; Songs recorded by Daniel O'Donnell, Big Tom, Larry Cunningham, Brian Coll, Declan Nearney, Margo, Philomena Begley; Formed, Johnny McCauley Trio. *Compositions include:* Among the Wicklow Hills; My Donegal Shore; 5000 Miles from Sligo; Just Pretending; Any Tipperary Town; Pretty Girl from Omagh; Destination Donegal. *Recordings:* From Ireland Country Style EP, which introduced Country 'n' Irish music. *Publications:* Skiff Rock, Beginner's Guitar Tutor, 1957. *Honours:* Honoured by Lord Mayor of Derry; 73rd birthday celebration featured many famous Irish artists; Lifetime Achievement Award, 1998. *Membership:* MCPS; PRS; BAC&S; IMRO. *Address:* 112 Preston Hill, Kenton, Harrow, Middlesex HA3 9SJ, England.

MCCLAIN, Charly (Charlotte Denise); b. 26 March 1956, Jackson, Tennessee, USA, Country vocalist; Songwriter; Actor. m. Wayne Massey, July 1984. *Career:* Sang with brother in Charlotte and the Volunteers, age 9; Worked on the mid-South Jamboree 1973–75; Changed name to Charly and modelled swimsuits, early 1970s; Toured with country singer OB McClinton; Signed to Epic, 1976; 39 Billboard country chart entries on Epic and Mercury Records until 1989; Collaborations: Johnny Rodriguez; Mickey Gilley; Wayne Massey; TV appearances include: Hart To Hart; CHIPS; Austin City Limits; Fantasy Island; Solid Gold; So You Want To Be A Star. *Recordings include:* Radio Heart, 1985; Paradise Tonight (with Mickey Gilley), 1983; Who's Cheatin' Who, 1980; Sentimental Ol' You, 1983; Dancing Your Memory Away, 1982; Albums: The Woman In Me, 1984; It Takes Believers (with Mickey Gilley), 1984; Surround Me With Love, 1981. *Honours:* Music City News, Most Promising Female Vocalist, 1981. *Address:* c/o John D Lentz, PO Box 198888, Nashville, TN 37219, USA.

MCCLARNON, Liz (Elizabeth Margaret); b. 10 April 1981, Liverpool, England. Vocalist. *Career:* Mem., Atomic Kitten, 1999–; UK Support tours 1999–2000; Co-spearheaded MTV Asia Awards, 2000; Pan-European breakthrough with Whole Again single; Guest at Celebrate South Africa Freedom Concert, London, 2001; Appearance, Party at the Palace, Buckingham Palace Jubilee celebrations, 2002. *Recordings:* Albums: Right Now, 2000 (reissue 2001); Feels So Good, 2002. Singles: Right Now, 1999; See Ya, 2000; I Want Your Love, 2000; Follow Me, 2000; Whole Again, 2001; Eternal Flame, 2001; It's OK, 2002; Tide Is High, 2002; Last Goodbye/Be With You, 2002. *Current Management:* Integral Management, 51–55 Highfield St, Liverpool L3 6AA, England. *Address:* c/o Innocent Records, Kensal House, 553–579 Harrow Rd, London W10 4RH, England. *Website:* www.atomickitten.com.

MCCLUSKEY, Andy; b. 24 June 1959, Wirral, Cheshire, England. Vocalist; Songwriter; Artiste Man; Prod. *Career:* Formed Id, 1977–78; Mem., Dalek I Love You, 1978; Co-founder, lead singer, Orchestral Manoeuvres In The Dark (OMD), 1978–98; Numerous tours, Europe, USA, Japan, Australia; Futurama Festival, Leeds, 1979; Supports to Talking Heads, Gary Numan, 1979; Festival of the 10th Summer, Manchester, 1986; Cities In The Park Festival, Prestwich, 1991; Support to Simple Minds, Milton Keynes Bowl, 1991; Songwriter, with Stuart Kershaw, for Atomic Kitten. *Compositions:* Whole Again (No. 1, UK), Atomic Kitten, 2001; You Are, Atomic Kitten. *Recordings:* Albums: Orchestral Manoeuvres In The Dark, 1980; Organisation, 1980; Architecture and Morality, 1981; Dazzle Ships, 1982; Junk Culture, 1984; Crush, 1985; The Pacific Age, 1986; In The Dark – The Best of OMD, 1988; Sugar Tax, 1991; Liberator, 1993; Walking on the Milky Way, 1996; Universal, 1996; Singles, 1998; Navigation (compilation), 2001. Singles: Electricity, 1979; Messages, 1980; Enola Gay, 1980; Souvenir, 1981; Joan of Arc, 1981; Maid of Orleans, 1982; Genetic Engineering, 1983; Locomotion, 1984; Talking Loud and Clear, 1984; Tesla Girls, 1984; So In Love, 1985; If You Leave (used in film Pretty In Pink), 1986; (Forever) Live and Die, 1986; Dreaming, 1988; Sailing On The Seven Seas, 1991; Pandora's Box, 1991; Stand Above Me, 1993; Dream of Me, 1993; Contributor, The Message of Love, Arthur Baker, 1989. *Current Management:* Direct Management Group, 947 La Cienega Blvd, Suite G, Los Angeles, CA 90069, USA.

MCCOO, Marilyn; b. 30 Sept. 1944, Jersey City, New Jersey, USA. Vocalist. m. Billy Davis Jr, 1969. *Education:* BS in Business Administration, UCLA, 1965. *Career:* Member, the Hi-Fi's; Vocalist, US harmony group Fifth Dimension (formerly the Versatiles, the Vocals), 1966–75; Appearances include: San Remo Festival, 1967; Bal Paree and Bambi Awards, Munich, Germany, 1970; Royal Albert Hall, London, 1972; Concert at the White House for President Nixon, 1973; Duo with Billy Davis Jr, 1976–80; Co-host, The Marilyn McCoo and Billy Davis Jr Show, CBS, 1977; Solo artist, 1980–; Television host, Solid Gold, 1981–87; Performance before Pope John Paul II, San Antonio, Texas with Billy Davis Jr; Theatrical performances include: Man of La Mancha; Anything Goes; Showboat, Broadway, 1995; Showboat, Chicago, 1996. *Recordings:* Albums: with Fifth Dimension: Up Up and Away, 1967; The Magic Garden, 1968; Stoned Soul Picnic, 1968; Age of Aquarius, 1969; Fantastic, 1970; Portrait, 1970; The July 5th Album, 1970; Love's Lines, Angles and Rhymes, 1971; Live!, 1971; Reflections, 1971; Individually and Collectively, 1972; Greatest Hits On Earth, 1972; Living Together, Growing Together, 1973; Earthbound, 1975; Greatest Hits, 1988; Marilyn McCoo Christmas, 2000; with Billy Davis Jr: I Hope We Get To Love In Time, 1977; The Two of Us, 1977; Marilyn and Billy, 1978; Solo: Solid Gold, 1983; The Me Nobody Knows, 1991; Singles: with Fifth Dimension: Up Up and Away, 1967; Carpet Man, 1968; Stoned Soul Picnic, 1968; Sweet Blindness, 1968; Aquarius/Let The Sunshine In, based on musical Hair (No. 1, USA), 1969; Wedding Bell Blues (No. 1, USA), 1969; Save The Country, 1970; One Less Bell To Answer, 1970; Never My Love, 1971; Last Night I Didn't Get To Sleep At All, 1972; If I Could Reach You, 1972; with Billy Davis Jr: You Don't Have To Be A Star (No. 1, USA), 1977; Your Love, 1977. *Honours:* Grammy Awards: 4 awards, 1968; 2 awards (with Fifth Dimension), 1970; 1 award (with Billy Davis Jr), 1977; Grand Prize, Tokyo Music Festival, with Billy Davis Jr, 1977; Hon. Doctorate, Talladega University, Alabama, 1988; Star on Hollywood Walk of Fame (with Fifth Dimension), 1991. *Current Management:* The Sterling/Winters Co, 16th Floor, 1900 Avenue of the Stars, Los Angeles, CA 90067, USA.

MCCREADY, Mike; Rock Musician (guitar). *Career:* Member, US rock group Pearl Jam, 1990–; Concerts include: Support to Alice In Chains, 1991; Lollapalooza Festival tour, 1992; Drop In The Park concert, Seattle, 1992; Bob Dylan 30th anniversary concert, Madison Square Garden, New York, 1992; Neil Young's Bridge School Benefit, with Elton John, Sammy Hagar, James Taylor, 1992; Support to Keith Richard and The Expensive Winos, New York, 1992; Concert appearances with Neil Young; Also member, tribute group Temple of The Dog, 1990; Group appears in film Singles, 1992. *Recordings:* Temple of The Dog, 1992; with Pearl Jam: Ten (No. 2, USA), 1992; Vs. (No. 1, USA), 1993; Vitalogy, 1994; No Code, 1996; Yield, 1998; Live on Two Legs, 1998; Riot Act, 2002; with Neil Young: Mirror Ball, 1995; with Screaming Trees: Dust, 1996; Singles: Alive, 1992; Even Flow, 1992; Jeremy, 1992; Contributor, Sweet Relief benefit album, 1993; Film soundtrack, Singles, 1992. *Honours:* American Music Award, Favourite New Artist, Pop/Rock and Hard Rock categories, 1993; Rolling Stone Readers' Awards, Best New American Band, Best Video, 1993; 4 MTV Awards, 1993; Highest 1-week album sales total in history, Vs., 1993. *Current Management:* Curtis Management, 417 Denny Way, Suite 200, Seattle, WA 98109, USA.

MCCULLOCH, Ian; b. 5 May 1959, Liverpool, England. Vocalist. *Career:* Founder, the Crucial Three, 1977; Group renamed Echo and The Bunnymen, 1978–88; Major appearances include: Futurama Festival, Leeds, 1979; Daze of Future Past, Leeds, 1981; WOMAD Festival, 1982; York Rock Festival, 1984; Solo artiste, 1988–; Founder, The Prodigal Sons, 1990; US tour, 1990; Founder, McCulloch's Mysterioso Show, 1992; Formed Electrafixion, with Will Sergeant; Re-formed Echo and the Bunnymen, 1999. *Recordings:* Albums with Echo and The Bunnymen: Crocodiles, 1980; Heaven Up Here, 1981; Porcupine, 1983; Ocean Rain, 1984; Songs To Learn and Sing, 1985; Echo and The Bunnymen, 1987; What Are You Going To Do With Your Life, 1999; Evergreen, 2000; Live in Concert, 2000; Flowers, 2000; Crystal Days, box set, 2001; Solo albums: Candleland, 1989; Mysterio, 1992; With Electrafixion: Album: Burned, 1995; Singles include: with Echo and The Bunnymen: Crocodiles, 1981; The Back Of Love, 1982; The Cutter, 1983; Never Stop, 1983; The Killing Moon, 1984; Seven Seas, 1984; Silver, 1984; Bring On The Dancing Horses, 1985; The Game, 1987; Lips Like Sugar, 1987; People Are Strange, from film The Lost Boys, 1988; Bedbugs and Ballyhoo, 1988; Pictures on my Wall, 1995; Nothing Lasts Forever, 1997; I Want To Be There When You Come, 1997; Don't Let it Get You Down, 1997; Get in the Car, 1998; Rust, 1999; Solo: September Song, 1984; Honey Drip, 1992; Lover Lover Lover, 1992; with Electrafixion: Zephyr, 1994; Never, 1995; Contributor, Last Temptation of Elvis compilation album, 1990. *Address:* c/o London Records, PO Box 1422, Chancellors House, Chancellors Rd, London W6 9SG, England.

MCCUSKER, John; b. 15 May 1973, Bothwell, Scotland. Musician (fiddle, tin whistle, cittern, accordion, keyboards); Composer; Prod. m. Kate Rusby. *Education:* Royal Academy, Glasgow, Scotland. *Career:* Began playing whistle aged 5, and fiddle aged 7; Played in youth orchestras; Joined a Ceilidh band, aged 12; Formed folk band Parcel O' Rogues with school friends, aged 14; Invited to join renowned Scottish folk group The Battlefield Band, aged 17; Recorded and toured internationally with The Battlefield Band; Has recorded 2 solo albums and has made guest appearances on over 100 albums; Produced albums for: Kate Rusby; Eliza Carthy; Cathie Ryan; Composed music with Kate Rusby for film Heartlands, 2002. *Recordings:* Albums: John McCusker, 1995; Yella Hoose, 2000; with Parcel O' Rogues: Parcel O' Rogues, 1987; with The Battlefield Band: After Hours, 1987; New Spring, 1991; Quiet Days, 1992; Threads, 1995; Across The Borders, 1997; Rain Hail Or Shine, 1998; Leaving Friday Harbor, 1999; Happy Daze, 2001; features on: Thirteen, Teenage Fanclub, 1993; Kate Rusby and Hathryn Roberts, 1995; Incholm, William Jackson, 1996; Easter Snow, Seamus Tansey, 1997; Donegal Rain, Andy Stewart, 1997; Eliza Carthy and The Kings of Calicutt, 1997; Hourglass, Kate Rusby, 1998; Sleepless, Kate Rusby, 1999; Little Lights, Kate Rusby, 2001;

Somewhere Along The Road, Cathie Ryan, 2001. *Honours:* Glenfiddich Spirit of Scotland Award for Music, 1999. *Website:* www.johnmccusker.demon.co.uk.

MCDANIEL, Mel Houston; b. 9 Sept. 1942, Checotah, Oklahoma, USA. Country vocalist; Songwriter; Musician (guitar). *Career:* Performer from age 14; Professional debut at 15 in talent contest, Okmulgee; Worked clubs in Oklahoma, Arkansas and Kansas; Worked in King X Club, Anchorage, Arkansas, 1970–72; Debut single Lazy Me written by J J Cale; Moved to Nashville without success, 1969; Returned as staff writer and demo singer for Combine Music, 1973; Performed at the Holiday Inn lounge; Signed to Capitol Records, 1976; Over 40 Billboard country chart entries on Capitol Records until 1989; Some singles credited as Mel McDaniels; Successful songwriting career in both pop and country; Grandest Lady of Them All used to celebrate Grand Ole Opry 60th anniversary; Continues to tour an average of 200 dates per year with own band Oklahoma Wind. *Compositions include:* Goodbye Marie; Roll Your Own; Grandest Lady of Them All; Goodbye Marie; I Could Sure Use This Feeling; I Just Want To Feel The Magic; Never Say Never. *Recordings include:* Baby's Got Her Blue Jeans On, 1984; Big Ole Brew, 1982; Stand Up, 1985; Let It Roll, 1985; Louisiana Saturday Night, 1981; Albums: Let It Roll, 1985; I'm Countryfied, 1981; Stand Up, 1985. *Honours:* Grammy Award, Best Country Vocal Performance – Male, 1984. *Membership:* Grand Old Opry, 1986. *Address:* c/o The Bobby Roberts Company Inc, 909 Meadowlark Lane, Goodlettsville, TN 37072, USA.

MCDILL, Bob (Robert Lee); b. 5 April 1944, Beaumont, Texas, USA. Songwriter. m. Nancy Whitsett, 6 Oct. 1971, 1 s., 2 d. *Education:* Lamar University, 1962–66. *Career:* Staff writer, Jack Music, Nashville, 1969–75; Hall Clement Publications, Nashville, 1975–84; Owner, writer, Ranger Bob Music, Nashville, 1984. *Compositions:* 25 US No. 1 hits include: for Don Williams: Say It Again; She Never Knew Me; Good Ole Boys Like Me; for Ronnie Milsap; Nobody Likes Sad Songs; for Dan Seals: Everything That Glitters; for Mel McDaniel: Baby's Got Her Blue Jeans On; for Waylon Jennings: Amanda. *Honours:* Distinguished Alumnus Award University, Lamar University, 1989; Composer of Year, Cash Box magazine, 1979, 1986; Approximately 40 awards from BMI, CMA, Nashville Songwriters Asscn; 11 ASCAP Awards; 2 Grammy Awards; Top Songwriter, World Record magazine, 1977; Inducted into Nashville Songwriters Asscn Hall of Fame, 1985. *Membership:* ASCAP; NARAS.

MACDONALD, Calum; b. 12 Nov. 1953, Lochmaddy, North Uist, Scotland. Musician (songwriter, percussion, drums). *Career:* Former member, Scottish celtic rock band, Runrig; International concerts include: Canada, 1987; Berlin, 1987; Support to U2, Murrayfield Stadium, Edinburgh, 1987; Support to Genesis, 1993; Support to Rolling Stones, 1995; Concerts at: Royal Concert Hall, Glasgow; Open-air concert, Loch Lomond. *Recordings:* Albums: Play Gaelic, 1978; Highland Connection, 1979; Recovery, 1981; Heartland, 1985; The Cutter and The Clan, 1987; Once In A Lifetime, 1988; Searchlight, 1989; The Big Wheel, 1991; Amazing Things, 1993; Transmitting Live, 1995; Mara, 1995; Long Distance, 1996; In Search of Angels, 1999; The BBC Archives, 1999; The Stamping Ground, 2001. *Honours:* Amazing Things, Environmental Album of the Year, 1993. *Current Management:* Marlene Ross Management, 55 Wellington St, Aberdeen AB2 1BX, Scotland.

MCDONALD, 'Country' Joe; b. 1 Jan. 1942, El Monte, California, USA. Vocalist; Musician (guitar). *Career:* Founder, folk group, Instant Action Jug Band, 1964; Group became Country Joe and The Fish, 1965–70; Concerts with Moby Grape, Howlin' Wolf, Led Zeppelin; Appeared at festivals: Monterey Festival, 1967; Miami Festival, 1968; Woodstock Festival, 1969; New Orleans Pop Festival, 1969; Solo artiste, 1971–; Concerts include: Bickershaw Festival, 1972; Concert with Grateful Dead, Boz Scaggs and Jefferson Starship, Vietnam Veteran's Project, 1982; Maine Arts Festival, 1989; Sporadic line-ups as The All-Star Band, Country Joe and The Fish; Also member, Energy Crisis and Barry Melton Band. *Recordings:* Albums: with Country Joe and The Fish: Electric Music For The Mind and Body, 1967; I Feel Like I'm Fixin' To Die, 1968; Together, 1968; Here We Are Again, 1969; Tonight I'm Singing For You, 1970; Solo albums: War War War, 1971; Country Joe, 1975; Paradise With An Ocean View, 1975; Something Borrowed, Something New, 1998. *Address:* c/o Tapestry Artists, 17337 Ventura Blvd, Suite 208, Encino, CA 91316–3956, USA.

MCDONALD, Dave; b. 1964. Musician (drums and drum machines); Prod. *Career:* Mem., Portishead, 1991–; Band signed to Go!Beat Records, 1993; Film, To Kill A Dead Man, shown in cinemas and projected on the MI5 building, London, 1995; Glastonbury Festival appearance, 1995; Live internet broadcast of New York concert, 1997. *Recordings:* Albums: Dummy, 1994; Herd of Instinct, 1995; Portishead, 1997; PNYC, 1998, Glory Times, 1998; Roseland, New York (DVD), 2002. Singles: Numb (EP), 1994; Sour Times, 1994; Glory Box, 1995; All Mine, 1997; Cowboys (EP), 1997; Over, 1997; Only You, 1998. *Honours:* Mercury Music Prize, 1994. *Address:* c/o Go Beat Records, The Fulham Palace, Bishops Ave, London SW6 6EA, England. *Website:* www.portishead.co.uk.

MCDONALD, J. Chris; b. 25 April 1954, Millington, Tennessee, USA. Musician (trombone); Arranger; Bandleader. m. Brenda Moore, 14 Feb. 1988,

1 s. *Education:* BS, Education, University of Tennessee, 1977. *Career:* Musical director, arranger, Miss Tennessee Pageant, Jackson, 1977–; Trombonist, Nashville Jazz Machine; Leader, Contraband, 1978–; Conductor, arranger, Brenda Lee, 1982–85. *Recordings:* Arranger for artists including: Lee Greenwood; Amy Grant; BeBe and CeCe Winans; Kenny Marks; Larnelle Harris. *Membership:* ASCAP; AFofM; NARAS.

MCDONALD, Michael; b. 2 Dec. 1952, St Louis, Missouri, USA. Vocalist; Musician (keyboards); Songwriter. m. Amy Holland, 1 s. *Career:* Regular session singer; Member, Steely Dan, 1974; Songwriter, keyboard player, Doobie Brothers, 1975–82; Concerts include: Great American Music Fair, 1975; Day On The Green, 1976; Canada Jam, 1978; Solo artiste, 1982–; Concerts include: Roy Orbison All-Star Benefit Tribute, 1990; Special guest, Tina Turner tour, 1990; Rock 'n' Soul Revue, New York, 1991; Benefit concert for family of late Jeff Porcaro (drummer with Toto), 1993. *Compositions include:* It Keeps You Runnin', Carly Simon, 1976; Co-writer, You Belong To Me, 1978; What A Fool Believes (No. 1, USA), 1979; Minute By Minute, 1979; Real Love, 1980; Take It To Heart, 1990; Collaborations with Kenny Loggins; Michael Jackson; Brenda Russell. *Recordings:* Albums: with The Doobie Brothers: Takin' It To The Streets, 1976; Livin' On The Fault Line, 1977; Minute By Minute (No. 1, USA), 1978; One Step Closer, 1980; Solo albums: That Was Then – The Early Recordings of Michael McDonald, 1982; If That's What It Takes, 1982; No Lookin' Back, 1985; Sweet Freedom, 1986; Take It To Heart, 1990; Blink of An Eye, 1993; Blue Obsession, 1997; In The Spirit, 2001; Other recordings (as writer and/or singer) include: Together (film soundtrack), 1979; Christopher Cross, Christopher Cross, 1979; High Adventure, Kenny Loggins, 1982; The Winner In You, Patti LaBelle, 1986; Anywhere You Go, David Pack, 1986; Decisions, The Winans, 1987; Back of My Mind, Christopher Cross, 1988; Love At Large (film soundtrack), 1990; The Offbeat of Avenues, Manhattan Transfer, 1991; Singles include: Let Me Go Love, with Nicolette Larson; I Keep Forgettin' (Every Time You're Near), 1982; Yah Mo B There, with James Ingram, 1984; Sweet Freedom, from film soundtrack Running Scared, 1986; Tear it Up, 1990; Hey Girl, 1993; Matters of the Heart, 1994; Appeared on: Ride Like The Wind, Christopher Cross, 1979; I'll Be Over You, Toto, 1986. *Honours:* Grammy Awards: Record of the Year, Song of the Year, Best Pop Vocal Performance, Best Vocal Arrangement, 1979; Ivor Novello Award, Best Film Theme, 1987. *Current Management:* Howard Kaufman, HK Management, 8900 Wilshire Blvd, Suite 300, Beverly Hills, CA 90211, USA.

MCDONALD, Richie; b. 6 Feb. 1962, Lubbock, Texas, USA. Country vocalist; Musician (guitar); Songwriter. *Career:* Began singing and writing music in school; Moved to Dallas and sang with award-winning band, Showdown; Sang on national US commercials, earning enough to move to Nashville to pursue career; Formed Texasee with Dean Sams, Keech Rainwater, Michael Britt and John Rich, 1992; Group became resident house band at the Wildhorse Saloon, Nashville; After subsequent name change to Lonestar, came to the attention of BMG and were signed to their BNA subsidiary; Released promotional six-track live CD, recorded at the Wildhorse; First country chart entry No News/Tequila Talkin' from debut album Lonestar, 1996; Same year duetted with Mindy McCready on the country hit Maybe He'll Notice Her Now; Sole featured lead vocalist on Lonestar's second album, Crazy Nights, prompting the departure of previous joint lead singer John Rich, 1998; Single, Amazed, from third album became huge international hit and career record to date, 1999; Has written a fair share of Lonestar's output as well as material for other country artists; By early 2000s, Lonestar estimated to be the most successful country group in the world. *Compositions include:* Everything's Changed; She's Always Right; I Couldn't Dream A Love Better Than This. *Recordings include:* No News, Tequila Talkin', Maybe She'll Notice Him Now (solo with Mindy McCready), 1996; Come Cryin' To Me, You Walked In, 1997; Say When, Everything's Changed, 1998; Amazed, Smile, 1999; I'm Already There, 2002; Albums include: Lonestar, 1995; Crazy Nights, 1997; Lonely Grill, 1999; I'm Already There, 2001. *Address:* c/o Country Music Asscn, 1 Music Circle S, Nashville, TN 37203, USA.

MACDONALD, Rory; b. 27 July 1949, Dornoch, Sutherland, Scotland. Vocalist; Musician (guitar, bass). *Career:* Founder member, Scottish folk group Runrig, 1973–; International concerts include: Canada; Berlin; Support to Murrayfield Stadium, Edinburgh, 1987; Concerts at: Royal Concert Hall, Glasgow; Open-air concert, Loch Lomond. *Recordings:* Albums: Play Gaelic, 1978; Highland Connection, 1979; Recovery, 1981; Heartland, 1985; The Cutter and The Clan, 1987; Once In A Lifetime, 1988; Searchlight, 1989; The Big Wheel, 1991; Amazing Things, 1993; Transmitting Live, 1995; Troubadours of British Folk Vol. 3, 1995; Mara, 1996; The Best of British Folk Rock, 1997; The BBC Archives, 1999; The Stamping Ground, 2001. *Current Management:* Marlene Ross Management, 55 Wellington St, Aberdeen AB2 1BX, Scotland.

MCELHONE, Johnny; b. 21 April 1963, Glasgow, Scotland. Musician (Bass); Prod. *Career:* Member, Altered Images, 1980–84; Joined Hipsway, 1984–88; Member, Texas, 1988–; Numerous tours, festivals and TV appearances. *Recordings:* Singles with Altered Images: Dead Pop Stars, 1981; Happy Birthday (No. 2, UK), 1981; I Could Be Happy, 1981; See Those Eyes,

1982; Pinky Blue, 1982; Don't Talk To Me About Love, 1983; Bring Me Closer, 1983; with Hipsway: The Honey Thief, 1986; Ask The Lord, 1986; Long White Car, 1986; with Texas: I Don't Want a Lover, 1989; Everyday Now, 1989; Alone With You, 1992; Tired of Being Alone, 1992; So Called Friend, 1993; So In Love With You, 1994; Say What You Want, 1997; Halo, 1997; Put Your Arms Around Me, 1997; Black Eyed Boy, 1997; In Our Lifetime, 1999; Summer Son, 1999; When We Are Together, 1999; In Demand, 2000; Inner Smile, 2001; Albums: with Altered Images: Happy Birthday, 1981; Pinky Blue, 1982; Bite, 1983; with Hipsway: Hipsway, 1986; with Texas: Southside, 1989; Mother's Heaven, 1991; Rick's Road, 1993; White on Blonde (No. 1, UK), 1997; The Hush (No. 1, UK), 1999; The Greatest Hits, 2000.

MCELHONE, Sean; b. 4 Jan. 1970, Leeds, Yorkshire, England. Musician (guitar, keyboards). 2 d. *Career:* Member, Bridewell Taxis; Television: ITV: Chart Show; Music Box; Radio: Radio 1, session, John Peel; Concerts: Reading Festival; Roundhay Park; Locomotive, Paris; Supported on tour: The Stone Roses; Happy Mondays; Inspiral Carpets. *Recordings:* Album: Invisible To You, 1991; Singles: Just Good Friends; Give In; Honesty; Spirit; Don't Fear The Reaper. *Membership:* Musicians' Union. *Current Management:* Music; Art; Computers. *Address:* 37 St Alban Rd, Leeds LS9 6LA, England.

MCENTIRE, Reba Nell; b. 28 March 1955, Chockie, Oklahoma, USA. Vocalist. m. (1) Charlie Battles, 1976, divorced; (2) Narvel Blackstock, 1989. *Career:* Singer with sister and brother as the Singing McEntires, 1972; Solo recording career (over 30m. album sales to date), 1976–; Film appearance, Tremors; 7 members of her band killed in plane crash, 1991. *Recordings:* Albums: Reba McEntire, 1977; Out of a Dream, 1979; Feel The Fire, 1980; Heart To Heart, 1981; Unlimited, 1982; Behind The Scenes, 1983; Just A Little Love, 1984; Have I Got A Deal For You, 1985; My Kind of Country, 1986; Whoever's In New England, 1986; What Am I Gonna Do About You, 1986; The Last One To Know, 1987; So So So Long, 1988; Merry Christmas To You, 1988; Reba, 1988; Sweet Sixteen, 1989; Live, 1989; Rumour Has It, 1990; For My Broken Heart, 1991; It's Your Call, 1992; Read My Mind, 1994; Starting Over, 1995; So Good Together, 1999; I'll Be, 2001; US Country No. 1 hits: Can't Even Get The Blues; You're The First Time I've Thought About Leaving; How Blue; Somebody Should Leave; Other hit singles include: (You Lift Me) Up To Heaven; Today All Over Again; For My Broken Heart; Whoever's In New England. *Current Management:* c/o Narvel Blackstock, Starstruck Entertainment, PO Box 121996, Nashville, TN 37212, USA.

MCERLAINE, Ally; b. 31 Oct. 1968, Glasgow, Scotland. Musician (guitar). *Career:* Member, Texas; Numerous tours, festivals and TV appearances. *Recordings:* Singles: I Don't Want a Lover, 1989; Everyday Now, 1989; Alone With You, 1992; Tired of Being Alone, 1992; So Called Friend, 1993; So In Love With You, 1994; Say What You Want, 1997; Halo, 1997; Put Your Arms Around Me, 1997; Black Eyed Boy, 1997; In Our Lifetime, 1999; Summer Son, 1999; When We Are Together, 1999; In Demand, 2000; Inner Smile, 2001; Albums: Southside, 1989; Mother's Heaven, 1991; Rick's Road, 1993; White on Blonde (No. 1, UK), 1997; The Hush (No. 1, UK), 1999; The Greatest Hits, 2000.

MCEVOY, Eleanor; b. 22 Jan. 1967, Dublin, Ireland. Vocalist; Musician (guitar, violin); Songwriter. *Education:* BA Mod, Music, Trinity College, Dublin; Started violin lessons, aged 8. *Career:* Played with National Symphony Orchestra of Ireland, 1988; Left to pursue solo career with major success on A Woman's Heart project; Numerous US and European tours with band; Performed for 80,000 in Dublin during US President Clinton's visit; Numerous TV appearances; Featured on soundtracks to TV series Clueless and films The Nephew and Some Mother's Son. *Compositions:* Only A Woman's Heart, title track of album. *Recordings:* Singles: Only A Woman's Heart, 1994; Precious Little, 1996; Please Heart You're Killing Me, 1999; Albums: A Woman's Heart, 1992; Eleanor McEvoy, 1994; What's Following Me? 1996; Snapshots, 1999; Yola, 2001. *Honours:* Irish Record Industry Awards, Best Solo Artist, 1992; Irish Recorded Music Asscn, Best New Artist, 1992; Featured tracks on Ireland's best ever selling album, A Woman's Heart, 1992; Hot Press Magazine Awards: Best Solo Performer, 1992; Best Songwriter, 1993; Irish National Entertainment Award, Best New Artist, 1993. *Membership:* IMRO, board mem.; IBEC Music Industry Group. *Current Management:* Real Good Management Ltd. *Address:* 17 Dame Court, Dublin 2, Ireland. *E-mail:* eleanor@eleanormcevoy.org. *Website:* www.eleanormcevoy.net.

MCFADDEN, Brian (Bryan); b. 12 April 1980, Dublin, Ireland. Vocalist. m. Kerry Katona, Jan. 2002, 1 d. *Career:* Mem., Westlife, 1999–; Numerous tours, festivals and television appearances. *Recordings:* Albums: Westlife, 1999; Coast To Coast (No. 1, UK), 2000; World of Our Own (No. 1, UK), 2001; Where Dreams Come True, 2001; Unbreakable: The Greatest Hits, 2002. Singles: Swear It Again (No. 1, UK), 1999; If I Let You Go, 1999; Flying Without Wings (No. 1, UK), 1999; I Have A Dream (No. 1, UK), 1999; Fool Again (No. 1, UK), 2000; Against All Odds (with Mariah Carey, No. 1, UK), 2000; My Love (No. 1, UK), 2000; What Makes A Man, 2000; Uptown Girl (for Comic Relief charity, No. 1, UK), 2001; Queen Of My Heart (No. 1, UK), 2001; World Of Our Own (No. 1, UK), 2002; Bop Bop Baby, 2002; Westlife Unbreakable, 2002. *Honours:* BRIT Awards, Best Pop Act, 2001, 2002.

Address: c/o RCA Records, 1540 Broadway, New York, NY 10036, USA. *Website:* www.westlife.co.uk.

MACFARLANE, Denis, (Dego, Tek 9); b. London, England. Prod; Remixer; DJ. *Career:* Member: 4 Hero; Nu-Era; Jacob's Optical Stairway; Co-founder: Reinforced Records, 1990; Black Records, 2000; Collaborations: Alex Attias; Roy Ayers; IG Culture; Jill Scott; Ursula Rucker. *Recordings:* Albums: with 4 Hero: In Rough Territory, 1991; Parallel Universe, 1995; Jacob's Optical Stairway (with Jacob's Optical Stairway), 1996; It's Not What You Think It Is (as Tek 9), 1996; Two Pages, 1998; Simply (as Tek 9), 2000; Creating Patterns, 2001; Singles: with 4 Hero: Mr Kirk's Nightmare, 1991; Earth Pioneers, 1997; Escape That, 1999; Les Fleurs, 2001. *Address:* c/o Reinforced Records, 387–389 Chapter Rd, London NW2 5NG, England.

MACFARLANE, Malcolm Douglas; b. 4 April 1961, Edinburgh, Scotland. Musician (guitar); Composer. *Education:* City of Leeds College of Music, 1983–86. *Career:* Member, Barbara Thompson's Paraphernalia, 1988–; Several European tours; World tours with Shakatak, 1992–; Formed Mulford/ MacFarlane group, 1994; First British tour, 1995. *Recordings:* with Barbara Thompson's Paraphernalia: Breathless; Everlasting Flame; with Mulford/ MacFarlane: Jamming Frequency, 1995. *Honours:* Eric Kershaw Memorial Prize, Leeds College of Music, 1984–86. *Membership:* Performing Rights Society.

MCGARRIGLE, Anna; b. 1944, Montréal, QC, Canada. Musician (keyboards, banjo, guitar, accordion); Vocalist. *Career:* Singer, performer in both French and English; Member, Mountain City Four, Montréal; Formed duo with sister Kate McGarrigle; Debut UK performance, 1976; Recent appearance, Cambridge Folk Festival, 1995; Barbican, 1996. *Compositions:* Songs recorded by artists including: Linda Ronstadt; Maria Muldaur; Emmylou Harris. *Recordings:* Albums include: Kate and Anna McGarrigle, 1976; Dancer With Bruised Knees, 1977; Pronto Monto, 1978; French Record, 1980; Love Over and Over, 1983; Heartbeats Accelerating, 1990; Matapedia, 1996; appears on: No More Shall We Part, Nick Cave & The Bad Seeds, 2001; Password, Geoff Muldaur, 2000. *Address:* c/o Concerted Efforts Inc, 59 Parsons St, West Newton, MA 02165, USA.

MCGARRIGLE, Kate; b. 6 Feb. 1946, Montréal, QC, Canada. Musician (keyboards, guitar). m. Loudon Wainwright III, 1 s., 1 d. *Career:* Singer, performer in both French and English; Member, Mountain City Four, Montréal; Formed duo with sister Anna McGarrigle; UK debut, 1976; Recent cocnert appearance, Cambridge Folk Festival, 1995. *Compositions:* Songs recorded by artists including: Linda Ronstadt; Maria Muldaur. *Recordings:* Albums include: Kate and Anna McGarrigle, 1975; Dancer With Bruised Knees, 1977; Pronto Monto, 1978; French Record, 1980; Love Over And Over, 1983; Heartbeats Accelerating, 1990; with Anna Mcgarrigle: Matapedia, 1996; Mcgarrigle Hour, 1998; with Loudon Wainwright III: Attempted Moustache, 1973; Unrequited, 1975; History, 1992; with Emmylou Harris: Wrecking Ball, 1995; Portraits, 1996; with Linda Ronstadt: Western Wall: The Tuscon Sessions, 1999; Linda Ronstadt Box Set, 1999; appears on: Password, Geoff Muldaur, 2000; Red Dirt Girl, Emmylou Harris, 2001; No More Shall We Part, Nick Cave & The Bad Seeds, 2001; record with Lou Reed. *Address:* c/o Concerted Efforts Inc, 59 Parsons St, West Newton, MA 02165, USA.

MCGARRY, David Graham; b. 18 Dec. 1955, Stoke-on-Trent, Staffordshire, England. Musician (keyboards). m. 9 May 1981, 2 d. *Education:* Leeds College of Music. *Career:* Television appearances include: Pebble Mill At One, BBC; Nightride, BBC; ITV Telethon; Toured with Lenny Henry and Ben E King; Musical Director at Alton Towers, 10 years. *Recordings:* Class, Linda Lewis; Style, Linda Lewis; Dreams of You, Saxtet. *Membership:* Musicians' Union; PRS; British Music Writers' Council Section of Musicians' Union. *Address:* 8 Castleton Rd, Lightwood, Stoke-on-Trent, Staffordshire ST3 7TD, England.

MCGARVEY, Patrick James; b. 2 Aug. 1971, Belfast, Northern Ireland. Musician (electric bass, guitar). *Education:* Basstech, grades 6 and 8 in bass. *Career:* Bassist, The Coal Porters (Sid Griffin's band), 1993–; Tours: All Europe, USA; Also live shows with Kate St John, 1995; Guitarist, bandleader, The Incredibly Strange Band; Television and radio apperances include: Channel 4, VH1, BBC Radio 1, GLR. *Compositions:* Featured on albums: All The Colours of The World; Chasing Rainbows; Santa Mira. *Recordings:* Land of Hope and Crosby, The Coal Porters, 1994; Los London, The Coal Porters, 1995. *Membership:* Musicians' Union. *Address:* PO Box 2539, London NW3 6DF, England.

MCGEOCH, John Alexander; b. 25 Aug. 1955, Greenock, Scotland. Musician (guitar, saxophone, keyboards); Composer. m. Denise Dakin, 14 Sept. 1988, 1 d. *Education:* BA Hons. *Career:* Continuous world tours, with various bands for last 18 years; Numerous television shows. *Recordings:* Albums: with Magazine: Magazine, 1978; Second Hand Daylight, 1979; The Correct Use of Soap, 1980; Maybe It's Right To Be Nervous Now, 2000; with Generation X: Kiss Me Deadly, 1981; with Siouxsie and The Banshees: Kaleidoscope, 1980; Ju Ju, 1981; A Kiss In The Dreamhouse, 1982; with Public Image Ltd: Happy?, 1988; 9, 1989; That What Is Not, 1991; with

Visage: Visage, 1980. *Membership:* PRS. *Current Management:* William Hunt. *Address:* 68 Neal St, Covent Garden, London WC2, England.

MCGINLEY, Raymond; b. 3 Jan. 1964, Glasgow, Scotland. Vocalist; Musician (guitar). *Career:* Member, The Boy Hairdressers; Founder member, Teenage Fanclub, 1989–. *Recordings:* Singles: Star Sign, 1991; The Concept, 1991; What You Do To Me (EP), 1992; Radio, 1993; Norman 3, 1993; Fallin', with De La Soul, 1994; Mellow Doubt, 1995; Sparky's Dream, 1995; Neil Jung, 1995; Have Lost It (EP), 1995; Ain't That Enough, 1997; I Don't Want Control Of You, 1997; Start Again, 1997; I Need Direction, 2000; Albums: A Catholic Education, 1990; Bandwagonesque, 1991; Thirteen, 1993; Grand Prix, 1995; Songs from Northern Britain, 1997; Howdy!, 2000. *Contributions to:* Sharks Patrol These Waters, 1995. *Address:* c/o Creation Records, 109 Regents Park Rd, London NW1 8UR, England.

MCGOLDRICK, Michael Brendan; b. 26 Nov. 1973, Manchester, England. Musician (uilleann pipes, low whistle, wooden flute); Composer. *Career:* Founder member of Manchester-based Celtic rock band Toss The Feathers; Formed Flook! with fellow flautists Brian Finnegan and Sarah Allen, 1995; Joined Scottish folk band Capercaillie, 1997; Helped form Lunasa; Collaborations: Jim Kerr; Youssou N'Dour; Alan Stivell; Kate Rusby; John McCusker; Afro-Celt Sound System; Idir; Karan Casey; Dezi Donnelly. *Recordings:* Albums: with Toss The Feathers: Live At The 32 Club, 1988; Columbus Eclipse, 1989; Awakening, 1991; TTF'94 Live, 1994; The Next Round, 1995; with Flook!: Flook! Live, 1997; with Lunasa: Lunasa, 1998; Otherworld, 1999; with Capercaillie: Beautiful Wasteland, 1997; Nadurra, 2000; solo: Champions of the North (with Dezi Donnelly), 1995; Morning Rory, 1996; Fused, 2000; At First Light (with John McSherry), 2001. *Honours:* All Ireland Championships, BBC Radio Two Young Tradition Award, 1995; BBC Radio Two Folk Awards, Best Instrumentalist, 2001. *Address:* c/o Vertical Records, 752 Argyle St, Glasgow, G3 8UJ, Scotland. *Website:* www.verticalrecords.co.uk.

MCGOVERN, Maureen; b. 27 July 1949, Youngstown, Ohio, USA. Vocalist; Actor; Songwriter. Divorced. *Career:* Recording Artist, concerts, stage appearances including Broadway, television and radio; Film appearances in The Towering Inferno and Airplane!; Joseph and The Cure For Boredom; Broadway debut in The Pirates of Penzance; Played Luisa in Nine; Starred with Sting in the Threepenny Opera; Mary in Brownstone; Appearances in South Pacific, The Sound of Music, Guys and Dolls, I do, I do; The Umbrellas of Cherbourne; Duet with Placido Domingo, A Love Until the End of Time, recorded with Philharmonia Virtuosi of New York; Performed, Celebrating Gershwin, 50th anniversary of his death; Revival of of Thee I Sing/Let 'Em Eat Cake, Brooklyn Academy of Music and Kennedy Center; Performed at George Gershwin Centennial Celebration, London Palladium; Television special, Maureen McGovern: Live at Wolftrap; Guest appearances with Boston Pops, PBS-Day Commemorative Concert with the National Symphony; Appeared with every US Symphony Orchestra; Host, television series, Girl's Night Out; Played Dr Berg in Pacific Blue for television; Recent theatre: Letters from 'Nam, The Lion in Winter, Dear World. *Compositions:* (for children) The Bengal Tiger's Ball; I Want to Learn to Fly. *Recordings:* Hit singles: The Morning After (No. 1, USA; Academy Award-winning Gold Record), 1973; The Continental, 1976; We May Never Love Like This Again (Academy Award winner); Can You Read My Mind; Another Woman In Love; State of the Heart; Naughty Baby; Christmas with Maureen McGovern; Baby I'm Yours; Out of this World: McGovern sings Arlen; Amen! A Gospel Celebration; The Music Never Ends: The Lyrics of Marilyn and Alan Bergman, The Pleasure of His Company; Works of Heart. *Honours:* Numerous Gold Records from USA, Canada, Australia, Japan, The Philippines; Grand Prize, Tokyo Music Festival, 1975. *Membership:* Vice-President, National Chairperson, Polymyositis/Dermatomyositis, Muscular Dystrophy Asscn. *Address:* 8530 Wilshire Blvd 200, Beverly Hills, CA 90211-3113, USA. *Telephone:* (310) 277-9137. *Fax:* (310) 277-6358. *E-mail:* mmprodsinc@aol.com. *Website:* www.maureenmcgovern.com.

MACGOWAN, Shane; b. 25 Dec. 1957, Kent, England. Musician (guitar); Vocalist. *Career:* Member, The Pogues, 1983–90; Support to Elvis Costello, British tour, 1984; Cambridge Folk Festival, 1985; US tours, 1986, 1988; Self Aid concert, Dublin, 1986; Glastonbury Festival, 1986; Fleadh '91, London, 1991; Chieftains Music Festival, London, 1991; Feile '91, Tipperary, Ireland, 1991; Solo artist, with backing group The Popes, 1993–; Film appearance, Straight To Hell, 1986. *Recordings:* Albums: with the Pogues: Red Roses For Me, 1984; Rum, Sodomy and The Lash, 1985; If I Should Fall From Grace With God, 1988; Peace and Love, 1990; Hell's Ditch, 1990; The Best of The Pogues, 1991; The Rest Of The Pogues, 1992; with The Popes: The Snake, 1994; Holloway Boulevard, 2000; Across The Broad Atlantic, 2002. Singles include: with The Pogues: A Pair Of Brown Eyes, 1985; Sally Maclennane, 1985; Dirty Old Town, 1985; Haunted, from film Sid And Nancy, 1986; A Fairytale Of New York (with Kirsty MacColl) (Number 2, UK), 1987; with The Dubliners: The Irish Rover, 1987; Fiesta, 1988; Yeah Yeah Yeah Yeah, 1988; Misty Morning, Albert Bridge, 1989; Summer In Siam, 1991; Jack's Heroes, 1990; with The Popes: The Church of The Holy Spook; The Woman's Got Me Drinking; Haunted, duet with Sinead O'Connor, 1995; You're The One, duet with Maire Brennan, for film soundtrack Circle of Friends, 1995;

Contributor, film soundtrack Straight To Hell, 1987; The Last Temptation of Elvis, Nordoff-Robbins charity record, 1990; Red Hot + Blue, AIDS awareness record, 1990; Nick Cave: Murder Ballads, 1996; Legends of Ireland, 1998.

MCGRATH, Bob (Robert Emmet); b. 13 June 1932, Ottawa, Illinois, USA. Vocalist. m. Ann L Sperry, 14 June 1958, 2 s., 3 d. *Education:* BMus, University of Michigan; Master's Degree, Manhattan School of Music. *Career:* Original host, Bob, on Sesame Street for 30 years; Tenor soloist on Sing Along With Mitch; Performed with: Robert Shaw Chorale; Fred Waring Pennsylvanians; Host for the International Children's Festival at Wolftrap for 10 years; Performed with 100 Symphony Orchestras; Has performed in over 800 concerts in the USA, Canada and Japan. *Recordings:* The Baby Record; Songs and Games For Toddlers; If You're Happy and You Know It Sing Along number 1 and number 2; Bob's Favourite Street Songs; Sing Me A Story. *Publications:* I'm A Good Mommy; You're A Good Daddy; Dog Lies; The Shoveller; Me Myself; Sneakers; Uh Oh! Gotta Go; Oops! Excuse Me Please!. *Honours:* Hon. Doctorate, Medaille College; Emmanuel Cancer Foundation Tribute; Variety Club Lifetime Honourary Mem.; Parent's Choice, American Library Asscn; National Chairperson, UNICEF Day; World Children's Day Foundation, UN General Assembly; Syracuse Symphony Asscn Achievement Award for Music Education; Canadian Recording Artist Gold Record, 1992, 1993. *Current Management:* Ken Greengrass, 38 E 57th St, New York, NY 10022, USA.

MCGRATH, Mark Sayers; b. 15 March 1968. Vocalist. *Education:* University of Southern California, degree in Communications. *Career:* Became band member of The Shrinky Dinx following unscheduled leap on stage at live gig; Group signed to Atlantic Records following circulation of self-made demo video; Act renamed Sugar Ray owing to threat of legal action prior to record releases; Built up world-wide fanbase through touring and TV appearances; Cameo in Fathers Day film, 1997. *Recordings:* Albums: Lemonade and Brownies, 1995; Floored, 1997; 14–59, 1999; Sugar Ray, 2001; Singles: Mean Machine, Iron Mic, 1995; Fly, RPM, 1997; Every Morning, Someday, 1999; Falls Apart, 2000; When It's Over, Answer The Phone, 2001. *Honours:* Second/third albums certified double/triple platinum by RIAA, respectively. *Address:* c/o PO Box 12018, Costa Mesa, CA 92627, USA. *E-mail:* management@sugarray.com. *Website:* www.sugarray.com.

MCGRAW, Tim, (Tim Smith); b. 1 May 1967, Delhi, Louisiana, USA. Country vocalist; Musician (guitar); Songwriter; Prod. m. Faith Hill, 6 Oct. 1996. *Education:* Northeast Louisiana University, sports scholarships. *Career:* Became involved in music when purchased guitar from a pawn-shop; Moved to Nashville and gigged around northeastern Louisiana and Jacksonville, Florida; While performing in clubs around Nashville, signed deal with Curb Records on strength of demo; Chart debut with Welcome To The Club, 1992; Released Indian Outlaw, a song using extracts of Lament of The Cherokee Reservation Indian, 1994; Track attracted criticism in USA for its alleged demeaning stereotypes of Native Americans, but received much airplay and became successful pop and country hit; Has charted consistently on both US pop and country chart, garnering many awards along the way; Produced other country artists including Jo Dee Messina. *Recordings include:* Just To See You Smile, 1997; It's Your Love (with Faith Hill), 1997; I Like It – I Love It, 1995; Don't Take The Girl, 1994, Not A Moment Too Soon, 1994; She Never Lets It Go To Her Heart, 1996; Everywhere, 1997; A Place In The Sun, 1999; Greatest Hits, 2000; Set This Circus Down, 2001. *Honours:* CMA Award, Vocal Event of the Year, It's Your Love (with Faith Hill), 1997; Billboard Country Artist of the Year, Male Country Artist of the Year; Country Albums Artist of the Year, Set This Circus Down; Country Album of the Year, Greatest Hits; Country Single Artist of the Year, 2001; American Music Awards, Favourite Male Country Artist, 2002, 2003, Favourite Country Album, for Set This Circus Down, 2002. *Current Management:* Image Management Group, 27 Music Sq. E, Nashville, TN 37203, USA. *Website:* www.timmcgraw.com.

MCGUIGAN, Paul 'Guigsy'; b. 9 May 1971, Manchester, England. Musician (bass). *Career:* Founder mem., Rain, with Paul Arthurs and Tony McCarroll; Joined by Liam Gallagher and changed band name to Oasis; Joined by Noel Gallagher; Debut performance, Boardwalk, Manchester, 1991; Support slots to The Milltown Brothers, BMX Bandits, The Verve, Liz Phair, The Real People, Dodgy; Signed to Creation Records, 1993; Numerous headline tours, television appearances and festival dates; Left band, 1999, during recordings for 2000 album Standing On The Shoulder Of Giants. *Recordings:* Albums: Definitely Maybe (No. 1, UK) 1994; What's the Story (Morning Glory) (No. 1, UK), 1995; Be Here Now (No. 1, UK), 1997; The Masterplan, boxed set, 1999; Standing On The Shoulder Of Giants (No. 1, UK), 2000. Singles: Supersonic, 1994; Whatever, 1994; Cigarettes and Alcohol, 1994; Shakermaker, 1994; Live Forever, 1994; Some Might Say (No. 1, UK, 1995); Wonderwall, 1995; Roll With It, 1995; Champagne Supernova, 1995; Don't Look Back in Anger (No. 1, UK, 1996); D'You Know What I Mean (No. 1, UK, 1997); Stand By Me; All Around the World (No. 1, UK, 1998); Go Let It Out (Number 1, UK), 2000; Who Feels Love?, 2000; Sunday Morning Call, 2000. *Honours:* BRIT Awards, Best British Newcomer, 1995; Best British Group, Best British Album, 1996.

MCGUINN, Roger, (James McGuinn, III); b. 13 July 1942, Chicago, Illinois, USA. Vocalist; Musician (guitar). m. Camilla. *Career:* Touring musician with: The Limelighters; Chad Mitchell Trio; Judy Collins; Bobby Darin; Founder member, The Byrds, 1964–73; Solo artiste, 1973–; Also member, McGuinn Clark and Hillman (with Gene Clark and Chris Hillman), 1978–79; Performances include: The Beach Boys Summer Spectacular, 1966; Monterey Pop Festival, 1967; Grand Ole Opry, 1968; Newport Festival, 1969; Bath Festival, 1970; Tours with Bob Dylan's Rolling Thunder Revue, 1975; Roy Orbison All-Star Tribute, 1990. *Recordings:* Albums: with the Byrds: Mr Tambourine Man, 1965; Turn! Turn! Turn!, 1965; Fifth Dimension, 1966; Younger Than Yesterday, 1967; The Notorious Byrd Brothers, 1968; Sweetheart of The Rodeo, 1968; The Ballad of Easy Rider, 1970; Untitled, 1970; Byrdmaniax, 1971; Farther Along, 1972; Best of The Byrds – Greatest Hits Vol. 2, 1972; History of The Byrds, 1973; The Byrds, 1990; Solo albums: Roger McGuinn, 1973; Peace On You, 1974; Cardiff Rose, 1976; Thunderbyrd, 1977; Back From Rio, 1991; Born to Rock and Roll, 1992; Nitty Gritty Dirt Band – Roger McGuinn Live, 1994; Live from Mars; Folk Den, Vols 1–4, 2000; Treasures From The Folk Den, 2001; with Clark and Hillman: McGuinn Clark and Hillman, 1979; with Hillman: McGuinn/Hillman, 1979; Singles: Mr Tambourine Man (No. 1, USA), 1965; All I Really Want To Do; Eight Miles High, 1966; 5D (Fifth Dimension), 1966; So You Want To Be A Rock 'n' Roll Star, 1967; Have You Seen Her Face, 1967; I Wasn't Born To Follow. *Honours:* Inducted into Rock and Roll Hall of Fame, 1991.

MCHUGH, Robert (Bob); b. 20 July 1946, Kearney, NJ, USA. Musician (Piano); Composer. m. Jane Belli, 28 June 1970, 1 s., 1 d. *Education:* BA, Music, Jersey City College; Private Study, Bill Manzi, Morris Nanton, Don Friedman, Hester Randolfi. *Career:* Performed in documentary, The Art of Worship, produced by Riverside Church, New York City, USA; Appearance on Around New York, WNYC, Concert's at Count Basic Theatre, Riverfest, New York Public Library, Lincoln Center. *Compositions:* Steamboat Rag; Rocky Rog Tune; Bus Boy Circus; Dream Street; Three Greek Dances; Baroque Piece; Buily and The Bean; Uptown; Summer Stride; Recuperation Tango, 1998. *Recordings:* Soring on Wings of Ivory and Black; Manhattan Sunrise; Interplay; MNB. *Honours:* ASCAP Popular Award, every year since 1989; Commissioned Composer for the New Jersey Music Teachers' State Piano Competition, 1998–99. *Membership:* ASCAP; NJEA; MTA. *Current Management:* Manduca Publications, PO Box 10550, Portland, ME 04104, USA. *Address:* 902 Lincoln Ave, Pompton Lakes, NJ 07442, USA.

MACINTOSH, Adrian; b. 7 March 1942, Tadcaster, England. Jazz Musician. m. Sheila Christie, 13 April 1974. *Career:* Early work with John Taylor Trio and Norma Winstone; Alan Elsdon Band, 1970; Joined Brian Leakes' Sweet and Sour, 1978; Joined Humphrey Lyttelton's Band, 1982; Work with Helen Shapiro, 1984–; Worked with many leading jazz names including: Sonny Stitt; Teddy Edwards; Jimmy Witherspoon; Harold Ashby; Nat Pierce; Scott Hamilton; Clark Terry; Warren Vache; Kenny Davern; Al Casey. *Recordings:* Humph and Wally Fawkes, 1983; Humph and Helen Shapiro, 1984; Humph, Al Casey and Kenny Davern, 1984; Humph At The Bulls Head, 1985; Humph and Buddy Tate, 1985; Humph Gigs, 1987; Humph and Lillian Boutté, 1988; Humph At Breda Jazz Festival, 1988; Humph Beano Boogie, 1989; Ken McCarthy Quartet (featuring Dick Pearce); Produced album by Brian Leake's Sweet and Sour, 1993; Drums on: Amnesiac, Radiohead (No. 1, UK), 2001. *Membership:* Musicians' Union; Chairman, Asscn of British Jazz Musicians.

MCINTOSH, Bradley John; b. 8 Aug. 1981, London, England. Vocalist; Actor. *Career:* Former mem., pop/R&B band, Krisp; Mem., S Club 7, 1998–; Group quickly achieved international success, following sales of TV series Miami 7, 1999, LA 7, 2000, and Hollywood 7, 2001, featuring the band's music, to nearly 100 countries; Also made nature TV series, S Club 7 Go Wild, 2000, and various TV specials; First British tour with S Club 7, 2001; Band renamed S Club, 2001. *Recordings:* Albums: S Club, 1999; 7 (No. 1, UK), 2000; Sunshine, 2001; Seeing Double, 2002. Singles: Bring It All Back (No. 1, UK), 1999; S Club Party, 1999; Two In A Million/You're My Number One, 1999; Reach, 2000; Natural, 2000; Never Had A Dream Come True (No. 1, UK), 2000; Don't Stop Movin' (No. 1, UK), 2001; Have You Ever (No. 1, UK), 2001; You, 2002. *Honours:* BRIT Awards, Best British Newcomer, 2000, Best British Single, for Don't Stop Movin', 2002; Record of the Year Award, for Don't Stop Movin', 2001. *Current Management:* 19 Management, Unit 32, Ransomes Dock, 35–37 Parkgate Rd, London SW11 4NP, England. *Website:* www.sclub.com.

MACISAAC, Ashley Dwayne; b. 24 Feb. 1975, Antigonish, Nova Scotia, Canada. Vocalist; Musician (violin); Composer. *Career:* Fiddle player from the Cape Breton tradition, rooted in Scottish folk music; Has great technique and, although sometimes criticised by purists for playing too fast and frenetically, flamboyant style has brought a solid fanbase; Hi How Are You Today? album was based on Cape Breton traditional music but introduced various other musical influences; Single release Sleepy Maggie (with vocals from Mary Jane Lamond) received much airplay in Canada, gaining national recognition as an artist; Follow-up album Fine Thank You Very Much is in the quintessential Cape Breton traditional style, but 2000 release Heltic Celtic explores electronic and ambient influences. *Recordings:* Single: Sleepy Maggie, 1997; Albums: Close To The Floor, 1992; Hi How Are You Today, 1995; Fine Thank

You Very Much, 1998; Helter's Celtic, 2000; features on: Feelings, David Byrne, 1997; Fire In The Kitchen, The Chieftains, 1998; Suas E!, Mary Jane Lamond, 1997; Spirit Trail, Bruce Hornsby, 1998; Hanging Garden OST, 1998. *Website:* www.ashley-macisaac.com.

MACK, Bobby; b. 19 June 1954, Fort Worth, Texas, USA. Vocalist; Musician (guitar); Music Prod. m. Pat Cullen, 24 May 1994, 1 s., 1 d. *Education:* University of Texas, Austin. *Career:* Delta Blue Festival, New Orleans Jazz Festival; Tours: Former USSR; Japan; New Zealand; Australia; Scandinavia; Europe; UK. *Recordings:* Bobby Mack and Night Train Albums include: Say What; Red Hot and Humid; Honeytrap; Sugar All Night; Live at J and J Blues Bar; Highway Man; produced Mississippi Bluesman Willie Foster, My Life; produced Mark Goodwin, I Found Joy; produced Texas Guitars Vol. I – The Women. *Publications:* Writer, Texas Blue Magazine. *Current Management:* Time Train Music. *Address:* 881 Lost Creek, Wimberley, TX 78676, USA.

MACK, Danny; b. 29 March 1943, Harvey, Illinois, USA. Vocalist; Musician (accordion, drums, trumpet, keyboards); Record Prod; Record Co Exec. m. Caroline Panczyck, 3 Nov. 1962, 1 s., 1 d. *Education:* Criminal justice; 15 years private study music instrumental, teaching, theory. *Career:* Bandleader, 1958–; Clubs circuit until 1977; Songwriting career began with first self-penned country recording on K-Ark, 1977; Recorded Fist Full of Dollars, Nashville, Tennessee; Formed Syntony Publishing BMI and Briarhill Records, 1984; WLS TV, TCI of Indiana; Guest appearances, Sig Sakowitz radio show. *Recordings:* Jesus Is The Reason For The Season (No. 1 Christmas hit); On The Right Road Again, 1994; Old Rockers Never Die, 1994. *Publications:* Chicago Tribune; Country and Western Corner; Radio and Record News; Indie Bullet; Star Quest Magazines. *Honours:* Indie Label of the Year, Producer of the Year, CMAA, 1992, 1993, 1994; Hon. Kentucky Col; Inspirational Record of the Year, CMA, USA, 1994; Song of Year, World Radio Network, Spain, 1994. *Membership:* Broadcast Music Inc; NARAS; Lifetime mem., Country Music Asscns of America. *Current Management:* The Danny Mack Music Group. *Address:* 3484 Nicolette Dr., Crete, IL 60417, USA.

MACK, James Joseph; b. 12 Nov. 1971, Kensington, London, England. Musician (percussion). *Education:* Guildhall School of Music and Drama; West London Institute of Higher Education. *Career:* World-wide tours and television appearances with: D:ream; Des'ree; Lonnie Liston Smith; C J Lewis; Rozalla; NYJO; Skin. *Recordings:* D:ream (second album); Skin; NYJO; Various television commercials include: American Express; Maxwell House; John Smiths Bitter. *Honours:* Performance diploma, Guildhall School of Music and Drama. *Membership:* Musicians' Union. *Address:* 28 Ashburnham Mansions, Ashburnham Rd, Chelsea, London SW10 0PA, England.

MACK, Warner (McPherson); b. 2 April 1938, Nashville, Tennessee, USA. Country Vocalist; Songwriter; Musician. *Career:* Performer, radio show, Louisiana Hayride; Successful solo career, late 1950s–; Regular tours, UK country clubs; First country artist to record national commercial for Coca-Cola. *Compositions include:* Tennessee Born, Mississippi Raised; Is It Wrong (For Loving You)? (US Country No. 1); The Bridge Washed Out. *Recordings include:* Sitting In An All Night Cafe; Talking To The Walls; How Long Will It Take?; These Crazy Thoughts; He Touched Me; Numerous albums include: The Country Touch, 1966; Drifting Apart, 1967; Love Hungry, 1970; You Make Me Feel Like A Man, 1971; Great Country, 1973; Prince of Country Blues, 1983; At Your Service, 1984; Early Years, 1998; Several compilation albums. *Current Management:* Capitol Advertising and Management, 1300 Division St #200, Nashville, TN 37203, USA.

MACKAY, David; b. 11 May 1944, Sydney, Australia. Record Prod; Composer; Musician (Keyboards). m. Brenda Anne Challis, 31 March 1973, 1 s., 1 d. *Education:* St Aloyisious College, Sydney, Australia; Conservatorium of Music, Sydney; Theory, Harmony, Arranging, Piano, Clarinet, privately studied in Melbourne; Modern Arranging, Guitar and Bass. *Career:* Producer of Records by: Blue Mink; Cliff Richard; New Seekers; Bonnie Tyler; Frankie Miller; Dusty Springfield; Johnny Hallyday; Demis Roussos; Sarah Jory; Cilla Black. *Compositions:* Theme Punderscores for: TV Programmes: Auf Wiedersehen Pet; Bread; Blott on the Landscape. *Honours:* Ivor Novello Award for Auf Wiedersehen Pet, 1983; AKIA Award, Best Cast Album of a Musical 1990. *Membership:* PRS; Repro; BAC&S; Professional Composers Guild. *Address:* Toftrees, Church Rd, Woldingham, Surrey CR3 7JX, England.

MACKAY, Robert Andrew; b. 12 July 1973, London, England. Composer; Musician (flute, guitar, bass); Vocalist; Actor. *Education:* BSc, Geology and Music, Keele University, 1995; MMus, Electroacoustic Composition, Bangor University, 1997; PhD, Electroacoustic Composition, in progress. *Career:* Performed in national stage production of Only Just, by Alec Davison, 1997; Session Musician, Wales, 1997–2001; Composer in Residence, Radio Bratislava, Slovakia, 1998–99; Bass Player, Gyroscope, 1998; Flute, guitar and bass player, Tystion, 1998–2002; Composer for multimedia events; Film appearances: Merlin; A Beautiful Mistake; TV appearances: Idot, Garej, Lois, Sesiwn Hwyr (all for Channel 4 Wales); Radio appearances for BBC Radio 1 and 3, incl. two John Peel Sessions and supporting P. J. Harvey live, as well as Late Junction and Hear and Now; Works performed in UK, France, USA and New Zealand. *Compositions:* Tempestuous Relationships, 1995; Sea

Pictures, 1997; Environs, 1997; Voicewind, 1998; Postcards from the Summer, 1999; Flute Melt, 2000; Augustine's Message, 2001; Need Without Reason, 2001; Joyce's Vision, 2002. *Recordings:* ICMC '98; Shrug Off Ya Complex. *Honours:* Prix Residence, Bourges Synthèse Festival, France, 1997; Single of the Week, Melody Maker, with Tystion, 1998; Special Prize, Hungarian Radio, 1999; Radio Cymru Rap Award, Album of the Year, 2000. *Membership:* PRS; PRC; Equity; SPNM; BMIC; SAN. *Address:* 239 Earlsfield Rd, Earlsfield, London SW18 3DE, England.

MCKEAN, Ian; b. 9 Jan. 1958, Hertford, Hertfordshire, England. Musician (guitar). *Education:* West Surrey College of Art and Design; City Literature Institute (Music Diploma). *Career:* with Twenty Flight Rockers: Reading Festival, 1986; Numerous live and studio sessions, BBC Radio 1; with Balaam and The Angel: 2 major British tours, 1988; 4 month tour, USA and Canada, 1988; Support to Aerosmith, Belfast and Wembley, 1989. *Recordings:* Albums: Days of Madness, 1989; No More Innocence, 1991; Prime Time, 1993; Single: Little Bit of Love, 1990. *Membership:* Musicians' Union; PRS. *Address:* 63 Eton Ave, London NW3 3ET, England.

MCKEE, Maria; b. 17 Aug. 1964, Los Angeles, California, USA. Vocalist; Songwriter. *Career:* Formed duo The Maria McKee Band with half-brother Bryan MacLean, later renamed the Brian MacLean Band; Founder member, Lone Justice; Concerts include: Support tour to U2; Solo artiste, 1987–. *Compositions include:* A Good Heart, Fergal Sharkey (UK No. 1), 1985. *Recordings:* Solo singles include: Show Me Heaven (No. 1, UK), 1990; I'm Gonna Soothe You, 1993; Albums: with Lone Justice: Lone Justice, 1985; Shelter, 1987; This World Is Not My Home, 1999; Solo albums include: Maria McKee, 1990; You Gotta Sin To Be Saved, 1993; Life Is Sweet, 1996; Ultimate Collection, 2000. *Current Management:* Fabulon Management, 1 McCrone Mews, Belsize Lane, London NW3 5BG, England.

MCKENNA, Mae; b. 23 Oct. 1955, Coatbridge, Scotland. Vocalist; Songwriter. m. James Woon, 17 Dec. 1977, 1 s. *Education:* A Level Music, Diploma, Music. *Career:* Recorded and toured UK and Europe as lead singer with folk rock band Contraband, 1971–75; Sung solo gaelic air on Ultravox tour, 1983; Solo singer, 1985; Backing singer for: Scritti Politti; Blur; Madness; Jason Donovan; Cliff Richard; ABC; Wet Wet Wet; Kylie Minogue; Rick Astley; Donna Summer; David Cassidy; Steps; Westlife. *Recordings:* Solo albums: Mae McKenna; Everything That Touches Me; Walk On Water; Nightfallers; Mirage and Reality; with Contraband: Contraband. *Membership:* Musicians' Union; Equity; PRS. *Current Management:* Keith Harris Music. *Address:* 204 Courthouse Rd, Maidenhead, Berkshire SL6 6HU, England.

MCKENNA, Rafe; Record Prod; Engineer; Mixer. *Career:* Prod., Engineer, Mixer for: David Essex; UFO; Magnum; Buggles; Elkie Brooks; Steve Hackett; Steve Howe; Wishbone Ash; Danny Wilson; Roger Daltrey; Giant; Depeche Mode; Thomas Dolby; Paul McCartney; Spandau Ballet; Gary Glitter; Bad Company; Big Country; Foreigner; The Corrs; Ash; Warm Jets; Electronic; Lewis Taylor; Ronan Keating; Madness; James Taylor Quartet; Zucchero; Marco Borsato; BB Mak; Dream Kids; UB40; Brian Kennedy; Eddi Reader. *Honours:* Numerous Platinum and Gold albums. *Current Management:* Stephen Budd Management Ltd, 109b Regents Park Rd, Primrose Hill, London NW1 8UR, England. *Website:* www.record-producers.com.

MCKENNITT, Loreena; b. Manitoba, Canada. Vocalist; Songwriter. *Career:* Won DuMaurier Search For Talent, 1978; Represented Canada at UNESCO in 1978 and 1985; Featured in festival productions as actor, singer and composer including: Shakespeare's The Tempest, 1982; The Two Gentlemen of Verona, 1984; Recorded debut album, 1985; Signed by Warner Music, 1991; Music featured in films: Women and Spirituality series; Jade; Highlander III; The Holy Man, Soldier; The Santa Clause; TV music for: Northern Exposure; Due South; Legacy; EZ Streets; Boston Public; Big Kelvin and Little Kelvin; Strange Luck. *Recordings:* Albums include: Elemental, 1985; To Drive The Cold Winter Away, 1987; Parallel Dreams, 1989; The Visit, 1991; The Mask and Mirror, 1994; The Book of Secrets, 1997; Live In Paris and Toronto, 1999. *Honours:* The Book of Secrets topped the Billboard World Music chart, reached number 1 on national album charts in Greece and Turkey; Juno Awards: Best Roots and Traditional Album: The Visit, 1992; The Mask and Mirror, 1995; Billboard Award: International Achievement, 1997. *Website:* www.quinlanroad.com.

MCKENZIE, Derrick; b. 27 March 1962, London, England. Musician (Drums). *Career:* Member, Jamiroquai; Numerous tours and TV appearances. *Recordings:* Singles: When You Gonna Learn, 1993; Emergency on Planet Earth, 1994; Space Cowboy EP, 1995; Cosmic Girl, 1996; Light Years, 1996; Alright, 1997; Deeper Underground, 1998; High Times, 1998; Canned Heat, 1999; Little J, 2001; Albums: Emergency on Planet Earth, 1993; Travelling Without Moving, 1996; Synkronized, 1999; A Funk Odyssey, 2001. *Honours:* Gold and Platinum Albums; Numerous MTV Video Music Awards.

MACKENZIE, Gisèle; b. 10 Jan. 1927, Winnipeg, Manitoba, Canada. Vocalist; Actress. Divorced, 1 s., 1 d. *Education:* Graduate Scholarship School; Royal Conservatory, Toronto, Canada. *Career:* Your Hit Parade, NBC; Jack

Benny Show; Gisèle MacKenzie Show, NBC; Sid Caesar Show. *Recordings:* Single: Hard To Get (No. 1); Albums: Getting To Know Gisele, 2000. *Membership:* SAG; AFTRA. *Current Management:* Samantha Group. *Address:* 300 S Raymond, Pasadena, CA 91105, USA.

MACKENZIE, Henry; b. 15 Feb. 1923, Edinburgh, Scotland. Musician (clarinet, saxophone). m. Barbara Holton, 17 Sept. 1976. *Career:* Featured soloist, clarinet, with Ted Heath, 18 years; 4 American tours including 2 at Carnegie Hall, New York, with Ted Heath; Concerts and radio appearances, Billy May and Nelson Riddle; Films with Henry Mancini; Also featured in White Mischief. *Recordings include:* Appears on: Give My Regards To Broad Street, Paul McCartney; When I'm Sixty-Four, The Beatles. *Honours:* Melody Maker Poll Winners Recording. *Address:* 27 The Glade, Epsom, Surrey KT17 2HN, England.

MCKENZIE, Julia Kathleen; b. 17 Feb. 1942, London, England. Actress; Vocalist. m. Gerald Hjert, 9 Sept. 1972. *Education:* Guildhall School of Music and Drama. *Career:* Television: Fresh Fields; French Fields; Julia and Company; Maggie and Her; Blott On The Landscape; Numerous dramas; Stage: 5 Sondheim musicals; National Theatre; 4 Alan Ayckbourn plays; Directing: Stepping Out; Steel Magnolias; Honk The Ugly Duckling; in New York, London, Tokyo, Denmark. *Recordings:* Albums include: The Musicals' Albums; Into The Woods; Side By Side By Sondheim; Unexpected Songs. *Publications:* Clothes Line. *Honours:* Swet Awards; Olivier Awards; Evening Standard Award; Emmy; Hon. Fellow of Guildhall; Dr of Letters, South Bank University. *Current Management:* April Young Ltd. *Address:* April Young Ltd, 11 Woodlands Rd, London SW13 0JZ, England.

MACKENZIE, Talitha; b. 3 April 1956, Oceanside, New York, USA. Vocalist; Musician (keyboards); Composer; Arranger; Actress; Dancer. m. Ian MacKenzie, 6 Sept. 1988, 2 s. *Education:* Connecticut College, 1974–76; New England Conservatory of Music, Boston, USA; Private study, Classical piano, 1960–78, Classical/Jazz Voice, 1977–80. *Career:* Concerts include: Ronnie Scott's, London; Chard Festival of Women in Music; WOMAD; Celts in Kent Festival, England; Edinburgh Festival Fringe; Celtic Connections Festival, Glasgow; Folk City, The Bottom Line, New York, USA; Vox Populi, Toronto; Cultures Canada, Ottawa; Winnipeg Folk Festival, Canada; Teatro Campoamor Oviedo; Juntos en Córdoba; WOMEX, Berlin; Melkweg, Amsterdam; Television includes: Arts and Parts, Don't Look Down, STV; Ex-S, Ainm a'Ghàidheil, Talla a'Bhaile; Sin Agad E, Brag, BBC Scotland; Global Jukebox, BSB; Radio includes: Nicky Campbell, BBC Radio 1; Mixing It, BBC Radio 3; Women's Hour, BBC Radio 4; Meridian, BBC World Service; All Things Considered, NPR, USA; The Usual Suspects, BBC Radio Scotland; Kaleidoscope, BBC Radio 4. *Compositions:* Wall of Sound (for National Museum of Scotland event, Museum of Sound), 2001. *Recordings:* St James Gate, 1985; Shantyman, 1986; Mouth Music, 1990; Sòlas, 1993; Spiorad, 1996; Theatre includes: Réiteach, (Proiseact Naiseanta); Russian Ritual Wedding, Harvard University. *Publications:* The Triangle Trade: African Influences in the Anglo-American Sea Shanty Tradition, 1984; Song of the Scottish Highlands, Scot, 1985. *Honours:* Billboard Song Contest for Owen's Boat, 1994. *Membership:* Musicians' Union; BMI; MCPS; PAMRA; British Equity. *Current Management:* Donald MacQueen, Winning Promotions, 96/1 South Gyle Wynd, Edinburgh EH12 9HJ, Scotland. *Address:* 33 Millar Cres., Edinburgh, EH10 5HQ, Scotland. *Website:* www.sonas.swinternet.co.uk.

MCKEOWN, Leslie; b. 12 Nov. 1955. Vocalist. *Career:* Lead singer, Bay City Rollers, 1973–78; Appearances include: British tour, 1974; Television series featuring the group, Shang-A-Lang, 1975–77; Saturday Night Variety Show, ABC, 1975; Solo artist, 1978–; Tours as Les McKeown's 70s Bay City Rollers. *Recordings:* with The Bay City Rollers: Hit singles include: Remember (Sha La La), 1974; Shang-A-Lang, 1974; Summerlove Sensation, 1974; All of Me Loves All of You, 1974; Bye Bye Baby (No. 1, UK), 1975; Give A Little Love (No. 1, UK), 1975; Money Honey, 1975; Saturday Night (No. 1, USA), 1976; I Only Want To Be With You, 1976; It's A Game, 1977; You Make Me Believe In Magic, 1987; Albums: Rollin' (No. 1, UK), 1974; Once Upon A Star (No. 1, UK), 1975; Wouldn't You Like It, 1975; Bay City Rollers, 1976; Rock 'N' Roll Love Letter, 1976; Dedication, 1976; It's A Game, 1977; Greatest Hits, 1978; Solo albums include: All Washed Up, 1978; Rollerworld: Live At The Budokan, 2001. *Current Management:* Brian Gannon Management, PO Box 106, Rochdale OL16 4HW, England.

MCKERRON, Charlie (Charles Alastair); b. 14 June 1960, London, England. Musician (fiddle); Composer. *Career:* Member: Capercaillie, 1985–; Group, along with original material, specialises in fusing traditional Gaelic songs with contemporary arrangements; Had first UK top 40 single in Gaelic, Coisich A Ruin (from A Prince Among Islands EP), 1992; Formed Big Sky band project with John Saich and cousin Laura McKerron; Big Sky formed from the Glasgow Celtic Grooves concerts and features many top traditional and roots musicians in its mix of traditional Celtic music and contemporary electronic instrumentation. *Compositions:* Contributed to the film Rob Roy; Collaborations include: Fish; The Pearl Fishers; Fred Morrison. *Recordings:* Albums: with Capercaillie: Crosswinds, 1987; Sidewalk, 1989; Delirium, 1991; Get Out, 1992; The Blood Is Strong, Secret People, 1993; Capercaillie, 1995; To The Moon, 1996; Beautiful Wasteland, 1997; Glenfinnan – Songs of The '45

(recorded 1995), 1998; Nàdurra, 2000; group feature on: Rob Roy OST, 1995; with Big Sky: Source, 2000; features solo on: Music of The Fiddle, 1981; Suilean Dubh, Tannas, 1999; Tacsi (TV series), 2000; Pray For Rain, Andrew P White, 2001. *Honours:* Daily Record Golden Fiddle award.

MACKEY, Steve; b. 10 Nov. 1966, Sheffield, England. Musician (bass guitar). *Career:* Mem., Pulp, 1987–; Numerous tours, television appearances and festival dates; Contribution to film soundtrack, Mission Impossible, 1996. *Recordings:* Albums: Freaks, 1987; Separations, 1992; His 'N' Hers, 1994; Different Class (No. 1, UK) 1995; This Is Hardcore (No. 1, UK), 1998; We Love Life, 2001; Hits, 2002. Singles: Master Of The Universe, 1987; My Legendary Girlfriend, 1990; Countdown, 1991; OU, 1992; Babies, 1992; Razzmatazz, 1993; Lipgloss, 1993; Do You Remember The First Time?, 1994; The Sisters (EP), 1994; Common People (No. 2, UK), 1995; Sorted For E's and Whizz/Misshapes (No. 2, UK), 1995; Disco 2000, 1995; Something Changed, 1996; Help The Aged, 1997; This Is Hardcore, 1998; A Little Soul, 1998; Party Hard, 1998; The Trees/Sunrise, 2001; Bad Cover Version, 2002. *Address:* c/o Island Records, 825 Eighth Ave, New York, NY 10019, USA. *Website:* www.pulponline.com.

MACKIE, (Mackie Jayson); Musician (drums). *Career:* Mem., Cromagnons, Bad Brains; Mem., Fun Lovin' Criminals, 1999–; Numerous tours, festivals and television appearances. *Recordings:* Albums: Loco, 2001; Bag Of Hits, 2002. Singles: Loco, 2001; Bump/Run Daddy Run, 2001. *Address:* c/o Chrysalis Group plc, The Chrysalis Bldg, Bramley Rd, London W10 6SP, England. *Website:* www.fun-lovin-criminals.co.uk.

MACKIE, Richard James; b. 6 Jan. 1960, Bolton, Lancashire, England. Composer; Artistic Dir; Musician (keyboards, saxophone). m. Christine Anne Waterhouse, 20 April 1985, 2 d. *Education:* Laban Centre For Movement and Dance. *Career:* Member of bands including: The Surgical Support Band; The Pharaohs; The Selecter; Extensive tours, UK and Europe; Replacement keyboard player for Madness; Appearances at Montreux Pop Festival and Saturday Night Live in New York; Theatre and radio productions, 1984–; Padmates (produced by Kate Rowland); Zeitgeist Times; Ron Koops Last Roadshow; Many compositions for dance and dance theatre. *Recordings:* Albums and single with The Selecter. *Address:* 44 Dallas Rd, Lancaster, Lancashire LA1 1TW, England.

MCKINNA, Iain; b. 27 Jan. 1955, Kilmarnock, Scotland. Prod; Musician (guitar, bass, keyboards); Songwriter; Recording Engineer; Programmer. 1 s. *Career:* Recording engineer, 1977–; First production released 1993; Engineer, Bay City Rollers, 1984; Own band The Harmonics; Producer, Solas, Talitha MacKenzie, 1994; Album by Mike Heron, 1996; Concerts include: Guitarist with Flying Colours, Level 42 tour, 1982; Toured with Talitha MacKenzie's band, as guitarist; Support Runrig, 1993; WOMAD '94; Womex, Berlin, 1994; Edinburgh Festival; Also played in Netherlands, Spain, Canada. *Recordings:* As producer, session musician, computer programmer: Solas, Talitha MacKenzie (No. 12, World Music Charts), 1994; Nectarine No 9; Spoonfed Hybrid. *Honours:* Best Song, Music In Scotland Trust, with own band The Harmonics, 1993. *Membership:* PRS; MCPS. *Current Management:* Offbeat Scotland. *Address:* 107 High St, Royal Mile, Edinburgh EH1 15G, Scotland.

MACKINTOSH, Andrew Kenneth; b. 20 May 1953, London, England. Musician (saxophone). m. Bonnie Sue 10 Jan. 1975, 1 s. *Career:* Played with: Maynard Ferguson; Buddy Rich; Quincy Jones; James Last; Involved in studio work in London. *Recordings:* Appeared on recordings by: Paul McCartney; Elton John; Bill Wyman; Elaine Paige; Melissa Manchester. *Membership:* PRS; Musicians' Union. *Address:* 27 Station Rd, South Norwood, London SE25 5AH, England.

MACKINTOSH, Gregor; b. 20 June 1970, Halifax, West Yorkshire, England. Musician (guitar). m. Mandy Taylor, 5 Aug. 1995, 1 d. *Career:* Festivals include: Rockamring; Dynamo; Roskilde; World-wide tours, television: Channel 4 Special; ITV's Chart Show; MTV; Viva TV; Noisy Mothers; Various radio, television world-wide; Soundtrack for Clarion Audio advertisements. *Recordings:* 5 albums including: Icon; Draconian Times; Host, 1999; Believe In Nothing, 2001; 3 singles including: The Last Time; Long Form video: Harmony Breaks. *Honours:* Kerrang, MTV Best video: Embers Fire, 1994. *Membership:* PRS; Musicians' Union. *Current Management:* Northern Music, Bradford. *Address:* 43 Cheapside Chambers, Cheapside, Bradford, West Yorkshire, England.

MACKNESS, Vanessa; b. Fordingbridge, Christchurch, England. Painter; Vocalist. 1 s. 1 d. *Education:* Degree, fine arts painting, Camberwell School of Art, late 1970s; Postgraduate, London University. *Career:* Played with artists including Derek Bailey; Barry Guy; Alexander Balanescu; Nishat Khan; Paul Lovens; Phil Minton; Concert tours include: Derek Bailey's Company Week, 1990; 1991; Duo with Barry Guy, Taktlos Festival, Switzerland, 1990; Irma, opera by Tom Phillips, USA, England, 1992; 10th Anniversary Minton-Weston Makhno Project, Bern, Basel, Zürich, Taktlos Festival, Switzerland, 1993; Solo performance, Total Music Meeting, Berlin, 1993; Soloist, Reiner Korff's composition for 35 musicians, Peter Edel Festival, Berlin, 1994; Jazz and More Festival '95, Munich, with Minton/Weston's Natural Formations, 1995;

Numerous interviews and recordings for radio include: Music In Our Time, Company With Derek Bailey, Radio 3, 1991; Impressions with Brian Morton, Radio 3, 1992; Trio with Butcher and Durrant, duo with John Butcher, 1996; Television includes 2 appearances Blue Peter; Duo with Phil Minton, 1991. *Recordings:* 3 CD compilations; Company '91, with Alexander Balanescu, Derek Bailey, Paul Lovens, Paul Rogers, John Zorn, Buckethead; Respirtus, duo with John Butcher; Vocals, Derek Bailey's String Theory, 2000. *Honours:* Awarded funding, concert tour, The Improvised Music Touring Scheme; Art Council Tour of England, with (bassist) Barry Guy, 1990. *Membership:* PRS. *Address:* c/o Incus Records, 14 Downs Rd, London E5 8DS, England.

MCLAREN, Malcolm Robert Andrew; b. 22 Jan. 1946, London, England. *Education:* Studied Fine Art, University of London. *Career:* Opened shop on King's Road with Vivienne Westwood (known as Sex), 1972; Created The Sex Pistols, 1974–79; Managed New York Dolls, USA, 1974; Created The Damned, with Chrissie Hynde; Gave first opportunities to Siouxsie and The Banshees, The Clash; Producer for artistes: Adam and The Ants; Bow Wow Wow; Boy George; Began solo recording career, 1981; Produced rap record, Buffalo Gals; Developed idea of World Music with Duck Rock, 1982; Developed film projects with Steven Spielberg, Hollywood, 1985; Paris album with Catherine Deneuve, 1994; Writing, producing musicals for cinema, stage; Candidate, Lord Mayor of London elections, 1999. *Compositions:* Music for advertising including theme for British Airways; Screenplay: The Great Rock 'N' Roll Swindle, 1979; Television musical: The Ghosts of Oxford Street, 1991. *Recordings:* Albums: Duck Rock, 1982; Fans, 1983; Waltz Darling, 1988; Paris, 1994; Paris The Ambient Album, 1996; Buffalo Gals Back to Skool, 1998; World Famous Supreme Team Show, 1998; Singles: Buffalo Gals, 1982; Soweto, 1983; Double Dutch, 1983; Madam Butterfly, 1984; Deep In Vogue, 1988; Something's Jumping In Your Shirt, 1989; Romeo and Juliet, 1991; Revenge of the Flowers, 1995; The Bell Song, 1997; Buffalo Gals Stampede, 1998; Opera House, 1998. *Membership:* Musicians' Union; PRS; SAG; SPAM. *Address:* 61 rue de Varenne, 75007 Paris, France.

MCLAUGHLIN, David Wallace; b. 13 Feb. 1958, Washington DC, USA. Musician (guitar, piano, mandolin, violin, bass, drums, percussion, banjo). m. Marilyn Gay Harman, 1 d. *Education:* Private lessons: piano, violin, classical guitar, mandolin. *Career:* Full time musician, 1978–; Carnegie Hall; Lincoln Centre; White House; Madison Square Garden; Library of Congress; Wolf Trap; Grand Ole Opry; Ambassador Auditorium; Knoxville Worlds Fair; TV appearances: TNN; PBS; CBS; Tours: USA; Canada; England; Africa; India. *Recordings:* with The Johnson Mountain Boys: Walls of Time, 1981; Working Close, 1982; Live At The Birchmere, 1983; We'll Still Sing On, 1984; Let The Whole World Talk, 1985; At The Old School House, 1988; Blue Diamond, 1990; Play Requests, 1986; with Crowe and McLaughlin: Going Back On Rounder; Contributed to: Adams County Banjo, Tom Adams, 2001. *Honours:* Awards from: IBMA; SPBGMA; WAMA. *Membership:* IBMA; WAMA; BMI; NARAS. *Current Management:* Shepherd Productions. *Address:* 18E Monmouth St, Winchester, VA 22601, USA.

MCLAUGHLIN, Dermot; b. 17 Aug. 1961, Derry, County Derry, Ireland. Irish Traditional Musician (fiddle). *Education:* Graduate, Trinity College, Dublin, Early and Modern Irish Language, Literature. *Career:* National Concert Hall, Dublin; Frequent radio and television appearances in Ireland; Concert tours and performances in: Ireland; UK; Europe; Nova Scotia; Record producer for Claddagh Records, specialist Irish label. *Publications:* Strad, 1991; O Riada Lecture, University College, Cork; Claddagh and Nimbus Records. *Honours:* Foundation Scholar of Trinity College, Dublin, 1981–86. *Membership:* Music Officer for the Arts Council, Dublin. *Address:* c/o The Arts Council, 70 Merrion Sq., Dublin 2, Ireland.

MCLAUGHLIN, John; b. 4 Jan. 1942, Yorkshire, England. Jazz Musician (guitar). *Education:* Piano and guitar studies. *Career:* Played with Alexis Korner; Georgie Fame; Graham Bond; Gunter Hampel; Played and recorded with John Surman; Dave Holland; Member, Tony Williams' band, Lifetime, 1969–70; As solo artist, recorded with Charlie Haden; Airto Moreira; Miles Davis; Founder, Mahavishnu Orchestra (with Billy Cobham, Jerry Goodman, Jan Hammer; later with Jean-Luc Ponty, Michael Walden), 1969–; Founder, Shakti, with Indian musicians L. Shankar and Zakir Hussain; Founder, One Truth Band, 1978; Formed trio with Larry Coryell and Paco De Lucia, 1978. *Compositions include:* Mediterranean Concerto, premiered with Scottish National Orchestra, Glasgow Jazz Festival, 1990. *Recordings:* Albums include: Solo/Mahavishnu Orchestra: Extrapolation, 1969; Devotion, 1971; My Goals Beyond, 1971; Inner Mounting Flame, 1971; When Fortune Smiles, 1972; Birds of Fire, 1973; Between Nothingness and Eternity, 1974; Apocalypse, 1974; Visions To The Emerald Beyond, 1975; Inner World, 1976; Electric Guitarist, 1978; Best Of, 1980; Belo Horizonte, 1981; Music Spoken Here, 1983; Live At The Royal Festival Hall, 1990; Greatest Hits, 1991; Que Alegria, 1992; After The Rain, 1995; The Heart of Things, 1997; Belo Horizonte, 1999; The Heart Of Things: Live In Paris, 2000; with Shakti: Shakti With John McLaughlin, 1975; Natural Elements, 1977 Remember Shakti, 1999; with Al Di Meola and Paco De Lucia: Friday Night In San Francisco, 1978; with One Truth Band: Electric Dreams, 1979; with Santana: Mclaughlin and Santana, 1994; Compilations: Compact Jazz, 1993; This is Jazz, Vol. 17, 1996.

MCLAUGHLIN, John I; b. 8 Jan. 1965, Glasgow, Scotland. Songwriter; Prod. *Career:* Writer and Producer, When the Lights Go Out with Five, 1998; Contributed tracks for Billie's debut album, 1998; Contributions to 911 albums The Journey and Moving On, 1997, 1998; Contributor to Matthew Marsden's debut album; Songwriter for pop/Motown act Mero; Collaborations with Graham Lyle, Lamont Dozier, The Full Crew, Steve DuBerry, Dave James, Paul Masterson. *Compositions include:* For 911: Love Sensation; Don't Make Me Wait; Bodyshakin'; The Journey; All I Want Is You; United Forever More, for Cliff Richard. *Current Management:* Backlash Music Management, 54 Carlton Pl., Glasgow G5 9TW, Scotland.

MCLEAN, Alexander James, (Bone); b. 9 Jan. 1978, West Palm Beach, FL, USA. Vocalist; Musician (bass guitar). *Career:* Puppeteer, Welcome Freshmen, on Nickelodeon satellite TV; Mem., Backstreet Boys, 1993–; Numerous tours and television appearances. *Recordings:* Albums: Backstreet Boys, 1996; Live in Concert, 1998; Backstreet's Back, 1998; Millennium, 1999; Black And Blue, 2000; Greatest Hits Chapter 1, 2001. Singles: We've Got It Goin' On, 1995; Quit Playing Games, 1998; I'll Never Break Your Heart, 1998; Everybody, 1998; As Long As You Love Me, 1998; Anywhere for You, 1998; All I Have to Give, 1998; I Want It That Way (No. 1, UK), 1999; Larger Than Life, 1999; Show Me The Meaning of Being Lonely, 2000; The One, 2000; Shape of My Heart, 2000; Drowning, 2001; The Call, 2001. *Honours:* MTV European Music Award, Best Pop Act, 1997, Best Group, 1999; Billboard Music Awards, Best Group, Best Adult Contemporary Group, 1998, Album of the Year, Artist of the Year, 1999; MTV Music Video Awards, Best Group Video, 1998, Viewer's Choice, for I Want It That Way, 1999; World Music Awards, Best-Selling Pop Group, 1999, 2000, Best-Selling R&B Group, 1999, 2000, Best-Selling Dance Group, 1999, 2000, Best American Group, 2000; American Music Awards, Favorite Pop/Rock Band, Duo or Group, 2000, 2001. *Website:* www.backstreetboys.com.

MCLEAN, Don; b. 2 Oct. 1945, New Rochelle, NY, USA. Vocalist; Musician (guitar, 5 string banjo); Composer. m. Patricia Shnier, 13 March 1987, 1 s., 1 d. *Education:* BBA, Iona College, 1965–68; Villanova University; Opera Bel Canto voice training, aged 12; Also learned from Josh White, Pete Seeger, Brownie McGhee. *Career:* Owner, Pres., Benny Bird Publishing Corpn, Inc, Don McLean Music, Starry Night Music; Mem., Hudson River Sloop Singers, 1969; Solo concert tours throughout USA, Canada, Australia, Europe, Far East; Numerous TV appearances. *Compositions:* Over 200 songs, incl.: American Pie (No. 1, USA), 1971; Tapestry, Vincent (Starry, Starry Night) (No. 1, UK), 1972; And I Love You So, 1971; Headroom, 1967, 1990; Castles In The Air, 1970; Dreidle, 1972; If We Try, 1972; Prime Time, 1978; Jerusalem, 1982; Angry Words, 1995; You're My Little Darlin, 1995; This Is America (Eisenhower), 1999; Film scores for Fraternity Row, Flight of Dragons. *Recordings:* Albums: Tapestry, 1970; American Pie (No. 1, USA), 1971; Don McLean, 1972; Playin' Favorites, 1973; Homeless Brother, 1974; Solo, 1976; Prime Time, 1977; Chain Lightning, 1979; Believers, 1982; Dominion, 1983; Love Tracks, 1988; Headroom, 1991; Favorites And Rarities, 1993; River Of Love, 1995; For The Memories, Vols I and II, 1996; Christmas Dreams, 1997; Starry Starry Night, 2001. Singles include: The Mountains Of Mourne, 1973; Wonderful Baby, 1975; Crying (No. 1, UK), 1980; Since I Don't Have You, 1981; Hit cover versions by: Perry Como (And I Love You So), 1973; Madonna (American Pie) (No. 1, UK), 2000. *Publications:* Songs of Don McLean, Vol. I, 1972, Vol. II, 1974. *Honours:* Israel Bonds Award, 1981; Over 40 Gold and Platinum discs world-wide. *Membership:* ASCAP; BMI; NARAS; AFTRA; Lotos Club; Coffee House, NYC; Groucho Club, UK. *Address:* c/o Atlantic Records, 1790 Avenue of the Americas, New York, NY 10104, USA.

MCLEAN, Jackie, (John Lenwood); b. 17 May 1932, New York, NY, USA. Musician (alto saxophone); Prof., African American Music. m. Clarice Simmons, 2 s., 1 d. *Education:* A & T College, Greensboro, North Carolina. *Career:* Performs regularly nationally at major concert halls; Tours Europe and Japan annually; USIS tour of South African countries: Namibia; Swaziland; Mozambique; Lesotho; South Africa (Johannesburg, Durban, Cape Town). *Compositions include:* Dig; Little Melonae; Minor March. *Recordings include:* Rhythm of The Earth; The Rites of Passage; Monuments; Contours; Jackie McLean and Co; New Soil; Dynasty; New Wine, Old Bottles; Hat Trick; Fire and Love; Nature Boy, 2000. *Honours:* Voted No. 1 alto saxophonist in Japan, Europe, America; Swing Journal Best Altoist, Downbeat Magazine Critics and Readers Poll, 1993, 1994, 1995; Awarded Officer of the Order of Arts and Letters medal by Jack Lang, Minister of Culture under Francois Mitterand. *Current Management:* Dollie McLean. *Address:* 261 Ridgefield St, Hartford, CT 06112, USA.

MACLEOD, James; b. 19 Aug. 1974, Sutton Coldfield, West Midlands, England. Musician (guitar, bass guitar); Vocalist; Composer; Lyricist. *Education:* King Edward VI School, Lichfield, ABRSM Grade 7 Theory. *Career:* Bass guitarist for Birmingham four-piece band, The Cantels, 1991; Performances incl. Birmingham Hummingbird club; As guitarist, performed national BBC Radio sessions and residencies at Ronnie Scott's Club, Birmingham, with Lou Dalgliesh Band, 1993; Composer, 1990s; Founder, with Martin Betts, alternative power pop band, The Macleods, 1998–, performing throughout UK. *Membership:* Musicians' Union. *Address:* 60 Cornfield Dr., Lichfield, Staffordshire WS14 9UG, England.

MCLEOD, Rory; b. 23 Jan. 1955, London, England. Vocalist; Songwriter; Poet; Storyteller; Musician (harmonica, guitar, trombone, percussion). 1 s. *Career:* Former Mexican circus clown and fire-eater; Played harmonica and guitar with Michelle Shocked; Ani Di Franco; Ali Farka Touré; Taj Mahal; Collaborated with Hassan Erraji; Kathryn Tickell; Paul Rodden; Eliza Carthy; Anam; The Oysterband; Radio and television appearances: BBC Radio 4 documentary; CH4 TV, After Image singing Farewell Welfare; Scottish Circus Physical Theatre Company as composer, musical director on Hey Big Nose, psychocomedy based on Punch and Judy. *Recordings:* Albums: Angry Love; Kicking The Sawdust; Footsteps and Heartbeats; Travelling Home; Lullabies For Big Babies, 1997; Mouth to Mouth, 2000; Single: I'm A Rebel Trying To Govern Myself (all self-produced, 1976–92); Compilation: The Disagreement Of The People. *Publications:* Poetry anthology: Apples and Snakes. *Honours:* Texas Harmonica Champion, 1981; Edinburgh Festival Busker of the Year. *Membership:* Musicians' Union; PRS; MCPS. *Address:* NE Music, 55 Lawe Rd, South Shields, Tyne and Wear NE3 3AL, England. *E-mail:* talkativemusic@dial.pipex.com. *Website:* www.rorymcleod.com.

MCLINTON, Delbert Ross; b. 4 Nov. 1940, Lubbock, Texas, USA. Vocalist; Songwriter; Musician (harmonica). m. Wendy Goldstein. *Career:* Recording artist with The Straightjackets and The Rondelles. *Compositions:* I Want To Love You; Two More Bottles of Wine; Giving It Up For Love; B Movie. *Recordings:* Albums: Victim of Life's Circumstances, 1975; Genuine Cowhide, 1976; Love Rustler, 1977; Second Wind, 1978; Keeper of The Flame, 1979; The Jealous Kind, 1980; Plain From The Heart, 1981; Live From Austin, 1989; I'm With You, 1990; Best Of..., 1991; Never Been Rocked Enough, 1992; Delbert McClinton, 1993; Let the Good Times Roll, 1995; The Great Songs – Come Together, 1995; One of the Fortunate Few, 1997; with T Graham Brown: Wine into Water, 1998; with Danny Gatton: Hot Rod Guitar, 1999; with Flying Burrito Brothers: Sons of the Golden West, 1999; Don't Let Go (compilation), 2000; Nothing Personal, 2001. *Honours:* In Top 20 Harmonica Players, Rolling Stone magazine, 1985. *Membership:* BMI. *Current Management:* Harriet Sternberg Management. *Address:* 4268 Hazeltine Ave, Sherman Oaks, CA 91423, USA.

MCMANUS, John Patrick; b. Enniskillen, Northern Ireland. Vocalist; Musician (bass, low whistle, Uilleann pipes, bodhran). *Career:* First TV appearance playing whistle with Matt Molloy of The Chieftains, aged 8; All-Ulster Champion on tin whistle aged 7–12; Formed rock band Mama's Boys with brothers Pat and Tommy and toured the world twice; Numerous TV appearances: Mama's Boys disbanded owing to Tom McManus' leukaemia, 1993; Tom died 1994; Changed musical direction and formed new act Celtus with brother Pat, 1995; Signed to Muff Winwood, Sony S2, 1996; Co-wrote Celtus' debut album; Debut performance dates for Celtus as support to Sheryl Crow at Royal Albert Hall, Wolverhampton Civic and Manchester Apollo; 2 tours followed with Paul Carrack; Played Womad Festival; Won Phil Lynott Best Album Award for Moonchild, Irish World Awards, 1998. *Recordings:* as Mama's Boys: Official Bootleg; Plug It In; Turn It Up; Mama's Boys; Power and Passion; Growing Up The Hard Way; Live Tonite; Relativity; With Celtus: Moonchild, 1997; Portrait, 1999; Live 2000, 2001; What Goes Around, 2001. *Membership:* PRS; Musicians' Union. *Current Management:* Lindy Benson, Shamrock Music Ltd, 9 Thornton Pl., London W1H 1FG, England.

MCMILLAN, Stuart; b. 1966, Glasgow, Scotland. Prod; Remixer; DJ. *Career:* Started career as a DJ in Glasgow; Met Orde Meikle and started putting on their own club nights, Atlantis and Slam; Formed the Slam production duo and Soma Records label; World-wide DJ; Collaborations: UNKLE; Remixed: Sunscreem; Mansun; Dave Angel; Phuture; Kym Sims; Member: Universal Principles. *Recordings:* Albums: Headstates, 1996; Alien Radio, Past Lessons – Future Theories (DJ-mixed compilation), 2001; Singles: Eterna, 1991; Positive Education, 1993; Snapshots, 1995; Dark Forces, 1996; Narco Tourists, Lifetimes, Alien Radio 2001. *Address:* c/o Soma Records, 342 Argyle St, Glasgow, G2 8LY, Scotland.

MCMURRAY, Rick; b. 11 July 1975, Larne, Co Antrim, Northern Ireland. Musician (drums, percussion). *Career:* Mem., Ash, 1992–; Numerous headline tours, UK festivals and television appearances; Record deal and tour of USA; Contributed track to film, A Life Less Ordinary, 1997. *Recordings:* Albums: Trailer, 1994; 1977, 1996; Live At The Wireless, 1997; Nu-Clear Sounds, 1998; Free All Angels, 2001; Intergalactic Sonic 7's: The Best Of Ash, 2002; Envy, 2002. Singles: Jack Names the Planets, 1994; Petrol, 1994; Uncle Pat, 1994; Kung Fu, 1995; Girl From Mars, 1995; Angel Interceptor, 1995; Goldfinger, 1995; Oh Yeah, 1996; A Life Less Ordinary, 1997; Jesus Says, 1998; Numbskull (EP), 1999; Wild Surf, 2001; Burn Baby Burn, 2001; Shining Light, 2001; Sometimes, 2001; Candy, 2001; Tokyo Blitz, 2002; There's A Star, 2002. *Honours:* Ivor Novello Award, Best Contemporary Song, for Shining Light, 2002. *Address:* Infectious Records, 1 Shorrolds Rd, London SW6 7TR, England. *E-mail:* rick@ash-official.com. *Website:* www.ash-official.com.

MCNABB, Ian; b. 3 Nov. 1962. Vocalist; Songwriter. *Career:* Founder member, Icicle Works; Recording debut, 1981; Founder, own record label Troll Kitchen; Solo artiste, 1992–. *Recordings:* Albums: with Icicle Works: The Icicle Works, 1984; The Small Price of a Bicycle, 1985; 7 Singles Deep, 1986; If You Want To Defeat Your Enemy Sing His Song, 1987; Blind, 1987; Permanent Damage, 1990; The Best Of, 1992; Also appears: with Mike Scott, Still Burning, 1997; with the Waterboys, Whole of the Moon, 1998; with Pspyched!, 1999; Solo: Truth and Beauty, 1992; Head Like A Rock, 1994; Merseybeast, 1996; A Party Political Broadcast On Behalf Of The Emotional Party, 1998; Live At Life, 2000; Ian McNabb, 2001; Waifs And Strays, 2001; The Gentleman Adventurer, 2002. Singles include: with The Icicle Works: Nirvana, 1982; Birds Fly (Whisper To a Scream), 1983; Love Is A Wonderful Colour, 1983; Hollow Horse, 1984; Understanding Jane, 1986; Who Do You Want For Your Love?, 1986; Evangeline, 1987; Little Girl Lost, 1988; Motorcycle Rider, 1990. *Website:* www.ianmcnabb.com.

MCNALLY, John; b. 30 Aug. 1941, Liverpool, England. Entertainer; Musician (guitar). m. Mary Hollywood, 27 June 1964, 1 s., 1 d. *Career:* Member, The Searchers; Every major media appearance including: Ed Sullivan Show; Royal Variety Show; Palladium Show. *Recordings include:* Sweets For My Sweet (No. 1, UK), 1963; Sugar And Spice, 1963; Needles and Pins (No. 1, UK), 1964; Don't Throw Your Love Away (No. 1, UK), 1964; When You Walk In The Room, 1964; Goodbye My Love, 1964. *Honours:* Runners-up to the Beatles in numerous 60s polls. *Current Management:* Alan Field Ltd. *Address:* 3 The Spinney, Bakers Hill, Hadley Common EN5 5BY, England.

MCNALLY, Stephen Patrick; b. 4 July 1978, Liverpool, England. Vocalist; Musician (guitar); Songwriter. *Career:* Co-founder: BBMak pop group, 1996; Signed to UK company Telstar; Gained large US popularity after licence deal with Hollywood/Disney; Performed to over 100m. US viewers through group's own TV specials; Supported Britney Spears on sell-out US tour followed by 28-date first headline US tour, 2000; UK shows with The Corrs, 2001. *Recordings:* Albums: Sooner Or Later, 2000; Singles: Back Here, Still On Your Side, 2000; Ghost of You and Me, 2001. *Honours:* Debut LP sales of over 1m. copies. *Address:* c/o Diane Young. *E-mail:* DaytimeENT@aol.com. *Website:* www.bbmak.co.uk.

MCNAMARA, Danny; b. 31 Dec. 1970, Huddersfield, England. Vocalist; Songwriter; Musician (guitar). *Career:* Member, Embrace; Obtained major label deals in UK and USA; Debut single released independently; Early support slots to Manic Street Preachers, 1997; Headline tours and TV appearances. *Recordings:* Singles: Fireworks, 1997; One Big Family, 1997; All You Good Good People, 1997; Come Back To What You Know, 1998; My Weakness Is None of Your Business, 1998; The Good Will Out, 1998; Hooligan, 1999; You're Not Alone, 2000; Save Me, 2000; I Wouldn't Wanna Happen To You, 2000; Wonder, 2001; Albums: The Good Will Out (Number 1, UK), 1998; Drawn From Memory, 2000; If You've Never Been, 2001; Fireworks (Singles 1997–2002), 2002.

MCNAMARA, Richard; b. 23 Oct. 1972, Huddersfield, England. Musician (Guitar); Backing Vocalist. *Career:* Member, Embrace; Obtained major label deals in UK and USA, 1996; Released debut single independently; Support slot to Manic Street Preachers, 1997; Headline tours and TV appearances. *Recordings:* Singles: Fireworks, 1997; One Big Family, 1997; All You Good Good People, 1997; Come Back To What You Know, 1998; My Weakness Is None of Your Business, 1998; The Good Will Out, 1998; Hooligan, 1999; You're Not Alone, 2000; Save Me, 2000; I Wouldn't Wanna Happen To You, 2000; Wonder, 2001; Albums: The Good Will Out (Number 1, UK), 1998; Drawn From Memory, 2000; If You've Never Been, 2001.

MCNEAL, Lutricia; b. Oklahoma, USA. Vocalist; Songwriter. *Career:* Teamed up with Swedish production team Rob 'n' Raz; Numerous appearances in Europe, USA and Britain. *Recordings:* Singles: Ain't That Just The Way, 1997; Someone Loves You Honey, 1998; Stranded, 1998; The Greatest Love You'll Never Know, 1998; 365, 1999; You'll Never Know, 2000; Albums: Ain't That Just The Way, 1998; My Side of Town, 1998; Watcha Been Doing?, 1999.

MCNEELY, Joel; b. Madison, WI, USA. Composer. *Education:* Composition, Interlochen Arts Academy; University of Miami; Eastman School of Music. *Compositions:* For television: Davy Crockett: Rainbow in the Thunder, 1988; Splash, Too, 1988; Parent Trap III, 1989; Parent Trap Hawaiian Honeymoon, 1989; Tiny Toon Adventures, 1990; Appearances, 1990; Frankenstein: The College Years, 1199; Lady Against the Odds, 1992; The Young Indiana Jones Chronicles, 1992; Buffalo Soldiers, 1997; Buddy Faro, 1998; Road Rage, 1999; Sally Hemings: An American Scandal, 1999; Santa Who?, 2000; Dark Angel, 2000; For film: You Talkin' to Me?, 1987; Polly, 1989; Samantha, 1991; Squanto: A Warrior's Tale, 1994; Iron Will, 1994; Terminal Velocity, 1994; Radioland Murders, 1994; Gold Diggers: The Secret of Bear Mountain, 1995; Flipper, 1996; Supercop, 1996; Vegas Vacation, 1997; Wild America, 1997; Air Force One (additional music), 1997; The Avengers, 1998; Soldier, 1998; Virus, 1999; Lover's Prayer, 2000. *Honours:* Emmy Award, The Young Indiana Jones Chronicles: The Scandal of 1920. *Membership:* ASCAP. *Current Management:* Blue Focus Management, 15233 Ventura Blvd, Suite 200, Sherman Oaks, CA 91403, USA.

MACNEIL, Rita; b. 28 May 1944, Nova Scotia, Canada. Vocalist; Songwriter. 1 s., 1 d. *Career:* Host, one hour weekly CBC TV Music entertainment show;

Concert tours Japan, Australia, UK, Sweden, USA, Canada. *Recordings:* Singles include: Working Man (Worldwide hit), 1990; Albums: Flying On Your Own, 1986; Reason To Believe, 1988; Now The Bells Ring, 1988; Rita, 1989; Home I'll Be, 1990; Thinking of You, 1992; Once Upon A Christmas, 1993; Vol. 1 – Songs From The Collection, 1994; Porch Songs, 1995; Joyful Sounds: A Seasonal Collection, 1996; Music of a Thousand Nights, 1997; with The Chieftans: Fire in the Kitchen; Celtic Colours International Festival, 1999. *Honours:* Order of Canada; 5 Hon. Doctorates; 3 JUNO Awards; 4 Canadian Country Music Awards; 3 Platinum albums; 3 Double Platinum albums; 1 Triple Platinum album; 1 Gold album; 1 Silver album. *Membership:* SOCAN; CMA; CARAS; ACTRA; AFofM. *Current Management:* Lupins Productions. *Address:* PO Box 183, Sydney, Cape Breton, Nova Scotia B1P 6H1, Canada.

MCREADY, Mindy; b. 30 Nov. 1975. Vocalist; *Recordings:* Singles: Guys Do It All The Time, 1996; What If I Do, 1997; Maybe He'll Notice Her Now, 1997; You'll Never Know, 1998; One in a Million, 1999; Albums: Ten Thousand Angels, 1996; If I Don't Stay the Night, 1997; I'm Not So Tough, 1999; Super Hits, 2000.

MCSHERRY, John; b. 1970, Belfast, Northern Ireland, UK. Musician (uilleann pipes, tin whistle, low whistle); Composer. *Career:* Formed Tamalin with brother Paul, cousin Kevin Dorris and sisters Tina and Joanne; Played in Donal Lunny's band Coolfin with Nollaig Casey, Sharon Shannon, Ray Fean and Graham Henderson; Part of Lunasa with Michael McGoldrick; Collaborations: Niamh Parsons; Nanci Griffith; Shaun Davey; Dan Ar Braz. *Recordings:* Albums: Rhythm and Rhyme (with Tamalin), 1997; Lunasa Live, Coolfin, 1998; At First Light (with Michael McGoldrick), 2001; features on: Loosely Connected (Niamh Parsons), 1992; Each Little Thing (Sharon Shannon), 1997; Waking Ned (Soundtrack), 1998; This Is My Father (Soundtrack), 1998; Blackbirds and Thrushes (Niamh Parsons), 1999. *Honours:* All Ireland Championship, three awards by age 15; Oireachtas Piping competition, youngest ever winner at 18. *Address:* c/o Vertical Records, 752 Argyle St, Glasgow, G3 8UJ, Scotland. *Website:* www.johnmcsherry.com.

MCTELL, Ralph; b. 3 Dec. 1944, Farnborough, Kent, England. Folk Vocalist; Songwriter; Musician (guitar). *Career:* Folk singer, 1960s–; Appearances, UK children's television including: Alphabet Zoo, Tickle On The Tum, 1980s. *Compositions include:* Streets of London, 1969; Zimmerman Blues, 1972. *Recordings:* Albums include: Eight Frames A Second, 1968; Spiral Staircase, 1969; My Side of Your Window, 1970; Not Till Tomorrow, 1972; Easy, 1973; Streets, 1975; Right Side Up, 1976; Ralph, Albert and Sydney, 1977; Slide Away The Screens, 1979; Love Grows, 1982; Sighs, 1987; Stealin' Back, 1990; The Boy With The Note, 1992; The Silver Celebration, 1992; Sand in Your Shoes, 1995; Songs For Six Strings Vol. II, 1996; Red Sky, 2001; Hit single: Streets of London (No. 2, UK), 1974. *Current Management:* Tickety-Boo Ltd. *Address:* The Boat House, Crabtree Lane, London SW6 6TY, England.

MCVICAR, Ewan Reynolds; b. 17 April 1941, Inverness, Scotland. Songwriter; Vocalist; Musician (guitar, banjo, autoharp); Author; Poet. m. Linda Rosemary Gammie, 30 April 1971. *Education:* Associate Member, Institute of Bankers in Scotland, 1959; Diploma in Social Work, Glasgow University, 1975; MSc (Scottish Children's Songs) by research, Edinburgh University, 1997–98. *Career:* Founded first folk club in Scotland, 1959; Toured and taught music in USA, 1965–67; Based in Glasgow, singing and writing, 1968–; Tour of Finland, 1980; Wrote show for the Glasgow-Nurnberg Twinning, 1985; Songmaker in Schools Project, 1991–; Mungo 200 Project with Amu Logotse, 1994–95; Scottish Arts Council, Writer in Residence, Craigmillar, Edinburgh, 1998–2000; Chair, Sangschule, Linlithgow, 1998; Co-animateur, Singers Gathering, Livingston, 1999. *Compositions:* Talking Army Blues, 1959; 20 songs commercially covered by other singers and groups; Shows written include: Salmon Spells; Church Bells; The Fyffes Banana Boat Show; Wrote 16 songs for The Singing Kettle Shows, 1990–98. *Recordings:* Gies Peace, 1987; Produced and released album, I Was Born In Glasgow, 1989; The New Songs of Fife, 1999. *Publications:* One Singer One Song, book, 1990; Streets, Schemes and Stages, book, 1991; Cod Liver Oil and The Orange Juice, book, 1993; Pictworks, booklet of Pictish poems and songs, 1999. *Honours:* Finalist, Songsearch, 1988. *Membership:* Musicians' Union. *Current Management:* Gallus Music.

MCVIE, Christine, (Christine Perfect); b. 12 July 1943, Birmingham, England. Musician (keyboards); Vocalist; Songwriter; Prod. m. (1) John McVie, divorced, (2) Eduardo Quintela, 18 Oct. 1986. *Career:* Member, Chicken Shack; Member, Fleetwood Mac, 1970–90; Numerous tours, concerts, television include: US Festival, San Bernadino, California; Shake The Cage tour, Europe, Australia, 1988; Wembley Stadium, with Jethro Tull, Hall and Oates, 1990; The Mask tour, 1990. *Compositions include:* Don't Stop; You Make Loving Fun. *Recordings:* Albums with Fleetwood Mac: Future Games, 1971; Bare Trees, 1972; Penguin, 1973; Mystery To Me, 1973; Heroes Are Hard To Find, 1974; Fleetwood Mac (No. 1, USA), 1975; Rumours (No. 1, UK and USA), 1977; Tusk (No. 1, UK), 1979; Fleetwood Mac Live, 1980; Mirage (No. 1, USA), 1982; Tango In The Night (No. 1, UK), 1987; Greatest Hits, 1988; Behind The Mask (No. 1, UK), 1990; 25 Years: The Chain (box set), 1992; Time, 1995; Solo: Christine McVie, 1984; Film soundtrack: A Fine

Mess, 1985; Contributor: Law and Order, Lindsey Buckingham, 1981; Rock, Rhythm and Blues, compilation album, 1989; Singles include: The Green Manalishi, 1970; Over My Head, 1976; Rhiannon (Will You Ever Win), 1976; Say You Love Me, 1976; Go Your Own Way, 1977; Dreams (No. 1, USA), 1977; You Make Loving Fun, 1977; Tusk, 1979; Sara, 1979; Think About Me, 1980; Hold Me, 1982; Gypsy, 1982; Oh Diane, 1983; Big Love, 1987; Little Lies, 1987; Everywhere, 1988; Solo: Got A Hold On Me, 1984; Love Will Show Us How, 1984. *Honours:* Melody Maker Female Vocalist of the Year, 1969; American Music Awards, Favourite Pop/Rock Group, Favourite Pop/Rock Album, 1978; Grammy, Album of the Year, Rumours, 1978; Star on Hollywood Walk of Fame, with Fleetwood Mac, 1979; BRIT Award, Outstanding Contribution, 1998. *Current Management:* Courage Management, 2899 Agoura Blvd, Suite 562, Westlake, CA 91361, USA.

MCVIE, John; b. 26 Nov. 1945, London, England. Musician (bass). m. Christine Perfect, divorced. *Career:* Member, Fleetwood Mac, 1967–; Solo artiste, 1992–; World-wide appearances include: Windsor Jazz and Blues Festival, 1967; Miami Pop Festival, 1968; Reading Festival, 1970; Bath Festival, 1970; US tour with the Eagles, 1976; US Festival, 1982; Reunion, Presidential Inaugural concert, Maryland, 1993. *Recordings include:* Albums: with Fleetwood Mac: Fleetwood Mac, 1968; Mr Wonderful, 1968; English Rose, 1969; Pious Bird of Omen, 1969; Then Play On, 1969; Blues Jam At Chess, 1969; Kiln House, 1970; Fleetwood Mac In Chicago, 1971; Black Magic Woman, 1971; Future Games, 1971; Bare Trees, 1972; Penguin, 1973; Mystery To Me, 1973; Fleetwood Mac (No. 1, USA), 1975; Rumours (No. 1, UK and USA), 1977; Tusk (No. 1, UK), 1979; Mirage (No. 1, USA), 1982; Tango In The Night (No. 1, UK), 1987; Behind The Mask (No. 1, UK), 1990; 25 Years: The Chain (box set), 1992; Time, 1995; The Dance (No. 1, USA), 1997; Solo album: John McVie's Gotta Band With Lola Thomas, 1992; Singles include: Black Magic Woman, 1968; Albatross (No. 1, UK), 1968; Mr Wonderful, 1968; man of The World, 1969; Oh Well, 1969; The Green Manalishi, 1970; Rhiannon, 1976; Say You Love Me, 1976; Go Your Own Way, 1977; Don't Stop, 1977; Dreams (No. 1, USA), 1977; You Make Loving Fun, 1977; Tusk, 1979; Sara, 1979; Hold Me, 1982; Oh Diane, 1982; Big Love, 1987; Seven Wonders, 1987; Little Lies, 1987; Everywhere, 1987; Save Me, 1990; Got A Hold On Me. *Honours:* American Music Awards: Favourite Band, Favourite Album, 1978; Grammy Award: Album of the Year, Rumours, 1978; Star on Hollywood Walk of Fame, 1979; Gold Ticket Award, Madison Square Garden, 1990; BRIT Award, Outstanding Contribution, 1998. *Address:* c/o Ernst and Young LLP, 1999 Avenue of the Stars, Suite 2100, Los Angeles, CA 90067, USA.

MADIGAN, Brian Alan; b. 27 June 1964, Enfield, Middlesex. Composer; Musician (drums, flute). m. Barbara Madigan. *Education:* BA, Middlesex Polytechnic, London, 1988–91. *Career:* Composer, Performer with Hot Savoury Souffles, 1991–93; Wise Wound, 1992–96; Madigan, 1997–99; Festival appearances, 1992–99. *Compositions:* Dance Notes; Coincidence; The Fisher King. *Membership:* SPNM; MU. *Address:* 12 Bladul Buildings, Bath BA1 5LS, England.

MADLINGOZI, Ringo, (Sindile Brian Madlingozi); b. 1964, Cape Town, South Africa. Vocalist; Songwriter. *Career:* At school, led acapella group which performed at community and youth functions; Became vocalist for the group Ikwezi, and later for Peto; Peto won national Shell Road to Fame talent competition, 1986; Prize led to the role of support act for King's Trust concert in Swaziland headlined by Eric Clapton; Moved to Johannesburg; Spent 1990s as member of Gecko Moon; Various studio session work for radio commercials, film, and album recordings including: Simply Red; The Power of One soundtrack (with Teddy Pendergrass); The Lion King soundtrack; Hugh Masekela; Caiphus Semenya; Oliver Mtukudzi; First solo album, 1996; Performs a Xhosa version of the title song of UB40's Cover Up album, 2002. *Recordings:* Vukani, 1996; Sondelani, 1997; Mamelani, Into Yam', 1999; Buyisa, 2000. *Honours:* Sondelani received double platinum sales award; FNB South African Music Awards, Best Adult Contemporary Performance (languages other than English and Afrikaans), Sondelani, 1998; Kora All-Africa Music Awards: Best Southern African Artist; Best Male Artist, 1998; Kora All Africa Music Award, Best Artist/Group in Southern Africa, 1999.

MADONNA, (Madonna Louise Veronica Ciccone); b. 16 Aug. 1958, Bay City, MI, USA. Vocalist; Songwriter; Actress. m. (1) Sean Penn, 1985, divorced 1989, 1 d. by Carlos Leon, (2) Guy Richie, 2000, 1 s. *Education:* University of Michigan, 1976–78. *Career:* Dancer, New York, 1979; Actress, 1980–; Solo singer, 1983–; Film appearances include: Vision Quest, 1985; Desperately Seeking Susan, 1985; A Certain Sacrifice, 1985; Shanghai Surprise, 1986; Who's That Girl?, 1987; Bloodhounds on Broadway, 1989; Dick Tracy, 1990; Shadows and Fog, 1992; A League of Their Own, 1992; Body of Evidence, 1993; Dangerous Game, 1993; Blue in the Face, 1995; Four Rooms, 1995; Girl 6, 1996; Evita, 1996; Kids Are Puny (voice, TV), 1998; The Next Best Thing, 2000; Star, 2001; Swept Away, 2002; Die Another Day, 2002; The Tulse Luper Suitcases, 2003; Numerous world-wide concerts, television appearances, 1983–; Television includes: In Bed With Madonna (documentary), 1991; Stage performances: Speed The Plow, Broadway, 1988; Up For Grabs, West End, London, 2002; Owner, Maverick record label. *Compositions include:* Co-writer, many of her own hits; Co-writer, Each Time You Break My Heart, Nick

Kamen, 1986. *Recordings:* Albums: Madonna, 1983; Like A Virgin (No. 1, UK and USA), 1984; True Blue (No. 1, UK and USA), 1985; Who's That Girl (soundtrack), 1987; Like A Prayer (No. 1, UK and USA), 1989; I'm Breathless (soundtrack to Dick Tracy), 1990; The Immaculate Collection, 1990; Erotica, 1992; Bedtime Stories, 1994; Something To Remember, 1995; Evita (soundtrack), 1997; Ray Of Light, 1998; Next Best Thing (soundtrack), 2000; Music, 2000; GHV2, 2001. Singles: Holiday, 1983; Lucky Star, 1984; Borderline, 1984; Burning Up, 1984; Physical Attraction, 1984; Everybody, 1984; Material Girl, 1985; Angel, 1985; Crazy For You (No. 1, USA), 1985; Like A Virgin (No. 1, USA), 1985; Dress You Up, 1985; Into The Groove (No. 1, UK), 1985; Gambler, 1985; Papa Don't Preach (No. 1, UK and USA), 1986; Open Your Heart (No. 1, USA), 1986; Live To Tell (No. 1, USA), 1986; True Blue (No. 1, UK), 1986; The Look Of Love, 1987; La Isla Bonita (No. 1, UK), 1987; Who's That Girl (No. 1, USA and UK), 1987; Causin' A Commotion, 1987; Spotlight, 1987; Like A Prayer (No. 1, UK and USA), 1989; Express Yourself, 1989; Cherish, 1989; Dear Jessie, 1989; Oh Father, 1990; Keep It Together, 1990; Vogue (No. 1, UK and USA), 1990; I'm Breathless, 1990; Hanky Panky, 1990; Justify My Love (No. 1, USA), 1990; Rescue Me, 1991; This Used To Be My Playground (No. 1, USA), 1992; Erotica, 1992; Deeper and Deeper, 1992; Bad Girl, 1993; Fever, 1993; Rain, 1993; I'll Remember, 1994; Secret, 1994; Take A Bow (No. 1, USA), 1994; Bedtime Story, 1995; Human Nature, 1995; You'll See, 1995; One More Chance, 1996; You Must Love Me, 1996; Don't Cry For Me Argentina, 1996; Another Suitcase In Another Hall, 1997; Frozen (No. 1, UK), 1998; Ray of Light, 1998; Drowned World, 1998; Power of Goodbye, 1998; Nothing Really Matters, 1999; Beautiful Stranger (theme song for film Austin Powers: The Spy Who Shagged Me), 1999; American Pie (for film American Pie, No. 1, UK), 2000; Music (No. 1, UK and USA), 2000; Don't Tell Me, 2000; What It Feels Like For A Girl, 2001; Die Another Day (theme song for film James Bond: Die Another Day), 2002. *Publications:* Sex, 1992. *Honours:* Numerous MTV Video Awards, including Vanguard Award, 1986; American Music Awards, Favourite Female Video Artist, 1987, Favourite Dance Single, 1991; Academy Award, Best Song, 1991; Juno Award, International Song of the Year, 1991; Grammy Award, Best Longform Music Video, 1992; BRIT Award, Best International Female, 2001; Numerous awards from Billboard, Vogue and Rolling Stone magazines. *Current Management:* Norman West Management, 9348 Civic Centre Dr., Beverly Hills, CA 90210, USA. *Address:* c/o Maverick Recording Co, 9348 Civic Center Dr., Beverly Hills, CA 90210, USA. *Website:* www.madonna.com.

MADSEN, Tue; b. 25 Jan. 1969, Hadsten, Denmark. Musician (Guitar); Prod. *Career:* Playing Guitar for 18 years. *Recordings:* Pixie Killers: One Size Fits All; Grope: Primates, 1994; Soul Pieces, EP, 1996; The Fury, 1996; Desert Storm, 1997. *Membership:* DMF. *Current Management:* Diehard, Vindegade 101, 5000 Odensec, Denmark. *Address:* Terp Skovvej 50, 8260 Vibij, Denmark.

MAEL, Ron(ald), (Ronald Day); b. 12 Aug. 1950, Culver City, Los Angeles, CA, USA. Musician (keyboards); Songwriter. *Education:* BA, Graphic Design, University of California, Los Angeles; Piano lessons, age 6–10. *Career:* Mem., various bands, incl. Moonbaker Abbey, Urban Renewal Project; Mem., Halfnelson, with brother Russell and others, 1971; Became duo, renamed Sparks, 1973–; Collaborations on music videos and soundtrack contributions, 1970s–80s; Numerous concert tours, television appearances world-wide. *Recordings:* Albums: Halfnelson, 1970; A Woofer In Tweeter's Clothing, 1973; Kimono My House, 1974; Propaganda, 1974; Indiscreet, 1975; Big Beat, 1976; Introducing Sparks, 1977; Number One In Heaven, 1979; Terminal Jive 1980; Whomp That Sucker, 1981; Angst In My Pants, 1982; Sparks In Outer Space, 1983; Pulling Rabbits Out Of A Hat, 1984; Music That You Can Dance To, 1986; Interior Design, 1988; Gratuitous Sax And Senseless Violins, 1994; Plagiarism, 1998; Balls, 2000; Lil' Beethoven, 2002. Singles include: This Town Ain't Big Enough For The Both Of Us (No. 2, UK), 1974; Amateur Hour, 1974; Never Turn Your Back On Mother Earth, 1974; Something For The Girl With Everything, 1975; Get In The Swing, 1975; Looks Looks Looks, 1975; The Number One Song In Heaven, 1979; Beat The Clock, 1979; When I'm With You, 1980; I Predict, 1982; Cool Places (with Jane Wiedlin), 1983; So Important, 1988; National Crime Awareness Week, 1993; When Do I Get To Sing My Way?, 1994; When I Kiss You (I Hear Charlie Parker Playin'), 1995; Now That I Own The BBC, 1996; This Town Ain't Big Enough For The Both Of Us (with Faith No More), 1997; More Than A Sex Machine, 2000. *Honours:* Various Gold discs. *Membership:* Sons of The Desert. *Current Management:* Eric Harle, DEF Management. *Address:* 21 Premier House, 313 Kilburn Lane, London W9 3EG, England. *Website:* www.allsparks.com.

MAEL, Russell, (Dwight Russell Day); b. 5 Oct. 1953, Culver City, Los Angeles, CA, USA. Vocalist; Songwriter. *Education:* Film school. *Career:* Mem., various bands, incl. Moonbaker Abbey, Urban Renewal Project; Mem., Halfnelson, with brother Russell and others, 1971; Became duo, renamed Sparks, 1973–; Collaborations on music videos and soundtrack contributions, 1970s–80s; Numerous concert tours, television appearances world-wide. *Recordings:* Albums: Halfnelson, 1970; A Woofer In Tweeter's Clothing, 1973; Kimono My House, 1974; Propaganda, 1974; Indiscreet, 1975; Big Beat, 1976; Introducing Sparks, 1977; Number One In Heaven, 1979; Terminal Jive 1980; Whomp That Sucker, 1981; Angst In My Pants, 1982; Sparks In Outer Space, 1983; Pulling Rabbits Out Of A Hat, 1984; Music That You Can Dance To,

1986; Interior Design, 1988; Gratuitous Sax And Senseless Violins, 1994; Plagiarism, 1998; Balls, 2000; Lil' Beethoven, 2002. Singles include: This Town Ain't Big Enough For The Both Of Us (No. 2, UK), 1974; Amateur Hour, 1974; Never Turn Your Back On Mother Earth, 1974; Something For The Girl With Everything, 1975; Get In The Swing, 1975; Looks Looks Looks, 1975; The Number One Song In Heaven, 1979; Beat The Clock, 1979; When I'm With You, 1980; I Predict, 1982; Cool Places (with Jane Wiedlin), 1983; So Important, 1988; National Crime Awareness Week, 1993; When Do I Get To Sing My Way?, 1994; When I Kiss You (I Hear Charlie Parker Playin'), 1995; Now That I Own The BBC, 1996; This Town Ain't Big Enough For The Both Of Us (with Faith No More), 1997; More Than A Sex Machine, 2000. *Honours:* Various Gold discs. *Current Management:* Eric Harle, DEF Management. *Address:* 21 Premier House, 313 Kilburn Lane, London W9 3EG, England. *Website:* www.allsparks.com.

MAGEE, Curtis; b. 12 Aug. 1965, Co. Tyrone, Northern Ireland. Country Vocalist; Musician. m. Lyn, 3 d. *Career:* Fronted own band for many years; Solo; Professional, 1990–; Tours include: UK; Ireland; Spain. *Compositions:* 30 Great Singalongs; 50 Xmas Hits; 20 Country Gospel; My Forever Friend; 20, Country Linde Dance; 21 Great Love Songs. *Recordings:* 13 Albums; 4 Videos. *Honours:* Numerous CMC Awards, Solo Act of the Year. *Membership:* BCMA. *Address:* 42 Greenhall Manor, Coleraine BT51 3GN, Northern Ireland.

MAGIC, Mick, (R. M. Lancaster); b. 21 April 1958, Wimbledon, England. Record Co Exec; Musician (guitar, keyboards); Composer; Partner: Samantha J Taylor. *Career:* Owner, Music and Elsewhere record label, promoting new bands especially underground bands; Studio work with own band; Appearance on BBC Radio 5. *Recordings include:* with Magic Moments At Twilight Time: Psychotron O, 1988; Zoen Nostalgia, 1989; White Hawk Atomic, 1992; Creavolution, 1996. *Publications:* The M and E Newsletter and Yearbook, United World Underground News. *Membership:* Mensa. *Current Management:* United World Underground, 6 Farm Court, Farm Rd, Frimley, Camberley, Surrey GU16 8TJ, England. *E-mail:* magic@uwunderground.fsnet.co.uk. *Website:* music-elsewhere.hypermart.net.

MAGOOGAN, Wesley; b. 11 Oct. 1951, London, England. Musician (saxophone). m. Marion Willett, 10 March 1973, 1 s., 1 d., deceased. *Education:* Royal Academy of Music. *Career:* Hazel O'Connor; The Beat (also known as The English Beat); Joan Armatrading; Elton John; Billy Ocean; Extensive world tours, 1978–. *Recordings:* Albums: with O'Connor/Magoogan: Will You; with The Beat: Special Beat Service, 1982; with Hazel O'Connor: Breaking Glass, 1980; Sons and Lovers, 1980; Cover Plus, 1981: with Joan Armatrading: Secret Secrets, 1985; Sleight of Hand, 1986; Shouting Stage, 1988; 2 albums with Billy Ocean; with Magnum: Sleepwalking, 1992. *Membership:* Royal Society of Musicians. *Current Management:* Simon Davies. *Address:* 5 Paddington St, Marylebone, London W1M 3LA, England.

MAGUIRE, Martie, (Martie Seidel); b. 12 Oct. 1969, York, PA, USA. Musician (fiddle); Vocalist; Songwriter. m. Gareth Maguire, Aug. 2001. *Career:* Mem., teen group, Blue Night Express, 1983–89; Joined two friends performing on the streets of Dallas, the Dixie Chicks, 1989–; Support slots for: Garth Brooks; Emmylou Harris; Loretta Lynn; Signed to Sony; Mix of traditional bluegrass with mainstream country music; Numerous stage shows. *Compositions include:* Cowboy Take Me Away; Ready To Run; You Were Mine. *Recordings include:* Albums: Shouldn't A Told You That, 1993; Wide Open Spaces, 1998; Fly, 1999; The Compact Dixie Chicks, 1999; Star Profile, 2002; Home, 2002. Singles include: I Can Love You Better, 1997; There's Your Trouble, 1998; Wide Open Spaces, 1998; Long Time Gone, 2002; Landslide, 2002. *Honours:* Country Music Asscn Awards, Music Video of the Year, Single of the Year, for Wide Open Spaces, Vocal Group of the Year, 1999, Entertainer of the Year, Album of the Year, for Fly, Vocal Group of the Year, Music Video of the Year, for Goodbye Earl, 2000; TNN Music Award, Group/Duo of the Year, 1999; ACM Awards, Album of the Year, for Fly, Favorite Duo or Group, 1999; American Music Awards, Favorite New Country Artist, 1999, Best Country Group, Best Country Album, for Home, 2003; Billboard Award, Favorite Country Artist, 1999; Grammy Awards, Best Country Album, for Wide Open Spaces, 1998, Best Country Performance By A Duo or Group With Vocal, 1998, 1999. *Address:* c/o Country Music Asscn, 1 Music Circle S, Nashville, TN 37203, USA. *Website:* www.dixiechicks.com.

MAHAL, Taj, (Henry St Clair Fredericks); b. 17 May 1942, Massachusetts, USA. Composer; Musician. m. Inshirah Geter, 23 Jan. 1976. *Education:* BA, University Massachusetts, Amherst, 1964. *Career:* Composer, musician, 1964–; Early concerts, Boston; Tours across USA; Europe; Africa; Australia; Actor in films: King of Ragtime; Sounder; Sounder II; Theatre appearance: Mule Bone. *Compositions:* Taj; Like Never Before; Film soundtracks: Sounder; Sounder II; Brothers; Television shows: Ewoks; The Man Who Broke A Thousand Chains; Brer Rabbit; The Hot Spot. *Recordings:* Albums: Taj Mahal, 1967; Natch'l Blues, 1968; Giant Step, 1969; The Real Thing, 1971; Happy Just To Be Like I Am, 1971; Recycling The Blues and Other Stuff, 1972; Sounder (film soundtrack), 1972; Ooh So Good 'n' Blues, 1973; Mo'Roots, 1974; Music Keeps Me Together, 1975; Satisfied 'n Tickled Too, 1976; Music Fuh Ya, 1977; Brothers (film soundtrack), 1977; Evolution, 1978; Taj Mahal and The International Rhythm Band, 1980; Big Blues, 1990;

Mule Bone, 1991; Like Never Before, 1991; An Evening of Acoustic Music, 1995; Dancing The Blues, 1995; Phantom Blues, 1996; Señor Blues, 1997; Shakin' a Tailfeather, 1997; Taj Mahal and the Hula Blues, 1998; Sacred Island, 1998; Kulanjan, 1999; Shake it to the One you Love the Best, 1999; Big Blues: Live at Ronnie Scott's; Shoutin' In Key: Live, 2000. *Honours:* Best Ethnic Music Award, Brothers, 1979; Bay Area Music Awards, Brothers, 1979; Grammy Award, Contemporary Blues Album, 2001. *Current Management:* Folklore Productions, 1671 Appian Way, Santa Monica, CA 90401, USA.

MAHAR, Eric Frederick; b. 11 Jan. 1959, Hamilton, Ontario, Canada. Music Prod; Music Consultant; Musician (guitar, banjo, harmonica). m. 11 June 1988. *Education:* Jazz Program, Humber College; Studied classical guitar at University of Toronto. *Career:* Solo guitarist; Theatre guitarist; R&B country guitarist for The Mercey Brothers; Marie Bottrell; Joan Kennedy; Television appearances: Tommy Hunter Show; CCMA Awards Show; Sunshine Country. *Recordings:* Producer and performer for various record labels. *Membership:* Musicians' Union.

MAIDMAN, Jennifer Jane; b. 24 Jan. 1958, Upminster, Essex, England. Record Prod; Songwriter; Musician (multi-instrumentalist). *Education:* Classical guitar; Piano; Music theory. *Career:* Producer for: Paul Brady; Pili Pili; Murray Head; Musician, tours with: Joan Armatrading, 1983; Murray Head, 1984–; Paul Brady, 1985–; Penguin Café Orchestra, 1985–; Boy George, 1988–89; David Sylvian, 1988; Currently with: Penguin Café Orchestra; Annie Whitehead; Paul Brady; Murray Head; Northern Lights; Robert Wyatt. *Compositions:* Songwriter, albums by Sam Brown and Boy George; Co-writer with Annie Whitehead. *Recordings:* Extensive session work includes: Paul Brady; Gerry Rafferty; Joan Armatrading; Shakespears Sister; Boy George; Sam Brown; David Sylvian; Albums include: with Penguin Café Orchestra: When In Rome; with Paul Brady: Back To The Centre; Primitive Dance; with Shakespears Sister: Hormonally Yours; with Annie Whitehead: Home, 1999; The Gathering, 2000. *Honours:* Back To The Centre, Best Album, Ireland, 1986–87. *Membership:* Musicians' Union; PRS; MCPS; PAMRA. *Current Management:* Positive Earth Music. *Address:* 22 Richford Rd, London E15 3PQ, England.

MAINES, Natalie Louise; b. 14 Oct. 1974, Lubbock, TX, USA. Vocalist; Songwriter. *Education:* Texas Tech; Berklee School of Music, Boston, MA. *Career:* Mem., the Dixie Chicks, 1995–; Signed to Sony; Mix of traditional bluegrass with mainstream country music; Numerous stage shows. *Compositions include:* Sin Wagon. *Recordings include:* Albums: Wide Open Spaces, 1998; Fly, 1999; The Compact Dixie Chicks, 1999; Star Profile, 2002; Home, 2002. Singles include: I Can Love You Better, 1997; There's Your Trouble, 1998; Wide Open Spaces, 1998; Long Time Gone, 2002; Landslide, 2002. *Honours:* Country Music Asscn Awards, Music Video of the Year, Single of the Year, for Wide Open Spaces, Vocal Group of the Year, 1999, Entertainer of the Year, Album of the Year, for Fly, Vocal Group of the Year, Music Video of the Year, for Goodbye Earl, 2000; TNN Music Award, Group/Duo of the Year, 1999; ACM Awards, Album of the Year, for Fly, Favorite Duo or Group, 1999; American Music Awards, Favorite New Country Artist, 1999, Best Country Group, Best Country Album, for Home, 2003; Billboard Award, Favorite Country Artist, 1999; Grammy Awards, Best Country Album, for Wide Open Spaces, 1998, Best Country Performance By A Duo or Group With Vocal, 1998, 1999. *Address:* c/o Country Music Asscn, 1 Music Circle S, Nashville, TN 37203, USA. *Website:* www.dixiechicks.com.

MAJID, Rashid al; b. Lebanon. Vocalist; *Recordings:* Albums: Ala Meen Til'abha; Paris Concert–Live; Tidhak El Dinya; Shamaat Hayati; Al Dinya Hzooz; Khalleihom Yinfa'oonak; Ana A'ibbek; Ya Ba'd Hal Dunia Laih; Fugadnaak; Oummi; Ti'ess Tawwek; Ayallah.

MAK, Wai-Chu Clarence; b. 1959, Hong Kong. Composer; Musician (Electronics, Guitar); Educator. *Career:* Composed music for various arts groups including professional performing ensembles, dance companies and theatres; Produced concert of electronic music, computer music, contemporary music; Head of Composition and Electronic Music, Hong Kong Academy for Performing Arts; Organized projects for creative music making in Hong Kong; Radio Presenter of creative music. *Compositions:* include the works for orchestra, voice, choir, electronic means, multimedia, chamber music, Chinese music ensemble and live computer music. *Membership:* Hong Kong Composers Guild; Composers and Authors Society of Hong Kong; International Computer Music Asscn. *Address:* School of Music, Hong Kong Academy for Performing Arts, 1 Gloucester Rd, Wan Chai, Hong Kong.

MAKAREVICH, Andrei Vadimovich; b. 11 Dec. 1954, Moscow, USSR. Composer; Vocalist; Artist. 1 s. *Education:* Moscow Institute of Architecture. *Career:* Founder, artistic dir, soloist, Machine of Time (first professional rock group in Russia), 1969–; Creator, presenter, Smak television programme; Drawings have been exhibited in Moscow, St Petersburg, Riga, Latvia, Caserta, Italy. *Honours:* Merited artist R.S.F.S.R. *Address:* ORT (Russian Public TV), Smak, Akademika Koroleva str. 12, 127000 Moscow, Russia. *Website:* www.mashina.ru.

MAKAROFF, Edouardo; b. Argentina. Vocalist; Musician (guitar); Composer. *Career:* Solo artiste; Composed and performed on many film soundtracks; Presenter, television shows, Buenos Aires, Argentina; Moved to France, 1990, as part of tango group Tango Mano; Conductor, orchestra at tango club Dancing de la Coupole; Founder-mem., Gotan Project, 1999–; World-wide Gotan Project tour, 2002, mixing video, pre-recorded and live performances; Collaborations with many tango musicians. *Recordings:* Albums: Solo: Twelve albums; with Gotan Project: La Revancha Del Tango, 2001. EPs: El Capitalismo Foraneo, 2000; Triptico, 2000; Santa Maria, 2001. *Address:* c/o XL-Recordings, 17–19 Alma Rd, London SW18 1AA, England. *E-mail:* yabastarecords@noos.fr. *Website:* www.gotanproject.com.

MAKAROV, Jüri; b. 3 April 1959, Tallinn, Estonia. Promoter. m. Tiina Makarov, 3 July 1985, 1 s., 2 d. *Education:* Tallinn Technical University, Economy; Tallinn Music College. *Career:* Promoter, for: Jethro Tull; Steve Hackett; EMF; Bob Geldof; Procul Harum; Faith No More; The Pogues; Samantha Fox; Bonnie Tyler, 1986–. *Current Management:* A S Makarov Muusik Management. *Address:* Regati PSt 1.6 K, 0019 Tallinn, Estonia.

MAKEBA, Miriam Zenzile; b. 4 March 1932, Prospect Township, Johannesburg, South Africa. Vocalist. m. (1) James Kubay, 1950, divorced 1952, 1 d., deceased 1985, (2) Sonny Pillay, 1959, (3) Hugh Masekela, 1964, divorced 1966, (4) Stokely Carmichael, 1968, divorced 1978, (5) Bageot Bah, 1980. *Education:* Methodist Training School, Pretoria. *Career:* Mem., Cuban Brothers, 1950; Manhattan Brothers, 1950s; Mem., touring show, African Jazz and Variety, 1957–59; Exiled from South Africa, 1960–90; Musical, King Kong; Starred in semi-documentary film, Come Back Africa; Worked on international club circuit in Europe, South America, Africa; Appearances at jazz festivals incl.: Montreux; Berlin; North Sea; Unofficial South African representative, Festac '77 festival, Lagos, Nigeria, 1977; Concert with Hugh Masakela, Botswana, 1982; Guest, Graceland tour with Paul Simon, 1987; Ambassador to FAO, 1999–. *Recordings:* Albums: Miriam Makeba, 1960; The World Of Miriam Makeba, 1962; The Click Song, 1965; Pata Pata, 1972; Live At Conakry, 1975; Festac 77, 1978; Greatest Hits From Africa, 1985; Sangoma, 1988; Welela, 1989; Eyes On Tomorrow, 1991; Miriam Makeba And The Skylarks, 1991; Malaisha, 1996; Meet Me At The River, 1996; Country Girl, 1997; Folk Songs From Africa, 1997; The Best Of Miriam Makeba And The Skylarks, 1998; Live From Paris And Conakry, 1998; Homeland, 2000; Sounds Of South Africa, 2001; Definitive Collection: Miriam's Choice, 2002. *Publications:* Makeba, My Story (autobiography), 1988. *Honours:* Dag Hammarskjold Peace Prize, 1986; Grammy Awards, Kora Award, Best Arrangement, 2001; Polar Music Prize, Royal Swedish Acad. of Music, 2002. *Current Management:* Sam Nole Management, 230 Park Ave, Suite 1512, New York, NY 10169, USA. *Address:* c/o Food and Agricultural Organization, UN Agency Bldg, North Maxwell Rd, PO Box 1628, Accra, Ghana.

MAKEM, Tommy; b. 4 Nov. 1932, Keady, County Armagh, Ireland. Vocalist; Actor. m. Mary Shanahan, 21 Sept. 1963, 3 s., 1 d. *Career:* Major concerts: Royal Albert Hall; Carnegie Hall; Lincoln Center; Sydney Opera House; Doothy Chandler Pavilion; Boston Symphony Hall; Tampa Performing Arts Center; Madison Square Gardens; Newport Folkfest's Most Promising Newcomer; Television appearances: Ed Sullivan Show; Arthur Godfrey Show; Johnny Carson Tonight Show; Today Show; Merv Griffin Show; Danny Thomas Show; Entertainment Tonight; Dublin Late Show; BBC Late Show; TV series, USA, England and Scotland. *Recordings:* Four Green Fields; Gentle Annie; Freedom's Sons; Rosie; Sing Me The Old Songs; The Winds Are Singing Freedom; The Winds of Morning; The Boys of Killybeg; Lord Nelson; Farewell To Carlingford; Summer Roads; Venezuela; Vancouver; Farewell To Nova Scotia; Sally O; True Love and Time; Better Times; Song Tradition; Two For The Early Dew; Live At The National Concert Hall. *Publications:* Tommy Makem's Ireland; The Clancy Brothers and Tommy Makem Song Book; The Tommy Makem Song Book. *Honours:* Grammy Award; Irish American Top 100 of the Year (5 years); Irish American Hall of Fame. *Current Management:* Bard Enterprises. *Address:* 2 Longmeadow Rd, Dover, NH 03820, USA.

MAKHENE, Blondie Keoagile Gerald; b. 16 Sept. 1955, White City Jabavu, Soweto, South Africa. Vocalist; Musician (guitar, piano). m. Agnes Mary, 18 Dec. 1979, 3 d. *Education:* Grade 4. *Career:* Concert In The Park, 1984; Mandela Welcome Concert, Soweto South Africa, 1990; Black Radio Exclusive Conference, New Orleans, 1992; Africa For AIDS Concert, Sun City, South Africa, 1993; Panafest, Ghana, Accra, 1994. *Recordings:* Weekend Special, Brenda Fassie debut album; Amaquabane featuring Blondie Makhene, 1990; Albums: Elakho Likhona, Pure Gold; Isencane, Platform 1; Amadamara, Freddy Gwala. *Honours:* Most Outstanding Person, Voice Education Centre, South Africa. *Membership:* Dorkay House.

MALACH, Bob; b. 23 Aug. 1954, Philadelphia, Pennsylvania, USA. Musician (saxophone, flute, clarinet). m. Janine Dreiding, 6 Jan. 1981, 1 s., 1 d. *Education:* Study with: Jow Allard; Harold Bennett; Eddie Daniels; David Weber; Keith Underwood. *Career:* Ben Sidran, 1977; Stanley Clarke, 1977–79; Stevie Wonder, 1980–85; Bob Mintzer, 1983; Horace Silver, 1986; Robben Ford, 1987; Steve Miller Band, 1987; Bill Cosby Show, 1987–92; Mike Stern, 1994. *Recordings include:* Patti Labelle; Lou Rawls; The O'Jays; Mose Allison; Regina Belle; Jean Carne; Marc Cohn; Georgie Fame; Robben Ford; The

Jackson 5; Soundtrack to Woman In Red (Stevie Wonder); Hoop Dreams; Miles Davis In Montreux; Solo albums: Mood Swing, 1997; After Hours, 1999. *Publications:* Swing Journal; Jazz Life; Ad Lib. *Membership:* AFofM; BMI. *Current Management:* Go Jazz.

MALE, Johnny; b. 10 Oct. 1963, Windsor, Berkshire, England. Musician (Guitar). *Career:* Member, Republica; Numerous TV appearances and festival dates; Contributed track, Are Friends Electric, to Gary Numan tribute album, 1997. *Recordings:* Singles: Out of This World, 1994; Bloke, 1994; Ready To Go, 1996; Drop Dead Gorgeous, 1996; From the Rush Hour With Love, 1998; Albums: Republica, 1996; Speed Ballads, 1998.

MALININ, Alexander; b. 16 Nov. 1958, Sverdlovsk. *Education:* Sverdlov Philharmonic School of Performing Arts; Ippolitov-Ivanov Conservatory, Moscow. *Career:* Soloist, military choir of Ural District, late 1970s; Played in Poyut Gitari (Singing Guitars) ensemble; Performed with Golubiye Gitari (The Blue Guitars) ensemble; Worked with Stas Namin; Toured USA, 1986; Recorded joint album with Dave Pomerantz, 1986, a single from which entered the Billboard Top Forty; World-wide tours; Television appearances include: Pesnya Goda and Stariye Pesni o Glavnom. *Recordings:* 11 albums. *Honours:* Grand Prix Prize, Yurmala Music Festival.

MALKMUS, Stephen; b. 30 May 1966, Santa Monica, CA, USA. Vocalist; Musician (guitar). *Career:* Founder, lead singer, rock group Pavement, 1989–2000; Tours: USA, Europe; Japan; Australia; New Zealand; UK and Ireland including Reading Festival, 1994; Headlined Big Cat Festival Tour, Europe 1995; Lollapolooza Tour, 1995. *Recordings:* Albums: Slanted and Enchanted, 1992; Westing By Musket and Sextant, 1993; Crooked Rain, 1994; Wowee Zowee, 1995; Brighten the Corners, 1997; Terror Twilight, 1999; Solo album: Stephen Malkmus, 2001; EPs, singles: Slay Tracks, 1989; Demolition Plot, 1990; Perfect Sound Forever, 1991; Trigger Cut, 1992; Watery Domestic, 1992; Cut Your Hair, 1994; Gold Soundz, 1994; Range Life, 1995; Rattled By La Rush, 1995; Father to a Sister of Thought, 1995; Pacific Trim EP; Stereo, 1997; Shady Lane EP, 1997; Carrot Rope, 1999; Spit on a Stranger, 1999. Solo single: Discretion Boogie, 2001. *Address:* c/o Big Cat Records, PO Box 3074, Chiswick, London W4 4ZN, England.

MALLEY, Matt; b. 4 July 1963, USA. Musician (bass). *Career:* Member, Counting Crows; Numerous headlining tours and TV appearances including MTV. *Recordings:* Singles: Round Here, 1994; Mr Jones, 1994; Rain King, 1994; Angels of the Silence (live), 1996; Albums: August and Everything After, 1993; Recovering the Satellites, 1996; Across a Wire: Live in New York, 1998; Long December, 1999; Daylight Fading, 1999; This Desert Life, 1999; Hard Candy, 2002.

MALLOZZI, Charlie; b. Parma, Italy. Record Prod; Mixer; Songwriter. *Career:* Writer, Producer with Marco Sabiu, known as Rapino Brothers; Moved to London, 1992; Mixer, producer of Pop/Dance music; Member of groups: Tabernacle; Rapination. *Recordings:* Albums for: Take That; Kylie Minogue; Dannii Minogue; Lulu; Kym Mazelle; Rozalla; Hit singles: Could It Be Magic, Take That; Rhythm of The Night, Corona; What Is Love, Haddaway; I Know The Lord, Tabernacle; Love Me The Right Way, Rapination and Kym Mazelle; Also produced singles for: Alicia Bridges; Heaven 17; Sparks. *Honours:* BRIT Award, Single of the Year, Take That; Triple Platinum album, Take That. *Current Management:* Stephen Budd Management. *Address:* 109B Regents Park Rd, London NW1 8UR, England.

MALMI, Jani; b. 1959. Jazz Musician; Record Prod. *Education:* Private study with John Abercrombie and John Scofield. *Career:* Began playing with various rock bands, 1970s; Bandleader, own quartet; Leader, Jani Malmi trio (with Jorma Ojanperä and Markku Ounaskari). *Recordings include:* Graffiti, 1988; One Leg Duck, 1995; As producer: Kosketuksia, 1995.

MALMSTEEN, Yngwie; b. 1963, Sweden. Rock Musician (guitar). *Career:* Played guitar from age 8; Founder, rock groups Powerhouse; Rising; Lead guitarist, Steeler, Los Angeles, 1983; Lead guitarist, Alcatrazz, 1983–84; Solo artiste, with own band, Rising Force, 1984–. *Recordings:* Albums: with Steeler: Steeler, 1983; with Alcatrazz: No Parole From Rock 'n' Roll, 1984; Live Sentence, 1984; Solo albums: Yngwie Malmsteen's Rising Force, 1984; Marching Out, 1985; Trilogy, 1986; Odyssey, 1988; Live In Leningrad, 1989; Eclipse, 1990; No Mercy, 1992; Concerto Suite for Electric Guitar, 1998; Live in Brazil, 1998; Facing the Animal, 1998; Inspiration, 1999; Alchemy, 1999; Double Live, 2000; War To End All Wars, 2000. *Current Management:* James Lewis Entertainment, 14 Deerfield Lane, Greenwich, CT 06831, USA.

MALO, Raul F. Martinez; b. 7 Aug. 1965, Miami, FL, USA. Vocalist, Musician (guitar, bass guitar, piano); Songwriter; Prod. m. Betty. *Career:* Played bass guitar in high school and joined several small bands; Mem., The Basics, 1987; Formed the Mavericks with Robert Reynolds, late 1980s; Became band's lead vocalist, 1990–2001; Group signed to MCA, 1991; Solo artiste, 2001–. *Recordings:* Albums: with The Mavericks: Mavericks, 1990; From Hell To Paradise, 1992; What A Crying Shame, 1994; Music For All Occasions, 1995; Trampoline, It's Now It's Live, 1998; Best Of The Mavericks, 2000; Solo: Today, 2001. Singles: Solo: I Think I Love You, 2002. Features on:

Flaco Jimenez, 1994; Jewel of The South, Rodney Crowell, 1995; Letter To Laredo, Joe Ely, 1995; Long Stretch of Lonesome, Patty Loveless, 1997; El Cancionero – Más Y Más, Los Lobos, 2000; Canto, Los Super Seven, 2001. *Honours:* with The Mavericks: Grammy Award, I Don't Care If You Love Me Anymore, 1996; CMA Awards, Top Vocal Group, 1995, 1996. *Current Management:* Positive Management, 33 Salisbury Rd, Larkhall, Bath BA1 6QZ, England. *Website:* www.raulmalo.com.

MALONE, Tom, (Bones); b. 16 June 1947, Honolulu, Hawaii, USA. Musician; Arranger; Prod. 2 d. *Education:* BS, Psychology, North Texas State University, 1969. *Career:* As student played with: Les Elgart; The Supremes; Little Stevie Wonder; Marvin Gaye; The Temptations; Gladys Knight and The Pips; Joined Woody Herman's big band; Tours USA, Europe with: Frank Zappa, 1972; Blood Sweat and Tears, 1973; Billy Cobham, 1975; Joined Gil Evans Orchestra, 1973; Tours, Europe, Japan, Far East; Tour, USA with The Band, appeared in film: The Last Waltz, 1976; Television: Musician, arranger, Saturday Night Live, 1975–85; Musical director, above programme, 1981–85; Played with CBS Orchestra, Late Night With David Letterman, 1993–; Appeared in film The Blues Brothers; Tours with The Blues Brothers Band, 1988–90; Appearing in film, Blues Brothers 2000, 1998. *Compositions include:* Theme song, Saturday Night Live; Comedy songs for Jim Belushi, Eddie Murphy, Billy Crystal; Arrangements for films: The Blues Brothers; Sister Act; Television: Saturday Night Live; CBS Orchestra. *Recordings include:* Solo album: Standards of Living, Tom 'Bones' Malone Jazz Septet, 1991; Eastern Standard Time, 1993; Recorded with artists including: Blues Brothers; Gil Evans Orchestra; Miles Davis and Quincy Jones; Blood, Sweat and Tears; Frank Zappa; Pat Metheny; Cyndi Lauper; Sister Act; Steve Winwood; David Sanborn; James Brown; Spinners; Barry Manilow; Glen Campbell; B. B. King; Billy Cobham; Lou Reed; Bonnie Tyler; Diana Ross; Carla Bley; Harry Connick Jr; Pink Floyd; Buddy Rich; Woody Herman; J Geils Band; George Benson; Paul Simon; Chaka Khan; Village People; Gloria Gaynor; Carly Simon. *Address:* c/o Late Show, CBS Orchestra, 1697 Broadway, New York, NY 10019, USA.

MALONE, Walter (Wally); b. 20 Sept. 1946, Pittsburgh, Pennsylvania, USA. Musician (bass); Vocalist; Entertainer. m. Peggy Jones, 20 Oct. 1968. *Career:* Principle bassist with Bo Diddley, West Coast, 1970–94; Bassist, Lady Bo, 1969–; Backing musician for: Lightning Hopkins; Richard Berry; Chuck Berry; The Olympics; Play: Tony N' Tina's Wedding, San Jose, 1997–98; Cable Car Theatre, San Francisco, 1998–99; Concerts include: HIC Arena, 1971; Monterey Jazz Festival, 1973, 1974; Greek Theatre, 1976; Boardwalk, 1988; Monterey Blues Festival, 1994, 1995, 1999; Tours: East Coast, 1960s; West Coast; Canada; Pacific Northwest, 1970s; Main Event European, No. 1, 1987; Bo Knows… NIKE Inc, endorsement, 1989; Television: Kenny Rogers, 1971; Donnie and Marie, 1976–77; Live concert, Sweden, 1987; Arts and Entertainment Special, world-wide coverage, 1990; Lady Bo and the BC Horns, South Bay Scene, USA, 1996. *Recordings:* Albums: The Mighty Bo Diddley: Ain't It Good To Be Free, USA, 1984; France, 1988; The Mighty Bo Diddley, Triple X Records, 1994; Lady Bo and The BC Horns, Shebo-Shebad, 2000; Video: I Don't Sound Like Nobody, Bo Diddley with Lady Bo and The Family Jewel, UK, 1992; Flashbacks: Vol. One, Soul Sensations, 1994; Say That You Love Me, Lady Bo and The BC Horns, 1997. *Publications:* Listed: The Complete Bo Diddley Sessions, by George R White, 1993. *Membership:* President, AFM Local 153, 1996; President, RMA of Northern California; President, Professional Musicians of California. *Address:* 14680 Bear Creek Rd, Boulder Creek, CA 95006, USA.

MANCHESTER, Melissa; b. 15 Feb. 1951, Bronx, New York, USA. Vocalist; Songwriter; Scriptwriter; Actress. *Career:* Staff writer, Chappell Music; Backing singer, Bette Midler; Solo artiste, 1973–; Actress and scriptwriter. *Recordings:* Albums: Home To Myself, 1973; Bright Eyes, 1974, 1974; Melissa, 1975; Better Days and Happy Endings, 1977; Singin', 1977; Don't Cry Out Loud, 1978; Melissa Manchester, 1979; For The Working Girl, 1980; Hey Ricky, 1982; Emergency, 1983; Mathematics, 1985; Midnight Blue, 1988; Tribute, 1989; If My Heart Had Wings, 1994; Melissa Manchester performs Pocahontas, 1995; The Colours of Christmas, 1997; Joy, 1997; The Essence of Melissa Manchester, 1997; Midnight Blue: The Encore Collection, 2001; Singles: Midnight Blue; Whenever I Call You Friend (co-written with Kenny Loggins), 1978; Dont Cry Out Loud, 1979; You Should Hear How She Talks About You, 1982. *Honours:* Grammy Award, Best Female Vocalist, 1982; NARAS Governors Award, 1997. *Current Management:* c/o Kevin DeRemer, Beacon Hill Entertainment, 5440 Carbin Ave, Tarzana, CA 91356, USA.

MANCINA, Mark; b. 1957, USA. Composer; Musician (guitar). *Education:* California State Fullerton and Golden West College. *Compositions:* For television: Space Rangers, 1993; Lifepod, 1993; The Outer Limits, 1995; Houdini, 1998; From the Earth to the Moon, 1998; The Strip, 1999; For film: Space Mutiny, 1988; Future Force, 1990; Where Sleeping Dogs Lie, 1992; Sniper (additional music), 1993; True Romance (with others), 1993; Speed, 1994; Monkey Trouble, 1994; Born Wild, 1995; Man of the House, 1995; Bad Boys, 1995; Assassins, 1995; Fair Game, 1995; Money Train, 1995; Twister, 1996; Moll Flanders, 1996; Con Air (with others), 1997; Speed 2: Cruise Control, 1997; Return to Paradise, 1998; Tarzan, 1999; Bait, 2001; Domestic Disturbance, 2001; Training Day, 2002. *Membership:* BMI. *Current*

Management: Gorfaine/Schwartz Agency Inc, 13245 Riverside Dr., Suite 450, Sherman Oaks, CA 91423, USA.

MANDRELL, Barbara; b. 25 Dec. 1948, Houston, Texas, USA. Vocalist; Musician (guitar). m. Ken Dudney, 1967. *Career:* Worked with Joe Maphis, Tex Ritter, Las Vegas; Founder member, The Mandrells; Recording artist, 1966; Joined Grand Ole Opry, 1972; Television series, Barbara Mandrell and The Mandrell Sisters, 1980–82. *Recordings:* Hit singles include: Sleepin' Single In A Double Bed; Years; I Was Country When Country Wasn't Cool; (If Loving You Is Wrong) I Don't Want To Be Right; Til You're Gone; One of a Kind Pair of Fools; Albums: Treat Him Right, 1971; A Perfect Match (with David Houston), 1972; The Midnight Oil, 1973; This Time I Almost Made It, 1974; This Is Barbara Mandrell, 1976; Midnight Angel, 1976; Lovers Friends and Strangers, 1977; Love's Ups and Downs, 1978; Moods, 1978; Just For The Record, 1979; Love Is Fair, 1980; Looking Back, 1981; Live, 1981; In Black and White, 1982; He Set My Life To Music, 1982; Spun Gold, 1983; Back To Back (with David Houston), 1983; Clean Cut, 1984; Meant For Each Other (with Lee Greenwood), 1984; Christmas At Our House, 1984; Get To The Heart, 1985; Moments, 1986; Sure Feels Good, 1987; I'll Be Your Jukebox Tonight, 1988; Morning Sun, 1990; No Nonsense, 1991; Key's In The Mailbox, 1991; Standing Room Only, 1994; Entertainer of the Year, 1995; Fooled by a Feeling, 1995; It Works for Me, 1997; Branson City Limits (live), 1998; Sisters in Song, 1999; Duelling Country, 2000; The Ultimate Collection, 2001. *Current Management:* Mandrell Inc, PO Box 800, Hendersonville, TN 37077, USA.

MANGESHKAR, Lata; b. 1929, Indore, India. Vocalist; Actress; Songwriter. *Career:* Indian film playback singer; Daughter of actor and singer Dinanath Mangeshkar, sister of Asha Bhosle; First sang in Kiti Hasaal, 1942; Has recorded thousands of songs in 14 Indian languages. *Recordings:* Albums: soundtracks: Sargam, 1979; Darr, 1993; Hum Aapke Hain Koun... !, 1994; Dilwale Dulhania Le Jayeng, 1995; Dil To Pagal Hai, 1997; Lagaan, 2001; solo: Lata In Concert – An Era In An Evening, 1997. *Honours:* Filmfare Awards, 1958, 1962, 1965, 1969 (refused to be considered for this award after 1969 to encourage new talent); Filmfare Lifetime Achievement Award, 1993; Filmfare Special Award, 1994; National Awards, Best Female Playback Singer, 1972, 1975, 1990; Maharasthatra State Award, Best Playback Singer, 1966, 1967; Bengal Film Journalist's Award, Best Female Playback Singer, 1964, 1967, 1968, 1969, 1970, 1971, 1973, 1975, 1981, 1985; Dada Saheb Phalke Award, 1989; Videocon Screen Lifetime Achievement Award, 1996; Rajiv Gandhi Award, 1997; Lux Zee Cine Lifetime Achievement Award, 1998; IIFA London, Lifetime Achievement Award, 2000; Noorjehan Award, 2001; Maharashtra Ratna, 2001; Key of the City of Georgetown, Guyana, 1980; Hon. Citizenship of Republic of Suriname, 1980; Hon. Citizenship of Houston, Texas, USA, 1987; Hon. Doctorate, Literature from Pune University, 1990; The Government of Madya Pradesh instituted an annual national music award in 1984 named The Lata Mangeshkar Award. *Address:* c/o Lata Mangeshkar Foundation, 45121 Cougar Circle, Fremont, CA 94539, USA.

MANGIONE, Chuck (Charles Frank); b. 29 Nov. 1940, Rochester, New York, USA. Jazz Musician (trumpet); Composer. 2 d. *Education:* MusB, Music Education, Eastman School of Music, University of Rochester, 1963. *Career:* Formed Jazz Brothers with Brother Gap, 1958–64; Director, Eastman Jazz Ensemble; Teacher, Eastman School of Music, 1968–72; Freelance musician with Maynard Ferguson and Kai Winding, 1965; Trumpeter, Art Blakey's Jazz Messengers, 1965–67; Formed Chuck Mangione Quartet, 1968; Guest conductor, Rochester Philharmonic Orchestra, 1970; Numerous concerts world-wide include: Europe; Japan; Australia; South America; Montréal Jazz Festival, 1986; Television appearances include: PBS specials; Grammy Awards Show, 1981; Guest star, Magnum PI; Film appearance: Paradise Blues, 1984. *Compositions include:* Hill Where The Lord Hides; Land of Make Believe; Bellavia; Give It All You Got (1980 Winter Olympics theme). *Recordings:* Albums include: Chuck Mangione Quartet, 1972; Chase The Clouds Away, 1975; Main Squeeze, 1976; Feels So Good, 1977; Children of Sanchez (film soundtrack), 1978; Fun and Games, 1980; Journey To A Rainbow, 1985; Bellavia, 1986; Classics, Vol. 6, 1989; Live at the Village Gate, Vol. 2, 1995; The Feeling's Back, 1999; Everything For Love, 2000; Finest Hour (compilation), 2000. *Honours:* Most Promising Male Jazz Artist, Record World, 1975; Numerous Gold and Platinum records; Grammy Awards; Emmy Award, Music Composition and Direction, Give It All You Got, 1980; Numerous Magazine Poll Wins; Hon. MusD, 1985; Georgie Award, Instrumental Act of Year, 1980; Regents Medal of Excellence, New York State, 1984; Jazz Music Campus Entertainment Award, NACA, 1987. *Current Management:* c/o Gates Music. *Address:* Gates Music Inc, 476 Hampton Blvd, Rochester, NY 14612, USA.

MANGO BOY. See: **MCBEAN, Colin.**

MANGRAM, Myles Edwin; b. 30 July 1956, Pueblo, Colorado, USA. Personal Man; Record Label Exec. m. Chea Rivera, 3 July 1994, 2 s. *Education:* BS, Music Science, Master, Business Administration, Entertainment, Law studies; Classical and Jazz training since age 5. *Career:* Founder, President, Tri-M Management (personal management company, consulting service); President, Black Lion Records Inc (independent record label); Professor, Music Business Studies; Professional musician and record producer with: Dizzy Gillespie; Tom Scott; Denver Symphony. *Recordings:* As producer: Alyssa Milano (Gold, Platinum discs); Anita Whitaker. *Publications:* Research reports, articles for. *Publications include:* Optic Music Magazine; Music Connection; Future Systems International. *Honours:* Outstanding Young Man of America Award; Colorado Schlars Award; Presidential Scholars Award. *Membership:* Conference of Personal Managers; Entertainment Law Society. *Address:* Myles E. Mangram, 5200 White Oak Ave, #31, Encino, CA 91316, USA.

MANGWANA, Sam; b. 1945, Kinshasa, Zaire. Vocalist; Musician (guitar); Songwriter. *Education:* Started singing in the Salvation Army choir. *Career:* Member: Tabu Ley Rochereau's Africa Fiesta, c. 1962; Franco's TPOK Jazz, 1972; Formed Festival des Maquisards with Dizzy Mandjeku, 1968; Set up La Belle Sonora label; Founder: African All Stars, 1976; Based in Abidjan, toured Africa, Europe and the USA; Lives in Paris. *Recordings:* Albums include: Sam and Les Maquisards, 1968; Sam and African All Stars Vols 1 and 2, 1982; Maria Tebbo, Rumba Music, 1991; Gallo Negro (featuring Papa Noel), 1998; Sam Mangwana Plays Dino Vangu, 2000. *Honours:* Sam Mangwana Plays Dino Vangu reached number 3 in the European World Music album charts, 2000. *Address:* c/o Alison Loerke, 12501 11th Ave NW, Seattle, WA 98177, USA.

MANI, (Gary Mounfield); b. 16 Nov. 1962, Manchester, England. Musician (bass). *Career:* Former member, Stone Roses; Numerous tours, TV and festival appearances; Joined Primal Scream, 1999. *Recordings:* with Stone Roses: Singles: Made of Stone, 1989; Fool's Gold, 1989; She Bangs the Drums, 1990; One Love, 1990; I Wanna Be Adored, 1991; Waterfall, 1992; I Am The Resurrection, 1992; Love Spreads (No. 2, UK), 1994; Ten Storey Love Song, 1995; Albums: The Stone Roses, 1989; The Second Coming, 1994; The Very Best Of The Stone Roses, 2002; with Primal Scream: Singles: Swastikka Eyes, 1999; Kill All Hippies, 2000; Accelerator, 2000; Miss Lucifer, 2002. Albums: XTRMNTR, 2000; Evil Heat, 2002. *Website:* www.primalscream.net.

MANIFOLD, Keith; b. 2 April 1947, Biggin-By-Hartington, Derbyshire, England. Musician (guitar); Vocalist; Agent; Country Music Consultant. m. Alice Nadin, 21 Nov. 1970, 2 d. *Career:* Television performances: Opportunity Knocks – Songwriters; Sing Country; Nationwide; Midlands; Sounds; Grampian Today; Border Today; Sons and Lovers; Radio performances: Radio 2; Local radio; Founder member, North West Promotions. *Recordings:* 20 albums include: Keith Manifold In Nashville. *Honours:* Billboard Best Solo Award '75; Nottingham Award For Special Achievement, Numerous Country Music Club Awards. *Membership:* Equity; Agents Asscn. *Current Management:* Keith Manifold Entertainment Services. *Address:* Trenton House, 30 Bank Rd, Matlock, Derbyshire DE4 3NF, England. *Telephone:* (1629) 584363. *Fax:* (1629) 584363. *Website:* www.keithmanifold.co.uk.

MANIGAT, Eval; b. 8 Dec. 1939, Haiti. Musician (bass, vibraphone); Composer; Arranger. Divorced, 1 s., 2 d. *Career:* Played with: Tropicana (Haiti); Weber Scott (Haiti); Vaccine; Karen Young Jazz Latin Band; Buzz; Chevere; Founder, band Tchaka; Fronts Many Ways (Latin-jazz ensemble); Appearances include: Montréal Jazz Festival; Ottowa Jazz Festival; Toronto Harbourfront summer festival; SOB, New York City; European tour, 1996. *Compositions include:* Contredanse, Karen Young, 1988. *Recordings:* Album: Africa, 1994. *Honours:* Juno Award, Global Recording, Canada, 1994. *Current Management:* Louise Matte. *Address:* CP 48015, 5678 Ave du Parc, Montréal, QC H2V 4S8, Canada.

MANILOW, Barry (Pinkus); b. 17 June 1946, Brooklyn, NY, USA. Vocalist; Musician (piano); Songwriter. *Education:* Advertising, New York City College; New York College of Music; Juilliard School of Music. *Career:* Film Editor, CBS; Writer, numerous radio and television commercials; Member, cabaret duo Jeanne and Barry, 1970–72; MD, arranger, producer for Bette Midler; Solo entertainer, 1974–; Numerous world-wide tours; Major concerts include: Gala charity concert for Prince and Princess of Wales, Royal Albert Hall, 1983; Arista Records 15th Anniversary concert, Radio City Music Hall, 1990; Royal Variety performance, London, 1992; Television film Copacabana, 1985; Numerous television specials and television appearances; Broadway show, Barry Manilow At The Gershwin, 1989; West End musical, Copacabana, 1994. *Recordings:* Albums include: Barry Manilow, 1973; Barry Manilow II, 1975; Tryin' To Get The Feelin', 1976; This One's For You, 1977; Barry Manilow Live (No. 1, USA), 1977; Even Now, 1978; Manilow Magic, 1979; Greatest Hits, 1979; One Voice, 1979; Barry, 1981; If I Should Love Again, 1981; Barry Live In Britain, 1982; I Wanna Do It With You, 1982; Here Comes The Night, 1983; A Touch More Magic, 1983; Greatest Hits Vol. II, 1984; 2.00 AM Paradise Café, 1984; Barry Manilow, Grandes Exitos En Espanol, 1986; Swing Street, 1988; Songs To Make The Whole World Sing, 1989; Live On Broadway, 1990; The Songs 1975–90, 1990; Because It's Christmas, 1990; Showstoppers, 1991; The Complete Collection and Then Some, 1992; Hidden Treasures, 1993; The Platinum Collection, 1993; Singin' with the Big Bands, 1994; Another Life, 1995; Summer of '78, 1996; Manilow Sings Sinatra, 1998; Here At The Mayflower, 2001; Ultimate Manilow, 2002. Hit singles include: Mandy (No. 1, USA), 1975; Could It Be Magic, 1975; I Write The Songs (No. 1, USA), 1976; Tryin' To Get The Feelin', 1976;

Weekend In New England, 1977; Looks Like We Made It (No. 1, USA), 1977; Can't Smile Without You, 1978; Copacabana (At The Copa), from film Foul Play, 1978; Somewhere In The Night, 1979; Ships, 1979; I Made It Through The Rain, 1981; Let's Hang On, 1981; Bermuda Triangle, 1981; I Wanna Do It With You, 1982; Read Em And Weep, 1983. *Honours:* Grammy Awards: Song of the Year, I Write The Songs, 1977; Best Male Pop Vocal Performance, Copacabana (At The Copa), 1979; Emmy Award, The Barry Manilow Special, 1977; American Music Awards, Favourite Male Artist, 1978–80; Star on Hollywood Walk of Fame, 1980; Tony Award, Barry Manilow On Broadway show, 1976; Hitmaker Award, Songwriters Hall of Fame, 1991; Platinum and Gold records. *Current Management:* Stiletto Entertainment, 5443 Beethoven St, Los Angeles, CA 90066, USA.

MANLEY, Colin William; b. 16 April 1942, Liverpool, Merseyside, England. Musician (guitar). m. Sheila Jones, 17 Jan. 1972, 1 s., 1 d. *Career:* 1960s tours: Tommy Roe; Gene Pitney; Last Beatles tour of UK with Tommy Quickly; Recent tours with: The Swinging Blue Jeans; Gerry Marsden; The Searchers; London Palladium Orchestra, 2 years; Television appearances: Lift Off, with Remo 4; Top of the Pops; Ready Steady Go; Crackerjack. *Compositions:* Lies, with Remo 4; Theme song, In The First Place, for re-release of the film Wonderwall, recorded in 1967, written and sung by self and produced by George Harrison. *Recordings:* Wonderwall album (with George Harrison); Smile In Germany, Remo 4. *Honours:* Third place in first Merseybeat Poll (behind The Beatles and Gerry Marsden); Winner, Best Instrumentalist, Beat Goes On magazine, 1996. *Membership:* Musicians' Union. *Current Management:* Hal Carter. *Address:* c/o Hal Carter, 101 Hazelwood Lane, Palmers Green, London N13 5HQ, England.

MANN, Aimee; b. 8 Sept. 1960, Richmond, VA, USA. Vocalist; Songwriter. m. Michael Penn, 1998. *Career:* Mem., Young Snakes; Lead singer, 'Til Tuesday, 1982–; Signed to Epic Records; Solo artiste, 1990–; Signed to Imago Records, then Geffen Records; Cameo appearance in film The Big Lebowski, 1998; Formed record label, SuperEgo Records, and music publishing label, Aimee Mann Music; Collaborations include: Elvis Costello, Jules Shear. *Recordings:* Albums: with 'Til Tuesday: Voices Carry, 1986; Welcome Home, 1987; Everything's Different Now, 1989; Coming Up Close: Retrospective, 1999; Solo: Whatever, 1993; I'm With Stupid, 1995; Bachelor No. 2, 2000; Lost In Space, 2002. Singles: Bachelor No. 2 (limited edn EP), 1999. *Contributions to:* Songs featured in Melrose Place (TV), Jerry Maguire (film), Cruel Intentions (film), Sliding Doors (film); Nine songs in soundtrack to film Magnolia, 1999. *Current Management:* Michael Hausman. *Address:* c/o SuperEgo Records, 48 Laight St, New York, NY 10013, USA. *Website:* www.aimeemann.com.

MANN, Jas (Jasbinder); b. 24 April 1970, Dudley, West Midlands, England. Vocalist; Musician (guitar). *Career:* Singer, The Sandkings, 1980s; Tours include: Support to Happy Mondays, Stone Roses; Lead singer, Babylon Zoo, 1994–; Concerts include: NME Brats, Midem, 1995; The Night The Earth Stood Still, London, 1995. *Recordings:* Albums: Boy With The X-Ray Eyes, 1996; King Kong Groover, 1998; Singles: Spaceman (International No. 1 hit), 1996; Animal Army, 1996; All The Money's Gone, 1998. *Honours:* Fastest selling debut single since the Beatles, with Spaceman, 1996. *Membership:* Musicians' Union. *Current Management:* Clive Black, Blacklist Entertainment Ltd. *Address:* 24–25 Elysium Gate, 126–128 New Kings Rd, London SW6 4LZ, England.

MANN, Manfred, (Michael Lubowitz); b. 21 Oct. 1940, Johannesburg, South Africa. Musician (keyboards); Songwriter. *Career:* Founder member, Mann-Hugg Blues Brothers, 1962; Became Manfred Mann, 1963–69; Concerts include Brighton Song Festival, 1965; Founder, Emanon, and Manfred Mann Chapter Three, 1969; Manfred Mann Earth Band, 1971–87; National and international tours with Free; Deep Purple; Savoy Brown; Blue Öyster Cult; Pink Pop Festival, Netherlands, 1977; Also taught at Goldsmith's College, London, late 1970s. *Recordings:* Albums with Manfred Mann: Five Faces of Manfred Mann, 1964; Mann Made, 1965; Mann Made Hits, 1966; As Is, 1966; Soul of Mann, 1967; Up The Junction, 1967; The Mighty Quinn, 1968; This Is Manfred Mann, 1971; Semi-Detached Suburban, 1979; The R&B Years, 1986; The Singles Plus, 1987; The EP Collection, 1989; The Collection, 1990; Ages of Mann, 1992; Two albums with Manfred Mann Chapter Three; with Manfred Mann's Earth Band: Manfred Mann's Earth Band, 1972; Get Your Rocks Off, 1973; Solar Fire, 1973; The Good Earth, 1974; Nightingales and Bombers, 1975; The Roaring Silence, 1976; The New Bronze Age, 1977; Watch, 1978; Angle Station, 1979; Chance, 1981; Somewhere In Africa, 1983; Budapest, 1983; Criminal Tango, 1986; Masque, 1987; Manfred Mann's Earth Band (13 CD box set), 1992; Solo albums: Manfred Mann's Plain Music, 1991; Ages of Mann, 1995; Soft Vengence, 1996; Wired, 2001; Hit singles include: 5–4–3–2–1 (theme for ITV pop show Ready Steady Go!), 1964; Do Wah Diddy Diddy (No. 1, UK and USA), 1964; Come Tomorrow, 1965; Oh No, Not My Baby, 1965; If You Got To Go, Go Now, 1965; Pretty Flamingo (No. 1, UK), 1966; Just Like A Woman, 1966; Semi-Detached Suburban Mr James, 1966; Ha! Ha! Said The Clown, 1967; Mighty Quinn (No. 1, UK), 1968; My Name Is Jack, 1968; Fox On The Run, 1969; Ragamuffin Man, 1969; Joybringer, 1973; Blinded By The Light (No. 1, USA), 1976; Davey's On The Road Again, 1978; Runner, 1984;

Contributor, film music including: What's New Pussycat?, 1965; Up The Junction, 1968.

MANN, Paul Duane; b. 15 March 1972, Carmarthen, Wales. Musician (Drums, Bass Guitar). *Career:* Llanelli Schools Orchestra, 1982; School Orchestras, 1985; Royal Air Force Drum Corps and Band, 1990; The Stone Dog, alternative rock band, 1993; Power House, hard rock, 1995; Blue Desert, country, 1996; Earth Angels, gospel, USA, 1996; Borda Line, country, 1997; Freelance sessions, drumming, 1990–94; Drum Tutor and Freelance Session Drummer, 1997–; Freelance Session Electric Bass Guitar and Upright Bass Fiddle, 1999; Bass player, Rattlebelly, a soul/blues band, and Cool Penguins, a gypsy jazz trio. *Membership:* Musicians' Union. *Address:* Brigadoon, Heol Ddu, Penymynydd, Llanelli, Carmarthen SA15 4RN, Wales.

MANN, Steve; b. 9 Aug. 1956, London, England. Musician (guitar, keyboards); Sound Engineer; Record Prod. *Education:* 1 year university studying electronic engineering; 8 years classical piano, 1 year classical guitar. *Career:* Joined Liar, toured UK and Europe, 1977; Joined Steve Swindells, appeared on Old Grey Whistle Test, 1980; Formed Lionheart, 1981; Toured UK with Tytan, 1983; Joined MSG, played Monsters of Rock Festival, European and USA tours, 1986; Joined Sweet, 1989; Toured: USA; Canada; Australia; Europe; Russia; Producer, engineer for: Shogun; Tora Tora; MSG; Rough Silk; Letter X; Sweet; Thunderhead; Spice. *Compositions:* Co-wrote Anytime (No. 2, USA AOR charts). *Recordings:* with Liar: Set The World On Fire, 1978; with Lionheart: Hot Tonight, 1984; with Tytan: Rough Justice, 1985; with MSG: Perfect Timing, 1987; Save Yourself, 1989; with Sweet: A, 1992; Glitz, Blitz and Hits, 1995. *Membership:* MCPS; PRS (associate mem.); Musicians' Union. *Address:* c/o Frida Park Studio, 30161 Hanover, Germany.

MANNING, Barbara Lynne; b. 12 Dec. 1944, San Diego, California, USA. Musician; Songwriter; Vocalist. *Education:* 4 years college. *Career:* Extensive tours, USA, Europe, 1990–. *Recordings:* 28th Day, 1985; World of Pooh, 1989; One Perfect Green Blanket, B Manning, 1990; Nowhere, S F Seals, 1994; Truth Walks In Sleepy Shadows, S F Seals, 1995; Barbara Manning Sings with the Original..., 1995; 1212, 1997; In New Zealand, 1999; Homeless Is Where The Heart Is, 2000; You Should Know By Now, 2000; Under One Roof, 2001. *Honours:* SF Goldie; SF Wammie, 1992; Bay Area Music Award, 1996. *Current Management:* Matador, 676 Broadway, New York, NY 10012. *Address:* PO Box 424762, San Francisco, CA 94142, USA.

MANNING, Roger Joseph, Jr; b. 27 May 1966, Inglewood, California, USA. Songwriter; Arranger; Record Prod; Musician (keyboards). *Education:* BMus, Jazz Studies, University of Southern California. *Career:* Keyboardist, Beatnik Beach, 1987–89; Keyboardist, songwriter, arranger, Jellyfish, 1990–94; Songwriter, arranger, producer, Imperial Drag, 1995–; Keyboardist, arranger, The Moog Cookbook, 1995–; Mutations, with Beck, 1998; Playing keyboards/ touring for Beck, 1999; Re-mixing other artists' work, including the French Band, Air. *Recordings:* Albums: with Beatnik Beach: Beatnik Beach, 1988; with Jellyfish: Bellybutton, 1990; Spilt Milk, 1993; with Imperial Drag: Imperial Drag, 1996; with The Moog Cookbook: The Moog Cookbook, 1996; The Moog Cookbook: Ye Olde Space Bande; with Beck: Mutations, 1998; Midnite Vultures, 1999; with Luscious Jackson: Electric Honey, 1999. *Honours:* Best Debut Album, with Beatnick Beach, 1988; Jellyfish, 1990. *Membership:* ASCAP. *Current Management:* Sharpe Entertainment Services, 683 Palerma Ave, Pacific Palisades, CA 90272, USA.

MANOV, Dragomir; Musician (guitar). *Career:* Lead guitarist, Concurent, 1986–; Numerous concerts, TV and radio appearances, Bulgaria. *Recordings:* Rock For Peace, 1988; Rock Festival In Mitchurin, 1989; The Black Sheep (rock collection), 1992; Something Wet (best-selling album, Bulgaria), 1994; The Best of Bulgarian Rock, 1995. *Honours:* First Prizes: Top Rock Band, Vidrin, 1989; Rock ring, Sofia, 1990; Top Rock Composition: The Cavalry, 1991; Group of the Year, The Darik Radio Countdown, 1994. *Address:* 40 St Stambolov Blvd, 1202 Sofia, Bulgaria.

MANSON, Marilyn, (Brian Warner); b. 5 Jan. 1969, Canton, Ohio, USA. Vocalist; Songwriter. *Career:* Numerous television appearances, tours and videos. *Recordings:* Singles: Touniquet, 1997; Dope Show, 1997; Beautiful People, 1997; Get Your Gunn; Rock Is Dead, 1999; Disposable Teens, 2000; Albums: Portrait of an American Family, 1994; Smells Like Children, 1995; Antichrist Superstar, 1996; Mechanical Animals, 1998; Last Tour On Earth, 1999; Holy Wood (In The Shadow Of The Valley Of Death), 2000; Genesis Of The Devil, 2001. *Website:* www.marilynmanson.com.

MANSON, Shirley; b. 3 Aug. 1966, Edinburgh, Scotland. Vocalist; Musician (guitar). *Career:* Mem., lead singer, Goodbye Mr McKenzie, Angel Fish; Mem., lead singer, Garbage, 1994–; Numerous tours, festivals, television and radio appearances. *Recordings:* Albums: Garbage, 1995; Version 2.0, 1998; Beautifulgarbage, 2001. Singles: Vow, 1994; Subhuman, 1995; Queer, 1995; Only Happy When It Rains, 1995; Stupid Girl, 1995; Milk, 1996; #1 Crush, 1997; Push It, 1998; I Think I'm Paranoid, 1998; Special, 1998; When I Grow Up, 1999; The Trick Is To, 1999; You Look So Fine, 1999; The World Is Not Enough (theme from James Bond: The World is Not Enough), 1999;

Androgyny, 2001; Breaking Up The Girl, 2001; Shut Your Mouth, 2002. *Current Management:* SOS Management, 106 Cleveland St, London W1 5DP, England. *Address:* c/o Mushroom Records, 1 Shorrolds Rd, London SW6 7TR, England. *Website:* www.garbage.com.

MANSOUR, Ahmad; b. 7 June 1960, Tehran, Iran. Musician (guitar). *Education:* Berklee College of Music, Boston, USA. *Career:* Radio and television: Boston; New York; France; Netherlands; Switzerland; Numerous tours and festivals throughout Europe. *Recordings:* 6 album releases as bandleader, featuring original compositions. *Membership:* BMI. *Current Management:* BMI. *Address:* 34 rue Maurice Braillard, 1202 Geneva, Switzerland.

MANSUR, Mallikarjun; b. 31 Dec. 1910, Mansur, India. Classical Vocalist. m. Gangambika Mansur, 1 s., 7 d. *Education:* Elementary education. *Career:* Joined drama co, 1919; Started sangeet lessons with Neela Kanth Bua, 1922; First gramophone record, 1933; Mem., Legislative Council, Karnataka State, 1985–. *Recordings include:* Albums: 16 Easy Songs; Look At Love; Almoraima; Le Prophete Cartouche R; Seven; Rumbero Soy; Angel Station; Now You Know; Last Pirates Psi Epsilon; Ngiyayifun'imali Yami; Resurrection; Grand Champion; Day In The Life; Urban Observer; Dma's Clubhouse; Reventon Tropical; Journees; This Much I Understand; Vocal, 1994; Raga Marwa, 1995; Legend Lives On, 1996. *Publications:* Sangeet Ratna; Ananna Rasayatre. *Honours:* Padmashri Award, 1970; Padmabhusan Award, 1975. *Address:* Mruthunjaya Nilava, A.I.R. Road, Dharwar, 580008, India.

MANTELS, Viv; b. 31 Oct. 1964, Diest, Belgium. Actress; Theatre, Music and Film Dir; Vocalist; Songwriter; Composer. *Career:* Radio (BRTN) Belgium; Film, USA, World-wide, 1999; TV, Europe, 1998. *Compositions:* Thinking of You, with Michel Herr; All Night Through, with Mal Waldron; No More Tears, with Mal Waldron. *Recordings:* Viv Mantels and Mal Waldron Trio, 1989; Alpha and Omega, Eluca, 1984. *Membership:* Jazz Educators, USA; National Asscn Teachers of Singing, USAS; Europe Vrouw and Musiek, Holland. *Current Management:* Lyons Management, Lorraine Lyons, Essex, England.

MANTLER, Karen; b. 1966, *Education:* Berklee College of Music, Boston. *Career:* Child of two famous jazz musicians; Joined the Carla Bley Band (mother) on Glockenspiel, 1977, toured Europe and the USA; Carnegie Hall, 1980; Guest Musician, Jazz Composers Alliance; Formed own band, rehearsed and toured; Joined Carla Bley Band on harmonica for European Tour, 1988; Knitting Factory with own band; Played on David Sanborn's Nith Music TV show; Toured alongside The Very Big Carla Bley Band; Joined father as assistant, Watt Works, promoted to General Manager; Montréal Jazz Festival; Played Synthesizer for Steve Swallow, 1991; Played organ with Motohiko Hino; Organ player, The Very Big Carla Bley Band, 1992, played Glasgow Jazz Festival, Umbria Jazz Festival, Italy; Left Watt Works, 1993; Played again with Motohiko Hino; Glockenspiel and Harmonica, band with Terry Adams, 1994; European Tour with Carla Bley Band; Worked with drummer Michael Evans as duo, gigs and recorded material; Another tour with Carla Bley Big Band, 1996; Regular appearances at Starbuck's Coffee House, 1997; Rejoined Carla Bley Big Band, 1997, tour of England, organ player in Fancy Chamber Music with Carla Bley. *Recordings include:* My Cat Arnold; Karen Mantler and her Cat Arnold get the Flu; Farewell; Karen Mantler's Pet Project, 2000; with Carla Bley: Escalator Over the Hill; Musique Mecanique; The Very Big Carla Bley Band; Big Band Theory; The Carla Bley Big Band Goes to Church; Others: The Watt Works Family Album; Carried Away, with Robbie Dupree; Swallow, with Steve Swallow; Sailing Stone, with Motohiko Hino; Folly Seeing All This, with Michael Mantler. *Address:* c/o Watt Works, PO Box 67, Willow, NY 12495, USA.

MANZAREK, Ray(mond Daniel); b. 12 Feb. 1939, Chicago, IL, USA. Musician (keyboards); Prod. *Education:* UCLA Film School. *Career:* Mem., The Doors, 1964–72; Solo artiste; Prod. for Los Angeles band X; Northern California Folk-Rock Festival, 1968; Hollywood Bowl (later released as video), 1968; Film documentary, The Doors Are Open, 1968; Documentary film, The Feast of Friends, 1969; Toronto Rock 'n' Roll Revival Show, 1969; Isle of Wight Festival, 1970; With surviving mems of The Doors played, Rock and Roll Hall of Fame, Cleveland, 1993; The Doors VH1 appearance, 2001; The Doors reunion tour, 2002–03; Co-founder, The Doors Music Co, Bright Midnight Records, 1997. *Recordings:* Albums: The Doors (No. 1, USA), 1967; Strange Days, 1967; Waiting For The Sun (No. 1, USA), 1968; Morrison Hotel, 1970; Absolutely Live, 1970; LA Woman, 1971; Other Voices, 1971; Weird Scenes Inside The Gold Mine, 1972; Full Circle, 1972; The Doors Box Set, 1997; Solo: The Golden Scarab, 1975; The Whole Thing Started With R 'n' R, 1975; Live At The Hollywood Bowl, 1987; The Doors: Myth and Reality, 1997. Singles include: Break On Through, 1967; Light My Fire (No. 1, USA), 1967; People Are Strange, 1967; Love Me Two Times, 1968; The Unknown Soldier, 1968; Hello I Love You (No. 1, USA), 1968; Touch Me, 1968; You Make Me Real, 1970; Love Her Madly, 1971; Riders On the Storm, 1971. *Publications:* Light My Fire: My Life With The Doors. *Current Management:* c/o Goldman and Knell, CPA's LLP, 1900 Avenue of the Stars, Suite 1040, Los Angeles, CA 90067, USA. *Address:* c/o Bright Midnight Records, Rhino Handmade, PO Box

30620, Tampa, FL 33630-0620, USA. *E-mail:* BMR@thedoors.com. *Website:* www.thedoors.com.

MAPFUMO, Thomas Tafirenyika Mukanya; b. Oct. 1945, Marondera, Zimbabwe. Musician (mbira, guitar); Vocalist; Songwriter. *Career:* Known as The Lion of Zimbabwe; Important figure in local Shona music, 1970s–; Singer, local bands including the Cosmic Dots and the Springfields; Began translating American songs into Shona, early 1970s; Founder, Hallelulah Chicken Run Band, 1973; Researcher, traditional Zimbabwean folk style music; Founder, Pied Pipers Band, 1977; Founder, Acid Band, 1977–; Government banned them from radio, Mapfumo imprisoned for subversion, 1977; Band renamed Blacks Unlimited, 1978; First tours, Britain, 1984; Europe, 1985. *Recordings:* Albums: Hokoya!, 1977; Gwindingwe, 1980; Mabesa, 1983; Congress, 1983; The Chimurenga Singles, 1983; Ndangariro, 1984; Mr Music, 1985; Chimurnega For Justice, 1986; Corruphon, 1989; Chamunorwa, 1990; Shumba, 1990; The Spirit of the Eagle, 1991; Shumba: Vital Hits of Zimbabwe, 1991; Hondo, 1994; Vanhu Vatema, 1994; Chumurenga: African Spirit Music, 1997; Gwindingwi Rine Shumba, 1997; Singles include: Morento; Ngoma Yarira. *Address:* c/o Free World Music Inc, 230 12th St, Suite 117, Miami Beach, FL 33139–4603, USA.

MARAZZI, Paul Thomas Leo; b. 24 Jan. 1975, Wanstead, London, England. Vocalist; Songwriter. *Career:* Relocated to Benidorm, Spain, aged 19; Career as club dancer before brief spell modelling for Christian Dior; Joined A1 pop group; Signed recording contract, 1999; Sell-out theatre tours of South-East Asia and UK, 2000–01. *Recordings:* Albums: Here We Come, 1999; The A List, 2000; Make It Good, 2002. Singles: Be The First To Believe, Summertime of Our Lives, Ready Or Not/Everytime, 1999; Like A Rose, Take On Me, Same Old Brand New You, 2000; No More, 2001; Caught In The Middle, 2002. *Honours:* BRIT Award, Best Newcomer, 2001; Also honoured at MTV Mandarin Music Awards. *Current Management:* c/o Byrne Blood Ltd. *Website:* www.a1-online.com.

MARCHANT, Colin; b. 27 Nov. 1937, Batley, England. Musician (drums). m. Joan Marchant, 1 s, 2 d. *Education:* Music Tuition at school. *Career:* Touring in 1960s with Gene Vincent, Danny Williams, Dusty Springfield, The Beatles and Rolling Stones; Working and living in Japan, 1968–71, 1972–; Working on Cabaret as back-up Musician.

MARDIN, Arif; b. 1932, Istanbul, Turkey. Prod. *Education:* Istanbul University; London School of Economics, England; Quincy Jones Scholarship, Berklee College of Music, Boston, USA; School of Jazz, Lenox, MA, 1958. *Career:* Played and arranged for local bands; Teacher, Berklee College of Music; Asst to Nesuhi Ertegun, Atlantic Records, 1963, became Studio Man., House Prod. and Arranger, Vice-Pres., 1969, Sr Vice-Pres.; Simultaneous independent Prod.; Worked with: Average White Band, Theresa Bazar, The Bee Gees, Brook Benton, Boy Meets Girl, Rachele Cappelli, Cher, Judy Collins, Phil Collins, Michael Crawford, Culture Club, Jackie DeShannon, Roberta Flack, Aretha Franklin, Steve Goodman, Daryl Hall, Eddie Harris, Richard Harris, Gordon Haskell, Donny Hathaway, Ofra Haza, Mikki Howard, Freddie Hubbard, Howard Jones, Margie Joseph, Chaka Khan, King Curtis, Charles Lloyd, Lulu, Les McCann, Melissa Manchester, Manhattan Transfer, Herbie Mann, Marilyn Martin, Bette Midler, Modern Jazz Quartet, Willie Nelson, Laura Nyro, John Oates, Danny O'Keefe, Scritti Politti, Andy Pratt, Maxi Priest, John Prine, The Rascals, Max Roach, Doug Sahm, Leo Sayer, Carly Simon, Dusty Springfield, Ringo Starr, Sonny Stitt, Dionne Warwick, Bebe and Cece Winans, Irene Worth, The Young Rascals. *Honours:* Hon. Doctorate, Berklee College of Music; Four Grammy Awards; Over 40 Gold and Platinum discs; Inducted, National Academy of Recording Arts and Sciences Hall of Fame, 1990; Shofar of Peace Amard from the Sephardic Hebrew Academy, 1992. *Address:* c/o Atlantic Records, 75 Rockefeller Plaza, New York, NY 10019, USA.

MARGARIT, Bernard; b. 19 Feb. 1956, Carcassonne, France. Musician (guitar); Composer. 1 s., 1 d. *Education:* Classical guitarist, The Academie, Toulouse. *Career:* International tours with Johnny Hallyday; Television shows with: Kim Wilde; Eddy Mitchell; Johnny Hallyday; French jazz concert tours with Jean Pierre LLabador; Remy Charmasson; Philippe Petrucciani. *Recordings:* Various recordings with Johnny Hallyday; Album: Friendship (all original compositions) with jazz guitarist Jean Pierre Llabador. *Membership:* SACEM; SPEDIDAM; ADAMI. *Current Management:* Edma Managements. *Address:* 13 rue du Stade, 11300 Limoux, France.

MARGOLIN, Bob; b. 9 May 1949, Boston, Massachusetts, USA. Blues Musician (guitar); Writer. *Education:* Graduated Boston University, 1970. *Career:* Seven years in Muddy Waters Blues Band; Leader, own blues band, 1980–. *Recordings:* 4 solo albums; Sideman on 30 albums with other blues players, 1974–96; Albums include: with the Band: The Last Waltz, 1978; with The Nighthawks, 1979; with Muddy Waters: Live At Mr Kellys, 1971; Woodstock Album, 1975; Hard Again, 1977; I'm Ready, 1977; Mississippi Muddy Waters Live, 1977; King Bee, 1980; with Johnny Winter: Nothin' But The Blues, 1977; The Johnny Winter Story, 1980; Solo Albums: Down in the Alley, 1993; My Blues and My Guitar, 1995; Up and In, 1997; Hold Me to It, 1999; Other session work includes: Henry Gray, Roy Roberts. *Publications:*

Senior writer, regular column for Blues Revue magazine. *Current Management:* Piedmont Talent, 1222 Kenilworth Ave, Charlotte, NC 28204, USA.

MARGUET, Christophe; b. 14 May 1965, Paris, France. Musician (drums). m. Isabelle, Aug. 1992. *Career:* Played with: Barney Wilen; Vincent Herring; Bud Shank; Alain Jean Marie; Claude Barthélémy; Daunik Lazro; Noël Akchoté; Didier Levallet; Tours: People's Republic of China; Egypt; Syria; Morocco; Cameroon; Own trio with Sebastien Texier (alto sax), Olivier Sens (double bass); Played with Marc Ducret, Yves Robert, Barry Guy, Kenny Wheeler, François Jeanneau, François Corneloup, Louis Sclavis, 1997–. *Recordings:* 2 with Georges Arvanitas: Gershwin; Ellington; Altissimo, Hubert Dupont Sextet; Amazonia, Nicolas Genest; Mr Claude, Claude Barthelemy Quartet, 1997; Resistance Poetique, Christophe Marguet Trio, 1997; Strophes, Sylvain Kassap Quartet, 1998; Animal Language, 49 Nord, 1999; Ça Commence Aujourd Hui, Louis Sclavis, 1999; Les Correspondances, Christophe Marguet Quartet, 2000. *Honours:* First Prize, Orchestra, First Prize, Composition, Concours de la Défense, 1995; Django d'Or for Resistance Poetique, Best CD of Year, 1997. *Current Management:* LMD Productions, 23 rue Parmentier, 93100 Montreuil, France. *Address:* 25 rue Jeanne d'Arc, 92600 Asnieres, France.

MARINO, Frank; b. 22 Aug. 1954, Canada. Rock Musician (guitar); Vocalist. *Career:* Founder, Mahogany Rush, 1970–80; Recorded under own name, 1981–82; Major concerts include: Heavy Metal Holocaust, Port Vale, UK, 1981. *Recordings:* Albums: with Mahogany Rush: Maxoom, 1971; Child of The Novelty, 1974; Strange Universe, 1975; Mahogany Rush IV, 1976; World Anthem, 1977; Live, 1978; Tales of The Unexpected, 1979; What's Next, 1980; Solo: The Power of Rock 'n' Roll, 1981; Juggernaut, 1982; Full Circle, 1986; Double Live, 1988; Eye Of The Storm, 2001; Also featured on Guitar Speak Vol. 2 (compilation album), 1990; From the Hip, 1993. *Current Management:* American Famous Talent Corporation, 816 W Evergreen, Chicago, IL 60622, USA.

MARKELIUS, Nike Maria; b. 29 Aug. 1962, Sweden. Songwriter; Musician; Vocalist. m. Rolf Markelius, 23 Aug. 1997, 2 d. *Education:* Studied singing; Digital Audio Editing. *Career:* Drummer and vocals in Swedish Rock Groups; Usch, tours in Denmark and Sweden, 1979–81; Tant Strul, Scandinavian tours, 1981–85; Roskilde Festival, Slottsparken, Helsingfors, 1985; Songwriter, Solo Performer, Theatre Music; Smisk, tours in Sweden, 1989–97; Puder, Teatter Tre, Stockholm, 2001–02; Singer in group, Nike, tours, 1992–97. *Compositions:* Hula Hula, 1987; Fandango, 1992; Several Theatre Plays, 1992–96; Music and Lyrics for Solo Album, Nike, 1996; Creating radio programme, 1998. *Recordings:* With Groups: 3 Singles, 4 Songs on Live Album with Usch, 1979–81; 3 Albums, Amazon, 1993, Jag Önskar Dig, 1994, Samlade Singlar, 1995; Several Singles with Tant Strul, 1981–85; Studio Project, Hula Hula, 1987; Solo Album, Nike, 1996. *Honours:* Kasper Priset, 1983; Scholarship, SKAP, 1992; Konstnärsnämnden, 1992–93, 1995–96, 1998; 1999; Stockholm City Artist Grant, 1997. *Membership:* STIM; SKAP; SAMI; SMF; Musikcentrum; DIVA. *Address:* Kattugglevägen 18, 123 52 Farsta, Sweden. *E-mail:* nike@divarecords.org. *Website:* www.divarecords.org/artistees/nike/.

MARKER, Steve; b. New York, USA. Musician (guitar, bass guitar, keyboards). *Career:* Co-founder, Smart Studios; Worked with Nine Inch Nails, L7; Mem., Garbage, 1994–; Numerous tours, festivals, television and radio appearances. *Recordings:* Albums: Garbage, 1995; Version 2.0, 1998; Beautifulgarbage, 2001. Singles: Vow, 1994; Subhuman, 1995; Queer, 1995; Only Happy When It Rains, 1995; Stupid Girl, 1995; Milk, 1996; #1 Crush, 1997; Push It, 1998; I Think I'm Paranoid, 1998; Special, 1998; When I Grow Up, 1999; The Trick Is To, 1999; You Look So Fine, 1999; The World Is Not Enough (theme from James Bond: The World is Not Enough), 1999; Androgyny, 2001; Breaking Up The Girl, 2001; Shut Your Mouth, 2002. *Address:* c/o Mushroom Records, 1 Shorrolds Rd, London SW6 7TR, England. *Website:* www.garbage.com.

MARKEY, Gerry, (Gerald Murphy); b. 13 Nov. 1963, Liverpool, England. Vocalist; Songwriter; Actor; Musician (guitar, piano, harmonica). *Education:* BA Hons, York University; PGCE, London University; AIL, Institute of Linguists. *Career:* Extensive tours: Europe; USA; Appeared on BBC TV performing: 95; Granada TV: St Joseph of Paradise Street; The Ballad of Dixie Dean; Talk To Me; Teacher, Art and Craft of Songwriting, Liverpool University; Project Co-ordinator, The European Song Project. *Recordings:* Oh John, 1984; Sweet Liberty, 1987; Marvellous Marvin Gaye, 1993; Ballad of Dixie Dean, 1981. *Honours:* PRS, John Lennon Award, Sweet Liberty, 1987; Second place, National Music Day Songwriter of 1993, Marvellous Marvin Gaye, 1993. *Membership:* Musicians' Union; BAC&S; Sound Sense; Equity; PRS. *Address:* The European Song Project, 12 Benson St, Liverpool L1 2ST, England.

MARKLEW, Leigh (Flare); b. 10 Aug. 1968. Musician (Drums). *Career:* Formed Spoilt Bratz with Shutty, Mark Yates and Tony Wright; Renamed as Terrorvision; Secured record deal, 1991; Support slot to the Ramones; Numerous headlining tours and TV appearances. *Recordings:* My House,

1992; Oblivion, 1994; Pretend Best Friend, 1994; Alice, What's The Matter, 1994; Bad Actress, 1996; Perseverance, 1996; Easy, 1996; Moonage Daydream, 1997; Josephine, 1998; Tequila, 1999; III Wishes, 1999; Albums: Formaldehyde, 1993; How To Win Friends and Influence People, 1994; Regular Urban Survivors, 1996; Shaving Peaches, 1998; Whales And Dolphins (compilation), 2001.

MARKOVIC, Milivoje; b. 20 March 1939, Zagreb, Yugoslavia. Musician (saxophone, clarinet); Composer; Conductor. *Education:* Law studies; Jazz Music Degree, Music Academy of Graz, Austria. *Career:* With Markovic-Gut Sextet performed at the Northsee Jazz Festival and toured Belgium, Germany, USSR, Hungary, Romania, Italy, Turkey, Bulgaria and Cuba; Numerous TV and radio appearances. *Compositions include:* Otpisani; Ballad in Escutabile; Stemi; YuN QMM; Suze. *Recordings include:* Markovic-Gut Sextet, 1980, 1981; Clark Terry Live in Belgrade with the Markovic-Gut Sectet, 1982; Message from Belgrade, 1984; Ernie Wilkins in Belgrade with Markovic-Gut Sextet; Machito and His Salsa Big Band. *Membership:* Composers Union of Yugoslavia, President, 1987–88. *Address:* Plato Jazz Club, Student TRG, Belgrade, Yugoslavia.

MARKS, Phillip; b. 22 June 1956, Manchester, England. Musician (Drums). *Education:* BA, Economics, Manchester University, 1982. *Career:* Recorded and toured England and Europe with his band Bark! (founder member); Organized, promoted, participated in numerous concerts, festivals in Manchester; Played in Grew Trio, Slip and Slant, trio; Played with musicians including Derek Bailey, Mattos, Lajonna Smith. *Recordings:* With Bark!: Celibacy, 1992; Harmfulodics, 1993; Our Traditional Values, 1994; With Grew Trio: Grew Trio, 1996. *Address:* 47 Parvet Ave, Droylsden, Manchester M43 7SD, England.

MARKS, Roger; b. 20 Feb. 1947, Tenby, Wales. Musician (trombone); Jazz Bandleader. m. (1) 1967–87, 2 s., (2) Susan, 14 March 1998. *Education:* Honiton Town Band. *Career:* Television appearance: Pebble Mill At One, BBC; Southern TV; German, Dutch, Yugoslavian television; Radio broadcast: Jazz Parade, Radio 2. *Recordings:* Somewhere Over The Rainbow, 1997; C'est Magnifique, 1998; Albums: with Rod Mason: Great Having You Around, 1978; After Hours, 1979; Stars Fell On Alabama, 1979; The Last Concert, 1980; Just The Five of Us, Roger Marks Quartet, 1989; Crazy Rhythm, Roger Marks Quartet and Bruce Turner, 1990; Dixie After Dark, Roger Marks Armada Jazz Band, CD 1994; Plato was a Good Parrot, 1995; Top Marks!, CD, 1996; Jazz Notes, BBC Radio 3, 1997. *Publications:* Roger Marks Discography, 1997. *Honours:* City of Plymouth Citation for Outstanding Contribution to the Arts. *Membership:* ABJM.

MARKS, Toby Anthony; b. 1 July 1964, London, England. Electronic Composer; Musician (guitar, keyboards, electronics, percussion); Composer. m. Sandra, 9 Sept. 1995. *Education:* University of Warwick, 1 year. *Career:* Performed in various bands and concerts in UK and Europe, 1978; Formed, Banco De Gaia (solo electronic project), performing world-wide, 1989–. *Recordings:* with Banco De Gaia: Maya, 1994; Last Train To Lhasa, 1995; Live At Glastonbury, 1996; Big Men Cry, 1997; The Magical Sounds of Banco De Gaia, 1999; Igizeh, 2000; 10 Years, 2002. *Membership:* MCPS; PRS; PPL; Musicians' Union. *Current Management:* None. *Address:* PO Box 1195, Cheddar, BS27 3YE, England.

MARLEY, Ziggy, (David Robert Nesta); b. 17 Oct. 1968, Kingston, Jamaica. Vocalist; Musician (guitar). *Career:* Leader, Ziggy Marley and the Melody Makers. *Recordings:* Hit single: Tomorrow People, 1988; Play The Game Right; Hey World; Conscious Party; One Bright Day; Jahmekya; Joy and Blues; Free Like We Want To Be; Fallen is Babylon; The Spirit of Music, 1999; The Best of Ziggy Marley and the Melody Makers; Live Vol 1, 2000. *Honours:* 2 Grammy Awards; NAACP Award; Group are UN Youth Environment Ambassadors. *Current Management:* William Morris Agency. *Address:* Ziggy Marley and the Melody Makers, 56 Hope Rd, Kingston 6, Jamaica.

MARLIN, Lene, (Lene Marlin Pedersen); b. 17 Aug. 1980. Vocalist; Musician (guitar); Songwriter. *Education:* Tromsdalen Videregaende Skole, Tromsø. *Career:* Signed to Virgin, 1997; Recorded first album while still at school; Heavy European promotion schedules throughout 1999–2000; Co-wrote songs for fellow Norwegian, Sissel, 2000; Preparing second solo album, 2001. *Recordings:* Albums: Playing My Game, 1999; Singles: Unforgivable Sinner, 1998; Sitting Down Here, 1999; Where I'm Headed (from film Bad Company), 2001. *Honours:* First single fastest selling in Norwegian history; Spelleman Awards: Best Artist; New Artist; Pop Artist; Best Song, 2000; MTV Europe Award, Best Nordic Act, 1999. *Address:* c/o Stageway Talent, Norway. *Website:* www.lenemarlin.com.

MARLO, Clair; b. New York, USA. Vocalist; Prod; Arranger; Songwriter; Composer. m. Alex Baker, 1 Nov. 1995, 1 d. *Education:* Berklee College of Music. *Career:* Tours: USA, 1980; USA, 1990; Far East, 1994; Television: Here's Johnny, The Philippines. *Recordings:* Let It Go, 1990; Behaviour Self, 1995; with Liquid Amber: Liquid Amber, 1994; Adrift, 1995; As producer: Just Ahead, Pat Coil, 1993; with Vox Mundi, 1997; with Primal Instinct, 1998;

Clair Marlo, 1999. *Honours:* 10 songwriting awards; one of the top two female producers in the USA, 1998; Freedom Award for film scoring, 1998. *Membership:* ASCAP; NARAS; AIMP; CC; Musicians' Union; SCL; AES. *Current Management:* Mike Gormley, LA Personal Development. *Address:* 950 N Kings Rd, #266, West Hollywood, CA 90069, USA.

MARR, Johnny, (John Maher); b. 31 Oct. 1963, Ardwick, Manchester, England. Musician (guitar). *Career:* Founder mem., The Smiths, 1982–87; Appearance, John Peel Show, BBC Radio 1, 1983; International tours and concerts; Began playing with Billy Bragg; Bryan Ferry; Paul McCartney; Talking Heads; The Pretenders; Played guitar in Midge Ure's band, Nelson Mandela's 70th Birthday Tribute, Wembley, 1988; Mem., The The, 1989; Founder mem., Electronic, with Neil Tennant, Bernard Summer, 1989–; Worked with Stex, Banderas, 1990; Formed, Johnny Marr and the Healers, 2000–, supported Oasis on European tour, 2000. *Recordings:* Albums: with The Smiths: The Smiths, 1984; Hatful Of Hollow, 1984; Meat Is Murder (No. 1, UK), 1985; The World Won't Listen, 1986; The Queen Is Dead, 1986; Louder Than Bombs, 1987; Strangeways Here We Come, 1987; Rank, 1988; Best... I (No. 1, UK), 1992; Best... II, 1992; Singles, 1995; The Very Best Of, 2001; with Electronic: Electronic, 1990; Raise The Pressure, 1996; Twisted Tenderness, 1999; with Johnny Marr and the Healers: Boomslang, 2003; Guitarist: Mind Bomb, The The, 1989; Behaviour, Pet Shop Boys, 1990; Dusk, The The, 1992; Bilingual, Pet Shop Boys, 1996; Preaching To The Converted, Billy Bragg, 1999; Crimson Moon, Bert Jansch, 2000. Singles include: with The Smiths: Hand In Glove, 1983; This Charming Man, 1983; What Difference Does It Make, 1984; Heaven Knows I'm Miserable Now, 1984; William It Was Really Nothing, 1984; How Soon Is (It) Now?, 1985; Shakespears Sister, 1985, That Joke Isn't Funny Anymore, 1985; The Boy With The Thorn In His Side, 1985; Bigmouth Strikes Again, 1986; Ask, 1986; Shoplifters of The World Unite, 1987; Panic, 1987; Sheila Take A Bow, 1987; Girlfriend In A Coma, 1987; I Started Something..., 1987; Last Night I Dreamt That Somebody Loved Me, 1987; There Is A Light That Never Goes Out, 1992; with The The: The Beat(en) Generation, 1989; Gravitate To Me, 1989; Armaggedon Days (Are Here Again), 1989; with Electronic: Getting Away With It, 1989; Get The Message, 1981; Feel Every Beat, 1991; Disappointed, 1992; Forbidden City, 1996; For You, 1996; Raise the Pressure, 1996; Second Nature, 1997; Late at Night, 1999; Vivid, 1999. *Current Management:* Ignition Management, 8A Wyndham Pl., London W1H 1PP, England.

MARS, Chris; b. 30 March 1965, London, England. Vocalist; Musician (keyboards, piano, guitar). *Education:* O-Level Music: guitar, piano. *Career:* A Flock of Seagulls, USA tour, 1986; Lead singer, The Happening, house band on Sky television, 1990–91; Live broadcast, Greater London Radio, Tim Smith Show, 1991; Solo tour, Norway, Switzerland, Germany, 1994–95. *Recordings:* Chris Mars (debut album) release due soon. *Membership:* Musicians' Union; PRS. *Address:* Cavendish Ave, Ealing, London W13 0JW, England.

MARS, Mick, (Bob Deal); b. 3 April 1955, Terre Haute, Indiana, USA. Rock Musician (guitar). m. Emi Canyn, 19 Sept. 1990. *Career:* Member, US heavy rock group Mötley Crüe, 1981–; World-wide concerts include: Tours with: Y & T, 1981, 1982; Kiss, 1983; Ozzy Osbourne, 1984; Iron Maiden, 1984; Cheap Trick, 1986; Theatre of Pain world tour, 1985–86; World tours, 1987, 1989; Major festivals: US Festival, 1983; Monsters of Rock festival, Castle Donington, 1984, 1991; Moscow Music Peace Festival, 1989. *Recordings:* Albums: Too Fast For Love, 1981; Shout At The Devil, 1983; Theatre of Pain, 1985; Girls, Girls, Girls (No. 2, USA), 1987; Dr Feelgood (No. 1, USA), 1989; Decade of Decadence (No. 2, USA), 1991; Till Death Do Us Part, 1994; New Tattoo, 2000; Singles: Stick To Your Guns, 1981; Looks That Kill, 1984; Too Young To Fall In Love, 1984; Smokin' In The Boys Room, 1985; Home Sweet Home, 1985; You're All I Need, 1987; Dr Feelgood, 1989; Kick Start My Heart, 1990; Without You, 1990; Don't Go Away Mad, 1990; Same Old Situation, 1990; Primal Scream, 1991; Contributor, Stars, Hear 'n' Aid charity record, 1985. *Publications:* The Dirt: Confessions of the World's Most Notorious Rock Band (with Mötley Crüe), 2001. *Honours:* Rolling Stone Poll Winners, Best Heavy Metal Band, 1991; American Music Award, Favourite Heavy Metal Album, 1991. *Current Management:* The Left Bank Organisation, 6255 Sunset Blvd, Suite 1111, Hollywood, CA 90028, USA.

MARSALIS, Branford; b. 26 Aug. 1960, New Orleans, Louisiana, USA. Jazz Musician (saxophone); Prod; Composer; Actor. *Education:* New Orleans Centre for Creative Arts; Southern University, Baton Rouge (with Alwin Bastite); Berklee School of Music, Boston. *Career:* Performed with: Art Blakey; Lionel Hampton; Clark Terry; Bu Blakey; Wynton Marsalis; Herbie Hancock; Sting; Grateful Dead; Albert Collins; Nils Lofgren; Leader of own band with Kenny Kirkland, Jeff Watts, Bob Hurst; Numerous world-wide tours; Major concerts include: Live Aid Concert, London, 1985; Nelson Mandela Concert, London, 1988; Jamaican Hurricane Relief Benefit Concert, Los Angeles, 1990; West Side Story, AIDS Project Los Angeles, 1992; Pori Jazz, Finland, 1995; Film roles: School Daze; Throw Mama From The Train; Television and radio appearances include: Bring On The Night, 1985; Host, New Visions, 1987; Story of a People, Expressions in Black, 1991; Host, Jazzset, radio series, 1992; Co-host, Best of Disney Music, 1992; Music Dir, Tonight Show, 1992; Composer and performer on numerous film and television scores; Founder, Marsalis Music label, 2002. *Recordings:* Scenes In The City, 1984; Romances For Saxophone, 1986; Bring On The Night, live album, 1986; Royal Garden Blues, 1986; Renaissance, 1987; Random Abstract, 1988; Trio Jeepy, 1989; Crazy People Music, 1990; Music From Mo' Better Blues, 1990; The Beautiful Ones Are Not Yet Born, 1991; I Heard You Twice The First Time, 1992; Bloomington, 1993; Buckshot Le Fonque, 1994; Dark Keys, 1996; Requiem, 1999; Contemporary Jazz, 2000; Creation, 2001; Footsteps Of Our Fathers (with quartet), 2002; Also performed on albums by Wynton Marsalis and Sting. *Honours:* 4 Grammy Awards, including Jazz Instrumental Album, Contemporary Jazz, 2001. *Current Management:* Anne Marie Wilkins, Wilkins Management.

MARSALIS, Wynton; b. 18 Oct. 1961, New Orleans, Louisiana, USA. Musician (trumpet). 3 c. *Education:* Trained in classical music, Juilliard School, New York, USA. *Career:* Played with New Orleans Philharmonic, age 14; Joined Art Blakey and the Jazz Messengers, 1980; Tour with Herbie Hancock, 1981; Formed own group with brother Branford Marsalis on tenor saxophone, 1982; Leader, Wynton Marsalis Septet; Appearances with New York Philharmonic; Cleveland Orchestra; Los Angeles Philharmonic; London Symphony Orchestra and other major European orchestras; Conductors include: Lorin Maazel; Zubin Mehta; Leonard Slatkin; Esa-Pekka Salonen; Held Saturday Jazz for Young People, Lincoln Centre, New York; Regularly conducts masterclasses in schools and holds private tuition; Regularly holds Jazz For Young People throughout each year; Artistic Dir, Jazz Dept, Lincoln Center, New York, 1990–. *Compositions:* include: Blood on the Fields, oratorio; In This House On This Morning, for septet; (At The) Octoroon Ball, for string quartet; Jazz/Syncopated Movements; Jump Start; Sweet Release, with Judith Jamison; Citi Movement/Griot New York, with Garth Fagan; Marcial Suite, engraved in Place du Marcial, France, 1998. *Recordings include:* Joe Cool's Blues, Wynton Marsalis Septet and Ellis Marsalis Trio, 1995; In This House On This Morning, 1994; Gabriel's Garden; Jazz for Young People; Jazz/Syncopated Movements, 1997; Goin' Down Home, 2001. *Honours:* Grand Prix du Disque, France; Edison Award, Netherlands; 4 Grammy Awards; Keys to many US cities; Numerous honorary Doctorates from US Universities; Named one of the USA's Most Influential People; Pulitzer Prize for Music, 1997; Concertos by Haydn, Hummel and Leopold Mozart; Grand Prix Du Disque, France; Named one of Time Magazine's Most Influential People Under 40; Grammy Awards in Jazz and Classical. *Current Management:* Management Ark. *Address:* c/o Shore Fire Media, 32 Court St, Brooklyn, NY 11201, USA.

MARSDEN, Gerry (Gerald); b. 24 Sept. 1942, Liverpool, Merseyside, England. Vocalist; Musician (guitar). m. Pauline Ann, 11 Oct. 1965, 2 d. *Career:* 33 years in music; Gerry and the Pacemakers, 1962–; 3 No. 1 hit singles with first 3 records; Numerous concerts and television shows world-wide; West End theatre: Charlie Girl; Pull Both Ends, (5 years). *Recordings:* Hit singles include: How Do You Do It (No. 1, UK), 1963; I Like It (No. 1, UK), 1963; You'll Never Walk Alone (No. 1, UK), 1963; I'm The One, 1964; Don't Let The Sun Catch You Crying, 1964; It's Gonna Be All Right, 1964; Ferry Cross The Mersey, 1965; I'll Be There, 1965; Walk Hand In Hand, 1965; Charity singles: You'll Never Walk Alone, The Crowd (No. 1, UK), 1985; Ferry Cross The Mersey, with Paul McCartney, The Christians & Holly Johnson (No. 1, UK), 1989; Albums include: How Do You Like It, 1963; Ferry Cross The Mersey, 1964; Girl On A Swing, 1966; Numerous compilations include: 20th Anniversary Album, 1983; Hit Singles Album, 1986; You'll Never Walk Alone, 1988; Gerry Cross the Mersey, 1995; Much Missed Man, 2001. *Publications:* I'll Never Walk Alone (autobiography). *Honours:* 2 BMI citations; Gold and Silver records; BASCA Gold Badge. *Membership:* Musicians' Union; Equity; PRS; Songwriters' Guild. *Current Management:* Derek Franks Organization/PIP.

MARSDEN, John Charles Stewart; b. 21 Nov. 1971, Melbourne, Australia. Vocalist; Musician (guitar); Songwriter. *Education:* Guitar lessons for two years. *Career:* Founding member of Melbourne band Wild Turkey, 1988; Nationwide tours with band; Performs in duo with drummer Kirk Syrett; Hosts Muso's Jam Nights encouraging new talent; Various minor acting roles in Australian TV and film productions. *Compositions:* Love That Kills; I Drove All Day; Burning Desire; Without You; Noon and Night; Surfin' Hearse; Mess Around Baby. *Recordings:* Albums: I Drove All Day, 1994; Love That Kills, 1997; Surfin' Hearse, 2001. *Membership:* APRA. *Current Management:* Wild Turkey Management Pty Ltd, PO Box 120, Kallista, Vic. 3791, Australia. *E-mail:* turkey_wild@hotmail.com. *Website:* www.wildturkeymusic.com.

MARSH, Barbara Lynn; b. Warwick, RI, USA. Vocalist; Songwriter; Musician (guitar, piano, mandolin). m. Peter Comley, divorced 1995, 28 April 1984. *Education:* AA, Pensacola Jr College; BA, Drama, Universty of West Florida; Choral Training, Woodham High Echoes; Certificate of Jazz, Popular Musicianship (studio), Goldsmiths College, London. *Career:* Mem., The Dear Janes, 1992–; Supported the Cranberries, Royal Albert Hall, 1995; Tours: UK, Ireland, Germany, Netherlands, 1993–95; London dates with Robyn Hitchcock, 1996–97; Toured USA with Robyn Hitchcock, 1997; Radio: Woman's Hour; Kaleidoscope; Loose Ends; Johnnie Walker; GLR; Recorded: Dangerous Dangerous Nuts, BBC Screen 2, Crazy For A Kiss; Acting; 2 episodes, Broadway Stories, 1994; Solo work, London, New York (live),

1980–92; Backing vocals, Anthony Thistlethwaite. *Recordings:* with The Dear Janes: Sometimes I, 1994; No Skin, 1996; Skirt, 2002. *Publications:* Poetry: The Panhandler, Literary Magazine, 1981; Pensacola, Florida, USA; The Auteur, magazine, London, 1992–93. *Honours:* Third Place National Forensics (intercollegiate), Informative Speaking, 1977; Finalist, Informative Speaking, 1978. *Membership:* PRS; Musicians' Union; MCPS; Poetry Society. *Current Management:* Steve Weltman Management. *Address:* 10C Porchester Sq., London W2 6AN, England.

MARSH, Henry; b. 8 Dec. 1948, Bath, Somerset, England. Composer; Musician (keyboards, guitar). m. Susan Norddahl, 1 April 1970, divorced, 2 s., 1 d. *Education:* O Level Viola. *Career:* First group, at Sherborne School (featured future actor Jeremy Irons on drums); Founder member, Sailor, 1970s; First musical, One Last Summer, opened in Atlanta; Writes music for television. *Recordings:* Hit singles with Sailor: Girls Girls Girls; A Glass of Champagne; Album with Sailor: Trouble – The Third Step. *Honours:* Joseph Jefferson Award, Chicago, for Best Original Music in Theatre Production, Comedy of Errors. *Membership:* PRS; MCPS. *Current Management:* Strawberry Hills Management. *Address:* The Red Cottage, Rood Ashton, Trowbridge, Wiltshire BA14 6BL, England.

MARSHALL, Christopher William; b. 18 Sept. 1956, Kolkata, India. *Education:* BSc, Hons, Manchester; Piano studies to age 16. *Career:* Semi-pro until 26; Keyboards with bands: Biddie and Eve; The Next Step; Angie; Started record label, Rhythm Shop Records, 1994, Dir, Rhythm Shop Productions Ltd, 2001–. *Compositions:* Television soundtracks: Ad Armageddon, BBC2; Zapruder Footage, BBC2; Broken Lives, BBC2; The No. 10 Show, Channel 4; Reputations: Hitchcock, BBC2, 1999; The Secret History of Hackers, Channel 4; Numerous albums library music; Co-writer, Your House Or My House, Samantha Fox, 1989. *Recordings:* As producer: Tracks by: Demis Roussos; Norman Wisdom; He Ain't Heavy, He's My Brother, Jonathan Paule; Blind Fool, Insane, Make Up, Dave Pop, 1998–99; Albums: with Tight Fit: Back To The 60s Vol. II, III; with Dream On Dream: Strangeways; with Hound Dog and The Megamixers: Junior Party Megamix, 1990. *Honours:* Gold, Platinum discs: Samantha Fox. *Membership:* APRS; Musicians' Union; MCPS; PRS; ANA; PPL. *Address:* 26 Weiss Rd, Putney, London SW15 1DH, England.

MARSHALL, Jamie; b. 8 July 1955, Doncaster, Yorkshire, England. Musician (guitar, keyboards); Vocalist; Songwriter; Composer. Partner, Helen Halliday. *Education:* Hons degree, Business Studies. *Career:* Over 3000 live concerts in places including: The Marquee Club; The Royal Festival Hall; Live show, Geneva radio to estimated 2m. people; Tour, Top of the Pops appearance with Don McLean, 1991; Radio 1; Radio 5; Sky TV. *Recordings:* Album: Even The Strongest Hearts, 1988; Troubletown (EP), 1990; Third recording in progress. *Current Management:* c/o Thump Thump Music, 1 York St, London W1H 1PZ, England. *Address:* Pound Corner, Pound Lane, Windlesham, Surrey GU20 6BP, England.

MARSHALL, John Stanley; b. 28 Aug. 1941, Isleworth, Middlesex, England. Musician (drums, percussion). m. Maxi Egger. *Education:* BA (Hons) Psychology, University of Reading; Studied music with Jim Marshall; Alan Ganley; Philly Joe Jones. *Career:* Freelance on London jazz scene; Played with Alexis Korner's Blues Incorporated, 1964; Graham Collier Sextet, 1965–70; Also played with John Surman; John McLaughlin; Dave Holland; Mike Westbrook; Graham Bond Organisation; Joe Harriot; Indo-Jazz Fusions; Keith Tippett's Sextet, Centipede; Alan Skidmore; Founder member, Nucleus, 1969; Montreux Festival (First Prize, 1970); Newport Festival, Village Gate, New York; Regular member, Mike Gibbs Orchestra, early 1970s; Left Nucleus to join Jack Bruce Band, 1971; Joined Soft Machine, 1972; Played with musicians including: Larry Coryell; Gary Burton; Mary Lou Williams; Ronnie Scott; Tubby Hayes; Ben Webster; Milt Jackson; Roy Eldridge; John Taylor; Norma Winstone; Volker Kriegel; Gordon Beck; Charlie Mariano; Jasper van't Hof; Philip Catherine; Joined Eberhard Weber's Colours, 1977–81; Worked with Gil Evans Orchestra; Ian Carr; Kenny Wheeler; Uli Beckerhoff; Anthony Braxton; Manfred Schoof; Joachim Kühn; Michel Portal; John Taylor; Alan Holdsworth; Norma Winstone; Gordon Beck; Jeff Clyne; Arild Anderson; John Abercrombie; John Surman Quartet; Brass Project; Mem., ATM trio, recordings and concerts, 2000–; Teacher, Jazz Faculty of the Royal Academy of Music, London. *Recordings:* Over 70 albums include: Elastic Rock, Nucleus, 1970; Harmony Row, Jack Bruce, 1971; Bundles, Soft Machine, 1975; Stranger Than Fiction, John Surman Quartet, 1994; Achirana, ATM, 2000. *Address:* 43 Combemartin Rd, London SW18 5PP, England.

MARSHALL, Oren Morris; b. 14 June 1966, Geneva, Switzerland. Musician (tuba, recorder, percussion). *Education:* Oboe, recorder, voice, Purcell School, 1977–79; Tuba, piano, Royal College of Music – JD, 1981–84. *Career:* Musician with every major orchestra in London, 1985; Jazz big bands include: Loose Tubes, 1984–90; Jazz Warriors, 1986; John Dankworth, 1995; Julian Joseph, 1994–95; Improvised music with: Company '92, with Derek Bailey; Say What Trio, with Steve Noble, Davey Williams, 1991–; World-wide tours, with London Brass, 1987–; Solo television appearances include: Wogan, BBC, 1987; South Bank Show, ITV, 1988; Performances with the Pan African Orchestra, UK and Ghana, 1991–94. *Recordings:* 10 albums with London

Brass; Other. *Recordings include:* Willcocks: Carols for Christmas, 1985; Mahler, Symphonies 9 and 10, Frankfurt Radio Orchestra, 1986; The Human Groove, Microgroove, 1988; London Brass: Christmas with the London Brass, 1990; Beyong the Groove: Contemporary Jazz, 1991; Antz Original Movie Score, 1998; Carols for Christmas Vol. 2; with The Paul Dunmall Octet, The Great Divide, 2001; Solo album: Time Spent At Traffic Lights (all compositions by Oren Marshall), 1995; Noble-Marshall-Buckley, Derek Bailey Trio, 1995; Mike Gibbs Band, 1993. *Honours:* ARCM (hons), 1983; FTCL, 1984; Shell/LSO Scholarship winner, 1987; Third prize, Geneva International Music Competition, 1991.

MARSTON, Steve; Musician (keyboards, multi-instrumentalist). *Career:* Mem., jazz funk quartet, D-Influence, 1990–; Support to Prince, Michael Jackson; Tours, television appearances; D-Influence also production team for R&B music; Group owns Freakstreet label. *Recordings:* Albums: Good 4 We, 1992; Prayer 4 Unity, 1995; London, 1997; D-Influence Presents D-Vas, 2002. Singles: I'm The One/The Classic, 1990; Midnite, 1995; Waiting, 1995. *Address:* c/o Dome Records Ltd, 59 Glenthorne Rd, London W6 0LJ, England.

MARTENS, Evert (Everardus Antonius Josephus Maria); b. 14 July 1956, Mill and St Hubert. 1 s. *Career:* Many TV and radio appearances. *Compositions:* Waltz for Rutger; La Copine; Where's My Key. *Recordings:* 4 CDs: After You're Gone; Just in Time; La Copine; Way to Go. *Honours:* First Prize, Capelino, Old Style Jazz Festival Breda, 1990. *Membership:* NTB; VAK; SENA; BUMA; STEMRA. *Address:* Sonsbeeksingel 11, 6814 AA Arnhem, Netherlands.

MARTENS, Hervé; b. 11 June 1963, Louvain, Belgium. Keyboard Player. *Career:* Member of Soulsister; Zap Mama World Tour, 2000. *Recordings:* Producer for Bobby Womack, Gibson Brothers and Sophie and So Four. *Honours:* Best Belgium Band Monte Carlo Award, 1988. *Membership:* Sabam; Zamu. *Address:* Kerkstraat 12, 3370 Boutersem, Belgium.

MARTIN, Barrie; b. 22 May 1944, London, England. Musician (baritone, tenor, alto saxophone). m. Elizabeth Gower, 5 Nov. 1976, 1 s., 2 d. *Education:* 5 years with Leslie Evans (private tutor). *Career:* Member, Quotations, Walker Brothers band for 2–3 years; All concert tours except last; Solo Spot, Sunday Night at London Palladium; Also as guest of Walker Brothers on German TV from Berlin; Played with Jet Harris' band: The Jet Blacks; One Night Stand, with Pete Murray, BBC TV, 1960s; Tours with: Roy Orbison; Brenda Lee; Duane Eddy; Little Richard; Englebert Humperdinck; Geno Washington and The Ram Jam Band; Working with Otis Grand and the Big Blues Band. *Recordings:* Solo, on Walker Brothers EP; Walker Brothers album: Portrait; Atlantic Soul Machine album: Coast To Coast. *Membership:* Musicians' Union. *Address:* 26 Halstow, Queens Cres., London NW5 4EH, England.

MARTIN, Beranger; b. 5 May 1960, Brugge, Belgium. Jazz Musician (Guitar; 2nd Instructor Piano). m. Elsie Tuyaerts, 1988, 2 s. *Education:* Jazz School, Dworp, Belgium. *Career:* On Tour in Sweden with Waso Quartet; with own trio, Beranger Trio; Toured in France, Germany and Netherlands; Guest Guitar Player in Australia. *Compositions:* LPs recorded with Gypsy Quintet, Piotto's; CD recorded with Big Band, Arena; Own CD for BRTN, Belgian TV. *Recordings:* Freelance Guitar Player; Swing-Jazz to Modern-Jazz and Gipsy Jazz; Guest Player on CDs. *Publications:* Cocktail, 1997. *Honours:* Jazz-Rally Hasselt, Best Solo Artist, 1990. *Current Management:* Kras Artist, Ghent Parcifal, Bruges Booking NTS, Knokke. *Address:* Sakramentstraat 8, 8300 Knokke-Reist, Belgium.

MARTIN, Bill; b. 9 Nov. 1938, Glasgow, Scotland. Songwriter; Music Publisher. m. 1972, 1 s., 3 d. *Education:* Royal Scottish Academy of Music. *Career:* Tours with The Drifters; Robert Parker; Winner, Eurovision Song Contest with Puppet On A String; Congratulations; All Kinds of Everything; Co-wrote UK No. 1 hits including: Puppet On A String, Sandie Shaw, 1967; Congratulations, Cliff Richard, 1968; Back Home, England World Cup Squad, 1970; Forever And Ever, Slik, 1976; All Bay City Roller hits including: Shang-A-Lang, 1974; Summerlove Sensation, 1974; Publisher of: Billy Connolly; Van Morrison; Sky-Songs; Writer, My Boy, for Elvis Presley; No. 1 songs world-wide. *Honours:* 20 Gold albums; 4 Platinum albums; 3 Ivor Novello Awards; 3 ASCAP Awards. *Membership:* BAC&S; PRS. *Address:* 225 Kensington High St, London W8 65A, England.

MARTIN, Billie Ray; b. Germany. Vocalist. *Career:* Singer with Electribe 101; Solo artiste. *Recordings:* Albums: Deadline For My Memories, 1995; 18 Carat Garbage, 2001. Singles: with Electribe 101: Talking With Myself, 1990; Solo: Your Loving Arms, 1995; Running Around Town, 1995; You and I (Keep Holding On), 1996; Imitation of Life, 1996; Space Oasis, 1996; Pacemaker, 1998; Honey, 1999; Crimes and Punishment, 1999. *Honours:* International Dance Music Award, Best New Dance Solo Artist, 1996. *Address:* c/o Mark Dean, East West Records, Electric Lighting Station, 46 Kensington Court, London W8 5DP, England.

MARTIN, Chris; b. 2 March 1977, Devon, England. Vocalist; Musician (guitar, piano), Songwriter. *Education:* University College, London. *Career:*

Mem., Coldplay, 1998–. *Recordings:* Albums: Parachutes, 2000; A Rush Of Blood To The Head, 2002. Singles: The Safety EP, 1998; Brothers and Sisters, The Blue Room EP, 1999; Shiver, 2000; Yellow, 2000; Trouble, 2000; Don't Panic, 2001; In My Place, 2002; A Rush Of Blood To The Head, 2002; The Scientist, 2002. *Honours:* BRIT Awards, Best Album, 2001, Best British Group, Best British Album, 2003; Grammy Award, Best Alternative Album, for Parachutes, 2001; MTV Award, Best UK and Ireland Act, 2002; Billboard Group of the Year, 2002; NME Award, Best Album, 2003. *Current Management:* Phil Harvey. *Address:* c/o Parlophone Records, 43 Brook Green, London W6 7EF, England. *Website:* www.coldplay.com.

MARTIN, Chris. See: **DJ PREMIER.**

MARTIN, Claire; b. 6 Sept. 1967, Wimbledon, London. Musician (Vocalist). *Education:* Doris Holford Stage School; Studied With Marilyn Johnson, Verona Chard. *Career:* Professional Singer Predominantly Jazz; Seven Years With LINN Records; Travelled Extensively In Europe, Asia; Worked For The British Council, Pakistan, Cyprus, Indonesia. *Compositions:* Years Apart; On Thin Ice; Jack and Sarah; The Waiting Game; Victim of Circumstance. *Recordings:* The Waiting Game; Devil May Care; Old Boyfriends; Offbeat; Make This City Ours; Take My Heart, 1999; Perfect Alibi, 2000; Every Now And Then, 2001. Vocals on: Stepping Stones, Martin Taylor, 2000; Easy The Hard Way, Mark Winkler, 2000; Honky Tonk Train Blues, Bob Zurke, 2001. *Honours:* British Jazz Awards, Rising Star, 1994, Best Vocalist, 1996, 1997. *Membership:* Equity; Musicians' Union. *Current Management:* James Taylor, Plant 3 Entertainments, PO Box 8403, Maybole, KA19 7YB. *Address:* Basement Flat, 61 Brunswick Pl., Hove, Sussex BN3 1NE, England.

MARTIN, Clive; b. 21 March 1963, London, England. Record Prod; Sound Engineer; *Recordings:* As Record Producer: Albums: with Reef: Replenish; Puressence album; with Echobelly: Insomniac (EP); with Les Negresses Vertes: Mlah (double Gold disc); Famille Nombreuse (Gold disc); with Hunters and Collectors: Ghost Nation (Platinum disc); As Sound Engineer: Soundtrack, David Byrne's The Last Emperor; with Youssou N'Dour; Echobelly, Everybody's Got One, 1994; Miquel Brown, So Many Men So Little Time, 1994; Drugstore, White Magic for Lovers, 1998; Llama Farmers, Dead Letter Chorus, 1999; As Assistant Engineer: Queen; Sting; The Cure; As Assistant to Flood: Jesus and Mary Chain; Matt Johnson; Soft Cell. *Honours:* Gold and Platinum albums; Academy Award, film soundtrack The Last Emperor. *Current Management:* Caroline Ryan. *Address:* Estate House, 921A Fulham Rd, London SW6 5HU, England.

MARTIN, Daniel-John; b. 25 Sept. 1965, Congleton, Cheshire, England. Jazz Musician (violin); Composer; Arranger. *Education:* Schola Cantorum (superieur) American School of Music; Didier Lockwood. *Career:* Tour with the 11tet de Violon Jazz; Theatre des Champs Elysées, France, Germany; Major French radio shows; TV: Le Cercle de Minuit; First festival, Jazz Violin, with Didier Lockwood; Jazz M6, TV; with Daniel Martin Group: Sunset; Baiser Solé; Petit Journal Montparnasse; Alligators. *Recordings:* Onxtet de Violon Jazz; Djeli Moussa (African music); Public Address (rock p-4 mati); Daniel-John Martin Group to be published. *Honours:* First Prize, Jazz Modern, Jazz Plus, Jazz Hot. *Membership:* General Secretary, Jazz and Violin Asscn.

MARTIN, Dey; b. 11 Sept. 1956, Los Angeles, CA, USA. Songwriter; Prod; Musician (guitar). *Education:* Composition Degree in Music BM, University of Hawaii; MM, University of California at Irvine, USA. *Career:* Backing Guitar, Polyphemus, Lollapalloosa Tour, 1995; Producer: Woodpecker, Lung Cookie, Jalopy Kinfolk, Music West, Vancouver, 1995; Songwriter, Solo Performer, mid 1980s; Owner: Naked Jain Records. *Compositions:* String Quartet, 1978; Three Images, text by EE Cummings for classical guitar, mezzo soprano vocal and piano, 1979; Berlin Wall, 1989. *Recordings:* Mr Monotony, producer. *Honours:* Young Composers, 1978–80. *Membership:* ASCAP, NAS, NARM. *Current Management:* Naked/Jain Records Inc, PO Box 4132, Palm Springs, CA 92263, USA. *Address:* 681 E Spencer Dr., Palm Springs, CA 92262, USA.

MARTIN, Eric; b. Oct. 1960. Vocalist. *Career:* Founder member, Eric Martin Band; Lead singer, Mr Big, 1989; Also member, side project Road Vultures. *Recordings:* Albums: with Eric Martin Band: Sucker For A Pretty Face, 1983; Eric Martin, 1985; with Mr Big: Mr Big, 1989; Lean Into It, 1991; Bump Ahead, 1993; Hey Man, 1996; Big, Bigger, Biggest: Very Best Of, 1997; with Working Man: Working Man, 1996; Deep House Party Vol. 4, 1996; with Sammy Hagar: Marching to Mars, 1997; with Gildas Arzel: Brazebeck, 1999; with Supersuckers: Teachers, 1999; Singles include: Green-Tinted Sixties Mind; To Be With You; I Love the Way You Love Me; Solo albums: I'm Only Fooling Myself, 2000. *Current Management:* Herbie Herbert Management, 2501 Third St, San Francisco, CA 94107, USA.

MARTIN, Sir George (Henry); b. 3 Jan. 1926, England. Music Industry Exec; Producer; Composer (retd). m. (1) Sheena Rose Chisholm, 1948, 1 s., 1 d., (2) Judy Lockhart Smith, 1966, 1 s., 1 d. *Education:* Guildhall School of Music and Drama. *Career:* Sub-Lieut, R.N.V.R., 1944–47; Worked in BBC Music Library, 1950; With EMI Records Ltd, 1950–65, produced all records featuring The Beatles and numerous other artists; Formed Associated

Independent Recording (AIR) Group of companies, 1965, Chair., 1965–; Built AIR Studios, 1969; Built AIR Studios, Montserrat, 1979; Completed new AIR Studios, Lyndhurst Hall, Hampstead, 1992; Company merged with Chrysalis Group, 1974, Dir, 1978–; Chair., Heart of London Radio, 1994–; Scored the music for 15 films incl.: the Beatles movies A Hard Days Night, Help! and Yellow Submarine; The Family Way; James Bond: Live and Let Die. *Publications:* All You Need Is Ears, 1979; Making Music, 1983; Summer of Love, 1994. *Honours:* Hon. Fellow, Guildhall School of Music; Hon. mem., Royal Acad. of Music; Hon. DMus, Berklee College of Music, Boston, 1989; Hon. MA, Salford, 1992; Grammy Awards, 1964, 1967 (two), 1973, 1993, 1996; Ivor Novello Awards, 1963, 1979; C.B.E. *Address:* c/o AIR Studios, Lyndhurst Hall, Hampstead, London NW3 5NG, England.

MARTIN, Juan; b. 1 Oct. 1943, Málaga, Spain. Concert Musician (guitar). m. Helen Foulds, 6 June 1973, 2 s. *Career:* World-wide solo tours; Tours with own Flamenco Dance Company; Played South Bank Centre, and The Barbican, London; Carnegie Hall, and the Lincoln Centre, New York; 18 date tours, including the Barbican, UK, 1993, 1995; Television includes: Wogan; Top of the Pops; Pebble Mill; Arts programmes; Radio recitals, BBC Radios 1–4; New York WNYC; Boston WGBH. *Recordings:* Hit single: Love Theme From The Thorn Birds, 1984; Exciting Sound of Flamenco, 1974; Romance, 1976; Olé Don Juan, Flamenco en Andalucia, 1977; Picasso Portraits, 1981; Serenade, 1984; Solo album, 1985; Painter In Sounds, 1986; Through The Moving Window, 1988; Andalucian Suites, 1990; Luna Negra, 1993; Musica Alhambra, 1998; Los Arte Flamenco, 1999; Through the Moving Window, 1999; El Alquimista (Alchemist), 2000. *Publications:* El Arte Flamenco de la Guitarra; Fifth Edition, La Guitarra Flamenca, video series; Folios: Exciting Sound of Flamenco; 12 Solos; Andalucian Suites. *Membership:* PRS; MCPS. *Current Management:* Flamencovision, PO Box 508, London N3 3SY, England.

MARTIN, Lynne; b. 6 Nov. 1957, Bedford, England. Musician (keyboards); Arranger; Musical Dir. 1 d. *Education:* College; Sat examinations of Associated Board of Royal Schools of Music. *Career:* Television appearances: Friday People, Border TV; Look Who's Talking; Laugh-In; Musical Director for numerous summer seasons and pantomimes throughout UK; Personal Musical Director for Derek Batey for 12 years; Also MD for artistes including Max Bygraves; Moira Anderson; Frank Carson. *Compositions:* Theme tune, Friday People, Border TV, 1982. *Recordings:* Numerous recording sessions. *Membership:* Musicians' Union; Equity. *Current Management:* Ray Cornell Artistes and Productions. *Address:* Applause House, 56 St Annes Rd, Blackpool, Lancashire, England.

MARTIN, Marie-Ange; b. 18 Jan. 1948, Bois Colombes, France. Jazz Musician (guitar, banjo, cello). *Education:* 8 years cello study. *Career:* Played swing and Dixieland music with Benny Waters, Bill Coleman, 1969–76; Bebop and modern jazz, 1976–84; Guitar Institute of Technology, Los Angeles, 1985; Guitarist with own quartet; Banjo player, Hot Kings; Cellist, cello quartet Cellofans, 1986–93; Tours of Asia, Australia, Eastern Europe, with Christian Escoude and Marcel Azzola, 1993–95; Banjo and cello player, Threepenny Opera, 1996. *Recordings:* Dixieland Parade; Cello Acoustics; Also recording music of Kurt Weil. *Honours:* Outstanding Award of the Year, Guitar Institute of Technology, Los Angeles, 1985. *Address:* 31 rue de Fontarabie, 75020 Paris, France.

MARTIN, Max; b. 26 Feb. 1971, Sweden. Vocalist; Songwriter; Music Engineer; Prod. *Career:* Mem. (as Martin White), Swedish heavy metal band, It's Alive; Songwriter, collaborating with Denniz Pop, Rami; Songs recorded by: 3T, Ace of Base, Bryan Adams, Christina Aguilera, Backstreet Boys, Gary Barlow, Bon Jovi, Dede, Céline Dion, Drain, E-Type, 5ive, Jessica Folker, George, Herbie, Leila K, Kahsay, Michele, *N'SYNC, Papa Dee, Rednex, Robyn, Safe, Solid Harmonie, Britney Spears, Westlife. *Compositions include:* ...Baby, One More Time, Britney Spears; 10,000 Promises, Backstreet Boys; As Long As You Love Me, Backstreet Boys; Don't Wanna Lose You Now, Backstreet Boys; Don't Want You Back, Backstreet Boys; Quit Playing Games, Backstreet Boys. *Recordings:* Album: with It's Alive: Earthquake Visions, 1993. *Honours:* Swedish Grammy Award (with Denniz Pop), 1998; ASCAP Songwriter of the Year Award, 1999, 2000. *Website:* www.tonos.com.

MARTIN, Michael Anthony; b. 9 Nov. 1960, London, England. Musician (piano, keyboards). 2 d. *Education:* Post graduate diploma; O'Level Music. *Career:* Keyboard player for Billy Paul; Aswad; Jean Carne; Cliff Richard; Television: Top of the Pops; Children's TV; 3 world tours with Aswad; Montreux Pop Festival; International AIDS Day; Nelson Mandela at Wembley. *Compositions:* Music for BBC, State of Europe. *Recordings:* with Aswad: Don't Turn Round; Production on Heartbeat, Aswad, No. 1 Japan; Roots Rocking: The Island Anthology, 1997; Big Up, 1997; with Elementals: Waking on Each Other; with Dr Seuss: Dr Seuss Green Eggs and Ham; Solo Album: Odyssey, 1998. *Honours:* Platinum disc, for album: Rise and Shine, Aswad. *Membership:* PRS; Musicians' Union.

MARTIN, Millicent; b. 8 June 1934, Romford, Essex, England. Actress; Vocalist. m. Marc Alexander, 26 Sept. 1977. *Career:* Side By Side By Sondheim (London, Los Angeles, Broadway); 42nd Street (Broadway, Las Vegas, Los Angeles); The Boyfriend (London, Broadway); King of Hearts

(Broadway); The Card (London); Shirley Valentine; Rise and Fall of Little Voice; Follies; The Rivals, England and USA; Moon Over Buffalo, USA; Television appearances: Moon and Son; Mainly Millicent; That Was The Week That Was (TW3); Downtown; LA Law; Coach; Upper Hand; Murphy Brown; Frasier. *Recordings:* Side By Side; King of Hearts; Our Man Crighton; Sondheim – A Celebration. *Honours:* TV Society Medal; Variety Club Award. *Current Management:* Sean Diamond, London Management. *Address:* 2–4 Noel St, London WC1, England.

MARTIN, Neil; b. 10 Dec. 1967, Great Britain. Musician (drums). *Education:* Studied with: Paul Robinson; Ed Soph; Bob Armstrong. *Career:* Extensive sessions and television, radio appearances; Jimmy Barnes Psyclone World Tour 95 (including support to The Rolling Stones), venues from 1,000–50,000 seaters. *Compositions:* Co-writer, track Stumbling, Psyclone album, Jimmy Barnes. *Recordings:* Album: Psyclone: Jimmy Barnes. *Membership:* Musicians' Union. *Address:* 2 Waddington Close, Enfield, Middlesex EN1 WB, England.

MARTIN, Peter (Philemon Winston); b. 28 Jan. 1948, Tuitts Village, Montserrat. Musician (drums, percussion); Vocalist. 2 d. *Education:* Courses in adult education. *Career:* First reggae gigs with Owen Grey, Alton Ellis, small tours of England, early 1970s; Studio musician, mid 1970s; Tours, England, Scotland, Wales, 1980s; Joined Steel and Skin, Art Company, played Danish Festival, 1983; Tour, Sweden, 1984; Recordings, gigs. tours, Europe, West Africa, Scandinavia; Tour with Dr Alban, 1992; Resident in Sweden, 1993; Taught rhythm and dance, Blå Hasten; Production of Benny The Boxer, Theatre X; Played Djembe on dance courses; Joined Afro Tiambo, West African Rhythm and dance group, 1994; Computer course, digital music recording; Sound, lighting engineer, Folkuniversitetet, theatre production, Ritten till havet; Teacher, Malmö Music High School; Television: Old Grey Whistle Test; Opportunity Works; Chinese Detective; WDR Rock Palace; MTV Live; Concerts: Ronny Lane Tour; Style Council Peace Concert, Brixton; Radio: Africa, Sweden, London; Festivals: Hultsfred; Roskilde; Tours/gigs with Jimmy Cliff; Style Council; Papa Dee; Red Mitchell; Eek-A-Mouse; Eddie Grant. Recordings include Dr Alban. *Honours:* Appearances, before Princess Margaret, London, 1978; Swedish royals, Stockholm, 1992. *Membership:* Musicians' Union; Svenska Musik Forbondet. *Address:* 21 Lavender Grove, Hackney, London E18 3LU, England.

MARTIN, Ricky, (Enrique Martin Morales); b. 24 Dec. 1971, San José, Puerto Rico. Vocalist; Actor. *Career:* Member, Menudo, 1984–89; Numerous tours and recordings; Acted in Mexican soap opera Alcanzar una Estrella II; Began releasing Spanish language albums; Role as bartender Miguel in General Hospital (US TV series); Played Marius in Broadway production of Les Misérables; Dubbed voice in Spanish version of Disney film Hercules; TV spokesperson for Puerto Rican tourism; Released first English language album, including a duet with Madonna; Numerous television appearances and tour dates. *Recordings:* Albums: Ricky Martin, 1991; Me Amarás, 1993; A Medio Vivir, 1995; Vuelve, 1998; Ricky Martin, 1999; Sound Loaded, 2000; La Historia, 2001. Singles: Maria, 1996; 1 2 3 Maria, 1997; La Copa De La Vida (Cup Of Life, official song of World Cup, France), 1998; Vuelve; Un Dos Tres; La Bomba, 1999; Livin' La Vida Loca (No. 1, UK and USA), 1999; She's All I Have Had, 1999; Shake Your Bon-Bon, 1999; Story (with Christina Aguilera); Private Emotion, 2000; She Bangs, 2000. *Honours:* Grammy Award, Best Latin Pop Album, 1999; American Music Award, Favourite Latin Artist, 2000. *Address:* c/o Sony Music Latin, 550 Madison Ave, New York, NY 10022, USA.

MARTIN, Roy; b. 10 July 1961, Liverpool, Merseyside, England. Musician (drums); Drum Tutor. m. Margie Yates, 20 June 1985, 2 d. *Career:* Concert tours: Played for: Modern English, 1986, 1990; Shalom Hanoch, 1987, 1988; Gavin Friday, 1992; Black, 1993; Diesel, 1993. *Recordings:* Drummer on: Jimmy Barnes: Flesh and Wood; Aretha Franklin: Jimmy Lee; Cock Robin: When Your Heart Is Weak; Black: Black; Film soundtrack (The Christians): Blame It On The Bellboy; Modern English: Pillow Lips, Joe Grushecky: Pumping Iron and Sweating Steel; Jim Hunter: Fingernail Moon (bass); Tractor: Worst Enemies; Very Best of British Dance Bands (clarinet and saxophone); Patricia Kaas: Rendez-Vous and Live; Recorded with: Viv Stanshall; Regina Belle; Billy Brannigan; Shalom Hanoch. *Current Management:* B and H Management, Lavender Cottage, Love Lane, Kings Langley, Hertfordshire WD4 9HN, England.

MARTIN, Sarah; b. 12 Feb. 1974. Vocalist; Musician (violin, recorder). *Career:* Member: Belle and Sebastian, 1996–; Curated Bowlie Weekend Festival with other band members, 1999. *Recordings:* Albums: If You're Feeling Sinister, 1996; The Boy With The Arab Strap 1998; Fold Your Hands Child – You Walk Like A Peasant, 2000; Storytelling, 2002. Singles: Dog On Wheels EP, Lazy Line Painter Jane EP, 3–6–9 Seconds of Light EP, 1997; This Is Just A Modern Rock Song EP, 1998; Legal Man, 2000; Jonathan David, I'm Waking Up To Us, 2001. *Honours:* BRIT Award, Best Newcomer, 1999. *Current Management:* Banchory Management, PO Box 25074, Glasgow G2 6YL, Scotland. *Website:* www.belleandsebastian.co.uk.

MARTIN, Tony; b. 19 April 1957, Birmingham, England. Vocalist; Songwriter. m. Mo, 18 Aug. 1990, 2 s., 1 d. *Career:* First show aged 7; Many local bands; Joined The Alliance, 1983; Signed with Warner Bros publishing,

1984; Released tracks on Bailey Bros Compilation Album; Joined Black Sabbath, 1987, 3 albums, 3 world tours; Left Black Sabbath, 1992; Signed with Polydor, 1992, solo album; Rejoined Black Sabbath, 1993, 2 albums, 2 world tours. *Recordings:* with Bailey Brothers: Vinyl Frontier; The Talisman; Forcefield II; Valley of The Kings; Blue Murder; with Black Sabbath: Eternal Idol, 1987; Headless Cross, 1989; Tyr, 1990; Cross Purposes, 1993; Forbidden, 1995; Solo: Back Where I Belong, 1992. *Current Management:* Albert Chapman. *Address:* Lethal Music UK Ltd, E9 Kenilworth Court, Hagley Rd, Birmingham B16 9NU, England.

MARTINO, Al; b. 7 Oct. 1927, Philadelphia, Pennsylvania, USA. Vocalist; Entertainer; Actor. m. Judith Stilwell, 10 Dec. 1968, 1 s., 2 d. *Career:* Played Johnny Fontaine in The Godfather, 1972; Tours in Australia, Germany, USA and Canada; Played in Godfather I and III yearly. *Recordings:* Spanish Eyes; Here In My Heart (No. 1, UK charts); Mary In The Morning; I Love You Because; Painted, Tainted Rose; Daddy's Little Girl; The Voice to Your Heart, 1993; Volare, 1993; Spotlight on Al Martino, 1996; In Concert, 1998; There Are Such Things, 1998; Style, 2000. *Honours:* Philadelphia Music Hall of Fame; Gold Disc, Spanish Eyes.

MARTUCCI, Vincent; b. 21 Oct. 1954, Medford, Massachusetts, USA. Composer; Arranger; Musician (piano); Educator. m. Elizabeth Lawrence, 21 Sept. 1981, 1 s., 1 d. *Education:* BA, Music, Colby College, Waterville, Maine; MM, Music State University of New York, Purchase, 2001; Alumnus, Berklee College of Music; Private studies with John Mehegan, Hal Galper, Dave Holland, Baikida Carroll. *Career:* Performed, synthesizer, film score, My Blue Heaven, with Steve Martin; Numerous tours, own group, Co-lead with Dan Brubeck, The Dolphins, in USA, Europe, South America, Canada; Redesign network themes, Travel Channel, Lifetime Medical Television; Showtime, children's TV series, 1989; Music Dir., pianist, arranger for numerous performers incl. Eileen Fulton, Laurel Massé, 1991–; Producer, Performer, Arranger, numerous theatrical productions with Baikida Carroll and McCarter Theatre, 1995. *Compositions:* Numerous tunes for The Dolphins; Scores for daytime drama As The World Turns, Guiding Light, Another World, 1992–. *Recordings:* Livingston Taylor, Life is Good, 1988; Dan Brubeck and the Dolphins, 3 CDs, 1989–99; Rory Black, Tornado, 1996. *Publications:* Introduction to Jazz Piano, 1997; Introduction to Blues Piano, 1997; Introduction to Rock Piano, 1997. *Honours:* 2nd Place, Billboard Song Contest, 1988; Jazz Category Finalist, Hennessey Jazz Search, 1990. *Membership:* ASCAP; AFTRA. *Address:* 29 Pleasant Ridge Dr., W Hurley, NY 12791, USA.

MARTY, Bobby, (Etienne Martens); b. 4 Oct. 1937, Brugge (Bruges), Belgium. m. Suffys Nicole, 8 Sept. 1963, 1 s., 1 d. *Education:* Private lessons, Dirigent Pol Horna; Bass Guitar and 1 Year Piano, age of 12 years. *Career:* Andrex; Ensemble Pol Horna; The Shamrocks; Luc Rène and the Jumps; Own show with the Bobby Marty Dancers, 1980–; Radio's in Belgium and France; TV in France; Concerts with trio Tea for Three, own songs and music of the 60s, played bass, singer. *Compositions:* Houtem Mijn Dorpje; De Bruggeling; Adieu Jacques Brel; La Maison Du Bonheur; Mon Amour; Ma Guitare et Quelques Chansons; Une Belle Nuit D'Hiver; Au Rendez-Vous des Artistes. *Recordings:* 18 singles, one album, two compilation albums in France, with other French artistes; Three solo albums: Bobby Marty International; Bobby Marty sings Elvis; Country Dreams. *Publications:* Flash, own magazine, 1989–. *Honours:* Golden Record, Rose Des Neiges; Silver Record for Johnny Laat je Jodel nog eens Horen (compilation of Johnny Hoes). *Address:* Molenwalstraat 8A, 8630 Houtem-Veurne, Belgium.

MARTYN, John, (Iain McGeachy); b. 11 Sept. 1948, New Malden, Surrey, England. Musician (guitar); Lyricist. m. Beverly Kutner (divorced). *Career:* Duo with wife Beverly; Toured regularly with full-time band. *Compositions include:* Solid Air; Angeline; May You Never, recorded by Eric Clapton. *Recordings:* Albums: London Conversation, 1968; The Tumbler, 1968; Stormbringer, 1970; The Road To Ruin, 1970; Bless The Weather, 1971; Solid Air, 1973; Inside Out, 1973; Sunday's Child, 1975; Live At Leeds, 1975; One World, 1977; So Far So Good, 1977; Grace and Danger, 1980; Glorious Fool, 1981; Well Kept Secret, 1982; The Electric John Martyn, 1982; Philentrophy, 1983; Sapphire, 1984; Piece By Piece, 1986; Foundations, 1987; The Apprentice, 1990; Cooltide, 1991; BBC Radio 1 Live In Concert, 1992; Couldn't Love You More, 1992; Live, 1995; The Church With One Bell, 1998; Live, 1998; Snooo, 1999; Live at Bristol, 1999; Dirty Down and Live: Shaw Theatre, London 1990, 1999; Glasgow Walker, 2000; Patterns In The Rain, 2001. *Address:* c/o Permanent Records, 22–23 Brook Mews, London W2 3BW, England.

MARUCCI, Mathew Roger, III (Mat); b. 2 July 1945, Rome, New York, USA. Musician (drums); Prod; Writer; Author. m. Diane Marie, 25 May 1982, 1 s., 1 d. *Education:* AAS, Retail Business Management, Auburn Community College, 1965; AA, Music, Sacramento City College, 1973. *Career:* Recording artist and jazz musician; Applied Music Instructor for American River College, Sacramento; Drummer for major jazz artists including Jimmy Smith, Kenny Burrell, James Moody, Eddie Harris, Les McCann, John Tchicai and Buddy De Franco; Appeared in feature film Uncle Joe Shannon and TV series Fantasy Island; Played on soundtracks for TV; Leader of Trio, Quartet and

Quintet. *Compositions:* Festival; Ulterior Motif; Who Do Voo Doo Suite; Blue Suspension; Danse Desire; Lifeline; Quiescence. *Recordings:* Who Do Voo Doo, 1979; Lifeline, 1981; Festival, 1982; Extensity, 1982; Avant-Bop, 1983; Body and Soul, 1991; Ulterior Motif, 1998. *Publications:* Contributor of articles in magazines for Modern Drummer; Percussive Notes; Percussion News; Sticks and Mallets; Upstrokes; Drum Instructors Only. *Membership:* Percussive Arts Society; Broadcast Music Inc. *Address:* Sacramento, CA, USA.

MARVIN, Hank (Brian Rankin); b. 28 Oct. 1941, Newcastle upon Tyne, England. Musician (Guitar); Songwriter. m. Carole, 2 s. *Career:* Lead Guitarist, Cliff Richard's backing group the Drifters, 1958; Group became the Shadows, 1959–. *Recordings include:* Albums: with the Shadows: The Shadows, No. 1, UK, 1961; Out of the Shadows, No. 1, UK, 1962; The Shadows Greatest Hits, 1963; Dance with the Shadows, 1964; The Sound of the Shadows, 1965; Shadow Music, 1966; Jigsaw, 1967; Established, 1958, 1968; Shades of Rock, 1970; 20 Golden Greats, No. 1, UK, 1977; Thank You Very Much, 20th Anniversary Reunion Concert, Cliff Richard and the Shadows, 1978; String of Hits, No. 1, UK, 1980; Change of Address, 1980; Hits Right Up Your Street, 1981; XXV, 1983; Moonlight Shadows, 1986; Simply Shadows, 1987; Steppin' To the Shadows, 1989; At Their Very Best, 1989; Reflections, 1990; Themes and Dreams, 1991; Shadows in the Night, 1993; Solo albums: Hank Marvin, 1969; Words and Music, 1982; Into the Light, 1992; Heartbeat, 1993; Would You Believe It... Plus, 1994; Hank Plays Cliff, 1996; Marvin At The Movies, 2000; Guitar Player, 2002. Hit singles: with the Shadows: Apache, No. 1, UK, 1960; Man of Mystery, 1960; FBI, 1961; Kon-Tiki, No. 1, UK, 1961; The Savage, 1961; Wonderful Land, No. 1, UK, 1962; Guitar Tango, 1962; Dance On, No. 1, UK, 1963; Foot Tapper, No. 1, UK, 1963; Atlantis, 1963; Shindig, 1963; Geronimo, 1963; Stingray, 1965; Don't Make My Baby Blue, 1965; Let Me Be The One, UK's Eurovision Song Contest entry, 1975; Don't Cry For Me Argentina, 1979; Cavatina (Theme From the Deerhunter), 1979; Riders in the Sky, 1980; Living Doll – charity version with Cliff Richard, No. 1, UK, 1986; Contributions to films include: Serious Charge, 1959; The Young Ones, 1961; The Boys, 1962; Summer Holiday, 1963; Wonderful Life, 1964; Finders Keepers, 1966; The Frightened City, 1961; The Deerhunter, 1979; The Third Man, 1981. *Honours:* CBS Arbiter Award, for Services to British Music, 1977; with the Shadows: NME Record of the Year, 1960; Gold Disc, Apache, 1962; Ivor Novello Awards: Best Musical Score, 1963; Special Award for 25 Years in the Music Business, 1983; Winners, Split Song Festival, Yugoslavia, 1967. *Address:* c/o Polydor Records, 72–80 Black Lion Lane, London W6 9BE, England.

MARWICK, Gavin; b. 29 Aug. 1969, Edinburgh, Scotland. Musician (fiddle). *Education:* Formal training with Angus Grant, Alastair Hardie, Tom Anderson, Davy Tulloch. *Career:* Mem., Iron Horse, 1988–; Festivals, tours, television and radio work across Europe, North America, Asia and Africa; Formed fiddle-led trio with Jonny Hardie, 1994; Founder mem., Burach, 1994; Occasional partnership with Leo McCann, 1999; Mem., Cantrip, 2002; Composer, recording artiste, teacher on ceilidh circuit; Teaching: short courses, Newcastle University Folk Degree Course; Celtic Connections Education Programme; Feis Rois; ALP; Recording sessions with: Old Blind Dogs; Wolfstone; Arz Nevez; Sogdiana; Talitha MacKenzie; The Humpff Family. *Compositions:* for the Traverse: Faith Healer, 1998; Heritage, 2001; for BBC the Gamekeeper: Highland Shorts; The Trestle At Pope Lick Creek; Outlying Islands. *Recordings:* with Iron Horse: The Iron Horse, 1991; Thro Water Earth And Stone, 1993; Five Hands High, 1994; Voice Of The Land, 1995; Demons And Lovers, 1997; with Jonny Hardie: Up In The Air, 1995; The Blue Lamp, 1999; with Burach: The Weird Set, 1995; with The Marwicks: Ceilidh Sets, 1998; with Cantrip: Silver, 2002. *Publications:* Contribution to The Balnain Collection. *Honours:* Belhaven Best New Folk Band, Burach, 1995; MRA for excellence, for Thro Water Earth and Stone, 1993. *Membership:* Musicians' Union; PRS; PAMRA. *Current Management:* Peter Stott, 11 Harling Dr., Troon, Ayrshire KA10 6NF, Scotland.

MARX, Richard Noel; b. 16 Sept. 1963, Chicago, Illinois, USA. Vocalist; Songwriter; Record Prod. m. Cynthia Rhodes, 8 Jan. 1989, 3 s. *Career:* Backing vocalist with Lionel Richie, 1982; Solo artiste, 1986–; Extensive tours throughout USA, Europe and Asia; Major concerts include: Farm Aid V, 1992; All-star benefit concert, Pediatric AIDS Foundation, 1992; Television and radio appearances world-wide. *Compositions:* Co-writer, What About Me?, recorded by Kenny Rogers; Co-writer, album tracks with Chicago; Philip Bailey; Co-writer, co-producer, with Randy Meisner; David Cole; Fee Waybill; Vixen; Poco; Kevin Cronin. *Recordings:* Hit singles: Don't Mean Nothing, 1987; Should've Known Better, 1987; Endless Summer Nights, 1988; Hold On To The Nights (No. 1, USA) 1988; Satisfied (No. 1, USA), 1989; Right Here Waiting, (No. 1, USA), 1989; Angelia, 1990; Too Late To Say Goodbye, 1990; Children of The Night, 1990; Hard To Believe, 1991; Keep Coming Back, 1991; Hazard, 1992; Take This Heart, 1992; Chains Around My Heart, 1992; Now and Forever (No. 1, USA), 1994; The Way She Loves Me, 1994; Nothing Left Behind Us, 1994; Hazard, 1997; Until I Find You Again, 1997; Keep Coming Back, 1997; As backing singer: with Lionel Richie: All Night Long; You Are; Running With The Night; Solo albums: Richard Marx, 1987; Repeat Offender (No. 1, USA), 1989; Rush Street, 1991; Paid Vacation, 1994; Flesh and Bone, 1997; Greatest Hits, 1997; Days Of Avalon, 2000. *Honours:* Billboard AC Artist of the Year, 1992; First male artist with four Top 3 hits

from debut album. *Membership:* ASCAP; SAG; AFTRA; AFofM. *Current Management:* The Left Bank Organization. *Address:* 9255 Sunset Blvd, Los Angeles, CA 90069, USA.

MARZEC, Andrzej; b. 3 Sept. 1944, Szczytniki, Poland, Promoter. m. Ewa Olinkiewicz, 31 March 1983, 1 s., 1 d. *Education:* Law, Warsaw University; Private lessons on piano. *Career:* Since 1969, Agent for top Polish Rock and Jazz acts: Niemen; Tomasz Stanko; Michal Urbaniak; 1980–, Promoting international acts in Poland including: Kraftwerk; Tangerine Dream; Klaus Schulze; Elton John; Tina Turner; Pat Metheny; Iron Maiden; Depeche Mode; Leonard Cohen; AC/DC; Metallica; David Byrne; Iggy Pop; Bob Dylan; Chris Rea; Jack Bruce; Beastie Boys. *Address:* Andrzej Marzec Concerts (AMC), Mickiewicza 27/69, 01562 Warsaw, Poland.

MASAKOWSKI, Steve; b. 2 Sept. 1954, New Orleans, Louisiana, USA. Jazz Musician (guitar). m. Ulrike Sprenger, 22 March 1982, 1 s., 1 d. *Education:* Berklee College of Music, Boston. *Career:* Extensive international travel with Dianne Reeves; Rick Margitza; Astral Project. *Recordings:* Direct AXEcess; What It Was; Friends; Mars; Appears on 28 albums: including Esquire Jazz Collection, 1995; Philip Manuel: Time for Love, 1995; Johnny Adams, Verdict, 1995; Astral Project: Astral Project, 1997; Jazz: Language of New Orleans, 1998. *Honours:* Voted Best Jazz Guitarist in New Orleans, Offbeat Magazine. *Current Management:* Scott Aiges, Arts International Group. *Address:* 516 S Rendon St, New Orleans, LA 70119, USA.

MASEK, Jiri; b. 15 June 1970, Prague, Czech Republic. Sound Engineer. m. Zuzana, 22 May 1992, 1 s., 1 d. *Career:* Sound Engineer, 28 records including many well-known Czech pop, folk and jazz groups and singers. *Recordings:* Zalman and Spol, 4 CDs, Czech Republic; Ivan Hajnis, CD, Sweden; Happy to Meet, CD, Ireland; Wild West, CD, Czech Republic; Relief, CD, Czech Republic. *Honours:* Folk and Country Awards, 1997, 1998, 1999; Stereo and Video Award, 1998. *Address:* Good Day Records, Vrsovická 74/699, Prague 10, 10000 Czech Republic.

MASEKELA, Hugh Rampolo; b. 4 April 1939, Witbank, Johannesburg, South Africa. Musician (trumpet); Bandleader. m. Miriam Makeba, 1964 (divorced). *Education:* Manhattan School of Music, New York. *Career:* Founder, The Merry Makers, 1955–; Joined African Jazz and Variety package tour, 1958; Joined cast of musical, King Kong, 1959; Formed the Jazz Epistles, 1959; Emigrated to USA, 1960; Formed own quartet, 1961; Signed to Motown Records, 1970; Formed Union of South Africa band, 1970; Played with Fela Kuti; Hedzollah Soundz; Herb Alpert; Major concerts include: Monterey Jazz Festival, 1967; Goin' Home concert, Lesotho, 1980; African Sounds for Mandela concert, Alexandra Palace, 1983; Graceland world tour, with Paul Simon, 1986. *Compositions include:* Music for Broadway show, Sarafina, 1989. *Recordings:* Jazz Epistles, 1959; Trumpet Africa, 1962; The Americanization of Ooga Booga, 1964; The Emancipation of Hugh Maskela, 1966; Promise of a Future, 1967; Coincidence, 1967; Maskela, 1968; Reconstruction, 1970; Home Is Where The Music Is, 1972; Your Mama Told You Not To Worry, 1974; I Am Not Afraid, 1974; The Boys Doin' It, 1975; The African Connection, 1975; Colonial Man, 1976; The Main Event, with Herb Alpert, 1978; Herb Alpert/Hugh Masekela, 1979; Home, 1982; Dollar Bill, 1983; Technobush, 1984; Waiting For The Rain, 1985; Tomorrow, 1987; Up Township, 1989; Back To The Future, 1998; Note of Life, 1999; Hugh Masakela's Latest, 1999; Hugh Masakela Is Alive and Well at the Whisky, 1999; Don't Go Lose It Baby, 1999; Lady, 1999; Colonial Man, 1999; Sixty, 2000; Time, 2002. *Honours:* Kora Award, Best Musician of the Year, 2002. *Current Management:* Sam Nole Management, 230 Park Ave, Suite 1512, New York, NY 10169, USA.

MASHBURN, Robin Arvil (Rob); b. 5 April 1942, Andrews, North Carolina, USA. Vocalist; Songwriter; Musician (guitar, bass). m. Catherine Stears Mashburn, 25 Sept. 1982, 2 s. *Career:* Grand Ole Opry: Wolftrap; Bele Chere; Tennessee Homecoming – Museum of Appalachia; University of Chicago; Georgia Mountain Fair. *Recordings:* Albums: The Picker; Another Place Another Time; Brother of Mine; It's Me Again Lord; Misty Mountain Music; The Picker's Best, CD. *Membership:* BMI; Bluegrass Music Asscn of North Carolina, South Carolina, Georgia. *Current Management:* Catherine Mashburn. *Address:* PO Box 1318, Andrews, NC 28901, USA.

MASON, Dave; b. 10 May 1947, Worcester, England. Musician (guitar). *Career:* Guitarist, The Hellions; Road manager, Spencer Davis Group; Founder member (with Steve Winwood), Traffic, 1967–68; Solo artist; Played with Eric Clapton's Derek and The Dominoes, 1970; Moved to USA, 1973; Recording with Fleetwood Mac. *Recordings:* Albums: with Traffic: Mr Fantasy, 1968; Solo: Alone Together, 1970; Dave Mason and Cass Elliot, 1971; Headkeeper, 1972; Dave Mason Is Alive!, 1973; It's Like You Never Left, 1973; Dave Mason, 1974; Split Coconut, 1975; Certified Live, 1976; Let It Flow, 1977; Mariposa De Oro, 1978; Old Crest On A New Wave, 1980; Some Assembly Required, 1981; Two Hearts, 1987; Long Lost Friend: The Best of Dave Mason, 1995; Will You Still Love Me?, 1998; Ultimate Collection, 1999; The 40,000 Headmen Tour (live), 1999; It's Like You Never Left, 2000; with Fleetwood Mac: Time, 1995; Various compilations. *Honours:* Gold discs.

MASON, Kerry; b. 31 March 1968, Dorking, Surrey, England. Vocalist; Songwriter; Performer. 1 d. *Education:* Singing lessons, Tona De Brett. *Career:* Singer, band Hed; Played all main festivals including: Glastonbury, Phoenix; 12 years' experience; Session singing. *Recordings:* Singles: Reigndance, 1994; Folklaw, 1995. *Membership:* Musicians' Union. *Current Management:* Timebomb. *Address:* PO Box No. 15, 63 Camden High St, London NW1 7JL, England.

MASON, Mila; b. 22 Aug. 1963, Dawson Springs, Kentucky, USA. Country vocalist. *Career:* Toured with country singer mother from an early age; Picture used by Kenner company on the Kenner toy jukebox, aged 6; Auditioned for a Bob Hope special singing I Can Feel The Earth Move, aged 8; Moved to Nashville and met songwriter Harlan Sanders (writer of hits for George Jones); Became demo singer for Sanders and other writers; Married at 19, temporarily abandoning career to raise two children, although marriage failed; Returned to Nashville to begin demo work again; Sang jingles and appeared in several music videos as well as developing own songwriting; Song co-written with Kostas came producer Blake Mevis' attention; Mevis set up showcase at a local club, 1995; This resulted in recording deal with Atlantic Records and release of debut album That's Enough of That, 1997; Appeared on the posthumous Patsy Cline duets album project singing Crazy Dreams, 1999. *Recordings include:* That's Enough of That, 1996; Dark Horse, 1997; Closer To Heaven; Albums include: That's Enough of That, 1996; The Strong One, 1998; Just A Peek, 2001. *Address:* c/o Country Music Asscn, 1 Music Circle S, Nashville, TN 37203, USA.

MASON, Nick; b. 27 Jan. 1945, Birmingham, England. Musician (drums). *Career:* Drummer, Pink Floyd, 1965–; Performances include: Rome International Pop Festival, 1968; Hyde Park, London, 1968; Bath Festival, 1970; Montreux Festival, 1971; Knebworth Festival, 1975; Films: Pink Floyd Live At Pompeii, 1972; The Wall, 1982; Autobiographical film, Life Could Be A Dream, 1985. *Recordings:* Albums: Piper At The Gates Of Dawn, 1967; A Saucerful of Secrets, 1968; More (film soundtrack), 1969; Ummagumma, 1969; Atom Heart Mother (No. 1, UK), 1970; Relics, 1971; Meddle, 1971; Obscured By Clouds, 1972; The Dark Side of The Moon (No. 1, USA), 1972; Wish You Were Here (No. 1, UK and USA), 1975; Animals, 1976; The Wall (No. 1, USA), 1979; The Final Cut (No. 1, UK), 1983; A Momentary Lapse of Reason, 1987; The Delicate Sound of Thunder, 1988; Shine On, 1992; The Division Bell (No. 1, UK) 1994; Pulse (No. 1, UK), 1995; Echoes: The Very Best Of Pink Floyd, 2001; Singles: Arnold Layne, 1967; See Emily Play, 1967; Money, 1973; Another Brick in The Wall (Number 1, UK and USA), 1979; When The Tigers Broke Free, 1982; Not Now John, 1983; Solo albums: Nick Mason's Ficticious Sport, 1981; Profiles, 1985; Producer, Music For Pleasure, The Damned, 1977. *Honours:* Outstanding Contribution To British Music, 1992. *Current Management:* Steve O'Rouke, EMKA Productions Ltd, 43 Portland Rd, London W11 4LJ, England.

MASONDO, David; b. KwaZulu Natal, South Africa. Vocalist; Musician (drums). *Career:* Started in church choir; Entertained guests at weddings and social functions; Joined The Groovy Boys, 1970; Drummer with The Young Brothers, 1973; Changed name to Soul Brothers after Moses Ngwenya joined the band, 1976; Various international tours; Recorded over 30 albums. *Recordings:* Albums include: Umshoza Wami, 1974; Isiphiwo, 1982; Xola, 1987; Jive Explosion, 1988; Impimpi, 1989; Isighebhezana, 1999; Induk' Enhle, 2001. *Honours:* FNB South African Music Award, Best Mbaqanga Performance; 15 gold discs, 5 platinum discs, several multiplatinum discs. *Address:* c/o Gallo, PO Box 2897, Parklands 2121, South Africa. *Website:* www.gallo.co.za.

MASSENBURG, George Y; b. 1947, Baltimore, MD, USA. Prod; Recording Engineer; Audio Equipment Designer. 1 s. *Career:* ITI Studios, Huntsville, MD; Chief engineer, Europa Sonar Studios, Paris, France, 1973–1974; Freelance engineer and equipment designer, 1973–74; Designer, builder and manager of recording studios; Founder and owner, George Massenburg Labs Inc, 1982–; Adjunct Prof., Recording Arts and Sciences, McGill University, Montreal, Canada; Visiting lecturer, University of California, Los Angeles, University of Southern California, Middle Tennessee State University; Worked with: Mary Chapin Carpenter, The Dixie Chicks, Earth Wind & Fire, Billy Joel, Journey, Little Feat, Kenny Loggins, Lyle Lovett, Aaron Neville, Randy Newman, Madeleine Peyroux, Linda Ronstadt, Michael Ruff, James Taylor, Toto. *Contributions to:* Professional journals and trade magazines. *Honours:* Academy of Country Music Award, Record of the Year, for The Trio, 1988; Mix Magazine TEC Awards, Producer and Engineer of the Year, for Little Feat, 1989; Engineer of the Year Award, for Linda Ronstadt, 1991; for Lyle Lovett, 1992; Grammy Awards, Producer, 1996, Best Engineered Non-Classical Record, 1990, Technical Achievement, 1998. *Address:* George Massenburg Labs Inc, PO Box 1366, Franklin, TN 37065, USA. *E-mail:* gmlinc@ix.netcom.com. *Website:* www.massenburg.com.

MASUKA, Dorothy, (Aunty Dot); b. 1937, Bulawayo, Rhodesia. Vocalist; Songwriter. *Career:* Started performing with the African Jazz and Variety Show, a travelling road show with Miriam Makeba and Hugh Masekela, aged 12; Started recording, 1951; Exiled from South Africa, 1960; Worked as a singer throughout Europe and Africa; Returned to Zimbabwe, 1980;

Performed several shows with The Golden Rhythm Crooners in Harare, 1989; Contributed to John Barry's soundtrack for Cry the Beloved Country, 1995. *Recordings:* Albums include: Hamba Notsokolo, Ingalo, 1988; Women of Africa Vol. 1, 1989; Pata Pata, 1990; Magumede, Mzilikazi, 2001. *Honours:* Pan-African Cultural Festival in Algiers, award winner, 1969.

MATHERS, Marshall Bruce, III. See: **EMINEM.**

MATHES, David Wayne; b. 23 April 1933, Steubenville, Ohio, USA. Music Industry Consultant; Record Prod; Musician (guitar). m. (1) Pauline Sexton, 25 Sept. 1955, 1 s., 1 d., (2) DeAnna S Newman Bass, 8 Sept. 1978, 1 step-d. *Education:* Electronics I and II, VoTech, Orlando, Florida; Florida Institute of Technology, Orlando; Advanced Electronics, Tennessee State University, Nashville; Musicianship correspondence course, Rutgers University, New Jersey; Advanced Songwriting Techniques, University of Tennessee. *Career:* On stage, country appearances with Warner Mack, Tommy Cash, Jim Ed Brown, The Rudy Sisters, Dottie West; Gospel stage appearances with the Hays Family, The Sextons, Tennessee Valley Quartet, The Frost Brothers, Jake Hess and the Imperials, The Swanee River Boys; TV appearances on Nashville Gospel, Maranatha, Sing Out America; The Music Machine; Radio appearances on Southern Gospel Hour, I Am Country Music; Sound Engineer on programmes including Johnny Cash Show, Jackie DeShannon, Ballad of the West and numerous commercials. *Compositions include:* My Love For You; Dreamers; Just A Simple Love Song; Who Can Mend a Broken Heart; Who Will Sing One Song For Me. *Recordings include:* Sounds of the Saved Soul, instrumental album; Produced: Man of the Street, Drusky; Shenandoah, The Four Guys; Just a Simple Love Song, DeAnna; Peg O My Heart, the Sgro Brothers; Golden Slippers, Smokehouse Band. *Publications:* Institute of Recording Arts and Sciences Home Study Course, 1987; Columns for Family Travel and Illinois Country Music Association, 1989; Columns for Masterpiece, 1997–98. *Honours:* Hon. Order of Kentucky Cols, 1975; Tennessee Ambassador, 1975; Hon. Lieut Col Aide de Camp, Alabama, 1986; Hon. Deputy Sheriff, Davidson County, Tennessee, 1975. *Membership:* Audio Engineering Society; Broadcast Music Inc; Country Music Asscn; National Entertainment Journalists' Asscn; American Federation of Musicians. *Current Management:* International Promotions Ltd.

MATHESON, Karen Elizabeth; b. 11 Feb. 1963, Oban, Argyll and Bute, Scotland. Vocalist. *Career:* Founder mem., Capercaillie; Group, along with original material, specialize in fusing traditional Gaelic songs with contemporary arrangements; Had first UK top 40 single in Gaelic, Coisich A Ruin (from A Prince Among Islands EP), 1992; Also worked on solo projects and appeared on L'Heritage de Celts, a French album with Donal Lunny and Dan Ar Braz; Project led to Matheson performing a Breton song, Que Naissant Les Enfants, with Dar An Braz and Elaine Morgan for France's entry in Eurovision Song Contest, 1996; Appeared in Rob Roy film singing an unaccompanied rendition of a Gaelic Lament; Performed on TV series Transatlantic Sessions with many well-known artists including: Emmylou Harris; The MacGarrigle Sisters; Mary Black; Collaborations with James Grant on solo albums and TV appearances. *Recordings:* Albums: with Capercaillie: Cascade, 1984; Crosswinds, 1987; Sidewaulk, 1989; Delirium, 1991; Get Out, 1992; The Blood Is Strong, Secret People, 1993; Capercaillie, 1995; To The Moon, 1996; Beautiful Wasteland, 1997; Glenfinnan—Songs of The '45 (recorded 1995), 1998; Nàdurra, 2000; group feature on: Rob Roy OST, 1995; Solo: The Dreaming Sea, 1996; Time To Fall, 2002; features on: L'Heritage De Celts, 1994; Finisterres, Dan Ar Braz, 1997; Zenith, Dan Ar Braz, 1998; Identities, Idir, 1999; Fused, Michael McGoldrick, 2000; Dawn of a New Century, Secret Garden, 1999; On The West Side, Donnie Munroe, 2000; Searchlight, Runrig, 2000; Sawdust In My Veins, James Grant, 2000; My Thrawn Glory, James Grant, 2000; Tacsi (TV series), 2000; Dreamcatcher, Secret Garden, 2001.

MATHEWS, Norman; b. 12 Sept. 1952, Rockford, Illinois, USA. Composer. *Education:* BA Hunter College, New York; MA, New York University. *Career:* Composer for Musical Theatre, Jazz, Concert Music. *Compositions:* Songs of a Poet; You Might As Well Live; Triumph of Night. *Recordings:* Songs of a Poet. *Honours:* ASCAP Standard Award, 1998, 1999. *Membership:* ASCAP; American Music Center; Dramatists Guild. *Address:* 667 W 161st St, Apt 3H, New York, NY 10032, USA.

MATHIESEN, Claus; b. 13 July 1957, Copenhagen, Denmark. Musician (clarinet, recorder). 1 s. *Education:* Classical education, Copenhagen; Turkish Art Music, Istanbul Conservatory. *Career:* Musician with Ildfuglen, 1979–83; Kefir, 1983–86; Fuat Saka Band, 1986–; Wild East, 1989–93; Oriental Mood, 1993–; Chochek Brothers, 1994–; All these bands merging Western and Balkan/Middle Eastern music. *Recordings:* with Fuat Saka Band: Nebengleis, 1989; Askaroz, 1991; Sen, 1994; with Anatolia: Anatolia, 1991; with Oriental Mood: Travels, 1994; Oriental Moods, 1996; Oriental Garden, 1998; with Nazê Botan: Akh Kurdistan, 1996; Kurdistan – The Forgotten World, 1998; with Chochek Brothers: Let's Chochek!, 1998. *Publications:* Contributor, Danish National Encyclopedia. *Membership:* DJBFA. *Address:* Mariendalsvej 32C, 2000 Copenhagen F, Denmark.

MATHIESON, Greg; b. 25 Feb. 1950, Los Angeles, California, USA. Arranger; Composer; Prod; Musician (keyboards). m. Barbara Price, 9 July 1983, 1 s. *Career:* Tours: Al Jarreau; Larry Carlton; Abraham Laboriel. *Recordings:* Baked Potato Super Live; For My Friends; with Al Jarreau: All Fly Home; This Time; Trouble In Paradise; with Bill Champlin: Burn Down The Night; Through It All; with Laura Branigan: Gloria; with Toni Basil: Mickey; with Sheena Easton: Telefone; Strut; Almost Over You; with Donna Summer: MacArthur Park; Heaven Knows; Live and More; with Barbra Streisand: Enough Is Enough; Songbird; Wet; with Abraham Laboriel: Dear Friends; Guidem; Frontline; Koinonia; with Manhattan Transfer: Extensions; Mecca For Moderns; Bodies and Souls; with Lee Ritenour: Banded Together; Earth Run; Collection; with Deniece Williams: When Love Comes; Hot On The Trail; Special Love; From The Beginning; with Rita Coolidge: Ann; with Rickie Lee Jones: Flying Cowboys; with Jimmy Cliff: Peace; with Steven Bishop: Bowling In Paris; with Umberto Tozzi: Gloria; Notte Rosa; Umberto Tozzi – Live; Le Une Cauzui; Equivacando; with David Hasselhoff: Crazy For You; with Helen Baylor: Live; with Tina Turner: Simply the Best; Keyboard player for: Larry Carlton; Ringo Starr; Joe Cocker; David Foster; Tom Jones; Billy Idol; Julio Iglesias; Nils Lofgren; Simple Minds; Film scores: American Flyer; Unfaithfully Yours; Midnight Express. *Honours:* One of select few producers to have top 2 singles in same week. *Current Management:* Wigwam. *Address:* 3724 Buena Park Dr., Studio City, CA 91604, USA.

MATHIESON, Ken; b. 30 June 1942, Paisley, Scotland. Musician (drums, zither); Arranger; Composer. m. with 2 s., 1 d. *Career:* Freelance musician; 15 year residency in Black Bull Jazz Club, Milngavie, Glasgow; Working and touring with leading UK and US jazz musicians including: George Chisholm; Tommy Whittle; John McLevy; Jack Emblow; Sonny Stitt; Johnny Griffin; Tal Farlow; Played with and wrote for Fat Sam's Band (Edinburgh-based jazz group touring world-wide), 1985–96; Leader, Picante (5 piece Bop and Latin band); Jazz Écosse All-Stars (6-piece Dixieland Band featuring top Scottish players and vocalist Fionna Duncan); Jazz Celebrities (7 piece mainstream band specialising in the music of Buck Clayton and Buddy Tate); Groovebusters (8/9 piece 'wee big-band' covering Jelly Roll Morton to Benny Golson); Latest venture a trio plus vocalist Lynn O'Neill dedicated to Brazilian music of all kinds; Organized first Glasgow International Jazz Festival, 1985; Frequent broadcaster on Jazz and World Music. *Recordings:* All Fat Sam's records. *Address:* 20 Kylepark Cres., Uddington, Glasgow, Scotland.

MATHIEU, Jean F; b. 11 Dec. 1948, Geneva, Switzerland. Composer; Musician (Guitar, Vocals, Drums, Bass). *Career:* Musicals, Bricelet Pradise; La Dame Aux Begonins; Films, Mort In Dimanche De Plvie; Locomemory; Show, Viva La Musica; Opera, Notes Par In Opera; Theatre, Flibuste. *Compositions:* Voyage Dans In Coeur Lorulant; Herakles Ducks Again. *Recordings:* Inguitarissable; Flibuste; Notes Par Un Opera. *Honours:* Journey Through A Burning Heart, Keyboards Contest; CRPLF Contest. *Current Management:* Jay Fm Productions. *Address:* 1205 Geneva, Switzerland.

MATHIEU, Mirielle; b. 24 July 1946, Avignon, France. Vocalist. *Career:* Television appearances include: Ed Sullivan TV Show; Andy Williams TV Show; International concerts include: Top Star Festival, 1972. *Recordings:* Albums: Mirielle Mathieu, 1968; You and I, with Paul Anka, 1979; Les Contes De Cri-Cri, 1985; Recontres De Femme, 1988; Greatest Hits, Vol. 1, 1989; Chante Piaf, 1994; L'American, 1995; Les Plus Grands Succes, Vols 1–3, 1995; Vous Lui Direz, 1995; In Meinem Traum, 1996; Rendezvous, 1997; Sings Ennio Morricone, 1999; Embrujo, 1999; Son Grand Numero; Hit singles include: Mon Credo; C'Est Ton Nom; Qu'Elle Est Belle; Funambule; Les Bicyclettes De Belsize.

MATHIS, Johnny (John Royce); b. 30 Sept. 1935, San Francisco, California, USA. *Education:* San Francisco State College. *Career:* Recording artist, 1964–; Tours world-wide. *Recordings include:* Singles: Wonderful! Wonderful!; Chances Are (No. 1, USA), 1957; Someone; The Twelfth of Never; It's Not For Me To Say; A Certain Smile; Misty; Winter Wonderland; There Goes My Heart; My Love For You; My One and Only Love; Let Me Love You; I'm Stone In Love With You; When A Child Is Born (No. 1, UK), 1976; Too Much, Too Little, Too Late, duet with Deniece Williams, (No. 1, USA), 1978; Other duets with Gladys Knight; Natalie Cole; Dionne Warwick; Stephanie Lawrence; Barbara Dickson; Nana Mouskouri; Albums: Johnny Mathis, 1956; Wonderful!, Wonderful!, 1957; Warm, 1957; Good Night, Dear Lord, 1958; Swing Softly, 1958; Open Fire, Two Guitars, 1959; Heavenly, 1959; Faithfully, 1960; Ride On A Rainbow, 1960; Johnny's Mood, 1960; I'll Buy You A Star, 1961; Portrait of Johnny, 1961; Live It Up, 1962; Rapture, 1962; Johnny, 1963; Romantically, 1963; I'll Search My Heart, 1964; Olé, 1965; Tender Is The Night, 1965; The Wonderful World of Make Believe, 1965; This Is Love, 1966; The Shadow of Your Smile, 1966; The Sweetheart Tree, 1967; Up, Up and Away, 1967; Johnny Mathis Sings, 1967; Love Is Blue, 1968; Those Were The Days, 1968; People, 1969; The Impossible Dream, 1969; Raindrops Keep Fallin' On My Head, 1970; The Long and Winding Road, 1970; Close To You, 1970; Love Story, 1970; You've Got A Friend, 1971; In Person, 1972; The First Time Ever I Saw Your Face, 1972; Make It Easy On Yourself, 1972; Me and Mrs Jones, 1973; Killing Me Softly With Her Song, 1973; I'm Coming Home, 1973; Song Sung Blue, 1974; The Heart of a Woman,

1974; Feelings, 1975; I Only Have Eyes For You, 1976; Sweet Surrender, 1977; When A Child Is Born, 1978; You Light Up My Life, 1978; Mathis Magic, 1979; Different Kinda Different, 1980; Friends In Love, 1982; A Special Part of Me, 1984; Right From The Heart, 1985; In The Still of The Night, 1989; How Do You Keep The Music Playing?, 1993; Celebration: Anniversary Album, 1995; All About Love, 1996; Because You Loved Me: Songs of Diane Warren, 1998; Romeo and Juliet, 1999; Mathis Magic, 1999; In the Still of the Night, 1999; Mathis On Broadway, 2000; Numerous Greatest Hits, Musical and Christmas compilations. *Current Management:* Rojon Production Inc, 3500 W Olive, Suite 750, Burbank, CA 91505, USA.

MATOLU-DODE, Papy-Tex; b. 28 June 1952, Kinshasa, Zaire. Vocalist. m. Ekofo-Wando, 21 Jan. 1989, 3 s., 8 d. *Education:* Itaga College, Kinshasa. *Career:* Singer, African Choc, 1968; Singer, African Choc (band name changed to Empire Bakuba), 1979–; Player, Etodle Filante, football team. *Compositions:* Sanda; Karibu; Sanco Yamawa; Welcome in Africa; Music Clarification. *Recordings:* Bakuba Show; Full Option; Surprise; Livre D'Or; La Belle Etoire. *Publications:* Sanda, 1973; Karibu, 1985; Bakuba Show, 1988; Full Option, 1997. *Honours:* Diplome of Performance for Development Initiative, 1995; Apid Certificate of Artistic Merit, 1987; Acknowledgement of Merit, Francophone Counsel of Songs, 1993. *Membership:* SONECA; SACEM; SABAM; SUIZA; BURIDA. *Address:* 69 rue Luapula, Commune de Kinghasa, Democratic Republic of Congo.

MATTACKS, David; b. 13 March 1948, London, England. Musician (drums). m. Caron Woods, 31 Dec. 1993. *Career:* Apprentice piano tuner; Mecca Big Band, 3 years; Played small jazz groups; Joined Fairport Convention, 1969; 7 albums; Tours of: UK; USA; Europe; Antipodes; Japan; Freelance musician, 1974–; Combines freelance work with re-formed Fairport Convention, mid 1980s–; International tours include: Europe; USA; Annual Oxfordshire Cropredy Festival; Drums and keyboards in concerts and recordings; Performed with artists including: Jethro Tull; Chris Rea; Joan Armatrading; Sandy Denny; Micky Jupp; Andy Fairweather-Low; Georgie Fame; Nick Heyward; Ashley Hutchings; Ralph McTell; The McGarrigles; The Swingles; Tours in UK, Europe, USA, with Richard Thompson Band, 1994–95; Recorded, played with: Liane Carroll; Everything But The Girl; Week's residency, Ronnie Scott's Club, London, with Liane Carroll Trio. *Compositions:* Television and film scores include: Death Wish 2; Green Ice; Give My Regards To Broad Street; Band of Gold (ITV); Love Hurts (Barbara Dickson); Time Bandits; McVicar; Lisztomania; Hussey; Hearts of Fire; Shoestring; Fox; Leo Sayer television series; Your Cheatin' Heart. *Recordings include:* Fairport Convention: Jewel In The Crown, 1995; Also with artists including: Joan Armatrading; Barbara Dickson; Elton John; Paul McCartney; Chris Rea; The Proclaimers; Jimmy Page; Alison Moyet; XTC; Beverley Craven; Richard Thompson; Gary Brooker; Elkie Brooks; John Gorka; Cat Stevens; Roger Daltrey; Mary Ann Redmond; Kimberly Rew; Recent. *Recordings include:* with Fairport Convention: Who Knows Where Time Goes?, 1997; with Richard Thompson: Celtschmerz, 1998; with Steve Ashley: Stroll on Revisited, 1999; with Steeleye Span: Horkstow Grange, 1999; with Paul McCartney: Run Devil Run, 1999.

MATTEA, Kathy; b. 21 June 1959, Cross Lane, West Virginia, USA. Country Vocalist; Musician (guitar). m. Jon Vezner. *Education:* University *Career:* Member, Bluegrass group Pennsboro; Tour guide, Country Music Hall of Fame, Nashville; Singer for demos and commercials; Backing singer, Bobby Goldsboro's roadshow, 1982; Solo recording artiste, mid-80s. *Recordings:* Singles: Street Talk; Love At The Five and Dime; Goin' Gone; 18 Wheels and A Dozen Roses; Life As We Knew It; Come From The Heart; Burnin' Old Memories; Where've You Been; Ready For The Storm; Among the Missing Albums: Kathy Mattea, 1984; From My Heart, 1985; Walk The Way The Wind Blows, 1986; Untasted Honey, 1987; Willow In The Wind, 1989; Time Passes By, 1991; Lonesome Standard Time, 1992; Good News Radio Special, 1994 Only Everything, 1995; Walking Away A Winner, 1995; Ready For The Storm – Favourite Cuts, 1995; Love Travels, 1997; The Innocent Years, 2000 *Honours:* Best Country Song of Year, Where've You Been. *Current Management:* Titley and Associates, 706 18th Ave S, Nashville, TN 37203 USA.

MATTHEWS, Cerys Elizabeth Phillip; b. 11 April 1969, Cardiff, Wales Vocalist; Songwriter; Musician (guitar). *Career:* Founder member, Catatonia 1992–2001; First release on Welsh Indie label Crai; Signed by Blanco Negro, 1996. *Recordings:* Albums: Way Beyond Blue, 1996; The Sublime Magic Of Catatonia, 1996; International Velvet (No. 1, UK), 1998; Equall Cursed and Blessed (No. 1, UK), 1999; Paper Scissors Stone, 2001; Greatest Catatonia Hits, 2002. Singles: For Tinkerbell (EP), 1993; Hooked (EP), 1994 Bleed/Do You Believe In Me, 1996; You've Got A Lot To Answer For, 1996 Mulder And Scully, 1998; Guest Vocalist, Ballad Of Tom Jones, with Space 1998; Strange Glue, 1998; Road Rage, 1998; Dead From The Waist Down 1999; Londinium, 1999; Karaoke Queen, 1999; Baby It's Cold Outside, wit Tom Jones, 1999; Stone By Stone, 2001.

MATTHEWS, Dave (David John); b. 9 Jan. 1967, Johannesburg, Sout Africa. Vocalist; Musician (guitar); Songwriter. *Career:* Owner of ATO Record label; Joined band TR3; Encouraged by local studio owner Ross Hoffman record solo, 1990; Employed musicians to first perform as The Dave Matthews Band, 1991; Rapid growth of fanbase through touring schedules; First album released on group's own Bama Rags label certified gold by RIAA; First national US tour in support of RCA debut album, 1994; Many world-wide concerts and festival appearances since including 2001 album tour; Group permits fans to tape-record shows for personal use; I Did It single officially released through Napster, 2001; Occasionally tours with Reynolds as acoustic duo. *Recordings:* Albums: Remember Two Things (live), 1993; Under The Table and Dreaming, 1994; Crash, 1996; Live At Red Rocks 8–15–95, 1997; Before These Crowded Streets, 1998; Live At Luther College '96 (Dave Matthews and Tim Reynolds), Listener Supported (live), 1999; Everyday, Live In Chicago 12–19–98, 2001; Singles: Recently (EP), 1994; What Would You Say, Jimi Thing, Ants Marching, 1995; So Much To Say, Too Much, 1996; Don't Drink The Water, 1997; Satellite, Crash Into Me, Crush, 1998; I Did It, The Space Between, Everyday, 2001. *Honours:* Grammy Awards: Best Rock Performance By A Duo Or Group With Vocal, 1997; US VH-1 Awards: Favourite Group; Must Have Album; Song of the Year, 2001; Top-grossing touring band in USA, 2000. *Address:* c/o Red Light Communications, 3305 Lobban Pl., Charlottesville, VA 22903, USA. *E-mail:* info@rlc.net. *Website:* www.dmband.com.

MATTHEWS, Donna Lorraine; b. 2 Dec. 1971, Newport, England. Musician; Songwriter. *Career:* Member of Elastica, 1992–99; Toured extensively world-wide including Reading Festival, 1994, Glastonbury, 1995, Big Day Out in Australia, 1996; Numerous television appearances including Top of the Pops; Solo artiste. *Recordings:* Stutter, 1993; Line Up, 1994; Connection, 1994; Albums include: Elastica (No. 1, UK), 1995; The BBC Sessions, 2001; Also vocals on: Seven More Minutes, The Rentals, 1999. *Honours:* NME Readers Award For Best New Band, 1994. *Current Management:* CMO Management International Ltd, Unit 32, Ransomes Dock, 35–37 Parkgate Rd, London SW11 4NP, England.

MATTHEWS, Iain; b. 16 June 1946, England. Songwriter; Vocalist. m. Veronique, 26 Feb. 1990, 1 s., 1 d. *Career:* Mem., The Pyramid, 1965; Founding mem., Fairport Convention, 1967; Mem., Matthews Southern Comfort; Solo, also Plainsong, 1972; Left performing for A&R: Island Records; Windham Hill, early 1980s; Returned to performance, after success at annual Fairport Convention, late 1980s; Moved to Austin, Texas, USA; Re-formed Plainsong; Started Hamilton Pool, Singing, songwriting collective, Austin Texas; Toured with Nanci Griffith, Other Voices Too, 1998. *Recordings:* with Fairport Convention: Fairport Convention, 1968; What We Did On Our Holiday, 1968; Unhalfbricking, 1968; with Matthews Southern Comfort: Matthews Southern Comfort, 1969; Second Spring, 1970; Later That Same Year, 1970; Best Of Matthews Southern Comfort, 1992; Best Of Matthews Southern Comfort, 1997; Solo: If You Saw Through My Eyes, 1970; Tigers Will Survive, 1971; Journeys From Gospel Oak, 1972; Valley Hi, 1973; Some Days You Eat The Bear, 1974; Go For Broke, 1976; Hit and Run, 1977; Stealin' Home, 1978; Siamese Friends, 1979; Discreet Repeat, 1980; Spot Of Interference, 1980; Shook, 1983; Walking A Changing Line (The Songs Of Jules Shear), 1988; Pure And Crooked, 1990; Nights In Manhattan, 1991; Orphans And Outcasts, 1991; Live Alone, 1993; Intimate Wash, 1993; The Soul Of Many Places, 1993; Skeleton Keys, 1993; Excerpts From Swine Lake, 1999; Orphans and Outcasts Vol. 3, 1999; Plainsong: In Search Of Amelia Earhart, 1972; And That's That, 1992; Plainsong On The Air, 1992; Dark Side Of The Room, 1992; Hi Fi: Demonstration Record, 1981; Moods For Mallards, 1982; The Dark Ride, 1994; Camouflage, 1995; God Looked Down, 1996; Nights In Manhattan, 1997; Voices Electric, 1994; Sister Flute, 1996; New Place Now, 1999. *Publications:* It's About Time (pictorial biography). *Membership:* NARAS. *Current Management:* Frank van den Meijden, Visserslaan 8, 4201-ZJ Copinchem, Netherlands. *Address:* PO Box 676, Buda, TX 78610, USA.

MATTHEWS, Jamie (James Lindsay); b. 15 May 1951, London, England. Musician (harmonicas, ukulele, percussion, jaws harp, whistle); Vocalist. *Education:* Church and school choirs. *Career:* Extensive tours, Far East, late 1960s; Europe and North America, 1980s; Major US tour with Daily Planet, including Telluride Festival, Colorado, 1995, 1996. *Recordings:* Parlour Games, John B Spencer; Sunday Best, John B Spencer; A Month of Sundays, double album, Johnny G; Clark's Secret, Daily Planet; The Big Scoop, Daily Planet. *Honours:* Guinness All-Ireland Busking Champion as Gentleman Jamie, 1986; with Daily Planet, awarded BBMA Best Progressive Bluegrass Band, 1995. *Address:* 5 Cleveland Row, Bathwick, Bath BA2 6QR, England. *Telephone:* (1225) 330842. *E-mail:* jamie@clark-kent.demon.co.uk. *Website:* www.dailyplanet.co.uk.

MATTHEWS, Julie; b. 2 April 1963, Sheffield, South Yorkshire, England. Vocalist; Songwriter; Musician (guitar, piano). *Career:* Seven years, piano bars throughout Europe, Middle East; Member, Albion Band, 1991–92, 1994–95; Female duo with Pat Shaw; Female duo with Chris While; Toured extensively throughout Europe, Canada; Many radio appearances, sessions; Cambridge, Edmonton festivals, 1995. *Compositions include:* Song: Thorn Upon The Rose, recorded by Mary Black. *Recordings:* with Pat Shaw: Lies and Alibis; Compilation: Intuition; with Albion Band: Captured; Albion Heart; Solo album: Such Is Life, 1995; with Chris While: Blue Moon On The Rise

(mini album); Piecework, 1998; Higher Potential, 1999; with Helen Watson: Somersault, 1998. *Membership:* PRS; MCPS; Musicians' Union. *Current Management:* Blue Moon Music; Circuit Music. *Address:* 130 Central Ave, Southport, Merseyside PR8 3ED, England.

MATTHEWS, Patrick; b. 1978. Musician (bass guitar). *Career:* Founding mem., The Vines, 1994–; Appearance, Sydney 2000 Olympic Festival; Australian tour, supporting You Am I, 2001; Record Beatles cover, I'm Only Sleeping, for film I Am Sam, 2001; Sign to Capitol Records, USA, Heavenly Records, UK; Short UK, US and Canadian tours, incl. Glastonbury Festival, England; Carling Weekend Festival, Reading, Leeds; Coachella Festival, Los Angeles; Troubadour, Los Angeles; Mercury Lounge, New York; WHFS Festival, Washington, 2002; Sign to EMI Australia, 2002; Television appearances: Top Of The Pops, Later With Jools Holland, The Late Show with David Letterman, 2002; Australian tour, late 2002; Performed, MTV Video Music Awards, 2002. *Recordings:* Albums: Highly Evolved, 2002. Singles: Factory, 2001; Sun Child/Hot Leather, 2002; Heavenly, 2002; Get Free, 2002; Highly Evolved, 2002. *Honours:* NME Award, Best Single, for Get Free, 2003. *Current Management:* Winterman and Goldstein Management, PO Box 545, Newtown, NSW 2042, Australia. *Address:* c/o Capitol Records, 1750 N Vine St, Hollywood, CA 90028, USA. *Website:* www.thevines.com.

MATTHEWS, Roderick Newton; b. 18 May 1956, London, England. Composer; Musician (guitar); Record Prod. m. Pamela Margaret Johnson, 14 Nov. 1992, 1 d. *Education:* Balliol College, Oxford; Grade 1 piano. *Career:* Produced records for small labels, including Troggs album, 1979–84; Produced for majors, including Roland Rat, Musical Youth, chart entries in Germany, Norway, 1984–86; Remixes include Manfred Mann; Session musician, 1987–92; Writing music for television (commercials, signatures, incidentals) 1988–; MD for Lenny Henry, 1989–91; Also appeared on soundtracks: French and Saunders; Absolutely Fabulous; Hello Mum; Alexei Sayle Shows; Lenny Henry; Rory Bremner; Harry Enfield; Girl Friday; Bad News; Blue Peter; Tracy Ullman; Newman and Baddiel; Fry and Laurie. *Compositions:* Written for 7 series of London's Burning; Newshounds (Screen Two), 1990; The Winston Pom; Funseekers (Comic Strip); Coffee Blues for Lenny Henry (in Lenny Live and Unleashed); Alexai Sayle: Shut Up; The Winjin Pom; Mary Whitehouse Experience, second series; Television commercials for Duracell; Burger King; Twix. *Recordings:* Played or sung on recordings including: Monkey, George Michael; Don't Make Me Wait, Bomb The Bass; Cross My Heart, Patsy Kensit and Eighth Wonder; ABC; Sinitta; Charles Aznavour; Rick Astley; Pepsi and Shirlee; England Football Squad; Comic Relief; John Parr, Running the Endless Mile; George Michael, Faith; Rick Astley, Hold Me in Your Arms; London's Burning (soundtrack compilation, with Simon Brint). *Membership:* PRS; MCPS.

MATTHEWS, Sarah; b. 22 June 1966, London, England. Vocalist. *Career:* Member, Rub Ultra; Radio 1 session; Appearance on Naked City (Channel 4); Festivals: Glastonbury; Phoenix, 1994; 4 British tours; Played NME Brats concert; XFM concert broadcast line. *Recordings:* EPs: Combatstrength Soap, 1994; Korporate Finger Tactic, 1994; Album: Liquid Boots and Boiled Sweets, 1995. *Membership:* Musicians' Union; PRS. *Current Management:* Nick Moore, Splash Management. *Address:* The Splash Club, 328 Gray's Inn Rd, Kings Cross, London W10, England.

MAULDIN, Jermaine Dupri; b. 23 Sept. 1972, Ashville, South Carolina, USA. Prod; Songwriter; Record Co Pres; *Recordings:* Warm It Up; Jump; Kris Kross; Understanding; Xscape: Just Kicking It; Funkdafied; Da Brat; Xscape: Feels So Good; Jermaine Dupri Presents Life in 1472, 1998; Jermaine Dupri Presents: 12 Soulful Nights; Singles include: Money Ain't a Thang, 1998; Sweetheart, 1998; Going Hone with Me, 1998; Party Continues, 1998; As Producer: Da Brat: Anuthatantrum, 1996; Mase: Harlem World, 1997; Aretha Franklin: Rose is Still a Rose, 1998; TLC: Fanmail, 1999; Men in Black, 1999. *Honours:* ASCAP: Best Song of Year, 1993. *Current Management:* Michael Mauldin. *Address:* 2849 Piedmont Rd, Atlanta, GA 30305, USA.

MAULIS, Zbynek; b. 24 April 1975, Kladno, Czech Republic. Musician (Bass Guitar). *Education:* Technical University, Prague, 2 years. *Career:* The Teplo, Rock and Roll group, 1992–; Brutus, Rock and Roll group, 1996–. *Compositions:* Want You Go With Me, Brutus, 1996. *Recordings:* Best of Brutus, 1997. *Address:* Na'm 1 Opletala 10, Kladno 4, 27204 Czech Republic.

MAUNICK, Jean-Paul, (Bluey); b. 1957, Mauritius. Prod; Musician (guitar); Songwriter. *Career:* Emigrated to London, 1967; Member: Light of the World, late '70s; Formed: Incognito with Paul 'Tubbs' Williams, 1979. *Recordings:* Albums: with Incognito: Jazz Funk, 1981; Inside Life, 1991; Tribes Vibes and Scribes, 1992; Positivity, 1993; 100° and Rising, 1995; Beneath The Surface, 1996; Blue Moods, 1997; No Time Like The Future, 1999; Life Stranger Than Fiction, 2001; Singles: Parisienne Girl, 1980; Incognito, 1981; North London Boy, 1982; Inside Life, Always There (featuring Jocelyn Brown), Crazy For You (featuring Chyna), 1991; Don't You Worry About A Thing, Change, 1992; Still A Friend of Mine, Givin' It Up, 1993; Pieces of a Dream, 1994; Everyday, I Hear Your Name, 1995; Jump To My Love, Out of the Storm, 1996; Nights Over Egypt, 1999. *Honours:* MOBO Award, Best Jazz Act, 2001. *Membership:* PRS; AURA. *Current Management:*

Ricochet, 5 Old Garden House, The Lantern Bridge Lane, London SW11 3AD, England. *Address:* c/o Talkin' Loud, Chancellor's House, 72 Chancellor's Rd, London W6 9QB, England.

MAURICE, (Glynn) Mike; b. 12 Feb. 1937, London, England. Musician (piano, guitar). Record Co Exec.; Artist Man.; Promoter. 1 s., 1 d. *Career:* Artist Manager, Purple Dreams; Managing Director, M & M Records; Promoter, Merlin's Cave Nite Club, first Western club, London; Club 21, London; Hangar Lane music venue, London; Originator, Richmont Bingo clubs, Reading; Lilly Road Bingo clubs, London; Auctioneer, Petticoat Lane, 1954–62; Stage act, mind reading and telepathy, 1957–68; Toured Europe, USA, Australia, Malaysia, Japan and Israel; Lecturer and demonstrator, clairvoyance, the paranormal and healing, Arthur Findlay College, Stanstead, London, 1968–82; Proprietor, M & M Recording Studios; M & M Video Studio. *Recordings:* released through M & M Recordings; M & M Records; M & M Video Agency. *Publications:* Original publisher, free newspapers, 1969; Local Express; Spiritualist News, Vision Journals; Life (biography) due for publication 1997. *Current Management:* M & M Management. *Address:* 79 Greenview Dr., Northampton NN2 7LE, England.

MAVIAN, Robert A, (Gibson Case); b. 29 Oct. 1936, New York, NY, USA. Bluegrass Musician; Performer; Songwriter. m. Barbara Lou Pearson, 18 Aug. 1962, 1 s., 1 d. *Education:* Doctorate Degree, Veterinary Medicine and Surgery. *Career:* Sideman performer with Peter Rowan; John Herald; Hazel Dickens; The Sykes Boys; Member, duo, The Case Brothers – Martin and Gibson; Leader, founder of the Horse Country Bluegrass Band; Performed, World Original WWVA Jamboree, Wheeling West Virginia; WSM Grand Ole Opry, Ryman Auditorium, Nashville, Tennessee; Winnipeg Folk Festival, Canada; Brandy Wine Mountain Music Convention Woodstown, New Jersey; Thomas Point Bluegrass Festival, Brunswick, Maine; Waterloo Bluegrass Festival, Stanhope, New Jersey; Berkshire Mt, Bluegrass Festival, Hillsdale, New York; WKCR-NYC; WFUV-NYC; WFDM-NJ; WHUS-Storrs, CT; WOWL-TV, Florence, Alabama. *Recordings:* As The Case Brothers – Martin and Gibson, Old Time Duets With Guitar and Mandolin; The Radio Album; Also: Collectors Edition, The Berkshire Mt Bluegrass Festival; Kenneth Brewer and His Melody Kings and Queens; The Cumberland Mountain Boys, single 78 RPM's. *Membership:* International Bluegrass Music Asscn; American Veterinary Medical Asscn; American Animal Hospital Asscn; New York State Veterinary Medical Society. *Address:* 168 Pines Bridge Rd, Ossining, NY 10562, USA.

MAX, Buddy, (Boris Max Pastuch); Recording Artiste; DJ. *Career:* America's Singing Flea Market Cowboy, F. Cowboy Junction Flea Market; Manager, Singing Flea Market Cowboy, Lecanto, Florida; Kingwood Play Boys Band, performed all over New Jersey, Pennsylvania, New York; Buddy Max Radio Show, WKia, WLBE, WKFL, WINV 1560 AM, AM Radio, Florida; TV: The Buddy Max Show; Country Western Bluegrass Show, 1969–. *Recordings include:* Buddy Max, 1980; The Great Nashville Star, 1984; The Story of Freda and Bud; Cowboy Junction Stars, 1985; Tribute to Challenger's Crew of 7, 1986; With Our Friends At Cowboy Junction, 1989; Little Circle B, 1990; Together – Our Masterpiece, 1991; I Love Miss America, 1992; The Life To Fame and Fortune, 1985. *Honours:* Gold Record, 1995; Inducted into Hall of Fame, 1997; Record John F Kennedy held in Smithsonian Institute, Washington, and John F Kennedy Library, Dallas; Statue of Liberty Award, Liberty Coin and Membership to Ellis Island. *Membership:* American Heart Asscn; American Lung Asscn; Girl Scouts of America; Citizens of Citrus County, Florida; Deaf Serv of Citrus County. *Address:* Cowboy Junction Flea Market, Hwy 44, Jctn 490, Lecanto, FL 34461, USA.

MAXI JAZZ; Vocalist; Rap Artiste; DJ. *Career:* Rapping world-wide; DJing; Running record label; Mem., Soul Food Café Band; Mem., Faithless, 1995–. *Recordings:* Albums: with Faithless: Reverence, 1996; Sunday 8pm, 1998; Saturday 3am, 1999; Testimony, Chapter 1, 1999; Back To Mine (compilation), 2001; Outrospective, 2001; Re-Perspective, 2002. Singles: with Faithless: Salva Mea, 1995; Insomnia, 1995; Don't Leave, 1996; Reverence, 1997; If Lovin' You is Wrong; Take the Long Way Home, 1998; God Is A DJ, 1998; Bring My Family Back, 1999; Why Go?; Muhammad Ali, 2001; We Come 1, 2001. *Honours:* Best International Act to Appear in Ireland, 2001. *Address:* Faithless Live Ltd, PO Box 17336, London NW5 4WP, England. *E-mail:* info@faithless.co.uk. *Website:* www.faithless.co.uk.

MAXWELL, (Maxwell Menard); b. 23 May 1973, Brooklyn, New York, USA. Vocalist. *Career:* Started his musical career with performances at Nell's night club in New York; Demo tape reached Sony Records resulting in record deal and release of debut album in April 1996; Collaborations: Leon Ware; Stuart Matthewman. *Recordings:* Albums: Maxwell's Urban Hang Suite, 1996; MTV Unplugged, 1997; Embrya, 1998; Now, 2001; Singles: Til The Cops Come Knockin', Ascension (Don't Ever Wonder), 1996; Sumthin' Sumthin', Whenever Wherever Whatever, 1997; Fortunate, 1999; Lifetime, Gotta Let You Know, 2001. *Honours:* Soul Train Awards, Best R&B Artist, 1997. *Address:* c/o Columbia Records, 550 Madison Ave, New York, USA.

MAXWELL, Thad James; b. 2 July 1945, Brooklyn, New York, USA. Musician (guitar, bass, steel guitar, drums). m. Jeanne Cornell, 1 s., 1 d.

Education: AA, Glendale College, 1987. *Career:* Guitarist, drummer, Tarantula, 1969–70; Bassist, various artists including: Ricky Nelson; Arlo Guthrie; Linda Ronstadt; Flying Burrito Brothers, 1970–80; Steel guitarist, guitarist, Mac Davis, 1973–. *Recordings include:* with Arlo Guthrie: Hobo's Lullabye, 1972; Last of The Brooklyn Cowboys, 1973; with Tarantula: Tarantula, 1969; Other. *Recordings include:* Horizon, The Carpenters, 1975; A Little Warmth, Steve Gillette, 1979; Sweet Country Suite, Larry Murray, 1971; Sierra, Sierra, 1977; Lead Free, B W Stevenson, 1972; Swampwater, Swampwater, 1970; with Flying Burrito Brothers: Tribute to Gram Parsons, 1995. *Membership:* AFofM; AFTRA. .

MAY, Brian; b. 19 July 1947, Twickenham, London, England. Musician (guitar); Vocalist; Composer; Prod. *Education:* Astronomy and Physics, Imperial College, London. *Career:* Guitarist, The Others; Smile; Guitarist, UK rock group Queen, 1970–; Numerous tours include: UK; USA; Australia; South America; Japan; Major concerts include: Rock in Rio Festival, Brazil, 1985; Live Aid, Wembley, 1985; Knebworth Festival, 1986; A Concert For Life, Wembley, 1992; Musical of Queen songs, We Will Rock You, West End, London, 2002–. *Recordings:* Albums include: Queen, 1973; Queen 2, 1974; Sheer Heart Attack, 1974; A Night At The Opera, 1975; News of The World, 1977; Jazz, 1978; Live Killers, 1979; The Game, 1980; Greatest Hits, 1981; Hot Space, 1982; The Works, 1984; The Complete Works, 1985; Live Magic, 1986; The Miracle, 1989; Innuendo, 1991; Greatest Hits II, 1991; Live At Wembley '86, 1992; Made In Heaven, 1995; Solo: Star Fleet Project, 1983; Back To The Light, 1992; Resurrection, 1994; Live at the Brixton Academy, 1994; Another World, 1998. *Contributions to:* Puttin' On The Style, Lonnie Donegan; All American Alien, Ian Hunter; Tribute To Muddy Waters; Singles include: Seven Seas In Rhye, 1974; Killer Queen, 1974; Bohemian Rhapsody (No. 1, UK), 1975; You're My Best Friend, 1976; Somebody To Love, 1976; We Are The Champions, 1977; Bicycle Race, 1978; Don't Stop Me Now, 1979; Love of My Life, 1979; Crazy Little Thing Called Love (No. 1, UK), 1979; Save Me, 1980; Play The Game, 1980; Another One Bites The Dust (No. 1, USA), 1980; Flash, 1981; Under Pressure (with David Bowie) (No. 1, UK), 1981; Radio Ga Ga, 1984; I Want To Break Free, 1984; It's A Hard Life, 1984; One Vision, 1985; A Kind of Magic, 1986; I Want It All, 1989; Breakthru, 1989; Innuendo (No. 1, UK), 1991; The Show Must Go On, 1991; These Are The Days Of Our Lives/Bohemian Rhapsody (No. 1, UK), 1991; Headlong, 1991; Heaven For Everyone, 1995; Too Much Love Will Kill You, 1995; Business, 1998; Driven By You, 1998; We Will Rock You, with Five (No. 1, UK), 2000. *Honours:* Ivor Novello Awards: Best Selling British Record, Bohemian Rhapsody, 1976; Outstanding Contribution To British Music, 1987; Gold Ticket, Madison Square Gardens, 1977; Britannia Award, Best British Pop Single 1952–77, 1977; American Music Award, Favourite Single, 1981; Silver Clef Award, Nordoff-Robbins Music Therapy Centre, 1984; BRIT Awards: Outstanding Contribution to British Music, 1990; Best British Single, 1991. *Current Management:* c/o Jim Beach, Queen Productions, 46 Pembridge Rd, London W11 3HN, England.

MAY, Derrick, (Mayday, Rhythim Is Rhythim); b. 6 April 1963, Detroit, Michigan USA. Prod; Remixer; DJ. *Career:* Founder Transmat Records; Credited with invention of techno genre as part of the Belleville Three (alongside Juan Atkins and Kevin Saunderson); World-wide DJ; Resident DJ at the Music Institute in Detroit in the early '90s; Collaborations: Juan Atkins, Kevin Saunderson, System 7, Carl Craig; Remixed: ABC, Funtopia, Yello, Inner City, DJ Rolando. *Recordings:* Albums: Innovator – Soundtrack For The Tenth Planet, 1992; Singles: Let's Go (as X-Ray), 1986; Nude Photo (as Rhythim Is Rhythim), 1987; Strings of Life (as Rhythim Is Rhythim), 1987; It Is What It Is (as Rhythim Is Rhythim), 1988; Beyond The Dance (as Rhythim Is Rhythim), 1989; The Beginning (as Rhythim Is Rhythim), 1990; Icon (as Rhythim Is Rhythim), 1993. *Current Management:* c/o Transmat Records, 1492 Gratoit Ave, Detroit, Michigan, USA.

MAY, Simon; b. 15 Aug. 1944. Composer. m. Rosie, 1 s., 3 d. *Education:* Choral Scholar, Degree modern languages, Cambridge University. *Career:* Taught German, French, Music, Kingston Grammar School, 8 years; Following commercial success of stage musical Smike (10,000 performances world-wide, BBC Christmas television production), became full-time composer; Songwriter, record producer, world-wide sales over 15m., include 10 UK top 20 hits; Songs recorded by: Cliff Richard; Amii Stewart; Nick Berry; The Pointer Sisters; Al Jarreau; Marti Webb; Anita Dobson; The Shadows; Richard Clayderman; Ruby Turner; Jonathan Butler; Stephanie De Sykes; Kate Robbins; Records produced for Amii Stewart include: Knock On Wood (No. 1, USA); Light My Fire. *Compositions:* Film: The Dawning; Television: EastEnders, BBC; Howard's Way, BBC; Trainer, BBC; Eldorado, BBC; The Holiday Programme, BBC; The Food and Drink Programme, BBC; Castaway 2000, BBC; Don't Try This At Home, LWT; Television Weekly, TVS; Olympic Theme, Thames; The Vet, BBC; People, BBC; Paramedics, BBC; Jobs For The Girls, BBC; The Trial of James Earl Ray, Channel 4; Swiss Family Robinson, 1997; Pet Rescue, 1997; Lion Country, 1997; Great Estates, Channel 4; A Place In The Sun, Channel 4; The Tribe; City Hospital; Musicals: Smike; Rick Van Winkel. *Publications:* William Shatner's Twist In The Tale. *Honours:* Novello Award, Every Loser Wins, Nick Berry, 1986; 3 TRIC Awards, Best TV Theme: EastEnders; Howard's Way; Trainer. *Membership:* PRS; Songwriters; BAC&S; Equity; Musicians' Union. *Current*

Management: Helstonleigh, 17 South Hill, Guildford, Surrey GU1 3SY, England.

MAY, Tina; b. 30 March 1961, Gloucester, England. Vocalist. m. Clark Tracey, 15 June 1989, 1 s. *Education:* BA, French, University of Wales; Studied singing from age 16, also at University (soprano). *Career:* Began by tours as singing actress, actress with own theatre co, Black Door; Full-time singer; Broadcasts, tours of Australia, Far East, Europe, UK with own quartet. *Recordings:* Never Let Me Go, 1992; Fun, 1993; It Ain't Necessarily So, 1994; Time Will Tell, 1995; Change Of Sky, 1998; N'oublie Jamais, 1998; One Fine Day, 1999; Live In Paris, 2000; I'll Take Romance, 2003; Recordings with own group; Various guest appearances on other recordings, incl. collaboration with Ray Bryant, 2003. *Honours:* Worshipful Company of Musicians, Outstanding Jazz Musician, 1993. *Membership:* Musicians' Union; Equity; Asscn of British Jazz Music; International Asscn of Jazz Educators. *Current Management:* Europa Jazz Live. *Address:* 6 Belgrove, Tunbridge Wells, Kent, England. *Telephone:* (1892) 516722. *Fax:* (1892) 536080. *E-mail:* jazz@davidjacobs.f9.co.uk. *Website:* www.tinamay.com.

MAYALL, John; b. 29 Nov. 1933, Macclesfield, Cheshire, England. Blues Vocalist; Songwriter; Musician (harmonica). *Education:* Manchester Art College. *Career:* Founder, The Blues Syndicate, 1962; John Mayall's Bluesbreakers, (members have included John McVie, Eric Clapton, Peter Green, Jack Bruce, Aynsley Dunbar, Mick Taylor, Mick Fleetwood), 1963–; Major concerts include: Uxbridge Festival, 1965; National Blues Festival, Windsor, 1967; Palm Springs Pop Festival, 1969; Newport Jazz Festival, 1969; Woburn Festival, 1969; Bath Festival, 1969; Regular tours, UK, USA, Australia, Europe; Launched own Crusade record label, 1969. *Recordings:* John Mayall Plays John Mayall, 1965; Blues Breakers, 1966; A Hard Road, 1967; Crusade, 1967; Diary of a Band, Vols 1 and 2, 1968; Bare Wires, 1968; Looking Back, 1969; Blues From Laurel Canyon, 1969; The Turning Point, 1969; Empty Rooms, 1970; USA Union, 1970; John Mayall – Live In Europe, 1971; Back To The Roots, 1971; Thru The Years, 1971; Memories, 1971; Jazz Blues Fusion, 1972; Moving On, 1972; Down The Line, 1973; Ten Years Are Gone, 1973; The Latest Edition, 1974; New Year New Band New Company, 1975; Time Expired Notice To Appear, 1975; John Mayall, 1976; A Banquet of Blues, 1976; Lots of People, 1977; Blues Roots, 1978; Bottom Line, 1979; No More Interviews, 1979; Road Show Blues, 1980; Behind The Iron Curtain, 1984; The Power of The Blues, 1987; Chicago Line, 1988; A Sense of Place, 1990; Wake Up Call, 1993; Cross Country Blues, 1994; Return of the Bluebreakers, 1994; Spinning Coin, 1995; Blues for the Lost Days, 1997; Padlock on the Blues, 1999; Rock the Blues Tonight, 1999; Live At the Marquee, 2000; Along For The Ride, 2001; Stories, 2002. *Honours:* Gold disc, The Turning Point, 1969.

MAYDAY. See: MAY, Derrick.

MAYOR, Simon; b. Sheffield, England. Musician (mandolin, mandola, mandocello, guitar, violin), Composer, Lyricist, Humourist. *Education:* Degree in Russian, Reading University. *Career:* Regular international concert touring includes: Vancouver Festival, Rudolstadt International Festival (Germany), Varazze International Mandolin Festival (Italy), Guest of Classical Mandolin Society of America Annual Conference, London's South Bank Festival, Cheltenham Literature Festival; Worked as broadcaster, BBC Radio 2, 4 and 5; Presented BBC Schools Radio music education programmes for six years; Written and performed many songs for children's programmes for BBC TV. *Recordings:* The Mandolin Album, 1990 (BBC Radio 2's Album of The Week); The Second Mandolin Album, 1991; Winter With Mandolins, 1992 (BBC World Service Album of The Week); The English Mandolin, 1995; Mandoliquents (The Simon Mayor Quintet), 1997; New Celtic Mandolin, 1998; Duos, with Hilary James; Albums feature approximately 50% original compositions; Also five albums of original songs for children in the Musical Mystery Tour series. *Publications:* The New Mandolin (original compositions in music and tablature), 1993; The Mandolin Tutor (Book/CD for beginners), 1995; New Celtic Mandolin (Celtic tunes with detailed teaching notes), 1998; Musical Mystery Tour (children's song book), 1992. *Membership:* Musicians' Union; Equity; PRS; MCPS. *Address:* c/o Acoustics Records, PO Box 350, Reading, Berks RG6 7DQ, England. *E-mail:* mail@mandolin.co.uk.

MAYS, L. Lowry; b. Texas, USA. Media Exec. *Career:* Founder, with Red McCombs, Chair. and CEO, San Antonio Broadcasting Co, 1972, acquired KEEZ-FM; Renamed Clear Channel Communications, 1975 (entertainment co, owning numerous radio and television stations, entertainment venues, advertising space world-wide; management and marketing cos); Created Clear Channel Sports, 1989. *Address:* c/o Clear Channel Communications, 200 Basse Rd, San Antonio, TX 78209, USA. *E-mail:* LLowryMays@ clearchannel.com. *Website:* www.clearchannel.com.

MAZETIER, Louis; b. 17 Feb. 1960, Paris, France. Jazz Musician (piano); Composer. m. Sophie Clement, 1 s., 1 d. *Education:* MD, Radiologist, University. *Career:* Member, Paris Washboard; Major festivals in France: Antibes; Marciac; Bayonne; Montauban; Festivals in Europe: Breda; Dresden; Plön; Tours, New Zealand; Australia; USA (including Moodus and Santa Rosa Festivals); Argentina; Uruguay; Japan. *Recordings:* 8 with Paris Washboard;

Duet with pianist Francois Rilhac; Duet with pianist Neville Dickie; Solo record; Duet with pianist Bernd Lhotzky. *Publications:* Many articles, various French Jazz Reviews, mostly about stride piano. *Honours:* Prix Sidney Bechet; Prix Bill Coleman, Academie de Jazz, 1992. *Address:* 3 rue Larrey, 75005 Paris, France.

MAZUR, Marilyn (Marie Douglas); b. 18 Jan. 1955, New York, NY, USA. Composer; Jazz Musician (percussion, drums, piano); Vocalist. 1 s. *Education:* Degree, Teaching Percussion, Royal Danish Music Conservatory, 1974–77. *Career:* Dancer, Creative Dance Theatre, 1971; Formed first band Zirenes, 1973; Played with Six Winds with Alex Riel; Miles Davis, 1985–88; Gil Evans Orchestra, 1986; Wayne Shorter, 1987; Jan Garbarek Orchestra, 1991–; Leader, own projects, Future Song, Pulse Unit, Primi Band; Performed all over the world; Played with Niels Henning Orsted Pedersen; Jasper van't Hof; Andreas Vollenweider; Kenneth Knudsen; Pierre Dorge; numerous others. *Compositions:* Well of Clouds, 1982; 30 magiske omkvæd, 1986; Bydansen (City Dance), 1989; Decemberdanse, 1992; Fjellslottet, 1992. *Recordings:* Albums include: Clouds, 1982; Rhythm-a-ning (with Gil Evans, Laurent Cugny), 1986; Aura (with Miles Davis, Palle Mikkelborg), 1989; Marilyn Mazur's Future Song, 1992; Future Song, 1997; Story of Multiplicity, 1998; Jon Balke with Magnetic North Orchestra, 1994; with Pulse Unit: Circular Chant, 1995; Feature on: New Spirits in Jazz Vol. 3, 1997; with Jan Garbarek, Rites, 1999. *Honours:* Ben Webster Prize, 1983; Jasa Prize, 1989; HK-Artist of the Year, 1994. *Current Management:* Hohensee/Bremme, Germany.

MAZWAI, Thandiswa, (Thandi); Vocalist. *Education:* Degree in International Relations and English. *Career:* Mem., kwaito band, Bongo Maffin, 1997–; World Wild Grooves tour, France, 2000; Performances in UK, Denmark, 2000; worked with: Skunk Anansie, Chaka Khan, Stevie Wonder, Boys II Men, Hugh Masekela. *Recordings:* Albums: Final Entry, 1996; The Concerto, 1998; IV, 1999; Bongolution, 2001. *Honours:* South African Music Award, Best Kwaito Artist, 1999; Kora Award, Best African Group, 2001; Gold disc, for Bongolution. *Address:* c/o Sony Music South Africa, 230 Jan Smuts Ave, Dunkeld West, 2196 Gauteng, South Africa.

MBANDE, Venacio Notico; b. 4 Oct. 1933, Chisiko, nr Zavala, Mozambique. Musician (xylophone, timbila); Composer; Performer; Master Instrument Maker. m. Alzira, 14 c. *Career:* Leading musician in Chopi xylophone and orchestration; Orchestra leader, Witwatersrand, South Africa, 1953–95; Demonstrator and lecturer in Chopi music, University of Pennsylvania, USA, 1973; Royal Conservatory of Music, The Hague, 1991, 1999; Zavala, Mozambique, 1995–; Performance in Royal Albert Hall, London with Dutch percussionists for BBC, 1995. *Compositions:* Numerous Mgodo xylophone orchestral suites. *Recordings:* Tapes held by International Library of African Music, Grahamstown, South Africa; Mozambique, Timbila Ta Venancio, CD, Germany, 1994; Musica Chope de Mozambique, Timbila ta Venancio, CD, Netherlands, 1999. *Honours:* African Arts Music Competition, Mgodo Xylophone Suite, USA, 1969; M'saho Competition, Chopie Xylophone, 1997–99, Mozambique. *Address:* PO Box No. 8, Quissico, Mozambique.

M'BANGO, Charlotte; b. 16 April 1960, Douala, Cameroon. Vocalist; Backing Vocalist. m. Mpacko Marcel, 4 Aug. 1984, 1 d. *Education:* Solfège; Piano. *Career:* Tours: Ivory Coast; Cameroon; Gabon; Burkina Faso; Togo; USA; Spain: Barcelona, Madrid, Valencia; London; France; Radio: Africa, France; Television: France, Belgium. *Recordings:* Nakossa Nostalgie, 1987; Konkai Makossa, 1988; Maloka, 1995; Masoma, 1996; Best of Makossa Vol. 2, 1998; with Paul Simon: Rhythm of the Saints, 1990. *Honours:* Gold Song, Palo Rabanne, 1989; Gold Lion, 1994. *Membership:* ADAMI; SACEM; SPEDIDAM; SFA; ACOP; AMF. *Address:* 10 Allée d'Amblonville, 77176 Savigny Le Temple, France.

MC SOLAAR; b. Dakar, Senegal. Rap Artiste; *Recordings:* Albums: Qui Sème Le Vent Récolte Le Tempo, 1993; Prose Combat, 1994; Paradisiaque, 1997; Le Tour De La Question, 1999; Cinquieme As, 2002. *Address:* c/o Eastwest Records: A&R Abteilung HipHop/Black Music, Postfach 106524, 20044 Hamburg, Germany. *Website:* www.solaarsystem.net.

MCA, (Adam Yauch); b. 15 Aug. 1967, Brooklyn, New York, USA. Rap Artiste; Musician (bass). m. Ione Skye, 1992. *Career:* Founder member, US rap/rock group The Beastie Boys, 1983–; Appearances include: Support to Madonna, Virgin Tour, 1985; Supports to Run DMC, Raisin' Hell Tour, 1986, Co-headliners with Run DMC, Together Forever Tour, 1987; Reading Festival, 1992; Made horror film, Scared Stupid; Film apperances: Krush Groove; Run-DMC film, Tougher Than Leather. *Recordings:* Singles include: She's On It; Fight For Your Right To Party; Albums include: Licensed To Ill (No. 1, USA), 1986; Paul's Boutique, 1989; Check Your Head, 1992; Ill Communication, 1994; Root Down, 1995; The In Sound From Way Out, 1996; Hello Nasty (No. 1, UK and USA), 1998; Sounds Of Science, 1999; Singles include: Fight For Your Right (To Party), 1987; No Sleep Till Brooklyn, 1987; She's On It, 1987; Girls/She's Crafty, 1987; Hey Ladies, 1989; Pass the Mic, 1992; Jimmy James, 1992; Get It Together/Sabotage, 1994; Sure Shot, 1994; Hey Ladies, 1997; Intergalactic, 1998; Body Movin', 1998; Remote Control, 1999; Alive, 1999. *Current Management:* Gold Mountain Entertainment, 3575 Cahuenga Blvd W, Suite 450, Los Angeles, CA 90068, USA.

MEADE, Bazil (Leonard Duncan); b. 4 May 1951, Montserrat. Musician (piano, Hammond organ). m. Andrea Encinas, 3 May 1980, 2 s., 2 d. *Career:* Founder and Principal, London Community Gospel Choir, 1982; Musical Director for numerous concerts including: The London Community Gospel Choir European Tours, 1984–93; Freddie Mercury Tribute Concert, 1991; George Michael British tour, 1991; HRH Queen Elizabeth's 60th Birthday concert, Royal Opera House; Stevie Wonder, Wembley; Luther Vandross, Royal Albert Hall, 1994; Gloria Gaynor, European Tour, 1994; Also Musical Director for: Amen Corner (theatre production), 1990; Royal Variety television shows for 5 years; Hallelujah Anyhow (film); Rock Gospel (television series); Desmonds (television series); Mama I Want To Sing, 1995. *Recordings:* with Paul McCartney: Give My Regards To Broad Street; with The London Community Gospel Choir: Live In Sweden; The London Community Gospel Choir Sings The Gospel Greats; Christmas With The London Community Gospel Choir; Hush and Listen; with Bobby Womack: No Matter How High I Get; Circle of Life (from Walt Disney's The Lion King). *Honours:* Greenbelt Award For Services To Gospel Music, 1986; Commonwealth Institute Award For Services To Gospel Music, 1986; BBC Award, Contribution To Gospel Music, 1987. *Membership:* Musicians' Union; PRS; MCPS. *Current Management:* Choir Connexion. *Address:* 9 Greenwood Dr., London E4 9HL, England.

MEAT LOAF, (Marvin Lee Aday); b. 27 Sept. 1951, Dallas, Texas, USA. Entertainer; Vocalist; Actor. m. Leslie Edmonds, 1975, 2 d. *Education:* University. *Career:* Appeared in films: The Rocky Horror Picture Show, 1975; Americathon, 1979; Scavenger Hunt, 1979; Roadie, 1980; Dead Ringer, 1981; The Squeeze, 1986; Out of Bounds, 1986; Motorama, 1990; Gun and Betty Lou's Handbag, 1991; Wayne's World, 1992; Leap of Faith, 1992; The Mighty, 1998; Black Dog, 1998; Fight Club, 1999; Crazy In Alabama, 1999; Outside Ozona, 1999; Plays: Hair; Rocky Horror; National Lampoon Show; More Than You Deserve; Rockabye Hamlet; Billy The Kid and Jean Harlow; As You Like It; Othello. *Recordings:* Hit singles include: You Took The Words Right Out Of My Mouth, 1978; Two Out Of Three Ain't Bad, 1978; Bat Out Of Hell, 1979; Dead Ringer For Love, 1981; Midnight At The Lost And Found, 1983; Modern Girl, 1984; Rock'n'Roll Mercenaries (with John Parr), 1986; I'd Do Anything For Love (But I Won't Do That) (Number 1, UK and USA), 1993; Rock And Roll Dreams Come Through, 1994; I'd Lie For You (And That's The Truth), 1995; Not A Dry Eye In The House, 1996; Is Nothing Sacred, featuring Patti Russo, 1999; Albums include: Featuring Stoney and Meat Loaf, 1970; Free For All (with Ted Nugent), 1976; Bat Out of Hell, 1977; Dead Ringer (No. 1, UK), 1981; Midnight At The Lost and Found, 1983; Bad Attitude, 1984; Hits Out of Hell, 1985; Blind Before I Stop, 1986; Meat Loaf Live, 1987; Bat Out Hell II: Back Into Hell (No. 1, UK and USA), 1993; Welcome To The Neighbourhood, 1995; Contributor, Pavarotti and Friends (Bosnia relief charity record), 1996; The Very Best Of, 1998. *Honours:* BRIT Award, 1993; Grammy, 1993. *Current Management:* The Left Bank Organization. *Address:* 9255 Sunset Blvd, 2nd Floor, W Hollywood, CA 90069, USA.

MEDLEY, Bill; b. 19 Sept. 1940, Santa Ana, California, USA. Vocalist. *Career:* Member, The Paramours; Founder member, The Righteous Brothers (with Bobby Hatfield), 1962–67, 1974–80; Concerts include: Support to the Beatles, US tour, 1964; Television includes: Shindig!; Scene At 6.30; Ready Steady Go; Discs A Go-Go; Solo career, 1967–73, 1981–; Opened Medleys Club, Los Angeles, 1982; Appearances, Cheers, NBC, 1990; Duet with Jennifer Warnes, for film Dirty Dancing, 1987; Returned to performing as Righteous Brothers. *Recordings:* Singles include: You've Lost That Lovin' Feelin', later used in film Top Gun (No. 1, UK and USA), 1964; Just Once In My Life, 1965; You Can Have Her, 1965; Justine, 1965; Unchained Melody (later used in film Ghost), 1965 (No. 1, UK, 1990); Ebb Tide, 1966; (You're My) Soul and Inspiration, 1966; Solo: (I've Had) The Time of My Life, duet with Jennifer Warnes, for film Dirty Dancing (No. 1, USA), 1987; He Ain't Heavy He's My Brother, 1988; Albums: with the Righteous Brothers: You've Lost That Lovin' Feelin', 1965; Right Now!, 1965; Some Blue-Eyed Soul, 1965; This Is New!, 1965; Just Once In My Life, 1965; Back To Back, 1966; Go Ahead and Cry, 1966; Soul and Inspiration, 1966; The Best of The Righteous Brothers, 1966; Sayin' Something, 1967; Greatest Hits, 1967; Greatest Hits Vol. 2, 1969; Give It To The People, 1974; The Righteous Brothers Greatest Hits, 1990; The Best Of..., 1990; The Very Best Of..., 1990; Anthology (1962–74), 1990; Solo: 100%, 1968; A Song For You, 1971; Sweet Thunder, 1981; Right Here and Now, 1982; I Still Do, 1984; Someone Is Standing Outside, 1985; Still Hung Up On You, 1985; Another Beginning, 1987; The Hard Side, 1987; Blue Eyed Singer, 1991; Smile, 1991; Christmas Memories, 1996; Almost Home, 1997; Contributor, film soundtracks: Cobra; Rambo III. *Honours:* Grammy Award, Best Pop Performance, 1987. *Current Management:* DBC Management, 131 Spinnaker Court, Marina del Rey, CA 90292, USA.

MEDLEY, Sue; b. 19 Aug. 1962, Nanaimo, British Columbia, Canada. Recording Artiste; Vocalist; Songwriter. *Career:* Toured Canada with: Bob Dylan; Dwight Yoakam; Tom Cochrane (as opening act); Television, radio appearances in Canada, including; half hour special, Adrienne Clarkson presents, CBC, spotlights on Much Music. *Recordings:* Albums: Sue Medley, 1990; Inside Out, 1992; Singles: Dangerous Times; Maybe The Next Time; That's Life; Love Thing; When The Stars Fall; Forget You; Jane's House; Inside Out. *Honours:* 5 West Coast Music Awards; 2 Juno Awards; 2

Songwriter Awards. *Membership:* AFofM; CARAS; SOCAN. *Current Management:* Marian Donelly Artist Management.

MEHLDAU, Brad; b. 23 Aug. 1970, Jacksonville, FL, USA. Jazz Musician (piano); Composer. *Education:* Berklee College of Music; New School, New York. *Career:* Solo artiste; Worked with: Peter Bernstein, Brian Blade, Jimmy Cobb, Larry Grenadier, Christopher Hollyday, Christian McBride, Joshua Redman, Jorge Rossy, Perico Sambeat, David Sanchez. *Recordings:* Albums: Introducing Brad Mehldau, 1995; Art Of The Trio, Vol. I, 1996; Art Of The Trio, Vol. II: Live At The Village Vanguard, 1998; Art Of The Trio, Vol. III: Songs, 1998; Elegiac Cycle, 1999; Art Of The Trio, Vol. IV: Back At The Vanguard, 1999; Places, 2000; Art Of The Trio, Vol. V: Progression; Largo, 2002. *Address:* c/o Warner Bros Jazz, 3300 Warner Blvd, Burbank, CA 91505, USA.

MEIJS, Norbert; b. 11 July 1952. Vocalist; Songwriter. m. Marianne, 2 s., 1 d. *Career:* Singer, Sophisticated Movement, 1968–71; Member of Plakband, 1973–74; Member of Teenager, 1977–78; Several Apperances as Singer, Songwriter, pseudonym Blackbyrd, 1993–99. *Compositions:* Louise; Calling Richard. *Recordings:* Baby, Hold on; Takin' My Time; Louise, recorded by the Ryes, 1999. *Membership:* BUMA; STEMRA; PALM. *Current Management:* Longboat Management. *Address:* Keerberg 71, 6267 DB, Cadier En Keer, Netherlands.

MEIKLE, Orde; b. 1964, Glasgow, Scotland. Prod; Remixer; DJ. *Career:* Started career as a DJ in Glasgow; Met Stuart McMillan and started putting on their own club nights, Atlantis and Slam; Formed the Slam production duo and Soma Records label; World-wide DJ; Collaborations: UNKLE; Remixed: Sunscreem; Mansun; Dave Angel; Phuture; Kym Sims. *Recordings:* Albums: Headstates, 1996; Alien Radio, Past Lessons – Future Theories (DJ-mixed compilation), 2001; Singles: Eterna, 1991; Positive Education, 1993; Snapshots, 1995; Dark Forces, 1996; Narco Tourists, Lifetimes, Alien Radio 2001. *Address:* c/o Soma Records, 342 Argyle St, Glasgow, G2 8LY, Scotland.

MEIKLEJOHN, Duncan Warner; b. 16 Dec. 1952, Edmonton, Alberta, Canada. Vocalist; Songwriter; Arranger; Prod; Musician (keyboards, guitars). 3 s. *Education:* Royal Conservatory, piano; Private vocal coach. *Career:* Concert appearances with: Michael Bolton; Sheena Easton; Dudley Moore; The Nylons; David Foster; 1994 Commonwealth Games Ceremonies. *Recordings:* Song of Songs; The Best Part (of You and Me); The Second Time Around; Paradise; Let The Spirit Live On. *Honours:* Hon. Mentions, Canadian Songwriting Contest. *Membership:* ACTRA; SOCAN. *Current Management:* Brass Ring Productions, PO Box 1266 Stn A, Kelowna, BC V1Y 7V8, Canada. *Telephone:* (250) 763-5502.

MEINE, Klaus; b. 25 May 1948, Germany. Vocalist. *Career:* Lead vocalist, German heavy rock group The Scorpions, 1971–; Regular world-wide tours; Support tours to Ted Nugent; Bon Jovi; Festivals and major concerts include: World Series of Rock, Cleveland, Ohio, 1979; US Festival, 1973; Reading Rock Festival, 1973; Rock in Rio, Brazil, 1985; Monsters of Rock, Germany, 1986; First Western rock band to play former USSR, Leningrad, 1989; Moscow Music Peace Festival, 1989; The Wall, with Roger Waters, Berlin, 1990; MTV New Year's Eve World Party, Berlin, 1990; Invited to meet President Gorbachev, at the Kremlin, 1991. *Recordings:* Albums: Lonesome Crow, 1972; Fly To The Rainbow, 1974; In Trance, 1975; Virgin Killer, 1976; Taken By Force, 1978; Tokyo Tapes, 1978; Lovedrive, 1979; Animal Magnetism, 1980; Blackout, 1982; Love At First Sting, 1984; World Wide Live, 1985; Savage Amusement, 1988; Best of Rockers and Ballads, 1989; Hurricane Rock, 1990; Crazy World, 1990; Face The Heat, 1993; Live Bites, 1995; Pure Instinct, 1996; Deadly Sting: The Mercury Years, 1997; Eye II Eye, 1999; Moment Of Glory, 2000; Acoustica, 2001; Hit singles include: There's No One Like You, 1982; Can't Live Without You, 1982; Rock You Like A Hurricane, 1984; Still Loving You, 1985; Rhythm of Love, 1988; Wind of Change (No. 2, UK), 1991; Face the Heat, 1993; Pure Instinct, 1996; Eye II Eye, 1999. *Honours:* ASCAP Award, Wind of Change, 1993. *Current Management:* Hard To Handle Management, 1133 Broadway, Suite 1301, New York, NY 10010, USA.

MEISNER, Randy; b. 8 May 1946, Scottsbluff, Nevada, USA. Musician (bass); Vocalist. *Career:* Member, The Dynamics, early 1960s; Member, Soul Survivors (later the Poor); Member, Poco, 1968–69; 1989; The Eagles, 1971–77; Solo artiste, 1977–; Member, Black Tie, 1990–. *Recordings:* Albums: with The Eagles: The Eagles, 1972; Desperado, 1973; On The Border, 1974; One of These Nights (No. 1, USA), 1975; Their Greatest Hits 1971–75 (No. 1, USA), 1976; Hotel California (No. 1, USA), 1976; Solo albums: One More Song, 1980; Randy Meisner, 1982; Meisner, Swan & Rich, 2001; Singles include: Take It Easy, 1972; Witchy Woman, 1972; Peaceful Easy Feeling, 1973; The Best of My Love (No. 1, USA), 1975; One of These Nights (No. 1, USA), 1975; Lyin' Eyes, 1975; Take It To The Limit, 1976; New Kid In Town (No. 1, USA), 1977; Hotel California (No. 1, USA), 1977; Life In The Fast Lane, 1977. *Honours:* Grammy Award, Best Pop Vocal Performance, Lyin' Eyes, 1976; American Music Awards, Favorite Band, 1977; Album of Year, Their Greatest Hits, National Asscn of Record Merchandisers, 1977. *Address:* c/o Geoffrey Blumenauer Artists, 11846 Balboa Blvd, Suite 204, Granada Hills, CA 91344, USA.

MEISSNER, Stan; b. 28 Aug. 1956, Toronto, Ontario, Canada. Songwriter. *Career:* Written songs recorded by: Céline Dion; Eddie Money; Rita Coolidge; B J Thomas; Ben Orr (from the Cars); Lee Aaron; Contributing composer for several television shows and films. *Recordings:* Albums: Dangerous Games, 1984; Windows To Light, 1986; Undertow, 1992; Metropolis, 1999. *Honours:* Gemini Award. *Current Management:* Meissner Music Productions Inc. *Address:* 162 Wychwood Ave, Toronto, ON M6C 2T3, Canada.

MELADZE, Valery; b. 1965, Batumi, Georgia. Vocalist; Songwriter. *Education:* Nikolayev Shipbuilding Institute, Ukraine, 1987. *Career:* Singer with group Dialogue, 1991–93; Formed group Mistikana, 1992; Solo career, singing songs written with brother, Konstantin, 1993–; Appeared at Rock Savania festival, 1993. *Recordings:* Albums: with Dialogue: In The Middle Of The World, 1991; Cry Of The Hawk, 1993; Solo: Saera, 1994; The Last Romantic, 1996; Live at Olympic Moscow, 1997. Singles: Don't Touch My Soul, You Violin; Saera; The Height Of Summer; Christmas Eve; You Are So Beautiful, 1996; Girls Of The Establishment, 1996. *Current Management:* FBI Music, Russia. *Website:* www.valerymeladze.ru.

MELANDER, Anders; b. 7 Jan. 1948, Stockholm, Sweden. Songwriter; Composer; Musician; Prod. *Education:* Philosophy and Foreign Languages, University of Lund, Sweden. *Career:* Band Leader, Bread, 1966–68; Musical Leader, Nationalteatern, 1970–75; Score Composer, SVT, 1976–; Songwriter, various artists; Member of CUE, 1997–. *Compositions:* Score for SVT WW2 drama serial recorded by Gothenburg Symphony Orchestra, 1994; News Themes for national network TV4, 1990–; Hallå Västindien, Vikingarna, 1981; Speedy Gonzales, Magnus Uggla, 1987. *Recordings:* Bread: singles and compilations, including Rough Lover; Nationalteatern: Early albums include: Livet är en fest, 1974; Jack the Ripper; Speedy Gonzales; Bängen Trålar; Solo releases: Good Luck, 1981; Ebba and Didrik, 1990; CUE: number 1 hit single: Burnin', 3 Platinum discs, 1997–98; Crazy, 2000; Album: Cue 2000; Singles: Sway, 2000, Hello, 2000. *Honours:* SKAP Honours, 1984; Grammis Award, 1997. *Membership:* Swedish Composers and Authors of Popular Music; Swedish Media Composers. *Address:* Sprängkullsgatan 10 B, 411 23 Göteborg, Sweden.

MELANIE B. See: **BROWN, Melanie Janice.**

MELANIE C. See: **CHISHOLM, Melanie Jayne.**

MELDER, Heinz; b. 16 Feb. 1951, Cologne, Germany. Sound Engineer; Music Prod. m. Anna Maria Melder, 20 Nov. 1976, 1 s. *Education:* Self-trained Sound Engineer, evening school education. *Career:* Manager, TMK, Musik Production, 1977–. *Recordings:* Numerous production in field of German popular music with leading artists. *Publications:* Eimol Prinz Zo Siu en Kolie Au Rhing. *Honours:* King Eagle Award, Airplay International Record Label of the Year, 1995–96. *Membership:* VDT; IFPI; GVL; GEMA. *Address:* TMK, Musik Production, Sebastian Str, 141 50735, Köln, Germany.

MELLE MEL, (Melvin Glover); Rap Artiste. *Career:* Founder member, Grandmaster Flash and The 3 MCs, 1977; Becomes Grandmaster Flash and The Furious Five, 1977–83; Founder, Grandmaster Flash, Melle Mel and The Furious Five, 1987. *Recordings:* Albums: The Message, 1982; Greatest Messages, 1984; Greatest Hits, 1992; Singles include: Freedom, 1980; The Adventures of Grandmaster Flash On The Wheels of Steel, 1981; The Message, 1982; White Lines (Don't Do It), 1983; Beat Street Breakdown Part 1, 1984; We Don't Work For Free, 1984; Sugarhill Work Party, 1984; Step Off, 1984; Pump Me Up, 1985; Vice, featured on soundtrack, Miami Vice, NBC, 1985; Featured on: I Feel For You, Chaka Khan (No. 1, UK), 1984; Also collaborated with: Duran Duran; Quincy Jones; The Last Poets; Bill Laswell.

MELLENCAMP, John; b. 7 Oct. 1951, Seymour, Indiana, USA. Vocalist; Musician (guitar); Songwriter. m. (1) Priscilla, 1 d.; (2) Victoria, 2 c.; (3) Elaine Irwin, 1 s. *Education:* Vincennes University. *Career:* Member, Crepe Soul, 1965; Snakepit Banana Barn, 1966; Glitter-rock group Trash, 1971; Solo artiste, 1975–; Adopted name Johnny Cougar, 1976; Formed The Zone, 1977; Changed name to John Cougar Mellencamp, 1983; Major concerts include: US Festival, 1983; Organizer, inaugural Farm Aid Festival, 1985; Also appeared in Farm Aid II – V, 1986–92; Concert For The Heartland, 1993; Numerous North American tours; Film appearances: Souvenirs, 1990; Falling From Grace (own project), 1992; Exhibition of paintings, 1991. *Recordings:* Albums: Chestnut Street Incident, 1976; The Kid Inside, 1977; A Biography, 1978; John Cougar, 1979; Nothin' Matters and What If It Did, 1980; American Fool, 1982; Uh-Huh, 1983; Scarecrow, 1985; The Lonesome Jubilee, 1987; Big Daddy, 1989; Souvenirs (film soundtrack), 1990; Whenever We Wanted, 1991; Human Wheels, 1993; Dance Naked, 1994; Mr Happy Go Lucky, 1996; John Mellencamp, 1998; Dance Naked Bonus CD, 1999; Rough Harvest, 1999; Cuttin' Heads, 2001; Hit singles: Ain't Even Done With The Night, 1981; Jack and Diane (No. 1, USA), 1982; Hurts So Good, 1982; Hand To Hold On To, 1983; Crumblin'Down, 1983; Pink Houses, 1984; Authority Song, 1984; Lonely Ol' Night, 1985; Small Town, 1985; R O C K In The USA, 1986; Paper In Fire, 1987; Cherry Bomb, 1988; Check It Out, 1988; Pop Singer, 1989; Get A Leg Up, 1991; Again Tonight, 1992; Now More Than Ever, 1992; Wild Night, 1994; Key West Intermezzo, 1996; Just Another Day, 1997; Your Life Is Now, 1998;

I'm Not Running Anymore, 1999; Contributor, A Very Special Christmas (charity album), 1987; Folkways – A Vision Shared (Woodie Guthrie tribute), 1988; Film soundtrack, Honeymoon In Vegas, 1992; As producer: Tracks for: Mitch Ryder; The Blasters; James McMurty. *Honours:* American Music Award, Favourite Male Artist (co-winner), 1983; Nordoff-Robbins Silver Clef, 1991; First US artist to have 2 Top 10 singles and No. 1 album simultaneously, 1982. *Current Management:* The Left Bank Organisation, 6255 Sunset Blvd, Suite 1111, Hollywood, CA 90028, USA.

MELLOR, David; b. 23 April 1955, Middlesborough, England. *Career:* Member of Evil Twin, With Karl Blake, 1987–; Recording and Performing As The Days of The Moon, 1993–. *Recordings:* The Black Spot; The Words and Music of David Mellor; The Prince. *Address:* PO Box 671, Beaconsfield, Bucks, HP9 1AX, England.

MELLY, (Alan) George (Heywood); b. 17 Aug. 1926, Liverpool, England. Jazz Vocalist; Critic. m. (1) Victoria Vaughn, 1955, divorced 1962, (2) Diana, 1963, 1 s., 1 step-d. *Education:* PhD, University of Liverpool. *Career:* Assistant, London Gallery, 1948–50; Singer, Mick Mulligan's Jazz Band, 1949–61; Cartoon strip writer with Trog, 1956–71; As critic for The Observer: Pop Music, 1965–67; Television, 1967–71; Films, 1971–73; Film scriptwriter, Smashing Time, 1968; Take A Girl Like You, 1970; Singer, John Chilton's Feetwarmers, 1974–2002; Concerts include: Royal Festival Hall; Royal Albert Hall; Edinburgh Festival; Television includes: Subject, This Is Your Life. *Recordings:* Albums include: George Melly and John Chilton's Feetwarmers: Best of Live; Anything Goes; Frankie and Johnny; Puttin' On The Ritz; The Pye Jazz Anthology, 2002. *Publications:* I Flook, 1962; Owning Up, 1965; Revolt Into Style, 1970; Flook By Trog, 1970; Rum Bum and Concertina, 1977; The Media Mob (with Barry Fantoni), 1980; Tribe of One, 1981; Great Lovers, (with Walter Dorin), 1981; Mellymobile, 1982; Scouse Mouse, 1984; It's All Writ Out For You, 1986; Paris and The Surrealists (with Michael Woods), 1991; Don't Tell Sybil, 1997; Hooked, 2000. *Honours:* Critic of the Year, IPC National Press Awards, 1970; Fellow, John Moores University; Dr, Middlesex and Glamorgan University; President, British Humanist Society, 1972–74; BT British Jazz Awards, 1998; Award for Lifetime Acheivement For Jazz. *Current Management:* Jack Higgins, Pear Tree Cottage, Weymarks, Bradwell on Sea, Essex CM0 7JB, England.

MELVOIN, Wendy Ann; b. 26 Jan. 1964, Los Angeles, California, USA. Musician (Guitar); Prod; Composer. *Career:* Joined Prince's Band as Guitar Player, 1982; Toured and recorded extensively; Appearance in film Purple Rain; Part of recording duo Wendy and Lisa with Lisa Coleman; Numerous TV appearances in Europe and the USA. *Compositions:* Musical scores for films including Dangerous Minds, Soul Food, Hav Plenty. *Recordings:* Albums: Wendy and Lisa, 1987; Fuit at the Bottom, 1988; Eroica, 1990; Girl Bros, 1998; Singles: Waterfall, 1987; Sideshow, 1988; Satisfaction, 1989; Appearances on Prince albums: 1999, 1982; Purple Rain (No. 1, USA), 1984; Around The World in a Day (No. 1, USA), 1985; Parade, 1986; Sign O' The Times, 1987; Recorded with artists including Seal, Joni Mitchell, kd lang, Sheryl Crow, Neil Finn. *Current Management:* Gold Mountain Entertainment. *Address:* c/o Renata Kanclerz, 2575 Cahuenga Blvd W, Suite 450, Los Angeles, CA 90068, USA.

MENEZES BASTOS, Rafael José de; b. 26 Dec. 1945, Salvador, Bahia, Brazil. Anthropologist; Ethnomusicologist; Musician (Guitar). m. (2) Silvia de O Beraldo, 17 Feb. 1984, 5 s., 5 d. *Education:* AB, Music, Federal University of Bahia, School of Music, 1964; Department of Music, University of Brasilia, 1965–68; MA, Social Anthropology, University of Brasilia, 1976; PhD, Social Anthropology, University of São Paulo, 1990; Postdoctoral Studies, Massachusetts Institute of Technology, 1992–94; Smithsonian Institution, 1994. *Career:* Anthropologist, 1975–80/ Member of the Advisory Board and it's first Vice-President, National Indian Foundation, 1999; Assistant Professor, Anthropology and Ethnomusicology, 1984–90; Associate Professor, 1990–; Member, Editorial Board, Federal University of Santa Catarina Press, 1991–92; Chairman, Graduate Programme, Social Anthropology, 1994–96. *Publications include:* A Musicológica Kamayura, 1978 and 1999 (2nd edition); Dioniso em Santa Catarina, editor, author of introduction and one article, 1993; Dissertations; Numerous articles in learned journals. *Membership:* Scientific Board, Brazilian Anthropological Asscn, 1990–92, Board of Trustees, 1996–98; International Council for Traditional Music, Liason Officer in Brazil, 1993–, Executive Board, 1997–99; Advisory Board, International Encyclopaedia of the Popular Musics of the World, 1993–; Advisory Board, The World of Music, 1997–. *Address:* Departamento de Antropologia, Universidade Federal de Santa Catarina, 88.040–900 Florinópolis, SC, Brazil.

MENSCH, Peter; b. 1948. Management Exec. *Career:* Joint founder and head, with Cliff Burnstein, Q-Prime Management; Has managed artistes and groups such as: AC/DC, Tal Bachman, Crazy Town, Def Leppard, Dokken, Fountains of Wayne, Garbage, Nina Gordon, Hole, Bruce Hornsby, Ivy, Madonna, Metallica, Queensyrche, Red Hot Chilli Peppers, Rush, Shania Twain, Smashing Pumpkins, Tesla, Vercua Salt, Warrior Soul; Q-Prime Management acquired part-ownership, with Zomba Music Publishing, of

Volcano Records, 1998. *Address:* Q-Prime Management, 3rd Floor, 9000 Sunset Blvd, Los Angeles, CA, USA.

MERCÉ, José, (Jose Soto Soto); b. 1955, Spain. Vocalist. *Career:* Well known singer, respected by flamenco aficionados; Appeal widened with release of Aire album, which remained within flamenco tradition but updated lyrical content to reach a contemporary audience. *Recordings:* Bandera de Andalucía, 1977; Carmen, 1983; Verde Junco, 1985; Caminos Reales Del Cante, 1987; Desnudando El Alma, 1994; Del Amanecer, 1998; Aire, 2000.

MERCEY, Larry Oliver Anthony; b. 12 Dec. 1939, Hanover, Ontario, Canada. Recording Artist. m. June, 19 May 1964, 1 s., 1 d. *Career:* Member, The Mercey Brothers, 1957–90; Solo artist, 1990–; Appeared Grand Ole Opry, Nashville, Tennessee. *Recordings:* 17 albums, including many number 1 hits; 2 Solo albums. *Honours:* 7 Juno Awards, Top Country Vocal Group; CF Martin Life Time Achievement Award; Canadian Country Music Awards, Top Vocal Group; Inducted into Canadian Country Hall of Fame, 1990. *Current Management:* Larry Mercey Productions. *Address:* 590 Hunters Pl., Waterloo, ON N2K 3L1, Canada.

MERCHANT, Natalie; b. 26 Oct. 1963. Vocalist; Songwriter; Musician (piano); Record Prod. *Education:* Jamestown Community College. *Career:* Founder, lead vocalist, 10,000 Maniacs, 1981–92; Concerts include: Tour with REM, USA, 1987; Cambridge Folk Festival, 1987, 1988; British tour, 1987; US tours, 1989, 1992; A Performance For The Planet, Maryland, 1990; Time Capsule Tour, 1990; Earth Day 1991 Concert, Massachusetts, 1991; National Earth Day, Hollywood Bowl, 1993; Television includes: Saturday Night Live; The Tonight Show; Late Night With David Letterman; MTV Drops The Ball '93; MTV's 1993 Rock 'n' Roll Inaugural Ball, Washington, 1993; Solo artiste, 1993–. *Recordings:* Albums: with 10,000 Maniacs: Secrets of The I Ching, 1983; The Wishing Chair, 1985; In My Tribe, 1987; Blind Man's Zoo, 1989; Hope Chest, 1989; Our Time In Eden, 1992; Solo albums: Tigerlily, 1995; Ophelia, 1998; Live in Concert, 1999; Motherland, 2001; Singles include: with 10,000 Maniacs: Like The Weather, 1988; What's The Matter Here, 1988; These Are Days, 1992; Candy Everybody Wants, 1993; Few and Far Between, 1993; Because The Night, 1993; Solo single: Carnival, 1995; Jealousy, 1996; Carnival, 1998; Break Your Heart, 1999. *Current Management:* Jon Landau Management, 40 W Elm St, Greenwich, CT 06830, USA.

MERCK, Alex; b. July 1956, Germany. Publisher; Musician (guitar); Composer. *Education:* Economics, Mainz University, Germany; Diploma, Professional Music, Berklec College of Music, Boston; Guitar and Composition Lessons. *Career:* Live tours with Raoul de Souza and as Solo Artist, 1984–86; Many TV appearances in Germany; Studio recordings, 1985–; TV-film scores, 1987–. *Compositions:* Molthe; Adios Buenos Aires. *Recordings:* Doy Days, album, 1986. *Publications:* Keyboards, Midi, Homgrecording, 1990, 1997. *Membership:* GEMA. *Address:* Trujanstr 18, 50678 Koeln, Germany.

MERCURY, Daniela, (Daniela Mercuri de Almeida Póvoas); b. 28 July 1965, Salvador, Bahia, Brazil. Vocalist; Songwriter; Dancer; Choreographer. *Career:* Performs in the energetic axé style; Member of dance group Salta, early 1990s; Backing singer in Gilberto Gil band and member of Companhia Clic; Toured internationally as a solo artist. *Recordings:* Albums: Compania Clic, 1990; Daniela, 1992; O Canto Da Cidade, 1993; Musica De Ruai, 1994; Feijao Com Arroz, Swing Da Cor, 1997; Electrica, 1998; Sol da Liberdade, 2000; Sou de Qualquer Lugar, 2001; features on: Da Licenca Men Senhor, Joao Bosco, 1996; Song Book, João Donato, 1999; Ofrenda, Pedro Guerra, 2001. *Honours:* Prêmio Sharp, Daniela, 1992.

MERRILL, Helen; b. 21 July 1930, New York, NY, USA. Vocalist. *Career:* First performed, 1944; Vocalist with Reggie Childs' orchestra 1946–47; Debut album released on EmArcy, 1954; Recorded regularly with trumpeter Clifford Brown; Short spell with Atco and Metrojazz, 1959; Moved to Italy for 4 years; Returned to USA briefly, recording with pianist Dick Katz on Milestone Records, mid 1960s; Relocated to Japan to concentrated on performing, early 1970s; Returned to USA by mid '70s and resumed recording career, releasing albums on Inner City, Owl and Antilles; Recorded for Verve; Tours widely. *Recordings:* Albums include: Don't Explain, Helen Merrill With Clifford Brown, 1954; Dream of You, 1956; The Nearness of You, Merrill At Midnight, 1957; You've Got A Date With The Blues, 1959; The Feeling Is Mutual, 1965; Shade of Difference, 1969; Sposin', 1971; Chasin' The Bird, 1979; Casa Forte, 1980; Collaboration, 1987; Alone Together, 1989; Clear Out of This World, 1991; Brownie – Homage To Clifford Brown, 1995; Jelena Ana Milcactic (aka Helen Merrill), 2000. *Current Management:* Abby Hoffer. *E-mail:* webmaster@helenmerrill.com. *Website:* www.helenmerrill.com.

MERRILL, Robbie; b. 13 June 1964, Lawrence, Massachusetts, USA. Musician (bass guitar). *Career:* Spent time in various covers bands until joining Godsmack, 1995; Recorded independent debut album for $2500 over 3 days with money borrowed from friend, 1996; Heavy local airplay on Boston-based WAAF radio station led to deal with Republic/Universal, 1998; Debut LP remixed/repackaged with eponymous title; Album banned by US Wal-Mart and K-Mart stores for profane content; US and European gigs in 1999 and 2000 including: Woodstock '99; Ozzfest; MTV's Return of The Rock tour;

Second album recorded in warehouse in Massachusetts, 2000; First major amphitheatre tour, 2001. *Recordings:* Albums: All Wound Up, 1997; Godsmack, 1998; Awake, 2000; Singles: Whatever, Keep Away, 1998; Voodoo, Bad Religion, 1999; Awake, 2000; Greed, Bad Magick, 2001. *Honours:* Whatever single spent record total of 33 weeks on Billboard Top 10; Boston Music Awards, Act of the Year, 2000 and 2001; Billboard Award, Rock Artist of the Year, 2001. *Address:* c/o Paul Geary, PGM, PO Box 9134, Boston, MA 02205, USA. *E-mail:* godsmack@pgmglobal.com. *Website:* www.godsmack.com.

MERRITT, Jymie, (James Raleigh); b. 3 May 1926, Philadelphia, Pennsylvania, USA. Jazz Musician (bass); Composer. m. (1) Dorothy Small, 1949 (divorced 1977), 5 s.; (2) Ave Maria Davis, 9 Sept. 1981. *Career:* Bass player with Art Blakey and The Jazz Messengers; Gregory and Maurice Hines; Max Roach; Dizzy Gillespie; Lee Morgan; Director, composer, Forerunner Jazz Organization and Orchestra, 1962–.

MERTA, Vladimir; b. 20 Jan. 1946, Prague, Czech Republic. Vocalist; Songwriter; Film Dir; Composer; Musician (guitar, flute). m. Lucie Lucka, 2 d. *Education:* CVUT, Faculty of Architecture; FAMU – Film Faculty, Academy of Musical Arts, Prague; LSU – People's School of Arts, Prague. *Career:* Performed at: Roskilde Festival, Denmark, 1988, 1990; Japan, 1991; Vancouver Folk Festival, 1992; Edinburgh Fringe, 1993; More Than Meets The Ear, London; South Bank Centre, London, 1994; Strasbourg, Mittleeuropa; Washington Folk Life Festival; Cheltenham Litterary Festival, 1995. *Compositions include:* Five television specials, Thru The Guitar Hole; One feature script, Opera In The Wineyard; Music for 15 cartoons; 10 pieces of theatre music. *Recordings:* Ballade de Prague, 1969; Vladimir Merta Live, Vols I and II, 1989, 1990; Svatky Trpelivosti, Chtit Chytit Vitr, Biti Rublem, 1993; Jewish choir Mispaha, Vols I and II, 1993, 1995; Sefardic Songs (with Jana Lewitova), 1996. *Publications:* Advantage Server (novel), 1987; Born In The Bohemia (complete lyrics), 1993; Folk Blues Guitar and Harmonica (with 3 hour VHS cassette), 1993; Troubadour In The Age of Global Village, 1994. *Honours:* Porta, 1986. *Membership:* OSA; INTERGRAM; SAI. *Current Management:* Z Agency, Zdenek Vrestal, Graficka 15, Prague 5, Czech Republic.

MESSINA, Jim; b. 5 Dec. 1957, Maywood, California, USA. Musician (guitar, bass); Vocalist; Record Prod; Engineer. *Career:* Recording engineer, member, Buffalo Springfield, 1968; Poco, 1968–70; Loggins and Messina, 1971–76; Built own studio, Gateway Studios, 1983. *Recordings:* Albums: with The Jesters: Jim Messina and The Jesters, 1967; The Dragsters, 1967; with Buffalo Springfield: Last Time Around, 1968; with Loggins and Messina: Kenny Loggins With Jim Messina Sittin' In, 1971; Loggins and Messina, 1973; Full Sail, 1973; On Stage, 1974; Mother Lode, 1974; So Fine, 1975; Native Sons, 1976; Solo albums: Finale, 1978; Oasis, 1979; Messina, 1981; One More Mile, 1981; Watching the River Run, 1996; with Poco: Legacy, 1989; Singles include: Your Mama Don't Dance, 1973; Thinking of You, 1973; My Music, 1973; Also recordings with: Hoyt Axton; Neil Young. *Membership:* ASCAP; AFTRA. *Current Management:* Steve Jensen, Direct Management, 947 N La Cienega, Los Angeles, CA 90069, USA. *Address:* c/o MCO Financial Management, PO Box 176, Los Olivos CA 93441–0176, USA.

MESSINA, Jo Dee Marie; b. 25 Aug. 1970, Framingham, Massachusetts, USA. Country vocalist. *Career:* Sang in country bands around New England area in teens; Performed at local talent shows, Nashville, aged 19; Brought to Curb Records by producer James Stroud; Signed to label, 1994; Debut album produced by Byron Gallimore and Tim McGraw; Debut singles Heads Carolina Tails California and You're Not In Kansas Anymore reached top ten on Billboard country singles chart, 1996; Considered quitting music business when subsequent releases were less successful; Return to chart success and popularlity, 1998–. *Recordings include:* Heads Carolina Tails California, You're Not In Kansas Anymore, 1996; I'm Alright, Bye Bye, Lesson In Leavin', 1998; Burn, 2000; Albums: Jo Dee Messina, 1996; I'm Alright, 1998; Burn, 2000. *Honours:* various including: CMA, Horizon Award, 1999; ACM, Top New Female Vocalist, 1999. *Address:* c/o Country Music Asscn, 1 Music Circle S, Nashville, TN 37203, USA. *Website:* www.jodeemessina.com.

METCALFE, Andy; b. 3 March 1956, Bristol, England. Musician (bass, keyboards); Prod. m. Lilian Metcalfe, 25 July 1992, 1 s. *Education:* Sussex University; A-level, degree in Music. *Career:* 12 albums, many tours with Robyn Hitchcock, 3 of whose albums produced, 1976–94; 3 years, 2 albums with Squeeze, 1985–88; 2 series MD Vic Reeves Big Night Out Channel 4, 1990, 1991. *Recordings:* Produced: The Reivers; Kimberley Rew; Julian Dawson; Edge Park; Robyn Hitchcock, 3 albums, 1976–94; Founder member, Soft Boys, 3 albums, 1976–79. *Honours:* Silver and Platinum discs with Squeeze. *Membership:* Musicians' Union (UK); American Musicians' Union. *Current Management:* Peter Jenner, Sincere Management. *Address:* c/o 421 Harrow Rd, London W10 4RD, England.

METHENY, Pat (Patrick Bruce); b. 12 Aug. 1954, Lee's Summit, Missouri, USA. Musician (guitar). *Education:* University of Miami, Florida. *Career:* Music Instructor at: University of Miami; National Stage Band Camps, Florida; Berklee College Music, Boston; Guitarist with Gary Burton Quintet; Music director and guitarist, Pat Metheny Group, 1978–; Tours throughout

USA; Europe; Canada; Japan; USSR; South America. *Compositions:* Film scores: The Falcon and The Snowman (with David Bowie), 1984; Twice In A Lifetime, 1985. *Recordings:* Albums include: Bright Size Life, 1976; Watercolours, 1977; Pat Metheny Group, 1978; New Chautauqua, 1979; American Garage, 1980; As Falls Wichita, So Falls Wichita Falls, 1981; Offramp, 1982; Travels, 1983; Rejoicing, 1983; Works, 1984; First Circle, 1984; Still Life (Talking), 1987; Works II, 1988; Letter From Home, 1989; Question and Answer (with Roy Haynes and Dave Holland), 1990; Song X (with Ornette Coleman); We Live Here, 1995; Quartet, 1996; Sign of Four, 1996; Imaginary Day, 1997; Passaggio Per Il Paradiso, 1998; A Map of The World, 1999; Last Train Home, 1999; Trio 99>00, 2000; Trio Live, 2001; Speaking Of Now, 2002. *Honours:* 6 Grammy Awards, 1982–2001; Boston Music Awards: Outstanding Jazz Album, Outstanding Guitarist, Outstanding Jazz Fusion Group, 1986; Magazine Awards and Poll Wins: Downbeat; Jazziz; Guitar Player; Also listed in Guitar Player magazine Gallery of Greats, 1982–86. *Address:* c/o Ted Kurland Associates, 173 Brighton Ave, Boston, MA 02134, USA.

METHOD MAN, (Clifford Smith), (Iron Lung, Hott Nikkels, Ticallion Stallion, Johnny Blaze); b. 1 April 1971, Staten Island, New York, USA. Prod; Rap Artiste. *Career:* Founder member: Wu Tang Clan; Released debut solo album, 1994; Appeared in Hype Williams' film Belly and How High (with Redman), 2002; Collaborations: Texas; LL Cool J; Redman; Notorious B.I.G.; Boyz II Men. *Recordings:* Albums: Enter The Wu-Tang Clan, 1993; Tical, 1994; Wu-Tang Forever, 1997; Tical, Judgement Day, The W, 2000; Blackout (with Redman), 2001; Singles: Release Yo' Delf, 1995; I'll Be There For You (with Mary J Blige), 1996; Break Ups To Make Ups, 1999; Da Rockwilder (with Redman), 2000; How High Part 2, 2002; Uzi (Pinky Ring), 2002. *Honours:* Grammy Award, Best Rap Performance By A Duo Or Group, I'll Be There For You (with Mary J Blige), 1996. *Address:* c/o Def Jam, 825, Eighth Ave, New York, USA.

METSERS, Paul; b. 27 Nov. 1945, Netherlands. Vocalist; Songwriter; Musician (guitar, dulcimer, mandocello). *Career:* Professional folk musician touring UK, Netherlands, Italy, Japan, Australia and New Zealand, 1980–89; Frequent radio coverage of songs and guest appearances. *Compositions include:* Farewell To The Gold, sung by various artists including Bob Dylan. *Recordings:* 5 albums. *Publications:* Song book. *Honours:* Voted in Top 10 of Best Male Folk Artists, Folk On 2 Poll; Featured in Guinness Book of Folk Music. *Membership:* Musicians' Union; PRS; MCPS; BAC&S. *Current Management:* P Brocklehurst. *Address:* Mint Cottage, Gilthwaiterigg Lane, Kendal, Cumbria LA9 6NT, England. *Telephone:* (1539) 724707. *E-mail:* paul@mintcottage.freeserve.co.uk. *Website:* www.sagemcrafts.freeserve.co.uk.

METZGER, Jon Frederick; b. 30 July 1959, Washington DC, USA. Musician. m. Linda Brookshire. *Education:* BMus, 1981, MMus, 1994, North Carolina School of the Arts. *Career:* US Information Agency Arts America Program Tours of the Near East, Northern and Sub Sahara, Africa, Central America; Concert Halls, Jazz Clubs, throughout the USA, Europe, Including East Coast Jazz Festival, Lincoln Center, Kennedy Center Constitutional Hall, Smithsonian Institute, Corcoran Gallery of Art, Blues Alley, One Step Down. *Compositions include:* Spiral Passages; On Verchiels Wings; Elephant Walk; The Spinner, I'll Always Be Loving you; Time Again; Credit Line; Mixed Up; Into The Light; Out of the Dark; My Lady. *Recordings:* While We're Young; The Spinner; Into The Light; Out of The Dark; Jon Metzger, Vibes. *Publications:* The Art and Language of Jazz Vibes, 1996. *Honours:* National Endowment for the Arts Grant, 1985; American Society of Composers, Authors, Publishers Popular Award, 1985–98. *Membership:* Artist, Clinician Musser; American Society of Composers, Authors, Publishers; International Asscn of Jazz Educators. *Current Management:* Percussion Events Registry Company, 8534 Coppertowne Lane, Dallas, TX 75243 8035, USA.

MEX, Paul; b. 25 Nov. 1962, St Albans, Hertfordshire, England. Record Prod; Musician. *Career:* Recording career producing and mixing for numerous artistes; As producer, over 500,000 record sales to credit, including Top 5 UK chart success; Business ventures: State Art; Mex One Recordings; DHE Enterprises. *Recordings:* with Poison No. 9: Lay All Your Love On Me; with United States of Europe: Free; with Son of Space: Magic Fly; with Man 2 Man: Malestripper; with Ugly As Sin: Terminal Love. *Honours:* Silver and Gold discs. *Membership:* PRS; MCPS; Musicians' Union. *Current Management:* Mex One Recordings. *Address:* Lower Ground Floor, 3 Eaton Pl., Brighton, East Sussex BN2 1EH, England.

MEYER, Patrice; b. 18 Dec. 1957, Saverne, France. Musician. *Career:* Member, Guitar Player in Hugh Hopper Band, 1989–, in Equip Out with Pip Pyle and Elton Dean; Member, Richard Sinclair's Band. *Recordings:* Patrice Meyer: Racines Croisées, 1983; Dromadaire Vicmaois, 1986; With Hugh Hopper: Mecano Pelorus, 1989; Carousel, 1994; Hooligan Romantics, 1993. *Address:* 12 Vieille Route, 77580 Voulangis, France.

MEYERS, Ken; b. 20 Aug. 1965. Vocalist; Musician (guitar, harmonica). *Education:* University of Lille III, France. *Career:* Support band for John Mayall, Calvin Russel, Bernard Allison, Peter Case; Numerous festivals and

concerts; Television and radio appearances; Solo artiste, 1998–, over 250 concerts in France. *Recordings:* Albums: Live, 1994; Some Unplugged Ones, Vol. I, 2001. *Membership:* SACEM. *Address:* 117 rue Lambrecht, Apt 22, 59500 Douai, France.

M'FOKO, Mansiamina, (Bopol Mansiamina); b. 26 July 1949, Kinshasa, Zaire. Artiste; Composer; Musician (Guitar). *Career:* Member, Orchestre Bamboula, represented Zaire in the festival of African music in Algeria, 1969; Founder, orchestra, Rock A Mambo, 1970; Member, orchestra, Africa Fiesta Sukisa with Dr Nico, 1970; Co-founder, orchestre, Continental, began writing and composing songs, released 3 singles, 1971; Member, orchestra, Afrisa and Tabu Leye, 1973–76; Founder, Ya Toupas with Ray Lema and Manuaku, accompanied the artist M'Pongo Love, 1976; Left for West Africa, met Sam Manguana-Lokassa and Dizzy Mandjeku, joined Africa All Stars, 1978; Began solo carer, released debut album, 1979; Arrived in France, 1982; Founder, 4 Etoiles with Nyboma-Syran Mbenza and Muta Mayi, 1983; Continued with solo career; Tours in most African countries, Europe and the USA. *Recordings:* 3 single releases; Albums: Pitié, je veux la reconciliation; Mariage forcé, Manuela.

MHLONGO, Busi; b. Inanda, KwaZulu Natal, South Africa. Vocalist; Songwriter. *Career:* Started singing in church and later joined choral groups; Won a Gallo Records talent contest, 1963; Appeared in stage and film productions of Alfred Herbert's African Jazz and African Follies; Lived in Portugal, America, Canada and Holland, continually performing; Collaborations: Osibisa; Ifang Bondi; Pops Mohamed; Amampondo; Brice Wassy. *Recordings:* Babemu, 1994; Urban Zulu, 1998. *Honours:* SAMA Awards: Best Female Artist; Best Adult Contemporary Album (African); Best African Pop Album, Urban Zulu, 2000; Urban Zulu also held number 1 position in European World Music Album Chart for two months.

MICENMACHER, Youval; b. 18 Oct. 1949, Paris, France. Musician (percussion); Actor. m. Arnelle de Frondeville, 9 Sept. 1983, 1 s., 1 d. *Career:* Co-founder, jazz group, Arcane V; L'Impossible Trio, 1986; Ichthyornis (duo), 1986; Played with: Michel Godard; Philippe Deschepper; Gérard Marais; Vincent Courtois; Louis Sclavis; Mohamad Hamam; Fawzi Al-Aiedy; Djamchid Chémirani; Pierre Seghers; Michel Touraille; Jean-Marc Padovani; Claude Barthélemy; Founder, company Solos Performces; Performances: Peau à Peau, Festival d'Avignon, 1983; Kaddish, Montpellier, 1984; La Braraque Rouge (jazz opera), 1985; Joueurs de Jazz, Festival de Marne-La-Vallée, 1987; Très Horas de Sol (jazz and flamenco), Festival Banlieues Bleues, 1987; Psyché, Opera by Lully, Festival d'Aix En Provence, 1987; Jubal, solo, 1988; Le Rôdeur, Festival de Marne-La-Vallée, tours of France, Austria, Hungary, 1989; Opéra-Goude, with solistes de l'Ensemble Intercontemporain, 1989; Jumelles, opera, 1990; Actor, percussionist, Black Ballad (with Archie Shepp, Dee Dee Bridgewater), 1991; Sud, 1992; Echange, musical, 1992; Around About Bobby, Festival de Banlieues Bleues, 1993; Mister Cendron (jazz opera), 1993; Ma Nuit Chez Lucy, musical, 1994; Hommage à Germaine Dulac, 1994; Numerous festivals with Quartet Opera de Gérard Marais, 1995; The Voice in Upper Galilee Festival, 1995. *Recordings:* Chants Hébreux D'Orient, 1994; Fera Fera, 1994; Tres Horas De Sol; Le Rodeur; L'Impossible Trio; Nimenio; Est; Lamidbar; Turkish Songs; Global Voices, 1998; Chant Spirit in Sound, 1999; Mediterranee. *Current Management:* Solos Performances. *Address:* 108 rue Gambetta, 94120 Fontenay-Sous-Bois, France.

MICHAEL, George, (Georgios Kyriacos Panayiotou); b. 25 June 1963, Finchley, London, England. Vocalist; Songwriter; Prod. *Career:* Singer, The Executive, 1979; Singer, pop duo Wham! with Andrew Ridgeley, 1982–86; Solo artiste, 1986–; World-wide appearances include: Live Aid, with Elton John, Wembley, 1985; Prince's Trust Rock Gala, 1986; Wham's 'The Final' concert, Wembley, 1986; Nelson Mandela's 70th Birthday Tribute, 1988; Rock In Rio II Festival, Brazil, 1991; A Concert For Life, tribute to Freddie Mercury, Wembley Stadium, 1992; Elizabeth Taylor AIDS Foundation Benefit, Madison Square Garden, New York, 1992; Dispute with Epic record label, and parent company Sony Entertainment, 1992–95; Television special, Aretha Franklin: Duets, 1993. *Recordings:* Albums: with Wham!: Fantastic (No. 1, UK), 1983; Make It Big (No. 1, UK and USA), 1984; The Final, 1986; Solo albums: Faith (No. 1, USA), 1987; Listen Without Prejudice, Vol. 1 (No. 1, UK), 1990; Older (No. 1, UK), 1996; Older and Upper, 1998; Ladies and Gentlemen: The Best of George Michael (No. 1, UK), 1998; Songs from the Last Century (No. 1, UK), 1999; Contributor, Duets, Elton John, 1991; Two Rooms, 1992; Hit singles include: with Wham!: Wham Rap, 1982; Young Guns (Go For It), 1982; Bad Boys, 1983; Club Tropicana, 1983; Wake Me Up Before You Go Go (No. 1, UK and USA), 1984; Freedom (Number 1, UK), 1984; Last Christmas, 1984; Careless Whisper (No. 1, USA and UK), 1984; Everything She Wants (No. 1, USA), 1984; Freedom, 1985; I'm Your Man (No. 1, UK), 1985; The Edge of Heaven (No. 1, UK), 1986; Solo: A Different Corner (No. 1, UK), 1986; I Knew You Were Waiting For Me, duet with Aretha Franklin, (No. 1, UK and USA), 1987; I Want Your Sex, 1987; Faith (No. 1, USA), 1987; Father Figure (No. 1, USA), 1988; One More Try (No. 1, USA), 1988; Monkey (No. 1, USA), 1988; Kissing A Fool, 1988; Praying For Time (No. 1, USA), 1990; Freedom 90, 1990; Waiting For That Day, 1990; Heal The Pain, 1990; Don't Let The Sun Go Down On Me, duet with Elton John (No. 1, UK and

USA), 1991; Too Funky, 1992; Five Live EP (No. 1, UK), 1993; Somebody To Love, with Queen, 1993; Jesus To A Child (No. 1, UK), 1996; Fast Love (No. 1, UK), 1996; Spinning The Wheel, 1996; Older, 1997; Star People, 1997; You Have Been Loved, 1997; Outside, 1998; As, with Mary J. Blige, 1999; If I Told You That, with Whitney Houston, 2000; Freeek!, 2002; Contributor, Do They Know It's Christmas?, Band Aid, 1985; Nikita, Elton John, 1985. *Publications:* Bare, with Tony Parsons (autobiography). *Honours:* BRIT Awards: Best British Group, 1985; Outstanding Contribution to British Music, 1986; Best British Male Artist, 1988; Best British Album, 1991; Best British Male Solo Artist, 1997; Ivor Novello Awards: Songwriter of the Year, 1985, 1989; Most Performed Work (Careless Whisper), 1985; Hit of the Year (Faith), 1989; Grammy, with Aretha Franklin, 1988; Nordoff-Robbins Silver Clef Award, 1989; American Music Awards: Favourite Pop/Rock Male Artist, Soul R&B Male Artist, Favourite Album, 1989; ASCAP Golden Note Award, 1992. *Address:* c/o Connie Filipello Publicity, 17 Gosfield St, London W1P 7HE, England.

MICHAEL, Richard Ewen; b. 24 July 1949, Stonehaven, Scotland. Jazz Educator. m. Morag, 12 Aug. 1972, 1 s., 2 d. *Education:* RSAMD, 1967–71. *Career:* Founder, Fife Youth Jazz Orchestra, 1976; Established Jazz Education in Fife and Scotland; Seminars giver throughout UK, Europe and in New York; One of architects of the Associate Board of Jazz Piano syllabus; Teacher, Beath High School, Cowdenbeath, 1974–. *Compositions:* Homecoming; The Shetland Suite; Young Persons Guide to the Jazz Orchestra; Jazz Suite for Vibes and Piano. *Recordings:* Homecoming; Shetland Suite; Dedication. *Publications:* Creative Jazz Education, 1987; Small Band Jazz for the Classroom, 1996; Various Associated Board jazz pieces; Jazz Beginnings, 1996. *Honours:* Music Teacher of the Year, 1984; Jr Band Winner of BBC Big Band Competition, as Director of Fife Youth Jazz Orchestra, 1994. *Membership:* SSTA; Musicians' Union. *Address:* 6 Dronachy Rd, Kirkcaldy, Fife KY2 5QI, Scotland. *E-mail:* r.e.michael@blueyonder.co.uk.

MICHAELIS, Pasquale, (Pasquale Michaux); b. 22 Oct. 1958, Auvelais. Musician (Saxophones, Clarinet, Keyboards, Hammond Piano, Electric Bass); Composer; Arranger; Vocalist. *Career:* Appearances with Deborah Brow Quartet; Art Farmer; Johnny Griffin Quartet; Kim Parker; Clark Terry Quartet; Toots, Matia Bazar; Drummin Man (P York); Adriano Celentano; D Geers; Bruce Adams/P Michaux Quintet; Hammond Swing Machine; J Halliday/T Jones/T Browne's Funk Machine. *Compositions:* My Angel's Eyes; I'll Remember You, Benny; Organology; Mild and Bourbon for Eddie Please. *Recordings:* Atmosphere; Remember Adolf Sax; Bob Lacemant Trio. *Honours:* Best Young Saxophonist, Belgium, 1979; Best Keyboards, Italy, 1985. *Membership:* SABAM' SIAE (Author and Lyric Society). *Address:* 8 rue E Deroover, 1081 Brussels, Belgium.

MICHAELS, Bret; b. 15 March 1963, Pittsburgh, Pennsylvania, USA. Vocalist. *Career:* Member, US rock groups: the Spectres; Paris; Lead vocalist, US rock group Poison, 1984–; Appearances include: Monsters of Rock Festival, Castle Donington, 1988, 1990; Solo tour, performing acoustic version of Poison material, 1991; Capitol Record's 50th anniversary gala, Hollywood, 1992; Solo participation, Lynyrd Skynyrd and Friends LYVE concert, Atlanta, 1993; The Tonight Show, NBC TV, 1993. *Recordings:* Hit singles with Poison: Talk Dirty To Me, 1987; I Won't Forget You, 1987; Nothin' But A Good Time, 1988; Fallen Angel, 1988; Your Mama Don't Dance, 1988; Every Rose Has its Thorn (Number 1, USA), 1988; Unskinny Bop, 1990; Something To Believe In, 1990; So Tell Me Why, 1991; Stand, 1993; Until You Suffer Some (Fire And Ice), 1993; Albums: with Poison: Look What The Cat Dragged In, 1986; Open Up and Say... Aah, 1988; Flesh and Blood, 1990; Swallow This Live, 1991; Native Tongue, 1993; Greatest Hits 1986–96, 1996; Letter from Death Row, 1998; Crack A Smile...And More, 2000; Power To The People, 2000; Guest on album by comedian Sam Kinison, Leader of The Banned, 1990. *Honours:* NARM Award, Best Selling Heavy Metal Album, Flesh and Blood, 1991. *Current Management:* H K Management, 8900 Wilshire Blvd, Suite 300, Beverly Hills, CA 90211, USA.

MICHEL, Pras, (Samuel Prazakiel Michel); b. 19 Oct. 1972, Haiti. Rap Artiste. *Career:* Member, Tranzlator Crew, with Lauryn Hill and Wyclef Jean; Renamed as The Fugees; Numerous television and live appearances; Began solo career. *Recordings:* With The Fugees: Singles: Boof Baf, 1993; Nappy Heads, EP, 1994; Vocab, EP, 1994; Ready or Not (No. 1, UK), 1996; The Score, 1996; Fu-Gee-La, 1996; Killing Me Softly (No. 1, UK), 1997; Rumble in the Jungle, 1997; Albums: Blunted on Reality, 1993; The Score, 1996; Solo: Singles: Ghetto Superstar (No. 2, UK), 1998; Another One Bites the Dust, 1998; Blue Angels, 1998; What'cha Wanna Do, 1998; Album: Ghetto Superstar, 1998. *Honours:* BRIT Award, Best International Group, 1997.

MICHELUTTI, Andrea; b. 20 Sept. 1962, Udine, Italy. Musician (drums). m. Amerita Moretti, 2 May 1992. *Education:* Graduate, Musicology, Bologna University, Italy; Conservatory of Music (percussion), Chatou, France. *Career:* Worked with: Art Farmer; Steve Grossman; Jerry Bergonzi; Ben Sidran; Harry Sweets Edison; Hal Crook; Jimmy Owens; Roger Guerin; Michelle Hendricks; Alain Jean-Marie; Paul Bollenback; Benny Golson, Jeffery Smith; Ricky Ford; Appearances, jazz festivals, concerts: Italy; France; Switzerland; Austria; Germany; Yugoslavia. *Recordings:* Orsa Minore, L Malaguti Qintet;

Tip of The Hat, La Malaguti Quintet, Sextet; L'Art d'Aimer, with Giovanni Licata Quintet; Les petits loups du Jazz, with Michelle Hendricks and Sylvain Beuf. *Address:* 33 rue Raymond Queneau, 92500 Rueil Malmaison, France.

MICHIELS, Paul; b. 15 June 1948, Belgium. Vocalist; Musician (guitar, keyboards); Composer. *Career:* Soulsister. *Compositions:* Soulsister: Repertoire; Changes, Tom Jones; The Way to Your Heart. *Recordings:* Soulsister: It Takes Two; Heat; Simple Rule; Live Savings; Swinging Like Big Dogs; The Very Best of Soulsister; Paul Michiels: The Inner Child; Forever Young. *Honours:* Golden Eye Award, 1992, 1993; World Music Award, Monaco, 1990. *Membership:* SABAM. *Current Management:* Johan P. Berckmans. *Address:* Mereldreef 3, 3140 Keerbergen, Belgium.

MIDDLETON, Darren; b. 4 Oct. 1972. Musician (guitar, keyboards). 1 d. *Career:* Last member to join Brisbane-based Powderfinger rock group 1992; Steadily built reputation on many Australian tours/festival appearances; International breakthrough with Odyssey Number Five album; Constant world-wide touring throughout 2000–01 ending with New Suburban Fables 2001 Australian shows; Also vocalist/guitarist in fun side-project Drag. *Recordings:* Albums: Parables For Wooden Ears, 1994; Double Allergic, 1996; Internationalist, 1998; Odyssey Number Five, 2000; Singles: Powderfinger Blue (EP), Transfusion (EP), 1993; Tail, Grave Concern, 1994; Save Your Skin, Mr Kneebone (EP), 1995; Pick You Up, D.A.F., Living Type, 1996; Take Me In, 1997; The Day You Come, Don't Wanna Be Left Out/Good-Day Ray, 1998; Already Gone, Passenger, 1999; My Happiness, 2000; Like A Dog, The Metre, 2001. *Honours:* ARIA Awards: Album of the Year; Song of the Year; Best Rock Album; Best Cover Artwork, 1999; six times platinum fourth album on Australian chart for 67 weeks by end of 2001; Only home-grown act ever to play more than 3 consecutive nights at Festival Hall, Australia. *Address:* c/o Republic Records, Australia. *Website:* www.powderfinger.com.

MIDDLETON, Tom, (Cosmos, The Mod Wheel, Tom 'The Jedi' Middleton); b. 1971 Devon, England. Prod; Remixer; DJ. *Education:* Classically trained cellist and pianist. *Career:* Co-founder Evolution/Universal Language Records (with production partner Mark Pritchard); Protégé of Aphex Twin; Presenter of weekly Deep Step Breakbeat Show on London radio station Kiss 100 FM; Member: Global Communication, Link, Jedi Knights, The Bays; Collaborations: Mark Pritchard, Jamie Odell; Remixed: Goldfrapp, Lamb, Depeche Mode, Ian Pooley, Pulp. *Recordings:* Albums: 76–14 (with Global Communication), 1994; New School Science (with Jedi Knights), 1996; Cosmos album, 2002; Singles: Auto Reload EP (with Global Communication), 1992; Maiden Voyage (with Global Communication), 1994; Antacid (with Link), 1995; May The Funk Be With You (with Jedi Knights), 1995; Catch The Break (with Jedi Knights), 1997; The Groove (with Global Communication), 1997; Summer In Space, 1999. *Current Management:* c/o Island Blue Records, 22 St Peter's Sq., London W6 9NW, England.

MIDDLETON, Tracey K; b. 20 Sept. 1966, Solihull, England. Musician (Accordion). *Education:* BA, Christ Church College, Canterbury; Guildhall School of Music with John Leslie; Royal School of Music, Piano, clarinet, theory with Dr Kevin Thompson. *Career:* Formed Amaryllis, accordion duo, with David Garwood, 1986; Provincial theatre work, 1986–95; Cheltenham International Music Festival, with Amaryllis, 1991; Chairman, Club Accord, Midlands UK accordion club, 1992–2002; Regular performer with Amaryllis at accordion festivals such as Autumn International Accordion Festival, 1990–93, 1996–99; Various folk festivals in England with Amaryllis, 1995–2002; Appearances at many folk clubs with Amaryllis, Folk dance weekly and weekend festivals; Numerous concerts at accordion clubs in England with Amaryllis; Workshops and lectures on the accordion and English and American folk dance music. *Recordings:* As Amaryllis: Here, There and Everywhere; Dance and Sing; Mendhams Maytime. *Publications:* Articles on English folk music in Accordion Times. *Membership:* Musicians' Union; English Folk Dance and Song Society; National Accordion Organisation. *Address:* 16 Norgrave Rd, Solihull, West Midlands B92 9JH, England.

MIDLER, Bette; b. 1 Dec. 1945, Paterson, New Jersey, USA. Vocalist; Actress; Comedienne. m. Martin von Haselberg, 1984, 1 d. *Education:* Theatre studies, University of Hawaii. *Career:* As actress: Cast member, Fiddler On The Roof, Broadway, 1966–69; Salvation, New York, 1970; Rock opera Tommy, Seattle Opera Company, 1971; Nightclub concert performer and solo artiste, 1972–; Numerous television appearances include: Ol' Red Hair Is Back, NBC, 1978; Bette Midler's Mondo Beyondo, HBO, 1988; Earth Day Special, ABC, 1990; The Tonight Show, NBC, 1991; Now, NBC, 1993; Seinfeld, NBC, 1995; Bette, CBS, 2000; Films include: Hawaii, 1965; The Rose, 1979; Jinxed!, 1982; Down and Out In Beverly Hills, 1985; Ruthless People, 1986; Outrageous Fortune, 1987; Big Business, 1988; Beaches, 1988; Stella, 1990; Scenes From A Mall, 1990; For The Boys (also co-producer), 1991; Hocus Pocus, 1993; What Women Want, 2000; Own company, All Girls Productions, 1989–. *Recordings:* Albums include: The Divine Miss M, 1972; Bette Midler, 1973; Songs For The New Depression, 1976; Broken Blossom, 1977; Live At Last, 1977; Thighs and Whispers, 1979; The Rose, film soundtrack, 1979; Divine Madness, film soundtrack, 1980; No Frills, 1984; Beaches, film soundtrack, 1989; Some People's Lives, 1991; Best Of, 1993;

Bette of Roses, 1995; Experience the Divine, 1997; Bathhouse Betty, 1998; From a Distance, 1998; Bette, 2000; Singles include: The Rose; Wind Beneath My Wings (No. 1, USA), from Beaches soundtrack, 1989; From A Distance, 1991. *Publications:* A View From A Broad; The Saga of Baby Divine. *Honours:* After Dark Award, Performer of the Year, 1973; Grammy Awards: Best New Artist, 1973; Best Female Pop Vocal Performance, The Rose, 1981; Record of the Year, Song of the Year, Wind Beneath My Wings, 1990; Special Tony Award, 1973; Emmy, Ol' Red Hair Is Back, 1978; Golden Globe Awards: The Rose, 1979; For The Boys, 1991; Contributor, We Are The World, USA For Africa, 1985; Oliver and Company, 1988. *Address:* c/o All Girls Productions, Animation Bldg, Suite 3B-10, 500 S Buena Vista, Burbank, CA 91521, USA.

MIGUEL, Luis; b. 1970, Puerto Rico. Vocalist. *Career:* Won first Grammy aged 15 for Me Gustas Tal Como Eres (duet with Sheena Easton), 1985; Duetted with Frank Sinatra on recording of Come Fly With Me for Sinatra's Duets Vol. 2 album, 1994; One of the biggest selling Latin solo artists of all time; Continues to tour internationally. *Recordings:* Albums include: Soy Como Quiero Ser, 1986; Un Hombre Busca Una Mujer, 1988; 20 Anos, 1990; Romance, 1991; Aries, 1993; Segunda Romance, 1994; El Concierto, 1995; Romance, 1997; Amarte Es Un Placer, 1999. *Honours:* seven Grammy awards; a star in the Hollywood Walk of Fame; 1990; European Excellence Award from Spain; First Latin artist to win Best Selling Artist award at the World Music Awards; MTV Award, Best International Video, 1992; Recognized by the Recording Industry Artists of America, 1994; sales of over 40m. records world-wide. *Website:* www.lacasadeluismiguel.com.

MIKE D, (Michael Diamond); b. 20 Nov. 1965, New York, USA. Rap Artiste; Musician (drums). *Career:* Member, the Young and Useless, 1979; Founder, US rap/rock group the Beastie Boys, 1983–; Appearances include: Support to Madonna, Virgin Tour, 1985; Support to Run-DMC, Raisin' Hell Tour, 1986; Co-headliners with Run-DMC, Together Forever Tour, 1987; Reading Festival, 1992; Film appearances: Krush Groove; Scared Stupid; Tougher Than Leather, with Run-DMC. *Recordings:* Singles: She's On It, 1987; Fight For Your Right To Party, 1987; No Sleep Till Brooklyn, 1987; Girls/She's Crafty, 1987; Hey Ladies, 1989; Pass The Mic, 1992; Sabotage/Get It Together, 1994; Sure Shot, 1994; Intergalactic, 1998; Body Movin', 1998; Alive, 1999; Albums: Licensed To Ill, 1986; Paul's Boutique, 1989; Check Your Head, 1992; Ill Communication, 1994; Root Down, 1995; The In Sound From Way Out, 1996; Hello Nasty (No. 1, UK and USA), 1998; Sound Of Science, 1999; Also appears on: Army of Me, Bjork; Special Brew; Notorious, Pimps Playas and Hustlas; Good Will Hunting; I'm The Bad Guy, Badwayz; So... How's Your Girl?, Handsome Boy. *Current Management:* Gold Mountain Entertainment, 3575 Cahuenga Blvd W, Suite 450, Los Angeles, CA 90068, USA.

MIKKELBORG, Palle; b. 6 March 1941, Copenhagen, Denmark. Musician (Trumpet); Composer; Conductor. m. Helen M Davies, 19 Aug. 1989. *Career:* Leader, Danish Radiojazz Group and Big Band, 1964–76; Riel/Mikkelborg Quintet, 1965–70; V8, 1970–75; Entrance, 1975–88; Heart to Heart Trio, 1985–88; Palle Mikkelborg Trio, 1989–; World-wide festival, radio and TV appearances as soloist and composer/conductor. *Compositions:* Maya's Veil, 1972; Te Faru, 1979; Pictures, 1983; So Many Come, So Many Go, 1983; Aura, dedicated to Miles Davis, 1984–85; Everything Has a Purpose, 1988; Soundscape, 1995; The Noone of Night, 1997; A Moon of Light, 1998. *Recordings:* The Mysterious Corona, 1967; Tempus Incertum Remanet, 1970; Heart To Heart; Hommage; Aura; Anything But Grey; The Gerden Is A Woman; Tread Lightly; Noone Of Night; The Voice Of Silence. *Honours:* First Prize, Montreaux, 1968; Jazz Musician of the Year, 1968; Lange-Müller Prize, 1976; 2 Grammy Awards, USA, 1990; Grammy Award, Denmark, 1993; Knight of the Order of Dannebrog, 1996; Wilhelm Hansen Composers Prize, 1997; Carl Nielsen and Anne Marie Carl Nielsen Prize of Honour, 1999; Nordic Council Music Prize, 2001. *Address:* Ellegaardsvaenge 5B, 2820 Gentofte, Copenhagen, Denmark.

MILANÉS, Pablo; b. 1943, Bayamo, Cuba. Vocalist; Musician (guitar); Songwriter. *Education:* Amadeo Roldán Conservatory, Havana, Cuba. *Career:* Joined vocal group El Cuarteto del Rey, aged 16; Formed Los Bucaneros, 1960s; Embarked on solo career; Prominent figure in Nueva Trova (popular song) movement, late 1960s; Songs recorded by many major Cuban artists, including Omara Portuonda. *Recordings:* Versos de José Marti, 1973; Canta A Nicolás Guillén, 1975; Pablo Milanes, 1976; No Me Pidas, 1977; Aniversario, 1979; Lilia Vera Y Pablo Milanes, 1981; El Guerrero, 1983; Querido Pablo, 1985; Buenas Dias América, Años Vol. 2, 1986; Comienzo Y Final De Una Verde Mañana, 1987; Proposiciones; Años Vol. 3, 1992; Origenes, 1994; Plegaria, 1995; Despertar, 1997; Los Días de Gloria, 2000.

MILENA, (Milena Slavova); b. 1966, Sofia, Bulgaria. Vocalist; Musician (guitar); Songwriter; Lyricist. m. Robert Page-Roberts. *Career:* Member, Review, Bulgaria, 1986–90; Formed own band, 1991–; Best selling female rock singer in Bulgaria; Numerous tours and concerts in Bulgaria and eastern Europe; Writes, plays and sings own compositions with backing band; Only Bulgarian artiste to record album in the UK. *Recordings:* with Review: Review, 1989; Solo: Ha-ha, 1991; The Scandal, 1993; Sold, 1995. *Honours:* Seven-times voted First Lady of Bulgarian Rock; Best Female Voice,

Bulgarian National Awards (Unison), 1994; Best Album, The Scandal. *Address:* c/o Union Media Ltd, 71 Evlogi Georgiev Blvd, Entr. A, Sofia 1142, Bulgaria.

MILES, Robert, (Roberto Concina); b. 3 Nov. 1969, Fleurier, Switzerland (Italian citizen). DJ; Songwriter; Prod. *Career:* Began as DJ in club near Venice; Director of Programming at an Italian radio station; Began producing own records; Worked as producer for Italian label Metromaxx. *Recordings:* Singles: Fable, 1996; One and One, 1996; Children, 1996; Freedom, 1997; Full Moon, 1998; Albums: Dreamland, 1996; 23 AM, 1997; Organik, 2001. *Honours:* BRIT Award, Best International Newcomer, 1997.

MILLAR, John Jhalib; b. 1 July 1951, Belfast, Northern Ireland. Musician (tabla, world percussion). 1 s., 1 d. *Education:* Studied at Tabla Alla Rakha Institute of Music, Mumbai, 1979–. *Career:* First studied tabla, London, 1972; Played with Steve Hillage Band, 1976; Member, Nic Turner's (Hawkwind) Sphynx; Member, Monsoon, 1982–83; Interviewed on Danish radio Copenhagen, 1980; Several compositions, contemporary percussion for major UK modern dance companies; Various sessions for television, dance scores include Chakrada, 1981; Composed with Barrington Pheloung, formed Akasa, 1988; Released 2 singles, 2 promo videos, 1 album, 1990; Guest appearance with Massive Attack, Roxy Club Bologna, Italy, 1995; Joined John Mayers Inov-Jazz Fusions, 1997. *Compositions:* Sitar In The Skye, BBC1 TV series Hamish Macbeth, 1996. *Recordings:* Ever So Lonely, Monsoon, (No. 12, UK charts), 1982; with Akasa: Kama Sutra, 1989; One Night In My Life, 1990; London Contemporary Dance Theatre, Under The Same Sun, 1983; Union Dance Company, Visions of Rhythm, 1985; Sangeet Sagar (Ocean of Music), CD, 1997. *Honours:* Associate mem., PRS. *Membership:* Musicians' Union; PRS; Mechanical Copyright Protection Society (MCPS). *Current Management:* Clifton-Wyatt Artistes Management, 1 Poets Rd, London N5 2SL, England. *Address:* 65 Bayham St, Camden Town, London NW1 0AA, England.

MILLAR, Robin; b. 18 Dec. 1951, London, England. Record Prod. 1 s., 1 d. *Education:* MA, Cambridge University; A Level Music; Grade 8 guitar. *Recordings:* As producer, arranger, musician, writer, include: with Lavine Hudson: Abraham, Martin and John, 1991; with Black: Comedy, 1991; I'm Not Afraid; with Latin Quarter and The Bhundu Boys: Radio Africa, 1991; with Patricia Kaas: Je Tu Dis Vous, 1993; Live album, 1994; with Ute Lemper: Espace Indecent, 1994; with Malcolm McLaren: Paris, 1994; with Randy Crawford: Rich and Poor; with The Christians: Ideal World; with The Bhundu Boys: True Jit; with Owen Paul: This Feeling; with Fine Young Cannibals: FYC; with The Style Council: Have You Ever Had It Blue; with Big Country: The Seer; with The Kane Gang: Big Sound Authority; with Everything But The Girl: Love Not Money; Eden; with Tom Robinson: Hope and Glory; with Bluebells: Forever Yours, Forever Mine; with Courtney Pine: Children of The Ghetto; Artists produced include: Sam Brown; Kate Bush; Wazis Djop; Herbie Hancock; Chris Rea; Juliet Roberts; Wayne Shorter; Jimmy Somerville; Working Week; Tom Robinson; Additional production and mixing credits include: Elvis Costello; Wazis Djop; Peter Gabriel; Gary Kemp; Maxi Priest; Gil Scott Heron; Sting; The Special AKA; Tolu; with Sade: Diamond Life (triple Platinum album); Singles: Your Love Is King; Smooth Operator; Sweetest Taboo; When Am I Going To Make A Living (triple Platinum album); Promise; Killer Blow (Absolute Beginners soundtrack). *Membership:* Re-Pro. *Current Management:* Dennis Muirhead, Muirhead Management, 202 Fulham Rd, Chelsea, London SW10 9PJ, England.

MILLER, Andy; b. 18 Dec. 1968, London, England. Musician (Guitar). *Career:* Joined Dodgy; Debut, Dodgy Club; Frequent live shows; Formed own record label, Bostin, 1991; Signed to A & M Records, 1992. *Recordings:* Singles: Staying Out For The Summer, 1994; So Let Me Go Far, 1995; Making The Most Of, 1995; In A Room, 1996; If You're Thinking Of Me, 1996; Good Enough, 1996; Found You, 1997; If You're Thinking of Me, 1998; Every Single Day, 1998; Albums: The Dodgy Album, 1993; Homegrown, 1994; Free Peace Sweet, 1996; Ace A's and Killer B's, 1998; Real Estate, 2001. *Website:* www.dodgy.co.uk.

MILLER, Bill (William Scott); b. 23 Jan. 1955, Neenah, Wisconsin, USA. Entertainer; Musician (guitar, flute). m. Renee Miller, 5 Aug. 1978, 2 s., 1 d. *Education:* College. *Career:* Tori Amos tour; Television appearances: Good Morning America; Austin City Limits. *Recordings:* Native Sons; Old Dreams and New Hopes; The Art of Survival; Loon Mountain Moon; Reservation Road; The Red Road; Raven in the Snow; Ghostdance. *Current Management:* Bob Burwell, William Morris Agency. *Address:* Bob Burwell, 1516 16th Ave S, Nashville, TN 37212, USA.

MILLER, Dominic James; b. 21 March 1960, Buenos Aires, Argentina. Musician (guitar); Songwriter. m. 12 April 1985, 3 s., 1 d. *Education:* Berklee College of Music; Guildhall School of Music. *Career:* Tours: World Party; Julia Fordham; King Swamp; Sting; Various television and radio appearances; Playing with Sting, touring and broadcasting, 1989–. *Compositions include:* Co-writer with Sting, Shape of My Heart, on Ten Summoners Tales album. *Recordings:* Solo: Second Nature, 2000; with The Pretenders: Packed; with Phil Collins: But Seriously; with Sting: Soul Cages; Ten Summoners Tales; Fields of Gold; with Paul Young: Other Voices. *Honours:* Guitar Album of the

Year, Sunday Times, 1983; Played on Sting's and Phil Collins' Grammy Awards. *Membership:* PRS. *Current Management:* In Between. *Address:* 5 Harley Pl., London W1 N1HB, England.

MILLER, Gary Alan; b. 24 Sept. 1966, Durham, England. m. Jane, 2 July 1994. *Career:* Founded folk-rock group The Whisky Priests with twin brother Glenn, 1985; Singer/Songwriter/Guitarist, The Whisky Priests, 1985–; Co-founded Mad Dogs And Englishmen, 2000–; Over 1000 live club and festival performances throughout Europe; Numerous radio and TV appearances including The Tube (Channel 4), TV Española (Spain), Good Morning Croatia; 18 official releases on own label Whippet Records, formed with brother. *Compositions:* Alice in Wonderland; A Better Man Than You; My Ship; Song for Ewan; Side by Side; Full Circle; The Man Who Sold His Town; Success Express; When the Wind Blows, Billy Boy; Ranting Lads; The Man Who Would Be King; He's Still My Son; This Village; Forever in our Hearts; Workhorse; Halcyon Days; The Durham Light Infantry; The Hard Men; Car Boot Sale; William's Tale; Legacy of the Lionheart; Shot at Dawn; Perfect Time; The Raven; Old Man Forgotten. *Recordings:* Albums: with The Whisky Priests: Nee Gud Luck, 1989; The First Few Drops, 1991; Timeless Street, 1992; Bloody Well Live!, 1993; The Power and the Glory, 1994; Bleeding Sketches, 1995; Life's Tapestry, 1996; Think Positive!, 1998; Here Come the Ranting Lads—Live!, 1999; Story Of My Life: Pye Anthology, 2002; with Mad Dogs And Englishmen: Going Down With Alice, 2000; Video: Here Come the Ranting Lads – Live!, 1999. *Membership:* PRS; MCPS; PPL; PAMRA; Musicians' Union. *Current Management:* Whippet Promotions, PO Box 72, York YO31 1YU, England. *Address:* 46 Milton St, York YO10 3EP, England. *Website:* www.whiskypriests.co.uk.

MILLER, Glenn Thomas; b. 24 Sept. 1966, Durham, England. Musician (Accordion). m. Stephanie, 1 s. *Career:* Accordion player and songwriter with The Whisky Priests, 1985–; Over 1,000 live club and festival appearances throughout Europe; 20 official recordings released; Radio shows throughout Europe and TV appearances including Channel 4's The Tube, and shows in Spain and Germany. *Compositions:* Positive Steps; Death of the Shipyards; The Ghost of Geordie Jones; Jenny Grey; Goblins; Farewell Jobling!; Lament for the Setting Sons; Success Road; Durham; Epitaph for a Working Class Couple. *Recordings:* Albums: Nee Gud Luck, 1989; The First Few Drops, 1991; Timeless Street, 1992; Bloody Well Live!, 1993; The Power and the Glory, 1994; Bleeding Sketches, 1995; Life's Tapestry, 1996; Think Positive!, 1998; Here Come the Ranting Lads! – Live!, 1999; Going Down With Alice, 2000. *Membership:* MCPS; PRS; PPL; PAMRA; Musicians' Union. *Current Management:* Whippet Promotions, PO Box 72, York YO31 1YU, England. *Address:* 14 Springfield Close, Stockton Lane, York YO31 1LD, England.

MILLER, Marcus; b. 14 June 1959, Brooklyn, NY, USA. Jazz Musician (bass); Record Prod. *Career:* Recording artiste, worked with Joshua Redman; Lalah Hathaway; M'shell Ndege Ocello; Countless other recording sessions; Record producer for artists including: Miles Davis; Luther Vandross; Chaka Khan. *Recordings:* Albums: Marcus Miller, 1984; The Sun Don't Lie, 1993; Tales, 1994; Live And More, 1998; M2: Power And Grace, 2001. *Current Management:* Patrick Rains and Associates, 1543 Seventh St, Third Floor, Santa Monica, CA 90401, USA.

MILLER, Mikel; b. 13 Oct. 1949, Toronto, ON, Canada. Vocalist; Songwriter; Musician (guitar). 1 d. *Career:* Live performances in clubs and festivals throughout Canada and the USA, 1970s–90s. *Compositions:* No More Trains, 1984; Hand In The Game, 1988; Slow Driftin' Song, 1989; The Key, 1992; Something You Never Knew, 1994; Pilgrim's Progress, 1995; The Compromise, 1998. *Recordings:* No More Trains, 1989; Another Day In Paradise, 1994; The Key, 1996; Rounder's Road, 1999; NXNE sampler, 1999; Yukon sampler RAIYA, 1999; A Norm Hacking Compilation, 1999; Yukon sampler, 2000; Yukon sampler, 2001; All Roads, 2002; One Voice (Tribute to Norm Hacking), 2002; Yukon sampler, 2003. *Publications:* Lost Moose Catalogue, 1990; Dirty Linen Magazine, 1999. *Membership:* Canadian Country Music Asscn; Folk Alliance; Recording Arts Industry Yukon Assn (RAIYA). *Current Management:* LEA/JEN Music, PO Box 5073, Whitehorse, YT Y1A 4S3, Canada. *Address:* PO Box 31467, Whitehorse, YT Y1A 6K8, Canada. *E-mail:* mallmiller@polarcom.com. *Website:* mikelmiller.polarcom.com.

MILLER, Ruth; b. 8 May 1962, Newark, Nottinghamshire, England. Songwriter; Vocalist; Musician (guitar). *Education:* Degree in Communications; Postgraduate Research. *Career:* Founder, Rutland Records, 1988; Member of PO!, including BBC Radio 1 session; Member of Ruth's Refrigerator, touring Europe. *Recordings:* with PO!: Little Stones, 1989; Ducks and Drakes, 1993; Not Marked on the Ordnance Map, 1996; Past Present Tense, 1997; Horse Blanket Weather, 1998; Ruth's Refrigerator: Suddenly A Disfigured Head Parachuted, 1990; A Lizard Is A Submarine On Grass, 1991. *Membership:* PRS; MCPS; PPL; Musicians' Union. *Address:* c/o Rutland Records, PO Box 132, Leicester LE2 3ZF, England.

MILLER, Steve; b. 5 Oct. 1943, Milwaukee, Wisconsin, USA. Vocalist; Musician (guitar); Songwriter. *Education:* Wisconsin University, 1961; Literature, Copenhagen University, Denmark; Studied guitar with Les Paul,

1948. *Career:* Member, Marksmen Combo, 1955; The Ardells (became Fabulous Night Train); Worked with Muddy Waters; James Cotton; Howling Wolf; Butterfield Blues Band; Member, World War Three Band (became Goldberg-Miller Blues Band); Founder, the Steve Miller Band, 1966–; Regular international appearances include: San Francisco State College Folk Festival, 1967; Monterey International Pop Festival, 1967; Northern California Folk-Rock Festival, 1968; Hollywood Music Festival, 1970; Knebworth Festival, 1975; Benefit for Texas Special Olympics, Dallas, 1990; Earth Day Sound Action benefit, 1992; All Our Colors – The Good Road benefit concert, California, 1992; Earth Day concert, Hollywood Bowl, 1992; Founder, record label Sailor Records, 1976. *Recordings:* Albums: with Steve Miller Band: Children of The Future, 1968; Sailor, 1968; Brave New World, 1969; Your Saving Grace, 1969; Number Five, 1970; Rock Love, 1971; Recall The Beginning... A Journey From Eden, 1972; Anthology, 1972; Fly Like An Eagle, 1977; Book of Dreams, 1977; Greatest Hits 1974–78, 1978; Abracadabra, 1982; The Steve Miller Band Live!, 1983; Italian X-Rays, 1984; Living In The 20th Century, 1986; Greatest Hits 1976–86, 1987; Born 2 Be Blue, 1988; The Best of Steve Miller 1968–73, 1990; Wide River, 1992; Box Set, 1994; The Very Best of Steve Miller, 1996; Greatest Hits, 1998; Singles include: The Joker (No. 1, USA), 1974 (No. 1, UK, 1990); Take The Money and Run; Rock 'n' Me (No. 1, USA), 1976; Fly Like An Eagle; Jet Airliner; Swingtown; Abracadabra (No. 1, USA), 1982. *Honours:* Platinum discs; Star on Hollywood Walk of Fame, 1987. *Current Management:* Scott Boorey Management, 325 Glen Arms Dr., Danville, CA 94526, USA.

MILLER, Steven; b. 8 Nov. 1956. Prod; Arranger; Engineer. *Education:* BA, Film and Music, San Francisco State University. *Career:* Vice-President: Windham Hill Records; Founder: Hip Pocket Records; RCA Novus Records; Windham Hill Jazz records; Produced, engineered: Manhattan Transfer; Juliana Hatfield; Medeski Martin and Wood; Paula Cole; Michael Hedges; Will Ackermann. *Recordings:* Albums include: December, George Winston; Vapor Drawings, Mark Isham; Suzanne Vega, Suzanne Vega; Talkin' Bout You, Diane Schuur; Temporary Road, John Gorka; Mortal City, Dar Williams. *Membership:* NARAS. *Current Management:* Greg Spotts Entertainment, 1124 Fifth St, Suite 304, Santa Monica, California 90403, USA. *Address:* 35 Montell St, Oakland, CA 94611, USA.

MILLINGTON-ROBERTSON, Janice Anita; b. 5 Nov. 1947, Barbados. Musician; Educator. m. Edward George Robertson, 17 April 1982, divorced, 1 s. *Education:* Queen's College, Barbados; University of the West Indies; Studied with father, James Millington, violinist, and mother, Odessa Millington, pianist; Also, piano with Gerald Hudson, and Jean Harvey; Violin with Sidney Griller and Trevor Williams; Studied at Royal Academy of Music, Berklee College of Music, Boston, Columbia University Teachers' College, Florida State University; Several masterclasses, conference presentations and workshops. *Career:* Performed for radio and TV; Own TV programme, 13 series; Recitals on violin and piano; Experimental work with piano and 2 violins including steelpan players in Trinidad; Developed calypso jazz idiom; Performed in clubs, concerts with popular and jazz musicians; Taught pop and jazz musicians for over 20 years; Author of reviews for local newspapers; Adjudicator, music festivals; Freelance lecturer, cultural topics; Cultural representative for Barbados in many music education and cultural seminars. *Recordings:* Janice Millington Plays; Xmas Time with Harrison College; The Romantic Spirit (video). *Publications:* Traditional Music and Its Place in Tourism, 1991; Many articles on Barbadian and Caribbean music; Contributor, Garland Encyclopaedia of World Music. *Honours:* NOW (National Organisation of Women) Award for contribution to education in Barbados; Bureau of Women Award for Development of Barbados; Scroll of Excellence, Harrison College. *Membership:* ARAM; GRSM; LRAM; ARCM (London) Certificate of Education, Management and Supervision (UWI); Corresponding Mem., Callaway International Resource Centre for Music Education; Advising Board Mem., Asscn of Professional Pianists and Teachers of the Americas; Barbadian Representative, International Society of Music Educators; Mem. of Incorporated Society of Musicians (UK). *Address:* PO Box 32W, Worthing, Christ Church, Barbados.

MILLS, Crispian; b. 18 Jan. 1973, London, England. Vocalist; Musician (guitar). *Career:* Founding mem., Objects of Desire, with Paul Winterhart and Alonza Bevan; Founding mem., the Kays, renamed Kula Shaker, with Jay Darlington; Numerous TV appearances and tours; Festival appearances incl. Knebworth with Oasis and Glastonbury; Guest vocals on Prodigy album, The Fat Of The Land, 1997; Solo artiste, 1999–; Founding mem., The Jeevas, 2002. *Recordings:* Albums: with Kula Shaker: K, 1996; Peasants, Pigs and Astronauts, 1999; with The Jeevas: 1-2-3-4!, 2002. Singles: with Kula Shaker: Tattva, 1996; Hey Dude, 1996; Govinda, 1996; Hush, 1997; The Sound of Drums, 1998; Mystikal Machine Gun, 1999; Shower Your Love, 1999. *Honours:* BRIT Award, Best British Newcomer, 1997. *Website:* www.crispianmills.com.

MILLS, Jeff, (Millsart, Purpose Maker); b. Detroit, Michigan, USA. Prod; Remixer; DJ. *Career:* Started career on Detroit radio station, WJLB, using DJ pseudonym The Wizard before collaborating with Mike Banks as part of Underground Resistance; Relocated to New York as resident DJ at the Limelight club; Founded Axis Records in New York; Collaborations: Mike

Banks; Robert Hood; Remixed: Maurizio; Lionrock; DJ Rolando; Put soundtrack to Fritz Lang's film, Metropolis, 2001. *Recordings include:* Albums: Sonic Destroyer (with X101), 1991; Waveform Transmission #1, 1992; Waveform Transmission #3, 1994; The Other Day, 1996; From the 21st, 1998, Lifelike, 2000; Metropolis, 2000; Every Dog Has Its Day, 2001; At First Sight, 2002; Singles: Take Me Away (with True Faith/Final Cut), 1991; Nation 2 Nation (with Underground Resistance); World 2 World (with Underground Resistance); Tranquilizer EP (with Robert Hood), 1993; Cycle 30, 1994; Purpose Maker, 1996; Every Dog Has Its Day, 2000; Metropolis, 2001. *Address:* c/o Axis Records, Dept 6277, 28 E Jackson Blvd, # 1910, Chicago, IL 60604, USA. *Telephone:* (312) 588-0528. *Fax:* (312) 588-0529. *E-mail:* info@axisrecords.com. *Website:* www.axisrecords.com.

MILLS, Mike; b. 17 Dec. 1958. Musician (bass). *Career:* Member, R.E.M., 1980–; International tours; Member, side project, Hindu Love Gods, 1986–90. *Recordings:* Albums: Chronic Town (mini album), 1982; Murmur, 1983; Reckoning, 1984; Fables of The Reconstruction, 1985; Life's Rich Pageant, 1986; Dead Letter Office, 1987; Document, 1987; Eponymous, 1988; Green, 1988; Out of Time (No. 1, UK and USA), 1991; The Best of R.E.M., 1991; Automatic For The People (No. 1, UK), 1992; Monster (No. 1, UK), 1994; New Adventures In Hi-Fi, 1996; Up, 1998; Star Profiles, 1999; Out of Time, 1999; Man On The Moon (soundtrack), 1999; Reveal (No. 1, UK), 2001; with Hindu Love Gods: Hindu Love Gods, 1990; Singles: with R.E.M.: The One I Love, 1987; Finest Worksong, 1988; Stand, 1989; Orange Crush, 1989; Losing My Religion, 1991; Shiny Happy People, 1991; Near Wild Heaven, 1991; Radio Song, 1991; Drive, 1992; Man On The Moon, 1992; The Sidewinder Sleeps Tonite, 1993; Everybody Hurts, 1993; Nightswimming, 1993; Find The River, 1993; What's The Frequency, Kenneth?, 1994; Bang And Blame, 1994; Strange Currencies, 1995; Crush With Eyeliner, 1995; Tongue, 1995; E-Bow The Letter, 1996; Bittersweet Me, 1996; Electrolite, 1996; Daysleeper, 1998; Lotus, 1998; At My Most Beautiful, 1999; The Great Beyond, 2000; Imitation Of Life, 2001; Tracks featured on film soundtracks: Batchelor Party, 1984; Until The End of The World, 1991; Coneheads, 1993; Other recordings with: Warren Zevon; Indigo Girls; Smashing Pumpkins; Liz Phair; Contributor, albums: Tom's Album; I'm Your Fan. *Honours:* Earth Day Award, 1990; Numerous MTV Music Video Awards; Billboard Awards: Best Modern Rock Artists, Best World Album, 1991; BRIT Awards: Best International Group, 1992, 1993, 1995; Grammy Awards: Best For Performance, Alternative Music Album, Music Video, 1992; Atlanta Music Awards: Act of the Year, Rock Album, Video, 1992; IRMA, International Band of the Year, 1992; Rolling Stone Critics Awards: Best Band, Best Album; Q Awards: Best Album, 1991, 1992; Best Act In The World, 1991, 1995. *Current Management:* REM/Athens Ltd. *Address:* 250 W Clayton St, Athens, GA 30601, USA.

MILLS, Richie; b. 13 Oct. 1971, Berkshire, England. Musician (drums). *Career:* Appeared in Short Film, When Animals Attack; Music Supplied for Major Drinks Television Commercial. *Compositions:* Freeze The Atlantic. *Recordings:* Cable; When Animals Attaack; Sub Lingual. *Membership:* Musicians' Union. *Current Management:* Furtive, 29 Charlotte Rd, London EC2A, England.

MILLS, Sam, (Samuel Peter Landrell-Mills); b. 15 June 1963, London, England, UK. Musician (guitar, programmer); Composer; Prod. *Career:* Member: 23 Skidoo; Tama (with Tom Diakite and Djanuno Dabo); Collaborations: Russell Mills; Paban Das Baul; Susheela Raman. *Recordings:* Singles: with 23 Skidoo: Ethics, 1979; Last Words, 1981; Tearing Up The Plans, 1982; Albums: Seven Songs (with 23 Skidoo), 1982; Real Sugar (with Paban Das Baul), 1997; Nostalgie (with Tama), 1999; Pearl and Umbra (Russell Mills and Undark), 2000; Salt Rain (Susheela Raman), 2001.

MILLS, Vincent Delano; b. 19 April 1960, Birmingham, England. Musician (guitar, electric bass guitar); Composer. *Career:* Performed with bands based in Birmingham and the Midlands area, late 1970s to 1990s, soul, funk, R&B, Jazz Big Bands, The Blue Pearls and numerous session gigs for Jazz combo's; Internationally: Toured USA with chart topping reggae artist Pato Banton's backing band the Reggae Revolution, 1992; East Coast tour, Florida and Georgia, 1992; West Coast tour, with performances at The Bob Marley Day Reggae Festival, concerts in California, Washington, Arizona, Canada, Hawaii and opening for Santana in Tijuana, Mexico; Performed with top Caribbean calypso/soca bands Nu-Vybes in St Kitts, 1995 and Small Axe, St Kitts Music Festival, 1999; Performed at Birmingham, Ludlow and Keswick Jazz Festivals, Black Music Festival, London. *Recordings:* Lead and Rhythm guitar on CD, Pan In Flight, Barcelona, Jamma. *Membership:* Musicians' Union.

MILSAP, Ronnie; b. 16 Jan. 1944, Robbinsville, NC, USA. Music Artist. m. Joyce. *Recordings:* Singles include: The Girl Who Waits on Tables, 1973; Please Don't Tell Me How, 1974; I'm a Stand By My Woman Man, 1976; Let My Love Be Your Pillow, 1976; Back On My Mind Again, 1978; Nobody Likes Sad Songs, 1979; Misery Loves Company, 1980; Smokey Mountain Rain, 1980; Any Day Now, 1982; Still Losing You, 1984; Only One Night of the Year, 1986; Make No Mistake, She's Mine, duet with Kenny Rogers, 1987; Button Off My Shirt, 1988; Woman in Love, 1989; Since I Don't Have You, 1991; LA to the Moon, 1992; True Believe, 1993; Albums include: Where My Heart Is, 1973; Night Things, 1975; Ronnie Milsap Live, 1976; It Was Almost Like A Song,

1977; Only One Love in My Life, 1978; Greatest Hits, Vol. 1, 1980; There's No Gettin' Over Me, 1981; Greatest Hits, Vol. 2, 1985; Lost in the Fifties Tonight, 1986; Christmas with Ronnie Milsap, 1986; Stranger Things Have Happened, 1989; Greatest Hits, Vol. 3, 1992; True Believer, 1993; Didn't We, 1996; Kentucky Woman, 1996; When It Comes To My Baby, 1996; Christmas in Dixie, 1997; Branson City Limits, 1999; Wish You Were Here, 2000. *Honours:* Grammy Awards: Best Country Male Vocal Performance, 1974, 1976, 1982, 1986, 1987, Country Song of the Year, 1984, Best Country Duet Performance, with Kenny Rogers, 1988; Billboard Awards: Best New Male Artist, 1974, Male Singles Artist of the Year, 1976, 1980, Overall Singles Artist of the Year, 1976, Bill Williams Memorial Award, Artist of the Year, 1976, Breakthrough Award, Outstanding Achievement, 1981; CMA Awards: Male Vocalist of the Year, 1974, 1976, 1977, Album of the Year, 1975, 1977, 1978, 1986, Entertainer of the Year, 1977; Numerous others. *Current Management:* Gold Mountain Entertainment, 1514 South St, Suite 100, Nashville, TN 37212, USA.

MINCHELLA, Damon; b. 1 June 1969, Liverpool, England. Musician (Bass). *Career:* Joined The Fanatics with Simon Fowler; When band split became Ocean Colour Scene; Secured indie record deal, but label taken over; Joined Paul Wellers backing band along with Fowler and Steve Cradock, while continuing with Ocean Colour Scene; Support slot to Oasis 1994 tour; Numerous TV appearances and radio play; Riverboat Song used as theme tune to TV series TFI Friday, 1996–2000; Several headlining tours. *Recordings:* Singles: The Riverboat Song, 1996; The Day We Caught The Train, 1996; 100 Mile High City; You've Got It Bad, 1996; The Circle, 1996; Travellers Tune, 1997; 100 Mile High City, 1997; Better Day, 1997; It's A Beautiful Thing, 1998; Profit In Peace, 1999; So Low, 1999; July/I Am The News, 2000; Up On The Downside, 2001; Albums: Ocean Colour Scene, 1992; Moseley Shoals, 1996; Marchin' Already, 1997; Mechanical Wonder, 2001; Songs For The Front Row, 2001. *Website:* www.oceancolourscene.com.

MINNELLI, Liza May; b. 12 March 1946, Los Angeles, CA, USA. Vocalist; Actress; Dancer. m. Peter Allen, 1967, divorced, (2) Jack Haley Jr, 15 Sept. 1974, divorced, (3) Mark Gero, 4 Dec. 1979, divorced, (4) David Guest, 2002. *Career:* Stage, film and television singer and entertainer; Major appearances include: Best Foot Forward (off-Broadway), 1963; Touring productions: Carnival; The Pajama Game; The Fantasticks; Performed with mother (Judy Garland), London Palladium, 1964; Broadway debut, Flora and The Red Menace, 1965; The Act, 1977; The Rink, 1984; The Ultimate Event, international tour with Frank Sinatra, Sammy Davis Jr, 1988; Film appearances: Charlie Bubbles, 1967; The Sterile Cuckoo, 1969; Cabaret, 1972; Tell Me That You Love Me Junie Moon, 1974; Lucky Lady, 1975; A Matter of Time, 1976; Silent Movie, 1976; New York, New York, 1977; Arthur, 1981; Arthur 2 – On The Rocks, 1988; Stepping Out, 1991; Television appearances include: Liza With A 'Z', 1972; Goldie and Liza Together, 1980; Baryshnikov On Broadway, 1980; The Princess and The Pea; Showtime, 1983; A Time To Live, 1985; Sam Found Out, 1988. *Recordings:* Albums: Best Foot Forward, 1963; Liza! Liza!, 1964; Flora, The Red Menace (soundtrack), 1965; The Dangerous Christmas Of Red Riding Hood, 1965; It Amazes Me, 1965; Live At The London Palladium, 1965; There Is A Time, 1966; Come Saturday Morning, 1969; New Feelin', 1970; Cabaret (soundtrack), 1972; Liza With A 'Z', 1972; Liza Minnelli The Singer, 1973; Live At The Olympia In Paris, 1973; Live At The Winter Garden, 1974; Liza Minnelli, 1975; Four Sider, 1977; Tropical Nights, 1977; The Act, 1977; Maybe This Time, 1978; Best Foot Forward, 1981; Liza Minnelli at Carnegie Hall, 1987; Lovely! Lively! Liza, 1987; Live From Radio City Music Hall, 1992; Gently, 1996; Rink (cast recording), 1999; Minnelli On Minnelli, 2000; Liza's Back, 2002; The Very Best of Liza Minnelli: Life Is A Cabaret!, 2002; with Judy Garland: Live At The London Palladium, 1964; with Pet Shop Boys: Results, 1989; Losing My Mind (single, first UK chart entry), 1989. *Honours:* Promising Personality Award, 1963; 2 Tony Awards, Best Foot Forward, 1965, The Act, 1977; Academy Award, Best Actress, for Cabaret, 1972; Emmy Award, Lisa With A 'Z', 1972; Golden Globe Award, Best Actress, for A Time To Live, 1985. *Current Management:* Krost/Chapin Management, Penthouse 1, 9911 W Pico Blvd, Los Angeles, CA 90035, USA. *Address:* c/o Angel EMI Guardian Records, 304 Park Ave S, New York, NY 10010, USA.

MINOGUE, Dannii (Danielle Jane); b. 20 Oct. 1971, Melbourne, Victoria, Australia. Vocalist; Actress; Television Presenter. *Career:* Actress: Australian TV drama series: Skyways, 1978; The Sullivans, 1978; All The Way, 1988; Home and Away, 1989; Variety Show: Young Talent Time, Australia, 1979–88; New Generation, Australia, USA, 1988; TV Presenter: Scoop; It's Not Just Saturday; Dannii on Safari, Disney; Co-host, Big Breakfast, UK, 1993; Fan T.C., UK, 1994; Cirque du Monde, Disney, 1996; Electric Circus, UK, 1996; Disney Villans, Disney, 1997; Film appearance: Secrets, 1992; Performances: Royal Children's Variety Performance, 1991; Cesme Festival, Turkey, 1992; Gay Pride Festival, London, 1993, 1994, 1997; Promotional tours of Australia, SE Asia, USA and UK; Unleashed Tour, UK and Ireland, 1998; Sydney Gay and Lesbian Mardi Gras, Australia, 1998, 1999; Musical: Grease, The Arena Spectacular, Australia, 1998; Chicago, London West End, 2000; Theatre: Journey to Macbeth, Edinburgh Festival, 1999. *Recordings:* Albums: Love and Kisses, 1991; Get Into You, 1993; Girl, 1997; Singles: 10 Top Ten singles, including: Love and Kisses, 1990; Jump To The Beat, 1991;

This Is It, 1993; All I Wanna Do, 1997; Major Composition: Success, 1991; Everything I Wanted, 1997; Everlasting Night, 1999; Contributor: NME Ruby Trax, British Spastic Society, 1992; The Gift of Christmas, Child Liners, 1995. *Honours:* Gold discs, UK and Australia; Young Variety Award (Australian Variety Club) 1989. *Membership:* Media, Entertainment and Arts Alliance, Australia; APRA. *Address:* c/o Jules Kulpinski, KDB Artists Pty Ltd, PO Box 26025, London SW10 9GD, England.

MINOGUE, Kylie (Ann); b. 28 May 1968, Melbourne, Vic. , Australia. Vocalist; Actress. *Career:* Actress, Australian television dramas: Skyways, 1980; The Sullivans, 1981; The Henderson Kids, 1984–85; Neighbours, 1986–88; Film appearances: The Delinquents, 1989; Streetfighter, 1994; BioDome, 1995; Cut, 2000; Sample People, 2000; Solo artiste, 1988–; Numerous tours, concerts, television and radio performances world-wide, incl.: Australian Royal Bicentennial Concert, 1988; John Lennon tribute, Liverpool, 1990; Cesne Music Festival, Turkey, 1992; Sydney Gay Mardi Gras, 1994, 1998; Prince's Trust Concert, 1994; T In The Park Festival, Glasgow, 1995; Launched own range of underwear, 2003. *Recordings:* Albums: Kylie (No. 1, UK), 1988; Enjoy Yourself (No. 1, UK), 1989; Rhythm Of Love, 1990; Let's Get To It, 1991; Kylie—Greatest Hits, 1992; Kylie Minogue, 1994; Kylie Minogue, 1997; Intimate And Live, 1998; Light Years, 2000; Hits+, 2000; Fever, 2001; Confide In Me (compilation), 2002. Singles include: Locomotion (No. 1, Australia), 1987; I Should Be So Lucky (Number 1, UK), 1988; Got To Be Certain, 1988; Je Ne Sais Pas Pourquoi, 1988; Especially For You, with Jason Donovan (No. 1, UK), 1988; Hand On Your Heart (No. 1, UK), 1989; Wouldn't Change A Thing, 1989; Never Too Late, 1989; Tears On My Pillow (No. 1, UK), 1990; Better The Devil You Know, 1990; Step Back In Time, 1990; What Do I Have To Do?, 1991; Shocked, 1991; If You Were With Me Now, with Keith Washington, 1991; Give Me Just A Little More Time, 1992; Confide In Me, 1994; Put Yourself In My Place, 1995; Where Is The Feeling, 1995; Where The Wild Roses Grow (duet with Nick Cave), 1995; Some Kind of Bliss, 1997; Did It Again, 1997; Breathe, 1998; Spinning Around (No. 1, UK), 2000; On A Night Like This, 2000; Kids, duet with Robbie Williams, 2000; Please Stay, 2000; Can't Get You Out Of My Head (No. 1, UK), 2001. *Honours:* Numerous Platinum, Gold and Silver discs; Six Logies (Australia); Six Music Week Awards (UK); Three Smash Hits Awards (UK); Three Australian Record Industry Asscn Awards; Three Japanese Music Awards; Irish Record Industry Award; Canadian Record Industry Award; World Music Award; Australian Variety Club Award; MO Award (Australian Showbusiness); Amplex Golden Reel Award; Diamond Award, (Belgium); Woman of the Decade (UK); MTV Video of the Year, Did It Again, 1998; BRIT Awards, Best International Female Solo Artist, Best International Album, for Fever, 2002; MTV Awards, Best Pop Act, Best Dance Act, 2002. *Current Management:* Terry Blamey Management, PO Box 13196, London SW6 4WF, England. *Website:* www.kylie.com.

MINOTT, Sugar (Lincoln); b. 25 May 1956, Kingston, Jamaica. Reggae Vocalist. *Career:* Billed as one of the African Brothers, 1970s; Success within UK reggae scene; Established own Youth Promotion/Black Roots promotion organization. *Recordings:* with the African Brothers: Collectors Item; Numerous solo albums include: Live Loving; Black Roots; Bittersweet; Ghetto-ology; Roots Lovers; Give The People; African Girl; Good Thing Going; With Lots of Extra; Herbman Hustling; Slice of The Cake; Wicked A Go Feel It; Leader of The Pack; Time Longer Than Rope; Sugar and Spice; Them Ah Wolf; Jamming In The Streets; African Soldier; Buy Off The Bar; Ghetto Youth Dem Rising; The Boss Is Back; A Touch of Class; Run Things; Breaking Free; International; Musical Murder; Easy Squeeze, 1999; Hit singles: Good Thing Going, 1981; Never My Love, 1981. *Address:* c/o Tempest Entertainment, 245 W 25th St, New York, NY 10001, USA.

MINTON, Philip Watcyn; b. 2 Nov. 1940, Torquay, Devon, England. Vocalist; Improvisor. 1 s., 3 d. *Career:* Performed at most improvised music festivals world-wide, with hundreds of musicians from many countries. *Recordings:* Songs From A Prison Diary, with Veryan Weston; Ammo, Dadada, with Roger Turner; Solo: Phil Minton, 2000. *Honours:* Voted Best Singer, Europe Jazz Forum Magazine, 1988. *Membership:* LMC; Musicians' Union; PRS; MCPS. *Current Management:* Margareta Peters, Zurich, Switzerland. *E-mail:* m_peters@dplanet.ch.

MISE, Marjan; b. 9 July 1952, Beograd, Croatia. Vocalist; Musician (drums). m. Dubravka, 22 Dec. 1973, 1 s., 1 d. *Education:* Elementary Musical School. *Career:* 16 years touring former USSR; Many performances in Europe; Many international festivals include: Vilach; Bratislava; Golden Orphei; Sopot; Slovenska Popeuka; Portoroz; Split. *Recordings:* 25 singles; 7 albums; 2 CDs; 2 compilations (in English). *Honours:* Many Croatian and foreign awards. *Membership:* Croatian Musical Union. *Current Management:* Croatian Musical Union.

MISHALLE, Luc; b. 6 Jan. 1953. Musician (Saxophones). 1 s. *Education:* Licenced Law, 1976, University Antwerp. *Career:* Theatre: Musical Director of Welfare State (UK); Dog Troop (NL); Internationale Nieuwe Scene (B); Music: Marakbar; Blindman Quartet; Galileo's Left Wing. *Compositions:* Mekoue; Urbanized; Akoestischo; Winterverhalen; Metropolis; Webl; Mdawa; Shark Dari. *Recordings:* Marakbar 'Live; Marockin' Antwerp; Blindman Poortenbos;

Galileo's Left Wing Live; Marockin' Stories; El Adoua; Al Harmoniah. *Current Management:* VZW de Krijtkring, Werfstraate, 1000 Brussels, Belgium. *Address:* 6 rue du Capitaine Linard, 1390 Grez-Doiceau, Belgium.

MÍSIA, (Susanna Alfonso); b. Oporto, Portugal. Vocalist. *Career:* Began singing Fado (Portuguese folk form) professionally, 1991. *Recordings:* Albums: Misia, 1991; Fado, 1993; Tanto Menos Tanto Mas, 1994; Garros Dos Sentidos, 1998; Paixões Diagonais, 1999; Ritual, 2001. *Honours:* Grand Prix de L'Acadamie Charles Cross, 1997. *Current Management:* Les Visiteurs Du Soir, 40 rue del la Folie Regnault, 75011, Paris, France. *Address:* c/o WEA, The Warner Building, 28 Kensington Church St, London W8 4EP, England. *Website:* www.misia-online.com.

MITCHELL, Alexander; b. 4 Nov. 1969, Minster, Kent, England. Musician (guitar, midi programming). *Education:* Goldsmiths College. *Career:* Guitarist with: Curve, 1991–94; Choob, 1993–95; Sparky Lightbourne, 1997–; Radio includes: John Peel Sessions for Radio 1; Concerts include: Glastonbury Festival; NME Stage; Major tours: USA; Europe; Japan; UK; Television includes The Beat; Now making Techno music, 2 EPs under name Choob. *Compositions:* with Choob: Little Girl, 1993; Choobular, 1994; as Sparky Lightbourne: EP, 1997; Sparky's Secret, 1998; Album, 1999; Chickin Lickin; Get Your Hands Off Me. *Recordings:* Albums: with Curve, 2 LPs: Doppelganger; Cuckoo; 2 EPs: Little Girl; Choobular. *Membership:* Musicians' Union; PRS; MCPS. *Current Management:* Andy Mack, Skint Records, 73a Middle St, Brighton. *Address:* 60 Crane House, Grummant Rd, Peckham, London SE15 5NG, England.

MITCHELL, Dryden; b. 15 June 1976, Redondo Beach, California, USA. Vocalist; Musician (guitar); Songwriter. *Career:* Played with local bands Crossover, Out of Order, Dragonphlie; Member: Alien Ant Farm, 1996–; Self-financed independent LP released to acclaim, 1999; Signed to Papa Roach's New Noize label; Second album released in conjunction with DreamWorks label, leading to major international breakthrough, 2000–01. *Recordings:* Albums: Greatest Hits, 1999; ANThology, 2001; Singles: $100 EP, 1996; Love Songs EP, 1998; Movies, Smooth Criminal, 2001. *Honours:* L.A. Music Award, Best Independent Album, 1999. *Address:* c/o New Noize, 2022 Cliff Dr #123, Santa Barbara, CA 93109, USA. *E-mail:* info@newnoize.com. *Website:* www.alienantfarm.com.

MITCHELL, Ian; b. 22 Aug. 1958, Downpatrick, Northern Ireland. Musician (Guitar); Vocalist. m. Wendy Antanaitis, 1992. *Career:* Began performing, aged 15; Joined Bay City Rollers, 1976, left, 1976; Founded Rosetta Stone, 1977; Formed Ian Mitchell Band, 1979; Appeared, Dinah Shore Show, Mike Douglas Show, Merv Griffin Show, Top of the Pops, all with Bay City Rollers; Own TV Programme, Fanfare, with Rosetta Stone. *Recordings:* With Bay City Rollers: Dedication, LP; With Rosetta Stone: Sunshine of Your Love; Try It On; Sheila; With the Ian Mitchell Band: Suddenly You Love Me; Hold On to Love; Boulevard LA; Solo: Edge Of The World, 2000. *Current Management:* Jeff Hubbard Productions. *Address:* PO Box 53664, Indianapolis, IN 46253, USA.

MITCHELL, John Lindsay; b. 24 Aug. 1967, Manchester, England. Writer; Musician (guitar); Vocalist. m. Clare Fiona Lindley. *Education:* Aberdeen College. *Career:* HM Forces, 1984–89; MOD Search and Rescue, 1990–91; Touring, Scottish Folk Festival Circuit, 1992–. *Compositions:* Leaving Carolina; Marie Celeste; Jamie Gows Farewell to Methadone; High and Low; Baroque Daydream; Squaddies Lament; Found on the Wave; The Fulmed. *Recordings:* Found on the Wave, 1996. *Membership:* PRS; PRC. *Current Management:* Marj Mitchell, 40 Hazelhead Gardens, Aberdeen. *Address:* Cairnwell Cottage, Newtonhill, Sonehaven, Kincardineshire, England.

MITCHELL, Joni, (Roberta Joan Anderson); b. 7 Nov. 1943, Fort McLeod, AB, Canada. Vocalist; Songwriter; Musician (piano, guitar, ukelele). m. (1) Chuck Mitchell, 1965, divorced, (2) Larry Klein, 1982. *Education:* Alberta College of Art, Calgary, 1962. *Career:* Duo with Chuck Mitchell, 1965; Solo singer, songwriter, 1966–; Major concerts incl.: Miami Pop Festival, 1968; Carnegie Hall, New York, 1969; Isle of Wight Festival, 1970; Tours, USA, Europe, with Jackson Browne, 1971; Bob Dylan's Rolling Thunder Revue, 1975; The Last Waltz (The Band's farewell concert), 1976; Playboy Jazz Festival, Hollywood Bowl, 1979; Roger Waters' The Wall, Berlin, 1990; Troubadours of Folk Festival, 1993; Exhibition of own paintings, Canada In The City exhibition, London, 1990. *Compositions:* Own album songs; Urge For Going, Tom Rush; Both Sides Now, Judy Collins; Woodstock, Crosby Still and Nash; This Flight Tonight, Nazareth. *Recordings:* Albums: Joni Mitchell (aka Song To A Seagull), 1968; Clouds, 1969; Ladies Of The Canyon, 1970; Blue, 1971; For The Roses, 1972; Court And Spark (No. 2, USA), 1974; Miles Of Aisles (live, No. 2, USA), 1974; Hissing Of Summer Lawns, 1975; Hejira, 1976; Don Juan's Reckless Daughter, 1977; Mingus, 1979; Shadows And Light (live), 1980; Wild Things Run Fast, 1982; Dog Eat Dog, 1985; Chalk Mark In A Rainstorm, 1988; Night Ride Home, 1991; Turbulent Indigo, 1994; Big Yellow Taxi (remixes), 1996; Hits, 1996; Misses, 1996; Taming The Tiger, 1998; Both Sides Now, 2000; Travelogue, 2002. Singles include: Big Yellow Taxi, 1970; Carey, 1971; You Turn Me On, I'm A Radio, 1972; Help Me, 1974; Free Man In Paris, 1974; Good Friends, duet with Michael McDonald, 1986; Guest vocalist, You've Got A Friend, James Taylor (No. 1, USA), 1971. *Honours:* Grammy Awards, Best Folk Performance, Clouds, 1970, Best Arrangement (with Tom Scott), 1975, Traditional Pop Vocal Album, 2001; Inducted into Juno Hall of Fame, 1981; Companion of the Order of Canada, 2002; 8 Gold discs. *Current Management:* Mind Over Management, 1505 W Second Ave, Suite 200, Vancouver, BC V6H 3Y4, Canada. *Address:* S. L. Feldman and Assocs, 1505 W Second Ave, Suite 200, Vancouver, BC V6H 3Y4, Canada. *Website:* www.jonimitchell.com.

MITCHELL, Neil; b. 8 June 1967, Helensborough, Scotland. Musician (keyboards). *Career:* Member, Wet Wet Wet, 1982–; Performances include: Greenpeace charity concert, Royal Albert Hall, 1986; Support to Lionel Richie, British tour, 1987; Prince's Trust Rock Gala, London, 1988–90; The Big Day (Channel 4), 1990; Edinburgh Castle, 1992; Nordoff-Robbins Music Therapy Centre, Royal Albert Hall, 1992; Live At The Royal Albert Hall 1992 (Channel 4), 1993. *Recordings:* Albums: Popped In Souled Out, 1987; Sgt Pepper Knew My Father, 1988; The Memphis Sessions, 1988; Holding Back The River, 1989; High On The Happy Side, 1992; Wet Wet Wet Live At The Royal Albert Hall, 1993; End Of Part One: The Greatest Hits, 1993; Picture This, 1995; 10, 1997; Singles include: Wishing I Was Lucky, 1987; Sweet Little Mystery, 1987; Angel Eyes (Home and Away), 1988; Temptation, 1988; With A Little Help From My Friends (No. 1, UK), 1988; Sweet Surrender, 1989; Broke Away, 1989; Hold Back The River, 1990; More Than Love, 1992; Goodnight Girl (No. 1, UK), 1992; Lip Service, 1992; Shed A Tear, 1993; Love Is All Around (No. 1, UK), 1994; She's All On My Mind, 1995; Julia Said, 1995; Don't Want To Forgive Me Now, 1995; Somewhere Somehow, 1995; If I Never See You Again, 1997; Yesterday, 1997. *Honours:* BRIT Award, Best British Newcomer, 1988. *Current Management:* The Precious Organisation, 14–16 Spiers Wharf, Port Dundas, Glasgow, Scotland.

MITCHELL-DAVIDSON, Paul; b. 29 Dec. 1946, Bristol, England. Composer; Arranger; Musician (all guitars, mandolin, banjo). *Career:* Various bands, 1960s; Monad, 1971–73; Maynard Ferguson Band, US tour, 1972; Paws For Thought, 1974; Freelance session musician, also musical director, radio and television, 1970s–; Played with many top UK and US jazz musicians; Major concert at RNCM, 1995. *Compositions:* All About Lions; Gaia; The Bestiary; Rhapsody For Duke; Solar Eclipse; Captain Corelli; Tubafication; Work for theatre, chamber, choral, orchestral music, jazz, dance, radio, television and commercial recording sessions. *Recordings:* Out of My Head; The Joy of Paranoia, with Lol Coxhill. *Honours:* BBC Marty Paich Award, 1991–92. *Membership:* PRS; APC; BMWC; MCPS; Musicians' Union. *Address:* 25 Bannerman Ave, Manchester M25 1DZ, England.

MITON, Gilles; b. 3 July 1962, Paris, France. Musician (baritone saxophone, flute). *Education:* National Conservatory, Versaille, 1980. *Career:* Television show, with Eddy Mitchell, Ray Charles, Michel Legrand; Played with: Claude Bolling; Michel Legrand; Ornical Band; Arturo Sandoval; Phil Woods; Johnny Griffin; Milky Sax; Lumiere; Laurent Cugny; Super Swing Machine, Gerard Badini; Jean-Loup Longnon; Philippe Baduoin; Antoine Hervé; Quoi de Neuf Doctor; Salena Jones; Dee Dee Bridgewater; Ray Charles; Arthur H; Charles Trenet; Michel Leeb; Le Grand Orchestre du Splendid; Manu Dibango; Sacha Distel; Eddy Mitchell. *Recordings:* Albums with: Charles Trenet; Le Grand Orchestre Du Splendid; Eddy Mitchell; Michel Legrand; Ornicar; Gerard Badini; Philippe Badouin; Quoi De Neuf Docteur; Salena Jones.

MIZE, Ben; b. 2 Feb. 1971, USA. Musician (drums). *Career:* Member, Counting Crows, 1994–; Numerous headlining tours and TV appearances. *Recordings:* Singles: Round Here, 1994; Mr Jones, 1994; Rain King, 1994; Angels of the Silence (live), 1996; Long December, 1999; Daylight Fading, 1999; Albums: August and Everything After, 1993; Recovering the Satellites, 1996; Across a Wire: Live in New York, 1998; Long December, 1999; Daylight Fading, 1999; This Desert Life, 1999; Hard Candy, 2002. *Website:* www.countingcrows.com.

MIZRAKI, Raf; Musician (drums, percussion, guitar, cello, dulcimer); Vocalist. *Education:* York University. *Career:* Plays with: The Dufay Collective; Arab music group, Arabesque; Soul band and various baroque orchestras; Member, The Carnival Band, 1990–; Appearances include: Glasgow Cathedral; Birmingham Symphony Hall; Barbican Centre; Arts theatres throughout UK; Plays material from: France; UK; Spain; Bolivia; USA; Croatia; Sweden. *Recordings:* Album with Maddy Prior: Christmas Carols. *Current Management:* Jim McPhee, Acorn Entertainments. *Address:* Winterfold House, 46 Woodfield Rd, Kings Heath, Birmingham B13 9UJ, England.

MKANDAWIRE, Wambali; b. Belgian Congo (Malawian). Musician (guitar); Vocalist; Songwriter. m. Wambui Muruiki, 1993, 1 d. *Career:* Mem., band, Pentagon; Mem., religious band, New Song, 1985–86, touring South Africa, Namibia and Zimbabwe; Solo artiste, 1988–; Founder, owner, Kajimete Arts Publishing. *Recordings:* Albums: first album, 1988; second album, 1989; third album, 1990; fourth album, 1992; Zani Muwone, 2000. *Address:* c/o Sheer Sound International, Sandhavon Office Park, Pongola Cres., Sandton, PO Box 3128, Parklands 2121, South Africa. *Website:* www.sheer.co.za.

MOBERG, Sten-Erik 'Pyret'; b. 20 Jan. 1947, Fröson, Sweden. Composer; Artist; Piano; Guitar. m. Karin Moberg-Hillmann, 2 s., 1 d. *Education:* Exam, Teachers' Training College, 1972; University Studies, Social Science and Pedagogics; Piano, Guitar and Song Studies. *Career:* The Threaten, TV, Theatre, 1966; The Helper, TV, Film, 1967; Hair, Sweden, Norway, 1968–70; The Diddlers, Tours in Ireland and England, 1966–70; Appearance at Olympia, Paris, 1978; TV appearances and tours in Europe. *Compositions:* Kärleken Ar Vit (Love is White), various Swedish songs; Another Year of Music; An Irish Saga, symphony. *Recordings:* Diddlers is Good For You, 1969; Hair, 1969; Kärleken Ar Vit, 1987; Another Year of Music, 1993. *Publications:* Ett Södermalm Som Gor Dig Varm (A South Part That Makes You Warm), 1987. *Honours:* STIM Award, 1990; Authors Union, 1991. *Membership:* SKAP; STIM; SAMI; Theatre Union.

MOBERLEY, Gary Mark; b. Sydney, New South Wales, Australia. Musician (keyboards); Composer; Writer; Programmer. *Education:* Grade 6, AMEB. *Career:* Live work/recorded with: The Bee Gees; The Sweet; John Miles Band; Terence Trent D'Arby; Prefab Sprout; Wet Wet Wet; The Damned; The Alarm; Hipsway; Jodie Watley; Girlschool; Drum Theatre; Sigue Sigue Sputnik; Little Richard; Haywoode; Nicole; Big Country (remix); Loose Ends; The Associates; Talk Talk; Kiki Dee; Band of Holy Joy; Toni Di Bart; Dangerous Grounds; Funkadelia; Steel Pulse; Trevor Horn; The JBs; ABC; Fine Young Cannibals; The Foundations; Jean Jacques Perrey; Live work with: Bee Gees; Paul Rodgers; Bonnie Tyler; Wilson Pickett; Eddie Floyd; Rufus Thomas; Ben E King; Arthur Conley; Andrew 'Junior Boy' Jones; Cookie McGhee; Texas Blues Summit; Memphis Blues Summit; 34 European tours; 9 American tours; 3 world tours; 4 albums of radio and TV themes used world-wide. *Address:* Flat 4, Grove End House, 150 Grove Terrace, London NW5 1PD, England.

MOBY, (Richard Melville Hall); b. 11 Sept. 1965, New York, NY, USA. Musician (guitar, drums, keyboards); Prod; Composer; Remixer. *Education:* Philosophy, University of Connecticut; Private classical education, 1976–83. *Career:* Production and remixes for: Metallica; Smashing Pumpkins; Michael Jackson; Depeche Mode; Soundgarden; Blur; David Bowie; Orbital; Prodigy; Freddie Mercury; Brian Eno; B-52's; Ozzy Osbourne; John Lydon; Butthole Surfers; Erasure; Aerosmith; OMD; Pet Shop Boys; Jon Spencer Blues Explosion; Tours: Lollapalooza, 1995; Red Hot Chili Peppers, 1995; Soundgarden, 1996; Big Top, 1997; Prodigy, 1993, 1995; Numerous solo tours, festivals, television and radio appearances; Owns tea shop, Teany, New York. *Recordings:* Albums: Moby, 1992; The Story So Far, 1993; Ambient, 1993; Early Underground, 1993; Move, 1994; Underwater, 1995; Everything Is Wrong, 1995; Everything Is Wrong: Non-stop DJ Mix By Evil Ninja Moby, 1996; Voodoo Child: The End Of Everything, 1996; Animal Rights, 1996; Rare: Collected B-Sides 1989–1993, 1996; I Like To Score, 1997; Play, 1999; Mobysongs, 2000; 18, 2002. Singles: Time's Up, 1990; Mobility, 1990; Voodoo Child, 1991; Go, 1991; Brainstorm; Drug Fits The Face; UHF; Instinct Dance; Drop A Beat; Moby; The Ultimate Go; Next Is The E; I Feel It (Next Is The E-Remix), 1993; Move, 1993; All That I Need Is To Be Loved, 1993; Hymn, 1994; Demons/Horses, 1994; The Original Go, 1994; Feeling So Real, 1994; Everytime You Touch Me, 1995; Into The Blue, 1995; Bring Back My Happiness, 1995; Dog Heaven, 1995; That's When I Reach For My Revolver, 1996; Come On Baby, 1997; James Bond Theme (Moby's Re-version), 1997; Honey, 1998; Run On, 1999; Bodyrock, 1999; Why Does My Heart Feel So Bad?, 1999; Natural Blues, 2000; Porcelain, 2000; Find My Baby, 2001; South Side, 2001; We Are All Made Of Stars, 2002; Extreme Ways, 2002; In This World, 2002; Full film score: Double Tap, 1997; Movie soundtrack contributions: Cool World, 1993; Heat, 1996; Scream, 1996; Joe's Apartment, 1996; Tomorrow Never Dies, 1997; The Saint, 1997; The Jackal, 1997; Spawn, 1997; Gattaca, 1998; Senseless, 1998; Rounders, 1998; Species II, 1998; Ever After, 1998; Blade, 1998; The Bumblebee Flies Anyway, 1998; Dangerous Beauty, 1998; Permanent Midnight, 1998; Playing By Heart, 1998; Any Given Sunday, 1999; Big Daddy, 1999; The Next Best Thing, 2000; The Beach, 2000. *Honours:* Everything Is Wrong, Album of the Year, Spin Magazine, 1995; Top 5 Albums of the Year, Village Voice, Entertainment Weekly and Go; Live Performer in Germany, 1995, Frontpage Magazine; MTV Award, The Web Award, 2002; Best Producer Award, Q Magazine, 2002; MTV Video Music Awards, Best Cinematography in a Video, for We Are All Made Of Stars, 2002. *Membership:* BMI; PMRS; AF of M; SAG; AFTRA. *Current Management:* c/o Mr Eric Härle, Deutsch-Englische Freundschaft Ltd, PO Box 2477, London NW6 6NQ, England. *Address:* c/o Mute, 429 Harrow Rd, London W10 4RE, England. *E-mail:* info@d-e-f.com. *Website:* www.moby.com.

MOD WHEEL, (THE). See: **MIDDLETON, Tom.**

MODEL 500. See: **ATKINS, Juan.**

MOFFATT, Hugh; b. 3 Nov. 1948, Fort Worth, Texas, USA. Country Vocalist; Songwriter; Musician (guitar, trumpet). *Education:* English degree, Rice University, Houston, Texas. *Career:* Singer, songwriter, Nashville, 1970s; Recording artist, 1974–; Formed band Ratz, early 1980s. *Compositions:* Just In Case, recorded by Ronnie Milsap, 1974; Old Flames Can't Hold A Candle To You (co-writer Pebe Sebert), recorded by Joe Sun, Dolly Parton, Foster and Allen; Wild Turkey (co-writer with Pebe Sebert), recorded by Lacy J Dalton;

Love Game, recorded by Jerry Lee Lewis; Praise The Lord and Send Me The Money, recorded by Bobby Bare; Why Should I Cry Over You, (co-writer Ed Penney), recorded by George Hamilton IV; Words At Twenty Paces, recorded by Alabama; Operas: King of The Clouds, with Michael Ching; Out of The Rain, with Michael Ching. *Recordings:* Putting On The Ratz (EP); Dance Me Outside, (album) duet with Katy Moffatt, 1992; Albums: Loving You, 1987; Troubadour, 1989; Live and Alone, 1991; The Wognum Sessions, 1992; The Way Love Is, 1992; The Life of a Minor Poet, 1996; Ghosts of The Music, 1998. *Address:* c/o Criterion Music, 6124 Selma Ave, Hollywood, CA 90028, USA.

MOFFATT, Katherine Louella (Katy); b. 19 Nov. 1950, Fort Worth, Texas, USA. Musician (guitar); Vocalist; Songwriter. *Education:* Sophie Newcomb College, 1968; St John's College, 1969–70. *Career:* Folk singer, 1967–68; Production assistant, announcer, television stations, 1970; Musician, singer, blues band Corpus Christi, 1970; Solo artiste, 1971–; On concert bills with: Muddy Waters; Everly Brothers; Willie Nelson; Warren Zevon; Musical film roles: Billy Jack; Hard Country; The Thing Called Love; Television and radio includes: Music City Tonight; Texas Connection; Nashville Now; Bobby Bare Show; National Public Radio; E-Town; World Cafe; Mountain Stage. *Compositions:* The Magic Ring; Kansas City Morning; Gerry's Song; Take Me Back To Texas; (Waiting For) The Real Thing; Didn't We Have Love; Co-writer, Walkin' On The Moon (with Tom Russell). *Recordings:* Singles include: Take It As It Comes, 1981; Under Loved and Over Lonely, 1983; Albums: Katy; Kissin' In The California Sun; Walkin' On The Moon; The Greatest Show On Earth; A Town South of Bakersfield; Hearts Gone Wild; Child Bride; Dance Me Outside; Sleepless Nights; Midnight Radio; Angel Town; Loose Diamond, 1999; Cowboy Girl, 2001. *Honours:* Record World Album Award, 1976; Cash Box Single Award, 1976; Best Singer-Songwriter, Fort Worth Weekly, 1997. *Membership:* AFofM; AFTRA; SAG; NARAS. *Address:* PO Box 334, O'Fallon, IL 62269, USA.

MOFFETT, Johnathan Phillip; b. 17 Nov. 1954, New Orleans, Louisiana, USA. Musician (drums); Musical Dir; Songwriter. m. Rhonda Bartholomew, 26 June 1976, 1 s., 1 d. *Career:* Drummer for artists including: Patti Austin; Cameo; Lionel Richie; Madonna; Tina Marie; Jermaine Jackson; Major tours and concerts with: The Jacksons, 1979–81, Victory Tour (also as set designer), 1984; Elton John world tours, 1988–89; Madonna, Virgin and Ciao Italia tours; George Michael, Rock In Rio Festival; Musical director for concerts by Jermaine Jackson, Michael Jackson; Numerous television and video appearances with: The O'Jays; Isaac Hayes; The Kane Gang; Cameo. *Recordings:* Albums include: Silk Electric, Diana Ross, 1982; Victory, The Jacksons, 1984; One More Story, Peter Cetera, 1988; Back To Avalon, Kenny Loggins, 1988; Also recorded with Julian Lennon; Richard Marx; Jody Watley; Chico de Barge; Brian Eno; Janet Jackson; Edgar Winter.

MOGENSEN, Grethe Stitz; b. 25 May 1937, Copenhagen, Denmark. Actress; Author; Playwright; Composer; Vocalist. m. Axel Busch-Jensen, 4 April 1964, 1 s., 1 d. *Education:* New Theatre Actors' School, Copenhagen. *Career:* Enlordag på Amàr, 1957; Champagnegaloppen, 1960, 1974; Farinelli, 1961; Guys and Dolls, 1992; No No Nanette, 1973; Company, 1972; Dollarprinssen, 1975; Piger tilsös, 1987; Sweeney Todd, 1988; Nitouche, 1989; Les Miserables, 1991; Cirkus Mikkelikski, 1991, 1997; Sommer i Tyrol, 1993; Mod mig på Cassiopeia, 1996; My Fair Lady, 1999; Films: Pigen i sogelyset, 1959; Bussen, 1963; Gift, 1966; Flagermusen, 1966; Tro, håb og Karlighed, 1984; Tango for tre, 1992; Singer, Denmark 1957–; Greenland 1967; Israel, 1978; USA, 1984. *Compositions:* Cirkus Mikkelikski; Granen, Nissen sad på loftet; Okker gokkar; Hvis Katten Kunne Vrinske; Dubbing for Walt Disney. *Recordings:* Enlordag på Amàr, 1959; Farinelli, 1961; En sondag på Amager, 1962; Dollarprinssen, 1964; Dyrene i Hakkebakkeskoven, 1963; Landmandsliv, 1965; Flagermusen, 1966; Shehvide, 1966; Bambi, 1970; Askepot, 1971; Pinoccio, 1971; Isyngelegeland, I–IV, 1967–87; Jul i Syngelegeland, I and II, 1971, 1979; Lidt af hvert, 1979; Cirkus Mikkelikski, 1981, 1996; Author of Teaterkattens Eventyr, 1993. *Honours:* Mogens Brandts Legat, 1960; Kiss Gregers, 1974; DPA's Haderslegat, 1991; Louis Halberstadt's Haderslegat, 1997. *Membership:* Danish Actors League; Danish Popular Authors. *Address:* Engstien 4, 2791 Dragor, Denmark.

MOGENSEN, Mogens Eddie; b. 31 March 1948, Odense, Denmark. Musician (fagot, bassoon). m. Nora Andrea Mogensen, 31 March 1972, 2 s., 1 d. *Education:* Det Fynske Musikkonservatorium, Odense, with Hagbard Knudsen. *Career:* Principal Bassoon, Royal Danish Orchestra, Copenhagen, 1972–; Teacher, Royal Danish Academy of Music, Royal Academy of Music. *Membership:* IDRS. *Address:* Landlyst Vaenge 61, 2635 Jshoj, Denmark.

MOGG, Phil; b. 1951, London, England. Rock Vocalist. *Career:* Founder member, UK rock group UFO, 1969–83; Re-formed twice, 1985, 1991; Regular world-wide tours. *Recordings:* Albums: UFO, 1971; UFO 2 – Flying, 1971; Live In Japan, 1972; Phenomenon, 1974; Force It, 1975; No Heavy Pettin', 1976; Lights Out, 1977; Obsession, 1978; Strangers In The Night, 1979; No Place To Run, 1980; The Wild, The Willing and The Innocent, 1981; Mechanix, 1982; Making Contact, 1982; Headstone, 1983; Misdemeanour, 1985; Ain't Misbehavin', 1988; High Stakes and Dangerous Men, 1992; Covenant, 2000; Hit singles include: Too Hot To Handle, 1977; Lights Out, 1977; Only You Can Rock Me, 1978; Rock Bottom, 1978; Doctor, Doctor 1979; Young Blood, 1980;

Lonely Heart, 1981; Solo albums: Edge of the World, 1997; Chocolate Box, 1999. *Current Management:* Singerman Entertainment, Penthouse West, 8833 Sunset Blvd, Los Angeles, CA 90069, USA.

MOHAMED, Pops; b. 10 Dec. 1949, Benoni, Johannesburg, South Africa. Musician (piano, synthesizer, programming, keyboards, kora, mbira, didgeridu, berimbau, marimba, percussion). Divorced, 2 s., 1 d. *Education:* Studied Jazz at FUBA, 1979–84; Studied traditional instruments, 1986–93. *Career:* Lead guitarist, Les Valiants, 1969–71; Band leader: The Dynamics: El Gringoes; Society's Children; Solo albums, 1975–; Black Disco, 1975; Night Express, 1976; Black Disco 3, 1978; Movement In The City, 1979; Award as original artist for Towntalk Show, 1979; Albums: BM Movement, 1980; Innercity Funk, 1981; Recording Engineer, 1981–87; Record Producer, 1988–95; Own record label Kalamazoo Music, 1993. *Compositions:* Lolly's Song; A New Hope!, 1995; African Sketches; A New Hope. *Recordings:* When In New York, 1993. *Publications:* Kalamazoo Music. *Membership:* Royal Schools and Federated Union of Black Arts. *Current Management:* Kalamazoo Music Productions. *Address:* 202 Bethlen, 13th St, Orange Grove, 2192 Johannesburg, Gauteng, South Africa.

MOLDEN, Nigel Charles; b. 17 Aug. 1948, Oxford, England. Music Co Dir. m. Hilary Julia Lichfield, 14 Aug. 1971, 3 s. *Education:* Bsc (Hons) London University; MSc Brunel University; PhD, Fairfax University; Piano Grade 2. *Career:* International General Manager, WEA Records, 1971–80; International Marketing Manager, Thorn EMI Video, 1980–84; Joint Chief Executive, TKO Magnum Music, 1994–. *Honours:* Freeman, City of London, 1990. *Membership:* FRSA; FCIM; FBIM; FinstD. *Address:* Ashcombe House, Deanwood Rd, Jordans, Buckinghamshire HP9 2UU, England.

MOLKO, Brian; b. 10 Dec. 1972. Vocalist; Musician (guitar, bass). *Education:* Studied Drama, Goldsmiths College, London. *Career:* Member, Placebo; Numerous television appearances; Live tours and numerous festival dates. *Recordings:* Singles: Come Home, 1996; 36 Degrees, 1996; Teenage Angst, 1996; Nancy Boy, 1997; Bruise Pristine, 1997; Pure Morning, 1998; You Don't Care About Us, 1998; Every You Every Me, 1999; Without You I'm Nothing, featuring David Bowie, 1999; Taste In Men, 2000; Slave To The Wage, 2000; Albums: Placebo, 1996; Without You I'm Nothing, 1998; Black Market Music, 2000. *Website:* www.placeboworld.co.uk.

MOLLER, Lars Alleso; b. 17 Sept. 1966, Copenhagen, Denmark. Musician (tenor saxophone); Composer. *Education:* Lessons with David Liebman, 5 years; BFA, New School, New York, 1989; Composer workshop with Bob Brookmeyer at Rytmekons Conservatory, 1996–98; Indian classical music studies, New Delhi, 1990–94. *Career:* Own groups, with Jimmy Cobb, Niels-Henning Orsted Pedersen, Billy Hart, Mads Vinding, Alex Riel, Jukkis Outila, Thomas Clausen and John Abercrombie, 1986–91; Concerts in Canada, USA, France, Italy, Sweden, Germany, Norway and India; Television and radio broadcasts in Europe and USA; Featured soloist with Jimmy Cobb Sextet, Hermeto Pascoal Group, European Youth Big Band and European Broadcasting Union Big Band; Also played with Holmes Brothers and various Danish bands such as Sound of Choice Ensemble, with Markus Stockhausen; Played with leading artists including: Lee Konitz, Jimmy Cobb, Adam Nussbaum, Art Blakey, Roy Haynes and David Liebman; Member, Den 3 Vej (composer workshop group); Leader, 18-piece group The Orchestra Big Band, 1997–98; Beijing Music Festival, 1998. *Compositions:* Works for small jazz groups, symphony orchestra, chamber orchestra, string quartet, big band and choir. *Recordings include:* Copenhagen Groove, with Niels-Henning Orsted Pedersen, 1989; Pyramid, 1993; Cross Current, 1995; Circles, 1996; Colours, with John Abercrombie, 1997; Kaleidoscope, Nazos/Jazz, 1998; Centrifugal, 2001. *Honours:* Hon. prize from Danish Jazz Beat and Folk Authors Society (DJBFA); Grammy Award, Best Danish Jazz Release, 2000; Danish Jazzmedia (JASA) Award, 2000. *Address:* Valdemarsgade 11, 1 tn, 1665 Copenhagen V, Denmark. *Website:* www.larsmoller.com.

MOLLISON, Deborah; b. 29 May 1958, England. Composer; Musician (piano). m. Gareth Mollison, 3 May 1986. *Education:* Piano and Composition, Royal Academy of Music; Master's degree, studied piano with Craig Sheppard, Lancaster University; Film Music course at UCLA; Classical composer; Tutor of Composition, Middlesex University. *Compositions:* Music for films: Stand Up The Real Glynn Vernon; Go On Make A Wish; Vampires; Television drama, The Gift of the Nile, Primetime TV; Sleeping With Mickey, BBC2; Before Your Eyes, BBC Wales; The Whistling Boy, BBC Wales; Television documentaries: Treasures At The South Pole, NBC; Thomas Cook On The Nile, Case TV; Connections 2, Discovery Channel; Given Half A Chance, Vanson Wardle Productions; Crossrail, London Transport Authority. *Honours:* Else Cross Prize, Royal Academy of Music; Song '92 UK Festival. *Membership:* PRS; BAC&S; Women In Film; Musicians' Union. *Current Management:* Soundtrack Music Management, 22 Ives St, Chelsea, London SW3 2ND, England.

MOLLOY, Matt; b. 12 Jan. 1947, Ballaghadareen Co. Roscommon, Ireland. Musician (flute, tin whistle). *Education:* Began studying flute, aged 8. *Career:* Mem., Bothy Band, c. 1974; Planxty, c. 1978; The Chieftains, 1979–; Collaborations: Paul Brady; Micheal O Suilleabhain; Donal Lunny; Irish

Chamber Orchestra; Publican in Westport. *Recordings:* with The Bothy Band: The First Album, 1975, Old Hag You Have Killed Me, 1976; with Planxty: After The Break, 1979, The Woman I Loved So Well, 1980; Solo: Matt Molloy (featuring Donal Lunny), 1976; The Heathery Breeze, 1981; The Gathering, 1981; Contentment Is Wealth (with Sean Keane), 1985; Stony Steps, 1988; The Fire Aflame (with Liam O Flynn and Sean Keane), 1992; Music At Matt Molloy's, 1992; Voyager (with Mike Oldfield), A Irmandade Das Estrellas (with Carlos Nunez), 1996; Shadows On Stone (featuring Steve Cooney, Christy Moore and Frankie Gavin), 1997; with The Chieftains: Water From The Well; Santiago; The Long Black Veil; Down The Old Plank Road: The Nashville Sessions, 2002; The Wide World Over: A 40 Year Celebration, 2002. *Honours:* All Ireland Flute championship, winner; TG4 National Traditional Award, 1999; with The Chieftains: Grammy Awards, Best Contemporary Traditional Album, for An Irish Evening – Live At The Grand Opera House, 1991, Best Traditonal Album, for Another Country, 1992, Best World Music Album, for Santiago, 1997. *Address:* c/o RCA Victor Group, 1540 Roadway, New York, NY 10036, USA. *Website:* www.irish.com.

MOLONEY, Paddy; b. 1938, Donnycarney, Dublin, Ireland. Folk Musician (uillean pipes, tin whistle). *Career:* Mem., Ceolteoiri Chaulann Folk Orchestra, led by Sean O'Raida, 1950s; Founder mem., Irish folk group, The Chieftains, 1964–; Collaborations with classical flute player, James Galway; Founding partner and exec. prod., Wicklow Entertainment, 1997–; Exec. prod. for: The Long Journey Home, 1998; Fire In The Kitchen, 1998; Imaginary Cuba, 1999; The Message, 1999; Wingspan, 1999. *Recordings:* Albums: Chieftains 1, 1964; Chieftains 2, 1969; Chieftains 3, 1971; Chieftains 4, 1973; Chieftains 5, 1975; Women Of Ireland, 1976; Bonaparte's Retreat, 1976; Chieftains Live, 1977; Chieftains 7, 1977; Chieftains 8, 1978; Chieftains 9, 1979; Boil The Breakfast Early, 1980; Chieftains 10, 1981; The Chieftains In China, 1984; Ballad Of The Irish Horse, 1985; Celtic Wedding, 1987; The Chieftains In Ireland (with James Galway), 1987; Year Of The French, 1988; Irish Heartbeat (with Van Morrison), 1988; A Chieftains Celebration, 1989; Chieftains Collection, 1989; The Celtic Connection – James Galway And The Chieftains, 1990; Bells Of Dublin, 1991; An Irish Evening, 1992; Another Country, 1992; The Celtic Harp (with Belfast Harp Orchestra), 1993; The Fire Aflame (with Sean Keane, Matt Molloy, Liam O'Flynn), 1993; Water From The Well; The Long Black Veil, 1995; Santiago, 1996; Tears of Stone, 1999; Down The Old Plank Road: The Nashville Sessions, 2002; The Wide World Over: A 40 Year Celebration, 2002. *Honours:* DMus, Trinity College, 1988; Hon. Chief of the Oklahoma Choctaw Nation, 1995; Six Grammy Awards. *Current Management:* S L Feldman and Assocs, 1505 W Second St, Suite 200, Vancouver, BC V6H 3Y4, Canada. *Address:* c/o RCA Victor Group, 1540 Roadway, New York, NY 10036, USA. *Website:* www.irish.com.

MOMCHIL; b. Bulgaria. Musician (keyboards); Vocalist; Songwriter; Arranger. *Career:* Keyboard player, new wave band Class, until 1993; Formed duo, Dony and Monchil, 1993–; Numerous tours, Bulgaria. *Recordings:* Albums: The Album!, 1993; The Second One, 1994. *Honours:* Orpheus National Music Awards: Best Single: The Little Prince; Best Video For Duo Or A Group. *Address:* c/o Union Media, 71 Evl Georgiev Blvd, Sofia 1142, Bulgaria.

MONAGHAN, Brendan; b. 3 April 1958, Newtownards, Co Down, Northern Ireland. Vocalist; Songwriter; Musician (guitar). m. Valerie McDonnell, 6 Sept. 1980, 2 s., 1 d. *Career:* Appearances with band The Cattle Company include major country festivals, Europe; Television and radio appearances, Ireland, Europe; USA; Cable television includes: Canada, USA; Solo appearances: Fiddler's Green International Festival, Co Down; Vlaardingen International Folk Festival, Netherlands, 2003; Music of the Rivers Festival, Florida. *Compositions:* I'm Right, You're Wrong, I Win. *Recordings:* with Cattle Company: Hero (debut album); Love to Be Loved; Big Town After Dark, 2000; Featured on album Alive In Belfast; Solo: Sister's Lament; Johnny Got Married; Precious Time, 2003; Single: Let Me In, 1999. *Honours:* Top Performance Award, International Country Music Festival, Netherlands; Publishers Award, Ray Shepherd Music, Efforts In Country Music; European Country Music Asscns, Best European Group, 1995; Audio Images 2000, 1997; Best Album, North America CMA International Awards, 1999; Best International Songwriter, North America CMA International Awards, 1999. *Membership:* PRS; International Songwriters Asscn; BMI, USA; United Song Makers. *Address:* 9 Stratford Dr., Bangor, Co Down BT19 6ZW, Northern Ireland. *Telephone:* (2891) 459350. *E-mail:* brendanmonaghan@ btopenworld.com. *Website:* www.brendanmonaghan.com.

MONDESIR, Michael Trevor Collins; b. 6 Feb. 1966, London, England. Musician (bass guitar); Composer. *Career:* Performed with Django Bates; Billy Cobham; Hermeto Pascoal; Pee Wee Ellis; Lenny White; Neneh Cherry; Jason Rebello; Annette Peacock; Bernard Purdie; Little Axe; Tackhead; Infinitum; Nikki Yeoh. *Recordings:* Keeping Time, Jason Rebello, 1992; Summer Fruits (and Unrest), Django Bates, 1993; The Traveller, Billy Cobham, 1994; Winter Truce (and Homes Blaze), Django Bates, 1995; Worotan, Oumou Sangare, 1996; Quiet Nights, Django Bates, 1998; Like Life, Django Bates, 1998. *Membership:* PRS; Musicians' Union. *Address:* 97A Hamlets Way, London E3 4TL, England.

MONDLOCK, Buddy (Robert); b. Chicago, USA. Vocalist; Musician (guitar); Songwriter. *Career:* Has had songs recorded by: Garth Brooks; Joan Baez; Nanci Griffith; Janis Ian; David Wilcox; Maura O'Connell; Peter Paul and Mary; Performed on Chicago club scene, 1980s; Moved to Nashville after securing publishing contract with EMI, mid-1980s; Appeared on Garth Brooks album No Fences, 1990; Co-wrote Tenderness with Janis Ian and played on her Revenge album, on which song appears, 1995; Nanci Griffith recorded Coming Down In The Rain on Grammy Award-winning Other Voices Other Rooms album; Peter Paul and Mary recorded The Kid on their Lifelines album. *Recordings:* On The Line, 1987; Buddy Mondlock, 1994; Poetic Justice, 1998; features on: No Fences, Garth Brooks, 1990; Revenge, Janis Ian, 1995; Around The Campfire, Peter Paul and Mary, 1998. *Honours:* Kerrville Folk Festival Award, 1987; Kerrville Music Award, Song of the Year, The Kid, 1996. *Current Management:* Bob Doyle and Associates, 1111 17th Ave S, Nashville, TN 37212, USA. *Website:* www.buddymondlock.com.

MONICA; b. 24 Oct. 1980, College Park, Atlanta, Georgia, USA. Vocalist; *Recordings:* Singles: Before You Walk Out of My Life, 1995; Why I Love You So Much, 1996; For You I Will, 1996; First Night, 1998; The Boy is Mine, with Brandy (No. 1, USA), 1998; Street Symphony, 1999; Inside, 1999; Angel of Mine, 1999; Albums: Miss Thang, 1995; The Boy is Mine, 1998.

MONK, Meredith Jane; b. 20 Nov. 1942, NY, USA. Composer; Choreographer; Dir; Vocalist; Filmmaker. *Education:* BA, Sarah Lawrence University, 1964; Honorary Doctorates, Bard College, 1988; University of the Arts, 1989; Juilliard School, 1998; S F Art Institute, 1999; Voice, Piano and Composition Study. *Career:* Creative Works Include, Vessel, 1971; Turtle Dreams, 1983; The Games, 1983; Book of Days, 1988; Facing North, 1990; Atlas, 1991; Three Heavens and Hells, 1992; Volcano Songs, 1994; American Archeology, 1994; The Politics of Quiet, 1996; Library of the Performing Arts Exhibition, Lincoln Center, 1996; Steppe Music, 1997; Magic Frequencies, 1997; Walker Art Center Exhibition, 1998. *Recordings:* Do You Be, 1987; Book of Days, 1990; Facing North, 1992; Atlas, An Opera In Three Parts, 1993; Monk and the Abbess, 1996; Volcano Songs, 1997. *Publications:* Art and Performance Meredith Monk, 1997. *Honours:* MacArthur Foundation Fellowship, 1995; Samuel Scripps Award, 1996; Sarah Lawrence Outstanding Allumma Award, 1996; Norton Stevens Fellow, 1993, 1994; Pentches Kritikev Preis for Best Record, 1981, 1986; Branders Creative Arts Award, 1974; Bessie Award for Sustained Achievement, 1985; National Music Theatre Award, 1986; Villager Award; Dance Magazine Award, 1993. *Membership:* ASCAP; American Music Center. *Current Management:* The House Foundation for the Arts Inc. *Address:* 228 W Broadway, New York, NY 10013, USA.

MONLEY, Julie (Julianne Margaret); b. 1 March 1954, Denver, Colorado, USA. Musician; Vocalist. m. Frederic Desmoulin, 27 Feb. 1987, 2 d. *Education:* Private lessons classical jazz. *Career:* Jazz Valley Festival, MJC club Dunkerque; Radio and television: France Music; Live radio: Vous En Moi; Radio shows in Denver. *Honours:* Second Prize, Tremplin Jazz, 1995; First Prize, Vocalist Jazz à Vienne, 1996. *Membership:* Jazz On The Blocks, Paris. *Address:* 69 Blvd Barbes, 75018 Paris, France.

MONRAD, Jan; b. 18 March 1951, Copenhagen, Denmark. Writer; Composer; Comedian. 1 s., 1 d. *Education:* Teachers' Seminarium. *Career:* Member of band Monrad and Rislund, with Saren Rislund; Several radio and television shows since 1977; Tours of Denmark and Greenland. *Compositions:* The Championship in Teddybear-Petting, 1993; The Statesman's Funeral, 1994. *Recordings:* 16 albums with Monrad and Rislund, 1976–; 1991, 1981; Jesus and Jens Vejmand, 1983; Dogstars Hospitalized, 1990; Goodbye Aage, 1994; 18 recordings and 1 video, 1976–. *Publications:* Black Sketches; Beske Barske Rimom Barn og Andre Kendisser. *Honours:* Danish Grammy Award, Entertainment Records, 1995. *Membership:* DJBFA; Dansk Solistforbund. *Address:* Toftojevej 27 B, 2720 Vanlose, Denmark.

MONTANARO, Miquieù (Michel François); b. 13 Aug. 1955, Hyères, France. Composer; Musician (flutes, saxophone, accordion, piano); Actor. m. Niké Nagy, 29 April 1981, 2 s., 1 d. *Education:* Teaching diploma, MA, Folk music. *Career:* First concert, Edinburgh, 1973; Tours, Hungary; Bulgaria; Austria; Italy; Portugal; USA; Indonesia; Algeria; Morocco; Tunisia; West Africa; Television: Hungary; Portugal; France (France 3, Cercle de Minuit, France 2); Radio: France Inter; France Culture; France Musique; Festivals include: Bamako; St Chartier; Nantes; Budapest; Comboscuro; Plays with: B Phillips; Kiss Tamàs; Konomba Traore; A Vitous; P Aledo; G Murphy; Téka; F Frith; Vujicsics; C Tyler; Sebastyén Màrta; P Neveu; Ghymes; F Richard; J Stivin; C Brazier; D Daumas; F Kop; D Regef; C Zagaria; K Ruzicka; Szabados; F Ulihr; P Vaillant; A Gabriel; J Lyonn Lieberman; L Andrst; J N Mabelly; D Phillips; Es Soundoussia; F Gaudé; S Pesce; Hayet Ayad; Christine Wodrascka; Samia Benchikh; Senem Diyici; René Sette; Mathieu Luzi; Nena Venetsanou; Sara Alexander; Michel Bianco; Carlo Rizzo; Corou de Berra; Wayal. *Compositions:* Cri, for symphonic orchestra and traditional instruments, 1997. *Recordings:* More than 40 include: Albums: Montanaro/ Collage, Bonton, 1990; Mesura and Arte del Danzare, 1992; Tenson – La Nef Des Musiques, Bleu Regard, 1993; Vents d'Est/Migrations, 1993; Montanaro/ Théâtre, 1994; Galoubet-Tambourin, Musiques d'Hier Et Aujourdhui, 1995;

with L'Ensemble Méditerranéen P Aledo: Fusion; D'île En Ile; Tres Corpos Una Alma; Java Sapto Raharjo, 1997; Vents d'Est Ballade pour une Mer qui Chante, 1997; Maurin des Maures, 1999. *Publications:* Video K7 Noir and Blanc with Konomba Traore, CNDP, France. *Membership:* ADAMI; SPEDIDAM; SACEM; SFA. *Current Management:* Sylvie Bondier. *Address:* Grande Fontaine, 83570 Correns, France.

MONTE, Marisa; b. 1967, Rio de Janeiro, Brazil. Vocalist; Musician (piano); Songwriter. *Education:* Studied music theory (drums, piano) as a child; Studied opera in Rome, 1986. *Career:* Made stage debut in Veludo Azul, Rio de Janeiro, 1987; Solo shows in São Paulo, 1990; Signed with World Pacific and released live album; Subsequent albums released internationally bringing regular tours to USA, UK, Europe and throughout Latin America. *Compositions:* Beija Eu; Ainda Lembro; Eu Sei; Tudo Pela Metade; Mustapha; Na Estrada; De Mais Ninguem; Bem Leve; Equanto Isso; Amor (I Love You); Nao Va Embora; Nao E Facil; Tema De Amor; Abololo; Gentileza; Agua Tambem E Mar. *Recordings:* Marisa Monte Ao Vivo, 1990; Mais, 1991; Green Blue Yellow Rose and Charcoal, 1994; Barulhinho Bom, 1996; Memories Chronicles and Declarations of Love, 2000; Café Brasil, 2001. *Honours:* Latin Grammy Award, Best Contemporary Pop Album, Memorias Cronicas E Declaracoes De Amor, 2001. *Current Management:* Monte Criacao E Producao Ltda. *Website:* www.marisamonte.com.br.

MONTENEGRO, Oswaldo; b. 15 March 1956, Rio de Janeiro, Brazil. Composer; Vocalist; Author and Dir, Musicals; Musician (guitar, piano). 1 s. *Education:* Communication Course, University of Brazil; Music, University of Rio de Janeiro. *Career:* Tours, Brazil, 1979–; TV, radio appearances, concerts, Portugal, until 1992; Shows in New Jersey; Connecticut; Boston; Miami; Orlando; Mount Vernon; Author and director, musical plays including: Veja Você Brasilia, 1981; Cristal, 1982; A Dança Dos Signos, 1983–87; Os Memestréis, 1985; Aldeia Dos Ventos, 1986; Vale Encantado, 1993; Noturno, 1993; Mayâ, 1992. *Compositions include:* Bandolins; Lua e Flor; Condor; Seo e Bia; Furtuição; Estrelas; Voz da Tela. *Recordings:* Trilhas, 1978; Poeta Maldito, Moleque Vadio, 1979; Oswaldo Montenegro Ao Viva, 1980; Asa De Lux, 1981; A Dança Dos Signos, 1982; Cristal, 1983; Os Menestréis, 1984; Drops De Hortelâ, 1985; Aldeia Dos Ventos, 1986; Oswaldo Montenegro, 1989; Ao Viva, 1990; Vida de Artista, 1991; Mulungo, 1992; Seu Francisco, 1993; Aos Filhos Dos Hippies, 1995. *Honours:* Third place of honour, with composition, Bandolins, TV Tupi Music Festival, 1979; First place of honour, with Agonia, TV Globo Brazilian Popular Music Festival, 1980; Gold Disc, Oswaldo Montenegro, 1989; Platinum disc, Visda de Artista, 1991. *Membership:* UBC; SBAT; Warner-Chappell. *Current Management:* Newton Montenegro. *Address:* R Viscondede Pirajá 51, ap 502, Ipanema, Rio de Janeiro, RJ, Brazil.

MONTGOMERY, John Michael; b. 20 Jan. 1965. Country vocalist; Musician (guitar); Songwriter. *Career:* Began performing on parents' country music shows, aged 5; Performed with local country bands, aged 15; Subsequently played with father Harold and brother Eddie (later of Montgomery Gentry country duo); Played the Austin City Saloon in Lexington, Kentucky, developing local following; Signed to Atlantic Records, 1992; Continued to have hits on both pop and country charts; 1993 pop and country hit I Swear reached No. 1 in US pop chart the following year in a recording by pop/R&B act All-4-One; Song subsequently became a favourite at wedding ceremonies. *Compositions include:* I Miss You A Little. *Recordings include:* I Swear, 1993; Sold (The Grundy County Auction Incident), 1995; I Can Love You Like That, 1995; I Love The Way You Love Me, 1993; Be My Baby Tonight, 1994; If You've Got Love, 1994. *Honours:* various including: CMA, Horizon Award, 1994; AMA Country Category, Favorite Newcomer, 1994; ACM: New Artist of the Year, Single of the Year, I Swear, 1994. *Address:* c/o Hallmark Direction Services, 1819, Broadway, Nashville, TN 37203, USA.

MONTREDON, Jean-Claude Pierre; b. 23 Sept. 1949, Martinique. Musician (drums); Composer. *Career:* Member, Frères Bernard Orchestra, Tropicana Orchestra; Drums for Marius Cultier and The Surfs; Formed trio with Alain Jean Marie, Winston Berkley; Performances in Barbados, Trinidad, 1972; Bilboquet, Paris jazz club, French Radio, 1973–75; Founder, Kominkayson, with Richard Raux, Michel Alibo, 1976; Appearances include: Palais de Congrès, Paris; Cultural Center, Martinique, 1976; Played with Didier Levellet Quintet, Chris McGregor, New Morning Jazz Club, Paris, 1977–; Rock concerts with Randy Weston, Claude Sommier, Michel Alibo, 1978–81; Tours, Finland, Sweden, West Africa, with Roland Brival, 1981; Played with Liquid Rock Stonne, Paris; Appearances include France Musique, classical radio station; Sermac Dance Workshop, Martinique, 1983; Jazz Festival, Barbados; Jazz and Folk Festival, Martinique, 1985; Caribbean Jazz Workshop, Berlin; Festival of Trinidad, 1986; Barbados Festival, with West Indies Jazz Band; Caribbean Jazz Workshop, 1987; Olympia, Paris, 1988; Tours, West Indies, South Africa, 1989; Founder, The Musical Corps of Martinique, 1990–94; Performs with own band Kominikayson, works with Luther François. *Recordings:* Malavoi, Tropicana Orchestre; Gisèle Baka; Al Lirvart and Didier Levallet Quintet; Brotherhood of Breath; Joby Bernabe; Doudou Guirand; 2 albums with The Caribbean Ensemble; West Indies Jazz

Band, 1990; 1992; Luther François, 1990. *Membership:* SACEM; SPEDIDAM; Congés Spectacle. *Address:* 131 rue de Rome, 75017 Paris, France.

MOODY, James; b. 26 March 1925, Savannah, GA, USA. Musician (Tenor, Alto, Soprano, Saxophone, Flute). m. Linda Petersen Moody, 3 April 1989. *Education:* US Air Force Band Theory, Composition with Dizzy Gillespie, Composition and Theory with Tom McIntosh with Michael Longo. *Career:* Teachings: Cornell University, Ithaca, New York; Harvard University, Cambridge, Massachusetts; Howard University, Washington, DC; Loyola University, New Orleans, Louisiana; Stanford University, Palo Alto, California; University of Alabama; University of Florida, Gainesville, Florida; Major Performances include: Dizzy Gillespie's 70th Birthday Celebration, televised; Requently appeared in USA, Egypt, Japan, Israel, Canada, Germany including Johnny Carson's Tonight Show and The Ben Sidran Show in New York; Carneo role, Clint Eastwood's film, Midnight in The Garden of Good and Evil; Radio: Voice of America, hosted by Willis Conover, numerous times; Interviews and concerts on many stations in USA and most European countries. *Compositions:* Moody's Mood for Love; Honey's Tune, with Linda Moody; Look Into My Eyes; It's a One-Way Road; Love, Where Are You?; Never Again; Simplicity and Beauty; The Television Song; You Better Believe It; Everyone Needs It; Coffee Break; He Whispered He Loved Her; Feelin' Low; Love Was the Cause; Put Your Shoes on Baby; I Saw a Flying Saucer; Hey Herbi; Where's Alpert?; Don't Throw Your Back Out-a Whack; Diskomblu-ba-late Me, Baby; What Do You Do; Moody's Theme; Shake, Rattle and Boogie. *Recordings:* Moody's Mood for Love, 1951; Last Train from Overbrook, 1958; Sweet and Lovely, 1989; Honey, 1991; Live at the Blue Note, 1995; Young at Heart, 1996; Moody Plays Mancini, 1997; Flute 'N the Blues, Chess; Never Again, Muse; Cookin the Blues, Cadet; Hey – Its James Moody, Argo; Compilations include: 1948–1949, 2000; 1949–1950, 2001. *Publications include:* Jazz Giants: A Visual Retrospective; The Eye of Jazz; Jazz is by Nat Hentoff; Jazz Styles: History and Analysis by Mark C Gridley; The Jazz Years: Earwitness to an Era by Leonard Feather; The Record Collector's Handbook by Alan Leibowitz. *Honours:* James Moody Day, 1993; 1996; Jamaica Hall of Fame, 1996; New Jersey Hall of Fame, 1996; International Hall of Fame, 1996; National Endowment for the Arts Jazz Masters Award, 1998. *Membership:* National Asscn of Recording Arts and Sciences, International Asscn of Jazz Educators; National Jazz Service Organization. *Address:* 36 Como St, Romford, Essex RM7 7DR, England.

MOOG, Robert Arthur; b. 23 May 1934, Flushing, New York, USA. Music Co Exec; Musical Instrument Designer. m. Shirley Leigh, 15 June 1958, 1 s., 3 d. *Education:* BS Physics, Queens College, 1957; BSEE, Columbia University, 1957; PhD Engineering Physics, Cornell University, 1965. *Career:* President, Moog Music Inc, 1954–77; President, Big Briar Inc, 1978; Vice-President, new product research, Kurzweil Music Systems, 1984–88; Designer, synthisizers, including Moog synthesizer, 1967; Mini-Moog, 1971; Polymoog, 1976; Pedal-operated Taurus system; Memory Moog; Exponents include: Walter Carlos; Keith Emerson; Jan Hammer; Rush. *Publications:* Contributor, professional journals. *Honours:* Hon. doctorates, Lycoming College, 1975; New York Polytechnic University, 1985; NARAS Trustees Award; Trendsetter Award, Billboard Magazine, 1970; Silver Medal, Audio Engineering Society, 1984; Fellow, Audio Engineering Society.

MOONEY, Gordon James; b. 27 May 1951, Edinburgh, Scotland. Piper; Musician; Planner; Businessman. m. 17 Apr. 1978, 1 s., 1 d. *Education:* BSc Town Planning, Dundee University; Highland bagpipes, border pipes, Northumbrian smallpipes from age 7. *Career:* Concerts include: Edinburgh International Festival; Sanders Tagare, Harvard, Boston; Old Songs Festival, USA; Tacoma University, USA; Québec Double Reed Convention; Vermont Bagpipe Festival; Television and radio appearances: Border TV; Canadian National Radio; BBC; Radio Scotland; Radio 4; World Service. *Recordings:* O'er The Border; Global Meditation; Song For Yarrow; Leading Figure, Scottish Music Revival. *Publications:* 3 collections of music; 1 tutor book. *Honours:* Scottish Arts Council Award, 1988; Billboard Award, 1993. *Membership:* MPRS; President of Lowland and Border Pipes Society. *Current Management:* Traditional music.

MOONEY, Tim; b. 6 Oct. 1958, Las Vegas, Nevada, USA. Musician (drums, keyboards, guitar); Songwriter. *Career:* Member of groups: Sleepers, 1977–79; Negative Trend, 1979–81; Toiling Midgets, 1982–92; American Music Club, 1992–95; Toured with Pearl Jam and Bob Dylan; Various BBC television appearances; Appeared at Reading and Glastonbury festivals. *Recordings:* with Sleepers: Seventh World, 1978; with Negative Trend: Beach Boulevard, Tooth and Nail, 1979; with Toiling Midgets: Sea of Unrest, 1982; Deadbeat, 1984; Son, 1992; with American Music Club: Mercury, 1993, San Francisco, 1994; with Li'l Tiger: Live, Work, Know, Growl, 1998; Session work includes: Once In A Blue Moon, Penelope Houston, 2000; Hurting Business, Chuck Prophet, 2000; Living And Forgetting, Glasstown, 2001. *Current Management:* Bennett Management, 549 14th Ave, San Francisco, CA 94118, USA.

MOORE, Abra; b. 8 June, Mission Bay, CA, USA. Vocalist; Songwriter; Musician (guitar). *Education:* University of Hawaii. *Career:* Founding Member, Poi Dog Pondering, Solo Artist, toured with Matthew Sweet,

Barenaked Ladies; Medeski, Martin and Wood, Third Eye Blind, Collective Soul, Lilith Fair and Big Head Todd and the Monsters; Session work includes: Rob Halverson; Appeared in feature films, Slacker and The Newton Boys; Sliding Doors, 1998; TV appearances on VH-1, E!, VH-1 (UK), CNN Showbiz Today; Live with Regis and Kathy Lee, Fox Live; Appearances on MTI and Westwood One Syndicated Radio. *Recordings:* Solo albums: Sing, 1995; Strangest Places, 1997; Singles: Four Leaf Clover, 1997; Don't Feel Like Cryin, 1997. *Contributions to:* national and international music magazines, newspapers and journals. *Membership:* AFTRA. *Current Management:* Tim Neece Management, 13101 Hwy 71 W, Austin, TX 78736, USA. *Address:* 13101 Hwy 71 W, Austin, TX 78736, USA.

MOORE, Alicia. See: PINK.

MOORE, Angelo (Christopher); b. 5 Nov. 1965, USA. Vocalist. *Career:* Member, Fishbone; Collaborations with rap artistes such as the Jungle Brothers; Numerous live appearances, including Lollapalooza in 1993. *Recordings:* Singles: Sunless Saturday, 1991; Everyday Sunshine, 1991; It's A Wonderful Life (Gonna Have A Good Time); Bonin' in the Boneyard EP; Albums: Fishbone, 1985; In Your Face, 1986; Truth and Soul, 1988; The Reality of our Surroundings, 1991; Give a Monkey a Brain and He'll..., 1993; Fishbone 101: Nuttasurusmeg, 1996; Chim Chim's Badass Revenge, 1996; Is Dr Madd Vibe: The Ying Yang Thang, 2000; Dr. Madd Vibe's Comprehensive Linkology, 2001.

MOORE, Bob Loyce; b. 30 Nov. 1932, Nashville, Tennessee, USA. Musician (bass); Record Prod. *Career:* Bassist for various artists including: Little Jimmy Dickens, 1949; Red Foley, 1950; Owen Bradley, 1951–66; Elvis Presley, 1963–71; Crystal Gayle, 1982–84; Co-owner, Monument Records, 1961–70; Record producer for Jerry Lee Lewis; George Jones; Johnny Cash; Boxcar Willie; Roy Orbison; President, K & K Productions, 1986–; President, Bob Moore Music, 1963–; Prolific studio musician, over 17,000 recording sessions for artists including: Kenny Rogers; Tammy Wynette; Don McLean; Hank Williams Jr; Tom Jones; Willie Nelson; Dolly Parton; Patsy Cline; Jim Reeves; Frank Sinatra; Simon and Garfunkel; Johnny Cash; Roy Orbison; Conway Twitty; Loretta Lynn; Brenda Lee; Ernest Tubb; Andy Williams; Connie Francis; The Statler Brothers; Clyde McFatter; Marty Robbins; Eddy Arnold; Kitty Wells; Solo recordings: This Our Joy And This Our Feast, 2000; Let Every Instrument Be Tuned For Praise, 2001. *Honours:* NARAS, Most Valuable Player Awards, 1979–82; Most Recording Session in History; AFofM; Numerous Superpicker Awards. *Membership:* AFofM; NARAS.

MOORE, Christy; b. 7 May 1945, Dublin, Ireland. Vocalist; Songwriter; Musician (guitar). *Career:* Solo folk performer, club circuit, Ireland and England, 1960s; Recording artiste, 1969–; Founder member, Planxty, 1969–75, 1979–80; Involved in Anti-Nuclear Roadshow, mid 1970s; Founder, Moving Hearts, 1981; Solo artiste, 1982–. *Recordings:* Albums: Paddy On The Road (with Dominc Behan), 1969; Prosperous, 1971; Whatever Tickles Your Fancy, 1975; Christy Moore, 1976; The Iron Behind The Velvet, 1978; Live In Dublin, 1978; The Spirit of Freedom, 1983; The Time Has Come, 1983; Ride On, 1984; Ordinary Man, 1985; Nice 'N' Easy, 1986; Unfinished Revolution, 1987; Voyage, 1989; Smoke and Strong Whiskey, 1991; The Christy Moore Collection, 1991; Live At The Point, 1994; Graffiti Tongue, 1996; Traveller, 1999; At The Point (Live), 2001; This Is The Day, 2001; with Planxty: After The Break, 1979; Woman I Loved So Well, 1980. *Current Management:* Mattie Fox Management, Derynell, Ballinlee, Co Longford, Ireland.

MOORE, Gary; b. 4 April 1952, Belfast, Northern Ireland. Musician (guitar). *Career:* Formed Skid Row, 1968; Formed Gary Moore Band, 1973; Guitarist with Thin Lizzy, 1974, 1977–79; Member, Colosseum II, 1975, 1977; Formed G-Force, 1979; Solo career, 1982–; Worked with various artists including: Phil Lynott; Ozzy Osbourne; Albert Collins; Albert King; B. B. King. *Recordings:* Singles include: Parisienne Walkways; Over The Hills and Far Away; Cold Day In Hell; Albums: with Skid Row: Skid Row, 1970; 34 Hours, 1971; with Gary Moore Band: Grinding Stone, 1973; with Thin Lizzy: Night Life, 1974; Black Rose, 1978; with Colosseum II: Strange New Flesh, 1975; Electric Savage, 1975; Wardance, 1977; with G-Force: G-Force, 1980; Solo: Back On The Streets, 1978; Corridors of Power, 1982; Victims of The Future, 1984; We Want Moore!, 1984; Run For Cover, 1985; Rockin' Every Night, 1986; Wild Frontier, 1987; After The War, 1989; Still Got The Blues, 1990; After Hours, 1992; Blues For Greeny, 1995; Desperado, 1997; Dark Days in Paradise, 1997; A Different Beat, 1999; Back To The Blues, 2001; Scars, 2002; Contributor, Tribute to Muddy Waters, 1993; Hit singles include: Parisienne Walkways, 1979; Empty Rooms, 1984; Out In The Fields, with Phil Lynott, 1985; Over The Hills And Far Away, 1986; Friday On My Mind, 1987; Still Got The Blues, 1990; Cold Day In Hell, 1992. *Current Management:* Part Rock Management, 53 Kings Rd, Suite 318, London SW10 0SZ, England.

MOORE, John Arlington; b. 5 Oct. 1938, Kingston, Jamaica. Musician (trumpet, piano); Entertainer. 3 s., 1 d. *Education:* Alpha, Jamaica Military Band; Berklee School, Boston, USA. *Career:* Played with Alpha Boy's Band; J M Band; Mapltoff Poole Band; Thaskatalites; Super Sonics; First tour, with Soul Vendors, England, 1967; with Super Sonic, 1969; Travelling world with Solomic Reggerstra. *Compositions:* Schooling The Duke; Something Special;

Tear Up; Ringo; Swing Easy; Rockfoot Rock; Sweet Sugar Candy; Somewhere In time; Where's The Love. *Recordings:* Album: Something Special; Single: Kibir La Dims. *Membership:* Jamaican Federation of Musicians; PRS. *Current Management:* Solomic Productions. *Address:* 173 Windward Rd Kingston 2, Jamaica.

MOORE, LeRoi; b. 7 Sept. 1961, Durham, North Carolina, USA, Musician (saxophone). *Education:* Classically trained; Studied tenor saxophone at James Madison University. *Career:* Member of high school bands; Spent ten years gigging in Charlottesville and Richmond, Virginia, with local jazz man John D'Earth prior to joining Dave Matthews Band, 1991; Rapid growth of fanbase through touring schedules; First album released on group's own Bama Rags label certified gold by RIAA; First national US tour in support of RCA debut album, 1994; Many world-wide concerts and festival appearances since including 2001 album tour; Group permits fans to tape-record shows for personal use; I Did It single officially released through Napster, 2001. *Recordings:* Albums: Remember Two Things (live), 1993; Under The Table and Dreaming, 1994; Crash, 1996; Live At Red Rocks 8–15–95, 1997; Before These Crowded Streets, 1998; Listener Supported (live), 1999; Everyday, Live In Chicago 12–19–98, 2001; Singles: Recently (EP), 1994; What Would You Say, Jimi Thing, Ants Marching, 1995; So Much To Say, Too Much, 1996; Don't Drink The Water, 1997; Satellite, Crash Into Me, Crush, 1998; I Did It, The Space Between, Everyday, 2001. *Honours:* Grammy Awards: Best Rock Performance By A Duo Or Group With Vocal, 1997; US VH-1 Awards: Favourite Group; Must Have Album; Song of the Year, 2001; Top-grossing touring band in USA, 2000. *Address:* c/o Red Light Communications, 3305 Lobban Pl., Charlottesville, VA 22903, USA. *E-mail:* info@rlc.net. *Website:* www.dmband.com.

MOORE, Malcolm Charles; b. 19 Jan. 1971, Chelmsford, Essex, England. Musician (bass guitar, double bassist); Vocalist; Songwriter. *Education:* City University, London; Guildhall School of Music. *Career:* Session bass player with Steve Martland, seen on Channel 4; BBC Symphony Orchestra; London Sinfonietta; London Philharmonic Orchestra; Tommy Chase Band; Tindersticks; Swordfish (Regular Radio 3 and Jazz FM); Elvis Costello; Spiritualized; Barry Adamson; Toured with: Westlife, A1, Girls Aloud, One True Voice; Performed in West End theatre productions: Rent, Fosse, The Lion King; Own group, themillionstars. *Recordings:* with Steve Martland: Crossing The Border; Patrol; Horses of Instruction; with Tindersticks: This Way Up; Horses of Instruction; with Swordfish: Living A Life; Frank and Walters, The Russian Ship; Lost Highway Soundtrack, Barry Adamson and David Lynch. *Membership:* Musicians' Union. *Current Management:* None. *Address:* 116 Skitts Hill, Braintree, Essex CM7 1AS, England. *E-mail:* mal@themillionstars.com.

MOORE, Mark; b. 1965 London, England. Prod; Remixer; DJ. *Career:* Began career as DJ at Phillip Sallon's Mud Club; Formed S-Express with Pascal Gabriel, 1988; Founder: Splish Records; Resident DJ at Chuff Chuff parties; Collaborations: William Orbit; Billie Ray Martin; Sonique; Remixed: Seal; Prince; Randy Crawford. *Recordings:* Albums: Original Soundtrack, 1990; Intercourse, 1991; Singles: Theme From S-Express, Superfly Guy, 1988; Hey Music Lover, Mantra For A State of Mind, 1989; Nothing To Lose, 1990; Find 'Em Fool 'Em Forget 'Em, 1992. *Current Management:* Ultra DJ Management, 29 City Business Centre, Lower Rd, London SE16 2XB, England.

MOORE, Nicky; b. 21 June 1952, Devon, England. Blues Vocalist; Musician (guitar, piano, harmonica). m. Maggie Moore, 5 Oct. 1974, 4 s., 1 d. *Education:* Exeter Cathedral/RSCM. *Career:* Rock bands: Hackensack; Tiger; Samson; Mammoth; Gerry Rafferty; Blues Corporation (current and future); Films: Hearts of Fire; Just Ask For Diamond; Numerous tours, television and radio appearances. *Recordings:* Tiger: Up The Hard Way; Going Down Laughing; Test of Time; Before The Storm; Mammoth: Don't Get Mad Get Even; I Just Got Back; Holding On; Samson Live In London, 2001; Numerous singles and videos. *Membership:* Musicians' Union. *Current Management:* Julia Ficken, Steppin' Out Ltd. *Address:* PO Box 216, Sevenoaks, Kent TN14 6ZQ, England.

MOORE, Sam; b. 12 Oct. 1935, Miami, Florida, USA. Vocalist; Entertainer. m. Joyce McRae, 26 March 1982. *Career:* Singer with Soul duo Sam and Dave; later solo artist; Television appearances include: (Solo) Best of Country; TNN Country News; Entertainment Tonight; Rhythm Country and Blues; Huey Lewis PBS Special; Roots of Country; In Concert Country; Music City Tonight; Good Morning America; Music City Today; Nashville Now; (as Sam and Dave) Ed Sullivan Show; Merv Griffin; Tonight Show; Hollywood Palace; Saturday Night Live; Midnight Special; Bandstand; Mike Douglas Show; Special appearances include: Host, The Pioneer Awards; The George Bush Rhythm and Blues Inaugural Gala; Rhythm Country and Blues, The Concert; Host, Miami Hard Rock Cafe Opening; Videos: Rainy Night In Georgia; Soul Man; Ordinary Man; Hey Joe; Films: One Trick Pony; Tapeheads; Tales of The City; Soul Man; Command performances for Queen Elizabeth II, England, and US President Jimmy Carter. *Recordings:* Hit singles include: Soul Man; Hold On I'm Coming; Soul Sister Brown Sugar; Rainy Night In Georgia, duet with Conway Twitty; I Thank You; Something Is Wrong With My Baby; Soothe Me; You Don't Know Like I Know; You Got Me Humming; Compilations include: Eleven Best, 2001; Soundtracks: White Men Can't

Jump; Soul Man; Tapeheads; Guest appearances on: Building The Perfect Beast, Don Henley; Human Touch, Bruce Springsteen; Soul Man, 1986; Great Outdoors, 1988; Conway Twitty Collection, 1994; Concert for the Rock and Roll Hall of Fame, 1996; Country Heartaches, 1997. *Honours:* Numerous Platinum and Gold records; Grammy, Soul Man, 1967; Rhythm and Blues Foundation Pioneer Award, 1991; Rock and Roll Hall of Fame Inductee, 1992. *Membership:* NARAS. *Current Management:* I'ma Da Wife Enterprises, Inc. *Address:* 7119 E Shea Blvd, Suite 109–436, Scottsdale, AZ 85254, USA.

MOORE, Sean; b. 30 July 1970, Pontypool, Gwent, Wales. Musician (Drums). *Career:* Member, Manic Street Preachers. *Recordings:* Singles: New Art Riot EP, 1990; You Love Us, 1991; Stay Beautiful, 1991; Love's Sweet Exile/Repeat, 1991; Slash N Burn, 1992; Motorcycle Emptiness, 1992; Theme From M.A.S.H., 1992; Little Baby Nothing, 1992; From Despair To Where, 1993; La Tristessa Durera, 1993; Roses In The Hospital, 1993; Life Becoming A Landslide, 1993; Faster/PCP, 1994; Revol, 1994; She Is Suffering, 1994; Everything Must Go, 1996; A Design for Life (No. 2, UK), 1996; Kevin Carter, 1996; Australia, 1996; If You Tolerate This Your Children Will Be Next (No. 1, UK), 1998; The Everlasting (No. 1, UK), 1998; You Stole The Sun From My Heart, 1999; Tsunami, 1999; Albums: Generation Terrorists, 1992; Gold Against The Soul, 1993; The Holy Bible, 1994; Everything Must Go, 1996; This Is My Truth, Tell My Yours, 1998; Know Your Enemy, 2001; Forever Delayed, 2002. *Honours:* BRIT Awards, Best British Group, 1997, 1999; Best British Album, 1997, 1999. *Address:* c/o Epic Records, 550 Madison Ave, New York, NY 10022-3211, USA. *Website:* www.manics.co.uk.

MOORE, Thurston; b. 25 July 1958, Coral Gables, FL, USA. Vocalist; Musician (guitar). m. Kim Gordon, 1 d. *Career:* Founder mem., US rock group, Sonic Youth, 1981–; Founding mem., Ciccone Youth, 1986–; Owner, record label, Ecstatic Peace!; Solo recording artiste, 1995–. *Recordings:* Albums: with Sonic Youth: Sonic Youth, 1981; Confusion Is Sex, 1983; Kill Yr Idols, 1983; Sonic Death: Early Sonic Youth 1981–83, 1984; Bad Moon Rising, 1985; E.V.O.L., 1986; Sister, 1987; Hold That Tiger, 1987; Daydream Nation, 1988; Goo, 1990; Dirty, 1992; Experimental Jet Set, Trash And No Star, 1994; Washing Machine, 1995; Just Leave Me, 1996; Piece For Jetsun Dolma, 1996; A Thousand Leaves, 1998; Root, 1999; Promise, 1999; NYC Ghosts & Flowers, 2000; Condo Painting: Life From A Different Angle, 2002; Murray Street, 2002; with Ciccone Youth: The Whitey Album, 1989; Solo: Psychic Hearts, 1995; Three Incredible Ideas, 2001; Other releases with Sonic Youth: Anagrama (syr1); Slaapkamers met Slagroom (syr2); Invito al Cielo (syr3); Goodbye 20th Century (syr4); Kim Gordon/Ikue Mori/DJ Olive (syr5); Contributed to film and television soundtracks: Pump Up The Volume, 1990; My So-Called Life, 1995; End Of Days, 1999; Singles include: Kool Thing, 1990; 100%, 1992; Youth Against Fascism, 1992; Sugar Kane, 1993; Bull In The Heather, 1994; Superstar, 1994; Sunday, 1998; Not Me, 1998. *Address:* c/o Gold Mountain Entertainment, Suite 450, 3575 Cahuenga Blvd W, Los Angeles, CA 90068, USA. *Website:* www.sonicyouth.com.

MOORE, Tim; b. 22 May 1958, Sussex, England. Musician (keyboard player); Composer; Prod. m. Venetia, 3 Jan. 1987, 2 s. *Education:* Piano since age 5, taught by father. *Career:* with Nik Kershaw: tours, television, videos; concerts include Live Aid, 1985, 1984–86; with Bee Gees: tours, recording, television includes Royal Variety Show, 1990–93; Tours with: Johnny Hallyday, 1994–95; Saga, 1988; East 17, 1995; Television appearances with Bros; Shakespears Sister. *Recordings:* Keyboards on albums with Nik Kershaw: The Riddle, 1984; Radio Musicola, 1986; Anthology, 1995; Keyboards/programming on albums with Bee Gees: High Civilization, 1991; Size Isn't Everything, 1993; Amy Fradon, Take Me Home, 1994; Other session work includes: Hall & Oates; Bonnie Raitt. *Membership:* Musicians' Union. *Current Management:* Debbie Haxton. *Address:* The Session Connection, 110–112 Disraeli Rd, Putney, London SW15, England.

MOORE, Vinnie; Rock Musician (guitar). *Education:* Jazz guitar. *Career:* Member, Vicious Rumours, 1985; Solo artiste, 1986–; Guitarist, Alice Cooper, Hey Stoopid tour, 1991. *Recordings:* Albums: with Vicious Rumours: Soldiers of The Night, 1985; Solo albums: Mind's Eye, 1986; Time Odyssey, 1988; Meltdown, 1991; Out of Nowhere, 1996; Maze, 1999; Live!, 2000; Defying Gravity, 2001. *Current Management:* Frank Solomon Management, PO Box 639, Natick, MA 01760, USA.

MORALES, David, (The Boss, Brooklyn Friends); b. 21 Aug. 1961, Brooklyn, New York, USA. Prod; Remixer; DJ. *Career:* Began DJ career at the Ozone Layer in New York and was guest at the legendary Paradise Garage club; Later resident at Better Days and Red Zone in New York; Member of the Def Mix production crew (alongside Frankie Knuckles and Satoshi Tomiie); In demand remixer since early '90s; Remixed: Mariah Carey, Jody Watley, U2, Jamiroquai, Luther Vandross, Incognito, Pet Shop Boys; Collaborations: Albert Cabrera, Juliet Roberts. *Recordings:* Singles: Congo (as The Boss), 1994; Philadelphia (as Brooklyn Friends), 1995; Needin' U, 1998; Needin' U II, 2001. *Current Management:* c/o Def Mix, 928 Broadway, Suite 400, New York, USA.

MORAN, Michael John; b. 18 July 1964, Birkenhead, England. Composer; Prod; Musician (electric guitar, keyboards); Programmer. *Education:* Diploma,

Light Music, Sandown College, Liverpool; BA, Popular Music and Recording, University College, Salford. *Career:* Mem., 16 Tambourines; Toured with: Squeeze; Hue and Cry; Wet Wet Wet; Tour Manager, 35 Summers tour with EMF; Manager, N-Trust (as Decent Exposure Management); Musical Dir, Jungle Book, Redgrave Theatre, Farnham; Sgt Pepper's Magical Mystery Trip, Liverpool Playhouse; Musical Dir, Rockin' Robin and the Babes, Halewood Pantomime Everyman Theatre, 1997–98. *Compositions:* Co-writer: It's Better To Love; Movies; Language of Love; Going Off Big Time (film music). *Recordings:* Album: How Green Is Your Valley, 16 Tambourines; As producer: Quiet Defiance, N-Trust; Singles: with 16 Tambourines: If I Should Stay; How Green Is Your Valley. *Membership:* PRS; Musicians' Union; MCPS. *Current Management:* Triple M Productions. *Address:* 31 Elmar Rd, Aigburth, Liverpool L17 0DA, England. *E-mail:* mike.moran@breathe.com.

MORAN, Mike; b. 4 March 1948, Leeds, Yorkshire, England. Composer; Musician (piano, clarinet). m. Lynda, 5 Sept. 1992, 1 d. *Education:* Royal College of Music. *Career:* Musician, arranger, record producer; As musician, arranger, worked with stars including: Paul McCartney; Stevie Wonder; Kate Bush; Paul Simon; Joe Cocker; George Harrison; Gladys Knight; Robert Plant; Cliff Richard; Carly Simon; Julio Iglesias; The Four Tops; Placido Domingo; Jose Carreras; Elvin Jones; Oliver Nelson; Leo Sayer; Lulu; Dusty Springfield; Kevin Ayers; Colin Blunstone; Chris de Burgh; Heart; Ozzy Osbourne; Chris Rea; Member of bands: Blue Mink; Stone The Crows; Gillan; Worked with Freddie Mercury; Took part in Wembley tribute to Freddie Mercury, 1994. *Compositions include:* Film music: Time Bandits; The Missionary; Water; Bloodbath At The House of Death; Whoops Apocalypse; The Bitch; Top Secret; Deathwish 3; Television music includes: Taggart, STV; Harry's Game, YTV; El CID, Granada; The Contract, YTV; Bookie, STV; Killer, STV; The Racing Game, YTV; The Krypton Factor, Granada; Love Story; The Kenny Everett Show, BBC; The Consultant, BBC; Print Out; Pop Quest, YTV; The Richard and Judy Show, Granada; Commercials include: TV Times; Kentucky Fried Chicken; Halifax Building Society; British Gas; Miss Selfridge; Co-writer, song on Innuendo album, Freddie Mercury; Collaborated on album Barcelona, with Freddie Mercury and Montserrat Caballe; More than 100 songs, recorded by: Freddie Mercury; Queen; George Harrison; Ian Gillan; Maggie Bell; Oliver Nelson; John Kongos; Extreme. *Honours:* Tric Best Music Award. *Membership:* Musicians' Union; PRS. *Current Management:* Triple M Productions.

MORAND, Roger; b. 30 Sept. 1958, Nogent sur Marne, France. Musician. 1 s., 1 d. *Education:* Music School, 6 years old; Classical Accordion; Professional 16 years old. *Career:* Television, MTV, Monte Carlo, FR3, A2, TF1, Arte, M6; Radio, BBC, Radio France, France Culture; Stage, Crawfish Festival, Ugly Day, Cajun Day, Feria de Nimes Jazzavienne, Festival Country, Mirande Nuit Cajun, Playing with Nathan Abshire, John Delafose, Dewey Balfa, Denis Mcgee, Marc Savoy, Corey Harris; Leader, Morand Cajun Band; Also plays Irish and Celtic accordion and music from the centre of France (Auvergne). *Recordings:* When I'm Up, 1993; Les Blues a Bébè, 1994; Nuit Cajun, 1995; Hey Ariba, 1997. *Contributions to:* musical journals and magazines. *Honours:* European Cup, Accordion. *Membership:* SACEM. *Address:* 3 Pl. du Doyen Gachon, 30610 Sauve, France.

MORELLO, Tom; b. 30 May 1964, New York, NY, USA. Musician (guitar). *Career:* Member of early band Lock Up; Mem., Rage Against the Machine, 1991–2000; Obtained major label deal; Support causes such as Fairness and Accuracy in Reporting, Rock for Choice and Refuse and Resist; Numerous tours incl. Lollapalooza; Tour with Wu Tang Clan; Collaboration with The Prodigy for soundtrack to film Spawn, 1997, and band contribution to soundtrack for Godzilla, 1998; Founder mem., Audioslave, 2002–. *Recordings:* Albums: with Rage Against the Machine: Rage Against The Machine, 1992; Evil Empire, 1996; The Battle Of Los Angeles, 1998; Renegades, 2000; Live And Rare, 2002; with Audioslave: Audioslave, 2002. Singles: with Rage Against the Machine: Killing In The Name, 1993; Bullet In The Head, 1993; Bombtrack, 1993; Freedom, 1994; Bombtrack Plus Live, 1994; Bulls On Parade, 1996; People Of The Sun (EP), 1997; Guerilla Radio, 1999; Sleep Now In The Fire, 2000; with Audioslave: Cochise, 2003. *Address:* c/o Epic Records, 550 Madison Ave, New York, NY 10022-3211, USA. *Website:* www.audioslave.com.

MORENO, Rita, (Rosa Dolores Alverio); b. Humacao, Puerto Rico. Actress; Vocalist; Entertainer. m. Leonard Gordon, 1 d. *Career:* Film, stage, television, concert performer, Films include: The King and I; West Side Story, 1962; Television: Starred in own TV series, sitcom version of 9 To 5; B L Stryker, 1989–90; The Top of The Heap, Fox Network series, 1991–92; Cosby Mystery Series, 1994; Performs concerts across USA with symphony orchestras for their Pops series; Performed at President Clinton's Inauguration, 1993; White House, 1993. *Recordings include:* Rita Moreno Sings; Warm, Wonderful and Wild; Shadow of a Bull; The Electric Company Album, 1972; Compilations include: Rita Moreno, 2000. *Honours:* Academy Award, West Side Story, 1962; The Golden Globe Award, Golden Apple, John Jefferson Award, Best Actress, Chicago's Theatrical Season, 1968; Grammy, The Electric Company Album, 1972; Tony, The Ritz (Broadway production), 1975; Emmys, The Muppet Show, 1977; Sarah Siddons Award, 1985; Star, Hollywood Walk of Fame, 1995. *Membership:* Presidents Committee on the

Arts and Humanities. *Current Management:* c/o Stan Scotland, JKE Services, 404 Park Ave S, 10th Floor, New York, NY 10016, USA. *Website:* www.ratm.com.

MORETTI, Fabrizio; b. 2 June 1980, Rio de Janeiro, Brazil. Musician (drums). *Education:* Dwight School, Manhattan. *Career:* Mem., The Strokes, 1998–. *Recordings:* Albums: Is This It, 2001. Singles: The Modern Age, 2001; Hard To Explain/New York City Cops, 2001; Last Nite/When It Started, 2001. *Honours:* NME Awards, Band of the Year, Best New Act, Album of the Year, 2001; BRIT Award, Best International Newcomer, 2002. *Current Management:* Ryan Gentles, Wiz Kid Management. *Address:* c/o RCA Records, 1540 Broadway, New York, NY 10036, USA. *Website:* www.thestrokes.com.

MORGAN, Charlie; b. 9 Aug. 1955, Hammersmith, London, England. Musician (drums, electronic percussion). m. Daniela Francesca James, 6 Oct. 1992, 1 d. *Education:* College de Genève; Piano lessons; Classes with James Blades. *Career:* Mostly freelance, 1973–84; Toured, recorded with Tom Robinson Band, 1979; 2 albums, tours with Judi Tzuke, 1980–81; Numerous recordings for Nik Kershaw, Tracey Ullman, Kate Bush; 14 month world tour, as drummer with Elton John, 1992–93; Tour with Elton John, Billy Joel, USA, 1994–95; Elton John World Tour, May 1995–. *Compositions:* Co-wrote television theme The Bill, ITV. *Recordings:* Edge of Heaven, Wham; 2 albums with Tracey Ullman; I Am The Phoenix, Judie Tzuke; Thunderdrome (Mad Max 2), Tina Turner; Iron Man, Pete Townshend; Oasis, Oasis; Out In The Fields, Gary Moore and Phil Lynott; Whose Side Are You On?, Matt Bianco; Rock and Roll Album, Johnny Logan; Human Racing, Nik Kerhsaw; Kane Gang album; Being There, Martyn Joseph; with Elton John: Live In Sydney (with the MSO); Made In England; Silver Bird, Justin Hayward; Go West, Go West; with Chris De Burgh: Spark To A Flame; This Way Up; Magic Ring, Clannad; Golden Days, Bucks Fizz; Theodore and Friends, The Adventures; Lionheart, Kate Bush; Cabaret (Live), Tom Robinson; Linda Thompson album, 1985; Nick Heyward album, 1985; Beverley Craven album tracks, 1991; Tasmin Archer album, 1992; The Glory of Gershwin, 1994; Plan 9, Cool Breeze, 2001. *Membership:* PRS; BAC&S; Musicians' Union.

MORGAN, Dennis William; b. 30 July 1952, Tracy, Minnesota, USA. Songwriter; Music Publisher. m. June Arnold, 27 July 1985. *Career:* Songwriter, Collins Music, 1969–73; Little Shop of Morgansongs, 1974–. *Compositions include:* Smoky Mountain Rain, Ronnie Milsap; I Wouldn't Have Missed It For The World, Ronnie Milsap; I Was Country When Country Wasn't Cool, Barbara Mandrell; I Knew You Were Waiting For Me, George Michael and Aretha Franklin; My Heart Can't Tell You Know, Rod Stewart; Jonny Lang, Lie to Me; Hank Thompson, Real Thing. *Honours:* Ivor Novello Award; 43 BMI Awards. *Membership:* CMA; Nashville Songwriters Asscn.

MORGAN, Edward Lee (Ed); b. 28 April 1941, Noel, Missouri, USA. Pres., Country Breeze Productions. m. Delores Arneta Shoemake, 1 s., 1 d. *Career:* Many No. 1 songs on independent charts in America; Songs published by other publishing companies. *Compositions include:* Shatter Me, recorded by several artists, played world-wide, 1987. *Publications:* Publishes monthly magazine: Midwest Newsbeat, for songwriters and artists. *Honours:* Golden Cross, for gospel label: Angel Star Records. *Membership:* BMI; Midwest Asscn of Music. *Address:* 1715 Marty, Kansas City, KS 66103, USA.

MORGAN, Huey (Hugh Angel Diaz); b. 8 Aug. 1968, Manhattan, NY, USA. Vocalist; Lyricist; Musician (guitar). *Career:* Founding mem., Fun Lovin' Criminals, 1993–; Numerous tours, festivals and television appearances. *Recordings:* Albums: Come Find Yourself, 1996; 100% Colombian, 1998; Mimosa – The Lounge Album, 1999; Loco, 2001; Bag Of Hits, 2002. Singles: The Grave And The Constant (EP), 1996; The Fun Lovin' Criminal, 1996; Scooby Snacks, 1996; King Of New York, 1997; I'm Not In Love, 1997; Love Unlimited, 1998; Big Night Out, 1998; Korean Bodega, 1999; Loco, 2001; Bump/Run Daddy Run, 2001. *Address:* c/o Chrysalis Group plc, The Chrysalis Bldg, Bramley Rd, London W10 6SP, England. *Website:* www.fun-lovin-criminals.co.uk.

MORGAN, Jeffrey; b. 20 March 1954, Spokane, WA, USA. Musician. *Education:* Liberal Arts, Music, Dance, Theatre, Philosophy of Aesthetics; Studied under Don Cherry, Karl Berger, Dumi Maraiere, Bert Wilson, Robert Gottlieb, Greg Steinke. *Career:* Concerts and festivals in Europe and USA; Experimental Theatre; Workshops for sound and installations. *Compositions:* Quasar-Mach, 1983; Snake Eyes, 1994; Near Vhana, 1997; Bitin Thru, 1997. *Recordings:* Albums: Quasar-Mach, 1983; Pokachevski Vol. I, 1990; Snake Eyes, 1994; Near Vhana, 1997; Bitin Thru, 1997; Dial: Log-Rhythms (with Keith Rowe), 1998; Ensemble Works 81/95, 1999; Electroshock, 1999; Quartz And Crow Feather, 2000; Sign Of The Raven, 2000; Magnetic Fields (with Bert Wilson), 2002; Dubbel Duo (with Peter Kowald), 2002. *Honours:* British Arts Council Performing Arts Grant, 1992. *Membership:* GEMA. *Address:* Lübecker Str 15, 50668 Cologne, Germany. *E-mail:* morgan@jeffreymorgan.net. *Website:* www.jeffreymorgan.net.

MORGAN, John Marshall; b. 3 May 1958, Clinton, Iowa, USA. Bandleader; Musician (saxophone); Composer; Teacher. m. Nancy Eichman, 15 March 1986, 2 s. *Education:* 3 Collegiate degrees, Masters; Drake University, Des Moines, Iowa, USA. *Career:* Sideman/arranger, The Russ Morgan Orchestra, The Don Hoy Orchestra; Leader, The John Morgan Band, 1984–; Saxophone guest artist with Drake Symphony Orchestra, Des Moines Municipal Band; Educator in Drake University Community School, 1986–; Des Moines School District, 1990–. *Publications:* The Instrumentalist Magazine. *Honours:* Drake Soloist Artist, 1981, 1987, WO1 Radio; Phi Kappa Lamda; Omicron Delta Kappa; Phi Mu Alpha. *Membership:* Macusa (National Asscn of Composers).

MORGAN, Loretta Lynn; b. 27 June 1959, Nashville, Tennessee, USA. Country Vocalist. 1 s., 1 d. *Career:* Two years touring with George Jones; Worked at Opryland, USA aged 18; Acting debut, Proudheart, Nashville Network film; Film, The Enemy Within, ABC; Television includes: Co-host, American Music Awards, 1995; CBS AM; The Ralph Emery Show; Entertainment Tonight; Late Night With David Letterman; 48 Hours; The Tonight Show; CBS 65 Years of The Grand Ole Opry; Austin City Limits; Hee Haw. *Recordings:* Albums: Leave The Light On, 1989; Something In Red, 1991; Classics, 1991; Watch Me, 1992; Trainwreck of Emotion, 1993; Merry Christmas From London, 1993; War Paint, 1994; Greatest Hits, 1995; Greater Need, 1996; Shakin' Things Up, 1997; Secret Love, 1998; Super Hits, 1998; The Essential, 1998; My Heart, 1999; Side By Side, 2000; I Finally Found Someone, 2001; Singles: We Both Walk, 1991; Back in Your Arms Again, 1995; I Didn't Know My Own Strength, 1995; Up on Santa Claus Mountain, 1995; By My Side, 1996; I Just Might Be, 1996; Go Away, 1997; I'm Not That Easy to Forget, 1998. *Honours:* CMA Awards, Vocal Event of the Year, with Keith Whitley, 1990; Album of the Year, Common Thread, 1994; TNN/Music City News Awards: Video Collaboration of the Year, with Keith Whitley, 1991; Female Artist of the Year, 1994; CMT: Female Vocalist of the Year, 1992. *Current Management:* Susan Nadler Management. *Address:* 1313 16th Ave S, Nashville, TN 37212, USA.

MORGAN, Tudur; b. 18 May 1958, Bangor, Gwynedd, Wales. Musician (acoustic guitar, bass, keyboards); Vocalist; Prod. m. Annwen Morgan, 18 Oct. 1986, 2 d. *Education:* Carmarthen Trinity College. *Career:* Television and radio appearances: Major television shows in Wales; BBC Pebble Mill; BBC Radio 2; Concerts throughout UK including London Albert Hall; Orkney Islands; Edinburgh Folk Festival and with Ronnie Drew of the Dubliners in Cardiff; Played with many top Welsh performers including Dafydd Iwan; Linda Healy; Plethyn; 4 Yn Y Bar; Mojo and Moniars; Iona ac Andy; John ac Alun; Tecwyn Ifan. *Recordings:* With numerous artists including: Branwen; Dafydd Iwan; Mojo; 4 Yn Y Bar; Linda Healy; Plethyn; Moniars and Dylan Parry; World Music album for Narada Media; Ellipsis Arts New York's Celtic Lullaby and World Music for Little Ears. *Membership:* MCPS; PRS; PRC; Musicians' Union. *Current Management:* Sblash. *Address:* c/o Sblash, Bryn Teg, 17, Brig y Nant, Llangefni, Ynys Mon, Gwynedd LL77 7EX, Wales. *E-mail:* TUDURM@aol.com.

MORGAN, Wayne; b. 15 Jan. 1970, Warrington, Cheshire, England. Musician (bass guitar). *Education:* 2 year foundation course. *Career:* Played in: Pele, 1993–; Supports include: Wet Wet Wet; Iggy Pop; Worked with major producers; Played bass, China Crisis tour. *Recordings:* 2 Pele albums, produced by Jon Heedy, Simon Vinestock; Various sessions include work for Gary Langan. *Membership:* Musicians' Union. *Current Management:* D L Management. *Address:* No. 3 Firshaw Rd, Meals, Wirral L47 5BD, England.

MORGANISTIC. See: **SLATER, Luke.**

MORILLO, Erick 'More'; b. 26 March 1971, New York, NY, USA. Prod; Remixer; DJ. *Education:* Center for Media Arts, Degree. *Career:* After a course in Technical Production and Engineering, released first single with reggae artist The General, 1992; Recorded for Strictly Rhythm label Reel 2 Real featuring The Mad Stuntman (Mark Quashie); Set up Subliminal Records, 1997; TV appearances include: MTV Europe's Most Wanted; Top of the Pops; The Big Breakfast; Numerous concerts and arena shows; Collaborations: Harry 'Choo Choo' Romero; Jose Nunez; Jocelyn Brown; Zig and Zag; Louie Vega; Remixed: Pete Heller; Madison Avenue; Whitney Houston. *Recordings:* Albums: Are You Ready For Some More (with Reel 2 Real), 1996; Albums: Live And More, 1996; The Subliminal Sessions Volume 1, 2001; Singles: with Reel 2 Real: The New Anthem, 1993; I Like To Move It, Go On Move, Can You Feel It, Raise Your Hands, 1994; Conway, 1995; Jazz It Up, Are You Ready For Some More, 1996; Come and Take A Trip (as Smooth Touch), 1994; Reach (with Lil' Mo Yin Yang), 1995; Fun (with Da Mob), 1998; Distortion (with Pianoheadz), 1998; Believe (with Ministers De La Funk), 1999. *Honours:* International Producer of the Year, Canada, 1994; Muzik Awards: Best Remixer (with Jose Nunez and Harry Romero), 1999; Best Ibiza Club, Subliminal Sessions at Pacha, 2001. *Current Management:* c/o Subliminal Records, 199 Hackensack Plank Rd, Weehawken, New Jersey, USA. *Address:* Positiva Records, 43 Brook St, London W6 7EF, England. *Website:* www.positivarecords.com.

MORISSETTE, Alanis; b. 1 June 1974, Ottawa, Canada. Vocalist; Songwriter. *Career:* Appeared in You Can't Do That (Canadian cable TV serial), aged 10; Signed contract as songwriter with MCA Publishing, aged 14; Solo recording artiste; Numerous concerts, festivals, television and radio appearances; Film appearance, Dogma, 1999. *Recordings:* Albums: Alanis,

1991; Now Is The Time, 1992; Jagged Little Pill (No. 1, UK and USA), 1995; Space Cakes (live), 1998; Supposed Former Infatuation Junkie, 1998; Alanis Unplugged (live), 1999; Under Rug Swept, 2002; Feast On Scraps: Inside Under Rug Swept, 2002. Singles: Fate Stay With Me; You Oughta Know, 1995; One Hand In My Pocket, 1995; Ironic, 1996; Head Over Feet, 1996; All I Really Want, 1996; Thank U, 1998; Joining You, 1999; So Pure, 1999; Vocal cameo on: Blowback, Tricky, 2001. *Honours:* BRIT Award, Best International Newcomer, 1996; Grammy Awards, Album of the Year, Best Rock Album; MTV European Music Award, Best Female Artist, 1996. *Current Management:* Third Rail Entertainment, 9169 Sunset Blvd, Los Angeles, CA 90069, USA. *Address:* c/o Maverick Recording Co, 9348 Civic Center Dr., Suite 100, Beverly Hills, CA 90210, USA. *Website:* www.alanismorissette.com.

MORRICONE, Ennio; b. 10 Nov. 1928, Rome, Italy. Composer. m. Maria Travia, 2 s., 2 d. *Education:* Studied trumpet and composition; Acad. of Santa Cecilia, Rome. *Career:* Composer for radio, television, film (incl. 'spaghetti' westerns), stage and concerts. *Compositions:* Scores and arrangements for vocalist Gianni Morandi, 1950s; Arrangement, Ogni Volta, Paul Anka, 1964; Film scores include: Il Federale, 1961; A Fistful of Dollars (under pseudonym Dan Savio), 1964; Battle of Algiers, 1966; Big Birds, Little Birds, 1966; 1900, 1976; Exorcist II, 1977; Days of Heaven, 1978; The Mission, 1986; The Untouchables, 1987; Frantic, 1988; Wolf, 1994; Disclosure, 1995; The Good, Bad and the Ugly; Once Upon a Time in the West; Partner; China is Near; Teorema; Decameron; Investigation of a Senior Citizen Above Suspicion; Orca; The Basilisks; For a Few Dollars More; The Five Man Army; Fraulein Doktor; The Guns of San Sebastian; A Fine Pair; Pardon; Let's Make Love; Once Upon a Time in the Country; Escalation; Grazie Zia; The Harem; La Cage aux Folles I, II and III; Cinema Paradiso; Casualties of War; Hamlet; Bugsy; City of Joy; The Bachelor; In the Line of Fire; A Pure Formality; Love Affair; Lolita; Phantom of the Opera; Bulworth; Canone Inverso. *Recordings:* Albums: Moses, 1977; Film Hits, 1981; Chi Mai, 1981; Film Music 1966–87, 1988; Chamber Music, 1988; The Endless Game, 1989; Live In Concert, 1989; The Very Best Of, 1992; Gothic Dramas 1996; Hawks and Sparrows, 1996; Secret of the Sahara, 1996; More than a Miracle, 1997; Desert of the Tartars, 1998; Corta Notte Dell Bambole Di vetro, 1998; Piume de Cristallo, 1999; Vite Strozzate, 1999; Stendhal Syndrome, 1999; Fourth King, 1999; Gli Occhi Freddi Della Paura, 2000; Il Segreto, 2000; Alzati Spia, 2000; Let's Go And Kill Comrades, 2001. Single: Chi Mai, theme to BBC's Life And Times Of David Lloyd George (Number 2, UK), 1981. *Current Management:* Gorfaine/Schwartz Agency Inc, 13245 Riverside Dr., Suite 450, Sherman Oakes, CA 91423, USA.

MORRIS, Doug; Record Co Exec; Songwriter; Prod. *Career:* Record Prod., songwriter, worked with: Tori Amos, Phil Collins, INXS, Led Zeppelin, Bette Midler, Stevie Nicks, The Rolling Stones, Pete Townsend; Founded Big Tree label, sold to Atlantic Records; Head, ATCO, Atlantic Records, Warner Music USA; Co-Chair., CEO, Warner Music Group, –1995; Helped create Interscope Records; Chair., CEO, Universal Music Group, 1995–, founded Universal Records; Founder, with Jimmy Iovine, Jimmy and Doug's Farm Club (project incorporating a record label, website and cable television show), 1999–; Joint owner, Pressplay (subscription-based music download website). *Compositions include:* Sweet Talkin' Guy, The Chiffons, 1966. *Address:* Universal Music Group, Universal Studios, 100 Universal City Plaza, Universal City, CA 91608, USA. *Website:* www.umusic.com; www.farmclub.com.

MORRIS, Johnny; b. 30 Oct. 1935, New York, NY, USA. Musician (Piano, Vocals); Orchestral Leader. m. (1) 2 s., 1 d., (2) Jean Farrell, 3 step-s. *Education:* BS, Music Education, Piano Major, State University of New York, 1958. *Career:* Pianist, Vocalist, Orchestral Leader; Performed with Jazz greats including Buddy Rich, Ruby Braff, Scott Hamilton, Roy Eldridge; Appearances with Jimmy Ryan's All Star Dixieland Band and at Kool Jazz Festival; TV appearances on the Today Show, GI Jive, From Jumpstreet. *Recordings include:* 3 albums with Buddy Rich; Alone Together (solo cassette); East Meets West (CD, Johnny Morris Quartet). *Address:* 321 Oenoke Ridge Rd, New Canaan, CT 06840, USA.

MORRIS, Lynn; b. 8 Oct. 1948, San Antonio, Texas, USA. Musician (banjo, guitar); Vocalist. m. Marshall Wilborn, 14 Oct. 1989. *Education:* BA, Art, Colorado College, Colorado Springs, USA; Studied classical and jazz guitar through school. *Career:* Began professionally in music, 1972; Performed in Europe; Asia; Canada; USA; Began Lynn Morris Band, 1988; Television appearances: Fire On The Mountain; Reno's Old Time Music Festival; Radio: WWVA on Wheeling Jamboree; WSM Grand Ole Opry, Nashville, Tennessee. *Recordings:* The Lynn Morris Band, 1990; The Bramble and The Rose, 1992; Mama's Hand, 1995; You'll Never Be the Sun, 1999; Also appeared on recordings by: Tom Adams; Kathy Killick; Mark Newton; Marshall Willborn. *Honours:* Twice, Female Vocalist (Traditional Category), Society for Preservation of Bluegrass Music in America; Twice, National Banjo Champion at Winfield, Kansas. *Membership:* IBMA Board of Directors, 6 years; International Bluegrass Music Asscn; Folk Alliance; Society For The Preservation of Bluegrass Music in America. *Current Management:* Mike Drudge, Class Act Entertainment, PO Box 771, Gallatin, TN 37066, USA.

MORRIS, Nathan Bartholomew 'Alex-Vanderpool'; b. 18 June 1971, USA. *Education:* Philadelphia High School of Creative and Performing Arts. *Career:* Mem., Boyz II Men, 1988–; Established Stonecreek label; Signed to Arista Records. *Recordings:* Albums: Cooleyhighharmony, 1993; II, 1995; Evolución, 1997; Nathan Michael Shawn Wanya, 2000; Full Circle, 2002. Singles: Motownphilly, 1991; I'll Make Love To You; On Bended Knee; One Sweet Day (with Mariah Carey, No. 1, USA). *Address:* c/o Arista Records, 6 W 57th St, New York, USA. *Website:* www.boyziimen.com.

MORRIS, Sarah Jane; b. 21 March 1959, Southampton, Hampshire, England. Vocalist; Songwriter; Actress. m. David J Coulter, 15 Aug. 1992, 1 s. *Education:* Central School of Speech and Drama for acting training. *Career:* Lead singer, The Republic, 1980–84; The Happy End, 1984–87; The Communards, 1985–87; Solo career includes 3 albums; Appearances include: Royal Albert Hall; Royal Festival Hall; Wembley Arena; Verona Arena; Venice Opera House; Support act to Simply Red, New Flame tour, 1989; Lead actress in Thin Air, BBC1; Lead Actress in film Expecting, Channel 4. *Compositions include:* I Am A Woman; Title track for television series The Mens Room, BBC, 1991–92; Music for film Expecting (Channel 4), 1995. *Recordings:* Don't Leave Me This Way, duet with Jimmy Somerville (No. 1, UK), 1986; Albums include: Sarah Jane Morris, 1988; Heaven, 1992; Blue Valentine, 1995; Fallen Angel, 1999. *Honours:* Freedom of the City of Verona; Best Newcomer, Italy, 1989. *Membership:* PRS; MCPS; Equity; Musicians' Union. *Current Management:* Ross Fitzsimmons, Kaliedoscope Music, 23 W Smithfield, London EC1A 9HY, England.

MORRIS, Stephen; b. 28 Oct. 1957, Macclesfield, Cheshire, England. Musician (drums). *Career:* Member, Joy Division, 1977–80; New Order, 1980–; The Other Two, with Gillian Gilbert, 1991–; Tours: UK; Europe; Australia; New Zealand; Far East; USA; South America; Concerts include: Glastonbury Fayre, 1981, 1987; Futurama Festival, Leeds, 1982; San Remo Festival, 1988; Reading Festival, 1989. *Compositions include:* with Gilbert: Numerous tracks for New Order; Television soundtracks: Making Out; Shooting Stars; Reportage; Common As Muck. *Recordings:* Albums: with Joy Division: Unknown Pleasures, 1979; Closer, 1980; Still, 1981; The Peel Sessions, 1988; Substance, 1988; Permanent, 1995; Heart And Soul (box set), 1998; Also featured on Short Circuit – Live At The Electric Circus, 1978; with New Order: Movement, 1981; Power, Corruption and Lies, 1983; Low Life, 1985; Brotherhood, 1986; Substance, 1987; Technique, 1989; BBC Radio 1 Live In Concert, 1992; Republic, 1993; The Best Of New Order, 1994; The Rest Of New Order, 1995; Get Ready, 2001; Back To Mine (compilation), 2002; with The Other Two: The Other Two and You, 1994; Superhighways, 1999; Singles: An Ideal For Living EP, 1978; with Joy Division: Transmission, 1979; Atmosphere, 1980; Love Will Tear Us Apart, 1980 (reissued 1983, 1995); with New Order: Ceremony, 1981; Procession/Everything's Gone Green, 1981; Temptation, 1982; Blue Monday, 1983 (remixed 1988, 1995); Confusion, 1983; Thieves Like Us, 1984; Murder, 1984; The Perfect Kiss, 1985; Subculture, 1985; Shellshock, 1986; State Of The Nation, 1986; Bizarre Love Triangle, 1986; True Faith, 1987; Touched By The Hand of God, 1987; Fine Time, 1988; Round and Round, 1989; Run-2, 1989; World In Motion, with England World Cup Football Squad (No. 1, UK), 1990; How Does It Feel?, 1992; Regret, 1993; Ruined In A Day, 1993; World, 1993; Spooky, 1993; 1963, 1995; 586, 1998; Crystal, 2001; 60 Miles An Hour, 2001; Here To Stay, 2002; with The Other Two: Tasty Fish, 1991; Selfish, 1993. *Website:* www.neworderweb.com.

MORRIS, Wanya Jermaine 'Squirt'; b. 29 July 1973, Philadelphia, PA, USA. Vocalist. *Education:* Philadelphia High School of Creative and Performing Arts. *Career:* Mem., Boyz II Men, 1988–; Established Stonecreek label; Signed to Arista Records. *Recordings:* Albums: Cooleyhighharmony, 1993; II, 1995; Evolución, 1997; Nathan Michael Shawn Wanya, 2000; Full Circle, 2002. Singles: Motownphilly, 1991; I'll Make Love To You; On Bended Knee; One Sweet Day (with Mariah Carey, No. 1, USA). *Address:* c/o Arista Records, 6 W 57th St, New York, USA. *Website:* www.boyziimen.com.

MORRISON, James; b. 11 Nov. 1962, Borrowa, NSW, Australia. Musician (Jazz Trumpet). m. Judi Morrison, 3 s. *Education:* NSW Conservatorium of Music. *Career:* Lecturer, NSW Conservatorium of Music, 1981; Formed Big Band with John, 1983; World Tour With Big Band; World Tour With Ray Charles and B. B. King, 1990; Performed For President Bush, Parliament House Canberra, 1992; Concert At Royal Albert Hall, London, 1994; Concert At Royal Opera House, 1995; Performed For President Clinton, Parliament House Canberra, 1996. *Recordings:* Jazz Meets The Symphony; Scream Machine, 2001. *Honours:* Australian Performer of the Year; Ricky May Performer of the Year Award. *Website:* www.jamesmorrison.com.

MORRISON, Lindy; b. 2 Nov. 1951, Sydney, Australia. Musician (drums). 1 d. *Education:* BA, Social Work, 1972. *Career:* Actor, Grin and Tonic Theatre and Popular Theatre Troupe, 1976–79; Drummer, Zero, 1979; Drummer, The Go-Betweens, 1980–90; Drummer, Cleopatra Wong, 1990–92; Major tours of USA, Europe and Australia, 1992–98; Musical Director, Regional Music Performances Festivals, Parades, Concerts, Theatre Shows. *Recordings:* Albums: Send Me A Lullaby, 1982; Before Hollywood, 1983; Spring Hill Fair, 1984; Liberty Belle and The Black Diamond Express, 1986; Tallullah, 1987; 16 Lovers Lane, 1988; Egg; Cleopatra's Lament. *Membership:* Artist Director of PPCA, 1993–2003; Music Council of Australia Board, 2000–03; National Coordinator, Support Act Ltd; Australian Musician Benevolent Society. *Address:* 291 Clovelly Rd, Clovelly 2031, Sydney, Australia.

MORRISON, Mark; b. 3 May 1972, Leicester, England. Soul Vocalist. *Career:* Solo recording artiste, 1994–; Tours include: Support to R Kelly, US tour, 1995; British tour, 1996. *Recordings:* Singles: Crazy, 1995; Let's Get Down, 1995; Return of The Mack (No. 1, UK), 1996; Trippin', 1996; Horny, 1996; Moan and Groan, 1997; Who's The Mack!, 1997; Best Friend, with Conner Reeves, 1999; Albums: Return of The Mack (No. 1, UK), 1996; Only God Can Judge Me, 1997. *Current Management:* JLM Management, Unit 8, 18 All Saints Rd, London W11 1HH, England.

MORRISON, Van (George Ivan); b. 31 Aug. 1945, Belfast, Northern Ireland. Vocalist; Songwriter; Composer; Musician. 1 d. *Career:* Founder, lead singer, Them, 1964–67; Solo artiste, 1967–; Appearances include: Knebworth Festival, 1974; The Last Waltz, The Band's farewell concert, 1976; Played with Bob Dylan, Wembley Stadium, 1984; Self Aid, with U2, Dublin, 1986; Glastonbury Festival, 1987; Prince's Rock Trust Gala, 1989; Performance, The Wall, by Roger Waters, Berlin, 1990; Concert in Dublin, with Bono, Bob Dylan, 1993; Phoenix Festival, 1995. *Recordings:* Singles include: Gloria/Baby Please Don't Go, 1964; Here Comes The Night, 1965; Brown-Eyed Girl, 1967; Moondance, 1970; Come Running, 1970; Domino, 1971; Blue Money, 1971; Wild Night, 1971; Jackie Wilson Said, 1972; Warm Love, 1973; Wavelength, 1978; Bright Side Of The Road, 1979; Did Ye Get Healed, 1987; Have I Told You Lately, 1989; Whenever God Shines His Light, with Cliff Richard, 1989; Real Real Gone, 1990; Days Like This, 1995; No Religion, 1995; The Healing Game, 1997; Precious Time, 1999; Back On Top, 1999; Albums include: Blowin' Your Mind, 1967; Astral Weeks, 1968; Moondance, 1970; His Band and Street Choir, 1970; Tupelo Honey, 1971; St Dominic's Preview, 1972; Hard Nose The Highway, 1973; It's Too Late To Stop Now, 1974; Tb Sheets, 1974; Veedon Fleece, 1974; This Is Where I Came In, 1977; A Period of Transition, 1977; Wavelength, 1978; Into The Music, 1983; Bang Masters, 1990; Common One, 1980; Beautiful Vision, 1982; Inarticulate Speech of The Heart, 1983; Live At The Opera House Belfast, 1984; A Sense of Wonder, 1984; No Guru, No Method, No Teacher, 1986; Poetic Champions Compose, 1987; Irish Heartbeat, 1988; Avalon Sunset, 1989; Best Of..., 1990; Bang Masters, 1990; Enlightenment, 1990; Hymns To The Silence, 1991; Too Long In Exile, 1993; Best Of..., Vol. 2, 1993; Days Like This, 1995; Songs of the Mose Allison: Tell Me Something, 1996; The Healing Game, 1997; Back on Top, 1999; The Skiffle Sessions: Live in Belfast 1998, 2000; You Win Again, 2000; Down The Road, 2002; Also recorded on albums: with The Band: Cahoots, 1971; The Last Waltz, 1978; with John Lee Hooker: Folk Blues, 1963; Mr Lucky, 1991; with Bill Wyman: Stone Alone, 1976; with Jim Capaldi: Fierce Heart, 1983; with Georgie Fame: How Long Has This Been Going On, 1996. *Honours:* Inducted into Rock and Roll Hall of Fame, 1993; BRIT Award, Outstanding Contribution to British Music, 1994; Q Award, Best Songwriter, 1995; Grammy Award, Best Pop Collaboration with Vocals, 1995; O.B.E., 1996. *Website:* www.vanmorrison.co.uk.

MORRISON, Will; b. 2 Feb. 1968, Tile Hill, Coventry, England. Musician (drums, percussion); Programmer. *Education:* Coventry University; Coventry School of Music, Drumtech, London. *Career:* Tours with Don Mescall supporting: Mary Coughlan; Davey Spillane; David Thomas; Richie Havens; The Dubliners; Festivals with Don Mescall: Phoenix; Larmer Bee; Berlin Music; Radio 1 Roadshows with Faun; Live Radio Sessions on Greater London Radio with: Philip French; Sugartrain; Don Mescall; Television includes: The Happening and Pot of Gold with Sugartrain; The Big City with Lisa Lamb Quartet. *Recordings:* State of The Arts EP; She Don't Know, Faun (featuring John Entwistle, Gordon Giltrap); Album: Here Be Dragons, Gargling With Brains. *Publications:* Working on drum tuition book: Learning To Read and Write. *Membership:* Musicians' Union. *Current Management:* Notes For Notes. *Address:* 12 The Old Orchard, Solomon Rd, Rainham, Kent ME8 8DT, England.

MORRISS, Mark; b. 18 Oct. 1971, Hounslow, Middlesex, England. Vocalist; Songwriter. *Career:* Founding mem., The Bluetones, 1994–; Release records on own label, Superior Quality Recordings, sell through Superior Quality Record Shop; Numerous tours, festivals, television and radio appearances. *Recordings:* Albums: Expecting To Fly, 1996; Return To The Last Chance Saloon, 1998; Science And Nature, 2000; The Singles 1995–2002, 2002. Singles: Return To Splendour, 1994; Nings Of Desire (EP), 1994; Are You Blue Or Are You Blind?, 1995; Bluetonic, 1996; Slight Return, 1996; Cut Some Rug, 1996; Marblehead Johnson, 1996; Solomon Bites The Worm, 1998; Sleazy Bed Track, 1998; 4-Day Weekend, 1998; If..., 1998; Mudslide, 2000; Keep The Home Fires Burning, 2000; Autophilia Or How I Learned To Stop Worrying And Love My Car, 2000. *Honours:* Gold disc for Return To The Last Chance Saloon. *Address:* c/o Mercury Records, Chancellors House, 72 Chancellors Rd, London W6 9QB, England. *Website:* www.bluetones.co.uk.

MORRISS, Scott; b. 10 Oct. 1973, Hounslow, Middlesex, England. Musician (bass guitar); Backing Vocalist; Songwriter. *Career:* Founding mem., The Bluetones, 1994–; Release records on own label, Superior Quality Recordings, sell through Superior Quality Record Shop; Numerous tours, festivals,

television and radio appearances. *Recordings:* Albums: Expecting To Fly, 1996; Return To The Last Chance Saloon, 1998; Science And Nature, 2000; The Singles 1995–2002, 2002. Singles: Return To Splendour, 1994; Nings Of Desire (EP), 1994; Are You Blue Or Are You Blind?, 1995; Bluetonic, 1996; Slight Return, 1996; Cut Some Rug, 1996; Marblehead Johnson, 1996; Solomon Bites The Worm, 1998; Sleazy Bed Track, 1998; 4-Day Weekend, 1998; If..., 1998; Mudslide, 2000; Keep The Home Fires Burning, 2000; Autophilia Or How I Learned To Stop Worrying And Love My Car, 2000. *Honours:* Gold disc for Return To The Last Chance Saloon. *Address:* c/o Mercury Records, Chancellors House, 72 Chancellors Rd, London W6 9QB, England. *Website:* www.bluetones.co.uk.

MORRISSEY, (Steven Patrick Morrissey); b. 22 May 1959, Davyhulme, Manchester, UK. Vocalist. *Career:* Founder mem., The Smiths, 1982–87; Appearances incl.: John Peel Show, Radio 1, 1983; Support to Altered Images, 1983; Solo artiste, 1987–. *Compositions include:* Co-writer (with Johnny Marr), all Smiths hits. *Recordings:* Albums: with The Smiths: The Smiths, 1984; Hatful Of Hollow, 1984; Meat Is Murder (No. 1, UK), 1985; The World Won't Listen, 1986; The Queen Is Dead, 1986; Louder Than Bombs, 1987; Strangeways Here We Come, 1987; Rank, 1988; Best... I (No. 1, UK), 1992; Best... II, 1992; Singles, 1995; The Very Best Of, 2001; Solo: Viva Hate (No. 1, UK), 1988; Bona Drag, 1990; Kill Uncle, 1991; Your Arsenal, 1992; Beethoven Was Deaf, 1993; Vauxhall And I (No. 1, UK), 1994; Southpaw Grammar, 1995; Maladjusted, 1997; My Early Burglary Years, 1998. Singles include: with The Smiths: Hand In Glove, 1983; This Charming Man, 1983; What Difference Does It Make, 1984; Heaven Knows I'm Miserable Now, 1984; William, It Was Really Nothing, 1984; How Soon Is Now, 1985; Shakespears Sister, 1985; That Joke Isn't Funny Anymore, 1985; The Boy With The Thorn In His Side, 1985; Big Mouth Strikes Again, 1986; Panic, 1986; Ask, 1986; Shoplifters of The World Unite, 1987; Sheila Take A Bow, 1987; Girlfriend In A Coma, 1987; I Started Something I Couldn't Finish, 1987; Last Night I Dreamt That Somebody Loved Me, 1987; There Is A Light That Never Goes Out, 1992; Solo singles include: Everyday Is Like Sunday, 1988; Suedehead, 1988; Last of The Famous International Playboys, 1989; Interesting Drug, 1989; Ouija Board, 1989; November Spawned A Monster, 1990; Piccadilly Palare, 1990; Our Frank, 1991; Sing Your Life, 1991; Pregnant For The Last Time, 1991; My Love Life, 1991; We Hate It When Our Friends Become Successful, 1992; You're The One For Me Fatty, 1992; Certain People I Know, 1992; Hold On To Your Friends, 1994; The More You Ignore Me The Closer I Get, 1994; Interlude, with Siouxsie, 1994; Boxers, 1995; Dagenham Dave, 1995; Boy Racer, 1995; Sunny, 1995; Alma Matters, 1997; Roy's Keen, 1997; Satan Rejected My Soul, 1998. *Honours:* Q Award, Best Songwriter, 1994. *Current Management:* Stiefel Phillips Entertainment, 9720 Wilshire Blvd, Suite 400, Beverly Hills, CA 90212, USA.

MORROW, Ian; Prod., Writer, Programmer. *Career:* Worked with Wet Wet Wet; Production work with Icelandic artist, Suala. *Recordings:* Wet Wet Wet: Holding Back the River, album, programming; High on the Happy Side, album, programming; Picture This, album, programming; Nightcrawlers, Push the Feeling On, production; Seal, Crazy, programming; Other session work includes: Capercailie; Emerson Lake & Palmer. *Current Management:* SARM Management. *Address:* The Blue Building, 42/46 St Luke's Mews, London W11 1DG, England.

MORTENSEN, Allan; b. 27 April 1946, Århus, Denmark. Vocalist; Composer; Actor. m. Titika, March 1967, divorced, 1 d. *Education:* Lithographer. *Career:* Singer, rock group Midnight Sun, 1971; Stage performances include lead parts in: Jesus Christ Superstar, 1972; Hair, 1972; Two Gentlemen of Verona, 1973; Godspell, 1979; Joseph and The Amazing Technicolour Dreamcoat, 1983; Odysseus, 1983; Tom Parker's Young Messiah, 1986–87; Singer, soul group 2nd Line, 1987–89. *Compositions:* Musicals: Thor, 1989; The Concert, 1991; The Three Musketeers, 1995. *Recordings:* Midnight Sun, 1971; Love Ambulance (as singer, composer), 1976; 2nd Line Live, 1988. *Honours:* The Amber Nightingale, Poland, 1987; Helexpo, Greece, 1991. *Membership:* Danish Artist Federation. *Current Management:* Danish Artist Management.

MORTIMER, Tony, (Anthony Michael Mortimer); b. 21 Oct. 1970, Stepney, London, England. Vocalist; Songwriter; Musician (piano). 1 d. *Career:* Began as Dancer for group Faith, Hope and Charity; Produced demo tape; Formed East 17; Signed record deal, 1992; Numerous television and live appearances; Duet with singer Gabrielle; Left band, 1996; Joined Sub Zero. *Recordings:* Singles: House of Love, 1992; Gold, 1992; Deep, 1993; West End Girls, 1993; It's Alright, 1993; Around The World, 1994; Steam, 1994; Stay Another Day (No. 1, UK), 1994; Let It Rain, 1995; Hold My Body Tight, 1995; Thunder, 1995; Do U Still, 1996; Someone To Love, 1996; If You Ever, with Gabrielle, 1996; Albums: Walthamstow, 1993; Steam, 1994; Up All Night, 1995; Around the World: The Journey So Far, 1996.

MORTON, Eddie; Vocalist; Musician (mandolin, accordion, guitar). *Career:* Member, Sub Zero, 1983; Formed The Trick, 1984; Extensive radio play, BBC1; Hits, Europe and Australia; Worked in production, songwriting with artists including: Phil Lynott; Slade; Ruby Turner; Rozalla; Steve Lillywhite; Roy Harper; Formed own band, 1988; Tours, Europe, UK, USA; Joined The

Adventure Babies, 1991; Founder member, The New Bushbury Mountain Daredevils, 1992–; Backing vocals, Slade album; Numerous television and radio performances; Producer, songwriting with dance artists. *Recordings:* Albums: with Sub Zero: Out of The Blue; with The Trick: My World; Heart of Hearts; with Rozalla: Heartbreaker; Sunny; Spirit of Africa; Perfect Kiss; as Morton: Keeper of The Light; with Adventure Babies: Adventure Babies; Laugh; Barking Mad; with Mack and The Boys: The Unknown Legends; As Eddie Morton: The Infinite Room; Way of The World; Black and Blue; with The New Bushbury Mountain Daredevils: Bushwacked; The Yellow Album; Bushbury Mountain. *Current Management:* c/o Jim McPhee, Acorn Entertainments. *Address:* Winterfold House, 46 Woodfield Rd, Kings Heath, Birmingham B13 9UJ, England.

MORTON, Nigel William; b. 23 Nov. 1953, Nairobi, Kenya. Man; Booking Agent; Consultant. m. Hilary Cooper, 26 Nov. 1977, divorced, 1 s., 1 d. *Career:* Journalist: Record Mirror; Sounds; Hi-Fi Weekly; Booking agent to various acts including: Carmel; Marillion; Wishbone Ash; Jimmy Cliff; Billy Bragg; Angelic Upstarts; Donovan; The Exploited; Pentangle; The Twinkle Brothers, 1978–84; Full time manager: New Model Army, 1982–91; Co-manager: The Almighty, 1987–90; Booking Agent, Consultant, Current clients include: Bruce Cockburn; Kate and Anna McGarrigle; Hot Tuna; The Ukrainians; Porcupine Tree; Test Department, 1992–; Negotiated recording contracts for New Model Army with: Quiet Records, 1982; Abstract Records, 1983; EMI Records, 1984; Negotiated publishing contracts for New Model Army with: Watteau Music, 1983; Warner-Chappell Music, 1986. *Address:* Forward Agency Booking, 132 Liverpool Rd, London N1 1LA, England.

MORTON, Peter Michael; b. 30 July 1964, Leicester, England. Vocalist; Musician (guitar); Songwriter. *Education:* Church choir; Busker until 1987. *Career:* Concerts throughout UK, Europe, North America; British Council Tours, Pakistan, Malaysia; Frequent guest, Folk On 2. *Compositions include:* Another Train. *Recordings:* Albums: Frivolous Love, 1987; One Big Joke, 1988; Urban Folk Vol. 1, 1989; Mad World Blues, 1992; Courage, Love, Grace, 1995. *Contributions to:* All Through The Year. *Honours:* Most Promising Newcomer, Folk Roots Magazine, 1987. *Membership:* PRS. *Current Management:* Small World Music. *Address:* PO Box 2259, London E17 4RD, England.

MORYKIT, Dmytro; b. 3 Dec. 1956, Northampton, England. Composer; Musician (piano, keyboards). m. Elaine Morykit, 2 Nov. 1985, 1 d. *Education:* BEd, University of Leicester; Classically trained on Piano from early age to LRAM; Studied with Graham Mayo. *Career:* Member of the National Student Theatre Company, 1978–80; Composer in Residence; Session musician with various rock bands; Freelance composer and musician. *Compositions:* Many for film, theatre, dance and public performance including music for The Wasteland by T. S. Eliot and original music for The Lion The Witch and The Wardrobe by C. S. Lewis; Commissioned by Amnesty International: The Unforgiving, 1997; Prisoners of Conscience, 1998. *Recordings:* The Unforgiving; From The Dungeons To The Skies. *Publications include:* Songs For Piano, 1982; The Enchanted, 1994. *Honours:* Best Original Music, National Student Drama Festival. *Membership:* Musicians' Union.

MOS DEF, (Dante Smith), (Dante Beze); b. 11 Dec. 1973, Brooklyn, New York, USA. Rap Artiste. *Career:* Began rapping, aged 9; Formed: Urban Thermo Dynamics with sister; Released first record, 1994; Joined the Native Tongues collective, leading to guest appearance on De La Soul's Big Brother Beat; Started recording solo material for independent label Rawkus; Formed rock group Black Jack Johnson; Collaborations: Jill Scott; A Tribe Called Quest; DJ Krush; Common; Talib Kweli; Scritti Politti; Ghostface Killah. *Recordings:* Albums: Mos Def and Talib Kweli Are Black Star, 1998; Black On Both Sides, 1999; Singles: The Universal Magnetic, Body Rock 1998; Umi Says, Miss Fat Booty – Part II, 2000. *Address:* c/o Rawkus Records, 676 Broadway, Fourth Floor, New York, USA.

MOSCA, Sal; b. 27 April 1927, Mount Vernon, New York, USA. Musician (piano). m. Stella C Di Gregorio, 2 s., 1 d. *Education:* 3 years New York College of Music and New York University; 8 years Lennie Taistano. *Career:* Alice Tulley Hall, solo recital; Carnegie Recital Hall, solo recital; Concertgebouw (Netherlands), solo recital; Solo recitals, Rotterdam, Maastricht, The Hague; Philharmonic Hall, West Berlin, with Warne Marsh, Kenny Clark, Eddie Gomez; 5 hour radio interview, WKCR. *Recordings:* 15 albums with Lee Konitz; Warne Marsh Quartet; Village Vanguard; Zinnia; 3 solo CDs: Interplay; Choice; Wave. *Honours:* ASCAP Pop Awards. *Membership:* ASCAP; AMRA; Local AFofM. *Address:* 5 S Fifth Ave, Mount Vernon, NY 10550–3108, USA.

MOSES, Jamie (James Michael); b. 30 Aug. 1955, Ipswich, Suffolk, England. Musician (guitar, bass guitar, keyboards); Vocalist; Musical Dir. m. Deborah Anne Webb, 30 Aug. 1983, 1 s., 1 d. *Education:* Redhill Technical College. *Career:* Tours with: Brian May; Bob Geldof; Eric Burdon; Broken English; S.O.S. Band; Bucks Fizz; The Hollies; Deana Carter; Stage appearances with: Paul Rodgers; Paul McCartney; Steve Lukather; Dave Stewart; Guns N' Roses; Fish; Chaka Khan; Curtis Stigers; Paul Young; Roger Chapman; Roger Taylor; Extreme; Kiki Dee; Television and radio with

artists including: The Pretenders; Olivia Newton-John. *Recordings:* Brian May Live At Brixton Academy; Another World; The Happy Club, Bob Geldof; Comin' On Strong, Broken English; I Used To Be An Animal, Eric Burdon; Various, Paul Young; Do You Really Want Me Back, Broken English; Merlin, Merlin; Turn Unstoned?, Roger Chapman; Other. *Recordings include:* Mike & The Mechanics; Tony Hadley. *Membership:* PRS; MCPS; Musicians' Union. *Address:* 32 William Rd, Caterham-On-The-Hill, Surrey CR3 5NN, England.

MOSES, Robert (Bob); Jazz Musician (drums, keyboards); Composer; Educator. *Career:* Leader, bands: Mozamba; Drumming Birds; Founder, owner, Mozown Records, 1975–; Worked with Jack DeJohnette; Keith Jarrett; David Sanborn; Rahsaan Roland Kirk; Gary Burton. *Recordings:* Albums include: with Larry Coryell: Free Spirit, 1967; Lady Coryell, 1969; with Steve Kuhn: Playground, 1967; Non Fiction, 1978; with David Liebman: Drum Ode, 1975; with Pat Metheny: Bright Size Life, 1975; with Compost: Compost, 1971; Life Is Round, 1973; with Free Spirits: Out of Sight and Sound, 1967; Solo: Bittersweet in the Ozone, 1975; Devotion, 1979; Family, 1980; When Elephants Dream of Music, 1982; Visit with the Great Spirit, 1983; The Story of Moses, 1987; Time Stood Still, 1993; Drumming Birds, 1993.

MOSLEY, Ian; b. 16 June 1953, Paddington, London, England. Musician (drums, percussion). *Education:* Guildhall School of Music. *Career:* Member, Curved Air; Gordon Giltrap Band; Steve Hackett; Member, orchestras for West End musicals: Hair; Jesus Christ Superstar; Member, UK progressive rock group Marillion, 1983–; Tours, UK; Europe; USA; Major concerts include: Milton Keynes Bowl, 1984; Nostell Priory Festival, 1984; Monsters of Rock Festival, Castle Donington, 1985; Colombian Volcano Appeal Concert, Royal Albert Hall, 1986; Welcome To The Garden Party, Milton Keynes Bowl, 1986. *Recordings:* Albums: with Gordon Giltrap: Peacock Party, 1980; Live, 1981; with Steve Hackett: Highly Strung, 1983; Till We Have Faces, 1984; with Marillion: Fugazi, 1984; Real To Reel, 1984; Misplaced Childhood (No. 1, UK), 1985; Brief Encounter, 1986; Clutching At Straws, 1987; B-Sides Themselves, 1988; The Thieving Magpie, 1988; Season's End, 1989; Holidays In Eden, 1991; A Singles Collection 1982–92, 1992; Brave, 1994; Marillion.com, 1999; Anoraknophobia, 2000; Made Again, Live, 2001; Anorak In The UK Live, 2002. Singles with Marillion include: Punch and Judy, 1984; Assassing, 1984; Kayleigh (No. 2, UK), 1985; Lavender, 1985; Heart of Lothian, 1985; Incommunicado, 1987; Sugar Mice, 1987; Warm Wet Circles, 1987; Freaks, 1988; Hooks In You, 1989; Uninvited Guest, 1989; Easter, 1990; Cover My Eyes (Pain and Heaven), 1991; No One Can, 1991; Dry Land, 1991; Sympathy, 1992; Beautiful, 1995; Other recordings with: Sally Oldfield; Darryl Way; Trace; Renaissance; Adrian Snell. *Current Management:* Rod Smallwood, Sanctuary Management. *Address:* Sanctuary House, 45–53 Sinclair Rd, London W14 0NS, England.

MOSS, Jon; b. 11 Sept. 1957, London, England. Musician (Drums). *Career:* Session drummer, Adam and the Ants, The Damned; Joined Sex Gang Children, with Boy George and Mikey Craig; Became Culture Club; Numerous TV appearances and several tours; Band split, 1987; Various solo projects; Band re-formed, 1998. *Recordings:* Singles: Do You Really Want To Hurt Me (No. 1, UK), 1982; Time (Clock of the Heart), 1982; Church of the Poisoned Mind, 1983; Victims, 1983; It's A Miracle, 1983; Karma Chameleon (No. 1, UK and USA), 1983; The War Song, 1984; The Medal Song, 1984; Move Away, 1986; I Just Wanna Be Loved, 1999; Your Kisses Are Charity, 1999; Albums: Kissing To Be Clever, 1982; Colour By Numbers, 1983; Waking Up With The House on Fire, 1984; From Luxury To Heartache, 1986; This Time, 1987; Greatest Moments (Live), 1998; Don't Mind If I Do, 1999; Culture Club Box Set, 2002.

MOSS, Mick (Mix); b. 25 May 1953, London, England. Prod; A&R Consultant. *Education:* BA Hons. *Career:* Worked with: The Farm; The La's; Elvis Costello; Pete Townshend; Sonya; Racey; The Troggs; Also worked with various members of The Clash; The Christians; Flock of Seagulls; Icicle Works; Tears For Fears; Suzi Quatro band; Lightning Seeds. *Recordings:* Producer, Engineer: Singles/EPs: Bread Not Bombs, (benefit single, Campaign Against the Arms Trade), 1986; What's Happening To Our Nation?, L8 Connexion (benefit single for MTUCURC); Free, Live Transmission, 1986; Are U In Pain?, Gaynor Rose Madder, 1987; Fading, Gaynor Rose Madder, 1987; Here Comes The Floor, Benny Profane, 1987; I Love You Liverpool, Steve May, 1988; Worse Year of My Life, Wild Swans, 1989; Soldier On, Wild Swans, 1989; This Is The Age, Pupils of Parkfield School Liverpool, 1989; Post Funk War, 25th of May, 1989; Cynthia Payne, The Hoovers, 1988; MDM: 4 singles, 2 albums, include: Take What You Want, 1988–94; Awakenings, The Senses, Oh Father, Ice Factory, 1990; Disease, Adams Family, 1991; Cinemascope, Syndicate, 1994; Greytown, Syndicate, 1995. *Publications:* Various articles in music magazines. *Membership:* PRS; MRF; IMF. *Address:* PO Box 25, Liverpool L17 8SX, England.

MOST, Mickie, (Michael Peter Hayes); b. 20 June 1938, Aldershot, Hampshire, England. Record Prod. *Career:* Toured, recorded as the Most Brothers with Alex Wharton, late 1950s; Solo artiste, South Africa, 1959–63; Successful RAK Producer, UK, 1964–; Head of RAK record label, 1969–; Successful RAK artists included Hot Chocolate; Alexis Korner's CCS; Smokie; Chris Spedding; Kim Wilde; New World; Suzi Quatro; Mud; Television appearances include:

Regular panelist, New Faces, UK television talent show, ATV, 1973–79; Presenter, television show, Revolver, ATV, 1978. *Recordings:* As producer: The Animals (7 hit singles); Lulu; Terry Reid; Jeff Beck; Donovan; Mary Hopkin; Julie Felix; Johnny Hates Jazz; Perfect Stranger; Herman's Hermits; Hot Chocolate; Brenda Lee; Also worked with Herman's Hermits; The Nashville Teens; Jimmy Page; Steve Harley; The Seekers; Rod Stewart; Nancy Sinatra. *Address:* c/o RAK Records, 43 Brook Green, London W6 7EF, England.

MOSUMGAARD, Niels Eliot; b. 20 Oct. 1961, Århus, Denmark. Songwriter; Musician (guitar, saxophone); Vocalist. m. Eva Baadsgaard, 18 May 1991, 2 s. *Career:* Songwriter, singer, Lars Liholt Band tour, 1984; Touring Denmark with own band, 1984–; Sideman, saxophone, guitar, blues, calypso and popular bands; Member, Calypsocapellet, 1984–87; Member, Sweethearts, 1989–91; Lyricist for several composers on independent scene in Danish and English; Lyricist for: Bamboo Brothers: Johnny Told Suzi, 1993 (music by Troels Skovgard); Inventor, personal mix of folk, ambient, ethnic and metal called Folkadelic; Working on album: N B Danish Lyrics, 1995.

MOTEN, Frank, Jr, (Tee Tah, Easy Mo'T'); b. 7 April 1967, New York, NY, USA. Prod; Composer. *Education:* Johnson C Smith University, student of Dizzy Gillespie. *Career:* TV appearances: Sesame Street, aged 4; Late Night with David Letterman; various commercials; Live performances include Carnegie Hall and The Apollo Theater; Various production projects; Recorded as Tee Tah, 1999–; Founder: OurGig.com, 2000. *Compositions:* Still Boppin/Night In Tunisia. *Recordings:* Singles: It Takes Two, Rob Base and DJ E–Z Rock, 1988; Together Forever, Lisette Melendez, 1991. *Current Management:* Prince Igor Management. *Address:* 233 E Erie St, Suite 2206, Chicago, Illinois 60611, USA. *Website:* www.ourgig.com.

MOTIAN, Stephen Paul; b. 25 March 1931, Philadelphia, Pennsylvania, USA. Musician (drums); Composer. *Education:* Private lessons; One year at Manhattan School of Music, New York. *Career:* Played with Bill Evans and with Lennie Tristano and Zoot Sims; Worked in '50s and '60s with Coleman Hawkins, Roy Eldridge, Oscar Pettiford, Thelonious Monk, Al Cohn and Zoot Sims; Formed trio with Keith Jarrett and Charlie Haden; Began releasing albums under own name; Formed Quintet with other musicians, the trio with Bill Frisell and Joe Lovano, 1980s; Formed Electric Be Bop Band 1980s, began performing and recording 1991; Toured in Europe and recorded with Trio 2000 and Trio 2000 + One, 1997; Further tours, 1998–99. *Compositions:* Over 50 compositions published and recorded. *Recordings include:* With Keith Jarrett: Eyes of the Heart; Death and the Flower; Life Between the Exit Signs; With Bill Evans: How My Heart Sings; Sunday at the Village Vanguard; New Jazz Conceptions; With Charlie Haden: The Ballad of the Fallen; Liberation Music Orchestra; With Bill Frisell: Rambler; With Paul Bley: The Paul Bley Quartet; Fragments; With Carla Bley: Tropic Appetites; Escalator Over the Hill; Other: Misterioso, 1986; Monk in Motian, 1988; Live in Tokyo, 1991; On Broadway Vol. 3, 1991; The Electric Be Bop Band, 1992; Flight of the Blue Jay, 1996; Trio 2000 + One, 1997; Electric Be Bop Band Play Monk and Powell, 1998. *Honours:* National Endowment for the Arts Grant, 1976; New York Foundation for the Arts Grant, 1987. *Current Management:* Hans Wendl, Berkeley, California, USA. *Address:* 467 Central Park W, New York, NY 10025, USA.

MOTION, David; b. 23 March 1959, Hamburg, Germany. Composer. Partner, Vera Hegarty. *Education:* G Gaunt; G Greed; Royal Academy of Music. *Career:* Recording engineer, 1982–84; Record producer, 1984–90; Composer. *Compositions:* Sally Potter's film Orlando; Television: Cardiac Arrest; Commercials: HSBC; Gaviscon; BMW; Ford Mondeo; Frontera; Tesco; Shell. *Recordings:* as producer: Since Yesterday, Strawberry Switchblade; Lean On Me, Red Box; Carmel; Chara; Toshihiko Takamizawa; Keyboards on: Shadow Behind The Iron Sun, Evelyn Glennie, 2000. *Honours:* D and AD Silver Award. *Current Management:* Bob Last. *Address:* Holdings Ecosse Ltd, 9/2 Tweeddale Court, 14 High St, Edinburgh EH1 1TE, Scotland.

MOTTIRONI, Adriano; b. 3 Nov. 1968, Rome, Italy. Composer; Sound Engineer. *Education:* Durham University. *Career:* Music, Sound Designing, Theatre Productions; Concert Promoter; Musical and Technical Advisor. *Compositions:* La Scoperta De L'America; Labyrinth; Romeo and Juliet; Sorry. *Address:* Via Dei Gigli 75B, 00040 Lavinio, Roma, Italy.

MOTTOLA, Thomas D. (Tommy); b. USA. Prod; Record Co Exec. m. (1) Mariah Carey, 1993, (2) Ariadna Thalía Sodi Miranda, 2000. *Career:* Record prod.; Joined CBS Records, 1987; Pres., Columbia Records; Chair. and CEO, Sony Music Entertainment Inc, 1998–2003; Left to establish own record company, in partnership with Sony Music Entertainment, 2003. *Address:* Sony Music Entertainment Inc, 550 Madison Ave, New York, NY 10022-3211, USA. *Website:* usa.sonymusic.com.

MOUFANG, David; b. 7 Sept. 1966, Heidelberg, Germany. Composer; Prod; Musician (guitar, keyboards, percussion). *Career:* Runs two record labels with Jonas Grossmanns, Source Records, 1992–, KM 20, 1996–. *Recordings:* Earth To Infinity, 1992; Big Rooms, Deep Space Network, 1993; Intergalactic Federation, Deep Space Network and Dr Atmo, 1993; Intergalactic Federation

2, 1994; Reagenz, with Jonah Sharp, 1994; View To View, with Rob Gordon, 1994; Kunststoff, 1995; Solitaire, 1995; Koolfang with Pete Namlook, 1995; Koolgang 2, 1995; Traffic (Live '95), Deep Space Network, 1996; Cymbelin, Move D, 1996; RO70/Move D, with Roman Flügel, 1996; Exploring the Psychdelic Landscape, 1996; Lips, with Tobacco Rot, 1997; Deep Space Network Meets Higher Intelligence Agency, 1997; A Day in the Life, 1997; RO70/Move D II, with Roman Flügel, 1997; Conjoint, Berger/Hodge/Moufang/Ruit, 1997; Out to Lunch, with Dan Jordan, 1998; Lost in Music, TV documentary, 1996. *Membership:* Sound Works Exchange (sponsored by the Goethe Institute and British Arts Council), 1995. *Current Management:* Source Records. *Address:* Kornmarkt 9, 69117 Heidelberg, Germany.

MOULD, Bob; b. 1960, New York, USA. Musician (guitar); Songwriter; Record Prod. *Career:* Co-founder, lead guitarist, rock group Hüsker Dü, 1979–87; Solo artiste, 1987–; Solo tour, 1991; Founder, guitarist, Sugar, 1992–. *Recordings:* Albums: with Hüsker Dü: Land Speed Record, 1981; Everything Falls Apart, 1983; Metal Circus, 1983; Zen Arcade, 1984; New Day Rising, 1985; Candy Apple Grey, 1986; Warehouse – Songs and Stories, 1987; Everything Falls Apart and More, 1993; Living End, 1994; Solo albums: Workbook, 1989; Black Sheets of Rain, 1990; The Poison Years, 1994; Bob Mould, 1996; Hubcap, 1996; The Last Dog and Pony Show, 1998; Modulate, 2002; with Sugar: Changes, 1992; Copper Blue, 1992; Good Idea, 1992; Helpless, 1992; If I Can't Change Your Mind, 1992; Beaster, 1993; FUEL (File Under Easy Listening), 1994; Your Favourite Thing, 1994; Believe What You're Saying, 1994; Gee Angel, 1994; Besides, 1995. *Current Management:* Granary Music, PO Box 4947, Austin, TX 78765, USA.

MOUNSEY, Paul Fraser; b. 15 April 1959, Irvine, Scotland. Composer; Prod; Arranger; Musician (piano). m. Dorinha Carelli, 8 July 1983. *Education:* Trinity College of London: GTCL, FTCL (composition), LTCL (piano). *Career:* Part-time lecturer: Goldsmith's College, London University, 1984–85; Songwriter, CBS (Sony) Brazil, 1986–; Producer, arranger, Sony (Brazil), EMI (Brazil) and Independents, 1987–; Musical Director, Play It Again Studios, São Paulo, Brazil, 1989–; Musical Director, Michael Nyman In Brazil, Concert, 1992; Appearances: BBC Radio Scotland, Scot FM, 1994. *Recordings:* Numerous songs; Soundtrack for mini-series: Procura-se, 1992; La Cigale Et La Fourmi, for soprano, oboe, piano, recorded and broadcast, BBC Radio 3; Nahoo, solo album, UK 1994, USA 1995; Nahoo Too, 1998; Nahoo 3: Notes From The Republic, 1999. *Publications:* Articles, Brazilian newspapers; Article: Music In Brazil, Contact (British music journal), No 31, Autumn 1987. *Address:* Iona Records, 27–29 Carnoustie Pl., Scotland St, Glasgow G5 8PH, Scotland; Mesa/Bluemoon Recordings, 209 E Alameda Ave, Suite 101, Burbank, CA 91502, USA.

MOUQUET, Eric; b. France. Musician. *Career:* mem., Deep Forest, with Michel Sanchez, 1991–; mem., Deo Dezi, with Guillain Joncheray; Collaborations with Abed Azrie, Peter Gabriel, Marcella Lewis, Wes Madiko, Jorge Reyes, Ana Toroja, Joe Zawinul; Concert, G7 show, France, 1996; World tour, 1996. *Recordings:* Albums: with Deep Forest: World Mix, 1994; Boheme, 1996; Comparsa, 1998; Made in Japan, 1999; Madazulu, 1997–98; with Deo Dezi: World Mix, 1994. Singles: with Deo Dezi: Ti Eliz Iza, 1994; La Jument de Mishao, 1994. *Honours:* MTV Award, Best Music Video, for Sweet Lullaby, 1993; Victoires de la Musique Awards, Best World Album, 1993, 1996; World Music Award for Most Sales in the World, 1995; Grammy Award, Best World Music Album, for Boheme, 1996. *Address:* c/o Sony Music France, 131 ave de Wagram, 75017 Paris, France. *E-mail:* deepforest@sonymusic.fr. *Website:* www.sonymusic.fr/deepforest/.

MOUSER, Richard; b. 4 June 1962, Santa Monica, California, USA. Musician (guitar); Record Prod; Engineer. 2 d. *Education:* Theory, Classical Guitar. *Career:* Support tours with 3 Dog Night; Huey Lewis and the News; Warrant; Michael Schenker Group; Melissa Manchester; Def Leppard; Queensryche; Wrote and produced jingles for numerous commercials. *Recordings:* Producer, engineer, mixer for albums by: Green Jelly; Corrosion of Conformity; Lucy's Fur Coat; LSD; The Coup de Grace; Black Market Flowers; The Ex-Idols; Jack Of Jill; Oleander; Blair Tefkin; Mixed album for: Imperial Tree; Mixed recordings by: Less Than Jake, Insane Clown Posse; Quickspace; Producer, The Generators, Schleprock; Engineer, Clawfinger. *Current Management:* Tapko Entertainment, 17337 Ventura Blvd, Suite 208, Encino, CA 91316, USA.

MOUSKOURI, Nana (Joanna); b. 13 Oct. 1934, Hania, Greece. Vocalist; Politician. m. (1) George Petsilas, divorced, 1 s., 1 d., (2) Andre Chapelle, 2003. *Education:* Diploma in piano and singing, Athens Academy of Arts; National Conservatory, Athens. *Career:* Regular European festival performances, late 50s; Regular television appearances, UK; UNICEF Ambassador, 1993–; Member, European Parliament, 1994–; Founder and president of the Focus On Hope Foundation. *Recordings:* Numerous albums, most recently: Dans Le Soleil Et Dans Le Vent, 2000; At Her Very Best, 2000; Hit singles include: Les Enfants du Piree; Weiss Rosen Aus Then; L'Enfant Au Tambour; Parapluies De Cherbourg (duet with Michel Legrand); Guantanamera; Only Love. *Honours:* Greek Broadcasting Festival Award; Golden Tulip Award; Barcelona Festival Award; Several Gold discs, 1959–;

Chevalier Des Arts Et Des Lettres; Chevalier De La Légion D'honneur, 1997. *Address:* 12 rue Gutenberg, 92100 Boulogne-Sur-Seine, France.

MOUTOUARI, Pierre; b. 3 April 1950, Kimuimba. Musician. 6 d. *Career:* National and International Musician; Manager, PM Production. *Compositions:* Missengué, on Le Retour de Pierre Moutouari; Assa, on Tout Bouge. *Recordings:* Le Retour de Pierre Moutouari; Tout Bouge. *Honours:* Gold Medal, Tunisia, 1973; Best Composer Prize, 1982; Prize, Zare, 1993. *Address:* PM Production, 37 rue Archambault, Bacongo, Brazzaville, Republic of Congo.

MOWER, Mike (Michael Henry); b. 9 June 1958, Bath, England. Composer; Musician (flutes, saxophones). m. Elizabeth Melia, 27 July 1994. *Education:* Royal Academy of Music, London. *Career:* Mike Mower Quartet (jazz), frequent broadcasts for BBC Radio, 1980–84; Wrote arrangements for BBC Radio Orchestra Big Band, 1984–86; Formed Itchy Fingers, jazz saxophone quartet playing his music, won Jazz Sounds '86, 1986–95; Band has toured 42 countries, playing all major European jazz festivals; Writes commissions for soloists and ensembles specializing in jazz/classical crossover style. *Compositions:* Numerous for wind instruments. *Recordings:* Albums: Producer, writer with Itchy Fingers saxophone quartet: Quark; Teranga; Itchy Fingers Live In Europe; Full English Breakfast; with flute player Kirten Spratt): Doodle and Flight; Triligence (titles taken from jazz sonatas for flute and piano by Mike Mower). *Contributions to:* Björk, Debut; Brendan Power Plays the Music from Riverdance, 1997; James Galway, Unbreak My Heart, 1999. *Honours:* Hon ARAM. *Membership:* Musicians' Union. *Address:* 56 Lessar Ave, London SW4 9HQ, England.

MOYET, (Genevieve) Alison (Jane); b. 18 June 1961, Billericay, Essex, England. Vocalist; Songwriter. 1 s., 1 d. *Education:* Musical Foundation, Southend Technical College; Musical Instrument Technology. *Career:* Singer with Yazoo, 1981–83; Solo singer, 1983–. *Recordings:* Albums: with Yazoo: Upstairs At Eric's, 1982; You and Me Both (No. 1, UK), 1983; Solo albums: Alf, 1984; Raindancing, 1987; Hoodoo, 1991; Essex, 1994; Hometime, 2002. Singles, 1995; The Essential Alison Moyet, 2001. Hit singles include: with Yazoo: Only You, 1982; Don't Go, 1982; The Other Side of Love, 1982; Nobody's Diary, 1983; Solo: Love Resurrection, 1984; All Cried Out, 1984; That Ole Devil Called Love, 1985; Is This Love?, 1987; Weak In The Presence Of Beauty, 1987; Love Letters, 1987; Whispering Your Name, 1994; Solid Wood, 1995; Guest vocal on: Nearly God, Tricky, 1996; Performed theme song for BBC drama Playing The Field, 1997–2002; Joined West End London cast of Chicago, 2001. *Honours:* BRITS Award, Best New Band, Yazoo, 1982; Rock and Pop Award, Best Female Artist, 1982; Brits Awards, Best Female Artist, 1984, 1987. *Current Management:* Motley Music Ltd. *Address:* 132 Liverpool Rd, London N1 1LA, England.

MOYSE, Nigel Arthur; b. 26 Feb. 1952, Dublin, Ireland. Musician (electric, semi-acoustic, acoustic guitar). m. Elizabeth McColl, 15 June 1974, 1 s., 1 d. *Education:* BA, Natural Sciences, Moderator, Trinity Collge Dublin; Piano, Municipal School of Music (Dublin); Guitar, with Louis Stewart. *Career:* John Stevens Away and Dance Orchestra; Folkus; Freebop; Ed Speight; Nigel Moyse Quartet; Mike Stock Band; The Flirtations, backing band; Bracknell; Camden; City of London; Sheffield Festivals; Folkus, National tour, 1984; Round House; ICA; Hyde Park; 100 Club; Universities; Clubs; Jazz venues; Jazz in Britain, BBC Radio III; Visiting music teacher, Eton College, Windsor, Berkshire. *Compositions:* Co-written with Ed Speight: The Dodder Suite, 1980; Complications, 1981; Solo: Tsk Tsk; Ballad For Mick; Martin's Dilemma, 1980; (All performed live and on Jazz In Britain, 1980, 1981). *Recordings:* Away: Integration, 1980; Mutual Benefit, 1994; Dance Orchestra: Ah, 1978; Some of: Conversation Piece, 1991; A Luta Continua, 1994; Folkus: The Life of Riley, 1984. *Membership:* Musicians' Union. *Address:* Flat 1, 10 Denbeigh Rd, Ealing, London W13 8PX, England.

MR BIGGS. See: **ISLEY, Ronald.**

MR C, (Richard West); b. 1964, London, England. Rap Artiste; Vocalist; Musician (guitar). *Career:* Joined The Shamen, 1991; Numerous TV appearances; Club gigs and dance nights; Owner, The End dance club. *Recordings:* Make It Mine, 1992; LSI (Love Sex Intelligence), 1992; Ebeneezer Goode (No. 1, UK), 1992; Boss Drum, 1992; Phorever People, 1994; Transamazonia, 1995; Destination Eschaton, 1995; Hemp, 1996; Move Any Mountain, 1996; Universal, 1998; U Nations, 1998; Albums: Boss Drum, 1992; Different Drum, 1994; Axis Mutatis, 1995; Hempton Manor, 1996; UV, 1998; Solo albums: Mr C. Presents Subterrain 100% Unreleased, 2000; Change, 2002.

MR G. See: **MCBEAN, Colin.**

MS DYNAMITE, (Niomi McLean-Daley); b. London, England. Vocalist; Rap Artiste; MC. *Education:* Acland Burghley school. *Career:* MC at rave parties; Presenter, Flava (Channel Four television show); Signed to Polydor, 2001; Appeared on Guns On Our Streets debate (Carlton Television), 2001; UK tour, 2002; Collaborations with: Eminem, So Solid Crew. *Recordings:* Albums: A Little Deeper, 2002; A Little Darker, 2003. Singles: Booo!; Dy-Na-

Mi-Tee; It Takes More, 2002; Put Him Out, 2002. *Honours:* MOBO Awards, Best UK Act, Best Single, Best Newcomer, 2002; Mercury Music Prize, for A Little Deeper, 2002; BRIT Awards, Best British Female Artist, Best Urban Act, 2003. *Address:* c/o Polydor, Universal Music, Stralauer Allee 1, 10245 Berlin, Germany. *E-mail:* msdynamite@deadlymedia.co.uk. *Website:* www.msdynamite.co.uk.

MTUKUDZI, Oliver Tuku; b. 1952, Zimbabwe. Vocalist; Musician (guitar); Songwriter. *Career:* Joined Wagon Wheels with Thomas Mapfumo, 1977; First single, Dzandimomotera, went gold; Formed Black Spirits, recording two albums a year; Sound referred to as Tuku music; Wrote and directed musical Was My Child, 1990s; Tours of Africa, Australia, America and Europe; Performed at WOMAD Reading, 1998 and 2001; Appeared in The Soul of Mbira and TV documentary Under The African Skies; Lead role in first local feature film, Jit, 1990; Appeared in and composed for film Neria; Has recorded more than 40 albums. *Recordings:* 44 albums, incl.: Africa, 1980; Ziwere, 1993; Tuku Music, 1998; Paivepo, 1999; Bvuma, 2000; Vhunze Moto, 2002. *Honours:* M-Net Award, Best Soundtrack, Neria; Zimbabwe Writers Union, honour for Was My Child; CAMA (Celebration of African Artists Ceremony) award, 2001; Kora Award, Best African Arrangement, 2002. *Website:* www.putumayo.com.

MUBARAK, Abdel Aziz el; b. Sudan. Vocalist; Musician (oud). *Education:* Institute of Music and Drama, Khartoum. *Career:* Popular solo artiste; Tours extensively in Africa and Arab States, including: Ethiopia; Somalia; Nigeria; Chad; Cameroon; Egypt; Kuwait; UAE; Member of trio with Abdel Gadir Salim and Mohammed Gubara; Regular television and radio appearances. *Recordings:* with Abdel Gadir Salim and Mohammed Gubara: The Sounds of Sudan, 1991. *Address:* c/o World Circuit Records, 106 Cleveland St, London W1P 5DP, England.

MUES, Jan; b. 8 Feb. 1955, Leuven, Belgium. Musician (Flugelhorn; Trumpet; Composer; Arranger). m. Marie Paule Branders, 12 Nov. 1976, 1 d. *Education:* Painting, Academy Des Beaux Arts, Antwerp, Belgium. *Career:* Laureate, 11th edition, The European Jazz Contest International, 1989; Soloist, Belgian Jazz Orchestra; Jazz Festival in Milan; Several Belgian Radio and TV appearances; Jazz Middelheim Festival, Antwerp, 1995. *Compositions:* Mystic Smile; Whippy Lippy; Why Do You Skip So Tippy; Hayday; Who's Watching Who; Lullaby For the Sun; I Hope the Guys Like It; Foolish Enter; Peter's Egg. *Recordings:* Mystic Smile, CD album. *Publications:* De Koning the Rijk. *Honours:* Fifth Annually Sabamprice. *Membership:* SABAM. *Current Management:* Jan Mües, Mannenberg 70, 3270 Scherpenheuvel, Belgium.

MUGGERUD, Lawrence. See: **DJ MUGGS.**

MUGGLETON, Paul Frank; b. 27 Feb. 1947, Queen Charlotte, London, England. Record Prod. Partner, Judie Tzuke, 2 s., 3 d. *Education:* University of Madrid, Faculty of Philosophy and Literature; Classical guitar, Madrid, 18 months. *Career:* All major tours with Judie Tzuke including tour of America with Elton John; Played to 450,000, Central Park, New York (with Judie Tzuke); Television includes: Top of the Pops; many other shows; Started Big Moon Records, 1996. *Recordings:* Co-producer with Mike Paxman: All Judie Tzuke albums, 1980–92, plus Welcome To The Cruise And Sports Car, 2001; Nick Kamen albums; Presently Scarlet. *Honours:* Song Award, Festival De Malaga, 1970. *Membership:* PRS; Musicians' Union. *Current Management:* Big Ocean Productions, 15–19 Cavendish Pl., London W1M 0DD, England. *Address:* Big Moon Records, PO Box 347, Weybridge, Surrey KT13 9WZ, England.

MUHL, Lars; b. 14 Nov. 1950, Århus, Denmark. Vocalist; Songwriter; Musician; Author. *Education:* Classical Piano, Jutland Conservatory of Music, 2 years. *Career:* Formed Warm Guns, Released 5 Albums in Europe and Australia, 1978; Solo Career, Released 5 Albums, 1986–; Songwriting for European Artists; Author of 4 Books. *Compositions:* One More Minute; Open Up My Heart; Regnfang. *Recordings:* The Glorious Art of Breakin Little Girls Hearts and Blowin Big Boys Brains, 1984; King of Croon, 1988; When Angels Fall, 1990; Kingdom Come, 1993; Mandolina, 1997; The Best of Muhl, 1998. *Honours:* DJBFA Prize of Honour, 1990; WCM Songwriters Million Certificate, 1996. *Membership:* DJBFA; Danish Artists Asscn. *Address:* Warner Chappell Music, Anker Heegaardsgade 2, 1572 Copenhagen, Denmark.

MÜHLEIS, Daniela; b. 27 April 1955, St Gallen, Switzerland. Vocalist; Musician (guitar, piano). m. Hans Georg Huber, 26 Sept. 1986, 1 adopted d. *Education:* Commercial school, commercial association, St Gallen; Music Lessons: guitar, piano. *Career:* Joined Cargo, 1979; National Country and Western Festival in Zürich, Open-Air Festival, St Gallen, 1981; Swiss finals, European Song Contest; Debut album, 1983; Band renamed, Daniela Mühleis and Band, 1984; Successful concerts, Switzerland, Italy; Country Festivals; Swiss television: Sonntagsmagazin, 1989; Holansky kapr Country Music Festival, Prague, 1989; International Country Festival, Geiselwind, 1990; German Cable TV: Offener Kanal Dortmund, 1991; PORTA Country Festival, Czech Republic, 1992; International Visagino Country Festival, Lithuania,

1993; Lithuanian television; Swiss TV: Country Roads; Video clip produced in Malta, 1994; Television: Switzerland, Malta; Own radio show in St Gallen, Country Music, 1984–97; International Rising Star Award, by North America Country Music Association International, 1999. *Recordings include:* Albums: Stage-fright, 1983; Die Sieger des 1 Country und Western Festivals Zürich, 1986; Far Away, 1987; Animals, 1990: Far Away, 1991; Better Life, 1993; Open Minds, 1997. *Honours:* Winner, Modern Country Music section, Swiss Country Open Air, 1985; SRI Selection, 1997. *Membership:* CMA, USA; CMFS, Switzerland; ECMA; NACMAI, USA; ECMA, Europe. *Current Management:* DMB. *Address:* Lehnackerstrasse 9a, 9033 Untereggen, Switzerland.

MUIR, Mike; Vocalist. *Career:* Member, Suicidal Tendencies; Numerous live gigs in USA; Also member, side project Infectious Grooves with Robert Trujillo, with Ozzy Osbourne guesting on debut album; Supported Blizzard of Oz No More Tears tour. *Recordings:* With Suicidal Tendencies: Suicidal Tendencies, 1983; Join the Army, 1987; How Will I Laugh Tomorrow When I Can't Even Smile Today, 1988; Controlled by Hatred, 1989; Lights, Camera, Revolution, 1990; F.N.G., compilation, 1992; The Art of Rebellion, 1992; Still Cyco After All These Years, 1993; Suicidal for Life, 1994; Prime Cuts, 1997; Friends and Family, compilation, 1998; Six the Hard Way, EP, 1998; FreeDumb, 1999; Free Your Soul And Save Your Mind, 2000; With Infectious Grooves: The Plague that Makes Your Booty Move, 1991; Sarsippius' Ark, 1993; Groove Family Cyco, 1994; Mas Borracho, 2000.

MUIRHEAD, Dennis Richard; b. 7 Oct. 1941, Dubbo, New South Wales, Australia. Lawyer. m. (1) Elizabeth, Dec. 1966, 3 s., (2) Angel, 10 Dec. 1988, 1 s., 1 d. *Education:* Law, University of Adelaide, South Australia. *Career:* Consultant Lawyer, Simons, Muirhead and Burton; CEO, Dennis Muirhead Company Ltd, Muirhead Management, 1982–; Management, business, legal services to record producers, engineers, studios, artists, songwriters; Clients include producers: Hugh Padgham; Jon Jacobs; Denis Woods; Colin Richardson; Richard Bennett; R S Field; Sun Studio Entertainment, Memphis; Australian jazz pianist and composer Paul Grabowsky; Missouri rockabilly singer, songwriter Billy Swan; Council Assisting the South Australian Royal Commission into the non-medical use of drugs; Chairman of City Roads (Crisis Intervention); Chairman, Institute for the Study of Drug Dependence; Founding Chairman and council member of The Music Managers' Forum; CEO, Muirhead Music and Hugely Music Publishing; Consultant in New Media. *Membership:* Country Music Assocn, NARAS, Nashville. *Address:* 202 Fulham Rd, London SW10 9PJ, England.

MULDAUR, Maria, (Maria Grazia Rosa Domenica d'Avato); b. 12 Sept. 1943, Greenwich Village, New York, USA. Vocalist. m. Jeff Muldaur, divorced 1972. *Career:* Member, Even Dozen Jug Band (with John Sebastian, Stefan Grossman, Joshua Rifkin, Steve Katz); Jim Kweskin Jug Band; US tour, 1975; European debut, 1975. *Recordings:* Albums: Maria Muldaur, 1973; Waitress In A Donut Shop, 1974; Sweet Harmony, 1976; Southern Winds, 1978; Open Your Eyes, 1979; Gospel Nights, 1980; There Is A Love, 1982; Sweet and Slow, 1984; Transblucency, 1985; Live In London, 1987; On The Sunny Side, 1991; Louisiana Love Call, 1992; Meet Me at Midnite, 1994; Jazzabelle, 1995; Fanning the Flames, 1996; Southland of the Heart, 1998; Swingin' in the Rain, 1998; Meet Me Where They Play the Blues, 1999; Music For Lovers, 2000; Richland Woman Blues, 2001; Singles include: Midnight At The Oasis; I'm A Woman. *Current Management:* Piedmont Talent, 311 Oakdale Rd, Charlotte, NC 28216, USA.

MULDOON, Mule (Paul Gerrard); b. 29 Oct. 1958, Huddersfield, Yorkshire, England. Musician (bass, guitar); Vocalist. m. C A Nester, 20 May 1995. *Career:* Own band, Muldoon Brothers; Appeared at many major country festivals throughout Europe; Appearances on British, Irish and Scandinavian television and radio. *Compositions:* Back O' The Barn; Following The Trail; Brandin' Time. *Recordings:* Back O' The Barn, by Muldoon Brothers. *Honours:* Most Promising Country Act, 1992. *Membership:* Musicians' Union. *Current Management:* International Artists Ltd. *Address:* 17 South Lane, Netherton, Wakefield, West Yorkshire WF4 4LL, England.

MULET, Sergio Roberto; b. 2 Nov. 1958, Montevideo, Uruguay. Musician (drums, congas, timbales, Brazillian percussion); Arranger; Music Teacher. m. Eloisa Valeria, 1 s., 2 d. *Education:* AMEB sixth grade; Many years of study on drums, congas and percussion (various styles). *Career:* Supported Gypsy Kings in Sydney, 1989; Many Australian TV appearances; Formed Sandunga (Australia's first Afro-Cuban band); Artistic Dir, Event Co-ordinator, Manly World Music Concert Series; Man. and Co-ordinator, Manly International Jazz Festival, 1998–. *Membership:* Australian Jazz Society. *Current Management:* Havana Entertainment. *Address:* 80 King St, Manly Vale, NSW 2093, Australia. *E-mail:* sergiomulet@yahoo.com. *Website:* sandunga.iuma.com.

MULLEN, Larry, Jr; b. 31 Oct. 1961, Dublin, Ireland. Musician (drums). *Career:* Founder member, drummer, rock group U2, 1978–; Regular national and international tours; Major concerts include: US Festival, 1983; The Longest Day, Milton Keynes, 1985; Live Aid, Wembley, 1985; Self Aid, Dublin, 1986; A Conspiracy of Hope (Amnesty International Tour), 1986; New

Year's Eve concert, Dublin (broadcast live to Europe), 1989. *Recordings:* Albums: Boy, 1980; October, 1981; War (No. 1, UK), 1983; Under A Blood Red Sky, 1983; The Unforgettable Fire (No. 1, UK), 1984; Wide Awake In America, 1985; The Joshua Tree (No. 1, UK and USA), 1987; Rattle and Hum, also film (No. 1, USA) 1988; Achtung Baby (No. 1, USA), 1991; Zooropa (No. 1, UK and USA), 1993; Passengers (film soundtrack), with Brian Eno, 1995; Pop, 1997; The Best of U2 1980–90, 1998; All That You Can't Leave Behind, 2000; The Best Of, 1990–2000. Singles include: Out of Control (No. 1, Ireland), 1979; Another Day (No. 1, Ireland), 1980; New Year's Day, 1983; Two Hearts Beat As One, 1983; Pride (In The Name of Love), 1984; The Unforgettable Fire, 1985; With Or Without You (No. 1, USA), 1987; I Still Haven't Found What I'm Looking For (No. 1, USA), 1987; Where The Streets Have No Name, 1987; Desire (No. 1, UK), 1988; Angel of Harlem, 1988; When Love Comes To Town, with B. B. King, 1989; All I Want Is You, 1989; The Fly (No. 1, UK), 1991; Mysterious Ways, 1992; Even Better Than The Real Thing, 1992; One, 1992; Who's Gonna Ride Your Wild Horses, 1992; Hold Me, Thrill Me, Kiss Me (from film Batman Forever), 1995; Theme from film soundtrack, Mission Impossible (solo with Adam Clayton), 1996; Discotheque (No. 1, UK), 1997; If God Will Send His Angels, 1997; The Sweetest Thing, 1998; Beautiful Day (No. 1, UK), 2000; Stuck In A Moment You Can't Get Out Of, 2001; Walk On, 2001; Electrical Storm, 2002. *Honours:* Grammy Awards, Album of the Year, for The Joshua Tree, 1987, Best Rock Album, for All That You Can't Leave Behind, 2001, Best Alternative Music Album, for Zooropa, 1993, Song of the Year, for Beautiful Day, 2000, Record of the Year, for Beautiful Day, 2000, for Walk On, 2001, Best Rock Performance By A Duo Or Group With Vocal, for The Joshua Tree, 1987, for Desire, 1988, for Achtung Baby, 1992, for Beautiful Day, 2000, for Elevation, 2001, Best Pop Performance By A Duo Or Group With Vocal, for Stuck In A Moment You Can't Get Out Of, 2001, Best Music Video, Long Form, for Zoo TV, Live From Sydney, 1994, Best Performance Music Video, for Where The Streets Have No Name, 1988; BRIT Awards: Best International Group, 1988–90, 1998, 2001; Outstanding Contribution Award, 2001; Best Live Album, 1993; World Music Award, 1993; Juno Award, 1993; Q Awards: Best Act In The World, 1990; 1992; 1993; Merit Award, 1994; American Music Award, Favorite Internet Artist of the Year, 2002; Ivor Novello Award, Best Song Musically and Lyrically, for Walk On, 2002; Golden Globe, Best Original Song, for The Hands That Built America (from film Gangs of New York), 2003; Gold and Platinum discs; Numerous magazine awards and poll wins. *Current Management:* Principle Management, 30–32 Sir John Rogersons Quay, Dublin 2, Ireland. *Website:* www.u2.com.

MÜLLER, Anders; b. 2 Feb. 1955, Copenhagen, Denmark. Musician (piano, keyboards); Composer; Arranger. m. Anne Macholm, 6 June 1987, 2 s. *Education:* Music Graduate, University of Copenhagen; Piano lessons with Ole Kock Hansen. *Career:* Leader, own jazz trio and quartets, 1975–; Member, orchestras led by Erling Kroner, Leif Johansson, Per Goldschmidt, 1979–92; Co-leader, jazz-rock group, Ariel, 1979–83; Appeared with New Music Orchestra as pianist, 1985, 1992; Conductor, 1990; Composer, 1985, 1988; Also worked with: Thad Jones; Eddie Bert; Red Rodney; Etta Cameron. *Compositions:* Tashmia; Woody's Blues, recorded by Lee Konitz. *Recordings:* with Erling Kroner; Leif Johansson; Ariel. *Honours:* First prize, Dunkerque Jazz Festival, with Soren Bogelund Quartet. *Membership:* DJBFA. *Current Management:* Mazurka Music. *Address:* Mazurka Music, Gammel Kongevej 78, 2 tv, 1850 Frederiksberg C, Denmark.

MULLER, Christoph H; b. France. Prod; Musician; Composer. *Career:* Owner, Ya Basta! Records, with Philippe Cohen Solal; mem. Boyz From Brazil, with Philippe Cohen Solal; Mem., band Gotan Project, 1999–; World-wide Gotan Project tour, 2002, mixing video, pre-recorded and live performances; Collaborations with many tango musicians. *Recordings:* Album: La Revancha Del Tango, 2001. EPs: El Capitalismo Foraneo, 2000; Triptico, 2000; Santa Maria, 2001. *Address:* c/o XL-Recordings, 17–19 Alma Rd, London SW18 1AA, England. *E-mail:* yabastarecords@noos.fr. *Website:* www.gotanproject.com.

MULLIGAN, Néillidh (Neil); b. 13 May 1955, Dublin, Ireland. Public Servant; Musician (Uilleann pipes). m. Sandra Ní Gharbháin, 6 Nov. 1993, 1 s., 1 d. *Education:* Taught by Tom Mulligan (father) and Leo Rowsome. *Career:* Played and toured many parts of the world including: Europe; America; New Zealand; Concerts in major cities; Many television and radio appearances home and abroad; Represented Ireland at various International Bagpipe Festivals. *Compositions include:* Barr Na Cúille; Tom Mulligan's Hornpipe; Wings of My Soul. *Recordings:* Albums: Barr Na Cúille, 1991; The Leitrim Thrush, 1997; Guest on other albums. *Contributions to:* piping publications. *Honours:* All-Ireland Champion at various age levels. *Membership:* Na Píobairí Uilleann; Folk Music Society of Ireland; Irish Traditional Music Archive. *Current Management:* Darina Ní Chuinneagáin, Allegro Music Agency.

MUMBA, Samantha Tamania Anne Cecilia; b. 18 Jan. 1983. Vocalist. *Education:* Billie Barry Stage School, Dublin, age 3–15. *Career:* Lead role in Dublin stage musical The Hot Mikado, 1998; Various Irish TV appearances followed; Signed with manager Louis Walsh after meeting in Dublin nightclub; Made first recordings while still at school; Scored in UK with first releases; Film appearance, The Time Machine, 2001. *Recordings:* Albums: Gotta Tell You, 2000; Singles: Gotta Tell You, Body II Body, 2000; Always Come Back To Your Love, Baby Come On Over, Lately, 2001. *Honours:* Smash Hits Award, Best New Female Artist, 2000. *Current Management:* Louis Walsh, Carol and Associates/WAR Management, 57 Meadowbank, Bushy Park Rd, Dublin 6, Ireland. *E-mail:* carolh@indigo.ie. *Website:* www.samanthamumba.com.

MUNDEN, David Charles; b. 2 Dec. 1943, Dagenham, Essex, England. Musician (drums); Vocalist. m. Andrée, 7 Dec. 1969, 1 s., 1 d. *Career:* Member, The Tremeloes; Toured world-wide: USA; South America; Australia; New Zealand; Iceland; South Africa; Middle East; Far East; Iceland; Germany; Eastern Bloc countries; Played with Beatles; Rolling Stones; Roy Orbison; Dusty Springfield; Television includes: Ready Steady Go; Top of the Pops; Sunday Night Live At The Palladium. *Recordings:* Twist and Shout; Do You Love Me (No. 1, UK), 1963; Someone, Someone; Candy Man; Here Comes My Baby; Silence Is Golden (No. 1, UK); Call Me Number One (No. 1, UK and world-wide); Helule Helule; Even The Bad Times Are Good; My Little Lady; Suddenly You Love Me; Me and My Life; I Shall be Released; Once on a Sunday Morning; Tremeloes played on Jeff Christie's No. 1 hit Yellow River; Albums: Shiner, 1974; As It Happened, 1983; Best of the Tremeloes, 1992. *Publications:* Guinness Book of Hit Records. *Honours:* Carl Alan Awards. *Membership:* Musicians' Union; Equity; PRS. *Current Management:* Stephen Colyer. *Address:* 25A Cliff Parade, Leigh-on-Sea, Essex SS9 1BB, England.

MUNKGAARD, Peer; b. 29 March 1965, Vejle, Denmark. Music Teacher; Freelance Musician (viola, violin). *Education:* Graduate, Esbjerg Kommunale Gymnasium, 1984; Studied viola with Gert Inge Andersson at the Music Academy in Esbjerg, 1987–93. *Career:* Danced folkdances since 1969; Played folk music (fiddle), 1973–; Danced on television show Les Lanciers, 1983; Danced in and played for numerous folkdance groups including Udöbt on their first tours in England; Danish representative on the Comhaltas Ceoltoiri Eireann European Tour, 1985; Instructor of folk dance and music at seminars, music schools and evening schools; Teacher of viola, violin, cello, chamber music, orchestras and choirs; Member of West Jutland Symphony Orchestra and the Jutland Sinfonietta; Assisted in various symphony orchestras and Esbjerg Ensemble; Also played in musicals including: The King and I, Showboat and the Phantom of the Opera. *Membership:* Danish Musicians' Union. *Current Management:* Det Klassiske Koncertbureau, Rorhaven 4, 8900 Randers, Denmark. *Address:* Peder Skrams Gade 5, II tv, 6700 Esbjerg, Denmark.

MUNRO, Donnie; b. 2 Aug. 1953, Uig, Isle of Skye, Scotland. Musician (guitar); Art Teacher. m. Andrée, 1980, 2 s., 1 d. *Education:* DA Hons, Dip Ed. *Career:* Member, Scottish folk group, Runrig, 1973–97; World-wide tours; Numerous television appearances; First Rector, University of the Highlands and Islands Project; Solo artiste, 1997–. *Recordings:* Albums: with Runrig: Play Gaelic, 1978; The Highland Connection, 1979; Recovery, 1981; Heartland, 1985; The Cutter And The Clan, 1987; Once In A Lifetime, 1988; Searchlight, 1989; The Big Wheel, 1991; Amazing Things, 1993; Townsmitting Live, 1995; Mara, 1996; Beat The Drum, 1999. *Contributions to:* Troubadours of British Folk, Vol. 3, 1995; Best of British Folk Rock, 1996; Solo: On The West Side, 1999; Across The City And The World, 2002. *Publications:* Going Home – The Runrig Story, Tony Morton. *Honours:* Rector, Edinburgh University, 1991–94; Dr h.c., 1994. *Membership:* Musicians' Union. *Current Management:* Marlene Ross Management, 55 Wellington St, Aberdeen AB2 1BX, Scotland.

MUPEMHI, Adrian, (Stoan); *Career:* Backing vocalist for Thebe; Mem., kwaito band, Bongo Maffin, 1996– World Wild Grooves tour, France, 2000; Performances in UK, Denmark, 2000; worked with: Skunk Anansie, Chaka Khan, Stevie Wonder, Boys II Men, Hugh Masekela. *Recordings:* Albums: Final Entry, 1996; The Concerto, 1998; IV, 1999; Bongolution, 2001. *Honours:* South African Music Award, Best Kwaito Artist, 1999; Kora Award, Best African Group, 2001; Gold disc, for Bongolution. *Address:* c/o Sony Music South Africa, 230 Jan Smuts Ave, Dunkeld West, 2196 Gauteng, South Africa.

MURCIA, Joey; b. 21 March 1948, Brooklyn, New York, USA. Musician (guitar). 1 s. *Education:* Graduate, Grove School of Music. *Career:* Session guitarist, 30 years; Major tours with: Benny Lattimore, support to James Brown, 1975; Bee Gees, Here At Last Tour, 1976, Spirits Having Flown Tour, 1979; Jay Ferguson, support to Foreigner, 1977; Andy Gibb, Shadow Dancing Tour, 1978; Performances with Ann Jillian include: Tahoe, Las Vegas, 1984; Trump Plaza, Atlantic City, 1989, 1990. *Compositions:* Cozumel, Jay Ferguson, 1978; Jennifer Slept Here, Joey Scarborough, theme for NBC series, 1985; Ann Jillian, theme for NBC series, 1990. *Recordings:* Albums: Clean Up Women, Betty Wright; Rockin Chair, Gwen McCrae; Lattimore III, Benny Lattimore; Monkey Grip Glue, Bill Wyman; Here At Last-Bee Gees Live, Bee Gees; Thunder Island, Jay Ferguson; But Seriously Folks, Joe Walsh; A Luxury You Can Afford, Joe Cocker; Grease, Frankie Valli; Saturday Night Fever, Bee Gees; Restless, Bellamy Brothers; with Andy Gibb: Flowing Rivers; Shadow Dancing; After Dark; Andy Gibb's Greatest Hits; Singles with Andy Gibb: I Just Want To Be Your Everything; Thicker Than Water; Shadow Dancing; Everlasting Love; Latimore, Straighten it Out: The Best of Latimore, 1995; Getting Down to Brass Tacks, 1995. *Honours:* 10

Gold Albums, with Bee Gees, Andy Gibb, Joe Walsh. *Membership:* AFofM, 30 years. *Current Management:* Have Mercy Music Inc. *Address:* 2080 W Hillcrest Dr., Suite # 106, Newbury Park, CA 91320, USA.

MURDOCH, Stuart; b. 25 Aug. 1968, Scotland. Vocalist; Musician (guitar); Songwriter. *Career:* Member: Belle and Sebastian 1996–; Collaborations: Future Pilot AKA; Arab Strap; Hefner; Curated Bowlie Weekend Festival with other band members, 1999. *Recordings:* Albums: Tigermilk, If You're Feeling Sinister, 1996; The Boy With The Arab Strap 1998; Fold Your Hands Child – You Walk Like A Peasant, 2000; Storytelling, 2002. Singles: Dog On Wheels EP, Lazy Line Painter Jane EP, 3–6–9 Seconds of Light EP, 1997; This Is Just A Modern Rock Song EP, 1998; Legal Man, 2000; Jonathan David, I'm Waking Up To Us, 2001. *Honours:* BRIT Award, Best Newcomer, 1999. *Current Management:* Banchory Management, PO Box 25074, Glasgow G2 6YL, Scotland. *Website:* www.belleandsebastian.co.uk.

MURPHY, Jamie; b. 1977. Musician (guitar); Vocalist; Songwriter. *Career:* Founder Member, Space, 1993; Numerous television appearances and headlining tours. *Recordings:* Singles: If It's Real, 1993; Money, 1995; Neighbourhood, 1996; Female of the Species, 1997; Me and You Vs the World, 1996; Dark Clouds, 1997; Avenging Angels, 1997; The Ballad of Tom Jones, with Cerys Matthews, 1998; Begin Again, 1998; Bad Days, 1998; Albums: Spiders, 1996; Remixes and B-Sides, 1996; Tin Planet, 1998; Greatest Hits, 2001.

MURPHY, John; b. 4 March 1965, Liverpool, England. Composer; Musician (guitar). *Career:* Session guitarist, worked with members of Japan, Propaganda; While working with Thomas Lang, began collaboration in composition with David Hughes. *Compositions:* with David Hughes: Films: Leon The Pig Farmer; Solitaire For 2; Clockwork Mice; Welcome To The Terrordome; Beyond Bedlam; A Feast At Midnight; Body Memories; Dinner In Purgatory; Destroying Angels; Proteus; Flame; Giving Tongue; Lock, Stock and Two Smoking Barrels; Stiff Upper Lips; The Real Howard Spitz; Television: White Men Are Cracking Up, BBC2; All The President's Women; Eunice The Gladiator (Channel 4); Where The Bad Girls Go, Granada; Black Velvet Band, Yorkshire. *Recordings:* Lock, Stock and Two Smoking Barrels. *Membership:* PRS; Musicians' Union. *Current Management:* Soundtrack Music Associates Ltd. *Address:* 22 Ives St, Chelsea, London SW3 2ND, England.

MURPHY, Robert Joseph; b. 3 June 1936, Summit, New Jersey, USA. Musician (saxophone, percussion). m. Judith Ann Miller, 3 Aug. 1962, 2 d. *Education:* BA, Brown University, 1958; LLB, Stanford University, 1963; Jazz Studies, Deanza College, Cupertino, California, 1972–75. *Career:* European tour, 1983, 1997; 3 times guest soloist, Kobe Jazz Festival Japan, 1991–93; Ranked number 16 among soprano soloists world-wide, Jazzology Readers Poll, 1985; On faculty of Stanford Jazz Workshop. *Compositions:* Red Neck Blues, musical condemnation of racism; To the Emerald Isle. *Recordings:* 11 albums with Natural Gas Jazz Band. *Publications:* Jazz theory text for Stanford jazz workshop. *Membership:* BMI.

MURPHY, Roisin; b. Dublin, Ireland. Vocalist; Composer; Prod. *Career:* Mem., and Turquoise Car Crash, The; Mem., Moloko, with Mark Brydon, 1995–. *Recordings:* Albums: Do You Like My Tight Sweater?, 1995; I Am Not A Doctor, 1998; Things To Make And Do, 2000; All Back To Mine, 2001. Singles: Where Is The What If The What Is The Why; Fe Fi Fo Fum For Me; The Moloko EP, 1995; Fun For Me, 1995; Dominoid, 1996; The Flipside, 1998; Sing It Back, 1999; The Time Is Now, 2000; Pure Pleasure Seeker, 2000; Indigo, 2000. *Address:* c/o Echo Records, Chrysalis Group PLC, The Chrysalis Bldg, Bramley Rd, London W10 6SP, England. *Website:* www.moloko.co.uk.

MURPHY, Terence James; b. 3 Oct. 1948, Dublin, Ireland. Musician (mandolin, banjo, guitar); Vocalist. m. Kristina Karlsson, 26 Oct. 1991, 1 s., 1 d. *Education:* Provincial High School of Music. *Career:* Tour of England, 1978; Netherlands, 1979 including television appearance; Tour of Germany with appearances on television and radio folk programmes, 1982; Touring and appearances on TV in Denmark, Sweden and Norway. *Recordings:* 4 albums with McEwan's Expotit: Hand Across The Water, 1979, McEwans, 1981, Highland Paddy, 1988, and McEwans, 1990; 3 Solo albums: Terry Murphy: A Dubliner In Denmark, 1982, Don't Bury Me 'Til I'm Dead, 1984; Jack of All Trades, 1986. *Membership:* DJBFA; Musicians' Union; Gramex. *Address:* Humlebaekgade 7 4 tv, 2200 Copenhagen, Denmark.

MURRAY, Andy; b. 31 July 1952, Isleworth, England. Composer; Songwriter; Musician (guitar, bass, keyboards). *Education:* University of Sussex; Royal Academy of Music. *Career:* Top 20 hit with Piranhas, 1982; Top of the Pops; Composer, television and video soundtracks; School and college music lecturer, examiner; Advisory consultant, Music Technology in Education. *Publications:* Music Matters, Notator Software Resource Packs, 1993; The Music IT Pack, 1997; New Music Matters 11–14, CD-ROMS, 1998; Music Technology in Action, 1998; Music Technology Inspected, 1999; ICT Activities for Music 11–14, 2002; Music Time Machine, 2002. *Honours:* BA; LRAM; BBC Song contest winner. *Membership:* PRS; Musicians' Union; NASUWT; ISM; NAME. *Address:* 69 Riley Rd, Brighton BN2 4AG, England.

MURRAY, Anne; b. 20 June 1945, Springhill, Nova Scotia, Canada. Vocalist. m. William M Langstroth, 20 June 1975, 1 s., 1 d. *Education:* BPhys, Education, University of New Brunswick, 1966; DLitt (hon), 1978; DLitt (hon), St Mary's University, 1978. *Career:* Recording artist, 1968–; World-wide tours; Television appearances: Singer, Singalong Jubilee, CBC television network, Canada; Numerous CBS US television specials, 1970–2000; Regular guest, Glen Campbell's Goodtime Hour. *Recordings:* Hits singles: Snowbird, 1970; Danny's Song, 1973; You Needed Me, 1978; He Thinks I Still Care (No. 1, USA country chart); Just Another Woman In Love; Could I Have This Dance, from film Urban Cowboy; A Little Good News, 1983; Nobody Loves Me Like You Do, duet with Kenny Loggins (No. 1, USA country chart), 1984; Albums: What About Me, 1968; This Way is My Way, 1969; Snowbird, 1970; Anne Murray, 1971; Talk It Over In The Morning, 1971; Annie, 1972; Danny's Song, 1973; Love Song, 1974; Country, 1974; Highly Prized Possession, 1974; Together, 1975; Keeping In Touch, 1976; Let's Keep It That Way, 1978; Hippo In My Tub (children's songs), 1977; New Kind of Feeling, 1979; I'll Always Love You, 1979 Somebody's Waiting, 1980; Where Do You Go To When You Dream, 1981; The Hottest Night Of The Year, 1982; A Little Good News, 1983; Heart Over Mind, 1984; Something To Talk About, 1986; Songs of The Heart, 1987; As I Am, 1988; Harmony, 1987; I Will, 1990; Yes I Do, 1991; Croonin', 1993; The Best... So Far, 1994; Anne Murray, 1996; An Intimate Evening with Anne Murray, 1997; What A Wonderful World, 1999; What A Wonderful Christmas, 2001; with Glen Campbell: Anne Murray and Glen Campbell, 1973. *Honours:* Numerous JUNO Awards, Top Female Vocalist, 1970–81; Grammy, Top Female Vocalist, 1978; Star on Hollywood Walkway of Stars, 1980; Inducted into Country Music Hall of Fame; Decorated Companion Order of Canada; Inducted into the Juno Hall of Fame, 1993. *Membership:* AFTRA; Asscn Canadian TV and Radio Artists; Executive mem., Canadian Save The Children Fund (Hon. Chairwoman, 1978–80). *Current Management:* Bruce Allen Talent, 68 Water St, Suite 406, Vancouver, BC V6B 1A4, Canada.

MURRAY, Neil; b. 27 Aug. 1950, Edinburgh, Scotland. Musician (bass guitar). *Education:* London College of Printing. *Career:* Member, Gilgamesh, 1973; Hanson, 1974; Colosseum II, 1975–76; National Health, 1976–77; Whitesnake, 1978–82; Gary Moore, 1982–83; Whitesnake, 1984–86; Vow Wow, 1987–89; Black Sabbath, 1989–90; Brian May Band, 1992–93; Black Sabbath, 1994–. *Recordings:* Albums include: with Whitesnake: Trouble, 1978; Lovehunter, 1979; Ready An' Willing, 1980; Live In The Heart of The City, 1980; Come An' Get It, 1981; Saints An' Sinners, 1982; Slide It In, 1984; Whitesnake 1987, 1987; Whitesnake's Greatest Hits, 1994; with Black Sabbath: Tyr, 1990; Forbidden, 1995. *Contributions to:* Gary Moore, Corridors of Power, 1982; Rockin' every Night, 1983; Victims of the Future, 1983; Brian May, Back to the Light, 1993; Another World, 1998; Twang!: A Tribute to Hank Marvin, 1996; Company Of Snakes, Here They Go Again (Live), 2001. *Current Management:* Bluefame Ltd. *Address:* 17 Hereford Mansions, Hereford Rd, London W2 5BA, England.

MURRAY, Phil; b. 18 Nov. 1953, North Shields, England. Writer; Performer. m. Allison Longstaff, 15 Aug. 1980, 2 s., 1 d. *Career:* Singer, songwriter with U Boat; Member of Blackie; Actor, television programmes including: Dempsey and Makepeace; Cats Eyes; Les Dawson Show; Many theatre tours; Personal Development author and presenter. *Recordings:* Album: End of My Time, U Boat; Single: Making A Bad Boy Good, U Boat; Also on albums: Talk Talk; Separate Holiday; Forever Again (love songs). *Publications:* Books: You Can Always Get What You Want; Before The Beginning Is A Thought; Empowerment, 1995; The 49 Steps to a Bright Life, 1996; Phil Murray Bites on Personal Development, 1997; You and Me Make Three, 1997; Staying Awake Forever, 1997; The Flow of Life, 1998. *Membership:* Equity; Musicians' Union; PRS; MCPS; PPS. *Current Management:* Perfect Words and Music. *Address:* 6 Church St, Isle of Wight, PO38 1SW, England.

MURRELL, David Evan (Dave); b. 22 Jan. 1952, London, England. Musician; College Lecturer (music); Arranger. m. Debora Anne Diamond, 5 July 1980, 2 d. *Education:* Art college; Humber College, Toronto, Canada. *Career:* Solo recordings, sessions, Transatlantic Records; Tours, Canada, USA with: Ken Tobias; Tommy Hunter; Ronnie Prophet; British artists: Psychic TV; Long John Baldry; Zoot Money; MD, arranger, World of Dance. *Recordings:* MD, Yamaha Jazz Connection; Film music: Words of Love, BBC, 1990; Long Way Home, ITV, 1991. *Membership:* Musicians' Union. *Address:* 37 Woodland Rd, Selsey, Sussex PO20 0AL, England.

MURTO, Janne; b. 26 Oct. 1964. Musician (saxophone, flutes). *Education:* Oulunkylä Pop/Jazz Conservatoire, 1982; Jazz Department, Sibelius Academy; Studied musical culture, Cuba. *Career:* Member, various big bands including Espoo Big Band; Big Bad Family, with Upi Sorvali; UMO Big Band; 10 years with Fiestacita (Afro-Cuban ensemble); Freelance musician for recording studios, radio and theatre; Current member, Paroni Paakunainen's Saxperiment Quartet; Kari Tenaken's Quintet.

MUSGRAVE, Gerard; b. 28 Aug. 1960, Bradford, England. Musician (Bass Guitar); Composer; Songwriter. 1 s., 1 d. *Education:* Private music lessons. *Career:* Appeared with Ruby Wax in Wax on Wheels, Channel 4 TV, 1990; Appearance, BBC2 Out of Our Heads, with Creation Roots, 1992; Appearances at Bradford Festival, Leeds Carnival, Huddersfield Carnival,

Music in the Sun Reggae Festival, Sheffield Don Valley. *Recordings:* Album, Troddin, 1999. *Membership:* PRS; MCPS; Musicians' Union. *Address:* 23 Wood End Court, West Bowling, Bradford BD5 8QL, England.

MUSHOK, Mike; b. 10 April 1970, Manhasset, New York, USA. Musician (guitar). *Education:* Electrical Engineering degree. *Career:* Previously worked with HVAC Applications; Formed Staind with Aaron Lewis and others; First live gig, 1995; Released self-financed debut album, 1996; Album sold 4,000 copies; Discovered by Fred Durst, 1997; Signed to Flip/Elektra; Presented to rock cognoscenti at Limp Bizkit gold record party for Three Dollar Bill Y'All $, 1998; Major breakthrough with unscheduled smash US No. 1 radio hit Outside; Appeared on bill for Korn-founded Family Values tours, 1999 and 2001; Headlined MTV's Return of the Rock tour, 2000. *Recordings:* Albums: Tormented, 1996; Dysfunction, 1999; Break The Cycle, 2001; Singles: Mudshovel, Just Go, 1999; Home, Outside, 2000; It's Been Awhile, Fade, 2001. *Honours:* Break The Cycle certified quadruple platinum by RIAA; It's Been Awhile topped Billboard Modern Rock Singles Chart for record-equalling 16 weeks; VH-1 Award, Your Song Kicked Ass But Was Played Too Damn Much prize, 2001; Guitar World Readers Poll, Best New Talent, Mike Mushok, 2000. *Address:* c/o The Firm, Inc, 9100 Whilshire Blvd, Suite 400W, Beverly Hills, CA 90212, USA. *Website:* www.staind.com.

MUSHROOM, (Andrew Vowles); b. 10 Nov. 1967, Bristol, England. Musician (keyboards); Prod. *Career:* Member, Massive Attack; Began as collective The Wild Bunch with Tricky, Goldie, Neneh Cherry and Nellee Hooper; Formed Massive Attack, 1986; Numerous club gigs and parties; Collaborations with Shara Nelson, Tricky, Horace Andy, Tracey Thorn of Everything But The Girl and Liz Fraser of Cocteau Twins. *Recordings:* Singles: Daydreaming, with Shara Nelson, 1990; Unfinished Sympathy, with Shara Nelson, 1991; Safe From Harm EP, 1991; Be Thankful/Hymn Of The Big Wheel, 1992; Sly, 1994; Protection, with Tracey Thorn, 1995; Karmacoma, 1995; Risingson, 1997; Teardrop, with Liz Fraser, 1998; Inertia Creeps, 1998; Angel/Group Four, 1998; 1 Against 1, 2002. Albums: Blue Lines, 1991; Protection, 1994; No Protection: Massive Attack vs Mad Professor, 1995; Mezzanine, 1998; The Singles Collection (box set), 1999; DVD compilation, 2001. *Honours:* BRIT Award, Best British Dance Act, 1996. *Website:* www.massiveattack.com.

MUSSANGO, Duke; b. 6 April 1980, Yaounde, Cameroon. Musician (drums). *Education:* Musical studies with Billy Mussango. *Compositions:* Numerous songs published. *Membership:* Socimada. *Address:* c/o Billy Mussango, PO Box 8363 Yaounde, Cameroon.

MUSTAINE, Dave; b. 13 Sept. 1961, La Mesa, CA, USA. Rock Vocalist; Musician (guitar); Songwriter. *Career:* Mem., Metallica, 1981–83; Founder mem., guitarist, songwriter, Megadeth, 1983–2002; World-wide tours; Concerts include: Monsters of Rock Festival, Castle Donington, 1988; Clash of The Titans Fest (with Slayer, Suicidal Tendencies, Testament), Wembley, 1990; Rock In Rio Festival, Brazil, 1991; Clash of The Titans, US tour (with Anthrax, Slayer, Alice In Chains), 1991. *Recordings:* Albums: Killing Is My Business and Business Is Good!, 1985; Peace Sells... But Who's Buying?, 1986; So Far So Good... So What?, 1988; Rust In Peace, 1990; Countdown To Extinction, 1992; Youthanasia, 1994; Rude Awakening, 2002. Hit singles: Wake Up Dead, 1987; Anarchy In The UK, 1988; No More Mister Nice Guy, 1990; Holy Wars, 1990; Hangar 18, 1991; Symphony of Destruction, 1992; Skin of My Teeth, 1992; Sweating Bullets, 1993; Breadline EP, 2000; Capitol Punishment: The Megadeth Years, 2000; World Needs A Hero, 2001; Other recordings: Contributor, film soundtracks: Super Mario Brothers, 1993; The Last Action Hero, 1993; Contributor, The Beavis and Butthead Experience. *Honours:* Doris Day Music Award; Genesis Award. *Current Management:* Lafitte Management, 1333 Ventura Blvd #204, Sherman Oaks, CA 91423, USA.

MYATT, Charlie; b. 24 June 1965, Bristol, England. Booking Agent. *Education:* Royal Holloway and Bedford New College; Clifton College, Bristol. *Career:* Ten years as agent with: The Levellers; Radiohead; The La's; Shampoo; Compulsion; Skunk Anansie; Longpigs; Suede; Supergrass. *Address:* 13 Artists, 36 Langham St, London W1N 5RH, England.

MYCKA, Katarzyna; b. 27 Oct. 1972, Leningrad, Russia. Musician (Marimba soloist). *Education:* Piano Diploma, Music School in Gdansk, Poland, 1979–85; Diploma with Distinction, 1985–91; Gdansk Academy of Music, 1991–95; Postgraduate Study, Music Academy, Stuttgart, Germany, 1993–95; Studied at Mozarteum, Salzburg, Austria, 1993–98; Soloist Class, Stuttgart Music Academy, 1995–97; Master's Degree in Music. *Career:* Winner in numerous competitions, First Prize Opole Percussion Competition, Poland, 1991; Prize, CIEM, Geneva, 1992; First Prize and Audience Prize Solo Marimba Competition, Luxembourg, 1995; First Prize First World Marimba Competition, Stuttgart, 1996; Final Round, International Percussion Competition ARD, Munich, 1997; Scholarship for Young Artists, Rotary Club, Stuttgart, 1997; Promotional Scholarship, Foundation of the Arts, Baden Wurttemberg, 1998; Festival Artist, First World Marimba Festival, Osaka, Japan, 1998; Numerous recordings for radio and TV in Germany and Poland; Masterclasses in Germany, USA, Poland, Switzerland, Luxembourg; Concerts in USA, Japan and Europe. *Recordings:* Solo CD, Katarzyna Mycka: Marimba Spirituel, 1997; Solo CD, Katarzyna Mycka: Marimba Dance, 1998. *Honours:* Ambassador of Polish Percussive Arts, Polish Percussive Arts Society, 1999. *Membership:* Percussive Arts Society, USA; Percussion Creative, Germany. *Address:* Tulpenstr 50, 70180 Stuttgart, Germany.

MYHRE, Wenche Synnöve; b. 15 Feb. 1947. Entertainer; Vocalist. m. Arthur Bucharot, 3 s., 1 d. *Career:* Musical, Wizard of Oz, 1965; Cabaret, Sweden, 1968, 1969–70, 1974, 1993; Appeared, German TV and personality shows, 1974–87; Played lead in Sweet Charity, Norway, 1989–90; Appeared, 4 films, TV films; Has 650 recorded and published songs; One-woman shows, 1978–98. *Recordings:* Lameg Vaere Ung, 1964; Beiss Nicht Gleich in Jeden Apfel, 1966; Jeg Og Du Og Vi To Og Mange Fler, 1972; Vi Lever, 1982–83; Er Steht Im Tor, 1969; Love A Go Go, 1967; Albums: Wenche Myhre, 1963; Sanger Fra Dengang, 1967; Powshow, 1970; Wenche, 1976; Vi Lever, 1983; Wenches Jul, 1991; Co-Wenches Beste, 1997. *Honours:* 5 Otto Awards, Germany, 1966–70; Midem Award, 1966–67; Silver Microphone, 1967; Norwegian Grammy, 1976; Silver and Gold Discs. *Address:* Venola 22, 1315 Nesoya, Norway.

MYLES, Heather; b. 31 July 1964, Riverside, California, USA. Vocalist; Songwriter; Musician (bass). *Education:* BA Business Administration. *Career:* Opened for Merle Haggard, 12 times; Charlie Daniels, 30 times; Extensive travel in Europe. *Recordings:* Albums: Just Like Old Times, 1992; Untamed, 1995; Sweet Little Dangerous (Live In London), 1996; Highways and Honky Tonks, 1998. *Honours:* Picked top 10 in Request Magazine, 1995–96. *Current Management:* Clyde Masters, Gehl Force Management, 1106 18th Ave S, Nashville, TN 37212, USA.

MYLLÄRI, Mika; b. 17 June 1966, Kokkola, Finland. Musician (trumpet); Composer. *Education:* Jazz Department, Sibelius Academy, 1986; Jazz Composition with Jukka Linkola, 1991. *Career:* Member, Espoo Big Band; Freelance musician with UMO Big Band; Formed own quintet, playing own material, 1990; Member, 10-man ensemble Zone, 1991–. *Honours:* Finnish Jazz Federation Award, Band of the Year, Mika Mylläri Quintet. *Address:* Dunckerinkatu 4 C 42, 00260 Helsinki, Finland.

MYROL, Keith; b. 19 July 1950, Maple Creek, Saskatchewan, Canada. Musician (guitar). m. Trish, 22 Jan. 1972, 1 s. 1 d. *Career:* The Myrol Brothers; Appearances: Capital Country CFAC TV Calgary; SCMA Awards Show 1990–94; 7 Sunday In the Park concerts; Right Tracks; Gold Rush Cafe; Saskatchewan Showcase of The Arts; CBC Arts Reel; Project Discovery. *Recordings:* Albums: The Singles Collection; Raisin' The Roof; Also on: Best of the West, Vols I and II, CFAC Country Showdown. *Honours:* SCMA: Non-Touring Band of the Year. *Membership:* CCMA; SCMA Hall of Fame. *Current*

Management: Agent: Cross Town Entertainment. *Address:* The Myrol Brothers, Box 969 Outlook, Saskatchewan S0L 2N0, Canada.

MYROL, Myles; b. 6 March 1957, Maple Creek, Saskatchewan, Canada. Musician (bass guitar). m. Diane, 31 July 1976, 1 s., 1 d. *Career:* The Myrol Brothers; Appearances: Capital Country CFAC TV Calgary; SCMA Awards Show, 1990–94; 7 Sunday In The Park concerts; Right Tracks; Gold Rush Cafe; Sask Showcase of the Arts; CBC Arts Reel; Project Discovery. *Recordings:* Albums: The Singles Collection; Raisin' The Roof; Also on: Best of the West, Vols I and II, CFAC Country Showdown. *Honours:* SCMA; Non Touring Band of the Year. *Membership:* CCMA; SCMA Hall of Fame. *Current Management:* Agent: Cross Town Entertainment. *Address:* The Myrol Brothers, Box 969 Outlook, Saskatchewan S0L 2N0, Canada.

MYROL, Rick; b. 30 May 1948, Maple Creek, Saskatchewan, Canada. Musician (guitar). m. Violet, 23 Nov. 1968, 2 s. *Career:* The Myrol Brothers; Appearances: Capital Country CFAC TV Calgary SCMA Awards Show, 1990–94; 7 Sunday In The Park apperances; Right Tracks; Gold Rush Cafe; Saskatchewan Showcase of the Arts; CBC Arts Reel; Project Discovery. *Recordings:* Albums: The Singles Collection; Raisin' The Roof; Also on: Best of West, Vols I and II, CFAC Country Showdown. *Honours:* SCMA: Non-Touring Band of the Year. *Membership:* CCMA; SCMA Hall of Fame. *Current Management:* Agent: Cross Town Entertainment. *Address:* The Myrol Brothers, Box 969 Outlook, Saskatchewan S0L 2N0, Canada.

MYSLIKOVJAN, Ivan; b. 24 Sept. 1960, Ostrava, Czech Republic. Musician (alto sax, electric wind instrument); Music Arranger; Composer; Teacher. m., 1 s. *Education:* Graduated, Conservatory of Ostrava, 1982; Jazz Studio, Prague, with Karel Velebny, 1981–82. *Career:* Studio musician and soloist; Appearances at jazz and pop festivals, clubs and concerts in Czech Republic and abroad; Numerous television and radio broadcasts; Teacher, bass clarinet and saxophone, improvisation lessons, Conservatory of Ostrava, 1982–86; Collaborations: Karel Ruzicka, Milan Svoboda, Jiri Stivin, Emil Viklicky, Tony Trishka, Breakfast Special, Second Grass, Patrick Bergman, Charlie 1, DJ Diome, Vandoren, Selmer, B. G. France, Pepé Mazan, Prague Philharmonic Orchestra, Prague Chamber Orchestra, Atlantis; Prod.: all his solo albums; Sax Horoscope Live in Prague Planetarium, 2002; Week-long festival of Czech Culture in Paris, 1995; Mem., jazz fusion group, Blue Birds; DJ project, Sax'o'phono. *Recordings:* Solo: Nice To Meet You, 1995; Information Of My Soul; Christmas Inspiration; Sax And Love; Sax Art; Sax Horoscope; The 4 Sea Sons; Sax 'N Dance, 2003; Soloist on more than 50 albums, incl.: Film Music Of Bernard Herrmann; Floodland. *Compositions:* Many jazz pieces, contemporary pieces. *Publications:* Modern School of Saxophone, 1998. *Current Management:* Viviane Management s.r.o., Lovosicka 768, 190 00 Prague 9, Czech Republic. *Telephone:* (2) 8658-1521. *E-mail:* ivan-sax@seznam.cz. *Website:* www.ivan-sax.com.

N

NABORS, James Thurston (Jim); b. 12 June 1930, Tuscaloosa, AL, USA. Entertainer; Actor; Musician (piano). *Education:* Business Degree, University of Alabama. *Career:* The Andy Griffith Show; Gomer Pyle USMC; The Jim Nabors Variety Hour; The Jim Nabors Show (TV); Las Vegas; Reno; Atlantic City; Various personal appearances across country. *Recordings:* 28 albums, 5 Gold, 1 Platinum including: Jim Nabors by Request, 1967; 16 Most Requested songs, 1989; Jim Nabor's Christmas Album, 1990; 22 Great Hymn and Country Favorites, 2000; When He Spoke, 2000; Featured on: The Best Little Whorehouse in Texas (Narrator), 1978. *Current Management:* William Morris Agency. *Address:* 151 El Camino, Beverly Hills, CA 91510, USA.

NAGAI, Yohei; b. 5 Nov. 1938, Tokyo, Japan. Specialist in Musical Instruments Research. *Education:* Engineering Department, Tokyo University; DEA, Acoustics, Marseilles University. *Career:* 38 years in Musical Instrument Research and Design Department, Yamaha Co Ltd, 3 years General Management of Research Laboratories. *Publications:* Numerous research papers on piano, wind instruments and electronic instruments. *Membership:* Acoustical Society of Japan; Acoustical Society of America; Acoustical Society of Europe. *Address:* 3–40–20 Sanarudai, Hamamatsu-shi, Japan.

NAIDENOV, Vassil; b. 3 Sept. 1950, Sofia, Bulgaria. Vocalist. *Education:* Music Academy, Sofia, Bulgaria. *Career:* Pop singer, No. 1 in list of Bulgarian National TV and radio for over 10 years; Tours: Germany; Belgium; Canada; Romania; Poland; Cuba; Republics of former USSR; First success with: Adaption, 1979. *Recordings:* 5 albums; 2 singles including Seven Times; Composes most of own material. *Honours:* Second place, Eurovision, Belgium; International prizes in Cuba, 1982; USSR; Belgium; Canada; The Golden Orpheus Festival: First prize, 1981; Second prize, 1982; Silver Orpheus, 1983; Prizes for television show, Melody of the Year, 1979, 1982–84, 1986. *Membership:* Union of Bulgarian Musicians. *Current Management:* Ivailo Manolov. *Address:* 91-A Vitosha Blvd, 1408 Sofia, Bulgaria.

NAIL, Jimmy, (James Michael Aloyisius Bradford); b. 1954, Newcastle upon Tyne, England. Vocalist; Actor. *Career:* Actor, UK television series, Auf Wiedersehen Pet, ITV; Co-writer, actor, Spender, BBC; Actor, Crocodile Shoes, BBC; Solo recording artiste, 1992–; Own company, Big Boy Productions. *Recordings:* Singles: Love Don't Live Here Anymore, 1985; Ain't No Doubt (No. 1, UK), 1992; Crocodile Shoes, 1994; Big River, 1995; Albums: Growing Up In Public, 1992; Crocodile Shoes, 1994; Big River, 1995; Crocodile Shoes II, 1996; The Nail File: The Best of Jimmy Nail, 1997; Tadpoles In A Jar, 2000; Appeared on: Gary Moore, We Want Moore, 1984; Greatest Hits of the 90s, 1994; Now That's What I Call Music, 1995; Evita, 1996; Carnival: Rainforest Foundation, 1997; Madonna, Selections from Evita, 1997. *Honours:* Great British Country Music Awards: Best Album, Best Song, 1996. *Current Management:* Fairwarning / Wasted Talent, London, England. *Address:* c/o East West Records, Electric Lighting Station, 46 Kensington Court, London W8 5DP, England.

NAINIA, Farid; b. Morocco. Vocalist; Musician (lothar, percussion). *Career:* Left Morocco for London, 1980s; Founder member of band MoMo (Music of Moroccan Origin); Act's fusion of North African Gnawa music with western-style drum kit, samples and contemporary dance styles (including house and garage) described as 'Dar'; Popular live band; Released first album, 2001. *Recordings:* Album: The Birth of Dar, 2001.

NAISSOO, Tonu; b. 18 March 1951, Tallinn, Estonia. Jazz Musician (piano); Composer. m. Kersti Johanson, 8 July 1977, 1 s., 1 d. *Education:* Diplomas in Theory of Music, Tallinn Music School, Estonia, 1970; Composition, Tallinn State Conservatory, Estonia, 1982; Post-graduate studies, Berklee College of Music, Boston, USA (scholarship), 1989–90. *Career:* Jazz pianist, bandleader (trio, quartet), solo pianist, 1967–; Keyboardist, pop/showgroup Laine, 1972–76; As solo artiste or with Tonu Naissoo Trio/Quartet: Jazz festivals, solo concerts, former USSR, 1978–89; Jazz pianist, sideman, international projects: EBU Big Band, Pori Jazz, Finland, 1985; Trio Eckert-Gaivoronski-Naissoo, Turku Jazz, Finland, 1992; Baltic Trio, Schleswig-Holstein Musik Festival, Germany, 1992; Vladimir Tarasov's Baltic Art Orchestra, Jazz Baltica, 1994; Munster Jazz Festival, Germany, 1994; Pianist, soloist, Alfred Schnittke's First Symphony, Symphony Orchestra of the USSR Ministry of Culture, 1987; Boston Symphony Orchestra, US premiere, 1988; Rotterdam Symphony Orchestra, Netherlands premiere, 1991; Pianist, entertainer, 1991–. *Compositions:* For films, television, theatre, 1969–; Jazz: First Flight, 1981; A Time There Was, 1983. *Recordings:* Tonu Naissoo Trio, 1968; Turning Point, 1980; Dedication, 1993. *Honours:* Music of the Year, Estonian Radio, 1991. *Membership:* Estonian Composers' Union, 1984. *Current Management:* Jazzkaar Festival Management. *Address:* Estonian Radio, Jazzkaar, Gonsiori 21, EE 0100 Tallinn, Estonia.

NAMYSOWSKI, Zbigniew; b. 9 Sept. 1939, Warsaw, Poland. Jazz Musician (trombone); Composer. m. Maria Magorzata Ostaszewska, 2 d., 1 s. *Career:* Trombone player with music groups Modern Dixielanders, 1957–59, Zygmunt Wichary Group, 1960, New Orleans Stompers, 1960–61, Jazz Rockers, 1961, Air Condition, 1980–82, Zbigniew Namysowski Quartet and Quintet, 1983–; Participant in festivals including: Students' Group Festival, Wrocaw (Award for the Best Soloist), 1957; International Jazz Festival, Prague (Award for the Best Soloist), 1964, Polish Songs Festival, Opole, and festivals in Bologna, 1961, 1964, Lugano, 1961, Frankfurt, 1964, Zürich, 1965, 1977, Tauranga, New Zealand, 1969, Mumbai, 1969, 1978, Paris, 1974, Ivrea, Italy, 1979, Montréal, 1984, Copenhagen, 1989, Århus, 1989, Red Sea Eilat, Israel, 1991, and others; Has toured in Denmark, USA, Italy, New Zealand, Australia, India, Netherlands, Greece, Canada, Mexico, Sweden, Norway, Switzerland. *Recordings include:* Polish Jazz–Zbigniew Namysowski Quartet; Kuyawiak Goes Funky; Zbigniew Namysowski with Symphony Orchestra; Song of the Pterodactil; Jasmine Lady; Song of Innocence; Double Trouble; Open; Without Talk; Adaptations of compositions by Mozart, Gershwin and Chopin for string quartet, clarinet and jazz band. *Compositions include:* Der Schmalz Tango, 1976; Convenient Circumstances, 1980; Speed Limit, 1981; Kuyawiak Goes Funky, 1984; After Perturbation, 1985; Quiet Afternoon, 1985; Double-Trouble Blues, 1985; Cuban Tango Mojito, 1986; Seven-Eleven, 1987; Western Ballade, 1992; Oriental Food, 1994; Mazurka Uborka, 1996. *Honours:* State Prize (First Class), 1984; Fryderyk (Polish music award for Best Polish Jazz Record of the Year—Zbigniew Namysowski Quartet and Zakopane Highlanders Band), 1995; Jazz Forum Awards, 1997, 1998; Gold Cross of Merit, 1974; Meritorious Activist of Culture Award, 1982. *Membership:* Polish Composer Assgn, 1972–. *E-mail:* quartet@poczta.onet.pl.

NAPOLEON, Marty; b. 2 June 1921, Brooklyn, New York, USA. Musician (piano). m. Marie Giordano, 15 May 1921, 1 s., 1 d. *Career:* Jazz pianist, 1941–; Played with numerous artistes including: Gene Krupa; Benny Goodman; Louis Armstrong's All-Stars; Bob Crosby's Bobcats; Red Norvo; Stan Getz; Lionel Hampton; Coleman Hawkins; Major concerts include: Odessa Jazz Festival, Texas; Berne Jazz Festival; Carnegie Hall (with Frank Sinatra); Command Performance at the White House with Lionel Hampton Sextet; Nice Jazz Festival; North Sea Jazz Festival; Downtown Jazz Festival, Toronto; Film appearances: Glenn Miller Story; All That Jazz; Tootsie; Raging Bull. *Recordings:* Charles Barnet; Louis Armstrong; Lionel Hampton, including Louis Armstrong, Hello Dolly, 1963. *Membership:* ASCAP.

NAS, (Nasir Jones), (Nas Escobar, Nasty Nas); b. 1973, Queensbridge, New York, USA. Rap Artiste. *Career:* Made first appearance aged 18 with Main Source on Live At The Barbecue, 1991; First solo effort Halftime appeared on Zebrahead soundtrack; Signed to Columbia with assistance of third Bass' MC Serch; Released debut album Illmatic, 1994; Collaborations: Will Smith; Puff Daddy; Missy Elliott; Notorious BIG; Mary J Blige; Allure; R Kelly. *Recordings:* Albums: Illmatic, 1994; It Was Written, 1996; I Am, 1999; Nastradamus, 2001; Singles: It Ain't Hard To Tell, 1994; If I Ruled The World, 1996; Hate Me Now, 1999; Nastradamus, 1999; Got Urself A Gun, 2002. *Address:* c/o Columbia Records, 550 Madison Ave, New York, USA.

NASCIMENTO, Milton; b. 26 Oct. 1942, Rio de Janeiro, Brazil. Vocalist; Songwriter; Composer; Musician (piano, accordion, guitar, bass guitar). *Career:* DJ, announcer, dir, Rádio Três Pontas, early 1960s; Composer, 1963–; Played, Carnegie Hall, 1994; Collaborations with: Art Blakey, Laudir De Oliviera, Deodato, João Gilberto, Herbie Hancock, Airto Moreira, Flora Purim, Charlie Rouse, Wayne Shorter, Roberto Silva. *Recordings:* Albums: Milton Nascimento (aka Travessia), 1967; Courage, 1968; Milton Nascimento, 1969; Milton, 1970; Clube Da Esquina–Milton Nascimento E Lo Borges, 1972; Milagre Dos Peixes, 1973; Milagre Dos Peixes–Gravado Ao Vivo–Milton Nascimento E Som Imaginário, 1974; Minas, 1975; Milton, 1976; Geraes, 1976; Clube Da Esquina 2, 1978; Journey To Dawn, 1979; Sentinela, 1980; Caçador De Mim, 1981; Missa Dos Quilombos, 1982; Anima, 1982; Milton Nascimento Ao Vivo, 1983; Encontros E Despedidas, 1985; A Barca Dos Amantes, 1986; Yauarete, 1987; Miltons, 1988; Txai, 1990; O Planeta Blue Na Estrada Do Sol, 1991; Angelus, 1993; Amigo, 1995; Nascimento, 1997; Tambores De Minas–Ao Vivo, 1998; Crooner, 1999; Gil E Milton, 2000; Gold, 2002. *Honours:* Festival of Brazilian Popular Music, Best Performer, 1965; Grammy Award, Best World Music Record of the Year, for Nascimento, 1998. *Address:* c/o WEA Latina, 5201 Blue Lagoon Dr., Suite 200, Miami, FL 33126, USA.

NASH, Graham; b. 2 Feb. 1942, Blackpool, Lancashire, England. Vocalist; Musician (guitar). m. Susan. *Career:* Touring musician with the Hollies; Member, Crosby Stills and Nash, 1968–; Also Crosby, Stills, Nash and Young; Also solo recording artiste; Performances include: Woodstock Festival, 1969; Altamont Speedway, with the Rolling Stones, 1969; Royal Albert Hall, 1970; Wembley Stadium, 1974; California benefit concerts with Jackson Browne,

1979; Anti-nuclear benefits, Madison Square Garden, 1979; Peace Sunday concert, Rose Bowl, California, 1982; Live Aid, Philadelphia, 1985; Madison Square Garden, New York, 1988; Amnesty International benefit concert, Chile, 1990; Television includes: Presenter, The Inside Track, interview show, cable TV, 1990. *Recordings:* Albums: with The Hollies: Stay With The Hollies, 1964; In The Hollies Style, 1964; The Hollies, 1965; Would You Believe?, 1966; For Certain Because, 1966; Evolution, 1967; Butterfly, 1967; The Hollies At Abbey Road, 2000; with Crosby Stills and Nash: Crosby Stills and Nash, 1969; Déjà Vu, 1970; 4-Way Street, 1971; So Far, 1974; Replay, 1981; Daylight Again, 1982; Allies, 1983; Innocent Eyes, 1986; American Dream, 1989; Live It Up, 1990; Solo albums: Songs For Beginners, 1971; Wild Tales, 1974; Earth and Sky, 1980; Innocent Eyes, 1986; with David Crosby: Graham Nash/David Crosby, 1972; Wind On The Water, 1975; Whistling Down The Wire, 1976; Crosby/Nash Live, 1977; The Best Of, 1978; Singles include: with The Hollies: Searchin', 1963; Stay, 1963; Just One Look, 1964; Here I Go Again, 1964; We're Through, 1964; Yes I Will, 1964; I'm Alive (No. 1, UK), 1965; Look Through Any Window, 1965; I Can't Let Go, 1966; Bus Stop, 1966; Stop! Stop! Stop!, 1966; On A Carousel, 1967; Carrie-Anne, 1968; Jennifer Eccles, 1968; Listen To Me, 1968; with Crosby, Stills, Nash & Young: Woodstock, 1970; Teach Your Children, 1970; Just A Song Before I Go, 1977; Wasted On The Way, 1982; with Neil Young, On the Beach, 1974; Zuma, 1975; with Carole King, Thoroughbred, 1976; In Concert, 1994. *Honours:* Grammy Award, Best New Artists, 1970. *Current Management:* Management Network Inc, 346 N Larchmont Blvd, Los Angeles, CA 90004, USA.

NASH, Johnny (John Lester); b. 9 Aug. 1940, Houston, Texas, USA. Vocalist; Actor. *Career:* Lead soprano, gospel choir; Film appearances include: Take A Giant Step, 1958; Key Witness, 1960; Singer on television variety show and as member, Teen Commandments (with Paul Anka and George Hamilton IV); Solo recording artiste, 1960s–70s; Now involved in recording and production. *Recordings:* Albums: Hold Me Tight, 1968; Let's Go Dancing, 1969; I Can See Clearly Now (No. 1, USA), 1972; My Merry-Go-Round, 1973; What A Wonderful World, 1977; Stir It Up, 1981; Johnny Nash, 1985; Here Again, 1986; Tears On My Pillow, 1987; The Very Best of Johnny Nash, 1995; The Best of Johnny Nash, 1996; Singles include: Let's Move and Groove Together, 1965; Hold Me Tight, 1969; You Got Soul, 1969; Cupid, 1969; Stir It Up (written by Bob Marley), 1971; I Can See Clearly Now, 1972; There Are More Questions Than Answers, 1972; Tears On My Pillow (No. 1, UK), 1975; What A Wonderful World, 1976; Rock Me Baby, 1985; Appears on: Bob Marley, Songs of Freedom, 1992; Rock to the Rock, 1998; Complete Bob Marley and the Wailers, 1998; Grosse Pointe Blank, Grosse Pointe Blank, 1997.

NASH, Paul; b. 19 Feb. 1948, New York, NY, USA. Composer; Dir, Manhattan New Music Project. m. Marta Danciu, 3 Oct. 1998. *Education:* Graduate Work, Public Management, New York University, 1992; BM, Composition, Berklee College of Music, 1969; MA, Composition, Mills College, 1976; Graduate Studies, University of California at Berkeley, 1986. *Career:* JVC Jazz Festival appearance, Carnegie Hall, with Manhattan New Music Project, 1997; New York club appearances at Sweet Basil, The Fez, New School. *Compositions:* Wind Over the Lake, San Francisco Chamber Symphony, 1989; Synchronicity, Manhattan New Music Project, 1991; Intimate Structures, for two actors and electronic tape, presented by Downtown Arts Festival, 1998; Collage (flute, violin, clarinet, trumpet and cello), commissioned and performed by St Luke's Chamber Ensemble, 1999. *Recordings:* Paul Nash: A Jazz Composers Ensemble, 1979; Night Language, 1984; Musical Heritage Society, 1987; Mood Swing, 1993; Second Impression, Soul Note 1985 Reissued, 1997; Soul of Grace, 1999. *Publications:* University of Northern Colorado (UNC) Jazz Press, Advance Music (Germany); A Practical Guide to Polyrhythms, 1980. *Membership:* BMI. *Address:* 400 W 43rd St 32-A, New York, NY 10036, USA.

NASH, Rob; b. 30 May 1956, Boston, Lincolnshire, England. Vocal Coach; Musician (keyboards, guitar). m. Nic Bagguley, 7 Nov. 1989, 3 s., 1 d. *Education:* Loughborough University; Ely Cathedral Chorister; Cambridge College of Arts and Technology. *Career:* Vocal coach to Michael Barrymore, for television series Barrymore; Jeremy Irons, for films The Lion King; Chorus of Disapproval; Work with Marc Almond; Simon Climie; Dion Estes; Stephanie Lawrence; Colin Blunstone; Nick Cave. *Recordings:* Albums: Phantom Of The Opera, A Touch Of Music In The Night, Michael Crawford; Weather In The Heart, Carmina; Solo: With Love; A Touch Of Music In The Night. *Honours:* Vivien Ellis Awards, 1990. *Membership:* Equity; Musicians' Union. *Current Management:* Bagmusic. *Address:* 31 Tyne St, St Werburgh, Bristol BS2 9UA, England.

NASH, Su-Elise; b. London, England. Vocalist. *Education:* Business, Middlesex University. *Career:* Mem., Mis-Teeq, 2001–, with Alesha Dixon and Sabrina Washington; Appeared, Party at the Palace, for Golden Jubilee celebrations, 2002. *Recordings:* Album: Lickin' On Both Sides, 2001. Singles: Why?, 2001; All I Want, 2001; One Night Stand, 2001; B With Me, 2002; Roll On, 2002. *Honours:* Platinum disc, for Lickin' On Both Sides; UK Garage Award, Best Artist, 2001; MOBO Award, Best Garage Act, 2002. *Address:* c/o Telstar Records, 107 Mortlake High St, London SW14 8HQ, England. *Website:* www.mis-teeq.co.uk.

NASTANOVICH, Bob; b. 1968, Rochester, New York, USA. Musician (Drums). *Career:* Member, Pavement; Released first EP on own label, soon obtained indie label deal; Numerous headlining tours; Appeared in cartoon Space Ghost Coast to Coast, 1997. *Recordings:* Singles: Perfect Sound Forever EP, 1990; Watery, Domestic EP, 1992; Trigger Cut, 1992; Cut Your Hair, 1994; Gold Soundz, 1994; Range Life, 1995; Rattled by La Rush, 1995; Father to a Sister of Thought, 1995; Pacific Trim EP, 1996; Stereo, 1997; Shady Lane EP, 1997; Spit on a Stranger, 1999; Carrot Rope, 1999; Albums: Slanted and Enchanted, 1992; Crooked Rain, Crooked Rain, 1994; Wowee Zowee, 1995; Brighten the Corners, 1997; Terror Twilight, 1999; with The Silver Jews: Starlite Walker, 1994.

NATCH, (Ian Mallett); b. 28 July 1945, Birmingham, England. Songwriter; Musician (bass guitar). Divorced, 3 s., 1 d. *Career:* Member, group Renegades; Toured extensively in Finland, Sweden, Germany and Italy; Television appearances in several countries, including San Remo Song Festival, 1966; Currently re-launching career. *Recordings:* Cadillac, Renegades; Several albums and singles recorded, 1960s; Compilations continue to be released. *Publications:* Cracking An Ancient Code. *Membership:* PRS; MCPS; Songwriting Guild. *Address:* La Louisiane, 4 Tynedale, Whitby, South Wirral L65 6RB, England.

NAUMOV, Julian; Musician (drums). *Career:* Member, Concurent, 1986–; Numerous concerts, television and radio appearances. *Recordings:* Rock For Peace, 1988; Rock Festival In Mitchurin, 1989; The Black Sheep (rock collection), 1992; Something Wet (best-selling album, Bulgaria), 1994; The Best of Bulgarian Rock, 1995. *Honours:* First Prizes: Top Rock Band, Youth Festival, Vidin, 1989; Rock Ring, Sofia, 1990; Top Rock Composition: The Cavalry, 1991; Group of the Year, The Darik Radio Countdown, 1994. *Address:* 40 St Stambolov Blvd, 1202 Sofia, Bulgaria.

NAWASADIO, Sylvie, (Kihanga); b. 8 Jan. 1965, Ixelles, Belgium. *Career:* Mem., Zap Mama, –1995; Mem., Barut Trio. *Compositions:* Sab Syl Ma. *Recordings:* Albums: with Zap Mama: Zap Mama; Sab Syl Ma; with Barut Trio: Ndugu Yangu; with Toni Child: The Woman's Boat; with Sally Nyolo: Tribu; Multiculti; Beti; with Kadja Nin: Free; with Uinckx: I Love My Job; with Jaques Higelin: Au Rex; Paradis Paen; with Arthur H.: Bachibouzouk; with H. Felix Thiéfaine: Le Bonheur De La Tentation; Other: Y-a-t'il Une Femme Noire Dans Cette Ville?, 1998; La Voix Dans Tous Ses États, 2000. *Honours:* Gold disc for album, Zap Mama, 1993; SABAM Prize, 1997. *Telephone and Fax:* (2) 411-62-09.

N'DOUR, Youssou; b. 1959, Dakar, Senegal. Musician; Vocalist; Songwriter. *Career:* Mem., Sine Dramatic, 1972; Orchestre Diamono, 1975; The Star Band (houseband, Dakar nightclub, the Miami Club), 1976–79; Founder, Etoile De Dakar, 1979; Re-formed as Super Etoile De Dakar, 1982–; International tours include support to Peter Gabriel, US tour, 1987; Owner, Jololi Records, recording studio, radio station, Thoissane nightclub, Dakar. *Recordings:* Albums: A Abijan, 1980; Xalis, 1980; Tabaski, 1981; Thiapathioly, 1983; Absa Gueye, 1983; Immigrès, 1984; Nelson Mandela, 1985; The Lion, 1989; African Editions Vols 5–14, 1990; Africa Deebeub, 1990; Jamm La Prix, 1990; Kocc Barma, 1990; Set, 1990; Eyes Open, 1992; The Best of Youssou N'Dour, 1994; The Guide, 1995; Gainde–Voices From The Heart Of Africa (with Yande Codou Sene), 1996; Immigrès/Bitim Rew, 1997; Inedits 84–85, 1997; Hey You: The Essential Collection, 1988–90; Best Of The 80s, 1998; Special Fin D'annee Plus Djamil, 1999; Joko, 2000; Lii, 2000; St Louis, 2000; Le Grand Bal, 2000; Nothing's In Vain (Coono Du Réér), 2002. Hit singles: Seven Seconds, duet with Neneh Cherry, 1994; How Come Shakin' The Tree, 1998; Recorded with: Paul Simon, Graceland, 1986; Lou Reed, Between Thought And Expression, 1992; Otis Reading, Otis! The Definitive Otis Reading, 1993; Manu Dibango, Wafrika, 1994; Cheikh Lo, Ne La Thiass, 1996; Alan Stivell, I Dour, 1998. *Address:* Nonesuch Records, Time Warner, 75 Rockefeller Plaza, New York, NY 10019, USA.

NEANDERTHAL, (THE). See: **SANCHEZ, Roger.**

NED B, (Ed Baden Powell); Musician (guitar, keyboards). *Career:* Mem., jazz funk quartet, D-Influence, 1990–; Support to Prince, Michael Jackson; Tours, television appearances; D-Influence also production team for R&B music; Group owns Freakstreet label. *Recordings:* Albums: Good 4 We, 1992; Prayer 4 Unity, 1995; London, 1997; D-Influence Presents D-Vas, 2002. Singles: I'm The One/The Classic, 1990; Midnite, 1995; Waiting, 1995. *Address:* c/o Dome Records Ltd, 59 Glenthorne Rd, London W6 0LJ, England.

NEDELCHEV, Boyko; b. 24 April 1965, Rousse, Bulgaria. Vocalist; Songwriter; Composer. *Career:* Singer, songwriter and composer with brother Deyan, 1987–; Appearances: Many festivals, concerts, television and radio appearances: Bulgaria; Russia; Kazakhstan; Mongolia; Egypt; Italy; Tour of Mediterranean; Romania. *Recordings:* A Plea To The World, 1990; A Game of Love, 1991; Madly In Love, 1992; The Best of Deyan and Boyko Nedelchev, 1993; Love and Dream, 1993; La Mia Musica, 1994; Love For Love, 1994; The Hits of Deyan and Boyko Nedelchev, 1995; Atlanta, 1996; Brothers, 1996; Gently News, 1997; Grande Amore, 1998. *Honours:* Awards received from: Contest for Youth Pop Singers, Bulgaria, 1988–89; Union of Bulgarian

Writers, 1989–90, 1992, 1996; Grand Prix, Nashville, USA, 1989; Golden Orpheus International Festival, Bulgaria, 1990, 1993–96; International Festival of Melody of the Friends, Ulan-Bator, Mongolia, 1990; Step To Parnasus International Festival, Moscow, Russia, 1994; Voice of Asia International Festival, Kazakhstan, 1995; International Song Festival, Cairo, Egypt, 1995–97; Silver Eros Festival, Bulgaria, 1996; Golden Stang International Festival, Romania, 1996; Love Duets Festival, Bulgaria, 1996; Annual National Music Awards, Bulgaria, 1996–98; South Pacific International Song Contest, Australia, 1998. *Membership:* FIDOF. *Address:* Lipnik Blvd 62, Entr G, Ap 16, 7005 Rousse, Bulgaria.

NEDELCHEV, Deyan; b. 16 Jan. 1964, Rousse, Bulgaria. Vocalist; Songwriter; Composer. *Career:* Singer, songwriter, composer with brother Boyko, 1987–; Signed 3 year contract with Poly Gram, South Africa; Appearances: Many festivals, concerts, television appearances and radio broadcasts: Bulgaria; Russia; Kazakhstan; Mongolia; Egypt; Italy; Tour, Mediterranean; South Africa. *Recordings:* Albums: A Plea To The World, 1990; A Game of Love, 1991; Madly In Love, 1992; The Best of Deyan and Boyko Nedeltchev, 1993; Love-dream; Dedication, 1993; Love For Love, 1994; La Mia Musica, 1994; The Hits of Deyan and Boyko Nedelchev, 1995; Brothers, 1996; Atlanta, 1996; Gently News, 1997; Grande Amore, 1998. *Honours:* Awards received from: Contest for Youth Pop Singers, Bulgaria, 1988–89; Union of Bulgarian Writers, 1989–90, 1992, 1996; Grand Prix, Nashville, USA, 1989; The Golden Orpheus International Festival, Bulgaria, 1990, 1993–96; International Festival of Melody of The Friends, Ulan-Bator, Mongolia, 1990; Step To Parnasus International Festival, Moscow, Russia, 1994; Voice of Asia International Festival, Kazakhstan, 1995; International Song Festival, Cairo, Egypt, 1995–97; Silver Eros Festival, Bulgaria, 1996; Golden Stang International Festival, Romania, 1996; Love Duets Festival, Bulgaria, 1996; Annual National Music Awards, Bulgaria, 1996, 1998; South Pacific International Song Contest, Australia, 1998. *Current Management:* Poly Gram, Johannesburg, South Africa. *Address:* Lipnik Blvd 62, Entr G, Ap 16, 7005 Rousse, Bulgaria.

NEECE, Timothy G; b. 2 Oct. 1946, Abilene, Texas, USA. Artiste Man. m. (1) Lynda Hunnicutt, 1 d.; (2) Deborah Chaffey, 12 June 1988. *Education:* BA, Business, McMurry University. *Career:* Manager, prior to release and through 3 albums for Christopher Cross; Bruce Hornsby and the Range; Charlie Sexton; Manager, Rickie Lee Jones during Flying Cowboys release. *Honours:* Launched careers of 2 Best New Artist Grammy Award Winners; Many Gold, Platinum awards world-wide for artistes managed.

NEFF, John; b. 13 March 1951, Birmingham, Michigan, USA. Recording Engineer; Prod; Instrumentalist; Musician. m. Nancy L B Neff, 2 s., 1 d. *Career:* Chief Engineer, David Lynch's Asymmetrical Studio; Re-Recording Mixer, The Straight Story, Mulholland Drive; Engineer, Walter Becker, Donald Fagen; Morning Radio Host. *Compositions:* The Straight Story; Mulholland Drive; Lux Vivens. *Recordings:* Lux Vivens; Kamakiriad; Eleven Tracks of Wuack; Coincidences and Likely Stories; Jimmy' Road; with Japancakes: If I Could See Dallas, 1999; Sleepy Strange, 2001. *Membership:* ASCAP; Audio Engineering Society. *Current Management:* Audio Engineering Services. *Address:* PO Box 931558, Hollywood, CA 90093, USA.

NEGRAO, Mario Borganovi; b. 18 Nov. 1945. Musician (drums, percussion, flute). m. Sonia Dias, 2 s. *Education:* Studies with maestro Guirra Peixe. *Career:* Drummer in showa with Brazilian artists including Chico Buarque Vinicius de Moraes, Quartet em CY, Leila Pinheiro, Baden Powell; Worked with ensembles including the Brazilian Symphony Orchestra, Rio Jazz Orchestra, Bebeto (Tamba Trio), Edson Lobo and Osmar Milito; Participated in shows in Brazil with Toquinho, Vinicius and Clara Nunes, in the Sistine Theatre with Chico Buarque, Italy, in Mexico with local orchestras, in Argentina, with Chico Buarque, Marilia Barbosa, Maria Creuza, Toquinho, Vicinius and MPB4. *Compositions:* Canela de Velho; Fruta Doce; Mata Mato; Joao Mole; Orelma de Onca; Farinma Seca; Respina Fundo e Zaratudo. *Recordings:* Solo album of his own compositions; With other artistes including Chico Buarque, Aresar de Voce, Calicz and Homenagem ao Malandao, Vinicius, Toquinho, Regna Très, Samba de Orly. *Honours:* Best Instrumental Recording in Originality, Critic of Panama State in Brazil, for solo album. *Address:* Rua Dois, Manga Larga, Itaipava, 92288 Petrópolis, Brazil.

NEGRIJN, Thomas; b. 19 Oct. 1959, Copenhagen, Denmark. Lead Vocalist; Musician (guitar). *Education:* Art glazier 7 years; H F Music School in Copenhagen. *Career:* Own first big band, Simcess, 1985–92; Played Roskilde Festival, Denmark, 5 times; Midfyn Festival, 6 times, including 2 times on biggest stage for 30,000 – 40,000 people; Many Danish television and radio appearances; Tours: Europe; Founder, new band Blink, 1995–; Released EP, toured Denmark, making new album. *Recordings:* with Simcess: Play With Your Life, 1988; The House, 1990; with Tam Tam Top: Secrets, 1993; with Blink: Blink, 1994. *Honours:* Title: John (Lennon) Award, Best Band, Copenhagen, 1987. *Membership:* Danish Society For Jazz Rock Folk Composers. *Current Management:* Off Beat, Norsgade 26–28, 8000 Århus C, Denmark. *Address:* Hjort Lorenzensgade 6 4tv, 2200 Copenhagen N, Denmark.

NEIL, Vince, (Vincent Neil Wharton); b. 8 Feb. 1961, Hollywood, California, USA. Vocalist. *Career:* Singer, Rock Candy; Member, US heavy rock group Mötley Crüe, 1981–92; World-wide concerts include: Tours with: Y&T, 1981, 1982; Kiss, 1983; Ozzy Osbourne, 1984; Iron Maiden, 1984; Cheap Trick, 1986; Theatre of Pain World Tour, 1985–86; World tours, 1987, 1989; Major festivals: US festival, 1983; Monsters of Rock Festival, Castle Donington, 1984; Moscow Music Peace Festival, 1989; Actor, film The Adventures of Ford Fairlane, 1990; Solo artiste, 1992–. *Recordings:* Albums: with Mötley Crüe: Too Fast For Love, 1981; Shout At The Devil, 1983; Theatre of Pain, 1985; Girls, Girls, Girls, 1987; Dr Feelgood (No. 1, USA), 1989; Decade of Decadence, 1991; Generation Swine, 1997; New Tattoo, 2000; Solo: Exposed, 1993; Carved In Stone, 1995; Singles: with Mötley Crüe: Stick To Your Guns, 1981; Looks That Kill, 1984; Too Young To Fall In Love, 1984; Smokin' In The Boys Room, 1985; Home Sweet Home, 1985; You're All I Need, 1987; Dr Feelgood, 1989; Kick Start My Heart, 1990; Without You, 1990; Don't Go Away Mad, 1990; Same Old Situation, 1990; Primal Scream, 1991; Solo hit: You're Invited But Your Friend Can't Come, from film Encino Man, 1992; Can't Change Me, 1993; Contributor, Stars, Hear 'n' Aid, 1985. *Publications:* The Dirt: Confessions of the World's Most Notorious Rock Band (with Mötley Crüe), 2001. *Honours:* Rolling Stone Readers Poll Winners, Best Heavy Metal Band, 1991; American Music Award, Favorite Heavy Metal Album, 1991. *Current Management:* Burt Stein Entertainment Co, 1514 South St, Suite 100, Nashville TN 37203, USA.

NEILL, Kevin; b. 25 July 1931, Manchester, England. Musician (lead electric guitar, acoustic guitar, trombone). m. Claire Cregan, 6 April 1953, 2 d. *Career:* Johnny Ray tour, 1954; Royal Command Performance, Oh Boy, 1959; Anthony Newley Tour, 1960; Don Lang and Frantic Five; Princess Margaret's state wedding ball, with Joe Loss Orchestra, Buckingham Palace; Accompanied Vera Lynn, Frankie Vaughan; Frankie Laine; Vic Lewis Orchestra; Eric Winstone Orchestra; BBC Northern Variety Orchestra; BBC Midland Orchestra; Karl Denver Trio, 26 years; Joined John Stokes to reform The Bachelors, 1996. *Compositions:* Points North; Singin' and Swingin'. *Recordings:* Hits with Karl Denver Trio: Wimoweh; Marcheta; Mexicali Rose; Love Me With All Your Heart; Still; Sleepy Lagoon; Just A Little Love; Never Goodbye (Eurovision Song Contest entry); Harry Lime Theme; Re-recorded all The Bachelors' hits, among others: Charmaine; Diane; Ramona; I Believe. *Honours:* Examiner, electric guitar, The London College of Music; Awarded Special Achievement Award from Irish World Newspaper, 1999. *Membership:* Vaudeville Golf Society; Variety Club Golf Society. *Address:* 69 Polefield Rd, Blackly, Manchester M9 7EN, England.

NELLY, (Cornell Haynes, Jr); b. Austin, TX, USA. Vocalist; Musician. *Career:* Founder mem., St Lunatics, 1993–; Solo artiste, 1999–; Signed to Universal Records; Official clothing line, Vokal; Film appearance, Snipes, 2002. *Recordings:* Albums: with St Lunatics: Free City, 2001; Solo: Country Grammar, 2000; Nellyville, 2002. Singles: Dilemma (with Kelly Rowland), 2002. *Honours:* Two Source Awards; MTV Video Music Award; Soul Train Award; American Music Awards, Favourite Rap/Hip Hop Artist, 2002; Fans' Choice Artist, 2003. *Address:* c/o Universal Music Group, Universal Studios, 100 Universal City Plaza, Universal City, CA 91608, USA. *Website:* www.nelly.net.

NELSON, Bonita Rae, (Bonnie Nelson); b. 4 Nov. 1949, Denver, Colorado, USA. *Career:* Ralph Emery Radio Show; Tenn Network Show, Nashville Now; German ZDE TV Special; Centecor Drug Programme; Donna Fargo Special; Girl in My Life, TV; NBC's Real People. *Recordings:* 9 albums; 16 singles; Double CD; 5 charted records nationally; Other. *Recordings include:* Willie Nelson. *Publications:* Book, It's Not Luck, It's God, 1998. *Honours:* Entertainer and Female Vocalist, Colorado and New York, State Country Music Asscn. *Address:* PO Box 25050, Nashville, TN 37202, USA.

NELSON, Matthew Edward; b. 20 March 1968, Colne, England. Vocalist; Songwriter. *Education:* Hotel and Catering Management, Manchester Polytechnic, 1988–89. *Career:* Lead singer with Milltown Brothers, appearing 5 times on television, touring Britain, USA, Europe and Japan, and appearing at various British Festivals. *Compositions:* Wrote songs for the BBC TV series, All Quiet On The Preston Front. *Recordings:* Albums: Slinky, 1991; Valve, 1993; The Best Of, 1997; Singles: Seems To Me, 1990; Apple Green, 1990; Which Way Should I Jump?, 1990; Here I Stand,1991; It's All Over Now Baby Blue, 1993; Sleepwalking, 1993; Turn Off, 1993; 5 Singles in UK Top 40. *Membership:* Performing Rights Society. *Address:* Forest House, Forest Lane, Barrowford, Nelson, Lancashire BB9 6QL, England.

NELSON, Shara; b. London, England. Vocalist; Songwriter. *Career:* Singer, Massive Attack; Solo artiste. *Recordings:* Albums: with Massive Attack: Blue Lines, 1991; Solo: What Silence Knows, 1993; Down That Road, 1994; Friendly Fire, 1995. Singles: with Massive Attack: Daydreaming, 1990; Unfinished Sympathy, 1991; Safe From Harm, 1991; Solo: Down That Road, 1993; One Goodbye In Ten, 1993; Uptight, 1994; Inside Out, 1994; Rough With The Smooth, 1995; I Fell; Appears on: Ref, Ref, 1994; Guru, Jazzmatazz Vol. 2, 1995; Air Cuba, Leap of Faith, 1999; Presence, All Systems Go, 1999. *Current Management:* Def Mix Productions, 938 Broadway, Suite 400, New York, NY 10010, USA.

NELSON, Tracy; b. 27 Dec. 1944, Madison, Wisconsin, USA. Vocalist; Musician. *Education:* 2 years college. *Career:* Lead singer, Mother Earth, 1968–73; Solo artiste, 1965–. *Recordings:* Albums: with Mother Earth: Living With The Animals, 1968; Make A Joyful Noise, 1969; Mother Earth Presents – Tracy Nelson Country, 1970; Satisfied, 1970; Bring Me Home, 1971; Tracy Nelson / Mother Earth, 1972; Poor Man's Paradise, 1973; Solo albums: Deep Are The Roots, 1965; Tracy Nelson, 1974; Sweet Soul Music, 1975; Time Is On My Side, 1976; Doin' It My Way, 1978; Homemade Songs, 1978; Come See About Me, 1980; In The Here and Now, 1993; I Feel So Good, 1995; Move On, 1996; Tracy Nelson Country, 1996; The Best of Tracy Nelson/Mother Earth, 1996; Ebony And Irony, 2001. *Honours:* Nashville Music Award, Best Blues Album, 1996. *Current Management:* Julie Devereux, Lucks Management, 817 18th Ave S, Nashville, TN 37203, USA; Agent: Ronnie Narmour, RNA, PO Box 19289, Austin, TX 78760, USA.

NELSON, Trevor; b. 7 Jan. 1964. DJ. *Career:* Founder, Madhatter sound system; DJ, Kiss FM Radio, London, later dir; DJ, Soul II Soul session, Africa Centre, later co-established Soul II Soul shop, London; Joined BBC Radio 1, 1996, presenting Rhythm Nation, 1996–, R&B Chart, 1997–; Head of A&R, EMI's Cooltempo label; Club DJ, sessions all over Europe; Video Jockey, MTV. *Honours:* MOBO Award, Best DJ, 1999. *Address:* c/o BBC Radio 1, London W1N 4DJ, England. *E-mail:* trevor.nelson@bbc.co.uk.

NELSON, Willie (Hugh); b. 30 April 1933, Abbott, Texas, USA. Country and Western Vocalist; Musician; Songwriter. m. Annie Marie Nelson, 3 s., 4 d. *Education:* Baylor University. *Career:* Salesman; Announcer; Host and DJ, Country music shows, Texas; Bass player, Ray Price's band; Formed own band; Appearances, Grand Ole Opry, Nashville, and throughout USA, 1964–; Tours: New Zealand; Australia; USA; Canada; Europe; Japan; Annual Fourth of July Picnics throughout USA, 1972–; Performed with: Frank Sinatra; Neil Young; Dolly Parton; Linda Ronstadt; ZZ Top; Waylon Jennings; Ray Charles; Santana; Joni Mitchell; Kris Kristofferson; Bob Dylan; Patsy Cline; Film appearances include: Electric Horseman, 1980; Honeysuckle Rose, 1980. *Compositions include:* Crazy, No. 1 for Patsy Cline; Hello Walls, No. 1 for Faron Young. *Recordings:* Albums: The Sound In Your Mind, 1976; The Troublemaker, 1976; Willie Nelson And His Friends, 1976; To Lefty From Willie, 1977; Willie Before His Time, 1978; Wanted/The Outlaw, 1978; The Willie Way, 1978; The Best Of Willie Nelson, 1978; Stardust, 1978; One For The Road, 1979; Willie And Family Live, 1979; Pretty Paper, 1979; Willie Sings Kristofferson, 1979; San Antonio Rose, 1980; Honeysuckle Rose, 1980; Family Bible, 1980; Tougher Than Leather, 1983; City Of New Orleans, 1984; Me And Paul, 1985; Highwayman, 1985; The Promised Land, 1986; Partners, 1986; Island In The Sea, 1987; Seashores Of Old Mexico, 1987; What A Wonderful World, 1988; A Horse Called Music, 1989; Highwayman II, 1990; Born For Trouble, 1990; Clean Shirt Waylon And Willie, 1991; Across The Borderline, 1993; Six Hours At Pedernales, 1994; Healing Hands of Time, 1994; Just One Love, 1995; Spirit, 1996; How Great Thou Art, 1996; Christmas With Willie Nelson, 1997; Hill Country Christmas, 1997; Teatro, 1998; Nashville Was The Roughest, 1998; The Very Best Of Willie Nelson, 1999; Night And Day, 1999; Forever Gold, 2000; Me And The Drummer, 2000; Milk Cow Blues, 2000; Rainbow Connection, 2001; Joy, 2001; The Great Divide, 2002; All The Songs I've Loved Before, 2002. *Honours:* 5 Grammy (NARAS) Awards; 8 CMA Awards; Nashville Songwriters Asscn, Hall of Fame, 1973; Playboy Hall of Fame, 1983; National Academy of Popular Music, Lifetime Achievement Award, 1983; 3 ACM Awards; Tex Ritter Songwriting Award, with Kris Kristofferson, 1984; 25 Platinum and Gold albums. *Current Management:* Mark Rothbaum and Associates. *Address:* c/o Mark Rothbaum and Assocs Inc, PO Box 2689, Danbury, CT 06813–2689, USA.

NELSON-SMITH, Simon; Musician (guitar). *Career:* Former member, Boys Wonder; Formed Corduroy for one-off gig; Decided to continue and obtained record deal; Several UK top ten hits. *Recordings:* Singles: Something in My Eye; The Frighteners; London, England; The Joker is Wild; Overhaul; Albums: Dad Man Cat, 1992; High Havoc, 1993; Out of Here, 1994; The New You, 1997.

NERNEY, Declan James; b. 20 May 1956, Drumlish, Ireland. Vocalist; Musician (guitar). *Career:* Played with Gene Stuart plus Brien Coll; Solo artiste; Played for interval BAA Senior Football Final, Crough Park, Dublin, 1990; 3 US tours, 1995; Australian tour. *Recordings:* Picture of My World; Going Places; 3 Way Love Affair; Walking On New Grass; Lucky I Guess; Let's Dance, Album; Part of The Journey. *Honours:* 4 Gold discs; Finalist, Person of the Year, 1994; Band of the Year, Irish World Awards, 1994. *Current Management:* Frank Kilbride. *Address:* Main St, Edgeworthstown, Co Longford, Ireland.

NESBO, Jo; b. Molde, Norway. Vocalist; Songwriter. *Education:* MBA (Master of Business Administration). *Career:* Singer, songwriter, Di Derre; 180 concerts, 1994–95. *Recordings:* Di Derre: Den Derre (Gold disc, Norway) 1992; Jenter and Sånn (Triple Platinum disc, Norway), 1994. *Current Management:* Artist Partner AS.

NESMITH, Robert Michael; b. 30 Dec. 1942, Houston, Texas, USA. Vocalist; Songwriter; Musician (guitar); Actor. *Career:* Folk duo, Mike and John, with John London, 1965; Member, The Monkees, 1966–69; Actor, Monkees television series, 1966–68; 33 1/3 Revolutions Per Monkee (NBC Special); Founder, First National Band, 1970; Re-formed as Second National Band, 1972; Founder, President, own Countryside and Pacific Arts Corporation, record labels, 1974; Financed and produced films Repo Man; Elephant Parts; Time Rider. *Recordings:* Albums with the Monkees: The Monkees (No. 1, USA and UK), 1966; More of The Monkees (No. 1, USA and UK), 1967; Headquarters (No. 1, USA), 1967; Pisces, Aquarius, Capricorn and Jones Ltd (No. 1, UK), 1967; The Birds, The Bees and The Monkees, 1968; Head (soundtrack), 1969; The Monkees Greatest Hits, 1969; The Monkees Present, 1969; Solo albums: The Wichita Train Whistle Sings, 1968; Magnetic South, 1970; Treason, 1972; And The Hits Just Keep On Comin', 1972; Pretty Much Your Standard Ranch Hash, 1973; The Prison, 1974; From A Radio Engine To The Photon Wing, 1977; Live At The Palais, 1978; Infinite Rider On The Big Dogma, 1979; Tropical Campfires, 1992; The Garden, 1994; Listen To The Band, 1997; Timerider–The Adventures Of Lyle Swann, 2000; Hit singles with the Monkees: Last Train To Clarksville (No. 1, USA), 1966; I'm A Believer (No. 1, USA and UK), 1966; (I'm Not Your) Steppin' Stone, 1967; A Little Bit Me, A Little Bit You, 1967; Alternate Title, 1967; Pleasant Valley Sunday, 1967; Daydream Believer (No. 1, USA), 1967; Valleri, 1968; Tear Drop City, 1969; Solo singles: Joanne, 1970; Silver Moon, 1971; Rio, 1977. *Publications:* The Prison, 1974. *Honours:* NARM Awards, Best Selling Group, Best Album, 1967; Emmy Award, Outstanding Comedy Series, 1967; 3 BMI Awards, 1968; Grammy Award, for video Elephant Parts, 1982; Monkees Day, Atlanta, 1986; Star on Hollywood Walk of Fame, 1989.

NESTOROVIC, Sascha; b. 27 Aug. 1964, Zagreb, Croatia. Musician (saxophone); Composer; Arranger. m. Vlasta Gyrura, 9 Nov. 1993. *Education:* Zagreb Academy of Music. *Career:* First alto in big band, Croatian State Television; Live concerts with Zagreb Saxophone Quartet, Muscora, Paris; World Saxophone Congress, Pesaro, Italy; Tours with Zagreb Jazz Portrait: Germany; Austria; Italy; France. *Recordings:* with Zagreb Saxophone Quartet: Croatian Contemporary Music for Saxophones; Zagreb 900; with Slovenian RTV Big Band: Peter Herbolzheimer; Moments Notice, Zagreb Jazz Portrait. *Honours:* Classical awards: Darko Lukic; Milka Trnina. *Membership:* Croatian Musicians' Union; Jazz Club Zagreb. *Current Management:* Vesna Vrandecic, Zitnjak 1, 10000 Zagreb. *Address:* Sascha Nestorovic, Kustossijanska 316, 10000 Zagreb, Croatia.

NETTLETON, Christopher; b. 25 Sept. 1968, Cardiff, Wales. Vocalist; Songwriter; Composer; Musician (guitar, keyboards). *Education:* 8 years, formal piano study. *Career:* Played with Hollyweird, 1989–92; Played with The Nubiles, 1993–98; Toured UK, 1994–97; Supported: Blur; Elastica; Oasis; Moist; Supergrass. *Recordings:* Mindblower, album; Layabout/Mother and Father; Without Waking; Tatjana; Kunta Kinté; Layabout vs Mindblower; singles with The Nubiles, 1995–98. *Membership:* Musicians' Union; Performing Rights Society. *Current Management:* Thirst Music Management. *Address:* c/o 5 Clare Court, Lime St, Bedford MK40 1NH, England.

NEUMANN, Bob; b. Chicago, Illinois, USA. Prod; Engineer; Musician (keyboards); Electronic Music Composer; Synthesist. m. Carolyn, 28 March 1992, 1 s., 1 d. *Education:* BSc, Electronic Engineering, BSEET; General Music Theory, Organ, Piano Training. *Career:* 25 years' performance experience, Chicago area pop bands; 18 years recording, composition; Owner, Project Studio, Lemont, Illinois. *Recordings:* 3 albums, 1 dance single released on independent labels; Beatbox-D; Neu Electro; 12 dance single: Juicy. *Publications include:* Discoveries column, Keyboard Magazine; KLEM. *Honours:* Discoveries Column Alumni, State Fair, Illinois Awards. *Membership:* EARS Society; Chicago BMI. *Current Management:* Neu Electro Productions, USA.

NEVILL, Brian Roy; b. 4 Jan. 1948, Wuppertal, Germany. Musician (drums, piano). Divorced. *Education:* Royal Society of Arts School Certificate. *Career:* Played with Graham Parker; Many recording sessions including The Flying Lizards, 1975–81; Television appearances with Kirsty McColl; Founder member, Shriekback; Member, Pigbag; Radio and television sessions with Shriekback, Pigbag; Worked in Brussels for one year; Live work with Virginia Astley, 1982–87; Formed record label, 1989; Recorded and played with numerous blues and rock 'n' roll visiting American artistes. *Recordings:* Albums: Lend An Ear, Pigbag; The Best Of Pigbag; The BBC Sessions, Pigbag, 1998; The Infinite, Shriekback; Blues and Stomps, Carl Sonny Leyland; The Panasonics; Eddie Angel's Guitar Party; Big Sixteen, Big Joe Louis and the Blueskings; Laugh It Up, Holly Golightly. *Publications:* Articles in Goldmine; Sleeve notes to album Soul Classics, The Best of Bell. *Membership:* PRS; MCPS; Musicians' Union. *Address:* 6 Lancaster Lodge, 83–85 Lancaster Rd, London W11 1QH, England.

NEVILLE, Alaric James; b. 28 July 1961, Derby, England. Sound Engineer; Record Prod; Musician (guitar). *Education:* BA, Fine Art, Leeds University. *Career:* Sound engineer to: Oysterband; The Ukrainians; Based at Woodhouse Studios, Hall Place, Leeds. *Recordings:* Produced artistes including Cud; Bridewell Taxis; The Ukrainians; Ringo's High; Ukranians, Kultura, 1996;

Lazer Boy, Forget Nothing, 1996; Oyster Band, Deep Dark Ocean, 1997; Here I Stand, 1999; Singles include: This Is The Voice, 1999; *Membership:* Musicians' Union. *Current Management:* Stolen Sounds. *Address:* Ivy Cottage, 36 School Lane, Chapel Allerton, Leeds L57 3PN, England.

NEVILLE, Art; b. 17 Dec. 1937, New Orleans, USA. Musician (piano); Vocalist. *Career:* Singer, pianist: The Neville Sound, 1962–68; The Meters, 1968–77; The Neville Brothers, 1977–; with the Meters: worked with Dr John; Robert Palmer; Labelle; European tour, support to the Rolling Stones, 1975; with the Neville Brothers: Amnesty International Concert, with Joan Baez, Sting, Peter Gabriel, Bryan Adams, 1986; Glastonbury Festival, 1990; Playboy Jazz Festival, 1991; Artists Against Hunger and Homelessness benefit, New Orleans 1992; American Music Festival, 1992; Summer Stage '92 concert series, New York, 1992; Berloni Foundation leukemia benefit concert, Modena, Italy, 1992. *Recordings:* Albums with the Meters: The Meters, 1969; Look-Ka Py Py, 1970; Rejuvenation, 1974; Fire On The Bayou, 1975; New Direction, 1977; Singles include: Sophisticated Cissy; Cissy Strut; Ease Back; Chicken Strut; Hand Clapping Song; Be My Lady; Albums with The Neville Brothers: The Neville Brothers, 1978; Fiyo On The Bayou, 1981; Neville-ization, 1984; Treacherous–A History of The Neville Brothers, 1987; Yellow Moon, 1989; Brother's Keeper, 1990; Family Groove, 1992; Very Best of the Neville Brothers, 1997; Live At Tipitani's 1982, 1998; Uptown Rulin', 1999; Solo albums: Mardi Gras Rock 'n' Roll, 1987; That Old Time Rock 'n' Roll, 1992; Art Neville – His Speciality Recordings, 1956–58, 1993; Also appears on: Red Hot + Blue: A Tribute to Cole Porter, 1991; Crescent City Soul, 1996; Gin Blossoms, Outside Lokking In, 1999; Organ-Ized, Organ-Ized, 2000. *Honours:* Best Pop Instrumental Performance, Healing Chant, 1990; Rolling Stone Critics Awards, Best Band, 1990. *Current Management:* Elevation Group Inc, 360 17th St, Suite 200, Oakland, CA 94612, USA.

NEVILLE, Charles; b. 28 Dec. 1938, New Orleans, USA. Musician (saxophone). *Career:* Tours South USA with various blues players, including: Jimmy Reed; Little Walter; Played with Joey Dee and The Starliters, 1962; Member, The Wild Tchoupitoulas, 1976–77; Member, The Neville Brothers, 1977–; Amnesty International Concert, with Sting, Peter Gabriel, Bryan Adams, Joan Baez, 1986; Nelson Mandela Tribute Concert, Wembley, 1990; Glastonbury Festival, 1990; Playboy Jazz Festival, Hollywood, 1991; American Music Festival, 1992; Berloni Foundation's Leukaemia benefit, Modena, Italy, 1992; Summer Stage 92 concerts, New York, 1992. *Recordings:* Wild Tchoupitoulas, 1976; The Neville Brothers, 1978; Neville-ization, 1984; Treacherous: A History of The Neville Brothers 1955–85, 1987; Yellow Moon, 1989; Brother's Keeper, 1990; Family Groove, 1992; Live on Planet Earth, 1994; Singles include: Healing Chant; Bird On The Wire; Contribution: In The Still of The Night, for album: Red Hot + Blue, 1990; Other session work includes: Dr. John; Maria Muldaur; Deep Rumba. *Honours:* Best Band, Rolling Stone magazine Critics awards, 1989; Grammy: Best Pop Instrumental Performance, Healing Chant, 1990; Downbeat Award, Best Blues/Soul/R&B Group, 1990. *Current Management:* Elevation Group Inc, 360 17th St, Suite 200, Oakland, CA 94612, USA.

NEVILLE, Cyril; b. 10 Jan. 1948, New Orleans, USA. Vocalist; Musician (percussion). *Career:* Member, The Neville Sound, 1962–68; Soul Machine, 1968–75; The Meters, 1975; The Wild Tchoupitoulas, 1976; The Neville Brothers, 1977–; Concerts include: Amnesty International Concert, with Joan Baez, Sting, Peter Gabriel, Bryan Adams, 1986; Nelson Mandela Tribute Concert, Wembley, 1990; Glastonbury Festival, 1990; Playboy Jazz Festival, Hollywood, 1991; American Music Festival, 1992; Berloni Foundation leukemia benefit concert, Modena, Italy, 1992. *Recordings:* Albums: Wild Tchoupitoulas, 1976; The Neville Brothers, 1978; Treacherous – A History of The Neville Brothers, 1987; Uptown, 1987; Yellow Moon, 1989; Brother's Keeper, 1990; Family Groove, 1992; Live on Planet Earth, 1994; Uptown Rulin': The Best of the Neville Brothers, 1999; New Orleans Cookin', 2000; Soulo, 2001; Singles include: Healing Chant; Bird On The Wire; In The Still of The Night; Appears on: Red Hot + Blue: A Tribute To Cole Porter, 1991; Other session work includes: Edie Brickell; Dr. John; Bob Dylan; Anders Osborne. *Honours:* Grammy Award: Best Pop Instrumental Performance, Healing Chant, 1990; Rolling Stone Critics Award, Best Band, 1989. *Current Management:* Elevation Group Inc, 360 17th St, Suite 200, Oakland, CA 94612, USA.

NEVIN, David Charles; b. 23 Sept. 1951, London, England. Musician (multi-instumentalist); Vocalist. *Career:* Musician for: Unit 4+2; Harmony Grass; Grass; Capability Brown; Sparrow; Divine; Radio and television appearances: Radio 1; Capital Radio; New Faces; Regional Radio; Concerts: Reading Festival; European festivals; Shirley Bassey tour includes Albert Hall. *Recordings:* Voice, Capability Brown; Matthew Fisher/Strange Days, Matthew Fisher, 1996. *Publications:* Numerous. *Membership:* PRS; Musicians' Union; BAC&S. *Address:* 69 Church Lane, Walthamstow, London E17 9RN, England.

NEW ELECTRO SOUND OF LONDON. See: **PILGREM, Rennie.**

NEWBURY, Mickey (Milton J, Jr); b. 19 May 1940, Houston, Texas, USA. Songwriter; Recording Artiste; *Compositions:* Swiss Cottage Place, recorded

by Roger Miller; Here Comes The Rain Baby, Eddy Arnold and Roy Orbison; Funny Familiar Forgotten Feelings, Don Gibson and Tom Jones; How I Love Them Old Songs, Carl Smith; Sweet Memories, Willie Nelson; Just Dropped In (To See What Condition My Condition Was In), Kenny Rogers and The First Edition; She Even Woke Me Up To Say Goodbye, Jerry Lee Lewis; San Francisco Mabel Joy, John Denver, Joan Baez, Kenny Rogers; I Dont Think About Her (Him) No More, Don Williams, Tammy Wynette; American Trilogy, Elvis Presley; Makes Me Wonder If I Ever Said Goodbye, Johnny Rodriguez; Blue Sky Shinin', Marie Osmond. *Recordings:* Albums: Harlequin Melodies, 1968; Mickey Newbury Sings His Own, 1968; Looks Like Rain, 1969; 'Frisco Mabel Joy, 1971; Heaven Help The Child, 1973; Live At Montezuma, 1973; I Came To Hear The Music, 1974; Lovers, 1975; Rusty Tracks, 1977; His Eye Is On The Sparrow, 1978; The Sailor, 1979; After All These Years, 1981; In A New Age, 1988; Sweet Memories, 1988; Mickey Newbury Collection, 1998; Lulled By The Moonlight, 2000; Stories From The Silver Moon Cafe, 2001. *Honours:* Nashville Songwriters International Hall of Fame, 1980.

NEWCOMB, Keith; b. 13 Oct. 1966, Yokosuka, Japan. Music Publishing Exec. *Education:* BBA, Belmont University, Nashville, Tennessee, 1989. *Career:* Music Publishing Executive and Consultant, 1987–96; Worked with top songwriters including: Paul Overstreet, Robb Royer, Jimmy Griffin, Stewart Harris, Jim Weather, Dean McTaggart, Delbert McClinton and others; Investment Broker, JC Bradford and Company, 1996–.

NEWCOMER, Carrie Ann; b. 25 May 1958, Dawajack, Michigan, USA. Vocalist; Musician (guitar, dulcimer); Songwriter. *Education:* Learnt flute as a child. *Career:* Singer-songwriter who uses folk country, jazz and blues influences; Began playing guitar at around age 14; Played dulcimer and was lead vocalist and songwriter in the folk trio Stone Soup (with guitarist Larry Smeyak and percussionist Dennis Leas), 1981–87; Released first solo album, 1991; Toured regularly and made appearances at events such as Newport folk festival; The Age of Possibility is one of the top ten best selling albums on Rounder Records. *Recordings:* with Stone Soup: Long Fields, 1984; October Nights, 1987; solo: Visions and Dreams, 1991; An Angel At My Shoulder, 1994; The Bird On The Wing, 1995; My Father's Only Son, 1996; My True Name, 1998; The Age of Possibility, 2000. *Website:* www.carrienewcomer.com.

NEWELL, Norman; b. 25 Jan. 1919, London, England. Lyricist; Former Record Prod. *Career:* Record prod., songwriter; worked with: John Barry; Shirley Bassey; Connie Francis; Al Martino; Vera Lynn; Mel Torme. *Compositions include:* More, from film Mondo Cane (over 5m. performances in USA and world hit, over 1,000 recordings); Portrait of My Love, (world hit). *Publications:* Many songs. *Honours:* Several BMI Awards; Golden Globe Award. *Membership:* PRS; BMI; BAC&S; MCPS. *Current Management:* Noel Gay Organisation (Charles Armitage). *Address:* 1 Albion Court, Galena Rd, Hammersmith, London W6 0QT, England.

NEWMAN, David; b. 11 March 1954, Los Angeles, CA, USA. Composer; Musician (violin); Conductor. *Education:* Classically trained. *Compositions:* For film: Frankenweenie, 1984; Vendetta, 1986; The Kindred, 1986; Critters, 1986; Throw Momma from the Train, 1987; My Demon Lover, 1987; Malone, 1987; The Brave Little Toaster, 1987; The War of the Roses, 1989; R.O.T.O.R., 1989; Little Monsters, 1989; Heathers, 1989; Gross Anatomy, 1989; Disorganized Crime, 1989; Bill & Ted's Excellent Adventure, 1989; The Runestone, 1990; Mr Destiny, 1990; Madhouse, 1990; Fire Birds, 1990; DuckTales: The Movie–Treasure of the Lost Lamp, 1990; The Freshman, 1990; Talent for the Game, 1991; Rover Dangerfield, 1991; Paradise, 1991; Don't Tell Mom the Babysitter's Dead, 1991; Bill & Ted's Bogus Journey, 1991; The Marrying Man, 1991; Other People's Money, 1991; That Night, 1992; The Itsy Bitsy Spider, 1992; The Mighty Ducks, 1992; Honeymoon in Vegas, 1992; Hoffa, 1992; Undercover Blues, 1993; The Sandlot, 1993; Coneheads, 1993; The Flintstones, 1994; The Air Up There, 1994; My Father the Hero, 1994; The Cowboy Way, 1994; I Love Trouble, 1994; Boys on the Side, 1995; Tommy Boy, 1995; Operation Dumbo Drop, 1995; Jingle All the Way, 1996; Big Bully, 1996; The Phantom, 1996; The Nutty Professor, 1996; Matilda, 1996; Out to Sea, 1997; Anastasia, 1997; Never Been Kissed, 1999; Bowfinger, 1999; Brokedown Palace, 1999; Galaxy Quest, 1999; The Flintstones in Viva Rock Vegas, 2000; Duets, 2000; The Nutty Professor II: The Klumps, 2000; Bedazzled, 2000; 102 Dalmatians, 2000; Dr Dolittle 2, 2001; The Affair of the Necklace, 2001; Death to Smoochy, 2002. *Honours:* Emmy Award, for The Young Indiana Jones Chronicles: The Scandal of 1920. *Membership:* BMI. *Current Management:* Blue Focus Management, 15233 Ventura Blvd, Suite 200, Sherman Oaks, CA 91403, USA.

NEWMAN, Randy; b. 28 Nov. 1943, Los Angeles, CA, USA. Vocalist; Songwriter; Musician (piano); Arranger. m. Gretchen Newman, 1 d. *Education:* Music Composition, UCLA. *Career:* Staff songwriter, Metric Music, 1962; Became staff arranger, prod., Warner Bros Records, 1967; Concerts include: Farm Aid, 1985; American Music Festival, Colorado, 1992. *Compositions include:* They Tell Me It's Summer, The Fleetwoods; I Don't Want To Hear It Anymore, Jerry Butler; I've Been Wrong Before, Cilla Black; Simon Smith and His Amazing Dancing Bear, Alan Price; Nobody Needs Your Love and Just One Smile, Gene Pitney; Mama Told Me (Not To Come), Three Dog Night (No. 1, USA); I Think It's Going To Rain Today (also recorded by

UB40); I Love L.A. (used to promote 1984 Olympic Games); Songs also recorded by artistes including Judy Collins; Harry Nilsson; Manfred Mann; Frankie Laine; Jackie DeShannon; Walker Brothers; As arranger: Is That All There Is?, Peggy Lee; for film: Ragtime, 1981; The Natural, 1984; Three Amigos!, 1986; Parenthood, 1989; Awakenings, 1990; Avalon, 1990; The Paper, 1994; Maverick, 1994; Toy Story, 1995; James and the Giant Peach, 1996; Michael, 1996; Cats Don't Dance, 1997; Pleasantville, 1998; A Bug's Life, 1998; Toy Story 2, 1999; Meet the Parents, 2000; Monsters, Inc., 2001; for television: The Marshall Chronicles, 1990; Cop Rock (ABC TV), 1991. *Recordings:* Albums: The Randy Newman Orchestra Plays Music From The Hit Television Series Peyton Place, 1966; Randy Newman, 1968; Twelve Songs, 1970; Randy Newman Live, 1971; Good Old Boys, 1974; Little Criminals, 1978; Born Again, 1979; Trouble In Paradise, 1983; Lonely At The Top, 1987; Land of Dreams, 1988; Music From The Motion Picture The Paper, 1994; Faust, 1995; Bad Love, 1999; The Best Of Randy Newman, 2001. Singles include: Short People (No. 2, USA), 1978; The Blues, duet with Paul Simon, 1983; Contributor, The Simpsons Sing The Blues, 1990; Producer: Classic Disney Vol. IV, 1997; A Bug's Life, 1998; two stage productions of Faust, La Jolla Playhouse, 1995, Goodman Theatre, Chicago, 1996. *Honours:* Grammy Awards, Best Instrumental Composition, 1984, Best Song Written for a Motion Picture, for A Bug's Life, for Toy Story 2, 2001; Emmy, music for Cop Rock, 1991; Frederick Loewe Award, 2001. *Membership:* ASCAP. *Current Management:* Gorfaine/Schwartz Agency Inc, 13245 Riverside Dr., Suite 450, Sherman Oakes, CA 91423, USA.

NEWMAN, Thomas; b. 29 October 1955, Los Angeles, CA, USA. Composer. *Education:* Music, University of Southern California; Yale University. *Compositions:* For television: Heat Wave, 1990; Those Secrets, 1992; For film: Revenge of the Nerds, 1984; Grandview, USA, 1984; Reckless, 1984; Real Genius, 1985; The Man with One Red Shoe, 1985; Desperately Seeking Susan, 1985; Girls Just Want to Have Fun, 1985; Gung Ho, 1986; Jumpin' Jack Flash, 1986; The Lost Boys, 1987; Light of Day, 1987; Less Than Zero, 1987; The Prince of Pennsylvania, 1988; The Great Outdoors, 1988; Cookie, 1989; Welcome Home, Roxy Carmichael, 1990; Naked Tango, 1990; Men Don't Leave, 1990; The Rapture, 1991; Deceived, 1991; Career Opportunities, 1991; The Linguini Incident, 1991; Fried Green Tomatoes, 1991; Whispers in the Dark, 1992; Scent of a Woman, 1992; The Player, 1992; Josh and S.A.M., 1993; Flesh and Bone, 1993; The War, 1994; The Shawshank Redemption, 1994; Little Women, 1994; The Favor, 1994; Threesome, 1994; Corrina, Corrina, 1994; Unstrung Heroes, 1995; How to Make an American Quilt, 1995; American Buffalo, 1996; Up Close & Personal, 1996; Phenomenon, 1996; The People vs Larry Flynt, 1996; Mad City, 1997; Red Corner, 1997; Oscar and Lucinda, 1997; Meet Joe Black, 1998; The Horse Whisperer, 1998; The Green Mile, 1999; American Beauty, 1999; Erin Brockovich, 2000; Pay It Forward, 2000; In the Bedroom, 2002. *Honours:* BAFTA, American Beauty; Grammy Award, American Beauty. *Membership:* BMI. *Current Management:* Gorfaine/Schwartz Agency Inc, 13245 Riverside Dr., Suite 450, Sherman Oaks, CA 91423, USA.

NEWSTED, Jason; b. 4 March 1963, Battle Creek, Michigan, USA. Rock Musician (bass). *Career:* Member, US heavy rock groups: Flotsam and Jetsam; Metallica, 1986–; 750 live appearances with Metallica, 1986–; Concerts include: Freddie Mercury AIDS Tribute, Wembley, 1992; Moscow Monsters of Rock Festival, 1991; Numerous world-wide tours, television and radio appearances. *Recordings:* with Flotsam and Jetsam: Flotsam and Jetsam, 1986; with Metallica: Garage Days Re-visited, 1987; Justice For All, 1988; Metallica (No. 1, UK and USA), 1991; Metallica VI: Load (No. 1, UK and USA), 1996; Reload (No. 1, USA), 1997; Phobos; Garage Inc; S&M, 1999; Singles include: Harvester Of Sorrow, 1988; One, 1989; Enter Sandman, 1991; The Unforgiven, 1991; Nothing Else Matters, 1992; Wherever I May Roam, 1992; Sad But True, 1993; Until It Sleeps, 1996; Hero Of The Day, 1996; Mama Said, 1996; The Memory Remains, 1997; The Unforgiven II, 1998; Fuel, 1998; Whiskey In The Jar, 1999; I Disappear, 2000. *Honours:* Grammy Awards, 1990–92; AMAs, 1992; MTV Award, 1992. *Membership:* AFofM San Francisco; ASCAP. *Current Management:* c/o Q-Prime Inc, 729 Seventh Ave, 14th Floor, New York, NY 10019, USA.

NEWTON, Allen; b. 30 Aug. 1950, Fort Worth, Texas, USA. Music Promoter. m. Frances, April 1983, 2 d. *Education:* Business degree. *Career:* 15 years in radio and television; Worked as: DJ; Music and programme director; Station manager; Newscaster; Sales manager; Programme producer; Owner, seven independent record labels and two publishing companies. *Membership:* BMI; ASCAP. *Address:* RT 1, Box 187-A, Whitney, TX 76692, USA.

NEWTON, (Carson) Wayne; b. 4 March 1942, Norfolk, Virginia, USA. Entertainer; Vocalist; Musician (trumpet, piano, guitars, violin, drums, valve trombone); Actor; Author. m. Kathleen McCrone, 9 April 1994, 1 d. *Career:* Performances include: Personal television specials; Fourth of July concert at Washington monument; USA tours; Total of 2000 television shows and films including: The Lucy Show; Jackie Gleason; Roseanne; Full House. *Recordings:* Danke Schoen; Red Roses For A Blue Lady; The Letter; Daddy Don't You Walk So Fast; 131 albums released; 300 singles; Sings The Hits Of The 70s, 1999. *Publications:* Autobiography – Once Before I Go. *Honours:* Entertainer of the Year (9 years); Presidential Awards; Ten Outstanding Men of America.

Membership: AFTRA; SAG; AFofM. *Address:* 3422 Happy Lane, Las Vegas, NV 89120, USA.

NEWTON, Tad (Robert Arthur William); b. 25 June 1946, Marlborough, Wiltshire, England. Jazz Musician (trombone); Vocalist. m. Anne Marie Newton, 2 Aug. 1969, 2 s., 2 d. *Education:* BA Hons, University of Southampton. *Career:* Bandleader, trombonist and vocalist, Tad Newton's Jazzfriends (7-piece dixieland and mainstream jazz band); Concert appearances include: Barbican Centre, Derngate Theatre, Royal Festival Hall, Wembley Conference Centre, major festivals; Also Jazz Promoter and Organizer. *Recordings:* Basin St To Harlem, 1988; Drivin', 1989; Jumpin' For Joy, 1991; Journey Thru' Jazz, 1994; Jazz Portraits, 1999. *Membership:* Musicians' Union. *Current Management:* TNJF Management. *Address:* 23 Windmill Ave, Blisworth, Northamptonshire NN7 3EQ, England. *E-mail:* tadnewton@fsmail.net. *Website:* www.jazzbandsuk.com.

NEWTON-JOHN, Olivia; b. 26 Sept. 1948, Cambridge, England. Vocalist; Actress. m. Matt Lattanzi, 1985, 1 d. *Career:* Moved to Australia, aged 5; Singer in folk group as teenager; Local television performer with Pat Carroll; Winner, National Talent Contest, 1964; Singer, actress, 1965–; Represented UK in Eurovision Song Contest, 1974; Music For UNICEF Concert, New York, 1979; Film appearances include: Grease, 1978; Xanadu, 1980; Two of a Kind, 1983; Own clothing business, Koala Blue, 1984–. *Recordings:* Albums: If Not For You, 1971; Let Me Be There, 1974; Music Makes My Day, 1974; Long Live Love, 1974; If You Love Me Let Me Know (No. 1, USA), 1974; Have You Ever Never Been Mellow, 1975; Clearly Love, 1975; Come On Over, 1976; Don't Stop Believin', 1976; Making A Good Thing Better, 1977; Greatest Hits, 1978; Grease (film soundtrack), 1978; Totally Hot, 1979; Xanadu (film soundtrack), 1980; Physical, 1981; 20 Greatest Hits, 1982; Olivia's Greatest Hits Vol. 2, 1983; Two of a Kind, 1984; Soul Kiss, 1986; The Rumour, 1988; Warm and Tender, 1990; Back To Basics: The Essential Collection 1971–92, 1992; Gaia – One Woman's Journey, 1995; More than Physical, 1995; Greatest Hits, 1996; Olivia, 1998; Back with a Heart, 1998; Highlights from the Main Event, 1999; Greatest Hits: First Impressions, 1999; Country Girl, 1999; Best of Olivia Newton John, 1999; Love Songs: A Collection: One Woman's Journey, 2000; Hit singles include: If Not For You, 1971; Banks Of The Ohio, 1972; What Is Life, 1972; Take Me Home Country Roads, 1973; Let Me Be There, 1974; Long Live Love, 1974; If You Love Me (Let Me Know), 1974; I Honestly Love You (No. 1, USA), 1974; Have You Never Been Mellow (No. 1, USA), 1975; Please Mr Please, 1975; Something Better To Do, 1975; Fly Away, duet with John Denver, 1976; Sam, 1977; You're The One That I Want, duet with John Travolta (No. 1, USA and UK, third-best selling single in UK), 1978; Summer Nights, duet with John Travolta (UK No. 1, 7 weeks), 1978; Hopelessly Devoted To You (No. 2, UK), 1978; A Little More Love, 1979; Deeper Than The Night, 1979; I Cant Help It, duet with Andy Gibb, 1980; Xanadu, with ELO (No. 1, UK), 1980; Magic (No. 1, USA), 1980; Physical (US No. 1, 10 weeks), 1981; Make A Move On Me, 1982; Heart Attack, 1982; Twist of Fate, from film soundtrack Two of a Kind, 1983; Back with a Heart, 1998; Grease (Remix), 1998; I Honestly Love You, 1998; Physical Remix 1999, 1999. *Honours:* O.B.E.; Grammy Awards: Record of the Year, 1974; Best Country Vocal Performance, 1974; Best Pop Vocal Performance, 1975; Numerous American Music Awards, 1975–77, 1983; CMA Award, Female Vocalist of Year (first UK recipient), 1975; Star on Hollywood Walk of Fame, 1981; Numerous other awards from Record World; Billboard; People's Choice; AGVA; NARM; Goodwill Ambassador, UN Environment Programme, 1989. *Current Management:* Bill Sammeth Organisation, PO Box 960, Beverly Hills, CA 90213, USA.

NGUYA-TRASA, Papy; b. 6 March 1973, Bas-Congo, Africa. Musician (guitar); Vocalist. *Education:* Musical interpretation, College of Arts. *Career:* Appearances at Musical Festival of Africa, 1996; Musical research performance, 1997; Festival of Jazz, 1999. *Compositions:* many performed but yet to be recorded. *Recordings:* Owala, 1994; Gaby Kwambamba, 1995; Let Them Say, 1996. *Honours:* Medal of Flying Musician of China, 1997. *Membership:* Asscn of Research Music. *Address:* Eglise Lagos-Rhema, 37/59 Av du 24 Novembre, Commune da la Ngombe, Kinshasa, Lingwala, Africa.

NGWENYA, Moses; b. Soweto, South Africa. Musician (keyboards, guitar, drums). *Career:* Drummer with The Crocodiles; Later worked with Intombi Zesi Manje Manje; Joined The Young Brothers, 1976; Act became Soul Brothers; Involved in production with own Black Moses Productions. *Recordings:* Albums include: Umshoza Wami, 1974; Isiphiwo, 1982; Xola, 1987; Jive Explosion, 1988; Impimpi, 1989; Isighebhezana, 1999; Induk' Enhle, 2001. *Honours:* FNB South African Music Award, Best Mbaqanga Performance; 15 gold discs, 5 platinum discs, several multiplatinum discs. *Address:* c/o Gallo, PO Box 2897, Parklands 2121, South Africa. *Website:* www.gallo.co.za.

NI MHAONAIGH, Mairead; b. 1959 Gaoth Dobhair, Co. Donegal, Ireland. Vocalist; Musician (fiddle). m. (1) Frankie Kennedy, deceased 1994, (2) Dermot Byrne. *Career:* Founding mem., Ragairne, with Frankie Kennedy; Recorded for RTE and performed at the Belfast Folk Festival; Played in USA with Kennedy, 1984–85; Founding mem., Altan, with Frankie Kennedy, 1987; First Irish traditional group to sign to a major label, Virgin Records, 1996;

Presented traditional music radio show, The Long Note; Presented TV series, The Pure Drop. *Recordings:* Albums: Ceol Aduaidh, 1983; Horse With A Heart, 1989; The Red Crow, 1990; Harvest Storm, 1992; Island Angel, 1993; The First Ten Years, 1996; Blackwater, 1996; Runaway Sunday, 1997; Another Sky, 2000; The Blue Idol, 2002. *Current Management:* c/o Tom Sherlock, 71 Carysfort Ave, Blackrock, County Dublin, Ireland. *Website:* www.altan.ie.

NI RIAIN, Nóirín; b. 12 June 1951, Limerick, Ireland. Vocalist; Musician (various Indian drones). m. Mícheál ó Súilleabháin, 27 June 1974, 2 s. *Education:* Dip Phil NuI; MA, BMus, Dip, CMSM. *Career:* Performed UN Conferences in Costa Rica; Rio De Janeiro; Copenhagen; Poland; India; Beijing, People's Republic of China, 1995; Worked with John Cage; Numerous world-wide television and radio appearances; Works extensively in Cathedral of St John the Divine, New York; Artist in residence, County of Laois, Ireland, 1999–2000. *Recordings:* Caoineadh Na Maighdine; Good People All; Vox De Nube; Soundings; Ple Hse Change; Gregorian Chant Experience; Stor Amhran; Darkest Midnight; Virgin's Lament. *Publications:* Im Bim Baboro; Stór Amhrán; Gregorian Chant Classics. *Current Management:* Personally managed. *Address:* Dromore House, Newport, Co Tipperary, Ireland.

NICHOLAS, James Hayden; b. 7 May 1956, Hobbs, New Mexico, USA. Musician (guitar); Songwriter. *Education:* University of Houston, 1975–76. *Career:* Guitarist, various bands, 1975–86; Lead guitarist, songwriter, Clint Black, 1987–; Guitar technician at: Dale Mullins Studios, Houston, 1977–81; Heck Music Co, 1981–82; Appearances with Clint Black include: Grand Ole Opry; CMA Awards Show; Tonight Show; Arsenio Hall. *Compositions include:* Better Man; Killing Time; Music City News. *Recordings:* Albums: with Clint Black include: Killing Time, 1989; Put Yourself In My Shoes, 1990; The Hard Way, 1992; No Time To Kill, 1993; One Emotion, 1994; Looking for Christmas, 1995; The Greatest Hits, 1996; Nothin' But The Taillights, 1997; D'lectrified, 1999; Greatest Hits Volume 2, 2001. *Website:* www.clintblack.com.

NICHOLAS, Julian Conan; b. 13 Jan. 1965, London, England. Musician (Saxophone); Composer. m. 1 d. *Education:* Hons Degree, York, 1986. *Career:* Saxophonist with Loose Tubes, 1989–91; Own group, Mountain People, 1989–98; Toured Europe extensively, 1989–98; Film score, Fools Gold, Brinksmat Robbery, LWT, 1992; Lecturer and Educationist, Bishop Otter College, West Sussex, 1993–96; Access to Music, 1992–98. *Compositions:* with W Woolf: A Thousand Ships; Mountain People; Food of Love; A Dawning; Madam, I'm Adam; Dear John. *Recordings:* Mountain People; RS001; Square Groove; Food of Love; Transformations; Everything You Do To Me. *Honours:* Twice Winner, Brighton Festival, Zap Award for Jazz, 1989, 1991. *Membership:* Musicians' Union; Performing Rights Society. *Current Management:* Aardvark, 1 Montague Pl., Brighton BN2 1JE, England. *Address:* 8A Powis Sq., Brighton, BN1 3HH, England.

NICHOLLS, Al (Alan Charles); b. 27 Feb. 1957, Wrexham, Wales. Musician (saxophone); Arranger. *Education:* City of Leeds College of Music. *Career:* Four years, Big Town Playboys, 1987–91; Numerous European tours; 2 US tours; Television includes: Jools Holland Happening; Pat Savak Show, USA; 3 years, King Pleasure and The Biscuit Boys, 1991–94; Elvis: The Musical, Prince of Wales Theatre, West End, 1996; Led own band, Blue Harlem, 1996–; Television includes: What's The Noise; Blue Peter; Ray Gelato Giants, 1994–; Freelance musician; Expanding career as solo jazz performer: clubs such as Shepperton Jazz Club, 100 Club, London Cheltenham Jazz Club; Festivals: Coventry, Soho, Llangollen; Returned to Big Town Playboys, 1999–. *Recordings:* Albums: Now Appearing, Big Town Playboys; Don't Mess With The Boogieman, Big Joe Duskin; Live At The Burnley Blues Festival, Champion Jack Dupree; The Full Flavour, Ray Gelato and The Giants; with King Pleasure and The Biscuit Boys: Live At Ronnie Scott's; Blues and Rhythm Revue; Hot News, Blue Harlem, CD, 1998; Ready To Rock, Big 6; We The Boys Will Rock Ya, Big 6; Get Off It and Rock It, Big 6; Just Can't Afford It, Mike Sanchez. *Honours:* Best Dep of the Year Award, for Hot News International, 1999. *Membership:* Musicians' Union; British Music Writers' Council. *Address:* 23 University Mansions, Putney, London SW15 1EP, England.

NICHOLLS, Billy (William Morris); b. 15 Febrary 1949, London, England. Vocalist; Songwriter; Prod. m. Anne Dupée, 2 s. 1 d. *Career:* Musical director for The Who: Roger Daltrey tour; Pete Townshend Psychoderelict tour; Own solo albums. *Compositions:* Can't Stop Loving You, Leo Sayer; Without Your Love, Roger Daltrey; Fake It, Pete Townshend; Music for the McVicar film. *Recordings:* Solo albums: White Horse; Love Songs; Under One Banner; with Pete Townshend: Who Came First, 1927; Rough Mix, 1977; Iron Man: a Musical, 1989; with Roger Daltrey: Celebration: The Music of the Who, 1994; McVicar, 1996; Martyrs and Madmen, 1997; Also recorded with: John Hammond; John Illsley; Phil Manzanera. *Address:* 16 Park Rd, E Twickenham, Middlesex TW1 2PX, England.

NICHOLLS, Craig; b. 1978. Vocalist; Musician (guitar). *Career:* Founding mem., The Vines, 1994–; Appearance, Sydney 2000 Olympic Festival; Australian tour, supporting You Am I, 2001; Record Beatles cover, I'm Only Sleeping, for film I Am Sam, 2001; Sign to Capitol Records, USA, Heavenly

Records, UK; Short UK, US and Canadian tours, incl. Glastonbury Festival, England; Carling Weekend Festival, Reading, Leeds; Coachella Festival, Los Angeles; Troubadour, Los Angeles; Mercury Lounge, New York; WHFS Festival, Washington, 2002; Sign to EMI Australia, 2002; Television appearances: Top Of The Pops, Later With Jools Holland, The Late Show with David Letterman, 2002; Australian tour, late 2002; Performed, MTV Video Music Awards, 2002. *Recordings:* Albums: Highly Evolved, 2002. Singles: Factory, 2001; Sun Child/Hot Leather, 2002; Heavenly, 2002; Get Free, 2002; Highly Evolved, 2002. *Honours:* NME Award, Best Single, for Get Free, 2003. *Current Management:* Winterman and Goldstein Management, PO Box 545, Newtown, NSW 2042, Australia. *Address:* c/o Capitol Records, 1750 N Vine St, Hollywood, CA 90028, USA. *Website:* www.thevines.com.

NICHOLLS, Jonathan Charles; b. 11 Dec. 1948, Northampton, England. Bandleader; Compere; Musician (bass guitar). m. Linda Joyce Singleton, 5 April 1969, 1 s. *Career:* Bandleader, top UK showband Mixed Feelings; Performed at leading international venues: New York Hilton; Bahrain Hilton; Gleneagles; Radio interview, The Tunnels of Arras 1917; Radio performance of play: Voices of The Fallen, BBC Radio 4. *Publications:* Cheerful Sacrifice – The Battle of Arras, 1917, 1992; Play: Voices of The Fallen, London, 1992–94. *Membership:* Musicians' Union. *Address:* 64 Wootton Dr., Hemel Hempstead, Herts HP2 6LB, England.

NICHOLS, Keith Charles; b. 13 Feb. 1945, London, England. Musician (Piano, Trombone); Arranger. m. Eve Nichols, 10 April 1976. *Education:* Guildhall School of Music. *Career:* Toured, 7 years, with jazz-comedy band, Levity Lancers, playing piano, trombone and tuba; Regular ragtime concerts, South Bank, as soloist and small ensembles; Member, Richard Sudhalter's New Paul Whiteman Orchestra, appearances in Philadelphia and Carnegie Hall, New York; Formed Midnite Follies Orchestra with Alan Cohen, 1977; Freelance, performing throughout UK, Europe and USA; Piano player, part of Hoagy Carmichael, in feature film soundtrack Bix; Lecturer, Jazz History, Royal Academy of Music; Performed music of Benny Goodman's 1938 Carnegie Hall Concert with Royal Academy Big Band; Recent tours of France, Scandinavia, Germany, Switzerland, Ireland, Egypt; Performed with Cotton Club at Royal Festival Hall, London. *Compositions:* Arrangements and transcriptions in 20s and 30s styles. *Recordings:* Numerous solo albums; Collaboration with Bing Crosby; Many albums as bandleader and sideman; CD, recreated music of Fletcher Henderson; Album of rare Duke Ellington and Fats Waller pieces; Featured on: Ace Of Rhythm, Louisiana Washboard Five, 2000. *Honours:* Great British Jr Champion, Accordion, 1960; GGSM, 1967; Hon. Associateship, Royal Academy of Music, 1998. *Address:* 33 Rosemary Dr., Ilford, Essex IG4 5JD, England.

NICKELL, Ylonda; b. 27 Sept. 1958, Napa, California, USA. Alto Saxophonist. m. Richie Cole, 1981, 1 d. *Career:* Performed with: Sonny Stitt, Freddie Hubbard, Mose Allison, Manhattan Transfer, Robert Cray and Willie Nelson; Performed at: Monterey Jazz Festival, Russian River Jazz Festival, Cotati Jazz Festival, Concerts-by-the-Sea, The Jazz Workshop, Roland's, Great American Music Hall, Yoshi's. *Recordings:* Alto Lady; Minnesota Sax. *Current Management:* Karen Kindig. *Address:* Karen Kindig, c/o The Blue Cat Agency, PO Box 399, Novato, CA 94948, USA.

NICKS, Stevie (Stephanie); b. 26 May 1948, Phoenix, AZ, USA. Vocalist; Songwriter. m. Kim Anderson, 29 Jan. 1983, divorced 1984. *Career:* Member, Fritz (with Lindsey Buckingham); Member, duo Buckingham and Nicks; Member, Fleetwood Mac, 1975–90; Solo artiste, 1981–; World-wide tours and concerts include: US tour with the Eagles, 1976; US Festival, San Bernardino, California, 1982; Shake The Cage tour, Europe, Australia, 1988; Mask tour, 1990. *Compositions include:* Rhiannon (Will You Ever Win); Dreams; Sara; Gypsy; Leather and Lace; Edge of Seventeen; I Can't Wait; The Other Side of The Mirror; Co-writer with Sandy Stewart: Seven Wonders; If Anyone Falls; Co-writer with Prince: Stand Back. *Recordings:* Albums: with Lindsey Buckingham: Buckingham Nicks, 1974; with Fleetwood Mac: Fleetwood Mac (No. 1, USA), 1975; Rumours (No. 1, UK and USA; 15m. sales), 1977; Tusk (No. 1, UK), 1978; Fleetwood Mac Live, 1980; Mirage (No. 1, USA), 1982; Tango In The Night (No. 1, UK), 1987; Greatest Hits, 1988; Behind The Mask (No. 1, UK), 1990; 25 Years—The Chain, 1992; Solo: Bella Donna, 1981; The Wild Heart, 1983; Rock A Little, 1985; The Other Side of The Mirror, 1989; Timespace – The Best of Stevie Nicks, 1991; Street Angel, 1994; Maybe Love Will Change Your Mind, 1994; Enchanted: The Works of Stevie Nicks, 1998; Trouble In Shangri-La, 2001. Singles include: with Fleetwood Mac: Rhiannon (Will You Ever Win), 1976; Say You Love Me, 1976; Go Your Own Way, 1977; Don't Stop, 1977; Dreams (No. 1, USA); You Make Loving Fun, 1977; Tusk, 1979; Sara, 1980; Hold Me, 1984; Oh Diane, 1983; Big Love, 1987; Little Lies, 1987; Everywhere, 1988; Solo: Stop Draggin' My Heart Around, with Tom Petty, 1981; Leather and Lace, duet with Don Henley, 1982; Edge of Seventeen, 1982; After The Glitter Fades, 1982; Stand Back, 1982; If Anyone Falls, 1982; Talk To Me, 1986; I Can't Wait, 1986; Rooms On Fire, 1989; Hard Game, 1994; Blue Denim, 1994; Also recorded with Kenny Loggins; Richie Vito; Tom Petty. *Honours:* American Music Awards: Favorite Pop/Rock Group, Favorite Pop/Rock Album, 1978; Grammy: Album of the Year, Rumours, 1978; Billboard Awards: Album of the Year, Group of the Year, 1977; Star on Hollywood Hall of Fame, with Fleetwood Mac, 1979; Gold

Ticket, Madison Square Garden, 1990; BRIT Award, Outstanding Contribution, 1998. *Address:* WEA Corpn, 79 Madison Ave, Floor 7, New York, NY 10016, USA.

NICOL, Ken (Kenneth Stephen); b. 27 May 1951, Preston, Lancashire, England. Musician (guitar); Vocalist; Writer. *Career:* Signed to CBS Records, 1974; Polydor until 1979; Played lead guitar and recorded with Al Stewart; Appeared live in USA, 1980–88; Currently member, Albion Band; Television appearances include: New Faces; This Morning; Pebble Mill; The Big Breakfast. *Recordings:* Easy Street, by Nicol and Marsh, 1974, 1976; Under The Glass, 1977; Nicol and Marsh, 1978; Living In A Spanish Town, 1993; Happy Accident, The Albion Band, 1998; Road Movies, 2001. *Membership:* Musicians' Union; PRS. *Current Management:* Ess'ntial Productions. *Address:* 298 Tag Lane, Ingol, Preston, Lancashire PR2 3UY, England.

NICOL, Simon; b. 13 Oct. 1950, Muswell Hill, London, England. Folk Musician (guitar, keyboards). *Career:* Founding mem., Fairport Convention, 1967–71, 1977–; Founder, guitarist, Albion Country Band, 1971; Appearances include: Royal Albert Hall, 1969; London Palladium, 1970; Tours, festivals, concerts, annual Fairport Convention reunion concerts, 1980–. *Recordings:* Albums: with Fairport Convention: Fairport Convention, 1968; What We Did On Our Holidays, 1969; Unhalfbricking, 1969; Liege and Lief, 1970; Full House, 1970; Angel Delight, 1971; Babbacombe Lee, 1971; A Bonny Band Of Roses, 1977; Moat On The Ledge, 1982; The Best Of…, 1988; Red And Gold, 1989; Fairport Convention, 1990; Them Five Seasons, 1991; Jewel In The Crown, 1995; Old-New-Borrowed-Blue, 1996; Who Knows Where The Time Goes?, 1997; Encore, Encore, 1997; Fiddlestix 1970–84: The Best of Fairport Convention, 1998; Fairport Convention, Woodworm Years, 1998; Wood And The Wire, 2000; XXXV, 2002; Heyday: BBC Radio Sessions 1968–69, 2002; with Albion Country Band: Battle of The Field, 1976; Prospect Before Us, 1977; Rise Up Like The Sun, 1978; Albion River Hymn March, 1979; Light Shining Albino, 1984; Shuffle Off, 1984. *Address:* c/o Woodworm Records Ltd, PO Box 37, Banbury, Oxfordshire OX16 8YN, England. *E-mail:* faircrop@aol.com. *Website:* www.fairportconvention.co.uk.

NICOLAS, Clovis; b. 13 March 1973, Abidjan, Ivory Coast. Musician (acoustic bass). *Education:* DEVG Philosophy; Jazz and classical music, Conservatoire of Music, Marseilles, 1993. *Career:* Played with Ted Curson; Peter King; Bobby Porcelli; Sandy Patton and Sara Lazarus, 1994; Plays with many French jazzmen including Jean-Pierre Arnaud; Philippe Renault; Pierre Drevet; Live in Paris, 1996; Played with Brad Mehldau, Belmondo Quintet, Stefano di Batista Quintet, Vincent Herring, Aldo Romano, Laurent de Wilde, Christian Escoude; *Compositions:* Groovy Globy, 1996; Li-Li Smiles Again, 1996; A Romance for JB, 1996. *Recordings:* Featured on album: Le Collectif Artistique du Cri du Port (Marseilles), 1995; Jean Christope Beney Quartet, 1997; Tenor Joke, JC Beney Quartet, 1997; Infinity, Belmondo Quintet, 1999; Le Douze, Temime Quartet, 1999; Baptiste Trotignon Trio, Fluide, 2000. *Honours:* First prize, International competition, Jazz Orchestras, Vienne, France, 1995; First Prize, Jazz Class Conservatoire de Marseille, 1996. *Address:* 9 rue Eugène Varlin, 75010 Paris, France.

NICOLS, Maggie; b. 24 Feb. 1948, Edinburgh, Scotland. Musician (Voice, Piano, Keyboards); Performer; Teacher; Composer. 1 d. *Education:* Apprenticeships to Dennis Rose and John Stevens. *Career:* dancer, Windmill Theatre, sang with Great Bebop Pianist, Dennis Rose; joined innovator John Steven's Spontaneous Music Ensemble; pioneer of Vocal and Instrumental Music Workshops, Oval House Theatre, 1970–; joined Keith Tippett's Centipede, formed duo with Julie Tippetts; co-founded Feminist Improvising Group; performed internationally at Major Festivals, Moers Music Festival, Berlin Jazz Festival, Bath and Bracknell Jazz Festivals; Radio appearances include Jazz In Britain; Television appearances in Germany, Italy, France and Switzerland. *Compositions:* Numerous. *Recordings:* Nearly 50 including Sweet and S'ours; Les Diaboliques; Nevergreens; Cats Cradle; Vocals on Loss Of Sexual Innocence OST, 1999. *Publications:* Many Interviews. *Honours:* A 60-piece orchestra playing own composition, Evolution Revolution. *Membership:* Musicians' Union; Equity; PRS; BAC&S; PAMRA. *Address:* 23 Nottingham House, Shorts Gardens, London WC2H 9AX, England.

NIEBLA, Salvador; b. 28 Dec. 1960, Ceuta, Spain. Musician (drums); Prod; Composer. *Education:* Conservatory Isaac Albeniz, Gerona; Berklee College of Music, Boston; Drummers Collective, New York; Berkley School of Music, Gerona. *Career:* Olympic Games, Barcelona, 1992; TV 1, Big Band; TV3, Big Band; Tours with: Orquesta Mondragon; La Trinca; Max Suwer Tigo; Salvador Niebla Natural Energy; Amargos-Benavent Group; Atila; Orquesta Mirasol. *Compositions:* J Manuel Serrat; Dyango; Moncho; La Barberia; Carlos Benavent; Sabandenos; J Albert Amargos; J Has Ikitflus; Alameda; Orquesta Mirasol. *Publications:* Guide for Pop and Rock Drums, 1998; The Virtual Drummer, 1999. *Honours:* Hon. Mem., Cuban Drummers Society, Percuba, 1997. *Membership:* SGAE; AIE; APE; AEMA; AMSC; Drummers Collective. *Current Management:* Odisea Productions. *Address:* c/ Rosselló, 217 2 1a, Barcelona, 08008, Spain.

NIELSEN, Ib Lund; b. 9 Oct. 1941, Vamdrup, Jylland, Denmark. Musician. m. Inge Holten Nielsen, 19 Dec. 1964, 2 s. *Education:* Bass Lessons with John

Nielsen; Dr-Radio Symphonic Orchestra, 1967–70. *Career:* Bass Player in Orchestra with Niels Husum Severel Radio AP; With Quartet, Quintet, Sextet, with the Nielshusum Septet; Bass Player in Leonardo Pedersens Jazz Kapel, 11 Piece Swing Band, 1970–. *Compositions:* Hic with Stormy's Quartet, 1960; Bass Relief, 1980. *Recordings:* Lockjaw, Sweets, 1976; Bass Relief, 1980; I Want A Roof, 1994. *Honours:* With Stormy's Quartet, Winner, Jazz Competition, Denmark, 1960. *Membership:* DMF; NDJ. *Address:* Hvidager 42, 2620 Albertslund, Denmark.

NIELSEN, Jens G; b. 1 Aug. 1951, Denmark. Musician (drums); Record Prod; Record Co Exec. *Career:* Member, Gnags; World-wide tours; Co-founder, Genlyd record label (bought by BMG); A&R Director, BMG, Denmark. *Recordings:* 20 Gnags albums; Producer, albums for various artistes. *Honours:* Danish Grammy, Mr Swing King, 1990. *Current Management:* Rock On, Denmark. *Address:* Rådhusstræde 4a, 1466 Copenhagen K, Denmark.

NIELSEN, Peter A. G; b. 17 Dec. 1952, Skjern, Denmark. Vocalist; Composer. m. Katrine Nyholm, May 1923, 1 s., 1 d. *Education:* Danish Literature, Århus University. *Career:* Founder, singer, songwriter, Gnags, 1966–. *Recordings:* Gnags, 20 albums. *Honours:* Grammy Award, Mr Swing King, 1990. *Current Management:* Rock On, Rådhusstræde 4 A, 1466 Copenhagen, Denmark. *Address:* Haraldsgade 23, 8260 Viby J, Denmark.

NIELSEN, Rick; b. 22 Dec. 1946, Rockford, Illinois, USA. Musician (guitar); Vocalist. *Career:* Member, various bands including Fuse; Sick Man of Europe; Founder member, US rock group Cheap Trick, 1969–; Appearances include: Concert, Tokyo, 1978; California Music Festival, Los Angeles, 1979; Reading Festival, 1979; British tour, 1980; Montreux Rock Festival, 1988; US tour with Robert Plant, 1988; US tour with Kiss, 1988; US tour with Heart, 1990; Solo performance, Concerto For Electric Guitar and Orchestra, Michael Kamen, with Rockford Symphony Orchestra, 1993. *Recordings:* Albums: Cheap Trick, 1977; Heaven Tonight, 1978; Cheap Trick At Budokan, 1979; Dream Police, 1979; Found All The Parts, 1980; All Shook Up, 1980; One On One, 1982; Next Position Please, 1983; The Doctor, 1986; Lap of Luxury, 1988; Busted, 1990; The Greatest Hits, 1991; Silver, 2001; Singles include: I Want You To Want Me, 1979; Ain't That A Shame, 1979; Dream Police, 1979; Voices, 1980; Everything Works If You Let It, 1980; If You Want My Love, 1982; Tonight It's You, 1985; Mighty Wings, used in film soundtrack Top Gun, 1986; Ghost Town, 1988; I Can't Stop Falling Into Love, 1990; Recordings with artistes including: Alice Cooper, Hall and Oates, John Lennon. *Current Management:* Silent Partner Management, Carnegie Hall, 154 W 57th St, Suite 828, New York, NY 10019, USA.

NIEMELÄINEN, Ilkka; b. 9 March 1956, Finland. Musician (guitar); Composer. *Education:* Guitar, musical theory, Helsinki Conservatory. *Career:* Writer, performer, electronic music with Otto Romanowski, Esa Kotilainen, 1970s; Founder, composer, musical director, Wasama Quartet, 1976–85; Concerts included: Ylioppilastalo, Tampere, Finland; Detroit Kool Jazz Festival; Founder, composer, musical director Instinct, 1985–; Represented Finland at EBU Festival, Kristianstad; Numerous concerts in Finland; Founder, trio IN2á3, with Pentti Lahti, Jukka Wasama, 1990. *Recordings:* Arranger, classical album for saxophonist Pentti Lahti. *Address:* Haukilahdenrata 21 D, 02170 Espoo, Finland.

NIEWOOD, Gerry (Gerard Joseph); b. 6 April 1943, Rochester, New York, USA. Musician (woodwind). m. Gurly Hulbert, 2 March 1972, 1 s., 1 d. *Education:* BM, Eastman School of Music, 1970. *Career:* Woodwind player with Chuck Mangione Quartet, 1968–76; Judy Collins, 1977–80; Simon and Garfunkel, 1982–83; Alto saxophonist, Radio City Music Hall, New York, 1979–; Saxophonist with Gerry Mulligan, 1980–; Liza Minnelli, 1984–; Freelance musician, 1986–; Concerts include: Simon and Garfunkel in Central Park, 1982; The Ultimate Event, with Frank Sinatra, Liza Minnelli, Sammy Davis Jr, 1989. *Compositions:* Floating, 1972; Joy, 1976. *Recordings:* Slow Hot Wind, 1975; Gerry Niewood and Timepiece, 1977; Share My Dream, 1986; Gerry Niewood/Alone, 1988; Recorded with artistes including: Liza Minelli, Liza Minelli at Carnegie Hall, 1981; Simon and Garfunkle, Concert in Central Park, 1982; Peggy Lee, Moments Like This, 1992; Randy Sandke, Awakening, 1998; Mark Murphy, Mark Murphy Sings Nat King Cole, 1999. *Honours:* Talent Deserving Wider Recognition, Downbeat Magazine, 1975, 1976. *Current Management:* Con Sona Music Inc. *Address:* 228 Bay Ave, Glen Ridge, NJ 07028, USA.

NIGAM, Sonu; b. Faridabad, Haryana, India. Vocalist; Actor. *Career:* Successful as both film playback singer and pop star; Spent childhood in Delhi, often singing at functions with father; Went to Mumbai to try and break into films, aged 18; Began by taking acting roles whilst attempting to become a playback singer; First found fame with song Achha Sila Diya Tune Mere Pyaar Ka from the film Bewafa Sanam; Other film offers followed along with the chance to record pop albums; Host of TV music show TVS Sa Re Ga Ma. *Recordings:* Albums: Sapnon Ki Baat, Deewana, Kismat, Yaad, 2001; features on soundtracks: Jeet, Papa Kehte Hain, 1996; Border, Tamanna, 1997; China-Gate, Dil Se…, Dulhe Raja, Jab Pyaar Kisise Hota Hai, Jeans, Keemat, 1998; Dillagi, Hum Saath-Saath Hain, Jaanwar, Mast, Shool, Taal, Vaastav, 1999; Chori Chori Chupke Chupke, Dhadkan, Fiza, Hadh Kar Di

Aapne, Har Dil Jo Pyar Karega, Jungle, Kahin Pyar Na Ho Jaaye, Kurukshetra, Kya Kehna, Mela, Phir Bhi Dil Hai Hindustani, Pukar, Refugee, Tera Jadoo Chal Gayaa, 2000; Dil Chahta Hai, One 2 Ka 4, Pyaar Ishq Aur Mohabbat, Pyaar Tune Kya Kiya.., Yaadein, 2001.

NIGHTINGALE, Annie; b. 1 April, London, England. DJ. Divorced, 1 s. *Career:* Journalist, several newspapers including London Daily Express and Cosmopolitan; TV Presenter, BBC's Old Grey Whistle Test, 1978–82; Worked as Radio 1 DJ, 1970s–present; Worked with nearly every major act and promoted acts such as The Police, U2, Duran Duran, Sex Pistols, Oasis, Portishead, Tricky and The Orb; Presenter, Sunday Night Request Show, 1982–94; Work for BBC World Service, Radio 4, Radio 5, British Forces Broadcasting; Presenter, Live Aid, Philadelphia, 1985; Presenter, Chill Out Zone, 1993–; Produced and presented numerous music documentaries world-wide. *Publications:* Chase the Fad, autobiography, 1981; Wicked Speed, 1999. *Honours:* First female DJ, BBC. *Membership:* Ambassador, The Prince's Trust.

NILES, Richard; b. 28 May 1951, Hollywood, California, USA. Composer; Prod; Arranger; Journalist; Broadcaster; Recording Artiste. *Education:* B Mus, Berklee College of Music, Boston. *Career:* Arranger for: Pet Shop Boys; Kate Dimbleby: Heather Small; Westlife; Samantha Mumba; Joe Cocker; Paul McCartney; Cher; Take That; Boyzone; Tears For Fears; Kiri Te Kanawa; Producer for: Pet Shop Boys; Hue and Cry; Dusty Springfield; Pat Metheny; The Troggs; Musical Director for TV series: David Essex; Leo Sayer; Michael Ball; Ruby Wax; Composer of numerous TV commercials; Broadcaster: Writer and presenter of New Jazz Standards, BBC Radio 2; Recording Artiste: Santa Rita, Black Box Records. *Compositions:* Recorded by: Ray Charles; Tina Turner; Hue and Cry; Bobby Womack; Deniece Williams; Spike Milligan. *Contributions to:* Making Music Magazine, London. *Honours:* Golden Rose of Montreux, Score for The Strike (Comic Strip). *Membership:* Musicians' Union; PRS; BMI; MPG. *Address:* Niles Productions, 34 Beaumont Rd, London W4 5AP, England.

NIMMERSJÖ, Conny; b. 20 March 1967, Angelholm, Sweden. Musician (guitar). 1 d. *Career:* Founder member, Bob Hund, 1991–; Performed more than 300 concerts around Scandinavia; Played at festivals including Roskilde, Lollipop, Ruisrock, Quartfestivalen and Hultsfred. *Compositions:* I Stället för Musik: Förvirring, 1996; Düsseldorf, 1996. *Recordings:* with Bob Hund: Bob Hund, 1993, 1994; Edvin Medvind, 1994; I Stället för Musik: Förvirring, 1996; Omslag: Martin Kann, 1996. *Honours:* Grammy Awards: Best Live Act, 1994, Best Lyrics, 1996. *Membership:* STIM; SAMI. *Address:* c/o Bob Hund Förlag, Råsundavägen 150, 169 36 Solna, Sweden.

NINO, Harold Michael; b. 29 Nov. 1950, New York, NY, USA. Musician (Guitar); Vocalist (Blues). m. Julie Hebner, 1 s. *Education:* Major in Music, Manhattan Community College; Studied at New School for Social Research; Private lessons with Robert Yelin and Ted Meckler. *Career:* Studio Musician, New York, 1977–82; Travelling road musician, 1978–; Appeared as regular on The Music Art Show, Huntsville, Alabama, 1978–79; Recorded 30-second commercial for Villa Esperanza; Appeared as extra in the film They Want To Know Too!. *Compositions:* You're Never Going to Understand, recorded by Oysters Rockefeller, 1996. *Recordings:* Past and Present, and Oysters Rockefeller, as member of blues band Oysters Rockefeller. *Honours:* Addy Award, for Villa Esperanza commercial, 1979. *Membership:* American Federation of Musicians, local branches; Blues Music Asscn; BMI. *Current Management:* O S Artists. *Address:* PO Box 6485, Springfield, IL 62708, USA.

NISBETT, Steve 'Grizzly'; Musician (drums). *Career:* Mem., Steel Pulse; Signed to Island Records, Elektra Records, MCA Records, Tuff Gong International; Television appearances include: Arsenio Hall, The Tonight Show with Jay Leno, Late Night with Conan O'Brien, The Keenan Ivory Wayans Show; Performed at the inauguration of President Bill Clinton, Washington, DC, 1993; Extensive world-wide tours; Band mems vary, currently nine-piece band; Performances with: Bob Dylan, Herbie Hancock, INXS, Bob Marley & the Wailers, Robert Palmer, Santana, Sting, The Stranglers, Peter Tosh, Stevie Wonder. *Recordings:* Albums: Handsworth Revolution, 1978; Tribute To The Martyrs, 1979; Caught You (aka Reggae Fever), 1980; True Democracy, 1982; Earth Crisis, 1984; Reggae Refreshers, 1985; Babylon The Bandit, 1985; State of Emergency, 1988; Victims, 1991; Rastafari Centennial, 1992; Smash Hits, 1993; Vex, 1994; Rastanthology, 1996; Rage & Fury, 1997; Sound System: The Island Anthology, 1996; Living Legacy, 1999. *Honours:* Grammy Award, for Babylon The Bandit. *Address:* Steel Pulse, 42 Upper Dean St, Digbeth, Birmingham, West Midlands B5 4SG, England. *E-mail:* info@steel-pulse.com. *Website:* www.steel-pulse.com.

NJIKENYA, Landry; b. 3 June 1970, Douala, Cameroon. Musician (percussion). 1 child. *Education:* Musical studies with Billy Mussango. *Compositions:* 45 published songs. *Membership:* Socimada. *Address:* c/o Billy Mussango, PO Box 8363 Yaounde, Cameroon.

NOBES, Roger Michael; b. 26 Dec. 1939, Abbots Langley, Hertfordshire, England. Musician (vibraphone, piano, drums); Arranger. m. Maureen Payne, 1 June 1987, 1 d. *Education:* Central School of Music. *Career:* Numerous

national and international tours with The Alex Welsh Band, The Dave Shepherd Quintet; Numerous tours with American artistes; Concert performers include: Festival Hall; Barbican Centre; Many radio and television appearances. *Recordings:* Recorded extensively with many bands and orchestras including The Roger Nobes Quartet. *Membership:* Musicians' Union. *Current Management:* Roma Enterprises. *Address:* 41 Manton Rd, Hitchin, Hertfordshire SG4 9NP, England.

NOBLE, Douglas; b. 9 July 1964, Edinburgh, Scotland. Guitar Instructor; Freelance Music Journalist. *Education:* BSc Psychology, Edinburgh University, 1985; ALCM, Classical guitar, London College of Music, 1986; LLCM (TD), Classical guitar, London College of Music, 1987. *Career:* Freelance music journalist, regular contributor to the Guitar Magazine (UK); Occasional contributor to Guitar Player (USA); Bass Player (USA); Contributions to several books on the electric guitar; Sleeve notes for several albums; Music Director for Univibes, international Jimi Hendrix magazine; Examiner, Rock School, Trinity College of Music. *Publications:* Instant Hendrix, book, 1988; Instant Peter Green, book, 1990. *Address:* 2F4 99 St Leonard's St, Edinburgh EH8 9QY, Scotland.

NOBLE, Stephen Francis Paterson; b. 26 March 1960, Wallingford, Oxfordshire, England. Musician (drums, percussion, musical saw, bugle). *Career:* Contemporary Music Network Tour, with Alex Maguire, 1994; Festivals: Glasgow Jazz, 1989–94; New Music America, New York, 1989; Sitges International Dance, 1991; Taklos (Swizz), 1990–92; London Jazz, 1993–94; Television and radio: Featured in On The Edge (series about improvisation), CH4; Live recording from Adrian Boult Hall, Birmingham, broadcast on Radio 3 (Impressions and Midnight Oil), with pianist Alex Maguire; Live broadcasts throughout Europe with various groups. *Compositions:* Commissioned by South Bank Centre, London to compose music for collaboration with Spanish Dance Company Mal Pelo, 1993. *Recordings:* Duo with Alex Maguire: Live At Oscar's; (voted one of top jazz albums of 1980s); Once, recordings from Derek Bailey's Company Week, featuring Bailey and Lee Konitz, 1987; The Shakedown Club. *Membership:* Musicians' Union; PRS. *Current Management:* Ping Pong Productions. *Address:* 13 Calthorpe St, London WC1X 0JP, England.

NOGALSKI, Rick; b. 15 Aug. 1964, Bolton, Lancashire, England. Musician (Guitar). *Education:* BSc, Electrical and Electronic Engineering, North Staffordshire Polytechnic; Guitar Institute, London, 1988–89. *Career:* Member, London Electric Guitar Orchestra, 1996–. *Recordings:* Kneel Down Like a Saint Gorilla and Stop; 17 Lumps of Cheese, Go!. *Address:* 37 Fulbourne Rd, Walthamstow, London E17 4AX, England.

NOLAN, J. William (Bill); b. 13 Nov. 1940, Derby, Connecticut, USA. Civil Rights Activist; Musicologist. m. Joan M Owens, 1962, 1 s. *Career:* Volunteer Radio Broadcaster for WPKN-FM, 1969–; Founder and Executive Director of The Rhythm and Blues Rock 'N Roll Society Inc, 1974; Founder of American Blues Movement, 1975; Volunteer helping Black African-American artists and sustaining music heritage. *Address:* c/o Rhythm and Blues Rock 'N Roll Society Inc, PO Box 1949, New Haven, CT 06510, USA.

NOLLI, Giorgio; b. 5 Feb. 1965, Merano, Italy. Musician, (percussion, congas, timbales). *Education:* Participated in various workshops in the UK. *Career:* Italian tour, pop band China Boy Hi, 1992; European tour, garage band Nicolette, 1993; Television appearance, James Whale Show, UK, 1993; Japanese tour, jungle group UK Tribe, 1995; Jonathan Ross's Big Big Talent Show, ITV, 1996; The Carmen Miranda Story, Jermyn Street Theatre, 1997. *Recordings:* Singles: I Want To Be Everything, China Boy Hi, 1992; There Isn't Any Way, China Boy Hi, 1993; Junglites, UK Tribe, 1995; Jungle Soul, UK Tribe, 1995. *Album:* Jungle *Membership:* Musicians' Union. *Address:* 29 Buckingham Rd, Harlesden, London NW10 4RP, England.

NOODLES, (Kevin Wasserman); b. 4 Feb. 1963, Los Angeles, California, USA. Musician (guitar). m. Jackie Wasserman, 1998, 1 d. *Career:* Resides in Tustin, Orange County, California; Member: Clowns of Death; Dirty Dot; Joined The Offspring, 1985; Privately pressed single took over 2 years to sell 1000 copies, 1987; Signed to independent labels, Nemesis and Epitaph, for 1988–95 releases; Major US breakthrough following heavy MTV/radio play rotation, 1994; Accused of betraying punk roots when signing to Columbia after dispute with former label, 1996; Consolidated world-wide success by scoring UK No. 1 hit single, 1999; Live shows include: Woodstock festival, 1999; KROQ Weenie Roast, 2000; European tour, 2001; Band gave lucky fan $1m. in Offspring prize draw, 2000; Member of side-project group Circus Penis. *Recordings:* Albums: The Offspring, 1989; Ignition, 1992; Smash!, 1994; Ixnay On The Hombre, 1997; Americana, 1998; Conspiracy of One, 2000; Singles: I'll Be Waiting, 1987; Baghdad EP, 1988; Come Out and Play (Keep 'Em Separated), Self-Esteem, 1994; Gotta Get Away, 1995; All I Want, Gone Away, 1997; Pretty Fly (For A White Guy), 1998; Why Don't You Get A Job?, The Kids Aren't Alright, She's Got Issues, 1999; Original Prankster, 2000; Want You Bad, Million Miles Away, 2001. *Honours:* Over 9m. copies of Smash album sold world-wide, best selling independent record of all time. *Current Management:* Jim Guerinot, Rebel Waltz Management, 31652 Second Ave, Laguna Beach, CA 92651, USA. *Website:* www.offspring.com.

NOONE, Peter; b. 5 Nov. 1947, Davyhulme, Manchester, England. Vocalist. m. Mireille Strasser. *Education:* Manchester School of Music and Drama. *Career:* Lead vocalist, Herman's Hermits, 1963–71; Solo artiste, 1971–; US tour, 1965; North American tour with The Who, 1967; Madison Square Garden, 1973; Member, The Tremblers, 1980; Actor, film: Mrs Brown You've Got A Lovely Daughter, 1968; Performed, play: The Canterville Ghost, US TV, 1966; Pinocchio, 1968; Business partnership with Graham Gouldman, studio production work, New York boutique, Zoo, 1968; Performed in Pirates of Penzance, Broadway and London, 1982–83; Video jockey, US Cable TV, 1990s. *Recordings:* Introducing Herman's Hermits, 1965; Herman's Hermits on Tour, 1965; The Best of Herman's Hermits, 1965; Hold On!, 1966; Both Sides of Herman's Hermits, 1966; Vol. III, 1968; I'm Into Something Good (No. 1, UK), 1964; Silhouettes, 1965; Wonderful World, 1965; Mrs Brown You've Got A Lovely Daughter (No. 1, USA), 1965; I'm Henry VIII, I Am (No. 1, USA), 1965; Just a Little Better, 1965; A Must To Avoid, 1965; Dandy, 1966; No Milk Today, 1966; There's A Kind Of Hush (All Over The World), 1967; Sleepy Joe, 1968; Sunshine Girl, 1968; Something's Happening, 1969; Years May Come Years May Go, 1970; Bet Yer Life I Do, 1970; Lady Barbara, 1970; Solo: Oh You Pretty Thing, 1971; One of the Glory Boys, 1982; Pirates of Penzance, 1986; I'm into Something Good, 1989. *Current Management:* DeLauro Management, Suite 1980, 875 Avenue of the Americas, New York, NY 10001, USA.

NORBY, Caecilie; b. 9 Sept. 1964, Frederiksberg, Denmark. Vocalist. *Education:* SKT Annae Gymnasium Music School, 1973–80; Music Theatre School, 1 year; Several Music Courses; Private Lessons in Singing and Piano. *Career:* Different Performing Groups, 1980–81; Lead Singer in the Funk Rock Band, Street Beat, 1981–84; Lead Singer in the recording band, Frontline, 1987; Lead Singer in One Two, together with colleague Nina Forsberg, 1993. *Compositions:* Several. *Recordings:* Frontline, 1985; Frontlife, 1986; One Two, 1986; My Corner of the Sky, 1996; Hvide Loegne, 1989; Getting Better, 1993; Caecilie Norby, 1995; Featured on Blue Box Vol. 2 Finest Jazz Vocal, 1998. *Honours:* Ben Webster Prize, 1987; Simon Spies Soloist Prize, 1995. *Membership:* Danish Artistes' Society; DJBFA. *Current Management:* PDH Management, Copenhagen, Denmark. *Address:* Absalonsgade 7A 1Tv, 1658 Copenhagen V, Denmark.

NORCROSS, Rick (Richard Charles); b. 23 March 1945, Waltham, Massachusetts, USA. Vocalist; Songwriter; Entertainer; Musician (guitar). *Education:* BA, Mass Communications, University of South Florida, Tampa, Florida, USA. *Career:* Solo artiste, 1963–80; 3 tours of England, 1965–75; Lead singer, Rick Norcross and The Nashfull Ramblers Western Swing Band, 1980–; Tours: Central Florida; New England Fair; Festival Circuit; Producer, 35 festivals and special events, 1974–. *Recordings:* Albums: Nashfull, 1980; Fairly Live, 1983; Tour du Jour, 1989; You Can't Get There From Here, 1991; Can't Catch A Rambler, 1994; The Legend of Scratch Leroux, 1995. *Publications:* Entertainment Editor, The Tampa Times, 1969–74. *Honours:* Vice-President, Yankee Festivals and Events Asscn. *Membership:* AFofM. *Current Management:* Airflyte Productions. *Address:* 216 Battery St, Burlington, VT 05401, USA.

NORMAN, Chris(topher); b. 25 Oct. 1950, Redcar, Yorkshire, England. Vocalist; Songwriter; Musician (guitar); Record Prod. m. Linda Heddle, 16 March 1970, 4 s., 2 d. *Career:* Lead singer, Kindness, Backing group to Peter Noone (ex Herman's Hermits), 1960s; Group later became Smokie, 1970s; Solo artiste, 1980s–; Produced number of records. *Recordings:* Hit singles: If You Think You Know How To Love Me, 1975; Don't Play Your Rock'N'Roll To Me, 1975; Something's Been Making Me Blue, 1976; I'll Meet You At Midnight, 1976; Living Next Door To Alice, 1976; Lay Back In The Arms Of Someone, 1977; It's Your Life, 1977; Needles And Pins, 1977; Oh Carol, 1978; Stumblin' In (with Suzi Quatro), 1978; Midnight Lady; This Time (We'll Get It Right); Recorded 16 albums, most recently: Full Circle, 1999; Album, 2001. *Honours:* 3 Bravo Awards, 1976–86; Golden Europa, 1986; CMT Europe, 1994. *Membership:* PRS; MCPS; BAC&S. *Current Management:* Bill Tuckey Music. *Address:* 20 Tor Bryan, Ingatestone, Essex, England.

NORMAN, David; b. 19 May 1962, London, England. Tour/Production Man; Sound Engineer. m. Suzanne Feit, 18 Oct. 1992. *Career:* Television and live credits include: The Arsenio Hall Show; Late Night with David Letterman Show; The Jon Stewart Show; MTV Beach House; Top of the Pops; Showtime at the Apollo; Kenny G 'Breathless' Tour; MTV Japan; The Far East Network; Woodstock, 1994; WOMAD Tour, 1994; Lowlands Festival. *Recordings:* Engineer on albums: Through The Fire, Peabo Bryson; Zingalamundi, Arrested Development; E'ssential, Bare E'ssentials. *Address:* 639 Gardenwalk Blvd, Suite 1632, College Park, GA 30349, USA.

NORMAN, Michael; b. 16 June 1970, Canada. Musician (Keyboards, Saxophones, Guitar, Vocals); Prod; Songwriter. *Education:* Jazz Diploma, Malaspina College, Canada. *Career:* Canadian Country Music Award shows with Lisa Brokop, 1993; Patricia Conroy, 1995, 1999; Patricia Conroy: Wild As The Wind, 1999. *Compositions:* Too Late; Bring It On; Put A Little Distance. *Recordings:* Girls Will Be Girls; Living Beyond Our Dreams; The Message, Alpha Yaya Diallo, 1999. *Honours:* BCCMA Keyboard Player of the Year,

1999. *Membership:* AFM; CCMA. *Address:* #102A 301 Maude Rd, Port Moody, BC Canada.

NORREEN, Claus; b. 5 June 1970, Charlottenlund, Denmark. Musician (keyboards, drum machines). *Career:* Worked with Soeren Rasted on film, Fraekke Frida; Formed Joyspeed; Changed name to Aqua; Obtained major record deal in Denmark; Numerous TV and live appearances. *Recordings:* Singles: Itsy Blitzy, as Joyspeed; Roses Are Red; Barbie Girl (No. 1, UK), 1997; Doctor Jones (No. 1, UK), 1998; Turn Back Time (theme from film Sliding Doors) (No. 1, UK), 1998; My Oh My, 1998; Good Morning Sunshine, 1998; Cartoon Heroes, 2000; Around The World, 2000; Lollipop; Albums: Aquarium, 1997; Bubble Mix, 1998; We Belong To The Sea, 2001.

NORREMOLLE, Jens; b. 12 Aug. 1956, Vejle, Denmark. Composer; Prod; Musician (keyboards). 1 s. *Education:* Teacher. *Career:* Various bands until 1987–; Composer, singer, keyboard player for Singing Zoo; Record producer for Anne Dorte Michelsen and Venter På Far, 1987–95. *Recordings:* with Anne Dorte Michelsen: Elskerindens Have; Den Ordlose Time; Min Karriere Som Kvinde (producer, arranger, musician); Also albums with Singing Zoo and Venter På Far. *Honours:* Best Band, 1988; Musikcafé Prize with Singing Zoo. *Membership:* DMF; DJBFA. *Current Management:* Warner Chappell, Denmark. *Address:* Blågårdsgade 17 IV left, 2200 Copenhagen N, Denmark.

NORRIS, Richard; b. 23 June 1965, London, England. Musician (keyboards, saxophone, drums); Prod; Remixer. *Education:* Liverpool University. *Career:* Member musical duo, The Grid; Met partner Dave Ball, recording Jack The Tab compilation, 1988; Recorded 4 albums, 11 singles; Tours, UK, 1991–; Japan, Thailand, Singapore, New Zealand, Australia, 1995; Producer, remixer, artistes including: Pet Shop Boys, Boy George, Marc Almond, Brian Eno, Billie Ray Martin, Black Grape, Happy Mondays, 1990–95; Director of Areeba Records; A&R Manager for Creation Records. *Recordings:* Albums: Electric Head, 1990; 456, 1992; Evolver, 1994; Music For Dancing, 1995; Singles: Floatation, 1990; A Beat Called Love, 1990; Figure Of 8, 1992; Heartbeat, 1992; Crystal Clear, 1993; Texas Cowboys, 1993; Swamp Thing, 1994; Rollercoaster, 1994; Diablo, 1995; Recorded with Joe Strummer for Grosse Point Blank film soundtrack, 1997; Bigg Buddha, Be Here Now, 12, 1994. *Honours:* Silver disc, Swamp Thing, 1994; Platinum disc (Australia), Swamp Thing, 1994; Silver disc, Evolver, LP, 1995. *Membership:* PRS; PPL; Musicians' Union. *Address:* Unit 204, Canalot Studios, 222 Kensal Rd, London W10, England.

NORRIS, Richard T; b. 9 Feb. 1966, Epping, Essex, England. Music Programmer; Writer; Recording Engineer. *Career:* Programmer, engineer for Bryan Ferry, including albums Taxi, Mamouna, 1990–95; Co-writer with Little Annie, 1989–94; Currently co-writing with Guy Pratt (Pink Floyd) under joint name Deep Cover. *Recordings:* Albums: Taxi, Bryan Ferry, 1993; Deboravation, Deborah Harry, 1993; Mix-ism, Mad Capsule Markets, 1994; Mamouna, Bryan Ferry, 1994; Grand Central, Deep Cover, from Hackers film soundtrack, 1995; Goodbye, Dubstar, 1997; Neapolis, Simple Minds, 1998; Invincible, Five, 2000; Interview With The Angel, Ghostland, 2001. *Current Management:* This Much Talent, 117 Church Rd, Barens, London SW13 9HL, England.

NORVELL, Loring L; b. 20 Jan. 1948, Norfolk, Virginia, USA. Composer; Arranger; Conductor. *Education:* Old Dominion University, 1974–78; MA, Radford University, 1979–80; DMA, Arizona State University, 1984–88. *Career:* Conductor, US Coast Guard Bands, Cape May, NJ and Governors Island, 1970–73; Conductor, Norfolk Savoyards, 1981–84; Conductor, Phoenix Pro-Musica Orchestra, 1985–93; Singer, Yesterdays Supper Club, 1985–99; Freelance Composer, Arranger, 1985–. *Compositions:* Festival Entrada; Oedipus Rex Ballet; Symphony For The Victims of War; 3 Woodwind Sonatas. *Honours:* Frequent Guest Conductor, Las Vegas Philharmonic, Flagstaff Symphony. *Membership:* American Music Center; American Composers' Forum. *Current Management:* Woody Norvell Music, 3728 E Joan De Arc, Phoenix, AZ 85032, USA.

NOTLEY, Wendy; b. 28 Oct. 1957, Australia. Vocalist; Songwriter; Musician (guitar); Teacher. *Education:* Diploma in Early Childhood Education. *Career:* Early childhood Teacher and Director, Yinbilliko School, Sydney, Australia; Teaching, Murawina Aboriginal multi-purpose Education Centre in Redfern, Sydney, for 4 years; Singer, songwriter, guitarist, co-producer, Growin' Up Strong, by Aunty Wendy's Mob. *Compositions:* Growin' Up Strong; Indigenous; We're Koori Kids; The Wheels On The Holden; Red, Black and Yellow; Wiradjuri and Bundjalung; Until The Fire Is Out; Dreamtime; There Was A Man; Stand Up; Noongar In The Bush; Melaleuca; Round The Campfire Tonight; We're Bininj kids. *Recordings:* Growin' Up Strong, Aunty Wendy's Mob. *Publications:* Author, 4 children's books, Teacher's Resource Book and Education Kit. *Membership:* Society of Authors. *Address:* 5/355 Glebe Point Rd, Glebe, Sydney, NSW 2037, Australia.

NOVA, Aldo; b. Canada. Rock Musician (guitar); Vocalist. *Career:* Solo recording artiste, 1980–. *Recordings:* Albums: Aldo Nova, 1982; Subject, 1984; Twitch, 1985; Blood On The Bricks, 1991; Nova's Dream, 1997; Also featured musician on albums: Bon Jovi, Bon Jovi, 1984; Blaze of Glory, Jon Bon Jovi,

1991; Falling into You, Céline Dion, 1996; Power Chords Vol. 3, 1997; Jon Bon Jovi, Destination Anywhere, 1998; La Ley, Uno, 2000; Garou, Seul, 2001.

NOVOSELIC, Kris; b. 16 May 1965, Croatia. Musician (bass). *Career:* Member, Nirvana, 1987–94; World-wide tours; Concerts include: Reading Festival, 1991, 1992; Transmusicales Festival, Rennes, France, 1991; Benefit concert, Washington State Music Coalition, 1992; Benefit concert, Tresnjevka Women's Group, Cow Palace, San Francisco, 1993; Founder, Sweet 75, 1995. *Recordings:* Albums: Bleach, 1989; Nevermind (No. 1, USA), 1991; Incesticide, 1993; In Utero (No. 1, UK and USA), 1993; Unplugged In New York, 1994; Singles, 1996; In Utero, 1998; Box, 1998; Singles include: Smells Like Teen Spirit, 1991; Come As You Are, 1992; Lithium, 1992; In Bloom, 1992; Oh, The Guilt, 1993; Heart-Shaped Box, 1993; All Apologies, 1993; Track, I Hate Myself and Wanna Die, featured on Beavis and Butthead Experience, 1993; Appears on: Live From The Battle In Seattle, The No WTO Combo, 2000. *Publications:* Come As You Are, Nirvana biography by Michael Azerrad. *Honours:* Platinum disc, Nevermind; Best Alternative Music Video, Best New Artist Video, Smells Like Teen Spirit, MTV Music Video Awards, 1992; Best International Newcomer, BRIT Awards, 1993.

NOWELS, Rick; Songwriter; Record Prod; Musician. *Education:* Music Major, University of California at Berkeley. *Career:* Prod. and songwriter; Worked with: Kelli Ali, Belinda Carlisle, Cher, The Corrs, Des'ree, Dido, Céline Dion, Geri Halliwell, Enrique Iglesias, Jewel, Ronan Keating, Madonna, Melanie C., New Radicals, Stevie Nicks, *NSYNC, Eros Ramazotti, Leeanne Rimes, Santana, Sonique, Texas. *Compositions:* Madonna, The Power of Good-bye, To Have and Not to Hold, Little Star; Céline Dion, Falling Into You; Robert Miles, One and One; Des'ree, Time, Get a Life; Anita Baker, Body and Soul; Belinda Carlisle, Heaven is a Place on Earth, Circle in the Sand, Leave a Light On, Live Your Life Be Free, In Too Deep, We Want the Same Thing, La Lune, Runaway Horses, Vision of You, Do You Feel Like I Feel?; Stevie Nicks, I Can't Wait, Rooms on Fire, Maybe Love Will Change Your Mind; Roachford, Naked Without You; The Corrs, Intimacy; Maria Nayler, Naked and Sacred; New Radicals, You Get What You Give; k. d. lang, Anywhere But Here; Mel C., Northern Star, I Turn To You (No. 1, UK), 2000; Enrique Iglesias, I Have Always Loved You; Ronan Keating, Life Is A Rollercoaster (No. 1, UK), 2000; Geri Halliwell, Scream If You Wanna Go Faster, 2001. *Honours:* ASCAP Awards; Grammy Award, Album of the Year, Falling Into You by Céline Dion, 1997. *Membership:* ASCAP. *Current Management:* Stephen Budd Management Ltd, 109b Regents Park Rd, Primrose Hill, London NW1 8UR, England. *Website:* www.record-producers.com.

NOYCE, Jonathan; b. 15 July 1971, Sutton Coldfield, England. Musician (bass guitar); Composer. m. Sara Joanna King, 15 July 1995. *Education:* North Herts College, Royal Academy of Music. *Career:* with Ian Anderson (Jethro Tull): Tours, USA, Canada, Europe; VH-1 radio broadcast, Secret Life; Television: Pebble Mill; What's Up Doc?; Videos; with C J Lewis: The White Room; with David Palmer: Concerts in Venezuela; Belgium; Estonia; Romania; Germany; Various concerts and recordings. *Recordings:* with Take That: Relight My Fire, 1993; with Al Green: Keep On Pushing Love, 1994; with Sister Sledge: Thinking of You (remix), 1993; with Diana Ross: Love Hangover (remix), 1994; with Joey Negro: Universe of Love, 1993; with David Palmer: Sgt Pepper; with Jethro Tull: J-Tull.Com, 1999. *Honours:* LRAM, Professional Certificate of Royal Academy of Music. *Membership:* Musicians' Union. *Address:* 1 Marcus Terrace, Wandsworth, London SW18 2JW, England.

NOYES, Cameron George Albert; b. 27 Feb. 1965, Edmonton, Alberta, Canada. m. Velveeta Krisp, 1 d. *Career:* Worked in musical or industry capacities with 800 artists including: Faith No More; King Sunny Ade; The Wailers; John Cale; Donovan; SNFU; Dead Kennedys. *Recordings:* Cable; Don't Care, Didn't Care; Yuppie Flux. *Honours:* IMBH, Award of Excellence, 1992. *Membership:* ARIA; PMIA; OTO. *Current Management:* Phantom Product Canada. *Address:* #104–1540 E Fourth Ave, Vancouver, BC, Canada.

NOZEDAR, Adele; b. 7 Aug. 1966, Yorkshire, England. Record Co Exec; Musician (piano, harp). m. Adam Fuest, 1 Aug. 1993. *Education:* Grade B Musical Theory. *Career:* Managing Director of Rhythm King Records, independent UK label founded in 1986 with Martin Heath; Co-founder of Renegade Software. *Honours:* Leslie Perrin Award for Public Relations in 1992. *Membership:* Musicians' Union; PRS. *Address:* c/o Rhythm King Records, 121 Salisbury Rd, London NW6 6RG, England.

N-TRANCE, (Dale Longworth); b. 19 June 1966, Middleton, Manchester, England. Musician (keyboards). *Education:* Degree, Sound Recording. *Career:* Sound engineer, leading PA company, most aspects of live sound (rock and roll, musicals, classical, television); Signed to PWL while working on the Hitman and Her. *Recordings:* Album: Happy Hour, 1999; Singles: Back To The Bass (unreleased); Set You Free; Turn Up The Power; Set You Free (re-released No. 2, UK); Tears in the Rain, 1999; Do Ya Think I'm Sexy?, 1999;

Paradise City, 1999; Shake Ya Body, 2000; As producer: 200% Energy, 1995; N Trance, Stayin' Alive, 1995; Now Dance '95, 1995; Dance '96 Supermix, 1996; goodtime disco Dance Hits, 1997; Euromix Vol. 3, 1997; Night at the Roxbury, 1998; House of Boogie, 1998. *Honours:* Best UK Dance Record, 1994; Platinum Disc, 1994; (both for Set You Free). *Membership:* Musicians' Union. *Current Management:* All Around The World. *Address:* All Around The World, 9–13 Penny St, Blackburn BB1 6HJ, England.

NUGENT, Ted; b. 13 Dec. 1949, Detroit, MI, USA. Rock Musician (guitar); Vocalist. *Career:* Founder, guitarist, The Amboy Dukes, 1966–75; Solo artiste, 1975–89; Formed Damn Yankees, 1989–; Appearances include: Reading Festival (UK debut), 1976; California Jam II Festival, Los Angeles, 1978; California Music Festival, with Van Halen, Cheap Trick, Aerosmith, 1979; World Series of Rock, Cleveland, with Aerosmith, Journey, Thin Lizzy, 1979; Whiplash Bash, Detroit, 1988; Volunteer Jam XIV, Nashville, 1991; Television includes: Miami Vice, NBC TV, 1984; Late Night With David Letterman, NBC TV, 1991. *Recordings:* Albums: with The Amboy Dukes: Call of The Wild, 1973; Tooth Fang and Claw, 1974; Solo: Ted Nugent, 1975; Free For All, 1976; Cat Scratch Fever, 1977; Double Live Gonzo, 1978; Weekend Warriors, 1978; State of Shock, 1979; Scream Dream, 1980; Great Gonzos – The Best of Ted Nugent, 1981; Intensities In Ten Cities, 1981; Nugent, 1982; Penetrator, 1984; Little Miss Dangerous, 1986; Anthology, 1986; If You Can't Lick 'Em, Lick 'Em!, 1988; Spirit of The Wild, 1995; Full Bluntal Nugity, 2001; Craveman, 2002; with Damn Yankees: Damn Yankees, 1990. *Honours:* Gold and Platinum discs. *Current Management:* Madhouse Management. *Address:* PO Box 15108, Ann Arbor, MI 48106, USA.

NUMAN, Gary, (Gary Webb); b. 8 March 1958, Hammersmith, London, England. Vocalist; Songwriter. *Career:* Singer, Tubeway Army, 1978–79; Billed as solo artiste, 1979–; Own record label, Numa Records, 1984–87; Extensive tours include: World tour, 1980; Annual British tours; Regular television appearances. *Recordings:* Albums: Replicas (No. 1, UK), 1979; The Pleasure Principle (No. 1, UK), 1979; Telekon (No. 1, UK), 1980; Living Ornaments 1979–80, 1981; Dance, 1981; I Assassin, 1982; New Man Numan—The Best of Gary Numan, 1982; The Plan, 1984; White Noise Live, 1985; Strange Charm, 1986; Exhibition, 1987; Metal Rhythm, 1988; Skin Mechanic, 1989; Outland, 1991; Machine + Soul, 1992; Best of 1979–83, 1993; Dream Corrosion, 1994; Exile, 1997; Dramatis Project, 2000; Pure, 2000; Contributor, Clues, Robert Palmer, 1980; White Noise, 1998; Black Heart, 1998; My Dying Machine, 1998; Exposure: The Best Of Gary Numan 1977–2002, 2002. Hit singles include: Are Friends Electric? (No. 1, UK), 1979; Cars (No. 1, UK), 1979; Complex, 1979; We Are Glass, 1980; I Die You Die, 1980; This Wreckage, 1981; She's Got Claws, 1981; Music For Chameleons, 1982; We Take Mystery (To Bed), 1982; White Boys and Heroes, 1982; Warriors, 1983; This Is Love; I Can't Stop; I Still Remember; Cars (E Reg Mix); with Bill Sharpe (Shakatak): Change Your Mind, 1985; New Thing From London Town, 1986. *Website:* www.numan.co.uk.

NÚÑEZ (MUÑOZ), Carlos; b. Spain. Musician (gaita, recorder, tin whistle); Composer. *Education:* Royal Conservatory, Madrid, studied Baroque Music. *Career:* Began playing the gaita (Galician bagpipes), aged 8; Invited to play as soloist with Lorient Symphony Orchestra, Britanny, aged 13; Studied at the Royal Conservatory of Music in Madrid, Received highest ever marks achieved for Baroque recorder; Brought new life to neglected Galician folk tradition by studying the style of Irish and Scottish pipers and bringing ornamentation into the playing of the pipes; Reached wider audience by collaborating with other Celtic musicians including: Chieftains; Dan Ar Braz. *Recordings:* Albums: A Irmandade Das Estrellas (Brotherhood of Stars), 1996; Os Amores Libres, Mayo Longo, 2000; features on: Treasure Island OST, 1989; The Long Black Veil, The Chieftains, 1995; Santiago, The Chieftains, 1996; Finisterres, Dan Ar Braz, 1997; Zenith, Dan Ar Braz, 1998; Silent Night – A Christmas In Rome, Paddy Moloney, 1998; Caminhos, Dulce Pontes, 1998; Bilbao Oh, Kepa Junkera, 1999. *Honours:* Folkest 2001, Special Award, Rome.

NUNN, Charles David; b. 14 Sept. 1954, Stellenbosch, South Africa. Pastor; Musician (pan flute); Vocalist. m. 8 Jan. 1982, 1 s., 2 d. *Career:* Performer, preacher, gospel music, and the Gospel of Jesus Christ; Star of the Week, Afrikaans Stereo; Several radio chat shows. *Recordings:* 2 albums of pan flute music; 1 album as vocalist. *Membership:* ASAMI. *Current Management:* Studio Nunn Ministries. *Address:* PO Box 4292, Secunda 2302, South Africa.

NYE, Cheryl; b. Montréal, QC, Canada. Vocalist; Songwriter; Model; Musician (keyboards). *Education:* BFA Music, Voice Major, Concordia University. *Career:* Sung anthems at: Toronto Skydome; Montréal Forum; Olympic Stadium; Lansdowne Park; Television: CBC; CFCF; Videotron; Télé-Métropole; RDS; CHRO; Radio-Québec; CFCL-CITO; CHNB-CKNY. *Recordings:* Singles: Never Give Up On A Dream; Heartbeat; Album: Loving You, 1993; With Goodbyes, 2001. *Honours:* B100 Pepsi Entertainer Award (USA). *Membership:* ACTRA; CCMA; SOCAN. *Current Management:* WE Communications. *Website:* www.cherylnye.com.

NYMAN, Michael; b. 23 March 1944, London, England. Composer. *Education:* Studied with Alan Bush at Royal Academy of Music, 1961–65; King's College, London, 1964–67; Studied with Thurston Dart. *Career:* Composer, writer and music critic, 1968–78; Lecturer, 1976–80. *Compositions include:* Soundtracks for Peter Greenaway films, 1976–91, including: The Falls, The Draughtsman's Contract, A Zed and Two Noughts, The Cook, The Thief, His Wife and Her Lover, Drowning By Numbers, Prospero's Books; Soundtracks for films by other dirs include: The Piano, 1992; A La Folie (Six Days, Six Nights), 1994; Carrington, 1994; The Diary of Anne Frank, 1995; The Ogre, 1996; Gattaca, 1997; Ravenous, 1998; Wonderland, 1999; The End of the Affair, 1999; Ballet scores for choreographers Lucinda Childs, Rosemary Butcher, Siobhan Davies, Karine Saporta, Plank and Stephen Petronio; Works for cabaret artiste Ute Lemper and the Balanescu Quartet; Concertos for John Harle, Julian Lloyd Webber, Elizabeth Chojnacka, Christian Lindberg; Other. *Compositions:* The Kiss (video-duet), 1984; The Man Who Mistook His Wife For A Hat (chamber opera), 1986; The Upside-down Violin, 1992; MGV (Musique a Grand Vitesse), 1993; Three Quartets, 1994; AET, 1996; Double Concerto for Saxophone and Cello, 1997; Cycle of Disquietude, 1998; The Commissar Vanishes, 1999. *Recordings include:* The Man Who Mistook His Wife For A Hat, 1987; String Quartet Nos 1–3, 1991; Songbook, 1992; The Essential Michael Nyman Band, 1992; Time Will Pronounce, 1993; Michael Nyman For Yohji Yamamoto, 1993; Noises, Sounds And Sweet Airs, 1994; The Piano Concerto/MGV, 1994; Michael Nyman—Live, 1994; Concertos, 1997; Enemy Zero, 1997; The Suit And The Photograph, 1998; The Commissar Vanishes, 1999. *Publications:* Libretto for Birtwistle's Dramatic Pastoral, Down By the Greenwood Side, 1968–69; Experimental Music: Cage and Beyond, 1974. *Address:* Michael Nyman Ltd, 83 Pulborough Rd, London SW18 5UL, England.

NYS, (Magthea) Sandy; b. 30 July 1959, Mechelen, Belgium. Graphic Designer. *Education:* Graphic Design, Art School; School for Electronic Music: SEM by Joris De Laet, Conservatorium Antwerpen. *Career:* Tours, Europe, with bands including: Klinik, Hybryds, 1983–; World-wide radio broadcast, in independent charts. *Recordings:* Music For Rituals – An Ongoing Musical Spiritual Quest; More than 10 album releases, more than 100 hours music registered at SABAM. *Publications:* More than 100 pages, official and underground press. *Honours:* Soundtrack for Aquaria of Antwerp Zoo. *Membership:* SABAM, Belgian copyright organization. *Current Management:* 3riort Vzw. *Address:* Julian Dillenstr 22, 2018 Antwerp, Belgium.

NYSTROM, Lene Grawford; b. 2 Oct. 1973, Tonsberg, Norway. Vocalist. *Career:* Joined Joyspeed; Changed name to Aqua; Secured record deal in Denmark; Numerous TV and live appearances in Scandinavia and UK. *Recordings:* Itsy Blitzy, as Joyspeed, 1989; Roses are Red; Barbie Girl (No. 1, UK), 1997; Doctor Jones (No. 1, UK), 1998; Turn Back Time (theme from film Sliding Doors) (No. 1, UK), 1998; My Oh My; Lollipop, 1998; Good Morning Sunshine, 1998; Cartoon Heroes, 2000; Around The World, 2000; Albums: Aquarium, 1997; Bubble Mix, 1998; We Belong To The Sea, 2001.

O

O CONGHAILE, Micheál; b. 14 March 1962, Galway, Ireland. Writer; Man.-Dir; Record Co Exec. *Education:* BA; MA; H Dip In Ed. *Education:* No formal, expert on Sean-nós (Irish language unaccompanied singing). *Career:* Author on 10 books in Irish language; Former college lecturer; Founder of Cló Iar-Chonnachta, Ireland's fastest growing traditional music label, 1985; Many national literary awards. *Publications:* Song collections: Croch Suas é; Up Seanamhach!. *Honours:* Elected member of Aosdána for outstanding contribution to the arts in Ireland. *Membership:* PRS; IMRO. *Address:* Cló Iar-Chonnachta, Indreabhán, Conamara, Co Galway, Ireland. *E-mail:* moccic@eircom.net.

Ó CONLUAIN, Proinsias; b. 17 Aug. 1919, Benburb, County Tyrone, Ireland. Radio Prod. m. Sheila Murphy, 2 Sept. 1947, 1 d. *Education:* Scholarship, Queen's University, Belfast. *Career:* Scriptwriter, Producer, Radio Éireann, 1947–60; Producer, RTÉ Radio, 1960–83; Numerous radio programmes, popular, folk, traditional music; Series included: The Ballad Tree; The Singer and The Song; Between The Jigs and The Reels; Gold-Dust On The Fiddle; Features, documentaries on traditional singers, musicians, collectors, including: Bunting; Hardebeck; Francis O Neill (The Captain from Chicago); Sam Henry (Coleraine); John Rea the Dulcimer Man (Glenarm); John Maguire (The Rosslea Pad); Robert Cinnamond (Glenavy); Mrs Eileen Keaney (Glenelly and Belfast); Founder, Pres., The O'Neill Country Historical Society. *Recordings:* Robert Cinnamond: You Rambling Boys of Pleasure, sleeve notes, 1975; Róise na nAmhrán, Songs of a Donegal Woman, 1994: Songs recorded Arranmore Island, Co Donegal, 1953; Introductions to Song Translations/Transcriptions. *Publications:* Articles on traditional music, musicians, in journals including: Irish Folk Music Studies; Dál gCais: The Journal of Clare, 1986; Dúiche Néill: The Journal of the O Neill Country Historical Society (editor). *Honours:* Jacob's Award, radio, 1979; Gradam Sean-Nós Cois Life, 1998. *Membership:* Founder mem., Irish Folk Music Society; Board mem., Irish Traditional Music Archive, 1993–95. *Address:* 75 Blackheath Park, Clontarf, Dublin 3, Ireland.

O CONNOR, Martin (Mairtin); b. 28 March 1955, Galway, Ireland. Musician (accordion). m. Sietske Van Minnen, 28 Dec. 1983, 1 s., 3 d. *Education:* Engineering. *Career:* Tours: America; Europe; Middle East; Hong Kong; Soloist, Bill Whelan's Seville Suite, with RTE Concert Orchestra, World Expo, Seville, 1993; Soloist in Riverdance; Featured in television documentaries: Bringing It All Back Home; River of Sound. *Compositions:* Music for 2 short films, many local theatre productions. *Recordings:* Solo albums: The Connachtman's Rambles; Perpetual Motion; Chatterbox (featuring own compositions); Featured as accordion player on: Riverdance, Bill Whelan, 1996; Golden Heart, Mark Knopfler, 1996; Eileen Ivers, So Far: The collection, 1979–95; Legends of Ireland, 1998; Ellen Cranitch, Karst, 1998; Maire Brennan, Whisper to the Wild Water, 1999; Retrospective, Mark O'Connor, 1999; Keeper Of The Flame, Luka Bloom, 2000; Os Amores Libres, Carlos Nunez, 2000; Little Lights, Kate Rusby, 2001; Dreamcatcher, Secret Garden, 2001. *Honours:* AIB (Allied Irish Bank) Traditional Musician of the Year, 1995. *Membership:* IMRO; Musicians' Union. *Current Management:* Annagh Music. *Address:* Annaghdown Pier, Annaghdown, Co Galway, Ireland.

O DOCHARTAIGH, Seoirse; b. 17 June 1946, Belfast, Northern Ireland. Teacher; Painter; Musician. *Education:* BA, Fine Arts; MA, University College, Cork. *Career:* Born into musical family, began with singing, later, guitar and tin whistle; Public performances increased 1970s, incl. television appearances and radio broadcasts; Tours to Germany, France, Netherlands, Ireland, UK, USA; Musical and artistic dir, own band, Dúlamán, 1995–. *Recordings:* Slán Agus Beannacht, 1988; Seoirse O Dochartaigh—Live, 1989; Bláth Buí, 1992; Amhráin Agus Bodhráin, 1994; Oíche Go Maidin, 1994; Dúlamán A' tSléibhe, 2002. *Publications:* Over 80 songs and instrumental pieces. *Honours:* Music prizes in the Oireachtas. *Membership:* FED; PRS; IMRO; PPI; MCPS. *Current Management:* H. Ponting, Auld of Clunie Farmhouse, Blairgowrie, Perthshire PH10 6RH, Scotland. *Telephone:* (1250) 884265. *Address:* Teach an tSrutháin, Ráth an Aonaigh Thiar, An Lathaigh, Co Dhún na nGall, Ireland. *Telephone:* (73) 23012.

Ó FARACHÁIN, Antaine; b. 6 Feb. 1959, Dublin, Ireland. Traditional Vocalist; Musician. *Education:* BEd. *Career:* Organizer, Sean-Nós Cois Life Festival; Guest at various music and vocal festivals including Sidmouth Folk Festival, Inishowen Singers Festival, Ennistymon Singers Festival, Willie Clancy Summer School, Milwaukee Irish Fest; Numerous radio and television appearances: The Pure Drop, Mountain Lark, Fleádh, Tinteán, Late Late Show, Síbín, Eurovision Song Contest, 1995. *Compositions:* Various songs in traditional style, in both Engish and Irish language. *Recordings:* Seachrán Sí, CD. *Honours:* Various prizes at Oireachtas na Gaeilge (Irish Cultural Festival). *Address:* 13 Bóthar Emmet, Cill Mhaighneann, Baile Átha Cliath 8, Dublin, Ireland.

Ó LIONÁIRD, Iarla; b. 1964, Cúil Aodha, County Cork, Ireland. Vocalist. *Education:* University College Dublin, studied Literature. *Career:* First performance, aged 5; First radio recording, aged 7; Member: Coir Cuil Aodha; Worked as teacher and, later, singing tutor at University College, Cork; Presenter of TV series The Pure Drop, 1989; Collaborations include: Peadar O Riada; Matt Molloy; Afro Celt Sound System; Shaun Davey. *Recordings:* Aislingi Ceoil (with Tony MacMahon and Noel Hill), 1993; Seven Steps To Mercy, 1997; I Could Read the Sky (featuring Sinead O Connor and Martin Hayes), 2000; features on Afro Celt Sound System Albums: Vol. 1 – Sound Magic, 1996; Vol. 2 – Release, 1999; Vol. 3 – Further In Time, 2001. *Address:* c/o Realworld Records. *E-mail:* records@realworld.on.net.

O MAONLAI, Liam; b. Dublin, Ireland. Vocalist; Musician (piano). *Career:* Member, punk group Congress (later became My Bloody Valentine), Dublin; Busker, duo Incomparable Benzini Brothers (with Fiachna O'Brainain), 1985; Founder member, Hothouse Flowers, 1986–. *Recordings:* Albums: with Hothouse Flowers: People (No. 2, UK), 1988; Home, 1990; Songs From The Rain, 1993; Best Of, 2000; with Def Leppard, Retro Active, 1993; with Sharon Shannon, Sharon Shannon, 1993; with Liam O'Flynn, Out to the Other Side, 1993; with the Rankin Family, North country, 1994; with ALT, Altitude, 1995; with Altan, Best of Altan, 1997; with Sharon Shannon, Spellbound: The Best of Sharon Shannon, 1999; with Maire Breatnach, Angels Candles, 1999; Singles: Don't Go, 1988; I Can See Clearly Now, 1990; Give It Up, 1990; Movies, 1990; Emotional Time, 1993; One Tongue, 1993; You Can Love Me Now, 1998. *Honours:* Street Entertainers of the Year Award, 1985. *Current Management:* Chris O'Donnell. *Address:* c/o London Records, PO Box 1422, Chancellors House, Chancellors Rd, London W6 9SG, England.

Ó SÚILLEABHÁIN, Micheál; b. County Tipperary, Ireland. Musician (piano); Composer; Conductor; Prod. *Education:* BMus, MA, University College Cork, Ireland; PhD, Queen's University Belfast. *Career:* Produced albums for artistes including: Noirin Ni Riain; Liam O'Flynn; Paddy Glackin; Lecturer at University College Cork, 1975–93; Chair of Music, University of Limerick, 1994–, Established course in traditional music; Founder: Irish World Music centre at University of Limerick; Visiting professor to Boston College, 1990; Produced a fiddle festival and founded archive for traditional music; Founder member of world music group Hiberno-Jazz; Contributed to RTE/BBC TV series Bringing It All Back Home, 1992; Wrote and presented TV series A River of Sound, 1995. *Compositions:* Lumen, interval entertainment at Eurovision Song Contest, 1995; Maranatha, vocal composition, commissioned by Cork International Choral Festival, premiered in 2000. *Recordings:* Albums include: Oro Damhnaigh, 1977; Cry of the Mountain, 1982; The Dolphin's Way (featuring Colm Murphy), 1987; Oilean (featuring Tony McMahon and Matt Molloy), 1989; Casadh (featuring Mel Mercier), 1990; Gaiseadh (with the Irish Chamber Orchestra), 1992; Becoming, 1998; Templum (featuring National Chamber Orchestra), 2001. *Address:* c/o Irish World Music Centre, University of Limerick, Limerick, Ireland. *Telephone:* (61) 202590. *Fax:* (61) 202589.

OAKENFOLD, Paul; b. 1964, London, England. DJ; Remixer; Recording Artiste; Prod. *Career:* Former chef; Began as DJ, Covent Garden, London, 1982; Resident, Heaven Club; Mem., Steve Hillage's collective System 7, 1990s; Numerous concerts, television and radio appearances; Produced and remixed for artistes including: Boy George, U2, Happy Mondays, Olive, Cure, Insider; Founder, owner, Perfecto Records. *Recordings:* Albums: Journeys by Stadium DJ, 1994; Journeys by DJ, Vol. 15: Paul Oakenfold in..., 1995; Journeys by DJ Marathon, 1996; Global Underground: Oslo, 1997; Fantazia Presents the House Collection, 1997; Cream Anthems '97, 1997; Global Underground: New York, 1998; Tranceport, 1998; Resident: Two Years of Oakenfold at Cream, 1999; A Sample from Essential Selection, Vol. 1, 2000; Another World, 2000; Travelling, 2000; Sampladelica: The Roots of Paul Oakenfold, 2000; Voyage into Trance, 2001; Swordfish (soundtrack), 2001; Ibiza, 2001; Bust A Groove, 2002; Bunkka, 2002; Perfecto Presents... Paul Oakenfold Travelling, 2000; Perfecto Presents... Paul Oakenfold in Ibiza, 2001. Singles: Southern Sun/Ready Steady Go, 2002. *Honours:* Q Award, Best Producer, 1990. *Current Management:* 140dB, 1 McCrone Mews, Belsize Lane, London NW3 5BG, England. *Website:* www.pauloakenfold.com; www.perfecto-fc.com.

OAKES, Richard; b. 1 Oct. 1976, Perivale, Middlesex, England. Musician (guitar); Songwriter. *Career:* Joined Suede to replace Bernard Butler as guitarist, 1995–; Numerous tours, festival dates and TV appearances. *Recordings:* Albums: Coming Up, 1996; Sci-Fi Lullabies, 1997; Head Music, 1999; A New Morning, 2002. Singles: Trash, 1996; Beautiful Ones, 1996; Saturday Night, 1997; Lazy, 1997; Filmstar, 1997; Electricity, 1999; She's In Fashion, 1999; Everything Will Flow, 1999; Can't Get Enough, 1999; Positivity, 2002; Obsessions, 2002. *Address:* c/o Sony Music Entertainment,

European Regional Office, 10 Great Marlborough St, London W1F 7LP, England. *Website:* www.suede.net.

OAKEY, Philip; b. 2 Oct. 1955, Sheffield, South Yorkshire, England. Vocalist; Musician (synthesizer). *Career:* Former hospital porter; Lead singer, Human League, 1978–; Concerts include: Support to Siouxsie and The Banshees, British tour, 1979; Support to Iggy Pop, European tour, 1980; Headline tours, UK, world-wide, 1980–. *Recordings:* Hit singles include: Empire State Human, 1980; Sound of The Crowd, 1981; Love Action, 1981; Open Your Heart, 1981; Don't You Want Me (No. 1, UK and USA), 1981; Being Boiled, 1982; Mirror Man, 1982; (Keep Feeling) Fascination, 1983; The Lebanon, 1984; Life On Your Own, 1984; Louise, 1984; Human (No. 1, USA), 1986; Love Is All That Matters, 1988; Heart Like A Wheel, 1990; Only Human, 1994; Tell Me When, 1995; One Man In My Heart, 1995; Filling Up With Heaven, 1995; Stay With Me Tonight, 1996; with Giorgio Moroder: Together In Electric Dreams, for film Electric Dreams, 1984; with All Seeing-I: 1st Man In Space, 1999; Albums: Reproduction, 1979; Travelogue, 1980; Dare! (No. 1, UK), 1981; Love and Dancing (remixed mini album), 1982; Hysteria, 1984; Crash, 1986; Greatest Hits, 1988; Romantic?, 1990; Octopus, 1994; Secrets, 2001. *Honours:* BRIT Award, Best Newcomer, 1982. *Current Management:* Huge and Jolly Management, 56–60 Islington Park St, London N1 1PX, England.

OAKLEY, Pete; b. 29 June 1962, Burton-on-Trent, Staffordshire, England. Musician (guitar); Vocalist; Songwriter. m. 12 April 1986. *Career:* Folk/blues guitarist; Many radio and television appearances including: BBC Radio 1, 2 and 5, World Service and European radio stations; Recordings for many local US and Australian radio stations; Tours, 1989–; Owner, 2 music shops, Pete Oakley Music. *Recordings:* Back Porch Blues; Old Guitars Never Lie; Ghost In The City. *Publications:* Various magazine contributions. *Membership:* British Actors Equity; PRS. *Current Management:* Pete Oakley Music. *Address:* 81 Horninglow Rd, Burton-on-Trent, Staffordshire DE14 2PT, England.

OANA, Augustin; b. 26 July 1942, Cabesti-Hunedoara, Romania. Folk Vocalist. m. 28 May 1972, 2 s. *Education:* Professional school in composition; Hunedoara Musical Assembly. *Career:* Several television and radio appearances, including Bucharest radio; Major concerts throughout Romania, and tours of Turkey and Austria; Adapted poems for folk music of region; Participated in many shows and television appearances with Bucharest Radio Orchestra. *Recordings:* Record of popular music. *Address:* Str Izvorul Muresului, Nr2 Block A-9, sc-E et4 ap73, Sector 4, Bucharest, Romania.

OATES, John; b. 7 April 1949, New York, USA. Vocalist; Songwriter; Musician (guitar). *Education:* Temple University. *Career:* Member, The Masters; Gulliver; Member, duo Hall and Oates, with Daryl Hall, 1969–; Appearances world-wide include: Live Aid, Philadelphia, 1985; Rainforest benefit concert, with Grateful Dead, Madison Square Garden, 1988; Earth Day, Central Park, New York, 1990; USA Harvest National Hunger Relief concert, 1991; The Simple Truth, benefit concert for Kurdish refugees, Wembley, 1991. *Compositions include:* Numerous hit songs co-written with Daryl Hall; Film soundtrack, Outlaw Blues, 1979; Co-writer, Electric Blue, Icehouse, 1988. *Recordings:* Albums: with Hall and Oates: Whole Oats, 1972; Abandoned Luncheonette, 1974; War Babies, 1974; Daryl Hall and John Oates, 1975; Bigger Than Both of Us, 1976; No Goodbyes, 1977; Beauty On A Back Street, 1977; Livetime, 1978; X-Static, 1979; Voices, 1980; Private Eyes, 1981; H2O, 1982; Rock 'n' Soul (Part 1), 1983; Big Bam Boom, 1984; Live At The Apollo, 1985; Ooh Yeah, 1988; Change of Season, 1990; Looking Back – The Best Of..., 1991; Atlantic Collection, 1996; Marigold Sky, 1997; Back to Back, 1998; Very Best Of, 2001; with Keith Martin, It's Long Overdue, 1995; with Icehouse, Man of the Colours/Code Blue, 1996; Pop in the 80s Vol. 1, 1999; US No. 1 singles include: Rich Girl, 1977; Kiss On My List, 1981; Private Eyes, 1981; I Can't Go For That (No Can Do), 1982; Maneater, 1982; Out of Touch, 1984; Numerous other hit singles including: She's Gone, 1974; You've Lost That Lovin' Feelin', 1980; Every Time You Go Away, 1980; Family Man, 1983; Say It Ain't So, 1983; Method Of Modern Love, 1985; Everything Your Heart Desires, 1988; Contributor: We Are The World, USA For Africa, 1985; Sun City, Artists Against Apartheid, 1985; The Last Temptation of Elvis, 1990; Two Rooms – Celebrating The Songs of Elton John and Bernie Taupin, 1991. *Honours:* American Music Awards: Favourite Duo or Band, 1983–85; 19 US Gold and Platinum discs (most successful duo in US recording history). *Current Management:* All Access Entertainment, 53 W 23rd St, 11th Floor, New York, NY 10010, USA.

OBA FUNKE. See: **KING BRITT.**

OBERG, Rolf Thomas; b. 15 March 1967, Helsingborg, Sweden. Vocalist; Musician (melodica, synthesizer). *Career:* Member, bob hund, 1991–; More than 300 concerts throughout Scandinavia; Played at festivals including Roskilde, Lollipop, Ruisrock, Quartfestivalen and Hultsfred; Member with Magnus Boman of electric and electronic duo, Instant Life. *Compositions:* I Stället för Musik: Förvirring, 1996; Düsseldorf, 1996. *Recordings:* with bob hund: bob hund, 1993, 1994; Edvin Medvind, 1994; I Stället för Musik: Förvirring, 1996; Omslag: Martin Kann, 1996; with Instant Life: I Turned My Best Friends into Slaves, CD, 1993; I Made Arrangements for World Peace,

1994. *Honours:* Grammy Awards: Best Live Act, 1994, Best Lyrics, 1996. *Membership:* STIM; SAMI. *Current Management:* Bob Hund Förlag, Råsundavägen 150, 169 36 Solna, Sweden.

OBI, Ben; b. 7 Oct. 1965, London, England. Prod. *Education:* College and University of Minnesota. *Career:* Producer, Alexander O'Neal, 1996; Produced, The Sunset Music Band and A Large Percentage of New Talent Emerging From Minneapolis. *Recordings:* Loversagain; Sex On The Beach; Sunset Celebration. *Membership:* ASCAP. *Current Management:* Savannah Street Music, 2325 Endicott St #202, St Paul, MN 55114, USA.

O'BRIEN, Ed(ward John); b. 15 April 1968, Oxford, England. Musician (rhythm guitar, percussion). *Education:* Economics, Manchester University. *Career:* Mem. and lead singer, On A Friday, 1987, renamed Radiohead, 1991–; Numerous tours, festivals and television appearances. *Recordings:* Albums: Pablo Honey, 1993; The Bends, 1995; OK Computer, 1997; Kid A, 2000; Amnesiac, 2001; I Might Be Wrong, 2001. Singles: Drill (EP), 1992; Creep, 1993; Anyone Can Play Guitar, 1993; Pop Is Dead, 1993; Stop Whispering, 1993; Itch (EP), 1994; My Iron Lung (EP), 1994; My Iron Lung, 1994; Live Au Forum (EP), 1995; High and Dry, 1995; Fake Plastic Trees, 1995; Just, 1995; Street Spirit (Fade Out), 1996; The Bends, 1996; Paranoid Android, 1997; Karma Police, 1997; No Surprises, 1997; Climbing Up The Walls, 1997; Airbag/How Am I Driving? (EP), 1998; Pyramid Song, 2001; Knives Out, 2001; I Might Be Wrong, 2001. *Honours:* Grammy Award, Best Alternative Rock Performance, 1998; Q Award, Best Act in the World Today, 2002. *Address:* c/o Parlophone Records, 43 Brook Green, London W6 7EF, England. *Website:* www.radiohead.com.

O'BRIEN, Steve, (Steve-O); Musician. *Career:* Founding mem., Fun Lovin' Criminals, 1993–99; Numerous tours, festivals and television appearances. *Recordings:* Albums: Come Find Yourself, 1996; 100% Colombian, 1998; Mimosa – The Lounge Album, 1999. Singles: The Grave And The Constant (EP), 1996; The Fun Lovin' Criminal, 1996; Scooby Snacks, 1996; King Of New York, 1997; I'm Not In Love, 1997; Love Unlimited, 1998; Big Night Out, 1998; Korean Bodega, 1999. *Address:* c/o Chrysalis Group plc, The Chrysalis Bldg, Bramley Rd, London W10 6SP, England.

O'BRIEN-OLUYEMI, Rebecca Jane; b. 4 Jan. 1966, Caerphilly, Wales. Vocalist. m. Emmanuel Valentine Oluyemi, 1 Dec. 1992. *Education:* Newham Community College, 1993–94; London Central St Martins School of Art and Design, 1994–97; Private lessons; Piano theory, 1995; Vocal training course and exam, with John Campbell. *Career:* Concerts with Thomas The Voice: The Africa Centre; The Bull and Bush; Camden Palace; Backing vocals with Sandra Tavernier. *Recordings:* Backing vocals, Tell Me Where; Nothing Compares To U; Backing vocals, Time Will Tell, Footsie Drummond; She Move Thru' The Fair, with Thomas The Voice. *Membership:* Musicians' Union. *Address:* 57 Talbot Walk, Church Rd, London NW10 9HU, England.

O'CARROLL, Sinéad Maria; b. 14 May 1978, Dublin, Ireland. Vocalist. *Career:* Member, B*Witched; Numerous tours and television appearances; Several hit singles. *Recordings:* Singles: C'est La Vie, 1998; Rollercoaster, 1998; To You I Belong, 1998; Blame it on the Weatherman, 1998; Jesse Hold On, 1999; Albums: B*Witched, 1998; Awake and Breathe, 1999.

OCASEK, Ric (Richard); b. 23 March 1949, Baltimore, Maryland, USA. Vocalist; Songwriter; Musician (guitar); Record Prod. m. Paulina Porizkova, 23 Aug. 1989. *Career:* Founder, singer, guitarist, The Cars, 1976–88; Appearances with the Cars include: Residency, The Rat club, Boston, 1977; European tour, 1978; Concert to 500,000 audience, Central Park, New York, 1979; US Festival, 1982; Founded Synchro Sound recording studio, Boston, 1981; Solo artiste, 1990–; Appearances include Earth Day, Central Park, New York, 1990. *Recordings:* Albums with The Cars: The Cars, 1979; Candy-O, 1979; Panorama, 1980; Shake It Up, 1982; Heartbeat City, 1984; The Cars' Greatest Hits, 1985; Door To Door, 1987; Solo albums: Beatitude, 1983; This Side of Paradise, 1986; Fireball Zone, 1991; Negative Theater, 1993; Quick Change World, 1993; Getchertikitz, 1996; Troublizing, 1997; Learner's Permit, 1999; Hit singles: with the Cars: Just What I Needed, 1978; My Best Friend's Girl, 1978; Good Times Roll, 1979; Touch and Go, 1980; Shake It Up, 1982; Since You're Gone, 1982; You Might Think, 1984; Magic, 1984; Drive, 1984; Hello Again, 1984; Why Can't I Have You?, 1985; Tonight She Comes, 1986; I'm Not The One, 1986; You Are The Girl, 1987; Solo singles: Emotion In Motion, 1986; The Next Right Moment, 1997; Record producer, artistes including: Bad Brains; Black 47; Guided By Voices; No Doubt; Hole; Jonathan Richman; The Wannadies; Weezer. *Honours:* Rolling Stone Best New Band of the Year, 1979; MTV Award, You Might Think, 1984. *Current Management:* Lookout Management, 2644 30th St, First Floor, Santa Monica, CA 90405, USA.

OCEAN, Billy, (Leslie Charles); b. 21 Jan. 1950, Trinidad. Vocalist; Songwriter. *Career:* Recording artiste, 1975–; International concerts include: Live Aid, Philadelphia, 1985. *Compositions include:* Co-writer, own hits: Loverboy; There'll Be Sad Songs; Get Outta My Dreams. *Recordings:* Albums: Nights (I Feel Like Getting Down), 1981; Inner Feeling, 1982; Suddenly, 1984; Love Zone, 1986; Tear Down These Walls, 1988; Greatest Hits, 1989; Time To

Move On, 1993; L.I.F.E., 1997; Emotions In Motion, 2002. Singles include: Love Really Hurts Without Me, 1976; Stop Me If You've Heard It Before, 1976; Red Light Spells Danger, 1977; Caribbean Queen (No More Love On The Run), also released as European Queen and African Queen (No. 1, USA), 1984; Loverboy, 1985; Suddenly, 1985; When The Going Gets Tough The Tough Get Going, used in film soundtrack The Jewel of The Nile (No. 1, UK), 1986; There'll Be Sad Songs (To Make You Cry), (No. 1, USA), 1986; Love Zone, 1987; Get Outta My Dreams (Get Into My Car) (No. 1, USA), 1988. *Honours:* Grammy Award, Best R&B Performance, 1985; American Music Awards: Favorite Male Video Artist, Favorite Single, 1988; ASCAP Award for Caribbean Queen, Most Played Song in USA, 1996. *Current Management:* LJE, 32 Willesden Lane, London NW6 7ST, England.

O'CONNELL, Carl; b. 24 Feb. 1965, Watford, Hertfordshire, England. Musician (keyboards); Programmer. *Education:* Grade II guitar; Formal jazz tuition. *Recordings:* Album: Is Nothing Sacred, Love Republic; Several Dox music albums; Production Assistant, several Mute Records remixes; Charity appearance with East 17. *Membership:* Musicians' Union; PAMRA. *Current Management:* Archangel Music, Ilford. *Address:* 16 Fortis Green, East Finchley, London N2 9EL, England.

O'CONNOR, Gerry; b. 20 July 1960, Tipperary, Ireland. Composer; Musician (banjo, guitar, violin). m. Marie, 13 May 1980, 1 s., 1 d. *Education:* Third level, UCD, Dublin. *Career:* Solo albums; Member, 4 Men and A Dog; Performances, television, radio: Britain; Europe; Scandinavia; Canada; USA; Australia; Workshop; Festivals; Tutor publications, book, cassette, video. *Recordings:* Time To Time; Trad At Heart; Funk The Cajun Blues; 4 Men and A Dog: Shifting Gravel; Dr A's Secret Remedies; Niamh Parsons: Loosen Up; Gordon Duncan: Circular Breath; Gaelic roots; Mighty Session; Mists of Morning; Moving Cloud: Foxglove; Other collaborations include: Maire Brennan; Luka Bloom. *Publications:* 50 Solos For Tenor Banjo; Tenor Banjo Techniques. *Honours:* International Radio Festival: Bratislava, 1989; Folk Album of the Year, 1991, (4 Men and A Dog). *Membership:* IMRO; PRS; MCPS. *Current Management:* Marie O'Connor, 46 Blarney Park, Kimmage, Dublin 12, Ireland; Jim Heaney CBM, 18 Dillons Ave, Whiteabbey, Co Antrim BT37 0SX, Northern Ireland.

O'CONNOR, Mark; b. 5 August 1961, Seattle, Washington, USA. Musician (violin, guitar, bass, mandolin). *Career:* Leader, own group, Nashville Strings; Musician with artistes including: Paul Simon; James Taylor; Dolly Parton; Willie Nelson; Chet Atkins; Randy Travis; Michael Brecker; Concerts include: Barbican Hall (with Yo-Yo Ma); Montreux Jazz Festival; Carnegie Hall, New York. *Recordings include:* Heroes, 1991; Johnny Appleseed (children's album with Garrison Keillor), 1995; Fiddle Concerto for violin and orchestra, 1995; Hot Swing, 2001; American Seasons, 2001. *Honours:* Winner, classical guitar competition, aged 11; Country Music Assen's Musician of the Year, 4 times; Grammy Award, New Nashville Cats. *Membership:* CMA.

O'CONNOR, Sinéad; b. 12 Dec. 1966, Glenageary, Ireland. Vocalist; Songwriter; Actress. m. John Reynolds, March 1989, 1 s. *Education:* Dublin College of Music; Singing lessons with Frank Merriman, Parnell School of Music, 1992. *Career:* Solo artiste, Dublin, 1985; Singer, Ton Ton Macoute, 1985; Solo artiste, 1986–; Concerts include: Tours, UK, Europe, USA, 1988; Year of The Horse World Tour, 1990; Glastonbury Festival, 1990; The Wall Benefit, Berlin, 1990; Amnesty International Benefit, Chile (duet with Peter Gabriel), 1990; Simple Truth Concert (for Kurdish refugees), Wembley, 1991; Bob Dylan 30th Anniversary; As actress: Hush-A-Bye-Baby (Channel 4), Dublin Film Festival, 1990; Ghost of Oxford Street (Channel 4), 1991; Television documentary: Sinead O'Connor – Coffee and Cigarettes, BBC TV, 1992. *Recordings:* Singles: Heroine, 1986; Troy, 1987; Mandinka, 1988; Jump In The River, 1988; Nothing Compares 2 U (No. 1, UK and USA), 1990; The Emperor's New Clothes, 1990; Three Babies, 1990; My Special Child, 1991; Thief of Your Heart, 1993; Fire On Babylon, 1994; Thank You For Hearing Me, 1994; Gospel Oak EP, 1997; This is a Rebel Song, 1997; This is to Mother You, 1997. Albums: The Lion and The Cobra, 1988; I Do Not Want What I Haven't Got (No. 1, UK), 1990; Am I Not Your Girl, 1992; Universal Mother, 1994; So Far... The Best of Sinead O'Connor, 1997; Faith And Courage, 2000; Sean-Nos Nua, 2002; Also featured on: Mind Bomb, The The, 1989; Red Hot + Blue, 1990; Two Rooms – The Songs of Elton John and Bernie Taupin, 1992; Rising Above Bedlam, Jah Wobble, 1992; Be Still, 1993; Across The Borderline, Willie Nelson, 1993; Long Black Veil, Chieftans, 1995; Long Journey Home, 1998. *Honours:* Grammy Award, 1991; Numerous Music and Video Awards, 1990; 3 MTV Awards, 1990; Billboard Music Award, 1990; BRIT Award, 1991. *Current Management:* Principle Management, 30–32 Sir John Rogersons Quay, Dublin 2, Ireland.

O'DAY, Anita Belle Colton; b. 18 Oct. 1919, Chicago, Illinois, USA. Vocalist. *Career:* Nightclub entertainer, Chicago, 1939–41; Singer, Gene Krupa's Orchestra, 1941–45; Stan Kenton, 1944; Woody Herman, 1946; Solo artiste, 1947–; Film appearances include: Gene Krupa Story, 1959; Jazz On A Summer's Day, 1960; Zigzag, 1970; Outfit, 1974; Concerts include: 50th Anniversary Concert, Carnegie Hall, 1985. *Recordings:* Solo albums include: Anita Sings; Pick Yourself Up; An Evening With Anita O'Day; Anita Sings The Winners; Lady Is A Tramp; Travellin' Light; At Mr Kelly's; Let Me Off

Uptown; Live in Concert Tokyo 1976; Singin' and Swingin'; The Night Has a Thousand Eyes; Live At The City, San Francisco 1979, 2001; Many compilation albums; Other recordings with Gene Krupa; Stan Kenton; Count Basie; Duke Ellington. *Publications:* Author: High Times, Hard Times, 1981. *Membership:* AFTRA; BMI; Screen Actors Guild.

ODDE, Knud; b. 25 Jan. 1955, Fröslev, Denmark. Musician (electric bass); Painter; Composer; Text Writer. *Education:* General Certificate of Education, Research Librarian. *Career:* Member, The Sods, 1977; Name changed to Sort Sol, 1980–2001; Toured: USA, 1982; Russia, 1988; Music for Danish Royal Ballet production of Hamlet, 1996; Solo Exhibition of paintings, DCA Gallery, New York, 1999. *Recordings:* Minutes to Go, 1979; Under En Sort Sol, 1980; Dagger and Guitar, 1983; Everything That Rises Must Converge, 1987; Flow My Firetear, 1990; Glamourpuss, 1993; Unspoiled Monsters, 1996; Blackbox, 1997; Snakecharmer, 2001; Circle Hits The Flame, 2002. *Publications:* Biography: Knud Odde by Henrik Wivel, 1994; Erich Von Stroheim, by Knud Odde, 1994. *Honours:* 3 (local) Grammy Awards, 1991; 5 Grammy Awards in 1994, with Sort Sol. *Address:* PO Box 613, Borups Alle 123, Copenhagen, Denmark. *Website:* www.knudodde.dk.

ODELL, Ann Mary; b. 18 April 1947, London, England. Musician (keyboards); Vocalist; Arranger. m. Stephen R Spurling, 17 June 1980, divorced 28 Nov. 1994, 2 s. *Education:* Royal Academy of Music, 1964–66, LRAM Diploma. *Career:* Ivy Benson Orchestra; QE2 Maiden Voyage, Anna Dell Trio, 1969; Session musician and arranger, 1972–81; Bryan Ferry World Tour, 1977; BBC Broadcasts, R2 Nightride and Roundabout own band Blue Mink, 1992–94; Television: Top of the Pops; Les Dawson Show; Little and Large; Currently, running Watermill Jazz Club, Dorking, Surrey; Agency, MIDI recording studio, Take Note Ltd. *Recordings:* with Blue Mink: Fruity; Blue Mink; with Bryan Ferry: Another Time, Another Place; In Your Mind; Bride Stripped Bare; Solo: Ann Odell; A Little Taste; Grand Slam, Chopyn; Original Evita album, Jesus Christ Superstar film soundtrack; Beatles, Beatles Tapes; London Symphony Orchestra, Silk Road Suit; Yvonne Elliman, The Best of Yvonne Elliman; John Gustafson, Goose Grease; Also contributed to recordings by: Murray Head; Japan; Shawn Phillips; David Sylvian; Pete Townshend. *Honours:* 5 Gold discs; Platinum disc; K-Tel Classic Rock Series with LSO. *Membership:* PRS; Musicians' Union; Assen of British Jazz Musicians. *Current Management:* Take Note Ltd. *Address:* 24 Dodds Park, Brockham, Betchworth, Surrey RH3 7LD, England.

ODELL, Roger Keith; b. 7 Dec. 1941, Epping, Essex, England. Musician (drums, percussion); Songwriter. m. Larraine, 18 Nov. 1968, 1 s., 1 d. *Education:* Private studies, leading to Grade 8, Guildhall School of Music, Honours. *Career:* Toured throughout the world in concert, with numerous appearances on television and radio. *Compositions:* Contributed to over 20 recordings by Shakatak, as drummer and songwriter; Co-writer, several top 20 UK hits including: Night Birds; Down On The Street; Recent releases include: with Shakatak: Live at Ronnie Scott's, 1998; Shinin On, 1998; Magic, 1999; Invitations, 1999; Christmas Dreams, 1999; Collection Volume 2, 2000; with Martini Grooves: Martini Grooves, 1999; Welcome to the Jazz Cafe, 1999. *Honours:* Tokyo International Song Festival, Silver Prize. *Membership:* PRS; International Percussion Society; Professional mem., BAC&S. *Current Management:* Les McCutcheon, Skratch Music Ltd. *Address:* 81, Crabtree Lane, London SW6 6LW, England.

ODGERS, Brian Norman, (Badger); b. 9 Feb. 1942, Forest Gate, London, England. Musician (bass, bass guitar); Teacher of Life, Yoga. m. Jahnet McIlwain, 12 Dec. 1976, 4 d. (3 by previous marriage). *Career:* Played with: Herbie Hancock; Chick Corea; Freddie Hubbard; Larry Carlton; Van Morrison; Georgie Fame on Herbie's 50th birthday; Television special in Los Angeles; Tours: 2 years Van Morrison; 6 months Andy Williams; 26 years Georgie Fame; 3 years Winifred Atwell; Television, radio appearances over 30 years with most UK and World stars, include: Tom Jones; Englebert Humperdinck; Elton John; Eric Clapton; Cliff Richard; Sarah Vaughan; Shirley Bassey; Neil Diamond; Tony Bennett; Abba; Andre Previn. *Recordings:* John McLaughlin: Extrapolation; Van Morrison: Enlightenment; Orginal Evita recording with Andrew Lloyd Webber; Roger Daltrey: White Horse; Jimmy Webb: Land's End; Georgie Fame: That's What Friends Are For; Marc Bolan: Cat Black; Roger Daltrey, Martyrs and Madmen; Sweet Thursday; Session musician for 20 years; Recorded with artistes from rock through jazz to light classical, including: Pete Atkin; Jane Birkin; Chris De Burgh; Serge Gainsbourg; Lou Reed; Al Stewart. *Honours:* Flavour of The Month Award, 3 times. *Membership:* Musicians' Union. *Address:* c/o Ronnie Scott's Club, Frith St, London W1, England.

O'DONNELL, Daniel; b. 12 Dec. 1961, Kincasslagh, Co Donegal, Ireland. Vocalist. m. Majella McLennan, 2002. *Career:* Backing vocalist for sister Margo O'Donnell, early 1980s; Tours, UK and Ireland, 1985–; Concerts include: Carnegie Hall, New York, 1991, 1997, Opera House, Sydney, 1996; Point Theatre, Dublin, NEC, Birmingham, 1997; Own television series, Ireland; Subject, This Is Your Life (BBC), 2000. *Recordings:* Albums: Two Sides Of Daniel O'Donnell, 1985; I Need You, 1986; Don't Forget To Remember, 1987; The Boy From Donegal, 1987; From The Heart, 1988; Thoughts Of Home, 1989; Favourites, 1990; The Last Waltz, 1990; The Very

Best Of..., 1991; Follow Your Dream, 1992; Christmas With Daniel, 1994; Especially For You, 1994; The Classic Collection, 1995; Irish Collection, 1996; Timeless (with Mary Duff), 1996; Songs Of Inspiration, 1996; I Believe, 1997; Love Songs, 1998; Greatest Hits, 1999; Live Laugh Love, 2001; Yesterday's Memories, 2002. Singles: I Just Want To Dance With You, 1992; Whatever Happened To Old Fashioned Love, 1993; Singing The Blues, 1994; Secret Love, 1995; Timeless, 1996; Footsteps, 1996; Give A Little Love, 1998; The Magic Is There, 1998; Uno Mas, 1999; The Way Dreams Are, 1999; Christmas Kiss, 1999; Light A Candle, 2000; 10 UK Country No. 1 hits; Videos include: Daniel O'Donnell Live In Concert, 1988; Thoughts Of Home, 1989; TV Show Favourites, 1990; An Evening With Daniel O'Donnell, 1990; Follow Your Dream, 1992; Daniel And Friends Live, 1993; Just For You, 1994; The Classic Concert, 1995; Christmas With Daniel, 1996; The Gospel Show, Live At The Point, 1997; Give A Little Love, 1998; Peaceful Waters, 1999; Faith And Inspiration, 2000; Live Laugh Love, 2001. *Publications:* My Story, 2000. *Honours:* M.B.E., 2002. *Address:* c/o Rosette Records, 103/105 Greenford Rd, Harrow, Middlesex, England.

OFFSET. See: **SLATER, Luke.**

O'FLYNN, Liam; b. 1945, County Kildare, Ireland. Musician (uillean pipes). *Career:* Born into family of traditional musicians; Founding member: Planxty; One of the first musicians to bring classical and traditional music together as soloist in Shaun Davey's The Brendan Voyage; Appeared on film soundtracks: Cal, 1992; The Field, 1990; A River Runs Through It, 1992; Collaborations: Mark Knopfler; Kate Bush; Enya; Sinead O'Connor; International tours; Performed at the first BBC Proms night of Irish music, 1999; Recorded over 50 albums. *Recordings:* Albums include: The Brendan Voyage, 1980; The Fine Art of Piping, 1989; Out To An Other Side, 1993; The Given Note, 1995; The Piper's Call, 1998. *Honours:* Golden Insignia of the University of La Coruna, Spain, 2000. *Address:* c/o Tom Sherlock, 71 Carysfort Ave, Blackrock, County Dublin, Ireland.

O'GRADY, Jenny; b. 30 Jan. 1949, Loughborough, Leicestershire, England. Vocalist; Vocal Coach. m. Robert Jolley, 1 s. *Education:* Royal College of Music, London. *Career:* Freelance singer, radio, television, film soundtracks, wide variety recordings from Royal Opera House to pop; Also established as leading vocal coach to actors, actresses, musical theatre in London's West End, tours, shows including: Phantom of The Opera; Cats; Les Miserables; Starlight Express; Joseph; Vocal contractor: West Side Story; Michael Ball recording; Albums: Sparks, Plagiarism, 1997; Message in a Bottle, Mesage in a Bottle, 1999; Messenger: The Story of Joan of Arc, 1999; As Director or Choirmaster: Michael Card, Unveiled Hope, 1997; City of Angels (original Soundtrack), 1998; Craig Armstrong, Plunkett and Macleane, 1999; Elton John, Muse, 1999; Pet Shop Boys, Nightlife, 1999; Look At Me, Geri Halliwell, 1999; Any Given Sunday, Any Given Sunday, 2000. *Honours:* ARCM; LRAM. *Membership:* Equity; Musicians' Union. *Address:* 2 Queens Rd, Barnet, Hertfordshire ENS 4DG, England.

O'GRUAMA, Aindrias; b. 9 May 1957, Dun Laoighaire, Ireland. Musician (guitar). *Career:* Guitar player with The Fatima Mansions; Many BBC radio and television sessions; Support to U2, Zoo TV tour; Tours of USA; MTV appearances. *Recordings:* Albums: Zerra (produced by Todd Rundgren); My Baby's Arm; Viva Dead Ponies; Valhalla Avenue; Lost In The Former West. *Honours:* Album of the Year, Hot Press Critics Poll, 1990. *Membership:* Musicians' Union. *Current Management:* Arthog Music Productions. *Address:* 49 Chartham Court, Brixton, London Sw9 7PT, England.

O'HIGGINS, David Charles; b. 1 Sept. 1964, Birmingham, England. Musician (saxophones); Composer. *Education:* Trumpet, drums, piano, at school; Music, City University, London. *Career:* Regular working groups: National Youth Jazz Orchestra, 1983–86; Leader, Dave O'Higgins Quartet/ Quintet, 1983–; Mezzoforte, 1986–89; Co-leader, Roadside Picnic, 1986–90; Leader, The Gang of Three, 1987–89; Leader, Dave O'Higgins and The Oblivion Brothers, 1989–91; Cleo Laine and The John Dankworth Quintet; Sax Appeal; Pizza Express Modern Jazz Sextet; Jason Rebello; Jim Mullen Quartet; Itchy Fingers; Clark Tracey Sextet; Martin Taylor's Spirit of Django; Stepping Stones; Tours include: Europe, Japan; Cuba; South Africa and Namibia; Tunisia; Sri Lanka; Bangladesh; Venues include: Montreux Jazz Festival, 1989; Havana Jazz Festival, 1993; Several residencies, Ronnie Scott's; New York's Visionez; Television includes: Wogan; Pebble Mill; Jonathan Ross Show; Appearance as busker, Mr Bean; Judge, YTV Young Jazz Musician of the Year; Many radio broadcasts. *Recordings:* with NYJO: Full Score; Concrete Cows; With An Open Mind; with Mezzoforte: No Limits; with Roadside Picnic: Roadside Picnic; For Madmen Only; with Jim Mullen: Soundbites; Rule of Thumb; with Jason Rebello: A Clearer View; with Sax Appeal: Flat Out; Let's Go; with Dave Higgins: All Good Things; Beats Working For A Living; with Clark Tracey: Full Speed Sideways; with Itchy Fingers: Full English Breakfast; with Martin Taylor: Spirit of Django; with John Dankworth: Live At Ronnie Scott's; with Matt Bianco: Another Time Another Place; with Simon Hale: East Fifteen; with Ray Charles: Strong Love Affair; with Stephane Grappelli: Celebrating Grappelli; with Colosseum: Breads and Circuses; with James Galway: Un-Break My Heart; with US3: Ordinary Day In An Unusual World. *Honours:* Best New Band, British Jazz

Awards, 1988, 1989; Cleo Laine Personal Award, 1990; BT British Jazz Awards, Best Tenor Sax, and Rising Star, 1995.

OILING, Matti; b. 20 Nov. 1942, Finland. Musician (drums). *Education:* State scholarship, to study Latin-American rhythms, 1976. *Career:* Formed the Happy Jazz Band, 1969; Now playing as Oiling Boiling; Played with brass band Rempsetti, 1980s; Also plays with UHO-Trio; Regular session player; Founded Samba School, Helsinki; Founded own drumming school, 1980; Concerts include: Australia, 1986; California and Hawaii with Richie Cole, 1987; First ever Jazz festival, Jakarta, Indonesia, 1989; Palm Springs, 1989; Opened the Oiling Boiling Jazz and Blues Club, Tallinn, Estonia, 1990. *Publications:* The Drummer's ABC (first drum tutor in Finnish language), 1969; Vol. II, 1975. *Honours:* Helsinki Medal, 1989. *Address:* Ristiniementie 40 A 7, 02320 Espoo, Finland.

OJANEN, Eero; b. 3 Jan. 1943, Finland. Musician (piano); Composer. *Career:* Played with: Juhani Vilkki's sextet, 1960s; Otto Donner Treatment, 1960s; Pianist, Pekka Pöyry, Montreux Festival, 1968; Concentrated on theatre and film work, 1970s; Currently playing improvised music with Jouni Kesti projects; Accompanist to numerous singers; Member, duo with bass player Teppo Hauta-Aho. *Compositions:* Väinämöinen's Music (cantata based on epic Kalevala), Pori Jazz Festival, 1974; Ballet, based on Aleksis Kivi's Seitsemän Veljestä (The Seven Brothers), 1980. *Honours:* Yrjö Award, Finnish Jazz Federation, 1968. *Address:* Mechelininkatu 16 A 7, 00100 Helsinki, Finland.

OJANPERÄ, Jorma; b. 24 March 1961, Alahärmä, Finland. Musician (bass). *Education:* Studied jazz, Oulunkylä Institute; Helsinki University music department; Sibelius Academy, Helsinki. *Career:* Performances with The National Theatre and symphony orchestras; Member, Pori Big Band, 1983; Regular bassist, Helsinki clubs: Groovy; Jumo; Orfeus; Played Bengt Hallberg's music, directed by Hannu Hoivula, 1989; Regular appearances at Pori Jazz Festival; Recently member of: The Seppo Kantonene Trio; Markku Johansson Quintet; Also plays with saxophonist Ion Muniz. *Address:* Rike 24 B, 07700 Koskenkylän Saha, Finland.

OKIN, Earl; b. 31 Jan. 1947, Carshalton, Surrey, England. Vocalist; Songwriter; Musician (guitar, piano, vocal trumpet); Comedian. *Education:* BA (Philosophy, English Literature), University of Kent, Canterbury. *Career:* Various television appearances world-wide including Belgium, Germany, Australia, UK; First UK television appearance, 1959; Edinburgh Festival, 1983–2000; Opening act with Paul McCartney and Wings, Van Morrison, Stéphane Grappelli; Tours of Brazil as Bossa Nova singer/songwriter; Presenter, MTV2. *Compositions:* Over 100 various songs; Classical pieces include a string quartet. *Recordings:* Singles include: Stop! and You Will Become Aware, 1969; Albums include: Bossa Britanica. *Publications:* Various articles, liner notes on opera and jazz. *Membership:* PRS; Musicians' Union; British Equity. *Current Management:* Spats Music Ltd. *Address:* 248 Portobello Rd, London W11 1LL, England. *E-mail:* spats@spats.demon.co.uk. *Website:* www.spats.demon.co.uk.

OL' DIRTY BASTARD, (Russell Tyrone Jones), (ODB, Big Baby Jesus); b. 15 Nov. 1968, Brooklyn, NY, USA. Rap Artiste. *Career:* Founder mem., Wu-Tang Clan, 1992–; Collaborations: Mariah Carey; GZA; Pras; Mya; Blackstreet; Kelis. *Recordings:* Albums: with Wu-Tang Clan: Enter The Wu-Tang Clan (36 Chambers), 1993; Return To The 36 Chambers, 1995; Wu-Tang Forever, 1997; Nigga Please, 1999; The W, 2001; Solo: The Trials And Tribulations Of Russell Jones, 2002. Singles: with Wu-Tang Clan: Protect Ya Neck, 1993; Shimmy Shimmy Ya, 1995; Triumph, 1997; Gravel Pit, 2000; Uzi (Pinky Ring), 2002; with Kelis: Got Your Money, 1999. *Address:* c/o Elektra Entertainment, 75 Rockefeller Plaza, New York, USA. *Website:* www.loud.com/wu/wu.html.

OLDFIELD, Mike (Michael Gordon); b. 15 May 1953, Reading, Berkshire, England. Musician (multi-instrumentalist); Composer. 3 s., 2 d. *Career:* Two world tours, 10 European tours, numerous world-wide television and radio appearances, including premiere concert of Tubular Bells II, Edinburgh Castle, 1992. *Recordings:* Albums: Tubular Bells (No. 1, UK), 1973; Hergest Ridge (No. 1, UK), 1974; Ommadawn, 1975; Incantations, 1978; Platinum, 1979; QE2, 1980; Five Miles Out, 1982; Crises, 1983; Discovery, 1984; Islands, 1987; Earthmoving, 1989; Amarok, 1990; Heaven's Open, 1991; Tubular Bells II, 1992; Elements, 1994; The Songs of Distant Earth, 1996; Voyager, 1996; XXV The Essential, 1997; Tubular Bells III, 1998; Guitars, 1999; Millennium Bell (album), 1999; Tres Lunas, 2002. Singles include: Tubular Bells, 1974; In Dulce Jubilo/On Horseback, 1975; Portsmouth, 1976; Guilty, 1979; Blue Peter, 1979; Moonlight Shadow, 1983; To France, 1984; Sentinel, 1992; Far Above The Clouds, 1999; Film score: The Killing Fields. *Honours:* Grammy Award, Tubular Bells.

OLIVA, Stéphan; b. 7 Jan. 1959, Montmorency, France. Jazz Musician (piano); Composer. m. Cathy Frantz, 14 Oct. 1982, 1 s. *Education:* Classical training, Ecole Normale De Musique De Paris. *Career:* Teacher, performer, Jah, Grim, Ajmi, Roy Hart Theatre (France); Concerts in jazz festivals with trios (with drums, bass, violin, saxophone); Selected to Biennale Des Jeunes

Createurs D'Europe De La Mediterranée, 1990; Selected to Jeunes Affiches '94, SACEM, 1994; Conferences: History of Jazz Piano, 1995; Trio Jade Visions, tribute to Bill Evans, 1995. *Recordings:* with trio: Novembre, 1991; Jade Visions, 1996; Tristano, 1999; Piano solo: Clair Obscur, 1994. *Honours:* Django D'Or, 1992. *Membership:* Archipel Mozaque (Montpellier). *Current Management:* Michel Lecomte. *Address:* 2 rue du Levant, 93100 Montreuil, France.

OLIVER, Tim; b. 6 Sept. 1959, England. Prod; Engineer. *Education:* BSc, Hons, Geology. *Career:* Freelance Engineer, 1981–; Sound Engineering, 1985–; Producer, 1990–. *Recordings:* Temper Temper, Temper Temper; Northern Soul, M People; Delightful, Happy Mondays; Definition of Sound, Definition of Sound; Superhighways, The Other Two; Gospel Oak, Sinead O'Connor; Live, New Order; Gene; Indigo Girls; Carlos Nunez, Os Amores Libres, 2000. *Contributions to:* Future Music magazine; The Mix magazine; Computer Music magazine. *Membership:* Musicians' Union. *Current Management:* Helium. *Address:* Carol Davies, 33 Salisbury Rd, Bath BA1 6QZ, England.

OLIVOR, Jane; b. 1947, Brooklyn, New York City, New York, USA. Vocalist. *Career:* Began in night clubs in New York City, early 1970s; Signed to Columbia Records, 1976; Cover of Some Enchanted Evening charted just prior to the release of second album, which became a best seller; Played major venues across America; Took long career break owing to husband's illness, and subsequent death in 1986; Returned to live performing, early 1990s; Resumed recording career by signing to Varese Sarabande label, 2000; Continues to tour extensively. *Recordings:* First Night, 1976; Chasing Rainbows, 1977; Stay The Night, 1978; The Best Side of Goodbye, 1980; In Concert, 1982; Love Decides, 2000; Songs Of The Season, 2001. *Current Management:* Ed Keane Associates, 32 St Edward Rd, Boston, MA 02128, USA. *E-mail:* missjaneo@aol.com. *Website:* www.members.com/missjaneo.

OLOMIDE, Koffi (Antoine); b. 13 Aug. 1956, Kisangani, Democratic Republic of Congo. Vocalist; Musician (guitar); Songwriter. *Education:* Commercial Science, Bordeaux; MA, Mathematics, University of Paris. *Career:* Began composing while a student; Composed for: Papa Wemba; Viva La Musica; Zaiko Langa Langa; Defao; Joined Viva La Musica as backing singer, late 1970s; Formed Quartier Latin, 1986; Invented Tcha Tcho style. *Recordings:* Albums include: Kiki Ewing, 1987; Henriquet, 1988; Elle Et Moi, 1989; Tcha Tcho, 1990; Pas De Faux Pas, Diva, 1992; Noblesse Oblige, 1993; Magie, 1994; V12, 1995; Wake Up, 1996; Loi, 1997; Ngounda, Ba La Joie, 1998; Droit De Veto, 1999; Live A Bercy, Force De Frappe, 2000. *Honours:* Best Singer award in Abidjan, 1998; Kora Awards, Best Male African Artist, 1998, 2002, Best Artist–Central Africa, 2002, Best Video–Africa, 2002. *Address:* Sonodisc, 85 rue Fondary, 75015 Paris, France.

OLSDAL, Stefan; b. 31 March 1974, Sweden. Musician (Guitar, Bass, Keyboards). *Career:* Played drums in school orchestra, 1987; Formed Ashtray Heart, with Brian Molko; Formed Placebo with Brian and Robert Schultzberg; Signed record deal, 1996; Numerous television appearances; Live tours and numerous major festival dates. *Recordings:* Singles: Come Home, 1996; 36 Degrees, 1996; Teenage Angst, 1996; Nancy Boy, 1997; Bruise Pristine, 1997; Pure Morning, 1998; You Don't Care About Us, 1998; Every You Every Me, 1999; Without You I'm Nothing, featuring David Bowie, 1999; Taste In Men, 2000; Slave To The Wage, 2000; Albums: Placebo, 1996; Without You I'm Nothing, 1998; Black Market Music, 2000. *Website:* www.placeboworld.co.uk.

OLSEN, Allan; b. 18 March 1956, Frederikshavn, Denmark. Vocalist; Songwriter. *Career:* Intensive touring, from mid-seventies; First, solo; 1988–, with own band; All major festivals, Denmark; Touring clubs all: Denmark; Germany; Iceland; National television programmes; Features in Q. *Recordings:* Norlan, 1989; Gaio, 1991; Pindsvin I Pigsko, 1992; Dalton (with colleagues Johnny Madsen and Lars Liholt), 1994: Dubble Live-Rygter Fra Randområderne. *Honours:* 1 Grammy, 1994; Denmark Labour Union Great Award of Culture. *Membership:* Danish Musicians' Union; DJFBA. *Current Management:* Keiser/Winther Management. *Address:* Mollevej 35, 9520 Skorping, Denmark.

OLSEN, Jørgen; b. 15 March 1950, Odense, Denmark. Vocalist; Musician (guitar); Songwriter. *Career:* Moved to Copenhagen, aged 12; Formed beat group The Kids, aged 15 with brother Noller; Released 3 singles; Supported The Kinks; Group became Olsen, 1970; Starred in Danish production of musical Hair, 1970; Scandinavian pop idol in the 1970s; Worked in education, 1990–94. *Recordings:* Albums (with Noller Olsen): Olsen, 1972; For What We Are, 1973; For The Children of The World (in conjunction with UNICEF), 1973; Back On The Tracks, 1976; You're The One, 1977; San Francisco, 1978; Dans – Dans – Dans, 1979; Rockstalgi, 1987; Greatest and Latest, 1994; Angelina, 1999; Wings of Love, 2000; The Story of The Olsen Brothers, 2000; Rockstalgi, 2001; Neon Madonna, 2001; Walk Right Back, 2001; Songs, 2002; solo: Det Stille Ocean, 1990; numerous Olsen Brothers singles. *Honours:* Eurovision Song Contest winner, Fly On The Wings of Love, 2000. *Current Management:* Steen Wittrock, International Personal Management, Store Kongensgade 46, 1264 Copenhagen K, Denmark. *Telephone:* 33-11-52-25. *Fax:* 33-13-19-50. *E-mail:* ipm-fib@mail.tele.dk.

OLSEN, Keith; b. Sioux Falls, SD, USA. Prod; Musician (bass guitar); Recording Engineer. *Career:* Founding mem., Ragamuffins, 1965, later Music Machine; Engineer, Sound City Studios, Los Angeles; Owner, Goodnight L.A. Studios, Los Angeles; Founder, publishing company, Bursen Music Group, 1996–; Dir, Professional Recording Products Division, Mackie Designs Inc, Seattle, 1999–; Worked with: The Babys, Bad Company, Russ Ballard, Pat Benatar, Kim Carnes, Sheena Easton, Emerson Lake & Palmer, Fleetwood Mac, Foreigner, Lou Gramm, Grateful Dead, Sammy Hagar, Heart, Journey, Loverboy, Eddie Money, Stevie Nicks, Ozzy Osbourne, Steve Perry, REO Speedwagon, Santana, Scorpions, Rick Springfield, Starship, 38 Special, Jethro Tull, Joe Walsh, Bob Weir, Whitesnake; Contributed to movie soundtracks: Flashdance, Footloose, Knotheads, Top Gun, Tron, Vision Quest. *Recordings include:* with Music Machine: Albums: (Turn On) The Music Machine, 1966; Bonniwell Music Machine; Single: Talk Talk, 1966. *Honours:* 39 Gold discs, 24 Platinum discs, 14 multi-Platinum discs. *Address:* c/o Bursen Music Group, 2611 Westwood Dr., Nashville, TN 37204, USA.

OLSEN, Noller (Niels); b. 13 April 1954, Odense, Denmark. Vocalist; Musician (guitar); Songwriter. *Career:* Moved to Copenhagen, aged 8; Formed beat group The Kids, aged 11 with brother Jørgen; Released 3 singles; Supported The Kinks; Group became Olsen, 1970; Appeared in Danish production of musical Hair, 1970; Scandinavian pop idol in the 1970s; Worked in education, 1990–94. *Recordings:* Albums (with Jørgen Olsen): Olsen, 1972; For What We Are, 1973; For The Children of The World (in conjunction with UNICEF), 1973; Back On The Tracks, 1976; You're The One, 1977; San Francisco, 1978; Dans – Dans – Dans, 1979; Rockstalgi, 1987; Greatest and Latest, 1994; Angelina, 1999; Wings of Love, 2000; The Story of The Olsen Brothers, 2000; Rockstalgi, 2001; Neon Madonna, 2001; Walk Right Back, 2001; Songs, 2002; numerous Olsen Brothers singles. *Honours:* Eurovision Song Contest winner, Fly On The Wings of Love, 2000. *Current Management:* Steen Wittrock, International Personal Management, Store Kongensgade 46, 1264 Copenhagen K, Denmark. *Telephone:* 33-11-52-25. *Fax:* 33-13-19-50. *E-mail:* ipm-fib@mail.tele.dk.

OLSON, Carla Beth; b. 3 July 1952, Austin, Texas, USA. Musician (guitar); Vocalist; Songwriter. m. Saul Davis, 7 June 1987. *Career:* Worked with Ry Cooder; Don Henley; Barry Goldberg; Gene Clark; Phil Seymour; Appearances include: Radio City Music Hall, New York; Tours, Europe, Japan; Film soundtrack contributions include: Real Genius; Blue City; Sylvester; Saturday Night Special; A Tiger's Tale. *Compositions:* Why Did You Stop (recorded by Percy Sledge); Number One Is To Survive (recorded with Gene Clark); Trail of Tears (co-writer with Eric Johnson); Midnight Mission (recorded with The Textones); Albums: So Rebellious a Lover, 1986; Too Hot for Snakes, 1991; Live, 1991; Within an Ace, 1993; Reap the Whirlwind, 1994; The Ring Of Truth, 2001; Honest As Daylight, 2001. *Membership:* AFTRA; NARAS; BMI. *Current Management:* Saul Davis Management, 11684 Ventura Blvd #583, Studio City, CA 91604, USA.

OLSSON, Mats Fredrik; b. 3 Nov. 1929, Stockholm, Sweden. Arranger; Composer; Conductor; Prod. m. Maj-Britt Elisabeth, 19 Aug. 1950, 2 s., 2 d. *Education:* BA, University of Stockholm, 1953; Cantors Exam, Uppsala Cathedral, 1948; Royal Academy of Music, Stockholm, 1949–51; Private studies, Counterpoint, Instrumentation, Composing and Conducting, 1950–55. *Career:* Professional Musician, Pianist, 1949–57; Arranger, Conductor, Radio Sweden, Swedish TV and record companies, 1957–; Musical Director, Stockholms Stadteater, 1963–65; Conductor, Eurovision Song Contest, 1966–72; Director, A&R, CBS Records, Sweden, 1970–77; Managing Director, Planet Records and Music, 1977–94; Arranger and composer for TV series, Notknäckarna, 1981–90. *Compositions:* Suite for Orchestra; Riksväg 13; Tunnel banepolka; Lappland; Ballet music; Film music; Pop songs; Adaptions of Swedish folk songs. *Recordings:* With Love From Sweden; LPs and CDs of Swedish pop and light music; Big band recordings; Arranger, Conductor, Producer for recordings by Swedish vocal artistes. *Honours:* SKAP Scholarship, 1959; Fred Winter Scholarship, 1986; Thore Ehrling Scholarship, 1991. *Membership:* STIM; SKAP; SAMI. *Address:* Gryningsvägen 28, 163 51 Spånga, Sweden.

O'MEARA, Joanne V; b. 29 April 1979, Essex, England. Vocalist; Actor. *Career:* Sang in local clubs in Romford, before scoring minor European hit with group 2-4 Family; Pre-fame mem., Solid Harmonie; Mem., S Club 7, 1998–; Group quickly achieved international success, following sales of TV series Miami 7, 1999, LA 7, 2000, and Hollywood 7, 2001, featuring the band's music, to nearly 100 countries; Also made nature TV series, S Club 7 Go Wild, 2000, and various TV specials; First British tour with S Club 7, 2001; Band renamed S Club, 2001. *Recordings:* Albums: S Club, 1999; 7 (No. 1, UK), 2000; Sunshine, 2001; Seeing Double, 2002. Singles: Bring It All Back (No. 1, UK), 1999; S Club Party, 1999; Two In A Million/You're My Number One, 1999; Reach, 2000; Natural, 2000; Never Had A Dream Come True (No. 1, UK), 2000; Don't Stop Movin' (No. 1, UK), 2001; Have You Ever (No. 1, UK), 2001; You, 2002. *Honours:* BRIT Awards, Best British Newcomer, 2000, Best British Single, for Don't Stop Movin', 2002; Record of the Year Award, for Don't Stop Movin', 2001. *Current Management:* 19 Management, Unit 32, Ransomes Dock, 35–37 Parkgate Rd, London SW11 4NP, England. *Website:* www.sclub.com.

ONDREICKA, Karol Michal; b. 3 Nov. 1935, Bratislava, Slovakia. Composer; Arranger; Musician. Divorced, 1 s. *Education:* Master, Philosophy, Faculty of Arts, Comenius University, Bratislava. *Career:* Leader, Combo 4, 1961–66, West Coast Jazz Quintet U5, 1975; Collaborated with Quartet pianist Ladislav Gerhardt, 1970–; Tours of Germany, Austria, Netherlands, Luxembourg, Poland, Switzerland and Greece; Performances at International Jazz Festivals in Prague, Bratislava and Athens; Appearances in clubs and festivals with: B. Rosengreen, H. Sachs, H. Beckmann, H. Koller, L. Harper, K. Wheeler, C. Mariano, W. Lackerschmid and T. Küppers. *Compositions:* The Musical Rabbit, 1974; Music for television series, Boy As Any Other One, 1976; 5-Part Suite From Our Mountains, 1979; Daddy, Mummy and Me, 1979. *Recordings:* with Combo 4: Jazz On The Stage, 1962; with the SP Karol Ondreicka Quartet: Reflections, 1965; with the Karol Ondreicka Trio: Slovak Jazz Mainstream, 1994; with Ladislav Gerhardt Quartet: A Sentimental Trumpet, 1970; Bratislava Jazz Days, 1976–82; Why Did We Get Married?, 1978, We Won't Marry Anymore, 1981. *Honours:* 3 Prizes, Czech Radio Bratislava for Arrangement, 1974, 1975, 1976; Prize, Lifelong Work and Jazz Promotion, Slovak Music Fund, 1990. *Membership:* Council, Music Fund, 1990–; Vice-President, Slovak Jazz Society, 1990–. *Current Management:* MIC, Medena 29, 811 02 Bratislava, Slovakia. *Address:* Azalkova 4, 821 01 Bratislava, Slovakia.

O'NEAL, Alexander; b. 14 Nov. 1954, Natchez, Mississippi, USA. Vocalist. *Career:* Singer, 1972–; Member, Flyte Time; Solo artiste, 1984–; Major concerts world-wide include: Prince's Trust Rock Gala, Birmingham, 1989; Simple Truth, Kurdish refugee benefit concert, Wembley Arena, 1991; World Song-Stylist Live Series, Tokyo, 1991. *Recordings:* Alexander O'Neal, 1985; Hearsay, 1987; My Gift To You, 1988; Hearsay All Mixed Up, 1988; All True Man (No. 2, UK), 1991; This Thing Called Love – Greatest Hits, 1992; Loves Makes No Sense, 1993; Lovers Again, 1997; Appeared on Affair, Cherrelle, 1988; Singles include: If You Were Here Tonight, 1985; A Broken Heart Can Mend, 1985; Saturday Love, 1986; Fake (R&B No. 1, USA), 1987; Criticize, 1987; The Lovers, 1988; What Can I Say To Make You Love Me, 1988; Christmas Song, 1988; Hitmix, 1989; All True Man, 1990; Sunshine, 1989; What Is This Thing Called Love, 1991; Shame On Me, 1991; Sentimental, 1992; Love Makes No Sense, 1992; In The Middle, 1993; All That Matters To Me, 1993; Grind, 1998; Criticize '98, 1998; Criticize '99, 1999; Lord Give Me Power, 1999; Duets with Cherrelle: Innocent, 1985; Never Knew Love Like This, 1987. *Honours:* Platinum disc, Hearsay, 1987. *Current Management:* Kuenstlermarketing GmbH, Hutteldorferstrasse 259/14, 1140 Vienna, Austria.

O'NEILL, Bernard Anthony; b. 4 Sept. 1961, Dublin, Ireland. Musician (double bass, cello, bass guitar, keyboards). *Education:* Associate of Royal Irish Academy of Music and Royal College of Music. *Career:* Teacher, composer, performer; Musical Director for numerous acts including: Rolf Harris; Viv Stanshall; Jon Spencer; Flower Sermon; Aqua Rhythms; Ether; Zumzeaux; Kimbara Brothers; Silly Sisters. *Recordings include:* with Zumzeaux: Wolf At Your Door, Live In Edinburgh; with Silly Sisters: No More To The Dance; with Andrew Cronshaw: The Language of Snakes; with Jon Spencer Band: Parlour Games; Echoes And Whispers, 2001. *Current Management:* Anne Pomerantz, Aqua Rhythms. *Address:* 5009 Riviera, Tampa, FL 33609, USA.

O'NEILL, John; b. 25 Feb. 1955, Romford, Essex, England. Musician (all saxophones, clarinet, flute, piano). m. Sylvie Sims, 26 July 1986, 1 s., 1 d. *Education:* BA, Modern Languages (French, German), Trinity College, Oxford, 1976; PGCE University of Reading, 1984. *Career:* with group Crosscurrents: BBC Radio 2, 1981; Bracknell Jazz Festival, 1983, 1984; Tour, Germany, Blueprint Jazz Orchestra, 1992; Musical director, arranger, saxophonist, Carlton TV series Shine On Harvey Moon, 1995. *Recordings:* Albums: The Jazz Method For Saxophone; The Jazz Method For Clarinet; The Jazz Method For Flute; The Jazz Method For Trumpet. *Publications:* The Jazz Method For Saxophone, 1992; The Jazz Method For Clarinet, 1993; The Jazz Method For Flute, 1994; The Jazz Method For Trumpet (with Steve Waterman), 1995; Also appeared on: Joined Up Talking, My Life Story, 2000. *Membership:* Musicians' Union; Equity. *Current Management:* Helen Stafford Management, 14 Park Ave, Bush Hill Park, Enfield, Middlesex EN1 2HP, England. *Address:* 103 South View Rd, Hornsey, London N8 7LX, England.

O'NEILL, Keith; b. 18 Feb. 1969, Liverpool, England. Musician (Drums). *Career:* Member, Cast; Early gigs supporting Elvis Costello and Oasis; Many headlining tours and festival appearances; Numerous TV appearances and radio sessions. *Recordings:* Singles: Finetime, 1995; Alright, 1995; Sandstorm, 1996; Walkaway, 1996; Flying, 1996; Free Me, 1997; Guiding Star, 1997; Live The Dream, 1997; I'm So Lonely, 1997; Beat Mama, 1999; Magic Hour, 1999; Albums: All Change, 1995; Mother Nature Calls, 1997; Magic Hour, 1999.

ONEIRO. See: CARTER, Derrick.

ONGALA, Remmy, (Ramazani Mtoro Ongala-Mungamba); b. 1947, Kivu, Congo. Vocalist; Musician (guitar); Songwriter. *Career:* Drummer and vocalist with Bantu Success; Later worked with Zairian bands: Success Mwachame; Mickey Jazz; Grand Mike Jazz; Joined Orchestra Makassy in Dar-Es-Salaam, 1978; Joined Orchestre Matimila, renaming it Orchestra Super Matimila; Joined WOMAD tour, 1988; Involved with Spirit of Africa AIDS relief project. *Recordings:* Nalilia Mwana, 1988; Songs For The Poor Man, 1989; Mambo, 1992; The Kershaw Sessions, 1994; Sema, 1996. *Honours:* Zanzibar Film Festival, Golden Dhow Award, Lifetime Achievement in Music.

ONO, Yoko; b. 18 Feb. 1933, Tokyo, Japan. Vocalist; Prod; Actress; Songwriter. m. John Lennon, 20 March 1969, deceased, 1 s. *Career:* Co-host, with John Lennon, Mike Douglas Show, 1972; Producer, film soundtrack, Imagine, 1988. *Recordings:* Albums with John Lennon/Plastic Ono Band include: Two Virgins, 1968; Life With The Lions, 1969; Wedding Album, 1969; Live Peace In Toronto, 1969; Sometime In New York City, 1972; Double Fantasy, 1980; Collection, 1982; Milk and Honey, 1984; Heart Play – Unfinished Dialogue, 1984; Reflections and Poetry, 1984; Solo albums: Fly, 1971; Feeling The Space, 1973; Approximately Infinite Universe, 1973; Seasons of Glass, 1981; It's Alright, 1982; Starpeace, 1985; New York Rock (original cast), 1995; Rising, 1996; A Story, 1997; Blueprint For A Sunrise, 2001. *Address:* c/o The Agency Group Ltd, 1775 Broadway, Suite 433, New York, NY 10019, USA.

ORANGE, Jason; b. 10 July 1970, Manchester, England. Vocalist. *Career:* Mem., UK all-male vocal group, Take That, 1991–96; Television incl.: Take That and Party (Channel 4), 1993; Take That Away documentary (BBC2), 1993; Take That In Berlin, 1994; Killer Net (Channel 4), 1998. *Recordings:* Albums: Take That And Party, 1992; Everything Changes (No. 1, UK), 1993; Nobody Else (No. 1, UK), 1995; Greatest Hits (No. 1, UK), 1996. Singles: Promises, 1991; It Only Takes A Minute, 1992; I Found Heaven, 1992; A Million Love Songs, 1992; Could It Be Magic, 1992; Why Can't I Wake Up With You, 1993; Pray (No. 1, UK), 1993; Relight My Fire (with Lulu, No. 1, UK), 1993; Babe (No. 1, UK), 1993; Everything Changes (No. 1, UK), 1994; Love Ain't Here Anymore, 1994; Sure (No. 1, UK), 1994; Back For Good (No. 1, UK), 1995; Never Forget (No. 1, UK), 1995; How Deep Is Your Love (No. 1, UK), 1996. *Honours:* Seven Smash Hit Awards, 1992; BRIT Award, Best British Single, 1994. *Current Management:* Nigel Martin-Smith, 41 S King St, Manchester M2 6DE, England.

ORBIT, William, (William Wainwright); b. 1 Oct. 1956, England. Prod; Remixer. *Career:* Mem., Torch Song, 1980s; Remixer for artistes incl.: Madonna, Prince, Human League, Erasure, Belinda Carlisle; Recorded own material under names, Strange Cargo, Bass-o-Matic; Founder, O Records. *Recordings:* Albums: with Torch Song: Wish Thing, 1984; Ecstasy, 1986; Toward the Unknown Region, 1995; Solo: Strange Cargo, 1987; Orbit, 1987; Strange Cargo II, 1990; Set The Controls For The Heart Of The Bass, 1990; Science And Melody, 1991; Strange Cargo III, 1993; Trance Europe Express 3, 1994; The Electric Chamber, 1995; Pieces In A Modern Style, 1995; Hinterland, 1995; Best Of Strange Cargo, 1996; Invisible, 1997; Harald (OST), 1997; Audio Visual (compilation), 1998; Pieces In A Modern Style, 2000. Singles: with Torch Song: Prepare to Energise, 1983; Don't Look Now, 1984; Ode to Billy Joe, 1985; Can't Find My Way Home, 1986; Solo: Young Blood (film theme music), 1985; Swamp Dog, 1987; Fool To Myself, 1987; Feel Like Jumping, 1987; Love My Way, 1987; Fire & Mercy, 1989; In The Realm Of The Senses, 1990; Fascinating Rhythm, 1990; Ease On By, 1990; Funky Love Vibrations, 1991; Science And Melody, 1991; Don't Wanna Know 'Bout Evil (as Spill, with Beth Orton), 1992; Go Getta Nutha Man, 1992; Water From A Vine Leaf, 1994; Sampler (as N-Gram Recordings), 1995; El Ninjo, 1995; Million Town, 1995; Scream, 1997; Barber's Adagio For Strings, 1999; Pieces In A Modern Style, 2000; Pavane Pour Une Infante Défunte, 2000. As remixer and prod.: S Express, Hey Music Lover, 1989; Prince, The Future, 1989; Jimmy Somerville, You Make Me Feel Mighty Real, 1989; The Cure, In Between Days, 1990; Oleta Adams, Circle Of One, 1990; Kraftwerk, Radioactivity, 1991; Seal, Killer, Crazy, 1991; The Shamen, Hyperreal, 1991; Madonna, Justify My Love, Erotica, 1992; Peter Gabriel, Us, 1992; Beth Orton, SuperPinkyMandy, 1993; One Dove, Breakdown, 1993; Kiss That Frog, 1993, Blood Of Eden, 1993; Depeche Mode, Walking In My Shoes, 1993; 18 Wheeler, The Hours And The Times, 1997; Dreadzone, Earth Angel, 1997; Blur, Bustin' and Dronin', 1998; Madonna, Ray Of Light (album), Frozen, Ray Of Light, The Power Of Goodbye, 1998; Melanie C., Northern Star, 1999; Sasha, Global Underground, 1999; Madonna, American Pie (No. 1, UK), 2000; All Saints, Pure Shores (No. 1, UK), 2000; Black Coffee (No. 1, UK), 2000. *Address:* c/o WEA Records, Time Warner, 75 Rockefeller Plaza, New York, NY 10019, USA. *Website:* www.williamorbit.com.

ORCHIN, Mark Alan; b. 3 Oct. 1957, London, England. Semi-professional Musician (guitar). m. Valerie Orchin, 6 Oct. 1979, 1 s., 1 d. *Career:* Lead guitar, late 70s band Possum and various pub, club bands; Currently playing folk/rock, guitar, mandolin with Touchstone; Playing for festivals, theatres, BBC Southern Counties; Recently played at Buddy Guy's, Chicago, USA; Duo with singer Bonnie Burden. *Recordings:* Albums: with Touchstone: The Night The Snow Came Down, 1991; One The Rum, 1995; Silently Calling, 1998; Wine Barrel Jigtarrel, 2001; Principal writer of all 4 albums. *Membership:* Musicians' Union. *Current Management:* Allwood Music. *Address:* PO Box 348, Haywards Heath, West Sussex RH17 7RB, England.

ORFORD, Tim; b. 10 March 1964, Cambridge, England. Sound Engineer; Programmer. *Education:* BSc Electronic Engineering. *Recordings:* Dina Carroll; EYC; Young Disciples; Carleen Anderson; Billie Curry; West End; Outlaw Posse; Watergates; Brand New Heavies; S'Express; PJ and Duncan; Sandals; Mary Kiani; Kym Mazelle; Marshall Jefferson; Alex Party; Mike; Rebecca Ryan; Grace; Kicks Like A Mule; Greatest 90s Dance Hits, 1996; Massive Dance Mix '96, 1996; Glen Scott, Without Vertigo, 1999; Kylie Minogue, Fever, 2001. *Address:* The Flat, Thornton, Kingston Hill, Kingston Upon Thames, Surrey KT2 7JX, England.

ORIGJANSKI; b. 13 Nov. 1963, Skopje, Macedonia. m. Magda Origjanska, 1 d. *Career:* Member, band Anastasia; Recorded 4 albums; Numerous concerts; Work on film Before The Rain. *Recordings:* Albums: Ikon; Mansarda; Before The Rain; Melourgia. *Honours:* Golden Lion Award, Venice, 1994. *Current Management:* Ivo Jankoski.

O'RIORDAN BURTON, Dolores Mary; b. 6 Sept. 1971, Limerick, Ireland. Vocalist; Songwriter; Musician (guitar, keyboards). m. Don Burton, July 1994. *Career:* Mem., lead singer, The Cranberries, 1990–; Numerous headlining tours, festivals, radio and television appearances. *Recordings:* Albums: with The Cranberries: Everybody Else Is Doing It, So Why Can't We? (No. 1, UK), 1993; No Need To Argue, 1994; To The Faithful Departed, 1996; Bury The Hatchet, 1999; Bury The Hatchet: The Complete Sessions, 2000; Wake Up And Smell The Coffee, 2001; Treasure Box, 2002; Stars: The Best Of 1992–2002, 2002; with Jah Wobble: Sun Does Rise, 1994; with Devil's Own: Devil's Own, 1997; with Amazing Grace: Amazing Grace, 1997; Legacy: A Tribute to Fleetwood Mac, 1998. Singles: Dreams, 1993; Linger, 1993; Zombie, 1994; Ode To My Family, 1994; I Can't Be With You, 1995; Ridiculous Thoughts, 1995; Salvation, 1996; Free To Decide, 1996; Promises, 1999; Animal Instinct, 1999; Just My Imagination, 1999; You And Me, 2000; Analyse, 2001; Time Is Ticking Out, 2002; This Is The Day, 2002; Stars, 2002. *Current Management:* Timeless Music Ltd. *Address:* The Cranberries, PO Box 180, Limerick, Ireland. *Website:* www.cranberries.com.

ORLANDO, Tony, (Michael Anthony Orlando Cassivitis); b. 3 April 1944, Manhattan, New York, USA. Vocalist. *Career:* Demo singer, 1960; Worked for music publishers, 1963–70; Lead singer, trio Dawn (later billed as Tony Orlando and Dawn), 1970–77; Own television series, CBS, 1974–75; Solo artiste, 1977–; Actor, television film: Three Hundred Miles For Stephanie, 1979; Lead role, musical, Barnum, 1981; Dawn reunion, 1990. *Recordings:* Hit singles with Dawn include: Candida, 1970; Knock Three Times (No. 1, USA and UK), 1971; What Are You Doing Sunday, 1971; Tie A Yellow Ribbon Round The Old Oak Tree (No. 1, UK and USA), 1973; Say Has Anybody Seen My Sweet Gipsy Rose, 1973; Steppin' Out (Gonna Boogie Tonight), 1974; He Don't Love You (Like I Love You) (No. 1, USA), 1975; Look In My Eyes Pretty Woman, 1975; Mornin' Beautiful, 1975; Cupid, 1976; Albums: Candida, 1970; Dawn Featuring Tony Orlando, 1971; Tuneweaving, 1973; Dawn's New Ragtime Follies, 1973; Golden Ribbons, 1974; Prime Time, 1974; Tony Orlando and Dawn II, 1975; He Don't Love You (Like I Love You), 1975; Greatest Hits, 1975; Skybird, 1975; To Be With You, 1976; Bless You and 17 Other Great Hits, 1997; Knock Three Times: Greatest Hits, 1997; Definitive Collection, 1998; Knock Three Times: Encore Collection, 1999. *Honours:* American Music Awards: Favorite Single, 1974; Favorite Pop/Rock Group, 1976; Tie A Yellow Ribbon Round The Old Oak Tree named one of BMI's Most Performed Songs, 1940–90, 1990. *Address:* c/o William Morris Agency, 1350 Avenue of the Americas, New York, NY 10019, USA.

O'ROURKE, Jim; *Career:* Collaborated with Sonic Youth, 1997, joined band, 2001. *Recordings:* Album: Murray Street, 2002. *Address:* c/o Smells Like Records, PO Box 6179, Hoboken, NJ 07030, USA. *Website:* www.sonicyouth.com.

OROZCO, Richard Gomez; b. 5 March 1973, San Antonio, Texas, USA. Vocalist; Songwriter; Musician. *Education:* Nuclear Medicine, Biology, Belmont University. *Career:* Music City Tonight, 1995; Austin City Limits, 1995. *Compositions:* Life Is Good; I Wish He Wouldn't Treat Her That Way. *Recordings:* Buscando Una Estrella, 1996; Don't Try To Find Me, 1998. *Current Management:* Refugee Management Inc. *Address:* c/o 209 10th Ave S, Cummins Station, Suite 347, Nashville, TN 37203, USA.

ORR EWING, Alastair; b. 28 Nov. 1964, Netheravon, England. Musician (harmonica); Teacher. *Education:* Aberdeen University, 1983–86; Studied under David Michelson, also known as Dr Midnight. *Career:* Rasp, Rebel Yell, National Student band Final, The Powerhaus, Islington, London, 1993; Glastonbury Cabaret Stage, harmonica duo 'et al', theatre stage with Midnight Specials harmonica band, June 1994. *Honours:* Runner-up, British Harmonica Championships, 1994; Accredited teacher, National Harmonica League. *Membership:* Musicians' Union. *Address:* 20 Santley St, London SW4 7BQ, England.

ORRALL, Robert Ellis; b. 4 May 1955, Winthrop, USA. Songwriter; Prod; Vocalist; Musician. *Career:* Artiste, RCA, 1980–84, 1991–93, Giant, 1993–94; Songwriter, Warner Brothers, 1980–84, Zomba, 1987–88, BMG, 1989–91, EMI, 1991–; Producer, Flying Colors, 1991, Orrall and Wright, 1993, Michael Peterson, 1997. *Compositions:* Next To You, Next To Me, 1990; What's It To You, 1994, 1997; From Here to Eternity, 1997. *Recordings:* Sweet Nothing, 1979; Fixation, 1981; Special Pain, 1982; Contain Yourself, 1984; Flying Colors, 1991; Orrall and Wright, 1993; Mistakes, 1998; with Michael Peterson: Michael Peterson, 1997; Drink, Swear, Steal and Lie, 1997; Being Human, 1999; with Wedding Day Music, Wedding Day Music, 1998; with Yankee Grey, All Things Considered, 1999; Untamed, 1999. *Honours:* ASCAP Country Awards, 1990, 1993, 1994; CMA Number One Awards, 1990, 1993, 1997; CMA Vocal Duo of the Year Finalist, 1994; World Festival Charleston Grand Award, Best Music Video, 1994; ASCAP Pop Award, 1995. *Membership:* ASCAP; AFTRA; CMA. *Current Management:* Alison Averbach Public Relations, 1229 17th Ave S, Nashville, TN 37212, USA. *Address:* 35 Music Sq. E, Nashville, TN 37203, USA.

ORTI, Guillaume; b. 8 Dec. 1969, Nyons, France. Musician (alto, soprano saxophone). *Career:* Member, Kartet; Urban Mood; Paintings; Altissimo; Frequent work with theatre and dance companies; Played with Steve Argüelles; Marc Ducret; Aldo Romano; Steve Lacy; Dominique Pifarely; Thierry Madiot; Noël Akchoté; Benoît Delbecq. *Recordings:* 22 include: Altissimo; With Kartet: Hask; Pression. *Membership:* Collectif HASK. *Address:* 4 rue Bretonneau, 75020 Paris, France.

ORTMANN, Carsten; b. 4 Aug. 1965, Copenhagen, Denmark. Television Prod; Musician (drums); Vocalist. *Education:* MA, Aesthetics and Culture, University of Århus; Singing, drumming and piano lessons; Institute of Music, University of Århus, three years. *Career:* Drummer in Picnic, 1986–96; Drums and percussion, Hunk Ai, 1986–89; Founder, drummer and singer, Fullface Storband, 1987–89; Drums, percussion and backing vocals, Shirtsville, 1989–91; Percussion and backing vocals, Tintin og HårtGirrerne, 1993–95; Singer, Guttermændene, 1989–. *Recordings:* with Hunk Ai: Hunk Ai, 1986; Alene Hjemme, 1989; with Picnic: Barking Up the Wrong Tree, 1987; Meat King, 1990; Reverse Ahead, 1992; Lemming Nation, 1995; with Shirtsville: Secrets 3, 1990; Girls Deserve the Best, 1991; with Tintin og Hårtgirrerne: Dance Crazy, 1994; Mad Guppies Fighting the Food Chain, 1995. *Address:* Nírreallé 30, 2 tv, 8000 Århus C, Denmark.

ORTON, Beth; b. Dec. 1970, Norwich, England. Vocalist; Songwriter; Musician (guitar). *Career:* Member of Duo, Spill; Appeared with group, Red Snapper; Worked with Chemical Brothers; Formed backing band with Ali Friend on double bass, Ted Barnes on guitar, Lee Spencer on keyboards and Wildcat Will on drums; Began to release own records; Worked with Terry Callier; Numerous live appearances and appearances at festivals including Cambridge Folk Festival with own band. *Recordings:* Singles: She Cries Your Name, 1997; Touch Me With Your Love, 1997; Someone's Daughter, 1997; Best Bit, 1997; Stolen Car, 1999; Concrete Sky, 2002. Albums: Trailer Park, 1996; Central Reservation, 1999; Central Reservation, 1999; Daybreaker, 2002; Guest Vocalist: Strange Cargo, Water From a Vine Leaf EP, William Orbit, 1994; Exit Planet Dust, Chemical Brothers, 1995; Hinterland, Strange Cargo, 1995; Plastic Compilation Vol. 2, 1998; Backing vocals on: Midnite Vultures, Beck, 1999; Lifetime, Terry Callier, 1999. *Honours:* BRIT Award, Best British Female Solo Artist, 2000. *Address:* c/o Astralwerks Records, 104 W 29th St, Fourth Floor, New York, NY 10001, USA. *Website:* www.bethorton.mu.

ORTON, Kenneth; b. 26 March 1934, Bedworth, Warwickshire, England. Musician (saxophones, woodwind); Teacher; Arranger; Writer. m. Jean Finlay, 1 June 1960, deceased 7 Dec. 1996, 1 d. *Education:* Technical College C&G; Dip Hons, London Art College; LLCM TD, London College of Music. *Career:* Qualified Electrical Engineer, 1955; Army Band, 1955–58; Performed with name Big Bands including: Syd Dean; Ken Turner; Geraldo; Soul Bands include: Ray King; Tours with name artistes, 1960s; Formed Don Ellis Connection Big Band, only band dedicated to the late Jazz Star; Retired from teaching, 1998; Re-formed Don Ellis Connection Orchestra, 1999. *Compositions:* 2 songs, recorded by Ray King; Major work reconstructing Don Ellis scores; Rearrange and set to lyrics (SATB choir) certain Ellis material, establish Don Ellis library in UK, personal interviews with jazz stars; Reconstructed all Ellis 1960s vocal arrangements for Karin Krog, and presented concert for Karin Krog, 1994. *Publications:* Don Ellis' Jazz Journal; Encyclopaedia of Pop Music; Who's Who In Jazz; Album liner notes. *Address:* 46 Coventry Rd, Bedworth, Warwickshire CV12 8NN, England. *E-mail:* k.orton@ntlworld.com.

ORZABAL, Roland; b. 22 Aug. 1961, Portsmouth, Hampshire, England. Vocalist; Songwriter; Musician (guitar, keyboards); Record Prod. *Career:* Member, ska group The Graduate; Founder member, Tears For Fears (with Curt Smith), 1981–; International tours include: Support to Thompson Twins, UK, 1982; British tour, 1985; US tour, 1990. *Compositions include:* Everybody Wants To Run The World (amended from hit single), theme for Sport Aid famine relief, 1986; Writer, producer (with Smith), Oleta Adams' album, Circle of One, 1990. *Recordings:* Albums: The Hurting, 1983; Songs From The Big Chair, 1985; The Seeds of Love (No. 1, UK), 1989; Tears Roll Down – Greatest Hits 82–92, 1992; Elemental, 1993; Raoul and The Kings of Spain, 1995; Saturnine, Martial and Lunatic, 1996; Songs from Big Chair, 1999; Hurting, 1999; Seeds of Love, 1999; with Oleta Adams, The Very Best of

Oleta Adams, 1998; Singles include: Pale Shelter, 1982; Mad World, 1982; Change, 1983; Mother's Talk, 1984; Shout (No. 1, USA), 1985; Everybody Wants To Rule The World (No. 1, USA), 1985; Head Over Heels, 1985; I Believe, 1985; Sowing The Seeds of Love, 1989; Woman In Chains (featuring Oleta Adams), 1989; Laid So Low, 1992; Breakdown, 1993; Break It Down Again, 1993; Raoul and The Kings of Spain, 1995; Secrets, 1996; Solo album: Tomcats Screaming Outside, 2001. *Honours:* Smash Hits Award, Most Promising New Act, 1982; BRIT Award, Best British Single, 1985; Ivor Novello Award, Songwriter of the Year, 1986; BMI Performance awards, Head Over Heels, 1991. *Current Management:* Debrah Baum, Whirlwind Entertainment, 15025 Greenleaf St, Sherman Oaks, CA 91403, USA.

OSBORN, Kassidy; b. Magna, Utah, USA. Country vocalist. *Career:* Member, country group SheDaisy (with sisters Kristyn and Kelsi). *Recordings include:* Little Good-Byes, 1999; Albums include: The Whole Shebang, 1999; Brand New Year, 2001; Knock On The Sky, 2002. *Address:* c/o PO Box 150638, Nashville, TN 37215–0638, USA. *Website:* www.shedaisy.com.

OSBORN, Kelsi; b. Magna, Utah, USA. Country vocalist. *Career:* Member, country group SheDaisy (with sisters Kassidy and Kristyn). *Recordings include:* Little Good-Byes, 1999; Albums include: The Whole Shebang, 1999; Brand New Year, 2001; Knock On The Sky, 2002. *Address:* c/o PO Box 150638, Nashville, TN 37215–0638, USA. *Website:* www.shedaisy.com.

OSBORN, Kristyn; b. Magna, Utah, USA. Country vocalist; Songwriter. *Career:* Member and lead vocalist, country group SheDaisy (with sisters Kassidy and Kelsi). *Recordings include:* Little Good-Byes, 1999; Albums include: The Whole Shebang, 1999; Brand New Year, 2001; Knock On The Sky, 2002. *Address:* c/o PO Box 150638, Nashville, TN 37215–0638, USA. *Website:* www.shedaisy.com.

OSBORNE, Jeffrey; b. 9 March 1948, Providence, Rhode Island, USA. Vocalist; Prod; Songwriter. *Career:* Singer, LTD (Love Togetherness and Devotion), 1970–82; Solo artiste, 1982–. *Recordings:* Albums: Jeffrey Osborne, 1982; Stay With Me Tonight, 1983; Don't Stop, 1984; Emotional, 1986; One Love One Dream, 1988; Only Human, 1991; Something Warm for Christmas, 1997; Ultimate Collection, 1999; That's for Sure, 2000; Can't Go Back on a Promise, 2000; Hit singles include: On The Wings of Love, 1982; Stay With Me Tonight, 1984; You Should Be Mine, 1986; Love Power (duet with Dionne Warwick), 1990; As singer and producer: Looking For Trouble, Joyce Kennedy, 1984. *Current Management:* Jack Nelson and Associates, PO Box 3718, Los Angeles, CA 90078–3718, USA.

OSBORNE, Joan; b. Anchorage, Kentucky, USA. Vocalist; Songwriter. *Career:* Performer, New York blues circuit, 1988; Solo recording artiste; Concerts include: Earth Day Concert with Midnight Oil, New York; Own record label, Womanly Hips Music. *Recordings:* Albums: Relish, 1995; Righteous Love, 2000; How Sweet It Is, 2002; Appeared with artistes including: Blues Traveller, 1990; Cracker, 1996; Spearhead, 1997; Randy Scruggs, 1998; Indigo Girls, 1999; Single: One of Us, 1995. *Address:* c/o DAS Communications, 83 Riverside, New York, NY 10024, USA.

OSBORNE, John Michael; b. 28 Sept. 1960, London, England. Agent; Record Co Owner. *Education:* Royal College of Art. *Career:* Owner, Slate Records; Own Management Company, John Osborne Management, looking after many top radio DJs. *Honours:* BEDA DJ of the Year, 1992; Disco International, 1992. *Current Management:* John Osborne Management. *Address:* PO Box 173, New Malden, Surrey KT3 3YR, England.

OSBORNE, Pete; b. 15 Sept. 1957, London, England. Musician (saxophones: alto, soprano, clarinet) Composer. m. Sally Bowring, 2 April 1983. *Education:* Studied with Professor Malcolm Ellingworth, classical, jazz, clarinet, saxophone. *Career:* Worked in: England; USA; Denmark; Belgium; Germany; Sweden; Italy; France; Concerts with: Herb Jeffries; Andy Sheppard; John Taylor, 1980; Georgie Fame; Andy Sheppard; Spirit Level, 1985; Bobby Shew; Mark Murphy, 1986; Radio broadcasts: with Rhythm Machine, Nightride, BBC Radio 2, 1987; with Lars Sjosten Trio, Radio Stockholm, 1989; Moved to Paris, concert with Liz McComb, 1991; 2 television shows: Taratata; Cercle De Minuit; 1 radio show, Billy Paul (Me and Mrs Jones), 1994; Concert, Elton John (MCM TV), Paris, 1995. *Compositions:* Jazz suite for Paris, and 50 original compositions (to be released) for jazz sextet. *Recordings:* with Billy Joel: Just The Way You Are, 1979; with James Brown: Album and video, 1991; Vanessa Paradis, 1992; Mc Solaar (Caroline Re-mix), 1993; with Cat Stevens: album, 1994; with Abbey Lincoln Trio: title film track, Tom Est Tout Seul, 1994. *Honours:* Best Saxophone Player, SW England, Bath Evening Chronicle, 1985, 1986, 1987. *Membership:* Musicians' Union, London; SACEM, France; SPEDIDAM. *Current Management:* Guy Fletcher. *Address:* 10 Margaret St, London W1N 7LF, England.

OSBOURNE, Ozzy (John); b. 3 Dec. 1948, Aston, Warwickshire, England. Vocalist. m. Sharon Arden, 4 July 1982, 1 d., 1 s. *Career:* Vocalist, Black Sabbath (formerly Earth), 1967–79; Numerous concerts world-wide include: Madison Square Garden, New York, 1975; Reunion concerts include: Live Aid, Philadelphia, 1985; Solo artiste, with own backing band Blizzard of Ozz,

1979–; US Festival, 1983; Rock In Rio festival, 1984; Monsters of Rock Festival, Castle Donington, 1986; Moscow Music Peace Festival, 1989; No More Tears world tour, 1992; Created highly successful yearly touring festival, Ozzfest, 1996; Has recorded with artistes including: Alice Cooper, Motörhead, Ringo Starr, Rick Wakeman; Television documentary series, The Osbournes, about the Osbourne family, MTV, 2002, second series due, 2003. *Recordings:* Hit singles: with Black Sabbath include: Paranoid; Iron Man; War Pigs; Never Say Die; Solo/with Blizzard of Ozz: Mr Crowley, 1980; Crazy Train, 1980; Bark At The Moon, 1983; So Tired, 1984; Shot In The Dark, 1986; The Ultimate Sin, 1986; Close My Eyes Forever, duet with Lita Ford, 1989; No More Tears, 1991; Perry Mason, 1995; Albums: with Black Sabbath: Black Sabbath, 1969; Paranoid, 1970; Sabbath Bloody Sabbath, 1973; Sabotage, 1975; Technical Ecstasy, 1976; Never Say Die, 1978; Numerous compilations; with Blizzard of Ozz/solo: Blizzards of Ozz, 1980; Diary of a Madman, 1981; Talk of The Devil, 1982; Bark At The Moon, 1983; The Ultimate Sin, 1986; Tribute, 1987; No Rest For The Wicked, 1988; Just Say Ozzy, 1990; No More Tears, 1991; Live and Loud, 1993; Ozzmosis, 1995; The Ozzman Cometh, 1997; OzzFest Vol. 1: Live, 1997; Diary of a Madman/Bark at the Moon/Ultimate, 1998; Down To Earth, 2001. *Honours:* Grammy Award, 1994, 2000. *Current Management:* Sharon Osbourne Management, PO Box 15397, Beverly Hills, CA 90209, USA.

OSCAR; b. South Africa. DJ; Musician. *Career:* Founding mem., kwaito band, Bongo Maffin, 1996–; World Wild Grooves tour, France, 2000; Performances in UK, Denmark, 2000; worked with: Skunk Anansie, Chaka Khan, Stevie Wonder, Boys II Men, Hugh Masekela. *Recordings:* Albums: Final Entry, 1996; The Concerto, 1998; IV, 1999; Bongolution, 2001. *Honours:* South African Music Award, Best Kwaito Artist, 1999; Kora Award, Best African Group, 2001; Gold disc, for Bongolution. *Address:* c/o Sony Music South Africa, 230 Jan Smuts Ave, Dunkeld West, 2196 Gauteng, South Africa.

OSLIN, K. T. (Kay Toinette); b. Crossett, Arkansas, USA. Country Music Vocalist; Songwriter; Actress. *Education:* Theatre Studies, Lon Morris College, Texas. *Career:* College drama; Folk singer in Houston; Touring and Broadway productions of: Hello Dolly; Promises, Promises; West Side Story; Began songwriting, 1978; Backing singer for Guy Clark; Signed Elektra Records, 1981; RCA Records, 1986; Fastest selling, highest charting country music debut album by woman (80s Ladies); Television appearances: Johnny Carson; Joan Rivers; Arsenio Hall; Oprah Winfrey; Own television specials; Television acting roles: Paradise; Evening Shade; Poisoned By Love; Film acting: The Thing Called Love; Host of Country Music Aids; Several Television commercials; Benefit concerts, 1993, 1994. *Compositions:* Songs: Do Ya?; Round The Clock Lovin'; Where Is A Woman To Go; 80s Ladies; Hold Me; Come Next Monday; Younger Men. *Recordings:* Albums include: 80s Ladies, 1988; This Woman, 1989; Love In A Small Town, 1990 (all sold 1m.); My Roots are Showing, 1996; Super Hits, 1997; At Her Best, 1998; Live Close By, Visit Often, 2001; Single: Hold Me, 1999. *Honours:* 3 Grammy Awards; Best Female Vocalist, CMA, 1988; Song of the Year, CMA 1988; Best Female Country Vocalist, ACM, 1989. *Current Management:* Moress-Nanas Management, 1102 18th Ave S, Nashville, TN 37212, USA.

OSMAN, Mat; b. 9 Oct. 1967, Welwyn Garden City, England. Musician (bass). *Career:* Mem., Geoff, 1985; Mem., Suave and Elegant, 1989; Mem., Suede, 1990–; Concerts include: Glastonbury Festival; Tours, UK, Europe; America; Japan; Television appearances include: Top of the Pops, BBC1; Later With Jools Holland, BBC2; The Beat, ITV; The Tonight Show, NBC; 12th BRIT Awards, Alexandra Palace, London. *Recordings:* Albums: Suede (No. 1, UK), 1993; Dog Man Star, 1994; Coming Up, 1996; Sci-Fi Lullabies, 1997; Head Music, 1999; A New Morning, 2002. Singles: The Drowners, 1992; Metal Mickey, 1992; Animal Nitrate, 1993; So Young, 1993; Stay Together, 1994; We Are The Pigs, 1994; The Wild Ones, 1994; New Generation, 1995; Trash, 1996; Beautiful Ones, 1996; Saturday Night, 1997; Lazy, 1997; Filmstar, 1997; Electricity, 1999; She's In Fashion, 1999; Everything Will Flow, 1999; Can't Get Enough, 1999; Positivity, 2002; Obsessions, 2002. *Honours:* Mercury Music Prize, 1993. *Current Management:* Interceptor Enterprises, The Greenhouse, 34–38 Provost St, London N1 7NG, England. *Address:* c/o Sony Music Entertainment, European Regional Office, 10 Great Marlborough St, London W1F 7LP, England. *Website:* www.suede.net.

OSMOND, Donny (Donald Clark); b. 9 Dec. 1957, Ogden, Utah, USA. Vocalist. m. Debra Glenn, 8 May 1978, 3 c. *Education:* Brigham Young University. *Career:* Singer with The Osmonds, from age 4, 1963–80; Solo singer, 1971–78, 1988–; Duo with sister Marie; Television includes: Co-star, Donny and Marie TV show, 1976–79; Osmonds Family show, 1980; Film appearance with Marie: Goin' Coconuts, 1978; Head of own television production company Night Star, 1980s; Also satellite television entrepreneur; Stage role, Joseph and His Amazing Technicolour Dreamcoat, Toronto, 1992–93. *Recordings include:* Singles: with The Osmonds: You Are My Sunshine; One Bad Apple (No. 1, USA); Yo-Yo; Down By The Lazy River; Crazy Horses; Goin' Home; Love Me For A Reason (No. 1, UK); Solo: Sweet and Innocent; Go Away Little Girl (No. 1, USA); Hey Girl; Puppy Love (No. 1, UK); Too Young; Why; Young Love (No. 1, UK); The Twelfth of Never (No. 1, UK); I'm In It For Love; Soldier of Love (No. 2, USA); with Marie Osmond: Make The World Go Away; I'm Leaving It All Up To You; Morning Side of The

Mountain; with Dweezil Zappa: Staying Alive, 1991; Albums: Numerous albums with The Osmonds; Solo albums: The Donny Osmond Album, 1971; Too Young, 1972; Portrait of Donny, 1972; My Best To You, 1972; Alone Together, 1973; A Time For Us, 1973; Love Me For A Reason, 1974; Donny, 1974; Discotrain, 1976; Donald Clark Osmond, 1977; Eyes Don't Lie, 1990; Christmas at Home, 1998; This Is The Moment, 2001; with Marie Osmond: I'm Leaving It All Up To You, 1974; Make The World Go Away, 1975; Donny and Marie – Featuring Songs From Their Television Show, 1976; Deep Purple, 1976; Donny and Marie: New Season, 1998; Goin' Coconuts, 1998; Contributor, Voice That Cares, American Red Cross charity record. *Honours:* Georgie Award, Best Vocal Team, with Marie Osmond, 1978; Numerous Gold discs. *Current Management:* Jill Willis, Renaissance Management, 1571 Lake Lucy Rd, Excelsior, MN 55331, USA.

OSMOND, Jimmy; b. 16 April 1963, Canoga Park, California, USA. Vocalist; Businessman. *Career:* Major UK hit with Long-Haired Lover From Liverpool, 1972; Rock impressario and restaurateur; Owner, Oz-Art advertising and design company; Promoter, Prince's Far East Tour; Assistant, Michael Jackson's Bad world tour; Owner, Osmond's family film and video centre, Utah, 1988–. *Recordings:* Singles: Long-Haired Lover From Liverpool (UK No. 1, 5 weeks), 1972; Tweedle Dee (No. 4, UK), 1973; I'm Gonna Knock On Your Door, 1974; Shine, 2001; Album: Killer Joe, 1973; Little Arrows, 1975. *Honours:* Youngest solo artiste (age 9) to top UK chart, 1972.

OSMOND, Marie; b. 13 Oct. 1959, Ogden, Utah, USA. Vocalist. m. (1) Stephen Craig, 1982 (divorced); (2) Brian Blosil, 28 Oct. 1986, 1 s., 2 d. *Career:* Member, family singing group The Osmonds, 1966–73; Also solo artiste, 1973–; Member, duo with brother Donny Osmond; Numerous television appearances include: Donny and Marie Show, 1976–79; Osmond Family Show, 1980; Marie, NBC, 1980; Maybe This Time, 1995; Donny & Marie, 1998–2000; Several Osmonds Christmas specials; Film appearance with Donny, Goin' Coconuts, 1978. *Recordings:* Singles with Donny Osmond: I'm Leaving It All Up To You (No. 2, UK); Morning Side of The Mountain; Make The World Go Away; Ain't Nothing Like The Real Thing; (You're My) Soul and Inspiration; Solo singles include: Paper Roses (No. 2, UK); Let Me In (No. 2, UK); You're Still New To Me; What Kind of Man; Albums with Donny Osmond: I'm Leaving It Up To You, 1974; Make The World Go Away, 1975; Donny and Marie – Songs From Their Television Show, 1976; Deep Purple, 1976; Donny and Marie – A New Season, 1977; Winning Combination, 1978; Solo albums include: Paper Roses, 1974; In My Little Corner of The World, 1974; Who's Sorry Now, 1975; This Is The Way That I Feel, 1977; I Only Wanted You, 1987; 25 Hits Special Collection, 1995. *Honours:* American Music Award, Best Country Band, Duo or Group, with Donny Osmond, 1976; Georgie Award, Best Vocal Team, with Donny Osmond, 1978; Best Country Duo of Year, with Dan Seals, 1986; Roy Acuff Community Service Award, 1988. *Current Management:* United Management, Suite 150, 3325 N University Ave, Provo, UT 84604, USA.

OSTERMANN, Flemming; b. 2 June 1947, Århus, Denmark. Musician (guitar); Vocalist; Prod. m. Annette Stenbjoern, 15 Aug. 1988, 2 s., 1 d. *Education:* Associate Professor, Rhythmic Music Conservatory, Copenhagen. *Career:* Tours with: Savage Rose, 1969–70; Cox Orange, 1972–76; Anne Linnet Band, 1977–80; Billy Cross and All Stars, 1980–95. *Recordings:* with Savage Rose; Cox Orange; Anne Linnet; Pia Raug; Billy Cross; Jens Rugsted; As producer: Keep The Light In Your Eyes, Lysdal & Rasmussen, 2000. *Publications:* Rhythmic Guitar For Beginners, 1995. *Membership:* Danish Music Society; DJBFA. *Address:* Brumleby 25, 2100 Copenhagen O, Denmark.

O'SULLIVAN, Gilbert (Raymond); b. 1 Dec. 1946, Waterford, Ireland. Vocalist; Musician (piano). *Education:* Art College, England. *Career:* Solo recording artiste, 1970–. *Recordings:* Albums: Himself, 1971; Back To Front, 1972; I'm A Writer Not A Fighter, 1973; Stranger In My Own Backyard, 1974; Greatest Hits, 1976; Southpaw, 1977; Odd Centre, 1980; 20 Golden Hits, 1981; 20 of The Very Best, 1981; Life and Rhymes, 1982; 20 Golden Pieces of Gilbert O'Sullivan, 1985; 16 Golden Classics, 1986; Frobisher Drive, 1988; Sounds of The Loop, 1993; Every Song Has Its Play, 1995; Live In Japan, 1993; By Larry, 1994; Singer Sowing Machine, 1998; Little Album, 2001; Singles include: Nothing Rhymed, 1970; We Will, 1971; No Matter How I Try, 1971; Alone Again (Naturally), (No. 1, USA), 1972; Ooh-Wakka-Doo-Wakka-Day, 1972; Clair (No. 1, UK), 1972; Get Down (No. 1, UK), 1973; Ooh Baby, 1973; Why Oh Why Oh Why, 1973; Happiness Is Me and You, 1974; Christmas Song, 1974; I Don't Love You But I Think I Like You, 1975; What's In A Kiss?, 1980. *Address:* c/o Park Promotions, PO Box 651k, Oxford OX2 9RB, England.

OTIS, Johnny, (John Veliotes); b. 28 Dec. 1921, Vallejo, California, USA. Musician (drums, piano, vibes); Bandleader; Record Co Owner; Songwriter; Promoter; Radio DJ; Talent Scout; Author. m. Phyllis Otis, 1941, 5 s., 3 d. *Career:* Drummer, Count Otis Matthew's West Oakland House Rockers, 1939; Member, Harlan Leonard's Kansas City Rockers, 1943; Founder, Barrelhouse R&B nightclub, Los Angeles (with Bardu Ali), 1948; Founder, California Rhythm and Blues Caravan group; DJ, central Californian radio stations KPFA, KPFB and KFCF, 1950s–; Host, television series, Johnny Otis Show, 8 years; Discovered artistes as talent scout including: Esther Phillips; Willie

Mae (Big Mama) Thornton; Etta James; Hank Ballard; Jackie Wilson; The Robins (later The Coasters); Owner, D16 Records and Blues Spectrum record label; Played with Big Joe Turner; Louis Jordan; Charles Brown; Joe Liggins; Roy Milton; Lester Young; Illinois Jacquet; Count Basie Orchestra. *Compositions include:* Every Beat of My Heart; Mistreatin' Blues; Willie and The Hand Jive; So Fine; Dance With Me Henry (The Wallflower); Double Crossin' Blues; Cupid's Boogie; Deceivin' Blues; Gee Baby. *Recordings:* Harlem Nocturne, 1945; Double Crossing Blues, 1950; Mistreatin' Blues, 1950; Ma, He's Making Eyes At Me, 1957; Willie and The Hand Jive, 1958; Country Girl, 1968; Spirit of The Black Territory Bands, 1994; Producer, recordings with Big Mama Thornton, Johnny Ace and Little Richard. *Publications:* Author: Listen To The Lambs, 1968; Upside Your Head! Rhythm and Blues On Central Avenue, 1993; Colours and Chords – The Art of Johnny, 1995; Johnny Otis – Red Beans and Rice and Other Rock and Roll Recipies, 1997; Rock & Roll Hit Parade, 2000; Watts Funky, 2001. *Honours:* Inducted into Rhythm and Blues Hall of Fame, Rock and Roll Hall of Fame. *Current Management:* Terry Gould, 4141 Shook Rd, Sebastopol, CA 94572, USA.

O'TOOLE, Gary (Gerald William John); b. 27 Sept. 1958, London, England. Musician (drums); Vocalist. *Education:* On stage, age 4, with parents, playing bass, drums. *Career:* played with China Crisis; Bucks Fizz; LW5; Papa D; Monroes (Norwegian tours); Orphy Robinson; 25th of May; Jean Aldebambo; Delfins (Portuguese band); Teaching at drum tech and writing part of curriculum (private lessons, degree level). *Recordings:* Roland tutorial video for TD7 (electronic kit); with Delfins: Ser Maior (1 track written on album); LW5: with Ripe For The Picking album. *Membership:* Musicians' Union. *Address:* 302 Essex Rd, Islington, London N1 3AU, England.

O'TOOLE, Steve; b. 4 April 1969, Chesterfield, England. Musician (Guitar). *Career:* Member of Slaughterhouse 5 and Enormous. *Compositions:* Pathetic; Things She Did; Wide Open; Cigerette Machine From God; My Type. *Membership:* Musicians' Union. *Current Management:* Beatific Management. *Address:* 31A Bishop St, Mansfield, Nottingham NG18 1HJ, England.

OTTEWELL, Ben; b. 1975, Chesterfield, England. Musician (guitar, bass); Vocalist. *Career:* Mem., Gomez, 1996–; Numerous concerts, festival, radio and television appearances. *Recordings:* Albums: Bring It On, 1998; Liquid Skin, 1999; Abandoned Shopping Trolley Hotline, 2000; In Our Gun, 2002. Singles: 78 Stone Wobble, 1998; Whippin' Piccadilly, 1998; Get Myself Arrested (EP), 1998; Bring It On, 1999; Rhythm and Blues Alibi, 1999; We Haven't Turned Around (in soundtrack to film, American Beauty), 1999; Machismo (EP), 2000. *Honours:* Mercury Music Prize, 1998. *Address:* c/o Hut Records, Kensal House, 553–579 Harrow Rd, London W10 4RH, England. *Website:* www.gomez.co.uk.

OTTO, John; b. Jacksonville, FL, USA. Musician (drums). *Education:* Learnt jazz drumming, age 17. *Career:* Played in jazz band until recruited for Limp Bizkit, 1994; Signed to Flip/Interscope on strength of demo tape; Live shows at concerts and festivals; Group spearheaded 'nu-metal' breakthrough in Europe, 2001. *Recordings:* Albums: Three Dollar Bill, Y'All $, 1997; Significant Other, 1999; Chocolate Starfish and The Hot Dog Flavored Water, 2000; New Old Songs (remix album), 2001; Singles: Faith, 1997; Nookie, Rearranged, 1999; Break Stuff, Take A Look Around (from Mission Impossible 2 OST), My Generation, 2000; Rollin', My Way, Boiler, 2001. *Honours:* Second and third albums both debuted at No. 1 on US chart; Significant Other sales in excess of 6m.; American Music Award, Favourite Alternative Artist, 2002. *Current Management:* The Firm Inc, 9465 Wilshire Blvd, Suite 500, Beverly Hills, CA 90212, USA. *Website:* www.limpbizkit.com.

OTWAY, John; Vocalist. *Career:* Began touring folk circuit with partner, Wild Willy Barrett, 1970–82; Numerous reunions and splits since; 25 years continuous touring; Television includes: Old Grey Whistle Test; Television commercials for R Whites Lemonade; Danepack Bacon; Radio credits include being banned by Radio 1 for inciting violence, 1981; Concerts include: Reading Festival, 1988; 2,000th concert, London Astoria. *Recordings:* Albums: with Willy Barrett: John Otway and Wild Willy Barrett, 1977; Deep and Meaningless, 1978; Way and Bat, 1980; All Balls and No Willy, 1983; Singles include: with Willy Barrett: Really Free, 1977; Solo: Green Green Grass of Home, 1980; Headbutts, 1981; Premature Adulation, 1995. *Publications:* Cor Baby That's Really Me (memoirs), 1990. *Current Management:* Matters Musical Ltd. *Address:* The Loft, Rear of 8 West St, Dorking, Surrey RH4 1BL, England.

OUZOUNOFF, Alexandre; b. 15 Nov. 1955, Suresnes, France. Musician (bassoon); Composer. m. 28 Aug. 1993, 1 d. *Education:* Student of Maurice Allard. *Career:* Trio Ozi (with C Villevieille, L Aubert), Festivals: France, Europe, Africa, Republic of Korea; Brazil; Middle East; Russia, 1976–96; Contemporary repertory Constitution; Solo bassoon recitals: Radio France; Centre Pompidou; IRCAM; Festival d'Automne à Paris; INA-GRM; MANCA (Strasbourg; GMEB (Bourges); GRAMW (Lyon); Germany; USA; Italy; Poland, 1979–87; Member, Blue Ensemble, contemporary jazz group (with T. Gubitsch, J. F. Jenny-Clarck, J. Schwartz), 1991–94; Appearances, festivals include: De La Butte Montmarte; Festival de Paris; Hyères; Presences 93/ Radio France; La Rochelle; Aix En Musique; Heures Musicales de Chatres;

Futurs Musiques; D'Automne; Prague; Presence 95/Radio France; Uzès; Breme; Théatre du Châtelet; Moscow-Idaho; Contemporary bassoon masterclasses, France and abroad, 1985–95. *Recordings include:* Jazz: Palissander's Night, 1988; Sokoa Tanz, 1991; with KOQ Trio: Made In Nigeria, 1993; Contemporary: with Jean Schwartz: Assolutamente, 1990; Canto, 1993; Destroy, 1990; with François Bousch: Espace-Temps, 1992; Classical: Heitor Villa Lobos, Trio d'Anches, 1989; Francis Poulenc, Trio d'Anches, 1991; Etienne Ozi, Trio d'Anches Ozi, 1991; André Caplet/Alberic Magnard, Trio d'Anches Ozi, 1994. *Publications:* Actually The Bassoon. *Honours:* First Prize, Music History, CNSM, Paris; Certificate, International Chamber Music Competition, Martigny (Switzerland). *Membership:* IDRS (International Double Reed Society). *Address:* 7 Pl. Victor Hugo, 94270 Kremlin Bicetre, France.

OVERETT, Kelly; b. England. Vocalist; Dancer. *Career:* Dancer, SL2; Singer, dance music group, Cappella, 1993–95. *Recordings:* Debut album: U Got To Know, 1994; Remixes, 1994 Singles with Cappella: U Got 2 Know, 1993; U Got To Let The Music (No. 2, UK), 1993; Move On Baby, 1994; Take Me Away, 1994; Move It Up, 1994; Tell Me the Way, 1995; As Kelly O: Follow Your Heart, 1995. *Address:* c/o Media, 5–7 Mandeville Pl., London W1M 5LB, England.

OVERON, Geoff(rey John); b. 26 Nov. 1953, Leicester, England. Musician (electric and acoustic guitar, bass guitar); Vocalist; Songwriter. *Education:* De Montfort University; Some private music tuition. *Career:* Turned professional in 1978; Played with: Eric Clapton, Muddy Waters' sideman, Ric Grech, backed Jimmy Witherspoon, jammed with the Van Morrison Band, played at Robert Cray's wedding; Recent tour dates with Thin Lizzy, The Animals, Taj Mahal; Currently, composing, recording and touring with the Geoff Overon Band; Session player, producer and impresario. *Compositions:* Loving With A Loaded Dice, with Ric Grech; If It Don't Come Easy, with Anthony Thistlethwaite (Waterboys/Saw Doctors). *Recordings:* Sessions for BBC and Central TV. *Honours:* Life President, Leicester Rhythm and Blues Society. *Membership:* British Music Writers' Council; Musicians' Union teacher and Registry of Electric Guitar tutors. *Current Management:* GO Productions and Promotions. *Address:* 12 Somerville Rd, Leicester LE3 2ET, England. *Telephone:* (116) 289-1919.

OVERWATER, Tony; b. 24 March 1965, Rotterdam, Netherlands. Musician (Acoustic Bass; Contrabass). 1 child. *Education:* Graduated with Hons, Royal Conservatory, The Hague, Netherlands, 1990. *Career:* Played at Ronnie Scott's, London, with David Murray; New Sea Jazz Festival with Yuri Honing Trio; Montréal Jazz Festival; Solo TV appearance in Reiziger in Muziek; Wrote music for documentary. *Compositions:* Le Petit Prince for double bass and mezzo soprano; Eter/Ether, for dancer/choreographer Anouk van Dijk. *Recordings:* Tony Overwater Up Close; Motion Music; Treya Quartet Plays; Gabriel Faure; Yuri Honing Trio: Sequel; Star Tracks; Scapes, Changes In Times, 2000. *Honours:* Podium Prize, Most Promising Musician of the Year, 1989. *Membership:* BIM. *Address:* 1e Molenweg 20, 1261 TD Blaricum, Netherlands.

OWEN, Huw Dylan; b. 20 May 1971, Nantwich, Cheshire, England. Social Worker. *Education:* Polytechnic of Wales; University of Glamorgan; All Wales Occupational Therapy Programme. *Career:* Lead singer with Y Celtiaid Anhysbus, 1987–89; Singer and mandolin player with folk rock group Gwerinos, 1988–95; Regular appearances on Welsh TV and Radio, 1988–; Lead singer and guitarist with folk punk group Defaid, 1989–92. *Compositions:* Composed 7 songs on the album Tocio Mogia, Defaid, 1992; Dolgellau, 1992; Hydref, 1992; 100,000,000, 1992; Llanfair Bryn Meurig, 1992; Gobaith, 1992; Fy Allwedd I Afallon, 1994. *Recordings:* Tocio Mogia, Defaid, 1992; Di-Didlan, Gwerinos, 1994; Lleuad Llawn, 1999. *Publications:* Editor of Welsh language magazine Sothach!, 1991–94. *Current Management:* Adloniant Alffa Entertainment. *Address:* Maesbrith, Dolgellau, Gwynedd LL40 1LF, North Wales.

OWEN, Mark; b. 27 Jan. 1972. Vocalist; Composer. *Career:* Mem., UK all-male vocal group, Take That, 1990–96; Solo artiste, 1996–; Television includes: Take That and Party (Channel 4), 1993; Take That Away (documentary, BBC2), 1993; Take That In Berlin, 1994; Mark Owen: Green Man (documentary, MTV), 1996; Mark Owen Story (Channel 4), 1997; MTV Live and Direct, 1997; I Love The 90s (BBC2), 2001; Winner, Celebrity Big Brother (Channel 4), 2002. *Recordings:* Albums: with Take That: Take That and Party, 1992; Everything Changes (No. 1, UK), 1993; Nobody Else (No. 1, UK), 1995; Greatest Hits (No. 1, UK), 1996; Solo: Green Man, 1996; with Physical Therapy: Casino, 1997. Singles: with Take That: Promises, 1991; It Only Take A Minute, 1992; I Found Heaven, 1992; A Million Love Songs, 1992; Could It Be Magic, 1992; Why Can't I Wake Up With You, 1993; Pray (No. 1, UK), 1993; Relight My Fire (with Lulu, No. 1, UK), 1993; Babe (No. 1, UK), 1993; Everything Changes (No. 1, UK), 1994; Love Ain't Here Anymore, 1994; Sure (No. 1, UK), 1994; Back For Good (No. 1, UK), 1995; Never Forget (No. 1, UK), 1995; How Deep Is Your Love (No. 1, UK), 1996; Solo: Child, 1996; Clementine, 1997; I Am What I Am, 1997. *Publications:* Mark Owen official magazine. *Honours:* Seven Smash Hit Awards, 1992; BRIT Award, Best British Single, 1994. *Membership:* PRS; Equity; MCPS. *Current Management:* Alex Kadis Management. *Address:* c/o Basement, 15 Grosvenor Rd, London E11 2EW, England.

OWEN, Randy Yeuell; b. 13 Dec. 1949, Fort Payne, Alabama, USA. Musician (rhythm guitar); Vocalist. m., 3 c. *Education:* Jacksonville State University. *Career:* Founder mem., country music group, Young Country, 1969, renamed Wild Country, 1972, renamed Alabama, 1977–. *Recordings:* Albums: Alabama, 1980; My Home's In Alabama, 1980; Feels So Right, 1981; Stars, 1982; Mountain Music, 1982; The Closer You Get, 1983; Roll On, 1984; 40 Hour Week, 1985; Alabama Christmas, 1985; The Touch, 1986; Greatest Hits, 1986; Just Us, 1987; Live, 1988; Tennessee Christmas, 1989; Southern Star, 1989; Pass It On Down, 1990; Greatest Hits Vol. 2, 1991; American Pride, 1992; Gonna Have A Party... Live, 1993; Cheap Seats, 1993; In The Beginning, 1994; In Pictures, 1995; From The Archives Vol. 1, 1996; Christmas Vol. 2, 1996; Live at Ebbets Field, 1997; Dancin' On The Boulevard, 1997; Twentieth Century, 1999; Alabama For The Record, 2000; When It All Goes South, 2001; Christmas, 2002. Singles include: I Want To Be With You; Tennessee River; Feels So Right; Love In The First Degree; Pass It On Down. *Honours:* Numerous Country Music Ass, Awards, 1981–84; Numerous Acad. of Country Music Awards, incl. Artist of the Decade, 1989; Numerous American Music Awards, incl. Award of Merit, 2003; Grammy Awards, for Mountain Music, 1983, for The Closer You Get, 1984; BMI President's Award, 2000; Numerous Billboard Awards. *Current Management:* Dale Morris and Assocs, 818 19th Ave S, Nashville, TN 37203, USA. *Website:* www.wildcountry.com.

OWENS, Buck (Alvis Edgar, Jr); b. 12 Aug. 1929, Sherman, Texas, USA. Country Vocalist; Songwriter; Musician (guitar). m. Bonnie Campbell, 1 s. *Career:* Musician, own radio programme with Ray Britten, 1946; Member, Mac's Skillet Lickers; Orange Blossom Playboys; Founder, own band the Schoolhouse Playboys; Session guitarist with artistes including: Sonny James; Wanda Jackson; Gene Vincent; Singer, musician with Tommy Collins; Recording artiste as Buck Owens, 1955–; Co-host, country music variety show Hee Haw, 1969; Retired from performing to run business interests, mid-1970s; Returned to recording and touring, 1988. *Compositions include:* Together Again, Emmylou Harris; Crying Time, Ray Charles. *Recordings:* US Country No. 1 hits include: Act Naturally, 1963; Love's Gonna Live Here, 1963; My Heart Skips A Beat, 1964; Together Again, 1964; I've Got A Tiger By The Tail, 1965; Before You Go, 1965; Waitin' In Your Welfare Line, 1966; Think of Me, 1966; Open Up Your Heart, 1966; Johnny B Goode, 1969; Streets of Bakersfield, 1988; Over 100 albums include: Under Your Spell Again, 1961; The Instrumental Hits of Buck Owens and The Buckaroos, 1965; I've Got A Tiger By The Tail, 1965; Carnegie Hall Concert, 1966; Buck Owens In London, 1969; Big In Vegas, 1970; I Wouldn't Live In New York City, 1971; The Songs of Merle Haggard, 1972; Hot Dog, 1988; Act Naturally, 1989; Duets: Half a Buck, 1996; In Japan (live), 1997; Tender Loving Care, 1997; Greatest Hits Vols 1 and 2, 1998, 40 Greatest Hits, 1999; Good Old Country, 2000; Young Buck, 2001. *Address:* c/o McFadden Artists, 818 18th Ave S, Nashville, TN 37203, USA.

OWENS, Ginny (Virginia Lee); b. 22 April 1975, Jackson Mississippi, USA. Vocalist; Musician (piano). *Education:* Bachelor of Music Education, Belmont University. *Career:* Performances at Lilith Fair and Sundance Film Festival; TV and radio appearances: Live With Regis and Kathie Lee; Ainsley Harriott Show; CNN Worldbeat; National Public Radio special; songs featured in TV series: Felicity; Charmed; Roswell. *Recordings:* Without Condition, 1999; Something More, 2002. *Honours:* Lilith Fair Talent Search, Nashville Winner, 1999; Dove Awards: New Artist of the Year, 2000; Best Enhanced CD, Without Condition, 2000; Inspirational Recorded Song of the Year, Blessed, 2001. *Current Management:* Rocketown Management, PO Box 1405, Franklin, Tennessee 37065, USA. *Address:* 404 Bridge St, Franklin, TN 37064, USA. *E-mail:* ginny@rocketownrecords.com. *Website:* www.ginnyowens.com.

OWENS, Jimmy (James Robert), Jr; b. 9 Dec. 1943, New York, USA. Jazz Musician (trumpet); Composer; Arranger. m. Lola Mae Brown, 18 March 1965. *Education:* MEd, University of Massachusetts, 1975. *Career:* Musician with Lionel Hampton, 1963–64; Slide Hampton, 1963; Hank Crawford, 1964–65; Charlie Mingus, 1964–65; Thad Jones/Mel Lewis Orchestra, 1965–66; Duke Ellington, 1968; Count Basie, 1968; Billy Taylor Quintet, David Frost, 1969–72; World-wide appearances as Jimmy Owens Plus; Panelist, New York State Council of Arts, 1978–81; Director, Jazzmobile Inc, jazz workshops, 1974–90; Blackarts, National Diaspora (board member), 1986–; Faculty member, SUNY, 1981–86; Panelist, National Endowment for Arts, 1972–76; 1990–; Panelist, Ohio Arts Council, 1981–82. *Recordings include:* Impressions of The Middle East, Herbie Mann, 1967; Coming At You, Junior Wells, 1968; Zawinul, Joe Zawinul, 1971; Spectrum, Billy Cobham, 1973; Cosmic Vortex, Weldon Irvine, 1974; Sound of a Drum, Ralph MacDonald, 1976; Inner Conflicts, Billy Cobham, 1978; Anthology, Yusef Lateef, 1994; Things to Come, Dizzy Gillespie, 1996; Pure Be-Bop, 1998; Autumn Jazz, 1999; The Best of Duke Ellington, 1999; Other collaborations include: Herbie Mann; George Benson; Eddie Harris. *Honours:* Drumbeat Award, Talent deserving wider recognition, 1967; Fellow, National Endowment Arts, 1980; Award for Excellence in Arts, Manhattan Borough, 1986. *Membership:* AFofM; BMI; National Jazz Service Organization; Jazz Foundation of America.

OXAAL, Adrian; Musician (guitar). *Career:* Mem., James, 1996–2001; Numerous tours, festival dates and television appearances; Farewell 'Getting Away With It' concert, Manchester Evening News Arena, Dec. 2001. *Recordings:* Albums: Whiplash, 1997; The Best Of James, 1998; Millionaires, 1999; B-Sides Ultra, 2001; Pleased To Meet You, 2001; Getting Away With It, 2002. Singles incl.: She's A Star, 1997; Tomorrow, 1997; Waltzing Along, 1997; Destiny Calling, 1998; Runaground, 1998; Sit Down (remix), 1998; I Know What I'm Here For, 1999; Fred Astaire, 1999; We're Gonna Miss You, 1999; Getting Away With It (All Messed Up), 2001. *Current Management:* Rudge Management, 1 Star St, London W2 1QD, England.

P

P. DIDDY. See: **COMBS, Sean.**

PAAKKUNAINEN, Seppo Toivo Juhani 'Baron'; b. 24 Oct. 1943, Tuusula, Finland. Jazz/Folk Composer; Arranger; Musician (flute, saxophone). m. Ritva Marjatta Ikävalko, 1 s., 1 d. *Education:* Sibelius Academy, Helsinki; Berklee College of Music, Boston, USA. *Career:* Member, jazz groups: Pori Jazz; Soulset; Tuohi Quartet; George Gruntz Concert Jazz Band; Braxtonia Project (with Anthony Braxton); Karelia; World-wide tours, including Norway Winter Olympics, Lillehammer, 1993–94 with artists Nils-Aslak Valkeapää and Juhan Anders Dær; Played with: Most top Finnish Jazz musicians; Charlie Mariano; Mal Waldron; Palle Mikkelborg; First Finnish Jazz musician to play Carnegie Hall, New York. *Compositions:* Mysterium Sacrum (opera), 1993–94; Amazon, 1994; Numerous works for orchestras, choirs and big bands. *Recordings:* Albums include: Plastic Maailma, 1971; with Edward Vesala: Nan Madol, 1974; Unisono, 1975; No Comments, 1975; Kissapa Uu, 1977; Baron Disco-Go, 1978; Kanteletar, 1980; Sami Luondu Gollerisku with Nils-Aslak Valkeapää, 1980; with Karelia: Nunnu, 1971; Tuohihiulu, 1981; Hyvää Joulua, 1981; Maanitus, 1983; with George Gruntz: Theatre, 1983; Karelia, 1986; Best of Karelia, 1990; Sápmi Lottázan with Nils-Aslak Valkeapää and Ingor Anette Ailu Gaup, 1992; with George Gruntz: George Gruntz Concert Jazz Band, 1981; Theatre, 1984; Dálveleaikkat Wintergames with Nils-Aslak Valkeapää, 1994; Saxperiment, 1997; 2 Compositions (Järvenpää), with Anthony Buxton and Ensemble Braxtonia, 1996. *Honours:* Gold Medal, Student Youth Festival, 1968; Best Ensemble, Montreux Jazz Competition (with Tuohi Quartet), 1971; Yrjö Award, Finnish Jazz Federation, 1973; Jazz Composer of Year, Helsinki Festival, 1981; Arrangers Prize, Nordring Competition, 1982; Prix Future, West Berlin Festival, 1989. *Membership:* Suomen Säveltäjät; ELVIS; Musicians' Union. *Address:* Katrillipolku 4 A, 04420 Järvenpää, Finland.

PACKHAM, Blair James; b. 23 April 1959, North Bay, Ontario, Canada. Vocalist; Songwriter; Composer; Musician (guitar). *Education:* BA with distinction in English, University of Toronto, Canada. *Career:* Leader, The Jitters, rock 'n' roll group, 1980s; Engineer, live recordings of Bryan Adams, Stevie Ray Vaughan; Television music composer. *Compositions:* Destiny Ridge; NHL Tonight, World Cup Soccer '94 television series. *Recordings:* The Jitters; Louder Than Words; Solo album: Everything That's Good, 2001. *Membership:* AFofM; Guild of Canadian Film Composers; Society of Canadian Composers Authors and Publishers. *Address:* 260 Adelaide St E, Suite 131, Toronto, ON M5A 1N1, Canada.

PACZYNSKI, Georges; b. 30 March 1943, Grenoble, France. Musician (drums). m. Sophie Tret, 24 April 1995, 1 d. *Career:* Represented France, Festival of Montreux, Festival of Zurich, 1968; Broadcasts, France Culture, with Black and Blue, Radio France, 1981, 1998–; Founded trio with Jean-Christophe Levinson and Jean-François Jenny-Clark, 1984; Une Histoire De La Batterie De Jazz, broadcast, France Culture, 1993; Professor, Conservatoire National de Cergy-Pontoise; Founded new trio with Philippe Macé and Ricardo del Fra, 1996; Founded trio with Edouard Ferlet and Yves Torchinsky; Concert historique à l'Ambassade de Pologne en France, 2002. *Compositions:* Over 22 pieces for percussion and piano, Paris, Zurfluh, 1985–2003. *Recordings:* Eight Years Old, 1992; Levin's Song, 1994. *Publications:* Thesis: Baudelaire Et La Musique, 1973; La Genèse Du Rythme Et L'Anthropologie Gestuelle, 1984; Book: Rythme Et Geste, Les Racines Du Rythme Musical, 1988; Une Histoire de La Batterie, Vol. 1, 1997; Une Histoire de La Batterie, Vol. 2, 2000; Dictionnaire du Jazz (co-author), 2000. *Honours:* Medal of the Society of Encouragement For Progress, 1989; Charge de Cours sur le jazz et le rythme au Conservatoire National Superieur de Lyon. *Address:* Georges Paczynski, 89 rue Nationale, 95000 Cergy-Village, France. *Telephone:* (1) 30-32-13-52. *Fax:* (1) 30-32-13-52.

PADEN, Jyrica; b. 3 Feb. 1955, Zagreb, Croatia. Composer; Musician (guitar); Vocalist. *Education:* University; 6 years classical guitar in music school. *Career:* 1,000 concerts in various groups, Croatia; 100 television appearances; Tour of former CCCP; Concerts in Netherlands, Germany. *Recordings:* About 30 albums; 10 hit singles with own group. *Honours:* Silver and Gold records; First Prize Arena-Fest, Pula. *Membership:* HGY (Croatian Music Union); DHS (Composers Union of Croatia). *Current Management:* Music Time, Zagreb. *Address:* Vidriceva 31, 91000 Zagreb, Croatia.

PADEN, Tom (Thomas) C; b. 13 Oct. 1956, Chattanooga, Tennessee, USA. Songwriter; Publisher; Musician (piano). m. Grace Michele Paden, 20 Nov. 1993. *Education:* BS in Business Management, University of Tennessee. *Career:* Staff writer for Starstruck Writer's Group, Reba McEntire's publishing company. *Compositions:* Numerous songs include: Same Time Each Year, national theme song for Ducko Unlimited. *Recordings:* Songs recorded by numerous artists including: Aaron Neville; Tammy Wynette; Restless Heart; Kenny Rogers; Lee Greenwood. *Membership:* NARAS;

Country Music Asscn; NSAI. *Address:* 3803 Bedford Ave, Nashville, TN 37215, USA.

PADGHAM, Hugh Charles; b. 15 Feb. 1955, London, England. Record Prod; Engineer; *Recordings:* As producer, engineer, mixer include: with Split Enz: Conflicting Emotions; Time and Tide; with The Police: Synchronicity; Ghost In The Machine; with Phil Collins: Face Value; Hello I Must Be Going; No Jacket Required; But Seriously; with Genesis: Genesis; Invisible Touch; with Sting: Ten Summoner's Tales; The Soul Cages; Fields of Gold–The Best of Sting; with Julia Fordham: Porcelain; Swept; with Melissa Etheridge: Yes I Am; Your Little Secret; No One Is To Blame, Howard Jones; Hysteria, Human League; English Settlement, XTC; Between Two Fires, Paul Young: Press To Play, Paul McCartney; Tonight, David Bowie; Two Rooms, Elton John and Bernie Taupin; Walkaway Joe (single), Trisha Yearwood; Clannad, 1996; Beth Hart Band, 1996; Bee Gees: Still Waters, 1997; Phil Collins: Hits, 1998; Julia Fordham: Collection, 1999; Mansun, Little Kix, 2000; Engineering/ mixing credits include: tracks from World Outside, Psychedelic Furs; Where's The Light, Toni Childs; Just Like Us, Robbie Neville; Nothing Like The Sun, Sting; Love and Affection, Joan Armatrading; Days of Open Hand, Suzanne Vega; Shakin' The Tree, Youssou N'Dour; The Scattering, Cutting Crew; My Nation Underground, Julian Cope; In The Air Tonight (88 Remix), Phil Collins; Abacab, Genesis; The Third, Peter Gabriel; Black Sea, Drums and Wires, XTC; with Hall and Oates: Starting All Over Again; H2O; Dead Man on Campus; Happy Texas; Yes. *Honours:* 4 Grammys; BRIT Awards; Music Week Award; TEC Award For Outstanding Creative Achievement. *Membership:* Re-Pro. *Current Management:* Dennis Muirhead, Muirhead Management, 202 Fulham Rd, Chelsea, London SW10 9PJ, England.

PADILLA, José; b. 1955, Spain. Prod; Remixer; DJ. *Career:* Began DJ career in Ibiza, 1975; Became resident DJ at the island's Café Del Mar; Compiled first Vol. of Café Del Mar CD series and several further editions; Collaborations: A Man Called Adam; Phil Mison; Seal; N'Dea Davenport. *Recordings:* Albums: Souvenir, 1998; Navigator, 2001; Singles: Who Do You Love (with Angela John), 1998; Adiós Ayer, 2001. *Address:* c/o East West Records, Electric Lighting Station, 46 Kensington Court, London W8 5DP, England.

PADOVANI, Jean-Marc; b. 2 Feb. 1956, Villeneuve les Avignon, France. Musician (saxophone); Composer. m. Françoise Piotelat, 9 March 1987, 2 s. *Education:* Philosophy; Conservatoire. *Career:* First part, Miles Davis, 1984; Many tours with his quartet including: France; India; South America; East Europe, 1989–91; Flamenco /Jazz show, Tres Horas de Sol. *Recordings:* Tres Horas de Sol, 1988; One For Pablo, 1989; Nîmeño, 1990; Mingus, Cuernavaca, 1991, 1996; Nocturne, 1994; Sud, 1995. *Current Management:* Didier Vuillecot, Le Jardin des Délices. *Address:* 208 rue de la Convention, 75015 Paris, France.

PAEFFGEN, Gilbert; b. 21 Jan. 1958, Würzburg, Germany. Musician (drums, hammered dulcimer); Composer. m. Bettina Paeffgen Hehl, 16 Feb. 1990, 1 s., 1 d. *Career:* Member, Aventure Dupont, 1983–93, over 500 performances; Expo Sevilla, Pabellón de la Suiza; Member, The Treya Quartet, 1997–; Numerous TV appearances. *Compositions:* Where are the Mountains in this Country; Seamen Without Sea; Golden Wings; Lena; Evening Train. *Recordings:* The Treya Quartet Plays Gabriel Fauré; Songs of Seas and Ferries; Ode; Cohabitation, Aventure Dupont; Evening Train, Dei Terro. *Honours:* Mentor, Swiss New Jazz Festival, 1997. *Membership:* Cimbalon Asscn. *Address:* Mattenstutz 2, 3053 Münchenbuchsee, Germany.

PAGE, Jimmy (James Patrick); b. 9 Jan. 1944, Heston, Middlesex, England. Musician (guitar); Songwriter. *Career:* Member, Neil Christian and the Crusaders, 1959; The Yardbirds, 1966–68; Concerts include: Dick Clark's Caravan of Stars, US tour, 1966; Rolling Stones '66 tour, 1966; Australia/Far East tour, 1967; Appearance in film Blow-Up, 1967; US and Japan tour, 1968; Founder, The New Yardbirds, 1968; Group becomes Led Zeppelin, 1968–80; Tours and concerts include: Royal Albert Hall, 1969, 1971; Madison Square Garden, 1970, 1976; Wembley Arena, 1971; Formed Led Zeppelin's own record label, Swan Song, 1974; Guitarist, Honeydrippers (with Robert Plant, Nile Rodgers, Jeff Beck), 1984–85; Guitarist, Coverdale/Page, with former Whitesnake singer David Coverdale, 1993; Guitarist, Page/Plant, with former Led Zeppelin singer, Robert Plant, 1994–. *Recordings:* Albums: with the Yardbirds: Over Under Sideways Down, 1966; Little Games, 1967; with Led Zeppelin (over 60m. copies sold): Led Zeppelin, 1969; Led Zeppelin II (No. 1, UK and USA), 1970; Led Zeppelin III (No. 1, UK and USA), 1970; Led Zeppelin IV (No. 1, UK and USA), 1971; Houses of The Holy (No. 1, UK and USA), 1973; Physical Graffiti (No. 1, UK and USA), 1975; Presence (No. 1, UK and USA), 1976; The Song Remains The Same (No. 1, UK), 1976; In Through The Out Door (No. 1, UK and USA), 1979; Coda, 1982; Remasters, 1990; The BBC Sessions, 1997; with Coverdale/Page: Coverdale/Page, 1993; with Page/

Plant: No Quarter, 1994; Walking Into Clarksdale, 1998; Masters, 1998; Before the Balloon Went Up, 1998 with The Honeydrippers: Honeydrippers Vol. 1, 1985; Solo: Deathwish II OST, 1982; Outrider, 1988; Live At The Greek, 2000; Rock And Roll Highway, 2000; Contributor, Suicide Sal, Maggie Bell, 1973; Now and Zen, Robert Plant, 1988; As session musician: Here Comes The Night, Them; Shout, Lulu; I Can't Explain, The Who; The Crying Game, Dave Berry; Is It True, Brenda Lee; Crosby Stills and Nash; Knebworth: The Album; Anthology, Joe Cocker. *Honours:* Outstanding Contribution to British Music, 1977; Q Magazine Merit Award (with Led Zeppelin), 1992. *Current Management:* Trinifold Management, 22 Harley House, Marylebone Rd, London NW1 4PR, England.

PAGE, Patti, (Clara Ann Fowler); b. 8 Nov. 1927, Claremore, Oklahoma, USA. Vocalist. m. Jerry Filicitto, 12 May 1990, 2 s., 3 d. *Career:* Discovered by Jack Rael, 1946; Signed to Mercury Records, 1947; Signed to Columbia Records, 1963. *Recordings:* 100 albums; 160 singles, including Tennessee Waltz; Christmas with Patti Page; Songs That Made Her Famous; The Patti Page Collection; Live at Carnegie Hall; Hush Hush Sweet Charlotte/ Gentle on My Mind; Compilations include: The Collection, 2001; Television appearances: Patti Page Oldsmobile Show, NBC; The Big Record, CBS; Patti Page Show, ABC (only musical performer with own series on all 3 US television networks); Actress, Elmer Gantry; Dondi; Boy's Night Out; Stage performances include Annie Get Your Gun. *Honours:* 14 Gold discs; Hollywood Walk of Fame; Country Music Walkway; Pioneer Award, ACM, 1980; Oklahoma Hall of Fame. *Membership:* Board of Directors, Academy of Country Music. *Current Management:* Jack Rael.

PAGE, Stuart; b. 12 May 1954, Leeds, West Yorkshire, England. Musician (guitar); Vocalist; Songwriter. 2 s.; 1 d. *Career:* Live appearance, Royal Albert Hall; BBC 2 Concert; Radio 2 airplay; Toured with many US country artists, Europe, UK, for last 11 years, including: Billie Jo Spears; James House; Albert Lee. *Recordings:* Wrote and performed music to ITV series A Brush With Ashley; New album due for release: Can't Sing The Blues. *Honours:* British Country Music Asscn, Band of the Year, 3 times. *Membership:* PRS; Royal Guild of Songwriters. *Current Management:* Milltown. *Address:* 26 East Parade, Bedford BD1 5HD, England.

PAICE, Ian Anderson; b. 29 June 1948, Nottingham, England. Rock Musician (drums); Writer. m. Jacky, 25 May 1976, 1 s., 2 d. *Education:* Technical College. *Career:* Founder, current member Deep Purple; Major concert headlining California Jam, 1973, to 350,000 people; Also played with Whitesnake and Gary Moore. *Recordings:* Albums include: Machine Head, 1972; Made In Japan, 1973; Deep Purple In Rock, 1970; Perfect Strangers, 1984; Purpendicular, 1996; Days May Come And Days May Go, 2000; Hit singles: include Smoke On The Water; Hush; Highway Star; Child In Time; Perfect Strangers. *Honours:* Biggest Selling Record Artist in USA, 1973. *Current Management:* Thames Talent, 45 E Putnam Ave, Suite 116, Greenwich, CT 06830, USA.

PAICH, David; b. 25 June 1954, Los Angeles, California, USA. Vocalist; Musician (keyboards). *Career:* Member, Rural Still Life; Support to artists including: Jackson Browne; Aretha Franklin; Barbra Streisand; Member, Toto, 1978–. *Compositions include:* Commissioned (with Toto) to write theme for Los Angeles Olympic Games, 1986; Songs include: Africa, co-written with Jeff Porcaro, 1983; Without You Love, 1987. *Recordings:* Albums: Toto, 1979; Hydra, 1979; Turn Back, 1981; Toto IV, 1982; Isolation, 1984; Dune (film soundtrack), 1985; Fahrenheit, 1986; The Seventh One, 1988; Past To Present 1977–90, 1990; Kingdom of Desire, 1992; Tambu, 1995; Sax for Lovers, 1996; Toto XX, 1977–97, 1998; Mindfields, 1999; Singles include: Hold The Line, 1979; Georgy Porgy, 1980; 99, 1980; Rosanna, 1982; Make Believe, 1982; Africa (No. 1, USA), 1983; I Won't Hold You Back, 1983; I'll Be Over You, 1986; Without Your Love, 1987; Pamela, 1988; Contributor, We Are The World, USA For Africa charity single, 1985; Backing musician, albums by Boz Scaggs: Silk Degrees, 1976; Down Two Then Left, 1977; Don Henley, Inside Job, 2000; Boz Scaggs, Dig, 2001. *Honours:* 6 Grammy Awards: Best Record, Best Album, Best Vocal Arrangement, Best Instrumental Arrangement, Best Engineered Recording, Best Producer (Toto) 1983. *Address:* c/o Fitzgerald-Hartley Co, 50 W Main St, Ventura, CA 93001, USA.

PAIGE, Elaine, (Elaine Bickerstaffe); b. 5 March 1951, Barnet, England. Vocalist; Actress. *Education:* Ada Foster Stage School. *Career:* West End theatre appearances: Hair, 1968; Jesus Christ Superstar, 1973; Grease (played Sandy), 1973; Billy (played Rita), 1974; Created roles of Eva Perón in Evita, 1978, and Grizabella in Cats, 1981; Abbacadabra (played Carabosse), 1983; Chess (played Florence), 1986; Anything Goes (played Reno Sweeney), 1989; Piaf, 1993–94; Sunset Boulevard (played Norma Desmond), 1995–96; The Misanthrope (played Célimène), 1998; The King and I, 2000. *Recordings:* Albums include: Sitting Pretty, 1978; Elaine Paige, 1981; Stages, 1983; Cinema, 1984; Love Hurts, 1985; Christmas, 1986; Memories: The Best Of Elaine Paige, 1987; The Queen Album, 1988; Elaine Paige: The Collection, 1990; Love Can Do That, 1991; An Evening With Elaine Paige, 1991; Elaine Paige And Barbara Dickson 'Together', 1992; Romance And The Stage, 1993; Piaf, 1994; Encore, 1995; Performance, 1996; From A Distance, 1997; On Reflection, 1998. Singles include: Memory, 1981; I Know Him So Well (duet

with Barbara Dickson, No. 1, UK), 1985; Contributions to soundtrack recordings, including: Nine, Anything Goes, Chess, Cats, Evita, Billy, The King And I; Appears on: Tim Rice Collection: Stage and Screen Classics, 1996; Christmas with the Stars Vol. 2, 1999. *Honours:* Eight Gold and four multi-Platinum albums; Society of West End Theatre Award, Best Actress in a Musical, Evita, 1978; Variety Club Awards for Showbusiness Personality of the Year, Recording Artist of Year, 1986; BASCA Award, 1993; Lifetime Achievement Award, National Operatic and Dramatic Asscn, 1999; O.B.E. *Address:* c/o E. P. Records, Sanctuary House, 45–53 Sinclair Rd, London W14 0NS, England. *Website:* www.elainepaige.com.

PAINE, Ed; b. 26 March 1949, Chatham, Kent, England. Musician (pedal steel guitar, dobro); Teacher. m. Beverley Paine, 24 May 1980. *Education:* Formal music theory. *Career:* Club, pub, college, theatre and festival appearances; Live and recorded local radio appearances and regional television appearances; Many recording sessions; Member of Country Cousins; Ned Porridge Band; Pan For Gold; Struck It Rich. *Compositions include:* The Tear In Daddy's Eye. *Recordings:* Sessions with many country bands including: Ned Porridge Band; Reg Haynes Outfit; Steve Scott Band; Memphis Roots; Pan For Gold. *Membership:* Musicians' Union. *Address:* Sundown, Lower Hartlip Rd, Hartlip, Sittingbourne, Kent ME9 7ST, England.

PÄIVINEN, Pertti 'Pepa'; b. 2 June 1955, Vantaa, Finland. Musician (saxophone, multi-instrumentalist). m. Marit Päivinen, 31 Jan. 1978, 2 s., 1 d. *Education:* Flute Study, Vantaa Music Institute, 1967–73; Theory and saxophone, Oulunkyla Pop-Jazz Conservatory, 1975–78. *Career:* Toured in Europe with Jukka Tolonen Band, 1979–80; Freelance work, television, theatre and teaching, 1980–85; Touring with Edward Vesala Sound and Fury, 1985–; UMO Big Band, 1985–; Saxophone quartet Saxperiment, 1989–; Tour with Anthony Braxton, 1988; Touring with own trio, 1998–. *Compositions:* Saxophobia; Umpsukkelis; Be Aware; Jisakki; Jakobe; Pohja-kosketus; We'll See; Mökö: Kuluk. *Recordings:* with Jukka Tolonen: Just Those Boys, 1980; with Edward Vesala: Death of Jazz, 1990; Invisible Storm, 1992; Nordic Gallery, 1995; with UMO: UMO Plays the Music of Muhal Abrams, 1986; Selected Standards, 1993; Green and Yellow, 1994; Umo Jazz Orchestra, 1998; Electrifying Miles, 1998; with Anthony Braxton: two compositions, 1988; with Saxperiment: Saxperiment, 1997; Pepa Päivinen Trio: Saxigon, 1998; Umpsukkelisk, 1999; Fun Faraway, 2002; with Jro Haarla Duo: Yarra, Yarra, 2001; with Jarmo Saari Filmtet: A Tribute to Finnish Cinema. *Honours:* Pekka Poyry Reward, 1984; Award from Finnish government for artistic working, 1998–2000; Finnish State Grant, 1998–2000; Georgie Award, 2000. *Membership:* Finnish Saxophone Society. *Address:* Kitarakuja 2, 01390 Vantaa, Finland.

PALLADINO, Pino; b. 17 Oct. 1957, Cardiff, Wales. Musician (electric bass guitar). m. Marilyn Roberts, 13 Oct. 1992, 1 s., 2 d. *Education:* 1 year classical guitar lessons, age 14. *Career:* Bass guitar for Paul Young, 1982–87; Recording sessions for artists including: Don Henley; Eric Clapton; Phil Collins; Elton John; Chaka Khan; Jeff Beck; Pete Townshend; Michael McDonald; John McLaughlin; Joan Armatrading. *Recordings:* No Parlez, Paul Young; Journeyman, Eric Clapton; But Seriously, Phil Collins; Building The Perfect Beast, Don Henley; Sowing The Seeds Of Love, Tears For Fears; Who Else, Jeff Beck; Pilgrim, Eric Clapton; Breakdown, Melissa Etheridge; Emotional Blends, Robbie McIntosh; Oltre, Claudio Baglioni; Naked Flame, Tony O'Malley; Human, Rod Stewart, 2000; Alone With Everybody, Richard Ashcroft, 2000; Reptile, Eric Clapton, 2001. *Publications:* Standing In The Shadows of Motown. *Current Management:* Keryn Kaplan, Principle Management. *Address:* 250 W 57th St, Suite 1502, New York, NY 10019, USA.

PALMER, Carl; b. 20 March 1950, Handsworth Wood, Birmingham, England. Musician (drums, percussion). m. Maureen Fraser, 4 March 1985, 1 d. *Education:* James Blades, Royal Academy; Gilbert Webster, Guildhall. *Career:* Founder member, Emerson Lake and Palmer (with Keith Emerson, Greg Lake), 1970–81; Founder member, Asia, 1982–86; Numerous world-wide concerts, television, radio appearances; ELP sold 30m. albums to date. *Recordings:* ELP: Singles: Fanfare For The Common Man (No. 2, UK), 1977; Albums: Emerson Lake and Palmer, 1970; Tarkus (No. 1, UK), 1971; Pictures At An Exhibition, 1971; Trilogy, 1972; Brain Salad Surgery, 1973; Welcome My Friends (3 disc set), 1974; Works, 1974; Works Vol. II, 1977; Love Beach, 1978; In Concert, 1979; Best Of, 1980; Asia: Asia, 1982; Alpha, 1983; Astra, 1985; Albums with: Atomic Rooster; Arthur Brown; Roger Daltrey; Chris Farlowe; Mike Oldfield; PM; Three; Solo: Percussion Concerto, 1995; One More Time–The Anthology, 2001. *Publications:* Applied Rhythms, Carl Palmer. *Honours:* Playboy Magazine Award, 1977; Hall of Fame, Modern Drummer Magazine, 1989. *Current Management:* Stewart Young, Part Rock Management.

PALMER, Dave, (Yorkie); Musician (bass); Backing Vocalist; Songwriter. *Career:* Member, Space, 1997–; Numerous world-wide tours and television appearances. *Recordings:* Singles: Dark Clouds, 1997; Avenging Angels, 1997; The Ballad of Tom Jones, with Cerys Matthews, 1998; Begin Again, 1998; Bad Days, 1998; Diary Of A Wimp, 2000; Album: Tin Planet, 1998; Greatest Hits, 2001.

PALMER, Florrie; b. 14 Nov. 1947, Broxted, Essex, England. Songwriter; Vocalist; Musician (keyboards). 1 s., 1 d. *Compositions:* Single: I Get Lonely; Nine to Five, retitled Morning Train (USA), Sheena Easton; The Heat is On, Agnetha Faltskog, ex-Abba singer; When He Shines, Sheena Easton (No. 1, USA), 1980; Various album tracks including: Halfway There; The Last One to Leave; I Want to Marry You. *Recordings:* I Get Lonely; The Mellen Bird, as Susie Mellen, 1973; Hi-fi Love. *Publications:* Never Final Till It's Vinyl, 1994. *Honours:* 9 to 5, Platinum Disc; Ivor Novello Award, Best Lyric of the Year, When He Shines. *Membership:* PRS. *Current Management:* Giles Hargreave, Hargreave Music Management, 15–16 Brooks Mews, London W1Y 1LF, England. *Address:* 28 Frogge St, Ickleton, Saffron Walden CB10 1SH, England.

PALMER, Ian; b. 3 March 1976, Birmingham, England. Musician (drums). *Career:* Tours: Russia, 1990; USA, 1991; Numerous radio, television sessions; Youngest endorser in world for Yamaha Corporation Sabian Cymbals, Vic Firth drumsticks; Clinic tours for Yamaha Drums and Sabian Cymbals, drums, 1993, 1994, 1995. *Publications:* Practice Techniques. *Honours:* BBC Radio Big Band Drummer of Year, 1992. *Membership:* Musicians' Union; Percussionists Society. *Current Management:* Ian Palmer Music. *Address:* 11A Hartopp Rd, Sutton Coldfield, West Midlands B74 2RQ, England.

PALMER, Robert (Alan); b. 19 Jan. 1949, Batley, West Yorkshire, England. Vocalist; Songwriter. *Career:* Member, Alan Bown Set; DaDa; Founder, Vinegar Joe, 1971–74; Solo artiste, 1974–; Member, Power Station, 1985; Regular UK, Europe and US tours; Television appearances include: Arsenio Hall Show; Des O'Connor Tonight; The Tonight Show. *Compositions include:* Film soundtrack, Sweet Lies, 1987. *Recordings:* Albums: with Vinegar Joe: Vinegar Joe; Rock 'n' Roll Gypsies; Six-Star General; Solo albums: Sneakin' Sally Through The Alley, 1974; Pressure Drop, 1975; Some People Can Do What They Like, 1976; Double Fun, 1978; Secrets, 1979; Clues, 1980; Maybe It's Live, 1982; Riptide, 1985; Heavy Nova, 1988; Addictions Vol. 1, 1989; Don't Explain, 1990; Addictions Vol. 2, 1992; Ridin' High, 1992; Honey, 1994; The Very Best Of, 1995; Don't Explain, 1999; Rhythm and Blues, 1999; Disturbing Behaviour, 1999; Nova, 1999; with Power Station: The Power Station, 1985; Hit singles include: Every Kinda People, 1978; Bad Case of Loving You, 1979; Johnny And Mary, 1980; Looking For Clues, 1980; Some Guys Have All The Luck, 1982; Addicted To Love (No. 1, USA), 1986; Hyperactive, 1986; I Didn't Mean To Turn You On (No. 2, USA), 1986; Simply Irresistible (No. 2, USA), 1988; She Makes My Day, 1988; Early In The Morning, 1988; I'll Be Your Baby Tonight, with UB40, 1990; Mercy Mercy Me/I Want You, 1991; Know Me By Now, 1994; with Power Station: Some Like It Hot, 1985; Get It On, 1985; Contributor, film soundtrack, Pretty Woman, 1990; A Matter of Feel, Brent Bourgeois, 1992. *Honours:* MTV Music Video Award, Addicted To Love, 1986; Grammy Awards: Best Male Rock Vocal Performance, Addicted To Love, 1987; Simply Irresistible, 1989. *Address:* c/o Universal Music Group, Universal Studios, 100 Universal City Plaza, Universal City, CA 91608, USA.

PALMER, Tim; b. 4 Oct. 1962, North Shields, England. Record Prod; Mixer. m. Nadine Marsh, 31 July 1995, 2 d. *Career:* Assistant, Utopia Studios; Engineer, Producer in England and USA for: Texas; David Bowie; Robert Plant; Pearl Jam; Tears For Fears; numerous others. *Recordings:* Now and Zen, Shaken and Stirred, Robert Plant; Tin Machine, Tin Machine 2, David Bowie; Elemental, Tears For Fears; Southside, Texas; Carved In Sand, The Mission; Ten, Pearl Jam; Reel Big Fish, Why Do They Rock so Hard; Michael Hutchence; American Pie; Gene Loves Jezebel, Voodoo Dollies: The Best of Gene Loves Jezebel; Legal Reins, Please, the Pleasure; tracks on All That You Can't Leave Behind, U2, 2000. *Membership:* Director, Re-Pro (British Record Producers Guild). *Current Management:* Sandy Roberton, Worlds End Management Inc. *Address:* 183 N Martel Ave, Suite 270, Los Angeles, CA 90036, USA.

PALMIERI, Edward (Eddie); b. 15 Dec. 1936, Spanish Harlem, New York, USA. Musician (piano, percussion); Composer. m. 1 July 1955, 1 s., 4 d. *Education:* Piano studies from age 8. *Career:* Started playing timbales in Chino y Sus Almas Tropicales band, aged 13; Switched to piano, 1951, and formed group with singer Joe Quijano; Became pianist in Johnny Segui's band, 1955; Joined Tito Rodriguez's Mambo Ochestra, 1958; Formed La Perfecta, 1961–68; Collaborations 1966–73 include: Tico All Stars; Fania All Stars; Harlem Drive; Cheo Feliciano; Went to Puerto Rico, 1980s; Formed Eddie Palmieri Orchestra; Returned to New York, late 1980s; Credited with creating the modern salsa; Played in numerous festivals including: North Sea Jazz Festival; Montréal Jazz Festival; Nice Jazz Festival; New Orleans; JVC Festival, New York; Muñeca featured in film Carlito's Way, 1993; Puerto Rico on Spike Lee's Crooklyn soundtrack, 1994; Contributed to HIV and AIDS video Breaking Silence, 1994. *Recordings:* Albums: La Perfecta; El Molestoso; Lo Que Traigo Es Sabroso; Enchando Pa'lante; Azucar Pa'Ti; Mambo Con Conga Es Mozambique; Palmiere and Tjader: El Sonido Nuevo; Molasses; Palmiere and Tjader: Bamboleate; Champagne; Justicia; Superimposition; Vamonos Pa'l Monte; Harlem River Drive; Live At Sing Sing, Vols 1 and 2; Sentido; Live At The University of Puerto Rico; The Sun of Latin Music; Unfinished Masterpiece; Lucumi Macumba Voodoo; Eddie Palmieri; Palo Pa'Rumba; Solito; La Verdad; Sueño; Llego La India Via Eddie Palmieri;

Palmas; Arete; Vortex; Jazz Latino Vol. I; El Rumbero del Piano; Live; Verdad: The Truth; Eddie's Concerto; Music Man; Salsa-Jazz-Descarga: Exploration; Live, 1999; The Best Of..., 1999. *Honours:* various including: Grammy Awards: Best Latin Album, 1975 and 1976; Best Tropical Latin Performance, 1984 1985 and 1987; Best Salsa Album, Masterpiece (with Tito Puente), 2001. *Membership:* Board of Governors, New York, National Asscn of Recording Arts and Sciences. *Current Management:* Edward Palmieri II Music Management, 1908 Parker St, Berkeley, CA 94704, USA.

PALUMBO, James; Nightclub Owner. *Education:* Eton College. *Career:* Former Exec. Merrill Lynch; Founder, Ministry of Sound club, London, 1991; Owner, Ministry of Sound Group, incorporating book and magazine publishing, fashion, a record label. *Address:* Ministry of Sound, 103 Gaunt St, London SE1 6DP, England. *Website:* www.ministryofsound.com.

PANDIT, Jasraj; b. 28 Jan. 1930, Hissar, Hariyana, India. Musician. m. Madhura Pandit, 1962, 1 s., 1 d. *Education:* DMus. *Career:* Studied under elder brother Maniram Pandit; Belongs to Mewati Gharana (school of music); Has conducted extensive research in Haveli Sangeet and presented the original Pure Haveli Sangeet with its devotional content intact; Has established an Ashram Motiram Sangeet Natale Academy with main object of propagating Indian classical music by teaching students free of charge; Mem., advisory board of radio and TV. *Compositions include:* works for opera, ballet and short films, including Kan Khani Sunyo Kare, Geet Govindam, Sur, Laya Aur Chhanda. *Publications:* Sangeet Saurabh. *Honours:* Rajiv Gandhi Award for professional excellence; Padma Bhushan; Sangeet Martand. *Address:* Rajkamal Bldg, 138 Shivaji Park, Mumbai 400016, India.

PANIO, John; b. 21 Feb. 1941, Ituna, Sask, Canada. Musician (guitar, keyboards, vocalist). m. Angeline R Panio, 1 s., 2 d. *Education:* Ba; MMus. *Career:* CKOS Television; CJGX Radio; Cable Regina; CKRM Radio; CKCK Television. *Compositions:* The Priest And The Cantor; Angeline; Pumpkin Kolomeyka; In The Spring; Playing Across Canada. *Recordings:* Dance With The Piano Birds; Songs of Sentiment; Songs of Joy; Celebrate Saskatchewan. *Honours:* Saskatchewan Music Educators Award. *Membership:* Canadian Country Music Asscn. *Current Management:* Panio Bros Band.

PANZU-NIOSI, Papy; b. 21 Jan. 1975, Kinshasa, Democratic Republic of Congo. Musician (guitar, piano). *Education:* Studied composition and musical writing. *Career:* TV and radio appearances, 1999. *Compositions:* Heritage; Testimony; Marriage; The Richness; Alleluia; Charity; Alienation; Lamb's Glory. *Honours:* Academic competition, 1997. *Membership:* Arts National Institute. *Address:* 114, Mayulu 114, Kinsangani II, Kinshasa, Democratic Republic of Congo.

PAPA DEE, (Daniel David Christopher Wahlgren); b. 13 July 1966, Gothenburg, Sweden. Vocalist; Reggae MC. *Education:* Church Choirs, Sweden. *Career:* Tours of Scandinavia with The Stonefunkers, 1987–89; Support to Steel Pulse Tour, USA, 1990; Support act for Ziggy Marley, London, 1991; Roskilde Festival with Papa Levi, 1991; Tour with backing band Protein Bubblers, Scandinavia, Europe, 1992–95. *Recordings:* Albums: Lettin' Off Steam, 1990; One Step Ahead, 1993; Original Master, 1994; Singles: Let The Music Play, 1988; Competition Is None, 1988; Microphone Poet, 1989; Ain't No Stopping Us, 1990; Beautiful Woman, 1990; Take It Easy, 1991; Ain't No Substitute, 1992; Runaround Girl, 1993; Mr Taxi Driver, 1993; I'd Rather Be With You, 1994; The First Cut Is The Deepest, 1995; Featured on recordings: Tribute To Martin Luther King, 1991; with The Stonefunkers: Hard As Kryptonite, 1990; Harder Than Kryptonite, 1991; No Problem '94, 1993; with Dayeene: Big Bad World; with 25th of May: Go Wild, 1992; with Timebomb Posse: Girls, 1992; with Brooklyn Funk Essentials: Single: The Creator Has A Master Plan, 1994; Album: Cool and Steady and Easy, 1994; with Leftfield: Leftism, 1995; Best of Acid Jazz, 1996; Brooklyn Funk Essentials, In the Buzz Bag, 1998; Make 'Em Like It, 2000; TITIYO: After The Rain, 1991/92; L O V E, 1991/92; My Body Says Yes, 1991/92. *Honours:* Swedish Dance Music Awards, Hip Hop Album of the Year, Best Male Vocalist, 1991; Best Male Vocalist, Best Pop Album, 1995. *Membership:* Swedish Musicians' Union. *Current Management:* William Derella, Track Management, NYC. *Address:* Entertainment Resource Group Ltd, 323 Park Ave S, Third Floor, New York, NY 10010, USA.

PAPA GEORGE, (George Papanicola); b. 9 May 1953, London, England. Songwriter; Blues Musician (guitar). *Career:* Opening act for Tina Turner, Hammersmith Apollo, 1983; Tours: Europe, Texas, Columbia; Appearances and interviews, UA TV (wire cable), 1995; Live radio GLR, local radio Wey-Valley 102–101 6FM. *Compositions include:* Co-writer with Ian Hunt: Heading South, title track, Ian Hunt; Guilty, for Paul Williams, 1995. *Recordings:* Papa George Live album, 1995. *Membership:* Musicians' Union; PRS.

PAPA NOEL, (Antoine Nedule Monswet); b. 25 Dec. 1940, Kinshasa, Democratic Republic of Congo. Vocalist; Musician (guitar); Songwriter. *Career:* First recording, 1957; Member: Rock-a-Mambo; Les Bantous de la Capitale; Orchestre African Jazz; TPOK Jazz until 1989; Kekele project, 2001; Collaborations: Sam Mangwana; Mose Fan Fan; Adan Pedroso;

International tours as part of Kekele and with Adan Pedroso including WOMAD Reading, 2000. *Recordings:* Bon Samaritain, 1984; Allegria, 1986; Heritage de Luambo (reunion with ex-members of TPOK Jazz), 1991; Haute Tension, 1994; Bel Ami, 2000; Rumba Congo, 2001, as part of Kekele: Mosala Makasi (with Adan Pedroso), 2001.

PAPA WEMBA, (Jules Shungu Wembadio Pene Kikumba); b. 14 June 1949, Kasai, Democratic Republic of Congo. Vocalist; Songwriter. *Career:* Began singing in church choir, 1966; Co-founder: Zaiko Langa Langa, 1969; Left to form Isife Lokole, 1974; Formed Viva La Musica with Ringo Starr, 1977; Worked with Koffi Olomide; Collaboration with Rochereau Tabu Ley's orchestra, Afrisa International, 1979. *Recordings include:* Zaiko Langa Langa Hits Inoubliables Vol. VIII, 1970–73; Yoka Lokole Dans Matembele Bangi, 1975–76; Papa Wemba and Koffi Olomide, 1978–79; Événement, 1981–82; Papa Wemba – Destiny Ya Moto, 1985; Papa Wemba, 1988; Le Voyageur, 1991; The Kershaw Sessions, 1994; Emotion, 1995; Molokai, 1998. *Honours:* Kinshasa newspaper Elima, Best Vocalist; Best Song of the Year, Mere Superiere, 1977. *Website:* www.papawemba.net.

PAPANDREOU, Elena; b. 7 March 1966, Athens, Greece. Musician (guitar). *Education:* Guitar, National Conservatory, 1985; Diploma in Advanced Studies in Musical Performance, Royal Northern College of Music, England, 1986. *Career:* Concerts world-wide; Soloist, State Orchestra of Athens, State Orchestra of Thessaloniki, Camerata Orchestra, Orchestra of Colours, Orchestra of Patras, Orchestra of Alessandria, Italy; Teacher, National Conservatory, Athens; Collaborations with: Evangelos Boudounis, Alirio Diaz, Roland Dyens, Stella Gadedi, Oscar Ghiglia, Leonidas Kavakos, Nikita Koshkin, Herbert Lippert, Yorgos Mouloudakis, Vasso Papantoniou, Gerardo Ribeiro, Nena Venetsanou. *Recordings:* Albums: Love Music for Solo Guitar, 1983; 22 Pieces for Solo Guitar, 1984; The New Excursion, 1986; Elena Papandreou, 1990; Elena Papandreou Live, 1992; Elena Papandreou, Guitar Recital, 1998; Leo Brouwer, Guitar Music Vol. 2, Elena Papandreou, 2001. *Honours:* First prize, Maria Callas competition, Greece; First prize, Gargnano competition, Italy; First prize, Alessandria competition, Italy; Guitar Foundation of America Competition, second prize, NAXOS prize; Spyros Motsenigos Prize, Academy of Athens, 1992. *Address:* Damareos 177, Athens 11632, Greece. *E-mail:* elpa@elenapapandreou.gr. *Website:* www.elenapapandreou.gr.

PAPER MACHE. See: CHANDLER, Kerri.

PAPERCLIP PEOPLE. See: CRAIG, Carl.

PARAMOR, Susan Marie; b. 9 July 1950, Torquay, England. Songwriter; Vocalist; Actress. m. Graham John Paramor, 1 s., 1 d. *Education:* 6 Years Community Theatre, Salisbury College of Arts; Head of Cathedral Choir, Cyprus. *Career:* Radio, Spire FM, 1996; BBC Radio, 1995–99; Stage Lead Soloist, Super Tramp; EastEnders; The Bill; The River; Dancing In The Dark; Maria Marten; The Spice of Life; Nelson. *Compositions:* Titanic, Street of Tears; Yours Truly Jack; Souls In Pain; Sisters of the Abyss; The Bridge of Hope; Call Me; Through The Window. *Honours:* Best Musical Director, SDA, 1996. *Membership:* Musicians' Union; British Actors Equity Asscn. *Current Management:* Parody Productions, The Stable Studio, Tinkers Cottage, Burcombe, Salisbury, Wiltshire SP2 0EN, England.

PARDESI, Silinder; b. 1 Sept. 1957, Kenya. Lead Vocalist. m. R K Bhooal, 1 s., 2 d. *Education:* BSc, MISTC; Classical Training in Vocals. *Career:* Formed 'Pardesi', 1982; Television broadcasts include, The Clothes Show, Motor Mouth, Def II; Recorded live sessions BBC's Network East, What's That Noise; Performed live in Finland, France, Switzerland, Belgium, Denmark and Italy; International Music Festivals. *Recordings include:* Albums, Shabad Gurbani and Geet Guran De; Pump Up The Bhangra; Full Badmashi; Planet Earth; No To Nasha; Bollywood Seduction; On A Dance Trip; Pump n' Up Again; Seduction 2. *Honours:* Winner, Asian Song Contest, 1986; Best Album of 1990; Best Track of 1990; Top Selling Album of 1990; Best Live Band of 1990; Outstanding Singing Achievement, 1995; Award for Achievement For Enhanced CD-ROM by His Excellency High Commissioner of India Lalit Mann Singh. *Membership:* MISTC; Musicians' Union. *Address:* 32 Ashdown Close, Ernestford Grange, Coventry CV3 2PT, England.

PARDY, Richard Alan; b. 17 April 1966, Grimsby, Lincolnshire, England. Musician (all saxophones, clarinet, flute, piano); Composer; Arranger; MD. m. 23 June 1993, 2 s. *Education:* Grade 8 clarinet, piano, theory; Studied clarinet with Jack Brymer and saxophone with Al Wood; 3 year Jazz/Pop degree course, Leeds, GCLCM; PGCE. *Career:* Tours include Ben E King, Marty Wilde, Cao Quin, Martha Reeves and the Vandellas, Drifters; Tributes to Carpenters, Steely Dan/Donald Fagen, Burt Bacharach, Big Bands/Jazz Combos; Pardy Quintet (appeared at South Bank International Jazz Festival); West End shows and touring shows in UK, Europe and World-wide; TV and radio: BBC Radio 1 and 2; Jazz/Capital FM; Pebble Mill; NZ TV; Film: Eyes Wide Shut (Cruise and Kidman), 1997. *Recordings:* Under the Orange Tree, CD; Session player on advertisement and film music; Featured soloist: Song for the United Nations; Just Can't Give It Up, Nirvana Remix-Hustler's Convention; Blue Lagoon; Living Planet, Lennon. *Publications:* Development/

Evolution of the Big Bands, 1987. *Honours:* Most improved and promising woodwind student, 1980, 1982. *Membership:* CASS; MU. *Current Management:* Richard Pardy Music.

PARFITT, Rick, (Rick Harrison); b. 12 Oct. 1948, Woking, Surrey, England. Musician (guitar); Vocalist. *Career:* Mem., the Highlights; Mem., UK rock group Status Quo (originally the Spectres), 1967–; Extensive tours world-wide; Concerts and festivals include: Reading Rock Festival, 1972, 1978, 1987; NEC Birmingham, before Prince and Princess of Wales (televised by BBC), 1982; Milton Keynes Bowl, 1984; Live Aid, Wembley, 1985; Support to Queen, Wembley Stadium, 1986; Knebworth Festival, 1986; Played four venues in 12 hours, entered in Guinness Book of Records, 1991. *Recordings:* Albums: Picturesque Matchstickable Messages, 1968; Spare Parts, 1969; Ma Kelly's Greasy Spoon, 1970; Dog of Two Heads, 1971; Piledriver, 1973; Hello, 1973; Quo, 1974; On The Level, 1975; Blue For You, 1976; Status Quo Live!, 1977; Rockin' All Over The World, 1977; If You Can't Stand The Heat, 1978; Whatever You Want, 1979; Just Supposin', 1980; Never Too Late, 1981; 1+9+8+2, 1982; To Be Or Not To Be, 1983; Back To Back, 1983; In The Army Now, 1986; Ain't Complaining, 1988; Rock 'Til You Drop, 1991; Live Alive Quo, 1992; Don't Stop, 1996; Whatever You Want, 1997; Under The Influence, 1999; Famous In The Last Century, 2000; Rockin' And Rollin', 2001; Heavy Traffic, 2002; Numerous compilations; Hit singles include: Pictures of Matchstick Men, 1968; Paper Plane, 1973; Caroline, 1973; Break The Rules, 1974; Down Down (No. 1, UK), 1975; Roll Over Lay Down, 1975; Rain, 1976; Mystery Song, 1976; Wild Side of Life, 1977; Rockin' All Over The World, 1977; Again and Again, 1978; Whatever You Want, 1979; Living On An Island, 1979; What You're Proposing, 1980; Lies, 1981; Something 'Bout You Baby I Like, 1981; Rock 'n' Roll, 1981; Dear John, 1982; Ol' Rag Blues, 1983; A Mess of The Blues, 1983; Marguerita Time, 1984; Rollin' Home, 1986; In The Army Now, 1986; Burning Bridges, 1989; Anniversary Waltz, 1990. *Honours:* Silver Clef Award, Nordoff-Robbins Music Therapy Centre, 1981; BRIT Award, Outstanding Contribution to British Music Industry, 1991. *Address:* c/o Universal Music Group, Universal Studios, 100 Universal City Plaza, Universal City, CA 91608, USA.

PARIS, Mica, (Michelle Warren); b. 27 April 1969, London, England. Vocalist. *Career:* Singer in church choir, early 1980s; Session singer, notably with Shakatak; Member, gospel group Spirit of Watts; Hollywood Beyond; Solo artiste, 1988–; Presenter, BBC Radio 2, 2001. *Recordings:* Singles: My One Temptation, 1988; Like Dreamers Do, 1988; Breathe Life Into Me, 1988; Where Is The Love, duet with Will Downing, 1988; Whisper a Prayer, 1993; Stay, 1998; Carefree, 1998; Albums: So Good, 1988; Contribution, 1990; Whisper A Prayer, 1993; Black Angel, 1998; Best Of, 2001; Appears on: Stereo MCs, Connected, 1992; Courtney Pine, To the Eyes of Creation, 1992; Brenda Russell, Soul Talkin', 1993; Omar, For Pleasure, 1995; Guru Jazzmatazz, Vol. 2: The New Reality, 1995.

PARISH, Alan Victor; b. 22 Oct. 1951, Edmonton, London, England. Musician (drums). Divorced, 2 s. *Education:* College. *Career:* Television and radio jingles; Played with Top 40 bands; Currently member of The Hamsters, 8 years; Numerous concerts, television and radio appearances; Toured UK and Europe. *Recordings:* On all Hamsters albums and video. *Address:* 8 Lillyville Walk, Rayleigh, Essex SS6 8UN, England.

PARISH, John (Scott Tracey); b. 11 April 1959, Yeovil, Somerset, England. Record Prod; Composer; Musician (guitar, drums, percussion); Vocalist. *Career:* Joined New Wave group Thieves Like Us, 1979; Group disbanded 1981; Founder, singer, guitarist, The Headless Horsemen, under pseudonym Scott Tracey; Frontperson, principal songwriter with experimental West Country band Automatic Dlamini, 1983–92 (with Polly Harvey and Robert Ellis); Began production career specialising in independent guitar groups; Associate lecturer, rock music and recording techniques, Yeovil College, 1991–94; Played in every PJ Harvey touring line-up, 1995–99; Also recorded with: Bettie Seevert; eels; Goldfrapp. *Compositions:* Two original scores for theatre productions; Music for Dance Hall at Louse Point, with lyrics by PJ Harvey, used for contemporary dance piece, toured Europe 1997; Original score for Rosie, Belgian film directed by Patrice Toye, 1998. *Recordings:* Producer, composer, performer with Automatic Dlamini, The D is for Drum, 1988; From a Diva to a Diver, 1992; Producer, composer, performer with PJ Harvey, Dance Hall at Louse Point, 1996; Producer: Kettle, The Chesterfields, 1986; Myth, Becketts, 1991; To Bring You My Love, PJ Harvey, 1995; Orbit, The Harvest Ministers, 1996; Low Estate, 16 Horsepower, 1997; United States, Elliot Green, 1997; Original soundtrack, Rosie, 1999; Special Appreciation Prize for Rosie score at Bonn International Film Music Biennale, 1999. *Membership:* PRS; Musicians' Union. *Current Management:* Sincere Management, 6B Bravington Rd, London W9 3AH, England.

PARIZO, Lisa; b. 20 May 1964, Lewiston, Maine, USA. Songwriter; Musician (guitar). *Education:* AS, Computer Technology. *Career:* Performed for Private Parties, 1990–98. *Compositions:* Life Should Be More, 1996; Anytime, Everytime, 1996. *Honours:* Certificate of Achievement, Between Now and Yesterday, 1997. *Membership:* Nashville Songwriters Asscn. *Address:* 2350 Shelter Creek Lane, San Bruno, CA 94066, USA.

PARK, Graeme; b. 4 Aug. 1963, Aberdeen, Scotland. DJ; Remixer; Musician. m. Anne-Marie Curtis. *Career:* DJ, Garage, Nottingham, 1982; Started Hacienda, Manchester, 1988; Saturday Night resident, Hacienda, 1988–; DJ world-wide including: Australia; South America; USA; Yugoslavia; Iceland. *Recordings:* Remixed acts including: Brand New Heavies; Inner City; New Order; ABC; Jan Hammer; Eric B; Dubstar; M People; K Klass; Ace Remix Vol. 16; Recent remixes include: Take Me Home and Murder On The Dancefloor, both by Sophie Ellis-Bextor, 2001. *Honours:* Dance-Aid DJ of Year, 1991, 1992, 1993. *Membership:* Musicians' Union. *Current Management:* Cream (DJ); Diesel (remixes, production).

PARKER, Alan; b. 26 Aug. 1944, England. Composer; Musician (guitar). m. Stephanie, 1 s., 1 d. *Education:* Studied classical guitar with Julian Bream, composition, orchestration, Royal Academy of Music, London. *Career:* Began as session guitarist, London's leading player, 1960s–70s; Artists worked with included: Stevie Wonder; Frank Sinatra; Elton John; Dusty Springfield; Andy Williams; Tony Bennett; Mick Jagger; David Bowie; Paul McCartney; John Lennon; Jimi Hendrix; John Denver; Johnny Cash; Dame Kiri Te Kanawa; Placido Domingo; Founder member, songwriter, Blue Mink; The Congregation. *Compositions:* Songs recorded by: Blue Mink; The Congregation; The Walker Brothers; Dusty Springfield; CCS; Arrangements for: Neil Diamond; John Denver; Dusty Springfield; The Walker Brothers; 21 films, 75 television productions include: What's Eating Gilbert Grape; Rhodes, BBC; Up on the Roof, Granada Films; Red Fox, LWT; Jaws 3; To Be The Best; Voice of The Heart; American Gothic; The Glory Boys; Dempsey and Makepeace; Firm Friends; Van Der Valk, Thames TV; Minder, Thames TV; Wild Justice; The Danedyke Mystery, Granada; Mirage; Philby Burgess and McClean; Moody and Peg; Mixed Doubles; Pop Quest, YTV; Children's ITV; Thames News; River Journeys, BBC TV; Oktober, ITV; Unknown Soldier, Carlton; Round Tower, ITV; Colour Blind, ITV; Nancherrow, BBC; Victoria And Albert; Movie scores include: Come See The Paradise; Angela's Ashes; Commercial jingles include: Kellogg's; Wrangler Jeans; Levi's Jeans; Volkswagen; Heinz; Citröen; Tuborg Lager; Mass performed at the Vatican, 1993; Work for music libraries. *Recordings:* Hits with Blue Mink and The Congregation; Session guitarist, soundtracks for composers: John Barry; John Williams; Jerry Goldsmith; Lalo Schiffrin. *Honours:* Ivor Novello. *Membership:* PRS; Musicians' Union. *Address:* Soundtrack Music Associates Ltd, 25 Ives St, Chelsea, London SW3 2ND, England.

PARKER, Ed; b. 16 July 1929, Goose Creek (now Baytown), Texas, USA. Country Vocalist; Musician (guitar). m. Carey Ruth Parker, 21 June 1962. *Education:* BS, MD, FBI National Academy. *Career:* Recording Artist; Live appearances, Bluegrass festivals, and guitar conventions; Film, Tomboy and the Champ. *Recordings:* Ed Parker Sings Just For You; From My Heart; I'd Like to Live It Again; One Ole Texan, Vol. 1; Still a Lot of Good Miles Left in Me. *Publications:* Policemen's Wives: Are They Important?, Texas Police Journal. *Honours:* Personality of the South; Country Music Asscn of America Hall of Fame; Airplay International Trailblazer Award, Leadership Award; International Star Music Award for Special Achievement. *Membership:* CMA; ACM; ROPE; CMOA. *Address:* PO Box 1032, Orange, TX 77631, USA.

PARKER, Graham; b. 18 Nov. 1950, London, England. Vocalist; Songwriter. *Career:* Member, R&B groups: The Black Rockers; Deep Cut; Vocalist, Graham Parker and The Rumour, 1975–80; Solo artiste, 1980–; Concerts include: British tour, support to Thin Lizzy, 1976; Support to Bob Dylan, 1978; US tour, support to Cheap Trick, 1979; Reading Festival, 1986; Rock 'n' roll revue US tour, 1989. *Recordings:* Albums: with Graham Parker and The Rumour: Howlin' Wind, 1976; Heat Treatment, 1976; Stick To Me, 1977; The Parkerilla, 1978; Squeezing Out Sparks, 1979; The Up Escalator, 1980; The Best of Graham Parker and The Rumour, 1980; Solo albums: Another Grey Area, 1982; The Real McCaw, 1983; Steady Nerves, 1985; Mona Lisa's Sister, 1988; Human Soul, 1989; Live! Alone In America, 1989; Struck By Lightning, 1991; Burning Questions, 1992; Passion Word—The Graham Parker Anthology 1976–91, 1993; Live on the Test, 1995; Squeezing Out Sparks/Live Sparks, 1996; The Last Rock and Roll Tour, 1997; Loose Monkeys, Spare Tracks and Lost Demos, 1999; Parkerilla, 1999; Master Hits: Graham Parker; Deepcut To Nowhere, 2001; Singles include: with the Rumour: Silly Thing, 1976; The Pink Parker EP, 1977; Hey Lord Don't Ask Me Questions, 1978; Solo: Temporary Beauty, 1982; Wake Up (Next To You); The Mona Lisa's Sister, 1988; Here It Comes Again, 1992; Christmas Cracker, 1994; 12 Haunted Episodes, 1995. *Address:* c/o RCA Records, Bedford House, 69–79 Fulham High St, London SW6 3JW, England.

PARKER, Mick; b. 12 June 1952, London, England. Musician (piano, keyboards, accordion); Composer. m. Angelika Helm, 25 July 1992, 1 s. *Education:* To degree level; All piano academy grades 1–8. *Career:* Toured with: Joan Armatrading, 1976–79; Billy Ocean, 1979–80; Linda Lewis, 1980–82; Television with all the above; Touring and recording for Gilbert O'Sullivan as MD, 1991–; Toured Japan with Linda Lewis, 1997. *Compositions:* Many jingles and film music, includes Merchant Ivory film Heat and Dust, 1985; Soundtrack for Thieftakers, ITV, 1996. *Recordings:* As producer: Single: So Macho, Sinitta, 1986; As arranger: Album: Aqaba Beach, Mory Kante, 1986; As musician: Album: Este Mundo, Gipsy Kings, 1992; with Gilbert O'Sullivan: Sounds of The Loop, 1992; Live In Japan, 1993; Singer

Sewing Machine, Gilbert O'Sullivan, 1996; Bare Bones, Wishbone Ash, 2000. *Honours:* Ampex Golden Reel Awards, Sinitta; Azucar Moreno. *Membership:* PRS; MCPS; Musicians' Union.

PARKER, Peter Paul; b. 31 Aug. 1964, Kingston, Surrey, England. Musician (bass); Songwriter. *Education:* Basstech College, Acton; Intermediate, Advanced Course. *Career:* Bassist, Heaven Can Wait, 1982–86; Recorded album, played Hammersmith Palais; Played with Thin Lizzy, Wolverhampton, Phil Lynott Tribute, 1994. *Compositions:* Album: Out of the Blue by Emily's Sister, written, recorded and produced, 1996. Single: One of a Kind/Special Friend by Emily's Sister (EP), written, recorded and produced, 1998. *Recordings:* Garden of Hope (EP), Afterlife, 1995; Out of the Blue, 1996. *Membership:* Musicians' Union; Guild of Master Songwriters. *Current Management:* Metro Music. *Address:* Metro Music Ltd, PO Box 75, Shepperton, Middlesex TW17 9NA, England.

PARKER, Ray, Jr; b. 1 May 1954, Detroit, Michigan, USA. Musician (guitar). *Career:* Member, houseband, 20 Grand Club, late 1960s; Toured with Detroit Spinners; Studio musician for Invicta Wax; Formed Raydio, 1977–; Solo artiste, 1982–. *Recordings:* Albums: as Raydio: Raydio, 1977; Rock On, 1979; as Ray Parker Jr and Raydio: Two Places At The Same Time, 1980; A Woman Needs Love, 1981; Solo albums: The Other Woman, 1982; Greatest Hits, 1982; Woman Out of Control, 1983; Chartbusters, 1984; Sex and The Single Man, 1985; After Dark, 1987; I Love You Like You Are, 1991; The Heritage Collection, 2000; Musician, albums by Stevie Wonder: Talking Book, 1972; Innervisions, 1973; Marvin Gaye, Master, 1961–84; Diana Ross, Greatest Hits The RCA Years; Boz Scaggs, My Time the Anthology 1969–97; Nona Hendryx, Transformation; Herbie Hancock, VSOP; Boz Scaggs, Dig, 2001; Singles include: Jack and Jill, 1978; A Woman Needs Love (Just Like You Do), 1981; The Other Woman, 1982; Ghostbusters (film theme) (No. 1, USA; No. 2, UK), 1984; I Don't Think That Man Should Sleep Alone, 1987; She Needs to Get Some, 1991; The Other Woman, 1993. *Honours:* Grammy Award, Best Pop Instrumental Performance, 1984. *Current Management:* Joseph Ruffalo Entertainment, 1728 Monte Cielo Court, Beverly Hills, CA 90210, USA.

PARKINSON, Bill; b. 28 Nov. 1941, Lancaster, England. Musician (guitar); Songwriter; Prod. m. Jennifer, 4 Dec. 1965, 2 d. *Career:* The Fourmost; P J Proby; Screaming Lord Sutch; The Savages; Tom Jones backing group: The Squires (3 years); Chuck Berry; Across The Beatles; Sammy Davis Jr; Shirley Bassey; Bobby Vee; Petula Clark; Vic Damone; Englebert Humperdink; Ted Heath Orchestra; Freddie Starr. *Compositions:* Neil Reid: Mother of Mine; Jimmy Osmond; Deep Purple: Theme to Mandrake Root. *Membership:* PRS; MCPS; Musicians' Union. *Address:* 2 Beech Pl., Epping, Essex CM16 5EJ, England.

PARKS, Van Dyke; b. 3 Jan. 1941, Hattiesburg, MS, USA. Vocalist; Songwriter; Prod; Musician (piano, clarinet). *Education:* American Boychoir School, Princeton, NJ; Carnegie Institute. *Career:* Child actor; Mem., Greenwood County Singers; Signed to MGM as songwriter for Walt Disney Studios, 1964, Warner Bros, 1966; Dir, Warner Bros Audio/Visual Services, 1970–71; Worked with: Fiona Apple, Tango Argentino, Tim Buckley, The Buena Vista Social Club, T Bone Burnett, The Byrds, Eliza Carthy, Peter Case, Cher, Natalie Cole, Judy Collins, Ry Cooder, Sheryl Crow, Kathy Dalton, The Everly Brothers, Kinky Friedman, Lowell George, Eliza Gilkyson, Arlo Guthrie, Harpers Bizarre, Peter Ivers, Leo Kottke, Little Feat, Mojo Men, Keith Moon, Aaron Neville, Randy Newman, Harry Nilsson, Phil Ochs, Sam Phillips, Bonnie Raitt, The Rembrandts, Stan Ridgway, Linda Ronstadt, Carly Simon, Mighty Sparrow, Bruce Springsteen, Ringo Starr, Syd Straw, Meryl Streep, Three Dog Night, U2, Jennifer Warnes, Victoria Williams, Brian Wilson, Steve Young. *Recordings:* Albums: Song Cycle, 1967; Discover America, 1971; Clang Of The Yankee Reaper, 1975; Jump!, 1982; Tokyo Rose, 1989; Moonlighting: Live At The Ash Grove, 1997; with Brian Wilson: Orange Crate Art, 1995. *Compositions include:* High Coin; Come To The Sunshine; For television: Chesapeake Borne; Polar Bears/Season of Fear; The Billy Crystal Comedy Hour; Alfred Hitchcock Mystery Theatre; Fairy Tale Theatre; The Marshal; Hallmark Hall of Fame; Movies of the Week; For film: Goin' South, 1978; Two Jakes; One Christmas; Wild Bill; Club Paradise; Bastard Out of Carolina; The Brave Little Toaster (three songs); Shadrach; Harland County; For theatre: Mother Courage by Brecht (Boston Shakespeare Theatre); Henry IV Part II (Kennedy Center); music for The Triumph of Love (Broadway). *Publications:* with Malcolm Jones: Jump; Jump Again; Jump on Over. *Address:* c/o Harcourt Brace, 525 B Street, Suite 1900, San Diego, CA 92101, USA.

PARLETT, Michael John; b. 19 July 1963, Bexleyheath, Kent, England. Musician (alto, soprano, tenor, saxophones, flute, percussion, windsynth); Prod. *Education:* BMus, Goldsmiths College, London; PGCE, Middlesex University. *Career:* Broadcasts on Radio 2, 1994; Tours with: Iona; Gail Thompson's Jazz Africa; Appeared on: Dave Taylor, Rock 'n' roll Show, Finland; Top of the Pops; European TV, Netherlands. *Recordings:* Sessions with: Lulu; Take That; Mica Paris; Eternal; Gabrielle; Yazz; Clive Griffin; Olu; David Grant; The Jones Girls; 911; M People; Geno Washington;

Currently working on solo album. *Membership:* Musicians' Union. *Current Management:* 61 Howland Way, Surrey Quays, London SW16 1HW, England.

PARNELL, Jack; b. 6 Aug. 1923, London, England. Jazz Musician (drums); Bandleader; Musical Dir. *Career:* Member, Radio Rhythm Club Sextet; Partnership with Vic Lewis as Lewis-Parnell Jazzmen, 1944–46; Member, Ted Heath's Big Band, 7 years; Musical Director, ATV, including Sunday Night At The London Palladium, 1960s; Musical Director, The Muppet Show; Bandleader, UK jazz circuit; Backing musician with touring US musicians, 1970s–, including: Barbra Streisand, Lena Horne. *Recordings:* Recent albums include: Big Band Show, 1976; Jack Parnell Plays Music of The Giants, 1975; Braziliana, 1977; 50 Big Band Favourites, 1984; Joe Williams, Here's to Life, 1993; Dick Sudhalter, After a While, 1994; Ted Heath, Very Best of Ted Heath, 1998; Ted Heath, Listen to my Music Vol. 3, 1999.

PARNELL, Lee Roy; b. 21 Dec. 1956, Abilene, Texas, USA. Country Musician (slide guitar). 1 s., 1 d. *Career:* Ten Feet Tall and Bulletproof tour, with Travis Tritt and Joe Diffie, 1994; Late Show With David Letterman; The Tonight Show; Live With Regis and Kathie Lee; Music City Tonight; Happy New Year America from the House of Blues; Miller Genuine Draft radio commercial; CocaCola Radio commercial; Theme song for 'The Road' radio and television programme. *Recordings:* We All Get Lucky Sometimes; On The Road; Love Without Mercy; Lee Roy Parnell; Every Night's a Saturday Night; Hits and Highways Ahead; Tell The Truth, 2001; Singles: Lucky Me Lucky You; You Can't Get There from Here. *Membership:* BMI; ACM; CMA. *Current Management:* Mike Robertson Management. *Address:* PO Box 120073, Nashville, TN 37212, USA.

PARR, John; b. 19 Nov. 1957, Nr. Sherwood Forest, Nottinghamshire, England. Vocalist; Songwriter; Prod. m. Sharon, 29 Aug. 1980, 2 s. *Education:* Guitar lessons. *Career:* Tours, 1985–, including tours with: Tina Turner; Bryan Adams; Toto; Heart; Beach Boys. *Recordings:* Hit singles: Naughty Naughty, 1985; St Elmo's Fire (world-wide No. 1), 1985; Rock 'N' Roll Mercenaries (with Meatloaf), 1986; Paris (with LSO and Philarmonic Choir); Miami Vice; As producer: Web Of Love, Sarah Jory, 1994; If I Love You, Sarah Jory, 1999; Movie soundtracks: 3 Men and A Baby; Quicksilver; American Anthem; The Running Man; St Elmo's Fire, 1985; Near Dark, 1987; Spruce Goose, 1986; Covers with: Tom Jones; The Monkees; Meatloaf; Roger Daltrey. *Honours:* ASCAP Award, Most Performed Song; MIDEM Award. *Membership:* PRS; MCPS; ASCAP; AFTRA; Equity; Musicians' Union. *Current Management:* Lou Howson, Bernie Fischbach. *Address:* Fischbach, 1925 Century Park E, Suite 1260, Los Angeles, CA 90067, USA.

PARRISH, Man; b. 6 May 1958, Brooklyn, New York, USA. Prod; Musician (keyboards); Man. *Education:* Dramatic Studies, American Academy of Dramatic Arts, New York, 1971. *Career:* 17 years in music business; Owner, production company, Man Made Productions, 1983–; Partner, Artist Management Company; Manager, Village People, 1988–93; Member of group Man 2 Man. *Recordings:* Singles: Hip Hop Be Bop, Man Parrish; Male Stripper, Man 2 Man; I Am What I Am, Gloria Gaynor (keyboards); Solo albums: Man Parrish, 1983; 2, 1996; Hip Hop Bee Bop (Don't Stop), 1996; The Best of Man Parrish: Heartstroke, 1996; Dream Man, 1998; Dreamtime, 1998; Producer/writer, approximately 50 recordings, including: Village People; Michael Jackson; Boy George; Gloria Gaynor; Omar Santana; Klaus Nomi. *Honours:* Billboard Award, Dance Artist; Bessie Smith Award. *Membership:* ASCAP; National Music Publishers; Harry Fox Agency. *Current Management:* AM:PM Entertainment. *Address:* 415 63rd St, Brooklyn, NY 11220, USA.

PARRY, J. Chris; b. 7 Jan. 1949, Wellington, New Zealand. Record Co Exec; Record Prod; Divorced, 1 s., 2 d. *Education:* HND Business Studies, 1974. *Career:* Professional drummer, 1968–71; A&R Manager, Polydor Records, 1974–78; Owner, Fiction Records, 1978–; Managing Director, Fiction Records, Fiction Songs; Managing Director, XFM Radio. *Recordings:* Albums: In The City, 1977, Modern World, 1977, All Mod Cons, 1978, all by The Jam; Various recordings, The Cure (as co-producer) including the albums: Japanese Whispers, 1983; The Top, 1984; Disintegration, 1989; Wish, 1992; Greatest Hits, 2001; Three Imaginary Boys, The Cure (as producer). *Membership:* BPI; Institute of Marketing. *Address:* 97 Charlotte St, London W1 1LB, England.

PARSONS, Alan; b. 1948. Musician; Record Prod; Engineer. *Career:* Former recording engineer, EMI Records; Founder, Alan Parsons Project, 1975–; The Alan Parsons Live Project have toured 19 different countries around the world since 1994. *Recordings:* Albums: with Alan Parsons Project: Tales of Mystery and Imagination, 1976; I Robot, 1977; Pyramid, 1978; Eve, 1979; The Turn of a Friendly Card, 1980; Eye In The Sky, 1981; Ammonia Avenue, 1983; Vulture Culture, 1984; Stereotomy, 1985; Gaudi, 1987; Instrumental Works – Best of Alan Parsons Project, 1983; Limelight – Best of (Vol. II), 1988; Try Anything Once, 1992; On Air, 1996; Definitive Collection; 1997; The Time Machine, 1999; Recording engineer, artistes including: The Beatles; Wings; Pilot; Cockney Rebel; Al Stewart; Pink Floyd. *Address:* c/o The Agency, 370 City Rd, London EC1V 2QA, England.

PARSONS, David John; b. 30 Aug. 1962, Colchester, Essex, England. Record Co Exec; Artist Man; Performer. m. Stephanie Bowyer, 5 Sept. 1992, 1

s. *Education:* BA Hons; Currently pursuing PhD. *Career:* Lead vocalist, Splat!, 1981–83; Owner, Ron Johnson Records, 1983–90; Director, Submission Records Ltd, 1987–90; Owner, Zung Records, 1994; Director, Too Pye Ahh Records, 1995; Lead vocalist, Chod, 1995. *Recordings:* 1936, The Ex; Mud On A Colon, Stump; Two Kan Guru, Big Flame; I Am John's Pancreas, A Witness; Dudley Dorite Wristwatch, Chod; Debut album, Wholesome Fish. *Honours:* Ron Johnson Records, Independent Label of the Year, 1986. *Membership:* PRS; MCPS; PPL. *Current Management:* Purple Skunk Management, The Basement, 19 Victoria Parade, Broadstairs, Kent CT10 1QL, England.

PARSONS, David Richard; b. 12 April 1959, Woking, England. Musician (guitar, violin); Songwriter. 1 s. *Education:* Violin tuition; Music O Level. *Career:* Member, Sham 69; Member, The Wanderers, with Stiv Bators on vocals; Arena, TV special with Sham 69. *Recordings:* With Sham 69: Albums: Tell Us The Truth; That's Life; Hersham Boys; The Game; Volunteer; Information Libre; Soapy Water and Mr Marmalade; Direct Action Day 21, 2001; All the singles including: Angels With Dirty Faces, 1978; If The Kids Are United, 1978; Hurry Up Harry, 1978; Questions And Answers, 1979; Hersham Boys, 1979; With The Wanderers: Only Lovers Left Alive, 1981; Solo Album: Reconcile. *Membership:* PRS; MCPS; Musicians' Union. *Address:* 30 Bois Hall Rd, Addlestone, Surrey KT 15 2JL, England.

PARSONS, Niamh; b. 1958, Dublin, Ireland. Vocalist. *Education:* Learned singing from father. *Career:* First sang with band Killera; Formed The Loose Connections with Dee Moore; Joined Arcady, 1992; Sang for President Clinton in 1999; Lecturer at the Ballyfermot School of Music. *Recordings:* Albums include: Loosely Connected, 1992; Loosen Up, Holding Up Half The Sky, 1997; Celtic Love Songs, 1998; Blackbirds and Thrushes, 1999; In My Prime, 2000. *Website:* www.niamhparsons.com.

PARTIS, Lee Valentine; b. 22 Feb. 1954, Romford, Essex, England. Musician (drums); Vocalist; Actor. 1 s. *Career:* Played with many bands including: Kirsty MacColl; Jah Wobble; Oysterband. *Recordings:* Numerous albums include: with Oysterband: Deserters, 1992; Holy Bandits, 1993; Trawler, 1994; with Kirsty MacColl: Desperate Character, 1981. *Current Management:* Forward Management. *Address:* 132 Liverpool Rd, London N1 1LA, England.

PARTON, Dolly Rebecca; b. 19 Jan. 1946, Locust Ridge, TN, USA. Country Vocalist; Actress. m. Carl Dean, 30 May 1966. *Career:* Singer, local radio, as child; Apperances include: Grand Ole Opry, Nashville, 1968–; Regular on Porter Wagoner Show; Regular recordings with Wagoner, 1967–74; Solo artiste, 1969–; Actress, films: 9 To 5, 1980; Best Little Whorehouse In Texas, 1982; Rhinestone, 1984; Steel Magnolias, 1990; Wild Texas Wind (NBC), 1990; Straight Talk, 1992; Host, own television shows, Dolly, 1976, 1987; TV special, Dolly Parton Christmas At Home (ABC), 1990; Founder Dollywood Foundation, 1988; Owner, Dollywood entertainment complex, incl. Dollyworld. *Compositions include:* I Will Always Love You (also recorded by Whitney Houston, for film The Bodyguard 1992). *Recordings:* Albums: with Porter Wagoner: Just The Two Of Us, 1969; Always, Always, 1969; Porter Wayne And Dolly Rebecca, 1970; Once More, 1970; Two Of A Kind, 1971; Solo: My Blue Ridge Mountain Boy, 1969; Joshua, 1973; New Harvest... First Gathering, 1977; Here You Come Again, 1978; Great Balls Of Fire, 1979; Dolly Dolly Dolly, 1980; 9 To 5 And Odd Jobs, 1980; Heartbreak Express, 1982; Best Little Whorehouse In Texas (soundtrack), 1982; Burlap And Satin, 1983; The Great Pretender, 1984; Rhinestone (soundtrack), 1984; Once Upon A Christmas, 1984; Greatest Hits, 1985; Trio (with Linda Ronstadt and Emmylou Harris), 1987; Rainbow, 1988; White Limozeen, 1989; Eagle When She Flies, 1991; Straight Talk (soundtrack), 1992; Slow Dancing With The Moon, 1993; Honky Tonk Angels (with Loretta Lynn and Tammy Wynette), 1993; Heartsongs: Live From Home, 1994; Something Special, 1995; Treasures, 1996; The Essential Dolly Parton, Vol. I; Hungry Again, 1998; Walking On Sunshine, 1999; The Grass Is Blue, 1999; Super Hits, 1999; Little Sparrow, 2001; Halos & Horns, 2002. Singles: Numerous US Country No. 1 hits include: Joshua, 1970; Jolene, 1974; I Will Always Love You, 1974 (also in 1982); Baby I'm Burnin', 1979; 9 To 5, 1981; Islands In The Stream, with Kenny Rogers, 1983; Think About Love, 1986; To Know Him Is To Love Him, 1987; Yellow Roses, 1989; Contributor, Heroes and Friends, Randy Travis, 1991. *Honours:* CMA Awards, Female Vocalist of the Year, 1975, 1976; American Music Awards, Favourite Country Album, 1978, Favourite Country Single, 1984, 1985; Grammy Awards, Best Female Country Artist, 1979, Best Country Vocal Performance, 1982, Top Country Album, 1981, 2001, Best Country Vocal, Duo or Group (with Ronstadt and Harris), 1988; ACM Record of the Year, 1983; AMA Best Country Single, 1983. *Current Management:* Maureen O'Connor, Rogers and Cowan, 10000 Santa Monica Blvd, Los Angeles, CA 90067, USA. *Address:* c/o RCA, 6 W 57th St, New York, NY 10019, USA. *Website:* www.dollywood.com.

PARTON, Stella; b. 4 May 1949, Locust Ridge, Tennessee, USA. Country Vocalist. *Career:* Radio debut with sister Dolly Parton, 1955; Featured on soundtrack of Dolly Parton's film Rhinestone; Actress, stage version, The Best Little Whorehouse In Texas. *Recordings:* Hit singles: I Want To Hold You In My Dreams Tonight; Standard Lie No. 1; Four Little Letters; Albums: I Want To Hold You In My Arms Tonight, 1975; Country Sweet, 1977; Stella Parton,

1978; Love Ya, 1979; So Far... So Good, 1982; Anthology, 1998. *Address:* c/o Joe Taylor Artist Agency, 2802 Columbine Pl., Nashville, TN 37204, USA.

PARTRIDGE, Andy; b. 11 Nov. 1953, Malta. Musician (guitar); Vocalist; Songwriter; Record Prod. *Career:* Guitarist, vocalist, XTC, 1977–; Appearances include: USA, Venezuela, SE Asia, Australia; Record as send-up 60s group, The Dukes of Stratosphear, 1985; XTC work as studio band only, 1982–; Producer, other bands, 1983–. *Recordings:* Hit singles: with XTC: Making Plans For Nigel, 1979; Generals And Majors, 1980; Sgt Rock (Is Going To Help Me), 1981; Senses Working Overtime, 1982; Mayor Of Simpleton, 1989; The Disappointed, 1992; Albums as XTC: White Music, 1978; Go 2, 1978; Drums and Wires, 1979; Black Sea, 1980; English Settlement, 1982; Waxworks – Some Singles, (1977–82), 1982; Mummer, 1983; The Big Express, 1984; The Compact XTC, 1986; Skylarking, 1986; Chips From The Chocolate Fireball, 1987; Oranges and Lemons, 1989; Nonsuch, 1992; Fossil Fuel, 1996; Transistor Blast, 1998; Apple Venus Volume I, 1999; Homespun, 1999; Wasp Star (Apple Venus Volume 2), 2000; Homegrown, 2001; Solo albums: Takeaway/The Lure of Salvage, 1980; as The Dukes of Stratosphear: 25 O'Clock, 1985; Psonic Psunspot, 1987; Transistor Blast, 1998; Apple Venus Vol. I, 1999; Homespun, 1999; Wasp Star (Apple Venus Vol. 2), 2000; Fuzzy Warbles 1 & 2; Coat Of Many Cupboards, 2002; with Martin Newell: The Greatest Living Englishman, 1993; Through the Hill, with Harold Budd, 1994; As producer: tracks by The Mission; The Lilac Time; Peter Blegvad; Wallflowers; Woodentops. *Honours:* Edison Award, 1982. *Current Management:* c/o Idea, St Annes, Foxhill, Wanborough, Nr Swindon, Wiltshire SN4 0DS, England.

PASCOAL, Hermeto; b. 22 June 1936, Lagoa da Canoa, Brazil. Multi-instrumentalist; Arranger; Composer. m. Ilza da Silva Pascoal, 30 July 1955, 3 s., 3 d. *Career:* Accordion, flute, with Quarteto Novo, to 1969; Solo artist, 1970–; Concerts with Hermeto Pascoal Group include Montreux Jazz Festival, 1978; With the Danish Radio Concert Orchestra, Copenhagen, 1989; With Symphonic, Berlin, 1989; Radio Big Band, 1992; with Special Big Band, London, 1994; Tours, Europe, USA; Television, radio: Brazilian TV; Sinfonia do Alto da Ribeira; Sound of Aura with: President Fernando Collor de Melo; Papa Joao Paulo II; Jo Soares; Clovodil; French TV with The Tubes. *Recordings:* Quarteto Novo, 1967; Hermeto, 1979; A Musica Livre De Hermeto Pascoal, 1973; Slaves Mass, 1976; Zabumbe-bum-a, 1978; Montreux ao Vivo, 1978; Cerebro Magnetico, 1980; Hermeto Pascoal and Grupo, 1982; Lagoa da Canoa Municipalo de Arapiraca, 1984; Brasil Universo, 1986; So Nao Toca Quem Nao Quer, 1987; Por Diferentes Caminhos/Piano solo, 1988; Festa Dos Deuses, 1992; Hermeta Pascoal E Grupo, 1992; Eu E Eles, 1999. *Honours:* Best Soloist, Associação Paulista de Criticos de Arte, Brazil, 1972; Best Group, Brazil, 1988; Best Cover and Best Tune: Pixitotina, Brazil, 1989; Concert of Year and Decade, Guardian, Q Magazine, 1994. *Membership:* SACEM, France. *Address:* Rua Victor Guisard 333, Jabour, Rio de Janeiro, RJ, Brazil.

PASCU, Ioan Gyuri; b. 31 Aug. 1961, Agnita, Romania. Teacher; Songwriter; Entertainer; Actor; Musician (guitar, drums); Writer; Radio, television producer. m. Daniela Marin, 15 Aug. 1993. *Education:* University of Cluj, Faculty of Philology; Private piano lessons. *Career:* Member, Divertis Group (humour, political satire shows) since 1990; Many radio and television shows, 1989–92; Soloist, 1991–; Established the Ioan Gyuri Pascu and The Blues Workers Band; International Jazz and Blues Festivals: Brasov, 1992; Bucharest, 1992; Russe, 1992; Brasov, 1993, 1994; International Rock Festivals: Bucharest, 1993; Dracula, Brasov, 1993; Skip Rock, Bucharest, 1994; International Pop Festival, Golden Stag, Brasov (record debut contest), 1993; Opened the Romanian tours of Beats International, 1993, Asia, 1994; Acted in Unforgettable Summer, by Lucian Pintilie (offically selected for Cannes film festival); TV specials: Stars Duel, 1993; VIP, 1993; Many Divertis Group shows, soloist in musical shows. *Compositions:* Over 30 songs; Original music for television shows: Teapa, 1993; Stars School, 1993. *Recordings:* It Could Be, 1992; Mixed Grill, 1993; The Machine With Jazzoline, 1994; Video: Divertis Group, 1995. *Publications:* Short stories in Apostrof (literature magazine), 1990; Cuvantul magazine (serial). Showman of the Year: Pop Rock and Show magazine; Major Personality of the Year, 1993; The Song of the Year, The Songwriter of the Year, Radio Contact, 1994; Record of the Year, Vox, Pop, Rock magazine. *Membership:* Divertis Cultural Asscn.

PASILLAS, José Antonio II; b. 26 April 1976. Musician (drums). *Career:* Started drumming in 1990; Formed group Incubus with school friends in Calabasas, California, 1991; Initially played small parties, graduating to support slots in Hollywood, California; Circulated demo tapes of Closet Cultivation and Incubus before independent album release, 1995; Group signed by Immortal/Epic; Built US and European following support slots on tours with: Sugar Ray; Black Sabbath; Korn; Drive reached #1 on US Modern Rock Chart, 2001; First Japanese and Australian live dates, 2001. *Recordings:* Albums: Fungus Amongus, 1995; S.C.I.E.N.C.E., 1997; Make Yourself, 1999; Morning View, 2001; Singles: Enjoy Incubus EP, 1997; Pardon Me, 1999; Stellar, When Incubus Attacks Vol. 1 EP, 2000; Drive, Wish You Were Here, 2001. *Honours:* Make Yourself album certified double platinum by RIAA; Billboard Award, Modern Rock Single of the Year, 2001. *Current*

Management: Steve Rennie, REN Management, California, USA. *Website:* www.enjoyincubus.com.

PASKIN, Layo; b. London, England. Prod; Remixer; DJ. *Career:* Opened London's The End nightclub with partner Mr C, 1995; Co-founder: End Recordings; Mem., Killer Loop (with Mr C); Layo and Bushwacka!. *Recordings:* Albums: Lowlife (with Bushwacka!), 1999; Night Works (with Bushwacka!), 2002. Singles: as Usual Suspects: Split Personality, 1997; Nightstalkin', 1998; with Bushwacka: Deep South, 1999; with Killer Loop: Someone, 1996; Broken, 1998; The Blue Hour, 2000; Organism, 2001. *Address:* c/o End Recordings, 18 W Central St, London WC1A 1JJ, England.

PASS, Liz (Elizabeth Ann); b. Mutare, Zimbabwe. Contemporary Gospel Artist. m. Rev Dr David B Pass, 1 Sept. 1973. *Education:* Bachelor of Music, Voice Performance; BA, Theatre, Communications. *Career:* Appeared on International TV with song: God Bless Africa; Tours, concerts, television appearances all over Africa, Europe, USA, South America. *Recordings:* God Bless Africa; Heart Cry For The Earth; Hymns For Africa; Christmas In Africa; African Collection; Under African Skies; Reach For Your Dreams; A Millennium Dream. *Publications:* Two song books. *Honours:* Top voice student, Biola University, 1980. *Membership:* ASAMI; SAMRO; SARREL.

PATTON, Mike; b. 27 Jan. 1968, Eureka, California, USA. Rock Vocalist. *Career:* Member, Mr Bungle; Lead singer, US rock group Faith No More, 1988–98; Regular international concerts include: Reading Festival, 1990; Support to Robert Plant, 1990; Monsters of Rock European festivals, 1990; Rock In Rio II, Brazil, 1991; Day On The Green, San Francisco, 1991; Phoenix Festival, 1993, 1995. *Recordings:* Hit singles include: From Out of Nowhere, 1990; Epic, 1990; Falling To Pieces, 1990; Midlife Crisis, 1992; A Small Victory, 1992; Everything's Ruined, 1992; I'm Easy, 1993; Albums: The Real Thing, 1989; Live At Brixton Academy, 1991; Angel Dust, 1992; King For A Day, Fool For A Lifetime, 1995; Adult Themes for Voice, 1996; Pranzo Oltranzis, 1997; Album of the Year, 1997; Faith No More, Greatest Hits, 1998; with Jerry Hunt, Song Drapes, 1999; Other projects include: with Fantomas: Fantomas, 1999; Director's Cut, 2001; with Tomahawk: Tomahawk, 2001. *Honours:* Bammy Awards, Outstanding Group, Male Vocalist, 1991. *Current Management:* Warren Entner Management, 5550 Wilshire Blvd, Suite 302, Los Angeles, CA 90036, USA.

PATTULLO, Gordon James; b. 8 Sept. 1961, Dundee, Scotland. Musician (accordion). m. June Elspeth McLaren, 17 Oct. 1984, 2 s., 1 d. *Education:* Dundee Accordion School of Music. *Career:* Concert tours world-wide with Andy Stewart Show, 1977–; Television appearances: 2 series for Andy's Party, Grampian TV; Thingummyjig, STV; Various Hogmanay shows for BBC TV, Grampian and Scottish TV. *Compositions include:* The Furrows End. *Recordings:* A Gordon For You; The Northlands; Scotland's Favourite; Here's Tae A Gordon; Accordion Favourites; Scotch On The Box; All The Best; Fair Play; Scottish Accordion Hits; Golden Sound of Scottish Music; A Scottish Celebration; Ceilidh Dance Party; A Guid Scots Night, 2000. *Honours:* Jr Accordion Champion of Scotland, 1974. *Membership:* Musicians' Union. *Address:* Tullybaccart Farmhouse, Coupar Angus, Blairgowrie, Perthshire PH13 9LA, Scotland.

PAUL, Amit Sebastian; b. 29 Oct. 1983, Boden, Sweden. Vocalist. *Education:* Kungsholmens school, Stockholm. *Career:* Picked to be member of A*Teens group following auditions at Leslie Kühler's dance school, 1998; Continued studies whilst pursuing musical career; Prestigious US support tours for *NSYNC and Britney Spears, 2000. *Recordings:* Albums: The Abba Generation, 1999; Teen Spirit, 2001; Singles: Mamma Mia, Super Trouper, Gimme! Gimme! Gimme!, Happy New Year, 1999; Dancing Queen, Upside Down, 2000; Halfway Around The World, Sugar Rush, 2001. *Honours:* Broke Swedish sales records with first album and single; World-wide sales of first album in excess of 3m.; Viva Music Awards, Best International Newcomer, 2000. *Address:* c/o Stockholm Records, Sweden. *Website:* www.stockholmrecords.com.

PAUL, Les, (Lester Polfus); b. 9 June 1915, Waukesha, WI, USA. Inventor; Musician (guitar). m. Mary Ford, deceased 1977, 3 s., 2 d. *Career:* Musician, numerous radio appearances, 1920s–30s; Formed Les Paul Trio, 1936; Recordings and television show with Mary Ford, 1950s; Chet Atkins, 1970s; Television includes: First television broadcast with orchestra, NBC, 1939; Documentary, The Wizard of Waukesha, 1980; Concerts include: Jazz At The Philharmonic concert with Nat 'King' Cole, 1944; Guitar Legends, Seville, Spain, 1992; Pioneer, multi-track tape recording; Inventor, first 8-track tape recorder; Inventor, sound-on-sound recording; Inventor, designer, Les Paul solid body electric guitar, for Gibson Guitars; Consultant, Gibson Guitar Corpn, Nashville. *Recordings:* Albums: with Mary Ford: New Sound Vols I and II; Les and Mary; Bye Bye Blues; The Hitmakers; Time To Dream; Lover's Luau; Warm and Wonderful; Bouquet of Roses; Swingin' South; Love Songs by Les Paul and Mary Ford, 1997; Blowing The Smoke Away From A Trail Of Hits, 2000; with Chet Atkins: Chester and Lester, 1977; Guitar Masters, 1978; Multi Trakin', 1979; Tiger Rag, 1984; All Time Greatest Hits, 1994; A Class Act, 1998; The World is Waiting, 1999; Solo: Early Les Paul, 1999; The V-Disc Recordings, 1999; The Millennium Collection, 2001; How

High The Moon, 2002; Other recordings with Bing Crosby; Andrews Sisters; Patti Smith. *Honours:* Grammy Award, for Chester and Lester, 1977; Hall of Fame Award, 1979.

PAUL, Oskar; Songwriter; Prod; Programmer. *Career:* Worked with as Prod. and Songwriter: Isabelle A, Marc Almond David Chavet, Hear'say, Emma Holland, Ladies First, Jamie Pearce, S Club 7, Steps; Worked with as Programmer: Curve, Depeche Mode, Seal, SJ. *Address:* c/o Stephen Budd Management Ltd, 109b Regents Park Rd, Primrose Hill, London NW1 8UR, England. *Website:* www.record-producers.com.

PAULIK, Dalibor; b. 22 Dec. 1953, Zagreb, Croatia. Composer; Musician (piano); Theatre Critic. m. Vesna Paulik, 7 June 1980, 1 s. *Education:* MSc, Theatrology; Professor, Music theatre; Secondary music school, private music seminars. *Career:* Croatian and international festivals of popular music; 500 concerts with popular Croatian singers; Music for theatre and television; Festivals in: Ireland; Latin America; Finland; Los Angeles; Croatia (Zagreb, Krapina, Split); Sarjevo; Songs for organizations: Stars of Hope (Sweden); World For Two (UK). *Compositions:* Over 200 include: Your Face In My Mirror; Goodbye Is Not For You; Love Is A Game; Never In My Life; Memories; The Violin Song; Stars of Hope; Today I'm Sad My Love; Together Forever; Dancing With The Moonlight. *Publications:* Scientific publications of HAZU; Who Is Who In Croatia; Directory of Croatian Composers Society. *Honours:* 20 at Croatian festivals; 1 in Ireland. *Membership:* Croatian Composers' Society (FIDOF).

PAULSEN, Michael Harbo; b. 23 March 1964, Jylland, Abenra, Denmark. Musician (drums). *Education:* With Classical Music Professor Bent Lylloff, Billyhart, Idriss Muhammed. *Recordings:* Sun Quartet; Two Bass Hit; Erik Brum Spreckelsen: I'll See You Soon. *Address:* Jakob Dannefaerdsvej 14 7th, 1973, FDB C, Denmark.

PAUSINI, Laura; Vocalist; Songwriter. *Career:* Appeared in Pavarotti & Friends concert, album, 1999. *Recordings:* Albums (some also available in Spanish and French): Laura Pausini, 1993; Laura, 1994; Le Cose Che Vivi, 1996; La Mia Risposta, 1998; Tra Te E Il Mare, 2000; Lo Mejor De Laura Pausini, 2002; From The Inside (in English), 2002. *Honours:* Festival de la Cancion Italiana, 1993; World Music Award, Best Selling Italian Artist; Premio Lo Nuestro, Most Promising Latin Artist. *Address:* c/o Atlantic Records, 1790 Avenue of the Americas, New York, NY 10104, USA. *E-mail:* info@laurapausini.com. *Website:* www.laurapausini.com.

PAXTON, Tom; b. 31 Oct. 1937, Chicago, Illinois, USA. Folk Vocalist; Songwriter; Author. m. Margaret Ann Cummings, 5 Aug. 1963, 3 d. *Education:* BFA, University of Oklahoma, 1959. *Career:* Folk recording artist, 1962–; Early concerts on Greenwich Village circuit; World-wide tours and concerts, 1960–; Board of directors, Kerrville Folk Festival, 1990. *Compositions include:* Lyndon Johnson Told The Nation; Talkin' Vietnam Pot Luck Blues; Leaving London; The Hostage (also recorded by Judy Collins). *Recordings:* Albums include: Ramblin' Boy, 1964; Ain't That News, 1965; Outward Bound, 1968; Morning Again, 1968; The Things I Notice Now, 1969; Tom Paxton 6, 1970; The Compleat Tom Paxton, 1971; How Come The Sun, 1971; Peace Will Come 1972; New Songs Old Friends, 1973; Something In My Life, 1975; Saturday Night, 1976; Heroes, 1978; Up and Up, 1980; The Paxton Report, 1981; In The Orchard, 1985; One Million Lawyers and Other Disasters, 1985; Even A Gray Day, 1986; And Loving You, 1988; Politics – Live, 1989; Storyteller, 1989; Suzy is a Rocker, 1992; Goin' to the Zoo, 1997; I Can't Help Wonder Where I'm Bound, 1999; Live From Mountain Stage, 2001; Under American Skies, 2001; Appears on: Tribute to Woody Guthrie, 1972; Newport Folk Festival, 1991; Where Have All the Flowers Gone, 1998. *Publications:* Ramblin' Boy and Other Songs, 1965; Tom Paxton Anthology, 1971; Politics, 1989; The Authentic Guitar of Tom Paxton, 1989; The Tom Paxton Children's Song Book, 1990; Author, children's books: Jennifer's Rabbit, 1988; Belling The Cat, 1990; Englebert The Elephant, 1990; Aesop's Fables Retold In Verse, 1988; Androcles and The Lion, 1991. *Membership:* ASCAP; AFTRA: AFofM; Screen Actors Guild; World Folk Music Asscn (Hon. Chairman of Board). *Current Management:* c/o Susan Martinez, Martinez Management and Media, PO Box 14901, University Station, Minneapolis, MN 55414, USA.

PAYNE, Dougie (Douglas); b. 14 Nov. 1972, Scotland. Musician (bass). *Career:* Mem., Travis, 1997–; Numerous tours, festivals and television appearances. *Recordings:* Albums: Good Feeling, 1997; The Man Who (No. 1, UK), 1999; The Invisible Band (No. 1, UK), 2001. Singles: U16 Girls, 1997; All I Want To Do Is Rock, 1997; Tied To The Nineties, 1997; Happy, 1997; More Than Us, 1997; Writing To Reach You, 1999; Driftwood, 1999; Why Does It Always Rain on Me?, 1999; Turn, 1999; Coming Around, 2000; Sing, 2001; Side, 2001. *Honours:* Q Magazine Award, Best Single, 1999; Select Magazine, Album of the Year, 1999; BRIT Awards, Best British Group, Best British Album, 2000, Best British Group, 2002. *Address:* c/o Independiente Ltd, The Drill Hall, 3 Heathfield Terrace, London W4 4JE, England. *Website:* www.travisonline.com.

PAYNE, Freda; b. 19 Sept. 1945, Detroit, Michigan, USA. Vocalist; Actress. m. Gregory Abbott, 1 Dec. 1976, 1 s. *Education:* Studied acting with Al Mancini; Detroit Institute of Musical Arts; Piano and Voice tuition. *Career:* Began singing career at age 17; Toured with Quincy Jones at such theatres as the Apollo in New York City and Regal Theatre in Chicago; Acting debut in the musical Hallelujah Baby, then as Linda in Lost in The Stars, in The Book of Numbers, Daddy Goodness, Ain't Misbehavin' and Sophisticated Ladies; Starred in the television special Freda Payne and The Stylistics, appeared in HBO's The Legendary Ladies of Rock and in the video Soul No 2 America's Music; Hosted her own TV talk show, Today's Black Woman; Has toured in UK, Germany and Japan; Starred in musical, Blues in the Night, 1990–91, and in the musical drama, Jelly's Last Jam by George C Wolf. *Recordings include:* Albums: Stares and Whispers; Supernatural High; Red Hot; Payne and Pleasure; Out of Payne Comes Love; I Hate Barney; An Evening with Freda Payne: Live; Live in Concert; Greatest Hits; Greatest Hits Live in Concert; Lost In Love, 2000; Come See About Me, 2001; Singles: Band of Gold (No. 1, UK), 1970; Bring The Boys Home; Deeper and Deeper; Cherish What's Dear To You; You Brought The Joy. *Honours:* Two Gold Singles; Best Ensemble Performance for Blues In The Night, Drama-Logue Award, 1990; Dame of Malta, Knights of Malta – The Sovereign Military and Hospital Order of St John of Jerusalem, 1994. *Address:* Embassy Artists/Full Circle Entertainment, 23500 Michigan Ave, Dearborn, MI 48124, USA.

PAYNE, John Devereux; b. 16 Dec. 1945, Virginia, USA. Musician; Music Teacher. m. Francine Rota, 3 s. *Education:* BA, Harvard University, 1972. *Career:* Played and recorded with Van Morrison, 1968; Bonnie Raitt, 1972–78; Led own Jazz Band, 1973–77; Toured with Dave Bromberg, 1973–74; Phoebe Snow, 1977; Toured with Michael Franks, 1978, 1979–; Directing, My Music School; Playing local Boston area jazz clubs. *Compositions:* Scenes From A Journey; Rush; Reaching. *Recordings:* with Van Morrison, Astral Weeks; with Bonnie Raitt, Give It Up; Bedtime Stories; John Paynes First Album; Razors Edge; with Krisanthi Pappas: My Backyard, 2000. *Honours:* Best of Boston Jazz Bands, 1970s. *Current Management:* John Payne Music Center, 9A Station St, Brookline, MA 02443, USA.

PAYNE, Les Alexander; b. 22 Aug. 1943, Newport, Isle of Wight, England. Vocalist; Songwriter; Musician (guitar, keyboards). m. (1) Brigitte Jean Wilson, 1965, divorced, 1971, 1 s., (2) Rosalind Jean Butler, 1974, divorced 1993, 2 s., (3) Pennie Hawkes, 1994, 1 step-s., 1 step-d. *Education:* Music, choir at school. *Career:* Concerts supporting artists including: Genesis; Nazareth; Rory Gallagher; Mott The Hoople; 40 date tour with Leo Sayer; Gary Moore; Radio includes: Record of the Week, Radio 1, 1974; Album and single of the week, Capitol; Power Play Luxembourg, 1979; Television includes: Sky; BBC; All ITV regions; Australian documentaries. *Recordings:* Who Am I?, 1971; I Can't Help To Feel The Love, 1974; Don't Say Goodbye, 1975; Who Do You Love, 1978; By Yourside, 1979; No Money, 1979; Exposure album, 1979; Who Will Be The Winner, (single in Japan), 1982; Single: Can't Cry For You, 1990; Album: 47 Summers. *Honours:* The Harp Beat Rock Plaque. *Membership:* PRS; Musicians' Union. *Address:* High Wycombe, Buckinghamshire, England.

PAYTON, Nicholas Edward; b. 14 Feb. 1972, Birmingham, England. Jazz Musician (saxophone, clarinet). m. *Education:* Leeds College of Music; Studied with Bob Wilber. *Career:* Toured with The Duke Ellington Orchestra; Lead alto saxophone with The Pasadena Roof Orchestra, The Charleston Chasers; Major jazz festivals in UK and Europe incl.: North Sea Jazz Festival, Pori Jazz Festival, Edinburgh, Cork, Breda; Extensive touring in USA and Europe; Major concerts at the Southbank Centre, London (International Jazz Orchestra), Kuala Lumpur, Hong Kong; Numerous appearances on television and radio; Performed with The Duke Ellington Orchestra, Bob Wilber, Kenny Davern, Spike Robinson, Marty Grosz, Mark Shane; Co-runs Swing Syndicate. *Recordings:* Henderson Stomp, 1993; Pleasure Mad, 1995; Steaming South, 1996; Rompin' With Buck, 1998; Swing That Music, 1998; What A Life, 1999; The Pasadena Roof Orchestra Live At Regents Park, 1999; Turn On The Heat, 2000; Misty Morning, 2001; If Dreams Come True, 2001; Smilin' Skies, 2002; Here And Now, 2002. *Address:* Halfway House, Grafton Mews, Chipping Campden, Gloucestershire GL55 6BW, England. *E-mail:* info@nikpayton.com. *Website:* www.nikpayton.com.

PAZ, Ania; b. 18 June 1966, Lima, Peru. Musician (Piano); Composer. *Education:* Bachelor of Music, University of Detmold, Germany; Master of Music, University of the Arts, Philadelphia, USA. *Career:* Performances at festivals including International Jazz Festival, Lima, 1996, Jazz Astwood Festivals, 1995, 1997, 1998, San Jose Jazz Festival, 1998; Numerous television appearances. *Compositions:* San Pedro de Macorrs; Classic Night; San Francisco. *Recordings:* Meta Arará. *Honours:* ASCAP Special award; Hon. Mention, USA Songwriting Contest, 1998; Plaque of Recognition, University of Missouri ALARA Conference. *Membership:* ASCAP. *Address:* c/o Blue Cat Agency, PO Box 399, Novato, CA 94948, USA.

PEACOCK, Olly; b. 1974, England. Musician (guitar, drums, percussion, piano). *Career:* Founding mem., Gomez, 1996–; Numerous concerts, festival, radio and television appearances. *Recordings:* Albums: Bring It On, 1998; Liquid Skin, 1999; Abandoned Shopping Trolley Hotline, 2000; In Our Gun,

2002. Singles: 78 Stone Wobble, 1998; Whippin' Piccadilly, 1998; Get Myself Arrested (EP), 1998; Bring It On, 1999; Rhythm And Blues Alibi, 1999; We Haven't Turned Around (in soundtrack to film, American Beauty), 1999; Machismo (EP), 2000. *Honours:* Mercury Music Prize, 1998. *Address:* c/o Hut Records, Kensal House, 553–579 Harrow Rd, London W10 4RH, England. *Website:* www.gomez.co.uk.

PEAKE, Ryan; b. 1 March 1973, Canada. Vocalist; Musician (guitar). *Career:* Mem., rock band, Nickelback, 1996–; Extensive touring of North America; Signed to EMI Canada and Roadrunner Records; Single, Yanking Out My Heart, used in soundtrack to film The Scorpion King, 2002. *Recordings:* Albums: Curb, 1996; The State, 1999; Silver Side Up, 2001. Singles: Hesher (EP), 1996; Breathe, 2000; Old Enough, 2000; Leader Of Men, 2000; How You Remind Me (No. 1, USA), 2002; Too Bad, 2002. *Honours:* Juno Awards, Best New Group, 2001, Best Group, Best Single, for How You Remind Me, Best Rock Album, for Silver Side Up, 2002; MuchMusic Video Awards, Best Video, for Too Bad, Best Rock Video, for How You Remind Me, 2002; Platinum discs. *Address:* c/o Roadrunner Records Inc, 902 Broadway, Eighth Floor, New York, NY 10010, USA. *Website:* www.nickelback.com.

PEARCE, Dave; b. 14 June. DJ. *Career:* Began as DJ on pirate radio, and in clubs; DJ, Radio Jackie, South London; Worked behind the scenes, BBC Radio London, late night show; Created BBC's first hip hop show; Helped create BBC's first dance show, Behind the Beat; Presenter, BBC GLR nightly dance show; A&R Director, Polydor Records; Established own label, Reachin Records; Joined Kiss FM at its establishment; Presented drivetime show with Gordon Mac, then presented The Dangerous Breakfast; Presenter, weekly music video guide on ITV networked Video View; Joined Radio 1, 1995, hosting Early Breakfast Show; Weekend Breakfast Presenter, 1997–99; Daily evening show, 1999–. *Recordings:* Compiler, Dance Anthems Vols 1 and 2.

PEARSON, John; b. 5 Oct. 1948, Liverpool, England. Musician (6- and 12-string guitar); Vocalist. *Career:* Television appearances: The Happening, 1991; National radio broadcasts: Paul Jones Blues Show, sessions, 1989, 1992, 2001; Major concerts include: Sonny Terry and Brownie McGhee; Alexis Korner; Louisianna Red; Davey Graham; Woody Mann; Jo Anne Kelly; Cephas and Wiggins. *Recordings:* Solo albums: Drive My Blues Away, 1989; Streamline Train, 1990; Busy Bootin', 1992 (with Roger Hubbard); Grasshoppers In My Pillow, 1995; John Pearson's Blues and Beyond: Rhythm Oil, 2000; Just Blowed In Your Town, 2002. *Current Management:* Last Days Recording. *Address:* PO Box 6002, Newbury, Berkshire RG14 6XD, England. *E-mail:* johnpearson@yahoo.com. *Website:* www.johnpearsonblues.com.

PEART, Neil; b. 12 Sept. 1952, Hamilton, ON, Canada. Musician (drums). *Career:* Member, Canadian rock group Rush, 1974–; Sell-out tours, USA; Canada; UK; Europe. *Recordings:* Albums: Fly By Night, 1975; Caress of Steel, 1975; 2112, 1976; All The World's A Stage, 1976; A Farewell To Kings, 1977; Archives, 1978; Hemispheres, 1978; Permanent Waves, 1980; Moving Pictures, 1981; Exit... Stage Left, 1981; Great White North, 1982; Signals, 1982; Grace Under Pressure, 1984; Power Windows, 1985; Hold Your Fire, 1987; A Show of Hands, 1988; Presto, 1989; Chronicles, 1990; Roll The Bones, 1991; Counterparts, 1993; Vapor Trails, 2002; Solo: Burning For Buddy, 1995; Test for Echo, 1996; Retrospective Vol. II, 1997; with Jeff Berlin, Crossroads, 1998; Different Stages (box set), 1998; Singles include: Spirit of Radio; Tom Sawyer; Closer To The Heart; New World Man; The Big Money; Countdown; Time Stand Still. *Honours:* Platinum discs; Juno Awards: Most Promising Group, 1975; Best Group, 1978, 1979; Group named Official Ambassadors of Music, Canadian Government, 1979; Gold Ticket, Madison Square Garden, New York, 1991. *Current Management:* Anthem Entertainment, 189 Carlton St, Toronto, ON M5A 2K7, Canada.

PEDERSEN, Karl-Erik; b. 17 Nov. 1960, Hobro, Jutland, Denmark. Vocalist; Songwriter; Musician (guitar, bass); Music Teacher. m. Anne Iben Hansen. *Education:* University. *Career:* Member, band Yellow Moon; Played concerts in: Denmark; Sweden; Finland; Iceland; Live concerts, national radio; Touring festivals, with Tears For Jeanie, 1998; Touring as a solo artist, 1998. *Compositions:* Songwriter for: Nikolaj and Piloterne, 1989; Björn Afzelius (Sweden), 1994; Kim C (Denmark), 1994; Music for films, documentaries with director Ole Henning Hansen; Albums: Tears For Jeanie, 1997; Fishjoint, 1997. *Recordings:* Album with Yellow Moon; Det Kinesiske Hav, 1989; Nitton År, 1994; Out There, 1997; You Gotta Believe It, 1997; Days, 1997; Crawling To You, 1998; with Naked Fish: Takin' It To The Bone, 2001. *Membership:* KODA; Danish Jazz Beat and Folk Authors; Danish Musicians' Union. *Current Management:* Warner/Chappell, Anker Heegårdsgade, 2 st.tv, 1572 Copenhagen V, Denmark. *Address:* Terp Skovvej 46, 8260 Viby J, Denmark.

PEDERSEN, Leonardo; b. Copenhagen, Denmark. Musician (saxophone, clarinet, flute); Songwriter. m. Annelise Pedersen, 15 Dec. 1972, 1 s., 1 d. *Career:* Formed first jazz band in 1958, becoming Leonardo Pedersen's Jazzkapel; Tours of Germany, Scandinavia, Eastern Europe, England, Italy, Scotland; Performed with numerous leading jazz artists including: Albert Nicolas, Ben Webster, Benny Waters, Al Grey, Bennie Bailey, Harry 'Sweets' Edison and Eddie 'Lockjaw' Davis; Appearances on national and international television and radio; Also played with: Barbarossa, 1978–88; Van Dango,

1986–89; The Original Danish Polcalypso Orchestra. *Recordings:* with Leonardo Pedersen's Jazzkapel: Danish Traditional Jazz, 1963; Leonardo Pedersen's Jazzkapel with Harry 'Sweets' Eddison, Eddie 'Lockjaw' Davis and Richard Boone, 1977; I Want A Roof, 1994; with Polcalypso: Karlekammeret, 1989, Polcalypso II, 1991; with Hans Knudsen Jumpband: So Long John, 1994; Jump In Focus, 1997; The Original Danish Polcalypso Orchestra featuring James 'Jamesie' Brewster, Live, 1996. *Current Management:* EPC Management, Ornevej 12, 2 th, 2400 Copenhagen NV, Denmark.

PEEL, John, (John Robert Parker Ravenscroft); b. 30 Aug. 1939, Heswall, Cheshire, England. Radio Presenter; DJ. m. Sheila, 4 c. *Career:* Radio broadcaster, WRR radio, Texas, KOMA, Oklahoma City, KMEN, California, 1960s; Broadcaster, own show The Perfumed Garden, on pirate radio station, Radio London, 1967; Broadcaster, BBC Radio One, 1967–; Known for promoting new and experimental music; Columnist, Radio Times; Presenter for BBC Radio 4, Offspring, 1995–97, Home Truths, 1998–. *Recordings:* Various Peel Sessions recordings taken from own Radio One show, incl.: Before The Fall; Winters of Discontent; The New Breed; Too Pure. *Honours:* Sony Award, Broadcaster of the Year, 1993; New Musical Express BRAT Award, 1994; Numerous hon. degrees; Hon. fellowship, John Moores University, Liverpool. *Address:* c/o BBC Radio One, Broadcasting House, London W1A 1AA, England.

PEGG, David; b. 2 Nov. 1947, Birmingham, England. Musician (bass guitar, guitar, mandolin); Prod. m. Christine, 12 Dec. 1966, 1 s., 1 d. *Education:* Six months piano lessons. *Career:* Mem., various Birmingham bands playing R&B; Double bass, Ian Campbell Folk Group; Mem., Fairport Convention, 1969–79, 1985–, Jethro Tull, 1979–96; Sessions, 1970s, with many folk artists including Nick Drake, John Martyn, Sandy Denny, Ralph McTell; Co-organizer, Cropredy Festival with Christine Pegg; Founder, owner, Woodworm Studios, 1978–. *Compositions:* Various with Fairport Convention. *Recordings:* with Fairport Convention: What We Did On Our Holidays, 1969; Unhalfbricking, 1969; Liege and Lief, 1970; Full House, 1970; Angel Delight, 1971; Babbacombe Lee, 1971; A Bonny Band Of Roses, 1977; The Best Of..., 1988; Red And Gold, 1989; Fairport Convention, 1990; Them Five Seasons, 1991; Jewel In The Crown, 1995; Old-New-Borrowed-Blue, 1996; Who Knows Where The Time Goes?, 1997; Encore, Encore, 1997; Fiddlestix 1970–84: The Best of Fairport Convention, 1998; Fairport Convention, Woodworm Years, 1998; Wood And The Wire, 2000; XXXV, 2002; Heyday: BBC Radio Sessions 1968–69, 2002; Recordings with Jethro Tull, 1979–96; Numerous session appearances; Recent. *Recordings* include: Philip Picket, Bones of All Men, 1998; Allan Taylor, Sometimes/Lady, 1998; Steve Ashley, Stroll On Revisited, 1999; Jethro Tull, The Best of Jethro Tull, 1999; Fallen Angels, Happy Ever After, 1999; Sally Barker, Another Train, 2000. *Honours:* Midland Beat Bassist of the Year, 1967; Grammy Award for Crest of a Knave, with Jethro Tull, 1988. *Membership:* Musicians' Union; MCPS; PAMRA. *Address:* c/o Woodworm Records Ltd, PO Box 37, Banbury, Oxfordshire OX16 8YN, England. *E-mail:* faircrop@aol.com. *Website:* www.fairportconvention.co.uk.

PELLEN, Jacques; b. April 1957, Brest, France. Musician (guitar). *Education:* University. *Career:* European tours, 1980–95; Celtic Procession (guest Kenny Wheeler), 1991; Europe Jazz Festival, Le Mans, 1994; Festival Quimper (guest Didier Lockwood); Zénith Paris, with Dan Ar Bras, 1995. *Recordings:* Celtic Progression, 1996; La Tombees De La Nuit, 2000; Sorserez (with Riccardo Del Fra); Condaghès, trio with Jacques Pellen, Paolo Fresu and Erik Marchand, 1998. *Address:* Bertrand Dupond, Ton All, 3 rue de Milad, 56630 Langonned, France.

PELLOW, Marti, (Mark McLoughlin); b. 23 March 1966, Clydebank, Scotland. Vocalist. *Career:* Lead singer, Wet Wet Wet, 1982–97; Performances include: Royal Albert Hall, Greenpeace charity concert, 1986; Prince's charity Tour, Royal Albert Hall, London, 1988–90; Nelson Mandela's 70th Birthday Tribute, Wembley, 1988; John Lennon Tribute Concert, Merseyside, 1990; Children In Need, BBC, 1991; Edinburgh Castle, 1992; Nordoff-Robbins Music Therapy Centre benefit, Royal Albert Hall, London, 1992; Live At The Royal Albert Hall 1992 (Channel 4), 1993; Appeared as Billy Flynn, musical Chicago, West End, London, 2002. *Recordings:* Albums: Popped In Souled Out, 1987; Sgt Pepper Knew My Father, 1988; The Memphis Sessions, 1988; Holding Back The River, 1989; High On The Happy Side, 1992; Wet Wet Wet Live At The Royal Albert Hall, 1993; End of Part One (Their Greatest Hits), 1993; Picture This, 1995; 10, 1997; Singles include: Wishing I Was Lucky, 1987; Sweet Little Mystery, 1987; Angel Eyes (Home and Away), 1988; Temptation, 1988; With A Little Help From My Friends (No. 1, UK), 1988; Sweet Surrender, 1989; Broke Away, 1989; Hold Back The River, 1990; Stay With Me Heartache, 1990; Make It Tonight, 1991; Goodnight Girl (No. 1, UK), 1992; More Than Love, 1992; Lip Sevice, 1992; Shed A Tear, 1993; Love Is All Around (No. 1, UK), 1994; Goodnight Girl, 1994; She's All On My Mind, 1995; Julia Said, 1995; Don't Want To Forgive Me Now, 1995; Somewhere Somehow, 1995; Morning, 1996; If I Never See You Again, 1997; Strange, 1997; Yesterday, 1997; Solo album: Smile, 2001; Solo single: Close To You, 2001. *Honours:* BRIT Award, Best British Newcomer, 1988. *Current Management:* The Precious Organisation, 14–16 Spiers Wharf, Port Dundas, Glasgow, Scotland.

PEMELTON, Bret; m. Diana Pemelton, 2 s. Gospel Vocalist. *Career:* Mem., Christian pop group, Dream of Eden; 2 major tours, USA; Television: CCM-TV, real videos (TBN); Explosion '95 (TBN); Numerous radio appearances. *Recordings:* 2 No. 1 singles: Wonderful Thing, 1993; Into The Here and Now, 1995. *Membership:* Gospel Music Asscn. *Current Management:* Brian A Mays, BMP Artists Management.

PENAVA, Pista (Pishta) Gordan; b. 29 Oct. 1967, Zagreb, Croatia. Vocalist; Musician (guitar); Songwriter; Television Host; Radio DJ; Journalist. *Education:* Faculty of Political Science, Journalism. *Career:* Singer, guitar player, Hard Time; Tours: Croatia; Slovenia; France; Appearances on MTV's Headbangers Ball. *Recordings:* Single cassette, 1992; Albums: Kiss My Ass and Go To Hell, 1992; Kad Poludim..., 1996; Compilation: Bijeli Put (1 song), 1993; Compilation: Cro Fest '94, Pop rock hit, 1994. *Honours:* Best Hard Rock Band of Croatia, Hard Time, 1992; Best Video Clip, Hit and Run, 1993. *Membership:* HGU (Croatian Musician Union); Zamp. *Address:* Aleja Pomoraca 11, 41000 Zagreb, Croatia.

PENDER, Mike, (Michael John Prendergast); b. 3 March 1942, Liverpool, England. Musician (guitar). *Career:* Member, lead guitarist, lead vocalist, The Searchers, early 1960s–85; Numerous tours and concerts; Left The Searchers to form Mike Pender's Searchers, 1985; Performing regularly all over UK, including Japan, South Africa and Australia; Active Fan Club providing quarterly magazine and merchandise. *Recordings:* UK No. 1 Hits: Sweets For My Sweet; Needles and Pins; Don't Throw Your Love Away; Other Hits include: When You Walk In The Door; Sugar and Spice; Farmer John; Some Day We're Gonna Love Again; Goodbye My Love; Love Potion No. 9; Numerous LPs and CDs including: Meet The Searchers, 1963; Sugar and Spice, 1963; It's The Searchers, 1964; Sounds Like Searchers, 1965; Take Me For What I'm Worth, 1965; Needles and Pins, 1974; The Searchers, 1979; Play For Today, 1981; 100 Minutes of The Searchers, 1982; The Searchers Hit Collection, 1987; The EP Collection, Vol. 1, 1989; 30th Anniversary Collection, 1992; The EP Collection, Vol. 2, 1992; Searchers, 2001. *Current Management:* The Small Concert Co, 5 Castleton Ave, Carlton, Nottingham NG4 3NZ, England.

PENDERGRASS, Teddy (Theodore); b. 26 March 1950, Philadelphia, Pennsylvania, USA. Vocalist; Musician (drums). m. Karen Still, 20 June 1987. *Career:* Member, Harold Melvin and The Blue Notes, 1969–76; Solo artiste, 1976–; Major appearances include: British tours, 1981, 1982; Live Aid, JFK Stadium, Philadelphia, 1985; Film debut, Soup For One, 1982. *Recordings:* Albums: with Harold Melvin: Harold Melvin and The Blue Notes, 1971; Black and Blue, 1975; Wake Up Everybody, 1976; All Their Greatest Hits, 1976; Solo: Teddy Pendergrass, 1977; Life Is A Song Worth Singing, 1978; Teddy, 1979; Teddy Live! (Coast To Coast), 1979; T P, 1980; It's Time For Love, 1981; This One's For You, 1982; Heaven Only Knows, 1983; Love Language, 1984; Workin' It Back, 1985; Greatest Hits, 1987; Joy, 1988; Teddy Pendergrass, 1989; Truly Blessed, 1991; This Christmas I'd Rather Have Love, 1998; Greatest Slow Jams, 2001; Close The Door, 2001; Singles include: with Harold Melvin: I Miss You; If You Don't Know Me By Now; Solo: The Whole Town's Laughing At Me; Close The Door; Turn Off The Lights; Love TKO; Hold Me, duet with Whitney Houston; Love 4 2; Joy; Dream Girl, from film soundtrack Soup For One, 1982; Duet with Lisa Fisher, Glad To Be Alive, from film soundtrack: The Adventures of Ford Fairlane, 1990; Contributor, Rubáiyát (Elektra's 40th Anniversary compilation), 1990. *Honours:* Platinum and Gold discs; American Music Award, Favourite Male Soul/R&B Artist, 1979. *Current Management:* Dream Street Management, 1460 Fourth St, Suite 205, Santa Monica, CA 90401, USA.

PENDLEBURY, Andrew Scott; b. 30 Nov. 1951, Melbourne, Australia. Musician (guitar). *Career:* Member, Australian band, The Sports; Recorded 8 albums; Toured England twice; First major tour, Graham Parker and The Rumour; Finished 3 nights at Hammersmith Odeon, London, England. *Compositions:* Who Listens to the Radio, 1979. *Recordings:* 8 sports albums including: Don't Throw Stones, 1979; 4 solo albums; with Peter Lawler, King Rooster, 1998. *Current Management:* Mushroom Records, ABC Music. *Address:* 34 Wellington St, Richmond 3121, Melbourne, Victoria, Australia.

PENG LIYUAN; b. Nov. 1952, Yuncheng, Shandong Province, People's Republic of China. Vocalist. *Education:* Shandong Acad. of Arts; Acad. of Music, People's Republic of China. *Career:* Solo singer, Qianwei Song and Dance Troupe of Ji'nan Military Command, 1980–84; Solo singer, Song and Dance Troupe, PLA Gen. Political Dept, 1984–. *Address:* Song and Dance Troupe, People's Liberation Army Gen. Political Dept, Beijing, People's Republic of China.

PENISTON, Cece; b. 6 September 1969, Dayton, Ohio, USA. Vocalist; Songwriter. *Education:* Phoenix College; Vocal lessons with Seth Riggs. *Career:* Crowned Miss Black Arizona as a student; Guest vocalist with rapper Overweight Pooch; Solo artiste, 1991–; International concerts, Philippines, Japan, USA, UK, Europe; Tours with: Joe Public; R Kelly; Levert. *Recordings:* Albums: Finally, 1992; Thought 'Ya Knew, 1994; I'm Movin' On, 1996; Winning Combination, 2000; Singles: Finally (No. 2, UK), 1991; We Got A Love Thing, 1992; I Like It, 1992; Keep On Walkin', 1992; Inside That I

Cried, 1992; Crazy Love, 1992; Keep On Walkin'; I'm In The Mood, 1994; Keep Givin' Me Your Love, 1995; Movin' On, 1996; Somebody Else's Guy, 1998; Nobody Else, 1998; He Loves Me 2, 1999; We Got A Love Thang, 1999; Guest vocalist, Female Preacher, Overweight Pooch. *Honours:* Gold discs, Finally, 1992. *Current Management:* Devour Management, 4840 Hollow Corner Rd #421, Culver City, CA 90230, USA.

PENN, Thomas Howard; b. 21 Nov. 1954, Cleveland, Ohio, USA. Artist Man; Concert Promoter. *Career:* Commenced under name Good Time Productions, 1974; Started out throwing keg parties; Dances and school promotions, progressed to national acts, 1974–; Acts include: Tower of Power; Ronnie Laws and Pressure; George Benson; Side Effect; Karma; Donald Byrd and the Black Byrds; Steel Breeze; Taxi; Curtis Salgado and the Stilletos; Pleasure; U-Krew; Seawind; Shock; Maya; Earth Wind and Fire; Vail Johnson; Alliance with T:T Promotions Inc, Portland, Oregon, 1978–; El Chicano; Tierra; Bruce Conte.

PENNEY, John; b. 17 Sept. 1968, Birmingham, England. Vocalist; Lyricist. *Career:* Vocalist, Ned's Atomic Dustbin, 1987–; Various large festivals world-wide include: Reading, 1990, 1991, 1993; Glastonbury, 1992; Phoenix, 1994; Tours: UK (11); Scandinavia (1); Europe (3); USA (9); Australia (3); Japan (3); Television: Top of the Pops (3 times); The Word (2); The Beat (5); Big Breakfast; Radio sessions: John Peel; Mark Goodier; Johnnie Walker. *Recordings:* God Fodder, 1991; Are You Normal?, 1992; 5.22, 1994; Brainbloodvolume, 1995; Kill Your Television, 1990; Until You Find Out, 1990; Happy, 1991; Trust, 1991; Long form videos: Nothing Is Cool, 1991; Lunatic Magnets, 1993; Singles: Saturday Night, 1993; Until You Find Out, 1993; Not Sleeping Around, 1992; Intact, 1992; All I Ask Of Myself Is That I Hold Together, 1995. *Publications:* Available For Panto, by Martin Roach, 1994. *Honours:* No. 1 US Modern Rock Single for Not Sleeping Around, 1993. *Membership:* Musicians' Union. *Current Management:* Tank Gilks. *Address:* Floor 4, Sony Music UK, 10 Great Marlborough St, London, England.

PEÓN, Mercedes, (Mercedes Peón Mosteiro); b. 1967, La Coruña, Spain. Vocalist; Musician (gaita, percussion); Composer. *Career:* Collects tunes, researches, teaches, lectures around the world to help preserve Galician folk tradition; Runs Discotrompo record label promoting Galician folk and traditional music; Organized several festivals including Federation of European Cultural Associations traditional music festival and Galicia Terra Unica; Previously member of Arjú before releasing solo material; Collaborations: Carlos Nunes; Xosé Manuel Budino; Manu Chao; Composed theme for Galician TV soap opera Mareas Vivas. *Recordings:* Single: Mareas Vivas; Albums: Isué, 2000; features on: Naciones Celtas II (Celtic Nations). *Honours:* Cídade Vella festival in Santiago de Compostela, special Jury Award; Santiago de Compostela Folk Days, Best Performer of Voice and Bagpipes; Lorient's Festival Interceltique, Macallan Award for Galician Pipers. *Website:* www.mercedespeon.com.

PEPA, (Sandra Denton); b. 9 Nov. 1969, Kingston, Jamaica. Rap Artiste; Songwriter; Prod. 1 c. *Career:* Formed US female rap duo Super Nature with Cheryl James, 1985; Signed to Next Plateau Records and group re-named Salt-N-Pepa, 1986; Group joined by DJ 'Spinderella', in form of Pamela Green, then Latoya Hanson and finally, in 1987, Dee Dee Roper; Signed to London Records, 1993; Signed to MCA Records, 1997; Created Jireh Records company with Cheryl James, 1997; Opened clothing store Hollywood, Atlanta, USA; Performances include: Youth Ball, Washington, DC, 1993; LIFEBeat AIDS benefit concert, 1993; Woodstock '94. *Recordings:* Albums: Hot Cool & Vicious, 1986; A Salt With A Deadly Pepa, 1988; Blacks' Magic, 1990; A Blitz of Hits: The Hits Remixed, 1990; Very Necessary, 1993; Brand New, 1997; Salt-N-Pepa... The Best Of, 2000. Singles include: as Super Nature: Showstopper, 1985; as Salt-N-Pepa: My Mike Sounds Nice, 1987; Push It (No. 2, UK), 1988; Shake Your Thang (It's Your Thing), 1988; Twist and Shout, 1988; Expression, 1990; Do You Want Me, 1991; Let's Talk About Sex (No. 2, UK), 1991; Let's Talk About AIDS (re-write of Let's Talk About Sex), 1992; You Showed Me, 1991; Start Me Up, 1992; Shoop, 1993; Whatta Man (with En Vogue), 1994; Ain't Nothin But A She Thing, 1995; Champagne, 1996; R U Ready, 1997; Gitty Up, 1998; Brick Track Vs Gitty Up, Pt I and II, 2000; Contributed to various compilations and film soundtracks. *Honours:* Platinum discs and Gold discs for albums and singles; Grammy for Best Rap Performance by a Duo or Group, for None Of Your Business, 1994; Three MTV Awards, 1994. *Address:* c/o CD Enterprises Inc, 7531 Leesburg Pike, Suite 201, Fallschurch, VA 22043, USA.

PERCIVAL, John Graham; b. 7 March 1938, Northampton, England. Musician (clarinet, saxophone, musical saw). m. Jane Allsop, 25 Aug. 1960, 3 d. *Career:* Appeared on television programmes Opportunity Knocks and Rising Stars, BBC TV; Ran own jazzband, Horace M Smith, 1971–87; Member, Bob Kerr Whoopee Band; Television appearances in Germany, Netherlands, France, Switzerland, Belgium, Sweden, Denmark, Russia. *Recordings:* as Horace M Smith: Hold That Tiger; with Bob Kerr Whoopee Band: Molotov Cocktails; Happy Daze; Videos: Live At The Half Moon; From Russia With Laughs; Films with Bob Godfrey: French Revolution; Happy Birthday Switzerland. *Membership:* Musicians' Union. *Address:* 20 Stoke Rd,

Blisworth, Northamptonshire NN7 3BZ, England. *Website:* www.whoopeeband.de.

PERCIVAL, Lynne; b. 24 Nov. 1954, Altrincham, Cheshire, England. Teacher; Vocalist; Musician (guitar, mandolin). *Education:* Masters Degree in Social Science. *Career:* Semi-professional singer, guitarist and mandolin player; Member, The Fluence Band, 1988–; Specialising in Irish traditional dance music and song, performing regularly in Northern England, local residencies and ceilidhs; Support to various artists including Dick Gaughan, Maria Tolly and Meliantu; Tours in Brittany, Berlin, Canada, Denmark, Hungary, Scotland and the Isle of Mull; Co-ordinator of Irish music promotions, Club Cheoil, Manchester. *Recordings:* Early singer and songwriter tapes; Goodwill (album of Polish tour), with Wild Bill Flatpick and The Bindle Stiffs, 1987; Children In Need Compilation, 1987; Guesting on various artists recordings, 1991–93. *Honours:* Voted second folk group in local poll, 1994. *Membership:* PRS; Musicians' Union. *Address:* 20 Alderfield Rd, Manchester M21 9JX, England.

PERCL, Ivica; b. 1 Jan. 1945, Zagreb, Croatia. Musician (guitar, harmonica). m. Mirjana, 8 Jan. 1972, 2 d. *Education:* Music secondary school. *Career:* Bass guitarist with groups: Mladi tehnicari, 1962; Kristali, 1963–64; Roboti, 1964–66; First Croatian protest singer, 1966; Festival of Shansone, Zagreb, 1967–71; Concerts include: Bulgaria; Russia; Finland, 1968–71; Playing protest songs, recording for Croatian radio station, Croatian television; Concerts, Boom Festival, 1972–74; Solo, 1979; Concerts on Days of Croatian Music; Advances in theatre, television as musician. *Compositions:* Over 200 include: 1966; Postovani profesore; Godine ratne, godine mirne; Izemedu tebe i mene; Kad zatvoris vrata iza sebe. *Recordings:* 7 singles; Albums: Stari Pjer, 1967–75; 30 Godina Starog Pjera, CD, 1998. *Honours:* Diploma of Soci 69, Russia, 1969; Katom, 1970; Labin, 1970. *Membership:* Croatian Asscn of Composers; Croatian Music Unit; Professional Asscn of Composers; Croatian Music Unit. *Address:* Vinogradska 17, 10 000 Zagreb, Croatia.

PEREIRA, Francis Martin Purcell; b. 1 May 1950, Singapore. Prod; Arranger; Musician (guitar). m. Ann Toh Swee Hua, 1 Jan. 1985. *Education:* Royal School of Music; Singapore Armed Forces Band (trombone); Gateway School of Audio Engineering. *Career:* Arranger, EMI, Singapore, 1975–83; Television Brunei; Played for Sultan of Brunei, 1985–87; Played for Cilla Black, local acts; First Asean Festival of Songs, 1986; Director, Shekinah Music Trading, 1992–. *Compositions:* Local acts; Film. *Compositions:* Eye of the Tiger. *Recordings:* Guitar Indigo Series; Guitar Latino Series; Guitar Memories; Different Class Harmonica Series; Sax with Love; Dijazz Series; Contemporary Saxophone, Vols I and II; Todos Latino; Guitarra Series, Hymns, Asia. *Honours:* Dr of Administration and Management Service; Conferred and Awarded by Golden Gates University; Affiliated Mem., Ferrum University, Virginia, USA; Ethnic Best Song Composition, 1982. *Current Management:* Shekinah Music Trading. *Address:* Blk 30 #07–17 Kallang Pl., 339159 Singapore.

PERES, Vivian; b. France. Musician (drums). *Career:* Participated in first Francofolies de la Rochelle; Leader, own group Traction Ailleurs; Worked at Béziers Conservatoire with René Nan; Founder member, La Campagnie du Jazz; Member, quartet Golem; Salsa group with Juan Quintana; Accompanist with numerous singers; Member, Slax; Mezcal Jazz Unit, European tour, 1994; Jazz Festival, Lithuania, 1994; Also performs with groups: Swing; Planete Jazz. *Honours:* Agfa Song Contest Winner, with group Traction Ailleurs, 1986.

PEREZ, Ivan; b. 11 Nov. 1964, Orange, France. Musician (guitar); Composer. *Education:* BPA Floriculture; Conservatoire de Music; Studied improvised music with bassist B Santacruz and saxophonist Andre Jaume. *Career:* Jazz Festivals: Avignon; Sorgues; Carpentras; Music for Florence Saul contemporary dance company; Member, duo with Frederic Duvivier; Trio with Colin McKellar and Tox Drohead; Trio with Simon Fayolle and Lionel Villard. *Address:* 80 rue Henri Durant, 84100 Orange, France.

PEREZ, Michel; b. 2 Jan. 1946, St Priest, France. Musician (guitar). m. Patricia Van Ginneken, 31 Dec. 1977, 1 s., 2 d. *Career:* Concert first part of Miles Davis, Vienne Festival, 1984; Nice Jazz Festival, 1984; Casino de Paris, 1989; Film in concert, Lyon, 1986; Around Midnight (Bertrand Taverner) with Herbie Hancock, Tony Williams, Wayne Shorter; Concert, first part of Zawinul Syndicate, 1992. *Recordings:* 2 with Spheroe: Spheroe, 1976; Primadonna, 1979; Kaleidoscope, 1982; Virgile, 1986; Orange, 1991; Toujours, Ron Carter, 1992; Film: Around Midnight, 1986. *Publications:* 3 compositions to be published in: Le Livre Du Jazz En France. *Address:* 19 rue de la Hacquière Pavillon, No. 68, 91440 Bures Sur Yvette, France.

PERKINS, John Sinclair; b. 3 Aug. 1945. Hindustani Musician (sitar). Divorced, 2 d. *Education:* Christ College, Finchley, London; Rycotewood College, Thame, Oxon; Leicester College of Art; Visva Bharati University, Bengal; Private Clarinet Lessons. *Career:* Television Appearances, BBC 1, BBC2, LWT, Children's Channel, Munich and Devon Educational Television; Local Radio, BBC Cornwall, Devon, Milton Keynes, Leicester; Concert

Appearances, London School of Contemporary Dance, Accompanist to Suriha Kumari; Tour of South Africa, Indian Academy of Durban; South West Arts Tour; Tour of West Midlands Schools and Hospitals; Huddersfield Contemporary Music Festival; Barbican, London with BBC Scottish Symphony Orchestra, 1998; Festivals, Glastonbury; Somerfield Folk; Badaun Festival, Uttar Pradesh, India, 2002; BBC Asianet Radio, 2002; Wells Cathederal; 2002; Eden Project, 2002; Waldorf Hotel, Aldwych, 2002. *Recordings:* Suns of Arqa. *Membership:* Musicians' Union. *Address:* 3 Ashleigh Villas, Plymouth Rd, Totnes, Devon TQ9 5PG, England. *Telephone:* (1803) 868687. *E-mail:* john@silver-sitar-co.fsnet.co.uk.

PERKINS, Walter; b. Feb. 1932, Chicago, Illinois, USA. Musician (drums). m. Barbara J Henderson, 6 d. *Education:* Cosmopolitan School of Music, Chicago. *Career:* Worked in Chicago, Illinois with musicians including Ahmad Jamal; Dinah Washington; Muddy Waters; Memphis Slim; Sarah Vaughan; Leader, own group, recorded under name MJT+3; Moved to New York City; Played, toured extensively with Carmen McRae; Played with major artists including: Billie Holiday; Della Resse; Art Farmer; Ernie Wilkins; Roland Kirk; Sonny Rollins; J J Johnson; Sonny Stitt; Teddy Wilson; Billy Taylor; Charles Mingus; Illinois Jacquet; Jimmy Rowe; George Duviver; Errol Garner; Played for King and Queen of England, Palladium, London, England; Numerous teaching jobs include: Public schools, New York; State Hospital; Federal funded, high schools, New York Board of Education system; Currently playing and teaching for Music for Young Audiences; Shared in co-op group with Shaw, Perkins, Holgate, featuring Marilyn Johnson; Performances include: Americana Hotel chain, USA, Caribbean; 2 Club Med resorts (Guadaloupe, Bahamas). *Recordings:* 40 albums with artists including: Gene Ammons; Donald Byrd; Rahsaan Roland Kirk; Jimmy Witherspoon; Ahmad Jamal; MJT+3; J J Johnson; Sonny Stitt; Sonny Rollins; Lucky Thompson; Art Farmer; Carol Sloan; Carmen McRae; Freda Payne; Josh White; Sunra; Booker Ervin; Yusef Lateef; Ray Bryant; Jaki Byard; Leo Wright; Gigi Gryce; Michael O'Bryant; Richard Williams; Hylton Ruiz; Clark Terry; George Terry; George Shearing; Milt Hinton; Ben Webster; Lightning Hopkins; Latest. *Recordings include:* Legends of Acid Jazz, 1998; with Ahmad Jamal, Priceless Jazz, 1998; Ballads for Trumpet, 1998; Impulsively Ellington: A Tribute, 1999; Great Jazz Artists Play Composition, 1999. *Honours:* US Army, Special Service, Germany; One Hundred Black Businessmens' Award. *Address:* 115–21 167th St, Jamaica, NY 11434, USA.

PERKIÖMÄKI, Jari; b. 13 April 1961, Finland. Musician (alto saxophone, reeds, flutes). *Education:* MA, Jazz programme, Sibelius Academy, 1989. *Career:* Joined Pori Big Band, aged 15; Represented Finland, EBU Big Band, 1981; Conductor, Pori Big Band; Own quartet, appearances included: Tampere Jazz Happening; Pori Jazz Festival; Debrecen Festival, Hungary; Member, Mika Mylläri; As soloist, tours, Sweden and Norway, 1987; As part of Jazz in Joiku project, including Kaamosjazz, Kalottijazz festivals, 1989; Conductor big band, Norway, on Nordic exchange programme, 1990. *Compositions include:* Music for 2 plays by Ilpo Tuomarila. *Honours:* Pekka Pöyry Award, 1985; Musician of the Year, RYTMI magazine, 1985; Thalia Award, for music to play Exit, 1988. *Address:* Reiherintie 1 H 103, 00870 Helsinki, Finland.

PERKO, Jukka; b. 18 Feb. 1968, Huittinen, Finland. Musician (alto and soprano saxophone). *Education:* Saxophone from 1982; Sibelius Academy, 1988. *Career:* Played Pori Jazz Festival, 1985; Played in Dizzy Gillespie 70th Anniversary Big Band, 1987; Tour with Dizzy Gillespie, 1988; Regular member, UMO (New Music Orchestra), 1989; Formed Jukka Perko Quartet; Finnish Jazz Federation Tour, 1990; Played with Horace Tapscott, Ultra Music Meeting workshop, Pori, 1990; Member, Perko-Pyysalo Poppoo, with Severi Pyysalo. *Recordings:* Albums: Portrait By Heart, Jukka Perko Quartet, 1990; Uuno Kailas, Perko-Pyysalo Poppoo, 1995. *Honours:* Yrjö Award, Finnish Jazz Federation, 1989. *Address:* Minna Canthinkatu 9 A 4, 00250 Helsinki, Finland.

PERREAU, Guy Jocelyn; b. 4 June 1950, Mauritius. m. Michol René, 18 May 1974, 1 s., 1 d. *Career:* Appeared in film Paul Et Virginie, filmed in Mauritius in late 1960s; Mimed One Sega Song; Many TV and radio appearances in Mauritius, Reunion and also Seychelles; Newspaper appearances. *Compositions:* Released 2 singles, 1977; Released 7 cassettes, 1991; Released CD 16 songs. *Recordings:* Released second album, 16 songs; Released third album, 1997; Best of Jocelyn Perreau Vol. I, 1999. *Honours:* Award for Best Entertainer for Radio and TV, Mauritius Broadcasting Corporation, 1974; Hon. Consul for Mauritius, 1986–96. *Membership:* SACEM, France; MASA, Mauritius. *Address:* Anse Aux Pins, Mahé, Seychelles, Indian Ocean.

PERRIN, Roland; b. 18 Jan. 1959, New York, NY, USA. Musician (piano); Composer; Arranger; Teacher. *Education:* BA Hons, Music, University of York, England. *Career:* Played in professional jazz/blues bands from age 15; Plays wide variety of music, specialising often in Afro-Cuban, Brazilian and South African Music; Played Mandela 70th birthday concert with Jonas Gwangwa, Wembley Stadium; Tours, sessions; Own band, Evidence, 1987–94; new band, The Blue Planet Orchestra, 1999. *Compositions:* With Evidence: Later; Kinacho; Golden Road; Salsa Diferente; Sleeping City; With South

African Friends: DP; With Beaujolais Band: The New World; El Monte; Sister Grace; Songs from the Cage (Big Band setting for Charles Bukowski poems), 2002. *Recordings:* Evidence, See You Later; It's A Triple Earth, Westway; Mark Ramsden, Above the Clouds; The Beaujolais Band, Mind How You Go; Talk, Talk and More Talk; Aster Aweke, Kabu; Dudu Pukwana, Cosmics '90; Brotherhood of Breath, In Memorium; Tumbaito, Otros Tiempos; Introducing The Blue Planet Orchestra, 1999; Mose, Congo Acoustic, 1999. *Publications:* 3 piano pieces for First Associated Board Jazz Piano Exams. *Address:* Basement Flat, 47A Waldram Park Rd, London SE23 2PW, England.

PERRO, Juan (Santiago Auseron); b. 25 July 1954, Zaragoza, Spain. Songwriter; Vocalist. m. Catherine François, 17 Nov. 1979. *Education:* Advanced studies, Philosophy, Madrid, 1972–77, Paris, 1977–78. *Career:* Songwriter, singer, Radio Futura, 1980–92; Frequent travels to Cuba, seeking roots of Afro-hispanic sound, 1984–; Released historic compilation of traditions Semilla del Son, 1992; Began touring as Juan Perro, with flamenco, jazz, rock musicians, 1993–94; First Juan Perro album, Havana, 1994. *Recordings:* (as Santiago Auseron) with Radio Futura: La Ley del Desierto, La Ley del Mar, 1984; De Un Pais En Llamas, 1985; La Cancion de Juan Perro, 1987; Escueladecalor, 1989; Veneno En La Piel, 1990; Tierra Para Bailar, 1992; as Juan Perro: Raices Al Viento (including Spanish, Cuban, British musicians), 1995; Serrat Eres Unico (producer), 1996; Mr Hambre, 2000. *Publications:* Articles on music, art and philosophy, to newspapers and magazines. *Honours:* Radio Futura acclaimed as Best Spanish Rock Band of the 1980s (voted by radio stations, rock magazines). *Membership:* Spanish Asscn of Interpreters and Authors; Mem., Independent Production Office, Animal Tour. *Current Management:* Animal Tour. *Address:* Corazón de Maria, No. 2, Ap 230, 28002 Madrid, Spain.

PERRONE, Marc; b. 8 Oct. 1951, Villejuif (Paris), France. Musician (diatonic accordion). m. Marie Odile Chantran, 27 June 1995. *Career:* Montparnasse, 1994; Olympia, Paris, 1995; Carnaval de Venise; Numerous foreign tours include: Africa; USA; Canada; South America; Asia; Japan, 1995; Films: La Trace, 1984; Un Dimanche à La Campagne, 1985; Maine Océan, 1986; La Vie Et Rien d'Autre, 1989; L-627, 1992. *Recordings:* Gabriel Valse, 1974; Perlinpinpin, 1974; Rondeaux Et Autres Danses Gasconnes à Samatan, 1976; Accordéons Diatoniques, 1979; Country Dances (Les Lendemains Qui Dansent), 1980; La Forcelle, 1983; La Trace (film score), 1984; Un Dimanche à La Campagne (film score), 1985; Velverde, 1988; Paris Musette, 1990; Cinéma Mémoire, 1993; Paris Musette Living It (Vol. 2), 1993; Jacaranda, 1995; Voyages, 2001. *Honours:* Prix de l'Academie Charles Cros for: La Forcelle. *Membership:* Administration Council of ADAMI. *Address:* 6 Ave Parmentier, 75011 Paris, France.

PERRY, André; b. 12 Feb. 1937, Verdun, Québec, Canada. Record Co Exec; Record Prod; Divorced, 2 c. *Career:* Founder, André Perry Productions, 1968–70; Son Québec, 1970–73; Founder, President, Groupe André Perry Inc, 1974–; André Perry Video, 1980–; Founder, on board of directors, Québec Assoc Record and Entertainment Industry; Independent Record Producers Association of Canada; Founder, Le Studio (recording studios); Music co-ordinator, Montréal Olympic Games, 1976; Record producer for: John Lennon; Charles Aznavour; Wilson Pickett; Numerous Canadian artistes. *Membership:* Audio Engineering Society; Pro-Can; Composers, Authors and Publishers Asscn of Canada; Canadian Recording Industry Asscn; Société d'Auteurs, Compositeurs et Editeurs de Musique.

PERRY, Barney (Blair); b. 2 Nov. 1953, Buffalo, New York, USA. Composer; Musician (guitar); Vocalist; Teacher; Minister. m. Ethlene Perry, 2 May 1982, 2 s., 2 d. *Education:* Education Administration, Buffalo State College; Business Management and Accounting, Howard University; Lay Pastor, Ministry, Canada Christian College; Music Composition and Performance education, Howard University and Washington DC; Advanced Instrumental Techniques, Classical Guitar, University of Buffalo; Electronic Music, Catholic University; Jazz Guitar with George Benson; Classical Guitar with Bill Harris and Oswald Rentucci; Symphonic Music with Russell Wollen and William Penn. *Career:* Activist for intellectual property rights, state courts and federal courts, New York and California; TV, Blair, Invitation to Dance Show; Numerous radio shows; Concerts and performances as soloist, quartet; Band and show with Herbie Hancock, Lenny Williams; Co-founder, Blackbyrds; Backing Guitarist, Donald Byrd, Phyllis Hyman, Bobbi Humphrey, Vivian Reed, Jack McDuff. *Compositions:* Walking in Rhythm; Nightlife; A Hot Day Today; Virgo Princess; Who is Blair. *Recordings:* Blair: Nightlife; Live at Lafayette Square; Flying Start; Hit the Open Man; Blackbyrds. *Honours:* Outstanding Citation of Achievement, BMI; Million Plus Performance Composer; Pop Music Award, BMI. *Membership:* BTF; UTLA; Musicians Local; NRA; Blessed Trinity Holy Name Society. *Current Management:* Enterprise Management, New York.

PERRY, Joe; b. 10 Sept. 1950, Boston, MA, USA. Musician (guitar). *Career:* Lead guitarist, US rock band Aerosmith, 1970–79, 1984–; Leader, Joe Perry Project, 1980–83; Concerts include: Support to the Kinks, Mott The Hoople, 1974; Schaefer Music Festival, Central Park, 1975; Reading Rock Festival, 1977; California Jam II Festival, 1978; Texas World Music Festival, 1978; Appearance in film: Sgt Pepper's Lonely Hearts Club Band, as the Future

Villain Band, 1978; California Music Festival, with Van Halen, Cheap Trick, Ted Nugent, 1979; World Series of Rock, with Journey, Ted Nugent, Thin Lizzy, 1979 Monsters of Rock Festival, Castle Donington, 1990; Guest voice, The Simpsons, Fox Television, 1990. *Recordings:* Albums: Aerosmith: 1973; Toys In The Attic, 1975; Get Your Wings, 1975; Rocks, 1976; Draw The Line, 1977; Greatest Hits, 1981; Done With Mirrors, 1985; Classic Live!, 1986; Permanent Vacation, 1987; Retrospective Gems, 1988; Pump, 1989; Pandora's Box, 1992; Get A Grip (No. 1, USA), 1993; Big Ones, 1994; Nine Lives(No. 1, USA), 1997; Little South of Sanity, 1998; Young Lust–The Aerosmith Anthology, 2001; O'Yeah! Ultimate Aerosmith Hits, 2002; with Joe Perry Project: Let The Music Do The Talking, 1980; I've Got The Rock 'n' Roll Again, 1981; Once A Rocker, Always A Rocker, 1983; The Best of the Joe Perry Project, 1999; Singles include: Dream On, 1973; Sweet Emotion, 1975; Walk This Way, 1975; Back In The Saddle, 1977; Draw The Line, 1977; Come Together, 1978; Walk This Way, with Run DMC, 1986; Dude (Looks Like A Lady), 1987; Angel, 1988; Rag Doll, 1988; Love In An Elevator, 1989; Janie's Got A Gun, 1989; What It Takes, 1990; The Other Side, 1990; Livin' On The Edge, 1993; Eat The Rich, 1993; Cryin', 1993; Crazy, 1994; Falling In Love, 1997; Hole In My Soul, 1997; I Don't Wanna Miss A Thing (No. 1, USA), 1998; Amazing. *Honours:* Grammy Award, 1991; American Music Awards, 1991. *Current Management:* Magus Entertainment, 584 Broadway, Suite 1009, New York, NY 10012, USA.

PERRY, Lee 'Scratch', (Rainford Hugh Perry); b. 1936, Hanover, Jamaica. Recording Artiste; Record Prod. *Career:* Also billed as Scratch and the Upsetter; Record scout, 1950s and 1960s; Prod. and songwriter for Delroy Wilson, 1963; Solo artiste, 1963–; Formed own label, Upsetter, 1968–. *Recordings:* Albums include: The Upsetter, 1969; Many Moods Of The Upsetter, 1970; Scratch The Upsetter Again, 1970; Prisoner Of Love—Dave Barker Meets The Upsetters, 1970; Africa's Blood, 1972; Battle Axe, 1972; Cloak And Dagger, 1972; Double Seven, 1973; Rhythm Shower, 1973; Blackboard Jungle, 1974; Kung Fu Meets The Dragon, 1974; DIP Presents The Upsetter, 1974; Revolution Dub, 1975; Scratch The Upper Ape, 1976; Jah Lion—Columbia Colly, 1976; Return Of The Super Ape, 1977; Roast Fish, Collie Weed And Corn Bread, 1978; Scratch On The Wire, 1979; Scratch And Company—Chapter 1, 1980; Return Of Pipecock Jackson, 1981; Heart Of The Ark, Vol. 1, 1982, Vol. 2, 1983; Megaton Dub, 1983; Megaton Dub 2, 1983; History Mystery And Prophecy, 1984; Black Ark In Dub, 1985; Battle Of Armagideon—Millionaire Liquidator, 1986; Time Boom X De Devil Dead, 1987; Satan Kicked The Bucket, 1988; Scratch Attack, 1988; Chicken Scratch, 1989; Build The Ark, 1990; Meets Bullwackie—Satan's Dub, 1990; Meets The Mad Professor, 1990; The Upsetter And The Beat, 1992; Soundz From The Hot Line, 1993; Black Art In Dub, 1993; Larks From The Ark, 1995; Experryments At The Grassroots Of Dub, 1995; Voodooism, 1996; Technomajikal, 1997; Dub Fire, 1998; Lick Shot, 1999; Lost Treasures Of The Ark, 2000; Techno Party, 2000; Station Underground, 2001; Divine Madness—Definitely!, 2001; Jamaican E.T., 2002; Sensimilla Showdown, 2002; Scratch, 2002; The Compiler, Vol. 1: Rude Walking, 2002; As prod.: Hurt So Good, Susan Cadogan; Police And Thieves, Junior Marvin; Punky Reggae Party, Bob Marley and The Wailers; Also with: Massive Attack, The Clash, The Heptones, Max Romeo, Junior Marvin, David Isaacs, The Untouchables, Junior Byles. *Website:* www.upsetter.net/scratch/.

PERRY, Steve; b. 22 Jan. 1953, Hanford, California, USA. Vocalist. *Career:* Member, Alien Project; Lead singer, Journey, 1977–87; Solo artiste, 1987–; Concerts include: Regular tours, USA, Japan and Europe; World Series of Rock, Cleveland, 1979; Mountain Aire Festival, 1981. *Recordings:* Albums: with Journey: Journey, 1975; Look Into The Future, 1976; Next, 1977; Infinity, 1978; Evolution, 1979; In The Beginning, 1979; Departure, 1980; Dream After Dream, 1980; Captured, 1981; Escape (No. 1, USA), 1981; Frontiers (No. 2, USA), 1983; Raised On Radio, 1986; Greatest Hits, 1988; Time 3, 1992; Trial By Fire, 1996; Solo albums: Street Talk, 1984; For the Love of Strange Medicine, 1994; Greatest Hits + Five Unreleased, 1998; with Laidlaw, The First Big Picnic, 1999; Hit singles: Lovin' Touchin' Squeezin', 1979; Any Way You Want It, 1980; Don't Stop Believin', 1981; Who's Crying Now, 1981; Open Arms (No. 2, USA), 1982; Separate Ways (World's Apart), 1983; Faithfully, 1983; Send Her My Love, 1983; Only The Young, 1985; Be Good To Yourself, 1986; Tracks for film soundtracks Tron; Vision Quest; Solo singles: Oh Sherrie, 1984; Foolish Heart, 1985; You Better Wait, 1994; Missing You, 1994; When You're in Love (For the First Time), 1998; Duet with Kenny Loggins: Don't Fight It, 1982; Contributor, We Are The World, USA For Africa, 1985. *Honours:* Bay Area Music Awards, Best Vocalist, Best Group, 1987; Numerous Platinum and Gold discs. *Current Management:* Third Rail Entertainment. *Address:* 10202 Washington Blvd, Tri-Star Bldg 26, Culver City, CA 90203, USA.

PERSSON, Nina Elisabet; b. 6 Sept. 1974, Örebro, Sweden. Vocalist; Songwriter; Musician (harmonica). *Career:* Mem., Green Camels; Mem., lead singer, The Cardigans, 1992–; Contributed tracks to films Romeo and Juliet and A Life Less Ordinary; Numerous concert tours, festivals, television and radio appearances. *Recordings:* Albums: Emmerdale, 1994; Life, 1995; First Band On The Moon, 1996; Other Side Of The Moon, 1998; Gran Turismo, 1998. Singles: Rise And Shine; Black Letter Day; Sick And Tired, 1995; Carnival, 1995; Hey! Get Out Of My Way; Lovefool (No. 2, UK), 1996; Been It,

1997; Your New Cuckoo, 1997; My Favorite Game, 1998; Erase/Rewind, 1999; Hanging Around, 1999; Gran Turismo Overdrive, 2000; with David Arnold: Theme From 'Randall & Hopkirk Deceased' (BBC1), 2000. *Honours:* Slitz Magazine, Best Band, 1994; BMI Best Song, 1997, Best Album, 1998, Best Group, 1996, 1998. *Current Management:* Motor, PO Box 53045, 400 14 Gothenburg, Sweden. *Address:* c/o Stockholm Records, Positionen 146, 115 74 Stockholm, Sweden. *Website:* www.cardigans.net.

PESCE, Serge; b. 7 Sept. 1959, Nice, France. Musician (guitar); Composer. *Career:* Performed with: Alan Vitous, Barre Phillips, Miquel Montanaro, Yves Rousguisto, Patrick Vaillant, Alex Grillo, Jean-Louis Ruf; Festival appearances at: Nantes, Toulon, Confolens, Uzeste, Avignon, Parthenay, St Chartier Miskols, Szeged, Hungary. *Compositions:* L'odore del caffe, guitar solo. *Recordings:* Guitare Attitude; Couples; Le Gaboulet, Tambourin – Ocora Radio France; Ballade Pour Une Mer Qui Chante, Vols 2 and 3; L'odore Del Caffè; Jazzd'aià; Tenson, with Alan Vitous and Miqueu Montanaro; Silence de faune, with Yves Rousguisto; Amb la doçor, Aguillera, Zagaria. *Publications:* Yes Bomb'ai. *Membership:* SACEM; SPEDIDAM; SACD; SFA. *Address:* Serge Pesce, Palais Théodore, 27 rue Théodore de Banville, 06100 Nice, France.

PETEJ, Peco Petar; b. 18 March 1949, Split, Croatia. Musician (drums, piano). m. Nada Vicic, 12 July 1973, 2 s. *Education:* College degree; Academy for Jazz Music and Theatre Arts, Graz, Austria. *Career:* Delfini, Split, 1972; Played with leading jazz musicians with Hans Koller Free Sound; Member, rock band Time, 1973–79; Moved to Britain, 1974; Played with Jackie McAuley Throat, 1975; The Foundations vocalist Collin Young; Zagreb Jazz scene, TV Big Band, 1979; Returned to London blues scene, 1990; Back to Croatia, war humanitarian work, 1991; Indexi Sarajevo, 1994. *Recordings:* 2100 recorded minutes for TV Big Band; Recorded over 150 albums with various artists; Original music, theatre play, Hamlet and Tarzan. *Honours:* Numerous Pop and Rock Festival Awards, jazz fairs, Zagreb, Slovenia, Germany; Original Music Theatre Award, 1994. *Membership:* Musicians' Union (UK); Croatian Music Union; Croatian Asscn of Orchestral Musicians. *Current Management:* Vladimir Mihaljek, Croatian Music Art.

PETERS, Mike; b. 25 Feb. 1963, St Asaph, Wales. Musician (guitar); Vocalist. *Education:* School Bands, Stripey. *Career:* Lead singer, The Alarm; 6 critically acclaimed world-wide albums; 14 Top 50 singles; Concerts include: Spirit of '86 (audience of 26,000), University of California, Los Angeles, world-wide broadcast on MTV; Percussionist with Colin Vearcombe, 2000–; Drummer with Lucky Luciano, 2001–. *Recordings:* with The Alarm: Albums: Declaration, 1984; Strength, 1985; Eye Of The Hurricane, 1987; Change, 1989; Standards, 1990; Raw, 1991; Greatest Hits Live, 2001; Singles: 68 Guns, 1983; Where Were You Hiding When The Storm Broke?, 1984; Absolute Reality, 1985; Spirit Of '76, 1986; Rain In The Summertime, 1987; A New South Wales, 1989; Raw, 1991; Solo recordings: Albums: Breathe, 1994; Second Generation Vol 1, 1996; Feel Free, 1996; Rise, 1998; Flatiron, History. *Publications:* The Words and Music of The Alarm. *Membership:* Musicians' Union; PRS. *Current Management:* Track Artist Management, UK/USA. *Address:* 7B Holland Rd, London W14 8HJ, England. *E-mail:* waferthin@hotmail.com. *Website:* www.waferthin.org.

PETERS, Rob; b. 4 Oct. 1954, Birmingham, England. Musician, (guitar, drums, percussion); Songwriter; Performer; Prod. *Education:* University of Exeter; Open University. *Career:* Songwriter, 1973–; Formed Dangerous Girls, 1978; Drummer with Here and Now, 1982–83; Drummer, Everything But The Girl, 1985–87; Session Drummer with Ruby Blue, 1987; Tour Manager, 1988–90; Percussionist with Boo Hewerdine, 1991–; Guitarist, 1996–. *Compositions:* Step Out; Man In The Glass; Dangerous Girls; Long Ride Home; Georgie's Back in Town. *Recordings:* Include, Fantasy Shift; Baby The Stars Shine Bright; Ignorance; Zinc. *Membership:* Musicians' Union; PRS; MCPS; PPL. *Address:* PO Box 81, Birmingham B30 2LF, England.

PETERSEN, Erik; b. 25 Jan. 1953, Uppsala, Sweden. Musician; Composer; Actor. 2 s., 1 d. *Education:* Sämus Malmö, Musikhögskolan, Stockholm. *Career:* Skottes Musikteater, Gävle, 1983–86; Den goda människan i Sezvan, Gävle, Drottningens Juvelsmycke, Dramaten, Den Perfekta Kyssen, Angered, Det Susar i Säven, Stockholm, Oliver Twist, Turteatern, Kärlekens himmelska helvete, Film. *Compositions:* Skrotsymfoni, 1999. *Recordings:* Den passionerade hästen, 1986; Propeller, 1997. *Membership:* SKAP. *Address:* Oxelvägen 38, 141 41 Huddinge, Sweden.

PETERSON, Gilles; b. 28 Sept. 1964, Switzerland. DJ. *Career:* Began DJ career aged 18, Jazz Rooms, Electric Ballroom, Camden, London; Regularly ran Sunday afternoon session at Dingwalls, Camden; Worked on Acid Jazz label, Talkin Loud label; DJ's at Bar Rumba and Atmapuri, Eve Club; Presenter, Radio 1. *Recordings:* The INCredible Sound Of…, 1999; Worldwide, 2000.

PETERSON, Oscar Emmanuel; b. 15 Aug. 1925, Montréal, Québec, Canada. Jazz Musician (piano). 3 s., 4 d. *Education:* Studied with Paul de Markey. *Career:* Weekly radio show; Johnny Holmes Orchestra, Canada, 1944–49; Appeared with Jazz at the Philarmonic, Carnegie Hall, 1949; World-wide tours 1950–; Leader of own trio, with Ray Brown, Irving Ashby, 1947–;

Later with Barney Kessel, Herb Ellis, Ed Thigpen, Sam Jones, Louie Hayes; Concert appearances with Ella Fitzgerald, UK, 1955; Stratford (Ontario) Shakespeare Festival; Newport Jazz Festival. *Compositions:* Canadiana Suite; Hymn To Freedom; Fields of Endless Day; City Lights (with Norman McLaren); Begone Dull Care; Salute to Johann Sebastian Bach; Music for films: Big North; Silent Partner. *Recordings:* with Billie Holiday; Fred Astaire; Benny Carter; Count Basie; Roy Eldridge; Lester Young; Ella Fitzgerald; Joe Pass; Niels Henning; Orsted Peterson; Dizzy Gillespie; Harry Edison; Clark Terry; Recent releases include: Oscar and Benny, 1998; Summer Night in Munich, 1999; Paris Jazz Concert, 1999; Live at the Blue Note, 1999; Live At The Barbican, 2000; Trail Of Dreams, 2000; Oscar's Ballads, 2001. *Publications:* Jazz Exercises and Pieces; Oscar Peterson New Piano Solos. *Honours:* Numerous, including 11 Hon. degrees, 1973–94; Edison Award, 1962; Officer, Order of Canada, 1972; Award of Merit, City of Toronto (twice); Companion, Order of Canada, 1984; American Jazz Hall of Fame, 1989; 7 Grammy Awards; Hall of Fame Awards: JUNO, 1982, Contemporary Keyboard, 1983, University of California, Berkeley, 1983; Best Jazz Pianist Award winner: Keyboard (5 times), Playboy (12 times), Downbeat (13 times), Contemporary Keyboard (5 times); Carnegie Hall Anniversary Medal; Charlie Parker Bronze Medal; Ville de Salon de Provence Medal. *Address:* Regal Recordings, 2421 Hammond Rd, Mississauga, ON L5K 1T3, Canada.

PETIT, Philippe; b. 23 Nov. 1954, Marmande, France. Jazz Musician (guitar); Composer. *Education:* Bordeaux Conservatory of Music. *Career:* Tours with Philip Catherine; Tal Farlow; Barney Wilen; Miroslav Vitous; Eliot Zigmund; With own group including: Michel Graillier; Alain Jean Marie; Riccardo Del Fra; Al Levitt; Aldo Romano; J F Jenny-Clark. *Compositions:* Sigmanialogie 21, for jazz quartet and symphony orchestra, 1985. *Recordings:* Parfums, 1977; For All The Life, 1979; La Note Bleue, with Barney Wilen, 1986; Impressions of Paris, with Miroslav Vitous, 1989; Solo: Guitar Reflections, 1991; Standards Recital, with Tal Farlow, 1993; Guitar Attitude, 1996. *Membership:* SACEM. *Address:* 16 rue Jacquemont, 75017 Paris, France.

PETRI, Michala; b. 7 July 1958, Copenhagen, Denmark. Musician (recorder). m. Lars Hannibal, 2 d. *Education:* Staatliche Hochschule für Musik und Theater, Hanover. *Career:* Recorder player; First concert as soloist in Tivoli, 1969; Since 1969 has given 2,000 concerts in the USA, Japan, Australia, Europe; Has played with Pinchas Zukerman, James Galway and Keith Jarrett; Performs frequently with Lans. *Recordings:* More than 30 albums. *Publications:* Ed. of several works for Wilhelm Hansen and Moeck. *Honours:* Several prizes. *Address:* Nordskraenten 3, 2980 Kokkedal, Denmark.

PETROV, Petar; Musician (bass). *Career:* Member, Concurent, 1986–; numerous concerts, TV, radio appearances, Bulgaria. *Recordings:* Rock For Peace, 1988; Rock Festival In Mitcurin, 1989; The Black Sheep (rock collection), 1992; Something Wet (best-selling album, Bulgaria), 1994; The Best of Bulgarian Rock, 1995. *Honours:* First Prizes: Top Rock Band, Vidin, 1989; Rock Ring, Sofia, 1990; Top Rock Composition: The Cavalry, 1991; Group of the Year, The Darik Radio Countdown, 1994. *Address:* 40 St Stambolov Blvd, 1202 Sofia, Bulgaria.

PETROV, Vadim; b. 24 May 1932, Prague, Czech Republic. Composer; Prof. of Composition. m. Marta Votápková, 26 June 1954, 1 s., 2 d. *Education:* Graduate, Department of Composition, Academy of Fine Arts, Prague, Czech Republic, 1956. *Career:* The Giant Mountains Fairy Tales; There Are Some Limits; The Romance of Water Spirit; The Good Old Band; Sonets Chi Seled in Stone; Pax Rerum Optima; The Swans' Lament; The Nightingale and Rose; The Twelve; Johan Doctor Faust Nocturno in G; Burlesque; The Valessian Intermezzo; Song of the Night; The Ditty. *Compositions:* Melancholical Waltz; Tango Habanero; Scherzo Poetico; Riva Dei Pini; Romans; The Silver Serenade; Russian Evangelium; Song for Jane Eyre; The Autumn Memory; Night Tango; Song of Hoping and Belief. *Recordings:* The Maple Violin; Lucy and Miracles; Anna Snegina; Don Quigxot; Don Jean and others. *Publications:* Czech and Slovak Composer, 1980; Film and Time, 1983; The Little Czechoslovak Encyclopedia, 1986. *Honours:* Award of The Asscn of Czechoslovak Composers; Czech Television, 1997; Svobodné Slovo, Prague, 1997. *Address:* Karasovská 833/6, 160 00 Prague 6, Czech Republic.

PETROV, Vassil; b. 1964, Sofia, Bulgaria. Musician; Vocalist. *Education:* Graduate, Academy of Popular Music, Sofia, 1990. *Career:* Best-selling Bulgarian pop and jazz star; Numerous jazz, popular music festivals; Best-selling recording artist, Bulgaria; Performances: Helsinki; Oslo; Stockholm; Belgrade; Winter Olympics, Lillehammer, Norway; Currently working with Villi Kazassyan's Big Band; Acoustic Version (Bulgaria's leading jazz group); Successful concerts with Pleven's Philharmonic Orchestra; Working on albums with composer Vassil Parmakov, lyricist Terry Kaliski; Plays and sings own compositions. *Recordings:* Only Bulgarian performer to release 3 albums in 1 year: The Other One; Castrol Presents: Vassil Petrov; Duet album with pianist Rumen Toskov; Petrov Sings Parmakoff, 1994. *Honours:* Number One Male Voice, Bulgaria, First Bulgarian National Music Awards; Orpheus: Best Male Vocalist; Best Hit of the Year; Best Album of the Year: The Other One.

PETROVIC, Bosko; b. 18 Feb. 1935, Bjelovar, Croatia. Musician (vibraphone); Composer; Record Prod; Author; Divorced, 1 s. *Career:* Zagreb Jazz Quartet; BP Convention; BP Club All Stars; Over 30 radio and television serials on jazz as author and MC; Over 80 albums as musician or producer; All major jazz festivals. *Compositions:* With Pain I Was Born, 1960; Keka Kolo, 1962; Green Mood, 1962; Sigurd's Garden, 1970; Green Lobster Dream, 1972; Valse for Jazz Mama, 1988; Fin de Siècle, 1998. *Recordings:* With Pain I Was Born, 1965; Swinging East, 1971; Mistery of Blues, 1974; Stabilisation Blues, with Clark Terry, 1982; Tiffany Girl, 1985; From Moscow To LA, 1986; What's New, with Joe Pass, 1989; Meet Us At The Bar, 1991; Bosko Petrovic Meets James Newton, 1993; Green Mood, 1995; Jazz Gala, with John Lewis, 1996; The Very Beginning, with Jerome Richardson, 1998. *Honours:* Annual Award For Music, J Slavenski, 1980; Town of Zagreb Award, 1989; Croatian Grammy Award Pórin, 1995; Government decoration, Danica of Croatia, 1996. *Membership:* Composers Asscn of Croatia. *Current Management:* Jazzette Records.

PETRUCIANNI, Louis; b. France. Musician (contrabass). *Education:* Studies with Chuck Israël, USA, 1980. *Career:* Played with Barre Phillips, 1975–80; European tour with brother Michel Petrucianni; Also played with Lenny White; Trio with brother Michel; Quartet with brother Philippe. *Recordings:* Solo albums: Loi's Blues; The Librarian; MisterLight; with Tony Petrucianni: Nuages; with Orchestre de Jazz du Languedoc-Rousillon: Dialogues; Recordings with numerous artists including: Bernard Lubat; Lee Konitz; Alain Jean-Marie; Philippe Petit.

PETTAN, Svanibor Hubert; b. 11 Feb. 1960, Zagreb, Croatia. Ethnomusicologist. m. Albinca Pesek, 20 Nov. 1992. *Education:* BA, University of Zagreb, 1983; MA, University of Ljubljana, 1988; PhD, University of Maryland, USA, 1992. *Career:* Music Editor, Radio Zagreb, 1984–88; Research Scholar, Institute of Ethnology and Folklore Research, Zagreb, 1988–98; Adjunct Staff, Universities of Zagreb, 1993–, and Maribor, 1995–; Assistant Professor, University of Ljubljana, 1995–, Assoc. Prof. 2001–; Visiting Scholar, Norway, 1994, 1996, and USA, 1998, 2001; Frequent guest lectures and conference participations. *Recordings:* Folk Songs and Dances of Banija, selection and sleeve notes, Croatia, Vols 2 and 3, 1988; Croatia: Traditional Music of Today selection and sleeve notes, 1998; Folk Revival in Slovenia, sleeve notes, 1998; Kosovo Roma, selection and sleeve notes, 2001. *Publications:* Lambada in Kosovo: A Profile of Gypsy Creativity, 1992; Selling Music: Rom Musicians and the Music Market in Kosovo, 1996; Making the Refugee Experience Different: Azra and the Bosnians in Norway, 1996; Music, Politics and War: Views from Croatia (ed.), 1998; Music and Minorities (ed.), 2001; Rom Musicians in Kosovo: Interaction and Creativity, 2002. *Membership:* Liaison Officer for Slovenia and Mem. Exec. Board, ICTM; SEM; ISME; Slovenian Musicological Society; Pres., Slovenian Folk Culture Society. *Address:* University of Ljubljana, Music Academy, Stari Trg 34, 1000 Ljubljana, Slovenia. *E-mail:* svanibor.pettan@guest.arnes.si.

PETTERS, John David; b. 13 April 1953, Stratford, London, England. Traditional and Swing Jazz Musician (drums); Bandleader. m. Teresa Mellerick, 26 April 1980, 2 s. *Career:* Formed New Dixie Syncopators, 1976; Worked with John Gill and Ronn Weatherburn, 1977; Joined Ken Sims Dixie Kings, 1979; Formed John Petters Swing Band, 1982; Opened Jazz Club, The Square, Harlow, Essex; American soloists include: Wild Bill Davison; Art Hodes; Kenny Davern; George Masso; Yank Lawson; Slim Gaillard; Al Casey; Billy Butterfield; British stars include: Georgie Fame; Ken Colyer; Monty Sunshine; Humphrey Lyttelton; Cy Laurie; Maxine Daniels; George Chisholm; Stage shows and concerts include: Queens of The Blues, 1986; Roarin' 20s Show, 1987; Concerts with Lonnie Donegan; George Chisholm; Yank Lawson; Legends of American Dixieland, 1988; Swinging Down Memory Lane, 1989; Legends of British Trad, 1991; This Joint Is Jumpin', 1993; Special Magic of Benny Goodman, 1994; Boogie Woogie and All That Jazz, 1994; Ran Honky Tonk Train, Severn Valley Railway, 1995; Formed National Traditional Mailing List; Director, Mundesley Jazz Weekend Festival, 1995; Drum Crazy show and workshops, 1996; Director, This Joint Is Jumping, Blackpool, 1996; Director, first Prestatyn Jazz 'n' Swing Forum, 1997; This Is Jazz, festival, Torquay, 1997; Now You Has Jazz Jazz Jazz, Pontins; Toured UK theatres with S'Wonderful, Gershwin centenary show, 1998; Toured with Hoagy – Old Music Master, Hoagy Carmichael centenary show, 1999. *Recordings include:* Live and Swinging, with Kenny Dalvern, 1985; Mixed Salad, with Wally Fawkes, 1986; Together Again, with Art Hodes and Wild Bill Davison, 1988; Swinging Down Memory Lane, with George Chisholm O.B.E. and Maxine Daniels, 1989; Rags Boogie and Swing, with Simon Holliday, 1989; Mixed Salad, 1990; The Legends of British Trad, 1991; Blowin' A Storm, 1991; This Joint Is Jumping, 1992; John Petter's Red Hot Seven, 1994; Walking With The King, 1994; Boogie Woogie and All That Jazz, with Duncan Swift, 1995; Makin' Whoopee, with John Petters Dixielanders; Swing Band, with Yank Lawson and Kenny Davern, 1996; Bechet Centenary Band, Blame It On The Blues, with Trevor Whiting, John Wurr, Martin Litson, Dave Green, 1997; It's Me, O Lord, 1998; Shades of Jazz, with John Cherry; It's Alright With Me, with Nick Dawson; S'Wonderful, John Petters Broadway Melodists, 1998; Hoagy – The Old Music Master, John Petters and His Music Masters, 1999; Goin' Bananas, John Petters Jazz 'n' Swing Band. *Publications:* History of Jazz Drumming, Jazz Journal, 1985. *Current*

Management: John Petters Entertainments. *Address:* PO Box 42, Wisbech, Cambridgeshire PE13 5RJ, England.

PETTY, Tom; b. 20 Oct. 1953, Gainesville, FL, USA. Vocalist; Musician (guitar); Songwriter. *Career:* Guitarist, with local groups Sundowners; Epics; Mudcrutch, 1971–; Founder, Tom Petty and The Heartbreakers, 1975–; Member, The Traveling Wilburys, with Bob Dylan, George Harrison, Roy Orbison, Jeff Lynne, 1988–; Film appearance: FM, 1978; Regular US and international tours; Concerts include: Knebworth Festival, 1978; Musicians United For Safe Energy (MUSE), Madison Square Garden, 1979; Peace Sunday (Anti-nuclear concert), Pasadena, 1982; US Festival, San Bernardino, 1982; Live Aid, Philadelphia, 1985; Farm Aid, 1985; Tours, Australia, New Zealand, Japan, supporting Bob Dylan, 1986; Amnesty International Concert, 1986; True Confesions Tour with Bob Dylan, 1986; Rock 'n' Roll Caravan tour, with Georgia Satellites, 1987; Bob Dylan 30th Anniversary Tribute, 1992. *Compositions include:* Never Be You, Roseanna Cash (No. 1, USA Country Chart), 1986. *Recordings:* Albums: with the Heartbreakers: Tom Petty and The Heartbreakers, 1976; You Gonna Get It!, 1978; Damn The Torpedoes, 1979; Hard Promises, 1981; Long After Dark, 1982; Southern Accents, 1985; Pack Up The Plantation, 1986; Let Me Up (I've Had Enough), 1987; Full Moon Fever, 1989; Into The Great Wide Open, 1991; Greatest Hits, 1993; Take The Highway, 1994; She's The One (film soundtrack), 1996; Echo, 1999; Anthology–Through The Years, 2000; The Last DJ, 2002; with The Traveling Wilburys: Traveling Wilburys, 1988; Vol. 2, 1989; Vol. 3, 1990; Solo: Wildflowers, 1994; Hit singles include: Breakdown, 1978; Don't Do Me Like That, 1980; Refugee, 1980; Insider, 1981; You Got Lucky, 1983; Change of Heart, 1983; Don't Come Around Here No More, 1985; Jammin' Me, 1987; I Won't Back Down, 1989; Runnin' Down A Dream, 1989; Free Fallin', 1989; Learning To Fly, 1991; Too Good To Be True, 1992; You Don't Know How It Feels, 1994; It's Good to be King, 1995; Walls, 1996; Also featured on: Stop Draggin' My Heart Around, Stevie Nicks, 1981; Give Peace A Chance, Peace Choir, 1991; Film theme, Band of The Hand, with Bob Dylan, 1986; Time Takes Time, Ringo Starr; 30th Anniversary Concert, Bob Dylan, 1993; 30 Years of Randy Newman, Randy Newman, 1998. *Honours:* Gold discs; MTV Music Video Award, Don't Come Around Here No More, 1985. *Current Management:* East End Management, 8209 Melrose Ave, Second Floor, Los Angeles, CA 90046, USA.

PEWNY, Michael; b. 11 Nov. 1963, Vienna, Austria. Boogie Woogie and Blues Musician (piano). *Education:* MBA; Private classical education on piano, started playing age 7. *Career:* First concert, Vienna, 1981; Several radio and television appearances, ORF, Austria; 3 US tours; Festivals include: Blues Spring Festival, Belgium, 1992; Le Nuits Jazz and Boogie Festival, Paris, 1993, 1994. *Recordings:* Left Hand Roller, featuring Dana Gillespie, 1990; Boogie On My Mind, featuring Sabine Ruzicka, 1992; Vienna Boogie Woogie, featuring Torsten Zwingenberger, 1994; Crazy Bout Boogie, 1996; Movin' To Chicago; 20th Anniversary, 2000. *Current Management:* Susy Records, Stefaniegasse, 10 + 14/12, Kaltenleutgeben, Austria.

PHILLIPPS, Martin John James; b. 2 July 1963, Wellington, New Zealand. Songwriter; Performer; Musician (guitar); Vocalist. *Career:* Member, bands: The Same, 1978–80; The Chills, 1980–92; Tours: Australasia; Europe; USA, late 1980s–early 1990s; Also played with The Clean (re-formed); Snapper; Pop Art Toasters; April Fools; Relaunched as Martin Phillips and The Chills, 1995–. *Recordings:* The Dunedin Double EP, 1982; The Lost EP, 1984; Albums: Kaleidoscope World (compilation), 1986; Brave Words, 1987; Submarine Bells, 1989; Love to Hate You, Erasure, 1991; Soft Bomb, 1992; Pop Art Toasters (EP), 1994; Heavenly Pop Hits (Best of. . .), 1994; Album: Sunburnt, 1996; Secret Box, 2001. *Honours:* New Zealand Music Awards: Top Group, 1987; Top Group, Album, Single, Songwriter, 1990. *Address:* PO Box 705, Dunedin Central, New Zealand.

PHILLIPS, Bill; b. 29 Aug. 1951, Taplow, Berkshire, England. Musician (bass). Divorced, 1 d. *Career:* Many European tours with Glitter; Television: Jools Holland; MTV; The Beat; Raw Soup; Reeves and Mortimer; British tour with: Alvin Stardust; Mud; Glitter Band, 1994–95. *Recordings:* Denim album: Back In Denim; First single: Shampoo. *Membership:* Musicians' Union. *Current Management:* Hal Carter. *Address:* 29 Egremont Gardens, Slough, Berkshire, England.

PHILLIPS, Dudley; b. 9 June 1960, Maidenhead, Berkshire, England. Musician (electric bass, bass); Composer. *Career:* Early experience with soul bands; World tour with Womack and Womack, Bill Withers, Mica Paris; Jazz touring with Annie Whitehead; Andy Sheppard; Orphy Robinson; Perfect Houseplants; Jazz festivals include: Montreux; North Sea; Montréal; Berlin; Numerous television and radio appearances; Projects include: Balanescu Quartet; London Sinfonietta; Orlando Consort; Ernestine Anderson; Ronny Jordan; Dave Valentin; Najma. *Compositions include:* Sextet for Vanessa Smith, for string quartet, electric bass and drums; Arrangement of early vocal music for Orlando Consort plus Perfect Houseplants; Writing for own jazz sextet. *Recordings:* 4 albums with Perfect Houseplants; Andy Sheppard's Moving Image; 2 with Orphy Robinson; 3 with Colin Town's Mask; 4 with June Tabor, most recently Quiet Eye, 2000; Also albums with: Annie Whitehead; John Etheridge; Tim Whitehead; Permission; Huw Warren,

Barrel Organ; Perfect Houseplants; Mark Lockheart band; Peter Sellers film with Andy Sheppard. *Honours:* First Perfect Houseplant's album voted Best Jazz Album of the Year. *Address:* 64 Weston Park, London N8 9TD, England.

PHILLIPS, (Holly) Michelle; b. 4 June 1944, Long Beach, California, USA. Vocalist; Actress. m. (1) John Phillips, 31 Dec. 1962, deceased, 2001, 2 s., 1 d., (2) Dennis Hopper, 1970, divorced. *Education:* Voice lessons. *Career:* Member of The Mamas and the Papas; 2 US tours; Films: Dillinger; Valentino; Bloodline; Let It Ride; Television appearances include: Knots Landing (6 years); Beverly Hills 90210; Lois and Clark; The New Adventures of Superman; Murder She Wrote. *Compositions:* Co-wrote California Dreamin'; Creque Alley. *Recordings:* Singles: California Dreamin', 1965; Monday Monday (No. 1, USA), 1966; I Saw Her Again, 1966; Words Of Love, 1967; Dedicated To The One I Love, 1967; Creeque Alley, 1966; Albums: If You Can Believe Your Eyes and Ears, 1966; Cass John Michelle Denny, 1966; Deliver, 1967; Presenting The Papas And The Mamas, 1968; Singles+, 1999; with Belinda Carlisle, Heaven on Earth, 1988. *Publications:* California Dreamin'. *Honours:* 4 Gold discs; Grammy Award. *Membership:* NARAS; ACOMPAS.

PHILLIPS, John Keith Andrew; b. 9 June 1961, Darlinghurst, Sydney, Australia. Composer; Prod; Musician (guitar, bass). m. Emily Humphries, 1 s., 1 d. *Education:* Latrobe University, Melbourne, Australia. *Career:* Founding Member, Easter, 1983–85; Not Drowning, Waving, 1984–95; Major Film Scores: Body Work, 1988; Proof, 1991; Say A Little Prayer, 1993; Greenkeeping, 1993; That Eye The Sky, 1994; What I Have Written, 1995; River St, 1996; Idiot Box, 1996; The Myth of Finger Prints, 1997; Contributor: Malcolm, 1985. *Recordings:* Another Pond; Little Desert; Cold and the Crackle; Claim; Tabaran; Circus; Stylin Up, by Christine Anu; Telek, by Telek; World Turning, by Yothu Yindi; Contributor recordings include Archie Roach, Monique Brumby, Hugo Race, Snog, Bloom, Big Bag, Solid. *Honours:* Aria Award, Proof, film soundtrack CD; Aria Award, Telek, album, 1997. *Current Management:* Loud and Clear Management, PO Box 276, Albert Park, 2306, Australia.

PHILLIPS, Josh; b. 12 Dec. 1962. Musician (keyboards). *Education:* Grade 7 piano, Guildhall School of Music syllabus, 1977. *Career:* Turned professional, 1982; Tours: Diamond Head, 1983–85; Heatwave, world tour, 1986–88; Big Country, Russia, Estonia, Europe, UK, 1988–90; Midge Ure, Europe, UK, 1991, 1992; Procul Harum, Europe, 1993–94; Steve Roux Band, UK and Europe, 1993–94; Moody Marsden Band, Europe, 1994–95; Gary Brooker All-Star Band Annual Charity Christmas Show, 1990–; Videos: Diamond Head Live; Big Country Live–Russia; Big Country East Berlin; Cliff Richard; Midge Ure; Heatwave; Moody Marsden; Procul Harum; Helen Hofner; Television appearances include: Wogan; Top of the Pops; Wired; Meltdown; Smash Hits Awards; Telethon with Sam Brown, Midge Ure; Various European pop and music shows; Currently recording with Mark Brzezicki, Tony Butler, Steve Roux. *Compositions:* Incidental television music; Meltdown ITV Rock Music Show; Comment; Music for various commercials. *Recordings:* Albums with Diamond Head; Heatwave; Big Country; Midge Ure; Pete Townshend; Tim Renwick; Bernie Marsden; Moody Marsden Band; The Hamsters; S.A.S. Band; Leo Sayer. *Current Management:* Judy Totton Publicity. *Address:* EBC House, 1A Ranelagh Gardens, London SW6 3PA, England.

PHILLIPS, Martyn John Courtenay; b. 24 Nov. 1960, UK. Record Prod; Recording Engineer; Musician (guitar, keyboards, viola). *Education:* BA, Hons, Engineering Science, Oxford University; Trained on viola, piano and guitar. *Career:* Recording Engineer, London, 1982; Synthesizer Programmer, 1983–; Record Producer, 1989–. *Compositions:* Dolphin Stories/Out of the Blue, music for TV series; Living with the Enemy, Title music; Songs for Lindy Layton, Akasa, Signs of Life, Deep. *Recordings:* Productions: The Beloved: Happiness, album, The Sun Rising, Hello, Time After Time, singles; Erasure: Chorus, album, single, Am I Right, single, Love to Hate You, single, Breath of Life, single; London Beat: In the Blood, album, Harmony, album, I've Been Thinking About You, single, A Better Love, single, You Bring On the Sun, single, Loved You Send Me Colours, single; Roachford: Only to Be with You, single, This Generation, single, Feel, album, How Can I? (Insecurity), single; Jesus Jones: Right Here, Right Now, single, Already, album, The Next Big Thing, single; The Christians: What's In A Word, single; Lindy Layton: Silly Games, single, Echo My Love, single; Programmer/Engineer, Soul II Soul: 1990: A New Decade, album; Was (Not Was): What's Up Dog, album, Spy in the House of Love, single, Walk the Dinosaur, single; Swing Out Sister: It's Better To Travel, album, Kaleidoscope World, album, Breakout, single, Surrender, single; Ronan Keating: The Way You Make Me Feel (single), 2000. *Address:* 12 Saville Rd, London W4 5NQ, England.

PHILLIPS, P. J; b. 24 July 1964, London, England. Musician (bass guitar); Vocalist. *Career:* World-wide tours include: World tour with Nina Hagen, 1980; Television and radio apperances include: with Taylor Dayne: This Morning, Granada TV; Wogan, BBC TV, 1990; with Curtis Stigers: Wogan, Top of the Pops, BBC TV (3 times), 1992; with Michael Ball: Top of the Pops, 1992; with Nina Hagen: Chameleon Varieté TV show, 1993; with Tom Jones: Top of the Pops, BBC TV, 1994; Vetton Bass, ZDF TV, 1995; Worked with Take That. *Membership:* Equity; Musicians' Union; PRS; BAC&S. *Current*

Management: Debbie Haxton, The Session Connection. *Address:* 110/112 Disraeli Rd, London SW15 2DX, England.

PHILLIPS, Roy; b. 5 May 1941, Parkstone, Poole, England. Musician (keyboards). *Education:* Piano lessons (5–10 years). *Career:* Had own band (trio): The Peddlars, 15 years; Worked Las Vegas, 15 seasons; 12 world tours; Regular television and radio world-wide; Ed Sullivan Show; BBC, ATV (England regularly). *Compositions:* Wrote complete album: Suite London; Heavy On The Light Side. *Recordings:* 15 albums; 83 singles; 2 No. 1 hits: Birth; Girlie; Appears on: Ollie Mitchell, Blast off, 1983; Groovy, 1997. *Honours:* No 1 Keyboards, England, 1971, 1972. *Membership:* PRS; Screen Writers Guild; Songwriters Guild. *Address:* PO Box 10, Paihia, Bay of Islands, New Zealand.

PHILLIPS, Shawn; b. 2 March 1943, Fort Worth, Texas, USA. Musician (guitar, keyboards, sitar). 1 d. *Career:* Film appearance, Run With The Wind; Lead singer, Broadway musical, Jesus Christ Superstar; Tours include: South Africa; Québec; Television includes: 4 appearances Midnight Special, CBS; In Concert, NBC. *Compositions include:* Co-writer, Sunshine Superman album, with Donovan. *Recordings:* Albums: Contribution, 1970; Second Contribution, 1971; Collaboration, 1972; Faces, 1973; Furthermore, 1974; Bright White, 1975; Do You Wonder, 1976; Rumplestiltskin's Resolve, 1977; Spaced, 1978; Transcendence, 1980; Best of Shawn Phillips, 1986; Beyond Here Be Dragons, 1988, reissued 2000; The Truth If It Kills, 1994; Another Contribution, 1995. *Honours:* Yamaha World Popular Song Festival; 3 Platinum discs for album Second Contribution. *Membership:* SOCAN; BMI. *Current Management:* Arlo Henning, Lodestone Management. *Address:* 10920 Irwin Ave S, Bloomington, MN 55437, USA.

PHILLIPS, Steve (Nicholas Stephen); b. 18 Feb. 1948, London, England. Vocalist; Musician (guitar). 2 d. *Career:* Semi-professional musician, 1961–86; Professional solo artist, 1986–; Also duo with Brendan Croker; collaborations with Paul Judge; Also, member, Notting Hillbillies, 1990; Own band, Steve Phillips and The Rough Diamonds. *Recordings:* The Best of Steve Phillips, 1987; Steel Rail Blues, 1989; with Notting Hillbillies: Missing Presumed Having A Good Time, 1990; Been A Long Time Gone, 1995; Just Pickin', 1996. *Membership:* PRS, PAMRA. *Current Management:* GTA, Wisteria House, 14 Glamorgan Rd, Hampton Wick, Surrey KT1 4HB, England.

PHIMISTER, Glen; b. 15 Sept. 1953, London. Recording Engineer. m. Hortensze. *Education:* Ealing Mead Academy, London. *Career:* Engineer, Unity Gain Studio and freelance; Previously with: Studios 301, Sydney; Air Studios, London; Trident Studios, London; Worked on various pop, rock, jazz and orchestral recordings, mid 1970s–; Worked on Sydney Olympics, 2000; TV work includes: Home and Away; The Farm. *Recordings:* Olivia Newton-John; INXS; Pseudo Echo; Prague Symphony Orchestra; Split Enz; Slim Dusty; David Campbell; Iota; Jazz Police. *Address:* 294a Livingstone Rd, Marrickville, New South Wales 2204, Australia.

PHOENIX, (David Michael Farrell); b. 8 Feb. 1977, Plymouth, MA, USA. Musician (bass guitar). *Education:* Taught guitar by mother. *Career:* Mem., high school group, The Snax; Joined Xero; Left band after completion of college; Rejoined group, now named Linkin Park, 2000; Numerous international appearances; Live shows include: Family Values, Ozzfest tours, KROQ Acoustic Christmas Concert 2001; TV specials include: Live At The Fillmore; Reverb. *Recordings:* Albums: Reanimation, 2002. Singles: Pts.Of.Athrty, 2002. *Honours:* Billboard Award, Best Modern Rock Artist, 2001; Rock Bear Awards, Best International Band, Best International Album, 2001; Kerrang! Award, Best International Newcomer, 2001; Rolling Stone Award, Best Hard Rock/Metal Band, 2001; MTV Awards, Best Group, Best Hard Rock, 2002. *Current Management:* Andy Gould Management, 8484 Wilshire Blvd #425, Beverly Hills, CA 90211, USA. *Website:* www.linkinpark.com.

PIATKOWSKI, Dionizy; b. 1954, Poznan, Poland. Critic; Jazz Historian; Journalist; DJ; Prod. m. Irena, 1 s., 2 d. *Education:* Postgraduate Studies, Journalism, 1984; MA, Ethnology, specialization in Music Folklore, Poznan University, 1978. *Career:* Music Journalist, Jazz Forum, Express Poznanski, Glos Wielkopolski, Wprost, Jazz a Go Go, Jazz Magazine; Freelance journalist for several jazz magazines in Europe and the USA; Leading jazz and music publicist, producer and organizer in Poland; Lecturer on Jazz, Black Music and Folklore, University of Graz, Poznan University, Pittsburgh University, USA; DJ and Producer, Polish radio stations, shows include Jazz Academy and Let's Play Folklore; Producer, Director and A&R, jazz festivals and concerts including Dave Brubeck, Stephane Grappelli, B. B. King, Jan Garbarek and Kronos Quartet; Man. Dir, Poznan Jazz Festival; Founder, Programme and Music Director, first Polish music radio station, Radio 88.4 Jazz/FM. *Publications:* Not Only Music; Fan Club Special; Komeda's Time; Jazz Giants; Blues, Punk, Disco; Encyclopaedia of Popular Music–Jazz; Numerous articles in Polish and international journals. *Membership:* International Asscn for Jazz Research, Austria; Friends of Polish Music, USA; International Jazz Hall of Fame, Pittsburgh University, USA. *Address:* Strzelecka 37, 62–050 Mosina, Poland.

PICCHIOTTI, Mark; Prod; Remixer; DJ. *Career:* Worked with: Adeva, Basstoy & The Absolute, Mariah Carey, Eternal, Enrique Iglesias, Michael Jackson, Jamiroquai, Kylie Minogue, Madonna. *Address:* c/o Stephen Budd Management Ltd, 109b Regents Park Rd, Primrose Hill, London NW1 8UR, England. *Website:* www.record-producers.com.

PICKERING, Mike; b. 21 Feb. 1959, Manchester, England. Musician (saxophone); Vocalist; Composer; DJ. *Career:* DJ, Manchester clubs; Singer, saxophonist, Quando Quango; Founder member, musician, songwriter, UK dance group M People, 1991–; Major concerts include: Glastonbury Festival, 1994. *Recordings:* Albums: Northern Soul, 1992; Elegant Slumming, 1993; Bizarre Fruit, 1994; Bizarre Fruit II, 1995; Fresco, 1997; Best Of M People, 1998; Hit singles: How Can I Love You More, 1991; One Night In Heaven, 1993; Movin' On Up (No. 2, UK), 1993; Don't Look Any Further, 1993; Renaissance, 1994; Sight For Sore Eyes, 1994; Itchycoo Park, 1995; Search For The Hero, 1995; Open Your Heart, 1995; Love Rendezvous, 1995; Just For You, 1997; Fantasy Island, 1997; Angel Street, 1998; Testify, 1998; Dreaming, 1999. *Honours:* Mercury Prize, Best Album, Elegant Slumming, 1994; BRIT Awards, Best Dance Act, 1994, 1995. *Current Management:* RD World Wide Management. *Address:* 37 Limerston St, London SW10 0BQ, England.

PICKERING, Phil; b. 27 June 1960, Pembury, Kent, England. Musician (bass guitar, didgeridoo, synthesizer). 3 s., 1 d. *Education:* Guitar tuition as teenager. *Career:* Webcore; Goat; Tribal Drift; Fun-Da-Mental; Lights In A Fat City; Zuvuya. *Recordings include:* Vane: Glamorous Boys, 1981; 2 Webcore albums: Webcore, 1987; Webcore Webcore, 1988; 1 Goat album: Goat; Tribal Drift: Like This!, 1992; Medicine Hat, 1992; 2 Zuvuya albums with Terence McKenna: DMT, 1994; Shamania, 1994; Zuvuya: The Goat Faced Girl, 1994; Driving The Monkey Insane, 1994; Moose Jaw, 1994; Away The Crow Road, 1994; The Trance End of Dreaming, 1994; Turn Around, 1994; Third Zuvuya album, 1997; Quadruped, Quadruped, 1995; Fun-Da-Mental: Seize the Time, 1995; Erotic Terrorism, 1998. *Membership:* PRS; Musicians' Union. *Current Management:* M.E.L.T. Music, Lescrow Farm, Fowey, Cornwall PL23 1JS. *Address:* Delerium Records, PO Box 1288, Gerrards Cross, Bucks SL9 9YB, England.

PICKETT, Wilson; b. 18 March 1941, Prattville, Alabama, USA. Vocalist; Musician (guitar). *Career:* Gospel singer; Lead singer, the Falcons, 1961; Solo artist, 1963–; Recent appearances include: Pori Jazz, Finland, 1995; Sardinia Blues and Jazz, Italy, 1997; Rock and Roll Hall of Fame and Museum, USA, 1998; Star Festival, Belgium, 1998; Blues Brothers 2000, 1998. *Recordings:* Albums: In The Midnight Hour, 1965; The Exciting Wilson Pickett, 1967; The Sound of Wilson Pickett, 1967; The Best of Wilson Pickett, 1967; I'm In Love, 1968; The Midnight Mover, 1968; Hey Jude, 1969; Wilson Pickett In Philadelphia, 1970; The Best of Wilson Pickett Vol. II, 1971; Mr Magic Man, 1973; Pickett In The Pockett, 1973; A Funky Situation, 1978; I Want You, 1979; The Right Track, 1981; American Soul Man, 1988; It's Harder Now, 1999; The Soul Of Wilson Pickett, 2001; Hit singles include: In The Midnight Hour, 1965; Don't Fight It, 1965; 634–5789, 1966; Land of 1,000 Dances, 1966; Mustang Sally, 1966; Everybody Needs Somebody To Love, 1967; I Found A Love, 1967; Funky Broadway, 1967; Stag-O-Lee, 1967; She's Lookin' Good, 1968; I'm A Midnight Mover, 1968; Hey Jude, 1969; Sugar Sugar, 1970; (Get Me Back On Time) Engine Number Nine, 1970; Don't Let The Green Grass Fool You, 1971; Don't Knock My Love, 1971; It's Harder Now, 1999. *Honours:* Inducted into Rock and Roll Hall of Fame, 1991. *Current Management:* Talent Source, 1560 Broadway, Suite 1308, New York, NY 10036, USA.

PICKFORD, Andrew Cliffe; b. 22 Oct. 1965, Kegworth, Nottinghamshire, England. Musician (electronic keyboards). *Career:* Solo artist, Electronic music; Concerts include: Derby Cathedral, Derby Assembly Rooms and Guildhall (several times); Radio and television: Interviews and broadcasts on BBC local radio; BBC Radio 1 including John Peel show; Formed Electronic Music and Musicians Association. *Recordings:* Albums: Replicant, 1993; Terraformer, 1994; Maelstrom, 1995 (all No. 1, Electronic music charts); 2 EPs; Dystopia, 1996; Xenomorph, 1996; Works Vol. 1, Works Vol. 2 (both live at Derby), 1997. *Membership:* PRS; Past Secretary, EMMA. *Current Management:* David Shoesmith, Centaur Discs Ltd, 40–42 Brantwood Ave, Dundee DD3 6EW, Scotland. *Address:* The Bryans, 89 Dundee Rd, West Ferry, Dundee DD5 3LZ, Scotland.

PIERCE, Jason; b. 19 Nov. 1965, Rugby, England. Musician (guitar); Vocalist. *Career:* Member, Spacemen 3; Formed Spiritualized; Worked with Dr John and Spring Heeled Jack; Numerous live dates including world tour; Concerts at Royal Albert Hall, London, and CN Tower, Toronto. *Recordings:* Singles: Run, 1991; Anyway That You Want Me, 1991; Let It Flow, 1995; Electricity, 1997; I Think I'm In Love, 1998; Come Together, 1998; Abbey Road EP, 1998; Stop Your Crying, 2001; Albums: Lazer Guided Melodies, 1992; Fucked Up Inside (live), 1993; Pure Phase, 1995; Ladies and Gentlemen We Are Floating In Space, 1997; Royal Albert Hall 10 October 1997 (live), 1998; Let It Come Down, 2001.

PIERSON, Kate; b. 27 April 1948, Weehawken, New Jersey, USA. Vocalist; Musician (organ). *Career:* Singer, musician, B-52's, 1976–. *Recordings:* Albums: B-52's, 1979; Wild Planet, 1980; Mesopotamia, 1982; Whammy!,

1983; Bouncing Off The Satellites, 1986; Cosmic Thing, 1989; Best Of The B-52's – Dance This Mess Around, 1990; Good Stuff, 1992; B Fifty Two's, Time Capsule, Greatest Hits, 1998; Associate, Associate, 1996; Singles include: Rock Lobster, 1980; Love Shack, 1989; Roam, 1990; Guest vocals on: Shiny Happy People, REM, 1991; Also appears on recordings by: Chicks On Speed; Iggy Pop; Matthew Sweet. *Current Management:* Direct Management Group, 947 N La Cienga Blvd, Los Angeles, CA 90069, USA.

PIG CITY. See: **CLARKE, Dave.**

PILC, Jean-Michel; b. 19 Oct. 1960, Paris, France. Musician (piano, keyboards); Composer. m. *Career:* Played in numerous concerts, festivals, tours to over 40 countries including Africa, Asia, Europe; Sideman with artistes incl.: Roy Haynes Quartet; Jean Toussaint (including Royal Festival Hall, London); Daniel Humair and Jean-François Jenny-Clarke; Michel Portal; Martial Solal; Aldo Romano; André Ceccarelli; Christian Escoude; Rick Margitza; Peter King; George Brown; Dave Liebman; Greg Hutchinson; Harry Belafonte; Michael Brecker; John Abercrombie; Adam Nussbaum; Omar Hakim; Jeff Watts; Dennis Irwin; Essie Essiet; Alvester Garnett; Leader with: Enrico Rava (trumpet), Marc Ducret (guitar), Mark Mondesir (drums); Composer, leader, arranger playing solo, in duo, trio and big band; Recent European tour, Germany, Switzerland, France; Moves to New York City, 1995; Plays in Sweet Basil, New York City, with his trio, 1999. *Compositions:* Music played throughout Europe, covered by many other artists; Many film scores. *Recordings:* Albums: Electrochoc, 1987; Funambule, 1989; Big One, 1993; For Edith Piaf and Charles Trenet, with Eric Le Lann/ Martial Solal, 1989; Prosodie, Aldo Romano, 1995; Life I Want, Jean Toussaint, 1995; From The Heart, André Ceccarelli, 1995; Richard Bona, 1999; Elisabeth Kontomanou, 1999; Welcome Home, 2002; Other recordings with: Elizabeth Kontomanou; Eric Le Lann; J-Loup Longnon. *Honours:* Django Reinhardt Prize, Académie du Jazz, France, 2000. *Current Management:* Jon Waxman Associates, 302 W 12th St, Suite 10B, New York, NY 10014, USA. *Address:* 262 Bergen St, Suite 2R, Brooklyn, NY 11217, USA.

PILGREM, Rennie, (Thursday Club, New Electro Sound of London, Tribal Underground); b. 15 Jan. 1961, London, England. Prod; Remixer; DJ. *Career:* Formed: Rhythm Section (with Ellis Dee), early 1990s; Duo were big live success on Rave scene; Founder: Thursday Club Recordings; Major figure in Nu Skool Breakz scene, late 1990s; Co-promoter: Friction night in London (alongside Adam Freeland); Collaborations: Ellis Dee; Arthur Baker; Will South; B.L.I.M.; Uberzone; Remixed: BT; Quivver; Kosheen. *Recordings:* Philadelphia Bluntz (with Philadelphia Bluntz), 1998; Selected Werks (compilation), 2000; Singles: Feel The Rhythm (with Rhythm Section), Check Out The Bass (with Rhythm Section), 1991; A Place Called Acid (as Thursday Club), 1996; Sister Sister (with Philadelphia Bluntz), Like No Other (with Arthur Baker), 1998; Eskimo (with B.L.I.M.), 2001. *Address:* c/o Thursday Club Recordings, 310 King St, London W6 0RR, England.

PILKINGTON, Stephen Roy; b. 5 Oct. 1946, Bakewell, Derbyshire, England. Music Dir; Musician (piano, organ). m. Patricia Anne Wall, 18 July 1970, 1 s., 1 d. *Education:* Royal Manchester College of Music, GRSM; ARMCM; LRAM; ARCO. *Career:* Music Director, many top star shows including: Royal Shows for Princess Royal, Princess Margaret, 1975–; Music Director for television series; Keyboard backing for television signature tunes and plays; Pianist for Welsh musical programmes. *Recordings:* Romance, solo piano ballads and orchestra accompaniment; Stephen Pilkington Organ Collection; Backing many Welsh recordings. *Membership:* Musicians' Union. *Address:* Glandwr Onest, Blaenffos, Boncath, Pembrokeshire SA37 0JB, Wales.

PINE, Courtney; b. 18 March 1964, London, England. Jazz Musician (saxophone). 1 s., 3 d. *Career:* International tours, with own reggae and acoustic jazz bands; Trio (with Cameron Pierre, Talvin Singh) opened for Elton John and Ray Cooper, The Zenith, Paris and Royal Albert Hall, London, European Tour, 1994; Teacher's Jazz European tour, 1996; Support to Cassandra Wilson, USA and Canada, 1996; Tours, Japan, South Africa and UK, 1996; Festivals in Europe, Japan, Thailand, 1996; Television appearances: Regular guest, Later With Jools Holland; Black Christmas, Channel 4; The White Room, 1996; Featured Artist on BBC's Perfect Day recording (No. 1, UK), 1997. *Recordings include:* Albums: Journey To The Urge Within, 1987; Destiny's Song, 1988; The Vision's Tale, 1989; Closer To Home, 1990; Within The Realms of Our Dreams; To The Eyes of Creation; Modern Day Jazz Stories, 1996; Underground, 1997; Another Story, 1998; Featured guest on: Wandering Spirit, Mick Jagger; Jazzmatazz, Guru; Jazzmatazz II – The New Reality, Guru; Summertime, track on The Glory of Gershwin (Larry Adler tribute album); Modern Answers To Old Problems, Ernest Ranglin, 2000. *Honours:* Mercury Music Prize, one of Albums of the Year, 1996; Best Jazz Act, MOBO, 1996, 1997. *Current Management:* c/o Nikki Neave, Tickety-Boo, The Boathouse, Crabtree Lane, London SW6 6TY, England.

PINK, (Alicia Moore); b. 8 Sept. 1979, USA. Vocalist; Songwriter. *Career:* Started singing and dancing in local bands, aged 13; Spotted at Philadelphia club Fever by MCA Records talent scout; After unsuccessful stints with manufactured groups Basic Instinct and Choice teamed up with producers LA Reid and Babyface. *Recordings:* Albums: Can't Take Me Home, 2000; M!ssundaztood, 2001. Singles: There You Go, 2000; Most Girls, 2000; You Make Me Sick, 2001; Lady Marmalade (with Christina Aguilera, Lil' Kim and Mya), 2001; Get The Party Started, 2001. *Honours:* MTV Video Award, Best New Artist; MTV Award, Best Song, for Get The Party Started, 2002. *Current Management:* Wrightstuff Management, USA. *Address:* c/o LaFace Records, 1 Capital City Plaza, 3350 Peachtree Rd, Suite 1500, Atlanta, GA 30326, USA. *Website:* www.pinkspage.com.

PINKSTON, Steven Ray; b. 12 Dec. 1960, Columbus, Ohio, USA. Record Prod; Engineer; Songwriter. m. Angie Akin, 30 Oct. 1993. *Education:* Belmont University, Nashville, Tennessee. *Career:* Concert tours: Linda Ronstadt; Steven Curtis Chapman; Shelley West; The Commodores; Geoff Moore and The Distance; ABC; Amy Grant. *Compositions:* Cleansing Rain, Kelli Reisen (No. 3, CCM hit); 50 albums include: 4Him; Commissioned; Angelo and Veronica; Brian White; J J Cale; Dallas Brass; Midnight Clear; Graham Maw; Videos: 4Him; Commissioned; Harvest; Brian White; Wellington Boone; Grace Lazenby; Becky Tirabassi. *Recordings include:* Natural Encounters, 1998; Mark Baldwin, In the pocket, 1999; Contemporary Christian Hits, 1999; Four Him, Basics of Life, 1999. *Membership:* GMA; NARAS. *Address:* PO Box 40784, Nashville, TN 37204, USA.

PITCH, Harry; b. 9 May 1925, Hull, Yorkshire, England. Musician (harmonica, trumpet). m. Ruby, 10 June 1946, 1 s., 1 d. *Career:* Session musician; Featured soloist at Sadlers Wells; Royal Festival Hall, with Hans Werner Henze; Barbican Centre with Carl Davis; Television includes: Playing for Last of Summer Wine, 25 years, Many radio series; Films with: Ron Goodwin; Laurie Johnson; James Horner; Geoff Love; One of the only harmonica players to move successfully from classical to jazz music; Many jazz broadcasts with various groups include Rhythm and Reeds, with Jack Emblow. *Compositions:* Recorded library music. *Recordings:* Hits with various artists, throughout 1960s–80s; Solo albums. *Membership:* Musicians' Union (Gold Card mem.). *Address:* Hunters Moon, Islet Rd, Maidenhead, Berks SL6 8HT, England.

PITCHFORD, Dean; b. 29 July 1951, Honolulu, Hawaii, USA. Songwriter; Screenwriter; Dir. *Education:* Yale University, 1972. *Career:* Actor, singer: Godspell, 1971–72; Pippin, 1972–75; The Umbrellas of Cherbourg, 1978; Songwriter, screenwriter, films: Fame, 1980; Footloose, 1984; Sing, 1988; Chances Are, 1989. *Compositions:* Songs: Fame, recorded by Irene Cara (No. 1, UK), 1980; Footloose, recorded by Kenny Loggins (No. 1, USA), 1984; Let's Hear It For The Boy, recorded by Deniece Williams (No. 1, USA), 1984; You Should Hear How She Talks About You, recorded by Melissa Manchester, 1982; After All; Almost Paradise; Holding Out For A Hero, recorded by Bonnie Tyler, 1984; All The Man That I Need, recorded by Whitney Houston, 1990; Love Moves In Mysterious Ways, recorded by Julia Fordham, 1992; Footloose, on Broadway, 1998. *Honours:* Academy Award, Fame; Golden Globe Award, Fame. *Membership:* BMI; NAS; NARAS.

PITICCO, Steve; b. 6 July 1961, Toronto, Ontario, Canada. Musician (lead guitar). m. Laurie Laporte, 25 April 1983, 1 s., 1 d. *Career:* Performs professionally with Fender Telecaster guitars; Formed own band, South Mountain, 1989; Toured with: Sweethearts of The Rodeo; Marty Stuart; Conway Twitty; Charlie Pride; Played shows supporting: Vince Gill; George Jones; Johnny Cash; Ricky Skaggs; Mid-Canada Television network, with South Mountain, 4 years; Picker, various bands, including South Mountain, on Canadian Country Music Awards' Annual Telecast, 1984–94; Tours in Canada and Europe, 1995. *Recordings:* 8 albums with South Mountain; Session player on recordings by: Patricia Conroy; Tracy Prescott; Don Neilson. *Honours:* 7 CCMA Instrumentalist of Year Awards, 1985–94; CCMA Rising Star Awards, 1991; CCMA Guitar Player of the Year, 1990–93. *Current Management:* Cathy Faint Entertainment Inc, 430 Signet Dr., Suite C, North York, ON M9L 2T6, Canada. *Address:* PO Box 64, Lot 7, County Rd 1, South Mountain, ON K0E 1W0, Canada.

PITMAN, Toby John; b. 27 Sept. 1971, Crawley, West Sussex, England. Musician (guitar). *Education:* Graduate Diploma, Guitar Institute of Technology, USA. *Career:* Appearances on television and radio include: Capital Radio programme, How Do They Do That, BBC, Glam Metal Detectives; Current member, funk/rock band Radio Jim. *Recordings:* Rock Guitar Album. *Membership:* Musicians' Union. *Address:* c/o E L Seeberg, Acremead, Framfield Rd, Blackboys, East Sussex TN22 5LR, England.

PITNEY, Gene; b. 17 Feb. 1941, Hartford, Connecticut, USA. Vocalist; Songwriter. m. Lynne, 21 Jan. 1967, 3 s. *Career:* Recording artiste, 1959–; Recorded albums in Italian and Spanish; Regular international tours. *Compositions:* Songs include: Loneliness, The Kalin Twins; Today's Teardrops, Roy Orbison; Rubber Ball, Bobby Vee; Hello Mary Lou, Ricky Nelson; He's A Rebel, The Crystals; Recorded with the Rolling Stones in 1964; Nessuno Mi Puo Guidicare, second place at San Remo Song Festival, 1966. *Recordings:* Albums: The Many Sides of Gene Pitney, 1962; Only Love Can Break A Heart, 1963; Pitney Sings Just For You, 1963; Blue Gene, 1964; Gene Pitney Meets The Fair Young Ladies of Folkland, 1964; I'm Gonna Be Strong,

1965; George Jones and Gene Pitney, 1965; The Great Songs of our Time, 1965; Nobody Needs Your Love, 1966; Young Warm and Wonderful, 1967; Just One Smile, 1967; Pitney Today, 1968; Pitney '75, 1975; Walkin' In The Sun, 1979; Pitney Espagñol, 1982; Love My Life Away, 1982; Half Heaven Half Heartache, 1983; Gene Pitney, 1984; The Definitive Collection, 1999; Sings Great Ballads, 2000; Various compilations; Singles include: I Wanna Love My Life Away, 1961; Town Without Pity, 1962; The Man Who Shot Liberty Valance, 1962; That Girl Belongs To Yesterday, 1962; Twenty Four Hours From Tulsa, 1963; Half Heaven Half Heartache, 1963; I'm Gonna Be Strong (No. 2, UK), 1964; I Must Be Seeing Things, 1965; Looking Through The Eyes of Love, 1965; Princess In Rags, 1965; Backstage, 1966; Nobody Needs Your Love (No. 2, UK), 1966; Just One Smile, 1966; Something's Gotten Hold of My Heart, 1967; Somewhere In The Country, 1968; Maria Elena, 1969; Shady Lady, 1970; Blue Angel, 1974; Gene Pitney, 1984; Something's Gotten Hold of My Heart, with Marc Almond (No. 1, UK), 1988; The Definitive Collection, 1999. *Honours:* Elected to Rock 'n' Roll Hall of Fame, 2002. *Membership:* ASCAP, BMI. *Current Management:* Pitney Music, c/o David P McGrath. *Address:* 6201 39th Ave, Kenosha, WI 53142, USA.

PIZZARELLI, John 'Bucky'; b. 9 Jan. 1926, USA. Jazz Musician (guitar). m. Ruth Litchult Pizzarelli, 9 Jan. 1954, 2 s., 2 d. *Education:* Studied with Peter and Robert Domenick. *Career:* Member, Vaughn Monroe Orchestra; White House concerts with Benny Goodman, Frank Sinatra; Staff musician with NBC; ABC; Skitch Henderson; Doc Severinson; Mitch Miller; Concerts and tours with artistes including: George Barnes and Les Paul; Stéphane Grappelli; Skitch Henderson; Bobby Short; Benny Goodman; Zoot Sims; Peter Appleyard; Barney Kessel and Charlie Byrd; Howard Alden; Festivals include: Umbria Jazz Festival; Newport Jazz Festival; Melon Jazz; Dick Gibson's Jazz Parties throughout USA; Faculty Member Emeritus, William Paterson College, Wayne, New Jersey. *Recordings:* Albums include: Green Guitar Blues; Buck Plays Bix; Bucky's Bunch; Cafe Pierre Trio; Love Songs; Solo Flight; One Morning In May, Sonatina, 2000; with Stéphane Grappelli: All Stars, 1978; Passion Guitars, April Kisses, 1999; Rare Delight Of You (with George Shearing), 2002; Also recorded with: George Barnes; Zoot Sims; Eddie Daniels; Benny Goodman; Joe Venuti. *Address:* 214 West Saddle River Rd, Saddle River, NJ 07458–2620, USA.

PLA, Roberto Enrique; b. Barranquilla, Colombia. Musician (percussion, timbales, bongos, congas, drums); Bandleader. m. Dominique Roome, 3 Oct. 1992. *Education:* Studied percussion with Pompelio Rodríguez; National University in Bogotá, 1964–. *Career:* Session musician with artists including Los Ocho De Colombia; Drummer with Orquesto Lucho Bermudez, 1968–78; Tours include Latin America and USA; Weekly television appearances, Colombian television; Moved to New York, 1978; Salsa session percussionist, bands including Orquesta La Inspiracion; Moved to London, 1979; Member, jazz-fusion band Cayenne; Founder member, bands including Valdez; Sondido De Londres (co-founder); Roberto Pla Latin Ensemble (12-piece all-star band); Numerous European festivals and television appearances, 1988; Concerts include: Boney M, World tour, 1982; Joe Strummer; Gonzalez, World tour; Arrow, US tour; Radio Futura; Slim Gaillard, Japan and Far East tour, 1987; Alfredo Rodriguez, North African tour; Sonny Southon, Europe, US tours, 1991–92; US3, Europe, Far East tours, 1993; Film apperances include: I Hired A Contract Killer (with Joe Strummer); Eat The Rich (with Motörhead). *Recordings:* Numerous albums include: Cumbia Dominique 1990; Danzas Delrenacimento, 2001; Recordings with artists including: Kate Bush; M People. *Current Management:* Salsa Boogie Productions. *Address:* 153 Shrewsbury Rd, London E7 8QA, England.

PLANETARY ASSAULT SYSTEMS. See: **SLATER, Luke.**

PLANKA, Pavel; b. 29 May 1962, Pilsn, Czech Republic. Musician. *Education:* Public School of Arts; Prague Conservatoire. *Career:* Performances with several top Czech ensembles, jazz, rock, pop, classical, orchestral, folk; Support to Rolling Stones, Voodoo Lounge. *Recordings:* Nerez, Ke Zdi, 1990; Tutu, Mr Jazz Man, 1991; Zuzana Navarová, Caribe, 1992; Vitacit, Mate Se Hnout; Hot line, Still Callin', 1993; Merinsky-Lewitova, Sefardske Pisne; Dan Barta Alice, Usta Hromu, 1994; Lucie, Cerny Kocky Mokry Zaby; Janek Ledecky, Jenom Tak; Michal Pavlicek, Na Kloboucku II, 1995; Tresnak-Korman-Koller, Kolaz; Roman Dragoun, Stin My Krve; Veleband All Stars Big-Band, 1996; Jarek Nohavica, Divne Stoleti; Musical, Hair, 1997; Daniel Hulka, Mise, 1998; Karel Gott, Souhvezdi Gott; Lucie Bila, Uplne Naha, 1999; Jaromir Nohavica, Moje Smutne Srdce, 2000; Marie Rottrova Podivej; Nerez, Ješte Jednou, 2001; Support Lesbians, Tune Da Radio, 2002. *Honours:* Prize, Authors Competition, Porta, 1986. *Address:* Plzenska 597, 349 01 Stribro, Czech Republic. *E-mail:* pavel.planka@volny.cz.

PLANT, Robert Anthony; b. 20 Aug. 1948, West Bromwich, Warwickshire, England. Vocalist; Songwriter. m. Maureen, 1 s. (deceased), 1 d. *Career:* Member, various R&B groups, including Listen; Band of Joy; Lead singer, UK heavy rock group Led Zeppelin (formerly the New Yardbirds), 1968–80; Appearances include: Carnegie Hall, 1969; Royal Albert Hall, 1969, 1971; Madison Square Gardens, 1970; Knebworth Festival, 1979; Sell-out tours, concerts, world-wide; Rock for Kampuchea concert, London, 1979; Reunion for Live Aid, Philadelphia, 1985; Formed Led Zeppelin's own label Swan Song

1974; Film: The Song Remains The Same, 1976; Solo artiste, 1980–; Member, The Honeydrippers (with Jimmy Page, Nile Rodgers, Jeff Beck), 1984–85; Currently member of Page/Plant, with Jimmy Page (former Led Zeppelin guitarist), 1994–. *Recordings:* Albums: with Led Zeppelin: Led Zeppelin I, 1969; Led Zeppelin II, 1969; Led Zeppelin III, 1970; Led Zeppelin IV, 1971; Houses Of The Holy, 1973; Physical Graffiti, 1975; Presence, 1976; The Song Remains The Same, 1976; In Through The Out Door, 1979; Coda, 1983; Remasters, 1993; Solo: Pictures At Eleven, 1982; The Principle Of Moments, 1983; Now And Zen, 1988; Manic Nirvana, 1990; Fate Of Nations, 1993; Divinity, 2000; Dreamland, 2002; with the Honeydrippers: The Honeydrippers Vol. 1, 1984; with Page/Plant: No Quarter, 1994; Walking Into Clarksdale, 1998; More Oar, 1999. Singles: Big Log, 1983; Little By Little, 1985; Tall Cool One, 1989; Hurting Kind, 1990; I Believe, 1993; 29 Palms/Whole Lotta Love, 1994; Contributor: Outrider, Jimmy Page, 1988; Last Temptation of Elvis (compilation), 1990. *Honours:* Ivor Novello Awards, Outstanding Contribution To British Music, 1977; Silver Clef Award, Nordoff-Robbins Music Therapy Foundation, 1990; Q Merit Award (with Led Zeppelin), 1992. *Address:* c/o Mercury Records, Chancellors House, 72 Chancellors Rd, London W6 9QB, England.

PLASTIKMAN. See: HAWTIN, Richie.

PLATT, Ted (Edward Stephen); b. 7 Oct. 1945, West Yorkshire, England. Musician (guitar, bass); Vocalist; Arranger. 1 d. *Education:* Music College, 1 year; Piano and Guitar Lessons; Arranging Techniques. *Career:* Tour with Jet Harris, 1963; Contrasts, 1965; Residencies in London, 1966; Resident guitarist and vocalist, Batley Variety Club, 1972–; Musical Director for Freddie Starr for 10 years and for Gene Pitney for 3 years; Rock and Roll Singer with tours of Australia. *Recordings:* Can't Get You Off of My Mind; Call Me; Ma He's Making Eyes At Me, by Lena Zavaroni. *Membership:* PRS; MCPS; BAC&S; Songwriters' Guild. *Current Management:* KSP (Leisure) Associates. *Address:* 19 Hyrst Garth, Batley, West Yorkshire WF1Y 7AD, England.

PLATT, Tony; b. 21 Jan. 1952, Yorkshire, England. Record Prod; Engineer. m. Jacqueline, 30 April 1974, 1 s., 1 d. *Career:* Trident Studios, London, England; Assistant Engineer, Island Studios, Basing Street, 1969–70; Recording Engineer for Bob Marley, Toots, Free, etc; Freelance, 1975–; Mutt Lange's Engineer on Highway to Hell, Backin Black, ACDC and Foreigner 4. *Recordings include:* Producer, Engineer, Marche ou Creve, Trust, 1981; Producer, Engineer, Shock Tactics, Samson, 1981; Producer, Engineer, One Vice at a Time, Krokus, 1982; Producer, Engineer, Another Perfect Day, Motörhead, 1983; Engineer, Co-Producer, Flick of the Switch, AC/DC, 1983; Remix, Producer, All Men Play on Ten, Manowar, 1984; Producer, Engineer, We Want Moore, Gary Moore, 1984; Producer, Engineer, Equator, Uriah Heep, 1984–85; Producer, Engineer, Brave the Storm, Shy, 1985; Producer, Engineer, Nightless City, VowWow, 1985; Producer, Engineer, Live and Dangerous, Krokus, 1986; Producer, Engineer, The Doctor, Cheap Trick, 1986; Producer, Engineer, Wired, Jeff Paris, 1986–87; Producer, BBC–Late Night in Concert, The Cult, 1987; Producer, Engineer, Cold Lake, Celtic Frost, 1988; Producer, Engineer, Love and War, Lillian Axe, 1988–89; Co-Producer, Engineer, Never Turn Your Back on the Blues, Moody Marsden Band, 1991; Producer, Engineer, The Ritual, Testament, 1992; Co-Producer, Engineer, Live in Hell, Moody Marsden Band, 1994; Co-Producer, Green and Blues, Bernie Marsden, 1995; Producer, Engineer, Eternity, Anathema, 1996; Producer, Engineer, Ten, 1997; Producer, Engineer, Mau Mau, 1997; Producer, Mixer, Huge Baby, 1997–98; Other productions include: Aswad; Dio. *Publications:* Contributer, Music Industry Management and Promotion, by Chris Kemp. *Membership:* Re-Pro; PAMRA. *Current Management:* NDM (UK), 2 Bloomsbury St, London WC1B 3ST, England, and, CMI (USA), 201 E 87th St, New York, 10128, USA. *Address:* Inch House, Lower St, Pury End, Towcester, Northants, NN12 7NS, England.

PLAYFORD, Robert; b. 25 March 1968, Ware, Hertfordshire, England. Record Prod; Engineer; Remixer; Programmer; Record Co Exec. *Career:* Formed Moving Shadow Music, 1990, pioneering and establishing Jungle music; Concerts: Orlando, Los Angeles, New York, 1992; Paris, 1994; Tokyo, US tour, Glastonbury Festival, 1995; Television and radio appearances: The Word; Interviews on BBC Radio 1, UK; Mars FM, Los Angeles; Radio Nova, Paris; Worked with: 2 Bad Mice, Audioweb, Babylon Zoo, Black Grape, David Bowie, Melanie C., Corduroy, Dom & Rob, Fugees, Garbage, Goldie, Lionrock, Marlo, Metalheads, Monday Michuru, Sly & Robbie, Ingrid Schroeder, Snowpony, Tin Star. *Membership:* Musicians' Union. *Current Management:* Stephen Budd Management Ltd, 109b Regents Park Rd, Primrose Hill, London NW1 8UR, England. *Address:* 55 Conifer Walk, Stevenage, Herts SG2 7QS, England. *Website:* www.record-producers.com.

PLIERS, (Everton Banner); b. 1965, Kingston, Jamaica. DJ; Recording Artist. *Career:* Recording with Black Scorpio; Recorded for numerous lables including: Pickout; Pioneer Musik; Jammys, Harry J and Studio One; Partner, in duo Chaka Demus and Pliers, 1991–. *Recordings:* Albums: with Chaka Demus and Pliers: Gal Wine, 1992; Ruff This Year, 1992; Chaka Demus and Pliers, 1992; Tease Me, 1993; She Don't Let Nobody, 1995; For Every Kinda People, 1997; Singles: Them a Watch Me, 1992; When I'm with You, 1993; Tease Me, 1993; She Don't Let Nobody, 1993; Twist And Shout (No. 1, UK),

1993. *Address:* c/o Free World Music Inc, 230 12th St, Suite 117, Miami Beach, FL 33139–4603, USA.

PLOTNIKOFF, Mike; *Career:* Audio Engineer, started at Vancouver's Little Mountain Sound; Sought after by the international music community; Worked with producers including Bruce Faibairn, Bob Rock, Chris Thomas; Mix credits include, How Do I Deal; Melos Modos; Elegantly Wasted; Balance; Day and Night; All For Love; Live Pay Per View For MTV and MUCH Music; Remixes for Sons of Freedom; Taste of Joy; Ginger; Rose Chronicles; Martina McBride; Delirium; The Devlins; Anne Murray; Sandbox; Econoline Crush; Wide Mouth Mason; Bloomsday. Recording Engineer. *Honours:* Monitor Awards finalist for Best Audio Production in Tape Originated Television Specials, 1996. *Address:* c/o Bruce Allen Talent, 406–68 Water St, Vancouver, BC V6B 1A4, Canada.

POE, David; b. 20 July 1969, Ann Arbor, Michigan, USA. Songwriter; Recording Artiste; Vocalist; Musician (guitar). m. *Education:* BS, Mass Communications, Miami University, Oxford. *Career:* Solo Performer, 1990–; Support Act for: Bob Dylan, Lisa Loeb, Ron Sexsmith, Jonathon Richman; Produced Debut Recording for Melissa Sheehan, Jenifer Jackson. *Compositions:* Blue Glass Fall; Moon; Reunion, from forthcoming solo debut; Blind Man, co-written with T-Bone Burnett. *Recordings:* David Poe, 1997; Glass Suit, 1996; Guitar on: Pose While It Pops, Barbara Brousal, 2000. *Current Management:* Pati DeVries, DeVries Entertainment 179 Franklin St, Fifth Floor, New York, N 10013, USA.

POHJOLA, Jussi Pekka; b. 13 Jan. 1952, Helsinki, Finland. Musician (bass); Composer. 3 s. *Education:* Studies in violin and piano, Sibelius Academy, Helsinki. *Career:* Member of Wigwam; Jukka Tolonen Band; Made In Sweden; UMO; Mike Oldfield, including European tour, 1979; Tours with Pori Big Band, 1980; Founder of several own bands; Tours throughout Scandinavia; Europe; USA; Japan. *Compositions:* Film music; Theatre music; Arrangements for different artists; One symphony, Sinfonia, 1989. *Recordings:* 12 solo albums, including Bialoipoikku The Magpie; Urban Tango; Jokamies; Space Waltz; Flight of The Angel; Heavy Jazz; Changing Waters; Everyman; Numerous recordings with several other artists. *Honours:* 2 Awards, Best Record of the Year, Finnish Broadcasting Company; Several state artist-grants including 15 year artist-grant. *Current Management:* Tapio Korjus, Rockadillo, Keskutori 7 A 11, 33100 Tampere, Finland. *Address:* Pisanniitty 4 B 14, 02280 Espoo, Finland.

POHJOLA, Mika (Antero); b. 1 Dec. 1971, Helsinki, Finland. Musician (jazz piano); Composer. *Education:* Classical Piano Degree, Vantaa Conservatory, 1987; Jazz Ed Degree, Swedish Royal Academy, 1992; BM, Berklee College of Music, 1994. *Career:* Tours of Europe, USA, Canada and Japan, 1993–; Performances in major New York clubs, 1995–; Blue Note debut, 1996; Radio Feature, Jazz Matazz, BBC World Service; TV appearances in Finland, Sweden, Estonia, UK, USA, Canada, Ukraine and Japan; Featured in recordings by Sophie Dunér, Johanna Grüssner Band, Gary Heckard, Stuck. *Compositions:* All original music on own releases. *Recordings:* Myths and Beliefs, 1996; On the Move, 1997; Announcement, 1998; Live at the Blue Note, 1999; Hur man räddar kärleken at annat, 1999; Sound of Village, 2001; The Music of Mika Pohjola, 2002; Landmark, 2002; Moomin Voices, 2003. *Honours:* The Downbeat Magazine Award, 1994; American-Scandinavian Society Award, 1996; Swedish Cultural Endowment, 1998. *Membership:* STIM, Sweden; TEOSTO, Finland. *Current Management:* MikaMusik. *Address:* 333 E 14th St, Ninth Floor, New York, NY 10003, USA.

POINTER, Anita; b. 23 Jan. 1948, East Oakland, California, USA. Vocalist. *Career:* Singer, Pointers (with sisters), San Francisco, 1969–71; Recorded as session singers with Boz Scaggs, Elvin Bishop, Taj Mahal, Dave Mason; Member, US female vocal quartet The Pointer Sisters, 1972–78; Continued as trio, 1978–; Concerts include: Midem Festival, 1974, 1993; Grand Ole Opry, 1974; Television includes: 25th Anniversary of American Bandstand, 1977; Welcome Home America! (Gulf forces tribute), 1991. *Recordings:* Best of Elvin Bishop: Tulsa Shuffle, 1969; The Pointer Sisters, 1973; Live At The Opera House, 1974; Steppin', 1975; Best Of, 1976; Having A Party, 1978; Energy, 1979; Priority, 1979; Special Things, 1980; Black and White, 1981; Jump – The Best Of, 1989; Right Rhythm, 1990; Only Sisters Can Do That, 1993; Solo album: Love For What It Is, 1987; Singles: Yes We Can Can, 1973; Fairytale, 1974; How Long, 1975; Fire, 1979; He's So Shy, 1980; Slow Hand, 1981; I'm So Excited, 1982; Automatic, 1984; Jump (For My Love), 1984; Neutron Dance (used in film Beverly Hills Cop), 1985; Dare Me, 1985; Be There (used in film Beverly Hills Cop II), 1987; Solo: Duet with Earl Thomas Conley: Too Many Times, 1986; Recordings with other artists include: Rockets; Ron Wood, Kenny Loggins; Earl Thomas Conley; Cold Blood; Working Girl; Taj Mahal. *Contributions to:* A Very Special Christmas, 1987; Rock Rhythm and Blues, 1989; Am I Cool Or What?, 1991; Charity singles: We Are The World, 1984; Voices That Care, 1991. *Honours:* Grammy Awards: Best Country Vocal Performance, 1974; Best Performance By Group, Best Vocal Arrangement, 1985; Billboard Awards: Top Dance Single and Album, 1984; American Music Awards: Favourite Soul/R&B Band, 1985; Favourite Soul/ R&B Video, 1985, 1986. *Address:* c/o The Sterling/Winters Co, Suite 1640, 1900 Ave of the Stars, Los Angeles, CA 90067, USA.

POINTER, June; b. 30 Nov. 1953, East Oakland, California, USA. Vocalist. *Career:* Singer, Pointers (with sisters), San Francisco, 1969–71; Recorded as session vocalists for Boz Scaggs; Taj Mahal; Dave Mason; Elvin Bishop; Kenny Loggins; Ray Charles; Cold Blood; Bruce Willis; Robert Foreman; Member, US female vocal quartet The Pointer Sisters, 1972–78; Continued as trio, 1978–; Concerts include: Midem Festival, 1974, 1993; Television includes: 25th Anniversary of American Bandstand, 1977; Welcome Home America! (Gulf forces tribute), 1991. *Recordings:* Albums: The Pointer Sisters, 1973; Live At The Opera House, 1974; Steppin', 1975; Best Of, 1976; Having A Party, 1978; Energy, 1979; Priority, 1979; Special Things, 1980; Black and White, 1981; Greatest Hits, 1982; So Excited, 1982; Break Out, 1984; Contact, 1985; Hot Together, 1986; Serious Slammin', 1988; Jump – The Best Of, 1989; Right Rhythm, 1990; Only Sisters Can Do That, 1993; Great R&B Female Groups, 1998; Solo album: Baby Sitter, 1983; Singles: with the Pointer Sisters: Yes We Can, 1973; Fairytale, 1974; How Long, 1975; Fire, 1979; Jump (For My Love), 1984; Neutron Dance (used in film Beverly Hills Cop), 1985; Dare Me, 1985; Be There (used in film Beverly Cop II), 1987; Solo album: Baby Sitter, 1983. *Contributions to:* A Very Special Christmas, 1987; Rock Rhythm and Blues, 1989; Am I Cool Or What?, 1991; Charity singles: We Are The World, 1984; Voices That Care, 1991. *Honours:* Grammy Awards: Best Country Vocal Performance, 1974; Best Performance by Group, Best Vocal Arrangement, 1985; Billboard Awards: Top Dance Single and Album, 1984; American Music Awards: Favourite Soul/R&B Band, 1985; Favourite Soul/R&B Video, 1985, 1986. *Address:* c/o The Sterling/Winters Co, Suite 1640, 1900 Avenue of the Stars, Los Angeles, CA 90067, USA.

POINTER, Ruth; b. 19 March 1946, Oakland, California, USA. Vocalist. m. Michael Sayles, 8 Sept. 1990. *Career:* Member, US female vocal quartet The Pointer Sisters, 1972–78; Continued as trio, 1978–; Recorded as a session vocalist for Bill Wyman, Oliver and Company, Rockets, Kenny Loggins, Iron Eagle 2; Céline Dion; Taj Mahal; Cold Blood; Concerts include: Midem Festival, 1974, 1993; Grand Ole Opry, 1974; Television includes: 25th Anniversary of American Bandstand, 1977; Welcome Home America! (Gulf forces tribute), 1991. *Recordings:* Albums: The Pointer Sisters, 1973; Live At The Opera House, 1974; Steppin', 1975; Best Of, 1976; Having A Party, 1978; Energy, 1979; Priority, 1979; Special Things, 1980; Black and White, 1981; Greatest Hits, 1982; So Excited, 1982; Break Out, 1984; Contact, 1985; Hot Together, 1986; Serious Slammin', 1988; Jump – The Best Of, 1989; Right Rhythm, 1990; Only Sisters Can Do That, 1993; Great R&B Female Groups: The 70s, 1998; Hit singles: Yes We Can, 1973; Fairytale, 1974; How Long, 1975; Fire, 1979; He's So Shy, 1980; Slow Hand, 1981; I'm So Excited, 1982; Automatic, 1984; Jump (For My Love), 1984; Neutron Dance (used in Beverly Hills Cop), 1985; Dare Me, 1985; Be There (used in Beverly Cop II), 1987; Contributor: A Very Special Christmas, 1987; Rock Rhythm and Blues, 1989; Am I Cool Or What?, 1991; Charity singles: We Are The World, 1984; Voices That Care, 1991. *Honours:* Grammy Awards: Best Country Vocal Performance, 1974; Best Performance By Group, Best Vocal Arrangement, 1985; Billboard Awards: Top Dance Single and Album, 1984; American Music Awards: Favourite Soul/R&B Band, 1985; Favourite Soul/R&B Video, 1985, 1986. *Address:* c/o The Sterling/Winters Co, Suite 1640, 1900 Avenue of the Stars, Los Angeles, CA 90067, USA.

POINTON, Mike; b. 25 April 1941, London, England. Musician; Vocalist; Writer; Broadcaster. *Education:* Elmwood School and Rose Bruford College of Speech and Drama, 1953–57; Private Piano Lessons. *Career:* Founded own band, 1950s; Worked with many European New Orleans style groups and American jazzmen and toured many countries; Documentaries for BBC Radio, including Swingtime For Hitler, 1987, Bunk and Bill, 1992, Preservation Hall, 1998; Up A Lazy River, with George Melly, 1998; Echoes of Harlem, with George Melly, 1999; Ride, Red, Ride, 2000; The Unknown Satchmo, 2001; Benny Carter at 95, 2002. *Recordings:* Barry Martyn's Band, 1961; Mezz Mezzrow/Cotton City Jazz Band, 1964; Young Olympia Brass Band, 1965; Eagle Brass Band, 1966; European Classic Jazz Band, 1983; British All-Stars, 1993; With Apex Jazzband of Northern Ireland, 1997; With Sammy Rimington and John Petters All Stars, 1999; Pat Hawes' All-Stars, 2000. *Address:* 11 Kings Court, Kings Rd, Wimbledon, London SW19 8QP, England.

POLAND, Chris; b. Dunkirk, NY, USA. Rock Musician (guitar, bass). *Career:* Mem., Megadeth; Mem., Circle Jerks; Mem., Damn The Machine, 1991–93; World tours with all three bands; Also worked with Ice T and Industrial Light and Sound. *Recordings:* with Megadeth: Killing Is My Business…; Peace Sells But Who's Buying?; Megadeah, 2000; Rude Awakening, 2002. Solo: Return To Metalopolis; with Damn The Machine: Damn The Machine, 1993. *Honours:* Platinum disc, Peace Sells But Who's Buying?; Gold disc, Killing Is My Business. *Membership:* AFTRA; ASCAP; AFofM. *Current Management:* Andy Somers, ICM; Jane Hoffman, Speed of Sound. *Address:* Speed of Sound, 626 Santa Monica Blvd, Suite 119, Santa Monica, CA 90401, USA.

POLCER, Ed (Edward Joseph); b. 10 Feb. 1937, Paterson, New Jersey, USA. Jazz Musician (cornet); Bandleader. m. Judy Kurtz, 9 May 1976, 3 s., 1 d. *Education:* BSE, Engineering, Princeton University; Music lessons with Professor James V Dittamo, Prospect Park, New Jersey. *Career:* Cornettist, Stan Rubin's Tigertown Five; concerts include: Carnegie Hall, Europe, Prince

Rainier, Grace Kelly wedding, 1955–56; Benny Goodman Sextet, 1973; Solo artist, band leader, international Jazz Festival circuit, 1975–; Owner, manager, bandleader, Eddie Condon's NY, 1975–85; Bandleader, 8 major US tours for Columbia Artists, several European tours, 1992–97; Congressional Ball, White House, by Presidential invitation, 1995; Business ventures: BlewZ Manor Productions, concerts, festivals, recordings. *Recordings:* Albums include: Ed Polcer–Live In Concert, 1988; with Ed Polcer's All Stars: Coast To Coast–Swinging Jazz, 1990; Some Sunny Day, 1991; Barbara Lea, 1992; A Night At Eddie Condon's, 1992; The Magic of Swing Street, 1993; A Salute To Eddie Condon, 1993; Jammin' A La Condon, 1994; At The Ball, with Jim Galloway, CD, 1998; The Magic Of Swing, 2000. *Publications:* Co-editor, Carmina Princetonia – The Song Book of Princeton University Centennial Edition, 1968. *Membership:* President, International Art of Jazz, 1982–89. *Current Management:* BlewZ Manor Productions Inc.

POLCHENKO, Yuri; b. 10 Oct. 1959, Kyiv, Ukraine. Vocalist; Songwriter; Prod; Musician (guitar). m., 1 s. *Education:* Kyiv Polytechinc Institute; Kyiv Jazz School. *Career:* Yunost (radio show), 1990; Promin, 1991; U Ozera (television show), 1996–97; Rock Existenzia Festival, 1997, 1998, 1999, 2000; Music for film: Night Saxophone, 1997, Resheto, 1998; Chas Ide (music video), 1999; Spirit of Woodstock Festival, 2000, 2002; Tericon 17, TV show. *Compositions:* Out of The Time, 1997; Chas Ide, 1998; Chekai, 1998. *Recordings:* Mist of Dance, 1997; Angels Sleep, 1998. *Address:* V. Pika 10, kv 46, 04111 Kiev, Ukraine. *E-mail:* nedesna@bigmir.net. *Website:* www.nebesna.bigmir.net.

POLEDOURIS, Basil; b. 21 Aug. 1945, Kansas City, MO, USA. Composer. *Education:* University of Southern California; California State University. *Compositions:* For television: The Interview, 1970; Congratulations, It's a Boy!, 1971; Three for the Road, 1974; The Andros Targets, 1977; A Whale for the Killing, 1981; Fire on the Mountain, 1981; Single Bars, Single Women, 1984; Amazons, 1984; Misfits of Science, 1985; The Twilight Zone, 1985; Island Sons, 1987; Prison for Children, 1987; Amerika, 1987; Intrigue, 1988; Lonesome Dove, 1989; Ned Blessing: The True Story of My Life, 1992; Zoya (theme), 1995; If These Walls Could Talk 2, 2000; Love and Treason, 2001; For film: Extreme Close-Up, 1973; Tintorera, 1977; Big Wednesday, 1978; Dolphin, 1979; 90028, 1979; The Blue Lagoon, 1980; Summer Lovers, 1982; Conan the Barbarian, 1982; Flyers, 1983; Protocol, 1984; Making the Grade, 1984; The House of God, 1984; Conan the Destroyer, 1984; American Journeys, 1984; Red Dawn, 1984; Flesh & Blood, 1985; Iron Eagle, 1986; RoboCop, 1987; No Man's Land, 1987; Cherry 2000, 1987; Wired, 1989; Farewell to the King, 1989; Flight of the Intruder, 1990; The Hunt for Red October, 1990; Quigley Down Under, 1991; Return to the Blue Lagoon, 1991; White Fang, 1991; Harley Davidson and the Marlboro Man, 1991; Wind, 1992; Robocop 3, 1993; Free Willy, 1993; Hot Shots! Part Deux, 1993; Lassie, 1994; On Deadly Ground, 1994; Serial Mom, 1994; The Jungle Book, 1994; Under Siege 2: Dark Territory, 1995; Free Willy 2: The Adventure Home, 1995; The War at Home, 1996; It's My Party, 1996; Celtic Pride, 1996; Amanda, 1996; Breakdown, 1997; Switchback, 1997; Starship Troopers, 1997; Les Misérables, 1998; Mickey Blue Eyes, 1999; For Love of the Game, 1999; Kimberly, 1999; Cecil B DeMented, 2000; Crocodile Dundee in Los Angeles, 2001. *Honours:* Emmy Award, Lonesome Dove. *Membership:* BMI. *Current Management:* Blue Focus Management, 15233 Ventura Blvd, Suite 200, Sherman Oaks, CA 91403, USA.

POLNAREFF, Michel; b. 3 July 1944, Nerac, France. Vocalist; Musician (piano, guitar); Songwriter. *Education:* Accomplished piano student during youth. *Career:* Signed to AZ Disques; Chose to work with UK musicians for highly acclaimed first recordings; Signed new US contract with Atlantic, scoring hit single, 1975; Sporadic but always well-received releases/performances since then; Wrote anthem for Modern Pentathlon Tournament of Monaco at request of Monaco's Principality, 2001. *Compositions:* theatre show scores: Rebelais, 1968; La Folie Des Grandeurs, 1971; film scores: L'Indiscret, 1969; Ça N'Arrive Qu'Aux Autres, 1971; Lipstick, 1976; La Vengeance Du Serpent À Plumes, 1985. *Recordings:* Albums include: Love Me Please Love Me, 1966; Le Bal Des Laze, 1968; Polnareff's, 1971; Tibilli, 1974; USA, 1975; Coucou Me Revoilou, 1978; Bulles, 1981; Télé 82, 1982; Incognito, 1985; Kama Sutra, 1990; Live At The Roxy, 1996; Nos Mots D'Amour (compilation), 1999. *E-mail:* michel@polnaweb.com. *Website:* www.polnaweb.com.

POLYGON WINDOW. See: **APHEX TWIN.**

PONCHO, Ildefonso; b. 30 Oct. 1954, Laredo, Texas, USA. Congas Vocalist. m. Stella Martinez, 15 July 1973, 2 s. *Career:* Klon; Monterey Jazz Festival; Long Beach Jazz Festival; Playboy Jazz Festival; Jazz Central B E T (58); Japanese tour; European tour. *Recordings:* 13 CDs released. *Publications:* Concord Jazz Picante. *Honours:* Many awards in USA. *Current Management:* Berkeley Agency, Poncho Sanchez Latin Jazz Band. *Address:* PO Box 59236 Norwalk, CA 90652, USA.

PONOMAREVA, Valentina; b. 10 July 1939, Moscow, Russia. m. Konstantin Gogunskiy, 7 Sept. 1985, 1 s. *Education:* Classical Music degree, Khabarovsk Institute of Arts, vocal and piano. *Career:* Soloist, Tula Jazz big band, 1967–70; Actress, singer, dancer, Moscow Gypsy Theatre Romen, 1971–78; Soloist, trio, Romen, 1973–84, international concerts, 1974–84; Metropolitan Opera, New York, 1976; Midem-76 Festival, Cannes, 1976; Edinburgh International Festival, 1977; Numerous national television and radio appearances, 1973–; Solo artiste, Russian and international concerts and tours, 1978–; Soviet Avantgarde Jazz Festival, Zurich, 1989; International workshop for free improvised music, Tokyo, Osaka, 1989; Huddersfield Contemporary Music Festival, UK, 1990; Voice Over Festival, London, 1990; International Music Festival, Davos, 1991; Europa Festival Jazz, Italy, 1991; Jazz Summer, Bolzano, 1991; USA seven-month tour, incl. Los Angeles, San Francisco, Chicago, Boston, New York, 1992; Musique Action Nancy, France, 1993; Fringe '99 International Festival, Edinburgh, 1999; Festival des Arts et du Cinema Russes, Cannes, 1999; Boheme Jazz Festival International, Moscow, 2001, 2002; International Odesa Jazz-Carnival, Odesa, 2001, 2002. *Recordings:* Solo: Fortune-teller, 1985; Intrusion, 1988; At Parting I Say, 1989; Temptation, 1989; Don't Rise My Recollection, 1990; Terra Incognita, 1990; Live In Japan, 1991; The Romances Of The Friends Of Mine, 1992; Dve Gitary, 1994; We Strangely Happen To Meet, 1997; Forte, 1999; The Russian Gypsy Queen 'Ochi Chiornye', 2001. *Membership:* Performing Right Society. *Current Management:* Valentina Ponomareva Musical Theatre, PO Box 45, Moscow 103104, Russia. *Telephone:* 291-9962. *Fax:* 234-1708. *Address:* 14 Malaya Bronnaya Str., Apt 19, Moscow 103104, Russia. *E-mail:* kosta@aha.ru.

PONOMARYOV, Olexander; b. 9 Aug. 1973, Khmelnitsky, Ukraine. Vocalist; Musician (piano). *Education:* Student, Third course, State Music Academy. *Career:* Joint concert with Patricia Kaas; Festivals: All-Ukrainian Chervona Ruta, first grant, 1993; International Festival, Slavonic Bazaar, second grant, 1994. *Recordings:* Album: My Love Has Grey Eyes. *Publications:* Articles on music items, Republican press. *Honours:* Grants: All Ukrainian Festival, 1993, International Festival, 1994; Best Newcomer, 1993; Best Ukrainian Singer in Popular Music, 1993–94. *Current Management:* Oleg Stupka, Kiev, Ukraine. *Address:* Zarichanska Str 14/1a Ap 35, 280017 Khmelnytskiy, Ukraine.

PONTIEUX, Loic; b. 10 June 1967, Harfleur, France. Musician (drums). m. 5 Jan. 1994. *Education:* Conservatoire, 5 years. *Career:* Drummer with many artists including: Michel Jonasz; Claude Nougaro; Didier Lockwood; Birelli Lagrene; Al Jarreau; Pascal Obispo; Veronique Sanson; Francis Cabrel; Mauranne; Maxime Le Forestier and Bernard Cavilliers. *Recordings:* Many with various artists including: Didier Lockwood; Bernard Cavilliers; Claude Nougaro; Birelli Lagrene; Solensi; Jean Michel Kajdan; Pascal Obispo; Idrissa Diop; Jean Jacques Milteau; Babik Reihardt; Grappelli Trio. *Address:* 4 bis, rue André Chénier, 92130 Issy les Moulineaux, France.

PONTY, Jean-Luc; b. 29 Sept. 1942, Avranches, France. Musician (jazz violin, synthesizers); Composer; Bandleader. m. Claudia Bosco, 6 Sept. 1966, 2 d. *Education:* Premier Prix (First Prize), violin, Conservatoire National de Musique, Paris. *Career:* Classical violinist to 1964; Jazz violinist, Europe, 1964–69; Night clubs, music festivals, in collaboration with the George Duke Trio, USA, 1969; Toured with own group, Europe, 1970–72; Moved to USA, 1973; Pioneer electric violin, jazz innovator; Headlined international concerts with own group, 1975–; Music festivals in USA include: Meadowbrook; Artpark; Wolf Trap; in Europe: Montreux; North Sea Festival; Paris Jazz Festival; Guest soloist, Montréal Symphony Orchestra, 1984; Toronto Symphony Orchestra, 1986; New Japan Philharmonic, 1987; New York Radio City Orchestra; 1990; Oklahoma Symphony Orchestra, 1995; Television includes: Soundstage; The Tonight Show; Solid Gold; Rock Concert; Fiddlers Three; Appearances in: Europe; Brazil; Chile; Venezuela. *Recordings:* (own productions) Albums include: Upon The Wings of Music; Aurora; Imaginary Voyage; Enigmatic Ocean; Cosmic Messenger; Jean-Luc Ponty – Live; Civilised Evil; A Taste For Passion; Mystical Adventures; Individual Choice; Open Mind; Fables; The Gift of Time; Storytelling; Tchokola (with African musicians); No Absolute Time; Life Enigman, 2001; The Rite of Strings (with Stanley Clarke, Al DiMeola); Jean-Luc Ponty with the George Duke Trio; With Kurt Edelhagen and His Orchestra; Live at Chene Park; Sonata Erotica; As; Far from the Beaten Paths; Also recorded with: Elton John; Honky Chateau, 1972; Frank Zappa and the Mothers of Invention, 1973; Mahavishnu Orchestra, 1974–75; Stephane Grappelli, 1996. *Current Management:* (USA) Mario Tirado, APA, 888 Seventh Ave, Suite 602, New York, NY 10106, USA; (Europe) Pascal Bernardin, Encore Productions, 6 rue du Mont Thabor, 75001 Paris, France.

POOK, Jocelyn; b. 14 Feb. 1960, Birmingham, England. Musician (viola, violin); Composer. *Education:* Performers Diploma, Guildhall School of Music and Drama; Postgraduate Year, GSMD in Orchestral and Early Music Studies. *Career:* Toured, played live with: The Communards, 1986–89; Lyle Lovett, 1994; The Cranberries, Meatloaf, 1995; Mark Knopfler, 1996; Laurie Anderson, Ryûichi Sakamoto; The Stranglers; Spiritualized, Michael Nyman, 1997. *Recordings include:* Peter Gabriel; PJ Harvey; Nick Cave; Paul Weller; This Mortal Coil; Eddi Reader; Co-Founder, Electra Strings; Performed in several theatre productions, Derek Jarman's Edward II, Midland Bank advertisement and regularly with Electra Strings on Later with Jools. *Compositions:* Composed extensively for theatre, dance and film; Dance

productions include: Strange Fish, 1993; MSM, 1994; DV8 Physical Theatre; Deluge, 1995; Overtigo Danse; Blight; Blow The Wind Southerly, selected for Orange mobile network advertising campaign; Score for Stanley Kubrick's film, Eyes Wide Shut; In A Land of Plenty, BBC TV series, 2001. *Recordings:* Blow the Wind – Pie Jesu, 1996–97; Deluge, 1997; Solo albums: Flood, 1999; Untold Things, 2001. *Honours:* Prix Italia, Strange Fish, film, 1994. *Membership:* Musicians' Union; Equity; PRS; MCPS. *Current Management:* Don Mousseau, 78 Greencroft Gardens, London NW6 3JQ, England. *Website:* www.jocelynpook.co.uk.

POOLE, Brian; b. 2 Nov. 1941, Barking, Essex, England. Vocalist. *Career:* Lead singer, Brian Poole and the Tremeloes, 1961–66; Appearances include: Tours with artists including: Roy Orbison; The Searchers; Freddie and The Dreamers; Dusty Springfield; PJ Proby; Gerry and The Pacemakers; NME Poll Winners Concert, Wembley, with the Beatles, Cliff Richard, 1964; Solo tour, Scandinavia, 1966; Formed new backing group, The Seychelles, 1969; Left music scene, 1969–88; Reunion with the Tremeloes, 1988; Member, The Corporation, with Reg Presley, Mike Pender, 1989; Appeared at Biggest 60s Party in Town, Olympia, London, 1991; Currently lead singer with Electrix. *Recordings:* Albums: Twist and Shout, 1963; Brian Poole and the Tremeloes, 1964; It's About Time, 1965; Brian Poole is Here, 1966; Silence is Golden, 1995; Time is on My Side, 1995; Twenty Miles, 1995; The World Of Brian Poole & The Tremeloes; Hit singles include: Twist and Shout, 1963; Do You Love Me? (No. 1, UK), 1963; I Can Dance, 1963; Candy Man, 1964; Someone Someone, 1964; Twelve Steps To Love, 1964; The Three Bells, 1965; I Want Candy, 1965; Good Lovin', 1965. *Current Management:* Brian Gannon Management, PO Box 106, Rochdale, Lancashire OL16 4HW, England.

POOLE, Chris; b. 23 June 1952, New York, USA. Musician (flutes, tenor saxophone); Composer. *Education:* BA, Berklee College of Music, Boston; First woman to complete Berklee's applied music programme; Studied with Gary Burton; Andy McGee; Joe Viola; James Newton. *Career:* Moved to Denmark from USA, 1975; Performed in jazz and latin bands; Numerous television and radio appearances; Solo performances, 1988–; Writer for theatre, film and modern dance including score for Troll, Norwegian film. *Recordings:* Chris Poole-Solo Flute, 1990; To The Powers That Be, with Pia Rasmussen, 1993; In Search of Solace, 1998; Breaking The Maelstrom. *Honours:* Bay Area Critics Award, Best Musical Score For A Drama, The Lady From The Sea, Berkeley Repertory Theater, USA, 1993. *Membership:* Danish Musicians' Union; Danish Asscn of Jazz and Rock Composers; Women In Music. *Address:* Jagtvej 229, 1th., 2100 Copenhagen Ø, Denmark. *Telephone:* 33799301. *E-mail:* Chrisp@post.tele.dk. *Website:* www.chrispoole.dk.

POOLEY, Ian, (Ian Pinnekamp, Ansicht); b. Mainz, Germany. Prod; Remixer; DJ. *Career:* Started producing tracks while still a student in Mainz; First releases were collaborations with DJ Tonka; Has released tracks on: Transmat; Plink Plonk; Definitive; Currently records for V2; Remixed: DJ Sneak; Daft Punk; Yello; Sven Vath; Modjo. *Recordings:* Albums: Meridian, 1998; Since Then, 2000; Singles: Rollerskate Disco, 1995; Chord Memory, 1996; What's Your Number, 1998; Coracao Tambor, 2000; Balmes (A Better Life), 2001. *Address:* c/o V2 Music Ltd, 131–133 Holland Park Ave, London W11 4UT, England.

POP, Iggy, (James Jewel Osterburg); b. 21 April 1947, Ypsilanti, Michigan, USA. Vocalist; Musician (guitar); Actor. *Education:* University of Michigan. *Career:* Formed Iguanas, High School band, 1962; Prime Movers, 1966; Concerts in Michigan, Detroit and Chicago; Formed The Stooges (originally the Pyschedelic Stooges), 1967; 3 albums, 1969–73; Solo artiste, 1976–; Collaborations with David Bowie, 1972–; Numerous tours and television appearances; Actor, films including: Sid and Nancy; The Color of Money; Hardware; Actor, television series, Miami Vice. *Compositions include:* Co-writer, China Girl, David Bowie. *Recordings:* Albums: with The Stooges: The Stooges, 1969; Jesus Loves The Stooges, 1977; I'm Sick of You, 1977; Solo albums: Fun House, 1970; Raw Power, 1973; Metallic KO, 1976; The Idiot, 1977; Lust For Life, 1977; TV Eye Live, 1978; Kill City, 1978; New Values, 1979; Soldier, 1980; Party, 1981; I'm Sick of You, 1981; Zombie Birdhouse, 1982; I Got The Right, 1983; Blah Blah Blah, 1986; Rubber Legs, 1987; Live At The Whiskey A Go Go, 1988; Death Trip, 1988; Raw Stooges, 1988; Raw Stooges 2, 1988; The Stooges Box Set, 1988; Instinct, 1988; Brick By Brick, 1990; American Caesar, 1994; Naughty Little Doggie, 1996; Heroin Hates You, 1997; King Biscuit Flower Hour, 1997; Your Pretty Face is Going to Hell, 1998; Sister Midnight, 1999; Avenue B, 1999; Iggy Pop, 1999; Hippodrome Paris '77 (live), 1999; Beat 'Em Up, 2001; Singles: Beside You, 1993; Wild America, 1993; Corruption, 1998; Appears on: Rock at the Edge, 1977; Low, David Bowie, 1977; Trainspotting, 1996; Death in Vegas, Contino Sessions, 1999; Contributor, Red Hot + Blue AIDs charity record. *Publications:* Autobiography, I Need More. *Current Management:* Art Collins Management, PO Box 561, Pine Bush, NY 12566, USA.

POPMAN. See: **LLOYD, Andrew Reginald.**

PORCARO, Steve; b. 2 Sept. 1957, Hartford, Connecticut, USA. Vocalist; Musician (keyboards). *Career:* Support musician to artists including: Jackson Browne; Aretha Franklin; Barbra Streisand; Jennifer Warnes; Jim Wilson;

Member, Toto, 1978–87. *Compositions:* Commissioned (with Toto) to write theme for Los Angeles Olympic Games, 1984. *Recordings:* Albums: with Toto: Toto, 1979; Hydra, 1979; Turn Back, 1981; Toto IV, 1982; Isolation, 1985; Dune (film soundtrack), 1985; Singles include: Hold The Line, 1979; Georgy Porgy, 1979; 99, 1980; Rosanna, 1982; Make Believe, 1982; Africa (No. 1, USA), 1983; I Won't Hold You Back, 1983; I'll Be Over You, 1986; Without Your Love, 1987; Contributor, We Are The World, USA For Africa charity single, 1985; Backing group, albums by Boz Scaggs: Silk Degrees, 1976; Down Two, 1977; Earth Wind and Fire, Elements of Love, 1990; Céline Dion, Let's Talk About Love, 1997; Take Six, Greatest Hits, 1999. *Honours:* Grammy Awards: Record of the Year, Album of the Year, Best Vocal Arrangement, Best Instrumental Arrangement, Best Producer (Toto), Best Engineered Recording, 1983. *Address:* c/o Fitzgerald-Hartley Co, 50 W Main St, Ventura, CA 93001, USA.

PORTASS, Nigel John; b. 23 Jan. 1943, Wisbech, Cambridgeshire, England. Musician (keyboards, saxophone, drums); Teacher. m. Dorothy Ann, 17 July 1965, 2 s. *Education:* Member, backing groups for visiting artistes including Chuck Berry; Gene Vincent; Georgie Fame; Van Morrison; Ronnie Scott; Matt Monro; Music tutor and lecturer at Boston College, 1964. *Membership:* Music Teachers' Assocn. *Address:* c/o Portass and Carter Music Shop, 26 Bridge Rd, Sutton Bridge, Spalding, Lincolnshire PE12 9UA, England.

PORTEJOIE, Philippe René Paul; b. 28 Dec. 1956, Niort, France. Musician (saxophone). m. Frederique Lagarde, 15 Sept. 1990, 1 s. *Education:* First Prize, CNSM, Paris. *Career:* Member duo Portejoie-Lagarde; 2 albums; 100 concerts, France; Italy; Belgium; Norway; Radio: Radio France (France Inter; France Musique); Premier alto saxophone, Big Band with Claude de Bolling. *Recordings:* 20 recordings include Musique Francaise Du XXe Siècle; Stéphane Grappelli; Strictly Classical; Saxomania Et Clark Terry; with Tsf: Ca Va Ca Va, 1996; with Claude Bolling: First Class 1991; Black Brown and Beige, 1993; Victory Concert, 1994; Cinema Dreams, 1996; Drum is a Woman, 1996; Tone Parallel to Harlem, 1999. *Honours:* Premier Prix d'Honneur à l'Unanité (Concours de Musique d'Ensemble de l'UFAM); Meilleur Formation Française (Musique de Chambre de Paris). *Membership:* Yehudi Menuhin Foundation; Professor, Conservatoire Superieur de Paris (CNR). *Address:* 48 Blvd Mission Marchand, 92400 Courbevoie, France.

PORTELLI, Rose-Marie; b. Toulon, France. Vocalist; Composer. *Education:* British and Irish folk music; American Jazz and Blues; Italian Gospel. *Career:* Appeared at Festival of Traditional Music, Birmingham, England, 1991; Olympia in 1994, Congrés Mondial Acadien, Canada, 1994, Fête de la Musique at American Center in Paris, 1995; Francofolies de la Rochelle, 1995; Disneyland in Paris, 1995; Tour of USA and Canada, 1995. *Recordings:* Marine Marine, 1993. *Publications:* Biography of Canadian singer, Fabienne Thibeau. *Honours:* First Prize for Interpretation, SACEM, 1992. *Membership:* SACEM. *Current Management:* Natasha Grandval, Dolphin Dreams Productions. *Address:* c/o Dolphin Dreams Productions, 98 Blvd Poniatowski, 75012 Paris, France.

PORTEOUS, Michael Lindsay; b. 2 Feb. 1948, The Mytertoun Menstrie, Clackmannanshire, Scotland. Ethnomusicologist; Musician (Jew's harp). *Career:* Several television appearances for various companies, and radio including several of own on folk instruments. *Compositions:* Dunblane, lament cassette; Farewell to Lizziewells. *Recordings:* Recordings with Heritage, 1978–93; Tell Tae Me, 1993; Greentrax, 1988; Tracks on various CD samplers, 1987–97; Cassettes. *Publications:* How to Play and Have Fun with the Jew's-Harp, 1990. *Honours:* Competition Certificates, Traditional Music Song Assocn, Scotland, 1976–97; Edinburgh Folk Festival, One Man Band Champion, 1982, 1983, 1984. *Membership:* MU; The Traditional Music and Song Assocn of Scotland. *Address:* Lindsay Porteous, Tron House, Culross, Fife, KY12 8JG, Scotland.

PORTER, Christopher; b. 4 May 1954, Southampton, Hampshire, England. Record Prod. m. Virginia Guarlez, 7 April 1977, 2 d. *Education:* Art College. *Career:* Began as engineer at Good Earth Studios under Tony Visconti, 1980; Early engineering success with Lynx and Junior Giscombe; Long-standing collaboration with George Michael; Co-producer with Tim Simenon for Whycliffe and Zan Jam. *Recordings:* Producer, Engineer: Singles/tracks include: Take That: Back For Good (No. 1, UK), 1995; Babe; George Michael: tracks for Red Hot and Dance; Elton John: Don't Let The Sun Go Down On Me; Some Other World; Aswad: On and On; Don't Turn Around; Beauty's Only Skin Deep; Wham: Wham Rap; Pet Shop Boys: Se A Vida É; Diana Princess of Wales: Tribute; Robbie Nevill: Wot's It to Ya; Music of the Heart; Albums: George Michael: Faith; Listen Without Prejudice, Part 1; Wham!: The Final; Make It Big; Hazel O'Connor, Breaking Glass film soundtrack; Recordings for: Living In A Box; Robbie Nevill; Hall and Oates; Debbie Gibson; Diana Ross; Omar; Breathe; Gary Moore; The Christians; The Alarm; Simple Minds; David Bowie; Dexy's Midnight Runners; Junior Giscombe; Boomtown Rats; Thin Lizzy; A Flock of Seagulls; Steps. *Current Management:* The Producers. *Address:* 45–53 Sinclair Rd, London W14 0NS, England.

PORTER, Henry L, (Bishop Henry Porter); b. 2 Jan. 1948, Sarasota, Florida, USA. Vocalist; Musician (piano, organ); Lecturer. m. Cynthia E Porter (Dr), 3 s., 1 d. *Education:* A&M University, Tallahassee, Florida; Yale University, New Haven. *Career:* TV appearances in series Reflection and as host of HLP Love Campaign. *Recordings:* City of Judah; Shout. *Recordings:* I Still Care; Just Good; Keep Making Tracks; The More I Travel This Road; The Love Campaign (TLC). *Membership:* American Assocn of University Professors; Yale Club; Ivy League Club. *Current Management:* Marie Watkins Music, Jewelstone Records, PO Box 49004, Sarasota 34230–6004, USA. *Website:* www.jewelstonerecords.com.

PORTER, K. C; b. 27 June 1962, Encino, CA, USA. Record Prod; Musician (keyboards). m. Aimée Porter, 1 d. *Education:* Music Study, CSUN University, 5 years. *Career:* Producer for Santana, Ricky Martin, Selena, Patti Labelle, Ednita Nazario, Los Fabulosos Cadillacs; Alan Azul; Laura Pausini. *Compositions:* Donde quiera que estés, 1992; Maria, 1995; La Bomba, 1997; El Farol, 1998. *Recordings:* Boyz II Men; Toni Braxton; Sting; Bon Jovi; Brian McKnight; Geri Halliwell; Montell Jordan; Lara Fabian; India; Az Yet (Producer of Spanish Crossover Versions). *Honours:* Many Gold/Platinum Awards; ASCAP/SESAC Writer Awards, 1994; Grammy Awards, 1998–99; Gold and Platinum Awards, BMI, Song of the Year, 1997–98. *Membership:* SAG; AFTRA; ASCAP; BMI; SESAC; NARAS; LARAS. *Current Management:* Tim McDaniels, c/o Lippman Entertainment. *Address:* 22315 Mulholland Hwy, Calabasas, CA 91302, USA.

PORTER, L. J. (Lisa Jean); b. 4 April 1960, New Orleans, LA, USA. *Education:* Cornish Music Institute. *Career:* TV commercials; Opening act on major stages for nationals including: B. B. King, Kenny G, Elvin Bishop; Voice overs, radio, locally. *Recordings:* Rollercoaster; Blue. *Address:* 11522 Northup Way, Bellevue, WA 98004, USA. *Website:* www.ljporter.com.

PORTNOW, Neil; b. New York, NY, USA. *Career:* Professional Musician, played with various bands; Studio Sideman, playing bass and guitar; President, Portnow-Miller Company Inc, own company, 1971; Manager, Talent Acquisition and Development, Screen Gems Publishing Group, 1972; Staff Producer, RCA Records, promoted to Executive Producer, 1977; Senior Vice-President, 20th Century Fox Records, 1979; Vice-President, Artists and Repertoire, EMI America Records, 1985; Senior Vice-President, West Coast Operations for Zomba Group of Companies including: Jive Records; Silvertone Records; Zomba Music Publishing; Zomba Management; Segue Music; Zomba Music Clearance, Music Supervision, Wired, motion picture, 1988; Music Supervisor for Frank Mancuso Jr's production of Permanent Record, Paramount Pictures, 1987. *Membership:* National Trustee, former National Vice-President, Board of Trustees, Recording Academy; former mem. and Treasurer, Board of Governors, Los Angeles Chapter, National Academy of Recording Arts and Sciences; Advisory Board, Songwriters Resources and Services; Team Captain, Los Angeles City of Hope Music Chapter. *Address:* Zomba, 9000 Sunset Blvd #300, Los Angeles, CA 90069 5803, USA.

PORTUONDO, Omara; b. Oct. 1930, Havana, Cuba. Vocalist; Dancer. *Career:* Joined her sister Haydee as a cabaret dancer at the Tropicana, 1945; Sang with sister in Loquibambla Swing with Cesar Portillode la Luz, Jose Antonio Mendez and Frank Emilio Flynn; Became known as The Fiancée of Filin (La novia del filin) after the Cuban music form combining bossa nova with American jazz influences known as feeling or filin; Founder member of Cuarteto Las D'Aida, 1952; Sang with Orquesta Aragón, 1970s; Appeared in the Wim Wenders documentary film Buena Vista Social Club; Collaborations: Ry Cooder; Ibrahim Ferrer; Afro-Cuban All-Stars. *Recordings:* recent Albums: Buena Vista Social Club, 1997; Buena Vista Social Club Presents Omara Portuondo, 2000; appears on Buena Vista Social Club Presents Ibrahim Ferrer, 1999; Distinto Diferente (with Afro Cuban All-Stars), 1999. *Address:* c/o World Circuit Ltd, First Floor, Shoreditch Stables, 138 Kingsland Rd, London E2 8DY, England.

POSH SPICE. See: **BECKHAM, Victoria.**

POST, Mike; b. 29 September 1944, San Fernando Valley, California, USA. Composer; Musician (guitar); Prod; Arranger. *Career:* Founder, Wellingbrook Singers; First Edition; Guitarist with Dick and Dee; Sammy Davis Jr; Dean Martin; Sonny and Cher; Musical Director, Andy Williams Show; Producer, Mac Davis Show. *Compositions:* Music scores and theme music for numerous television shows including: Rockford Files; LA Law; Hill Street Blues; The A-Team; Magnum PI; Doogie Howser, MD; Quantum Leap; Hardcastle and McCormick; Riptide; NYPD Blue; Law and Order; Silk Stalkings; Wiseguy; Hunter; News Radio; The Commish; Blossom; Hooperman; White Shadow; Renegade. *Recordings include:* As producer and/or arranger: Photograph, Mason Williams; Various albums by Ray Charles; Nine To Five, Dolly Parton; I Could've Been A Sailor, Peter Allen; Greatest American Hero, Joey Scarbury (also as musician and writer), 1981; As musician: All I Really Want To Do, Cher, 1965; Sandman, Herb Pedersen, 1977; *Compilations:* Television Theme Songs, 1982; Music From LA Law and Otherwise; NYPD Blue–The Best Of, 1999. *Honours:* Numerous Grammy Awards for: Rockford Files; LA Law; Hill Street Blues; Greatest American Hero; Murder 1, 1995–6. *Current*

Management: Gorfaine/Schwartz Agency Inc, 13245 Riverside Dr., Suite 450, Sherman Oaks, CA 91423, USA.

POTGER, Keith; b. 2 March 1941, Columbo, Sri Lanka. Vocalist; Musician (guitar); Man. *Career:* Founder mem., folk/pop group The Seekers, with Athol Guy and Bruce Woodley, later joined by Judith Durham; Success following concert, Palladium, England, 1964; Group split, 1968; Formed the New Seekers, 1969, left group 1970; Music manager, 1971–. *Address:* c/o Shelley Bovey, 90 Above Town, Glastonbury, Somerset BA6 8JG, England.

POTTER, (Allen) Dale; b. 28 April 1929, Puxico, Missouri, USA. Country Musician (fiddle). 1 s., 1 d. *Education:* Few lessons, fiddle, aged 12. *Career:* Radio appearances, Poplar Bluff, Missouri, and Blytheville, Arkansas; Played on Grand Ole Opry, 1948–62; Tours with Carl Smith; Webb Pierce; Cowboy Copas; Red Sovine; George Jones; Roger Miller; Played on Phillip Morris country Music Show, with Little Jimmy Dickens, George Morgan; Played throughout Eastern, Western and Southern USA; Led 5 piece band, Honolulu, Hawaii, 1970s; Now retired. *Compositions:* Fiddlesticks Boogie, 1954; Fiddle Patch, 1954; Arrangements: Faded Love; Maidens Prayer; Orange Blossom Special, 1979–80. *Recordings:* 8 albums; Recorded with Chet Atkins and Country All Stars; Bill Monroe; Ernest Tubb; Hank Williams Sr; Webb Pierce; Red Foley; Carl Smith; Mac Wiseman; Fiddlesticks Boogie and Fiddle Patch, with Chet Atkins and Country All Stars; Everly Brothers; Marty Robbins; Charline Arthur; Hank Locklin; Marty Robbins; Faron Young. *Honours:* Award, Grand Ole Opry, for Outstanding Contribution To Country Music; Inducted into Western Swing Society Hall of Fame, 1988. *Membership:* Musicians' Union; ROPE. *Address:* PO Box 351, Puxico, MO 63960, USA.

POUGET, Nelly; b. 19 May 1955, Dijon, France. Musician (saxophone); Composer. *Education:* Classique Conservatoire; School of Art, Beaune. *Education:* Conservatoire, Dijon. *Career:* Festival de Jazz de Dudelange; AMR Geneve; Festival Frankfurt; Festival du Mans; International tours; Television and radio appereances: FR3 TV Bourgogne Franche Comte; RFI Radio Interview; RTL Luxembourg; Radio Monte Carlo, Interview, Los Angeles Trilogy. *Recordings:* Albums (own compositions): Le Dire, 1991; Le Vivre, 1993; Vidéomusic, Nelly Pouget Quartet Live, 1996; Le Voir, 1997; Fraîcheur Cuivrée, solo record, in CD and Vidéomusic, 1999. *Publications:* Le Monde; The Wire; Liberation. *Honours:* Le Dire, four key Review, Telerama. *Membership:* SACEM France. *Current Management:* Minuit Regards.

POULIOT, George Stephen; b. 12 June 1954, North Hollywood, California, USA. Record Prod; Sound Engineer; Composer. m. Erica Gardner, 7 May 1989. *Education:* Sherwood Oaks College. *Career:* Recording engineer, Steve Pouliot Music, 1979–; Sound engineer for Rita Coolidge and Dwight Yoakam; Also collaborated with: Bonnie Bramlett; Peaches & Herb; Robin Pearl. *Compositions:* Songwriter for: Micky Martin; Billy Burnett. *Recordings:* As engineer: Behind The Mask, Fleetwood Mac, 1990; As producer: Rick Vito, 1991; The Honest, 1991. *Honours:* Grammy, 1978; Gold and Platinum discs. *Membership:* BMI.

POUSSI, Moussa; b. 5 May 1962, Niamey, Niger. Vocalist; Songwriter; Dancer. m. Adama Tahirou, 29 Dec. 1988, 2 s., 3 d. *Education:* Four years musical training as vocalist, arranger, orchestrator, Centre de Formation et de Promotion Musicales, Hadj Taya. *Career:* Solderer; Comic actor; Musician; Began as entertainment singer in night clubs; Became leader of many orchestras in Niamey; Concerts in Nigeria, Côte d'Ivoire, Burkina Faso and Mali; Leader, Le Degara-Band, Niamey. *Compositions:* Over thirty compositions including Adama; Tchirey; Nafissa; Kokaina; Waimo; Sibo; Toro. *Recordings:* Three compilation albums, Vols I, II and III, 1988; Toro, 1991, CD, 1994. *Honours:* First Prize, Concours de Musique Nigerienne Moderne, 1987. *Membership:* Nigerian Asscn of Musicians. *Address:* PO Box 11203, Niamey, CFPM, Niger.

POWELL, Claire-Louise; b. Norfolk, England. Vocalist; Actress; Prod. *Career:* Lead singer, Pentangle; Lead singer, Sugar Mice; Cabaret at La Parisien; Ma Kindley's Musical Extravaganza; Extensive musicals, film, television, radio and opera Don Giovanni; Director, Osiris Productions; Director, Chucklefactory; Production Executive, Sound Pound; Casting Consultant, Good Vibrations. *Recordings:* Cabaret Cage; Poison Dwarf; Sacred Songs of Scotland; Rock Opera 1; Soul Sounds, Mellow Yellow. *Honours:* Le Sarlation, Most Outstanding Female Vocalist, 3 years running. *Current Management:* Bill Richards Personal Management.

POWELL, Don; b. 10 Sept. 1950, Bilston, Warwickshire, England. Musician (drums). *Career:* Member, UK rock group Slade (formerly N'Betweens, Ambrose Slade), 1966–; Concerts include: First British tour, 1972; Fanfare For Europe festival, London Palladium, 1973; Great British Music Festival, 1978; Reading Festival, 1980; Film appearance: Flame, 1974. *Recordings:* Albums: Beginnings (as Ambrose Slade), 1969; Play It Loud, 1970; Slade Alive, 1972; Slayed, 1973; Sladest, 1973; Old New Borrowed Blue, 1974; Slade In Flame (soundtrack), 1974; Nobody's Fool, 1976; Slade Alive Vol. 2, 1978; Return To Base, 1979; Slade Smashes, 1980; Till Deaf Do Us Part, 1981; We'll Bring The House Down, 1981; Slade On Stage, 1982; The Amazing Kamikaze Syndrome, 1983; Slade's Greats, 1984; Rogue's Gallery, 1985; Crackers, 1985;

You Boyz Make Big Noize, 1987; Wall of Hits, 1991; Keep On Rockin', 1996; Fantastic World of Spaghetti Westerns, 1999; Slade II, 2001; Digital Transfers include: Original Rock and Roll Classics, 1996; Jerry Lee Lewis, Great Balls of Fire, 1997; Jennie C Riley, Harper Valley PTA, 1997; As Producer, Merry Soulful Christmas, 1996; Heartthrob Hits, 1998; UK No. 1 singles: Coz I Luv You, 1971; Take Me Back 'Ome, 1972; Mama Weer All Crazee Now (later recorded by Mama's Boys, Quiet Riot), 1972; Cum On Feel The Noize (later covered by Oasis), 1973; Skweeze Me Pleeze Me, 1973; Merry Christmas Everybody, 1973; Other hits: Get Down And Get With It, 1971; Look Wot You Dun, 1972; Gudbuy T'Jane, 1972; My Friend Stan, 1973; Everyday, 1974; Bangin' Man, 1974; Far Far Away, 1974; Thanks For The Memory, 1975; In For A Penny, 1975; We'll Bring The House Down, 1981; My Oh My, 1983; Run Run Away, 1984; All Join Hands, 1984; Radio Wall Of Sound, 1991. *Honours:* Hon. Fellow, University of Wolverhampton, 2002. *Address:* c/o Polydor (UK), 72 Black Lion Lane, London W6 9BE, England.

POWELL, James Michael; b. 25 March 1973, London. Musician (drums). *Education:* Tuition from John Parish. *Career:* Numerous Tours with Georgie Fame; Stephen Duffy; Alan Price; Van Morrison; Lloyd Cole; Orchestra for Whistle Down The Wind and Mamma Mia. *Recordings:* Relationships, Georgie Fame, 2001. *Membership:* Musicians' Union. *Address:* 4 Thornbury Rd, London SW2 4DH, England.

POWELL, Owen; b. 9 July 1967, Cambridge, England. Musician (guitar). Member, various bands including Y Crumblowers, Colour 45, The Family; Member, Catatonia, 1995–2001; Signed to Blanco Y Negro, 1996. *Recordings:* Albums: Way Beyond Blue, 1996; The Sublime Magic of Catatonia, 1996; International Velvet (No. 1, UK), 1998; Equally Cursed and Blessed (No. 1, UK), 1999; Paper Scissors Stone, 2001; Greatest Catatonia Hits, 2002. Singles: Bleed/Do You Believe In Me, 1996; Mulder and Scully, 1998; Road Rage, 1998; Strange Glue, 1998; Londinium, 1999; Karaoke Queen, 1999; Stone By Stone, 2001.

POWELLS, Jimmy; b. 18 March 1947, Arbroath, Scotland. Musician (mandolin, guitar); Vocalist. 2 s. *Career:* Mem., folk groups, Town Choice, Carterbar. *Recordings:* Albums: Romantic Mandolin/Mandolin Moments; Mandolin Magic, 2000. *Address:* 55 Langdale Dr., Cramlington, Northumberland NE23 8EL, England.

POWER, Brendan; b. 20 Feb. 1956, Mombasa, Kenya. Musician (chromatic and diatonic harmonica). m. Lorraine Power, 26 June 1991. *Education:* BA, English, Religious Studies; MA, Religious Studies. *Career:* Top New Zealand session harmonica player; Came to Britain, 1992; In band for Riverdance; Irish TV series: A River of Sound. *Compositions:* Jig Jazz; The Real Blues Reel. *Recordings:* State of The Harp; Harmonica Nights; Digging In; Harmonica After Hours; New Irish Harmonica; Played on Sting album: Ten Summoners Tales; also recordings by Mary Black; Andy Irvine. *Publications:* Harping On, articles on harmonica playing. *Honours:* All-Ireland Champion, 1993. *Membership:* Musicians' Union (UK).

POWER, John (Timothy); b. 14 Sept. 1967, Liverpool, England. Vocalist; Songwriter; Musician (guitar). m. Belinda Stone, 21 Sept. 1996, 2 c. *Career:* Bassist with the LA's; Singer/Songwriter, Guitarist, Cast. *Compositions:* All tracks on album All Change including Promised Land, Sandstorm, Fine Time, Walk Away. *Recordings:* with The La's: Singles: There She Goes, 1988 (reissued 1990, 1997); Timeless Melody, 1990; Feelin' 1991; Albums: The La's, 1990; Breakloose—Lost La's 1984–87, 2001; with Cast: Singles: Fine Time, 1995; Alright, 1995; Sandstorm, 1996; Walkaway, 1996; Flying, 1996; Free Me, 1997; Guiding Star, 1997; Live The Dream, 1997; I'm So Lonely, 1997; Beat Mama, 1999; Magic Hour, 1999; Albums: All Change, 1997; Magic Hour, 1999. *Membership:* PPL; PRS; Musicians' Union. *Current Management:* Rock 'n' Roll Management. *Address:* Studio 2, 108 Prospect Quay Point, London SW18 1PR, England.

POWER, Niall; b. 14 Nov. 1957, Ireland. Musician (drums). m. Michelle, 4 Feb. 1991, 1 s. *Education:* Three years music theory in school. *Career:* 20 years, professional drummer with various Irish groups, solo artists; Tours with Bob Geldof and The Vegetarians of Love, 1990–; Hazel O'Connor, live album and tour, 1994; Also: Marianne Faithfull; Johnny Logan; Stepaside. *Recordings:* with Bob Geldof: Les Enfants Touche, 1985; Happy Club, 1994; with Hazel O'Connor: live album, 1994; LA Confidential, 2001; Various singles, television themes, jingles. *Membership:* Musicians' Union. *Current Management:* MDO Productions. *Address:* Northwood Lane, Bewdley, Worcestershire DY12 1AS, England.

POWERHOUSE. See: **GONZALEZ, Kenny.**

POWERPILL. See: **APHEX TWIN.**

POWERS, Stephen H; b. 22 Aug. 1951, Rockford, Illinois, USA. Record Prod; Entrepeneur. *Education:* Massachusetts Institute of Technology; Private music tutors. *Career:* Founder, Manager, Charlotte's Web Performing Arts Center, Rockford, Illinois, 1992–; Founder, President, Mountain Railroad Records Inc, 1974; Producer, over 50 folk, blues, rock, reggae albums; Director of Entertainment, Los Angeles Olympics, 1984; Director, A & R, Capitol Records, Hollywood, 1984–87; Worked with artists including: The Beach Boys; Duran Duran; Duane Eddy; The Eurythmics; Bryan Ferry; Tina Turner; Founder, President, Chameleon Music Group, 1987–92; Co-founder, CEO, Drive Entertainment Inc, 1993–. *Recordings:* Producer, Singer In The Storm, Holly Near; 9 1/2 Weeks (soundtrack); Executive Producer, Mad Max III (soundtrack); The Healer, John Lee Hooker (Grammy Award winner), 1991. *Honours:* Producer of the Year, Wisconsin Music Awards, 1982; Independent Executive of the Year, Los Angles Music Council, 1991. *Membership:* NARAS; National Academy of Songwriters (Board of Directors); Country Music Asscn; NAIRD; NARM. *Address:* c/o Drive Entertainment Inc, 10351 Santa Monica Blvd, Suite 404, Los Angeles, CA 90025, USA.

POZGAJEC, Branko; b. 23 July 1950, Zagreb, Croatia. Vocalist; Musician (flute). m. Margita Pozgajec, 16 April 1983, 1 s., 1 d. *Education:* Graduate, Economics, university; High School of Music. *Career:* 29 years, professional singing, playing; 24 years leading Drugi Nacin, famous Croatian rock group; More than 1,800 concerts in Croatia and abroad; Numerous TV shows and radio appearances. *Compositions include:* The Right Words (Prave Rijeci); Dilemmas (Dileme); Again (Opet); Promise Me Springtime (Obecaj Mi Proljece); I'd Like To Get Back (Htio Bih Vratiti). *Recordings:* 5 singles, 4 albums with Drugi Nacin. *Membership:* Croatian Composers Union; Croatian Artists Union; Croatian Musicians' Union, vice-pres., 1998–.

PRATT, Guy Adam; b. 3 Jan. 1962, London, England. Musician (bass guitar); Record Prod; Songwriter. *Career:* Tours and television appearances with: Icehouse; Bryan Ferry; Scritti Politti; Pink Floyd; Coverdale/Page; Womack and Womack; Bobby Womack and Jeff Beck; Currently writing stage musical with Gary Kemp. *Recordings:* with Madonna: Like A Virgin; Hanky Panky; with Robert Palmer: Riptide; Don't Explain; with Bryan Ferry: Bête Noire; Mamounia; with Pink Floyd: The Division Bell; Delicate Sound of Thunder; Pulse; Ain't No Doubt, Jimmy Nail; Storyville, Robbie Robertson; Power Station, Power Station; History, Michael Jackson; The Orb, The Orb; Communion, Debbie Harry; Toy Matinee, Third Matinee; Dream Academy; Junior Reid, Long Road; Last Action Hero; Pink Floyd, Division Bell; Ted Hawkins, Ted Hawkins Story; In Dreams, In Dreams; Natalie Imbruglia, White Lillies Island; Ronan Keating, Ronan; Naimee Coleman, Bring Down The Moon. *Membership:* PRS; Musicians' Union. *Current Management:* Paul Toogood. *Address:* Lancaster House, 14–16 St Marks Rd, London W11 1QU, England.

PREISS-HARRIS, Patricia Ellen; b. 19 May 1950, New York, USA. Musician (piano); Composer; Educator. m. William Harlow Harris. *Education:* BA, MA, Harvard University, Cambridge; New England Conservatory, 1970–71; California Institute of The Arts, 1987; Private Studies With Vera Appleton, Charlie Banacos, Dave Holland; Creative Music Studio. *Career:* Pianist Regularly Appearing At Hyam Regency Hotel and Private Functions, 190–99; Appearances At Colleges and Night Clubs Throughout The USA and Europe; Solo and Ensemble Performances; Educator, Private Piano Teacher. *Compositions:* Messages; Invocations; Complete Enlightenment For Chamber Ensemble and Speaker; Dozens of Jazz Tunes; Love Remembered. *Recordings:* Jamaica's Album; Trust In Love; Massachusetts. *Publications:* Frontiers of Improvisation. *Honours:* Music Merit Scholarship, 1985–86; Artists Grantee, Northern Berkshire Council On The Arts, 1983; Performance Grantee, Cambridge Arts Council. *Membership:* ASCAP; The Schubert Club.

PRESCOTT, Peter James; b. 20 Oct. 1956, Erith, Kent, England. Vocalist. m. Wendy Patricia Lewsley, 22 April 1978, 2 d. *Career:* Singer for 23 years; 6 albums; Further 7 compilation albums; Appearances on 6 television shows in Europe; Several major festivals, Switzerland and Austria. *Recordings:* Album with Forcefield (with Cozy Powell, Neil Murray and Ray Fenwick); 2 albums with Paul Sinden: Turn It Up, 1993; Mean Business, 1995; 3 albums with Swiss band Sergeant; Time Stands Still, album with band Passion Play. *Publications:* Over 70 songs published. *Membership:* Musicians' Union; PRS; MCPS. *Address:* 157 Bulverhythe Rd, St Leonards on Sea, East Sussex TN38 8AF, England.

PRESENCER, Gerard; b. 12 Sept. 1972, London, England. Musician (trumpet, piano); Composer. *Career:* Jazz musician and session player; Played trumpet from age 10, first performing with National Youth Jazz Orchestra, aged 11; Performed and recorded with many jazz artists and ensembles including: Roadside Picnic; Clark Tracey; Pizza Express Modern Jazz Sextet; Charlie Watts Quintet; Dankworth Generation Band; Pete King; Gail Thompson's Gail Force; Stan Tracey; Tina May; Martin Taylor; Tim Garland; Ian Barnes; Don Weller; Made a number of solo albums and led own Quartet; Regular session work, both as an individual and as a member of the Horny Horns (with Denis Rollins and Michael Smith); Appearances on a wide range of artists' recordings including: The Brand New Heavies; Tina Turner; Tindersticks; Gabrielle; Beverley Knight; Incognito; Joni Mitchell. *Recordings:* Albums: Platypus, 1998; The Optimist, 2000; Dreams (with Tony Coe), 2001; features on: Brand New Heavies albums: The Brand New Heavies, 1990; Brother Sister, 1994; Shelter, 1997; Alec and John Dankworth Generation Band albums: Nebuchadnezzar, 1994; Rhythm Changes, 1995; Martin Taylor albums: Years Apart (Martin Taylor's Spirit of Django), 1996; Gold, 1997;

Celebrating Grappelli, 1998; Tim Garland albums: Enter The Fire, 1997; Made By Walking, 2000; Pete King Quartet albums: Speed Trap, 1996; Lush Life, 1999; From One Charlie, Charlie Watts, 1991; Hand On The Torch, US3, 1993; Fun, Tina May, 1993; Live At The QEH, Stan Tracey, 1994; 100 Degrees and Rising, Incognito, 1995; For Heaven's Sake, New Stan Tracey Quartet, 1996; Wildest Dreams, Tina Turner, 1996; Young Mind – Old Hands, Alan Barnes and Brian Lemon, 1997; 10, Wet Wet Wet, 1997; Curtains, Tindersticks, 1997; A Dotty Blues, Alan Barnes, 1998; Prodigal Sista, Beverley Knight, 1998; Peasants Pigs and Astronauts, Kula Shaker, 1999; Rise, Gabrielle, 2000; Still, Field of Blue, 2000; Both Sides Now, Joni Mitchell, 2000.

PRESLEY, Reg, (Reginald Ball); b. 12 June 1943, Andover, Hampshire, England. Vocalist; Songwriter. *Career:* Lead singer, The Troggs (formerly The Troglodytes), 1964; Tours, concerts include: Star Scene 66, with Walker Brothers, Dave Dee Dozy Beaky Mick and Tich, 1966; Regular live work, USA, UK; Concert for Hillsborough soccer disaster fund, Sheffield, 1989. *Compositions include:* I Can't Control Myself; With A Girl Like You; Give It To Me. *Recordings:* Albums: From Nowhere... The Troggs, 1966; Trogglodynamite, 1967; Best of The Troggs, 1967; Love Is All Around, 1968; The Troggs Tapes, 1972; Vintage Years, 1976; Live At Max's Kansas City, 1980; Athens Andover, 1991; Archeology (1966–76), 1992; Best of the Troggs, 1994; Athens, Georgia and Beyond, 1996; Singles include: Wild Thing (No. 1, USA) (later used for Lion Bar commercial; ITV show Gladiators; theme for film Major League), 1966; With A Girl Like You (No. 1, UK), 1966; I Can't Control Myself, 1966; Any Way That You Want Me, 1967; Give It To Me, 1967; Night of The Long Grass, 1967; Hi Hi Hazel, 1967; Love Is All Around (covered by REM; No. 1 hit for Wet Wet Wet, used in film 4 Weddings and A Funeral, 1994), 1967; Little Girl, 1968. *Current Management:* Stan Green Management, PO Box 4, Dartmouth, Devon TQ6 0YD, England.

PRESTON, Billy; b. 9 Sept. 1946, Houston, Texas, USA. Musician (keyboards); Vocalist. *Career:* Solo singer, keyboard player, 1962–; Keyboard player, Plastic Ono Band (with John Lennon), 1969–71; Backing musician for numerous artists including: The Beatles; Ray Charles; Little Richard; Aretha Franklin; Sam Cooke; Mahalia Jackson; Martha Reeves; Luther Vandross; Stephen Stills; George Harrison; Ringo Starr; The Crusaders; Delaney and Bonnie. *Recordings:* Singles include: That's The Way (God Planned It), 1969; Will It Go Round In Circles, 1973; Nothing For Nothing, 1974; with The Beatles: Get Back (No. 1, UK and USA), 1969; Let It Be (No. 1, USA), 1970; with Syreeta: With You I'm Born Again (No. 2, UK), 1979; Solo Albums include: Whole New Thing, 1977; Behold, 1979; Fastbreak, 1979; Late At Night, 1979; Billy and Syreeta, 1980; The Way I Am, 1981; Universal Love, 1980; Pressin' On, 1982; The Best of Billy Preston, 1988; Minister of Music, 1995; Words and Music, 1996; Universal Love, 1997; Music From My Heart, 2001; Featured on other albums including: No Reason To Cry, Eric Clapton; Mad Dogs and Englishmen, Joe Cocker; Blood On The Tracks, Bob Dylan; Beat and Soul, Everly Brothers; I Heard That!, Quincy Jones; Sometime In New York City, John Lennon and Yoko Ono; Exile on Main Street, Rolling Stones; Songs from a Parent to a Child, Art Garfunkel. *Address:* c/o Embassy Artists/Full Circle Entertainment, 23500 Michigan Ave, Dearborn, MI 48124, USA.

PRICE, Adrian; b. 11 March 1967, Colchester, Essex, England. Musician (drums). m. Joanna Snelling, 17 June 1995. *Education:* Trinity College of Music, London. *Career:* Drummer, Scissormen; Live concerts, UK, Europe; Singles promoted on BBC Radio 1, Greater London Radio (GLR); German, French, Eastern European radio; Videos shown on British television and MTV. *Recordings:* Single: Burst/Sever, Scissormen; Glee (EP), Scissormen; Album: Mumbo Jumbo, Scissormen. *Membership:* Musicians' Union; PRS. *Current Management:* Diversity, 34B Haven Green, London W5 2NX. *Address:* c/o Welwyn House, 28 Wash Lane, Clacton, Essex CO15 1DU, England.

PRICE, Alan; b. 14 April 1941, Fatfield, County Durham, England. *Career:* Formed Alan Price Combo, 1958; Formed the Animals, 1963; Left the Animals, 1965; Formed Alan Price Set, 1965; Formed Alan Price and Friends, 1968–69; Teamed up with Georgie Fame, many television appearances, 1971–74; Acted in Alfie Darling, 1975; 2 British tours; Director, Fulham Football Club, 1978; British tour, 1979; Series of shows, BBC2, 1980; Formed own record label Key Records, 1981; Appeared in Andy Capp, Manchester, London, 1982; Re-formed Animals, 1983; Tour: Canada; USA; Hawaii; Japan; France; UK; 2 concerts, Royal Albert Hall; Wembley, with The Police, New Year's Eve, 1983; 21st Anniversary Tour, 1986; Travelling Man Tour, 1987; Liberty Tour, 1990–91; Greatest Hits Tour, 1992–93; Current band, Alan Price and the Electric Blues Company. *Compositions:* include: The House That Jack Built; Jarrow Song; Just For You; Composer, film scores, theatre music, and commercials; Film scores include: O Lucky Man, 1973; The Plague Dogs, 1982; Britannia Hospital, 1982; Whales of August, 1988; Theatre music: Home, 1970; Early Days, 1980; Musical: Andy Capp, 1982; Television appearances: Turtles' Progress; World's End; Fame Is The Spur; A Night On The Tyne; The Chalk Face. *Recordings:* Hit singles include: with The Animals: House of The Rising Sun (No. 1, UK and USA), 1964; Don't Let Me Be Misunderstood, 1965; We've Gotta Get Out of This Place, 1965; with Alan

Price Set: I Put A Spell On You, 1966; Hi-Lili Hi-Lo, 1966; Simon Smith And His Amazing Dancing Bear, 1967; The House That Jack Built, 1967; Don't Stop The Carnival, 1968; Rosetta, with Georgie Fame, 1971; Jarrow Song, 1974; Just For You, 1978; Baby Of Mine, 1979; Goodnight Irene; Changes, 1988; Albums: Metropolitan Man; Performing Price; Shouts Across The Street; Travelling Man; Liberty; Covers; A Gigster's Life For Me; A Rock 'N' Roll Night At The Royal Court Theatre, 2000; Geordie Boy—The Anthology, 2002; Based On A True Story, 2002. *Honours:* BAFTA Award, 1973; Inducted into American Rock and Roll Hall of Fame, 1994. *Current Management:* Cromwell Management, 4–5 High St, Huntingdon, Cambs PE28 3TE, England.

PRICE, James; b. 20 Nov. 1959, Copenhagen, Denmark. Composer; Orchestrator; Conductor. m. Kirsten, 14 Nov. 1992, 1 s. *Education:* Composition, Royal Danish Academy of Music, 1979–84. *Career:* Debut, 1979; Musical Director, Arranger and Pianist; Revues, Vaudevilles, Musicals including Nitouche, Sound of Music, HMS Pinafore, Annie Get Your Gun, Cabaret, Annie; Host in television show; Around a Piano; Compositions for theatre, radio, television, film. *Compositions:* Ved Frokosten (Opera-Monologue, Royal Theatre, 1983); Underscore for TV Serials: Two People in Love; Karrusel; Musicals: Tordenskiold; Livsens Ondskab. *Recordings:* Tordenskiold, 1994. *Honours:* Wilhelm Hansens Grant, 1992; Revue Composer of the Year, 1983, 1996. *Membership:* Danish Songwriters' Guild; Danish Conductors' Society. *Current Management:* Nordiska Strakosch Teater-Förlaget, Gothersgade 11, 4 1123 Copenhagen K, Denmark.

PRICE, Kelly; b. Queens, New York, USA. Vocalist. *Career:* Received musical foundation in church; Began as backing vocalist and moved into vocal arranging and writing; Signed deal as an artist in own right with Island Black Music, 1997–; Collaborations: Puff Daddy; Faith Evans; Whitney Houston; Brian McKnight. *Recordings:* Albums: Soul of a Woman, 1997; Mirror Mirror, 2000; One Family, 2001; Singles: Friend of Mine, 1997; Secret Love, 1999; You Should've Told Me, Love Sets You Free, 2000. *Honours:* Kora Award, Best Female African Diaspora Artist, 2002. *Address:* c/o Island/Def Jam, 825 Eighth Ave, New York, USA.

PRICE, Mark; Musician (drums). m. Jude, 1 d. *Career:* Fmr mem., Right Said Fred, All About Eve; Mem., Del Amitri, 1997–. *Recordings:* Albums: Hatful Of Rain/Lousy With Love, 1998; Can You Do Me Good?, 2002. Singles: Don't Come Home Too Soon, 1998; Cry To Be Found, 1998; Just Before You Leave, 2002. *Address:* c/o A & M Records Inc, 595 Madison Ave, New York, NY 10022, USA. *Website:* www.delamitri.com.

PRICE, Mark; b. 10 Aug. 1959, Nelson, Lancashire, England. Musician (drums); Writer; Programmer. m. Lise Regan, 26 Jan. 1989, 1 s. *Education:* BA Hons, Graphic Design. *Career:* Producer/Programmer; Nik Kershaw, 3 world tours; Numerous television appearances and Live Aid; Bryan Ferry; All About Eve: 4 albums and tours; The Cure: album tracks; Julianne Regan: album; Peter Murphy: American tours; Joined Del Amitri, 1997; World tour, 1997–98. *Compositions:* Co-writer, musician, 4 albums: All About Eve; Co-writer album: Never Swallow Stars; Jingles and commercials. *Recordings:* All About Eve albums: All About Eve; Scarlet and Other Stories; Touched By Jesus; Ultraviolet; Appears on: Amy Grant, Amy Grant, 1977; Tin Huey, Contents Dislodged During Shipment, 1979; Feelabeelia, East to West, 1985; Archers of Loaf, Icky Mettle, 1994; Cure, Wide Mood Swings, 1996; Pere Ubu Datapanik in the Year Zero, 1996; Del Amitri, Hatful of Rain, 1999; Eileen Rose, Shine Like It Does, 2001. *Membership:* Musicians' Union; PRS. *Current Management:* Lise.

PRICE, P. J; b. 8 July 1964, Houston, Texas, USA. Vocalist; Songwriter; Musician (guitar, keyboards). 2 s. *Career:* Various radio releases; Television appearances: Solo artiste on Entertainment Unlimited; Owner, Priceless Records; Owner, Taste of Texas Music. *Recordings:* Album: P J Price, 1994; Singles: Runnin' On Love; What's A Heart Like Yours. *Honours:* Star of Tomorrow, Airplay International, 1993–94; Best Female Indie and Album of the Year, World Country Music Network, 1994; No. 1, GSCMA European Chart, 1995. *Membership:* GSCMA; NCMO. *Current Management:* Priceless Promotions. *Address:* 111 Pine Valley, Huntsville, TX 77340, USA.

PRICE, Ray Noble; b. 12 Jan. 1926, Perryville, Texas, USA. Country Vocalist; Musician (guitar). *Career:* Appeared as the Cherokee Cowboy, local radio station; Joined the Big D Jamboree, 1949; Member, Grand Ole Opry; Formed own band, The Cherokee Cowboys; Toured extensively, appeared on all major network radio and television shows; Appeared with artists including Oscar Peterson, Barbara Mandrell, Patsy Cline, Kris Kristofferson; Hank Williams; Semi-retired, 1973–78; Returned to recording until 1980s; Film appearance, Honkytonk Man. *Recordings:* Over 100 hit singles; US Country No. 1 hits include: Crazy Arms; My Shoes Keep Walking Back To You; For The Good Times; Release Me (later recorded by Englebert Humperdinck); Other hits: Talk To Your Heart; Don't Let The Stars Get In Your Eyes; Faded Love (duet with Willie Nelson); Numerous albums include: Heart Songs, 1957; Faith, 1960; Night Life, 1964; Born To Lose, 1967; For The Good Times, 1970; This Time Lord, 1974; Help Me, 1977; San Antonio Rose (with Willie Nelson), 1980; Ray Price, 1981; Town and Country, 1981; Tribute To Willie and Kris,

1981; Diamonds In The Stars, 1981; Loving You, 1982; Somewhere In Texas, 1982; Master of The Art, 1983; Portrait of a Singer, 1985; Welcome To The Country, 1985; A Revival of Old Time Singing, 1987; The Heart of Country Music, 1987; Just Enough Love, 1988; Sometimes A Rose, 1992; Memories That Last (with Faron Young), 1992; The Old Rugged Cross, 1993; Christmas Gift for You, 1993; Release Me, 1995; Sings A Tribute To The Great Bob Wills, 1996; Prisoner Of Love, 2000; Various compilations. *Honours:* Country Music Hall of Fame, 1996. *Current Management:* James R Doran, Original Artists Agency. *Address:* 1031 E Battlefield, Springfield, MO 65807, USA.

PRICE, Rick; Vocalist; Songwriter; *Recordings:* Heaven Knows, 1992; Tambourine Mountain, 1995; Another Place, album, 1999. *Honours:* Apra Award, Song of Year, Heaven Knows, 1992; Australian Music Awards, Song of Year, Walk Away Renee, 1993, Album of Year, Heaven Knows, 1993; Advance Australia Foundation, 1993; Australia Export Award, 1993; Singapore Music Award, Song of Year, Heaven Knows, 1993. *Address:* c/o RCM International, Lennox House, 229 Lennox St, Richmond, Victoria 3121, Australia.

PRIDE, Charley Frank; b. 18 March 1938, Sledge, Mississippi, USA. Musician (guitar); Vocalist. *Career:* Former baseball player; Recording artiste, 1965–; First appeared at Grand Ole Opry, 1967. *Recordings:* 29 US Country No. 1 hits; Singles: The Snakes Crawl At Night; Just Between You and Me; Is Anybody Goin' To San Antone?; Crystal Chandelier; Kiss An Angel Good Mornin'; Albums include: Country Charley Pride, 1966; Songs of Pride... Charley That Is, 1968; I'm Just Me, 1971; Pride of America, 1974; Charley, 1975; The Happiness of Having You, 1975; Sunday Morning With Charley Pride, 1976; She's Just An Old Love Turned Memory, 1977; Someone Loves You Honey, 1978; Burgers and Fries, 1978; You're My Jamaica, 1979; There's A Little Bit of Hank In Me, 1980; Roll On Mississippi, 1981; Charley Sings Everybody's Choice, 1982; Live, 1982; Night Games, 1983; The Power of Love, 1984; After All This Time, 1987; I'm Gonna Love Her On The Radio, 1988; In Person (Special Music), 1989; Moody Woman, 1989; Amy's Eyes, 1990; Classics With Pride, 1991; My Six Latest and Six Greatest, 1994; Branson City Limits (live), 1998; Various compilations include: 36 All Time Greatest Hits, 1996; The Essential Charley Pride, 1997; 30 Years of Pride, 1999; Special Collectors Edition, 3 Vols, 1999; A Tribute To Jim Reeves, 2001. *Honours:* Grammy, Best Country Record (Male), Just Between You and Me. *Current Management:* Cecca Productions Inc, 3198 Royal Lane #200, Dallas, TX 75229, USA.

PRIEST; Vocalist; Musician; Prod. *Career:* Released cassette-only recordings on Anti-Pop Recordings label; Mem., The Anti-Pop Consortium, 1997–2002; Supported DJ Shadow's US tour, 2002; Solo artiste, 2002–; Collaboration with Matthew Shipp; Prod., remixer; Joint founder, Anti-Pop Records. *Recordings:* Albums: with Anti-Pop Consortium: Tragic Epilogue, 2000; Arrhythmia, 2002. Singles: with Anti-Pop Consortium: Diagonal Ryme Gargantua (EP), 2000; What Am I?, 2000; Lift, 2000; The Ends Against The Middle (EP), 2001; Ghostlawns, 2002. *Current Management:* Amaechi Uzoigwe, Ozone Music. *Address:* c/o Warp Records Ltd, Spectrum House, 32–34 Gordon House Rd, London NW5 1LP, England. *Website:* www.warprecords.com.

PRIEST, Mathew; b. 3 April 1970, Birmingham, England. Musician (drums). *Career:* Formed Dodgy with Nigel Clarke (left band, 1998); Joined by Andy Miller; Frequent live shows and festival appearances; Formed own record label, Bostin, 1991; Signed to A & M records, 1992; Presenter, BBC Greater London Radio (GLR), 1997–99. *Recordings:* Singles: Staying Out For The Summer, 1994; In A Room, 1996; Good Enough, 1996; Found You, 1997; If You're Thinking of Me, 1998; Every Single Day, 1998; Feather Cuts And Monkey Boots, 2000; Albums: The Dodgy Album, 1993; Homegrown, 1994; Free Peace Sweet, 1996; Ace A's and Killer B's, 1998; Real Estate, 2001.

PRIEST, Maxi, (Max Elliot); b. 1962, London, England. Reggae Vocalist. *Career:* Former carpenter, builder of sound systems; Tour with UK reggae group Saxon International Sound System; DJ; Solo artiste; Appeared with artists including Aswad, Roberta Flack, Shabba Ranks, Dennis Brown, Pieces of a Dream, including Sensual Embrace album, 2001. *Recordings:* Albums: You're Safe, 1985; Intentions, 1986; Maxi, 1987; Bona Fide, 1990; The Best of Me, 1991; Man with the Fun, 1996; Live in Concert, 1996; CombiNation, 1999; Singles: Strollin' On, 1986; In The Springtime, 1986; Crazy Love, 1986; Some Guys Have All The Luck, 1987; Wild World, 1988; Close To You (No. 1, USA), 1990; Space in My Heart; Housecall, 1991; Groovin' in the Midnight, 1992; Waiting in Vain, 1993; Dreaming; One More Chance, 1993; That Girl, 1996; Watching the World Go By, 1996.

PRIESTLEY, Brian; b. 10 July 1946, Manchester, England. Writer; Musician. *Education:* BA, Hon, French; Diploma of Education, Leeds University. *Recordings:* You Taught My Heart To Sing, 1996; Love You Madly, with Louise Gibbs, 1999. *Publications:* Mingus, A Critical Biography, 1982; Jazz Piano, 6 Vols, 1983–90; Charlie Parker, 1984; John Coltrane, 1987; Jazz – The Essential Companion (with Ian Carr and Digby Fairweather), 1987; Jazz on Record, A History, 1988; Jazz – The Rough Guide (with Ian Carr and Digby Fairweather), 1995. *Contributions to:* Reviews and articles; The Gramophone; New Grove Encyclopedia of Jazz; The Cambridge Companion to the Piano; The International Directory of Black Composers;

Liner notes for recordings by artist including: Charlie Parker, Charles Mingus, Thelonius Monk, Ben Webster, Duke Ellington, Ella Fitzgerald, Lionel Hampton. *Literary Agent:* Barbara Levy. *Address:* 120A Farningham Rd, Caterham, Surrey CR3 6LJ, England.

PRIESTLEY, Mark; b. 13 July 1963, Kabwe, Zambia. Musician (saxophone, guitar); Vocalist; Songwriter. 1 s. *Education:* BA; MA. *Career:* Various studio session work; Member of Jon Strong Band, From The Underworld, Bassa Bassa, and Dr Fray; Concert appearances include: Glastonbury Festival, 1990; WOMAD Festival, 1990; Edinburgh Fringe Festival, 1991; Live radio sessions on Radio 1. *Recordings:* with Cassandra Complex, The Word and Kay Field; as Producer: Bassa Bassa (album); Not In My Back Yard (album). *Membership:* Musicians' Union. *Current Management:* Bassa Bassa Collective. *Address:* PO Box 10, Christ Church Mount, Leeds LS12 3NH, England.

PRIESTMAN, Henry; b. 21 July 1958, Liverpool, England. Vocalist; Songwriter. *Career:* Member, The Christians, 1984–; Appearances include: Liver Aid Ethiopian Famine benefit, Liverpool, 1985; Support to Fleetwood Mac, British tour, 1988; John Lennon Tribute Concert, Merseyside, 1990; Regular UK and European tours. *Compositions:* Songs recorded by the Christians. *Recordings:* Albums: The Christians, 1987; Colour (No. 1, UK), 1990; Happy In Hell, 1992; The Best of The Christians, 1993; with the Yachts: Yachts, 1979; Yachts without Radar, 1989; with Echo and the Bunnymen, Echo and the Bunnymen, 1987; 1988 Summer Olympic Album; with Lightning Seeds, Cloudcuckooland, 1989; with Mike Peters, Feel Free, 1996; with Ian McNabb: Waifs and Strays, 2000; with Enemy Within: Death Blues, 2000; Singles include: Forgotten Town, 1987; Hooverville (They Promised Us The World), 1987; When The Fingers Point, 1987; Ideal World, 1988; Born Again, 1988; Harvest For The World, 1988; Words, 1989; The Bottle, 1993; Contributor, Ferry 'Cross The Mersey, Hillsborough football disaster benefit, 1989. *Current Management:* Eternal Management, 55 Lark Lane, Liverpool L17 8UW, England.

PRIMO. See: **DJ PREMIER.**

PRIMORAC, Vanja; b. 1 Jan. 1966, Zagreb, Croatia. Promoter; Man; Booking Agent; Prod. 1 s. *Education:* University of Theatre and Film Art, Political Science; Mid-school, piano. *Career:* Columnist, musical critic, promotional work, 1985–; Manager, several highly-rated Croatian, Slovenian, American/English artists; producer, manager, first Yugoslavian alternative music festival: Offestum; Work with Siouxie and The Banshees, Laurie Anderson, Tuxedomoon, The Young Gods; First private promoter in ex-Yugoslavia. *Honours:* Japan Award for Festival Design. *Membership:* Croatian (HGU, HGS). *Current Management:* Media Nova Promotions, N L Jain. *Address:* Via Delle Murina 19, 50053 Empoli (Florence), Italy; Podvrsje 2, Zagreb 41000, Croatia.

PRIMROSE, Neil; b. 20 Feb. 1972, Scotland. Musician (drums). *Career:* Mem., Travis, 1997–; Numerous tours, festivals and television appearances. *Recordings:* Albums: Good Feeling, 1997; The Man Who (No. 1, UK), 1999; The Invisible Band (No. 1, UK), 2001. Singles: U16 Girls, 1997; All I Want To Do Is Rock, 1997; Tied To The Nineties, 1997; Happy, 1997; More Than Us, 1997; Writing To Reach You, 1999; Driftwood, 1999; Why Does It Always Rain on Me?, 1999; Turn, 1999; Coming Around, 2000; Sing, 2001; Side, 2001. *Honours:* Q Magazine Award, Best Single, 1999; Select Magazine, Album of the Year, 1999; BRIT Awards, Best British Group, Best British Album, 2000, Best British Group, 2002. *Address:* c/o Independiente Ltd, The Drill Hall, 3 Heathfield Terrace, London W4 4JE, England. *Website:* www.travisonline.com.

PRINCE, (Prince Rogers Nelson), (The Artist, TAFKAP, Symbol); b. 7 June 1958, Minneapolis, Minnesota, USA. Vocalist; Songwriter; Prod. m. Mayté, 1996. *Career:* Previously billed as Prince, The Artist Formerly Known as Prince (AFKAP) and Symbol; Leader, Prince and The Revolution; Singer, with own backing group the New Power Generation, 1991–; Numerous tours, concerts; Own recording studio and record label, Paisley Park; Currently billed as The Artist. *Recordings:* Singles include: I Wanna Be Your Lover, 1979; 1999, 1983; Little Red Corvette, 1983; When Doves Cry (No. 1, USA), 1984; Purple Rain, 1984; Let's Go Crazy (No. 1, USA), 1984; Raspberry Beret, 1985; Kiss, 1986 (No. 1, USA); Sign O' The Times, 1987; If I Was Your Girlfriend, 1987; U Got The Look, 1987; I Could Never Take The Place of Your Man, 1987; Alphabet Street, 1988; Batdance, (No. 1, USA), 1989; Thieves In The Temple, 1990; Gett Off!, 1991; Cream (No. 1, USA), 1991; Money Don't Matter 2 Nite, 1992; Sexy MF, 1992; Controversy, 1993; The Most Beautiful Girl In The World (No. 1, UK), 1994; Gold, 1995; Betcha By Golly Wow, 1996; The Greatest Romance Ever Sold, 1999; Albums include: For You, 1978; Dirty Mind, 1979; Controversy, 1979; Prince, 1979; 1999, 1983; Purple Rain, 1984; Around The World In A Day, 1985; Parade, 1986; Sign O' The Times, 1987; Lovesexy, 1988; Batman (soundtrack), 1989; Graffiti Bridge (soundtrack), 1990; Diamonds and Pearls, 1991; Symbol, 1992; Hits 1 and 2 (compilations), 1993; Come, 1994; The Black Album (recorded 1987), 1994; The Gold Experience, 1995; Emancipation, 1996; Chaos and Disorder, 1996; New Power Soul, 1998; Rave Un2 The Joy Fantastic, 1999; The Very Best of Prince (compilation), 2001; As producer: Child of The Sun, Mayté, 1996.

Honours: Academy Award, Best Original Score, Purple Rain, 1984; 3 Grammy Awards, 1985; BRIT Awards: Best International Artist, Best Soundtrack (Purple Rain), 1985; Best Soundtrack (Batman), 1990; Best International Male Artist, 1992, 1993, 1995, 1996; Q Award, Best Songwriter, 1990. *Current Management:* Paisley Park Enterprises, 7801 Audoban Rd, Chanhassen, MN 55317, USA.

PRINCE, Anna Lou; Composer; Music Publisher; Recording Artist; Construction Co Exec. 3 c. *Education:* Diploma, Carolina School of Broadcasting, 1966; Zion Diploma, Israel Bible School, Jerusalem, 1970; Diploma, SW Technical College, 1970; MusD, London Institute of Applied Research, 1991; Diplomatic Diploma, Academy Argentina de Diplomacia, 1993. *Career:* Songwriter, Hank Locklin Music Co, Nashville, 1963–70; Entertainer, World's Fair, Knoxville, Tennessee, 1982; Partner, Owner, Prince wholesale Bait Co, Canton, North Carolina, 1976–82; Prince TV Co, 1986–94; Music Publisher, Broadcast Music Inc, Nashville, 1982–; Member, Production Staff, Talent Co-ordinator, TV Series Down Home, Down Under, 1989–90; Over 20 songs recorded; Appeared, Grand Ole Opry; Executive Producer, Host, Music show and TV talk show, Real Heroes of Country Music, 1996–; Candidate for County Commissioner, Macon County, 1984. *Recordings:* I Feel A Cry Coming On, 1965; Best Part of Loving You, 1969; Anna, 1969; I'm In Love with You, 1995; We're Making Memories, 2000. *Honours:* Order of Knight of Templars (Dame); Lofsensic Order (Dame); Maison Internationales des Intellectuals; Hon. Doctorates. *Membership:* BMI; Nashville Songwriters Asscn; Country Music Asscn; Songwriters Guild of America. *Address:* 313 Gallatin Rd S, Madison, TN 37115, USA. *Website:* futureheroesofcountrymusic.com.

PRINCE BUSTER, (Cecil Bustamante Campbell); b. 28 May 1938, Kingston, Jamaica. Vocalist; Record Prod. *Career:* Boxer; Worked for Clement 'Coxsone' Dodd's Down Beat sound system; Founded Voice Of The People sound system, Wild Bells, Islam, Buster's Record Shack labels, and numerous record stores; Worked with artistes including: Big Youth, Dennis Brown, Alton Ellis, John Holt; Toured the UK, mid-1960s. *Recordings:* Albums: On Tour, 1966; Ten Commandments, 1967; Judge Dread Rock Steady, 1967; Wreck A Pum Pum, 1968; She Was A Rough Rider, 1969; Big Five, 1972; Contributed to: Prince Buster Record Shack Presents The Original Golden Oldies Vol. 3; I Feel The Spirit (various artists), 1963; Pain In My Belly (various artists), 1966. Singles: Al Capone (Guns Don't Argue); Black Head Chinaman; Ten Commandments; Judge Dread, 1967; Madness; Ghost Dance; Johnny Cool; Shepherd Beng Beng; Wreck a Pum Pum, 1968; Rough Rider, 1969; Whine and Grine; Burkes Law. *Address:* 127 Orange St, Kingston, Jamaica.

PRINCE PICHO, (Emmanuel Volel); b. 24 April 1942, Port-au-Prince, Haiti. Vocalist; Actor; Musician (guitar, keyboards). 1 s., 2 d. *Education:* College, Hotel Management; Music studies, New-Sewell Music Conservatory, Washington, DC. *Career:* Appearances include: Cable TV channel 45; Cable TV channel 33; Annual guest at Marvin Gaye Festival, African festival, Washington DC; Performed at benefit for homeless. *Recordings:* Numerous albums for Henri Debs record company, Guadaloupe, FWI; Also for Marc Recors, New York, USA. *Publications:* Numerous articles, Montgomery Journal, La Nacion. *Honours:* Masons of Washington DC Award. *Membership:* New Sewell Music Conservatory. *Current Management:* Edwardo Semperegui, Espectaculor Productions.

PRINE, John; b. 10 Oct. 1946, Maywood, Illinois, USA. Vocalist; Songwriter. *Career:* Began writing folk songs as teenager; Regular on Chicago club circuit, 1970; Recording artiste, 1972–; Founder, president, Oh Boy record label, 1980; US tour supporting Bonnie Raitt, 1991; Summer Stage '92 concert, Central Park, New York, 1992; Cambridge Folk Festival, 1992; Cameo film appearance, Falling From Grace, 1992; Appearances with artists including: Steve Goodman, Bonnie Raitt, Nancy Griffith, David Olney, Randy Scruggs. *Compositions include:* Love Is On A Roll, Don Williams (US Country No. 1), 1980. *Recordings:* Singles include: Take A Look At My Heart, 1992; Albums: John Prine, 1972; Diamonds In The Rough, 1972; Sweet Revenge, 1973; Common Sense, 1975; Prime Prine – The Best Of, 1977; Bruised Orange, 1978; Pink Cadillac, 1979; Storm Windows, 1980; Aimless Love, 1984; German Afternoons, 1986; John Prine Live, 1988; The Missing Years, 1991; A John Prine Christmas, 1993; The John Prine Anthology – Great Days, 1993; Lost Dogs and Mixed Blessings, 1995; Live on Tour, 1997; In Spite of Ourselves, 1999; Souvenirs, 2000. *Honours:* Grammy Award, Best Contemporary Folk Album, The Missing Years, 1991. *Current Management:* Al Bunetta Management, 33 Music Sq. W, Suite 102A, Nashville, TN 37203, USA.

PRIOR, Maddy; b. Blackpool, England. Folk Vocalist; Songwriter. m. Rick Kemp, 2 c. *Career:* Founder member, lead singer, folk group, Steeleye Span, 1970–; Member, The Carnival Band; Solo artiste, 1978–; Collaborations with Tim Hart, guitarist, and Nick Holland, keyboard player. *Recordings:* Solo albums: Woman In The Wings, 1978; Changing Winds, 1978; Hooked On Winning, 1982; Going For Glory, 1983; Happy Families, 1991; Sing Lustily and with Good Cheer, 1994; Year, 1994; Hang Up Sorrow and Care, 1996; Flesh and Blood, 1998; Ravenchild, 2000; Ballads And Candles, 2001; All albums recorded by Steeleye Span; 4 albums with Tim Hart; Guest vocalist on numerous albums including: Albion River Hymn March, Albion Band, 1979; Shearwater, Martin Carthy, 1972; Too Old To Rock and Roll, Jethro Tull, 1976; Streets, Ralph McTell, 1975; Incantations, Mike Oldfield, 1978; Silly Sisters, June Tabor, 1976; First Light, Richard and Linda Thompson, 1978; Troubadours of British Folk, 3 Vols, 1995. *Current Management:* Jim McPhee, Acorn Entertainments. *Address:* Winterfold House, 46 Woodfield Rd, Kings Heath, Birmingham B13 9UJ, England.

PRITCHARD, Peter Andrew; b. 13 Aug. 1955, London, England. Musician (bass guitar, double bass). m. Chrystella Maria Nicholas, 6 Oct. 1978, 1 s., 1 d. *Education:* Private tuition, Trinity College of Music. *Career:* Member of Flying Saucers with numerous appearances on German, Dutch and British television and radio; Tours with Chuck Berry, Bill Haley, Scotty Moore, D J Fontana, and The Jordonaires; Film, Blue Suede Shoes. *Compositions:* 10 compositions. *Recordings:* Several singles and albums with Flying Saucers including: The Rawking Sandy Ford, 1994; Albums and singles with Avengers include: She Walks Right In, 2001; CD with the Jordonaires. *Membership:* Musicians' Union. *Address:* 56 King Edwards Rd, Edmonton, London N9 7RP, England.

PROBY, P. J, (James Marcus Smith); b. 6 Nov. 1938, Houston, Texas, USA. Vocalist; Songwriter. *Career:* Founder, The Moondogs, 1958; Work as demo singer, recording under names: Jett Powers, Orville Wood; Appeared on Beatles TV Special, London, 1964; British tours, 1965, 1966; Stage performances include: Catch My Soul (rock version of Othello), West End, 1970; Elvis (musical), 1977; Cabaret circuit and recording career continued to 1991. *Recordings include:* Hold Me, 1964; Together, 1964; Somewhere, 1965; I Apologise, 1965; Let The Water Run Down, 1965; That Means A Lot, 1965; Maria, 1965; You've Come Back, 1966; Niki Hoeky, 1967; Yesterday Has Gone, with Marc Almond, 1996; Albums include: I Am PJ Proby, 1965; Three week hero, 1969; Elvis, 1978; I am P. J. Proby/P. J. Proby, 1996; Legend, 1997; Heroes, 1998; Phenomenon/Believe It or Not, 1998. *Honours:* Best Musical of the Year, Elvis, 1977.

PROCHAZKA, Jiri; b. 23 May 1969, Prague, Czech Republic. Guitar; Keyboards; Drums; Computers; Music Teacher. m. Vladimira Prochazkova, 3 July 1990, 1 d. *Education:* Musical Psychology. *Career:* Tramp Po Cesku 1–8, video; Unlimited Warriors, videogame. *Recordings:* Unlimited Warriors, videogame. *Publications:* Unlimited Warriors, videogame. *Address:* Jiri Prochazka, Olbramovicka 715/2, 142 00, Prague 4, Czech Republic.

PROFESSOR GRIFF, (Richard Griffin); Rap Artiste. *Career:* Member, US rap group Public Enemy, 1984–89; Concerts include: Support to the Beastie Boys, US tour, 1987; Support to LL Cool J, European tour, 1987; Brixton Academy, London, 1990; Solo artiste, 1989–. *Recordings:* Albums: with Public Enemy: Yo! Bum Rush The Show, 1987; It Takes A Nation Of Millions To Hold Us Back, 1988; There's a Poison Goin' On, 1999; with Two Live Crew, Back at Your Ass for the Nine-4; Revolverlution, 2002; Solo albums: Pawns In The Game, 1990; Kao's II Wiz-7-Dome, 1991; Disturb N Tha Peace, 1992; Blood of the Profit, 1998; And the Word Became Flesh, 2001; Singles: Rebel Without A Pause, 1987; Bring The Noise, 1988; Don't Believe The Hype, 1988; Night of The Living Baseheads, 1988; Black Steel In The Hour of Chaos, 1988; Fight The Power, theme for film Do The Right Thing, 1989; Welcome To The Terrordrome, 1990; Jail Sale, 1991; Verdict, 1991; Verbal Intercourse, 1992; Sista Sista, 1992; Ole Bitch U Worryz, 1998.

PROKOP, Michal; b. 13 Aug. 1946, Prague, Czech Republic. Vocalist; Composer; Musician (guitar, harmonica). m. Nina, 1972, 1 s., 1 d. *Education:* High School of Economics, 1968; Faculty of Philosophy, Charles University, Prague, 1992. *Career:* Rock Singer, 1967–90; Member of Parliament, 1990–92; Deputy Minister of Culture, 1992–95; Member of Parliament, 1996–98; TV Talk Show Host, I Mean It Well, 1998–; Director, European City of Culture (Prague) initiative, 2000. *Recordings:* Albums: Blues in Soul; Mesto Er; Holubi Dante; Kolej Yesterday; Nic Ve Zlým; Nic v Dobrým; Snad Nam Naše Deti Prominou; Az Si Pro Mne Prijdou; Cerný Ovce (Black Sheep). *Honours:* Melodia Award, Czechoslovakia, 1988; L'Ordre des Arts et des Lettres, France, 1995. *Address:* Na Hanspaulce 3, 160 00 Prague, Czech Republic.

PROPHET, Ronnie; b. 26 Dec. 1928, Hawksbury, Ontario, Canada. Entertainer; Musician (guitar); Vocalist. m. Glory-Anne, 26 April 1986, 2 s. *Career:* Duo with wife, Glory-Anne; Ronnie Prophet World Tour; USO tour, England; Germany; Netherlands; Tours with Kenny Rogers; Johnny Cash; Emmylou Harris; Tammy Wynette; Janie Fricke; Appearances include: Calgary Stampede; Wembley Country Music Festival (7 years); Caesar's Palace, Sands Hotel, Las Vegas; Television appearances include: Johnny Carson Show; Co-host, Canadian Country Music Awards, 1988–90; Host, Rocky Mountain Inn; Host, Grand Ole Country (6 years); Host, Ronnie Prophet Show; Host, Music Hall America; Host, Ronnie Prophet Entertains. *Recordings:* 32 albums; The Phantom; No Holiday In LA; Ronnie Prophet, 1977; I'm Gonna Love Him out of You, 1983; Sure Thing, 1987. *Honours:* CCMA, 1976, 1980, 1984; Juno Awards, 1977, 1978; TV Country Show of the Year, Canada, 1977–80; Angel Award, St Jude Children's Research Hospital; ASCAP Awards for 3 songs as chart records for more than 10 weeks each.

Membership: AFofM; ACTRA; ROPE. *Current Management:* Prophet Productions.

PROWSE, Ian; b. 10 Jan. 1967, Ellesmere Port, England. Musician; Songwriter. *Career:* Seven full headline tours as lead singer, songwriter with: Pele; Support tours with: Del Amitri and the Pogues; Numerous television and live radio appearances; 3 Radio 1 playlists; Composed all three Pele albums. *Recordings:* Albums: Pele: Fireworks; The Sport of Kings; Alive, Alive-O. *Membership:* PRS; Musicians' Union. *Current Management:* Target Management, London; D L Management, Liverpool. *Address:* 2 Forge Rd, Little Sutton, Wirral, Cheshire L66 3SQ, England.

PRYCE, Guto; b. 4 Sept. 1972, Cardiff, Wales. Musician (bass guitar). *Career:* Mem., Catatonia, 1992–93; Mem., Super Furry Animals, 1996–; Early releases on small indie label before obtaining major indie label deal; Numerous tours in the UK and internationally; Many festival appearances. *Recordings:* Albums: with Super Furry Animals: Fuzzy Logic, 1996; Radiator, 1997; Guerrilla, 1999; Mwng, 2000; Rings Around The World, 2001. Singles: with Catatonia: For Tinkerbell (EP), 1993; Llanfairpwllgwyngyllchwyndrobwl... (EP), 1995; Moog Droog (EP), 1995; God! Show Me Magic, 1996; If You Don't Want Me To Destroy You, 1996; The Man Don't Give A Fuck, 1996; Hometown Unicorn, 1996; Something 4 The Weekend, 1996; The International Language of Screaming, 1997; Hermann Loves Pauline, 1997; Demons, 1997; Play It Cool, 1997; Ice Hockey Hair, 1998; Northern Lights, 1999; Fire In My Heart, 1999; Do Or Die, 2000; Juxtaposed With U, 2001; Rings Around The World, 2001. *Address:* c/o Epic Records, 550 Madison Ave, New York, NY 10022-3211, USA.

PRZYGODDA, Johannes Pit; b. 2 June 1968, Luthe, Germany. Musician; Composer; Textwriter. *Career:* Some Pieces For Film and Music In Germany, 1980s; Working In Hamburg, With Band, Go Plus, 1990–; Experimental Music, Together With Burkhard Beins, Rudi Mahall, Michal Griener; Making Film Music. *Compositions:* Schwerelos; Definitiv; Song For Brian; Superfreunde. *Recordings:* Go Plus; La Montanara; Largo. *Current Management:* Kitty Yo, Torstrasse 172, 10115 Berlin. *Address:* Oelmuehle 2, 20357 Hamburg, Germany.

PSYCHE. See: **CRAIG, Carl.**

P'TAAH. See: **BRANN, Chris.**

PUEYRREDON, César; b. 7 July 1952, Buenos Aires, Argentina. Vocalist; Composer; Musician (keyboards). m. Cecilia Garcia Laborde, 27 Nov. 1979, 1 s., 1 d. *Education:* University; Composition, UCA (Universidad Católica Argentina). *Career:* Member, group Banana, tours, Argentina, Uruguay, Chile, Paraguay, 1969–84; Tour, Central America, 1977; Solo artiste (as César 'Banana' Pueyrredon), tours, Argentina, Uruguay, Paraguay, Chile, Colombia, 1984–; 12 concerts, Teatro Opera, 1989; Opened for Sting, Uruguay, 1990. *Recordings include:* with Banana: Negra No Te Vayas De Mi Lado, 1971; Conociéndote, 1973; Aún Es Tiempo De Soñar, 1979; Solo albums: Asi De Simple, 1984; Solo Un Poco Mas, 1985; Esta En Vivo, 1986; Mas Cerca De La Vida, 1987; Ser Uno Mismo, 1988; Tarde O Temprano, 1990; Zo Anos, 1991; Armonia, 1992; De La Ternura A La Pasión, 1993. *Honours:* Premio Santa Clara de Asis. *Membership:* SADAIC (composers' society). *Current Management:* Abraxas Producciones Internacionales.

PUFF DADDY. See: **COMBS, Sean.**

PUGACHEVA, Alla Borisovna; b. 5 April 1949, Moscow, USSR. Vocalist. m. (1), (2) Filipp Kirkorov, 1 d. *Education:* M. Ippolitov-Ivanov Music High School; A. Lunacharsky State Institute of Theatrical Arts. *Career:* Debut as soloist of Lipetsk vocal-instrumental group, 1970; Singer with bands, New Electron, Moscovites, Happy Fellows, Oleg Lundstrem Jazz orchestra, 1971; Soloist, Veselye Rebyata Ensemble, 1973–78; Appearances in many films; Several concert programmes; Tours in France, Germany, India, Italy, Switzerland, USA and other countries; Christmas Reunion concerts, 1988–; Founded Song Theatre, 1988, Alla Co., 1993, Alla Magazine, 1993; Repertoire includes: numerous songs by popular Soviet composers such as R. Pauls, A. Muromtsev, A. Zatsepin and others, also songs of her own. *Honours:* Third Prize, All-Union Competition of Pop Artists, Moscow, 1974; Grand Prix International Competition, Golden Orpheus, Bulgaria, 1975; International Festival, Sopot, 1978; USSR People's Artist, Ovation Prize, 1994 (last one awarded); State Prize of Russia, 1995. *Address:* Tverskaya-Yamskaya str., Apt. 57, Moscow, Russia.

PULLEN, Doug; b. 9 April 1957, Loring, Maine, USA. Pop Music Writer. m. Teresa, 1 s. *Education:* Bachelor in Journalism, Texas Technical University, 1975. *Career:* Journalist, El Paso Times; El Paso Herald and Post; Kalamazoo Gazette; Metro Times, Detroit; Flint Journal; MusicHound, rock, country, blues; R&B album guides. *Membership:* National Music Critics Assćn. *Address:* Flint Journal, 200 E First St, Flint, MI 48502, USA.

PULSFORD, Nigel; b. 11 April 1965, Newport, Gwent, Wales. Musician (guitar). *Career:* Former Member, Future Primitive, changed name to Bush;

Obtained major US record deal; Numerous US tours and lots of radio play; UK gigs and festival dates. *Recordings:* Singles: Little Things, 1995; Comedown, 1995; Swallowed, 1997; Greedy Fly, 1997; Cold Contagious, 1999; Albums: Sixteen Stone, 1994; Razorblade Suitcase, 1996; Deconstructed, 1997.

PUOLIS, Rolandas; b. 20 Nov. 1969, Lithuania. Artist Man; Broadcaster. *Education:* Vilnius Technical University. *Career:* Lithuanian radio and television DJ, 1987–92; Manager, rock group BIX, 1991–. *Recordings:* Blind Soldiers, Best Record in Lithuania, 1991; Labomba, 1992; Doozgle, Best CD, Lithuania, 1994. *Honours:* Band of the Year, 1991, 1992, 1994; Science of Things, 2001; Golden State, 2000. *Address:* PO Box 552, 2024 Vilnius, Lithuania.

PURIM, Flora; b. 6 March 1942, Rio De Janeiro, Brazil. m. (1), 1 d., (2) Airto Moreira, 19 March 1972, 1 d. *Education:* University of California, Long Beach; Graduate, California State University. *Recordings:* As composer/lyricist with Airto Moreira: Seeds On The Ground, 1970; Natural Feelings, 1969; Free, 1971; Fingers, 1972; Identity, 1975; Promises of The Sun, 1976; Solo albums: Virgin Land, 1972; Butterfly Dreams, 1973; Stories To Tell, 1974; Open Your Eyes You Can Fly, 1976; 500 Miles High In Montreux, 1976; Encounter, 1977; Nothing Will Be As It Was Tomorrow, 1977; Queen of the Night, 1992; Milestone Memories, 1994; Now Go Ahead and Open Your Eyes, 1994; Speed of Light, 1995; Perpetual Emotion, 2001; Wings Of Imagination, 2001; Sings Nascimento, 2002; with Chick Corea: Return To Forever, 1972; Light As A Feather, 1973; with Carlos Santana: Welcome, 1973; Borboletta, 1974; with Airto Moreira, Neville Potter: San Francisco River, 1972; with McCoy Tyner: Search for Peace, 1974; with George Duke: Love Reborn, 1973; Feel, 1974; with Airto Moreira: Alue, 1969; with Hermeto Pascoal: We Love, 1970; A Brazilian Love Affair; with Ernie Hood: Mountain Train, 1974; with Duke Pearson: How Insensitive, 1969; It Could Only Happen With You, 1970; with Airto and Deodato: Deodato/Airto In Concert, 1973; That's What She Said, Everyday Every Night, Humble People, 1985; The Magicians; The Sun Is Out, 1987; Producer, with Moreira: I'm Fine How Are You, 1977. *Honours:* Downbeat Critics Poll, Established Singer, 1974–76, 1978; Record World, Top Female Jazz Artist, 1974, 1976; Cash Box Award, Top New Female Jazz Artist, 1974. *Current Management:* A Train Management, PO Box 29242, Oakland, CA 94604, USA.

PURPOSE MAKER. See: **MILLS, Jeff.**

Q

Q-TIP, (John William Davis), (The Lone Ranger); b. 20 Nov. 1970, Brooklyn, NY, USA. Rap Artiste. *Career:* Founded A Tribe Called Quest, 1988; Part of the Native Tongues collective with De La Soul and Queen Latifah; Collaborations: Lucy Pearl; Slick Rick; Mos Def; Jay-Z; Janet Jackson; Deee-Lite. *Recordings:* Albums: with A Tribe Called Quest: People's Instinctive Travels and The Paths of Rhythm, 1990; The Low End Theory, 1991; Midnight Marauders, 1993; Beats Rhymes and Life, 1996; The Love Movement, 1998; solo: Amplified, 1999; Singles: with A Tribe Called Quest: Description of a Fool, 1989; Bonita Applebum, 1990; Can I Kick It?, 1990; Scenario, 1992; Award Tour, 1993; 1nce Again, 1996; Find A Way, 1998; Stressed Out, 1998; solo: Vibrant Thing, 1999; Breathe and Stop, 1999. *Address:* c/o Arista Records, Cavendish House, 423 New King's Rd, London SW6 4RN, England.

QUATRO, Suzi, (Susan Kay); b. 3 June 1950, Detroit, MI, USA. Vocalist; Songwriter; Musician (bass, drums, piano); Actor; Presenter. m. (1) Len Tuckey; (2) Rainer Haas, 22 Oct. 1992, 1 s., 1 d. *Career:* Over 30 years as entertainer, 1964–; Numerous world-wide concert tours and stage appearances; Various acting, presenting and voiceover work on radio and TV including: Chat show, ITV; Happy Days; Annie Get Your Gun (West End); Author and star of stage musical about Tallulah Bankhead, Tallulah Who; Presenter, Rockin' With Suzi Q, BBC Radio 2, 1998–; Subject of This Is Your Life, 1999. *Recordings:* 16 hit singles include: Can The Can (No. 1, UK), 1973; 48 Crash, 1973; Daytona Demon, 1973; Devil Gate Drive (No. 1, UK), 1974; The Wild One, 1974; If You Can't Give Me Love, 1978; Stumblin' In, with Chris Norman, 1978; She's In Love With You, 1979; Albums include: Suzi Quatro, 1973; Quatro, 1974; Your Mama Won't Like Me, 1975; Aggro Phobia, 1977; If You Knew Suzi, 1978; Suzi and Other 4 Letter Words, 1979; Rock Hard, 1980; Greatest Hits, 1980; Main Attraction, 1982; The Wild One, 1990; Oh Suzi Q, 1990; The Latest and Greatest, 1992; Unreleased Emotion, 1998; The Best of Suzi Quatro, 1998; Original Hits, 2000; Naked Under Leather, 2001. *Honours:* Numerous Best Female Artist Awards, UK, Europe, Australia, Japan.

QUAYE, Finley; b. 1974, Edinburgh, Scotland. Vocalist. *Education:* BTEC in Music Production, Manchester. *Career:* Worked with: A Guy Called Gerald; Graham Massey; Rainbow Tribe; Solo artiste, 1996–. *Recordings:* Albums: Maverick A Strike, 1997; Vanguard, 2000; Singles: Ultra Stimulation (EP), 1997; Sunday Shining (EP), 1997; Even After All, 1997; It's Great When We're Together, 1997; Your Love Gets Sweeter, 1998; Spiritualized, 2000. *Honours:* BRIT Award, Best Male Solo Artist, 1998. *Address:* c/o Epic Records, 10 Great Marlborough St, London W1V 2LP, England.

QUEEN BEE. See: **LIL' KIM.**

QUEEN LATIFAH, (Dana Owens); b. 18 March 1970, East Orange, NJ, USA. Rap Vocalist. *Career:* Worked with female rap act, Ladies Fresh; Recorded with producers Dady-O, KRS-1, DJ Mark the 45 King and members of De La Soul; Moved to Motown Records; Began acting career with film Living Single; Other film appearances incl.: Jungle Fever, 1991; House Party 2, 1991; Juice, 1992; My Life, 1993; Set It Off, 1996; Hoodlum, 1997; Sphere, 1998; Living Out Loud, 1998; The Bone Collector, 1999; Bringing Out the Dead, 1999; The Country Bears, 2002; Brown Sugar, 2002; Chicago, 2002; Bringing Down the House, 2003; Established own label and management company, Flavor Unit; Guest appearance on Shabba Ranks's single, Watcha Gonna Do; Other recording collaborations with De La Soul and Monie Love. *Recordings:* Singles: Wrath Of My Madness, 1990; How Do I Love Thee, 1990; Ladies First, 1990; Mama Gave Birth To The Soul Children, 1990; Find A Way, with Coldcut, 1990; Come Into My House, 1993; U.N.I.T.Y., EP, 1994; Just Another Day, EP, 1994; Mr Big Stuff, 1997; It's Alright, 1997; Paper, 1998. Albums: All Hail The Queen, 1989; Latifah's Had It Up 2 Here, 1989; Nature Of A Sista, 1991; Black Reign, 1993; Queen Latifah and Original Flava Unit, 1996; Order In The Court, 1998.

QUERALT, Stephen Paul; b. 4 Feb. 1968, Oxford, England. Musician (bass guitar). 1 s. *Career:* Bass guitarist, rock band Ride; Concerts include: Main support act, Reading Festival, 1992; Television: 3 appearances, Top of the Pops, BBC; Recorded 2 Top 10 albums and 1 Top 20 album. *Recordings:* Singles: with Ride: Ride EP, 1990; Play EP, 1990; Fall EP, 1990; Today Forever, 1991; Leave Them All Behind, 1992; Twisterella, 1992; Birdman, 1994; Albums: with Ride: Nowhere, 1991; Going Blank Again, Ride, 1992; Carnival of Light, Ride, 1994; Live Light, 1995; Tarantula, 1996; Poptopia! 90s Power Pop Classics, 1997; OX4, 2001; with Sharks Patrol These Waters: Sharks Patrol These Waters, 1995. *Current Management:* Ben Winchester, Primary Talent. *Address:* OMC, Suite 1, 2nd Floor, 65 George St, Oxford OX1 2BE, England.

QUIBEL, Robert Henri Maurice; b. 12 Oct. 1930, Le Havre, France. Musician (double bass); Arranger; Dir. m. Madeleine Saumon, 23 March 1955, 1 s., 1 d. *Education:* Petit Séminaire de Rouen. *Career:* Bass player with Berny Bennett; Jacques Helian; Claude Bolling, 1961–63; Backing for various French artistes including: Maurice Fanon; Jacques Martin; Musical director, director of house band on Dimanche-Matin, weekly French TV programme (France 2), 1980–. *Recordings:* The Flight of The Ox-Pecker, Claude Bolling, 1963; Various recordings for children include: Le Petit Ménestral, Lucien Adès; Various title songs and jingles for Dimanche-Matin. *Honours:* Grand Prix de la Chanson Comique, Les Cuisses de Grenouille by Fernand Raynaud, 1965. *Membership:* SACEM; SDRM; SACD. *Address:* 2 rue Ronsard, 95560 Baillet-En-France, France.

QUILLEY, Denis Clifford; b. 26 Dec. 1927, Islington, London, England. Actor; Vocalist. m. Stella Chapman, 27 Aug. 1949, 1 s., 2 d. *Education:* Studied singing with Ernst Urbach. *Career:* Candide, West End Production; The Boys from Syracuse; Privates on Parade, Piccadilly Theatre; La Cage aux Folles, Palladium; Non-musical work includes: Many seasons at National Theatre; Peter Hall season at The Old vic; National Theatre Season; Films: Masada; Evil Under the Sun; Murder on the Orient Express; Privates on Parade. *Recordings:* Grab Me A Gondola; Boys from Syracuse; High Spirits; Mark and Mabel in Concert at Drury Lane; Showboat; Shows Collection; BBC's Tribute to Jerry Herman; Candide (London Cast Recording), 2000. *Honours:* SWET Award for Comedy Performance of the Year for Privates on Parade. *Current Management:* Bernard Hunter. *Address:* 22 Willow Rd, Hampstead, London NW3 1TL, England.

QUILLIVIC, Jean; b. 10 Jan. 1960, Rabat, Morocco. Composer; Musician (saxophone). m. Josiame Robakowski, 2 s., 2 d. *Education:* BA, Sciences, Brest; BA, MA, Musicology, Paris. *Career:* CIM School of Jazz, Paris, 1985; First alto saxophone in Pierre Sellin Big Band, 1985–; Formed group Oxyde de Cuivre, 1987; Formed own group Jean Quillivic Quartet, 1988; Concerts in festivals, summer tours, 1989–. *Recordings:* Prise de Bec, Zap, 1989; La Femme à La Valise, Jean Quillivic Quartet, 1990; En Public Au Fourneau 95, Oxyde de Cuivre, 1995. *Membership:* SACEM. *Current Management:* Promoart. *Address:* B P 27, 29470 Plougastel, Dadulas, France.

QUIN, Andrew James; b. 12 Aug. 1960, London, England. Composer; Musician (keyboards, percussion); Music Lecturer. m. Anne Perrett, 20 Aug. 1983, 1 s., 1 d. *Education:* BA, Music, Electronics, Keele University, 1982. *Career:* 25 albums for Dewolfe, 1984–; Freelance lecturer, Music Technology, universities and conservatories throughout UK; Currently Manchester Metropolitan University; Regular jazz performer in Midlands; Broadcasts in 36 countries, all continents; Television documentary, Quest, 1985. *Recordings:* Albums: Mirage, 1985; The Cutting Edge, 1987; Four Minus One, 1988; The Corporate Net, 1995; Colours Of Classical Piano, 1997; Television themes: Something To Treasure, 1988; Central Weekend, 1985; Scandal, 1988; Commercials: Fairy Snow, 1989; Canderel, 1990; Webster's Bitter, 1991; Lynx Deodorant, 1992. *Membership:* Musicians' Union; PRS; APC. *Current Management:* De Wolfe Ltd. *Address:* De Wolfe Ltd, 80–88 Wardour St, London W1V 3LF, England.

QUINCY, Dave; b. 13 Sept. 1939, Battle, Sussex, England. Musician (saxophone); Composer; Music Publisher. m. Patricia Ann (Patti) Quincy, 1 d. with second wife (3 marriages). *Career:* First tour, Little Richard, Sam Cooke, 1962; British tour as member of Jet Harris' group (ex-Shadows); Extensive tours with rock and jazz groups, 1960s; Began recording with band IF, 1969; Material now to be released in compilation album, Forgotten Roads, 1995; Work, tours, recordings, many Jazz Fusion projects. *Compositions:* Material in IF compilation, 1995. *Recordings:* IF, Vols 1–4, 1969–72. *Membership:* PRS; BAC&S; MCPS; Musicians' Union; Jazz Umbrella.

QUINN, Edwin Henry; b. 17 July 1963, Portsmouth, Hampshire, England. Musician (drums). 1 s., 1 d. *Education:* School lessons, orchestras and bands. *Career:* Member of Dakinis, with various session work; Drummer, indie band Blow Up, 1990–92; Tours of UK and Paris showcase concerts; Video for single, World, filmed for Music Box, MTV Europe. *Recordings:* Album: Amazon Eyegasm, 1991; Single: World. *Current Management:* Sarah Heyworth Independent PR. *Address:* 67 Cobden Rd, Brighton, East Sussex BN2 2TJ, England.

QUINN, Eimear; b. 18 Dec. 1972, Dublin, Ireland. Vocalist. *Education:* Degrees in Town Planning and Music; Piano Lessons; Degree in Music Studies. *Career:* Lead Voice with Anuna Vocal Group; Vocalist with Anuna, Irish Mediaeval Vocal Group; Sang Lead in London with Riverdance The

Show; Toured Australia and Scandinavia as solo act. *Recordings:* The Voice, Eurovision Winner, 1996; Winter, Fire and Snow (EP), 1996; Caccini's Ave Maria; Omnis, with Anuna, 1996; Through The Lens Of A Tear, 2002. *Honours:* Winner, Eurovision Song Contest, Oslo, 1996. *Current Management:* 24 Merchants Quay, Dublin 8, Ireland.

QUINN, Mick; b. 17 Dec. 1969. Musician (bass guitar). *Career:* Member, Supergrass, 1994–; Concerts include: Support to Blur, Alexandra Palace; British tour, with Shed Seven, 1994; T In The Park Festival, Glasgow, 1995.

Recordings: Album: I Should Coco (No. 1, UK), 1995; In It For The Money (reached No 2), 1997; Supergrass, 1999; B-Side Trax, 2000; Life On Other Planets, 2002. Singles: Caught By The Fuzz, 1994; Mansize Rooster, 1995; Lenny, 1995; Alright (No. 2, UK), 1995; Going Out, 1996; Richard III (No. 2, UK), 1997; Sun Hits The Sky, 1997; Late In The Day, 1997; Pumping on Your Stereo, 1999; Moving, 1999; Mary, 2000; Grace, 2002. *Honours:* Q Award, Best New Act, 1995. *Current Management:* Courtyard Management, 22 The Nursery, Sutton Courtenay, Abingdon, Oxfordshire OX14 4UA, England. *Website:* www.supergrass.com.

R

RABIN, Trevor; b. 13 Jan. 1954, Johannesburg, South Africa. Musician (guitar, keyboards); Songwriter; Record Prod. m. Shelley May, 17 Aug. 1979, 1 s. *Education:* Orchestration with Walter Mony; 8 years of piano studies. *Career:* Formed band, Rabbitt, age 14; Several tours, film and television appearances; Moved to England, 1977; Solo artiste, tours and television, 1977–; Member, progressive rock group, Yes, 1982–; International concerts include: US tour, 1987; Yesshows tour, 1991; Wembley Arena, 1991. *Compositions include:* Films: The Glimmer Man, 1996; Con Air, 1997; Enemy of the State, 1998; Homegrown, 1998; Armageddon, 1998; Jack Frost, 1998; Whispers, 1999; Deep Blue Sea, 1999; Whispers: An Elephant's Tale, 2000; Gone in Sixty Seconds, 2000; The 6th Day, 2000; Remembering the Titans, 2000; American Outlaws, 2001; The One, 2002; Other: Owner of a Lonely Heart; Yes (world-wide No. 1 hit). *Recordings:* Albums: Solo: Trevor Rabin, 1978; Face To Face, 1979; Wolf, 1981; Can't Look Away, 1989; 2 albums with Rabbitt; with Yes: 90125, 1983; 9012 Live – The Solos, 1986; The Big Generator, 1987; Union, 1991; Yesstory, 1991; Hit singles with Yes: Owner of a Lonely Heart; Leave It; It Can Happen; Rhythm of Love; Lift Me Up. *Publications:* Instructional guitar video. *Honours:* Grammy Award, Best Instrumental Performance, Cinema, 1985. *Membership:* AFTRA; Musicians' Union. *Current Management:* Tony Dimitriades, East End Management. *Address:* 8209 Melrose Ave, Second Floor, Los Angeles, CA 90046, USA.

RABINOWITZ, Harry; b. 26 March 1916, South Africa. Conductor; Composer; Musical Dir. m. (1) Lorna Thurlow Anderson, 15 Dec. 1944, divorced 2000, 2 d., 1 s., (2) Mary C. Scott, 18 March 2001. *Education:* University of the Witwatersrand; Guildhall School of Music, London. *Career:* Corporal, SA Forces, 1942–43; Conductor, BBC Radio, 1953–60; Head of Music, BBC Television Light Entertainment, 1960–68; LWT, 1968–77; Freelance conductor, composer; Conductor: Hollywood Bowl, 1983–84, Boston Pops, 1985–92, London Symphony Orchestra, Royal Philharmonic Orchestra, Carnegie Hall, 1996, Merchant Ivory 35th Anniversary Celebration; Conductor for films: Chariots of Fire; Manhattan Project; Heat and Dust; The Bostonians; Maurice; Time Bandits; Return to Oz; L'Argent; Camille Claudel; Ballad of the Sad Café; J'Embrasse Pas; La Voix; Pour Sacha; Les Carnassiers; Howard's End; The Ark and the Flood; Tractions; The Remains of the Day; Shirley Valentine; Business Affair; Grosse Fatigue; Le Petit Garçon; The Flemish Board; Mantegna et Fils; La Fille de d'Artagnan; Death and the Maiden; Jefferson in Paris; Nelly and Mr Arnold; Secret Agent; The Stupids; The Proprietor; Star Command; La Belle Verte; Surviving Picasso; The English Patient; Tonka; Amour Sorcier; My Story So Far; City of Angels; Place Vendôme; A Soldier's Daughter Never Cries; Message in a Bottle; Cotton Mary, 1999; The Talented Mr Ripley, 2000; The Golden Bowl, 2000; Possession, 2001; The Music Box; Le Divorce, 2002; Bon Voyage, 2003; Conductor for television: New Faces, 1987–88; Paul Nicholas Special, 1987–88; Julia MacKenzie Special, 1986; Nicholas Nickleby; Drummonds; The Insurance Man; Absent Friends; Simon Wiesenthal Story; Marti Caine Special; Alien Empire; Battle of the Sexes; Conductor for theatre: World premieres of Cats, Song and Dance. *Recordings:* As Time Goes By, 1992; Battle Of The Sexes, 1999; The Music Of Duke Ellington (with Johnny Mathis); The Music Of George Gershwin (with Jack Jones); Radio City Christmas Album; Phil Woods: I Remember; Collaborated with: Michael Crawford, Sarah Brightman, José Carreras, Vangelis, Dave Grusin. *Compositions:* Reilly Ace of Spies; Agatha Christie Hour; The Great Depression; Memento Mori; D. W. Griffiths, Father of Film. *Honours:* MBE, 1978; BASCA Gold Award, 1986; Radio and Television Industries Award, 1984; Allmusic Lifetime Contribution Gold Award, 1990; Freeman City of London, 1996. *Membership:* Composers' Guild; BAC&S. *Address:* 11 Mead Rd, Cranleigh, Surrey GU6 7BG, England. *Telephone:* (1483) 278676. *E-mail:* mitziscott@aol.com.

RADCLIFFE, Mark; b. 1958, Bolton, Lancashire, England. DJ; Presenter. m. 1 c. *Education:* English and American Studies, Classic Civilization, Manchester University. *Career:* Jr Asst Prod., Piccadilly Radio, Manchester, 1979; Producer, Radio 1, Saturday Live and John Peel session, 1983; Head of Music, Piccadilly Radio, 1985; Began DJ work; Popular Music Producer, BBC North, including Martin Kelner on Radio 2 and In Concert series for Radio 1; Presenter, Hit the North evening programme, Radio 5, 1990; Out on Blue Six, indie show, 1991; Returned to Radio 1, 4 evenings weekly show, 1993; Stand-in, Radio 1 Breakfast Show with Lard, 1996; Breakfast Show presenter, 1997; Afternoon show, Radio 1, 1998–; Other radio work includes: How Tickled Am I, BBC Radio 4, 1999–; Hope I Die Before I Get Old, BBC Radio 2, 1999–2000; Heroes Or Zeroes, BBC Radio 2, 2001; TV work includes: Pop Upstairs Downstairs, UK Play, 1998; Next, BSkyB, 2001; Match Of The Nineties, BBC, 2001; Drums/vocals for the Shirehorses, 1996–. *Recordings:* The Worst Album In The World Ever….Ever!, 1997. *Honours:* Sony Radio Award, Best Specialist Music Programme, 1992. *Address:* c/o BBC Radio 1, London W1N 4DJ, England. *Website:* www.bbc.co.uk/radio1.

RADLEY, Kate; b. 19 Feb. 1965. Musician (keyboards). m. Richard Ashcroft. *Career:* Member, Spiritualized; Numerous live dates including world tour; Concerts at Royal Albert Hall, London and CN Tower, Toronto, Canada; Left band, 1999; Worked on Richard Ashcroft's solo album, Alone With Everybody, 2000. *Recordings:* Singles: Anyway That You Want Me, 1991; Run, 1991; Let It Flow, 1995; Electricity, 1997; I Think I'm In Love, 1998; Abbey Road EP, 1998; Album: Ladies And Gentlemen We Are Floating In Space, 1997.

RAE, Dashiell; b. 10 Jan. 1956, New Jersey, USA. Composer; Musician (flute, piano); Vocalist. *Education:* Eastman School of Music, New York. *Career:* Orchestral musician, principal flautist, soloist, New York; Moved to London, 1985; Worked with Julia Fordham (keyboards, flute, backing vocals), 1989–; Worked with: Level 42; The Style Council; Womack and Womack; Midge Ure; Aztec Camera; Paul Young; Colin Towns; Became composer film and television music, 1992. *Compositions include:* Film: Keys; The Queen's House; The Docket Box; Tea and Bullets; Television: Hidden Hands; Art and The CIA, CH4; The Dream, BBC Wales; Children's Ward, Granada; Last Days At Forchwen, BBC Wales; Touch, BBC Wales; Commercials: Onken Yogurt, 1994; Various: Sky Sport, 1993; Anglia, Survival, 1994; Channel Islands TV News Theme, 1994–; Promos for BBC, ITV; Classical. *Compositions:* La Chasse (piano duet); Misere (string orchestra). *Recordings include:* Solo piano album: Songs Without Words, 1985; Also appears on: Rattled, with Rattlers, 1985; Swept, with Julia Fordham, 1991; Wings of the Dove, 1997. *Membership:* Musicians' Union; PRS; Equity (UK); AFTRA; ASCAP; Women in Film and TV (UK). *Current Management:* Soundtrack Music Management, 22 Ives St, London SW3 2ND, England.

RAESIDE, Diane Lesley Cameron; b. Scarborough, Ontario, Canada. Country/Blues Vocalist. *Education:* Canadian Academy for the Performing Arts, Ian Garrett. *Career:* Professional singer from age 18; Concert appearances throughout Ontario, and Zevenbergen Festival, Netherlands, 1995; Television appearance: Be A Star, Nashville Network. *Recordings:* Album: Crazy Infatuation, 1992; Since You Went Away, 1995; Singles: Turning Into Strangers; Half A Heart; I'll Cry About That Tomorrow; Run For Your Money; Just Another Day; Take Me In Your Arms Tonight; Love Is Where The Good Times Are; Crazy Infatuation; Last Date; Some Rivers Run Dry; Slow Dance; This Time of Year, Singing Songs of Love (All-star charity single). *Honours:* Labatts-Guinness Travel Bursary; Numerous Song Contests; RPM Big Country Award, Outstanding New Artist, 1992. *Membership:* Songwriters Asscn; Canadian Country Music Asscn. *Address:* 23 Timgren Dr., Scarborough, ON M1R 3R4, Canada.

RAFFERTY, Gerry; b. 16 April 1947, Paisley, Scotland. Vocalist; Songwriter; Musician (guitar). *Career:* Member, The Humblebums, 1968–70; Founder member, Stealers Wheel, 1972–75; Solo artist, 1978–. *Recordings:* Albums: with the Humblebums: The New Humblebums, 1969; Open Up The Door, 1970; with Stealers Wheel: Stealers Wheel, 1973; Solo albums: Can I Have My Money Back?, 1971; City To City, 1978; Night Owl, 1979; Snakes and Ladders, 1980; Sleepwalking, 1982; North and South, 1988; Right Down The Line – The Best of Gerry Rafferty, 1990; A Wing and A Prayer, 1993; Over My Head, 1995; Clowns to the Left, Jokers to the Right, 1997; Don't Count Me Out, 1998; Baker Street, 1999; Greatest Hits and More, 2001; Singles include: with Stealers Wheel: Stuck In The Middle With You, 1973; Solo: Baker Street (No. 2, USA), 1978; Right Down The Line, 1978; Home and Dry, 1979; Night Owl, 1980; Days Gone Down (Still Got The Light In Your Eyes), 1980; Get It Right Next Time, 1980; Contributor, film soundtrack Local Hero, with Mark Knopfler, 1983; Producer, Letter From America, The Proclaimers, 1987. *Honours:* 2 Ivor Novello Awards, Best Song, Best Pop Song, 1979. *Address:* c/o Asgard Agency, 125 Parkway, London NW1 7PS, England.

RAFFIT, Jean-Paul; b. 2 Aug. 1964, Patiers, France. Musician (guitar). *Education:* First year university; 3 years with private guitar teacher. *Career:* Jazz festivals: Montréal with B Sandoval; Kalamata (Greece) with B Sandoval; Dortmund; Bonn; Frankfurt; Petit Journal; Passage Nordouest; Cartou Cherie; Television: Nulle Part Ailleurs (Canal+) with Eric Lareine; Cercle de Minuit (France 2). *Recordings:* Albums: with B Sandoval: Camino del Alba, 1992; Caracola, 1993; Vida, 1994; Album with S Lopez, 1993; All The Generics, 1994–95; Graffiti (with 9 original compositions), 1995; Antenne Ouverte A La Conscience (video). *Publications:* Jean-Paul Raffit, Un Amour de Guitare, 1995; Flash, 1995. *Honours:* ffff (telerada) for Vida (album with B Sandoval). *Membership:* SACEM; SPEDIDAM. *Current Management:* Michel Guilhem. *Address:* Plaisance, 09100 Madiere, France.

RAFIATOU, Fifi, (Rafiatou Bellow-Adjani); b. 2 Oct. 1963, Atakpame, Togo. Vocalist; Composer. 1 s., 1 d. *Career:* Backing singer in Togo; Member, National Presbyterian Choir; International concerts with Papa Wemba; Alpha Blondy; Ossibissa; Miriam Makeba; Masa; Performed at St Martin Black

Festival. *Compositions:* Ibama; Ahe; Ile; Wawa; Ikoule. *Publications:* Priere Pour La Paix, 1980; Nwassa, 1985; Djofe, 1990; Motus, 1997. *Honours:* Pan-African Fair of Art and Music Award, 1990; First Prize, Afrovision, 1991; Spring Festival of Dion-Yang. *Membership:* SACEM; ADAMI. *Current Management:* c/o Georges Konila Figah, Discorama Production, PO Box 12629 Lomé, Togo.

RAHMAN, A(llah) R(akha), (A. S. Dileep Kumar); b. 6 Jan. 1966, Chennai, India. Vocalist; Musician (keyboards); Composer. *Education:* Western Classical Music, Trinity College of Music, Oxford University. *Career:* Son of well-known film music director K. A. Sekar; Converted to Islam, adopting the name A. R. Rahman, 1988; Performed with Illaiyaraja's troupe, aged 11; Later with the orchestra of M. S. Vishwanathan and Ramesh Naidu; Accompanied Zakir Hussain and Kunnakudi Vaidanathan on world tours; Career in advertising; Composed more than 300 jingles winning many awards; Also won award for the theme music to Madras Telegu Academy's Spirit of Unity Concerts; Established studio, Panchathan Record Inn, 1989, developed into one of India's most advanced recording studios; Collaborations include: Nusrat Fateh Aki Kahn; Apache Indian; L. Shankar; Zakir Hussain; Kunnakudi Vaidyanathan; Kadri Gopalnath; Vikku Vinayakram; David Byrne; Talvin Singh. *Compositions:* Over 60 films, incl.: Roja, 1992; Pudhiya Mugaml; Gentleman; Kizhaku Seemaiyilae; Duet; May Maadham; Kadhal Desam; Dil Se..; Mani Ratham; Taal; Lagaan; Fiza; Bombay; Legend of Bhagat Singh, 2002; Musical: Bombay Dreams, 2001. *Recordings:* Albums include: Deen Isai Malai, 1988; Set Me Free, 1992; Vande Mataram, 1997; Jana Gana Mana, Live In Dubai, 2000; soundtracks include: Roja, Vaishnavar, 1992; Uzhavan, Thiruda, Thiruda, Pudhiya Mugam, Kizhakku Cheemayilae, Nippu Ravva, Mawaali Raj, Gentleman, Ashokan, 1993; Duet, Kadhalan, Karuthamma, May Maadham, Pavithra, Super Police, Vandicholai Chinraasu, 1994; Bombay, Gang Master, Indira, Muthu, Rangeela, 1995; Anthimandaari, Fire, Indhiyan, Love Birds, Mr Romeo, 1996; Daud, Iddaru, Iruvar, Kabhi Na Kabhi, Minsaara Kanavu, Ratchakan, 1997; 1947/Earth, Dil Se..., Doli Saja Ke Rakhna, Jeans, 1998; En Swasa Kaatre, Kadhalar Dhinam, Muthalvan, Padaiyappa, Pukar, Sangamam, Taal, Thakshak, 1999; Alai Payuthey, Kandukondain Kandukondain, Rhythm, Thenaali, Zubeidaa, 2000; Alli Arjuna, Lagaan, One 2 Ka 4, Parthale Paravasam, Star, 2001; Bombay Dreams, 2002. *Honours:* SuMu Music Award, 1993; R. D. Burman Awards, 1993, 1995; National Awards, Roja, 1993, Best Music Direction, Minsara Kanavu, 1998; Filmfare Awards, 1992–2002; Screen-Videocon Awards, Kadhal Desam, 1997, Minsara Kanavu, Vande Mataram, 1998, Taal, 2000; Cinema Express Awards, Roja, 1993, Gentleman, 1994, Kadhalan, 1995, Kadhal Desam, 1997, Jeans, 1999; Zee Awards, Zee Sangeet Award, Dil Se.., 1999, Zee Cine Award, Taal, 2000, Zee Gold Bollywood Award, Taal, 2000; MTV-VMA Award, Dil Se Re (from Dil Se..), 1999; International India Film Award, Taal, 2000; Padma Shree Award. *Website:* www.arrahman.com.

RAIMON, (Raimon Pelegero Sanchis); b. 2 Dec. 1940, Xàtiva, Spain. Vocalist; Songwriter. m. Annalisa Corti, 22 Aug. 1966. *Education:* University Graduate, Contemporary History; Elemental studies. *Career:* Tours: France, Mexico; USA; Argentina; Japan; Concerts include: Olympia Theatre, Paris, 1966, 1969, 1974; Teatro Español, Madrid, 1988; Many appearances, Barcelona, Valencia; Television includes: Especial Raimon, TVE, 1984; Raimon previously banned during Franco Dictatorship to 1977; Live broadcast, Festival of La Mercè, Barcelona, 1987; Live recital, Raimon, 30 Anys d'al Vent, Barcelona, TV3, TVE2, 1993. *Compositions include:* Al Vent; Diguem No; Jo Vinc d'un Silenci; Com Un Puny. *Recordings include:* Raimon, 1963, 1964; A L'Olympia, 1966; Diguem No, 1971; Catalonian Protest Songs, 1971; T'Adones Amic, 1974; Raimon, 1977; Quan L'Aigua Es Queixa, 1980; Entre La Nota I El So, 1984; Canta Ausiàs March, 1989; Cançons, 1993; Integral, 1993; Spain, 1994; Cancons, 1996; Anthology of 120 Songs, 1996. *Publications:* Canzoni Contro, 1971; Poemes I Cançons, 1973; Poemas y Canciones, 1976; Les Hores Guanyades, 1983; D'Aquest Viure Insistent, 1986; Les Paraules Del Meu Cant, 1993. *Honours:* Grand Prix Francis Carco, Académie Du Disque, Paris, 1967; City of Barcelona Prize, 1982; Fundació Jaume Primer, Barcelona, 1987; Aportació Musical, Valencia, 1993; The Best Show of the Year, Barcelona, 1994; Premi Nacional de Música, 1993; Grand Prix, Nouvelle Academie Du Disque, Integral Raimon, France, 1994. *Current Management:* Annalisa Corti. *Address:* Plaça Bonsuccès, 7 atc 2a, 08001, Barcelona, Spain.

RAINEY, Ron Paul; b. 3 Feb. 1946, East Stroudsburg, Pennsylvania, USA. Artist Man. *Career:* Concert agent, International Famous Agency (now International Creative Management), New York City, 1969–71; Vice-President, concert department, Agency For The Performing Arts, New York City and Los Angeles, 1971–73; Chairman, chief executive officer, Magna Artists Corporation, Los Angeles, 1974–81; President, chief executive officer, Ron Rainey Management Inc, Beverly Hills, California, 1981–. *Address:* 315 S Beverly Dr., Suite 206, Beverly Hills, CA 90212, USA.

RAINWATER, Keech; b. 24 Jan. 1963, Plano, Texas, USA. Country Musician (drums, banjo, percussion). *Career:* Had minor hits on independent label 16th Avenue as member of Canyon, 1988–90; Formed Texasee with Dean Sams, Richie McDonald, Michael Britt and John Rich, 1992; Group became resident house band at the Wildhorse Saloon, Nashville; After

subsequent name change to Lonestar, came to the attention of BMG and were signed to their BNA subsidiary; Released promotional six-track live CD, recorded at the Wildhorse; First country chart entry No News/Tequila Talkin' from debut album Lonestar, 1996; Single, Amazed, from third album became huge international hit and career record to date, 1999; By early 2000s, Lonestar estimated to be the most successful country group in the world. *Recordings include:* No News, Tequila Talkin', 1996; Come Cryin' To Me, You Walked In, 1997; Say When, Everything's Changed, 1998; Amazed, Smile, 1999; I'm Already There, 2002; Albums include: Lonestar, 1995; Crazy Nights, 1997; Lonely Grill, 1999; I'm Already There, 2001. *Address:* c/o Country Music Asscn, 1 Music Circle S, Nashville, TN 37203, USA.

RAITT, Bonnie Lynn; b. 8 Nov. 1949, Burbank, CA, USA. Musician (guitar, piano). *Education:* Radcliffe College. *Career:* Performer, blues clubs, USA East Coast; Concerts include: MUSE concert, Madison Square Garden with Bruce Springsteen, Jackson Browne, Carly Simon, The Doobie Brothers, 1979; Roy Orbison Tribute Concert with artists including: Whoopi Goldberg; kd lang; Bob Dylan; B B King, 1990; Performances with artists including: Stevie Wonder, Bruce Springsteen, Aretha Franklin, Willie Nelson, Elton John; Recorded with: Altan; Paul Brady; Jackson Browne; The Chieftains; Vince Gill; Emmylou Harris; John Hiatt; John Lee Hooker; The Judds; B. B. King; Sonny Landreth; Little Feat; Maria Muldaur; John Prine; Roy Orbison. *Recordings:* Albums include: Bonnie Raitt, 1971; Give It Up, 1972; Takin' My Time, 1973; Streetlights, 1974; Home Plate, 1975; Sweet Forgiveness, 1977; The Glow, 1979; Green Light, 1982; Nine Lives, 1986; Nick of Time, 1989; The Bonnie Raitt Collection, 1990; Luck of The Draw, 1991; Road Tested, 1995; Fundamental, 1998; Silver Lining, 2002. Singles include: Something to Talk About, 1991; Not the Only One, 1992; Burning Down the House, 1996. *Honours:* Nine Grammy Awards, incl. Album of Year; Best Rock Vocal Performance; Best Female Pop Vocal Performance; Best Traditional Blues Performance (with John Lee Hooker).

RAITT, John Emmet; b. 29 Jan. 1917, Santa Ana, California, USA. Actor; Vocalist. m. Rosemary Kraemer, 2 s., 1 d. *Education:* BA University of Redlands, California; Private music lessons. *Career:* Oklahoma; Carousel; 3 Wishes For Jamie; Magdelena; Carnival In Flanders; Pajama Game (Broadway and film); Annie Get Your Gun; Zorba; On A Clear Day; Summer Chevy Show; Bell Telephone Hour; 25 Years of Summer Stock; Concerts: A Joyful Noise – Musical Jubilee. *Recordings:* Oklahoma; Carousel 1945, 1965; Showboat; Highlights of Broadway; The Best of John Raitt; Broadway Legend; Under Open Skies; Mediterranean Magic; 3 Wishes For Jamie; Annie Get Your Gun. *Honours:* Hon Dr, University of Redlands and Pepperdine and Boston Conservatory; Theater Hall of Fame, New York; Hollywood Walk of Fame. *Current Management:* James Fitzgerald Ent. *Address:* 4300 Prominade Way #121 P, Marina Del Rey, CA90292, USA.

RAKSIN, David; b. 4 Aug. 1912, Philadelphia, Pennsylvania, USA. Composer; Conductor; Author; Prof. m. Joanne Kaiser, 19 Sept. 1959, divorced, 2 s., 1 d. *Education:* University of Pennsylvania; Private music lessons with William Happich, Harl McDonald, Isador Freed, Arnold Schoenberg. *Career:* Went to Hollywood, worked with Charlie Chaplin, music for Modern Times, 1935; Scored over 100 films, including: Laura; The Bad and The Beautiful; Several hundred radio shows; Approximately 400 television programmes; Conducted major orchestras. *Compositions:* Music from films: Laura; Forever Amber; The Bad and The Beautiful; Composed text and music, conducted premiere of Oedipus Memneitai (Coolidge Commission from Library of Congress). *Publications:* 7 articles published by Library of Congress; Book of Songs, 1996. *Honours:* Career achievement awards from: ASCAP; Composers and Lyricists Guild. *Membership:* President, Composers and Lyricists Guild of America; Board of Directors, ASCAP; President, Society for Preservation of Film Music (appointed by the Librarian at Congress to the National Film Preservation Board).

RALPH, Mark; b. 2 May 1974, Stoke-on-Trent, Staffordshire, England. Musician (guitar). *Career:* Long term member of Max The Sax, 12-piece jazz funk band; Featured on We Are Family by Sister Sledge, 1993 remixes; Worked with Sure Is Pure, on further dance remixes. *Recordings:* We Are Family, Sister Sledge; Lost In Music, Sister Sledge; Manha De Brasil, Max The Sax; Reload, Tom Jones, 1999; Nightlife, Pet Shop Boys, 1999. *Current Management:* Nigel Woodcock. *Address:* 73 Rothesay Ave, Newcastle-under-Lyme, Staffordshire ST5 2LQ, England.

RALPHES, Paul Stuart; b. 23 Feb. 1962, Shrewsbury, England. Record Prod; Songwriter; Musician (bass, guitar). m. Rosana Ferrao, 7 Dec. 1991. *Education:* BA in Film, University of Warwick, 1984. *Career:* Producer, songwriter, musician, Bliss, 1987–92; Tours with: Van Morrison; Paul Simon; Gipsy Kings; Chris Isaak; Worked with: Rupert Hine; Jon Kelly; John Shaw; Hugh Jones; Currently producer, writer, Duke Baysee. *Recordings:* As producer, writer, musician: Loveprayer, Bliss, 1989; Change In The Weather, Bliss, 1991; Sugar Sugar, Duke Baysee, 1994; Do You Love Me?, Duke Baysee, 1995; Siderado, Skank, 1999; Cidade Negra, Cinquante, 2000. *Honours:* Best International Act, Bliss, Italy, Brazil, 1989. *Membership:* PRS; Musicians' Union. *Current Management:* Pulso Productions. *Address:* Rua Sao

Felan 94, Jardim Marapendi, Barra Da Tijuca, 22630–170 Rio de Janeiro, RJ, Brazil.

RALPHS, Mick; b. 31 March 1944, Hereford, England. Musician (guitar); Songwriter. 2 s., 1 d. *Career:* Founder member, Mott The Hoople, 1969–73; Founder member, Bad Company, 1973–83; Toured world-wide; Tour with Dave Gilmour (Pink Floyd), 1984; Solo recording artiste, 1983; Re-formed Bad Company, 1986–. *Compositions include:* Can't Get Enough; Movin' On; Feel Like Makin' Love (co-writer with Paul Rodgers). *Recordings:* Singles with Mott the Hoople: Rock 'n' Roll Queen, 1972; All the Young Dudes, 1972; Honaloochie Boogie, 1973; All the Way from Memphis, 1973; Roll Away the Stone, 1973; Albums: Mott the Hoople, 1969; Mad Shadows, 1970; Wild Life, 1971; Brain Capers, 1971; All the Young Dudes, 1972; Mott, 1973; Greatest Hits, 1976; Mott Anthology, 1998; All the Way From Stockholm, live in 1971, 1999; Live Dudes, 2000; Albums with Amazing Blondell: Blondell, 1973; Mulgrave Street, 1974; Singles with Bad Company: Can't Get Enough; Feel Like Makin' Love; Young Blood; If You Need Somebody; Holy Water; Here Comes Trouble; Hey Hey; Hammer of Love; Albums: Bad Company, 1974; Straight Shooter, 1975; Run With The Pack, 1976; Burnin' Sky, 1977; Desolation Angels, 1979; Rough Diamonds, 1982; 10 from 6, 1985; Fame and Fortune, 1986; Dangerous Age, 1988; Holy Water, 1990; Here Comes Trouble, 1992; The Best of Bad Company Live – What You Hear Is What You Get, 1993; Company of Strangers, 1995; The Original Bad Co Anthology, 1999; Solo: Take This, 1983. *Honours:* Gold and Platinum albums with Bad Company; Grammy Award, 1975; Hon. Col of Louisiana, with Bad Company. *Membership:* Musicians' Union; PRS. *Current Management:* Gremlin Productions. *Address:* PO Box 148, Fincham, Norfolk PE33 9EH, England.

RAMAGE, Andrew; b. 24 Sept. 1949, Edinburgh, Scotland. Musician (guitar, bass: contra). m. Anita, 11 April 1975. *Education:* Diploma British Display Society, Telford College. *Career:* BBC TV; RME TV; STV; Grampian TV; Tours: Bermuda; Bangladesh; Iceland; Norway; Denmark; Netherlands; Switzerland; Morocco; Ireland; Radio BBC Scotland; Radio Tay; Radio Forth; Radio Moray Firth; Radio Heartland; Radio Clyde. *Recordings:* Golden Bird Vols 1 and 2, 1968; Bitter Withy Sampler, 1973; Bridging The Gap, 1983; Two For The Road, 1986; Silver Darlings, 1988; Dancing On A Wave, 1989; Naturally, 1991; Family Ties, 1993; Scotland The Brave, 1995; Songs You Heard Tonight, 1999. *Honours:* RBI, 1970; Glenfarg Quaich, 1980. *Membership:* Musicians' Union. *Address:* Sunnyside House, Drunzie, Glenfarg, Perthshire PH2 9PE, Scotland.

RAMAN, Susheela; b. 20 July 1973, London, England. Vocalist. *Career:* Tamil parents from South India; Moved to Australia, 1977; Learnt and gave recitals of South Indian classical music; Branched out into blues-based music as a teenager; Went to India to study with Shruti Sadolikar, 1995; Returned to England, 1997; Recorded with Sam Mills, 2000. *Recordings:* Salt Rain, 2001. *Honours:* BBC Radio 3 Awards for World Music, Best Newcomer, 2002.

RAMAZZOTTI, Eros; b. 28 Oct. 1963, Rome, Italy. Vocalist; Musician (guitar); Songwriter. *Career:* Participated in Castrocaro Music Festival, 1981; Led to signing first record deal and relocation to Milan; Released first single, 1982; Won Best Young Artist award at San Remo Festival, 1984; First album release, 1985, a major success throughout Europe; Achieved instant cult status in Italy; Musica E album reached an international audience, 1988; Promoted album In Ogni Senso with European / American tour culminating with world-wide broadcast of Barcelona concert, 1991; Created own management company, Radiorama, 1993; Signed new contract with BMG International. *Recordings:* Cuori Agitati, 1985; Nuovi Eroi, 1986; In Certi Momenti, 1987; Musica E, 1988; In Ogni Senso, 1990; Eros In Concert, 1991; Tutte Storie, 1993; Dove C'e Musica, 1996; Eros, 1997; Eros Live, 1998; Stile Libero, 2000. *Honours:* MTV Music Award, Best Italian Singer, 1996; Echo Award, Germany, Best International Singer, 1997; Dove C'e Musica album sales over 6m. world-wide. *Current Management:* c/o Radiorama, Milan, Italy. *Website:* www.erosramazzotti.net.

RAMIREZ, Humberto; b. 31 Jan. 1963, San Juan, Puerto Rico. Musician (trumpet); Composer; Prod; Arranger. m. Ivette Maritza Negron, 16 Jan. 1988, 1 s., 1 d. *Education:* Escuela Libre de Musica, San Juan, Puerto Rico; Berklee College of Music, Boston, MA, Bachelor of Music. *Career:* Concerts played at Madison Square Garden; Hollywood Bowl; Miami Arena; Blue Note Jazz Club; Blues Alley; Tours: Spain, Mexico City, USA, Canada and Europe. *Recordings:* Jazz Project; Aspects; Portrait of a Stranger; Canciones de Amor; Best Friends, 1999. *Honours:* 5 Gold records; 4 Platinum records; Diplo Award Best Jazz Recording, 1992; TU Musica Award, Best Jazz Recording, 1994, 1995, 1996; 8 Gold and 6 Platinum Records. *Membership:* NARAS; ASCAP. *Current Management:* Nilpo Music Inc. *Address:* PO Box 9020924, San Juan, 00902–0924 Puerto Rico.

RAMIREZ, Juan; b. 17 Oct. 1947, London, England. Flamenco Musician (guitar); Songwriter. m. Marsha, 15 April 1972. *Education:* Studied flamenco guitar, dance accompaniment, Spain and London. *Career:* Full time 1974–; Formed internationally renowned Viva Flamenco Dance Company, 1976; Performed at Royal Albert Hall; Barbican; Royal Festival Hall, London; Film appearance: The Curse of The Pink Panther, 1983; World's largest production

of Carmen, 1992; Numerous television appearances. *Compositions include:* Just Love. *Recordings:* with Marc Almond: The Desperate Hours; with Gary Barlow: Stronger; 12 Months 11 Days; with Vanessa Mae: Pasha. *Membership:* Musicians' Union. *Address:* 122B Wood Vale, London SE23 3EB, England.

RAMIREZ, Karen; b. 1972, Islington, London, England. Vocalist. *Career:* Began work as vocalist for producers, Souled Out, worked on their album; Solo artiste. *Recordings:* Singles: Looking for Love, 1998; Troubled Girl, 1998; If We Try, 1998; Album: Distant Dreams, 1998.

RAMONE, Phil; b. 5 Jan. 1939, New York, USA. Record Prod; Musician (violin). m. April 1984, 3 s. *Education:* Juilliard School of Music, New York; Doctor Musicology, Berklee College of Music, Boston; Doctor Musicology, Five Towns College, New York. *Career:* Founded own studio, A & R Recording, New York, 1961; Theatre credits include: Chicago; Hair; Little Shop of Horrors; Starlight Express; The Wiz; Film credits include: A Star Is Born; Flashdance; Ghostbusters; Midnight Cowboy; Reds; Yentl; Shampoo; Television credits include: Liza With A Z; Raffi On Broadway; Extreme; Liza Live From Radio Music Hall; The Jim Henson Hour; The Academy Awards; The Grammy Awards; Simon and Garfunkel Concert, Central Park; Show Business. *Recordings include:* As producer: The Stranger, 52nd Street, Glass Houses, Songs From The Attic, Innocent Man, Billy Joel; Flashdance (soundtrack); A Star Is Born, Yentl, Barbra Streisand; One Trick Pony, Still Crazy After All These Years, 50 Ways To Leave Your Lover, Slip Slidin' Away, Paul Simon; Too Late For Goodbyes, Valotte, Julian Lennon; Send In The Clowns, Judy Collins; Alice's Restaurant, Arlo Guthrie; The Look of Love, Dusty Springfield; Leaving On A Jet Plane, Peter Paul and Mary; Duets I and II, Frank Sinatra; also producer for Elton John; Gloria Estefan; Sinead O'Connor; Barry Manilow; Jon Secada; Paul McCartney; Dionne Warwick; Art Garfunkel; Chicago; Stephen Sondheim; Burt Bacharach; George Michael; Michael Bolton; Michael Amarte; Donny Osmond. *Honours:* 8 Grammy Awards; Emmy Award; Numerous Platinum and Gold discs; TEC Hall of Fame, 1992; 3M Visionary Award, 1994; Eyes On NY Award, 1994; Rock Walk Award, 1994; Songwriters Hall of Fame. *Membership:* Former President, New York Chapter, NARAS; NATAS; AFTRA; AFofM; ASCAP; BMI; SESAC; SAG. *Current Management:* Peter Asher Management. *Address:* 644 N Doheny Dr., Los Angeles, CA 90069, USA.

RANADE, Ashok Da; b. 25 Oct. 1937, India. m. Hamida Ebrahim. *Education:* LLB, MA, English Literature, MA, Marathi Literature, University of Bombay; Hindustani Vocal Classical Training with Pt Gajanauruo Joshi and others. *Career:* All India Radio, Mumbai; Lecturer, English and Marathi, Siddharth College of Commerce and Economics; First Director of University Music Centre, Mumbai, 1968–83; Associate Director, Archives and Research Centre, Ethnomusicology, American Institute of Indian Studies, 1983–84; Deputy Director, Theatre Research and Ethnomusicology, National Centre for Performing Arts, Mumbai, 1984–94; Conducts many workshops and courses in voire culture singing, music appreciation and ethnomusicology; Numerous seminars. *Compositions:* Composed music for Akar, International Exhibition of Calligraphy, New Delhi, 1988; Discovery of India, Nehru Centre, Mumbai, 1989; Composed music for plays and films; Composed and compered many thematical musicpresentations. *Recordings:* Cassettes: Baithakchi Lavani, 1989; Devgani, 1991. *Publications include:* Lok Sangget Shastra, 1975; On Music and Musicians of Hindustan, 1984; Marathi Stage Music, 1986; Keywords and Concepts: Hindustani Classical Music, 1990; Music and Drama in India, 1991; Essays in Indian Ethnomusicology, 1998. *Honours:* Appointed National Lecturer in Music, University Grants Commission, New Delhi, 1990–91; Appointed, Tagore Chair, M S University of Baroda, 1994–95; Awarded Master Krishnarao Phulambrikar Puraskar, Maharashtra Sahitya Parishad, 1998; Award for Music Research, Music Forum, Mumbai, 1998. *Address:* 7 Dnyanadevi, Sahitya Sahawas, Kalanagar, Kalelkar Marg, Mumbai 400051, India.

RANALDO, Lee; b. 3 Feb. 1956, Glen Cove, NY, USA. Artist; Poet; Musician (bass guitar). *Education:* BFA SUNY, Binghampton. *Career:* Soloist, performer with Glenn Branca and Rhys Chatham; Founding mem., Sonic Youth, 1981–; Founding mem., Ciccone Youth, 1986–; Duo performances: spoken word/film/music called Drift, with filmmaker Leah Singer. *Recordings:* Albums: with Sonic Youth: Sonic Youth, 1981; Confusion Is Sex; Sonic Death—Early Sonic Youth 1981–83; Kill Yr Idols; Bad Moon Rising; E.V.O.L., 1986; Sister, 1987; Hold That Tiger, 1987; Daydream Nation, 1988; Goo, 1990; Dirty, 1992; A Thousand Leaves, 1998; NYC Ghosts & Flowers, 2000; Condo Painting: Life From A Different Angle, 2002; Murray Street, 2002; with Ciccone Youth: The Whitey Album, 1989; Other releases with Sonic Youth: Anagrama (syr1); Slaapkamers met Slagroom (syr2); Invito al Cielo (syr3); Goodbye 20th Century (syr4); Kim Gordon/Ikue Mori/DJ Olive (syr5); Contributed to film and television soundtracks: Pump Up The Volume, 1990; My So-Called Life, 1995; End Of Days, 1999. *Publications:* Road Movies: Poems, 1998; Bookstore; Jrnls 80s (poems), 1999; Moroccan Journal (with Leah Singer), 2001. *Membership:* AFofM. *Current Management:* ICM. *Address:* c/o Smells Like Records, PO Box 6179, Hoboken, NJ 07030, USA. *Website:* www.sonicyouth.com.

RANDALL, Alan; b. 10 June 1934, Bedworth, England. Entertainer. m. Mary Laird, 1 s., 1 d. *Career:* Wrote script, starred in, musical play, Turned Out Nice Again; World entertainer; Royal Variety Shows; Guest artist, Rolling Stones; World cruises; Radio and television appearances world-wide; Featured in Beatles video, Free As A Bird, 1995; Summer season, Blackpool North Pier, 2002. *Compositions:* Where Does Father Xmas Hang His Stocking; Mr Banjo Man; Football, Football; Lottery Millionaire. *Recordings:* Albums, The Vibraphone Entertainer World of Alan Randall, 1996; I Remember George; Songs From World War 2; Who Do You Think You A Kidding My Hitler. *Publications:* George Formby Biography, 1974. *Honours:* Top Commercial Award, 1982. *Membership:* Variety Club of Great Britain; Grand Order of Water Rats. *Current Management:* United Kingdom Entertainment. *Address:* 104 Hickley Rd, Nuneaton CV11 6LS, England.

RANDAZZO, Teddy; b. 13 May 1935, New York, NY, USA. Composer; Musician; Actor. m. Rosemary Randazzo, 4 s., 3 d. *Education:* Private music studies. *Career:* Appeared on Ed Sullivan TV show 7 times, and in 4 films, Rock Rock Rock, The Girl Can't Help It, Mister Rock and Roll, and, Hey, Let's Twist; Appearances at various clubs including: Copacabana, Blaisdell Arena, Hawaii, and Araneta Colosseum, Philippines. *Recordings:* Goin' Out of My Head; Hurt So Bad; Pretty Blue Eyes; It's Gonna Take A Miracle; I'm On The Outside Looking In; Have You Looked Into Your Heart; Big Wide World; You're So Right For What's Wrong; Also recorded with: Connie Francis; Joe Simon. *Membership:* BINI. *Address:* 5254 Oak Island Rd, Orlando, FL 32809, USA.

RANDOLPH, 'Boots' (Homer Louis); b. 3 June 1927, Paducah, Kentucky, USA. Musician (tenor saxophone). m. Dee Barber, 17 Sept. 1947, 1 s., 1 d. *Education:* High School and Army Band. *Career:* Concerts all over USA and Canada; Most variety television shows, including: Ed Sullivan; Jimmy Dean; Jackie Gleason; Boston Pops with Arthur Feedler; TNN-Nashville Network. *Recordings:* Yakety Sax, as composer and musician; Recorded 43 albums, most recently Songs for the Spirit, 2000. *Honours:* 8 years Playboy All Star Jazz Poll. *Membership:* AFofM; AFTRA. *Current Management:* Gerard W. Purcell, New York, NY, USA. *Address:* 964 Second Ave, New York, NY 10022–6304, USA.

RANEY, Sue; b. 18 June 1939, McPhearson, Kansas, USA. Vocalist. m. Carmen Fanzone, 14 Dec. 1985. *Career:* Child star, recording debut aged 16; Performed world-wide, with stars including Don Rickles; Dean Martin; Bob Hope; Henry Mancini; Michel Legrand; Guest faculty member, Dick Grove School of Music. *Recordings:* Over a dozen albums; Songs For a Raney Day; Ridin' High; In Good Compnay, 1995; Flight of Fancy (Lyrics of Alan and Marilyn Bergman); When Your Lover Has Gone, 1997; Dreamsville (The Music of Henry Mancini); Autumn In The Air, 1998. *Membership:* Society of Singers. *Current Management:* Jim DiGiovanni, F Sharp Productions Ltd, 157 W 57th St, New York, NY, USA.

RANGE, Heidi; b. 23 May 1982, Liverpool, England. Vocalist. *Career:* Mem., Atomic Kitten; Solo artiste; Mem., Sugababes, 2001–; Signed to Island Records, 2001. *Recordings:* Album: Angels With Dirty Faces, 2002. Singles: Freak Like Me, 2002; Round Round, 2002. *Honours:* Q Award for Freak Like Me, 2002; BRIT Award, Best Dance Act, 2003. *Address:* c/o Island Records, 825 Eighth Ave, New York, NY 10019, USA. *Website:* www.sugababes.com.

RANKIN, Dusty; b. 8 Feb. 1924, Birchip, Victoria, Australia. Vocalist; Songwriter; Musician (guitar). m. Mary, 14 May 1957, deceased 1993, 2 d. *Career:* Worked in TV, Melbourne, 1950s; Recorded for Hadley, 1964; Recorded for Selection Records, 1980; Own show, Starnite, throughout Victoria; Toured with Skuthorpe's and Queensland Wild West Rodeos around Australia, 3 times; Toured with Athol McKoy Show, 1962; First Recordings for Columbia EMI Records, 1948. *Compositions:* Songs released on 13 compilation albums; 2 song albums (books). *Recordings:* 4 albums: Family Bible; The Country I Love; A Portrait of Dusty Rankin; Sunset Valley Calling; 5 EPs – Red Wing Smooth 'N Country; Dusty Rankin and Bernadette; Intimate Style of Dusty Rankin; Family Bible; 1 cassette, Best of Dusty Rankin; 20 of The Best – Dusty Rankin, 1999; After 50 Years, with Val Phelan. *Honours:* Won Australian Amateur Hour, 1946; Inducted into Hands of Fame, Tamworth, NSW, 1980; Inducted into Avenue of Honour Bamera, SA, 1985; Golden Guitar, Tambourine Mountain, Queensland, 1988; Inducted into Roll of Renown, Tamworth, NSW, 1996. *Membership:* Australian Performing Rights Asscn. *Address:* PO Box 113, Birchip, Vic 3483, Australia.

RANKIN, Mark; b. Glasgow, Scotland. Vocalist. *Career:* Vocalist, Scottish rock group Gun, 1989–; Concerts include: Support to Rolling Stones; Urban Jungle Tour, Europe, 1990; Support to Simple Minds, 1990; Support to Def Leppard, UK, 1993; International tours as headline act. *Recordings:* Albums: Taking On The World, 1989; Gallus, 1992; Swagger, 1994; 0141 632 6326, 1997; Singles: Better Days, 1989; Shame On You, 1989; Money, 1989; Inside Out, 1990; Word Up, 1994; Don't Say It's Over, 1994. *Current Management:* G R Management, 974 Pollockshaw Rd, Glasgow G41 2HA, Scotland.

RANKS, Shabba, (Rexton Gordon); b. 17 Jan. 1966, Sturgetown, Jamaica. Reggae/Ragga Vocalist. *Career:* Club artiste as DJ Don, early 1980s; Solo artiste, mid-1980s; Prolific local recording artiste, Caribbean; Support to Bobby Brown, USA, 1992. *Recordings:* As Raw As Ever, 1991; Rough and Ready Vol. 1, 1992; Xtra Naked, 1992; Mr Maximum, 1992; Love Punanny Bad, 1993; No Competition, 1993; A Mi Shabba, 1995; Shine Eye Gal, 1995; Holding On, 1998; King of Dancehall, 1998; Get Up Stand Up, 1998; Loverman, 1999; Shabba Ranks and Friends, 1999; Greatest Hits, 2001; Hit singles: She's A Woman (with Scritti Politti), 1991; Housecall (with Maxi Priest), 1991; Mr Loverman, used in film soundtrack Deep Cover, 1993; Slow and Sexy, 1992; What'cha Gonna Do? (with Queen Latifah), 1993; Family Affair, used in film soundtrack Addams Family, 1993. *Honours:* Grammy Awards: Best Reggae Album, As Raw As Ever, 1992; Xtra Naked, 1993; 2 Caribbean Music Awards, 1992; 6 International Reggae Awards, 1992. *Current Management:* Shang Artist Management, 850 Seventh Ave, Suite 500, New York, NY 10019, USA.

RANSOME, Steve; b. 24 Aug. 1961, London, England. Musician (keyboards); Composer; Record Prod. m. Shirley Peterson, 8 April 1994. *Education:* Advanced Jazz tuition, Grangewood School in London; Qualified Yamaha Music Teacher. *Career:* ATV Production Assistant, 1977–78; Played keyboards in various bands at Wembley, Peterborough and Glasgow Festivals; Toured UK, Ireland, Europe and America; Appeared on BBC TV, ITV, MTV, Channel 4 TV and Cable TV; Yamaha demonstration concerts given; Played at Bahai Festivals, the University circuits in Scotland and on most radio stations; Owns recording studio. *Compositions include:* About 12 television themes and soundtracks; Arranger for 1988 special Olympics theme. *Recordings:* Single: Peace Moves, world-wide release; Many major artists as production assistant. *Publications:* Peace Moves; Storming The Gates; Bahai Song Book Vol. 1. *Membership:* PRS; MCPS; Musicians' Union. *Address:* Donfield House, Backmill by Turriff, Aberdeenshire AB53 8ET, Scotland.

RAPHAEL, (Rafael Martos); b. 5 May 1942, Jaén, Spain. Vocalist. m. Natalia Figueroa, 1972, 2 s., 1 d. *Career:* First prize, Salzburg Festival (children's singing competition) age 9; Winner, numerous subsequent competitions; Professional debut, Madrid, 1960; Represented Spain, Eurovision Song Contest, 1966, 1967; International concerts, USA (including Broadway debut, 1974); USSR; Japan; Australia; Concerts include: 25th Anniversary open air concert, Bernabé Stadium, Madrid, 1985; Film appearances: Cuando Tú No Estás; The Hobo. *Recordings include:* Los Hombres Lloran También, 1964; Hotel De L'Universe, 2001; Yo Soy Aquel, 2001; Maldito Raphael, 2001. *Honours:* First Prize, Salzburg Singing Competition; Numerous Platinum and Gold discs. *Address:* c/o Arie Kaduri Agency Inc, 16125 NE 18th Ave, North Miami Beach, FL 33162, USA.

RASE, Bill; b. 25 Oct. 1926, Long Beach, CA, USA. Orchestra Leader. m. Shirley Bishop, 24 Aug. 1952, 2 d. *Education:* Sacramento State College; General music courses. *Career:* Vocalist, Eddie Halter Orchestra, 1946–48; Orchestra leader, Bill Rase Orchestra, 1948–; Over 8,000 engagements, backed Bob Hope, Cab Calloway shows; DJ, The Bill Rase Show, KCRA Radio-Sacramento, 1952–64; Producer, host, The Bill Rase Show (talent show), KCRA TV, Channel 3, over 500 shows in nine years; Children's show host, Bosun Bill and Popeye Show, over 2,600 shows in four years; Impersonated Bing Crosby, Network Eddie Cantor Show, 1962; Opened recording video production studio, Bill Rase Productions Inc, 1965–; Vocalist, Rainbow Records, Era Records, Esar Records. *Membership:* Sacramento Musicians' Asscn. *Address:* 955 Venture Ct, Sacramento, CA 95825, USA.

RASMUSSEN, Pia; b. 10 Nov. 1954, Århus, Denmark. Musician (piano); Composer; Music Teacher. *Education:* Cand Phil, Musicology, Copenhagen University. *Career:* Pianist and composer, all-woman groups Sosterrock and Lilith, 1976–83; Composer for documentaries, films and theatre; Solo concerts, piano, synthesizers, 1991–; Duo with flautist Chris Poole, 1992–; Teacher, Department of Musicology, Århus University. *Recordings:* Album: To The Powers That Be; Theme song, Nordic Women's Conference, Oslo, 1988. *Publications:* Blues For Klaver, Vols 1 and 2 (educational books on blues piano). *Membership:* DJBFA; Danish Musicians' Union; Women In Music. *Address:* Skolesvinget 8, 8240 Risskov, Denmark.

RASOANAIVO, Hanitra; b. 1 Oct. 1964, Antananarivo, Madagascar. Vocalist; Dancer; Musician (percussion); Songwriter. m. Ian Anderson. *Career:* Lead singer and founding member of Tarika, 1994; Band toured USA and Europe; Performed with: Weave; Gogmagogs; Women of Africa collaboration (with Oumou Sangare, Sally Nyolo and Sibongile Khumalo), performing on tour, 1998; Working on project to build an arts centre in Antananarivo. *Recordings:* Albums include: Bibiango, 1994; Avelo, 1997; Son Egal (produced by Simon Emmerson), 1997; D, 1998; Soul Makassar, 2001. *Honours:* Indie Award, USA, 1998; Tarika voted one of the ten best bands in the world by Time Magazine, October 2001. *Current Management:* Rogue Productions, PO Box 337, London N4 1TW, England.

RASTED, Peter; b. 28 July 1958, Copenhagen, Denmark. Musician (trumpet, flugelhorn); Arranger; Conductor. m. Annette Frandsen, 2 s. *Education:* Royal Academy of Music, Copenhagen. *Career:* Several big bands: Kluvers Big Band, Blast, The Franks, Cordero and Los Gran Daneses;

Theatre appearances in Ålborg and Århus; Danish Television Show, Showbisserne; Studio sessions. *Recordings:* With Blast: All recordings except Blast; SKO/Torp: I Ain't Got Too Many Problems; Cordero and Los Gran Daneses: Del Norte Y Tropical. *Address:* Sandogade 4, 8200 Århus N, Denmark.

RASTED, Soeren; b. 13 June 1969, Blovstrod, Denmark. Musician (keyboards, drum machines). *Career:* Worked with Claus Norreen on film Fraekke Frida; Formed Joyspeed; Changed name to Aqua; Obtained major label deal in Denmark; Numerous TV and live appearances. *Recordings:* Singles: Itsy Blitzy, as Joyspeed; Roses Are Red; My Oh My; Barbie Girl (No. 1, UK), 1997; Doctor Jones (No. 1, UK), 1998; Lollipop; Turn Back Time (theme from film Sliding Doors) (No. 1, UK), 1998; Good Morning Sunshine; Albums: Aquarium, 1997; Bubble Mix, 1998; We Belong To The Sea, 2001.

RATCLIFFE, Simon; b. England. DJ; Prod; Songwriter. *Career:* Mem., Basement Jaxx, 1994–; Co-founder, owner, Atlantic Jaxx records, 1994–; Remixes for acts, incl. Pet Shop Boys, Roger Sanchez, Lil' Mo Yin Yang; Worked with vocalist Corrina Josephs; Numerous gigs and television appearances. *Recordings:* Albums: Atlantic Jaxx (compilation), 1997; Remedy, 1999; Rooty, 2001. Singles: Samba Magic, 1995; Fly Life, 1997; Same Old Show/Automatic, 1998; Red Alert, 1999; Rendez-vu, 1999; Jump 'n' Shout, 1999; Bingo Bango, 2000; Jus 1 Kiss, 2001; Romeo, 2001; Where's Your Head At?, 2001; Get Me Off, 2002. *Honours:* BRIT Award, Best British Dance Act, 2002. *Address:* c/o Astralwerks Records, 104 W 29th St, Fourth Floor, New York, NY 10001, USA. *Website:* www.basementjaxx.co.uk.

RATHBOURNE, Andie; b. 8 Sept. 1972, Blacon, Chester, England. Musician (drums). *Career:* Joined Mansun, 1996; Numerous TV appearances and live gigs; Appearance at Glastonbury Festival, 1997. *Recordings:* Singles: Egg Shaped Fred, 1996; Stripper Vicar, 1996; Wide Open Space, 1996; She Makes My Nose Bleed, 1997; Taxloss, 1997; Closed For Business, 1997; Legacy, 1998; Six, 1999; I Can Only Disappoint U, 2000; Electric Man, 2000; Albums: Attack of the Grey Lantern, 1997; Six, 1999; Little Kix, 2000.

RATZER, Karl; b. 4 July 1950, Vienna, Austria. Musician (guitar); Composer; Vocalist. *Career:* Member, C Department, 1969; Gipsy Love, 1970; High Voltage (later known as Rufus and Chaka Khan), USA; Based in USA, 1972–81; Worked with: Chet Baker; Eddie Gomez; Joe Chambers; Steve Gadd; Joe Farrell; Sal Nistico; Bob Mintzer; Johnny Griffin; Clark Terry; Art Farmer; Fritz Baver; Lee Konitz; James Moody; Chaka Khan; Jenny Evans; Formed band project, Beat The Heat, 1991; Recordings, tours, Europe; Festivals include: Indianapolis; Tampa; Birmingham; Chicago; New York; New Orleans; Atlanta; Played Seventh Avenue Club, New York. *Recordings:* Live In Paris (I and II), Chet Baker; with Ray Mantilla: Nightbird; Conception; Tune Up; Rainforest, Jeremy Steig; Land of Dreams, Eddie Lockjaw Davis; Solo albums: In Search of The Ghost; Street-Talk; Fingerprints; Serenade; Happy Floating; Electric Finger; Dancing On A String; Fool For Your Sake; That's Jazz; Gitarre; Gitarrenfever; Gumbo Dive; Waltz For Ann; Bayou; Coasting; Saturn Returning. *Current Management:* Mr Kiss, Agency For Music and Art. *Address:* Vienna Hilton, Top 1719–1721, Landstrasser Hauptstrasse, 1030 Vienna, Austria.

RAULIN, Francois; b. 17 March 1956, Annecy, France. Musician (piano); Composer. 3 s. *Education:* Mathematics; Piano lessons from age 9. *Career:* Founder, Association Grenoble Espace Musical (AGEM), 1981; Duo, with pianist Pascal Lloret, tour, France, 1981; Studied African music, 1980–83; Pianist, La Marmite Infernale, 1982; Tours, France; Festivals include: Paris; Le Mans; Nancy; Milan, 1982; Zürich, 1984; Moers, 1984; Hofheim, 1985; Nickelsdorf, 1986; Tours: Algeria; Germany; Switzerland; Italy; Austria; Member, Louis Sclavis Group, 1985; Festivals world-wide include: All over Europe; Canada; Japan; India; Turkey; Algeria; Mexico; Festival appearances with Claude Barthelemy, Jean-Marc Padovani, 1986; Antoine Herve, 1988; Philippe Deschepper, 1992; Solo performances at festivals including: Grenoble; Lausanne; Geneva; Cologne, 1992–; Tours with trio and quartet. *Compositions include:* Quelque Chose Du Sud, with Maurice Merle; Battleship Potemkin (film music); with Louis Sclavis: Chamber Music, 1988; Clarinettes; Indigène, 1989; Duke On The Air, 1990; Face Nord, with Mathilde Monnier's Dance Company, 1991; Vue Sur Tower Bridge (Travelling) (co-writer), 1992; Work for 5 Pianos, 1993; Hit Parada, Jean Mereu, 1993; Les Violences de Rameau, with Louis Sclavis, 1993, reissued 2001; Music for theatre, film and dance, with Louis Sclavis, J Mereux, A Gibert. *Recordings include:* Chine; Rouge; First Flush; Duke on The Air. *Honours:* Winner, Biennale, Barcelona (with Louis Sclavis Quartet), 1988. *Current Management:* Marion Piras, Montpellier, France. *Address:* 686 Ave Saint Jean, 38360 Noyarey, France.

RAUX, Richard; b. 17 July 1995, Perigaux, France. Musician (saxophone, flute); Composer; Bandleader. m. Helena, 25 May 1970, 1 s., 1 d. *Education:* Bac Philo; 2 years university; Saxophone, Phil Woods; Flute, Caratgt; Composition, G Russell. *Career:* Played, recorded with Eddy Louis; Magma; Luther Allisson; Kenny Clarke; Mal Waldron; Charlie Haden; Memphis Slim; Dizzy Gillespie; Roy Burrowes Sextet; John Greaves; Festivals, concerts, clubs, Telé France; Nice, 1991, 93; London; Berlin; Jazz teacher, saxophone,

flute. *Recordings:* Feel Good At Last, Richard Raux Quartet; S Murray; Eddy Louis; Under The Magnolias, Richard Raux Quartet, 1989; Live At The Dreyer, Roy Burrowes, Mal Waldron; Won't Rain in California, Sonny Rhodes, 1996; House Rent Party, 1998. *Address:* 2 Chemin du Mopulin, 95550 Bessancourt, Nr Paris, France.

RAVEN, Eddy, (Edward Garvin Futch); b. 19 Aug. 1944, Lafayette, Louisiana, USA. Musician; Vocalist; Songwriter. 2 s. *Education:* College. *Career:* Staff writer, La Louisiane, Lafayette; Worked with: Hank Williams Jr; Alabama; Tracy Lawrence; George Strait; Reba McEntire; Alan Jackson; Charlie Daniels; Stevie Ray Vaughan; The Judds; George Jones; Conway Twitty; Merle Haggard; Dolly Parton; Roy Acuff; Barbara Mandrell; Marty Robbins; Television appearances: Co-host, Yesteryear, TNN; Founder, own publishing company; Staff writer on: La Louisianne, 1963–69; Acriff Rose, 1970–83. *Compositions:* Country Green, Don Gibson; Touch The Morning, Don Gibson; Good Morning Country Rain, Jeannie C Riley; Thank God For Kids, Oak Ridge Boys. *Recordings:* Hit Singles: Bayou Boys; I Got Mexico; Shine Shine Shine; I'm Gonna Get You; Joe Knows How To Live; 'Til You Cry; In A Letter To You; Albums: That Cajun Country Sound, 1969; This Is Eddy Raven, 1976; Eyes, 1979; Desperate Dreams, 1981; Thank God For Kids, 1984; I Could Use Another You, 1984; Love and Other Hard Times, 1985; Right Hand Man, 1986; Temporary Sanity, 1989; Greatest Country Hits, 1990; Right For Flight, 1991; Wild Eyed and Crazy, 1994; 4 Best Of/Greatest Hits compilation albums; 4 Christmas compilation albums; Live At Billy Bob's, 1998; Living In Black And White, 2001. *Membership:* ASCAP; BMI; AFTRA; AFofM; Lifetime mem., Songwriters Asscn; Tennessee Film and Entertainment Commission. *Address:* PO Box 2476, Hendersonville, TN 37077, USA.

RAVEN MAIZE. See: **LEE, Dave.**

RAWLINGS, David Todd; Vocalist; Musician (guitar). m. Gillian Welch. *Education:* Berklee School of Music, Boston, Massachusetts. *Career:* Met Gillian Welch whilst both students at Berklee; T-Bone Burnett heard performance in Nashville and produced Revival album, release solely under Welch's name, 1996; Appeared solo on many film soundtracks including: O Brother Where Art Thou?; Down From The Mountain; Songcatcher; The Horse Whisperer; Appearances on Dwight Yoakam and Gram Parsons tribute albums; Guested on albums by: Mark Knopfler; Ryan Adams; Steve Earle; Songs, many co-written with Welch, recorded by acts including: Ryan Adams; Christine Collister; Nitty Gritty Dirt Band; Laurie Lewis; Alison Krauss and Union Station. *Recordings:* Albums: Revival, Hell Among The Yearlings, 1996; Time (The Revelator), 2001; features on: Horse Whisperer OST, 1998; Beneath My Wheels, Kevin Welch, 1999; Mountain, Steve Earle and Del McCoury, 1999; Swing Set, Ani DiFranco, 2000; O Brother Where Art Thou? OST, 2000; Sailing To Philadelphia, Mark Knopfler, 2000; Rich From The Journey, Kimmie Rhodes, 2000; Sebastopol, Jay Farrar, 2001; Down From The Mountain OST, 2001.

RAWLS, Lou; b. 1 Dec. 1935, Chicago, Illinois, USA. Vocalist. *Career:* Briefly member, gospel group, the Pilgrim Travellers; Solo artiste, 1958–; Also actor; Voiceovers, Budweiser beer commercials. *Recordings:* Albums: Lou Rawls Sings, 1962; Black and Blue, 1963; Tobacco Road, 1963; Nobody But Lou Rawls, 1965; Lou Rawls and Strings, 1965; Live!, 1966; Soulin', 1966; Merry Christmas Ho! Ho! Ho!, 1967; Feeling Good, 1968; You're Good For Me, 1968; The Way It Was— The Way It Is, 1969; Your Good Thing, 1969; You Made Me So Very Happy, 1970; Bring It On Home To Me, 1970; Natural Man, 1971; Silk and Soul, 1972; All Things In Time, 1976; Unmistakably Lou, 1977; When You Hear Lou, You've Heard It All, 1977; Live, 1978; Let Me Be Good To You, 1979; Sit Down and Talk To Me, 1980; Shades of Blue, 1981; Now Is The Time, 1982; When The Night Comes, 1983; Close Company, 1984; Love All Your Blues Away, 1986; At Last, 1989; Portrait of The Blues, 1992; Greatest Hits In Concert, 1993; Seasons 4 U, 1998; I'm Blessed, 2001; Christmas Will Be Christmas, 2001. *Current Management:* The Brokaw Co. *Address:* 9255 Sunset Blvd, Suite 804, Los Angeles, CA 90069, USA.

RAYE, Collin, (Floyd E. Wray); b. 22 Aug. 1960, De Queen, Arkansas, USA. Vocalist. *Career:* Television appearances include: 3 Tonight Shows; Street Justice, television series; 3 Regis and Kathy; Kathy Lee Xmas special. *Recordings:* Albums: All I Can Be, 1990; In This Life, 1992; Extremes, 1994; I Think About You, 1995; Christmas The Gift, 1996; The Walls Came Down, 1998; Counting Sheep, 2000; Singles: That's My Story, 1993; Man and My Word, 1994; My Kind of Girl, 1994; One Boy One Girl, 1995; Not That Different, 1995; Someone You Used to Know, 1998; On The Verge, 1999; Couldn't Last A Moment, 2000; Counting Sheep, 2000; Tracks, 2000; Can't Back Down, 2001. *Membership:* SAG; AFTRA. *Current Management:* Scott Dean Management, 612 Humboldt St, Reno, NV 89509–1606, USA; William Morris Agency, 2100 West End Ave, Suite 1000, Nashville, TN 37203, USA.

RAYMONDE, Simon; b. 3 April 1963, London, England. Musician (bass, keyboards). m. 1 c. *Career:* Joined Cocteau Twins, 1983; Collaboration with 4AD collective This Mortal Coil; Collaboration with pianist Harold Budd; Band collaborated on Spooky's Found Sound, 1996; Began singing with own band, 1997. *Recordings:* Lullabies, 1982; Peppermint Pig, 1983; Sunburst and

Snowblind, 1983; Pearly Dewdrops' Drops, 1984; Aikea-Guinea, 1985; Tiny Dynamite, 1985; Echoes in a Shallow Bay, 1985; Love's Easy Tears, 1986; Iceblink Luck, 1990; Evangeline, 1993; Frosty the Snowman, 1993; Bluebeard, 1994; Twinlights, 1995; Otherness, 1995; Tishbite, 1996; Violaine, 1996; Albums: Treasure, 1984; The Pink Opaque, 1985; The Moon and the Melodies, 1986; Blue Bell Knoll, 1988; Heaven or Las Vegas, 1990; Four Calendar Café, 1993; Milk and Kisses, 1996; Stars And Topsoil, 2000; Solo: Blame Someone Else, 1997.

REA, Chris; b. 4 March 1951, Middlesbrough, Cleveland, England. Vocalist; Songwriter; Musician (guitar). m. Joan, 1980. *Career:* Member, Magdelene, 1973–75; Name changed to The Beautiful Losers, 1975–76; Solo artist, 1977–; Appearances include: Great British Music Festival, Wembley, 1978; Regular UK and European tours. *Compositions include:* Film score, Soft Top Hard Shoulder, 1993; Songs on all his albums. *Recordings:* Albums: Whatever Happened To Benny Santini?, 1978; Deltics, 1979; Tennis, 1980; Chris Rea, 1982; Water Sign, 1983; Wired To The Moon, 1984; Shamrock Diaries, 1985; On The Beach, 1986; Dancing With Strangers (No. 2, UK), 1987; The Best of Chris Rea – New Light From Old Windows, 1988; The Road To Hell (No. 1, UK), 1989; Auberge (No. 1, UK), 1991; God's Great Banana Skin, 1992; Expresso Logic, 1993; The Very Best Of, 1994; Contributor, Hank Marvin Guitar Syndicate, Hank Marvin, 1977; Duets, Elton John, 1993; La Passione, 1996; The Blue Café, 1998; Working on It, 1998; Dancing Shoes, 1998; King Of The Beach, 2001; Dancing Down The Stony Road, 2002. Hit singles include: Fool (If You Think It's Over), 1979; I Can Hear Your Heartbeat, 1983; Stainsby Girls, 1985; On The Beach, 1986; Let's Dance, 1987; Driving Home For Christmas, 1988; The Road To Hell (Part 2), 1989; Tell Me There's A Heaven, 1990; Auberge, 1991; Winter Song, 1991; Nothing To Fear, 1992; Julia, 1993; Featured on Do They Know It's Christmas, Band Aid II (No. 1, UK), 1989. *Honours:* Melody Maker Award, Best Newcomers, with the Beautiful Losers, 1975. *Current Management:* Real Life Ltd, 122 Holland Park Ave, London W11 4UA, England.

READ, Mark Daniel; b. 7 Nov. 1978, Kingston, Surrey, England. Vocalist; Musician (piano, drums); Songwriter. *Career:* Toured world-wide performing cover versions with parents' group throughout youth; Won Best Young Performer award whilst representing England at Romanian Song Festival; Cruise ship entertainer and small acting roles prior to joining A1 pop group; Signed recording contract, 1999; Sell-out theatre tours of South-East Asia and UK, 2000–01. *Recordings:* Albums: Here We Come, 1999; The A List, 2000; Make It Good, 2002. Singles: Be The First To Believe, Summertime of Our Lives, Ready Or Not/Everytime, 1999; Like A Rose, Take On Me, Same Old Brand New You, 2000; No More, 2001; Caught In The Middle, 2002. *Honours:* BRIT Award, Best Newcomer, 2001; Also honoured at MTV Mandarin Music Awards. *Current Management:* c/o Byrne Blood Ltd. *Website:* www.a1-online.com.

READER, Eddi; b. 29 Aug. 1959, Glasgow, Scotland. Vocalist. 2 s. *Career:* Lead singer, Fairground Attraction; Later, solo artiste; Tours: UK; Europe; America; Japan; Television appearances include: Top of the Pops; Later With Jools Holland. *Recordings:* Albums: with Fairground Attraction: First of a Million Kisses, 1988; Ay Fond Kiss, 1990; Solo albums: Mirmama, 1992; Eddi Reader, 1994; Candyfloss and Medicine, 1996; Angels and Electricity, 1999; Simple Soul, 2001; Singles include: Perfect, with Fairground Attraction (No. 1, UK), 1988; Find My Love, with Fairground Attraction, 1988; Patience Of Angels, 1994; Nobody Lives Without Love, 1995; Town Without Pity, 1996. *Honours:* BRIT Awards: Best Single, Best Band, Best British Female Artist. *Membership:* Equity; Musicians' Union. *Current Management:* Douglas Kean, Interface Management. *Address:* 37 Oxford Gardens, London W4 3BN, England.

READER, Mark; b. 21 March 1960, Liverpool, England. Musician (guitar); Vocalist. 1 s. *Education:* Classical guitar, classical piano. *Career:* Television with Bill Le Sage, Alec Dankworth, Alan Ganley in Body Talk; Composed music for: Bitsa; We Are The Champions; Is That A Fact?; Words and Pictures; Guitarist, Liverpool Empire with P J Proby; Now fronting guitarist, singer, Strider. *Compositions:* for Bitsa: Hurry Up; For We Are The Champions: Hang On Steve, Uphill Champs; for Strider: She's The One; The Loser; Spare Me The Pain; Finding A Way; Seasons With You; UFO. *Membership:* Musicians' Union; Equity; PRS (associate mem.). *Address:* 7 Thorndale Rd, Waterloo, Liverpool L22 9QP, England.

REBELLO, Jason Matthew; b. 29 March 1969, Carshalton, Surrey, England. Jazz Musician (piano). *Education:* Degree, Guildhall School of Music and Drama. *Career:* Concerts with Halle Orchestra; Played with Wayne Shorter, Freddie Jackson, Claire Martin, Gerard Presencer, Tony Remy and Mica Paris; Television presenter, Artrageous. *Recordings:* Albums: A Clearer View, 1990; Keeping Time, 1993; Make It Real, 1995; Last Dance. *Honours:* The Wire Jazz Album of the Year; Perrier British Jazz Pianist of the Year. *Membership:* Freemason. *Current Management:* Alex Hardee, Concorde International Artists. *Address:* 101 Shepherds Bush Rd, Hammersmith, London W6 7LP, England.

REBERT, Jeph(rey) L; b. 10 June 1959, Carlisle, Pennsylvania, USA. Musician (drums, percussion); Vocalist; Senior Transportation Planner. *Education:* Pennsylvania State University, 1982; Continuing Education courses, 1987–; Private instruction: Piano; Snare Drum; Kit Drums; Class instruction: Percussion, West York Area High School music programme. *Career:* Percussionist, West York Area High School: Symphonic Band; Jazz Ensemble; Pit Orchestra; Drill Team; White Rose Drum and Bugle Corps; York City Concert Band; Pennsylvania State University Blue Band; Phi Mu Alpha Sinfonia Ensembles; Kit drummer, various local rock and lounge acts, 1975–85; Kit drummer and percussionist, 35 local and regional bands, 1989–; Percussionist, Pit Orchestra, The Actors Company of Pennysylvania, 1993; Performances: Bethlehem PA Music Festival (with Namaste), 1997; Lancaster PA Celebration of Cultures Festival (with Namaste), 1996–2000. *Recordings:* Loose Cannons, Peace of Mind, producer and musician, 1995; Single, Symptoms of Depression (compilation), 1995; Namaste, Colonial Pagoda, musician, 1997; features on compilations: Zigarettes, 1998; Breakfast With NPR, 1999. *Membership:* National Asscn of Rudimental Drummers, 1976–80; Percussive Arts Society, 1980–83; Phi Mu Alpha Sinfonia, alumni mem.; Penn State Blue Band, alumni mem. *Address:* 59 N Lehman St, York, PA 17403, USA.

REDBONE, Leon; Vocalist; Musician (guitar). 2 d. *Career:* Performer world-wide, 1973–; Numerous television, film and radio performances, 1976–. *Recordings:* Albums: On The Track, 1975; Double Time, 1977; Champagne Charlie, 1978; From Branch To Branch, 1981; Red To Blue, 1986; No Regrets, 1988; Christmas Island, 1988 (re-released 1989–91); Sugar, 1990; Up A Lazy River, 1992; Whistling In The Wind, 1994; Any Time, 2001; So Relax, track used in British Rail commercials; Live And Kickin', 1999; Anytime, 2001. *Honours:* Gold disc, On the Track, 1975; Silver Lion, 1989; London International Advertising Award, 1989. *Membership:* AFofM; SAG; AFTRA; Equity. *Current Management:* Beryl Handler. *Address:* 2169 Aquetong Rd, New Hope, PA 18938–2169 USA. *Website:* www.leonredbone.com.

REDDING, Noel David; b. 25 Dec. 1945, Folkestone, Kent, England. Musician (bass, rhythm guitar); Vocalist. *Education:* Harvey Grammar School, Folkestone, Kent; Folkestone Art College; Violin lessons at school. *Career:* Professional musician aged 17; Guitarist, The Burnettes, The Loving Kind; Bass player, The Jimi Hendrix Experience, 1966–69; Own band, Fat Mattress, 1969–70; Member, Road, 1971; Solo artiste, session musician, 1974–. *Recordings:* Albums with Jimi Hendrix Experience: Are You Experienced, 1967; Electric Ladyland, 1968; Axis Bold As Love, 1967; Songs include: Little Miss Strange; She's So Fine; Hey Joe; Voodoo Chile; Crosstown Traffic; Foxy Lady; Wind Cries Mary; All Along The Watchtower; with Fat Mattress: Fat Mattress, 1969; Fat Mattress 2, 1970; Road, Road, 1971; with Noel Redding Band: Clonakilty Cowboys, 1975; Blowin', 1976; Other. *Recordings include:* Martin Darvill & Friends, Greatest Show On Earth, 2000. *Publications:* Noel Redding's Bass Method Book (tutor); Are You Experienced? (co-author with the late Carol Appleby). *Honours:* Rock 'n' Roll Hall of Fame Inductee, 1992; Numerous others. *Membership:* ASCAP; Equity. *Current Management:* Ian Grant. *Address:* Owl House, Byers Lane, South Godstone, Surrey KH9 8SL, England. *Telephone:* (1342) 892074.

REDDOG, Jeff Higgins; b. 28 Feb. 1954, Alexandria VA, USA. Vocalist; Musician (guitar). *Career:* Blues Player, Southeast USA. *Compositions:* Four albums. *Address:* PO Box 7032, Marietta GA 30065, USA.

REDDY, Helen; b. 25 Oct. 1942, Melbourne, Victoria, Australia. Vocalist; Actress. m. (1) Jeff Wald, (2) Milton Robert Ruth, 1 s., 1 d. *Education:* UCLA Extension College. *Career:* Singer, 1966–; Numerous concerts world-wide; Actress, films: Airport, 1975; Pete's Dragon, 1977; Television host, Midnight Special, 1970s; Campaign work for women's political movement and women in prison. *Recordings:* Albums: I Don't Know How To Love Him, 1971; Helen Reddy, 1971; I Am Woman, 1972; Long Hard Climb, 1973; Love Song For Jeffrey, 1974; Free and Easy, 1974; No Way To Treat A Lady, 1975; Greatest Hits, 1975; Music Music, 1976; Ear Candy, 1977; We'll Sing In The Sunshine, 1978; Live In London, 1979; Reddy, 1979; Take What You Find, 1980; Play Me Out, 1981; Imagination, 1983; Take It Home, 1984; Very Best Of, 1993; When I Dream, 1996; Center Stage, 1998; Christmas, 2001; Hit singles: I Don't Know How To Love Him, 1971; I Am Woman, 1972; Delta Dawn, 1973; Angie Baby, 1974; I Can't Hear You No More, 1976. *Honours:* Numerous Gold and Platinum records; LA Times, Woman of the Year, 1975; NAACP Image Award, 1974; Maggie Award, 1976; Humanitarian Award, B'nai B'rith, 1975. *Address:* Helen Reddy Inc, 820 Stanford St, Santa Monica, CA 90403, USA.

REDMAN, (Reggie Noble), (Dr Trevis, Funk Docta Spock); b. Newark, New Jersey, USA. Rap Artiste. *Career:* First appeared on friend Erick Sermon's group EPMD's Hardcore and Headbanger; Signed to Def Jam on strength of those performances; Released debut album, 1992; Starred in How High film with Method Man, 2002; Collaborations: LL Cool J; Adam F; Lil' Cease; Dave Hollister; D'Angelo; De La Soul. *Recordings:* Albums: Whut? Thee Album, 1992; Dare Iz A Darkside, 1994; Muddy Waters, 1997; Doc's Da Name, 1998; Blackout (with Method Man), 2000; Malpractice, 2001; Singles: Blow Your Mind, 1992; Tonight's Da Night, 1994; Whateva Man, 1997; I'll Bee

Dat, 1999; Da Rockwilder (with Method Man), 2000; Smash Sumthin' (with Adam F), 2001. *Address:* c/o Def Jam, 825, Eighth Ave, New York, USA.

REDMOND, Melaine; b. 25 Oct. 1962, Putney, London. Session Vocalist. m. Brian Tench, 2 s. *Career:* World Tours with: Duran Duran, Bill Wyman and The Rhythm Kings, Bob Geldof; Recordings with: Duran Duran; Bill Wyman and The Rhythm Kings; Boy George; Apache Indian; Television Work with: Duran Duran; The The; Bill Wyman; Dolly Parton; Sting; Dana Int; Gigs with: Adam Ant; Patsy Kensit; Johnny Marr; Jingles include: set of 5 advertisements for Mazda Car Co. *Recordings:* 3 albums including: Struttin Our Stuff; Any Way The Wind Blows. *Membership:* Musicians' Union. *Current Management:* Session Connection and Hobsons Agencies. *Address:* 61 Dysart Ave, Kingston, Surrey KT2 5RA, England.

REECE, Alex; b. 18 Feb. 1970, London, England. Jungle DJ and Prod. *Career:* Early releases on Goldie's Metalheadz label; Additional recordings as Jazz Juice, Lunar Funk and Original Playboy. *Recordings:* Basic Principles, 1995; I Want You, 1995; Chill Pill; Detroit; Jazz Juice; A Nu Era; Touch Me; Pulp Fiction; Ibiza; Jazz Master; UR; Rough Cut; Atlantic Drama; Out of Time; Others; Album: So Far, 1996; Singles: Feel the Sunshine; Candles; I Want You/B-Boy Flavour, 1995; Acid Lab, 1996; Candles, 1996; As Producer: Platinum Breakz, 1996; Rawworks, for Laurent Garnier, 1996; Jungle Jazz, 1996; In Flux (remixing), 1997; Incredible Sound of Drum 'n' Bass, with Goldie, 1999; Remixer of: Mandalay, Solace, 2001. *Honours:* Best Jungle Single, Pulp Fiction, Dance Awards, Kiss FM, 1995. *Membership:* PRS; Musicians' Union. *Address:* c/o Island Records, 825 Eighth Ave, 24th Floor, New York, NY 10019, USA.

REECE, Damon; b. 16 Feb. 1967. Musician (drums). *Career:* Member, Spiritualized; Numerous live dates including world tour; Concerts at London Royal Albert Hall and CN Tower, Toronto. *Recordings:* Singles: Anyway That You Want Me, 1991; Run, 1991; Let It Flow, 1995; Electricity, 1997; I Think I'm In Love, 1998; Abbey Road EP, 1998; Albums: Lazer Guided Melodies, 1992; Fucked Up Inside (live), 1993; Pure Phase, 1995; Ladies and Gentlemen We Are Floating In Space, 1997; Royal Albert Hall October 10 1997 (live), 1998; with Lupine Howl: The Carnivorous Lunar Adventures Of. . ., 2001; The Bar At The End Of The World, 2002.

REED, Brett; b. 1972. Musician (drums). *Career:* Joined Rancid; Numerous live shows. *Recordings:* Singles: Rancid, 1993; Radio, Radio, Radio, 1994; Roots Radicals, 1995; Time Bomb, 1995; Ruby Soho, 1996; Bloodclot, 1998; Hooligans, 1998; Brad Logan, 1998; Albums: Rancid, 1993; Let's Go, 1994; And Out Come the Wolves, 1995; Life Won't Wait, 1998; Other collaborations include: Peter Garland; Wayne Kramer.

REED, Jerry, (Jerry Hubbard); b. 20 March 1937, Atlanta, Georgia, USA. Country Musician (guitar); Vocalist; Composer; Actor. *Career:* Session guitarist, Nashville; Solo country artiste, 1967–; Duets with Chet Atkins, 1970s; Regular television appearances with Glen Campbell, 1970s; Film appearances include: W W And The Dixie Dance Kings, 1975; Gator, 1976; Smokey and the Bandit, 1977. *Compositions include:* Crazy Legs, Gene Vincent; Misery Loves Company, Porter Wagoner; A Thing Called Love, Johnny Cash; Guitar Man, Elvis Presley; Hits include: Amos Moses; When You're Hot, You're Hot; Lord Mr Ford; She Got The Goldmine (I Got The Shaft); Albums include: Tupelo Mississippi Flash, 1967; Alabama Wild Man, 1969; Cookin', 1970; Georgia Sunshine, 1971; When You're Hot, You're Hot, 1971; Ko Ko Joe, 1972; Jerry Reed, 1972; Hot A Mighty, 1973; Lord Mr Ford, 1973; Half and Half, 1974; Red Hot Picker, 1975; Uptown Poker Club, 1975; Smell The Flowers, 1975; Me and Chet, 1976; Eastbound and Down, 1977; Both Barrels, 1978; In Concert, 1980; Guitar Man, 1997; Pickin, 1999; RCA Country Legends, 2001. *Address:* Jerry Reed Enterprises, PO Box 3586, Brentwood, TN 37024, USA.

REED, Leslie David; b. 24 July 1935, Westfield, Woking, Surrey, England. Composer; Arranger; Conductor; Musician (piano). m. June Williams, 21 May 1960, 1 d. *Education:* Personal music tutor, age 5; London College of Music exams. *Career:* Joined John Barry Seven, 1958; Wembley Concerts; Television appearances include: Drumbeat; Oh Boy; Six Five Special; Ready Steady Go (conductor); Gadzooks; Rolf Harris Show; International Pop Proms; New Faces (panellist); Juke Box Jury. *Compositions include:* for Tom Jones: It's Not Unusual (No. 1, UK), 1965; I'm Coming Home (No. 2, UK), 1967; Delilah (No. 2, UK), 1968; Daughter Of Darkness, 1970; for Engelbert Humperdinck: The Last Waltz (No. 1, UK), 1967; Les Bicyclettes De Belsize; for Des O'Connor: I Pretend (No. 1, UK), 1968; Other. *Compositions include:* There's A Kind of a Hush; Love Is All; Tell Me When; Here It Comes Again; I'm Coming Home; 24 Sycamore; Everybody Knows. *Recordings include:* As arranger, conductor: Green Green Grass of Home, Tom Jones (No. 1, UK), 1966; You've Got Your Troubles, The Fortunes; Hits recorded by Dave Clark Five; P J Proby; Sammy Davis Jr; Connie Francis; Film soundtrack CDs: Mars Attacks; Little Voice; Parting Shots. *Honours:* Jimmy Kennedy Award, 1993; Freedom of City of London, 1994; 110 Gold discs; 10 Ivor Novello awards; O.B.E., 1998. *Membership:* PRS; Vice-President, BAC&S; Ambassador, FIDOF. *Current Management:* Donna L Ford, Rebecca Music Co Ltd. *Address:* Terwick Pl., Rogate, Nr Petersfield, Hampshire GU31 5BY, England.

REED, Lou, (Louis Firbank); b. 2 March 1943, Freeport, Long Island, NY, USA. Vocalist; Songwriter; Musician (guitar); Poet; Journalist. m. Sylvia Morales, 14 Feb. 1980. *Career:* Founder member, lead singer, songwriter, Velvet Underground, 1964–70, 1993–; Tours as part of Andy Warhol's Exploding Plastic Inevitable show; Solo artiste, 1971–93; Appearances include: Montréal World Fair, 1967; Crystal Palace Garden Party, 1973; Reading Festival, 1975; Nelson Mandela – An International Tribute, Wembley Stadium, 1990; John Lennon Tribute Concert, Liverpool, 1990; Glastonbury Festival, 1992; Bob Dylan 30th Anniversary Concert, New York, 1992; Conductor, Metal Machine Music Orchestra, playing his music. *Recordings:* Albums: with the Velvet Underground: The Velvet Underground and Nico, 1967; White Light, White Heat, 1968; The Velvet Underground, 1969; Loaded, 1970; Solo albums: Lou Reed, 1972; Transformer, 1973; Berlin, 1973; Rock 'n' Roll Animal, 1974; Sally Can't Dance, 1974; Lou Reed Live, 1975; Metal Machine Music, 1975; Coney Island Baby, 1976; Rock and Roll Heart, 1976; Walk On The Wild Side—The Best of Lou Reed, 1977; Street Hassle, 1978; Take No Prisoners, 1979; The Bells, 1979; Vicious, 1979; Growing Up In Public, 1980; Rock And Roll Diary, 1980; The Blue Mask, 1982; Transformer, 1982; Legendary Hearts, 1983; Rock Galaxy, 1983; New Sensations, 1984; Mistrial, 1986; Retro, 1989; New York, 1989; Songs For Drella—A Fiction (with John Cale), 1990; Magic And Loss, 1992; Set The Twilight Reeling, 1996; The Raven, 2003; Also appears on: Sun City single, Artists Against Apartheid, 1985; Soul Man (with Sam Moore), theme for film Soul Man, 1987; Duets album, Rob Wasserman, 1988; Victoria Williams benefit album, 1993; Set the Twilight Reeling, 1996; Live, in Concert, 1997; Ecstacy, 2000. *Publications include:* Between Thought and Expression (poetry), 1992. *Honours:* Q Magazine Merit Award, 1991; Knight of the Order of Arts and Letters, France, 1992; Inducted into Rock 'n' Roll Hall of Fame (with Velvet Underground), 1996. *Membership:* AFofM; Screen Actors Guild. *Current Management:* Sister Ray Enterprises, 584 Broadway, Suite 609, New York, NY 10012, USA.

REESE. See: **SAUNDERSON, Kevin.**

REESE, Della, (Deloreese Patricia Early); b. 6 July 1931, Detroit, Michigan, USA. Gospel Vocalist. m. (1) Vermont Adolphus Bon Taliaferro (divorced), (2) Leroy Basil Gray (divorced), (3) Franklin Thomas Lett Jr. *Education:* Wayne University. *Career:* Choir singer, 1938–; Singer with Mahalia Jackson, 1945–49; Clara Ward; Lead singer, Meditation Singers; Erskine Hawkins Orchestra, 1956; Solo artist, 1957–; Organized gospel group at Wayne University; Numerous television appearances include: Jackie Gleason; Ed Sullivan; McCloud; The Love Boat; The A-Team; Charlie and Co; Crazy Like A Fox; MacGyver; Guest host, The Royal Family, 1991; The Tonight Show; Della; Nightmare In Badham County; Ain't Misbehavin'; Blues In The Night; The Last Minstrel Show. *Recordings:* Singles: And That Reminds Me; In The Still of The Night; Don't You Know; Not One Minute More; Someday (You'll Want Me To Want You); Bill Bailey; Albums include: Special Delivery, 1961; The Classic Della, 1962; Waltz With Me Della, 1964; Let Me Into Your Life, 1975; The Classical Della, 1980; Della By Starlight, 1982; I Like It Like That, 1984; Sure Like Lovin' You, 1985; And Brilliance, 1990; Voice of an Angel, 1996; My Soul Feels Better Right Now, 1998; All Of Me, 2000; Sure Like Lovin' You, 2000. *Honours:* Voted Most Promising Singer of Year, 1957. *Current Management:* William Morris Agency, 151 El Camino Dr., Beverly Hills, CA 90212, USA.

REES-JONES, John; b. 9 Nov. 1948, Cardiff, Wales. Musician (double bass, electric upright bass, bass guitar). *Career:* Toured and recorded with Keith Tippett's Centipede, including many other top jazz and rock musicians; Appeared with numerous artists including Yehudi Menuhin, Vilhem Tausky and Roger Norrington; Since 1970s, has worked in theatre, cabaret, studio and in jazz fields; Deputised in many West End Shows including Me and My Girl, Crazy for You, Miss Saigon and Guys and Dolls at the National Theatre; Worked in concert and in cabaret with Richard Stilgoe, Peter Skellern, Vera Lynn, Benny Green, Roy Castle, Helen Shapiro and Anita Harris; Performed on TV's South Bank Show with Petula Clark, the Noel Edmonds Show and on Soldier Soldier; Numerous other TV and radio appearances in the UK and abroad; Toured with the Inkspots, 1988–89, and with the Glenn Miller Orchestra UK; Visiting teacher, Bass Guitar and Bass, Eton College; Worked with many top jazz musicians including Slim Gaillard, Herb Ellis, Barney Kessell, Charlie Byrd, Scott Hamilton, Harry 'Sweets' Edison; Toured, recorded and appeared on TV as part of Giants of Jazz, including Kenny Ball and Acker Bilk, 1993. *Recordings include:* Septeber Energy, 1999. Member, 100 Club All Stars; Deputiser, Humphrey Lyttelton Band; Worked in most European countries, Hong Kong, Pakistan, Argentina and Uruguay. *Address:* May Cottage, 39 Slough Rd, Datchet, Berkshire SL3 9AL, England.

REEVES, Del (Franklin Delano); b. 14 July 1933, Sparta, North Carolina, USA. Country Vocalist; Songwriter; Musician (multi-instrumentalist); Artiste Man. *Career:* Own radio show, aged 12; Own TV show, California, 1950s; Solo recording artiste, 1961–; Regular appearances at Grand Ole Opry, 1958–; Host, numerous TV shows; Film appearances include: Second Fiddle To An Old Guitar; Artist Manager, 1992–; Discovered Billy Ray Cyrus. *Recordings:* Over 50 country hits include: Girl On A Billboard; Looking At The World Through A Windshield; Good Time Charlies; The Philadelphia Phillies; Duet with Penny DeHaven, Bobby Goldsboro, Billie Jo Spears; Albums include: Girl On A Billboard, 1965; Mr Country Music, 1966; Our Way of Life, with Bobby Goldsboro, 1967; Running Wild, 1968; Big Daddy Del, 1970; Friends and Neighbours, 1971; Truckers Paradise, 1973; With Strings and Things, 1975; By Request, with Billie Jo Spears, 1976; Del Reeves, 1979; Baby I Love You, 1988; Greatest Hits, 1994; Gospel, 1996; 20 Golden Good Time, 1996; Let's Go To Heaven Tonight. *Address:* Joe Taylor Artist Agency, Nashville, TN, USA.

REEVES, Martha; b. 18 July 1941, Eufaula, Alabama, USA. Vocalist; Musician (piano, tambourine). Divorced, 1 s. *Education:* 12th Grade graduate, Motown University; Lee Strassberg's Theatre Institute. *Career:* Professional Entertainer; Began as Martha LaVaille, Blues singer; Lead singer, Martha Reeves and The Vandellas; Recent appearances include: Leeza; Dick Clark Specials; Beverly Sills Special; Motown 25 Special; Dusty Springfield Specials; Ed Sullivan; K T Oslin Show; Dinah Shore; Merv Griffin; Mike Douglas; American Bandstand; Saturday Night Live; Dick Cavett; Flip Wilson; The Legendary Ladies of Rock and Roll; Music featured in films including: Thelma and Louise; Good Morning Vietnam; Carrie; Tours of USA, other countries; Performances for Charitable organizations include: Arthritis Foundation; Make A Wish Foundation; March of Dimes; Easter Seals Telethon; Detroit Music Hall; Pat Boone's Telethon; Jerry Lewis' Telethon. *Compositions:* Love Is Like A Heatwave; Nowhere To Run; Dancing In The Street. *Recordings include:* Come and Get These Memories, 1963; Love Is Like A Heat Wave, 1963; A Love Like Yours, 1963; Quicksand, 1963; Live Wire, 1964; In My Lonely Room, 1964; Dancing In The Street (No. 1), 1964; Wild One, 1964; Nowhere To Run, 1965; Love (Makes Me Do Foolish Things), 1965; You've Been In Love Too Long, 1965; My Baby Loves Me, 1966; I'm Ready For Love, 1966; Jimmy Mack, 1967; Third Finger, Left Hand, 1967; Honey Chile, 1967; Live Wire!: The Singles 1962–72, 1993; Dancing in the Street: Their Greatest Hits, 1995; Motown Milestones, 1995; Best Of, 1999. *Publications:* Autobiography, Dancing In The Street (Confessions of a Motown Diva); Martha Reeves Exclusive Newsletter. *Honours:* Dick Clark, Soul of America Award, 1992; Rhythm and Blues Foundation Pioneer Award, 1993; Black Women In Publishing Award, 1994; Rock and Roll Hall of Fame, 1995; Alabama Music Hall of Fame, 1995; Superbowl halftime, 1998; performed for President Clinton, Christmas Tree Lighting, 1998. *Membership:* AFTRA; Screen Actors Guild, spokesperson for Rite-Aid; Breast Cancer Foundation. *Current Management:* Ace Lichtenstein, Ideal Entertainment Inc, Suite 1908, 875 Avenue of the Americas, New York, NY 10001, USA.

REEVES, Thomas W, Jr (Tom); b. 14 Feb. 1953, Boston, Massachusetts, USA. Sound Engineer; Mobile DJ; Musician (electric bass). m. Carol Reeves, 23 Jan. 1998, 1 s., 1 d. *Education:* ATI Technical Institute; School of Contemporary Music, Brookline, Massachusetts; Cabrillo College, California. *Career:* Owner, Cat's Voice Productions; Assistant Manager, Vibrations, 1988; DJ, Encore Entertainment, Newbury, Massachusetts, 1989–; Producer, Sound Block Studios, Salem, New Hampshire, 1990–; Owner, Engineer, Cat's Voice Productions, Massachusetts, 1990–; Owner, Reel Adventures II Recording Studio; Representative, Market America Inc; Manager, Member, Protex Blues Band, 1991; Marketing Agent, Tennie Komar, Fine and Devine. *Recordings:* Producer, M C Chill, 1990; Clean Shot, 1988–; One Groove At A Time, 1991; The Mangled Ducklings, 1993; Hot, Moist, Pink and Stinky, 1993; Paul Wilcox, Signature, 1996. *Membership:* American Federation of Musicians; ASCAP; DJs of America; Brotherhood of Electrical Workers; National Asscn of Independent Record Distributors; National Asscn of Music Merchants. *Address:* 114 Kennebunk Pond Rd, Lyman, ME 04002–7719, USA.

REFOY, Mark Gerard; b. 3 July 1962, Windsor, Berkshire, England. Songwriter; Musician (guitar). *Career:* Played guitar, Spacemen 3, 1989; Played guitar, Spiritualized, 1990–94; Musician, singer, songwriter, own band Slipstream. *Recordings:* Albums as guitarist: Recurring, Spacemen 3; with Spiritualized: Lazer Guided Melodies, 1992; Pure Phase, 1995; Slipstream, 1995; Be Groovy or Leave, 1997; Side Effects, 1998. *Membership:* Musicians' Union; PRS. *Address:* c/o Slipstream – Che Trading, PO Box 653, London E18 2NX, England.

REGAN, Julianne; b. England. Vocalist; Musician (bass). *Career:* Former music journalist; Backing singer, The Mission; Bass player, Gene Loves Jezebel; Lead singer, All About Eve, 1986–. *Recordings:* with All About Eve: Albums: All About Eve, 1987; Scarlet and Other Stories, 1989; Touched By Jesus, 1991; Circle Dance, 1991; Ultraviolet, 1992; Winter Words, Hits and Rarities, 1992; Singles: Our Summer, 1987; Flowers In Our Hair, 1987; Every Angel, 1988; Martha's Harbour, 1988; What Kind Of Fool, 1988; Farewell Mr Sorrow, 1991. *Address:* c/o Polar Union, 45–53 Sinclair Rd, London W14 0NS, England.

REICHMANN, Silke; b. 1 March 1966, Frankfurt, Germany. Musician (hurdy-gurdy). *Education:* University Kassel, Germany; Tuition in hurdy-gurdy and flute; Cornet at Conservatory Frankfurt; Hurdy-gurdy Master Class with Valentin Clastrier, Improvisation with Helmut Eisel. *Career:* Musician, Folk Dance Coach with Die Hummel, 1982–86; Teacher, Workshops in Germany, Netherlands, France, 1983–; Musician in Folk and World Music Band, Trio Grande, 1984–; with Paul Engel, World Premiere in Philharmonic Hall, Munich, 1987; solo Radio Broadcasts, Berlin, 1994; special concert for

the visit of Germany's President Dr Roman Herzog, 1996; Member of EU World Music Project, Kaleidoscop, touring in Sweden, Norway and Finland, 1998; concert at Reception of Minister of Women's Affairs, International Women's Day, 1999; Teacher for hurdy-gurdy, Music School, Berlin, 1999–. *Compositions:* Mazurka des amis; Laisser tomber!; Symbati; Zwei Lieben; Ghostdance; Vielfaches Fuer Aspe. *Recordings:* with Trio Grande: Nabucodonosor, 1990; Bagage, 1994; PiloPao, 1998; with Madre: Ghostdance on Mesmerismo; 1997. *Honours:* First prize at the Hurdy Gurdy Duo Competition, St Chartier France, 1991. *Membership:* ProFolk; GEMA; GVL. *Current Management:* World Music, Valentin Reinbold, Gorrisstrasse 9, 50674 Koeln, Germany. *Address:* Pasteurstrasse 4, 10407 Berlin, Germany.

REID, Antonio 'LA'; Record Co Exec; Prod; A&R; Musician. *Career:* Prod., Boys II Men, Whitney Houston; Co-Founder, Co-Pres., LaFace Records, 1989–2000; Pres. and CEO, Arista Records, 2000–. *Honours:* Grammy Award, Producer. *Address:* c/o Arista Records, 6 W 57th St, New York, NY 10019, USA. *Website:* www.arista.com.

REID, Charlie; Vocalist; Songwriter. *Career:* Formed The Proclaimers, with twin brother Craig, 1983; Played pubs, Edinburgh, Inverness; British tour with The Housemartins; Television debut, The Tube, 1987; Signed to Chrysalis Records, 1987; First single No. 3 in charts; 145 performances, 18 countries, 1988–89; Recorded in Nashville, 1991; Song, I'm Gonna Be (500 miles), theme song to film Benny and Joon, 1993; Tour, USA, included Madison Square Gardens, 1993; Tour: Venezuela; Costa Rica; Brazil; Malaysia; Slovakia; Austria; Canada; Germany; Netherlands; Norway. *Recordings:* (own compositions) Albums: Sunshine On Leith, 1988; This Is The Story, 1994; Hit The Highway, 1994; Persevere, 2001; The Proclaimers: The Best Of..., 2002. Singles: Throw The R Away, 1987; Letter From America, 1987; Make My Heart Fly, 1988; I'm Gonna Be (500 Miles), 1988; Sunshine On Leith, 1988; King of The Road, 1990; Let's Get Married, 1994; What Makes You Cry, 1994; These Arms of Mine, 1994. *Honours:* Platinum disc, Sunshine On Leith. *Current Management:* Braw Music Management. *Address:* 78 Pentland Terrace, Edinburgh EH10 6HF, Scotland.

REID, Craig; Vocalist; Songwriter. *Career:* Formed The Proclaimers, with twin brother Charlie, 1983; Played pubs, Edinburgh, Inverness; British tour with The Housemartins; Television debut, The Tube, 1987; Signed to Chrysalis Records, 1987; First single No. 3 in charts; 145 performances, 18 countries, 1988–89; Recorded in Nashville, 1991; Song, I'm Gonna Be (500 miles), theme song to film Benny and Joon, 1993; Tour, USA, included Madison Square Gardens, 1993; Tour: Venezuela; Costa Rica; Brazil; Malaysia; Slovakia; Austria; Canada; Germany; Netherlands; Norway. *Recordings:* (own compositions) Albums: Sunshine On Leith, 1988; This Is The Story, 1994; Hit The Highway, 1994; Persevere, 2001; The Proclaimers: The Best Of..., 2002. Singles: Throw The R Away, 1987; Letter From America, 1987; Make My Heart Fly, 1988; I'm Gonna Be (500 Miles), 1988; Sunshine On Leith, 1988; King of The Road, 1990; Let's Get Married, 1994; What Makes You Cry, 1994; These Arms of Mine, 1994. *Honours:* Platinum disc, Sunshine On Leith. *Current Management:* Braw Music Management. *Address:* 78 Pentland Terrace, Edinburgh EH10 6HF, Scotland.

REID, Junior (Delroy); b. 1965, Kingston, Jamaica. Reggae Vocalist; Record Prod. *Career:* First recording, aged 13; Member, Voice of Progress group; Solo recording artist, early 1980s, and 1989–; Singer, Black Uhuru, 1985–88; Founder, own record label JR Productions and own recording studio; Record producer, leading artists including: Junior Demus, Ninjaman, Dennis Brown and Gregory Isaacs. *Recordings:* Albums include: with Voice of Progress: Mini-Bus Driver; with Black Uhuru: Brutal, 1986; Positive; Solo albums: Boom Shack A Lack; Back To Back; Original Foreign Mind; Visa, 1994; Junior Reid and the Bloods, 1995; Listen to the Voices, 1996; Big Timer, 2000; Also appears on: Lovegod, Soup Dragons; Two for One, Ninjaman; Nothing Like This, Dennis Brown; Not a One Man Thing, Gregory Isaacs; Rass Portraits, Gregory Isaacs; Streetsoul, Guru, 2000; Singles include: Jailhouse; Sister Dawn; Pallaving Street; Give Thanks and Praise; Boom Shack A Lack; Stop This Crazy Thing (with Coldcut); I'm Free (with the Soup Dragons); One Blood, 1990; Actions Speak Louder Than Words, 1991; Rappa Pam Pam, 1993. *Address:* c/o Zoe Productions, 450 Broome St, Eighth Floor, New York, NY 10013, USA.

REID, Terry (Terrance James); b. 13 Nov. 1949, Huntingdon, Cambridgeshire, England. Vocalist; Musician (guitar, piano). 2 d. *Career:* Toured with: The Rolling Stones; The Hollies; Scott Walker; The Small Faces; Paul Jones; Cream; The Beach Boys; Jethro Tull; Del Shannon; Television includes: Whistle Test; Lulu; David Frost. *Compositions:* Recorded by: Crosby Stills and Nash; Cheap Trick; The Hollies; Arrival. Solo albums include: Bang Bang You're Terry Reid, 1968; Seed Of Memory, 1971; Rogue Waves, 1979; The Hand Don't Fit The Glove, 1985; The Driver, 1991; Terry Reid (compilation), 1992. *Membership:* PRS. *Address:* Hollyoaks, 1a Rectory Rd, Bluntisham, Huntingdon, Cambs PE17 3LN, England.

REID, Vernon; b. England. Musician (guitar). m. Mia McLeod, 6 April 1991. *Education:* Ted Dunbar; Rodney Jones; Manhattan Community College, 2 years. *Career:* Musician with Defunk; Decoding Society; Founder, member, funk rock group Living Colour, 1985–95; Tours include: with Rolling Stones, North America, 1989; Miracle Biscuit Tour, USA, 1990; Lollapalooza Tour, 1991; Stained In The UK tour, 1993; Concerts include: Host, benefit concert, Black Rock Coalition, Los Angeles, 1989; Earth Day, Central Park, 1990; Reading Festival, 1990; Phoenix Festival, 1993; Photography exhibition, Once Upon A Time, Called Now, Chicago, 1991. *Compositions include:* Writer, producer, tracks for B B King, 1990. *Recordings:* Albums: Vivid, 1988; Time's Up, 1991; Biscuits, 1991; Stain, 1993; Super Hits, 1998. *Contributions to:* Primitive Cool, Mick Jagger, 1986; Talk Is Cheap, Keith Richard, 1988; Funk of Ages, Bernie Worrell, 1988; Singles include: Cult of Personality, 1989; Glamour Boys, 1989; Type, 1990; Love Rears Its Ugly Head, 1991; Solace of You, 1991; Leave It Alone, 1993; Also played on sessions for: Jack Bruce; Tracy Chapman; Santana. *Honours:* Elvis Award, Best New Band, International Rock Awards, 1989; MTV Awards, Best New Artist, Best Group Video, Best Stage Performance, 1989; Grammy Award, Best Hard Rock Performance, 1990; Rolling Stone Critics Poll Winners, Best Band, 1991. *Membership:* Black Rock Coalition. *Current Management:* Jim Grant, JGM, Suite 1C, 39A Gramercy Park N, New York, NY 10010, USA.

REID, Wilson; b. 28 Feb. 1961, Accra, Ghana. Vocalist; Musician (guitar). *Education:* Qualified teacher. *Career:* Lead singer, songwriter, Death Bang Party, 1986–94; 2 major UK college tours; Headlined London Town and Country Club, 2 times, 1993; Headlined Marquee Club several times; 2 successful runs, Edinburgh Fringe Festival, 1993, 1994; Appeared on Julian Clary's Best of the Fest, CH4, 1993; Singer and Guitarist with The Tarantinos, completing two nationwide tours. *Publications:* Thrills, Pills and Backache: The Hank Williams Story, 1995. *Membership:* Musicians' Union; Equity. *Current Management:* DBP Productions. *Address:* 842 Garratt Lane, London SW17 0NA, England.

REID DICK, William F; b. 19 July 1952, London, England. Audio Prod; Engineer. m. Lorna Hewitt, 5 June 1982. *Career:* CBS Studios, Whitfield Street, West Indies, 1972–73; Ramport Studios, London, 1973–83; Freelance, 1983–95. *Recordings:* with Thin Lizzy: Jailbreak; Johnny The Fox; Live and Dangerous; with Saxon: Wheels of Steel; Strong Arm of The Law; Motörhead: Iron Fist; also Carlene Carter; Curved Air; Roger Daltrey. *Honours:* 2 Platinum, 5 Gold, 6 Silver albums; Ampex Gold Reel Award. *Membership:* Re-Pro; PRS. *Address:* No. 1, 35 Wemyss Rd, Blackheath, London SE3 0TG, England.

REIFF, Soren, (Reiff, Jr); b. 22 Oct. 1962, Butterup, Denmark. Musician (guitar, keyboard, bass); Prod. *Education:* Music College, Holstebro, 1982. *Career:* Toured Europe and USA with different artists and as a solo artist, 1989–98; Guitarist in TV houseband appearing in around 200 talkshows, Meyerheim and Co, 1991–94; Played with Robert Palmer, Randy Crawford, Paul Young, Toots Thielemanns, Jamie Walters, Curtis Stigers, Bonnie Tyler, Robin Beck and Suzi Q, 1991–98; Played in houseband on TV show Don't Forget Your Toothbrush, Denmark, 1995; Played in houseband on Safari TV show, 1996; Musical Director of houseband on It's Saturday Night, Denmark, 1997; Appeared on 199 shows with Danish trio, Linie 3, 1997–98. *Recordings:* Numerous recordings with Tower of Power, Michael Brecker and Madness 4 Real and artists from the UK, Scandinavia, Japan, India and Mexico; Guitar sample CD, 1998. *Membership:* Board Mem., Music Highschool of Jyderup, Denmark, 1998. *Current Management:* Ballroom.

REIMERS-WESSBERG, Marianne; b. 6 Aug. 1957, Stockholm, Sweden. Music Publisher. m. H G Wessberg, 1 s., 2 d. *Education:* BA, Musicology, German, Economics. *Career:* Editor, Music Teachers' Magazine, Musik Kultur, 1983–88; Managing Director, Reimers AB, 1990–. *Publications:* Lyssna ar Silver, Spela ar Guld, (To Listen Is Silver – To Play Is Gold), 1991. *Membership:* Music Publishers Asscn; STIM; Swedish Music Information Center. *Address:* PO Box 15030, 5 16115 Bromma, Sweden.

REISIG, Bernd; b. 10 March 1963, Frankfurt, Germany. Media Man. *Education:* Engine Fitter; Children's Male Nurse. *Career:* Founded concert agency; Artists: Purple Schulz; Bruce Cockburn; Extrabeit, 1984; Founded music publishing agency, 1985; Founded management agency, 1987; Represent artists: Nena; Badesalz; Thomas Koschwitz; Matthias Beltz; Christian Kahrman; Founded RMG Merchandising and RMG Music Entertainment, 1993; Represent artists: Nena; The Stroke; Mellow D; McDowell-Tarr; Dan; Several dance projects; Share in radio station, Radio 01, 1994; Share in advertising agency Koschwitz-Kommunikation; Share in television production company Feedback. *Honours:* Several Gold records, Grimme-Preis. *Membership:* IFPI; GEMA. *Address:* Reisig Media GmbH, Lersnerstrasse 23, 60322 Frankfurt/Main, Germany.

REISSIG, Heiko Christian; b. 19 Feb. 1966, Wittenberge, Germany. Vocalist (Tenor); Actor; Dir. *Education:* Diplomas, University of Music and Theatre, Leipzig, Berlin and Munich, 1990–97; Diploma of Teaching in Voice. *Career:* Opera Singer and Actor, Komische Oper, Berlin; Oper Leipzig; Theater Hof, Görlitz and other venues in Germany; Actor, film and TV; Singer, numerous festivals and concert tours abroad including Japan, Mexico and Austria. *Membership:* International Yehudi Menuhin Society, London, 1997–; President of the International Society Supporting Young Stage Artists

(ISSA), BühnenReif, Germany, 1997–. *Address:* Richard-Sorge Strasse 11, 10249 Berlin, Germany.

RENAUD, Norman Joseph; b. 11 Aug. 1938, Durban, South Africa (British citizen). Author; Composer; Musician (acoustic, electric guitar, casiotone keyboards, piano, percussion); Singer; Songwriter. m., 3 s., 3 d. *Education:* Technical College; City University. *Career:* Radio and television performances, in UK and worldwide; Vocalist and orchestral musician. *Recordings:* Ballads; Standards, Popular styles, Rock 'n' Roll; Soul; Dance; Country and Western styles, Popular styles, Jazz, Motown song styles; R&B. *Publications:* Currently compiling own songs and music. *Membership:* Guild of International Songwriters and Composers, England. *Current Management:* Renaud Music. *Address:* No. 17 Corbiere House, Fifth Floor, De Beauvoir Estate, Balmes Rd, London N1 5SR, England. *Telephone:* (20) 7923-1527.

RENAULT, Nathalie; b. 26 Nov. 1966, Paris, France. Musician (banjo and trumpet). *Education:* Fine Arts: National Superior Beaux-Arts School of Paris and University of Arts, Paris; Conservatory of Music, Clamart, Hauts-de-Seine. *Career:* Concerts: International Music Festival, Riga, Latvia; Centre Cuturel Francais, Skopje, Macedonia; Jazz Festival, Corinth, Greece; Malmö Festival, Sweden; Cromwell Festival, Upton Upon Severn, UK; Oude Stijl Jazz Festival, Breda, Netherlands; 12 tage Jazz, Frankfurt, Germany; Dixie Jazz Festival, Sargans, Switzerland; Jazz Festival, Vannes; Jazz Band Ball, Paris, France; Nice Jazz Festival, Nice, France. *Recordings:* with female jazz (old style) band Certains L'Aiment Chaud (Some Like It Hot): 1 cassette, 1985; 1 cassette, 1991; Albums: J'ai Deux Amours, 1995; April In Paris, 2002. *Honours:* Sidney Bechet Prize, Jazz Academy, Paris, France, 1992. *Address:* 4 rue Des Pommiers, 93500, Paris, France.

RENBOURN, John; b. 8 Aug. 1944, Marylebone, London, England. Musician (guitar). *Education:* Kingston Art School; Dartington College, Devon. *Career:* Collaborations with: Bert Jansch; Stefan Groossman; Robin Williamson; Founder, groups Pentangle; John Renbourn Group; Ship of Fools; Played at Carnegie Hall; New York Town Hall; Central Park Concert; Sydney Opera House; Royal Albert Hall; Festival Hall; Les Cousins. *Recordings:* Sir Johnalot; Lady and The Unicorn; Black Balloon; Nine Maidens; Wheel of Fortune; Live in America; BBC Live in Concert, 2001. *Publications:* Guitar Pieces; Guitar Styles; Medieval Renaissance Anthology. *Membership:* The Galpin Society. *Current Management:* Folklore Inc, 1671 Appian Way, Santa Monica, CA 90401, USA.

RENDELL, Don; b. 4 March 1926, Plymouth, England. Musician (saxophone, flute, clarinet). m. Joan Ruth Yoxall, 27 March 1948, 1 d. *Career:* Oscar Rabin Band, 1948–49; Founder member, John Dankworth Seven, 1950–53; Ted Heath Orchestra, 1955–56; Stan Kenton, 1956; Own Quartet, Quintet, Sextet, 1957–; Woody Herman Anglo-American Herd, 1959; Recordings with all the above; International jazz festivals: Antibes, 1968; BBC2 TV, Greenwich, 1979; Brecon, 1991; Villeneuve, 1992; Professor, Jazz Saxophone, Guildhall School Music and Drama. *Compositions:* 100 include: On The Way; Antibes; Euphrates; Calavinas. *Recordings:* 5 albums as Rendell/Carr 5; Solo albums: Space Walk, 1971; Earth Music, 1979; Don Rendell Big 8: If I Should Lose You, 1992; with Jimmy Deuchar, Showcase, 2001. *Publications:* Flute Method; Saxophone Selection; Sax Skills (video). *Membership:* Founder mem., Clarinet and Saxophone Society (CASS); Asscn of British Jazz Musicians. *Address:* 23 Weir Hall Gardens, Edmonton, London N18 1BH, England.

RENE, Tawamba; b. 27 July 1962, Bangassou, Central African Republic. Author; Composer; Vocalist. m. Fozen Brigitte, 1 s., 1 d. *Career:* Dancer, Johny Tezano, 1987–91; Many Television and Radio Programs; Festivals. *Compositions include:* Bibi Kitoko; Palauce Sonkouss; Bjamena; Sambara Reko; Kibindo Lauce; Tika Kolela. *Recordings:* Bibi Kotoko; Confiance Perdue; Palauce Sonkouss; Bjamena; Sambara Perko; Kibindo Lauce; Tika Kolela. *Current Management:* Jack Palance, Tawamba Rene S/C Aamont PO Box 4562, Yaoundé, Cameroon.

RENLIDEN, Ivan; b. 27 Sept. 1936, Sweden. m. Sonja, 27 Oct. 1956, 1 s., 1 d. *Education:* Student, 1956; Academy of Music, Stockholm, Musical Teacher, 1964, Diploma of Piano, 1964. *Career:* Musical Leader, Arranger and Pianist, major stages in Stockholm; Almost 1000 Radio and TV Programs, lots of recordings with popular Swedish artists. *Recordings:* Svenska Melodier; Ivan Renliden Spelar Ivan Renliden; Ain't Misbehavin; Spectrum; Ivan Renliden Spelar Chopin. *Honours:* Cultural Prize of Stockholm, 1975. *Membership:* STIM; SAMI. *Address:* Ullerudsb 79, 12373 Farsta, Sweden.

RENO, Mike; b. Canada. Vocalist; Songwriter. *Career:* Member, Moxy; Founder member, Canadian rock group, Loverboy, 1980–89; Extensive tours, USA, Canada; Support to Def Leppard, European tour, 1988. *Compositions:* Co-writer, with Bryan Adams, Jon Bon Jovi, Richie Sambora, for Loverboy tracks. *Recordings:* Albums: Loverboy, 1980; Get Lucky, 1981; Keep It Up, 1983; Lovin' Every Minute of It, 1985; Wildside, 1987; Big Ones (compilation), 1989; Six, 1997; Live, Loud And Loose, 1982–86, 2001; Singles: Turn Me Loose; The Kid Is Hot Tonite; Working For The Weekend; Hot Girls In Love; Lovin' Every Minute of It. *Honours:* Multi-platinum records for all 5 studio albums; JUNO Awards: Album of the Year, Loverboy, 1981; Get Lucky, 1982; Single of the Year, Turn Me Loose, 1981; Group of Year, 1981; 1982; Composer of the Year (with Paul Dean), 1981; Tribute To West Coast Music Awards: Best Group, 1981; 1982; Best Album: 1981, 1982; Song of the Year, The Kid Is Hot Tonite, 1981; Most Promising Act, 1981; International Achievement Award, 1984; Rock Band of Year, 1981. *Current Management:* Lou Blair Management Inc. *Address:* No. 407–68 Water St, Vancouver, British Columbia V6B 1A4, Canada.

RESCALA, Tim, (Luiz Augusto); b. 21 Nov. 1961, Rio de Janeiro, Brazil. Composer; Arranger; Musician (piano). m. Claudia Mele, 24 June 1995, 1 d. *Education:* Piano with Maria Yêda Cadah; Composition with Hans-Joachim Koellreutter, Master's degree at University of Rio de Janeiro. *Career:* Works with serious music and pop music; Musical producer at TV Globo since 1988. *Compositions:* Scores for over 50 stage productions; Compositions played in Brazil; France; Canada; Belgium; USA; United Kingdom; Music for films with director Eduardo Coutinho; Music for Berimbuu and Tape, Cliché Music; Salve O Brasil!, Ponto, Linha E Plano. *Recordings:* Cliché Music (with popular songs and a suite for instruments); Album, Estudio da Glória (electroacoustic music). *Honours:* First Prize in Villa-Lobos Competition; Mambembe Prize (theatre), 1983, 1993; Prize of Rio de Janeiro Municipality to write an opera. *Membership:* Estúdio da Glória (co-founder). *Address:* Estúdio da Glória, Rua Candido Mendes 53/104, Glória Cep 20.241, Rio de Janeiro, RJ, Brazil.

REUBEN, Cyril; b. 30 April 1930, Bangor, North Wales. Musician (woodwind); Music Shop Retailer. m. Sylvia, 22 Dec. 1958, deceased, 1 s., 1 d. *Education:* University College of North Wales. *Career:* Member, orchestras of: Geraldo; Squadronaires; Jack Parnell; Concerts, tours include: Frank Sinatra; Liza Minelli; Shirley MacLaine; Johnny Mathis; Bing Crosby; Sarah Vaughan; Liberace. *Recordings:* Records with: The Beatles (The Beatles/The White Album, No. 1, UK and USA, 1968); The Carpenters; Music for television series include: Thunderbirds; Stingray; Captain Scarlett; Films include: Jesus of Nazareth; Fall of The Roman Empire; In Hannibals Footsteps. *Membership:* Musicians' Union. *Address:* Woodwind, Derek Rd, Maidenhead, Berkshire SL6 8NT, England.

REVELL, Graeme; b. 23 Oct. 1955, Auckland, New Zealand. Composer. *Education:* University of Auckland. *Compositions:* For television: Bangkok Hilton, 1989; Psycho IV: The Beginning, 1991; Dune, 2000; For film: Dead Calm, 1989; Spontaneous Combustion, 1989; Till There was You, 1990; Child's Play 2, 1990; Love Crimes, 1991; Until the End of the World, 1991; Traces of Red, 1992; Deadly, 1992; The People Under the Stairs (additional music), 1992; The Hand That Rocks the Cradle, 1992; Hear No Evil, 1993; Ghost in the Machine, 1993; The Crush, 1993; Body of Evidence, 1993; Boxing Helena, 1993; Hard Target, 1993; Street Fighter, 1994; S.F.W., 1994; No Escape, 1994; The Crow, 1994; Killer: A Journal of Murder, 1995; Tank Girl, 1995; The Basketball Diaries, 1995; Mighty Morphin Power Rangers: The Movie, 1995; The Tie That Binds, 1995; Strange Days, 1995; From Dusk Till Dawn, 1996; Race the Sun, 1996; The Craft, 1996; Fled, 1996; The Crow: City of Angels, 1996; Suicide Kings, 1997; Chinese Box, 1997; The Saint, 1997; Spawn, 1997; Phoenix, 1998; Bride of Chucky, 1998; The Big Hit, 1998; The Negotiator, 1998; Lulu on the Bridge, 1998; Strike, 1998; The Siege, 1998; Idle Hands, 1999; Buddy Boy, 1999; Three to Tango, 1999; Bats, 1999; The Insider (additional music), 1999; Pitch Black, 2000; Gossip, 2000; Attraction, 2000; Titan A.E., 2000; Red Planet, 2000; Double Take, 2001; Blow, 2001; Tomb Raider, 2001; Collateral Damage, 2001; High Crimes, 2002. *Membership:* BMI. *Current Management:* Blue Focus Management, 15233 Ventura Blvd, Suite 200, Sherman Oaks, CA 91403, USA.

REVERE, Paul; b. 7 Jan. 1938, Caldwell, Idaho, USA. Musician; Comic; Businessman. m. Sydney Revere, 1980, 1 s., 1 d. *Career:* Formed Paul Revere and The Raiders, 1960; Television, hosted: Where The Action Is, with Dick Clark, 1965–66; Happening, 1968–69; 2 appearances, Ed Sullivan Show. *Recordings:* Kicks; Indian Reservation; Just Like Me; Good Thing; Louie Louie; Hungry; Ups and Downs; Him Or Me; Just Like Us; Super Hits, 2000; Mojo Working, 2000. *Honours:* Northwest Music Awards; Hall of Fame; Numerous Gold Records. *Current Management:* Robert Norman/Fred Lawrence at International Management. *Address:* 8942 Wilshire Blvd, Beverly Hills, CA 90211, USA.

REYES, Fernando; b. 4 Feb. 1939, Conil De La Frontera, Cádiz, Spain. Flamenco Vocalist; Flamenco Musician (guitar). m. Gillian Carol Hamling, 29 March 1975, 1 s., 1 d. *Education:* Private musical tuition, Spain. *Career:* Performed throughout: Spain; Europe; Canada; USA; Asia; Played for Antonio and Paco Romero and The King and Queen of Belgium; Toured with: Los Paraguayos; Performances include: Madison Square Gardens; Palais De Beaux Arts; Royal Albert Hall; Royal Festival Hall; Sadlers Wells; Covent Garden; Queen Elizabeth Hall; Fairfield Hall; Purcell Room; Numerous provincial festivals; Sang in opera Carmen in UK and Germany; Television includes: Opportunity Knocks; Blue Peter; Barrymore; Good Stuff; Collector's Lot; Live musical soundtrack for film, Pain Is…, 1998; also various film scores; Broadcast on Virgin Radio. *Compositions:* Words and music various songs. *Recordings:* Albums: Spanish, South American music; Flamenco Songs;

Spanish Popular Songs; CDs: Encuentros; Flamenco; Flamenco Gypsy. *Honours:* Various medals, trophies, awards, flamenco competitions in Spain. *Membership:* Musicians' Union. *Current Management:* Gillian Reyes. *Address:* 19 Fairmount Rd, London SW2 2BJ, England. *Telephone:* (20) 8671-1317.

REYNOLDS, Debbie (Mary Frances); b. 1 April 1932, El Paso, Texas, USA. Actress; Vocalist; Entertainer. m. (1) Eddie Fisher, 26 Sept. 1955, divorced, 1959, 1 d.; m. (2) Harry Karl, 25 Nov. 1960, divorced 1973; m. (3) Richard R Hamlett, 1985. *Career:* Nightclub act, mid 1960s–; Headlines casino circuit, including Reno, Tahoe, Las Vegas, Atlantic City; London Palladium; Tours average 42 weeks a year; Over 30 films include: Three Little Words; Two Weeks With Love; Singin' In The Rain; The Unsinkable Molly Brown; The Tender Trap; Divorce American Style; Theatre includes: Irene, 1973; Annie Get Your Gun; Woman of the Year, 1983; National tour, The Unsinkable Molly Brown, 1989; Founded Debbie Reynolds Professional Rehearsal Studios, North Hollywood, late 1970s; Currently establishing Hollywood Motion Picture and Television Museum, in the Debbie Reynolds Hollywood Hotel and Casino. *Recordings:* Abba Dabba Honeymoon (from Two Weeks With Love); Tammy; 5 videos Debbie/Am I That Easy to Forget?, 1996; Cocktail Hour, 2001; Post sessions producer: Baltimore Consort: Tunes from the Attic, 1997. *Publications:* Debbie My Life (co-written with David Patrick Colombia), 1987. *Honours:* National Hon. Presented by Girl Scouts USA, 1966–69; National Film Award, Humanitarian Award, National Film Society; Celebrity Hall of Fame Award, National Asscn for Mental Health; Hollywood Hall of Fame, Hollywood Historic Trust and Chamber of Commerce. *Membership:* Supporter, fund raiser, Girl Scouts; Founder-president of the Thalians. *Address:* c/o Stan Scotland, JKE Services, 404 Park Ave S, 10th Floor, New York, NY 10016, USA.

REYNOLDS, (Lee) Allen; b. North Little Rock, Arkansas, USA. Country record producer; Songwriter; Music publisher. *Education:* Rhodes College, Memphis, English student. *Career:* Began songwriting partnership with long-term collaborator and friend Dickey Lee at college; Moved to Texas; Joint composition I Saw Linda Yesterday became US hit for Lee, 1962; Composition about day job in a bank, Five O'Clock World, subsequently a Top 5 US pop hit for the Vogues; Moved to Nashville and began production work, including Don Williams' recording of I Recall A Gypsy Woman; Purchased Jack's Tracks Recording Studio in Nashville, 1976; Set up self-contained recording and publishing operation; Own recording career, 1978; Productions include: Crystal Gayle; Kathy Mattea; O'Kanes; Bobby Bare; George Hamilton IV; Daniel O'Donnell; Randy VanWarmer; Hal Ketchum; Emmylou Harris; all of Garth Brooks' country albums; Songs recorded by artists including: Waylon Jennings; Johnny Russell; Marianne Faithfull. *Compositions include:* Catfish John; Everybody's Reaching Out For Someone; Five O'Clock World; I Saw Linda Yesterday; Ready For The Times To Get Better; Somebody Loves You; We Should Be Together. *Honours:* Sales of albums produced for Garth Brooks surpass the 100m. mark; BMI 'Millionair' Award for over 1m. radio performances of compositions Ready For The Times To Get Better and Five O'Clock World; Inducted into Nashville Songwriters Asscn Inc (NSAI) Hall of Fame with long time associate and friend Dickey Lee, 2000. *Address:* c/o Jack's Tracks Recording Studio, 1308 16th Ave S, Nashville 37212, USA.

REZNOR, Michael Trent; b. 17 May 1965, Mercer, PA, USA. Rock Musician; Vocalist. *Career:* Founder member, lead vocalist, US rock group Nine Inch Nails, 1989–. *Recordings:* Albums: Pretty Hate Machine, 1990; Broken (mini album), 1992; Fixed, 1992; Downward Spiral, 1994; Children of the Night, 1996; Perfect Drug, 1997; Fragile, 1999; Things Falling Apart, 2000; Singles include: Head Like A Hole, 1990; Compiler, film soundtrack Natural Born Killers, 1995. *Current Management:* John Malm, Conservative Management, 2337 W 11th St, Suite 7, Cleveland, OH 44113, USA.

RHYS, Gruff; b. 18 July 1970, Haverfordwest, Wales. Vocalist; *Career:* Member, Super Furry Animals; Recorded 2 EPs on indie label, then obtained major indie label deal; Numerous tours in the UK and abroad; Began as techno outfit but became more psychedelic and progressive rock; Appeared at numerous festivals. *Recordings:* Singles: Llanfairpwllgwyngyllgogerychwyndrobwl… EP, 1995; Moog Droog, 1995; God! Show Me Magic, 1996; If You Don't Want Me To Destroy You, 1996; The Man Don't Give a Fuck, 1996; Hometown Unicorn, 1996; Something 4 The Weekend, 1996; The International Language of Screaming, 1997; Hermann Loves Pauline, 1997; Demons, 1997; Play it Cool, 1997; Ice Hockey Hair, 1998; Northern Lights, 1999; Fire In My Heart, 1999; Do Or Die, 1999; Juxtaposed With U, 2001; (Drawing) Rings Around The World, 2001; Albums: Fuzzy Logic, 1996; Radiator, 1997; Guerrilla, 1999; Mwng, 2000; Rings Around The World, 2001.

RHYS-JONES, Merlin; b. 15 June 1958, Brighton, Sussex, England. Musician (guitar); Songwriter; Arranger. *Career:* Recorded with Lipservice; Toured with Ian Dury and The Music Students, 1983; Ian Dury and The Blockheads, 1992, 1994–95; Ellis, Beggs and Howard, 1989; Television includes: The Tube with Ian Dury; Sight and Sound; Martin Dobson's Main Course, Capital Radio. *Recordings:* Albums with Ian Dury: 4000 Weeks Holiday; Apples; Bus-Drivers Prayer and Other Stories (includes some co-writes); Warts and Audience (Live Blockheads at Brixton Academy); Guitar on Strange Liquid, Recoil, 2000; Several sessions for television shows; Currently teaching at Musicians Institute, Wapping. *Membership:* Publishing agreement with Mute Song; Musicians' Union; PRS. *Address:* Flat 21, 318 Hornsey Rd, London N7 7HE, England.

RHYTHIM IS RHYTHIM. See: MAY, Derrick.

RIBOT, Marc; b. 21 May 1954, Newark, New Jersey, USA. Musician (guitar). *Education:* Studied with Frantz Casseus. *Career:* Moved to New York, 1978; Member, Realtones/Uptown Horns Band, 1979–83; Member, John Lurie's Lounge Lizards, 1984–89; Freelance musician, 1989–; Played with Jack MacDuff; Wilson Pickett; Chuck Berry; Solomon Burke; Tom Waits; Elvis Costello. *Recordings:* Albums: with Tom Waits: Rain Dogs; Big Time; Frank's Wild Years; with John Zorn: Cynical Hysterical Tour; Kristellnacht; with Elvis Costello: Spike; Mighty Like A Rose; Kojak Variety; Numerous solo albums include: Rootless Cosmopolitans, 1990; Shrek, 1994; Don't Blame Me, 1995; Shoe String Symphonettes, 1997; Prosthetic Cubans, 1998; A Yo I Killed Your God, 1999; Muy Divertido, 2000; Saints, 2001; Also recordings with: The Lounge Lizards; John Lurie; Evan Lurie; Solomon Burke; The Jazz Passengers; David Sanborn; Caetano Veloso; Marianne Faithfull; Laurie Anderson; T-Bone Burnett; Sam Philips; Alain Bashung; Joe Henry. *Current Management:* Emcee Artist Management. *Address:* 189 Franklin St, Suite 294, New York, NY 10013, USA.

RICE, Melanie Ailene; b. 4 Nov. 1957, Philadelphia, Pennsylvania, USA. Vocalist; Musical Contractor. *Education:* Rowan College; BA, Music, University of Delaware. *Career:* Tours: Opening act for: Joan Rivers; Smokey Robinson; Shecky Greene; David Brenner; Susan Anton; George Kirby; Bobby Vinton; Backing vocalist for: Grover Washington; James Darren; Joe Piscopo; Bobby Rydell; Various Casino Hotel appearances as solo act. *Recordings:* Solo: He Loves She Loves, 2000. *Honours:* John Phillip Sousa Award. *Membership:* NACE. *Current Management:* Melanie Rice Entertainment, Inc. *Address:* 2511 Huntingdon Pike, Huntingdon Valley, PA 19006, USA.

RICE, Sir Tim, (Miles Bindon); b. 10 Nov. 1944, Amersham, Buckinghamshire, England. Writer; Broadcaster. m. Jane Arterata McIntosh, 1974, divorced 1990, 1 s., 1 d. *Education:* Lancing College. *Career:* EMI Records, 1966–68; Norrie Paramor Organisation, 1968–69; Founder, Director, GRRR Books Ltd, 1978–; Pavilion Books Ltd, 1981–97; Appearances on TV and radio including Just A Minute, Radio 4; Creative Works: Lyrics for stage musicals (with Andrew Lloyd Webber): Joseph and the Amazing Technicolour Dreamcoat, 1968; Jesus Christ Superstar, 1970; Evita, 1976; Cricket, 1986; Other musicals: Blondel, with Stephen Oliver, 1983; Chess, with Benny Andersson and Bjorn Ulvaeus, 1984; Tycoon, with Michel Berger, 1992; Selection of songs, Beauty and the Beast, with Alan Menken, 1994; Heathcliff, with John Farrar, 1996; King David, with Alan Menken, 1997; Aida, with Elton John, 1998; Lyrics for musical films: Aladdin, with Alan Menken, 1992; The Lion King, with Elton John, 1994, theatre version, 1997; Lyrics for songs with other composers including Paul McCartney, Mike Batt, Freddie Mercury, Graham Gouldman, Marvin Hamlisch, Rick Wakeman, John Barry; Hit singles (as composer) include: Don't Cry For Me Argentina, Julie Covington (No. 1, UK), 1977, covered by Madonna, 1996; I Know Him So Well, Elaine Paige & Barbara Dickson (No. 1, UK), 1984, covered by Steps, 2001; Can You Feel The Love Tonight?, Elton John, 1994. *Publications:* Song books from musicals; Guinness Book of Hit Albums, co-author; Guinness Book of British Hit Singles, co-author; Fill Your Soul, 1994; Cricket Writer, National Newspapers and Cricket Magazines. *Honours:* Academy Award, Golden Globe, Best New Song, A Whole New World, 1992 for Can You Feel The Love Tonight, with Elton John, 1994, and for You Must Love Me with Andrew Lloyd Webber, 1996; Gold and platinum records in numerous countries; 11 Ivor Novello Awds; 2 Tony Awards; 5 Grammy Awards; Kt, 1994. *Membership:* Chairman, Stars Organisation for Spastics, 1983–85; Shaftesbury Avenue Centenary Committee, 1984–86; President, Lords Taverners, 1988–90; Dramatists' Saints and Sinners, Chairman, 1990; Cricket Writers; Foundation for Sport and the Arts, 1991–; Garrick Club; Groucho Club; MCC. *Address:* 31 The Terrace, Barnes, London SW13 0NR, England.

RICH, John; b. 7 Jan. 1974, Amarillo, Texas, USA. Country vocalist; Musician (pedal steel guitar, bass guitar). *Career:* Began career as singer and performer in the bluegrass field; Formed Texasee with Dean Sams, Keech Rainwater, Michael Britt and Richie McDonald, 1992; Originally shared lead vocal duties in band with McDonald; Group became resident house band at the Wildhorse Saloon, Nashville; After subsequent name change to Lonestar, came to the attention of BMG and were signed to their BNA subsidiary; Released promotional six-track live CD, recorded at the Wildhorse; First country chart entry No News/Tequila Talkin' from debut album Lonestar, 1996; By the time of group's second album release, Crazy Nights, effectively sidelined as Richie McDonald became Lonestar's sole featured lead vocalist, despite previously shared duties and penning band successes Come Cryin' To Me and Say When; Left band to pursue solo career, 1998; Continued association with BNA label and first solo album, produced by friend and veteran songwriter Sharon Vaughan, Underneath The Same Moon contained debut single I Pray For You. *Recordings include:* with Lonestar: No News, Tequila Talkin', 1996; Come Cryin' To Me, 1997; solo: I Pray For You;

Albums: Underneath The Same Moon. *Address:* c/o Country Music Asscn, 1 Music Circle S, Nashville, TN 37203, USA.

RICHARD, Sir Cliff, (Harry Rodger Webb); b. 14 Oct. 1940, Lucknow, India. Vocalist; Musician (guitar). *Education:* Riversmead School, Cheshunt. *Career:* Leader, Cliff Richard and the Shadows; First successful record, Move It, 1958; Later, solo artiste; Regular international concert tours, 1958–; Films include: Serious Charge, 1959; Expresso Bongo, 1960; The Young Ones, 1961; Summer Holiday, 1962; Wonderful Life, 1964; Finders Keepers, 1966; Two a Penny, 1968; His Land, Take Me High, 1973; Own television series, BBC and ITV; Frequent television and radio appearances; various repertory and variety seasons; Stage appearances in musicals: Time, Dominion Theatre, London, 1986–87; Heathcliff, Hammersmith Apollo, London, 1996–97. *Recordings:* First single, Move It, 1958; Over 120 singles to date including: Living Doll (No. 1, UK), 1959; Please Don't Tease (No. 1, UK), 1960; I Love You (No. 1, UK), 1960; The Young Ones (No. 1, UK), 1962; Bachelor Boy/The Next Time (No. 1, UK), 1963; Summer Holiday (No. 1, UK), 1963; The Minute You're Gone (No. 1, UK), 1965; The Day I Met Marie, 1966; Congratulations (No. 1, UK), 1968; Power To All Our Friends, 1973; Miss You Nights, 1975; Devil Woman, 1976; We Don't Talk Anymore (No. 1, UK), 1979; Carrie, 1980; Daddy's Home, 1981; Living Doll, with The Young Ones (No. 1, UK), 1986; All I Ask Of You, with Sarah Brightman, 1986; Some People, 1987; Mistletoe And Wine (No. 1, UK), 1988; The Best Of Me, 1989; I Just Don't Have The Heart, 1989; Saviour's Day (No. 1, UK), 1990; The Millennium Prayer (No. 1, UK), 1999; Somewhere Over The Rainbow/What A Wonderful World, 2001; Over 50 albums include: 21 Today, 1961; The Young Ones, 1961; Summer Holiday, 1963; 40 Golden Greats, 1977; Love Songs, 1981; Private Collection, 1988; The Album, 1993 (all No. 1 in UK charts); The Whole Story, 2000; Wanted, 2001; The Singles Collection, 2002. *Publications:* Questions, 1970; The Way I See It, 1972; The Way I See It Now, 1975; Which One's Cliff?, 1977; Happy Christmas from Cliff, 1980; You, Me and Jesus, 1983; Mine to Share, 1984; Jesus, Me and You, 1985; Single-Minded, 1988; Mine Forever, 1989; My Story: A Celebration of 40 Years in Showbusiness, 1998. *Honours:* O.B.E., 1980; Ivor Novello Award for Outstanding Achievement, 1989; Knighted, 1995; Top Box Office Star of Great Britain, 1962–63, 1963–64; Gold discs for Living Doll, The Young Ones, Bachelor Boy, Lucky Lips, Congratulations, Power to All Our Friends, Devil Woman, We Don't Talk Anymore, Daddy's Home, Mistletoe and Wine; 32 Silver discs; Platinum disc for Millennium Prayer, 1999. *Membership:* Equity. *Current Management:* Cliff Richard Organisation. *Address:* c/o PO Box 46c, Esher, Surrey KT10 0RB, England. *Website:* www.cliffrichard.org.

RICHARD, Marc; b. 22 Nov. 1946, Neuilly-Sur-Seine, France. Jazz Musician (saxophone, clarinet); Composer; Arranger. *Education:* 3 years of courses for arrangement. *Career:* Played cornet with Haricots Rouges, 1963; Played saxophone and clarinet with many different bands including: Irakli; François Biensan; Founder, Anachronic Jazz Band, 1976; Played as sideman in Paris for many years with prominent jazzmen, including: Cab Calloway; Dee Dee Bridgewater; Harry Edison; Teacher, Jazz History, various schools. *Recordings:* Anachronic Jazz Band, Vol. 1, 1977; Vol. 2, 1980; Also appears on: Duke Ellington Complete Edition Vol. 1; Accident, John Greaves, 1982; Bix Beiderbecke, Vols 2, 4, 5, 7, 8, 1994–96; Solo: After You've Gone. *Address:* 21 Allée de Fontainebleau, 75019 Paris, France.

RICHARD, Zachary; b. 8 Sept. 1950. Vocalist; Songwriter; Poet; Musician (guitar, piano, cajun accordion, harmonica). m. Claude Thomas, 11 Jan. 1992. *Education:* BA, summa cum laude, Tulane University, 1972. *Career:* Innovator, Cajun and Zydeco Musical Styles; Composer and Prod., TV documentaries: Against the Grain, 2002; Contre vents, contre mareés, 2002. *Recordings:* Albums: Bayou des Mystères, 1976; Mardi Gras, 1977; Migration, 1977; Allons Danser, 1978; Live in Montréal, 1979; Vent D'Été, 1980; Zack Attack, 1984; Zack's Bon Ton, 1986; Mardi Gras Mambo, 1988; Women in the Room, 1990; Snake Bite Love, 1992; Cap Enragé, 1996; Who Stole My Monkey; Come on Sheila; Cap Enragé; La Ballade de Jean Batailleur; Coeur Fidèle, 2000; High Time, 2001. *Publications:* Poetry: Voyage de Nuit, 1986; Faire Récolte, 1997; Anthology: Travailler C'est Trop Dur, 1999; Feu, 2000; Conte Cajun, 2000; Silver Jubilee, 2000; High Time, 2001. *Honours:* Prix de la Jeune Chanson Francaise, 1980; Prix Miroir de Québec, 1996; Officier de l'Ordre des Arts et Lettres, 1996; 2 Certified Gold Canadian Awards, 1978; Felix de l'ADISQ, 1997, 1998, 1999, 2000; Certified Platinum Canadian, 1997; Prix Littéraire Champlain, 1998; Prix Roland Gasparic, 2001. *Current Management:* Claude Thomas, PO Box 1378, Scott Lane 70583, 318, 2699926, USA. *Website:* www.zacharyrichard.com.

RICHARDS, Aled; b. 5 July 1969, Camarthen, Wales. Musician (drums). *Career:* Member, The Hepburns; Member, Catatonia, 1996–2001; Numerous festival appearances and live gigs; Many appearances on music shows on TV and radio. *Recordings:* Albums: Way Beyond Blue, 1996; The Sublime Magic of Catatonia, 1996; International Velvet (No. 1, UK), 1998; Equally Cursed and Blessed (No. 1, UK), 1999; Paper Scissors Stone, 2001; Greatest Catatonia Hits, 2002. Singles: Bleed/ Do You Believe In Me, 1996; Mulder and Scully, 1998; Road Rage, 1998; Strange Glue, 1998; Londinium, 1999; Dead From The Waist Down, 1999; Karaoke Queen, 1999; Stone By Stone, 2001.

RICHARDS, Andy; Prod; Programmer; Musician (keyboards). *Career:* As Programmer and Keyboard Player has worked with Trevor Horn and Stephen Lipson on many projects including: Frankie Goes to Hollywood, Propaganda, Grace Jones; Other Artists include: George Michael, The Pet Shop Boys, Chris De Burgh, Def Leppard, Wet Wet Wet, Cher, Ronan Keating, Annie Lennox and Tina Turner; As Producer and Programmer clients include: Alphaville; Prefab Sprout; The Pet Shop Boys; Fuzzbox; OMD; T'Pau; Dusty Springfield; Boyzone; Seal; Orchestral Manoeuvers in the Dark; Art of Noise; Genesis. *Current Management:* SARM Management, The Blue Building, 42/46 St Luke's Mews, London W11 1DG, England.

RICHARDS, Claire; b. 17 Aug. 1977, Hillingdon, Middlesex, England. Vocalist. *Career:* Mem., girl group, TSD; Mem., Steps, 1997–2001; Popular with UK teen audience; Numerous television appearances, incl. Steps To The Stars; Tours, incl. Gold–Greatest Hits tour, 2001; Mem., duo, H and Claire, with fellow Steps mem., Ian Watkins, 2002–. *Recordings:* Albums: with Steps: Step One, 1998; Steptacular, 1999; Buzz, 2000; Gold, 2001; The Last Dance, 2002; with H and Claire: Another You Another Me, 2002. Single: with H and Claire: All Out Of Love, 2002. *Honours:* BRIT Award, Best Selling Live Act, 2000. *Address:* c/o Zomba Records Ltd, Zomba House, 165–167 Willesden High Rd, London NW10 2SG, England. *Website:* www.stepsofficial.com.

RICHARDS, Dick, (Richard Boccelli); b. Philadelphia, Pennsylvania, USA. Musician (drums); Vocalist. *Career:* Original member, Bill Haley's Comets, 1954–55; Influential in early development of rock 'n' roll; First rock band to headline a film; Theatre and film actor (as Richard Boccelli). *Recordings:* Rock Around The Clock; See You Later Alligator; Crazy Man Crazy; Shake Rattle and Roll; Rock The Joint; Mambo Rock; Rudy's Rock; Florida Twist; Shimmie Minnie; with Bill Haley: From the Original Master Tapes, 1985; Decca Years and More, 1991; We're Gonna Rock Around The Clock, 2001. *Publications:* Rock Around The Clock; Stage Clear; We're Gonna Party; Never Too Old To Rock; Let's All Rock Together; Now Dig This. *Honours:* Best Vocal group of 1953 Rock and Roll Hall of Fame; Gold records. *Address:* Rock It Concerts, Bruno Mefer Platz 1, 80937 Munich, Germany.

RICHARDS, Eddie, (Jolly Roger); b. Amersham, Buckinghamshire, England. Prod; Remixer; DJ. *Career:* Started as a DJ at the Camden Palace in London; Instrumental in introducing House music to the UK as resident DJ at the Clink Street parties, 1988; Founder: Dy-na-mix DJ agency; Lunar Records; Collaborations: Mr C; Richie Hawtin; Kid Bachelor; Remixed: The Shamen; Orbital. *Recordings:* Singles: as Jolly Roger: Acid Man, 1988; Why Can't We Live Together, 1989; as Eddie Richards: Love Is/House, 2001. *Current Management:* Dy-na-mix.com. *E-mail:* eddierichards@dy-na-mix.com.

RICHARDS, Eric (Thomas); b. 21 July 1953, Alnwick, England. Musician (bass guitar, piano, guitar). 2 d. *Education:* City of Leeds College of Music; BA, Durham University; Jazz and Light Music, Newcastle College of Arts and Technology. *Career:* with Gloria Gaynor: British tour, live television; with Dudu Pukwana's Zila: Tours, television and radio: UK, Europe, Africa; UK radio with Lloyd Ryan; Rhythm on Two, with Tony Evans Orchestra. *Recordings:* with Dudu Pukwana: Live At The 100 Club, 1981; Life In Bracknell and Willisau, 1983; Zila, 1986; Cosmics Chapter 90, 1990; with Lloyd Ryan: Circular Storm, 1989; Four Songs... From Under Mount Nephim, 1997; Smilin Samba, with Selma Garcia, 1998. *Publications:* The Music Factory (bass guitar instrumental workbooks). *Honours:* LTCL (flute). *Address:* Rastenburger Str 17, 44369 Dortmund, Germany.

RICHARDS, Keith, (Keith Richard); b. 18 Dec. 1943, Dartford, Kent, England. Musician (guitar); Vocalist; Songwriter. m. (1) Anita Pallenberg, 1 s., 1 d.; (2) Patti Hansen, 1983, 2 d. *Education:* Sidcup Art School. *Career:* Member, The Rolling Stones, 1962–; Co-writer with Mick Jagger, numerous songs (often under psuedonym The Glimmer Twins); Appearances include: First British tour, 1963; Debut US tour, 1964; Free concert, Hyde Park, 1969; Free concert, Altamont Speedway, 1969; Knebworth Festival, 1976; Played with Chuck Berry, Chicago Blues Festival, 1986; Steel Wheels North American tour, 1989; Final world tour, 2002–03. *Recordings:* Albums include: The Rolling Stones, 1964; The Rolling Stones No 2, 1965; Out of Our Heads, 1965; Aftermath, 1966; Between The Buttons, 1967; Their Satanic Majesties Request, 1967; Beggar's Banquet, 1968; Let It Bleed, 1969; Get Yer Ya-Ya's Out, 1969; Sticky Fingers, 1971; Exile On Main Street, 1972; Goat's Head Soup, 1973; It's Only Rock 'n' Roll, 1974; Black and Blue, 1976; Some Girls, 1978; Emotional Rescue, 1980; Still Life, 1982; Steel Wheels, 1989; Flashpoint, 1991; Stripped, 1, 1995; Bridges to Babylon, 1997; No Security, 1999; Forty Licks, 2002; Also: Hail Hail Rock 'n' Roll (with Chuck Berry), 1987; Talk is Cheap, 1988; Main Offender, 1992; Live at the Hollywood Palladium with the Expensive Winos, 1991; Singles include: Not Fade Away, 1964; It's All Over Now (No. 1, UK), 1964; Little Red Rooster (No. 1, UK), 1964; The Last Time (No. 1, UK), 1965; (I Can't Get No) Satisfaction (No. 1, UK and USA), 1965; Get Off Of My Cloud (No. 1, UK and USA), 1965; Nineteenth Nervous Breakdown, 1966; Paint It Black (No. 1, UK and USA), 1966; Let's Spend The Night Together/Ruby Tuesday, 1967; Jumping Jack Flash (No. 1, UK), 1968; Honky Tonk Woman (No. 1, UK and USA), 1969; Brown Sugar (No. 1, USA), 1971; Tumbling Dice, 1972; Angie (No. 1, USA), 1973; It's Only Rock'n'Roll, 1974; Fool To Cry (No. 1, USA),

1978; Emotional Rescue, 1980; She's So Cold, 1980; Start Me Up, 1981; Going To A Go-Go, 1982; Undercover Of The Night, 1983; Harlem Shuffle, 1986; Mixed Emotions, 1989; Love Is Strong, 1994; Like A Rolling Stone, 1996. *Honours:* with Rolling Stones include: Grammy, Lifetime Achievement Award, 1986; Inducted into Rock and Roll Hall of Fame, 1989; Q Award, Best Live Act, 1990; Ivor Novello Award, Outstanding Contribution To British Music, 1991; Songwriters Hall of Fame, 1993. *Current Management:* Jane Rose, 1776 Broadway Suite 507, New York, NY 10019, USA. *Website:* www.rollingstones.com.

RICHARDS, Red (Charles); b. 19 Oct. 1912, Brooklyn, New York, USA. Jazz Musician (piano); Vocalist. m. Dorothy, 6 Aug. 1942. *Education:* Studied Classics, 6 years. *Career:* Played at Savoy Ballroom with Tab Smith, 4 years; Co-leader, Saints and Sinners with Vic Dickenson; Tours as solo artist, trio, quartet: USA; Canada; Europe; Australia; Played with: Sidney Bechet; Muggsy Spanier; Mezz Mezzrow; Frank Sinatra; Wild Bill Davison; Jimmy McPartland. *Recordings include:* Big Reunion, Fletcher Henderson; Stanley Dances series with Buster Bailey; Dreamy; My Romance; Echoes of Spring, 1998; Guest musician, Marion McPartland's Piano Jazz series, No. 11; Featured on All Star Jazz, 1995; Ladies Sing the Blues 1945–57, 1997; Swingville All Stars: Memphis Blues, 1997; Muggsy Spanier: Live at the Hangover Club in San Francisco, 1997; Stuyvesant Stompers: Dr Jazz, 1997; Dinah Washington: Slick Chick: On the Mellow Side, 1997. *Honours:* Grand Pris Disque de Jazz, Hot Club de France, 1994. *Membership:* AFofM. *Current Management:* Russ Dantzler, 328 W 44th St, New York, NY 10036, USA. *Address:* 3944 Paulding Ave, Bronx, New York, NY 10466, USA.

RICHARDSON, Garth John; b. 23 July 1958, Toronto, Ontario, Canada. Record Prod. m. Jennifer Quinn, 7 Oct. 1989, 2 d. *Education:* Fanshawe Music College. *Career:* Engineer, Canada; Producer, USA; Producer for: Rage Against The Machine; L7; The Melvins; Ugly Kid Joe; POL; Houdini; Chase the Sun; State; Engineer for: Red Hot Chili Peppers; Ozzy Osbourne; Kiss; Mötley Crüe; Alice Cooper; American Man; Bulletboys; Also worked on recordings by: Mary Margaret O'Hara; Bonfire; The Neville Brothers. *Current Management:* Tap/KO Entertainment.

RICHARDSON, Kevin Scott; b. 3 Oct. 1971, Lexington, KY, USA. Vocalist. *Career:* Qualified ballroom dancing instructor; Mem., Backstreet Boys, 1993–; Numerous tours and television appearances. *Recordings:* Albums: Backstreet Boys, 1996; Live in Concert, 1998; Backstreet's Back, 1998; Millennium, 1999; Black And Blue, 2000; Greatest Hits Chapter 1, 2001. Singles: We've Got It Goin' On, 1995; Quit Playing Games, 1998; I'll Never Break Your Heart, 1998; Everybody, 1998; As Long As You Love Me, 1998; Anywhere for You, 1998; All I Have to Give, 1998; I Want It That Way (No. 1, UK), 1999; Larger Than Life, 1999; Show Me The Meaning of Being Lonely, 2000; The One, 2000; Shape of My Heart, 2000; Drowning, 2001; The Call, 2001. *Honours:* MTV European Music Award, Best Pop Act, 1997, Best Group, 1999; Billboard Music Awards, Best Group, Best Adult Contemporary Group, 1998, Album of the Year, Artist of the Year, 1999; MTV Music Video Awards, Best Group Video, 1998, Viewer's Choice, for I Want It That Way, 1999; World Music Awards, Best-Selling Pop Group, 1999, 2000, Best-Selling R&B Group, 1999, 2000, Best-Selling Dance Group, 1999, 2000, Best American Group, 2000; American Music Awards, Favorite Pop/Rock Band, Duo or Group, 2000, 2001. *Website:* www.backstreetboys.com.

RICHARDSON, Mark; b. 28 May 1970, Leeds, England. Musician (drums). *Career:* Founder mem., Skunk Anansie, 1994–2001; Signed to indie label One Little Indian, 1994, Virgin Records, 1996; Numerous headlining tours, festival appearances, television and radio shows. *Recordings:* Albums: Paranoid and Sunburnt, 1995; Stoosh, 1996; Post Orgasmic Chill, 1999. Singles: Little Baby Swastikkka, 1994; Selling Jesus, 1995; I Can Dream, 1995; Charity, 1995; Weak, 1996; All I Want, 1996; Twisted (Everyday Hurts), 1996; Hedonism, 1997; Brazen (Weep), 1997; Charlie Big Potato, 1999; Secretly, 1999; Lately, 1999. *Address:* c/o Virgin Records America Inc, 338 N Foothill Rd, Beverly Hills, CA 90210, USA. *Website:* www.skunkanansie.com.

RICHEY, David Andrew; b. 21 Sept. 1965, Edgbaston, Birmingham, England. Musician (guitar); Composer; Actor; Playwright. m. Gillian MacKenzie, 4 June 1988, 1 d. *Career:* Lead guitarist, vocalist with many bands including YZI; Founder member, Aquila; Wayzgoose; Lyra and The Fianna; Created Dave Richey Music, Media Music Production company, 1993; Appeared numerous stage plays, pantomimes; Writer, plays include: The Thorn In The Rose; Directed several plays, wrote and starred in The Parkie; Writer, composer, numerous songs and instrumentals. *Membership:* Musicians' Union; SPAM. *Current Management:* Gill MacKenzie. *Address:* Sonas, Calgary, Isle of Mull, Scotland.

RICHIE, Lionel; b. 20 June 1949, Tuskegee, Alabama, USA. Vocalist; Songwriter; Musician (piano); Actor; Record Prod. m. Diane Alexander, 1996. *Education:* BS, Econs, Tuskegee University, 1971. *Career:* Member, the Commodores, 1968–82; Support tours with The Jackson 5, 1973; The Rolling Stones, 1975; The O'Jays, 1976; Numerous other concerts; Solo artiste, 1982–; Concerts include: Closing ceremony, Olympic Games, Los Angeles, 1984; Live Aid, Philadelphia, 1985. *Compositions:* Hit songs with the Commodores:

Sweet Love, 1975; Just To Be Close To You, 1976; Easy, 1977; Three Times A Lady (No. 1, USA and UK), 1979; Sail On, 1980; Still (No. 1, USA), 1980; Oh No, 1981; for Kenny Rogers: Lady (No. 1, USA), 1981; for Diana Ross: Missing You, 1984; Solo hits: Endless Love, film theme duet with Diana Ross (No. 1, USA), 1981; Truly (No. 1, USA), 1982; All Night Long (No. 1, USA), 1983; Running With The Night, 1984; Hello (No. 1, USA and UK), 1984; Stuck On You, 1984; Penny Lover (co-writer with Brenda Harvey), 1984; Say You Say Me (No. 1, USA), 1986; Dancing On The Ceiling, 1987; Love Will Conquer All, 1987; Ballerina Girl, 1987; My Destiny, 1992; Don't Wanna Lose You, 1996; Contributor, We Are The World (co-writer with Michael Jackson), USA For Africa (No. 1 world-wide), 1985. Recordings: Albums with the Commodores: Machine Gun, 1974; Caught In The Act, 1975; Movin' On, 1975; Hot On The Tracks, 1976; Commodores, 1977; Commodores Live!, 1977; Natural High 1978; Greatest Hits, 1978; Midnight Magic, 1979; Heroes, 1980; In The Pocket, 1981; Solo albums: Lionel Richie, 1982; Can't Slow Down, 1983; Dancing On The Ceiling, 1986; Back To Front, 1992; Louder Than Words, 1996; Time, 1998; Renaissance, 2001; Encore—Greatest Hits, 2002. Solo singles: All Night Long, 1985; Do It To Me, 1992; My Destiny, 1992; Ordinary Girl, 1996; Don't Wanna Lose You, 1996. Honours: ASCAP Songwriter Awards, 1979, 1984–96; Numerous American Music Awards, 1979–; Grammy Awards: Best Pop Vocal Performance, 1982; Album of the Year, 1985; Producer of the Year (shared), 1986; Lionel Richie Day, Los Angeles, 1983; 2 NAACP Image Awards, 1983; NAACP Entertainer of the Year, 1987; Academy Award, Best Song, 1986; Golden Globe, Best Song, 1986. Current Management: John Reid. Address: 505 S Beverly Dr., Suite 1192, Beverly Hills, CA 90212, USA.

RICHMAN, Guy Charles; b. 3 June 1965, Rush Green, England. Musician (drums). m. Alison Murray, 20 June 1994. Education: Taught by Maz Abrams and Bobby Armstrong. Career: Concert dates with Kylie Minogue, 1995; World tours and television appearances with: Black; Patricia Kaas; British tours with: Joe Longthorne (including television); Sister Sledge; Odyssey; Harold Melvin. Recordings: Black; Boy George; Bucks Fizz; Patricia Kaas; Joe Longthorne; Two People; Sister Sledge; Odyssey; Howard Jones. Membership: Musicians' Union. Address: 53 St Marys Lane, Upminster, Essex RM14 2QU, England.

RICHMOND, Kim; b. 24 July 1940, Champaign, Illinois, USA. Musician; Composer; Arranger. m. Chris Zambon, 5 April 1989. Education: Graduate, University of Illinois, 1963; BA, Music Education; BM, Music Compilation. Career: Written and conducted original musical scores for several television series including: Kojak; Harry O; ABC Movie of the Week; Composed new works for concert stage (mostly jazz); Arranger and music director for singers including: Ann Jillian, Buddy Greco, Helen Reddy and Johnnie Ray; Arranged for many acts including Pat Boone, Dianhann Carroll, Thelma Houston, Jaye P Morgan, Kaye Ballard; Written for jazz groups of Stan Kenton, Buddy Rich, Louis Bellson, Stan Getz; Toured with Percy Faith Orchestra in Japan and Australia, several years; Freelance studio work, TV shows, theatre orchestras, concerts and other musical activities in Los Angeles; Artist-in-Residence, Australia's University of Sydney Music Conservatorium Jazz Studies programme; Occasional jazz radio host; Writes articles and reviews for jazz magazines. Compositions include: (for large concert jazz ensemble) Augustana, Trump Card I; Trump Card II; Viridian; Range; Variations; All Together; Back A Tad; Bhakti; Big Mama Louise; The Big Sur; Brain Trouble; Chester's Way; Chic-a-brac; City of LA; Clear Command; Continued Obscurity; Fantasia For Alto Sax and Jazz Orchestra (3 movements); Firebush (3 movements); Flapjacks and Maple Syrup; Franz; Gems; Image; Blues and Likeness; Mayo; Melon Bells; Nicé; Old Acquaintances; Osage Autumn; Passages; Planos; Realization for guitar and jazz orchestra (3 movements); Soft Feelings; Sojourn; 3 Refractions; Tributaries; White Tornado; Wind Chimes; Wind-up; Trains; (for small jazz ensemble) Range; Tracks; Cal 20; Common Denominator; Data Bank; Trains; Corrective Measures; (Classical compositions) Centunia for symphony orchestra; Movements for brass quintet, strings and percussion; Mixtures for brass quintet and others. Recordings: (as a leader): Look At The Time; Range; Passage; Looking In Looking Out; Ballads, 2001; many others for other leaders. Membership: AFofM; ASCAP; ASMAC; NARAS; RMA; Pacific Composers Forum; Chamber Music Society. Address: 6248 Rogerton Dr., Hollywood, CA 90068, USA.

RICHRATH, Gary; b. 18 Oct. 1949, Peoria, Illinois, USA. Musician (guitar); Songwriter. Career: Guitarist, songwriter, US rock group REO Speedwagon, 1971–92; Richrath, 1992–; Live concert, Denver (first stereo concert broadcast), 1981; Anti-drug concert Users Are Losers, Miami, Florida, 1990. Recordings: Albums: with REO Speedwagon: REO Speedwagon, 1971; R.E.O. T.W.O., 1972; Ridin' The Storm Out, 1973; Lost In A Dream, 1974; This Time We Mean It, 1975; R.E.O., 1976; REO Speedwagon Live/You Get What You Play For, 1977; You Can Tune A Piano But You Can't Tuna Fish, 1978; Nine Lives, 1979; A Decade of Rock 'N' Roll 1970–80, 1980; Hi Infidelity (No. 1, USA), 1981; Good Trouble, 1982; Wheels Are Turning, 1984; Best Foot Forward, 1985; Life As We Know It, 1987; The Hits, 1988; A Second Decade of Rock 'N' Roll 1981–91, 1991; Ballads, 1999; with Richrath: Only The Strong Survive, 1992; Hit singles include: Time For Me To Fly, 1978; Take It On The Run, 1981; Keep On Loving You (No. 1, USA), 1981; Don't Let Him Go, 1981; Keep The Fire Burnin', 1982; Can't Fight This Feeling (No. 1, USA), 1985;

That Ain't Love, 1987; In My Dreams, 1987. Honours: Gold, Platinum discs. Current Management: Baruck-Consolo Management, 15003 Greenleaf St, Sherman Oaks, CA 91403, USA.

RICKFORS, Mikael; b. 4 Dec. 1948, Sweden. Vocalist; Musician (guitar, piano); Songwriter. m. Mia, 2 s., 1 d. Career: Concert tours; Television (Europe, USA). Compositions: Yeah Yeah, recorded by Cyndi Lauper; Blue Night, Percy Sledge; Daughter of The Night, Carlos Santana; The Last Wind, Touch, Carla Olson; Recorded by the Hollies: Don't Leave The Child Alone; They Don't Realise I'm Down. Recordings: with the Hollies: Romany, 1972; Out on The Road, 1972; Mikael Rickfors, 1975; The Wheel, 1976; Kickin' a Dream, 1979; Tender Turns Tuff, 1981; Rickfors Live, 1981; Blue Fun, 1983; Hearthunters, 1985; Rickfors, 1986; Vingar, 1988; Judas River, 1991; Happy Man Don't Kill, 1997; Greatest Hits, 1999; The Mikael Rickfors Years, 2000. Address: c/o Polygram Records, Stockholm, Sweden.

RIDGELEY, Andrew; b. 26 Jan. 1963, Windlesham, Surrey, England. Vocalist; Musician (guitar). m. Keren Woodward, 1 s. Career: Member, The Executive, 1979–80; Member duo, Wham! with George Michael, 1982–86; Most successful English pop group of 1980s; World-wide tours and concerts include: Club Fantastic Tour, 1983; World tour, 1984; US tour, 1985; First western pop band to play in People's Republic of China, 1985; Farewell concert, 'The Final' concert, Wembley, 1986; Solo artiste, actor and racing driver, 1986–; Performed at Rock in Rio II, with George Michael, 1991. Recordings: Albums: with Wham!: Fantastic (No. 1, UK), 1983; Make It Big (No. 1, UK and USA), 1984; The Final, 1986; If You Were There, 1997; Solo album: Son of Albert, 1990; Singles include: Young Guns (Go For It), 1982; Wham Rap!, 1982; Bad Boys, 1983; Club Tropicana, 1983; Wake Me Up Before You Go Go (No. 1, UK), 1984; Careless Whisper (No. 1, UK and USA), 1984; Last Christmas, 1984; Freedom (No. 1, UK), 1984; Everything She Wants (No. 1, USA), 1985; I'm Your Man (No. 1, UK), 1985; The Edge of Heaven (No. 1, UK), 1986; Solo single: Shake, 1990. Honours: BRIT Awards: Best Newcomer Group, 1985; Outstanding Contribution To British Music, 1986.

RIDGWAY, Stanard; b. 5 April 1956, Los Angeles, California, USA. Vocalist; Songwriter; Composer. m. Pietra Wexstun, 17 May 1981, 1 s. Education: College. Career: Singer, Wall of Voodoo; Television appearances include: The Tube, Top of the Pops. Compositions: Songs include: Camouflage; The Big Heat; Mexican Radio; Calling Out To Carol. Recordings: with Wall of Voodoo: Wall of Voodoo, 1979; Dark Continent, 1980; Call of The West, 1981; Solo recordings: The Big Heat, 1985; Mosquitos, 1990; Party Ball, 1991; Songs That Made This Country Great, 1992; Anatomy, 1999. Membership: BMI. Current Management: S.R. Dis-Information. Address: PO Box 9524, Los Angeles, CA 90295–1924, USA.

RIDING, Jules; b. 22 May 1949, Cheltenham, Gloucestershire, England. Christian Musician; Vocalist. m. Lynn Gousmett, 11 May 1980, 2 s., 2 d. Education: First year university, Auckland, New Zealand. Career: Full-time professional, 1988–; Founder, Elkanah School of Music Ministry, 1995. Recordings: Albums: On This Night, 1984; Heartstrings, 1987; Revelation, 1991; Homecoming, 1992; The Fisherman, 1994; Kids Time, 1997; Amazing Sacrifice, 1998. Publications: Don't Let Poor Nellie Starve, poetry, 1975; New Zealand Lamb, poetry, 1981. Honours: New Zealand Music Awards, Gospel Album of the Year, 1984, 1987. Membership: APRA, New Zealand.

RIDLEY, Larry (Laurence Howard, II); b. 3 Sept. 1937, Indianapolis, Indiana, USA. Musician; Music Educator. m. Magdalena Ridley, 1 d. Education: BS, Music Education, Indiana University, 1955–59; New York University, 1971; MA, State University of New York, 1993. Career: Associate Professor of Music, Livingston College of Rutgers University, New Jersey, 1971–; Chairman, Department of Music, Rutgers University, 1972–80; Professor Emeritus, Rutgers University, 1999; Artist-in-Residence, colleges in USA and South Africa; Bandleader, Jazz Legacy Ensemble; Recordings and international performances with numerous leading musicians including: Dizzy Gillespie; Duke Ellington; Art Farmer; Thelonious Monk; Dinah Washington; Benny Goodman; Dexter Gordon; Benny Carter; Herbie Hancock; Freddie Hubbard; Mercer Ellington; Sonny Rollins; Philly Joe Jones; Chet Baker; Kenny Burrell; Stephane Grappelli; Roy Haynes; Lee Morgan; Jazz Artist-in-Residence, Schomburg Centre/New York Public Library since 1993. Honours: Chair., Jazz Panel, National Endowment Arts, 1976–78; National co-ordinator, NEA Jazz Artists in School pilot programme, 1978–82; Mem., National Asscn Jazz Educators (advisory board, 1981–); Mid Atlantic Arts Foundation Living Legacy Jazz Award, 1997; Inducted into the International Assccn of Jazz Educators Hall of Fame, 1998; Downbeat Magazine, Jazz Education Hall of Fame, 1999. Address: 3 Stuyvesant Oval, Suite 9B, New York, NY 10009, USA.

RIDLEY, Tim; b. 5 Aug. 1967, Portsmouth, Hampshire, England. Teacher; Musician (keyboards, drums, percussion). Education: Royal Academy of Music. Career: Keyboard player, Brotherhood of Man, 1989–; Teacher, drums and percussion, 1989–96, Assistant Master, teaching music and music technology, 1996–, Marlborough College, Wiltshire; Keyboard player, The Sounds of The Supremes Show, 1993–; Keyboard player, composer, Mentaur. Compositions: Daedalus (musical), 1988; Ongoing film commission; Requiem

Mass, 1988. *Recordings:* Darkness Before Dawn, Mentaur, 1995; Live In Germany, The Sounds of The Supremes, 1995. *Honours:* LRAM, 1984; GRSM, 1985. *Membership:* Rollercoaster Club of Great Britain. *Current Management:* Videoscope Productions. *Address:* Marlborough College, Marlborough, Wiltshire SN8 1PA, England.

RIEL, Alex; b. 13 Sept. 1940, Copenhagen, Denmark. Musician (drums). *Education:* Private lessons with Borge Ritz; 1 semester with Allan Dawson, Berklee School of Music, Boston, USA. *Career:* Founder, Alex Riel Trio; Member, Niels Lan Doky Trio; Freelance solo musician; Television appearances with: Nancy Wilson; Manhattan Transfer; Stan Getz; Bill Evans; Eddie Gomez; Toots Thielemans; Gerry Mulligan; Roland Kirk; Niels Henning Orsted Petersen; Played concerts with: John Scofield; Michel Petrucianni; Dizzy Gillespie; Wayne Shorter; Dollar Brand; Archie Shepp; Don Cherry; Videos: Bill Evans Trio In Oslo, 1967; Niels Lan Dorky Trio, Close Encounter, 1992. *Recordings include:* In A Way, Alex Riel Trio, 1966; Emerge, Alex Riel Trio, 1993; Unriel, 1998; Rielatin', 2000; Recorded as guest musician with numerous artistes including: Dexter Gordon; Ben Webster; Gary Burton; Thomas Clausen; Palle Mikkelborg; Karin Krog; Archie Shepp; Toots Thielmans; Jean Luc Ponty; Eddie Lockjaw Davis; Marilyn Mazur; Stéphane Grappelli. *Honours:* Danish Jazz Musician of Year, 1965; Palace Jazz Award, 1991. *Membership:* Dansk Musiker Forbund.

RIENIETS, Andrea; b. Feb. 1963, Shepparton, Victoria, Australia. Vocalist; Songwriter; Composer. *Education:* BA, Communications; Theatre, Opera Singing, Choir Studies, Jazz Drumming. *Career:* 17 scores for stage; Founder/ Director of Before You Were Blonde choir, 1991–96; Guest Director, Sing It Up BIG, Indigenous Australian Choir, 1997–98; WOMAD, 1997. *Compositions:* Wooden Child, 1995; Love of a Lifetime, 1995; Something So Simple, 1998. *Recordings:* Fluently Helvetica, 1995; Something So Simple, 1998. *Current Management:* Gorgeous Girl Records. *Address:* PO Box 10059, Adelaide BC Eighth, Australia 5000.

RIGBY, Paul Julian; b. 21 Dec. 1968, Blackburn, Lancashire, England. Musician (drums, piano); Bandleader. *Education:* Studied at Salford University, Bretton Hall and University of North Texas, Higher Diploma in Popular Music with Recording, and BA Honours in Popular Music; PGCE. *Career:* Played with Georgie Fame; Kenny Baker; Mark Nightingale; Bobby Shew; Maynard Ferguson; Appeared in shows and musicals; Toured extensively with Wigan Youth Jazz Orchestra and Northern Jazz Orchestra; Tutor for Lancashire School Jazz Orchestra; Lecturer of Popular Music. *Recordings:* with Northern Jazz Orchestra; Good News; with Wigan Youth Jazz Orchestra: Aim For The Heart; One More Time; Check It Out. *Membership:* Musicians' Union. *Address:* Clairville, Manor Rd, Darwen, Lancashire BB3 2SN, England.

RILEY, Howard; b. 16 Feb. 1943, Huddersfield, Yorkshire, England. Musician (piano); Composer. *Education:* BA, 1964, MA, 1966, University of Wales; MMus, Indiana University, USA, 1967; MPh, York University, 1970. *Career:* Festival, Club, TV, Radio appearances as Pianist (solo and group), throughout Europe and USA, 1967–. *Recordings:* 60 solo albums, incl.: Synopsis, 2000; Overground, 2001; Airplay, 2001. *Publications:* The Contemporary Piano Folio, 1982. *Honours:* UK/USA Bicentennial Arts Fellowship, 1976. *Address:* Flat 2, 53 Tweedy Rd, Bromley, Kent BR1 3NH, England. *Telephone:* (20) 8290-5917.

RILEY, Jeannie C, (Jeannie Carolyn Stephenson); b. 19 Oct. 1944, Anson, Texas, USA. Vocalist. m. Mickey Riley, 1 d. *Recordings:* Hit singles: Harper Valley PTA (No. 1, USA), 1969; The Girl Most Likely; There Never Was A Time; The Back Side of Dallas; The Rib; Good Enough To Be Your Wife; When Love Has Gone Away; Return To Harper Valley; Albums: Yearbooks and Yesterdays, 1968; Things Go Better With Love, 1969; Songs of Jeannie C Riley, 1969; Country Girl, 1970; Generation Gap, 1970; Jeannie, 1972; Down to Earth, 1973; Jeannie C Riley and Fancy Friends, 1977; From Harper Valley to the Mountain Top, 1981; Here's Jeannie C, 1991; Praise Him, 1995; Good Old Country, 2000. *Honours:* Grammy Award, 1968; CMA Record of Year, 1969; Music Operators of America Award, 1969; Gold disc, Harper Valley PTA (6m. copies sold), 1969. *Current Management:* Morningstar Public Relations, PO Box 83, Brentwood, TN 37027, USA.

RILEY, Marc, (Lard); b. 10 July 1961, Manchester, England. Musician (guitar, bass, keyboards); Prod; Presenter. m. 2 d. *Career:* Member, The Fall; Left band, formed The Creepers; PR for labels such as 4AD and Factory; Guest, Hit the North, with Mark Radcliffe, Radio 5; Researcher and Producer for Radio; Joined Mark Radcliffe on Radio 1 evening slot, 1993, stand-in on the breakfast show, 1996, permanent presenter on Breakfast Show, 1997, afternoon show, 1998–. *Recordings:* with The Fall: Live At The Witch Trials, 1979; Dragnet, 1979; Grotesque (After The Gramme), 1980; Slates, 1981; Hex Enduction Hour, 1982; with The Shirehorses: The Worst Album In The World Ever...Ever!, 1997. *Address:* c/o BBC Radio 1, London W1N 4DJ, England. *Website:* www.bbc.co.uk/radio1.

RILEY, Teddy; b. 8 Oct. 1967, Haarlem, New York, USA. Musician (multi-instrumentalist); Record Prod. *Career:* Considered pioneer of 'New Jack Swing'; Member, groups: Guy; Blackstreet; Musician for various artists including: Kool Moe Dee; Heavy D; Michael Jackson; Roy Brown; Own recording studio, Future Records. *Recordings:* Over 30 Platinum albums as producer; Albums include: with Michael Jackson, Dangerous, 1991; Blood on the Dance Floor, 1997; Invincible, 2001; also: Don't Be Cruel, Bobby Brown; with Wreckx 'N' Effects, Hard or Smooth, Rap's New Generation; Make It Last Forever, Keith Sweat; Personal, Men of Vision; Another Level, Blackstreet; Get on the Bus; Ill Na Na, Foxy Brown; Make It Reign; G-Funk Classics, Nate Dogg; Hurricane; Other recordings for: Heavy D; James Ingram; Jazzy Jeff and The Fresh Prince; Profyle; K-Ci and Jo-Jo; As musician: U Blow My Mind, Blackstreet, 1995. *Current Management:* ICM, 40 W 57th St, New York, NY 10019, USA.

RILEY, Terry Mitchell; b. 24 June 1935, Colfax, CA, USA. Composer; Musician (piano); Raga Vocalist. m. Ann Yvonne Smith, 1958, 3 c. *Education:* San Francisco State University; MA, University of California; Private studies with Duane Hampton, Adolf Baller and Pandit Pran Nath. *Career:* Taught music composition and North Indian Raga, Mills College, 1971–83; Freelance composer and performer, 1961–; Launched Minimal Music movement with composition and first performance of In C, 1964. *Compositions include:* The Harp of New Albion for Solo Piano in Just Intonation; Salome Dances for Peace (string quartet); Cadenza on the Night Plain; Sunrise of the Planetary Dream Collector; Sri Camel, a Rainbow in Curved Air; In C; The Ten Voices of the Two Prophets; Persian Surgery Dervishes; Jade Palace (for large orchestra), 1989; June Buddhas, 1991; The Sounds (concerto for string quartet and orchestra), 1991; The Saint Adolf Ring (chamber opera), 1992; Ritmos and Melos, 1993; El Hombre (piano quintet), 1993; Ascension (solo guitar), 1993; The Heaven Ladder, 1996; Three Requiem Quarters, 1997; Autodreamographical Tales, 1997. *Honours:* John Simon Guggenheim Prize, 1980. *Address:* c/o ASCAP, ASCAP Bldg, 1 Lincoln Plaza, New York, NY 10023, USA.

RIMES, (Margaret) LeAnn; b. 28 Aug. 1982, Jackson Mississippi, USA. Country vocalist. m. Dean Sheremet, 23 Feb. 2002. *Career:* Encouraged by father, part-time guitarist Wilbur Rimes, was singing and tap dancing at age 2 and winning talent shows, aged 5; Parents recorded an album to sell at gigs, aged 7; Released first commercial album on Nor Va Jack label, recorded at legendary producer Norman Petty's studio in Clovis, New Mexico, aged 11; One of album tracks Blue, written by Texas DJ and country artist Bill Mack, and very much in the style of Patsy Cline came to the attention of record executive Mike Curb, resulting in immediately signing to his Curb label; Blue re-recorded with a 50s retro feel and appeared on the album of the same name, 1996; Album reached #1 on US country chart and #3 on pop charts; Singles and album sales to date over 20m., on both pop and country charts; How Do I Live from the film Con Air became most successful US single of all time, completing 69 straight weeks on Billboard pop chart, 1997–95; Single also stayed in UK Top 40 for 30 weeks; More recent material has tended to be aimed more at the pop/AOR market with artist no longer desiring to be regarded as a country act; Has garnered many major music awards and appeared as self in films: Holiday In Your Heart, 1997; Dill Scallion, 1999; Coyote Ugly, containing UK chart-topping theme Can't Fight The Moonlight, 2000; Started litigation against Curb Records, 2000; Case eventually resolved; Filed lawsuit against father and his partner alleging they stole $7m. of earnings, 2000. *Recordings include:* One Way Ticket (Because I Can), Unchained Melody, Blue, 1996; How Do I Live, On The Side of Angels, 1997; Written In The Stars (with Elton John), 1999; I Need You, Can't Fight The Moonlight, 2000; Albums include: Blue, 1996; You Light Up My Life – Inspirational Songs, 1997; Sittin' On Top of The World, 1998; LeAnn Rimes, 1999; I Need You, God Bless America, 2001; Twisted Angel, 2002. *Address:* c/o Country Music Asscn, 1 Music Circle S, Nashville, TN 37203, USA. *Website:* www.rimestimes.com.

RINGO, Sheena; b. 15 Nov. 1978, Fukuoka, Japan. Vocalist; Musician (piano, bass guitar); Songwriter. m. Junji Yayoshi, 2001. *Education:* Trained as classical pianist and ballerina. *Career:* Member of various semi-professional groups including The Marvelous Marbles before signing as solo artist to Toshiba-EMI; First live tour of Japan, 2000; Temporary career break owing to pregnancy, 2001. *Recordings:* Albums: Muzai Moratorium, 1999; Shoso Strip, 2000; Singles: Kofukuron, Kabukicho No Jyoou, 1998; Kokode Kiss Shite, Honnou, 1999; Gips, Tsumi To Batsu, 2000; Mayonaka Wa Jyunketsu, 2001. *Honours:* Annual Music Quest, Award of Excellence, 1996. *Address:* c/o Solid Bond Corp/Toshiba-EMI Ltd. *Website:* www.toshiba-emi.co.jp/ringo/english.

RINTOUL, Laura Jane; b. 3 Oct. 1950, Perth, Scotland. Vocalist; Musician (accordion, recorder). *Education:* HNC, Napier College, Edinburgh, Scotland. *Career:* Medical Scientist, then trained in Glasgow from 1985; Concert tour of Japan in 1989; First broadcast on BBC Radio Scotland, 1988 appearing regularly since then; Presenter, local radio, Festival of Remembrance, Perth, 1992; Appeared on Grampian TV, 1994. *Recordings:* As guest artist on: A Ceilidh From Aberfeldy, and Gather, from the Clan MacGregor Celebration Concerts. *Honours:* Silver Pendant, Edinburgh Gaelic MOD, 1987; Gold Medal, Arbroath Music Festival, 1991; Glasgow, 1992; Scots Songs Silver Medal, Perth, 1993. *Membership:* Musicians' Union; Perthshire Musical

(Competition) Festival Asscn. *Address:* 18 Low Rd, Cherrybank, Perth PH2 0NF, Scotland.

RISDON, Ronald Valentine; b. 14 Feb. 1950, Dorking, Surrey, England. Artist Man; Television and Film Prod. m. Jane Risdon, 15 June 1972, 1 s. *Career:* Bassist, then guitarist, with Marjorine, including UK, Europe tours, 1968–; Re-named Jungle Jim, 1972; Tours, North Africa, UK and Europe; Television and radio: Europe, UK, Channel Islands; Manager of various acts including: Tag, Ignorance, Heat featuring T J Felton, Treana, Craig Thomson, actor, Lucy, Gita, Blackout; Co-owner, production company Everyday Productions. *Recordings:* Singles: I Live, 1968; Big Fat Orangoman, (Top 20, UK, No. 1, France, Germany); Manager, recording artists 1980–; Released: Tag, USA; Ignorance, USA; Treana, USA; Rain; Manages record producers: G Young and K Holland; Manages Songwriters: Young/Morris, A Hayman, Holland/Palmer/Wilcocks. *Membership:* PRS; BAC&S. *Current Management:* Showcase Management International, 33 Mandarin Pl., Grove, Oxfordshire OX12 0QH, England. *Address:* SMI, 3217 Overland Ave, Suite 7115, Los Angeles, CA 90034, USA. *E-mail:* selectevents@mediaone.net.

RITCHIE, Billy (Darrell, Jr); b. 11 Sept. 1986, High Point, North Carolina, USA. Vocalist; Songwriter. m. Michelle Ritchie, 6 Sept. 1990, 1 d. *Education:* BA, Communications, Gardner-Webb College, 1990; Minor in Music, Gardner-Webb College, 1990. *Career:* Full time concert artist; Songwriter; Over 500 concerts, 1991–. *Recordings:* Albums: Stand and Believe, 1992; No Turning Back, 1993; Big Time, 1995. *Membership:* Gospel Music Asscn; BMI. *Current Management:* Darrell Ritchie Concerts. *Address:* 1071 Colgan Court, Lawrenceville, GA 30244, USA.

RITENOUR, Lee; b. 11 Jan. 1952, Los Angeles, California, USA. Jazz Musician (guitar). *Career:* Session player, as Captain Fingers, mid 1970s; Also jazz fusion solo artiste; Played with Herbie Hancock; Steely Dan; Eddie Henderson; Stanley Clarke; Member, Friendship (with Don Grusin). *Recordings:* Albums: First Course, 1974; Guitar Player, 1975; Captain Fingers, 1975; The Captain's Journey, 1978; Gentle Thoughts, 1978; Sugarloaf Express, 1978; Feel The Night, 1979; Friendship, 1979; Rit, 1981; Rio, 1982; Rit 2, 1983; Banded Together, 1983; On The Line, 1984; Harlequin, with Dave Grusin, 1985; American Flyers, 1986; Earth Run, 1986; Portrait, 1987; Festival, 1988; Wes Bound, 1993; Larry and Lee with Larry Carlton, 1995; Alive in LA, 1997; This is Love, 1998. *Address:* c/o GRP Records, 33 Broadwick St, London W1V 1FR, England.

RIVERA, Chita; b. 23 Jan. 1933, Washington, DC, USA. Actress; Vocalist; Dancer. m. Anthony Mordente. *Education:* American School of Ballet, New York. *Career:* Performs in nightclubs and cabarets around the world; Stage appearances include: Call Me Madam; Guys and Dolls; Can-Can; Seventh Heaven; Mister Wonderful; West Side Story; Father's Day; Bye Bye Birdie; Threepenny Opera; Flower Drum Song; Zorba; Sweet Charity; Born Yesterday; Jacques is Alive and Well and Living in Paris; Sondheim—A Musical Tribute; Kiss Me Kate; Ivanhoe; Chicago; Bring Back Birdie; Merlin; The Rink, 1984; Jerry's Girls, 1985; Kiss of the Spider Woman, 1993; Television includes: Kojak and the Marcus Nelson Murders, 1973; The New Dick Van Dyke Show, 1973–74; Kennedy Center Tonight—Broadway to Washington!; Pippin, 1982; The Mayflower Madam, 1987. *Honours:* Tony Awards, 1984, for Best Actress in a Musical, 1993. *Address:* c/o Gayle Nachlis, William Morris Agency, 1325 Avenue of the Americas, New York, NY 10019, USA.

RIVERA, Sandy; b. San Diego, California, USA. Prod; Remixer; DJ. *Career:* Founder: Blackwiz Records, 1992; Deep Vision Records; Remixed: Moloko Eddie Amador; Ladysmith Black Mambazo; Member: Kings of Tomorrow; Soul Vision; Collaborations: Everything But The Girl; Jose Burgos; Julie McKnight. *Recordings:* Albums: It's In The Lifestyle (with Kings of Tomorrow), 2000; Singles: with Kings of Tomorrow: Fade II Black, 1997; Tear It Up, 2000; Finally, 2001; Tracey In My Room (as Soul Vision with EBTG), 2001. *Address:* c/o Defected Records, 14–15 D'arblay St, London W1F 8DY, England.

RIVERS, Johnny; b. 7 Nov. 1942, New York, NY, USA. Musician; Vocalist; Songwriter. *Career:* President, top record and publishing company, singer and songwriter by age 25; Started American discotheque craze at Whiskey A Go Go, Los Angeles, 1963; Appeared La Riviera, with Nancy Wilson, 1966; First rock and roll act to play Copacabana, New York; Formed record company, Soul City Records; Currently owner, manager, Rivers Music; Influenced the careers of The Mamas and Papas; Lou Adler; Glen Campbell; Al Wilson; Wolfman Jack; Brought together Hal Blaine, Joe Osborn, Larry Knectel, creators of 1960s–70s West Coast Sound; Special guest on Memphis Horns 25th Anniversary Concert, 1992. *Recordings:* Hits include: Memphis; Maybelline; Mountain of Love; Seventh Son; Midnight Special; Secret Agent Man; Poor Side of Town; Baby, I Need Your Lovin'; Tracks of My Tears; Summer Rain; Look To Your Soul; Rockin' Pneumonia and The Boogie Woogie Flu; Sea Cruise; Blue Suede Shoes; Help Me Rhonda; Swayin' To The Music (Slow Dancin'); Curious Mind (Um Um Um Um Um Um); Last Train to Memphis; Albums include: Back At The Whisky (Live), 2001; As Producer: Jimmy Webb and The Fifth Dimension: Up, Up and Away. *Honours:* 2 Grammys; BMI Awards. *Membership:* BMI; ASCAP; AFTRA; AFofM. *Current Management:* American Concert and Touring Company, Nashville, Tennessee; Variety Artists, San Luis Obispo, California. *Address:* Soul City Records Inc, 12358 Ventura Blvd # 342, Studio City, CA 91604, USA.

RIVERS, Sam; b. 21 Sept. 1977, Jacksonville, FL, USA. Musician (bass guitar). m. Kinter, Feb. 2001. *Education:* Arlington Middle School, Jacksonville; Douglas Anderson School of the Arts; Learnt tuba at Middle School. *Career:* Joined Limp Bizkit, 1994; Signed to Flip/Interscope on strength of demo tape; Striking live shows at concerts and festivals; Group spearheaded 'nu-metal' breakthrough in Europe, 2001. *Recordings:* Albums: Three Dollar Bill, Y'All $, 1997; Significant Other, 1999; Chocolate Starfish and The Hot Dog Flavored Water, 2000; New Old Songs (remix album), 2001; Singles: Faith, 1997; Nookie, Rearranged, 1999; Break Stuff, Take A Look Around (from Mission Impossible 2 OST), My Generation, 2000; Rollin', My Way, Boiler, 2001. *Honours:* Orville H. Gibson Guitar Award, Best Rock Bass Player, 2000; American Music Award, Favorite Alternative Artist, 2002. *Current Management:* The Firm Inc, 9465 Wilshire Blvd, Suite 500, Beverly Hills, CA 90212, USA. *Website:* www.limpbizkit.com.

RIX, (Leon) Luther; b. 11 Feb. 1942, Lansing, Michigan, USA. Musician (percussion, drums); Composer. m. Ellen Garrett, 14 May 1973, 1 s. *Education:* MusB, Indiana University, 1963; Postgraduate, Jordan Conservatory of Music, Indianapolis, 1964–65. *Career:* Percussionist with Indianapolis Symphony Orchestra, 1965–67; Winter Consort, 1968; Doc Severinsen, 1970; Drummer with Bette Midler, 1971–72; Manhattan Transfer, 1974–75; Mary Travers, 1975–76; Bob Dylan, 1975–76; Leonard Cohen, Laura Branigan, 1976; Peter, Paul and Mary, 1978; Freelance musician, 1979–; Drummer with Rosenhontz, 1986–; Richard Reiter Swing band, 1987–; Crossing Point, 1990–; Musician, shows include: The Wiz; Grease; Barnum; Little Shop of Horrors. *Compositions:* Boogaloother, 1972; Like A Beautiful Song, 1980; Tightrope (also arranger), 1969; Compositions recorded by Genya Raven; Buzzy Lindhart; Kaleidoscope. *Recordings include:* with Loudon Wainwright III: Fame and Wealth, 1983; Tommy (original Broadway cast), 1993; with Bob Dylan: Greatest Hits Vol. 3, 1994; With Labelle: Something Silver, 1997; also: Topaz; Bette Midler. *Membership:* ASCAP; AFTRA; BMI; AFofM.

RIZZO, Carmen; b. 8 April 1964, Akron, Ohio, USA. Record Prod; Engineer. m. 11 Dec. 1993. *Career:* Engineer, mixer, co-writer, programmer, for latest Seal album. *Recordings:* Albums for: Seal; Prince; Ray Charles; Chris Connelly (Ministry); Wendy and Lisa; Melanie C; Robbie Robertson; Freak Power; Human Nature; Phil Collins; MC Lyte. *Membership:* ASCAP; NARAS. *Current Management:* Greg Spotts Management (USA); Worlds End Ltd (England). *Address:* 421 Hudson St, Suite #216, New York, NY 10014, USA.

ROACH, Archie; b. 1956, Framlingham, Victoria, Australia. Vocalist; Songwriter. Partner, Ruby Hunter, 5 c. *Career:* Singer, songwriter; Performed extensively across Australia; Appeared at 3 WOMADelaide festivals, with Paul Kelly; Frente; Jimmy Barnes; Weddings Parties Anything; Crowded House; Numerous Aboriginal cultural festivals including: Sydney's Survival Day Concerts; Nambundah, New South Wales; Bogong Moth; Brunswick Koori Arts, Victoria; Oyster Cove, Tasmania; Cape York, Queensland; US tour, support to Joan Armatrading and Bob Dylan, 1992; Guest (with Ruby Hunter), Corrobee Festival Festival, Southbank Centre, London, 1993; British tour, 1993; UK visit with Robyn Hitchcock and The Egyptians, 1994; Berlin Independence Festival, 1994; Support to Suzanne Vega, Australia, 1994; Other appearances include AFL Grand Final, 1994; Performed before Prime Minister Paul Keating, football game, Alice Springs; Documentary: Land Of The Little Kings, SBS, 2000. *Recordings:* Albums: Charcoal Lane, 1990; Jamu Dreaming, 1994; Looking for Butter Boy, 1997. *Publications:* Anthology of lyrics: You Have The Power, 1994. *Current Management:* Julie Hickson. *Address:* 25 Overend St, Brunswick, VIC 3056, Australia.

ROACH, Max(well Lemuel); b. 10 Jan. 1924, Elizabeth City, North Carolina, USA. Jazz Musician (percussion). m. (1) Mildred Wilkinson, 14 Jan. 1949, 1 s., 1 d., (2) Abbey Lincoln, 3 March 1963 (divorced). *Education:* Manhattan School of Music, New York City; MusD (hon), New England Conservatory of Music, 1982. *Career:* Jazz percussionist with Charlie Parker, 1946–48; Also played with Thelonious Monk; Bud Powell; Dizzy Gillespie; Sonny Rollins; Eric Dolphy; Co-leader, Max Roach-Clifford Brown Quintet; Appearances include: Paris Jazz Festival, 1949; Newport Jazz Festival, 1972; Producer; Director; Choreographer; Professor of Music, University of Massachusetts, 1973–. *Compositions:* Freedom Now suite. *Recordings:* Albums include: Percussion Bitter Sweet; It's Time; Drums Unlimited; Speak Brother Speak; The Loadstar; Conservations; Long As Your Living; Survivors; The Long March; Jazz In 3/4 Time; Scott Free; To The Max!, 1991; Max and Dizzy (with Dizzy Gillespie), 1989 Mop Mop, 1995; Festive Journey, 1996; Bejing Trio, 1998; Max Roach Trio, 1999; Les Incontournables, 2000; The Complete Mercury Max Roach Plus Four, 2000. *Honours:* Down Beat Awards: Best Record of the Year, 1956; Down Beat Poll Winner, 1955, 1957–60, 1984; Metronome Poll Winner, 1951–54. *Membership:* Organizer, Jazz Artists Guild Inc; Officier des Arts et des Lettres; Hon. Mem.,

American Academy. *Current Management:* Max Roach Productions. *Address:* Suite 14-E, 415 Central Park W, New York, NY 10025, USA.

ROACHFORD, Andrew; Vocalist; Musician (keyboards, percussion). *Career:* Performer, Soho jazz clubs, London, aged 14; Founder, own band Roachford, 1987–; Toured with Terence Trent D'Arby, The Christians, 1988. *Recordings:* Albums: Roachford, 1988; Get Ready!, 1991; Feel, 1997; The Roachford Files, 2000; Singles include: Cuddly Toy, 1989; Family Man, 1989; Get Ready!, 1991; Only To Be With You, 1994; The Way I Feel, 1997; Also: Beckology, with Jeff Beck, 1991. *Current Management:* Pure Management, 6 Chingford Rd, London E17 4PJ, England.

ROADHOUSE, JOHNNY; b. 13 Jan. 1921, Sheffield, Yorkshire, England. Musician (saxophone, woodwind). Divorced, 2 s., 2 d. *Career:* 35 years BBC Staff Musician (Principal); Freelance Syphony Orchestras: Halle; Liverpool Philharmonic; 30 years in orchestra accompanying television series: Good Old Days; Many tours with top international artists including: Tony Bennett, Vic Damone; Recordings, radio series with Nigel Ogden (Organist Entertains series). *Membership:* Musicians' Union. *Address:* 262 Brantingham Rd, Manchester M21 0Q2, England.

ROAR, Finn; b. 21 July 1937, Kolding, Denmark. Composer; Educator; Musician (piano, saxophone); Vocalist. m. Gisela Moberg, 8 April 1960, 3 s., 1 d. *Education:* MA, Music, French; Music studies with Professor Arne Skjold Rasmussen. *Career:* Bandleader (FR 5) for radio programmes; Leader and composer, fusion group Beaver Service, 1974–; Television appearances: Denmark, SF; Many concert tours to primary schools (More Jazz To The Children); First director, Danish Conservatory of Jazz, Latin, Rock Music, 1985–88; Festivals in Denmark and France; Co-founder, Radio Jazz; Member of presidency, Rhythmic Folk College. *Recordings:* Ants In My Ears, 1981; More Jazz To The Children, 1985; U-Spring (concerto for big band), 1990; Black Messiah (oratorio), 1994; Once There Was A Carnival (opera), 1995; In omnibus caritas (cantata), 1996; Where is my… (cantata), 2002. *Publications:* Actual Music, 1975; Have You Heard, 1975; Beaver Service, 1976; From Gregorian Chant To Rock, Western Music History, Blue Book, 1981. *Membership:* DJBFA; IAJE. *Current Management:* Beaver Records, Copenhagen, Denmark. *Address:* Udbakken 21, 2750 Ballerup, Denmark. *E-mail:* finnroar@get2net.dk. *Website:* www.finnroar.dk.

ROBBINS, Dennis Anthony; b. Hazelwood, North Carolina, USA. Musician (guitar). m. Helen Hughs, 2 d. *Career:* US Marines, toured Viet Nam, 1968; Joined the Rockets, 1976; Moved to Nashville, record deal on MCA Records, first country album released, 1985; Signed to Warner Brothers with new band, Billy Hill, 1988; First artist signed to Giant Records, 1992; Writer, performer for Warner/Chappell, 1994–. *Compositions include:* Do You Love Me, Just Say Yes, Highway 101 (No. 1) 1987; Church On Cumberland Road, Shenandoah; Two of a Kind, Working On A Full House, Garth Brooks; Finally Friday, by both Earl Thomas Connelly, George Jones; Paris Tennessee, Tracy Lawrence; I'm Just A Rebel, by both Confederate Railroad, Joy Lynn White; Home Sweet Home, Dennis Robbins; Film soundtracks: Rolling Dice (used in Pink Cadillac); Looking For A Thing Called Love (used in A Thing Called Love); I Can't Help Myself (used in My Blue Heaven). *Recordings:* Albums: The First of Me, 1986; I Am Just a Rebel, 1989; Man with a Plan, 1992; Born Ready, 1994; Singles: Mona Lisa on Cruise Control, 1993; Travelin' Music, 1994; Also appears: with Rockets: Love Transfusion, 1977; Rockets, 1979; No Ballads, 1980; Back Talk, 1981.

ROBERSON, LaTavia; b. 1 Nov. 1981, Houston, TX, USA. Vocalist; Songwriter. *Career:* First TV appearance on Ed McMann's Star Search, aged nine; Package model for Pro-Line Hair Corpn, 1989–98; Various other national TV and print advertising work; Joined GirlsTyme vocal group, 1992, with Beyoncé Knowles, Kelly Rowland and LeToya Luckett; Group renamed Something Fresh then The Dolls before settling on Destiny's Child; Signed to Columbia Records, 1996; Acrimonious split from group, February 2000; Formed new group Anjel with fellow former Destiny's Child mem., LaToya Luckett. *Recordings:* Albums: with Destiny's Child: Destiny's Child, 1998; The Writing's On The Wall, 1999. Singles: with Destiny's Child: No No No (with Wyclef Jean), 1997; With Me (with Timbaland), 1998; She's Gone (with Matthew Marsden), 1998; Get On The Bus (from film Why Do Fools Fall In Love), 1999; Bills Bills Bills (No. 1, USA), 1999; Bug-A-Boo (No. 1, USA), 1999; Say My Name (No. 1, USA), 2000; Jumpin' Jumpin', 2000; Contributions to film soundtracks including, Men In Black, Romeo Must Die, Life; with Anjel: 10 Things I Hate About You, 2001. *Address:* c/o 581 Records/ So So Def/Columbia, 550 Madison Ave, New York, NY 10022-3211, USA. *Website:* www.sonymusic.com.

ROBERT, George (Paul); b. 15 Sept. 1960, Geneva, Switzerland. Musician (alto and soprano sax, clarinet, piano). m. Joan Yap, May 1991. *Education:* 9 years classical clarinet studies, Conservatory, Geneva; Bachelor of Arts, Jazz Composition and Arranging, cum laude, Berklee College of Music, 1985; Master of Music, Manhattan School of Music, 1987. *Career:* Toured Europe with own quartet, 1983, performed at Montreux Jazz Festival; Lead alto sax, MSM Big Band; Formed George Robert/Tom Harrell Quintet, 1987, toured throughout USA, Canada and Europe; Freelance musician with many groups

including Lionel Hampton and Toshiko Akiyoshi Jazz Orchestras, Buster Williams, Ray Drummond, Ron McClure; First Swiss jazz musician to lead successful career in USA; Formed George Robert Quartet, worked with Clark Terry, numerous tours including 16-week world tour in top jazz clubs with Clark Terry; Continued freelance work; Teacher and Jazz Clinician, USA, Canada and Europe; George Robert/Tom Harrell Quintet performed at IAJE Conference, Washington DC, 1991; Performed in numerous top clubs as leader; Director, Swiss Jazz School, Berne, 1995; Organized USA tour for SJS Big Band, 1998; Also performed at Cully Jazz Festival; Toured with own big band, 18 concerts throughout Europe, 1998; Teacher, Interlaken Jazz Workshop teaching and performing with leading names including Billy Hart, Phil Woods, Lionel Hampton, Tony Bennett, Benny Green, 1999. *Recordings include:* With George Robert Quartet: First Encounter, with Ron McClure, 1985; Looking Ahead, 1989; Live at the Q-4, with Clark Terry, 1991; Jazz on the Mountain, with Clark Terry, 1992; The Good Things in Life, with Clark Terry, 1994; Voyage, 1995; Inspiration (Live), 2000; With George Robert/Tom Harrell Quintet: Sun Dance, 1988; Lonely Eyes, 1989; Live in Switzerland, 1990; Visions, 1991; Cape Verde, 1993; George Robert with the Metropole Orchestra, 1995; The Summit, with Phil Woods, Kenny Barron, Ray Drummond and Bill Goodwin, 1999. *Honours:* Down Beat Awards: Outstanding Performance, 1983, Best College Band, 1987. *Membership:* ASCAP; SUISA; American Federation of Musicians. *Address:* Wiesengrundweig 11, 3047 Bremgarten, Switzerland.

ROBERTS, Austin; b. 19 Sept. 1945, Newport News, Virginia. Songwriter; Artist; Prod; Publisher. *Career:* Approximately 60 hits world-wide including No. 1's (7 in USA); Songs featured, films and television series; Wrote and sang many of the Scooby-Doo songs; Wrote musicals: Damon's Song; Rachinof; Formed Hot House Music, 1992; Two Top 10 singles as recording artist. *Compositions:* Hits include: When You Put Your Heart In It; Honor Bound; Strong Heart; IOV; My Night To Howl; Desesperados; You Lie; Songs recorded by: Reba McEntire; Kenny Rogers; Crystal Gayle; Michelle Wright; Lee Greenwood; Oak Ridge Boys; Charley Pride; Lulu; Julio Iglesias; Glen Campbell; Tanya Tucker; Sonny and Cher; Dan Seals; Englebert Humperdinck; Vicky Carr; Loverboy; Billy Crash Craddock; The Osmonds; Rosa Reeves; Marta Sanchez. *Honours:* Grammy Award; Music City News Award; NSAI Award; Numerous ASCAP Airplay Awards; 1 German Grammy Award; 4 JUNO Awards; SESAC Airplay Award. *Current Management:* Scramblers Knob Studio. *Address:* 1000 Scramblers Knob, Franklin, TN 37064, USA.

ROBERTS, Graham Andrew; b. 3 Feb. 1964, Northampton, England. *Education:* Royal Academy of Music. *Career:* Numerous concerts, television, radio, for BBC, ITV, various European stations; Tours, USA, Europe, Far East. *Recordings:* with Grahamphones: Let's Do It Again, 1990; with Pasadena Roof Orchestra: Breakaway, 1991; Swing That Music, 2000; with Swing Sisters: Swing, 1992; Take Me Back, 1994; with Tetra Guitar Quartet: By Arrangement, 1993; Pasadena, 1994. *Honours:* Winner, Julian Bream Guitar Competition, 1988. *Current Management:* Hothouse Entertainments. *Address:* 7 Wychwood Close, New Duston, Northampton, England.

ROBERTS, J. Patricia; b. 17 Feb. 1954, Aberdeen, Scotland. Scottish Traditional Vocalist; Musician (Celtic harp (clarsach), guitar). *Education:* Born Hamilton Academy, 1966–72; BSc, DipEd, Stirling University, 1977; Studied clarsach briefly with Sanchia Pielou. *Career:* Science teacher and guidance counsellor in high school, 1977–93; Appeared: Lorient Celtic Folk Festival; QE2; Burns' Suppers in Munich, Germany and Stavanger, Norway; USA, 2002; Radio interviews on Radio Bretagne, Radio Forth; Television appearance, Carols for Christmas (BBC). *Recordings:* Just As I Am, 1993; Glamis, A Trysting Place; Patricia Roberts and Lorna Swan. *Membership:* Musicians' Union, Scotland. *Address:* 113 Lothian Cres., Causewayhead, Stirling FK9 5SE, Scotland. *Telephone:* (1786) 465065. *E-mail:* patriciaroberts@totalise.co.uk. *Website:* www.patriciaroberts.com.

ROBERTS, Mark; b. 3 Nov. 1969, Colwyn Bay, Wales. Musician (guitar). *Career:* Member, Welsh-language band, Y Cyrff, –1991; Founder member, Catatonia, 1992–2001; First release on Welsh Indie label Crai; Signed to Blanco Y Negro, 1996; Numerous tours and festival appearances; Many TV appearances. *Recordings:* Albums: Way Beyond Blue, 1996; The Sublime Magic of Catatonia, 1996; International Velvet (No. 1, UK), 1998; Equally Cursed and Blessed (No. 1, UK), 1999; Paper Scissors Stone, 2001; Greatest Catatonia Hits, 2002. Singles: For Tinkerbell (EP), 1993; Hooked (EP), 1994; Bleed/Do You Believe In Me, 1996; You've Got A Lot To Answer For, 1996; Mulder and Scully, 1998; Road Rage, 1998; Strange Glue, 1998; Dead From The Waist Down, 1999; Londinium, 1999; Karaoke Queen, 1999; Stone By Stone, 2001.

ROBERTS, Rudy; b. 9 April 1966, Nantes, France. Rock Musician (guitar). *Education:* American School of Modern Music, Paris. *Career:* Squealer, 1991, French support tour with UDO; Member, Starmania/Tycoon, 1993–95; Solo artist, 1991–; Numerous concerts, France, Belgium, Switzerland, Canada, played to over 1m. people; Played with: Stuart Hamm; Jonathon Mover; Electric guitar teacher, Vitré Conservatory of Music; Demonstrator for Jackson guitars; Hughes and Kettner amplifiers. *Recordings:* with Squealer

This Is What The World Is About, 1991; with Starmania: Starmania; Solo albums: Passion Colors, 1993; Rudy Roberts Live, 1994. *Publications:* Instruction video, Plans and Techniques Hard Rock. *Honours:* Guinness World Record Holder, Non-stop guitar playing (50 hours); Ninth Victoires de la Musique Award, Best Live Show, Starmania, 1994. *Membership:* SACEM; SPEDIDAM. *Current Management:* Pierrick Morin, Move On Productions. *Address:* 7 rue Baudrairie, 35500 Vitré, France.

ROBERTS, Stephen; b. 27 March 1958, London, England. Musician (drums). m. Philippa Jane, 26 May 1991. *Career:* In 1980 formed legendary New Wave of British Heavy Metal group: Silverwing, with brother Dave; Toured with Diamond Head and Phil Lynott, split 1983; Formed Pet Hate; released 2 albums; Toured USA and Canada; Appeared on Channel 4's ECT; Formed Wild Ones, 1989; Released 1 album; Session musician with Belinda Carlisle and Rick Astley, including appearances on Wogan and at San Remo Festival, 1990; Currently with No Fit State. *Recordings:* with Silverwing: Rock and Roll Are Four Letter Words, 1980; Sittin' Pretty, 1981; Alive and Kicking, 1982; with Pet Hate: The Bride Wore Red, 1984; Bad Publicity, 1985: with Wild Ones: Writing On The Wall, 1991; with No Fit State: Welcome To..., 1995. *Membership:* Musicians' Union. *Current Management:* Triumphant Productions. *Address:* 1 Waterloo St, Stockport SK1 3DB, England.

ROBERTSON, Brian; b. 12 Sept. 1956, Glasgow, Scotland. Rock Musician (guitar). *Career:* Guitarist, UK rock group Thin Lizzy, 1974–78; Concerts include: Regular UK and European tours; Reading Festival, 1974, 1975, 1977; US tour, supporting Bachman-Turner Overdrive, 1976; Briefly with Graham Parker and The Rumour, 1977; Founder, Wild Horses, 1978–81; Guitarist, UK heavy metal group Motörhead, 1982. *Recordings:* Albums: with Thin Lizzy: Nightlife, 1974; Fighting, 1975; Jailbreak, 1976; Johnny The Fox, 1976; Bad Reputation, 1977; Live and Dangerous (No. 2, UK), 1978; Japanese Compilation, 1980; Adventures of Thin Lizzy, 1981; Life, 1983; Dedication, 1991; with Motörhead: Another Perfect Day, 1983; Singles: with Thin Lizzy: Still In Love With You, 1975; The Boys Are Back In Town, 1976; Jailbreak, 1976; Cowboy Song, 1976; Don't Believe A Word, 1977; Dancin' In The Moonlight, 1977; Rosalie, 1978; with Motörhead: I Got Mine, 1983; Shine, 1983; Other collaborations include: Eric Burdon; Shane MacGowan & The Popes; Frankie Miller; B.A. Robertson. *Honours:* Gold disc, Jailbreak, 1976.

ROBERTSON, Donald Irwin; b. 5 Dec. 1922, Beijing, People's Republic of China. Composer; Musician (piano); Vocalist. m. (1) Ella Lucille Dinning, 2 Aug. 1946, divorced, 1 s. (deceased), 1 d., (2) Irene Symsk, 1 Jan. 1962, 2 s. *Education:* AA, University of Chicago, 1943. *Career:* Moved to USA, 1927; Freelance songwriter, musician, singer, 1944–. *Recordings:* Featured on albums by numerous artists including: Elvis Presley; Bob Dylan; Willie Nelson; Dinah Shore; Nat King Cole; Waylon Jennings; Dolly Parton; Perry Como; Eddy Arnold; Roy Clark; Loretta Clark. *Honours:* Inducted, Walkway of Stars, Country Music Hall of Fame, 1967; 2 BMI Awards, 1954; Billboard Award, 1964; 17 ASCAP Awards, 1955–84; Nashville Songwriters Asscn International Hall of Fame, 1972. *Membership:* AFTRA; ASCAP; AFofM; NARAS; NSAI; Songwriters Guild of America.

ROBERTSON, Robbie (Jaime); b. 5 July 1944, Toronto, Ontario, Canada. Musician (guitar); Vocalist. *Career:* Guitarist, singer with The Band (formerly the Hawks), 1964–78; Long association with Bob Dylan; As backing band for Bob Dylan, appearances include: Don't Look Back British tour, 1965; Royal Albert Hall, 1966; Isle of Wight Festival, 1969; US tour, 1974; Performances as The Band include: Watkins Glen Festival, with the Grateful Dead, Allman Brothers, 1973; Producer, film The Last Waltz, film of final Band concert, 1977; Film appearance, Solo career, 1978–. *Compositions:* Much of Band's material including: 4% Pantomime (co-written with Van Morrison). *Recordings:* Singles: with the Band: The Weight, used in film Easy Rider, 1968; Up On Cripple Creek, 1970; Don't Do It, 1972; Solo singles include: Somewhere Down That Crazy River, 1988; Albums with The Band: The Basement Tapes (with Bob Dylan), 1967; Music From Big Pink, 1968; The Band, 1969; Stage Fright, 1970; Cahoots, 1971; Rock of Ages, 1972; Moondog Matinee, 1973; Before The Flood (with Bob Dylan), 1974; Northern Lights Southern Cross, 1976; Best Of..., 1976; Islands, 1977; The Last Waltz, 1978; Solo albums: Robbie Robertson, 1987; Storyville, 1991; Music For The Native Americans, 1994; Contact from the Underworld of Red Boy, 1998; Producer, Beautiful Noise, Neil Diamond, 1976; Contributor, Planet Waves, Bob Dylan, 1974; Beauty, Ryûichi Sakamoto, 1989; Rainbow Warriors, Greenpeace charity album, 1979; Contributor, film soundtracks: Raging Bull; King of Comedy; The Color of Money; Also appeared on recordings by: Eric Clapton; John Hammond; Emmylou Harris; B. B. King; Joni Mitchell; Tom Petty; Carly Simon; Ringo Starr. *Honours:* The Band, inducted into Canadian Hall of Fame, 1989. *Current Management:* Addis Wechsler and Associates, 955 S Camillo Dr., Third Floor, Los Angeles, CA 90048, USA.

ROBIN, Thierry (Titi); b. 26 Aug. 1957, France. Composer; Musician (guitar; ud –atre de la Ville de Paris; Arabic World Institute; UNESCO; Most European festivals including: Transmusicales; WOMAD; Angoulême; WOMEX; Tours: Japan; Africa; Indian Ocean; Europe; USA; Canada; North Africa; Middle East; Appearances include European TV: Arte Megamix, FR3;

TVS; France Inter; France Musique; Europe 1. *Recordings:* Luth et Tablá, 1985; An Henchoû Treùz, 1990; Trio Erik Marchand, 1991; Gitans, 1993; Regard Nu, 1996; Payo Michto, 1997; Kali Gadji, 1998; Un Ciel de Cuivre, 2000. *Honours:* Grand Prix de l'Academie Charles Cros, 1990. *Membership:* SACEM. *Current Management:* Guillaume Dubois.

ROBINS, Reed W; b. 4 June 1957. Prod; Engineer; Vocalist; Musician (piano, guitar, bass); Composer. m. Sevgi Ercan. *Education:* BA, Virginia Commonwealth University. *Career:* Television Performances, Commercial With Ray Charles, Richard Tucker Galas, Pavarotti; Many Performances In Carnegie Hall including The American Premiere of Paul McCartney's Liverpool Oratorio at Carnegie. *Compositions:* Tommys; Jack and The North West Wind; The Painter. *Recordings:* Songs of Jimi Hendrix For Solo Jazz Piano; Music For Film and Theatre Vol. I; My Happiness. *Membership:* ASCAP; American Music Center. *Current Management:* Changing Tones Corporation, 874 Broadway Suite 901, New York, NY 10003–1222, USA.

ROBINSON, Barry; b. 10 Sept. 1963, Bushey, Watford, Hertfordshire, England. Musical Dir; Composer; Conductor; Arranger; Musician (piano, keyboards). *Education:* Honours Graduate, Composition and arranging, Grove School of Music, Los Angeles. *Career:* Music for Television includes: Big Stage Indie Awards; Come Dancing; Variety Club Awards; Children In Need; The Accountant; Tours with: The Three Degrees; Rose Royce; The Supremes; Kiki Dee; Joe Longthorne; Helen Shapiro; West End Shows: Saturday Night Fever; Smokey Joe's Cafe; Fame; musical supervisor, Jesus Christ Superstar; Kat and The Kings. *Compositions:* Composer, arranger, Midas Touch, game show, Central Television. *Membership:* PRS. *Current Management:* Emma Darrell, Roger Hancock Ltd. *Address:* 4 Water Lane, London NW1 8NZ, England.

ROBINSON, Chris(topher Mark); b. 20 Dec. 1966, Atlanta, GA, USA. Rock Vocalist; Songwriter. m. Kate Hudson, 2001. *Career:* Founding mem., US rock group, Mr Crowe's Garden, later renamed The Black Crowes, 1984–; Major concerts include: Support tours to Heart, 1990; Robert Plant, 1990; ZZ Top, 1991; Memphis In May Festival, 1991; Monsters of Rock Festival, Castle Donington, 1991; Glastonbury Festival, 1993; Phoenix Festival, 1993; Solo artiste, 2002–. *Recordings:* Albums: with The Black Crowes: Shake Your Money Maker, 1990; The Southern Harmony and Musical Companion, 1992; Amorica, 1994; Three Snakes and One Charm, 1996; Sho Nuff: The Complete Black Crowes, 1998; By Your Side, 1999; Live At The Greek, 2000; Tribute To A Work In Progress: Greatest Hits 1990–1999, 2001; Lions, 2001; Live, 2002; Solo: New Earth Mud, 2002. *Honours:* Rolling Stone magazine, Best New American Band, Best Male New Singer, 1991. *Current Management:* Angelus Entertainment, 9016 Wilshire Blvd, Suite 3461, Beverly Hills, CA 90211, USA. *Address:* c/o V2 Records, 14 E Fourth St, New York, NY 10012, USA. *E-mail:* info@theblackcrowes.com. *Website:* www.blackcrowes.com.

ROBINSON, Orphy; b. 13 Oct. 1960, London, England. Jazz Musician (vibraphone, drums, percussion, keyboards); Composer. 1 s. *Education:* Hackney College; Hackney and Islington Youth Band. *Career:* Played with Savanna; Courtney Pine; Andy Sheppard; Balanescu String Quartet; Mica Paris; David Murray; Jazz Warriors; Lead soloist, Shivanova, 1990–; Solo artiste, 1990–. *Recordings:* I Can't Turn Away, Savanna; In and Out of Love, Imagination; Journey To The Urge Within, Courtney Pine; Out of Many One People, Jazz Warriors; When Tomorrow Comes, The Vibes Describes, Orphy Robinson; Introductions In The Dark, Andy Sheppard; Suite de Lorenzo, Ensemble Bash; Singles include: Life; Makes A Change; Film soundtracks: Men of The Month; Bloodrights. *Honours:* British Jazz Awards, Most Promising Newcomer, 1989; Best Miscellaneous Instrumentalist, 1993. *Membership:* PRS; Musicians' Union. *Address:* c/o Coalition Music and Media, Devonshire House, 12 Barley Mow Passage, London W4 4PH, England.

ROBINSON, Pat; b. 7 April 1948, USA. Songwriter; Vocalist; Musician (guitar, piano). 2 d. *Compositions:* You Got Away With Love, recorded by Percy Sledge; Civilised Man, Joe Cocker; No Promise No Guarantee, Laura Branigan; Jokers Are Wild, Gene Clark; *Recordings:* . *Contributions to:* Wave of the Hand: The Best of Carla Olson, 1995; Honest As Daylight, 2001; Textones, Through The Canyon, 1989; Back In Time, 1990; Cedar Creek, 1998; Revenge of the Nerds, 1998. *Membership:* BMI. *Current Management:* Saul Davis. *Address:* c/o Saul Davis, 11864 Ventura Blvd, #583, Studio City, CA 91604, USA.

ROBINSON, Rich(ard S.); b. 24 May 1969, Atlanta, GA, USA. Musician (guitar). *Career:* Founding mem., US rock group, Mr Crowe's Garden, later renamed The Black Crowes, 1984–; Major concerts include: Support tours to Heart, 1990; Robert Plant, 1990; ZZ Top, 1991; Memphis In May Festival, 1991; Monsters of Rock Festival, Castle Donington, 1991; Glastonbury Festival, 1993; Phoenix Festival, 1993. *Recordings:* Albums: Shake Your Money Maker, 1990; The Southern Harmony and Musical Companion, 1992; Amorica, 1994; Three Snakes and One Charm, 1996; Sho Nuff: The Complete Black Crowes, 1998; By Your Side, 1999; Live At The Greek, 2000; Tribute To A Work In Progress: Greatest Hits 1990–1999, 2001; Lions, 2001; Live, 2002. *Honours:* Rolling Stone magazine, Best New American Band, Best Male New Singer, 1991. *Address:* c/o V2 Records, 14 E Fourth St, New York, NY 10012, USA. *E-mail:* info@theblackcrowes.com. *Website:* www.blackcrowes.com.

ROBINSON, Ross; b. 1969. Record Producer; Musician (guitar). *Career:* Mem. and prod., thrash metal group Detente; Debut as Prod., Korn's first album, Korn, 1995; Prod. of albums by: Amen, At The Drive In, Deftones, Glassjaw, Korn, Limp Bizkit, Sepultura, Slipknot, Soulfly, Vanilla Ice, Vex Red; Owner and Pres., record label, I Am Recordings. *Recordings:* with Detente: Recognize No Authority, 1983. *Address:* c/o I Am Recordings UK, Kensal House, 553 Harrow Rd, London W10 4RH, England. *E-mail:* ross@iamrecordings.com. *Website:* www.iamrecordings.com.

ROBINSON, Smokey (William); b. 19 Feb. 1940, Detroit, Michigan, USA. R&B Soul Vocalist; Songwriter; Prod. m. Claudette, 7 Nov. 1959, 2 c. *Career:* Singer with The Matadors; Singer with The Miracles, 1954–72; Also billed as Smokey Robinson and The Miracles, 1967–72; Solo artiste, 1973–; Executive producer, composer, film Big Time, 1977; Appearances on television specials: Smokey Robinson 25th Anniversary Special, ABC, 1981; Motown 25th Anniversary special, NBC, 1983; Motown 30 – What's Goin' On, 1990; Aretha Franklin – Duets, 1993. *Compositions include:* Most recordings with the Miracles until 1968; Other hits include: The Way You Do The Things You Do, The Temptations, 1964; Co-writer, My Guy, Mary Wells (No. 1, USA), 1964; My Girl, Temptations (No. 1, USA), 1965. *Recordings:* Albums: The Fabulous Miracles, 1963; The Miracles On Stage, 1963; Doin' Mickey's Monkey, 1964; Going To A Go-Go, 1966; Make It Happen, 1967; Special Occasion, 1968; Time Out For..., 1969; What Love Has Joined Together, 1970; A Pocketful of Miracles, 1970; One Dozen Roses, 1971; Flying High Together, 1972; Solo albums: Smokey, 1973; Pure Smokey, 1974; Smokey's Family Robinson, 1976; Deep In My Soul, 1977; Love Breeze, 1978; Smokin', 1979; Where There's Smoke, 1979; Being With You, 1981; Smoke Signals, 1986; One Heartbeat, 1987; Love Songs, 1988; Love, Smokey, 1990; Double Good Everything, 1991; Ballads, 1995; Our Very Best Christmas, 1999; Intimate, 1999; Anthology, 2001; Singles include: with the Miracles: Shop Around, 1961; You've Really Got A Hold On Me, 1963; The Tracks of My Tears, 1965; Going To A Go-Go, 1966; I Second That Emotion, 1967; If You Can Wait, 1968; Baby Baby Don't Cry, 1969; The Tears of a Clown (No. 1, USA), 1970; Solo: Cruisin', 1980; Being With You (No. 1, UK), 1981; Just To See Her, 1987; Contributor, We Are The World, USA For Africa, 1985; Recorded duets with Barbara Mandrell; Kenny G; Dolly Parton; Rick James. *Honours:* Inducted into Rock and Roll Hall of Fame, 1987; Grammy Award, Best R&B Vocal Performance, 1988; Grammy Living Legend Award, 1989; Inducted into Songwriters Hall of Fame, 1990; Soul Train Heritage Award, 1991; Motor City Music Award for Lifetime Achievement, 1992. *Current Management:* Jeff Wald Entertainment, Suite 840, 12424 Wilshire Blvd, Los Angeles, CA 90025, USA.

ROBINSON, Tom; b. 1 June 1950, Cambridge, England. Songwriter; Broadcaster. 1 s. *Career:* Joined first band Café Society, London, 1973; Album produced by Ray Davies of The Kinks, 1975; Left Café Society, formed Tom Robinson Band (TRB), 1976; Chart success, concerts for Rock Against Racism, world tours, 1977–78; Formed Sector 27, 1979; US tour with Police, 1981; Lived and worked in East Germany, 1982; Further chart success, 1983–84; Tours of USA, Australia, 1985; Purchased recording studio, 1985; Tours of Japan, Italy, UK 1987; Hit show Private View, Edinburgh Fringe, 1987; Presenter, BBC World Service, Radio 1, 1988; Re-formed Tom Robinson Band, 1989; Tours throughout UK, Europe, Canada, USA, Australia, 1991–95; Presenter, BBC Radio 4 series, The Locker Room, 1992–95; Heineken Festival, Leeds, 1995; Presents, The Evening Sequence, BBC6 Music. *Compositions include:* Co-writer with Peter Gabriel: Bully For You; Merrily Up On High, 1979; Atmospherics: Listen To The Radio, 1983; Co-writer with Elton John: Sartorial Eloquence; Elton's Song; Never Gonna Fall In Love Again, 1979–80; Composed music for: More Lives Than One, BBC2 TV, 1985; with Jakko Jakszyk: Hard Cases, Central TV, 1988; Lyrics for It's About Time, Manu Katché, 1991. *Recordings:* Singles include: 2–4–6–8 Motorway, 1977; Glad To Be Gay, 1978; War Baby, 1983; Atmospherics: Listen To The Radio, 1983; Hard, 1994; Albums include: Café Society, 1975; Power In The Darkness, 1978; TRB Two, 1979; Sector 27, 1981; North By Northwest, 1982; Cabaret 79, 1982; Hope and Glory, 1984; Still Loving You, 1986; We Never Had It So Good (with Jakko Jakszyk) 1990; Living In A Boom Time, 1992; Love Over Rage, 1994; Having It Both Ways, 1996; Holidays in the Sun, 1997; Smelling Dogs, 2001. *Honours:* Gold Winner with You've Got to Hide Your Love Away, UK Sony Awards, 1997. *Address:* PO Box 3185, London SW18 3JG, England. *Website:* www.tomrobinson.com.

ROBISON, Emily Burns, (Emily Erwin); b. 16 Aug. 1972, Pittsfield, MA, USA. Musician (guitar, banjo, dobro, fiddle, mandolin, keyboards); Vocalist; Songwriter. m. Charlie Robison, 1 May 1999. *Career:* Mem., teen group, Blue Night Express, 1983–89; Joined two friends performing on the streets of Dallas, the Dixie Chicks, 1989–; Support slots for: Garth Brooks; Emmylou Harris; Loretta Lynn; Signed to Sony; Mix of traditional bluegrass with mainstream country music; Numerous stage shows. *Compositions include:* You Were Mine. *Recordings include:* Albums: Shouldn't A Told You That, 1993; Wide Open Spaces, 1998, Fly, 1999; The Compact Dixie Chicks, 1999; Star Profile, 2002; Home, 2002. *Singles include:* I Can Love You Better, 1997; There's Your Trouble, 1998; Wide Open Spaces, 1998; Long Time Gone, 2002. *Honours:* Country Music Asscn Awards, Music Video of the Year, Single of the Year, for Wide Open Spaces, Vocal Group of the Year, 1999, Entertainer of the Year, Album of the Year, for Fly, Vocal Group of the Year, Music Video of the

Year, for Goodbye Earl, 2000; TNN Music Award, Group/Duo of the Year, 1999; ACM Awards, Album of the Year, for Fly, Favorite Duo or Group, 1999; American Music Awards, Favorite New Country Artist, 1999, Best Country Group, Best Country Album, for Home, 2003; Billboard Award, Favorite Country Artist, 1999; Grammy Awards, Best Country Album, for Wide Open Spaces, 1998, Best Country Performance By A Duo or Group With Vocal, 1998, 1999. *Address:* c/o Country Music Asscn, 1 Music Circle S, Nashville, TN 37203, USA. *Website:* www.dixiechicks.com.

ROCHEMAN, Manuel David; b. 23 July 1964, Paris, France. Musician (piano); Composer. m. Beatriz España, 15 April 1991, 1 s., 1 d. *Education:* Piano, with Alberto Neuman (CNR de Paris); Jazz with Martial Solal. *Career:* Appearances with own trio: Radio-France, 1984; Festival de Jazz Paris, 1984, 1986; Montpellier, 1986; Antibes-Juan-Les Pins, 1988; Grande Parade Du Jazz, Nice, 1992; JVC Halle That Jazz, 1992; Auditorium Du Châtelet, 1993; Festival Cervantino and Palacio de Bellas Artes (Mexico), 1993, 1994; Tours: Belgium; Switzerland; East European countries, 1993–95; Jazz Festivals: Cannes, 1996; Malta, 1996; Montréal, 1996; Copenhagen, 1997; Århus, 1997; New Morning in Paris, with George Mraz and Al Foster, 1998, Toured USA and Canada, 2000, South America, 2001; Also played with Jean-Luc Ponty; Anthony Ortega; Johnny Griffin. *Compositions:* Concerto for piano and orchestra, 1988; San Felipe, for jazz band and philharmonic orchestra, 1995; Concerto For Piano and Orchestra, 1999. *Recordings:* Albums: Trio Urbain, 1989; White Keys, 1992; Tropic City, 1995; Come Shine, with George Mraz and Al Foster, 1998; I'm Old Fashioned, 2000. *Honours:* Prix Boris Vian, 1991; Django D'Or, 1992; Prix Django Reinhardt, 1998. *Membership:* SACEM; SPEDIDAM; ADAMI. *Address:* 14 rue Camille Pelletan, 93600 Aulnay-Sous-Bois, France.

ROCK, Bob; Prod. *Career:* Played In Punk Band, The Payolas, In 1987 changed name to Rock and Hyde; Worked alongside producer Bruce Fairbairn; Producer, secured gigs with Blue Murder, Loverboy, The Cult, Motley Crue, David Lee Roth, Cher; Teamed up with Metallica, 1991. *Recordings include:* Sonic Temple; A Little Ain't Enough; Bitter, Sweet and Twisted; Keep The Faith; The Cult; Subhuman Race; Load; Eight Arms To Hold You; Tal Bachman; On A Day Like Today; Load; Reload; Garage Inc; American Hi-Fi. *Address:* c/o Bruce Allen Talent, 406–68 Water St, Vancouver BC V6B 1A4, Canada.

ROCKY, (Darren Rock); b. 25 Sept. 1967, Hayes, London, England. Prod; Remixer; DJ. *Career:* Started DJ career with partner Diesel; Formed X-Press 2 with Ashley Beedle and Diesel, 1993; Signed to Junior Boy's Own label; Co-founder: Low Pressings Records; Member: Ballistic Brothers; Problem Kids; Remixed: Cevin Fisher; Fatboy Slim; River Ocean. *Recordings:* Albums: Ballistic Brothers vs The Eccentric Afro's, 1995; London Hooligan Soul (with Ballistic Brothers), 1995; My First Acid House (with Problem Kids), 2001; X-press-2, 2002; Muzikizum, 2002. Singles: Muzik X-Press, London X-Press, Say What, 1993; Rock 2 House, 1994; The Sound, 1995; Tranz Euro Express, 1996; Blacker (with Ballistic Brothers), 1997; AC/DC, 2000; Smoke Machine, Muzikizum, 2001; #lazy (featuring David Byrne), 2002. *Honours:* Muzik Awards, Best Producers, X-Press 2, 2001. *Membership:* MCPS/PRS. *Address:* c/o Skint Records, 73A Middle St, Brighton, Sussex, BN1 4BA, England.

RODE, Birgitte; b. 26 Feb. 1956, Copenhagen, Denmark. Vocalist; Musician (keyboards). m. Claus Hvass, 14 June 1992, 1 s. *Education:* Academy of Music, Alborg, Denmark. *Career:* Roskilde Festival; Tours: UK; California, USA; France; Norway; Germany; Sweden; Denmark; Television appearances: Live Aid; Grand Prix-Slovenia; National and international television and radio. *Compositions:* Sculptural Music. *Recordings:* with Johnny Og De Kolde Dæmoner: Paraneuropa; with Walk The Walk: Walk The Walk; Feet On The Ground; Frog Dance. *Publications:* The International Discography of New Wave; Dansk Rock. *Honours:* 4 National Music Council Awards, 1991–94. *Membership:* National Musicians Society; DJBFA. *Current Management:* Zing Zing Music Production and Management.

RODGERS, Nile; b. 19 Sept. 1952, New York, USA. Musician (guitar); Record Prod. *Career:* Member, New World Rising, 1960s; Founder member, Big Apple Band, 1972–76; Became Chic, 1977–; Also solo artiste and record producer; Member, The Honeydrippers, with Robert Plant, Jimmy Page, Jeff Beck; Leader, own trio, Outloud; Co-founder, Ear Candy record label, 1999. *Recordings:* Albums: with Chic: C'Est Chic, 1978; Risqué, 1979; The Best of Chic, 1980; Real People, 1982; Take It Off, 1982; Tongue In Chic, 1982; Believer, 1983; Freak Out, 1987; Chic-Ism, 1992; Solo albums: Adventures In The Land of The Good Groove, 1983; B-Movie Matinee, 1985; Singles include: Dance Dance Dance, 1977; Everybody Dance, 1978; Le Freak (No. 1, USA), 1978; I Want Your Love, 1979; Good Times (No. 1, USA), 1979; My Forbidden Lover, 1979; My Feet Keep Dancing, 1980; Soup For One, 1982; Jack Le Freak, 1987; Chic Mystique, 1992; As writer, producer with Bernard Edwards: Norma Jean, Norma Jean Wright, 1977; He's The Greatest Dancer, Sister Sledge, 1979; We Are Family, Sister Sledge, 1979; Love Somebody Today, Sister Sledge, 1979; Upside Down, Diana Ross, 1980; Diana, Diana Ross, 1982; Why, Carly Simon, 1982; Record producer for artists including: David Bowie; Madonna; Duran Duran; Aretha Franklin; Jeff Beck; Mick Jagger; Al Jarreau; Grace Jones; Johnny Mathis; Marta Sanchez.

RODGERS, Paul; b. 17 Dec. 1949, Middlesborough, Cleveland, England. Vocalist; Songwriter; Musician (guitar, piano). 1 s., 2 d. *Career:* Singer, with Roadrunners; Brown Sugar; Founder member, Free, 1968–73; Concerts include: US tour, 1969, 1971–73; Hollywood Music Festival, Staffordshire, 1970; Isle of Wight Festival, 1970; Tours of UK and Japan, 1972; Formed Peace, 1971; Founder member, singer, Bad Company, 1973–83; Toured UK, Europe, USA, Japan and Australia; Played with Eric Clapton, Jimmy Page and Jeff Beck on The Ronnie Lane ARMS appeal concert tour, 1983; Founder member, singer, The Firm, 1984–86; Toured Europe and USA 1985–86; Founder member, singer, The LAW, 1991; Miscellaneous Concerts include: Atlantic Records 40th anniversary party, 1988; Guitar Legends, Expo '92, Seville, Spain, 1992; Gibson Night of 100 Guitars, Wembley, London, 1994; Elvis Tribute, Memphis, 1994; Woodstock '94, USA; Began solo career; Formed new bands, Paul Rodgers, 1993–; Toured Europe, USA and Japan. *Recordings include:* With Free: Albums: Tons of Sobs, 1968; Free, 1969; Fire and Water, 1970; Highway, 1971; Free Live, 1971; Free at Last, 1972; Heartbreaker, 1973; The Free Story, 1973; Best of Free, 1991; Walk In My Shadow – An Introduction To Free, 1998; Singles: All Right Now; My Brother Jake; Little Bit of Love; Wishing Well; With Bad Company: Albums: Bad Co, 1974; Straight Shooter, 1975; Run With the Pack, 1976; Burnin' Sky, 1977; Desolation Angels, 1979; Rough Diamonds, 1982; 10 From 6, 1985; The Original Bad Co Anthology, 1999; Singles: Can't Get Enough; Feel Like Making Love; Young Blood; Movin' On; Hey Hey; Hammer of Love; With The Firm: Albums: The Firm, 1985; Mean Business, 1986; Singles: Radio-active; All The King's Horses; With The Law: Album: The Law, 1991; Single: Laying Down the Law; As Solo Artist: Cut Loose, 1983; Muddy Waters Blues, 1993; The Hendrix Set, 1993; Live (The Loreley Tapes), 1995; Now, 1997 (also released as double album Now and Live); Electric, 1999; Muddy Water Blues, 1999; Hit single, Soul of Love, 1997; Various contributions to compilation albums. *Honours:* With Free: ASCAP Award for 1m. radio plays; Gold Disc: Single: All Right Now; With Bad Company: Grammy Award, 1975; Gold/ Platinum albums with Bad Company; Hon. Col of Louisiana 1977; Solo: UK Silver Disc: Album: Muddy Water Blues. *Membership:* Musicians' Union; PRS; MCPS. *Address:* c/o Gremlin Productions, PO Box 216, Diss, Norfolk PE22 2TY, England.

RODNEY, Godfrey Winston, (Burning Spear); b. 1 March 1945, St Ann's Bay, Jamaica. Vocalist; Songwriter. m. Sonia Marlene Thompson, 13 Sept. 1981, 1 s., 3 d. *Career:* Singer, songwriter, reggae group Burning Spear; Career began recording for Studio One label, 1969; Releases for Island Records, 1970s; Toured with bands including: UB40; Talking Heads; The Clash; Tour USA from East to West coast; TV appearance Bet, Rockers; Many radio appearances world-wide; Rendered Estimated Prophet on Dedicated, Grateful Dead tribute album, 1991. *Recordings:* 20 albums include: Burning Spear; Rocking Time; Marcus Garvey; Man In The Hills; Garvey's Ghost; Hail H I M, 1981; Farover, 1982; Resistance, 1984; Mek We Dweet, 1990; Jah Kingdom, 1992; The World Should Know, 1993; Rasta Business, 1995; Best Of The Fittest, 2001. *Honours:* Musicians Merit Award, Album of the Year, 1990; Martin's International Reggae Award for Most Educational Entertainer of the 1980s, 1991; Album of the Year, Best Arranger (reggae), Caribbean Music Awards; Best Reggae Album, NAIRD Indie Awards, 1992; 4 IRMA Awards, including Best Music Video, 1995; Bob Marley Award Entertainer of the Year; International Reggae Hall of Fame; Marcus Garvey Humanitarian Award. *Membership:* PRS; ASCAP. *Current Management:* Burning Music Production. *Address:* 130–34 231th St, Laurelton, NY 11413, USA.

RODRIGUEZ, Arabella Sabina; b. Norfolk, England. Recording and Mixing Engineer. 1 s., 1 d. *Education:* Piano, Harmony, Violin, Flute. *Career:* Sound Engineer, 1986–. *Recordings:* Credits as Engineer include: Motörhead; Scritti Politti; Soul II Soul; Black Rain; Caron Wheeler; Manu Dibango; Angelique Kidjo; D-Influence; East 17; Sinead O'Connor; Natacha Atlas; Tama; Jack Roberts; Busi Mholongo; Ghostland. *Membership:* Repro; PRS; MCPS. *Current Management:* Stephen Budd Management, 109 B Regent's Park Rd, London NW1 8UR, England. *Address:* 106 Albion Rd, London N16 9AD, England.

RODRIGUEZ, Johnny (Juan Raoul Davis); b. 10 Dec. 1951, Sabibal, Texas, USA. Country vocalist; Songwriter; Musician (guitar). *Career:* Performed with high school rock band The Spocks, late 1960s; Discovered by Tom T Hall and Bobby Bare while performing at Alamo Village Amusement Park, Brackettville, Texas, 1971; Moved to Nashville; Worked as guitarist with Tom T Hall's band; Signed to Mercury Records; First chart appearance, 1972; Most successful Chicano country singer of all time, recording in both English and Spanish; peak period early to mid-1970s but continued to chart until 1989; Appeared in TV show Adam-12, 1974; Movies include: Rio Diablo; Nashville Girl (aka Country Music Daughter/New Girl In Town), 1976; La Bamba Party; The Runaway Barge (aka River Bandits), 1975; Charity work includes helping underprivileged Mexican-American children through the Life Enrichment Center. *Compositions include:* Dance With Me (Just One More Time); Down On The Rio Grande; Ridin' My Thumb To Mexico. *Recordings include:* Pass Me By (If You're Only Passing Through), 1972; That's The Way Love Goes, 1973; Just Get Up and Close The Door, 1975; You Always Come Back (To Hurting Me), 1973; Love Put A Song In My Heart, 1975; I Just Can't Get Her Out My Mind, 1975; Albums: Introducing Johnny Rodriguez, 1973; All I Ever Meant To Do Was Sing, 1973; Greatest Hits. *Honours:* various

including: ACM, Most Promising Male Vocalist, 1972; Cash Box, New Male Vocalist, Singles and Albums, 1973; Music City News, Most Promising Male Vocalist, 1973 and 1974; Billboard, Trendsetter Award, 1973; Cash Box, Upcoming Male Award, 1973; Record Review, Most Promising Male Vocalist, Album Charts and Singles Chart, 1973. *Address:* c/o Fat City Artists, 1226 17th Ave S, Suite 2, Nashville 37212, USA.

ROE, Tommy; b. 9 May 1942, Atlanta, Georgia, USA. Entertainer; Musician (guitar); Songwriter; Music Publisher. *Career:* Performances and concerts world-wide; Appearances, all major television and radio shows in 1960s; Sold 40m. records. *Recordings:* Hit Singles: Sheila; Sweet Pea; Dizzy; Everybody (all Gold discs); Hooray For Hazel; It's Now Winter's Day; Jam Up; Jelly Tight; Albums include: 12 in a Roe; Tommy Roe's Greatest Hits; Dizzy: The Best of Tommy Roe; Golden Legends, 2000; High Profile, 2000. *Honours:* 4 Gold Singles; Georgy Award; BMI Awards. *Membership:* Society of Singers; Academy of Country Music. *Current Management:* Dave Hoffman. *Address:* PO Box 26037, Minneapolis, MN 55426, USA.

ROEL, (Anne) Charlotte; b. 3 Dec. 1964, Copenhagen, Denmark. Vocalist. m. Floyd Adams III, 21 July 1990. *Education:* Manhattan School of Music, New York City. *Career:* Solo performer, 1992–; Concerts: Copenhagen Gospel Rock Festival; Opstand Festival; Glumsö Gospel Festival; Västervik Gospel Festival, Sweden; Performed; Montmartre; Copenhagen Jazz House; Huset; KB Hallen; Radio: Strax, Denmark National Radio; More Than Music; Tjek Listen; Danish local radio; NIK Kolding; Radio Roskilde; Naestved Radio; Copenhagen FM; Radio Ballerup; Swedish radio; KFUM Sweden; Television: KKR/TV Charlotte Roel – A Musical Portrait; Norwegian TV; Hello Norden; Hostess, producer, The Five Blind Boys of Alabama. *Recordings:* Single: Perfect Love (No. 1, Denmark), 1994; Debut album, 1995. *Membership:* DAF (Danish Artist Society). *Current Management:* William B Proven Productions. *Address:* Nörre Sögade 33 A 1, 1370 Copenhagen K, Denmark.

ROESER, Donald (Buck Dharma); b. 12 Nov. 1947. Musician (guitar); Vocalist. *Career:* Lead guitarist, vocalist, US rock group Blue Öyster Cult, 1971–; Concerts: US tours, including support to Alice Cooper, 1972; World tour, 1978 Monsters of Rock Festival, Castle Donington, 1981; British tour, 1989. *Recordings:* Singles include: (Don't Fear) The Reaper, 1976; Albums: Blue Öyster Cult, 1972; Tyranny and Mutation, 1973; Live On Your Feet Or On Your Knees, 1975; Agents of Fortune, 1976; Spectres, 1978; Some Enchanted Evening, 1978; Mirrors, 1979; Cultosaurus Erectus, 1980; Fire of Unknown Origin, 1981; ETL (Extra-Terrestrial Live), 1982; Club Ninja, 1986; Imaginos, 1988; Career of Evil: The Metal Years, 1990; Live 1976, 1994; Cult Classic, 1994; The Curse Of The Hidden Mirror, 2001; Soundtrack, horror film Bad Channels, 1992; Solo album (as Buck Dharma): Flat Out; with Blotto, Collected Words, 1994; with Summerdaze, Summerdaze, 1997. *Honours:* Platinum disc, (Don't Fear) The Reaper. *Current Management:* Steve Schenck.

ROGERS, David; b. 3 Jan. 1963, Dartford, Kent, England. Composer (keyboards); Programmer; Prod. m. Sue Ward, 21 Nov. 1992, 2 s. *Education:* Hons, Comparative Physiology, London University. *Career:* Founder member, Daybreak Productions, 1987; Numerous television, radio appearances including: BBC Radio 1; TV AM; Pebble Mill; Top of the Pops; Kent Rocks; Noel's House Party; Live and Kicking. *Compositions:* 346 works published by 1995; Works include: Mr Blobby; Light of Summer; Peanuts; Steady; Blobby – The Album; The Dream; Boing; Probe. *Honours:* Ivor Novello, Best Selling Song, Mr Blobby, 1993. *Membership:* Musicians' Union; PRS. *Address:* Carlin Music/Destiny Music, Iron Bridge House, Bridge Approach, London NW1 8BD, England.

ROGERS, Kenny (Kenneth David); b. 21 Aug. 1938, Houston, Texas, USA. Country Vocalist; Songwriter. m. Wanda Miller. *Career:* Member, The Scholars, 1955; Founder, Ken-Lee record label (with brother Lelan); Jolly Rogers record label; Bass player, Bobby Doyle Three, 1962; Member, New Christy Minstrels, 1967; Founder member, First Edition, 1967–74; Featured in television films: The Gambler; The Gambler II; The Gambler Returns; Documentary, Kenny Rogers and The American Cowboy; Established Dreamcatcher Entertainment, 1998; European Concert Tour, 1999; AandE's Live By Request, TV concert, 1999. *Compositions include:* Sweet Music Man, recorded by Billie Jo Spears, Anne Murray, Tammy Wynette, Dolly Parton, Millie Jackson. *Recordings:* Albums: with First Edition: The First Edition, 1967; The First Editions Second, 1968; The First Edition '69, 1969; Ruby, Don't Take Your Love To Town, 1969; Something's Burning, 1970; Fools (film soundtrack), 1970; Tell It All Brother, 1971; Transition, 1971; The Ballad of Calico, 1972; Backroads, 1972; Monumental, 1973; Rollin', 1974; Solo albums include: Kenny Rogers, 1976; Love Lifted Me, 1976; Daytime Friends, 1977; Every Time Two Fools Collide (with Dottie West), 1978; Love Or Something Like It, 1978; The Gambler, 1978; Gideon, 1980; Share Your Love, 1981; Love Will Turn You Around, 1982; We've Got Tonight, 1983; Eyes That See In The Dark, 1983; What About Me?, 1984; The Heart of The Matter, 1985; Short Stories, 1986; I Prefer The Moonlight, 1987; Something Inside So Strong, 1989; Some Prisons Don't Have Walls, 1991; Back Home Again, 1992; She Rides Wild Horses, 1999; After Dark, 1999; There You Go Again, 2000; The Way It Used To Be, 2001; Sing You A Sad Song, 2001; Hit singles include: Ruby Don't Take Your Love To Town; Something's Burning;

Lucille (No. 1, UK); She Believes Me; You Decorated My Life; Coward of The County (No. 1, UK); Lady (No. 1, USA); I Don't Need You; Morning Desire (US Country No. 1); Tomb of The Unknown Love (US Country No. 1); Duets include: Don't Fall In Love With A Dreamer, with Kim Carnes; What About Me, with James Ingram and Kim Carnes; Make No Mistake She's Mine, with Ronnie Milsap; We've Got Tonight, with Sheena Easton; Islands In The Stream, with Dolly Parton; Contributor, We Are The World, USA For Africa, 1985. *Publications:* Making It In Music (co-author with Len Epland). *Honours:* 4 Grammys; 11 People's Choice Awards; 8 Academy of Country Music Awards; 11 Platinum Albums; 1 Platinum Single; numerous Gold Albums and Singles; Sammy Cahn Lifetime Achievement Award, 1999; Diamond Award, RIAA, 1999; LeRoy Neiman Award For Artistic Excellence, 1999. *Current Management:* Kragen and Co, 1112 N Sherbourne Dr., Los Angeles, CA 90069, USA.

ROGERS, Robert; b. 27 Jan. 1926, London, England. Bandleader; Musician (guitar); Vocalist. m. Olive, 23 Sept. 1950, 1 s. *Career:* Over 200 TV Tonight shows with Ted Taylor Four; Don Lang's Frantic Five; 6.5 Special; Saturday Club and Country Club on radio; Hundreds of radio shows as Sounds Bob Rogers; Own series, The Towncriers; Things Are Swinging; Skinnerette in the Frank Skinner TV Shows, BBC, 1995–99; ITV, 2000–. *Recordings:* 11 albums; Session guitarist with artists including: John Barry Seven; Adam Faith; Freddy and The Dreamers; Les Reed; Banjo player with artistes including: Mike Daniels Delta Jazzmen; Sid Phillips; Joe Henderson. *Address:* 11 Darwin Close, Orpington, Kent BR6 7EP, England. *Telephone:* (1689) 858164.

ROGERS, Roy; b. 28 July 1950, Redding, California, USA. Prod; Musician (slide guitar). m. Gaynell Toler Rogers, 28 April 1984, 1 s., 1 d. *Education:* BA, History, Hayward State University, California. *Career:* Member, Delta Rhythm Kings; Producer/musician, John Lee Hooker, 1989–; World-wide tours, major jazz festivals; Numerous television and radio shows including John Lee Hooker special, Rock Steady Late Show, UK; Performed with: Carlos Santana; Miles Davis; Albert Collins; B. B. King; Bonnie Raitt; Robert Cray. *Compositions:* The Healer, with John Lee Hooker. *Recordings:* Solo albums: Chops Not Chaps; Slidewinder; Blues On The Range; Slide Zone; Slide of Hand; Slide Zones; with Norton Buffalo: R&B; Travelin' Tracks; Rhythm and Groove, 1996; Everybody's Angel, 1999; Soundtracks: The Hot Spot; One Flew Over The Cuckoo's Nest. *Honours:* Best Emerging Blues Artist, Jazz Times Critics Poll, 1990; NARAS Award of Recognition. *Membership:* AFofM; NARAS; BMI. *Current Management:* Blue Muse Inc. *Address:* PO Box 598, Novato, CA 94948, USA.

ROGERS, Tim (Timothy Adrian); b. 20 Sept. 1969, Kalgoorlie, WA, Australia. Vocalist; Musician (guitar); Songwriter; Prod. m. Rocío García Rodríquez, 1999. *Education:* Arts and Law, Australian National University. *Career:* Founding mem., lead singer, Australian rock band, You Am I, with brother Jaimmes and Nick Tischler, 1989–; First performance, The Cave, Surry Hills, 1990; Numerous world-wide tours; Formed The Brides, later renamed The Twin Set, to back his solo career, 1999–; Appeared in film, Holy Smoke. *Recordings:* Albums: with You Am I: Sound As Ever, 1994; Hi Fi Way (No. 1, Australia), 1995; Hourly, Daily (No. 1, Australia), 1996; # 4 Record (No. 1, Australia), 1998; Saturday Night, 'Round Ten, 1999; Dress Me Slowly, 2001; Deliverance, 2002; solo, with The Twin Set: What Rhymes With Cars and Girls, 1998. Singles: with You Am I: Snake Tide (EP), 1991; Goddamn (EP), 1991; Can't Get Started (EP), 1992; Coprolalia (EP), 1993; Adam's Ribs; Berlin Chair; Someone Else's Crowd (limited edition EP); Jaimmes Got A Gal; When You Got Dry; Cathy's Clown; Jewels And Bullets; Purple Sneakers, 1995; Mr Milk, 1995; Soldiers, 1996; Good Mornin'; Tuesday; Trike; What I Don't Know 'Bout You, 1998; Rumble, 1998; Heavy Heart, 1998; Damage; Get Up; Kick Hole In The Sky; Dirty Deeds Done Dirt Cheap; Trouble. *Honours:* Gold discs; ARIA Awards, incl. Best Alternative Release, 1995; Six Industry Awards, 1996. *Address:* c/o BMG Australia Ltd, 194 Miller St, North Sydney, NSW 2060, Australia. *Website:* www.youami.com.au.

ROGERS, Tony; Musician (mellotron, organ, piano); Backing Vocalist. *Career:* Mem., The Charlatans, 1999–; Signed to Beggars Banquet Records, later Universal Records; Numerous tours, festivals, television and radio appearances. *Recordings:* Albums: Some Friendly (No. 1, UK), 1990; Between 10th And 11th, 1992; Up To Our Hips, 1995; The Charlatans (No. 1, UK), 1995; Tellin' Stories (No. 1, UK), 1997; Melting Pot: The Best Of The Charlatans, 1998; Us And Us Only, 1999; Songs From The Other Side, 2000; Wonderland, 2001; Live It Like You Love It, 2002. Singles: Indian Rope, 1990; The Only One I Know, 1990; Then, 1990; Me In Time, 1991; Over Rising, 1991; Weirdo, 1992; Tremelo Song, 1992; Can't Get Out Of Bed, 1994; Autograph, 1994; I Never Want An Easy Life If Me And He Were Ever To Get There, 1994; Jesus Hairdo, 1994; Crashin' In, 1994; Just Lookin', 1995; Just When You're Thinkin' Things Over, 1995; One To Another, 1996; North Country Boy, 1997; How High, 1997; Tellin' Stories, 1997; My Beautiful Friend, 1999; Forever, 1999; Impossible, 2000; Love Is The Key, 2001; A Man Needs To Be Told, 2001; You're So Pretty—We're So Pretty, 2002. *Honours:* Gold, Silver and Platinum discs. *Address:* The Charlatans, PO Box 134, Sandbach, Cheshire CW11 1YS, England. *E-mail:* cat@thecharlatans.net. *Website:* www.thecharlatans.net.

ROKER, Ron; b. 23 Jan. 1941, Lincoln, England. Composer; Songwriter; Record Prod; Publisher. m. Karol Roker, 7 Sept. 1977, 1 s., 1 d. *Career:* Founder, lead vocalist, own group, 1960s (with guitarist Albert Lee); Toured, worked with various headliners; Turned to writing and producing; Co-writers include: Gerry Shury; Barry Blue; Lynsey De Paul; Roger Greenaway; Howard Greenfield; Formed own publishing and producing company, Karon Productions. *Recordings:* Top 10 hits include: Rupert, Jackie Lee; Storm In A Teacup, The Fortunes; Do You Wanna Dance, Barry Blue; Dance Little Lady Dance, Tina Charles; Guilty, The Pearls; US Top 20 hits: Guilty, First Choice; Up In A Puff of Smoke, Polly Brown; Devils Gun, CJ and Co; Funk Theory, Rokotto and BT Express; Do You Believe In Love At First Sight, Dionne Warwick; Honey Honey, Sweet Dreams. *Honours:* Composer, Never Giving Up, performed by Sweet Dreams, 1983 Eurovision Song Contest (placed sixth). *Membership:* IPA; Term, BAC&S Council. *Current Management:* Karon Productions. *Address:* c/o Karon Productions, 20 Radstone Court, Hill View Rd, Woking, Surrey GU22 7NB, England.

ROLLINS, Henry; b. 13 Feb. 1961, Washington DC, USA. *Education:* American University. *Career:* Singer, punk rock group, Black Flag, 1981–86; Concerts include: Support tours to The Exploited; The Damned; Christmas On Earth Festival, Leeds; Leader, Henry Rollins Band, 1986–; Regular tours and concerts include: World tour, 1991; Publisher, 1984–; Actor in films including The Chase, 1994 and Johnny Mnemonic, 1995. *Compositions include:* End To End, 1985; Hallucination of Grandeur, 1986; Works, 1988; Knife Street, 1989; One From None, 1991; Now Watch Him Die, 1993; Get Him In The Van: On the Road with Black Flag, 1994. *Recordings:* Albums include: with Black Flag: Everything Went Black, 1982; Damaged, 1982; Slip It In, 1984; Loose Nut, 1985; The Process of Weeding Out, 1985; In My Head, 1985; Who's Got The Ten, 1986; with Henry Rollins Band: Hot Animal Machine; Drive By Shooting, 1987; Life Time, 1988; Do It, 1989; Hard Volume, 1989; Turned On, 1990; The End of Silence, 1992; Electro Convulsive Therapy, 1993; The Weight, 1994; Everything, 1996; Black Coffee Blues, 1997; Think Tank, 1998; Live in Australia, 1999; Get Some Go Again, 2000; A Rollins In The Wry, 2001; Nice, 2001; Spoken works include: Short Walk On A Long Pier, 1987; Live At McCabe's, 1992; Deep Throat, 1992; The Boxed Life, 1993. *Contributions to:* Details; Face; Interview; Melody Maker; Sounds; Village Voice. *Current Management:* 3 Artist Management, 2550 Laurel Pass Ave, Los Angeles, CA 90046, USA.

ROLLINS, (Theodore Walter) Sonny; b. 7 Sept. 1930, New York, USA. Jazz Musician (saxophone); Composer. m. Lucille Rollins, 7 Sept. 1957. *Education:* Private music teachers. *Career:* Modern Jazz innovator; Numerous television appearances including solo saxophone on Tonite Show; Annual concert tours of Europe, Japan, USA by Sonny Rollins and Concert Orchestra, 1973–. *Compositions include:* Oleo; Doxy; Duke of Iron; Way Out West; Concerto For Tenor Sax and Orchestra; Soundtrack: Alfie. *Recordings:* Recent releases: This Is What I Do, 2000. *Publications:* Sonny Rollins: Journey of a Jazzman; Open Sky: Sonny Rollins and His World of Improvisation by Eric Nisenson, 2000. *Honours:* Hon. Dr of Arts, Bard College; Guggenheim Fellow, 1972; Inducted, several Halls of Fame; Tufts University Lifetime Achievement Award, 1996; Hon. Doctorate of Music, Long Island University, 1998; Hon. Doctorate of Arts, Wesleyan University, 1998; Hon. Doctorate of Fine Arts, Duke University, 1999; Hon. Doctorate of Music, New England Conservatory, 2002. *Current Management:* Ted Kurland Associates; Lucille Rollins. *Address:* Route 9 G, Germantown, NY 12526, USA.

ROLLO, (Roland Armstrong); Prod. *Career:* Prod. of British house music; Established own label Cheeky Records, 1991; Produced Felix's single, Don't You Want Me, 1992; Began remixing numerous artists incl. Pet Shop Boys, Gabrielle, M People, Wonderstuff, Ian Wright, Björk, Simply Red; Produced hit singles for Out Tribe and High on Love; Founding mem., Faithless, 1995. *Recordings:* Albums: As remixer: Pet Shop Boys: Absolutely Fabulous, Disco 2, Can You Forgive Her; Black Grape, Get Higher; As producer and remixer: Olive, You're Not Alone; Sliding Doors (film soundtrack); As co-producer: Dido, No Angel (No. 1, UK), 2001; with Faithless: Reverence, 1996; Sunday 8pm, 1998; Saturday 3am, 1999; Testimony, Chapter 1, 1999; Back To Mine (compilation), 2001; Outrospective, 2001; Re-Perspective, 2002. Singles: with Faithless: Salva Mea, 1995; Insomnia, 1995; Don't Leave, 1996; Reverence, 1997; If Lovin' You is Wrong; Take the Long Way Home, 1998; God Is A DJ, 1998; Bring My Family Back, 1999; Why Go?; Muhammad Ali, 2001; We Come 1, 2001. *Address:* Faithless Live Ltd, PO Box 17336, London NW5 4WP, England. *E-mail:* info@faithless.co.uk. *Website:* www.faithless.co.uk.

ROMAN-SMITH, Lu Lu; b. 6 May 1946, Pilot Point, Texas, USA. Vocalist; Songwriter. Divorced, 2 s. *Career:* Gospel and Country music and contemporary Christian singer; Appearances include: Grand Ole Opry (21 years); One Woman Show, Branson, Missouri, for 3 years; Cast member, television show, Hee-Haw, 1968–; Presidential Inaugural Event for Ronald Reagan, 1980; Featured artist, Bob Hope Charity Benefits, 1988–91; Pat Boone Celebrity Spectacular, 1991; Television includes: The Love Boat; The Tony Orlando Show; The Mike Douglas Show; Sally Jesse Raphael; Nashville Now; The 700 Club; Music City Tonite; Ralph Emory Show; Featured headliner, numerous state fairs. *Recordings:* Now Let Me Sing, 1974; One Day At A Time, 1975; Love Coming Down, 1976; Lulu's Testimony, 1978; Sing

For My Friends, 1979; You Were Loving Me, 1984; Take Me There, 1986; Hymns That Light The Way, 1987; Joy, 1988; Key To The Kingdom, 1990; Best Friend, 1991; King of Whom I Am; Two More Hands. *Contributions to:* King's Gold, 1992; Operation Angel Wings, 1993. *Honours:* Dove Award, Best Album By A Secular Artist, You Were Loving Me, 1985. *Membership:* CCMA; GMA. *Current Management:* Century II Promotions, PO Box 40707, Nashville, TN 37204–0707, USA. *Address:* Rainey Steele, 1300 Division St, Suite 206, Nashville, TN 37203, USA.

ROMBOLA, Tony; b. 24 Nov. 1964, Norwood, Massachusetts, USA. Musician (guitar). m. Sue, 3 c. *Career:* Formerly in The Crushed Tomatoes; Joined Godsmack group, 1995; Recorded independent debut album for $2,500 over three days with money borrowed from friend, 1996; Heavy local airplay on Boston-based WAAF radio station led to deal with Republic/Universal, 1998; Debut LP remixed/repackaged with eponymous title; Album banned by US Wal-Mart and K-Mart stores for profane content; US and European gigs in 1999 and 2000 including: Woodstock '99; Ozzfest; MTV's Return of The Rock tour; Second album recorded in warehouse in Massachusetts, 2000; First major amphitheatre tour, 2001. *Recordings:* Albums: All Wound Up, 1997; Godsmack, 1998; Awake, 2000; Singles: Whatever, Keep Away, 1998; Voodoo, Bad Religion, 1999; Awake, 2000; Greed, Bad Magick, 2001. *Honours:* Whatever single spent record total of 33 weeks on Billboard Top 10; Boston Music Awards, Act of the Year, 2000 and 2001; Billboard Award, Rock Artist of the Year, 2001. *Address:* c/o Paul Geary, PGM, PO Box 9134, Boston, MA 02205, USA. *E-mail:* godsmack@pgmglobal.com. *Website:* www.godsmack.com.

ROMCESCU, Mircea; b. 5 Feb. 1957, Bucharest, Romania. Musician (violin, piano, guitar); Songwriter; Vocalist. m. Olimpia Panciu Romcescu, 20 Nov. 1986. *Education:* Special School of Music 'George Enesco', 1964–76; Academy of Music 'Ciprian Porumbescu', 1976–80. *Career:* Concerts, tours, television, radio, with own group Academica; Big Band arranging, directing; Film music; Studio musician, producer; Owner, 16 track digital studio; Violin soloist, Academy's Symphony Orchestra, 1980. *Recordings:* Albums: Academica, 1980; Music Is My Life, 1981; Olimpia, 1983; Words Against Words, 1989; Free, 1993. *Honours:* Composer of the Year, 1982; Billboard Song Contest, 3 times. *Membership:* Danish Composer's Union; Romanian Composer's Union. *Current Management:* Claes Cornelius, Mega Records. *Address:* Hyttemestervej 16, Fensmark, 4700 Naestved, Denmark.

ROMER, Hanne; b. 29 July 1949, Copenhagen, Denmark. Composer; Conductor; Musician (guitar, saxophone). 2 d. *Education:* Composing, arranging, conducting, Dick Grove School of Music, Los Angeles, 1983. *Career:* Founder, singer, guitarist, all-woman rock group, Hos Anna, 1975–81; Hexethyl Big Band, 1978–81; Duo with pianist Marietta Wandell; Conductor, several choirs and big bands; Leader, Nordic All-Women Big Band, 1994–; Tours throughout Denmark and Finland. *Compositions:* Piano feature, for Danish Radio Light Music Orchestra, 1985; Saxophone Concert, 1987; Several Symphonic poems; Music for string orchestras, choirs, big bands and jazz ensembles. *Recordings:* 4 albums with Hos Anna; with Marietta Wandall: Akijava, 1990; Ametyst, 1994; with the Nordic All-Women Big Band: Somewhere In Time, 1994; with the Hanne Romer Quartet: Come Rain Or Come Shine, 1994. *Address:* Amanda Music, Kirkepladsen 8 B, 6200 Åbenraa, Denmark.

ROMMEL, Bernd; b. 10 June 1967, Waiblingen, Germany. Musician (drums). m. Monika, 1 d. *Education:* Music High School (MHS, Graz, Austria) with jazz diploma. *Career:* Several R&B projects throughout Germany including: White Bread; Paddy Corn Band; Member, Lizl, 1990; Member, The Solutions, 1991; Member, Blues Pumpm, 1992. *Recordings:* with Lizl: Talk About Jobsharing; All Blues Pumpm productions, (1993–) including: Single: Men From Milwaukee, 1993; Album: Living Loving Riding, 1994. *Honours:* Winner, Bigband Contest Festival with High School Big Band, Graz, Austria. *Membership:* AKM; Austromecha; LSG. *Current Management:* Peter Steinbach, RGG Music, Favoritenstr 53/2/6/18, 1100 Vienna, Austria.

ROMO, Olle; b. 3 July 1958, Stockholm, Sweden. Programmer; Engineer; Musician (drums). m. Mary Beth Romo, 11 Oct. 1991, 1 d. *Education:* Stockholm Music Conservatory. *Career:* Two Eurythmics world tours as drummer; Recording career as drummer, programmer, engineer. *Recordings:* Contributions (as drummer/programmer): Feargal Sharkey, 1985; Eurythmics, Savage, 1987; Shakespears Sister, Sacred Heart, 1989; Eurythmics, We Too Are One, 1989; Neville Brothers, Brother's Keeper, 1990; Pulp, Different Class, 1996; Alisha's Attic, Alisha Rules the World, 1996; Shania Twain, Come On Over, 1997; Bryan Adams, MTV Unplugged, 1997; Pulp, This is Hardcore, 1998; Céline Dion, These Are Special Times, 1998; Also programmer for Backstreet Boys. *Membership:* Musicians' Union. *Current Management:* Tony Quinn, 7 Hz Productions.

RONCHETTI, Francesco; b. 18 Feb. 1962, Florence, Italy. Vocalist; Composer; Performer. m. Lyall Forsyth Harris, 1 Oct. 1998. *Education:* University, Master degree; DMus, DAMS, University of Bologna, Italy. *Career:* Member of vocal trio, Trinovox; Appearances on German television and radio, 1994; Concerts in Germany, Switzerland, Austria (Berlin, Lübeck, Stuttgart, Basel, Vienna, Innsbruck), Finland, Italy, 1994–97; Soundtrack for

radio play, Bavarian State Radio, 1995; Voice specialist, teacher; Speaker at many international conferences in the field; Collaborations with established American and Italian singers, composers, musical producers; Frequent broadcast of music by Trinovox on Italian National Radio; Founded acoustic improvisational duo, The Dedications, 1999; Several North Californian tours; Founded artistic company, Ars Una. *Recordings:* Albums: with Trinovox: Incanto, 1994; Voices, (Trinovox, Sarband, The Bulgarian Voices), 1994; Earborn, Trinovox and Various Artists, 1994; Mediterranea, 1997. *Publications:* Articles: Pop-Rock Singing, in Suonare Uno Strumento, 1989; Tell Me How He Sings..., in Imparerock, 1994; The Sound of Colors, book and CD of poetry, paintings and original music. *Honours:* with Trinovox: Premio Quartetto Cetra, Italian National Award for Vocal Artists, 1994. *Membership:* SIAE; GEMA; SIEM; Contemporary A Cappella Society of America. *Current Management:* Ulrich Balss, Jaro Records, Bismarckstr 43, 28203 Bremen 1, Germany.

RÖNNBLOM, Anders F; b. 9 May 1946, Stockholm, Sweden. Vocalist; Songwriter; Musician (guitar); Designer. *Education:* Graduate from College, 1966; Art and Design School, 1972. *Career:* First recording in 1959; Played with numerous bands in the 1960s with recordings, 1963–66; Debut album under own name in 1971; Currently 20 albums released. *Recordings include:* Jag Kysste Henne Våldsamt; Europa Brinner; Det Är Inte Snön Som Faller. *Publications:* Publishing own magazine, Mac Art and Design. *Current Management:* Studio Matchbox. *Address:* c/o Studio Matchbox, Roslagsgatan 11, 11355 Stockholm, Sweden.

RONSTADT, Linda; b. 15 July 1946, Tucson, Arizona, USA. Vocalist. *Education:* Arizona State University. *Career:* Sang with sisters in the Three Ronstadts; Founder member, the Stone Poneys; Solo career, 1968– ; Performed in operas: The Pirates of Penzance; La Boheme. *Recordings:* Hit singles: You're No Good (No. 1, USA); I Can't Help It; Somewhere Out There, duet with James Ingram (film theme to An American Tail), 1987; Don't Know Much, duet with Aaron Neville (No. 2, USA), 1989; Albums: Hand Sown, Home Grown, 1969; Silk Purse, 1970; Linda Ronstadt, 1971; Don't Cry Now, 1973; Heart Like A Wheel, 1974; Prisoner In Disguise, 1975; Hasten Down The Wind, 1976; Simple Dreams, 1977; Living In The USA, 1978; Mad Love, 1980; Pirates of Penzance, 1981; Get Closer, 1982; What's New, 1983; Lush Life, 1984; For Sentimental Reasons, 1986; Trio (with Emmylou Harris and Dolly Parton), 1987; Canciones De Mi Padre, 1987; Cry Like A Rainstorm, Howl Like The Wind, 1989; Winter Light, 1994; Feels Like Home, 1995; Dedicated to the One I Love, 1996; We Ran, 1998; A Merry Little Christmas, 2000. Compilations include: 5 Stone Poney tracks on Different Drum, 1974. *Honours:* Grammy Award, Best Female Country Vocal, I Can't Help It. *Current Management:* Peter Asher Management, 644 N Doheny Dr., Los Angeles, CA 90069, USA.

ROSE, Axl, (William Bailey); b. 6 Feb. 1962, Lafayette, IN, USA. Rock Vocalist. m. Erin Everly, 28 April 1990, annulled 1991. *Career:* Mem., US heavy rock group, Guns N' Roses, 1985–97; Regular international tours include: Support to Iron Maiden, USA, 1987, 1988; Mötley Crüe, USA, 1987; The Cult, USA, 1987; British tour, 1988; Support to Aerosmith, USA, 1988; Get In The Ring tour, with Skid Row, 1991; World tour, 1992; Major concerts include: Monsters of Rock, Castle Donington, 1988; Farm Aid IV, 1990; Rock In Rio, Brazil, 1991; A Concert For Life (Freddie Mercury Tribute), Wembley, 1992; National Bowl, Milton Keynes, 1993. *Recordings:* Albums: Appetite For Destruction (No. 1, USA), 1987; G 'N' R Lies, 1988; Use Your Illusion I (No. 2, USA, UK) and II (No. 1, USA, UK), 1991; The Spaghetti Incident, 1993; Live Era '87–'93, 1999. Singles: Live ?1*! Like A Suicide, 1986; Welcome To The Jungle, 1987; Sweet Child O'Mine (No. 1, USA), 1988; Night Train, 1989; Paradise City, 1989; Patience, 1989; Knockin' On Heaven's Door (used in film soundtrack, Days of Thunder), 1990; You Could Be Mine (used in film soundtrack, Terminator 2), 1991; Don't Cry, 1991; Live And Let Die, 1991; November Rain, 1992; Yesterdays, 1992; Ain't It Fun, 1993; Since I Don't Have You, 1994; Sympathy For The Devil (used in film soundtrack, Interview With the Vampire), 1995; Live Era, 1999. *Honours:* American Music Awards, Favourite Heavy Metal Single, Favourite Heavy Metal Artist and Album, 1989, Favourite Heavy Metal Artists, 1992; Several MTV Awards; World Music Award, Best Selling Hard Rock Artists of the Year, 1993; Rolling Stone and Billboard magazine awards. *Current Management:* Big FD Management, 510 S Coast Hwy, Laguna Beach, CA 92651–2406, USA. *Website:* www.gnronline.com.

ROSE, David Richard; b. Chatham, Ontario, Canada. Promoter; Musician (drums). 3 d. *Education:* 3 years study in Electronics. *Career:* Agent for 3 years; Promoter for 4 years; Owner of promotion company, Rose Concert Productions Inc, producing many concerts including Blue Rodeo, Jefferson Starship, Procol Harum, 54–40; Rusty; King, Cobb Steelie; Change of Heart; Big Sugar; Nazareth. *Membership:* CCMA; CARAS; CAE; SOCAN. *Address:* Rose Concert Productions Inc, Box 23053, London, ON N6A 5N9, Canada.

ROSE, Dennis Peter; b. 9 Feb. 1947, Brooklyn, New York, USA. Musician (guitar, bass, harmonica); Recording Engineer; Prod. *Career:* Session musician for Phil Spector, 1962, on: Bob B Sox and The Blue Jeans; Zip A Dee Do Dah; Albums with: Surf Band: The Centurions; Del-fi: Surfers Pajama Party;

Shepard Records: Surf War; Other Surf compilation records; Radio KFWB Surf Battle at Deaville Castle Club, Santa Monica; No. 4, West Coast Battle of the bands, Pismo Beach, California; Second annual Teen-Age Fair, Hollywood Paladium; Backed up: Sonny and Cher; Jimmy Reed; John Lee Hooker; at the Pavilion, Huntington Beach and Marina Palace, Seal Beach; Solo Blues Album Project; Cowabunga! The Surf Box; Produced, recorded many R&B, Rock, Gospel, Jazz acts at own studio: Golden Goose Recording; Blues Album Project, studio in Costa Mesa, California. *Honours:* Platinum record: Bullwinkle P11, used for Academy Award winning: Pulp Fiction. *Membership:* ASCAP. *Address:* Golden Goose Productions, 2074 Pomona Ave, Costa Mesa, CA 92627, USA.

ROSE, Michael 'Bammie'; b. 28 Sept. 1942, Jamaica. Musician (flute, tenor, alto, soprano saxophones). m. Cynthia, 1 s., 2 d. *Career:* Cymande, 1973; Paul Simon, 1987; Budely, 1989; Five Guys, 1993; Aswad Jazz Warriors; Jazz Jamaica; Soul II Soul. *Recordings:* Aswad; Soul II Soul; Jazz Jamaica; Elliott Caine, Le Supercool, 2000. *Address:* 26 Blincoe Close, London SW19 5PP, England.

ROSEN, Hilary B; *Education:* International Business, George Washington University, 1981. *Career:* Worked for Governor Brendan Byrne, transition teams of Senators Bill Bradley and Dianne Feinstein; Owned consulting company; Vice-Pres., Liz Robbins Assocs lobbying company; Joined Recording Industry Asscn of America (RIAA—trade group representing the US recording industry), 1987, Chair. and CEO, 1998–; Involved in the establishment of the Secure Digital Music Initiative, the passage of the Digital Performance Rights Act, the US ratification of the World Intellectual Property Organization treaties regarding copyright laws, the adoption of the Digital Millennium Copyright Act. *Honours:* Recipient, American Civil Liberties Union Torch of Liberty. *Membership:* Founding board mem., Rock the Vote; Board mem., Ford's Theatre, Human Rights Campaign Foundation, Kaiser Family Foundation, LifeBeat, Meridian International Center, National Cancer Foundation, National Music Council, Y.E.S. to Jobs. *Address:* Recording Industry Asscn of America (RIAA), 1330 Connecticut Ave NW, Suite 300, Washington, DC 20036, USA. *Website:* www.riaa.com.

ROSENTHAL, David Michael; b. 1 Jan. 1961, New York, USA. Musician (keyboards); Prod; Orchestrator; Composer; Synthesizer Programmer. m. Michelle Christo, 11 Sept. 1999. *Education:* BA in Professional Music, Berklee College of Music, Boston, 1981. *Career:* World Tours: Rainbow: Straight Between The Eyes, 1982–83; Bent Out of Shape, 1983–84; Little Steven, Voice of America; Robert Palmer, Heavy Nova; Cyndi Lauper: Japan Tour, 1991; True Colors, 1986–87; Enrique Iglesis, Vivir, 1997; Billy Joel and Elton John, Face To Face, 1994–95, 1998; Billy Joel: River of Dreams, 1993–95; Greatest Hits World Tour, 1998–99; Two Thousand Years Tour, 1999–2000; Numerous TV and video appearances. *Compositions:* Producer and songwriter for Red Dawn, Never Say Surrender; Orchestrator for Yngwie Malmsteen's Millennium Concerto Suite. *Recordings:* Albums: Billy Joel: The Complete Hits Collection, 1997; Greatest Hits Vol. III, 1997; A Voyage On The River of Dreams, 1994; Yngwie Malmsteen: Millennium Concerto Suite, 1998; Inspiration, 1997; Archives, 2001; Vinnie Moore: Defying Gravity, 2001; Niji-Densetsu, Legends of Rainbow, 1998; Departure: Open Your Mind, 1998; Departure, 1998; Good Rats, Tasty Seconds, 1996; Dream Theater, A Change of Seasons, 1995; Red Dawn, Never Say Surrender, 1993; Deborah Blando, A Different Story, 1991; Steve Vai, Passion and Warfare, 1990; Whitesnake, Slip of The Tongue, 1989; Nicole McCloud: Jam Packed, 1989; Love Town, 1998; Donna Allen, Heaven Goodwin, 1988; Stacy Lattisaw: Very Best of Stacy Lattisaw, 1998; Personal Attention, 1987; Rainbow: The Very Best of Rainbow, 1997; Finyl Vinyl, 1986; Bent Out of Shape, 1983; Straight Between The Eyes, 1982; Roger Glover, Mask, 1984; Hit Singles: Billy Joel, Hey Girl; Will To Power, Baby I Love Your Way/Freebird Medley; Stacy Lattisaw, Let Me Take You Down; Donna Allen, Joy and Pain; Rainbow: Stone Cold; Street of Dreams; Can't Let You Go. *Publications:* Multi-Keyboard Master Class with David Rosenthal; Macintosh, MIDI and Music: The Open Door; Columnist for Keyboard Magazine and Electronic Musician. *Honours:* Keyboard Magazine Reader's Poll Winner, 1993; Berklee College of Music, Distinguished Alumnus Award, 1994. *Membership:* BMI; American Federation of Musicians. *Current Management:* Nocturnal Productions Inc.

ROSENTHAL, Phil; b. 30 Sept. 1948, New Haven, Connecticut, USA. m. Elizabeth Sommers, 4 Sept. 1977, 1 s., 1 d. *Education:* BA, English Literature, University of Chicago, 1970. *Career:* Lead singer, guitarist, bluegrass band The Seldom Scene, including concerts: The White House; The Kennedy Centre; Philadelphia Folk Festival; Prairie Home Companion radio; Many television, radio appearances, 1977–86; Singer, guitarist, banjo player, The Sommers Rosenthal Family Band, 1993–; Founder, President, American Melody Records, 1986–. *Recordings:* 7 albums, The Seldom Scene, 1977–86; Producer, engineer, 17 albums, 1985–; Solo recordings: Indian Summer, 1978; A Matter of Time, 1981; Turkey In The Straw, 1985; The Paw Paw Patch, 1987; Chickens In The Garden, 1991; Comin' Round The Mountain, 1994; The Green Grass All Around, 1995; Animal Songs, 1996; This Land Is Your Land, 1999; Folk Song Lullabies, 2001. *Honours:* Official Connecticut State Troubadour, 1994; 4 Parents' Choice Awards; 3 American Library Asscn Awards for solo children's music recordings, 1985–. *Membership:*

International Bluegrass Music Asscn. *Current Management:* American Melody. *Address:* PO Box 270, Guildford, CT 06437, USA.

ROSKO, Emperor, (Mike Pasternak); b. 26 Dec. 1942, Los Angeles, California, USA. DJ; Broadcaster. *Education:* 1 year college. *Career:* Radio Monte Carlo; Europe No 1; Radio Caroline; Radio Luxembourg, France and 208 UK; Radio 1 BBC; Virgin Radio; Nostalgie FM and many others. *Honours:* Best DJ (UK), Billboard; Top DJ, RandR. *Current Management:* Brian Jones (USA); Tim Jibson, International Marketing (UK). *Website:* www.emperorrosko.com.

ROSNELL, Esko 'Raisin'; b. 23 June 1943, Pori, Finland. Musician (drums). *Career:* Drummer with Leo Kähkönen's dance band, 1964; Tour of USSR with band; Played in groups led by: Otto Donner; Pekka Pöyry; Eero Koivistoinen; Played first Montreux Jazz Festival with Esa Pethmen's Quintet, 1967; Appearances with Heikki Sarmanto in: Scandinavia; Yugoslavia; Poland; Czechoslovakia; USA; 2 visits to Cuba in Government's cultural exchange programme; 2 visits to England with UMO (New Music Orchestra); Member, UMO, 1975–; Work in radio, television, theatre, recording studios. *Recordings include:* To A Finland Station, Dizzy Gillespie; Other recordings with UMO and own quartet. *Honours:* Best drum solo, Montreux Jazz Festival, 1967. *Address:* Gyldenintie 14 B, 00200 Helsinki, Finland.

ROSS, Andrew David; b. 24 Feb. 1960, Bromley, Kent, England. Prod; Songwriter; Musician (guitar). m. Dina Burnstock, 18 Sept. 1994. *Education:* Art School. *Career:* Formed band Immaculate Fools; Television appearances and tours of UK, Europe, USA; Tours and television appearances with: Howard Jones; Tom Robinson; Basia; Other television broadcasts with: Nik Kershaw; Robert Palmer. *Recordings:* with Immaculate Fools: Immaculate Fools; Tragic Comedy; Dumb Poet; Another Man's World; The Toy Shop; with Miguel Bosé: The Sign of Cain; with Howard Jones: Igy; Working In The Back Room; with Tori Amos: Crucify; with Propaganda: 1234; with Nan Vernon: Manta Ray. *Membership:* Musicians' Union; PRS; MCPS. *Address:* 4 Wellfield Ave, London N10 2EA, England.

ROSS, Brian; b. 13 Feb. 1943, Chicago, Illinois, USA. Record Prod; Financier; Musician (keyboards). 2 s. *Education:* UCLA (USC Law School); 25 years classical music training. *Career:* Chairman, CEO, Starborn Records and International Music Commission; Placing talent in over 50 countries world-wide for 30 years; Licensing of masters and music publishing rights to labels and music firms, USA and other countries; Produced records for: CBS/Sony; Phonogram; Warner Bros; RCA/BMG; A&M and MCA Record labels. *Recordings:* Producer, publisher, Music Machine, Talk Talk, 1966; Released children's version of We Are The World, written by Michael Jackson, Lionel Richie; Publisher, I'm On Fire, Barry White; Licensed La Bamba, Ritchie Valens. *Honours:* Gold record, Barry White, The Message Is Love. *Membership:* National Academy Recording Arts and Sciences; AFTRA; Musicians' Union; Japan America Society; Asian Business League. *Address:* 3884 Franklin Ave, Los Angeles, CA 90027–4661, USA.

ROSS, Diana; b. 26 March 1944, Detroit, Michigan, USA. Vocalist; Entertainer; Actress; Fashion Designer. m. (1) Robert Ellis Silberstein, 1971, 3 d.; (2) Arne Ness, 23 Oct. 1985, 1 s. *Career:* Backing singer, the Temptations, Marvin Gaye, Mary Wells; Lead singer, Diana Ross and The Supremes; Solo artiste, 1969–; Appearances include: Opening ceremonies, Football World Cup, USA, 1994; Rugby World Cup, South Africa, 1995; Film appearances: Lady Sings The Blues, 1972; Mahogany, 1975; The Wiz, 1978; Television specials: An Evening With Diana Ross, 1977; Diana, 1980; Christmas In Vienna, 1992; Business ventures: Diana Ross Enterprises Inc; Anaid Film Productions; RTM Management Corp; Chondee Inc. *Recordings:* Singles include: with The Supremes: Where Did Our Love Go (No. 1, USA), 1964; Baby Love (No. 1, UK and USA), 1964; Come See About Me (No. 1, USA), 1964; Stop! In The Name Of Love (No. 1, USA), 1965; Back In My Arms Again (No. 1, USA), 1965; I Hear A Symphony (No. 1, USA), 1965; You Can't Hurry Love (No. 1, USA), 1966; You Keep Me Hangin' On (No. 1, USA), 1966; Love Is Here And Now You're Gone (No. 1, USA), 1967; The Happening (No. 1, USA), 1967; In And Out Of Love, 1967; Love Child (No. 1, USA), 1968; I'm Gonna Make You Love Me, with The Temptations, 1969; Someday We'll Be Together (No. 1, USA), 1969; Solo singles include: Reach Out And Touch, 1970; Ain't No Mountain High Enough (No. 1, USA), 1970; Remember Me, 1971; I'm Still Waiting (No. 1, UK), 1971; Surrender, 1971; Touch Me In The Morning (No. 1, USA), 1973; All Of My Life, 1973; Theme From Mahogany (Do You Know Where You're Going To) (No. 1, USA), 1975; Love Hangover (No. 1, USA), 1976; The Boss, 1979; Upside Down (No. 1, USA), 1980; My Old Piano, 1980; Work That Body, 1982; Muscles, 1982; Missing You, 1985; Chain Reaction (No. 1, UK), 1986; When You Tell Me That You Love Me, 1991; One Shining Moment, 1992; Your Love, 1993; Not Over You Yet, 1999; Duets include: You Are Everything, with Marvin Gaye, 1973; Endless Love, with Lionel Richie (No. 1, USA), 1981; Albums include: Diana Ross, 1970; Lady Sings The Blues, 1972; Touch Me In The Morning, 1973; The Boss, 1979; Why Do Fools Fall In Love?, 1981; Eaten Alive, 1984; Silk Electric, 1982; Chain Reaction, 1986; Ain't No Mountain High Enough, 1989; The Force Behind The Power, 1991; Motown's Greatest Hits, 1992; Live... Stolen Moments, 1993;

One Woman – The Ultimate Collection, 1993; The Remixes, 1994; Take Me Higher, 1995; Very Special Christmas, 1998; Every Day is a New Day, 1999; Voice Of Love, 2000; Gift Of Love, 2000. *Publications:* Secrets of a Sparrow (autobiography), 1993. *Honours:* Citations: Vice-President Humphrey; Mrs Martin Luther King, Rev Abernathy; Billboard award: Record World award, World's Outstanding Singer; Grammy Award, 1970; Female Entertainer of the Year, NAACP, 1970; Golden Globe, 1972; Antoinette Perry Award, 1977. *Current Management:* RTC Management, PO Box 1683, New York, NY 10185, USA.

ROSS, Ricky; b. 22 Dec. 1957, Dundee, Tayside, Scotland. Vocalist; Songwriter. *Career:* Founder member, Deacon Blue, 1985–94; Concerts include: Reading Festival, 1988; John Lennon Tribute Concert, Liverpool, 1990; The Big Day Festival, Glasgow, 1990; Glastonbury Festival, 1990; Currently solo recording artiste. *Recordings:* Albums: with Deacon Blue: Raintown, 1987; When the World Knows Your Name (No. 1, UK), 1989; Ooh Las Vegas, 1990; Fellow Hoodlums, 1991; Whatever You Say, Say Nothing, 1993; Our Town: The Greatest Hits (No. 1, UK), 1994; Walking Back Home, 1999; Homesick, 2001; The Very Best Of, 2001; Solo: What You Are, 1996; New Recording, 1997; This Is The Life, 2002. Singles include: with Deacon Blue: Dignity, 1987; When Will You Make My Telephone Ring, 1988; Chocolate Girl, 1988; Real Gone Kid, 1988; Wages Day, 1989; Fergus Sings the Blues, 1989; Queen Of The New Year, 1989; I'll Never Fall in Love Again, 1990; Your Swaying Arms, 1991; Twist And Shout, 1991; Your Town, 1992; I Was Right And You Were Wrong, 1994; Solo: Radio On, 1996; Compiler: The Tree and The Fish and the Bird and The Bell (tribute by Glaswegian bands to photographer Oscar Marzaroki), 1991. *Current Management:* CEC Management. *Address:* 4 Warren Mews, London W1P 5DJ, England.

ROSSDALE, Gavin; b. 30 Oct. 1967, London, England. Vocalist; Musician (guitar). *Career:* Former Member, Future Primitive, changed name to Bush; Obtained US record deal; Much US radio play and numerous US headlining tours; British tours and festivals. *Recordings:* Singles: Little Things, 1995; Comedown, 1995; Swallowed, 1997; Greedy Fly, 1997; Cold Contagious, 1999; Albums: Sixteen Stone, 1994; Razorblade Suitcase, 1996 Deconstructed, 1997; Science Of Things, 2000; Golden State, 2001.

ROSSELL, Marina; b. 17 Jan. 1954, Barcelona, Spain. Vocalist. *Education:* Guitar, Solfege. *Career:* Professional singer, 1970–; *Appearances include:* Concerts: Theatre de la Ville, Paris, 1981–87; Festival Tenco, San Remo, Italy, 1982; Moscow, 1985; Bogotá, 1988; Festival Utono Musicale, Como, Italy, 1989; Cuban International Festival, 1994; Concert For Peace, San Sebastian, 1995; International tour, Mexico, Paris, Lisbon, Netherlands, Cuba, Canary Isles, Malaga, Pamplona, Barcelona, Sitges, 1994; Bolivian Pro-Native Concert, 1995; Television includes: TVE (Spanish National TV), 1981; Concert, TVE, 1992; Film: El Vicari d'Olot, 1981; Collaborations with composers including: Georges Moustaki; Tomatito; Antoni Ros Marbà; Manzanita; Maria del Mar Bonet; Joan Bibloni; Pau Riba. *Recordings include:* Llegendes de Catalunya, 1975; Si Volieu Escolatar, 1977; Penyora, Premio Fotogramas, Vol. 1, 1978; Festival Internacional, Vol. 1, 1979; Cos Meu Recorda, 1982; Victoria (Banda Sonora Pelicula), 1983; Maremar – Lluis Llach, 1985; Barca del Temps, Disco de Oro, 1986; Les Millors Cançons de Marina Rossell, 1990; Cinema Blau, 1990; Marina, 1993; Gracies (Recopilaciones), 1994; Cinema Blau + La Gavina, 1994; Y Rodara El Mundo, 2000. *Honours:* Silver Shot Award, 1979; Award, Best Catalan record of the Year, R-4, 1981; Best Catalan Record of the Year R-4, for Rosa De Foc (Fire Rose), 1989. *Current Management:* Josep Sanz, JSB Management. *Address:* Calle Llauder, 161–3er. 2a., 08302 Mataró, Barcelona, Spain.

ROSSELSON, Leon; b. 22 June 1934, London, England. Songwriter; Vocalist; Musician (guitar). m. Rina Picciotto, 27 Sept. 1959, 2 d. *Education:* BA Hon Cantab (English Literature); Grade VI Piano. *Career:* Member, Galliards Folk Group, 1959–61; BBC radio Easy Beat and Saturday Club, solo performer, 1961–; Folk clubs; Arts centres; Universities; Concert halls, including Festival Hall, Royal Albert Hall; Tours: Belgium; Netherlands; Australia; Canada; USA; Songs for television programme That Was The Week That Was; Songs for stage production of They Shoot Horses Don't They?, 1973; Television includes: All You Need Is Love; The Oxford Road Show; World Turned Upside Down, singles charts, Billy Bragg, 1985; Ballad of a Spycatcher, Indie singles charts, 1987. *Recordings:* Solo albums: Songs For Sceptical Circles, 1967; A Laugh A Song And A Handgrenade, 1968; Hugga Mugga, 1971; That's Not The Way It's Got To Be, 1974; Palaces Of Gold, 1975; Love Loneliness And Laundry, 1976; If I Knew Who The Enemy Was, 1979; For The Good Of The Nation, 1981; Temporary Loss Of Vision, 1984; Bringing The News From Nowhere, 1986; I Didn't Mean It, 1988; Rosselsongs, 1989; Wo Sind Die Elefanten?, 1991; The Happiness Counter, 1992; Intruders, 1995; Perspectives, 1997; Harry's Gone Fishing, 1999; The Last Chance (EP), 2002. *Publications:* Bringing The News From Nowhere, 125 selected songs, 1993. *Membership:* MCPS; PRS; Musicians' Union; Writers' Guild. *Address:* 28 Park Chase, Wembley Park, Middlesex HA9 8EH, England. *Website:* www.fishdesign.com/rosselson/.

ROSSER, Hamish; b. 1978. Musician (drums). *Career:* Mem., The Vines, 2001–; Short UK, US and Canadian tours, incl. Glastonbury Festival,

England; Carling Weekend Festival, Reading, Leeds; Coachella Festival, Los Angeles; Troubadour, Los Angeles; Mercury Lounge, New York; WHFS Festival, Washington, 2002; Sign to EMI Australia, 2002; Television appearances: Top Of The Pops, Later With Jools Holland, The Late Show with David Letterman, 2002; Australian tour, late 2002; Performed, MTV Video Music Awards, 2002. *Recordings:* Albums: Highly Evolved, 2002. Singles: Factory, 2001; Sun Child/Hot Leather, 2002; Heavenly, 2002; Get Free, 2002; Highly Evolved, 2002. *Honours:* NME Award, Best Single, for Get Free, 2003. *Current Management:* Winterman and Goldstein Management, PO Box 545, Newtown, NSW 2042, Australia. *Address:* c/o Capitol Records, 1750 N Vine St, Hollywood, CA 90028, USA. *Website:* www.thevines.com.

ROSSI, Francis (Mike); b. 29 May 1949, Peckham, London, England. Musician (guitar); Vocalist. *Career:* Founder member, UK rock group Status Quo, 1967–; Extensive tours world-wide; Concerts, festivals include: British Great Western Festival; Reading Festival, 1972, 1978, 1987; NEC Birmingham, before Prince and Princess of Wales, (televised by BBC); Milton Keynes Bowl, 1984; Live Aid, Wembley Stadium, 1985; Support to Queen, Wembley Stadium, 1986; Played 4 venues in 12 hours, entered in Guinness Book of Records, 1991. *Recordings:* Albums: Picturesque Matchstickable Messages, 1968; Spare Parts, 1969; Ma Kelly's Greasy Spoon, 1970; Dog of Two Heads, 1971; Piledriver, 1973; Hello, 1973; Quo, 1974; On The Level, 1975; Blue For You, 1976; Status Quo Live!, 1977; Rockin' All Over The World, 1977; If You Can't Stand The Heat, 1978; Whatever You Want, 1979; Just Supposin', 1980; Never Too Late, 1981; 1+9+8+2, 1982; To Be Or Not To Be, 1983; Back To Back, 1983; In The Army Now, 1986; Ain't Complaining, 1988; Rock 'Til You Drop, 1991; Live Alive Quo, 1992; Don't Stop, 1996; Whatever You Want, 1997; Under The Influence, 1999; Famous In The Last Century, 2000; Rocking And Rolling, 2001; Heavy Traffic, 2002; Numerous compilations. Hit singles include: Pictures of Matchstick Men, 1968; Ice In The Sun, 1969; Paper Plane, 1973; Caroline, 1973; Break The Rules, 1974; Down Down (No. 1, UK), 1975; Roll Over Lay Down, 1975; Rain, 1976; Mystery Song, 1976; Wild Side of Life, 1977; Rockin' All Over The World, 1977; Again and Again, 1978; Whatever You Want, 1979; Living On An Island, 1979; What You're Proposing, 1980; Lies, 1981; Rock 'n' Roll, 1981; Something 'Bout You Baby I Like, 1981; Dear John, 1982; Ol' Rag Blues, 1983; A Mess of The Blues, 1983; Marguerita Time, 1984; Rollin' Home, 1986; In The Army Now, 1986; Burning Bridges, 1989; Anniversary Waltz, 1990; Contributor, Do They Know It's Christmas?, Band Aid, 1984. *Honours:* Silver Clef Award, Nordoff-Robbins Music Therapy Centre, 1981; BRIT Award, Outstanding Contribution To The British Music Industry, 1991; World Music Award, Outstanding Contribution To Music, 1991. *Address:* c/o Universal Music Group, Universal Studios, 100 Universal City Plaza, Universal City, CA 91608, USA.

ROSSINGTON, Gary; b. 4 Dec. 1951, Jacksonville, Florida, USA. Musician (guitar); Songwriter. *Career:* Musician, US rock group, Lynyrd Skynyrd, 1970–77, 1987–; Rossington-Collins Band (with Allen Collins) later The Rossington Band, 1979–88; US tour, support to The Who, 1973; Knebworth Festival, 1976; Serious injuries in plane crash, 1977; Volounteer Jam Reunion, 1987; Farm Aid V, 1991; 20th Anniversary, Lynyrd Skynyrd and Friends LYVE (pronounced Live), cable TV pay-per-view performance, 1993; Inaugural Freebird Festival, 1993. *Recordings:* Albums with Lynyrd Skynyrd: Pronounced Leh-nerd Skin-Nerd, 1973; Second Helping, 1974; Nuthin' Fancy, 1975; Gimme Back My Bullets, 1976; One More For The Road, 1976; Street Survivors, 1977; Skynyrd's First and Last, 1978; Gold and Platinum, 1980; Best of The Rest, 1985; Legend, 1987; Southern By The Grace of God/Lynyrd Skynyrd Tribute Tour, 1988; Lynyrd Skynyrd, 1991, 1991; The Last Rebel, 1993; Endangered Species, 1994; Freebird, 1996; Lyve, 1998; Edge of Forever, 1999; Then And Now, 2000; with the Rossington-Collins Band; Anytime Anyplace Anywhere, 1980; This Is The Way, 1981; Love Your Man, 1988; Singles include: Sweet Home Alabama, 1974; Free Bird, 1975; What's Your Name, 1978. *Address:* c/o Alliance Artists Ltd, 6025 The Corners Parkway, Suite 202, Norcross, GA 30092, USA.

ROTH, David Lee; b. 10 Oct. 1955, Bloomington, Indiana, USA. Rock Vocalist. *Career:* Singer, Red Ball Jets; Founder member, US rock group Van Halen, 1975–85; Support tours with UFO; Santana; Black Sabbath; Regular headlining US and world-wide tours; Major concerts include: California Music Festival, 1979; US Festival, 1982, 1983; Monsters of Rock Festival, Castle Donington, 1984; Solo artiste, 1985–; US tour, 1986; British tour, 1988; World tour, 1991. *Recordings:* Albums: with Van Halen: Van Halen, 1978; Women and Children First, 1980; Fair Warning, 1981; Diver Down, 1982; 1984, 1983; Live Anthology, 1975–81, 2000; Solo albums: Eat 'Em and Smile, 1986; Skyscraper, 1988; A Little Ain't Enough, 1991; Your Filthy Little Mouth, 1994; DLR Band, 1998; Singles with Van Halen include: You Really Got Me, 1978; Running With The Devil, 1978; Dance The Night Away, 1979; And The Cradle Will Rock, 1980; (Oh) Pretty Woman, 1982; Dancing In The Street, 1982; Jump (No. 1, USA), 1984; Panama, 1984; I'll Wait, 1984; Hot For Teacher, 1984; Solo singles: California Girls, 1985; Just A Gigolo/I Ain't Got Nobody, 1985; Yankee Rose, 1986; Goin' Crazy, 1986; Just Like Paradise, 1988; Stand Up, 1988; A Lil' Ain't Enough, 1991; Sensible Shoes, 1991; Slam Dunk, 1998. *Honours:* Numerous Platinum discs; MTV Music Video Award,

1984. *Current Management:* Diamond Dave Enterprises. *Address:* c/o Eddie Anderson, 11288 Ventura Blvd, Suite 430, Studio City, CA 91606, USA.

ROTHERAY, Dave; b. 9 Feb. 1963, Hull, England. Musician (guitar). *Career:* Member, The Beautiful South; Numerous TV appearances and live gigs; Numerous appearances at festivals. *Recordings:* Singles: Song For Whoever, 1989; You Keep It All In, 1989; A Little Time (No. 1, UK), 1990; Old Red Eyes Is Back, 1992; We Are Each Other, 1992; Bell Bottomed Tear, 1992; Good As Gold, 1994; One Last Love Song, 1994; Prettiest Eyes, 1994; Everybody's Talkin', 1994; Pretenders To The Throne, 1995; Rotterdam (Or Anywhere), 1996; Don't Marry Her, 1996; Liar's Bar, 1997; Perfect 10, 1998; Dumb, 1999; The River, 2000; Albums: Welcome To The Beautiful South, 1989; Choke, 1990; 0898, 1992; Miaow, 1994; Carry On Up The Charts: The Best of The Beautiful South, 1994; Blue Is The Colour, 1996; Quench, 1998; Painting It Red, 2000; Solid Bronze: Great Hits, 2001. *Address:* The Beautiful South, PO Box 87, Hull, East Yorkshire HU5 2NR, England. *Website:* www.beautifulsouth.co.uk.

ROTHERY, Steve; b. 25 Nov. 1959, Brampton, South Yorkshire, England. Musician (guitar). *Career:* Member, UK progressive rock band, Marillion, 1980–; Tours; UK; Europe; North America; Major concerts include: Theakston Festival, 1982; Reading Festival, 1982, 1983; Nostell Priory Festival, 1982, 1984; Glastonbury Festival, 1984; Support to Rush, Radio City Music Hall, New York, 1983; Monsters of Rock Festival, Castle Donington, 1985; Welcome To The Garden Party, Milton Keynes Bowl, 1986. *Recordings:* Albums: Script For A Jester's Tear, 1983; Fugazi, 1984; Real To Reel, 1984; Misplaced Childhood, 1985; Brief Encounter, 1986; Clutching At Straws, 1987; B-Sides Themselves, 1988; The Thieving Magpie, 1988; Season's End, 1989; Holidays In Eden, 1991; A Singles Collection 1982–92, 1992; Brave, 1994; Afraid of Sunlight, 1995; Blueprint of the World, 1995; Made Again, 1996; This Strange Engine, 1997; Radiation, 1998; Clutching At Straws, 1999; Marillion.com, 1999; Made Again (Live), 2001; Anorak In The UK Live, 2002. Singles include: Market Square Heroes, 1982; He Knows You Know, 1983; Garden Party, 1983; Punch and Judy, 1984; Assassing, 1984; Kayleigh (No. 2, UK), 1985; Lavender, 1985; Heart of Lothian, 1985; Incommunicado, 1987; Sugar Mice, 1987; Warm Wet Circles, 1987; Freaks, 1988; Hooks In You, 1989; Uninvited Guest, 1989; Easter, 1990; Cover My Eyes (Pain and Heaven), 1991; No One Can, 1991; Dry Land, 1991; Sympathy, 1992. *Current Management:* Hit and Run Music Ltd. *Address:* 30 Ives St, London SW3 2ND, England.

ROTTEN, Johnny. See: **LYDON, John.**

ROUCAN, Jean-Yves; b. 2 June 1962, Neuilly Sur Seine, France. Musician (drums). 1 s., 1 d. *Education:* CIM, Paris; Berklee School of Music, Boston, USA. *Career:* Jazz drummer, Triode, 1986–87; Formed own trio with M Bismut and B Paillard, 1987–; Concerts include: Nîmes Festival, 1988; Béziers Festival, 1989; Radio France Festival, 1991; Radio: France Inter, France Musique, other FM stations, 1992; Television: 4 regional shows, France 3, 1991–92; Worked with: R. Beirach; D. Liebman's Quest; P. Motian; D. Holland; B. Frisell; J. Lovano; D. Humair; Currently, freelance jazz drummer, Plays with Passage (big band); Plays with Interplay Collectif, Switzerland. *Recordings include:* Triode Jazz Quartet; Socco, Trio Paillard-Bismut-Roucan, 1992; With Interplay Collectif: S. Duner Project. *Honours:* First Prize, Concours International de Vienne, France. *Address:* 56 rue Saint Sebastien, 75011 Paris, France.

ROUGVIE, Jeff James; b. 4 March 1963, Quincy, Massachusetts, USA. Dir of A&R and Special Projects. *Education:* Art School; Hartford Art School, 1984. *Career:* Signings: Sugar; Golden Smog; Alejandro Escovedo; Martin Zellar; Morphine; Resposible for catalogue development: Badfinger; Big Star; David Bowie; Elvis Costello; Bill Hicks. *Recordings:* As Producer: Ned Kelly, 1970; Jimmy Buffett, Rancho Deluxe, 1975; Born to Choose, 1993; Chitty Chitty Bang Bang, 1997; Across 10th Street, 1997. *Address:* Rykodisc A & R, Shetland Park, 27 Congress St, Salem, MA 01970, USA.

ROUNDS, James; b. 16 Oct. 1951, Tokyo, Japan. Musician (guitar); Songwriter. *Education:* BA, English, Dickinson College, Carlisle, PA, USA, 1973. *Career:* Played on stage with John Lee Hooker, Charlie Gracie and others. *Compositions:* Go Man Go, Charlie Gracie, with the Jordanaires, 1988; Where Everybody Stays, in the film, Liars Club, 1991. *Recordings:* The Metropolitans, LP, 1996. *Honours:* Help Heal LA Award, 1992; Music City (Nashville) Award for R&B Category, 1988. *Membership:* ASCAP Writer and Publisher. *Current Management:* Bristol Music. *Address:* 515 Rosedale Ave, Nashville, TN 37211, USA.

ROUNDS, Michelle; Vocalist; Songwriter. *Career:* Sydney, Australia, 1989–93; Suva, Fiji, 1993–96; Auckland Area, Aotearoa, 1996–99. *Recordings:* Never Been In Love Before, 1992; Draw Blood, 1994; Contrasts, 1996; Culture Cross, 1998; Era Bini Tu, 1998. *Honours:* Vakalutuivoce Award for Best Female Artist and Best Album; Award from Mai Time. *Current Management:* Polyphony Entertainment, Australia. *Address:* PO Box 172, Hunters Hill, 2110 Sydney, Australia.

ROUSSIN, Didier Jean; b. 1 Nov. 1949, St Mandé, France. Musician (classical, electric and acoustic guitars, banjo, dobro, percussion); Writer; Artistic Advisor; Artistic Dir; Guitar Teacher. *Education:* Conservatoire d'Ivry Sur Seine; Brevet d'Enseignement, Ecole Normale de Musique de Paris. *Career:* Played, recorded with singers: Renaud; Monique Morelli; Gérard Pierron; Backed American jazz accordionists: Art Van Damme, Frank Marocco; Guitarist for Jo Privat, last 13 years; Duo, with jazz accordionist Daniel Colin; Member, several groups including: Denécheau Jâse Musette; Paris-Musette; Les Primitifs du Futur; Robert Santiago's Latino-Américain; Played or recorded with jazzmen and bluesmen: Georges Arvanitas; Marcel Azzola; Steve Lacy; Bernard Lubat; Jean-Claude Fohrenbach; Pierre Michelot; Jean-Jacques Milteau; Bobby Rangell; Benny Waters; Dominique Pifarely; Co-author, French television documentary Le Blues du Musette (La Sept). *Recordings:* Juju Doudou, Dominique Cravic; Night and Day Rue de Lappe, with Jo Privat; Jazz Experience; Quel Temps Fait-il à Paris, with Daniel Colin; Denécheau Jâse Musette à Paris, with Daniel Denécheau, Robert Santiago; with Paris Musette: Vent d'Automne Vol. 3. *Publications:* CD booklets for Musette re-releases; Co-author, book L'Argot des Musiciens. *Contributions to:* Jazz Swing Journal; Modal; Trad Mag; Journal de la Cité de la Musique; Accordéon Magazine; Guitare et Claviers. *Honours:* Grand Prix du Disque de l'Académie Charles Cros, for Paris Musette Vol. I (musician, artistic advisor); Grand Prix de la Littérature Musicale de l'Académie Charles Cros, for Histoires de l'Accordéon, with François Billard. *Current Management:* Madeleine Juteau, 20, Route de Sorel, 28500 Montreux, France.

ROWBOTTOM, Simon; b. Wallasey, England. Vocalist. *Career:* Vocalist, Boo Radleys, 1989–99. *Recordings:* Albums: Ichabod and I, 1989; Everything's Alright Forever, 1992; Giant Steps, 1993; Learning To Walk, 1994; Wake Up (No. 1, UK), 1995; C'mon Kids, 1996; Solo albums under name of Eggman: First Fruits; Kingsize, 1998; Singles include: I Hang Suspended, 1992; Lazarus, 1993; Barney (And Me...), 1994; Wake Up Boo, 1995; Find The Answer Within, 1995; It's Lulu, 1995; From The Bench At Belvedere, 1995; What's In The Box, 1996; C'mon Kids, 1996; Ride The Tiger, 1997; Free Huey, 1998. *Honours:* Select and NME magazines, Album of the Year, 1993. *Address:* c/o Creation Records, 10 Westgate St, London E8 3RN, England.

ROWLAND, Broz (Henry Cottrell); b. 30 July 1949, Dallas, Texas, USA. Prod; Songwriter; Musician (guitar, bass, keyboards, drums). *Education:* BA, Communication in the Audio Visual Arts, University of Colorado, 1978. *Career:* Member, Blue Pearl band, 1978; Formed Alpha Wave, 1980; Member, Modern Kids, 1982; Producer, co-songwriter, Bodyhouse album with Allen Ginsberg, 1986; Formed The Pilots, 1990; Joined Flying Perfect, 1994. *Recordings:* You Know It's Coming (single and album), Alpha Wave, 1980; Album with Modern Kids, 1982; Co-mixer, Lonnie Hill single, You Got Me Runnin', 1986; Writer, producer, Dreams, Visions and Nightmares, The Pilots, 1992; Producer, co-writer, debut album by Flying Perfect, 1995; Producer, debut solo album, John Guillot (former partner in The Pilots), 1995; with Rowland Brothers, No Sleep for the Dreamers, 1998. *Honours:* Quarter Finalist, American Song Festival, 1980; KBCO Eighth Boulder Music Invitational, 1984; Houston International Film Festival, 1986. *Membership:* ASCAP. *Address:* High Kite Productions, 1245 Elizabeth St, Denver, CO 80206, USA.

ROWLAND, Kelly (Kelendria); b. 11 Feb. 1981, Atlanta, GA, USA. Vocalist. *Career:* Founding mem., GirlsTyme vocal group, 1989, with Beyoncé Knowles, later joined by LaTavia Roberson and LeToya Luckett; Group renamed Something Fresh then The Dolls before settling on Destiny's Child; Signed to Columbia Records, 1996; Numerous TV appearances, including Tonight Show, Donnie & Marie, Regis & Kathie Lee, Rosie O'Donnell; Live performances include: Soul Train Awards; Tour with Christina Aguilera, 2000; United We Stand concert, USA, 2001; Acting roles include guest appearance on TV sitcom Taina; Simultaneous solo career, 2001–. *Recordings:* Albums: with Destiny's Child: Destiny's Child, 1998; The Writing's On The Wall, 1999; Survivor, 2001; Eight Days Of Christmas, 2001; This Is The Remix, 2002; Solo: Simply Deep, 2003. Singles: with Destiny's Child: No No No (with Wyclef Jean), 1997; With Me (with Timbaland), 1998; She's Gone (with Matthew Marsden), 1998; Get On The Bus (from film Why Do Fools Fall In Love), 1999; Bills Bills Bills (No. 1, USA), 1999; Bug-A-Boo (No. 1, USA), 1999; Say My Name (No. 1, USA), 2000; Jumpin' Jumpin', 2000; Independent Women (from film Charlie's Angels, No. 1, UK, USA), 2000; Survivor, 2001; Bootylicious, 2001; Emotion, 2001; Eight Days Of Christmas, 2001; Solo: Dilemma (with Nelly), 2002; Contributions to film soundtracks, including Men In Black, Romeo Must Die, Life. *Honours:* Billboard Awards, Artist of the Year, Group of the Year, Hot 100 Singles Artist of the Year, Hot 100 Group of the Year, 2000; American Music Awards, Favorite Soul/R&B Group, 2001, Favorite Pop/Rock Album, for Survivor, Favorite Pop/Rock Band, Duo or Group, 2002; Grammy Awards, Best R&B Song, Say My Name, Best R&B Performance by a Duo or Group with Vocal, Say My Name, 2001; NAACP Image Award for Outstanding Duo or Group, Say My Name, 2001; Best R&B Video MTV Video Award, Say My Name, 2001; Sammy Davis Jr Award for Entertainer of the Year, Soul Train Awards, 2001; BRIT Award, Best International Group, 2002; 13 Gold, Platinum and multi-Platinum Awards. *Address:* c/o Mathew Knowles, Music World Entertainment, 9898 Bissonnet, Suite 625, Houston, TX 77036, USA. *Website:* www.destinyschild.com.

448

ROWLAND, Kevin; b. 17 Aug. 1953, Wolverhampton, West Midlands, England. Vocalist; Musician (guitar). *Career:* Member, Lacy and The Lovers; The Killjoys; Lead singer, Dexy's Midnight Runners, 1978–; Solo artiste, 1988–. *Recordings:* Albums: with Dexy's Midnight Runners: Searching For The Young Soul Rebels, 1980; Too-Rye-Ay, 1982; Geno, 1983; Don't Stand Me Down, 1985; The Very Best of Dexy's Midnight Runners, 1991; It Was Like This, 1996; Solo albums: The Wanderer, 1988; My Beauty, 1999; Singles: with Dexy's Midnight Runners: Dance Stance, 1979; Geno (No. 1, UK), 1980; There There My Dear, 1980; Keep It, 1980; Plan B, 1981; Show Me, 1981; Liars A To E, 1981; The Celtic Soul Brothers, 1982, reissued 1983; Come On Eileen (No. 1, UK and USA); Jackie Wilson Said, 1982; Let's Get This Straight From The Start, 1982; This Is What She's Like, 1985; The Celtic Soul Brothers; Because of You (television theme, Brush Strokes, BBC TV), 1986; Solo: Walk Away, 1988; Concrete And Clay, 1999.

ROWLANDS, Tom; b. 11 Jan. 1971, England. Musician. *Education:* Manchester University. *Career:* Formed first band, Ariel; Formed, The Dust Brothers, with Ed Simons; Formed, The Chemical Brothers, 1989–, with Ed Simons. *Compositions:* Exit Planet Dust, album; Dig Your Own Hole, album; Block Rockin Beats; Setting Sun; Leave Home. *Recordings:* Albums: Exit Planet Dust, 1995; Live At The Social, Vol. 1, 1996; Dig Your Own Hole (No. 1, UK), 1997; Brothers Gonna Work It Out (DJ mix album), 1998; Surrender (No. 1, UK), 1999; Come With Us, 2002. Singles: Song To The Siren, 1993; 14th Century Sky (EP), 1994; My Mercury Mouth (EP), 1994; Leave Home, 1995; Life Is Sweet, 1995; Loops Of Fury (EP), 1996; Night Shift, 1996; Special Brew, 1996; Setting Sun (No. 1, UK), 1996; Block Rockin Beats (No. 1, UK), 1997; Electronic Battle Weapons, 1997; Elektrobank, 1997; Hey Boy, Hey Girl, 1999; Let Forever Be, 1999; Out Of Control, 1999; Music: Response, 2000; It Began In Afrika, 2001; Starguitar, 2002; Come With Us/The Test, 2002; American (EP), 2003. *Honours:* Grammy Award, 1997; BRIT Award, Best British Dance Act, 2000. *Current Management:* Robert Linney, 1 Cowcross St, London EC1M 6DR, England. *Address:* c/o Astralwerks Records, 104 W 29th St, Fourth Floor, New York, NY 10001, USA. *Website:* www.astralwerks.com/chemical/home/chemical.html.

ROWLES, Greg; b. 6 Sept. 1965, Fredericksburg, Virginia, USA. Entertainer; Musician (guitar, bass guitar, pedal-steel guitar). m. Brandee Ann Courtney, 31 Dec. 1992, 1 d. *Education:* Gemanna College Graduate (Business Administration). *Career:* Performances include: Ed McMahon's Star Search Male Vocalist Champion; Grand Ole Opry Live; Music City Tonight; TNN Country News; Opryland Showpark, 1992–94; Tours, shows with Sammy Kershaw, Martina McBride, 1994–. *Compositions:* Professional songwriter signed with Music For The Future, 1995–. *Honours:* Spokesperson in Tennessee for child abuse prevention. *Membership:* Nashville Union. *Current Management:* (Agent) Buddy-Lee Attractions. *Address:* Williams Bell and Associates, Inc, 707 18th Ave S, Nashville, TN 37203, USA.

ROWLES, Stacy Amanda; b. 11 Sept. 1955, Hollywood, California, USA. Musician (horns). *Career:* Major concerts: Monterey Jazz Festival, 1973; Wichita Jazz Festival, with Clark Terry All-Star Band, 1975; All-Women's Quintet, US tour, 1985; Charlie Hayden Liberation Orchestra, 1986; Performed at Woody Herman 50th Anniversary Tribute Concert, Hollywood, 1986; Freelance musician, 1987–; Member, Maiden Voyage, all-female jazz orchestra; Performed at Nice Jazz Festival, 1989. *Recordings:* Nels Cline; Ray Brown; Donald Bailey; Jimmy Rowles; Sweets Edison; Merv Griffin; Albums: Tell It Like It Is, 1984; Me and the Moon, 1993. *Honours:* Best Flugelhorn Soloist, Orange Coast College Jazz Festival, 1973, 1974.

ROWNTREE, Dave, (David Alexander De Horne); b. 8 May 1964, Colchester, Essex, England. Musician (drums). m. 16 June 1994. *Education:* HND Computer Science, Woolwich; Lessons in bagpipes, drums. *Career:* Formed Idle Vice; Played in clubs for 2 years, France; Member, Blur; Extensive television, radio includes: Top of the Pops; Later With Jools Holland; Concerts include Alexandra Palace; Reading Festival, 1993, 1999; Glastonbury Festival, 1994, 1998; Mile End, 1995; V97, 1997; All UK arenas, 1997; T In The Park, 1999; Leeds Festival, 1999. *Recordings:* Blur: Albums: Leisure, 1991; Modern Life Is Rubbish, 1993; Parklife, 1994; The Great Escape, 1995; Blur, 1997; 13, 1999; The Best of Blur, 2000; Singles: She's So High, 1990; There's No Other Way, 1991; Bang, 1991; Popscene, 1992; For Tomorrow, 1993; Chemical World, 1993; Sunday Sunday, 1993; Girls and Boys, 1994; To The End, 1994; Parklife, 1994; End of a Century, 1994; Country House (No. 1, UK), 1995; The Universal, 1995; Stereotypes, 1996; Charmless Man, 1996; Beetlebum (No. 1, UK), 1997; Song 2, 1997; On Your Own, 1997; MOR, 1997; Tender, 1999; Coffee and TV, 1999; No Distance Left To Run, 1999; Music Is My Radar, 2000. *Honours:* Four Platinum discs, Parklife; 3 Platinum discs, The Great Escape; Platinum disc, Blur; BRIT Awards: Best Single, Album, Video, Band, 1995; Q Awards, Best Album, 1994, 1995; Q Awards, 1999; Platinum disc, 13. *Current Management:* CMO Management, Unit 32, Ransomes Dock, 35–37 Parkgate Rd, London SW11 4NP, England.

ROY, Stephane; b. 2 July 1959, Québec, Canada. Composer. m. Claudine Jomphe, 1 s., 1 d. *Education:* BA, 1988, MA, 1990, Doctorate, 1994, University of Montréal. *Career:* Professor, Queens University, Kingston, Canada,

1993–94; Guest Composer, son Mu 95 Concert, Paris, 1995; Guest Composer, Los Andes University, Colombia, 1995; Guest Lecturer, Conservatoire Superieur de Mons, Belgium, 1996; Professor, University of Montréal, 1993–97; Guest Composer, FIMAV, 1998. *Compositions:* Paysages Interieurs; Mimetismo; Crystal Music; Inaccessible Azur; Trois Petites Histoires Concretes. *Recordings:* Crystal Music; Mimetismo; Paysages Intérieurs; Ondes Arborescences; Resonances D'Arabesques; Kaleidos, 1996. *Publications include:* Functional and Implicative Analysis of Ombres Blaches of Francois Bayle; La Serie Schonberg; Form and Referential Citation in a Work By Francis Dhomont. *Honours:* Hon. Mention, International Computer Music Competition Ars Electronica; First Prize, 14th Luigi Russolo International Competition; First Prize, 1993 Noroit Prize. *Membership:* Canadian Music Centre; International Computer Music Assocation; Canadian Electroacoustic Community. *Address:* 8627 Joseph, Brentwood, MO 63144, Missouri, USA.

ROYAL, Billy Joe; b. 3 April 1942, Valdosta, Georgia, USA. Vocalist. *Career:* Nightclub singer, Savannah, Georgia; Recording artiste, 1962–. *Recordings:* Hits include: Down In The Boondocks; I Knew You When; Cherry Hill Park; Burned Like A Rocket; I'll Pin A Note On Your Pillow; I Miss You Already; Members Only, duet with Donna Fargo; Albums: Down In The Boondocks, 1965; Billie Joe Royal, 1965; Hush, 1967; Cherry Hill Park, 1969; Looking Ahead, 1987; The Royal Treatment, 1987; Tell It Like It Is, 1989; Out of The Shadows, 1990; The Best of Billy Joe Royal, 1995; Golden Hits, 1996; Stay Close to Home, 1998; Now And Then, Then And Now, 2000; Drift Away, 2001.

ROYAL HOUSE. See: **TERRY, Todd.**

ROZALLA, (Rozalla Sandra Miller); b. 18 March 1964, Ndola, Zambia. Vocalist. *Career:* Support act, Michael Jackson; Support act, Alexander O'Neal; Numerous UK/US television appearances including: Wogan; Big Breakfast; Arsenio Hall. *Recordings:* Albums: Everybody's Free; Look No Further; Feelin' Good, 1998; Singles: Born To Luv Ya, 1990; Everybody's Free, 1991; You Gotta Have Faith, 1991; Are You Ready To Fly, 1992; Don't Go Lose It Baby, 1998; Everybody's Free Remix, with RHV, 2001. *Honours:* Best African Artiste; Diamond Award, Best 12 Single; Silver album, Silver single. *Membership:* Musicians' Union. *Current Management:* DMA. *Address:* c/o Concorde International Artistes, Concorde House, 101 Shepherds Bush Rd, London W6 7LP, England. *Website:* www.rozalla.com.

RUBEL, Mark; b. 1 May 1958. Musician (bass guitar); Record Prod; Engineer; Studio Owner; Recording Instructor. *Career:* Freelance and Studio Musician, 1978–; Bassist, Captain Rat and the Blind Rivets, 1980; Bassist, J B Hutto and the Hawks, 1980; Has produced and recorded numerous artists, including Hum, Poster Children, Menthol, Alison Krauss, Adrian Belew, Mojo Nixon, Shiner. *Membership:* Prod. Committee, NARAS. *Current Management:* Gary Taylor Management, Canada. *Address:* Pogo Studio, 35 Taylor St, Champaign, IL 61820, USA.

RUBIE, Stephen Mark; b. 14 Oct. 1952, Marlow, Buckinghamshire, England. Musician (flute, saxophone); Jazz Club Proprietor. *Education:* University College Hospital, Dental School, London; Flutes with William Bartlett, Principal with BBC Concert Orchestra, Trinity College, London; Jazz theory, harmony, with Peter Ind. *Career:* Professional freelance, 1974–; Toured Italy, 1975; Peripatetic teacher, 1978–85; Proprietor, 606 Jazz Club, 1976–; Leader, 606 Club Big Band, 1985–90; Bandleader, Jazz/Latin sextet, Samara, 1991–; Featured flute player, Julian Joseph Big Band, BBC Prom, live broadcast, 1995; African band, Amabutho, live television in Germany, 1995; Appeared on BBC2 TV series, Jazz 606, 1998. *Membership:* Musicians' Union; Equity. *Address:* 10A Stadium St, London SW10 0PT, England.

RUBIN, Joel; b. 17 Oct. 1955, Los Angeles, USA. Musician (clarinet); Ethnomusicologist. *Education:* California Institute of the Arts, 1973–75; BA, State University of New York, 1978; PhD, City University, London, 2001. *Career:* Including film, television and radio appearances: Gewandhaus Leipzig, 1993; Berlin Philharmonic, 1994; Tonhalle Zurich, 1996; Cité de la Musique, Paris, 1996; Co-Author, Musical and Research Consultant, A Tickle in the Heart, 1996. *Recordings:* Bessarabian Symphony, 1994; Zeydes un Eyniklekh, 1995; Beregovskis Khasene, 1997; Hungry Hearts, 1998. *Publications:* Kol Rino, The Voice of Jubilation; Mazltov: Jewish American Wedding Music for Clarinet; Klezmer-Musik; Jewish Musical Traditions, 2001. *Honours:* State University of NY, Most Outstanding Student, 1978; German Record Critics Prize, 1992, 1995; Artur Brauner Prize, 1996; Prix Europa, 1996; 18th Bavarian Film Prize, 1996. *Membership:* Society for Ethnomusicology; International Council for Traditional Music; American Folklore Society; College Music Society; International Clarinet Society. *Current Management:* Jewish Cultural Programming and Research, Emser Str. 39a, 10719 Berlin, Germany.

RUBIN, Rick; b. 10 March 1963, Long Beach, New York, USA. Record Prod; Record Co Exec. *Education:* BFA, New York University, 1985. *Career:* Owner, founding president, Def Jam Recordings, 1984–88; Def American Recordings, 1988–; Director, co-producer, film Tougher Than Leather, 1987. *Recordings include:* As producer: Radio, LL Cool J, 1985; License To Ill, Beastie Boys, 1986; Raising Hell, Run DMC, 1986; It Takes A Nation, Public Enemy, 1986;

Electric, The Cult, 1987; Blood Sugar Sex Magic, Red Hot Chili Peppers, 1992; Tom Petty, Wildflowers, 1994; One Hot Minute, Red Hot Chili Peppers, 1995; South Park: Chef Aid, The South Park Album, 1998; Rancid, Brad Logan, 1998; Black Crowes, Sho' Nuff, 1998; Sheryl Crow, Globe Sessions, 1998; Sweet Child O' Mine, 1999; Kula Shaker, Peasants, Pigs and Astronauts, 1999; Red Hot Chili Peppers, Californication, 1999; Melanie C, Northern Star, 1999; Beastie Boys, Sounds of Science, 1999; Also: Johnny Cash; Eagle-Eye Cherry; American Head Charge; Krishna Das; Macy Gray; Paloalto. *Honours:* Numerous Gold and Platinum discs as producer; Rolling Stone Award, Hot Producer of Year, 1988; Joel Weber Award, New Music Seminar, 1990. *Address:* c/o American Recordings, 3500 W Olive Ave, Suite 1550, Burbank, CA 91505, USA.

RUBINI, Michel; b. 3 Dec. 1942, Los Angeles, California, USA. Musical Dir; Composer; Musician; Record Prod. *Career:* Musical director for: Johnny Mathis, 1968; Nancy Wilson, 1969–70; Producer, arranger for Sonny and Cher, 1971–73; Artist, producer, Motown Records, 1975–78; Worked with numerous artists including: Elvis Presley; John Lennon; Diana Ross; Quincy Jones; Linda Ronstadt. *Compositions:* Numerous television and film soundtracks. *Recordings:* Solo albums: Secret Dreams, 1988; Secret Dreams: Improvisations I–VII, 1995; The Hunger, original soundtrack, 1995; Theme from Joe's Death, 1995; As record producer: Stoney End, Barbra Streisand; California Dreamin', Johnny Mathis; All I Ever Need Is You, Sonny and Cher; Country Class, Jerry Lee Lewis; So Fine, Loggins and Messina. *Honours:* BMI Writers Award, 1985. *Membership:* BMI; Composers and Lyricists Guild.

RUBIO, Paulina; b. 1970, Mexico. Vocalist, Actress. *Career:* Began singing career in children's dancing and singing group Timbiriche, formed by producers for the Mexican TV network Televisa, 1981; Began acting in soap operas and TV series, 1998; Left Timbiriche and recorded first solo album, 1992; Continues to combine singing and acting careers, appearing in the popular soap Pobre Niña Rica and the film Bésame en la Boca. *Recordings:* Albums: La Chica Dorada, 1992; 24 Kilates, 1993; Tiempo Es Oro, 1995; Planeta Paulina, 1996; Paulina, 2000; Border Girl (in English), 2002.

RUDD, Raphael; Musician; Composer; Songwriter; Arranger. *Education:* BM, MM, Manhattan School of Music. *Career:* Orchestrated Final Scene of the Score to the Who Film, Quadrophenia, 1979; Arranged Horns on Pete Townshend's Hit Single, Rough Boys, 1980; Touring Member, Renaissance and Annie Haslam Band as Keyboardist, 1982–92. *Recordings:* R Rudd: Reflections, 1983; R Rudd: Skydancer, 1991; Raphael Rudd: The Awakening, with Pete Townshend, Phil Collins and Annie Haslam, 1997; Joyfest, 1998; Oceanic Concerts, with Pete Townshend, 2001. *Honours:* Artist of the Year, Oakside/Bloomfield Cultural Center, New Jersey, 1996. *Membership:* American Harp Society. *Current Management:* Rob Findlay, Headfirst Management.

RUFFIN, Bruce; b. 17 Feb. 1952, St Catherine, Jamaica. Musician (guitar, piano). 3 d. *Education:* Studied for LLB (Law), England; Grade 3 piano. *Career:* Discovered in Vere John's Talent Contest, Jamaica; Member, The Techniques; Songs inspired by Duke Reid, owner Treasure Isle Label; Formed The Shades, 1969; Joined Inner Circle Band; Concerts include: Support to Stevie Wonder, Carib Theatre, 1969; UK and European tours; Guest of Czechoslovakian Government at Bratislav Song Festival, 1973; Hit single as solo artist; Television appearance: Top of the Pops, 1971; Formed Chain Reaction, 1977; Signed to RCA Records, 1979–81; Formed Slick Records and Smash Music, 1980–; Working with: Record, Publishing and Management Company, 1982–; Managing Director, Jeunesse Cosmetics Ltd; Yak Yak Babywear Company. *Compositions:* Hits include: with The Techniques: Love Is Not A Gamble; My Girl; It's You I Love; Run Come Celebrate; Man of My Word; There Comes A Time; Find Yourself A Fool; Solo: Dry Up Your Tears; Bitterness of Life; Mad About You; Long About Now; Free The People; with Chain Reaction: Never Lose and Never Win. *Recordings:* Other hit singles include: as solo artiste: Rain; Candida; with The Techniques: Queen Majesty; You Don't Care. *Contributions to:* King Kong Compilation, 1981; Techniques, Run Come Celebrate: Their Greatest Hits, 1993; as publisher, Smash Music: Holding On To Love; Fuchi; The Best Of 1967–71, 2001. *Membership:* PRS; BAC&S; ASCAP; MCPS. *Current Management:* BRM Music Consultancy Ltd; BRM Music Publishing Ltd; Genius Management Agency Ltd. *Address:* 89a High Rd, Wood Green, London N22 6BB, England.

RUFFIN, Jimmy; b. 7 May 1939, Collinsville, Mississippi, USA. Vocalist. *Career:* Session singer, early 1960s; Commercial breakthrough, major US, UK hit, What Becomes of The Broken-Hearted, 1966. *Recordings:* Albums: Top Ten, 1967; Ruff 'n' Ready, 1969; The Groove Governor, 1970; I Am My Brother's Keeper (with David Ruffin), 1970; Jimmy Ruffin, 1973; Love Is All We Need, 1975; Sunrise, 1980; Best of ERC Records, 1995; 20th Century Masters, 2001; Singles include: What Becomes of The Broken-Hearted, 1966; I'll Say Forever My Love; It's Wonderful; Hold On To My Love, 1980; Turn To Me (duet with Maxine Nightingale), 1982; There Will Never Be Another You, 1985. *Address:* c/o Barry Collings Entertainments, 21a Clifftown Rd, Southend-on-Sea, Essex SS1 1AB, England.

RUFFNER, Mason; b. 29 Nov. 1952, USA. Musician (guitar); Vocalist. *Career:* Support tours with: U2; Jimmy Page; Ringo Starr; Crosby Stills and Nash. *Recordings:* Solo albums: Mason Ruffner; Gypsy Blood; Evolution; You Can't Win, 1999; Other. *Recordings include:* Oh Mercy, Bob Dylan; Acadie, Daniel Lanois; Moonshine Cherries. *Current Management:* Davis McLarty. *Address:* Rt 2 Box 592, Wimberley, TX 78676, USA.

RUFFY, (Glen) David; b. 23 March 1952, York, England. Musician (drums); Programmer; Composer. m. Jennifer, 24 June 1995, 2 d. *Career:* Major tours: Sinead O'Connor; Adam Ant; Aztec Camera; Ruts; Edwyn Collins; Yazz; WaterBoys; World Party; Martin Stephenson; Concerts with Mica Paris; Kirsty MacColl; Prefab Sprout. *Recordings include:* with Ruts: Babylons Burning; In A Rut; West One; Jahwar; Rude Boys; The Crack; Grin and Bear It; Animal Now; Rhythm Collision Remixes; with Sinead O'Connor: My Special Child; Damn Your Eyes; Year of The Horse (video); Three Babies; with Kirsty MacColl: Titanic Days; What Do Pretty Girls Do?; Tropical Brainstorm, 2000; with Aztec Camera: High Land Hard Rain; Knife; with Pigeonhead: Flash Bulb Emergency; It's Like the Man Said. *Membership:* PRS; MCPS; Musicians' Union. *Current Management:* Southside Management; Agent: Grip. *Address:* 20 Cromwell Mews, London SW7, England.

RUHLMANN, Jean-Jacques; b. 18 May 1952, Nogent-le-Rotrou, France. Musician (saxophone, clarinet); Composer. *Education:* CAPES Musicologie at the Sorbonne; C A Jazz. *Career:* Played with musicians including: J Thollot; F Jeanneau; J Gilson; E Watson; A Mangelsdorf; A Hervé; Michael O'Neil; B Renaudin; F Moerman; J F Jenny-Clark; Performed at many festivals in France; Belgium; Netherlands; Germany; Colombia; Tunisia; Spain. *Recordings:* Albums: Evensong, Michael O'Neil; Valses Manouches, with F A Moerman; Ciel De Traine (as a sideman); Windows, J J Ruhlmann Big Band. *Current Management:* M T Ruhlmann. *Address:* 3 rue des Poupardieres, 28400 Nogent le Rotrou, France.

RUNDGREN, Todd; b. 2 June 1948, Philadelphia, Pennsylvania, USA. Vocalist; Songwriter; Musician (guitar); Record Prod. *Career:* Member, Woody's Truck Stop; Founder member, The Nazz, 1967–70; Solo recording artiste, 1970–; Formed progressive rock group Utopia, 1974–. *Recordings:* Albums: with The Nazz: Nazz, 1968; Nazz Nazz, 1969; Nazz III, 1970; with Utopia: Todd Rundgren's Utopia, 1974; Another Live, 1975; Ra, 1977; Oops! Wrong Planet, 1977; Adventures In Utopia, 1980; Deface The Music, 1980; Swing To The Right, 1982; Utopia, 1982; Oblivion, 1984; Solo albums: Runt, 1970; The Ballad of Todd Rundgren, 1971; Something / Anything?, 1972; A Wizard, A True Star, 1973; Todd, 1974; Initiation, 1975; Faithful, 1976; Hermit of Mink Hollow, 1978; Back To The Bars, 1978; Healing, 1981; The Ever Popular Tortured Artist Effect, 1983; A Cappella, 1985; POV, 1985; Anthology – Todd Rundgren, 1988; Nearly Human, 1989; Second Wind, 1991; No World Order, 1993; No World Order Lite, 1994; The Individualist, 1995; With a Twist, 1997; Up Against It, 1998; Live in Chicago 1991, 1999; Singles, 1995; One Long Year, 2000; Record producer, Bat Out of Hell, Meat Loaf, 1977; Also producer/engineer, recordings by New York Dolls; Grand Funk Railroad; Hall and Oates; XTC; The Band. *Current Management:* Panacea Entertainment Management. *Address:* 2705 Glendower Ave, Los Angeles, CA 90027, USA.

RUNGE, Jens (Christian); b. 28 Nov. 1961, Malaysia. Musician (guitar); Vocalist. *Career:* Toured Scandinavia with Hanne Boel, 1989, 1993, 1994, 1996, 1997, 1998; Sanne Salomonsen, 1990, 1991, 1992, 1995; Kasper Winding, 1987, 1988, 1989, 1990; Anne Linnet, 1988, 1989, 1991, 1992; Toured Europe with Hanne Boel, 1995; Played at Roskilde Festival with Hanne Boel, 1989, 1993, 1998, Sanne Salomonsen, 1992, 1995, Anne Linnet, 1989. *Recordings:* Hanne Boel: Dark Passion, 1990; Misty Paradise, 1994; Silent Violence, 1996; Need, 1998; Kasper Winding: No 5, 1989; Blue Isis: Kalder Pa Tiden, 1989; Paris Paris: Paris Paris, 1986; Love Construction: Caught in the Act, 1988. *Membership:* The Danish Artist Union. *Address:* Ahlefeldtsgade 22 3 sal, 1359 Copenhagen K, Denmark.

RUOCCO, Joanne; b. 26 May 1961, New Jersey, USA. Musician (drums, percussion). m. Douglas Newbery, 30 Sept. 1989. *Education:* Graduate, New Jersey; BA, Music, Fine Art, Farleigh Dickenson University, New Jersey. *Recordings:* Duke Ellington Orchestra (Mercer Ellington); Chuck Berry; Bobby Womack; J Geils Band; Ron Wood; Hollywood Beyond; Jellybean; Mick Hucknell (Simply Red); The Style Council (Paul Weller). *Membership:* Musicians' Union; AFofM. *Current Management:* Independent. *Address:* 7 Linwood Rd, Harpenden, Hertfordshire AL5 1RR, England.

RUPIC, Hrvoje; b. 2 March 1970, Zagreb, Croatia. Musician (percussion). *Education:* Latin Percussion, Drum Teaching Studios, London. *Career:* Founder and leader of latin-jazz group, Cubismo; Over 50 recorded CDs in jazz, rock, pop, latin and other music; Collaboration, concerts and recordings with Toots Thielemans, Philippe Catherine, Bob Mover, Gianni Basso, Yolanda Duke, Mind Games; Workshops for hand-drumming and Afro-Cuban rhythms; Teacher for hand-drumming at Classical Academy, Zagreb. *Recordings:* Cubismo: Cubismo; Viva La Habana; Csaba Deseo, The Swinging Violin; Mind Games, Pretty Fonky; Bob Mover, Yesterdays; Soul Fingers, Live

In BP Club. *Honours:* STATUS (Croatian Musicians' Union Award), 1996–97; Porin (Croatian Discography Award); 7 awards with Cubismo for numerous recordings. *Membership:* HGU, Croatian Musicians' Union; HUOKU, Croation Asscn of Orchestral and Chamber Musicians; HZSU, Croation Asscn of Freelance Artists. *Address:* Petrova 51, 10000 Zagreb, Croatia.

RUSBY, Kate Anna; b. 4 Dec. 1973. Vocalist; Musician (guitar, piano, fiddle); Songwriter. m. John McCusker. *Career:* Spent some time with all-female folk group The Poozies; As solo artist performs traditional songs and own folk-influenced material. *Recordings:* Singles: Cowsong, 1998; Albums: Kate Rusby and Kathryn Roberts, 1995; Hourglass, 1997; Sleepless, 1999; Little Lights, 2001; 10, 2002; with The Poozies: Come Raise Your Head, 1997; Infinite Blue, 1998; features on: Yella Hoose (with John McCusker), 2000; Evolving Tradition, 1995; Evolving Tradition #2, 1996. *Honours:* BBC Folk Album of the Year, Sleepless, 1999. *Address:* c/o Pure Records, PO Box 174, Penistone, West Yorkshire, S30 6P, England. *Website:* www.katerusby.com.

RUSCHKOWSKI, André; b. 25 March 1959, Berlin, Germany. Composer. *Education:* PhD, Musicology, Humboldt University, Berlin, 1993. *Career:* Composer in Residence, several studios for electronic music including Berlin, Budapest, Paris, Vienna; Lecturer, Electronic Music and Music of the 20th Century, Music University Mozarteum Salzburg, Austria, 1992–, Technische Universität Berlin, University of Cologne; Professor for Electronic Music, Director, Electronic Music Studio, Composition Department. *Compositions:* Zeichen, for tape, 1989; Nasca, for tape, 1993; Succubus Quartet, for tape, 1994; Salzburgtrum, for flute, violin and percussion and tape, 1995–98; Four Short Studies, for tape, 1995; Sonama, for flute, violin and percussion, 1996; Karabontara, for piano and tape, 1996; Arara and Araku, for percussion and tape, 1997; Trakl Cycle (In blauem Kristall, Weisser Scheaf, Dunkle Stunde, Unter steinernen Bogen, 1997) for soprano, flute, clarinet, violin, cello, piano and tape, Les pas intérieurs, for female dancer, percussion and tape, 1997; Arion, Dione, Cento, Boreas, for tape, 1998; Doxa, for female dancer, video, percussion and tape, 1999. *Recordings:* Numerous. *Publications:* Soundscapes, 1990; Electronic sound synthesis and musical discoverings, 1998. *Honours:* Prize of the City of Varese, Italy, 1990, Bourges, France, 1985, 1989; International Competition for Audio Art, Paris, 1997; Prize, Composition Competition for Computer Music, Braunschweig, 1998; Sonic Circuits, American Composers Forum, 1998. *Membership:* Vice-President, Austrian Society for Electroacoustic Music; International Computer Music Asscn. *Address:* Strauss Str 3, 83457 Bayerisch Gmain, Germany.

RUSKIN, Tommy; b. 15 July 1942, Kansas City, Missouri, USA. Musician (drums). m. 11 Feb. 1963, 1 s. *Education:* School band and orchestra. *Career:* Played with: Roy Johnson; Marilyn Maye; Sammy Tucker; Gary Foster; Mike Metheny; Pat Metheny; Julie Turner (wife); Clark Terry; Zoot Sims; Herb Ellis; Carl Fontana; Scott Hamilton; Bill Watrous; Warren Vaché; Jack Sheldon; Jay McShann. *Recordings:* Mike Methany: Day in Nightout; Gary Foster: Kansas City Connections; Marilyn Maye: The Second of Maye; Jay McShann: Warm. *Membership:* Musicians' Union. *Address:* 7225 Outlook, Overland Park, KS 66204, USA.

RUSSELL, Brenda, (Brenda Gordon); b. 8 April 1949, Brooklyn, New York, USA. Vocalist; Songwriter; Musician; Prod. m. Brian Russell, 14 Sept. 1974, divorced, 1 d. *Career:* Toured with: David Sanborn; Billy Ocean; Jeffrey Osborne; Television appearances: Good Morning America; Today Show; Arsenio Hall; Late Show; British Music Shows, Germany, Sweden; Pat Sajek Show, USA; Toured as singer (pre-solo career) with Mac Davis; Elton John; Television background work: Sonny and Cher Show. *Compositions:* Songs recorded by: Herb Alpert; Ray Charles; Joe Cocker; Rita Coolidge; Earth Wind and Fire; Roberta Flack; Chaka Khan; Johnny Mathis; Diana Ross; Donna Summer; Dionne Warwick; Oleta Adams; Regina Belle; Peabo Bryson; Alex Bugnon; Don Grusin; Layla Hathaway; George Howard; Bunny Hull; Jermaine Jackson; Walter Jackson; Al Jarreau; Koinonea; Ivan Lins; Byron Miller; Ann Murray; Phil Perry; Anita Pointer; Rufus; Patrice Rushen; Tom Scott; Marilyn Scott; Tavares; Luther Vandross; Tata Vega; Sudao Watanabe; Kirk Whalum; David Williams; Pauline Wilson; Phillipe Wynne. *Recordings:* Albums: Brenda Russell, 1979; Two Eyes, 1983; Love Life, 1980; Get Here, 1988; Kiss Me With the Wind, 1990; Soul Talkin', 1993; Paris Rain, 2000; Singles include: So Good So Right; Piano In The Dark. *Current Management:* Turner Management Group. *Address:* 3500 W Olive Suite 770, Burbank, CA 91505, USA.

RUSSELL, George Allen; b. 23 June 1923, Cincinnati, Ohio, USA. Composer; Theoritician; Bandleader; Musician (piano). m. Alice Norbury, 4 Aug. 1981, 1 s. *Education:* Wilberforce University High School; Private Study with Stephan Wolpe. *Career:* Performances with large and small ensembles world-wide, including Tokyo; Paris; London; Scandinavia; Italy; Germany; Portugal; United States; Radio and television: Broadcasts for BBC; Broadcasts in Sweden; Norway; Denmark; Japan; Finland; Germany; Italy; Commissions from National Endowments for the Arts; Massachusetts State Council on the Arts; Swedish Radio; The British Council; Cité de la Musique; Glasgow International Festival; Rocella Ionica; New England Presentors; Relache New Music; Norwegian Cultural Fund; BMI; Bradeis University; Member of faculty, New England Conservatory of Music, 1969–; Seminars

and lectures world-wide. *Recordings include:* African Game; Living Time; Vertical Form VI; All About Rosie; Ezz-Thetic; Stratusphunk; Cubano Be-Cubano Bop; A Bird in Igor's Yard; Uncommon Ground; Listen to the Silence; Time Spiral; Electronic Sonata for Souls Loved by Nature; It's About Time; At Beethoven Hall. *Honours:* MacArthur Foundation Fellow; Guggenheim Fellow; National Endowment for the Arts American Jazz Master; Guardian Milestone Award. *Membership:* Mem. International Society of Contemporary Music; American Federation of Musicians; Foreign Mem., Swedish Royal Academy of Music. *Current Management:* Serious Speakout, Windsor House, Fourth Floor, 83 Kingsway, London WC2B 6SD. *Address:* c/o Concept Inc, #182, 1770 Massachusetts Ave, Cambridge, MA 02140, USA.

RUSSELL, Graham Cyril; b. 11 June 1950, Nottingham, England. Vocalist; Musician (piano, guitar); Composer. m. Jodi Varble, 7 June 1986, 1 s., 1 d. *Career:* Singer, Co-founder group, Air Supply, (most successful Australian group); World-wide tours, 1975–, including People's Republic of China, 1995; World-wide television and radio appearances. *Recordings:* 17 albums released, including: Yours Truly, 2001; 9 Top 5 songs, US charts, including: Lost In Love, 1980; All Out Of Love, 1980; The One That You Love, 1981; Even The Nights Are Better, 1982; 25m. albums sold to date. *Honours:* Song of Year, 1980; American Music Awards, Artist of Year, 1980. *Membership:* BMI; 2 Million Plays Club. *Current Management:* Barry Siegel. *Address:* 10345 W Olympic Blvd, Suite 200, Los Angeles, CA 90064, USA.

RUSSELL, Jack Patrick; b. 5 Dec. 1960, Montebello, California, USA. Vocalist. m. Jana Whisenant, 19 Sept. 1991, 1 s. *Career:* Vocalist with rock group Great White; Support tours with: Whitesnake, UK, 1984; Judas Priest, USA, 1984; Dokken, USA, 1986; Night Ranger, 1987; Ratt, 1987; Twisted Sister, 1987; Whitesnake, 1987–88; Kiss, 1991; Co-headline tour with Tesla, 1989–90; Headline tours USA, 1992–95. *Recordings:* Albums: Great White, 1984; Shot In The Dark, 1986; Once Bitten, 1987; Recovery Live, 1987; Twice Shy, 1989; Hooked, 1990; Psycho City, 1992; Best of Great White, 1994; Sail Away, 1994; Can't Get There From Here, 1999; Latest And Greatest, 2000; various live recordings. *Current Management:* Premier Talent Agency; Wildcat Management. *Address:* c/o Siegl, Feldstein, Duffin and Vuylstehe, Inc, 10345 W Olympic Blvd, Los Angeles, CA 90064–2524, USA.

RUSSELL, John William Edward; b. 19 Dec. 1954, London, England. Improvising Musician (guitar). *Education:* Private lessons. *Career:* Crossing Bridges, TV, radio include: Channel 4; Radio 3; Radio 4; Local radio; Concerts, festivals, tours include: East, West Europe, North America. *Compositions:* QuaQua. *Recordings:* 20 albums and CDs. *Publications:* Essays, interviews in: Musics; Rubberneck; The Wire. *Honours:* Arts Council development bursary. *Membership:* London Musicians' Collective. *Current Management:* Mopomoso. *Address:* 23B Charteris Rd, London N4 3AA, England.

RUSSELL, Leon, (Hank Wilson); b. Lawton, Oklahoma, USA. Musician (guitar, piano, trumpet); Vocalist. m. Mary McCreary, Jan. 1976, 1 s., 1 d. *Career:* Multi-instrumental session musician; Regular member, Phil Spector's Wall of Sound session crew, 1962; Pianist, television series Shindig!, NBC TV; Built own recording studio, 1967; Appeared in film Mad Dogs and Englishmen, 1970; Played with Bob Dylan; Rolling Stones; Eric Clapton; Major concerts include: Concert For Bangladesh, Madison Square Garden, 1971; New Orleans Jazz and Heritage Festival, 1991; American Music Festival, with Neville Brothers, Randy Newman and Warren Zevon, 1992; Owner, video production company. *Compositions include:* Co-writer, singer, theme to Flesh and Blood, NBC TV; Delta Lady, recorded by Joe Cocker; A Song For You, recorded by The Carpenters, Donny Hathaway; This Masquerade, recorded by George Benson; Co-writer, Superstar, recorded by The Carpenters. *Recordings:* Albums: Asylum Choir, 1968; Leon Russell, 1970; Leon Russell and The Shelter People, 1971; Asylum Choir II, 1972; Carney, 1972; Leon Live, 1973; Hank Wilson's Back, 1973; Stop All That Jazz, 1974; Will O'The Wisp, 1975; The Wedding Album, 1976; Make Love To The Music, 1977; Americana, 1978; Willie and Leon (with Willie Nelson), 1979; The Live Album, 1981; Hank Wilson Vol. II, 1984; Anything Can Happen, 1992; Hank Wilson Vol. 3, 1998; Face in the Crowd, 1999; Blues: Same Old Song, 1999; Life and Love, 1999; Guitar Blues, 2001; Singles include: Tight Rope; Bluebird; Lady Blue; Back To The Island; As session musician: A Taste of Honey, Herb Alpert; Mr Tambourine Man, The Byrds. *Honours:* Grammy, Record of the Year, This Masquerade, 1976; Several Gold discs.

RUSSELL, Mark J; Composer. m. Joanne Whitworth, 10 May 1997. *Education:* Hons Degree, Film Music and Composition. *Career:* Joined BBC Television's music department for three years, then left to start own recording studio; As Musican and arranger has worked with Tanita Tikaram, Julia Fordham and acclaimed Chinese flautist Guo Yue, with whom he appeared in concerts throughout Europe and Australia; Writer and presenter of BBC Radio 3's music programme Mixing It which covers jazz through to world music and experimental techno, drum and bass. *Compositions include:* For Film: Saving Grace (director Nigel Cole: Fineline); For television: The Prince of Atlantis (BBC/Canal+ Ravensburger); The Peter Principle (Hat Trick/BBC, director, Nick Woods); A Horse's World (Wall To Wall/Channel Four, director, Steve Ruggi); Barnados Children (BBC, director Michael Davies); For Whom

The Bull Tolls (Tiger Aspect/Channel Four); Fragile Earth (Channel Four); Love Me Love Me Not (TVS); Comic Relief (BBC, director, Michael Davies); Crimestoppers (Carlton Television); Poets News (BBC, director, Michael Davies); Granada on Sunday (Granada Television); Dispatches: The Marchioness Tragedy, Dispatches: Lorries, Dispatches: Child Prostitution, Dispatches: Privateers, (Channel Four, director Alex Sutherland); Kingdoms of Survival (Anglia Television); Network First: Going to Chelsea (Hartswood/ Carlton, director Michael Davies); Wildlife Showcase (BBC, director Tania Dorrity); Lifeline (BBC); It Happened Next Year (BBC); Style Challenge (BBC); Cold Feet (Three series, Granada); The Red Baron (BBC); Officers and Gentlemen (BBC); Passion Killers (Granada); Wonderful You (Hartswood); Playing the Field (Tiger/Aspect); For BBC Radio: Superman I, Batman, Spiderman, Independence Day, Superman II (all directed by Dirk Maggs, first four recorded and released). *Address:* c/o Soundtrack Music Associates Ltd, 25 Ives St, Chelsea, London SW3 2ND, England.

RUSSELL, Paul Stuart Rupert; b. 13 Feb. 1934, Nuthall, Nottingham, England. Musician (drums, New Orleans style). m. June Vivian Hill, 25 Jan. 1958, 3 s., 1 d. *Education:* Leicester School of Architecture; Study of drumming in New Orleans, casual basis. *Career:* Member, Mercia Jazz Band (Nottingham), 1954–58; Then musician with various bands: Mike Casimir; Chris Blount; Chris Burke; Spirits of Rhythm (own band); Oriole Brass Band (own band); Dave Donohoe; Louisiana Joymakers; Worked with Sammy Rimington, accompanied many visiting Americans including: Alton Purnell; Kid Thomas; Louis Nelson; Benny Waters; Herb Hall; Sam Lee; Captain John Handy; Played at Jazz Festivals in New Orleans; Nice; Ascona; Lugano; Milan; Breda; Cork; Gent; Currently with The Teddy Fullick Quintet and the Frank Brooker New Orleans Swingtet. *Recordings:* With Dave Donohoe, Jimmy Noone Jr. *Membership:* Musicians' Union; ARCUK. *Address:* 105 Kimberley Rd, Nuthall, Nottingham NG16 1DD, England.

RUTHERFORD, Mike; b. 2 Oct. 1950, Guildford, Surrey, England. Musician (guitar, bass); Record Prod. *Career:* Musician, Genesis, 1970–; Also solo artiste, 1980–; Founder, producer, Mike and the Mechanics, 1986–; Numerous world-wide tours and major concerts including: Philharmonic Hall, New York; Madison Square Gardens, New York; Giants Stadium, New York; LA Forum. *Recordings:* Albums: with Genesis: Foxtrot, 1972; Selling England By The Pound, 1973; Genesis Live, 1973; The Lamb Lies Down On Broadway, 1974; Trick of The Tail, 1976; Wind and Wuthering, 1977; Seconds Out, 1977; And Then There Were Three, 1978; Duke, 1980; Abacab, 1981; Three Sides Live, 1982; Genesis, 1983; Invisible Touch, 1986; We Can't Dance, 1991; Calling All Stations, 1997; Not About Us, 1997; Turn it On Again: The Hits, 1999; Archives Vol. 1, 1967–75, 1999; Archives Vol. 2, 1976–92, 2001; with Mike and The Mechanics: Mike and The Mechanics, 1986; The Living Years, 1988; Word of Mouth, 1991; Beggar On A Beach of Gold, 1995; Hits, 1996; Solo albums: Small Creep's Day, 1980; Acting Very Strange, 1982; Singles: with Genesis: Follow You Follow Me, 1978; Turn It On Again, 1980; Abacab, 1981; Mama, 1983; That's All, 1983; Illegal Alien, 1983; Invisible Touch, 1986; In Too Deep, 1986; Land Of Confusion, 1986; Tonight Tonight Tonight, 1987; Throwing It All Away, 1987; No Son Of Mine, 1991; I Can't Dance, 1992; Jesus He Knows Me, 1992; Abacab; Follow You Follow Me; Mama; Illegal Alien; Invisible Touch; Land of Confusion; Tonight Tonight Tonight; That's All; Turn It On Again; with Mike and The Mechanics: Silent Running, 1986; All I Need Is A Miracle, 1986; The Living Years, 1989; Word Of Mouth, 1991; Over My Shoulder, 1995; Beggar On A Beach of Gold, 1995; Another Cup Of Coffee, 1995; Now That You've Gone, 1999; Also recorded on: Voyage of The Acolyte, Steve Hackett, 1975; with John Verity: Interrupted Journey, 1983; Truth of The Matter, 1985. *Honours:* Golden Ticket, Madison Square Gardens, 1986; First group, 5 Top 5 US singles from 1 album, 1986; Band of the Year, Rolling Stone Readers Poll, 1987. *Current Management:* Hit and Run Music, 30 Ives St, London SW3 2ND, England.

RUTHERFORD, Paul William; b. 29 Feb. 1940, Greenwich, London, England. Musician (trombone, euphonium). *Education:* RAF Musical Services; Guildhall School of Music Services. *Career:* Five years, RAF Music Services; Leading member, avant garde jazz in UK; Numerous festivals in UK; International television, radio. *Recordings:* Solo albums: Sequences 72 and 73, 1972; Gentle Harm of the Bourgeoisie, 1974; Rogues, 1998; Rottor, 1998; Iskra 1903, 2001; Played with the Tony Oxley Sextet; Mike Westbrook Bands; Spontaneous Music Ensemble; Globe Unity Orchestra; London Jazz Composers Orchestra. *Honours:* Melody Maker Poll, 3 years consecutively. *Membership:* Musicians' Union. *Address:* Flat 2, 67A Shooters Hill Rd, Blackheath, London SE3 7HS, England.

RUTKOWSKI, Louise; b. 15 March 1964, Paisley, Scotland. Vocalist. *Career:* Worked with: Sunset Gun; This Mortal Coil; The Kindness of Strangers; Nellee Hooper; Dave Stewart. *Recordings:* 1 album and 3 singles with Sunset Gun, 1984–86; 2 albums with This Mortal Coil, 1984–86; 1 album with The Kindness of Strangers, 1990–93; 1 album with The Hope Blister, 1998; Currently performing Short Stories, the songs of Randy Newman; Six Songs, 2001. *Membership:* PRS. *Address:* c/o Arts Council of England, Music Department, 14 Great Peter St, London SW1P 8NQ, England.

RUTTEN, Leo; b. 25 Dec. 1957, Tongeren, Belgium. Engineer (two-row, three-row melodeon, bagpipes, hurdy-gurdy, flutes, saxophone). m. Lieve Veulemans, 9 July 1988, 2 s., 2 d. *Education:* Industrial Engineer Degree, Khlim Diepenbeek; Summer course with Wilfrid Moonen, Riccardo Tesi, Hurdy-Gurdy with Evelyne Girardon. *Career:* Former Hurdy-Gurdy and Melodeon Player with Limburgs Dansorkest, 1984–93; TV Program 'De Milieu-Karavaan', 1987; Concert Zoo Leipzich DDR, 1988; Concert Brin Radio 3, 1993; Concert Festival St Chartier, 1993, France; Former member, SLEMP; Current member, Peper and playing with Poescafe, Concert Poescafe Ancienne Belgique, Brussels, 1998. *Compositions:* Biesenwals; Wals Voor Mathilde; De Groene Wants; De Gebroken Duimlus; Alvers in De Lucht. *Recordings:* Volksmuziek, 1985; Limburgsdans Orkest, 1990; Folk Music from Belgium, 1997; Poescafe, 1997. *Membership:* Belgian Bagpipe Player Asscn. *Address:* Rooierheide Straat 11, B3530 Diepenbeek, Belgium.

RYAN, Barbara; b. 29 May 1950, Colombo, Sri Lanka. Vocalist; Celtic Musician (guitar, bouzouki, bodhran). m. David B Ryan, 2 s. *Education:* BA, George Washington University, 1971; Studied voice with Lida Brodenova, Jane White, Rilla Mervine. *Career:* Founder, traditional Celtic music group, Iona, 1986; Performed at major Celtic festivals throughout the USA; Solo work includes broadcasts on Voice of America; Singing for the National Geographic Explorer special series; Vocal coach, 1988–; Founder, Potomac Celtic Festival, 1994. *Recordings:* Back To Our Roots, 1992; Holding Our Own, 1994; Nutmeg and Ginger, 1996; The Sound Of Iona, 1998; Compilations: Celtic Festival, Live, 1996; Takoma Park Folk Festival, 1997. *Membership:* Folk Alliance; Celtic Women International; Washington Area Music Asscn. *Current Management:* Barnaby Productions Inc, PO Box 11160, Burke, VA 22009 1160, USA.

RYAN, Lee; b. 17 June 1983, Chatham, Kent, England. Vocalist. *Career:* Mem., UK band, Blue, 2001–; UK tour, 2002. *Recordings:* Albums: All Rise, 2001; One Love, 2002. Singles: All Rise, 2001; Too Close (No. 1, UK), 2001; If You Come Back (No. 1, UK), 2001; Fly By II, 2002; Sorry Seems To Be The Hardest Word, 2002. *Honours:* Multi-Platinum discs, for All Rise, 2001; Smash Hits Awards, Best Newcomer, 2001, Best Live Act, Best UK Band, 2002; Interactive Music Award, Artist of the Year, 2002; BRIT Award, Best British Newcomer, 2002. *Address:* c/o Virgin Records Ltd, 553–579 Harrow Rd, London W10 4RH, England. *Website:* www.officialblue.com.

RYDELL, Bobby, (Robert Ridarelli); b. 26 April 1942, Philadelphia, Pennsylvania, USA. Vocalist; Musician (drums). *Career:* Drummer, Teen Club television show, 3 years; Duo with Frankie Avalon, 1954; Member, Rocco and the Saints; Solo artiste, 18 Top 40 hits, 1959–63; Film appearance, Bye Bye Birdy; Cabaret and club singer. *Recordings:* Albums include: Rydell At The Copa, 1961; Bobby Rydell/Chubby Checker, 1961; Bobby's Biggest Hits, 1961; All The Hits, 1962; Top Hits of 1963, 1964; Forget Him, 1964; The Best of Bobby Rydell, 2000; Bobby's Biggest Hits, 1999; Now And Then, 2000; Singles include: Fatty Fatty; Kissin' Time; Wild One; Sway; Volare; Forget Him. *Current Management:* Fox Entertainment, 1650 Broadway, Suite 503, New York, NY 10019, USA.

RYDER, Paul; b. 24 April 1964. Musician (bass guitar). *Career:* Mem., Happy Mondays, 1985–93; Tours, UK, Europe, USA; Support tours to: New Order, UK, 1987; Jane's Addiction, US, 1990; Concerts include: Glastonbury Festival, 1990; Great British Music Weekend, Wembley, 1990; Feile Festival, Tipperary, 1990; Cities In The Park Festival, Prestwich, 1990; Re-formed, 1999. *Recordings:* Albums: Squirrel And G-Man Twenty-Four Hour Party People Plastic Face Carnt Smile (White Out), 1986; Bummed, 1988; Pills 'N' Thrills And Bellyaches (No. 1, UK), 1990; Live, 1991; ...Yes Please!, 1992; Happy Mondays Greatest Hits, 1999. Singles: Madchester Rave On (EP); Step On, 1990; Kinky Afro, 1990; Judge Fudge, 1991. *Honours:* Best Indie Act, DMC World DJ Awards, 1991. *Address:* c/o London Records, PO Box 1422, Chancellors House, Chancellors Rd, London W6 9SG, England. *Website:* www.londonrecords.co.uk.

RYDER, Shaun; b. 23 Aug. 1962, Little Hulton, Lancashire, England. Vocalist. 1 d. *Career:* Mem., lead singer, Happy Mondays, 1985–93; Tours, UK, Europe and USA; Support tours to: New Order, UK, 1987; Jane's Addiction, USA, 1990; Concerts include: Glastonbury Festival, 1990; Great British Music Weekend, Wembley, 1990; Feile Festival, Tipperary, 1990; Cities In The Park Festival, Prestwich, 1990; Featured in film, The Ghost of Oxford Street (Channel 4), 1990; Founder mem., Black Grape, 1993–98; Re-formed Happy Mondays, 1999; Concerts include: T In The Park Festival, Glasgow, 1995; Numerous television and radio appearances. *Recordings:* Albums: with Happy Mondays: Squirrel And G-Man Twenty-Four Hour Party People Plastic Face Carnt Smile (White Out), 1986; Bummed, 1988; Pills 'N' Thrills And Bellyaches, 1990; Live, 1991; Yes Please!, 1992; Loads, 1995; Happy Mondays Greatest Hits, 1999; with Black Grape: It's Great When You're Straight... Yeah! (No. 1, UK), 1995; Stupid, Stupid, Stupid, 1997; Solo: Planet Groove–The Shaun Ryder Session (selected tracks), 2000; Clowns And Pet Sounds, 2002. Singles: with Happy Mondays: Freaky Dancing, 1986; Delightful, 1986; Tart Tart, 1987; 24 Hour Party People, 1987; Wrote For Luck, 1988; Lazyitis, 1989; WFL, 1989; Madchester Rave On EP, 1989; Step On, 1990; Kinky Afro, 1990; Loose Fit/Bob's Yer Uncle, 1991; Judge Fudge,

1991; Stinkin' Thinkin', 1992; Sunshine And Love, 1992; The Boys Are Back In Town, 1999; with Black Grape: Reverend Black Grape, 1995; In The Name Of The Father, 1995; Kelly's Heroes, 1995; England's Irie, 1996; Fat Neck, 1996; Get Higher, 1997; Marbles, 1998. *Honours:* Best Indie Act, DMC World DJ Awards, 1991. *Address:* c/o Fairwarning/Wasted Talent, The Plaza, 535 Kings Rd, London SW10 0SZ, England.

RYGERT, Göran T; b. 1 May 1935, Tranås, Sweden. m. (1) 2 s., (2) Janet A Rybka, 19 Sept. 1997. *Education:* Master of Architecture, Chalmers University of Technology, Göteborg, Sweden; Private, with Torsten Rygert (father), Music Director and Composer. *Career:* Arranger and Composer, field of song – ballad and folk music; String Bass Musician, Swedish song – ballad artists, in many folk music orchestras, Sweden and USA; Appearances in Swedish, American and Russian Radio and TV; many song festivals; Producer, many song books, Freelance Editor, Warner/Chappell Music Scandinavia AB, Sweden. *Compositions:* A number of songs with words by Swedish Poets and Writers. *Publications:* Ölands Folkliga Visor och Melodier Genom Tiderna, 1987; Visor Kring Bordet, 1993; Festvisor, 1994; many other song-books, 1994–2002. *Honours:* Royal Gustav Adolf's Academy Prize, 1991; Kalmar County Council Cultural Award, 1997. *Membership:* Hon. Mem., Visans Vänner; Swedish Composers of Popular Music; Georgia Music Industry Asscn; Balalaika and Domra Asscn of America. *Address:* 4390 Ivywood NE, Marietta, GA 30062, USA. *E-mail:* rygert@mindspring.com.

RYPDAL, Terje; b. 23 Aug. 1947, Oslo, Norway. Musician (piano, guitar); Composer. m. Elin Kristin Rypdal, 15 June 1988, 3 s., 1 d. *Education:* Grunnfag in Music, University of Oslo; Composition Studies with Finn Mortensen. *Career:* Musician with The Vanguards, 1962–67; The Dream, 1967–69; Jan Garbarek Group, 1969–71; Leader, own groups, 1971–. *Compositions:* 6 symphonies, 2 operas. *Recordings:* Albums include: Bleak House, 1968; Ved Sorevatn (on album of Baden Baden Free Jazz Meeting), 1969; Terje Rypdal, 1971; What Comes After, 1974; Whenever I Seem To Be Far Away, 1974; Odyssey, 1975; After The Rain, 1976; Waves, 1978; Descendre, 1980; To Be Continued, 1981; Eos, 1984; Chaser, 1986; Works, 1989; Undisonus, 1990; QED, 1993; If Mountains Could Sing, 1995; Nordic Quartet (with John Surman, Karin Krog, Vigleik Storaas), 1995; Skywards, 1997; Double Concerto/Fifth Symphony, 2000; Selected Recordings, 2002; Also collaborated with: Robert Wyatt; Ketil Bjornstad. *Honours:* Deutscher Schallplattenpreis. *Membership:* Norwegian Composers Guild. *Address:* c/o ECM Records, 1540 Broadway, New York, NY 10036-4098, USA.

SAADIQ, Raphael, (Raphael Wiggins); b. 14 May 1966, Oakland, CA, USA. Vocalist; Prod. *Career:* Formed vocal trio Tony! Toni! Toné! with brother Dwayne and cousin Timothy Christian, 1988; Founder: Pookie Records; Formed Lucy Pearl with Dawn Robinson (En Vogue) and Ali Shaheed Muhammad (A Tribe Called Quest), 2001; Joi replaced Robinson, 2001; Collaborations: Q-Tip; Snoop Doggy Dogg; Willie Max; Vanessa Williams; D'Angelo; Bilal; Whitney Houston; Angie Stone. *Recordings:* Albums: with Tony! Toni! Toné!: Who?, 1988; The Revival, 1990; Sons of Soul, 1993; House of Music, 1996; with Lucy Pearl: Lucy Pearl, 2000; Singles: with Tony! Toni! Toné!: Little Walter, 1988; The Blues, Oakland Stroke, Feels Good, It Never Rains (In Southern California), 1990; Whatever You Want, House Party II, 1991; If I Had Not Loot, Anniversary, My Ex-Girlfriend, 1993; Lay Your Head On My Pillow, Leavin', 1994; Let's Get Down, 1996; Thinking of You, 1997; solo: Ask of You, 1995; Get Involved (with Q-Tip), 1999; with Lucy Pearl: Dance Tonight, Don't Mess With My Man, 2000. *Address:* c/o Virgin Records, 304 Park Ave, New York, USA.

SABER, Danny; b. 22 Dec. 1966, New York, NY, USA. Prod; Musician (bass). *Career:* Producer; Bass guitarist and songwriter, Black Grape; Numerous live tours and festival appearances including Tribal Gathering and Reading festivals, 1997. *Recordings:* Singles: Reverend Black Grape, 1995; England's Irie, 1996; Fat Neck, 1996; Get Higher, 1997; Marbles, 1998; Albums: It's Great When You're Straight... Yeah, 1995! (No. 1, UK); Stupid, Stupid, Stupid, 1997; Producer of recordings by: U2; Marilyn Manson; The Rolling Stones; The Charlatans; David Bowie; Public Enemy; John Lydon; Garbage; Dave Navarro; Agent Provocateur.

SABINA, Leslie Michael; b. 21 Sept. 1958, Nebraska, USA. Prof. of Music. m. Evelyn May Rennie, 1 s., 1 d. *Education:* BMus, University of Toronto, 1981; BEd, University of Windsor, 1986; MM, University of Miami, 1984; PhD, Michigan State University, 1992. *Career:* Music Professor, University of Windsor, 1988–90; St Bonaventure University, 1991–; Honorary Visiting Fellow, University of York, 1998; Jazz Performances With Dizzy Gillespie, J C Heard, Joe Williams, Billy Eckstine, Della Reese, The Temptations. *Compositions:* 47 Jazz Compositions. *Recordings:* JC Heard Jazz Orchestra; Joe Coughlin. *Honours:* PROCAN Jazz Composers Award, 1986, 1988; PROCAN Jazz Composer of the Year, 1988; ASCAP Composition Award, 1995–99. *Membership:* ASCAP; IAJE; College Music Society; North American Saxophone Alliance. *Address:* St Bonaventure University, St Bonaventure, NY 14778, USA.

SABIU, Marco; b. Forli, Italy. Record Prod; Mixer; Songwriter. *Career:* Writer, Producer with Charlie Mallozzi, known as Rapino Brothers; Moved to London, 1992; Classically trained pianist; Programmer, mixer, producer of Pop/Dance music; Member of groups: Tabernacle; Rapination. *Recordings:* Albums for: Take That; Kylie Minogue; Dannii Minogue; Lulu; Kym Mazelle; Filippa Giordano; Rozalla; Hit singles: Could It Be Magic, Take That; Rhythm of The Night, Corona; What Is Love, Haddaway; I Know The Lord, Tabernacle; Love Me The Right Way, Rapination and Kym Mazelle; I Love My Radio, Taffy; T'pau, Red; Also singles for: Alicia Bridges; Heaven 17; Sparks. *Honours:* BRIT Award, Single of Year, Take That; Triple Platinum album, Take That. *Current Management:* Stephen Budd Management. *Address:* 109B Regents Park Rd, London NW1 8UR, England.

SADASHIGE, Yuzuru; b. 12 May 1966, Chiba, Japan. Composer. m. Wendy Griffiths, 4 Sept. 1998. *Education:* Bachelor of Law, Tokyo University, Japan, 1989; Bachelor of Music, Composition, Berklee College of Music, Boston, USA, 1993; Master of Music, Composition, Manhattan School of Music, New York, USA, 1995; Masterclasses with Ned Rorem, Lucal Foss, Robert Starer. *Career:* Co-Founder, Co-Artistic Director, NeWorks, contemporary music group; Composer In Residence, American Chamber Music Festival at Edsvik, Sweden, 1999; Assistant Conductor, Pianist, Golden Fleece Chamber Opera, 1995; US Premiere of Maurice Ohana's Three Stories of Honorable Flower, 1996; Pianist for ballet classes, Rehearsal Pianist for Musical Theatre; Pianist, Scott Wolson's Folk-Rock CD, Anything Left to Say; Jazz/Pop Pianist/ Keyboardist, Arranger for bands, sessions and parties. *Compositions:* Third Tribe, for flute, djembe drums and piano, 1992; Electric Ice Dream, for clarinet quartet, 1996; Fractured Skies, 1998; eX-s-Tet, for clarinet, 2 violins, viola, cello, piano, 1999; Concert music performed throughout USA and Mexico by Civic Orchestra of Chicago; ONIX New Music Ensemble; The New York Clarinet Quintet; NewEar Ensemble of Kansas City; Synchronia of St Louis; Numerous commissions; Theatre scores, Dance scores; Film score for ANA: Portrait in Days, 1995. *Honours:* Hon. mention, Percussive Arts Society, 1992; Hon. mention, Vienna Modern Masters, 1993; Brian M Israel Award, Society for New Music, 1996. *Membership:* ASCAP; American Music Center; Actors' Company Theatre. *Address:* 364 14th St, No. 2, Brooklyn, NY 11215, USA.

SADE, (Helen Folasade Adu); b. 16 Jan. 1959, Ibadan, Nigeria. Vocalist; Songwriter. *Education:* St Martin's School of Art, London. *Career:* Member, Arriva; Member, Pride; Singer, founder, own band, Sade, 1983; Appearances include: Montreux Jazz Festival, 1984; Live Aid, Wembley Stadium, 1985; Film appearance: Absolute Beginners, 1987. *Recordings:* Singles: with Sade include: Your Love Is King, 1984; When Am I Going To Make A Living, 1984; Smooth Operator (co-writer), 1984; The Sweetest Taboo, 1985; Is It A Crime?, 1986; Never As Good As The First Time, 1986; Love Is Stronger Than Pride, 1988; Paradise, 1988; No Ordinary Love (used in film Indecent Proposal), 1993; Feel No Pain, 1993; By Your Side, 2000; King Of Sorrow, 2001; Albums: Diamond Life (No. 2, UK), 1984; Promise (No. 1, UK), 1985; Stronger Than Pride, 1988; Love Deluxe, 1992; Best Of, 1994; Lovers Rock, 2000; Contributor, film soundtrack Absolute Beginners, 1987. *Honours:* BRIT Awards, Best British Album, for Diamond Life, 1985, Best New Artist, 1986; Black Music Award, 1992; American Music Award, Favourite Adult Contemporary Artist, 2002; Grammy Award, Pop Vocal Album, for Lovers Rock, 2002; O.B.E., 2002. *Current Management:* Roger Davies Management, 15030 Ventura Blvd, Suite 772, Sherman Oaks, CA 91403, USA.

SADIER, Laetitia; b. 6 May 1968, Paris, France. Vocalist; Musician (keyboards, guitar, trombone); Songwriter. *Career:* Member: Stereolab, 1991–; Monade; Son Alex with band member Tim Gane; Collaborations: High Llamas; Mouse On Mars; Ui; Brigitte Fontaine; Luna; Blur; Herbie Mann. *Recordings:* Albums include: Peng!, 1992; Transient Random Noise Bursts With Announcements, 1993; Mars Audiac Quintet, 1994; Music For The Amorphous Body Study Center, 1995; Emperor Tomato Ketchup, 1996; Dots and Loops, 1997; Cobra and Phases Group Play Voltage In The Milky Night, 1999; The First of The Microbe Hunters, 2000; Sound-Dust, 2001. *Current Management:* Martin Pike c/o Duophonic Ultra High Frequency Disks. *Website:* www.stereolab.co.uk.

SAFARI, Jean Bosco, (Jean Vijdt); b. 10 May 1954, Rwanda. Vocalist; Songwriter. 1 s., 1 d. *Career:* Band member of a O; Solo artist, originally as Kid Safari; Billed as Jean Bosco Safari, 1995–; *Recordings:* Wow, 1991; Romantic Heroes, 1993; Little Boy Blue, 1995; Visions Of Home. *Honours:* Gold album: Romantic Heroes. *Membership:* SABAM; ZAMU. *Current Management:* Tempo Belgium, Time Lecompte. *Address:* Krijslaan 61, 9000 Ghent, Belgium.

SAFFRON, (Samantha Sprackling); b. 1969, Nigeria. Vocalist. *Career:* Former ballet dancer; Lead singer, N-Joi; Lead singer, Republica, 1994–. *Recordings include:* with N-Joi: Anthem, 1990; with Republica: Album: Republica, 1997; Speed Ballads, 1998; Hit singles: Ready To Go, 1997; Drop Dead Gorgeous, 1997; From Rush Hour With Love, 1998; Guest vocals on: Fat Of The Land, Prodigy (No. 1, UK and USA), 1997; Drums Are Dangerous, The Drum Club. *Current Management:* Rise Management Ltd, PO Box 9788, London W10 5WN, England.

SAGER, Carole Bayer; b. 1946, New York, NY, USA. Songwriter; Vocalist. m. Burt Bacharach. *Education:* High School of Music and Art, New York. *Career:* Songwriter, 1960s; Recording artiste, 1972–. *Compositions:* Groovy Kind of Love (recorded by Patti Labelle, The Mindbenders, Phil Collins); That's What Friends Are For (raised $1m. for AIDS charity, recorded by Dionne Warwick and Friends); Co-writer, Midnight Blue (recorded by Melissa Manchester; When I Need You (recorded by Leo Sayer); They're Playing Our Song, with Marvin Hamlisch; Arthur's Theme, with Burt Bacharach (recorded by Christopher Cross); Nobody Does It Better, Carly Simon (James Bond theme); On My Own, Patti Labelle, Michael McDonald; Also composed songs for: Roberta Flack; Taja Sevelle; Neil Diamond; Aretha Franklin; The Monkees; Andrea Bocelli; Céline Dion. *Recordings:* Albums: Carole Bayer Sager, 1977; Too, 1978; Sometimes Late at Night, 1981; Singles: You're Moving Out Today; Stronger Than Before (co-written with Bette Midler). *Honours:* Academy Award, Arthur's Theme.

SAGOV, Margo Leona; b. 22 Dec. 1952, Cape Town, South Africa (British). Musician (guitar); Vocalist; Songwriter; Prod; Studio Designer. m., divorced. *Education:* Registered architect; Studied Architectural Association, London. *Career:* Founder member, group Amazulu; Guitarist, backing vocalist, 1982–86; Signed to Towerbell Records, 1984; Island Records, 1984–86; Desert Songs, ATV Music Publishing, 1984–89; Toured extensively, UK, Europe; Television appearances include: Top of the Pops; The Young Ones; Tube; Radio sessions: John Peel; Annie Nightingale; David Jensen. *Recordings:* with Amazulu: Cairo, 1984; Smiley Stylee, 1984; Excitable, 1985; Moonlight Romance; Don't You Just Know It, 1985; Too Good To Be Forgotten, 1986; with Clicking The Mouse: I Must Be Dreaming; Numerous sessions include: Happiness, The Beloved, 1990; Zeke Manyika. *Membership:* Musicians' Union; Equity; ACTT as sound recordist; ARB. *Address:* 10 Brookfield Mansions,

Highgate West Hill, London N6 6AS, England. *Telephone:* (20) 8340-6189. *Fax:* (20) 8348-2148. *E-mail:* margosagov@aol.com.

SAINSBURY, Roy; b. 12 April 1942, Birmingham, England. Musician (guitar). m. Wendy Sainsbury, 2 s., 1 d. *Education:* Studied guitar with Reg Bishop and Jack Toogood. *Career:* Appeared on BBC Radio 2, Night Ride, Jazz Parade; Played with BBC Midland Radio Orchestra and New Millionaires Band; Solo appearances: BBC Radio 2 Arts Programme; Television in Netherlands and Malta. *Compositions:* Love and Sunshine; Crieff Melody; Wendy's Blues. *Recordings:* Album: Gentle Guitar; I've Got It Bad (with Jane Christie). *Membership:* Musicians' Union. *Current Management:* Norman Phillips Agency, Birmingham, England. *Address:* 185 Birches Rd, Codsall, Wolverhampton WV8 2JW, England.

ST CLAIR, Frank Creel; b. 17 Nov. 1936, Jacksonville, Texas, USA. Publisher; Writer; Recording Artist; Musician (guitar). m. Barbara Mae Young, 29 Oct. 1963, 4 s., 3 d. *Education:* Fine Arts, Kilgore College, 1968–70; Graphic Arts, Texas State Technical Institute, Waco, 1970–72; Commercial Art, Tyler College, 1978–80; Understudied with Jack Rhodes, Curly Putman and others. *Career:* Third Army Special Services, Touring Southeast USA; KLIV, Tyler, Texas; WFLB TV, Fayetteville, North Carolina; Major TV Stations in Deep South, 1955–70; Performed as singer in night clubs and stage shows throughout Texas, 1957–. *Compositions:* My Heart and Mind are at War, 1964; Portrait of a Fool, 1964; Guitar Bum, 1966; Mr Blues, 1966; Night Bird, 1969; This Is Life, 1969; I Hope My Guilt Don't Show, 1970; Pollution of the Mind, 1980; Good Times Are Fleeting Things, 1982. *Membership:* BMI; Country Music Asscn; MCPS, London. *Address:* Rr 5 Box 1635, Henderson, TX 75652, USA.

ST JAMES, Rebecca; b. 26 July 1977, Sydney, Australia. Christian Recording Artist. *Education:* High school music group; Coaching by Norris Brannstrom. *Career:* Carman's Revival In The Land Tour, 1991; Bryan Duncan's Slow Revival Tour, 1995; Dove Awards, Family TV Network, 1995; Side By Side Tour, 1995. *Recordings:* Refresh My Heart, 1991; Rebecca St James, 1994; Remix Album, 1995; One Way (Forefront compilation), 1995; Transform, 2000. *Publications:* Cover stories: Brio Magazine; Campus Life. *Membership:* BMI; GMA. *Current Management:* Ambassador Agency; David Smallbone Management. *Address:* PO Box 1741, Brentwood, TN 37024, USA.

ST JOHN, Kate Elinor Margaret; b. 2 Oct. 1957, London, England. Musician (oboe, saxophone); Vocalist; Composer; Arranger. m. Sid Griffin, 28 July 1993. *Education:* BSc Music, City University; Oboe at Guildhall. *Career:* Member, Ravishing Beauties, 1981–82; Member, Dream Academy, 1983–91; Oboe/saxophone session player in many bands; Member, Channel Light Vessel, 1994; Member, Van Morrison's live and recording band, 1991–95; Toured with Nigel Kennedy, 1998. *Compositions include:* For television: Harry Enfield's Television Show; Harry Enfield and Chums. *Recordings:* Albums: with Dream Academy: The Dream Academy; Remembrance Days; A Different Kind of Weather; Somewhere In The Sun (compilation); with Channel Light Vessel: Automatic, 1994, Excellent Spirits, 1996; Solo albums: Indescribable Night, 1995; Second Sight, 1997; Hit single: Life In a Northern Town, Dream Academy; Singer with Roger Eno: The Familiar, 1993; Co-producer, Russian artist Boris Grebenschikov, 1995. *Membership:* Musicians' Union; PRS; MCPS. *Current Management:* Mark Vernon, Firebrand. *Address:* 12 Rickett St, London SW6 1RU, England.

SAINTE-MARIE, Buffy; b. 20 Feb. 1941, Saskatchewan, Canada. Vocalist; Songwriter; Musician (keyboards, guitar, mouthbow, computer). 1 s. *Education:* PhD, Fine Arts, University of Massachusetts (undergraduate, Philosophy). *Career:* Solo concerts world-wide, 1963–; Symphony concerts with: Calgary Symphony; National Arts Centre Orchestra; Vancouver Opera Symphony; Toured with various bands major cities, hundreds of Indian reservations, indigenous area world-wide; TV includes: Sesame Street, Children's Television Workshop, 1970s–1980s. *Recordings:* 19 albums include: Sweet America, 1976; Coincidence and Likely Stories, 1992; Up Where We Belong, 1996. *Honours:* Academy Award as songwriter, Up Where We Belong, from film An Officer and A Gentleman; Billboard Best New Artist, 1964; Premico Award, Italy, 1972; Queen Elizabeth Jubilee Medal; Academy Award, 1981; Charles De Gaulle Grand Prix, Best International Artist, 1994; Saskatchewan Lifetime Achievement Award, 1994; Canada JUNO Hall of Fame, 1995. *Membership:* ASCAP; AFofM. *Current Management:* Jack Lentz, Einstein Brothers. *Address:* 20 Duncan St, Toronto, ON M5H 3G8, Canada.

SAKAMOTO, Ryûichi; b. 17 Jan. 1952, Tokyo, Japan. Musician; Composer; Actor. m. Akiko Yano, 1979. *Education:* Composition and electronic music, Tokyo College of Arts; Masters degree, 1976. *Career:* Founder, Yellow Magic Orchestra, 1978; Worked with David Sylvian, 1982–83; Solo recording artiste, composer, 1982–; Actor, composed soundtrack, film, Merry Christmas Mr Lawrence, 1983; Composed soundtracks for films: The Sheltering Sky; The Last Emperor (with David Byrne, Cong Su), 1987; Femme Fatale; Worked with leading musicians incl. Adrian Belew, Andy Partridge, Iggy Pop, Brian Wilson, Thomas Dolby, Robbie Robertson, Madonna; Conductor, arranger, music for Olympic Games opening ceremony, Barcelona, Spain, 1992. *Recordings:* Albums: B-2 Unit, 1980; Hidariudeno (A Dream Of The Left

Arm), 1981; Coda, 1983; Ongaku Zukan (A Picture Book Of Music), 1984; Esperanto, 1985; Miraiha Yarô (A Futurist Chap), 1986; Media Bahn Live, 1986; Oneamisno Tsubasa (The Wings Of Oneamis), 1986; Illustrated Musical Encyclopedia, 1986; Neo Geo, 1987; Playing The Orchestra, 1988; Tokyo Joe, 1988; Sakamoto Plays Sakamoto, 1989; Grupo Musicale, 1989; Beauty, 1989; Heartbeat, 1991; Neo Geo, with Iggy Pop, 1992; Sweet Revenge, 1994; Soundbites, 1994; Hard To Get, 1995; 1996, 1996; Music For Yohji Yamamoto, 1997; Smoochy, 1997; Discord, 1998; Love Is The Devil, 1998; Raw Life, 1999; Intimate, 1999; Space, 1999; BTTB, 1999; Gohatto, 1999; Complete Index of Gut, 1999; Cinemage, 2000; Casa, 2002. Singles include: Bamboo Houses, with David Sylvian, 1982; Forbidden Colours, with David Sylvian, 1983; Field Work, with Thomas Dolby, 1986; Risky, 1988; We Love You, 1991; Moving On, 1994; Prayer/Salvation, 1998; Anger, 1998. *Publications:* Otowo Miru, Tokiwo Kiku (Seeing Sound and Hearing Time), with Shôzo Omori; Seldom-Illegal; Contributor, Album, Public Image Limited; Esperanto, Arto Lindsey. *Honours:* Academy Award, for The Last Emperor, 1987. *Current Management:* David Rubinson Management, PO Box 411197, San Francisco, CA 94141, USA.

SALIM, Abdel Gadir; b. Kordofan Province, Sudan. Vocalist; Musician (oud); Teacher. *Education:* Institute for Music and Drama, Khartoum. *Career:* Headmaster in Chad; Regular national television and radio appearances popularizing traditional folk music; British tour with Abdel Aziz el Mubarak and Mohammed Gubara, 1986. *Recordings:* with Mubarak and Gubara: The Sounds of Sudan, 1991. *Address:* c/o World Circuit Records, 106 Cleveland St, London W1P 5DP, England.

SALISBURY, Peter; b. 24 Sept. 1971, Bath, Avon, England. Musician (drums). *Career:* Founder Member, The Verve, 1990; Obtained record deal, 1991; Support dates to The Black Crowes; Played 1994 Lollapalooza tour; Band splits, 1995, then reforms; Numerous live dates including 1997 Reading Festival; Band splits again, 1999. *Recordings:* Singles: She's A Superstar, 1992; Gravity Grave, 1992; All in the Mind, 1992; Slide Away, 1993; Blue, 1993; This is Music, 1995; On Your Own, 1995; History, 1995; Bittersweet Symphony (No. 2, UK), 1997; Lucky Man, 1997; The Drugs Don't Work (No. 1, UK), 1997; Albums: A Storm in Heaven, 1993; No Come Down, 1994; A Northern Soul, 1995; Urban Hymns (No. 1, UK), 1997; Drummer on: Alone With Everybody, Richard Ashcroft, 2000.

SALLEY, Jerry; b. Tennessee, USA. Vocalist; Songwriter; Prod. m. 3 d. *Career:* Regular performer, Nashville Showcase Circuit; 5 appearances, Grand Ole Oprey; Regular television appearances; Over 100 songs commercially recorded; Staff writer, Warner Chappell; Instructor, music business, Belmont University; Frequent panelist in music industry forums; Backing vocals on: Love Letters, Leslie Satcher, 2000. *Compositions:* I Fell In The Water, John Anderson (Top 5); Breakin' New Ground, Wild Rose (Top 10); His Strength Is Perfect, Real Life Conversations, Stephen Curtis Chapman; Tracy Byrd; Roger Brown and Swing City; Songs for: Patty Loveless; The Hutchins; Woody Lee; Rhonda Vincent. *Honours:* Dove Award, for His Strength Is Perfect, 1990; 4 SESAC National Performance Activity Awards. *Membership:* Gospel Music Asscn; Country Music Asscn; Nashville Songwriter's Asscn; SESAC. *Current Management:* SESAC. *Address:* 55 Music Sq. E, Nashville, TN 37203, USA.

SALMINEN, Simo; b. 16 Dec. 1956, Finland. Musician (trumpet, flugelhorn). *Career:* Played with Tapiola Big Band; Paradise (dance orchestra); UMO (New Music Orchestra); Went to USA, 1978; Played with Thad Jones/Mel Lewis band; Buddy Rich; Machito; Eddie Palmieri; Mike Oldfield; Gladys Knight and The Pips; 1 year in Broadway show; Returned to Finland, 1983; Teacher, Oulunkylä Jazz and Pop Institute; Played in UMO; Led UMO in performance of music of Bob Moses, 1984; Leader, Arctic Big Band, 1987–. *Recordings:* Albums with: Espoo Big Band; UMO; Mel Lewis; Buddy Rich. *Address:* Hämeentie 72 A 7, 00550 Helsinki, Finland.

SALMINEN, Teemu Tapio; b. 5 June 1953, Helsinki. Musician (saxophones, clarinet, flutes). m. Eija Salminen. *Education:* Sibelius Academy. *Career:* Played in UMO Jazz Orchestra, 1976–; Played in several small groups; Teemu Salminen Quartet, Jukka Jukkis Octet, Quintet, Quartet, Jarmo Savolainen Nonet, Edward Vesala Group, Jukkis Uotila Quartet; Teacher, Sibelius Academy, Music Education, Jazz Department. *Compositions:* Mystery; Yes, Please; Gaudi. *Recordings:* 16 with the UMO Jazz Orchestra including, Selected Standards; Day Dreamin; Lady In Green; Green and Yellow; Electrifying Miles; Linkola's Orchestral Works, 1997. *Membership:* Musicians' Union; Flute Players Asscn; Jazz Players Asscn. *Address:* Tollinpolku 1B 20, 00410 Helsinki, Finland.

SALT, (Cheryl James); b. 8 March 1964, Brooklyn, New York, USA. Rap Artiste; Songwriter; Prod. 1 d. *Career:* Formed US female rap duo Super Nature with Sandra Denton, 1985; Signed to Next Plateau Records and group re-named Salt-N-Pepa, 1986; Group joined by DJ 'Spinderella', in form of Pamela Green, then Latoya Hanson and finally, in 1987, Dee Dee Roper; Signed to London Records, 1993; Signed to MCA Records, 1997; Created Jireh Records company with Sandra Denton, 1997; Performances include: Youth Ball, Washington, DC, 1993; LIFEBeat AIDS benefit concert, 1993; Woodstock '94. *Recordings:* Albums: Hot Cool & Vicious, 1986; A Salt With A

Deadly Pepa, 1988; Blacks' Magic, 1990; A Blitz of Hits: The Hits Remixed, 1990; Very Necessary, 1993; Brand New, 1997; Salt-N-Pepa... The Best Of, 2000. Singles include: as Super Nature: Showstopper, 1985; as Salt-N-Pepa: My Mike Sounds Nice, 1987; Push It, 1988; Shake Your Thang (It's Your Thing), 1988; Twist and Shout, 1988; Expression, 1990; Do You Want Me, 1991; Let's Talk About Sex, 1991; Let's Talk About AIDS (re-write of Let's Talk About Sex), 1992; You Showed Me, 1991; Start Me Up, 1992; Shoop, 1993; Whatta Man (with En Vogue), 1994; None Of Your Business, 1994; Ain't Nothin But A She Thing, 1995; Champagne, 1996; R U Ready, 1997; Gitty Up, 1998; Brick Track Vs Gitty Up, Pt I and II, 2000; Contributions to various compilations and soundtrack albums. *Honours:* Platinum discs and Gold discs for albums and singles; Grammy for Best Rap Performance by a Duo or Group, for None Of Your Business, 1994; Three MTV Awards, 1994. *Address:* c/o CD Enterprises Inc, 7531 Leesburg Pike, Suite 201, Fallschurch, VA 22043, USA.

SALT, Jack (John Robert); b. 30 Jan. 1920, Stafford, England. Musician (alto, baritone saxophones, clarinet, violin, viola). m. Katherine Barbara Barnard, 19 Aug. 1948, 4 s. *Education:* Private music tuition. *Career:* Sandy Powell Road Show, 1941; Alan Green, 1942; Waldini Gypsy Band, including Ensa overseas tour of War Zones: North Africa; Middle East; Far East; Europe, 1943–49; Wally Fry, 1949; Don Rico, 1952; Benny Freedman, 1953–63; Model Railways specialist, 1957–94; Television and radio broadcasts: BBC; All India Radio; Radio Solent; Radio Victory; Southern TV; Currently, Havant Symphony Orchestra. *Publications:* Featured in Frontline Theatre, Waldini; Mentioned in Life and Death of Peter Sellers, Evans. *Honours:* Italy Star; Burma Star; 1939/45 War and Victory Medals. *Membership:* Musicians' Union; National Federation of Musical Societies. *Address:* 171 Fratton Rd, Portsmouth, Hampshire PO1 5ET, England.

SALUT, Christian 'Ton-Ton'; b. 2 Feb. 1953, Montauban, France. Jazz Musician (drums, percussion). 2 d. *Education:* Literature, University of Toulouse; Certificate of Completion, Drummers Collective, New York City. *Career:* Founder, Ton-Ton Quartet, 1980–84; Accompanist for soloists including: Sonny Stitt; Siegfried Kessler; Guy Lafitte; Michel Roques; Founder, Drumpact, 1986–; Tours: Germany; Switzerland; Austria; Netherlands; Denmark; Spain; Africa (Cameroon, Nigeria); Festivals with Drumpact include: Hyères; Madrid; Berlin; Marciac; Visits and concerts, Boston, New York; Tour with Drumpact and Ballet-Theatre Le Baobab, of Yaoundé; Freelance musician with Christian Escoudé; Jack Walrath; Glenn Ferris; Hein Van de Geyn; Also played with: Magali Piétri; Yéko-Lé-Bop; Black 'n' Blue; Big Band 31 (including festivals: Vienna, Nice, Ramatuelle, Tarbes); Concerts, tours with: Christian Escoudé; Lou Bennett; Tony Pagnao; Jay Cameron; Daniel Huck; Peter King; Ted Curson; Eric Lelann; Andrew White; Turk Mauro; Jazz teacher, Conservatoire National de Région de Toulouse; Festival of Saint-Louis, Senegal, 1997–98. *Compositions:* Creation for a Double Trio, in festival, Jazz sur Son 31, 1997; Ali Aba, 1994; Train Fou, 1997. *Recordings:* with Drumpact: Journey Into The World; Percussion Unlimited; New Music; with Big Band 31: Big Band; Billie; Nobody Knows, with Magali Pietri; Mauresaca, Jazz Time Big Band; Samantha's Dance, Steve Mabry, 1993; Ali-Aba, 1993; Abdu Salim Quintet, 1995; Street Music, Sonny Simmons, 1997; Don't Stop the Carnival, Hip Jazz Trio, 1997; Be Hip Be Bop, 2001. *Membership:* UMJ (Union of Jazz Musicians). *Current Management:* Jazz Unit. *Address:* 8 rue Lakanal, 31000 Toulouse, France.

SALUZZI, Dino; b. 20 May 1935, Campo Tanta, Argentina. Musician (bandoneon, flute); Composer. *Career:* Several European, US and South American tours including with George Gruntz, Mark Egan, Charlie Haden, Palle Mikkelbourg, Bob Moses and Enrico Rava. *Recordings:* Kultrum; Once Upon a Time; Volver; Andina; Other session work includes: Gato Barbieri; Leon Ciego; Enzo Favata. *Current Management:* Karen Kindig, c/o Blue Cat Agency, PO Box 399, Novato, CA 94948, USA.

SAMBORA, Richie; b. 1 July 1959. Musician (guitar); Vocalist; Songwriter. *Career:* Guitarist, US rock group Bon Jovi, 1983–; Appearances include: Regular world-wide tours; Donington Monsters of Rock Festival, 1987; Moscow Music Peace Festival, 1989; Solo US tour, 1991; Solo appearance, Late Night With David Letterman, 1991; Solo performance, KISS Radio's 13th Anniversary Concert, Massachusetts, 1992; Numerous hit compositions with Jon Bon Jovi and Desmond Child. *Recordings:* Singles include: with Bon Jovi: You Give Love A Bad Name (No. 1, USA), 1986; Livin' On A Prayer (No. 1, USA), 1986; Wanted Dead Or Alive, 1987; Bad Medicine (No. 1, USA), 1988; Born To Be My Baby; I'll Be There For You (No. 1, USA), 1989; Lay Your Hands On Me, 1989; Living In Sin, 1989; Miracle, 1990; Keep The Faith, 1992; Bed of Roses, 1993; In These Arms, 1993; I'll Sleep When I'm Dead, 1993; I Believe, 1993; These Days, 1996; Solo: The Wind Cries Mary (featured in film The Adventures of Ford Fairlane); Ballad of Youth; Albums with Bon Jovi: Bon Jovi, 1984; 7800° Fahrenheit, 1985; Slippery When Wet, 1986; New Jersey, 1988; Keep The Faith, 1992; Crossroads, 1994; These Days, 1995; Wild In The Streets, 2000; Crush, 2000; One Wild Night: Live 1985–2001, 2001; Solo albums: Stranger In This Town, 1991; Undiscovered Soul, 1999; Contributor to Tribute To Muddy Waters album, 1993; Undiscovered Soul, 1998. *Honours:* Best Stage Performance, MTV Music Video awards, 1987; All

Bon Jovi albums Gold or Platinum status. *Current Management:* c/o Bon Jovi Mgmt, 248 W 17th St Apt 501, New York, NY 10011–5330, USA.

SAMKOPF, Kjell; b. 6 April 1952, Baerum, Norway. Composer; Musician (percussion). m. Mona Walderhaug, 23 July 1994, 2 s. *Education:* Diploma in Composition, 1977, Degree in Percussion, 1978, Norwegian State Academy of Music; Studied jazz vibraphone at the Berklee College of Music, Boston, Massachusetts, 1979. *Career:* Timpanist, Trondheim Symphony Orchestra, Norway, 1974–75; Freelance Percussionist with the Norwegian Opera Orchestra and the Oslo Philharmonic Orchestra, 1975–82; Teacher of Percussion, East Norway Conservatory, 1979–85; Head of Percussion Department, 1988–, currently Professor, Norwegian State Academy of Music. *Compositions:* Associations, for large orchestra with live electronics and 4-channel tape, 1984; Invention No 5, for solo percussion and electronics, 1981; Aqua, for tape and two percussionists, 1986; Tide, for 5 tapes, 1990; Harstad, for symphonic band and percussion soloist, 1991; Did You Sing This For Grieg?, electroacoustic, 1993; Mårådalen Walk, electroacoustic, 1994; Bergen, for woodwind quintet and two percussion players, 1996. *Recordings:* Invention No 5; On The Way; Because of GH; Intention, solo percussion with electronics; Asphyxy; Positive Frustrations; Waltz Around The Circle; Intention; Blues Extract (with Sandvika Storband); Aqua (with Rob Waring Duo); Did You Sing This For Grieg?, electroacoustic; Self-Portrait; Invention No 3, solo piece for snare drum; Tokke Kraftverk; Mårådalen Walk, electroacoustic; Mountain Listening, 1998. *Publications:* Practical Drum Method, Vols 1a, 1b, 2, 1981. *Honours:* Concours International de Composition de la Ville du Havre, Special Mention of the Jury for Harstad. *Membership:* Vice-President, Society of Norwegian Composers, 1988–90; President of the Board, Norwegian Music Information Centre, 1994–95. *Address:* Rudshagen 8, 3430 Spikkestad, Norway.

SAMS, Dean; b. 3 Aug. 1966, Garland, Texas, USA. Country vocalist; Musician (keyboards, harmonica); Songwriter. *Education:* Southwest Texas State University. *Career:* Attended college for three years before moving to Nashville to pursue a career in country music, late 1980s; Secured a job at Opryland Theme Park singing in Country Music USA show; Had 16-track recording studio, engineered and produced demos for self and others; Formed Texasee with Richie McDonald, Keech Rainwater, Michael Britt and John Rich, 1992; Group became resident house band at the Wildhorse Saloon, Nashville; After subsequent name change to Lonestar, came to the attention of BMG and were signed to their BNA subsidiary; Released promotional six-track live CD, recorded at the Wildhorse; First country chart entry No News/ Tequila Talkin' from debut album Lonestar, 1996; Single, Amazed, from third album became huge international hit and career record to date, 1999; By early 2000s, Lonestar estimated to be the most successful country group in the world; Developed parallel career outside of Lonestar; Co-wrote I'm Willing To Try from Joe Diffie's Life's So Funny album, 1995; Regular collaborations with other Nashville writers; Appeared in the film New Horizons directed by Tony Tarantino, 2001. *Compositions include:* I'm Willing To Try. *Recordings include:* No News, Tequila Talkin', 1996; Come Cryin' To Me, You Walked In, 1997; Say When, Everything's Changed, 1998; Amazed, Smile, 1999; I'm Already There, 2002; Albums include: Lonestar, 1995; Crazy Nights, 1997; Lonely Grill, 1999; I'm Already There, 2001. *Address:* c/o Country Music Asscn, 1 Music Circle S, Nashville, TN 37203, USA.

SAMSING, Freddy; b. 29 June 1946, Copenhagen, Denmark. Musician (Cathedral organ). m. Anita Hyldgård Samsing, 11 Oct. 1997, 1 s., 2 d. *Education:* Royal Danish Academy of Music, Copenhagen, studied conducting. *Career:* International concert player, Northern Europe; Solo appearances on TV and Radio; Solo appearances with almost all Danish Symphony Orchestras. *Recordings:* As Soloist/Accompanist: Works by Albinoni, Bach, Vivaldi, Monteverdi; Trio with two outstanding trumpet players, Hovaldt and Son; Solo trumpet by the Royal Danish Orchestra. *Honours:* Jury Mem., International Organ Competition, Odense, Denmark. *Membership:* DOKS. *Address:* Fangel Bygade 34, Fangel 5260, Odense 5, Denmark.

SAMUEL, Julie; b. 15 May 1949, London, England. Music Man. Widow, 1 d. *Education:* Italia Conti Stage School, London. *Career:* Began as actress, singer, 1962; Appeared in over 100 television shows, 10 films, numerous stage plays; Started Music Management, 1980; Now Artist manager for rock group Mexico 70; Sarah Cracknell (vocalist with Saint Etienne); Janey Lee Grace (recording artist, television presenter, DJ for Virgin Radio); Donna Air, Janey Hoy, Vicky Taylor (vocal act from Byker Grove). *Honours:* Silver discs, So Tough; Fox Base Alpha; Platinum album, Smash Hits '91. *Current Management:* Diamond Sounds Music Management, The Fox and Punchbowl, Burfield, Old Windsor, Berks Sl4 2RD, England.

SAMUELS, Elaine Mary; b. 17 Sept. 1962, Hampton, Middlesex, England. Vocalist; Songwriter; Folk, Blues, Bluegrass Musician (guitar, banjo, cittern, dulcimer, bodhran). m. Michael Paul Samuels, 23 July 1982, 1 s. *Education:* Electrical Engineering Degree. *Career:* Featured on HTV singing own songs; Appearances: Wire TV; BBC radio stations: Kent; Cambridge; Essex; Oxford; Suffolk; Kingston FM; Wey Valley Radio; Atlantis Radio, Belgium; Played at: Barbican; Marquee; Weavers; Half Moon; Mean Fiddler; Tour throughout UK, including Glastonbury, 1995. *Recordings:* Albums: Solo: Obsession; Reach Out

For Me; Blue Skies; Dragonfire; with Now and Then: New Country; Best of British Bluegrass, Vol. 1. *Honours:* Second place, Leicester's Live At The Y (song competition). *Membership:* Musicians' Union. *Address:* 55C Sheen Rd, Richmond, Surrey TW9 1YH, England.

SANBORN, David; b. 30 July 1945, Tampa, Florida, USA. Musician (alto saxophone). *Career:* Member, Paul Butterfield group; Leading session player with artists including: David Bowie; James Taylor; Stevie Wonder; Albert King; Dean Brown; Linda Ronstadt; Solo recording artiste, 1975–. *Recordings:* Albums: Taking Off, 1975; David Sanborn, 1976; Promise Me The Moon, 1977; Heart To Heart, 1978; Hideaway, 1980; Voyeur, 1981; As We Speak, 1982; Backstreet, 1983; Straight To The Heart, 1984; Double Vision (with Bob James), 1986; A Change of Heart, 1987; Close Up, 1988; Another Hand, 1991; Upfront, 1992; Hearsay, 1994; Pearls, 1995; Songs From The Night Before, 1996; Inside, 1999; Love and Happiness, 1999; Camel Island, 1999; I Told U So, 1999; Inside, 1999; Recent Singles: Got to Give it, 1994; Everything Must Change, 1995. *Honours:* Grammy Award, Voyeur, 1982. *Address:* c/o Patrick Rains and Associates, 1543 Seventh St, Third Floor, Santa Monica, CA 90401, USA.

SANBOWER, Jack Douglas; b. 14 Sept. 1960, Waynesboro, Pennsylvania, USA. Bluegrass Musician (banjo, guitar, bass). m. Albina Marie, 19 Feb. 1983, 1 s., 1 d. *Education:* AA Degree Data Processing. *Career:* Performed at Bluegrass festivals, USA, include: Gettysburg, Pennsylvania; Bass Mountain, North Carolina; Lazy River, New York; Wind Gap, Pennsylvania; Wellsboro, Pennsylvania; Leader, No Leeway Band. *Recordings:* Four Leaf Clover Breakdown, 1983; Before The Weekend's Over, 1986; Jack In the Box, 1989; Traveling Down This Lonesome Road, 1991; Just Monkeyin' Around, 1990; Throwing Caution To The Wind, 1991; Finger Pickin' For Supper, 1992; Let Loose, 1993; Thinking of Old Memories, 1994; Live At The Pocono Mountain Bluegrass Festival, 2000; Same Ole Fools, 2002. *Membership:* International Bluegrass Music Asscn; Tri-State Bluegrass Asscn. *Address:* 14461 Edgemont Rd, Smithsburg, MD 21783, USA. *E-mail:* Noreeway@aol.com. *Website:* noleeway.cjb.net.

SANCHEZ, David, (José David Sanchez DeLeon); b. 3 Sept. 1968, Hato Rey, Puerto Rico. Jazz Musician (tenor/soprano saxophones). *Education:* Psychology, University of Puerto Rico; Rutgers University. *Career:* Dizzy Gillespie and The United Nation Orchestra, 1991–92; An Evening with Dizzy Gillespie and Miriam Makeba, 1992; Dizzy Gillespie Diamond Jubilee Tribute Concerts, 1992; Phillip Morris Superband Tour, 1992; Member, Slide Hampton and The Jazzmasters, 1993–95; Leader, David Sanchez Quintet, 1994–99; Leader, David Sanchez Sextet, 1999–. *Recordings:* With Dizzy Gillespie: To Bird With Love, 1992; Bird Songs, recorded 1992, released 1997; With Slide Hampton and The Jazzmasters, To Diz With Love, 1993; With Roy Hargrove's Crisol, Habana, 1997; With Roy Haynes, Praise, 1998; As leader: The Departure, 1994; Sketches of Dreams, 1995; Street Scenes, 1996; Obsesion, 1998; Solo albums: Melaza, 2000; Y Sus Corridos Bravos, 2001; Travesia, 2001. *Membership:* AFofM; BMI. *Current Management:* Charismic Productions, 2604 Mozart Pl. W, Washington, DC 20009, USA.

SANCHEZ, Michel; b. France. Musician. *Career:* mem., Deep Forest, with Eric Mouquet, 1991–; Solo career; Collaborations with Abed Azrie, Peter Gabriel, Marcella Lewis, Wes Madiko, Jorge Reyes, Ana Toroja, Joe Zawinul; Concert, G7 show, France, 1996; World tour, 1996. *Recordings:* Albums: with Deep Forest: World Mix, 1994; Boheme, 1996; Comparsa, 1998; Made in Japan, 1999; Madazulu, 1997–98; Solo: Windows, 1995. *Honours:* MTV Award, Best Music Video, for Sweet Lullaby, 1993; Victoires de la Musique Awards, Best World Album, 1993, 1996; World Music Award for Most Sales in the World, 1995; Grammy Award, Best World Music Album, for Boheme, 1996. *Address:* c/o Sony Music France, 131 ave de Wagram, 75017 Paris, France. *E-mail:* deepforest@sonymusic.fr. *Website:* www.sonymusic.fr/deepforest/.

SANCHEZ, Paco; b. 7 June 1956, Murcia, Spain. Musician (drums). *Education:* University of Human Sciences; Paris VII Conservatory. *Career:* Played with the International Orchestra of Tchicai John in Denmark and Morocco; Played in West Africa; Benin; Festival of Brazzville, Bangui; Trio Soledad, France. *Recordings:* Soledad, with Carlos Acciari and Michel Fernandez, 1996; Itinerances, 1996; Narvalo, Gypsy Flamenco Music, 1998; Danza Fuego, Flamenco Poetry, 1998; Adam Del Monte, Heart and Soul: Romantic Dedications, 1999. *Honours:* First Excellency Prize. *Membership:* SACEM. *Current Management:* RDC Records. *Address:* 16 rue du Transvaal, 75020 Paris, France.

SANCHEZ, Roger, (The S-Man, Roger S, Funk Junkeez, The Neanderthal); b. 1 June 1967, New York, NY, USA. Prod; Remixer; DJ. *Career:* Began as a New York club DJ; Progressed to producing, recording for Strictly Rhythm in New York; Founder: R-Senal Records; Presents weekly radio show on London radio station Kiss 100 FM; Collaborations: Armand Van Helden; Todd Terry; Judy Cheeks; Kathy Sledge; Remixed: Juliet Roberts; Incognito; Brand New Heavies; Michael Jackson. *Recordings:* Albums: First Contact, 2001; Singles: Luv Dancin' (as Underground Solution), 1991; Time 2 Stop (as The S-Man), 1994; Got Funk (as Funk Junkeez), 1997; I

Never Knew (with Cooly's Hot Box), 1999; Another Chance, 2001. *Address:* c/o Defected Records, 14–15 D'arblay St, London W1F 8DY, England.

SANDERS, Kevin Bruce; b. 22 May 1962, Torquay, Devon, England. Freelance Musician (double bass, bass guitar); Arranger. m. 6 June 1987, 1 d. *Education:* College; Private classical double bass tuition. *Career:* Started with Dennis Rowland Trio; Later joined Lawrie Dixon Trio; Since worked with: Mornington Lockett; Kathy Stobart; Don Weller; Michael Hashim; Tony Lee; Stan Grieg; Worked with Dave Thompson Quartet, 1992–94; Lectured in bass studies at Dartington College of Arts; Runs successful 7-piece soul and blues review Rhythm Machine and contemporary jazz ensemble. *Recordings:* Rayas Pictures, 1992. *Honours:* Musicians' Union Award, Most Promising Bass Player, 1984. *Membership:* Musicians' Union. *Current Management:* Music à la Carte Ent. Services; Bette Holman (For Rhythm Machine). *Address:* 30 Elm Park, Paignton, Devon TQ3 3QH, England.

SANDERS, Tim Bryan; b. 16 April 1962, Stoke-on-Trent, Staffordshire, England. Vocalist; Songwriter. m. Jynine James, 1 May 1993, 3 s. *Education:* Music and Law Studies at Cauldon College; Guitar tuition; Private tuition for music reading, Cauldon College. *Career:* Formed the City Zones in 1979; Re-formed in 1992; Appeared in BBC Radio live sessions; Appeared on television with Toyah; Supported many early 1980s artists; Actor, Joy Swift's original Murder Weekends, German Satellite TV and BBC TV, 1990–91; Movie soundtrack co-written and recorded by Legendary Lonnie, 1994–95. *Compositions:* Don't Stop Me Now, co-written with Muchin/Ainsworth/O'Dowd, 1996. *Recordings:* La Maison De L'Amour, The City Zones, 1992; Live At The BBC, The City Zones, 1992; Born To Win; Knock Me Down Pick Me Up; Pain of Love; When I Dream; Spoils of Humanity; Past Shadows; Knock Me Down Pick Me Up, Legendary Lonnie, 1994; Sexual Affection, Stacy Grant, 2001. *Publications:* Collections of works. *Honours:* Presentation Disc for sales of La Maison De l'Amour and Pain of Love (released by Jynine James and Peter Frampton), Mr and Mrs Music Publishing, 1992, 1993. *Membership:* PAMRA; PRS; MCPS. *Current Management:* Fast Tracks Records; Mr and Mrs Music Publishing; Djamus Ltd. *Address:* c/o Fast Tracks Records, 11 Maen Gwyn, Tan-y-Gopa Parc, Abergele, Clwyd, LL72 7BZ, Wales.

SANDIRA; b. 27 Aug. 1958, Opotiki, New Zealand. Musician (percussion); Vocalist; Programmer. *Education:* Musical tuition with Nemoi Aquam (Speedy). *Career:* Tours of UK, Europe, with: The Shamen; Loop Guru; Counterfeit Stones; Denise Black and the Kray Sisters; Television and radio with above; Played Phoenix Festival as Sandira; Festivals include: Glastonbury; WOMAD; Reading; Phoenix. *Recordings:* Singles: Solo: Ishmar Du Bach; Single by Loop Guru, 1995; Caroline Lavelle; William Orbit; Apple Head; Also featured on albums by Labi Siffre; Loop Guru. *Membership:* Musicians' Union. *Current Management:* None. *Address:* 14 Drayton Rd, London NW10 4EL, England.

SANDKE, Randy; b. 23 May 1949, Chicago, Illinois, USA. Composer; Arranger; Musician (trumpet). m. Karen Kelly, 15 Sept. 1990. *Education:* University of Chicago Lab School; Indiana University; Studied TPT with Renold Shilke, Vince Penzerella; Arranging with Oliver Nelson; Composing with Henry Brant and Easley Blackwood. *Career:* TPT with Benny Goodman, 1985–86, with Buck Clayton, 1986–90; Concord Recording Artist, 1993–; Written several suites for Carnegie Hall Jazz Band; Performed on soundtracks of 3 Woody Allen films. *Compositions:* Orphic Mystery, 1997; Overture For the Year 2000, 1997. *Recordings:* NY Stories, 1986; I Hear Music, 1993; Get Happy, 1994; The Chase, 1995; Calling All Cats, 1996; Awakening, 1997; Count Basie Remembered, 1998; Rediscovered Louis And Bix, 2000. *Publications:* Introduction to Metatonal Music, 1997; Bix Beiderbecke From a Musician's Perspective, 1998; Annual Review of Jazz Studies. *Membership:* NARAS; IAJRC; Musicians' Union Local 802. *Address:* 213 1/2 Bergen St, Brooklyn, New York, 11217, USA.

SANDOVAL, Arturo; b. 6 Nov. 1949, Artemisia, Cuba. Musician (trumpet); Prof. m. Marianela, 17 Oct. 1975, 1 s. *Education:* National Music Institute, Havana, Cuba. *Career:* Full Professor (tenure), Florida International University; Musician; Appearances: with Irakere, 1972–81; World tours, 1980–; United Nations Band; Sandoval Group, 1981; Dizzy Gillespie, 1987–91; Television includes: Super Bowl Halftime Event, 1995; King Orange Disney New Year's show, 1995; Tonight Show; David Letterman; Arsenio Hall; HBO; CNN; Summit of The Americas, Grammy Awards; Academy Awards with Céline Dion. *Recordings:* Live At Royal Festival Hall, Dizzy Gillespie; Danzón; Flight To Freedom; Dream Come True; I Remember Clifford; Latin Train; The Classical Album; Swinging; Sandoval's Hot House; Perez Family soundtrack; Mambo Kings Soundtrack; Americana, 1999; LA Meetings, 2001. *Publications:* Hal Leonard 4 Trumpet Method Books. *Honours:* Grammy, Best Latin Album, Irakere II; Danzón; 2 Billboard International Jazz, Jazz Central Station Best Latin Jazz Artist Award; Disney Music Hall of Fame, 1994; 4 Scholarships given in his name at various USA universities. *Membership:* ITG; IAJE; NARAS. *Current Management:* Carl Valldejuli, Turi's Music Ent Inc. *Address:* 103 Westward Dr., Miami Springs, FL 33166, USA.

SANDREN, Heikki; b. 1 June 1960, Finland. Musician (drums). *Education:* Clarinet and drums; Sibelius Acadmey, Helsinki. *Career:* Began in music shop, early 1980s; Became professional musician; Member, Pekka Toivanen quartet; Played for Severi Pyysalo's No Hope Band; Stayed with Pyysalo's re-formed band The Front; Played on tour with leading Finnish trumpeter Markku Johansson. *Address:* Lönnrotinkatu 23 B 31, 00120 Helsinki, Finland.

SANDRESKY, Eleanor; b. 5 Oct. 1957, NC, USA. Composer; Musician (piano). m. Dan Russell Dryden. *Education:* North Carolina School of Arts; Wisconsin Conservatory of Music; Eastman School of Music; Yale University School of Music. *Career:* Performed with Philip Glass Ensemble, 1991–; Co Artistic Director, Producer, Music at the Anthology, NY; Freelance Composer, Pianist, NY. *Compositions:* Mathematically Inclined; It's Come Undone; Regarding Women; My Goddess. *Recordings:* La Belle et le Bete; Complete Works of William Russell. *Honours:* Ascap Special Award, 1998, 1999; Grants from Meet the Composer Jerome Foundation and NYSCA; Most Promising Composer Award, from Yale School of Music. *Membership:* American Music Centre; American Composers Forum; ASCAP. *Address:* 81 Warren St, New York, NY 10007, USA.

SANDS, Colum; b. 26 May 1951, Newry, Ireland. Vocalist; Songwriter; Musician. m. Barbara Wendel, 3 May 1978, 3 s., 1 d. *Career:* Tours with Sands Family, 1972–, USA (including Carnegie Hall), Canada, Ireland, England, Germany, Belgium, France, Spain, Portugal, Netherlands, Switzerland, Austria, Italy, Poland, Luxembourg. *Compositions:* Solo albums: Unapproved Road, 1981; March Ditch, 1989; All My Winding Journeys, 1996; with Sharon Aviv, Talking To The Wall, 2002; Guest appearance: The Man With The Red Guitar, Anthony John Clarke, 1999; Songs include: Whatever You Say, Say Nothing; Almost Every Circumstance; The Man with the Cap; Looking the Loan of a Spade. *Publications:* Between the Earth and the Sky, song book, 2001. *Honours:* Living Tradition Award, Glasgow, 1996. *Membership:* PRS; MCPS. *Current Management:* Spring Records. *Address:* 50 Shore Rd, Rostrevor, County Down, BT34 3EW, Ireland.

SANDS, Tommy; b. 19 Dec. 1945, Mayobridge, Co Down, Northern Ireland. Vocalist; Songwriter; Musician (guitar, whistle, banjo, bodhran). m. Katrine Bescond, 1 s., 1 d. *Education:* Latin, Philosophy, Newry St Colman's College, St Patrick's Carlow. *Career:* Began playing with Sands Family, first album, 1968; Concerts, Carnegie Hall, New York, USA, 1972; Federick Palast, Berlin, 1974; Moscow Olympic Stadium, solo; Numerous world tours including appearances with Miriam Makeba; Harry Belafonte; Pete Seeger; Mikis Theodorakis. *Compositions:* There Were Roses; Daughters and Sons; Dresden; Music of Healing, with Pete Seeger; Sudako and 1000 Paper Cranes; Sarajevo, with Vedran Smailovic and Joan Baez. *Recordings:* 5 solo albums: Singing of the Times, 1985; Beyond the Shadows, 1992; Down By Bendys Lane, 1993; Hedges of County Down, 1994; The Hearts A Wonder, 1995; To Shorten The Winter, 2001; 20 albums with the Sands Family. *Publications:* Tommy Sands Song Book, 1986. *Honours:* Best Irish Single of the Year, There Were Roses, 1986; Living Tradition Award, 1995. *Membership:* PRS; MCPS; MIMA. *Current Management:* Katrine Bescond, Spring Records.

SANGARE, Oumou; b. 1968, Bamako, Mali. Vocalist; Songwriter. m. Ousmane Haidara, 1 c. *Career:* Began singing age 5; First performance, Stade des Omnisports, age 6; Member, National Ensemble of Mali; Djioliba percussion, 1986–89; Solo artiste, with own backing group, 1989–; Concerts: Regular tours, West Africa; Europe; First US concert, 1994; Radio includes: BBC Radio 1 session, Andy Kershaw; Television includes: The Late Show, BBC2; Campaigner, Women's Rights, Mali. *Recordings:* Moussolou (Women), 1990; Ko Sira (Marriage Today), 1993; Worotan, 1996; Appears on: African Blues, 1998; Beloved, 1998; Also recording with Ali Farka Touré; Trilok Gurtu. *Honours:* Best Selling African Album of Year, Moussolou, 1990; European World Music Album of the Year, Ko Sira, 1993; Performance of the Year, 1993; Numerous African Music Awards. *Current Management:* Wim Westerweldt. *Address:* c/o World Circuit Records, 106 Cleveland St, London W1P 5DP, England.

SANLUCAR, Manolo; b. 24 Nov. 1943, Sanlucar De Barrameda, Cádiz, Spain. Composer; Musician (Flamenco guitar). *Education:* Learnt to play guitar with father (famous Flamenco guitarist). *Career:* Musical Director, Sevillanas a Carlos Saura, film; La Gallarda, Rafael Alberti. *Compositions:* Medea, composed for Ballet Nacional de España; Tauromagia; Solea. *Honours:* Prize Spanish Guitarist, Record World, USA, 1978; First Prize, Concurso Mundial de Guitarra, Italy, 1972; National Music Prize, Caja Madrid Flamenco Festival, 2001. *Current Management:* Intercambio de Cultura y Arte. *Address:* Calle Carretas, 14-5 I-5, 28012 Madrid, Spain.

SANSOM, Frank Roger Charles; b. 3 Dec. 1946, London, England. Co Dir. m. Frances Sansom, 27 March 1976, 2 s., 1 d. *Education:* Christopher Wren, Gloucestershire and Wimbledon College of Art; Jack Jackson: Ready Steady Go; 6 5 Special. *Career:* Art Director, BandC Records, 1971; Marketing Director, Charisma Records, 1973–78; Management, 1979–81; Set up First Bill Ltd (First Independent Tele-Sales Team), 1981; First Strike, 1985; Sold companies to Stylus Music, 1987; TV Marketing Consultant, 1987–90; Managing Director, shareholder, Pulse Records launched 1990–95.

Membership: BPI. *Address:* 53A Hereford Rd, Bayswater, London W2 5BB, England.

SANTANA, Carlos; b. 20 July 1947, Autlán de Navarro, Mexico. Musician (guitar); Vocalist. m. Deborah, April 1973. *Career:* Played Tijuana nightclubs; Founder, Santana Blues Band, 1966, playing club circuit, San Francisco; Numerous concerts, world tours, television and radio appearances, incl. Woodstock, 1969; Performed or recorded with: Mike Bloomfield, Al Kooper, Buddy Miles, McCoy Tyner, Jose Feliciano, Herbie Hancock, Wayne Shorter, Alice Coltrane, Aretha Franklin; Prod., music for La Bamba, 1986; Solo artiste, 1987–; Founder, Guts and Grace label, 1989. *Recordings:* Albums: with Santana Band: Santana, 1969; Abraxas, 1970; Santana III, 1971; Caravanserai, 1972; Welcome, 1973; Greatest Hits, 1974; Borboletta, 1974; Lotus, 1975; Festival, 1976; Amigos, 1976; Moonflower, 1977; Inner Secrets, 1978; Marathon, 1979; Zebop!, 1981; Shango, 1982; Beyond Appearances, 1985; Freedom, 1987; Viva Santana, 1988; Spirits Dancing In The Flesh, 1990; Milagro, 1992; Sacred Fire, 1993; Dance Of The Rainbow Serpent, 1995; Live At Fillmore 1968, 1997; Best Of Santana, 1998; Supernatural, 1999; The Essential Santana, 2002; Shaman, 2002; Solo: Carlos Santana And Buddy Miles, Live!, 1972; Love, Devotion, Surrender (with Mahavishnu John McLaughlin), 1973; Illuminations (with Alice Coltrane), 1974; Orness, Silver Dreams–Golden Reality, 1979; Swing Of Delight, 1980; Havana Moon, 1983; Blues For Salvador, 1987; Brothers, 1994; Evolution: Original Recordings, 1995; Acapulco Sunrise, 1999; Numerous collaborations, contributions and guest appearances. *Honours:* CBS Records, Crystal Globe Award; Grammy Awards, incl. Best Rock Instrumental Performance, 1989, Song of the Year, Record of the Year, Pop Performance of the Year, Rock Performance of the Year, Rock Instrumental Performance, Rock Album, 2000; NARAS tribute concert and induction into Hollywood Rock Walk; Bay Area Music Award, Outstanding Guitarist, 1992; Nosotros Golden Eagle Legend Award, 1992; Billboard Magazine Century Award, 1996; Chicano Music Award, Latino Music Legend of the Year, 1997; Inducted, Rock 'n' Roll Hall of Fame, Hollywood Walk of Fame, 1998; Numerous Gold and Platinum discs. *Current Management:* Santana Management, PO Box 10348, San Rafael, CA 94912–0348, USA. *Website:* www.santana.com.

SANTIAGO, Joey; b. 10 June 1965, Manila, Philippines. Musician (guitar). *Career:* Formed The Pixies with Frank Black; Early support slots to Throwing Muses; Numerous tours and festival dates; Some television appearances; Band split, 1993; Worked with Frank Black on his solo material; Formed The Martinis, with David Lovering, 1995. *Recordings:* Singles: Gigantic, 1988; Monkey Gone to Heaven, 1989; Here Comes Your Man, 1989; Velouria, 1990; Dig for Fire, 1990; Planet of Sound, 1991; Head On, 1991; Debaser, 1997; Albums: Come on Pilgim, 1987; Surfer Rosa, 1988; Doolittle, 1989; Bossanova, 1990; Trompe le Monde, 1991; Death To The Pixies, 1997; Complete B-Sides, 2001; with Frank Black: Singles: Hang On To Your Ego, 1993; Headache, 1994; Albums: Frank Black, 1993; Teenager Of The Year, 1994.

SANZ, Alejandro; b. 18 Dec. 1968, Madrid, Spain. Vocalist. *Career:* Signed to WEA Latina, 1991. *Recordings:* Albums: Viviendo Deprisa, 1991; Si Tú Me Miras, 1992; 3, 1995; Más, 1997; Básico, 1998; El Alma Al Aire, 2000; MTV Unplugged, 2001; El Concierto Tour Mas 98, 2002; Canta Como, 2002. *Honours:* Amigo Awards, Best National Male Artist, 1997, Special Tribute, 1998; Ondas Awards, Best National Artist, 1997, Best Song for Corazón Partío, 1998; World Music Awards, Best Selling Spanish Artist, 1999; Premios Gardel de la Música, Best Male Artist, Album of the Year, 2002; Latin Grammy Awards, Record of the Year, for Y Solo Se Me Ocurre Amarte, Album of the Year, for MTV Unplugged, Song of the Year, for Y Solo Se Me Ocurre Amarte, 2002. *Address:* WEA Latina, 5201 Blue Lagoon Dr., Suite 200, Miami, FL 33126, USA. *Website:* www.alejandrosanz.com.

SAPUNDZIJEV, Mary; b. 16 Feb. 1965, Melbourne, Vic. , Australia. Musicologist; Composer; Songwriter; Librettist. *Education:* BA, Music Major, 1986, BA Hons, Music, 1988, PhD, Music, 1997, Monash University. *Career:* Artistic Dir, folk dance co, 1984–92; Film appearance, The John Sullivan Story, 1979; Stage appearance, Sale of the Century, 1983–86; Production Asst, ethnic radio, Victoria; Dancer and co-organizer, cultural festivals throughout Australia. *Publications:* Politics in Music—Music of Politics: The Choral Miniature Repertoire of First Generation Macedonian Composers (PhD dissertation); Motivation, Function and Value (article in IRASM), 2002. *Honours:* Shared Ernst Morawetz Prize for Music, Monash University, 1987; Australian Postgraduate Research Award, 1988–91. *Fax:* (3) 9877-3810.

SARA K; b. 16 May 1956, Dallas, Texas, USA. Vocalist; Songwriter; Musician (4-string guitar). 1 d. *Education:* Art, music studies. *Career:* Chesky recording artist; PBS Radio Australia; Mountain Stage; US and international airplay. *Recordings:* Gypsy Alley; Closer Than They Appear; Play On Words; Tell Me I'm Not Dreamin', 1995; Hobo; 1997; No Cover, 1999; What Matters, 2001; with Glad I'm A Girl: Glad I'm A Girl, 1997; Postman (music from the motion picture), 1997. *Honours:* Gypsy Alley, received 8 awards from New Mexico Music Industry Coalition including Best Album, 1990; Audio-Ohr award, Grammy, Play On Words album, 1994. *Current Management:* Chesky Records, New York, NY, USA. *Address:* PO Box 696, Ruidoso, NM 88345, USA.

SARIC, Stanko; b. 26 June 1960, Stitar, Croatia. Musician (tambura – Tours all around the world: USA; Canada; Australia; Western Europe. *Recordings:* Patriotic songs: Don't Touch My Fields; Croatia In Me; Singing The Song About Croatia; Other popular songs: Crying Because of You; Tena; Marijana; High Road; Anica; To Whom Could I Give My Young Years; 13 albums; Christmas Songs; Classical Music. *Honours:* 10 Golden Records, many other awards. *Membership:* Croatian Musical Union. *Current Management:* Josip Ivanovic. *Address:* Zlatni Dukati, Zatisje 8E, 41000, Zagreb, Croatia.

SARJEANT, Derek; b. 7 June 1930, Chatham, Kent, England. Folk Vocalist; Musician (concertina, guitar, trumpet). m. (1) Diane Doherty, 23, Sept. 1966, 2 s., (2) Hazel King, 10 Sept. 1977, 1 s., 1 d. *Education:* Kingston College. *Career:* Member, jazz bands, leader, Golden Gate Jazzmen, 1950s; Pioneer, British Folk revival, 1960s; Organizer, one of Britain's largest Folk clubs, Surbiton and Kingston for 14 years; Assisted with Organisation of English Folk Dance and Songs Society's First Folk Festival, 1965; Radio and television, all British stations including: Hootenanny Show; Folk In Focus; Television commercials on all British independent channels, also USA; Tours solo, also with wife, Hazel: Folk clubs, concerts, festivals in UK, Europe, America; Work as session musician; Teaches Folk guitar at Adult Education Centre. *Recordings:* 24 albums, British and German labels. *Publications:* Books with records: How Do You Do, stages 1–5 (English Folk Songs For German Schools). *Honours:* First English Folk singer booked in Dublin Folkclub, 1962; Melody Maker Folk Medal of Year, Best First Record, Derek Sarjeant Sings English Folk Songs, 1962; Represented Britain, British Week, Stockholm, Sweden, 1968. *Membership:* Musicians' Union. *Current Management:* Assembly Artistes. *Address:* 4 Coneygar House, Coneygar Park, Bridport, Dorset DT6 3BA, England.

SARJEANT, Hazel; b. 11 Oct. 1948, London, England. Folk Vocalist; Musician (guitar, concertina). m. Derek Sarjeant, 10 Sept. 1977, 1 s., 1 d. *Education:* Wimbledon College of Art; St Martin's College of Art; BA (Fine Arts); Trained in various choirs. *Career:* Resident singer, Surbiton Folkclub, 6 years; Frequent tours, concerts, festivals, folkclubs, UK, Europe and USA; National radio and television; Film music for USA. *Recordings:* 14 albums, cassettes, UK and German labels. *Honours:* BA Fine Arts; Winner, National Folk and Beat Final, Hammersmith Town Hall, 1967. *Membership:* Musicians' Union; Royal College of Church Music. *Current Management:* Assembly Artists. *Address:* 4 Coneygar House, Coneygar Park, Bridport, Dorset DT6 3BA, England.

SARMANTO, Heikki; b. 22 June 1939, Finland. Composer; Musician (piano). *Education:* Music and language, Helsinki University and Sibelius Academy, 1962–64; Lessons with Margaret Chaloff, Berklee College of Music, Boston, USA, 1968–71. *Career:* Regular visits to East Coast of USA; Own ensemble became UMO (New Music Orchestra); Played Jazz Mass, Newport Festival, 1979. *Compositions include:* New Hope Jazz Mass (premiered in New York); Jazz Mass; Jazz opera; Songs to words by Finnish poets including: Edith Södergran; Laura Vita; Eino Leino; 3 suites for soloists: Maija Hapuoja; Juhani Aaltonen; Pekka Sarmanto; Suomi, suite for jazz ensemble and strings; Passions of Man, ballet suite; Music for radio stories by Robert Shure: Man With A Sax; Felix The Great; Hearts (commissioned by WHO), 1995. *Recordings include:* Distant Dreams; The Traveller; Tales of Max; Orchestral Works. *Honours:* First prize, Jazz composition contest, Minneapolis, 1961; Yrjö Award, Finnish Jazz Federation, 1970. *Address:* Kankurinkatu 8 B 14, 00150 Helsinki, Finland.

SARMANTO, Pekka; b. 15 Feb. 1945, Finland. Musician (bass). *Education:* Sibelius Academy. *Career:* One of Finland's most recorded artists; Played with: Eero Koivisoinen, 1965–; Long term partnership playing with brother Heikki Sarmanto; Played at The Groovy Club, with artists including: Benny Carter; Toots Thielmans; Clifford Jordan; Joe Newman; Bob Berg; Tom Harrell; Member of UMO (New Music Orchestra), 1975–; Accompanist to numerous visiting foreign musicians; Festival appearances include: Warsaw; London; Paris; Newport; Montréal; Soloist, performance Heikki Sarmanto's suite, Song For My Brother, 1982; Duo with Juhani Aaltonen, 1980s. *Recordings include:* To A Finland Station, with Dizzy Gillespie and Arturo Sandoval, 1982; with Umo Jazz Orchestra: Umo Jazz Orchestra, 1998; One More Time, 2000; Transit People, 2001; with Thad Jones: That Jones Mel Lewis and Umo, 1998. *Honours:* Yrjö Award, Finnish Jazz Federation, 1978. *Address:* Albertinkatu 5 B 27, 00150 Helsinki, Finland.

SÁROSI, Bálint; b. 1 Jan. 1925, Csikrákos, Harghita, Romania. Ethnomusicologist. m. Benkö Jolán, 18 Oct. 1952, 2 d. *Education:* PhD, University; Composition and Musicology, Liszt Ferenc High School of Music, Budapest, Hungary. *Career:* Research Fellow, Institute for Musicology, Budapest, 1956–, Director, Ethnomusicological Section, 1974–, retired, 1988; Lectures on folk music, Hungarian Radio, weekly programme, 1969–87; Guest Professor, University of Innsbruck, 1985–86, University of Göttingen, 1989, 1994; Invited Lecturer, most countries of Europe and USA, Japan, Armenia and Samarkand, Jerusalem. *Recordings:* Hungarian Instrumental Folk Music, 3 discs, 1980; Anthology of Hungarian Folk Music V and VI, 1993, 1995. *Publications:* Die Volksmusikinstrumente Ungarus, 1967; Gypsy Music, 1978; Folk Music, 1986; Sackpfeifer Zigeunermusikanten, 1999. *Honours:* Erkel

Prize, 1976; Order of Labour, Golden Degree, 1988; Middle Cross of the Order of Hungarian Republic, 1995; Presidential Gold Medal, 2000. *Membership:* Executive Board, International Council for Traditional Music, 1978–91. *Address:* Aldás u 11, 1025 Budapest, Hungary.

SARPILA, Antti Juhani; b. 11 June 1964, Helsinki, Finland. Musician (clarinet, saxophones). m. Minna Niemela, 23 April 1994, 3 s. *Education:* Private studies with Bob Wilber, USA, 1981–83. *Career:* Freelance Jazz Musician; Performances as soloist with different jazz orchestras world-wide including Tribute to Benny Goodman Concert at the Carnegie Hall, New York and Royal Ellington Concert at Royal Festival Hall, London. *Compositions:* Around 100 published compositions and arrangements, mostly recorded. *Recordings:* Numerous recordings under own name and around 50 recordings as guest musician including: Peter Meyer; Ralph Sutton; Allan Vache; Bob Wilber. *Honours:* George Award, Finnish Jazz Federation, 1997. *Membership:* Finnish Composers and Authors Society. *Address:* Museokatu 26 A 14, 00100 Helsinki, Finland.

SARSTEDT, Peter; Folk Vocalist; Songwriter. m. Joanna. *Recordings:* Albums: Peter Sarstedt, 1969; PS..., 1979; Up Date, 1981; Asia Minor, 1987; Never Say Goodbye, 1987; Where Do You Go To, 2000; The Legends Collection, 2001; with Eden Kane and Robin Sarstedt: Worlds Apart Together, 1973; Singles: I Am A Cathedral; Where Do You Go To My Lovely (No. 1, UK), 1969; Frozen Orange Juice, 1969; Beirut; Love Among The Ruins, 1982; Appears on: Acoustic Highway Collection, 1996. *Address:* c/o Jason West Agency, Kings Lynn, Norfolk, England.

SARTORIUS, Paula; b. 18 Feb. , New York, USA. Artist Man. *Education:* BA, Fordham University. *Career:* Artist Manager, Side One Management, for: Los Lobos; Luscious Jackson.

SASH!, (Sascha Lappessen); b. 1971, Wuppertal, Germany. DJ; Prod. *Career:* Electrical Engineer; Started as DJ; Began producing as Sash!, with Thomas Lüdke and Ralf Kappmeier; Numerous gigs, television appearances and hit singles throughout Europe; Remixer for Jean-Michel Jarre and Dr Alban. *Recordings:* Singles: It's My Life, 1996; Ecuador, 1997; Erotmania 97, 1997; Stay, 1997; Encore Une Fois, 1997; La Primavera, 1998; Mysterious Times, 1998; Ma Baker, 1998; Colour the World, 1998; Adelante, 1999; Just Around The Hill, 2000; With My Own Eyes, 2000; Albums: It's My Life, 1997; Life Goes On, 1998; Trillennium, 2000.

SASHA, (Alexander Coe); b. 4 Sept. 1969, Bangor, Wales. Prod; Remixer; DJ. *Career:* Began DJ career at the Hacienda in Manchester, then Shelly's in Stoke; World-wide DJ; Various mix compilations for Renaissance and Global Underground labels; Collaborations: Brian Transeau; Maria Nayler; Charlie May; Remixed: Urban Soul; M People; Mr Fingers; Madonna; Seal. *Recordings:* Album: Airdrawndagger, 2002. Singles: Appolonia (as BMEX), 1992; Arkham Asylum, 1996; Be As One (with Maria Nayler), 1996; Xpander, 1999; Scorchio (with Darren Emerson), 2000. *Honours:* Muzik Awards, Best DJ, 2001. *Current Management:* Ornadel Management. *Address:* c/o BMG UK & Ireland Ltd, Bedford House, 69–79 Fulham High St, London SW6 3JW, England. *Website:* www.djsasha.com.

SASSETTI, Bernardo; b. 24 June 1970, Lisbon, Portugal. Musician (piano); Jazz Composer. *Education:* Graduate, Lisbon Academy of Music. *Career:* Played with major jazz names including: John Stubblefield; Andy Sheppard; Frank Lacy; Al Grey; Art Farmer; Kenny Wheeler; Freddie Hubbard; Paquito d'Rivera; Benny Golson; Eddie Henderson; The United Nation Orchestra; Concerts in France; Spain; Italy; USA; South Africa; UK, including Ronnie Scott's, London. *Recordings:* Album: Salssetti, 1995; Andy Hamilton, Jamaica By Night, 1994; Carlos Martins, Passagem, 1997. *Honours:* Various local awards. *Membership:* Mem., Professor, Jazz School of HCP, Lisbon. *Current Management:* Paulo Santos Gil. *Address:* Rua Das Pracas, 66–1-DRT-1200, Lisbon, Portugal.

SATRIANI, Joe; b. 1956, Long Island, New York, USA. Musician (guitar, banjo, harmonica); Educator. *Career:* Founder member, The Squares; Member, Greg Kihn Band; Solo artiste, 1984–; British tour, 1995; Guitar tutor to rock musicians Steve Vai, Kirk Hammett. *Recordings:* with Greg Kihn Band: Love and Rock 'N' Roll, 1986; Solo: Joe Satriani (EP), 1984; Not of This Earth, 1986; Surfing With The Alien, 1987; Dreaming II, 1988; Flying In A Blue Dream, 1990; Joe Satriani, 1995; Crystal Planet, 1998; Engines Of Creation, 2000; Live In San Francisco, 2001. *Honours:* Several Grammy Awards. *Current Management:* Bill Graham Management. *Address:* PO Box 429094, San Francisco, CA 94142–9094, USA.

SAUMAIWAI, Chris Thompson; b. 14 Aug. 1943, Cleveland, Ohio, USA. Businesswoman; Ethnomusicologist; Composer; Poet. m. 2 s., 1 d. *Education:* Cleveland Baldwin Wallace College; Cleveland Institute of Music; Private composition student of Donald ERB, 1958–61; George F Strickling, CHHS Choir, 1959–63; Voice, Carmela Caffarelli, 1959–63; Oboe, Harvey McGuire, 1961–63; Music theory and composition, Baldwin Wallace Conservatory of Music, 1961–65; Music theory and composition, Cleveland Institute of Music, 1963–65. *Career:* Various hotels in Fiji, Hawaii and New Zealand as part of

Counterstroke EWI benefit concerts including Suva Travelodge, Centra Suva, Wellington Park Royal Hotel, New Zealand; Also sang at Trigger Prince Kuhio Hotel, Honolulu. *Compositions:* Haiko Spring, Song Cycle; Sonnet II, Prayer of St Francis; The Waking; The Pasture; Supper Stew Blues; Could I Have Loved You More; Not Me Baby; Settler's Blues. *Publications:* Groves Dictionary of Music Vol. 12 Melanesia, Fiji; Music of Sem Conference, 1981; Fijian Lullabies and Games, Honolulu; Fiji Society, 1966; Music and Dance of Fiji Musical; Urban Fijian Musical Attitudes and Ideals (Music Cultures in Contact), 1993, Melbourne. *Membership:* Muphi Epsilon Soroptimist International; Society for Ethnomusicology (life member). *Address:* PO Box 1206, Suva, Fiji.

SAUNDERS, Cameron; b. 18 Feb. 1973, Cuxhaven, England. Musician. m. Louise Latham, 22 May 1994. *Education:* BA, Social Anthropology, King's College, Cambridge. *Career:* Mem., New Atlantic (1989–93); Extensive tours, UK, especially Scotland; Television: Hitman and Her, 1992; Top of the Pops, 1992; Radio: BBC Radio 1; Capital Radio; World Service; Interviews; Debut broadcast, Radio Berlin International (club of). *Recordings:* I Know, 1992; Global, 1995. Singles: Sunshine After The Rain, 1995; I Know, 1999. *Honours:* Scottish Clubscene 1992: Best Newcomer, Runner-up best dance band. *Membership:* Musicians' Union; PRS. *Address:* 16 Shirdley Cres., Ainsdale, Southport PR8 3RR, England.

SAUNDERS, Eddie (Edward John); b. 6 July 1965, London, England. Lead Vocalist; Composer; Lyricist; Musician (percussion, various other instruments). *Career:* Founder member, lead vocalist, Push; Lead and back-up vocals, Groove Nation; Extensive live appearances UK, Europe; Live work with the above, also: Reuben Wilson (Push was his UK pick-up band); Omar; Leon Ware; Jo Cang; Boogie Back All Stars; Support to Curtis Mayfield; Airto and Flora Purim; Maceo Parker; Average White Band. *Recordings:* Traffic, track on Acid Jazz and Other Illicit Grooves compilation (first ever Acid Jazz record), 1988; Further recordings with Push; Talbot/White; Jo Cang; Galliano; Groove Nation; Steve Beresford, Cue Sheets. *Membership:* PRS; Musicians' Union; MCPS. *Current Management:* Represented by Alexis Grower, McGrath and Co. *Address:* 18 Dartmouth Park Ave, London NW5 1JN, England.

SAUNDERS, Gerry (Gerald Ivor Ewart); b. 3 Nov. 1929, Plymouth, Devon, England. Musician (percussion); Radio Presenter; Writer. *Career:* ENSA, 1943–45; Theatre Pit, 1945–47; RAF, 1947–49; Big band/Orchestra tours, 1949–55; Magazine proprietor, broadcasting, writing, 1955–65; Musical/club proprietor (6 clubs), music/stage producer, jazz tours, 1965–80; Musical/stage tours, writing, band management, broadcasting, 1980–93; National Executive, South East District Council; Chairman Bournemouth Branch, Musicians' Union; Radio presenter; Writer; Jazz tours, 1980–. *Publications:* Playtime Entertainment Newspaper; Editor and Publisher, Secretary, Editor, Video Record. *Membership:* National Executive Musicians' Union; Chairman, British Citizens Band Confederation; Chief Executive, National Citizens Band Confederation; Chairman, Bournemouth Branch, Musicians' Union; Director, Coastal Radio, community radio station. *Address:* 12 Lincoln Ave, Springbourne, Bournemouth, Dorset BH1 4QS, England.

SAUNDERS, Mark; b. 20 March 1959, Basingstoke, Hampshire, England. Mixing Engineer; Record Prod; *Recordings:* Albums: Raw Like Sushi, Neneh Cherry; Wild, Erasure; Maxinquaye, Tricky; Singles: with The Cure: Lullaby; Lovesong; with The Farm: Groovy Train; with Lisa Stansfield: This Is The Right Time; Erasure: Little Respect; Wild!; Blue Savannah; Star; Buffalo Stance, Neneh Cherry; Rapture, Siouxsie and the Banshees; Madder Rose, Tragic Magic; David Byrne, Feelings; John Lydon, Psycho's Path; Depeche Mode, Strangelove (remix); Cathy Dennis; The Chamelons; Coldcut; Laptop; Madness; The Mission. *Address:* The Smoothside Organisation, Ashbank, Heyford Rd, Middleton Stoney, Oxfordshire OX6 8SH, England.

SAUNDERS, Roger; b. 9 March 1947, Barking, Essex, England. Musician (guitar, piano). *Career:* Member, Medicine Head, Freedom; Television includes: Top of the Pops; Jonathan Ross; Concerts include: Wembley Stadium; Wembley Arena; Tours throughout USA, including Madison Square Gardens, New York; Middle East including Dubai, Bahrain; Europe including Germany, France, Italy, Spain, Norway, Denmark, Sweden, Finland; Concerts with: Medicine Head; Gary Glitter; Peter Skelton; Duane Eddy; Chicken Shack; Numerous recordings; Over 600 songs published. *Membership:* PRS; MCPS; Songwriters Guild; Musicians' Union. *Address:* Barking, Essex, England.

SAUNDERSON, Kevin, (Reese, E-Dancer); b. 5 Sept. 1964, Brooklyn, New York, USA. Prod; Remixer; DJ. *Career:* Formed the Belleville Three with Juan Atkins and Derrick May; Founder: KMS Records; Member: Inner City; The Reese Project; Collaborations: Santonio Echols; Juan Atkins; Paris Grey; Remixed: Pet Shop Boys; Paula Abdul; New Order. *Recordings:* Albums: with Inner City: Paradise, 1989; Fire, 1990; Praise, 1992; with The Reese Project: Faith, Hope and Clarity, 1993; as E-Dancer: Heavenly, 1998; Singles: as Reese: Just Another Chance, 1987; Rock To The Beat, 1987; The Groove That Won't Stop, 1988; with Inner City: Big Fun, 1988; Good Life, 1988; Pennies From Heaven, 1992; Ahnonghay, 1994; Buena Vida (Good Life), 1998; Good Love, 2001; with The Reese Project: Direct Me, 1991; as E-Dancer: Heavenly, 1998. *Address:* c/o Play It Again Sam, 338A Ladbroke Grove, London W10 5AH, England.

SAVAGE, Rick; b. 2 Dec. 1960, Sheffield, England. Rock Musician (bass); Vocalist. *Career:* Bass player, UK rock group Def Leppard, 1977–; International concerts include: Support tours with Sammy Hagar; AC/DC; Ted Nugent; Reading Rock Festival, 1980; World tour, 1983; Monsters of Rock Festival, Castle Donington, 1986; World tour, 1988; Freddie Mercury Tribute Concert, Wembley, 1992. *Recordings:* Albums: On Through The Night, 1980; High 'n' Dry, 1981; Pyromania, 1983; Hysteria, 1987; Adrenalize, 1992; Retroactive, 1993; Vault 1980–95, 1995; Slang, 1996; Getcha Rocks Off, 1997; X, 2002; with others: Wild One: The Best of Thin Lizzy, 1996; Deseo de Oir Tu Voz, 1996; Europe, 1997. Singles include: Photograph, 1983; Rock of Ages, 1983; Foolin'; Animal, 1987; Pour Some Sugar On Me, 1987; Love Bites (No. 1, USA), 1988; Rocket, 1989; Make Love Like A Man, 1992; Let's Get Rocked, 1992; Stand Up (Kick Love Into Motion); Heaven Is, 1993; Two Steps Behind, featured in film soundtrack The Last Action Hero, 1993; When Love and Hate Collide, 1995; Slang, 1996; Goodbye, 1999; Now, 2002. *Honours:* American Music Awards: Favourite Heavy Metal Album, Favourite Heavy Metal Artists, 1989. *Current Management:* Q-Prime Inc. *Address:* 729 Seventh Ave, 14th Floor, New York, NY 10019, USA. *Website:* www.defleppard.com.

SAVANNAH, Jonn; b. 13 Jan. 1957, Nairobi, Kenya. Musician. m. Marie. *Education:* 1 year college; Grade 4 piano. *Career:* Toured with: Tina Turner; Squeeze; Van Morrison; Session work; Backing vocals, Kylie Minogue, Light Years, 2000; No. 3 hit, Germany, 1984; Signed publishing deal with EMI UK, 1994. *Recordings:* The Catch: 25 Years (No. 3, Germany). *Membership:* PAMRA; Musicians' Union; MCPS. *Address:* Little Barn, Plaistow Rd, Loxwood, West Sussex RH14 0SX, England.

SAVOLAINEN, Jarmo Tapio; b. 24 May 1961, Iisalmi, Finland. Composer; Musician (piano, keyboards). m. Helena Haaranen, 1 d. *Education:* Jazz and composition studies, Berklee College of Music, Boston, USA. *Career:* Member, various groups including: Finnforest; Blue Train; Formed own nine-piece ensemble and quartet; Duos with Make Lievonen, 1988; Seppo Kantonen, 1990; Major jazz festivals world-wide, including Jukkis Uotila Quintet, Paris, 1984; EBU Big Band, Pori Jazz, 1985; Kalott Jazz and Blues Festival, 1995; Television appearances on many European national networks. *Compositions:* Music for big bands, theatre and films. *Recordings:* Blue Dreams, 1987; Songs For Solo Piano, 1990; First Sight, 1992; True Image, 1995; Another Story, 1997; John's Sons, 1998; Grand Style, 2000; First Sight, 2000; Times Like These, 2002; with Klaus Suonsaari: Something in Common, 1998; with Jukkis Uotila: Hunters & Gatherers, 2000. *Honours:* Jazz Musician of the Year, Finland, 1994. *Membership:* Finnish Light Music Composers. *Address:* Porvoonkatu 17 B 25, 00510 Helsinki, Finland.

SAWHNEY, Nitin; b. 1964, Kent, England. Musician (keyboards, guitar); Remixer; Prod; Composer. *Education:* Liverpool University, Law. *Career:* Solo recordings feature influences of many cultures, including Indian, Flamenco, Jazz, Dance; Also composed for commercials, TV and film soundtracks; Prod. and remixed other artists' work; Actor, comedian: Secret Asians double act; Goodness Gracious Me (BBC); Toured with the James Taylor Quartet; Formed, The Jazztones; Worked with Talvin Singh in the Tihai Trio; Musical Dir, Theatre Royal (Stratford East), London; Provided music for the National Theatre; Composed music for documentary series, The Sikhs; Written for films: The Dance of Shiva; Split Wide Open; Written and prod. for Amar and Aya; Songs recorded by: Sinead O'Connor, Shara Nelson; Remixed: Mandalay; Khaled; Mondo Gross; Worked on Sir Paul McCartney's project, The Fireman; Urban Prophecies, a commission for the Proms, premiered at the Albert Hall, conducted by Cameron Sinclair, featuring Joanne MacGreggor (piano) and Aref Durvesh (tabla), 2000. *Recordings:* Albums: Spirit Dance, 1993; Migration, 1995; Displacing The Priest, 1996; Introduction To Nitin Sawhney; Beyond Skin, 1999; Prophesy, 2001; features on: Drum The Bass, Shri, 1997; Intro, Mandalay, 2000; Ayeshteni, Natacha Atlas, 2001; Dallali, Cheb Mami, 2001. *Honours:* The South Bank Show Award for Popular Music, 2000; BBC Radio 3 Award for World Music, Boundary Crossing, 2002. *Current Management:* Worldwide Management. *E-mail:* spiritdancetour@aol.com. *Website:* www.nitinsawhney.com.

SAWTELL, Paul; b. 1 May 1959, Stourbridge, West Midlands, England. Arranger; Composer; MD; Musician (piano). *Education:* Classical training. *Career:* Numerous BBC Radio Sessions; Television Shows with Tom Jones; Shirley Bassey; Neil Sedaka; Worked with Peter King; Dick Morrisey; Jim Mullen; Norma Whinstone. *Compositions:* Over 200 Pieces. *Recordings:* 10 albums. *Address:* 20 Seymour Rd, Stourbridge, West Midlands, DY9 8TB, England.

SAYER, Ron James; b. 24 Oct. 1970, Wisbech, Lincolnshire, England. Musician (guitar, bass); Vocalist; Songwriter; Teacher. *Education:* BA Hons in Music; Grade 8 Electric Guitar, Grade 8 Bass Guitar. *Career:* Bassist, composer with: Monster; Spider Murphy; Played live concert broadcast on Friday Rock Show, Radio 1; Sound City 1992; Toured supporting: Quireboys; Skin; Mr Big; L7; Mini-tour with Monster and Supercircus, including Royal

Standard, London; Currently guitarist with Purple Ronnie. *Recordings:* Radio broadcast concert included: So Here It Is; Innocence; What Would U Do; My Mind's Treasure; released on Rock The Canary album. *Honours:* Guitarist of the Year, 1996–97. *Membership:* Musicians' Union; PRS; Guild of International Songwriters and Composers (GISC). *Address:* 27 Morris Rd, North Walsham, Norfolk NR28 0EJ, England.

SAYYID, M; Vocalist. *Career:* Released cassette-only recordings on Anti-Pop Recordings label; Mem., The Anti-Pop Consortium, 1997–2002; Supported DJ Shadow's US tour, 2002; Solo artiste, 2002–; Technical advisor, film Hurricane Streets. *Recordings:* Albums: Tragic Epilogue, 2000; Arrhythmia, 2002. Singles: Diagonal Ryme Gargantua (EP), 2000; What Am I?, 2000; Lift, 2000; The Ends Against The Middle (EP), 2001; Ghostlawns, 2002. *Current Management:* Amaechi Uzoigwe, Ozone Music. *Address:* c/o Warp Records Ltd, Spectrum House, 32–34 Gordon House Rd, London NW5 1LP, England. *Website:* www.warprecords.com.

SCABIES, Rat, (Chris Miller); b. 30 July 1957, Kingston Upon Thames, Surrey, England. Musician (drums). *Career:* Member, groups Rat; London SS; Member, UK punk rock group, The Damned, 1976–77; Appearances include: Mont de Marsan punk festival, France, 1976; Support to Sex Pistols, Anarchy In The UK Tour, 1976; First UK punk band to play USA, 1977; Member, the White Cats, 1978; Rejoined the Damned, 1979–89; Regular international concerts include: Christmas On Earth Festival, Leeds, 1981; Farewell tour UK, 1989; UK reunion tour, 1991; Member, side project Naz and the Nomads, 1988. *Recordings:* Albums with the Damned: Damned, Damned, Damned, 1977; Music For Pleasure, 1977; Machine Gun Etiquette, 1979; The Black Album, 1980; The Best Of, 1981; Strawberries, 1982; Phantasmagoria, 1985; Anything, 1986; Light At The End of The Tunnel, 1987 Not of this Earth, 1996; Boxed Set, 1999; Eternal Damnation Live, 1999; with Naz and the Nomads: Give Daddy The Knife, Cindy, 1988; Singles with The Damned: New Rose, 1976; Neat Neat Neat, 1977; Love Song, 1979; Smash It Up, 1979; Grimly Fiendish, 1985; The Shadow of Love, 1985; Is It A Dream, 1985; Eloise, 1986; Gigolo, 1987; Alone Again Or, 1987.

SCAGGS, Boz; b. 8 June 1944, Ohio, USA. Musician (guitar); Vocalist. *Career:* Member, groups The Marksmen; The Ardells; Formed R&B group, The Wigs; Folk singer in Europe, successful in Sweden; Joined Steve Miller Band, 1967; Solo artiste, 1968–. *Recordings:* Albums: Boz, 1966; Boz Scaggs, 19069; Moments, 1971; Boz Scaggs and Band, 1971; My Time, 1972; Slow Dancer, 1974; Silk Degrees, 1976; Two Down Then Left, 1977; Middle Man, 1980; Hits!, 1980; Other Roads, 1988; Some Change, 1994; Come on Home, 1997; Fade into Light (Japan bonus track), 1999; Dig, 2001; Hit singles include: Lowdown (No. 3, USA); What Can I Say?; Lido Shuffle; I'll be the One. *Current Management:* HK Management, 8900 Wilshire Blvd, Suite 300, Beverly Hills, CA 90211, USA.

SCARTH, Andrew; Record Prod; *Recordings:* Recordings for: Levellers; Heather Nova; Blameless; Skunk Anansie; Killing Joke; Mundy; Credit to the Nation; Addict; Underworld; Mainstream; Diamond Head; Bad Company; As Engineer: Howard Jones: Dream Into Action; Cross That Line; Prefab Sprout, Two Wheels Good; Tina Turner, Foreign Affair; Tesla, Time's Makin' Changes: The Best of Tesla; Drain STH, Freaks of Nature; Backyard Babies; Bob Geldof; Honeymoon Suite. *Current Management:* One Management Ltd, 43 St Alban's Ave, London W4 5JS, England.

SCARY SPICE. See: **BROWN, Melanie Janice.**

SCAVONE, Sam John; b. 12 July 1926, New York, USA. Musician (trumpet). m. (1) Esther Scavone, divorced 1961, 1 s., 1 d., (2) Marion Scavone, 1965, divorced 1973, 1 s., 1 d. *Education:* Hartnet School of Music, 1948–50. *Career:* Trumpeter, jazz groups, 1943–; Played with numerous artists including: Buddy Morrow; Woody Herman; Tito Puente; Xavier Cugat; Sammy Kaye; Tex Beneke; Charlie Spivak; Les Elgart.

SCHAC,K, Michael E. K; b. 11 May 1966, St Miklaas, Belgium. Musician (drums); Songwriter. *Education:* Economics, Degree in Marketing. *Career:* Blue Blot, 1987; Drummer, with Clouseau, 1995–97; Roland Demoband, 1992; Blue Blot Tour, 1992–94; Groovemania and Clouseau, 1995; Demonstrator, Sabian – Vic Firth Endorser – Slingerland Clinician, 1997. *Compositions:* Blue Blot: Pretty Good; New Blunk; Groovemania: Posativity; Mich van Hautem, Jacky; Beasone. *Recordings:* Blue Blot Albums, 1990–94; Orphan; September Rain; True Blue, Calvin Owens, 1993; De 7 Drumzonden; Live for Life, 1993; Drum Editor, Meetmusic, 1992–97. *Honours:* Drumvideo of the Year, 1996. *Membership:* SABAM, Uradex, Zamu, Belgium. *Current Management:* King IS, Leuvensesteemweg 120A, 3290 Diest, Belgium. *Address:* Eikstraat 49, 1981 Hofstade, Belgium.

SCHAFFER, Jan E. T; b. 24 Sept. 1945, Stockholm, Sweden. Musician. *Education:* University. *Career:* Professional from 1970–; Played on records with Abba (27 numbers); 10 solo albums (1 with Toto); Many television programmes. *Compositions:* About 120. *Recordings:* Hallmans Affair; Bersellii; Park and Electric Banana Band; Leif Strand: Year; Zodiac.

Publications: Play Guitar, with R Gustavsson. *Membership:* STIM; SAMI. *Address:* Dr Abrahamsu 43, 16152 Bromma, Sweden.

SCHECHTMAN, Saul; b. 4 Sept. 1924, Winchester, Connecticut, USA. Conductor; Composer. m. Carolyn Raney, 31 July 1952, 2 d. *Education:* BA, Brooklyn College, New York, 1947; Piano and French Horn, Greenwich House Music School; Theory, Brooklyn College; Orchestral Conducting, Juilliard School of Music. *Career:* Music Director, Bronx Symphony Orchestra, 1953–56, Bergen Philharmonic, New Jersey, 1956–60; Omnibus Programme, 1954–57; Original Cast, Carnival, 1961–63; Hello, Dolly, New York, 1966–70; How To Succeed, Paris, 1964; Orchestra Piccola, Baltimore, 1976–80. *Compositions:* Diaspora Variations for Orchestra; Incidental music for Auntie Mame, original play and film. *Recordings:* Carnival; Hello, Dolly, cast album, issued 1967; How to Succeed in Business, French production cast album. *Publications:* Recreations for Piano, 1967; Capriccio for Organ, 1968; Diaspora Variations for Orchestra, 1994. *Honours:* Juilliard Fellowship in Orchestral Conducting, 1949–51. *Membership:* ASCAP. *Address:* 134 Cathedral Ave, Hempstead, NY 11550, USA.

SCHEINER, Elliot; Music Dir; Prod; Engineer; Musician (percussion). *Career:* Percussionist, bands incl. Jimmy Buffett's Coral Reefers; Asst to Phil Ramone, A&R Recording, 1967, becoming engineer; Independent Engineer and Prod., 1973–; Co-Music Dir, DH1, 2002–; Authority on 5.1 Surround Sound mixing and DVD audio; Worked with: Aerosmith, George Benson, The Eagles, Fleetwood Mac, John Fogerty, Bruce Hornsby, Billy Joel, B. B. King, Ricky Martin, Steely Dan, Sting, Van Morrison. *Honours:* Four Grammy Awards. *Address:* c/o DH1 Studios, Woolworth Center, 233 Broadway, 22nd Floor, Suite 2200, New York, NY 10279, USA. *E-mail:* elliot@dh1.tv. *Website:* www.dh1.com.

SCHENKER, Michael; b. 10 Jan. 1955, Savstedt, Germany. Musician (guitar). *Career:* Founder, German heavy rock group The Scorpions, 1971–; Member, UFO, 1973–78; Rejoined Scorpions, 1979; Formed own band, The Michael Schenker Group, later called MSG, 1979–; Contributor, Contraband recording project (with members of Shark Island, Vixen, Ratt, LA Guns), 1991. *Recordings:* Albums: with the Scorpions: Lonesome Crow, 1972; Lovedrive, 1979; with UFO: Phenomenon, 1974; Force It, 1975; No Heavy Pettin', 1976; Lights Out, 1977; Strangers In The Night, 1977; Obsession, 1978; Deadly Sting : The Mercury Years, 1997; with MSG: The Michael Schenker Group, 1980; MSG, 1981; One Night At Budokan, 1982; Assault Attack, 1982; Built To Destroy, 1983; Rock Will Never Die, 1984; Perfect Timing, 1987; Save Yourself, 1989; Never Ending Nightmare, 1992; The Michael Schenker Life Story, 1997; Unforgiven, 1999; Written in Sand, 1999; The Unforgiven World Tour: Live, 1999; Unplugged (live), 1999; Adventures of the Imagination, 2000; Be Aware Of Scorpions, 2001; with Contraband: Contraband, 1991.

SCHENKER, Rudolph; b. 31 Aug. 1948, Germany. Musician (guitar); Songwriter. *Career:* Founder member, German heavy rock group The Scorpions, 1971–; World-wide tours; Concerts include: Support to Ted Nugent, USA, 1979; World tour, 1982; Support to Bon Jovi, USA, 1984; Leningrad, Russia, 1989; Festivals include: World Series of Rock, Cleveland, Ohio, 1979; Reading Rock Festival, 1983; US Festival, 1983; Rock In Rio, Brazil, 1985; Moscow Music Peace Festival, 1989; Roger Waters' The Wall spectacular, Berlin, 1990; Invited to meet President Gorbachev at the Kremlin, 1991. *Recordings:* Albums: Lonesome Crow, 1972; Fly To The Rainbow, 1974; In Trance, 1975; Virgin Killer, 1976; Taken By Force, 1978; Tokyo Tapes, 1978; Lovedrive, 1979; Animal Magnetism, 1980; Blackout, 1982; Love At First Sting, 1984; World Wide Live, 1985; Savage Amusement, 1988; Best of Rockers and Ballads, 1989; Hurricane Rock, 1990; Crazy World, 1990; Face The Heat, 1993; Live Bites, 1995; Deadly Sting: The Mercury Years, 1997; Moment Of Glory, 2000; Acoustica, 2001; Singles include: Can't Live Without You; No One Like You; Still Loving You; Rhythm of Love; Wind of Change, Eye II Eye, 1999. *Current Management:* McGhee Entertainment, 8730 Sunset Blvd, STE 175, Los Angeles, CA 90069, USA.

SCHICK, Ignaz; b. 9 Sept. 1972, Germany. Musician (saxophone, electronics, experimental music). *Education:* Academy of Fine Arts, Munich; Studied with Josef Anton Riedl. *Career:* Toured, played concerts and festivals of experimental music, 1989–; Festivals include, Bonner Herbst, Donaueschingen, Autumn Concerts, Graz, Austria, FEAM, Berlin; Radio broadcasts with Swiss radio DRS, Bavarian radio BR2; Collaboration with Mathias Bauer, Tony Buck, Jason Kahn, Tarwater, Kalle Laar. *Compositions:* Che; Die Wueste Bleibt Leer; Liebe Macht Blind; Koerper Im Abseits; Tools And Tales Against Radio Agents; Puppy Love; Perm; Vononoch. *Recordings:* Albums: Kratzen, 1990; Kaeseplatte, 1991; Donaueschingen, 1995; Lonely Woman, 1997; Tales And Tools Against Radio Agents, 1997; Nuts, 1998; Petit Pale, 2001; Singles: Perlon, 2000. *Honours:* Foerderstipendium fur Musik, 1994. *Membership:* GEMA; GVL; JIM. *Current Management:* Zangi Music, Weserstr 22, 10247 Berlin, Germany.

SCHIFRIN, Lalo; b. 21 June 1932, Buenos Aires, Argentina. Musician (piano, keyboards); Composer; Educator; Arranger. *Education:* Sociology, Law, University; Classical piano; Studied with Olivier Messiaen, Paris

Conservatoire. *Career:* Represented Argentina, Paris International Jazz Festival, 1955; Founded Argentina's first big band; Played with Dizzy Gillespie, including European tour with Jazz At The Philharmonic Ensemble, 1960–62; Also played with Quincy Jones; Jimmy Smith; Tutor, Composition, University of California, Los Angeles, 1968–71. *Compositions:* 2 suites for Dizzy Gillespie: Gillespiana; New Continent; Film music includes: The Cincinnati Kid, 1965; Bullitt, 1968; Dirty Harry, 1971. *Recordings:* Albums include: New Fantasy, 1966; Towering Toccata, 1977; Black Widow, 1976; Free Rides, 1979; Guitar Concerto, 1985; Anno Domini, 1986; Mission – Anthology, 1994; Gillespiana, 1996; Masters of Mayham, 1997; Rush Hour, 1998; Cantos Aztecas, 1999; Mannix, 1999; Jazz Goes To Hollywood, 2000; Esperanto, 2000; Intersections, 2001; with Jimmy Smith: Verve Jazz, 1972; The Cat Strikes Again, 1980; with Eddie Harris: Bossa Nova, 1962; with Quincy Jones: Plays Hip Hits, 1963; with Paul Horn: Dream Machine, 1978. *Address:* c/o Ted kurland, 173 Brighton Ave, Boston, MA 02134, USA.

SCHMIDT, Bjarne Gregers; b. 3 Nov. 1957, Copenhagen, Denmark. Musician (tenor banjo, Irish bouzouki, guitar). *Education:* Piano lessons; Sound Engineering Course, 1996; Musical Studies, Ireland. *Career:* Foxhunters, band, Skagen Festival, 1986; Live appearance, Danish Radio, 1987, 1989, 1991, 1992, 1996, 1997; Scandinavian Tour with Irish top acts, Mary Bergin and Mick Conneely Gin Whistle and Fiddle, 1991; Live at TV-Stop, 1993, Telemark Festival Norway, 1997. *Compositions:* The Moth in the Lampshade; Happy Days, 1997. *Recordings:* Same Old Story, contributor, 1990; Folk music in Denmark 1, 1992; Folk music in Denmark 2, 1993; Trad Lads, Happy Days, 1997; Eck D'Ville, Contributor, 1997; Folk music of Denmark, 1997. *Publications:* Trad Lads, Happy Days, 1997; Eck D'Ville, 1997. *Current Management:* Martin O'Hare, Selvedje Allé 19, 2500 Valby, Denmark.

SCHMIDT-HOLTZ, Rolf; Record Co Exec. *Career:* Journalist, Television correspondent, Editor-in-Chief and Publisher, magazines, newspapers, Television Exec.; Chief Creative Officer, Bertelsmann; Chair. and CEO, BMG, 2001–. *Address:* c/o BMG, 1540 Broadway, New York, NY 10036, USA. *E-mail:* info@bmg.com. *Website:* www.bmg.com.

SCHMIT, Timothy B; b. 30 Oct. 1947, Sacramento, California, USA. *Career:* Member, folk trio, Tim, Tom and Ron, 1962; Member, groups: The Contenders; New Breed; Glad; Member, Poco, 1970–77; Member, The Eagles, 1977–. *Recordings:* Albums: with Poco: Poco, 1970; Deliverin', 1971; From The Inside, 1971; A Good Feelin' To Know, 1973; Crazy Eyes, 1973; Seven, 1974; Cantamos, 1974; Head Over Heels, 1975; The Very Best of Poco, 1975; Poco Live, 1976; Rose of Cimarron, 1976; Indian Summer, 1977; With The Eagles: The Long Run (No. 1, USA), 1979; Live, 1980; Eagles Greatest Hits, 1982; The Best of The Eagles, 1985; Solo albums: Playin' It Cool, 1981; Timothy B, 1987; Singles include: Heartache Tonight (No. 1, USA), 1979; I Can't Tell You Why, 1980; Seven Bridges Road, 1981. *Honours:* Grammy Award, Best Rock Vocal Performance, Heartache Tonight, 1980; American Music Awards, Favourite Band, Favourite Album, 1981. *Address:* c/o William Morris Agency, 1350 Avenue of the Americas, New York, NY 10019, USA.

SCHMITT, Al; Music Co Dir; Prod; Music Engineer; Mixer. *Career:* Worked at Apex Studios, New York; Independent engineer, Atlantic Records, Prestige Records, Radio Records; Staff Prod. for label, RCA Records; Staff Engineer, RCA studio; Music Dir, DH1 Studios, 2001–; Worked with: Jefferson Airplane, David Benoit, George Benson, Tony Braxton, Dee Dee Bridgewater, Les Brown, Ray Charles, Natalie Cole, David Grusin, Al Jarreau, Doctor John, Quincy Jones, Diana Krall, Madonna, Luis Miguel, John Raitt, Kenny Rankin, Joe Sample, Diane Schuur, Frank Sinatra, Steely Dan, Barbra Streisand, Luther Vandross, Vanessa Williams, Yasuka Agawa. *Honours:* Nine Grammy Awards, Best Engineering, 1962, 1976, 1977, 1978, 1982, 1991, 1996, 2002; Two Latin Grammy Awards, Best Engineering, 2000; Over 150 Gold and Platinum albums; Inducted, Technical Excellence and Creativity Awards Hall of Fame, 1997. *Address:* c/o DH1 Studios, Woolworth Center, 233 Broadway, 22nd Floor, Suite 2200, New York, NY 10279, USA. *E-mail:* al@dh1.tv. *Website:* www.dh1.com.

SCHNEIDER, John; b. 8 April 1954, Mount Kisco, New York, USA. Vocalist; Actor. *Career:* Performed in musicals since age 14; Actor, television series the Dukes of Hazzard, 1979–85; Country artiste, 1981–89; Television includes: Grand Slam, 1990–; Smallville, 2000–; Films include: Snow Day, 2000. *Recordings:* Hits: US Country No. 1 hits include: I've Been Around Enough To Know; Country Girls; What's A Memory Like You (Doing In A Love Like This)?; You're The Last Thing I Needed Tonight; Albums: Now Or Never, 1981; Dukes of Hazzard cast album, 1982; Quiet Man, 1982; If You Believe, with Jill Michaels, 1983; Too Good To Stop Now, 1984; Trying To Outrun The Wind, 1985; A Memory Like You, 1986; Take The Long Way Home, 1986; You Ain't Seen The Last of Me, 1987; Biggest Hits for the Highway, compilation, 1997. *Current Management:* Lee S. Mimms and Associates, 2644 E Chevy Chase Dr., Glendale, CA 91206, USA.

SCHNEIDER, Maria; b. 27 Nov. 1960, Windom, Minnesota, USA. *Education:* BM, Theory and Composition, University of Minnesota; Studied, University of Miami; Master in Jazz and Contemporary Media, Eastman

School of Music. *Career:* Led own orchestra, Maria Schneider Jazz Orchestra, New York, 1993–, performing weekly; Conducted jazz orchestras throughout Sweden, Norway, Finland, Germany, Denmark, Holland, France, Spain and Italy. *Compositions:* El Viento, Carnegie Hall Jazz Orchestra, 1994; Scenes from Childhood, Monterey Jazz Festival, 1995. *Recordings:* Evanescence, 1992; Coming About, 1995; Manhattan School of Music, Live at Montreux 1997; Allegresse, 2000; Dejan Terzic, Four of One. *Address:* 50W 72nd St #510, New York, NY 10023, USA.

SCHOCK, Gina; b. 31 Aug. 1957, Baltimore, MD, USA. Musician (drums). *Career:* Joined the Go-Go's (formerly The Misfits), 1980–85; Formed House of Schock; The Go-Go's re-formed briefly for PETA benefit concert, 1990; Mem., re-formed Go-Go's, 1994, Shows in Las Vegas; The Go-Go's re-formed, 2000–, for an album and tours, including US tour with B-52's. Albums: Beauty And The Beat (No. 1, USA), 1981; Vacation, 1982; Talk Show, 1984; Return To The Valley Of The Go-Go's, 1994; God Bless The Go-Go's, 2001; Contributor, Tame Yourself (animal rights benefit album), 1991; with House of Schock: House of Schock, 1988. *Current Management:* c/o Left Bank Management, 9255 Sunset Blvd, West Hollywood, CA 90069, USA. *E-mail:* gogos@beyondmusic.com. *Website:* www.gogos.com.

SCHOELINCK, Roland; b. 3 Jan. 1951, Anderlues, Hainaut, Belgium. m. Lefevre Chantal, 2 s., 1 d. *Career:* Director, private music school; Composer, Arranger and Performer, jazz, classical and popular music and studio work; Works: Ballet music, Arranger and Composer for Gerard Corbiau's film, L'annee de l'éveil. *Compositions:* Toots Concerto, harmonica and symphony orchestra; Safety First, official safety hymn; Complicity, flute, piano (jazzy); 1 Symphony; 1 Symphony Poem; 1 String Quartet; 1 Wind Quintet; Pieces for Solo Piano; Dr Theodore, for symphony orchestra, 1998; Lions Ceremony; Bouglione Parade; Concerto Pur Cor et Orchestre; Horn Concerto. *Recordings:* Safety First; Dolphin Tears; Complicity; Toots Concerto. *Publications:* Sur La Voie de l'improvisation, 1996; Easy to Write, 1997; Petit Livre de Jazz, 1 and 2, 1997; Complicity, 1997; 26 Airs de Gilles, piano. *Membership:* Belgian Composers Union; SABAM. *Address:* 6 Chemin Brulotte, B-7063, Neufvilles, Belgium. *E-mail:* roland.schoelinck@skynet.be. *Website:* users.skynet.be/roschoel/.

SCHOLZ, Drazen; b. 25 June 1961, Zagreb, Croatia. Musician (drums). m. 28 June 1986, 1 d. *Career:* Promise of Spring; Parliament; Film: Some Like It Hot; Le Cinema; Parni Valjak (Steam Roller). *Recordings:* with Parni Valjak: Live In ZKM (Unplugged); Parni Valjak – All 15 Years (3 LPs live), 1990; Dream Hunters, 1990; Awakenings, 1994. *Honours:* 7 Porin Awards (Croatian equivalent of Grammy) with Parni Valjak. *Membership:* HGU (Croatian Music Union). *Current Management:* Nenad Drobnjak, Miramarska 15b, Zagreb, Croatia. *Address:* Laginjina 9, 41000 Zagreb, Croatia.

SCHOLZ, Tom; b. 10 March 1947, Toledo, Ohio, USA. Vocalist; Musician. *Education:* Masters, Mechanical Engineering, Massachusetts Institute of Technology. *Career:* Founder, rock group Boston, 1976; British tour, 1979; Seven-year absence from recording; US tour, 1987. *Recordings:* Albums: Boston, 1976; Don't Look Back, 1978; Third Stage (No. 1, USA), 1986; Walk On, 1994; Greatest Hits, 1997; Corporate America, 2002; Singles include: More Than A Feeling, 1976; Long Time, 1977; Peace of Mind, 1977; Don't Look Back, 1978; Amanda (No. 1, USA), 1986; We're Ready, 1987; Can'tcha Say, 1987. *Honours:* Platinum and Gold discs; Best-selling debut album all-time, 16m. copies. *Address:* c/o Boston, PO Box 6191, Lincoln Center, MA 01773, USA.

SCHON, Neal; b. 27 Feb. 1954, San Mateo, California, USA. Musician (guitar); Vocalist. *Career:* Guitarist with Carlos Santana; Founder, Azteca; Founder member, US rock group Journey, 1973–87; Member, HSAS, 1984; Bad English, 1988–91; Hardline, 1992–; Partnership with Jan Hammer, 1981–82. *Recordings:* with Santana: Santana, 1972; Santana/Abraxas/Santana, 1997; Santana/Abraxas/Santana, 1998; with HSAS: Through The Fire, 1984; with Jan Hammer: Untold Passion, 1981; Here To Stay, 1982; with Bad English, Bad English, 1989; Backlash, 1991; Solo: Beyond The Thunder, 1995; Electric World, 1997; Piranha Blues, 1999; Voice, 2001; Hit singles include: with Journey: Who's Crying Now; Don't Stop Believin'; Open Arms; Separate Ways (Worlds Apart); After The Fall; Send Her My Love; Suzanne; Be Good To Yourself; Albums: Evolution, 1979; Escape, 1981; Frontiers, 1983; Greatest Hits, 1988; Escape/Frontiers/Infinity, 1998; with Bad English: When I See You Smile (No. 1, USA), 1990; Straight To The Heart, 1991. *Current Management:* Bill Thompson Management. *Address:* 2051 Third St, San Francisco, CA 94107, USA.

SCHÖNBERG, Claude-Michel; b. 6 July 1944, France. Composer. m. Béatrice Szabo, 1979, 1 s., 1 d. *Career:* Record Producer for EMI France; Composer, songs and musicals, 1967–. *Compositions:* Musicals include: La Révolutions Française, 1973; Les Misérables, 1980–84; Miss Saigon, 1985–86. *Recordings:* Producer: Les Misérables, London cast recording; Miss Saigon, London cast recording; Martin Guerre, London cast recording. *Honours:* Tony Awards; Grammy Awards; Evening Standard Awards.

SCHREURS, Dirk; b. 23 May 1966, Neerpelt, Belgium. Prof. of Jazz/Popular Music, Piano; Musician (piano). m. Vera Kerckhoven, 28 July 1990. *Education:* Master Degree in Arts and Humanities, University of Louvain; Master Degree in Teaching; Assistant, Faculty of Arts, University of Louvain; Master Classes with John Abercrombie and Dave Kikoski, Trilok Gurtu. *Career:* Keyboardist with Real Deal, DSWB 4, Jan Mues Quartet, Jive Talk, Marco Ruggiero Band; Appearances on Belgian Radio and TV; Prof. of Jazz/Popular Music, Prof. of Piano, Brussels Royal Conservatory. *Compositions:* Over 200 compositions and arrangements in various styles. *Recordings:* Flexibility, 1992; Beyond Ballads, 1993; From Blues to Funk, 1995; The Joy of Rhythm 'N Jazz, 1996. *Publications:* Author, Jazzics; A Book on Jazz Theory, Analysis and Improvisation, 1993. *Honours:* Touch Down, composition selected for publication, 1994–95. *Membership:* SABAM; ZAMU; Zavelhof Cultural Society. *Current Management:* Dirk Schreurs, Don Boscostraat 98, 3940, Hechtel, Belgium.

SCHULTZ, Debra Kay; b. 30 Oct. 1955, Holden, West Virginia, USA. Gospel Vocalist. m. Robert A Schultz, 13 Dec. 1974, 2 s. *Education:* Vocal lessons, Robert Turner; Several years of piano. *Career:* Appearances, gospel concerts, Gospel TV stations, throughout USA; Radio stations internationally. *Recordings:* Radio singles: Lord You're My Strength, 1991; Don't Lift The Anchor, 1992; I Just Found Jesus, 1993. *Honours:* King Eagle Award, Christian Female Artist of the Year, Airplay International, 1994–95. *Membership:* Gospel Music Asscn (GMA). *Address:* PO Box 88 Rt 17, Sharples, WV 25183, USA.

SCHULTZ, Eric; b. 11 Sept. 1960, Los Angeles, California, USA. Musician (guitar, electric bass); Composer; Arranger; Teacher. *Education:* BA, Humanities, California State University, Northridge, USA; Composition, California State University, Northridge; Guitar studies with Ralph Towner; Joe Diorio; John Abercrombie; Ron Escheté. *Career:* Professional jazz player, 1982; Resident Paris, 1986–; Worked regularly with some of greatest drummers in jazz: Oliver Johnson; Barry Altschul; Sunny Murray; Frank Butler; Alan Jones; Peter Perfido; ESP with Paul Carman, 1984–85; Onzy Matthews Quartet, Peter Perfido/Andy Laster Group; Eric Schultz Trio (with Oliver Johnson, Jack Gregg), 1991–; Eric Schultz Nonet; Jean Michel Couchet/Eric Schultz Quartet, 1993–; Eric Schultz Space and Time Ensemble, 1995; Viviane Ginapé/Eric Schultz duo. *Recordings:* Eric Schultz Space And Time Ensemble, 1995. *Membership:* SACEM. *Current Management:* Space and Time Productions. *Address:* 8 rue de la Pompe, 94410 St Maurice, France.

SCHULTZ, Irma; b. 1 Oct. 1965, Stockholm, Sweden. Vocalist; Songwriter; Actress. *Education:* Special Music School, 6 years; Drama School, 4 years. *Career:* Tours of Sweden and Many Television Shows; Background Vocals on 40 Albums in Sweden including: The Leather Nun; Lolita Pop; Ulf Lundell; Actress in The Black Rider by Waits, Wilson and Bourroughs at the Royal Dramatic Theatre; 10 Television Productions, Leading Role in Kvällspressen, 1992; 3 Movies for Cinema. *Compositions:* Stureplan; Precis som du; Andas Fritt. *Recordings:* Da Staden Vaknat, 1989; Irma, 1991; Tröst för Stygga Barn, 1993; Andas Fritt, 1995; A Bird That Whistles, Songs of Joni Mitchell, 1996. *Honours:* Scholarships, STIM, SKAP; Grammy Award, Best Female Artist in Sweden, 1989. *Current Management:* Sony Music AB, Box 20037, 16102 Bromma, Sweden. *Address:* Erstagatan 20, 116 36 Stockholm, Sweden.

SCHULZE, Erich; b. 1 Feb. 1913, Berlin, Germany. *Career:* Editor; Chairman. *Publications:* Include, Collection of Case Law Reports On Copyright, With Comments; Commentary On German Copyright Law With Regard to International Law and Community Law In The EU Member States; Commentary On Social Security For Self Employed Artists Act; Germany Copyright In Works of Music and The Development of Mechanical Music; Music and Poetry, 50 Years of The German Copyright Society; Music and Law – The Composers Royalties; Collection of Forms for Protection of Industrial and Intellectual Property. *Honours:* Cross of Knight Commander of Papal Order of Silvester, 1962; Hon. Cross of Republic of Austria, 1965; Officers Cross of Order of Merit, 1967; Bavarian Order of Merit, 1971; Commanders Cross of The Order of Merit, 1978; Bela Bartok Medal, 1980; Cross of Knight Commander of the Papal Order of Gregorius With Star, 1986; Supreme Order of Merit, 1988; Richard Strausse Medal, 1989; Gold Medal Confederation Internationale Des Societes d'Auteurs et Compositeurs, 1990; Agustin Lara Award, 1991; Golden Score of The Forderkreis, 1995. *Address:* Dr Hans Staub Strasse 3, 82031 Grunwald, Germany.

SCHUUR, Diane; b. 1953, Seattle, WA, USA. Vocalist. m. Dave Schuur. *Career:* Performances include: White House; Monterey Jazz Festival; Hollywood Bowl; Moscow Symphony; Tours: Europe; Japan; Far East; Israel; South America. *Recordings:* Albums: Pilot of My Destiny, 1982; Schuur Thing, 1985; Timeless, 1986; Diane Schuur and the Count Basie Orchestra, 1987; Talkin' About You, 1988; Pure Schuur (No. 1, Billboard contemporary jazz chart), 1991; Blues For Schuur, 1997; The Best of Diane Schuur, 1997; Music Is My Life, 1999; Friends For Schuur, 2000; Swingin' For Schuur, with Maynard Ferguson, 2001; Friends for Schuur, 2000; Midnight, 2003. *Honours:* 2 Grammy Awards, 1987–88; Manhattan Assocn of Cabarets and Clubs Award, 1997; Bagley Wright Award, 1997; First Annual Ella Fitzgerald Award from the Montréal International Jazz Festival, 1999; Helen Keller Achievement

Award, 2000. *Current Management:* Paul Cantor Enterprises, 33042 Ocean Ridge, Dana Point, CA 92629–1708, USA.

SCHWARTZ, Stephen; b. 6 March 1948, New York, NY, USA. Songwriter; Composer. *Education:* Piano and composition, Juilliard School of Music; BFA, Drama, Carnegie Mellon University, 1968. *Career:* Prod., RCA Records; Prod., Original Cast album of Godspell; Runs ASCAP Foundation musical theatre workshops. *Recordings:* Reluctant Pilgrim, 1997; Uncharted Territory. *Compositions:* Title song, play Butterflies Are Free, Broadway, 1969; For musicals: Music and lyrics, Godspell, 1971, Pippin, 1972, The Magic Show, 1974, The Baker's Wife, 1976, Children Of Eden, 1991; Lyrics, Rags, 1986; Music, Working, 1978, Personals; For film: Score, Pocahontas (with Alan Menken), 1995, The Hunchback of Notre Dame (with Alan Menken), 1996; Songs, The Prince of Egypt; For television: Geppetto. *Publications:* The Perfect Peach. *Honours:* Two Grammy Awards, for Godspell; Drama Desk Award, Best Dir, Working; Academy Awards, Original Musical or Comedy Score and Original Song, for Pocahontas (with Alan Menken), Original Song, for When You Believe, from The Prince of Egypt, 1999; ASCAP Award, Most Performed Motion Picture Song. *Membership:* ASCAP Foundation, board mem.; Council of the Dramatists' Guild. *Current Management:* c/o Harry Fox Agency, 711 Third Ave, New York, NY 10017, USA. *E-mail:* schwartz@stephenschwartz.com. *Website:* www.stephenschwartz.com.

SCHWISBERG, Arnold; b. 17 Nov. 1961, Montréal, Québec, Canada. m. Kathrine Brodie, 2 s. *Education:* BA, BSc, LLB, Queens Faculty of Law, Kingston, Ontario, Canada. *Career:* Founder and Owner, President, Jazz Inspiration Records. *Address:* 2001 Sheppard Ave, Suite 808, Toronto, ON, Canada.

SCHWISBERG, David; b. 20 July 1966, Montréal, Québec, Canada. *Education:* Economics and Marketing. *Career:* Co-Owner, Vice-President, Jazz Inspiration Records, independent jazz label. *Address:* 5510 Robinson Ave, Suite 206, Montréal, QC, Canada.

SCOCCO, Mauro; b. 11 Sept. 1962, Stockholm, Sweden. Artist; Composer. *Career:* Sales in Scandinavia: 600,000 albums; 4 Swedish Grammy Awards; numerous other awards. *Recordings:* Sarah, single, topped every list in Sweden. *Current Management:* Diesel Music. *Address:* Diesel Music, Blasieholmsg 2a, 1148 Stockholm, Sweden.

SCOFIELD, John; b. 26 Dec. 1951, Ohio, USA. Jazz Musician (guitar); Composer. *Education:* Berklee College of Music, Boston. *Career:* Began playing in local R&B groups; Solo artiste, 1970s–; Played with Billy Cobham; Gary Burton; Dave Liebman; Charlie Haden; Jack DeJohnette; McCoy Tyner; Marc Johnson; French National Orchestra; Mike Gibbs Orchestra; Member, Miles Davis' group, 1983–85. *Recordings:* Albums include: John Scofield Live, 1977; Rough House, 1978; Who's Who, 1979; Bar Talk, 1980; Shinola, 1981; Out Like A Light, 1981; Electric Outlet, 1984; Still Warm, 1987; Blue Matter, 1987; Loud Jazz, 1987; Flat Out, 1989; Pick Hits Live, 1989; Time On My Hands, 1990; Slo Sco, 1990; Meant To Be, 1991; Blue Matter, 1991; Grace Under Pressure, 1992; What We Do, 1993; Bump, 2000; Steady Groovin', 2000; Works For Me, 2001; Uberjam, 2002; with Miles Davis: Decoy, 1984; You're Under Arrest, 1985; Star People, 1989; Groove Elation, 1996; with Herbie Hancock: The New Standard, 1996; Also recorded with Gerry Mulligan; Chet Baker; John Abercrombie. *Current Management:* Ted Kurland Assocs, 173 Brighton Ave, Boston, MA 02134, USA.

SCOTT, Al; Record Prod. *Career:* Musician, Recording, session work; Live Sound for: The Jam; Little Feat; Fleetwood Mac; Composer and arranger; Record producer, with close links with Vinyl Solution. *Recordings:* Albums: Angels and Cigarettes, Eliza Carthy, 2000; The Levellers: Levelling The Land; Cud: Slip Away; Dogs D'Amour: Uncharted Heights of Disgrace; Oyster Band: Holy Bandits; Tom Robinson: Love Over Rage; Cherry Bombz: Live; Derek B: Bullet From A Gun; Bomb The Bass: Love So True; Betty Boo: Where Are You Baby; Eddie Grant: Gimme Hope Joanna; Eric B and Rakim: Paid In Full; Mad For It; Fruit Cocktail; Best Album in the World Ever; Ted Hawkins: The Ted Hawkins Story; Other artists including: Mae; Suicide Twins; Bizarre Inc; Gunshot; War; Catch My Soul. *Current Management:* XL Talent. *Address:* Studio 7, 27A Pembridge Villas, London W11 3EP, England.

SCOTT, Clive Kenneth; b. 24 Feb. 1945, Coventry, England. Musician (keyboards); Prod; Writer. m. Ann Constance, 18 June 1994, 1 s. *Education:* Church choir to pop groups. *Career:* Keyboard player, co-writer for Jigsaw, 1968–81; Independent writer producer. *Recordings:* with Apollo 100: Joy; with Candlewick Green and St Etienne: Who Do You Think You Are, 1974; with Jigsaw: Sky High, 1975; The Very Best of Jigsaw; with Bad Boys Inc: Walking On Air; Disco Remix Project, Vols 5 and 6, 1997; Other recording work includes: OTT; Chuck Jackson; Edwin Starr; Upside Down; Gemini; The Nolans. *Publications:* Music for video and film includes Shape Challenge fitness videos. *Honours:* Gold discs, Sky High; Ivor Novello Certificate of Honour. *Membership:* Songwriters Guild; PRS. *Current Management:* Chas Peate, Belsize Music. *Address:* 29 Manor House, Marylebone Rd, London NW1 5NP, England.

SCOTT, David Andrew; b. 20 Aug. 1964, Falkirk, Scotland. Songwriter; Musician (guitar; keyboards); Vocalist. m. Julie Parker, 19 Aug. 1989. *Education:* Graphics, Falkirk College; Glasgow School of Art. *Career:* Appeared on Indie compilation, 1984; Other recordings as Chewy Raccoon and Hearts and Minds; Film and television commissions; Founder, My Dark Star record label to release records by The Pearlfishers, 1991–; Major concert appearances include: Scottish Fleadh, 1992; T In The Park, Glasgow, 1994; Celtic Connections, Royal Concert Hall, 1995. *Recordings:* Sacred (EP), The Pearlfishers, 1991; Hurt (EP), The Pearlfishers, 1991; Za Za's Garden, The Pearlfishers, 1994; Producer, The Gentle Waves, 2000; Session work with Robin Laing, 1999. *Membership:* PRS; Musicians' Union. *Current Management:* My Dark Star Records. *Address:* PO Box 1, Glasgow G3 6TZ, England.

SCOTT, Don E; b. 12 Feb. 1937, Canada. Vocalist; Songwriter; Musician (guitar, steel guitar, mandolin, harmonica, dobro, drums). m. Marie, 1 s., 2 d. *Education:* Diplomas in Real Property Management, Public Relations, Interpersonal Skills, Economics and Social Philosophy. *Career:* Television, Radio, Video and Stage Performances; Businessman and Consultant. *Compositions:* Over 600 Songs. *Recordings:* The Real Deal; Beginnings; Room In My Heart. *Honours:* Numerous awards and prizes in songwriting and singing; also numerous honours for community services. *Membership:* Songwriters' Asscn of Canada. *Current Management:* The Management Centre, 13808, 110A Ave, Edmonton, AB T5M 2M9, Canada.

SCOTT, Hammond; b. 15 May 1950, Alexandria, Louisiana, USA. Record producer; Attorney. *Education:* Dr of Law. *Career:* Co-owner, Black Top Records Inc (internationally distributed and recognized blues, R&B and roots label); Produced over 100 albums; Served as personal manager of blues artist Clarence 'Gatemouth' Brown, 1970s; Former writer, Living Blues Magazine; Hosted radio show on WWOZ FM, New Orleans, for 5 years; Produced recordings by R&B artists including: Buckwheat Zydeco; WC Clark; Albert Collins; Robert Ward; Solomon Burke; Maria Muldaur; Earl King; Snooks Eaglin; Bobby Parker; Neville Brothers; Anson Funderburgh and the Rockets, Former Prosecutor, District Attorney's Office of Harry Connick Sr; Neville Brothers; Bobby Radcliff; Bobby Parker; Robert Ward; Ronnie Earl; Earl Gaines. *Honours:* Numerous W. C. Handy Awards. *Address:* 5340 Camp St, New Orleans, LA 70115, USA.

SCOTT, Jill; b. Philadelphia, USA. Vocalist; Poet. *Career:* Started career reading poetry until spotted by local hip hop outfit The Roots; Wrote lyrics for their Grammy Award-winning first single You Got Me; Performed with Canadian cast of stage musical Rent; Collaborations: Eric Benet; Will Smith; Common; 4 Hero. *Recordings:* Albums: Who Is Jill Scott? Words and Sounds Vol. 1, 2000; Experience, 2001; Singles: Gettin' In The Way, 2000; A Long Walk, The Way, Thickness, 2001. *Address:* c/o Hidden Beach Recordings, 3030 Nebraska Ave Penthouse Suite, Santa Monica CA 9404, USA. *Website:* www.hiddenbeach.com.

SCOTT, Lydia; b. 9 Aug. 1953, Montréal, QC, Canada. Country Recording Artist; Musician (guitar). *Education:* Montréal University. *Career:* Six Top 30 Chart singles nationally. *Compositions:* The Moon She Knows; True Love; I Could Love You; As Good As You Look. *Recordings:* Isn't It Always Love; You Can Crash Here. *Honours:* Talent Contest Winner, 1989; BC Award, Female Vocalist of the Year, 1999. *Current Management:* Publicity: Jodi Smith. *Address:* #704 2121 W 44th Ave, Vancouver, BC V6M 2G5, Canada.

SCOTT, Malcolm; b. 20 Aug. 1964, San Francisco, California, USA. Musician (drums, percussion, guitar); Songwriter; Vocalist. m. Dominique Atkins, 26 Aug. 1994. *Education:* Berkshire Centre Performing Arts; Musicians Institute, London. *Career:* Musician for: The Cure; Pretenders; Belinda Carlisle; Buddy Curtiss; McAlmont; Jimmy Nail; Vanessa Mae; Skunk Anansie; Take That; Michelle Gayle; Grace. *Recordings:* Lovesongs End, Grace; I Will Be With You. *Membership:* Musicians' Union. *Current Management:* Mickey Curbishley; Agent: Session Connection. *Address:* 16 Lynfield Court, 161 Devonshire Rd, London SE23 3ND, England.

SCOTT, Matthew James; b. 11 Oct. 1967, London, England. Musician (piano); Composer. *Career:* Resident pianist, The Vortex, 1994–95; Regular appearances on London jazz/pop circuit, London jazz festivals, 1994–95; Clubs include: The 606; The Orange; The King's Head, Upper Street; Chat's Palace. *Compositions:* L'Esquisse, film soundtrack, 1995; Trio for strings, 1995; The Land Girls, film soundtrack, 1998; The Mrs. Bradley Mysteries, BBC drama serial, 2000. *Recordings:* Singles: The Whole of The Moon, 1985, reissued 1991; Fisherman's Blues, 1989; And A Bang On The Ear, 1989; Album: Improvisations For Solo Piano, 1995; Standards, 1995. *Contributions to:* Wonderful Town, London cast recording, 1986; Snoopy, original London cast recording, 1998. *Current Management:* Paddy French. *Address:* 249 Goswell Rd, London EC1V 7JD, England.

SCOTT, Mike; b. 14 Dec. 1958, Edinburgh, Scotland. Vocalist; Songwriter; Musician (guitar). *Career:* Lead singer, groups: Another Pretty Face, 1979–81; The Red and The Black, 1982; The Waterboys, 1983–93; Solo artiste, 1994–; Tours, UK, USA and Japan, 1995; Glastonbury Festival, 1995; UK, Europe,

Japan, 1997. *Recordings:* Albums: with The Waterboys: A Pagan Place, 1984; This Is The Sea, 1985; Fisherman's Blues, 1988; Room To Roam, 1990; The Best of The Waterboys, 1991; Dream Harder, 1993; Secret Life of Waterboys, 1994; Rock In The Weary Land, 2000; Solo albums: Bring 'Em All In, 1995; Still Burning, 1997; Whole of the Moon, 1998; with Characters: Characters, 1997; with Angel Grant: Album, 1998. *Publications:* Jungleland, 1977–80. *Honours:* Ivor Novello Award for composition, The Whole of The Moon, 1992. *Current Management:* Strawberry Management Ltd, 112 Maxwell Ave, Glasgow G61 H11, Scotland. *Website:* www.mikescottmusic.com.

SCOTT, Rick; b. 14 July 1948, New Jersey, USA. Vocalist; Songwriter; Actor; Musician (dulcimer, whimmydiddle, guitar, trombone, tuba, Japanese flute). *Career:* Pied Pumkin String Ensemble, 1975–76; Pied Pear, 1976–83; Rick Scott Band, 1985–86; Concert tours throughout Canada, USA, Australia, Asia as solo family performer; Starred in numerous stage plays, musicals including: Barnum (title role); The Late Blumer and Angry Housewives. *Recordings:* 10 recordings including 3 albums for children; The Electric Snowshoe, 1989; Rick Around the Rock, 1992; Philharmonic Fool, 1995. *Honours:* Pacific Music Industry Award, Best Children's Album, 1997. *Membership:* AFofM; SOCAN; ACTRA; Canadian Actors Equity. *Current Management:* Ms Valley Hennell, Manager. *Address:* 2736 W 13 Ave, Vancouver, BC V6K 2T4, Canada.

SCOTT, Tommy; b. 18 Feb. 1966. Vocalist; Songwriter. *Career:* Founder Member, Space; Original bass player, until 1997; Numerous television appearances and live dates. *Recordings:* Singles: If It's Real, 1993; Money, 1995; Neighbourhood, 1996; Female of the Species, 1997; Me and You vs The World, 1997; Dark Clouds, 1997; Avenging Angels, 1997; The Ballad of Tom Jones, with Cerys Matthews, 1998; Begin Again, 1998; Bad Days, 1998; Diary Of A Wimp, 2000; Albums: Spiders, 1996; Remixes and B-Sides, 1996; Tin Planet, 1998; Greatest Hits, 2001.

SCOTT, Toni Lee; b. 15 Jan. 1933, San Francisco, California, USA. Vocalist. m. Angelo Ligi, 26 Dec. 1989. *Career:* Professional singer, from age 14; Member, Bob Scobey's Band; Bob Crosby's Band; Television shows: This Is Your Life; Johnny Carson; Steve Allen; Tennessee Ernie Ford; Mike Douglas; Radio shows across the country; Clubs include: Stardust, Las Vegas; Riviera, Las Vegas; Roundtable, New York; Mr Kelly's, Chicago; Sherman House, Chicago; Mr T's, Chicago; Pigalle, Chicago; Cafe Continental, Chicago; Memory Lane, Los Angeles; Purple Onion, San Francisco; Other appearances include: Chicago Tribune Music Festival, Chicago; Codac Benefit, Phoenix. *Recordings:* Albums: San Francisco; Goody Goody; Something's Always Happening On The River, 1959; Volume Lonely, 1963; Songs of My Friends, 1996. *Publications:* A Kind of Loving, (autobiography). *Honours:* Fade To Gold Award, Entertainer of the Year – Cerebral Palsy; Woman of the Year, Heart Asscn. *Membership:* Society of Singers; Women In Music Business. *Current Management:* Terri Tilton Management; Agent: Prince SF Productions. *Address:* 6 Haverhill Court, Novato, CA 94947, USA.

SCOTT, Tony; b. 3 Oct. 1973, Paramaribo, Suriname. Rap Artiste; Dancer; Vocalist; Composer. *Career:* First hit and recording, 1987; 10 Top 10 hits; Worked with Candy Dulfer. *Recordings:* Pick Up The Pieces, 1987; Top 10 hit singles: The Chief, 1988; That's How I'm Living, 1988; Gangster Boogie, 1989; Get Into It, 1990; Greenhouse Effect, 1991; The Bigband, 1992; Love and Let Love, 1992; with Candy Dulfer: Albums: Big Girl, 1995. *Honours:* Dance Artist Award, 1989, 1990; 5 Gold singles. *Membership:* FNV Kunstenbond. *Current Management:* Hans Van Pol Management. *Address:* PO Box 9010, 1006 AG Amsterdam, Netherlands.

SCOTT-HERON, Gil; b. 1 April 1949, Chicago, Illinois, USA. Vocalist; Songwriter. *Education:* Lincoln University, Pennsylvania, USA. *Career:* Co-founder, The Midnight Band, 1972–; Major concerts include: Phoenix Festival, 1995. *Compositions include:* The Revolution Will Not Be Televised, Labelle; Home Is Where The Hatred Is, Esther Phillips. *Recordings:* Albums: Small Talk at 125th and Lenox, 1970; Pieces of a Man, 1971; Free Will, 1972; Winter In America, 1974; The Revolution Will Not Be Televised, 1974; The First Minute of a New Day, 1975; From South Africa To South Carolina, 1975; It's Your World, 1976; Bridges, 1977; Secrets, 1978; The Mind of Gil Scott-Heron, 1979; 1980, 1980; Real Eyes, 1980; Reflections, 1981; Moving Target, 1982; The Best of Gil Scott-Heron, 1984; Amnesia Express, 1990; Spirits, 1994; Minister of Information, 1994; Evolution And Flashback, 1999; Singles include: The Bottle, 1973; Johannesburg, 1976; B-Movie, 1982; Fast Lane, 1982; No Exit, 1982; Re-Ron, 1984. *Publications:* Author, novels: The Vulture; The Nigger Factory; Book of poetry.

SCOTT-LEE, Lisa; b. 5 Nov. 1975, St Asaph, Wales. Vocalist. *Education:* Italia Conti stage school, London. *Career:* Former professional dancer, dance instructor; Mem., Steps, 1997–2001; Popular with UK teen audience; Numerous television appearances, incl. Steps To The Stars; Tours, incl. Gold–Greatest Hits tour, 2001; Solo artiste, 2001–. *Recordings:* Albums: Step One, 1998; Steptacular, 1999; Buzz, 2000; Gold, 2001; The Last Dance, 2002. *Honours:* BRIT Award, Best Selling Live Act, 2000. *Address:* c/o Zomba Records Ltd, Zomba House, 165–167 Willesden High Rd, London NW10 2SG, England. *Website:* www.stepsofficial.com.

SCREECHY, Jah, (Elton Loye Sinclair); b. 9 Feb. 1958, Jamaica. Vocalist; DJ. *Education:* College diploma; City and Guilds. *Career:* Mechanical Engineering; Television appearances: Top of the Pops; Radio 1 Road Show, Margate; Ritzy Night Club, Streatham; Stage shows and personal appearances, England, France and Germany. *Recordings:* Walk and Skank, 1984; Shadow Move, Hop Scotch, 1985; On A Ragga Tip, 1992. *Membership:* Musicians' Union; PRS. *Current Management:* James Augustus (Jessus). *Address:* Oxford House Studio, Oxford House, Derbyshire St, Bethnal Green, London E2, England.

SCRUGGS, Earl; b. 6 Jan. 1924, Cleveland County, North Carolina, USA. Country Musician (banjo). *Career:* Member, Bill Monroe's Bluegrass Boys, 1944–48; Co-founder, Flatt and Scruggs show with Lester Flatt, 1948; Regular radio and television appearances include: Folk Sound USA; Concerts include: Newport Folk Festival, 1960; Leader, Earl Scruggs Revue, 1969–; Concerts include: Wembley Country Music Festival, 1972. *Compositions:* Foggy Mountain Breakdown. *Recordings include:* Foggy Mountain Breakdown, from film Bonnie and Clyde; The Ballad of Jed Clampett, theme for television series The Beverly Hillbillies; Albums: with Earl Scruggs Revue: include: Duelling Banjos, 1973; Family and Friends, 1972; Anniversary Special Vol. I, 1975; Family Portrait, 1976; Bold and New, 1978; Today and Forever, 1979; Top of The World, 1983; Can You feel it in Your Soul, 1999; Earl Scruggs And Friends, 2001; Several collections of Flatt and Scruggs; WithBill Monroe: 16 Gems, 1996; Early Years, 1998. *Publications:* Author, Earl Scruggs and The 5-String Banjo. *Honours:* Artist of the Year, Hi-Fi Institute, 1975; Best Country Instrumental Group, Billboard Magazine, 1975; Certificate of Appreciation, Governor of Tennessee, 1978; Earl Scruggs Day, for contribution to American Music, 1980; Gibson Hall of Fame, 1981; Country Music Asscn Hall of Fame, 1985; Hon. Mem., Lieutenant Governors Staff, State of Tennessee, 1987; Order of the Long Leaf Pine Award, Governor of North Carolina, 1988; Hall of Honour, International Bluegrass Music Asscn, 1991; National Medal of Arts, presented by George Bush, 1992. *Membership:* Country Music Asscn. *Current Management:* Louise Scruggs, PO Box 66, Madison, TN 37116, USA.

SEAL, (Henry Samuel); b. 19 Feb. 1963, Paddington, London, England. Vocalist; Songwriter. *Career:* Singer, Adamski, 1990; Solo artiste, 1991–; Concerts and tours: Red Hot and Dance, AIDS benefit concert, London, 1991; Amnesty International's Big 30, 1991; Freddie Mercury Tribute, A Concert For Life, Wembley, 1992; Support to Rolling Stones, 1994. *Recordings:* Solo albums: Seal (No. 1, UK), 1991; Seal, 1994; Human Being, 1998; Seal, 1999; Singles: Killer, with Adamski (No. 1, UK), 1990; Solo singles: Crazy (No. 2, UK), 1991; Future Love Paradise, 1991; The Beginning, 1991; Prayer For The Dying, 1994; Kiss From A Rose, 1995; If I Could, 1995; I'm Alive, 1995; Don't Cry, 1996; Fly like an Eagle, 1997; Human Beings, 1998; Lost my Faith, 1999; Killer, 1999; Featured vocals on: Navigator, Jose Padilla, 2001; Featured on film soundtracks: Toys, 1991; Indecent Proposal, 1993. *Honours:* Ivor Novello Award, Best Contemporary Song, Killer, 1991; Q Award, Best New Act, 1991; Variety Club of Great Britain's Recording Artist of 1991; BRIT Awards: Best Male Artist, Best British Album, Best British Video, 1992; 3 Grammy Awards, including Best Record, Best Song, 1996; Ivor Novello Awards: Best Contemporary Song, International Hit of the Year, Crazy, 1992. *Current Management:* Third Rail Entertainment, 9169 Sunset Blvd, Los Angeles, CA 90069, USA.

SEALS, Dan; b. 8 Feb. 1950, McCamey, Texas, USA. Country Vocalist; Songwriter. *Career:* Partnership with John Ford Coley, 1967–80; Originally billed as Southwest FOB, then as England Dan and John Ford Coley; Solo artiste, 1980–. *Recordings:* As England Dan and John Ford Coley: Hit singles include: I'd Really Love To See You Tonight; Nights Are Forever Without You; Albums: Smell of Incense (as Southwest FOB), 1968; England Dan and John Ford Coley, 1971; Fables, 1971; I Hear The Music, 1976; Nights Are Forever, 1976; Dowdy Ferry Road, 1977; Some Things Don't Come Easy, 1978; Dr Heckle and Mr Jive, 1978; Just Tell Me If You Love Me, 1980; Solo hits include: Meet Me In Montana, with Marie Osmond (US Country No. 1), 1985; Bop; Everything That Glitters (Is Not Gold); You Still Move Me; I Will Be There; Three Time Loser; One Friend; Addicted; Big Wheels In The Moonlight; Love Thing; Fired Up; Albums: Stones, 1980; Harbinger, 1982; Rebel Heart, 1983; San Antone, 1984; Won't Be Blue Anymore, 1985; On The Front Line, 1986; Rage On, 1988; On Arrival, 1990; Walking The Wire, 1992; The Songwriter, 1992; My Baby's Got Good Timing, 1994; Fired Up, 1994; In A Quiet Room, 1995; In A Quiet Room II, 1998; Back To Back, 2001. *Current Management:* Morningstar Management, PO Box 1770, Hendersonville, TN 37077, USA.

SEALS, Troy; b. 16 Nov. 1938, Big Hill, Kentucky, USA. Songwriter; Musician (guitar). m. Jo Ann Campbell. *Career:* Guitarist, club bands, Ohio, 1960s; Formed duo with Jo Ann Campbell; Moved to Nashville as songwriter; Session guitarist and solo artiste. *Compositions:* There's A Honky Tonk Angel (Who'll Take Me Back In), recorded by Elvis Presley, Conway Twitty (US Country No. 1); Pieces of My Life, recorded by Elvis Presley; We Had It All (co-written with Donnie Fritts), recorded by Rita Coolidge, Brenda Lee, Scott Walker, Waylon Jennings; Feeling (co-written with Will Jennings and Don Goodman), recorded by Loretta Lynn and Conway Twitty (US Country No. 1);

Storms (co-written with Max Barnes), recorded by Randy Travis; Seven Spanish Angels (co-written with Eddie Setser), recorded by Willie Nelson and Ray Charles (US Country No. 1). *Recordings:* Solo albums include: Now Presenting Troy Seals, 1973; Troy Seals, 1976. *Contributions to:* James Brown's Original Funky Divas, 1998; Lonnie Mack, Road Houses and Dance Halls; Con Hunley, I Don't Want to Lose You; Bob Ruzicka, Soft Rocker; Dobie Gray; Doug Kershaw; Lonnie Mack; Randy Travis.

SEALY, Denice; b. 25 Nov. 1964, London, England. Backing Vocalist. *Education:* Vocal Studies, University of East London. *Career:* Greenbelt Christian Festival, with Bryan Powell, 1989–91; Hammersmith Odeon, with Jennifer Holliday, 1993; EMI Music Conference, with Kenny Thomas, 1993; Wembley Arena, with Dina Carroll, 1994; with Carleen Anderson, British tour, 1993; Motor Traders Awards, 1995; with D C Lee, UK promo tour, 1995; Television: The Beat; The Late Show, 1993; Virgin Records Music Anniversary, 1994; Pebble Mill, 1995; Backing vocals, World (Pentecostal Conference), Jerusalem, Israel, 1995. *Recordings:* Albums: I Think of You, Bryan Powell, 1992; Michelle Gayle, 1993; Nu Inspirational Album, Soul Stirrings; Backing vocals on: Mama, The Spice Girls (No. 1, UK), 1997. *Membership:* Musicians' Union. *Current Management:* c/o Mixed Music Ltd. *Address:* 2 The Spinney, Dyke Rd Ave, Hove, Sussex BN3 6QT, England.

SEAMONE, Joyce Evelyn; b. 21 May 1946, Bridgewater, Nova Scotia, Canada. Vocalist; Songwriter; Entertainer. m. Gerald Ivan Seamone, 12 Sept. 1964, 3 d. *Career:* Toured Canada, early 1970s; Television appearances, Countrytime, Canadian National TV show; Headliner, exhibitions and clubs in Eastern Canada; Currently performing in Eastern Canada. *Recordings:* Testing 1–2–3, 1972; Merry Christmas From Joyce Seamone, 1972; Stand By For A Special Announcement, 1973; I Can See It In His Eyes, 1976; The Other Side of Me, 1994; Instructional Line, Dance video, 1995. *Honours:* Gold Record, Testing 1–2–3, 1973; CHFX-FM, Country Music Hall of Fame, Halifax, Nova Scotia, Canada. *Membership:* CCMA; SOCAN; ECMA; MIANS; SAC. *Current Management:* Gerald Seamone. *Address:* RR2 New Germany, Nova Scotia B0R 1E0, Canada.

SEARLE, Richard; Musician (bass). *Career:* Former Member, Doctor and the Medics; Several television appearances; Formed Corduroy for one-off gig; Decided to continue and obtained record deal; Several UK top ten hits. *Recordings:* Singles: with Doctor and the Medics: Spirit in the Sky (UK number 1); Burn; with Corduroy: Something in My Eye; The Frighteners; London, England; The Joker is Wild; Overhaul; Albums: Dad Man Cat, 1992; High Havoc, 1993; Out of Here, 1994; The New You, 1997; Clik!, 1999.

SEATE, Tshepo, (Appleseed); b. Zimbabwe. *Education:* Degree in Quantity Surveying. *Career:* Mem., kwaito band, Bongo Maffin, 1996–; World Wild Grooves tour, France, 2000; Performances in UK, Denmark, 2000; worked with: Skunk Anansie, Chaka Khan, Stevie Wonder, Boys II Men, Hugh Masekela. *Recordings:* Albums: Final Entry, 1996; The Concerto, 1998; IV, 1999; Bongolution, 2001. *Honours:* South African Music Award, Best Kwaito Artist, 1999; Kora Award, Best African Group, 2001; Gold disc, for Bongolution. *Address:* c/o Sony Music South Africa, 230 Jan Smuts Ave, Dunkeld West, 2196 Gauteng, South Africa.

SEBASTIAN, John; b. 17 March 1944, New York, USA. Vocalist; Musician (guitar, harmonica, autoharp). *Career:* Founder member, The Lovin' Spoonful, 1965–68; Appearances include: British tour, 1966; Beach Boys Summer Spectacular, Anaheim, 1966; State Fairs tour, 1966; Solo artiste, 1969–; Appearances include: Woodstock Festival, 1969; Isle of Wight Festival, 1970; Tours as one-man show, 1970s; Session musician for artistes including: Stephen Stills; Rita Coolidge; Everly Brothers; Host, The Golden Age of Rock 'N' Roll, AandE cable channel, 1991; Actor, episode, Married With Children, Fox TV, 1992. *Compositions include:* Music for television and films: Welcome Back, for Welcome Back, Kotter, ABC TV, 1976; The Care Bears; Strawberry Shortcake; The Jerk II, NBC TV. *Recordings:* Albums: with The Lovin' Spoonful: Do You Believe In Magic, 1965; Daydream, 1966; What's Shakin', 1966; Hums of The Lovin' Spoonful, 1966; The Best of The Lovin' Spoonful, 1967; Everything Playing, 1968; The Best of The Lovin' Spoonful Vol. 2, 1968; Very Best of Lovin' Spoonful, 1998; Solo albums: John B Sebastian, 1970; John Sebastian Live, 1970; Cheapo Cheapo Productions Present, 1971; The Four of Us, 1971; The Tarzana Kid, 1974; Welcome Back, 1976; Tar Beach, 1993; John Sebastian, 1995; I Want My Roots, 1996; King Biscuit Flower Hour Live, 1996; Chasin' Gus' Ghost, 1999; with Doors: Greatest Hits, 1996; with Peter Paul and Mary: Around the Campfire, 1998; with Secret Sessions: Secret Sessions, 1999; Live, 2000; Faithful Virtue, 2000; Hit singles include: with Lovin' Spoonful: Do You Believe In Magic, 1965; You Didn't Have To Be So Nice, 1966; Daydream, 1966; Did You Ever Have To Make Up Your Mind, 1966; Summer In The City (No. 1, USA), 1966; Rain On The Roof, 1966; Nashville Cats, 1967; Darling Be Home Soon, 1967; Six O'Clock, 1967; She's Still A Mystery, 1967; Money, 1968. *Current Management:* c/o David Bendett, 2431 Briar Crest Rd, Beverly Hills, CA 90210, USA.

SEBASTIAN, Mark Douglas; b. 20 Feb. 1951, New York, NY, USA. Performer; Songwriter; Screenwriter; Film Prod; Musician (guitar, bass, keyboards). *Education:* Kim Stanley Drama Study; Piano study, New York.

Career: Performances: New York clubs: Gaslight; Wetlands; Lone Star; Theatre Music: La Mama; Television; Solid Gold; Cheers; Wizards and Warriors; Los Angeles clubs: The Strand; Wadsworth Theatre; Also performing member, Second City Emperor (Santa Monica group). *Compositions:* Summer In The City (Lovin' Spoonful, 1966) (No. 1, USA), song co-written with (brother) John Sebastian and Steve Boone, used in film Die Hard – With A Vengeance, 1996. *Honours:* 3 Gold records. *Membership:* BMI; ASCAP; SAG; AFTRA. *Address:* c/o BMI, Los Angeles, California, USA.

SEBESTYÉN, Márta; b. 1961, Budapest, Hungary. Vocalist; Musician (recorder); Songwriter. *Career:* Sings, researches and promotes roots music of Hungary and Transylvania; Grew up surrounded by folk music, mother had studied with composer Zoltan Kodaly and collected folk songs; Started singing at Budapest 'dance houses' while still at school; Joined Sebö Halmos group, 1975; Became part of Hungary's leading folk group Muszikás, 1980; Also sang with renowned group Vujicsics; Appeared in musical based on the life of King Stephen, 1984; Toured internationally with Muzsikás. *Recordings:* Albums: Transylvanian Portraits, 1993; Kismet, 1996; with Karoly Cserepes: Hungarian Christmas Songs, 1984; Loverecord, 1985; Emigration, 1986; with Muzsikás: The Prisoner's Song, 1986; Muzsikás, 1987; Blues For Transylvania, 1991; Maramaros – The Lost Jewish Music of Transylvania, 1993; The Bartok Album, 1999; with Vujicsics: Serbian Music From Southern Hungary, 1988; features on: East Wind, Andy Irvine and Davy Spillane, 1992; Boheme, Deep Forest, 1995; Coolfin, Donal Lunny, 1998; The English Patient OST, 1996; Flirt OST, 1996; American Rhapsody, 2001. *Honours:* Hungarian Female Singer of the Year, 1984; Liszt Award, 1991.

SECADA, Jon; b. 10 April 1961, Havana, Cuba. Vocalist; Songwriter; Prod. *Education:* Master's degree, Jazz Vocal Performance, University of Miami. *Career:* Central and South America Tour, 1994; US Tour, 1995; World Cup, 1994; X-Mas in Washington, 1994; National Anthem World Series, 1992; Grease, Broadway, 1995; Lifebeat concert, 1994. *Recordings:* Albums: Jon Secada, 1992; Heart Soul and A Voice, 1994; Si Te Vas, 1994; Frank Sinatra Duets II: The Best Is Yet To Come, 1994; Heart Soul and Voice, 1994; Amor, 1995; Secada, 1997; Better Part Of Me, 2000; The Gift, 2001; Singles include: Just Another Day, 1992; Mental Picture, 1995; Where Do I Go From You?, 1995; Whipped, 1995; If I Never Knew You, 1995; Too Late too Soon, 1997. *Honours:* Grammy: Best Latin Pop Album: Otro Dia Mas Sin Verte, 1992; Alumnus of Distinction, University of Miami. *Membership:* National Academy of Recording Arts and Sciences. *Current Management:* William Morris Agency, 151 El Camino Dr., Beverly Hills, CA 90212, USA; Estefan Enterprises, 6205 Bird Rd, Miami, FL 33155, USA.

SECK, Cheick Amadou Tidiane; b. 11 Dec. 1953, Segou, Mali. Musician (keyboards, African percussion); Vocalist. 1 s. *Education:* BEPC, Diplome Institut National des Arts; Learned lear organ and solfege in church. *Career:* Concert with Jimmy Cliff, 1977; African and European tours with The Ambassadors of Mali and Salif Keita; World Tour with Amina, 1992–93; Printemps de Bourges Festival; Television Show: Taratata; Cercle De Minuit; Nulle Part Ailleurs, France. *Recordings:* Salif Keita: Soro; Amen; Graham Haynes: The Griots Footstep; Joe Zawinul: Next; Hank Jones, Cheick Tidiane Seck: My People; The Madenkas; with Toure Kunda: Mouslai, 1996; Ceci N'Est Pas Une Compilation, 1998; with Tama: Nostalgie, 1999; Sekou Diabete Bembeya; Nahawa Doumbia; Ousmane Koyate Band; Tama; Toure Kunda; Joe Zawinul. *Honours:* Emission: Pollen by Jean Louis Foulquier; Articles: Liberation/Bingo. *Membership:* SACEM; SPEDIDAM. *Current Management:* Jacques Sajuan, Polygram Music, 20 rue des Fosses St Jacques, 75005 Paris, France.

SEDAKA, Neil; b. 13 March 1939. Vocalist; Songwriter. m. Leba Margaret Strassberg, 11 Sept. 1962, 1 s., 1 d. *Education:* Graduate, Juilliard School of Music. *Career:* Solo performer, world-wide, 1959–; Television appearances include: NBC Special, 1976. *Compositions include:* Breaking Up Is Hard To Do; Stupid Cupid; Calendar Girl; Oh! Carol; Stairway To Heaven; Happy Birthday Sweet Sixteen; Laughter In The Rain; Bad Blood; Love Will Keep Us Together; Solitaire; The Hungry Years; Lonely Night (Angel Face). *Recordings:* Albums include: In The Pocket; Sedaka's Back; The Hungry Years; Steppin' Out; A Song; All You Need Is The Music; Come See About Me; Greatest Hits, 1988; Oh! Carol and Other Hits, 1990; Timeless, 1992; Calendar Girl, 1993; Tuneweaver, 1995; The Immaculate, 1997; Tales of Love, 1999; Timeless Classics Live, 2001; Very Best Of, 2001. *Honours:* Songwriters' Hall of Fame, 1980; Platinum album, Timeless, 1992; Numerous Gold records; Various industry awards. *Membership:* AGVA; AFofM; AFTRA. *Address:* c/o Neil Sedaka Music, 201 E 66th St, Suite 3N, New York, NY 10021, USA.

SEDGWICK, Amanda; b. 7 Oct. 1970, Stockholm, Sweden. Musician; Songwriter; Composer. *Education:* Royal Swedish University College of Music, Stockholm. *Career:* Toured Sweden; Appeared on Swedish Television and Radio, including Live Broadcasts. *Compositions:* Volt, 3 movement suite for jazz group, string quartet and woodwinds. *Recordings:* Volt, 1996; Contributor to So Many Stars, 1996 and Kalabra, 1997. *Honours:* Debut of the Year, Swedish National Radio. *Membership:* Swedish Society of Popular Music Composers; Swedish Performing Rights Society. *Address:* Stromkarlsvagen 74, 167 62 Bromma, Sweden.

SEEGER, Michael; b. 15 Aug. 1933, New York, NY, USA. Vocalist; Musician; Folklorist. m. (1) Marjorie L Ostrow, 20 Dec. 1960, divorced, 3 c., (2) Alice L Gerrard, 16 Aug. 1970, divorced, (3) Alexia Smith, 27 Aug. 1995. *Career:* Founder member, New Lost City Ramblers, 1958–; Strange Creek Singers, 1968–76; Bent Mountain Band, 1981; Guest lecturer, English department, University of California, Fresno, 1974; Performs Appalachian vocal and instrumental music in variety of styles, radio, TV, USA and abroad; Numerous record albums and documentary recordings from traditional folk musicians and dancers. *Recordings:* Old Time Country Music, 1991; Southern Banjo Sounds, 1998; Vertie's Dream, Jones And Leva, 2000. *Honours:* First prize, banjo, Galax Virginia Old Time Fiddlers Convention, 1958; National Endowment for the Arts grantee, 4 times; Visiting scholar, Smithsonian Institute, 1983; Guggenheim Fellow, 1984; Ralph J. Gleason Memorial Award Rex Foundation, 1994. *Current Management:* Folklore Productions, 1671 Appian Way, Santa Monica, CA 90401–3293, USA. *Address:* PO Box 1592, Lexington, VA 24450–1592, USA.

SEEGER, Peggy; b. 17 June 1935, New York, USA. Vocalist; Songwriter; Musician (guitar, piano, 5-string banjo, autoharp, Appalachian dulcimer, English concertina). m. Ewan MacColl, 25 Jan. 1978, 2 s., 1 d. *Education:* Radclyffe College. *Career:* Concerts include: (in USA) Boston Orchestra Hall; Carnegie Hall; Australia; New Zealand; Canada; UK; Sweden; USSR; France; Belgium; Netherlands; People's Republic of China; Many television and radio appearances; Tours since 1955. *Compositions:* Ballad of Springhill; Gonna Be An Engineer. *Recordings:* 19 solo albums; Major participation in over 100 other albums; Recent releases include: Love Will Linger On, 2000; Almost Commercially Viable, 2000. *Publications:* ; with Ewan MacColl: Travellers' Songs of England and Ireland; Doomsday In The Afternoon; Solo: Peggy Seeger Song Book: Forty Years of Songmaking; The Essential Ewan MacColl Song Book. *Honours:* Italia Prize for participation in BBC Radio Ballad: Singing The Fishing. *Membership:* Musicians' Union; USA and UK. *Current Management:* Josh Dunson.

SEEGER, Pete; b. 3 May 1919, New York, USA. Folk Musician (banjo, guitar); Composer. m. Toshi, 20 July 1943, 1 s., 2 d. *Education:* Harvard College, 1936–38. *Career:* Folk singer/musician for 56 years; World-wide tours across 35 countries; Collaborated on anti-Fascist and labour songs; National Director, People's Songs Inc, 1945; Formed the Weavers, 1948; appeared, until blacklisted from, on national radio and television networks; Assisted Newport Folk Festivals; Produced educational short films, Folklore Research Films; TV and film appearances: To Hear My Banjo Play, 1946; Rainbow Quest, 1965; Tell Me That You Love Me, Junie Moon, 1970. *Compositions include:* Turn, Turn, Turn; Where Have All The Flowers Gone; If I Had A Hammer (with Lee Hays); Kisses Sweeter Than Wine (with the Weavers); Also popularized Guantanamera, We Shall Overcome. *Recordings include:* Abiyoyo, 1967; Rainbow Race, 1971; The World of Pete Seeger, 1973; Live at Newport, 1993; Kisses Sweeter than Wine, 1996; Link in the Chain, 1996; God Bless the Grass, 1998; American Favorite Ballads, Vols 1, 2, 3, 4, 5; If I had a Hammer: Songs of Hope and Struggle, 1998; Pioneer of Folk, 1999; Pete Seeger's Greatest Hits, 2000; Live In Lisbon, 2000; In Prague (Live, 1964), 2001. *Publications:* American Folk Ballads, 1961; The Bells of Rhymney, 1964; How To Play The Five String Banjo, Henscratches and Flyspecks, 1973; The Incompleat Folksinger (with Charles Seeger), 1973; The Foolish Frog, 1973; Where Have All The Flowers Gone (autobiography), 1993; Co-writer with Robert Reiser: Abiyoyo, 1983; Carry It On, 1986; Everybody Says Freedom, 1990. *Honours:* Westchester People's Action Committee, Peace and Justice Award to Toshi and Peter Seeger, 1990; NEA National Medal of Arts, 1994; Kennedy Center Honours, 1994. *Membership:* AFofM. *Current Management:* Harold Leventhal. *Address:* Room 1218, 250 W 57th St, New York, NY 10107, USA.

SEGER, Bob; b. 6 May 1945, Dearborn, Missouri, USA. Vocalist; Songwriter; Musician (keyboards). *Career:* Member, The Town Criers; Doug Brown and The Omens, 1965–66; Leader of own bands: The Last Heard, 1966–67; The Bob Seger System, 1967–70; The Silver Bullet Band, 1976–; Regular US tours. *Recordings:* Albums: Ramblin' Gamblin' Man, 1969; Noah, 1970; Mongrel, 1970; Brand New Morning, 1971; Smokin' OP's, 1972; Back In '72, 1973; Seven/Contrasts, 1974; Beautiful Loser, 1975; Live Bullet, 1976; Night Moves, 1977; Stranger In Town, 1978; Against The Wind (No. 1, USA), 1980; Nine Tonight, 1981; The Distance, 1983; Like A Rock, 1986; The Fire Inside, 1991; Greatest Hits, 1995; It's A Mystery, 1995; Singles include: Ramblin' Gamblin Man, 1969; Katmandu, 1975; Night Moves, 1977; Mainstreet, 1977; Still The Same, 1978; Hollywood Nights, 1978; We've Got Tonight, 1979; Fire Lake, 1980; Against The Wind, 1980; You'll Accomp'ny Me, 1980; Tryin' To Live My Life Without You, 1981; Shame On The Moon (No. 2, USA), 1983; Even Now, 1983; Roll Me Away, 1983; American Storm, 1986; Like A Rock, 1986; Shakedown (No. 1, USA), from film soundtrack Beverley Hills Cop II, 1987; The Real Love, 1991; It's A Mystery, 1995; Turn the Page, 1995; Night Moves, 1997; Also contributor to: Risky Business, 1983; Teachers, 1984; Miami, for television series Miami Vice, 1986; A Very Special Christmas benefit album, 1987; Let It Roll, Little Feat, 1988; Armageddon, 1998; Guilty: 30 Years of Randy Newman, 1998. *Honours:* Numerous Platinum discs; Grammy Award, Best Rock Performance, 1981; Star on Hollywood Walk of Fame, 1988; Governors Award, NARAS, 1992; Motor City Music Awards,

Musician of the Year, Outstanding National Rock 'n' Pop Album, 1992. *Current Management:* Punch Enterprises, 567 Purdy, Birmingham, MI 48009, USA.

SEGLEM, Karl; b. 8 July 1961, Ardalstangen, Norway. Musician (tenor saxophone); Composer; Arranger. *Education:* Private music lessons. *Career:* Toured Norway and abroad with jazz and folk bands, 1985–; Now one of foremost saxophone players, Norway; Working with own music based on Norwegian folk music; Numerous television and radio appearances; Concert tours: USA; Japan; UK; Germany. *Recordings:* with Isglem: To Steg, Null G; with Utla: Juv; Brodd; Dans; Solo album: Rit: Tya; And Spir. *Honours:* Edvard Prize, 1998. *Membership:* TONO; NOPA; GRAMO; Norwegian Musician Asscn. *Address:* Hammerstads gt 48, 0363 Oslo, Norway.

SEGUNDO, Compay, (Maximo Francisco Repilado Muñoz); b. 18 Nov. 1907, Siboney, Oriente, Cuba. Vocalist; Musician (guitar, armónico, clarinet). *Career:* Invented seven-stringed guitar called an armónico; Collaborations: Quinteto Cuban Stars; Cuarteto Hatuey; Miguel Matamoros; Los Compadres (with Lorenzo Hierrezuelo); Name originated from his part as second voice in the duo Los Compadres – compay being a diminutive of compadre and segundo meaning second (or harmony) voice against Hierrezuelo's lead vocal (Compay Primero); Retired, 1970s; Began performing again with Cuarteto Patria in the 1980s; Performed and recorded in Spain, mid-1990s, before working on the Buena Vista Social Club album; Appeared in Wim Wenders' documentary film Buena Vista Social Club. *Recordings:* recent Albums: Antología, 1995; Buena Vista Social Club, 1997; Calle Salud, 1999; Las Flores de la Vida, 2000; Yo Vengo Aquí, 2001; Duets, 2002. *Current Management:* International Music Network, 278 Main St, Gloucester, MA 01930, USA. *Website:* www.imnworld.com.

SEINE, Johannes Hendricus; b. 30 March 1946, Amsterdam, Netherlands. Man.-Dir; Artist Man; Agent. m. Annette Washington, 17 Dec. 1971, 2 s. *Career:* Manager, Amsterdam bands, 1964; Producer Dutch radio 3 Vara Drive-in show, 1969; Producer, Radio Northsea Mobile Show, 1972; Managing Director, Europop; Manager, agent for: American Gipsy; Lois Lane; Boney M; Doop; Tours organized with: Divine; Inner Circle; Latoya Jackson; Tower of Power; Capella; Prodigy. *Current Management:* Europop. *Address:* Gaelstraat 1b, 2013 CE Haarlem, Netherlands.

SELIGMAN, Matthew; b. 14 July 1955, Cyprus. Musician (bass guitar). *Career:* The Soft Boys, 1979–80; The Thompson Twins, 1981–82; Thomas Dolby, 1982–84; Toured USA, Europe, with Thomas Dolby, 1984; Performed at Live Aid with David Bowie, 1985; Session bassist, London, 1986–94; Radio Science Orchestra, 1994–98. *Compositions:* Co-writer of: The Brightest Star; Now and Forever; Motorcycle; Neon Sisters; Slipping You The Midnight Fish; Daddy; Stabbed In The Heart Again. *Recordings:* English Garden, Bruce Woolley and The Camera Club, 1979; Drip Dry Zone, SW9, 1980; with The Soft Boys: Underwater Moonlight, 1980; Lope At The Hive, 1981; Invisible Hits, 1983; The Soft Boys 1979–81, 1994; Black Snake Diamond Rock, Robyn Hitchcock, 1981; In The Name of Love, The Thompson Twins, 1982; Magic's Wand, Whodini, 1982; with Thomas Dolby: Blinded By Science, 1982; The Flat Earth, 1983; Retrospectacle, 1994; A Moral Tale, Sophie Cherie, 1983; Absolute Beginners, David Bowie, 1985; Dancing In The Street, David Bowie and Mick Jagger, 1985; Be My Enemy, The Waterboys, 1986; with Transvision Vamp: Tell That Girl To Shut Up, 1988; Baby I Don't Care, 1989; with Morrissey: Yes I Am Blind, 1989; East West, 1989; Build It Up, June Mitchell, 1989; April Moon, Sam Brown, 1990; with Sinead O'Connor: The Value of Ignorance, 1989; Fire On Babylon, 1994; God Must Live In New York City, 1998; China, Tori Amos, 1991; with The Stereo MCs: Elevate My Mind, 1990; All Night Long, 1992; The End, 1992; Nan Vernon: Manta Ray, 1994; with The Radio Science Orchestra: Theme From The Electronic City; The Architect; Beachcombing Man; The Brightest Star, 1995; with Ghostland: Blue, 1998; Free, 1998; Interview With The Angel, 2001; with Moog Poets: Space Galleon; with Grace Jones and the Radio Science Orchestra: Strange Weather; As Producer: Crazy, The Pop Guns, 1991. *Membership:* Musicians' Union. *Address:* 39 Essex St, London WC2R 3AT, England.

SELLAM, Philippe; b. 24 Oct. 1960, Algeria. Musician (saxophone). *Career:* Concerts with: John Scofield; Gil Evans; European Union Radio Big Band; Michel Portal; Many tours, Africa. *Recordings:* with Gil Evans; Laurent Cugny; Henri Salvador; French National Jazz Orchestra; Michel Legrand; 3 records with own band African Project. *Honours:* Best Soloist, Concours National De Jazz De Paris La Defense, 1987.

SELLAR, Gordon Maxwell; b. 13 June 1947, Glasgow, Scotland. Musican (bass guitar, guitar). m. Julie, 22 March 1975, 1 s., 1 d. *Career:* Band member: Beggar's Opera; The Alex Harvey Band; The Denny Laine Band; Jackie Lynton Band; The Freddie Starr Band. *Compositions:* Featured on 2 Gordon Neville albums. *Recordings include:* Joseph and His Amazing Technicolour Dreamcoat; Evita; Robson and Jerome, 1995, including Unchained Melody (No. 1, UK) and Up On The Roof (No. 1, UK). *Membership:* Musicians' Union. *Address:* 2 Clewer Court Rd, Clewer Village, Windsor, Berks SL4 5JD, England.

SELLERS, Joey Elton; b. 5 May 1962, Phoenix, Arizona, USA. Musician (trombone); Composer. *Education:* BS, Music Education, State University, Arizona; Studied improvisation with Warne Marsh; Chuck Mahronic; Bobby Shew; Gary Foster. *Career:* Merv Griffin with Side Street Strutters, 1984; US Presidents dinner, 1986; Numerous radio broadcasts; Brass quintets, I and II, St Louis Brass; Trombone with California Arts Trombone Quartet. *Recordings:* Joey Sellers Jazz Aggregation: Something For Nothing; Pastels, Ashes; Malby/Sellers Quartet: Cosas; Kim Richmond/Clay Jenkins Ensemble: Range; Commission for Gil Evans Fellowship: Seeds; Trumpet Summit for Summit Records featuring: Bobby Shew; Alan Vizzetti; Vince D'Marino; Satoko Fujii Orchestra. *Honours:* Gil Evans Fellowship in Jazz Composition. *Membership:* BMI; AFofM. *Current Management:* Walrus Publishing; Balquidder Music. *Address:* 4243 E Fifth St, 1, Long Beach, CA 90814, USA.

SELWAY, Phil(lip James); b. 23 May 1967, Hemingford Grey, Cambridgeshire, England. Musician (drums). m. Kate. *Education:* English and History, Liverpool Polytechnic. *Career:* Mem. and lead singer, On A Friday, 1987, renamed Radiohead, 1991–; Numerous tours, festivals and television appearances. *Recordings:* Albums: Pablo Honey, 1993; The Bends, 1995; OK Computer, 1997; Kid A, 2000; Amnesiac, 2001; I Might Be Wrong, 2001. Singles: Drill (EP), 1992; Creep, 1993; Anyone Can Play Guitar, 1993; Pop Is Dead, 1993; Stop Whispering, 1993; Itch (EP), 1994; My Iron Lung (EP), 1994; My Iron Lung, 1994; Live Au Forum (EP), 1995; High and Dry, 1995; Fake Plastic Trees, 1995; Just, 1995; Street Spirit (Fade Out), 1996; The Bends, 1996; Paranoid Android, 1997; Karma Police, 1997; No Surprises, 1997; Climbing Up The Walls, 1997; Airbag/How Am I Driving? (EP), 1998; Pyramid Song, 2001; Knives Out, 2001; I Might Be Wrong, 2001. *Honours:* Grammy Award, Best Alternative Rock Performance, 1998; Q Award, Best Act in the World Today, 2002. *Address:* c/o Parlophone Records, 43 Brook Green, London W6 7EF, England. *Website:* www.radiohead.com.

SELWYN, Esmond Wayne; b. 19 Feb. 1948, London, England. Musician (guitar). m. Veronica, 27 July 1975, 3 s. *Education:* BA, German and French, Kings College, London; Personal tuition from master musicians: Ivor Mairants, Tal Farlow. *Career:* Professional musician from age 12; Varied career especially in Jazz includes: Private party, Frank Sinatra, Savoy Hotel, 1975; Malta Jazz Festival, opposite Chick Corea and Elvin Jones, 1993; Tour with Salena Jones, Thailand, 1994. *Recordings:* Matt Bianco: Tequila; Melanie Marshall: Cocktail; Robin Jones Quartet: Eye of The Hurricane; Don Rendell. *Publications:* Jake Lee Arrives; The Jakes Progress; Included in Guildhall Guitar Syllabus. *Membership:* Musicians' Union. *Address:* Min Y Dyffryn, The Green, Gresford, Wrexham, Clwyd LL11 7BB, Wales.

SEMENOFF, Sasha; b. 20 Sept. 1924, Riga, Latvia. Orchestra Leader, Violinist. m. Sylvia, 2 s. *Education:* Handel Music Conservatory, Munich. *Career:* Music Contractor, Las Vegas, since 1959; Romantic Strings, Merv Griffin Show, 1972; Television film, Pleasure Palace; Movies, Vegas Vacation, Casino and Honeymoon in Vegas. *Compositions:* The Song I Wrote For You, 1974; Remember; Sasha Nova; Just One More Time; Bat-Yam. *Recordings:* Live Album with Elvis Presley, International Hotel, Las Vegas, 1969–70. *Membership:* American Federation of Musicians; Screen Actors Guild. *Address:* 2125 Michael Way, Las Vegas, NV 89108 3171, USA.

SEN DOG, (Senen Reyes); b. 20 Nov. 1965, Cuba. Vocalist. *Career:* Member, Cypress Hill; Numerous tours including Lollapalooza; Collaboration with Pearl Jam on the film soundtrack Judgement Night, 1993; Left band, 1995. *Recordings:* Singles: Phuncky Feel One, 1991; Hand on the Pump, 1991; Latin Lingo, 1991; Insane the Brain, 1993; We Ain't Goin' Out Like That EP, 1994; Throw Your Set in the Air, 1995; Albums: Cypress Hill, 1991; Black Sunday, 1993; Cypress Hill III: Temples of Boom, 1995; Live At The Fillmore, 2000.

SENATOR, Ronald; b. 17 April 1926, London, England. Composer; Author. m. Miriam Brickman. *Education:* Marlborough College, Oxford University; London University; Trinity College of Music. *Career:* Film Work, Music for Peter Greenaways Lightning; Incidental Music for Stage. *Compositions:* Include, Trotsky; Insects. *Honours:* Pulitzer Prize, 1991. *Membership:* PRS; ASCAP; BAC&S; BMI. *Address:* 81 Hillcrest Ave, Yonkers, NY 10705, USA.

SENFLUK, Jerry (Jaromir); b. 17 March 1946, Prague, Czechoslovakia. Jazz Musician (clarinet). m. Jirina, 7 June 1973, 1 s. *Education:* Piano and Elementary Theory of Music, 1952–60; Clarinet, by Mr Karel Dlouhy, 1969–61; Intonation, 1959–61; Conservatoire in Prague, 1961–67. *Career:* Frequent bookings in West Germany, worked with a band accompanying Freddie Kohlman, and with Savoy Gang, swing quartet, 1975–77; Founded Hallmark Swingtet, Berlin, 1979–84; West End venues and composing, London, England, 1985–90; With pianist Mick Pyne, guitarist Nils Solberg, double bassist John Rees-Jones and drummer Rex Bennett, formed Capital Swing, 1991; Yves 'Little Fats' Guyot and Eric Luter, residencies at Hotel Ermitage Golf near Gstaad, Switzerland, 1991–94; Radio Appearances: BBC2, Jazz Parade, 1993; BBC 2, Jazz Notes, 1994. *Compositions:* Pas De Chat; Air Condition Breakdown. *Recordings:* From East to West, 1974; We Swing – Take It From Me, 1995; Swing Express, 1997. *Membership:* Musicians' Union;

Asscn of British Jazz Musicians. *Address:* 280 Lordship Lane, Dulwich, London SE22 8LY, England.

SENIOR, Russell; b. 18 May 1961, Sheffield, England. Musician (guitar, violin). *Career:* Mem., Pulp, –1996; Numerous tours, television appearances and festival dates; Contribution to film soundtrack, Mission Impossible, 1996; Founding mem., Venini, 1999–2000. *Recordings:* Albums: with Pulp: It, 1983; Freaks, 1987; Separations, 1992; His 'N' Hers, 1994; Different Class (No. 1, UK) 1995. Singles: with Pulp: My Lighthouse/Looking For Life, 1983; Everybody's Problem/There Was, 1983; Little Girl (With Blue Eyes), 1985; Dogs Are Everywhere (EP), 1986; They Suffocate At Night, 1986; Master Of The Universe, 1987; My Legendary Girlfriend, 1990; Countdown, 1991; OU, 1992; Babies, 1992; Razzmatazz, 1993; Lipgloss, 1993; Do You Remember The First Time?, 1994; The Sisters (EP), 1994; Common People (No. 2, UK), 1995; Sorted For E's and Whizz/Misshapes (No. 2, UK), 1995; Disco 2000, 1995; with Venini: Carnival Star, 1999; Postcard, 2000; Unshaker (EP), 2000.

SEPE, Daniele; b. 17 April 1960, Naples, Italy. Musician (wind instruments). *Education:* Graduated, flute, Conservatorio Sanpietro A Masella, Naples. *Career:* Formed group, Gruppo Operaio 'E Zezi Di Pomigliano; Appeared festivals: Rennes; Martigues; Bonn, 1976; Played at festivals including: Les Allummes, Nanates; Vignola; Atina; Ravenna; Horizontal Radio Linz; Rai Stereonette; Audio Box; DOC; Radiotresuite. *Compositions include:* Arrangements for groups including: Little Italy; Bisca; Walhalla; Degrado; Music for theatre, ballet, cinema. *Recordings:* Malamusica, 1983; L'Uscita dei Gladiatori, 1991; Plays Standards and More, 1991; Vite Perdite, 1993; Spiritus Mundi, 1995; Contribututions to: Roberto Murolo, Tu Si Na Cosa Grande, 1995. *Publications:* L'Italia Del Rock; Encyclopedia Del Rock. *Honours:* Academia International Del Tango. *Current Management:* Roberto Balassoue. *Address:* Daniele Sepe, Via Manzoni 191, 80123 Naples, Italy.

SERGENT, Carole; b. 22 Jan. 1962, Montargis, Loiret, France. Vocalist; Entertainer; Author; Composer; Actress. 1 d. *Education:* CIM; ARIAM. *Career:* Festivals: Jacques Brel; Jazz Amiens; Jazz Montlouis; Printemps Bourges; Choralies; Jazz Paris; Tourtour Paris; Jazz Sous Les Pommiers; Estival; France Television 2; MCM Telsat; 1988–; 673rd concert, 1997. *Recordings:* Albums: Chant Du Corps, 1994; Cherche Passion, 1997. *Honours:* Ellipse d'Or Canal, 1992. *Membership:* SACEM. *Current Management:* J Fallot. *Address:* 45 rue Jussieu, 78150 Le Chesnay, France.

SERMILÄ, Jarmo Kalevi; b. 16 Aug. 1939, Hämeenlinna, Finland. Composer; Musician (trumpet, flugelhorn). m. Ritva, 6 Nov. 1962. *Education:* Studied with Frantisek Kovaricek, Prague; Master's degree, University of Helsinki, 1975; Composer's diploma, Sibelius Academy, 1975. *Career:* Worked for Finnish Broadcasting Company (YLE); Director, YLE Experimental Studio, 1973–79; Jazz improvising on trumpet, 1970s–; Played with Czech artists, Emil Vicklicky, Rudolf Dasek; Artistic Director, Time of Music Festival, late 1988–99. *Compositions:* Avant-garde, electro-acoustic music; Music for chamber groups; Ballets and orchestral works. *Recordings:* Quattro Rilievi; At Bizarre Exits; Random Infinities. *Honours:* Janacek Medal, 1978; Music Reward of the City of Hämeenlinna, 1981; Smetana Medal, 1984; State Grant for Composing, 1990–. *Membership:* Finnish Composers' Society. *Address:* Niittykatu 7 A 7, 13100 Hämeenlinna, Finland.

SERNEHOLT, Marie Eleonor; b. 11 July 1983, Stockholm, Sweden. Vocalist. *Education:* Rytmus school, Stockholm. *Career:* Picked to be member of A*Teens group following auditions at Leslie Kühler's dance school, 1998; Continued educational studies whilst pursuing musical career; Prestigious US support tours for *NSYNC and Britney Spears, 2000. *Recordings:* Albums: The Abba Generation, 1999; Teen Spirit, 2001; Singles: Mamma Mia, Super Trouper, Gimme! Gimme! Gimme!, Happy New Year, 1999; Dancing Queen, Upside Down, 2000; Halfway Around The World, Sugar Rush, 2001. *Honours:* Broke Swedish sales records with first album and single; World-wide sales of first album in excess of 3m.; Viva Music Awards, Best International Newcomer, 2000. *Address:* c/o Stockholm Records, Sweden. *Website:* www.stockholmrecords.com.

SERVI, Jo; b. 17 May 1970, Aylesbury, Buckinghamshire, England. Vocalist; Actor. *Career:* Session singer, 1988–; Steel pan player, singer, Radcliffe Rollers Steel Band; Television: Saturday Superstore, 1986; Barrymore, 1993; Performed Tommy, Marquee, with the Who, 1993; Backing vocalist, duo, Sister-Brother; Lead singer, keyboards, The Bizz, 1993; Wind Parade, 1994; Joined Southlanders vocal quartet, 1995. *Membership:* Musicians' Union; Equity. *Current Management:* Richard Starnowski Casting; Jackie Palmer Agency. *Address:* 2 Bateman Dr., Brookhurst, Aylesbury, Buckinghamshire WP21 8AF, England.

SESSOMATO. See: **LEE, Dave**.

7TH PLAIN, (THE). See: **SLATER, Luke**.

SEVERINSEN, Doc (Carl H.); b. 7 July 1927, Arlington, Oregon, USA. Musician; Music Dir. m. Emily Marshall, 1980, 2 s., 3 d. *Career:* Musician with: Ted Fio Rito, 1945; Charlie Barnet, 1947–49; Also with Tommy Dorsey; Benny Goodman; House band, Steve Allen Show, NBC, 1954–55; NBC Orchestra for Tonight Show, 1962–; MD, 1967–; Partner, Severinsen-Akwright Co. *Recordings:* Albums include: Brass Roots, 1971; Facets, 1988; Night Journey; Doc Severinsen and Friends; Ja-Da; Two Sides of Doc Severinsen; Brass on Ivory; Skyliner; Doc Severinsen and Xebron; Doc Severinsen with Strings; The Very Best of Doc Severinsen. *Current Management:* Brentwood Management Group, 11812 San Vicente Blvd #200, Los Angeles, CA 90049, USA.

SEVERSON, Paul Thomas; b. 18 Aug. 1928, Fargo, North Dakota, USA. Composer; Arranger; Musician (piano, trombone); Educator. m. (1) Marie Proft, (2) Shirley Jean Thompson, divorced, 1 s., 1 d., (3) Karen Louise Schwankel, 1 s. *Education:* BMus, 1950, MusM, 1951, Northwestern University, Evanston, Illinois, USA. *Career:* Performed with various orchestras including Stan Kenton Orchestra, Hal McIntyre Orchestra, Chicago Theatre Orchestra and Chicago Civic Symphony, 1951–54; Performed with artists including Stan Getz, Dizzy Gillespie, Louis Armstrong, Zoot Simms, Art Van Damme, Ella Fitzgerald and Al Hirt; Solo trombonist and arranger, CBS Studios, 1954–62; Composer, arranger, producer, Dick Marx Associates, 1962–73; President, Severson Enterprises, 1975–84; Director, Musical Industry programme, Moorhead (Minnesota) State University, 1984–91; Leader, Great American Ballroom Band, 1980–91; Music Director, Red River Dance and Performing Co, 1980–96; Leader, Paul Severson and Friends Jazz Quintet, 1995–; Leader, composer, arranger, Pianist, Mood Indigo orchestra, 1996–; Composer/arranger with the Jazz Arts Group Big Band. *Compostions:* Over 3000 compositions and arrangements in the broadcast and publishing media; Music for commercials including Chevrolet, McDonalds, Kelloggs, Sears and Wrigley; 4 network television themes; 22 music scores for films; Portrait of Stan Kenton, 1994. *Recordings:* Albums: with Paul Severson Quintet and Septet; And That's That, Jazz Arts Big Band; 3 arrangements and Portrait of Stan Kenton; Four Freshmen. *Publications:* Co-author, Brass/Wind Artistry – Know Your Instrument, Know Your Mind. *Honours:* Hollywood Advertising Club Grand Slam Award, 1965; Silver medal, Advertising Federation, 1988; 5 Clio Awards; Outstanding Advisor Award, Moorhead State University; Lifetime Achievement Award, Minnesota State University, 2000; Lifetime Achievement Award, Jazz Arts Group, 2000. *Address:* PO Box 535, Ranier, MN 56668–0535, USA.

SEXTON, Charlie; b. 11 Aug. 1968, San Antonio, Texas, USA. Vocalist; Songwriter; Musician (guitar). *Career:* Toured with David Bowie, numerous appearances with Letterman, Conan O'Brien; Acted in Thelma and Louise; Last Ride, with Mickey Rourke and Lori Singer; Recorded with Steve Earle. *Compositions:* Contributed to film soundtracks: Thelma and Louise, True Romance, Beverly Hills Cop II, Air America. *Recordings:* Solo Artist: Pictures for Pleasure, 1985; Charlie Sexton, 1989; Arc Angels, 1992; Under the Wishing Tree, 1995; Contributions on albums, as Member of the band, by Bob Dylan, Don Henley, Keith Richards, Ron Wood; Lucinda Williams; Double Trouble; Michael Fracasso. *Current Management:* Tim Neece Management, 13101 Hwy 71 W, Austin, TX 78736, USA. *Address:* 13101 Hwy 71 W, Austin, TX 78736, USA.

SEXTON, Will; b. 10 Aug. 1970. Musician (guitar). *Career:* Bassist for WC Clark Bires Band, performed and recorded with Stevie Ray Vaughan, Speedy Spaks, Joe Ely, Stephen Stills, Waylon Jennings, Steve Earle; Alejandro Escovedo; Frontman for the Kill; Member of the Sexton Sextet. *Current Management:* Tim Neece Management, 13101 Hwy 71 W, Austin, TX 78736, USA. *Address:* 13101 Hwy 71 W, Austin, TX 78736, USA.

SEYMOUR, Nick; b. 9 Dec. 1958, Benalla, Victoria, Australia. Musician (bass). *Career:* Member, Crowded House; Numerous early acoustic gigs in restaurants and clubs; Numrous headlining tours, festival dates and TV and radio appearances; Farewell gig at Sydney Harbour Bridge and Opera House, 1996; Band split; Formed Akimbo. *Recordings:* Singles include: World Where You Live, 1986; Crowded House EP, 1986; Something So Strong, 1987; Don't Dream It's Over, 1987; Sister Madly, 1988; It's Only Natural, 1991; Fall At Your Feet, 1991; Weather With You, 1991; Four Seasons In One Day, 1992; Pineapple Head, 1993; Locked Out, 1993; Distant Sun, 1993; Nails in My Feet, 1994; Instinct, 1996; Not The Girl You Think You Are, 1996; Everything is Good For You, 1996; Albums: Crowded House, 1986; Temple of Low Men, 1988; Woodface, 1991; Together Alone, 1993; Recurring Dream: The Best of Crowded House, 1996; with Akimbo: Invasion Of The Happy People, 1998; On Top, 2000.

SEYMOUR, Patrick; b. 11 Dec. 1958, Reading, Berkshire, England. Composer; Musician (keyboard); Prod. *Education:* BA Music, Oxford University. *Career:* Film composer, songwriter; World tours with The Eurythmics, 1986, 1989. *Compositions:* Film scores: The Feast of All Saints; Tricks; The End of Summer; Northern Lights; Co-writer: Revival, When Tomorrow Comes, Eurythmics; You're History, Shakespears Sister. *Recordings:* Keyboard player on albums with Eurythmics: Revenge, 1986; We Too Are One, 1989; with The Pretenders: Get Close; with The Jayhawks: Smile, 2000; Other albums by: Mick Jagger; Bob Dylan. *Current Management:* Anxious Music Ltd. *Address:* 147 Crouch Hill, London N8 9QH, England.

SFECI, Paolo; b. 15 May 1955, Zagreb, Croatia. Musician (drums). m. Gordana Farkas, 2 d. Career: Groups: Aerodrom; Parni Valjak; Boa. Recordings: 1 album with Aerodrom; 14 albums with Parni Valjak; 4 albums with Boa. Honours: President, Croatian Musicians' Union. Membership: EC, Croatian Performers Rights Collecting Society); EC, Porin Music Awards; Croatian Musicians' Union. Address: Al V Ruzdjaka 37, 10000 Zagreb, Croatia.

SHABALALA, Joseph; b. 28 Aug. 1940, Ladysmith, South Africa. Vocalist; Dancer; Songwriter. Career: Founding member and leader: Ladysmith Black Mambazo; First recording contract, 1970; Released 28 albums since; Performed at Nobel Peace Prize ceremony at the request of Nelson Mandela and FW de Klerk, 1993; Performed at Mandela's presidential inauguration, 1994; Associate professor of ethnomusicology, University of Natal; Part-time lecturer, University of California, Los Angeles; Recordings featured in TV advertisements: Heinz Beans; IBM; 7Up. Recordings: Albums include: Journey of Dreams, 1988; Two Worlds One Heart, 1990; Gift of The Tortoise, 1993; Thuthukani Ngoxolo, 1996; Heavenly (including Dolly Parton and Bonnie Raitt), 1997; The Star and The Wise Man (including Paul Simon and Dolly Parton), 1998; The Chillout Sessions, 2002; featured on soundtracks: The Lion King Part 3; Coming To America; A Dry White Season; Moonwalker; Cry the Beloved Country; featured appearances include: Graceland, Paul Simon, 1986; Conversation Peace, Stevie Wonder, 1995; Treasures, Dolly Parton, 1996. Honours: Grammy Award, Best Traditional Folk Recording, Shaka Zulu, 1987; JEFF Award, Best Original Musical Score, Nomathemba stage production; Kora Award, Special Judges' Award for Contribution to African Music, 2000; SAMA Award, Best Zulu Album, Lihl'lxhiba Likagogo, 2001. Address: c/o Gallo, PO Box 2897, Parklands 2121, South Africa. Website: www.mambazo.com.

SHACKLETON, Danny J; b. 7 April 1966, Wegberg, Germany. Engineer; Prod; Programmer; Writer; Musician (keyboards). Education: 4 years art college. Career: Freelance engineer, producer, studios throughout UK, for several years; Programmed for various projects including specialist jazz ventures, library music; Taught Music Technology to A Level; Various chart entries for albums, singles; Major jazz pieces due completion, July, 1995; Various dance projects, 1995. Membership: Musicians' Union. Current Management: Fairview Music. Address: c/o Fairview Studio, Willerby, Hull HU10 6DP, England.

SHADY, Slim. See: **EMINEM.**

SHAFER, Whitey (Sanger D.); b. 24 Oct. 1934, Whitney, TX, USA. Songwriter. m. Lyndia Shafer. Education: Whitney High School. Career: Signed publishing contract with Blue Crest Music Publishing, Nashville, 1967; Signed contract with Acuff-Rose Music; Inducted, Songwriters Hall of Fame, 1989; Songs recorded by: Moe Bandy, Lefty Frizzell, Jack Greene, Merle Haggard, George Jones, The Oak Ridge Boys, Johnny Rodriguez, Johnny Russell, Connie Smith, George Strait, Keith Whitley. Recordings: Albums: I Never Go Around Mirrors; So Good For So Long. Compositions include: Solo: Between My House And Town; I'm A New Man In Town; Soft Lights And Hard Country Music; I Can't Get Over You To Save My Life; I Wonder Do You Think Of Me; Overnight Success; Lefty's Gone; I Never Knew; Dream Painter; Lord Is That Me?; Honky Tonk Amnesia; Soft Lights & Hard Country Music; You Babe; Overnight Success; Birmingham Turnaround; with Lefty Frizzell: That's The Way Love Goes; Bandy The Rodeo Clown; I Never Go Around Mirrors; I Can't Get Over You to Save My Life (with Lefty Frizzell); Lucky Arms (with Lefty Frizzell); with Darlene Shafer: Does Fort Worth Ever Cross Your Mind; with Lyndia Shafer: All My Ex's Live In Texas; with Dallas Frazier: The Baptism Of Jesse Taylor; Tell Me My Lying Eyes Are Wrong; with A. L. Owens: I Just Started Hatin' Cheatin' Songs Today. Address: c/o Nashville Songwriters Foundation, PO Box 121775, Nashville, TN 37212-1775, USA.

SHAFRANOV, Vladimir 'Vova'; b. 1948, Leningrad, Russia. Musician (piano). Education: Piano, violin lessons from age 4; Piano diploma, Rimsky-Korsakov Conservatory, 1962. Career: Played with various bands throughout USSR; Became Israeli citizen, 1973; Became Finnish citizen, 1980–; Worked in Finnish jazz trios with Eero Koivistoinen; Represented Finland at Middleheim Festivals, Belgium, 1978; Ljubljana, 1979; Lived and worked in New York, 1983–; Performed duos, trios in local clubs with American jazz artists including : Ron Carter; Eddie Gomez; Mark Johnson; Al Foster; Mel Lewis. Recordings: Album with Al Foster and George Moraz; White Nights, 1992.

SHAGGY, (Orville Richard Burrell); b. 22 Oct. 1968, Kingston, Jamaica. Vocalist; Songwriter. Career: Left Jamaica to live with mother in Brooklyn, New York, USA, aged 18; Former Gulf War veteran with US Marines; Scored New York reggae/dancehall hits with independent label releases: Mampie; Big Up; Period in military followed by world-wide #1 hit Oh Carolina after track licensed to UK label Greensleeves; Signed record-breaking deal with Virgin UK lasting to 1997; New contract with MCA after hit soundtrack duet with Janet Jackson, 1998; Opening act for Backstreet Boys' US tour, 2001; Co-owner: Big Yard record label (with manager Robert Livingston and others);

Collaborations: Rayvon; Ricardo 'RikRok' Ducent; Grand Puba; Wayne Wonder. Recordings: Albums: Pure Pleasure, 1993; Original Doberman, 1994; Boombastic, 1995; Midnite Lover, 1997; Ultimate Shaggy Collection, 1999; Hotshot, 2000; The Best Of Shaggy, Vol. I, 2002; Lucky Day, 2002. Singles: Mampie; Big Up; Oh Carolina, Soon Be Done, 1993; In The Summertime, Boombastic, 1995; Why You Treat Me So Bad, Something Different/The Train Is Coming, That Girl (with Maxi Priest), 1996; Piece of My Heart, 1997; Luv Me, Luv Me (with Janet Jackson, from How Stella Got Her Groove Back OST), 1998; Hope (from For Love of The Game OST), 1999; Dance and Shout, It Wasn't Me, Angel, Freaky Girl, 2001. Honours: Grammy Award, Best Reggae Album, 1996; Billboard Music Awards, Male Artist of the Year; Male Albums Artist of the Year, 2001, Best-Selling Album 2001, for Hotshot; BRIT Award, International Male Solo Artist, 2002. Address: c/o MCA Records, 1755 Broadway, Eighth Floor, New York, NY 10019, USA. Website: www.shaggyonline.com.

SHAIMAN, Marc; b. 22 October 1959, Newark, NJ, USA. Composer; Compositions: For television: What's Alan Watching Now?, 1989; From the Earth to the Moon, 1998; Jackie's Back!, 1999; Bette, 2000; For film: When Harry Met Sally..., 1989; Misery, 1990; Scenes from a Mall, 1991; City Slickers, 1991; The Addams Family, 1991; Mr Saturday Night, 1992; Sister Act, 1992; A Few Good Men, 1992; Heart and Souls, 1993; Sleepless in Seattle, 1993; Addams Family Values, 1993; Speechless, 1994; City Slickers II: The Legend of Curly's Gold, 1994; North, 1994; Stuart Saves His Family, 1995; Forget Paris, 1995; The American President, 1995; Mother, 1996; Ghosts from the Past, 1996; The First Wives Club, 1996; Bogus, 1996; In & Out, 1997; George of the Jungle, 1997; Patch Adams, 1998; My Giant, 1998; Simon Birch, 1998; The Out-of-Towners, 1999; South Park: Bigger, Longer and Uncut, 1999; The Story of Us, 1999; The Kid, 2000; One Night at McCool's, 2000; What's the Worst That Could Happen?, 2001. Membership: ASCAP. Current Management: Blue Focus Management, 15233 Ventura Blvd, Suite 200, Sherman Oaks, CA 91403, USA. Website: shaiman.filmmusic.com.

SHAKESPEARE, Robbie; b. 27 Sept. 1953, Kingston, Jamaica. Reggae Musician (bass); Prod. Career: Member, US rhythm partnership, Sly and Robbie, with Sly Dunbar, 1975–; Prolific session musician with artists including: Peter Tosh; Bunny Wailer; Black Uhuru; Grace Jones; Bob Dylan; Ian Dury; Joan Armatrading; Horace Andy; Mikey Dread; Gregory Isaacs; Augustus Pablo; Formed own label, Taxi; Tours with Black Uhuru. Recordings: Sly and Robbie Present Taxi, 1981; A Dub Extravaganza, 1984; Language Barrier, 1985; Sly and Robbie Meet King Tubby, 1985; Reggae Greats, 1985; The Sound of Taxi, Vol. 1, 1986; Vol. 2, 1986; Rhythm Killers, 1987; Taxi Fare, 1987; Uhuru In Dub, 1987; The Summit, 1988; Hardcore Dub, 1989; Silent Assassin, 1990; Remember Precious Times, 1993; Dubmission, 1996; Honorary Citizen, Peter Tosh, 1997; Raw: The Best of Lady Saw, 1998; Doin' it Right, Freddie McKay, 1999; Story of Jamaican Music, 2000; Dub Fire, 2000. Current Management: Starline Entertainment, 1045 Pomme de Pin Lane, New Port Richey, FL 34655, USA.

SHAKIRA, (Shakira Isabel Mebarak Ripoll); b. 2 Feb. 1977, Barranquilla, Colombia. Vocalist; Songwriter. Career: Signed recording contract with Sony Music Colombia, 1990, when 13 years old; Released first album, Magia, 1991; Subsequent albums won her success in Latin America and Spain; Appeared for three years in Colombian television drama, El Oasis; First album in English, Laundry Service, was released in 2002. Recordings: Albums: Magia, 1991; Peligro, 1993; Pies Descalzos, 1996; ¿Dónde Están Los Ladrones?, 1998; Laundry Service, 2002; Washed And Dried: Laundry Service Limited Edition, 2002. Honours: Latin Grammy Awards, Best Female Vocal Performance, 2000, Best Music Video, for Suerte, 2002; Five MTV Video Awards, 2002. Current Management: Sony Music. Address: c/o Sony Music Entertainment, 10 Great Marlborough St, London W1F 7LP, England. Website: www.shakira.com.

SHALIT, Jonathan Sigmund; b. 17 April 1962, London, England. Career: Saatchi and Saatchi; Shalit Global Entertainment and Management, Shalit Global Music/Riot Recordings; Devised and presented Charlotte Church; Manager: Jamelia, Claire Sweeney, Ruthie Henshall, Esther McVey, Anthea Turner, James Alexander, Big Brovaz. Recordings: The Glory Of Gershwin (featuring Larry Adler, produced by George Martin). Publications: Me and My Big Mouth, Larry Adler; Walking On Air, Trevor Jones; Paula's Story. Membership: Music Manager's Forum; Queen's Club; Freeman of the City of London; Liveryman of the Worshipful Co of Coach Makers and Coach Harness Makers. Address: Shalit Global Entertainment and Management, 7 Moor St, Soho, London W1D 5NB, England. Telephone: (20) 7851-9155. Fax: (20) 7851-9156.

SHAMBORGUER, Naima; b. 18 April 1943, Detroit, MI, USA. Song Stylist. m. George Shamborguer, 3 s., 2 d. Education: Wayne State University. Career: Performs Professionally, Night Clubs, Festivals, Playhouses, Concerts, Privately and Publicly; Conducted Vocal Workshops in Technique and Song. Honours: Voted Number One Jazz Vocalist in The Detroit Area, 1989; Spirit of Detroit Award, 1994. Current Management: George Lee, 19760 Hartwell, Detroit, Michigan 48235, USA.

SHANK, Bud (Clifford); b. 27 May 1926, Dayton, Ohio, USA. Musician (alto saxophone). m. Linda Alexander Shank, 14 May 1994. *Education:* 3 years, University of North Carolina; UNC; Private studies, New York, Los Angeles. *Career:* Played in big bands of Charlie Barnet, late 1940s, Stan Kenton, late 1950s; with Howard Rumsey's Lighthouse All Stars, also trumpet ace Shorty Rogers, 1950s; Club, university, festival appearances, North and South America, Europe, Japan, studio work, 1960s–70s; Formed world renowned LA Four, with Ray Brown, Jeff Hamilton, Laurindo Almeida, recordings, tours, 1970s–80s; Performed with orchestras including: Royal Philharmonic; New American Jazz; Gerald Wilson Big Band; Stan Kenton's Neophonic; Duke Ellington; Created multimedia jazz performance The Lost Cathedral; Expanded Bud Shank Jazz Workshop and festival in Port Townsend, Washington; Works with sextet and quartet world-wide; Collaborated with koto player Kimio Eto and sitar player Ravi Shankar. *Recordings:* 126 as leader or co-leader, many others as sideman/featured artist; Recent. *Recordings include:* Silver Storm, 2000; Also classical works by: Bach; Faure; Debussy; Ravel; Scriabin; Several scores for films and television. *Publications:* Autobiography in progress; Quarterly newsletter, Budnotes. *Honours:* Multiple Playboy Poll; NARAS; Theme International. *Membership:* ASCAP; IAJE. *Current Management:* Linda Alexander Shank.

SHANKAR, Anoushka; b. London, England. Musician (sitar, piano); Conductor. *Education:* Learned the sitar from her father, Ravi Shankar. *Career:* Debut performance at 13 years old, New Delhi; Signed to Angel/EMI Classics, 1997; Performances in Europe, America and Asia, incl.: Tours with Ravi Shankar's ensemble; First solo tour in 2000; Fundraising concert for the Tibet Foundation Peace Garden, 2000; Ramakrishna Centre, Kolkata, 2000; Siri Fort Auditorium, New Delhi (as conductor), 2001; World Economic Forum, New York, 2002; Rainforest Foundation Benefit Concert, Carnegie Hall, 2002. *Recordings:* Albums: Anoushka, 1998; Anourag, 2000; Live at Carnegie Hall, 2002; contributions to albums by Ravi Shankar. *Publications:* Bapi: The Love of My Life (biography of Ravi Shankar), 2002. *Honours:* British Parliament House of Commons Shield, 1998. *Current Management:* Sulivan Sweetland, 28 Albion St, London W2 2AX, England. *Address:* Angel Records, 304 Park Ave S, Fourth Floor, New York, NY 10010, USA. *E-mail:* anoushka@ravishankar.org. *Website:* www.anoushkashankar.com.

SHANKAR, Ravi; b. 7 April 1920, Varansi, India. Musician (sitar). m. Sukanya, 23 Jan. 1989, 1 s., 2 d. *Education:* Studied under Ustad Allaudin Khan of Maihar. *Career:* International career as solo sitarist; Former dir of music, All-India Radio; Founded National Orchestra, All India Radio; Founder, Dir, Kinnara School of Music, Mumbai, 1962, Los Angeles, 1967; Concerts world-wide (except East and South Africa); Major festivals include: Edinburgh; Woodstock; Monterey. *Compositions include:* Concerto No. 1 for Sitar and Orchestra, 1971; Concerto No. 2 for Sitar and Orchestra, 1981; Film scores: Pather Panchali; Charlie; Chappaqua; Ghandhi; Music for television production, Alice In Wonderland; Opera-ballet, Ghanashayam, 1989; Kalyan, 2001; Mood Circle, 2002. *Recordings:* Over 50 albums include: Concertos 1 and 2 for Sitar and Orchestra, Raga Jageshwari, 1981; Homage To Mahatma Ghandhi, 1981; West Meets East (with Yehudi Menuhin and others); In London (live), 1999; In New York, 2000; Full Circle: Carnegie Hall, 2000; In San Francisco, 2001; Collected, 2001. *Publications:* My Music My Life (autobiography), 1968; From India, 1997; Mantram: Chant of India, 1997; Raga Jogeshwari, 1998. *Honours:* Fellow, Sangeet Natak Academy, 1976; Padma Vibushan, 1981; Elected to Rajya Sabha (Indian Upper House), 1986; Magisaysay; Grand Prize, Fukuoka, Japan; 12 hon. doctorates world-wide; Grammy Award, 2000; K.B.E., 2001. *Address:* c/o Sulivan Sweetland, 28 Albion St, London W2 2AX, England.

SHANNON, Sharon; b. 1968, Corofin, County Clare, Ireland. Traditional Musician. *Education:* German and Irish, Cork University. *Career:* Musician with the Waterboys, Room To Roam tour and album; Also played with Adam Clayton; Van Morrison; Sinead O'Connor; Dennis Bovell; Solo recording artiste, 1991–; Regular festival appearances including Glastonbury, Cambridge and Isle of Wight; Tours of USA, Europe, Australia, New Zealand, Hong Kong, Japan. *Recordings:* Albums: Sharon Shannon, 1991; Out The Gap, 1994; Each Little Thing, 1997; The Diamond Mountain Sessions, 2000; Live In Galway, 2001. Appears on: Her Infinite Variety: Celtic Woman, 1998; Coolfin, 1998; Finisterres, 1999; Moods Box Set, 1999. *Current Management:* Top Floor Management, 7–9 Sweetman's Ave, Blackrock, County Dublin, Ireland.

SHAPER, Harold David (Hal); b. 18 July 1931, Cape Town, South Africa. Author; Composer; Music Publisher. m. Pippa Marsh, 2 s., 2 d. *Education:* Attorney-at-Law, Cape Bar, 1955. *Career:* Founder, Sparta Florida Music Group and Prestige Elite Records Ltd, London; Writer of many Hollywood film songs. *Compositions include:* Softly as I Leave You (Frank Sinatra and Elvis Presley); Adaptation and libretto of opera La Bohème: Noir. *Publications:* A Prince of Liars, poetry; Book and lyrics of musical opera Cyrano, 1996; Wrote poetic epitaph on Enoch Sontonga's National Monument; Contributed to President Mandela's Heritage Day tribute Speech. *Honours:* British Academy Awards for musicals Treasure Island and Great Expectations; Freedom of the City of London, 1989; Lord of Stoke Bruerne; Hon. MA, Creative Literature, Cape Town University; Hon. DMus, University

of New York at Long Island. *Membership:* Queens Club; Hurlingham; Chelsea Arts; Memorial Society; British Academy of Songwriters, Composers and Authors. *Address:* Waterlane House, Wynberg Park, Cape Town, South Africa.

SHAPIRO, Helen; b. 28 Sept. 1946, Bethnal Green, London. Vocalist. *Education:* Vocal lessons, Maurice Berman Singing Academy, London. *Career:* Solo recording artiste, aged 14; Numerous radio and television appearances by age 15; Tours world-wide including: UK, supported by the Beatles, 1963; UK/Ireland, with The Beach Boys, 1967; Far East, 1964; Poland, 1965; Concerts include: Concerts with own band, 1963–98; British Song Festival, Brighton, 1966; Gospel concert with Cliff Richard, Royal Albert Hall, 1991; Humph 'n' Helen Show with Humphrey Lyttelton, 1984–2001; Solid Silver Sixties Tour with The Searchers and Swinging Blue Jeans, 1998; Gospel concerts in UK and Europe; Television includes: Sunday Night At The London Palladium; Thank Your Lucky Stars; Albion Market, ITV, 1985–86; Subject of This Is Your Life, ITV, 1995; Film appearance: It's Trad Dad, 1962; Play It Cool, 1992; Theatre includes: I'll Get My Man, 1967; West End musicals: The French Have A Song For It; Oliver; Theatre: Cabaret, 1982; Goose Pimples, 1982; Ello Ello Ello, 1982; One For The Road, 1985; Seesaw, 1987; Numerous pantomimes as principal boy. *Recordings:* Albums: Tops With Me, 1962; It's Trad, Dad (film soundtrack), 1962; Helen's Sixteen, 1963; Helen Hits Out, 1964; All for the Love of Music, 1978; Straighten Up and Fly Right, 1983; Echoes of the Duke, 1985; Helen 'n' Humph, 1990; The Pearl, 1990; Helen Shapiro 25th Anniversary Album, 1991; Kadosh, 1992; Nothing But The Best, 1995; The Essential Helen Shapiro, 1997; Enter Into His Gates, 1997; The Best of the 80s, 1997; Helen Shapiro, 1997; Helen 'n' Humph Mark II, 1998; Helen Shapiro at Abbey Road, 1998; By Request, 1998; Simply Shapiro, 2000; Gospel Collection, 2002; Hit singles include: Don't Treat Me Like A Child, 1961; You Don't Know (No. 1, UK), 1961; Walkin' Back To Happiness (No. 1, UK), 1961; Tell Me What He Said (No. 2, UK), 1962; Little Miss Lonely, 1962. *Publications:* Walking Back to Happiness, autobiography, 1993. *Honours:* NME Reader's Poll Winner, Best British Female Singer, 1961; 1 Gold disc, 3 Silver Discs; BASCA Gold Badge of Merit, 1991. *Current Management:* John Robert Williams Productions. *Address:* PO Box 423, Chislehurst, Kent BR7 5TU, England.

SHARAM, (Sharam Tayebi); b. 12 Aug. 1970, Iran. Prod; Remixer; DJ. *Career:* Relocated to Washington DC, USA; Formed Deep Dish and founded Deep Dish/Yoshitoshi Records with partner Dubfire, 1992; Released BT's A Moment of Truth, 1993; Signed to Tribal Records, 1993; Moved to Deconstruction, 1996; Collaborations: Danny Tenaglia; John Selway; Everything But The Girl; Remixed: Madonna; De'Lacy; Billie Ray Martin; Joi Cardwell; Dusted; Sven Vath; The Shamen; Eddie Amador. *Recordings:* Albums: Junk Science, 1998; Singles: A Feeling (as Moods), 1992; Sexy Dancer (as Quench), 1993; The Dream, 1994; Love Songs (as Chocolate City), Stay Gold, 1996; The Future of The Future, 1998. *Honours:* Grammy Award, Remixer of the Year, 2001. *Address:* c/o BMG UK & Ireland Ltd, Bedford House, 69–79 Fulham High St, London SW6 3JW, England.

SHARDA, Anju; b. 17 March 1969, Perivale, Middlesex, England. Vocalist; Songwriter. *Education:* BA Hons, Communication Studies; A level Music; Grade 8 violin. *Career:* Member, Cardiff-based trio Banana Cat (later Glorious), 1991; Television: Band appeared on Rough Mix, 1992; Dance Energy, BBC2, 1993; Left Glorious, 1993; Co-writing deal with Simon and Diamond Dougal, 1994; Co-writing deal with Jon Moss (ex-Culture Club), 1995. *Recordings:* Backing vocals, album: The Lick, Definition of Sound, 1992; Releases with 3rd Core: Singles: Mindless And Broken, 2000; Albums: Pandemic, 2000. *Membership:* Musicians' Union; PRS. *Current Management:* Sue Carling. *Address:* 13 Elvendon Rd, London N13 4SJ, England.

SHARKEY, Feargal; b. 13 Aug. 1958, Londonderry, Northern Ireland. Vocalist. *Career:* Member, The Undertones; Numerous hit singles and live appearances, television and radio appearances; Band split, 1983; Worked with Vince Clarke (of Erasure) on project The Assembly, 1983; Began solo career with numerous TV appearances; A & R man. *Recordings:* With The Undertones: Singles: Teenage Kicks, 1978; Jimmy Jimmy, 1979; Here Comes The Summer, 1979; My Perfect Cousin, 1980; Wednesday Week, 1980; It's Going to Happen, 1981; Crisis of Mine; You're Welcome; Albums: Teenage Kicks, 1978; Undertones, 1979; Hypnotised, 1980; Positive Touch, 1981; The Sin of Pride, 1983; Peel Sessions, 1986; The Very Best of The Undertones, 1994; Singles: As & Bs, 2001; With The Assembly: Single: Never Never, 1983; Solo: Singles: A Good Heart (No. 1, UK), 1985; You Little Thief, 1985; I've Got News For You, 1991; Albums: Feargal Sharkey, 1985; Wish, 1988; Song from the Mardi Gras, 1991.

SHARKIMAXX. See: **FELIX DA HOUSECAT.**

SHAW, Donald Patrick; b. 6 May 1967, Ketton, Leicestershire, England. Musician (keyboards, accordion); Composer. *Career:* Founder member: Capercaillie; Group, along with original material, specialise in fusing traditional Gaelic songs with contemporary arrangements; Had first UK top 40 single in Gaelic, Coisich A Ruin (from A Prince Among Islands EP), 1992; Produced and performed on fellow Capercaillie members' solo albums: Karen Matheson, The Dreaming Sea, 1996; Michael McGoldrick, Fused, 2000;

Written music for television documentaries, dramas and the feature film Rob Roy. *Recordings:* Albums: with Capercaillie: Cascade, 1984; Crosswinds, 1987; Sidewalk, 1989; Delirium, 1991; Get Out, 1992; The Blood Is Strong, Secret People, 1993; Capercaillie, 1995; To The Moon, 1996; Beautiful Wasteland, 1997; Glenfinnan – Songs of The '45 (recorded 1995), 1998; Nàdurra, 2000; group feature on: Rob Roy OST, 1995; features solo on: L'Heritage De Celts, 1994; The Dreaming Sea, Karen Matheson, 1996; Finisterres, Dan Ar Braz, 1997; Zenith, Dan Ar Braz, 1998; Identities, Idir, 1999; Suilean Dubh, Tannas, 1999; Ru-Ra, Tannas, 2000; Sawdust In My Veins, James Grant, 2000; My Thrawn Glory, James Grant, 2000; Fused, Michael McGoldrick, 2000; Source, Big Sky, 2000; Magaid A Phipir, Rory Campbell, 2000; Tacsi (TV series), 2000. *Honours:* All Britain Accordion Champion, 1984.

SHAW, Ian; b. 2 June 1962, North Wales. Jazz Vocalist; Musician (piano, trumpet). *Education:* 8 piano grades (Trinity College of Music); BMus, King's College, London. *Career:* Plays regularly Ronnie Scott's London; Tours, UK, Europe; Worked with Kenny Wheeler; John Taylor; Carol Grimes; Ruby Turner; Mari Wilson; TV includes Top of the Pops; Pebble Mill; Jools Holland's The Happening; The Jack Dee Show; The Late Show; Radio: Kaleidoscope; Nicky Campbell (Radio One); Major US Tour, 1997. *Recordings:* Lazy Blues Eyes, album of jazz love songs with Carol Grimes, 1990; Ghostsongs, Live at Ronnie Scott's, 1992; Zebra, guest singer with Yello, 1994; Taking It To Hart, a tribute to Rodgers and Hart, 1995; Famous Rainy Day, 1996; The Echo of a Song, 1996; In A New York Minute, 1999; Soho Stories, 2001. *Publications:* Making It In The Music Business, 1993. *Honours:* Perrier Award, Edinburgh, 1991. *Membership:* Equity. *Current Management:* Dr Darren Crowdy, 42 Elsham Rd, London W14 8HB, England.

SHAW, Paul John; b. 20 Feb. 1962, Dartford, Kent, England. Composer; Musician (keyboards, guitar); Programmer; Prod. m. Jacqueline Ives (Shaw), 2 July 1994. *Career:* Started business, Daybreak Productions, with David Rogers, 1987; Success with library music ever since; Regular CD-I and CD-ROM work; Conferences, television and radio including: Mr Blobby; BBC Radio; BBC Pebble Mill; Top of the Pops; Live and Kicking; House Party. *Compositions:* 345 published works co-written with David Rogers; Mostly library music (production): Peanut Vendor, 1987; Mr Blobby, 1995; Light of Summer, 1995; Mr Blobby, The Album, 1995–96. *Publications:* Various interviews in industry publications; PRS yearbooks. *Honours:* Ivor Novello, Best Selling Song, 1993; Various corporate awards for Mr Blobby. *Membership:* Musicians' Union; PRS. *Address:* Carlin Music/Destiny Music, Iron Bridge House, Bridge Approach, London NW1 8BD, England.

SHAW, Sandie, (Sandra Goodrich); b. 26 February 1947, Dagenham, Essex, England. Vocalist; Songwriter; Record Prod. m. (1) Jeff Banks; (2) Nik Powell. *Education:* Pschychodynamic Psychology, university. *Career:* International recording artist, singer, composer and producer; numerous hit singles, over 30 years; Winner, Eurovision Song Contest, 1967; Semi-retirement, 1970s; Relaunched music career with Morrissey, 1984; Numerous concerts, television and radio appearances world-wide; Founder, Arts Clinic, psychological counsellor, writer and lecturer. *Compositions:* Numerous collaborations with Chris Andrews. *Recordings:* Hit singles include: (There's) Always Something There To Remind Me (No. 1, UK), 1964; Long Live Love; Message Understood; Girl Don't Come; Tomorrow; Nothing Comes Easy; Puppet On A String; Monsieur Dupont; Hand In Glove (with Morrissey and The Smiths); Most 1960s hits self-produced; Recent Albums: Choose Life, 1983; Sandie/ Me Sandie Shaw, 1996; The Pye Anthology, 2000; Appears on: Docudrama, 1996 (Star Pimp); Kill the Lights, 1997 (Lowercase). *Publications:* The World At My Feet (partly autobiographical); Stress in Rock Musicians: The Phenomena of Fame and its Psychological Effect on the Developmental Processes of Artists. *Honours:* Eurovision Song Contest Winner, Puppet On A String, 1967; International Ambassador for Women Aid, United Nations, 1985; Professor of Music, Royal Society of Musicians, 1998. *Membership:* Royal Society of Musicians. *Address:* c/o Negus-Fancey Co, 78 Portland Rd, London W11 4LQ, England.

SHAW, Tommy; b. 11 Sept. 1953, Montgomery, Alabama, USA. Musician (guitar); Vocalist; Songwriter. *Career:* Guitarist, Styx, 1975–89; Damn Yankees, 1989–; Also member of side project Shaw Blades (with Jack Blades), 1995; World-wide tours and concerts. *Recordings:* Albums: with Styx: Crystal Ball, 1976; The Grand Illusion, 1977; Pieces of Eight, 1978; Cornerstone, 1979; Paradise Theater (No. 1, USA), 1980; Kilroy Was Here, 1983; Caught In The Act, 1984; Brave New World, 1999; Styx World (Live), 2001; with Damn Yankees: Damn Yankees, 1990; Don't Tread, 1992; with Shaw Blades: Hallucination, 1995; Singles: with Styx: Sail Away; Babe (No. 1, USA); The Best of Times; Too Much Time On My Hands; with Damn Yankees: Coming of Age; High Enough; Come Again; Where You Goin' Silence Is Broken, from film Nowhere To Run, 1993. *Honours:* Motor City Music Award, Outstanding National Rock/Pop Single, 1992. *Current Management:* Madhouse Management, PO Box 15108, Ann Arbor, MI 48106, USA.

SHEA, George Beverly; b. 1 Feb. 1909, Ontario, Canada. Soloist. m. Karlene Aceto, 1 s., 1 d. *Education:* Annesley College, Ottawa; Houghton College, Houghton. *Career:* Radio Broadcasting, Singing on WMCA and WHN, 1929–38; Clerk, Mutual of New York Insurance Co, 1929–38; Announcer, Staff

Soloist, WMBI Chicago, 1938–44; Soloist, ABC's Club Time, 1944–52; Soloist, Billy Graham Evangelistic Association, 1947–; Soloist, Hour of Decision, Radio Broadcast, 1950–; Recording Artiste, RCA and Word Records, 1951–. *Compositions:* Then Sings My Soul, 1968; Songs That Lift The Heart, 1972; Then Sings My Soul, 1984. *Honours:* Grammy Award, National Academy of Recording Arts and Sciences, 1965; Elected Gospel Music Asscn Hall of Fame, 1978; Elected Religious Broadcasting Hall of Fame, 1996. *Address:* c/o Media Relations, PO Box 9313, Minneapolis, Minnesota 55440, USA.

SHEA, Pat; b. 7 Dec. 1957, Buffalo, New York, USA. Vocalist; Songwriter; Musician (guitar, piano). *Career:* Grand Prize Winner, TNN's Be A Star Talent Show, 1991; Appearances on Nashville Now, with Ralph Emery; Made Video Special at Billy Bobs in Texas for TNN's On Stage Show; Opening Act for Holly Dunn, Emmylou Harris, Tanya Tucker, Lee Greenwood, Sawyer Brown, John Berry. *Compositions:* The Lord May Take Me. *Recordings:* The Lord May Take Me, single; The Road Less Travelled, album. *Honours:* Grand Prize Winner, Be A Star Talent Show, 1991. *Membership:* ASCAP. *Address:* PO Box 991, Orchard Park, NY 14127, USA.

SHEARING, George Albert; b. 13 Aug. 1919, London, England. Musician (piano); Composer. m. Beatrice Bayes, 1 May 1941 (divorced), 1 d., (2) Eleanor Geffert. *Education:* Linden Lodge School for the Blind, London. *Career:* Musician with Harry Parry; Stéphane Grappelli; Leader, own quintet, with members including Gary Burton, Joe Pass, Cal Tjader; Later played in trio, duo and as solo artiste; Played with Marian McPartland; Hank Jones; Peggy Lee; Carmen McRae; Frequent collaborations with Mel Tormé; Appearances at: London Symphony Pops Concerts, 1986, 1987; London Palladium, 1987; Concord Jazz Festival, Japan, 1987; Vice-President, Shearing Music Corporation. *Compositions:* Numerous popular songs including Lullaby of Birdland. *Recordings:* Albums include: Latin Escapade, 1956; Velvet Carpet, 1956; Black Satin, 1957; Burnished Brass, 1957; White Satin, 1960; The Shearing Touch, 1960; Satin Affair, 1961; Jazz Concert, 1963; My Ship, 1974; The Way We Are, 1974; Continental Experience, 1975; 500 Miles High, 1977; On Target, 1979; On A Clear Day, 1980; Bright Dimensions, 1984; Grand Piano, 1985; More Grand Piano, 1986; Breakin' Out, 1987; Piano, 1989; Paper Moon: Songs Of Nat King Cole, 1995; Christmas With The George Shearing Quintet, 1998; Back To Birdland (Live), 2001; Duets, 2002; Rare Delight Of You (with John Pizarelli), 2002; with Peggy Lee: Americana Hotel, 1959; with Stéphane Grappelli: The Reunion, 1976; with Carmen McRae: Two For The Road, 1980; with Marian McPartland: Alone Together, 1981; with Mel Tormé: An Evening With Mel Tormé And George Shearing, 1982; Top Drawer, 1983; An Elegant Evening, 1986; with Barry Tuckwell: George Shearing and Barry Treadwell Play The Music Of Cole Porter, 1986; with Hank Jones: The Spirit of 1761, 1989. Singles: September In The Rain; Lullaby of Birdland; Let Their Be Love (with Nat 'King' Cole). *Honours:* Voted Top English Pianist, 1941–47; Winner, All-American Jazz polls; American Academy of Achievement, Golden Plate Award, 1968. *Membership:* BMI; Board directors, Guide Dogs For The Blind, San Rafael, Hadley School for the Blind, Winnetka, Illinois. *Current Management:* Joan Shulman. *Address:* 103 Avenue Rd, Suite 301, Toronto, ON M5R 2G9, Canada.

SHEEHAN, Billy; b. Musician (bass). *Career:* Founder member, rock group Talas, 1980–83; Bass player, David Lee Roth, 1985–88; Founder member, Mr Big, 1989–. *Recordings:* Albums: with Talas: Talas, 1980; Sink Your Teeth Into That, 1982; Live Speed On Ice, 1983; The Talas Years, 1990; with David Lee Roth: Eat 'Em and Smile, 1986; Skyscraper, 1988; with Mr Big: Mr Big, 1989; Lean Into It, 1991; Solo: Compression, 2001; Singles include: with Dave Lee Roth: Yankee Rose; Goin' Crazy; Just Like Paradise; with Mr Big: Green-Tinted Sixties Mind; To Be With You. *Current Management:* Herbie Herbert Management, 2501 Third St, San Francisco, CA 94107, USA.

SHEHAN, Steve; b. 18 Jan. 1957, Fort Eustis, Virginia, USA. Composer; Musician (percussion, bass, keyboards). *Education:* Classical piano and guitar, Balinese gamelan. *Career:* Concerts and recordings with: Didier Lockwood, 1978–2002; John McLaughlin, 1981; Yves Montand, 1982; Alan Stivell, 1982; Jacques Higelin, 1983; Magma, 1984; Michael Jonasz, 1984; Veronique Samson, 1984; Kim Wilde, 1984; Richard Horowitz, 1985–98; Gipsy Kings, 1987–89; Amina, 1987–2002; Leonard Bernstein, Carnegie Hall, 1989; Peter Gabriel's band and Akiro Inoué, 1989; Les Polyphonies Corses, 1989–90; Le Mystere des voix Bulgares, 1991; Paco de Lucia's band, 1991; David Sylvian, Riyochi Sakamoto, 1991; Jon Hassel, John Cage, Manu Dibango, 1991–92; Wasis Diop, 1992–2002; Liane Foly, 1986–96; Paul Winter, 1995; Zazie, 1997–98; Simon Shehan, 2000; Bob Dylan, 2000; Paul McCartney, 2001; Nitin Sawhney, 1998–2002; Paul Simon, 1998–2002; Michaël Brecker, 1999; Jerry Douglas, 1999; Alan Simon, 2000–02; Cheb Mami, 2001; Angun, 2002; Supertramp, 2002; Ray Charles, 2002; Zucherro, 2002; Tracy Chapman, 2002; Joe Cocker, 2002; Natacha Atlas, 2002; Cirque du Soleil, 2002; Rokia Traore, 2002; Billy Preston, 2002; Fleetwood Mac, 2002; Carla Bruni, 2002; Film music with: Elliot Goldenthal, 1991; Gabriel Yared (L'AMANT); Costa Gravas; Jonathan Dem; Several fashion shows, as composer and performer: with Antonio Miro, 1989–92, with Yves Saint Laurent, 1989; Own publishing and production and record label: Safar Production Inc; Mem. trio, Hadouk. *Compositions:* Ballet music for Ismaël Ivo, 1997–2000; Ballet Jazz Art; 1999, 2000. *Recordings:* Impressions de Voyages, 1984; Arrows, 1989; Assouf, with

Baly Otmani, 1994, 1997; Figaro Si!, 1995; Indigo Dreams, 1995; Safar – A Journey, 1997; Versecrets, 1997; Awham, with Youssef el Idrissi, 1998; Amok, 1998; Plenitude, 1998; Alif, with Omar Farouk Tekbilek, 2001; Roads, 2002; with Hadouk: Shamanimal, 1997, Now, 2002; Ikewan, 1997; Producing and arranging Omar Farouk Tekbilek with Natacha Atlas, 2000. *Publications:* Arrows, 1990; Assouf, 1994; Indigo Dreams, 1995; Safar, 1997; Ikewan, 1997; Assarouf, 1997; Versecrêt, 1997; Awham, 1998; Amok, 1998; Plenitude, 1998. *Membership:* SACEM; SDRM; BMI; SPEDIDAM. *Current Management:* Safar. *Address:* 11 rue des Dahlias, 45300 Dossainville, France. *E-mail:* steve.shehan@wanadoo.fr. *Website:* www.steveshehan.com.

SHELDON, Kenny Herbert; b. 1 May 1923, Berlin, Germany. Orchestra Leader; Conductor; MC; Musician (trumpet, piano, drums, vibraphone). m. Rita Levy, 21 Feb. 1961. *Education:* New York University; Columbia University; Juilliard; Manhattan School of Music. *Career:* Entertainer, orchestra leader, Kenny Sheldon and his Swing and String Orchestra, in nightclubs, resorts, country clubs, colleges, hotels, 1947–; Starred, Stars and Styles, New York; Television: Quantum Leap (NBC), 1989; Peaceable Kingdom (CBS), 1989. *Recordings:* Album: Dance Around the World with Kenny Sheldon Orchestra; Prod.: Theme From Love Story, with Andy Williams. *Membership:* Fellow, AFofM. *Address:* 1420 N Fuller Ave, Suite 304, Los Angeles, CA 90046, USA.

SHELLEY, Steve; b. 23 June 1962, Midland, MI, USA. Prod. *Career:* Mem., Sonic Youth, 1985–; Founded, Smells Like Records, 1992. *Recordings:* Albums: E.V.O.L., 1986; Sister, 1987; Hold That Tiger, 1987; Daydream Nation, 1988; Goo, 1990; Dirty, 1992; A Thousand Leaves, 1998; NYC Ghosts & Flowers, 2000; Condo Painting: Life From A Different Angle, 2002; Murray Street, 2002; Other releases with Sonic Youth: Anagrama (syr1); Slaapkamers met Slagroom (syr2); Invito al Cielo (syr3); Goodbye 20th Century (syr4); Kim Gordon/Ikue Mori/DJ Olive (syr5); Contributed to film and television soundtracks: Pump Up The Volume, 1990; My So-Called Life, 1995; End Of Days, 1999. *Address:* c/o Smells Like Records, PO Box 6179, Hoboken, NJ 07030, USA. *Website:* www.sonicyouth.com; www.smellslikerecords.com.

SHELTON, Ricky Van; b. 12 Jan. 1952, Grit, Virginia, USA. Country Vocalist; Songwriter. m. Bettye Witt, 4 Aug. 1986. *Career:* Previous employment includes: Pipefitter; Plumber; Car salesman; Country singer, 1985–. *Recordings:* Hits include: US Country No. 1s include: Somebody Lied, 1987; Life Turned Her That Way, 1987; Don't We All Have The Right, 1987; I'll Leave This World Loving You; From A Jack To A King; Living Proof; Rockin' Years, with Dolly Parton, 1991; Albums: Wild-Eyed Dream, 1987; Loving Proof, 1988; Ricky Van Shelton Sings Christmas, 1989; Ricky Van Shelton III, 1990; Backroads, 1991; Don't Overlook Salvation, 1992; Greatest Hits Plus, 1992; Love and Honor, 1994; Ultimately Fine, 1994; Making Plans, 1998. *Honours:* CMA Awards: Horizon Award, 1988; Male Vocalist of Year, 1989; Nashville Network Viewer's Choice: Male Vocalist of Year, Album of Year, 1989. *Membership:* Country Music Assn; Academy of Country Music. *Current Management:* Michael Campbell and Associates, 6424 Bresslyn Rd, Nashville, TN 37205–3047, USA.

SHEPHERD, Ben; b. 20 Sept. 1968, Okinawa, Japan. Musician (bass). *Career:* Former mem., March of Crimes; Mem., US heavy rock group, Soundgarden, 1990–97; Numerous tours and festival appearances. *Recordings:* Albums: Badmotorfinger, 1991; Superunknown, 1994; Down on the Upside, 1996; A-Sides, 1997. Singles: Rusty Cage; Spoonman; The Day I Tried To Live; Black Hole Sun; Fell on Black Days; Pretty Noose; Burden in My Hand; Blow Up The Outside World; Ty Cobb; Bleed Together. *Address:* c/o A&M Records, Interscope Records, 2220 Colorado Ave, Santa Monica, CA 90404, USA. *Website:* www.soundgardenonline.co.uk.

SHEPHERD, Jean (Ollie Imogene); b. 21 Nov. 1933, Paul's Valley, Oklahoma, USA. Country vocalist; Songwriter; Musician (bass). m. Hawkshaw Hawkins, deceased 1963. *Career:* Formed all-girl band, the Melody Ranch Girls, late 1940s; Debut single Help penned by Hank Thompson who discovered group, 1948; Worked with Red Foley's Ozark Jubilee, 1955–57; Husband died in same plane crash as fellow country stars Patsy Cline and Cowboy Copas, 5 March 1963; Debut country hit A Dear John Letter (with Ferlin Huskey), #1 country, #4 pop, 1953; Forty five country chart entries mostly on Capitol and United Artists, until 1978. *Recordings include:* A Dear John Letter (with Ferlin Huskey), 1953; Slippin' Away, 1953; A Satisfied Mind, 1955; Beautiful Lies, 1955; Forgive Me John (with Ferlin Huskey), 1953; Albums: Heart We Did All That We Could, 1967; Many Happy Hangovers, 1966; I'll Take The Dog (with Ray Pillow), 1966. *Honours:* Cash Box, Top Female Singer, 1959. *Membership:* Grand Ole Opry, 1955. *Address:* c/o Jim Chase, Ace Productions, PO Box 292725, Nashville, TN 37229, USA.

SHEPHERDSON, Paul; b. 23 June 1941, Hull, England. Musician (drums); Drama Teacher; Dir, Drama and Stage Musicals. m. Sandra Nicholl, 13 July 1963, 1 s., 1 d. *Education:* Piano, 5 years. *Career:* Member, Mike Peters Florida Jazz Band; Supporting Kenny Ball Band; Roy Williams; Terry Lightfoot Band; Backing residental musician to most cabaret acts including: Marti Caine; The Nolans; Norman Collier; Faith Brown; Currently, own band with Martin Jones. *Compositions:* Co-writer, various musicals for local

performance. *Membership:* Musicians' Union. *Address:* 73 The Wolds, Castle Park, Cottingham, Nr Hull HU16 5LQ, England.

SHEPPARD, Andy; b. 20 Jan. 1957, Bristol, Avon, England. Jazz Musician (saxophones). *Education:* Clarinet, saxophone, flute and guitar. *Career:* Musician with: Sphere; Klaunstance; Lumiere (French Big Band); Urban Sax; Paul Dunmall; Keith Tippett; Leader, own band, 1987; Founder, Soft On The Inside Big Band, 1990; Founder, Co-motion, 1991–. *Recordings:* Albums: Andy Sheppard, 1987; Introductions In The Dark, 1989; Soft On The Inside, 1990; 66 Shades of Lipstick (with Keith Tippett), 1990; In Co-Motion, 1991; Inclassifiable (with Nana Vasconcelos and Steve Lodder), 1995; Songs With Legs (with Carla Bley), 1995; Dancing Man and Woman, 2000; Nocturnal Tourist, 2002; with Sphere: Present Tense, 1988; Guest musician with Judie Tzuke: Ritmo, 1983; Turning Stones, 1989. *Current Management:* Serious Speakout, 42 Old Compton St, London W1V 5PB, England.

SHEPPARD, Rodney Charles; b. 25 Nov. 1967. Musician (guitar). m. Gretchen, 1 s. *Career:* Played colleges and parties with local group The Tories; Group became The Shrinky Dinx; Signed to Atlantic Records following circulation of self-made demo video; Act renamed Sugar Ray owing to threat of legal action prior to record releases; Built up world-wide fanbase through touring and TV appearances; Cameo in Fathers Day film, 1997. *Recordings:* Albums: Lemonade and Brownies, 1995; Floored, 1997; 14–59, 1999; Sugar Ray, 2001; Singles: Mean Machine, Iron Mic, 1995; Fly, RPM, 1997; Every Morning, Someday, 1999; Falls Apart, 2000; When It's Over, Answer The Phone, 2001. *Honours:* Second/third albums certified double/triple platinum by RIAA respectively. *Address:* c/o PO Box 12018, Costa Mesa, CA 92627, USA. *E-mail:* management@sugarray.com. *Website:* www.sugarray.com.

SHEPPARD, T. G, (William Neal Browder); b. 20 July 1944, Humboldt, Tennessee, USA. Country vocalist; Songwriter, Musician (guitar, saxophone, piano). *Career:* Moved to Memphis, 1960; Worked as backup singer with Travis Wammack's band; Recorded High School Days as Brian Stacey for Atlantic, 1966; Brief stint as record promoter for Stax label; First charted on pop and country chart with Devil In The Bottle for Motown's country subsidiary, Melodyland, 1974; Collaborations: Karen Brooks; Clint Eastwood; Judy Collins; Hits (including 14 #1s) continued on Warner/Curb and Columbia until 1991; Currently tours with band named after hit recording Slow Burn. *Compositions include:* Tryin' To Beat The Morning Home. *Recordings include:* Tryin' To Beat The Morning Home, 1975; Last Cheater's Waltz, I'll Be Coming Back For More, 1979; Party Time, I Loved 'Em Every One, 1981; Albums: 3/4 Lonely, 1979; Finally!, 1982; Greatest Hits, 1983. *Current Management:* R J Kaltenbach Personal Management, 641 Lindsay Ct, Dundee, IL 60118, USA.

SHERMAN, Richard S; b. New York, USA. Record and Video Co Exec. m. Linda Jordan, 1 s., 1 d. *Education:* BS, 1948; LLB, 1950; LLM, 1951. *Career:* National Sales Manager, Product Manager, Mercury Records Corporation, Chicago, 1962–67; National Sales Manager, Warner Bros Records, Los Angeles, 1967–761; Product Manager, Sales Manager, Motown Record Corporation, Los Angeles, 1971–74; Executive Vice-President, Sales Hollywood, California, 1981–85; Director, West Coast Ops, Bell Records, Los Angeles, 1974–75; Senior Vice-President, Sales, Distribution Executive, Casablanca Records, 1975–81; Senior Vice-President, Sales, Distribution, Marketing, Motown Records, 1981–85; Senior Vice-President, Sales, Distribution, JCI, Agoura Hills, California, 1985–87; President, August Moon Productions, 1987–. *Membership:* NARAS. *Address:* 9908 Alegria Dr., Las Vegas, NV 89144, USA.

SHERMAN, Sandy; b. 7 March, New York, USA. Songwriter; Lyricist. m. Michael Sherman, 1 c. *Education:* BA, Brooklyn College, City University of New York; Master of Science, Major in Education, minor in Music. *Career:* Composed songs for many films and TV shows including Police Academy 4, Ghost Fever, The Substitute, Walker Texas Ranger, X Files, In the Line of Duty; Writer of children's songs for Disney, and for Shari Lewis's Lamb Chop Play Along; Lyricist, The Little Witch of Wichita. *Compositions:* He Delivers; Fast Asleep; Nighty Night; Dancing Arms; The Good News Is...; Dancin' Up a Storm, for Stacy Lattisaw; Big Rig Christmas Tree for Truckers Christmas; Cast A Stone Upon the Water; E.S.P.; When You Go Dancin'. *Honours:* Contribution to album, certified Gold by RIAA; Songwriter of the Year Award, Tennessee Songwriters' Assscn; The Little Witch of Wichita, Winner of the City of Los Angeles Cultural Affairs Department Theater Competition, 1995. *Membership:* ASCAP; Society of Composers and Lyricists. *Address:* PO Box 4445, Palos Verdes, CA 90274, USA.

SHERRY, Rachel Patricia; b. 16 March 1960, Nottingham, England. Musician (harp); Vocalist. m. John Byron, 25 Sept. 1993. *Education:* Birmingham University; Royal Academy of Music. *Career:* Appearances at Purcell Room and Queen Elizabeth Hall; Concert tours to France, Italy, Spain and throughout UK; Numerous television appearances as actress, singer and harpist; 4 programmes of music for harp and voice for BBC Radio and numerous broadcasts with BBC Singers. *Recordings:* Rachel Sherry – Voice and Harp; New album due for release, 1996. *Publications:* Folk Songs For Voice and Harp, in preparation. *Membership:* Musicians' Union; Equity

Current Management: Alexander Personal Management. *Address:* 16 Roughdown Ave, Hemel Hempstead, Hertfordshire HP3 9BN, England.

SHERWOOD, John Torrance; b. South Africa. Composer; Prod; Musician (guitar); Engineer. *Education:* Architectural Association of Architecture; Studied classical guitar with Patrick Bashford and Hector Quine. *Compositions:* Soundtracks: Rumours of Rain, CH4, 1992; Spoilt For Choice, BBC2, 1993; Trouble, CH4, 1993. *Recordings:* Albums: As guitarist with Haysi Fantaysee: Battle Hymns For Children Singing; As engineer with P M Dawn: of The Heart of The Soul and of The Cross; Single: Set Adrift On Memory Bliss; As engineer: Project One and Irresistible Force: Outlaw Posse: My Afro's On Fire. *Honours:* Gold records for PM Dawn: Set Adrift On Memory Bliss; Of The Heart of The Soul and of The Cross. *Membership:* Musicians' Union; PRS. *Current Management:* Paradox Productions. *Address:* PO Box 3083, London N1 8NZ, England.

SHIJI, (Awoyinka); b. 23 Oct. 1969, London, England. Vocalist; Songwriter; Musician (keyboards, percussion). *Education:* BEng (hons), Mechanical Engineering; MSc, Product Design. *Career:* Finalist, Sony Dance Music Search, 1993; Concerts: Ronnie Scott's, 1995; Orange, 1995; WKD, 1995. *Recordings:* Facets (Debut EP); My Lover's Embrace, 1997. *Membership:* MCPS; PRS; Musicians' Union. *Current Management:* Ivy Records. *Address:* 15 Reynardsons Court, High Rd, London N17 9HX, England.

SHILKLOPER, Arkady; b. 17 Oct. 1956, Moscow, Russia. Musician (horn). m. Olga Goloborodko, 22 July 1981, 1 s., 1 d. *Education:* Moscow Gnesin Institut, 1976–81. *Career:* Bolshoi Theatre Orchestra, 1978–85; Moscow Philharmonic Orchestra, 1985–89; Freelance musician (jazz, classical, folk), since 1990; Hornplayer (also alphorn, corno du caccio); Jazz podium; Jazz time; Jazz kwadrat. *Recordings:* with Pago Libre: Titles, 1996; Wake Up Call, 1998; Sheffield Jazz Experience, 1996; with Karl Berger: No Man Is An Island, 1996; with Misha Alperin: North Story, 1998. *Membership:* International Horn Society. *Address:* Osennij Blvd 6–526, Moscow, 121609, Russia.

SHINKARUK, Irina Volodimirivna; b. 31 July 1979, Fastiv, Kiev, Ukraine. Vocalist. *Education:* Musical College, Zhitomyr-city, Ukraine, 1995–97; Zhitomir State Pedagogical Institute, 1995–. *Career:* Film: Cheremhove Vihola, 1993; Tours of Ukraine, 1994; Concert of The Prizewinners, at International Competition: The Voice of Asia, 1994; Tours: France; Germany; Hungary, other countries, 1994; Television show: Ukraine, Spring, Slavutich (commemorating Chernobyl), 1995. *Compositions:* Mermaid's Week, 1993; I'm Like a Bird, 1996. *Recordings:* I'm Like a Bird (14 Songs of the Period), 1993; The Fifth Season Of The Year (The Season of Love), 1995; Step Towards the Summer, 1996; Best composition: The Moon Talisman (Misyachniy Oberig). *Publications:* The Stars of Chervona Ruta Academy, 1993. *Honours:* First Prize: Chervona Ruta, 1993; Grand Prize, International Festival, Bilostotsky Malvi, Poland, 1993; Diploma FIDOF vth International Festival, The Voice of Asia, 1994. *Membership:* FIDOF. *Current Management:* Vlodimir Shinkaruk. *Address:* 102 B Ten Str, Apt 65, Zhytomyr 262024, Ukraine.

SHINODA, Mike Kenji; b. 11 Feb. 1977, Agoura, CA, USA. Vocalist. *Education:* Illustration, Pasadena Art College of Design. *Career:* Founding mem., Xero; Renamed Hybrid Theory and signed to Warner Bros, Spring 2000; Further name change to Linkin Park prior to first record releases; Numerous international appearances; Live shows include: Family Values, Ozzfest tours, KROQ Acoustic Christmas Concert 2001; TV specials include: Live At The Fillmore; Reverb. *Recordings:* Albums: Hybrid Theory, 2000; Reanimation, 2002. Singles: Hybrid Theory (EP), 2000; One Step Closer, 2001; Crawling, 2001; Papercut, 2001; In The End, 2001; Pts.Of.Athrty, 2002. *Honours:* Billboard Award, Best Modern Rock Artist, 2001; Rock Bear Awards, Best International Band, Best International Album, 2001; Kerrang! Award, Best International Newcomer, 2001; Rolling Stone Award, Best Hard Rock/Metal Band, 2001; MTV Awards, Best Group, Best Hard Rock, 2002. *Current Management:* Andy Gould Management, 8484 Wilshire Blvd #425, Beverly Hills, CA 90211, USA. *Website:* www.linkinpark.com.

SHIPSTON, Roy; b. 25 Aug. 1951, London, England. Musician (keyboards); Vocalist; Composer; Arranger; Record Prod. m. Julia Diane Twigg, 23 Nov. 1968, divorced 1994, 1 s., 1 d. *Education:* ABRSM Finals: Theory of Music, Pianoforte. *Career:* Music journalist, Disc and Music Echo, 1969–71; Musician, 1971–; Member, Formerly Fat Harry; Leader, own bands: Rococo; The Legendary Brats; Future; Performed on more than 30 albums; Sessions with Peter Green (including Alone With The Blues, 2000); Carl Palmer (ELP); Mike Harrison (Spooky Tooth); Chris Thompson; Peter Cox (Go West); Jake Sollo (Osibisa); Biddu; Jim Diamond; Now member, First Light; Co-owner, The Mill Recording Studios, Cookham, Berkshire; 1989–94; Clients included: Elton John; George Harrison; Chris Rea; Clannad. *Honours:* 2 BASF/Studio Master Awards; Music Week Top European Engineer Award; 3M Award. *Membership:* PRS; Musicians' Union. *Current Management:* Rococo Productions. *Address:* 2 Selwyn Court, Church Rd, Richmond, Surrey TW10 5LR, England.

SHIPWAY, Nigel Howard; b. 29 March 1953, Reading, Berkshire, England. Musician (percussion, timpani, mallets). *Education:* Studied percussion, composition with James Blades, Royal Academy of Music; Reg Barker, principal percussionist, Royal Opera House; Studied with Bobby Christian, USA. *Career:* Film appearances: Hunchback; The Wall; Return To Oz; Musical performances: Principal percussionist, Cats, New London Theatre, 20 years; National Symphony Orchestra, for 25 years; Academy of St Martins in the Fields; English Chamber Orchestra; Played on film scores: The Far Pavilions; Knight's Move; The Tall Guy; Morons From Outer Space; The Honorary Consul; The Killing Fields; Gangster No. 1; Knight's Move; Appearances with: The Moody Blues; Pink Floyd; Bob Geldof; Gene Pitney; Dionne Warwick; Bob Hoskins; José Carreras; Kiri Te Kanawa; Placido Domingo; Frankie Laine; The Pointer Sisters; Billy Daniels. *Compositions:* 44 studies for timpani; Style Studies For Xylophone; Concert Marimba Etude. *Recordings:* Over 1,000 listings with: National Symphony Orchestra; English Chamber Orchestra; Royal Opera House Orchestra; Alyn Ainsworth Orchestra; Ron Goodwin Orchestra. *Publications:* Articles: Talking Drums; Percussive Notes. *Membership:* Founding Pres. (UK Chapter), Percussive Arts Society; Royal Society of Musicians; Fellow of the Royal Society of Arts. *Current Management:* MAS. *Address:* Masters Yard, 180A South St, Dorking, Surrey RH4 2ES, England.

SHIRE, David Lee; b. 3 July 1937, Buffalo, New York, USA. Composer. m. (1)Talia Rose Coppola, 29 March 1970, divorced, 1 s., (2) Didi Conn, 11 Feb. 1984, 1 s. *Education:* BA, Yale University, 1959. *Compositions:* Film scores include: The Conversation, 1973; The Taking of Pelham 1–2–3, 1974; Farewell, My Lovely, 1975; All the President's Men, 1977; Saturday Night Fever, 1977; Norma Rae, 1979; Return To Oz, 1985; TV scores include: Raid on Entebbe, 1977; The Kennedys of Massachusetts; Sarah Plain and Tall, 1991; Rear Window, 1999; Theatre scores include: Starting Here, Starting Now, 1975; Baby, 1983; Closer Than Ever, 1989; Big, 1996. *Recordings:* Recorded songs include: What About Today?, 1965; The Promise, 1978; It Goes Like It Goes, 1979; With You I'm Born Again, 1979; Albums include: Saturday Night Fever, 1977; Starting Here, Starting Now, 1975; Baby, 1984; Return to Oz, 1985; Closer Than Ever, 1989; David Shire at the Movies, 1991; Big, 1996. *Honours:* Academy and Grammy Awards. *Membership:* Composers and Lyricists Guild of America; Academy of Motion Picture Arts and Sciences; National Academy of Television Arts and Sciences; Dramatists Guild of America, council mem. *Address:* 19 Ludlow Lane, Palisades, NY 10964, USA.

SHIVY, Sylvia Massy; Prod; Engineer; Mixer. *Career:* Prod., Zoo Records; Worked with: Johnny Cash, Cowboy Mouth, Cyclefly, The Deadlights, Deftones, Dig, Econoline Crush, Firewater, Glueleg, Green Jelly, Greta, Horsehead, Insolence, Luscious Jackson, Lollipop Lust Kill, Loudermilk, Love & Rockets, Lustra, Machines of Loving Grace, Oingo Boingo, Powerman 5000, Artist formerly known as Prince, Red Hot Chili Peppers, R.E.M., Seigmen, Sevendust, Skunk Anansie, System Of A Down, Tallman, Tom Petty and the Heartbreakers, Tool, Toy Shop, Virgos; Founded RadioStar Studios. *Current Management:* McDonough Management. *Address:* RadioStar Studios, Weed Palace Theater, 180 Main St, Weed, CA 96094, USA. *E-mail:* sylvia@radiostarstudios.com. *Website:* www.radiostarstudios.com.

SHOCKED, Michelle; b. 24 Feb. 1962, Dallas, TX, USA. Vocalist; Songwriter; Musician (guitar). m. 4 July 1992. *Education:* BSc, University of Texas, Austin. *Career:* World-wide tours, 1987–; Concerts include: Heineken Festival, Leeds, 1995. *Recordings:* Short Sharp Shocked, 1988; Captain Swing, 1989; Arkansas Traveller, 1992; Kind Hearted Woman, 1994; Mercury Poise, 1996; Artists Make Lousy Slaves, 1996; Good News, 1998; Deep Natural, 2002. *Membership:* NARAS; Rhythm and Blues Foundation. *Current Management:* Janine Natter, Codikow Carroll Guido and Groffman, New York. *Address:* 828 Royal St #520, New Orleans, LA 70116, USA.

SHORE, Howard; b. 18 Oct. 1946, Toronto, ON, Canada. *Education:* Berklee School of Music. *Career:* Mem., rock group Lighthouse; Wrote scores for theatre and radio; Musical Dir, Saturday Night Live NBC); Collaborations with: David Cronenberg, Peter Jackson. *Compositions:* I Miss You, Hugs and Kisses, 1978; The Brood, 1979; Scanners, 1981; Videodrome, 1983; Nothing Lasts Forever, 1984; After Hours, 1985; Fire with Fire, 1986; The Fly, 1986; Heaven, 1987; Nadine, 1987; Dead Ringers, 1988; Big, 1988; Signs of Life, 1989; She-Devil, 1989; The Local Stigmatic, 1989; An Innocent Man, 1989; Made In Milan, 1990; Naked Lunch, 1991; The Silence of the Lambs, 1991; A Kiss Before Dying, 1991; Prelude to a Kiss, 1992; Single White Female, 1992; Philadelphia, 1993; Mrs Doubtfire, 1993; M. Butterfly, 1993; Sliver, 1993; Guilty As Sin, 1993; Late Night with Conan O'Brien (TV theme), 1993; Nobody's Fool, 1994; The Client, 1994; Ed Wood, 1994; Seven, 1995; Moonlight and Valentino, 1995; White Man's Burden, 1995; That Thing You Do!, 1996; Crash, 1996; Before and After, 1996; The Truth About Cats & Dogs, 1996; Striptease, 1996; Looking For Richard, 1996; Cop Land, 1997; The Game, 1997; Gloria, 1999; Existenz, 1999; Analyze This, 1999; Dogma, 1999; High Fidelity, 2000; The Yards, 2000; Cell, 2000; Ester Kahn, 2000; The Score, 2001; The Lord of the Rings: The Fellowship of the Ring, 2001; Panic Room, 2002; Spider, 2002; The Lord of the Rings: The Two Towers, 2002; Gangs of New York, 2002. *Membership:* ASCAP. *Current Management:*

Gorfaine/Schwartz Agency Inc, 13245 Riverside Dr., Suite 450, Sherman Oaks, CA 91423, USA.

SHORROCK, Glenn; b. 30 July 1944, Rochester, Kent, England. Vocalist. *Career:* Vocalist with The Twilights, Axiom, then Esperanto before international success with Little River Band (formerly Mississippi), 1975–83; 1988–; Also solo career. *Compositions:* Help Is On Its Way, 1976; Home On Monday, 1977; Cool Change, 1979. *Recordings:* Albums: Little River Band, 1975; After Hours, 1976; Diamantina Cocktail, 1977; Sleeper Catcher, 1978; First Under The Wire, 1979; Backstage Pass, 1980; Time Exposure, 1981; Greatest Hits, 1982; Monsoon, 1988; Too Late To Load, 1989; Get Lucky, 1990; Reminiscing – The 20th Anniversary Concert, 1995; Little River Band Greatest Hits, 2000; solo: Villain of The Peace, 1983; The First 20 Years, 1985; with The Twilights: '64–'69; with Axiom: '69–'71. *Honours:* ARIA, Hall of Fame, 1991. *Membership:* APRA; board mem. 1980–98. *Current Management:* Talentworks Pty Ltd, Suite 1a, 663 Victoria St, Abbotsford, VIC 3067, Australia.

SHORTER, Wayne; b. 25 Aug. 1933, Newark, New Jersey, USA. Musician (saxophone). *Education:* BA, New York University, 1956. *Career:* Saxophonist with: Art Blakey, 1959–63; Miles Davis, 1964–70; Weather Report, 1970–86; Solo artiste, 1962–; Recent appearances include: London Jazz Festival, 2001. *Recordings:* Solo albums: Freeform, 1962; Search For a New Land, 1964; Night Dreamer, 1964; Some Other Stuff, 1964; Ju Ju, 1987; Speak No Evil, 1965; All Seeing Eye, 1966; Adam's Apple, 1967; Schizophrenia, 1968; Odyssey of Iska, 1970; Super Nova, 1970; Shorter Moments, 1972; Wayne Shorter, 1974; Moto Grosso Felo, 1975; Native Dancer, 1975; The Soothsayer, 1980; Etcetera, 1981; Wayning Moments, 1984; Second Genesis (reissue) 1984; Atlantis, 1985; Best Of..., 1988; Introducing... ; Phantom Navigator, 1987; Joy Ryder, 1988; High Life, 1994; Portrait, 2000; with Weather Report: Weather Report, 1971; I Sing The Body Electric, 1972; Sweetnighter, 1973; Mysterious Traveller, 1974; Tail Spinnin', 1975; Black Market, 1976; Black Market/Heavy Weather, 1978; Mr Gone, 1978; 8.30, 1979; Night Passage, 1980; Weather Report, 1982; Procession, 1983; Domino Theory, 1984; Sportin' Life, 1985; This Is This!, 1986; Greatest Hits, 1991; with Miles Davis: In Berlin, 1964; ESP, 1965; Miles Smiles, 1967; The Sorcerer, 1967; Nefertiti, 1968; Miles In The Sky, 1968; Filles De Kilimanjaro, 1968; In a Silent Way, 1969; Bitches Brew, 1970; Live Evil, 1972; Big Fun, 1974; Water Babies, 1977; Circle In The Round, 1979; with Joni Mitchell: Don Juan's Reckless Daughter, 1977; Mingus, 1979; Wild Things Run Fast, 1982; Dog Eat Dog, 1985; Chalk Mark In a Rain Storm, 1988; Night Ride Home, 1991; Panthalassa: The Music of Miles Davis, 1998; Sketches of Spain/ Kind of Blue, 1998; Also featured on recordings by: Airto; Stanley Clarke; Don Henley; Herbie Hancock; Freddie Hubbard; Jaco Pastorius; Rolling Stones; Sanatana; Steely Dan; Joe Zawinul. *Address:* c/o The Jazz Tree, 648 Broadway, Suite 703, New York, NY 10012, USA.

SHOVELL, (Andrew Lovell); b. 11 Feb. 1969, Jamaica. Musician (percussion). *Career:* Member, M People; Numerous live dates and television appearances; Song, Search for the Hero used in TV advertisement. *Recordings:* Singles: Colour My Life; Padlock; One Night in Heaven; Excited; Moving on Up; Open Your Heart; Search for the Hero; Just for You; Fantasy Island; Angel St; Testify; Albums: Elegant Slumming, 1994; Northern Soul, 1995; Love Rendezvous, 1995; Bizarre Fruit, 1995; Fresco, 1997; Best Of, 1998; Percussion on It Began In Afrika, Chemical Brothers, 2001. *Honours:* BRIT Award, Best Dance Band, 1992; Mercury Music Prize, 1993.

SHPORTKO, Victor; b. 30 Oct. 1944, Dniepropetrovsk, Ukraine. Vocalist. m. Natalia Biezko, 29 Oct. 1977, 1 s., 1 d. *Education:* Kiev Institute of Culture; Dniepropetrovsk Music Institute. *Career:* Tours: Canada; USA; Belgium; Poland; Czechoslovakia; Germany; Greece; Appears regularly on Ukrainian television and radio. *Recordings:* 3 Ukrainian cassettes. *Honours:* Singer Laureate International Competitions. *Membership:* Ukrainian Musical Societies. *Current Management:* Nicholas Tarasinko, 3A Horkogo St, Kiev, Ukraine. *Address:* 125A Horogo St, Apartment 109, Kiev 252006, Ukraine.

SHREEVE, Mark; b. 2 June 1957, Great Yarmouth, Norfolk, England. Composer; Musician (keyboards, synthesizers, guitar). *Education:* Studied architecture. *Career:* UK Electronica Festival, 1983, 1984, 1990; EMMA Festival, 1994; KLEM Festival, Netherlands, 1995. *Compositions:* Songs include: Touch Me, 1986; I Surrender, 1987; True Devotion, 1988 (all recorded by Samantha Fox). *Recordings:* Albums: Phantom, 1980; Embryo, 1980; Thoughts Of War, 1981; Assassin, 1983; Legion, 1985; Crash Head, 1988; Nocturne, 1995; Soundtracks include: Turnaround, 1986; Buy and Cell, 1988; Honor Bound, 1989. *Honours:* Gold, Silver discs, UK, USA; ASCAP Awards, various songs. *Membership:* PRS. *Current Management:* Virtual World Ltd. *Address:* 155 Prince George Ave, Southgate, London N14 4TD, England.

SHRIEVE, Michael; b. 6 July 1949, San Francisco, California, USA. Musician (drums). m. Cindy Weintraub, 1 May 1982, 1 s. *Education:* BA, San Mateo Jr College; BA studies with Anthony Cirome. *Career:* Long involvement as drummer/percussionist with Santana; Recorded with artists such as: The Rolling Stones; Steve Winwood; David Crosby; Also with experimental jazz musicians: Stomu Yamashta; Klaus Schulze; John McLaughlin; Bill Frisell;

One of first to experiment with electronic drums, 1973–. *Compositions include:* (for film and television) The Tempest; The Bedroom Window. *Recordings:* with Santana: Santana; Abraxas; Woodstock; Santana III; Caravansérail; Welcome; Lotus; Barboletta; with Steve Winwood: Automatic Man; with Stomu Yamashta: Go; with David Crosby: If Only I Could Remember My Name; with John McLaughlin: Love Devotion and Surrender; with The Rolling Stones: Emotional Rescue; Tattoo You; with Bill Frisell: Fascination, reissued 2001; Solo: Stiletto, 1989; Two Doors, 1995. *Honours:* Melody Maker; Modern Drummer. *Membership:* BMI; NARAS; Percussive Arts Society. *Current Management:* CMP Records. *Address:* 4756 University Village Pl. NE #288, Seattle, WA 98105, USA.

SHUMAN, Earl Stanley; b. 2 Aug. 1923, Boston, Massachusetts, USA. Songwriter (lyrics); Music Publisher. m. Margaret Stein, 25 Nov. 1956, 2 s., 1 d. *Education:* BA, Yale College, 1945. *Career:* Appeared with George Gibbs on The Perry Como Show, 1953, Jackie Gleason Show, 1953, Red Buttons Show, 1953. *Compositions:* Seven Lonely Days; Banjo's Back in Town; I Am; Left, Right, Out of Your Heart; Theme For a Dream; Starry-Eyed; Most People Get Married; Caterina; Hotel Happiness; Hey There Lonely Boy (Girl); The River; My Shy Violet; Young New Mexican Puppeteer; Clinging Vine; Close to Cathy; I've Been Here; Time, Time; Leaves are the Tears of Autumn; Off-Broadway Production, Secret Life of Walter Mitty, 1964; Movie Title Songs: Disorderly Orderly; Carpetbaggers; Judith; Dondi; Situation Hopeless But Not Serious. *Publications:* Bat Out of Hell, Meatloaf, 1977. *Honours:* Gold Record, Hey There Lonely Girl, 1970; Country Music Award, Leaves Are The Tears of Autumn, 1970; Platinum Record, Bat Out of Hell, 1978. *Membership:* ASCAP; NARAS; SGA. *Current Management:* Music Sales Publishing Inc. *Address:* Earl/Peg Music Co, 111 E 88th St, Apt 3 B, New York, NY 10128, USA.

SHUTTLEWORTH, David, (Shutty); b. 20 March 1967, Keighley, Yorkshire, England. Musician (drums). *Career:* Formed Spoilt Bratz with Tony Wright, Mark Yates and Leigh Marklew; Became Terrorvision; Secured record deal, 1991; Support slot to the Ramones; Numerous headlining tours and TV appearances. *Recordings:* Singles: My House, 1993; Oblivion, 1994; Pretend Best Friend, 1994; Alice, What's The Matter, 1994; Bad Actress, 1996; Perseverance, 1996; Easy, 1996; Moonage Daydream, 1997; Josephine, 1998; Tequila (No. 2, UK), 1999; III Wishes, 1999; Albums: Formaldehyde, 1993; How To Win Friends and Influence People, 1994; Regular Urban Survivors, 1996; Shaving Peaches, 1998; Whales And Dolphins (compilation), 2001; Good To Go, 2001.

SHVEDOVA, Irina; b. 28 April 1959, Kishivev, Moldova. Vocalist. Divorced, 1 d. *Education:* Kiev State Institute of Theatre Art; Music School, Kiev. *Career:* Lead role, children's radio play, 1968; Ukrainian pop concert, 1986; Diploma, Song of the Year, 1990, 1991; Hit '93, Russian competition; 10 Years on stage live, 1996. *Compositions:* America Separating, 1990; The White Waltz, 1991; Jordano, 1991; The Witch, 1992; Stay Cool, 1994; Faeton, 1998. *Recordings:* The Witch, 1993, 1994, CD, 1995; We'll Meet Again, 1996; Faeton, forthcoming. *Membership:* Theatre Artists Union, Ukraine. *Current Management:* Anton Klimov. *Address:* Frumenskaya na 6, 27/1, ap 50, 119196 Moscow, Russia.

SIBERIL, Sog; b. 1 Feb. 1955, France. Musician (Celtic guitar). 1 s. *Career:* Guitarist, 20 years; Member: Sked, 1975; Kornog, 1980; Gwerz, 1980; Pennou Skoulm, 1989; Kemia, 1989; Orion, 1992; La Rouchta, 1992; Numerous concerts and festivals all over Europe and America. *Recordings:* 1 solo album: Digor, 1993; 15 albums with other bands, including 5 with Kornog, 3 with Gwerz; with Den Quintet, Just Around The Window, 2001. *Honours:* Prix Academie du Disque Charles Cros: Gwertz, 1987, Le Sours Du Scorff, 1995.

SIBERRY, Jane; b. 12 Oct. 1955, Toronto, Ontario, Canada. Vocalist; Songwriter; Musician (piano, guitar). *Education:* BSc, University of Guelph (Ontario). *Career:* Guest at Peter Gabriel's Real World recording week, 1994; Co-wrote and performed closing title track in film: The Crow; 5 world tours; Contributing artist on Hector Zazoo's project, Songs From The Cold North Seas; Wrote, performed Calling All Angels, for Wim Wender's film Until The End of The World. *Recordings:* Albums: Jane Siberry, 1981; No Borders Here, 1983; The Speckless Sky, 1985; The Walking, 1987; Bound By The Beauty, 1989; When I Was a Boy, 1993; Maria, 1995; Teenager, 1997; Child: Music for the Christmas Season (live), 1997; Lips: Music For Saying It, 1999; Tree: Music for Films and Forests, 1999; Hush, 2000; City, 2001; Singles: Temple, 1993; Lovin' Cup, 1995. *Honours:* Casby (Canadian People's Choice Award); Album and Producer of the Year, 1986; Now Magazine Songwriter of the Year, 1995. *Current Management:* Bob Blumer Management. *Address:* 2700 Rutherford Dr., Los Angeles, CA, USA.

SIDDIQUI, Khalid; b. 14 Feb. 1970, Oxford, England. Vocalist; Musician (guitar, lap steel, mandolin). *Education:* University of East London. *Career:* Founded Doleboy Cowboy record label, 1990; Releases own material, other bands' material, and re-issues; British tour, 1993; Television: Kilroy; Radio: GLR; Mark Radcliffe, BBC Radio 1; Working/production with other bands; Currently tours London only. *Recordings:* City of Circles; Spend Monday Evening With; Angry Young Women Don'tcha Just Love 'Em; God's Outlaw; Man With Cock; Background Music On Paper; Various other bands productions include: Tribute To Johan Penson, Yupe Yeah. *Publications:* Contributor: Alcohol and Actors – Their Uses and Abuses; Surviving Performance Poetry Vol. III: Modernists; Various fanzines. *Honours:* Best Soundtrack (University of Westminster) Musical accompaniment (Jackson Comedy com). *Membership:* Pub-Orientation Rock National Organ. *Current Management:* Doleboy Cowboy Music. *Address:* 14 Westbury Rd, Feltham, Middlesex TW13 5HQ, England.

SIEBINGER, Manfred; b. 6 Dec. 1956, Salzburg, Austria. Concert Promoter. *Education:* Press-distribution; Advertising Agency; High School of Music. *Career:* Promoter, with local acts, 1984; Jazz/folk groups; Singer, songwriter; Acts produced by Broadway Musical Company, New York; Promoter, Lucio Dalla; Donovan; Gilbert Becaud; Stéphane Grappelli; Golden Gate Quartet; Paco De Lucia; Canadian Brass; Jaco Pastorius; The Dubliners; Dave Brubeck; Kris Kristofferson; Golden Earring; Blues Pumpm; Chris Barber; Pasadena Roof Orchestra; Flying Pickets, 1986–94. *Current Management:* PO Box 165, 5024 Salzburg, Austria.

SIFFRE, Labi; b. Bayswater, London, England. Vocalist; Musician (guitar). *Education:* Studied music harmonics. *Career:* Member, various soul bands in Cannes, France; Solo artiste, late 1960s–. *Recordings:* Albums: Labi Siffre, 1970; Singer and The Song, 1971; Crying, Laughing, Loving, Lying, 1972; So Strong, 1988; Make My Day, 1989; Singles: It Must Be Love (later recorded by Madness), 1971; Crying, Laughing, Loving, Lying, 1971; Watch Me, 1972; (Something Inside) So Strong, 1987; Guest vocals: Harmony Train, Sally Barker, 2000. *Current Management:* Mismanagement, 754 Fulham Rd, London SW6 5SH, England.

SIIKASAARI, Eerik; b. 8 Oct. 1957, Kotka, Finland. Musician (bass). *Education:* Piano, electric and acoustic bass; Oulunkylä; Diploma, Sibelius Academy. *Career:* Appeared with Jukkis Uotila Quartet, Middelheim Festival, Belgium, 1978; Association with Seppo Paakkunainen's Karelia, 1980–; Plays regularly with bands: Jukka Perko Quartet; Trio Töykeät; Espoo Big Band; Jukka Linkola Quintet; Perko-Pyysalo Poppoo; Concerts with Karelia and big bands in France, Switzerland, Germany, UK, USA. *Recordings include:* Kudos. *Honours:* First prize, with Trio Töykeät, Belgian jazz contest, 1988; Yrjö Award, Finnish Jazz Federation, 1995. *Address:* Apollonkatu 23 B 55, 00100 Helsinki, Finland.

SILAG, Marc; b. 22 May 1953, New York, USA. Tour Production Man; Artist Man. m. Susan Brown. *Education:* College. *Career:* General Manager, Bitter End, New York, 1974; Stage Manager, Bottom Line Theatre, New York, 1975–77; Tour, Artist Manager, 1977–; Tour, Production Manager for: Michael Urbaniak; John McLaughlin; David Sanborn; Herb Alpert; Patti Labelle; Pat Metheny Group; Paul Simon; Simon and Garfunkel; Personal Manager for: Ladysmith Black Mambazo; Chris Botti; Musical contractor, The Capeman, Broadway. *Recordings:* Co-ordinator: Graceland, Paul Simon (New York only); Rhythm of The Saints, Paul Simon; Various recordings with: David Sanborn; Ladysmith Black Mambazo; Chris Botti. *Publications:* Musician Magazine; Record Engineer and Producer. *Membership:* AFM; AFTRA. *Current Management:* Right Side Management. *Address:* 1674 Broadway #4C, New York, NY 10019, USA.

SILSON, Alan; b. 21 June 1951, Bradford, West Yorkshire, England. Musician (lead guitar); Vocalist. m. Angela, 11 July 1986, 1 d. *Career:* Founder member, Smokie; Television: Top of the Pops; Old Grey Whistle Test; Television and radio appearances in Germany; Norway; Denmark; Sweden; Ireland; Australia. *Compositions include:* Boulevard of Broken Dreams (number 1 album, Scandinavia, 6 weeks). *Recordings:* Numerous albums including: Pass It Round, 1975; Midnight Cafe, 1976; Bright Lights and Back Alleys, 1977; The Other Side of The Road, 1979; Strangers In Paradise, 1982; Boulevard of Broken Dreams, 1990; 20 top 20 hits, including If You Think You Know How To Love Me, 1975; I'll Meet You At Midnight, 1976; Living Next Door To Alice, 1976; Lay Back In The Arms of Someone, 1977; Needles And Pins, 1977; Oh Carol, 1978. *Honours:* Silver, Gold, Platinum discs world-wide. *Membership:* Musicians' Union; PRS; MCPS; PPL; BAC&S.

SILVANO, Judi; b. 8 May 1951, Philadelphia, Pennsylvania, USA. Vocalist; Composer. m. Joe Lovano, 30 Sept. 1984. *Education:* Pennsylvania Ballet School; Murray Louis/Alwin Nikolais Dance Theatre School; Graduated, cum laude, Temple University College of Music, 1974; BMI Composers Workshop; Private study with Anne Marie Moss (voice), Mark Murphy (voice), Kirk Nurock (theory), Yolanda Picucci Radlowski (flute). *Career:* Member, Group Motion Dance Troupe, Residency, Berlin Arts Festival, 1975; First European Tour and live recording at Amiens, France, with Joe Lovano, Worlds, 1989; Montréal Jazz Festival, European Tours, Montreux, Switzerland, Scandinavia, Italy, Paris, Festivals, 1991–98; BET Jazz Showcase, Judi Silvano Vocalise Band, 1997; Concerts at Carnegie Hall, Lincoln Center, Chicago Symphony Hall, Canadian Jazz Festivals with Joe Lovano Ensembles; Faculty, Rutgers University and BANFF Jazz Workshop, 1999. *Compositions:* Bass Space and Left Behind with Joe Lovano; Ecstasy, Isadora, 23rd St, Calypso, on Dancing Voices CD; Heuchera Americana, It's So Amazing, At Home, Bass Space on Vocalise; Nature of Life, American Festival of American Composers. *Recordings:* As Leader: Vocalise, CD;

Dancing Voices; Songs I Wrote or Wish I Did, 2000; With Joe Lovano: Universal Language; Celebrating Sinatra; Rush Hour; Worlds; With Kenny Werner: Paintings. *Honours:* Top 10 Vocalist, Down Beat magazine, 1995. *Membership:* AFTRA; Internatiohal Asscn of Women Composers, New York; Composers Concordance. *Address:* PO Box 218, Salisbury Mills, NY 12557, USA.

SILVER, Ken(neth M.); b. 23 March 1948, Philadelphia, Pennsylvania, USA. Musician (saxophone, clarinet); Bandleader. m. Judith Lipkin, 2 Nov. 1978, 2 s. *Education:* BSEd, 1969, MEd, 1971, Temple University; Studied clarinet with Ronald Reuben and Harold Karabell. *Career:* Performed at over 4000 Charity Balls, galas, corporate and social events since 1970; Performed a local, state and national inaugurals. *Honours:* Played for President Clinton and also for mayors, governors. *Current Management:* Entertainment Solutions Inc. *Address:* Suite 525, Fox Pavilion, Jenkintown, PA 19046, USA.

SILVERLIGHT, Terry; b. 15 Jan. 1957, Newark, New Jersey, USA. Composer; Prod; Musician (drums); Arranger. m. Judy, 7 Sept. 1995. *Education:* Princeton University; Piano with Olga Von Til; Percussion with Morris Lang. *Career:* Songs aired on TV Shows Melrose Place, Pacific Palisades, Beverly Hills 90210, The Guiding Light, CNN Lifestyles, Jag, Clueless, Seventh Heaven, The Sopranos; TV appearances as drummer with Roberta Flack and Marvin Hamlish at the White House, Peabo Bryson, Natalie Merchant on the Rosie O'Donnell Show, Sheena Easton, Barry Miles, Al DiMeola, Stephen Stills. *Compositions:* All That Matters, Louise; Chasin' a Dream, Nancy Wilson; All I Wanna Do, Carl Anderson; Love's The Key, Maria Amada; Take My Love For Real, Yasuko Agawa and Philip Ingram. *Recordings:* Played drums on records for Billy Ocean, Mel Tormé, Laura Nyro, Anne Murray, Tom Jones, Barry Miles, Phil Woods, Stephanie Mills, George Benson, David Matthews, Don Johnson, Freddie Jackson, Eric Kloss, Jonathan Butler, Melba Moore, David Sancious; Bobby Belfry; Odyssey; Jeffrey Osborne. *Publications:* The Featured Drummer, instruction book, 1981. *Honours:* Platinum Disc for All That Matters; Numerous Gold and Platinum discs as drummer. *Membership:* ASCAP.

SILVESTRI, Alan; b. 26 March 1950, New York, NY, USA. Composer. *Education:* Berklee College of Music. *Career:* Collaborations with: Howard Deutch, Stephen Hopkins, Mick Jackson, Nancy Meyers, Donald Petrie, Robert Zemeckis. *Compositions:* The Doberman Gang, 1972; The Mack, 1973; Starsky and Hutch (TV), 1975; The Amazing Dobermans, 1976; Chips (TV), 1977; The Fifth Floor, 1980; Romancing the Stone, 1984; Summer Rental, 1985; Fandango, 1985; Back to the Future, 1985; Cat's Eye, 1985; No Mercy, 1986; Flight of the Navigator, 1986; Amazing Stories (TV), 1986; American Anthem, 1986; The Clan of the Cave Bear, 1986; The Delta Force, 1986; Overboard, 1987; Critical Condition, 1987; Predator, 1987; Outrageous Fortune, 1987; My Stepmother Is An Alien, 1988; Mac and Me, 1988; Who Framed Roger Rabbit, 1988; She's Out of Control, 1989; Tales from the Crypt (TV), 1989; The Abyss, 1989; Back to the Future Part II, 1989; Downtown, 1990; Back to the Future Part III, 1990; Young Guns II, 1990; Predator 2, 1990; Father of the Bride, 1991; Dutch, 1991; Back to the Future–The Ride, 1991; Soapdish, 1991; Shattered, 1991; Ricochet, 1991; Stop! Or My Mom Will Shoot, 1992; Death Becomes Her, 1992; Ferngully: The Last Rainforest, 1992; The Bodyguard, 1992; Sidekicks, 1992; Judgment Night, 1993; In Search of the Obelisk, 1993; Grumpy Old Men, 1993; Cop and a Half, 1993; Super Mario Bros, 1993; Richie Rich, 1994; Clean Slate, 1994; Blown Away, 1994; Forrest Gump, 1994; The Quick and the Dead, 1995; The Perez Family, 1995; Judge Dredd, 1995; Father of the Bride Part II, 1995; Grumpier Old Men, 1995; Sgt Bilko, 1996; Eraser, 1996; The Long Kiss Goodnight, 1996; Fools Rush In, 1997; Volcano, 1997; Contact, 1997; Mouse Hunt, 1997; The Odd Couple II, 1998; The Parent Trap, 1998; Holy Man, 1998; Practical Magic, 1998; Stuart Little, 1999; Reindeer Games, 2000; What Lies Beneath, 2000; Cast Away, 2000; What Women Want, 2001; The Mexican, 2001; The Mummy Returns, 2001; Serendipity, 2001; Show Time, 2002; Lilo And Stitch, 2002; Stuart Little 2, 2002; Maid In Manhatten, 2002; Pirates Of The Carribean, 2003; Polar Express, 2003. *Honours:* Saturn Awards for Best Music, Predator, 1988, Back to the Future Part II, 1991; Cable Ace Award for Best Original Score, Tales from the Crypt TV series, 1990; BMI Richard Kirk Award for Outstanding Career Achievement, 1995; Grammy Award for Best Instrumental Composition, Cast Away, 2002; ASCAP Henry Mancini Award for Lifetime Achievement, 2002. *Membership:* BMI. *Current Management:* Gorfaine/ Schwartz Agency Inc, 13245 Riverside Dr., Suite 450, Sherman Oaks, CA 91423, USA. *Website:* www.alan-silvestri.com.

SIMARD, Bernard; b. 27 Aug. 1959, Valleyfield, Québec, Canada. Musician (guitar); Vocalist. m. 8 July 1994, 1 s., 1 d. *Career:* Member: La Bottine Souriante; Gwazigan, 1996; Tours include USA, Canada, Europe, 1984–87; Member, Manigance; Tours of France, 1988–90; Current member, Cabestan; First part of Raymond Léveque, 1994; Television includes: Ad Lib (Québec), BBC (UK). *Recordings include:* with La Bottine Souriante: La Traversée de l'Atlantique, 1986; Nouvelle Manigance, 1991; Tracks also featured on Down Home, Vols I and II, 1986; with Cabestan: Tempête Pour Sortir; St Laurent-Sur-Oust, 1995; with Christian Maes: Coup de Vent, 1998; with Gwazigan: Dessus La Fougère; Y'Avait Du Monde. *Membership:* SOCAN. *Current Management:* Micmac Musik, 24 Quai De La Fosse, 44000 Nantes, France.

SIMINS, Russell; b. 1964, Long Island, NY, USA. Musician (drums). *Career:* Mem., Jon Spencer Blues Explosion, 1990–. *Recordings:* Albums: with Jon Spencer Blues Explosion: Jon Spencer Blues Explosion, 1992; Crypt Style, 1992; Extra Width, 1993; Mo' Width, 1994; Orange, 1994; Experimental Remixes, 1995; Now I Got Worry, 1996; Controversial Negro, 1997; Rocketship, 1997; ACME, 1998; Magical Colours, 2000; Plastic Fang, 2002; Solo: Public Places, 2000. Singles: The Sound Of The Future Is Here Today, 1992; Shirt-jac, 1992; Son Of Sam, 1992; Big Yule Log Boogie, 1992; Train 3, 1993; Bellbottoms, 1995; Get With It, 1996; 2 Kindsa Love, 1996; Wail, 1997; Rocketship, 1997; Talk About The Blues, 1998. *Address:* c/o Mute Records, 136 W 18th St, New York, NY 10011, USA.

SIMMONS, Gene, (Chaim Witz); b. 25 Aug. 1949, Haifa, Israel. Musician (bass guitar); Vocalist; Actor; Songwriter. *Education:* ABA, Sullivan College, SUNY, 1970; BA, Richmond College, CUNY, 1972. *Career:* Founder, Wicked Lester, 1972; Founder member, US rock group Kiss, 1973–; Regular UK, US, European and world-wide tours; Actor, films: The Runaway, 1984; Never Too Young To Die, 1986; Trick Or Treat (with Ozzy Osbourne); Dead Or Alive, 1986; Kiss Attack of The Phantom; Inventor, Axe bass guitar, 1980; Established Simmons record label, 1988–. *Compositions:* Many for Kiss. *Recordings:* Albums: Kiss, 1974; Hotter Than Hell, 1974; Dressed To Kill, 1975; Alive!, 1975; Destroyer, 1976; The Originals, 1976; Rock and Roll Over, 1976; Kiss Alive II, 1977; Love Gun, 1977; Double Platinum, 1978; Dynasty, 1979; Kiss Unmasked, 1980; Music From The Elder, 1981; Creatures of The Night, 1982; Lick It Up, 1983; Animalize, 1984; Asylum, 1985; Crazy Nights, 1987; Smashes, Thrashes and Hits, 1988; Hot In The Shade, 1989; Revenge, 1992; Kiss Alive III, 1993; Unplugged, 1996; Greatest Kiss, 1997; Carnival of Souls: The Final Sessions, 1997; Kiss, The Second Coming I and II, 1998; Psycho Circus, 1999; First Kiss, Last Licks, 1999; Solo album: Gene Simmons, 1978; Singles include: Rock 'N' Roll All Nite, 1975; Beth, 1976; Detroit City, 1976; Hard Luck Woman, 1976; Calling Dr. Love, 1977; Christine Sixteen, 1977; Rocket Ride, 1978; I Was Made For Lovin' You, 1979; A World Without Heroes, 1981; I Love It Loud, 1982; Lick It Up, 1983; Heaven's On Fire, 1984; Tears Are Falling, 1985; Heaven's On Fire; Crazy Crazy Nights, 1967; Reason To Live, 1987; Hide Your Heart, 1989; Forever, 1990; God Gave Rock and Roll To You, featured in film Bill and Ted's Bogus Journey, 1992; Contribution, Runaway, to album Hear 'N' Aid (charity project for Ethiopian famine relief), 1986. *Honours:* Footprints at Grauman's Chinese Theater, Hollywood, 1976; Gold Ticket, Madison Square Garden, 1979; Inducted into Hollywood's Rock Walk; Kiss Day proclaimed, Los Angeles, 1993; Numerous Gold and Platinum records. *Current Management:* Entertainment Services Unlimited, Main St Plaza 1000, Suite 303, Voorhees, NJ 08043, USA. *Address:* c/o Doc McGhee, McGhee Entertainment, 8730 Sunset Blvd, Suite 175, Los Angeles, CA 90069, USA.

SIMON, Carly; b. 25 April 1945, New York, NY, USA. Composer; Vocalist; Musician (piano, guitar). m. (1) James Taylor, 3 Nov. 1971, divorced 1983, 1 s., 1 d., (2) James Hart, 23 Dec. 1987. *Education:* Sarah Lawrence College, 2 years; Studied with Peter Seeger. *Career:* Singer, composer, recording artist, 1971–; Appeared in film No Nukes, 1980; Television appearances include: Carly In Concert – My Romance, 1990. *Compositions:* Opera, Romulus Hunt; Film scores: Working Girl; Heartburn; This Is My Life; Postcards From The Edge. *Recordings:* Albums include: Carly Simon, 1971; Anticipation, 1972; No Secrets (No. 1, USA), 1973; Hotcakes, 1974; Playing Possum, 1975; The Best of Carly Simon, 1975; Another Passenger, 1976; Boys In The Trees, 1978; Spy, 1979; Come Upstairs, 1980; Torch, 1981; Hello Big Man, 1983; Spoiled Girl, 1985; Coming Round Again, 1987; Greatest Hits Live, 1988; My Romance, 1990; Have You Seen Me Lately?, 1991; Letters Never Sent, 1994; Clouds In My Coffee 1965–95, 1996; Film Noir, 1997; The Bedroom Tapes, 2000; Also appeared on albums by James Taylor; Lee Clayton; Mick Jones; Nils Lofgren; Tom Rush; Jesse Colin Young; Hit singles: Anticipation, 1971; You're So Vain (No. 1, USA), 1972; The Right Thing To Do, 1973; Haven't Got Time For The Pain, 1974; Nobody Does It Better, 1977; You Belong To Me, 1978; Vengeance, 1979; Jesse, 1980; Why, 1982; Coming Around Again, 1986; Let The River Run, from the movie Working Girl, 1989; Featured vocal on: Kissing With Confidence, Will Powers, 1983; Recorded with numerous artists including Paul McCartney; Luther Vandross; Mick Jagger; Linda Ronstadt; Michael McDonald; John Forte; Janet Jackson. *Publications:* Children's books: Amy The Dancing Bear, 1988; The Boy of The Bells, 1990; The Fisherman's Song, 1991; The Nighttime Chauffer, 1993; Midnight Farm, 1997. *Honours:* Grammy, Best New Artist, 1971; Academy Award, Let The River Run, 1989; Golden Globe. *Membership:* Songwriters Hall of Fame. *Current Management:* c/o Lee Phillips, Manatt Phelps and Phillips, 11355 W Olympic Blvd, Los Angeles, CA 90064, USA.

SIMON, Edward; b. 27 July 1969, Comunidad Cardom, Falcon State, Venezuela. Jazz Musician (piano). m. Maria A Simon, 19 Feb. 1994. *Education:* The University of the Arts, music performance, classical piano (not completed); The Manhattan School of Music, music performance, jazz piano (not completed). *Career:* Member, Bobby Watson's Horizon, 1988–92; Played with Greg Osby; Kevin Eubanks; Paquito D'Rivera; Herbie Mann; Charlie Sepulveda; Jerry Gonzalez; Currently member, The Terence Blanchard Quartet. *Recordings:* Albums: Solo: Beauty Within, 1994; Edward Simon, 1994; La Bikina, 1998; with Kevin Eubanks: The Searcher, 1989;

Promise of Tomorrow, 1990; with Greg Osby: Mind Games, 1988; Season of Renewal, 1989; Man-Talk, 1990; with Bobby Watson: The Inventor, 1990; Post Motown Bop, 1991; Present Tense, 1992; Midwest and Shuffle, 1993; with Herbie Mann: Caminho de Casa, 1990; with Dave Binney: Point Game, 1990; with Victor Lewis: Family Portrait, 1992; Know It Today, Know It Tomorrow, 1993; with Claudio Roditi: Two of Swords, 1991; with Craig Handy: Split Second Timing, 1992; with Charlie Sepulveda: Algo Nuestro, 1993; with Terence Blanchard: Romantic Defiance, 1995; The Heart Speaks, 1996; Wandering Moon, 2000; with Carl Allen: The Pursuer, 1994; with Terell Stafford: Time To Let Go, 1995; with Mark Shim: Turbulent Flow, 2000; with Marlon Simon: Rumaba A La Potato, 2000; with John Patitucci: Communion, 2001. *Honours:* Third Finalist, The Thelonious Monk International Jazz (Piano) Competition. *Membership:* NARAS; BMI. *Current Management:* c/o Timothy Patterson, Split Second Timing. *Address:* 104 W 70th St, #11-C, New York, NY 10023, USA.

SIMON, Paul; b. 13 Oct. 1941, Newark, New Jersey, USA. Vocalist; Composer. m. (1) Peggy Harper (divorced), 1 s., (2) Carrie Fisher (divorced), (3) Edie Brickell, 30 May 1992, 2 s., 1 d. *Education:* BA, Queens College; Postgraduate, Brooklyn Law School. *Career:* Duo, Simon and Garfunkel, with Art Garfunkel, 1964–71; Appearances with Garfunkel include: Monterey Festival, 1967; Royal Albert Hall, 1968; Reunion concerts: Central Park, New York, 1981; US, European tours; Solo artiste, 1972–; Appearances include: Anti-war Festival, Shea Stadium, New York, 1970; Farm Aid V, 1992; Hurricane Relief concert, Miami, 1992; Born At The Right Time Tour; Tour, Europe and Russia; Television includes: Paul Simon Special, 1977; Paul Simon's Graceland – The African Concert, 1987; Paul Simon – Born At The Right Time, 1992; Film appearances: Monterey Pop, 1968; Annie Hall, 1977; All You Need Is Cash, 1978; One Trick Pony, 1980; Steve Martin Live, 1985. *Compositions include:* The Sound of Silence; Homeward Bound; I Am a Rock; Mrs Robinson; The Boxer; Bridge Over Troubled Water; Cecilia; Slip Slidin' Away; Late In The Evening; You Can Call Me Al; The Boy In The Bubble; Graceland; Paul Simon, Songs From The Capeman, 1997. *Recordings:* Albums: with Art Garfunkel: Wednesday Morning 3AM, 1964; Sounds of Silence, 1965; Parsley Sage Rosemary and Thyme, 1967; The Graduate (film soundtrack), 1967; Bookends (No. 1, UK and USA), 1968; Bridge Over Troubled Water (No. 1, UK and USA), 1970; Simon and Garfunkel's Greatest Hits, 1972; Breakaway, 1975; Watermark, 1978; Collected Works, 1981; The Concert In Central Park, 1982; Various compilation albums; Old Friends (box set), 1998; Singles: The Sound Of Silence (No. 1, USA), 1965; Homeward Bound, 1966; I Am A Rock, 1966; A Hazy Shade Of Winter, 1966; At The Zoo, 1967; Scarborough Fair, 1968; Mrs. Robinson (No. 1, USA), 1968; The Boxer, 1969; Bridge Over Troubled Water (No. 1, UK and USA), 1970; Cecilia, 1970; El Condor Pasa, 1970; America, 1972; Solo albums: Paul Simon, 1972; There Goes Rhymin' Simon, 1973; Live Rhymin': Paul Simon In Concert, 1974; Still Crazy After All These Years (No. 1, USA), 1975; Greatest Hits Etc, 1977; One-Trick Pony, 1980; Hearts and Bones, 1983; Graceland (No. 1, UK), 1986; Negotiations and Love Songs, 1988; Rhythm of The Saints (No. 1, UK), 1990; Paul Simon's Concert In The Park, 1991; Paul Simon 1964–93, 1993; Paul Simon – Songs From The Capeman, 1997; Shining Like A Natural Guitar (Greatest Hits), 2000; You're The One, 2000; Solo hit singles include: Mother And Child Reunion, 1972; Me And Julio Down By The Schoolyard, 1972; Kodachrome, 1973; Take Me To The Mardi Gras, 1973; American Tune, 1973; 50 Ways To Leave Your Lover (No. 1, USA), 1975; Still Crazy After All These Years, 1976; Slip Slidin' Away, 1977; Late In The Evening, 1980; Allergies, 1983; You Can Call Me Al, 1986; The Boy In The Bubble, 1986; The Obvious Child, 1990. *Publications:* The Songs of Paul Simon, 1972; New Songs, 1975; One-Trick Pony (screenplay), 1980; At The Zoo (for children), 1991. *Honours:* Grammy awards: two for The Graduate soundtrack, 1968, six for Bridge Over Troubled Water, 1970, two for Still Crazy After All These Years, 1986, one for Graceland, 1987; Emmy Award, Paul Simon Special, NBC, 1977; Inducted into Rock and Roll Hall of Fame, with Art Garfunkel, 1990; Antoinette Perry Award, The Capeman, Best Original Score Written For The Theatre 1997–98; Doctorate of Music, Berklee College of Music, 1986; Doctorate of Music, Queens College, 1995; Doctorate of Music, Yale University, 1996. *Address:* Paul Simon Music, 1619 Broadway, Suite 500, New York, NY 10019, USA.

SIMONE, Nina, (Eunice Waymon); b. 21 Feb. 1933, Tryon, North Carolina, USA. Vocalist. *Education:* Juilliard School of Music, New York. *Career:* Singer, clubs, Philadelphia; Recording artist, 1959–; Active in civil rights movement, early 1960s; Presenter, BBC Radio 2, 2000. *Recordings:* Albums: Little Girl Blue, 1950; Nina Simone At The Town Hall, 1959; At Newport, 1960; Forbidden Fruit, 1961; Nina Simone At The Village Gate, 1961; Sings Ellington, 1962; Nina's Choice, 1963; Nina Simone At Carnegie Hall, 1963; Folksy Nina, 1964; In Concert, 1964; Broadway... Blues... Ballads, 1964; I Put a Spell On You, 1965; Tell Me More, 1965; Pastel Blues, 1965; Let It All Out, 1966; Wild Is The Wind, 1966; Nina With Strings, 1966; This Is, 1966; Nina Simone Sings The Blues, 1966; High Priestess of Soul, 1967; Sweet 'N' Swinging, 1967; Silk and Soul, 1967; 'Nuff Said, 1968; And Piano, 1969; To Love Somebody, 1969; Black Gold, 1970; Here Comes The Sun, 1971; Heart and Soul, 1971; Emergency Ward, 1972; It Is Finished, 1972; Gifted and Black, 1974; I Loves You Porgy, 1977; Baltimore, 1978; Cry Before I Go, 1980; Nina Simone, 1982; Fodder On My Wings, 1982; Live At Vine Street, 1987; Live At Ronnie Scott's, 1988; Nina's Back, 1989; In Concert, 1992; A Single

Woman, 1993; After Hours, 1995; In Concert, 1996; Saga of the Good Life and Hard Times, 1997; At Newport, 1998; Misunderstood, 2000; Various compilations; Singles include: I Loves You Porgy; Gin House Blues; Forbidden Fruit; Don't Let Me Be Misunderstood; I Put a Spell On You; Ain't Got No – I Got Life; To Love Somebody; To Be Young Gifted and Black; My Baby Just Cares For Me.

SIMONS, Ed(ward); b. 9 June 1970, England. Musician. *Education:* Medieval History, Manchester University. *Career:* Formed, The Dust Brothers, with Tom Rowlands; Formed, The Chemical Brothers, 1989–, with Tom Rowlands. *Compositions:* Exit Planet Dust, album; Dig Your Own Hole, album; Block Rockin Beats; Setting Sun; Leave Home. *Recordings:* Albums: Exit Planet Dust, 1995; Live At The Social, Vol. 1, 1996; Dig Your Own Hole (No. 1, UK), 1997; Brothers Gonna Work It Out (DJ mix album), 1998; Surrender (No. 1, UK), 1999; Come With Us, 2002. Singles: Song To The Siren, 1993; 14th Century Sky (EP), 1994; My Mercury Mouth (EP), 1994; Leave Home, 1995; Life Is Sweet, 1995; Loops Of Fury (EP), 1996; Setting Sun (No. 1, UK), 1996; Block Rockin Beats (No. 1, UK), 1997; Electronic Battle Weapons, 1997; Elektrobank, 1997; Melting Pot, 1998; Action, 1999; Hey Boy, Hey Girl, 1999; Let Forever Be, 1999; Out Of Control, 1999; Action with Liquid Todd (producer), 1999; Music: Response, 2000; It Began In Afrika, 2001; Starguitar, 2002; Come With Us/The Test, 2002; American (EP), 2003. *Honours:* Grammy Award, 1997; BRIT Award, Best British Dance Act, 2000. *Current Management:* Robert Linney, MBL, 1 Cowcross St, London EC1M 6DR, England. *Address:* c/o Astralwerks Records, 104 W 29th St, Fourth Floor, New York, NY 10001, USA. *Website:* www.astralwerks.com/chemical/home/chemical.html.

SIMPSON, Jim; b. 27 Jan. 1938, Westminster, London, England. Music Co Exec; Record Prod; Journalist; Musician (trumpet). 1 s. *Education:* Tuition with Dougie Roberts; Dennis Darlowe. *Career:* Played with Locomotive, 1964–69; Managed Black Sabbath, 1969–71; Recorded and toured with American Bluesmen: Lightnin' Slim; Homesick James; Doctor Ross; Snooky Pryor, through 1970s; Began Birmingham International Jazz Festival, 1985; BT British Jazz Awards, 1987; Bruce Adams/Alan Barnes Quintet, 1995; Managing Director, Big Bear Music Group. *Recordings:* with Locomotive: Rudi's In Love; 5 albums with King Pleasure and The Biscuit Boys; with Black Sabbath: Black Sabbath; Paranoid; with The Quads: There Must Be Thousands. *Publications:* Launched jazz national magazine The Jazz Rag, 1986. *Honours:* British Jazz Award, Jazz CD of the Year, 1994. *Current Management:* Big Bear Music. *Address:* PO Box 944, Edgbaston, Birmingham B16 8UT, England.

SIMPSON, Kerri; b. 15 Nov. 1960, Melbourne, Australia. *Career:* Performed, toured, nationally and internationally in New Orleans, Chicago, London, Barcelona, Blues, Gospel, Alternative Dance; Regular House Artist, ABC TV's Big Gig, 1989–91; International supports for Kylie Minogue, 1991; Charlie Musselwhite, 1991; The Church, 1995. *Compositions:* Veve; Ah Jole; Higher; Jaguar; I Wonder; Very Popular; Shed; Billy Cowboys; Cry Mercy. *Recordings:* Veve, 1992; Veve (remix by Ollie Olsen); Albums: The Arousing, 1995; Speak, 1996; Higher; Turkey Necklasso, 1996; Psy Harmonica, Vol. 1; Confessin' The Blues, 1998; Vodou – Songs of The Spirits, 2001. *Honours:* Featured Artist, Fritz Radio Berlin, 1991. *Membership:* MU; Australian Performing Rights Asscn. *Current Management:* Maverick Arts Management. *Address:* PO Box 780, Brunswick Lower, VIC 3058, Australia.

SIMPSON, Martin Stewart; b. 5 May 1953, Scunthorpe, Lincolnshire, England. Vocalist; Musician (guitar, banjo); Composer; Songwriter. m. Jessica Ruby Radcliffe, 1985. *Career:* Folk musician; Started playing guitar, aged 12, and banjo soon after; Performed professionally from age 15; Recorded first album, Golden Vanity, at 22 and toured supporting Steeleye Span; Worked with June Tabor for over a decade and recorded 3 albums together; Relocating to the USA with American wife; Worked with many folk greats including: Martin Carthy; Dave Mattacks; Ashley Hutchings; Simon Nicol; Richard Thompson; Also performed more recently with musicians from diverse backgrounds including: Wu Man (Chinese pipa player); Bob Brozman; Debashish Bhattacharya; Cool and Unusual album draws on Celtic, American and Afro-American music, featuring David Lindley, Joe Phelps and members of Tarika; Acclaimed album Bramble Briar concentrates on English folk material. *Recordings:* Golden Vanity, 1976; Special Agent, A Cut Above (with June Tabor), 1981; Grinning In Your Face, 1983; Nobody's Fault But Mine, 1985; True Dare Or Promise (with Jessica Simpson), 1987; Leaves of Life, 1989; When I Was On Horseback, 1991; A Closer Walk With Thee, 1994; Smoke and Mirrors, Red Roses, 1995; Band of Angels, Music For The Motherless Child, 1996; Live, Cool and Unusual, 1997; The Bramble Briar, 2001; features on: Larkrise To Candleford, 1980; Aqaba, June Tabor, 1988; Abyssinians, 1989. *Honours:* BBC Radio 2 Folk Awards: Best Instrumentalist; Best Album, Bramble Briar, 2002. *Current Management:* Herschel Freeman Agency Inc, 7684 Apahon Lane, Germantown, TN 38138, USA. *E-mail:* hfreeman@ixlmemphis.com. *Website:* www.martinsimpson.com.

SIMPSON, Valerie; b. 26 Aug. 1946, Bronx, New York, USA. Vocalist; Songwriter. m. Nickolas Ashford, 1974. *Career:* Performing and songwriting duo, with husband Nickolas Ashford; Worked with Marvin Gaye singing on

recordings in place of Tammi Terrell; Solo artiste, 1971–73. *Compositions:* Co-writer with Nickolas Ashford: Never Had It So Good, Ronnie Milsap; One Step At a Time, Maxine Brown, The Shirelles; Let's Go Get Stoned, Ray Charles; Songs include: Ain't No Mountain High Enough; You're All I Need To Get By; Reach Out and Touch Somebody's Hand; Remember Me; Solid. *Recordings:* Solo albums: Exposed!, 1971; Valerie Simpson, 1972; with Nickolas Ashford: Keep It Comin', 1973; Gimme Something Real, 1973; I Wanna Be Selfish, 1974; Come As You Are, 1976; So So Satisfied, 1977; Send It, 1977; Is It Still Good To Ya?, 1978; Stay Free, 1979; A Musical Affair, 1980; Performance, 1981; Street Opera, 1982; High-Rise, 1983; Solid, 1984; Real Love, 1986; Love Or Physical, 1989; As producer: The Boss, Diana Ross, 1979; The Touch, Gladys Knight, 1981; Gladys Knight, Ultimate Collection, 1997; Supremes: Ultimate Collection, 1997; Motown 40 Forever, 1998; Martha and the Vandellas, Ultimate Collection, 1998; Marvelettes Ultimate Collection, 1998; Contributed to numerous sessions as vocalist, including: Blood Sweat & Tears; Donald Fagen; Four Tops; Quincy Jones; Gladys Knight & The Pips; Al Kooper; Diana Ross; David Sanborn; Paul Simon; Steely Dan. *Current Management:* Hopsack and Silk Productions, 254 W 72nd St, Suite 1A, New York, NY 10023, USA.

SINATRA, Nancy; b. 8 June 1940, Jersey City, New Jersey, USA. Vocalist; Writer. *Education:* Lessons in music, dance, drama. *Career:* Appearances include: Sinatra/Elvis Presley television special, 1959; Recording debut, 1961; 10 appearances, Ed Sullivan Show; Numerous TV specials including Movin' With Nancy, 1967; Sold over 8m. records world-wide; Film appearances include: Wild Angels; Speedway (with Elvis Presley), 1968. *Recordings:* Albums: Boots, 1966; How Does That Grab You Darlin', 1966; Nancy In London, 1966; Sugar, 1967; Country My Way, 1967; Movin' With Nancy, 1968; Nancy and Lee (with Lee Hazlewood), 1968; Nancy, 1969; Woman, 1970; Nancy's Greatest Hits, 1970; This Is Nancy Sinatra, 1971; Did You Ever (with Lee Hazlewood), 1972; All-Time Hits, 1988; Lightning's Girl – The Very Best of Nancy Sinatra, 1988; One More Time, 1995; Sheet Music: Collection of her Favorite Love Songs, 1998; Greatest Hits, 2000; Singles include: These Boots Are Made For Walkin' (International No. 1 hit); How Does That Grab You Darlin'; Sugar Town; Something Stupid, with father Frank Sinatra (No. 1, UK); You Only Live Twice (theme to James Bond film); Jackson (with Lee Hazlewood); Did You Ever (with Lee Hazlewood); For My Dad. *Publications:* Frank Sinatra My Father, 1985; Frank Sinatra – An American Legend, 1995. *Current Management:* John Dubuque, Dublen Entertainment Group, 330 Merwin Ave, Unit # F1, Milford, CT 06460, USA. *Address:* c/o Delsener/ Saleter, 27 E 67th St, New York, NY 10021, USA.

SINCLAIR, Cynthia; b. 17 Nov. 1951, Philadelphia, Pennsylvania, USA. Musician; Record Co Exec. *Education:* BA, Boston University, 1973; BMus, Berklee College of Music, 1983; Postgraduate, Santa Monica College, 1998–2002. *Career:* Founder, Myoho Records, Boston, 1984–; Assistant Cameraperson, Young Musicians' Foundation, Beverly Hills, California, 1996; Singer/Songwriter, Red Hot to Icy Blue, No Exit, The Blues Make Good Lovers, Black in Back in Style; Member, Joe Vento Big Band Jazz Orchestra, tour of college stadiums, 2001–02. *Compositions:* Composer/Arranger, Outside You; Singer/Arranger, Good Morning Heartache; Prelude to a Kiss; Composer/Lyricist, over 50 published songs. *Membership:* Group Leader, Women's Issues, Soka Gakkai International, Boston, 1986–88; ASCAP; NARAS; Mensa. *Address:* PO Box 462, Santa Monica, CA 90406, USA.

SINFIELD, Peter John; b. 27 Dec. 1943, Fulham, London, England. Divorced. *Career:* King Crimson, writer, producer, 1969–72; Roxy Music, Producer, 1973; Solo album, 1974; Greg Lake, Co-writer, co-producer, 1974–80; Songwriting with Andy Hill, Albert Hammond, Bill Livsey and others, 1981–. *Compositions:* King Crimson: In the Court of the Crimson King; 21st Century Schizoid Man; I Talk to the Wind; Emerson Lake and Palmer: Karnevil 9; Pirates; Greg Lake: C'est La Vie; I Believe in Father Xmas; The Land of Make Believe, for Bucks Fizz (No. 1, UK), 1982; Allstars, 2001; Rain or Shine, for Five Star; Don't Walk Away; Have You Ever Been in Love, for Leo Sayer; Keep Each Other Warm, for Barry Manilow; Peace in Our Time, for Cliff Richard; Waiting in the Wings, for Diana Ross; As Dreams Go By, for Bette Midler; Think Twice; Call the Man, for Céline Dion. *Honours:* Ivor Novello Awards for Best Song, Have You Ever Been in Love, 1981, Think Twice, 1992; Call The Man, 30m. album sales; Solo album: Still, 1973. *Membership:* PRS; BAC&S Council, Chair of IT Committee. *Current Management:* David Ravden, MGR Ltd, 55 Loudoun Rd, St Johns Wood, London NW8 0DL, England.

SINGER, Ray; b. 4 July 1946, Tonbridge, Kent, England. Record Prod; Film Music Supervisor; Musician (percussion). m. Janine Turkie, 20 Sept. 1987, 1 s., 2 d. *Education:* London Film School. *Career:* Singer: Television appearances: Juke Box Jury; Thank Your Lucky Stars; Gadzooks!; As percussionist toured with David Knopfler, Germany, 1992; Tours with Cinema, guest appearance on EastEnders; As film music supervisor: Another Country; Civvies; A Perfect Spy. *Recordings:* Producer: Peter Sarstedt: Where Do You Go To My Lovely; Frozen Orange Juice; Child: It's Only Make Believe; Japan: Assemblage; Robin Sarstedt: My Resistance Is Low; David Knopfler; Small Mercies; Produced music to over 100 TV commercials. *Honours:* Gold records; Ivor Novello Award, Best TV Series Music for Civvies.

Membership: PRS; Musicians' Union; Equity. *Current Management:* Soundtrack Music Management, 22 Ives St, Chelsea, London SW3 2ND, England.

SINGH, Gary; b. 31 Jan. 1969, California, USA. Composer; Media Artist; Author. m. K Yamaguchi. *Education:* BA, San Jose State University. *Career:* Musica Works Broadcast and Performed in Asia, South American, Europe, USA; Published Short Fiction; Mail Art Displays, World-wide. *Publications:* Cyberthuggee and the Ridiculous World Over, 1996. *Honours:* American College Theater Festival Meritorious Achievement for Sound. *Membership:* International Computer Music Asscn. *Address:* 5580 Copeland Lane, San Jose, CA 95124, USA.

SINGH, Talvin; b. 1970, London, England. *Career:* Head of Omni Records; Tabla Player; Composer and Arranger; Worked with artists including Björk, Sun Ra and Future Sound of London; Worked on projects with numerous other Asian artists, including Osmani Soundz, Amar and Milky Bar Kid; Host at Anokha club, and at Blue Note Club; Solo artiste, 1997–; Producer, One World One Drum percussion album; Played on Björk's world tour. *Recordings:* Albums: Anokha: Soundz of the Asian Underground, 1997; O.K., 1998; Ha, 2001; Back To Mine, 2001; Vira (with Rakesh Chaurasia), 2002. Singles: Anokha Sampler, 1997; O.K., mixes, 1998; Traveller, 1998. *Honours:* Winner, Mercury Music Prize, 1999. *Address:* c/o Sona Rupa Ltd, 103 Belgrave Rd, Leicester, Leicestershire LE4 6AS, England.

SINGH, Tjinder; Vocalist; Songwriter; Musician (guitar, dholki). 1 s. *Career:* Mem., General Havoc, –1991; Founding mem., Cornershop, 1992–; Mem., Clinton; Founder, owner, Meccico label, 1998–. *Recordings:* Albums: with Cornershop: Hold On It Hurts, 1994; Woman's Gotta Have It, 1995; When I Was Born For The 7th Time, 1997; Handcream For A Generation, 2002; with Clinton: Disco And The Halfway To Discontent, 1998. Singles: with Cornershop: In The Days Of Ford Cortina (EP), 1993; Lock Stock & Double Barrel (EP), 1993; Readers' Wives (EP), 1993; Born Disco, Died Heavy Metal, 1994; Jullander Shere, 1995; Wog (The Western Oriental Mixes), 1996; Butter The Soul, 1996; Good Ships, 1997; Brimful Of Asha, 1997; Sleep On The Left Side, 1998; Lessons Learned From Rocky I To Rocky III, 2002; with Clinton: Jam Jar, 1995; Superloose, 1996; Superloose (The Automator Remixes), 1997; David D. Chambers; Buttoned Down Disco; People Power In The Disco Hour. *Address:* c/o Oasis Productions, 36 W 20th St, New York, NY 10011, USA. *Website:* www.cornershop.com.

SIOUX, Siouxsie, (Susan Dallion); b. 27 May 1957, Bromley, Kent, England. Vocalist. *Career:* Singer, Siouxie and the Banshees, 1976–; Film appearances: Punk Rock Movie (with The Clash, Sex Pistols, Generation X), 1978; Out of Bounds, 1986; Tours, UK, Europe, USA; Concerts include: Royal Albert Hall, 1983; Lollapalooza US tour, 1991; The Ritz, New York, 1992; Heineken Festival, Leeds, 1995; Also formed The Creatures, 1981. *Recordings:* Singles: with the Banshees: Hong Kong Garden, 1978; The Staircase (Mystery), 1979; Playground Twist, 1979; Happy House, 1980; Christine, 1980; Spellbound, 1981; Fireworks, 1982; Dear Prudence, 1983; Swimming Horses, 1984; Cities In Dust, 1985; This Wheel's On Fire, 1987; Peek a Boo, 1988; Kiss Them For Me, 1991; Face To Face, 1992; with the Creatures: Mad Eyed Screamers, 1981; Miss Then Girl, 1983; Right Now, 1983; Albums: with the Banshees: The Scream, 1978; Join Hands, 1979; Kaleidoscope, 1980; Once Upon a Time, 1981; A Kiss In The Dreamhouse, 1982; Nocturne, 1983; Hyena, 1984; Tinderbox, 1986; Through The Looking Glass, 1987; Peepshow, 1988; Superstition, 1992; Twice Upon a Time – The Singles, 1992; The Rapture, 1995; with the Creatures: Feast, 1983; Second Floor, 1998; Sad Cunt, 1998; Exterminating Angel, 1998; Bestiary Of... The Creatures, 1998; Eraser Cut, 1998; Say Pt 1, 1999; Say Pt 2, 1999; Say, 1999; Hybrids, 2001; Collaboration with Morrissey: Interlude, 1994. *Current Management:* Mission Impossible Management, 102A Western Rd, Hove, East Sussex BN3 1FA, England.

SIRACUSA, Gérard; b. 6 Oct. 1957, Tunis, Tunisia. Musician (drums, percussion); Composer. m. Sophie Schneider, 28 Sept. 1984, 1 s., 1 d. *Education:* Higher level studies in Science; Gold Medal, Percussion, National Conservatory, Rueil-Malmaison, France. *Career:* Goah, 1974; G S Duo with André Jaume, 1975; Trios with Raymond Boni and Michel Redolfi, 1976; Blaguebolle (musical theatre), 1974–78; Groupe de Recherche et d'Improvisation Musicales de Marseille (GRIM), 1978–84; Molto Mobile, 1980; Touchers (percussion quartet), 1981–83; Solo percussionist, 1981–86; G S Quartet, 1985; G S Alma Ata Quintet, formed for Banlieues Bleues Festival, 1986–87; Ensemble Musique Vivante, 1982–87; Un Drame Musical Instantané, 1982–84; 1991–94; Solibrius, solo percussion, 1986–; Claude Barthélémy – G S Quintet/Nonet, formed for Vandoeuvre-les-Nancy Festival, 1988–91; Collectif Incidences, 1990–94; G S Trio, 1991; Pied de Poule, 1991–93; Bûcher des Silences, formed for Moers Festival, 1991–; Trio Bal(l)ade, 1993–95; Duo with Valentin Clastrier, 1995; Radio: L'Heure Bleue, by Philippe Carles, France Musique, Radio France, 1992; Transversales, by Xavier Prévost, France Musique, Radio France, 1997; Musiques nouvelles: profils de passeurs, by Frédéric Deval, Radio Suisse Romande, 1998; Television: Megamix, with Valentin Clastrier, ARTE, 1994; Fête de la Musique, ARTE, 1995. *Compositions:* Jardins de Paille, 1982; Titchak, 1985;

Kaling, 1990; Pas Oui C'Est Non, 1993; M'Arco Polo, 1989; Ballade Sur Une Autoroute Et Ses Sept Bretelles, with Jean-Marie Maddeddu, 1994; Diptères, with Daniel Petitjean, 1993; Les Matins De Blanche, 1993; Les Petits Endroits Du Corps, 1994; 3 Minutes De Gloire, 1994; Le Dîner Percutant, 1993; Special Percussion, 1997; Discontinuo, 1997; Music for Radio France Culture: Les Chiennes, 1987; Nationalité Française, Special Percussion 1988; Executeur 14, 1989; L'Argent, 1994; Le long voyage vers le jour, 1997; Les demeurés, 1997; Ah, Vous Dirai-je..., 1998; Les histoires du Prince Oreille au Salon du livre Jeunesse de Montreux, 1998. *Recordings:* Musique Pour 8 – L'Oc, with André Jaume, 1982; Anna S Et Autres Histoires, with Trio MRS, 1983; Jardins De Paille, 1982; Terra, Michel Doneda, 1985; Slumberland, 1986; Kind Lieder, 1991; What a Time, Michael Riessler, 1991; Hérésie, Valentin Clastrier, 1992; Crasse Tignasse, 1993; Hélose, 1993; Jamais Tranquille, 1993; Le Bûcher Des Silences, 1994; Les Tentations d'Abelard, 1995; Stations Avant L'oubli, 1998; La Jardinière De Légumes, 1999. *Honours:* First Prize, Academie Charles Cros, for Le Bûcher Des Silences, 1995. *Membership:* SACEM; SPEDIDAM; ADAMI; SACD. *Current Management:* En L'Air Asscn. *Address:* 27 rue des Papillons, 93100 Montreuil, France.

SISQÓ, (Mark Andrews), (Sisqo The Golden Child, Dru Nasty); b. 1977, Baltimore, Maryland, USA. Vocalist. *Career:* Originally worked as a dancer; Formed group Dru Hill with college friends, named after Druid Hill Park in Baltimore; First release Tell Me from the soundtrack of film Eddie; After two hit albums, group decided to pursue solo projects; Successful solo career 1999–; Starring alongside Will Smith in Wild Wild West; Collaborations: Foxy Brown; Mya; Kelly Price. *Recordings:* Albums: with Dru Hill: Dru Hill, 1997; Enter The Dru, 1998; solo: Unleash The Dragon, 1999; Return of Dragon 2001; Singles: with Dru Hill: In My Bed, 1997; How Deep Is Your Love, 1998; solo: Got To Get It, 1999; The Thong Song, Incomplete, Unleash The Dragon, 2000; Dance For Me, 2001. *Honours:* Billboard Award, Male Artist of the Year, 2000. *Address:* c/o Def Jam, 825 Eighth Ave, New York, USA. *Website:* www.sisqo.com.

SISSAY, Lemn; b. 1967, Billinge, Manchester. Poet. *Career:* BBC Radio 4, Pick of the Week, 1994; Various appearances on BBC, Channel 4 and other British Stations. *Compositions:* Tape recordings: Blackwise, 1988; Homeland, including 2 poems, 1988. *Recordings:* The Flag, 1996; Are You Listening, 1992; Move On, 1993; Earth Flower, 1993; Advice For The Living, 2000. *Publications:* Books: Perceptions of the Pen, 1985; Tender Finger in a Clenched List, 1988; Elevator, 1999; Records: The Flag, 1996; Collaborations include: Leftfield, Izit. *Current Management:* Lounge Records, Oberhafenstr 1, 3 OG, 20097 Hamburg, Germany.

SISTER BLISS, (Ayalah Bentovim); b. 1970, London, England. Musician (keyboards, violin, piano); Remixer; DJ; Prod. *Education:* Classically trained pianist. *Career:* DJ at London's Bar Industria club; Founding mem., Faithless, 1995–. *Recordings:* Albums with Faithless: Reverence, 1996; Sunday 8pm, 1998; Saturday 3am, 1999; Testimony, Chapter 1, 1999; Back To Mine (compilation), 2001; Outrospective, 2001; Re-Perspective, 2002. Singles: with Faithless: Salva Mea, 1995; Insomnia, 1995; Don't Leave, 1996; Reverence, 1997; If Lovin' You is Wrong; Take the Long Way Home, 1998; God Is A DJ, 1998; Bring My Family Back, 1999; Why Go?; Muhammad Ali, 2001; We Come 1, 2001; Solo: Sister Sister, 2000. *Honours:* Best International Act to Appear in Ireland, 2001. *Membership:* MCPS/PRS. *Address:* Faithless Live Ltd, PO Box 17336, London NW5 4WP, England. *E-mail:* info@faithless.co.uk. *Website:* www.faithless.co.uk.

SITBON, Franck; b. 15 May 1957, Paris, France. Musician (keyboards); Vocalist. m. Brigitte Silverio, 3 July 1982, 2 s. *Education:* Private piano lessons, from age 6–15. *Career:* Tour, West Coast of United States, 1979–81; Returned to Paris, Played at Casino De Paris with Nicole Croiselle; Tour with Bernard Lavilliers, 1986; With Jacques Higelin, 1989; Played Italy with Pino Danielle; Tours, Tahiti, New Caledonia, with Patrick Bruel, 1992; Bercy, with Patrick Bruel, 1994. *Recordings:* Serge Guirao: Enchanteur, 1988; Nicole Croiselle: Black and Blanche, 1990; Joelle Ursule: Comme Dans Un Film, 1993; with Richard Galliano: Gallianissimo, 2001. *Publications:* Method Up Clavies, 1991. *Membership:* SACEM; SPEDIDAM. *Address:* 34 rue des Bordes, 94490 Ormesson, France.

SIXX, Nikki, (Frank Carlton Serafino Ferrano); b. 11 Dec. 1958, San Jose, California, USA. Musician (bass); Songwriter. *Career:* Member, groups: London; Christmas; Founder member, US heavy rock group Mötley Crüe, 1981–; World-wide concerts include: Tours with: Y&T, 1981, 1982; Kiss, 1983; Ozzy Osbourne, 1984; Iron Maiden, 1984; Cheap Trick, 1986; Theatre of Pain World Tour, 1985–86; World tours, 1987, 1989; Major concerts: US festival, 1983; Monsters of Rock Festival, Castle Donington, 1984; Moscow Music Peace Festival, 1989. *Recordings:* Albums: Too Fast For Love, 1981; Shout At The Devil, 1983; Theatre of Pain, 1985; Girls Girls Girls (No. 2, USA), 1987; Dr Feelgood (No. 1, USA), 1989; Decade of Decadence (No. 2, USA), 1991; Til Death Do Us Part, 1994; Generation Swine, 1997; Live: Entertainment or Death, 1999; New Tattoo, 2000; Singles: Stick To Your Gun, 1981; Looks That Kill, 1984; Too Young To Fall In Love, 1984; Smokin' In The Boys Room, 1985; Home Sweet Home, 1985; You're All I Need, 1987; Dr Feelgood, 1989; Kick

Start My Heart, 1990; Without You, 1990; Don't Go Away Mad, 1990; Same Old Situation, 1990; Primal Scream, 1991; Hooligan's Holiday, 1994; Misunderstood, 1994. *Publications:* The Dirt: Confessions of the World's Most Notorious Rock Band (with Mötley Crüe), 2001. *Honours:* Rolling Stone Readers Poll Winners, Best Heavy Metal Band, 1991; American Music Award, Favourite Heavy Metal Album, 1991. *Current Management:* The Left Bank Organisation, 9255 Sunset Blvd, Suite 1111, Hollywood, CA 90069–3309, USA.

SIXX-SCHMULEWITZ, Aaron; b. 4 Aug. 1947, Feldafing, Germany. Record Co Man.-Dir. m. Lynda M Jones, 18 Aug. 1977, 1 s., 1 d. *Education:* Bachelor of Arts, University of California at Los Angeles (UCLA). *Career:* Record Executive with: 1973–74, United Artists Records, European A & R Director; 1975–77, Arista Records, Director, International Operations; 1978–, Aura Records, Music and Entertainment, Managing Director. *Address:* 1 Liverpool Rd, London W5 5NZ, England.

SIZE, Roni; Musician (keyboards, drums, programming); Prod. 1 s. *Career:* Began as DJ in clubs; Co-founder, Full Cycle Records, 1993; Creative leader of Bristol-based collective, Reprazent, with record deal on Talkin' Loud; With Reprazent, numerous performances at concert venues and festivals worldwide. *Recordings:* with DJ Die, Music Box; Agility; Solo: Jazz Thing; with Reprazent: Reasons For Sharing (EP), 1996; New Forms, 1997; In The Mode, 2000; Touching Down, 2002. *Honours:* Mercury Music Prize, for New Forms, 1997. *Address:* c/o Kas Mercer, Talkin' Loud, Chancellors House, Chancellors Rd, London W6 9QB, England. *Website:* www.ronisize.com.

SJOBLOM, Titti; b. 29 Aug. 1949, Stockholm, Sweden. Vocalist. m. Ehrling Eliasson, 2 s. *Education:* Private Singing Lessons; Musicology. *Career:* Played, Maria Magdalena in Jesus Christ Superstar, 1972; Own Children Shows, 1980s on Television; Tours Every Year, Entertainment Parks, Restaurants, Churches; Entertained UN Troops. *Compositions:* Trumman; Det Tanker; Dar Utanfor. *Recordings:* Sjung Med Oss Mamma; 10 LPs; 4 CDs; For Sjal Och Hjarta. *Honours:* Expressens Best Television Entertainment for Children, 1964; Perne Paddock Award, 1994. *Membership:* Chair. of Board, Forsvarets Faltartist Forening (Entertainers of the Swedish Armed Forces). *Current Management:* Own Company and Label, Seaflower Music. *Address:* Seaflower Music, Box 7, 87032 Ullanger, Sweden.

SJOSTEN, Lars; b. 7 May 1941, Oskarshamn, Sweden. Jazz Musician (piano); Composer; Arranger. m. Lilly, 24 April 1976. *Education:* Piano and Harmony privately. *Career:* Played with Dexter Gordon, Chet Baker, Lee Konitz, Lars Gullin and many more legendary jazz musicians; Played with Lars Gullin, 1960–76; Led own groups, numerous records and radio/television programmes; Tours and festivals in Scandinavia and Europe; Composing and Arranging Commissions for Big Band. *Compositions:* In Confidence; Denile; Thorgeirs Sang; The Inner Voice; Tidigt; Gasoline My Beloved; From Reliable Sources; The Comeback of a Tradesman; Tale of Two Trees. *Recordings:* Select Notes, 1981; Bells, Blues and Brotherhood, 1983; Dedicated to Lee, w Lee Konitz, 1983, 1995; Roots and Relations, 1989; Lars Sjosten Quartet in Moscow, 1990; In Confidence, 1990; I Love You So, with Rolf Ericson, 1997. *Honours:* Jan Johansson, 1969; Two Golden Disques, 1981, 1989; Income Guarantee, 1990; Lars Gullin Prize, 1997. *Membership:* Musicians' Union; Asscn of Swedish Jazz Musicians; Musikcentrum. *Current Management:* Musikcentrum, Chapmansgatan 4, 11236 Stockholm, Sweden. *Address:* Filipstadsbacken 70, 123 43 Farsta, Sweden.

SKAGGS, Ricky Lee; b. 18 July 1954, Cordell, Kentucky, USA. Recording Artist; Musician (guitar, banjo, mandolin, fiddle, telecaster, mandocaster). m. Sharon White, 4 Aug. 1981, 2 s., 2 d. *Career:* Member of Ralph Stanley and the Clinch Mountain Boys, 1970; Country Gentlemen, 1974; Formed own band Boone Creek, 1975; Emmylou Harris' Hot Band, 1977; Whites, 1980; Solo artist 1981–; Host of own radio series, Simple Life With Ricky Skaggs; Television appearances include: Host, TNN Nashville Now; Co-host, TNN Viewer's Choice Awards. *Recordings:* 12 US No. 1 singles, 1981–89; Albums: Waitin' For The Sun To Shine, 1981; Highways and Heartaches, 1982; Don't Cheat In Our Hometown, 1983; Country Boy, 1984; Favourite Country Songs, 1985; Live In London, 1985; Love's Gonna Get Ya!, 1986; Comin' Home To Stay, 1988; Kentucky Thunder, 1989; My Father's Son, 1991; Ricky Skaggs Portrait, 1992; Super Hits, 1993; Solid Ground, 1995; Bluegrass Rules, 1997; Ancient Tones, 1999; Soldier of the Cross, 2000; History Of The Future, 2001. *Honours:* Ralph Stanley Dove Award, 1982; 8 Grammy Awards, 1984–2001; 8 Academy of Country Music Awards including Best Touring Band, 1983–87; Edison Award, Netherlands, 1987; 8 Country Music Asscn Awards; 6 Music City News Awards; Artist of The Decade, BBC Radio 2, UK; Best Country Guitarist, Guitar Player Readers Poll, 1987–89; Best Country Instrumentalist, Playboy Readers Poll (twice); Gospel Voice Diamond Award, 1993; Bluegrass Instrumentalist Group of the Year, with Kentucky Thunder, 1998 and 1999. *Membership:* AFTRA; AFofM. *Current Management:* RS Entertainment Inc. *Address:* 320 Rockland Rd, Hendersonville, TN 37075, USA.

SKARBEK, Sacha J; b. Epsom, Surrey, England. Prod; Musician (keyboards); Songwriter. *Education:* BA Hons, Music, Oxford. *Career:* Tours:

Europe, with Double Vision; UK with Jamiroquai, Original Son; UK with Sister Sledge, Fekisha; BBC Interview, with Innocent Lies; Tour, USA, What The Funk; Various concerts with Dana Brown. *Recordings:* Keyboard player: Seven Seconds, Youssou N'Dour and Neneh Cherry; Keyboard player: Let It Last, Carleen Anderson; Producer, writer: Desire and Somewhere, Pauline Henry; Keyboard player, writer: Album: Original Son; Other session work includes: Samantha Mumba; Culture Club; Amanda Ghost; Ginuwine. *Current Management:* Alan Edwards; Clem Chan. *Address:* Poole Edwards, Charlotte St, London W1, England.

SKELLERN, Peter; b. 14 March 1947, Bury, Lancashire, England. Musician (piano); Vocalist; Songwriter. *Education:* Honours graduate, Guildhall School of Music, 1968. *Career:* Member, March Hare (recorded as Harlan County), 1971; Wrote and performed 6 autobiographical programmes for BBC TV; Series of musical plays, Happy Endings; Host, chat show, Private Lives, 1983; Formed Oasis with Julian Lloyd Webber, Mary Hopkin, Bill Lovelady, 1984, 1996. *Recordings:* Peter Skellern With Harlan County, 1971; Peter Skellern, 1972; Not Without a Friend, 1973; Holding My Own, 1974; Hold On To Love, 1975; Hard Times, 1976; Skellern, 1978; Astaire, 1979; Still Magic, 1980; Happy Endings, 1981; Introducing Right From The Start, 1981; A String of Pearls, 1982; Oasis, 1984; Best of Peter Skellern, 1985; Love Light, 1987; Sentimentally Yours, 1996; The Masters, 1997; Singles include: You're a Lady, 1972; Love Is The Sweetest Thing, with the Grimethorpe Colliery Band, 1978. *Honours:* Best MOR Album, Music Trades Asscn, 1979.

SKI, (Dominic Oakenfull); b. 28 Jan. 1971, Sevenoaks, Kent, England. Musician (keyboards, zither); Prod; Writer. *Education:* City University, London; Music lessons with Keith Rusling, Kent; K B Wizard, London. *Career:* Keyboard player, writer, producer for the K-Creative, 1991–93; Raw Stylus, 1993; Palm Skin Productions, 1993; Thats How It Is, 1994; Galliano, 1994, 1995; Solo artiste as Ski, 1993–; Writer, jingles for various radio commercials; Television appearances include Gimme 5; Top of the Pops; Later With Jools Holland; The Beat. *Recordings:* Albums: QED, K-Creative, 1992; The Plot Thickens, Galliano, 1994; Marla Glen (second album), 1995; Pushing, Raw Stylus, 1995; Galliano (fourth album), 1996; Solo album: Life Changes, 2001; Singles: Justify, Ski featuring Chesere, 1994; Realise Your True, Ski with Ife, 1994; Theme from Millennium Falcon, 1994. *Publications:* Fender Rhodes, A Brief History, 1994. *Current Management:* Guy Tresize, GT Management, Unit B7, 8/9 Hoxton Sq., London, England.

SKIFS, Björn Nils Olof; b. 20 April 1947, Vansbro, Sweden. Vocalist; Performer; Composer. m. Pernilla, 20 May 1988, 2 s. *Education:* College. *Career:* Major concert tours and television shows, 1970–; Eurovision Song Festival, 1978 and 1981; Musicals and 3 major films (screenplay, leading role); Strul, 1986; Joker, 1989; Drömåken, 1993. *Recordings:* 13 albums, 1967–87, including: Hooked On a Feeling (No. 1, USA, 1974); Never My Love (Top 10, USA, 1974); Michaelangelo (No. 1, Scandinavia, 1975–76). *Current Management:* Desert AB, Box 103, 70142 Orebro, Sweden.

SKILLINGS, Muzz, (Manuel Skillings); b. 6 Jan. 1960, New York, USA. Musician (bass). *Career:* Member, Living Colour; Backed Mick Jagger on Primitive Cool album, 1986; Mick Jagger produced demo, which obtained them record deal; Support slots live to Rolling Stones; Left band, 1993. *Recordings:* Singles: Cult of Personality, 1988; Glamour Boys, 1988; Type, 1990; Love Rears Its Ugly Head, 1990; Solace of You, 1991; Talkin' Loud and Saying' Nothing, 1991; Albums: Vivid, 1988; Time's Up, 1990; Biscuits, 1991; Other appearances include: This What I Do, Sir Mack Rice, 2000; Brand New Man, Freddie Scott, 2001.

SKIN, (Deborah Ann Dyer); b. 3 Aug. 1967, London, England. Vocalist. *Education:* Furniture Design, Teeside Polytechnic. *Career:* Founder mem., Skunk Anansie, 1994–2001; Signed to indie label One Little Indian, 1994, Virgin Records, 1996; Numerous headlining tours, festival appearances, television and radio shows; Solo artiste, 2001–, working on solo album; Contributed songs to films: Timecode 2000, Princess and the Warrior. *Recordings:* Albums: Paranoid and Sunburnt, 1995; Stoosh, 1996; Post Orgasmic Chill, 1999. Singles: Little Baby Swastikkka, 1994; Selling Jesus, 1995; I Can Dream, 1995; Charity, 1995; Weak, 1996; All I Want, 1996; Twisted (Everyday Hurts), 1996; Hedonism, 1997; Brazen (Weep), 1997; Charlie Big Potato, 1999; Secretly, 1999; Lately, 1999. *Address:* c/o Virgin Records America Inc, 338 N Foothill Rd, Beverly Hills, CA 90210, USA. *Website:* www.skunkanansie.com.

SKINNER, Harry; b. 30 April 1958, Barking, Essex, England. Musician (guitar); Vocalist; Composer; Songwriter. m. Elizabeth Vango, 4 May 1991, 1 s., 1 d. *Education:* Southampton University, 1995–97; RMSM, Kneller Hall, Twickenham; Bournemouth and Poole College, Poole. *Career:* Oboist with Rhine Staff Band RTR, 1976–81; Formed band, Manitou, touring UK, Gemany and Japan; Formed band The Producers; Appeared at Colne Blues Festival, Burnley Blues Festival, Monighan, Templebar, Shepton Mallet and at festivals throughout Europe; Live radio session, BBC Radio 2, 1994; Tours of UK, Germany, France, Belgium and Ireland. *Recordings:* Single: Tasmania, 1984; Albums: with Manitou: Manitou At The Electric Drum I and II, 1987; Looking For The Lost, 1991; with The Producers: Escape From Muswell Hell,

1991; Ain't No Love In The World, 1993; For This Night Only, 1994; Nearly Wired, 1996; Really Wired, 1996; Arizona. *Membership:* Musicians' Union; Associate Mem., PRS; MCPS. *Current Management:* Dave Saunders, Mojo Management / Mojo Records UK. *Address:* 77 Haviland Rd, Boscombe, Bournemouth, Dorset BH7 6HJ, England.

SKINNER, Mike, (The Streets); b. 1979, Birmingham, England. Prod; MC; Musician (keyboards). *Career:* Garage Prod., MC and musician as The Streets; Signed to Locked On label, 2000; Numerous live appearances. *Recordings:* Albums: Original Pirate Material, 2002. Singles: Has It Come To This?, 2001; Let's Push Things Forward, 2002; Weak Become Heroes, 2002; Don't Mug Yourself, 2002. *Address:* c/o 679 Recordings, Second Floor, 172A Arlington Rd, London NW1 7HL, England. *Website:* www.the-streets.co.uk.

SKIPPER, Svend; b. 22 April 1947, Naestved, Denmark. Musician (piano); Conductor; Composer; Arranger. m. Ghita Noerby, 15 July 1984. *Education:* Studied piano, solfeggio, conducting, Royal Danish Conservatory, 1970–77. *Career:* Musical Director, all Danish theatres, Directed musicals: The Peanuts; No No Nanette; Promises Promises; Showboat; Pal Joey; Oliver; They're Playing Our Song; Chicago; My Fair Lady; Orpheus In The Underworld; Parisian Life; Beggar's Opera (Weill); Jesus Christ Superstar; Teenage Love (Finn Savery); Starting Here Starting Now; Sunday In The Park With George; Sweeney Todd; Side By Side By Sondheim; A Little Night Music; En Spurv I Tranedans (Danish vaudeville, 1880); I'm Getting My Act Together; Les Miserables, Odense and Copenhagen; Conducted all Danish symphony orchestras; Also Danish Light Music Orchestra playing jazz, rock, musicals, Indian, classical repertoire; Concerts, television and radio appearances in Denmark and Sweden; Performed with instrumentalists and singers including: Birgit Nilsson; Elizabeth Soderstroem; Anne Sofie von Otter; Indian violinist, Supramaniam; Hubert Laws; Ben Webster; Harry 'Sweets' Edison; Bob Rockwell; Doug Rayney; Touring Europe with pioneer jazz/classical Skipper-Lund-Simonsen Trio (piano, flute, bass); Own recording studio, The Holtewood Studio; Song coach for Danish version of Prince of Egypt; Conductor, Evita, recorded with Bournemouth Sinphonietta (conducting), The Little Mermaid, drama theatre, 1998. *Compositions:* Composer for Danish films, television series, songs, signatures, 8 minute comic opera, Bread; Arranger: orchestra, theatre, live and recorded music. *Recordings:* More than 100, including musicals: The Peanuts; Starting Here Starting Now; Oliver; Les Miserables, Danish cast, Spanish cast; Miss Saigon, Danish cast. *Membership:* Danish Conductors Society; DJBFA. *Address:* Pindehuggervang 19, 2840 Holte, Denmark.

SKIRVING, Mark Antony; b. 13 March 1966, Wednesday, West Midlands, USA. Vocalist; Musician (saxophone). 1 s. *Career:* 40 television appearances world-wide; Played with: B. B. King; Cab Calloway; Slim Gaillard; Matt (Guitar) Murphy; Steve Cropper; Donald Dunn; Eddie Floyd; Several small film appearances. *Recordings:* 5 albums: King Pleasure and the Biscuit Boys; This Is It; Better Beware; King Pleasure and the Biscuit Boys Live at Ronnie Scott's; Blues and Rhythm Revue, Vol. 1. *Membership:* Birmingham Jazz Festival Board; British Jazz Awards Committee. *Current Management:* Jim Simpson, Big Bear Music. *Address:* Big Bear Music, PO Box 944, Edgbaston, Birmingham B16 8UT, England.

SKOLNICK, Alex; b. 29 Sept. 1968, Berkeley, California, USA. Rock Musician (guitar). *Education:* Studied with Joe Satriani. *Career:* Toured and recorded with US heavy rock group Testament; Toured with Stu Hamm; Recorded with Michael Manring. *Recordings:* Albums with Testament: The Legacy, 1987; The New Order, 1988; Practice What You Preach; Souls of Black; The Ritual, 1992; Signs of Chaos: The Best of Testament, 1997; First Strike Still Deadly, 2001; with Michael Manring: Thank; with Savatage: Handful of Rain, 1994; with Attention Deficit: Attention Deficit, 1998; Idiot King, 2001; Compilations: Guitars That Rule The World; Guitars Practicing Musicians. *Publications:* Columnist for magazines: Guitar; Guitar Player; Guitar World. *Membership:* ASCAP. *Current Management:* Marcy Straw, CMA (Creative Music Alternatives). *Address:* Alex Skolnick, c/o CMA, 2608 Ninth St, Berkeley, CA 94710, USA.

SKOVBYE, Kim Lind; b. 10 Jan. 1955, Copenhagen, Denmark. Musician (harp, guitar, violin, bouzouki, mandolin, recorder); Composer; Songwriter. Partner, Anne Ostrup, 2 s., 2 d. *Education:* Private lessons from age 9; 3 years study at Danish Music Academy. *Career:* 10 years teaching children; 7 years, teaching music and drama, adult training college; 10 years as street musician with the juggler and singer Heramn; Several television and radio shows; Two big concerts at the Tivoli; Several shows and tours with keyboard player, Klaus Schonning, Denmark, Germany and Netherlands. *Compositions:* Skygge Boxer (songs), 1986; Barsebeck (songs), 1987; Scandinavia (instrumental), 1990; Heartland (instrumental), 1992; Aftermath (instrumental), 1993; Ask and Riana (children), 1994; Mountains of Fire (song), 1995; Coming Albums: Wayfarer, 1995; Lord of The Rings, Part 1, 1996; Eventide, 2000; The Fullmoon Concert, 2000; Hvidt Sa Vidt, 2001; Film music: Holografi, 1988; Landscapes of Childhood, 1992; The Glassheart, 1989; Song of a Tiger, 1989. *Honours:* Awards from Danish Jazz Beat Folk Society. *Current Management:* The New Agency. *Address:* Strandvejen 324, 3060 Espergaerde, Denmark.

SLABAK, Jan; b. 24 March 1941, Kelcany, Kyjova, Czechoslovakia. Musician (trumpet); Composer; Conductor; Band Master. m. (1) Jitka Janowskova, 18 Nov. 1960, (2) Ivana Soutalova, 22 July 1976, 1 s., 1 d. *Education:* State Conservatoire (Academy of Music), Brno; Janacek's Academy of Music Arts, Brno. *Career:* State Philharmonic Orchestra, Brno; Moravanta of Jan Slabak; Many film, TV, radio appearances. *Compositions:* 210 compositions for brass band, published and recorded on LPs, MCs, and CDs. *Publications:* Hundreds of reviews and contributions, Kaoje Kdo, 1991–92; Mijosua ic Moravanka, 1997. *Honours:* TV Prize, 1973; Ministry of Culture, 1975; Golden Key, Cleveland, USA, 1978; 3 times Golden Disc, 1980, 1985, 1991; 1 Platinum Disc, 1995; 1 Diamond Disc, 1996. *Membership:* OSA; Chair, Competition juries. *Address:* Sosnova 18, Brno 63700, Czech Republic.

SLASH, (Saul Hudson); b. 23 July 1965, Stoke-on-Trent, Staffordshire, England. Rock Musician (guitar). m. Renee Suran, 10 Sept. 1992. *Career:* Mem., US heavy rock group, Guns N' Roses, 1985–97; International tours include: Support to Iron Maiden, USA, 1987, 1988; Mötley Crüe, USA, 1987; The Cult, USA, 1987; British tour, 1988; Support to Aerosmith, USA, 1988; Get In The Ring tour, with Skid Row, 1991; World tour, 1992; Major concerts include: Monsters of Rock, Castle Donington, 1988; Farm Aid IV, 1990; Rock In Rio II, Brazil, 1991; A Concert For Life (Freddie Mercury Tribute), Wembley, 1992; National Bowl, Milton Keynes, 1993; Lead singer, Slash's Snakepit, 1994–. *Recordings:* Albums: with Guns N' Roses: Appetite For Destruction (No. 1, USA), 1987; G 'N' R Lies, 1988; Use Your Illusion I (No. 2, USA, UK) and II (No. 1, USA, UK), 1991; The Spaghetti Incident, 1993; Live Era '87–'93, 1999; with Slash's Snakepit: It's Five O'Clock Somewhere, 1995; Ain't Life Grand, 2000. Singles: with Guns N' Roses: Live ?1*! Like A Suicide, 1986; Welcome To The Jungle, 1987; Sweet Child O'Mine (No. 1, USA), 1988; Night Train, 1989; Paradise City, 1989; Patience, 1989; Knockin' On Heaven's Door (used in film soundtrack, Days of Thunder), 1990; You Could Be Mine (used in film soundtrack, Terminator 2), 1991; Don't Cry, 1991; Live And Let Die, 1991; November Rain, 1992; Yesterdays, 1992; Ain't It Fun, 1993; Since I Don't Have You, 1994; Sympathy For The Devil (used in film soundtrack, Interview With the Vampire), 1995; Live Era, 1999; Contributor: Nobody's Child (Romanian Angel appeal), 1990; Black and White, Michael Jackson, 1991; Brick By Brick, Iggy Pop, 1990; Dangerous, Michael Jackson, 1991; Coneheads (film soundtrack), 1993; Tribute To Muddy Waters, 1993; Believe In Me, Duff McKagan, 1993; Also: Cheap Trick; Alice Cooper; Bob Dylan. *Honours:* American Music Awards, Favourite Heavy Metal Single, Favourite Heavy Metal Artist and Album, 1989, Favourite Heavy Metal Artist, 1992; Several MTV Awards; World Music Award, Best Selling Artist of the Year, 1993; Rolling Stone and Billboard Magazine Awards. *Current Management:* Big FD Entertainment, 510 South Coast Hwy, Laguna Beach, CA, 92651–2406, USA. *Website:* www.gnronline.com.

SLATER, John; b. 12 Jan. 1957, London, England. Artist Man; Tour Man. *Education:* 1 year Electronics at Essex University. *Career:* Stage Manager at Edinburgh Playhouse, 1976–77; Sound Engineer, 1977–80, Radio Presenter, BRMB Radio Birmingham, hosting and producing Indie and Rock evening show, 1980–91, with 1500 interviews, 200 sessions and 50 concert recordings; Compered Donington Monsters of Rock Festival in 1991; Currently in partnership with Danny Kenny managing various bands. *Address:* PNG World-wide, Westminster Court, 10 Park Rd N, Birmingham B6 5UJ, England.

SLATER, Luke, (Offset, Clementine, Morganistic, Planetary Assault Systems, The 7th Plain); b. Reading, Berkshire, England. Prod; Remixer; DJ. *Career:* Started to DJ at London's Troll club, 1988; Worked in Jelly Jam Records shop in Brighton, East Sussex; First recordings appeared on shop's own label; Subsequently recorded for labels including: Djax; Peacefrog; GPR; Currently signed to Novamute; Remixed: Madonna; Depeche Mode; Ballistic Brothers; Slam. *Recordings:* Albums: Fluids Amniotic (as Morganistic), 1994; Freek Funk, 1997; Wireless, 1999; Alright On Top, 2002; as 7th Plain: My Yellow Wise Rug, The Four Cornered Room, 1994; as Planetary Assault Systems: The Drone Sector, 1998; Atomic Funkster, 2001; Singles: as Planetary Assault Systems: In From The Night, Booster, 1995; solo: Love, 1997; All Exhale, 1999; Body Freefall, Electronic Inform, 2000. *Address:* c/o Mute Records, 429 Harrow Rd, London W10 4RE, England.

SLEDGE, Percy; b. 25 Nov. 1941, Leighton, Alabama, USA. Soul Vocalist. *Career:* Singer, The Esquires Combo; Solo recording artiste. *Recordings:* Albums include: When a Man Loves a Woman, 1966; Warm and Tender Soul, 1966; The Percy Sledge Soul, 1967; Take Time To Know Her, 1968; I'll Be Your Everything, 1974; If Loving You Is Wrong, 1986; Percy, 1987; Wanted Again, 1987; Blue Night, 1994; Percy Sledge, 1994; Wanted Again, 1998; Behind Closed Doors, 2001; Singles: When a Man Loves a Woman, 1966; It Tears Me Up, 1967; Out of Left Field, 1967; Take Time To Know Her, 1968. *Honours:* Blues Foundation Soul/Blues Album of the Year, for Blue Night, 1996. *Current Management:* Artists International Management, 9850 Sandalfoot Blvd #458, Boca Raton, FL 33428, USA.

SLEEN, Harm van; b. 31 Dec. 1965, Utrecht, Netherlands. Bass. m. Kerstin Lucia Venhuizen, 16 Aug. 1995, 1 d. *Education:* Bass, Hilversums Conservatory, 1989. *Career:* Played with various pop groups, 1980–89;

Recorded single with Burt and the Brand New Lifestyle, 1989; Played with Jaap Dekker's Jazz and Boogie Set, 1989–93; Playing with Capelino and with Mr Boogie Woogie and the Fire Sweep Blues Band. *Compositions:* Take Me To Swine Lane; Goodbye; Gossip; Bad Day; If You Went Away; Trouble; Lovin On My Mind; Holy Boogie; Young Boys and Girls (On the Old Side of Town). *Recordings:* Relite! Revelation, 1993; Capelino, Way To Go, 1997; Mr Boogie Woogie and The Fire Sweep Blues Band, Live At the Pub, 1997. *Publications:* Mag Die Radio War Harder?!!, 1993. *Address:* Glanerschans 28, 3432 ES Nieuwegein, Netherlands.

SLICK, Grace; b. 30 Oct. 1939, Evanstown, Illinois, USA. Vocalist; Songwriter; Entertainer. m. (1) Gerald Robert Slick, 26 Aug. 1961 (div), 1 d.; (2) Skip Johnson, 25 Nov. 1976. *Education:* Finch College, 1957–58. *Career:* Singer of Great Society, 1965–66; Jefferson Airplane, 1966–72; Jefferson Starship (later known as Starship), 1972–; Major concerts including Woodstock and Altamont; Most television shows, including Ed Sullivan and Johnny Carson. *Recordings:* Solo albums: Manhole; Dreams; Welcome To The Wrecking Ball; Software; Albums with Jefferson Airplane/Starship include: Surrealistic Pillow; Earth; Modern Times; Winds of Change; Blows Against The Empire; Dragon Fly; Freedom At Point Zero; Nuclear Furniture; Red Octopus; Windows Of Heaven; Singles include White Rabbit; Somebody To Love; We Built This City On Rock 'n' Roll; Nothing's Going To Stop Us Now. *Publications:* Grace Slick, biography by Barbara Rosa, 1978. *Honours:* 4 Bay Area Music Awards, Best Singer. *Membership:* AFofM. *Current Management:* Trudy Green, HK Management. *Address:* 8900 Wilshire Blvd #300, Beverly Hills, CA 90211–1906, USA.

SLIGER, Robert Earl; b. 31 Oct. 1962, Detroit, Michigan, USA. Vocalist; Songwriter; Composer; Prod; Educator; Musician (guitar, piano, keyboards, drums). *Education:* Community College of the Air Force, USA; USAF Chorale with Martha Daige (Dir), Denver, Colorado, 1980; Voice instruction with: Bill White and Sid Wright, Austin, Texas, 1981; Tom Prebble, Torejon, Spain, 1982; Gene Nice, Pensacola Civic Opera, Florida, 1985; Vaccai, Italian Opera (English); Chris Beatty, Tennessee, 1991; Thomas Appell, California, 1997. *Career:* Tenor/MC, USAF Air Force Chorale, 1980–81; Lead singer, background, with Star Fire, 1982; Tenor, Gospel Quartet, W Germany, 1983; Lead singer, background, with Angel Band, 1990–92; Producer, lead and background singer, with Liberty-N-Justice, 1991–93; Lost In Eden tour, with Liberty-N-Justice, 1993; Filmed 2 music videos with Liberty-N-Justice: All Your Love, 1992; We Are Family, 1993; Solo career, 1993–; Radio interview, WQFL, WGSL, Rockford, Illinois, 1995; Tenor, Mendelssohn's Elijah, Bradley Community Chorus and Chamber Orchestra, Bradley University, IL, 1996; Lead vocalist, with Marvin Lee Zilch, 1997–98. *Compositions:* Songs: Christ You Share, 1991; Through The Night, 1992; You're Not Alone, 1993; LORD Jesus Christ, 1993; In Your Arms, 1993; Dr Werking's Office, 1993; Your Open Door, with Marvin Zilch, 1994; When You're Needing A Friend, with Marvin Zilch, 1994; Show The Way, 1995; Majestic, instrumental, 1995; When I Walk With You (Road to Emmaus), 1997. *Recordings:* with Liberty-N-Justice: Armed With The Cross, 1992; Big Guns, 1994; with Angel Band: Down To Earth, 1992; Down To Earth (remastered), 1993; solo: EP, The Practices, 1998; The Aunt Gloria Project, 1999; with Marvin Zilch: LOVE, 1999. *Publications:* How To Read The Holy Bible – The Basics, 1988. *Honours:* Weigel Music Award Scholarship, Tennessee Temple University, 1986. *Membership:* Gospel Music Asscn; ASCAP. *Current Management:* C & R Productions. *Address:* PO Box 10763 Austin, Texas 78766, USA.

SLIJNGAARD, Ray; Rap Artiste; Songwriter. *Career:* Rapper, Belgian dance music group 2 Unlimited, 1991–. *Recordings:* Albums: No Limits, 1993; Real Things, 1994; Hits Unlimited, 1995; Singles: Get Ready For This, 1991; Twilight Zone, 1992; Workaholic, 1992; No Limits (No. 1, UK), 1993; Tribal Dance, 1993; Faces, 1993; Let The Beat Control Your Body; The Real Thing, 1994; No One, 1994. *Address:* c/o Michel Maartens, CBA Artists, PO Box 1495, 1200 BL Hilversum, Netherlands.

SLOANE, Carol; b. 5 March 1937, Providence, Rhode Island, USA. Jazz Vocalist. m. Edward 'Buck' Spurr, 30 Nov. 1986. *Education:* Business College. *Career:* Professional singer from age 14, with Ed Drew's Dance Band; Tours with Larry Elgart Orchestra, 1958–60; Singer with Hendricks (Dave) Lambert and Ross Trio, 1960; Shared bills with Bill Cosby, Woody Allen, Lenny Bruce, Richard Pryor, 1960s; Singer with Tonight Show Band, Johnny Carson's Tonight Show; Supper club work, regular public radio show, North Carolina, 1981–85; Moved to Boston, 1986; DJ, WGBH, 1986–95; Played Starlight Roof, Boston, 1985; Signed with Concord Jazz, 1991; Featured artist, Pre-Fujitsu/Concord Jazz Festival party, honouring Carl Jefferson (president, Concord Jazz), 1993; 10 consecutive appearances festival season, Japan; DJ, National Public Radio Station, WICN in Worcester Massachusetts, 2000–. *Recordings include:* Albums: A Night of Ballads (duets with Don Abney), 1984; But Not For Me (with Tommy Flanagan, George Mraz, Al Foster, Frank Wess), 1986; Love You Madly, (with Richard Rodney Bennett, Kenny Barron, Kenny Burrell), 1988; The Real Thing (with Phil Woods, Grady Tate, Mike Renzi, Rufus Reid), 1989; Heart's Desire (Stef Scaggiari, John Lockwood, Colin Bailey), 1990; Concord All Stars On Cape Cod, (Scott Hamilton and Dave McKenna), 1991; Sweet and Slow (with Frank Wess, Tenor Sax), 1992; Concord Christmas (Mel Torme, Rosemary Clooney, Various Artists), 1993;

When I Look In Your Eyes (with Bill Charlap, Steve Gilmore, Ron Vincent), 1994; The Songs Carmen Sang (with Phil Woods, Bill Charlap, Michael Moore, Ron Vincent), 1995; The Songs Ella and Louis Sang with Clark Terry, 1996; Romantic Ellington with Benny Golson, DRG, 1999; I Never Went Away, 2001. *Current Management:* Buck Spurr. *Address:* Spurr Marketing Group, 215 Salem St, Woburn, MA 01801, USA.

SLUIJS, Ben; b. 6 March 1967, Antwerp, Belgium. Musician (jazz saxophone). 2 d. *Education:* 5 years classical saxophone education; Antwerp Jazz Studio with John Ruocco, 5 years; Brussels Conservatory with Steve Houben, 1 year. *Career:* Played with Big Bands, BRT, BB, Yellow City Big Band, Act Big Band, Brussels Jazz Orchestra; Philip Catherine Trio; Represented Belgium, EBU Big Band in Slovenia; Knitting Factory, New York; Montréal Jazz Festival with Actium, 1997. *Recordings:* Till Next Time with the Ben Sluijs Quintet, 1991; Reminiscense, with the Miriam Alter Quintet, 1994, Chromatic History, with Octurn, 1994; Silent Walk, with the Miriam Alter Quintet, 1996; Ocean, with Octurn, 1996; Hamp Digs Ham, with the François Descamps octet, 1997; Food for Free, with the Ben Sluijs kwartet, 1997; Candy Century with the Ben Sluijs kwartet, 1999; Paolo Radini Live, 1999. *Honours:* Jack Van Poll Award, 1991. *Address:* Antoon Van Dyckstraat 14, 2018 Antwerp, Belgium.

SLUSHER, Michael Dennis; b. 13 Nov. 1949, Oliver Springs, Tennessee, USA. Musician (trombone); Arranger; Prod. *Education:* Brevard Community College, 1967–69; BS, North Texas State University, 1975. *Career:* Musician, Elvis Presley, 1977–79; Resident musician, venues in Las Vegas, 1977–82; Producer, arranger, Take Cover Enterprises, Beverly Hills, 1983–86; Associate Producer, television and radio commercials, 1984–86; Independent producer, arranger, Seattle, 1986–; Musician with artistes including: Frank Sinatra; Sammy Davis Jr; Tony Bennett; Righteous Brothers; Tom Jones; Glen Campbell; Paul Anka; Pearl Bailey; Also played for orchestras with: Tommy Dorsey; Si Zentner; Tex Beneke; Thad Jones; Mel Lewis.

SMALE, Joanne R. Muroff; b. 20 June 1949, Brooklyn, New York, USA. Production, Publicity, Promotion Exec. *Education:* BA Psychology, University of Miami. *Career:* President: Joanne Smale Productions Ltd, 1980–; Vice-President, Dark Light Music Ltd; Owner, Listening House Booking Agency, 1974–80; Publicist, numerous theatre productions; music industry events; Charity and benefit events include: Rekindle The Light Festival, 1988; Arts Against Apartheid, Toronto, 1990; Industry and media organizations include: True North Records; Sam The Record Man; Began Canadian representation for events including: New Music Seminar (New York); The International Music and Media Conference (Montreux, Switzerland); American Video Conference and Awards (Los Angeles); Publicist: Road Movies, CBC-TV; In The Key of Oscar, documentary, CBC-TV; Co-producer, with National Film Board, The Un-Canadians. *Honours:* 6 Gold, 2 Platinum albums for work with: Rough Trade; Murray McLauchlan; Bruce Cockburn. *Membership:* Videofact; Vice-President, Canadian Independent Recording Producers Asscn (CIRPA); Canadian Independent Film Caucus (CIFC); Canadian Women in Radio and Television (CWRT). *Address:* Joanne Smale Productions Ltd, 51 Bulwer St, Toronto, ON M5T 1A1, Canada.

SMALL, Heather; Vocalist. *Career:* Singer, soul group, Hothouse; Lead singer, UK dance group M People, 1991–; Major concerts include: Glastonbury Festival, 1994. *Recordings:* Albums: Northern Soul, 1992, 1995; Elegant Slumming, 1993; Bizarre Fruit, 1994; Bizarre Fruit II, 1995; Fresco, 1997; Testify, 1999; Hit singles: How Can I Love You More, 1991; One Night In Heaven, 1993; Movin' On Up, 1993; Don't Look Any Further, 1993; Renaissance, 1994; Sight For Sore Eyes, 1994; Itchycoo Park, 1995; Search For The Hero, 1995; Open Your Heart, 1995; Love Rendezvous, 1995; Just For You, 1997; Angel Street, 1998; Testify, 1998; Dreaming, 1999; Solo: Proud, 2000; Holding On, 2000; You Need Love Like I Do, duet with Tom Jones, 2000; Solo album: Proud, 2000. *Honours:* Mercury Prize, Best Album, Elegant Slumming, 1994; BRIT Awards: Best Dance Act, 1994, 1995. *Current Management:* RD World-wide Management, 37 Limerston St, London SW10 0BQ, England.

SMIETANA, Jarek Zdzislaw; b. 29 March 1951, Krakow, Poland. Musician (guitar). m. Anna Smietana, 21 July 1978, 1 d. *Education:* Studied Class Composition and Arranging, Academy of Music, Katowice, Poland. *Career:* One of the major jazz musicians in Poland; First Band, Extra Ball, formed 1974; One of the most successful European jazz groups. *Compositions:* A Few Warm Words; Follow the Fellow; Flowers in Mind; Children of Time; Sounds and Colours. *Recordings:* Ballads and Other Songs, 1996; Jarek Smietana Quintet Live, 1996; Phone Consultations, 1997; Songs and Other Ballads, 1998; Art Farmer Plays Standards, 1998; Speak Easy, 1999. *Publications:* Jazz Songs by Smietana. *Honours:* No 1 Jazz Guitarist in Poland, prizes every year since 1983; Fryderyk, Polish Music Award, 1998. *Membership:* Polish Jazz Society. *Address:* c/o Sound Music, Os 2 Pulku Loniczego 13/118, 31867 Krakow, Poland.

SMITH, Bryan Christopher; b. 21 Dec. 1954, St Albans, Hertfordshire, England. Recording Engineer; Prod; Programmer; Musician (guitar, keyboards). m. Denise, 6 July 1974, 1 s., 1 d. *Career:* Red Bus Records,

1980–82; Member, French Impression, 1984–86; Member, The Big Push, 1992–; Founded Farm Factory Studios, 1990; Support tours: Jools Holland; Cool Notes; Member, Hello, 1993. *Recordings:* Musician, engineer, programmer for: Move Your Skin; And Why Not; Amazing Colossal Men: Buddy's Song; Chesney Hawkes; Also recorded Jon Anderson/Frances Dunnery, 1991; Steve Harley demos, 1994. *Honours:* Gold disc, Chesney Hawkes: The One and Only (hit single from Buddy's Song). *Membership:* PRS. *Current Management:* Paul Loasby, One Fifteen Management. *Address:* The Gallery, 28/30 Wood Wharf, Horseferry Pl., London SE10 9BT, England.

SMITH, Carl; b. 15 March 1927, Maynardsville, Tennessee, USA. Country vocalist; Songwriter; Musician (guitar); Actor. m. (1) June Carter (Cash), 1952, divorced; (2) Goldie Hill, 1957, 1 d. *Career:* Entered talent contest age 13, 1944; Early radio experience at WROL, Knoxville; Bass player and occasional vocalist with Skeets Williamson Band, 1949; Sang with Archie Campbell's band on WROL radio shows Audition for Peer International Music led to spot on Grand Ole Opry as a guest of Hank Williams, March 1950; Signed to Columbia Records, 1950; Charted 93 times on Billboard country chart singles, 1951–78; Later hits Hickory/MGM and ABC/Hickory labels; Feature film appearances include: The Badge of Marshal Brennan, 1957; Buffalo Gun, 1961; From Nashville With Music, 1969; That's Country, 1977; Hosted TV series: Four Star Jubilee, late '50s; Carl Smith's Country TV Show, 1960s; Semi-retired; Father of Carlene Carter; Nicknamed 'The Country Gentleman'. *Compositions include:* I Overlooked An Orchid; Ten Thousand Drums; Mr Moon. *Recordings include:* Let Old Mother Nature Have Her Way, 1951; (When You Feel Like You're In Love) Don't Just Stand There, Are You Teasing Me, 1952; Hey Joe!, 1953; Loose Talk, 1954; Your Name Is Beautiful, 1958; Ten Thousand Drums, 1959; Albums: There Stands The Glass, The Tall Tall Gentleman, 1964; Man With A Plan, 1966; Satisfaction Guaranteed (compilation), 1996. *Address:* c/o Country Music Asscn, 1 Music Circle S, Nashville, TN 37203, USA.

SMITH, Chad; b. 25 Oct. 1962, St Paul, MN, USA. Musician (drums). *Career:* Mem., Red Hot Chili Peppers, 1988–; Numerous tours, festivals and television appearances; Simultaneous mem., of Honeymoon Stitch. *Recordings:* Albums: with Red Hot Chili Peppers: Mother's Milk, 1989; Mother's Milk Gold, 1989; Blood Sugar Sex Magik, 1991; What Hits!?, 1992; One Hot Minute, 1995; Under The Covers, 1998; Californication, 1999; By The Way, 2002; with John Fogerty, Blue Moon Swamp, 1997; with Private Parts: Private Parts, 1997; with Leah Andreone: Alchemy, 1998. Singles: with Red Hot Chili Peppers: Abbey Road (EP), 1988; Higher Ground, 1989; Taste the Pain, 1989; Give It Away, 1991; Under The Bridge, 1992; Suck My Kiss, 1992; Breaking the Girl, 1993; If You Have to Ask, 1993; Soul 2 Squeeze (EP), 1994; My Friends, 1995; Aeroplane, 1996; Love Rollercoaster, 1997; Warped, 1998; Scar Tissue, 1999; Behind the Sun, 1999; Around The World, 1999; Otherside, 1999; Californication, 2000; Road Trippin', 2001; The Zephyr Song, 2002; Contributor, The Beavis and Butthead Experience, 1993. *Honours:* MTV Music Video Awards, 1992; Grammy Awards, Best Hard Rock Song, for Give It Away, 1993, Best Rock Song, for Scar Tissue, 2000; American Music Award, Favorite Alternative Artist, 2000; MTV Awards, Best Live Act, Best Rock, 2002. *Current Management:* Lindy Goetz Management, 11116 Aqua Vista, Suite 39, Studio City, CA 91602, USA. *Address:* c/o Rockinfreakapotamus, The Red Hot Chili Peppers Official Fan Club, PO Box 801, Rockford, MI 49341, USA. *Website:* www.redhotchilipeppers.com.

SMITH, Connie, (Constance June Meador); b. 14 Aug. 1941, Elkhart, Indiana, USA. Country vocalist; Songwriter; Musician (guitar, piano). m. (1) Jerry Smith, (2) Marty Stuart, 8 July 1997. *Career:* Early appearances with Floyd Miller's Square Dance Band as a teenager; Weekly appearances on West Virginia local TV: Saturday Night Jamboree, WSAZ TV Huntington; Big Red Jubilee, Parkersburg; Discovered by country writer-performer Bill Anderson, 1963; Signed by RCA; Billboard country chart debut with Once A Day, 1964; No other solo female country artist has spent longer than the eight weeks at #1 this release achieved; Followed by nearly 50 entries, mostly for RCA; Movies appearances: Second Fiddle To A Steel Guitar, 1965; The Las Vegas Hillbillys, 1966; The Road To Nashville, 1967; Hell On Wheels, 1967; The Hi-Lo Country, 1998; Became Christian and recorded gospel material as well as country, early 1970s–. *Compositions include:* I'll Come Running. *Recordings include:* Once A Day, 1964; Ain't Had No Lovin', 1966; Just One Time, 1971; The Hurtin's All Over, 1966; Cincinnati Ohio, 1967; Albums: Connie Smith, 1965; Cute 'n' Country, 1965; Miss Smith Goes To Nashville, 1966; Downtown Country, 1967; Born To Sing, 1966. *Honours:* CMA, Song of the Year, Once A Day, 1971. *Membership:* Grand Ole Opry, 1971. *Address:* c/o Fat City Artists, 1226 17th Ave S, Suite 2, Nashville, TN 37212, USA.

SMITH, Curt; b. 24 June 1961, Bath, Avon, England. Musician (bass guitar); Vocalist. *Education:* College. *Career:* Professional musician since age 18; Member, Graduate, 1979; Member of duo Tears For Fears, 1981–90; Solo artiste, 1991–; Concert band Mayfield, first album Mayfield, 1998. *Recordings:* Acting Your Age, Graduate, 1979; with Tears For Fears: The Hurting, 1982; Songs From The Big Chair, 1985; Seeds of Love (No. 1, UK), 1989; Tears Roll Down (compilation), 1992; Songs from the big Chair (UK bonus tracks), 1999; Hurting (UK bonus tracks), 1999; Seeds of Love (UK bonus tracks), 1999; Solo albums: Soul On Board, 1993; Aeroplane, 2000;

Singles include: Mad World, 1982; Change, 1983; Pale Shelter, 1983; The Way You Are, 1983; Mother's Talk, 1984; Shout (No. 1, USA), 1984; Everybody Wants To Rule The World (No. 1, USA; No. 2, UK), 1985; Head Over Heels, 1985; I Believe, 1985; Sowing The Seeds of Love, 1989; Woman In Chains, 1989; Advice For The Young At Heart, 1990. *Membership:* in UK: Musicians' Union; PRS; in USA: AFTRA; BMI.

SMITH, Geoff; b. 11 May 1966, Tynemouth, England. Songwriter; Musician (piano). m. Nicola Walker Smith, 16 Sept. 1989, 2 s. *Education:* BA, Hons, Nottingham University, 1987; MPhil, Oxford University, 1989; PhD, Huddersfield University, 1996. *Recordings:* Albums: Gas Food Lodging, 1993; Fifteen Wild Decembers, 1994; Black Flowers, 1997; with Mono: Formica Blues, 1997; with Gap Mangione: Planet Gap: Big Band, 1998; with Burning Bush: Klezmer and Hassidic Music, 1998. *Publications:* Co-author, American Originals, 1994; Interviews with Harold Rudd, Philip Glass, Steve Reich. *Honours:* Debut album selected as Top 40 Album of the Year, BBC Music Magazine; Youngest Composer to be signed by Sony Classical in the history of the label. *Current Management:* Keith Armstrong. *Address:* Kitchenware, St Thomas' St Stables, Newcastle Upon Tyne, NE1 4LE, England.

SMITH, James Edward; b. 2 Aug. 1952. Jazz Musician (guitar). m. Gloria C. Smith, 2 s., 2 d. *Education:* BA, University of New Mexico, 1974; MM, Wisconsin Conservatory of Music, 1980. *Career:* Chairman, Fine and Performing Arts, Central St University; Adjunct, Associate Professor of Jazz Guitar, University of Cincinnati College, Conservatory of Music, 1984–; Four National Public Radio Broadcasts, 1992. *Compositions:* Song For Om, 1992. *Recordings:* Cincinnati Seven. *Publications:* Jazz Guitar: Theory and Technique, 1982; Bebop Riffs, 1990; Guitarists Guide To Technique, 1992; Chord Thesaurus For Jazz Guitar, 1994. *Honours:* Outstanding Service To Jazz Education, 1988, 1997. *Membership:* IAJE; AAUP. *Current Management:* Smith Management, 4189 Sugar Leaf, Dayton, OH 45440, USA.

SMITH, Josh; b. 10 July 1979, Middletown, Connecticut, USA. Blues Musician (guitar). *Education:* Private study, 9 years. *Career:* Member, band, the Rhinocats, 1993–; Opened for bands including Buddy Guy; The Fabulous T-Birds; Allman Brothers Band. *Recordings:* CD: Born Under a Blue Sign, 1995; Woodsheddin, 1996; With High Karate: High Karate, 1998; with One Eighty: Crackerjack, 1998. *Honours:* Best Blues Band, State of Florida, Florida Jam Magazine, Jammy Awards, 1994. *Membership:* ASCAD. *Current Management:* Dan Cohen, Musicians Exchange. *Address:* 8920 N W 14th St, Pembroke Pines, FL 33024, USA.

SMITH, Karen M; b. 23 July 1958, Chicago, Illinois, USA. Artist Development; Record Co Exec. m. A J Smith, 5 May 1994. *Education:* 2 years college. *Career:* Currently owner, Glow In The Dark Rehearsals, (rehearsal space in Chicago); Owner, record company TOW Records, Chicago; Consultant for Ex-Idols; PO! Executive Producer for: Wait For Light; S Is For Space. *Honours:* Gottlieb Award, Best Rehearsal Studio, 1994. *Membership:* NAMM; NARAS. *Address:* PO Box 740, Oak Park, IL 60303, USA.

SMITH, Keely; b. 9 March 1932, Norfolk, Virginia, USA. Vocalist; Actor. m. Louis Prima, 1953, divorced 1961. *Career:* Joined Louis Prima's band aged 16, 1948; Married Prima at 21 and settled in Las Vegas and virtually invented the 'lounge act'; After Decca contract expired, signed to Capitol as a solo artist at the insistance of Prima, securing position as a major vocalist, 1956; Appeared in films: Thunder Road (with Robert Mitchum), 1958; Senior Prom, 1958, Hey Boy Hey Girl, 1959, both with Prima; Prior to divorce, signed with Dot (again recording own albums alongside those with Prima); Joined Reprise in 1964 before semi-retirement; Re-emerged with Fantasy Records album, 1985; Currently signed to Concord Jazz; Occasional live performances in Las Vegas. *Recordings:* I Wish You Love, 1957; Politely, 1958; Swingin' Pretty, 1959; Because You're Mine, 1959; Be My Love, 1960; Swing You Lovers, 1960; Dearly Beloved, 1961; What Kind of Fool Am I, 1961; Cherokeely Swings, 1962; Keely Smith Wishes You A Merry Christmas, 1963; Little Girl Blue Little Girl New, 1964; Keely Smith Sings The Lennon and McCartney Song Book, 1965; That Old Black Magic, 1965; I'm In Love Again, 1985; Swing Swing Swing, 2000; Keely Sings Sinatra, 2001. *Current Management:* Suzy Frank. *Address:* c/o Concord Records, PO Box 845, Concord, California, 94522, USA. *Website:* www.keelysmith.com.

SMITH, Laura; b. 18 March 1952, Ontario, Canada. Vocalist; Songwriter; Musician (guitar). *Career:* Contributor: albums, Chieftains, 1997; Far Cry From Leaving, Terry Kelly, 1996; Fire In The Kitchen, 1998. *Recordings:* Between the Earth and My Soul; It's a Personal Thing; Agnes Browne, soundtrack, with Ed Shearmur. *Honours:* ECMA Female Artist, 1996; ECMA Album, 1996; Gemini Award for Best Performance, 1997; Vanity Pressed: A Collection, 1998. *Membership:* SOCAN; CARAS; ECMA; AVLA. *Current Management:* Jones and Co. *Address:* 5212 Sackville St, Suite 100, Halifax, NS, B3J 1K6, Canada.

SMITH, Mark 'Hitman'; b. 20 Oct. 1972, Doncaster, Yorkshire, England. Freelance Prod. and Remixer; Programmer; Musician (keyboards). *Education:* High Melton College, Doncaster; Piano, Royal School of Music. *Career:* Producer, remixer, for Music Factory Records; Commercial DJ. *Recordings:*

Mixes include: Rock 'N' Roll Dance Party, Jive Bunny; Nolans Hitmix; Hot Chocolate Hitmix; Glamma; Paradox; Remixes include: Kylie Minogue; 2 Unlimited; Kelly Marie. *Publications:* Contributor, Mixology Magazine. *Membership:* Musicians' Union. *Current Management:* Saint Productions, PO Box 1295, New Rossington, Doncaster DN11 0GF. *Address:* 5/7 Fitzwilliam St, Parkgate, Rotherham, South Yorkshire S62 5EP, England.

SMITH, Mark E(dward); b. 5 March 1957, Salford, Manchester, England. Vocalist; Songwriter; Musician (guitar). m. Brix (Laura Elise Smith), divorced 1990. *Career:* Founder, The Fall, 1977–. *Recordings:* Albums include: Live At The Witch Trials, 1979; Dragnet, 1979; Totale's Turns (It's Now Or Never), 1980; Grotesque (After The Gramme), 1980; Slates, 1981; Hex Enduction Hour, 1982; Room To Love, 1982; Perverted By Language, 1983; The Wonderful and Frightening World Of..., 1984; This Nation's Saving Grace, 1985; Bend Sinister, 1986; The Frenz Experiment, 1988; I Am Kurious Oranji, 1988; Seminal Live, 1989; Extricate, 1990; 458489, 1990; 458489: B Sides, 1990; Shiftwork, 1991; Code Selfish, 1992; The Infotainment Scan, 1993; Sinister Waltz, 1996; The Marshall Suite, 1999; The Unutterable, 2000; Are You Are Missing Winner, 2001; Singles: Fiery Jack; How I Wrote Elastic Man; Totally Wired; There's a Ghost In My House; Victoria; Hit The North; Why Are People Grudgful?; F-'oldin' Money; Guest vocal, Telephone Thing, Coldcut, 1990; I Want You, Inspiral Carpets, 1994. *Publications:* Play: Hey! Luciani. *Address:* c/o Permanent Records, 22–23 Brook Mews, London W2 3BW, England.

SMITH, Michael; b. 19 Jan. 1967, Bridport, Dorset, England. Musician (saxophone). *Education:* City of Leeds College of Music; Guildhall School of Music and Drama, London. *Career:* Saxophonist, Brand New Heavies, 1990–93; Saxophone and flute, Jamiroquai; Extensive recording, world-wide touring with above acts; Television appearances include: Top of the Pops; The Word; The Beat; MTV's Most Wanted; In-house arranger, Acid Jazz Records. *Recordings:* Arranger for: Corduroy; Mother Earth; James Taylor Quartet; Solo album: The Whole Thing, 1993; Recorded every release with The Brand New Heavies including: Never Stop, 1992; Dream On Dreamer, 1994; Back To Love, 1994; Midnight At The Oasis, 1994; You've Got A Friend, 1997; Album: with Jamiroquai: Space Cowboy. *Membership:* PRS; MCPS. *Current Management:* Richard H Smith. *Address:* 14D Wilde St, London WC2B 4AG, England.

SMITH, Mike; b. 6 Dec. 1943, London, England. Record Prod; Songwriter; Vocalist; Musician (keyboards). *Education:* Trinity College, London. *Career:* Lead singer, keyboard player with: Dave Clark 5; Writer all songs; Writer, producer, television commercials and themes; Record producer, 2 Top 5 albums with Michael Ball. *Recordings:* with Dave Clark 5: Bits And Pieces, 1963; Glad All Over (Number 1, UK), 1964; Catch Us If You Can, 1966; with Michael Ball: Michael Ball; Always; One Careful Owner. *Membership:* PRS; BAC&S. *Current Management:* Graham Carpenter, Pachuco Management, Priestlands, Letchmore Heath, Herts WD2 8EW, England.

SMITH, Mike (Michael John); b. 16 Nov. 1946, Edgware, Middlesex, England. Artist Man; Music Publisher; Television and Film Production Co Owner. m. Sally James, 22 July 1978, 3 s. *Career:* Producer, Assistant Head Light Entertainment, LWT, 1968–76; Head of A & R, Decca Records, 1976–78; General Manager, Vice-President, GTO Records, 1978–80; Own companies: Yellow Balloon Productions Ltd; Mike Music Ltd; Yellow Balloon Music; Yellow Balloon Records; Universal Media Management Ltd; Unitapes UK Ltd; Unismart Ltd; Fishtanc Ltd. *Recordings:* As manager or producer: Rick Wakeman; Bruce Foxton; Adam and The Ants; Billy Ocean; The Moody Blues; The Smurfs; The Dooleys; Rolf Harris; Hazel O'Connor. *Honours:* Tokyo Music Festival Award; Award Winning Producer of London Bridge television programme; 30 Gold and Silver discs as producer, manager of established acts. *Membership:* Musicians' Union; ACCA; PRS. *Address:* Freshwater House, Outdowns, Effingham, Surrey KT24 5QR, England.

SMITH, Patti; b. 30 Dec. 1946, Chicago, IL, USA. Vocalist; Songwriter; Musician (guitar); Poet; Author. m. Fred 'Sonic' Smith, 1 March 1980, deceased 1994, 2 s. *Career:* Journalist, Rock magazine, 1970; Creem magazine, 1971; Solo artiste, 1972–; Concerts include: Support to New York Dolls, 1972; Formed Patti Smith Group, 1974; UK debut, 1976; European tour, 1976; Sporadic appearances, 1988–; Poetry performance, New Year's Day Extravaganza, New York, with Yoko Ono, 1975. *Recordings:* Albums: Horses, 1975; Radio Ethiopia, 1976; Easter, 1978; Wave, 1979; Dream Of Life, 1988; Gone Again, 1996; Peace And Noise, 1997; Gung Ho, 2000; Land 1975–2002, 2002; Guest vocalist on albums: Secret Treaties, Blue Oyster Cult, 1974; Agents of Fortune, Blue Oyster Cult, 1976; The Whole Thing Started With Rock 'N' Roll, Ray Manzarek, 1975; Nervous Night, The Hooters, 1985; New Adventures In Hi-Fi, REM (No. 1, UK), 1996; Contributor, film soundtrack, Until The End Of The World, 1991. Singles: Gloria; Hey Joe; So You Want To Be A Rock And Roll Star; Dancing Barefoot; Because The Night. *Publications:* Poetry: Seventh Heaven, 1971; Kodak, 1972; Witt, 1973; Feb Babel, 1979; Cowboy Mouth (play, with Sam Shepard), 1972; Woolgathering (short stories), 1993. *Current Management:* Rascoff/Zysblat Organization Inc, 110 W 57th St, Third Floor, New York, NY 10019–3319, USA.

SMITH, Rob(ert Kevin); b. 17 Dec. 1960, West Yorkshire, England. Musician (saxophone, keyboards, percussion). m. Sarah Stone, 12 May 1990, 2 d. *Education:* Nottingham University; King's College, London. *Career:* with Four Quartets: Appeared on HTV, 1987; Appeared at 'Outside In' jazz festivals in 1988 and 1993; Brecon Jazz Festival, 1984–; 2 Arctic songs with London Sinfonietta Voices, 1994; Lecturer, composition, Bath Spa University College; Musical Director, Wonderbrass, Community Jazz Orchestra. *Compositions:* Anonymous Twentieth Century, 1998; Toccata Lachrymal Tenebrae, 2001; Gwen John Suite, 2002. *Recordings:* with Heavy Quartet: Poum, 1988; A Screaming Tradition, 1989; Short Stories, 1991; with The Diggers: Imbolc, 1993; with Wonderbrass: Daisy Roots, 2001; Musicals: Race, 1989; Starcross'd, 1991; Dangerous Acquintances, 1997; Carnivore, Heavy Quartet, 1995; Delete Memory, 2001; Film scores: The Knowledge, 1996; The Confectioner, 1997; Minim, 1999; Overland, 2001. *Publications:* 2 articles on trip to Gambia, Taplas, 1992. *Membership:* PRS; Society for Promotion of New Music. *Current Management:* HQ Enterprises, Cardiff, Wales. *Address:* 26 Burlington Terrace, Llandaf, Cardiff CF5 1GG, Wales.

SMITH, Robert; b. 8 Nov. 1960, Cheshire, England. Musician (percussion). m. Tina, 1 s., 1 d. *Career:* Played with Bad Habits pop group; Made several television and radio recordings; Theatre work. *Recordings:* With Fodens Motor Works Band. *Honours:* Best Percussionist, Buxton Music Festival, 1984, 1985, 1986. *Membership:* Musicians' Union. *Address:* 17 Christleton Ave, Crewe, Cheshire CW2 8TD, England.

SMITH, Ruthie Elaine Foster; b. Manchester, England. Musician (saxophones); Vocalist; Composer. *Education:* BA English/Music Honours, York University. *Career:* Member, Stepney Sisters, one of first feminist rock bands, 1974–76; Founder member, all women's jazz band The Guest Stars; World tours, jazz festivals, clubs including Ronnie Scott's; Also played with Mervyn Africa and Bryan Abrahams in South African band District Six; Toot Sweet with Jim Dvorak; Jazz in Britain, television, tours financed by The British Council; Served on Greater London Arts Council panel, 2 years. *Recordings:* 3 albums with The Guest Stars; 2 recordings with District Six; Live recordings for BBC; Currently working with Toot Sweet Jazz Band, featuring Frances Knight and Julia Doyle. *Honours:* Jazz Bursary, Arts Council of Great Britain, to compose and perform a jazz suite. *Membership:* Musicians' Union. *Address:* 2a Banning St, Greenwich, London SE10 9PH, England.

SMITH, Spencer John; b. 8 Feb. 1967, City of London, England. Musician (drums). *Career:* Member, North of Cornwallis; Concerts include support to Nico; Member, East Village, 1986–90; Recorded 4 singles; Member, Saint Etienne, 1992; Tours include: UK; Japan; Canada; USA; Europe; Television includes: Top of the Pops (4 times); Later With Jools Holland; The Word (2 times); Festivals include: Glastonbury; Sweden; Denmark; Radio includes: Evening session, BBC Radio 1. *Recordings:* with East Village: 4 singles; Albums: Dropout; Hotrod Hotel; with St Etienne: 4 singles; 1 track on album Tiger Bay. *Honours:* Silver Disc, So Tough; Gold Disc, Too Young To Die, 1997. *Membership:* Musicians' Union; PRS. *Current Management:* Heavenly Management, 47 Frith St, London W1V 5TE, England.

SMITH, Stephen Bowden; b. 17 Oct. 1946, Oxford, England. Musician (electric, string bass). *Education:* Studied electric bass with Joe Hubbard (theory and practice). *Career:* Cruise ships orchestra with Geraldo's Navy, 1969–70; P&O ships Orsova, Oriana (own trio), 1972; Michel Heuser Trio, Gstaad, Switzerland, 1972; Tour with Hindukush, Switzerland, 1974; Tommy Hawkins Band, Hammersmith Palais, 1977; John Burch Trio, London Playboy Club, 1977–78; Season and UK concerts with Matt Monro, 1978; Concerts with Vera Lynn, 1980; Accompanying jazz musicians including: Red Rodney; Tal Farlow; Slim Gaillard; Red Holloway; Harold Land; Ray Alexander; Spike Robinson; Oliver Jones; Dick Morissey; Radio, recordings, European tours, with Stutz Bear Cats, 1984; Concerts, Spanish television with Iris Williams, 1987; Tours, television, concerts, with Vince Hill, 1988; Jazz clubs, festivals, with Butchers Brew, 1993; Tour of USA with Vince Hill, 1995–96; Cruise on flagship Oriana with the Groove Company, 1997. *Compositions:* Severn Borsa Nova; Purple Parrot Road; Jive For The Cider Insid 'er (Inside); The Mango Tango; Rio Yeo Samba. *Recordings:* The Session, Whisky Time, with Diana Jarrett-Harris Trio. *Current Management:* Smith. *Address:* 23 Westbury Cres., Oxford OX4 3RZ, England.

SMITH, Toby; b. 29 Oct. 1970, London, England. Musician (keyboards). *Career:* Member, Jamiroquai; Numerous tours and TV appearances. *Recordings:* Singles: When You Gonna Learn, 1993; Too Young To Die, 1993; Emergency on Planet Earth, 1994; Space Cowboy EP, 1995; Virtual Insanity, 1996; Cosmic Girl, 1996; Light Years, 1996; Alright, 1997; Deeper Underground (No. 1, UK), 1998; High Times, 1998; Canned Heat, 1999; Albums: Emergency on Planet Earth, 1993; Travelling Without Moving, 1996; Synkronized, 1999; A Funk Odyssey, 2001. *Honours:* Gold and Platinum Albums; Several MTV Video Music Awards.

SMITH, Tommy; b. 27 April 1967, Edinburgh, Scotland. Musician (tenor saxophone); Composer. *Education:* Berklee College of Music, Boston, USA, 1984–86. *Career:* Hired as sideman to Gary Burton, 1986; Record deal, 1989

Began recording under own name with guest musicians; Returned to Scotland, mid-1990s; Recorded with James Talley, Gary Burton, Red Krayola; Songs performed by Garth Brooks, Marty Brown, Engelbert Humperdinck, Tracy Lawrence, Josh Logan. *Recordings:* Albums: Forward Motion: The Berklee Tapes, 1984; Step By Step, 1988; Peeping Tom, 1990; Standards, 1991; Misty Morning and No Time, 1994; Sound of Love, 1999; Into Silence, 2002. *Address:* c/o Spartacus Records Ltd, PO Box 3743, Lanark ML11 9WD, Scotland.

SMITH, Wendy; b. 31 May 1963, Middlesbrough, Cleveland, England. Vocalist; Musician; Voice Movement Therapist. *Career:* Member, Prefab Sprout, 1982–; Extensive tours: Europe; UK; Japan; Numerous television appearances; Practitioner of Voice Movement Therapy, trained with Paul Newham, founder of Voice Movement Therapy. *Recordings:* Albums: Swoon, 1984; Steve McQueen, 1985; From Langley Park To Memphis, 1987; Protest Songs, 1988; Jordan: The Comeback, 1990; Life of Surprises: The Best of Prefab Sprout, 1992; Andromeda Heights, 1997; with Bryan Savage: Cat Food, 1996; with James Bignon: What a Mighty God We Serve, 1996; with Special Delivery: This is Special Delivery, 1996; Numerous hit singles including: When Love Breaks Down, 1985; Cars And Girls, 1988; The King Of Rock'n'Roll, 1988; Carnival 2000, 1990; The Sound Of Crying, 1992; If You Don't Love Me, 1992; Life Of Surprises, 1993; Prisoner Of The Past, 1997. *Honours:* 6 Gold discs. *Membership:* International Network of Voice Movement Therapy Associates. *Current Management:* Keith Armstrong, Kitchenware Records. *Address:* 7 The Stables, St Thomas St, Newcastle Upon Tyne NE41 8DU, England.

SMITH, Will (Willard C, II); b. 25 Sept. 1968, Philadelphia, PA, USA. Vocalist; Rap Artiste; Actor. m. (1) Sheree Zampino, 1 s., (2) Jada Pinkett, 1997, 1 s. *Career:* Formed duo, DJ Jazzy Jeff and the Fresh Prince; Star of TV sitcom, The Fresh Prince of Bel Air, 1990–; Films: Where the Day Takes You, 1992; Made in America, 1993; Six Degrees of Separation, 1993; Bad Boys, 1995; Independence Day, 1996; Men in Black, 1997; Enemy of the State, 1999; Wild Wild West, 1999; Legend of Bagger Vance, 2000; Ali, 2002; Men in Black II, 2002. *Recordings:* Albums: With DJ Jazzy Jeff: He's the DJ, I'm the Rapper, 1988; And In This Corner..., 1989; Homebase, 1991; Code Red, 1993; Rock the House, 1997; Greatest Hits, 1998; Solo: Big Willie Style, 1997; Willennium, 1999; Born To Reign, 2002. Singles: With DJ Jazzy Jeff: Parents Just Don't Understand; I Think I Could Beat Mike Tyson, 1989; Summertime, 1991; Boom! Shake the Room (No. 1, UK), 1993; Solo: Just Cruisin', 1997; Men in Black (No. 1, UK), 1997; Gettin' Jiggy With It (No. 1, USA), 1998; Just The Two Of Us, 1998; Miami, 1998; Wild Wild West (No. 1, USA), 1999; Boy You Knock Me Out, with Tatyana Ali, 1999; Will 2K, 1999; Freakin' It, 2000. *Honours:* Grammy Awards, with DJ Jazzy Jeff, Best Rap Performance, 1988, 1991; Grammy Award, Best Rap Solo Performance, 1998; MTV Music Video Awards, Best Male Video, Best Rap Video, 1998; American Music Awards, Favorite Pop/Rock Male Artist, Favorite Album, Favorite Male Soul/R&B Artist, 1998, Favourite Pop/Rock Male Artist, 2000. *Address:* c/o Ken Stovicz, Creative Artists Agency, 9830 Wilshire Blvd, Beverly Hills, CA 90212, USA.

SMYTH, Jimmy (James Patrick); b. 22 April 1958, Navan, Ireland. Musician (guitar, keyboards); Vocalist; Prod. m. Jenny Newman, 22 March 1994. *Education:* Father (music teacher, RIAM, Dublin). *Career:* Toured with: The Kinks; Thin Lizzy; Bob Dylan; Rory Gallagher; Bon Jovi; Played guitar with: Bogey Boys; Toni Childs (all world tours); Van Morrison; Paul Brady; Don Baker; Numerous television appearances world-wide, including performance at Grammy Awards Ceremony, 1989. *Compositions:* Co-wrote 6 songs on Toni Child's album The Woman's Boat; Many songs covered. *Recordings:* 2 albums as singer, guitarist with The Bogey Boys; Played on over 150 major release albums including Daniel O'Donnell: Love Hope and Faith, 1998; Winter's Tale: Winter's Tale, 1998; Lisa Stansfield, Face Up, 2001. *Honours:* Twice voted in Top 5 guitarists in Ireland, Hot Press magazine. *Membership:* Musicians' Union; ASCAP; IMRO; MCPS. *Current Management:* Bob Brimson, 2 Tynings Terrace, Bath, Avon, England. *Address:* Thatched Cottage East, Upper Stand, Malahide, Co Dublin, Ireland.

SNIDER, Dee; b. 15 March 1955, New York, USA. Rock Vocalist; Lyricist. *Career:* Founder, vocalist, US rock group Twisted Sister; Sold over 8m. albums world-wide, 1983–87; Numerous world-wide tours; Major concerts include Monsters of Rock Festival, Castle Donington; Founder member, vocalist, Desperado, with Bernie Torme; Founder member, Widowmaker, 1991–; Television includes: Host, Heavy Metal Mania, MTV (now known as Headbangers Ball); Radio includes: Host, Dee Snider's Metal Nation, WRCN; Defendant for rock music and lyrics, US Senate hearings, 1985. *Recordings:* Albums: with Twisted Sister: Under The Blade, 1982; You Can't Stop Rock and Roll, 1983; Stay Hungry, 1984; Come Out and Play, 1985; Love Is For Suckers, 1987; Big Hits and Nasty Cuts: The Best of Twisted Sister; Live at Hammersmith, 1994; Early Works, 1999; with Widowmaker: Blood and Bullets, 1992; Stand By For Pain, 1994; Thunderbolt: A tribute to AC/DC, 1998; with Strangeland (executive producer): Strangeland, 1998; with Bernie Torme: White Trash Guitar, 1999; Never Let The Bastards Wear You Down, 2000; Singles: with Twisted Sister: I Am; I Wanna Rock; The Kids Are Back; Leader of The Pack; We're Not Gonna Take It; You Can't Stop Rock 'N' Roll;

You Want What We Got. *Current Management:* c/o Music For Nations Records, 333 Latimer Rd, London W10 6RA, England.

SNOOP DOGG, (Calvin Broadus), (Snoop Doggy Dogg); b. 20 Oct. 1972, Long Beach, California, USA. Rap Artiste. *Career:* Worked with Warren G and Domino; Began collaboration with Dr Dre; Numerous live appearances including Lollapalooza in 1997; EP with Rage Against the Machine; Worked with K-Ci and JoJo on You Lift Me Up; Contributed to soundtrack for film Men in Black; Movie cameo roles in The Show, 1995, Half Baked, 1998, Ride, 1998, Caught Up, 1998. *Recordings:* Singles: What's My Name, 1993; Gin and Juice, 1994; Snoop's Upside Your Head, 1996; We Just Wanna Party With You, 1997; The Dogfather, 1998; Da Game Is To Be Sold Not To Be Told, EP, 1998; Still a 'G' Thang, 1998; The Baller Doggy Dogg, 1999; Doggy Dogg World, 1999; Woof, 1999; Still D.R.E., with Dr. Dre, 2000; Albums: Doggystyle, 1993; Tha Doggfather, 1996; Da Game Is To Be Sold Not To Be Told, 1998; Top Dogg, 1999; The Last Meal, 2000; Paid Tha Cost To Be Da Boss, 2002. *Website:* www.snoopdogg.com.

SNOW, Phoebe (Laub); b. 17 July 1952, New York, NY, USA. Vocalist. *Education:* Piano studies, guitar. *Career:* Performer, New York clubs, 1970s; Solo recording artist, 1974–; Tours with Paul Simon; Played and recorded with Stan Getz, Donald Fagen and Michael McDonald. *Recordings:* Albums include: Phoebe Snow, 1974; Second Childhood, 1976; It Looks Like Snow, 1976; Never Letting Go, 1977; Against The Grain, 1978; Best of 1981; Rock Away, 1981; Something Real, 1989; I Can't Complain, 1998; The Very Best Of, 2001. *Address:* c/o The Agency Group, 1775 Broadway, Suite 433, New York, NY 10019, USA.

SNOWBOY, (Mark Cotgrove); b. 3 July 1961, Hadleigh, Essex, England. Musician (Latin percussion); Recording Artist. *Education:* Graphics, Southend-on-Sea Technical College; Private music lessons (initially with Robin Jones). *Career:* Television appearances: A13: The Road To Somewhere (documentary on self and two other Essex musicans); Festival of Brighton; Sampled Here and Now, documentary; The Pier; Pebble Mill; Tours: Japan, 1991, 1993; Europe, 1994; World tours with: Lisa Stansfield, including Rock In Rio, Brazil 1993; Basia; James Taylor Quartet; Producer, various bands, sessions, remixes. *Recordings:* Albums: with Snowboy and the Latin Section: Ritmo Snowbo, 1989; Descarga Mambito, 1992, 1996; Something's Coming, 1994, 1996; Best Of..., 1995; The World Of..., 1995; Mambo Rage, 1998; The Soul Of Snowboy, 2000; Afro-Cuban Jazz, 2000; Beyond The Snowstorm, 2001; Singles include: Casa Forte, 1999; Theme tune, Artrageous, BBC2, 1993. *Membership:* Musicians' Union; PRS; MCPS; BPI. *Current Management:* Alex Hardee, Concorde Artists. *Address:* Concorde House, 101 Shepherds Bush Rd, London W6 7LP, England.

SNOWDEN, John Robert; b. 17 Feb. 1968, Darlington, County Durham, England. Musician (jazz specialist guitar, bass). *Education:* Salford College of Technology; Graduate diploma in band musicianship (performance passed with distinction). *Career:* Various jazz combos, Salford College Big Band, 1989; Adaptation (cruiseship MV La Palma), 1990; National Youth Jazz Orchestra, 1991; Summer season, world cruise on board QE2, backing Neil Sedaka; Vic Damone; Iris Williams; Doug Cameron; Jimmy Tarbuck; with Rob Charles Orchestra; London Pops Orchestra; One Hundred Years of the Great British Musical, introduced by David Jacobs, recorded by BBC Radio 2; The Sound and Style of James Last, national tour, 1994; Mike James Sound, including a Tribute To Nat King Cole, Birmingham Town Hall, 1994; Summer season and winter season on QE2, backing top artists; John Oliver Sound summer season, 1994; Ray McVay Orchestra, Blackpool Tower Ballroom, 1995; Teaching, Wigan, Bolton Education Authorities, 1994–95; Self-employed guitar/keyboard teacher. *Membership:* Musicians' Union. *Address:* 2 St Margarets Grove, Acklam, Middlesborough, England.

SNYMAN, Neil (Jean Corneille); b. 3 Nov. 1956, Bellville, South Africa. Prod; Engineer; Musician (multi-instrumentalist). m. 17 Dec. 1977, 1 s., 1 d. *Education:* Higher National Diploma for Technicians, Electrical Engineering. *Career:* Specialist in Zulu ethnic recordings; Four featured documentaries on activities, all filmed, broadcast on South African television, 1994–. *Recordings:* Recorded Ladysmith Black Mambazo for Rugby World Cup, 1995; For album Anthems: Swing Low; Sosholoza; World In Union. *Honours:* SABC Artes Awards, for traditional music. *Membership:* ASAMI; SAMRO. *Current Management:* Direct.

SOARES, João Paulo; b. 24 July 1969, Beira, Mozambique. Vocalist; Graphic Designer; Writer. *Education:* 12 years, legal education. *Career:* Solo artiste as Johnny, 1990; Lead singer, composer, Selva Urbana, 1994–. *Recordings:* Lovers (Amor Sem Fim), 1991; Island Girl (Rapariga Da Ilha), 1991; My Dreams (Meus Sonhos), 1992; Lime Light (Sonhar Bem Alto), 1993; Street Boys (Putos Da Rua), 1994; Wonderful Tonight (Esta Noire Foi Maravilhosa), 1994; Urban Jungle (Selva Urbana), 1994. *Publications:* World Music (Musica Do Mundo), 1993. *Membership:* SPA (Portuguese Authors Society). *Current Management:* JPP Productions. *Address:* Av Paulo Vi-Lote 60–2-Fte, PO Box 59–2041 Rio Maior, Portugal.

SOARES-PEIXOTO, Rogerio; b. 9 May 1954, Rio de Janeiro, Brazil. Musician (guitar, percussion); Vocalist. 2 c. *Career:* Concerts on stage; Radio reports on local stations; Festivals and open-air appearances. *Recordings:* With band, Rogerio Soares-e Sveiro Azul, CDs: Rogerio Soares-e-Saveiro Azul; Sentindo a caricia do vento. *Membership:* GEMA. *Address:* Bromeis str 4a, 34125 Kassel, Germany.

SOENEN, Geert; b. 25 April 1963, Wervik, Belgium. Piano Teacher; Conductor. m. Elly Deflo, 8 Oct. 1988. *Education:* Higher Degree for Chamber Music, Conservatory of Gent, Belgium; Orchestral Conducting Degree, Conservatory of Den Haag, Netherlands. *Career:* Soloist, played on trumpet and piano, classical, popular and chamber music; Conductor, Accademia Amanti Dell'Arte, The Symphony Orchestra of Flanders, The Prague Philharmonic Chamber Orchestra; Conductor of Symphonic Youth and Music Orchestra East of Flanders. *Compositions:* Arrangements for Pitti Polak, Raymond Van Het Groenewoud, for proms with symphony orchestra. *Address:* Mispelbilk 14, 9030 Mariakerke-Gent, Belgium.

SOERENSEN, Kim Hougaard; b. 21 May 1956, Haldum, Denmark. Composer; Lyricist; Journalist; Music Theatre Critic. *Education:* Journalism, Danish University, 1981; Private lessons by Danish composers. *Career:* Keyboard player, numerous Danish pop and rockbands, 1980–90; Composer, lyricist, Danish National Concert musical, The Egtved Chronicle, tour, 1993. *Recordings:* The Egtved Chronicle, 1993. *Publications:* Songs From The Egtved Chronicle, 1993. *Honours:* The Cultural Award, 1993; The VAF Foundation Award, 1993. *Membership:* Danish Jazz, Folk and Rock Composers; Danish Board of Journalists.

SOIRAT, Philippe; b. 11 March 1961, Menton, France. Jazz Musician (drums). *Education:* Jazz Academy, Monaco; Centre Musical Contemporain, Nice. *Career:* Concerts with: J R Monterose; Warren Bernhardt; Barney Wilen; John Stubbelfield; Duke Jordan; Ray Brown; Walter Bishop Jr; Bob Mover; Alain Jean-Marie; Jacky Terrasson; Georges Cables; LaVelle; James Moddy; Lou Donaldson; Horace Parlan; Emmanuel Bex; Jimmy Gourley; Dee Dee Bridgwater; Larry Schneider; Andy Laverne; Enrico Rava; Eric Lelann; Tours: Turkey (Armen Donelian Trio), 1990; France (Lee Konitz Quartet), 1992; Viet Nam, Thailand, Malaysia, Singapore (Laurent de Wilde, Ira Coleman, Eric Barret), 1993; Australia, New Zealand (Laurent de Wilde Quartet), 1995; Portugal (Carlos Barretto Quintet); Canada (Yannick Rieu Quartet); Singapore, Brunei, Poland (Laurent de Wilde Trio), 1995; Africa (Belmondo Quintet), 1996. *Recordings include:* What Is The Color of Love?, Yannick Rieu Quartet; Passione, Barney Wilen Quintet; Alone Together, Georges Cables Trio; Going Up, Carlos Barretto Quintet.

SOLEM, Phil; Vocalist; Songwriter; Musician. *Career:* Member, Great Buildings since late 1970s; Member, The Rembrandts, 1991–. *Recordings:* The Tremblers, with Peter Noone, 1980; With Great Buildings: Apart from the Crowd, 1981; Gone, with Dwight Yoakum, 1995; Testimonial Dinner, with XTC, 1995; Compilation, Friends, 1995; Disney's Music from The Park, 1996; Oneman, with Dex Dickerson, 1997; Albums with the Rembrandts: The Rembrandts, 1991; Untitled, 1992; LP, 1995; Lost Together, 2001; Poptopia! 80s Power Pop Clasics, 1997; Poptopia! 90s Power Pop Classics, 1997; with Mango Jam: Preserves, 1998; Singles: That's Just The Way It Is Baby; Johnny Have You Seen Her; I'll Be There For You (theme for television series Friends), 1995; This House is not a Home, 1995. *Honours:* ASCAP and BMI Awards, 1995–97; LA Music Award. *Membership:* ASCAP; SAG. *Current Management:* Under discussion. *Address:* 9744 Wilshire Blvd, Suite 305, Beverly Hills, CA 90212, USA.

SOLIS, Marco Antonio; b. Michoacan, Mexico. Vocalist; Songwriter. m. Beatriz, divorced. *Career:* First group, Los Hermanitos Solis, aged 12; Formed Los Bukis, 1970s; Songwriter for singers including ex-wife and Marisela; Wrote for Mexican soap operas Amor en Silencio and El Alma no Tiene Color; Compositions recorded by singers including: Lucero; Enrique Iglesias; Solo career, 1995–. *Recordings:* Albums include: En Pleno Vuelo, 1996; Marco, 1997; Romantico Instrumental, Trozos De Mi Alma, 1999; Mas De Mi Alma, En Concierto Vol. 1, 2001. *Honours:* Pride of SESAC award, 2000. *Website:* www.marcomusic.com.

SOLO, Sal; b. Hatfield, England. Vocalist; Songwriter; Broadcaster. *Career:* Lead singer, Classix Nouveaux, 1979–85; Major tours, numerous hit singles in approximately 30 countries; Lead Singer, Rockets, Italy, 1984–92; Solo career, 1984–; Host, radio shows, 1988–. *Recordings:* Guilty, Night People, 1981; Is It a Dream, La Verité, 1982; Secret, Imperception, Under The Sun, 1983; San Damiano, Heart and Soul, 1985; Look At Christ, 1991; Another Future, 1992; Through Ancient Eyes, 1994; Anno Domini, 1999; Producer: Living in Oblivion: Living in Oblivion Vol. 1, 1993; Hardest Hits Vol. 4, 1994; Our Friends Electric, Our Friends Electric, 1996. *Publications:* For God's Sake, 1993. *Honours:* Various Gold and Silver discs; CACLB Radio Award, 1990. *Membership:* Christian Music Assccn. *Current Management:* Falcon Stuart, 59 Moore Park Rd, London SW6 2HH, England.

SOMACH, Denny; b. 30 Sept. 1952, Allentown, Pennsylvania, USA. Prod; Record Co Exec. m. Kathy Levinsky Somach, 25 May 1995, 2 s., 1 d.

Education: BA, Moravian College. *Career:* Radio announcer, Station WSAN, Allentown, 1971–75; Program director, 1975; Announcer, music director, Station WYSP-FM, Philadelphia, 1975–81; Record producer; Television producer: Hot Spots; USA Network, 1982–84; Rock 'n' Roll Show, CBS, 1982; John Debella Show, 1990; Radio producer, Psychedelic Snack, 1985–; Ticket To Ride, 1985–; Legends of Rock, 1985–; Don Kirshner's History of Rock 'n' Roll, 1990; Producer, President, Denny Somach Productions, 1979–; President, Cinema Records, 1986–; President, founder, Musicom International, 1992. *Recordings:* Albums produced for: Dave Mason, 1987; Patrick Moraz, 1987; Johnny Winter, 1988; Eric Johnson, 1990; Barbara Mandrell, It Works for Me, 1997; Alan Parsons, Definitive Collection, 1997. *Publications:* Ticket To Ride, 1989. *Honours:* Grammy, Best Rock Instrumentalist, Eric Johnson, Cliffs of Dover. *Membership:* NARAS. *Address:* 812 W Darby Rd, Havertown, PA 19083, USA.

SOMERS, Lynn Marie; b. 15 April 1961, Jeanette, Pennsylvania, USA. Contemporary Christian Vocalist; Puppeteer. m. Frederick A Somers, 25 May 1984, 1 d., 1 s. *Education:* BA, Psychology, Asbury College, 1983; 2 Masters degrees from United Seminary, Dayton, Ohio, 1986, 1988; Two PhDs, Faith Formation, The Unrow Institute and University; Private vocal instruction, High School, college, seminary; Piano, guitar lessons as child, youth; MA, Theological Studies, Vocal performance emphasis. *Career:* Television appearance, Crosslink (United Theological Seminary), 1985; Radio interviews: Canada, 1989; WAMN, Princeton, West Virginia, 1995, Off the Cuff show on WSNJ, Bridgeton, New Jersey, 1996; Programmes in churches, prisons, community and retirement homes; TV appearances: 60 Live Show with WBPH, Bethlehem, Pennsylvania, 1997; Edited version of Genesis video aired on WGCB, Red Lion, Pennsylvania and ACTV, Reading, Pennsylvania, 1997; Various tours through 30 states over 19 years. *Recordings:* We Are The Reason, 1986; God's House/Our House, 1992; The Gift of a Child, 1997. *Publications:* Video: Bible Stories From Genesis, for children; Puppets and Music, 1992; Dear Jesus, I wanna talk to you... My Home is Broken, story colouring book, 1996; Lynn Somers and Friends Character Coloring Book, 1996; Hand of the Master, puppet scriptbook, 1996; Various articles in publications, including Quarter Notes. *Membership:* Gospel Music Assccn; Fellowship of Christian Puppeteers; Christian Educators Fellowship; Asscn of Professors and Researchers in Religious Education. *Current Management:* Hand of The Master Ministries Inc (own non-profit ministry). *Address:* Lynn Somers and Friends, 103 Glen Court, Ephrata, PA 17522, USA.

SOMERVILLE, Jimmy; b. 22 June 1961, Glasgow, Scotland. Vocalist; Songwriter. *Career:* Founder member, Bronski Beat, 1984–85; Formed The Communards, with Richard Coles, 1985–89; Tours include: UK Wedge tour, with Paul Weller and Billy Bragg, 1986; European tour, 1986; Solo artiste, 1989–; Concerts include: Red Hot and Dance AIDS benefit concert, 1991. *Recordings:* Albums with Bronski Beat: The Age of Consent, 1984; Hundreds and Thousands, 1985; with the Communards: Communards, 1986; Red, 1987; Solo albums: Read My Lips, 1990; The Singles Collection, 1984–90, 1991; Dare To Love, 1995; Manage the Damage, 1999; Rootbeer, 2000; Very Best Of, 2001; Hit singles: with Bronski Beat: Smalltown Boy, 1984; Why?, 1984; I Feel Love, 1985; with the Communards: You Are My World, 1985; Disenchanted, 1986; Don't Leave Me This Way, (No. 1, UK), 1986; So Cold The Night, 1986; Tomorrow, 1987; Never Can Say Goodbye, 1987; For a Friend, 1988; There's More To Love, 1988; Solo singles: Comment Te Dire Adieu, 1989; You Make Me Feel, 1990; Read My Lips, 1990; To Love Somebody, 1990; Run From Love, 1991; Hurts So Good, 1995; Heartbeat, 1995; By Your Side, 1995; Safe, 1997; Dark Sky, 1997; Something to Live For, 1999; Other. *Recordings include:* Track on Red Hot + Blue, AIDS benefit compilation, 1990; Gimme Shelter, Voice of The Beehive (for Putting Our House In Order charity), 1993. *Current Management:* Solar Management, 42–48 Charlbert St, London NW8 7BU, England.

SON OF SCIENTIST. See: **IG CULTURE.**

SONDHEIM, Stephen Joshua; b. 22 March 1930, New York, NY, USA. Composer; Lyricist. *Education:* BA, Williams College, 1950. *Compositions:* Incidental Music: The Girls of Summer, 1956; Invitation to a March, 1961; Twigs, 1971; Lyrics: West Side Story, 1957; Gypsy, 1959; Do I Hear a Waltz?, 1965; Candide, (additional lyrics) 1973; Music and Lyrics: A Funny Thing Happened on the Way to the Forum, 1962; Anyone Can Whistle, 1964; Evening Primrose, 1966; Company, 1970; Follies, 1971; A Little Night Music, 1973; The Frogs, 1974; Pacific Overtures, 1976; Sweeney Todd, 1979; Merrily We Roll Along, 1981, 1997; Sunday in the Park With George, 1984; Into the Woods, 1987; Assassins, 1991; Passion, 1994; Anthologies: Side by Side by Sondheim, 1976; Marry Me a Little, 1980; You're Gonna Love Tomorrow, 1983; Putting It Together, 1992; Film: Stravinsky, 1974; Reds, 1981; Dick Tracy, 1990; Compilations include: Celebrating Sondheim, 2000. *Membership:* President, Dramatists Guild, 1973–81; American Academy and Institute of Arts and Letters. *Address:* c/o Sarah Douglas, 393 W 49th St, New York, NY 10019, USA.

SONIQUE, (Sonia Clarke); b. 21 June 1965, London. Vocalist; Prod; DJ. *Career:* Vocalist with S-Express; Started as a DJ in the '90s, singing over the records; Resident DJ for Manumission in Ibiza; Solo recording career 1998–.

Recordings: Albums: Hear My Cry, 2000; Serious Sounds of Sonique (Mixed multi-artist compilation), 2000; Singles: I Put A Spell On You, 1998; It Feels So Good, 1998; Sky, 2000. *Honours:* BRIT Award, Best British Female Artist, 2001. *Membership:* MCPS/PRS. *Address:* c/o Serious Records Ltd, First Floor, Tudor House, Llanvanol Rd, Finchley Rd, London NW2 2AQ, England.

SONNEBORN, Daniel Atesh; b. 31 Oct. 1949, Illinois, USA. Composer; Prod; Musician; Musical Dir. m. Patrizia Pallaro, 2 s. *Education:* BA, 1982, MA, 1984, University of California; PhD, UCLA, 1995. *Career:* Consultant, Educator, 1975; Project Director, Drumming at the Edge of Magic, 1988–92; Co-Producer, Remembrance, 1991; Theatre, Opera, Film Composer, USA and Europe, 1970–; Executive Co-Producer, Available Sound, 1995. *Recordings:* Jumping Over The Fence: XA:A Vietnam Primer; Delta Prime. *Publications:* Co-Author, Planet Drum; Sufi Music. *Honours:* Best Show of the Year, 1973; La Drama Critics Circle, 1971, 1972; International Herald Tribune; Department of Music Fellowship, 1984, 1985; Presidents Fellowship. *Membership:* Society for Ethnomusicology; International Council for Traditional Music. *Address:* 2386 I St, Petaluma, CA 94952, USA.

SORRELL, Jonathan Lindsay; b. 19 Oct. 1961, Salisbury, Wiltshire, England. Composer; Record Prod; Musician (keyboards); Programmer. m. Miriam Grech, 24 June 1994. *Education:* Piano Diploma, 1976; A Level Music, 1978; BMus Degree, 1984. *Career:* Chorister, St Paul's Cathedral, 1970–75; Keyboard player for Trevor Horn, 1984–85; Keyboard player, arranger for David Dundas, 1988–95; Freelance session musician, 1985–95; Composer, television and film commercials, 1986–95. *Compositions:* Chart Show theme, ITV; You Bet theme, LWT; Survival logo, Anglia; Star Test, CH4; Starchamber Titles; Commercials for: American Airlines; Commerical Union; BMW Cars. *Recordings:* Albums with artistes including: Frankie Goes To Hollywood; Propaganda; Tears For Fears; Def Leppard; Eddie Howell; Film music: Little Shop of Horrors; The Bear; Lord of The Flies; Music Box; Freddie As F.R.O.T.; Television music: ITV, LWT, CH4 television logos; BBC World News; Dark City; Sleepers; White Goods. *Membership:* PRS; BAC&S. *Current Management:* Jeff Wayne Music Ltd. *Address:* The Cottage, 26 High St, Prestwood, Nr Great Missenden, Bucks HP16 9ED, England.

SOSSIN, Stephen Mark; b. 28 Sept. 1956, Hartford, Connecticut, USA. Music Prod; Musician (guitar, bass, keyboards, violin). *Education:* Business, Computers, Manchester College; Heil/Sound Engineering; Studied with Al DiMeola and Mike Ruff; Pursuing advanced degree; Special Major Programme, California University, 1997. *Career:* Early performing career with artists including: Mike Ruff (keyboards, songwriter), 1986; Tom Chapin (saxophone, horns), 1971–76; Established songwriter in original music scene, New England, 1975–; Founder, Vizion productions studio, world class digital recording facility, photo, video services; Began artist development programme, 1983–; Works mainly with emerging artist, custom writing for individual's voice; Founder-Producer, New Vizion Studios. *Compositions:* Thats Why I Ran, Dianne Glynn, 1996. *Recordings:* with Bonnie Lynn: Embrace of My Heart, 1993; with Dianne Glynn: I Can't Find The Words, 1995; Thats Why I Ran, 1996; Take My Hand, 1996. *Publications:* Listed in Mixmaster Directory; Northeast Mix Plus; Recording Industry Sourcebook; Instage; Songwriters Market. *Honours:* Knight Chevalier Medal; National Patriotism Medal; AFP; Capitol Records Promotional Awards. *Membership:* Independent Producer's Guild; NE; United States Naval Institute. *Current Management:* John Carpino; Agent: Caroline Hayes.

SOUL BOY. See: **TENAGLIA, Danny.**

SOUND PATROL. See: **CARTER, Derrick.**

SOUQUES, Laurent; b. 27 Oct. 1963, Paris, France. Musician (double bass); Composer. *Education:* Conservatoire National Supérieur de Musiques et de Dance, Paris. *Career:* Jazz Festival, Franche Comté, 1986, 1987, 1989; Jazz Festival Suedine Bleue (Dijon), 1986; Jazz Festival Aiguillon, 1990; Jazz clubs in Paris, 1991–95; Jazz Festival Banlieue Bleue, with G Russell, Living Time Orchestra, 1993; Banlieue Bleue, G Russell, Cité de la Musique, 1995; JUC Halle That Jazz, Paris, 1995. *Compositions:* Film music; Syndrome de l'Espion – Zooleil, N Joyeux; Paris des Freres Tenebres, Muriel Mazieres. *Recordings:* Just Back From New Orleans, 1989; G Russell for Radio France, 1993, 1995; Fire Beat, Ralph Thomas Sextet, 1996; Un Charivari Entre Chien Et Loup Skymninsgslandet, 1998. *Address:* 10 rue Saint Jean, 75017 Paris, France. *E-mail:* loso@free.fr.

SOUSA, (Duane) 'Beans'; b. 22 July 1951. Musician (bass); Vocalist. m. Barbara Runnion, 8 April 1989, 1 s. *Career:* Bassist for major country and rock artists: Lacy J Dalton; Phoebe Snow; Larry Hosford; Studio work for major recording companies including CBS, MCA, Capitol and Shelter Records. *Recordings include:* Dream Baby, Lacy J Dalton; Solo album: You Don't Know. *Membership:* AFofM. *Address:* 906 30th Ave, Santa Cruz, CA 95062, USA.

SOUTH, Joe, (Joe Souter); b. 28 Feb. 1940, Atlanta, Georgia, USA. Musician (guitar); Vocalist; Songwriter. *Career:* Session guitarist, Nashville, 1960s; Recording sessions include: Aretha Franklin; Wilson Pickett; Marty

Robbins; Eddy Arnold; Bob Dylan; Simon and Garfunkel; Solo artiste, 1962–. *Compositions include:* Games People Play, Billy Joe Royal and Boots Randolph; Untie Me, The Tams; Down In The Boondocks, Billy Joe Royal; I Knew You When, Billy Joe Royal; These Are Not My People, Freddy Weller; Birds of a Feather, Paul Revere and The Raiders; Hush, Deep Purple. *Recordings:* Albums include: Introspect, 1968; Don't It Make You Want To Go Home, 1969; Walkin' Shoes, 1970; So The Seeds Are Growing, 1971; Midnight Rainbows, 1975; Look Inside, 1976; Anthology 1968–75, 2001; Other. *Recordings include:* Blonde On Blonde, Bob Dylan, 1966; Sound of Silence, Simon and Garfunkel, 1966; Aretha Arrives, Aretha Franklin, 1967; Lady Soul, Aretha Franklin, 1968; Dan Baird, Buffalo Nickel, 1996; Jazz Singers, 1919–94, 1998; Rock Classics of the 60s, 1998.

SPACEY-FOOTE, Gary Martin; b. 15 Dec. 1961, Weybridge, Surrey, England. Musician (saxophone, flute, percussion, drums). m. Carrie Spacey-Foote, 17 Aug. 1991. *Education:* Some percussion tutorage with Danny Cummings. *Career:* Two world tours, Joan Armatrading; Television appearances with Bee Gees; Tom Jones; Recording, touring, with Nightrains; The Hipjoints; Maroon Town; House of Rhythm; Jamiroquai; Kiss of Life; Espiritu; Lionel Moyst. *Recordings:* with The Hipjoints: Rock Hopper; Chillin'; with Lionel Moyst Sextet: Chillin'. *Contributions to:* Martini Grooves, 1998; Duboniks, On the Vibe, 1998; Chris Bangs, Dazzle, 1999. *Membership:* Musicans' Union; PRS. *Current Management:* c/o Carrie Spacey-Foote, 34 Hampden Rd, Kingston on Thames, Surrey KT1 3HG, England.

SPANG-HANSSEN, Simon Cato; b. 13 April 1955, Hellerup, Denmark. Musician (saxophone); Composer. m. Mariane Bitran, 23 Jan. 1987, 1 s. *Career:* Tours with: John Tchicai and Strange Brothers, Scandinavia, Germany, Italy; Andy Emler's Mega-Octet, Europe; French National Jazz Orchestra, 1991–94, Europe; Leader of Quartet, Muluankh; Duo with Denis Badault, France, Denmark, Central Africa. *Recordings:* Darktown Highlights; Ten By Two; Because Forever; Mardi Gras, Chez Toi; Instant Blue, 1998; Wondering, 1999; Identified, 1999. *Honours:* Ben Webster Prize, 1978. *Membership:* Union de Musicians de Jazz (Paris). *Current Management:* Blue Line Productions, Mr Bourgaut, Mr Vautrot. *Address:* 5 rue Leon Giraud, 75019 Paris, France.

SPARROW, Edwin Harold James; b. 28 Jan. 1943, Harrogate, Yorkshire, England. Musician (drums, timpani, percussion, Latin percussion). *Education:* Piano with Evelyn Gunnar; ARCM; LTCL; LLCM; Timpani with Lewis Pocock, Trinity College. *Career:* Many years in France, worked with top light entertainment artistes including: Johnny Hallyday; Sylvie Vartan; Charles Aznavour; Appeared in film Les Jeunes Loups, directed by Marcel Carné; Appeared with Kevin Ayers; Mike Oldfield; Nico and others connected with The Velvet Underground; Gerry Rafferty, 1970s; Closely connected with Ballet Rambert; London Contemporary Dance Theatre; Contemporary Dance and Therapy in UK; Featured on: June The 1st, 1974; Bannamour, Kevin Ayers; Banana Follies, Kevin Ayers, 2000. *Address:* Harrogate, North Yorkshire, England.

SPARROW, Willy; b. 29 Aug. 1960, Buenos Aires, Argentina. Musician. *Education:* Walter Malosseti Jazz School; Berklee School. *Career:* Chacarita Festival; DSPS Festival; Other Festivals in Madrid, Barcelona, Hamburg, Lyon, Amsterdam, Brighton. *Recordings:* Magic Band; The Impossibles; Missing Band; Stalking; Cobble Stones; Jazz Allcovers; Toko; Niks; Horizon Meeting. *Membership:* Argentine Musicians' union; Dutch Musicians' union. *Current Management:* Siza Records. *Address:* Makassarstraat 38–1, Amsterdam, Netherlands.

SPEAKE, Martin John; b. 3 April 1958, Barnet, Hertfordshire, England. Musician (alto saxophone); Jazz Educator; Composer. m. Rachel Cutler, 6 Jan. 1990, 1 d. *Education:* A Level Music; Classical saxophone, Trinity College of Music, LTCL, FTCL diplomas. *Career:* Tours of West Africa, Latin America, Europe, with saxophone quartet Itchy Fingers; Tours of Indonesia, Philippines, Croatia, UK, with 7-piece Fever Pitch, own quartet, and duo with guitarist Phil Lee; Various radio and television appearances. *Recordings:* Albums: with Itchy Fingers: Quark; Teranga; In Our Time, Martin Speake Group; Entertainment USA, Billy Jenkins; Midnight Sun, Flora Purim and Airto Moreira; Solo album: Secret, 2001. *Honours:* Schlitz Young Jazz Musicians Winner, with Itchy Fingers, 1986. *Membership:* Musicians' Union. *Address:* 1 Mawson House, Baldwins Gardens, London EC1N 7SD, England.

SPEARE, Paul; b. 10 Dec. 1955, Romford, Essex, England. Musician (saxophone, flute); Arranger; Prod; Lecturer. m. Paula Davies, 27 July 1985, 1 d. *Education:* London College of Music; Birmingham Polytechnic. *Career:* Member, Dexy's Midnight Runners, 1980–82; Q-Tips British tour, 1982; Elvis Costello, USA, UK, and European tours, 1983; Manager, Expresso Bongo Studios, Tamworth, 1985–94; Leader, Expresso Bongo Orchestra, 1988–94; Lecturer, Popular Music, Lewisham College, London, 1995–. *Recordings:* Singles include: Show Me, 1981; Liars A–E, 1981; Celtic Soul Brothers, 1982; Come On Eileen, Too-Rye-Ay, Dexy's Midnight Runners, 1982; Punch The Clock, Elvis Costello, 1983; Free Nelson Mandela, Special AKA, 1984; Keep Moving, Madness, 1984; Hold Back The Night, KWS/The Tramps, 1992; Nick Lowe and his Cowboy Outfit, 1984; Terminal Power Company, Run Silent,

Run Deep, 1992. *Membership:* Musicians' Union. *Current Management:* Mr R Speare. *Address:* 314 Upminster Rd N, Rainham, Essex RM13 9RY, England.

SPEARRITT, Hannah Louise; b. 1 April 1981, Great Yarmouth, England. Vocalist; Actor. *Education:* National Youth Music Theatre. *Career:* Moved to London aged 16 to appear in West End production of Bugsy Malone; Various TV acting work, incl. The Cater Street Hangman; Mem., S Club 7, 1998–; Group quickly achieved international success, following sales of TV series Miami 7, 1999, LA 7, 2000, and Hollywood 7, 2001, featuring the band's music, to nearly 100 countries; Also made nature TV series, S Club 7 Go Wild, 2000, and various TV specials; First British tour with S Club 7, 2001; Band renamed S Club, 2001. *Recordings:* Albums: S Club, 1999; 7 (No. 1, UK), 2000; Sunshine, 2001; Seeing Double, 2002. Singles: Bring It All Back (No. 1, UK), 1999; S Club Party, 1999; Two In A Million/You're My Number One, 1999; Reach, 2000; Natural, 2000; Never Had A Dream Come True (No. 1, UK), 2000; Don't Stop Movin' (No. 1, UK), 2001; Have You Ever (No. 1, UK), 2001; You, 2002. *Honours:* BRIT Awards, Best British Newcomer, 2000, Best British Single, for Don't Stop Movin', 2002; Record of the Year Award, for Don't Stop Movin', 2001. *Current Management:* 19 Management, Unit 32, Ransomes Dock, 35–37 Parkgate Rd, London SW11 4NP, England. *Website:* www.sclub.com.

SPEARS, Billie Jo; b. 14 Jan. 1937, Beaumont, Texas, USA. Vocalist. *Career:* Country singer, 1952–; Regular recording artiste, 1964–; Television includes: Louisiana Hayride; Leader, own band, Owlkatraz. *Recordings:* Hits include: Blanket On The Ground; Mr Walker, It's All Over; What I've Got In Mind; Sing Me An Old-Fashioned Song; Misty Blue; I Will Survive; Numerous albums include: The Voice of Billie Jo Spears, 1968; Mr Walker It's All Over, 1969; Miss Sincerity, 1969; With Love, 1970; Country Girl, 1970; Just Singin', 1972; Blanket On The Ground, 1974; Billie Jo, 1975; What I've Got In Mind, 1976; By Request (with Del Reeves), 1976; If You Want Me, 1977; Everytime I Sing a Love Song, 1977; Lonely Hearts Club, 1978; Love Ain't Gonna Wait For Us, 1978; I Will Survive, 1979; Standing Tall, 1980; Special Songs, 1981; Del and Billie Jo (with Del Reeves), 1982; BJ – Billie Jo Spears Today, 1983; We Just Came Apart At The Dreams, 1984; Unmistakeably, 1992; Voice Of, 2000; Look What They've Done To My Song, 2001; Country Stars And Stripes, 2001; with Guy Clark: Craftsmen, 1995. *Address:* c/o Joe Taylor Artist Agency, 2802 Columbine Pl., Nashville, TN 37204, USA.

SPEARS, Britney Jean; b. 2 Dec. 1981, Kentwood, Louisiana, USA. Vocalist. *Career:* Presenter, Mickey Mouse Club; Solo artiste, 1998–; Numerous tours, television and radio appearances; Owner, southern grill restaurant, Nyla; Film appearance: Crossroads, 2002. *Recordings:* Albums: Baby One More Time, 1998; Oops!... I Did It Again (No. 1, USA), 2000; Britney, 2001. Singles: Baby One More Time (No. 1, UK and USA), 1998; Sometimes, 1999; (You Drive Me) Crazy, 1999; Born To Make You Happy (No. 1, UK), 2000; From The Bottom Of My Broken Heart, 2000; Oops! I Did It Again (No. 1, UK), 2000; Lucky, 2000; Stronger, 2000; Don't Let Me Be The Last To Know, 2001; I'm A Slave For You, 2001; Overprotected, 2002; I'm Not A Girl Not Yet A Woman, 2002. *Honours:* MTV Europe Music Awards, Best Female Artist, Best Breakthrough Act, Best Pop Act, Best Song, for Baby One More Time, 1999; Several MTV Video Music Awards, 1999; Billboard Music Award, 2000; American Music Awards, Favourite New Artist, 2000. *Address:* Zomba Records Ltd, Zomba House, London NW10 2SG, England. *Website:* www.britney.com.

SPECTOR, Phil (Harvey Phillip); b. 26 Dec. 1940, Bronx, New York, USA. Record Prod; Composer; Musician. m. Ronnie Spector (divorced). *Career:* Member, The Teddy Bears; The Spectors Three; Formed Philles Records, 1961–66; Produced albums for Beatles' Apple label; Formed Phil Spector International. *Compositions:* Co-writer, with Ben E King, Spanish Harlem; Young Boy Blues. *Recordings:* As producer for artists including: LaVern Baker; Ruth Brown; Billy Storm; Twist and Shout, The Top Notes; Corrina Corrina, Ray Petersen, 1960; Pretty Little Angel Eyes, Curtis Lee; I Love How You Love Me, Paris Sisters; Work with the Crystals and the Ronettes includes: He's a Rebel, 1962; Then He Kissed Me, 1963; Be My Baby, 1963; Baby I Love You, 1963; River Deep Mountain High, 1966; Black Pearl, Sonny Charles and The Checkmates; Albums: by John Lennon; The Plastic Ono Band; Imagine; Sometime In New York City; George Harrison: All Things Must Pass; Concert For Bangladesh; Leonard Cohen: Death of a Ladies Man, 1977; Ramones: End of The Century, 1980; Compilations: A Christmas Gift To You, 1963; Phil Spector Wall of Sound, Vol. 1: The Ronettes, 1975; Vol. 2: Bob B Soxx and The Blue Jeans, 1975; Vol. 3: The Crystals, 1975; Vol. 4: Yesterday's Hits Today, 1976; Vol. 5: Rare Masters, 1976; Vol. 6: Rare Masters, Vol. 2, 1976; The Phil Spector Story, 1976; Echoes of The Sixties, 1977; Phil Spector 1974–79, 1979; Wall of Sound, 1981; The Early Productions, 1958–61; Twist and Shout: Twelve Atlantic Tracks Produced by Phil Spector, 1989; John Lennon, Anthology, 1998; All Time Greatest Movie Songs, 1998; Gene Pitney, All-Time Greatest Hits, 1999; Ramones, Hey! Ho! Let's Go: The Anthology, 1999. *Honours:* Q Awards, 1999.

SPECTOR, Ronnie, (Veronica Bennett Spector Greenfield); b. 10 Aug. 1943, New York, USA. Vocalist. m. (1) Harvey Phillip (Phil) Spector, (2) Jonathan Greenfield, 16 Jan. 1982, 5 c. *Career:* Dancer, New York, 1962–63;

Lead singer, choreographer, dancer, The Ronettes (originally Ronnie and The Relatives), 1962–67; Appearances include: Group Scene '64 Tour, support to The Rolling Stones, 1964; Solo artiste, 1969–; Writer, 1988–90. *Recordings:* Albums: with the Ronettes: Presenting The Fabulous Ronettes, 1965; Solo albums: Siren, 1981; Unfinished Business, 1987; Dangerous, 1996; Hit singles with The Ronettes: Be My Baby, 1963; Baby I Love You, 1964; The Best Part of Breaking Up, 1964; Do I Love You, 1964; Walking In The Rain, 1964; She Talks to Rainbows, 1999; Contributor, A Christmas Gift For You compilation album, 1963. *Publications:* Be My Baby (autobiography), with Vince Waldron, 1990. *Honours:* Gee-Gee Awards, 16 Magazine, 1963, 1964; Inducted into New York Music Hall of Fame, 1982; Gold discs, 1963–65; Grammy Award, Walking In The Rain, 1964. *Current Management:* GreenSpec Properties, Suite 233, 39B Mill Plain Rd, Danbury, CT 06811, USA.

SPEDDING, Paul Brian; b. 28 Sept. 1945, Birmingham, England. Musician (drums). *Career:* Various Jazz Festivals Throught UK and Europe; Stage, Royal Festival Hall with Fats Domino Band; Capital Radio Jazz Festival; Worked with Olympia Brass Band, Tuxedo BB. *Recordings:* The John Handy Memorial; Dan Pawson's Buddies. *Honours:* Musical Prize Breda, Holland. *Membership:* Musicians' Union. *Address:* 34 Old Tannery Court, Severnside South, Bewdley, Worcestershire DY12 2DS, England.

SPEECH, (Todd Thomas); b. 1968, Milwaukee, Wisconsin, USA. Vocalist; Lyricist. *Education:* Art Institute of Atlanta. *Career:* Originally kmown as DJ Peech; Formed gangsta rap act DLR (Disciples of a Lyrical Rebellion), renamed Secret Society; Evolved into hip hop act Arrested Development, 1988–; Performances include: MTV Drops The Ball '93, 1992; MTV Unplugged, 1992; Lollapalooza '93 US Tour, 1993. *Recordings:* Singles include: Tennessee, 1992; People Everyday, 1992; Revolution (used in film soundtrack Malcolm X), 1993; Mr Wendal, 1993; Ease My Mind, 1994; Albums: 3 Years, 5 Months and 2 Days In The Life Of…, 1993; Unplugged, 1993; Hoopla, 1999; Best Of Arrested Development, 1999; Producer, Dropping H20 On The Fiber, Gumbo, 1993. *Honours:* Grammy Awards: Best New Artist, Best Rap Group, 1993; Soul Train Award, Best Rap Album, 1993; 7 Atlanta Music Awards, 1993. *Current Management:* Entertainment Resources International Inc, 9380 SW 72nd St, #B-220, Miami, FL 33173, USA.

SPEIDEL, Paul; b. 15 Feb. 1965, Kenmare, North Dakota, USA. Jazz and Blues Musician (guitar); High School Jazz Programme Dir. m. Adlin Quiles, 1 June 1991. *Education:* BA, Augustana College, 1986; MMus, University of Northern Colorado, 1990. *Career:* Freelance guitarist, bassist in Chicago, Denver, Boston; Vocal performances with University of Northern Colorado Vocal Jazz I; Performances with Patti Page; Gerry Beaudoin; Jeff Benedict; Terry Cooke; Ted Pilzecker; Numerous musical shows; 3 tours, Latin and Central America with the Latin Continental Singers as Instrumental Director; Currently guitarist with the Monique Weiss Quartet; Guiarist, vocalist with the Paul Speidel Band. *Publications:* CD reviewer in bi-monthly No Name Jazz News. *Honours:* Illinois State Scholar, Colorado National Scholar. *Membership:* International Asscn of Jazz Educators; Boston Jazz Society; Boston Blues Society; Gospel Music Asscn; Music Educators National Conference. *Current Management:* PSB Management. *Address:* 130 Academy Ave, Providence, RI 02908, USA.

SPEIRS, Fraser; b. 4 Oct. 1949, Glasgow, Scotland. Vocalist; Musician (harmonica). *Education:* Medical Illustrator, University of Glasgow. *Career:* Concert appearances with: Love and Money; Tam White; Carla Laula Band; Rab Noakes; Radio credits: Radio Clyde; Radio 2 Nightride, with David Pringle Band; Television credits: All Kinds of Country, STV. *Recordings:* Album with: Del Amitri; Fish; The Soup Dragons; Carol Kidd; Lloyd Cole and The Commotions; Love and Money; Carol Laula; Humpff Family; King Hash; Kindness of Strangers; Rod Clements; James Grant; Macalias; Donnie Munro; Theme tune to Your Cheatin' Heart. *Membership:* Musicians' Union. *Address:* 53 Marywood Sq., Glasgow G41 2BN, Scotland.

SPENCER, John B; b. 5 June 1944, West London, England. Vocalist; Musician (guitar); Bandleader; Record Prod; Novelist. m. Lou, 26 Feb. 1966, 3 s. *Career:* Pubs, clubs, concert halls, festivals, throughout Europe, 1976–; Featured, interviewed, Channel 4 documentary: Living With The Blues, 1990; Radio broadcasts: Andy Kershaw Show, Radio 1, several occasions; Member: John Spencer's Louts; Spencer's Alternative; John B Spencer Band; Parlour Games; The Goods; Also worked with: Martin Simpson's Flash Company; Home Service; Toured with Fairport Convention. *Compositions:* One More Whiskey, Will This House Be Blessed, Forgotten The Blues, covered and recorded by many folk artists; Cruisin' On a Saturday Night, hit in Sweden for Jerry Williams; Outside the Wall and Bluebird recorded by Norma Waterson, 1998–99; Stockholm Sick Blues, The YoYos, 2000. *Recordings:* The Last LP, 1978; Out With a Bang, 1986; Break and Entry, 1989; Parlour Games, 1990; Sunday Best, 1992; Left Hand of Love, 1998; Appeared on: True Dare Or Promise, 1988; Blues Brittanica, 1993; The Wish and The Way, 1993; with Martin Simpson's Flash Company: Bluebird, 2000. *Publications:* Novels: The Electronic Meat Market, 1975; A Case For Charley, 1984; Charley Gets The Picture, 1985; Quake City, 1995; Perhaps She'll Die, 1997; Tooth and Nail, 1998; Stitch!, 1999; Grief!, 2001. *Membership:* Musicians' Union; PRS;

MCPS. *Current Management:* Jim Driver. *Address:* PO Box 4215, London SE23 2QD, England.

SPENCER, Jon; b. 1966, Hanover, NH, USA. Musician (guitar). m. Cristina Martinez. *Career:* Mem., Boss Hog, Pussy Galore; Founder mem., Jon Spencer Blues Explosion, 1990–. *Recordings:* Albums: with Boss Hog: Drinkin', Lechin' and Lyin', 1989; Cold Hands, 1990; Boss Hog, 1995; with Jon Spencer Blues Explosion: Jon Spencer Blues Explosion, 1992; Crypt Style, 1992; Extra Width, 1993; Mo' Width, 1994; Orange, 1994; Experimental Remixes, 1995; Now I Got Worry, 1996; Controversial Negro, 1997; Rocketship, 1997; Acme, 1998; Magical Colours, 2000; Plastic Fang, 2002. Singles: with Boss Hog: Girl Positive (EP), 1993; with Jon Spencer Blues Explosion: The Sound Of The Future Is Here Today, 1992; Shirt-jac, 1992; Son Of Sam, 1992; Big Yule Log Boogie, 1992; Train 3, 1993; Bellbottoms, 1995; Get With It, 1996; 2 Kindsa Love, 1996; Wail, 1997; Rocketship, 1997; Talk About The Blues, 1998; Vocals on: Bow Down To The Exit Sign, David Holmes, 2000. *Address:* c/o Mute Records, 136 W 18th St, New York, NY 10011, USA.

SPIDER JOHNSON, (Etienne); b. 5 Oct. 1963, London, England. Musician (drums, bass, guitar); Vocalist. 1 d. *Education:* Disc cutting course with LTS, Denmark Street, London; Electronics at Hackney College. *Career:* with Potato 5: World tour, 1989; Extensive television coverage; with The Deltones: European tour, 1991; with Nutty Boys (Madness); Crunch European tour, 1991; British tour, 1992; with Humble Souls: European tour and television coverage, 1993–94; Humble Souls and Night Trains World tour, 1994. *Recordings:* Do The Jerk, Potato 5, 1989; Five Alive, Potato 5, 1990; Silent River, Deltones, 1991; Crunch, Nutty Boys, 1991; Gone He's Gone, Stop Playing Around, Wendy Walker, 1991; Thoughts and Sound Paintings, 1993–94; Sleazeball, Night Trains, 1994. *Honours:* BPI International Reggae Award, 1992; Best Newcomer, for Wendy Walker. *Membership:* MCPS; PRS. *Current Management:* Concorde International. *Address:* Concorde House, Shepherds Bush Rd, London W12, England.

SPILLANE, Davy; b. 1959, Dublin, Ireland. Musician (uillean pipes, whistle). *Career:* Began playing pipes, aged 13; Founder member of Moving Hearts; Released several solo albums on Tara; Formed the Davy Spillane Band; Signed to Sony, 1993; Launched label, Burrenstone Records, 2000; Soloist in Riverdance; Currently an instrument maker; Collaborations: Elvis Costello; Bryan Adams; Kate Bush; Van Morrison; Tim Finn; Baba Maal; Afro Celt Sound System; Starred in film Traveller; Featured on film soundtracks: Lamb; Wuthering Heights; Eat the Peach; Rob Roy; Michael Collins. *Recordings:* Out of The Air (featuring Rory Gallagher), Atlantic Bridge, 1988; The Storm (with Moving Hearts), 1989; Shadow Hunter, 1990; Pipedreams, A Place Among The Stones, 1994; Sea of Dreams, 1998. *Honours:* Grammy Award, Best New Age Album, Celtic Solstice, Paul Winter and Friends, 2000. *Website:* www.davyspillane.com.

SPILLANE, John; b. 1961, Cork, Ireland. Vocalist; Songwriter. *Career:* Former member of traditional band Nomos; Songs recorded by artists including: Sinead Lohan; Karen Casey; Christy Moore; Has toured France, Italy, Ireland and the USA. *Recordings:* with Nomos: I Won't Be Afraid Anymore, 1995; Set You Free, 1997; solo: The Wells of The World, 1997; Will We Be Brilliant Or What?, 2002. *Honours:* Realta Irish song contest, winner (with Louis de Paor), 2001. *Current Management:* Verge Management, Henry A Crosbie Business Centre, Ossory Rd, Dublin 1, Republic of Ireland. *Website:* www.johnspillane.ie.

SPINDERELLA, (Dee Dee (Deidre) Roper); b. 3 Aug. 1971, New York, USA. DJ; Prod. 1 c. *Career:* Joined US female rap duo Salt-N-Pepa, 1987, as DJ 'Spinderella'; Signed to London Records, 1993; Signed to MCA Records, 1997. *Recordings:* Albums: A Salt With A Deadly Pepa, 1988; Blacks' Magic, 1990; Very Necessary, 1993; Brand New, 1997; Salt-N-Pepa... The Best Of, 2000. Singles include: Push It, 1988; Shake Your Thang (It's Your Thing), 1988; Twist and Shout, 1988; Expression, 1990; Do You Want Me, 1991; Let's Talk About Sex, 1991; Let's Talk About AIDS (re-write of Let's Talk About Sex), 1992; You Showed Me, 1991; Start Me Up, 1992; Shoop, 1993; Whatta Man (with En Vogue), 1994; Ain't Nothin But A She Thing, 1995; Champagne, 1996; Gitty Up, 1998; Brick Track Vs Gitty Up, Pt I and II, 2000; Contributions to various compilations and soundtrack albums. *Honours:* Platinum discs and Gold discs for albums and singles; Grammy for Best Rap Performance by a Duo or Group, for None Of Your Business, 1994; Three MTV Awards, 1994. *Address:* c/o CD Enterprises Inc, 7531 Leesburg Pike, Suite 201, Fallschurch, VA 22043, USA.

SPINELLI, Philip Antony; b. 30 March 1950, Newcastle upon Tyne, England. Musician (drums, keyboards); Vocalist. m. Biliana Mancheva, 19 Oct. 1994, 1 s. *Education:* Berklee College, Boston, USA; Masterclass with Bob Armstrong, PIT, London. *Career:* Founder member, Brand X; Tours with Atomic Rooster; Edwin Starr; Rick Kenton (Roxy Music); Session work with: Chris Wood (Traffic); Pino Palladino; Several UK television appearances; Performed for HM The Queen and Royal Family, Buckingham Palace. *Recordings:* Albums: Brand X: First album (with Phil Collins); Locust: Alpha Waves; Singles with Atomic Rooster. *Membership:* Performing Rights Society.

Current Management: Data Sound. *Address:* 19 Wharfdale, Hemel Hempstead, Herts HP2 5TQ, England.

SPINETTI, Henry Anthony George; b. 31 March 1951, Cwm, South Wales. Musician (drums). Divorced, 2 s. *Career:* Tours, concerts include: Eric Clapton, 1979–82, 1993, 1995; Tina Turner, 1984, 1985, 1990; Joan Armatrading, 1972, 1990; Neil Sedaka, 1974; Andy Fairweather-Low, 1970–76; Procol Harum, 1994; Bill Wyman, 1993, 1994; Television appearances include: Top of the Pops; Radio includes: Wembley Concert with Tina Turner, 1990. *Recordings:* Albums include: with Joan Armatrading: Show Some Emotion, 1977; To The Limit, 1978; Rough Mix, Townsend and Lane, 1977; City To City, Gerry Rafferty, 1978; with Eric Clapton: Just One Night, 1979; Another Ticket, 1981; All The Best, Paul McCartney; Gone Troppo, George Harrison, 1982; Willie and The Poor Boys, 1985; Best of Dark Horse, 1989; All Day Thumbsucker Revisited, 1995; Blue, with Eric Clapton, 1999; Painting Signs, with Eric Bibb, 2001; Film soundtracks include: Lethal Weapon; Color of Money. *Membership:* Musicians' Union.

SPITERI, Sharleen Eugenie; b. 7 Nov. 1967, Glasgow, Scotland. Vocalist; Musician (guitar, piano, organ, harmonica). 1 d. *Career:* Formed Texas with John McElhone, 1988. *Compositions:* Albums: Southside, 1989; Mothers Heaven, 1991; Ricks Road, 1993; White On Blonde, 1997; The Hush, 1999. *Recordings:* Singles: I Don't Want a Lover, 1989; Everyday Now, 1989; Alone With You, 1992; Tired of Being Alone, 1992; So Called Friend, 1993; You Owe It All To Me, 1993; So In Love With You, 1994; Say What You Want, 1997; Halo, 1997; Black Eyed Boy, 1997; Put Your Arms Around Me, 1997; Insane/ Say What You Want, with Wu Tang Clan, 1998; In Our Lifetime, 1999; Summer Son, 1999; When We Are Together, 1999; In Demand, 2000; Inner Smile, 2001; Albums: Southside, 1989; Mothers Heaven, 1991; Ricks Road, 1993; White On Blonde, 1997; The Hush, 1999; The Greatest Hits, 2000; Guest vocals on: Bad Time, The Jayhawks, 1995. *Honours:* Capital Radio, Best Female Vocal; Malta Music Prize, Best Intl; Ivor Novello Award, Best Collection of Songs, 1998. *Current Management:* G R Management, 974 Pollokshaw Rd, Shawlands, Glasgow G41 2HA, Scotland.

SPIZZ, Julian, (Spizzman); b. 17 Sept. 1968, Florence, Italy. Vocalist; Composer; Performer. *Education:* Studies in field of experimental singing. *Career:* Member, Trinovox; Appearances in major German televison and radio programmes, 1994; Concerts in major German, Swiss, Austrian towns (Berlin, Bremen, Lübeck, Stuttgart, Basel, Vienna, Innsbruck), 1994–95; Soundtrack, radio play, Bavarian State radio, 1995. *Recordings:* Albums: Incanto, Trinovox, 1994; Voices, Trinovox; Sarband, The Bulgarian Voices, 1994; Earborn, Trinovox and Various Artists, 1995. *Honours:* Italian National Award, vocal artists: Quartetto Cetra (with Trinovox), 1994. *Membership:* SIAE; GEMA. *Address:* c/o Ulrich Balss, Jaro Records, Bismarck 43, 28203 Bremen 1, Germany.

SPORTY SPICE. See: **CHISHOLM, Melanie Jayne**.

SPRINGER, Scott; b. 1 April 1959, Birmingham, Alabama, USA. Vocalist; Musician (guitar, bass guitar). m. Helen C Akin, 2 Aug. 1980, 2 s., 1 d. *Career:* Tour with band Halo, USA, Canada, 1989–93; Jesus Music, 1990; 6 Christian Radio No. 1 songs, USA. *Recordings:* Halo; Heaven Calling; Hello Forever, 1993; Rock Power Praise. *Publications:* CCM; Release. *Membership:* BMI. *Current Management:* Halo Productions Inc. *Address:* 311 Cherokee Dr., Clanton, AL 35046, USA.

SPRINGFIELD, Rick, (Richard Springthorpe); b. 23 Aug. 1949, Sydney, Australia. Vocalist; Musician (guitar, piano); Actor. *Career:* Member, Jordy Boys; Rock House; MPD Band; Zoot; Solo artiste, 1972–; Also television actor; Guest appearances include: The Rockford Files; Wonder Woman; The Six Million Dollar Man; Leading role, General Hospital; Actor, film, Hard To Hold, 1984. *Recordings:* Albums include: Beginnings, 1972; Comic Book, 1974; Heroes, 1974; Wait For The Night, 1976; Working Class Dog, 1981; Success Hasn't Spoiled Me Yet, 1982; Living In Oz, 1983; Tao, 1985; Rock of Life, 1988; Karma, 1998; VH-1: Behind The Music, 2000; Singles include: Human Touch; Speak To The Sky; Jessie's Girl (No. 1, USA), 1981; I've Done Everything For You; Don't Talk To Strangers; Love Somebody, used in film Hard To Hold; Bruce. *Current Management:* Ron Weisner Entertainment, PO Box 261640, Encino, CA 91426, USA.

SPRINGSTEEN, Bruce; b. 23 Sept. 1949, New Jersey, USA. Vocalist; Songwriter; Musician (guitar). m. (1) Julianne Phillips (divorced), (2) Patti Scialfa, 1 s., 1 d. *Career:* Recording artist, 1972–; Formed own band, The E-Street Band, 1974; Numerous national and world-wide tours, include: MUSE No-Nukes Concerts, 1979; The River tour, 1980; Born In The USA tour, 1984; Tunnel of Love Express tour, 1988; Amnesty International Human Rights Now! tour, 1988; North American tour, 1992; Numerous benefit and charity concerts. *Compositions:* Numerous songs include: Born To Run; Blinded By The Light (also recorded by Manfred Mann); Fire (recorded by the Pointer Sisters); Because The Night (recorded by Patti Smith); Badlands; Hungry Heart; Dancing In The Dark; Born In The USA; I'm On Fire; I'm Goin' Down; Fire; Pink Cadillac; Cover Me; 57 Channels and Nothin' On; Better Days; Glory Days. *Recordings:* Albums: Greetings From Asbury Park, 1973; The

Wild The Innocent and The E Street Shuffle, 1973; Born To Run, 1975; Darkness On The Edge of Town, 1978; The River (No. 1, USA), 1980; Nebraska, 1982; Born In The USA (No. 1, USA and UK), 1984; Live 1975–85 (No. 1, USA), 1986; Tunnel of Love (No. 1, USA and UK), 1987; Human Touch (No. 1, UK), 1992; Lucky Town, 1992; In Concert – MTV Plugged, 1993; Greatest Hits, 1995; The Ghost of Tom Joad, 1995; Live In New York City, 2001; The Rising, 2002; Contributor, We Are The World, USA For Africa, 1985; Sun City, Artists Against Apartheid, 1986; Singles include: Hungry Heart, 1980; Dancing In The Dark, 1984; Cover Me, 1984; I'm On Fire, 1985; Born In The USA, 1985; My Hometown, 1985; I'm Going Down, 1985; War, 1986; Brilliant Disguise, 1987; Tougher Than The Rest, 1988; Chimes of Freedom, 1988; 57 Channels, 1992; Streets of Philadelphia, 1994; Secret Garden, 1995; My Hometown, 1998; Tougher Than the Rest, 1999; Lonesome Day, 2002. *Honours:* 2 Grammy Awards: Best Male Rock Vocalist, 1984, 1987; BRIT Award, Best International Solo Artist, 1986; Inducted, Rock 'n' Roll Hall of Fame, 1988; Numerous Platinum and Gold discs; Academy Award, Best Original Song In a Movie, Streets of Philadelphia, 1994. *Current Management:* Jon Landau Management, 40 W Elm St, Greenwich, CT 06830, USA. *Website:* www.brucespringsteen.net.

SPRUNG, Roger; b. 29 Aug. 1930, New York, USA. Folk Vocalist; Musician (5-string banjo); Teacher; Entertainer. m. Nancy, 24 May 1990, 2 d. *Career:* Tour with Kay Starr; Jimmy Dean TV Show; An American Experience TV Show; Dean Martin TV Show; Garry Moore Show; Appearances include: Philadelphia Folk Festival; Lincoln Center, New York; Carnegie Hall, New York. *Recordings:* 46 including: Bluegrass Gold, Vols 1–2, 1976; The Philadelphia Folk Festival, 1977; 44th Annual Galax Fiddler's Convention, 1980; Pound Ridge Fiddler's Celebration, 1981; Irish Grass, 1983; The Irish Bluegrass Connection, 1983; Southwest Winds, 1983; Let's Pick, 1988; Thyme and Beyond, 1989; Stompin' Stuff, 1990; Recordings in the Library of Congress and Smithsonian/Folkway. *Honours:* World Champion 5 string banjo player. *Current Management:* Sprung Enterprises. *Address:* 7 Papoose Hill Rd, Newtown, CT 06470, USA.

SPRY, Bro, (Crispin Luke Robinson); b. 3 Nov. 1966, London, England. Musician (congas, shakers, djembs, drumkit, percussion). Separated, 2 d. *Education:* City and East London College; Kent University; Studied with Bobby Sanabria, USA; John Amira, USA; Bob Armstrong, UK; Robin Jones, UK. *Career:* First recordings with: Manassah; Soul II Soul; Yazz; Youth; Young Disciples; Signed to Polygram as part of Galliano, 1991–; Live work: Tours with Galliano include: Europe; Japan; Australia; USA; Hong Kong; Scandinavia; Marvin Gaye Tribute Concert (feauring: Al Jarreau; George Duke; Pointer Sisters; Chaka Khan; Leon Ware; Wah Wah Watson; Chuck Rainey; James Gadson), 1992; Roy Ayers, 1995; Straight No Chaser Jazz Festival, Bheki Mselku. *Recordings:* First and second albums: Soul II Soul; 3 albums with Galliano, include various compositions; Adam F; Lamb; Roni Size; Valerie Etienne. *Membership:* Musicians' Union. *Current Management:* Steve Baker, Worldchief Management, 132 Liverpool Rd, London N1, England.

SQUAREPUSHER. See: **JENKINSON, Tom.**

SQUIRE, Chris; b. 4 March 1948, London, England. Musician (bass). *Career:* Founder member, UK progressive rock group Yes, 1968–; Concerts include: Support to Cream, farewell concert, Royal Albert Hall, 1968; Support to Janis Joplin, Royal Albert Hall, 1969; Montreux TV Festival, 1969; Support to The Nice, Royal Festival Hall, 1970; Reading Festival, 1975; Yesshows '91 – Round The World In 80 Dates Tour, 1991. *Recordings:* Albums: Yes, 1969; Time and a Word, 1970; The Yes Album, 1971; Fragile, 1971; Close To The Edge, 1972; Yessongs, 1973; Tales From Topographic Oceans, 1973; Relayer, 1974; Yesterdays, 1975; Going For The One, 1977; Tormato, 1978; Drama, 1980; Classic Yes, 1982; 90125, 1983; 9012 Live – The Solos, 1986; The Big Generator, 1987; Union, 1991; Yesstory, 1991; Keys to Ascension, 1996; Open Your Eyes, 1998; Ladder, 1999; Magnification, 2001; Keys To The Studio Ascension, 2001; Solo album: Fish Out of Water, 1975; Singles with Yes include: Roundabout; Wonderous Stories, Going For The One; Owner of a Lonely Heart; Leave It; It Can Happen; Cinema; Love Will Find a Way; Rhythm of Love; Lift Me Up. *Honours:* Gold Ticket, Madison Square Garden, 1978; Grammy Award, Best Rock Instrumental Performance, Cinema, 1985. *Current Management:* Big Bear Management, 9 Hillgate St, London W8 7SP, England.

SQUIRE, John; b. 24 Nov. 1962, Broadheath, Greater Manchester, England. Musician (guitar); Vocalist; Songwriter. *Career:* Mem., the Stone Roses, 1984–96; Formed, The Seahorses, 1997–99; Solo artiste, 2001–. *Recordings:* Albums: with the Stone Roses: The Stone Roses, 1989; Turn Into Stone, 1992; Second Coming, 1994; The Very Best Of The Stone Roses, 2002; with The Seahorses: Do It Yourself, 1997; Solo: Time Changes Everything, 2002. Singles: with the Stone Roses: Made of Stone, 1989; She Bangs The Drums, 1989; Fool's Gold/What The World Is Waiting For, 1989; Elephant Stone, 1990; One Love, 1990; I Wanna Be Adored, 1991; Waterfall, 1992; I Am The Resurrection, 1993; Love Spreads, 1994; Ten Storey Love Song, 1995; Begging You, 1995; with The Seahorses: Love Is The Law, 1997; Love Me And Leave Me, 1997; You Can Talk To Me, 1997; Blinded By The Sun, 1997; Solo: Joe

Louis, 2002. *Address:* c/o Hall or Nothing Publicity, 11 Poplar Mews, Uxbridge Rd, London W12 7JS, England. *Website:* www.johnsquire.com.

STAFF, Bryan Alastair; b. 16 May 1950, Christchurch, New Zealand. DJ; Rock Music Journalist; Photographer. *Education:* BA Linguistics, Auckland University; Commercial radio. *Career:* Became an announcer, age 19, commercial radio; Specialised in local music, largely ignored on radio otherwise; Formed punk label, Ripper Records; In Auckland continued as rock writer, reviewer, photographer to date; Ran Ripper Records which began with New Zealand's first punk album: AK79, 1979; Ripper produced 5 albums, given over next 5 years. *Publications:* Co-author with Sheran Ashley: The Record Years, a history of New Zealand record labels. *Membership:* Recording Industry Asscn of New Zealand. *Address:* PO Box 5154, Wellesley St, Auckland, New Zealand.

STAFFORD, Jo; b. 12 Nov. 1920, Coalinga, California, USA. Vocalist. m. Paul Weston. *Career:* Member, country music act, with sisters; Freelance singer on radio with vocal group, The Pied Pipers; Appeared, radio with Tommy Dorsey, 1939–42; Solo recording artiste, 1940s–60s; Recorded spoof albums with husband as Jonathan and Darlene Edwards; Retired from public performance, 1959; Founder, own Corinthian record label. *Recordings include:* Singles: Little Man With a Candy Cigar; Manhattan Serenade; For You; Yes Indeed (duet with Sly Oliver); Candy (with Johnny Mercer); That's For Me; Serenade of The Bells; Some Enchanted Evening; Tennessee Waltz; My Darling My Darling (with Gordon McRae); Whispering Hope (with Gordon McRae); Make Love To Me; Shrimp Boats; Keep It a Secret; Jambalaya; You Belong To Me; Spotlight on Jo Stafford; Numerous albums, 1953–, including several with Gordon McRae; The Two Of Us, 2001.

STAFFORD, Simon; b. Sheffield, England. Musician (bass). *Career:* Member, The Longpigs. *Recordings:* Singles: Happy Again, 1995; She Said, 1995; Jesus Christ, 1995; Far, 1996; On and On, 1996; Lost Myself, 1996; Blue Skies, 1999; The Frank Sonata, 1999; Albums: The Sun Is Often Out, 1996; Mobile Home, 1999; Also features on: Late Night Final, Richard Hawley, 2001.

STAGG, Mark Jeffrey; b. 26 May 1961, Sheffield, Yorkshire, England. Prod; Engineer; Programmer; Remixer. *Education:* Manchester School of Sound Recording. *Career:* Member of bands: Lionrock; Pro-Gress; Much studio work includes: Production: Eskimos and Egypt; Sparks; Pro-Gress; MC Tunes; Engineering: K-Klass; Lionrock; The Grio; Björk; TC 1992; Rednex; Erasure; Remixing: Nitzer Ebb; The Shamen; Supreme Love Gods; Sweet Mercy. *Recordings:* Co-writer and engineer, Rhythm is a Mystery, K-Klass (Top 3 Hit UK). *Membership:* Musicians' Union; PRS. *Current Management:* DEF. *Address:* 21 Premier House, 313 Kilburn Lane, London W9 3EG, England.

STAINTON, Christopher Robert; b. 22 March 1944, Sheffield, Yorkshire, England. Musician (bass, piano). m. Gail Ellyn Travi, 25 June 1970, 1 d. *Career:* Tours and recordings with: Joe Cocker, 1966–72, 1988–92; Concerts include: Woodstock; Tours and recordings with Eric Clapton, 1979–85, 1993–. *Recordings:* Albums include: with Joe Cocker: With a Little Help From My Friends, 1968; Joe Cocker, 1969; Mad Dogs and Englishmen, 1971; Something To Say, 1973; with Eric Clapton: Just One Night, 1980; Money and Cigarettes, 1983; with The Who: Quadrophenia, film soundtrack, 1979; Other recordings with: Jimmy Smith; Alvin Lee; Maddy Prior; Leon Russell; Spooky Tooth; Marianne Faithfull; Ian Hunter; Jim Capaldi; Gary Brooker; Bryn Haworth; Stephen Bishop. *Membership:* PRS. *Current Management:* Roger Forrester Management. *Address:* 18 Harley House, Regent's Park, London NW1 5HE, England.

STAKENAS, Virgis; b. 10 Aug. 1953, Lithuania. Country Vocalist; Songwriter; Musician; Prod. m. Ramute Stakeniene, 1 d. *Education:* Siauliai University; Siauliai Music School. *Career:* Produced Country Music Festivals In Lithuania; Played In More Than 40 Big Country, Bluegrass, Pop Music Festivals in USA, Canada, Holland, Germany, Denmark, Sweden, Czechoslovakia, Poland, Russia, Latvia, Estonia, Lithuania. *Compositions:* More Than 250 Songs, 1973–98. *Recordings:* Life; The Evening; Here Is Your Home; Siauliai; Song-Book; Jumbo; 615. *Publications:* Balades, 1995. *Honours:* Too Numerous. *Membership:* International Bluegrass Music Asscn. *Address:* Musos 7, Vijoliu k, LT 5400, Siauliu r, Lithuania.

STALEY, Layne Thomas; b. 22 Aug. 1967, Bellevue, Washington, USA. Rock Vocalist. *Career:* Lead singer, US rock groups: Alice In Chains; Mad Season; Appearances with Alice In Chains: Clash of The Titans, 1991; Support tour, Van Halen, 1991; Support tour, Ozzy Osbourne, 1992; Brazil, 1993; Lollapalooza, 1993. *Recordings:* Albums: with Alice In Chains: Facelift, 1990; Sap, 1991; Dirt, 1992; Jar of Flies, 1994; Alice In Chains, 1995; Unplugged, 1996; Music Bank, 1999; Live, 2000; with Mad Season: Above, 1995; Also appears on: Working Class Hero, 1995; Another Brick in the Wall, 1995; Faculty, 1998. *Honours:* MTV Award, Would. *Current Management:* Susan Silver Management, 207 First Ave S, Third Floor, Seattle, WA 98104, USA.

STALLINGS, Felix. See: **FELIX DA HOUSECAT.**

STAMPLEY, Joe Ronald; b. 6 June 1943, Springhill, Louisiana, USA. Country vocalist Musician (guitar, piano, ukulele); Songwriter. *Career:* First recorded for Imperial Records, 1957; Lead vocalist and member of pop/rock group the Cutups, 1960; Later known as the Uniques, 1963; US hit with Not Too Long Ago, 1965; Solo, early 1970s; Staff writer for Gallico Music; Many country hits mostly on Epic Records, occasionally with Moe Bandy, 1971–89; Moe and Joe collaborations included controversial parody of Boy George, Where's The Dress, 1984; Continues to perform with band, The Tennessee Fat Cats. *Compositions include:* Bring It On Home To Your Woman; How Lucky Can One Man Be; If You Touch Me. *Recordings include:* Soul Song; All These Things; Just Good Ol' Boys (with Moe Bandy); Roll On Big Mama; I'm Still Loving You; Albums: Soul Song, 1973; Take Me Home To Somewhere, I'm Still Loving You, 1974; All These Things, 1976; Just Good Ol' Boys (with Moe Bandy), 1979. *Honours:* Two CMA Awards, Vocal Duo of the Year (with Moe Bandy); Louisiana Hall of Fame; Texas Country Music Asscn Hall of Fame. *Address:* c/o PO Box 150006, Nashville, TN 37215, USA.

STAN, Mircea; b. 2 Oct. 1943, Romania. Musician (trombone). *Education:* 11 years study at Music High School and Conservatory in Bucharest, 1958–69. *Career:* Moved to Finland, 1970s; Formed own quartet, 1972; Ran several groups including: Sextet formed for Pori Festival, 1978; Trombone quartet, toured Finland, 1980s; Played in UMO (New Music Orchestra); Also in bands run by: Heikki Sarmanto; Edward Vesala; Seppo Paakunainen; Taught trombone at Sibelius Academy; Coaches amateur jazz bands. *Recordings:* Album: Para Los Trombones, with own sextet, late 1980s; Also appears on: Mau-mau, Edward Vesala, 1982; Thad Jones, Mel Lewis and UMO; Anthony Braxton. *Address:* Käsityöläisenkatu 25 E, 00750 Helsinki, Finland.

STAN, Ollie; b. 28 May 1969, Kronstadt, Germany. Composer; Arranger; Musician (keyboards); Prod. *Education:* Over 10 years lessons: piano, rhythm/percussion. *Career:* Tour with group: Bang!, Germany, with Dr Alban; 2 Unlimited; DJ Bobo, Mega Dance Festival, 1994. *Recordings:* Papa Winnie: You Are My Sunshine, 1994; Go: Your Body My Body, 1994; Bang! You Know I Know, 1994; Slavik/Kemmler: Indian Spirits (Dance Mixes), 1994; Powersound and Lori Glori: Freedom Forever, 1995. *Honours:* Gold, prospective Platinum for: Papa Winnie. *Address:* c/o Advance Music, Ovelgönnerweg 13, 21335 Luneburg, Germany.

STANCHEV, Georgi; b. 1 June 1951, Sofia, Bulgaria. Composer; Arranger; Lyricist; Prod. m. Tsvetanca Georgieva, 3 Dec. 1976, 1 s., 2 d. *Career:* Solo vocalist, guitarist, Diana Express, 1979–81; Festivals, television; Tours: USSR, Cuba, Germany, 1984; Hungary, 1987; USSR, Romania, Israel, 1988; USSR, 1989; Worked with Hungarian group The Times, recording and performing, 1986; President, Georgia-Venice Music House; Executive Musical Director, Peak Music Record Company. *Compositions include:* Soul; Whisper. *Recordings:* First single, 1980; Whisper, 1982; Third single, 1982; Albums: Lovers, 1983; A Handful of Sands, 1985; Be a Star Up To The End, 1991; Venice, 1995. *Honours:* Best Song of Year, Soul, 1980; Prizes, Bulgarian Television, Knoque Festival, Belgium, 1982; Prize, Dresden Festival, 1983; Best Singer, Caven, Ireland, 1984; Performer's Prize, Valletta, Malta, 1984; Grand Prize, Composer, Siofok, Hungary, 1986; Best Singer, Best Album of Year, 1991. *Address:* Suhodolska str, 2 bl, 122 vh A, ap4, 1373 Sofia, Bulgaria.

STANDAERT, Luc; b. 17 Jan. 1958, Ghent, Belgium. Music Publisher; Artist Man. m. Tine Lecompte, 3 April 1981. *Education:* Architecture; Scenography. *Career:* Scenographer, 1979–82; Show Director, Tour Manager, 1982–88; Music Publisher, Artist Manager, 1988–; Business ventures: Tempo BVBA; Tempo Media Nv; Yellow House BVBA; Taste My Music. *Compositions:* Publisher of songs performed by: Arno; Dinky Toys; Francis Goya; Viktor Lazlo; Jack Radics; Jean Bosco Safari; Music for films includes: Koko Flanel; Daens; Marie. *Publications:* Vrije Radio In Vlaanderen, 1986. *Membership:* SABAM; URBEM; BVBI. *Address:* Krijgslaan 61, 9000 Gent, Belgium.

STANGER, William John Nigel; b. 16 Jan. 1943, Newcastle upon Tyne, England. Architect; Developer; Musician (saxophone, keyboards). 2 d. *Education:* Oxford University, Newcastle University, MA (Oxon), BA, BArch. *Education:* Piano, 1947–; Saxophone, 1959–; School education. *Career:* Performed with various bands in London including: Alexis Korner, John Mayall Bluesbreakers, Alan Price Set, Herbie Goins, Night Timers, 1963–66; Performed with Newcastle Big Band (with Sting), East Side Torpedoes, Little Mo, 1996–; Currently with Crosbys; Various television and radio broadcasts. *Recordings:* with John Mayall: Live At Klooks Kleek; with Alan Price: Any Day Now; Album with Newcastle Big Band; with Alexis Korner: Bootleg Him, 1993. *Membership:* ARCUK; Musicians' Union; Equity. *Address:* 51 Brandling Pl. S, Jesmond, Newcastle upon Tyne NE2 4RU, England.

STANLEY, Bob; b. 25 Dec. 1965, Horsham, Sussex, England. Musician (keyboards, programming); Prod. *Career:* Journalist, writer, NME, Melody Maker, MOJO; Founding mem., Saint Etienne, 1988–; Worked with guest vocalists, joined by Sarah Cracknell, 1991; Launched own label, Emidisc. *Recordings:* Albums: with Saint Etienne: Foxbase Alpha, 1991; So Tough, 1993; You Need A Mess Of Help To Stand Alone (compilation), 1993; Tiger Bay, 1994; I Love To Paint (compilation), 1995; Fairytales From Saint Etienne

(compilation), 1995; Too Young To Die (compilation), 1995; Casino Classics (compilation), 1996; Continental (compilation), 1997; Good Humor, 1998; The Misadventures Of Saint Etienne (soundtrack), 1999; Built On Sand (compilation), 1999; Sound Of Water, 2000; Interlude (compilation), 2001; Smash The System (compilation), 2001; Finisterre, 2002; Singles: with Saint Etienne: Only Love Can Break Your Heart, 1990; Kiss And Make Up, 1990; Nothing Can Stop Us, 1991; Join Our Club, 1992; Avenue, 1992; You're In A Bad Way, 1993; Hobart Paving/Who Do You Think You Are?, 1993; I Was Born On Christmas Day (with Tim Burgess), 1993; Pale Movie, 1994; Like A Motorway, 1994; Hug My Soul, 1994; Reserection (with Etienne Daho), 1995; He's On The Phone, 1995; Xmas '95 (EP), 1995; Angel/Burnt Out Car, 1996; Valentines Day '97 (EP), 1997; Sylvie, 1998; The Bad Photographer, 1998; Bronx Dogs Mixes, 1998; Lose That Girl, 1998; Xmas '98 (EP), 1998; Lover Plays The Bass, 1999; Places To Visit (EP), 2000; Saturday, 1999; How We Used To Live, 2000; Heart Failed (In The Back Of A Taxi), 2000; Boy Is Crying, 2001; Asleep At The Wheels Of Steel (EP), 2002; Action, 2002; contribution to Gone, David Holmes, 1996; Tell Me Why, Paul Van Dyk, 2000. *Address:* c/o Mantra Recordings, 17–19 Alma Rd, London SW18 1AA, England. *Website:* www.saint.etienne.net.

STANLEY, Damian Mark; b. 18 Aug. 1967, Nottingham, England. Prod; Writer; Engineer; Musician (keyboards). *Career:* Recording artist with Mad; Overview; The Deadbeats; Owner, Spacehopper Recordings and Ill Communications; Remixes: Moodswings; Whycliffe; Turntable Orchestra; Ashley Beadle; Jimi Polo; Alabama 3 (DIY Dub); Humdrum (soundtrack to film Hackers); Chrissie Hynde; Sly and Love Child; Chumbawamba; Mind the Gap and Leena Conquest; Recording artist as MAD; Overview, The Deadbeats; DIY, DEA, Love Brothers; Remixes for: Secret Knowledge; Century Falls; Owner, Spacehopper Records and DIY Communications. *Membership:* PRS; MCPS. *Address:* Spacehopper, PO Box 350, Nottingham NG3 6DF, England.

STANLEY, Ian Charles; b. 28 Feb. 1957. Record Prod; Musician (keyboards). *Career:* Keyboard Player, Tears For Fears; Produced Tracks for Lloyd Cole & The Commotions; A-ha; Pretenders; Human League; Saturnine; Tori Amos; Mozaic; Jimmy Nail; Rialto; The Aloof and Ultra; Worked with Republica; Barenaked Ladies; Natalie Imbruglia. *Compositions:* Everybody Wants To Rule The World. *Recordings:* with Tears For Fears including: Shout (Number 1, USA), 1985; Everybody Wants To Rule The World (Number 1, USA), 1985; Head Over Heels, 1985; I Believe, 1985; Shout; Everybody Wants To Rule The World; Into The Fire. *Current Management:* Isisglow Ltd, The Wool Hall, Castle Corner, Beckington, Somerset BA3 6TA, England.

STANLEY, Paul, (Paul Eisen); b. 20 Jan. 1950, Queens, New York, USA. Vocalist; Musician (guitar). *Career:* Member, guitarist, US rock group Kiss, 1973–; Appearances include: Debut, Academy of Music, New York, 1973; Numerous tours include UK, 1976; US Dynasty Tour, 1979; Palladium, New York, 1980; US tour, with Cheap Trick, 1988; Marquee Club, 1988; US tour, 1990; Revenge '92 Tour, 1992; Concert, Palace of Auburn Hills, Missouri, recorded for video, album, Kiss Alive III, 1992. *Compositions:* Many for Kiss. *Recordings:* Albums: Kiss, 1974; Hotter Than Hell, 1974; Dressed To Kill, 1975; Destroyer, 1976; The Originals, 1976; Rock and Roll Over, 1976; Kiss Alive II, 1977; Double Platinum, 1978; Dynasty, 1979; Kiss Unmasked, 1980; Music From The Elder, 1981; Creatures of The Night, 1982; Lick It Up, 1983; Animalize, 1984; Asylum, 1985; Crazy Nights, 1987; Smashes Thrashes and Hits, 1988; Hot In The Shade, 1989; Revenge, 1992; Kiss Alive III, 1993; Unplugged, 1996; Psycho Circus, 1998; Box Set, 2001; Solo album: Paul Stanley, 1978; Contributor, Hear 'N' Aid, charity project for Ethiopian famine relief, 1986; Numerous singles include: Rock 'N' Roll All Nite; Beth; Detroit Rock City; I Was Made For Lovin' You; I Love It Loud; Lick It Up; Heaven's On Fire; Tears Are Falling; Crazy Crazy Nights; Reason To Live; Hide Your Heart; Forever; God Gave Rock and Roll To You, used in film Bill and Ted's Bogus Adventure, 1992. *Honours:* Footprints at Grauman's Chinese Theatre, 1976; Gold Ticket, Madison Square Garden, 1979; Inducted into Hollywood's Rock Walk, 1993; Kiss Day proclaimed in Los Angeles, 1993; Numerous Gold and Platinum discs. *Current Management:* Entertainment Services Unlimited, Main St Plaza 100, Suite 303, Voorhees, NJ 08043, USA. *Address:* c/o Doc McGhee, McGhee Entertainment, 8730 Sunset Blvd, Suite 175, Los Angeles, CA 90069, USA.

STANNERS, Malcolm James; b. 27 Dec. 1965, Derby, England. Sound Engineer; Programmer; Prod. *Education:* Higher Diploma, Musical Instrument Technology. *Career:* Sound Engineer, Programmer, Paradise Studios, London, England, 1988–89; Clients include: Boy George, Bill Wyman, Errol Brown; Films: Madame Suzatska; Incredibly Strange Picture Show; Studio Owner, 4 Real Studios, 1989–; Dance Music Producer and Artist; Co-Founder, Salt Tank, London Records. *Recordings include:* Singles: Ease the Pressure, 1991; Ethereal EP, 1992; 4 EPs, 1993–94; Peel Session EP, 1994; Eugina, 1996; Swell, 1996; Album: Science and Nature, 1996; Wavebreaks, 1998; The Energy, 2001; Compilation Albums: Cafe Del Mar 2; Ministry of Sound; Cream; In the Mix 96; Horizons; Chill Out 2; Trance Europe Express; Essential Mix 2; Remixes: Sueño Latino; Chakra; Paul Van Dyk; Orbital; Chicane; Man With No Name; Hawkwind; TV Incidental Music: Grandstand, Euro 1996; Home Front; EastEnders; Hollyoaks; Wish You Were

Here; Tomorrow's World. *Honours:* Reached Top 5, twice, Indie Singles Chart; Top 10, Indie Album Chart; Top 40, UK Singles Chart. *Membership:* MCPS; PRS. *Current Management:* Doug Smith Associates, London, England. *Website:* www.salttank.co.uk.

STANSFIELD, Lisa; b. 11 April 1966, Rochdale, Lancashire, England. Vocalist. *Career:* Television presenter, Razzamatazz, ITV, 1982–1986; Formed Blue Zone, 1984; Singer, Coldcut, 1989; Solo singer, 1989–; Tours and concerts include: All Around The World Tour, 1990; Arista Records 15th Anniversary concert, 1990; Prince's Trust Rock Gala, Wembley Arena, 1990; Rock In Rio II, Brazil, 1991; Simple Truth benefit concert for Kurdish Refugees, Wembley Arena, 1991; Red Hot and Dance AIDS benefit concert, London, 1991; Amnesty International's Big 30 Concert, ITV, 1991; Dance Energy Christmas House Party, BBC2, 1992. *Compositions:* Tracks on own albums co-written and produced. *Recordings:* Albums: Affection (No. 2, UK), 1989; Real Love, 1991; So Natural, 1993; Lisa Stansfield, 1997; Swing, 1999; Never, Never Gonna Give You Up, 1999; Face Up, 2001; Biography (Greatest Hits), 2003. Singles include: with Coldcut: People Hold On, 1989; Solo: This Is The Right Time, 1989; All Around The World (No. 1, UK; R&B No. 1, USA), 1989; Live Together, 1990; What Did I Do To You, 1990; You Can't Deny It, 1990; This Is The Right Time, 1990; Change, 1991; All Woman, 1992; Time To Make You Mine, 1992; Set Your Loving Free, 1992; Someday (I'm Coming Back), from film The Bodyguard, 1993; In All The Right Places, 1993; So Natural, 1993; Make It Right, 1994; Real Thing, 1997; Lisa Stansfield, EP, 1998; Remixes, 1998; 831, 2001; Featured vocalist, Do They Know It's Christmas (reworked), Band Aid II (No. 1, UK), 1989; Contributor, Red Hot and Blue AIDS benefit record, 1990. *Honours:* Variety Club of Great Britain, Recording Artist of 1989, 1990; BRIT Awards: Best Newcomer, 1990; Best Female Artist, 1992; Ivor Novello Awards: Best Contemporary Song Award, 1990; International Hit of the Year, 1991; Nordoff-Robbins Music Therapy Charity, Best Newcomer, 1990; Rolling Stone Critics Poll Winner, Best British Female Singer, 1990; ASCAP Award, All Around The World, 1991. *Current Management:* Big Life Management. *Address:* 15 Little Portland St, London W1N 5DE, England. *Website:* www.lisa-stansfield.com.

STAPLES, Neville; Vocalist; Musician (percussion). *Career:* Member, The Special AKA, 1978–81; Numerous tours and television appearances; Debut album produced by Elvis Costello; Established own record label, 2-Tone; Left Band, formed Fun Boy Three; Rejoined new version of Spcials, 1990s. *Recordings:* with Specials: Singles: Gangsters, 1979; A Message to You Rudi, 1979; Too Much Too Young (No. 1, UK). 1980; Rat Race, 1980; Do Nothing, 1980; Stereotype, 1980; Ghost Town (No. 1, UK), 1981; Albums: The Specials, 1979; More Specials, 1980; Specials Singles, 1991; Skinhead Girl, 2000; Stereotypes As & Bs, 2000; Conquering Ruler, 2001; With Fun Boy Three: Singles: The Lunatics Have Taken Over the Asylum, 1981; It Ain't What You Do, with Bananarama, 1982; The Telephone Always Rings, 1982; Tunnel Of Love, 1983; Our Lips Are Sealed, 1983; Albums: Fun Boy Three, 1982; Waiting, 1983.

STAPLEY, Jay; b. 13 April 1957. Musician (guitar); Prod; Writer. m. 5 June 1990, 2 d. *Career:* Session and live work, London, 1979–; 2 world tours and albums with Roger Waters (formerly of Pink Floyd); Tubular Bells II tours with Mike Oldfield; Tours and albums with Westernhagen. *Recordings:* 4 solo albums; Also appears on: When the Wind Blows, with Roger Waters, 1987; Kiss My Soul, with Roger Chapman, 1996; Phoenix, with Toyah, 1997; Schwarz Oder Weiss, with Klaus Schulze, 1998; Just Good Stuff, Just Good Stuff, 1998; with Nigel Dick: All Stars And All Sorts, 2000. *Publications:* Articles on technical subjects in trade press. *Membership:* PRS; MCPS. *Address:* 11 Glenthorne Rd, Friern Barnet, London N11 3HU, England.

STAPP, Petra Rebecca; b. 29 Nov. 1964, Castleford, England. Vocalist; Songwriter; Musician (acoustic guitar). m. Timothy Alan Bigelow. *Career:* Singer, Songwriter, Carbolic Smokeball Company; Partnership with C Cahill, Wrote Songs, Performed; Record Deal with Round Tower of Dublin, 1995; Support to Nils Lofgren, Paul Carrack, Martin Carthy, Ric Sanders, Vikki Clayton. *Compositions:* I Hope It Will Be You. *Recordings:* Album, Remedy; Backing Vocals on: The Bean King, Curtis E. Johnson. *Membership:* PRS; MCPS. *Current Management:* Claire Hudson Management. *Address:* 25 Spa Rd, Gloucester, Gloucestershire GL1 1UY, England.

STARDUST, Alvin, (Bernard William Jewry); b. 27 Sept. 1942, London, England. Vocalist. *Career:* Solo singer, as Shane Fenton, early 1960s; Comeback as Alvin Stardust, 1973; Chart success, 1970s–80s; Presenter, performer, BBC TV; Actor, Hollyoaks, Channel 4, 1995–96. *Recordings:* Albums: It's All Happening, 1963; Good Rockin' Tonight, 1974; Greatest Hits: Alvin Stardust, 1977; I'm a Moody Guy, 1982; I Feel Like... Alvin Stardust, 1984; 20 of The Best, 1987; The Alvin Stardust Story, 2001; Latest And Greatest, 2001; Singles include: My Coo-Ca-Choo (No. 2, UK), 1973; Jealous Mind (No. 1, UK), 1974; Red Dress, 1974; You You You, 1974; Tell Me Why, 1974; Good Love Can Never Die, 1975; Pretend, 1981; I Feel Like Buddy Holly, 1984; I Won't Run Away, 1984; So Near To Christmas, 1984. *Current Management:* Roy Massey Management. *Address:* 40 Salisbury Dr., Cannock, Staffs, WS12 5YP, England.

STARR, Edwin, (Charles Hatcher); b. 21 Jan. 1942, Nashville, Tennessee, USA. Vocalist. *Career:* Formed vocal group Future Tones, 1957; Member, Bill Doggett Combo, Solo artist, 1965–; Motown recording artist, 1967–75; Based in UK, 1980s; Collaborations with the Style Council; Worked with Ian Levine's Motor City Records, 1989–91. *Recordings:* Singles include: Contact; Agent Double-O-Soul; Stop Her On Sight (SOS); 25 Miles; Stop The War Now; Funky Music Sho Nuff Turns Me On; Albums: Soul Master, 1968; 25 Miles, 1969; Just We Two, with Blinky, 1969; War and Peace, 1970; Involved, 1971; Hell Up In Harlem, 1974; Free To Be Myself, 1975; Edwin Starr, 1977; Afternoon Sunshine, 1977; Clean, 1978; HAPPY Radio, 1979; Stronger Than You Think I Am, 1980; 20 Greatest Motown Hits, 1986; Where Is The Sound, 1991; Timeless Energy, 1996; 20th Century Masters, 2001. *Current Management:* Lilian Kyle. *Address:* 118 Derby Rd, Bramcote, Nottinghamshire NG9 3HP, England.

STARR, Lucille; b. St Boniface, Manitoba, Canada. Entertainer; Vocalist; Musician (guitar, bass). m. (1) Bob Reagan, 19 Sept. 1955, divorced, 1 s.; (2) Bryan Cunningham, 16 April 1978, 1 step-s., 1 step-d. *Education:* Studied classical (voice). *Career:* First Grand Ole Opry Tour with Hank Snow, 1961; 4 television shows in Los Angeles; Yodelling for Cousin Pearl on Beverly Hillbillies. *Recordings:* Hits include: The French Song; Jolie Jacqueline; Colinda; Yours; Crazy Arms; Pepères Mill; First Time I've Ever Been In Love; Freight Train; Leaving It Up To You; Send Me No Roses; Collaborations include: Sylvia Tyson, 1994. *Honours:* Several Platinum and Gold records; First lady inducted in Hall of Honour (Canada); Hall of Fame, Canada; Street named Lucille Starr Drive in Vancouver, BC, Canada; Inducted into Walkway of Stars, Hall of Fame, Nashville, Tennessee, 1997. *Membership:* AFTRA; Television Screen Actors Guild; Musicians' Union; Canadian Country Music Asscn. *Current Management:* Cardinal Records.

STARR, Ringo, (Richard Starkey); b. 7 July 1940, Dingle, Liverpool, England. Musician (drums). m. (1) Maureen Cox, 1965, divorced, 2 s., 1 d.; m. (2) Barbara Bach, 1981. *Career:* Member, Rory Storm and The Hurricanes, Liverpool; Member, The Beatles, 1962–70; Appearances, Hamburg, 1962; World-wide tours, 1963–; Attended Transcendental Meditation Course, Maharishi's Academy, Rishkesh, India, 1968; Co-founder, Apple Corps Ltd, 1968; Solo artiste, 1969–; Narrator, children's television series, Thomas The Tank Engine; Film appearances include: A Hard Day's Night; Help!; Candy; The Magic Christian. *Recordings:* Albums include: with The Beatles: Please Please Me, 1963; With The Beatles, 1963; A Hard Day's Night, 1964; Beatles For Sale, 1965; Help!, 1965; Rubber Soul, 1966; Revolver, 1966; Sgt Pepper's Lonely Hearts Club Band, 1967; The Beatles (White Album), 1968; Yellow Submarine, 1969; Abbey Road, 1969; Let It Be, 1970; At The Beeb, 1994; Anthology 1, 1995; Anthology 2, 1996; Anthology 3, 1996; 1 (Number 1, UK and USA), 2000; Solo albums: Sentimental Journey, 1969; Beaucoups of Blue, 1970; Ringo, 1973; Goodnight Vienna, 1974; Blasts From Your Past, 1975; Ringo's Rotogravure, 1976; Ringo The Fourth, 1977; Bad Boy, 1977; Stop and Smell The Roses, 1981; Old Wave, 1985; StarrStruck – Ringo's Best (1976–83), 1989; Time Takes Time, 1992; Ringo Starr & His All-Star Band: The Anthology, 2001; Solo singles include: It Don't Come Easy; Back Off Boogaloo; Photograph; You're Sixteen; Oh My My; Snookeroo; Only You. *Honours:* (with the Beatles) BPI Awards: Best British Album (Sgt Pepper's Lonely Hearts Club Band), Best British Group, 1952–77, 1977; Inducted into Rock and Roll Hall of Fame, 1980. *Current Management:* David Fishof Presents, 252 W 71st St, New York, NY 10023, USA.

STATHAM, Robert; b. 4 April 1959, Bournemouth, Dorset, England. Musician (fretless bass guitar). *Education:* Certificate of Advanced Studies, Jazz/Rock, Guildhall School of Music. *Career:* Played with John Etheridge; Dick Heckstall-Smith; Ed Jones; Paz – Keith Emerson; Theo Travis; Radio broadcasts with Paz; Ed Jones; Theo Travis; Tours with Ed Jones; Theo Travis. *Compositions:* Featured on Ed Jones album; also Ed Jones radio broadcasts, Jazz Today, 1989. *Recordings:* Ed Jones; Paz; Kelvin Christiane; Theo Travis; Totally Wired compilation (acid jazz); Bop Brothers compilation: ...And Sisters, 2000. *Membership:* Musicians' Union; PRS. *Address:* 90 Bridge Lane, Golders Green, London NW11 0EL, England.

STAVNSTRUP, Jens Peter Fjeder; b. 18 Oct. 1963, Naestved, Denmark. Vocalist; Songwriter. 1 d. *Compositions:* Power Flower; Rain; Love Junkie. *Recordings:* Velvet Revolution, The Savage Affair; Shiner, Shiner. *Address:* Kinavej 11 I, 2300 Copenhagen S, Denmark.

STEAD, Dave; b. 15 Oct. 1966, Huddersfield, Yorkshire, England. Musician (drums). *Career:* Member, The Beautiful South. *Recordings:* Singles: Song For Whoever, 1989; You Keep It All In, 1989; A Little Time (No. 1, UK), 1990; My Book EP, 1990; Old Red Eyes Is Back, 1992; We Are Each Other, 1992; Good As Gold, 1994; One Last Love Song, 1994; Prettiest Eyes, 1994; Everybody's Talkin', 1994; Rotterdam (Or Anywhere), 1996; Don't Marry Her, 1996; Liar's Bar, 1997; Perfect 10, 1998; Dumb, 1999; How Long Does A Tear Take To Dry?, 1999; The River, 2000; Albums: Welcome To The Beautiful South, 1989; Choke; 1990' 0898, 1992; Miaow, 1994; Carry On Up The Charts: The Best of The Beautiful South, 1994 (No. 1, UK); Blue Is The Colour, 1996; Quench, 1998; Painting It Red, 2000; Solid Bronze: Great Hits, 2001. *Address:* The

Beautiful South, PO Box 87, Hull, East Yorkshire HU5 2NR, England. *Website:* www.beautifulsouth.co.uk.

STEELE, Kevin; b. Cleveland, Ohio, USA. Vocalist; Songwriter; Musician (harmonica). *Career:* Lead singer, US rock group Roxx Gang; Performances include: Things You've Never Done Before World Tour, 1990; US Tour, 1991; The Voodoo You Love, US Tour, 1996–97; Television and radio apperances include: Various videos, MTV; BBC TV; Z-Rock coast to coast radio broadcast. *Compositions:* Soundtrack to Playboys, Girls of South Beach, 1997. *Recordings:* Things You've Never Done Before; Love 'Em and Leave 'Em; The Voodoo You Love, 1996; Mojo Gurus, 1997; Roxx Gang: Old, New, Borrowed and Blue, 1998; Drinking TNT & Smokin' Dynamite, 2000. *Current Management:* Brett Steele, Steele Management. *Address:* 7002 124th Terrace N, Largo, FL 33773, USA.

STEELE, Tommy, (Thomas Hicks); b. 17 Dec. 1936, Bermondsey, London, England. Actor; Vocalist. m. Ann Donoghue, 1960, 1 d. *Career:* First stage appearance, Empire Theatre, Sunderland, 1956; First London appearance, Dominion Theatre, 1957; Major roles include: Buttons, Rodgers and Hammerstein's Cinderella, Coliseum, 1958; Tony Lumpkin, She Stoops To Conquer, Old Vic, 1960; Arthur Kipps, Half a Sixpence, Cambridge Theatre, 1963–64; The same, Broadhurst Theatre, New York, 1965; Truffaldino, The Servant of Two Masters, Queen's, 1969; Dick Whittington, London Palladium, 1969; Meet Me In London, Adelphi, 1971; Jack Point, The Yeoman of The Guard, City of London Festival, 1978; The Tommy Steele Show, London Palladium, 1973; Hans Andersen, 1974, 1977; One-man show, Prince of Wales, 1979; Singing In The Rain (also director), 1983; Some Like It Hot, 1992; What a Show, Prince of Wales Theatre, 1995; Film appearances: Kill Me Tomorrow, 1956; The Tommy Steele Story; The Duke Wore Jeans; Tommy The Toreador; Light Up The Sky; It's All Happening; The Happiest Millionaire; Half a Sixpence; Finian's Rainbow; Where's Jack?; Television: Writer, actor, Quincy's Quest, 1979. *Compositions:* Composed, recorded, My Life My Song, 1974; A Portrait of Pablo, 1985. *Recordings:* Compilations: The Decca Years, 1999; Best Of, 2000; Hit singles include: Rock With The Caveman, 1956; Singing The Blues (No. 1, UK), 1956; Butterfingers, 1957; Water Water/Handful Of Songs, 1957; Nairobi, 1958; Come On Let's Go, 1958; Little White Bull, 1959; What A Mouth, 1960. *Publications:* Quincy, 1981; The Final Run, 1983; Rock Suite – An Elderly Person's Guide To Rock, 1987. *Honours:* O.B.E., 1979. *Current Management:* James Kelly, International Artistes Ltd, 235 Regent St, London W1R 8AX, England.

STEEVES, Paulette; b. 25 Nov. 1955, Whitehorse, Yukon Territories, British Columbia, Canada. Songwriter; Musician (guitar); Vocalist. Divorced. 2 s., 1 d. *Education:* 1 year Canadian Academy vocal music (grant from Native American Foundation). *Career:* Formed The Mother and Child Band, with son Jesse (banjo, washboard, singer), son Dustin (harmonica, Indian hand drums), daughter Marina (tub base, spoons, tambourine, singer); Appearances: Hamilton Festival of Friends, 1992; Klienburg Binder Twine Festival, 1993; Festival of The Islands, 1993, Gananoque; Ridgetown Fair, 1993; Own Honeysuckle Records label; Workshops for making home made recycled instruments. *Recordings:* Heart For Sale; Cotton Fields. *Membership:* SOCAN; NSWA; CAIIA. *Address:* The Mother and Child Band, Box 442, Johnson, AR 72741, USA.

STEFANI, Gwen Renee; b. 3 Oct. 1969, Fullerton, CA, USA. Vocalist. m. Gavin Rossdale, 14 Sept. 2002. *Career:* Founding mem., lead singer, US group, No Doubt, 1987–. *Recordings:* Albums: with No Doubt: No Doubt, 1992; Beacon Street Collection, 1994; Tragic Kingdom, 1995; Return Of Saturn, 2000; Rock Steady, 2001; Collaborations: Good (with Gameface), 1997; Dirty Boogie (with Brian Setzer), 1998; Greatest Hits (with Sublime), 1999. Singles: Just A Girl, 1995; Don't Speak (No. 1, UK), 1997; New, 1999; Ex-Girlfriend, 2000; Simple Kind Of Life, 2000; Bathwater, 2000; Hella Good, 2002; Tour (EP), 2002; Underneath It All, 2002; Solo: Let Me Blow Your Mind (with Eve), 2001. *Honours:* Grammy Award, Best Rap/Sung Collaboration, 2002. *Current Management:* Spark Management, 100 Wilshire Blvd, Suite 1830, Santa Monica, CA 90405, USA. *Address:* c/o Interscope Records, 2220 Colorado Ave, Santa Monica, CA 90404, USA. *Website:* www.nodoubt.com.

STEINBERG, Billy; Songwriter. Current: Songs recorded by: Ace Of Base, Amber, Atomic Kitten, The Bangles, Meredith Brooks, Melanie C, The Corrs, Celine Dion, Whitney Houston, Ronan Keating, Cyndi Lauper, Madonna, Robert Miles, The Pretenders, Tina Turner. *Address:* c/o Stephen Budd Management Ltd, 109b Regents Park Rd, Primrose Hill, London NW1 8UR, England. *Website:* www.record-producers.com.

STEINCKE, Viggo; b. 15 Nov. 1951, Viborg, Denmark. Musician (guitar, bass); Composer. *Career:* Several live performances on Danish radio. *Recordings:* with Coma: Financial Tycoon, 1977; Amoc, 1980; Love and Madness, 1986; with Colours of Blue: Colours of Blue, 1989; Workshop, 1994. *Honours:* North Jutland Country Music Award, 1991. *Membership:* KODA; Danish Music Foundation. *Current Management:* Honor Agency. *Address:* Schleppegrellsgade 11, 9000 Ålborg, Denmark.

STEINER, Fred(erick); b. 24 Feb. 1923, New York, NY, USA. Composer; Conductor; Musicologist. m. Shirley Laura Steiner, 2 d. *Education:* Institute of Musical Art, New York City; BM, Oberlin Conservatory of Music, Ohio, 1943; PhD, Musicology, University of Southern California, 1981. *Career:* Composer, Conductor, radio in New York City; Music Director, radio programme This Is Your FBI; To Los Angeles, 1947; Many other radio programmes; First TV work, Columbia Broadcasting System, 1950; First film work, 1950; Major TV credits include Andy Griffith, Danny Thomas, Gunsmoke, Have Gun Will Travel, Hogan's Heroes, Rocky and Bullwinkle Show, Movie of the Week, Fractured Fairy Tales, Rawhide, Star Trek, Twilight Zone, Hawaii Five-O, Dynasty, Amazing Stories, Tinytoons; Major film credits include: Della, First To Fight, Hercules, The Man From Del Rio, Run For The Sun, St Valentine's Day Massacre, Time Limit, Shipwreck, The Color Purple; Lecturer, History and Art of Film Music, University of Southern California, 1984–89, College of Santa Fe, 1990–93. *Compositions:* Perry Mason Theme; Navy Log March; Dudley Doright Theme; Five Pieces for String Trio; Tower Music for Brass and percussion; Pezzo Italiano for cello and piano; Act Without Words, for percussion ensemble; Indian Music for Viola and Piano; Transcriptions and pieces for TV and film. *Recordings:* King Kong, conductor, motion picture score by Max Steiner; Great American Film scores; Music from the Paramount TV Series Star Trek. *Publications:* Foreword, in Music on Demand (by R R Faulkner), 1983; Music for Star Trek, in Wonderful Inventions (by Iris Newsom), 1985; Fred Steiner on Film Music, in Film Score (by Tony Thomas), 1991; Interlude, in Hollywood Holyland (by Ken Darby), 1992. *Contributions to:* Journal of the Arnold Schoenberg Institute; Film Music Notebook; Quarterly Journal of the Library of Congress; New Grove Dictionary of American Music; Dictionary of American Biography; New Grove Dictionary of Music and Musicians; Record Album Notes. *Honours:* City of Los Angeles Special Recognition Certificate; Award of Merit, Film Music Society. *Membership:* Academy of Motion Picture Arts and Sciences; American Musicological Society; AFofM; ASCAP; Society of Composers and Lyricists; Board of Advisors, Film Music Society. *Address:* 1086 Mansion Ridge Rd, Santa Fe, NM 87501, USA.

STEINKE, Gord; b. 11 July 1959, North Battleford, Saskatchewan, Canada. Musician (bass guitar, acoustic guitar); Songwriter. m. Deb, 7 June 1985, 1 c. *Education:* BA in Journalism and Communications. *Career:* Appeared on numerous television shows in Canada with own band Hidden Agenda; Major concerts include Classic Rock Weekend with Deep Purple, George Thorogood, Rick Derringer and Nazareth, 1997. *Recordings:* Larger Than Life, Inner City, 1982; Something Wrong, Gord Steinke, 1997. *Honours:* Recognition award, International Songwriting Competition. *Membership:* ACTRA; SOCAN; ARIA. *Address:* PO Box 57217, 2010A Sherwood Dr., Sherwood Park, AB T8A 5L7, Canada.

STEINMETZ, Hugh; b. 15 Feb. 1943, Copenhagen. Composer; Conductor; Musician (trumpet). m. Anna Lise Malmros, 1 s. *Education:* MA, University of Copenhagen. *Career:* Trumpet Player, Composer, Conductor, 1959–60; Composer, Soloist, The Danish Radio Jazz Group, The Contemporary Jazz Quintet, Cadentia Nova Danica; Latest Groups, Hugh Steinmetz Octet and Communio Musica. *Compositions:* Include Fujiama; Gizzy; Sound Like Arnoldi; Nisshinbo; Afrodisiaca; Stars and Mirrors; Mandra; Magic Waters; Relief; Traffic War Victims; Memory of a Face; Opus Statium; Electric Dancer; Flower Power; Global Community; Many Faces; Ah-Wah-Pah. *Recordings include:* Action; Nu; Afrodisiaca; City Music; Gate of Changes; Special Alloy; Collaborations include: Sunny Murray. *Honours:* Danish Jazz Musician of the Year, 1966; Legacies From Danish State Art Foundation, 1967, 1997, 1998, 1999, 2000, 2001, 2002. *Membership:* Danish Musicians' union; KODA; DJBFA; Tone Art. *Current Management:* Anna Lise Malmros. *Address:* Hyldegårdsvej 7, 1 tv, 2920 Charlottenlund, Copenhagen, Denmark. *E-mail:* hugh@steinmetz.dk.

STEINVIG, Peter; b. 20 July 1955, Ronne, Denmark. Musician (organ); Music Dir. m. Anette, 2 s., 3 d. *Education:* Ba, University of Copenhagen; MA, Royal Danish Music Conservatory; Duke University. *Career:* Music Director, Organist, Karlslunde Strandkirke; Gospel Choirleader and Clinician; Founder, KEFAS, 1975–; Originator, Copenhagen Gospel Festival, 1992–; Performances With Edwin Hawkins, Andrae Crouch, Richard Smallwood; Touring USA, 1994, England, 1996, 1998. *Recordings:* Blessed Be The Rock; Copenhagen Gospel Festival Live, 1997–99. *Publications:* 88 Salmer and Sange, Hymnbook; Dig Til Aere, Song Book. *Membership:* Danish Guild of Organists; DOKS. *Address:* Toftenholmen 18, 2690 Karlslunde, Denmark.

STEPHENSON, Larry Lee; b. 24 Oct. 1956, Harrisonburg, Virginia, USA. Musician (mandolin, guitar). *Career:* Four years with Bill Harrell and The Virginians; Five years with The Bluegrass Cardinals; Six years with The Larry Stephenson Band; Tours: The Middle East; Europe; Japan; Travelled USA, Canada; Appearances: Nashville Network; Grand Ole Opry; Many Bluegrass Festivals world-wide. *Recordings:* Albums: 5 with Bill Harrell; 3 with The Bluegrass Cardinals; 8 with The Larry Stephenson Band; including: Everytime I Sing a Love Song, 1988; Far Away in Tennessee, 1995; On Fire, 1998; Two Hearts On The Borderline, 2001; Heavenward Bound, 2001; Featured musician on about 25 other Bluegrass albums. *Membership:*

International Bluegrass Music Asscn; BMI, Writer and Publisher; Musicians' Union.

STEPHENSON, Robert; b. 30 June 1953, Dublin, Ireland. Music Promoter; Artist Man; Agent. *Education:* Belvedere College; Roscrea College; Blackrock College; Psychology, Trinity College, Dublin, Ireland. *Career:* Sense of Ireland Festival, London, 1980; Organizer of Irish rock festivals in London, 1986–90; Paris, 1992; Manager of bands, tour organizer, agent and promoter; Managing Director of Treasure Island Promotions, Media, Music, Discs; Acts on record label: Dr Millar; Ruby Horse. *Address:* Bartra Lodge, Harbour Rd, Dalkey, Co Dublin, Ireland.

STEPHENSON, Wilfredo; b. 27 Feb. 1948, Lima, Peru. m. Maria, 21 June 1988, 3 s., 2 d. *Education:* BA, Economics, Howard University, USA; Economic Studies, Stockholm University; Computers, NM School, Stockholm, Sweden; Piano, Lima Musical Conservatory; Private music lessons, diverse known percussionists, incl. Sabu Martinez, Pello Elafrokan, Anga, Tata Guiness. *Career:* Reader, Hot Salsa, Swedish Salsa Group, toured Scandinavia, Europe and USA, 1979–95; Percussionist with Aston Reymers Riivaler, 1981–86; Co-owner, Rub a Dub Records and Studios, 1988–97; Co-Producer, Rub a Dub Catalogue (19 productions with Salsa, Afro, Flamenco and World Music), 1997. *Compositions:* Lana Turkaleza, 1997. *Recordings:* Ensemble of Salsa Percussion, solo LP, 1981; Hot Salsa, 1979; Maldito Primitivo, 1985; Hot Salsa Meets Swedish Jazz, 1988; Lamowosbacuba, 1989; Ilusiones, 1992; With Friends for Friends, 1995; First Summer, 1998. *Honours:* Swedish Grammy for Per Mernberg. *Membership:* STIM; SAMI; SKAP; Swedish Socs for Musicians. *Address:* Alkallevagen 2, 13933 Varmdo, Sweden.

STERIAN, Valeriu; b. 21 Sept. 1952, Rîmnicu Sárat, Romania. Vocalist; Musician (guitar, drums). m. Lucia Sterian, 4 Aug. 1976, 1 s. *Education:* Psychologist; Music School. *Career:* Folk-rock group, Vali and Carmen, 1973; Lead singer, guitar, rock group, 1975–; Valeriu Sterian and Compania de Sunet; Tours: Romania; Bulgaria; Hungary; Poland; Russia; Norway; Germany; France; England. *Recordings:* Albums: Folk, 1977; Antirazbolnica, 1979; Veac XX, 1982; Nimic Fara Oameni, 1989; Noati in Norway, 1990; Vino Doamne, 1991; S-A Votat Codul Penal, 1993; Evenimentul Zilei, 1994. *Publications:* Vox Pop Rock, Romania. *Current Management:* Valerian Sterian Studio, B'inisor, Compania de Sunet SRL. *Address:* Str Ion Címpineanu-27, Ap 75, Sect L, Bucharest, Romania.

STES, Walter; b. 24 Jan. 1950, Heist-Aan-Zee, Belgian. Musician (bass). m., 3 c. *Education:* Law Studies, 2 years; Oriental Philology, 2 years; Classical Education, Double Bass. *Career:* Musical Director, Theatre Arena, Ghent, 1975–85; Musical Director, Royal Ballet of Flanders, 1985–90; Leader, Blues band, Red Rooster; Sales Manager, EAITC (prod. of stringed instruments). *Recordings:* Albums: Straight From the Heart; Bluesin' Up; On the Move; Never Alone. *Address:* St Anna Straat 60, 9820 Bottelare, Belgium.

STEVENS, Cat. See: ISLAM, Yusuf.

STEVENS, Craig Ronald; b. 30 Sept. 1959, Syracuse, New York, USA. Vocalist. m. Mary L Sinclair, 30 Aug. 1986. *Education:* MS; BA; AAS. *Career:* Touring artist, session musician, RCA Canada and Wurlitzer; Contract artist, keyboardist for Thrill of a Lifetime, Canada, 1982. *Recordings:* Just Another Night, 1980, 1981; Live At The Grand, 1983; Terminal Barber Shop, 1984; Risin' Child, 1994. *Publications:* Poems On The Road, 1983. *Honours:* Excellence In Music Education, 1992. *Membership:* GMA; ASCAP; CAPAC (SOCAN). *Current Management:* Capitol Management. *Address:* Division St, #1300, Suite 200, Nashville, TN 37203, USA.

STEVENS, Dane; b. 31 July 1942, Colchester, Essex, England. Country Vocalist; Songwriter; Musician (guitar). m. Kathleen Marian, 9 April 1985, 3 s., 1 d. (previous marriage). *Career:* 20 years, working professional; Solo ariste, working in country music clubs, major country festivals; Local radio interviews; Radio plays; Tours nationwide. *Compositions:* Original songs for albums; Songs recorded by The Haleys; Jolene and Barry. *Recordings:* Albums: TBL: New Country; Across The Miles; We Danced, 1998; Love Is My Life, 2000. *Honours:* Best Act, Country Music Club. *Membership:* PRS. *Current Management:* Contact Direct. *Address:* 139 Harwich Rd, Colchester, Essex CO4 3DB, England.

STEVENS, Michael Jefry; b. 13 March 1951, New York, USA. Musician (piano); Composer; Educator. *Education:* Masters degree, Queens College, NYC; Masters degree, Jazz Performance. *Career:* Extensive tours, Italy, Spain, Germany, Denmark, with Stevens Siegel and Ferguson trio and the Lily White Band; Various other tours including David Clayton Thomas Band; Worked with: Cecil Bridgewater; Dakota Staton; Charnott Moffett; Mark Whitfield; Ira Sullivan; Harold Vick; Ralph Lalama; Billy Drewes; Mark Feldman; Pheeroan Aklaff; Leo Smith; Gerry Hemingway; Phil Haynes; Perry Robinson; Ed Schuller; Thomas Chapin; Herb Robertson; Mark Whitecage; Billy Martin; Dave Douglas; Blood Sweat and Tears; The Platters; Carlos Patato Valdez; Jeff Andrews; Frank Gambale; Jaco Pastorius; Suzanne Vega; Head, keyboard department, National Guitar Summer Workshop; Musical Director, Music Theatre Ensemble, Barnard College, 1980–84. *Compositions:*

Music for vocal and instrumental ensembles, dance, music-theatre, film. *Recordings:* with Mark Whitecage and Liquid Time: Liquid Time; Live At Brandeis; with Jim Finn: Jim Finn; Talking With Angels; with Tim Ferguson Trio: Habitat; Dedication; Vagabond Blues; with The Lily White Band: Somewhere Between Truth and Fiction; with Phil Haynes/Michael Stevens: Music For Percussion and Piano; with The Mosaic Sextet: Today This Moment; Live At Brandeis; with Stevens/Siegel/Ferguson: One of a Kind; with Mark Whitecage/Michael Jefry Stevens: Duo Improvisations; Live At Greenwich House; Haiku, 1995; Elements, 1996; Points of View, 1996; Short Stories, 1998. *Honours:* BMI Composers Workshop; Eurie Blake Scholar. *Membership:* BMI; Minnesota Composers Forum.

STEVENS, Michael William; b. 26 Jan. 1957, Wisbech, Cambridgeshire, England. Artist; Musician (saxophone, keyboards). *Education:* Birmingham School of Music, 1975–79. *Career:* MD, Take That; Bill Withers, Member, LA mix; Toured as support act with: The Temptations; Dionne Warwick; Freddie Jackson. *Recordings:* 2 solo albums: Light Up The Night, 1988; Set The Spirit Free, 1990; Soloist on hits by: Cathy Dennis; Glen Goldsmith; Tom Jones; David Grant; 911; Black Box; Juliet Roberts; Adeva; Eternal. *Honours:* ARCM; ABSM. *Membership:* PPL; PRS, MU. *Current Management:* Sue Carling, Mike Stevens Music. *Address:* 13 Elvendon Rd, London N13 4SJ, England.

STEVENS, Mike; b. 9 Oct. 1957, Sarnia, Ontario, Canada. Musician (harmonica). m. Jane Gosselin, 8 Nov. 1986, 1 s. *Education:* Electrical Instrumentation at college. *Career:* First played The Grand Ole Opry, guest of Jim and Jesse, 1989; Guested over 100 times since; Tours: Canada; USA; Japan; Bahamas; Mexico. *Recordings:* Harmonica, 1990; Blowing Up a Storm, 1992; Life's Railway To Heaven, 1994; Joy, 1998; With Mike Stevens Project: Normally Anomaly, 1998; The World Is Only Air, 2000. *Publications:* Mike Stevens Harmonica Techniques For Bluegrass and Beyond. *Honours:* Recording of the Year, Central Canada, Bluegrass, 1990; 5 times Entertainer of the Year, Central Canada, Bluegrass; Best Selling Album, PRC, 1992; Made a Kentucky Col, 1994. *Membership:* SOCAN; CMRAA; HFA; AFofM; NARAS; CARAS. *Current Management:* Jim McReynolds, 560 Zieglers Rd, TN 37066, USA. *Address:* 1595 Blackwell Rd, Sarnia, ON N7X 1A4, Canada.

STEVENS, Paul; b. 30 June 1969, Hammersmith, London, England. Musician (guitars: electric, acoustic, classical); Electronics and Sound Engineer. *Education:* Chelmsford College of Further Education, Anglia Polytechnic; Colchester Music College, 1980–85; Martin Smith LLCM, 1985–94. *Career:* Parallel careers as musician and electronics/sound engineer; Sessions in London, Essex and Suffolk; Many live performances with bands including: Real Lives (early version of Blur); Hot Wired; Customs Men; Colours; Dream Age; Empathy; Product Design and Engineering Manager for Trace Elliot, designed several ranges of guitar and bass amplifiers for Trace Elliot, 1994–, Orange and Gibson, 1998–. *Recordings:* Produced solo work of guitar instrumentals, 1991; Session for U2: I Can't Help Falling In Love (remix at SARM West), 1992; Producer for: Empathy, Universal (EP), 1995. *Honours:* HNC Electronic Engineering, 1990. *Membership:* Musicians' Union; Institute of Incorporated Engineers. *Current Management:* Trace Elliot Ltd. *Address:* Blackwater Trading Estate, Maldon, Essex CM9 4GG, England.

STEVENS, Rachel Lauren; b. 9 April 1978, North London, England. Vocalist; Actor. *Education:* Drama college; London School of Fashion. *Career:* Worked in fashion PR; Mem., S Club 7, 1998–; Group quickly achieved international success, following sales of TV series Miami 7, 1999, LA 7, 2000, and Hollywood 7, 2001, featuring the band's music, to nearly 100 countries; Also made nature TV series, S Club 7 Go Wild, 2000, and various TV specials; First British tour with S Club 7, 2001; Band renamed S Club, 2001. *Recordings:* Albums: S Club, 1999; 7 (No. 1, UK), 2000; Sunshine, 2001; Seeing Double, 2002. Singles: Bring It All Back (No. 1, UK), 1999; S Club Party, 1999; Two In A Million/You're My Number One, 1999; Reach, 2000; Natural, 2000; Never Had A Dream Come True (No. 1, UK), 2000; Don't Stop Movin' (No. 1, UK), 2001; Have You Ever (No. 1, UK), 2001; You, 2002. *Honours:* BRIT Awards, Best British Newcomer, 2000, Best British Single, for Don't Stop Movin', 2002; Record of the Year Award, for Don't Stop Movin', 2001. *Current Management:* 19 Management, Unit 32, Ransomes Dock, 35–37 Parkgate Rd, London SW11 4NP, England. *Website:* www.sclub.com.

STEVENS, Richard William; b. 17 Aug. 1962, Wegberg, Germany. Musician (drums). *Education:* Private jazz tuition, Tommy Chase, John Stevens. *Career:* Performed with: Dennis Bovell; Linton Kwesi Johnson; George Clinton; Own group: Well Red; Own project: Drumhead. *Recordings:* Simply Red; Joan Armatrading; Oleta Adams; Boy George; Dido; Dexy's Midnight Runners; Jim Diamond; Mica Paris; Keziah Jones. *Current Management:* Copasetic Records. *Address:* 102 Ulleswater Rd, London N14 7BT, England.

STEVENS, Shakin', (Michael Barratt); b. 4 March 1948, Ely, Cardiff, South Wales. Vocalist; Songwriter. *Career:* Enjoyed much success touring for many years with his band, the Sunsets; Starred in the multi-award-winning West End musical, Elvis, which ran for 19 months from 1977; Signed as solo artiste with Epic Records world-wide, 1978; First UK Top 30 single, Hot Dog, charted in 1980; First European chart entry, Marie Marie, in 1980; First UK No. 1, later a major international hit, This Ole House, 1981; 38 hit singles, 36 of which were consecutive, throughout the 1980s and 1990s; UK hits: Four No. 1 hits, three No. 2 hits, 12 Top 5 hits, 15 Top 10 hits, 25 Top 20 hits, 30 Top 30 hits and 32 Top 40 hits (success was mirrored across Europe and world-wide); Musical collaborations incl. Bonnie Tyler, Roger Taylor, Hank Marvin, Albert Lee; Tours, personal appearances and television performances world-wide; Most successful hit-maker of the 1980s in the UK, with more weeks in the charts (254 in the 1980s alone) than any other international recording artiste; His work has been covered by many artists, incl. Eddy Raven (A Letter To You), Sylvia (Cry Just A Little Bit), No. 1 and No. 9 in the Nashville charts, Barry Manilow (Oh Julie), US hit in 1982. *Recordings:* Albums (UK): Shakin' Stevens Take One!; This Ole House; Shakin' Stevens; Shaky (No. 1, UK), 1981; Give Me Your Heart Tonight; The Bop Won't Stop; Greatest Hits; Lipstick, Powder And Paint; Let's Boogie; A Whole Lotta Shaky; There's Two Kinds Of Music—Rock 'N' Roll; The Epic Years. UK hit singles include: Hot Dog, 1980; Marie Marie, 1980; This Ole House (No. 1, UK), 1981; You Drive Me Crazy, 1981; Green Door (No. 1, UK), 1981; It's Raining, 1981; Oh Julie (No. 1, UK), 1982; Shirley, 1982; I'll Be Satisfied, 1982; The Shakin' Stevens EP, 1982; It's Late, 1983; Cry Just A Little Bit, 1983; A Rockin' Good Way (To Mess Around And Fall In Love), duet with Bonnie Tyler, 1984; A Love Worth Waiting For, 1984; A Letter To You, 1984; Teardrops, 1984; Breakin' Up My Heart, 1985; Lipstick Powder And Paint, 1985; Merry Christmas Everyone (No. 1, UK), 1985; Turning Away, 1986; Because I Love You, 1986; A Little Boogie Woogie (In The Back Of My Mind), 1987; What Do You Want To Make Those Eyes At Me For?, 1987; Feel The Need In Me, 1988; Love Attack, 1988; I Might, 1990; The Best Christmas Of Them All, 1990; Radio, 1992. *Honours:* 30 Top 30 hits in a decade, unsurpassed by any other artist; Best Musical of 1977; Best Singer/ Performer, MIDEM; Chartmaker Award for four simultaneous singles in the German chart; Numerous Gold and Platinum discs world-wide; First double platinum single ever to an international artiste, Sweden; Shares with the Beatles and Elton John the distinction of being the most successful British chart performer of a decade; Gold Badge Award, British Acad. of Composers and Songwriters, for contribution to the music industry, 2000; Guiness Book of British Hit Singles, Number One Gold Award, 2002. *Current Management:* Sue Davies, The HEC Organisation, PO Box 184, West End, Woking, Surrey GU24 9YY, England. *E-mail:* contactus@shakinstevens.com. *Website:* www.shakinstevens.com.

STEVENS, Steve; b. New York, USA. Musician (guitar). *Career:* Lead guitarist, Billy Idol, 1981–88; Solo artiste, and leader of own group Atomic Playboys; Also worked with Michael Jackson; Ric Ocasek; Steve Lukather; Thompson Twins. *Recordings:* with Billy Idol: Don't Stop, 1981; Billy Idol, 1982; Rebel Yell, 1983; Whiplash Smile, 1986; Vital Idol, 1987; Idol Songs – 11 of The Best, 1988; Solo: Steve Stevens' Atomic Playboys, 1989; Flamenco A Go-Go, 1999; Steve Stevens, 2000; Other. *Recordings include:* Bad, Michael Jackson, 1987; Lukather, Steve Lukather, 1989; Chalk Mark in a Rain Storm, Joni Mitchell, 1988; Don't Explain, Robert Palmer, 1990; Hit singles with Billy Idol include: Hot In The City; White Wedding; Without a Face; Rebel Yell; To Be a Lover; Don't Need a Gun; Sweet Sixteen; Mony Mony Live; Hot In The City; Other singles include: Dirty Diana, Michael Jackson. *Address:* c/o Weidenbaum Ryder and Co, 720 Palisade Ave, Englewood Cliffs, NJ 07632, USA.

STEVENSON, Jeffrey; b. 14 Jan. 1947, Leeds, Yorkshire, England. Musician (guitar, piano); Vocalist; Songwriter. m. Cecile Louise McDonald, 30 Aug. 1969, 2 d. *Career:* Played role of Woof, Canadian production of musical, Hair, 1970; Singer, guitarist, co-writer, television series Spider, BBC; Support to Labi Siffre in concert; Staff writer for programme Watch, BBC TV; Numerous and television radio gigs. *Compositions:* Over 80 titles published / recorded. *Recordings:* Spider; Recorded with Marty Wilde; One Day, 2000. *Membership:* Musicians' Union; Songwriters Guild; PRS; MCPS. *Address:* 30 Chiswick Village, London W4 3BY, England.

STEVE-O. See: **O'BRIEN, Steve.**

STEWART, Al; b. 5 Sept. 1945, Glasgow, Scotland. Vocalist; Songwriter; Musician (guitar). m. Kristine Russell, 18 May 1991, 1 d. *Career:* Solo artist, 1967–; Appearances include: Royal Festival Hall, 1967; US tour, 1974; Cambridge Folk Festival, 1989. *Recordings:* Singles include: Midnight Rocks; License To Steal; Albums: Bedsitter Images, 1967; Love Chronicles (featuring Jimmy Page), 1969; Zero She Flies, 1970; Orange, 1972; Past Present and Future, 1974; Modern Times, 1975; Year of The Cat, 1976; Time Passages, 1978; Carrots, 1980; Live/Indian Summer, 1981; Russians and Americans, 1984; Last Days of The Century, 1988; Rock The World, 1990; Rhymes In Rooms – Al Stewart Live Featuring Peter White, 1993; Between The Wars (with Laurence Juber), 1995; Seemed Like a Good Idea, 1996; Live at the Roxy, 1997; Acoustic Evening, 1998; Down In The Cellar, 2000. *Current Management:* c/o Steve Chapman, Chapman and Co, PO Box 5549, Santa Monica, CA 90409, USA.

STEWART, Dave; b. 9 Sept. 1952, Sunderland, Tyne and Wear, England. Musician (guitar, keyboards); Songwriter; Composer. m. Siobhan Fahey, 1

Aug. 1987, divorced, 1 s. *Career:* Musician, Harrison and Stewart (with Brian Harrison); Longdancer; The Catch, 1977; Renamed The Tourists, 1979–80; Formed Eurythmics with Annie Lennox, 1980–89; re-formed 1999; Worldwide concerts include Nelson Mandela's 70th Birthday Tribute, Wembley, 1988; As solo artiste: Nelson Mandela Tribute concert, Wembley, 1990; Amnesty International Big 30 concert, 1991; Founder, Spiritual Cowboys, 1990–92; Vegas, with Terry Hall, 1992–93; Founder, own record label Anxious Records, 1988; Owner, The Church recording studio, 1992; Producer, session musician, for artistes including Bob Dylan; Mick Jagger; Tom Petty; Daryl Hall; Bob Geldof; Boris Grebenshikov; Sinead O'Connor; Feargal Sharkey. *Compositions:* All Eurythmics songs co-written with Lennox; Theme for Jute City, BBC1; Co-writer, film score Motorcycle Mystics; Co-writer with Gerry Anderson, music for children's series GFI, 1992. *Recordings:* Albums: with The Tourists: The Tourists, 1979; Reality Affect, 1979; Luminous Basement, 1980; with Eurythmics: In The Garden, 1981; Sweet Dreams (Are Made of This), 1982; Touch (No. 1, UK), 1983; 1984 (For The Love of Big Brother), film soundtrack, 1984; Be Yourself Tonight, 1985; Revenge, 1986; Savage, 1987; We Too Are One (No. 1, UK), 1989; Eurythmics Greatest Hits (No. 1, UK), 1991; Eurythmics Live 1983–89, 1992; Peace, 1999; with the Spiritual Cowboys: Dave Stewart and The Spiritual Cowboys, 1990; with Vegas: Vegas, 1992; Solo: Greetings From The Gutter, 1994; Film soundtrack: De Kassiere, with Candy Dulfer, 1990; Hit singles include: with the Tourists: I Only Want To Be With You, 1979; So Good To Be Back Home, 1979; with Eurythmics: Sweet Dreams (Are Made of This) (No. 1, USA), 1983; Love is a Stranger, 1983; Who's That Girl?, 1983; Right By Your Side, 1983; Here Comes The Rain Again, 1984; Sex Crime (1984), 1984; Would I Lie To You?, 1985; There Must Be An Angel (Playing With My Heart) (No. 1, UK), 1985; Sisters Are Doin' It For Themselves, with Aretha Franklin, 1985; It's Alright (Baby's Coming Back), 1986; When Tomorrow Comes, 1986; Thorn In My Side, 1986; The Miracle Of Love, 1986; Missionary Man, 1986; Beethoven (I Love To Listen To), 1987; Shame, 1987; I Need A Man, 1988; You Have Placed a Chill In My Heart, 1988; Revival, 1989: Don't Ask Me Why, 1989; The King And Queen Of America, 1990; Angel, 1990; Love Is a Stranger, 1991; Sweet Dreams, 1991; I Saved the World, 1999; 17 Again, 1999; Solo: Lily Was Here, with Candy Dulfer, 1990; Contributor, Rock The World, 1990; Give Peace a Chance, Peace Choir, 1991; Videos: Eurythmics Live; Sweet Dreams; Savage. *Honours:* MTV Music Awards, Best New Artist Video, Sweet Dreams, 1984; BRIT Awards: Best Producer, 1986, 1987, 1990; Oustanding Contribution, 1999; Grammy, Best Rock Performance, Missionary Man, 1987; Ivor Novello Awards: Songwriters of the Year (with Annie Lennox), 1984, 1987; Best Song, It's Alright, 1987. *Current Management:* Miss Management, 16101 Ventura Blvd, Suite 301, Encino, CA 91436, USA. *Address:* c/o East West Records, Electric Lighting Station, 46 Kensington Court, London W8 5DP, England.

STEWART, Don(ald George); b. 8 Jan. 1935, Sterling, Illinois, USA. Musician; Music Industry Exec; Composer. m. Susan Ann Trainer, 13 June 1963, divorced 1979, 1 d. *Education:* MusB, Indianana University, 1960; Postgraduate Studies, Manhattan School, 1960–62; School of Jazz, 1958–60; Studied with Ray Harris, Bernhard Heiden, Gunther Schuller. *Career:* Second Clarinet, Birmingham Symphony Orchestra, Alabama, 1954–56; Florida Symphony, Orlando, 1963; Played with numerous jazz ensembles including Ornette Coleman, David Baker, Sammy Davis, 1957–65; Woodwind, orchestras, New York, 1967–72; Founder, Boehm Quintette, New York City, 1968–88; Music Assistant, New York State Council on the Arts, 1972–75; Freelance Copyist, 1958–88; Founder, President, Trillenium Music Co, 1986–; President, Opera North, Norwich, Vermont, 1987–89; Founder, Treasurer, Chamber Music America, New York, 1977–81; Panellist, Vermont Council on the Arts, 1976–78. *Compositions:* Piccolo Concerto, 1973; August Lions, for youth orchestra, 1978; Song of Arion, 1985; First Blue Symphony, 1988; Book of Sliding Things, 1989; Green Mountain Christmas Card, opera, 1995; Never Seek To Tell Thy Love, for voice and ensemble, 1998; Transcriber, composer, arranger. *Recordings:* Numerous on several labels. *Membership:* ASCAP; American Federation of Musicians; American Society of Music Copyists, Board of Directors 1970–87, Treasurer, 1984–87; American Music Centre; Music Publisher's Asscn; Retail Print Music Dealers Asscn, 1995–. *Address:* Trillenium Music, PO Box 88, Tunbridge, VT 05077, USA.

STEWART, Jimmy (James Otto); b. 8 Sept. 1935, San Francisco, California, USA. Musician (guitar); Prod; Composer; Writer. m. Terri Tilton, 22 April 1988. *Education:* AA, College of San Mateo, 1957; BA, Chicago School of Music, 1960; Certificate, Berklee School of Music, 1964; Private studies. *Career:* Featured soloist with: Los Angeles Philharmonic; Dallas Symphony Orchestra; St Louis Symphony Orchestra; San Francisco Light Opera; Guitarist with artists including: Ray Charles, Stan Getz, David Grisman, Dave Grusin, Michael Jackson, Quincy Jones, Herbie Mann, Shelly Manne, Gary McFarland, Carlos Santana, Sonny Stitt, Gabor Szabo; Musical director for: Lainie Kazan; Chita Rivera; Andy Williams; Vocal coach for: Linda Ronstadt; Juice Newton; Lee Ritenour; Master class tutor at: Dick Grove School of Music; Musicians Institute of Technology; Audio/Video Institute of Technology, Hollywood; University of Southern California. *Compositions include:* classical pieces, music for commercials, television, films. *Recordings:* Solo albums include: Fire Flower, 1977; The Touch, 1986; Blues Trax, 1992; The Art, History and Style of Jazz Guitar, 1993; The Complete Jazz Guitarist, 1994; Tribute To Classical Guitar, 1995; Also recorded with artists including:

Gabor Szabo (7 albums, including The Sorcerer, 1967); Burt Bacharach; James Brown; Sammy Davis Jr; Neil Diamond; Barbra Streisand; Everly Brothers; Maurice Jarre; Dusty Springfield; Featured on 1,200 recordings; Memorabilia, 1998. *Publications:* 21 guitar books include: Mode Mania, 1992; Heavy Metal Guitar, 1992; The Art History and Style of Jazz Guitar, 1993; The Complete Jazz Guitarist, 1994; Tribute To Classical Guitar, 1995; Numerous song books; contributor to Guitar Player, Recording Engineer and Producer magazine; Wes Montgomery Jazz Guitar Method, 1968. *Honours:* Alabama Jazz Hall of Fame; Decade of Service, Guitar Player Magazine; Communicator Award, Crystal Award of Excellence, 1998. *Membership:* ASCAP; NARAS; IAJE; AFM.

STEWART, Jon Randall; b. 14 Feb. 1949. Vocalist; Musician (guitar, mandolin). *Career:* Lead guitar, harmony, vocals for Emmylou Harris with The Nash Ramblers, 1990–95; Opening act for Mary Chapin Carpenter, 1995; Signed with Asylum Records, 1998. *Compositions:* Just Like You. *Recordings:* Albums: What You Don't Know, 1995; Emmylou Harris and The Nash Ramblers of The Ryman; Cold Coffee Morning, 1999; Willin', 2000; Singles include: Baby Make The Sun Go Down, 2000. *Honours:* Grammy Award, Emmylou Harris and The Nash Ramblers, 1992. *Current Management:* M Hitchcock Management. *Address:* PO Box 159007, Nashville, TN 37215, USA.

STEWART, Rod (Roderick David); b. 10 Jan. 1945, Highgate, North London, England. Vocalist. m. (1) Alana Collins, 1970; (2) Rachel Hunter, 1990, 1 s., 2 d. *Career:* Singer with: Steampacket; Shotgun Express; Jeff Beck Group, 1967–69; Concerts include: British tour with Roy Orbison, 1967; US tours, 1967, 1968; The Faces, 1969–75; Appearances include: Reading Festival, 1972; UK, US tours, 1972; Solo artiste, 1971–; Solo appearances include: Rock In Rio, Brazil, 1985; Vagabond Heart Tour, 1991–92. *Recordings:* Singles include: Reason To Believe; Maggie May (No. 1, UK and USA), 1971; (I Know) I'm Losing You; Handbags and Gladrags; You Wear It Well (No. 1, UK), 1972; Angel; Farewell; Sailing (No. 1, UK), 1975; This Old Heart of Mine; Tonight's The Night (Gonna Be All Right) (No. 1, USA), 1976; The Killing of Georgie (Parts 1 and 2); Get Back; The First Cut Is The Deepest; I Don't Want To Talk About It (No. 1, UK), 1977; You're In My Heart; Hot Legs; D'Ya Think I'm Sexy? (No. 1, UK and USA), 1978; Passion; Young Turks; Tonight I'm Yours; Baby Jane (No. 1, UK), 1983; What Am I Gonna Do; Infatuation; Some Guys Have All The Luck; Love Touch; Every Beat of My Heart; Downtown Train; Rhythm of My Heart; This Old Heart of Mine; Have I Told You Lately; Reason To Believe; Ruby Tuesday; All For Love, with Sting and Bryan Adams (No. 1, USA), 1994; You're The Star; Albums include: 2 with Jeff Beck; 4 with the Faces; Solo albums: Every Picture Tells a Story, 1971; Never a Dull Moment, 1972; Atlantic Crossing, 1975; A Night On The Town, 1976; Foot Lose and Fancy Free, 1977; Blondes Have More Fun, 1978; Foolish Behaviour, 1980; Tonight I'm Yours, 1981; Camouflage, 1984; Love Touch, 1986; Out of Order, 1988; The Best Of, 1989; Downtown Train, 1990; Vagabond Heart, 1991; Lead Vocalist, 1992; Unplugged... and Seated, 1993; A Spanner In The Works, 1995; When We Were the New Boys, 1998; Human, 2000; It Had To Be You... The Great American Songbook, 2002; Numerous compilations. *Honours:* BRIT Awards, Lifetime Achievement Award, 1993; First artist to top US and UK singles and album charts simultaneously, 1971. *Address:* c/o Warner Bros Records, 3300 Warner Blvd, Burbank, CA 91505, USA. *Website:* www.wbr.com/rodstewart/.

STEWART, Tommy; b. 26 May 1966, Flint, Michigan, USA. Musician (drums). *Career:* Previously in Lillian Axe and various covers groups; Joined Boston-based band Godsmack for short period, 1995; Returned, replacing Joe Darko, 1997; Group secured deal with Republic/Universal following heavy airplay of first single on local WAAF-FM station, 1998; US and European gigs in 1999 and 2000 including: Woodstock '99; Ozzfest; MTV's Return of The Rock tour; Second album recorded in warehouse in Massachusetts, 2000; First major amphitheatre tour, 2001. *Recordings:* Albums: Godsmack, 1998; Awake, 2000; Singles: Whatever, 1998; Awake, 2000; Greed, Bad Magick, 2001. *Honours:* Whatever single spent record total of 33 weeks on Billboard Top 10; Boston Music Awards, Act of the Year, 2000 and 2001; Billboard Award, Rock Artist of the Year, 2001. *Address:* c/o Paul Geary, PGM, PO Box 9134, Boston, MA 02205, USA. *E-mail:* godsmack@pgmglobal.com. *Website:* www.godsmack.com.

STIEF, Bo; b. 15 Oct. 1946, Copenhagen, Denmark. Musician (bass guitar, double bass); Composer; Bandleader; Teacher. 1 s., 2 d. *Career:* Bass player, 1963–; Began as bass player for touring soloists including: Dexter Gordon; Chet Baker; John Scofield; Don Cherry; Stan Getz; Dizzy Gillespie; Member of: Entrance; Midnight Sun; Leader, own band Chasing Dreams, 1980–; Major tours, festivals throughout Europe; Also played with: Miles Davis; Toots Thielmans; Joe Henderson; Larry Coryell; Alex Riel; Clark Terry; Archie Shepp; Yusef Lateef; Gato Barbieri; Art Farmer; Terje Rypdal; Jan Garbarek; George Russell; Astrid Gilberto; Zoot Sims; Carla Bley; AMO; Recent collaborations with: Just Friends; Palle Mikkelborg; Barbara Thompson; Ernie Watts; Jasper van't Hof Quartet; Lena Ericsson; Vince Nilsson Quartet. *Compositions:* Simple Song; Miss Julie, used for UN educational film. *Recordings:* Albums: with Bo Stief Chasing Dreams: Hidden Frontiers; 1987; Chasing Dreams, 1994; Also played on over 500 albums including: Aura, Miles Davis, Palle Mikkelborg, 1985; Anything But Grey, Palle Mikkelborg, 1992;

Ernie Watts, Jasper van't Hof Quartet, 1993. *Honours:* Jazz Musician of the Year, 1988; Composers Award of Honour, DJBFA, 1990. *Address:* Kaermindevej 11, 2820 Gentofte, Denmark.

STIGERS, Curtis; b. 1968, Boise, Idaho, USA. Jazz Vocalist; Songwriter; Musician (clarinet, saxophone). *Education:* Classical training in clarinet. *Career:* Mem., local punk and blues bands; Later played in blues groups, New York; Discovered in jazz trio; Solo artiste, 1991–. *Recordings:* Album: Curtis Stigers, 1992; Time Was, 1995; Brighter Days, 1999; Baby Plays Around, 2001; Secret Heart, 2002. Singles include: I Wonder Why, 1991; You're All That Matters to Me, 1992; Never Saw a Miracle, 1992; To Be Loved; Contributor, Tapestry Revisited—A Tribute To Carole King, 1996. *Current Management:* C. Winston Simone, 1790 Broadway, 10th Floor, New York, NY 10019, USA.

STILLS, Stephen; b. 3 Jan. 1945, Dallas, Texas, USA. Vocalist; Musician (guitar). m. Veronique Sanson, Jan. 1971. *Career:* Member, Au Go Go Singers; Buffalo Springfield, 1966–68; Crosby Stills and Nash, 1968–; (also as Crosby Stills Nash and Young); Manassas, 1971–74; Performances include: with Buffalo Springfield: Monterey Festival, 1967; with Crosby Stills and Nash: Woodstock, 1969; Royal Albert Hall, 1970; Festival of Hope, New York, 1972; Wembley Stadium, 1974; Night of The Hurricane 2 benefit concert, Texas, 1976; Last Waltz concert, San Francisco, with The Band, 1976; US tour, 1979; Anti-nuclear benefits, Madison Square Garden, 1979; No Nukes benefit concert, Hollywood Bowl, 1980; Film, No Nukes, 1980; Live Aid, Philadelphia, 1985; Amnesty International benefit, Chile, 1990; Hurricane Andrew benefit, Miami, 1992; Royal Albert Hall, 1992; Imua Hawaii, 1992. *Recordings:* with Buffalo Springfield: Buffalo Springfield, 1967; Stampede, 1967; Buffalo Springfield Again, 1967; with Crosby Still and Nash: Crosby Stills and Nash, 1969; Déjà Vu, 1970; 4-Way Street, 1971; So Far, 1974; Daylight Again, 1982; What Goes Around, 1983; Allies, 1983; American Dream, 1989; Live It Up, 1990; Looking Forward, 1999; Solo albums: Stephen Stills, 1970; Stephen Stills 2, 1971; Stills, 1975; Stephen Stills – Live On Atlantic, 1976; Illegal Stills, 1976; Still Stills – The Best of Stephen Stills, 1977; Thoroughfare Gap, 1978; with Manassas: Manassas, 1972; Down The Road, 1973; with Stills/Young: Long May You Run, 1976; Singles include: with Buffalo Springfield: For What It's Worth, 1967; Bluebird, 1967; Rock 'n' Roll Woman, 1967; with Crosby Stills and Nash: Suite – Judy Blue Eyes, 1969; Woodstock, 1970; Ohio, 1970; Just a Song Before I Go, 1977; Wasted On The Way, 1982; Southern Cross, 1982; Solo: Love The One You're With, 1971; Other session work includes: Hoyt Axton; Joan Baez; The Bee Gees; Eric Clapton; Judy Collins; Rita Coolidge; Joni Mitchell; Bill Withers. *Honours:* Grammy Award, Best New Artist, Crosby Stills and Nash, 1970; Best International Group, Melody Maker Poll, 1971. *Current Management:* Management Network, 14930 Ventura Blvd #205, Sherman Oaks, CA 91403, USA.

STING, (Gordon Matthew Sumner); b. 2 Oct. 1951, Wallsend, Newcastle upon Tyne, England. Vocalist; Musician (bass guitar); Actor; Songwriter. m. (1) Frances Tomelty, 1 May 1976, divorced 1984, 1 s., 1 d.; (2) Trudie Styler, 20th Aug. 1992, 2 s., 2 d. *Career:* School teacher, Newcastle, 1975–77; Singer, songwriter, bass player, The Police, 1977–86; Solo artiste, 1985–; Numerous world-wide tours, television and radio, with the Police and solo; actor in films: Quadrophenia, 1980; Secret Policeman's Other Ball, 1982; Brimstone and Treacle, 1982; Dune, 1984; The Bride, 1985; Plenty, 1985; Julia and Julia, 1988; Stormy Monday, 1988; The Adventures of Baron Munchausen, 1989; Broadway Performance, Threepenny Opera, 1989; Lock Stock and Two Smoking Barrels, 1998. *Recordings:* Hit singles include: with The Police: Roxanne, 1979; Can't Stand Losing You, 1979; Message In A Bottle (No. 1, UK), 1979; Walking On The Moon (No. 1, UK), 1979; So Lonely, 1980; Don't Stand So Close To Me (No. 1, UK), 1980; De Do Do Do, De Da Da Da, 1980; Invisible Sun, 1981; Every Little Thing She Does Is Magic (No. 1, UK), 1981; Spirits In The Material World, 1981; Every Breath You Take (No. 1, UK and USA), 1983; King Of Pain, 1983; Wrapped Around Your Finger, 1983; Synchronicity II, 1983; Solo hits include: Spread A Little Happiness, 1982; Walking On The Moon; Message In a Bottle; So Lonely; Roxanne; De Do Do Do, De Da Da Da; Every Little Thing She Does; Every Breath You Take; Invisible Sun; Can't Stand Losing You; Don't Stand So Close To Me; If You Love Somebody, 1985; Russians, 1985; We'll Be Together, 1987; Fragile, 1988; An Englishman In New York, 1988, remixed 1990; All This Time, 1991; If I Ever Lose My Faith In You, 1993; Fields of Gold, 1993; Love Is Stronger Than Justice, 1993; All For Love, with Rod Stewart & Bryan Adams (No. 1, USA; No. 2, UK), 1994; When We Dance (No. 2, UK), 1994; Cowboy Song (with Pato Banton), 1985; Let The Soul Be Your Pilot, 1986; Roxanne 97, 1987; Brand New Day, 1999; Desert Song, 2000; After The Rain Has Fallen, 2000; Albums: with the Police: Outlandos D'Amour, 1977; Regatta De Blanc, 1979; Zenyatta Mondatta, 1980; Ghost In The Machine, 1981; Synchronicity, 1983; Bring On The Night, 1986; Sting & The Police—The Very Best Of, 2002; Solo: The Dream of The Blue Turtles, 1985; Nothing Like The Sun, 1987; The Soul Cages, 1991; Ten Summoner's Tales, 1994; Mercury Falling, 1996; Brand New Day, 1999; All This Time, 2001; Contributor, Tower of Song (Leonard Cohen tribute), 1995. *Honours:* 13 Grammy Awards (with Police and solo); Q Award, Best Album, 1994; BRIT Awards, Best Male Artist, 1994, Outstanding Contribution, 2002; Ivor Novello Award, International Achievement, 2002.

Membership: PRS. *Current Management:* Firstars, 1 Water Lane, Camden Town, London NW1 8NZ, England.

STIPE, (John) Michael; b. 4 Jan. 1960, Decatur, Georgia, USA. Vocalist; Songwriter; Record and Film Prod. *Career:* Member, R.E.M., 1980–; International concerts include: Earth Day Concert, Maryland, 1989; Green World tour, 1989; A Performance For The Planet concert, 1990; European tour, 1992; Owner, film and video companies C-00 and Single Cell Pictures; Owner, vegetarian restaurant, Grit, Athens, GA. *Recordings:* Chronic Town (mini album), 1982; Murmur, 1983; Reckoning, 1984; Fables of The Reconstruction, 1985; Life's Rich Pageant, 1986; Dead Letter Office, 1987; Document, 1987; Eponymous, 1988; Green, 1988; Out of Time, 1991; Monster, 1995; Up, 1998; Star Profiles, 1999; Out of Time, 1999; Reveal, 2001; Singles: The One I Love, 1987; Stand, 1989; Orange Crush, 1989; Losing My Religion, 1991; Shiny Happy People, 1991; Near Wild Heaven, 1991; Radio Song, 1991; Drive, 1992; Man On The Moon, 1992; The Sidewinder Sleeps Tonite, 1993; Everybody Hurts, 1993; Nightswimming, 1993; Crush With Eyeliner, 1994; What's The Frequency Kenneth?, 1994; Bang And Blame, 1994; Tongue, 1995; Strange Currencies, 1996; Bittersweet Me, 1996; E-Bow The Letter, 1996; Daysleeper, 1998; Lotus, 1998; At My Most Beautiful, 1999; The Great Beyond, 2000; Imitation Of Life, 2001; Tracks featured on film soundtracks: Batchelor Party, 1984; Until The End of The World, 1991; Coneheads, 1993; Recordings with: Indigo Girls, 1988; Syd Straw, 1989; Billy Bragg, 1991; Neneh Cherry, 1991; Contributor, Disney compilation, Stay Awake, with Natalie Merchant, 1988; Tom's Album, 1991; I'm Your Fan (Leonard Cohen tribute), 1991; Producer, artistes including: Swell; Chickasaw Muddpuppies; Opal Fox Society; Co-producer, film Desperation Angels, with Oliver Stone; Being John Malkovich, 1999. *Honours:* Earth Day Award, 1990; Numerous MTV Music Video Awards, Billboard Awards, 1991; BRIT Awards: Best International Group, 1992, 1993, 1995; Grammy Awards: Best Pop Performance, Alternative Music Album, Music Video, 1992; Atlanta Music Awards, 1992; IRMA Band of the Year, 1993; Rolling Stone Critics Awards, 1993; Q Awards: Best Album, 1991, 1992; Best Act In The World, 1991, 1995. *Current Management:* REM/Athens, 250 W ClaytonSt, Athens, GA 30601, USA.

STOCK, Michael; b. 3 Dec. 1951, Margate, Kent, England. Songwriter; Record Prod; Musician. m. Frances Roberta, Dec. 1975, 2 s., 1 d. *Education:* University of Hull. *Career:* Signed first publishing deal, 1970; Member of bands: Mirage, 1976–84; Nightwork, 1981–84; Founder, partner, writing/production team Stock Aitken Waterman, 1984–93; Relocated to new studios, started new production company and Love This Records, 1994. *Recordings:* As writer/producer, artists include: Princess; Hazell Dean; Dead or Alive; Bananarama; Mel and Kim; Rick Astley; Kylie Minogue; Jason Donovan; Donna Summer; Cliff Richard; Sybil; Kym Mazelle; Sonia; Big Fun; Sinitta; Jocelyn Brown; Nicki French; Power Rangers; Robson and Jerome; Scooch. *Honours:* BPI Best Producer, 1988; IVN Songwriter of Year 3 times; BMI Award, 4 times. *Membership:* PRS; BAC&S. *Address:* c/o Love This International, Hundred House, 100 Union St, London SE1 0NL, England.

STOCKLEY, Miriam; b. Johannesburg, South Africa. Vocalist. *Career:* Solo recording artiste; Backing vocalist for top recording stars: Kylie Minogue; Jason Donovan; Brian May; Deniece Williams; Cliff Richard; Chaka Khan; Ronan Keating; Freddie Mercury; Robert Plant; Paul Young; Dina Carroll; B*Witched; Tina Turner; Boyzone; Sarah Brightman; Tom Jones; Mike Oldfield; Appeared on tribute to Freddie Mercury, Brian May tour; Worked extensively with Stock, Aitken and Waterman; Television includes: Spitting Image; Kenny Everett; Beatrix Potter's Peter Rabbit theme song; Perfect Day. *Compositions:* Solo album, Miriam, 1999. *Recordings:* As Praise: Only You, used in Fiat commercial (No. 3, UK), 1991; 4 albums as Adiemus, with Karl Jenkins: First album: Songs of Sanctuary (No. 3, classical charts, Spain; Gold record Germany, Holland, Japan, UK), 1995–2000; Solo album, Miriam, 1999. *Honours:* Sarie Award for Best South African Recording Artiste. *Membership:* PRS; MCPS; GVL; PAMRA. *Current Management:* David Stopps, Friars Management Ltd. *Address:* 33 Alexander Rd, Aylesbury, Buckinghamshire HP20 2NR, England.

STOCKMAN, Shawn Patrick 'Slim'; b. 26 Sept. 1972, USA. *Education:* Philadelphia High School of Creative and Performing Arts. *Career:* Mem., Boyz II Men, 1988–; Established Stonecreek label; Signed to Arista Records. *Recordings:* Albums: Cooleyhighharmony, 1993; II, 1995; Evolución, 1997; Nathan Michael Shawn Wanya, 2000; Full Circle, 2002. Singles: Motownphilly, 1991; I'll Make Love To You; On Bended Knee; One Sweet Day (with Mariah Carey, No. 1, USA). *Address:* c/o Arista Records, 6 W 57th St, New York, USA. *Website:* www.boyziimen.com.

STOICA, Laura; b. 10 Oct. 1967, Alba-Iulia, Romania. Vocalist; Entertainer; Actress. m. Florin Ionescu, 31 Oct. 1992. *Education:* Baccalaureat, Electrical Engineering; 5 year course, Diploma in Performing Arts (theatre, musical, pop music); Diploma, Performing Classical Music; Licence, Professional Music Interpretation. *Career:* Lead singer, Riff, Semnal M. to 1988; Solo artiste, 1987–; Lead singer, Laura Stoica Band, 1993–; Over 40 live appearances, national, international, television and radio; TV specials include: 5 O'Clock Tea, 1991, 1993–95; Bucharest International, 1990, 1993; Talk Show with

Laura Stoica, 1993–95; Mamaia, 1991–95; Charity for Romanian children with AIDS and orphans, 1993, 1994; Radio specials include: Talk shows, 1991–95; Laura Stoica Live, 1992–95; Unplugged, 1995; Founder, President, Laura Stoica Charity Trust, 1993. *Recordings include:* Single: An Actor In My Life, 1992; Album: The Fire, 1994. *Honours:* City Song Trophy, 1988; Mamaia Trophy, 1990, 91; Bucharest International Award, 1990; Golden Stag International Record Trophy, 1992; Pop, Rock and Show Award, 1991, 92, 93; Radio Contact Award, 1992; Bregenz International Pop Music Award, 1992. *Membership:* Romanian Guild of Songwriters and Composers.

STOIKOV, Dimitar; b. 22 March 1931, Varna, Bulgaria. Musician (accordion). m. Stanka Stoikova, 25 Aug. 1955, 2 s. *Education:* College of Harmony and Composition, Varna. *Career:* Film profile on Bulgarian TV; Participation in radio programmes; Concerts in Macedonia, Serbia, Turkey, Slovenia, Czech Republic, Russia, Germany. *Compositions:* Over 900 folk compositions. *Recordings:* Over 150 records including 7 albums, 8 singles, 4 cassettes and 1 CD, Imperishable Gleeds, 1999. *Honours:* SS Cyril and Methodius Order; Gold medals, prizes at folk festivals. *Membership:* Musicauter Sofia, Bulgaria. *Address:* 13a Sv Dimitar Salounski St, Vinitsa, 9022 Varna, Bulgaria.

STOIKOV, Youri; b. 1 March 1962, Varna, Bulgaria. Composer; Musician (Keyboards). m. Savina Stoikova, 9 July 1994. *Education:* Higher Humanitarian Education, St Kliment Ochridski State University, Sofia, Bulgaria; Varna College of Musical Harmony and Composition, with Petke Mechkev. *Career:* First and Second Festivals of Electronic Music, Getse Delchev, Bulgaria, shown on national TV; Member, Jury, Diskovery 1994–96 Festival, Varna. *Recordings:* Window to the Soul, cassette, 1988; Things, cassette, 1990; Transfiguration, 1992; The Legends, 1996. *Publications:* Series of articles on electronic music, 1988–89, Varna. *Honours:* First Prize for Song dedicated to the Sea, Maritime Navigation Competition, Bulgaria, 1992; Jury's Prize, Badalona, Spain. *Membership:* Musicautor, Sofia. *Address:* Ap 28, Bl 43 b Chaika, Varna 9005, Bulgaria.

STOKER, Richard; b. 8 Nov. 1938, Castleford, Yorkshire, England. Composer; Author; Painter; Poet. m. Dr Gillian Patricia Watson, 10 July 1986. *Education:* Huddersfield School of Music and School of Art, 1953–58; Royal Academy of Music, with Lennox Berkeley, 1958–62; Composition with Nadia Boulanger, Paris, 1962–63; Mendelssohn Scholarship, 1962–63; Also private study with Britten, Benjamin, Fenby and Truscott; Professor of Composition, RAM, 1963–87. *Career:* Composition Teacher to Paul Patterson, Joe Jackson, Malcolm Singer, the late Paul Reade and others; Performing pianist, BBC radio, television and CDs. *Compositions include:* Song lyrics and music, orchestral, choral, 3 overtures, chamber music, jazz preludes, operas; Films and theatre music; Tribute to Hoagy Carmichael, with Fazarro and Earl Okin, South Bank, 1981. *Recordings include:* Album with Susan Fazarro, Chandos; Sonatina for Clarinet and Piano, Chandos; 2 CD Tribute to Hoagy Carmichael; Complete piano works, Eric Parkin; Complete guitar music, Martin Vishnick, 1999; Priory, vocal and duo piano works, 1999–2000; ASC Records Ltd, 3 CD songs: Royal, JJ, Saydisc. *Publications:* Open Window—Open Door, autobiography; Regency 'Words without Music' (outposts); Between the Lines; Portrait of a Town, filmed 1983); Tanglewood, 1994; Diva – A Novel, 1995; Collected Short Stories, 1997; 3 plays; Numerous lyrics and numerous poems in more than 30 anthologies; Numerous stories in anthologies. *Contributions to:* magazines and journals; Editor, Composer Magazine, 1969–80. *Honours:* Mendelssohn Scholarship, 1962; Dove Prize RAM, 1962; Associate Royal College of Music, 1962; Associate, RAM, 1965, Fellow, 1971, Royal Academy of Music; Justice of the Peace, 1995–; 3 Editor's Awards, National Society of Poetry, USA. *Membership:* Executive Committee, Composers' Guild, 1969–74, 1974–80; Asscn of Professional Composers, 1977–99, Promotions Committee, 1995–; BASCA, Professional Mem., 1979–95; Executive committee, British Academy of Composers and Songwriters, 1999–; PRS, 1962–; MCPS, 1970; Founder Mem., RAM Guild, 1986–, Executive Committee, 1994–, Hon Treasurer, 1995–; Magistrates' Asscn, 1995; U3A, 1993–; Founder Mem., Atlantic Council of the UK, 1994; Euro-Atlantic Group, 1994–; PEN International; English PEN, 1996–; Royal Society of Literature, 1997–. *Current Management:* Ricordi and Co Ltd. *Address:* c/o Ricordi and Co Ltd, BMG, 210 New Kings Rd, London SW6 4NZ, England.

STOKES, Mary Teresa; b. 25 Aug. 1962, Dublin, Ireland. Vocalist. m. Brian Palm, 14 Feb. 1994. *Education:* BA, Psychology; MA by Research; 10 years classical singing, to Grade 5. *Career:* Formed blues band The Mary Stokes Band, 1988 (now 5-piece); Performed concerts in Ireland, Europe, USA; Backed: John Lee Hooker; Fats Domino; Carey Bell; Lowell Fulson; B. B. King; Radio and television appearances: Ireland; BBC; UTV; Began composing, 1993. *Recordings:* 3 albums; 3 singles. *Honours:* Smithwicks Hot Press Best Newcomer Award, 1989.

STOKKEBYE, Peter; b. 22 Aug. 1975, Copenhagen, Denmark. Musician. *Education:* Drum School, Music School, Copenhagen. *Career:* Played with Blink on a Tour to Seoul in Republic of Korea; Concert with 50,000 People on Live Television; Several Radio Programs and Television Shows. *Recordings:* Prunes, 1996–97; Secret Garden; Standing on the Hill; Get High, 1998.

Honours: Gold Record, Republic of Korea, 1997. *Membership:* Danish Musicians' union. *Current Management:* Sundance Records. *Address:* Nivaavaenge 196, 2990 Nivaa, Denmark.

STOLTING, Arnold Hugo; b. 12 Aug. 1969, Georgetown, Guyana. Vocalist; Songwriter; Prod. *Education:* National Institute of Broadcasting, Toronto. *Career:* Productions aired on Radio World-wide; Producer for Songwriter demo tapes; Produces professional recording artistes and involved with development of new talent; President, CEO, Canadance Music Records/Productions/Publishing. *Compositions:* Numerous compositions in styles of Dance, R&B, Pop, Reggae, HipHop, Rap. *Recordings:* Think I'm In Love, Hugo; Hey Pretty Boy; Give It To Me Baby, Azz; In the Distance, Sona; Summatime, Blakborough. *Membership:* SOCAN; CMRRA. *Current Management:* Canadance Music. *Address:* 36–3430 Finch Ave E, Toronto, ON M1W 2R5, Canada.

STONE, Angie; b. Columbia, South Carolina, USA. Vocalist; Songwriter. *Career:* Daughter of a gospel singer, started singing in church choir with father; Member of rap trio The Sequence on Sugarhill records; Reached the attention of Prince protégé Jill Jones and was recruited to work on her album; Formed vocal trio Vertical Hold; Solo career 1999–; Collaborations: Mantronix; Lenny Kravitz; D'Angelo; Omar; Mary J Blige; Guru; Alicia Keys; Prince; Gerry DeVeaux. *Recordings:* A Matter of Time (with Vertical Hold), 1993; Head First (with Vertical Hold), 1995; Black Diamond, 1999; Mahogany Soul, 2001; Singles: with The Sequence: Funk You Up, 1980; Funky Sound (Tear The Roof Off), 1981; I Don't Need Your Love, 1982; with Vertical Hold: Summertime, 1988; Seems You're Much Too Busy, ASAP, 1993; Love Today, 1995; solo: Everyday, 1997; No More Rain (In This Cloud), Life Story, 1999; Keep Your Worries (with Guru), 2000; Brotha, 2001. *Honours:* Soul Train Award, Best R&B/Soul New Artist, 2000; Kora Award, Best Video–Diaspora, 2002. *Address:* c/o Arista Records, 6 W 57th St, New York, USA. *Website:* www.angiestoneonline.com.

STONE, Brian; b. 28 Aug. 1949, Lewisham, England. Musician (drums, percussion). m. Christine Ann Stone, 1 s., 3 d. *Education:* Guildhall with Gilbert Webster, Trevor Tompkins; Trinity College with Michael Skinner. *Career:* Varied freelance work; Some summer seasons at Pontins; Various West End clubs; Big Band and group work; Percussion teacher; Guildhall Examiner and London College Examiner. *Compositions:* Independance Day, 1985; Circus Rush, 1985. *Honours:* National Award, Ballroom Dancing, 1965; National Award Latin American Dancing, 1968; LTCL, 1979; QTS, 1992. *Membership:* Musicians' Union; National Asscn of Percussion Teachers; NASUWT. *Address:* 9 Church St, Ellesmere, Shropshire SY12 0HD, England.

STONE, Doug; b. 19 June 1956, Nashville, Tennessee, USA. Musician (piano, electric guitar, acoustic guitar, bass, mandolin, drums); Mechanic. *Career:* Eight-year tenure with Sony Nashville; Signed with Atlantic Records. *Recordings:* Numerous, including, (I'd Be Better Off) In A Pine Box; Fourteen Mintues Old; In A Different Light; Too Busy Being In Love; Why Didn't I Think Of That; Make Up In Love, 1999; These Lips Don't Know How To Say Goodbye; Come In Out Of The Pain. *Honours:* Grammy Award; Best Male Vocal Performance; Horizon Award; Academy of Country Music Awards; TNN Music City News Awards; Platinum and Gold Records. *Current Management:* Atlantic Records. *Address:* c/o Trifecta Eng, 209 10th Ave S, Suite 302, Nashville, TN 37203, USA.

STONE, Ronald William; b. 27 March 1959, Merseyside, England. Record Prod; Engineer; Programmer; Musician (guitar); Songwriter. *Education:* Art College. *Career:* Member, Afraid of Mice, 1978; Backing musician for China Crisis, 1982; Formed Freeze Frame, 1984 (hits in Europe, Japan, Australia); Producer/Engineer for: Easterhouse; Throwing Muses; The Pixies; Oceanic; River City People; Audioweb; Pete Wylie; Shack; Sarah Cracknell; Mansun; Christians; Live sound: Easterhouse; Jason Donovan; WOMAD 1996, 1997; Connie Lush; Sian James; Lotus Eaters; Producer/soundtracks for TV/Cinema commercials: Gas; Electricity; Tea; Yves St Laurent; Consultant A & R for major record labels; Music for BBC TV series, Birdman, 1999. *Compositions:* Numerous songs published. *Recordings:* Producer/engineer for Say Something Good, River City People; All works by Oceanic, 1991–93; Singles including Wide Open Space and album, Attack of the Grey Lantern, by Mansun (Gold disc). *Honours:* Gold and Silver discs as producer, engineer. *Current Management:* Area 51 Management. *Address:* TMW House, 12 Princess Terrace, Balls Rd, Birkenhead, Merseyside L43 5RB, England.

STONE, Sly, (Sylvester Stewart); b. 15 March 1944, Dallas, TX, USA. Songwriter; Musician (drums, guitar); Prod. *Career:* Mem., The Stewart Four, several other bands; Songwriter (under name Sylvester Stewart) and Prod., Autumn Records; Formed band, The Stoners, 1966; Formed band, Sly and the Family Stone, 1967; Signed to Epic; Appeared at Woodstock, Monterey festivals; Worked with: The Beau Brummels, Bobby Freeman, Mojo Men, The Tikis. *Recordings:* Singles: with The Stewart Four: On The Battlefield For My Lord; Solo: Long Time Away; with Sly and the Family Stone: I Ain't Got Nobody, 1967; Dance To The Music, 1968; Everyday People, 1969; Family Affair; Albums: A Whole New Thing, 1967; Dance To The Music, 1968; Life, 1968; Stand!, 1969; There's A Riot Going On, 1971; Fresh, 1973; Small Talk,

1974; High On You, 1975; Heard Ya Missed Me, Well I'm Back, 1976; Back On The Right Track, 1979; Ain't But The One Way, 1982; Greatest Hits; Anthology.

STONE, Tony (Anthony George); b. 21 Dec. 1930, Weston-Super-Mare, England. Musician (multi-instrumentalist); Music Teacher. m. Shirley Winifred Parker, 31 Aug. 1955, 3 s. *Career:* Solo keyboard player; Saxophonist with dance bands, big bands, jazz bands, orchestras, pit orchestras; Bandleader, arranger, composer, teacher; Appearances on BBC Radio and commercial television; Currently leader of New Parkway Showband, 1985–. *Compositions:* The Comet; Dancing; Moonrise; Freeway; Life Goes On; My Special Xmas Wish; Chocolate Cha-Cha; Eileen; Continuation Waltz; Encounters; Easy Walk; Coleford Jaunt; Marguerite; Loneliness. *Membership:* Musicians' Union. *Address:* Horfield School of Music, 22 Wellington Hill, Horfield, Bristol BS7 8SR, England.

STONEBRIDGE; b. Stockholm, Sweden. Record Prod; DJ; Songwriter. *Career:* Formed Swemix, DJ service and promotion group, late 1980s; Formed BTB record label, 1992; Formed Stoney Boy Music record label, 1997; Signed as artist to Hed Kandi, UK, 2002; Increasing success as producer and songwriter. *Compositions include:* Jacey John's Freestyle Dub, 1990; Back It Up, 1994; Satisfy My Love, 1994; Earthbeat, 1996; Boy You Knock Me Out, 1997; The Beach, 1999; Calling, 2000; Something About You, 2001. *Recordings include:* All Nite Long, 1999; Sometimes, 2002; Artist Album, 2003; As producer: Show Me Love, Robin S.; Make My Love, Shawn Christopher; Satisfy My Love, Sabrina Johnston; Boy You Knock Me Out, Tatyana Ali and Will Smith; The Beach, Coco and StoneBridge; Numerous remix credits include: Escape, Enrique Iglesias; I Turn To You, Melanie C. (No. 1, UK), 2000; Inner Smile, Texas; Wish I Could Fly, Roxette. *Honours:* Best DJ, Sweden, 2001; Best Remixer, Swedish Dance Awards, 1991, 1993, 1994, 1996; Best 12', Winter Music Conference, 1994. *Membership:* STIM. *Current Management:* StoneBridge Productions. *Address:* Stonebridge Productions, Eremitvagen 6, 112 64 Stockholm, Sweden. *Website:* www.stoneyboy.com.

STONER, Joel; b. 13 Jan. 1964, Sewickley, Pennsylvania, USA. Recording Engineer; Prod. m. Clare B McDonald, 10 Feb. 1991, 1 s. *Education:* Berklee College of Music, Boston. *Career:* Recording and mixing multi-platinum albums including: Fishbone; Susanna Hoffs; Kazo Matsui; Keiko Matsui; Roxx Gang; Steve Stevens; Music for film, television and commericals in all styles for major record labels and film companies. *Contributions to:* professional magazines including Billboard and Mix. *Address:* 1567 Fair Ave, Simi Valley, CA 93063, USA.

STORAAS, Vigleik; b. 9 Feb. 1963, Bergen, Norway. Musician (piano, synthesizer). m. Astrid Vasseljen, 3 June 1994, 1 s., 1 d. *Education:* College; Jazz Department, Conservatory. *Career:* Festival appearances with Karin Krog, John Surman and Terje Rypdal in England and Italy. *Compositions:* Co-wrote many compositions including Nordic Quartet. *Recordings:* Nordic Quartet (with John Surman, Karin Krog, Terje Rypdal), 1995; Other albums with artists including: Bjorn Alterhaug; Soyr; Norma Winstone. *Membership:* Norsk Musikforbund; NJF; FNJ, Norway. *Address:* Bromstadekrh 21C, 7046 Trondheim, Norway.

STOREY, Michael Andrew; b. 26 Oct. 1936, Wakefield, Yorkshire, England. Entertainment Agent. m. Margaret Storey, 7 June 1965, 1 s., 1 d. *Career:* RAF Travel Agent; Entertainment Agent, 1971–; 20 years as broadcaster, BBC Radio Leeds; Vice-Chairman of British Country Music Association. *Membership:* British Country Music Asscn; Entertainment Agents Asscn. *Address:* Mike and Margaret Storey Entertainment, 59 Knowl Rd, Golcar, Huddersfield, West Yorkshire HD7 4AN, England.

STORRY, Richard; b. 8 Sept. 1965, Ontario, Canada. Composer; Musician (guitar, keyboards). *Education:* Royal Academy of Music. *Career:* Television appearances: Motormouth; Heno; S4C; Telethon; Sky; Radio broadcasts: Radio 2; Classic FM; GLR; Performed at: Coliseum; St James' Palace; Riverside Studios; Tours throughout UK with the Tetra Guitar Quartet including South Bank Centre; West End; Accompanist for West End singers and Recreation Theatre Company's The Rivals; Music Consultant and tutor for Uncle Vanya; Adjudicator, public speaker. *Compositions:* Musicals: A Musical Term; Arthur; Spellbyte; Kennedy. *Recordings:* Tetra By Arrangement; Tetra play Vivaldi's Four Seasons; Carmen, 1999. *Honours:* GRSM (Hons); LRAM; DipRAM; Julian Bream Prize; Lady Holland Award. *Membership:* PRS; BAC&S; MCPS; PAMRA. *Current Management:* LA Management International. *Address:* 52 Junction Rd, Gillingham, Kent ME7 4EQ, England.

STOTZEM, Jacques; b. 17 July 1959, Verviers, Belgium. Musician (acoustic guitar). 1 s. *Career:* Major concerts include: Guitar Festival of Liege, 1983, 1985; Inner Circle Concert, Los Angeles, USA, 1994; International Guitar Tour, Germany, 1994; Belga Jazz Festival, 1994; Clinics for: Fishman Transducers and Lowden Guitars, in Europe; Direction, Fingerstyle Workshops in Europe; Concerts during the Namm Show, Los Angeles, 1996, 1997; International Jazz Festival of Montréal, Québec, 1997; International Guitar Festival of Birkenhead, England, 1997; International Acoustic Guitar

Night, Germany, 1997; Japan Tour, 1998; Concert Tour, Taiwan, 2002. *Recordings:* Last Thought Before Sleeping, 1982; Training, 1985; Words From The Heart, 1988; Clear Night, 1991; Straight On, 1993; Two Bridges, 1995; Different Ways, 1996; Fingerprint, 1997; Connections, 2000; Sur Vesdre, 2002. *Publications:* Selections from Two Bridges, Straight On and Clear Night, 1996. *Membership:* ASIA (Asscn of Stringed Instrument Artisans). *Address:* Jacques Stotzem, 24 rue Francval, 4800 Lambermont, Belgium. *E-mail:* jaques@stotzem.com. *Website:* www.stotzem.com.

STOVEY, Martin Trevor; b. 27 Feb. 1971, Bushey, Hertfordshire, England. Musician (keyboards); Songwriter; Arranger. *Education:* HNC Civil Engineering. *Career:* Kings College, Cambridge, 1990–92; Flavour of the Month at Borderline, 1993; Lindsey Wesker Show (Kiss FM). *Recordings:* Driftings; Oh La La; Love Season; Chosen Child; Populus; I Witness, as Sykes, 2000. *Membership:* Musicians' Union. *Address:* 66 Milton Dr., Borehamwood, Hertfordshire WD6 2BB, England.

STRACHAN, Matthew James; b. 11 Dec. 1970, London, England. Composer; Musician (piano). *Education:* Dartington College of Arts, Devon. *Career:* Musical Director of stage shows: Flora The Red Menace; Godspell; You don't Have To Say You Love Me. *Compositions include:* Music written or arranged for television: The Detectives; The Hypnotic World of Paul McKenna; The Jasper Carrott Trial; The Ward; What's Cooking?; Scratchy and Co; Who Wants To Be A Millionaire?; The People Versus; Compositions for Theatre: Simpleton of the Unexpected Isles; The Good Woman of Setzuan; The Fly. *Membership:* PRS; FRS; MCPS. *Current Management:* Blaze Music. *Address:* Upper Flat, 162 George Lane, London E18 1AY, England.

STRADLIN, Izzy, (Jeffrey Isabelle); b. 8 April 1961, Lafayette, IN, USA. Rock Musician (guitar). *Career:* Mem., US heavy rock group, Guns N' Roses, 1985–91; Regular national and international tours include: US support tours, Iron Maiden; Mötley Crüe; The Cult; Aerosmith; Get In The Ring tour, with Skid Row, 1991; Major concerts include: Monsters of Rock, Castle Donington, 1988; Farm Aid IV, 1990; Rock In Rio II, Brazil, 1991; Founder, Izzy Stradlin and the Ju Ju Hounds, 1992–. *Recordings:* Albums: with Guns N' Roses: Appetite For Destruction (No. 1, USA), 1987; G 'N' R Lies, 1988; Use Your Illusion I (No. 2, USA, UK) and II (No. 1, USA, UK), 1991; with the Ju Ju Hounds: Izzy Stradlin and the Ju Ju Hounds, 1992; 117°, 1998; Ride On, 1999. Singles: with Guns N' Roses: Live ?1*! Like A Suicide, 1986; Welcome To The Jungle, 1987; Sweet Child O'Mine (No. 1, USA), 1988; Night Train, 1989; Paradise City, 1989; Patience, 1989; Knockin' On Heaven's Door (used in film soundtrack, Days of Thunder), 1990; You Could Be Mine (used in film soundtrack, Terminator 2), 1991; Don't Cry, 1991; with the Ju Ju Hounds: Pressure Drop, 1992. *Honours:* American Music Awards, Favourite Heavy Metal Single, Favourite Heavy Metal Artist and Album, 1989; Rolling Stone and Billboard magazine awards. *Address:* c/o Geffen Records, 9130 Sunset Blvd, Los Angeles, CA 90069–6197, USA.

STRAHAN, Derek William; b. 28 May 1935, Penang, Malaysia. Composer; Writer; Actor; Vocalist; Dir; Prod. Divorced, 1 s., 1 d. *Education:* BA, Cantab Modern Languages, Cambridge University. *Career:* Singer, Songwriter, topical songs, TV appearances ABCTV, This Day Tonight, ATN7 Breakfast Show, 1970; Actor, Number 96, 1974; Actor, film, Fantasy, 1990; Actor, leading role, Inspector Shanahan Mysteries (Cult of Diana), 1992; Radio Presenter, Words and Music, Eastside Radio FM, 1984–. *Compositions:* Concert Music: String Quartet No 1, The Key, 1981; Clarinet Quintet No 1 in D, The Princess 1981; Rose of the Bay, song cycle, 1987; String Trio No 1 in F, 1987; Escorts Trio, 1989; China Spring Cello/Piano, 1989; Atlantis, Flute/Piano, 1990; Solo Cello Suite No 1, 1991; Solo Cello Suite No 2, 1992; Atlantis Variations for Piano, 1992; Voodoo Fire, Trio, 1994; Eden in Atlantis, Soprano/Flute/Piano, 1995; Clarinet Concerto No 1, 2001. *Recordings:* Film music: 30 documentaries including: Shell's Australia, 13 part, 1969–73; Aliens Among Us and Garden Jungle, 1974; Artisans of Australia, 4 part, 1985; Feature films, Leonora, 1985; Fantasy, 1990; Cult of Diana, 1992. *Membership:* Australian Music Centre, represented composer; APRA; Music Arrangers Guild of Australia; Australian Writers Guild; Media Entertainment and Arts Alliance. *Current Management:* Revolve Pty Ltd. *Address:* PO Box 1003, Marrickville, NSW 2204, Australia. *E-mail:* dstrahan@revolve.com.au. *Website:* www.revolve.com.au.

STRAIT, George; b. 18 May 1952, Poteet, Texas, USA. Country Vocalist. m. Norma, 1 d. *Education:* Agriculture, SW Texas State University. *Career:* Solo singer, with own band, Ace In The Hole, formed at college; Recording artist, Nashville, 1981–; Film appearance, The Soldier. *Recordings:* 31 US Country Singles include: Fool Hearted Memory, 1982; Amarillo By Morning, 1983; You Look So Good In Love, 1984; Does Fort Worth Ever Cross Your Mind, 1985; Nobody In His Right Mind Would've Left Her, 1986; Am I Blue, 1987; Famous Last Words of a Fool, 1988; Baby's Gotten Good At Goodbye, 1989; Ace In The Hole, 1989; Love Without End, 1990; I've Come To Expect It From You, 1990; Drinking Champagne, 1991; When Did You Stop Loving Me, 1993; Easy Come, 1993; I'd Like to Have That One Back, 1993; Lovebug, 1994; Man in Love with You, 1994; Big One, 1994; You Can't Make a Heart Love, 1994; Murder on Music Row, with Alan Jackson, 2000 Albums include: Strait Country, 1981; Strait From Your Heart, 1982; Right Or Wrong, 1983;

Does Fort Worth Ever Cross Your Mind?, 1984; Something Special, 1985; Merry Christmas Strait To You, 1986; No 7, 1987; Ocean Front Property, 1987; If You Ain't Lovin' (You Ain't Livin), 1988; Beyond The Blue Neon, 1989; Livin' It Up, 1990; Chill of An Early Fall, 1991; Holding My Own, 1992; Pure Country, 1992; Lead On, 1995; Strait Out of The Box, 1996; Blue Clear Sky, 1996; Carrying Your Love with Me, 1997; One Step at a Time, 1998; Always Never the Same, 1999; Merry Christmas Wherever You Are, 1999; George Strait, 2000; Latest Greatest Straitest Hits, 2000; The Road Less Travelled, 2001. *Honours:* CMA Awards: Entertainer of the Year, 1989, 1990; Male Vocalist of the Year, 1985, 1986, 1996, 2000; Album of the Year, 1985, 1996, 2000; Single of the Year, 1996; Vocal Event of the Year, 2000; ACM Awards: Entertainer of the Year, 1990; Male Vocalist of the Year, 1984, 1985, 1989; American Music Award: Top Country Vocalist, 1991; SRO Touring Artist of Year, 1990. *Membership:* ACM; CMA. *Current Management:* Erv Woolsey Co, 1000 18th Ave S, Nashville, TN 37212, USA.

STRAND, Arthur John Philip; b. 8 Oct. 1948, Finchampstead, Berkshire, England. Musician (fretboards, lute, flamenco); Composer. *Education:* SE Berks College; Private cornet tuition. *Career:* Six Minus Two; Sketch; Misty; Concerts, deps, sessions; BBC radio and TV (sound only); US Forces Europe tours and residencies; Songwriting, composing; Studio installation, promotion; Own record label; Folk Session Singarounds, Acoustic. *Compositions:* 164 songs, 1964–94; 150 instrumental melodies; four fusion longer works, one orchestral work, 1985; Supplied sequence for Figure of Eight on Flowers in the Dirt album, Paul McCartney. *Recordings:* As bassist: If Not For You, Olivia Newton-John. *Publications:* Poem, Time Itself Imploded, Poetry Now, 1996; Editor, Escutcheon Magazine, 1997–. *Membership:* ABJM; BAC & S; Musicians' Union; GISC; F/MBF; PPL; Lute Society; Peña Flamenca; MCPS; PRS; PAMRA; ISA; ASCAP; MU. *Current Management:* Escusson Deux. *Address:* Escutcheon Media, 7 Grove Close, Nine Mile Ride, Wokingham, Berkshire, England.

STRANDBERG, Orjan; b. 22 Aug. 1956, Stockholm, Sweden. Composer; Lyricist; Musician (guitar). m. Carina Strandberg, 3 July 1981, 1 d. *Career:* Musician, TV, 1970; Dice, progressive rock group, 1974; Dice, first album, 1978; Touring to Sweden and Denmark, until 1980; Signed by Peer Music as Songwriter; JetSet, new group, 2 singles released; Fulltime Composer, commercials and industry, 1980–; Responsible for Swedish script and lyrics for Walt Disney's World On Ice, 1989–. *Compositions:* Commercials and industrial assignments. *Recordings:* Albums: with Dice: Dice, 1978; The Four Riders of the Apocalypse, 1992; Live Dice, 1993; Singles: with JetSet: Rock 'n' Roller Skates, 1980; Diamonds for My Hands, 1980; As Producer, Arranger: All Up to You, by World Youth Choir, 1989. *Publications:* Grönsakernas Hemliga Liv (The Secret Life of Vegetables), 1986; several papers on music and copyright between 1990 and today. *Honours:* Several awards; Silver Screen Award, 1985. *Membership:* Board Mem., Swedish Society of Popular Music Composers; Board Mem., Swedish Performing Rights Society; Chairman, Swedish Society of Media Composers; Swedish Artists' and Musicians Organisation. *Current Management:* Vision and Sound AB.

STRANDBERG, Paul Bocciolone; b. 21 July 1949, Malmö, Sweden. Musician. *Career:* Guitar and Cornet player; Formed Scaniazz ensemble, regular performances in Malmö and throughout Sweden; Festival appearances throughout Europe, 1975–77; Tours of Holland, Belgium, Germany, England; Played in pop and folk group playing guitar and banjo, many appearances on radio and TV; Started Absalon Orchestra, '20s style dance music band, played Breda festival, 1987; Played New Orleans Jazz and Heritage festival with Scaniazz, 1982; Band disbanded, 1987; Played cornet, Peruna Jazzmen, tours of Holland and Germany, 1983; Teacher, Jazz Institute of Malmö; Participated in events organized by Malmö College of Music; Board Member of new jazz club; Founded Paul and his Gang, 1990; Tours of Hungary and Czech Republic and at European jazz festivals including International Dixieland Festival in Dresden, Germany, 1997; Chicago, USA and Toronto, Canada, 2000; Regular tours in Europe with Hot House Jazzmen and also Original Jazzmakers; Sousaphone with Swing Kings quartet. *Recordings include:* With Scaniajazz: Some Like it Hot, 1977; Messin' Around, 1980; Sunset Café Stomp, 1982; In New Orleans, 1982; Jazzfestival Dresden, 1985–86; With Absalon Orchestra: Reaching for Someone, 1985; Stardust, 1986; Paul and His Gang: Jazzfestival Breda, 1982; Futuristic Rhythm, 1994; Hot House Jazzmen: Storyville's Sensation, 1994; Anthology; Hot House Jubilee, 1999. *Publications:* Essays and reviews of classical jazz in periodicals. *Honours:* Certificate of Merit, City of New Orleans, 1982; Cultural Award, Malmö, 1989; Grant, Arts Council of Sweden, 1991, 1994; Winner, Competition for Jazz Bands in Breda, Holland, 1992. *Address:* Aengelholmsgatan 10B, 214 22 Malmö, Sweden.

STRAND-HOLM, Klaus; b. 6 May 1951, Praestoe, Denmark. Musician; Vocalist; Prod. m. Karin Maud Mortensen, 7 April 1985. *Career:* Released 25 albums and 40 singles, many in Danish charts, 1969–; Appearances on television. *Recordings:* Den Bedste Pige; Lad mig Vaere den; Der' Rock, Der' Pop; 60'er musik; Herstedvester; Bank 3 gange; Oresund; Herlig Herlig; Ring Ring; Ska'det vaere os to; 25 Rode Roser; Vi Maa Passe Bedre Paa Vor Jord, with Klaus and Servants, 1999; Naar Et Hjerte Slaar, Jeg Vil leve.

Membership: Dansk Musiker Forbund; KODA; NCB; DPA. *Address:* Stadionvej 15, 4720 Praestoe, Denmark.

STRAVATO, William; b. 1 June 1968, Fondi, Italy. Musician (guitar). *Education:* Degree in English and Spanish Language and Literature; Graduated, Guitar Institute of Technology, Hollywood, USA. *Career:* Studio and live session work for Italian pop singers; Columnist, Axe guitar magazine. *Recordings:* Album: Survivor. *Address:* Viale Europa 29, 00042 Anzio, Rome, Italy.

STRAYBLOVA, Blanka; b. 1952, Prague, Czech Republic. Musician; Composer; Vocalist. *Career:* Played in several important alternative rock groups; Member, The Rock and Joces Extempore Band, 1978–; Innumerable concerts; Toured London, Hungary; Founder, MCH Band. *Recordings:* with The Extempere Band: 9 albums; with MCH Band: 7 albums. *Address:* Romek Hanzlik Via Unijazz, Jindrisska 5, 110 00 Prague 1, Czech Republic.

STREET, Karen Jane; b. 13 Dec. 1959, Burton-On-Trent, England. Musician (saxophone, accordion, clarinet, flute). *Education:* Bath College of Higher Education; Welsh College of Music and Drama. *Career:* Member, The Fairer Sax; Member, Saxtet (saxophone quintet); Member, Mike Westbrook Orchestra; Extensive tours; Television and radio appearances include: Wogan; Jim'll Fix It; Blue Peter; Forty Minutes; Radio 3; Nightride; Woman's Hour. *Recordings:* Diversions; Saxpressions; Comparing Notes; Safer Sax. *Publications:* Streetwise; Easy Street; Dizzy Duets; Fairer Sax Album 1 and 2; Streetbeats; All Because of You. *Address:* 14 Janice Grove, Yardley Wood, Birmingham B14 4DP, England.

STREET, Stephen; b. 29 March 1960, London, England. Record Prod; Musician (guitar, bass, keyboards). m. Sarah, 14 Aug. 1987, 2 s., 1 d. *Career:* Recording Engineer, Island Records, 1980s; Freelance, after working with The Smiths on 3 albums, 1980s; Co-wrote and Produced Morrissey's First Solo LP, Viva Hate, 1988; Pursued Production career, Indie Music Genre including: Blur, Sleeper, The Cranberries, Psychedelic Furs, Triffids, The Pretenders; Shed Seven. *Compositions:* with Morrissey: Viva Hate, album; Suedehead; Singles: Everyday Is Like Sunday; Last of the Famous International Playboys; Interesting Drug. *Recordings:* The Smiths: The Queen is Dead; Strangeways Here We come; Morrissey: Viva Hate; The Cranberries: Everybody Else is Doing It; No Need to Argue; Wake Up And Smell The Coffee; Greatest Hits; Sleeper: The It Girl; Pleased To Meet You; Blur: Leisure; Modern Life Is Rubbish; Parklife; The Great Escape; The Pretenders: Last of the Independents, The Isle of View; Viva El Amor; Shed Seven: Let It Ride; Lloyd Cole & The Negatives: Negatives; The Webb Brothers: Maroon; The Promise Ring: Wood/Water; Suede: A New Morning. *Honours:* Q Magazine, Best Producer, 1995. *Membership:* Re-Pro. *Current Management:* Gailforce Management, 24 Ives St, London SW3 2ND, England.

STREETS, (THE). See: **SKINNER, Mike.**

STREISAND, Barbra Joan; b. 24 April 1942, Brooklyn, NY, USA. Vocalist; Actress; Dir; Prod; Writer; Composer; Philanthropist. m. (1) Elliot Gould, 1963, divorced 1971, 1 s., (2) James Brolin, 1998. *Career:* Actress since age 15; Recording artiste, 1962–; Concerts include: Support to Liberace, Hollywood Bowl, 1963; Madison Square Garden (as part of first tour for 27 years), recorded for later release, 1994; Stage performances include: Nightclub debut, Greenwich Village, 1961; New York theatre debut, Another Evening With Harry Stoones, 1961; I Can Get It For You Wholesale, 1962; Funny Girl, New York 1964, London, 1966; Film appearances: Funny Girl, 1968; Hello Dolly!, 1969; On a Clear Day You Can See Forever, 1970; The Owl and the Pussycat, 1971; What's Up Doc?, 1972; Up the Sandbox, 1972; The Way We Were, 1973; For Pete's Sake, 1974; Funny Lady, 1975; A Star is Born (also prod.), 1976; The Main Event (also prod.), 1979; All Night Long, 1981; Yentl (also writer, dir, prod.), 1984; Nuts (also prod., composer), 1987; The Prince of Tides (also dir, prod.), 1990; The Mirror Has Two Faces, 1996; Television specials: My Name Is Barbra, 1965; Color Me Barbra, 1966; Belle of 14th Street, 1967; A Happening in Central Park, 1968; And Other Musical Instruments, 1973; One Voice, 1976; Barbra Streisand – The Concert (HBO, also prod., co-dir), 1994; Exec. prod., Silence: The Margarete Cammermeyer Story (NBC), 1995. *Recordings:* 58 albums incl.: The Barbra Streisand Album, 1963; The Second Barbra Streisand Album, 1963; The Third Album, 1964; My Name Is Barbra, 1965; People, 1965; Color Me Barbra, 1966; Je M'Appelle Barbra, 1967; Barbra Streisand: A Happening In Central Park, 1968; What About Me?, 1969; Stoney End, 1970; Barbra Joan Streisand, 1972; Classical Barbra, 1974; The Way We Were, 1974; Lazy Afternoon, 1975; A Star Is Born, 1976; Superman, 1977; Songbird, 1978; Wet, 1979; Guilty (with Barry Gibb), 1980; Memories, 1981; Emotion, 1984; The Broadway Album, 1986; One Voice, 1986; Til I Loved You, 1989; Just For The Record, 1991; Butterfly, 1992; Back To Broadway, 1993; Barbra Streisand – The Concert, 1994; The Concert – Highlights, 1995; Mirror Has Two Faces, 1996; Higher Ground, 1997; A Love Like Ours, 1999; Timeless, 2000; Christmas Memories, 2001; The Essential Barbra Streisand, 2002; Duets, 2002; Soundtracks include: Funny Girl, 1968; Yentl, 1983; Nuts, 1987; The Prince of Tides, 1991. *Honours:* NY Critics Award, Best Supporting Actress, for I Can Get It For You Wholesale, 1962; Variety Poll Award, Best Foreign Actress, for Funny Girl, UK, 1966; Academy Awards, Best Actress, Funny Girl, 1968, Best Composition (joint winner), Evergreen, 1976; Special Tony Award, for Funny Girl, 1970; Golden Globe Awards, Best Actress, Funny Girl, 1968, Best Picture, Best Director, Yentl, 1984; Emmy Awards, Five for My Name Is Barbra, 1966, five for Barbra Streisand: The Concert, 1994; Three Cable Ace Awards, Barbra Streisand: The Concert, 1994; Peabody Awards, My Name Is Barbra, 1966, Barbra Streisand: The Concert, 1994; Grammy Awards, Best Female Vocalist, 1963, 1964, 1965, 1977, 1986, Best Songwriter (with Paul Williams), 1977; Awarded 37 Gold and 21 Platinum discs. *Address:* c/o Martin Erlichman Assocs, Inc, 5670 Wilshire Blvd, Suite 2400, Los Angeles, CA 90036, USA. *Website:* www.barbrastreisand.com.

STUART, Gareth Ian; b. 26 March 1963, Bracknell, Berkshire, England. Recording Engineer; Lecturer; Musician (clarinet, saxophone, guitar). m. Amanda Jane, 23 Sept. 1989, 1 s. *Education:* Guildhall School of Music (part time), CCAT, Surrey University. *Career:* Recording studio owner, engineer, 1986–; Partner, Zigzag Music Productions, 1992–; Sound projectionist for Tim Souster (Equalisation and trumpet concerto); Equale Brass, Chelmsford Festival, Philharmonia, Queen Elizabeth Hall; Sinetone Generator Operator for Stockhausen 'Mixtur' with BBC Symphony Orchestra, Barbican. *Recordings:* Sin Ti Por El Alma Adentro, for album Culture Electroniques, Julio D'Escrivan; Lady of The Grave, Faith; My Guitar, Bongo Blister; Hold On Tight, Bob and The Bearcats; Rollin' To The Jukebox Rock, Bob And The Bearcats. *Publications:* Articles on recording equipment, Sound On Sound, 1987–89. *Honours:* Clarinet (Grade 8); Alto Saxophone (Grade 8); Piano (Grade 6); GMus, Distinction; PG Dip (Tonmeister), Surrey University. *Membership:* Associate APRS; Musicians' Union; MCPS. *Address:* Zigzag Music Productions, Croeso, Church Lane, Hilton, Huntingdon, Cambs PE18 9NH, England.

STUART, George K; b. 25 Jan. 1951, Edinburgh, Scotland. Musician (drums, percussion). 1 s. *Career:* Tour with band Scottie, 1975; Support to Showaddywaddy, Shakin' Stevens, and Hello; German tour of American airbases, 1974 and 1976; Television appearance: Arrows, Granada TV, (with Scottie), 1976; Radio appearances with Scottie; Member, Distraction, 1993–. *Recordings:* with Scottie: Happy Together, 1975; Sweet Rock 'N' Roll, 1976; The Time Has Come, 1976; with West Side Strut: Nothing I Can Do, 1978. *Membership:* Musicians' Union. *Address:* 9 Victoria Rd, Victoria Park, Newton Grange, Edinburgh EH22 4NN, Scotland.

STUART, Glenn Douglas; b. 8 May 1932, Elmira, New York, USA. Musician (lead trumpet). m. Laverne, 4 Nov. 1981, 1 s., 2 d. *Education:* BS, Ithaca College; MA New York University. *Career:* Played trumpet with orchestras: Tony Pastor; Richard Hayman; Noro Morales; Ralph Marterie; Vaughn Monroe; Les and Larry Elgart; Tommy Tucker; Hank Levy; Jimmy Dorsey; Stan Kenton, Don Ellis, 1965–; Tours: Canada; Bermuda; Japan; Hawaii; Europe, with Don Ellis, 1969, 1977; Jazz Festivals include: Monterey; New Port; North Sea; Montreux; Pacific; Antibes; Television, films include: Emmy Awards Banquet; Ed Sullivan Show; Shirley Maclaine Special; Mission Impossible; French Connection I and II; Soupy Sales Special, California; Played with artists including: The Supremes; Frankie Avalon; Joe Williams; Jack Jones; Frankie Valli; Chubby Checker; Cleo Laine; Johnny Mathis; Jose Feliciano; Steve Lawrence; Phyllis Diller; Pat Boone; Louis Armstrong; Paul Anka; Teaches trumpet, schools, colleges, California; Lecturer, clinics, universities, colleges. *Recordings include:* Featured on album: Autumn, Don Ellis; Single: Child of Ecstasy, Don Ellis. *Publications:* The Art of Playing Lead Trumpet. *Honours:* Featured soloist at International Trumpet Guild, 1977. *Membership:* NA of Jazz Educators. *Address:* 21682 Ocean Vista Dr., Laguna Beach, CA 92651, USA.

STUART, James Hamish; b. 8 Oct. 1949, Glasgow, Scotland. Vocalist; Musician (guitar, bass); Writer. m. Lyn, 2 May, 1 s., 2 d. *Education:* 3 grades piano. *Career:* Began recording with Dream Police, 1969; Average White Band, 1972–82; Numerous tours, television shows, 1972–82; Tours with Chaka Khan, David Sanborn, numerous writing, production credits, 1982–87; 2 world tours, 5 albums with Paul McCartney. *Recordings:* Pick Up The Pieces (No. 1, USA), 1975, Person To Person, A Love of Your Own; Queen of My Soul; Schoolboy Crush, on 8 Average White Band albums; Flowers In The Dirt; Off The Ground; Paul Is Live; Tripping The Light Fantastic; Unplugged; Albums with Paul McCartney; Atlantic Starr: If Your Heart Isn't In It; Chaka Khan: Whatcha Gonna Do For Me; David Sanborn: Love and Happiness; Solo albums: Sooner Or Later, 1999. *Honours:* Many Gold, Platinum discs with: Average White Band; Chaka Khan; Paul McCartney. *Membership:* ASCAP; AFTRA; PRS. *Current Management:* Ramon Hervey. *Address:* New York, Los Angeles, USA.

STUART, Marty; b. 30 Sept. 1958, Philadelphia, Pennsylvania, USA. Vocalist; Musician (guitar, mandolin). *Career:* Concerts include No Hats Tour, 1992; Television: Marty Party, TNN, 4 shows; The Music of The Wild West, TNN Special, 1993. *Recordings:* Hillbilly Rock, 1989; Little Things; Tempted, 1991; Burn Me Down; Till I Found You; Western Girls (all Top 10); Once Upon a Time, 1992; This One's Gonna Hurt You, 1992; Love and Luck, 1994; Marty Party Hit Pack, 1995; Honky Tonkin's What I Do Best, 1996; The Pilgrim, 1999; Singles: Hey Baby, 1993; Kiss Me I'm Gone, 1994; That's What Love's

About, 1994; Sweet Love, 1997; Session work includes: Pam Gadd; Alison Moorer; Johnny Russell; Billy Bob Thornton. *Honours:* CMA Award, Vocal Event, with Travis Tritt, 1992; Grammy Awards: Best Vocal Collaboration, with Travis Tritt, 1993; Best Country Instrumental, with Bob Wills, 1994. *Membership:* Inducted into Grand Ole Opry, 1992. *Current Management:* Rothbaum and Garner. *Address:* 119 17th Ave S, Nashville, TN 37203, USA.

STUBER, William Charles; b. 25 Sept. 1951, Rochester, NY, USA. Prod; Engineer; Musician (percussion); Arranger. m. Irene Stuber, 1 s. *Education:* Recording Institute of America; Stonybrook University; Cleveland Institute of electronics. *Career:* KONP; KCTS; NZOK; KZAM; ISIW; KZFM; KBPI; King Television; KIRO Television. *Compositions:* Devotion; Love's Heavenly Dream. *Recordings:* Include, Hall and Oates; Rachael Sweet; Nitty Gritty; Supersonics; Ted Nugent; The Hooters; Heart; Jesse Colin Young; Sammy Hagar; Judas Priest; London Ballet; Moscow Ballet. *Publications:* Love's Heavenly Dream, 1995; Devotion, 1996; Ultimate Love, 1997; Gems of The Seven Color Rays, 2000. *Honours:* Seattle's Best Recordings, 1979. *Membership:* RIAA. *Address:* 2076 Taylor Cutoff Rd, Sequim, WA 98382, USA.

STYLUS TROUBLE. See: **HELLER, Pete.**

SUBBULAKSHMI, Madurai Shanmugavadivu; b. 16 Sept. 1916, Madurai, India. Classical Karnatic Musician. m. Sri T. Sadasivam, 1940. *Career:* Recitals with her mother, Guru Veena Shanmugavadivu, 1928–32; Gave solo performances and became a leading musician before age 18; Acted title role in Hindi film Meera; Numerous benefit performances, donated royalties from many of her records to social and religious causes; Represented Karnatic music at Edinburgh Festival, 1963; Concerts in London, Frankfurt, Geneva, Cairo; Seven-week tour of USA, 1966; Performed in Tokyo, Bangkok, Hong Kong, Manila, Singapore, Malaysia, New York, Pittsburgh, Moscow; Pres., Chennai Music Conference, 1968; National Prof. (Music), 1990–; National Research Prof., 1995–; Prod. Emeritus, All India Radio and Doordarshan, 1979–; Life mem., International Music Council, 1981; Trustee Indira Gandhi National Centre for Arts. *Honours:* Hon. DLitt, Ravindra Bharati University, 1967, Shri Venkateswara University, 1971, Delhi University, 1973, Madhya Pradesh University, 1979, Banaras Hindu University, 1980, Chennai University, 1987, Tirupati, 1989, Madurai Kamaraj University, 1994; President's Award for Karnatic Music, 1956; Ramon Magsaysay Award for Public Service, Philippines, 1974; Melvin Jones Fellowship Award for outstanding humanitarian services, 1986; Indira Gandhi Award, 1990; Woman of the Year Award, International Women's Asscn, 1992; Swaralaya Puraskaram–Delhi Award, 1997; Sangeet Natak Acad. Fellowship, 1974; Padma Bhushan, 1954; Padma Vibhushan, 1975; Hon. title Sangeetha Khalanidhi, Sapthagiri Sangeetha Vidwanmani, 1975, Thanipperum Kalaignyar, 1980, Gayaka Ratnam, 1990. *Address:* 'Sivam-Subham', 11 First Main Rd, Kotturpuram, Chennai 600085, India.

SUGAR, (Zacharia Hajishacalli); b. 8 July 1954, London, England. Musician (bouzouki, Cypriot flute); Prod. m. Androulla, 24 July 1977, 2 d. *Education:* BTec, Electronics; Master classes, bouzouki, Greece. *Career:* Toured with Boy George's Jesus Loves You Band; Concerts include: Town and Country; Ronnie Scott's; Royal Festival Hall; Television and radio appearances: The Word; BSB; Birds of a Feather, BBC; Rhythms of The World, BBC; The Green Line, CH4; Andy Kershaw Show, BBC Radio 1; Les Nuils, French TV; Cyprus TV and radio performances; Runs ethnic music recording studio. *Recordings:* Produced and recorded 4 Greek albums for ARC Music; Bouzouki player on Mathilda May album; Yamaha instruments for sampling bouzouki for new synth; Bouzouki player on 4 tracks for Boy George; Composer, producer, Cypriot Flute of Sugar; Composer, music for film, The Odyssey. *Publications:* Cypriot Flute of Sugar; Turning Point, Angela, 2001; Haji-Mike album. *Membership:* Musicians' Union; PRS; MCPS. *Address:* 7 Bulwer Rd, Edmonton, London N18 1QL, England. *Telephone:* (20) 8803-2058. *E-mail:* sugarstudio@hotmail.com.

SUGGS, (Graham McPherson); b. 13 Jan. 1961, Hastings, Sussex, England. Vocalist. m. Bette Bright, 1982. *Career:* Singer, Madness, 1977–88; Appearances include: 2-Tone Tour, UK, 1979; Twelve Days of Madness Tour, 1980; Far East Tour, 1981; Prince' Trust Royal Gala, 1982; Greenpeace benefit, London, 1983; Solo artiste, 1988–; Regular comedy host, Mean Fiddler Club, North London; Manager, The Farm; Presenter, Night Fever, TV Quiz, Channel 5, 1997–; Team Captain, A Question Of Pop (BBC1), 2000–01; Film appearances: Dance Craze, 1981; Take It Or Leave It, 1981; Madstock–The Movie, 1992; Musical based on Madness songs, Our House, 2002. *Recordings:* Albums: with Madness: One Step Beyond, 1979; Absolutely, 1980 Seven, 1981; Complete Madness, 1982; The Rise and Fall, 1982; Madness, 1983; Keep Moving, 1984; Mad Not Mad, 1985; Utter Madness, 1986; Divine Madness, 1992; Madstock!, 1992; Wonderful, 1999; The Heavy Heavy Hits, 1999; Our House: The Original Songs, 2002; Solo: The Lone Ranger, 1995. Singles: with Madness: The Prince, 1979; One Step Beyond, 1979; My Girl, 1980; Night Boat to Cairo, 1980; Baggy Trousers, 1980; Embarrassment, 1980; Return of The Los Palmas Seven, 1981; Grey Day, 1981; Shut Up, 1981; It Must Be Love, 1982; Cardiac Arrest, 1982; House of Fun (No. 1, UK), 1982; Driving In My Car, 1982; Our House, 1982; Tomorrow's (Just Another Day), 1982; Wings Of A Dove, 1983; The Sun And

The Rain, 1983; Michael Caine, 1984; One Better Day, 1984; Yesterday's Men, 1985; Waiting For The Ghost, 1986; Lovestruck, 1999; Johnny The Horse, 1999; Solo: I'm Only Sleeping, 1995; Camden Town, 1995; Cecilia, 1996; Guest vocalist, Piccadilly Palace, Morrissey, 1990. *Honours:* Singles Artists of the Year, NME, 1980; Ivor Novello Award, Best Pop Song, 1983. *Website:* www.madness.co.uk.

SUGIYAMA, Kazonori; b. 18 Aug. 1950, Tokyo, Japan. Prod. m. Emi Fukui, 11 Aug. 1981. *Education:* BS, Waseda University, Tokyo, also postgraduate study; MA, Boston University, Massachusetts, USA, 1977. *Career:* New York Representative, Jazz Division, Toshiba EMI, 1990–93; US Representative, Executive Producer, DIW/Avant Records, 1991–; Executive Producer, Tzadik Records, 1995–; Advisory Board, New Grove Dictionary of Jazz, 1997. *Recordings:* Bud and Bird/Gil Evans, Engineer, 1988; V/Ralph Peterson Jr, Producer, 1990; Big Band and Quartet, David Murray, Producer, 1992; Produced many other artists including: George Adams; Derek Bailey; Steven Bernstein; Greg Cohen; Joe Henderson; John Patton. *Publications:* Autobiography of Miles Davis, Japanese Translator, 1989. *Honours:* Grammy Award, 1988; Jazz Album of the Year (producer), 1990; Album of the Year in Japan, Best Production, 1992. *Membership:* NARAS. *Address:* 93 Mercer St 3W, New York, NY 10012, USA.

SULTON, Kasim Anthony; b. 08 Dec. 1955, New York, USA. Musician (bass guitar, guitar, keyboards); Vocalist. m. Laurie Rampulla, 1 s., 2 d. *Career:* Joined band, Utopia as bassist and vocalist, 1976; Bassist with Joan Jett, 1986; Bassist with Hall and Oates, 1990; Guitarist with Meat Loaf, 1993; Bassist, musical director, Meat Loaf, 1998. *Compositions:* Set Me Free; Love Is The Answer; Mated. *Recordings:* 10 Utopia Albums, 1976–86; Meat Loaf, Bat Out of Hell, 1 and 2; Joan Jett, I Hate Myself For Loving You; Céline Dion, Falling Into You; Kasim Sulton, Kasim; Todd Rundgren, One Long Year, 2000. *Honours:* Best Video and Grammy Award, 1995, 1996. *Membership:* American Federation of Musicians; American Federation Radio and Television Artists. *Address:* PO Box 060 106, Staten Island, New York 10306, USA.

SUMMER, Donna, (Donna Adrian Gaines); b. 31 Dec. 1948, Boston, Massachusetts, USA. Vocalist; Songwriter; Actor; Artist. m. (1) Helmut Sommer, 1971, divorced, 1 d., (2) Bruce Sudano, 1980, divorced, 2 d. *Career:* Singer, various groups, Boston; Appeared in musicals, Munich, Germany, 1968–74; Also worked as model and backing singer; Solo singer, 1975–; Major appearances include: Music For UNICEF Concert, New York, 1979; 50th American Presidential Gala, 1985; American Music Awards Concert Series, Yokohama, Japan, 1991; Actress, film Thank God It's Friday, 1978; Playwrite; As artist: exhibition of paintings and lithographs, New York, Miami, Chicago, and has sold close to $1m. worth of art. *Recordings:* Albums: Love To Love You Baby, 1976; A Love Trilogy, 1976; Four Seasons of Love, 1976; I Remember Yesterday, 1977; Once Upon a Time, 1978; Greatest Hits, 1978; Live and More, 1978; Bad Girls, 1979; On The Radio, 1980; The Wanderer, 1980; Donna Summer, 1982; She Works Hard For The Money, 1983; Cats Without Claws, 1984; All Systems Go, 1987; Another Place and Time, 1989; Best of Donna Summer, 1990; The Donna Summer Anthology, 1993; VH-1: Live And More And Encore, 1999; Hit singles include: Love To Love You Baby, 1976; I Feel Love (No. 1, UK), 1977; Deep Down Inside, from film The Deep, 1977; I Love You, 1978; Love's Unkind, 1978; Last Dance, 1978; MacArthur Park (No. 1, USA), 1977; Heaven Knows, 1979; Hot Stuff (No. 1, USA), 1979; Bad Girls (No. 1, USA), 1979; Dim All The Lights, 1979; No More Tears (Enough Is Enough), duet with Barbra Streisand (No. 1, USA), 1979; On The Radio, from film Foxes, 1980; The Wanderer, 1980; Love Is In Control (Finger On The Trigger), 1982; She Works Hard For The Money, 1983; Dinner With Gershwin, 1987; This Time I Know It's For Real, 1989; I Don't Want To Get Hurt, 1989; State of Independence, 1995; The Donna Summer Anthology, 1993; Donna Summer Christmas Spirit, 1994; Also recorded with: Rosie O'Donnell; Quincy Jones; Gene Simmons; Liza Minnelli. *Honours:* Academy Award, Best Original Song, Heaven Knows, 1979; Grammy Awards: Best Rhythm and Blues Vocal Performance, 1979; Best Rock Vocal Performance, 1980; Best Inspirational Performance, 1984, 1985; American Music Awards: Favourite Female Disco Artist, Disco Single, Disco Album, 1979; Favourite Female Pop/Rock Artist, Favourite Pop/Rock Single, Favourite Female Soul/ R&B Artist, 1980; Star on Hollywood Walk of Fame, 1992; Hon. Doctorate of Fine Arts, University of Massachussetts, 1997; Best Dance Recording, Carry On, 1997; Hon. mem. of The Golden Key National Honor Society, University of Massachusetts, 1997; Guest speaker at American Medical Women's Asscn, 1999. *Current Management:* Moress/Nanas Entertainment; 1102 18th Ave S, Nashville, TN 37212, USA.

SUMMER, Henry Lee; b. 7 May 1960, Evansville, Indiana, USA. Vocalist; Songwriter; Record Prod; Musician (multi-instrumentalist). *Education:* Western Wyoming University. *Career:* National support tours with: Stevie Ray Vaughan; Don Henley; Eddie Money; Richard Marx; .38 Special; Chicago; Cheap Trick; The Doobie Brothers; The Allman Brothers; REO Speedwagon; Also played Indiana State Fair, with John Mellencamp, 1988; Farm Aid IV, with John Mellencamp, Willie Nelson, Guns N' Roses, Neil Young, Bonnie Raitt, Indiana, 1990; Television appearances: David Letterman; Arsenio Hall; Charlie Rose; Guest VJ-MTV, Rock Line. *Recordings:* Albums: Stay With Me,

1984; Time For Big Fun, 1986; Henry Lee Summer, 1988; I've Got Everything, 1989; Way Past Midnight, 1991; Slam Drunk, 1993; Smoke And Mirrors, 1999; Tracks for various film soundtracks including Iron Eagle II and Twins. *Publications:* Song book collections. *Honours:* BMI Award, Hey Baby, 1991. *Membership:* BMI; AFTRA; AFofM. *Current Management:* James Bogard Associates. *Address:* 7608 Teel Way, Indianapolis, IN 46256, USA.

SUMMERS, Al; b. 9 Sept. 1957, Somerset, England. Musician; Composer. m. Gillian Rosemary Summers, 26 Sept. 1992, 1 step-s. *Education:* Dartington College. *Career:* Composition, teaching; Various theatre, some radio; Classical jazz blues and avant garde performances; Session work; Publications on music theory and contributions to journals on teaching theory. *Compositions:* Several hundred compositions for community projects; Early works mostly chamber ensembles and unusual combinations of instruments. *Membership:* Musicians' Union; RGT; SPAM. *Current Management:* Ian Grant, Action Sales, Westbury Trading Estate, Wiltshire, England. *Address:* 61 Bratton Rd, Westbury, Wiltshire BA13 3ES, England. *Telephone:* (1373) 864721. *E-mail:* gill.summers@virgin.net.

SUMMERS, Andy, (Andrew Somers); b. 31 Dec. 1942, Poulton-Le-Fylde, Lancashire, England. Musician (guitar); Vocalist. *Career:* Guitarist, vocalist, The Police, 1977–86; Numerous world-wide tours, television, radio appearances with the Police; Began solo recording career, 1987–; Live music director, The Dennis Miller Show, US television, 1992; Writer, film scores: Weekend At Bernie's; 2010. *Recordings:* Hit singles with The Police: Roxanne, 1979; Can't Stand Losing You, 1979; Message In A Bottle (No. 1, UK), 1979; Walking On The Moon (No. 1, UK), 1979; So Lonely, 1980; Don't Stand So Close To Me (No. 1, UK), 1980; De Do Do Do, De Da Da Da, 1980; Invisible Sun, 1981; Every Little Thing She Does Is Magic (No. 1, UK), 1981; Spirits In The Material World, 1981; Every Breath you Take (No. 1, UK and USA), 1983; King Of Pain, 1983; Wrapped Around Your Finger, 1983; Synchronicity II, 1983; Albums: with The Police: Outlandos D'Amour, 1977; Regatta De Blanc, 1979; Zenyatta Mondatta, 1980; Ghost In The Machine, 1981; Synchronicity, 1983; Solo albums: I Advance Masked, with Robert Fripp, 1982; XYZ, 1987; Mysterious Barricades, 1988; Golden Wire, 1989; Charming Snakes, 1990; World Gone Strange, 1991; Synaesthesia, 1995; The Last Dance of Mr X, 1998; Strings of Desire, 1998; Green Chimneys, 1999; Peggy's Blue Skylight, 2000; Session work includes: Joan Armatrading; Kevin Ayers; David Bedford; Toni Childs. *Honours:* Grammy Awards, with the Police. *Current Management:* Firstars/Talent Bank Management, Bugle House, 21A Noel St, London W1V 3PD, England.

SUMNER, Bernard; b. 4 Jan. 1956, Salford, Lancashire, England. Vocalist; Musician (guitar, keyboards). *Career:* Member, Joy Division, 1977–80; Futurama Festival, Leeds, 1979; European tour, 1980; Member, New Order, 1980–; World-wide tours including Australia; New Zealand; Far East; USA; South America; Concerts include: Glastonbury Festival, 1981, 1987; Futurama Festival, 1982; San Remo Festival, 1988; Monsters of Art tour, with PIL and Sugarcubes, 1989; Reading Festival, 1989; Electronic, 1989; Support to Depeche Mode, Los Angeles Dodgers Stadium, 1990; Cities In The Park Festival, 1991. *Recordings:* Albums: with Joy Division: Unknown Pleasures, 1979; Closer, 1980; Still, 1981; Substance, 1988; The Peel Sessions, 1988; Permanent, 1995; Heart And Soul (box set), 1998; Also featured on Short Circuit – Live At The Electric Circus, 1978; with New Order: Movement, 1981; Power Corruption and Lies, 1983; Low Life, 1985; Brotherhood, 1986; Substance, 1987; Technique (No. 1, UK), 1989; BBC Radio 1 Live In Concert, 1992; Republic, 1993; The Best Of New Order, 1994; The Rest Of New Order, 1995; Get Ready, 2001; Back To Mine (compilation), 2002; with Electronic: Electronic, 1991; Raise the Pressure, 1996. Singles: with Joy Division: Atmosphere, 1979; Transmission, 1980; Love Will Tear Us Apart, 1980; with New Order include: Ceremony, 1981; Procession/Everything's Gone Green, 1981; Temptation, 1982; Confusion, 1983; Blue Monday, 1983; Thieves Like Us, 1984; The Perfect Kiss, 1985; Subculture, 1985; Shellshock, from film soundtrack Pretty In Pink, 1986; Bizarre Love Triangle, 1986; True Faith, 1987; Touched By The Hand of God, 1987; Fine Time, 1988; Round and Round, 1989; World In Motion, with England Football Squad (No. 1, UK), 1990; How Does It Feel?, 1992; Regret, 1993; World (The Price of Love), 1993; Ruined In A Day, 1993; Spooky, 1993; 1963, 1995; Crystal, 2001; 60 Miles An Hour, 2001; Here To Stay, 2002; with Electronic includes: Getting Away With It, featuring Neil Tennant, 1989; Get the Message, 1991; Feel Every Beat, 1991; Disappointed, 1992; Forbidden City, 1996; For You, 1996; Vivid, 1999; Guest vocals on: Out Of Control, Chemical Brothers, 1999; Features on: XTRMNTR, Primal Scream, 2000. *Current Management:* Rebecca Boulton, Prime Management, Ducie House, Ducie St, Manchester, England. *Website:* www.neworderweb.com.

SUMRONGTHONG, Bussakorn; b. 29 Nov. 1962, Thailand. Asst Prof. *Education:* BA, Chulalongham University; MPhil, DPhil, University of York. *Career:* Guest Lecturer; Presentations On Television; Chairman, Secretary, Chulalongkorn University; Judge, Thai Musical Ensemble Competition, The Golden Television Awards, Drawing Competition; Lecturer, Assistant Professor, Chulalongkorn University. *Compositions:* Hudan Mus-Javanese Piece On Thai Xylophone; Homnong Sakura: Composition for the New Millennium; The Thai and European Perspective Concert. *Recordings:*

Manmongkol. *Honours:* First Prize, Best Thai Xylophone Player, 1984. *Membership:* International Council of Traditional Music. *Address:* Faculty of Fine and Applied Arts, Chulalongkorn University, Bangkok 10330, Thailand.

SUN, Hongjun; b. 6 Dec. 1934, Liaoyang District, Liaoning Province, People's Republic of China. Musician (accordion). m. Cui Min, 1 Oct. 1957, 2 s., 2 d. *Education:* ShenYang Musical College. *Career:* Attended PLA China, Liaoning Military Organization, 1956; Attended Fu Shun song and dance ensemble, assigned as accordion player, 1959; Chief, Main Editor, Fushun Office, Chinese National Music, 1979; Programmed Russian Red Army song and dance ensemble, many others. *Compositions:* North East Drum and Wind Music, 1986; Chao Xian Folk Songs, 1991. *Recordings:* 100 Man Folk Songs of China; Xi Bo Music; Chaoxian Folk Songs; North East Drum and Wind Music. *Publications:* National Folk Musician essay, 1995. *Honours:* Man Musical Essay, First Festival of Asian Pacific Society for Ethnomusicology. *Membership:* Cui Min; Sun Like; S Dongke; Sun Qiuke; Xiake. *Address:* 5 E Sixth Rd, Xinfu District, Fushun, Liaoning Province 7677423, People's Republic of China.

SUN, Joe; b. 25 Sept. 1943, Rochester, Minnesota, USA. Musician; Songwriter. m. Inka Sun Paulsen, 10 Oct. 1965. *Education:* Brown School of Broadcasting, Minneapolis, 1967. *Career:* National promotions director, Ovation Records, Nashville, 1976–78; Recording artist, 1978–82; Touring musician, songwriter, 1987–; Actor, film Marie – A True Story, 1986. *Recordings include:* Heartbreak Saloon. *Honours:* Most Promising New Country Artist, Billboard, 1979.

SUND, John; b. 6 Jan. 1957, Copenhagen, Denmark. Musician (guitar); Composer. *Career:* Debut at age 18 as soloist with the Danish Radio Big Band, 1976; Mem., Creme Fraiche Big Band, broadcasting in radio and television, 1978; Permanent mem., Danish Radio Jazzgroup, incl. appearances at Montmartre, 1976–80; Mem. and Contributor to Danish Radio Workshop/Palle Mikkelborg, 1978–80; Formed own band, John Sund Group, with others incl. American trumpet player, Tim Hagans, 1977–79; Own trio, Trigon, broadcast on DR television, 1982; Played with Bo Stief, Thomas Clausen, Alex Reel, Mads Vinding, Debbie Cameron, South Indian musicians Ganesh and Kumaresh, Mariam Mursal, among others; Currently leading jazz/ethnic-fusion ensemble, Special Venture, and world/fusion group Acoustic Sense; Co-leading the jazz/world quartet, World on a String, with violinist Bjarke Falgren. *Compositions:* Fusion Symphony, extended suite of eight compositions, 1993. *Recordings:* with the Neumann Brothers, 3 x Neumann: Song Hits From 1920–70, 1977; with Creme Fraiche Big Band: Creme Fraiche, 1978; with Richard Boone and Debbie Cameron: Brief Encounter, 1978; Yadam: Cosas De La Vida, 2001; Ayi Solomon: Back Home, 2002; Solo: John Sund And The Danish Radio Big Band—Fusion Symphony, 1995; with Special Venture: Special Venture, 1999; John Sund and Acoustic Sense—New Gems, 2003. *Honours:* Jacob Gades Grant, 1977. *Membership:* Society of Danish Jazz, Rock and Folk Composers (DJBFA); KODA; Danish Musicians' Union. *Current Management:* Copenhagen Concerts, Holmbladsgade 35, 2300 Copenhagen S, Denmark. *Website:* www.johnsund.dk.

SUNDING, Per Gunnar; b. 23 Nov. 1967, Lund, Sweden. Vocalist; Songwriter; Prod; Musician (bass). *Career:* Formed Eggstone with Maurits Carlsson and Patrik Bartosch in 1986; Eggstone founded Tambourine Studios with Tore Johansson and Anders Nordgren in 1991; Studios used by St Etienne and the Cardigans; Founded Vibrafon Records in 1995. *Recordings:* with Eggstone: Albums: In San Diego, 1992; Somersault, 1994; Vive La Différence, 1997; with Wannadies: The Wannadies, 1990; Aquanautic, 1992; Be a Girl, 1995; Bagsy Me, 1997; Yeah, 2000; Singles include: You And Me Song, 1996; Hit, 1997; Shorty, 1997; Yeah, 2000; Producer: 3 Bob Hund albums; 1 Ray Wonder album; Co-producer and co-lyricist on Wannadies album Bagsy Me. *Membership:* SKAP. *Current Management:* Marcantonio Management. *Address:* Tambourine Studios, Sofielundsv. 57, 214 34 Malmö, Sweden.

SUONSAARI, Klaus; b. 7 Nov. 1959, Finland. Musician (drums); Composer. *Education:* Piano lessons from age 6; Drums from age 14; Studied at Lahti Conservatory; Eastman School of Music, Rochester, USA; Berklee College of Music, Boston, USA; Private studies with: Billy Higgins; Jeff Hamilton; Alan Dawson; Kauko Saari; Jorma Alanne. *Career:* Living, working in New York, 1985–; Played with musicians including: Bob Berg; Niels-Henning Orsted-Pedersen; Ray Drummond; Tom Harrell; Mike Mainieri; Niels Lan Doky; Muhal Richard Abrams; International appearances in USA; Canada; UK; Scandinavia; Central Europe; Performances with: Jerry Bergonzi; Randy Brecker; Geri Allen; Joe Henderson; Toots Thielemans; David Sanborn. *Recordings include:* Inside Out, 1995; Something In Common, 1998; With Every Breath I Take, 1999. *Honours:* Buddy Rich Jazz Masters Award, 1983; Quincy Jones Jazz Masters Award, 1984; Artist of the Year Award, Finland, 1992. *Membership:* Local 802; AFofM; AFL; CIO; Associated Musicians of Greater New York. *Current Management:* Charlie Elliott Talent Group 7 Fourth St, Suite 43, Petaluma, CA 94952, USA. *Address:* 652 Blvd E, Weehawken, NJ 07087–6811, USA.

SURNOCK, Richard William; b. 19 Oct. 1932, Chicago, Illinois, USA. Musician. m. Lynn Margaret Kennaugh, 16 May 1964, 1 s., 2 d. *Education:* Los Angeles City College. *Career:* Musician with: Buddy Rich, 1956; Mort Sahl and Joanie Sommers, 1958; Murry Arnold, 1960; Jim McDonald Trio, 1965–; Billy Daniels, 1970; Peggy Lee, 1980; Mickey Rooney Show, 1988; Page Cavanaugh, 1990; Palisades Symphony, 1990–.

SUTCLIFFE, Jess (Jeremy); b. 25 Nov. 1958, London, England. Recording Engineer; Prod. m. Shari Lee Inoue, 25 July 1987, 1 s., 1 d. *Career:* Tape Operator and Assistant Engineer, London Recording Studios, 1977; Independent First Engineer, 1979; Engineer for Vangelis, 1982–86; Recording Engineer for films, records, and TV commercials; Freelance Engineer and Producer, 1987; Moved to Los Angeles, 1988. *Recordings:* Artists include: Vangelis; Toto; Manu Dibango; Warren Hill; Aretha Franklin; Jon and Vangelis; Carlene Carter; Sheila E; Quincy Jones; Patti LaBelle; Willie Nelson; Patti Austin; Gary Numan; Elvis Costello; Sheena Easton; Wall of Voodoo; The Fall; Handel's Messiah; Meat Loaf; Toto; Film scores include: The Bounty; Boyz 'n the Hood. *Honours:* Platinum records; Grammy-winning records. *Membership:* NARAS. *Current Management:* Belgravia Music. *Address:* Belgravia Music, 22647 Ventura Blvd, Suite 301, Woodland Hills, CA 91364, USA.

SUTTON, Chris; b. 25 Dec. 1960, Essex, England. Vocalist; Songwriter; Musician (piano, keyboards). m. Elaine Sutton, 1 d. *Career:* First solo album with 22, produced by Motown producer Dennis Lambert; Support to James Brown, Wembley Arena, London; 2 Top 100 singles, Germany airplay. *Compositions:* That's Her Way, 1994; However Long It Takes, 1994; Miracle, 1994. *Recordings:* That's Her Way; However Long It Takes; COCO, with COCO; Album: Songs Into The Light; Recorded with Paul McCartney, George Michael and Mark Knopfler; Singer, Knee Deep in the Hoopla album, Starship. *Membership:* PRS. *Address:* c/o BME Records, Postbox 450224, 50877 Cologne, Germany.

SUTTON, Graham Paul; b. 1 April 1972, Stratford, London, England. Songwriter; Vocalist; Prod; Musician (multi-instrumentalist). *Career:* Formed Bark Psychosis, 1987; Left school and home to pursue music at 16; Recorded several independently released and critically acclaimed EPs; Signed to Circa Records; Worked with: Lee Harris, Paul Webb of Talk Talk under name Orang; Also records under name Boymerang: Soul Beat Runna; Mind Control; Still. *Recordings:* Albums: Bark Psychosis: Hex, 1994; Independency, 1994; Game Over, 1997; also appears on: White Squall; Fields and Waves; Inventing the Abbotts; Balance of the Force; Event Horizon. *Membership:* Musicians' Union; PRS; MCPS. *Current Management:* Mike Collins. *Address:* 40 Abbotsford Gardens, Woodford Green, Essex IG8 9HW, England.

SUTTON, Ralph; Recording Engineer; Mixer; Re-mixer. *Education:* Recording Institute of America; University of California, Los Angeles. *Career:* Runner, Second Engineer, City Recorders; Engineer, Chateau Recording Studios; Electra Asylum Recording Annex; Motown Hitsville, U.S.A., 1982–86; Lionshare Recording Studios; The Tracking Place, 1995–96; Chief Engineer and Dir of Studio Operations, Wonderland Recording Studios; Worked with: Norman Brown, C4, Chicago, George Duke, The Four Tops, Marvin Gaye, Howard Hewett, Whitney Houston, Julio Iglesias, Rick James, Kansas, Kenny Loggins, Tina Marie, Missing Persons, Mötley Crüe, Yoshiaki Ochi, Jeffrey Osborne, Lionel Richie, Smokey Robinson, Frank Sinatra, Barbra Streisand, The Temptations, Dionne Warwick, Stevie Wonder; Contributed to film soundtracks: Bamboozled, BAPS, The Big Chill, Dangerous Ground, Eddie, Get Crazy, John Q, The Last Dragon, Sprung. *Honours:* Adlib Magazine, Superior Record of the Year in the Best Engineering Section. *Membership:* National Asscn of Recording Arts and Sciences, board of govs. *Current Management:* C Management.

SVARE, Jorgen Christian; b. 28 Dec. 1935, Copenhagen, Denmark. Musician. 2 s., 1 d. *Career:* Clarinet Player, Local Bands, 1950s'; Founder Member, Papa Bue's Viking Jazz Band, 1956; Played and Toured World-wide, 30 years; Own quartet, 1986–95; Club Owner, Jazz Club, Slukefter Jazzhus, Tivoli Gardens, Copenhagen, 1994–97; Co-leader of Stolle and Svare Jazz Quintet, 1995–. *Compositions:* Slukefter Blues. *Recordings:* Over 60 Albums with Papa Bue; 6 albums with quartet; 1 album with Stolle and Svare Jazz Quintet, 1998. *Honours:* Sorens Penge, Denmark, 1996. *Membership:* Danish Society of Band Leaders. *Address:* Peder Hvitfeldts Straede 11, 1173 Copenhagen K, Denmark.

SVEINSSON, Kjartan (Kjarri); b. Iceland. Musician (keyboards). *Career:* Mem., Icelandic band, Sigur Rós; Signed to MCA/Universal, USA, FatCat Records, UK; Music featured in film, Vanilla Sky, 2001; North American tour, 2001; European tour, 2002. *Recordings:* Albums: Von; Agœtis Byrjun, 2000; ( ), 2002. Singles: Ny Batteri, 2000; Svefn-G-Englar, 2001; Contributed to: Angels of the Universe (soundtrack), 2001. *Honours:* Shortlist Music Prize, 2001. *Address:* c/o FatCat Records, PO Box 3400, Brighton BN1 4WG, England. *Website:* www.sigur-ros.com.

SVENINGSSON, Johan Magnus; b. 4 April 1972, Falköping, Sweden. Musician (bass guitar); Songwriter. *Career:* Founding mem., The Cardigans,

with Peter Svensson, 1992–; Contributed tracks to films Romeo and Juliet and A Life Less Ordinary; Numerous concert tours, festivals, television and radio appearances. *Recordings:* Albums: Emmerdale, 1994; Life, 1995; First Band On The Moon, 1996; Other Side Of The Moon, 1998; Gran Turismo, 1998. Singles: Rise And Shine; Black Letter Day; Sick And Tired, 1995; Carnival, 1995; Hey! Get Out Of My Way; Lovefool (No. 2, UK), 1996; Been It, 1997; Your New Cuckoo, 1997; My Favorite Game, 1998; Erase/Rewind, 1999; Hanging Around, 1999; Gran Turismo Overdrive, 2000; with David Arnold: Theme From 'Randall & Hopkirk Deceased' (BBC1), 2000. *Honours:* Slitz Magazine, Best Band, 1994; BMI Best Song, 1997, Best Album, 1998, Best Group, 1996, 1998. *Current Management:* Motor, PO Box 53045, 400 14 Gothenburg, Sweden. *Address:* c/o Stockholm Records, Positionen 146, 115 74 Stockholm, Sweden. *Website:* www.cardigans.net.

SVENNINGSSON, Uno; b. 1 July 1959, Jönköping, Småland, Sweden. Vocalist; Songwriter. m. Carina Bihli, 11 Sept. 1993, 1 s. *Career:* Singer, songwriter, rock group Freda, 1983–93; Solo artist, 1994–; Numerous tours, television and radio appearances, major Swedish programmes. *Recordings:* En Människa, 1984; Välkommen Hero, 1986; Tusen Eldar, 1988; Undan För Undan, 1990; Alla Behöver, 1993; Freda Samling, 1993; Uno, 1994. *Honours:* Swedish Grammy Award, Best Rock Group, 1991; RockBjörnen Award, Best Male Artist, 1994; The Mozart Prize, Best Male Artist, 1994. *Current Management:* The Record Station. *Address:* The Record Station, BMG Ariola, PO Box 1026, 17221 Sundbyberg, Sweden.

SVENSSON, Anders Peter; b. 18 Oct. 1974, Jönköping, Sweden. Musician (guitar); Composer. *Education:* Music College, Jönköping, 1991–93. *Career:* Founding mem., The Cardigans, 1992–; Contributed tracks to films Romeo and Juliet and A Life Less Ordinary; Numerous concert tours, festivals, television and radio appearances. *Recordings:* Albums: Emmerdale, 1994; Life, 1995; First Band On The Moon, 1996; Other Side Of The Moon, 1998; Gran Turismo, 1998. Singles: Rise And Shine; Black Letter Day; Sick And Tired, 1995; Carnival, 1995; Hey! Get Out Of My Way; Lovefool (No. 2, UK), 1996; Been It, 1997; Your New Cuckoo, 1997; My Favorite Game, 1998; Erase/Rewind, 1999; Hanging Around, 1999; Gran Turismo Overdrive, 2000; with David Arnold: Theme From 'Randall & Hopkirk Deceased' (BBC1), 2000. *Honours:* Slitz Magazine, Best Band, 1994; Swedish Government Export Prize, 1997; Best Composer, 1998; BMI Best Song, 1997, Best Album, 1998, Best Group, 1996, 1998. *Membership:* Society for Swedish Composers of Pop Music. *Current Management:* Motor, PO Box 53045, 400 14 Gothenburg, Sweden. *Address:* c/o Stockholm Records, Positionen 146, 115 74 Stockholm, Sweden. *Website:* www.cardigans.net.

SVIRIDOVA, Alena; b. 14 Aug. , USSR. Vocalist; Actor. *Career:* Solo artiste; Numerous acting roles incl.: Buro Shchastya (television series). *Recordings:* Albums: Rozovoye Flamingo; Liniya Zhizni, 2000. *Membership:* Russian Union of Writers. *Current Management:* Nox-Music. *Website:* www.sviridova.ru.

SWALLOW, Steve; b. 1940, New York, NY, USA. Musician. *Education:* Studied piano with Howard Kasschau, and trumpet; Composition, Yale University. *Career:* Tours and recordings with Paul Bley, Jimmy Giuffre Trio and George Russell Sextet, 1960; Performances with other noted jazz musicians; Joined Art Farmer Quartet, 1964; Toured with Stan Getz Quartet, 1965–67; Joined Gary Burton Quartet, 1968; Took up electric bass; Teacher, Berklee College of Music, 1974–76; Performed with Dizzy Gillespie, George Benson, Herbie Hancock and played on numerous recordings with other musicians; Joined Carla Bley Band, 1978, numerous recordings and tours; Toured and recorded with John Scofield, 1980–84, and produced many recordings; Production for numerous artists including Andy Sheppard, Karen Mantler, Lew Soloff; Numerous tours with Paul Bley, Ernie Watts, Allen Ginsberg; Reunited with Jimmy Giuffre and Paul Bley, 1989, numerous tours; Contributions to numerous recordings, 1993; Many concert appearances with Carla Bley, Jimmy Giuffre, Andy Sheppard, 1994; Numerous tours with many artists, 1994–98; Played with Harvard University Jazz Band. *Recordings include:* Deconstructed; Real Book; Go Together; Swallow; Duets; Carla; Home; Hotel Hello; Always Pack Your Uniform On Top, 2000; With Carla Bley: Night-Glo; Sextet; With John Scofield: Shinola; Out Like a Light. *Honours:* National Endowment for the Arts Grant, 1976; First Place, Downbeat International Critics' Poll, Electric Bass, 1983–; Readers' Poll, 1985–; Winner, Jazz Times Poll, Electric Bass, several times. *Address:* c/o Watt Works, PO Box 67, Willow, NY 12495, USA.

SWAN, Billy; b. 12 May 1942, Cape Giardeau, Missouri, Canada. Vocalist; Songwriter; Musician (guitar, bass, keyboards). m. Marlu, 2 d. *Career:* Musical Director, Filmography: A Thing Called Love, coached River Phoenix; Wild At Heart, acted and sang; Songwriter, Willie Nelson and Kris Kristofferson; Assistant Music Director, Great Balls of Fire; As You Like It, Scored and played singing minstrel; Toured with: T Bone Burnett; Kinky Friedman and The Texas Jewboys; Billy Joe Shaver; Black Tie; Harry Dean Stanton and Kris Kristofferson. *Recordings:* Albums: I Can Help; Rock 'n' Roll; Billy Swan; Four; You're OK, I'm OK; I'm Into Lovin' You; Black Tie; Recent Releases: Billy Swan's Best, 1993; Vinyl Junkie Country, Undying Love, 1995; The Sun Studio Story: Rockabilly B; Lonely Weekends, 1995; Bop To Be, 1995; Billy Swan Live, 1996; Billy Swan, Choice Cuts, 1997; The Best of Billy Swan,

1997; Billy Swan – collectibles, 1997; I Can Help/Rock 'n' Roll Moon and Billy Swan/Four – See For Miles, 1997; Like Elvis Used To Do, 2000. *Current Management:* Dennis Muirhead, Muirhead Management, 202 Fulham Rd, Chelsea, London SW10 9PJ, England. *Address:* Chelsea, London SW10 9PJ, England.

SWAN, Ren; Mix Engineer; Engineer. *Career:* Engineering work for Jon Douglas on: Salt 'N' Pepa, Champagne 7; Michelle Gayle, Do You Know, Sensational; Remix of Clementine for Mark Owen with Grant Mitchell (3 UK charts); Worked on albums by: Gary Barlow, Dee Ellington, Conner Reeves, All Saints; Remixed, Above the Law, The Evil That Men Do; Engineering and mixing credits include: George Michael, Older; Eternal, including: Stay, Oh Baby I, Good Thing; Michael Jackson, Wanna Be Starting Something mix; De La Soul, Ring Ring; Aswad, Close to You, 7 and 12 remix; Pet Shop Boys, Where The Streets Have No Name 7; Other engineering work for: Rick Astley; The Beloved; Betty Boo; Boyzone; Dina Carroll; Tom Jones; Kylie Minogue; 911; Tina Turner. *Address:* SARM Productions, SP2 Holdings Ltd, The Blue Building, 42/46 St Luke's Mews, London W11 1DG, England.

SWAN LAKE. See: **TERRY, Todd.**

SWANSON, David James; b. 15 Aug. 1951, Edinburgh, Scotland. Musician (percussion). 1 d. *Education:* Studied with James Catherwood privately; 1 year music course at college. *Career:* Played with many jazz stars including: Joe Temperley; Roy Williams; Kenny Davern; Buddy DeFranco; Tal Farlow; Louis Stewart; Tour of Middle East with Demis Roussos; Television appearances with: Tam White; Benny Waters; Healing Force; Craig McMurdo; Radio with George Chisholm; Recent tour with Herb Geller; Featured in Edinburgh Jazzfest with Alex Shaw Trio, 1997; Tutor with Fyjo and Nyjos; Member, Jack Duff Quintet; Member, Freddy King Quintet; Member, Edinburgh Light Orchestra. *Membership:* Chairman, Edinburgh Branch, Musicians' Union. *Address:* c/o Musicians' Union, 1 Seafield Rd E, Edinburgh, Scotland.

SWINFIELD, Raymond; b. 14 Dec. 1939, Sydney, Australia. Musician (saxophone, clarinet, flutes). m. Rosemarie, Sept. 1970, divorced 1991. *Career:* Played on recordings by: Quincy Jones; Robert Farnon; Henry Mancini; Pat Williams; Ella Fitzgerald; The Beatles; Phil Woods; Michel Legrand; Kiri Te Kanawa; Stéphane Grappelli; Johnny Mercer; J J Johnson; Bjork; Everything But The Girl; Mel Torme. *Compositions:* Sydney Suite; Rain Curtain; Caroline; Thinking On It. *Recordings:* Albums: Rain Curtain; The Winged Cliff; Angel Eyes. *Honours:* Own albums listed amongst jazz records of the Year in Gramophone Jazz Journal magazines. *Membership:* PRS; British Jazz Musicians. *Address:* c/o Musicians' Union, National Office, 60/62 Clapham Rd, London SW9 0JJ, England.

SWING KIDS. See: **GONZALEZ, Kenny.**

SYKES, John; b. 29 July 1959, Reading, Berkshire, England. Rock Musician (guitar); Songwriter. *Career:* Guitarist, UK rock groups Streetfighters; Tygers of Pan Tang, 1980–81; Thin Lizzy, 1982–83; Concerts include: British tour, 1982; Tours, Europe, Japan, 1983; Reading Festival, 1983; Monsters of Rock European tour, 1983; Guitarist, Whitesnake, 1984–86; Tours, UK, Europe, 1984; US tours with Dio and Quiet Riot, 1984; Rock In Rio (largest ever rock festival), 1985. *Compositions:* Co-writer with David Coverdale: Still of The Night; Is This Love?. *Recordings:* Albums: with Tygers of Pan Tang: Spellbound, 1981; Crazy Nights, 1981; with Thin Lizzy: Thunder and Lightning, 1983; with Whitesnake: Slide It In, 1984; Whitesnake, (No. 2, USA), 1987; Solo: Loveland, 1997; Best of John Sykes, 1998; Please Don't Leave Me, 1999; Chapter One, 2000; Out Of My Tree, 2000; Singles: with Thin Lizzy: Hollywood; Cold Sweat; Thunder and Lightning; The Sun Goes Down; with Whitesnake: Give Me More Time; Standing In The Shadow; Love Ain't No Stranger. *Honours:* Platinum and Gold discs. *Current Management:* Music Group Management. *Address:* 3500 W Olive, Suite 950, Burbank, CA 91505, USA.

SYLVAIN, Dominique; b. 17 Nov. 1959, New York, USA. Haitian Vocalist; Author; Composer. 1 d. *Education:* DEA, degree in Anthropology; Studied piano, guitar, percussion, voice. *Career:* Concerts include: L'Espace Julien (Marseilles), 1993; Pollen France Inter, 1994; L'Opus Café (Paris); Festival d'Été de Besauçon, 1995; 2 broadcasts for France Inter radio; Television appearances: Antenne 2; RFO. *Recordings:* Reconnais, 1994. *Honours:* First Prize, Choreography and Interpretation, FFD, 1990. *Membership:* SACEM; ADAMI; SACED. *Current Management:* Myriam Willis. *Address:* Axile 37 rue Doudeauville, 75018 Paris, France.

SYLVESTRE, Frédéric; b. Angouleme, France. Musician (guitar, synthesizer guitar). *Career:* Played with artists including: Eddy Louiss; Martial Solal; Christian Escoudé; Marcel Azzola; Michel Graillier; Bernard Lubat; Alain Jean-Marie; Pepper Adams; Albi Cullaz; Tania Maria; Claude Cagnasso; Aldo Romano; Marc Bertaux; Jacques Vidal; Eric Le Lann; Gérard Marais; Jean-Louis Chautemps; Sacha Distel; Philip Catherine; Didier Levallet; Marcel Azzola; Jimmy Gourley; Georges Arvanitas; Luigi Trussardi. *Recordings:* Five Compact, Claude Cagnasso Big Band; with the Dolphin

Orchestra: Prologue; Olympia Live; Rencontre; with Jacques Vidal: Premier Grand Cru; 2+; Hommages; Trio Live; Capricorne; with Martial Solal Big Band: Martial Solal Big Band Joue André Hodeir; Big Band de Guitares de Gerard Marais, Gerard Marais; Music Band, Teddy Lasry; Dolores, Jean-Marc Jafet; Gipsy Waltz, Christian Escoudé Octet; Salena Jones Sings Cole Porter; Holidays, Christian Escoudé; News of Bop, Jacques Vidal Quintet; Trio Sur Seine, with Marcel Azzola. *Address:* 31 rue de Fontarabie, 75020 Paris, France.

SYLVIAN, David, (David Batt); b. 23 Feb. 1958, Beckenham, Kent, England. Vocalist; Musician (guitar). *Career:* Singer, guitarist, Japan, 1977–82; Solo artiste, 1982–; Member, Rain Tree Crow (with 3 members of Japan), 1991. *Recordings:* Albums: with Japan: Adolescent Sex, 1978; Obscure Alternatives, 1978; Quiet Life, 1980; Gentlemen Take Polaroids, 1980; Assemblage, 1981; Tin Drum, 1981; Oil On Canvas, 1983; Exorcising Ghosts, 1984; Solo albums: Brilliant Trees, 1984; Alchemy, An Index of Possibilities, 1985; Gone To Earth, 1986; Secrets of The Beehive, 1987; Plight and Premonition, with Holger Czukay, 1988; Flux and Mutability (with Holger Czukay), 1989; Weather Box, 1989; Ember Glance, The Permanence Memory (with Russell Mills), 1991; with Rain Tree Crow: Rain Tree Crow, 1991; with Robert Fripp: The First Day, 1993; Damage, (with Robert Fripp) 1994; Guest singer, Dreams of Reason Produce Monsters, Mick Karn, 1987; Dead Bees on a Cake, 2000; Approaching Silence; Everything And Nothing, 2000; Singles include: with Japan: Life in Tokyo, 1979; The Art of Parties, 1981; Quiet Life, 1981; Ghosts, 1982; Cantonese Boy, 1982; Night Porter, 1982; Canton, 1983; Solo: Red Guitar, 1984; The Ink In The Well, 1984; Pulling Punches, 1984; Taking The Veil, 1986; Let The Happiness In, 1987; I Surrender; Godman; with Ryûichi Sakamoto: Forbidden Colours, from film Merry Christmas Mr Lawrence, 1983. *Current Management:* Opium (Arts) Ltd, 49 Portland Rd, London W11 4LJ, England.

SYMBOL. See: **PRINCE.**

SZABO, Richard Wayne; b. 16 March 1956, Newark, New Jersey, USA. Musician (trumpet); Bandleader. *Education:* BA, Music Education, Fairleigh Dickinson University, Madison, New Jersey, USA. *Career:* Played in bands of Maynard Ferguson; Buddy Rich; Ray Anthony; Sammy Kaye; Guy Lombardo; Tito Puente; Billy May; Xavier Cugat; Frank Sinatra Jr; Appeared or recorded with: Melissa Manchester; The Grass Roots; Mel Torme; Johnny Desmond; Margaret Whiting; Helen Forrest; Regis Philbin; The Four Tops; The Four Lads; The Four Aces; The Chordettes; Author (screenplay): College Inc, 1984; Traffic Vigilante, 1986; Music director, Station WPCN-AM Radio, Pennsylvania, 1988. *Recordings:* Manhattan At Dusk, 1994; Best of Both Worlds; Big Bands 80s, Various Artists Vols 3 and 4; Jumpin' On The Bandstand. *Honours:* Listed in Who's Who in Entertainment. *Membership:* Songwriters Hall of Fame; NARAS; AFofM; AFTRA; IJAE. *Current Management:* Al Bauman, Fame Management, 939 Kimball St, Philadelphia, PA 19147, USA.

SZAWLOWSKI, William Stephen; b. 24 March 1955, Montréal, Québec, Canada. Record Prod; Engineer; Arranger; Writer. m. Margaret Lilliane Boutet, 6 Sept. 1975, 2 s. *Career:* Assistant recording engineer, 1974–75; Recording engineer, 1976–83; President, SCI Productions, Record Producer, 1984–90; Independent Record Producer, Engineer, Arranger, 1991–. *Recordings:* Producer for: Marjo; Marie-Carmen; Ray Lyell; Engineer for: April Wine; Aldo Nova; Frank Marino; Robbie Robertson; Helix; Luba; Teaze; Murray Head; Walter Rossi; Cirque du Soleil; Diane DuFresne; Kashtin; Pagliaro; Nanette Workman. *Honours:* 27 Gold and Platinum discs; ADISQ Award, Best Engineer, 1987. *Membership:* SOCAN. *Address:* 7195 Mauriac St, Brossard, QC J4Y 1T8, Canada.

SZCZESNIAK, Mieczyslaw Wojciech; b. 9 July 1964, Kalisz, Poland. Vocalist. *Education:* Academy of Music, Katowice. *Career:* Many television and radio appearances, concerts and recitals, Poland and abroad; Pop and jazz festivals include: Jazz Jamboree, Warsaw; Gospel festivals. *Recordings include:* Niby Nowy, 1990. *Honours:* Sopot Festival, 1989; Bresenz Intertalent, 1989; Golden Orpheus, 1990; Cesmè Festival, 1990; Golden Record of Nashville (FIDOF) 1990. *Membership:* STOMUR (Polish Society of Pop Musicians); PSJ (Polish Society of Jazz). *Address:* Plac Wolnica 11/11, 31–060 Krakow, Poland.

SZE, Jean Yi-Ching; b. 14 May 1956, Shanghai, People's Republic of China. Composer; Zheng Performer. m. Ming Xiao, 26 Nov. 1994. *Education:* Graduate, Shanghai Conservatory of Music, 1984; Bachelor, College of St Elizabeth, USA, 1988; Master, Virginia Tech, USA, 1992. *Career:* Composer and Zheng Performer; Organic Chemist. *Compositions:* Shi, string quartet; Mountain, electric violin, zheng, bamboo flute; Autumn, string orchestra, with bamboo flute; Flute Solo; Eastern View and Tradition Suite, violin and zheng; A Spring Morning at Miao Mountain, bamboo flute and zheng; Three Poems of Tang Dynasty, soprano, bamboo flute, yang qing, zheng, ban hu and pipa; The Sword and the Silk, 2000; The Pearl and the Thread, 2001. *Honours:* Second Prize, Shanghai National Music Competition, 1983. *Membership:* American Music Center; American Society of Composers, Authors and Publishers;

American Chemical Society. *Address:* 13 Joann Court, Monmouth Junction, NJ 08852, USA.

SZE, Kwan Leung; b. 11 Dec. 1938, People's Republic of China. Musician. m. Chi Wan Sze Siu, 1 s. *Education:* Tianjin Conservatory of Music, People's Republic of China. *Career:* The Choir of Hong Kong, Professional Teacher, Conductor; Radio Television Hong Kong; Hong Kong Chinese Folk Song Group; Recital, 1982, 1983; Professor, Tsing Hua College Music Department. *Publications:* Chorus and Chorus Conductor; The Great Singers In Record. *Membership:* Hong Kong Ethnomusicology Society. *Address:* Flat A, Kam Fai Building, 20 Waterloo Rd, Kowloon, Hong Kong.

SZÖRÉNYI, Levente; b. 26 April 1945, Gmunden, Austria (Hungarian citizen). Musician (guitar); Composer; Songwriter. m., divorced. *Education:*
College of Music. *Career:* Worked with János Bródy, 1965–; Pop musician with Mediterrán and Balassa, 1963–64, with Illés, 1965–73; Dance participant Még fáj minden csók (song festival), 1966; Founding mem. Fonográf, 1974–81; Retd. from theatre, 1984. *Compositions include:* Human Rights (oratory), 1968; Kömíves Kelemen (rock ballad), 1982; István a Király (rock opera), 1983; Fehér Anna (rock ballad), 1988; Fénylé Ölednek édes Örömében (Innin and Dumuzi—oratory), 1989; Soundtracks include Ezek a fiatalok, 1967; Extázis 5-7-ig, 1969; Eltávozott a nap; Locsolókocsi Pókfoci; A Koncert, 1982; István a Király, 1983; Attila Isten kardja (opera), 1993; Veled Uram! (opera), 2000; Ének a csodaszarvasról, 2001. *Honours.* First Prize, Hungarian Radio Amateur Competition, 1965; SZOT (Trade Union) Award, 1981; Composer of the Year, 1983; Erkel Ferenc Award 1983; KISZ (Youth Organization) Award. *Address:* Mátru u. 9, 1029 Budapest, Hungary.

T

TABOR, June; b. 31 Dec. 1947, Warwick, Warwickshire, England. Folk Vocalist. *Career:* Singer of contemporary and traditional songs; Various collaborations with: Martin Simpson, Maddy Prior (as Silly Sisters), Oysterband, Huw Warren, Savourna Stevenson. *Recordings:* Albums: Silly Sisters (with Maddy Prior), 1976; Airs And Graces, 1976; Ashes And Diamonds, 1977; A Cut Above, 1980; Abyssinians, 1983; The Peel Sessions, 1986; Aqaba, 1988; No More To The Dance (with Maddy Prior), 1988; Some Other Time, 1989; Aspects (compilation), 1990; Freedom And Rain (with Oysterband), 1990; Angel Tiger, 1992; Anthology (compilation), 1993; Against The Streams, 1994; Singing The Storm (with Savourna Stevenson), 1996; Aleyn, 1997; On Air, 1998; A Quiet Eye, 1999; Rosa Mundi, 2001. *Current Management:* Speaking Volumes Ltd, Huntingdon Hall, Crown Gate, Worcester WR1 3LD, England. *Telephone:* (1905) 611323. *Fax:* (1905) 619958. *E-mail:* chris@speakingvolumes.co.uk. *Website:* www.junetabor.com.

TACUMA, Jamaaladeen, (Rudy MacDaniel); b. 11 June 1956, Hempstead, NY, USA. Musician (double bass); Composer. *Education:* Double bass from age 13. *Career:* Session musician, 1977–; Played with Charles Earland; Ornette Coleman's band Prime Time; Jeff Beck; Jayne Cortez (poet); Solo recording artiste, 1983–; Founder, own dance band Cosmetic, 1983–; Founder member, Golden Palominos; Concerts include: Recital with the Ebony String Quartet, Carnegie Hall, 1985. *Recordings:* Albums: Solo: Showstopper, 1983; Renaissance Man, 1984; Music World, 1987; Juke Box, 1989; Boss of The Bass, 1993; Sound Symphony, 1994; Intense, 1995; Journey into Gemini Territory, 1996; Dreamscape, 1998; Live in Cologne, 1998; Meet The Podium Three, 2000; with Cosmetic: So Tranquilizin', 1984; with Ornette Coleman/Prime Time: Dancing In Your Head, 1977; Body Meta, 1978; Of Human Feelings, 1979; Opening At The Caravan of Dreams, 1985; In All Languages, 1987; with James Blood Ulmer: Tales of Captain Black, 1978; As producer: (I Want To) Squeeze You Hold You, Willy De Ville, 1983. *Honours:* Downbeat Poll, Talent Deserving Wider Recognition (most votes ever), 1981.

TADMAN, Tad (Paul); b. 19 Oct. 1969, Sutton, Surrey, England. Musician (bass guitar). *Education:* Wimbledon School of Art. *Career:* Member, Nutty Boys; Television appearances: TXT, ITV; The Big E, ITV; 100% programme, BBC; Radio sessions on BBC and GLR. *Recordings* include: It's OK I'm a Policeman, Nutty Boys (EP and video), 1992. *Membership:* Musicians' Union. *Current Management:* Universal, Railton Rd, London SE24, England. *Address:* c/o PO Box 3087, London NW5 3DZ, England.

TAFJORD, Stein Erik; b. 2 Nov. 1953, Langevag, Norway. Musician (tuba). m. 1 Sept. 1973–93, 3 d. *Education:* Norwegian State Academy of Music. *Career:* Norwegian Radio Symphony Orchestra; Carla Bley Scandinavian Orchestra; Lester Bowie; David Murrey's Jazz Baltica Ensemble; The Brazz Brothers; Soloist, several TV and radio productions in Europe, USA. *Recordings:* Participated on approximately 120 recordings, 16 with own band. *Honours:* Jazz Musician of the Year, Norway, 1991. *Membership:* Norwegian Musicians' Union.

TAFKAP. See: **PRINCE.**

TAHA, Rachid; b. 1958, Oran, Algeria. Rai Vocalist; Songwriter. *Career:* Family emigrated to France, 1968; Founding mem., Carte de Séjour, 1981–89; Solo artiste, 1991–; Numerous tours, live performances and festival appearances world-wide. *Recordings:* Albums: with Carte de Séjour: Rhoromanie, 1984; Deux Et Demi, 1986; Solo: Barbès, 1990; Rachid Taha, 1993; Olé Olé, 1995; Carte Blanche, 1997; Diwân, 1998; 1 2 3 Soleil (with Khaled and Faudel); Ach Adani; Made In Medina, 2000; Live, 2001. *Honours:* World Music Album of the Year, France, 2000. *Address:* c/o FKO Music, 18 rue de Reuilly, 75012 Paris, France. *Website:* www.rachidtaha.com.

TALBOT, Jamie Robert; b. 23 April 1960, London, England. Musician (saxophone, clarinet, flute). m. Clare, 4 Nov. 1988, 1 s. *Education:* Centre for Young Musicians, RCM (briefly). *Career:* Worked with: Stan Tracy; John Dankworth; Cleo Laine; Gil Evans; Ella Fitzgerald; Nelson Riddle; Frank Sinatra; Shorty Rogers; Natalie Cole. *Recordings:* Altitude, Jamie Talbot Sextet; Live At Ronnie Scott's, Stan Tracey; Genesis, Stan Tracey; Suddenly Last Tuesday, Clark Tracey; Also recorded with: Richard Ashcroft; Joni Mitchell; Tindersticks; Kirsty MacColl; George Michael; Tom Jones. *Address:* 34 Elmers End Rd, Anerley, London SE20 7SN, England.

TALBOT, Joby; b. 25 Aug. 1971, Wimbledon, London. Composer; Arranger; Musician (piano, oboe); Conductor. m. Claire Burbridge. *Education:* Guildhall School of Music and Drama; University of London. *Career:* Composer of Concert Music for Goups, London Sinfonietta; RRC Philharmonic; Britten Sinfonia Crouch End Festival Chorus; Keyboard Player, Arranger with The Divine Comedy, 1993–; Composer of Television and Film Music for BBC, 1996–. *Compositions:* Incandescence; Luminescence; Young Musician of the

Year Theme; Tomorrow's World Theme; League of Gentlemen Theme, BBC TV, 1999–2000. *Recordings:* The Divine Comedy: Albums: Casanova, 1996; Fin De Siecle, 1998; A Secret History (compilation), 1999; Singles: Something For The Weekend, 1996; Becoming More Like Alfie, 1996; The Frog Princess, 1996; Everybody Knows, Except You, 1997; The Certainty of Chance, 1998; Generation Sex, 1998; I've Been To A Marvellous Party, 1998; National Express, 1999. *Honours:* BBC Young Composer of the Year, 1996; BMus and MMus With Distinction. *Membership:* Musicians' Union; PRS. *Current Management:* Amos Barr Music Management, 10 Huntley Close, High Wycombe HP13 5PQ, England. *Address:* 16 Denman Rd, Peckham, London SE15 5NP, England.

TAMINIAUX, Eric; b. 13 March 1963, La Hestre, Belgium. *Education:* Germanic Languages College, 1981–84; Three years, Music School. *Career:* First Band, 17 years old; Singer, guitarist, Halloween, support act for various Belgian bands, 1983–94; Singer, guitarist, Check Point Charlie, support act for French band Miossec, 1994–. *Compositions:* With Halloween: Somebody Else Is You, 1991; Nameless People's Hotel, 1993; With Check Point Charlie, 12 Tracks Recorded. *Membership:* Belgian Society of Authors, Composers and Publishers. *Current Management:* Keylight. *Address:* c/o Keylight, rue Amerique 79, 6120 Ham Sur Heure, Belgium.

TAMPIER, Karel; b. 24 June 1946, Ceské Budejovice, Czech Republic. Composer; Songwriter. Divorced, 3 d. *Education:* Piano lessons, 9 years. *Career:* Leader, Guitar, Mandolin Player, Bluegrass Group, Bobri, 1970–84; Leader, Piano, Zridlo (The Source), 1979–85; Countryfuga, family group with wife and 3 daughters, 1989–93; Concerts in clubs and festivals in Czechoslovakia; About 100 songs recorded in Czech radio; 10 performances in Czech and Slovak TV; Music for Theatre; New music group, De Tampier, 1999; Music for TV films. *Compositions:* Proc Jsem Mrtev? (Why Do I Death?); Postel (The Bed) – Song and Musical. *Recordings:* Bobri, 1977–80, 1994; De Tampier, 1999. *Honours:* Czech Country and Folk Festival, Porta: Main prizes for interpretation, 1978, 1979, 1980; Main prize for songwriter, 1984. *Address:* Karel Tampier, Staromestská 9, 37004 Ceské Budejovice, Czech Republic.

TAMS, John Murray; b. 16 Feb. 1949. Vocalist; Musician (guitar, melodeon, fiddle, banjo, harmonica); Actor; Songwriter; Prod. *Career:* Regular on the British folk scene for many years before recording first solo album, 2000; Played trumpet in a brass band as a child but is known in folk circles as vocalist/guitarist; Member: Ashley Hutchings' Albion Band, 1976–87; Leader: Home Service (folk rock band); Musical Director for the National Theatre production of the Mysteries; Launched record label No Masters Co-operative with Jim Boyes; Actor and theatrical producer; Associate Director of Crucible Theatre, Sheffield; Produced radio dramas; Appeared in and composed music for TV series Sharpe. *Recordings:* Unity, 2000; Home, 2002; with Albion Band: The Prospect Before Us, 1977; Rise Up Like The Sun, 1978; Larkrise To Candleford, 1980; 1990, 1990; with Home Service: Home Service, The Mysteries, 1985; Alright Jack, 1986; features on: Son of Morris OST, 1976; Raggedy Rawney OST, 1988. *Honours:* Radio 2 Folk Award, Album of the Year, Unity, 2001; Froots Magazine Critics Poll, Album of the Year, third place, Unity, 2000.

TAÑÓN, Olga; b. 13 April 1967, Santurce, Puerto Rico. Vocalist. *Career:* First sang with Orchestra Las Nenas de Ringo Y Jossie; Joined Chantelle; First solo album, 1992; Sales of over 2.5m. records; Tours internationally. *Recordings:* Sola, 1992; Mujer De Fuego, 1993; Siente El Amor, 1994; Exitos Y Mas, 1995; Nuevos Senderos, 1996; Llevame Contigo, 1997; Te Acordaras De Mi, 1998; Olga Viva – Viva Olga, 1999; Yo Por Ti, 2001. *Honours:* various including: Asscn of Entertainment Critics of New York, Ace Award, 1994; ASCAP award, 1993; Billboard International Latin Music Awards, Female Album of the Year, 1998; Grammy Awards, Best Merengue Album, 2000 and 2001. *Website:* www.olgatanon.com.

TANT, Jean-Christophe; b. 12 Feb. 1962, Lille, France. Vocalist; Composer; Musician (guitar). *Education:* Degree, Plastic Arts; Academy of Music, Lille. *Career:* Performed at festivals including: Montréal; Munchen-Gladbach; Edinburgh; Lille; Jelena Gora; Jazz Valley, Paris; Singapore; Television appearances: France: FR3, M6, A2; Poland, Channel 1; Radio appearances: France Inter, Europe 2, Frequence Nord. *Honours:* Golden Nono (Wazemmes), France. *Membership:* SACEM. *Current Management:* Lyse Bochner.

TAPIO, Jorma Ilmari; b. 6 Aug. 1957, Mikkeli, Finland. Musician (alto saxophone, bass clarinet, flutes, percussion). *Education:* Piano, private lessons, aged 6; Violin, flutes and saxophone at music school; Lessons from Pekka Pöyry, Juhani Aaltonen and Edward Vesala. *Career:* Member, trio Lavantairyhmä, 1980–82; Member, traditional tango band, rock groups and big bands; Own tapes for radio, television documentaries, theatre, film pieces and dance performances; Numerous tours with Krakatau; Tours, recordings, television appearances and two documentary films with Edward Vesala; Founder, own group Rolling Thunder, 1995–97; Also solo appearances. *Recordings:* with Krakatau: Ritual, 1988; with Edward Vesala's Sound and Fury: Lumi, 1985; Ode To The Death of Jazz, 1989; Invisible Storm, 1991; Nordic Gallery, 1994. *Address:* Agricolankuja 2 C 96, 00530 Helsinki, Finland.

TARDLEY, Ken; b. 5 Oct. 1949, Rotherham, Yorkshire, England. Musician (dobro); Bandleader; University Lecturer. m. Lorretta Tardley, 12 Aug. 1982, 1 d. *Education:* BSc Hons, Chemistry, MSC, Systems Analysis, PGCE; Elkins College, West Virginia, 1990, 1995. *Career:* Member, US band, Muleskinner, 1990–92; Member, Sound In Mind, 1985–93; Member, Generation Gap, 1992–94; Toured USA, 1994; DJ, WTHO radio, Thompson, Georgia, USA; Curator, Dalebilly Museum, Airdale Drive, Howarth. *Recordings:* Riding Down The Canyon, Sound In Mind, 1989; Muleskinner, 1990. *Publications:* Staff writer, British Bluegrass News. *Honours:* King of The Dalebilly Dobro Players, 1995. *Membership:* Founder mem., British Bluegrass Music Asscn. *Current Management:* Loretta Tardley. *Address:* 65 Gledholt Bank, Huddersfield, West Yorkshire HD1 4HE, England.

TARKAN, (Tarkan Tevetoglu); b. 17 Oct. 1972, Alzey, nr Frankfurt, Germany. Vocalist. *Education:* Karamürsel Music High School, studied Turkish classical music; Continued music studies in Istanbul, Turkey. *Career:* Moved to Turkey with family, aged 14; Hugely popular in Turkey, 1993–95; Rest period followed owing to pressure of celebrity status; Commenced studies at Baruch College, New York, 1995; Returned to recording, 1997; European breakthrough with Simarik single, 1999; National military service followed by short tour of Latin America, 2000; Fronted Pepsi TV commercial, 2001; Concerts in Turkey, 2001; Now resides Manhattan, New York. *Recordings:* Albums: Yine Sensiz, 1993; A-Acayipsin, 1995; Ölürüm Sana, 1997; Tarkan, 1999; Karma, 2001; Singles (international releases): Simarik, Sikidim, Bu Gece, 1999; Kuzu Kuzu, 2001. *Honours:* World Music Awards, Best Selling Turkish Act, 1999; Asscn of Turkish Journalists, Most Successful Turkish Artist; Turkish album sales estimated to be in excess of 10m. *Address:* c/o Mehmet Sögütoglu, Istanbul Plak, Turkey. *Website:* www.tarkanfancenter.com.

TASHIAN, Barry M; b. 5 Aug. 1945, Oak Park, Illinois, USA. Vocalist; Musician (guitar); Songwriter. m. Holly Paige Kimball, 2 s. *Education:* Boston University; Private lessons in guitar, piano and voice. *Career:* Founder, 60s Rock Band, Barry and The Remains; Appeared Ed Sullivan Christmas Show, CBS Television, 1965; Hullabaloo, NBC, 1966; Epic Recording Artists; Travelled with The Beatles as opening act, summer tour of USA, 1966; Regional chart single hits in the Boston, New England area. *Compositions:* Why Do I Cry; Two Ways To Fall; Ooh Las Vegas; Spinning Straw Into Gold; Heaven With You; Long Train of Fools. *Recordings:* The Remains: 10 Albums with Emmylou Harris; 5 Albums with wife, as Barry and Holly Tashian; Other. *Recordings include:* Charlie Louvin; Marty Stuart; Gram Parsons; Nanci Griffith; Suzy Bogguss. *Publications:* Ticket To Ride: The Extraordinary Diary of The Beatles Last Tour. *Honours:* Boston Music Award, 1990; Indie Album of the Year, 1996. *Membership:* AFM; BMI; IBMA. *Current Management:* Tashian Music, PO Box 150921 Nashville, TN 37215, USA.

TASHIAN, Holly P; b. 8 Jan. 1946, New York, USA. Vocalist; Songwriter; Musician (guitar). m. Barry Tashian, 1 Nov. 1972, 2 s. *Education:* BA Psychology, 1 year graduate; Private lessons, violin, piano, voice. *Career:* As act Barry and Holly Tashian; Television: Grand Ole Opry Live; American Music Shop; Backstage Opry; Radio: Grand Ole Opry; Prairie Home Companion. *Compositions:* Songs recorded by Nashville Bluegrass Band and Ty England; Daniel O'Donnell; Roland White; Jody Stecher; Kate Brislin. *Recordings:* Albums: Trust In Me; Live In Holland; Ready For Love; Straw Into Gold; Harmony; Recordings with: Nanci Griffith; Delia Bell. *Honours:* NAIRD (National Asscn of Independent Record Distributors); Country Album of the Year, Straw Into Gold, 1995. *Membership:* ASCAP; AFofM; IBMA; NARAS; Folk Alliance. *Current Management:* Tashian Music. *Address:* Tashian Music, PO Box 150921, Nashville, TN 37215, USA.

TATE, Geoff; Vocalist. *Career:* Lead singer, US rock group Queensrÿche, 1981–. *Recordings:* Albums: Queen of The Reich (EP), 1983; The Warning, 1984; Rage For Order, 1985; Operation – Mindcrime, 1988; Empire, 1990; Promised Land, 1994; Hear in the Now Frontier, 1997; Operation: Mindcrime, 1999; Live Evolution, 2001; Singles include: Silent Lucidity; Best I Can; Jet City Woman. *Current Management:* Q-Prime Inc, 729 Seventh Ave, 14th Floor, New York, NY 10019, USA.

TAUPIN, Bernie; b. 22 May 1950, Lincolnshire, England. Songwriter. *Career:* Long-term songwriting partnership with Elton John, 1967–. *Compositions:* As co-writer with Elton John: Albums with Elton John: All albums, 1969–77; Too Low For Zero, 1983; Sleeping With The Past, 1989; Two Rooms – Celebrating The Songs of Elton John and Bernie Taupin, 1992; Solo: Bernie Taupin, 1970; Taupin, 1971; He Who Rides The Tiger, 1980; Tribe, 1987; Numerous hits include: Don't Let The Sun Go Down On Me; Crocodile Rock; Rocket Man; Sacrifice; Goodbye Yellow Brick Road; Bennie & The Jets; Your Song; Candle In The Wind; Don't Go Breaking My Heart;

Sorry Seems To Be The Hardest Word; Daniel; Saturday Night's Alright For Fighting; I'm Still Standing; Other co-compositions: Skyline Pigeon, Roger Cook, 1968; I Can't Go On Living Without You, 1969; Snookeroo, 1975 These Dreams, Heart, 1985. *Honours:* Ivor Novello Awards: Best Song, Daniel, 1974; Sacrifice, 1991; MTV Award, Special Recognition Trophy, 1987; Inducted into Songwriters Hall of Fame, 1992. *Current Management:* Lippman Entertainment, 8900 Wilshire Blvd, Suite 340, Beverly Hills, CA 90211, USA.

TAVERNER, Tony; b. 20 Sept. 1951, London, England. Prod; Engineer. m. Ruth, 4 c. *Career:* Engineered Duran Duran's US No 1 single, Ordinary World and The Wedding Album, and Thank You, albums; Co-Produced and Engineered, Warren Cuccurullo's solo album project; Engineered and Produced 2 chart topping albums in Spain with Duncan Dhu; Worked with Mikel Erentxun and Diego Vasallo; Senior Engineer, Maison Rouge Studios in London, 1977–88; Engineer, various albums, with Jeff Beck, 1973–99; Teamed-up with songwriter, producer, Simon Ellis (Spice Girls, S Club 7). *Recordings:* Sound mixing on 2 Spice Girl videos; Sex Chips and Rock N Roll; TV series: Taggart; The Turnaround; Other. *Recordings include:* Jeff Beck; Bill Wyman & The Rhythm Kings; Mick Taylor; The Damned; Cutting Crew. *Honours:* Numerous Gold and Platinum album awards. *Current Management:* Film and TV: Soundtrack Music Associates Ltd, 25 Ives St, Chelsea, London SW3 2ND, England; *Records:* Pachuco Management, The Blue Building, 42–46 St Lukes Mews, London W11 1DG, England.

TAYLER, Stephen William; b. 20 Sept. 1953, High Wycombe, Buckinghamshire, England. Recording and Mixing Engineer; Prod; Programmer; Musician (various). *Education:* New College School (Choir); Shrewsbury School (Music Scholarship); Royal College of Music (ARCH). *Career:* Trident Studios: House Engineer, 1974–80; Freelance engineer, musician, producer, programmer, 1980–; Worked on over 120 album projects. *Recordings:* Engineer / mixer for: Tina Turner; Stevie Nicks; Peter Gabriel; Bob Geldof; Rush; Howard Jones; The Fixx; Others. *Honours:* Numerous include: Ampex Golden Reel; 2 BASF/Studio Awards for Excellence. *Membership:* Re-pro; Musicians' Union. *Address:* c/o Chimera Records, 41 Rosebank, Holyport Rd, London SW6 6LQ, England.

TAYLOR, Andy; b. 16 Feb. 1961, Tynemouth, England. Musician (guitar). m. Tracey Wilson, 29 July 1982. *Career:* Guitarist, Duran Duran, 1979–86; Guitarist, Power Station, 1985; Solo artiste, 1986; Concerts include: UK tour, support to Hazel O'Connor, 1980; Edinburgh Festival, 1980; US tour, support to Blondie, 1982; MENCAP charity, concert, attended by HRH the Prince and Princess of Wales, 1983; Live Aid, Philadelphia, 1985; Television appearance, Miami Vice, NBC, 1985. *Recordings:* Albums: with Duran Duran: Duran Duran, 1981; Carnival, 1982; Seven and The Ragged Tiger, 1983; with Power Station: The Power Station, 1985; Solo: Thunder, 1987; Singles with Duran Duran include: Planet Earth, 1981; Girls On Film, 1981; My Own Way, 1981; Hungry Like The Wolf, 1982; Save a Prayer, 1982; Is There Something I Should Know (No. 1, UK), 1983; Rio, 1984; Union of The Snake, 1984; New Moon On Monday, 1984; The Reflex (No. 1, UK and USA), 1984; The Wild Boys, 1984; A View To A Kill, Bond film theme (No. 1, USA), 1985; with Power Station: Some Like It Hot, 1985; Get It On, 1985; Communication, 1985; Solo: Take It Easy, 1986; When The Rain Comes Down, 1986; Lola, 1990. *Contributions:* Anne Runolfsson, At Sea, 1997; By Jeeves, original cast recording, 1997; Engineer, Songs of Rodgers and Hammerstein, 1999; Producer: Shouting The Odds, Contempt, 2001. *Honours:* Best Group, Daily Mirror/BBC TV Nationwide/Radio 1 Awards, 1983; Grammy Awards, Best Video Short and Album, 1984; BRIT Award, Best British Music Video, Wild Boys, 1985; Ivor Novello, International Hit of the Year, 1985; Star on Hollywood Walk of Fame, 1993.

TAYLOR, Caroline; b. 25 March 1965, Auburn, New York, USA. Musician; Composer. *Career:* Performed with Nikki Yeoh, Chris Lineham's Popcorn Club. *Compositions:* CT Blues; Deep Blue Sea; Mum's Cove; Chickenbutt; Blues for Sarah; Groovin' Low; For The Moment. *Recordings:* For The Moment. *Current Management:* Mike Curtis, 17 Havelock Rd, Tonbridge, Kent TN9 1JE, England. *Address:* 4B Younge Park, London N4 3NT, England.

TAYLOR, Christopher Gordon; b. 24 Nov. 1966, Birmingham, England. Musician (keyboards, drums); Composer; Arranger. *Career:* Musical Director for Central Television: Central Weekend; Keyboards, MD, Ruby Turner, 1988–95; MD, Accompanist, many top UK cabaret artists; Musical Director for Sheila Ferguson, 1996; Musical Director for the Three Degrees and The Supremes, 1997; Oh What a Night, The Musical, Opera House, 1997; Worked with: Rose Royce; Heatwave; Jools Holland; Gloria Gaynor; Leo Sayer; Boyzone; Peter Andre; And many top UK cabaret artists. *Compositions:* Gardener's World, BBC, 1990; Central Weekend, Central TV, 1993; Home Run, Central TV, 1993; Sunday Supplement, Central TV, 1993; Millionaires, 1995; Wednesday Night Live, 1998; Many video soundtracks. *Recordings:* Producer/Musician on album, Responsible, Ruby Turner. *Membership:* Musicians' Union; British Music Writers' Council; PRS; MCPS; PAMRA. *Current Management:* Grosvenor Records. *Address:* 16 Grosvenor Rd, Handsworth Wood, Birmingham B20 3NP, England.

TAYLOR, Crispin Luke; b. 1 July 1961, London, England. Musician (drums, percussion). m. Rosamond Howe, 26 March 1994, 2 d. *Career:* Concerts include: Montreux Jazz Festival (twice); Nice Jazz Festival, twice; Glastonbury Festival, four times; Television appearances: The Word and Pebble Mill, with Seal; Top of the Pops, with Galliano; Dance Energy and Motormouth, with Definition of Sound. *Recordings:* with Galliano: The Plot Thickens; Joyful Noise Unto The Creator; A Thicker Plot; with Urban Species: Spiritual Love; Listen; with Oui 3: Oui Love You; Tracks/singles: Long Time Gone, Twyford Down, both with Galliano, 1994; Wear Your Love Like Heaven, Definition of Sound (No. 12, UK charts); Let It Last, Carleen Anderson; Mathar, Indian Vibes; As co-writer, producer: Scratchmo, 1988; Same Feeling, Mica Paris, 1988. *Honours:* 2 Silver discs. *Membership:* PRS. *Current Management:* Pump Music. *Address:* 9A Yerbury Rd, London N19 4RN, England.

TAYLOR, Gary Anthony; b. 18 Jan. 1951, Los Angeles, California, USA. Vocalist; Songwriter; Musician (keyboards). 2 s., 1 d. *Education:* 5 years college (Psychology major). *Career:* Working in studios; Began songwriting early 80s; Signed to A & M Records, 1983; Virgin Records, 1988; Written, produced records for numerous artists; Radio and television commercials; solo artist, 1988–. *Compositions:* Good Love (Anita Baker); I'm Coming Back (Lalah Hathaway); Square One (Ray Parker Jr); One Day At A Time (Vanessa Williams); Songs also recorded by: Grover Washington Jr; Vesta Williams; Chico Debarge; Joyce Kennedy; The Whispers; Mac Band; Jennifer Holliday; Stephanie Mills. *Recordings:* Albums: Compassion, 1988; Take Control, 1990; Square One, 1993; The Mood of Midnight, 1995; Love Dance, 1998; Under the Nightlight, 2001; Singles: Eye to Eye, 1993; Hold Me Accountable, 1994; In and Out of Love, 1994; Restless, 1994; Special, 1995. *Current Management:* Steven Ivory.

TAYLOR, Graeme David; b. 2 Feb. 1954, Stockwell, London, England. Musician (guitar, mandolin, banjo, piano). m. Sue Meldon, 20 July 1974, 1 d. *Education:* Music O'Level, Piano lessons to Grade 4. *Career:* Tours with Gryphon, Europe, USA, supporting Yes, 1971–; Many television appearances include: Jim'll Fix It; Magpie; All BBC radio channels in 1 week; Tours in Albion Band with: Billy Connolly; Julie Covington; Theatre work: National Theatre productions, Lark Rise To Candleford; The Mysteries; Other theatre include: Cats; Joseph and The Technicolour Dreamcoat; Television includes: This Is Your Life with Rolf Harris. *Recordings:* Albums include: with Gryphon: Gryphon, 1973; Red Queen to Gryphon Three, 1974; Midnight Mushrumps, 1974; Raindance, 1975; with Albion Band: Prospect Before Us, 1977; Rise Up Like The Sun, 1978; Larkrise to Candleford, 1980; with Home Service: Mysteries, 1998; Alright Jack, 1998; Many of own compositions on these recordings; Collaborated on record with: John Tams; Ashley Hutchings; Linda Thompson. *Membership:* Musicians' Union; PRS. *Current Management:* London Musicians. *Address:* 15 Eastway, Morden, Surrey SM4 4HW, England.

TAYLOR, James; b. 12 March 1948, Boston, MA, USA. Vocalist; Songwriter. m. Kathryn Walker, 1985. *Career:* First album, produced by Peter Asher, Apple Records, London, 1968; Signed to Warner Brothers Records; Moved to California, with Peter Asher, 1969; Films: Two Lane Blacktop, 1971; No-Nukes, 1980; Tours, USA: 1971, 1974–77, 1979–87, 1990–92, 1994; Tours: Far East, Australia, 1981; Italy, 1985; Australia, Europe, Brazil, 1986; Australia, New Zealand, 1988; Europe, 1992; Far East, Australia, 1995; Concerts include: Carnegie Hall, 1975; No-Nukes concert, 1979; Rock In Rio, Rio De Janeiro, 1985; Festivals, Munich, Nurburgring, Berlin, Germany, 1986; Phoenix Festival, 1995; Television includes: Live In Concert, Atlanta, 1981; Working, PBS TV, 1981. *Recordings:* Albums: James Taylor, 1968; Sweet Baby James, 1970; Mud Slide Slim, 1971; One Man Dog, 1972; Walking Man, 1974; Gorilla, 1975; In The Pocket, 1976; Greatest Hits, 1976; JT, 1977; Flag, 1979; Dad Loves His Work, 1981; That's Why I'm Here, 1985; Never Die Young, 1988; New Moon Shine, 1991; James Taylor (Live), 1993; In The Hands of The Inevitable, 1995; Original Flying Machine, 1996; Hourglass, 1997; Live at the Beacon Theatre, 1998; October Road, 2002. Singles include: Carolina In My Mind, 1969; Something's Wrong, 1969; Sweet Baby James, 1970; Fire and Rain, 1970; Country Road, 1971; You've Got A Friend (by Carole King), 1971; Long Ago and Far Away (with Joni Mitchell), 1971; Don't Let Me Be Lonely Tonight, 1972; One Man Parade, 1973; Mockingbird (with Carly Simon), 1974; Walking Man, 1974; Mexico, 1975; Rainy Day Man, 1975; You Make It Easy, 1976; Stop Thinkin Bout That, 1992; Copperline, 1995; Line 'Em Up, 1997; Jump Up Behind Me, 1998; Whole Lotta Live, 2000; Appeared on No-Nukes album, 6 tracks, 1979; In Harmony, Sesame Street album, 1980; Producer, guitarist, singer, (sister) Kate Taylor's single, 1977, album, 1988. *Honours:* Grammy Awards, 1972, 1978, 2002. *Current Management:* Peter Asher Management, 644 N Doheny Dr., Los Angeles, CA 90069, USA.

TAYLOR, Jeremy; b. Newbury, Berkshire, England. Vocalist; Composer; Entertainer. *Education:* French, Italian, Oxford University. *Career:* Taught at Eton College; Taught in South Africa; Wrote hit show, Wait A Minim, West End (two years) and Broadway; Worked with Sydney Carter, Spike Milligan; One man shows throughout South Africa. *Recordings include:* Ag Please Daddy (No. 1, South Africa), now unofficial national anthem; Jobsworth. *Current Management:* Jim McPhee, Acorn Entertainments. *Address:*

Winterfold House, 46 Woodfield Rd, Kings Heath, Birmingham B13 9UJ, England.

TAYLOR, John Michael; b. 24 March 1934, Retford, Nottinghamshire, England. Musician (trumpet, piano, keyboards, organ). *Education:* Piano lessons, 1 year, aged 9; Trumpet lessons, 1 year, aged 12. *Career:* Mike Taylor Jazzmen, 1956–59; Micky Askman Ragtime Jazzband, 1959–63; Appearances: Morecambe and Wise Show; 2 appearances: Thank Your Lucky Stars; Kent Walton Show; BBC Jazz Club; Midland Allstars, 1964–66; Second City Jazzmen, 1969–75; Accompanied various American stars including: Billy Butterfield; Wild Bill Davidson; Eddie Miller; Bud Freeman; Art Hodes; Earl Warren; Kenny Daverne; John Handy; Derby Big Band, 1976–79; Burton MU Big Band, 1977–80; All That Jazz Parade band, 1984–89; Festivals: Tilburg; Giethoorn; Breda; Kassel; 2 times Ascona Jazz Festival; 3 times Upton Jazz Festival; 2 times Bude; Keswick; Edinburgh; Duke Ellington Conference, Harlem, 1985–94; German tour; Several London Night at the Cotton Club shows with: Doc Cheetham; Benny Waters; Adelaide Hall; Bertice Reading; Herb Jeffries; Juanita Brooks; Hi-Life Parade Band, 1989–; Ascona Festival; 3 times Cork Jazz Festival; 2 times Bude Festival; Keswick Festival; Freelance musician, on piano, trumpet, with numerous groups. *Membership:* Musicians' Union. *Address:* 1 Redblock Field, Lichfield, Staffordshire WS14 0AB, England.

TAYLOR, Jon T-Bone; b. 29 Aug. 1963, London, England. Blues and Jazz Musician (guitar). *Education:* Guildhall School of Music. *Career:* Leader of Bop Brothers, 1986–2000; Guitarist with Tim Richards' bands Roogalator and Grooveyard; Daniel Smith Blues Band and Duo, 2000–; Toured with Charlie Sayles; Champion Jack Dupree; Mojo Buford; Lefty Dizz; Dick Heckstall-Smith. *Recordings:* Strange News, Bop Brothers, 1995; Bop Brothers... and Sisters, with Earl Green, Dana Gillespie and Ruby Turner, 1998; Bop Brothers... and Sisters, with Deitra Farr, Taka Boom and Connie Lush, 2000; Dreamtime, with Daniel Smith Blues Band, 2002; You're Not Far Away, with John Stapelton and The Big Easy, 2002. *Membership:* Musicians' Union. *Current Management:* Abacabe Ltd. *Address:* 10 Messaline Ave, London W3 6JX, England.

TAYLOR, Linda Christina; b. 27 July 1950, Cleveland, England. Vocalist; Songwriter; Impressionist. m. Jeff Taylor, 28 Oct. 1968, 1 s. *Education:* Piano, Professor Larman, Bedford; Voice, Jean Knight, London. *Career:* Backing vocals, albums: Chris Rea; Tom Jones; Céline Dion; Gary Moore; Kylie Minogue; Doctor John; Mike and The Mechanics; Julien Clerc; ABC; Paul Young; Jimmy Nail; Sting; Johnny Hallyday; Zucchero; Fish Tree Water Blues; Then Jerico; Sam Brown; Bananarama; Tours with: Go West; Art of Noise; Jocelyn Brown; Marvin Gaye; EPO (Japan); Chris Rea; Impressions: Spitting Image; Prime Suspect III; Crazy Horse, Paris; Television Commercials. *Compositions:* Angel; Everybody Knows; Taylor Made, (solo album, 1981); Morrisey/Mullen, 1981; Cayenne, Gary Numan, Bill Sharpe; Every Waking Hour; You and Me Just Started, 1981. *Honours:* Platinum disc, Angel, 1990; Gold discs: Chris Rea, Breathe. *Membership:* Equity; Musicians' Union; PAMRA; PRS. *Current Management:* Isobel Griffiths; Hobsons Singers. *Address:* 61 Sutherland Ave, Maida Vale, London W9 2HF, England.

TAYLOR, Martin; b. 20 Oct. 1956, Harlow Essex, England. Musician (guitar, banjo, flute); Composer. *Career:* Son of guitarist and double bassist Will 'Buck' Taylor; Played guitar from age 4 and gigged with father's dance band in early teens; Performed with Sonny Dee's All Stars, aged 15; Various stints at Pontin's holiday camp and various cruise liners followed; Played with Alan Elsdon, Dave Shepherd, Bob Bryan and led own quartet, mid 1970s; Began long musical association with Stéphane Grappelli, involving many world-wide tours, 1979; Worked with: Ike Isaacs; Louis Stewart; Peter Ind; Dave Newton; David Grisman; Led own trio and quartet, early 1990s; Made Django Reinhardt-influenced Spirit of Django album, 1994; Subsequently toured and recorded with band named Spirit of Django; Recorded Nitelife album in Nashville with musicians including: Kirk Whalum; Jim Horn; Chester Thompson; Viktor Krauss, 2001. *Recordings:* Skye Boat, 1981; Sarabanda, 1987; Don't Fret, 1990; Change of Heart, 1991; Artistry, 1993; Spirit of Django, 1994; Portraits, 1995; Years Apart, 1996; Gypsy, 1998; Two's Company, 1999; Nitelife, 2001; features on Stéphane Grappelli albums: At The Winery, 1981; Jealousy and Other Great Standards, 1988; Menuhin and Grappelli Play..., 1991; Reunion, 1993. *Website:* www.martintaylor.com.

TAYLOR, Mick; b. 17 Jan. 1948, Hemstead, England. Musician (guitar). *Career:* Guitarist, John Mayall's Bluesbreakers, 1960s; Played National Jazz and Blues Festival, 1968; Lead guitarist, Rolling Stones, 1969–75; Film: Gimme Shelter (including Altamont Concert), 1969; Recorded, toured with Bob Dylan; Currently, session player, solo artist. *Recordings:* Bare Wires, John Mayall's Bluesbreakers, 1968; Albums with the Rolling Stones: Let It Bleed (No. 1, UK), 1969; Get Yer Ya Ya's Out (No. 1, UK), 1970; Sticky Fingers (No. 1, UK), 1971; Exile On Main Street (No. 1, UK), 1972; Goat's Head Soup (No. 1, UK), 1973; It's Only Rock and Roll; Singles: Honky Tonk Women, 1969; Brown Sugar, 1971; Tumbling Dice, 1972; Angie, 1973; It's Only Rock And Roll, 1974; with Bob Dylan: Infidels; Empire Burlesque; Solo: Mick Taylor, 1979; Stranger In This Town, 1990; Too Hot for Snakes, 1991; Coastin' Home, 1995; Live at 14 Below, 1995; A Stone's Throw, 2000; Also appears with: John Mayall; Carla Olson; Knights of the Blues Table; Video with John Mayall and The Bluesbreakers, Blues Alive, 1983. *Honours:* Rock and Roll Hall of Fame (with Rolling Stones); Numerous domestic and international Gold, Platinum records. *Address:* 156 Fifth Ave, Suite 434, New York, NY 10010, USA.

TAYLOR, (Nigel) John; b. 20 June 1960, Birmingham, Warwickshire, England. Musician (bass, guitar); Songwriter. 1 d. *Career:* Founder member, Duran Duran, 1978–; Member, Power Station, 1985; Performances include: Edinburgh Festival, 1980; British tour, supporting Hazel O'Connor, 1980; British tour, 1981; MENCAP charity concert, attended by HRH the Prince and Princess of Wales, 1983; Live Aid, Philadelphia, 1985; Guest appearance, Miami Vice, NBC, 1985; The Secret Policeman's Third Ball, London, 1987; An Acoustic Evening With Duran Duran, Birmingham Symphony Hall, 1993. *Recordings:* Albums: with Duran Duran: Duran Duran, 1981; Carnival, 1982; Seven and The Ragged Tiger, 1983; Arena, 1984; So Red The Rose, 1985; Notorious, 1987; Big Thing, 1988; Decade, 1990; Duran Duran (The Wedding Album), 1993; Thank You, 1995; Medazzaland, 1997; Greatest, 1998; with Power Station: The Power Station, 1985; Solo: Feelings Are Good and Other Lies, 1997; Singles with Duran Duran: Planet Earth, 1981; Girls On Film, 1981; My Own Way, 1981; Save A Prayer, 1982; Hungry Like The Wolf, 1982; Is There Something I Should Know (No. 1, UK), 1983; Rio, 1983; Union of The Snake, 1983; New Moon On Monday, 1984; The Reflex (No. 1, UK and USA), 1984; The Wild Boys, 1984; A View To A Kill, theme from Bond film (No. 1, USA), 1985; Notorious, 1986; Meet El Presidente, 1987; I Don't Want Your Love, 1988; All She Wants, 1989; Do You Believe In Shame, featured in film Tequila Sunrise, 1989; Violence of Summer (Love's Taking Over), 1990; Serious, 1990; Ordinary World, 1993; Come Undone, 1993; Too Much Information, 1993; Electric Barbarella, 1997; with Power Station: Some Like It Hot, 1985; Communication, 1985; Solo: I Do What I Do, theme from film 9 1/2 Weeks, 1986; Contributor, Do They Know It's Christmas?, Band Aid, 1984. *Honours:* BRIT Award, Best British Music Video, 1985; Ivor Novello Award, International Hit of the Year, 1985; Star on Hollywood Walk of Fame, 1993. *Current Management:* The Left Bank Organisation, 9255 W Sunset Blvd, Second Floor, Los Angeles, CA 90069, USA.

TAYLOR, Robin; b. 17 May 1956, Copenhagen, Denmark. Composer; Musician (guitar, bass, keyboards, percussion); Prod. *Education:* Academy for Free and Commercial Art, Copenhagen. *Career:* Member of several local rock groups, 1970s; First radio appearance, 1978; In collaboration with keyboard player Jan Marsfeldt, 1988–98; Record debut, 1991; Composer, film music; Founder: experimental jazz/rock fusion group, Taylor's Universe, 1993–98; Taylor's Free Universe, 2000–; Member, Avant-garde Big Band Communio Musica, led by Hugh Steinmetz, 1996–97. *Recordings:* Solo albums: Essay, 1991; Cloze Test Terror, 1992; Heart Disc, 1999; The Båndbix Tapes, 2000; Edge of Darkness, 2000; Samplicity, 2001; with Taylor's Universe: Taylor's Universe, 1994; Pork, 1996; Experimental Health, (with Karsten Vogel), 1998; with Communio Musica: Special Alloy, 2000; with Taylor's Free Universe: File Under Extreme, 2002. *Honours:* Danish Arts Foundation work grants. *Membership:* Danish Musicians' Union; Danish Jazz Beat and Folk Authors (DJBFA). *Current Management:* Marvel of Beauty Records, Listedvej 40, 3. mf., DK-2770 Kastrup, Denmark. *E-mail:* marvelofbeauty@hotmail.dk.

TAYLOR, Roger, (Roger Meddows-Taylor); b. 26 July 1949, Kings Lynn, Norfolk, England. Musician (drums); Vocalist; Prod. *Education:* Biology. *Career:* Drummer, Smile; Drummer, UK rock group Queen, 1970–; Founder, The Cross, 1987–; Numerous tours include: UK; USA; Australia; South America; Japan; Major concerts include: Rock In Rio, Brazil, 1985; Live Aid, Wembley, 1985; Knebworth Festival, 1986; Concert For Life, Wembley, 1985; Musical of Queen songs, We Will Rock You, West End, London, 2002–. *Recordings:* Albums include: Queen, 1973; Queen 2, 1974; Sheer Heart Attack, 1974; A Night At The Opera, 1975; A Day At The Races, 1977; Jazz, 1978; Live Killers, 1979; The Game, 1980; Flash Gordon (soundtrack), 1981; Greatest Hits, 1981; Hot Space, 1982; The Works, 1984; The Complete Works, 1985; A Kind of Magic, 1986; The Miracle, 1989; Innuendo, 1991; Live At Wembley '86, 1992; Made In Heaven, 1995; Queen Rocks, 2000; with the Cross: Shove It!, 1988; Solo: Fun In Space, 1981; Strange Frontier, 1984; Happiness?, 1994; Electric Fire, 1998; Singles include: Seven Seas of Rye, 1974; Killer Queen, 1974; Bohemian Rhapsody (No. 1, UK), 1975; Now I'm Here, 1975; You're My Best Friend, 1976; Somebody To Love, 1976; We Are The Champions, 1977; Bicycle Race, 1978; Don't Stop Me Now, 1979; Love of My Life, 1979; Crazy Little Thing Called Love, 1979; Play The Game, 1980; Save Me, 1980; Another One Bites The Dust (No. 1, USA), 1980; Flash, 1981; Under Pressure, with David Bowie (No. 1, UK), 1981; Radio Ga Ga, 1984; I Want To Break Free, 1984; It's A Hard Life, 1984; Hammer To Fall, 1984; One Vision, 1985; A Kind of Magic, 1986; Friends Will Be Friends, 1986; I Want It All, 1989; Breakthru, 1989; Innuendo (No. 1, UK), 1991; Headlong, 1991; Too Much Love Will Kill You, 1995; Heaven For Everyone, 1995; Pressure On, 1998; We Will Rock You (with Five) (No. 1, UK), 2000. *Honours:* Britannia Award, 1976; Gold Ticket, Madison Square Gardens, 1977; American Music Award, 1981; Silver Clef Award, Nordoff-Robbins Music Therapy Centre, 1984; Ivor Novello Award, Outstanding Contribution to British Music, 1987; BRIT Awards: Outstanding Contribution to British

Music, 1990; Best British Single, 1991. *Current Management:* c/o Jim Beach, Queen Productions, 46 Pembridge Rd, London W11 3HN, England.

TAYLOR, Steve; b. 9 Dec. 1957, Brawley, California, USA. Recording Artist; Songwriter; Prod; Film maker. m. Debbie L Taylor, 16 March 1985. *Education:* BA Music, Colorado University, Boulder, USA. *Career:* Recording artist; Producer, Co-writer for Newsboys. *Recordings:* I Want To Be A Clone, 1983; Meltdown, 1984; On The Fritz, 1985; I Predict 1990, 1987; Chagall Guevara, 1991; Squint, 1993; Liver, 1995; Video: Squint: Movies From The Soundtrack, 1994; Producer, Co-writer, The Newsboys: Not Ashamed, 1992; Going Public, 1994; Take Me To Your Leader, 1996; Producer, Guardian: Buzz, 1995; Producer, Sixpence None the Richer, 1997. *Honours:* Three Dove Awards; 2 Billboard Music Video Awards (as artist and director); CCM Magazine, Producer of the Year, 1994; 1995. *Current Management:* Proper Management, PO Box 23069, Nashville, TN 37202, USA.

TAYLOR, Steven Vernard; b. 24 Dec. 1950, Norton, Virginia, USA. Prod; Dir A&R, RCM Recordings. *Education:* BMus, Opera, University of Tennessee, Complete Recording Workshop, Los Angeles Valley College. *Career:* 16 years touring as vocalist, musician; Engineered for Jimmy Buffett, Michael McDonald, Jeff Berlin; Assistant to director on Grammy winner: Boys of Summer (Don Henley); Musical consultant for television shows: Gimme A Break; Facts of Life; Diff'rent Strokes; One Day At A Time. *Recordings:* Unknown Soul (producer); Sugar Jones; Argument Clinic (producer); Choral Collection; Women Of Faith; Truth; First Call; Alleluia Worship Band; Gary Sadler. *Honours:* Commendation by Texas Governor Ann Richards for internationally aired song: Dear Mr President, Dear Mr Gorbachev (producer/promoter). *Address:* PO Box 4735 Austin, TX 78765–4735, USA.

TAYLOR, Tot; b. 15 July 1957, Cambridgeshire, England. Prod; Composer; Songwriter. *Career:* Founder, own Compact Organization record label; Songwriter, Producer for Mari Wilson, Virna Lindt, early 1980s. *Compositions:* Music for Absolute Beginners, 1986; Started Poppy Records, 1996; Picasso's Women, for the Royal National Theatre. *Recordings:* Producer: Just What I Always Wanted, Mari Wilson, 1982; World of Leather, 1995; Producer, Bachology, 1995; Released six albums under own name, 1981–95; Waterland, soundtrack, 1997; Macbeth, soundtrack, 1997; Music For The Left Handed, 1998; Whipsnade, 1999; Film soundtrack, The Shatterer, 1999; Pop Folk Jazz, 2000; The Remainder of Honey Weeks, 2000; Film soundtrack, Dream, 2001; Theatre soundtracks: The Tempest, Blood Royal. *Honours:* DandAD Award, Best Sound Design, 2000. *Current Management:* LPA. *Address:* PO Box 562, London N10 3LJ, England. *Telephone:* (20) 7482-5036. *E-mail:* poppy@poptel.org.

TAYLOR, Will; b. 30 Nov. 1968, DeKalb, Illinois, USA. Composer; Arranger; Musician (jazz violin, viola). m. Julie A Noble, 4 April 1992, 1 s., 1 d. *Education:* University of Texas at Austin. *Career:* Arranger, Musician, Ian Moore, Eddie Harris, 8 1/2 Souvenirs, Sara Hickman, Toni Price, Betty Elders; Sue Young; David Rice; Toured with the Turtle Island String Quartet, 1991. *Compositions:* Raga; Blues for Fritz; Tigris. *Recordings:* Reel Life, 1993; Simple Gifts, 1994; Live from Austin, 1996. *Membership:* ASCAP; AFM. *Address:* 613 Fletcher, Austin, TX 78704, USA.

TAYLOR-GOOD, Karen; b. El Paso, Texas, USA. Vocalist; Songwriter. *Career:* Began as folk singer: Austin, Texas; Europe; Radio, television commercials: United Airlines; McDonalds; Heinz; Backing singer for: Willie Nelson; Merle Haggard; Randy Travis; Roy Rogers; George Jones; Now Solo artist on Mesa Records; Songwriter for Warner Chappell; Represented USA, Musical Peace Mission to USSR, 1988. *Compositions:* Songs written for: Laura Branigan; Patty Loveless; Melanie; Nana Mouskouri; Diamond Rio. *Recordings:* Solo album: On Angels Wings, 2001; Sang on soundtracks: Best Little Whorehouse In Texas; Smokey and the Bandit; Main solo success with: How Can I Help You Say Goodbye. *Honours:* Best New Female, ACM; New Folk Winner, Kerrville Festival, 1992; Songwriter of Year, SESAC, 1994; 2 CMA Awards (all for How I Can I Help You Say Goodbye); Music Video Awards, SESAC and Music Row Magazine. *Membership:* Founding mem., Planet Earth Project. *Current Management:* SESAC. *Address:* 55 Music Sq. E, Nashville, TN 37203, USA.

T-BOZ. See: WATKINS, Tionne Tenese.

TCHANDO, (Salvador Embalo); b. 22 March 1957, Bafata, Guinea-Bissau. Composer; Musician (guitar); Vocalist. *Education:* Second level, Economics, Superior Economic Institute of Lisbon. *Career:* Guitarist, backing singer for N'kassa Kobra; Issabari; Hanne Boel; Kaba Mane; Lead singer for Zebra; Continental Heat; Solo artiste, 1991–; Television apperances: Afrika Musika and MCM (Paris); Special 'Tchando', TVE (Bissau); Radio appearances: RFT; RDN; Africa No 1. *Compositions:* Music for theatre in Denmark. *Recordings:* Albums: Solo album: Naton, released 1994; with Kabe Mane: Chefo Mae Mae; Kungha; with Hanne Boel: Dark Passion. *Membership:* Danish Musicians' and Composers' Union; Koda. *Address:* Bispeengen 11, 2 th, 2000 Frederiksberg, Denmark.

TE, Carlos; Composer; Lyricist; Musician (guitar). m. Olga Fortes, 1 s., 1 d. *Education:* Degree, Philosophy, Oporto University. *Career:* Worked with Rui VeLoso, writing and producing records, 1979–; Collaborations with Trovante, 1983, Gabriela Schaff, 1983, Jáfumega, 1982, 1983, CLÃ, writing and producing, 1995, Mãozinha, 1997, Santos and Pecadores, 1999. *Compositions:* Chico Fininho; Porto Covo; Porto Sentido; Nao Há Estrelas No Céu; A Paixão; Lado Lunar; GTI; Novas Babilónias. *Recordings:* Mingos and Os Samurais; Auto da Pimenta; Kazoo; Lado Lunar; Avenidas. *Publications:* Ar de Rock, 1980; Rui VeLoso, 1987; Mingos and Os Samurais, 1990; Auto da Pimenta, 1991; Avenidas, 1998. *Honours:* Best Album of the Year, 1980; Best Song of the Year, Caras magazine and Nove Gente magazine, 1998. *Membership:* SPA. *Current Management:* EMI Publishing, Portugal. *Address:* Praceta Joao Moreira Bastos 468, 4400 Vila Nova de Gaia, Portugal.

TEE TAH. See: **MOTEN, Frank, Jr.**

TEE-BIRDD, Jamaka, (Richard Anthony Johnson); b. 15 Sept. 1952, Kingston, Jamaica. Musician (keyboards, guitar, percussion); Publisher. m. Celia Caiz. *Education:* Kingston College, 1967–71; College of Art, Science and Technology, 1972–73. *Career:* Member, bands: Bare Essentials; Zap-Pow; In-Crowd; Soul Syndicate; Burning Spear; Judy Mowatt; Bunny Wailer; Boris Gardiner; Top Notch; Roots Radics; Home T; Performed on Reggae Sunsplash I–V, X, XI, reggae Sunsplash Pay Per View, 1991; Tours: USA; Europe; Africa; South America; Japan; Israel. *Compositions:* Jamdown Rock, song used on radio and TV to advertise The First Reggae Sunsplash. *Recordings:* Albums: with Zap-Pow: Now; LoveHits; ZapPow; with Soul Syndicate: Harvest Uptown-Famine Downtown; Was Is and Always; Friends of Soul Syndicate; FM, Freddie McGregor; with In-Crowd: His Majesty Is Coming; Man From New Guinea; Best of In-Crowd; with Burning Spear: Far Over; Fittest of The Fittest; Resistance; People of The World; Live In Paris; Jah Kingdom; with Israel Vibration: Forever; Vibes Alive; IV; Free to Love; On the Rock; Dub-the-Rock; Live Again; IV Dub; Cry Blood, Charlie Chaplin; Party, Yellowman; World Peace Three, Radically Radics, Roots Radics; with Bare Essentials: Back-a-Yard; No Loafin'; Soca With You; with various artists; Reggae For Kids; RORXX (Reggae On The Rocks X), Tee-Bird Showcase; Heart Monitor. *Publications:* Jamaka comic magazines, Jamaka serial cartoon in the Star daily newspaper. *Honours:* Co-arranger of The Jamaica Festival Song Competition's first and only female performed winning song Mek Wi Put Things Right. *Membership:* PRS; JFM; Musicians' Union (UK). *Current Management:* RAS Records. *Address:* 2447 Linden Lane, Silverspring, MD 20910, USA.

TEIMOSO. See: **DA SILVA, Rui.**

TEK 9. See: **MACFARLANE, Denis.**

TEMIZ, Okay; b. 11 Feb. 1939, Ankara, Turkey. Musician (percussion). 1 s. *Education:* Conservatory. *Career:* World tours: USA, Europe, India, with Don Cherry, Karnata Ka College of Percussion, Oriental Wind, Okay Temiz Magnetic Band. *Recordings:* Music For Axaba, 1974; Oriental Wind; 12 records, 1947–86; Fis Fis Tziganes, 1992; Fish Market, 1993; Don Cherry/Bobo Stainson/Okay Temiz, 1993; Ranarop, Gjallarhorn, 1998; Peregrina World, 1999; Hammage An Istanbul, 2000. *Honours:* Year of The Musician, Istanbul, 1971. *Membership:* Swedish and Finnish Jazz Organization. *Current Management:* Denis Leblond, 99 Ave de Clichy, 75017 Paris, France; Orane Senly, Artalene, 15 Passage de la Main d'Or, 75001, Paris, France; Werner Oberender, PO Box 1926, 5450 Neuvied 1, Germany.

TEMPEST, Joey; b. 19 Aug. 1963, Stockholm, Sweden. Vocalist; Songwriter. *Career:* Co-founder, rock group Force, 1982; Won national rock talent contest, Sweden; Recorded two albums for Swedish market; Renamed Europe, 1985–92; Solo artist, 1993–; International tours. *Recordings:* Albums: with Europe: Wings of Tomorrow, 1985; The Final Countdown, 1986; Out of This World, 1988; Prisoners In Paradise, 1991; Super Hits, 2000; Solo: A Place To Call Home, 1995; Azalea Place, 1999; Hit singles include: with Europe: Carrie; The Final Countdown (No. 1, UK), 1986; Rock The Night; Cherokee; Superstitious. *Current Management:* Rascoff/Zysblat Organisation, 110 W 57th St, New York, NY 10019, USA.

TEMPLETON, David J; b. 18 June 1960, Chicago, Illinois, USA. Composer; Performer; Musician (piano, guitar). *Education:* University of Washington; Studied jazz improvisation under Bill Smith; studied film scoring under Hummie Mann. *Career:* Concerts, Seattle Paramount Theatre, 1985; Columbia River Grand Coulee, 1993; Chateau Saint Michelle, 1997, 1998, 1999. *Compositions:* Promise; Elisha; Only With You. *Recordings:* Albums, Time Alone; Promise; The Deepest Water; Change. *Membership:* ASCAP; NARAS. *Address:* Mason Ridge Records, PO Box 942, Seahurst, WA 98062 0942, USA.

TEMPLIN, Ray; b. 27 Jan. 1947, Chicago, Illinois, USA. Musician; Actor; Writer. m. Trish, 19 May 1968, 1 s., 1 d. *Education:* 2 years, University of Illinois. *Career:* 30 years professional musician, bandleader specializing in stride piano; Major jazz festivals in USA, concerts, guest artist appearances; 20 years voice-over, acting, including cartoon and television voice; 5 seasons

as piano playing proprietor of Ray Templin's Bar, on Matlock (NBC). *Compositions:* Jam '38 A Theatrical Experience, theatrical production. *Recordings:* Ray Templin – Piano Man; Ray Templin – Swingology; Crazy 'Bout Fats, Ray Templin's Chicagoans; Dueling Banjomania, 1997; Calling All Jitterbugs, 1998; Flash At The Piano, 1999. *Membership:* AFM; SAG; AFTRA: ASCAP. *Current Management:* The Bigley Agency.

TEMS, Michael James Anthony (Mick); b. 3 Jan. 1950, London, England. Vocalist; Musician. *Career:* Member, Welsh traditional group Swansea Jack, 1973–78; Member, Welsh traditional group Calennig, 1978–; Television includes: The Folk Club, BBC Wales, 1975; Torth y Fara, 1982; Folk On The Move, HTV, 1983; Trade Winds, BBC Wales, 1985; Fastest to Frisco, BBC Wales, 1986; Evening News, Dunedin, New Zealand, 1990; Celtic Magic, HTV, 1990; Gwerin, S4C, 1995. *Recordings:* Solo: Gowerton Fair, 1977; with Swansea Jack, The Seven Wonders, 1978; with Calennig: Songs and Tunes From Wales, 1980; You Can Take a White Horse Anywhere, 1983; Dyddiau Gwynion Ionawr, 1985; Dwr Glan, 1990; Trade Winds, 1994; A Gower Garland, 2000; Numerous compilations, most recently Celtic Waves, 2001. *Membership:* Equity; Musicians' Union; MCPS; PAMRA; NUJ; CDdWC; COTC. *Address:* 1 Ty Clwyta Cottages, Cross Inn, Llantrisant, Rhondda Cynon Taf CF72 8AZ, Wales.

TENAGLIA, Danny, (Soul Boy); b. New York, USA. Prod; Remixer; DJ. *Career:* Began as a DJ in New York; relocation to Miami during the '80s led to production work; Returned to New York, 1990; Resident DJ at Vinyl in New York; Collaborations: Peter Daou; Liz Torres; Celeda; Remixed: Deep Dish; East 17; D*Note; Pet Shop Boys; Faithless; Kings of Tomorrow; Depeche Mode. *Recordings:* Albums: Hard and Soul, 1995; Tourism, 1998; Singles: Harmonica Track (as Soul Boy), 1991; Bottom Heavy, 1994; Look Ahead (with Carol Sylvan), 1995; Music Is The Answer (Dancin' and Prancin'), 1998; B (with Datar), 2000; Fever Rising (with Cass and Slide), 2001. *Website:* www.dtenaglia.com.

TENKANEN, Kari; b. 20 Feb. 1963, Finland. Musician (alto, soprano saxophone, clarinet). *Education:* Clarinet lessons age 6–10; Jazz, summer camp held by Oulunkylä Pop/Jazz Conservatoire, 1980. *Career:* Member, Espoo Big Band, 10 years; Small ensembles include Jani Malmi Quartet, 5 years; Founder, own quintet. *Recordings:* Appears on: John Adams, I Was Looking At The Ceiling, 1998. *Address:* Mechelininkatu 15 A 15, 00100 Helsinki, Finland.

TENNANT, Neil Francis; b. 10 July 1954, North Shields, Northumberland, England. Vocalist; Songwriter; Prod. *Education:* History, North London Polytechnic. *Career:* Mem., Dust, 1970–71; Worked in publishing, 1975–; Founder mem., West End, renamed Pet Shop Boys, 1981–, with Chris Lowe; Film: It Couldn't Happen Here, 1988; Numerous television appearances; Tours: Europe, Hong Kong, Japan, UK, USA, Canada; Host (with Chris Lowe), Simon Bates Show, BBC Radio One, one week, 1991, 1992; Launched record label, Spaghetti, 1991; Prod., songwriter, artistes incl.: Dusty Springfield, Patsy Kensit, Liza Minnelli, Boy George, Electronic; Musical, Closer to Heaven (written with Chris Lowe and Jonathan Harvey), West End, London, 2001. *Recordings:* Albums: Please, 1986; Disco—The Remix Album, 1986; Actually, 1987; Introspective, 1988; In Depth (Japan only), 1989; Behaviour, 1990; Discography, 1991; Very, 1993; Very Relentless, 1993; Disco 2, 1994; Alternative, 1995; Bilingual, 1996; Originals (Please, Actually, Behaviour box set), 1997; Bilingual Special Edition, 1997; Essential Pet Shop Boys, 1998; Nightlife, 1999; Please—Further Listening 1984–1986, 2001; Actually—Further Listening 1987–1988, 2001; Introspective—Further Listening 1988–1989, 2001; Behaviour—Further Listening 1990–1991, 2001; Very—Further Listening 1992–1994, 2001; Bilingual—Further Listening 1995–1997, 2001; Release, 2002; Disco 3, 2003. Singles: West End Girls; Opportunities; Suburbia; Love Comes Quickly; It's A Sin; What Have I Done To Deserve This?; Rent; Heart; Always On My Mind; Domino Dancing; Left To My Own Devices; It's Alright; So Hard; Being Boring; Where The Streets Have No Name (I Can't Take My Eyes Off You)/How Can You Expect To Be Taken Seriously; Jealousy; DJ Culture; DJ Culture Remix; Was It Worth It; Can You Forgive Her; Go West; I Wouldn't Normally Do This Kind Of Thing; Liberation; Yesterday When I Was Mad; Absolutely Fabulous; Before; Se A Vida E; Single Bilingual; A Red Letter Day; Somewhere; I Don't Know What You Want But I Can't Give It Anymore; New York City Boy; You Only Tell Me You Love Me When You're Drunk; Home And Dry; I Get Along; Writer, singer, Electronic: Getting Away With It, 1989; Patience Of A Saint, 1991; Disappointed, 1992. *Publications:* Pet Shop Boys, Annually; Pet Shop Boys Versus America; Pet Shop Boys, Literally, 1990. *Honours:* Ivor Novello Awards, 1987, 1988; BPI Award, Best Single, 1987; Best Group, 1988; Berolina, Germany, 1988. *Address:* Pet Shop Boys Partnership, 8 Pembridge Studios, 27a Pembroke Villas, London W11 3EP, England. *Website:* www.petshopboys.co.uk.

TENNILLE, Toni; b. 8 May 1943, Montgomery, Alabama, USA. Vocalist. m. Daryl Dragon, 14 Feb. 1974. *Career:* Co-writer and performer, musical Mother Earth, San Francisco, 1972; Formed duo, The Captain and Tennille, with Daryl Dragon, 1972–80; Tour with Beach Boys, 1972; Performed at White House dinner, in honour of Queen Elizabeth II, 1976; Musical variety show,

The Captain and Tennille, ABC TV, 1976; Solo artiste, 1980–; Appeared in Broadway show, Stardust, 1991; Nevada Ambassador for the Arts, 1998; Stage performance in The Rainmaker. *Recordings:* Albums: with The Captain and Tennille: Love Will Keep Us Together, 1975; Song of Joy, 1976; Come In From The Rain, 1977; Captain and Tennille's Greatest Hits, 1978; Dream, 1978; Make Your Move, 1980; Twenty Years of Romance, 1995; Solo albums: More Than You Know, 1984; Moonglow, 1986; All of Me, 1987; Never Let Me Go, 1992; Things Are Swingin', 1994; Tennille Sings Big Band, 1998; Incurably Romantic, 2001; Hit singles include: Love Will Keep Us Together (No. 1, USA), 1975; The Way I Want To Touch You, 1975; Lonely Night (Angel Face), 1976; Shop Around, 1976; Muskrat Love, 1976; Can't Stop Dancin', 1977; You Never Done It Like That, 1978; Do That To Me One More Time (No. 1, USA), 1980. *Honours:* Grammy Award, Record of the Year, Love Will Keep Us Together, 1976; Juno Awards, Best International Single, Love Will Keep Us Together, Canada, 1976. *Current Management:* Cheri Ingram Co, 3575 Cahuenga Blvd, Suite 600, Los Angeles, CA 90068, USA.

TERMINATOR X, (Norman Rogers); DJ; Rap Artiste. *Career:* Member, US rap group Public Enemy, 1984–90; Concerts include: Support to the Beastie Boys, USA, 1987; Support to LL Cool J, European tour, 1987; Tour of a Black Planet, 1990; Solo artiste, 1990–; Manager, The Entourage (hip hop club), Long Island, New York, 1986. *Recordings:* Albums: with Public Enemy: Yo! Bum Rush The Show, 1987; It Takes A Nation of Millions To Hold Us Back, 1988; Fear of a Black Planet, 1990; Muse Sick 'n' Hour Mess Age, 1994; There's A Poison Goin' On, 1999; Revolverlution, 2002; Solo: Terminator X and The Valley of the Jeep Beets, 1991; Singles: Rebel Without A Pause; Bring The Noise; Don't Believe The Hype; Night of The Living Baseheads; Black Steel In The Hour of Chaos; Fight The Power, theme song for film Do The Right Thing; Welcome To The Terrordome; 911 Is A Joke; Brothers Gonna Work It Out; Want To Be Dancin'; Homey Don't Play That; Juvenile Delinquentz; It All Comes Down to Money; Under The Sun; Do You Wanna Go Our Way?. *Current Management:* Malik Entertainment Management, PO Box 310, Roosevelt, NY 11575, USA.

TERRY, Todd, (Swan Lake, Royal House, Gypsymen); b. 18 April 1967, Brooklyn, New York, USA. Prod; Remixer; DJ. *Career:* Originally part of Masters At Work with Kenny Dope before achieving legendary house music producer status in his own right using various pseudonyms; Founder: Freeze Records; Sound Design Records; Collaborations: Kenny Dope; Roland Clark; T La Rock; Remixed: Martha Wash; Janet Jackson; Jamiroquai; Everything But The Girl; Michael Jackson; Kylie Minogue; The Corrs. *Recordings:* Albums: To The Batmobile – Let's Go, 1988; Resolutions, 1999; Singles: Can You Party (as Royal House), 1988; Bango – To The Batmobile (as Todd Terry Project), 1988; Dreams of Santa Anna (as Orange Lemon), 1989; Jumpin', 1993; Bounce To The Beat, 1995; Keep On Jumpin', 1996; Something Goin' On, 1997; Let It Ride, 1999; Babarabatiri (as Gypsymen), 2001; Raining, 2001. *Address:* In House/Sound Design Records, c/o Ministry of Sound, 103 Gaunt St, London SE1 6DP, England.

TETTEH-LARTEY, Benny; b. 29 Sept. 1965, Mayfield, Dalkieth, Scotland. Vocalist; Songwriter; Musician. m. Lesley Moss, 15 Sept. 1999, 1 s., 2 d. *Career:* Began 1987, several different bands; Uses 8-string acoustic guitar; Solo career; Appeared unofficially at T in the Park festival, and was asked to return; Numerous live sessions and interviews on BBC Radio Scotland's Ghetto Blasting, The Usual Suspects, Radio Forth, Scot FM; Played alongside Nick Harper at 12 Bar Club in London, 1999. *Compositions:* Head in the Sand, 1998; Injustice, 1997; Song to Papa, 1996; In the Same Boat, 1987. *Recordings:* Single: Roses Are Red, 1998; Album: Don't Be Sad, 1998; Rough Cut, 2001. *Honours:* BBC Scotland Tympanali Award (songwriter showcase), for Injustice, 1998. *Membership:* MCPS; PRS; Musicians' Union. *Current Management:* BTL Management. *Address:* 50 Paradykes Ave, Loanhead, Midlothian EH20 9LD, Scotland.

THAIN, Laurie Anne; b. 18 Feb. 1955, New Westminster, British Columbia, Canada. Vocalist; Songwriter; Musician (guitar). *Education:* BA, Physical Education and Theatre. *Career:* Concert artist specialising in the intimate singer/songwriter approach; Writer and producer of numerous custom entertainment shows and corporate events; Concerts, opening shows for Lee Greenwood; Gary Morris; Rita MacNeil; Pam Tillis; World-wide tours. *Recordings:* Hopeless Romantic, 1984; Matters of The Heart, 1987; Stages, 1992; 5 song EP, Preview, of album No 4, 1997. *Honours:* Winner, Canadian National, Du Maurier Search For Stars. *Membership:* Canadian Country Music Asscn; AFofM. *Address:* #205, 6359 198th St, Langley, BC V2Y 2ES, British Columbia, Canada.

THALÍA, (Ariadna Thalia Sodi Miranda); b. 27 Aug. 1971, Mexico City, Mexico. Actress; Vocalist. m. Tommy Mottola, 2000. *Career:* Mem., children's group Din-Din; Mem., Timbiriche, 1984; Solo artiste, 1990–; Film appearances: Vamos al baile, 1996; Mambo Café, 1999; Television appearances: soap operas La pobre señorita Limantour, Quinceañera, Luz y sombra, Maria Mercedes, Marimar, Maria la del barrio; Co-host, VIP de noche. *Recordings:* Albums: with Din-Din: Four albums; with Timbiriche: Three albums; Solo: Thalia I, 1990; Mundo De Cristal, 1991; Love, 1992; Marimar, 1994; En Extasis, 1995; Amor A La Mexicana, 1997; Arrasando,

2000; Thalia II, 2002. *Honours:* Platinum disc. *Address:* EMI Latin, EMI Group PLC, 4 Tenterden St, Hanover Sq., London W1A 2AY, England. *Website:* www.thalia.com.

THANDI. See: **MAZWAI, Thandiswa**.

THANGER, Hakan; b. 23 Oct. 1943, Boo, Stockholm, Sweden. Musician (electric bass, guitar); Vocalist. Divorced. *Career:* Contributor, Swedish Eurovision Song Contest; Played and written songs and arrangements for many artists from Sweden including: Lill Babs; Jerry Williams; Family Four and others. *Compositions:* Dagar Jag Ner I Min Källare. *Recordings:* More than 500 studio recordings. *Membership:* STIM; SAMI; SKAP; TSO. *Address:* Sverkersgatan 6, 3tr, 126 51 Stockholm, Sweden.

THAYIL, Kim; b. 4 Sept. 1960, Seattle, WA, USA. Musician (guitar). *Education:* Philosophy Degree, University of Washington. *Career:* Mem., US heavy rock group, Soundgarden, 1984–97; Numerous live tours and festival appearances. *Recordings:* Singles: Nothing to Say; Flower; Loud Love; Hands All Over; Get on the Snake; Jesus Christ Pose; Outshined; Rusty Cage; Spoonman; The Day I Tried to Live; Black Hole Sun; Fell on Black Days; Pretty Noose; Burden in My Hand; Blow Up the Outside World; Ty Cobb; Bleed Together; Albums: Ultramega OK, 1988; Louder than Love, 1989; Badmotorfinger, 1991; Superunknown, 1994; Down on the Upside, 1996; A-Sides, 1997; Guitar on: The No WTO Combo, Live From The Battle In Seattle, 2000; Wellwater Conspiracy, Scroll And Its Combinations, 2001. *Address:* c/o A&M Records, Interscope Records, 2220 Colorado Ave, Santa Monica, CA 90404, USA. *Website:* www.soundgardenonline.co.uk.

THEMIS, John; b. 13 Oct. 1954. Prod; Musician (guitar); Writer; Musical Dir. m. Anne Lawrence, 14 Jan. 1981, 1 s., 2 d. *Education:* BSc Marketing, Management. *Career:* UK television appearances include: Aspel; Jonathan Ross; Terry Wogan; The Big E; The Word; The Chart Show; Pebble Mill; BPM; Top of the Pops; Jools Holland Show; Brian Conley Show; Lily Savage Show; The Box; MTV Live; US appearances include: Tonite With Jay Leno; The Ru Paul Show; The John and Lisa Show; French appearances include: Le Nuils; Tarata; Couscous; C'est Nous; Also television in Germany; Belgium; Argentina; Russia; Chile; Japan; Concerts include: Hammersmith Odeon; Festival Hall; Ronnie Scott's; Pride Festival, Brockwell Park, 250,000 people; International concerts include: Canada, Romania, Japan; Musical director, songwriting partner, guitarist with Boy George, for 4 years; Played with Chris de Burgh, on Room In This Heart, BBC TV; Also worked with: Dannii Minogue; Lavine Hudson; Paul Young; Wendy and Lisa; Tim Rice; Nigel Kennedy; Jason Donavon; Kim Wilde; Ray Simson; London Chamber Orchestra. *Compositions include:* What Took You So Long (Emma Bunton); Please Stay (Kylie Minogue). *Recordings:* Albums; Sirens; Ulysses and The Cyclops; English Renaissance; As musician, producer: with Boy George; Chris de Burgh; Suggs; Blair; Cher; Evolution; Simon Climie; Lippy Lou; Malcolm MacLaren; The Grid; Billy Ray Martin; Eve Gallagher; Elton John; Pet Shop Boys; George Michael; The Beloved; Gary Kemp; Barry Manilow; Orchestral Manoeuvres In The Dark; Bad Boys Inc; Spice Girls; Gary Barlow; Eternal; Sophie Ellis-Bextor; Dido; Boyzone; Gabrielle; Charlotte Church; Bond; Emma Bunton; S Club 7; Five; Producer, Voices (single), Junior Reid. *Honours:* Ulysses, Album of the Month, British Guitarist Magazine. *Address:* 46 The Limes Ave, London N11 1RH, England.

THERRIEN, Lucie; b. 21 Aug. 1945, Newport, VT, USA. Vocalist; Musician (piano, guitar, ethnic instruments). *Education:* MA, UNH; Ecole Des Beaux Arts. *Career:* PBS Television, PBS Radio, Good Day Show, Radio Québec and France; Television 5 International, Radio Canada; Television and Radio in Québec; Cultural Exchanges and Performances Over 4 Continents. *Compositions:* Cousins; Memere. *Recordings:* Noel c'est l'amour; Cousins; Pot Pourri Folklorique; Un Tresor. *Membership:* Le Conseil Francophone de la Chanson; NH Council of the Arts; NH Humanities Council. *Current Management:* French American Music Ent, PO Box 4721, Portsmouth, NH 03802 4721, USA.

THIGPEN, Edmund Leonard; b. 28 Dec. 1930, Chicago, IL, USA. Musician. Widower, 1 s., 1 d. *Education:* Los Angeles City College. *Career:* Joined the Cootie Williams Band, 1951; Worked with Dinah Washington, Johnny Hiodges Band, avant-garde group of Gil Melle, Trois of Bud Powell, Jutta Hipp, Billy Taylor, 1954–58; Joined Oscar Peterson Trio, 1959–65; Travelled world-wide; Founded the Advanced School of Contemporary Music, Toronto, Canada; Worked in recording studios making jingles, performing on television and movie soundtracks, 1967; Founded own group, Action-Reaction; Worked as teacher and clinician. *Recordings:* More than 50 albums, most recent release It's Entertainment, 1998. *Publications:* Ed Thigpen Talking Drums; Rhythm Analysis and Basic Co-ordination; Rhythm Brought to Life; Ed Thigpen on Jazz Drumming; The Essence of Brushes. *Membership:* The Percussive Arts Society; International Asscn of Jazz Educators. *Address:* Bagerstraede 3, Second Floor, 1617 Copenhagen, Denmark.

THISTLETHWAITE, Anthony Silvester; b. 31 Aug. 1955, Leicester, England. Musician (saxophone, multi-instrumentalist). *Career:* Busking, Paris, 1979–80; Member, The Waterboys, 1982–91; The Saw Doctors,

1993–95; Moved to St Petersburg, Russia, 1995; Currently working with top Russian bands Aquarium and DDT. *Recordings:* with The Waterboys: The Waterboys, 1983; A Pagan Place, 1984; This Is The Sea, 1986; Fisherman's Blues, 1989; Room To Roam, 1990; Rock In The Weary Land, 2000; Solo albums: Aesop Wrote A Fable, 1993; Cartwheel, 1995; Other recordings with Bob Dylan; Donovan; Johnny Thunders; Psychedelic Furs; World Party; Mission; Fairground Attraction: Sharon Shannon; Eddi Reader; Robyn Hitchcock; Ian McNabb; Solo: Cartwheel, 1995; Crawfish and Caviar, 1997. *Membership:* Musicians' Union. *Address:* c/o Purpleteeth Productions, PO Box 2666, London W14 0ZT, England.

THOMAS, B. J. (Billie Joe); b. 7 Aug. 1942, Hugo, Oklahoma, USA. Vocalist; Songwriter; Entertainer. m. Gloria Richardson, 9 Dec. 1968, 3 d. *Career:* Lead singer, The Triumphs; Opened for acts including Roy Orbison; The Dave Clark Five; the Four Tops; Solo artiste; Toured with Dick Clark Caravan of Stars; Regular appearances Ed Sullivan Show, nightclubs, concert halls; Became 60th member, Grand Ole Opry; B J Thomas Celebrity Theater, Tennessee Smoky Mountains. *Recordings:* Albums include: Peace In The Valley; Love Shines; Great American Dream; Shining; All Is Calm, All Is Bright; Throwin' Rocks At The Moon; Nightlife; Midnite Minute; I Believe; You Call That A Mountain, 2000; Singles include: I'm So Lonesome I Could Cry; Mama; The Eyes of a New York Woman; Hooked On A Feeling; Raindrops Keep Fallin' On My Head (from Butch Cassidy and the Sundance Kid soundtrack); It's Only Love; I Just Can't Help Believin'; No Love At All; Rock and Roll Lullabye; As Long As We Got Each Other (theme from series Growing Pains); Somebody Done Somebody Wrong; Broken Toys (adopted as theme tune by child abuse agencies); What Ever Happened To Old Fashioned Love; New Looks From An Old Lover; The Whole World's In Love When You're Lonely. *Publications:* Home Where I Belong; In Tune. *Honours:* 5 Grammy Awards; 2 Dove Awards; 5 Platinum, 11 Gold albums: Lifetime Achievement Award, U C Berkeley; Academy Award, 1970; Country Song of the Year, 1975. *Membership:* AFTRA; SAG; Grand Ole Opry; AFofM; CMA; NARAS; National Songwriters' Asscn. *Current Management:* Michael Goldstein, Goldwest, 9125 Otto St, Downey, CA 90240, USA; Agent: Lee Farmer, Marathon Attractions.

THOMAS, Daniel; b. 11 Jan. 1970, Brixton, London, England. Musician (keyboards); Vocalist; Songwriter. *Career:* Backing vocals for: Luther Vandross; Elton John; Carleen Anderson; Deuce; Eternal; Erasure; David Essex; Jools Holland; Features on: Ready Or Not, M&S Presents The Girl Next Door, 2001; Played keyboards for: Sir Harry Secombe (Crystal Rose Show); IDMC; Bryan Powell; Ricky Grundy; Music Director for London Community Gospel Choir and Choir Director; Also teacher of vocal techniques. *Membership:* Musicians' Union; Black Gospel Asscn. *Current Management:* Basil Meade, Choir Connexion. *Address:* 9 Greenwood Dr., Highams Park, London E4 9HL, England.

THOMAS, Irma (Lee); b. 18 Feb. 1941, Pontchatoula, Louisiana, USA. Vocalist. *Career:* R&B singer known as The Soul Queen of New Orleans. *Recordings:* Albums: Wish Somone Would Care, 1964; Take A Look, 1968; In Between Tears, 1973; Live, 1977; Soul Queen of New Orleans, 1978; Safe With Me, 1979; Hip Shakin' Mama, 1981; The New Rules, 1986; The Way I Feel, 1988; Simply The Best, 1991; True Believer, 1992; Turn My World Around, 1993; Walk Around Heaven, 1993; The Story of My Life, 1997; My Heart's In Memphis, 2000. *Address:* c/o Emile Jackson, PO Box 26126, New Orleans, LA 70186, USA.

THOMAS, Patrice; b. 17 March 1961, Besancon, France. Musician (guitar). *Education:* Diplome d'Etat Jazz. *Career:* Performed at festivals: Montpellier; Mulhouse; Calvi; Milan; Nancy; Concerts at Maison de Radio France, Paris; Radio and TV: TF1; Fr3; France Musique; France Culture; France Inter. *Recordings:* CDs: Isis; Portraits. *Honours:* Soloist, first prize, Ninth Jazz Challenge, Paris (Défense). *Membership:* UMJ; Teacher, Ecole de Musique, Montbeliard. *Address:* Refranche, 25330 Amancey, France.

THOMAS, Patrick; b. 27 July 1960, Oxford, England. Musician (keyboards); Composer; Prod. *Education:* BA, hons, Psychology, Open University; Private Classical Piano Lessons; Studied with Mary Howell-Pryce, St Edmund Campion School, Oxford. *Career:* Paris with Chuck Berry, Continental Drift, 1989; London with Derek Bailey, Eugene Chadbourne, Keith Rowe, 1990; London with John Zorn, Bucket Head, Paul Lovens, 1991; Germany with Tony Oxley, Sirone, Larry Stabbins, Manfred Schoof, 1992; Glasgow with Lol Coxhill, 1993; Berlin Jazz Festival with Bill Dixon, 1994; London Jazz Cafe with Thurston Moore, Lee Renaldo, 1996; Solo, Copenhagen, 1997; Austria Graz Music Protocol, with And, 1997; CMN Tour, with Butch Morris; London Sky Scraper; Vancouver Jazz Festival, with Eugene Chadborne and Alex Ward, 1998; Cologne, Germany with Celebration Orchestra, 1998; Uncool Festival, Switzerland, with Scatter, 1999. *Compositions:* Ensemble WX7e Turntables Dialogue (with interruptions); Pulse, for drum machine and two percussionists; Reflex, for ensemble and computers. *Recordings:* With Tony Oxley Quartet, Incus, 1992; Lol Coxhill, Halim Nato, 1993; One Night in Glasgow, Scatter, 1994; Company 91, 3 Vols, 1994; Mike Cooper Island Songs, 1995; Celebration Orchestra, The Enchanted Messenger, 1996; Tones of Life, Guidance, 1997; Solo Album, Remembering, 1998; Total Tuesday, Hellington

Country, 1998; And, Intakt, 1998; Hard Edge, with Rhys Chatham, 1999; Powerfield, EEE, 1999. *Publications:* Islam's Contribution to Jazz and Improvised Music, 1993; Upside Down (The Myth of Jazz History), 1998. *Honours:* Arts Council of Great Britain Jazz Bursary for 3 Electro-accoustic Compositions. *Membership:* Performing Rights Society; London Musicians Collective. *Address:* 5 Saint Omer Rd, Cowley, Oxford OX4 3HB, England.

THOMAS, Rhozanda, (Chilli); b. 27 Feb. 1971, Atlanta, GA, USA. Vocalist; Choreographer. 1 s. *Career:* Professional Dancer, Damian Dame; Mem., TLC, 1991–; Appeared in film Have Plenty; Started own publishing company, T-Ron Music. *Recordings:* Albums: Ooooooohhh... On The TLC Tip, 1992; Crazysexycool, 1994; Fanmail, 1999; 3D, 2002. Singles: Ain't 2 Proud 2 Beg, 1991; Baby Baby Baby, 1992; What About Your Friends, 1992; Get It Up, 1993; Creep (EP), 1994; Diggin' On You, 1995; Red Light Special, 1995; Waterfalls, 1995; Future/Off, 1997; No Scrubs, 1999; Silly Ho, 1999; Unpretty, 1999; Dear Lie, 1999; Girltalk, 2002. *Honours:* Grammy Awards, Best R&B Performance by Duo/Group, Best R&B Album, for Crazysexycool; Two Lady of Soul Awards; Two Billboard Music Awards; Three Soul Train Awards; Blockbuster Entertainment Award; Four MTV Music Video Awards, for Waterfalls. *Address:* LaFace Records, 1 Capital City Plaza, 3350 Peachtree Rd, Suite 1500, Atlanta, GA 30326, USA.

THOMPSON, Christopher Hamlet; b. 9 March 1947, Hertford, Hertfordshire, England. Musician. m. Maggie, 4 Jan. 1995, 1 s. *Education:* BSoc Science, Teaching Certificate. *Career:* Professional musician, 1972–; Joined Manfred Mann's Earth Band, 1975–86; Formed own band Night, 1979; Extensive tours throughout USA, Europe: With Manfred Mann's Earth Band, 1975–86; With Night, 1979–83; Working in Europe, under own name, 1986–; with The Alan Parsons Project; Singer, TV product campaigns: Rank Xerox; Mandate; De Beers; ADT; Bayer; Tennents Pilsner; Twix; Kelloggs Cornflakes; The Daily Mail; Peugeot 205; Abbey National; Budweiser. *Recordings:* with Manfred Mann's Earth Band: The Roaring Silence, 1976; Watch, 1978; Angel Station, 1979; Chance, 1980; Somewhere In Africa, 1982; Live In Budapest, 1983; Criminal Tango, 1986; The Best Of, Remastered, 1998; Blindin', 2000; Singles: Blinded By The Light; Davy's On The Road Again; Solo albums: Radio Voices, 1983; High Cost of Living, 1986; Beat of Love, 1989; Hits in Germany with: The Challenge, 1989; The Joker, 1991; Florida Lady, 1994; Songs and vocals to albums by: The Doobie Brothers; Tina Turner; Elton John; Roger Daltrey; Jefferson Starship; Brian May; Barbara Dickson; Ozzy Osbourne. *Membership:* PRS; SAG; Equity. *Current Management:* Horst Zwipp, Feedback Music.

THOMPSON, Danny Henry; b. 4 April 1939, Teignmouth, S Devon, England. Musician (double bass, trombone). m. Sylvia Thompson, 2 step-s., 1 s. *Education:* Salesian College Grammar. *Career:* Alexis Korner, 1964–67; Roy Orbison Tour, 1964; Recording sessions, 1960s including Marianne Faithfull; Incredible String Band; Nick Drake; Donovan; Co-Founded Pentangle, 1968; Own trio with John McLaughlin, 1966; Tubby Hayes Quartet, Phil Seamen Quartet, Studio Work including Bert Jansch; Rod Stewart, Kate Bush, Talk Talk, 1970s, 1980s; Formed own band, Whatever, 1989, toured, 1992–97; Studio work, 1990s to present includes: Tasmin Archer; Sally Barker; Billy Bragg; Boo Hewerdine; Ian McNabb; David Sylvian; Norma Waterson. *Compositions:* Take 3 Girls Theme, Light Flight; Musing Mingus; Til Minne Au Jan; Children of the Dark; Pitfalls; New Rhythms; No Love is Sorrow; Passion to Protect, film; Swedish Dance; Fair Isle Friends. *Recordings:* Sweet Child Basket of Light; Whatever; Whatever Next; Elemental; Whatever's Best; Dizrhythmia; Songhai; Solid Air; Live at Leeds, with John Martyn; The Pentangle; Industry; Spirit of the Century, with Peter Gabriel, 2002. *Publications:* Video Basically Speaking. *Honours:* Hugo, Chicago International Film Festival; Ivor Novello Award, theme for Take 3 Girls (BBC), 1969; Grammy Award, for Blind Boys of Alabama. *Address:* 43 Mount View, Rickmansworth, Herts WD3 2BB, England. *Telephone:* (1923) 777512. *Fax:* (1923) 777512. *E-mail:* dannynorelation@aol.com.

THOMPSON, Gail; b. 15 June 1958, London, England. Musician (saxophone, clarinet); Composer; Conductor. m. Tim May, 10 May 1994. *Education:* Studied at school. *Career:* Tenor saxophone, West End hit show Bubbling Brown Sugar, 1977; Music teacher, South East London Technical College, 1977; Manageress, Macari's Music Shop, Charing Cross Rd, 1980; Formed Jazz Funk band The Gail Thompson Approach, featured Camden Jazz Week, 1980; Founded Women In Music, 1986; Established Sax Council tuition school; Created Gail Force, 1986; Founded the Jazz Warriors, with Courtney Pine, 1986; Played regularly with Charlie Watts Big Band, Art Blakey's Jazz Messengers; Founded Music Work Resource Centre, music school, 3,000 members; Joined Greater London Arts, The Arts Council of Great Britain advisory panels, 1987; Presented, judged Schlitz Beer, Virgin Records competition; Television: Presented jazz programmes with Russell Davies, BBC2, 1878; Sang solo with Reggae Philharmonic Orchestra, Highway, ITV, 1990–91; Travelled Africa, studying African music, 1988; Set up Frontline Productions to promote Jazz music; MC, various major jazz festivals; Reggae Philharmonic Orchestra, on Highway, ITV, 1990–91; Vocalist, panellist, The Music Game Show, Channel 4, 1992; Films: Tell Me That You Love Me, BBC1, 1991; Close My Eyes (cinema and video release), 1991; Administrator, Britain's first National Music Day with Harvey Goldsmith, 1992; Director,

Jazz Services, 1992; Freelance Consultant, music schools, projects, 1992; Chairman, Arts Council Jazz Committee; ACGTS Music Panellist, 1993; Founder and Chief Executive, Turnaround Project for music media and film for the disabled; Jazz Africa appearances at Berlin Jazz Festival; Recorded live album, 1997. *Compositions:* Commissioned by BBC2, composition for Midland Big Band, featuring Courtney Pine, performed, televised, Royal Albert Hall; Various compositions commissioned include: Royal Opera House Covent Garden, featuring Stan Tracey, Andy Sheppard, 1989; Jazz Africa (suite), by Apples and Snakes, 1991; TV themes for Carlton TV. *Recordings:* Album: Gail Force Big Band; Jazz Africa Big Band, 1996; Jadu, 1998. *Membership:* Chairperson, Arts Council Jazz Review; Started Jazz in Women Festival, 1997. *Address:* 5 St Faiths Rd, West Dulwich, London SE21 8JD, England.

THOMPSON, Hank (Henry William); b. 3 Sept. 1925, Waco, Texas, USA. Country Vocalist; Songwriter; Musician (guitar, harmonica). m. Ann. *Career:* Own radio series, Hank – The Hired Hand, 1942; Founder member, the Brazos Valley Boys, 1946; Recording artiste, 1949–; First country artist recording in stereo, 1959; Tutor, School of Country Music, Claremore, Oklahoma, 1973. *Recordings:* Country hits include: (I've Got) A Humpty Dumpty Heart; Whoa Sailor; The Wild Side of Life (US Country No. 1); Waiting In The Lobby of Your Heart; Rub-A-Dub-Dub; Breakin' The Rules; Honky Tonk Girl; The Blackboard of My Heart; Breakin' In Another Heart; She's Just A Whole Lot Like You; Oklahoma Hills; Where Is The Circus?; The Older The Violin The Sweeter The Music; Mr Honky Tonk The King of Western Swing; Numerous albums include: Songs of The Brazos Valley, 1953; Hank!, 1957; Songs For Rounders, 1959; Live At The Golden Nugget (first live-in-concert country album), 1961; A Six Pack To Go, 1961; Just An Old Flame, 1967; Cab Driver – A Salute To The Mills Brothers, 1972; Movin' On, 1974; Brand New Hank, 1978; Take Me Back To Texas, 1980; Hank Thompson, 1986; Here's To Country Music, 1988; Various compilation albums; Hank Thompson and Friends, 1997; Seven Decades, 2000. *Honours:* Inducted into Country Music Hall of Fame, 1989; Inducted into Nashville Songwriter's Hall of Fame, 1997. *Current Management:* D D Bray Management. *Address:* c/o Hank Thompson Enterprises, 5 Rushing Creek Court, Roanoke, TX 76262, USA.

THOMPSON, John Alexander; b. 15 Aug. 1942, Philadelphia, Pennsylvania, USA. Reverend; Gospel Vocalist; Choir Leader; Songwriter. *Career:* Founder: Sunlight Jubilee Juniors, 1955; Johnny Thompson Singers, 1965; Pennsylavania District F B H Choir, 1970; Sanctificaton, 1983; Member, Philadelphia Mass Choir and Gospel Music Preservation Alliance Choir; Johnny Thompson Singers, numerous tours, Europe and Africa, including: First Gospel act to play Montreux Festival, with Bessie Griffin, 1972; First Black Gospel act to produce own video, 1980; First Gospel act behind Iron Curtain, Poland, 1981; First Black American Gospel act to play Russia, Bulgaria and Egypt; Countless television and radio appearances, Europe; Performed with numerous Gospel acts including: Marion Wlliams; Bessie Griffin; Dorthy Love-Coates; Reverend James Cleveland; Evangelist Shirley Caesar; Dorothy Norwood. *Compositions include:* The Creation; Stranger On The Road; Get Up My Brother; If I Perish; Hold Out; Happy On My Way; There Must Be A Reason; If You Gonna Pray; Wrote several Gospel plays. *Recordings:* Albums: with The Johnny Thompson Singers: I'm On My Way To Zion, 1972; Philadelphia, 1975; Live At Montreux, 1977; Lord I Belong To You, 1982; Gospel At The Opera, 1985; Gospel Christmas, 1986; Spirit of Gospel, 1987; Swing Low Sweet Chariot, 1988; Oh Happy Day!, 1990; 25 Years, 1990; Hand In Hand, 1993; Glory Glory Hallelujah, 1995; with The Pennsylvania District F B H Choir: Look Over Your Shoulders, 1974; Live At Lausanne, 1977. *Honours:* Prix Mahalia Jackson, Philadelphia, 1975. *Membership:* National Convention of Gospel Choirs and Choruses; Gospel Minister, Gospel Music Workshop of America; Choral Director, Wynnefield Academy, Philadelphia. *Current Management:* Freddy J Angstmann. *Address:* Fronhof 100, 8260 Stein am Rhein, Switzerland.

THOMPSON, Keith; b. 29 Jan. 1956, Worcester, England. Blues and Rock Musician (electric and acoustic guitar, harmonica, piano, bass). m. Janette Kathleen Thompson, 26 June 1982, 1 s., 2 d. *Career:* Tours include: Netherlands, 1989; Denmark, 1990; UK, 1992, 1993, 1994 including appearances at The Mean Fiddler, London; The Standard, London; Greenbelt Festival, Bedfordshire; Crossrhythms Festival, Devon; Crossfire Festival, Liverpool; Road Dreams music for Tortworth TV shown on Channel 4, 1991, 1992. *Recordings:* Against The Odds, 1991; Young Hearts, 1992; Voice From Heaven, 1994; Reputation, 1996; Strange Brew, 1998; Also collaborated with: Alex Lawton-Johnston. *Honours:* Songwriter of the Year, 6 Counties Festival, 1990. *Membership:* Musicians' Union; PRS; MCPS. *Address:* 46 Libertus Rd, Cheltenham, Gloucestershire GL51 7EP, England.

THOMPSON, Linda, (Linda Peters); b. London, England. Vocalist; Songwriter. m. Richard Thompson, divorced, 3 c., partner Steve Kenis. *Career:* British tour as member of folk group Albion Band, 1972; Duo with Richard Thompson, 1972–82; Appearances include: Reading Festival, 1975; Regular British tours; Co-writer, appeared in The Mysteries, 1975; Solo artiste, 2000–. *Compositions include:* Co-writer (with Betsy Cook): Telling Me Lies (recorded by Emmylou Harris; Linda Ronstadt; Reba McEntire).

Recordings: Albums: with Richard Thompson: Henry The Human Fly, 1972; I Want To See The Bright Lights Tonight, 1974; Hokey Pokey, 1975; Pour Like Silver, 1975; First Light, 1978; Sunnyvista, 1979; Shoot Out The Lights, 1982; Solo: One Clear Moment, 1985; Give Me A Sad Song, 2000; Fashionably Late, 2002; Contributed to Ashley Hutchings, Guv'nor, Vol. 3, 1999; David Thomas, Mirror Man, 1999; Cathal McConnell, Long Expectant Comes Last, 1999. *Address:* c/o Topic Records Ltd, 50 Stroud Green Rd, London N4 3EF, England.

THOMPSON, Richard; b. 3 April 1949, London, England. Vocalist; Songwriter; Musician (guitar). m. Linda Peters, divorced. *Career:* Founding mem., folk group, Fairport Convention, 1968–71; Concerts include: Folk Meets Pop, Royal Albert Hall, 1969; Royal Festival Hall, with Joni Mitchell, 1969; Bath Festival of Blues and Progressive Music, 1970; London Palladium, 1970; Partnership with wife, Linda, 1972–82; Concerts include: Reading Festival, 1975; Fairport Convention reunion concert, 1980; South Yorkshire Folk Festival, 1982; Also appeared together in groups Albion Country Band; Hokey Pokey; Sour Grapes; Solo artiste, 1982–; Regular world-wide appearances include: Guitar Legends, Seville, Spain, 1992; Cropredy Festival, 1992, 1995. *Recordings:* with Fairport Convention: Fairport Convention, 1968; What We Did On Our Holidays, 1969; Unhalfbricking, 1969; Liege and Lief, 1970; Full House, 1970; with Linda Thompson: I Want To See The Bright Lights Tonight, 1974; Hokey Pokey, 1975; Pour Like Silver, 1975; First Light, 1978; Sunnyvista, 1979; Shoot Out The Lights, 1982; Small Town Romance, 1982; Solo: Henry The Human Fly, 1972; Guitar Vocal, 1976; Strict Tempo, 1981; Hand Of Kindness, 1983; Across A Crowded Room, 1985; Daring Adventures, 1986; The Marksman (soundtrack to BBC drama series), 1987; Live, Love, Larf And Loaf, 1987; Amnesia, 1988; Rumour And Sigh, 1991; Sweet Talker, 1992; Watching The Dark—The History Of Richard Thompson, 1993; You? Me? Us?, 1996; Industry, 1997; Mock Tudor, 1999; Action Packed, 2001; The Old Kit Bag, 2003; Also featured on: Love Chronicles, Al Stewart, 1969; Drunk With Passion, The Golden Palominos, 1991; The Hunter, Jennifer Warnes, 1992; 99.9°F, Suzanne Vega, 1992. *Honours:* New Music Awards, Solo Artist, Songwriter of the Year, Life Achievement Trophy, 1991; Q Award, Best Songwriter, 1991. *Current Management:* Gary Stamler, Suite 2400, 1801 Century Park E, Los Angeles, CA 90067, USA.

THOMPSON, Richard E. 'Butch'; b. 28 Nov. 1943, Stillwater, Minnesota, USA. Musician (piano, clarinet). m. Mary Ellen Niedenfuer, 20 July 1991. *Education:* BA, University of Minnesota. *Career:* Clarinetist, Hall Brothers Jazz Band, 1962–94; Pianist, leader, Butch Thompson Trio in residency, National Public Radio, 1974–86; World Tours as pianist include Cairo, Egypt, 1994; 1997, 1998; European festivals, appearances with orchestras include: Hartford Symphony; Minnesota Orchestra; St Louis Symphony and many more; National tour of off-Broadway show, Jelly Roll, 1994–97; Major US jazz festivals, 1968–. *Compositions include:* Ecuadorean Memories; Yancey On My Mind; Eduadorean Suite, for piano and orchestra, premiered with Minnesota Orchestra in 1998. *Recordings include:* 10 solo CDs, including Thompson Plays Joplin, 1998; Bethlehem After Dark, 2000; Over 100 more recordings, 25 as leader or soloist. *Honours:* Pianist on Grammy winning Verve CD, Doc Cheatham and Nicholas Payton, 1997. *Membership:* American Federation of Musicians, local 30–73. *Current Management:* Zajonc/Valenti Management. *Address:* PO Box 7023, Ann Arbor, MI 48107, USA.

THOMPSON, Robert Scott; b. 17 Feb. 1959, California, USA. Recording Artist; Engineer; Prod; Vocalist; Musician (keyboards, guitar, computer music). m. Debra Mobley. *Education:* Campbell College; University of Oregon; University of California; Compostion and Computer Music With Bernard Rands, Roger Reynolds, Joji Yuasa and F Richard Moore. *Recordings:* Deeper In The Dreamtime; The Strong Eye; Ginnungagap; Shadow Gazing; Air Friction; The Silent Shore; Frontier; Fountainhead, Cloud Cover; Elemental Folklore; Summer Evening; Blue Day. *Publications:* The Stronge Eye; Shadow Gazing; The Silent Shore; Frontier. *Honours:* Bourges Electro Acoustic, 1984; Fulbright Scholar, 1991; Luiy Russolo, 1994; Irino Prize, 1996. *Current Management:* Aucourant Records. *Address:* PO Box 2231, Roswell, GA 30075, USA.

THOMPSON, Teddy; b. 1976. Vocalist; Musician (guitar); Songwriter. *Career:* Son of British folk-rockers Richard and Linda Thompson; First recording singing backing vocals on father's You? Me? Us? album, 1996; Support slot on subsequent promotional tour; Debut album containing 10 self-penned songs released on Virgin, 2000. *Recordings:* solo: Teddy Thompson, 2000; on Richard Thompson albums: You? Me? Us?, 1996; Celtschmertz, 1998; Mock Tudor, 1999; features on: Psycho soundtrack, 1998; Poses, Rufus Wainwright, 2001. *Current Management:* c/o Chris Blake, Blake and Bradford, London, England.

THOMPSON, Wayne; b. 28 July 1947, Toronto, Ontario, Canada. Artist Man; Theatrical Prod. m. Wendy Cochrane, 24 July 1971, 2 s. *Education:* BA, University of Toronto, Political Science, Economics. *Career:* Manager for several major artists; Currently manager for: The Barra MacNeils, Sydney, Nova Scotia. *Membership:* Director, Pacific Music Industry Asscn.

THOMSON, Colin; b. 6 July 1937. University Teacher; Researcher; Musician (all saxophones, piano, drums). m. Maureen Margaret Green, 1 Sept. 1962, 2 s., 2 d. *Education:* BSc, PhD, Chemistry, Leeds University. *Career:* Member, Eric Thomson Band, 1953–65; Colin Thomson Big Band, 1974–; Colin Thomson Jazz Quartet; Co-Director, Fife Youth Jazz Orchestra, 1975–80; Director, St Andrews Music Centre Big Band, 1992–. *Publications:* 130 Scientific publications. *Honours:* Chairman, Asscn for International Cancer Research. *Membership:* Musicians' Union. *Address:* 12 Drumcarrow Rd, St Andrews KY16 8SE, Scotland.

THOMSON, Kenny; b. 18 March 1944, Irvine, Scotland. Musician (accordion). m. Cathy Rowan, 3 Oct. 1970, 2 s. *Education:* Studied for 3 years with Robert McAdamson, Cumnock. *Career:* Played with small local bands from age 10; Started radio broadcasting with BBC Radio Scotland, 1976; Currently, leader of The Wardlaw Scottish Dance Band. *Recordings:* 3 recordings of Scottish Country Dances for the Royal Scottish Country Dance Society. *Membership:* Musicians' Union. *Address:* 20 Walker Court, Cumnock, Ayrshire KA18 1TF, Scotland.

THORDARSON, Gunnar; b. 4 Jan. 1945, Holmavik, Iceland. Composer; Prod. m. Sigrun Toby Herman, 2 s., 3 d. *Education:* Counterpoint lessons. *Career:* Record producer and writer, 1966–; Member, group Hljomar, 1963–69; Member, Trubrot, 1969–73; Record producer, over 100 records; Written hundreds of television commercials, music for 3 Icelandic films and scores for two musicals. *Compositions:* 440 songs as songwriter; Songs recorded by various artists; Work performed by Icelandic Symphony Orchestra. *Recordings:* Himinn Og Jörd, 1981; Borgar Bragur, 1986; Islensk Alpydulög, 1980; Reykjavikurflugur, 1986; I Loftinu, 1987; Ungir Mennà Uppleid, 1997. *Publications:* Film music: Pitt Fyrsta, 1994; Agnes, 1996. *Honours:* Hon. Prize for Service in Icelandic Music, 1997; Arts Grant from Government, 1997. *Membership:* STEF, Iceland; FIH, Iceland. *Address:* Aegisgata 10, Reykjavík 101, Iceland.

THORDSEN, Hanne; b. 6 Dec. 1954, Copenhagen, Denmark. Vocalist; Composer; Writer; Actress. m. (1) Keld Jakobsen, (2) Lasse Aagaard Nielsen, 1988, 2 d. *Education:* As social worker and Kindergarten teacher. *Career:* Singer with group Knap and Nap, (mainly Irish and Scottish folk music and some blues); Formed folk-rock group Freja; Performed at festivals including: Roskilde, Skagen and Tonder; Television appearance in 1984 and some radio broadcasting, 1993; Appeared as Salene in musical Atlantis at Östre Gasvark. *Recordings:* Kom Nu, Freja, 1988; Participant on the album Folkemusik Til Oerne; Atlantis (album of the musical), 1995. *Membership:* DJBFA. *Current Management:* Morten Grunwald, Östre Gasvark Theatre, Denmark. *Address:* Gl Mejerivej 14 D, 3050 Humlebaek, Denmark.

THORHALLSSON, Olafur Gaukur; b. 11 Aug. 1930, Iceland. Musician (guitar); Composer; Conductor; Prod; Teacher. m. (1) 1 s., 4 d., (2) Svanhildur Jakobsdottir, 8 June 1963, 1 s., 1 d. *Education:* Classical guitar lessons; Composition, Music Academy of Reykjavik, 1985; Composition, 1984, Composition for films and video, 1988, Grove School of Music, Los Angeles, USA; Guitar Institute, Hollywood, 1993. *Career:* Musician, Bandleader, Composer and Arranger on numerous shows, stage, television and radio; Own TV show, Icelandic State Television, 1968–71; Concerts with international vocal groups include The Mills Brothers, The Platters, The Delta Rhythm Boys; Arrangements for different kinds of groups, orchestras and artists including Björk; Head of own music school (mainly guitar), 1975–; Participated on over 100 albums as composer, lyricist, arranger, conductor, producer, musician. *Compositions:* Music for Icelandic feature films; Documentaries, TV shows and plays; Popular songs over 30 years. *Recordings:* 11 albums with own band or orchestra, 1968–94. *Publications:* Author of educational material including books and cassettes, mainly for guitar students. *Membership:* Icelandic Musicians' Union; Performing Rights Society of Iceland; Jazzvakning. *Address:* Sidumula 17, 108 Reykjavik, Iceland.

THORHALLSSON, Robert; b. 12 Aug. 1971, Husavik, Thingeyjarsysla, Iceland. Musician (trumpet, saxophone, drums, double bass, electric bass). *Education:* Jazz music graduate on electric bass; Tuition on double bass, trumpet and saxophone. *Career:* Played in shows staged in Iceland, Superstar 1995–96; World premiere of Jim Cartwright's Stone Free; The Beatles' Sergeant Pepper's Lonely Hearts Club Band staged by the Icelandic Symphony, 1997. *Recordings:* Crougie dou là, 1995; Merman, 1996; Superstar, 1995; Stone Free, music from a play, 1996; Love, live recordings from Stone Free, 1996. *Publications:* Superstar, 1995; Stone Free, 1996; Merman, 1996. *Honours:* Gold Albums, 1996, 1997; Platinum album, 1997. *Membership:* Icelandic Musicians' Asscn (FIH). *Address:* Sigluvogur 15, 104 Reykjavik, Iceland.

THORN, Tracey; b. 26 Sept. 1962. Vocalist; Songwriter. *Education:* Hull University. *Career:* Member, trio, Marine Girls; Forms duo Everything But The Girl with musician Ben Watt, 1983–; Appearances include: Regular British tours, 1984–; World Tour, 1990, including Japan; Friends of the Earth Benefit Concerts, 1990; Red Hot and Dance AIDS Benefit Concert, 1991; UK and US Tours, 1993–95; World tour, 1996–97 including Japan and Australasia. *Compositions:* Writer, co-writer with Ben Watt, and Massive Attack, of own material for trio, duo and solo work. *Recordings:* Albums: Solo album: A Distant Shore, 1982; with Marine Girls: Beach Party, 1980; Lazy Ways, 1983; with Everything But The Girl: Eden, 1984; Everything But The Girl (USA only), 1984; Love Not Money, 1985; Baby, The Stars Shine Bright, 1986; Idlewild, 1988; The Language of Life, 1990; World-wide, 1991; Essence and Rare (Japan only), 1992; Acoustic, 1992 (USA only); Home Movies – Best of Everything But The Girl, 1993; Amplified Heart, 1994; Walking Wounded, 1996; Temperamental, 1999; Back To Mine (mix album), 2001; with Massive Attack: Better Things, 1994; Protection, 1995; Guest singer, albums by Style Council; Go Betweens; Lloyd Cole; Adam F; Deep Dish; Singles include: with Everything But The Girl: Night And Day, 1982; Each and Every One, 1984; Come On Home, 1986; I Don't Want To Talk About It, 1988; Missing, 1995; Walking Wounded, 1996; Wrong, 1996; Missing, 1999; Blame, 2000; Contributor with Massive Attack, film soundtrack for Batman Forever, 1995. *Current Management:* JFD Management, 106 Dalling Rd, London W6 0JA, England.

THOROGOOD, George; b. 31 Dec. 1952, Wilmington, Delaware, USA. Blues Musician (guitar). *Career:* Former baseball player; Formed own group the Destroyers, 1973–; Opened for the Rolling Stones, 1981; Appeared at Live Aid with Albert Collins, 1985. *Recordings:* Albums: George Thorogood and The Destroyers, 1978; Move It On Over, 1978; Better Than The Rest, 1979; More George Thorogood and The Destroyers, 1980; Bad To The Bone, 1982; Maverick, 1985; Live, 1986; Born To Be Bad, 1988; Let's Work Together, 1995; Rockin' My Life Away, 1997; Half a Boy Half a Man, 1999; Live in 1999; Anthology, 2000. *Current Management:* Mike Donahue Management, PO Box 807, Lewisburg, WV 24901, USA.

THORPE, Anthony John; b. 20 July 1945, London, England. Musician (guitar); Writer; Vocalist; Actor. m. Shirley Atherton, 14 Feb. 1968, 1 s. *Education:* St Ignatius' College, London. *Career:* Guitarist, arranger, Wee Willie Harris; Tommy Steele (including West End); Guitarist, singer, Rubettes, 1970s; Guitarist, singer, The Firm, 1980s; Writer, actor, Cooger and Dark two-man show, Edinburgh Fringe; Blues Band Gas Company, John Caira Band; Also worked with Tony Crombie, Gary Boyle, Mike Walker, Tal Farlow, Jimmy Smith and Denny Laine. *Recordings:* 7 albums with The Rubettes; Lead vocals on two hit singles; Hits include: I Can Do It, 1975; Baby I Know, 1977; with The Firm: Arthur Daley, 1982; Solo album: Illusions and Dangerous Prayer. *Publications:* Concert reviews, The Guardian, 1980s. *Membership:* Musicians' Union; PRS. *Address:* 143 Marsden Rd, Burnley, Lancashire BB10 2QW, England.

THORUP, Jesper; b. 9 June 1952, Copenhagen, Denmark. Composer; Vocalist; Musician (drums). *Education:* Music lessons with Alex Riel, Hans Fülling, Ed Thigpen. *Career:* Dana Gillespie (UK); The Rustics (USA); Mal Waldren Trio (USA); Benny Waters (USA); Peter Thorup and Jesper Band; Paul Millins (UK); Sam Mitchel Blue Vikings (UK/Denmark); Dexter Gordon; Jackie McLean; Danish Grand Prix; Danish Radio Jazzgroup. *Compositions:* Composed and recorded with: Annegrete: Hvem Sir; Duggen Falder: Drops: Koernes Sang; Aorta: Havnerfunk. *Honours:* First prize, Best Soloist, Dunquerque International Jazz Festival, France, 1975. *Membership:* DMF; DJFBA. *Address:* Fabritius Alle 16, 2930 Klampenborg, Denmark. *Website:* www.jesperthorup.dk.

THOUMIRE, Simon John; b. 11 July 1970, Edinburgh, Scotland. Musician (concertina); Composer. *Career:* Started at 16 years old with Seannachie, 1989; Formed duo with Ian Carr; Television performance on Aly Bain's Shetland Session; First tour USA, 1990; Formed Simon Thoumire Three, 1992; Television: Aly Bains Transatlantic Sessions, 1995; Formed duo with Fergus McKenzie. *Recordings:* with Seannachie: Take Note, 1987; Devil's Delight, 1992; Hootz, Simon Thoumire and Ian Carr, 1990; Waltzes For Playboys, Simon Thoumire Three, 1994; Exhibit A, Simon Thoumire and Fergus MacKenzie, 1995; Celtic Connections Suite, 1998; March, Strathspey & Surreal; Music For A New Scottish Parliament, 1999; The Big Day In, with David Milligan, 2001. *Honours:* BBC Radio 2 Young Tradition Award, 1989; Folk Roots, Most Innovative Performance, 1989. *Membership:* Musicians' Union. *Current Management:* Hootz! Productions. *Address:* 17 Redford Dr., Edinburgh EH13 0BL, Scotland.

THRALE, Carlos Heinrich; b. 3 Aug. 1962, London, England. Musician (guitar). *Education:* BA Hons, Nottingham Trent University; ARCM, Royal College of Music. *Career:* Session musician for: Mica Paris; Freeze; Dr Egg; Sugar Bullet; Radio and television commercials; Also lecturer, Course co-ordinator, Popular Music. *Publications:* Guitar Theory and Technique, video and book, EMI, 1985. *Membership:* Musicians' Union. *Current Management:* Spencer Wells. *Address:* 12 Grove Rd, Bingham, Nottinghamshire NG13 8DY, England.

3-D, (Robert Del Naja); b. 21 Jan. 1965, Brighton, England. Vocalist. *Career:* Member: Massive Attack; Numerous club shows and parties; Collaborations: Shara Nelson; Tricky; Horace Andy; Madonna; Tracey Thorn, Everything But The Girl; Liz Fraser, Cocteau Twins; Damon Albarn, Blur; One Day At A Time features on soundtrack to Ordinary Decent Criminal film,

2000. *Recordings:* Albums: Blue Lines, 1991; Protection, 1994; No Protection (Massive Attack vs Mad Professor), 1995; Mezzanine, 1998; Singles Collection Box Set 1990–98, 1998; 100th Window, 2003. Singles: Daydreaming (with Shara Nelson), 1990; Safe From Harm (EP), 1991; Sly, 1994; Protection, 1995; Karmacoma, 1995; Risingson, 1997; Teardrop (with Liz Fraser); Inertia Creeps; Angel/Group Four, 1998; 1 Against 1, 2002. *Honours:* BRIT Award, Best British Dance Act, 1996. *Website:* www.massiveattack.co.uk.

THROB, (Robert Young); Musician (guitar). *Career:* Member, Primal Scream; Numerous tours and festival appearances; Collaborations with DJ Andrew Weatherall, vocalist Denise Johnson, Jah Wobble and Alex Paterson of The Orb; Contributed track to the film Trainspotting, co-written by Irvine Welsh, 1996. *Recordings:* Singles: Loaded EP, 1990; Come Together EP, 1990; Don't Fight It, Feel It, 1991; Movin' On Up, 1991; (I'm Gonna) Cry Myself Blind, 1994; Jailbird, 1994; Rocks/Funky Jam, 1994; Rocks Off, 1994; The Big Man and the Scream Team Meet the Barmy Army Uptown (from Trainspotting), 1996; Star, 1997; Burning Wheel, 1997; Kowalski, 1997; If They Move, Kill 'Em, 1998; Albums: Sonic Flower Groove, 1987; Primal Scream, 1989; Screamadelica, 1991; Give Out But Don't Give Up, 1994; Echo Dek, 1997; Vanishing Point, 1997. *Honours:* Mercury Music Prize Winner, 1992.

THROCKMORTON, Sonny (James Fron); b. 2 April 1941, Carlsbad, NM, USA. Songwriter; Musician (bass guitar). *Career:* Country music songwriter; Worked for small record company, 1961–62; Played bass for Carl and Pearl Butler, 1964–66; Signed to Capitol, Mercury, MCA, Warner Bros; 17 No. 1 hits; Songs recorded by: George Burns, Johnny Duncan, Emmylou Harris, Alan Jackson, Millie Jackson, the Judds, Jerry Lee Lewis, George Strait. *Recordings:* Albums: The Last Cheater's Waltz, 1978; Southern Train, 1986; Ten Number Ones, 1986. *Compositions:* I Feel Like Loving You Again; I Had a Lovely Time; Thinking Of A Rendezvous; I'm Knee Deep In Loving You; If We're Not Back In Love By Monday; Middle Age Crazy; When Can We Do This Again; Smooth Sailing; Fadin' In Fadin' Out; Lovin' You Lovin' Me; I Wish You Could Have Turned My Head (and Left My Heart Alone); I Wish I Was Eighteen Again; Last Cheater's Waltz; It's A Cheatin' Situation; The Way I Am; Trying To Love Two Women; Friday Night Blues; Why Not Me; Where The Cowboy Rides Away; She Can't Say That Anymore; Stand Up; Made for Loving You. *Honours:* Nashville Songwriters' Association, Songwriter of the Year, 1978, 1979, 1980; BMI Songwriter of the Year (with others), 1980; Inducted, Nashville Songwriters Hall of Fame, 1987. *Membership:* Nashville Songwriters' Asscn. *Current Management:* c/o Riata Talent, PO Box 15345, Austin, TX 78761, USA. *E-mail:* randywillis@riatatalent.com. *Website:* www.riatatalent.com.

THUNDERBITCH. See: **KELIS.**

THURSDAY CLUB. See: **PILGREM, Rennie.**

TICALLION STALLION. See: **METHOD MAN.**

TICKELL, Kathryn Derran; b. 8 June 1967, England. Musician (northumbrian pipes, fiddle); Composer. *Career:* Plays traditional folk material from the North-East of England and composes own tunes; Started playing Northumbrian Smallpipes aged 9; Recorded The Long Tradition TV documentary, 1987; Performed on the Sting hit Fields of Gold; Performed with Jimmy Nail at City Hall, Newcastle; Composed, performed and recorded Music For A New Crossing with jazz saxophonist Andy Sheppard (commissioned for the opening of the Gateshead Millennium Bridge), broadcast live on the Last Night of the Proms, 2001. *Recordings:* Albums: On Kielderside, 1984; Borderlands, 1986; Common Ground, 1988; The Kathryn Tickell Band, 1991; Signs, 1993; The Gathering, 1997; The Northumberland Collection, 1998; Debateable Lands, 1999; Kathryn Tickell and Ensemble Mystical, 2000; Music For A New Crossing, 2001; Back To The Hills, 2002. *Current Management:* Karen McWilliams, PO Box 130, Morpeth, Northumberland NE65 7WD, England. *E-mail:* info@kathryntickell.com. *Website:* www.kathryntickell.com.

TIELENS, Louis, (Country Lewis); b. 2 Aug. 1942, Beringen, Belgium. Broadcaster. m. Germa Baelen, 6 Aug. 1984, 1 s., 1 d. *Education:* College. *Career:* DJ 'Country Lewis'; Retired manager, Radio Animo; Retired Station Manager, Radio Loksbergen; Producer, syndicated country music programmes, De Bazuin non-profit organization; With wife, producer, gospel programme Good News. *Membership:* Executive Committee, Country and Western Asscn, Belgium. *Address:* Pauwenlaan 23, 3583 Paal-Beringen, Belgium.

TIERS, Wharton; b. 11 Feb. 1953, Philadelphia, Pennsylvania, USA. Prod; Musician (drums, keyboards, guitar); Songwriter; Engineer. *Education:* BA, English, Villanova University, Pennsylvania. *Career:* Producer, engineer, Indie records, 1980s–90s; Over 120 records produced; Member, Laurie Anderson's Band; Glenn Branca's Band; Played with: Theatrical Girls; Glorious Strangers; Played on US network. *Recordings:* Albums as producer: 6 albums with Sonic Youth, most recently A Thousand Leaves, 1998; with Dinosaur Jr: Just Like Heaven; You're Living All Over Me; with Gumball:

Special Kiss; Unsane; Urban Discipline, Biohazard; In The Meantime, Helmet; God Knows It's True, Teenage Fanclub; Anaesthesia, Dean Wareham; Primitive Origins, Prong; Headkick Facsimile, Cop Shoot Cop; Pussy Gold 5000, Pussy Galore; Solo. *Recordings include:* Brighter then Life, 1996; Twilight of the Computer Age, 1999. *Current Management:* Susan Sidel Management.

TIFFANY, (Tiffany Renee Darwish); b. 2 Oct. 1971. Vocalist. m. Bulmaro Garcia, 1992, separated, 1 s. *Career:* Signed to MCA Records, 1986; Numerous tours, television and radio appearances; Voice of Judy Jetson in The Jetsons Movie, 1990; Contributions on various tribute and charity albums. *Recordings:* Albums: Tiffany, 1987; Hold An Old Friend's Hand, 1988; New Inside, 1990; Dreams Never Die, 1993; All The Best, 1995; Tiffany's Greatest Hits, 1996; The Color Of Silence, 2000. Singles: Danny, 1987; I Think We're Alone Now, 1987; Could've Been, 1987; I Saw Him Standing There, 1988; Feelings Of Forever, 1988; All This Time, 1988; Radio Romance, 1989; Hold An Old Friend's Hand, 1989; It's The Lover (Not The Love), 1989; New Inside, 1990; Here In My Heart, 1990; If Love Is Blind, 1993; I'm Not Sleeping, 2000. *Current Management:* The Artist Network. *Address:* c/o Jive Records, Zomba Recording Corpn, 137–139 W 25th St, New York, NY 10001, USA. *Website:* www.tiffanymusic.com.

TIGER, Flower; b. 29 Sept. 1934, Baojing County, Hunan Province, People's Republic of China. Composer. m. Zhang Xiangming, 20 Oct. 1968, 2 s. *Education:* Graduated, Minzu Normal school of Jishou City, studied under Professor of Music Liu Tianlin; Graduated, Composition, Shanghai Conservatory, studied with He Luding, Sha Hankun, Liu Zhuang, Deng Erjing. *Career:* Professional Composer, ensembles at central, provincial and prefectural levels; Over 100 published; Many televised or broadcast by stations at central and local levels. *Compositions:* Beautiful Peacock, Please Fly Back Soon; The Charming Moonlight of Tujia Home Villages; many other ethnic minority folk songs. *Recordings:* Hunting in Wuling Mountains; Grand Chorus in Praise of National Unity; Wind and Percussion Concerto; Miao Music Dance; Polyphonic Piano Suite for Chinese Folk Songs; The Drum of Blood. *Publications:* Beacon fire in Miao Borders, 1988; A New Song Anthology of National Art, 1990. *Honours:* Expert, with special subsidies from the government, 1993–; 2 Medals from the USA, while lecturing; 2 National Music Prizes, 1983, 1988. *Membership:* Chinese Musicians' Asscn; Vice-President, China Minorities Music Society. *Address:* 11 Wenyi Rd, Jishou City, Hunan Province, 416000 People's Republic of China.

TIGGER. See: **LYONS, Ken.**

TIJSSENS, Michael Warren; b. 27 March 1961, Amersfoort, Netherlands. Lyricist; Screenwriter; Playwright. m. Dyna Justin, 26 Sept. 1987, 2 s. *Education:* Royal Academy of Dramatic Art; Sorbonne University. *Career:* Numerous roles as actor, singer, writer, director, dramatist and producer; Now writing for artists in music business; Has worked with: Bob Geldof, Rick Smith, Karl Hyde, Lou Reed, Tom Waits. *Recordings:* Joint Venture; Tropical Corridor; Blanc Nègre; Sens Unique Show; Destination Tomorrow. *Publications:* Rendez-Vous; Cahiers de Prospero; Theatre Public. *Honours:* Prix d'Honneur, Institut Radiodiffusion Suisse. *Membership:* SACEM; SACD; ATLF. *Current Management:* Media Writers and Translators. *Address:* 13 Blvd de la Marne, 77420 Champs-Sur-Marne, France. *E-mail:* contact@mwtexts.com.

TIKARAM, Tanita; b. 12 Aug. 1969, Münster, Germany. Vocalist; Songwriter; Musician (guitar). *Career:* Moved to UK, 1982; Songwriter, 1987–; Support tour, Warren Zevon, 1988; Major international tours, 1989, 1992. *Recordings:* Albums: Ancient Heart, 1988; The Sweet Keeper, 1990; Everybody's Angel, 1991; Eleven Kinds of Loneliness, 1992; Lovers In The City, 1995; Singles: Good Tradition, 1988; Twist In My Sobriety, 1988; Cathedral Song, 1989; World Outside Your Window, 1989; Only The Ones We Love, 1991; I Might Be Crying, 1995; The Cappuccino Songs, 1998. *Current Management:* Stephen Budd Management, 109B Regents Park Rd, London NW1 8UR, England.

TIKHONOV, Dimitri; b. 6 Aug. 1964, Vladivostok, Russia. Keyboard; Vocal; Composer. m. Juliette Alix, 12 Aug. 1994, 1 s. *Education:* Jazz School, St Petersburg, Russia. *Career:* Composer, Keyboarder and Singer of the group, Nom, St Petersburg, 1987–94; Tours over Western Europe, Italy, Czechoslovakia, France, Germany, Switzerland and Hungary; Nom video demonstrated on BBC2, MTV, M6, MCM, TV channels; Solo career as composer and bass, Geneva Opera's Choir, 1995–. *Compositions:* Nom, Masters of the USSR; Ape's Snout, 1995; Nom, Made in Europe, 1997. *Recordings:* Brutto, Nom, LP, CD, 1989; To Hell With It, LP, Super Disc, 1990; Senka – Mosgaz, LP, CD, 1992, 1994; Live is Game, CD, Ultracompact, 1995; In the Name of Mind, CD, 1995, 1996; Les Sons De Carton, solo, 1997; Some Original Melodies, 1998; The Songs of Cartoon, 1999; Jban D – soundtrack from the film of NOM, 2000; What a Wonderful Liver, 2000. *Honours:* Skotinorap, Best Alternative Video of Russia, 1993; Nina-2, Grand Prix Exotica, 1994; Ukr Blues, Best Low Budget Video, 1996. *Address:* Tikhonov Dimitri, 9 rue du Mont-Blanc, 74100 Ville-La-Grande, France.

TILBROOK, Glenn; b. 31 Aug. 1957, London, England. Vocalist; Musician (guitar); Songwriter. *Career:* Founder member, Squeeze, 1974–; Longstanding writing partnership with Chris Difford; Performances include: US tours, 1978–; Reading Rock Festival, 1978; Dalymount Festival, Dublin, 1980; Jamaica World Music Festival, 1982; Support to Fleetwood Mac, US tour, 1990; Crystal Palace Bowl, 1991; Support to Bryan Adams, British tour, 1992. *Compositions include:* Co-writer, with Elvis Costello, From A Whisper To A Scream, 1981; Songs for musical, Labelled With Love, 1983. *Recordings:* Albums: Squeeze, 1978; Cool For Cats, 1979; Argy Bargy, 1980; East Side Story, 1981; Sweets From A Stranger, 1982; Singles 45's and Under, 1982; Cosi Fan Tutti Frutti, 1985; Babylon and On, 1987; Frank, 1989; A Round and A Bout, 1990; Greatest Hits, 1992; Some Fantastic Place, 1993; Ridiculous, 1995; Six of One, 1997; Domino, 1998; Live at Royal Albert Hall, 1999; Singles include: Take Me I'm Yours, 1978; Cool For Cats, 1979; Up The Junction, 1979; Slap And Tickle, 1979; Another Nail In My Heart, 1980; Pulling Mussels From A Shell, 1980; Labelled With Love, 1981; Black Coffee In Bed, 1982; Annie Get Your Gun, 1982; Last Time Forever, 1985; Hourglass, 1987; This Summer, 1995; Solo albums: The Incomplete Glenn Tilbrook, 2001; Singles: Parallel World, 2000; This Is Where You Ain't, 2001. *Current Management:* Firstars, 3520 Hayden Ave, Culver City, CA 90232, USA.

TILBURY, John; b. 1 Feb. 1936, London, England. Musician (piano). 1 s., 2 d. *Education:* Royal College of Music, and privately with James Gibb; Warsaw Conservatory with Zbigniew Drzewecki. *Recordings:* Cage: Sonatas And Interludes; Feldman: Complete Solo Piano Music; Skempton: Solo Piano Music; Christian Wolff: Early Piano Music; Cornelius Cardew: Early Piano Music; Many recordings as member of AMM Free Improvisation group including: Tunes Without Measure Or End, 2001. *Address:* 158 Middle St, Deal, Kent CT14 6LW, England.

TILLIS, Mel (Lonnie Melvin); b. 8 Aug. 1932, Tampa, Florida, USA. Country Vocalist; Songwriter; Musician (guitar, fiddle). *Education:* University of Florida. *Career:* Began performing, recording, 1956–57; Toured extensively with The Statesiders, 1960s–70s; Numerous tours and television appearances; Recorded duets with Glen Campbell and Nancy Sinatra; Film apperances: WW and The Dixie Dance Kings; Smokey and The Bandit 2; Murder In Music City; Uphill All The Way; Owned several publishing companies; Also cattle breeder. *Compositions include:* I'm Tired; Tupelo County Jail; I Ain't Never (all hits for Webb Pierce); Lonely Island Pearl, Johnny and Jack; Heart Over Mind, Ray Price; Ten Thousand Drums, Carl Smith; Detroit City (co-written with Danny Dill) Bobby Bare, 1963; The Snakes Crawl At Night, Charley Pride, 1966; Ruby Don't Take Your Love To Town, Johnny Darrell, 1967 (Also hit for Kenny Rogers and The First Edition, 1969). *Recordings:* US Country No. 1 hits: I Ain't Never; Good Woman Blues; Heart Healer; I Believe In You; Coca Cola Cowboy; Southern Rains; Other hits include: Life Turned Her That Way; Stateside; These Lonely Hands of Mine; Send Me Down To Tucson, featured in film Every Which Way But Loose; Take My Hand; Numerous albums include: Heart Over Mind, 1961; Stateside, 1966; Mr Mel, 1967; One More Time, 1970; Mel Tillis, 1972; Sawmill, 1973; M-M-Mel and The Statesiders, 1975; Are You Sincere, 1979; The Great Mel Tillis, 1979; Southern Rain, 1980; M-M-Mel Live, 1980; It's A Long Way To Daytona, 1982; After All This Time, 1983; New Patches, 1984; California Road, 1985; Four Legends (with Jerry Lee Lewis, Webb Pierce, Faron Young), 1985; Branson City Limits (live), 1999; Brand New Mister Me; I Believe in You; M-M-Mel Live; Also recorded with: Glen Campbell; Nancy Sinatra; Sherry Bryce. *Publications:* Stutterin' Boy, The Autobiography of Mel Tillis (with Walter Wager). *Honours:* Inducted into Nashville Songwriters International Hall of Fame; 1976; CMA Entertainer of the Year, 1976. *Address:* c/o Mel Tillis Enterprises, PO Box 1626, Branson, MO 65615, USA.

TILLIS, Pam (Pamela Yvonne); b. 24 July 1957, Plant City, Florida, USA. Country vocalist; Musician (guitar, piano); Songwriter; Actor. m. Bob DiPiero. *Education:* University of Tennessee; Studied classical piano. *Career:* Member of group Billy Hill; Debut appearance with father, country vocalist Mel Tillis, and family on stage of the Grand Ole Opry singing Tom Dooley, aged 8; Performed solo at Nashville's Exit/In during teens; At 16, car crash shattered face in 30 places requiring five years of surgery; Formed first band High Country Swing Band at University, also appearing in duo with Ashley Cleveland; After college, worked for father's publishing company, Sawgrass Music, achieving first cut I'll Meet You On The Other Side of The Morning for Barbara Fairchild; Left for San Francisco and formed the Pam Tillis Band; Returned to Nashville singing backing vocals in father's band, 1978; Achieved another cut, When I Get Around To It by Gloria Gaynor; Debut album for Warner Brothers: Beyond The Doll Of Cutey, 1983; Brief spell of three months in England before returning to Nashville to continue songwriting; Debut single on Billboard country chart Goodbye Highway, 1984; Subsequent Warners singles struggled sales-wise; Signed to Tree Publishing, cuts on Chaka Khan So Close and the Forester Sisters Drawn To The Fire; Signed to Arista Records, 1989; Career took off following year Don't Tell Me What To Do reaching country chart top 5; Continued to be highly successful throughout 1990s with hit albums and singles and a clutch of awards; Appearances in TV series: LA Law, 1986; Hot Country Nights, 1991; Diagnosis Murder, 1993; Promised Land, 1996; Also appeared in The Thing Called Love film, 1993, and TV films: XXXs and OOOs, 1994; The Best of Country, 1995.

Compositions include: Cleopatra – Queen of Denial; Spilled Perfume; Mi Vida Loca; Put Yourself In My Place; Someone Else's Trouble Now. *Recordings include:* Don't Tell Me What To Do, 1990; One of Those Things, Maybe It Was Memphis, 1991; Shake The Sugar Tree, 1992; Mi Vida Loca, When You Walk In The Room, Spilled Perfume, 1994; In Between Dances, 1995; All The Good Ones Are Gone, Land of The Living, 1997; Albums include: Put Yourself In My Place, 1991; Sweetheart's Dance, 1994; Greatest Hits, 1997; Thunder and Roses, 2001. *Honours:* CMA, Female Vocalist of the Year, 1994. *Address:* c/o Country Music Assocn, 1 Music Circle S, Nashville, TN 37203, USA. *Website:* www.pamtillis.com.

TILLMAN, Floyd; b. 8 Dec. 1914, Ryan, Oklahoma, USA. Country Vocalist; Songwriter; Musician (mandolin, banjo, guitar). *Career:* Performed as member of Adolph Hofner; Mack Clark; Blue Ridge Playboys, 1930s; Solo artiste, 1939–60; One of first country artists to use electric guitar; Now semi-retired. *Compositions:* It Makes No Difference Now, hit for Bing Crosby, Gene Autry; Slippin' Around, recorded by numerous artists including Ernest Tubb, Jimmy Wakeley. *Recordings:* Hits include: They Took The Stars Out of Heaven (US Country No. 1); GI Blues; Drivin' Nails In My Coffin; I Love You So Much It Hurts; Albums include: Let's Make Memories, 1962; Country, 1967; Dream On, 1968; I'll Still Be Loving You, 1969; Floyd Tillman and Friends, with Willie Nelson and Merle Haggard, 1982; Crazy Cajun Recordings, 1999; Best Of, 1999. *Honours:* Inducted into Nashville Songwriters Assocn Hall of Fame, 1970; Inducted into Country Music Hall of Fame, 1984; Crazy Cajun Recordings, 1999; Best of Floyd Tillman, 1999.

TILLOTSON, Paul; b. 18 Dec. 1964, Boise, Idaho, USA. Musician (piano); Composer. *Education:* AAS, Edmonds CC, 1985; University of Miami, 1986; Bachelor of Music, William Patterson, 1989. *Career:* North Sea Jazz Festival; Montreux Jazz Festival; Gene Harris Jazz Festival. *Compositions:* Simple Pleasures; Tulips; Big Valley; Tidbits; Tebadadeda; Loungin' @ The Evelyn; Chartreuse; Seltzer. *Recordings:* The Paul Tillotson Trio: Tulips; Live At The Lock; Tidbits; Sweet Mystery; Tasty Morsels; Drinkin' Wine With Pauli; Duck Callin' Man; Funky Good Time. *Membership:* Local 802. *Address:* 316 E Sixth St # B1, New York, NY 10003, USA.

TILSTON, Stephen Thomas Gregory; b. 26 March 1950, Liverpool, England. Musician (guitar); Songwriter. m. Maggie Boyle, 27 Jan. 1984, 1 s., 3 d. *Education:* Trained as graphic artist. *Career:* Solo, also duo with Maggie Boyle; Member, Ship of Fools, with John Renbourn; Guitarist, Ballet Rambert. *Recordings:* Acoustic Confusion, 1971; Collection, 1973; Songs From The Dress Rehearsal, 1977, In For A Penny, 1983; Life By Misadventure, 1987; Swans At Goole, 1990; Of Moor and Mesa, 1992; And So It Goes, 1995; All Under the Sun, 1996; Solorubato, 1998; The Greening Wind, 1999. *Membership:* British Longbow Society. *Current Management:* Alan King. *Address:* 78 Sydenham Park, London SE26 4DP, England.

TILTON, Martha Ellen; b. 14 Nov. 1915, Corpus Christi, Texas, USA. Vocalist. m. James L Brooks, 3 May 1953, 2 s., 1 d. *Education:* Piano lessons. *Career:* Carnegie Hall Concert, Benny Goodman, 1937; Philco Radio Hall of Fame programme; Radio, with Paul Whiteman Orchestra, 4 years, mid 1940s; Alka Seltzer Program CBS, 8 years; Martha Tilton, Count Maskey Show, National Broadcasting Company, 6 years; Capitol Records; Decca Records; Two overseas tours with Jack Benny, Larry Adler; Ingrid Bergman, during World War II: South Pacific, 1943; Germany, 1944. *Recordings:* Complete Standard Transcriptions, 2000; Liltin' Miss Tilton, 2000. *Honours:* Academy of Television Arts and Sciences: Most Outstanding Female Personality, 1959–60, 1960–61; For Dedication and Service to the City, City Council Los Angeles, 1983; National Academy of Arts and Sciences, Hall of Fame Award, 1987. *Membership:* American Federation Television and Radio Artists; American Guild of Variety Artists. *Address:* 2257 Mandeville Canyon Rd, Los Angeles, CA 90049, USA.

TIMBALAND, (Timothy Mosley); b. Norfolk, Virginia, USA. Prod; Remixer; Songwriter. *Career:* Came to prominence as a writer on Aaliyah's One In A Million album; Went on to work with Missy Elliott, producing her debut album Supa Dupa Fly, 1997; One of the most in-demand producers in Hip Hop and R&B; Production credits include: Destiny's Child; Jay-Z; Usher; The Lox; Collaborations: Missy Elliott; Ginuwine; Magoo; Bubba Sparxx. *Recordings:* Albums: Welcome To Our World (with Magoo), 1997; Tim's Bio, 1998: We At It Again (with Magoo), 2000; Singles: Clock Strikes (with Magoo), 1998; Lobster and Shrimp (with Jay-Z), 1998; Here We Come, 1999. *Address:* c/o Virgin Records, Kensal House, 553–579 Harrow Rd, London W10 4RH, England.

TIMBERLAKE, Justin Randall; b. 31 Jan. 1981, Memphis, TN, USA. Vocalist; Songwriter; Actor. *Career:* Started vocal training aged 8; Guest appearance at Grand Ole Opry, 1991; Early TV appearances: Star Search, 1992; The Mickey Mouse Club, 1993–94; Mem., *NSYNC vocal quintet, 1995–; Signed to BMG Ariola Munich, 1997; First headline US tour, 1998; Acting roles: Model Behavior, 2000; various TV films. *Recordings:* Albums: with *NSYNC: *NSYNC, 1998; Home For Christmas, 1998; No Strings Attached, 2000; Celebrity, 2001; Solo: Justified, 2002. Singles: with *NSYNC: I Want You Back, 1997; Tearin' Up My Heart, 1997; Let The Music Heal Your

Soul (various artists charity single credited to Bravo All Stars), 1999; Music Of My Heart (with Gloria Estefan), 1999; Bye, Bye, Bye, 2000; I'll Never Stop, 2000; It's Gonna Be Me, 2000; This I Promise You, 2000; Pop, 2001; Gone, 2001. *Honours:* Presented with keys to City of Orlando, 2000; American Music Award, Favorite Pop/Rock Band, Duo or Group, 2002. *Address:* c/o Wright Entertainment Group, PO Box 590009, Orlando, FL 32859–0009, USA. *Website:* www.nsync.com.

TIMMY C, (Tim Commerford); Musician (bass). *Career:* Member, Rage Against The Machine; Obtained major label record deal; Involvement in various causes such as Fairness and Accuracy in Reporting, Rock for Choice and Refuse and Resist; Numerous tours including Lollapalooza; Tour with Wu Tang Clan; Contributed to soundtrack for film Godzilla, 1998. *Recordings:* Singles: Killing In The Name, 1993; Freedom, 1994; Bombtrack Plus Live, 1994; People of the Sun EP, 1997; Albums: Rage Against the Machine, 1992; Evil Empire, 1996; Renegades, 2000. *Website:* www.ratm.com.

TINETA, (Tineta Michelle Couturier); b. 24 Aug. 1972, Red Deer, Alberta, Canada. Vocalist; Songwriter; Musician (guitar, piano, drums). *Career:* Solo artist, 1989–; Support act for Steve Wariner, Pam Tillis; Major concerts: Grand Ole Opry, 1989; Big Valley Jamboree, Craven, Saskatchewan; Big Valley Jamboree, Camrose, Alberta. *Compositions:* Slippin Away; Love On The Line; Let's Make Up; It's Rainin'; Too Bad So Sad; Walkin' That Line; That's What Love's About. *Recordings:* Albums: Love On The Line; Drawn To The Fire. *Membership:* CCMA; SOCAN; CMN; CARAS; ARIA. *Current Management:* Keith and Dawnalyn Couturier. *Address:* PO Box 5039, Drayton Valley, AB T7A 1R3, Canada.

TINSLEY, Boyd Calvin; b. 16 May 1964. Musician (violin). *Education:* Walker Middle School, Charlottesville; University of Virginia, History graduate; Tutored by Isador Saslav, concertmaster of Baltimore Symphony Orchestra. *Career:* Part-time model including work for: JanSport; Tommy Hilfiger; Gucci; As teenager helped found the Charlottesville-Albermarle Youth Orchestra; Formed duo Down Boy Down, 1987; Changed name to The Boyd Tinsley Band when augmented by other musicians; Became permanent member of The Dave Matthews Band following regular guest appearances, around 1992; Rapid growth of fanbase through touring; First album released on group's own Bama Rags label certified gold by RIAA; First national US tour in support of RCA debut album, 1994; Many world-wide concerts and festival appearances, including 2001 album tour; I Did It single officially released through Napster, 2001. *Recordings:* Albums: Remember Two Things (live), 1993; Under The Table and Dreaming, 1994; Crash, 1996; Live At Red Rocks 8–15–95, 1997; Before These Crowded Streets, 1998; Listener Supported (live), 1999; Everyday, Live In Chicago 12–19–98, 2001; Singles: Recently (EP), 1994; What Would You Say, Jimi Thing, Ants Marching, 1995; So Much To Say, Too Much, 1996; Don't Drink The Water, 1997; Satellite, Crash Into Me, Crush, 1998; I Did It, The Space Between, Everyday, 2001. *Honours:* Grammy Awards: Best Rock Performance By A Duo Or Group With Vocal, 1997; US VH-1 Awards: Favourite Group; Must Have Album; Song of the Year, 2001; Top-grossing touring band in USA, 2000. *Address:* c/o Red Light Communications, 3305 Lobban Pl., Charlottesville, VA 22903, USA. *E-mail:* info@rlc.net. *Website:* www.dmband.com.

TIPLER, Paul; Record Prod; Engineer; *Recordings:* As producer, co-producer, albums include: Mars Audiac Quintet, Stereolab; Dream of 100 Nations, TransGlobal Underground; Weird's Bar and Grill, Pop Will Eat Itself; Duniya, Loop Guru; In Love With, Mambo Taxi; Chocolate Revenge, Voodoo Queens; As engineer: Eat Yourself Whole, Kingmaker; Suspira, Miranda Sex Garden; Peggy Suicide, Julian Cope; Elastica, Elastica; Stereolab, Fluorescences; Cybele's Reverie; Mars Audiac Quintet; Emperor Tomato Ketchup; TransGlobal Underground, Psychic Karaoke; Vibrators, We Vibrate; Primo, Dr Feelgood; Singles with: Kingmaker; Shriek; Fun-Da-Mental; Pop Will Eat Itself; Back To The Planet; Jah Wobble; New Fast Automatic Daffodils. *Current Management:* Stephen Budd Management, 109B Regents Park Rd, London NW1 8UR, England.

TISO, Wagner; b. Tres Pontas, Minas Gerais, Brazil. Musician (piano, keyboards); Composer; Arranger; Conductor; Musical Dir. m. Giselle de Andrade Goldoni, 2 d. *Career:* Soundtracks: O Guarani, Norma Bengell, 1995; A Ostra e o Vento, Walter Lima Jr, 1997; Television: Meu Marido, Walter Lima Jr, TV Globo; O Sorriso do Lagarto, Roberto Talma, TV Globo; Suites: Suite Tom Jobim, 1995; Cenas Brasileiras, 1995; Stage apperances: Soloist, Rhapsody In Blue, 1997; Encontro de Violoncellos, 1997; Numerous concert and festival appearances include: Montreux Jazz Festival, with Flora Purim, Airto Moreira and Ron Carter (1974), and in 1982; Festival de Música Latina, Cuba, 1983, and Paris, 1986; Festival de Música Brasileira, Rome, 1984; Jazz festivals in São Paulo, Berlin, Montmartre and Rio de Janeiro. *Compositions include:* Coraçao de Estudante, for film Jango; Chorata, suite for piano and orchestra; Lenda Ao Boto; Choro de Mae; Cafezais Sem Fim. *Recordings include:* Wagner Tiso, 1978; Baobab, 1990; O Livro de Jó, 1993; Brazilian Scenes, 1997; Crooner, 1999; Millenium, 1999. *Publications:* Wagner Tiso Ao Vivo na Europa, 1982; Giselle, 1986; A Floresta Amazônica (Villa Lobos), 1987; Cine Brasil (original soundtracks), 1989; Wagner Tiso Ao Vivo, with Rio Cello Ensemble, 1995. *Honours:* Best Arranger, for Sentinela, Milton

Nascimento, 1981; Best Instrumental recording, Todas as Teclas, with Cesar Camargo Mariano, 1983; Best Soundtracks: Jango, 1984, Chico Rei, 1987. *Membership:* AMAR; OMB. *Current Management:* Giselle de Andrade Goldoni, Tres Mineiro Produçoes Artisticas Ltda. *Address:* Rua Cesário Alvim 55/107 Bla, Humaitá, 22261–030 Rio de Janeiro, RJ, Brazil.

TISSENDIER, Claude; b. 1 Oct. 1952, Toulouse, France. Musician (saxophones, clarinet). *Education:* 6 years Conservatoire. *Career:* All major jazz festivals in France; Member, Claude Bolling Band, 22 years; Leader, own band, Saxomania, 12 years. *Recordings:* Benny Carter, 1988; Spike Robinson, 1989; Phil Woods, 1991; Guy Lafitte, 1993; Marlene Verplanck, 1994; Clark Terry, 1995; 20 albums with Claude Bolling, 1978–2001, most recently: Paris Swings, 2001. *Honours:* Sidney Bechet Prize, 1987; Best Jazz Recording Prize, 1986, 1988; Bill Coleman Prize, 1989; Django d'Or, 1996. *Address:* 5 rue Gracieuse, 75005 Paris, France.

TITELMAN, Russ; b. 16 Aug. 1944, Los Angeles, California, USA. Record Co Exec; Record Prod. m. Carol Wikarska, 10 May 1978. *Career:* Vice-President, A & R Department, and record producer, Warner Brothers Records, New York, 1971–. *Recordings include:* As producer: with Randy Newman: Sail Away, 1972; Good Old Boys, 1974; Little Criminals, 1977; with Ry Cooder: Paradise and Lunch, 1973; with James Taylor: Gorilla, 1975; In The Pocket, 1976; with Rickie Lee Jones: Rickie Lee Jones, 1979; Pirates, 1981; with Paul Simon: Heart and Bones, 1983; with George Benson: 20/20, 1985; with Steve Winwood: Back In The High Life, 1986; Higher Love, 1986; with Miriam Makeba: Sangoma, 1988; with Eric Clapton: Journeyman, 1989; Monkees, Anthology, 1998; Love Shouldn't Hurt, 1998; Very Best of Meatloaf, 1998; Clapton Chronicles, 1999; Also featured on recordings of: Rufus and Chaka Khan; Ladysmith Black Mambazo; Little Feat; George Harrison; B-52s; Brian Wilson. *Honours:* Numerous Grammy Awards with: Rickie Lee Jones; Rufus and Chaka Khan; Steve Winwood; Eric Clapton. *Address:* c/o Warner Brothers Records, 75 Rockefeller Plaza, New York, NY 10019, USA.

TITIYO, (Titiyo Jah); b. Sweden. Vocalist; *Recordings:* Albums: Titiyo, 1991; This Is Titiyo, 1993; Extended, 1998; Come Along, 2002. *Honours:* Three Swedish Grammy Awards, Best Female Artist. *Address:* c/o Diesel Music AB, PO Box 12 745, Kungsholmsgatan 23, 11294 Stockholm, Sweden. *Website:* www.titiyo.com.

TIVEY, Caroline (Cara); b. 19 Feb. 1959, Wellingborough, Northamptonshire, England. Musician (piano); Backing Vocalist. m. Micky Harris, 10 Oct. 1988. *Education:* Grade 8 piano, Birmingham School of Speech and Drama. *Career:* Worked with: Fine Young Cannibals; Everything But The Girl; Fuzzbox; Billy Bragg; The Lilac Time; Blur; Michael Stipe (REM); Stephen Duffy; Numerous world-wide tours; Television appearances include: Top of the Pops; The Tube; The Word; Hootenanny; Letterman; The Late Show; MTV. *Recordings:* with Everything But The Girl: Baby The Stars Shine Bright; with The Lilac Time: and Love For All; The Astronauts; The Laundry; with Billy Bragg: Workers Playtime, 1988; Don't Try This At Home, 1991; William Bloke, 1996; Reaching to the Converted, 1999; The Internationale; with Ted Chippington: She Loves You; Man In A Suitcase. *Honours:* No. 1 charity single with Billy Bragg, She's Leaving Home, 1988. *Membership:* Musicians' Union. *Address:* Flat 1, 48 Somers Rd, Malvern Link, Worcestershire WR14 1JB, England.

TOBIN, Karen; b. Drexel Hill, Pennsylvania, USA. Vocalist; Songwriter; Musician (guitar). m. Tim Boyle, divorced, 2 d. *Education:* College degree in Applied Science Education; Vocals, Bryn Mawr Conservatory of Music. *Career:* Recording artist with Arista; Atlantic Records; Nashville; Video; CMT; TNN. *Compositions:* Co-writer, Holdin' Back The Tears, L A Cowboys; Don't Want To Give Up On Love, Sam Harris. *Recordings:* Album: Carolina Smokey Man. *Contributions to:* Bellevue Cadillac, Prozac Nation; Boston Pops Orchestra, Dash of Pops; Vocals on: John Stewart, Wires For The Bunker, 2000. *Membership:* AFTRA; SAG; CMA. *Current Management:* Les Oreck, Weisberg and Associates Management. *Address:* 4451 Canoga Dr., Woodland Hills, CA 91403, USA.

TOCANNE, Bruno; b. 19 March 1955, Paris, France. Jazz Musician (drums); Bandleader. 2 s. *Education:* Primary School Teacher studies, University; Private lessons with jazz drummers; Workshops with Steve Lacy. *Career:* Bandleader, Bruno Tocanne Réunion; Appearances include: Montréal Jazz Festival; Zagreb Jazz Festival, 1985; Belgrade Jazz Festival, 1985; Tour, Poland, 1992; TF1-France 2, France 3, 1993; Festival Radio-France, 1995; France-Musique (radio), 1995. *Recordings:* Albums: Hors-Sèrie, B Tocanne, S Domancich, Philippe Sellah, Michel Saulvier, 1992; Odessa, Bruno Tocanne Réunion, S Domacich, P Rogers, Erci d'Enfert; Funérals, Sophia Domanisch Trio and Paul Rogers, John Greaves, 1994. *Membership:* Vice-President, UMJ (Union of Jazz Musicians), 1993–. *Current Management:* Asscn Jazzland. *Address:* 80 rue de Stalingrad, 78800 Houilles, France.

TOD, A; b. New York, NY, USA. Vocalist; Musician (bass). *Career:* Vocalist, musician, Cop Shoot Cop, 1988–; Several international tours, Japan; Europe; USA; Appearances at Reading Festival, 1992, 1994; World tour, 1993; Recorded radio session for John Peel, BBC Radio 1, 1992. *Recordings:*

Albums: Consumer Revolt, 1990; White Noise; Ask Questions Later; Release, 1994; EPs: Headkick Facsimile; Piece Man; Suck City. *Contributions to:* Teleconned: We Want the Air; Firewater, Ponzi Scheme; Clay Pigeons; Foetus, Null And Void, 1998. *Address:* c/o Big Cat Records, PO Box 3074, Chiswick, London W4 4ZN, England.

TODOROV, Dimo; Musician (guitar). *Career:* Member, Concurent, 1986–; Numerous concerts, TV and radio appearances, Bulgaria. *Recordings:* Rock For Peace, 1988; Rock Festival In Mitchurin, 1989; The Black Sheep (rock collection), 1992; Something Wet (best-selling album, Bulgaria), 1994; The Best of Bulgarian Rock, 1995. *Honours:* First Prizes: Top Rock Band, Youth Festival, Vidin, 1989; Rock ring, Sofia, 1990; Top Rock Composition: The Cavalry, 1991; Group of the Year, The Darik Radio Countdown, 1994. *Address:* 40 St Stambolov Blvd, 1202 Sofia, Bulgaria.

TOIVANEN, Pekka; b. 27 Sept. 1961, Finland. Musician (tenor saxophone). *Education:* Piano from age 10; Clarinet lessons from age 12. *Career:* Concerts with Kulttis Big Band; Brushane Big Band; Joined jazz department, Sibelius Academy, Helsinki, 1983; Formed own quartet, 1987. *Compositions:* Works for big bands, include Breakfast, commissioned by UMO, 1990. *Honours:* Winners, Finnish Jazz Federation band competition, 1987; Second place, Karlovy Vary contest, 1988. *Address:* Agricolankatu 7 D 94, 00530 Helsinki, Finland.

TOLJA, Davor; b. 31 May 1957, Rijeka, Croatia. Vocalist; Musician (keyboards); Songwriter; Arranger. *Education:* 4 years technical study, Rijeka University; 6 years piano, musical school. *Career:* Keyboard player, group: Vrijeme Zemlja; Leader, author, player, singer, group Denis and Denis; Currently solo singer, composer, arranger, musician, producer; Owner, small recording studio. *Recordings:* with Vrijeme I Zemlja: Vrijeme I Zemlja, 1979; with Denis and Denis: Cuvaj Se, 1984; Ja Sam Lazljiva, 1985; Budi Tu, 1988; Solo: Stari Macak, 1990. *Honours:* Gold discs for albums: Cuvaj Se; Ja Sam Lazljiva; Best Pop Album of the Year, Rock (music magazine), Cuvaj Se, former Yugoslavia, 1984; Many pop festival awards for songs and arrangements; As a Composer participated at Eurosong, Dublin, Ireland with song Probudi Me by Group ENI, 1997. *Membership:* CMU (Croatian Music Union). *Address:* Strossmayerova 11, 51000 Rijeka, Croatia.

TOLLY, Maria; b. 10 Feb. 1933, Islington, London, England. Composer; Writer. m. Valeriano Rocca, 1 March 1958, divorced 1980, 3 s., 1 d. *Education:* Degree Modern Languages, 1954; Computer Music, Electronics, Music Courses, Dartington College, 1991–95. *Career:* Mezzo-soprano touring Mauritius with Rae Woodland, John Lawrenson, Paul Ferris, 1977; Lead singer, Ballet Rambert's Cruel Garden (Christopher Bruce, Lindsay Kemp), 1979, 1980; Composer, performer, Theatre, 1983–89; Singer, songwriter, guitarist, tours Belgium; Netherlands; USSR; Germany; Cuba; Yugoslavia, Italy, Czechoslovakia, 1985–90; Performer, composer, Compact Theatre, 1990–92; Performer, composer, Electro-acoustic concerts, 1992–95; Festivals in London and Sheffield, 1993–97; Composed electro-acoustic music for new ballet Women Unbound, performed by Conundrum Dance Company, premiered at The Place, followed by tour of the UK, 1997; Songwriter, Musical Director for Banner Theatre's new production Redemption Song, premiered in Birmingham followed by tour of the UK, 1997; Musical Director, Telling Tales new production Rise and Run touring UK, 1998; Composed music for small children's dance classes, 1999–2000; Performed own songs at Central Hall Westminster and Hackney Empire with dance interpretations by Lisa Grivello and Suzette Rocca; Oral History Recordings for Museum on London Waterways; Musical Director, Bonner Theatre, 2002–. *Compositions:* Music for the under 5s to be used in schools. *Recordings:* 3 albums, original songs: Gonna Get Up, Voices, Up To Here, 1985–88; Dance drama: About Time, 1991; Musical play: Mrs Columbus Speaks Out, 1992; Play: Cargo, 1999; New works performed, Dartington Summer School; Morley College, 1993–95. *Publications:* Article in Women Live, used in syllabus of Women's Studies, 1989; Chapter, songwriting, Taking Reality By Surprise, Women's Press Ltd, 1990. *Honours:* Winner, GLC Songwriting Competition, Victor Jara Song Competition, 1983; Winner, competition for the composition, Dreams, 1998; Millennium Award to compose music for 3–5 year-olds in schools, 2001. *Membership:* Equity; Writers Guild of Great Britain. *Address:* 91 Percival Rd, Enfield, Middlesex, EN1 1QT, England.

TOLONEN, Jukka Jorma; b. 16 April 1952, Helsinki, Finland. Musician (guitar, piano); Composer. m. Liisa-Elina, 17 July 1992, 3 s., 1 d. *Education:* Piano lessons from age 8; Sibelius Academy, 1971–72. *Career:* Member, Tasavallan Presidentti, 1967–74; Formed Jukka Tolonen Band, 1976; Also worked with: Bill's Boogie Band (with Bill Öhström); Piirpauke; Christian Sievert and Gilberto Moreira; Several concert tours: Germany; Switzerland; England; Scandinavia; Concerts: Moscow; Estonia; Georgia; Tatarstan; Festivals include: Montreux Jazz Festival; Reading Rock Festival; Roskilde Rock Festival; Television shows, Scandinavia and Germany; Old Grey Whistle Test, England. *Recordings:* 9 solo albums, including: Tolonen, 1974; Crossection, 1976; Impressions, 1977; Mountain Stream, 1980; 8 band albums; 4 acoustic guitar duo albums; Also collaborated with: Charlie Mariano; Edward Vasala. *Honours:* Yrjö Award, Finnish Jazz Federation, 1972. *Membership:* Musicians' Union (Sweden).

TOMATITO, (José Fernández Torres); b. 1958, Almeria, Andalucía, Spain. Musician (guitar); Composer. *Career:* Flamenco Guitarist; Began musical career in Málaga playing in Tablaos (Flamenco nightclubs); Accompanied Camarón De La Isla for many years; Collaborations: Paco De Lucia; Jose Mercé; Pansequito; Enrique Morente; Carmen Linares; Appeared on numerous flamenco albums; Participated in several film scores and composed music for the German film Bin Ich Schoen; Movie appearances: Sevillanas, 1992; Flamenco (De Carlos Saura), 1995; Vengo, 2000. *Recordings:* Albums: Rosas De Amor, 1987; Barrio Negro, 1991; Guitarra Gitana, 1996; Spain (with Michel Camilo), 2000; Paseo De Los Castaños, 2001.

TOMICH, Michael Robert; b. 24 Feb. 1948, Chiswick, London, England. Musician (bass guitar). m. Anita Kaarinä Viero, 15 Dec. 1971. *Education:* Nescot College, Ewell, Surrey; Stafford College, Kensington; Acoustic guitar, Harrow School of Music. *Career:* Played with many acts 150 different acts, 1966–83; Constant tours of UK, Europe and USA; Numerous television appearances and radio broadcasts; Acts include: Clyde McPhatter; The Isley Brothers; Bonzo Dog Doo Dah Band; The Skatalites; Joan Armatrading; Peter Banks; Bill Bruford; Heron; Karl Wallinger; Atomic Rooster; Pickettywitch; The Gods; If; The Fantastics. *Recordings:* Early records with: Pickettywitch; Album: Diamond of Dreams, Heron; Many session recordings. *Honours:* Wycombe Radio Personality, 1994. *Membership:* Wycombe Hospital Radio Asscn. *Address:* 10 Sandford Gardens, High Wycombe, Buckinghamshire HP11 1QT, England.

TOMIIE, Satoshi, (Loop 7, Black Shells); b. 1966, Tokyo, Japan. Prod; Remixer; DJ. *Career:* Formed first band in Tokyo, early 1980s; Met Frankie Knuckles at a fashion party and joined the Def Mix crew; Collaborations: Frankie Knuckles; Robert Owens; Diane Charlemagne; Remixed: Madonna; Simply Red; Janet Jackson; Michael Jackson; Gabrielle. *Recordings:* Albums: Full Lick, 2001; Singles: Tears (with Frankie Knuckles), 1989; And I Loved You (with Arnold Jarvis), 1990; The Anthem (as Black Shells), 1994; Darkness, 1998; Inspired, 2000; Love In Traffic, Up In Flames, 2001. *Address:* c/o Sony Music, 550 Madison Ave, New York, USA.

TOMMEY, Glenn; b. 27 Aug. 1951, Ross-On-Wye, Herefordshire, England. Recording Engineer; Prod; Composer; Arranger; Musician (guitar, keyboards, drums). m. Carolyn Jane Kellett, 1 Aug. 1981, 3 s. *Education:* Newton Park College, Bath; Newton Park College, Bath; University of Bristol, Certificate in Education (Music). *Career:* Resident Engineer, Crescent Studios, Bath, 1974–87; Freelance Engineer, 1987–; Projects for CBS/Sony, Tokyo; Toshiba/EMI, Tokyo; Peter Gabriel IV, 1982; XTC; Big Express, 1984; Fossil Fuel, 1996; Stranglers; Rupert Holmes; Korgis; Icehouse; Currently, lecturer in music dedicated micro-technology at Bath College of Higher Education. *Honours:* Best Recorded Album of the Year, Precious, Hajime Mizoguchi, 1990. *Membership:* Musicians' Union. *Address:* 99 Fairfield Park Rd, Fairfield Park, Bath, Avon BA1 6JR, England.

TOMPKINS, David Mark; b. 12 Aug. 1963, Lincoln, England. Musician (double bass, bass guitar). *Education:* First Class Mathematics Degree, 1984; Jazz studies, 1987–90. *Career:* Performed with rock band Niadem's Ghost, 1984–86; Concerts include headlining at The Marquee Club, London; Studied Jazz, 1987–90; Member of D'semble, 1990–; Played with Martin Taylor in 1993; Member, Book Of Days, 1999–. *Recordings:* In Sheltered Winds, Niadem's Ghost, 1985; D'Semble, D'Semble, 1992. *Honours:* Featured in Best New Band Reader's Poll with Niadem's Ghost, 'Sounds' magazine, 1986. *Membership:* Musicians' Union. *Address:* 2 Dawlish Rd, Chorlton, Manchester M21 8XR, England.

TONE THEORY. See: **CARTER, Derrick.**

TONG, Des; b. 30 April 1951, Woking, Surrey, England. Music Prod; Musician (bass guitar). 1 s, 1 d. *Career:* Played bass guitar with Sad Café; Producer, Time Warp for Damian; Worked with: Real Thing; Lisa Stansfield; Joe Cocker; Alvin Stardust; Cissy Stone; Ruby Turner; Engelbert Humperdinck; Inez and Charlie Foxx; The Jacksons; Music Producer for US Gold. *Recordings include:* Sad Café, The Politics of Existing; Anthology, 2001; Hit singles include: Every Day Hurts, 1979; My Oh My, 1980; Producer, Ultimate Party Animal Album. *Honours:* Siver disc, Time Warp. *Membership:* PRS. *Current Management:* Cissy Stone. *Address:* 108 Kingsbury Rd, Erdington, Birmingham B24 8QU, England.

TONG, Pete; b. 30 July 1960, Dartford, England. DJ; A&R Exec. *Career:* Became DJ aged 15; Freelance DJ on leaving school; Worked at Blues and Soul and Black Music, 1979–83; Radio broadcaster, Radio Invicta, Capital Radio and Radio London; Radio 1; Originally on Peter Powell show, now DJ with own dance music show; Head of A & R, London/Ffrr Records. *Recordings:* Albums: Ministry of Sound—The Annual, Vol. I, 1995, Vol. II, 1996, Vol. III, 1997; Ministry of Sound—Dance Nation, Vol. I, 1995, Vol. II, 1996, Vol. III, 1997, Vol. IV, 1997, Vol. V, 1999; Essential Mix, 1996, 1996, 1998, 2000, 2001; Essential Selection, Winter, 1997, Spring, 1998, Spring, 1999, Ibiza, 1999, Spring, 2000, Ibiza, 2000; Pete Tong's Essential Collection, 1997; Platinum On Black: The Final Chapter, 1998; Ministry of Sound–Clubber's Guide to Ibiza, 1998; Essential Millennium, 1999; Human Traffic (film soundtrack),

1999; The Beach (film soundtrack), 2000; Twisted Beats, 2001. *Address:* c/o London Records, PO Box 1422, Chancellors House, Chancellors Rd, London W6 9SG, England. *Website:* www.trustthedj.com/petetong.

TONG, Simon; Musician (guitar, keyboards). *Career:* Mem., The Verve, 1996–99; Numerous live dates including headlining slot at Reading Festival, 1997; Mem., The Shining, 2002–. *Recordings:* Albums: with The Verve: Urban Hymns (No. 1, UK), 1997; with The Shining: True Skies, 2002. Singles: with The Verve: Bittersweet Symphony, 1997; Lucky Man, 1997; Drugs Don't Work (No. 1, UK), 1997; with The Shining: Quicksilver; I Wonder How; Young Again. *Honours:* with The Verve: BRIT Awards, Best British Group, Best British Album, 1998. *Website:* www.theshiningarehere.com.

TONTOH, Frank; b. 22 May 1964, Kumasi, Ghana. Musician (drums); Writer; Composer. *Education:* 2 years study, piano, Trinity College of Music. *Career:* Member, Osibisa, for 4 years; Aztec Camera, 4 years; Tanita Tikaram, 8 months; Also played with: Tasmin Archer; Level 42; Omar; Mica Paris; Zucchero; Roachford; Courtney Pine; Jason Rebello; Edwyn Collins; Misty Oldland; Irene Grandi. *Recordings:* Aztec Camera: Stray; Misty Oldland: Supernatural; Kimiko Yamashita: Love and Hate; Tony Remy: 2 albums; Theme to Wired, TV programme; Kiko Veneno: 2 albums (Gold); Bachology: 1 album; Gang of Four: 100 Flowers Bloom, 1998; Jarabe de Palo: Depende, 1998.

TOPAZ, Rona Lisa; b. 4 Sept. 1965, New York, USA. Vocalist; Actress; Songwriter; Musician (keyboards). m. 19 Feb. 1988, separated, 1992. *Education:* Associate Applied Sciences Degree, Performing Arts, Five Towns College; City and Guilds, Theatre Skills. *Career:* Recording sessions for Lloyd Clarke; Gary Louca; Sebastian; No Go Productions; Friction; District Six; Kezi O'Neal; Leighton Carter; Musicals include: Destiny; Say Why; Ensemble, Un Ballo In Maschera, for Capital Opera Company; Lead vocalist, solo artist for over 100 events including: Edinburgh Festival Fringe; Highbury Festival; Glasgow Big Day Festival, 1991; Supported 4 Men and A Dog, Glasgow Mayfest, 1992; Shape Arts Festival; International Jazz Day; Fitzrovia Festival; Television includes: Highway, ITV; Kazukos Karaoke Klub, Channel 4; Plays, films; Member, Artists In Exile, 2001. *Compositions include:* Lyricist, No Second Chances, recorded 1991. *Recordings:* Lead vocals, Visualize, 1992. *Publications:* Lyrics: The Divisions Are Fine, London Voices Anthology. *Honours:* Second Prize, Croydon Music Festival; Hon. Mention, Brixton Songwriting Competition. *Membership:* Musicians' Union; Women In Music. *Current Management:* Solomon Artists Management International. *Address:* c/o 30 Clarence Rd, Southend-on-Sea, Essex SS1 1BD, England.

TORK, Peter, (Peter Halsten Thorkelson); b. 13 Feb. 1944, Washington DC, USA. Musician (bass, guitar, keyboards); Vocalist; Actor. *Career:* Folk musician with Au Go Go Singers, Los Angeles; Member, The Monkees, 1966–68; 1986–89; Actor, Monkees comedy television series, 1966–68; 33 1/3 Revolutions Per Monkee, TV Special, NBC; Monkees film, Head, premiere 1968; Founder, own groups: Release, 1969; The New Monks, 1981; High school teacher, Santa Monica, early 1970s; Rejoined Monkees, 1986–89; Cameo appearance, The Brady Bunch Movie, 1995. *Recordings:* Albums: The Monkees (No. 1, USA and UK), 1966; More of the Monkees (No. 1, USA and UK), 1967; Headquarters (No. 1, USA), 1967; Pisces, Aquarius, Capricorn and Jones Ltd (No. 1, UK), 1967; The Birds, The Bees and The Monkees, 1968; Then and Now, 1986; Pool It, 1987; Anthology, 1998; Greatest Hits, 1999; Hit singles: Last Train To Clarksville (No. 1, USA), 1966; I'm A Believer (No. 1, USA), 1966; (I'm Not Your) Steppin' Stone, 1967; A Little Bit Me, A Little Bit You, 1967; Alternate Title, 1967; Pleasant Valley Sunday, 1967; Daydream Believer (No. 1, USA), 1967; Valleri, 1968; Solo albums: Stranger Things Have Happened, 1994; Two Man Band, 1996; Once Again, 2001. *Honours:* NARM Awards, Best Selling Group, Best Album, 1967; Emmy, Outstanding Comedy Series, 1967; 3 BMI Awards, 1968; Monkees Day, Atlanta, 1986; Star on Hollywood Walk of Fame, 1989. *Address:* c/o Nationwide Entertainment Services, 2756 N Green Valley Parkway, Suite 449, Las Vegas, NV 89014–2100, USA.

TORRENCE, Dean; b. 10 March 1940, Los Angeles, California, USA. Vocalist. *Education:* Graphics Degree. *Career:* Member, duo Jan and Dean (with Jan Berry), 1957–66; 1973–; Solo artiste, 1966–; Performances include: Dick Clark's Stage Show, Michigan State Fair, 1959; American Bandstand, 1959; New York, with The Animals, Chuck Berry, Del Shannon, 1964; Launched Kittyhawk Graphics, 1967; Member, Legendary Masked Surfers, 1972; California Surfer's Stomp Festival, 1973; Subject of biopic, Dead Man's Curve, 1978. *Recordings:* Albums: with Jan and Dean: Jan and Dean Take Linda Surfin', 1963; Surf City and Other Swingin' Cities, 1963; Drag City, 1964; Dead Man's Curve/The New Girl In School, 1964; The Little Old Lady From Pasadena, 1964; Ride The Wild Surf, 1964; Command Performance/Live In Person, 1965; Jan and Dean Meet Batman, 1966; One Summer Night – Live, 1982; Solo album: Save For A Rainy Day, 1967; Singles: with Jan and Dean include: Linda, 1963; Surf City (No. 1, USA), 1963; Drag City, 1964; Dead Man's Curve, 1964; The New Girl In School, 1964; The Little Old Lady (From Pasadena), 1964; Ride The Wild Surf, 1964; Catch A Wave, 1964; Popsicle, 1966. *Contributions to:* Hard Rock Café: Surf, 1998; Also recorded

with: The Beach Boys; Walter Egan. *Current Management:* Bill Hollingshead Productions, 1720 N Ross St, Santa Ana, CA 92706, USA.

TORREZ, Juan Pablo; b. 17 Aug. 1946, Cuba. Musician (trombone). m. Elsa Torres, 30 Dec. 1988, 1 s. *Career:* Member, Cuban Orchestra of Modern Music, with Paquito d'Rivera, Artuo Sandoval, Chuco Valdes, 1970s; Played with: Dizzie Gillespie; Don Cherry; Gato Barbieri; Mongo Santamaria; Slide Hampton; Astor Piazolla; Steve Gadd; Paquito D'Rivera; Arturo Sandoval; Hilton Ruiz; Cachao; Nestor Torres; Chocolate Armentaros; Giovanni Hidalgo; Travels throughout Spain; Portugal; France; Switzerland; Italy; Germany; Poland; Mexico; USA; Canada; Currently resident in Miami, USA. *Recordings:* Over 20 include: Trombone Man; From John To Johnny; For Elsa; Banana Split; Foot Tapping; Folklore Mexicano, 2000; Inspiracion de Juan Gabriel, 2001; El Truinfador, 2001. *Membership:* ITA; National Academy Recording. *Current Management:* Elsa Torres. *Address:* 635 SW 13 Ave, Miami, FlL 33135, USA.

TORROJA, Ana; b. 28 Dec. 1959, Madrid, Spain. Vocalist. *Career:* Mem., Mecano, with José and Nacho Cano, 1980–; Simultaneous solo career, 1992–. *Recordings:* Albums: with Mecano: Mecano, 1982; ¿Dónde Está El País De Las Hadas?, 1983; Ya Viene El Sol, 1984; En Concierto, 1985; Lo Ultimo De Mecano, 1986; Entre El Cielo Y El Suelo, 1986; Descanso Dominical, 1988; Aidalai, 1991; Ana José Nacho, 1998; Solo: Puntos Cardinales, 1997; Pasajes De Un Sueño, 2000; Girados En Concierto (with Miguel Bosé), 2000. *Address:* c/o Sony Music Entertainment, European Regional Office, 10 Great Marlborough St, London W1F 7LP, England. *Website:* www.anatorrojaweb.com.

TORU, Mitsui; b. 31 March 1940, Saga, Japan. Prof. of Music and English. *Career:* Lecturer, Aichi University, 1964–68; Lecturer, 1969–71, Associate Professor, 1971–83, Professor, 1983–, Kanazawa University. *Publications:* Karaoke Around The World; Global Technology, Local Singing. *Membership:* The International Musicological Society; International Asscn For The Study of Popular Music. *Address:* Graduate Program In Music, Kanazawa University, Kanazawa, Ishikawa 920–1164, Japan.

TOUNKARA, Djelimady; b. 1947, Kita, Mali. Musician (guitar); Songwriter. *Career:* Born into a griot family; Member: Orchestre Misira; National A; Pioneer Jazz (first modern dance bands in Mali); Super Rail Band, early 1970s; Later played with acoustic trio Bajourou; Director and conductor with Super Rail Band. *Recordings:* Albums include: Djali Madi Tounkara and Rail Band, 1983; Mansa (with Rail Band), 1995; In Griot Time (compilation), 2000; Sigui, 2001. *Publications:* One of the subjects of Banning Eyre's book In Griot Time. *Honours:* BBC Radio 3 Awards for World Music Award, Best African Artist, 2002. *Address:* c/o Alison Loerke, 12501 11th Ave NW, Seattle, WA 98177, USA.

TOURE, Ali Farka; b. 1939, Gourmararusse, Mali. Musician (guitar, n'jurkel, njarka); Farmer. *Career:* Formerly, river ambulanceman, Mali; Member, Niafunke District Troupe (music and dance group), 1960s; Sound engineer, Radio Mali, late 1960s; Professional solo artiste, 1974–; Regular tours: UK; Europe; USA; Africa; Major concerts include: US tour with Ry Cooder, 1994; West Africa, Europe, USA, 1995; Womad Festival, Reading, 1995; New Orleans Jazz Festival; London Jazz Festival; Major role against music piracy in Mali; Part-ownership, EMI Mali and Bamako recording studio. *Recordings:* 6 albums, France, 1980s; 4 albums on World Circuit: Ali Farka Toure, 1988; The River, 1990; The Source, 1992; Talking Timbuktu, with Ry Cooder (No. 1, Billboard World Music Charts), 1994; Radio Mali sessions 1970–80, 1996; Niafunké, 1999; As producer: Album for Lobi Traore (Album of Year, Le Monde), 1994; Also appears on: African Blues, 1998; Alkibar, Afel Bocoum, 1999. *Honours:* Grammy, Talking Timbuktu, 1994; European World Music Album of Year, Talking Timbuktu, 1994. *Address:* c/o World Circuit Records, 106 Cleveland St, London W1P 5DP, England.

TOURNAS, Kostas; b. 23 Sept. 1949, Tripolis, Greece. Musician (guitar); Vocalist; Composer; Lyricist; Prod; Recording Studio Owner. m. Maria, 4 Dec. 1977. *Education:* Harmony; Synthesis; Guitar. *Career:* many tours, Greece and Cyprus; Club appearances; Host or guest, radio and television talk shows; Owner, City Studios, Athens. *Compositions:* More than 500 titles released since 1971. *Recordings:* Aperanta Horafia (Endless Fields); Kiries Kai Kirioi (Ladies and Gentlemen) Duets; Poll/Anthrope (Man). *Publications:* Kostas Tournas' Songs (sheet music and lyrics of his best). *Honours:* Gold, Platinum records; Lyric awards. *Membership:* AEPI Greece; ETE Greece; FIA. *Address:* 133 Kafkassou St, Kipseli, Athens, 11364, Greece.

TOUSSAINT, Jean-Baptiste Nazaire; b. 27 July 1960, Aruba, Netherlands Antilles. Jazz Musician (tenor and soprano saxophone). *Education:* Saxophone at Miami State, with Charles Cox; Associate degree, Berklee College of Music, Boston, USA. *Career:* Member, Art Blakey's Jazz Messengers, 1982–86; Concerts world-wide include: Jazz Mobile, New York, 1982; Residency, Ronnie Scott's, 1985; Concerts with John Dankworth Band, UK, 1983; Camden Jazz Festival, 1986; Teacher, Guildhall School of Music, 1987–; Formed own bands Jean Toussaint Quartet, 1987; Nazaire, 1992; Tours of Europe and Middle East with Max Roach, 1989; Member, Julian Joseph's band, 1992–94; Also worked with Jason Rebello; Bheki Mseleku; Lenny White, UK, Europe and USA, 1995; Numerous world-wide television and radio appearances, 1982–. *Recordings:* Albums: with Art Blakey's Jazz Messengers: The New York Scene, 1984; Live At Kimballs, 1985; Blue Night, 1985; Solo: Impressions of Coltrane, 1987; Silvershine (with Andy Hamilton), 1990; What Goes Around, 1991; The Language Of Truth (with Julian Joseph), 1991; Who's Blues, 1992; Reality, 1993; Jamaica By Night (as producer), 1994; Life I Want, 1995; Metropolis, 1998; Back To Back, 1998; Live At Ronnie Scott's, 2000; Coast To Coast, 2000; The Street Above The Underground, 2001; Blue Black, 2002. *Membership:* MCPS; PRS: Broadcast Music Inc. *Current Management:* Agent: Fish Krish. *Address:* c/o Fish Krish, 6 Carlton House, 319 West End Lane, London NW6 1RN, England.

TOWNEND, Richard James Patrick; b. 4 July 1948, London, England. Musician (banjo, guitar, fiddle). *Career:* Formed first school bluegrass group in UK; Played at: Royal Albert Hall; Hammersmith Odeon; Cambridge Folk Festival; Appeared on BBC radio and television folk and country music programmes; Also on Kaleidoscope, BBC Radio 4; Partner in Wadhurst Bluegrass Day Venture. *Recordings:* Make The Old Times New, with Rosie Davis, 1995; The Echo Mountain Band, 1975, (reissued 1995); Fraces on the Frets, 1997. *Membership:* Musicians' Union; British Bluegrass Music Asscn. *Address:* 2 Fairview Cottages, Balaclava Lane, Wadhurst, East Sussex TN5 6EQ, England.

TOWNSHEND, Peter Dennis Blandford; b. 19 May 1945, Isleworth, London, England. Musician (guitar) Composer; Publisher; Author. m. Karen Astley, 1968, 1 s., 2 d. *Education:* Ealing Art College. *Career:* Mem., UK rock group, The Who, 1964–84; Solo artiste, 1979–; Appearances include: National Jazz and Blues festival, 1965, 1966, 1969; Monterey Pop Festival, 1967; Rock At The Oval, 1972; Farewell tour, 1982–83; Live Aid, Wembley, 1985; Reunion tour, 1989; Films include: Tommy; Quadrophenia; The Kids Are Alright; Owner, Eel Pie Recording Ltd, 1972–; Established Eel Pie (bookshops and publishing), 1972–; Established Meher Baba Oceanic (UK archival library), 1976–81; Ed., Faber and Faber, 1983–. *Compositions include:* Rock operas, Tommy, 1969; Quadrophenia, 1973; Numerous songs for The Who. *Recordings:* Albums: with The Who: My Generation, 1965; A Quick One, 1966; The Who Sell Out, 1968; Direct Hits, 1968; Tommy (rock opera), 1969; Live At Leeds, 1970; Who's Next, 1971; Meaty Beefy Big And Bouncy, 1971; Quadrophenia, 1973; Odds And Sods, 1974; The Who By Numbers, 1975; The Story Of The Who, 1976; Who Are You, 1978; The Kids Are Alright (film soundtrack), 1979; Face Dances, 1981; Hooligans, 1982; It's Hard, 1982; Rarities Vols 1 and 2, 1983; Once Upon A Time, 1983; The Singles, 1984; Who's Last, 1984; Who's Missing, 1987; Two's Missing, 1987; Who's Better Who's Best, 1988; Joined Together, 1990; 30 Years Of Maximum R&B, 1994; My Generation: The Very Best Of The Who, 1996; The BBC Sessions, 2000; Solo: Who Came First, 1972; Rough Mix, 1977; Empty Glass, 1980; All The Best Cowboys Have Chinese Eyes, 1982; Scoop, 1983; White City, 1985; Another Scoop, 1987; The Iron Man, 1989; Psychoderelict, 1993; The Best Of Pete Townshend, 1996; Pete Townshend Live, 1999; Lifehouse Elements, 2000; The Oceanic Concerts, 2001; Singles include: with The Who: I Can't Explain, 1965; Anyway Anyhow Anywhere, 1965; My Generation, 1965; Substitute, 1966; I'm A Boy, 1966; Happy Jack, 1967; Pictures of Lily, 1967; I Can See For Miles, 1967; Pinball Wizard, 1969; See Me Feel Me, 1970; Won't Get Fooled Again, 1970; Join Together, 1972; Who Are You, 1978; You Better You Bet, 1981; Contributor, Sun City, Artists Against Apartheid, 1985. *Publications:* Horse's Neck, 1986. *Honours:* BRIT Lifetime Achievement Award, 1983; Living Legend Award, International Rock Awards, 1991; with The Who: Gold Ticket, Madison Square Garden, 1979; Ivor Novello Award, Contribution to British Music, 1982; British Phonographic Industry Award, 1983; BRIT Award, Contribution to British Music, 1988; Inducted into Rock 'n' Roll Hall of Fame, 1990; Tony Award for Tommy score, 1993; Grammy Award for original cast recording Tommy, 1993; Dora Mavor Moore Award for Tommy in Toronto, 1994; Olivier Award, Tommy, London, 1997; Q Lifetime Achievement Award for The Who. *Address:* PO Box 305, Twickenham TW1 1TT, England.

TOWNSHEND, Simon John; b. 10 Oct. 1960, Ealing, London, England. Songwriter; Musician (guitar, piano); Vocalist. m. Janie Harris, 15 July 1978, 2 s., 1 d. *Career:* First record contract, Warner Bros, age 14; Founder member, On The Air, with Mark Brzezicki, Tony Butler (Big Country), 1980; Solo artiste, Polygram USA; Founder member, Animal Soup, with Zak Starkey; Sung part of Newsboy in Tommy, The Who; Singer, Rise, Rise on Smash The Mirror. *Compositions include:* Until Tomorrow; The Way It Is; Girl In New York; Ecstasy Heaven. *Recordings:* Solo: When I'm A Man, 1974; Janie, 1975; Turn It On, 1976; Ready For Action, 1980; I'm The Answer, 1984; Barriers, 1986; Albums: Sweet Sound, 1984 (produced by brother Pete Townshend); Moving Target, 1986; Among Us, 1997. *Contributions to:* Who's Serious: The Symphonic Music; British Rock Symphony. *Membership:* Musicians' Union; ASCAP; PRS; PARMA. *Current Management:* Stir Management. *Address:* 20 Woodgrange Ave, Ealing Common, London W5 3NY, England.

TOZER, Faye; b. 14 Nov. 1975, Northampton, England. Vocalist. *Career:* Cabaret career, incl. residency at London Hilton Hotel; Mem., Steps, 1997–2001; Popular with UK teen audience; Numerous television

appearances, incl. Steps To The Stars; Tours, incl. Gold–Greatest Hits tour, 2001; Host, Proms In The Park concert, performing solo with BBC Philharmonic Orchestra, 2001; Solo artiste, 2002–. *Recordings:* Albums: with Steps: Step One, 1998; Steptacular, 1999; Buzz, 2000; Gold, 2001; The Last Dance, 2002. Singles: Solo: Someone Like You (with Russell Watson), 2002. *Honours:* BRIT Award, Best Selling Live Act, 2000. *Address:* c/o Zomba Records Ltd, Zomba House, 165–167 Willesden High Rd, London NW10 2SG, England. *Website:* www.stepsofficial.com.

TRAASDAHL, Jan Ole; b. 21 Aug. 1958, Odense, Denmark. Assoc; Prof.Musician (piano); Composer; Educator. m. Hanne Mulvad, 21 Nov. 1981. *Education:* MA, Musicology, University of Århus, Denmark; Studies, Berklee College of Music, Boston, 1981. *Career:* Performed and recorded with many international jazz soloists, including Thad Jones, Richard Boone and Bent Jaedig; Conducted Big Bands and musicals; Composed music for Big Bands, vocal choirs and theatre. *Recordings:* Panta Rei, 1984; Stig Moller, 1994; Musam Big Band, 1995; Video, TVE Rio de Janeiro, 1995. *Publications:* Rhythmic Music Education, 1996; Music Education In A Multicultural Society, 1999. *Membership:* Vice-President, Musicians' Union, Copenhagen, 1996. *Address:* Oster Farimagsgade 45A, 2100 Copenhagen K, Denmark.

TRACEY, Clark; b. 5 Feb. 1961, London, England. Musician (drums); Composer; Arranger. m. Tina May, 15 June 1989, 1 s. *Career:* Toured with Stan Tracey: USA; India; Australia; Middle East; Europe; 1978–; Own group to Far East; Many television and radio appearances; Solely jazz concerts; Own group toured Far East and Europe. *Compositions:* Stiperstones Suite, for own quintet, 1988; Current original album: Full Speed Sideways, for own sextet; Playing In The Yard, with Charlie Rouse and Stan Tracey; Suite for Quintet at Finnish Festival, 1997; Recent. *Recordings include:* Stability, 2001. *Honours:* British Jazz Award, Best Drummer Category; Best Drummer Category, British Jazz Awards, 1997. *Membership:* PRS; MCPS; PPL; Musicians' Union. *Current Management:* Bernard Lyons, 73 Eglantine Ave, Belfast BT9 7EU, Northern Ireland; David E Jacobs, 6 Belgrove, Tunbridge Wells, Kent, England. *Address:* 8 Oliver Rd, Hemel Hempstead, Hertfordshire HP3 9PY, England.

TRAERUP, Birthe; b. 9 Oct. 1930, Kolding, Denmark. Assoc; Prof.; Musicologist. m. Erik Elias, 1966, 1 s. *Education:* MA, Musicology, Serbocroatian Linguistics and Literature, University of Copenhagen, 1959; Short-stay studies, Yugoslavia, Bulgaria, Albania, Greece, Poland, Czechoslovakia, Hungary, 1963–; Ethnomusicological studies in Yugoslavia, 1954–55, 1959–61. *Career:* Research Assoc., Danish Folklore Archives, Dept of Ethnomusicology, Copenhagen, 1961–64, 1967–68; Consultant, South Slavic Linguistics and Literature, Royal Library of Copenhagen, 1967–86; Adjunct Prof., 1968–72, Assoc. Prof., Ethnomusicology, 1972–97, Institute of Musicology, University of Copenhagen; Radio programmes and lectures on music of the Balkans, Denmark and other European countries; Research projects on songs, instrumental music in the Muslim community, Gora, Kosovo, folk music of Albanian population, studies on Karol Szymanowski and Denmark. *Publications include:* East Macedonian Folk Songs, 1970; Makedonske folkesange, 1983. *Contributions to:* Numerous contributions to musicological journals. *Honours:* Study Scholarships, 1954–55, 1959–61; Order of Merit, Jugoslavia Esperanto-Ligo, 1964; Hon. Mem., Udruzenje Folklorista Srbije, 1972; Interval Signal Prize, Radio Denmark, 1972; Order of Merit, Ministry for Culture and Art, Poland, 1983. *Address:* Birkevang 158, 3250, Gilleleje, Denmark. *E-mail:* birthe.traerup@get2net.dk.

TRAMP, Mike; b. 14 Jan. 1961, Denmark. Vocalist; Vocalist. *Career:* Vocalist, Danish rock group Mabel; Vocalist, songwriter, White Lion, 1985–92; Vocalist, songwriter, Freak of Nature, 1992–; Numerous tours: UK; Europe; USA. *Recordings:* Albums: with White Lion: Fight To Survive, 1985; Pride, 1987; Big Game, 1989; Mane Attraction, 1991; Capricorn, 1998; Remembering White Lion, 1999; with Freak of Nature: Freak of Nature, 1993; Gathering of Freaks, 1994; Also featured on Sahara, House of Lords, 1990. *Current Management:* Wyatt Management World-wide. *Address:* 10797 Onyx Circle, Fountain Valley, CA 92708, USA.

TRANCHART, Romain; b. 9 June 1976, Paris, France. Musician (piano, guitar); Prod. *Education:* Studied guitar at the American School of Modern Music, Paris, France. *Career:* Lived in Mexico, Algeria and Brazil before relocating to Paris aged 16; Temporarily with rock band Seven Tracks before releasing underground hit single as Funk Legacy; Co-founder of group Modjo, record label Modjo Music (with Yann Destagnol). *Recordings:* Album: Modjo, 2001; Singles: Lady (Hear Me Tonight), 2000; Chillin', 2001; What I Mean, 2001. *Honours:* Modjo first French group to score UK number 1 hit. *Current Management:* Modjo Music. *E-mail:* matt@modjo.com.

TRANS-X, (Pascal Leguirand); b. Paris, France. Composer; Lyricist; Vocalist; *Recordings:* New Age albums: Minos; De Harmonia; Gregorian Waves; As Incanta: Ishtar; Voice of The Cybicle; Dance albums: Trans-X; Living On Video/Vivre Sur Video (2m. copies sold world-wide); On My Own. *Honours:* Best Dance Artist, Adisq-Québec; Platinum record, Living On Video. *Membership:* SGAE (Spain). *Current Management:* Michel Huygen (Onira International).

TRAORE, Boubacar; b. 1940, Kayes, Mali. Vocalist; Musician (guitar); Songwriter. *Career:* Began composing at an early age; Acted in theatre, 1957–58; Started Les Pionniers Jazz, early 1960s; Also appeared on radio show, Les Auditeurs du Dimanche; Earned a living as a tailor, shop keeper and agricultural agent, training orchestras at night; After 20 years absence, invited to perform on Mali TV, 1987; Relocated to France after wife's death, 1989; Recorded two albums and toured Europe and USA; Collaborations include: Ali Farka Toure; Toumani Diabate; Keletigui Diabate; Habib Koite; Returned to settle in Bamako, 1991. *Recordings:* Albums include: Mariama, 1990; Kar Kar, 1992; Les Enfants De Pierrette, 1995; Sa Golo, 1996; Maciré, 1999; Je Chanterai Pour Toi, 2002. *Address:* c/o Alison Loerke, 12501 11th Ave NW, Seattle, WA 98177, USA. *E-mail:* loerkeali@aol.com.

TRAORE, Koniba; b. 1958, Koutiala, Mali. m. Kone Kadia, 1 s., 3 d. *Education:* Music classes with others at local, regional and national level. *Career:* Orchestral music, 1978–; Biennial competitions and national level, song and dance, 1982, 1984, 1986; Numerous TV appearances and on national radio; Participant, various festivals, including Moscow and Paris. *Compositions:* Ni bè joro, 1996; Balani, 1998. *Honours:* Biennial Artistic Prize, Bamako, 1984; Talabé Prize, Bamako, 1997. *Address:* s/c A Diabate, PO Box 86, Koutiala, Mali.

TRAORE, Rokia; b. 26 Jan. 1974, Bamako, Mali. Vocalist; Musician (guitar); Songwriter. *Career:* Received support from Ali Farka Toure, 1997; Appeared in concert with Habib Koite and Oumou Sangare and recorded first album; Toured USA and Europe, 2000; UK TV appearance on Later With Jools Holland, 2001. *Recordings:* Albums: Mouneissa, 1998: Wanita, 2000. *Honours:* Mouneissa sold 40,000 copies in Europe; Radio France Internationale, African Discovery award, 1997; Kora Award, Most Promising Female, 2001.

TRAVERS, Pat; b. 1954, Toronto, Canada. Musician (guitar); Songwriter; Vocalist. *Career:* Member, The Band; Founder, Pat Travers Band, London, 1976–; Concerts include: Reading Rock Festival, 1976; Worked with Nicko McBain; Scott Gorham; Pat Thrall; Tommy Aldridge; Michael Shrieve. *Recordings:* Albums: Pat Travers, 1976; Makin' Magic, 1976; Putting It Straight, 1977; Heat In The Street, 1978; Go For What You Know – Live, 1979; Crash and Burn, 1980; Radio Active, 1981; Black Pearl, 1982; Hot Shot, 1984; School of Hard Knocks, 1990; Blues Tracks, 1992; Just A Touch, 1993; Blues Magnet, 1994; Halfway to Somewhere, 1995; Lookin' Up, 1996; King Biscuit Live, 1997; Summerdaze '97, compilation, 1997; Whiskey Blues, 1997; Blues Tracks, 1998; Born Under a Bad Sign, 1998; Boom Boom, 2000; Don't Feed The Alligators, 2000. *Current Management:* Don Barnard Management, PO Box 300023, Fern Park, FL 32730, USA.

TRAVIS, Randy, (Randy Bruce Traywick); b. 4 May 1959, Marshville, North Carolina, USA. Country Vocalist; Songwriter; Musician (guitar). m. Lib Hatcher (Mary Elizabeth Robertson), 1991. *Career:* Played local clubs with brothers; Resident, Charlotte nightclub owned by Lib Hatcher, 1977; Early recordings as Randy Traywick; Resident singer, as Randy Ray, Nashville Palace, 1992; Name changed to Randy Travis, 1985–; Joined Grand Ole Opry, 1986. *Recordings:* US Country No. 1 hits: On The Other Hand; Diggin' Up Bones; Forever and Ever, Amen; I Won't Need You Anymore (Always and Forever); Gone Too Long; I Told You So; Honky Tonk Moon; Deeper Than The Holler; Is It Still Over; It's Just A Matter of Time; Hard Rock Bottom of Your Heart; Forever Together; Look Heart No Hands; This Is Me; Whisper My Name; Before You Kill Us All; Out of My Bones; Hole; Albums: Randy Ray Live At The Nashville Palace, 1982; Storms of Life, 1986; Always and Forever, 1987; Old 8 X 10, 1988; An Old Time Christmas, 1989; No Holdin' Back, 1989; Heroes and Friends (duets with Merle Haggard, George Jones, Loretta Lynn, Dolly Parton, Tammy Wynette and B. B. King), 1990; High Lonesome, 1991; Greatest Hits Vols 1 and 2, 1992; This Is Me, 1994; Full Circle, 1996; You and You Alone, 1998; A Man Ain't Made of Stone, 1999; Inspirational Journey, 2000; Live: It Was Just A Matter of Time, 2001. *Honours:* Grammy Award, Best Country Newcomer, 1986; Male Vocalist of the Year, Country Music Asscn, 1988. *Current Management:* Lib Hatcher-Travis Management, 1610 16th Ave S, Nashville, TN 37212, USA.

TRAVIS, Theo (Theodore John); b. 7 July 1964, Birmingham, England. Musician (tenor and soprano saxophones and flute); Composer. m. Madelyn J Cohen, 24 May 1992. *Education:* BMus, Manchester University; Grade 8 flute; Saxophone to BMus Final recital standard. *Career:* Toured Spain with NYJO, 1985; Leader, Theo Travis Band; Also performed with John Etheridge; Jim Mullen; John Marshall; Slim Gaillard; Radio includes: Jazz Parade, BBC Radio 2, playing original compositions, 1993; Interview, WKCR-FM, New York; Toured Japan with Mick Karn, 1997; Arts Council Tour for improvising trio with John Marshall (drums) and Mark Wood (guitar), 1998. *Compositions:* Broad Street Changes Suite for jazz septet, commissioned by West Midlands Arts; Commissioned by Derby Metro Cinema to write with Dave Sturt new music for Hitchcock silent film, The Lodger. *Recordings:* Solo: 2 AM, 1993; View From The Edge, 1994; Heart Of The Sun, 2001; with The Other Side: Dangerous Days, 1995; Secret Island, 1996; with Marshall Travis Wood, Bodywork, 1998; Guest appearances: Porcupine Tree, Mick Karn and Dick Heckstall-Smith. *Honours:* Financial Times Best Newcomer, 1993; Best

British CD, View From The Edge, 1994. *Membership:* Musicians' Union; PRS; Equity. *Address:* 20 Strathmore Gardens, Finchley, London N3, England.

TRENT, Tammy; b. 11 April 1968, Grand Rapids, Michigan, USA. Musician (drums, percussion). m. Trent Lenderink, 18 Aug. 1990. *Education:* 1 year college. *Career:* Signed to Rex Music, Brentwood, Tennessee. *Recordings:* Debut album, 1995; First radio single: Your Love Is 4 Always (No. 1, Christian Hits Radio charts); Albums: Tammy Trent, 1996; You Have My Heart, 1997; Set You Free, 2000. *Membership:* BMI. *Current Management:* Lenderink Management. *Address:* 1271 House Rd, Belmont, MI 49306, USA.

TRETOW, Michael Bo; b. 20 Aug. 1944. Recording Engineer. m. Lilian B, 1 s., 1 d. *Education:* Degree, Electronic Engineering, 1966. *Career:* Recording Engineer, around 40 Gold Records for early work; Engineer, all ABBA albums: Ring Ring, 1973; Waterloo, 1974; Abba, 1975; Greatest Hits, 1976; Arrival, 1976; The Album, 1978; Voulez Vous, 1979; Greatest Hits Vol. 2, 1979; Super Trouper, 1980; The Visitors, 1981; The First Ten Years, 1982; Abba Gold, 1992; More Abba Gold, 1993; Singles Collection, 2001; Independent Engineer and Producer, 1980–; Composer, music for film and video, and commercials. *Compositions:* Swedish TV Station Call. *Recordings:* Hubba Hubba Zoot Zoot, 1981; Den Makalösa Manicken, 1986. *Honours:* Gold Camera Award, 1988; International TV, Cinema and Radio Award, 1988; Monaco Radio Contest, 1989. *Membership:* SSES. *Address:* Virvelvindsvagen 8, 161 28 Bromma, Sweden.

TRETTINE, Caroline Anne Halcrow; b. 4 Sept. 1958, Kingston-on-Thames, Surrey, England. Vocalist; Songwriter; Musician (guitar); Systems Analyst. *Education:* BA Hons, Bristol University, English with French. *Career:* Singer, writer, guitarist with Blue Aeroplanes, 1984–85; Solo artiste, tours with: Billy Bragg; Christy Moore; Radio: Radio 1 sessions for Richard Skinner; Bob Harris, 1985–95; Member, Library of Love, 1995. *Compositions include:* Sleep With Me; Guilty; Hope. *Recordings:* with Blue Aeroplanes: Action Painting EP: Le Petit Cadeau de Don Juan, 1985; Be A Devil EP, 1990; Solo album: Ten Light Years, 2001. *Membership:* PRS; Musicians' Union. *Current Management:* Sincere Management, 421 Harrow Rd, London W9, England.

TREVISAN, Luciano (Fricchetti); b. 25 Sept. 1959, Venice, Italy. Musical Man; Promoter; Publisher. *Education:* DAMS, Bologna University. *Career:* Involved in Cultural Association, ARCI Manager; Record Distributors until 1986; Partner in record company, Materiali Sonori; Promoter, live events; Artist manager, 1989–; Partner, Ossigeno, Music Publishing Company, 1993–; Partner, Evolution Music, 1995; Alma Music, 2000–. *Publications:* Compra O Muori (book). *Honours:* Gold and Platinum records for album: Na Bruta Banda by Pitura Freska; Gold Record, Gran Calma, Pitura Freska. *Membership:* Publisher Mem., SIAE. *Current Management:* Pitura Freska; Skardy; Farenheit 451; Fabio Furian. *Address:* Via Marovich, 5–30030 Mestre Venezia, Italy.

TREWAVAS, Peter; b. 15 Jan. 1959, Middlesbrough, Cleveland, England. Musician (bass). *Career:* Member, The Metros; Bassist, UK progressive rock group Marillion, 1982–; Tours, UK; Europe; North America; Concerts include: Theakston Festival, 1982; Reading Festival, 1982, 1983; Nostell Priory Festival, 1982, 1984; Glastonbury Festival, 1983; Support to Rush, New York's Radio City Music Hall, 1983; Milton Keynes Bowl, 1984; Monsters of Rock Festival, Castle Donington, 1985; Colombian Volcano Appeal Concert, 1986; Welcome To The Garden Party, 1986. *Recordings:* Albums: Script For A Jester's Tear, 1983; Fugazi, 1984; Real To Reel, 1984; Misplaced Childhood, 1985; Brief Encounter, 1986; Clutching At Straws, 1987; B-Sides Themselves, 1988; The Thieving Magpie, 1988; Holidays In Eden, 1991; A Singles Collection 1982–92, 1992; Brave, 1994; Afraid of Sunlight, 1995; Made Again, 1996; This Strange Engine, 1997; Radiation, 1998; Marillion.com, 1999; Anorak In The UK Live, 2002; with Transatlantic: Smpte, 2000; Singles include: Market Square Heroes, 1982; He Knows You Know, 1983; Garden Party, 1983; Punch and Judy, 1984; Assassing, 1984; Kayleigh (No. 2, UK), 1985; Lavender, 1985; Heart of Lothian, 1985; Incommunicado, 1987; Sugar Mice, 1987; Warm Wet Circles, 1987; Freaks, 1988; Hooks In You, 1989; Uninvited Guest, 1989; Easter, 1990; Cover My Eyes (Pain and Heaven), 1991; No One Can, 1991; Dry Land, 1991; Sympathy, 1992. *Current Management:* Hit and Run Music Ltd, 30 Ives St, London SW3 2ND, England.

TRIBAL UNDERGROUND. See: PILGREM, Rennie.

TRIBBLE, (Brian Evans); b. 20 March 1953, Coventry, England. Musician (bass, keyboards, guitar); Vocalist. Divorced, 5 s., 1 d. *Career:* Partner, Horizon Recording Studios; Extensive session work, touring with rock bands in Europe and the USA; Member, rock, reggae and jazz outfits in West Indies; Recording for numerous labels; Advertising and video soundtrack work; Member, Chainsaw; Rumrunners; The Trial; Owner/Manager, STI/Pro-Audio; Graphic design work, arrangements, session work; Playing, programming and production of samples for dance producers; Promoter for new artists; Audio producer. *Compositions include:* The Last Great Bank Raid; The Hellpits of Nightfang; City Life; Accident Victim; Rock 'n' Roll Gambler; Werewolf; And many more as co-composer with other musicians. *Recordings include:* Police and Politicians; Devil's Daughter; Bolt From The Black; Pissed Again; Twisted and Dysfunktional; And many more with other artists/compilations.

TRICKY, (Adrian Thaws); b. Bristol, England. Rap Artiste; Songwriter. *Career:* Rapper, Wild Bunch; Solo artiste with singer Martina; Regular collaborations as singer/writer with Massive Attack; Leader, recording project Nearly God (duets with Björk, Alison Moyet, Terry Hall, Neneh Cherry), 1996; Concerts include: T In The Park Festival, Glasgow, 1995; Reading Festival, 1995. *Recordings:* Single: Overcome, Wild Bunch; Solo singles: Aftermath, 1993; Ponderosa, 1994; Overcome, 1995; Black Steel, 1995; The Hell EP, 1995; Pumpkin, 1995; Grassroots, 1996; Poems, 1996; Makes Me Wanna Die, 1997; 6 Minutes, 1998; For Real, 1999; Albums: with Massive Attack: Blue Lines, 1991; Protection, 1995; Solo albums: Maxinquaye (No. 1, UK), 1995; Nearly God, 1996; Pre-Millennium Tension, 1996; Angels with Dirty Faces, 1998; Juxtapose, 1999; BlowBack, 2001. *Honours:* Face Magazine, Best Album of the Year, Blue Lines, 1991; Gold disc, Maxinquaye, 1995; Q Award, Best Producer, 1995. *Current Management:* Fruit Management. *Address:* Unit 104, Saga Centre, 326 Kensal Rd, London W10 5BZ, England.

TRITT, Travis; b. 9 Feb. 1963, Maretta, Georgia, USA. Country Vocalist; Songwriter. m. Theresa, 12 April 1997. *Career:* Recording artiste, 1990–; Recorded, toured with Marty Stuart, included No-Hats Tour. *Compositions include:* Here's A Quarter (Call Someone Who Cares); Help Me Hold On, 1990; Anymore, 1991; Tell Me I Was Dreaming, 1994; Ten Feet Tall and Bulletproof, 1994; More Than You'll Ever Know, 1995. *Recordings include:* Anymore; Lord Have Mercy On The Working Man; Albums: Country Club, 1990; It's All About To Change, 1991; T-R-O-U-B-L-E, 1992; A Travis Tritt Christmas: Loving Time of Year, 1992; Rhythm, Country and Blues; The Restless Kind; Greatest Hits – From The Beginning, 1995; No More Looking Over My Shoulder, 1998; Down The Road I Go, 2000; The Lovin' Side, 2002. *Publications:* Ten Feet Tall and Bulletproof, autobiography, 1992. *Honours:* CMA Horizon Award, 1991; Grammy Award, 1992. *Current Management:* Falcon Goodman Management. *Address:* 1012 16th Ave S, Nashville, TN 37212, USA.

TROCMÉ, Elisa Andréa; b. 21 Aug. 1955, Pennsylvania, USA. Musician (counter-bass, Bb clarinets, other wind instruments). 2 s., 1 d. *Education:* History, French popular arts and traditions, EHESS, Paris; Private music lessons, workshops with B Vitet; Tamia; Steve Lacy; Michel Fano; George Benjamin; Robert Aitken; Georges Aperghis; Toru Takemitsu; Barre Phillips. *Career:* Instrument making with B Vitet; Music Education Program with P Maretan, Paris, 1978; Irving Plaza/BCBG, New York, 1980; Le Grand Rex; New Morning; Centre Georges Pompidou; Musée d'Art Moderne; Grand Palais dance, music, plastic arts creations; Improvised music and dance encounters, Toulouse, 1992–; Art Wars, La Mama, Theater, New York, 1980; Cinema de Minuit, directed by Patricia Bardon, ProdA2, Paris, 1984; The Weapons of The Spirits, directed by Pierre Sauvage (prize-winning documentary, Cannes, 1987; 666, Julie West video-dance production, S Rougier, Paris, 1985. *Publications:* Clarinette magazine; Translations for Télérama; L'Événement du Jeudi; L'Humanité; Melody Maker. *Honours:* Oscar de Mécémat (P Mariétam). *Membership:* ESEM (Euro Semionar of Ethnomusicology). *Current Management:* Christianne Bories. *Address:* 282 Route de Seysses, 31100 Toulouse, France.

TROTT, Milton; b. 4 Nov. 1958, Adelaide, South Australia. Television and Film Composer; Musician (keyboards); Creative Consultant. *Education:* Classical Piano, Violin, Cello, Guitar, Drums, Flute. *Career:* Keyboard Player/ Songwriter/Producer; Numerous local bands session too; Member, Prestigious Arts Education, 1982; Team (SA Govt), Music/Multimedia, 1985; Winner, Pot Luck, TV Talent Quest, 1989; Mr Music, Theatrespots, 1986; Musician, Magick Circus, Soundtracks TV Documentaries, 1988. *Compositions:* Sugar is Sweet, 1982; The Greens, 1984; H2O, 1983. *Recordings:* Music CD, Aurora Australis, 1995. *Honours:* Young Composers Award, 1983. *Membership:* Australian Screen Composers Asscn; Australian Performing Right Asscn. *Address:* Post Office Aldgate, SA 5154, Australia.

TROUT, Walter Cooper; b. 6 March 1951, Atlantic City, New Jersey, USA. Musician (guitar, harmonica, trumpet). m. Marie Braendgaard, 3 s. *Education:* College, 1 year; Classical trumpet, 7 years. *Career:* Played with John Lee Hooker, Big Mama Thornton, Joe Tex, Pee Wee Crayton, 1979–80; Lead guitarist, harmonica, Canned Heat, 1984–89; Lead guitar, John Mayall's Bluesbreakers, 1984–89; Formed the Walter Trout Band, 1989; Name change to Walter Trout and the Radicals, 1998. *Recordings:* With Canned Heat: The Boogie Assault, 1981; Heat Brothers '84, 1984; John Mayall's Bluesbreakers: Behind The Iron Curtain, 1985; The Power of The Blues, 1987; Chicago Line, 1988; Life In The Jungle, 1992; Walter Trout Band: Life In The Jungle, 1989; Prisoner of a Dream, 1990; The Love That We Once Knew, 1990; No More Fish-Jokes Live, 1992; Radio Records, 1992; Transistion, 1992; Motivation of Love, 1992; No More Fish-Jokes Live, 1992; Tremble, 1994; Still Got The Blues, 1994; Tellin' Stories, 1994; Breaking The Rules, 1995; Where Blues Meets Rock, 1995; Jeffology (tribute to Jeff Beck), 1995; Tribute to Stevie (tribute to Stevie Ray Vaughan), 1996; Walter Trout, 1998; Livin' Everyday, 1999; Live Trout, 2000; Go The Distance, 2001; Blue Christmas, 2001. Blues Revue, cover story, October 2000. *Honours:* BBC Listeners' Poll, All Time

Greatest Guitarists 1993, voted # 6 of 20; Guitarist of the Year, Best Independent Rock Album, LA Music Awards; Best Blues/R&B Performer, Orange County. *Membership:* ASCAP. *Current Management:* Fish-Net Productions Inc, 4933 W Craig Rd, Suite 228, Las Vegas, NV 89130, USA. *Address:* PO Box 246, Huntington Beach, CA 92648, USA.

TROW, Zane Roderick; b. 25 Jan. 1956, London, England. Composer; Preformer; Artistic Dir. *Career:* Composer in Residence, Civilian Theatre; Composer, Performer, Common Stock Theatre Company; Artistic director, Nextwave Festival; Chairman, Contemporary Music Events Company. *Compositions:* The Wolves; Hot Time; Dream Mamma. *Recordings:* Big River. *Honours:* Numerous Grants, Australian Council for the Arts. *Membership:* Actors Equity; PRS. *Address:* Lot 15, Clifton Dr., North Maclean, Queensland 4280, Australia.

TROWER, Robin; b. 9 March 1945, Southend, Essex, England. Musician (guitar). *Career:* Founder member, The Paramounts, 1962–66; Founder member, Procul Harum, 1967–71; Solo artiste, 1971–; Formed Jude; Miami Founder, Robin Trower Band; Founder, band BLT, 1981; Pop Festival, 1968; Palm Springs Pop Festival, 1969; Toronto Rock Festival, 1969; Atlantic City Pop Festival, 1969; Isle of Wight Festival, 1970. *Recordings:* Albums with Procul Harum: Procul Harum, 1967; Shine On Brightly, 1968; A Salty Dog, 1969; Home, 1970; Solo: Twice Removed From Yesterday, 1973; Bridge of Sighs, 1974; For Earth Below, 1975; Robin Trower Live, 1976; Long Misty Days, 1976; In City Dreams, 1977; Caravan To Midnight, 1978; Victims of The Fury, 1980; Back It Up, 1983; Beyond The Mist, 1985; Passion, 1987; Portfolio, 1987; Take What You Need, 1988; No Stopping Anytime, 1989; In the Line of Fire, 1990; 20th Century Blues, 1994; New Haven 1977; King Biscuit Flower Hour, 1996; Someday Blues, 1997; Go My Way, 2000. *Current Management:* Stardust Management, 4600 Franklin Ave, Los Angeles, CA 90027, USA.

TRUBETSKY, Tonu (Prince); b. 24 April 1963, Revala, Tallinn, Estonia. Vocalist; Composer; Poet; Writer; Actor; Video Dir. m. Anu Trubetsky, 28 May 1988, 1 s., 2 d. *Education:* Diver, Engineer forces; Rock 'n' Roll High School. *Career:* Lead singer, Vennaskond, 1984–; Lead singer, Felis Ultramarinus, 1986; Prince Trubetsky and JMKE, 1986; The Un Concern, 1988; Solo artist, 1993; Business venture: Vennaskond Ltd; Films: Soda (Waw), 1987; Hysteria (Hysterics), 1993; Videos with Vennaskond: Elagu Proudhon! (Long Live Proudhon!), 1994; Riga My Love, 1995. *Recordings:* with Vennaskond: Ltn Schmidt'i Pojad (The Sons of Lieutenant Schmidt), 1991; Girl In Black, 1991; Rockpiraadid (The Rock Pirates), 1992; Usk. Lootus. Armastus (Faith. Hope. Love), 1993; Vaenlane Ei Maga (The Enemy Is Not Sleeping), 1995; Voluri Tagasitulek (Return of the Wizard), 1994; Inglid Ja Kangelased (Angels and Heroes), 1995. *Publications:* Books: Pogo, 1989; Inglid Ja Kanglased (Angels and Heroes), 1992; Anarhia (Anarchy), 1994; Daam Sinises (Lady In Blue), 1994. *Honours:* Levijaagup, 1990; 2 Gold records, 1993. *Address:* Vennaskond, PO Box 2225, 0035 Tallinn, Estonia.

TRUE, Roger; b. 2 June, Greensboro, NC, USA. Country Vocalist; Musician (guitar). *Career:* City Stage Celebration; The Lexington Barbecue Festival; Summerfield Founder's Day Celebration; Clubs: The Blind Tiger; Kilroy's; Playing, Piedmont Triad; International Country Music Fan Fair, Nashville; Starred and sang in motion picture, The Dam. *Recordings:* Crazy Arms; There Stands the Glass; Your Cheatin' Heart; Walk Through This World With Me; Tonight the Bottle Let Me Down; El Paso; Before the Next Teardrop Falls; Good Hearted Woman; Take This Job and Shove It; Don't Rock the Jukebox; We'll Burn that Bridge; Friends in Low Places, many more. *Honours:* Most Promising Vocal of Tomorrow Third Place, North Carolina Country Music Assocation, 1993; NCCMA Award Winner. *Membership:* BMI; ASCAP. *Current Management:* Webb Pierce Enterprises, 1521 Clayton Ave, Nashville, TN 37217, USA.

TRUESDALE, Tommy; b. 17 Nov. 1947, Annbank, Ayr, Scotland. Vocalist; Entertainer; Actor; Radio Presenter. m. Marjory, 9 Feb. 1972. *Career:* Television appearances: One Night Stand, Scottish TV, 1965; The Best Disco In Town, Scottish TV, 1979; The Singer and the Song, BBC, 1981; Various television and radio interviews; British headliner, Great Scottish Country Music Festival, Wonderwestworld, Ayr, 1994; Radio presenter, prod., Radio West. *Recordings:* Albums: C'mon Everybody, 1979; Sings Country, 1985; The Best of T. T. Album, 1990; A Tree In The Meadow, 1993; Favourites, with The Sundowners, 1998; Tommy Truesdale Favourites, 2000; Single: The United Men of Ayr, 2000. *Contributions to:* Columnist, Country Music News and Roots Magazine, Ayrshire World Newspaper. *Honours:* Scottish Country Music Fellowship Award, Top Male Vocalist, 1989, 1990. *Membership:* British Country Music Asscn. *Address:* 3 McColgan Pl., Ayr KA8 9PU, Scotland.

TRUJILLO, Robert; Musician (bass). *Career:* Member, Suicidal Tendencies; Numerous live dates in USA; Member, side project, Infectious Grooves, with Mike Muir and other guest musicians; Ozzy Osbourne featured as guest on debut album; Support slot to Blizzard of Oz No More Tears tour. *Recordings:* With Suicidal Tendencies: Suicidal Tendencies, 1983; Join the Army, 1987; How Will I Laugh Tomorrow When I Can't Even Smile Today, 1988; Controlled by Hatred, 1989; Lights, Camera, Revolution, 1990; F.N.G., compilation, 1992; The Art of Rebellion, 1992; Still Cyco After All These Years, 1993; Suicidal for Life, 1994; Prime Cuts, 1997; Friends and Family, compilation, 1998; Six the Hard Way, EP, 1998; FreeDumb, 1999; With Infectious Grooves: The Plague that Makes Your Booty Move, 1991; Sarsippius' Ark, 1993; Groove Family Cyco, 1994; Mas Borracho, 2000.

TRUSSARDI, Louis; b. 6 June 1938, Clichy, France. Musician (contrebass). m. Martine Teyssier, 31 Jan. 1972, 3 s. *Education:* 2 years, Conservatory de Versailles. *Career:* Played with: Chet Baker; Kenny Clarke; Dizzy Gillespie; Stéphane Grappelli; 'Philly' Joe Jones; Art Taylor; Louis Hayse; Richie Cole; Teddy Edwards; Frank Morgan; Milt Jackson; Art Simmons; Dusco Boy Kovic. *Recordings:* Solo album: Vendredi 14; Also recorded with: Maurice Vander; 'Philly' Joe Jones; Kenny Clarke; Stéphane Grappelli; Chet Baker. *Membership:* SACEM. *Address:* 3 rue d'Ablis, 78660 Prunay en Yvelines, France.

TSE, Nicholas, (Nicholas Tse Ting Fung); b. 29 Aug. 1980, Hong Kong. Vocalist; Actor. *Education:* Professional vocal training in Japan, 1996. *Career:* Son of famous actor parents Patrick Tse Yin and Deborah Lai; Moved with family to Vancouver, Canada, aged 7; Teen-pop star and high profile actor; Film roles include: Young and Dangerous – The Prequel, 1998; Gen-X Cops, 1999; Time and Tide, 2000; Master Q, 2001; Co-directed: Heroes In Love, 2001; Records in Mandarin and Cantonese languages. *Recordings:* Albums: My Attitude, Fun, 1997; Horizons, Music Video Karaoke, 1998; Believe, Grateful For Your Love, Most Wanted, 1999; Zero Distance, Understand, 20 Twenty, Viva, Viva Live, 2000; Senses, Jade Butterfly, 2001. *Honours:* Hong Kong Film Award, Best New Actor, 1999; Numerous local awards for music; World Music Award, 2002. *Address:* c/o Fitto Entertainment Co Ltd, 28/F Emperor Group Centre, 288 Hennessy Rd, Wanchai, Hong Kong.

TSENOVA, Julia; b. 30 July 1948, Sofia, Bulgaria. Composer; Musician (piano). m. Stefan Sandulov, 1 d. *Education:* Piano, Musical Academy in Sofia, 1972; Composition, 1974; Associated Professor Dean, Department of Pop and Jazz Music, 1997. *Career:* Pianist and Composer. *Compositions:* Symphony; Movement for Orchestra; Cantus Firmus a Due; That Means all Gods. *Honours:* Many awards for chamber, choir and children's music. *Membership:* Union of Bulgarian Composers; International Society for Contemporary Music. *Address:* Vassil Levski 4, 1000 Sofia, Bulgaria.

TSHMALA, Mufubela; b. 11 March 1957, Ilebok Kasai Occidental, Congo. Researcher; Musician (flute, guitar); Vocalist; Composer. m. Petronie Mbombo Malumba, 1988, 4 s., 3 d. *Education:* Graduated, Administration and Management of Cultural Enterprises. *Career:* Composed music for film, La Pipe, 1983; Composed jingles for African Radio, 1983; Numerous TV and radio appearances, and work as Producer; Puppeteer and drag artist; Played in nightclubs and hotels, Kinshasa; Flautist; Teacher of Music; Researcher into traditional and modern mixing techniques; Guitarist, Flautist and Singer in group, Msumuenu. *Compositions:* Music for Le Refuge; Music for Le Crapeaud Chez Ses Beaux Parents; Revue Noire à Kinshasa No 21, 1996. *Recordings:* Naza Balado Te, 1982; Many contributions with various groups. *Publications:* La Vie de Robert le Diable, lyric drama, Colmar, France, 1984. *Honours:* First Prize, Orchestration, Festival of Central African Music, 1982; Festpam, 1996; Brazzaville Festijazz, Kinshasa, 1999. *Membership:* Asscn des Musiques de Recherche du Congo. *Address:* PO Box 14110, Kinshasa, Africa.

TSISKARIDZE, Kakha; b. 4 June 1976, Batumi, Republic of Georgia. Musician (drums, piano, percussion); Vocalist. *Education:* Batumi Musical College. *Career:* Several Concerts with S Pavliashvili on the major stages of Georgia, Russia, Miami, USA. *Compositions:* Several, Jazz, Soul, Funk, AC Jazz. *Recordings:* debut album, Is Erti (The One), 1999. *Honours:* The Best Drummer of the Jazz Music Festival, Batumi, 1992; Drummer of the Year, Margarette Festival, 1996; Best Drummer of the Year (Georgia), 1996. *Membership:* Dianaland Club, Batumi. *Address:* Gincharadzo St N 14, 384515 Batumi, Republic of Georgia.

TSUI, Trix Ko-Chuan; b. 20 Oct. 1953, Taipei, China (Taiwan). Musician (guitar) Concert Promoter; DJ. m. Farie Hsiu-Ching Le, 1 Dec. 1979, 1 d. *Education:* Graduate, World College of Journalism and Communication. *Career:* Concert Promoter, Stage Manager: Chick Corea's Acoustic and Electric Band; Lee Ritnour; Brecker Brothers; Peabo Bryson and Patti Austin; Stage Manager: INXS; B. B. King; Hard Rock Cafe, Taipei, 1992–94; Leader, guitarist: Rock City Band, 1971–80; Diplomats, 1980–93; Now house band of Hard Rock Cafe, Taipei, Name changed back to Rock City Band, 1994–95; Radio DJ, BBC, TBC; Technical Director, Gibson and Digitech; Musical Cosultant, Taipei Communicating Arts (from the system of MIT). *Recordings:* Producer debut album by Miss Jade Lee: Hermits; Blindman Pop Group: Eden; Welfare Foundation's tribute single and collection of: International Family Years. *Publications:* Columnist for: Non-Classical Music Magazine; Audio and CD Shopper; Liberty Time newspaper. *Membership:* Musical Mountain Communication. *Address:* 3F No. 16, Alley 88, Sec 2, Pao-Fu Rd, Yung-Ho, Taipei, China (Taiwan).

TUCKER, David; b. 23 July 1960, Manchester. Musician. *Education:* General music theory, composing and synchronising music for film and video.

Career: Guitarist, New Wave pop groups; Improvising guitarist, Allan Tomlinson Trio, Scatter, The Guided Muscle; Radio appearances; Principal conductor for the London Improvisers Orchestra. *Recordings:* Mellatron; The Fall.

TUCKER, Maureen; b. 1945, New Jersey, USA. Musician (drums). *Career:* Musician, Velvet Underground, 1965–71; Solo artiste, 1982–; Residency, Café Bizarre; House band, Andy Warhol's Factory arts collective, New York; Member, Warhol's multimedia show, The Exploding Plastic Inevitable, 1966; Concerts include: Montréal World Fair, Canada, 1967; Reunions with Velvet Underground, France, 1990; Wembley, London, 1993. *Recordings:* with The Velvet Underground: The Velvet Underground and Nico, 1967; White Light, White Heat, 1968; The Velvet Underground, 1969; Loaded, 1970; VU, 1985; Peel Slowly And See, 1993; The Quine Tapes, 2001; Various compilations and collections; Solo albums: Playing Possum, 1982; Moejadkatebarry, 1987; Life In Exile After Abdication, 1989; I Spent A Week There The Other Night, 1991; Dogs Under Stress, 1994. *Honours:* Inducted into Rock 'n' Roll Hall of Fame (with Velvet Underground), 1996.

TUCKER, Paul; b. 1969, Cambridge, England. Musician; Songwriter. *Education:* Newcastle University. *Career:* Member, The Lighthouse Family, 1994–; Television includes: Top of the Pops. *Recordings:* Album: Ocean Drive, 1995; Postcards from Heaven, 1997; Whatever Gets You Through The Day, 2001; Singles: Lifted, 1995; Ocean Drive (used for film soundtrack Jack and Sarah), 1995; High, 1997; Out Of Space, 1998; Free/One, 2001. *Current Management:* Kitchenware, 7 The Stables, St Thomas St, Newcastle-Upon-Tyne, Tyne and Wear NE1 4LE, England.

TUCKER, Tanya; b. 10 Oct. 1958, Seminole, Texas, USA. Country Vocalist. *Career:* Singing at country fairs as a teenager; Recording artist, 1972–; Regular concerts include: Grand Ole Opry; Film appearance: Jeremiah Johnson (with Robert Redford). *Compositions include:* Save Me; Leave Them Boys Alone (co-writer with Hank Williams Jr). *Recordings:* Hits include: Delta Dawn; Jamestown Ferry; What's Your Mama's Name?; Lizzie and The Rainman; San Antonio Stroll; Here's Some Love; I Won't Take Less Than Your Love (with Paul Davis and Paul Overstreet); Strong Enough To Bend; If It Didn't Come Easy; Dream Lover (duet with Glen Campbell); Albums: Delta Dawn, 1972; What's Your Mama's Name?, 1973; Would You Lay With Me, 1974; Lovin' and Learnin', 1975; Tanya Tucker, 1975; Here's Some Love, 1976; You Are So Beautiful, 1977; Ridin' Rainbows, 1977; TNT, 1978; Tear Me Apart, 1979; Dreamlovers, 1980; Should I Do It?, 1981; Changes, 1982; Live, 1982; Love Me Like You Used To, 1987; Strong Enough To Bend, 1988; Tennessee Woman, 1990; Greatest Hits – Encore, 1990; What Do I Do With Me, 1991; Lizzie and The Rainman, 1992; Hits, 1992; Can't Run From Yourself, 1992; Fire To Fire, 1995 Complicated, 1997; 20 Greatest Hits, 2000; Country Classics, 2001; featured on Biggest Country Duets of the 80s, 1998; Paul Davis: Sweet Life His Greatest Hit Single, 1999. *Honours:* CMA Female Vocalist of Year, 1991. *Address:* c/o Tanya Tucker Inc, 109 Westpark Dr., Suite 400, Brentwood, TN 37027–5032, USA.

TUDOR-POLE, Edward; b. 6 Dec. 1956, London, England. 1 s. *Education:* Yardley Court Tonbridge, KESW, RADA. *Career:* Touring and recording with own band, Tenpole Tudor; Acting career: Films include: the Great Rock and Roll Swindle; Absolute Beginners; Sid and Nancy; Kull the Conqueror; Theatre: The Admirable Crichton; The Rocky Horror Show; The Deep Blue Sea; TV: Top of the Pops; presented The Crystal Maze. *Compositions:* Recorded: Who Killed Bambi (Sex Pistols); Swords of 1000 Men; Throwing the Baby Out with the Bathwater; Wunderbar; Three Bells in a Row; Ted Ain't Dead; Compilation: Swords Of A Thousand Men, 2001; To Her Majesty, 2002; He's Got a Moustache, 2002. *Honours:* Silver disc for Swords of 1000 Men, 1981. *Address:* c/o Jane Brand, ICM, 76 Oxford St, London W1N 0AX, England.

TULLY, Nigel; b. 22 July 1943, Barnsley, Yorkshire, England. Bandleader; Vocalist; Musician (guitar, saxophone). m. Prue Lyell, 29 Sept. 1978, 1 s., 1 d. *Education:* MA, University of Oxford; Private tuition with Pat Crumly, saxophone. *Career:* Bandleader, The Dark Blues, 1962–; Completed 3,500 live concerts, 1998; Highlights include 21st and 40th birthday parties for HRH Prince Charles at Buckingham Palace. *Recordings:* Overdue, 1983; Live At Ashdown, 1985; 25 and Going For Gold, 1988; Midsummer Dance, 1992. *Membership:* Fellow, British Computer Society; Liveryman, Worshipful Company of Musicians. *Current Management:* Dark Blues Management Ltd. *Address:* 30 Stamford Brook Rd, London W6 0XH, England.

TUREK, Jan; b. 19 Oct. 1957, Most, Czech Republic. Composer. m. Hana Pegrímková, 26 June 1982, 1 s., 1 d. *Education:* University of Economics; Private study of classical guitar. *Career:* More than 60 scenic music compositions for drama and puppet shows including realization. *Compositions:* There Was a Town in Prairie, 1994; The House with 7 Circles, 1995; The Royal Seconds, 1996; Kiss the Aunt, 1999; The Tiger, 1999; Absurd Person Singular, 2000; Beauty and the Beast (musical), 2000; Am and Ea, 2001; Legend of Maribyla, 2001; Don't Drink the Water, 2002. *Recordings:* Fairy Tales of Mr Fairy-Tale, 1995; Dilia, Prague. *Current Management:* F

Agency, Zizkova 1616, 434 01 Most, Czech Republic. *Address:* Hasicska 147, 434 01 Most-Vtelno, Czech Republic. *E-mail:* turekvtelno@volny.cz.

TURNER, Carl; b. 2 June 1969, Wolverhampton, England. Writer; Prod; Musician (keyboards). *Education:* 2 years OND, Graphic Design, Stafford College; 2 years HND, Wolverhampton College. *Career:* Three major British tours; Two major US tours; One major European tour; Six appearances, Top of the Pops; Other television appearances: Hangar 17; The Big Breakfast; The Beat; The Chart Show. *Recordings:* Such A Feeling, 1991; Playing With Knives (No. .4, UK); 1992; I'm Gonna Get You (No. 3, UK), 1992; Took My Love, 1993; Southern Harmoneers, He'll Make a Way, 1995; Do I, Gifted, 1997. *Honours:* Music Week Award, Top Dance Single, 1991. *Membership:* Musicians' Union; PRS. *Current Management:* Antony Johnson. *Address:* BGA, Unit 1B, Hollins Business Centre, Rowley St, Stafford ST16 3RH, England.

TURNER, Geraldine Gail; b. 23 June 1950, Brisbane, Australia. Actress; Vocalist. m. Brian Castles-Onion, 31 Dec. 1993. *Education:* Diploma in Education, Queensland; Singing, Queensland Conservatoire, two years; Classical ballet training, ten years. *Career:* Internationally renowned in cabaret and as Sondheim interpreter; Performed in Australia, England, Canada, USA and Africa; Starred in musicals: Oliver!; Chicago; Anything Goes; Company; Sweeney Todd; A Little Night Music; Into The Woods; Ned Kelly; Guys and Dolls; Plays: Don's Party; Present Laughter; Summer of The Seventeenth Doll; Operas and operettas: La Belle Helénè; HMS Pinafore; The Mikado; Film appearances: Careful He Might Hear You; Summerfield; Numerous television appearances. *Recordings:* The Stephen Sondheim Song Book; Torch Songs – and Some Not So Tortous; Once In A Blue Moon; Gala Night; One Life To Live; When We Met; Cast albums include: Anything Goes; Chicago. *Honours:* Order of Australia (OAM), 1988; Green Room Awards, for Oliver!, 1984, and Anything Goes, 1989; Mo Awards, for Sweeney Todd, 1988, and Anything Goes, 1989. *Membership:* Federal President, Australian Actors' Equity, four years. *Current Management:* Robyn Gardiner Management, 397 Riley St, Surry Hills, NSW 2010, Australia.

TURNER, Howard; b. 24 Feb. 1959, Thornage, Holt, England. Prod; Engineer; Musician (guitar, vocals); Songwriter; Studio Designer. *Education:* BA Hons, UEA, Norwich; PGCE, UEA, Norwich. *Career:* Began Raven Recording as recording studio, 1984; Producer, Engineer for Pete DeFreitas (Echo and The Bunnymen) on Sex Gods project; Developed reputation as freelance Indie/Rock producer and engineer; Sold studios, 1991; Acquired interest in Swamp Studios, 1992; Created Raven Recording Services and Studio Wizard Organization (studio design company); Major studio installations include: GWBB (London); The Cutting Rooms (Manchester); The Temple (Malta); Numerous television and radio appearances; Sold Swamp Studios, 1998; New studios under construction; Extending into corporate training and consultancy (studio technique and design). *Recordings:* 4 albums as musician under name The Nivens; As producer/engineer, includes albums by: Jacob's Mouse; Red Harvest; Jazz Butcher; Perfect Disaster; The Pollen; Bad Manners; Close Lobsters; Girlschool; Eden; Green On Red; Other recordings for Captain Sensible and The Damned; New artists: Crome Yellow; New album, Nivens. *Membership:* APRS; MPG; PRS; MCPS. *Current Management:* Studio Wizard, County School, Dereham, Norfolk NR20 5LE, England.

TURNER, Ike (Izear), Jr; b. 5 Nov. 1931, Clarksdale, Mississippi, USA. Vocalist; Songwriter; Musician (guitar). m. Tina Turner (Annie Mae Bullock), 1958, divorced 1978. *Career:* Founder, Kings of Rhythm band; Session guitarist, on recordings by B. B. King; Howlin' Wolf; Johnny Ace; Duo, Ike and Tina Turner, 1960–78; One of most popular acts on R&B tour circuit, 1960s; Concerts include: with Rolling Stones, 1966; Newport 69 Festival, 1969; Support to Rolling Stones, US tour, 1969; Built Bolic Sound Recording Studio, 1970. *Recordings:* Albums: with Ike and Tina Turner: Live! The Ike and Tina Turner Show, 1965; River Deep, Mountain High, 1966; In Person, 1969; Outa Season, 1969; The Hunter, 1969; Come Together, 1970; Workin' Together, 1971; Live At Carnegie Hall, 1971; 'Nuff Said, 1970; Feel Good, 1972; Nutbush City Limits, 1974; Solo: My Confessions, 1988; My Blues Country, 1997; Here And Now, 2001; The Sun Sessions, 2001; Singles include: with Kings of Rhythm: Rocket 88, 1951; with Ike and Tina Turner: It's Going To Work Out Fine, 1961; River Deep Mountain High, 1966; A Love Like Yours, 1966; I Want To Take You Higher, 1970; Proud Mary, 1971; Nutbush City Limits, 1973; Baby Get It On, 1975. *Honours:* Rocket 88 widely credited as first rock 'n' roll record; Rock and Roll Hall of Fame, with Tina Turner, 1991.

TURNER, Joe Lynn; b. USA. Vocalist. *Career:* Vocalist, rock groups: Fandango, 1977–80; Last Kiss, 1979; One Night Stand, 1979; Cadillac, 1980; Rainbow, 1980–85; Yngwie Malmsteen, 1987–89; Deep Purple, 1990–91; Also solo recording artiste. *Recordings:* Albums: 4 albums with Fandango, 1977–80; with Rainbow: Difficult To Cure, 1981; Best Of, 1981; Straight Between The Eyes, 1982; Bent Out of Shape, 1983; Finyl Vinyl, 1986; Hit singles include: I Surrender, 1981; Can't Happen Here, 1981; Stone Cold, 1982; Solo albums: Fandango, 1982; Rescue You, 1985; Nothing Changes, 1995; Under Cover, 1997; Hurry Up and Wait, 1999; with Yngwie Malmsteen: Odyssey, 1988;

Live In Leningrad, 1989; Heaven Tonight, 1999; with Deep Purple: Slaves and Masters, 1990. *Address:* c/o American Talent Group, 221 W 57th St, Eighth Floor, New York, NY 10019, USA.

TURNER, Juliet; b. 16 July 1973, Tummery, County Tyrone, Northern Ireland. Vocalist; Musician (guitar); Songwriter. *Education:* Trinity College, Dublin. *Career:* Began performing at university; Recorded first album in Scotland, 1996; Led to support slots for acts including: Tracy Chapman; Natalie Merchant; U2; Brian Kennedy; Second album sold 40,000 copies in Ireland; Collaboration with John Spillane on single Will We Be Brilliant Or What?; Signed to EastWest, 2000. *Recordings:* Let's Hear It For Pizza, 1996; Burn The Black Suit, 2000. *Current Management:* Nally Management, Derek Nally, 39, Silverstream Ave, Stameen, Drogheda, Co Louth, Ireland. *E-mail:* dereknally@oceanfree.net. *Website:* www.julietturner.com.

TURNER, Lee; b. Jacksonville, Florida, USA. Musician (piano); Composer; Arranger; Music Publisher. m. Dianne Gross, 3 s. *Education:* University of Florida; Southern Baptist Theological Seminary. *Career:* Professional pianist since high school; Studio work, Nashville and Jacksonville; Regular television and radio appearances, dances, shows and concerts; Accompanist and soloist; Appeared with The Dream Weavers, Ed Sullivan Show; Minister of music, 29 years; Director, choirs and groups, religious and secular; Owner, publishing company, TurnerSong, 1981–. *Compositions include:* Into The Night, The Dream Weavers. *Recordings include:* It's Almost Tomorrow, The Dream Weavers; Rhapsody in Stained Glass, solo piano; There's a Meetin' Here Tonight, musical; Make Every Day a Good Day!; I Love a Piano; I Still Love a Piano. *Honours:* Annual ASCAP Award, 1974–. *Membership:* ASCAP; AFofM. *Address:* 4263 San Jose Blvd, Jacksonville, FL 32207, USA. *Website:* www.turnersong.com.

TURNER, Nik; b. 26 Aug. 1940, Oxford, England. Musician (saxophone, flute); Vocalist; Composer; Arranger; Teacher. *Career:* Formed Hawkwind, 1969; Television and radio appearances: Top of the Pops, 1972; BBC Live John Peel at Paris Theatre, 1972; Tours of Europe, 1972–76; Left Hawkwind 1976; Formed Inner City Unit/Sphynx, 1976; Nik Turner's Fantastic All Stars, 1988; Nik Turner's Space Ritual, 1994; US tours 1994, 1995; Numerous radio appearances. *Recordings:* with Hawkwind: 8 albums, most recently Conscience Of Hawkwind, 2000; Numerous samplers; 6 singles include: Silver Machine (No. 1, UK), 1972; with Inner City Unit: 6 albums, 3 singles; with Sphynx: 1 album, 1978; with Nik Turner's Space Ritual: 5 albums, USA, video, 1994/95; with Nik Turner's Fantastic All Stars: Kubano Kickasso. *Membership:* Musicians' Union. *Current Management:* Money Talks Management. *Address:* Cadillac Ranch, Pencraig Uchaf, Cwm Bach, Whitland, Dyfed SA34 0DT, Wales.

TURNER, Roger; b. 3 Feb. 1946, Whitstable, Kent, England. Musician (drums, percussion). m. Sara Ljungberg, 24 July 1992, divorced, 1 d. *Education:* BA, English Literature, Philosophy, University of Sussex. *Career:* Tours: USA; Canada; Australia; Europe; Festival concerts from the Berlin Jazz Fest to Macao; BBC Midnight Oil; Television in Australia, France, UK. *Recordings:* I Have No Feelings, Annette Peacock; Ammo, Phil Minton; The Recedents; Solo: Blur Between; Mouth Full of Ecstasy, Phil Minton Quartet; Birthdays, with John Russell; In the Tradition, with Alan Silva and Johannes Bauer; Shot In The UK, with Steve Beresford. *Honours:* Arts Council of Great Britain, Bursary Awards, 1980–83. *Membership:* London Musicians' Collective. *Current Management:* Fabe/Koschik. *Address:* 34 Lancaster Rd, London W11 1QR, England.

TURNER, Scott; b. 23 Aug. 1931, Sydney, Nova Scotia, Canada. Prod; Writer; Publisher; Divorced, 1 s., 1 d. *Education:* BA, BSc, University of Dubuque, 1955; 1 year Graduate School, Texas Tech University. *Career:* Lead guitarist, writer for Tommy Sands and the Raiders, 1957–60; Guy Mitchell, 1960–61; Eddie Fisher, 1961–63; Joined writer and producer, A & M Records, 1963; General Manager, Central Songs, Hollywood; Executive Producer, Country division, Liberty and Imperial Records, 1964; Independent Producer for Slim Whitman, Del Reeves and Jimmy Clanton, 1976; Also worked with: Sandy Nelson; Artie Kane; Composer of over 350 recorded songs including co-written songs with many leading artists; Music Director for numerous television shows; Composer of many background tracks and songs in films. *Recordings:* Numerous songs recorded by various artists including: Roy Clark; Nilsson; Herb Alpert; Dean Martin; Tammy Wynette; Jimmy Dean; The Del Vikings; Skeets MacDonald; Gene Vincent, including: Shutters and Boards; Please Mr Music Man; Does He Love You Like I Do; She's My Baby. *Address:* 524 Doral Country Dr., Nashville, TN 37221, USA.

TURNER, Tina, (Annie Mae Bullock); b. 26 Nov. 1939, Brownsville, Tennessee, USA. Vocalist; Songwriter. m. Ike Turner, 1958, divorced 1978. *Career:* Member, Ike and Tina Turner, 1958–78; World-wide tours include: Support to Rolling Stones, British tour, 1966, US tour, 1969; European tour, 1971; Newport Festival, Solo artiste, 1978–; US tour, 1981; Support to Lionel Richie, British tour, 1984; Rock In Rio Festival, Brazil, 1985; Live Aid, Philadelphia, 1985; European tour, 1985; Prince's Trust Gala, London, 1986; World tours, 1987, 1990; Record 182,000 audience attend concert, Rio De Janeiro, 1988; First woman to play Palace of Versailles, France, 1990; Film appearances: Tommy, 1974; Mad Max – Beyond Thunderdome, 1985; Life story documented in film What's Love Got To Do With It?, 1992. *Compositions include:* Nutbush City Limits. *Recordings:* Albums with Ike Turner: Live! The Ike and Tina Turner Show, 1965; River Deep, Mountain High, 1966; Outa Season, 1969; The Hunter, 1969; Come Together, 1970; Workin' Together, 1971; Live At Carnegie Hall, 1971; 'Nuff Said, 1971; Feel Good, 1972; Nutbush City Limits, 1974; Solo albums: The Acid Queen, 1975; Private Dancer, 1984; Mad Max – Beyond The Thunderdome, 1985; Break Every Rule (No. 1 in nine countries), 1986; Live In Europe, 1988; Foreign Affair (No. 1, UK), 1989; Simply The Best, 1991; What's Love Got To With It (film soundtrack), 1993; Wildest Dreams, 1996; Dues Paid, 1999; Twenty Four Seven, 1999; Hit singles include: with Ike Turner: It's Gonna Work Out Fine, 1961; Poor Fool, 1962; River Deep, Mountain High, 1966; I Want To Take You Higher, 1970; Proud Mary, 1971; Nutbush City Limits, 1973; Solo: Let's Stay Together, 1983; What's Love Got To Do With It? (No. 1, USA), 1984; Better Be Good To Me, 1984; Private Dancer, 1984; We Don't Need Another Hero, theme for film Thunderdome (No. 2, USA), 1985; One of The Living, 1985; It's Only Love, with Bryan Adams, 1985; Typical Male (No. 2, USA), 1986; Two People, 1986; What You Get Is What You See, 1987; The Best, 1989; I Don't Wanna Lose You, 1989; Steamy Windows, 1990; Be Tender With Me Baby, 1990; It Takes Two, duet with Rod Stewart, 1990; Way of The World, 1991; I Don't Wanna Fight, 1993; Goldeneye (film theme), 1995; On Silent Wings, 1996; Missing You, 1996; In Your Wildest Dreams, 1996; When the Heartache is Over, 1999; Whatever You Need, 2000; Contributor, We Are The World, USA For Africa, 1985. *Publications:* I Tina (autobiography). *Honours:* Grammy Awards: Record of the Year; Song of the Year; Best Female Vocal Performance; Best Female Rock Vocal, 1985; American Music Awards: Favourite Soul/R&B Female Artist, and Video Artist, 1985; Best Female Pop/Rock Artist, 1986; MTV Music Video award, 1985; Star on Hollywood Walk of Fame, 1986; Rock and Roll Hall of Fame, with Ike Turner, 1991; World Music Award, Outstanding Contribution To The Music Industry, 1993. *Current Management:* Roger Davies Management, 15030 Ventura Blvd, Suite 772, Sherman Oaks, CA 91403, USA.

TUTUNJIAN, Nancy M; b. 7 Dec. 1959, Needham, Massachusetts, USA. Vocalist; Songwriter; Actress. *Education:* Associated degree in Business; 2 years college to learn to read music. *Career:* Regional theatre; Series of concerts sponsored by WNGN-FM, New York; Numerous festival, concert appearances all over USA; Guest on Jericho cable show; Power Hour cable show; Numerous phoned radio interviews, USA; Own record company, Paraclete Records. *Compositions include:* Numerous contemporary Christian songs (lyrics and music); Three one-act Biblical theatre pieces (book, lyrics and music). *Recordings include:* Songs For The Bridegroom, 1992; Christmas Glow, 1994. *Honours:* Trailblazers Award, International Airplay Asscn; Hon. Mention Certificate; Billboard Songwriting Contest. *Membership:* BMI as songwriter, publisher. *Current Management:* Paraclete Music Ministries. *Address:* PO Box 473, Watertown, MA 02272–0473, USA.

TWAIN, Shania; b. 28 Aug. 1965, Timmins, Ontario, Canada. Country Vocalist; Songwriter. m. Robert 'Mutt' Lange. *Career:* Regular television performances on CMT and TNN. *Compositions:* Songwriting partnership with Mutt Lange (husband). *Recordings:* Albums: Shania Twain, 1993; The Woman In Me, 1995; Come On Over, 1997; On The Way, 1999; Wild and Wicked, 2000; Complete Limelight Sessions, 2001; Singles: Any Man of Mine, 1995; You're Still The One, 1998; When, 1998; From This Moment On, 1998; That Don't Impress Me Much, 1998; Man I Feel Like A Woman, 1999; Don't Be Stupid, 2000. *Honours:* CMT Europe, Rising Video Star of the Year, 1993; Grammy Awards, Best Female Country Vocal Performance, Best Country Song, 2000; American Music Awards, Favorite Female Pop/Rock Artist, Favorite Female Country Artist, 2000. *Current Management:* Jon Landau Management, 40 W Elm St, Greenwich, CT 06830, USA.

TWEED, Karen; b. 27 May 1963, London. Musician (accordion); Composer. *Education:* BA, Leeds Polytechnic, 1985; Studied Under Lawry Eady and John Whelan). *Career:* Kathryn Tickell Band, until 1993; All Female Folk Band, The Poozies and Anglo Swedish Ensemble, Swap; May Morning, 2001. *Compositions:* Walking up in Wonderful Wark. *Recordings:* Chantoozies, 1993; Dansoozies, 1995; Infinite Blue, 1998; Fyace, 1997; Swap, 1997. *Membership:* MU; PAMRA; PRS. *Current Management:* Brass Tacks Agency, PO Box 1162, Sheffield S8 0JY, England.

TYAS, Michael; b. 21 June 1957, Durham City, England. Musician (bass, guitar, mandolin, dulcimer); Vocalist. m. Margaret Tyas, 26 Sept. 1992, 1 d.

Career: Worked in amateur folk groups in North East England; Professional musician, 1991–; Joined the Whisky Priests, 1989–95; Formed: The Wickermen, 1998; Solo career within folk roots music, 2000–; Toured 14 European countries; Appeared on Anglia and Tyne Tees TV, BBC Radio 1 and 2, and on national radio in Belgium, Holland and Germany. *Compositions:* Geronimo's Blues; The Scissorman; Leap of Faith; England My England. *Recordings:* 5 albums with The Whisky Priests including 1 live album; Lyricist for one recorded song, Here Come The Ranting Lads, Live!, 1999. *Address:* Chilton, County Durham, England.

TYLER, Bonnie; b. 8 June 1951, Skewen, Wales. Vocalist. m. Robert Sullivan, 14 July 1973. *Career:* Lead vocalist, local bands; Solo artiste, 1976–; First solo female artist to enter UK album charts at No. 1. *Recordings:* Lost In France, 1976; It's A Heartache, 1978; Natural Force, 1978; Faster Than The Speed of Night, 1983; Total Eclipse of The Heart, 1983; Holding Out For A Hero, 1985; Secret Dreams, 1986; Hide Your Heart, 1987; Bitterblue, 1991; The Best Of, 1993; Free Spirit, 1996; All In One Voice, 1998; Greatest Hits, 2001; Also recorded with: Shakin Stevens; Steve Hackett; Rick Derringer; Mike Oldfield; Rick Wakeman; Nelson Miranda & Rochester. *Honours:* Winner, Yamaha World Song Contest, 1978; Best Female Vocalist, Echo, 1994; Variety Club of Great Britain, 1984. *Current Management:* David Aspden Management. *E-mail:* d.aspden@virgin.net.

TYLER, Stephen, (Stephen Tallarico); b. 26 March 1948, New York, USA. Vocalist; Musician (harmonica). *Career:* Singer, US rock band Aerosmith, 1970–; Concerts include: Support to the Kinks, Mott The Hoople, 1974; Schaefer Music Festival, New York, 1975; Reading Rock Festival, 1977; California Jam Festival II, 1978; Texas World Music Festival, 1978; Appearance as the Future Villain Band in film Sgt Pepper's Lonely Hearts Club Band, 1978; California Music Festival, with Van Halen, Cheap Trick, Ted Nugent, 1979; World Series of Rock with Journey, Ted Nugent, Thin Lizzy, 1979; Monsters of Rock Festival, Castle Donington, 1990; Television includes: MTV 10th anniversary special, ABC TV, 1991; Saturday Night Live, NBC TV, 1993. *Recordings:* Albums: Aerosmith, 1973; Toys In The Attic, 1975; Get Your Wings, 1975; Rocks, 1976; Draw The Line, 1978; Night In The Ruts, 1980; Greatest Hits, 1981; Rock In A Hard Place, 1982; Classic Live!, 1986; Done With Mirrors, 1986; Permanent Vacation, 1987; Pump, 1989; Pandora's Box, 1992; Get A Grip, 1993; Little South Of Sanity, 1998; Young Lust–The Aerosmith Anthology, 2001; O'Yeah! Ultimate Aerosmith Hits, 2002. Singles include: Dream On; Last Child; Walk This Way; Dude (Looks Like A Lady); Angel; Rag Doll; Love In An Elevator; Janie's Got A Gun; What It Takes; Livin' On The Edge; Eat The Rich; Cryin'; Amazing; Guest vocal: Love Makes The World, Carole King, 2001. *Honours:* Inducted into Hollywood's Rock Walk; 3 Boston SKC Music Awards, 1990; American Music Awards, 1991; Grammy, Best Rock Performance, 1991; Rolling Stone and Billboard magazine awards; Platinum discs. *Current Management:* Magus Entertainment, 584 Broadway, Suite 1009, New York, NY 10012, USA.

TYRRELL, John William; b. 14 March 1961, Melbourne, Australia. Drums; Man. *Career:* Manager and Drummer, Abba Tribute Band, Björn Again (with Rod Leissle), 1988–; Toured 50 countries world-wide, performed over 3,000 shows. *Recordings:* A Little Respect/Stop; Santa Claus Is Coming to Town; So You Win Again; Flashdance – What a Feeling; Albums: Live At The Royal Albert Hall. *Membership:* UK Music Union. *Address:* 48 Fernhead Rd, Maida Vale, London W9 3EW, England.

TYSON, Liam, (Skin); b. 7 Sept. 1969, Liverpool, England. Musician (guitar). *Career:* Member, Cast; Support gigs with Elvis Costello and Oasis; Record deal with Polydor. *Recordings:* Singles: Finetime, 1995; Alright, 1995; Live the Dream, 1998; Guiding Star, 1998; Sandstorm, 1998; Walkaway, 1998; Beat Mama, 1999; Magic Hour, 1999; Albums: All Change, 1995; Mother Nature Calls, 1997; Magic Hour, 1999; Beetroot, 2001.

TZUKE, Judie; b. 1955, London, England. Vocalist; Songwriter. *Education:* Drama. *Career:* Solo artiste; Songwriting partnership with Mike Paxman, 1975. *Compositions include:* These Are The Laws, with Mike Paxman; Give Me The Love, recorded by Elton John. *Recordings:* Albums: Welcome To The Cruise, 1979; Sports Car, 1980; I Am The Phoenix, 1981; Road Noise, 1982; Shoot The Moon, 1983; Ritmo, 1983; Judie Tzuke, 1985; The Cat Is Out, 1985; Turning Stones, 1989; Left Hand Talking, 1991; BBC Live in Concert, 1995; Wonderland, 1996; Under the Angels, 1997; Very Best Of, 2001.

U

UI CHEALLAIGH, Aine; b. 29 Oct. 1959, Belfast, Northern Ireland. Vocalist; Musician (violin); Teacher. 2 s. *Education:* Degree, diploma, University College Dublin; City of Belfast School of Music. *Career:* Many broadcasts on RTE Radio and Television; BBC Radio; Solo singer, Riverdance–The Show, by Bill Whelan; Teacher, English, Irish and Music. *Recordings:* Solo albums: In Two Minds, 1992; Roots Of Riverdance, 1997. *Honours:* Oireachtas Gold Medal, 1990, 1992. *Address:* Ring, Co Waterford, Ireland.

UKIC, Zoran; b. 31 May 1962, Split, Croatia. Musician (drums); Record Prod; Man. m. Vesna, 30 June 1984, 1 s., 1 d. *Career:* with Daleka Obala: Faraway Coast tours, 1990, 1993–95; Zagreb Salata, D Dvornik, N Belan, Daleka Obala, 1992; Television show 7 Noc. *Recordings:* with Daleka Obala: Faraway Coast, 1990; Ludi Mornari Dolaze U Grad (Crazy Sailors Come On The Town); MRL, E (Dirty), 1993; Morski Pas (Shark), 1994. *Publications:* Blue and Green, Croatian Rock Encyclopedia. *Honours:* The Best Debutant, Split Festival, 1990. *Membership:* Croatian Musicians' Union. *Address:* Zoran Ukic, Teutina 15, 5800 Split, Croatia.

ULRICH, Lars; b. 26 Dec. 1955, Copenhagen, Denmark. Musician (drums). *Career:* Former tennis player; Compiler, New Wave of British Heavy Metal album with Geoff Barton, 1979; British tour with Diamond Head; Member, US heavy rock group Metallica, 1981–; World-wide tours include: Masters of Puppets world tour, 1986–87; US tour, 1988; Damaged Justice British tour, 1989; World tours, 1991–; Also tours with Raven; Ozzy Osbourne; Twisted Sister; Motörhead; Major concerts include: Monsters of Rock Festival, Castle Donington, 1985, 1987, 1991; German Monster of Rock festivals, 1987; Monsters of Rock, Europe and US tours, 1988, 1991; Day On The Green, Oakland, 1991. *Recordings:* Albums: Kill 'Em All, 1983; Ride The Lightning, 1984; Master of Puppets, 1986; ...and Justice For All, 1988; Metallica (No. 1, UK and USA), 1991; Live Shit, 1993; Singles: Garage Days Revisited (EP), 1987; Harvester of Sorrow, 1988; One, 1989; Enter Sandman, 1991; The Unforgiven, 1991; Nothing Else Matters, 1992; Wherever I May Roam, 1992; Sad But True, 1992; Stone Cold Crazy, track featured on Rubáiyát (Elektra's 40th anniversary compilation); Until It Sleeps, 1996; Hero Of The Day, 1996; Mama Said, 1996; The Memory Remains, 1997; The Unforgiven II, 1998; Fuel, 1998; Whiskey In The Jar, 1999; I Disappear, 2000. *Honours:* Platinum and Gold discs; Grammy Awards: Best Heavy Metal Performance: One, 1989; Stone Cold Crazy, 1991; The Unforgiven, 1992; Grammy Award, Hard Rock Performance, 2000; American Music Award, Favourite Heavy Metal Artist, 1993; Bay Area Music Awards: Outstanding Album, 1992; Outstanding Metal Album, Outstanding Group, Outstanding Drummer, 1993; Rolling Stone Readers Poll Winners, Best Heavy Metal Band, 1993. *Current Management:* Q-Prime Inc. *Address:* 729 Seventh Ave, 16th Floor, New York, NY 10019, USA.

ULRICH, Shari; b. 17 Oct. 1951, Marin County, California, USA. Composer; Musician (violin, mandolin, piano, guitar); Vocalist; Television Host. m. 29 April 1989, 1 d. *Education:* 1 year college; Violin training, grades 3–13. *Career:* Member, Pied Pumpkin String Ensemble, 1972–76; Hometown Band, 1976–78; UHF (Ulrich, Bill Henderson, Roy Forbes), 1989–; Solo artist, 1978–; Composer: theme music, several Canadian television series, documentaries; Pieces for Sesame Street; Host Future Scan 1984, 1985; Host, Inside Trax, 1989–94. *Recordings:* Two albums with Pied Pumpkin, 1974, 1975; Hometown Band: Flying, 1976; Hometown Band, 1977; Raffi: Bananaphone, 1994; Solo albums: Long Nights, 1978; One Step Ahead, 1980; Talk Around Town, 1982; Every Road, 1989; The View From Here, 1998; with UHF: UHF, 1990; UHF II, 1994. *Honours:* Juno Awards, 1977, 1981; B.C. Entertainment Hall of Fame, 2002. *Membership:* Vice-Pres., Songwriters' Asscn of Canada, AFofM; ACTRA; SOCAN. *Address:* PO Box 152, Bowen Island, BC V0N 1G0, Canada.

ULRIK, Hans (Jensen); b. 28 Sept. 1965, Copenhagen, Denmark. Musician (saxophone, flute). *Education:* 2 years, Berklee College of Music, Boston, USA, 1984–86. *Career:* Founder, own band Hans Ulrik Quartet; Member, Marilyn Mazur Future Song; Tours: Europe, mostly Scandinavia; Numerous television and radio appearances. *Recordings:* Day After Day (with Gary Peacock, Adam Nussbaum, John Abercrombie); Strange World (with Marilyn Mazur); Jazz And Mambo, 2000; Shortcuts: Jazzpar Combo, 2000. *Honours:* Best Soloist, Leverkusen International Jazz Competition, Germany, 1988. *Current Management:* The Danish Jazz League. *Address:* Den Danske Jazzkreds, Kjeld Langes Gade 4 A, 1367 Copenhagen K, Denmark.

ULSTRUP, Thomas Videro; b. 31 Aug. 1968, Frederiksberg, Denmark. Musician (moog synthesizers, keyboards, modified piano); Composer; Agent; Teacher. *Education:* Teacher's Academy of Art, Music and Multimedia; High Schools of Jazz and Rock; Private tuition. *Career:* Member of various experimental groups in Copenhagen, 1984–92; Solo key performances; Co-founder with Las Nissen of Gone Fishin', 1989–96; Solo, duo and trio member and recording artist; Founder of Native Music Denmark, 1997; Radio Host, Copenhagen radio-jazz show Alternative Music; Toured with The Sun

Mountain Experience, Caribbean, 1998. *Compositions:* 10 x Cai, 1988; Jack Daniels, 1994; Meditations, 1998. *Recordings:* with Gone Fishin': Gone Fishin', 1994; Adventure: Once Upon a Time..., 1998; Alternative music: Sound Environment, 1998. *Publications:* Native Music Compilation Vols I and II, 1998; Alternative Music – Soundenvironment. *Honours:* Gold Talent Prize, Berlingske Tidende, 1988. *Membership:* Gramex; Danish Jazz and Folk Authors (DOBFA); Composers in Denmark (KODA). *Current Management:* Native Music. *Address:* H/F Grænsen 8, Finsensvej 263, 2720 Vaniose, Denmark.

ULVÆUS, Björn Kristian; b. 25 April 1945, Gothenburg, Sweden. Songwriter; Musician (guitar); Vocalist. m. Agnetha Fältskog, 1971, divorced 1979. *Career:* Songwriter with Benny Andersson, 1966–; Duo with Andersson as The Hootennanny Singers; Partner in production with Andersson at Polar Music, 1971; Mem., Swedish pop group, Abba, 1973–82; Winner, Eurovision Song Contest, 1974; World-wide tours; Concerts include: Royal Performance, Stockholm, 1976; Royal Albert Hall, London, 1977; UNICEF concert, New York, 1979; Wembley Arena, six sell-out performances, 1979; Reunion with Abba, Swedish TV's This Is Your Life, 1986; The Story of Abba (Channel 4), 1991; Film: Abba: The Movie, 1977; Continued writing and producing with Andersson, 1982–; Produced musical Mamma Mia!, with Andersson, West End, London, 1999–. *Compositions include:* Abba songs (with Benny Andersson); Musicals: Chess (with lyrics by Tim Rice), 1983; The Immigrants, 1994; Mamma Mia! (with Andersson), 1999. *Recordings:* Albums: with Andersson: Happiness, 1971; with Abba: Waterloo, 1974; Abba, 1976; Greatest Hits, 1976; Arrival, 1977; The Album, 1978; Voulez-Vous, 1979; Greatest Hits Vol. 2, 1979; Super Trouper, 1980; The Visitors, 1981; The Singles: The First Ten Years, 1982; Thank You For The Music, 1983; Absolute Abba, 1988; Abba Gold, 1992; More Abba Gold, 1993; Forever Gold, 1998; The Definitive Collection, 2001. Singles include: with Abba: Ring Ring, 1973; Waterloo (No. 1, UK), 1974; Mamma Mia (No. 1, UK), 1975; Dancing Queen (No. 1, UK and USA), 1976; Fernando (No. 1, UK), 1976; Money Money Money, 1976; Knowing Me Knowing You (No. 1, UK), 1977; The Name Of The Game (No. 1, UK), 1977; Take A Chance On Me (No. 1, UK), 1978; Summer Night City, 1978; Chiquitita, 1979; Does Your Mother Know?, 1979; Angel Eyes/Voulez-Vous, 1979; Gimme Gimme Gimme (A Man After Midnight), 1979; I Have A Dream, 1980; On and On and On, 1981; Lay All Your Love On Me, 1981; One Of Us, 1981; When All Is Said and Done, 1982; Head Over Heels, 1982; The Day Before You Came, 1982; Under Attack, 1982; Thank You For The Music, 1983. *Honours:* with Abba: Gold discs; Best-selling group in history of popular music, Guinness Book of Records, 1979; World Music Award, Best Selling Swedish Artist, 1993; Ivor Novello Award, Special International Award (with Benny Andersson), 2002. *Address:* Södra Brobänken 41A, Skeppsholmen, 111 49 Stockholm, Sweden. *Website:* www.abbasite.com.

ULVESETH, Sigurd; b. 13 July 1953, Bergen, Norway. Musician (acoustic bass). m. Eli, 13 March 1981, 2 s., 1 d. *Career:* Many tours, different jazz groups; Appearances, radio and television shows; Own quartet featuring Adam Nussbaum, drums. *Recordings:* Sigurd Ulveseth Quartet: To Wisdom The Prize (with Adam Nussbaum, Knut Rüsmas; Dug Arnesen); Played on 13 other albums. *Honours:* Jade Prize, 1990. *Membership:* Norwegian Jazz Society. *Current Management:* Vaakleivbrotet 7, 5062 Bones, Norway.

UNCLE KRACKER, (Matthew Lynford Shafer); b. 6 June 1974, Mount Clemens, MI, USA. DJ; Vocalist; Songwriter. m. Melanie, 2 d. *Career:* Owns Mount Clemens tyre store run by father, and Sunny's Tavern bar in suburban Detroit; Befriended Kid Rock, 1987; Recruited to Kid Rock's Twisted Brown Trucker touring group as DJ following release of Rock's album Grits Sandwiches For Breakfast, 1991; Became Rock's co-producer/co-songwriter; Achieved success with solo side project recorded whilst on tour; Many solo TV and live appearances backed by Twisted Brown Trucker group, 2001. *Recordings:* Albums: Double Wide, 2000; No Stranger To Shame, 2002. Singles: Follow Me, 2001; Yeah Yeah Yeah, 2001. *Address:* c/o Top Dog/Lava/Atlantic Records, USA. *Website:* www.unclekracker.com.

UNDERDOG, (THE). See: JACKSON, Trevor.

UNDERWOOD, Charles Jeremy; b. 14 Aug. 1956, Leicester, England. Musician (saxophone). *Education:* BA Hons, Fine Art; Associated Board exams (Grade 8 clarinet). *Career:* Professional musician, 1984–; Member, John Martyn Band, 1991–; Tours: UK; Europe; USA; Glastonbury Festival; Edinburgh Festival; Bath Festival; Member, British jazz group Spirit Level, 1989–; Member, Andy Sheppard's Big-Comotion Band, also Carla Bley's Very Big Band. *Recordings:* with John Martyn: Couldn't Love You More, 1992; No Little Boy, 1993; with Andy Sheppard: Rhythm Method, 1993; Delivery Suite, 1994; Other collaborators include: Gail Thompson. *Membership:* PRS; MCPS. *Address:* 9 Lucas House, Argyle Walk, Kings Cross, London WC1, England.

UNKNOWN, (THE). See: **CARTER, Derrick.**

UNTOUCHABLES. See: **GONZALEZ, Kenny.**

UOTILA, Jukkis; b. 23 Aug. 1960, Finland. Musician (drums); Composer. *Career:* Jazz concerts, 1976–; Played and recorded with artists including: Gil Evans; McCoy Tyner; Joe Henderson; Chet Baker; Moved to New York, 1980; Worked with artists including: Randy Brecker; Eliane Elias; Ted Curson; Mike Stern; Dave Samuels; Returned to Finland; Bandleader, Jukkis Uotila Band; Performed world-wide, including festivals at Montreux, Detroit, Paris; Head of Jazz Department, Sibelius Academy, Helsinki, 1986–; Bandleader, with band featuring: Mike Stern, Bob Berg, Lars Jansson, Lasse Danielsson; Tours of Scandinavia and Germany. *Recordings:* with Bob Rockwell: No Rush, 1985; On the Natch, 1985; with Chet Baker: When Sunny Gets Blue, 1986; with Joe Bonner: Lost Melody, 1987; with Doug Raney Quintet, 1988; with Stockholm Jazz Orchestra: Soundbites, 1997; Tango, 1999; Solo: Hunters And Gatherers, 2000. *Address:* Laivurinkatu 35 B 35, 00150 Helsinki, Finland.

UPTON, Eddie; b. 4 Oct. 1944, Brighton, Sussex, England. Folk Vocalist; Musician (concertina, harmonica, percussion). *Education:* BA (Hons) Politics, Sussex University. *Career:* Full time folk performer, 1980–, specializing in traditional English songs, music and dance; Former member, Albion Dance Band and Etchingham Steam Band, both with Ashley Hutchings; Co-founder, artistic director, Folk South West, the folk development society for South West of England. *Compositions:* Suite of song arrangements celebrating Somerset's River Parrett, 1997. *Recordings include:* The Prospect Before Us, Albion Dance Band; A Tale of Ale, Various Artists; Music For Christopher Columbus and His Crew, St Georges Canlona; Prospect Before Us, with Albion Band; Guv'nor, Vol. 2, 1996; The BBC Sessions, 1998; Solo album: First Orders; where the Parrett Winds Peaceful, 1997. *Publications:* Caedmon Capers – A Collection of New Folk Dances and Folk Dance Tunes. *Membership:* Folklore Society; English Folk Dance and Song Society; Equity; Musicians' Union; Performing Rights Society, 1997. *Address:* 2 Hayes Cottages, Stocklinch, Ilminster, Somerset TA19 9JG, England.

URBAN, Stan; b. 10 Jan. 1944, Dundee, Scotland. Musician (piano); Vocalist. m. (1) Erika Kuhnert, 3 Sept. 1963, divorced 1984, 2 s., (2) Annette Wetterberg, 29 March 1986, deceased 1987, 1 adopted s., (3) Evelyn Jetzschmann, 15 April 1996. *Career:* Rock 'n' roll pianist; Formed own band of German musicians, following tour of Germany with Long John Baldry, 1962; Lived and played in Ibiza, late 60s to 1984; Scandinavia recommended by Robert Plant; Tours of Scandinavia, 1981–. *Recordings:* Single: Little Queenie, 1982; Albums: Rock 'N' Roll Cocktail, 1982; M'Roccan Rollers, 1986; Live, 1988; Through My Door, 1992; Can't Hold On Can't Let Go, 1995; The Devil Made the Boogie, 1997; Dundee Jivin', 2003. *Address:* Skaering Sandager 18, 8250 Egå, Denmark. *Telephone:* 86228474. *Fax:* 86228474.

URE, Midge (James); b. 10 Oct. 1953, Glasgow, Scotland. Vocalist; Songwriter; Prod; Dir. 4 d. *Career:* Member of bands: Slik; Rich Kids; Thin Lizzy (US tour only); Visage; Formed Ultravox; Also solo artist; Trustee of Live Aid; Musical Director, Prince's Trust, 1987–88; Musical Director, special 40 minute set, Nelson Mandela Concert; Directed video Monument for televison special; Director of videos for: Ultravox; Visage; Fun Boy Three; Bananarama; Phil Lynott; Monsoon; Midge Ure/Mick Karn; Midge Ure; Martha Ladly; Truth; Andrew Strong. *Compositions include:* Levis advertisements music, with Christopher Cross, 1987; Writer/co-writer, many hit songs; Film music: Max Headroom; Turnaround; Playboy Late Night Theme; October 22 AKG; Went To Lonely Island. *Recordings include:* Albums: with Visage: Visage, 1980; Anvil, 1982; with Ultravox: Vienna, 1980; Rage In Eden, 1981; Quartet, 1982; Lament, 1984; The Collection, 1984; U-Vox, 1986; Solo albums: The Gift, 1985; Answers, 1988; Pure, 1991; Breathe, 1996; Went To Coney Island, 2000; Move Me, 2001; Little Orphans, 2001; Singles include: with Slik: Forever And Ever (No. 1, UK), 1976; with Rich Kids: Rich Kids, 1978; with Ultravox: Sleepwalk, 1980; Vienna, 1981; All Stood Still, 1981; The Thin Wall, 1981; The Voice, 1981; Reap The Wild Wind, 1982; Hymn, 1982; Visions In Blue, 1983; We Came To Dance, 1983; Dancing With Tears In My Eyes, 1984; Lament, 1984; Love's Great Adventure, 1984; All Fall Down, 1986; Solo hits include: No Regrets, 1982; If I Was (No. 1, UK), 1985; That Certain Smile, 1985; Call Of The Wild, 1986; Cold Cold Heart, 1991; Contributor, producer, co-writer (with Bob Geldof), Do They Know It's Christmas?, Band Aid (No. 1, UK), 1984; Also singles with: Slik, Rich Kids, Visage and as solo artist; Produced records for: Antrix; Ronny; Cold Fish; Phil Lynott; Pete Godwyn; Modern Man; Fatal Charm; Steve Harley; Strasse; The Messengers; Rodeo; Visage; Ultravox; Michel Van Dyke; Countermine. *Honours:* Winner of Ivor Novello and Grammy Awards. *Current Management:* Richard Beck, CMO Management, Unit 32, Ransomes Dock, 35–37 Parkgate Rd, London SW11 4NP, England.

URTREGER, René; b. 6 July 1934, Paris, France. Musician (piano); Bandleader; Composer. m. (1), 1 d., (2) Jacqueline Fornari, 1 s. *Education:* Studied classical music from age 6; Serious study after war from age 11; Promoted Charlie Parker's music from age 13. *Career:* Concerts and festivals throughout the world, 1953–; Starts working at 19 with Don Byas-Buck Clayton Band, 1953; Worked with: Dexter Gordon; Zoot Sims; Stéphane Grappelli; Allen Eager; Stan Getz; Dizzy Gillespie; J. J. Johnson; Double Six; Current trio with Pierre Michelot and Kenny Clarke; House pianist for (Nicole) Barclay Records, France, 1954–65; European tours as pianist within Miles Davis Quartet, 1956; Miles Davis Quintet, 1957; Break from jazz music, 1967–77, touring with Sacha Distel and Claude Francois; Returned to jazz ensembles, 1977; Pianist with Sonny Stitt's French tour, 1982. *Recordings:* Numerous recordings include albums with: Lionel Hampton; Chet Baker; Bobby Jaspar; Hubert Fol; Maurice Meunier; Lester Young; Kenny Clarke; Michael Hausser; Stéphane Grappelli, Gary Burton, Stan Getz, Miles Davis, Pat Metheny and Stuff Smith; Film music: Ascenseur Pour L'Echafaud, within Miles Davis Quintet; Le Poulet (Oscar short film, 1965); Other albums include: Recidive, 1978; Humair/Urtreger/Michelot (H.U.M.) Trio, 1979; Collection Privée, 1981; En Direct Du Festival D'Antibes, 1981; Jazzman, 1985; Masters, 1987; Avec Chet Baker, 1989; Serena, 1990; Chet Baker in Paris, 1998; Film: René Urtreger/Homme De Jazz, 1991; Saint Germains Des Presents, Telefilm by J. Ch. Averty, 1993; Victoires de le Musique, HUM Trio, 2000. *Honours:* Winner, National Jazz Tournament, 1953; Prix Django Reinhardt, L'Academie Du Jazz, 1961; Prix Boris Vian, L'Academie Du Jazz, for album Jazzman, 1985; L'Ordre Des Arts And Lettres, 1988; Grand Prix, SACEM, 1993. *Address:* 44 rue Charles de Gaille, 61 400 Mortangne, France.

USHER, (Usher Raymond); b. 1978, Chattanooga, Tennessee, USA. Vocalist. *Career:* Appearances include Oprah Winfrey Show (TV) and the American Music Awards as part of Black Men United; Movie appearances include: The Faculty, 1998; Light It Up, 1999. *Recordings:* Singles: Can U Get Wit It, 1994; Think of You, 1995; The Many Ways, 1995; Comin For X-Mas, 1995; My Way, 1997; Nice and Slow (No. 1, USA), 1998; You Make Me Wanna (No. 1, UK), 1998; U Got It Bad, 2001; Pop Ya Collar, 2001; Albums: All About U, 2000; 8701, 2001.

USSING, Joachim; b. 9 Oct. 1952, Copenhagen, Denmark. Musician (bass player); Composer. m. Henriette Rolffes Becker, 13 Feb. 1989, 1 s., 1 d. *Career:* Toured Scandinavia, television appearances with: Moirana; Phantom Band; Lone Kellermann and Rockband; Jomfru Ane; Doraz; Small Talk; Big Talk; Anne Grete; Peter Abrahamsen; Peter Viskinde, from 1974–95. *Recordings:* First album: Terje, Jesper, Joachim, 1970 (released 1991). *Honours:* Platinum disc, Natten Blir Til Dag, Lone Kellermann and Rockband. *Membership:* DMF; DJBFA; KODA; GRAMEX; NCB. *Current Management:* DMA. *Address:* Vendersgade 23, 1363 Copenhagen, Denmark.

UTADA, Hikaru, (Cubic U); b. 19 Jan. 1983, New York, USA. Vocalist; Songwriter. m. Kazuaki Kiriya, 2002. *Education:* American School, Tokyo; Columbia University, New York, 2001. *Career:* Daughter of record prod., Teruzane Utada, and early '70s Japanese pop/enka vocalist, Keiko Fuji; Recorded demos in downtime at father's studio, releasing them in USA under alias Cubic U; First Japan releases as Hikaru Utada, 1999, while continuing education in Tokyo; Simultaneously maintained US and Japanese careers under respective names; Hosted own radio shows in Japan incl. Tres Bien Bohemian. *Recordings:* Albums: Precious (as Cubic U), 1998; First Love, 1999; U3*Star (live), 2000; Distance, 2001. Singles: Close To You (as Cubic U), 1998; Moving On Without You, 1999; First Love, 1999; Automatic/Time Will Tell, 1999; Addicted To You, 1999; Wait And See, 2000; For You/Time Limit, 2000; Can You Keep A Secret, 2001; Final Distance, 2001; Traveling, 2001. *Honours:* First Love album sales in excess of a record 9.5m. copies in Japan; World Music Award, Best Selling Asian Artist, 2000. *Address:* c/o Toshiba-EMI, 3-taku, Room 2–2–17, Akasaka Minato-Ku, Tokyo 107–8510, Japan. *Website:* www.toshiba-emi.co.jp/hikki.

UTLEY, Adrian; b. 1958. Musician (guitar). *Career:* Former mem., Big John Patton, Jazz Messengers; Mem., Portishead, 1991–; Signed to Go!Beat Records, 1993; Film, To Kill A Dead Man, shown in cinemas and projected onto the MI5 building, London, 1995; Glastonbury Festival appearance, 1995; Live internet broadcast of New York concert, 1997; Played guitar on: Reload, Tom Jones, 1999; Felt Mountain, Goldfrapp, 2000. *Recordings:* Albums: Dummy, 1994; Herd of Instinct, 1995; Portishead, 1997; PNYC, 1998, Glory Times, 1998; Roseland New York (DVD), 2002. Singles: Numb (EP), 1994; Sour Times, 1994; Glory Box, 1995; All Mine, 1997; Cowboys (EP), 1997; Over, 1997; Only You, 1998. *Honours:* Mercury Music Prize, Best Album, 1994. *Address:* c/o Go Beat Records, The Fulham Palace, Bishops Ave, London SW6 6EA, England. *Website:* www.portishead.co.uk.

UTTERBACK, Joe; b. 8 Oct. 1944, Hutchinson, Kansas. *Education:* DMA, University of Kansas. *Career:* Gigs in the Jazz Centers of Kansas City, St Louis, New York City, San Francisco; Solo Jazz Piano Concerts, USA. *Compositions:* Tuxedo Blues; Three Spirituals For Organ in Jazz Styles; Three Spirituals For Piano; Dr Joes Long Ragtime Special. *Recordings:* Blues and Ballads at the Movies; Christmas on the Mountain; Night and Day, Gershwin: Porgy and Bess Jazz Suite; Joe Utterback; Night Train. *Publications:* Knockin at your Door; Voluntaries; Jazz Piano Starter Set; Beautiful Night. *Honours:* Annual ASCAP Award. *Membership:* ASCAP; AGO, College Music Society. *Current Management:* Jazzmuze Inc. *Address:* 50 Crooked Trail, Rowayton, CT 06853, USA.

V

VACHÉ, Warren Webster; b. 27 Nov. 1914, Brooklyn, NY, USA. Musician (string bass); Bandleader. m. 18 Sept. 1948, 2 s. *Career:* Worked, played with: Bobby Hackett; Wild Bill Davison; Pee Wee Russell; Max Kaminsky; Sons are both jazz musicians: Warren Jr, cornet; Allan, clarinet; Leader, own 7-piece jazzband, The Celebratin' Seven; Tours: Germany; Switzerland; Netherlands; France; Also US and international jazz festivals. *Recordings:* Jazzology; Swingin' and Singin'; The Music of Harry Barris; The Music of Isham Jones, 1998; Diamond Cut Productions—The Marvelous Melodies of Peter Mendoza; Vintage Vallee; Eddy Duchin And His Central Park Casino Orchestra; JAZZ: It's A Wonderful Sound, 2002; Ray Noble Plays Ray Noble, 2003. *Publications:* This Horn For Hire, biography of Pee Wee Erwin; Crazy Fingers, biography of Claude Hopkins; Back Beats and Rim Shots, Biography of Johnny Blowers, 1997; Jazz Gentry (anthology jazz articles), 1999; The Unsung Songwriters, 2000; Sittin' In With Chris Griffin, 2003; Editor, Jersey Jazz (monthly publication, New Jersey Jazz Society), 18 years. *Membership:* Life mem., American Federation of Musicians; Life and founding mem., New Jersey Jazz Society; Founder, American Jazz Hall of Fame; Co-founder, American Federation of Jazz Societies. *Address:* 836 W Inman Ave, Rahway, NJ 07065, USA. *E-mail:* vachesr@aol.com.

VAERNES, Knut; b. 1 April 1954, Trondheim, Norway. Musician (guitar); Composer; Bandleader; Record Co Exec. 1 s. *Education:* Master of Arts; Master of Music. *Career:* 15 years as professional musician; Concerts include: All national jazz festivals; Tours in Europe; British tour with Cutting Edge, including Ronnie Scott's, 1983; Numerous television appearances; Extensive touring; Played with Jan Garbarek, Jon Christensen, Oslo, 1982; Head of jazz record label Curling Legs. *Recordings:* Albums: with Cutting Edge: Cutting Edge; Our Man In Paradise; Duesenberg; Solo albums: Admisson For Guitars and Basses, 1992; Roneo, 1993; Trio, 1995; Film music, with Jan Garbarek, 1981. *Membership:* Musicians' Union. *Address:* Vidarsgt. 9A, 0452 Oslo, Norway.

VAI, Steve; b. 6 June 1960, Long Island, New York, USA. Musician (guitar). *Education:* Tutored by Joe Satriani; Jazz and Classical music, Berklee College of Music, Boston. *Career:* Lead guitarist, Frank Zappa, 1979–84; Built own recording studio, 1984; Lead guitarist with Alcatrazz, 1985; David Lee Roth, 1986–89; Whitesnake, 1989–90; Also solo artiste; World-wide concerts and television/radio appearances with the above include: World Series of Rock, USA; Monsters of Rock, UK; Super Rock, Germany; Film appearance: Crossroads. *Recordings:* Albums include: with Frank Zappa: Tinseltown Rebellion, 1981; You Are What You Is, 1981; Shut Up and Play Yer Guitar, 1981; Ship Arriving Too Late, 1982; The Man From Utopia, 1983; Thing Fish, 1984; Jazz From Hell, 1986; Guitar, 1988; You Can't Do That On Stage Anymore, 1988; with Alcatrazz: Disturbing The Peace, 1985; with David Lee Roth: Eat 'Em and Smile, 1986; Skyscraper, 1988; with Whitesnake: Slip of The Tongue, 1989; Solo albums: Flex-able, 1984; Passion and Warfare, 1990; Sex and Religion, 1993; Alien Love Secrets, 1995; Fire Garden, 1996; Flex-Able Leftovers, 1998; The Ultra Zone, 1999; The 7th Song, 2000; Alive In An Ultra World, 2001. *Current Management:* C. Winston Simone Management, 1790 Broadway, New York, NY 10019, USA.

VAIL, Frederick Scott; b. 24 March 1944, San Francisco, California, USA. Recording Studio Exec. m. Brenda Joyce Howard, 18 June 1972, divorced 1977. *Education:* California State University, 1962–64; Industrial College of the Armed Forces, 1963; Voluntary State Community College, Nashville, 1980–81. *Career:* Radio announcer, Sacramento, 1958–62; Frederick Vail Productions, 1962–66; Producer, sales manager, Teen-age Fair Inc, 1966–69; Artist manager, Beach Boys, 1969–71; Promotion Manager, Capitol Records, 1972–73; President, Frederick Vail and Associates, 1974–80; President, General Manager, Treasure Isle Recording Studios, 1980–; Consultant, Promotion and Marketing: Waylon Jennings, 1974–75; GRT Records, 1976–78; RSO Records, 1978–79; Lecturer, numerous colleges and universities; Event producer for: Beach Boys; Glen Campbell; Righteous Brothers; Four Seasons; Dave Clark Five; The Crickets. *Recordings:* Producer for: B. B. King; Isaac Hayes; Billy Preston; Carla Thomas; Lee Atwater; Red Hot + Blue compilation. *Publications:* Contributing author: Beach Boys – The California Myth, 1978; Beach Boys – Heroes and Villains, 1987; Contributor to Mix Magazine. *Honours:* 7 Gold, 2 Platinum discs. *Membership:* NARAS, Board of Governors, 1981–83; CMA. *Address:* Treasure Isle Recording Studios, Nashville, Tennessee, USA.

VALDES, Chucho; b. 9 Oct. 1941, Quivican, Cuba. Jazz Musician (piano, keyboards); Bandleader. *Career:* Son of Bebo Valdes; Began playing piano, aged 3; Leader of own group by age 16; Formed: Orquesta Cubana de Música Moderna, 1967; Founder: Irakare, the top Cuban jazz orchestra, 1973; Collaborations incl.: Cesoria Evora. *Recordings:* Albums: with Chucho Irakare: Felicidad, 1991; Live At Ronnie Scott's, 1993; Exuberancia, 1994; Indestructible, 1998; Babalu Aye, 1999; Yemayà, 2002; Toda Cuba, 2002; with

Arturo Sandoval and Chucho Valdes Quartet: Straight Ahead, 1994; Solo: Solo Piano, 1993; Grandes Momentos De La Música Cubana, 1994; Pianissimo, 1997; Briyumba Palo Congo, 1999; Live At The Village Vanguard, 2000; Invitación, 2000; Bele Bele En La Habana, 2001; Fantasia Cubana, 2002; Canciones Inéditas, 2002. *Honours:* Latin Grammy Award, Best Pop Instrumental Album, for Canciones Inéditas, 2002. *Address:* c/o International Music Network, 278 Main St, Gloucester, MA 01930, USA.

VALDY, Paul Valdemar Horsdal; b. 1 Sept. 1945, Ottawa, Canada. Vocalist; Songwriter; Musician (guitar); Prod. m. Kathleen Mary Fraser, 13 Aug. 1986, 2 s. *Education:* Usgar Collegiate, St Pat's College; Private music lessons; Victoria School of Music. *Career:* Appearances: International Pop Song Festival, Sopot, Poland, 1975; CBC TV Super Special Simulcast, Valdy and The Hometown Band, 1976; Expo '86, Vancouver; Festival Cervantino, Mexico, 1987; Olympic Arts Festival, Calgary, '88; World's Fair, Seville, Expo '92; Royal Gala, Melbourne Music Festival, Australia, 1995. *Recordings:* Albums: Country Man, 1971; Landscapes, 1972; Family Gathering, 1974; Valdy and The Home Town Band, 1976; Hot Rocks, 1978; 1001, 1979; Valdy's Kid Record, 1981; Notes From Places, 1986; Heart At Work, 1993. *Publications:* The Best of Valdy. *Honours:* 2 Juno Awards; BMI Song of the Year, Landscapes, 1974. *Membership:* AFofM, local 247; NSAI; SAC; FEPRA; CARAS; CIRPA. *Current Management:* Paquin Entertainment Group. *Address:* 1067 Sherwin Rd, Winnipeg, Manitoba R3H 0T8, Canada.

VALENSI, Nick; b. 16 Jan. 1981, New York, NY, USA. Musician (guitar). *Education:* Dwight School, Manhattan. *Career:* Mem., The Strokes, 1998–. *Recordings:* Albums: Is This It, 2001. Singles: The Modern Age, 2001; Hard To Explain/New York City Cops, 2001; Last Nite/When It Started, 2001. *Honours:* NME Awards, Band of the Year, Best New Act, Album of the Year, 2001; BRIT Award, Best International Newcomer, 2002. *Current Management:* Ryan Gentles, Wiz Kid Management. *Address:* c/o RCA Records, 1540 Broadway, New York, NY 10036, USA. *Website:* www.thestrokes.com.

VALENTIN, David Peter; b. 29 April 1952, USA. Recording Artist; Musician (flute). *Education:* High School Music and Art; One year Bronx Community College. *Career:* First artist on GRP Records; 17 albums recorded. *Compositions:* Over 30 compositions; Film soundtracks; Ghost music, Bill Cosby Show; Title track, album with Arturo Sandoval (Grammy award-winning album). *Honours:* Voted Best Flute, 6 years consecutively, Jazz Iz Magazine; Entertainer of Year, NHAMAS, 1993; Vista 2000 Excellence In The Arts, 1995. *Current Management:* Carl Valldejuli, Turi's Music Inc, 193 Westward Dr., Miami Springs, FL 33168, USA. *Address:* 154 Harding Park, New York, NY 10473, USA.

VALENTINE, Kathy; b. 7 Jan. 1959, Austin, TX, USA. Musician (bass guitar). m. Steven, 1 d. *Career:* Mem., Textone; Joined the Go-Go's, 1980–85; The Go-Go's re-formed briefly for PETA benefit concert, 1990; Mem., re-formed Go-Go's, 1994, Shows in Las Vegas; Formed, the Bluebonnets, 1992–94; re-named the Delphines, 1994–; The Go-Go's re-formed, 2000–, for an album and tours, including US tour with B-52's. Albums: Beauty And The Beat (No. 1, USA), 1981; Vacation, 1982; Talk Show, 1984; Return To The Valley Of The Go-Go's, 1994; God Bless The Go-Go's, 2001; Contributor, Tame Yourself (animal rights benefit album), 1991. *Current Management:* c/o Left Bank Management, 9255 Sunset Blvd, West Hollywood, CA 90069, USA. E-mail: gogos@beyondmusic.com. *Website:* www.gogos.com; www.delphines.com.

VALLANCE, Jim; b. 31 May 1952. Songwriter. m. Rachel Paiement, 1 s. *Education:* Private study, piano, cello. *Compositions:* for Aerosmith: Other Side; Ragdoll; Eat The Rich; for Bryan Adams: Heaven; Run To You; Summer of '69; Cuts Like A Knife; for Heart: What About Love; for Joe Cocker: When The Night Comes; for Tina Turner: It's Only Love; Back Where You Started; for Glass Tiger: Don't Forget Me When I'm Gone; for Bonnie Raitt, No Way To Treat A Lady; for Roger Daltrey, Rebel; for Ozzy Osbourne: Just Want You; Also wrote songs with: Lita Ford; Joan Jett; Motley Crue; Diane Warren; Alice Cooper. *Honours:* 4 Juno Awards, Composer of the Year, (Canadian equivalent of Grammy); 3 BMI Awards (USA); More than 50 Gold and Platinum album awards (USA, Canada, Japan, UK, Germany). *Membership:* SOCAN (Canada); ASCAP (USA); Board of Directors, PROCAN, 1987–90; Advisory Board, Songwriters Asscn of Canada, 1990–; Director of Canadian Society of Composers, Authors and Publishers, 1996–98, 2000–. *Current Management:* Rondor Music. *Address:* c/o Barbara Vander Linde, Rondor Music, 360 N La Cienega Blvd, Los Angeles, CA 90048, USA.

VALLDEJULI, Carl Cats; b. 9 March 1962. Recording Artist Man. *Education:* Marine Biochemist, BS, MS; Piano; Music Theory. *Career:* Produced, co-ordinated world-wide concert tours. *Recordings:* Assistant and executive producer on over 10 albums including: Arturo Sandoval; Dave Valentin, including Sunshower, 1999; Ed Calle. *Honours:* IAJE; NARAS;

World Relief; Billboard; Grammy. *Membership:* Trustee NARAS. *Address:* Quiet Storm Inc, 2830 SW Lejeune Rd, Coral Gables, FL 33134–6602, USA.

VALLEJO, Ramón M; b. 20 June 1963, Honduras. Vocalist; Musician (trombone, percussion). *Education:* Musicianship at Cit Lit; Brass at Kensington and Chelsea College of Private Tutors. *Career:* Band leader, 2 Latin bands; Tours, Europe; Radio shows on news radio GLR, Jazz FM; Backing vocals for Matt Bianco; Own show in London, played with major world famous Latin players. *Compositions:* Numerous, all salsa, rumba, merengue rhythms. *Recordings:* Albums: Shango; The Story So Far, with Terry Seabrook's Cubana Bop, 1998. *Membership:* Musicians' Union; PRS. *Current Management:* RVR Promotions. *Address:* Mid Basement, 32 Queen's Gate Gardens, London SW7 5RR, England.

VALLI, Frankie, (Frank Castelluccio); b. 3 May 1937, Newark, New Jersey, USA. Vocalist. *Career:* Member, Four Seasons, 1954–77; 1980s; Solo artiste, 1958–. *Recordings:* Albums: with The Four Seasons: Sherry and 11 Others, 1962; Ain't That A Shame and 11 Others, 1963; The 4 Seasons Greetings, 1963; Born To Wander, 1964; Dawn and 11 Other Great Songs, 1964; Rag Doll, 1964; Entertain You, 1965; The Four Seasons Sing Big Hits By Bacharach, David and Dylan, 1966; Working My Way Back To You, 1966; Lookin' Back, 1967; Christmas Album, 1967; Genuine Imitation Life Gazette, 1969; Edizione D'Oro, 1969; Chameleon, 1972; Streetfighter, 1975; Inside You, 1976; Who Loves You, 1976; Helicon, 1977; Reunited Live, 1981; Solo, 1967; Timeless, 1968; Inside You, 1975; Close Up, 1975; Story, 1976; Frankie Valli Is The Word, 1978; The Best of Frankie Valli, 1980; Heaven Above Me, 1981; Off Seasons, 2001; Singles include: with the Four Seasons: Spanish Lace; Sherry; Big Girls Don't Cry (used in film soundtrack Dirty Dancing); Walk Like A Man; Dawn (Go Away); Rag Doll; The Night; Who Loves You; December 1963 (Oh What A Night), (No. 1, USA and UK), 1976; East Meets West (with the Beach Boys), 1984; Solo singles include: (You're Gonna) Hurt Yourself; Can't Take My Eyes Off You; I Make A Fool of Myself; To Give (The Reason I Live); You're Ready Now; My Eyes Adored You; Grease, 1978; Swearin' To God; Our Day Will Come; Fancy Dancer; Where Did We Go Wrong (with Chris Forde); Walk Like a Man, 1999. *Current Management:* International Creative Management, 8942 Wilshire Blvd, Beverly Hills, CA 90211, USA.

VAN BAVEL, Boudewijn; b. 9 Jan. 1952, Breda, Netherlands. Prod; Composer. 1 s. *Education:* Rotterdam; Music High, Rotterdam, 1975; Sound Engineering, 1989. *Career:* Producer, composer, Black Lee, Breda, Netherlands, 1973–79; Managing Director, Bo Easy Studios, Breda, 1980–89; Managing Director, Artists and Business, Rotterdam, 1990; Managing Director, Sky Trance International (studios and theatre), Hilversum, Netherlands, and Antwerp, Belgium, 1990–. *Recordings:* California Fried Scene, Black Lee, 1979; I Got To Spend More Time, Bo Easy, 1983. *Current Management:* Sky Trance International, Hilversum. *Address:* PO Box 64, 1200 AB Hilversum, Netherlands.

VAN BEST, Peter; b. 15 Oct. 1951, Kaatsheuvel, Netherlands. Music Publisher; Organizer; Songwriter; Vocalist. *Education:* School of Music (singing, piano). *Career:* Castlebar International Song Contest 1986 (RTE); Cavan International Song Contest 1988; Artemare Italy 1992; Europa Song France 1992 (Radio France); Europa Song Brussels 1993; Top Artist Show Italy, 1993; Midem Showcase 1994; Invited guest 70th anniversary in Paris of Peter Ustinov, 1991. *Compositions:* 25 years songwriting; own compositions published world-wide. *Honours:* Fidof (Festival Federation) Awards, 1988, 1990. *Membership:* BUMA/Stemra; BAC&S; FIDOF; SENA. *Current Management:* Best Music. *Address:* Crispijnstraat 9, 5171 CH Kaatsheuvel, Netherlands.

VAN DEN BRINK, Bert; b. 24 July 1958, Geldrop, Netherlands. Composer; Arranger. m. Medy Doves, 1 s. *Education:* Private lessons, since age 5 years; Classical Music, Utrecht Conservatory, with Herman Uhlhorn. *Career:* Teacher, Jazz music, Utrecht Conservatory; Played with Dee Dee Bridgewater, Toots Thielemans, Denise Jannah, Philip Catherine, Chet Baker, Nat Adderly, Rick Margitza, Charlie Mariano. *Compositions:* Wondering Why. *Recordings:* Live at Montréal Dee Dee Bridgewater, 1990; Deepest to Dearest, solo album; Hazy Hugs, Amstel Octet with Guest Chet Baker; Denise Jannah Albums; Also appears on: In Montreux, Dee Dee Bridgewater; Live, Philip Catherine; Dialogues, Lee Konitz; Chez Toots, Toots Thielemans. *Honours:* First Prize, International Concours for Visually Handicapped Musicians, Hungary. *Current Management:* Brink Productions BV, Akkerse Straat 6A, 4061 BH, Ophemert, Netherlands. *Address:* Brink Productions BV, Akkerse Straat 6A, 4061 BH, Ophemert, Netherlands.

VAN DORT, Elizabeth (Liz); b. 3 March 1968, Melbourne, Australia. Vocalist; Composer. *Education:* BA, Social Anthropology, University of Melbourne; HSC, Classical Singing; AMEB. *Career:* Vocalist, composer, various film and television projects; Vocalist, composer, Faraway; Vocalist, Sting and the Radioactors. *Membership:* APRA; MCPS. *Current Management:* i-sage, PO Box 2237, St Kilda West, Vic. 3182, Australia. *Website:* www.lizvandort.com; www.farawaymusic.com.

VAN DYKE, Leroy Frank; b. 4 Oct. 1929, Pettis County, Missouri, USA. Country Music Performer. m. Gladys Marie Daniels, 25 June 1980, 3 s., 1 d. *Education:* Graduate, Journalism, Animal Science, University of Missouri; Graduate, Reppert's School of Autioneering. *Career:* Support for show by Marilyn Monroe; Tours regularly, USA and abroad; Played Las Vegas; Plays various venues, especially agricultural events (fairs, rodeos, livestock events); Television includes: Regular member, Red Foley's Ozark Jubilee, ABC TV; Host, Leroy Van Dyke Show; Star, film, What Am I Bid?; Radio: Co-host, Country Crossroads. *Recordings include:* Auctioneer; Walk On By, compilation, 2000. *Honours:* Billboard magazine, Biggest Ever Country Hit, Walk On By, 1994. *Membership:* CMA; ACM; NATD; IEBA; IAFE. *Current Management:* Leroy Van Dyke Enterprises, Gladys Van Dyke. *Address:* 29000 Hwy V, Smithton, MO 65350, USA.

VAN HALEN, Alex; b. 8 May 1955, Nijmegen, Netherlands. Musician (drums). *Career:* Formed US rock group Van Halen, with brother Eddie 1974–; Support tours with UFO; Santana; Black Sabbath; Regular headlining tours, USA and world-wide; Major appearances include: First US tour, 1978; California Music Festival, 1979; US Festival, 1982, 1983; Monsters of Rock, Castle Donington, 1984; Monsters of Rock US tour (with Metallica, Scorpions), 1988; Texas Jam, 1988. *Recordings:* Albums: Van Halen, 1978; Van Halen II, 1979; Women and Children First, 1980; Fair Warning, 1981; Diver Down, 1982; 1984, 1983; 5150 (No. 1, USA), 1986; OU812 (No. 1, USA), 1988; For Unlawful Carnal Knowledge (No. 1, USA), 1991; Right Here Right Now, 1993; Balance, 1995; Twister, 1996; Best of Van Halen, 1996; Van Halen 3, 1998; Van Halen Box, 1978–84, 2000; Singles include: You Really Got Me, 1978; Runnin' With The Devil, 1978; Dance The Night Away, 1979; And The Cradle Will Rock, 1980; (Oh) Pretty Woman, 1982; Dancing In The Street, 1982; Jump (No. 1, USA), 1984; Panama, 1984; I'll Wait, 1984; Hot For Teacher, 1984; Why Can't This Be Love, 1986; Love Walks In, 1986; Dreams, 1986; When It's Love, 1988; Finish What Ya Started, 1988; Feels So Good, 1989; Poundcake, 1991; Top of The World, 1991; Right Now, 1992. *Honours:* Numerous Platinum discs; Grammy Award, Best Hard Rock Performance, 1992; American Music Award, Favourite Hard Rock Album, 1992; Band awarded Gold Ticket, Madison Square Gardens, 1988; Inducted into Hollywood Rock Walk, 1991; MTV Video Awards, 1984, 1992. *Current Management:* SRO Management Inc, 189 Carlton St, Toronto, ON M5A 2K7, Canada.

VAN HALEN, Eddie; b. 26 Jan. 1957, Nijmegen, Netherlands. Rock Musician (guitar). m. Valerie Bertinelli, 11 April 1981, 1 s. *Education:* Piano lessons, Pasadena City College. *Career:* Founding mem., US rock group Van Halen, with brother Alex 1974–; Support tours to UFO; Santana; Black Sabbath; Regular headlining tours, USA and world-wide; Major appearances include: First US tour, 1978; California Music Festival, 1979; US Festival, 1982, 1983; Monsters of Rock Castle Donington, 1984; Monsters of Rock US tour (with Metallica, Scorpions), 1988; Texas Jam, 1988. *Recordings:* Albums: Van Halen, 1978; Van Halen II, 1979; Women and Children First, 1980; Fair Warning, 1981; Diver Down, 1982; 1984, 1983; 5150 (No. 1, USA), 1986; OU812 (No. 1, USA), 1988; For Unlawful Carnal Knowledge (No. 1, USA), 1991; Right Here Right Now, 1993; Balance, 1995; Twister, 1996; Best of Van Halen, 1996; Van Halen 3, 1998; Van Halen Box, 1978–84, 2000; Also appears on: Legend of 1900; Private Life; Wild Life; Singles include: You Really Got Me, 1978; Running With The Devil, 1978; Dance The Night Away, 1979; And The Cradle Will Rock, 1980; (Oh) Pretty Woman, 1982; Jump (No. 1, USA), 1984; Panama, 1984; I'll Wait, 1984; Hot For Teacher, 1984; Why Can't This Be Love, 1986; Dreams, 1986; Love Walks In, 1986; When It's Love, 1988; Finish What Ya Started, 1988; Feels So Good, 1989; Poundcake, 1991; Top of The World, 1991; Right Now, 1992; Contributor, Beat It, Michael Jackson (No. 1, USA), 1983. *Honours:* Numerous Platinum discs; Grammy Award, Best Hard Rock Performance, 1992; American Music Award, Favourite Hard Rock Album, 1992; MTV Music Video Awards, 1984, 1992; Band awarded Gold Ticket, Madison Square Gardens, 1988. *Current Management:* SRO Management Inc, 189 Carlton St, Toronto, ON M5A 2K7, Canada.

VAN HELDEN, Armand; b. 1972, Boston, Massachusetts, USA. DJ; Remixer/Prod. *Career:* Member, X-Mix Productions, Boston; Began remixing many Euro-pop acts; Began parallel solo career; Now remixes numerous top acts as well as releasing own records. *Recordings include:* Singles: Witch Doktor, 1994; Armand Van Helden, 1994; Psychic Bounty Killas, 1996; The Funk Phenomena, 1996; Ain't Armand, 1997; Ultrafunkula/Reservoir Dogs, 1997; Old School Junkies, 1997; Welcome to the Meat Market, 1997; Ghetto House Groove, 1998; 2 Future 4 U EP, 1998; You Don't Know Me (No. 1, UK), 1999; Flowerz, 1999; Koochy, 2000; Albums: Old School Junkies, 1996; Da Club Phenomena, 1997; Enter the Meatmarket, 1997; Armand Van Helden Phenomenon, 1999; 2 Future 4 U, 1999; Killing Puritans, 2000; Gandhi Khan, 2001; Repro, 2001; As Remixer/Producer: Latin Thang: Latin Thang, 1994; This Is Strictly Rhythm Vol. 4, 1994; Rest of New Order, 1995; Jimmy Somerville: Heartbeat, 1995; This Is Strictly Rhythm, Vol. 5, 1995; Mega Dance Party, 1995; Platinum On Black Vol. 2, 1996; Digitized, 1996; C J Bolland: Analogue Theatre, 1996; Tori Amos: Professional Widow, 1996; Best Girl Power Album Ever, 1997; Decade of Ibiza, 1997; DJ Icey: Funky Breaks, 1997; Jocelyn Brown: It's Alright I Feel It, 1997; Sneaker Pimps: Spin Spin

Sugar, 1997; Apollo Four Forty: Ain't Talkin' 'Bout Dub, 1997; Henry Street Bombs Vol. 2, 1998; Tuff and Jam: Speed Garage Underground, 1998.

VAN HOVE, Fred; b. 19 Feb. 1937, Antwerp, Belgium. Musician (piano, church organ, accordion). m. (2) Mie Van Cakenberghe, 2 April 1986, 3 s. *Education:* Piano, Theory, Harmony, Music Academy. *Career:* Free improvised music: Concerts, radio, TV; Festivals: Europe, Japan, USA, Canada, People's Republic of China, South Africa, Morocco. *Compositions:* for mixed instrument groups and improvising soloists; for Big Band and own groups: MLB III, Piano Kwartet, Nonet. *Recordings:* More than 60: Lust; Pyp; Suite for B-City; Flux, 1998; Passing Waves, 1998. *Honours:* Cultural Ambassador of Flanders, 1996, 1997. *Membership:* Wim wzw, Asscn for Improvised Music, Antwerp, Chairman. *Current Management:* Mie, St Vincentiusstr 61, B2018 Antwerp, Belgium.

VAN OLDEREN, Martin; b. 3 Jan. 1931, Netherlands. Blues Promoter; Record Prod; Radio Broadcaster. m. Carolien Van Der Kamp, 13 March 1957, 1 s., 1 d. *Career:* Organized concert featuring Memphis Slim, Little Brother Montgomery, Lightning Slim, Whispering Smith, 1971; Started Chicago Blues Festival, 1970–; Organized Blues Estafette, Utrecht, 1979–81; Amsterdam Blues Festival, Meervaart, annual event; Established Oldie Blues, own blues record label reproducing 78s, 1970; Compiled archive on blues music, including 15000 photos; Writes texts for CD covers; Broadcaster, own radio programme Bluesnachten (Blues Nights), VRPO, 1972–; Personal agent for blues artists playing in Holland including: Bo Diddley; Muddy Waters; Sonny Terry; Doctor Ross; B. B. King. *Publications:* Boogie Woogie and Blues Collector. *Membership:* President, Dutch Blues and Boogie Organisation. *Current Management:* Martin Van Olderen Blues Promotions. *Address:* Maasdrielhof 175, 1106 NG Amsterdam, Zuidoost, Netherlands.

VAN POL, Hans; b. 6 Aug. 1955, Amsterdam, Netherlands. Personal Man; Talent Scout. *Education:* Literature and Law, University of Amsterdam; Private singing and dancing lessons for 4 years. *Career:* First Gold recording as solo singer with children's choir, 1964; Singer with various rock, wave and ska bands, 1973–78; Member of Small Talk, touring through Europe, 1978–80; Member of Dutch band, Vulcano, 1980–85; Now Manager, 1985–. *Recordings:* 5 albums and 15 singles. *Honours:* 2 Gold albums; Popularity Award, 1983. *Membership:* Dutch Music Manager Asscn. *Address:* PO Box 9010, 1006 AA Amsterdam, Netherlands.

VANCEUNEBROUCK-WERTH, Richard; b. 1952, Seattle, WA, USA. Prod; Composer; Musician (keyboards, percussion). *Education:* Studied under electronic music pioneer Vladimir Ussachevsky, University of Utah. *Career:* Performed internationally with touring groups, 1970–77; Tangerine Dream's first North American tour, 1977; First performance, Seattle Symphony Orchestra, 1982; Composer, film and special event soundtracks, 1980–; First commissioned work, IBM, Paramount, Disney, 1981; National broadcasts include CTV (Canada), ABC; First commissioned operatic work, Seattle's Floating Opera, 1987; Produced AFFINITY Project, release new Beethoven work, 1989; Producer, composer, St Elmo's Choir; Tangerine Dream, 1989–. *Recordings:* with Tangerine Dream: Music From The 21st Century; with R. V. Werth and S. Chatelaine: AFFINITY; with Floating Opera: Seraphim Suite; with St Elmo's Choir: Syrenes; White Stocking Day; with R. Kotta: Alive, Alive-O; Many others. *Honours:* NAMA, Best New Age Group, 1989; Commissions: Seattle Opera; National Endowment for the Arts, Seattle, Tacoma, Vancouver BC, Edmonton, Canada Arts Commissions. *Membership:* ASCAP; BMI; NAMA; International Producer's Guild. *Current Management:* Omega Organisation International. *Address:* PO Box 33623-WWIM, Seattle, WA 98133–0623, USA.

VANDENBROUCQE, Gérard; b. 15 May 1961, France. Musician (violin). *Education:* Lessons with Pierre Cuuaz; J L Pino; Didier Lockwood. *Career:* Television: Antenne 2; M6; Europe 1; Appearances at: Montréal Festival, 1993; SOPS, New York; Radio France Inter. *Recordings:* Tango, Violin Onztet. *Membership:* Asscn Jazz et Violon. *Current Management:* c/o JMS, 12 rue Bouchut, 75015 Paris, France. *Address:* 12 rue Lazare Carnot, 92140 Clamart, France.

VANDENDRIESSCHE, Johan; b. 30 May 1958, Leuven, Belgium, Musician (saxophone, flute, bass clarinet, drums, bass guitar, keyboard); Teacher of Jazz History and Harmony (Conservatorium GENT) and Woodwinds. m. Hilde Pollet, 8 Dec. 1991, 1 s., 1 d. *Education:* Degree of Excellence, Conservatorium of Leuven; Private lessons, Jazz; Musicology, KUL, Leuven. *Career:* Appearances with Belgium Radio and TV Orchestras; BRT Big Band; BRT Jazzorkest/Philharmonic Orchestra; Euro/Jazz Orchestra; Own Band, Milkshake Banana, played in jazz festivals in Atlanta, USA, Montreux, Switzerland, Århus, Denmark; Concerts with Randy Crawford and John Miles as a soloist in Belgium and Holland; WDR Big Band, Cologne, Germany, with Clare Fisher; with Calvin Owens: That's Your Booty; Own bands Jive Talk and The Demagogue Reacts. *Compositions:* Move; Nathalie; Cool Bird; ISIRO. *Recordings:* With Milkshake Banana, ACT Bigband, Caude Maurane, Soulsister, Claude Nougaro, Indochine, Johan Verminnen. *Publications:* Articles on jazz in KNACK magazine, 1981–82. *Honours:* First

Prize, International Jazz Contest, Hoeilaart, 1979. *Current Management:* BVBA VDDR. *Address:* Groenstraat 33, 3110 Rotselaar, Belgium.

VANDROSS, Luther; b. 20 April 1951, New York, USA. Vocalist; Songwriter; Arranger; Prod. *Career:* Member, Listen My Brother (musical theatre workshop), Harlem, 1973; Session singer (recordings and commercials), arranger, 1974–80; Leader, own group, Luther, 1976–77; Solo artiste, 1980–; Regular international concerts. *Compositions include:* Fascination, David Bowie; You Stopped Lovin' Me, Roberta Flack. *Recordings:* Albums: Luther, 1976; This Close To You, 1977; Solo albums: Never Too Much, 1981; Forever For Always For Love, 1982; Busy Body, 1984; Give Me The Reason, 1986; Any Love, 1988; The Best of Luther Vandross, 1989; Power of Love, 1991; Never Let Me Go, 1993; Songs, 1994; This is Christmas, 1995; Your Secret Love, 1996; I Know, 1998; Smooth Love, 2000; Luther Vandross, 2001; Hit singles include: with Change: A Lover's Holiday, 1980; Searching, 1980; Solo hits: Never Too Much, 1983; The Night I Fell In Love, 1985; Give Me The Reason, from film Ruthless People, 1986; Stop To Love, 1987; I Really Didn't Mean It, 1987; So Amazing, 1987; There's Nothing Better Than Love, duet with Gregory Hines, 1987; Any Love, 1989; She Won't Talk To Me, 1989; Here and Now, 1990; Power of Love/Love Power, 1991; Don't Want To Be A Fool, 1991; The Best Things In Life Are Free, duet with Janet Jackson, from film Mo' Money, 1992; The Rush, 1992; Endless Love, duet with Mariah Carey, 1994; Love The One You're With, 1995; Always And Forever, 1995; Ain't No Stopping Us Now, 1995; Going in Circles, 1995; I Can Make It Better, 1996; Are You Using Me?, 1998; Heart of a Hero, 1999; Sessions as backing singer include: Young Americans, David Bowie, 1974; Songs For The New Depression, Bette Midler, 1975; Sounds and Stuff Like That, Quincy Jones, 1978; Le Freak, Chic, 1978; We Are Family, Sister Sledge, 1978; Other sessions for Ringo Starr; Carly Simon; Chaka Khan; Average White Band; Vocal arranger, No More Tears, Donna Summer and Barbra Streisand, 1979; Producer, recordings by Aretha Franklin; Dionne Warwick; Diana Ross; Whitney Houston; Contributor, Voices That Care (Red Cross charity record), 1991; The Heart of a Hero (AIDS research benefit record), 1992. *Honours:* MVP Background Singer, 1977–80; Grammy Awards: Best R&B Vocal Performance, 1991, 1992; Best R&B Song, 1992; Soul Train Music Awards: Best Male R&B Album, 1987, 1992; Best Male R&B Single, 1990; American Music Awards: Favourite Soul/R&B Male Artist, 1988, 1990, 1992, 2002; Favourite Soul/R&B Album, 1992; NAACP Image Awards: Best Male Artist, 1990; Best Male Vocalist, Best Album, 1992; Luther Vandross Day, Los Angeles, 1991. *Current Management:* The Left Bank Organization. *Address:* 6255 Sunset Blvd, Suite 1111, Hollywood, CA 90028, USA.

VANGELIS, (Evangelos Papathanassiou); b. 29 March 1943, Volos, Greece. Musician (keyboards); Composer; Conductor. *Education:* Acad. of Fine Arts, Athens; Classical music with Aristotelis Coudourof. *Career:* Mem., Formynx, 1960s; Mem., Aphrodite's Child, with Demis Roussos; Composer, Paris, 1972; Built Nemo recording studio, London, 1974; Partnership with Jon Anderson as Jon and Vangelis, 1980–84. *Compositions:* Music scores for French wildlife films, 1972; Heaven and Hell, Third Movement, theme for Carl Sagan's TV series Cosmos (BBC1), 1981; Film scores: Chariots of Fire; Antarctica; Blade Runner; Missing; Mutiny On The Bounty; Wonders of Life; Wild and Beautiful; Francesco; 1492 – Conquest of Paradise; Bitter Moon; Cavafy; All tracks on solo albums self-composed, played and produced. *Recordings:* Albums: with Aphrodite's Child: 666; Solo: L'Apocalypse Des Animaux, 1972; Heaven and Hell, 1976; Albedo 0.39, 1976; Spiral, 1977; Reprise 1990–1999, 2000; Mythodea–Music For The NASA Mission, 2001; Beauborg, 1978; China, 1979; Chariots of Fire (soundtrack), 1981; Soil Activities, 1984; Mask, 1985; Opera Sauvage, 1987; Direct, 1988; Themes, 1989; 1492 – Conquest of Paradise, 1992; Voices, 1995; El Greco, 1995; Oceanic, 1997; Spiral, 1997; Mythodea (Music for the NASA Mission: 2001 Mars Odyssey), 2001; As Jon and Vangelis: Short Stories, 1980; The Friends of Mr Cairo, 1981; Private Collection, 1983; The Best of Jon and Vangelis, 1984; Page of Life, 1991. Singles include: with Aphrodite's Child: Rain and Tears; Solo: Heaven and Hell, Third Movement, 1981; Chariots of Fire (No. 1, USA), 1982; with Jon Anderson: I Hear You Now, 1980; I'll Find My Way Home, 1982; State Of Independence, 1984; Also featured on Polar Shift charity album, 1991. *Honours:* Academy Award, Best Original Score, Chariots of Fire, 1982. *Address:* c/o Sony Classical, 550 Madison Ave, New York, NY 10022-3211, USA. *Website:* www.vangelisworld.com.

VANIAN, Dave, (David Letts); b. 12 Oct. 1956. Vocalist. *Career:* Former grave digger; Vocalist, UK punk rock group, The Damned, 1976–77; Appearances include: Mont de Marsan punk festival, France, 1976; Support to the Sex Pistols, Anarchy In The UK Tour, 1976; First UK punk group to play US dates, 1977; Member, Doctors of Madness, 1978; The Damned re-formed, 1981; Member, side projects: Naz and the Nomads, 1988; Dave Vanian and the Phantom Chords, 1990, 1995; The Damned reunion tour, 1991. *Recordings:* Albums: with the Damned: Damned Damned Damned, 1977; Music For Pleasure, 1977; Machine Gun Etiquette, 1979; The Black Album, 1980; The Best Of, 1981; Strawberries, 1982; Phantasmagoria, 1985; Anything, 1986; Light At The End of Tunnel, 1987; Peel Sessions, 1990; Not of This Earth, 1996; Eternal Damnation Live, 1999; Molten Lager, 2000; with Naz and the Nomads: Give Daddy The Knife, Cindy, 1988; Singles include:

with The Damned: New Rose, 1976; Neat Neat Neat, 1977; Problem Child, 1977; Don't Cry Wolf, 1977; Love Song, 1979; Smash It Up, 1979; I Just Can't Be Happy Today, 1979; The History Of The World, 1980; Lovely Money, 1982; Thanks For The Night, 1984; Grimly Fiendish, 1985; The Shadow of Love, 1985; Is It A Dream, 1985; Anything, 1986; Eloise (No. 3, UK), 1986; Gigolo, 1987; Alone Again Or, 1987.

VANNELLI, Joseph Anthony; b. 28 Dec. 1950, Montréal, Québec, Canada. Prod; Arranger; Musician (keyboards). *Education:* 3 years university; Private music lessons. *Career:* Worked with: Gino Vannelli; Gary Morris; David Meece; Kudasai; Marilyn Scott; Jimmy Haslip; Don Sebesky and The Royal Philharmonic Orchestra; Gregory Hines; Co-producer, commercials including Pontiac; Honda; Owner, recording studio; Concerts include Gino Vannelli's World Tour, 1990–92; Television includes: Arsenio Hall Show, European television; Juno Award Show, Canada; Dick Clark Night Time; Documentary on rain forests of Costa Rica. *Recordings:* Crazy Life, 1973; Powerful People, 1974; Storm At Sunup, 1975; The Gist of The Gemini, 1976; Brother To Brother, 1978; Nightwalker, 1981; Black Cars, 1985; Big Dreamers Never Sleep, 1987; Inconsolable Man, 1991; Gino Vannelli Live In Montréal, 1992; Yonder Tree, 1995; Man in the Moon, 1996; Sexogroove, 1998; Voices in Harmony, 1998; Never Knew, 1998; Sweetest Day of May, 1999; Awakening, with Joseph Curiale, 2000. *Publications:* REP Magazine; Midi Magazine; Keyboard Magazine, Japan. *Current Management:* Diane Ricci. *Address:* 28205 Agoura Rd, Agoura Hills, CA 91301, USA.

VANROBAEYS, Filip; Musician (fiddle, harp, guitar, whistles, badhan). *Career:* Member, Group The Swigshift; Dranouter Festival, 1995; Den Ekster, 1996, 1997; Labadoux Festival, 1997; Paulus Festival, 1997; Sloanthe Festival, 1997; Gooik Festival 2002, 1997; De Brakke Grond, Amsterdam, 1997; Foleys Irish Pub, Ghent; Radio 1, De Groote Boodschap; Several Regional Radio and Television Appearances. *Compositions:* Jumpin The Fences; Dirty Wally; Friends Sadness; Something to Fear; Shut the Pub; A Whistler's Wedding. *Recordings:* Tales From the Great Whiskey Book, 1996. *Honours:* Government Medal, Flute, 1986; Second Place, Youth Soloist Festival, 1986; Finale, Westtalent, 1995. *Membership:* Volksmuziekfederatie, Belgium. *Current Management:* KAFT Productions, Akkerwindelaan 20, 8791 Beveren-Leie, Belgium. *Address:* c/o Barrierestraat 49, 8940 Wervik, Belgium.

VARIS, Francis; b. 4 Feb. 1957, Clamart, France. Musician (accordion). m. Françoise Niay. *Education:* Musicological License, Paris VIII University. *Career:* Tours and European jazz festivals with: American guitarist Tal Farlow, 1983; Brazilian singer Nazaré Pereira, 1985–; Saxophone player Lee Konitz, 1986–89; The Paris-Musette, Tokyo, Montréal, 1991–; Own group Bolovaris. *Recordings:* Cordes Et Lames, 1983; Medium Rare, with Lee Konitz, 1986; Accordion Madness, with accordionist Kenny Kotwitz, 1989; Paris-Musette 1 and 2, 1991, 1993; Bolovaris, 1994; Ombre, with Romane, 1998; Identities, with Idir, 1999; Ivory Port, with Jacques Bolognesi, 1999; Ciranda, with Marcio Faraco, 2000. *Honours:* Grand Prix du Disque de l'Academie Charles Cros. *Current Management:* Alain Brisemontier. *Address:* Le Moulin, 49800 Sarrigné, France.

VARSANYI, Juraj; b. 14 May 1961, Bratislava, Slovakia. Musician (drums, percussion, cimbalom). *Education:* People's Conservatory of Bratislava. *Career:* International tours; Many TV and radio shows with: Vus-Orchestra, Gravis, Knock-Out, Jully's Orchestra, Just Jazz, Bratislava Jazz Days, 1991; Burg Mautendorf Jazzwettbewerb-Aut; Hajnal Quintet, 1987; Varsanyi Habsburg-Wedding, 1993. *Recordings:* Vus LP, 1983; Gombitova and Gravis LP, 1986; Knock Out, LP, 1987; Gravis, LP, 1989; Varsanyi, LP, 1991; La Rubia, CD, 1995; Slovak Jazz Anthology, CD, 1992. *Honours:* Gorizia, International Festival Contest, 1986; Second Prize, Slovak Jazz Festival, 1995. *Membership:* Slovak Jazz Society, 1989/90–. *Current Management:* Slovak Jazz Society, Jakubovo nam. 12, Bratislava, Slovakia. *Address:* Varsanyi Juraj, Hlavna 20, 90044 Tomasov, Slovakia. *Fax:* (2) 4595-8555. *E-mail:* georg@vav.sk.

VARTAN, Sylvie; b. 15 Aug. 1944, Iskretz, Bulgaria. m. (1) Johnny Hallyday, 1965, divorced, 1980, 1 s., (2) Tony Scotti, 1984, 1 d. *Education:* Lycée Hélène-Boucher, Paris. *Career:* Singing debut in duet with Frankie Jordan (panne d'essence), national tours, 1961–, international tours, 1965–, including Paris Olympia, 1961, 1962, 1963, 1964 (with The Beatles), 1967, 1968, 1970, 1972, 1996, 1999; Palais des Congres, Paris, 1975–76, 1977–78, 1983; Palais des Sports, Paris, 1981, 1991; Casino de Paris, 1995, Las Vegas, USA, 1982, Los Angeles, USA, 1983, Atlantic City, USA, 1984 and Sofia, Bulgaria, 1990; Songs include: Tous mes copains, En ecoutant la pluie, I'm Watching, Si je chante, La plus belle pour aller danser, Quand tu es la, Par amour par pitié, 2'35 de bonheur, Le Kid, Comme un garçon, La Maritza, La chasse a l'homme, Loup, Dilindam, L'heure la plus douce de ma vie, Pour lui je reviens, Mon père, J'ai un problème (with Johnny Hallyday), Toi le garçon, Bye bye Leroy Brown, la drole de fin, Qu'est-ce qui fait pleurer les blondes?; Le temps du swing, Petit rainbow, I don't want the night to end, Nicolas, Merveilleusement desenchantee, L'amour c'est comme une cigarette, Aimer, Des heures de desir, Double exposure, Virage, Femme sous influence, C'est fatal, Qui tu es, Je n'aime encore que toi, Sensible; *Recordings:* L'Essentiel, 2001; TV appearances include: Show Averty, 1965; Jolie poupee, 1968; Doppia

coppia, 1969; Sacha Sylvie Show, 1969; Sylvissima, 1970; Top a Sylvie Vartan, 1972, 1972; Top a Sylvie et Johnny, 1973; Je chante pour Swanee, 1974; Sylvie, 1975; Punto e Basta, 1975; Dancing Star, 1977; La Maritza, 1990; Sylvie sa vie, 1994; Irrésistiblement... Sylvie, 1998; Qu'est-ce qui fait rêver Sylvie?, 2000; Mausolée pour une garce, 2001; Films: Un clair de lune a Maubeuge, 1962; D'ou viens-tu Johnny?, 1963; Cherchez l'idole, 1964; Patate, 1964; Les poneyttes, 1967; Malpertuis, 1971; Mon amie Sylvie, 1972; L'ange noir, 1994. *Publications:* Si je chante, 1981; Beauty Book, 1985. *Honours:* Triomphe des variétés award, 1970; Chevalier des Arts et des Lettres, 1985; Chevalier de l'ordre national du mérite, 1987; Chevalier de l'ordre du Cavalier de Madara, Bulgaria, 1996; Chevalier dans l'ordre de la legion d'Honneur, 1998. *Address:* c/o Charley Marouani, 37 rue Marbeuf, 75008, Paris, France.

VASCONCELLOS, Joe; b. 9 March 1959, Santiago, Chile. Musician (percussion); Vocalist; Composer. m. Irene Gonzalez Peña, 1 March 1985. *Education:* College (Brazil, Ecuador, Japan, Italy); Conservatorio Musicale Nicolo Paganini, Genoa, Italy. *Career:* with Maria Creuza, Musician (percussion): Tours throughout Brazil; Argentina; Uruguay; Spain; USA; As Joe Vasconcellos (Singer with own band): all national territory Chile; TV appearances: Sabado Gigante, Chile. *Recordings:* As vocalist of Congreso: Viaje Por La Cresta del Mundo; Ha Llegado Carta; Joe Vasconcellos: Esto Es Solo Una Canción; Verde Cerca; Toque, 1995; Vivo, 1999; Major composition: Hijo Del Sol Luminoso. *Honours:* with Congreso: Best Group (Chile). *Membership:* Sociedad Chilena Del Derecho De Autor. *Current Management:* Galo Producciones S A. *Address:* Hernando de Aguirre 944, Providencia, Santiago, Chile.

VASCONCELOS, Monica; b. 13 Nov. 1966, São Paulo, Brazil. Musician; Vocalist; Lyricist. *Education:* São Paulo University, Brazil. *Career:* Started singing at 17; Bars, parties, backing vocals for record producers; Joined vocal, drama group, Beijo, 1987; Toured Brazil, Sang on television and radio; Recorded with musicians in London, Roland Perrin, Ashley Slater, John O'Neall; Sang with Tim Garland, Christine Tobin, Jacqui Dankworth; Own band, toured England; Supported Gilberto Gil, Barbican Hall. *Compositions:* Sabonete Do Mato; Mudanca Oragao; Ivan Da Caverna; Vestidinho; Guizim; Xotemo; Bossa Zangada; Outono; Maracatu Do Pomso; Samba Da Ponte; Atabaque. *Recordings:* Beijo; Nois, 1994; Nois Dois, 1999. *Membership:* Musicians' Union.

VASIK, Cassandra; b. Chatham, Ontario, Canada. Musician (acoustic guitar); Entertainer. *Education:* 3 year diploma, Fanshawe College, London, Ontario. *Career:* Member, Little Egypt; Moved to Toronto; Receptionist, independent record label; Member, Lost, acoustic trio; Television: Christmas With The Troops, performing to United Nations Peace Keeping Troops, Europe and Middle East, 1992; Ear To The Ground; Canada Day; Spotlight; Winterlude '93; Friday Night With Ralph Benmergui; Video, Sadly Mistaken, No. 1, Outlaws and Heroes, Much Music: Tours with: Randy Travis; The Nitty Gritty Dirt Band; Clint Black; Steve Wariner; Vince Gill; Van Shelton; Marty Stewart. *Recordings:* Albums: Wildflowers; Feels Like Home; Different, 2000; Singles: It Comes Back To You; Which Face Should I Put On Tonight; Those Stars; Wildflowers; Sadly Mistaken; Fortune Smiled; Roll Like A Wheel; Almost Like You Cared. *Honours:* 2 JUNO Awards, Country Female Vocalist, 1991, 1993; Vista Rising Star Award, CCMA, 1992; CCMA Award, Vocal Collaboration (with Russell de Carle), 1993; Commemorative Medal for the 125th Anniversary, Confederation of Canada, 1993. *Membership:* CARAS; SOCAN; CCMA; ACTRA. *Current Management:* John W. Edwards, Renaissance Music and Entertainment.

VAUGHN, Danny; b. New York, USA. Vocalist; Lyricist. *Career:* Singer, rock group Waysted, 1987; Tours include Europe, supporting Iron Maiden, 1987; Singer, lyricist, rock group Tyketto, 1988–; Concerts include: L'Amour, Brooklyn; NYC Cat Club, supporting Skid Row; Numerous US State Fairs; Tours and festivals, Europe, USA, 1991–. *Recordings:* Albums: with Waysted: Save Your Prayers, 1987; with Tyketto: Don't Come Easy, 1990; Strength In Numbers, 1994; Shine, 1995; Take Out And Served Up Live, 1996; Inishmore, 1998; Also featured on Union, Yes, 1991. *Address:* c/o Music For Nations Records, 333 Latimer Rd, London W10 6RA, England.

VAZQUEZ, Roland; b. 4 July 1951, Pasadena, California, USA. m. Susan Botti, 1988, 1 d. *Education:* MM, Manhattan School of Music, 1985; Member, Manhattan School of Music Jazz Faculty, Ensembles and Composition. *Career:* Leader and Sideman, numerous recordings, on US and international jazz radio, 1979–; Appearances as Composer/Leader at major jazz festivals and venues throughout the USA, and in Canada, Scandinavia and Central America. *Compositions:* 57 compositions recorded and published for jazz quintet, octet, tentet, big band, and chamber group. *Recordings:* Albums as Composer/Leader: Urban Ensemble: The Music of Roland Vazquez, 1979; Feel Your Dream, 1982; The Tides of Time, 1988; No Separate Love, 1991; Best of the LA Jazz Ensemble, 1994; Further Dance, 1997. *Honours:* National Endowment for the Arts grant, 1977; Meet the Composer, 1986, 1997; Arts International, 1997. *Membership:* ASCAP; NARAS; IAJE; AFIM. *Address:* 924 West End Ave No. 1, New York, NY 10025, USA.

VEAR, Anthony Craigy 'Watts'; b. 4 Dec. 1970, Middlesbrough, England. Musician (drums, percussion). *Career:* At 14, 3 years' working mens' clubs; Theatre premieres of: Assassins; Stephen Sondheim; Manchester; Little Shop of Horrors; 5 tours with Cholmondelys Dance Company; World tours with: Renegade Soundwave, 1994; The Wolfgang Press, 1995; Concerts in Los Angeles with Tom Jones, 1994. *Recordings:* Albums include: Funky Little Demons, 1993–94; Tom Jones: The Lead and How To Swing It, 1994. *Honours:* Included in exhibition at New Rock and Roll Museum, Cleveland, USA. *Membership:* Musicians' Union; LMC; SAL, UK. *Address:* Basement Flat, 5 Gilmore Rd, London SE13 5AD, England.

VEDDER, Eddie (Edward Mueller); b. 23 Dec. 1966, Evanston, IL, USA. Vocalist. *Career:* Lead singer, US rock group Pearl Jam, 1991–; Concerts include: Support tour, Alice In Chains, 1991; Lollapalooza Festival tour, 1992; Drop In The Park concert, Seattle, 1992; European tour, 1992; Bob Dylan 30th anniversary concert, Madison Square Garden, 1992; Band appears in film Singles, 1992; Support to Keith Richards and The Expensive Winos, 1992; Rock For Choice benefit concert, Los Angeles, 1993; Concert appearances with Neil Young. *Recordings:* Albums: with Pearl Jam: Ten, 1992; Vs. (No. 1, USA), 1993; Vitalogy (No. 1, USA), 1994; Merkin Ball, 1995; No Code (No. 1, USA), 1996; Yield, 1998; Live on Two Legs, 1998; Binaural, 2000; Live, 2000; Riot Act, 2002; Singles include: Alive, 1992; Even Flow, 1992; Jeremy, 1992; Daughter, 1993; Dissident, 1994; Spin The Black Circle, 1994; Merkinball, 1995; Who You Are, 1996; Given To Fly, 1998; Wishlist, 1998; Nothing As It Seems, 2000; Contributor, Singles film soundtrack, 1992; Sweet Relief album, 1993; Dead Man Walking, film soundtrack, 1996; Tibetan Freedom Concert, 1997. *Honours:* American Music Award, Favourite New Artist, Pop/Rock and Hard Rock categories, 1993; Rolling Stone Readers Awards: Best Male Singer, Best New American Band, Best Video, 1993; 4 MTV Video Awards; Highest 1-week album sales total in history, Vs., 1993. *Current Management:* Curtis Management, 417 Denny Way, Suite 200, Seattle, WA 98109, USA.

VEE, Bobby, (Robert Velline); b. 30 April 1943, Fargo, North Dakota, USA. Vocalist. *Career:* Founder, US group The Shadows, 1958; Solo singer, 1960–; World-wide appearances include: Hollywood Bowl, with Jerry Lee Lewis, Brenda Lee, The Shirelles, 1961; British tour with The Crickets, 1962; Dick Clark's Caravan of Stars US tour, 1963; British tour with Dusty Springfield, The Searchers, 1964; British tour, with Dusty Springfield, The Searchers, The Zombies, 1965; British tour, with Del Shannon and Brian Hyland, 1988; Annual appearances, Buddy Holly Memorial Concerts; Giants of Rock 'n' Roll, Wembley Arena, with Little Richard, Duane Eddy, 1992; Film appearances: Play It Cool, 1962; Just For Fun, 1963. *Recordings:* Albums: Bobby Vee, 1961; Bobby Vee Sings Hits of The Rockin' 50s, 1961; Take Good Care of My Baby, 1962; Bobby Vee Meets The Crickets, 1962; A Bobby Vee Recording Session, 1962; Golden Greats, 1962; Merry Christmas From..., 1962; The Night Has A Thousand Eyes, 1963; Bobby Vee Meets The Ventures, 1963; Bobby Vee Sings The New Sound From England, 1964; Come Back When You Grow Up, 1967; Just Today, 1968; Nothing Like A Sunny Day, 1972; The Bobby Vee Singles Album, 1980; Favorites, 1997; Down the Line, 1999; The EP Collection, 1999; Hit singles include: Devil Or Angel, 1960; Rubber Ball, 1961; More Than I Can Say, 1961; Take Good Care of My Baby (No. 1, USA), 1961; How Many Tears, 1961; Run To Him, 1961; Sharing You, 1962; A Forever Kind of Love, 1962; The Night Has A Thousand Eyes, from film Just For Fun, 1963; Charms, 1963; Come Back When You're Grown Up, 1967. *Current Management:* DHM – Dave Hoffman Management. *Address:* PO Box 26037, Minneapolis, MN 55447, USA.

VEGA, Louie, (Little Louie Vega, Groovebox); b. 12 June 1965, New York, USA. Prod; Remixer; DJ. *Career:* Began as a DJ in New York, 1980s; Starting doing mixes for artists including The Cover Girls; Worked with Todd Terry before teaming up with Kenny 'Dope' Gonzalez as Masters At Work; Duo also recorded as Nu Yorican Soul; Co-founder: MAW Records; Collaborations: India; Marc Anthony; Jocelyn Brown; James Ingram; Stephanie Mills; Remixed: Debbie Gibson; St Etienne; Shanice; Tito Puente; Barbara Tucker; Jamiroquai; Atmosfear; Incognito; Luther Vandross; Ce Ce Peniston; Martha Wash; Ballistic Brothers. *Recordings:* Albums: Nu Yorican Soul, 1997; with Masters at Work: Our Time Is Coming, 2002. Singles: Ride On The Rhythm (with Marc Anthony), 1991; I Can't Get No Sleep (as Masters At Work), 1992; Deep Inside (as Hardrive), 1993; Love and Happiness (as River Ocean), 1994; The Nervous Track (as Nu-Yorican Soul), 1994; I Am The Black Gold of The Sun (as Nu-Yorican Soul), 1996; What A Sensation (as Kenlou), 1996; To Be In Love, 1997; Brasilian Beat, 1998. *Address:* c/o Strictly Rhythm, 920 Broadway 1403, New York, USA.

VEGA, Suzanne Nadine; b. 11 July 1959, Santa Monica, CA, USA. Vocalist; Songwriter; Musician (guitar). m. Mitchell Froom, 17 March 1995, divorced 2003. *Education:* High School For The Performing Arts, New York; Barnard College, New York. *Career:* Folk singer, songwriter, 1982–; Began performing at Greenwich Village; World-wide concerts include: Royal Albert Hall, London, 1986; Prince's Trust Benefit Concert, Wembley Arena, 1986; Carnegie Hall, New York, 1987; Cambridge Folk Festival, 1991; Woody Guthrie Tribute, Central Park, New York, 1992; Berloni Foundation concert (for leukemia patients), Modena, Italy, 1992. *Recordings:* Albums: Suzanne Vega, 1985; Solitude Standing, 1987; Days of Open Hand, 1991; 99.9°F, 1992; In Concert,

1993; Nine Objects of Desire, 1996; Songs In Red And Gray, 2001; Hit singles include: Marlene On The Wall, 1986; Luka, 1987; Tom's Diner, 1987; Book of Dreams, 1990; 99.9°F, 1992; Blood Makes Noise, 1992; When Heroes Go Down, 1993; No Cheap Thrill, 1997; Book And A Cover, 1998. *Contributions to:* Deadicated (Grateful Dead tribute album), 1991; Tom's Album, 1991; Pavarotti and Friends, 1993; Tower of Strength (Leonard Cohen tribute album), 1995. *Honours:* Grammy, Art Direction, 1990; MTV Award, Best Female Video, Luka, 1988; New York Music Awards, Best Alternative Music Artist, joint Best Rock Album, 1992. *Current Management:* M+ Management, 632 Broadway, New York, NY 10012, USA.

VEJSLEV, Jakob; b. 25 July 1957, Copenhagen, Denmark. Musician (guitar); Composer. m. Astrid Dyssegaard, 24 July 1987, 1 s. *Career:* Played harmonica from age 13; Guitar, 1975–; Full-time guitarist with several groups and musicians (free jazz, fusion, latin, rock), Copenhagen, 1977–; Composed jazz, classical music, worked with own trio and duo, 1985–; Moved to Norway to work as composer, musician and music teacher, 1992–. *Compositions:* Flute quartet in 8 movements, 1992; Trio (trombone, violin and marimba), 1993; Piece for 10 instruments, 1994. *Recordings:* News: Stereo Magasin; Arranger, soloist: Håndslag Til Frank, 1987; Arranger, soloist: Til Dine Ojnes Åndmusik, 1990. *Membership:* Danish Jazz, Beat and Folk Composer Asscn; KODA (Danish Composers Copyright Asscn); Norwegian Jazz Asscn. *Current Management:* Warner Chappell.

VEJSLEV, Tony; b. 25 Oct. 1926, Copenhagen, Denmark. Composer; Vocalist; Musician (guitar). m. Benthe Kolding, 19 Oct. 1954, 1 s. *Education:* Teacher. *Career:* Concerts in Denmark; Radio broadcasts, 1938–; Television appearances, 1949–. *Recordings:* Tony Vejslev Synger, 1983; Haandslag Til Frank, 1988; Til Dine Oejnes Aaandemusik, 1990; 50 Danske Viser Og Sange, 1993; Old Poems – New Songs, 2001. *Publications:* 19 Jaegerviser 1953, 1967; 26 Viser, 1987; Fem Farum Digte, 1988; 18 Danske Sange, 1990; 50 Danske Viserog, 2002. *Honours:* KODA; Dansk Musikraad; Scholarships. *Membership:* Danish Jazz, Beat and Folk Authors; Prize of Honour, Danish Jazz, Beat and Folk Authors, 1998. *Current Management:* Olafssongs, Paarupvej 44, Græsted, Denmark. *E-mail:* fo@olafssongs.dk.

VELGHE, Rudy; b. 4 Jan. 1960, Oudenaarde, Belgium. Violin; Nyckelharpa; Guitar; Composer; Arranger. *Education:* Licence Degree, History, Rug-State University, Ghent, Belgium. *Career:* Professional Musician, 1987–; Founder Member, Celtic band, Orion; Composed and arranged music for different short films and TV programmes; Performed in many shows on radio and TV/BRT, RTB, BBC, Irish Radio; Studio musician, with many artists. *Compositions:* Wailing Reel; Restless Home; Shores of Marsannay; Reel of Notes. *Recordings:* Histoires de Rue; 1990; Blue Room; Restless Home; Dao Dezi; 1995; Orion 1990, 1996; About to Go. *Current Management:* VZW Worm Productions ASBL, 136 Chaussée de Wemmel, 1090 Brussels, Belgium.

VELOSO, Caetano Emanuel Vianna Telles; b. 7 Aug. 1942, Santo Amaro da Purificação, Bahia, Brazil. Vocalist, Musician (guitar), Songwriter. *Career:* Won a lyric competition in mid 1960s with Um Dia; Signed to the Philips label; Part of MPB (Musica Popular Brasileira) new wave of young artists along with artists such as Gal Costa and Gilberto Gil; Experimental nature of Veloso's music was not favoured by the military dictatorship, resulting in arrest, 1968; Two months in prison before going into exile in London; Returned to Brazil, 1972; His great knowledge of old Brazilian songs led to him reviving the careers of older musicians, including Luiz Gonzaga; Hosted a TV show with Chico Buarque in 1980s. *Recordings include:* Albums: Alegria, Alegria, 1967; Domingo, 1967; Caetano Veloso, 1967; Atrás do Trio Eléctrico, 1969; Caetano E Chico – Ao Vivo Na Bahia, 1972; Araçá Azul, 1973; Jóia, 1975; Doces Barbaros, 1976; Bicho, 1977; Maria Bethania and Caetano Veloso Ao Vivo, 1978; Cinema Transcendental, 1979; Outras Palavaras, 1981; Cores Nomes, 1982; Uns, 1983; Velo, 1984; Caetano, 1987; Estrangeiro, 1989; Muito, 1990; Circulado, 1992; Tropicália 2, 1994; Fina Estampa En Vivo, 1995; Divina Estampa, 1996; Tieta Do Agresta, 1997; Livros, 1998; Noites Do Norte, 2001. *Honours:* Latin Grammy Award, Best MPB Album, Livros, 2000; Grammy Award, Best World Music Album, Livros, 2000. *Address:* c/o Universal Do Brasil Ltda, PO Box 37133, 22622–970 Rio de Janeiro, RJ, Brazil. *Website:* www.caetanoveloso.com.br.

VENIER, Glauco; b. 8 Sept. 1962, Sedegliano, Udine, Italy. Musician (piano); Composer. *Education:* Berklee College of Music, Boston, Massachusetts, 1991; Graduated, Performance Major in Organ, Conservatory of Music, Udine, Italy, 1985; Studied privately with Franco D'Andrea, Enrico Rava, Hal Crook, Ray Santisi, George Garzone. *Career:* Private Piano Instructor, Udine, 1985–90; Music Educator, several grammar schools, 1985–90; Educator, Conservatory of Music, Gorizia, Italy, 1993–98; Performed with: Kenny Wheeler, Lee Konitz, Jack Walrath, Enrico Rava, Paolo Fresu, Valery Ponomarev, Flavio Boltro, Hal Crook, George Garzone, Massimo Urbani, Stefano Di Battista, Gianni Basso, Chriss Speed, Matt Garrison, Abe Laboriel Jr.; Roberto Dani. *Recordings include:* Massimo De Mattia, Poesie Pour Pasolini, 1993, The Silent Drama, 1995; Enrica Bacchia, Ancora, 1995; Monografie By New Age (compilation), 1996; Diego Sandrin, Millionaire, 1996; Tamara Obrovac, Triade, 1996; Enzo Pietropaoli, Stolen Songs, 1998; Fondazione Luigi Bon, Il Vieli, Il Dragon e Il Cavalir, Music for Fairytale By

Glauco Venier, 1998; Klaus Gesing and Glauco Venier Play Bach, 2000; Ides of March (with Lee Konitz), 2001; Gorizia (with Kenny Wheeler), 2001. *Honours:* Semifinalist, Martial Solal Piano Jazz Competition, Paris, 1989; Finalist, Thelonious Monk Piano Jazz Competition, Washington, 1989; Berklee College of Music Achievement Scholarship, 1991; Best Group, Glauco Venier Trio, Jazz Festival in Vienne, France, 1997. *Current Management:* Orpheus Management, via Giberti, Verona, Italy. *Address:* Via Castelliere No. 6, Gradisca di Sedegliano, Udine, Italy. *E-mail:* orpheus@serenacom.net.

VENTO, Joseph; b. 16 Dec. 1926, Los Angeles, California, USA. Composer; Conductor; Band Leader. *Education:* Composition, Film-Scoring, Psychology, University of South Califonia; Optometry, Philosophy, Fresno State College; Piano, composition, Juilliard School; Conducting, New England Conservatory of Music. *Career:* Accordion Solo, Radio KFI, Los Angeles, The William Tell Overture, 10 years old, 1937; Films, Counterpoint, Man's Favorite Sport, This Earth is Mine, The Competition, Guide for a Married Man, Made in Paris, Girl Happy, Those Lips Those Eyes. *Compositions:* The Three Suns; I Can't Forget; Our Love is Gone; City of The Angles; Sacro Sanctum; Warsaw Connection; Sarah Suite; Ole Joe, 1997; Joes Bach, 1997. *Recordings:* Artist of The Three Angels, Twilight Time; Joe Vento Golden Hits, Vol. I and II; Surfside Records; Bells of Christmas; The Best of Joe Vento; The Best of The Three Suns; Film Soundtrack, True Friends. *Publications:* I Can't Forget, 1939; City of The Angels, 1968; Sacro Sanctum, 1979; Love Is Gone, 1995; Edulerp III, 1995. *Contributions to:* Midi'ing in Music Composition, Moorpark College, 1991; Nurturing Music in the Nineties. *Honours:* Best Accordionist Grand Prize, 1939. *Membership:* ASCAP; ASMAC; AFofM, New York and Los Angeles; NARAS; American Academy of Sciences; Disabled American Veterans, SR, CDR; Music Teachers' National Asscn, USA. *Current Management:* S V Enterprises. *Address:* 419 Mark Dr., Simi, CA 93065, USA.

VERA, Billy; b. 28 May 1944, Riverside, California, USA. Vocalist; Actor; Songwriter; Prod; Music Historian. m. (1) Barbara, Jan. 1966, (2) Rosalee, 30 April 1988, 1 s., 1 d. *Education:* 1 year, Fordham University, Bronx, New York. *Career:* Concerts: Peppermint Lounge, New York City, 1963; Apollo Theater, 2 times, 1968; Dick Cavett Show, 1968; Steve Allen Show, 1969; NYC Academy of Music, 13 times, 1972–75; Madison Square Garden, 1972; Howard Theater, Washington DC, 1979; Johnny Carson Show, 9 times, 1986–89; Films: Buckaroo Banzai; Blind Date; The Doors; Television: Wise Guy; Alice; Scarecrow and Mrs King; Knot's Landing. *Compositions:* Recorded by: Ricky Nelson: Mean Old World; Barbara Lewis: Make Me Belong To You; Dolly Parton: I Really Got The Feeling; Bonnie Raitt: Papa Come Quick. *Recordings:* Storybook Children, 1967; With Pen In Hand, 1968; I Can Take Care of Myself, 1981; At This Moment, 1987; Out of the Darkness, 1994; Oh What A Night, 1996; Other collaborators include: James Brown; Judy Clay; Lou Rawls. *Publications:* Liner notes to over 200 historical albums. *Honours:* Gold Prize, Tokyo Music Festival, 1981; ASCAP Award, 1987; Star on Hollywood Walk of Fame, 1988; George Peabody Award for Excellence in Broadcasting, 1994. *Membership:* Trustee, Rhythm and Blues Foundation; ASCAP; AFTRA; SAG; AFofM. *Current Management:* Danny Robinson Agency for the Performing Arts. *Address:* 9200 Sunset Blvd, Los Angeles, CA 90069, USA. *Website:* www.billyvera.com.

VERA, Stephane; b. 11 May 1965, Paris, France. Musician (drums). *Education:* 1 year Right University, World Music; Boulogne Conservatory, Jazz-Rock School. *Career:* Gilbert Becaud; Dany Brillant; Jeane Manson; Vivian Reed; David Koven; I Muvrini; Karim Kacel; Eric Lelann; Ultra Marine; Angelique Kidjo; Jacky Quartz; Idrissa Diop; Yvan Dautin; Georges Macintosh. *Recordings:* Dany Brillant; Jacky Quartz; Imurvine; Karim Kacel; Richard Bona, Scenes from My Life, 1999; Film: Le Nouveau Monde, 1994. *Publications:* Drummer's Magazine, Paris; VAC Magazine. *Membership:* SACEM; SPEDIDAM; SDRM. *Current Management:* Marouani Charley, Becaud's agent; Ginibrej. *Address:* 27 rue D'Herblay, 78700 Conflans, Ste Honorine, France.

VEREEN, Ben; b. 10 October 1946, Miami, FL, USA. Vocalist; Actor; Entertainer. *Career:* Broadway productions include: The Chimney Man in musical, Jelly's Last Jam, 1993; Sweet Charity; Hair; Jesus Christ Superstar; Pippin; Grind; I'm Not Rappaport; A Christmas Carol, 1995; One-man show, concert tours, throughout USA including Las Vegas; Atlantic City; Lake Tahoe; Also Europe; Asia; Caribbean Islands; Movies include: Sweet Charity, 1969; Funny Lady, 1975; Why Do Fools Fall In Love?, 1998; I'll Take You There, 1999; Television includes: The Fresh Prince of Bel Air; The Nanny; Webster; New York Undercover; Star Trek – The Next Generation; Intruders; They Are Among Us; Silk Stockings; Own series, Tenspeed and Brownshoe, 1980; JJ Starbuck; Booker; Louis Armstrong – Chicago Style; Roots; Ben Vereen: His Roots; The Jesse Owens Story; Ellis Island; All That Jazz; Funny Lady; In demand speaker on lecture circuit; Formed organization, Celebrities For a Drug Free America, 1991; Currently developing performing arts center, Chicago; Appears on Once Upon A Forest, 1993. *Honours:* Israel's Humanitarian Award, 1978; NAACP, Image Award, 1978; 1979; Eleanor Roosevelt Humanitarian Award, 1983; Victory Award, 1990; Tony for Best Actor, Pippin; American Guild of Variety Artists: Entertainer of the Year; Rising Star; Song and Dance Star; Hon. Doctorates: Emerson College, Boston; St Francis College, Brooklyn; Columbia College, Chicago. *Address:* c/o Stan

Scotland, JKE Services, 404 Park Ave S, 10th Floor, New York, NY 10016, USA.

VERHAEREN, Gert J. M; b. 30 July 1973, Neerpelt, Belgium. Vocalist; Songwriter; Musician (guitar, bass guitar); Sequencer. *Career:* Main concerts with band named Ivy: 1996: Zeezicht, Antwerp, Belgium; Geuseltpop Festival, Maastricht, Netherlands; Electric Ladyland Festival, Maarheze, Netherlands; Airpop-Festival, Heerlen, Netherlands; 1997: Absolutely Free Festival, Ghent, Belgium; with band named Supergum: 1997: Support act for The Paranoiacs, Overpelt, Belgium; 1998: Absolutely Free Festival, Ghent, Belgium; Eurorock Festival, Neerpelt, Belgium; Hangarock Festival, Lo-reninge, Belgium. *Recordings:* with band Ivy: Bo(o)s(e); Goozehand; Liquid Courage; Watermelon; with band Supergum: Airplane, 1997; Eating Bullets; Last Song; Local Hero, 1998; Indecision; Airplane (engineless); Bitch!, 1999; Doctor Y; Surfin' Suspect. *Honours:* Finalist, Rock Competition, Het Licht Van Eindhoven, Eindhoven, Netherlands, 1996. *Membership:* SABAM. *Current Management:* Kattestraat 17, 3900 Overpelt, Belgium.

VERITY, John; b. 2 May 1944, Bradford, Yorkshire, England. Vocalist; Musician (guitar); Record Prod. m. Karen, 10 Dec. 1994, 2 s., 1 d. (from previous relationships). *Career:* Guitarist, various groups, 1960s; Leader, John Verity Band, 1969–73; Support tours with: Jimi Hendrix; Canned Heat; Janis Joplin; Lead vocalist, Argent, 1973–76; Member, Phoenix; Charlie; John Coughlan's Diesel Band; Numerous concerts world-wide, including: Fender Stratocaster 40th Anniversary Concert, Manchester, 1994; Strat Pack, Australia Day, London, Hippodrome, 1995; Built own recording studio; Full time record producer; Producer, guitarist, vocalist, Saxon; John Parr; Motörhead; Ringo Starr; Russ Ballard; Tank; The Zombies; Colin Blunstone; Matthew Fisher. *Recordings:* Albums: with Verity/John Verity Band: John Verity Band, 1972; Interrupted Journey, 1983; Truth of The Matter, 1985; Rock Solid, 1989; Hold Your Head Up, 1994; with Argent: Circus, 1975; Counterpoints, 1975; Hold Your Head Up, 1978; with Phoenix: Phoenix, 1976; In Full View, 1979; with Charlie: Good Morning America, 1981. *Membership:* MRCS; PRS. *Current Management:* Verity Associates. *Address:* 5A Greta Heath, Burton-In-Lonsdale, via Carnforth, Lancashire LA6 3LH, England.

VERLAINE, Tom, (Thomas Miller); b. 13 Dec. 1949, New Jersey, USA. Vocalist; Musician (guitar). *Career:* Member, The Neon Boys; Goo Goo; Founder member, Television, 1973–78; Solo artiste, 1979–; Re-formed Television, 1991–; Glastonbury Festival, 1992; European Festivals, Japanese and US tours, 1992. *Recordings:* Albums: with Television: Marquee Moon, 1978; Adventure, 1979; The Blow Up, 1990; Television, 1993; Solo albums: Tom Verlaine, 1979; Dreamtime, 1981; Words From The Front, 1982; Cover, 1984; Flash Light, 1987; Warm and Cool, 1992; The Miller's Tale, 1996; Singles: with Television: Marquee Moon, 1977; Prove It, 1977; Other recordings: Guitarist, Hey Joe, Patti Smith, 1974; Gung Ho, Patti Smith, 2000. *Honours:* Rolling Stone Magzine Critics Award, Comeback of the Year, Television, 1993. *Current Management:* Basement Music, 6 Pembridge Rd, London W11 3HL, England.

VERLY, François; b. 5 April 1958, Paris, France. Jazz Musician (piano, tablas, drums, percussion). 1 d. *Education:* BEPC-Bac D. *Career:* Many concerts on television and radio; World tours, jazz festivals: Canada; Mexico; Colombia; Ecuador; India; Hong Kong; Europe; East Europe; Africa; Plays with Michel Portal, David Friedman and Martial Solal. *Recordings:* Andy Emler, National French Jazz Orchestra, 1986, 1987; Marc Ducret; Antoine Hervé; Padovani; Denis Badault; Fawsi Al Aiedy; Nguyen Lê; Emmanuel Bex, Mauve, 2000. *Honours:* First prize, Percussion, Creteil, 1978; First Prize, piano soloist, Défense, 1986. *Current Management:* Opus 31, 78 rue Chateaubriand, 34070 Montpelier, France.

VERNEY, Frannie; b. 14 May 1963, Buckinghamshire, England. Vocalist; Arranger; Composer; Musician (piano, percussion). *Education:* Grade VIII piano, 1975; Purcell School for Young Musicians; GSMD Diploma in Jazz and Studio Music, 1994. *Career:* Radio appearances include: BBC Radio 5, BBC Radio Scotland, Newstalk AM; Tours throughout Europe; Repeat performances at prestigious Jazz venues throughout Britain including: Jazz Cafe, Royal Festival Hall Foyer, Bull's Head Barnes, Chicken Shed Theatre, Jazz Club Ascot, Edinburgh Festival Fringe, West Wales Jazz Festival, Vortez Jazz Club, Covent Garden Festival, Cork International Jazz Festival, Greenwich and Docklands Jazz Festival; Performs original and arranged Jazz Fusion material with her band, The Big Idea; Bandleader and Promoter of successful party band, Happy Feet, who have played all over Britain and in Europe at numerous venues including: Cumberland Hotel, London, RAC Club, Epsom, St Anton am Arlberg, Austria; Also performs as Soloist, with duos, performs, writes and arranges for smaller bands and acapella groups. *Membership:* PRS; MCPS; BAC&S; Musicians' Union. *Address:* c/o Epicurean Music, London, England.

VERNHETTES, Dan (Daniel); b. 20 May 1942, Paris, France. Musician (trumpet, cornet); Vocalist. m. Lill, 1965. *Career:* Main early influence, King Oliver; Interest developed in trumpeters of Swing era, most recently in music from New Orleans; Founder, Jazz O'Maniacs, 1966; Cornet player, bandleader, Six Cats, 1990–93; Member, Eddie Louis' Multicolor Fanfare,

1991–93; Leader, second trumpet, Swing Feeling (30s–40s jazz orchestra), 1992; Currently, trumpet player, singer, bandleader, Vintage Jazzmen (New Orleans-style sextet), 1992; Also, member, Olivier Franc orchestra, specialising in music of Sidney Bechet; Formed Brother D Blue Band, 1999. *Recordings include:* Various records, 1960s; Vintage Jazzmen, 1995, live, 1999; Swing Feeling with Screamin' Jay Hawkins and Spanky Wilson, 1995; Swing Feeling Live in Langen, 1998; Vintage Jazzmen and Reverend Garrett; Vintage Jazzmen and Brian Lewis; Vintage Jazzmen of France in New Orleans; New Orleans Gospel Live, Tori Robinson and the Vintage Jazzmen. *Honours:* Prix Sidney Bechet De L'Académie de Jazz, 1997. *Current Management:* Bertrand Henrion. *Address:* 45 rue Roger Buessard, 94200 Ivry-Sur-Seine, France. *Telephone:* (1) 64-31-56-16.

VERNON, Mike; b. 20 Nov. 1944, Harrow, Middlesex, England. Record Prod; Songwriter. 2 d. *Education:* Croydon College of Art. *Career:* Production Assistant, then Staff Producer, Decca Record Company, 1962–66; Founder, producer, Blue Horizon Label, 1966; Editor, R&B Monthly (early Blues Fanzine); Independent record producer, 1968; Formed Indigo Records, 1992; Became Code Blue (through East/West), 1994; Artists included Sherman Robertson, The Hoax, Jay Owens, Bo Diddley, John Primer and Eric Bibb; Headed Blueside Label, 1998. *Recordings:* As producer: Singles include: with Fleetwood Mac: Albatross; Need Your Love So Bad; Man of The World; with David Bowie: The Laughing Gnome; with Focus: Hocus Pocus; Sylvia; with Bloodstone: Natural High; with Roachford: Family Man; Albums by numerous artistes include: Level 42; John Mayall's Bluesbreakers; David Bowie; Fleetwood Mac; Focus; Ten Years After; Savoy Brown; Rocky Sharpe and The Replays; Edwin Starr; Dr Feelgood; Sherman Robertson; Jimmy Witherspoon; Climax Blues Band; Joe Cocker; Danza Invisible; Renaud Hantson; Candye Kane; Eugene Bridges; Jerry McCain; Six Was Nine; Bo Diddley; Eric Bibb. *Honours:* 10 Gold records; 6 Silver; WC Handy Award, 1987–88. *Membership:* Associate Mem., Re-Pro; PRS. *Current Management:* Worlds End (America) Inc, 183 N Martel Ave, Suite 270, Los Angeles, CA 90036, USA.

VERSAILLES, Fred; b. 15 June 1958, Versailles, France. Prod; Composer. m. Line Alloet, 1984, 2 d. *Education:* University of Nantere, Economics. *Recordings:* NTM, first single: Le Monde De Demain; Albums: Authentik; Incontrolables; Native; Paris Groove Up; Dis Bonjour A La Dame; Other. *Recordings include:* Axel Bauer. *Honours:* Victoire de la Musique, France, for: Native, 1994. *Membership:* Co-manager, Zbing Publishing. *Address:* 16 rue de Saint Denis, 95160 Montmorency, France.

VESALA, Edward; b. 15 Jan. 1945, Mantyharju, Finland. Musician (percussion); Composer. *Career:* Member, Tuohi Quartet, Montreux Jazz Festival, 1971; Joined Jan Garbarek's trio, 1972; Played jazz workshops, festivals throughout Europe; Worked with Tomasz Stanko, Stanko-Vesala Quartet, 1974–78; Solo percussionist, Finland and Europe, including Prague and Le Mans Jazz festivals; Teacher, Helsinki Theatre College; Bandleader, current group Sound and Fury. *Compositions include:* Music for Shakespeare plays; Aleksis Kivi's Seven Brothers; National epic, Kalevala. *Recordings:* Albums: Solo: Nan Madol; Heavy Life; with Sound and Fury: Lumi; Ode To The Death of Jazz; Invisible Storm; Nordic Gallery; Tomasz Stanko, Balldyna, 2000. *Honours:* Best Jazz Ensemble, (with Tuohi Quartet), Montreux Jazz Festival, 1971; Yrjö Awards, Finnish Jazz Federation, 1972, 1980. *Address:* Seilimäki 25 C, 02180 Espoo, Finland.

VIBSKOV, Per (Nielsen); b. 23 May 1962, Viborg, Denmark. Composer; Prod; Musician (bass). *Career:* Bass player with: Peyote, 1978–85; Rosegarden, 1986; Janes Rejoice, 1986–87; TAO, 1988–; Bayou Brothers, 1990–94; Bass player, producer, Home Sweet Home, 1994–; Bass fiddle player with Luksus, 1996–; Roskilde Festival, 1998. *Recordings:* with Peyote: For Sent Igen, 1984; with Janes Rejoice: Wievs To Keep, 1987; with TAO: Senor Maski, 1995; with Home Sweet Home: Divine, 1996. *Honours:* Prize for application, Efterslaegten, 1994. *Membership:* Danish Jazz, Beat, and Folk Authors. *Address:* Viktoriagade 10 ITV, Copenhagen V, Denmark.

VICH, Michal; b. 5 Nov. 1952, Prague, Czechoslovakia. Vocalist; Musician (guitar); High School Dir. m. Vera Vichova, 3 March 1977, 1 d. *Education:* School of Economics, Prague; Prague Musical School; J Jezek Conservatoire, guitar and voice studies. *Career:* Musician, recital group Vpred; Member, artistic group, The Prague Five; Film music for the films of T Vorel, including: Olda's Party, 1988; Kour, musical, 1990; La Serra, opera, Prague, 1994; Songs for the Children. *Compositions:* Kour, film soundtrack, 1990; La Serra, opera score, 1994. *Recordings:* Kour, film soundtrack, 1990; La Serra, opera, 1994; Albums: Monday Tells To Tuesday, 1995; Oh, The Sails, Where Are They? (with members of the Czech Philharmonic Orchestra), 1997. *Publications:* Books for children: Monday Tells to Tuesday, 1995; Oh, The Sails, Where Are They?, 1996. *Honours:* Oh, The Sails, Where Are They? selected as one of the best books of the year, 1996. *Membership:* The Protective Syndicate of Authors (Czech Republic). *Address:* 252 62 Unetice 84, Okr Prague Za'pad, Czech Republic.

VICKHOFF, Björn Ture; b. 9 May 1946, Växjö, Sweden. Singing Songwriter (guitar). m. Eva-Marie Vickhoff, 1 s., 1 d. *Education:* MA, Gothenburg University; Individual Musician Degree, Gothenburg University. *Career:*

Kosmiskt Eko, an opus for TV (music, lyrics and performance); Film music to Samtidigt en Fredag; TV-serie music to Flykten; Appearances in Scandinavian TV and radio. *Recordings:* LP: Fiskdikt Och Fågelsång; Riv Alla Stängsel, with Göteborgs Visgrupp, Kosmiskt Eko, with Åke Parmerud; Huset vid Havet, Än Finns Det Tid, CD: Fantastico. *Publications:* Än Finns Det Tid, with Ulf Marken, anthology with environmental songs; Música Popular Brazileira, an academic thesis. *Honours:* STIM Award; Gothenburg City Award; Art Society Award. *Membership:* SKAP; SAMI; Musikcentrum Väst; Yrkestrubadurernas Förening; Visans Vänner. *Address:* Björn Vickhoff, Småkullav 23, 424 70 Olofstorp, Sweden.

VICKREY, Dan; b. 26 Aug. 1966, Walnut Creek, California, USA. Musician (guitar). *Career:* Member, Counting Crows; Numerous headlining tours and TV appearances including MTV. *Recordings:* Singles: Round Here, 1994; Mr Jones, 1994; Rain King, 1994; Angels of the Silence (live), 1996; Albums: August and Everything After, 1993; Recovering the Satellites, 1996; Across a Wire: Live in New York, 1998; Long December, 1999; Daylight Fading, 1999; This Desert Life, 1999; Hard Candy, 2002.

VIDAL, Jacques Henri; b. 13 Oct. 1949, Athis-Mons, France. Musician (double bass); Composer; Teacher. m. 13 April 1993, 1 s. *Education:* National Versailles Academy of Music. *Career:* Formation of Christian Vander's group, Magma, 1970; Leader, Trijoums, 1976; Tour, France, with American drummer Philly Joe Jones, 1977; Played with guitarist Frederic Sylvestre, 1978; Jacques Vidal Quintet (Michel Graillier, piano, Florin Niculescu, violin, Frederic Sylvestre, guitar, Simon Goubert, drums), 1995; Television series as musician/actor. *Compositions:* Music for theatre. *Recordings:* Return, with Christian Escoudé and A Romano, 1979; Be Bop, Pepper Adams and B Altschul, 1979; Live A L'Olympia, J P Debarbat, 1979; A Live In Paris, Glenn Ferris, 1980; Rencontre, J P Debarbat, 1981; Music Band, Teddy Lasry, 1983; Under The Magnolias, Richard Raux, 1989; with Frederic Sylvestre: Premier Grand Cru with J L Chautemps, 1980; 2 Plus, with Eric Lelann, 1982; Hommages, with Eric Lelann, A Jean-Marie, 1983; Trio Live, S Huchard, 1986; Capricorne, 1989; As bandleader: Bass For Ever, 1995; News of Bop, Jacques Vidal Quintet, 1995. *Membership:* SACEM; SACD; ADAMI. *Address:* 2 Bis Cité Popincourt, 75011 Paris, France.

VIDOVIC, Ana; b. 8 Nov. 1980, Karlovac, Croatia. Musician (guitar). *Education:* Music Academy, Zagreb. *Career:* Performing solo and with orchestras in music centres, Warsaw, Vienna, Salzburg, Budapest, Tel-Aviv, Paris, London, Oslo, Århus, Bergen, Rome, Bari, Vaduz, Copenhagen; Had a television documentary made about her. *Recordings:* 3 CDs, Sony, 1993; London BGS Records, 1996; Guitar Recital, 1996; Croatia Records, 1998. *Address:* Donja Jelsa 61, HR 470–00 Karlovac, Croatia.

VIG, Butch; b. 8 Dec. 1957, Viroqua, Wisconsin, USA. Record Prod; Musician (drums). *Career:* Record prod., various artists; Mem., group, Spooner; Founding mem., Garbage, 1994–; Numerous tours, festivals, television and radio appearances. *Recordings:* Albums: Garbage, 1995; Version 2.0, 1998; Beautifulgarbage, 2001. Singles: Vow, 1994; Subhuman, 1995; Queer, 1995; Only Happy When It Rains, 1995; Stupid Girl, 1995; Milk, 1996; #1 Crush, 1997; Push It, 1998; I Think I'm Paranoid, 1998; Special, 1998; When I Grow Up, 1999; The Trick Is To, 1999; You Look So Fine, 1999; The World Is Not Enough (theme from James Bond: The World is Not Enough), 1999; Androgyny, 2001; Breaking Up The Girl, 2001; Shut Your Mouth, 2002; As producer: Nevermind, Nirvana; Siamese Dream, Smashing Pumpkins; Remixes for U2, Nine Inch Nails, House of Pain, Depeche Mode, Ash, Chainsaw Kittens. *Current Management:* SOS Management, 106 Cleveland St, London W1 5DP, England. *Address:* c/o Mushroom Records, 1 Shorrolds Rd, London SW6 7TR, England. *Website:* www.garbage.com.

VIKEDAL, Ryan; b. 9 May 1975, Canada. Musician (drums). *Career:* Mem., rock band, Nickelback, 1998–; Extensive touring of North America; Signed to EMI Canada and Roadrunner Records; Single, Yanking Out My Heart, used in soundtrack to film The Scorpion King, 2002. *Recordings:* Albums: The State, 1999; Silver Side Up, 2001. Singles: Breathe, 2000; Old Enough, 2000; Leader Of Men, 2000; How You Remind Me (No. 1, USA), 2002; Too Bad, 2002. *Honours:* Juno Awards, Best New Group, 2001, Best Group, Best Single, for How You Remind Me, Best Rock Album, for Silver Side Up, 2002; MuchMusic Video Awards, Best Video, for Too Bad, Best Rock Video, for How You Remind Me, 2002; Platinum discs. *Address:* c/o Roadrunner Records Inc, 902 Broadway, Eighth Floor, New York, NY 10010, USA. *Website:* www.nickelback.com.

VILLEGER, André Franucin Raymond; b. 12 Aug. 1945, Rosny L/Bois, France. Musician (saxophone). 1 s., 1 d. *Career:* Festivals: Nice; Antibes; Paris; Marciac; Saragosse; London; Madrid; Carthage; Bayonne; Trinidad; Fort De France. *Recordings:* Albums: Something To Live For, 1986; A Villeger Connections, 1991; Also appears: with Claude Bolling: Jazz Gala; Live at the Meridien; Bolling Plays Ellington; Tone Parallel to Harlem; Paris Swings, 2001. *Honours:* Prix Sidney Bechet 1973 (Academie Du Jazz). *Membership:* Los Angeles Jazz Society. *Address:* 28 rue du Gibet, 95100 Argenteuil, France.

VINCENT, Amanda; b. 20 Jan. 1958, Perth, Australia. Musician (keyboards). *Education:* BMus, composition; University of Western Australia. *Career:* Tours with: Eurogliders, UK, USA, Philippines, Australia, 1980–87; Tim Finn, Australia, New Zealand, 1986; The Thompson Twins, UK, Ireland, USA, Canada, 1987; Boy George, UK, Europe, Australia, 1987–93; Jenny Morris, UK, Europe, Australia supporting Prince, 1990; Gang of Four, UK, USA, Canada, 1991; Billy Bragg, Australia, New Zealand, Japan, 1992; Black, UK, Turkey, 1993; Yazz, UK, 1994. *Compositions include:* Music for Strollers, ballet, Human Veins dance theatre, Canberra, 1980; Music, Fields of Fire, ABC TV, 1987; Music, The Collector, cinema and television, 1994; Music for TV documentary: The Feelgood Factor, 1995. *Recordings:* with Tim Finn: Escapade, 1983; Les Patterson Saves The World (soundtrack), 1987; with Eurogliders: Pink Suit Blue Day, 1981; This Island, 1983; Absolutely, 1985; with Jenny Morris: Animal Magic, 1986; Body and Soul, 1987; Shiver, 1989; with Boy George: Clause 28 (single), 1988; Boyfriend, 1989; High Hat, 1988; Tense Nervous Headache, 1988; Don't Try This At Home, 1991; Bloke On Bloke, 1997; Spiritual High, Moodswings featuring Chrissie Hynde, (single) 1991. *Honours:* 1 Platinum, 2 Gold albums, 1 Gold single; Second Prize, New York Film, TV awards, video: Heaven, Euroglider (single), 1985; Best Single, Heaven, Australia, 1985. *Membership:* PRS; MCPS; Musicians' Union. *Address:* Flat 5, 15A Cricklewood Broadway, London NW2 3JX, England.

VINCENT, Eric; b. 27 June 1946, Force, France. Vocalist; Musician (guitar, violin). m. 4 March 1987. *Education:* Conservatory. *Career:* Performed in more than 120 countries: Brooklyn Auditorium, New York, USA; World Congress Center, Atlanta, USA; Opera Manaus, Brasil; National Folk Festival of Adelaide, Australia; Theatre Municipal Manoi, Viet Nam. *Compositions:* CD: Un Pays Quelquepart; Luca; Harmoniques; Voyage Pour L'Immediat; Haiti Kimbe. *Recordings:* Operation Boule De Neige; Je Suis Fatigue. *Publications:* Cest Comme Ça, 1987; Iles, 1987; Reflets France, 1992; Sans Borne, 1990. *Membership:* SCPP; SACEM; ADAMI; SPEDIDAM. *Address:* Madura, 11 bd de la Bastille, 75012, Paris, France.

VINCENT, Julian Francis Vincent; b. 19 Jan. 1943, London, England. University Prof. m. Elizabeth May, 22 June 1968, 1 d. *Education:* MA, Cambridge University; PhD, DSc, Sheffield University. *Career:* Concerts at Purcell Room as Solo Recitalist; Appearances at 100 Club; TV appearances for BBC, ITV and Radio RTE, with tenor banjo; Organizer, Reading Banjo Festival, 1983–. *Recordings:* Stomp Off, Tenor Banjo with Paramount Theatre Orchestra. *Publications:* Banjoists' Broadsheet, journal. *Address:* 93 Redhatch Dr., Earley, Reading RG6 5QN, England.

VINDING, Mads; b. 7 Dec. 1948, Copenhagen, Denmark. Musician (bass). *Career:* Professional at age 16; House bass player, Montmartre jazz club, Copenhagen; Worked with many jazz masters including: Herbie Hancock, Wayne Shorter, Stan Getz, Gary Burton, Hank Jones, Dexter Gordon, Bob Brookmeyer, Ben Webster, Benny Goodman, Dizzy Gillespie, Quincy Jones, Johnny Griffin, Eddie 'Lockjaw' Davis, Gerry Mulligan, Tony Williams, Ed Thigpen, Sir Roland Hanna, Dollar Brand, Clark Terry, Monty Alexander and Toots Thielemans. *Recordings:* Numerous albums include: Solo albums: Danish Design, 1974; The Kingdom (Where Nobody Dies), 1997; with Ed Thigpen: Action-Re-Action, 1974; Mr Taste, 1991; with Tony Williams and Wlodek Gulgowsky, Pop-Workshop, 1974; with Kai Winding: Trombone Summit, 1980; with Doug Raney: Guitar Guitar Guitar, 1985; with Dexter Gordon and Herbie Hancock: Cinema Jazz, 1986; The Other Side of Midnight, 1986; with Hanne Boel and Jorgen Emborg: Shadow of Love, 1987; with Roland Hanna and Jesper Thilo: This Time It's Real, 1987; with Thomas Clausen Trio: She Touched Me, 1988; Psalm, 1995; with Sven Asmussen: Fiddler Supreme, 1989; with Thomas Clausen Trio and Gary Burton: Cafe Noir, 1991; Flowers and Trees, 1992; with Danish Radio Big Band: Endangered Species, 1993; with Trine Lise Væring: When I Close My Eyes, 1996; with Jesper Thilo: Jesper Thilo Meets Thomas Clausen, 1997; with Bob Brookmeyer: Old Friends, 1998; with Great Jazz Trio: Great Standards Vols 1–5, 1998; Daddio Don, 2000; Other albums with Duke Jordan; Johnny Griffin; Ernie Wilkins; Kenny Drew; Hank Jones. *Address:* Bogevej 8, 3500 Voerlose, Denmark.

VINTON, Bobby (Stanley Robert); b. 16 April 1935, Canonsburg, Pennsylvania, USA. Vocalist. *Career:* Played trumpet with The Tempos; Formed own band; Became solo singer, 1962–; Sold over 30m. records worldwide; Actor, films Surf Party; Big Jake; The Train Robbers; Numerous television appearances including host of weekly variety show, 1975–78; Major concerts include: The Biggest Show of Stars For 1960, with Chubby Checker and Brenda Lee; Dick Clark's Caravan of Stars, US tour, 1961; New Zealand tour with Gene Pitney, 1962; Carnegie Hall, 1974; Opened The Bobby Vinton Blue Velvet Theater, Branson, Missouri, 1993. *Recordings:* US No. 1 singles: Roses Are Red; Blue Velvet; There! I've Said It Again; Numerous other hits include: Blue On Blue; My Heart Belongs To Only You; Clinging Vine; L-O-N-E-L-Y; I Love How You Love Me; Coming Home Soldier; Every Day of My Life; My Melody of Love; Blue Velvet (No. 2, UK), re-issued 1990; Albums: Roses Are Red, 1962; Bobby Vinton Sings The Big Ones, 1963; Blue Velvet, 1963; Bobby Vinton's Greatest Hits, 1964; Tell Me Why, 1964; Bobby Vinton Sings For Lonely Nights, 1965; Satin Pillows And Careless, 1966; Please Love Me Forever, 1968; Take Good Care of My Baby, 1968; I Love How You Love Me, 1969; Vinton, 1969; Bobby Vinton's Greatest Hits of Love, 1970; My Elusive Dreams, 1970; Every Day of My Life, 1972; Sealed With A Kiss, 1972; Bobby Vinton's All-Time Greatest Hits, 1972; Melodies of Love, 1974; Bobby Vinton Sings The Golden Decade of Love, 1975; Heart of Hearts, 1975; The Bobby Vinton Show, 1976; The Name of Love, 1977; Timeless, 1990; Duet with George Burns on album, As Time Goes By, 1993; A Very Merry Christmas, 1994; Kissin' Christmas, 1995; Branson City Limits, 1998; Blue On Blue, 2000. *Honours:* Bobby Vinton Day, Chicago, 1975; Hon. citizen, Chicago, City's Certificate of Merit, 1975: Hon. doctorate of Music, Duquesne University, 1978; Several Gold discs.

VIRTANEN, Heikki; b. 4 Sept. 1953, Finland. Musician (bass). *Education:* Studied Contrabass and Musicology. *Career:* Member, jazz-rock group, Tasavallen Presidentti, early 70s; Concerts with Juhani Aaltonen; Jarmo Savolainen; Severi Pyysalo; Jukkis Uotila, 1980s–; Bass player, Conjunto Baron (with Seppo Paakkunainen); Bassist for Olli Ahvenlahti, backing singer Vesa-Matti Loiri on Olli Ahvenlahti's compositional projects; Featured on recordings by: Charlie Mariano; Jukka Tolonen. *Honours:* Yrjö Award, Finnish Jazz Federation, 1987. *Address:* Töölöntorinkatu 7, 00260 Helsinki, Finland.

VISCONTI, Tony; b. 1944, Brooklyn, NY, USA. Record Prod; Musician (guitar, bass guitar, double bass, tuba, piano, keyboards). m. (2) May Pang, divorced 2000. *Education:* Guitar with Leon Block. *Career:* Jazz musician, duo Tony and Sigrid; Joined Richmond Organization, Essex Music, working in England; Signed Tyrannosaurus Rex (later T-Rex); Independent Prod.; Mem. band, The TV Show; Worked with: Argent, Badfinger, Richard Barone, David Bowie, Carmen, Dandy Warhols, Gasworks, Gentle Giant, Mary Hopkin, Marsha Hunt, Luscious Jackson, Legend, Ralph McTell, Mercury Rev, Moody Blues, The Move, Omaha Sheriff, Osibisa, Tom Paxton, Procol Harum, Sarstedt Brothers, Sparks, Strawbs, Surprise Sisters, Thin Lizzy, T-Rex, Wings, Kristeen Young. *Address:* c/o The Looking Glass Studios, 632 Broadway, 9th Floor, New York, NY 10012, USA. *Website:* www.tonyvisconti.com.

VISKINDE, Peter; b. 14 Nov. 1953, Copenhagen, Denmark. Musician (guitar); Composer. m. Susan Kjeldsen, 23 June 1992, 2 s., 2 d. *Career:* Musician, 1974–; Member of groups Buffalo; Hualsospillemandene; Malurt Doraz; Also recorded as solo artist. *Recordings:* Two albums with Buffalo; Two albums with Hualsospillemandene; Seven albums with Malurt; Five solo albums, 1986, 1993, 1994, 1998 and 2000; Seven albums with Big Fat Snake, 1991–2000. *Membership:* DJBFA. *Current Management:* Århus Musikkontor, Mindegade 10, 8000 Århus C, Denmark.

VITEK, Pavel; b. 30 Sept. 1962, Olomouc, Czech Republic. Vocalist; Actor; Composer; Lyricist. *Education:* Academy of Musical Art (Faculty of Dramatic Art); Conservatoire, Musical Singing. *Career:* Theatre Musicals: Pop Festival, 1984; Gypsies Go To Heaven, 1986; Some Like It Hot, 1987; Dracula, 1995–; TV Films: Creation of the World, 1988; About 100 various TV shows including own recital, To Find My World, 1988; Many video clips; Radio: 1994–96; Own talk show on radio frequence 1. *Compositions:* Scent of Your Skin, 1992; This Time I Love You Much Better, lyrics, 1993; Garden of Wishes, 1994; Amen With You, 1995; Heaven Full of Stars, lyrics, 1995. *Recordings:* Albums: She's Got Her Day, 1988; Scent of Your Skin, 1992; Garden of Wishes, 1994; Lucky Star, 1995; Dracula, 1996. *Honours:* Second Prize, OIRT Festival Budapest, 1988; Prize of Finland, The Midnight Sun Song Festival, 1992. *Membership:* Czech Asscn of Authors; Intergram. *Current Management:* Nota Bene Musical Londy'nska' 53, Prague 2, 12000, Czech Republic. *Address:* Pavel Vitek, Nota Bene Musical, Londy'nska' 53, 12000 Prague 2, Czech Republic.

VIVES, Carlos, (Carlos Alberto Vives Restrepo); b. 7 Aug. 1961, Santa Marta, Departamento del Magdalena, Colombia. Vocalist; Actor. *Career:* Appeared in seven television series, Colombia; Formed band, La Provincia, 1991–; Established Gaira Música Local label; Film appearance: La Estrategia del Caracol, 1994. *Recordings:* Albums: Clásicos De La Provincia, 1993; La Tierra Del Olvido, 1995; Tengo Fe, 1997; El Amor De Mi Tierra, 1999; Déjame Entrar, 2001; Colección De Oro, 2002. *Honours:* Two Latin Grammy Awards, Best Contemporary Tropical Album, for Déjame Entrar, Best Tropical Song, 2002. *Address:* Gaira Producciones, Calle 103 A, No. 18-02, Bogotá, Colombia. *E-mail:* gaira@colomsat.net.co. *Website:* www.carlosvives.com.

VOLCKE, Ivan; Musician (guitar, badhan, brass pedals). *Career:* Member, The Swingshift; Dranouter Festival, 1995; Den Ekster, 1996, 1997; Labadoux, 1997; Paulus Festival, 1997; Sloanthe Festival, 1997; Gooik Festival 2002, 1997; De Brakke Grond, Amsterdam, 1997; Foleys Irish Pub, Ghent; Radio 1 De Groote Boodschap; Several Regional Radio and Television Appearances. *Compositions:* Jumpin The Fences; Dirty Wally; Friends Sadness; Something to Fear; Shut the Pub; A Whistler's Wedding. *Recordings:* Tales From the Great Whiskey Book, 1996. *Honours:* Government Medal, Flute, 1986; Second Place, Youth Soloist Festival, 1986; Finale, Westtalent, 1995. *Membership:* Volksmuziekfederatie, Belgium. *Current Management:* KAFT Productions, Akkerwindelaan 20, 8791 Beveren-Leie, Belgium. *Address:* c/o Barrierestraat 49, 8940 Wervik, Belgium.

VOLCY, Jean-Marc; b. 29 Jan. 1966, Anse Royal, Seychelles. Cultural Officer; Musician (guitar, banjo, percussion); Vocalist. m. Eudoxie Volcy, 4 d. *Education:* Degree in Voice Training. *Career:* TV appearance, RFO, Reunion Island, 1994; Festival des Flaurallis Reunion Island, 1994; Radio appearance, RFI Bamako, 1993; MBF, 1995, 1996, 1997. *Compositions:* Musical Director, Three, musical play, 1995, 1996, 1997. *Recordings:* Debut album, soundtrack Sanmoi Swar Lo Zil St Pierre; Oseselwa and Sega of Seychelles. *Publications:* Debut album, Vandreni Sen and Musique Traditionelle Des Seychelles. *Honours:* Winner, Grand Prix D'Afrique Decouvert Des RFI, 1993; Winner, Festival Creole Song Contest, 1993, 1996. *Address:* Volcy c/o NAC, National Arts Council Mahe, Seychelles.

VOLKSORKEST, Brabants; b. Nov. 1978, *Career:* Concerts, Television and Radio appearances, Belgium, Netherlands, Germany, France, Spain, Italy, Denmark, England, Ireland, Czechoslovakia, Hungary, Canada, USSR (Russia, Moldavia, Armenia, Mari Republic, Chuvash Republic); Mali, Kenya, Uganda, Cuba, Brazil. *Recordings include:* Brabantse Volksmuziek; Volksmuziek uit Brabant en de Kempen; Volksmuziek uit Brabant en de Vlaamse gewesten; Flemish Folk Music, Vol. 1 and Vol. 2; Rozenland; De Liedboeken, Vol. 1 and Vol. 2; Belgian Folk Music; Le Printemps de la Cornemuse; Harbalorifa: 25 jaar Omroep Brabant; Café B. *Honours:* La Cithare d'Argent (Paris 1979); Europa Preis für Volkskunst, 1989. *Current Management:* Egide Vissenaekens.

VOLLENWEIDER, Andreas; b. 4 Oct. 1953, Zurich, Switzerland. Musician (harp, multi-instrumentalist). m. Beata, 27 Oct. 1973, 2 s., 1 d. *Career:* Composer of numerous musical productions for theatre, film and ballet; Alvin Atley Company on world tour with ballet based on own music. *Compositions:* Ace Verde, anthem of European Peace Movement, 1983; Pearls and Tears, anthem in black townships of South Africa, 1990. *Recordings:* Behind the Gardens; Caverna Magica; White Winds; Down to the Moon; Dancing with the Lion; Book of Roses; Eolian Minstrel; Live; Kryptos; Pavarotti and Friends II; Cosmopoly, 1999. *Honours:* Edison Award, 1983; Grammy Award, 1987; World Music Award, 1992. *Address:* Impact Music Inc, Zollikerstr 144, 8008 Zurich, Switzerland.

VOLLMER, Brian Joseph; b. 30 June 1955, Kitchener, Ontario, Canada. Vocalist. m. Lynda Cowgill, 10 Aug. 1991, 1 d. *Education:* Bel canto method of singing. *Career:* Vocalist, heavy rock group Helix; Several tours with Helix to Europe; Tours, North America; Appearances numerous TV shows, MTV. *Recordings:* Albums: White Lace and Black Leather, 1978; Breaking Loose, 1979; No Rest For The Wicked, 1982; Walking The Razor's Edge, 1984; Long Way To Heaven, 1985; Wild In The Streets, 1988; Back For Another Taste, 1990; It's A Business Doing Pleasure, 1992; Half Alive, 1998; Best of Helix: Deep Cuts, 1999; Solo albums: When Pigs Fly, 1999. *Honours:* Heavy Metal Video of Year, Running Wild In The 21st Century. *Current Management:* William Seip Management. *Address:* 52 Terrence St, London, ON N52 1C4, Canada.

VOROS, George Ladislaus; b. 5 March 1958, Swaziland. Musician (drums); Drum Teacher. *Education:* Grade 8 Music Theory, Royal Schools; Military Band Certificate. *Career:* Member, South African bands: Neil Solomon; E'Void; Wozani; Numerous South African television appearances and sessions; Worked with Jimmy James and The Vagabonds, UK; Member, Stu Page Band, UK; Television: Stars In Your Eyes; Private drum studio, The Drum Workshop, 5 years. *Recordings:* The Love We Can Share, World Vision (charity single); Album: Come and Dance, Wozani. *Publications:* Book on drums, practice and performance, endorsed by Virgil Donati, Steve White and others. *Honours:* Best British Country Band, Stu Page Band, 1994. *Membership:* Musicians' Union (registered teacher). *Address:* Hayter and Shone Ltd Music Publishers, 19 Grove Hill, South Woodford, London E18 2JB, England.

VRAIT-WRIGHT, Silvi; b. 28 April 1951, Kehra, Estonia. Vocalist; Music Teacher; English Teacher; Actress. 1 s. *Education:* Tartu University, Estonia, graduate, English, Philology, Language, Literature, 1974; Children's Music School, piano. *Career:* Lead singer, Fix (Estonia), 1976–83; Solo artist, 1983–; Rock opera; Porgy and Bess (Bess) by George Gershwin; Television specials: Light and Shade; Silvi and Her Friends; Silvi Vrait Sings, Eurovision Song Contest, 1994. *Recordings:* Albums: Silvi Vrait, 1985; Embrace, 1988; English Children's Songs; Single: Like The Sea, 1994; Album: Cosy and Warm, 1994. *Current Management:* Rock Hotel Management. *Address:* Astangu 22–61, 00035 Tallinn, Estonia.

VRIENDS, Peter; b. 31 Oct. 1963, Rotterdam, Netherlands. Musician (midi instruments). *Career:* Co-owner, record company essential dance music; Co-owner, record company basic beat recordings; Owner and Engineer, recording studio; Producing own compositions; Producing productions for third parties, mixing great variety of dance mix albums. *Compositions:* Pot of Gold; Joy; Love; Follow Your Heart; Emotional Travellogue, album; Quadripart Project, 1995. *Honours:* Best House Record of the Year, Benelux, Pot of Gold, 1991. *Membership:* SENA; IFPI, Stermra, Buma. *Address:* Essential Dance Music BV, Nieuwe Binnenweg 19, 3014 GB Rotterdam, Netherlands.

VUJICA, Matija; b. 19 July 1963, Metkovic, Croatia. Vocalist. *Education:* Faculty of Economics, Zagreb; Private piano lessons. *Career:* Vocalist with group Gracia, 1990–; Concerts, tours and rock festivals all over Croatia, Austria, Germany, Slovenia and Sweden; Many television and radio appearances. *Recordings:* Hit singles: Rolana; Zaplesimo; Albums: Gracia; Vrijeme Snova (Time of Dreams); Jer Tu Ima Neki Crni Vrag (Black Devil Spies Upon Us All); Dancetheria; Forte Forte. *Publications:* Croatian Awards: Ethno Dance Award 1994; Most Original Look, 1994. *Membership:* Croatian Musical Union (HGU).

VUKAN, George; b. 21 Aug. 1941, Budapest, Hungary. Composer; Musician. *Education:* Liszt Academy of Music; Medical University Budapest. *Career:* Concerts include Classical and Jazz, with his trio and solo; Guest artist, all around Europe; Played with Philly Joe Jones, Clifford Jordan, Linda Hopkins, Annette Lowman, Frank Foster, Clarck Terry, Kenny Wheeler; Played with his creative art Jazz trio in Sevilla at World Expo; Composer; Conductor; Ferenc Liszt, Ferenc Erkel Chamber Orchestras, Hungarian Symphonica Orchestra; Written music for more than 140 films, three ballets, opera, symphonic works, concertos, chamber music compositions, 150 psalms, music to theatrical performances, television, radio and films; Pianist member, founder, quartet, 1997–. *Compositions:* Missa Ad Dominum Jesum Christum. *Honours:* Include, Hilikon Prize, 1957; Press Award Montreux, 1968; Composer Award of The Hungarian Record Producing Company, 1970; Balázs Bèla Prize, 1978; Artist Prize of The Hungarian Radio, 1981; Erkel Ferene Prize, 1991; Lyra Prize, Little Cross of Hungarian Republic, 1996. *Address:* Határör UT 19/B 8, 1122 Budapest, Hungary.

VUVU, J. L; b. 12 Dec. 1968, Uige, Angola. Musician (keyboards); Songwriter. 2 s. *Education:* Car mechanic. *Career:* Street musician in Zaire (as Abute Bango Likonga); Club musician in Angola (as Parisien J L); Tour of Zaire; Residency in Cafe Rio; Now relocated to UK as dance musician. *Recordings:* Debut album being recorded, own compositions. *Publications:* Listed in Zairians and Angolans. *Membership:* Musicians' Union. *Current Management:* Basky-Capitao, Love Life M P M. *Address:* 82A Plashet Rd, Plaistow, London E1 0RQ, England.

VYVÉRE, Pascale; b. 31 May 1966, Brussels; Belgium. Vocalist; Composer; Songwriter; Musician (piano, accordion); Actress. *Education:* Fine Arts Degree; Musical Theory, Harmony, Piano, Song Writing, Singing and Performing Lessons. *Career:* Festivals: Botanique, Brussels, 1993, 1994, 1997; Francofolies, Spa, 1994, 1997; Festival De Marne, 1993, 1999; Chorus Des Hauts-De-Seine, 1994; Many concerts in France, Belgium and Switzerland; Roles in: Chants De Femmes, Film, R Olivier, 1994; La Voix Humaine, J Cocteau, 1996; La Dame De Chez Maxim, G Feydeau, 1996; Les Poules, 1997–99; Les Miroirs d'Ostende, P Willems, 1998, 2000; Les Feux de Babel, 1998–99. *Compositions:* Words and/or music of many French songs. *Recordings:* Single: Solo, 1994; Contributor, album: J G Coulange, Enfin Seul, 1994; Solo album: Je Vous Attends, 1997. *Honours:* Prize Sentier Des Halles and Prize Adiam-92, Tremplin Chorus Hauts-De-Seine, 1993; Prize Auditeurs France-Inter/RTBF/RSR, 1994. *Membership:* SABAM, Brussels. *Current Management:* Tango, ASBL, 5 Av Des Vanneaux, 1420 Braine-L'Alleud, Belgium.

WAAKTAAR, Pål, (Pål Garnst); b. 6 Sept. 1961, Manglerud, Oslo, Norway. Musician (guitar); Vocalist; Composer. m. Lauren. *Career:* Mem., A-Ha, 1983–94; Mem., Savoy; Band re-formed, 1999–; Numerous tours world-wide, television and radio appearances. *Recordings:* Albums: Hunting High And Low, 1985; Scoundrel Days, 1986; Stay On These Roads, 1988; East Of The Sun West Of The Moon, 1990; Deadlines: The Hits Of A-Ha, 1991; Memorial Beach, 1993; Minor Earth Major Sky, 2000; Lifelines, 2002. Singles: Take On Me (No. 1, USA), 1985; The Sun Always Shines On TV (No. 1, UK), 1985; Train Of Thought, 1986; Hunting High And Low, 1986; I've Been Losing You, 1986; Cry Wolf, 1986; Manhattan Skyline, 1987; The Living Daylights (theme music for James Bond film), 1987; Stay On These Roads, 1988; The Blood That Moves The Body, 1988; Touchy!, 1988; You Are The One, 1988; Crying In The Rain, 1990; I Call Your Name; Dark Is The Night; Can't Take My Eyes Off You (for film soundtrack Coneheads); Angel. *Honours:* Eight MTV Music Video Awards, for Take On Me and The Sun Always Shines On TV, 1986; BMI Award, One Million Broadcast Performances, for Take On Me, 1991; World Music Award, Best Selling Norwegian Artist of the Year, 1993. *Current Management:* Bandana Management, London, England. *Address:* c/o WEA Germany, Warner Music Germany Group, Oberbaumbrücke 1, 20457 Hamburg, Germany. *Website:* www.a-ha.com.

WADE, Terri (Teresa); b. 3 March 1957, Staffordshire, England. Vocalist; Entertainer. m. David Bryan, 6 Oct. 1987, 1 s. *Education:* College of Further Education. *Career:* Sang for Mecca, Top Rank Dance bands; Touring bands, session work for local studios; Backing vocals with: Peabo Bryson; Career as Terri Wade, 1980–; Television: Walk on parts: Crossroads; Keynotes; Sky Star Search; New Faces, 1986; Hippodrome, London; Stringfellows to promote Single Girl; Interviewed on radio stations all over country; Performed over 1,000 live shows. *Recordings:* Light, 1982; Single Girl, 1985, number 11 (Gay Top 20). *Honours:* Best Vocalist, NSSCEP, 1986, South Skeffs, 1990. *Membership:* Musicians' Union; Equity. *Current Management:* Ray Stanton Entertainments. *Address:* 294 Ash Bank Rd, Werrington, Stoke-on-Trent ST9 0JS, England.

WAGER, Henrik Rickard; b. 14 March 1969, Manchester, England. Vocalist. *Education:* Birmingham University; Birmingham Conservatoire. *Career:* Founder member, Brave New World, 1992–93; Ascension, 1993–94; Singer with The Flying Pickets; Performed on Warning Tour, 1994; 5 Alive In '95 Tour; Happy Birthday, 1996; Director, Inner Sanctum Studio; Inner Sanctum Productions; Director of Ulum Jingle Shed. *Membership:* Musicians' Union; Equity.

WAGHORN, Gary; b. 9 May 1949, Chatham, Kent, England. Musician (guitar, banjo). m. Linda Evans, 15 Aug. 1970, 1 d. *Career:* Lead guitarist for Bonnie Tyler; Lead guitarist, vocalist, Slack Alice; Lead guitarist, backing vocals, Mountain Child. *Recordings:* Album: Diamond Cut, Bonnie Tyler; 6 singles with Bonnie Tyler; Single: Night Pilots, Mountain Child. *Membership:* PRS; Musicians' Union.

WAGNER, Bill (William); b. 12 Feb. 1920, Warsaw, Indiana, USA. Record Prod; Trumpet Arranger. m. Vicki, 23 May 1942, 2 d. *Education:* Mechanical Engineering, Purdue University; Pilot, US Air Force. *Career:* Personal Manager for The Four Freshmen; Pete Christlieb; Page Cavanaugh; Si Zentner; Vicki McClure; Faunda Hinton; Michael Dees; Sandy Graham; Over 100 record dates for: Serenade In Blue, USAF Band, Washington DC. *Compositions:* 5 jingles (musak); Airmen of Note, USAF Band. *Recordings:* Producer of over 1,000 records to date with various artistes including: 23 albums, The Four Freshmen; 2 albums, Sandy Graham; 3 albums, Page Cavanaugh, 1989; John Klemmer: Priceless Jazz, 1999; Jerry Herman, Jerry's Girls, 1999. *Membership:* NARAS; AFTRA; AGMA. *Address:* 14343 Addison St, #221, Sherman Oaks, CA 91423, USA.

WAGNER, Heribert; b. 24 Dec. 1952, Vienna, Austria. Musician (Violin); Composer. 1 s. *Education:* Violin, since aged 7; Conservatory of Vienna and Enschede, Netherlands. *Career:* WDR-TV appearance, Live from Berlin Jazz Festival; Dutch TV, NL3, Jazz uit het BIM-Huis; North Sea Festival, The Hague; Montreux Jazz Festival; Jazzfest, Vienna; Nürnberg Ost-West; Nancy Jazz Pulsations; Stuttgarter Jazztage. *Compositions:* Gaia, a Story for Jazzgroup and Symphony Orchestra, Donemus, Amsterdam; Homage; 5; Ballad for a Lonesome Guy Somewhere on This Earth; Horizontal Curve. *Recordings:* LP, To Be Continued, with New Association; CD, Four Wheel Drive, with New Association; Disco Compacto, with Trio Famoso. *Honours:* Jaromir Prize, Netherlands, 1988. *Membership:* BUMA; BIM; NTR. *Current Management:* Art in Music. *Address:* Altingstraat 38, The Hague, Netherlands.

WAGNER, Kurt; b. 1958, Bethseda, Maryland, USA. Vocalist; Musician (guitar); Songwriter. *Education:* Art School, Memphis, Tennessee, USA.

Career: Lead vocalist and main songwriter of loose collective known as Lambchop; One of the main bands in the alternative country or Americana movement, their music mixes country, soul, folk and jazz; Brought up in Nashville, went to art school in Memphis and spent time in Montana before returning to Nashville; Formed Posterchild, Act renamed Lambchop owing to existence of another band The Poster Children, 1992. *Recordings:* Albums: with Lambchop: I Hope You're Sitting Down/Jack's Tulips, 1994; How I Quit Smoking, Hank, 1996; Thriller, 1997; What Another Man Spills 1998; Nixon, 2000; Is A Woman, 2002; with Josh Rouse: Chester, 1999 features on: Salesman and Bernadette, Vic Chesnutt, 1998; Kathleen Lague Kathleen Lague, 1999.

WAGNER, Windy; b. 6 Dec. 1971, Los Angeles, CA, USA. Vocalist. *Career* Vocals for Walt Disney Records, Baywatch, Fame LA, Various Television Commercials. *Recordings:* Vocals On Trine Rein; Walt Disney Records; 1 Braxton; Melanie C. *Honours:* Los Angeles Music Award, Best Female Vocalist. *Membership:* SAG; AFTRA; LA Singers United. *Current Management:* Kelly Coleman Esq. *Address:* PO Box 17551, Beverley Hills, C. 90209, USA.

WAGONER, Porter; b. 12 Aug. 1930, West Plains, Missouri, USA. Country Vocalist; Songwriter. *Career:* Worked at radio station; Cast member television series Ozark Jubilee; Recording artist, 1954; Regular member Grand Ole Opry, 1957–; Television series with own band The Wagonmasters 1960s–70s; Co-host with singers Norma Jean, Dolly Parton; Regular recording partnership with Dolly Parton, 1967–74; Regular tours and concerts with Al Girls Band. *Recordings:* 81 Country hit singles include: A Satisfied Mind (U Country No. 1); Eat Drink and Be Merry; Your Old Love Letters; Sorrow O The Rocks; Misery Loves Company (US Country No. 1); The Green Gree Grass of Home (later recorded by Tom Jones and Elvis Presley); The Col Hard Facts of Life; The Carroll County Accident; Duets with Dolly Parton The Last Thing On My Mind; Just Someone I Used To Know; Daddy Was A Old Time Preacher Man; If Teardrops Were Pennies; Please Don't Sto Loving Me (US Country No. 1); Albums include: A Satisfied Mind, 1956; Slice of Life, 1962; Old Log Cabin For Sale, 1965; The Thin Man From Wes Plains, 1965; The Bottom of The Bottle, 1968; Howdy Neighbour Howd 1970; The Farmer, 1973; Porter, 1977; Today, 1979; Natural Wonder, 198 One For The Road, 1983; Porter Wagoner, 1986; with Norma Jean: Porte Wagoner Show, 1963; In Person, 1964; Live – On The Road, 1966; with Dol Parton: Just Between You and Me, 1968; Just The Two of Us, 1969; Alway Always, 1969; Porter Wayne and Dolly Rebecca, 1970; Once More, 1971; Th Right Combination, 1972; Together Always, 1972; Love and Music, 1973; W Found It, 1973; Porter 'N' Dolly, 1974; Say Forever You'll Be Mine, 197 Porter Wagoner and Dolly Parton, 1980; The Best I've Ever Been, 200 *Honours:* CMA Awards: Vocal Group of the Year, 1968; Vocal Duo of the Yea 1970, 1971. *Address:* c/o Porter Wagoner Enterprises, PO Box 29078 Nashville, TN 37229, USA.

WAGSTAFF, Paul (Wags); b. 28 Dec. 1964, Stockport, Cheshire, Englan Musician (Guitar). *Career:* Member, Black Grape; Numerous tours a festival appearances including Tribal Gathering and Reading festivals, 199 *Recordings:* Singles: Reverend Black Grape, 1995; In The Name of T Father, 1995; Kelly's Heroes, 1995; England's Irie, 1996; Fat Neck, 1996; G Higher, 1997; Marbles, 1998; Albums: It's Great When You're Straight Yeah (No. 1, UK), 1995; Stupid, Stupid, Stupid, 1997.

WAHLBERG, Ulf; b. 11 April 1951, Stockholm, Sweden. Prod; Musici (Keyboards). m. Catherina, 1 s., 2 d. *Education:* Five years Piano; Two yea music. *Career:* Ola Hakansson, The Group Secret Service, 1979; Produc 1979–. *Compositions:* Som Stormen River Oppet Hav; Heden. *Recordin* Secret Service; Freestyle; Susan Alfvengren; Magnum Bonum; Martin; Al Lake Of Tears, Forever Autumn, 1999. *Publications:* Popcorn; Jukeb *Honours:* Swedish Grammy as Producer, 1986. *Membership:* STIM; SA SKAP. *Current Management:* XTC Productions AB, PO Box 2065 125 Alvsjo, Sweden.

WAILER, Bunny, (Neville O'Riley Livingston); b. 10 April 19 Kingston, Jamaica. Vocalist; Songwriter. *Career:* Harmony singer, songwrit and occasional lead singer, reggae group Bob Marley and the Wailers, 196 and 1970s; Solo recording artist, on own Solomonic record label, 197 *Recordings:* Albums include: with the Wailers: Catch A Fire; Burnin'; S albums: Blackheart Man; Protest; Struggle; In A Fathers House; Bu Wailer Sings The Wailers; Tribute To The Hon. Robert Nesta Marley; Rock Groove; Hook Line and Sinker; Roots Radics Rockers Reggae; Marketpla Bunny Wailer Live; Roots Man Skanking; Rule Dancehall; Liberat Gumption; Hall of Fame: A Tribute to Bob Marley's 50th, 1995; Complete I Marley and the Wailers, 1998; with Bob Marley: Rock to the Rock, 19

Dubdisco, 1999; Communication, 2000. *Address:* c/o Performers of the World, 8901 Melrose Ave, Second Floor, West Hollywood, CA 90069, USA.

WAINWRIGHT, Loudon, III; b. 5 Sept. 1946, Chapel Hill, North Carolina, USA. Vocalist; Songwriter; Musician (guitar). m. Kate McGarrigle, 2 c., divorced 1977. *Education:* Studied acting, Carnegie Mellon University, Pittsburgh. *Career:* Singer, folk clubs, New York and Boston, 1968; Recording artiste, 1969–; Founding mem., Spinal Tap; Concerts incl.: Support to Everly Brothers, UK; Cambridge Folk Festival, 1972; Royal Festival Hall, 1992; Television incl.: The Jasper Carrott Show; Original musician/sidekick on David Letterman Show; Conan O'Brien; Compositions for ABC Nightline; Several episodes, M.A.S.H.; Episode, Soldier Soldier; Own show, Loudon and Co (BBC Scotland); Played Hal Karp in Undeclared (TV series, Fox/Dreamworks); Episode, Ally McBeal; Stage performances: The Birthday Party; Pump Boys and Dinettes; Caryl Churchill's Owners at the Young Vic; Films: The Slugger's Wife; Jacknife; 28 Days; Radio: NPR in USA continues to commission topical songs on events and individuals in the news. *Compositions include:* Dead Skunk; Your Mother and I; I wish I was A Lesbian; YK2; Glad To See You've Got Religion; The Man Who Couldn't Cry; Swimming Song; Motel Blues; Be Careful, There's A Baby In The House; The Picture, 1992; Dreaming, 1995. *Recordings:* Albums: Loudon Wainwright III, 1970; Album II, 1971; Album III, 1972; Attempted Moustache, 1973; Unrequited, 1975; T-Shirt, 1976; Final Exam, 1978; A Live One, 1979; Fame and Wealth, 1983; I'm Alright, 1985; More Love Songs, 1986; Therapy, 1989; History, 1992; Career Moves, 1993; One Man Guy: Best Of Loudon Wainwright III, 1994; Grown Man, 1996; Little Ship, 1998; BBC Sessions, 1998; Social Studies, 1999; Last Man On Earth, 2001. *Current Management:* The Rosebud Agency, PO Box 170429, San Francisco, CA 94117, USA.

WAINWRIGHT, Rufus; b. 22 July 1973, Rhinebeck, New York, USA. Vocalist; Musician (piano); Songwriter. *Education:* McGill University, studied classical music, 1991. *Career:* Son of Kate McGarrigle and Loudon Wainwright III; Sang backing vocals on tour with mother and aunt (folk duo Kate and Anna McGarrigle), 1980s; Dropped out of university to perform own songs in and around Montréal; Cut demo, 1997; Signed record deal with DreamWorks; Tours North America, Britain and Europe. *Compositions:* I'm A-Runnin'; Millbrook; Cigarettes and Chocolate Milk. *Recordings:* Rufus Wainwright, 1998; Poses, 2001. *Current Management:* Ron Stone, Gold Mountain Entertainment. *Address:* c/o DreamWorks Records, 9268 W Third St, Beverly Hills, CA 90210, USA. *Website:* www.rufuswainwright.com.

WAITE, John; b. 4 July 1955, England. Vocalist; Songwriter; Musician (bass, harmonica). *Career:* Member, The Babys, 1976–81; Solo artiste, 1981–; Singer, Bad English, 1989–91. *Recordings:* Albums: with The Babys: The Babys, 1976; Broken Heart, 1977; Head First, 1978; Union Jacks, 1980; On The Edge, 1980; Anthology, 1981; Solo albums: Ignition, 1982; No Brakes, 1984; Mask of Smiles, 1985; Rovers Return, 1987; The Essential, 1991; Temple Bar (USA only), 1995; with Bad English: Bad English, 1989; Backlash, 1991; Solo: The King Biscuit Flower Hour, 1999; These Times are Hard for Lovers; with Ian McDonald, Driver's Eyes, 1999; Figure In A Landscape, 2001; Singles: Solo: Missing You (No. 1, USA); Change; with Bad English: When I See You Smile (No. 1, USA). *Current Management:* Gold Mountain Entertainment. *Address:* 120 W 44th St, Suite 704, New York, NY 10036, USA.

WAITS, Tom; b. 7 Dec. 1949, Pamona, CA, USA. Vocalist; Songwriter; Musician (piano, accordion); Actor. m. Kathleen Brennan, 31 Dec. 1981, 1 s., 1 d. *Career:* Recording artiste, 1973–; Concerts incl.: Ronnie Scott's jazz club, 1976; London Palladium, 1979; The Black and White Night—Roy Orbison and Friends, 1987; Actor, films incl.: Paradise Alley; Wolfen; Stone Boy; One From The Heart; The Outsiders; Rumblefish; The Cotton Club; Down By Law; Cold Feet; The Fisher King; At Play In The Fields Of The Lord; Queen's Logic; Bram Stoker's Dracula; Coffee and Cigarettes. *Compositions include:* Ol' 55, The Eagles, 1974; Angel Wings, Rickie Lee Jones, 1983; Downtown Train, Rod Stewart, 1990; One From The Heart (film soundtrack), 1981; Night On Earth (contribution to film score), 1992; Co-writer, musical, Frank's Wild Years, 1986; Theatre: The Black Rider, 1989; Alice, 1992; Woyzeck, 2002. *Recordings:* Albums: Closing Time, 1973; The Heart Of Saturday Night, 1974; Nighthawks At The Diner, 1975; Small Change, 1976; Foreign Affairs, 1977; Blue Valentine, 1978; Heartattack And Vine, 1980; Bounced Checks, 1981; One From The Heart, 1982; Swordfishtrombones, 1983; Anthology, 1983; The Asylum Years, 1984; Rain Dogs, 1985; Frank's Wild Years, 1987; Big Time, 1988; The Early Years, 1991; The Early Years Vol. 2, 1992; Night On Earth, 1992; Bone Machine, 1992; The Black Rider, 1993; Beautiful Maladies, 1998; Mule Variations, 1999; The Dime Store Novels Vol. 1, 2001; Used Songs 1973–80, 2001; Alice, 2002; Blood Money, 2002; Numerous contributions and guest appearances. *Honours:* Grammy Award, Best Alternative Music, Bone Machine, 1993; Contemporary Folk Performance, 2000. *Address:* c/o Anti-Inc, 2798 Sunset Blvd, Los Angeles, CA 90026, USA. *Website:* www.officialtomwaits.com.

WAKEFIELD MILLSAPS, Wilma; b. 13 Feb. 1949, Monroe Co, Tennessee, USA. Vocalist; Songwriter; Musician (guitar). m. Bill Millsaps, 13 Nov. 1967, 1 s., 1 d. *Education:* Apprenticed under Tommy Scott. *Career:* Travelled extensively across USA with husband Bill Millsaps and their Snowbird

Mountain Band; Appears twice weekly on satellite TV on Snowbird Mountain Bluegrass. *Recordings:* Albums include: Legendary Friends of The Snowbird Mountain Band, with John Hartford, Uncle Josh Graves, Benny Martin, others. *Publications:* Bluegrass Unlimited, by Dr Ivan Tribe, 1992. *Membership:* BMI; IBMA. *Current Management:* Bill Millsaps. *Address:* PO Box 85, Robbinsville, NC 28771, USA.

WAKEMAN, Adam; b. 11 March 1974, Windsor, Berkshire, England. Musician (keyboards); Vocalist; Musical Dir. *Education:* All eight practical and theory Associated Board exams, 1993–94. *Career:* Toured most of Europe, America, South America, UK, with Wakeman band alongside father, Rick, 1995; Performing Musical Dir, Cirque Surreal, touring UK; Toured with: Artful Dodger, 2001, Victoria Beckham, 2001–02; Musical Dir, Atomic Kitten, 2002–03. *Recordings:* Albums: Wakeman with Wakeman; No Expense Spared; Romance Of A Victorian Age; The Official Bootleg; Tapestries, 1995; Vignettes, 1996; Return To The Centre Of The Earth, 1999; Tales Of Future And Past, 2001; Solo: Soliloquy; 100 Years Overtime; Real World Trilogy, 1997; The Classical Connection, 2000; Neurasthenia; Contribution to Yes tribute album, with new band Jeronimo Road. *Membership:* Musicians' Union; PRS. *Current Management:* DW Management, Barn Business Centre, 14 Hall Rd, Haconby, Lincs PE10 0UY, England. *E-mail:* dwmanagers@aol.com. *Website:* www.adamwakeman.com.

WAKEMAN, Dusty; b. 31 Aug. 1953, Houston, Texas, USA. Musician (bass guitar); Record Prod; Engineer. m. Szu Wang, 5 April 1986. *Education:* University of Texas; Studied music with Jamie Faunt. *Career:* Mixer, engineer, bassist, numerous recordings, 1986–; Bassist, Michelle Shocked British tour, 1989. *Recordings:* Mixer, engineer, producer, bassist on albums by: Dwight Yoakam; Rosie Flores; Lucinda Williams; Buck Owens; Michelle Shocked; Los Lobos; Jackson Browne; Wynton Marsalis; Tom Russell; Ralph Stanley; American Pie; Giant Sand; Steve Forbert; Heather Myles. *Honours:* 2 Grammy Awards: Cryin', Roy Orbison/kd lang, 1987; Ain't That Lonely Yet, Dwight Yoakam, 1993. *Current Management:* Bonnie Simmons. *Address:* PO Box 5895, Berkeley, CA 94705, USA.

WAKEMAN, Rick; b. 18 May 1949, London, England. Musician (keyboards). *Career:* Member, UK progressive rock group Yes, 1971–74, 1976–80, 1990; International concerts include: Yesshows '91 – Round The World in 80 Dates tour, 1991; Film: Yessongs, 1973; Solo artiste, 1974–. *Compositions include:* Score for Phantom of The Opera, 1991. *Recordings:* Albums: with Yes: Fragile, 1971; Yessongs, 1973; Tales From Topographic Oceans, 1973; Going For The One, 1977; Union, 1991; Yesstory, 1991; Solo albums: The Six Wives of Henry VIII, 1973; Journey To The Centre of The Earth, 1974; The Myths and Legends of King Arthur and The Knights of The Round Table, 1975; White Rock, 1976; No Earthly Connections, 1976; Criminal Record, 1977; Rhapsodies, 1979; 1984, 1981; Beyond The Planets, 1984; The Gospels, 1987; Soundtrack to 1982 World Cup film Golé!, 1983; Themes, 1998; A Tribute to the Beatles, 1998; Natural World Trilogy, 1999; Selections from Journey to he Centre of the Earth, 1999; Preludes to a Century, 2000; Stella Bianca, 2000; Recollections, 2000; as Anderson Bruford Wakeman Howe: Anderson Bruford Wakeman Howe, 1989. *Honours:* Gold Ticket, Madison Square Garden, 1978. *Current Management:* BDA, Bryson House, Chiltern Rd, Culceth, Warrington, Cheshire WA3 4LL, England.

WALDEN, Chris; b. 10 Oct. 1966, Hamburg, Germany. Composer; Arranger (Trumpet). m. Beate Walden, 15 March 1996, 1 d. *Education:* Music University, Cologne, 1988–93; MA Composition, 1994. *Career:* Feature Films, Schtonk, 1992; Ein Mann Fuer Jede Tonart, 1992; Lilien in der Bank, 1992; Engel Ohne Fluegel, 1993; Late Show, 1998; 20 TV Movies; Director, German Movie Award Show, 1995–98. *Compositions:* Ticino, suite for big band; A Deadly Vision, suite for symphony orchestra; Opus 3, for orchestra. *Recordings:* Smokie, 1994' Ticino, 1995; Harlem Gospel Singers, 1998. *Honours:* Ernst Fischer Prizes, 1993, 1997. *Membership:* GEMA; ASCAP; SCL. *Current Management:* Alan Davis, Legal Representation. *Address:* 8491 Sunset Blvd No. 340, Los Angeles, CA 90069, USA.

WALDEN, John 'White Boy'; b. 23 Oct. 1948, London, England. Musician (harmonica); Blues singer. m. Natalie Marjory Gellineau, 26 Dec. 1982, 1 s., 1 d. *Career:* Took up harmonica when child; Started to play blues aged 13 with Bespoke Tailor Unit; Several European tours with John Walden Workshop, late 1960s; Madison Blues Band, 1990s; Re-formed John Walden's Blues Band, 1997. *Recordings:* Many sessions, soundtracks, commercials; John Walden's Blues Band, CD, 1997; Collaborators include: Brian Green. *Honours:* Acknowledged as one of the World's best blues harmonica players; Medal Winner, European Harp (Harmonica) Festival, Trossingham, Germany, 1996. *Membership:* Musicians' Union. *Address:* 90 Shooters Hill Rd, Blackheath, London SE3 8RL, England.

WALDEN, Myron; b. 18 Oct. 1973, Miami, Florida, USA. Musician (alto saxophone); Songwriter; Arranger. *Education:* La Guardia High School of Music and Art; Harlem School of the Arts; Manhattan School of Music. *Career:* Performed and recorded with Ron Carter; Benny Golson; Winard Harper; Eddie Henderson; Kevin Hays; Mulgrew Miller. *Recordings:* Night Watch, Winard Harper; Be Yourself, Ravi Coltrane; Brian Blade; Phil Woods;

International Who's Who in Popular Music

Akilli, Ravi Coltrane; Bop, Carl Allen and Vincent Herring; Solo albums: Like A Flower Seeking The Sun, 1999. *Honours:* Young and Upcoming Artist, Yamaha Corporation, 1990; Saxophonist of the Year, Harlem School of The Arts. *Current Management:* c/o Preston Powell, Jazzateria Inc, 112 W 72nd St, #2F, New York, NY 10023, USA.

WALDEN, Narada Michael; b. 23 April 1952, Kalamazoo, Michigan, USA. Vocalist; Musician (drums, keyboards); Record Prod; Songwriter. m. Anukampa Coles. *Education:* West Michigan University, 1970–72. *Career:* Drummer, with John McLaughlin, 1974–76; President, Perfection Light Productions, 1976–; Recording artist, songwriter, producer, 1976–; Board of Directors, Bay Area Music Awards, San Francisco, 1992. *Recordings:* Solo albums: Garden of Love Light, 1977; I Cry, I Smile, 1978; Awakening, 1979; The Dance of Life, 1979; Victory, 1980; Confidence, 1982; Looking At You, Looking At Me, 1983; The Nature of Things, 1985; Divine Emotion, 1985; with John McLaughlin: Apocalypse, 1974; Visions of The Emerald Beyond, 1975; Inner Worlds, 1976; Other recordings as musician: Teaser, Tom Bolin, 1975; Wired, Jeff Beck, 1976; My Spanish Heart, Chick Corea, 1976; Jaco Pastorius, Jaco Pastorius, 1976; Black Market, Weather Report, 1976; Loading Zone, Roy Buchanan, 1977; Velvet Darkness, Allan Holdsworth, 1977; Exposure, Robert Fripp, 1979; Oneness, Santana, 1979; Clarke Duke Project 2, Stanley Clarke, 1983; Patti Austin, Patti Austin, 1984; Teaser, Angela Bofill, 1984; Who's Zoomin' Through, Aretha Franklin, 1985; Through The Storm, Aretha Franklin, 1989; As musician and producer: Hero, Clarence Clemons, 1985; While The City Sleeps, George Benson, 1986; As producer: with Sister Sledge: Love Somebody Today, 1980; All American Girls, 1981; Rose is Still a Rose, Aretha Franklin, 1998; Ladies and Gentlemen, George Michael, 1998; Definitive Collection, Angela Bofill, 1999; Best of Bond... James Bond, 1999; Love Songs, Jefferson Airplane, 2000; with Whitney Houston: Whitney Houston, 1985; I'm Your Baby Tonight, 1990; Other artists include: Phyllis Hyman; Gladys Knight; Mica Paris; Regina Belle; Al Jarreau. *Honours:* NARAS Award: Songwriter of the Year, 1986; Grammy, 1986; ASCAP Awards: Producer of the Year; Songwriter of the Year; Publisher of the Year, 1987; Billboard Magazine: Producer of the Year, 1986, 1987.

WALDEN, Natan; b. 3 Nov. 1947, Bystrzyca, Klodska, Poland. Musician (bass, keyboards); Composer. m. Ewa Kryger-Walden, 5 Jan. 1974, 1 s., 1 d. *Education:* MFA, Music Education, Lund University, Sweden, 1982; Music Producer Degree, Malmö Academi of Music, Sweden, 1985. *Career:* Poland: Nastolatki (Teenagers); Bassplayer with legendary singer, Niemen; USA: Live work, studio work commercials with Billy Cobham and Valerie Simpson; Sweden: Studio work, theatre-musical, Röda Orm; Animalen; Blood Brothers; TV and live works with Toots Thielemans; Nestor Marconi; Lill Babs, Eurovision Song Contest; Musical Director, many TV shows on Swedish TV; Many theme songs for TV serials, Sköna Söndag; Vem Tar Vem; Helt Apropa; In Denmark: The Most; Bassplayer, in live concert versions of a musical Chees; with 3 different orchestras: Danish Radio Orchestra; Odense Symphonic Orchestra; Sonderjisk Symphonic Orchestra. *Honours:* Golden Rose Montreux for music production of The Prize; Finalist for Outstanding Achievement in Popular Arts; International Emmy Awards, 1987. *Membership:* Swedish Society of Popular Music Composers. *Current Management:* Wiktor Kubiak Management. *Address:* 14 Henrietta St, London WC2, England.

WALICKI, Peter Englundh; b. 4 Feb. 1950, Denmark. Musician (drums, keyboards); Songwriter; Vocalist. m. Hanne Jakobsen, 11 May 1974, 1 s., 1 d. *Education:* Music Teacher, Danish Music School. *Career:* Scool Band, 1960; Doctor Phill, 1967; Several Dance bands on DFDs, 1971; Golden Diamond, 1980; Grethe Ingmann and Sunset, 1984; A/S Rockkompagniet, 1985; Hit the Hay, 1996; A/S Rockkompagniet, 1998. *Compositions:* Ann Mari, 1975; Habet Er Gront, 1977; Dancing Dynamite, 1996. *Recordings:* Ann Mari, 1975; Habet Er Gront, 1977; A/S Rockkompagniet Several Songs, 1985–98; Nikki Hokey, 1982; Mooreen, 1982. *Publications:* TV Show, Rock Palazt, ZDF Germany with Joe Bank's Rock Medicine Show, 1986. *Membership:* KODA; NBC; DMF. *Current Management:* Strike Records, own company. *Address:* Peter Englundh Walicki, Lysholm Alle 64, 4690, Haslev, Denmark.

WALKER, Billy; b. 14 Jan. 1929, Ralls, Texas, USA. Musician (guitar); Vocalist. m. Bettie, 6 Feb. 1978. *Career:* Toured with Elvis Presley, Texas, 1954; Performances include: Hollywood Bowl; Las Vegas; Hee Haw; Nashville Now; Crook and Chase; Grand Ole Opry Show, 1960–; Music City Tonight; Yesteryear; The Nashville Network; The Statler Brothers; Jimmy Dean Show; Dick Clark's American Bandstand; Billy Walker's Country Carnival, 3 years; 32 State Fairs; Tours: Austria; Bermuda; England; Guam; Hawaii; Ireland; Italy; Japan; Republic of Korea; Philippines; Japan; Spain; Sweden; Switzerland; Germany. *Recordings:* Over 100 chart records; 32 Top 10 hits; No. 1 hit singles: Funny How Time Slips Away; Charlie's Shoes; Cross The Brazos At Waco; A Million and One; When A Man Loves A Woman; Sing Me A Love Song Too Baby; Also: She Goes Walking Through My Mind; In Del Rio; Gone Our Endless Love; Curtains On The Window; Come A Little Bit Closer; Word Games; If I'm Losing You; Don't Stop In My World; Adam's Side (most requested wedding song, USA); Latest albums: Larger Than Life; Billy Walker, 1999; Autumn Memories, 1999; Bobby Vinton, 1999. *Publications:* Larger Than Life (autobiography), 1998. *Current Management:* Bettie Crook,

Artist Management. *Address:* PO Box 618, Hendersonville, TN 37077-0618, USA.

WALKER, Clay, (Ernest Clayton, Jr); b. 9 Aug. 1969, Beaumont, Texas, USA. Country vocalist; Musician (guitar); Songwriter. *Education:* Taught guitar by father, aged 9. *Career:* Played bars in local Beaumont, Texas area from age 16 before gigging more extensively in Louisiana, Oklahoma and New Mexico; Spotted by record producer James Stroud while performing as resident singer at Neon Armadillo bar, Beaumont; Stroud helped secure recording contract with Giant Records; Debut single What's It To You became his first No. 1 hit, 1993; Achieved four platinum albums, two gold albums and has sold over 8m. albums; Has landed a song on Billboard's year-end Top 10 country list for five consecutive years, unmatched by any artist in same period. *Compositions include:* Live Until I Die; Rumor Has It; Who Needs You Baby. *Recordings include:* Rumor Has It, 1997; This Woman and This Man, 1995; Live Until I Die, 1993; What's It To You, 1993; Dreaming With My Eyes Wide Open, 1994; If I Could Make A Living, 1994; Albums include: Clay Walker, 1993; If I Could Make A Living, 1994; Hypnotise The Moon, 1995; Rumor Has It, 1997; Greatest Hits, 1998; Live Laugh Love, 1999; Say No More, 2001. *Current Management:* c/o The Erv Woolsey Agency, 1000 18th Ave S, Nashville 37212, USA. *Website:* www.claywalker.com.

WALKER, Eddie; b. 31 Oct. 1948, Middlesbrough, England. Vocalist; Musician (guitar); Songwriter. m. Judith Ann, 22 March 1969, 1 s. *Education:* Charles Trevelyan Technical College, Newcastle. *Career:* Concert, folk festiva and club appearances throughout UK, Germany, Belgium, Netherlands, Italy Austria, Denmark, Slovenia, Croatia, Switzerland, Ireland, Luxembourg Hong Kong, Bangkok, New Zealand; Television and radio appearances: Tyne Tees TV; BBC Radio 2; BBC Radio Scotland. *Recordings:* Solo albums Everyday Man, 1977; Castle Cafe, 1981; Red Shoes On My Feet, 1983 Picking My Way, 1985; with guitarist John James: Carolina Shout!, 1990 Sidesteppin, 1993; Live At The Albert Hole!, solo video album, 1996; Mind To Ramble, 2000. *Honours:* Winner of Songwriter Competition, Stolen My Hear Away, 1982; Northumbria Trophy for Songwriting, 1975; Slough Arts Festival Solo Winner, 1977. *Membership:* PRS; MCPS. *Address:* 33 The Grove Brookfield, Middlesbrough, Cleveland TS5 8DT, England.

WALKER, Junior (Autrey Dewalt, II); b. 1942, Blythesville, Arizona, USA Musician (saxophone); Vocalist. *Career:* Founder, Junior Walker and The Al Stars, 1961–; Concerts include: Miami Pop Festival, 1968; Jazz and Blue Festival, Ann Arbor, Michigan, 1972; American Bandstand's 25th Anniversar Special, ABC TV, 1977. *Recordings:* Albums: Shotgun, 1965; Soul Session 1966; Road Runner, 1966; Home Cookin', 1969; Greatest Hits, 1969; What Does It Take To Win Your Love, 1970; A Gasses, 1970; Rainbow Funk, 197 Peace and Understanding Is Hard To Find, 1973; Sax Appeal, 1977; Whoppe Bopper Show Stopper, 1977; Blow The House Down, 1981; Greatest Hit 1982; Shake and Fingerpop, 1996; Uno Dos Tres: Latin Jazz Grooves, 199 Singles: Shot Gun (No. 1, US R&B Chart), 1965; Do The Boomerang, 196 Shake and Fingerpop, 1965; (I'm A Roadrunner), 1966; How Sweet It Is (To Be Loved By You), 1966; Money (That's What I Want) Part 1, 1966; Pucke Up Buttercup, 1967; Shoot Your Shot, 1967; Come See About Me, 1968; H City Pt 2, 1968; Home Cookin', 1969; What Does It Take (To Win Your Lov (No. 1, US R&B), 1969; These Eyes, 1969; Gotta Hold On To This Feelin 1970; Do You See My Love (For You Growing), 1970; Take Me Girl, I'm Read 1971; Walk In The Night, 1972; Way Back Home, 1973; Guest on: Urge Foreigner, 1981.

WALKER, Mark Robert Thomas; b. 7 March 1962, London, Englan Musician (drums); Lyricist; Songwriter; Journalist. m. Claire Cooper, 6 Au 1988, 1 s., 2 d. *Education:* BEd Hons. *Career:* Tours with the Tin Gods, U Europe; Appeared at Lausanne Festival, Switzerland, 1991; Televisio Hangar 17, BBC1; Radio: Live sessions for Capital Radio and GLR wi Peachey Keen and World of Leather; TV appearances: House band drumm for the Jack Dee Show; National Lottery Show; Blue Peter; This Mornin Nightfever; London Tonight; The Big Stage and the Esther Show with R Harris; Solo Performer of drum shows and clinics; British tours with R Harris including Glastonbury Festival, 1997–2000; Ireland, 1999; Capetow South Africa, 2000; Solo performer of The Have-A-Go Drum Sho appearances include GMTV, This Morning; Rhythmsticks 1998, 1999, 200 Festival Hall; National Music Show, Wembley; BBC Music Live; Mad Abo Music, Docklands Arena; Duo Drum 'n' Didg, appearances inclu Rhythmsticks 1999 and Horniman Museum; Drumming in London West E production, Walt Disney's The Lion King. *Recordings:* St Mark's Place, Wo of Leather (debut album); The Coronation Street Album; Invisible History The Black Celt, Martin Okasili; Private Party, Akin; Numerous recordi sessions with producers Robin Miller; Faney; Colin Fairley, Jeff Fost Composed theme tune for Airdrum (cartoon series); With Rolf Harr Albums: Bootleg 1 and 70/30; Single: Christmas in the Sun; Fine D *Publications:* The Court of King Rolf – a tribute book to Rolf Harris, 20 Regular features writer for Rhythm magazine, including series, The Sec Diary of a Session Drummer Aged 33 3/4; The Rudiments of Time; Rhyt Beginners. *Membership:* Musicians' Union; PAMRA; PAS. *Curr Management:* Active Entertainment Management. *Address:* 165 Green La London SE9 3SZ, England.

WALKER, Scott, (Noel Scott Engel); b. 9 Jan. 1944, Hamilton, Ohio, USA. Vocalist; Songwriter; Musician (bass). m. Mette Teglbjaerg, divorced, 1 d. *Education:* Fine Arts foundation course; Double bass lessons. *Career:* Member, The Routers, 1963; Member, Dalton Brothers, 1964; Member, Walker Brothers, 1965–67; Regular television appearances; Concerts include: British tour with Roy Orbison and Lulu, 1966; British tour with the Troggs, 1966; Far East tour with Yardbirds and Roy Orbison, 1967; British tour with Jimi Hendrix, 1967; Solo artiste, 1967–; British tour, 1968; Weekly show, BBC, 1969; Walker Brothers Reunion, 1975–78. *Recordings:* Albums: with the Walker Brothers: Take It Easy With The Walker Brothers, 1966; Portrait, 1966; Images, 1967; No Regrets, 1976; Lines, 1977; Nite Flights, 1978; After The Lights Go Out, 1990; No Regrets – The Best of The Walker Brothers, 1992; Solo albums: Scott, 1967; Scott 2 (No. 1, UK), 1968; Scott 3, 1969; Scott 4, 1970; Til The Band Comes In, 1971; The Moviegoer, 1972; Any Day Now, 1973; Stretch, 1974; We Had It All, 1974; Scott Walker Plays Jacques Brel, 1981; Climate of Hunter, 1984; Boy Child, 1990; Tilt, 1995; Pola X, 1999; Hit singles: with the Routers: Let's Go, 1963; with The Walker Brothers: Make It Easy On Yourself (No. 1, UK), 1965; My Ship Is Coming In, 1966; The Sun Ain't Gonna Shine Any More, (No. 1, UK) 1966; No Regrets, 1976; Solo: Joanna, 1968; Lights of Cincinnati, 1969; As producer: Punishing Kiss, Ute Lemper, 2000; We Love Life, Pulp, 2001. *Current Management:* Negus-Fancey Co, 78 Portland Rd, London W11 4LQ, England.

WALKER SMITH, Nicola; b. 18 Feb. 1964, Batley, West Yorkshire, England. Vocalist. m. Geoff Smith, 16 Sept. 1989, two s. (twins). *Education:* BA Hons, Music, Electronics, Keele University, 1987; MA Music Theatre, Birmingham University, 1988. *Career:* World-wide concert appearances; Television and radio includes: In Tune, BBC Radio 3; Midnight Oil; Music In Our Time; The Late Show, BBC2; Other radio broadcasts world-wide; Performances include: Spindle And Shuttle, by Phillip Flood, 1992. *Recordings:* Albums: The Garden, 1991; Gas Food Lodging, 1993; Fifteen Wild Decembers, 1995; Black Flowers, with the Geoff Smith Band, 1997; L'imboscata, with Franco Battiato, 1997. *Publications:* American Originals (co-author with Geoff Smith), 1994. *Honours:* Winston Churchill Fellowship, 1992. *Current Management:* Keith Armstrong, Kitchenware, St Thomas' St Stables, Newcastle upon Tyne NE1 4LE, England. *Address:* 25 Exeter Close, Chippenham, Wiltshire SN14 0YG, England.

WALLACE, Angus; b. 7 April 1968, Guilsborough, Northants, England. *Education:* Media Productions, School of Recording, Brixton, London, 1987; MA, Sound Design, 2002. *Career:* Own Recording Studio, age 18. *Recordings:* Album tracks for: Love and Rockets; David J; Unisex; Wishbone Ash; Spiritualized; The Fall; Natacha Atlas (Transglobal Underground); Live Drums, recorded for The Prodigy; I Don't Need a Gun. *Honours:* Ampex Golden Reel Award, 1994; Gold Disc, world-wide sales, Fiend with Violin by The Fall, 1996. *Current Management:* GMM Management, Coton, NN6 8RF, England. *Address:* Far Heath, Guilsborough, Northants, NN6 8RH, England.

WALLACE, Robert Andrew; b. 21 Nov. 1951, Glasgow, Scotland. Musician (pipes). 1 s., 1 d. *Career:* Member, folk band Whistlebinkies, 1974–; Appeared on television and radio with RSNO, Scottish Ensemble, John Cage, Yehudi Menuhin. *Recordings:* 5 albums with Whistlebinkies; Solo albums: Chance Was A Fine Thing, 1982; Piper of Distinction, 1990; Also features on: On The West Side, Donnie Munro, 2000. *Publications:* Glasgow Collection of Bagpipe Music. *Honours:* Gold Medal, Oban, 1985; Bratach Gorm (Blue Banner), London, 1989. *Membership:* Musicians' Union; CPA; Piobaireachd Society.

WALLEME, Christophe; b. 1964. Musician (acoustic bass). *Education:* Private lessons with M Kazoran; Hein Van de Guyn; Césarius Alvim; Training with: QUEST; Kenny Barron's rhythm section. *Career:* Member, PRYSM; Manuel Rocheman Trio; David Patois Trio, Quintet; Sarah Lazarus Quartet; Lois Winsberg Quintet; Jean-Pierre Como Quintet; Jean-Loup Longnon Sextet and Big Band; Played numerous clubs, Paris; Festivals, France; Played with: Tom Harrell; Ted Curson; Jean-Loup Longnon; Rick Margitza; Sylvain Beuf; Eric Barret; Richard Galliano; Philip Catherine; Christian Escoudé; N'Guyen Lee; Stephanie Crawford; Walter Davis Jr; Barry Altschul; René Urtreger; Michel Graillier; Alain Jean-Marie; Georges Arvanitas; Jacky Terrasson; Jean-Pierre Como; Denuis Badault; Bob Mover; George Brown; Aldo Romano; Teacher, EDIM, 1986–. *Recordings:* Bop For Sale, Ludovic de Preissac Quintet, 1989; Correspondence, Daniel Beaussier Quartet, 1990; Ciao Mon Coeur, Elizabeth Caumont, 1993; Sanscrit, Daniel Beaussier Quartet, 1993; Impro Primo, Sylvain Beuf Quartet, 1993; Cyclades, Jean-Loup Lognon Big Band, 1994; PRYSM, PRYSM, 1995; Tropic City, Manuel Rocheman Trio, 1995; Express Paris-Rome, Jean-Pierre Como Quintet, 1996; Louis Winsberg Quintet. *Honours:* Soloist Award, La Défense National Jazz Contest, 1988; First Prize, Jazz Et Polar Contest, 1991; First Prize, La Défense National Jazz Contest, 1994. *Address:* 16 rue des Eglantines, 91130 Ris-Orangis, France.

WALLER, Paul; b. 1961, London, England. Record Prod.; Remixer; Programmer; Songwriter. 2 s, 1 d. *Recordings:* Björk; Soul II Soul; Naughty By Nature; Lisa Stansfield; Baby Face; Eric Clapton; Elton John; Heather Small; The Spice Girls; Art Of Noise; Louise; Shola Ama. *Membership:*

Musicians' Union. *Current Management:* Paul Kennedy, 1 2 One Management, PO Box 6627, London N22 4JZ, England.

WALLGREN, Henrik; b. 10 Sept. 1965, Gothenburg, Sweden. Vocalist; Songwriter. m. Katarina Wallgren, 24 June 1988, 2 d. *Career:* Formed ORO, 1990; For Gothenburg Film Festival: Metropolis, 1994; Total King Kong, 1996; Joined Den Fule, 1994; Solo album, 1996. *Compositions:* New Music to Mother Curage, 1994; New Music to Nosferatu, 1995. *Recordings:* Milk and Concrete, 1990; Iron-Storm, 1992; Ragamedon... 2048, 1993; Quake!, 1995; Walk On By, 1996. *Honours:* Grammis, 1993; City of Gothenburg Prize, 1997. *Membership:* Swedish Composers of Popular Music. *Current Management:* Musikcentrum Väst Pjurgardsgatan 13, 414 62 GBG Sweden. *Address:* Pl. 1039, 430 85 Branne, Sweden.

WALLINGER, Karl; b. 19 Oct. 1957, Prestatyn, Wales. Vocalist; Musician (multi-instrumentalist); Record Prod; Arranger; Songwriter. *Career:* Member, groups Quasimodo; Zero Zero; Out; Invisible Body Club; Member, The Waterboys, 1983–86; Founder, World Party, 1986; Concerts include: Launch of Greenpeace – Rainbow Warriors album, with Peter Gabriel, Annie Lennox, Moscow, 1989; Reims Music Festival, France, 1990. *Recordings:* with The Waterboys: Singles: The Whole of The Moon, 1985; with World Party: Ship of Fools, 1987; Is It Like Today, 1993; All I Gave, 1993; Albums: with The Waterboys: A Pagan Place, 1984; This Is The Sea, 1985; with World Party: Private Revolution, 1987; Goodbye Jumbo, 1990; Bang!, 1993; Egyptology, 1997; Dumbing Up, 2001; Compilation: Whole of The Moon: The Music of The Waterboys, 1998; Co-writer, She's The One, Robbie Williams (No. 1, UK), 1999. *Honours:* Q Award, Best Album, Goodbye Jumbo, 1990. *Current Management:* Pure Management, 39 Bolton Gardens, London SW5 0AQ, England.

WALSH, Greg; b. England. Record Prod. *Career:* Producer for: Heaven 17; Tina Turner; Xymox; Chicago; Elkie Brooks; Lucio Battisti; British Lions; Trainspotting; Ron. *Recordings:* with Heaven 17: Singles: Let Me Go, 1982; Temptation (No. 2, UK), 1983; Come Live With Me, 1983; Crushed By The Wheels Of Industry, 1983; Sunset Now, 1984; This Is Mine, 1984; And That's No Lie, 1985; Albums: The Luxury Gap, 1983; How Men Are, 1984; with Tina Turner: Let's Stay Together, 1983. *Current Management:* Gary Davison, The Liaison and Promotion Co. *Address:* 70 Gloucester Pl., London WH1 3HL, England.

WALSH, Joe; b. 20 Nov. 1947, Wichita, Kansas, USA. Vocalist; Musician (guitar, keyboards); Record Prod. *Education:* Kent (Ohio) State University. *Career:* Member, James Gang; Solo artiste, and with own group Barnstorm, 1971–; Member, The Eagles, 1976–81; Tour of Australia, New Zealand, Japan, 1976; 2 US tours, 1977; 2 European tours, 1977; Canadian tour, 1978; Self-nominated for Vice-President, 2 US presidential campaigns; Joined with the Eagles for the Hell Freezes Over tour and album, world tour spanning 3 years and 5 countries. *Recordings:* Albums: with The James Gang: Yer Album, 1969; James Gang Rides Again, 1970; Thirds, 1971; Live In Concert, 1971; with The Eagles: Hotel California (No. 1, USA), 1976; The Long Run (No. 1, USA), 1979; Eagles Live, 1980; Hell Freezes Over, 1994; Selected Works 1972–1999, 2000; Solo/with Barnstorm: Barnstorm, 1972; The Smoker You Drink..., 1973; So What, 1974; You Can't Argue With A Sick Mind, 1976; But Seriously Folks, 1978; There Goes The Neighbourhood, 1981; You Bought It, You Name It, 1983; The Confessor, 1985; Got Any Gum, 1987; Ordinary Average Guy, 1991; Songs For A Dying, 1992; Look What I Did! – The Joe Walsh Anthology, 1995; Robocop (soundtrack), 1995; Look What I Did!: The Joe Walsh Anthology, 1995; Greatest Hits: Little Did He Know, 1997; 20th Century Masters Millennium Collection, 2000; with Ringo Starr: Vertical Man, 1998; with Randy Newman: Guilty: 30 Years of Randy Newman; Hit singles: with The Eagles: Hotel California (No. 1, USA), 1977; Life In The Fast Lane, 1977; Heartache Tonight (No. 1, USA), 1979; The Long Run, 1980; Seven Bridges Road, 1981; Solo hit: Life's Been Good, 1978. *Honours:* Grammy Awards: Records of the Year, Hotel California, 1978; Best Vocal Arrangement, New Kid In Town, 1978; Best Rock Vocal Performance, Heartache Tonight, 1980; American Music Awards: Favourite Pop/Rock Album, 1977, 1981; Favourite Pop/Rock Band, 1981. *Current Management:* David Spero Management. *Address:* 1679 S Belvoir Blvd, Cleveland, OH 44121, USA.

WALSH, Peter; b. England. Record Prod. *Career:* Producer for: Simple Minds; China Crisis; Boomtown Rats; Alphaville; The Church; Scott Walker; Peter Gabriel; Miguel Bose; The Charlatans; Pulp. *Current Management:* Gary Davison, The Liaison and Promotion Co. *Address:* 70 Gloucester Pl., London W1H 3HL, England.

WALSH, Steve; b. 1951, St Joseph, Missouri, USA. Vocalist; Musician (keyboards); Songwriter. *Career:* Member, US rock group, Kansas, 1972–80; 1986–; Also solo artiste. *Recordings:* Albums: with Kansas: Kansas, 1974; Songs For America, 1975; Masque, 1975; Leftoverture, 1976; Point of No Return, 1977; Two For The Show, 1978; Monolith, 1979; Audio-Visions, 1980; Power, 1986; In The Spirit of Things, 1988; At the Tower Theatre in Philadelphia, 1998; Somewhere To Elsewhere, 2000; Solo album: Schemer Dreamer; Glossolalia, 2000. *Honours:* UNICEF Deputy Ambassador of

Goodwill, 1978. *Current Management:* Entertainment Services Unltd. *Address:* Main St Plaza 1000, Suite 303, Voorhess, NJ 08043, USA.

WALTER, Rémy; b. 1 Sept. 1964, Paris, France. Vocalist; Actor; Record Prod. 1 d. *Education:* Exam as an arranger (SACEM). *Career:* Producer, 1986–; First International success: Etienne by Guesh Patti; Producer, 20 singles and 7 albums; Formed own record label; Actor in 6 films, 1979. *Recordings:* Albums include: Ziskakan: Kasasnicola; Rosina de Peira: Anveit; Pascal Mathieu: En Attendant Des Jours Pires; A3: Les Fous Du Large; Clément Masdonoar: Anastasia; First solo album: Face To The Ground, 1995. *Honours:* Clément Masdonoar: Anastasia, Best World Music Record of Year, Le Monde, 1990. *Membership:* GRAF; SACEM. *Current Management:* Safta Jaffery. *Address:* 1 Prince of Wales Passage, 117 Hampstead Rd, London NW1 3EF, England.

WALTERS, Dez; b. 1 Oct. 1948, Llysfaen, North Wales. Musician (guitar, banjo); Songwriter; Vocalist. 3 d. *Career:* Began, early teens in rock band; Worked playing country music in: Middle East; America; Canada; Europe; Backing musician and support act to: Billie Jo Spears: Jim Glaser; Ronnie Prophet; UK and European tours; Song in film: Too Young To Die; 3 songs appeared on STV Show, 1994, 1995; Various radio stations, UK. *Compositions:* Writer, most of own material. *Recordings:* Here's Looking At You; Wide Brimmed and Legless, 1995; Ladies Man, 1995; Mare Veris; Totally Covered, 2001; videos: Choice Cuts, 2000; Live In Tuscon, 2001. *Honours:* Scotland's No. 1 Country Band, 1994, 1995; Various awards, country clubs nationwide. *Membership:* Equity; Musicians' Union.

WALTERS, Hannelore Liesemarie (Fil); b. 31 Jan. 1970, Dartford, Kent, England. Vocalist; Songwriter; Lyricist. *Education:* Studied violin, aged 9–12; Currently learning piano. *Career:* Member, various bands from age 16; Singer, songwriter, lyricist, Back To The Planet, 6 years; Appearances radio and television; Signed to London Records, 1993; Continuous concerts, England, Europe, 6 years; Festivals include: Glastonbury; Phoenix; Reading. *Recordings:* 2 cassettes, 1991; 1992; Singles include: Teenage Turtles, 1993; A Small Nuclear Device, 1994; Albums: Mind and Soul Collaborators, 1993; Messages After The Bleep, 1994. *Current Management:* Westbury Music Ltd. *Address:* 8 Roberts Rd, Belvedere, Kent DA17 6NP, England.

WANDALL, Marietta; b. 21 Nov. 1956, Copenhagen, Denmark. Jazz Musician (piano); Composer; Music Teacher. m. Kristian Sparre Andersen, 5 Nov. 1988, 2 d. *Education:* Private teachers; University of Copenhagen. *Career:* Played piano, synthesizer in jazz ensembles, including Crystal Quintet (with Marylin Mazur); Concerts in Denmark, Norway, Finland; Solo pianist at several Copenhagen Jazz Festivals; Duo concerts with Chris Poole (flute); Jazz duo with Hanne Romer (saxophone), 1980–; Numerous appearances on Danish radio and television; Piano teacher in digital piano-lab. *Recordings:* with Hanne Romer: Akijava, 1990; Ametyst, 1994. *Address:* C F Richsvej, 101 C, 2000 Frederiksberg, Denmark.

WANGFORD, Hank (Samuel Hutt); b. 15 Nov. 1940, Wangford, Suffolk, England. Country Vocalist; Musician (guitar); Doctor. *Education:* Medicine, Cambridge University. *Career:* Became singer, London pub circuit, 1976–; Founder, Sincere Management; Sincere Products; Presenter, 2 country music television series, Channel 4; Stage show, Radio Wang; Also Senior Medical Officer, Family Planning Clinic, London. *Recordings:* Chicken Rhythm; Cowboys Stay On Longer; Albums: Live Hank Wangford, 1982; Hank Wangford, 1985; Rodeo Radio, 1985; Stormy Horizons, 1990; Hard Shoulder To Cry On, 1993. *Publications:* Author (as Sam Hutt): Hank Wangford Vol. III – The Middle Years, 1989. *Current Management:* FAB, 132 Liverpool Rd, London N1 1LA, England.

WARD, Bill; b. 5 May 1948, Birmingham, England. Musician (drums). *Career:* Drummer, UK heavy rock group Black Sabbath (formerly Earth), 1967–80, 1983; Concerts include: Hollywood Music Festival, 1970; Madison Square Garden, New York, 1975. *Recordings:* Albums; Black Sabbath, 1970; Paranoid, 1970; Master of Reality, 1971; Black Sabbath, Vol. 4, 1972; Sabbath Bloody Sabbath, 1974; Sabotage, 1975; We Sold Our Souls For Rock 'n' Roll, 1976; Technical Ecstacy, 1976; Never Say Die, 1978; Heaven and Hell, 1980; Live At Last, 1980; Born Again, 1983; Black Sabbath, Reunion, 1998; Solo Album: Two Hands Clapping, 1999 Singles: Evil Woman, 1970; Paranoid, 1970; Iron Man, 1972; Never Say Die, 1978; Hard Road, 1978; Neon Knights, 1980.

WARD, John Robert; b. 28 June 1964, Halesworth, Suffolk, England. Vocalist; Songwriter; Musician (guitar, bodhran, bass guitar, harmonica). m. Lynne, 3 Feb. 1996, 1 s., 1 d. *Education:* Lowestoft College. *Career:* Bass player, singer in rock and pop bands, 1980s; Full-time acoustic singer/songwriter, 1988–; TV appearance at Cambridge Folk Festival; Elected, Folk Section, Committee of Musicians' Union; Times feature and interview, 1996. *Recordings:* The Shrinking World, album, 1988; Water on the Stone, CD, 1992; Billy Bragg and Friends, contributor, 1996; Waking Dreams, CD, 1998. *Membership:* PRS; PPL; PAMRA; Musicians' Union. *Address:* PO Box 59, Lowestoft, Suffolk NR33 8EA, England.

WARE, Martyn; b. 19 May 1956. Musician; Record Prod. *Career:* Founder mem., Human League, 1977–80; Founder mem., production team, British Electronic Foundation (BEF), 1980, renamed Heaven 17, 1981–88; Worldwide tours, numerous television and concert appearances; Independent record prod.; Worked with: Marc Almond, Terence Trent D'Arby, Erasure, Lena Fiagbe, Pauline Henry, Sanna Kurki-Suonio, Alison Moyet, Conner Reeves, Joe Roberts, Scritti Politti, Shabba, Tina Turner, Urban Cookie Collective, Mario Vasquez, Paul Weller. *Recordings:* Albums with Human League: Reproduction, 1979; Travelogue, 1980; with BEF: Music For Stowaways, 1981; Music Of Quality And Distinction Vol. 1, 1982, Vol. 2, 1991; with Heaven 17: Penthouse And Pavement, 1981; Heaven 17, 1982; The Luxury Gap, 1983; How Men Are, 1984; Endless, 1986; Pleasure One, 1986; Teddy Bear, Duke & Psycho, 1988; Higher And Higher, 1993; Bigger Than America, 1996; Retox/Detox, 1999; Live At Last, 1999; Temptation: Live In Concert, 2001; with Vince Clarke (as The Clarke & Ware Experiment): Pretentious, 2000; Spectrum Pursuit Vehicle, 2001. Singles: with Human League: Being Boiled, 1978; The Dignity Of Labour, 1979; Empire State Human, 1980 with BEF: Music For Stowaways (EP), 1980; Family Affair, 1991; with Heaven 17: We Don't Need This Fascist Groove Thang, 1981; I'm Your Money, 1981; Play To Win, 1981; Penthouse And Pavement, 1981; Height Of The Fighting, 1982; Let Me Go, 1982; Temptation (No. 2, UK), 1983; Come Live With Me, 1983; Crushed By The Wheels Of Industry, 1983; Sunset Now, 1984; This Is Mine, 1984; And That's No Lie, 1985; The Foolish Thing To Do, with Jimmy Ruffin, 1986; Contenders, 1986; Trouble, 1987; The Ballad Of Go Go Brown, 1988. *Current Management:* Stephen Budd Management Ltd, 109 Regents Park Rd, Primrose Hill, London NW1 8UR, England. *Website:* www.record-producers.com.

WARE, Nicholas Stewart; b. 5 April 1963, Burnham, Buckinghamshire, England. Project Man., Videoconferencing. *Education:* O Level Music, High Wycombe Music CTRE, Baritone and alto saxophone, bass guitar. *Career:* Bucks Cyjo, 1982–88; Herman Nush Windtunnel Experience, 1988–89 Saxophonist, musical director, arranger, soul/blues band Straight Eight, 1990–; Bucks Symphonic Ensemble, 1990–94. *Recordings:* Session recording with No No Fear, 1987, 1989, 1990; with Orbitone: All Day; Set Me Free Optimism; with Straight Eight: It's A Cover Up (album), 1991. *Address:* Rectory Court, High Wycombe, Buckinghamshire HP13 7DH, England.

WARINER, Steve; b. 25 Dec. 1954, Noblesville, Indiana, USA. Musician (bass); Songwriter; Vocalist. *Career:* Bass player with Dottie West; Bob Luman; Chet Atkins; Solo artiste, 1978–. *Compositions include:* I'm Already Taken, Conway Twitty; Several songs recorded by Bob Luman. *Recordings:* US Country No. 1 hits: All Roads Lead To You; Some Fools Never Learn; You Can Dream On Me; Love's Highway; Small Town Girl; Lynda; The Weekend Duets include: The Hand That Rocks The Cradle, with Glen Campbell; That's How You Know When Love's Right, with Nicolette Larson; Albums: Steve Wariner, 1982; Midnight Fire, 1983; One Good Night Deserves Another, 1985 Life's Highway, 1985; Down In Tennessee, 1986; It's A Crazy World, 1987 Should Be With You, 1988; I Got Dreams, 1989; I Am Ready, 1991; Drive, 1993; No More Mr Nice Guy, 1996; Christmas Memories, 1999; Burnin' the Roadhouse Down, 1998; Two Teardrops, 1999; Faith in You, 2000; Love Wins; Plano Texas Girl; Where Did I Go Wrong; with: T Graham Brown Wine into Water, 1998; Clint Black, D'Lectrified, 1999; Kieth Urban, 1999 *Honours:* CMA Vocal Event Award, Restless, 1991. *Address:* Steve Wariner Productions, 1103 16th Ave S, Nashville, TN 37212, USA.

WARNES, Jennifer; b. 3 March 1947, Seattle, Washington, USA. Vocalist. *Career:* Singer, 1967–; Theatre appearance, Hair, Los Angeles, 1968 *Recordings:* Albums: I Can Remember Everything, 1968; See Me, Feel Me, Touch Me, Heal Me, 1969; Jennifer, 1972; Shot Through The Heart, 1979 The Best Of…, 1982; Famous Blue Raincoat, 1987; Just Jennifer, 1992; The Hunter, 1992; Also featured on: The Mason Williams Ear Show, Mason Williams, 1967; Everybody's Angel, Tanita Tikaram, 1991; For Our Children, with Jackson Browne, 1991; Singles include: Right Time of The Night, 1976 Know A Heartache When I See One, 1979; It Goes Like It Goes, 1980; Where We Belong, duet with Joe Cocker, for film An Officer and A Gentleman (No. 1, USA), 1982; All The Right Moves, for film All The Right Moves, 1983 (I've Had) The Time of My Life, duet with Bill Medley, for film Dirty Dancing (No. 1, USA), 1987; Albums include: Shot Through the Heart, 1979; The Best of Jennifer Warnes, 1982; Famous Blue Raincoat, 1987; with Chris Hillman Like a Hurricane, 1998; with Michael Martin Murphy: Wildfire 1972–1998; with Jim Billie: Alligator Tales, 1998; The Well, 2001. *Honours:* Academy Awards: It Goes Like It Goes, 1980; Up Where We Belong, 1983; (I've Had) The Time of My Life, 1988; (all for Best Original Song); Grammy Awards: Best Pop Performances, Up Where We Belong, 1983; (I've Had) The Time of My Life, 1987. *Current Management:* Donald Miller, 1246 Kling, Studio City, CA 91604, USA.

WARREN, Diane; b. 1956, California, USA. Songwriter. *Education:* Film Studies, Cal State University. *Compositions include:* If I Could Turn Back Time, Cher; Solitaire, Laura Branigan; If You Asked Me To, Céline Dion; Get Weak, Belinda Carlisle; Rhythm of The Night, Debarge; Look Away, Chicago; Who Will You Run To, Heart; When I'm Back On My Feet Again, Michael Bolton; Not A Dry Eye In The House, Meat Loaf; Also composed

Gloria Estefan, Al Green, Olivia Newton-John, Roy Orbison, Joe Cocker, Christina Aguilera; *NSYNC. *Honours:* ASCAP Songwriter of the Year, 1990, 1991, 1993; Billboard Singles Publishers of the Year, 1990, 1993; ASCAP Voice of Music Award, 1995.

WARREN, (Robert) Huw; b. 18 May 1962, Swansea, West Glamorgan, Wales. Musician (piano, accordion, keyboards); Composer. *Education:* Studied classical piano and cello at young age; Degree in Music, London. *Career:* Crosses many genre boundaries including: Jazz; Folk; Contemporary Classical; World Music; Early musical experiences included playing organ in working men's clubs, South Wales; Moved to London to study for a music degree, 1980; Involved with the British experimental music scene and London jazz musicians; Collaborated with musicians from: Brazil; Democratic Republic of the Congo; Iran; Indian sub-continent; Began long-running collaboration with June Tabor, late 1980s; Co-founder: Perfect Houseplants (with Mark Lockheart and Dudley Phillips); Collaborations include: Billy Bragg; Christine Tobin; The Orlando Consort; Mose Se Fan Fan (African guitarist). *Compositions:* commissions include: Riot for Piano Circus; Steamboat Bill Jr (new score for the Buster Keaton film); Music for a production of Jean Cocteau's Monologues, Lyric Theatre, London. *Recordings:* Albums: A Barrel Organ Far From Home, 1997; Infinite Riches In A Little Room, 2000; with Perfect Houseplants: Perfect Houseplants, 1993; Clec, 1995; Snap Clatter, 1997; Extempore (with Orlando Consort), 1998; New Folk Songs, 2000; with June Tabor: Some Other Time, 1989; Aqaba Topic, 1990; Angel Tiger, 1992; Against The Streams, 1994; Aleyn, 1997; A Quiet Eye, 2000; Rosa Mundi, 2001; with Maddy Prior and June Tabor: No More To The Dance, 1988; features on: Through Rose Coloured Glasses, Mark Lockheart, 1998; Mirmama, Eddi Reader, 1992; Busy Listening, Steve Arguelles, 1994; Entertainment USA, Billy Jenkins, 1994; Tales From The Sun, Tim Garland, 1995; Mayfest 95, Billy Jenkins and the Fun Horns of Berlin, 1995; Aililiu, Christine Tobin, 1995; Yell of the Gazelle, Christine Tobin, 1996; East Meets West 95, Billy Jenkins and the Fun Horns of Berlin, 1996; Circuits, Steve Arguelles, 1998; House of Women, Christine Tobin, 1998. *Website:* www.huwwarren.com.

WARWICK, (Marie) Dionne; b. 12 Dec. 1940, East Orange, New Jersey, USA. Vocalist. m. Bill Elliott, deceased, 2 s. *Education:* Hartt College of Music, Hartford, Connecticut; MMus. *Career:* Singer, gospel groups The Drinkard Singers; The Gospelaires; Solo singer, 1962–; Association with songwriters Bacharach and David, originally as demo and backing singer, 1961–72; Numerous concerts, tours and benefit shows world-wide; Television includes: Top of the Pops; Thank Your Lucky Stars; Ready Steady Goes Live!; The Bacharach Sound; It's What's Happening Baby; The Divine Dionne Warwick; Ed Sullivan Show; Host, Solid Gold, 1980, 1984–86; Host, A Gift of Music, 1981; Sisters In The Name of Love, 1986; Dionne and Friends, 1990; Actress, film Slaves, 1969. *Recordings:* Albums: Presenting Dionne Warwick, 1964; Make Way For Dionne Warwick, 1964; The Sensitive Sound of Dionne Warwick, 1965; Dionne Warwick In Paris, 1966; Here Where There Is Love, 1967; On Stage and In The Movies, 1967; The Windows of The World, 1967; Valley of The Dolls, 1968; Promises Promises, 1969; Soulful, 1969; Dionne, 1972; From Within, 1972; Just Being Myself, 1973; Then Came You, 1975; Track of The Cat, 1976; A Man and A Woman, with Isaac Hayes, 1977; No Night So Long, 1980; Hot, Live and Otherwise, 1981; Friends In Love, 1982; Heartbreaker, 1982; So Amazing, 1983; Without Your Love, 1985; Reservations For Two, 1987; Dionne Warwick Sings Cole Porter, 1990; Friends Can Be Lovers, 1993; Aquarela Do Brazil, 1995; Hits from Stage and Screen, 1997; Dionne Sings Dionne, 1998; I Say A Little Prayer For You, 2000; Numerous compilation albums; Hit singles include: Anyone Who Had A Heart, 1964; Walk On By, 1964; A Message To Michael, 1966; Alfie, 1967; I Say A Little Prayer, 1967; Do You Know The Way To San José, 1968; This Girl's In Love With You, 1969; I'll Never Fall In Love Again, 1970; Then Came You, with The Spinners (No. 1, USA), 1974; I'll Never Love This Way Again, 1979; Heartbreaker, with Barry Gibb (No. 2, UK), 1982; All The Love In The World, 1983; That's What Friends Are For (AIDS charity record), with Stevie Wonder, Gladys Knight, Elton John (No. 1, USA), 1985; Featured on numerous film soundtracks including: A House Is Not A Home, 1964; What's New Pussycat?, 1965; Valley of The Dolls, 1968; The April Fools, 1969; Slaves, 1969; The Love Machine, 1971; After You, 1980; The Woman In Red, 1984; Contributor, charity records: We Are The World, USA For Africa, 1985; Forgotten Eyes, 1990; Lift Up Every Voice and Sing, 1990; That's What Friends Are For, 1993; Sunny Weather Lover, 1993; What the World Needs Now, 1998. *Honours:* Top Selling Female Artist, NARM, 1964; Grammy Awards: Best Female Pop Vocal Performance, 1969, 1970, 1980; Best Contemporary Vocal Performance, 1971; Best Female R&B Vocal Performance, 1980; Best Pop Performance, Duo or Group, 1987; Song of the Year, 1987; Star on Hollywood's Walk of Fame, 1985; NAACP Key of Life Award, 1990; CORE Humanitarian Award, 1992; Nosotros Golden Eagle Humanitarian Award, 1992; Award from City of New York for contributions to AIDS research, 1987; DIVA Award, 1992; Platinum and Gold discs. *Address:* c/o Brokaw Company, 9255 Sunset Blvd, Suite 804, Los Angeles, CA 90069, USA.

WARWICK, Ricky; b. Belfast, Northern Ireland. Vocalist; Rock Musician (guitar). m. Vanessa Warwick. *Career:* Member, New Model Army, Def

Leppard; Founder member, UK heavy rock group The Almighty, 1988–; Major concerts include: Monsters of Rock Festival, Castle Donington, UK, 1982. *Recordings:* Albums: with The Almighty: Blood Fire and Love, 1989; Blood Fire and Live, 1990; Soul Destruction, 1991; Powertrippin', 1993; Crank, 1995; Just Add Life, 1996; Almighty Almighty, 2000; Psycho Narco, 2001; with Def Leppard, 1999; Hit single: Free 'N' Easy, 1991. *Current Management:* Triple T Management Co, 21 Napier Pl., London W14 8LG, England.

WASHBURN, Dan; b. 28 May 1956, Coburg, Ontario, Canada. Vocalist; Songwriter; Musician (bass). m. Jane, 15 Dec. 1984, 3 s., 1 d. *Career:* Lead singer, South Mountain, 1992; Concerts, as lead singer and bassist, South Mountain: Netherlands; Germany; Switzerland; Belgium; Canada; Appeared with: Marty Stuart; Waylon Jennings; Toby Keith; Merle Haggard; Prairie Oyster; Various television shows in above mentioned countries; Appeared, CCMA Awards Show, 1993. *Recordings:* Played on soundtrack for Into The Fire, 1990; South Mountain album: Where There's A Will, 1995; Session bassist, singer, many Canadian country, folk, blues albums. *Membership:* AFofM; Canadian Country Music Asscn. *Current Management:* Katherine Faint, Agent, Savannah Music Group. *Address:* 768 Chamberlain St, Peterborough, ON K9J 4M3, Canada.

WASHINGTON, Sabrina; b. London, England. Vocalist; Rap Artiste; Songwriter. *Career:* Mem., lead singer, Mis-Teeq, 2001–, with Alesha Dixon and Su-Elise Nash; Appeared, Party at the Palace, for Golden Jubilee celebrations, 2002. *Recordings:* Album: Lickin' On Both Sides, 2001. Singles: Why?, 2001; All I Want, 2001; One Night Stand, 2001; B With Me, 2002; Roll On, 2002. *Honours:* Platinum disc, for Lickin' On Both Sides; UK Garage Award, Best Artist, 2001; MOBO Award, Best Garage Act, 2002. *Address:* c/o Telstar Records, 107 Mortlake High St, London SW14 8HQ, England. *Website:* www.mis-teeq.co.uk.

WATERHOUSE, David Boyer; b. 13 July 1936, Harrogate. University Prof; Musician (Piano, Highland Bagpipes). m. Naoko Matsubara, 1 s. *Education:* MA, King's College, Cambridge, 1963; LRAM, 1956, Piano pupil of M Denny (pupil of Tobias Matthay), Highland Bagpipes with P/M John Wilson. *Career:* Research Assistant, Cambridge Institute of Criminology, 1959–60; Research Fellow, Center for Asian Arts, University of Washington, 1964–66; Assistant Professor, 1966–70, Associate Professor, 1970–75, Professor, 1975–, Department of East Asian Studies; Consultant to numerous museums, publishers on Asian art and other subjects; Solo performance of Highland bagpipes, ensemble with the 48th Highlanders of Canada. *Publications include:* Harunobu and his Age: The Development of Colour Printing in Japan, 1964; Japanese Woodblock Prints from the J Bruce Varcoe Collection, 1976; Early Japanese prints in the Philadelphia Museum of Art, 1983; Dance of India, editor, 1998; Numerous contributions to books including The New Grove Dictionary of Music and Musicians, 2001; Encyclopaedia of Music in Canada, 1992; Numerous articles including those on Japanese music, Buddhist music and Highland bagpipes. *Membership:* International Council for Traditional Music; Pipers' Society of Ontario; Pipes and Drums Asscn, 48th Highlanders of Canada; Fellow, Royal Society of Canada; Fellow, Royal Asiatic Society; Society for Asian Music, USA; Society for Ethnomusicology, USA; Toyo Ongaku Gakkai, Japan. *Address:* 324 Coral Terrace, Oakville, ON L6J 4C4, Canada.

WATERMAN, Pete; b. 15 Jan. 1947. Songwriter; Record Prod; Record Co Exec. *Career:* Soul DJ; Promoter, record producer and remixer, for artistes including Adrian Baker; Susan Cadogan; Member, group, Agents Aren't Aeroplanes, 1984; Member, songwriting and production team Stock/Aitken/ Waterman (SAW), with Matt Aitken and Mike Stock, 1984–93; Founder, own PWL record label, 1988; Founder, 3 record labels, PWL America, PWL Continental, PWL Black, 1991–; The Hit Man And Her, ITV, 1988–92; Judge, Pop Idol (ITV1), 2001; Popstars–The Rivals (ITV1), 2002. *Recordings:* Albums: Hit Factory; Hit Factory Vol. 2, 1988; Hit Factory Vol. 3, 1989; The Best of Stock, Aitken and Waterman, 1990; Hit singles: As co-writer, producer: You Spin Me Round, Dead Or Alive (No. 1, UK), 1984; Say I'm Your Number One, Princess, 1985; Showing Out, Mel and Kim, 1986; Venus, Bananarama (No. 1, USA), 1986; So Macho, Sinitta, 1986; Respectable, Mel and Kim (No. 1, UK), 1987; Never Gonna Give You Up (No. 1, UK and USA), Rick Astley, 1987; Together Forever, Rick Astley (No. 1, USA), 1988; with Kylie Minogue: I Should Be So Lucky (No. 1, 12 countries), 1988; Got To Be Certain, 1988; The Locomotion, 1988; Especially For You, duet with Jason Donovan (No. 1, UK), 1988; Hand On Your Heart (No. 1, UK), 1989; Better The Devil You Know, 1990; Rhythm of Love, 1993; 50+1, 1998; with Steps: Steptacular, 2000; Also recordings for: Jason Donovan; Divine; Hazell Dean; Sonia; Brother Beyond; Big Fun; Donna Summer. *Current Management:* PWL Management International, 4–7 The Vineyard, off Sanctuary St, London SE1 1QL, England.

WATERS, Peter Russell; b. 4 Aug. 1953, Broken Hill, Australia. Concert/ Jazz Musician (piano). m. Sybille Waters, 29 Aug. 1997, 1 d. *Education:* Piano studies in Adelaide with Rolland May and Clemens Leske, and in London with Peter Walfisch. *Career:* Concert Pianist, Salzburg Gestival with Gundula Janowitz; Solo and duo recitals with Janowitz in Paris, Vienna, Berlin,

London, Lyon, Rome, Stockholm, Cologne, Frankfurt, Munich, Zurich and numerous festivals; Bach Festival Schaffhausen, 1985; Numerous tours, live concerts and recordings in Europe and South America, 1992–; Musical Director, Solo Pianist, exchange project with St Petersburg and Switzerland; Solo tour with Orchestre de Lille, 1997; Formed Treya Quartet with Sardinian Trumpeter Paolo Fresu. *Recordings:* CD, Gates Beyond, music of John Adams, Ravel and Satie; Treya Quartet plays Gabriel Fauré. *Honours:* ABC FM Best Classical Recording in Australia, for Gates Beyond, 1997. *Membership:* Tonkünstlerverein, Switzerland; World Wildlife Fund. *Current Management:* Jacqui Howard. *Address:* Rothalde 333, 9055 Bühler, Switzerland.

WATERS, Roger; b. 6 Sept. 1944, Great Bookham, Surrey, England. Vocalist; Musician (bass); Composer. *Education:* Regent Street Polytechnic, London. *Career:* Founder mem., Pink Floyd, 1965–83; Performances include: Rome International Pop Festival, 1968; Hyde Park, London, 1968; Bath Festival, 1970; Montreux Festival, 1971; Knebworth Festival, 1975; Films: Pink Floyd Live At Pompeii, 1972; The Wall, 1982; Solo artiste, 1983–; Performance of The Wall, Berlin, 1990; Guitar Legends, Seville, Spain, 1991. *Recordings:* Albums: Piper At The Gates of Dawn, 1967; A Saucerful of Secrets, 1968; More (film soundtrack), 1969; Ummagumma, 1969; Atom Heart Mother (No. 1, UK), 1970; Meddle, 1971; Relics, 1971; Obscured By Clouds, 1972; The Dark Side of The Moon (No. 1, USA), 1973; Wish You Were Here (No. 1, UK and USA), 1975; Animals, 1976; The Wall (No. 1, USA), 1979; The Final Cut, 1983; Echoes: Best Of, 2001; Solo albums: Music From The Body (film soundtrack), 1970; The Pros and Cons of Hitch Hiking, 1984; When The Wind Blows, 1986; Radio KAOS, 1987; The Wall – Live In Berlin, 1990; Amused To Death, 1992; In The Flesh Live, 2000; Also appears on: Vagabond Ways, Marianne Faithfull, 1999; Madcap Laughs, Syd Barrett, 1999; Legend of 1900, 1999; Singles include: See Emily Play, 1967; Another Brick In The Wall (No. 1, USA and UK), 1979; Run Like Hell, 1980; When The Tigers Break Free, 1982; Not Now John, 1983; Solo: 5.01 AM (The Pros and Cons of Hitch-Hiking), 1984; Radio Waves, 1987; The Tide Is Turning (After Live Aid), 1988. *Honours:* with Pink Floyd: Silver Clef Award, Nordoff-Robbins Music Therapy Centre, 1980; Ivor Novello Award, Outstanding Contribution To British Music, 1992.

WATERSON, Norma, (Norma Christine Carthy); b. 15 Aug. 1939, Kingston-upon-Hull, Humberside, England. Vocalist. m. Martin Carthy. *Career:* Mem., seminal folk group, The Watersons (line-up included sister Lal, brother Mike and husband Martin Carthy), 1960s; Toured with daughter Eliza Carthy, Lal Waterson and Lal's daughter Maria as the Waterdaughters, 1980s; Formed another family band Waterson: Carthy (including Norma, Martin Carthy and daughter Eliza), 1990s; Solo artiste, 1996–. *Recordings:* Albums: with The Watersons: New Voices, Frost and Fire, 1965; Watersons, A Yorkshire Garland, 1966; For Pence and Spice Ale, 1975; Sound Sound Your Instruments, 1977; Greenfields, 1981; with Lal Waterson: A True Hearted Girl, 1977; with Waterson-Carthy: Waterson-Carthy, 1994; Common Tongue, 1997; Broken Ground, 1999; Solo: Norma Waterson, 1996; The Very Thought Of You, 1999; Bright Shiny Morning, 2000. *Honours:* O.B.E., 2003. *Address:* c/o Topic Records Ltd, 50 Stroud Green Rd, London N4 3EF, England.

WATES, Matt (Matthew James); b. 1964. Musician (saxophone, flute, clarinet); Composer. *Education:* Berklee College of Music, 1988. *Career:* Jazz musician, arranger and composer; Recorded with: Roadside Picnic; PAZ; Sax Appeal; NYJO; The Michael Garrick Big Band; Recorded three albums, including many orignal compositions, as leader of The Matt Wates Sextet; Appeared with many top jazz musicians including: Bucky Pizzarelli; Humphrey Lyttelton; Georges Arvanitas; Helen Shapiro; John Colianni; Don Weller; Bobby Wellins; Dusko Goykevich; Duncan Lamont; Ian Shaw; Norma Winston; Peter King. *Recordings:* Albums: with Matt Wates Sextet: Relaxin' At The Cat, 1993; Two, 1996; Smallbill's Garage, 1999; with PAZ: Dancing In The Park, 1995; Samba, Samba, 2000; Laying Eggs, 2001; with Itchy Fingers: Full English Breakfast, 1993; with Roadside Picnic: La Famille, 1995; features on: Meteors Close At Hand, Michael Garrick, 1995; Mellow Mania, Liz Fletcher, 1997; Live In The Park, Liz Fletcher, 1999. *Honours:* BT British Jazz Awards: Rising Star Award, 1997; Best Small Group, Matt Wates Sextet, 2001. *E-mail:* mattwates@hotmail.com.

WATKINS, Ian 'H'; b. 8 May 1976. Vocalist. *Career:* Former holiday camp children's entertainer; Mem., Steps, 1997–2001; Popular with UK teen audience; Numerous television appearances, incl. Steps To The Stars; Tours, incl. Gold–Greatest Hits tour, 2001; Mem., duo, H and Claire, with fellow Steps mem.–Claire Richards, 2002–. *Recordings:* Albums: with Steps: Step One, 1998; Steptacular, 1999; Buzz, 2000; Gold, 2001; The Last Dance, 2002; with H and Claire: Another You Another Me, 2002. Single: with H and Claire: All Out Of Love, 2002. *Honours:* BRIT Award, Best Selling Live Act, 2000. *Address:* c/o Zomba Records Ltd, Zomba House, 165–167 Willesden High Rd, London NW10 2SG, England. *Website:* www.stepsofficial.com.

WATKINS, Tionne Tenese, (T-Boz); b. 26 April 1970, Des Moines, Iowa, USA. Vocalist. *Career:* Began as singer in Church choir; Mem., lead singer, TLC, 1991–; Acting role in film, Belly, 1998; Owner, Shee Inc, Grunge Girl Music; Co-owner, line of clothes, Grungy Glamorous; Released solo song, Touch Myself, for film, Fled. *Recordings:* Albums: Ooooooohhh... On The TLC

Tip, 1992; Crazysexycool, 1994; Fanmail, 1999; 3D, 2002. Singles: Ain't 2 Proud 2 Beg, 1991; Baby Baby Baby, 1992; What About Your Friends, 1992; Get It Up, 1993; Creep (EP, No. 1, USA), 1994; Diggin' On You, 1995; Red Light Special, 1995; Waterfalls (No. 1, USA), 1995; Future/Off, 1997; No Scrubs (No. 1, USA), 1999; Silly Ho, 1999; Unpretty (No. 1, USA), 1999; Dear Lie, 1999; Girltalk, 2002. *Publications:* Thoughts (poems), 1999. *Honours:* Grammy Awards, Best R&B Performance by Duo/Group, Best R&B Album, for Crazysexycool; Two Lady of Soul Awards; Two Billboard Music Awards; Three Soul Train Awards; Blockbuster Entertainment Award; Four MTV Music Video Awards, for Waterfalls. *Address:* LaFace Records, 1 Capital City Plaza, 3350 Peachtree Rd, Suite 1500, Atlanta, GA 30326, USA.

WATSON, Andy; b. 20 June 1958, Enfield, England. Session Musician (guitar). m. Pam Watson, 20 Aug. 1983. *Education:* Crawley and Swindon Technical College; London College of Music; Royal College of Music; Leeds College of Music. *Career:* Sessions for YTV; BBC; Channel 4; Royal Philharmonic Orchestra; West End Shows: Joseph and The Amazing Technicolour Dreamcoat; Les Miserables; Sunset Boulevard; Anything Goes; Ross Mitchell Band and Singers. *Recordings:* Solo album: Sweeping Statement, 1989; with Ross Mitchell & His Band: Dance Fever, 1998; Dancing With Time, 2000. *Publications:* Author, Join The Dots column, Guitarist magazine. *Honours:* Associate, Royal College of Music; Graduate, Leeds College of Music. *Membership:* Musicians' Union; PRS; MCPS. *Address:* Chelmsford, Essex, England.

WATSON, Bobby (Robert Michael), Jr; b. 23 Aug. 1953, Lawrence, USA. Musician (alto saxophone); Composer; Bandleader. m. Pamela Watson, 11 Sept. 1976, 1 s., 1 d. *Education:* BM, Theory and Composition, University of Miami. *Career:* Musical director with Art Blakey and The Jazz Messengers, 1977–81; Member, Leads Horizon, 1980–; Alto with Zahir Batin, 1980–; Alto with Art Blakey and The Jazz Messengers, 1981–; Alto with Mickey Bass Quartet, 1981–; Member, 28th Street Saxophone Quartet, 1983–; Lead alto with Panama Francis and The Savoy Sultans, 1983–; Lead alto with The Duke's Men, 1987–; Performs with Charlie Mingus Epitaph Project, 1989–; Alto with Smithsonian Jazz Masterworks Orchestra, 1982; Lead alto Carnegie Hall Jazz Orchestra, 1992; Premiered Tailor Made big band, 1993; Tours: Brazil; Europe; Japan; Canada; North America; Caribbean; Italy; Netherlands; Scotland; Germany; England; Cyprus; Every major jazz festival in Europe; Own publishing company, Lafiya Music, 1979–; Record label, New Note Records, 1983–. *Compositions:* Over 100. *Recordings include:* As leader: Post-Motown Bop; No Question About It; The Inventor; The Year of The Rabbit; Love Remains; Round Trip; All Because of You; Gumbo; Jewel; Live At Someday In Tokyo, 2000; *Recordings with artists including:* Bill Cosby; Art Blakey and The Jazz Messengers; 29th Street Quartet; Duke Ellington; Charlie Mingus; Cornelius Kreusch. *Honours:* Recipient of National Endowment Composers Grant, 1980; Downbeat Critics Poll Wins: Best Alto Saxophonist, 1989–92; Jazz Musician of the Year, 1990. *Current Management:* Timothy Patterson, Split Second Timing. *Address:* 104 W 70th St, Apt 11C, New York, NY 10024, USA.

WATSON, (Gary) Gene; b. 11 Oct. 1943, Palestine, Texas. Country vocalist; Songwriter; Musician (guitar). *Career:* Formed first band, Gene Watson and the Other Four, with brothers and cousins, Houston, Texas, aged 14; Debut single Autumn In June on Wide World Records; Also recorded for Stonewall Records; Country chart debut, Bad Water, on Resco Records, 1975; Signed to Capitol, 1975; Nearly 50 Billboard country chart singles on labels including Capitol; MCA; Epic; Warner Bros; Continues to record on independent label and tour with own band, the Farewell Party Band. *Recordings include:* Love In The Hot Afternoon, 1975; Paper Rosie, 1977; Should I Come Home (Or Should I Go Crazy), 1979; Fourteen Carat Mind, 1981; You're Out Doing What I'm Here Doing Without, 1983; Albums: Love In The Hot Afternoon, 1975; Should I Come Home, 1979; Sometimes I Get Lucky, 1983. *Address:* c/o Adams and Green Entertainment Agency, 2011 Masters Lane, Missouri City, TX 77459, USA.

WATSON, Jamie; b. 3 June 1954, Canada. Recording Engineer; Pro Musician (guitar, drums, keyboards). m. Beverley Watson, 26 March 199_ *Education:* George Watsons College; Edinburgh Art College. *Career:* Member Solos; Major British tour support to The Tourists, 1979; Currently owns and runs Chamber Recording Studio in Edinburgh. *Recordings:* Singles: Talking Pictures, Solos; Single by Persian Rugs; Album and other records on various independent labels; As producer: Foil; Eugenius; Long Fin Killie; Snow Patrol. *Membership:* PRS; MCPS. *Address:* 120A W Granton Rd, Edinburgh EH_ 1PF, Scotland.

WATSON, Jeff; b. 4 Nov. 1959, Sacramento, California, USA. Musician (guitar); Vocalist; Writer; Record Prod; Sound Engineer. *Career:* Guitarist, US rock group, Night Ranger, 1982–91; Guitarist, Mothers Army; Television appearances include: American Bandstand (4 times); Solid Gold; Tours world wide; 10m. albums sold. *Recordings:* Albums: with Night Ranger: Dawn Patrol, 1982; Midnight Madness, 1983; Seven Wishes, 1985; Big Life, 1987; Man In Motion, 1988; Live In Japan, 1990; Seven, 1998; Live In Japan, Greatest Hits, Live, 1999; Solo: Lone Ranger, 1992; Around The Sun, 199_ with Steve Morse: Southern Steel; with Chris Isaak: San Francisco Day_

Forever Blue; with Mothers Army: Mothers Army I and II; 3 No. 1 videos with Night Ranger. *Honours:* Multiple Platinum and Gold albums. *Membership:* BMI; AFTRA; JASRAC. *Current Management:* Bruce Cohn Management, 15140 Sonoma Hwy, Glenellen, CA 93442, USA. *Address:* 120 Sunnyside, #149 Mill Valley, CA 94941, USA.

WATSON, Russell; b. 1974, Salford, England. Singer (Tenor). *Career:* Professional singer, 1996–; Numerous television and radio appearances; Concert performances incl. Wembley Arena, Royal Albert Hall, Carnegie Hall, Sydney Opera House, opening ceremony of the Commonwealth Games, Manchester, 2002; Sang Pelagia's Song from film, Captain Corelli's Mandolin, 2001; Sang theme tune to Star Trek Enterprise, television series, 2002. *Recordings:* Albums: The Voice, 2000; Encore, 2001; Reprise, 2002. Singles: Swing Low '99 (official England Rugby Team song), 1999; Barcelona (with Shaun Ryder), 2000; Someone Like You (with Faye Tozer), 2002. *Honours:* Platinum discs. *Address:* 3www Web Services Ltd, Dept F, Glenfield Park, Site 2, Suite 505, Blakewater Rd, Blackburn, Lancashire BB1 5QH, England. *E-mail:* info@russellwatson.co.uk. *Website:* www.russellwatson.com.

WATT, Ben; b. 6 Dec. 1962. Musician (guitars, keyboards); Vocalist. Songwriter. *Education:* Hull University. *Career:* Solo artiste, 1981–82; Formed duo, Everything But The Girl, with singer Tracey Thorn, 1983–; Appearances include: Regular British tours, 1984–; World Tour 1990, including Japan; Friends of the Earth Benefit Concerts; Red Hot and Dance AIDS Benefit Concert, 1991; UK and US Tours, 1993–95; World Tour, 1996–97, including Japan and Australasia. *Compositions:* Writer, co-writer with Tracey Thorn, of own material for duo and solo work. *Recordings:* Albums: Solo album: North Marine Drive, 1983; with Everything But The Girl: Eden, 1984; Everything But The Girl (USA only), 1984; Love Not Money, 1985; Baby, The Stars Shine Bright, 1986; Idlewild, 1988; The Language of Life, 1990; World-wide, 1991; Essence and Rare (Japan only), 1992; Acoustic, 1992 (USA only); Home Movies – Best of Everything But The Girl, 1993; Amplified Heart, 1994; Walking Wounded, 1996; Temperamental, 1999; Back To Mine, 2001; with Deep Dish: future of the Future, 1998; Junk Science, 1999; Lazy Dog, 2000; With Splendour, Splendour, 1999; with Next Best Thing, Next Best Thing, 2000; Singles include: Everything But The Girl: Each and Every One, 1984; Come On Home, 1986; I Don't Want To Talk About It, 1988; Missing, 1995; Walking Wounded, 1996; Wrong, 1996; Single, 1996; Five Fathoms, 1999. *Current Management:* JFD Management, 106 Dalling Rd, London W6 0JA, England.

WATTS, Andy; b. Macclesfield, England. Musician (shawn, Flemish bagpipes, clarinet, recorders, curtal); Vocalist. *Education:* History of Music, Cambridge University; Guildhall School of Music and Drama; Royal Conservatory, The Hague, Netherlands. *Career:* Recorder teacher; Freelance musician with early music groups; Musical Director, Medieval Players; Baroque and classical bassoon with: The Orchestra of The Age of The Enlightenment; The English Baroque Soloists; The Academy of Ancient Music; Teacher, baroque bassoon, Royal Academy of Music; Founder member, The Carnival Band, 1984–; Appearances include: Glasgow Cathedral; Birmingham Symphony Hall; Barbican Centre; Arts theatres and centres; Plays material from: Sweden; Croatia; USA; Bolivia; Spain; UK; France. *Recordings include:* Album with Maddy Prior: Christmas Carols; Also recorded with Frances Eustace; Colin Lawson; Lisa Beznosiuk and Nigel North. *Current Management:* c/o Jim McPhee, Acorn Entertainments. *Address:* Winterfold House, 46 Woodfield Rd, Kings Heath, Birmingham B13 9UJ, England.

WATTS, Charlie (Charles Robert); b. 2 June 1941, Islington, London, England. Musician (drums). *Career:* Member, Blues Incorporated; Member, Rolling Stones, 1962–; Numerous tours and concerts include: National Jazz and Blues Festival, 1963; First British tour, 1963; Group Scene British tour, 1964; Debut US tour, 1964; Free concert, Hyde Park, 1969; Free concert, Altamont Speedway, 1969; Knebworth Festival, 1976; Steel Wheels North American Tour, 1989; Final world tour, 2002–03; Films include: Ladies and Gentlemen The Rolling Stones, 1976; Let's Spend The Night Together, 1983; Co-founder, record label, Rolling Stones Records, 1971. *Recordings:* Albums include: The Rolling Stones, 1965; The Rolling Stones No 2, 1965; Out of Our Heads, 1965; Aftermath, 1966; Between The Buttons, 1967; Their Satanic Majesties Request, 1967; Beggar's Banquet, 1968; Let It Bleed, 1969; Get Yer Ya-Ya's Out, 1969; Sticky Fingers, 1971; Exile On Main Street, 1972; Goat's Head Soup, 1973; It's Only Rock and Roll, 1974; Black and Blue, 1976; Some Girls, 1978; Emotional Rescue, 1980; Tattoo You, 1981; Still Life, 1982; Steel Wheels, 1989; Flashpoint, 1991; Stripped, 1995; Long Ago and Far Away, 1996; Forty Licks, 2002. Hit singles include: It's All Over Now; Little Red Rooster; Get Off of My Cloud; (I Can't Get No) Satisfaction; 19th Nervous Breakdown; Ruby Tuesday; Jumping Jack Flash; Honky Tonk Women; Let's Spend The Night Together; Brown Sugar; Miss You; Start Me Up; Emotional Rescue; Harlem Shuffle; Going To A Go-Go; Paint It Black; Angie; Undercover of The Night; She's So Cold; Solo: Charlie Watts/Jim Keltner Project, 2000. *Honours:* with Rolling Stones include: Silver Clef, Nordoff-Robbins Therapy, 1982; Grammy Award, Lifetime Achievement Award, 1986; Inducted into Rock and Roll Hall of Fame, 1989; Q Award, Best Live Act, 1990; Ivor Novello Award, Outstanding Contribution to British Music, 1991. *Current*

Management: Rupert Loewenstein, 2 King St, London SW1Y 6QL, England. *Website:* www.rollingstones.com.

WATTS, Trevor Charles; b. 26 Feb. 1939, York, Yorkshire, England. Musician (alto, soprano saxophones, piano, percussion). 2 s., 1 d. *Career:* Founder member, Spontaneous Music Ensemble; Amalgam; Moiré Music; Celebration Band, Burma; India; Caribbean; USA; Canada; Venezuela; Mexico; Botswana; South Africa; Lesotho; Colombia; Ecuador; Bolivia; Malaysia, People's Republic of China; First group to play Burma for 10 years; Arte Television show, 1994; Collaborated with traditional musicians, Khartoum International Festival, Sudan, 1996; Collaborations with Afro-Venezuelan Barlovento musicians, 1992, 1995; Toured in Cameroon, West Africa; Festivals with Moiré Music: San Fransisco Jazz Fest, 2001, Chicago World Music Fest, 2001, Monterey Jazz Fest, 2002. *Compositions:* Bracknell Festival Commission: Mr Sunshine, 1984. *Recordings:* with M M Drum Ork: A Wider Embrace; with Moiré Music: With One Voice; Intakt, 1995; Live at the Athens Concert Hall, 2000; with The Celebration Band: Trevor Watts & The Celebration Band, 2001; Life and Music, 2003. *Publications:* Music Outside, Ian Carr, 1973; Leonard Feathers Encyclopaedia of Jazz; Innovations in British Jazz, Vol. 1, 1999. *Membership:* PRS; MCPS; Musicians' Union; PAMRA. *Address:* Moire Music, 20 Collier Rd, Hastings, East Sussex TN34 3JR, England. *Telephone:* (1424) 443424. *Fax:* (1424) 443424. *E-mail:* moire@watts900.freeserve.co.uk. *Website:* trevorwatts.whistlingmule.com; thecelebrationband.whistlingmule.com.

WAVERLY, Josie; b. USA. Entertainer. m., 2 s. *Career:* Plays 150–180 dates a year, with band: Genuine Country; Appearances with country artists including: John Michael Montgomery; Lorrie Morgan; Tracy Lawrence; Charlie Daniels; Randy Travis; Neal McCoy; John Anderson; Sawyer Brown; Doug Stone. *Recordings:* CD and cassette: Who Cries This Time. *Honours:* Citizen of the Year. *Membership:* CMA; ASCAP; BMI; NAFE. *Current Management:* Nancy Carroll Agency. *Address:* PO Box 19468, Sarasota, FL 34276, USA.

WAY, Bryan Douglas; b. 20 Jan. 1953, Cornerbrook, Newfoundland, Canada. Vocalist; Songwriter. 1 s., 1 d. *Education:* Academic, English Literature. *Career:* Appearances: Oprey North; Tommy Hunter Show; Ronnie Prophet Show; Global TV; Day By Day Show; Country Music Showcase; Mountain Festival; Hiram Walker Canadian Songwriter Tour; Producer: Pieces Of Life, Jimmy Payne, 2000. *Compositions:* Goodbye To The Rain, recorded by Roger Whittaker; Your Memory Lays Down With Me, recorded by James Owen Bush; End of Money, written and recorded by Bryan Way, played on 70 European radio stations. *Publications:* Country Music News; Billboard; Canadian Composer. *Membership:* CCMA (Canadian Country Music Asscn); NSAI (Nashville Songwriters' Asscn International). *Current Management:* Penelope Talent Agency; Suzanne Gaudette Management; Publisher: Songcraft Communications. *Address:* 20 Gamble Ave, Suite 105, Toronto, ON M4K 2G9, Canada.

WAY, Pete; Musician (bass). *Career:* Founder member, UFO, 1969–83; Founder member, Waysted, 1983–88; Rejoined UFO, 1991–; UK and world-wide tours with both bands. *Recordings:* Albums: with UFO: UFO, 1971; UFO 2 – Flying, 1971; Live In Japan, 1972; Phenomenon, 1974; Face It, 1975; No Heavy Pettin', 1976; Lights Out, 1977; Obsession, 1978; Strangers In The Night, 1979; No Place To Run, 1980; The Wild, The Willing and The Innocent, 1981; Mechanix, 1982; High Stakes and Dangerous Men, 1992; with Waysted: Vices, 1983; The Good The Bad The Waysted, 1985; Solo recordings: Amphetamine, 2001.

WAYBILL, Fee, (John Waldo); b. 17 Sept. 1950, Omaha, Nebraska, USA. Vocalist. *Education:* Drama student. *Career:* Lead singer, The Tubes, 1972–; Regular international tours and concerts including: Knebworth Festival (with Frank Zappa and Peter Gabriel), 1978; KUPD U-Fest, Phoenix, 1993; Band appeared in film Xanadu, 1980. *Recordings:* Albums: Read My Lips, 1984; Don't Be Scared by These Hands, 1996; With The Tubes: The Tubes, 1975; Young and Rich, 1976; The Tubes Now, 1977; What Do You Want From Live, 1978; Remote Control, 1979; Completion Backwards Principle, 1981; TRASH (Tubes Rarities and Smash Hits), 1982; Inside Outside, 1983; Love Bomb, 1986; Solo album, Read My Lips, 1984; Singles: White Punks On Dope, 1975; Don't Touch Me There, 1976; Prime Time, 1979; I Don't Want To Anymore, 1981; She's A Beauty, 1983; Tip of My Tongue, 1983; The Monkey Time, 1983; Piece By Piece, 1985; Other recordings: Richard Marx, Richard Marx, 1987; Contributor, film soundtrack Nobody's Perfect, 1990; Days In Avalon, Richard Marx, 2000. *Address:* c/o Geoffrey Blumenauer Artists, 11846 Balboa Blvd, Suite 204, Granada Hills, CA 91344, USA.

WAYNE, Jeff; b. New York, NY, USA. Composer; Arranger. *Education:* Journalism Graduate; Juilliard School of Music, New York; Trinity College of Music, London. *Career:* Member, The Sandpipers, 1960s; Arranger, The Righteous Brothers; Composer for TV commercials, 1970s; Producer, musical director, David Essex, 1970s. *Compositions include:* A Tale of Two Cities, 1969. *Recordings:* War of The Worlds, 1978; War of The Worlds: Highlights, 1981; Spartacus, 1992; Ulladubulla: War Of The Worlds Remix Album, 2000; Contributor, Beyond The Planets, Rick Wakeman and Kevin Peek, 1984.

WAYNE, John Phil; b. 14 July 1946, West Kensington, London, England. International Concert Musician (guitar, keyboards, bass, drums); Vocalist; Actor. Partner, Ludivine Blondin, Jan. 1989, 1 d. *Education:* Radio Telegraphy for Planes and Ships (HMS); Private music tuition, 1 year. *Career:* Sideman with Wild Bill Davis; David Bowie; Tom Jones; John Littleton; Stéphane Grappelli; 5 days with Count Basie; Solo artist and Trio, 1975; Arranger, replaced Quincy Jones for a year, 1978; Conducted The Paris Opera Musicians; Solo concerts: Most international festivals and concerts (jazz); Tours: Africa; Europe; Television, radio, newspapers, magazines, world-wide; Played with: Shirley Bassey; Memphis Slim; Babik Reinhardt; Christian Escoude; Willy Mabon; Sugar Blue; Vic Pitts; Jerome Van Jones; Bruce Grant; Sangoma Everett; Jack Greg; Yos Zoomer; Business: Longsongs Music Ltd. *Recordings:* Let's Rock, 1968; Nunchaku, 1974; Nostalgia, 1980; Broadway By Night, 1981; 1981 Guitar Solo, 1981; John Phil Wayne Live In Europe, 1986; Fairy Queen, 1987; Heavy Metal of The '90s, 1991; Express X, 1992; Trio Compilation, 1995; Solo Compilations, 1995; Music for films, 1970–. *Honours:* Godfather of the International Monte Carlo Racing Car; Twice Best Jazz Guitarist, First Prize Jazz, USA, 1980–82. *Membership:* PRS; MCPS; Musicians' Union; SACEM; SGVA; Steam Train Companies. *Current Management:* Longsongs Music Ltd, 21–23 Greenwich Market, London SE10 9HZ, England.

WAZIMBO, (Benfica Humberto Carlos); b. 1948, Chibuto, Mozambique. Vocalist; Songwriter. *Career:* Member: The Silverstars, 1964; The Geiziers; Grupo Radio Mocambique, 1975; Orchestra Marrabenta Star de Mocambique, lead vocalist, 1979; Song, Nwahulwana, used in Microsoft commercial and film The Pledge, 2001. *Recordings:* with Orchestre Marrabenta Star de Mocambique: Independence, 1985; Marrabenta Piquenique, 1996; solo: Makweru, 1997; Nwahulwana, 2001. *E-mail:* records@piranha.de. *Website:* www.piranha.de.

WEATHERALL, Andrew (Andy); b. 6 April 1963, Windsor, Berkshire, England. Prod; Remixer; DJ. *Career:* Began DJ career at Danny Rampling's Shoom club night; Remixed Primal Scream's Loaded and went on to produce their Mercury Music Prize-winning Screamadelica album; Co-founder: Boy's Own fanzine; Founder: Sabres of Paradise; Emissions Audio Output; Rotter's Golf Club Recordings; Collaborations: Terry Farley; Keith Tenniswood; Jagz Kooner; Member: Bocca Juniors; Sabres of Paradise; Two Lone Swordsmen; Remixed: Texas; Primal Scream; Future Sound of London; My Bloody Valentine; The Orb. *Recordings:* Albums: Sabresonic (with Sabres of Paradise), 1993; Haunted Dancehall (with Sabres of Paradise), 1994; Stay Down (with Two Lone Swordsmen), 1998; Tiny Reminders (with Two Lone Swordsmen), 2001; Singles: Raise (with Bocca Juniors), 1990; Smokebelch (with Sabres of Paradise), 1993; Wilmot (with Sabres of Paradise), 1994; Rico's Helly (with Two Lone Swordsmen), 1996; A Bag of Blue Sparks (with Two Lone Swordsmen), 1998. *Address:* c/o Warp Records, Spectrum House, 32–34 Gordon House Rd, London NW5 1LP, England.

WEAVER, Blue (Derek); b. 11 March 1947, Cardiff, Wales. Prod; Musician (keyboards). m. Ann, 24 June, 1 d. *Education:* Piano Lessons; Cardiff College of Music and Drama. *Career:* Keyboard player, Amen Corner, tours with artists including Jimi Hendrix, Pink Floyd, Hermans Hermits, The Nice, Status Quo, 1965–70; Member, The Stawbs, 1970–73; Also session work included: T Rex; Lou Reed; Family; Alice Cooper; Graeme Edge (Moody Blues); Member, Mott The Hoople, US tour supported by Queen, first rock band to play Broadway, 1973–74; Also played keyboards for Streetwalkers; Member, Ian Hunter/Mick Ronson Band, European tour, 1974–75; US resident, member Bee Gees, 1975–82; Keyboard player, co-producer, co-writer, 6 consecutive No. 1 records, USA; Also session work; Returned to London, 1982; Played keyboards, produced, programmed computers for artists including: Pet Shop Boys; Art of Noise; Stevie Wonder; Miguel Bose; Duran Duran; Propaganda; The Damned; Billy Ocean; Swing Out Sister; Five Star; Own digital studio; Tutor, popular music, Westminster University, London. *Compositions include:* Co-wrote songs for Bee Gees; Commercials include jingles for Labatts, music for Volkswagen; Videos; Film soundtracks for Palace Pictures. *Recordings:* Amen Corner including: Gin House Blues, 1967; World Of Broken Hearts, 1967; Bend Me Shape Me, 1968; High In The Sky, 1968; If Paradise Is Half As Nice (No. 1, UK), 1969; Hello Suzie, 1969; Strawbs, 1970–73; Get It On, T Rex; Mott The Hoople Live; Berlin, Lou Reed; Bee Gees, 1974–82; Keyboards on albums by: Chicago; Stephen Stills; Neil Young; McGuinn Clark Hillman; The Osmonds; John Cougar Mellencamp; KC and the Sunshine Band, 1999. *Honours:* Emmy, music on Calder Racetrack; BMI 2m. performance song co-written with Barry Gibb: Our Love. *Membership:* PRS; BMI; BAC&S; Musicians' Union; Re-Pro. *Address:* 12 South Parade, Bedford Park, London W4 1JU, England.

WEBB, Eric Loder; b. 27 May 1921, Bedford, Bedfordshire, England. Musician (bass, guitar, steel guitar). m. 2 s., 1 d. *Career:* Wartime: Ralph Readers Gang Shows; Own band: Beginners Please, 1947; BBC Radio, 1948; Showtime, BBC, 1949; Geraldo Orchestra, Bermudiana Hotel, Bermuda, 1960–70. *Membership:* Musicians' Union. *Current Management:* Colin Bryant Entertainments, Poole, Dorset, England. *Address:* Cuckoo Cottage, Green Bottom, Colehill, Wimborne, Dorset BH21 2LW, England.

WEBB, Sarah Anne; b. 1971. Vocalist. *Career:* Mem., lead singer, jazz funk quartet, D-Influence, 1990–; Support to Prince, Michael Jackson; Tours, television appearances; D-Influence also production team for R&B music; Group owns Freakstreet label; Session work with: Seal, Digable Planets, Keziah Jones. *Recordings:* Albums: Good 4 We, 1992; Prayer 4 Unity, 1995; London, 1997; D-Influence Presents D-Vas, 2002. Singles: I'm The One/The Classic, 1990; Midnite, 1995; Waiting, 1995. *Current Management:* The Third Rail, 70 Hurlingham Rd, London SW6 3RQ, England. *Address:* c/o Dome Records Ltd, 59 Glenthorne Rd, London W6 0LJ, England.

WEBBE, Simon Solomon; b. 30 March 1979, Manchester, England. Vocalist. *Career:* Mem., UK band, Blue, 2001–; UK tour, 2002. *Recordings:* Albums: All Rise, 2001; One Love, 2002. Singles: All Rise, 2001; Too Close (No. 1, UK), 2001; If You Come Back (No. 1, UK), 2001; Fly By II, 2002; Sorry Seems To Be The Hardest Word, 2002. *Honours:* Multi-Platinum discs, for All Rise, 2001; Smash Hits Awards, Best Newcomer, 2001, Best Live Act, Best UK Band, 2002; Interactive Music Award, Artist of the Year, 2002; BRIT Award, Best British Newcomer, 2002. *Address:* c/o Virgin Records Ltd, 553–579 Harrow Rd, London W10 4RH, England. *Website:* www.officialblue.com.

WEBBER, Mark; b. 14 Sept. 1970, Chesterfield, Derbyshire, England. Musician (guitar). *Career:* Mem., Pulp, 1995–; Numerous tours, television appearances and festival dates; Contribution to film soundtrack, Mission Impossible, 1996. *Recordings:* Albums: Different Class (No. 1, UK) 1995; This Is Hardcore (No. 1, UK), 1998; We Love Life, 2001; Hits, 2002. Singles: Common People (No. 2, UK), 1995; Sorted For E's and Whizz/Misshapes (No. 2, UK), 1995; Disco 2000, 1995; Something Changed, 1996; Help The Aged, 1997; This Is Hardcore, 1998; A Little Soul, 1998; Party Hard, 1998; The Trees/Sunrise, 2001; Bad Cover Version, 2002. *Address:* c/o Island Records, 825 Eighth Ave, New York, NY 10019, USA. *Website:* www.pulponline.com.

WEBBER, Stephen; b. 14 April 1958. Composer; Prod; Prof; Musician (guitar). m. Susan Matthews, 1 Aug. 1981, 2 d. *Education:* BM, University of North Texas; MM, WKU; Guitar Studies with Sharon Isbin, Aspen, and John Johns, Vanderbilt. *Career:* Owner, Mid South Recording Studios, 1987–94; Professor of Record Production and Music Production for TV and Film, Berklee College of Music, 1994–; Music Director, Americana, 1997–; Music Director, National Tour, off Broadway, Cotton Patch Gospel; Bandleder, Stephen Webber Swing Band; Guitar, Cumberland Consort. *Compositions:* Zoetrobics, produced and conducted soundtrack at Lucasfilm's Skywalker ranch; I'm in the Truth Business, documentary; TV series theme music, Art Hysteria and Integrated Science. *Recordings:* As Guitarist: Timeless, 1988; Hymns, 1990; Cumberland Consort, 1992; Angel Christmas, 1994; Producer: He Calms the Storm in Me, Brenda Stuart, 1992; No Solid Ground, Donna Carey, 1993; Kevin Gallagher, 1994; Manhattan Guitar Duo, 1997 *Publications:* Interview with George Martin for Mix magazine, 1996; Active Monitor Comparison Study, Cover story, Electronic Musician, 1997 Riverdance feature for Mix, 1997. *Honours:* Outstanding New Leader Award Berklee College of Music, 1995; Emmy Award, Outstanding Achievement Individual Excellence/Composer, Southern region, 1997. *Membership* NARAS; AES; AFM; GFA. *Current Management:* Willow Shade Records.

WEBER, Eberhard; b. 22 Jan. 1940, Stuttgart, Germany. Musician (bass guitar, double bass). m. Maja, 28 June 1968. *Education:* Studied violoncello Career: Member: Dave Pike Set, 1972–73; Volker Kriegel Spectrum, 1973–75 Eberhard Weber Colours, 1975–81; United Jazz and Rock Ensemble, 1975–87 Collaborations include: Jan Garbarek, 1982–; Kate Bush; Monty Alexander Pat Metheny; Stephane Grappelli; World-wide solo performances; Compose of music for TV and film, 1975–. *Recordings:* The Colours of Chloe, 1973 Yellow Fields, 1975; The Following Morning, 1976; Silent Feet, 1977; Flui Rustle, 1978; Little Movements, 1980; Later That Evening, 1982; Chorus 1984; Works, 1985; Orchestra, 1988, Pendulum, 1993; Endless Days, 2001 *Honours:* German Phono Academy Awards: Artist of the Year; Record of th Year, Colours of Chloe, 1975. *Membership:* Union of German Jazz Musician (UDJ). *Current Management:* Bremme and Hohensee, Hauptstrasse 25, 6911 Heidelberg, Germany. *Website:* www.bremme-hohensee.de/weber_e.htm.

WECKL, Dave; b. 8 Jan. 1960, St Louis, MO, USA. Drums. m. Joyce, 6 Ma 1989, 1 d. *Education:* 2 Years Jazz Studies Program, Marching Bands Colleg *Career:* Stage: Simon and Garfunkel, Paul Simon, Chick Corea, Brecker Bro Michel Camit, Mike Stern, Dave Weckl Band; TV: Tonight Show with Chic Corea; Arsenio Hill Show with Chick Corea; Mag: On covers of Moder Drummer Jazz Is and Downbeat. *Compositions:* Co-writer, 4 solo record *Recordings:* with Chick Corea Elektric Band; Robert Plant (Honey Drippers Diana Ross (Swept Away); Dave Grusin; Chick Corea Akoustic Band; So Albums: Rhythm of the Soul, 1998; Synergy, 1999; Transition, 2000; T Zone, 2001. *Publications:* Instructional – On Warner Bros, 1988; Back Basics, Next Step, 1989; Working It Out, I and II, 1994; The Ultimate Pl Along, I and II, 1994, 1995. *Honours:* Grammy, Chick Corea Akoustic Ban 1988; Best Electric Jazz Drummer, Modern Drummer, 1987–92. *Curre Management:* Ron Moss Management Agency. *Address:* 2635 Griffith Pa Blvd, LA, CA 90039, USA.

WEEDON, Bert; b. 10 May 1920, East Ham, London, England. Musician (guitar); Guitar Tutor. *Career:* Session musician, 1950s–; Member, touring groups of Django Reinhardt; Stéphane Grappelli; Featured soloist, Mantovani; Played with numerous artistes including: Ted Heath; Jimmy Shand; Leader, own quartet, 1956; Television appearances: Residency, 5 O'Clock Club, ITV; Subject, This Is Your Life, 1992; Radio appearances: 3 shows per week, BBC Show Band; Guitar tutor, 1950s–; Play In A Day tutor books once used by Eric Clapton, George Harrison, Pete Townsend. *Recordings:* Guitar Boogie Shuffle (No. 1, UK), 1959; Apache, 1960; Numerous albums include: King Size Guitar, 1960; The Romantic Guitar of Bert Weedon, 1970; Rockin At The Roundhouse, 1971; The Gentle Guitar of Bert Weedon, 1975; 22 Guitar Greats, 1976; Guitar Favourites, 1983; Mr Guitar, 1984; Once More With Feeling, 1988; Encore!, 1990; Compilations include: The Bert Weedon Collection, 2000; Featured musician, hundreds of records by artists including: Marty Wilde; Cliff Richard; Adam Faith; Billy Fury; Tommy Steele; Laurie London; Alma Cogan; Dicky Valentine; Frank Sinatra; Rosemary Clooney, 1950s–. *Publications:* Numerous guitar tuition books, courses, videos, including: Play In A Day (2m. copies sold, most successful guitar tutor book ever); Play Every Day.

WEEKES, Alan Noel; b. 25 Dec. 1958, London, England. Musician (guitar); Tutor; Prod; Composer. m., 1 s. *Education:* Guildhall School of Music and Drama, post-graduate. *Career:* Founder mem., pop band, La Famille, jazz band, Jazz Jamaica; Original mem., Jazz Warriors; Television appearances incl.: Channel 4 club mix; Black on Black; Party at the Palace; Top of the Pops; Switch; Pebble Mill; The White Room; Late Show; Tours: Japan; West Indies; First Lucia Jazz Festival; Africa; Europe with Jazz Jamaica, Sound Advice and Asley Slater's Big Lounge; Appeared, Proms, BBC radio at Hyde Park, London. *Compositions:* Composer, performer, Breath (series of music commissioned by Arts Council), Shaw Theatre, 1992; Just a Dream (album), 1996. *Recordings:* with Sugar Minor, Carol Thompson, Trevor Walters, Jean Adebambo, Jacky Mitto, Janet Kay, Art Blakey, Dick Heckstall-Smith, Courtney Pine; Recent recordings with: Jazz Jamaica, Byron Wallen's Sound Advice, Jazz Warriors, Jazz Jamaica All Stars, Soothsayers, Hugh Massicela, Alan Weekes' Jazz Quartet. *Honours:* Best Jazz Band award, with Jazz Jamaica All Stars, BBC Radio 3. *Membership:* Musicians' Union. *Address:* 28 Valerian Way, London E15 3DF, England.

WEEKS, Clifford M; b. New York, NY, USA. Arranger: Composer; Musician (trombone); Teacher. 1 s., 1 d. *Education:* CAGS in Educational Administration, Boston State College, 1977; Professional Diploma in Arranging and Composition, Berklee College of Music, 1962; Bachelor of Music (magna cum laude), 1963, Master of Music, 1975, Boston Conservatory of Music. *Career:* Teacher, Assistant Principal, Adminstrative Assistant and Cluster Co-ordinator in Boston public schools; Conductor, All-City Jazz band and college jazz bands; Musical Arranger, Greater Bostonians and various professional artists. *Compositions:* Triptych For Tuba and Piano; Four jazz/ stage band compositions. *Recordings:* Triptych For Tuba and Piano, recorded by Karl Megules, 1975. *Honours:* Fellow, Boston University; Omega Man of the Year, Omega Psi Phi Fraternity, 1972. *Address:* 20 Fells Ave, Medford, MA 02155, USA.

WEIDNER, Tim; Mix Engineer; Engineer; Programmer. *Career:* Worked with Seal on the Spacejam Soundtrack; Worked with Trevor Horn for The Art of Noise and Seal. *Recordings:* Tina Turner, Wildest Dreams; Seal, Seal I, Seal II, Human Being, Kiss From a Rose (Engineer), Prayer For the Dying (Engineer, Programmer), Future Love Paradise (Engineer); Janet Jackson and Luther Vandross, Best Things in Life Are Free (Engineer, Remixer); Mike Oldfield, Tubular Bells II (Engineer, Mixed, Programmer), 1992; Shara Nelson, I Fell (Engineer, Mixed); Brand New Heavies, Back To Love (Engineer, Mixed); Sweetback; Art of Noise: Seduction of Claude Debussy, 1999; Frames, Dance the Devil, 1999; Genesis: Turn it on Again: The Hits, 1999; Other. *Recordings include:* XTC; Steve Howe. *Address:* SARM Productions, SP2 Holdings Ltd, The Blue Building, 42/46 St Luke's Mews, London W11 1DG, England.

WEILAND, Scott; b. 27 Oct. 1967, Cleveland, USA. Vocalist. *Career:* Member, Stone Temple Pilots; Numerous headlining tours and television appearances. *Recordings:* Singles: Sex Type Thing, 1992; Plush, 1993; Vasoline, 1994; Interstate Love Song, 1994; Trippin' on a Hole in a Paper Heart, 1996; Big Bang Baby, 1996; Albums: Core, 1992; Live, 1992; Purple Ltd, 1994; Purple, 1994; Tiny Music... Songs from the Vatican Gift Shop, 1996; No. 4, 1999; Shangri La Dee Da, 2001.

WELCH, Ed; b. 22 Oct. 1947, Oxford, England. Composer; Arranger; Musician (piano). m. Jane, April 13 1968, 2 s., 1 d. *Education:* Trinity College London; Music Scholar, Trinity College of Music, London, GTCL, LTCL, Mus Ed. *Career:* Staff arranger, plugger, orchestrator, United Artists Music, 1967–76; Freelance composer, 1977–; Guest conductor with all major British Orchestras; Musical Director for television series. *Compositions:* 250 recorded songs; 3 musicals; over 200 television themes, incidentals, including: Films: The Thirty Nine Steps, 1974; The Snow Goose, 1976; Television: Shillingbury Tales, 1980; Blockbusters, 1983; Catchphrase, 1985; TV AM News, 1986; Knightmare, 1986; $64,000?, 1989; One Foot In The Grave, all series, BBC,

1989–2000; Jim Henson's Animal Show (all music), 1994; The National Lottery, 1994; Wolves Witches Giants, 1995. *Membership:* BAC&S; PRS; Musicians' Union; BAFTA Jury. *Address:* c/o Welcome Music Ltd, Redhills, Stokenham, Nr Kingsbridge, Devon TQ7 2SS, England.

WELCH, Gillian Howard; b. 1968, California, USA. Vocalist; Musician (guitar, banjo); Songwriter. m. David Rawlings. *Education:* Berklee School of Music, Boston, Massachusetts. *Career:* Born into a musical family (parents scored the music for TV comedy The Carol Burnett Show); Listened to bluegrass and early country music as a child and, whilst studying at Berklee, began performing in this style along with her own material as part of a duo with fellow student David Rawlings; Heard by T-Bone Burnett whilst performing in Nashville; He produced the duo's Revival album, 1996; Featured solo on film soundtracks including: O Brother Where Art Thou?; Down From The Mountain; Songcatcher; The Horse Whisperer; Appeared on Dwight Yoakam and Gram Parsons tribute albums; Guested on albums by: Mark Knopfler; Ryan Adams; Nanci Griffith; Steve Earle; Songs recorded by artists including: Ryan Adams; Cindy Church; Christine Collister; Emmylou Harris; Alison Krauss; Union Station. *Recordings:* Albums: Revival, 1996; Hell Among The Yearlings, 1996; Time (The Revelator), 2001; features on: Gringo Honeymoon, Robert Earl Keen, 1994; Horse Whisperer OST, 1998; Other Voices Too, Nanci Griffith, 1998; Beneath My Wheels, Kevin Welch, 1999; Mountain, Steve Earle and Del McCoury, 1999; Swing Set, Ani DiFranco, 2000; O Brother Where Art Thou? OST, 2000; Heartbreaker, Ryan Adams, 2000; Sailing To Philadelphia, Mark Knopfler, 2000; Rich From The Journey, Kimmie Rhodes, 2000; Sebastapol, Jay Farrar, 2001; Down From The Mountain OST, 2001.

WELCH, Justin Stephen; b. 4 Dec. 1972, Nuneaton. Musician (drums). *Career:* Drummer With Psychedelic Rockers Spitfire; Joined Justine Frischmann, 1992; Formed Band, Elastica, 1992; Toured Extensively Worldwide; Television Performances Included Top of the Pops. *Recordings:* Album, Elastica (No. 1, UK), 1995; EP, Elastica, 1999; Album, The Menace, 2000; The BBC Sessions, 2001; Singles: Stutter, 1993; Line Up, 1994; Connection, 1994; Waking Up, 1995; Mad Dog, 2000. *Honours:* NME Readers Award for Best New Band, 1994. *Current Management:* Chris Morrison, CMO Management International Ltd, Unit 32 Ransomes Dock, 35–37 Parkgate Rd, London SW11 4NP, England.

WELCH, Sean; b. 12 April 1965, Enfield, England. Musician (Bass). *Career:* Member, The Beautiful South. *Recordings:* Singles: Song For Whoever, 1989; You Keep It All In, 1989; A Little Time (No. 1, UK), 1990; My Book EP, 1990; Let Love Speak Up Itself, 1991; Old Red Eyes Is Back, 1992; We Are Each Other, 1992; Bell Bottomed Tear, 1992; Good As Gold, 1994; One Last Love Song, 1994; Prettiest Eyes, 1994; Everybody's Talkin', 1994; Rotterdam (Or Anywhere), 1996; Don't Marry Her, 1996; Liar's Bar, 1997; Perfect 10, 1998; Dumb, 1999; How Long's A Tear Take To Dry?, 1999; Closer Than Most, 2000; The River, 2001; Albums: Welcome To The Beautiful South, 1989; Choke, 1990; 0898, 1992; Miaow, 1994; Carry On Up the Charts: The Best of The Beautiful South (No. 1, UK), 1994; Blue Is The Colour, 1996; Quench, 1998; Painting It Red, 2000; Solid Bronze: Great Hits, 2001. *Address:* The Beautiful South, PO Box 87, Hull, East Yorkshire HU5 2NR, England. *Website:* www.beautifulsouth.co.uk.

WELDEN, Judy Ann; b. 1 April 1938, Buffalo Valley, Pennsylvania, USA. Vocalist; Songwriter; Promoter; Musician (piano). m. William Blecha, 28 Dec. 1983, 1 s., 2 d. *Education:* Voice and piano lessons. *Career:* Singer, songwriter and entertainer; Member of numerous bands; Owner, 2 record labels; Performed at festivals in many countries. *Compositions:* Too Old Blues; Woman of the 90s; Hurry Up Sunrise; I'm Hittin' The Road; Love Conquers All; Shelter in the Rain. *Recordings include:* Come on Home; Fishin' For A New Love; You Are There For Me; Daddy's Army Whistle; Every Day's A Holiday; Confusion, What's The Solution; Grandma's Quilts; Grace; Chasing A Dream; Forever Grateful, 2000. *Publications:* 68 Unforgettable Days in Europe, 1998. *Honours:* First Place Vocal Award, 1990; Hollywood Song Jubilee, 1992; Woman of the Year in Arts, 1998; Most Promising Female Vocalist, New Gospel Division, 1999; Modern Country Album of the Year, Judy Welden Country Hits, 1999; Female International Recording Artist of the Year, 1999; American Horizon Award, 1999; Horizon Co-Writer Award (Best of Texas), Grandma's Quilts and Confusion (What's The Solution), with Terrance Alan and Mia Heylen, 1999; ICMAG, Promoter of the Year, Artist of the 20th Century, Hall of Fame, 2000. *Membership:* CGMA; DCDJA; ECMA; ICMAG; LSSCMA. *Current Management:* Well Done Promotions. *Address:* 692 SE Port St Lucie Blvd, Port St Lucie, FL 34984, USA.

WELDING, Paul Daniel; b. 14 May 1971, St Helens, England. Record Prod; Remixer. *Career:* Dance music record producer; Various radio appearances on local stations; 2 appearances on television; Remixes for major record companies and also DJ at The Opera House, Toronto, Canada. *Recordings:* 3 record releases: Void 1 and 2; Rebound; As Foundation: Prisoner Of Love; Various remixes including: Sounds of Blackness; Crystal Waters; Lisa M. *Membership:* Musicians' Union. *Current Management:* John Slater, Ken Grogan, Deep Management. *Address:* 85 Central Dr., Haydock, St Helens W11 0JE, England.

WELDON, Joel; b. 1958. Vocalist; Songwriter. m. 1986–95, 1 s., 1 d. *Career:* Major touring artist in contemporary Christian music. *Recordings:* Mistaken Identity, 1985; Terror and Love, 1987; Pure Adventure, 1988; Wisdom Street, 1989; Cross The World, 1990; Catch Fire America, 1991; Rock It, 1993; Rise Up America, 1994. *Current Management:* Brian A Mayes, BMP Artist Management.

WELLER, Martin William Charles; b. 28 Oct. 1961, Bristol, England. Vocalist; Songwriter; Musician (guitar); Arranger. 1 d. *Education:* City and Guilds, Industrial Heating and Welding; Guitar and singing lessons. *Career:* Support to: Benny Gallagher; Isaac Guillory; Clive Gregson; Counterfeit Stones; Tours include: UK; France; Germany; Cyprus; Television appearances include: Cable TV; London Weekend Television; Local radio includes: Eclipse; Mercury; London News Radio. *Compositions:* Many unpublished. *Recordings:* Singles: The Good Die Young, 1984; Maggie, 1990; With Clive Frampton: Frampton Weller, 1997. *Honours:* Finalist, Hammersmith Rock Festival, 1985; Selected to play German Festival, 1995. *Membership:* Musicians' Union.

WELLER, Paul; b. 25 May 1958, Woking, Surrey, England. Vocalist; Songwriter; Musician (guitar, piano). m. Dee C Lee, Dec. 1986. *Career:* Founder, singer, guitarist, The Jam, 1976–82; Concerts include: Reading Festival, 1978; Great British Music Festival, 1978; Pink Pop Festival, 1980; Loch Lomond Festival, 1980; Founder, The Style Council, 1983–89; Appearances include: Miners benefit concert, Royal Albert Hall, London, 1984; Live Aid, Wembley Arena, 1985; Film: JerUSAlem, 1987; Founder, The Paul Weller Movement, 1990; Solo artiste, 1990–; UK and international tours; Phoenix Festival, 1995; T In The Park Festival, Glasgow, 1995; Own record label, Freedom High. *Compositions include:* My Ever Changing Moods; Shout To The Top; The Walls Come Tumbling Down; Have You Ever Had It Blue, for film Absolute Beginners; It Didn't Matter; Wanted; Sunflower; Wild Wood; The Weaver. *Recordings:* Albums: with The Jam: In The City, 1977; This Is The Modern World, 1977; All Mod Cons, 1978; Setting Sons, 1979; Sound Affects, 1980; The Gift, 1982; Dig The New Breed, 1982; Snap!, 1983; Greatest Hits, 1991; Extras, 1992; Live Jam, 1993; The Singles: Box Set, 2001; Illumination, 2002; The Sound Of The Jam, 2002; The Jam At The BBC, 2002; with Style Council: Introducing The Style Council, 1983; Café Bleu, 1984; Our Favourite Shop, 1985; Home and Abroad, 1986; The Cost of Loving, 1987; Confessions of a Pop Group, 1988; The Singular Adventures of The Style Council, 1989; Here's Some That Got Away, 1993; Solo albums: Paul Weller, 1992; Wild Wood, 1993; Live Wood, 1994; Stanley Road, 1995; Heavy Soul, 1997; Modern Classics, 1998; Helioscentric, 2000; Days Of Speed, 2001; EPs and Singles: with The Jam: In The City, 1977; This Is The Modern World, 1977; David Watts/A Bomb In Wardour Street, 1978; Down In The Tube Station At Midnight, 1978; Strange Town, 1979; Eton Rifles, 1979; Going Underground/Dreams of Children (No. 1, UK), 1980; Start! (No. 1, UK), 1980; That's Entertainment, 1981; Funeral Pyre, 1981; Absolute Beginners, 1981; Town Called Malice/Precious (No.1, UK), 1982; Just Who Is The 5 O'Clock Hero, 1982; The Bitterest Pill, 1982; Beat Surrender (No. 1, UK), 1982; with The Style Council: Speak Like A Child, 1983; Money Go Round, 1983; Long Hot Summer, 1983; A Solid Bond In Your Heart, 1983; My Ever Changing Moods, 1984; You're The Best Thing, 1984; Shout To The Top, 1984; Walls Come Tumbling Down, 1985; The Lodgers, 1986; Have You Ever Had It Blue, 1986; It Didn't Matter, 1987; Wanted, 1987; Promised Land, 1989; Solo singles: Into Tomorrow, 1991; Uh Huh Oh Yeh, 1992; Sunflower, 1993; Wild Wood, 1993; The Weaver, 1993; Hung Up, 1994; Out Of The Sinking, 1994; The ChangingMan, 1995; You Do Something To Me, 1995; Broken Stones, 1995; Peacock Suit, 1996; Brushed, 1997; Friday Street, 1997; Mermaids, 1997; Brand New Start, 1998; Wild Wood (remixes), 1999; Hung Up, 1999; Sweet Pea, My Sweet Pea, 2000. *Honours:* Ivor Novello Award; BRIT Awards: Best Male Artist, 1995, 1996. *Current Management:* Solid Bond Management, 45–53 Sinclair Rd, London W14 0NS, England. *Address:* c/o Independiente Ltd, The Drill Hall, 3 Heathfield Terrace, London W4 4JE, England. *Website:* www.paulweller.com.

WELLER, Timothy James; b. 30 Dec. 1969, Tunbridge Wells, Kent, England. Musician (drums, percussion). m. Aliza Colman, 28 Nov. 1992. *Education:* University of London, Kings College; Drummers Collective (New York); Bob Armstrong (London). *Career:* Tours with: McKoy; Federation; Eddie Floyd; Ashley Flowers; Colin John; Performed with: Izit; Zeke Manyika; Jerry Dammers; Roger Beaujolais; Maxi Jazz; Daniel Walker; Giles Martin. *Recordings:* Original soundtracks for: The Confessional (David Puttnam), 1995; Johnny and The Dead (LWT), 1995; Albums, singles with: Teenie Hodges; Zeke Manyika and Jalal; McKoy; Paul Reid; tracks with: Black Box Recorder; Raissa; Barry Adamson. *Honours:* Drummer of the Year, Joe Hubbards School, Pearl Drums, 1993. *Current Management:* Sound Advice Management. *Address:* C104, Faircharm Trading Estate, 10 Creekside, London SE8 3DX, England.

WELLINGS, Clive; b. 20 Sept. 1953, Burton Upon Trent, England. Musician (drums); Massage Therapist. *Education:* BA Hons. *Career:* Drummer for: Nasty Sandwich; Midnight Sun, Bracknell Jazz Festival, 1978; Hydra; The Fabulous Falling Angels; The Royal Monkeys; Lacewing Bomber, support to Great White, 1987; The Young Outlawz; Wild Angel; Lipstick Daggers; Twisted; Secret Society; Also various session recordings. *Recordings:* with Lacewing Bomber: Feelin' Electric; with The Fabulous Falling Angels: Unsung Heroes. *Membership:* Musicians' Union. *Current Management:* 1A Musical Promotions. *Address:* 76 Hamilton Rd, Reading, Berkshire RG1 5RD, England.

WELLINGS, George; b. 13 Jan. 1941, Wolverhampton, Staffordshire, England. Musician (saxophones, clarinets, flutes). m. Maureen Glenn, 23 Dec. 1967, 1 d. *Career:* In backing orchestras for many American and British stars including: Johnny Mathis; Jack Jones; Four Tops; O'Jays; Englebert Humperdinck; Gene Pitney; Shirley Bassey; Matt Monro; Pat Boone; Variety artistes include: Morecambe and Wise; Bruce Forsyth; Des O'Connor. *Membership:* Musicians' Union.

WELLMAN, Samuel Edison; b. 15 May 1951, Anderson, Indiana, USA. Prof; Composer; Musician (Piano). m. Deborah Eileen Moyer, 12 June 1971, 4 s., 2 deceased, 3 d. *Education:* BA, Music Education, Lenoir Rhyne College; MM, Music Theory, DM, Composition, Florida State University. *Career:* College Professor, Warner Southern College, Lake Wales, Florida, 1974–92, Liberty University, Lynchburg, Virginia, 1992–; Concert Pianist and Accompanist; Church Pianist and Organist, 1962–. *Compositions:* Over 860 works. *Publications:* Four American Pieces, 1991; Anna Magdalena Revisited, 1993; Hometown, USA, 1997; Hymn Favourites, 1997; Beyond Boundaries, 2002. *Honours:* Commissioned Composer, Florida State Music Teachers' Asscn, 1989. *Membership:* American Composers Alliance; Music Teachers' National Asscn; American Music Center. *Address:* 125 Temple Circle, Lynchburg, VA 24502, USA.

WELLS, Kitty, (Muriel Ellen Deason); b. 30 Aug. 1919, Nashville, Tennessee, USA. Vocalist. m. Johnnie Wright, 30 Oct. 1937, 1 s., 2 d. *Career:* Founder member, the Deason Sisters, 1935–37; Regular radio programme, Nashville; Later billed as Johnnie Wright and The Harmony Girls, then the Tennessee Mountain Boys; Took name Kitty Wells, 1943; Solo recording artist, 1949–; Became member of Grand Ole Opry, 1951; Extensive world-wide tours, 1950s–70s; Toured as The Kitty Wells and Johnny Wright Family Show, 1963–; Hosted own television show, 1969–; First UK appearance, Wembley Festival, 1974. *Recordings:* Over 80 country hits; US Country No. 1 singles include: It Wasn't God Who Made Honky Tonk Angels, 1952; One By One (with Red Foley), 1954; Heartbreak USA, 1961; Albums include: Solo: Country Hit Parade, 1956; After Dark, 1959; Queen of Country Music, 1962; Kitty Wells, 1966; Country Heart, 1969; Your Love Is The Way, 1970; Pledging My Love, 1971; I've Got Yesterday, 1972; Sincerely, 1972; Yours Truly, 1973; Forever Young, 1974; with Red Foley: Golden Favourites, 1961; Together Again, 1967; with Johnnie Wright: We'll Stick Together, 1969; Heartwarming Gospel Songs, 1972; Christmas with Kitty Wells, 1996; Country Spotlight, 1996, Queen of Country, 1996; God's Honky Tonk Angel, 2000; with Roy Drusky: Kitty Wells and Roy Drusky, 1987; Various compilations. *Honours:* Female Country Artiste, Billboard, 1953–65; Inducted into Country Music Hall of Fame, 1976; Named Queen of Country Music, 1952; First female country singer to have No. 1 record, 1952. *Current Management:* Wright's Enterprises, 240 Old Hickory Blvd, Madison, TN 37115, USA.

WELLS, Robert Henry Arthur; b. 7 April 1962, Stockholm, Sweden. Composer; Musician (Piano and Vocal). Engaged to Maria Sköld. *Education:* Adolf Fredriks Music School, 1969–78; Academy of Music, 1978–82; Private piano lessons, 1969–78. *Career:* Professionally working in Scandinavia and Russia, 1987–; Toured with different bands and singers, 1977–87; Featuring in major TV-shows; Played for Swedish Royalties several times; Concerts and TV performances in USA and Canada, 1998–99. *Recordings:* Upp Pa Berget, 1987; The Way I Feel, 1988; Rhapsody in Rock I, 1989; Rhapsody in Rock II, 1990; Norman Vs Wells, 1991; Rhapsody in Rock III, 1993; Nordic Rhapsody, 1996; Boogie Woogie Norman and Wells, 1996; Rhapsody In Rock Complete, 1998. *Honours:* Gold Record, 1998. *Address:* Gurtman and Murtha, 450 Seventh Ave, New York, NY 10123, USA.

WELSFORD, Andy Wells; b. 14 March 1959, Bristol, England. Musician (drums). 1 d. *Education:* Technical college. *Career:* Drummer with Meat Loaf, 1985–86; March Violets, 1987; Romeo's Daughter, 1989; Then Jerico, 1994; World tours, television and radio appearances, videos; Sessions for Roxette; Whitney Houston; John Parr; Dee Lewis; Daniel Weaver; Andy Leek. *Recordings:* 2 albums, Romeo's Daughter; 1 track, album, Meat Loaf; 1 album, Then Jerico. *Current Management:* Grahame Perkins, Session Connection, B & H Musicians. *Address:* 20 Clementina Rd, London E10 7LS, England.

WELTY, Ron; b. 1 Feb. 1971, Long Beach, California, USA. Musician (drums). m. Erica, 1 s. *Education:* California trade school, Electronics graduate. *Career:* Played alto saxophone and drums in high school bands; Previously FQX band member; Joined The Offspring, 1987; Privately pressed single took over 2 years to sell 1,000 copies, 1987; Signed to independent labels, Nemesis and Epitaph, for 1988–95 releases; Major US breakthrough following heavy MTV/radio play rotation, 1994; Accused of betraying punk roots when signing to Columbia after dispute with former label, 1996; Consolidated world-wide success by scoring UK No. 1 hit single, 1999; Live shows include: Woodstock festival, 1999; KROQ Weenie Roast, 2000;

European tour, 2001; Band gave lucky fan $1m. in Offspring prize draw, 2000; Drummer with side-project group Spinning Fish, 1990–. *Recordings:* Albums: The Offspring, 1989; Ignition, 1992; Smash!, 1994; Ixnay On The Hombre, 1997; Americana, 1998; Conspiracy of One, 2000; Singles: I'll Be Waiting, 1987; Baghdad EP, 1988; Come Out and Play (Keep 'Em Separated), Self-Esteem, 1994; Gotta Get Away, 1995; All I Want, Gone Away, 1997; Pretty Fly (For A White Guy), 1998; Why Don't You Get A Job?, The Kids Aren't Alright, She's Got Issues, 1999; Original Prankster, 2000; Want You Bad, Million Miles Away, 2001. *Honours:* Over 9m. copies of Smash album sold world-wide, best selling independent record of all time. *Current Management:* Jim Guerinot, Rebel Waltz Management, 31652 Second Ave, Laguna Beach, CA 92651, USA. *Website:* www.offspring.com.

WELZ, Joey, (Joseph Welzant); b. 17 March 1940, Baltimore, Maryland, USA. Vocalist; Musician (piano); Record Prod; Record Co Exec. 1 s, 1 d. *Education:* Degree in Broadcasting, Harford College, 1978. *Career:* Pianist, Bill Haley and the Comets, 1960s–80s; Played with Beatles; Link Wray; Roy Buchanan; Re-formed Original Comets, 1981; Numerous world-wide tours and television appearances; A & R executive, Canadian American Records, 1966–70; Palmer Records, Detroit, 1971–73; Music City Records, Nashville, 1974–81; Caprice Records, Pennsylvania, 1982–4; President, Caprice International Records, 1984–; Canadian American Records, 1989–; President/owner, Rock Mill Studios, Pennsylvania, 1990–. *Compositions include:* Hey Little Moonbeam; Baby Let Your Head Hang Down; Candle In The Wind; Forever; Everyday For The Rest of My Life; Universal Love; One Stormy Love; In The Middle Of The Night Time; Hey Baby; Life on Mars, 1997; Your Love Means Everything, with Amy Beth; A Ring Between Us, with Amy Beth; Rang-a-Tang Boogie. *Recordings:* Over 100 singles and 75 albums; Hits include: One Way Ticket; 16 Ways; Where Would I Be; Rock-A-Billy; Shake Rattle and Roll; Summertime Blues; Blue Collar Love; Last Kiss; Lonesome Traveller; Forever and A Day; Spanish Rose From Mexico; Summer Place, 1996; You Don't Own Me, 1997; Recent album releases include: The Turn Of The Century, 2000; Radio Rock, 2000; Song And Dance Man, 2001; Rock And Roll Remembers, 2001. *Honours:* Top 25 Rock Pianist, Keyboard Magazine, 3 times; One of Top Rock Pianists, DIB, London, 1971; Country Rock Pioneer Award; EIA Award, Most Promising Country Male Vocalist; CMA Award, Video of Year, 1993; Independent Country Male Vocalist of Year; Legendary Performer of Year; Songwriter of Year; Inductee and Gold Charter Mem., Rock and Roll Hall of Fame. *Membership:* ASCAP. *Current Management:* Caprice International Records. *Address:* PO Box 808, Lititz, PA 17543, USA.

WENER, Louise; b. 1966, Ilford, Essex, England. Vocalist; Songwriter. *Education:* Politics and English degree, Manchester University. *Career:* Lead singer, Sleeper, 1993–98; Support tours with: Blur; Manic Street Preachers; Major concerts include: Heineken Festival, Leeds, 1995; T In The Park, Glasgow, 1995; Glastonbury Festival, 1995; Feile Festival, Ireland, 1995; Milton Keynes Bowl (with REM, The Cranberries, Radiohead), 1995; Also toured in Japan; Television includes: Later With... Britpop Now, BBC2, 1995; Tours with: Elvis Costello, 1996; Brixton Academy, 1996–97; Milton Keynes Bowl, 1996. *Compositions:* What Do I Do Now?, 1995; Sale of The Century, 1996; Nice Guy Eddie, 1996; She's A Good Girl, 1997. *Recordings:* Albums: Smart, 1995; It Girl, 1996; Pleased To Meet You, 1997. Singles: Delicious, 1994; Inbetweener, 1995; Vegas, 1995; What Do I Do Now?, 1995; Sale Of The Century, 1996; Nice Guy Eddie, 1996; Statuesque, 1996; She's A Good Girl, 1997; Romeo, 1997. *Publications:* Goodnight Steve McQueen (novel), 2002. *Honours:* Gold Disc, 1996; Platinum Disc, 1996. *Membership:* PRS; MU; PAMRA. *Current Management:* Geoff Wener, Big Brother Management, 15 Pratt Mews, London NW1 0AD, England.

WENNIKE, Ole B; b. 15 May 1958, Copenhagen, Denmark. Musician; Composer. 1 s. *Career:* Founder, Copenhagen Based The Sandmen, 1985–92, support gigs in Copenhagen for Nico, Jeffrey Lee Pierce, Long Ryders, 1985–86; USA Tour, 1989, London's Borderline, 1989; Founder, Copenhagen Based Nerve, 1995, support gigs in Copenhagen for David Bowie. *Compositions:* Western Blood, House in the Country, Heart of Steel, 1989; 5 mins Past Loneliness, Can't Cry No More, 1993; Slave Song, 1994. *Recordings:* The Sandmen Albums: Western Blood, 1988; Sleepy Head, 1993; In the House of Secrets, 1994; Nerve Album: Speedfreak Jive, 1996. *Honours:* Danish Grammy, 1993; Gold Record, Denmark. *Current Management:* Rock-On APS. *Address:* Rosenörns Alle 6, 4Tv, 1634 Copenhagen V, Denmark.

WENTZEL, Magni; b. 28 June 1945, Oslo, Norway. Musician (classical guitar); Jazz Vocalist. m. 28 April 1976, divorced 1986, 1 s. *Career:* Numerous national and international performances; Regular appearances on Norwegian television and radio. *Education:* Private teachers, Norway and abroad. *Recordings:* As guitarist: with Radio Symphony Orchestra; with Einar Iversen's Trio: That Old Feeling/My One and Only Love, 1959; Magni Wentzel Plays, 1969; Guitar and Flute, with Torkil Bye, 1975; Sofies Plass, 1983; All Or Nothing At All, 1986; with Art Farmer: My Wonderful One, 1988; with Roger Kelleway and Red Mitchell: New York Nights, 1991; with Roger Kelleway and Niels H. O. Pedersen: Come Away With Me, 1993; with Roger Kelleway and Mads Vinding: Turn Out the Stars, 1996; Gershwin: Porgy & Bess, 2000; Divergence, 2002. *Honours:* Gamleng Prize; Buddy Award, Norwegian Jazz Federation. *Membership:* Norsk Musikerferbund (Norwegian

Musicians' Union). *Current Management:* The Norwegian Jazzscene. *Address:* Neuberggt 6 A, 0367 Oslo, Norway. *E-mail:* magniwentzel@hotmail.com.

WÉRGLER, Arne Niels; b. 30 Oct. 1943, Copenhagen, Denmark. Vocalist; Songwriter. m. Asa Didriksen, 27 May 1989, 2 d. *Career:* Singer and songwriter; President, The Danish Society for Jazz, Rock and Folk Composers. *Address:* Danish Society for Jazz, Rock and Folk Composers, Gråbrodretorv 16, 1154 Copenhagen K, Denmark.

WERMAN, Thomas Ehrlich; b. 2 March 1945, Newton, Massachusetts, USA. Record Prod; Musician (guitar, percussion). m. 25 Aug. 1968, 1 s., 2 d. *Education:* BA, Columbia College; MBA Columbia Business School. *Career:* A & R Epic Records, 1970–82; Senior Vice-President, A & R Elektra Records, 1982; Independent producer, 1983–; Signed: REO Speedwagon; Ted Nugent; Cheap Trick; Molly Hatchet; Boston; The Producers; Mother's Finest. *Recordings:* Produced: Ted Nugent; Cheap Trick; Molly Hatchet; Twisted Sister; Jeff Beck; Poison; Mötley Crüe; Kix; LA Guns; Jason and the Scorchers; Lita Ford; Gary Myrick; The Supersuckers; Blue Oyster Cult; The Cult; Dokken; Krokus. *Honours:* 13 RIAA Platinum records, 9 Gold records. *Membership:* NARAS. *Address:* 11818 Laurel Hills Rd, Studio City, CA 91604, USA.

WERNICK, Peter, (Dr Banjo); b. 25 Feb. 1946, New York, USA. Musician (banjo); Author; Teacher; Music Asscn Exec. m. Joan (Nondi) Leonard, 29 June 1974, 1 s. *Education:* BA, Columbia College, 1966; PhD Sociology, Columbia University, 1973. *Career:* Country Cooking, Ithaca, New York, 1970–76; Rambling Drifters, Denver, Colorado, 1976–78; Hot Rize, Boulder, Colorado, 1978–90; Pete Wernick's Live Five, 1992–; US and international tours with Hot Rize; Appeared on Austin City Limits; Grand Ole Opry; Nashville Now; Prairie Home Companion; President, IBMA (International Bluegrass Association). *Recordings:* Writer, performer, No. 1 hit songs: Ruthie; Just Like You; Albums: Solo albums: On A Roll; Dr Banjo Steps Out; with Hot Rize: Untold Stories; Take It Home; Traditional Ties; In Concert; with Five Live: I Tell You What!. *Publications:* Bluegrass Banjo, 1974; Bluegrass Song Book, 1976; How to Make a Band Work, 1991; Acutab Transcriptions, Vol. I, 1996; I Tell You What, 1996; with Tony Trischka: Early Years, 1998; with Marshall Wilborn: Brass and Piano, 1999; Choice Picks, 2000; Also appears on: Been A Long Time, Si Kahn, 2000; Music From Rancho De Ville, Charles Sawtelle, 2001. *Honours:* IBMA Entertainer of the Year with Hot Rize, 1989. *Membership:* President IBMA; ASCAP; NARAS. *Current Management:* Keith Case Associates, Nashville, Tennessee. *Address:* 59 Music Sq. W, Nashville, TN 37203, USA.

WERTICO, Paul David; b. 5 Jan. 1953, Chicago, Illinois, USA. Musician (drums, percussion); Instructor and Clinician. m. Barbara Ungerleider, 22 Aug. 1986, 1 d. *Education:* 2 years at College; Scholarship, Western Illinois University. *Career:* Member, Pat Metheny Group, 1983–; Tours include: US and world-wide tours as clinician, 1986–; North American tours with the Simon and Bard Group, 1980–82; world-wide tours with the Pat Metheny Group, 1983–; Tour of Argentina, with Pat Metheny, Ernie Watts and Charlie Haden, 1986; Also California, Japan and Hong Kong apperances, 1988; Tour of Japan with Special EFX, 1991; Tour of Germany and Poland with the Paul Wertico Trio, 1994; Member, Pat's Secret Story Band, performing in 18 countries world-wide; Tour of Denmark with the Niels Lan Doky Band, 1999; Performed with numerous jazz artists including: Larry Coryell; Lee Konitz; Herbie Mann; Terry Gibbs; Buddy DeFranco; Lew Tabakin; Art Porter; Jaco Pastorius; Chico Freeman; Ron Carter; Alan Pasqua; Ramsey Lewis; Dave Liebman; Eddie Harris; Sam Rivers; Bob Mintzer; Jay McShann. *Recordings include:* Albums: Solo/bandleader: The Yin and The Yout; Live in Warsaw!; Don't Be Scared Anymore, 2000; as co-leader: Earwax Control; Spontaneous Composition; 2 LIVE; BANG!; The Sign of Four; Union; State of the Union; with Pat Metheny/Pat Metheny Group: First Circle, 1984; Still Life (Talking), 1987; Letter From Home, 1989; Secret Story, 1992; The Road To You, 1993; We Live Here, 1995; Quartet, 1996; Imaginary Day, 1997; Appeared on three Pat Metheny videos; Film soundtrack The Falcon and the Snowman, with Pat Metheny; Albums with artists including: Paul Winter; Kurt Elling; John Moulder; Bobby Lewis; Ken Nordine; Ellen McIlwaine; Jerry Goodman; Terry Callier; Niels Lan Doky. *Publications:* Columnist, Drums and Drumming magazine; DRUM! magazine; Drum Tracks magazine; Modern Drummer magazine; Contributor, Thinking In Jazz; Instructional videos on drumming and percussion: Fine Tuning Your Performance; Sound Work of Drumming. *Honours:* Eight Grammy Awards with Pat Metheny/Pat Metheny Group, (three for Best Jazz Fusion Performance, four for Best Contemporary Jazz Performance), one Grammy Award, Best Rock Instrumental; NARAS Outrageous Recording Award, 1990; NAIRD Best Rock Record Award, with Ellen McIlwaine, 1981; Fourth in Electric Jazz Drummer Reader's Poll, Modern Drummer Magazine, 1997; Fusion Drummer of the Year, DRUM! Magazine Reader's Poll, 1997; Second in Electric Jazz Drummer, Reader's Poll, Modern Drummer Magazine, 1998; Best Electric Group (Pat Metheny Group), Reader's Poll, Downbeat Magazine, 1997–99. *Membership:* Chicago Federation of Musicians; National Academy of Recording Arts and Sciences, Broadcast Music Inc (BMI), Harry Fox Agency Inc. *Current Management:* Ungerleider Artist Management. *Address:* 8728 N Drake, Skokie, IL 60076, USA.

WEST, Leslie, (Leslie Weinstein); b. 22 Oct. 1945, Queens, NY, USA. Musician (guitar). *Career:* Guitarist, Vagrants; Founder mem., US rock group, Mountain, 1968–85; Concerts include: Woodstock Festival, 1970; European tour, support to Deep Purple, 1985; Also recorded as West, Bruce, Laing (with Jack Bruce, Corky Laing), 1974; Song Nantucket Sleighride used as theme for TV series, World In Action, Weekend World, (LWT), 1970s–80s. *Recordings:* Albums: Mountain Climbing, 1979; Nantucket Sleighride, 1971; Flowers of Evil, 1971; The Road Goes On Forever – Mountain Live, 1972; Best Of…, 1973; Twin Peaks, 1974; Avalanche, 1974; Go For Your Life, 1975; Dodgin' the Dirt, 1994; Over The Top, 1995; As Phat as It Gets, 1999, Sessions, 1999; Guitar on: New Day Yesterday, Joe Bonamassa, 2000. *Address:* c/o Skyline Music, PO Box 31, Lancaster, NH 03584, USA.

WEST, Steve; b. 1967, Richmond, Virginia, USA. Musician (Drums). *Career:* Joined Pavement, 1992; Numerous headlining tours; Appeared in cartoon Space Ghost Coast to Coast, 1997. *Recordings:* Singles: Trigger Cut, 1992; Cut Your Hair, 1994; Gold Soundz, 1994; Range Life, 1995; Rattled by La Rush, 1995; Father to a Sister of Thought, 1995; Pacific Trim EP, 1996; Stereo, 1997; Shady Lane EP, 1997; Spit on a Stranger, 1999; Carrot Rope, 1999; Albums: Slanted and Enchanted, 1992; Crooked Rain, Crooked Rain, 1994; Wowee Zowee, 1995; Brighten the Corners, 1997; Terror Twilight, 1999.

WESTBROOK, Kate (Katherine Jane); b. Guildford, Surrey, England. Vocalist; Songwriter; Librettist; Painter. m. (1) 1 s., 2 d., (2) Mike Westbrook, 23 Sept. 1976. *Education:* Bath Academy of Art; Reading University; London University, Institute of Education. *Career:* Joined Mike Westbrook Brass Band, 1974; Mike Westbrook Orchestra, 1979; formed Westbrook and Company, 1998; Tours: Europe; Far East; Australia; Canada; Co-author with Mike Westbrook of theatre, dance pieces including: The Ass, 1985; Pier Rides, 1986; London Bridge Is Broken Down, 1987; Platterback, 1998; Jago (opera), 2000; Played role of Anna in Seven Deadly Sins, by Brecht/Weill, with LSO, Barbican, London, 1989–90; Sang Big Band Rossini, Royal Albert Hall, Proms, 1992; Good Friday 1663, television opera, libretto by Helen Simpson (Channel 4), 1995; Soloist, KlangWettReligion with Heribert Leuchter's Lux Orchestra, Germany, 2001; Exhibitions of paintings in UK and USA, Europe and Australia, 1963–. *Compositions:* with Kate Westbrook Ensemble: Revenge Suite, Bloomsbury Festival, 1985; with Kate Westbrook and the Skirmishers; Even/Uneven, 1994; Nijinska (music by Errolyn Wallen), 1998. *Recordings include:* Solo album: Goodbye Peter Lorre, 1992; Duo with Mike Westbrook, Stage Set, 1996; Love Or Infatuation, 1997; Bar Utopia, with Mike Westbrook Orchestra, 1997; The Orchestra of Smith's Academy, 1998; Glad Day, 1999; Platterback, 1999; The Dance Band, 2001. *Honours:* Diaspason d'Or, Goodbye Peter Lorre; Also for Love For Sale with The Westbrook Trio, 1992. *Membership:* Musicians' Union; PRS; SACEM. *Current Management:* MYOM. *E-mail:* janinka@myom.fsnet.co.uk.

WESTBROOK, Mike (Michael John David); b. 21 March 1936, High Wycombe, Buckinghamshire, England. Composer; Musician (piano); Bandleader. m. Katherine Jane (Kate), 23 Sept. 1976, 1 s., 1 d. (by previous marriage). *Education:* NDD, Plymouth College of Art; ATD, Hornsey College of Art. *Career:* Formed first band, Plymouth Art School, 1958; Led groups including: Mike Westbrook Brass Band, 1973–; Mike Westbrook Orchestra, 1974–; The Westbrook Trio, 1982–; Kate Westbrook/Mike Westbrook Duo, 1995–; Westbrook & Company, 1998–; New Westbrook Orchestra, 2001–; Tours: Britain; Europe; Australia; Singapore; Hong Kong; Canada; New York. *Compositions:* Music for theatre, opera, dance, radio, television, films. *Recordings include:* Marching Song, 1967; Metropolis, 1969; Tyger (A celebration of William Blake), 1971; Citadel/Room 315, 1974; The Westbrook Blake, 1980; On Duke's Birthday, 1984; Love For Sale, 1986; Big Band Rossini, 1987; Off Abbey Road, 1988; Bean Rows and Blues Shots, 1991; Coming Through Slaughter (opera), 1994; Bar Utopia, 1995; Blues For Terenzi, 1995; Cable Street Blues, 1997; The Orchestra of Smith's Academy, 1998; Platterback, 1999; Classical Blues, 2001; Television score: Caught On A Train, 1980; Cinema: Moulin Rouge, 1990; with Kate Westbrook: The Cortege, 1979; London Bridge Is Broken Down, 1987; Measure For Measure, 1992; Chanson Irresponsible, 2001; Music theatre with Kate Westbrook includes: Mama Chicago, 1978; Westbrook Rossini, 1984; The Ass, 1985; Pier Rides, 1987; Quichotte, 1989; Good Friday 1663, (TV opera), 1995; Stage Set, 1996; Love or Infatuation, 1997; Platterback, 1998, Jago (opera), 2000; L'ascenseur/ he Lift, 2002. *Honours:* O.B.E., 1988. *Membership:* Musicians' Union; Duke Ellington Society. *Current Management:* John Clare Society. *Address:* Brent House, Holbeton, Nr Plymouth, Devon PL8 1LX, England. *E-mail:* admin@westbrookjazz.co.uk. *Website:* www.westbrookjazz.co.uk.

WESTERGAAD MADSEN, Dicte (Benedicte); b. 9 Sept. 1966, Denmark. Vocalist; Songwriter; Musician. *Career:* Formed band, Her Personal Pain, 1989; Numerous Danish club tours, including Roskilde Festival, 1991, 1994, 1997, 2000; Popkomm, Germany, 1997; Sopot Festival, Poland, 1997; Actress in film Smukke Dreng (Beautiful Boy), 1992; Lead Actress in play by Hotel Pro Forma, 1998; Wrote and performed music for play Searching Hamlet, 2002; Founder, record label, Velvet Recording, 2003. *Recordings:* Albums: with Her Personal Pain: Songs From Cinema Cafe, 1992; Solo: Between Any Four Walls, 1994; Voodoo Vibe, 1996; This Is Cool, 2000. Singles: with Her Personal Pain: contributions to Secrets II Live, 1990; Rock Love and

Understanding (Amnesty International), 1991; Solo: Make It Alright, 2003; contribution to: Gaa Ikke Over Sporet (Don't Pass the Trail, Danish National Railways), 1997. *Honours:* Grammy, Best New Name, 1992. *Current Management:* Århus Musikkontor. *Address:* Åarhus Musikkontor, Aps – Skole Bakken 7, 8000 Århus C, Denmark.

WESTERGAARD, Torben; b. 9 Oct. 1960, Århus, Denmark. Musician (bass guitar); Composer. *Education:* Musicians' Institute, Los Angeles; New School, New York. *Career:* Plays in own groups and freelance work in many music styles, Jazz, Brazilian, Pop, Funk, Latin; Studio Musician. *Recordings:* Own albums: What I Miss, 1990; Brazilian Heart, 1996; Featured on: Dig This Samba, Hendrik Meurkens & Manfredo Fest, 1998. *Honours:* Outstanding Bass Player of the Year, Musicians' Institute, 1985. *Membership:* DJBFA. *Current Management:* B M Productions. *Address:* Ragnhildsgade 74 2th, 2100 Copenhagen, Denmark.

WESTFALL-KING, Carmen Sigrid; b. 24 Aug. 1962, Burlington, Ontario, Canada. Vocalist; Songwriter; Musician (guitar). m. Kenny King, 27 May 1989, 1 d. *Education:* Recording Arts. *Career:* Television apperances include: Tommy Hunter Show, CBC Canada; Global TV Network; Opened concerts for Vince Gill; Waylon Jennings; Mary Chapin Carpenter; Michelle Wright; Dan Seals; Kitty Wells. *Recordings:* Your Old Girlfriend; You're An Angel; I Wanna Hear It From You; Talk Around Town (all Top 10, Canada). *Honours:* Country Awards, Outstanding New Artist, 1989. *Membership:* SOCAN; CCMA. *Current Management:* Jerry Knight. *Address:* 1050 Barnardo Ave, Peterborough, ON K9H 5X2, Canada.

WESTFIELD, Steve; b. 2 May 1965, Massachusetts, USA. Vocalist; Songwriter; Musician (guitar). *Education:* University of Massachusetts. *Career:* Singer, songwriter, guitarist, Pajama Slave Dancers, 1981–; Singer, songwriter, guitarist, Steve Westfield Slow Band, 1993–; Tour, Europe, Sebadoit, 1995–96. *Recordings:* with Pajama Slave Dancers: All You Can Eat, 1982; Problems of Sects, 1983; Blood, Sweat and Beers, 1984; Pajama Beach Party, 1984; Heavy Petting Zoo, 1985; Full Metal Underpants, 1989; It Came From The Barn, 1996; It's Heartbreak the Sells, 1999; with Steve Westfield Slow Band: Mangled, 1994; Reject Me… First, 1996; Underwhelmed, 1998. *Current Management:* c/o Andy Doherty, 63 Endicott St #9, Boston, MA 02113, USA.

WESTLAKE, David; b. 26 Dec. Musician (drums). *Career:* Mem., Sneaker Pimps, 1995–; Band founded Splinter Recordings, 1999. *Recordings:* Albums: Becoming X, 1996; Splinter, 1999; Bloodsport, 2002. Singles: 6 Underground (EP), 1996; Roll On, 1996; Tesko Suicide, 1996; Spin Spin Sugar, 1997; Post Modern Sleaze, 1997; 6 Underground, 1998; Low Five, 1999; Ten To Twenty, 1999; Sick, 2002. *Address:* c/o Tommy Boy Music, 902 Broadway, New York, NY 10010, USA. *E-mail:* parmesanchic@aol.com. *Website:* www.sneakerpimps.com.

WESTWOOD, Elizabeth Rose; b. 29 Nov. 1963, Washington DC, USA. Vocalist; Musician. *Education:* Art School, Washington DC. *Career:* Singer with Westworld; Radio and television appearances includes Top of the Pops; Tours; Singer in Moondogg. *Recordings:* Hit singles: Sonic Boom Boys, 1987; Ba-Na-Na-Bam-Boom, 1987; Where The Action Is, 1987; Albums: with Westworld: Where The Action Is; Beat Box Rock 'n' Roll; Movers and Shakers. *Membership:* PRS; Musicians' Union. *Current Management:* Proper Management. *Address:* 93 Rivington St, London EC1, England.

WESTWOOD, Tim; b. 3 Oct. 1967, London, England. DJ. *Career:* Rap DJ for radio and clubs including: Pirate radio, LWR and Kiss FM, 1984–87; Capital FM, 1987–94; Presenter and producer of the Radio 1 Rap Show and producer of the Radio 1 Reggae Dancehall Nite Show, BBC Radio 1, 1994–. *Recordings:* Compiler, Vol 1, 2001; Westwood 2, 2001; Owner, Justice Productions, independent TV and radio production company for Radio 1 Rap Show and Radio 1 Reggae Show; Producer, General Levi and London Posse. *Honours:* Sony Radio Award, Best Specialist Music Programme, 1990–91, 1996, 1999. *Membership:* Radio Academy. *Current Management:* Justice Production. *Address:* PO Box 689, London SW6 6HW, England.

WETTON, John; b. 12 June 1949, Derby, England. Vocalist; Songwriter; Musician (bass, keyboards). m. Jill Briggs, 10 July 1987. *Education:* Bournemouth College; Brother Robert, organist, choirmaster. *Career:* Member, Family, 1971–72; King Crimson, 1973–75; Roxy Music, 1975; Uriah Heep, 1976; UK, 1978–79; Solo artiste, 1980; Member, Asia, 1982–91; Solo artiste, 1991–. *Recordings:* with Family: Fearless, 1971; Bandstand, 1972; with King Crimson: Larks Tongues In Aspic, 1973; Starless and Bible Black, 1974; Red, 1974; USA, 1975; Night Watch, 1998; Collectors' King Crimson Vol. 1; with Roxy Music: Viva!, 1976; with UK: UK, 1978; Danger Money, 1979; Live Roxy Music Album, 1999; with Asia: Asia, 1982; Alpha, 1983; Astra, 1985; Then and Now, 1990; Solo album: Battle Lines, 1994; Chasing The Deer, 1998; Live in Tokyo, 1998; Monkey Business, 1999; Arkangel, 1997; Live At The Sun Plaza Tokyo, 2001. *Honours:* Three ASCAP Awards; 40 Gold and Platinum discs. *Membership:* PRS; National Academy of Songwriters; ASCAP. *Current Management:* Carr/Sharpe Entertainment. *Address:* 932 Wilshire Blvd, Suite 200, Beverly Hills, CA 90212, USA.

WETTRE, Petter; b. 11 Aug. 1967, Sandefjord, Norway. Musician (saxophone). 1 s. *Education:* Berklee College of Music, Boston, USA, 1989–92. *Career:* Several Norwegian tours with Nordic Jazz Quartet and Petter Wettre Quartet; Appeared at Konigsberg Jazz Festival with Petter Wettre Quartet, 1993; Oslo Jazz Festival, 1994; Recorded for Norwegian National Broadcasting 2 times; Appeared on several TV shows including: Amandas How; Tawde P; Melody Grand Prix; Freelance musician with artists including: Shirley Bassey; Magui Wenjzel; Lilh Babs; Jon Eberson; Jon Christensen; Several commercials for Norwegian radio and TV; Also runs various clinics and workshops; Currently member of: Petter Wettre Quartet, Horns For Hire, All Stars, and Oystein Sevags. *Recordings include:* Works with Jan Werner; Stephen Ackles; The Stavanger Gospel Choir; Solvi Hansen. *Honours:* Outstanding Achievement Award, Berklee College of Music. *Address:* Bergliotsveg 1B, 0575 Oslo, Norway.

WHARTON, Darren Dean; Musician (keyboards, guitar); Vocalist; Songwriter. *Career:* Keyboard player with Phil Lynott, 1980; Member, Thin Lizzy, 1981–83; Concerts include: Tours of UK; Scandinavia; Europe; Japan; Reading Rock Festival, 1983; Monsters of Rock Festival, Germany, 1983; Founder member, Dare, 1987–91. *Recordings:* Albums with Thin Lizzy: Chinatown, 1980; Adventures of Thin Lizzy, 1981; Renegade, 1981; Thunder and Lightning, 1983; The Boys Are Back In Town, 1983; Thin Lizzy Live, 1992; Wild One: The Very Best of Thin Lizzy, 1996; One Night Only, 2000; with Dare: Out of The Silence, 1988; Blood From Stone, 1991; with Phil Lynott: Solo In Soho, 1980.

WHEATLEY, Martin Russell; b. 29 Aug. 1958, London, England. Musician. m. Angela, 3 s. *Education:* BA, Colchester College; MA, University College, London. *Career:* Broadcasts on Radio and Television, BBC and Commercial; Concert Appearances at the Purcell Room and Queen Elizabeth Hall; Extensive Touring of Canada, USA, including Hawaii; Specialist in acoustic fretted instruments playing in authentic early styles, jazz, blues, ragtime, Hawaiian. *Recordings:* New Orleans Hop Scop Blues, with Bent Persson and Alain Marquet; Charleston Mad, with Neville Dickie; Syncopated Jamboree, I Like To Do Things For You, The Henderson Project, Harlem's Arabian Nights, all with Keith Nichols; with Roger Eno, Long Walk, 2000; with Hula Bluebirds: Stowaways In Paradise.

WHEELER, Tim(othy); b. 4 Jan. 1977, Downpatrick, Co Down, Northern Ireland. Musician (guitar); Vocalist. *Career:* Founding Mem., Ash; Early releases on indie label; Numerous headline tours, UK festivals and television appearances; Record deal and tour of USA; Contributed track to film, A Life Less Ordinary, 1997. *Recordings:* Albums: Trailer, 1994; 1977, 1996; Live At The Wireless, 1997; Nu-Clear Sounds, 1998; Free All Angels, 2001; Intergalactic Sonic 7's: The Best Of Ash, 2002; Envy, 2002. Singles: Jack Names the Planets, 1994; Petrol, 1994; Uncle Pat, 1994; Kung Fu, 1995; Girl From Mars, 1995; Angel Interceptor, 1995; Goldfinger, 1995; Oh Yeah, 1996; A Life Less Ordinary, 1997; Jesus Says, 1998; Numbskull (EP), 1999; Wild Surf, 2001; Burn Baby Burn, 2001; Shining Light, 2001; Sometimes, 2001; Candy, 2001; Tokyo Blitz, 2002; There's A Star, 2002. *Honours:* Ivor Novello Award, Best Contemporary Song, for Shining Light, 2002. *Address:* Infectious Records, 1 Shorrolds Rd, London SW6 7TR, England. *E-mail:* tim@ash-official.com. *Website:* www.ash-official.com.

WHELAN, Bill, (William Michael Joseph Weldon); b. 1950, Ireland. Composer. *Career:* Toured and recorded with Planxty for 2 years; Composer in residence at the Yeats festival, Abbey Theatre, Dublin; Collaborations include: Andy Irvine; The Dubliners; Kate Bush; Soundtracks include: Lamb (co-written with Van Morrison); Some Mother's Son, 1996; Dancing At Lughnasa. *Compositions include:* The Seville Suite, 1992; The Spirit of Mayo, 1993; Riverdance, 1995; Music for 15 Yeats International Theatre Festival plays in Dublin. *Honours:* Riverdance single stayed at number 1 for 18 weeks in Ireland, went platinum in the USA and Ireland; Grammy Award, Best Musical Show Album, Riverdance, 1997; Billboard Awards, Top World Music Artist, 1996, 1997. *Website:* www.billwhelan.com.

WHELAN, Gary (Gaz); b. 12 Feb. 1966. Musician (drums). *Career:* Mem., Happy Mondays, 1985–93; Tours, UK, Europe, USA; Support tours to: New Order, UK, 1987; Jane's Addiction, US, 1990; Concerts include: Glastonbury Festival, 1990; Great British Music Weekend, Wembley, 1990; Feile Festival, Tipperary, 1990; Cities In The Park Festival, Prestwich, 1990; Re-formed, 1999. *Recordings:* Albums: Squirrel And G-Man Twenty-Four Hour Party People Plastic Face Carnt Smile (White Out), 1986; Bummed, 1988; Pills 'N' Thrills And Bellyaches (No. 1, UK), 1990; Live, 1991; ...Yes Please!, 1992; Happy Mondays Greatest Hits, 1999. Singles: Madchester Rave On (EP); Step On, 1990; Kinky Afro, 1990; Judge Fudge, 1991. *Honours:* Best Indie Act, DMC World DJ Awards, 1991. *Address:* c/o London Records, PO Box 1422, Chancellors House, Chancellors Rd, London W6 9SG, England. *Website:* www.londonrecords.co.uk.

WHELAN, Gavan; Musician (drums). *Career:* Founder mem., James, 1983–90; Numerous tours, festival dates and television appearances. *Recordings:* Albums: Stutter, 1986; Strip Mine, 1988; One Man Clapping, 1989; Gold Mother, 1990; as Prod.: Alive, 2001. Singles incl.: Jimone (EP),

1983; Jim 2 (EP), 1985; How Was It For You, 1990; Come Home, 1990; Lose Control, 1990.

WHILE, Christine Mills; b. 22 Dec. 1955, Barrow-in-Furness, England. Vocalist; Musician (guitar); Songwriter. m. Joe While, 18 Oct. 1974, divorced 1993, 1 s., 1 d. *Career:* Lead vocalist: The Albion Band, 1993–97; Duo with Julie Matthews; Tours: UK; USA; Australia; Europe; Numerous television and radio appearances; Performed at Cambridge and Edmonton festivals. *Compositions:* 100 Miles, 1992; Young Man Cut Down In His Prime, co-written with Julie Matthews, 1996; The Light In My Mother's Eye, 1999. *Recordings:* Albums: Solo album (own compositions): Look At Me Now; Blue Moon On The Rise (EP), with Julie Matthews: In The Big Room, 1996; Piecework, 1997; Higher Potential, 1999; Stages (live), 2000; with the Albion Band: Acousticity; Albion Heart; Vocals on: Songbird, Christine Collister, 2000. *Membership:* MCPS; PRS; Musicians' Union. *Current Management:* Blue Moon Music. *Address:* PO Box 291, Southport, PR8 3GY, England.

WHITAKER, Michael Whiteley; b. 26 May 1948, Ploughley, Oxfordshire, England. Musician (keyboards, harmonica, percussion); Vocalist. m. Helen, 15 Aug. 1969, 2 s. *Education:* Newcastle College of Arts and Technology School of Music. *Career:* Member of Halfbreed; European tour with Leo Sayer; British tour with Curved Air; Television and radio appearances: Tube; Geordie Scene; In Concert, BBC Radio 1. *Recordings:* 4 albums; 2 releases for North East labels; 12 singles. *Publications:* Out Now (Rock fanzine). *Membership:* PRS; Equity; Musicians' Union. *Current Management:* Bill Dixon Agency. *Address:* 58 Hedley St, Gosforth, Newcastle upon Tyne NE3 1DL, England.

WHITE, Adam Peter; b. 22 Sept. 1948, Bristol, England. Journalist. *Career:* Reporter, news editor, Music Week, 1974–77; International Editor, Billboard, 1978–80; Managing Editor, Billboard, 1981–83; Editor-in-Chief, Billboard, 1983–85; New York Bureau Chief, Radio and Records, 1985–88; London correspondent, Rolling Stone, 1988–89; International Editor-In-Chief, Billboard, 1989–. *Publications:* The Billboard Book of Gold and Platinum Hits, 1990; Co-author, The Billboard Book of No 1 Rhythm and Blues Hits, 1993. *Address:* Billboard, Endeavour House, 189 Shaftesbury Ave, London WC2H 8TJ, England.

WHITE, Alan; b. 26 May 1972, London, England. Musician (drums). *Career:* Mem., Oasis, 1995–; Numerous headlining tours, television appearances and festival dates; Concert, Finsbury Park, London, 2002. *Recordings:* Albums: What's The Story (Morning Glory) (No. 1, UK), 1995; Be Here Now (No. 1, UK), 1997; The Masterplan, 1998; Standing On The Shoulder Of Giants (No. 1, UK), 2000; Familiar To Millions (Live), 2001; Heathen Chemistry, 2002. Singles include: Wonderwall (No. 2, UK), 1995; Roll With It (No. 2, UK), 1995; Champagne Supernova, 1995; Don't Look Back In Anger (No. 1, UK), 1996; D'You Know What I Mean (No. 1, UK), 1997; Stand By Me (No. 2, UK), 1997; All Around the World (No. 1, UK), 1998; Go Let It Out (No. 1, UK), 2000; Who Feels Love?, 2000; Sunday Morning Call, 2000; Stop Crying Your Heart Out, 2002; Little By Little/She Is Love, 2002; The Hindu Times, 2002. *Honours:* NME Awards, Best UK Band, Artist of the Year, 2003. *Current Management:* Ignition Management, 54 Linhope St, London NW1 6HL, England. *Website:* www.oasisnet.com.

WHITE, Andrew Nathaniel, III; b. 6 Sept. 1942, Washington, District of Columbia, USA. Musician (saxophone, oboe, English horn, bass); Recording Engineer; Composer; Arranger; Conductor; Musicologist; Lecturer; Publisher; Impresario. m. Jocelyne H J Uhl. *Education:* BMus Music Theory, Howard University, Washington, 1964. *Career:* Jazz saxophonist, JFK Quintet, 1960–64; New Jazz Trio, 1965–66; Oboist, English horn player, Center of Creative and Performing Arts, 1965–67; Principal oboe and English horn, American Ballet Theater, 1968–70; Electric bassist, Stevie Wonder and Motown Records, 1968–70; Fifth Dimension, 1970–76; Weather Report (recordings), 1970–73; The Jupiter Hair Company, 1971–; Solo debut, Carnegie Hall, 1974; Jazz saxophonist, Elvin Jones, 1980–81; Beaver Harris, 1983–. *Compositions include:* Concerto, 1963; Concertina, 1963; Shepherd Song, 1963; Andrew With Strings, 1987; A Jazz Concerto (5 versions), 1988. *Recordings:* 42 self-produced recordings; Collaborations include: JFK Quartet; McCoy Tyner; Gerry Rafferty; Bobby Watson. *Publications include:* Saxophone Transcriptions – The Works of John Coltrane, 14 vols; The Eric Dolphy Series Limited; The Charlie Parker Collection, 4 vols; The Andrew White Transcription Series; Big Band Series; Small Band Series; Andy's Song Book; Chamber Music Series; Saxophone Recital Series; Saxophone Etudes; Saxophone Trios, Quartets, Quintets; 2 Symphonies For 8 Saxophones; 4 Jazz Duets; 4 Jazz Trio Sonatas; 12 Jazz Miniatures; Books on improvisation, professionalism, practice, transcription, jazz education, self-production, Coltrane's music; 5 comedy books; Autobiography, Everybody Loves The Sugar – The Book, 2001; Contributor, numerous articles to trade journals; Staff writer, Saxophone Journal. *Honours:* Numerous study grants; Conductor, Dean Dixon Memorial Award, 1984; Washington Area Music Asscn Award, 1985. *Membership:* International Double Reed Society; Pi Kappa Lambda. *Current Management:* Andrew's Musical Enterprises Inc. *Address:* 4830 South Dakota Ave NE, Washington, DC 20017, USA.

WHITE, Andy; b. 28 May 1962, Belfast, Ireland. Vocalist; Songwriter; Musician (guitar, bass guitar). m. Christine, 26 Aug. 1995, 1 s. *Education:* Degree in English, Robinson College, Cambridge. *Recordings:* Religious Persuasion, 1985; Rave on Andy White, 1986; Kiss the Big Stone, 1988; Himself, 1990; Out There, 1992; Destination Beautiful, 1994; Teenage, 1996; andywhite.compilation, 1998; Speechless, 2000; Andy White, 2001; With Liam Ó Maonlaí and Tim Finn as ALT: Altitude, 1995; Bootleg, 1995. *Publications:* The Music of What Happens, 1998. *Honours:* Hot Press Irish Songwriter of the Year, 1993. *Current Management:* c/o Madeleine Seiler, 5 Wellington Gardens, Oakley Rd, Dublin 6, Ireland.

WHITE, Barry; b. 12 Sept. 1944, Galveston, Texas, USA. Vocalist; Musician (keyboards, drums). *Career:* Singer with The Upfronts and The Majestics; Drummer, road manager, for Earl Nelson, 1966; Manager, producer, Love Unlimited, 1968; Solo singer (originally as Barry Lee), 1965–; Founder, own production company, Soul Unlimited Productions; Television appearances include: Late Night With David Letterman; Arsenio Hall Show; Ally McBeal; Major concerts include: First Annual Gospel Festival, Jerusalem, 1983; Regular world-wide tours. *Recordings:* Albums: with Love Unlimited: Love Unlimited, 1972; Under The Influence Of..., 1974; Rhapsody In White, 1974; Together Brothers (soundtrack), 1974; Solo: I've Got So Much To Give, 1973; Stone Gon', 1974; Can't Get Enough (No. 1, USA), 1974; Just Another Way To Say I Love You, 1975; Let The Music Play, 1976; Is This Whatcha Wont?, 1976; Barry White Sings For Someone Your Love, 1977; Barry White The Man, 1978; The Man, 1979; The Message Is Love, 1979; I Love To Sing The Songs I Sing, 1979; Barry White's Sheet Music, 1981; Change, 1982; Heart and Soul, 1985; The Right Night and Barry White, 1987; The Man Is Back!, 1990; Love Is The Icon, 1994; Staying Power, 1999; What a Groove, 1999; My Musical Bouget, 1999; Your Heart And Soul, 2000; Hit singles include: with Love Unlimited: Walkin' In The Rain With The One I Love, 1972; Solo: I'm Gonna Love You Just A Little More Baby, 1973; Can't Get Enough of Your Love Babe (No. 1, USA), 1974; You're The First The Last My Everything (No. 1, UK), 1974; What Am I Gonna Do With You?, 1975; You See The Trouble With Me, 1976, sampled for Black Legend, same title (No. 1, UK), 2000; It's Ecstasy When You Lay Down Next To Me, 1977; Just The Way You Are, 1979; Sho' You Right, 1987; Staying Power, 1999. *Honours:* American Music Award, Favourite Male Soul/R&B Artist, 1976; Hon. degree, Recording Arts and Sciences, UCLA, 1980; Grammy Award Best Traditional R&B Vocal; Grammy Award, Best Male R&B Vocal. *Current Management:* SDM Management, 740 N La Brea Ave, First Floor, Los Angeles, CA 90038, USA.

WHITE, Freddie; b. 22 Sept. 1951, Cobh, Cork, Ireland. Vocalist; Songwriter; Musician (guitar). m. Ann O'Sullivan, 31 March 1979, 1 s., 1 d. *Career:* Concerts: Olympia Theatre; National Concert Hall; National Stadium; Television appearances: Late Late Show; Pat Kenny Show; Kelly Show; Live At Three. *Recordings:* Albums: Freddie White, 1979; Do You Do, 1981; Long Distance Runner, 1985; Close To You, 1991; Straight Up, 1993; My Country, 1999. *Honours:* Hot Press, Best Folk Specialist, 1981. *Membership:* PRS. *Current Management:* Madeleine Seiler. *Address:* 5 Wellington Gardens, Dublin 6, Ireland.

WHITE, Melvyn Arthur; b. 1 Dec. 1963, Norwich, England. Musician (bass guitar). m. Amanda Ross, 5 Dec. 1992, 2 s. *Career:* Broadland Radio, 1985; Radio Manchester, 1991; Supported Jools Holland, 1991; Member, group Law; Supported Nils Lofgren and Steve Marriott. *Recordings:* Only One Night Away, Gospel Truth, 1988; Jackie Dee, Law, 1990. *Honours:* UK Band of Year, Runner up, with Law, 1991. *Membership:* Musicians' Union. *Address:* 16 Marsh Rd Upton, Nr Acle, Norwich, Norfolk NR13 6BS, England.

WHITE, Peter; b. 20 Sept. 1954, Luton, Bedfordshire, England. Musician; Composer. *Career:* 20 years, Al Stewart; Tours, recordings, with Basia; Solo tours, recordings, 1990–. *Recordings:* Reveillez-Vous, 1990; Excusez-Moi, 1991; Promenade, 1993; Caravan of Dreams, 1996; Songs of the Season, 1997; Perfect Moment, 1998; With Al Stewart: Year of The Cat, 1974; Time Passages, 1978; Midnight Rocks, 1980; With Basia: Time and Tide, 1987; London Warsaw New York, 1990; The Sweetest Illusion, 1994; Basia, 1998; With Shippen Wise; Standing Outside In The Rain, 1990; With Roberto Perera: In the Mood, 1999; Other. *Recordings include:* Philip Bailey; Rick Braun; Richard Elliot; Snowy White; Dave Koz. *Honours:* BMI Adult Contemporary Song of the Year, Time Passages, 1978. *Membership:* BMI; AFofM. *Current Management:* Chapman and Co Management. *Address:* PO Box 15906, North Hollywood, CA 91615, USA.

WHITE, Snowy (Terence Charles); b. 3 March 1948, Devon, England. Musician (guitar); Vocalist. *Career:* Guitarist with Peter Green; Guitarist with Pink Floyd (touring band); Thin Lizzy, 1979–81; Tours, Europe, UK, Japan, USA, Australia, 1979–81; Solo artiste, 1982–. *Recordings:* Albums: with Thin Lizzy: Chinatown, 1980; Renegade, 1981; Adventures of Thin Lizzy, 1981; Solo: White Flames, 1984; Snowy White, 1985; That Certain Thing, 1987; Change My Life, 1991; Little Wing, 1998; Melting, 1999; Singles: with Thin Lizzy: Chinatown; Killers Live (EP); Solo: Bird of Paradise, 1983; Recordings with Peter Green include: Songbook, 2000; Clown, 2000; Time Traders, 2001; with Roger Waters: In The Flesh Live, 2000.

WHITE, Tony Joe; b. Oak Grove, Louisiana, USA. Songwriter. *Care[...]* Toured with rock bands including Creedence Clearwater Revival, 197[...] Toured extensively throughout Europe, including shows with Joe Cocker a[...] Eric Clapton, 1991–92. *Compositions:* Rainy Night in Georgia; Produced h[...] for: Tina Turner, Joe Cocker, Etta James, Waylon Jennings, John Anderso[...] Isaac Hayes, Roy Orbison, Kris Kristofferson, Charlie Rich, Chet Atki[...] Hank Williams Jr, Jessi Colter, Christine McVie, Ray Charles, Aret[...] Franklin and Wild Cherry. *Recordings:* Polk Salad Annie; For Ole Tim[...] Sake; I've Got A Thing About You, Baby; The Path of a Decent Groove; La[...] Placid Blues, album; with Kerouac: Kicks Joy Darkness, 1997; Beginnin[...] 2001. *Current Management:* RD World-wide Management BV, Keizersgrac[...] 683, Amsterdam 1017 DW, Netherlands.

WHITE, Will; Musician. *Career:* Member of Propellerheads, with Al[...] Gifford. *Recordings:* Albums: Bang On!, 1997; Decksandrumsandrockandro[...] 1998; Singles: On Her Majesty's Secret Service (with Shirley Bassey), 199[...] Dive, 1997; Take California (EP), 1997; Spybreak (EP), 1997; Histo[...] Repeating (with Shirley Bassey), 1997; Other. *Recordings include:* with F[...] Static: Crash And Burn, 2001; with Jungle Brothers: VIP, 2000. *Address:* Wall of Sound, Office 3, 9 Thorpe Close, London W10 5XL, England.

WHITEHEAD, Alan; b. 24 July 1945, Oswestry, Shropshire, England. Ma[...] Agent; Musician (drums). m. Louise Burton, 17 Dec. 1978, divorced, 2[...] *Career:* Drummer, Marmalade, 1967–78; 14 Hit records, Marmalade; Start[...] own company, disco act promotion, 1979; Founder, manager, Mel and Kim[...] major hit records); dance group Body Check; robotic acts: Arbie The Rob[...] Adam and Eve; magician Marc Oberon; Bought out by Mecca Leisure, 198[...] Current owner, largest Glamour Shows agency in Europe, including: T[...] Sunday Sport Roadshow; The Dreamboys, 1988–; Touring girl roadshow[...] Europe; The Far East; Japan; Australia; Managed artists in partnership w[...] Ben Findon and Steve Rowland; Founder, Fit Management, with Stevie 'V[...] Lange and Bill Smith. *Recordings:* Marmalade: Lovi[...] Things; Wait For Me Mary Ann; Ob-La-Di Ob-La-Da; Baby Make It So[...] Reflections of My Life; Rainbow; Cousin Norman; Ra Dancer; Back On t[...] Road; Falling Apart At The Seams; Compilations include: Reflections Of T[...] Marmalade, 2001. *Honours:* Pop Group of the Year, 1968; Various Gold dis[...] *Membership:* British Institute of Management; Fellow, The Agents Asso[...] *Address:* 79 The Ryde, Hatfield, Hertfordshire, AL9 5DN, Englan[...] *Telephone:* (1707) 267883. *Fax:* (1707) 267247. *E-mail:* alan.whitehead.u[...] yahoo.com.

WHITEHEAD, Tim; b. 12 Dec. 1950, Liverpool, England. Jazz Musicia[...] (saxophone). m. Linda Jones, 26 June 1978, 2 s., 2 d. *Career:* Member, Loo[...] Tubes (modern jazz orchestra), 1984–89; Founder, Tim Whitehead Quart[...] Tim Whitehead Band; Regular recordings on BBC radio, including Apple[...] Jazz Festival, 1995; Numerous tours, concerts include: Brecon Jazz Festiv[...] 1992; London Jazz Festival, 1994; PORI International Jazz Festival, Finlar[...] 1995; Regular appearances at Ronnie Scott's Club, London; Televi[...] apperances include: Wogan, BBC TV, 1986, 1987; Bath Festival, BBC2 T[...] 1987; with Loose Tubes, New Year's Day, Granada TV, 1988; 30 Years[...] PORI, Finnish TV, 1995; Also performed, toured, broadcast with: Ian Car[...] Nucleus; Graham Collier; Jim Mullen's Meantime; Breakfast Ban[...] Woodworks; Martin Drew Quartet. *Compositions:* Nine Sketches for Sc[...] Saxophone, 1996; Soundtracks; Heart and Soul. *Recordings:* with Ti[...] Whitehead Band: English People, 1983; Decision, 1988; with Tim Whitehea[...] Quartet: Authentic, 1991; Silence Between Waves, 1994, 1995; Person[...] Standards, 1999; with Loose Tubes: Loose Tubes; Delightful Precipice; Op[...] Letter; Other. *Recordings include:* Water's Edge, Breakfast Band; Firedan[...] Richard Bailey; Pictures of You, Harry Beckett; Aural Sculpture, T[...] Stranglers; Live In London, Maria Muldaur; Permission, with Pe[...] Fairclough, Mike Walker and Dudley Phillips, 1997; with Colin Riley: Tid[...] 2001. *Honours:* Young Jazz Musician, 1977; Arts Council Commission, Silen[...] Between Waves, GLA, 1992; Commissioned by Jazz Umbrella/Arts Council[...] compose Nine Sketches for Solo Saxophone for London Jazz Festival on t[...] South Bank, 1996; BBC Music Magazine, Critics' Choice of the Year, Person[...] Standards; Andrew Milne Award for Jazz, Soundtracks, 1998; Pet[...] Whittingham Award Tides (with Colin Riley), 2000. *Membersh[...] Chairperson, Co-founder, Jazz Umbrella (London Jazz Musicia[...] Cooperative). *Current Management:* Basho Music, 18 Linhope St, Lond[...] NW1 6HT, England. *Address:* 5 Willowbank, Ham, Richmond, Surre[...] England. *Website:* www.timwhitehead.co.uk.

WHITEHOUSE, Cedric John; b. 24 March 1944, Walsall, West Midland[...] England. Musician (guitar). m. Peggy Whitehouse, 27 Feb. 1987, 2[...] *Education:* A Level Music. *Career:* Session guitarist, 1971–; Television sho[...] include: Golden Shot; New Faces, 1974–80; Pebble Mill at One; Radio sessio[...] include: BBC Radio Orchestras, 1974–76; Radio 2; Archers, 1975–76; Writin[...] producing artists, and television commercials, 1980–95. *Recordings:* Abo[...] 1000 television shows as session guitarist; Stringz And Saxy Things, wi[...] Snake Davis & Bob Wilson, 1999; Current production work includes: Ru[...] Turner (Gershwin Album); Howard McCrary; Chaka Khan. *Honours:* Mec[...] Bandleader of the Year, 1976, 1977, 1978; Carl Alan Award, 198[...] *Membership:* Musicians' Union. *Address:* Pool House, Pirton, Worcs, Englan[...]

WHITFIELD, George William; b. 29 Feb. 1964, Worcester, England. Musician (accordion); Vocalist. *Education:* Warwick University. *Career:* Accordion player, vocalist with Pressgang, 1988; Solo appearances; Work with outcast band, WOB, Steve Hunt; Pressgang played 180 concerts: England (including Glastonbury Festival); Germany; Belgium; France; Wales; USA (including SXSW Festival), 1994. *Recordings:* with Pressgang: Rogues, 1989; Albums: with Pressgang: Burning Boats, 1994; with Outcast Band: Devil's Road, 1993; Steve Hunt: Head The Heart and The Hand, 1993; with Roy Bailey, Coda, 2000. *Membership:* Musicians' Union; PRS. *Current Management:* Vox Pop, Reading, England; Berlin Consert, Max Biere Strasse, Berlin, Germany. *Address:* c/o Vox Pop, 1 Donnington Gardens, Reading, Berks, England.

WHITFIELD, Mark Adrian; b. 6 Oct. 1966, New York, NY, USA. Musician (guitar). 2 s. *Education:* BMus, Berklee College of Music, Boston. *Career:* Appearances include: The Tonite Show; Good Morning America; The Today Show; CNN Showbiz Today; CBS Sunday Morning. *Recordings:* Albums: The Marksman; Patrice; Mark Whitfield; True Blue; Seventh Avenue Stroll; Forever Love; Take the Ride, 1999; Raw, 2000; Soul Conversation, 2000. *Publications:* Mark Whitfield Guitar Transcriptions. *Honours:* Hon. Mayor of Baton Rouge, Louisiana, USA. *Current Management:* Paul Tannen. *Address:* 38 Laurel Ledge Court, Stamford, CT 06903, USA.

WHITMAN, Slim, (Otis Dewey Whitman Jr); b. 20 Jan. 1924, Tampa, Florida, USA. Vocalist; Musician (guitar). m. Geraldine Crist, 1941, 1 s. *Career:* Recording artist, 1949–; Weekly appearances on Louisiana Hayride radio show; Joined in 1955 with regular appearances on Grand Ole Opry; Film appearance, Disc Jockey Jamboree, 1957; Recorded 25th Anniversary concert, Empire Theatre, Liverpool, England, 1973; Toured with son Byron, 1977–; First Country and Western singer to headline the London Palladium, 1956; Celebrated 50 years in showbusiness in 1998. *Recordings:* Hit singles include: Love Song of The Waterfall; Indian Love Call (No. 1, UK, 11 weeks), 1955; China Doll; Cattle Call; Tumbling Tumbleweeds; Serenade; Happy Anniversary; Numerous albums include: Slim Whitman Sings and Yodels, 1954; Slim Whitman, 1958; Once In A Lifetime, 1961; A Lonesome Heart, 1967; Slim, 1969; 25th Anniversary Concert, 1973; The Very Best of Slim Whitman (No. 1, UK), 1976; Home On The Range, 1977; Red River Valley (No. 1, UK), 1977; Ghost Riders In The Sky, 1978; Just For You, 1980; Songs I Love To Sing, 1980; Mr Songman, 1981; Till We Meet Again, 1981; Country Songs, City Hits, 1982; Angeline, 1984; Magic Moments (with Byron Whitman), 1990; Cow Poke, 1992; Traditional Country, with Byron Whitman, 1999; Legendary, 2000. *Honours:* BCMA, Best International Male Vocalist, 1978–80. *Address:* c/o Tessier-Marsh Talent, 505 Canton Pass, Madison, TN 37115, USA.

WHITMORE, Andrew David; b. 31 March 1962, Coventry, England. Prod; Musician (keyboards); Studio player. m. 27 Sept. 1988, 1 s., 1 d. *Education:* Grade 8 piano; Grade 5 cello; Grade 5 theory. *Career:* Member, Terence Trent D'Arby band, keyboard player; Now accomplished programmer, producer. *Compositions:* Co-wrote with Peter Andre, No 1 single, Flava, 1996. *Recordings:* Albums: MN8 (production); East 17; Paris Paris, Malcolm McLaren; Peter Andre, 3 tracks, Natural album; Kavana Productions, 3 tracks; S-Man Classics: The Essential Sanchez, 1998; Barrington Levy, Living Dangerously (synthesizer and drums), 1998; Other collaborations include: Cathy Dennis; Des'ree; Erasure. *Membership:* PRS; MCPS. *Current Management:* Stephen Budd Management. *Address:* 39 Greystoke Parr Terrace, Ealing, London W5 1JL, England.

WHITTAKER, Roger; b. 22 March 1936, Nairobi, Kenya. Vocalist; Whistler; Musician (guitar); Songwriter. *Education:* Medicine; Biology; Biochemistry. *Career:* Former teacher and part-time folk singer; Recording artist, 1961–; Television includes: This And That, Ulster TV; Own series, BBC TV; Concerts include: Knokke Music Festival, Belgium, 1967; Launched UNESCO songwriting competition, 1975; World-wide record sales exceed 40m. Copies. *Recordings:* Singles include: Mexican Whistler (No. 1 throughout Europe), 1967; The Leavin' (Durham Town), 1969; I Don't Believe In If Anymore, 1970; New World In The Morning, 1971; The Last Farewell (over 11m. copies sold), 1975; The Skye Boat Song, with Des O'Connor, 1986; Over 70 albums, including compilations and special German language recordings, 1965–; Recent. *Recordings include:* Legendary, 2001. *Publications:* So Far So Good, with Natalie Whittaker. *Honours:* B'nai B'rith Humanitarian Award, 1975. *Current Management:* Tembo Entertainments. *Address:* 223 Regent St, London W1R 7DB, England.

WHITWAM, Jan Barry; b. 21 July 1946, Prestbury, Cheshire, England. Musician (percussion, guitar). m. Anne Patricia, 19 Jan. 1987, 1 s., 1 d. *Education:* 2 years drum tuition. *Career:* Original member, Herman's Hermits, 39 years; 150 major US tours with Herman's Hermits; 50 World tours; Numerous major concerts including Royal Command Performance; Television appearances: Top of the Pops; Ready Steady Go (UK); Danny Kay; Dean Martin; Jackie Gleason; Merv Griffin; Ed Sullivan; Hullabaloo; Shindig (USA); Film appearances: Hold On, 1966; Mrs Brown You've Got A Lovely Daughter, 1967. *Recordings:* 23 hit singles, UK; 24 hit singles, USA; Best-selling records in world, 1965; 60m. records sold to date; Hits include: I'm

Into Something Good (No. 1, UK), 1964; Mrs. Brown You've Got A Lovely Daughter (No. 1, USA), 1965; I'm Henry The Eighth I Am (No. 1, USA), 1965; Silhouettes, 1965; Wonderful World, 1965; No Milk Today, 1966; Something's Happening, 1968. *Honours:* NME Award winner; Keys to 25 cities, USA; 8 Gold albums; 9 Gold singles. *Membership:* Musicians' Union; Equity. *Current Management:* Barry Whitwam Management. *Address:* 26 S Park Rd, Gatley, Cheadle, Cheshire SK8 4AN, England.

WHYTE, Gordon; b. 22 May 1971, Glasgow, Scotland. Freelance Musician (keyboards, guitar, bodhran); Vocalist; Songwriter. *Education:* Master of Engineering (MEng), 1993; Strathclyde University, Glasgow. *Career:* Session work for: Rick Wakeman; Noel Richards; Ian White; Established Leader of Christian Worship for conferences and festivals, including: Spring Harvest; Greenbelt; Carberry Festivals; Songwriting partnership with Susan Lennartson established 1994. *Recordings:* Debut album with Susan Lennartson: Wind of Life, 1995. *Membership:* Musicians Christian Fellowship (MCF). *Current Management:* Gordon Whyte. *Address:* 31 Dunchurch Rd, Paisley PA1 3JW, England.

WICKENS, Paul (Wix); b. 27 March 1956, Chelmsford, Essex, England. Record Prod; Musician (keyboards). m. Margo Buchanan, 31 Jan. 1992. *Education:* O and A Level Music; Piano grades. *Career:* Recorded with: The Pretenders; Dave Stewart; Mike and The Mechanics; Céline Dion; Nik Kershaw; Boy George; Status Quo; Alison Moyet; John Hiatt; The The; Prefab Sprout; The Kane Gang; Emmylou Harris; Linda Ronstadt; Jackson Browne; Bonnie Raitt; Performed live with: Joni Mitchell; Jon Bon Jovi; Ry Cooder; The Kane Gang; The Chieftains; Bob Dylan; Jim Diamond; Worked with Paul McCartney, 5 albums, 2 world tours including Maracana Stadium, Brazil (record breaking concert), 1989–; Buckingham Palace House Band, Party at the Palace (Queen's Jubilee concert), 2002; Production credits include: The Kane Gang; Jim Diamond; The Big Dish; Freddie McGregor; Mel Garside; Carmel; Alisha's Attic; Shakin Stevens; Texas; Kevin Coyne; Edie Brickell; Leann Rimes; Tasmin Archer, including Sleeping Satellite, No. 1, UK charts. *Membership:* Musicians' Union; PRS; MCPS; MPG. *Address:* c/o Marshall Arts, Leeder House, 6 Erskine Rd, London NW3, England.

WICKHAM, Steve; b. 28 Oct. 1960, Dublin, Ireland. Musician (violin). m. (1) Barbara Kernal, (2) Heidi Ansell, Aug. 1996. *Education:* College of Music. *Career:* With U2, tour Ireland, European dates, 1982; Television, touring: the Waterboys, 1986–89; Touring and Television: Texas Kellys, 1990–92. *Compositions:* Score for Abbey Theatre production of Caoineadh Art O'Laoghaire, 1998. *Recordings:* Elvis Costello: Spike, 1988; Texas Kellys, 1992; Waterboys: This Is The Sea Fisherman's Blues, 1987; Room To Roam, 1989; U2: War, 1982; Sinead O'Connor: The Lion and The Cobra, 1987; Karl Wallinger, World Party, 1988; Sharon Shannon, 1991; Sweet White Water, City Of Tribes,1997; Cry From The Heart, 2000; all by Deirdre Cunningham; Other collaborators include: Maria McKee; In Tua Nua. *Publications:* Sofa So Good, 1991. *Honours:* Hot Press Musician of the Year, 1986. *Membership:* IMRO. *Current Management:* Traci Gordon.

WIDMARK, Anders; b. 25 Nov. 1963, Uppsala, Sweden. Musician (piano); Composer. *Education:* Royal Academy of Music, Stockholm. *Career:* Professional pianist, 1986–; Collaborated with Stockholm Jazz Orchestra, The Swedish Radio Jazz Orchestra, Eddie Harris, Bob Brookmeyer, Clark Terry, Rebecka Törnqvist, Bengt-Arne Wallin; Soloist, performances with Sundsvall Symphony Orchestra and Uppsala Chamber Soloists; The Uppsala Stadsteater, composing music for plays, 1 year. *Recordings:* Solo Albums: Sylvesters sista resa, 1991; Anders Widmark and the Soul Quartet, 1993; Holly Hannah, 1994; Freewheelin', 1995; Anders Widmark, 1996; Anders Widmark Trio – Psalmer, 1997; Carmen, 2000; Contributor: Dreams, Bob Brookmeyer and Stockholm Jazz Orchestra, 1989; A Night Like This, Rebecka Törnqvist, 1993; Obsession! Live at Fasching, Egil Bop Johansen, 1994; Quel Bordel, Christian Falk, 1999. *Membership:* STIM; SKAP. *Current Management:* NW Produktion, Björngardsgatan 9A, 11852 Stockholm, Sweden. *Address:* Karlsborgsvagen 10, 121 50, Johanneshov, Sweden.

WIEDLIN, Jane; b. 20 May 1958, Oconomowoc, Wisconsin, USA. Vocalist; Musician (guitar); Songwriter; Fashion Designer. *Career:* Founder mem., US all-female group the Go-Gos (formerly The Misfits), 1978–85; Numerous international tours; Mem., Sparks, 1984; Solo artiste, 1985–93; The Go-Go's re-formed briefly for PETA benefit concert, 1990; Mem., re-formed Go-Go's, 1994, Shows in Las Vegas; The Go-Go's re-formed, 2000–, for an album and tours, including US tour with B-52's; Film appearance: Bill and Ted's Excellent Adventure, 1989. *Recordings:* Albums: with the Go-Go's: Beauty and The Beat (No. 1, USA), 1981; Vacation, 1982; Talk Show, 1984; Greatest, 1991; Return To The Valley of The Go-Go's, 1994; God Bless The Go-Go's, 2001; Contributor, Tame Yourself (Animal Rights benefit album), 1991; Solo: Jane Wiedlin, 1985; Fur, 1988; Tangled, 1990; Very Best of Jane Wiedlin, 1993; Kissproof World, 2000. Singles: with the Go-Gos: Our Lips Are Sealed, 1981; We Got The Beat (No. 2, USA), 1982; Beauty and The Beat, 1982; Solo: Blue Kiss, 1986; Inside A Dream, 1988; Rush Hour, 1988; World on Fire, 1990; The Whole World Lost Its Head, 1995. *Compositions include:* Our Lips Are Sealed (co-writer with Terry Hall). *Current Management:* c/o Left Bank

Management, 9255 Sunset Blvd, West Hollywood, CA 90069, USA. *E-mail:* gogos@beyondmusic.com. *Website:* www.janewiedlin.com; www.gogos.com.

WIENEUSKI, Matthew; b. 20 Sept. 1965, London, England. Composer; Filmmaker; Musician (saxophone, flute). *Education:* Bristol University, English degree. *Career:* European tour, 1993; Japan, 1994; Screenplays: Hardcore Nation; The Kabbalist of Lincoln. *Compositions:* D*votions; The Garden of Earthly Delights. *Recordings:* Albums under D*note: Babel; Criminal Justice. *Membership:* PRS. *Address:* Dorado Records, 76 Brewer St, London W1R 3PH, England.

WIGGS, Josephine Miranda Cordelia; b. 26 Feb. 1963, Letchworth, Hertfordshire, England. Musician (bass guitar); Composer. *Education:* BA, Hons, London; MA, Philosophy, Sussex.; Studied cello, 6 years. *Career:* Bass player and backing vocalist with Perfect Disaster, 1987–90; Bass, vocals, guitar, cello, drums, with The Breeders, 1990–; Bass player with Ultra Vivid Scene, US tour, 1990; Honey Tongue (solo project with Jon Mattock, Spacemen 3, Spiritualized), 1992–. *Recordings:* with Perfect Disaster: Asylum Road, 1988; Up, 1989; Heaven Scent, 1990; with Breeders: Pod, 1990; Last Splash, 1993; Nude Nudes, Honey Tongue, 1992; Guest appearances on recordings by: Dusty Trails, Luscious Jackson, Amy Ray. *Publications:* Breeders Digest, official Fanclub newsletter. *Honours:* Platinum Award for US sales, Last Splash; BRIT Award, Best Single, for Cannonball, 1993. *Current Management:* Janet Billig, Manage This, 154 W 57th St, #828, New York, NY 10019, USA. *Address:* Fairfield House, Biggleswade, Bedfordshire SG18 0AA, England.

WIGGS, Pete; b. 15 May 1966, Reigate, Surrey, England. Musician (keyboards, programming); Prod. *Career:* Founding mem., Saint Etienne, 1988–; Worked with guest vocalists, joined by Sarah Cracknell, 1991; Launched own label, Emidisc. *Recordings:* Albums: with Saint Etienne: Foxbase Alpha, 1991; So Tough, 1993; You Need A Mess Of Help To Stand Alone (compilation), 1993; Tiger Bay, 1994; I Love To Paint (compilation), 1995; Fairytales From Saint Etienne (compilation), 1995; Too Young To Die (compilation), 1995; Casino Classics (compilation), 1996; Continental (compilation), 1997; Good Humor, 1998; The Misadventures Of Saint Etienne (soundtrack), 1999; Built On Sand (compilation), 1999; Sound Of Water, 2000; Interlude (compilation), 2001; Smash The System (compilation), 2001; Finisterre, 2002; Singles: with Saint Etienne: Only Love Can Break Your Heart, 1990; Kiss And Make Up, 1990; Nothing Can Stop Us, 1991; Join Our Club, 1992; Avenue, 1992; You're In A Bad Way, 1993; Hobart Paving/Who Do You Think You Are?, 1993; I Was Born On Christmas Day (with Tim Burgess), 1993; Pale Movie, 1994; Like A Motorway, 1994; Hug My Soul, 1994; Reserection (with Etienne Daho), 1995; He's On The Phone, 1995; Xmas '95 (EP), 1995; Angel/Burnt Out Car, 1996; Valentines Day '97 (EP), 1997; Sylvie, 1998; The Bad Photographer, 1998; Bronx Dogs Mixes, 1998; Lose That Girl, 1998; Xmas '98 (EP), 1998; Lover Plays The Bass, 1999; Places To Visit (EP), 2000; Saturday, 1999; How We Used To Live, 2000; Heart Failed (In The Back Of A Taxi), 2000; Boy Is Crying, 2001; Asleep At The Wheels Of Steel (EP), 2002; Action, 2002; contribution to Gone, David Holmes, 1996; Tell Me Why, Paul Van Dyk, 2000. *Address:* c/o Mantra Recordings, 17–19 Alma Rd, London SW18 1AA, England. *Website:* www.saint.etienne.net.

WILBER, Bob, (Robert Sage); b. 15 March 1928, New York, NY, USA. Bandleader; Composer; Arranger; Writer; Musician (clarinet, soprano, alto, tenor saxophones). m. Joanne Horton, 2 s., 1 d. *Education:* BA, State University, New York; Juilliard, Eastman, Manhattan schools; Teachers: Sidney Bechet; Lennic Tristano; Leon Russianoff. *Career:* Subbed for Sidney Bechet, Nice Festival, 1948; Also leading bands at Savoy, Storyville clubs, Boston; Played with: Bobby Hackett; Benny Goodman; Jack Teagarden; Eddie Condon; Founding member, World's Greatest Jazz Band, 1969; Began Soprano Summit with Kenny Davern, 1973–78; Re-formed as Summit Reunion, 1990; Performed, recorded with jazz artists including: Duke Ellington; Billy Strayhorn; Louis Armstrong; Sidney Bechet; Performed, presented Carnegie Hall Tribute to Benny Goodman; Premiered orchestral version of Duke Ellington's Queens Suite; Toured with Bechet Legacy Band; Helped organize New York jazz Repertory Company; Director, Smithsonian Jazz Repertory Ensemble; Leads big band in Benny Goodman re-creations; Musical Director: The Cotton Club; Soloist, Pittsburgh, Baltimore, Colorado Symphony Orchestras; Recorded chamber music by Brahms, Beethoven, Mozart. *Compositions:* The Piscean Suite; Portraits In Jazz. *Recordings:* Over 1,500 titles include: Saxophones on: Horns A-Plenty; Recent releases include: Fletcher Henderson's Unrecorded Arrangements, 2000; Vital Wilber, 2000; Moments Like This, 2000; Nostalgia. *Publications:* Autobiography: Music Was Not Enough, 1987. *Honours:* Grammy Award, music for film: The Cotton Club, 1985; Hon. Doctorate of Music, Hamilton College, 1998. *Membership:* ASCAP; Rotary; Senior Statesman of Jazz.

WILDE, Danny; Vocalist; Songwriter; Musician. *Career:* Member, Great Buildings; The Rembrandts, 1991–; Also solo artiste. *Recordings:* Solo Albums: Danny Wilde; Any Man's Hunger; The Boyfriend; With The Rembrandts: Rembrandts, 1991; Untitled, 1992; LP, 1995; Spin This!, 1998; Lost Together, 2001; Singles: That's Just The Way It Is Baby; Johnny Have You Seen Her?; I'll Be There For You (theme for television series Friends),

1995. *Current Management:* Mogul Entertainment Group. *Address:* 9744 Wilshire Blvd, Suite 305, Beverly Hills, CA 90212, USA.

WILDE, Kim, (Kim Smith); b. 18 Nov. 1960, Chiswick, London, England. Vocalist. *Education:* Art school. *Career:* Backing singer to father Marty; Solo artiste, 1980–; Sold 6m. discs world-wide in 18 months, 1981–82; AIDS benefit concert, Wembley, 1987; Support to Michael Jackson, Bad world tour, 1988; Performed at World Music Awards, Monaco, 1992. *Recordings:* Albums; Kim Wilde, 1981; Select, 1982; Catch As Can Can, 1983; Teases and Dares, 1984; The Very Best of Kim Wilde, 1985; Another Step, 1986; Close, 1988; Love Moves, 1990; Love Is, 1992; The Singles Collection 1981–93, 1993; Now and Forever, 1995; Breaking Away, 1995; The Gold Collection, 1996; Original Gold, 1999; The Kim Wilde Collection, 2001; Hit singles include: Kids In America, 1981; Chequered Love, 1981; Water On Glass, 1981; Cambodia, 1981; View From A Bridge, 1982; Rage To Love, 1985; You Keep Me Hangin' On (No. 1, USA), 1986; Another Step (Closer To You), duet with Junior, 1987; Say You Really Want Me, 1987; Rockin' Around The Christmas Tree, with Mel Smith (for Comic Relief), 1987; You Came, 1988; Never Trust A Stranger, 1988; Four Letter Word, 1988; Love Is Holy, 1992; If I Can't Have You, 1994. *Contributions to:* Rock The World charity record, 1990; Let It Be, Ferry Aid (Zeebrugge ferry disaster benefit). *Honours:* BRIT Award, Best British Female Artist, 1983; Played female lead in West End production of Pete Townshend's Tommy, 1996. *Current Management:* Big M Productions Ltd. *Address:* Thatched Rest, Queen Hoo Lane, Tewin, Hertfordshire AL6 0LT, England.

WILDE, Marty, (Reginald Smith); b. 15 April 1939, Greenwich, London, England. Vocalist. m. Joyce Baker, 2 Dec. 1959, 2 s., 2 d. *Career:* Performed as Reg Patterson, and with The Hound Dogs; Changed name, with backing group The Wildcats, 1957; Television appearances include: Off The Record, 1957; Oh Boy!, ITV, 1958; Host, Boy Meets Girls, 1959; Group Scene 1964, Regular British tours, including Group Scene 1964, with Rolling Stones, 1964; Formed the Wilde Three, vocal trio, with Justin Haywood, 1965; Rock 'n' Roll Road Show, British tour with Bert Weedon, 1977; AIDS benefit, with son Ricky and daughter Kim, Wembley, 1987; Film appearances: The Helions, 1961; What A Crazy World, 1964; Theatre: Bye Bye Birdie, London production, 1961. *Compositions include:* Co-writer (with Ronnie Scott), Ice In The Sun, Status Quo; Jesamine, The Casuals; Co-writer (with Ricky Wilde), Kim Wilde, 1981–. *Recordings:* Albums: Diversions, 1969; Good Rocking, Now and Then, 1973; Solid Gold, 1994; It's Been Nice, 1996; Born To Rock 'n' Roll, 1999; The Best Of Marty Wilde; Hit singles include: Endless Sleep, 1958; Donna, 1959; A Teenager In Love, 1959; Sea of Love, 1959; Bad Boy, 1960; Little Girl, 1961; Rubber Ball, 1961; Jezebel, 1963. *Current Management:* Joyce Wilde. *Address:* Thatched Rest, Queen Hoo Lane, Tewin, Hertfordshire AL6 0LT, England.

WILDER, Alan; b. 1 June 1959, London, England. *Career:* Joined Depeche Mode, 1982; Numerous world tours including Pasadena Rose Bowl, California; TV and radio appearances world-wide; Left band, 1995. *Recordings:* Singles: Leave in Silence, 1982; Meaning of Love, 1982; Love in Itself, 1983; Everything Counts, 1983; Get the Balance Right, 1983; Blasphemous Rumours, 1984; Master and Servant, 1984; Shake the Disease, 1985; It's Called a Heart, 1985; Stripped, 1986; Question of Lust, 1986; Never Let Me Down Again, 1987; I Want You Know, 1988; Behind the Wheel, 1988; People are People, 1988; Personal Jesus, 1989; Enjoy the Silence, 1990; Policy of Truth, 1990; Heavens in Motion, 1990; A Heart, 2990; But Not Tonight, 1990; World in My Eyes, 1990; A Question of Time, 1991; Condemnation, 1993; Walking in My Shoes, 1993; One Caress, 1993; In Your Room, 1994; Albums: Construction Time Again, 1983; Some Great Reward, 1984; Catching Up With Depeche Mode, 1985; Black Celebration, 1986; Music for the Masses, 1987; Violator, 1990; Songs of Faith and Devotion, 1993; Depeche Mode, 1995; Producer of Recoil: Liquid, 2000; Strange Hours, 2000; One Night In Paris (DVD), 2002. *Website:* www.depechemode.com.

WILDHORN, Frank N; b. 29 Nov. 1958, New York, USA. Composer; Prod. 1 s. *Education:* College. *Career:* Long-term relationship with Warner Brothers Pictures to develope and compose both musical feature-length animated films and live-action projects; Creative Director of Atlantic Theatre. *Recordings:* Theatrical productions of: Jekyll and Hyde; The Scarlet Pimpernel; Victor/Victoria; Svengali; The Civil War; Over 200 songs. *Publications:* Song books: Jekyll and Hyde (romantic highlights and The Gothic Musical Thriller; The Scarlet Pimpernel; Linda Eder's albums: Linda Eder; So Much More; Something to Believe In; Christmas Stays The Same, 2000; A Little Bit of Heaven (single); Jung, Gift, 1998; Scarlet Pimpernel, Encore, 1999; Broadway in Love, 2000. *Honours:* Numerous Platinum, Gold discs; ASCAP writing awards. *Membership:* ASCAP; NAS; DGA; WGA. *Current Management:* Mark Shimmel Management, 8899 Beverly Blvd, Suite #100, Los Angeles, CA 90048, USA.

WILFRIED, (Scheutz); b. 24 June 1950, Bad Goisern, Austria. Vocalist; Actor. m. Marina, 15 April 1982, 1 s. *Education:* Trades Academy, English French studies. *Career:* Three No. 1 hits in Austria; 17 hits (studio); One live double LP and CD; Tours in Austria, Germany, France; About 10 films in major roles. *Recordings:* Run Rabbit Run; Highdelbeeren; Ziwui Ziwui; Mar

Oh Mary; Ikarus; Compilation: Grossten Hits Aus 20 Jahren, 1998; Television, film music: St Benedikt.

WILK, Bradley; b. 5 Sept. 1968, Portland, OR, USA. Musician (drums). *Career:* Mem., Rage Against the Machine, 1991–2000; Obtained major label record deal; Involvement in various causes incl. Fairness and Accuracy in Reporting, Rock for Choice and Refuse and Resist; Numerous tours incl. Lollapalooza; Tour with Wu Tang Clan; Contribution to soundtrack for film Godzilla, 1998; Founder mem., Audioslave, 2002–. *Recordings:* Albums: with Rage Against the Machine: Rage Against The Machine, 1992; Evil Empire, 1996; The Battle Of Los Angeles, 1998; Renegades, 2000; Live And Rare, 2002; with Audioslave: Audioslave, 2002. Singles: with Rage Against the Machine: Killing In The Name, 1993; Bullet In The Head, 1993; Bombtrack, 1993; Freedom, 1994; Bombtrack Plus Live, 1994; Bulls On Parade, 1996; People Of The Sun (EP), 1997; Guerilla Radio, 1999; Sleep Now In The Fire, 2000; with Audioslave: Cochise, 2003. *Address:* c/o Epic Records, 550 Madison Ave, New York, NY 10022-3211, USA. *Website:* www.audioslave.com.

WILKIE, Chris; b. 25 Jan. 1973, Gateshead, England. Songwriter; Musician (Guitar). *Career:* Member of British popgroup, Dubstar. *Compositions:* Anywhere; Just A Girl; I Will Be Your Girlfriend; Can't Tell Me; It's Clear; When You Say Goodbye; Wearchest; Week In, Week Out. *Recordings:* Stars; Not So Manic Now; Dubstar; Cathedral Park; Anxious; I (Friday Night), 2000; Albums: Disgraceful, 1995; Goodbye, 1997; Make It Better, 2000. *Honours:* Gold Disc for Disgraceful, album, 1996. *Current Management:* Stevo Pearce, Some Bizarre. *Address:* 124 New Bond St, London W1Y 9AE, England.

WILKINS, Keith Allen; b. 12 Sept. 1974, Farmington Hills, Michigan, USA. Musician (drums, clarinet); Lyricist. *Education:* 1 year Music Business Management; 4 years clarinet; 1 year drum class. *Career:* Studio drummer, lyricist, consulting manager; Wrote 2 songs with Donn Hecht, 1994; Collaborated with many musicans; Drummer in local concerts; Guest, television show, Dave's Garage. *Compositions:* Always, 1993; Hard Promises, 1993; News For You Baby, 1993; Everytime I Cry, 1995; Together, 1995; Good Lovin' Gone Bad, 1995; You're A Part of Me, 1996; Could It Be You, 1996; Down By The Ocean Shore, 1996; They'll Come A' Runnin', 1996; Magic Moment, 1996. *Recordings:* Music of America, 1993; Hollywood Gold, 1993; America Sings, 1995. *Publications:* Lock and Load magazine, 1993; Stars magazine, 1995; Jam magazine, 1995. *Honours:* Songwriter's Guild of America, Composer and Lyricist Certificate, 1999; Music Business Seminars Ltd, Diploma in Music Business Management, 1999. *Membership:* Charter mem., Rock 'N' Roll Hall of Fame and Museum; BMI; Nashville Songwriters Asscn International (NSAI); South West Virginia Songwriters Asscn (SVSA); Memphis Songwriters Asscn (MSA); Songwriters Guild of America (SGA); Florida Music Asscn (FMA); National Academy of Songwriters (NAS); Songwriters of Wisconsin (SOW); Rock Out Censorship (ROC); Central Florida Musicians Asscn; American Federation of Musicians (AFofM); The National Academy of Recording Arts and Sciences Inc; Housequake Recording Studios. *Address:* KAM Lyric Writing, 11124 64th Terrace N, Seminole, FL 33772, USA.

WILKINS, Mark Thomas; b. 14 Dec. 1956, Seattle, Washington, USA. Music Organization Exec. *Education:* BA Education, 2 teaching credentials, CSULA; Sherwood Oaks Experimental College, LACC, CSULA. *Career:* Member, Quincy Jones Workshops; Head of Promotion, Mystic Records, 1983–90; Founder, Affiliated Independent Record Labels (AIR Co), and International Record Promotion (IRP), 1990–93; Co-founder, CEO, Independent Network (Indy Net), 1993–; CEO, IMRA; AIM, ILTPA. *Recordings:* with Mandrill: Love Attack; with Bandit: 1 World 1 People. *Publications:* Soundtrack Mag; Author: Music Biz 411 (USA); 411 International (Europe, Asia); The Right Way To Run A Record Label, 1996; Forms and Contracts For Success, 1996; International Success In The Music Business, 1996. *Honours:* Innovations In Music. *Membership:* Founder, CEO, The Independent Network; Vice-President, Independent Music Asscn (IMA); Co-founder, Independent Music Retailer's Asscn (IMRA); Independent Live Talent Presenter's Asscn (ILTPA); Asscn of Independent Media (AIM).

WILKINSON, Alan James; b. 22 Aug. 1954, Ilford, Essex, England. Musician (soprano, alto, baritone saxophones). Vocalist. Partner, Gina Southgate. *Education:* BA Hons Degree Fine Art, Leeds Polytechnic, 1975–78. *Career:* Joined Crow, with Matthew Coe (aka Xero Slingsby), drummer Paul Hession, 1978; Art Bart and Fargo with Hession (toured in Europe), 1979; Trio with Akemi Kuniyoshi and Hession, 1982; Tour, Europe with drummer Steve Hubback; Duo with Hession, played 10th Free Music Festival, Antwerp and Netherlands, 1983; Art Initiative, Eindhoven; Started Termite Club, Leeds; Derek Bailey's Company, 1987; Italy, 1988, 1993; Sound Symposium, St Johns, Newfoundland, with Hession, Wilkinson, Fell, 1994; Radio 3, Jazz Today, 1987; Mixing It, 1993; CBC: Two New Hours, 1994. *Recordings:* with Hession, Wilkinson, Fell: Bogey's, 1991; foom! foom!, 1992; The Horrors of Darmstadt, 1994; The Saxophone Phenomenon, 1992; Registered Firm, 1998; with John Law Quartet: Exploded on Impact, 1992; Live solo recordings: Seedy Boy, 1994. *Publications:* Featured in: Penguin Guide To Jazz On CD; Guinness Encyclopedia of Popular Music. *Honours:* Several ACGB and ACE touring and study awards, 1985–95; LAB travel grant, 1994. *Membership:*

Musicians' Union; Director London Musicians Collective. *Address:* 36 Arbor Court, Queen Elizabeth's Walk, London N16 0QU, England.

WILKINSON, Gary; Record Prod; *Recordings:* Records Produced and Remixed: Fire Island; Farley and Heller; The Farm; Sunscreen; Janet Jackson; Roach Motel; Jimmy Somerville; Happy Mondays; M People; Pet Shop Boys; Run DMC; U2; *Recordings:* As Remixer/Producer: Inspiral Carpets, Life, 1990; The Farm, Spartacus, 1991; New Order, Regret, 1993; One Dove, Morning Dove White, 1993; Kylie Minogue, Confide in Me, 1994; Janet Jackson, Runaway, 1995; Michael Jackson, Blood on the Dance Floor, 1997; Sneaker Pimps, Spin Spin Sugar, 1997; Glasgow Gangster, Deeva Feeva, 1999; Badly Drawn Boy, 2000. *Current Management:* One Management Ltd, 43 St Alban's Ave, London W4 5JS, England.

WILKINSON, Peter; b. 9 May 1969, Liverpool, England. Musician (bass). *Career:* Fmr mem., Cast; Early tours supporting Elvis Costello and Oasis; Numerous headlining tours; Festival appearances; TV and radio appearances; Founding mem., Aviator, 2002–. *Recordings:* Albums: with Cast: All Change, 1995; Mother Nature Calls, 1997; Magic Hour, 1999; Beetroot, 2001; with Aviator: Huxley Pig—Pt 1, 2002. Singles: with Cast: Finetime, 1995; Alright, 1995; Free Me; Live the Dream, 1998; Guiding Star, 1998; Sandstorm, 1998; Walkaway, 1998.

WILLIAM-OLSSON, Staffan; b. 13 Dec. 1959, Gothenburg, Sweden. Jazz Musician (guitar); Composer; Arranger. 1 d. *Career:* Member, Norwegian hard-rock group Sons of Angels, 1989–91; Tours, USA, UK, Germany; Band disbanded, 1991; Now working with Norwegian soul/jazz group The Real Thing. *Recordings:* Albums: with Sons of Angels: Sons of Angels, 1990; with The Real Thing: The Real Thing, 1992; The Real Thing In New York, 1993; A Perfect Match, 1994; Shades of Blue, 1996; Contribution to: Jukka Linkola, Pegasos, 1996; Matz Nilsson, Moonroom. *Address:* Eikev 5, 1181 Oslo, Norway.

WILLIAMS, Andy; Musician (drums). *Career:* Mem., UK band, Sub Sub, late 1980s; Changed band name to Doves, 1998; Tours in UK and USA; Signed to Heavenly Recording, 2000. *Recordings:* Albums: with Doves: Lost Souls, 2000; The Last Broadcast, 2002. Singles: with Sub Sub: Ain't No Love (Ain't No Use); Firesuite; with Doves: Cedar (EP), 1998; Sea Song (EP), 1999; Here It Comes (EP), 1999; The Cedar Room, 2000; Catch The Sun; The Man Who Told Everything; There Goes The Fear, 2002. *Address:* c/o Heavenly Recording, PO Box 607, London SW6 4YY, England. *Website:* www.doves.net.

WILLIAMS, Andy (Howard Andrew); b. 3 Dec. 1928, Wall Lake, Iowa, USA. Vocalist. *Career:* Member, quartet with his three brothers; Own US radio shows; Backed Bing Crosby in film Going My Way, 1944; Other film appearances: Kansas City Kitty, 1944; I'd Rather Be Rich, 1964; Worked as The Williams Brothers, with Kay Thompson (pianist, singer), 1947–48; Solo singer, 1952–; Featured artist, Tonight Show, 2 years; Own weekly variety show, 1962–71. *Recordings:* Albums include: Moon River and Other Great Movie Themes; Days of Wine and Roses; The Wonderful World of Andy Williams; Dear Heart; Born Free; Love Andy; Honey; Happy Heart; Home Loving Man; Love Story; Solitaire; The Way We Were; Reflections; Greatest Love Classics; Christmas Album; Under Paris Skies; Branson City Limits; Christmas Treasures, 2001; Singles include: Canadian Sunset; Butterfly; I Like Your Kind of Love (duet with Peggy Powers); Lips of Wine; Are You Sincere; Promise Me Love; The Hawaiian Wedding Song; Lonely Street; The Village of St Bernadette; Can't Get Used To Losing You; Hopeless; A Fool Never Learns; (Where Do I Begin) Love Story; Solitaire; Almost There; Can't Take My Eyes Off You; Music To Watch Girls By.

WILLIAMS, Brad; b. 13 April 1968, Clatterbridge, England. Musician (guitar, bass, keyboards); Vocalist; Prod; Programmer. *Career:* Musician, 17 years; Performer, 12 years; Recording artist, 10 years; Teacher, 9 years; Exodus 1992 British tour supporting Mike Peters and The Poets of Justice; Subsequent recording and touring as guitarist in his band; Live performance, interview, regular airplay, Wirral Community Radio, 1995; Interview, Mersey Community Radio, 1995. *Recordings:* Over 50 original compositions by Mike Peters; The Next Sound You Hear, 1991; Upon a Jazz Top: Christmas Holiday Series, 1999; Piano on: Drew Phelps, Round To it, 2000. *Membership:* Musicians' Union. *Address:* c/o Paul Brown, The Image Business Ltd, Orleans House, Edmund St, Liverpool L3 9NG, England.

WILLIAMS, Claude; b. 22 Feb. 1908, Muskogee, Oklahoma, USA. Jazz Musician (violin, guitar). *Career:* Musician for 77 years; Played with: Charlie Parker; Lester Young; Mary Lou Williams; Oklahoma Blue Devils; The Pettifords Band; Andy Kirk; Don Byas; Buddy Tate; Lloyd Cole; Nat King Cole; Count Basie; Jay McShann; Sir Roland Hanna; Grady Tate; Ruth Brown; Bill Easley; Earl May; First recorded guitarist with Basie, 1936; Musician and bandleader, 1960s–70s; Concerts included Newport in New York; Monterey Festival; Played in Black and Blue, Paris and New York, 1980s; World-wide tours and concerts including: Carnegie Hall; President Clinton inaugural events, 1992; Jazz festivals at New Orleans; Monterey; Newport; Jazz Triumph, Puerto Rico; Master of The Folk Violin US Tour, 1994–95. *Recordings include:* Swing Time In New York; Man From Muskogee (with Jay McShann); Call For The Fiddler; Live At J's, Vols 1 and 2; King of Kansas City, 2000; Swingin' the Blues; Recorded and toured with Statesmen of Jazz (including Milt Hinton, Benny Waters, Jane Jarvis), 1994–95; Featured soloist, Lincoln Center Jazz Orchestra, directed by Wynton Marsalis, 1995. *Honours:* Best Guitarist of Year, Downbeat, 1936; First Inductee, Oklahoma Jazz Hall of Fame; Charlie Christian Jazz Award, Black Liberated Arts Inc (only recipient ever), 1994; Distinguished Achievement Award, Amherst University, 1995. *Current Management:* Russ Dantzler, Hot Jazz Management. *Address:* Suite 4FW, 328 W 43rd St, New York, NY 10036, USA.

WILLIAMS, Dar, (Dorothy Snowden); b. 19 April 1967, Mount Kisco, New York, USA. Vocalist; Musician (guitar); Songwriter. *Education:* Wesleyan University, Connecticut, BA in Theatre and Religion. *Career:* Has had material recorded by Joan Baez; Active in environmental issues and set up Snowden Environmental Trust. *Recordings:* Albums: I Have No History, 1990; All My Heroes Are Dead, 1991; The Honesty Room, 1993; Mortal City, 1996; End of Summer, 1997; Cry Cry Cry (with Lucy Kaplansky and Richard Shindell), 1998; The Green World, 2000; Out There Live, 2001; The Beauty of the Rain, 2003; features on Gone From Danger (with Joan Baez), 1997; Badlands – Bruce Springsteen Tribute, 2000. *Current Management:* c/o AF Entertainment, 29 Haines Rd, Bedford Hills, NY 10507, USA.

WILLIAMS, (David) Paul (Gifford), (Terry Day); b. 3 Sept. 1940, Kingston, Surrey, England. Composer; Music Prod. m. Rosalind Anne Burns, 3 Sept. 1965, 1 s., 2 d. *Education:* MA, Cambridge University; Royal College of Music; Jesus College, Cambridge. *Career:* BBC Senior Producer, 1980; Sony Award winner, McCartney, BBC series, 1988; Composer for film, television; Worked with Phil Manzanera on Nowomowa album, 1988; TV music, House of Gristle, BBC TV, 1994; BBC TV Out of This World, 1994; Mysteries, BBC TV, 1997–98; Growing Places, BBC TV, 1999. *Compositions:* Over 1,200 published for television, films. *Recordings:* 22 albums. *Honours:* 3 Sony radio awards, 1988, 1990, 1992; Stemra Award, Netherlands, 1994. *Membership:* BACS; PRS; Musicians' Union. *E-mail:* paul@paulwilliamsmusic.com.

WILLIAMS, Deniece, (Deniece Chandler); Vocalist. *Career:* Solo gospel/soul singer; Joined Stevie Wonder's backing group, Wonderlove; Recording artiste, including many duets with Johnny Mathis; Recorded first gospel album 1988. *Compositions:* Numerous including songs recorded by: Merry Clayton; The Emotions; The Whispers; Frankie Valli. *Recordings:* Albums: This Is Niecy, 1976; I'm So Proud, 1983; Let's Hear It For The Boy, 1984; Hot On The Trail, 1986; Water Under The Bridge, 1987; So Glad I Know, 1988; As Good As It Gets, 1989; Special Love, 1989; Lullabies to Dreamland, 1991; Love Solves It All, 1996; This Is My Song, 1998; Love Songs, 2000; Singles: Free (No. 1, UK), 1976; That's What Friends Are For, 1977; Too Much Too Little, Too Late, duet with Johnny Mathis (No. 1, USA), 1978; Let's Hear It For The Boy (No. 1, USA), 1984; Why You Wanna Do Me, 1996; Great Is Thy Faithfulness, 1996. *Address:* c/o Pyramid Entertainment Group, 89 Fifth Ave, Seventh Floor, New York, NY 10003, USA.

WILLIAMS, Don; b. 27 May 1939, Floydada, Texas, USA. Songwriter; Vocalist; Musician (guitar). *Career:* Member, Strangers Two; Pozo-Seco Singers; Solo artiste, 1971–; Film appearances: W W and The Dixie Dancekings; Smokey and The Bandit 2. *Recordings:* Albums: with the Poco-Seco Singers: Time, 1966; I Can Make It With You, 1967; Shades of Time, 1968; Solo albums: Don Williams Vols 1–3, 1973, 1974; You're My Best Friend, 1975; Harmony, 1976; Visions, 1977; Country Boy, 1977; Expressions, 1978; Portrait, 1979; I Believe In You, 1980; Especially For You, 1981; Listen To The Radio, 1982; Yellow Moon, 1983; Cafe Carolina, 1984; New Moves, 1986; Traces, 1987; One Good Well, 1989; As Long As I Have You, 1989; True Love, 1990; Currents, 1992; I've Got a Winner in You, 1993; Lord I Hope This Day Is Good, 1993; I Turn the Page, 1998; Various compilations; Singles include: Amanda; The Shelter of Your Eyes; I Recall A Gypsy Woman; You're My Best Friend; Tulsa Time; Till The Rivers All Run Dry; Some Broken Hearts Never Mend; Lay Down Beside Me; I Believe In You; If I Needed You (duet with Emmylou Harris); Good Ol' Boys Like Me; An Evening with Don Williams, Best of Live, 1994; Borrowed Tales, 1995; Flatlands, 1996; Pretty Little Baby Child, 1998. *Address:* c/o Don Williams Productions, PO Box 160206, Nashville, TN 37216, USA.

WILLIAMS, Doug; b. 22 Oct. 1950, Chicago, USA. Vocalist; Musician (bass guitar). 3 d. *Career:* Powerhouse, 1975–76; My Old School, 1985; Missing in Action; Marcia Hines Band; Renee Geyer Band; Hip Hop, 1988; Duffhead, 1990; The Black Mass, 1992; The Rockmelons, 1992; D Williams and the Black Mass, 1993. *Compositions:* Feel So Good, 5 Track EP, 1993; Stronger Together (The Rockmelons), lead vocals; Love is Gonna Bring You Home (The Rockmelons), lead vocals; Doug Williams L R Mix, 2000; 2 track EP, Walking on Thin Ice, second track (original) Fall into Love, 2000. *Recordings:* The Rockmelons, lead vocals; Form One Planet; My Island Home; Peter Andre; Kate Ceberano, backing vocals; Grace Knight, backing vocals; Swoop, backing vocals; Also worked with: Buddy Guy; Phil Guy. *Honours:* Chosen to sing to President Bill Clinton, Australia, 1996. *Membership:* APRA, Australia. *Current Management:* Milly Petriella, Playworks Entertainment Management. *Address:* PO Box 448, Crows Nest, NSW 2065, Australia.

WILLIAMS, Enid; Musician (bass guitar); Vocalist. *Career:* Founder mem., heavy metal band Painted Lady, with Kim McAuliffe; Joined by Kelly Johnson and Denise Dufort, 1978, band renamed Girlschool; Introduced to management deal with Bronze label by Lemmy from Motörhead, 1980; Supported Motorhead on their Overkill tour; Left band, 1981; Formed band, Framed; Worked with Dave Parsons, Biddu; Joined band, Moho Pack; Appeared in Fay Weldon's The Small Green Space and her own opera, The Waterfall; Teacher, performance and vocal skills; Formed band Strangegirls, with Toyah, Denise Dufort and Kim McAuliffe; Rejoined Girlschool, mid-1990s. *Recordings:* Albums: Demolition, 1980; Hit 'N' Run, 1981; Live, 1995; Race With The Devil (Live), 1998; Live On The King Biscuit Flower Hour, 1998; Can't Keep A Good Girl Down, 1999; Very Best Of Remastered, 2002; 21st Anniversary: Not That Innocent, 2002. Singles: Take It All Away; Race With The Devil; St Valentine's Day Massacre (EP with Motörhead, as Headgirl); Please Don't Touch, 1981; Hit And Run, 1981; C'mon Let's Go, 1981. *Address:* c/o PO Box 33446, London SW18 3XN, England. *Website:* www.girlschool.co.uk.

WILLIAMS, Geoffrey; b. 25 April 1964, London, England. Songwriter; Vocalist; Musician (guitar); *Compositions:* Songs for Beverly Hills 90210 album; Eternal; Colour Me Badd; The Drop, album, 1997. *Recordings:* Albums: The Drop, 1997; Lost in Dinosaur World, 1997; Prisoner of Love, 1997; Singles: It's Not a Love Thing, 1992; Drive, EP, 1996; I Guess I Will Always Love You, 1996; Sex Life, 1997; Deliver Me Up, 1997; Also worked with: Jimmy Somerville; Alison Limerick; Shaun Escoffery. *Membership:* Musicians' Union. *Current Management:* Hands On Management. *Address:* 3 Lambton Pl., London W11 2SH, England.

WILLIAMS, J. Owen; b. 1 Feb. 1959, Ireland. Vocalist; Songwriter; Musician (acoustic guitar). *Education:* Irish traditional music. *Career:* Glastonbury Festival, 1992, 1993; Milan, Turin festivals, Italy, 1992, 1993; Live radio sessions for Greater London Radio (GLR); London gig residency. *Recordings:* Albums: Ribbonmen, 1991; Sean One Shoe, 1994. *Membership:* Musicians' Union; PRS. *Current Management:* Freddie Daniels, Runaway Music. *Address:* 18c Alwyne Pl., Islington, London N1 2NL, England.

WILLIAMS, Jez; Musician (guitar); Songwriter. *Career:* Mem., UK band, Sub Sub, late 1980s; Changed band name to Doves, 1998; Tours in UK and USA; Signed to Heavenly Recording, 2000. *Recordings:* Albums: with Doves: Lost Souls, 2000; The Last Broadcast, 2002. Singles: with Sub Sub: Ain't No Love (Ain't No Use); Firesuite; with Doves: Cedar (EP), 1998; Sea Song (EP), 1999; Here It Comes (EP), 1999; The Cedar Room, 2000; Catch The Sun; The Man Who Told Everything; There Goes The Fear, 2002. *Address:* c/o Heavenly Recording, PO Box 607, London SW6 4YY, England. *Website:* www.doves.net.

WILLIAMS, John Towner; b. 8 Feb. 1932, Flushing, NY, USA. Composer. *Education:* Studied Music, UCLA and Juilliard School, New York. *Career:* Pianist, Columbia Pictures; Jazz Pianist, working with Henry Mancini on television scores; Worked solo on television soundtracks before progressing to film scores; Work with orchestras includes the American Film Orchestra, Boston Pops Orchestra, 1980–93; Cincinnati Pops, London Symphony Orchestra, Movin' Dream Orchestra, National Philharmonic Orchestra; Has also worked with the Chieftains, Ray Conniff, Sally Harmon and others. *Compositions:* Film scores: The Secret Ways, 1961; Diamond Head, 1962; None But The Brave, 1965; How To Steal A Million, 1966; Valley Of The Dolls, 1967; The Cowboys, 1972; The Poseidon Adventure, 1972; Tom Sawyer, 1973; Earthquake, 1974; The Towering Inferno, 1974; Jaws, 1975; The Eiger Sanction, 1975; Family Plot, 1976; Midway, 1976; The Missouri Breaks, 1976; Raggedy Ann And Andy, 1977; Black Sunday, 1977; Star Wars, 1977; Close Encounters Of The Third Kind, 1977; The Fury, 1978; Jaws II, 1976; Superman, 1978; Dracula, 1979; The Empire Strikes Back, 1980; Raiders Of The Lost Ark, 1981; E.T.: The Extra Terrestrial, 1982; Return Of The Jedi, 1983; Indiana Jones And The Temple Of Doom, 1984; The River, 1985; Space Camp, 1986; The Witches Of Eastwick, 1987; Empire Of The Sun, 1988; 1941, 1989; Always, 1989; Born On The Fourth Of July, 1989; Indiana Jones And The Last Crusade, 1989; Stanley And Iris, 1990; Presumed Innocent, 1990; Home Alone, 1990; Hook, 1991; JFK; Far and Away; Home Alone 2: Lost In New York; Jurassic Park, 1993; Schindler's List, 1993; Sabrina, 1995; The Reivers, 1995; Nixon, 1996; Sleepers, 1996; Rosewood, 1996; Land Of The Giants, 1997; Seven Years In Tibet, 1997; The Lost World: Jurassic Park, 1997; Amistad, 1997; Lost In Space, 1997; Time Tunnel, 1997; Saving Private Ryan, 1998; The Phantom Menace, 1999; Angela's Ashes, 1999; Harry Potter And The Sorcerer's Stone, 2001; Attack of the Clones, 2002; Minority Report, 2002; Harry Potter And The Chamber Of Secrets, 2002; Catch Me If You Can, 2002. *Recordings:* Recordings of film scores: John Williams Plays The Movies, 1996; Music From The Star Wars Saga, 1999; Jane Eyre, 1999; Compilations: Themes From Academy Award Winners; Over The Rainbow: Songs From The Movies, 1992; John Williams Conducting The Boston Pops, 1996; The Hollywood Sound, 1997; From Sousa To Spielberg; Best Of John Williams, 1998; Treesong, 2001; Call Of The Champions (official theme of 2002 Winter Olympics, Salt Lake City), 2001; John Williams Trumpet Concerto, 2002; American Journey, 2002. *Honours:* Five Academy Awards for Best Music, Original Score (for Fiddler on the Roof, Jaws, Star Wars, E.T., Schindler's List); Six BAFTA Awards, incl. Best Score (for Empire of the Sun), 1988; Two

Emmy Awards; Three Golden Globes; 16 Grammy Awards. *Address:* c/o Michael Gorfaine, Gorfaine & Schwartz, 13245 Riverside Dr., Suite 450, Sherman Oaks, CA 91423, USA. *Website:* www.johnwilliams.org.

WILLIAMS, John Charles; b. 8 Feb. 1941, Hammersmith, London. Composer; Arranger; Musician. m. Frances Margaret, 3 s., 1 d. *Education:* Acton Technical College, 1957–59. *Career:* Leader, Resident Big Band, Marquee Club, London, 1961–63; Formed Octet, 1969 and Big Band, 1973; Ensembles include saxophone quartet Changing Face, 1976–78, Trio Spectrum, 1985, Baritone Band, 1985; Played and recorded with Keith Tippett, Alan Cohen, Don Rendell; Instituted annual Summer Music Festival, Shropshire. *Compositions:* Four pieces for Jazz Soloists and Orchestra; Out of Focus; When Summers End Is Nighing; Tenorama, 2001. *Recordings:* Year of The Buffalo; Spotlite; Five Housman Settings and other jazz works; Other collaborations include: Centipede; New Perspectives; with John Williams' Baritone Band: Spotlite. *Membership:* Musicians' Union. *Current Management:* All Electric Theatre Productions, Unit 6, 94 Charlton Rd, Andover, Hants SP10 3JY, England. *Address:* Leasowes Bank Farm, Ratlinghope, Shrewsbury SY5 0SW, England.

WILLIAMS, Leroy Anthony; b. 4 Sept. 1962, London, England. Musician (drums, percussion). 1 s. *Career:* Played with: Five Star; Level 42; Simple Minds; Talk Talk; Hi Tension; Aswad; Roni Ben-Hur. *Recordings:* There's A Reason, Hi Tension. *Membership:* Musicians' Union. *Current Management:* Session Connection. *Address:* 12c Parkfield Cres., Harrow, Middlesex HA2 6JZ, England.

WILLIAMS, Linda; b. 7 July 1947, Anniston, Alabama, USA. Musician (guitar, banjo, mouth harp); Vocalist; Songwriter. m. Robin Williams, 2 June 1973. *Education:* BA Michigan State University; Piano lessons. *Career:* Began together, 1973; Worked with Garrison Keillor's Home Companion, as semi-regulars, 1975–; Numerous appearances, Grand Ole Opry, Nashville, Tennessee; Numerous television appearances include: Austin City Limits; Disney Specials; TNN Shows; Played all major festivals in USA, Canada; Two tours: Europe, UK; Carnegie Hall, 1987. *Compositions:* Songs recorded by: Emmylou Harris; Tom T Hall; George Hamilton IV; Holly Near; Tim and Molly O'Brien; The Seldom Scene. *Recordings:* 14 albums including, Devil of a Dream; Close As We Can Get; with Robin Williams: In The Company Of Strangers, 2000. *Publications:* Song Book of Original Pieces, Vol. 1, 1979. *Honours:* Peabody Award, Broadcasting, for work on a Prairie Home Companion, 1980. *Membership:* Country Music Asscn; International Bluegrass Music Asscn; The Folk Alliance.

WILLIAMS, Lucinda; b. 26 Jan. 1953, Lake Charles, LA, USA. Vocalist; Songwriter. *Career:* Played folk clubs in Texas; Solo artiste; Signed to Folkways Records; Signed to Rough Trade Records, 1988; Appeared on various tribute albums; Song, Still I Long For Your Kiss, for the film The Horse Whisperer, 1998. *Recordings:* Albums: Ramblin' On My Mind, 1979; Happy Woman Blues, 1980; Lucinda Williams, 1988; Sweet Old World, 1992; Car Wheels On A Gravel Road, 1998; Essence, 2001. *Honours:* Grammy Awards, Best Songwriter, 1994, Best Female Rock Vocal Performance, for Get Right With God, 2002. *Address:* c/o Lost Highway Records, Universal Music Group, Universal Studios, 100 Universal City Plaza, Universal City, CA 91608, USA. *Website:* www.lucindawilliams.com.

WILLIAMS, Marcus Christian; b. 25 Oct. 1965, Rochdale, England. Musician (bass guitar). *Education:* Art College, 1 year. *Career:* Tours: with Julian Cope in UK, Europe and Japan; with The Mighty Lemon Drops in UK (twice), Europe and USA and Canada (3 times); with Blue Aeroplanes in UK and Europe; with The Madonnas in UK; with Kirsty MacColl in UK, USA and Canada; Various appearances on television, radio and at festivals, with artists including Nick Heywood; Alison Moyet; Terry Wogan. *Recordings:* 4 albums with The Mighty Lemon Drops; 3 albums with Blue Aeroplanes, including: Cavaliers, 2000; 1 album with Hectors House; Played on two Lisa Stansfield albums. *Contributions to:* Don Diego, This Must Be Heaven, 1998, Isaac Curry, Lavender Bull, 1998, James Bignon, On the Other Side of Through, 1998, Heaven Belongs to You, 1999, as drummer; Various singles and sessions. *Membership:* Musicians' Union; PRS. *Address:* 5 Dralda House, Keswick Rd, London SW15 2JL, England.

WILLIAMS, Mason; b. 24 Aug. 1938, Abilene, Texas, USA. Composer; Writer; Performer; Musician (guitar); Vocalist. m. (1), 1 d., (2), (3), 1993. *Education:* Music major, Oklahoma City University, 3 years. *Career:* College student/folk singer, 1959–61; US Navy, 1962–63; Hollywood folk singer, songwriter, sideman, 1964–65; Television Writer, Smothers Brothers, Andy Williams, Glenn Campbell and Petula Clark, 1966–69; Musical performances at clubs, concerts, festivals, symphony orchestra, television, 1972–; Current concerts: Mason Williams and Friends, Symphonic Bluegrass, of Time and Rivers Flowing, X-Mas and Pop Shows. *Recordings:* 3 Folk, 1960–63; 6 Folk Anthologies and Them Poems, 1963–65; 5 Warner Bros LPs, 1968–71; Classical Gas, hit single, 1968; Albums: Fresh Fish, 1978; Of Time and Rivers Flowing, 1984; Classical Gas with Mannheim Steamroller, Pop, 1987; A Gift of Song, CD X-Mas, 1992; Of Time and Rivers Flowing, CD, 1996, reissued, 2000. *Publications:* The Mason Williams Reading Matter, 1969; Flavors, 1971; The

FCC Report, 1969; The Music of Mason Williams, 1992; 14 limited editions. *Honours:* 2 Grammy Awards; 1 Emmy Award; 1 Writers Guild Award; Hon. DMus, Oklahoma City University, 1995; Special Citation of Achievement for Classical Gas, BMI, 1999; University of Oregon, Distinguished Service Award, 1999; State of Oregon, Musicians Laureate, 2000. *Membership:* AFofM; AFTRA; WGAW; NARAS; NAS; SGA. *Address:* PO Box 5105, Eugene, OR 97405, USA.

WILLIAMS, Melanie Joy; b. 28 Oct. 1964, London, England. Vocalist; Songwriter. *Education:* Languages; English; History. *Career:* Television appearances: Top of the Pops; The Word; The Beat; Lily Savage; Passion; The O-Zone. *Recordings:* Albums: Temper Temper; Human Cradle, 1995; Singles: Ain't No Love (Ain't No Use), collaboration with Sub Sub (No. 3, UK), 1993; Everyday Thang, 1994; You Are Everything, 1995. *Honours:* Silver disc (UK); Gold disc (Australia). *Membership:* Musicians' Union; Equity. *Current Management:* Paul Craig, Sound Management. *Address:* 222 Lambolle Pl., London NW3 4PG, England.

WILLIAMS, Mervyn; b. 8 May 1957, St James, Jamaica. Audio Engineer. Fiancée, Kaye Troy E Janagalee, 1 s., 2 d. *Education:* Aquarius recording studio, studios overseas. *Career:* Several tours with Burning Spear. *Recordings:* with Jimmy Cliff; Burning Spear; Beres Hammond; Judy Mowatt; Mikey Dread; Roots Radics; Dwight Pinkney; Delroy Wilson; Vocalist on Tiger, Ras Portraits, 1997. *Honours:* Jamaica Federation of Music (JFM). *Membership:* MFM. *Address:* 3 Tunbridge Dr., Kingston 19, Jamaica.

WILLIAMS, Michelle; b. 1 Dec. 1980, Rockford, IL, USA. Vocalist. *Career:* Joined Destiny's Child group, February 2000; Numerous TV and live performances, including tour with Christina Aguilera, 2000; Appeared at United We Stand concert, USA, 2001; Simultaneous solo career, 2001–; Released solo gospel album, 2002. *Recordings:* Albums: with Destiny's Child: Survivor, 2001; Eight Days Of Christmas, 2001; This Is The Remix, 2002; Solo: Heart To Yours, 2002. Singles: with Destiny's Child: Independent Women (from film Charlie's Angels, No. 1, UK, USA), 2000; Survivor, 2001; Bootylicious, 2001; Emotion, 2001; Eight Days Of Christmas, 2001. *Honours:* American Music Awards, Favorite Soul/R&B Group, 2001, Favorite Pop/Rock Album, for Survivor, Favorite Pop/Rock Band, Duo or Group, 2002; Grammy Awards, Best R&B Song, Say My Name, Best R&B Performance by a Duo or Group with Vocal, Say My Name, 2001; NAACP Image Award for Outstanding Duo or Group, Say My Name, 2001; Best R&B Video MTV Video Award, Say My Name, 2001; Sammy Davis Jr Award for Entertainer of the Year, Soul Train Awards, 2001; BRIT Award, Best International Group, 2002; MOBO Award, Best Gospel Act, 2002; Gold, Platinum and multi-Platinum Awards. *Address:* c/o Mathew Knowles, Music World Entertainment, 9898 Bissonnet, Suite 625, Houston, TX 77036, USA. *Website:* www.destinyschild.com.

WILLIAMS, Otis Clayborn; b. 30 Oct. 1941, Texarkana, Texas, USA. Vocalist; Songwriter; Prod. m. 28 Jan. 1982, 1 d. *Career:* Member, Temptations; Television specials; Motown revue tours; Countless tours. *Recordings:* 51 albums (31 gold and platinum records); Singles: My Girl, 1965; Cloud Nine, 1968; Get Ready, 1969; Ball Of Confusion, 1970; Papa Was A Rolling Stone, 1972; Just My Imagination, 1973. *Publications:* Temptations, life story written by Otis Williams. *Honours:* Rock 'n' Roll Hall of Fame; Star On Hollywood Boulevard; 31 Gold, Platinum records. *Membership:* ASCAP. *Current Management:* William Morris, Star Direction Management. *Address:* 9255 Sunset Blvd, Suite 610, Los Angeles, CA 90069, USA.

WILLIAMS, Pharrell; b. Virginia, USA. Prod; Remixer; Songwriter; Musician. *Career:* Formed The Neptunes production duo, with Chad Hugo, 2000–; Formed recording act, N.E.R.D. (Nobody Ever Really Dies), 2001–; Co-founder, Star Trak Entertainment label; Worked with: Air, Mary J. Blige, Foxy Brown, Jay-Z, Kelis, Ludacris, Mystikal, Nelly, No Doubt, *NSYNC, Ol' Dirty Bastard, Britney Spears, Justin Timberlake, Usher. *Recordings:* with N.E.R.D.: Albums: In Search Of..., 2001. Singles: Lapdance, 2001. *Honours:* Source Award, Producer of the Year, The Neptunes, 2001; MOBO Award, Best Producer, The Neptunes, 2002. *Address:* c/o Virgin Records, 304 Park Ave S, Fifth Floor, New York, USA. *Website:* www.n-e-r-d.com.

WILLIAMS, Philip; b. 18 Oct. 1962, England. Musician (bass guitar); Vocalist. *Education:* BEC in Business; Diploma in Jazz and Light Music, Chichester. *Career:* Tours and various television appearances including, Kim Wilde; Walk On Fire; Curtis Stigers; Jordinaires; Greg Parker; Tony Hadley; Gary Barlow; Rick Wakeman; Vonda Shepherd. *Recordings:* with Tony Hadley: Tony Hadley, 1997; True, 2001; with Rick Wakeman: Return To The Centre Of The Earth, 1999. *Membership:* Musicians' Union. *Current Management:* Session Connection. *Address:* 62 New Rd, Staines, Middlesex TW18 3DA, England.

WILLIAMS, (Randall) Hank, Jr; b. 26 May 1949, Shreveport, Louisiana, USA. Country Vocalist; Musician. m. Mary Jane Williams, 2 s., 3 d. *Career:* Performer since aged 8; Debut appearance Grand Ole Opry, 1960; Recording debut aged 14; Recorded with father Hank Williams; Connie Francis; Toured with band, the Cheatin' Hearts; Recorded as Luke The Drifter, 1960s–70s;

Career halted by mountaineering accident, 1975–77. *Recordings:* 64 albums include: Your Cheatin' Heart (film soundtrack), 1964; Living Proof, 1974; Hank Williams Jr and Friends, 1976; 14 Greatest Hits, 1976; One Night Stands, 1977; The New South, 1977; Family Tradition, 1979; Rowdy, 1981; Hank Live, 1987; Born To Boogie, 1987; Pure Hank, 1991; Maverick, 1992; Out of Left Field, 1993; Hog Wild, 1995; Wham Bam Sam, 1996; Stormy, 1999; Hank Williams Jr. & Friends, 2000; *Compilations* include: The Bocephus Box, 2000; Essential, 2001; *Singles* include: Long Lonesome Blues; Standing In The Shadows (US Country No. 1); All My Rowdy Friends (Have Settled Down), 1981; Recorded with numerous artists including: Ray Charles; Willie Nelson; John Lee Hooker; Johnny Cash; Reba McEntire; Huey Lewis; Tom Petty; Waylon Jennings; George Jones; George Thorogood; Travis Tritt. *Publications:* Living Proof (with Michael Bane). *Honours:* 5 Entertainer Awards for country music; Youngest songwriter to win BMI citation, age 16; Emmy, Monday Night Football theme, ABC, 1990; Grammy Award, There's A Tear In My Bear, 1990; Gold Medal, International Film and TV Festival, New York; Platinum and Gold albums. *Membership:* BMI; ASCAP; NEA; CMA; NARAS; ACM; AMA; AFTRA; SAG. *Current Management:* Merle Kilgore Management, 2 Music Circle S, Nashville, TN 37203, USA.

WILLIAMS, Robbie (Robert Peter); b. 13 Feb. 1974, Stoke-on-Trent, Staffordshire, England. Vocalist. *Career:* Mem., UK all-male vocal group, Take That, 1990–95; Solo artiste, 1995–; Signed contract with EMI, 2002; Television includes: Take That and Party (Channel 4), 1993; Take That Away documentary (BBC2), 1993; Take That In Berlin, 1994. *Recordings:* Albums: with Take That: Take That And Party, 1992; Everything Changes, 1993; Greatest Hits, 1996; Solo: Life Thru A Lens, 1997; I've Been Expecting You, 1998; The Ego Has Landed (USA), 1999; Sing When You're Winning, 2000; Swing When You're Winning, 2001; Escapology, 2002. *Singles* with Take That: It Only Takes A Minute, 1992; I Found Heaven, 1992; A Million Love Songs, 1992; Could It Be Magic, 1993; Pray, 1993; Relight My Fire (with Lulu), 1993; Babe, 1993; Why Can't I Wake Up With You, 1993; Love Ain't Here Anymore, 1994; Everything Changes, 1994; Sure, 1994; Back For Good, 1995; Never Forget, 1995; Solo: Freedom, 1996; Old Before I Die, 1997; Lazy Days, 1997; South Of The Border, 1997; Angels, 1997; Let Me Entertain You, 1998; Millennium, 1998; No Regrets, 1998; Strong, 1999; She's The One/It's Only Us, 1999; Rock DJ, 2000; Kids (with Kylie Minogue), 2000; Supreme, 2000; Let Love Be Your Energy, 2001; Eternity/Road To Mandalay, 2001; Better Man, 2001; Somethin' Stupid (with Nicole Kidman), 2001; Feel, 2002. *Publications:* Robbie Williams: Somebody Someday, 2001. *Honours:* Smash Hits Awards, seven in 1992, one in 1996, Best Male, 1998; BRIT Awards, Best British Single, 1994, 1996, 1999, 2000, 2001, Best British Male Solo Artist, 1999, 2001, 2002, 2003; MTV Award, Best Male, 1998. *Membership:* Equity; Musicians' Union; MCPS; PRS; ADAMI; GVC; AURA. *Current Management:* IE Music Ltd, 59A Chesson Rd, London W14 9QS, England. *Address:* c/o EMI Group PLC, 4 Tenterden St, Hanover Sq., London W1A 2AY, England. *Website:* www.robbiewilliams.com.

WILLIAMS, Robin; b. 16 March 1947, Charlotte, North Carolina, USA. Musician (guitar, banjo, mouth harp); Vocalist; Songwriter. m. Linda, 2 June 1973. *Education:* BA, Presbyterian College. *Career:* Solo artiste, 1969–73; Began with Linda (wife), 1973; Worked with Garrison Keillor's Prairie Home Companion, as semi-regulars, 1975–; Numerous appearances: Grand Ole Opry, Nashville, Tennessee; Numerous television appearances include: Austin City Limits; Disney Specials; TNN Shows; Played all major festivals in USA, Canada; Toured Europe, UK, 2 times, played Carnegie Hall, 1987. *Recordings:* 14 albums, lates, Devil of Dream; with Linda Williams: In The Company Of Strangers, 2000; Appears on: My Life, with Iris Dement, 1993; Songs recorded by Emmylou Harris; Tom T Hall; George Hamilton IV; Holly Near; Tim and Molly O'Brien; The Seldom Scene. *Publications:* Song Book of original pieces, Vol. I, 1979. *Honours:* Peabody Award for Broadcasting, for work on Prairie Home Companion, 1980. *Membership:* Country Music Asscn; International Bluegrass Music Asscn; The Folk Alliance. *Current Management:* Music Tree. *Address:* 1414 Pennsylvania Ave, Pittsburgh, PA 15233, USA.

WILLIAMS, Tim; b. 11 Aug. 1948, California, USA. Songwriter; Musician (Multi Instrumentalist). m. Johanne Deleevw, 2 s. *Career:* Coffee Houses; Concerts; Signed with Epic Records, 1968. *Compositions:* My Heart Can't Take Another Rodeo; Trying to Rope the Wind; Au Contraire Mon Frere. *Recordings:* Blues Full Circle, 1969; Writing This Song, 1977; Enough to be Remembered, 1982; Riverboat Rendezvous, 1995; Creole Nightingale, 1996; Indigo Incidents, 1997. *Honours:* Magazine Awards; Betty Mitchell Theatre Award. *Current Management:* Cayuse Music. *Address:* 833 17th Ave SE, Calgary, AB T2G 1J2, Canada.

WILLIAMS, Victoria Ann; b. 23 Dec. 1958, Shreveport, Louisiana, USA. Vocalist; Songwriter; Musician (guitar, banjo, dulcimer, piano, mandolin, harmonica). m. Mark Olson, 22 Dec. 1993. *Education:* 2 years' college; Some music theory, college; Piano aged 8–10. *Career:* Solo recording artiste, 1987–; Appearances include: Tonight Show with Johnny Carson; Also with Jay Leno; David Letterman with Dave Pirman; Today Show; Good Morning America; Dave Stewart Show; Politically Incorrect, Comedy Channel; MTV Host twice. *Recordings:* Albums: Happy Come Home, 1987; Swing The Statue, 1990; Sweet Relief (compilation of own compositions recorded by artists including

Lou Reed, Michael Penn, Evan Dando, Lucinda Williams, Michelle Shock, Jay Hawks, Michael Scott, Maria McKee; Pearl Jam, Soul Asylum), 1993; Loose, 1994; This Moment Live In Toronto, with the Loose Band, 1995; Gas, Food and Lodging (film soundtrack), 1995; Lilith Compilation, from tour, 1997; Musings of a Creek Dipper, 1998; The Original Harmony Ridge Creek Dippers, 1998; Pacific Coast Rambler, 1998; Zola and the Tulip Tree, 1999; Water to Drink, 2000; Backing vocals for recordings by: The Jayhawks; Giant Sand; Jimmie Dale Gilmore; Tammy Rogers; Ron Surrey; Jim White. *Membership:* US Musicians' Union; AFTRA; SAG. *Current Management:* Danny Heaps, PO Box 23, Pioneertown, CA 92268, USA.

WILLIAMSON, Astrid; b. 28 Nov. 1968, Shetland Islands, Scotland. Musician (piano, guitar); Vocalist. *Education:* BA, Music, Royal Scottish Academy. *Career:* British tour with Suede; Support to Bryan Ferry; Melody Maker tour. *Recordings:* with Goya Dress: Singles: Bedroom Cinema, 1995; Crush, 1995; Glorious, 1996; Albums: Rooms, 1996; with Hope Blister, Smile's OK, 1998; with Electronic: Vivid Pt. 2; Late at Night Pt. 1 and 2, 1999; Solo: Boy For You, 1998. *Current Management:* Nick Moore, Splash Management. *Address:* 328 Grays Inn Rd, Kings Cross, London WC1X 8BZ, England.

WILLIAMSON, Cris; b. 15 Feb. 1947, Deadwood, South Dakota, USA. Vocalist; Songwriter; Musician (keyboards, guitar). *Education:* BA, University of Denver; 7 years piano, 7 years voice. *Career:* Performances include 3, Carnegie Hall, New York (2 sell-outs); Newport Folk Festival; 25 years touring include Europe; Australia; Russia; Several documentary scores; 3 film scores; Play, Blue Fish Cove (Last Summer Of), feature song, Don't Lose Heart. *Recordings:* Albums: Artistry of Cris Williamson, 1963; The World Around Cris Williamson, 1965; Cris Williamson, Ampex, 1971; The Changer and The Changed, 1974; Live Dream, 1977; Strange Paradise, 1978; Lumiere, 1981; Blue Rider, 1982; Meg and Cris at Carnegie Hall, 1983; Portrait, 1983; Prairie Fire, 1984; Snow Angel, 1985; Wolf Moon, 1988; Country Blessed, 1989; The Best of Cris Williamson, 1990; Circle of Friends, 1991; Postcards From Paradise, (with Tret Fure), 1993; Between The Covers (with Tret Fure); Radio Quiet, 1999; Ashes, 2001. *Honours:* Parents Choice Award, Lumiere, 1982; Cable Car Award, Outstanding Recording Artist, 1983; 1990; City and County of San Francisco, State of California Honour Award, Outstanding Performer and Musician, 1988. *Membership:* AFofM; AFTRA. *Current Management:* Tam Martin, Beachfront Bookings. *Address:* PO Box 970, Marcola, OR 97454–0970, USA.

WILLIAMSON, Harry; b. 12 May 1950, Ilfracombe, Devon, England. Composer; Musician (guitar); Prod. Divorced, 1 d. *Education:* Physics, London University; Chorister at Exeter Cathedral; seventh grade piano and guitar. *Career:* Collaborated with Anthony Phillips (Genesis), 2 albums; Worked with Gong and Mother Gong, including tours USA, Europe, 1979–; Currently part of Far From The Madding Crowd, with Australian singer Liz Van Dort. *Compositions include:* Nuclear Waste, featuring Sting. *Recordings:* with Sphynx: Xitintoday; with Anthony Phillips: Tarka (No. 1, New Music Charts), 1988; The Gypsy Suite; 12 albums with Mother Gong/Gong; Far From The Madding Crowd; Solo: Life In The World Unseen, 2001. *Membership:* PRS; MCPS; Musicians' Independent Producer, USA, 1986. *Membership:* PRS; MCPS; Musicians' Union. *Address:* PO Box 2237, St Kilda West, Melbourne, Victoria 3182, Australia.

WILLIAMSON, John Robert; b. 1 Nov. 1945, Victoria, Australia. Vocalist; Songwriter. m., 2 c. *Career:* Singer songwriter, in a career spanning over 30 years, selling over 2.5m. albums. *Compositions include:* Love Is A Good Woman; True Blue; Home Among The Gum Trees; Prettiest Girl In The Kimberley; This Is Australia Calling; Raining Of The Rock; Rosewood Hill. *Recordings:* 29 albums. *Publications:* Books and songbooks. *Honours:* Numerous Golden Guitars, for Album of the Year, Biggest Selling Album of the Year, Male Vocalist of the Year, Song of the Year, Heritage Award, Video Clip of the Year, Inducted to Roll of Renown, 1997; Numerous MO Awards, for Best Male Country Performer of Previous Year, Best Country Performer, Most Successful Attraction of the Year; Two ARIA Awards, Best Australian Country Record; Advance Australia Award, for contribution to the arts and environment; Advance Australia Foundation Ambassadorship; A.M. *Membership:* Australian Conservation Foundation; Bush Heritage Fund; Australian National Museum; Country Music Asscn of Australia, Chair., 2003–; Landcare Australia. *Address:* PO Box 399, Epping, NSW 1710, Australia. *Telephone:* (2) 9868-3888. *Fax:* (2) 9868-1501. *E-mail:* trueblue@ozemail.com.au. *Website:* www.johnwilliamson.com.au.

WILLIAMSON, (John Robert) Graeme; b. Montréal, QC, Canada. Musician (guitar); Vocalist; Songwriter. m. Iris Jamieson, 10 June 1995. *Education:* MA, Glasgow University. *Career:* Frequent live television CBC (national) television and local television, 1984–85; Radio: Live concert broadcasts and tours, Canada; Retired from live performance, 1985. *Compositions:* Might As Well Be On Mars; Every Man and Every Woman Is A Star; Let Your Light Shine; Rubber Girl. *Recordings:* 3 tracks, album, 1970; Albums with Pukka Orchestra: Pukka Orchestra, 1984; Dear Harry, 1993; Palace of Memory, 1986. *Honours:* Casby Award (Canada), 1984. *Membership:* SOCAN (Canada). *Address:* 38 Victoria Crescent Rd, Glasgow G12 9DE, Scotland.

WILLIS, Doug. See: LEE, Dave.

WILLIS, Gary Glen; b. 28 March 1957, Longview, Texas, USA. Musician (electric bass); Composer. m. Pamela Nichols, 11 April 1991. *Education:* Kiljore Jr College; East Texas State University; North Texas State University. *Career:* Co-founder, co-leader of Tribal Tech, with Scott Henderson, 1983–; Annual tours: USA; Europe; South America; Performed, recorded with: Allan Holdsworth; Wayne Shorter; Hubert Laws; Wayne Johnson; Tim Weston & Shelby Flint. *Recordings:* Albums: Tribal Tech; Spears, 1985; Dr Hee, 1987; Nomad, 1989; Tribal Tech, 1991; Illicit, 1992; Face First, 1993; Reality Check, 1995; No Sweat, 1997; Bent, 1998. *Publications:* Instructional Video: Progressive Basics, 1991; Book: Lessons With The Greats For Bass, 1995.

WILLOUGHBY, Brian; b. 20 Sept. 1949, Glenarm, Co Antrim, Northern Ireland. Musician (guitar). *Education:* Post-graduate level French. *Career:* Toured and recorded with: The Strawbs, Mary Hopkin, Cathryn Craig, Nanci Griffith, Joe Brown, Roger Whittaker, New World, Brian Connolly, Jim Diamond, The Monks, Monty Python, and numerous other artistes. *Contributions to:* Musicians Only guitar reviews; Fender Frontline article on guitar tunings. *Honours:* Gold disc, The Monks. *Membership:* Musicians' Union; Institute of Linguists. *Address:* 47 Manygate Lane, Shepperton TW17 9EQ, England.

WILLS, Mark, (Daryl Mark Williams); b. 8 Aug. 1973, Cleveland, Tennessee, USA. Country vocalist. *Career:* Won Buckboard Country Music Showcase talent show at 17, leading to regular spot; Continued there for five years, augmented by demo work in Atlanta area and, eventually, demo work in Nashville; Secured deal with Mercury Records after being spotted at a Buckboard show by songwriter Carson Chamberlain and writer/performer Keith Stegall; The pair produced moderately successful self-titled debut album, 1996; Continued to sell consistently, making regular visits to Billboard singles and albums chart; Took unusual step of covering contemporary R&B hits, Brian McKnight's Back At One and Brandy's Almost Doesn't Count, on Permanently album, 2000. *Recordings include:* Jacob's Ladder, 1996; Places I've Never Been, 1997; I Do (Cherish You), Don't Laugh At Me, 1998; Wish You Were Here, She's In Love, 1999; Back At One, 2000; Albums include: Mark Wills, 1996; Wish You Were Here, 1998; Permanently, 2000; Loving Every Minute, 2001. *Address:* c/o Country Music Asscn, 1 Music Circle S, Nashville, TN 37203, USA. *Website:* www.markwills.com.

WILSON, Allan; b. 5 Sept. 1949, London, England. Conductor. m. 25 Jan. 1986, 2 d. *Education:* State University of New York; Studied trumpet, composition, conducting, London's Royal Academy of Music. *Career:* Teacher, Conducting, orchestral training, State University of New York; Lecture recitals, Britain; USA; Canada; Appearances as trumpet player; Specialist conductor, film soundtrack music; Film credits include: by Colin Towns: The Puppet Master; Fellow Traveller; Wolves of Willoughby Chase; Bellman and True; Knights and Emeralds; by Chris Young: The Dark Half; Hellbound: Hellraiser II; by Basil Polidouris: Lassie; by Loek Dikker: Body Parts; Television music includes: by Colin Towns: Clarissa; Capital City; The Fifteen Streets; Blind Justice. *Recordings include:* Conductor: Many film soundtracks include: The Fly II, 1989; Sundown, 1989; Sleepy Hollow, 1999; Classical works by Mozart, Holst, Wagner, with orchestras and ensembles such as: National Studio Orchestra; London Wind Ensemble; Munich Symphony Orchestra; Hungarian State Orchestra; The Mercury Players; Festival Brass of London; Symphonie-Orchester Graunke. *Current Management:* Soundtrack Music Management. *Address:* 22 Ives St, Chelsea, London SW3 2ND, England.

WILSON, Ann; b. 19 June 1951, San Diego, California, USA. Vocalist. 1 d. *Career:* Member, groups Ann Wilson and The Daybreaks; Bordersong; The Army; Renamed White Heart; Later became Heart, 1974–; UK debut, London, 1976; Regular US and international tours with artistes including Queen; Tears For Fears; Michael Bolton; Cheap Trick; Black Crowes; Concerts include: California Jam II Festival, 1978; Bread and Roses Festival, 1981; Benefit concert for local environmental groups, Seattle, 1990; Benefit for Seattle centre for victims of child abuse, 1992; Also member of side project The Lovemongers; Performed with Alice In Chains, animal rights benefit concert, Los Angeles, 1992. *Recordings:* Albums: with Heart: Dreamboat Annie, 1975; Little Queen, 1977; Magazine, 1978; Dog and Butterfly, 1978; Bebe Le Strange, 1980; Private Audition, 1982; Passionworks, 1983; Heart (No. 1, USA), 1985; Bad Animals, 1987; Brigade, 1990; Rock The House Live!, 1991; Desire Walks On, 1993; The Road Home, 1996; Hit singles include: Magic Man, 1976; Barracuda, 1977; Straight On, 1978; Tell It Like It Is, 1981; How Can I Refuse, 1984; What About Love?, 1985; Never, 1985; These Dreams (No. 1, USA), 1986; Nothin' At All, 1986; If Looks Could Kill, 1986; Alone (No. 1, USA), 1987; Who Will You Run To, 1987; There's The Girl, 1988; What About Love, 1988; All I Wanna Do Is Make Love To You, 1990; Stranded, 1990; Will You Be There (In The Morning), 1993; Solo single: The Best Man In The World, from film The Golden Child, 1987; Duet with Robin Zander: Surrender To Me, from film Tequila Sunrise, 1989; with The Lovermongers: Battle of Evermore, from film Singles, 1992; Albums: Whirlygig, 1997; Here is Christmas, 1998; Guest vocalist, Sap (EP), Alice In

Chains, 1992. *Contributions to:* Heats, Smoke, 1998; Renaissance Album, 1998; Love Shouldn't Hurt, 1998; Golden Child, 1998; Treason, Spinning, 2001. *Current Management:* Borman Entertainment Inc, 1250 Sixth St, Suite 401, Santa Monica, CA 90401, USA.

WILSON, Brian; b. 20 June 1942, Inglewood, CA, USA. Musician (bass, keyboards); Vocalist; Composer; Songwriter; Prod. *Career:* Founder member, the Beach Boys, 1961–; Retired from live performance, to concentrate on composing and recording, 1964–; Appearances include: Australian tour, 1964; Headlines Million Dollar Party, Honolulu, 1964; US tour, 1964; Established Brother Records label, 1967; Concert at International Center, Honolulu, 1967; Plays with Beach Boys, Whiskey-A-Go-Go, Los Angeles, 1970; Filmed for NBC Special, 1976; Presenter, Don Kirshner's Second Annual Rock Music Awards, Hollywood, 1976; 15th Anniversary Beach Boys show, 1976; Rejoins band for US concerts, 1989; Solo appearance, China Club, Hollywood, 1991; Documentaries include: Prime Time Live, ABC, 1991; I Just Wasn't Made For These Times, BBC, 1995. *Compositions:* Many hit songs include: Caroline No; Co-writer, California Girls; Good Vibrations; Fun Fun Fun. *Recordings:* Albums include: Surfin' Safari, 1962; Surfer Girl, 1963; Little Deuce Coupe, 1963; Shut Down Vol. 2, 1964; All Summer Long, 1964; Surfin' USA, 1965; Beach Boys Party, 1966; Pet Sounds, 1966; Beach Boys Today!, 1966; Smile, 1967; Surfer Girl, 1967; Smiley Smile, 1967; Wild Honey, 1968; 15 Big Ones, 1976; The Beach Boys Love You, 1977; Solo albums: Brian Wilson, 1988; I Just Wasn't Made For These Times, 1995; Presents Pet Sounds Live, 2002; Pet Projects—The Brian Wilson Productions, 2003; Contributor, vocals for film soundtrack Shell Life. Singles include: Surfin' USA; Surfer Girl; Little Deuce Coupe; In My Room; I Get Around; When I Grow Up To Be A Man; Dance Dance Dance; Producer: Help Me Rhonda; Barbara Ann; Caroline No; Sloop John B; God Only Knows; Good Vibrations; Wouldn't It Be Nice; Friends; Do It Again; I Can Hear Music; Brian Wilson, 1988; Sweet Insanity, 1990; I Just Wasn't Made for These Times, 1995; Orange Crate Art, 1995; Imagination, 1998; Live At the Roxy Theatre, 2000. *Honours:* Rock and Roll Hall of Fame, 1988; Special Award of Merit, 1988. *Current Management:* Elliott Lott, Boulder Creek Entertainment Corp, 4860 San Jacinto Circle W, Fallbrook, CA 92028, USA.

WILSON, Brian Scott; b. 12 Nov. 1962, Massachusetts, USA. Composer; Conductor; Jazz Musician (piano). m. Ruth, 1 s. *Education:* BMus, New England Conservatory; MA, University of Chicago; DMus, University of Arizonia. *Career:* Professor of Music, Composer in Residence, Hartwick College, NY, 1992–; Faculties, Hartwick College Summer Music Festival and Institute in Oneonta. *Recordings:* Orchestral, My Mother's Irises; Wandering The River; The First Sea Shell; The Flat Top Roof; Symphony No. 1, Desert Scenes; Symphony No. 2, Modes of Transportation; Band, Fastfare; Melting Pot; Choral, Jabberwocky; Three Songs of Nature; Joy; Wings; Chamber Music Including, The Avanti Feels Glued to the Road; Sentiments; Tuba Cat Fanfare; Avinu Malkaynu; Musicals including, The Birds; Speak of The 20s; The Knights; Operas including, Agamemnon; incidental music to Medea; The Bachal. *Honours:* Include, Winner of the International Trombone Asscn Composition Competition, 1998; Fellowship to Composers Conference Center for New Music, Duquesne University; James Madison Flute Choir Composition Competition Prize; ASCAP Distribution Award. *Membership:* Include, American Composers Forum; American Music Center; ASCAP; College Band Directors National Asscn; Conductors Guild; Kappa Kappa Psi; Phi Mu Alpha; Pi Kappa Lambda. *Address:* 1 Tilton Ave, Oneonta, NY 13820, USA.

WILSON, Cassandra; b. Jackson, Mississippi, USA. Jazz Vocalist. *Education:* Listening to father, Herman B Fowlkes, jazz musician. *Career:* Started playing guitar aged 6; Songwriting at 12; Solo performer as folk and blues singer, turned to jazz; Regular collaborations with saxophonist Steve Coleman; Signed to Blue Note Records. *Recordings:* Albums include: Point of View, 1986; Days Aweigh, 1987; Blue Skies, 1988; Jumpworld, 1990; She Who Weeps, 1991; Blue Light 'Til Dawn, 1993; New Moon Daughter, 1996; Blue Moon Rendezvous, 1998; Traveling Miles, 1999; Belly Of The Sun, 2002; Also featured vocalist on other artist's works, including: Doug Hammond; Dave Holland; Angelique Kidjo; Wynton Marsalis; Courtney Pine; The Roots; Chris White. *Current Management:* Dream Street Management, 1460 Fourth St, Suite 205, Santa Monica, CA 90401, USA.

WILSON, Damian Augustine Howitt; b. 11 Oct. 1969, Guildford, Surrey, England. Vocalist; Songwriter; *Recordings:* Albums: with Landmarq: Solitary Witness, 1992; Infinity Parade, 1993; The Vision Pit, 1995; with Threshold: Wounded Land, 1993; with LaSalle, 1994; Vocals for: Ayreon: Universal Migrator, 2000; Ayreonauts Only, 2001; Contributions to: Tribute to the Late Joseph T, 1996. *Honours:* Best Vocalist, Classic Rock Society, 1993.

WILSON, Dennis Edward; b. 22 July 1952, Greensboro, North Carolina, USA. Musician (trombone). m. Rebecca Elvert, 12 July 1986, 1 s. *Education:* MusB in Education, Berklee College of Music, Boston, 1974. *Career:* Trombonist, Musical director, Lionel Hampton Orchestra, 1974–76; Teacher, Choral director, NY schools, 1976–77; Trombonist arranger, Count Basie Orchestra, 1977–87; Music production manager, Count Basie Enterprises, 1987–; Trombonist, arranger, Frank West Orchestra, 1990–; Also arranger, conductor, Manhattan Transfer, Blee Blop Blues, 1985; Trombonist, Dizzy Gillespie Orchestra, 1988; Creator, executive producer, Count Basie Orchestra Big Band Festival; Also collaborated with: Mel Torme; Ella Fitzgerald; Buddy Guy; Sarah Vaughan; Bill Doggett; Milt Jackson. *Membership:* National Asscn of Jazz Educators.

WILSON, Gerald Stanley; b. 4 Sept. 1918, Shelby, Mississippi, USA. Musician (trumpet, piano); Arranger; Composer; Orchestrator; Bandleader. m. Josefina Villaseñor, 4 Sept. 1950, 1 s., 3 d. *Education:* Cass Tech, Detroit, Michigan, USA; Private Tutorial. *Career:* Local bands, Detroit; Joined Jimmie Lunceford Orchestra, as trumpeter, arranger, 1939–42; Moved to Los Angeles; Arranger, trumpeter, Les Hite, Benny Carter, Phil Moore; World War II, Joined Count Basie band, trumpeter, arranger, 1948–49; Trumpeter for Dizzy Gillespie, 1949; Arranged for artists including: Ella Fitzgerald; Nancy Wilson; Ray Charles; Bobby Darin; Dinah Washington; Carmen McRae; Sarah Vaughan; Benny Goodman; Cab Calloway; The Platters; Eartha Kitt; Billy Eckstine; Jean Luc Ponty; Performed, with Al Hirt, Carnegie Hall, 1965; Musical director, Redd Foxx Variety series, 1978; Leader, composer, arranger, own orchestra; Member, faculty, University of California, Los Angeles; Festivals include: Chicago Jazz, 1994; Playboy Jazz, 1995. *Compositions include:* Royal Suite In Seven Movements; Imagine My Frustration, featured Broadway hit: Sophisticated Ladies; Piece for symphony orchestra, 1972; filmscores include: Where The Boys Are, 1960; Love Has Many Faces, 1960; Paco, 1964; Viva Tirado (recorded by El Chicano), no 1, 1968. *Recordings include:* Lomelin, 1981; Jessica, 1982; Calafia, 1984; Jenna, 1989; State Street Sweet, 1994; Suite Memories, 1996; Theme from Monterey, 1998; Complete Pacific Jazz Recordings, 2000. *Honours:* American Jazz Masters Fellowship Grant, 1990; Paul Robeson Award; Music archived by Library of Congress, Washington DC. *Membership:* AFM; NARAS; ASMAC; Los Angeles Jazz Society; Board Governors, National Academy, Recording Arts and Sciences.

WILSON, Joe; b. 7 Feb. Musician (bass guitar). *Career:* Mem., Sneaker Pimps, 1995–; Band founded Splinter Recordings, 1999. *Recordings:* Albums: Becoming X, 1996; Splinter, 1999; Bloodsport, 2002. Singles: 6 Underground (EP), 1996; Roll On, 1996; Tesko Suicide, 1996; Spin Spin Sugar, 1997; Post Modern Sleaze, 1997; 6 Underground, 1998; Low Five, 1999; Ten To Twenty, 1999; Sick, 2002. *Address:* c/o Tommy Boy Music, 902 Broadway, New York, NY 10010, USA. *E-mail:* parmesanchic@aol.com. *Website:* www.sneakerpimps.com.

WILSON, Joe Lee; b. 22 Dec. 1935, Bristow, Oklahoma, USA. Jazz Vocalist; Composer; Musician (guitar, piano, percussion). m. Jill Carlyon Christopher, 13 Dec. 1976, 2 d. *Education:* Piano lessons age 5–10; Sang Baptist Gospel church, age 5–16; Major in voice, Los Angeles Conservatory of Music, 1955; City College, 1956–58. *Career:* Played with: Sonny Rollins; Freddie Hubbard; Lee Morgan; Jackie MacLean; Roy Brooks; Pharoah Sanders; Frank Foster; The Collective Black Artists' Ensemble; Roy Haynes; Milt Jackson; Rashied Ali; Miles Davis; Archie Shepp; Innovator, the Jazz Loft Movement, 1973–78; Organized Live Loft Festivals; Appeared Newport New York Jazz Festival, 1973; Numerous television shows include: Showcase '68, NBC; DJ, broadcasting live jazz scenes; Leader, own jazz band; Travelled to Europe; Middle East; Africa; Far East; Played Ronnie Scott's, 1978; Clubs, concerts, festivals, France, England; Humphrey Lyttelton's BBC Radio programme; Special guest, Satchmo concert, Royal Festival Hall; Tonight In Town, BBC1 TV; Performed with Dizzy Gillespie, Marciac Festival, 1986. *Compositions:* Nice and Easy; Come and See; The Shadow; Lyrics to Milestones; Blues Ain't Nothing; Sphirlov; Children's Suite – Makes You Feel You're Real. *Recordings:* Albums: Living High Off Nickels and Dimes; Mr Joe Lee Wilson In The Great City; Without A Song; What Would It Be Without You, reissued 2000; Things Gotta Change, Archie Shepp; Secrets From The Sun; Shout For Trane; with Archie Shepp: A Touch of The Blues; Cry of My People; The Shadow; Acid Rain. *Honours:* 5 Downbeat magazine awards; ASCAP Song award; NBC Showcase winner, 1968. *Address:* 41 rue St Louis En l'Ile; 75004 Paris, France.

WILSON, Mari; b. 29 Sept. 1957, London, England. Vocalist. *Career:* Six hit singles, hit album, 1981–84; Television and concert tours: UK; Europe; USA; with 12 piece band the Wilsations; Jazz/pop career includes: Regular Ronnie Scott's Clubs appearances; Theatre, television, radio, DJ on Greater London Radio; Theatre acting: Sweet Charity; Chainsaw Manicure; Performer: Perhaps, Perhaps, Perhaps, theme to TV sitcom Coupling, BBC2, 2000–01. *Recordings:* Hit singles: Just What I've Always Wanted, 1982; Cry Me A River, 1983; Theme tune to Dance With A Stranger, 1984; Albums: Show People, 1983; The Rhythm Romance, 1992. *Membership:* Musicians' Union; Equity; PRS; MCPS. *Current Management:* Music: BPR, 36 Como St, Romford, Essex RM7 7DR, England; Acting: Macfarlane Chard Associates, 7/8 Little Turnstile, London WC1V 7DX, England.

WILSON, Mary; b. 3 June 1944, Greenville, Mississippi, USA. Vocalist; Entertainer. m. Pedro A Ferrer, 11 May 1973, 2 s. (1 deceased), 1 d. *Education:* Glee Club and Choir in High School; Professional vocal lessons, 1970–92. *Career:* Member, Supremes, 1961–77; World tours; 15 appearances on Ed Sullivan Show; Only American act with 5 consecutive number 1 hits; 12 number 1 hits; Broke record for sales; Broke racial barriers for blacks and

women; Epitomized the Motown Sound. *Recordings:* Where Did Our Love Go (No. 1, USA), 1964; Baby Love (No. 1, UK and USA), 1964; Come See About Me (No. 1, USA), 1964; Stop! In The Name of Love (No. 1, USA), 1965; Back In My Arms Again (No. 1, USA), 1965; I Hear A Symphony (No. 1, USA), 1965; My World Is Empty Without You, 1965; You Can't Hurry Love (No. 1, USA), 1966; You Keep Me Hangin' On (No. 1, USA), 1966; Love Is Here and Now You're Gone, 1967; The Happening (No. 1, USA), 1967; Reflections, 1967; Love Child, 1968; I'm Gonna Make You Love Me (with the Temptations), 1968; Someday We'll Be Together (No. 1, USA), 1969; Up The Ladder To The Roof, 1970; Stoned Love, 1970; River Deep Mountain High (with the Four Tops), 1970; Nathan Jones, 1971; Floy Joy, 1972; Solo: Red Hot, 1979; Walk The Line, 1992; U, 1995; Numerous compilations. *Publications:* Dreamgirl: My Life As A Supreme, 1986; Supreme Faith: Someday We'll Be Together, 1990. *Honours:* Star, Hollywood Walk of Fame; Inductee, Rock 'N' Roll Hall of Fame, 1988; Several awards, recording, recognition from music industry; Organizations include NAACP. *Current Management:* Duryea Entertainment. *Address:* 54 Danbury Rd, Suite 367, Ridgefield, CT 06877, USA.

WILSON, Nancy; b. 16 March 1954, San Francisco, California, USA. Vocalist; Musician (guitar). m. Cameron Crowe. *Career:* Member, Bordersong; Solo folk singer; Member, US rock group Heart, 1974–; UK debut, London, 1976; Regular US and international tours with artists including Queen; Tears For Fears; Michael Bolton; Black Crowes; Cheap Trick; Major concerts include: California Jam II Festival, 1978; Bread and Roses Festival, Berkeley, 1981; Benefit concert for local environmental groups, Seattle, 1990; Also member, side project The Lovemongers; Film appearances: Fast Times At Ridgemount High; The Wild Life. *Recordings:* Albums: with Heart: Dreamboat Annie, 1975; Little Queen, 1977; Magazine, 1978; Dog and Butterfly, 1978; Bebe Le Strange, 1980; Private Audition, 1982; Passionworks, 1983; Heart (No. 1, USA), 1985; Bad Animals, 1987; Brigade, 1990; Rock The House Live!, 1991; Desire Walks On, 1993; The Road Home, 1996; Here Is Christmas, 1998; Whirlygig, 1998; Solo: Live At McCabe's Guitar Shop, 1999; Meant To Be (with Ramsey Lewis), 2002. Singles: Magic Man, 1976; Barracuda, 1977; Straight On, 1978; Tell It Like It Is, 1981; How Can I Refuse, 1983; What About Love?, 1985; Never, 1985; These Dreams (No. 1, USA), 1986; Nothin' At All, 1986; If Looks Could Kill, 1986; Alone (No. 1, USA), 1987; Who Will You Run To, 1987; There's The Girl, 1987; What About Love, 1988; All I Wanna Do Is Make Love To You, 1990; Stranded, 1990; Will You Be There (In The Morning), 1993; Almost Paradise (duet with Mike Reno, from film Footloose), 1984; Battle of Evermore (with the Lovermongers, from film Singles), 1992. *Contributions to:* Simpsons, Yellow Album (vocals), 1998; Golden Child, Golden Child, 1998; Collaborated with: The Rockfords; Supertramp; Randy Meisner; Holly Knight. *Current Management:* Borman Entertainment Inc, 1250 Sixth St, Suite 401, Santa Monica, CA 90401, USA.

WILSON, Peter, (Emerson Peters); b. 28 July 1956, Newport, Isle of Wight, England. Musician (piano); Composer; Arranger; Teacher. *Education:* Royal Artillery Band, 1972–77; City of Leeds College of Music, 1977–78; Trinity College of Music, London, 1978–82. *Career:* Keyboards for Helen Shapiro and Neil Reid including television and radio; Freelance pianist ballet, dance, cocktail, bands, 1982–; First keyboards for Robin Cousins tour of UK, Electric Ice, 1984; First keyboards for rock opera, Jeanne, and musical Judy, 1985; Keyboards for Bruce Forsyth, Val Doonican, Michael Barrymore other cabaret acts, 1981–83; Teacher, Blackheath Conservatoire of Music 1981–83; Member, Tower Hamlets Strings Project, 1981–92; Teacher, Arts Educational College, 1983–85; Director, Greenwich Strings Project, 1993–. *Compositions:* Overture and suite for string orchestra; 1 Symphony for string orchestra, 2 horns and oboe; The Pirate Suite for strings and piano; The Wild West Suite for strings and piano; 3 piano suites, 1 piano sonata and many small pieces. *Publications:* Stringpops; Ragtime Preludes; Go Canon Go; Palm Court Trios; Fanfares; The 2001 Piano Collection. *Honours:* 2 awards of The Van Someren-Godfrey Gold Medal, Royal Artillery Band; Hannah Brook Prize for piano at TCM; Scholarship at TCM, 1981–82; LTCL, LGSM AMusTCL. *Membership:* Musicians' Union; Radio Society of Great Britain. *Address:* 74 Coleraine Rd, Blackheath, London SE3 7PE, England.

WILSON, Reuben; b. 9 April 1935, Mounds, Oklahoma, USA. Musician (Hammond B3 Organ). *Career:* Tour with Guru and Jazzmatazz II, 1993. *Recordings:* Ronnie's Bonnie; Inner City Blues; We're In Love; Walk On By On Broadway; Love Bug; Groovy Situation; Blue Mode; Set Us Free; Cisco Kid; Bad Stuff; Sweet Life; Gotta Get Your Own; Straight No Chaser; The Lost Grooves; Giant Steps; Hot Rod; Blue Breaks Vol. 2; Orange Peel; Shades of Red; Hip Hop Bop! NY Funkies; Live at SOB's; Organ Donor; Organ Grooves II; Down With It; Sampled Recordings: Hand On The Torch: I Got It Goin' On, US3; Ill Matic: Memory Lane: NAS; Inner City Blues; Tribe Called Quest; Also contributed to recordings by: Bob Beldon; Fatback Band; Grant Green. *Current Management:* c/o Preston Powell, Jazzateria Inc. *Address:* 11 W 72nd St, #2F, New York, NY 10023, USA.

WILSON, Roger; b. 22 July 1961, Leicester, England. Folk Musician; Songwriter. Divorced, 1 d. *Education:* BA, Graphic Design. *Career:* Solo 1986–; Urban Folk, 1990–; Touring with the House Band, 1995–98; Wood Wilson, Carthy, 1997–. *Compositions:* Ultrasound, The Zakynthos Jig; Payday; Indian Tea; Sick of the Working Life; Many Re-workings of Fo

Songs Including Hey Joe; Delia; Fair and Tender Lovers; Ramble Away, Two Sisters. *Recordings:* The Palm of your Hand; Stark Naked; Wood, Wilson, Carthy; Urban Folk Volumns I and II; Rockall; October Song. *Address:* 71 Lothair road, Leicester, LE2 7QE, England.

WILSON, Tony; b. 1950, England. Prod; Journalist. *Career:* Regional television newsreader and presenter; Founder, Factory Records, 1976; Signed bands including: Joy Division, New Order, Happy Mondays; Opened The Haçienda nightclub, 1987; Factory Records closed, 1992; Contributed to film of his book, 24 Hour Party People, 2001; Founder, Red Cellars record label, with Warren Bramley, 2002. *Publications:* 24 Hour Party People, 2002. *Address:* c/o Channel 4 Books, 124 Horseferry Rd, London SW1P 2TX, England.

WIMBISH, Doug; b. 22 Sept. 1956, Hartford, Connecticut, USA. Musician (Bass). *Career:* Joined Living Colour, 1993. *Recordings:* Singles: Leave It Alone, 1993; Nothingness, 1993; Ausländer, 1993; Bi, 1993; Sunshine of Your Love, 1994; Albums: Stain, 1993; Pride, 1995; Other session work includes: Audio Active; Herb Alpert; Bomb The Bass; Gary Clail; George Clinton; Depeche Mode; Will Downing; Billy Idol; Freddie Jackson; Mick Jagger; Al Green; Keith LeBlanc; Little Axe; Madonna; Joe Satriani; Carly Simon; Tackhead; Solo: Trippy Notes For Bass, 1999.

WINDRICH, Erik Rudolph; b. 5 Feb. 1960, Netherlands. Vocalist; Songwriter; Musician (multi-instrumentalist). 2 d., 2 step-s., 1 step-d. *Education:* University entrance (South Africa). *Career:* Evoid, 1982–86; Campus tour, 1984; Operation Hunger, Ellis Park Stadium, South Africa, 1985; Gold selling debut album, 3 hit singles, 1987–90; European tours; Regional radio UK, with The Vision Thing, 1992–; Work in progress with Ear Productions. *Compositions:* with Evoid: Shadows; Taximan; I Am A Fadget; with The Vision Thing: Fist In The Air; Wyah; Brother Sistem. *Recordings:* with Evoid: Evoid; Here Comes The Rot; A Space In Which To Create; with The Vision Thing: The Vision Thing. *Honours:* Sarie Award, South Africa, 1984. *Membership:* SAMRO; PRS; PPL; Musicians' Union; COBRA. *Current Management:* Sack The Management. *Address:* PO Box 572, Harrow, Middlesex HA1 3XA, England.

WINK, Josh, (Joshua Winkelman, Winks, Winx, Size 9); b. Philadelphia, Pennsylvania, USA. Prod; Remixer; DJ. *Career:* After meeting King Britt, duo recorded Tribal Confusion for Strictly Rhythm label; Co-founder: Ovum Records (with King Britt); World-wide DJ with club residencies in Philadelphia, New York and London; Collaborations: King Britt; Ursula Rucker; Remixed: Slam; Mood II Swing; Moby. *Recordings:* Singles: Tribal Confusion (as E-Culture), 1991; I'm Ready (as Size 9), Hypnotizin', Higher State of Consciousness, Don't Laugh (as Winx), 1995; Thoughts of a Tranced Love, 1996; How's Your Evening So Far? (with Lil' Louis), 2000. *Current Management:* Elite Music Management, PO Box 3261, Brighton, East Sussex BN2 4WA, England. *Website:* www.ovum-rec.com.

WINN, Tony Ellis; b. 15 Aug. 1949, Ilford, Essex, England. Vocalist; Songwriter; Performance Poet; Musician (guitar, banjo). m. Rebecca Jane Stewart, 30 May 1987, 2 s. *Career:* Member, 2 touring bands; Currently mainly solo performances at folk clubs, festivals, arts centres around UK, including the Edinburgh Fringe Festival; Appearances include: TV AM; Live local radio performances; Recordings played on local and national radio; Formed new band Mamwf, 1995. *Recordings:* Albums: Between Venus and Mars, 1993; Short Stories; Mice On A Cheese, 1997; Singing in the Bath; Satan's 200; Singles: Motorway Maniac/Rubbish; Shadows In The Night/ Secretly Admiring You. *Membership:* Musicians' Union. *Current Management:* Freefall Records, 21 London Rd, Kelvedon, Essex CO5 9AR, England.

WINSTON, George; b. 1949, Hart, Michigan, USA. Solo Musician (piano, guitar). *Career:* Solo piano, guitar concerts; Producer, recordings by Hawaiian slack key guitarists for Dancing Cat Records. *Recordings:* Solo piano albums: Ballads and Blues, 1972; Autumn, 1980; Winter Into Spring, 1982; December, 1982; Summer, 1991; Forest, 1994; Soundtracks: The Velveteen Rabbit (solo piano with narration by Meryl Streep), 1985; Sadako and The Thousand Paper Cranes (solo guitar with narration by Liv Ullmann) 1995; Linus and Lucy The Music of Vince Guaraldi, 1996; Plains, 1999; Remembrance: A Memorial Benefit, 2001. *Current Management:* Dancing Cat Productions, Inc. *Address:* PO Box 639, Santa Cruz, CA 95061, USA.

WINTER, Edgar; b. 28 Dec. 1946, Beaumont, Texas, USA. Musician (multi-instrumentalist); Composer. m. Monica Winter, 23 March 1979. *Career:* Member, various groups: Black Plague; Johnny Winter's group (brother); Founder, White Trash, 1971; Founder, the Edgar Winter Group, 1972; Session musician with: Meat Loaf, Dan Hartman, Bette Midler, Tina Turner, 1981–. *Recordings:* Albums: with Johnny Winter: Second Winter, 1970; Johnny Winter And..., 1970; with White Trash: Edgar Winter's White Trash, 1971; Roadwork, 1972; with the Edgar Winter Group: They Only Come Out At Night, 1973; Shock Treatment, 1974; The Edgar Winter Group With Rick Derringer, 1975; Recycled, 1977; The Edgar Winter Album, 1979; Standing On Rock, 1981; Solo album: Entrance, 1975; Jasmine Nightdreams, 1975; Not a Kid Anymore, 1994; The Real Deal, 1996; Live in Japan, 1998; Winter

Blues, 1999; Hits You Remember, 2000; Singles include: with White Trash: Keep Playin' That Rock and Roll; I Can't Turn You Loose; with the Edgar Winter Group: Frankenstein; Free Ride; Hangin' Around; River's Risin'; Easy Street. *Current Management:* Hooker Enterprises International, 5958 Bosch Dr., Malibu, CA 90265, USA.

WINTER, Johnny (John Dawson, III); b. 23 Feb. 1944, Beaumont, Texas, USA. Vocalist; Songwriter; Musician (guitar, harmonica); Record Prod. *Career:* Member, various bands, including Black Plague; Gene Terry and the Downbeats; Founder, leader, own band, 1968–; Appearances include: Newport '69 Festival, 1969; Newport Jazz Festival, 1969; Texas International Pop Festival, Dallas, 1969; Atlanta International Pop Festival, 1970; Royal Albert Hall, 1970; Bath Festival, 1970; San Francisco Blues Festival, 1987; Riverwalk Blues Fest, Fort Lauderdale, 1988; Highway 61 Revisited, 1992; Live In NYC '97, New York, 1997. *Recordings:* Albums: The Progressive Blues Experiment, 1969; Johnny Winter, 1969; The Johnny Winter Story, 1969; Second Winter, 1970; Johnny Winter And/Live, 1971; Nothin' But The Blues, 1977; White Hot and Blue, 1978; Raisin' Cain, 1980; Guitar Slinger, 1984; Serious Business, 1985; Third Degree, 1985; Winter of '88, 1988; Let Me In, 1991; White Hot Blues, 1997; Livin' The Blues, 1998; Black Cat Blues, 1999; Back In Beaumont, 2000; No Time To Live, 2001; with Edgar Winter (brother): Entrance, 1970; White Trash, 1971; Roadwork, 1972; Jasmine Nightdreams, 1975; Together, 1976; Together Live, 1977; with Muddy Waters: Hard Again, 1977; I'm Ready, 1977; King Bee, 1980; Guest musician, Mr Lucky, John Lee Hooker, 1991; Live In NYC '97, 1998. *Honours:* Gold disc, Johnny Winter and – Live, 1974. *Membership:* BMI; Musicians' Union. *Current Management:* Slatus Management, 208 E 51st St, New York, NY 10022, USA.

WINTER, Paul Theodore; b. 31 Aug. 1939, Altoona, Pennsylvania, USA. Musician (saxophone); Composer; Bandleader; Recording Artist. m. Chez Liley, 1 Sept. 1991. *Education:* BA, English composition, Northwestern University; Private studies with John Monti, Joe Allard. *Career:* Concert, recording artist, 1961–; Performed 2,300 concerts, 37 countries; Recorded 31 albums; Paul Winter Sextet won Intercollegiate Jazz Festival, 1961; State Department tour, 23 Latin American countries, 1962; Founded Paul Winter Consort, 1967; Founded Living Music Records, 1980; Played numerous environmental events including Global Forum, Oxford, 1988; Global Forum, Moscow, 1990; Earth Summit, Rio, 1992; Global Forum, Kyoto, 1993. *Recordings include:* The Paul Winter Sextet, 1961; Jazz Meets the Bossa Nova, 1962; Jazz Premiere: Washington, 1963; NewJazz on Campus, 1963; Jazz Meets the Folk Song, 1963; The Song of Ipanema, 1963; Rio, 1963; The Winter COnsort, 1968; Something in the Wind, 1969; Road, 1970; Icarus, 1972; Common Ground, 1977; Callings, 1980; Earth Mass, 1981; Sunsinger, 1983; Concert for the Earth, 1984; Canyon, 1985; Wintersong, 1986; Whales Alive, 1987; Earthbeat, 1988; Wolf Eyes, 1989; Earth: Voices of a Planet, 1990; Solstice Live, 1992; Spanish Angel, 1993; Prayer For The Wild Things, 1994; Canyon Lullaby, 1997; Brazilian Days, 1998; Celtic Solstice, 1999; Journey with the Sun, 2000. *Honours:* Grammy Awards, 1993, 1994, 1999, 2000; Global 500 Award, United Nations; Award of Excellence from UN's Environmental Programme; Joseph Wood Krutch Medal, US Humane Society; Alumni Merit Award, Northwestern University, 1996; Hon. DHL, Juniata College; Governor's Distinguished Arts Award, State of Pennsylvania. *Current Management:* International Music Network, 2 Main St, Fourth Floor, Gloucester, MA 01930, USA. *Address:* Living Music, PO Box 72, Litchfield, CT 06759, USA.

WINTER-HART, Paul; b. 19 Sept. 1971, London, England. Musician (drums). *Career:* Mem., The Objects of Desire, renamed The Kays, then Kula Shaker, –1999; Numerous TV appearances and live festival gigs. *Recordings:* Albums: K, 1996; Peasants, Pigs and Astronauts, 1999. Singles: Tattva, 1996; Hey Dude, 1996; Govinda, 1996; Hush, 1997; Sound of Drums, 1998; Mystical Machine Gun, 1999; Shower Your Love, 1999.

WINTHER, Jens; b. 29 Oct. 1960, Næstved, Denmark. Musician (trumpet); Composer; Bandleader. m. Trine Ulla Abildgård, 2 s., 2 d. *Career:* with Ernie Wilkins: Almost Big Band, 1980; Solo trumpeter, Danish Radio Big Band, 1982–89; Moved to New York to join a two-year Jazz Composers Workshop and played with groups and musicians including: Toshiko Akoishi Band, Eddie Palmieri, Kenny Barron, Max Roach, Tito Puente, Marie Bauza Orchestra, George Mraz, Xavier Cugat Orchestra, 1989–91; Major projects (writing and playing) for Danish Radio Big Band; Own music played with WDR, SWR, HR, NDR, RIAS, big bands in Germany, Finland, Sweden, Norway; Fulltime Composer and Trumpet Soloist, 1991–. *Compositions:* The Beginning, Now, The Future, Beyond, 1996; The Four Elements, 1996 Facing The Sun, 1998; Angels for choir and big band, 1998; The Eagle, 1999; Pluto and Beyond, 2001. *Recordings:* JW/Danish Radio Big Band, 1991; with JW Group: Scorpio Dance with Al Foster, 1991; The Planets, 1995; The 4 Elements, big band composition, 1996, CD, 1997; Pieces for symphony orchestra; Angels, 1998; The Escape, 1998; Jazz In Concert, live, 2000; with Jens Winther Trio, Standards, 2000. *Honours:* International Competition of Jazz Themes in Monaco, First Prize, 1990, 1991, 1996, Second Prize, 1988, 1997; Grammy for Best Danish Jazz Recording of the Year, 1996; Award

Danish National Arts Foundation, 1998. *Membership:* DJBFA. *Address:* Sotoften 6B, 2680 Solrod Strand, Denmark.

WINWOOD, Muff (Mervyn); b. 15 June 1943, Birmingham, England. Musician (bass); Music Co Exec. *Career:* Folk/blues soloist; Member, Muff-Woody Jazz Band (with brother Steve); Rhythm and Blues Quartet; Member, Spencer Davis Group, 1963–67; Concerts include: National Jazz and Blues Festival, 1965, 1966; Grand Gala du Disques, Amsterdam, 1966; British tours with: The Rolling Stones, 1965; The Who, 1966; The Hollies, 1967; Management Executive, West End Promotions; Executive, CBS Records; Currently Managing Director, Sony Soho Square (S²) Records, London. *Recordings:* Albums: Their First LP, 1966; The Second Album, 1966; Autumn '66, 1966; Singles include: Strong Love, 1965; Keep On Running (No. 1, UK), 1966; Somebody Help Me (No. 1, UK), 1966; Gimme Some Lovin', 1966; I'm A Man, 1967; Producer, Sutherland Brothers Band, Sutherland Brothers Band, 1972; Sparks, Kimono My House, 1974; Sparks, Propaganda, 1974; Kevin Ayers, Yes We Have No Mananas, 1976; Steve Winwood: 20th Century Masters, album, 1999. *Honours:* Carl Alan Award, Most Outstanding Group, 1966. *Current Management:* Sony Soho Square Records, 10 Great Marlborough St, London W1V 2LP, England.

WINWOOD, Steve; b. 12 May 1948, Birmingham, Warwickshire, England. Musician (keyboards, guitar); Vocalist; Songwriter. *Career:* Founder mem., Spencer Davis Group, 1963–67; Performances include: National Jazz and Blues Festival, 1965, 1966; Grand Gala du Disques, Amsterdam, 1966; British tours with The Rolling Stones, 1965; The Who, 1966; The Hollies, 1967; Traffic, 1967–68, 1970–75; Blind Faith, 1969; Concerts include: Hyde Park, 1969; Madison Square Garden, 1969; Concerts include: Zurich Rock Festival, 1968; Hollywood Festival, 1970; Headliners, Reading Festival, 1973; Solo artiste, 1977–; ARMS benefit concert, Royal Albert Hall, 1983; US tour, with Robert Cray, 1991. *Recordings:* Albums: with The Spencer Davis Group: Their First LP, 1966; The Second Album, 1966; Autumn '66, 1966; with Traffic: Mr Fantasy, 1968; Traffic, 1968; John Barleycorn Must Die, 1970; The Low Spark of High Heeled Boys, 1972; When The Eagle Flies, 1974; with Blind Faith: Blind Faith (No. 1, UK and USA), 1969; Solo albums: Steve Winwood, 1977; Arc of a Diver, 1981; Talking Back To The Night, 1982; Back In The High Life, 1986; Refugees of The Heart, 1990; The Finer Things, box set, 1995; Junction Seven, 1997; Singles include: with Spencer Davis Group: Keep On Running (No. 1, UK), 1966; Somebody Help Me, 1966; Gimme Some Lovin', 1966; I'm A Man, 1967; with Traffic: Paper Sun, 1967; Hole In My Shoe, 1967; Solo: Freedom Overspill, 1986; Roll With It, 1989; One and Only Man, 1990; I Will Be Here, 1991; Reach for the Light, 1995; Spy in the House of Love, 1997; Solos include: Higher Love (No. 1, UK), 1986; The Finer Things, 1987; Valerie, 1987; Roll With It (No. 1, USA), 1988; Don't You Know What The Night Can Do, 1988; Holding On, 1989; One and Only Man, 1989; Other session work includes: Lou Reed, Berlin, 1973; John Martyn, Inside Out, 1973; Viv Stanshall, Men Opening Umbrellas Ahead, 1974; Marianne Faithfull, Broken English, 1979; Talk Talk, The Colour of Spring, 1986; Paul Weller, Stanley Road, 1995. *Honours:* Grammy Awards: Record of the Year, Best Pop Vocal Performance, Higher Love, 1987; Gold discs. *Address:* Helter Skelter, Third Floor, 18 Bond St, Brighton BN1 1RD, England.

WIRE, Nicky, (Nicky Jones); b. 20 Jan. 1969, Tredegar, Gwent, Wales. Musician (Bass). *Career:* Member, Manic Street Preachers. *Recordings:* Singles: New Art Riot EP, 1990; You Love Us, 1991; Motorcycle Emptiness, 1992; Theme From M.A.S.H., 1992; From Despair To Where, 1993; La Tristessa Durera, 1993; Roses In The Hospital, 1993; Faster/PCP, 1994; Revol, 1994; She Is Suffering, 1994; A Design for Life (No. 2, UK), 1996; Everything Must Go, 1996; If You Tolerate This Your Children Will Be Next, 1998; The Everlasting, 1998; You Stole The Sun From My Heart, 1999; Tsunami, 1999; The Masses Against The Classes (No. 1, UK), 2000; So Why So Sad, 2001; Ocean Spray, 2001; Let Robeson Sing, 2001; Albums: Generation Terrorists, 1992; Gold Against The Soul, 1993; The Holy Bible, 1994; Everything Must Go (No. 1, UK), 1996; This Is My Truth, Tell Me Yours (No. 1, UK), 1998; Know Your Enemy, 2001; Forever Delayed, 2002. *Honours:* BRIT Awards, Best British Group, 1997; 1999; Best British Single, 1997; 1999. *Address:* c/o Epic Records, 550 Madison Ave, New York, NY 10022-3211, USA. *Website:* www.manics.co.uk.

WISE, Denny; b. 12 Sept. 1947, Bedford, Bedfordshire, England. Bandleader; Vocalist; Musician; Composer. m. Teresa Wise, 16 Aug. 1955, 1 s., 1 d. *Education:* Intermediate, Leicester Collge of Art and Technology; Piano and vocal lessons. *Career:* Radio appearances include: BBC; Capital Radio; Local stations; Television appearances in Germany. *Recordings:* Wise One; Time; with Marian Davies (A Toast To Gilbert O'Sullivan (Denny Wise Sings). *Publications:* Wise One; Love In The Night; Where Did We Go Wrong. *Membership:* Musicians' Union; Variety and Allied Entertainments Council. *Current Management:* Wise & Wicket Promotions Ltd. *Address:* 65 Shawley Way, Epsom Downs, Surrey KT18 5PD, England.

WISEFIELD, Laurence Mark (Laurie); b. London, England. Musician (guitar, electric and acoustic, slide, banjo); Vocalist; Songwriter. m. Patricia France Rousseau, 26 May 1986. *Career:* Formed group Home, 1971–73; Joined Al Stewart Band, 1973; Member, group Wishbone Ash, 1974–86; Joined Tina

Turner Band, 1987; Solo performance, Night of the Guitars; Tours: Joe Cocker, Night Calls tour; Tom Jones Show; Roger Chapman Band, 1991; Eros Ramazzotti, 1994; 14 month world tour with Tina Turner, Break Every Rule Tour, including live album, video, Christmas special, Live In Rio, numerous television appearances. *Recordings:* 3 albums with Home, 1971–73; 9 studio albums, 2 live albums, with Wishbone Ash; Live album with Tina Turner; Albums: Night of Guitars; UNO, Roger Chapman; SAS Band. *Honours:* Platinum, Gold albums. *Membership:* Musicians' Union; PRS; MCPS; PAMRA. *Address:* c/o Loz Ltd, 56 Forest Court, Snaresbrook, London E11 1PL, England.

WISEMAN, Debbie; b. 10 May 1963, London, England. Composer; Conductor. m. Tony Wharmby, 21 Sept. 1987. *Education:* Saturday Exhibitioner, Trinity College of Music, 1977–81; Kingsway Princeton/Morley College, 1979–81; GGSM, Guildhall School of Music and Drama, 1984. *Career:* Freelance composer and conductor. *Compositions:* Music for film and television productions including: Wilde; Tom and Viv; Haunted; The Guilty; Lighthouse; Warriors; Female Perversions; The Dying of The Light; The Good Guys; The Project; The Upper Hand; The Churchills; Serious and Organised; The Second Russian Revolution; Little Napoleons; Children's Hospital; What Did You Do In The War, Auntie?; The Cuban Missile Crisis; Vet's School; The Missing Postman; Tom's Midnight Garden; My Uncle Silas, 2001; Othello, 2001. *Recordings:* Wilde; Tom and Viv; Haunted; Lighthouse; Special performance of original composition with The Debbie Wiseman Collection, St John's Smith Square, London, 1989; Wilde, 1997; Featured works on BBC Radio 3 series The Music Machine and Every Note Paints A Picture; Tom's Midnight Garden; A Week In Politics; People's Century; Animal Planet; Warriors; Absolute Truth; The Fairy Tales of Oscar Wilde. *Honours:* David Taylor Memorial Prize, Trinity College of Music, 1981; Television and Radio Industries Club Award for TV Theme Music of the Year (The Good Guys), 1993; Women in Film and Television Awards; Royal Television Society Award, Warriors, 2000. *Membership:* Performing Right Society; British Academy of Film and Television Arts; Musicians' Union; British Academy of Composers and Songwriters. *Current Management:* Music Matters International, Crest House, 102–104 Church Rd, Teddington, Middlesex, England.

WISNIAK, Alain; b. 23 Sept. 1947, Boulogne, Seine, France. Composer; Arranger; Prod. m. Mariline Raichenbach, 25 March 1975, 1 s., 1 d. *Education:* Marguerite Long piano school; Harmony with André Hodeir. *Career:* Musician for sessions and tours with major French pop artists; Co-Prod., Writer for Bob Sinclair III. *Recordings:* Show theme for television series Maguy; Producer, composer, Cerrone's Supernature album; Soundtracks for films: La Femme Publique; L'Année Des Méduses; On Peut Toujours Rever; Victoire De La Musique, 1992; Medaille De La SACEM. *Membership:* Sociétaire Définitif; SACEM. *Current Management:* Tralala Music, 14 Blvd Emile Augier, 75116 Paris, France. *Address:* 16 rue Paira, 92190 Meudon, France.

WITHERS, Bill; b. 4 July 1938, Slab Fork, West Virginia, USA. Vocalist; Songwriter. m. Denise Nicholas. *Career:* Began work with Ford, IBM, Lockheed Aircraft Corporation; Recording artiste, 1970–; Appearances include: British tour; Summer Jazz Explosion '92, 1992; Valley Forge Music Fair, 1992; 2 tribute concerts for Eddie Kendricks, organized by Bobby Womack, California, 1992. *Recordings:* Albums: Just As I Am, 1971; Still Bill, 1972; Bill Withers Live At Carnegie Hall, 1973; The Best of Bill Withers, 1975; Making Music, 1975; Naked and Warm, 1976; Menagerie, 1977; 'Bout Love, 1979; Bill Withers Greatest Hits, 1981, 1988; Watching You, Watching Me, 1985; Ain't No Sunshine, 1997; Top Bill, 1999; Singles include: Ain't No Sunshine, 1971; Grandma's Hands, 1971; Lean On Me (No. 1, USA), 1971; Use Me, 1972; Lovely Day, 1977, remixed 1988; with Grover Washington: Just The Two of Us, 1981; with Ralph McDonald: In The Name of Love, 1984; Other. *Recordings include:* The Crusaders; Al Green; Don Henley; The Isley Brothers; Quincy Jones; Gladys Knight; Bobby Womack; Lovely Day, 1988. *Honours:* Grammy Awards: Best R&B Song, 1982, 1988; Gold discs for: Still Bill, 1972; Menagerie, 1977; Lean On Me, 1987. *Address:* c/o Associated Booking Corporation, 1995 Broadway, Suite 501, New York, NY 10023, USA.

WITHERS, Pick; b. 4 April 1948, Leicester, England. Musician (Drums). *Career:* Member, Dire Straits; Obtained major label deal and subsequent management contract; Support slot on Talking Heads European Tour, 1979; Numerous headlining tours and TV appearances; Left band, 1982. *Recordings:* Singles: Sultans of Swing, 1978; Lady Writer, 1979; Romeo and Juliet, 1981; Skateaway, 1981; Tunnel of Love, 1981; Private Investigations, 1982; Albums: Dire Straits, 1978; Communiqué, 1979; Making Movies, 1980; Love Over Gold (No. 1, UK), 1982; Sultans of Swing: The Very Best Of, 1998. Contributed to: Bert Jansch, Rare Conundrum, 1977; Ralph McTell, Right Side Up, 1978; Bob Dylan, Slow Train Coming, 1979.

WITTER, Rick; b. 23 Nov. 1972, Stockport, Cheshire, England. Vocalist. *Career:* Two Top of the Pops appearances; Reading Festival; Four British tours; Three European tours; Roskilde '95 (Denmark); Sellout Far East tour; Various appearances on music programmes; MTV live concert; Extensive press coverage. *Recordings:* Singles: Mark/Casino Girl, 1994; Dolphin,

Speakeasy, 1994; Ocean Pie, 1994; Where Have You Been Tonight, 1995; Going For Gold, 1996; Bully Boy, 1996; On Standby, 1996; Chasing Rainbows, 1996; She Left Me On Friday, 1998; Disco Down, 1999; Devil in Your Shoes, 1999; She Left Me on Friday; Heroes; Cry For Help, 2001; Albums: Change Giver, 1995; Maximum High, 1996; Let It Ride, 1998; Truth Be Told, 2001. *Honours:* Gold disc, 25,000 sales: Changegiver. *Membership:* PRS; Musicians' Union. *Current Management:* Cut Throat Management; Polydor. *Address:* PO Box 77, Coventry CV7 9Y2, England.

WITTMAN, William; b. 16 Sept. 1952, Richmond-on-Thames, Surrey, England. Record Prod. m. Barbara Solomon, 23 Aug. 1975, 1 s. *Career:* Mixer, record producer, New York, 1978–87; RCA Records, 1987–90; CBS Records, 1990–. *Recordings:* As producer include: with Cyndi Lauper: She's So Unusual, 1982; Hat Full of Stars, 1992; 12 Deadly Cyns, 1995; with Graham Parker: Steady Nerves, 1985; Passion Is No Ordinary Word, 1993; with Fixx: Calm Animals, 1988; Ink, 1991; with Lloyd Cole: Negatives, 2000. *Membership:* NARAS.

WOBBLE, Jah, (John Wardle); b. London, England. Musician (bass). *Career:* Member, Public Image Ltd (PIL), 1978–80; Founder, Human Condition; Jah Wobble's Invaders of The Heart. *Compositions:* The River, Kucheng concerto performed by the Royal Liverpool Philharmonic Orchestra. *Recordings:* Albums: with PIL: Public Image Ltd, 1978; Metal Box, 1979; Second Edition, 1980; Solo: Rising Above Bedlam, 1991; Take Me to God, 1994; Heaven and Earth, 1995; Spinner, with Brian Eno, 1995; The Inspiration of William Blake, 1996; Requiem, 1997; Umbra Sumus, 1998; Celtic Poets, 1998; Deep Space, 1999; Full Moon Over The Shopping Mall, 2000; Passage To Hades, 2001. Hit singles include: Public Image, PiL, 1978; Death Disco, PiL, 1979; Visions Of You, with Sinead O'Connor, 1992; Becoming More Like God, 1994; The Sun Does Rise, 1994; Also collaborated with: Holger Czukay; Gary Clail; Bill Laswell; Dub Syndicate; The Orb; Primal Scream; The Wolfgang Press. *Current Management:* c/o 30 Hertz, PO Box 11177, London E2 0DS, England.

WOIWOD, Bill (William); b. 27 Oct. 1919, London, England. Musician (clarinet, bass clarinet, flute, alto flute, piccolo). m. Joan Jenner, 8 July 1950. *Education:* Trinity College; Guildhall School of Music; London College of Music. *Career:* Featured soloist, Edmundo Ros LA Orchestra, 26 years; 9 concert tours, Scandinavia; Royal Command Performance, 1962; State Visit of Queen, 1956; 3 seasons, Monte Carlo; 5 tours Japan, Okinawa, Singapore; 81 television appearances, including 9 abroad; 904 BBC broadcasts. *Recordings:* 118 for Edmundo Ros Orchestra, Decca Studios; Teacher of woodwind for: ILEA, 15 years; Havering and Essex, 10 years; Brentwood School, 12 years.

WOLANIN, Vincent M; b. 13 Dec. 1947, Philadelphia, Pennsylvania, USA. Prod. and Management Exec. m. Illona Koch Dove, 27 July 1981, 2 d. *Education:* BS Philadelphia University, 1969; Grad school, Union College, 1971; Accordion, piano. *Career:* President/CEO Topnotch Entertainment Corp; Holds musical trademarks for Studiolive Sound TM, Thoughts TM, Topnotch; Founder, Topnotch Music, Records; Former Professional Athlete; Creator, Executive Producer, Supercollossal TM Show; Head, TopNotch Management Company. *Recordings:* Producer, Breaking Through album, 1995; Producer, Angry Room, Lyndal's Burning; Producer, Lingerie, Natalia. *Publications:* Created ads for Spin Magazine, April, May, 1996. *Honours:* Gold and Platinum discs for various albums and records; Platinum disc: Holy Water, Bad Company; Gold discs: Dangerous Age, Bad Company; Here ComesTrouble, Bad Company; Exposed, Vince Neil, Japan, 1993; Silver disc, for Breakin' Through, 1996. *Membership:* NARM (National Assn of Recording Merchandises) NARAS (National Academy Recording Arts/Science); Grammy Voting Member. *Current Management:* Topnotch Entertainment Corp, Topnotch Music and Records. *Address:* PO Box 1515, Sanibel Island, FL 33957–1515, USA.

WOLF, (THE). See: **KORN, Daniel.**

WOLFSON, Mark; b. 1 Sept. 1951, Chicago, Illinois, USA. Record Prod; Sound Engineer; Songwriter. *Career:* Record Production, Sound Engineer, Artist Development; Clients include: Natalie Cole; Jane Child; Stone Temple Pilots; Kimberly Bass; Producer: Film soundtracks; Television music. *Recordings:* (As producer) with UB40: Something Wild; with Talking Heads: Stop Making Sense; Lifetime Piling Up; Also producer for Jane Child; School of Fish; Stone Temple Pilots; Natalie Cole, Everlasting, 1987; Sound Engineer for: Sir Mix-A-Lot; Talking Heads; Smokey Robinson; Ice-T; Natalie Cole; Thelma Houston; Phil Everly; Melle Mel; Kim Carnes; Celia Cruz; Jane Child; Michael Des Barres; Film soundtracks include: Philadelphia; Silence of The Lambs; That Thing You Do; 12 Bucks; Police Academy; Police Academy III; Down and Out In Beverly Hills; K2; Television commercials include: Burger King; Coors; Toyota; 7 Up; Pizza Hut; Circle K. *Honours:* 25 Multi-Platinum, Platinum and Gold Records. *Membership:* NARAS. *Address:* 11684 Ventura Blvd, Suite 134 Studio City, CA 91604, USA.

WOLLO, Erik; b. 6 Jan. 1961, Norway. Composer; Prod; Musician (guitar, synthesizer). 1 s. *Career:* Professional artist, 1980–; Rock, jazz, classical music; Music for film, theatre, ballets, multimedia; Mostly electronic/

synthesizer music, also strings, woodwinds, orchestra; Producer other artists; Building own Wintergarden Studio. *Compositions:* Formations, 1982; Buteo Buteo, 1986; Eb Brottsjo, 1986; Solar, 1986; Windows, 1988; Pre sense, 1990; Vidder, 1992; Cairns, 1992; Music for ballet: Pyramider, 1986; Jeg Dromte, 1992; Music for theatre: Motspillerne, 1988, 1991; Aldri Verden, 1992; Fossegrimen, 1992; Abiriels Love, music for theatre, 1996; Maunushymnen, 1997. *Recordings:* Albums: Where It All Begins, 1983; Dreams of Pyramids, 1984; Traces, 1985; Silver Beach, 1986; Images of Light, 1990; Solstice, 1992; Fossegrimen, 1995; Albums with other artists: Celeste: Design By Music, 1984; Wiese/Wollo/Waring: Trio, 1984; New Music Composer's Group: In Real Time, 1992; Transit, 1996; Dimension D, Exile, 1997; Solo album: Guitar Nova, 1998. *Membership:* NOPA; Ny Musikk. *Current Management:* Monumental Records. *Address:* Blomsterveien 10, 1636 Fredrikstad, Norway.

WOLSTENHOLME, Chris Tony; b. 2 Dec. 1978. Musician (bass guitar). *Career:* Spent pre-teen years in Manchester, England; Formed group Gothic Plague in adopted hometown of Teignmouth, aged 13; Group became Fixed Penalty then Rocket Baby Dolls before finally settling on name Muse; Released two 1,000-copy EPs on UK independent label Dangerous; Signed to Madonna's US label Maverick following lauded UK In The City '98 and New York CMJ festival appearances; Rapid rise to fame followed; Live shows include: Ill-fated Woodstock '99 US festival; Headline slots at UK's Leeds, Reading and T In The Park festivals, 2000; European tours, 2001. *Recordings:* Albums: Showbiz, 1999; Origin of Symmetry, 2001; Hullabaloo, 2002. Singles: Muse EP, 1998; Muscle Museum EP, Uno, Cave, 1999; Sunburn, Unintended, 2000; Plug In Baby, New Born, Bliss, Hyper Music/Feeling Good, 2001; Dead Star In Your World, 2002. *Honours:* NME Award, Best Newcomer, 2000; Kerrang! Award, Best British Band, 2001. *Current Management:* Taste Media/SJP Management, 263 Putney Bridge Rd, London SW15 2PU, England. *Website:* www.muse-official.com.

WOMACK, Bobby; b. 4 March 1944, Cleveland, Ohio, USA. Vocalist; Songwriter; Musician (guitar). m. Barbara Cooke, 1965, divorced 1970. *Career:* Member, The Womack Brothers (later known as The Valentinos); Support to James Brown, US tour, 1962; Guitarist, Sam Cooke, 1960; Session work, 1965; Solo artiste, 1968–; Regular UK and US tours; Concerts include: New Orleans Jazz Festival, 1992. *Compositions include:* It's All Over Now (UK No. 1 for Rolling Stones); Numerous songs for Wilson Pickett including: 634–5789; I'm A Midnight Mover; I'm In Love. *Recordings:* Albums: Fly Me To The Moon, 1968; The Womack Live, 1971; Communication, 1972; Understanding, 1972; Across 110th Street, 1973; Facts of Life, 1974; Looking For Love Again, 1974; Bobby Womack's Greatest Hits, 1974; I Don't Know What The World Is Coming to, 1975; Safety Zone, 1976; BW Goes C&W, 1976; Home Is Where The Heart Is, 1976; Pieces, 1978; Roads of Life, 1979; The Poet, 1981; The Poet II, 1984; So Many Rivers, 1985; Womagic, 1987; The Last Soul Man, 1987; Lookin' For A Love (1968–75), 1993; I Still Love You, 1993; I Wanna Make Love To You, 1993; Soul Seduction Supreme, 1994; Back To My Roots, 1999; Traditions, 1999; Soul Sensation Live, 2000; Producer, Now Look, Ron Wood, 1974; Contributor, Sun City, Artists Against Apartheid, 1985; Dirty Work, The Rolling Stones, 1986; Coast To Coast, Paul Shaffer, 1989; Nearly Human, Todd Rundgren, 1989; Guitarist on recordings by artists including: King Curtis; Ray Charles; Wilson Pickett; Joe Tex; Aretha Franklin; Dusty Springfield; Janis Joplin; Singer, duets with Patti Labelle; Altrina Grayson; Shirley Brown; Lulu. *Address:* c/o Nick Cowan, Bobby Womack and Co, 9595 Wilshire Blvd #502, Beverly Hills, CA 90210, USA.

WOMACK, Lee Ann; b. 19 Aug. 1966, Jacksonville, TX, USA. Country vocalist. m. Jason Sellers, 1990, divorced. *Education:* South Plains Jr College, Levelland, Texas; Bellmont University, Nashville. *Career:* Joined college band Country Caravan; After studying music business at Bellmont University, worked as intern at MCA Records in A & R department; Became a parent after marriage to fellow country singer Jason Sellers; Started to write songs, perform at artist showcases and sing on demo sessions; Signed by Tree Publishing in Nashville, 1995; Wrote material with Bill Anderson, Mark Wright, Ed Hill and husband Sellers; Signed by MCA Records, 1996; Self-titled album produced first country chart entry Never Again Again, highly praised for its adherence to a hardcore country sound; Subsequent recordings moved away from strict traditional approach, but were critically well-received and chart success continued for remainder of the decade; Recorded I Hope You Dance with backing vocals from Sons of The Desert, 2000; Song charted internationally, becoming career record; Lyrical content inspired a best-selling book celebrating the joy of living and the possibility of dreams; Disowns hit dance remix of track. *Recordings include:* The Fool, You've Got To Talk To Me, 1997; Albums include: Lee Ann Womack, 1997; Something Worth Leaving Behind, 2002. *Honours:* CMA Awards: Single of the Year, Song of the Year, I Hope You Dance, 2000; Female Vocalist of the Year, 2001. *Address:* c/o Country Music Assn, 1 Music Circle S, Nashville, TN 37203, USA. *Website:* www.leeannwomack.com.

WONDER, Stevie, (Steveland Morris); b. 13 May 1950, Saginaw, Michigan, USA. Vocalist; Musician (multi-instrumentalist); Composer. m. Syreeta Wright, 1970, divorced, 3 c. *Education:* Michigan State School for the Blind, 1963–68. *Career:* Motown recording artist (initially as Stephen

Judkins), 1963–70; Founder, president, music publishing company, Black Bull Music Inc; Founder, Wonderdirection Records Inc; Taurus Productions; Numerous concerts include: Midem Festival, France, 1974; Night of The Hurricane II (hurricane relief concert), Houston, 1976; Peace Sunday, Rose Bowl, 1982; Nelson Mandela's Birthday Tribute, Wembley, 1988; Film appearances include: Bikini Beach, 1964; Muscle Beach Party, 1964. *Compositions include:* It's A Shame, Detroit Spinners, 1970; Productions include: Lovin' You, Minnie Riperton, 1975. *Recordings:* Hit singles include: Fingertips Part 2 (No. 1, USA), 1963; Uptight (Everything's Alright), 1966; I Was Made To Love Her, 1967; For Once In My Life, 1968; My Cherie Amour, 1969; Yester-Me, Yester-You, Yesterday, 1969; Signed Sealed Delivered I'm Yours, 1970; Heaven Help Us All, 1970; Never Had A Dream Come True, 1970; We Can Work It Out, 1971; Superwoman, 1972; Superstition (No. 1, USA), 1973; You Are The Sunshine of My Life (No. 1, USA), 1973; Higher Ground, 1973; Living For The City, 1973; He's Misstra Know-It-All, 1973; Don't You Worry 'Bout A Thing, 1974; You Haven't Done Nothin' (No. 1, USA), 1974; Boogie On Reggae Woman, 1975; I Wish (No. 1, USA), 1976; Sir Duke (No. 1, USA), 1977; Another Star, 1977; As, 1977; Send One Your Love, 1979; Master Blaster, 1980; Lately, 1981; Happy Birthday, 1981; That Girl, 1982; Ebony and Ivory, duet with Paul McCartney (No. 1, USA and UK), 1982; I Just Called To Say I Love You (No. 1, USA and UK), 1984; Part-Time Lover (No. 1, USA), 1985; Don't Drive Drunk, 1985; Overjoyed, 1986; Get It, 1988; Keep Our Love Alive, 1990; Gotta Have You, 1991; Fun Day, 1991; These Three Words, 1991; For Your Love, 1995; Tomorrow Robins Will Sing, 1995; Treat Myself, 1995; Kiss Away Your Tears, 1996; Albums include: The 12 Year Old Genius, 1963; Up Tight Everything's Alright, 1966; Down To Earth, 1967; I Was Made To Love Her, 1967; Greatest Hits, 1968; For Once In My Life, 1969; My Cherie Amour, 1969; Signed Sealed and Delivered, 1969; Greatest Hits Vol. 2, 1971; Music of My Mind, 1972; Talking Book, 1972; Innervisions, 1973; Fulfillingness' First Finale, 1974; Songs In The Key of Life, 1976; Journey Through The Secret Life of Plants, 1979; Hotter Than July, 1980; Woman In Red (soundtrack), 1984; Love Songs, 1984; In Square Circle, 1985; Characters, 1987; Music From The Music Jungle Fever (soundtrack), 1991; Conversation Peace, 1995; Natural Wonder, 1996; Song Review, 1996; At The Close Of A Century, 1999; Contributor, I Feel For You (No. 1, UK) Chaka Khan, 1984; There Must Be An Angel (No. 1, UK), The Eurthymics, 1985; That's What Friends Are For, Dionne Warwick and Friends (No. 1, USA), 1986; Hallelujah!, Quincy Jones, 1992. *Honours:* Numerous Grammy Awards, including Lifetime Achievement Award, 1990; Edison Award, 1973; NARM Presidential Award, 1975; Inducted into Songwriters Hall of Fame, 1983; Numerous American Music Awards, including Special Award of Merit, 1982; Academy Award, Best Song, 1984; Gold Ticket, Madison Square Garden, 1986; Soul Train Heritage Award, 1987; Inducted into Rock 'n' Roll Hall of Fame, 1989; Nelson Mandela Courage Award, 1991; IAAAM Diamond Award for Excellence, 1991; Lifetime Achievement Award, National Academy of Songwriters, 1992; NAACP Image Award, 1992; Numerous other charity and civil rights awards. *Current Management:* Stevland Morris Music, 4616 Magnolia Blvd, Burbank, CA 91505, USA.

WOOD, Jeffrey; b. 5 Sept. 1950, Chicago, Illinois, USA. Record Prod; Recording Artist; Composer. m. Carine F Verheyen, 16 Nov. 1992. *Education:* BA, University of Illinois; 12 years piano and composition, Helen Beidel. *Career:* Produced over 30 major recording artists including: Luka Bloom; The Housemartins; The Origin; Pauline Black; Penelope Houston. *Recordings include:* Twist of Destiny; The Surrendering Room; 3 feature film soundtracks. *Current Management:* Steve Moir Company. *Address:* 46 Hillside Ave, Mill Valley, CA 94941, USA.

WOOD, Michael Stefan; b. 12 April 1954, Hyde, Cheshire, England. Head of Music and Expressive Arts Faculty, School. m. Anita Jane, 25 May 1991. *Education:* Music at University of Hertfordshire, recorder with Evelyn Nallen, guitar/lute, Ian Gammie. *Career:* Formed folk band: The Brighthelmstones, 1969; Semi finalists National Folk Rock Fest, 1972; Album, 1971; Co-founded Wilbury Jam, 1977; Folk/cabaret in band play guitars, mandolin, banjo, recorder, clarinet, violin, trombone, horn; Played Krummhorn as part of Drake Anniversary, TVS, 1988; Similar, BBC radio, 1988. *Recordings:* Album: Brighthelmstones, 1971; Wilbury Jam: A Good Spread, 1980; A Second Helping, 1991. *Honours:* Dip Mus LTCL (Performers Recorder) LLCM ALCM. *Membership:* Musicians' Union. *Address:* 52 Chanctonbury Rd, Burgess Hill, West Sussex RH15 9EY, England.

WOOD, Patte; b. 29 Jan. 1949, Seattle, Washington, USA. Musician (Piano); Arts Admin. *Education:* Studies in Piano Performance, Harpsichord and Music Theory, 1956–75; BA, Music, San Jose State University, 1972; Studies in Fine Art Administration, 1979–81, Fine Art Photography, 1978–89; MA Candidate, 1997–. *Career:* Instructor, Piano Performance and Accompanist, San Francisco Bay Area, 1965–76; Administrative Director, Stanford University Center for Computer Research in Music and Acoustics, 1984–95; Visiting Scholar, Stanford University, 1995–99; Director, Blue Ridge Association for Community, Culture, Art and Technology, Eagle Rock, Virginia, 1999–; Solo Performances at festivals and concerts; Coproducer, numerous music projects; Consultant for numerous musical conferences. *Publications:* Early History of the Center for Computer Research in Music

and Acoustics, 1988; Conversations with John Robinson Pierce, 1991; Interview with French composer Jean-Claude Risset, 1992–98. *Honours:* National Piano Auditions, Outstanding and Superior Grades, 1956–66; International Standing, Superior Grade, 1967; Community Action Grant, AAUW, 1999. *Membership:* International Computer Music Asscn; Bay Area New Music Coalition, 1986–90; ICMA Commission Awards Selection Panel, 1992; Officer, Board of Directors, ICMA, 1992–2000; Advisory Board, Electronic Music Foundation, 1995. *Address:* 572 Poorhouse Rd, Lexington, VA 24450, USA. *E-mail:* patte@rockbridge.net.

WOOD, Paul, (Paul Richard Woodcock); b. 16 Nov. 1964, Romford, Essex, England. Vocalist. *Career:* Played with The Ray Ward Trio; Worked with artists including: Don Lusher; George Chisholm; Kenny Ball; Terry Lightfoot; Appeared at venues including: Pizza Express; Cafe Loire; Royal Festival Hall; Royal Ascot; Various radio and television includes: 2 hour radio broadcast from The Film Festival Hall, Cannes, France; Currently with Glenn Miller Memorial Orchestra, 1987–; Concert tours in France, Switzerland, Spain, Italy, Germany, Belgium, Austria, including Sporting Club, Monte Carlo, before Prince Rainier and Princess Caroline; Works regularly with various bands on the Continent; Played many Liberation Concerts; Spa Belgium; Toulon, France; Lille (25,000 people); Nice Jazz Festivals. *Recordings:* 4 albums with Glenn Miller Orchestra include: Recorded Live The Sporting Club Monte Carlo; 2 albums with Lex Van Wel and His Swing Orchestra. *Honours:* Freedom of The City of London. *Membership:* Musicians' Union; The Coda Club. *Current Management:* Lex Van Wel, PO Box 1436, 5602 BK Eindhoven, Netherlands.

WOOD, Ronnie (Ronald); b. 1 June 1947, Hillingdon, London, England. Musician (guitar, bass). 1 s. *Career:* Musician, Jeff Beck Group, 1967–69; Concerts include: National Jazz and Blues Festival, 1967, 1968; Newport Jazz Festival, 1969; Member, The Faces, 1969–75; Reading Jazz Festival, 1972; Buxton Festival, 1974; Member, The Rolling Stones, 1975–; US tour, 1975; Knebworth Festival, 1976; The Band's Last Waltz Farewell Concert, San Francisco, 1976; Film, Ladies and Gentlemen, The Rolling Stones, 1977; Played Knebworth Festival as The New Barbarians (with Keith Richards), 1979; Live Aid, JFK Stadium, Philadelphia, 1985; Played with Bo Diddley as the Gunslingers; Tours: North America, 1987; Japan, 1988; Germany, Italy, Spain, 1988; Sang at Bob Dylan 30th Anniversary Tribute, Madison Square Garden, 1992; Final world tour, 2002–03. *Recordings:* Albums with The Faces: First Step, 1970; Long Player, 1971; A Nod's As Good As A Wink... To A Blind Horse, 1971; Coast To Coast Overture and Beginners, 1974; with The Rolling Stones: Made In The Shade, 1975; Black and Blue, 1976; Love You Live, 1977; Some Girls, 1978; Emotional Rescue, 1980; Tattoo You, 1981; Still Life, 1982; Undercover, 1983; Dirty Work, 1986; Steel Wheels, 1989; Voodoo Lounge, 1994; Forty Licks, 2002; Solo: I've Got My Own Album to Do; Now Look; Mahoney's Last Stand; 1234; Live at the Ritz; Slide on This; Slide on Live; Live And Eclectic, 2000; Singles: with The Faces: Stay With Me, 1972; Cindy Incidentally, 1973; Pool Hall Richard, 1974; You Can Make Me Dance Or Sing Or Everything, 1974; with The Rolling Stones: Fool To Cry, 1976; Miss You (No. 1, USA), 1978; Emotional Rescue, 1980; Start Me Up, 1981; Going To a Go-Go; Undercover of The Night; Dancing In The Street (No. 1, UK), 1985; Mixed Emotions, 1989. *Honours:* Silver Clef, Nordoff-Robbins Music Therapy, 1982; Madison Square Garden Hall of Fame, 1984; Grammy, Lifetime Achievement Award, 1986; Ivor Novello, Outstanding Contribution To British Music, 1991. *Current Management:* Rupert Loewenstein, 2 King St, London SW1Y 6QL, England. *Website:* www.rollingstones.com.

WOOD, Roy; b. 8 Nov. 1947, Birmingham, England. Vocalist; Musician (guitar); Songwriter. *Career:* Member, Mike Sheridan and the Nightriders; Singer, guitarist, The Move, 1966–72; Appearances include National Jazz and Blues Festival, 1966; 14-Hour Technicolour Dream, with Pink Floyd, Alexandra Palace, 1967; Isle of Wight Festival, 1968; Founder member, Electric Light Orchestra (ELO), 1971–72; Founder, lead singer, Wizzard, 1972–75; Concerts include: London Rock 'n' Roll Festival, 1972; Reading Festival, 1972; Also formed The Wizzo Band; The Helicopters; Writer, producer, various artists including Darts, 1977; Performed at Heartbeat '86 benefit concert, 1986; Cropredy Festival, 1995. *Compositions include:* Night of Fear; I Can Hear The Grass Grow; Blackberry Way; Hello Susie; See My Baby Jive. *Recordings:* UK Top 10 singles include: with The Move: Night of Fear, 1967; I Can Hear The Grass Grow, 1967; Flowers In The Rain (first song ever played on BBC Radio 1), 1967; Fire Brigade, 1968; Blackberry Way (No. 1, UK), 1969; Hello Susie, 1969; Brontosaurus, 1970; California Man, 1972; with ELO: 10538 Overture, 1972; with Wizzard: Ball Park Incident, 1973; See My Baby Jive (No. 1, UK), 1973; Angel Fingers (No. 1, UK), 1973; I Wish It Could Be Christmas Every Day, 1973; Rock 'n' Roll Winter, 1974; Are You Ready To Rock, 1975; Solo singles include: Dear Elaine, 1973; Forever, 1973; Going Down The Road, 1974; Oh What A Shame, 1974; Albums with The Move: Move, 1968; Shazam, 1970; Looking On, 1970; Message From The Country, 1971; with ELO: Electric Light Orchestra, 1972; with Wizzard: Wizzard Brew, 1973; Introducing Eddy and The Falcons, 1973; with The Wizzo Band: On The Road Again, 1977; Super Active Wizzo, 1977; Solo albums: Boulders, 1973; Mustard, 1976; Main Street, 2000; Starting Up, 1987; Various compilation albums; Contributor, Arrested (album of Police covers by various artists and the Royal Philharmonic Orchestra), 1983. *Address:* RO-LO Productions, 35 Dillotford Ave, Coventry CV3 5DR, England.

WOODLEY, Bruce; b. 25 July 1942, Melbourne, Australia. Vocalist; Musician (guitar). *Career:* Founder mem., folk/pop group The Seekers, with Keith Portger and Athol Guy, later joined by Judith Durham; Success following concert, Palladium, England, 1964; Group split, 1968. *Address:* c/o Shelley Bovey, 90 Above Town, Glastonbury, Somerset BA6 8JG, England.

WOODLEY, Mark Kenneth; b. 5 Sept. 1953, Brantford, Ontario, Canada. Songwriter; Musician (piano); Vocalist; Motivator. m. Elaine, 18 June 1977, 1 s., 2 d. *Education:* Leadership Training. *Career:* Toured through Canada, USA, UK, 1981–; National television in Canada. *Recordings:* Taken By Force, Image 7, 1987; More Like You, Image 7, 1985; Breaking Ground, Listen, 1981; Edify The Church, 1991. *Membership:* SOCAN; GMA. *Current Management:* YES International Inc. *Address:* 7 Painters Rd, RR7, Brantford, ON N3T 5L9, Canada.

WOODRUFF, Bob; b. 14 March 1961, Suffern, New York, USA. Vocalist; Songwriter; Musician (guitar, drums). *Career:* Television appearances include: Music City Tonight, Nashville Network; TNN Country News; Inside Country, Ontario, Canada; The Road, Tribune Entertainment; Country Road Frutigen, Switzerland. *Recordings:* Albums: Dreams and Saturday Nights, 1994; Desire Road, 1997; Singles: Alright, 1994; Hard Liquor Cold Women Warm Beer, 1994. *Honours:* Charleston International Film Festival Silver Award, Best Country Music Video, for Alright, 1994. *Membership:* CMA; NARAS; AFTRA; AFofM. *Current Management:* Jim Della Croce Management, 1229 17th Ave S, Nashville, TN 37212, USA.

WOODS, John William; b. 23 July 1967, Cheltenham. *Career:* Ektos; Quest; Universe; Bristol Exposure; Pandemonium; Vibes Alive; Sutra; Obsession; Obsessed; Hyperbolic; Pleasuredome; Kinetic; Tick Tock; Own Record Label, Junkie Vinyl. *Recordings:* Tearin' My Love Apart; Funky Man; Seatrching For A Beat; Drive Me Crazy; Just Be Good; Hidden Dreams; Everything Starts Now; Only You/Funky Man. *Membership:* MCPS; PRS; PPL. *Address:* 18A High St, Shirehampton, Bristol, BS11 0DX, England.

WOODS, Philip Wells; b. 2 Nov. 1931, Springfield, Massachusetts, USA. Musician (Alto Saxophone, Clarinet); Composer. m. Jill Goodwin, 20 Dec. 1985, 1 s., 2 d. *Education:* Lessons with Harvey Larose, Springfield; Manhattan School, New York, 1948; Juilliard Conservatory, 1948–52. *Career:* Appearances with Benny Goodman, Buddy Rich, Quincy Jones, Thelonious Monk, Michel Legrand, Dizzy Gillespie and others; Appearing with own bands, Phil Woods Quintet, Phil Woods Little Big Band, Phil Woods Big Band; Featured, soundtracks of films including It's My Turn; Bandleader, Composer, Arranger and Soloist. *Compositions include:* Three Improvizations for Saxophone Quartet; Sonata for Alto and Piano; Rights of Swing; The Sun Suite; Fill the Woods with Light; I Remember; Deer Head Sketches. *Recordings include:* Images, with Michel Legrand, 1976; I Remember, Phil Woods Quartet, 1979; Dizzy Gillespie Meets Phil Woods Quintet; Evolution, Phil Woods Little Big Band; An Affair to Remember, Phil Woods Quintet; The Rev and I, with Johnny Griffin; Elsa, 1998; Porgy and Bess, 1999; Voyage, 2001. *Honours:* Down Beat Magazine New Star Award, 1956, Critics' Poll Winner, alto saxophone, 1975–79, 1981–90, 1992, Readers' Poll Winner, alto saxophone, 1976–95; Grammy Award, Images with Michel Legrand, 1976, for More Live, Phil Woods Quartet, 1982, 1983; National Asscn of Jazz Educators Poll Winner, alto saxophone, 1987, Phil Woods Quintet, 1987; East Stroudsburg University Hon. Degree, 1994; Induction into American Jazz Hall of Fame, 1994. *Membership:* Delaware Water Gap Celebration of the Arts; Board of Directors, Al Cohn Memorial Jazz Collection; American Federation of Musicians; International Asscn of Jazz Educators. *Address:* PO Box 278, Delaware Water Gap, PA 18327, USA.

WOODWARD, Keren; b. 2 April 1961, Bristol, Somerset, England. Vocalist. *Career:* Worked at BBC; Singer, all-female group, Bananarama, 1981–; Numerous concerts, television and radio performances. *Recordings:* Albums: Deep Sea Skiving, 1983; Bananarama, 1984; True Confessions, 1986; Wow!, 1987; Greatest Hits Collection, 1988; Pop Life, 1991; Please Yourself, 1993; Very Best Of, 2001; Ultraviolet, 1996; The Very Best Of, 2001; Exotica, 2001; I Found Love, 2002. Singles: Aie A Mwana, 1981; It Ain't What You Do (with Fun Boy Three), 1982; Really Sayin' Somethin', 1982; Shy Boy, 1982; Shy Boy, 1982; Na Na Hey Hey Kiss Him Goodbye, 1983; Robert De Niro's Waiting, 1984; Cruel Summer (featured in film The Karate Kid), 1984; Venus (No. 1, USA), 1986; I Heard A Rumour, 1987; Love In The First Degree, 1987; I Want You Back, 1988; Nathan Jones, 1988; Help! (with comedy duo French and Saunders, for Comic Relief charity), 1989; Only Your Love, 1990; Long Train Running, 1991; Preacher Man, 1991; Tripping On Your Love, 1991; Movin' On, 1992; Venus, 1993; More More More, 1993; Please Yourself (EP), 1993; Every Shade Of Blue, 1995; Take Me To Your Heart, 1996; Waterloo, 1998; Contributor: Do They Know It's Christmas?, Band Aid (Ethiopian famine relief, No. 1, UK), 1984; Let It Be, Ferry Aid (Zeebrugge ferry disaster benefit, No. 1, UK), 1987; Do They Know It's Christmas?, Band Aid II (No. 1, UK), 1989; Rock The World, benefit album, 1990. *Address:* c/o Mission Control

Artists Agency, Unit 50 City Business Centre, St Olav's Ct, Lower Rd, London SE16 2XB, England.

WOOLEY, Sheb (Shelby F.); b. 10 April 1921, Eric, Oklahoma, USA. Actor; Musician (fiddle, harmonica, acoustic guitar); Songwriter; Comedian. m. Linda S Dotson, 30 Dec. 1985, 2 d. *Career:* Over 80 major films, including: High Noon; Outlaw; Josie Wales; War Wagon; Rio Bravo; Rocky Mountain; Giant; Television appearances include: Original cast member, Hee Haw; Rawhide, 7 years; American Bandstand; Mod Squad; Murder She Wrote; Hootnanny Hoot; The Lone Ranger; Ed Sullivan Show. *Recordings:* Hit singles include: The Purple People Eater (100m. sales including covers); That's My Pa; Are You Satisfied; Sweet Chile; White Lightnin'; as Ben Colder: Fifteen Beers Ago; Almost Persuaded; Harper Valley PTA; Albums include: That's My Pa, 1998. *Honours:* CMA Comedian of the Year, 1968; 2 Golden Boot Awards; 7 Western Heritage Awards, 1966–; Second fastest selling record ever, The Purple People Eater. *Membership:* ASCAP; CMA; NARAS; ROPE; ACM; AFM; SAG; AFTRA. *Current Management:* Linda Dotson, Circuit Rider Talent and Management. *Address:* 123 Walton Ferry Rd, Hendersonville, TN 37075–3616, USA.

WOOLWAY, Colin; b. 24 Jan. 1959, London, England. Musician (drums); Teacher. m. Lucy MacArthur, 22 July 1995. *Career:* Theatre tours: Godspell; Rocky Horror Show; 1978–80; English tour with The Enid, 1984; with Suzi Quatro: 5 Australian tours, 2 Japan tours, Russian tour, constant television appearances, 1985–93; Top Clinician for Zildjan Cymbals; Clinician for Sonor Drums, teaching at Drumsense studio. *Publications:* Drumsense, Vols 1–3, (drum tutors); 4 musician joke books. *Current Management:* Hayter and Shone, Publisher. *Address:* Flat 8, Highview House, 1 Highview Rd, Upper Norwood, London SE19 3SS, England.

WORLLEDGE, Terry; b. 31 Jan. 1945, Essex, England. Musician (guitar, harmonica); Vocalist; Songwriter; Prod; Engineer. m. Jean, 10 Oct. 1964, 2 d. *Career:* Member, Country Shack; Member, Jackson Queen; Numerous appearances, Wembley Country Music Festival; Television and radio appearances: BBC; ITV; Radio: BBC Radio 2. *Recordings:* Albums include: with Country Shack: Your Country Needs You; Portrait; Which Way Is Gone?; BBC Compilation album: 20 Country Greats; with Jackson Queen: Jackson Queen (EP); On The Rewind; On The Rewind, 2001. *Honours:* British Country Music Asscn, Most Promising Act, 1980; Radio 2 Country Club, Best Band during 3 years as producer. *Membership:* Musicians' Union; BCMA; PRS; PAMRA. *Address:* Pipers, Maypole Rd, Tiptree, Essex CO5 0EP, England. *E-mail:* terryworlledge@onetel.net.uk.

WORRALL, Sean; b. 6 June 1966, Leicester, England. Artist; Record Label Owner; Magazine Editor; Concert Promoter; Vocalist; Musician (bass player); Fashion Designer. *Education:* West Surrey College of Art. *Career:* Editor, Organ Magazine; Toured extensively; Many radio, television appearances; Several album covers, videos. *Recordings:* Sophie Magic, Angel Cage; Late Developer, Rhatigan; Bullseye, Cardiacs; Redoubtable, Deathblanket, Goosebumps. *Publications:* Organ Magazine; Organ Videozine. *Honours:* The Golden Bassoon for Services to Punk Rock, 1994. *Membership:* The Yous Family. *Address:* Unit 205, The Old Gramophone Works, 326 Kensal Rd, London W10 5BZ, England.

WORTLEY, Barry George; b. 19 May 1951, Norwich, Norfolk, England. Musician (drums, guitar); Vocalist. m. Susan Read, 4 Oct. 1986, 5 s. *Career:* Member: The Aytons, 1966–68; Norma and The Shade of Pale, 1968–71; Edentree (touring comedy/showband), 1972–75; Fresh 1975–; Winner, ITV's New Faces, 1978; (name changed to Monte Carlo for last 12 of Song For Europe and Dooley's Tour Support Band, name returned to Fresh); Currently a trio working functions and summer seasons. *Recordings:* Valentino; Win A Few, Lose A Few; Home Again. *Honours:* Music Award, Ljubljana Song Festival, Yugoslavia, 1979. *Membership:* Musicians' Union. *Current Management:* Anglia Artistes, Nicky Walker Entertainments and Leisure Services. *Address:* 105 Netherwood Green, Norwich, Norfolk NR1 2RJ, England.

WORTLEY, J; b. 5 June 1971, Grimsby, Lincolnshire, England. Vocalist; Songwriter; Musician (guitar). *Career:* Joined Illustrious Gy, 1989; Signed to Arista Records, 1991; Toured with Squeeze in UK; Appeared: Going Live (BBC); Several ITV programmes; Played live, Steve Wright In The Afternoon, BBC Radio 1; Recently signed with MCA, as Giant Killers. *Recordings:* Singles: Twenty Questions; Anytime At All; I'm Very; Album: No No No. *Membership:* Musicians' Union. *Current Management:* J Cooke, Fatcat Management. *Address:* 81 Harley House, Marylebone Rd, London NW1 5HT, England.

WRAIGHT, Jeffrey Charles; b. 17 Aug. 1954, West Sussex, England. Musician (keyboards, bass guitar); Vocalist; Arranger; Composer; Musical Dir; Co Dir, Entertainments Agency and Management. *Education:* A Level Music; Some piano lessons; Studied with Cyril Winn. *Career:* Accompanied many modern jazz artists, 1973–79; Experimental free jazz workshop, Reading, 1977–79; Television broadcasts from Bracknell Jazz Festival, 2 years running; Soulstice, Funk Jazz group recording with Tony Visconti; Founder member of early Punk group Billy and the Conquerors; Joined big band on QEII, 1979, became band leader of own band on the same ship; Several television appearances; Worked with: The Batchelors; Bob Monkhouse; Tommy Dorsey Orchestra; Peter Gordeno; Joe Loss; Faith Brown; Elaine Delmar; Lorna Dallas; Started business venture in 1983 becoming Heartrate Entertainments, 1989–; Keyboard player, vocalist, arrangements for A Tribute To The Blues Brothers, London West End, 1992; Musical Director, and rewriter of show, 1994–. *Recordings include:* Soulstice, Tony Visconti; Several live sessions by Pendulum; Some recordings for BBC TV and Radio including several Blues Brothers appearances. *Publications:* Critique on the music of Miles Davis (in preparation). *Honours:* John Dankworth Award for Best Instrumentalist Under 25 (Piano), 1977. *Current Management:* Heartrate Entertainments. *Address:* 3 Seacroft, 9 Lansdowne Rd, Worthing, Sussex BN11 4NA, England.

WRAY, John; b. 16 Jan. 1943, Ramshaw, England. Co Dir; Musician (keyboards). m. Karen Anne Western, 9 July 1986, 1 s., 1 d. *Education:* Private tuition. *Career:* Owner, Spennymoor Variety Club; Band leader, John Ray Set; Director, Air Entertainments Agency; Producer, tours: Simply The Best; Moscow Ballet 2a Classique. *Recordings:* Owner, Bullseye Recording Studios. *Current Management:* Air Entertainments. *Address:* 17 Clyde Terrace, Spennymoor, Co Durham DL16 7SE, England.

WRAY, Walter; b. 7 Feb. 1959, Portsmouth, Hampshire, England. Vocalist; Songwriter; Musician (guitar). m. Joanne Redfearn, 1 April 1989, 1 d. *Education:* Sheffield University; Guitar and piano lessons, BA dual Hons, Music/English. *Career:* Two albums with band Junk; Joined rock band King Swamp, 1988; 2 albums, and tours of USA and Europe; Currently solo artist. *Recordings:* Albums: with Junk: Cuckooland, 1986; Drop City Souvenirs, 1987; with King Swamp: King Swamp, 1988; Wiseblood, 1990; Solo: Foxgloves and Steel Strings, 1992; Heaven Is On Our Side, 1993. *Membership:* Musicians' Union; PRS. *Current Management:* JFD Management, 106 Dalling Rd, Hammersmith, London W6 0JA, England.

WRETZKY-BROWN, D'Arcy; b. 1 May 1968, South Haven, MI, USA. Musician (bass guitar). *Career:* Mem., Smashing Pumpkins, 1989–99; Numerous headlining tours, television and radio sessions. *Recordings:* Albums: Gish, 1991; The Peel Sessions, 1992; Siamese Dream, 1993; Pisces Iscariot, 1994; Mellon Collie And The Infinite Sadness (No. 1, USA), 1995; The Aeroplane Flies High, 1996; Adore, 1998; Greatest Hits, 2001; Earphoria, 2002; Vieuphoria (DVD), 2002. Singles: Lull (EP), 1992; Today, 1994; Cherub Rock (EP), 1994; Disarm, 1994; I Am One (EP), 1994; Bullet With Butterfly Wings, 1995; Thirty Three, 1996; Zero, 1996; End Is The Beginning Is The End, 1997; Perfect, 1998.

WRIGHT, Chely; b. 25 Oct. 1970, Kansas City, Missouri, USA. Country vocalist; Musician (guitar). *Career:* Formed own band County Line; Moved to Branson, Missouri, securing a job singing on the Ozark Jubilee before finishing high school; Moved to Nashville and landed a job impersonating country artists by age 18; Signed to Mercury after coming to the attention of producer Harold Shedd; Records performed moderately until move to MCA Records, 1997; Let Me In album gave first real taste of success on both country singles and album charts; Turned further away from traditional country sound heard in earlier work and recordings have become more sophisticated and uptown, culminating in the complex Never Love You Enough, 2001; Latterly has been recording and writing with friend and fellow artist Brad Paisley, including the hit duet Hard To Be A Husband – Hard To Be A Wife. *Recordings include:* Single White Female, It Was, 2000; Hard To Be A Husband – Hard To Be A Wife (with Brad Paisley), 2001; Albums include: Right In The Middle of It, 1996; Let Me In, 1997; Single White Female, 1999; Never Love You Enough, 2001. *Honours:* ACM, Top New Female Vocalist, 1995. *Address:* c/o Country Music Asscn, 1 Music Circle S, Nashville, TN 37203, USA. *Website:* www.chely.com.

WRIGHT, David; b. 2 Feb. 1958, Colombo, Sri Lanka. Local Government Officer. m. Nicola, 4 July 1987, 2 s. *Education:* Degree, Environmental Sciences. *Career:* Solo performer and with band The Thomas Wright Affair; Live performance, BBC Radio Bristol, Somerset Sound, 1993; Canny Wizard Stage, Glastonbury, 1994, 1995; Castle Park Stage, Bristol Sound City, 1995; Mean Fiddler, Acoustic Room, London, 1996, 1997. *Compositions:* Kathy's Eyes, 1996; Sign Your Life Away, 1996; Lost in the Wilderness, 2000; Distant Trains, 2000; Shotgun, 2000. *Recordings:* Self-produced albums: Kathy's Eyes, 1996; Lost in the Wilderness, 2000. *Honours:* Glastonbury Festival Canny Wizard Stage, 1994, 1995; Radio 1 FM Park Stage for Bristol Sound City, 1995; Ashton Court Festival, Bristol, 1995, 1998. *Membership:* PRS; PAMRA; Musicians' Union. *Address:* PO Box 743, Bristol BS99 5GU, England. *E-mail:* 113040.3101@compuserve.com. *Website:* www.blueballonrecords.com.

WRIGHT, Dennis; b. 12 Dec. 1926, Rochdale, Lancashire, England. Musician (drums); Arranger. m. Auidrey Elsie Jones, 8 Sept. 1986, 4 s. *Education:* George Evans arranging course; Glenn Miller booklet. *Career:* Played radio broadcast, 1947; Further broadcasts Rink Ballroom, Sunderland; Own trio accompanied artists at Wetherals Night Club, Sunderland, include: Bobby Bennett; Donald Peers; Mike Sarne; Lance Percival; Bertice Reading; Bill Pertwee; Frankie Vaughan (big band); Valerie Masters; Vince Hill; Lena

Martell; Dorothy Squires; Dick Emery. *Recordings:* Newcastle broadcast, 1947; Local band, Henfield, Sussex, recorded. *Current Management:* Sunrise Management, Forest Green, Dorking, Surrey, England.

WRIGHT, Eugene Joseph; b. 29 May 1923, Chicago, Illinois, USA. Musician (bass); Composer. m. Jacqueline Winters, 29 May 1945, divorced 1954, 1 s., 1 d., m. (2) Phyllis Lycett, 10 Aug. 1962. *Education:* Tilden Tech, Chicago, 1938. *Career:* Bandleader, Dukes of Swing Orchestra, 1943–46; Bassist with Count Basie Orchestra; Gene Ammons/Sonny Stitt Quintet; Buddy DeFranco; Red Norvo; Arnett Cobb; Cal Tjader; Dave Brubeck; Monty Alexander, 1947–72; Billie Holiday, US and European tours, 1954; Duo, Money Tree, 1975–86; Bandleader, Eugene J Wright Ensemble, 1986–; Private music teacher, 1969–; Performed with B. B. King Blues Band, Linda Hopkins International Jazz Festival, Switzerland, 1988; Performed with Dave Brubeck Quartet, US State Dinner (for Presidents Reagan and Gorbachev), Moscow, 1988. *Recordings include:* Monty Alexander; Count Basie; Dave Brubeck Quartet. *Publications:* Bass Solos; Modern Music For Bass; Jazz Giants. *Honours:* Playboy Jazz Poll Award, 1964–66; Outstanding Voluntary Service Award, Los Angeles Human Relations Commission, 1988. *Membership:* NARAS; AFofM. *Address:* c/o Dukes of Swing Record Company, Hollywood, California, USA.

WRIGHT, Finbar; b. 26 Sept. 1959, Kinsale, Co Cork, Ireland. Tenor singer. m. Angela, 23 Nov. 1990, 1 s., 1 d. *Education:* BD; HDE; Studied with Ileana Cotrubas and Veronica Dunne. *Career:* Australian Tour, performed with Melbourne Symphony Orchestra, Spring 1994; Performed with Montserrat Caballe, Dublin, 1993; USA tour, Spring 1995. *Compositions:* Blackwind 1998. *Recordings:* Albums: Because; Whatever You Believe; Live Tribute To John McCormack; Lift The Wings; I Give My Heart; Another Season; With The Irish Tenors: Live In Belfast, 2000; Ellis Island, 2001. *Honours:* IRMA Best MOR Artist, 1992; IRMA Best Male Artist, 1993. *Membership:* IMRO *Current Management:* Barleyfield Music, Barleyfield House, Farran, Co Cork Ireland. *Website:* www.finbarwright.com.

WRIGHT, Michelle; b. 1 July 1961, Chatham, Ontario, Canada. Vocalist; Songwriter; Musician (guitar). *Career:* Radio: Grand Ole Opry Debut, 1992 TV: Tonight Show with Jay Leno, 1992; The Women of Country; Prime the CBC Specials, Michelle, 1991; Songs and Secrets, 1996; Co-Host, TNN Music City News Awards, 1994; Host, 1995; CCMA Awards Show; ACM and CMA Awards Shows, 1992–96. *Recordings:* Do Right By Me, 1988; Michelle Wright 1990; Now and Then, 1992; The Reasons Why, 1994; The Power of Peace 1996; Star of Wonder, 1996; For Me It's You, 1996; Greatest Hits, 2000 Singles: One Good Man, 1994; Nobody's Girl, 1996. *Honours:* Top Femal Vocalist, 1989; Top Female Vocalist, 1991; Artist of the Year, 1991; To Country Single, Take It Like a Man, 1992; Top Female Vocalist, 1993; Artis of the Year, 1993; Top Country Album, Now and Then, 1993; Top Countr Single, He Would Be Sixteen, 1993; Top Female Vocalist, 1994; Top Femal Vocalist, 1995; Hon. Spokesperson for Special Olympics, 1996. *Membership* National Academy of Recording Arts and Sciences, Academy of Countr Music; Country Music Asscn; Canadian Country Music Asscn; Canadia Academy of Recording Arts and Sciences. *Current Management:* Savanna Music, 209 10th Ave S, Suite 528, Nashville, TN 37203, USA.

WRIGHT, Nod (Alexander James); b. 14 June 1966, Hertfordshir England. Musician (drums, percussion, guitar, keyboards). *Education:* Nort Herts College. *Career:* Member, Fields of The Nephilim, now known a Rubicon; Numerous European tours; 2 American tours; Reading Festiva 1987, 1988; Loralei Festival (Germany); Chart show videos; Top of the Pop BBC Radio Live; Drums and Percussion. *Recordings:* Fields of The Nephili Discography, 1984–91; Rubicon, 1992–95; Co-wrote, produced, album Dawnrazor; The Nephilim; Elizium; Revelations; What Starts Ends; Roo 101; One More Nightmare, 2000. *Honours:* Best Album and Band, Melo Maker Readers Poll. *Membership:* PRS; Musicians' Union; BPI. *Address:* 5 Regent St, Stotfold, Herts SG5 4EA, England.

WRIGHT, Rick; b. 28 July 1943, London, England. Musician (keyboard *Career:* Member, Pink Floyd, 1965–80; 1986–; Performances include: Ron International Pop Festival, 1968; Hyde Park, London, 1968; Bath Festiva 1970; Montreux Festival, 1971; Knebworth Festival, 1975; Films: Pink Floy Live At Pompeii, 1972. *Recordings:* Albums: Piper at the Gates of Dawn, 196 A Saucerful of Secrets, 1968; More (film soundtrack), 1969; Zabriskie Poin (film soundtrack), 1969; Ummagumma, 1969; Atom Heart Mother, 197 Relics, 1971; Meddle, 1971; Obscured By Clouds, 1972; The Dark Side of T Moon, 1973; Wish You Were Here (No. 1, UK and USA), 1975; Animals, 197 The Wall (No. 1, USA), 1979; A Momentary Lapse of Reason, 1987; T Delicate Sound of Thunder, 1988; Shine On, 1992; The Division Bell, 199 Pulse, 1995; Echoes: The Best Of, 2001; Solo: Wet Dream, 1977; As Zee (wi Dee Harris): Identity, 1984; Solo: Broken China, 1996; Singles include: S Emily Play, 1967; Another Brick In The Wall, 1979; Run Like Hell, 198 When The Tigers Break Free, 1982; Learning To Fly, 1987; On The Turni Away, 1987; 1 Slip, 1988. *Honours:* Best Group Video, MTV Music Awar 1988; Ivor Novello Award, Outstanding Contribution To British Music, 199 Rock and Roll Hall of Fame, 1995. *Current Management:* Steve O'Rour

EMKA Productions Ltd, 43 Portland Rd, Holland Park, London W11 4LJ, England.

WRIGHT, Tony; b. Bradford, Yorkshire, England. Vocalist. *Career:* Singer, UK rock group Terrovision (formerly the Spoilt Bratz), 1986–; Support tours with The Ramones; Motörhead; Television apperances include: Top of the Pops. *Recordings:* Albums: Formaldehyde, 1993; How To Make Friends and Influence People, 1994; Regular Urban Survivors, 1996; Shaving Peaches, 1998; Good To Go, 2001; Whales And Dolphins: The Very Best Of Terrorvision, 2001; Singles: Oblivion, 1994; Middleman, 1994; Pretend Best Friend, 1994; Alice What's The Matter, 1994; Some People Say, 1995; Perseverance, 1996; Tequila, 1999; III Wishes, 1999. *Current Management:* JPR Management, The Power House, 70 Chiswick High Rd, London W4 1SY, England.

WU, Vanness; b. USA. Actor; Vocalist. *Career:* Actor, Taiwanese television series, Meteor Garden, based on Japanese cartoon strip, Boys Are Prettier Than Flowers; Mem., boy band, F4 (Flowers 4). *Recordings:* Album: Meteor Rain, 2002. *Address:* Sony Music Entertainment (Taiwan) Ltd, c/o Sony/ATV Music Publishing Asia, Suite 2801-13, 28th Floor, Citic Tower, No. 1 Tim Mei Ave, Admiralty, Hong Kong.

WU BAI; b. 1968, Chaiyi Province, Taiwan (China). Actor; Musician; Vocalist; Songwriter. *Career:* Appeared in films: A Beautiful New World, 1998; The Personals; Time and Tide, 2000; Singer, songwriter with China Blue, 1993–.

WYATT, Robert; b. 28 Jan. 1945, Bristol, England. Composer; Vocalist. m. Alfreda Benge, 26 July 1974, 1 s. *Career:* Featured in full-length profile, Catalan Television, mid-1980s; Various radio programmes, Europe, USA; Several recordings own pieces including: Old Rottenhat, solo CD; EPS, Box set of mini albums. *Compositions:* Heaps of Sheeps, with Alfreda Benge, 1997; September 9th; Alien; Out of Season; A Sunday in Madrid. *Recordings:* Matching Mole/Little Red Record; Rock Bottom; Ruth Is Stranger Than Richard; Dondestan (with poems by Alfreda Benge), compilation, mid-80s; Shleep, CD, 1997; Hapless Child, with Mike Mantler and Carla Bley, 1976; Drummer on recordings by: Kevin Ayers; Syd Barrett; Hatfield & The North, Soft Machine. *Publications:* MW, with J M Marchetti. *Honours:* Grand Prix Du Disque, Academie Charles Cros. *Membership:* PRS; MCPS; Musicians' Union; PAMRA. *Current Management:* Hannibal/Ryko.

WYKES, Debsey; b. 21 Dec. 1960, London, England. Vocalist; Songwriter; Musician (bass). *Career:* Six years with all girl band Dolly Mixture; Support tours with The Undertones, Bad Manners, The Jam, Dexy's Midnight Runners; Films: Dolly Mixture documentary, director Simon West, 1983; Backing vocals, Saint Etienne, 2 years; British tours, European tour, US tour; Television includes: Top of the Pops; Something Else; The Word; Later With Jools Holland; The Beat; Glastonbury; Radio sessions: Dolly Mixture, John Peel session, Radio 1, 1979; Kid Jensen sessions, 1981, 1982. *Recordings:* 4 singles, 1980–83; Double album: Demonstration Tapes, 1983, re-released 1995; with Captain Sensible: 6 singles include: Happy Talk (No. 1, UK charts), 1982; with Coming Up Roses: I Said Ballroom (mini album); Various backing vocals: Saint Etienne; Duetted on: Who Do You Think You Are?; Backing vocals on: Sylvie, 1998; The Bad Photographer, 1998; with Birdie: Singles: Folk Singer, 1999; Let Her Go, 1999; Such A Sound, 2000; Sidewalk, 2001; Albums: Some Dusty, 1999; Triple Echo, 2001.

WYLIE, Pete; Vocalist; Songwriter; Musician (guitar). *Career:* Mem., Crucial Three; Founding mem., Wah! Heat, later renamed Wah!, 1979–84; Mem., Sinful, 1986; Mem., Pete Wylie and Wah! the Mongrel, 1991; Solo artiste; Mem., Mighty Wah!, 1998–. *Recordings:* Albums: with Wah!: Nah Poo: The Art Of Bluff, 1981; Wah! The Maverick Years 1981–1982, 1982; A Word To The Wise Guy, 1984; The Way We Wah! (compilation), 1984; with Sinful: Sinful, 1987. Singles: with Mighty Wah!: Heart As Big As Liverpool (EP), 1998. *Address:* Disgraceland, PO Box 154, Liverpool L17 8YR, England. *E-mail:* themightywah@hotmail.com. *Website:* www.petewylie.com.

WYMAN, Bill, (William George Perks); b. 24 Oct. 1936, Lewisham, London, England. Musician (bass). m. (1) Diane Cory, 1959, divorced 1968, 1 s., (2) Mandy Smith, 1989, divorced 1991, m. (3) Suzanne Accosta, 1993, 3 d. *Career:* Member, The Rolling Stones, 1962–93; Owner: WGW Holdings; Ripple Productions; Ripple Records; Ripple Music; WGW Enterprises; Wytel Music; KJM Nominees; Sticky Fingers Restaurant; Numerous Rolling Stones tours and concerts 1963–90; ARMS Tour, UK and USA, 1983; Willie and the Poor Boys, 1985; Bill Wyman's Rhythm Kings, 1989–2000. *Recordings:* Albums include: The Rolling Stones, 1964; The Rolling Stones, No 2, 1965; Out of Our Heads, 1965; Aftermath, 1966; Between The Buttons, 1967; Their Satanic Majesties Request, 1967; Beggar's Banquet, 1968; Let It Bleed, 1969; Get Yer Ya-Ya's Out, 1969; Sticky Fingers, 1971; Exile On Main Street, 1972; Goat's Head Group, 1973; It's Only Rock and Roll, 1974; Black and Blue, 1976; Some Girls, 1978; Emotional Rescue, 1980; Still Life, 1982; Primitive Cool, 1987; Steel Wheels, 1989; Flashpoint, 1991; solo: Monkey Grip, 1974; Stone Alone, 1976; Green Ice (film soundtrack), 1981; Bill Wyman; Digital Dreams, 1983; Stuff, 1991; Struttin' Our Stuff; Anyway the Wind Blows, 1999; Groovin' 2000;

Double Bill, 2001; Blues Odyssey, 2001; Singles include: Come On; I Wanna Be Your Man; Get Off of My Cloud; 19th Nervous Breakdown; Let's Spend The Night Together; It's All Over Now; Little Red Rooster; (I Can't Get No) Satisfaction; Jumping Jack Flash; Honky Tonk Women; Brown Sugar; Miss You; Ruby Tuesday; Paint It Black; Going To A Go-Go; Emotional Rescue; It's Only Rock 'n' Roll; Harlem Shuffle; Start Me Up; Angie; Undercover of The Night; Harlem Shuffle; solo: (Si Si) Je Suis Un Rock Star; Come Back Suzanne; A New Fashion. *Publications:* Stone Alone—The Story of a Rock and Roll Band (with Ray Coleman), 1990; Wyman Shoots Chagall, 2000; Bill Wyman Blues Odyssey (with Richard Havers, 2001; Rolling With The Stones (with Richard Havers), 2002. *Honours:* Lord of the Manor or Gedding and Thornwoods, Suffolk, 1968–; Silver Clef Award, Nordoff-Robbins Music Therapy, 1982; Grammy Lifetime Achievement Award, 1986; Inducted into Rock and Roll Hall of Fame, 1989; Q Award, Best Live Act, 1990; Prince's Trust Award, 1991; Ivor Novello Awards, Outstanding Contribution To British Music, 1991; Literary Award, Memphis Blues Foundation, 2002. *Address:* c/o Ripple Productions, 344 Kings Rd, London SW3 5UR, England. *Website:* www.billwyman.com.

WYNENS, Rene; b. 21 Aug. 1954, Bouwel, Belgium. Musician (drums); Television and Film Figuration. m. Helsen Anita, 6 Sept. 1974, 1 s. *Education:* Private lessons, by drummer Jan Cuyvers and Academie of Music Herentals. *Career:* Figuration in different professional films: Brylcream Boulevard; Karakter; Elixir d'Anvers; Gastons War; Left Luggage; Sono Pazzo Di Iris Blond; De Bal; Lijmen Het Been; Iedereen Beroemd; Music Clip For Nova Star; Different television productions for several TV stations and production houses; TV soaps: Wittekerke; Familie; Levensgevaar; Vennebos; Dokters; Gaston Berghmansshow '98 I and II; De Kampioenen; Engeltjs; Sitcom with Walter Baele; Founder, drummer and contact person of rock and roll/beatgroup, Big Problem. *Recordings:* Album CD, Big Problem 1; Album CD, Big Problem Rockers Look Out; Album CD, Big Problem Look Out Again. *Membership:* Belgian Drumclub; Dutch Slagwerkkrant; Modern Drummer. *Current Management:* Big Problem, PO Box 27, 2200 Herentals, Belgium.

WYNNE, Michael Alexander; b. West Kirby, Merseyside, England. Composer; Songwriter; Record Prod; Arranger; Musician (electric, acoustic guitars, mandolin, banjo). *Education:* BA, Newcastle University. *Career:* Part-time recording, live work, with Irish group Flynn and Wynne; Tours include Holland, Germany, Singapore; Worked in Karachi, 1989; Producer, live all-star show, and pop album, singer Mohammed Ali Shiakhi; Also film score composition; Producer, dance album, New York, 1993; Television apperance with band Posh Monkeys, UK. *Compositions:* Composed musical Baby and 3 Devils. *Recordings:* Shiakhi Speaks (Karachi); The Wise Guys (Abbey Road). *Membership:* Musicians' Union; PRS; BAC&S. *Address:* c/o Wilson Barca, 13–14 Dean St, London W1V 5AH, England.

WYNONNA, (Wynonna Judd); b. 1966. Country Vocalist; Musician. *Career:* Member, Country duo, The Judds, with mother Naomi, 1984–90; Solo artiste, billed as Wynnona, 1991–; Most successful country duo, as the Judds, with 15m. album sales; Undefeated, all 3 major US Country Awards, 8 consecutive years; Co-founder, booking agency Pro-Tours, 1988. *Recordings include:* Singles: Had A Dream For The Heart, 1983; Mama He's Crazy, 1984; Why Not Me, 1984; Girls' Night Out, 1985; Rockin' With The Rhythm of The Rain, 1986; Let Me Tell You About Love, 1989; Love Can Build A Bridge, 1990; No One Else on Earth, 1992; My Strongest Weakness, 1992; Only Love, 1993; Healing, 1994; Rock Bottom, 1994; When Love Starts Talkin', 1997; Love Like That, 1999; Can't Nobody Love You Like I Do…, 1999; Albums include: with The Judds: The Judds, 1984; Why Not Me?, 1985; Rockin' With The Rhythm of The Rain, 1986; Heartland, 1987; Greatest Hits, 1988; River of Time, 1989; Love Can Build A Bridge, 1990; The Judds Collection, 1991; The Essential, 1996; Solo albums: Wynonna, 1992; Tell Me Why, 1993; Revelations, 1996; The Other Side, 1997; New Day Dawning, 2000; Guest vocals on recordings by: Huey Lewis; Kelly Price; Kenny Rogers; Brady Seals; Tammy Wynette. *Honours:* 7 Grammy Awards; 4 ACM Awards, Best Duet, 1984–89; 3 CMA Awards, Best Vocal Duo, 1988–91. *Current Management:* William Morris. *Address:* c/o The Judd House, 325 Bridge St, Franklin, TN 37064, USA.

WYSOCKI, Jon; b. 17 Jan. 1971, Northampton, MA, USA. Musician (drums). *Career:* Invited to join Staind rock group by friend and guitarist Mike Mushok; First gig with band, 1995; Released self-financed debut album, 1996; Album sold 4,000 copies; Discovered by Fred Durst, 1997; Signed to Flip/Elektra; Presented to rock cognoscenti at Limp Bizkit gold record party for Three Dollar Bill Y'All $, 1998; Major breakthrough with unscheduled smash US No. 1 radio hit Outside; Appeared on bill for Korn-founded Family Values tours, 1999, 2001; Headlined MTV's Return of the Rock tour, 2000. *Recordings:* Albums: Tormented, 1996; Dysfunction, 1999; Break The Cycle, 2001. Singles: Mudshovel, 1999; Just Go, 1999; Home, 2000; Outside, 2000; It's Been Awhile, 2001; Fade, 2001; For You, 2001. *Honours:* Break The Cycle certified quadruple platinum by RIAA; It's Been Awhile topped Billboard Modern Rock Singles Chart for record-equalling 16 weeks; VH-1 Award, Your Song Kicked Ass But Was Played Too Damn Much prize, 2001. *Address:* c/o The Firm Inc, 9465 Wilshire Blvd, Suite 500, Beverly Hills, CA 90212, USA. *Website:* www.staind.com.

X

X (CROSS), Alan; b. 8 March 1958, London, England. Prod; Writer; Musician (keyboard). *Education:* BA; Diploma, Architecture Pt III Professional; Grade 5 Theory. *Career:* Founder mem., Chakk; Signed to MCA Records/Publishing, 1985; Signed solo publishing deal with Warner Chappell; Writer and prod.; International DJ; Composer, film soundtracks. *Recordings:* Set Me Free, Clubland; So In Love/Real Deal, Judy Cheeks; Lost, 1996; Decibel, 1996; Down 2 Da Disco, 1999; Come N Geddit, 1999; The Carry On Gang, 1999. *Current Management:* XTRAX. *Address:* PO Box 966, London SE11 5SA, England.

XIMENES, Charlson Pedro Vasconcelos; b. 8 May 1965, Sao Caitano, Pernambuco, Brazil. Performer; Songwriter; Musician (guitar, bass, drums, saxophone); Vocalist. *Education:* Songwriting, Music in the Making, Music History, Morley College, London. *Career:* Radio broadcasts: Radio Bitury; Belo Jardim; Garanhuns Difusora; 97.7 São Paulo, Brazil; WMRZ Radio Miami, USA. Television appearances: Belezinha the Clown TV Show; Brazil tour with Universitaria TV crew. *Recordings:* With Flying Squad (Esquadrilha Da Fumaça): Tora Tora Tora, 1984; With Deja Vu: Black Angel, 1987; Love Me Tonite, 1988; Collision Course, 1998; With Nando Lynch: Never Around, 2000. *Honours:* Amateur Theatre Background Music Award, Brazil, 1980; Second Prize, Northeastern Popular Music Festival, Belo Jardim Pe, Brazil. *Membership:* Musicians' Union. *Website:* www.charlson.org.uk; www.audiosurge.com; www.presscafe.com.

Y

YA, Kid K, (Manuela Kamosi); b. 1973, Zaire. Rap Artiste. *Career:* Moved to Belgium, aged 11; Mem., Antwerp-based rap group Fresh Beat; Mem., Technotronik; Rapping partnership with MC Eric. *Recordings:* Albums: with Technotronik: Pump Up The Jam, 1990; Trip On This: Remixes, 1990; Body To Body, 1991; Solo: One World Nation, 1992. Singles: Pump Up The Jam (Number 2, UK), 1989; Get Up (Before The Night Is Over) (No. 2, UK), 1990; This Beat Is Technotronik, 1990; Rockin' Over The Beat, 1990; with Hi Tek: Spin That Wheel, 1990; Solo: Awesome, 1991; Let This Housebeat Drop, 1992; That Man, 1993; with Robi-Rob's Clubworld: Shake That Body, 1996. *Current Management:* ARS Productions. *Address:* Singel 5, 2550 Kontich, Belgium.

YAGNIK, Alka; b. India. Vocalist. *Career:* Indian film playback singer; Musically trained from an early age; All India Radio artist in Kolkata; Won a Sugam Sangeet award, aged 11; Sang a few lines in film Payal Ki Jhankar, 1979; First full song on film was a duet with Amit Kumar, Hum Tum Rahenge, in Hamari Bahu Alka but the film was delayed; First release was Mere Angne Mein from Laawaris, 1981; Sang regularly for most of the top directors throughout the 1980s; Became established as one of the top playback singers with massive hit Ek Do Teen, 1988. *Recordings:* soundtracks include: Mera Jawaab, 1985; Biwi Ho To Aisi, Qayamat Se Qayamat Tak, Tezaab, 1988; 100 Days, Saajan, Afsana Pyar Ka, Akayla, 1991; Deewana, Khiladi, Raju Ban Gaya Gentleman, 1992; Darr, Hum Hain Rahi Pyaar Ke, Anari, 1993; Akele Hum Akele Tum, Barsaat, Coolie No 1, Karan Arjun, 1995; Gupt, Ishq, Judaai, Pardes, Yes Boss, 1997; China-Gate, Ghulam, 1998; Baadshah, Dil Kya Kare, Dillagi, Hum Aapke Dil Mein Rehte…, Hum Dil De Chuke Sanam, Hum Saath-Saath Hain, Jaanam Sanjha Karo, Taal, 1999; Champion, Deewane, Dulhan Hum Le Jayenge, Har Dil Jo Pyar Karega, Josh, Kahin Pyaar Na Ho Jaaye, Kaho Naa… Pyaar Hai, Refugee, 2000; Albela, Bas Itna Sa Khwaab Hai, Choori Choori Chupke Chupke, Daman, Dil Chahta Hai, Ek Rishtaa – The Bond of Love, Kasoor, Lagaan, One 2 Ka 4, Pyaar Ishq Aur Mohabbat, Pyaar Tune Kya Kiya, Rahul, Yaadein, 2001. *Honours:* 4 Filmfare Awards; 2 National Awards.

YAMAKOSHI, Brian Seiji; b. 29 Dec. 1957, Chicago, Illinois, USA. Musician (koto – Music theory, guitar, piano, and koto training. *Career:* Television appearances: Numerous in Japan; Concon C'est Nous (France); NHK Television and radio, Japan; BBC Radio. *Recordings:* Snowflake, Peter Gabriel; Akiko Yano, Akira Inoue; World Diary, with Tony Levin, Manu Katché, Shanker, 1996. *Membership:* ASCAP; JASRAC; SACEM. *Current Management:* Ms Naoto Tsunoi.

YANG, Mu; b. 16 Aug. 1949, Fuzhou, People's Republic of China. Ethnomusicologist. *Education:* BA and Diploma in Musicology, Central Conservatory of Music, Beijing, People's Republic of China, 1983; PhD, Ethnomusicology, University of Queensland, Australia, 1990. *Career:* Violinist, Composer, Conductor, 1971–78; Music Editor and Programme Producer, National Broadcasting Service, Beijing, 1983–85; Sessional Lecturer, Project Director, Research Fellow in Ethnomusicology, Monash University, Melbourne, 1990–95; Visiting Fellow, Australian National University, Canberra, 1995–98; Research Fellow, Northern Territory University; Australia, 1999–2002. *Publications:* Chinese Musical Instruments: An Introduction, 1993; Articles in Music Research (Beijing), Musicology Australia, Ethnomusicology, International Journal of Music Education, Yearbook for Traditional Music, Asian Music, Journal of the Central Conservatory of Music (Beijing). *Honours:* Jaap Kunst Prize, Society for Ethnomusicology, USA, 1998. *Membership:* Society for Ethnomusicology; International Council of Traditional Music; Musicological Society of Australia; Asscn for Chinese Music Research, USA. *Address:* School of Southeast Asian and Australian Studies, Northern Territory University, Darwin, NT 0909, Australia.

YANKOVIC, 'Weird' Al (Alfred); b. 23 Oct. 1959, Lynwood, California, USA. Musician (accordion); Songwriter; Performer; Actor. *Education:* BA, Architecture, California Polytechnic San Luiz Obispo, California; Accordion lessons. *Career:* As Weird Al, 15 years of successful parodies of pop classics; Concert appearances; Television and radio appearances: including own Showtime and MTV specials; 3 best-selling home videos; Film: UHF, 1989. *Recordings include:* Ricky, 1983; Weird Al Yankovic In 3-D, 1984; Dare To Be Stupid, 1985; Polka Party, 1986; Fat (parody of Michael Jackson: Bad), 1988; Greatest Hits, 1988; Peter And The Wolf, 1988; UHF (soundtrack), 1989; Off The Deep End, featuring the hit Smells Like Nirvana, 1992; The Food Album, 1993; Apalooza, 1993; Bad Hair Day, 1996; Running with Scissors, 1999; Hit single: Eat It, 1984; Like A Surgeon, 1985; Compilation albums: Greatest Hits, 1989; Greatest Hits Vol. 2, 1994. *Publications:* The Authorized Al, autobiography by Al Yankovic and Tino Insana, 1985. *Honours:* Grammy Awards: Best Comedy Recording, for Eat It, 1984; Best Video: Fat, 1988. *Membership:* NARAS; BMI; AFofM. *Current Management:* Jan Levey,

Imaginary Entertainment. *Address:* 923 Westmount Dr., Los Angeles, CA 90069, USA.

YANNI, (Yanni Chryssomallis); b. 1955, Kalamata, Greece. Composer; Musician (keyboards). *Education:* Psychology degree, Minnesota. *Career:* Keyboard player with US progressive rock group Chameleon; Composer, leader, own orchestra; Recent concerts include: The Acropolis, Athens, 1993; Royal Albert Hall, London, 1995; Taj Mahal, India, 1997; Forbidden City, People's Republic of China, 1997. *Recordings:* Albums include: Keys To Imagination, 1986; Out of Silence, 1987; Chameleon Days, 1988; Niki Nana, 1989; Reflections of Passion, 1990; In Celebration of Life, 1991; Dare To Dream, 1992; Yanni – Live At The Acropolis, 1993; Tribute, 1997; Winter Light, 1999; Snowfall, 2000; Soaring Free, 2000; If I Could Tell You, 2000. *Honours:* 2 Grammy Awards. *Current Management:* CPRA Inc, 1712 Cypress Row Dr., West Palm Beach, FL 33411, USA.

YARED, Gabriel; b. 7 Oct. 1949, Beirut, Lebanon. Composer. *Career:* Composer of film scores. *Compositions:* Miss O'Gynie And The Flower Man, 1974; Every Man For Himself, 1979; Malevil, 1981; Invitation Au Voyage, 1982; Sarah, 1983; The Moon In The Gutter, 1983; Hanna K., 1983; Adieu Bonaparte, 1984; Dangerous Moves, 1984; Fire On Sight, 1984; Nemo, 1984; Flagrant Desire, 1985; Scout Toujours…, 1985; Betty Blue, 1986; Désordre, 1986; Beyond Therapy, 1987; Agent Trouble, 1987; The Veiled Man, 1987; Les Saisons Du Plaisir, 1988; Clean And Sober, 1988; Camille Claudel, 1988; Tennessee Nights, 1989; Romero, 1989; Vincent & Theo, 1990; Tatie Danielle, 1990; Sheherazade, 1990; The King's Whore, 1990; The Lover, 1991; Map Of The Human Heart, 1992; L'Instinct De L'Ange, 1992; The Ark And The Deluge, 1992; IP5: The Island Of Pachyderms, 1992; The Girl In The Air, 1992; The Groundhogs, 1993; Low Profile, 1994; Poorly Extinguished Fires, 1994; Wings Of Courage, 1995; Hercule Et Sherlock, 1996; The English Patient, 1996; La Dame Du Cirque, 1996; Tonka, 1997; Premier De Cordée, 1998; City Of Angels, 1998; The Talented Mr Ripley, 1999; Message In A Bottle, 1999; The Next Best Thing, 2000; Autumn In New York, 2000; Lisa, 2001; Possession, 2002; L'Idole, 2002. *Honours:* Academy Award, Best Original Dramatic Score, for The English Patient, 1996; Golden Globe, Best Original Score, for The English Patient, 1996. *Address:* c/o Gorfaine-Schwartz Agency, 13245 Riverside Dr., Suite 450, Sherman Oaks, CA 91423, USA.

YARLING, Nicole; b. 31 July 1957, Brooklyn, NY, USA. Musician (Violin, Vocals). m. John Yarling. *Education:* BA, Baruch College; MA, Columbia University; Private Instruction in Violin, Composition and Arranging. *Career:* Freelance, Formed Ensemble Strings, 1981–84; Formed R&B Rock Band Little Nicky and the Slicks, 1985; Featured Soloist with Jimmy Yarling, 1990–94; Walden Wood Concert, 1993; Tribute to Ella Fitzgerald, 1997; JVC – Jazz Festival, 1998. *Recordings:* Strings Attached, 1984; Little Nicky and the Slicks, 1988; Fruitcakes, 1994; Afro Blue Band, 1997; N Yarling, 1999; Also appears on: Terrance Simien, Positively Beadhead, 1999; Tom Lippincott, Painting The Slow Train Brown, 2001; Yochanan Mascaro, Restoration, 2001. *Membership:* AFTRA. *Current Management:* John Levy Enterprises, 1828 Coolidge Ave, ALTadena, CA 91001, USA. *Address:* 690 Siesta Key Circle #2018, Deerfield Beach, Florida 33441, USA.

YARROW, Peter; b. 31 May 1938, New York, USA. Vocalist; Songwriter; Film and Television Prod. *Career:* Member, Peter Paul and Mary, 1960–; Television specials: 25th Anniversary Special, PBS, 1985; A Holiday Celebration, PBS, 1988; Peter Paul and Mommy Too, PBS, 1993; Co-founder, Kerrville Folk Festival, Texas; Founding member, board of directors, Newport Folk Festival; Television Specials, Lifelines, PBS, 1995. *Compositions:* Author/co-author songs include: Puff The Magic Dragon; Light One Candle; Day Is Done; The Great Mandala; Torn Between Two Lovers. *Recordings:* 16 albums with Peter Paul and Mary; 4 solo albums; Compilations include: Songs Of Conscience And Concern, 1999. *Honours:* Allard K Lowenstein Award (for Human Rights, Peace and Freedom); Vista Citizen Action Leadership Award; Kate Wolf Memorial Award, The World Folk Music Asscn; Grammy Awards, 1962, 1963, 1969. *Membership:* Board of Directors: Center for Global Education, North American Congress on Latin America, Friends of Vista. *Current Management:* Walk Street Management. *Address:* 1639 B Electric Ave, Venice, CA 90291, USA.

YASINITSKY, Gregory Walter; b. 3 Oct. 1953, San Francisco, California, USA. Composer; Musician (saxophone); Educator. m. Ann Marie Kelley, 15 Jan. 1977, 1 d. *Education:* AA Music, College San Mateo, 1973; San Francisco State University, BM, Composition, 1976, MA, 1978; DMA, Composition, Eastman School of Music, Rochester, New York, 1995; Composition studies: Joseph Schwantner; Wayne Peterson; Lou Harrison; Samuel Adler; Robert Morris; Saxophone studies with Ramon Ricker, Joe Henderson, Donald Carroll, James Matheson, Jerry Vejmola. *Career:* Professor of Music, Co-ordinator, Jazz Studies, Washington State Univesity, 1982–; Lecturer in

Music, San Jose State University, 1978–82; San Francisco State University, 1977–81; Lecturer, Jazz Studies, 1977–80; Principal saxophonist, Spokane Symphony, 1991–; Orchestral saxophonist with: San Francisco Symphony; Oakland Symphony; Cabrillo Festival Orchestra; Performances as jazz saxophonist with: Sarah Vaughan; Lionel Hampton; Stan Getz; Clark Terry; Louis Bellson; Randy Brecker; Tom Harrell; Gary Burton; Mark Isham; Art Lande; Performances, clinics, workshops throughout USA, Canada, Japan, Europe. *Compositions:* Over 90 works published. *Publications:* Articles for: Jazz Educators Journal; Band World; New Ways; Aftertouch; Saxophone Symposium. *Honours:* Mullen Award Excellence in Teaching, Washington State University, 1989; Jazz Fellowship, US National Endowment for the Arts, 1986; ASCAP Special Awards for Composition, 1986–. *Membership:* ASCAP; IAJE; MENC. *Address:* NW 485 Robert St, Pullman, WA 99163, USA.

YATES, Mark (Sark); b. 4 April 1968. Musician (guitar). *Career:* Joined Spoilt Bratz with Shutty, Leigh Marklew and Tony Wright; Renamed as Terrorvision; Major label deal, 1991; Support slot to Ramones; Numerous headlining tours and TV appearances. *Recordings:* Singles: My House, 1993; Oblivion, 1994; Pretend Best Friend, 1994; Alice, What's The Matter, 1994; Bad Actress, 1996; Perseverance, 1996; Easy, 1996; Moonage Daydream, 1997; Josephine, 1998; Tequila, 1999; Albums: My House, 1993; Formaldehyde, 1993; How to Win Friends and Influence People, 1994; Regular Urban Survivors, 1996; Shaving Peaches, 1998; Good To Go, 2001; Whales And Dolphins: The Very Best Of Terrorvision, 2001.

YEARWOOD, Trisha; b. 19 Sept. 1964, Monticello, Georgia, USA. Country Vocalist. *Education:* Belmont University. *Career:* Session singer, Nashville, 1985–; Discovered by, support tours with Garth Brooks, 1991. *Recordings:* Albums: Trisha Yearwood, 1991; Hearts In Armor, 1992; The Song Remembers When, 1993; The Sweetest Gift, 1994; Thinking About You, 1995; Everybody Knows, 1996; Song Book (A Collection of Hits), 1997; Where Your Road Leads, 1997; Real Live Woman, 2000; Inside Out, 2001; Backing vocals, No Fences, Garth Brooks; Tower of Strength (Leonard Cohen tribute album), 1995. *Honours:* Best New Country Artist, American Music Award, 1991; Country Music Asscn, Female Vocalist of the Year, 1997; British Country Music Award, Female Vocalist of the Year, 1997; Grammy Awards for: Best Country Vocal Collaboration; Best Female Country Performance, 1998; Academy of Country Music Award, Top Female Vocalist, 1998; Country Music Asscn Award, Female Vocalist of the Year, 1998. *Current Management:* Force Inc. *Address:* 1505 16th Ave S, Nashville, TN 37212, USA.

YELLOW SOX. See: **DIESEL.**

YEN, Jerry; Actor; Vocalist. *Career:* Actor, Taiwanese television series, Meteor Garden, based on Japanese cartoon strip, Boys Are Prettier Than Flowers; Mem., boy band, F4 (Flowers 4). *Recordings:* Album: Meteor Rain, 2002. *Address:* Sony Music Entertainment (Taiwan) Ltd, c/o Sony/ATV Music Publishing Asia, Suite 2801-13, 28th Floor, Citic Tower, No. 1 Tim Mei Ave, Admiralty, Hong Kong.

YEN, Wen-Hsiung; b. 26 June 1934, Tainan, China (Taiwan). Musician (piano, erhu); Composer; Conductor. m. Yuan Yuan, 6 Jan. 1961, 3 s. *Education:* BA, National Taiwan Normal University; MA, Chinese Culture University; MA, University of California at Los Angeles, PhD, candidate; Cultural Doctorate, Philosophy and Music, World University; Studied Piano with Qing-Yan Zhou, Fu-Mei Lee, Composition with Paul Chihara Hsu, Chang-Houei and Mike Mitacek. *Career:* Radio appearance, Taiwan, 1967, 1990; TV appearance, Channel 62, 1992; Leading Chinese Music Orchestra of Southern California, for An Evening of Chinese Music and Dance; Professor and Instructor, colleges and universities; Video, with Chinese American Musicians' Association of Southern California; Video, Chinese Performing Arts Association of America; Conductor, Chinese Music Orchestra of Southern California, Chinese Art and Culture Festival, CA, 2002. *Publications:* Taiwan Folk Songs, Vol. I, 1967, Vol. II, 1969; A Dictionary of Chinese Music, 1967; A Collection of Wen-Hsiung Yen's Songs, 1968, Vol. II, 1987, Vol. III, 2002; Chinese Musical Culture and Folk Songs, 1989; Silk and Bamboo Expresses Emotion of Meaning, 2000. *Honours:* Outstanding Teacher, Confucius Commemorative Day Ceremony, Los Angeles, 1984; National Taiwan Normal University Alumni Asscn of Southern California. *Membership:* Overseas Chinese Affairs Commission; International Council for Traditional Music; Society for Ethnomusicology; Society for Asian Music. *Address:* 615 Las Turnas Dr., #B, Arcadia, CA 91007, USA.

YEO, Oscar, (Port); b. 28 June 1929, London, England. Musician (drums); Vocalist; Graphic designer. m. Gay Clarke, 16 Sept. 1964, 2 s. *Education:* Private violin tuition as child. *Career:* Known as Port, pre-1960; Founder member, Eric Silk's Southern Jazz Band; Broadcasts include: Albert Hall, Festival Hall concerts, include Festival of Britain, 1950–54; Freelanced music; Graphic design to 1959; Professional musician until 1963; Semi-professional, 1963–. *Membership:* Musicians' Union.

YEOH, Nicola Beng Ean; b. 24 May 1973, London, England. Musician (piano); Composer; Arranger; Band Leader. *Education:* A Level Music, Centre

Young Musicians Weekend Arts College. *Career:* Courtney Pine Band, 1991–94; Neneh Cherry, 1993; The Roots, 1994; Eddie Harris, 1996; Jools Holland, TV Show, Later, 1993; Arsenio Hall, show, USA, 1993; Infinitum, own band, featuring Keith Le Blanc and Michael Mondesir, Radio 3 Broadcast, 1993; Composer in Residence for NYJOS, 1998–99; Commission of Quiet Freedom, 1998. *Compositions:* Commissioned: Six as 1, 1996; Speechmix X-ploration, 1997; Be-Bop, 1997; Entwined, for pianist Joanna MacGregor, 1997; Infinitum, Big Band, 12 piece, 1997; Common Denominator, commissioned by LAB, 1998; Two Rainbows, 1998; 4 Pieces for Cello and Piano, commissioned by Norfolk and Norwich Jazz Festival, 1999. *Recordings:* Red, Hot and Cool, with The Roots and Roy Ayers. *Membership:* PRS; PAMRA; MU. *Current Management:* Beng Ean Productions, 1 Rodney House, Donegal St, London N1 9QF. *Address:* 67 Dyne Rd, London NW6 7DR, England.

YERNJAKIAN, Lilit; b. 8 Feb. 1950, Yerevan, Armenia. Musician (piano); Musicologist. m. V Gasparian, 2 s. *Education:* Yerevan State Conservatory, 1968–73. *Publications:* Traditional Genres of Monody and The Present, 1987; Armenian Musicians, 1990; Mythopoetic Sources of Ashoog Dastgahus, 1990; From The History of Armenian-Persian Musical Ties, Yerevan, 1991; Hymn to the Sun, Yerevan, 1998. *Membership:* Union of Composers of Armenia. *Address:* Nalbanian St N47 Ap 19a, 375025 Yerevan, Armenia.

YETNIKOFF, Walter R; b. 11 Aug. 1933, Brooklyn, New York, USA. Record Co Exec. m. June Yetnikoff, 24 Nov. 1957, 2 s. *Education:* BA, Brooklyn College, New York Bar, 1953; LLB, Columbia University, 1956. *Career:* Lawyer, New York, 1958–61; Attorney, CBS Records, 1961–65; General attorney, CBS Group, 1965–69; Vice-Pres., International Division, CBS, 1969–71; Pres., CBS International, 1971–75; Pres., CBS Group, 1975–. *Membership:* International Federation of Producers of Phonograms and Videograms.

YOAKAM, Dwight; b. 23 Oct. 1956, Pikeville, Kentucky, USA. Country Vocalist; Musician (guitar); Songwriter. *Education:* History and Philosophy Ohio University. *Career:* Country singer, 1978–; Also played with Los Lobos Concerts include: UK and US tours; Tours with Buck Owens; Farm Aid VI Indiana, 1993. *Recordings:* Albums: Guitars, Cadillacs, 1986; Hillbilly Deluxe 1987; Buenas Noches From A Lonely Room, 1988; Just Looking For A Hit 1989; If There Was A Way, 1990; La Croix D'Amour, 1992; This Time, 1993 Gone, 1996; Under the Covers, 1997; Come on Christmas, 1997; A Long Way Home, 1998; La Croix d'Amour, 1999; dwightyoakamacoustic.net, 2000 Tomorrow's Sounds Today, 2000; South Of Heaven, West Of Hell, 2001 Singles: Honky Tonk Man, 1986; Guitars, Cadillacs, 1986; Little Sister, 1987 Streets of Bakersfield, duet with Buck Owens, (No. 1, USA Country charts) 1988; Always Late (With Your Kisses), 1988; I Sang Dixie (No. 1, USA Country charts), 1989; Suspicious Minds, from film soundtrack, Honeymoon In Vegas, 1992; Fast As You Can, 1993; Dwight Live, 1995; These Arms, 1998 *Honours:* 5 Platinum discs; One Multi Platinum disc; Gold disc; Academy of Country Music, Best New Male Artist, 1986; Music City News Country Award, Best Vocal Collaboration, with Buck Owens, 1988. *Current Management:* Borman Entertainment, 1250 Sixth St, Suite 401, Santa Monica, CA 90401, USA.

YOGESWARAN, Manickam; b. 3 March 1959, Sri Lanka. Vocalist Musician (South Indian flute, drums). *Education:* Accountancy, CIMA; Learn by Guru-Sisya method. *Career:* Concert vocalist, musician, Indo-pop music Lead singer, Dissidenten, European tours, 1993–; Concerts include Commonwealth Institute, 1992; Paris Music Festival, 1993; Music Guimet Paris, 1994; Music Festival, Chennai, India, 1995; Visiting Lecturer for Music Workshop Skills, Goldsmiths College, University of London, England *Recordings:* Background score, documentary Serendipity; 7 albums, 1990–9 Singer, Duets With Automobiles (Shobana Jeyasing Dance Company Romance With Footnotes; Tamil Classics; Collaborations include: Learning Curve, DJ Rap, 1998; Untold Things, Jocelyn Pook, 2001. *Publications* Currently compiling video: South Indian Drumming. *Honours:* Kalai Mamani London Sri Murugan Temple; Suranaya Devan, Oslo Music Asscn; Regular appearances in the December Music Festival, Chennai, 1994–. *Membership* Musicians' Union. *Address:* 29 Firdene, Tolworth, Surrey KT5 9QQ, England.

YORKE, Thom (Thomas Edward); b. 7 Oct. 1968, Wellingborough Northamptonshire, England. Vocalist; Musician (guitar, keyboard) Songwriter. *Education:* English and Art, Exeter University. *Career:* Mem. an lead singer, On A Friday, 1987, renamed Radiohead, 1991–; Also designer record sleeves; Numerous tours, festivals and television appearance *Recordings:* Albums: Pablo Honey, 1993; The Bends, 1995; OK Computer (No 1, UK and USA), 1997; Kid A (No. 1, UK and USA), 2000; Amnesiac, 2001 Might Be Wrong, 2001. Singles: Drill (EP), 1992; Creep, 1993; Anyone Can Play Guitar, 1993; Pop Is Dead, 1993; Stop Whispering, 1993; Itch (EP), 1993 My Iron Lung (EP), 1994; My Iron Lung, 1994; Live Au Forum (EP), 1995 High and Dry, 1995; Fake Plastic Trees, 1995; Just, 1995; Street Spirit (Fade Out), 1996; The Bends, 1996; Paranoid Android, 1997; Karma Police, 1997; No Surprises, 1997; Climbing Up The Walls, 1997; Airbag/How Am I Driving (EP), 1998; Pyramid Song, 2001; Knives Out, 2001; I Might Be Wrong, 2001 Contributor, Help (Bosnia Relief Album), 1995; guest vocalist with Drugstore on White Magic for Lovers, and El President, 1998; guest vocalist with Velvet Goldmine, 1998; MTV's 120 Minutes Live, 1998; Other collaborations incl.: UNKLE, 1998; P. J. Harvey, 2000. *Honours:* Grammy Award, Best Alternative Rock Performance, 1998, Best Alternative Music Album, 2000; Q Award, Best Act in the World Today, 2002. *Current Management:* Courtyard Management, 21 The Nursery, Sutton Courtenay, Abingdon, Oxfordshire OX14 4UA, England. *Address:* c/o Parlophone Records, 43 Brook Green, London W6 7EF, England. *Website:* www.radiohead.com.

YOUNG, Adrian; b. 26 Aug. 1969, Long Beach, CA, USA. Musician (drums). 1 s. *Career:* Mem., US group, No Doubt, 1989–. *Recordings:* Albums: No Doubt, 1992; Beacon Street Collection, 1994; Tragic Kingdom, 1995; Return Of Saturn, 2000; Rock Steady, 2001. Singles: Just A Girl, 1995; Don't Speak (No. 1, UK), 1997; New, 1999; Ex-Girlfriend, 2000; Simple Kind Of Life, 2000; Bathwater, 2000; Hey Baby, 2001; Hella Good, 2002; Tour (EP), 2002; Underneath It All, 2002. *Address:* c/o Interscope Records, 2220 Colorado Ave, Santa Monica, CA 90404, USA. *Website:* www.nodoubt.com.

YOUNG, Angus; b. 31 March 1959, Glasgow, Scotland. Rock Musician (guitar). *Career:* Guitarist, heavy rock group AC/DC, 1973–; Numerous tours world-wide; Major concerts include: Reading Rock Festival, 1978; Monsters of Rock Festival, Castle Donington, 1981, 1984; European rock festivals, Hungary, Switzerland, Belgium, Germany, 1991; Concert, Moscow, 1991; Over 80m. albums sales to date. *Recordings:* Singles include: Rock 'n' Roll Damnation, 1978; Highway To Hell, 1979; Touch Too Much, 1980; Rock 'n' Roll Ain't Noise Pollution, 1980; You Shook Me All Night Long, 1980; Back In Black, 1981; Let's Get It Up, 1982; For Those About To Rock (We Salute You), 1982; Guns For Hire, 1983; Nervous Shakedown, 1984; Shake Your Foundations, 1986; Who Made Who, 1986; Heatseeker, 1988; Thunderstruck, 1990; Moneytalks, 1990; Are You Ready, 1991; That's The Way I Wanna Rock 'n' Roll, 1993; Big Gun (used in film The Last Action Hero), 1993; Hard As A Rock, 1995; Albums: High Voltage, 1975; TNT, 1975; High Voltage, 1975; Dirty Deeds Done Cheap, 1976; Let There Be Rock, 1977; Powerage, 1978; If You Want Blood You've Got It, 1978; Highway To Hell, 1979; Back In Black, 1980; For Those About To Rock (We Salute You), 1981; Flick of The Switch, 1983; Fly On The Wall, 1985; Who Made Who, 1986; Blow Up Your Video, 1988; The Razor's Edge, 1990; Live, 1992; Ballbreaker, 1995; Private Parts, 1997; Bonfire, 1997; Stiff Upper Lip, 2000; Satellite Blues, 2001. *Current Management:* Hard To Handle Management, 1133 Broadway, Suite 1301, New York, NY 10010, USA.

YOUNG, Christopher; b. 28 April 1957, Red Bank, NJ, USA. Composer; Musician (drums). *Education:* University College of Los Angeles. *Compositions:* For television: Norma Jean and Marilyn, 1996; Max and Helen, 1990; Last Flight Out, 1990; Hider in the House, 1989; Vietnam War Story: The Last Days, 1989; American Harvest, 1987; Vietnam War Story, 1987; The Twilight Zone, 1985; For film: The Power, 1980; Highpoint, 1980; The Dorm That Dripped Blood, 1981; Wheels of Fire, 1984; The Oasis, 1984; Wizards of the Lost Kingdom, 1985; Def-Con 4, 1984; A Nightmare on Elm Street Part 2: Freddy's Revenge, 1985; Trick or Treat, 1986; Torment, 1986; Getting Even, 1986; Invaders from Mars, 1986; Hellraiser, 1987; Flowers in the Attic, 1987; Hellbound: Hellraiser II, 1988; Haunted Summer, 1988; Bat-21, 1988; The Fly II, 1989; Bright Angel, 1991; Jennifer Eight, 1992; The Vagrant, 1992; Rapid Fire, 1992; Dark Half, 1993; Judicial Consent, 1994; Dream Lover, 1994; Murder in the First, 1995; Tales from the Hood, 1995; Species, 1995; Virtuosity, 1995; Copycat, 1995; Unforgettable, 1996; Set It Off, 1996; Head Above Water, 1996; Murder at 1600, 1997; Man Who Knew Too Little, 1997; Rounders, 1998; Hard Rain, 1998; Hush, 1998; Urban Legend, 1998; Entrapment, 1999; In Too Deep, 1999; Hurricane, 1999; Bless the Child, 2000; Big Kahuna, 2000; Wonder Boys, 2000; The Gift, 2001; Sweet November, 2001; The Glass House, 2001; Bandits, 2001; The Shipping News, 2001. *Membership:* BMI. *Current Management:* Blue Focus Management, 15233 Ventura Blvd, Suite 200, Sherman Oaks, CA 91403, USA. *Website:* www.christopher-young.com.

YOUNG, Jesse Colin, (Perry Miller); b. 11 Nov. 1944, New York, NY, USA. Vocalist; Musician (guitar, bass). *Career:* Began as folk singer, New York; Founder member The Youngbloods, 1965–72; Appearances include: Sky River Rock Festival; Lighter Than Air Fair, 1968; Solo career, 1973–; Appeared, No Nukes, Madison Square Garden, New York, with Bruce Springsteen, Doobie Brothers, Jackson Browne, 1979. *Compositions include:* Get Together, recorded by Dave Clark Five, 1970. *Recordings:* Albums: with The Youngbloods: The Youngbloods, 1967; Earth Music, 1967; Elephant Mountain, 1969; Best of The Youngbloods, 1970; Rock Festival, 1970; Ride The Wind, 1971; Good 'n' Dusty, 1971; Sunlight, 1971; High On A Ridgetop, 1972; Get Together, 1972; Darkness, Darkness (compilation), 1998; Solo: The Soul of a City Boy, 1964; Youngblood, 1964; Song For Juli, 1973; Light Shine,

1974; Songbirds, 1974; On The Road, 1974; Love On The Wing, 1974; American Dreams, 1978. *Current Management:* Skyline Music, PO Box 31, Lancaster, NH 03584, USA.

YOUNG, John; b. 31 May 1956, Romford, Essex, England. Musician (keyboards); Songwriter. *Education:* Head Chorister, Liverpool Metropolitan Cathedral; Grade VIII Piano; A Level Music. *Career:* Tours: Uli Jon Roth – Electric Sun world tour, 1985; Robin George, UK, 1986; Roy Wood, UK, Asia, Europe, 1987–90; Paul Rodgers and Kenny Jones (billed as The Law), UK, 1991; Bonnie Tyler world tour, 1994–; Also member, MTV band, 1988. *Recordings:* Albums by Batisti; Steeleye Span; Various unsigned artists including own Project Cathedral, 1986–89; Crime of Passion, John Wetton, 1994; Live album, 1995; Qango, Live In The Hood, 2000. *Membership:* PRS. *Current Management:* The Control Group. *Address:* Chapel Mews, 68 Crewe Rd, Alsager, Cheshire ST7 2HA, England.

YOUNG, Neil; b. 12 Nov. 1945, Toronto, ON, Canada. Vocalist; Songwriter; Musician (guitar). m. Pegi Young, 1 s., 1 d. *Career:* Lead singer, The Squires; Co-founder, Buffalo Springfield (with Stephen Stills), 1966–69; Support to Rolling Stones, Hollywood Bowl, 1966; CAFF Charity concert, 1967; Support tours to Steve Miller Band, 1967; Iron Butterfly, 1968; Solo artiste, with own backing group, Crazy Horse, 1969–; Joined Crosby Stills and Nash, to become Crosby Stills Nash and Young, 1969–74; Tours include: US tour, 1969; Support to Rolling Stones, 1969; European tour, 1970; European tour with Booker T. and the MGs, 1993; US tour with Pearl Jam, 1995; Major concerts include: Royal Festival Hall, 1973; The Last Waltz (the band's farewell concert), 1976; Miami Music Festival, 1977; Live Aid, Philadelphia, 1985; Farm Aid II, 1987; Nelson Mandela–An International Tribute, Wembley, 1990; Farm Aid V, 1992; Bob Dylan's 30th Anniversary concert, Madison Square Garden, 1992; Reading Festival, 1995; Writer, dir, films: Rust Never Sleeps (also recorded soundtrack), 1979; Human Highway, 1982. *Recordings:* Albums: with Buffalo Springfield: three albums; with Crosby Stills Nash and Young: Déjà Vu (No. 1, USA), 1970; Four Way Street (No. 1, USA), 1971; So Far (No. 1, USA), 1974; with Stills/Young Band: Long May You Run, 1970; Solo (with Crazy Horse): Neil Young, 1969; Everybody Knows This Is Nowhere, 1969; After The Goldrush, 1970; Crazy Horse, 1971; Loose 1972; Harvest, 1972; Journey Through The Past, 1972; Time Fades Away, 1973; On The Beach, 1974; Tonight's The Night, 1975; Zuma, 1975; American Stars 'N' Bars, 1977; Decade, 1977; Crazy Moon, 1978; Comes A Time, 1978; Rust Never Sleeps, 1979; Live Rust, 1979; Hawks And Doves, 1980; Re-ac-tor, 1981; Trans, 1982; Everybody's Rockin', 1983; Old Ways, 1985; Landing On Water, 1987; Life, 1987; This Note's For You, 1988; American Dream, 1988; Eldorado, 1989; Freedom, 1989; Ragged Glory, 1990; Left For Dead, 1990; Arc-Weld, 1991; Harvest Moon, 1992; Lucky Thirteen, 1993; Unplugged, 1993; Sleeps With Angels, 1994; Mirror Ball, 1995; Dead Man (music from and inspired by the motion picture), 1996; Broken Arrow, 1996; Year Of The Horse, 1997; Crazy Moon And Bonus Tracks, 1997; Silver And Gold, 2000; Road Rock, 2000; Are You Passionate?, 2002. *Honours:* Grammy Award, Best New Artists (with Crosby Stills Nash and Young), 1970; Melody Maker Poll Winner, Best International Group, 1971; MTV Video Award, 1989; Rolling Stone Critics Award, Best Album, 1989; Bay Area Music Award, Outstanding Album, 1993; Q Award, Best Live Act, 1993. *Current Management:* Elliot Roberts, Lookout Management, 1460 Fourth St, Suite 210, Santa Monica, CA 90401, USA.

YUAN ENFENG; b. 22 Jan. 1940, Shaanxi Province, People's Republic of China. Folk Vocalist. m. Sun Shao, 1 s., 2 d. *Education:* Dong Yangshi Elementary School, Xian. *Career:* Joined Cultural Troupe of Provincial Broadcasting Station, 1951; Participated in over 3,000 performances, including numerous solo concerts and 1,000 radio and TV programmes; Appearances abroad include Romania, Bulgaria, fmr Czechoslovakia, fmr USSR, Japan, Thailand, Philippines and USA; Hon. Dir and Chair., Folk Music Section, Shaanxi Broadcasting Station, 1986–; Vice-Chair., Shaanxi TV Station; Mem., Chinese Musicians' Asscn; Mem. of Board, Shaanxi Branch, Chinese Cultural Exchange Centre; Mem. of many official organizations; TV film: Silver Bell. *Compositions:* (with Sun Shao) Millet Is Delicious And Caves Are Warm; Nowhere Is Better Than Our North Shaanxi; 300 songs recorded. *Publications:* Song books. *Honours:* State Actress Award, 1987; May Day Labour Medal Award, 1993. *Address:* Folk Music Section, Provincial Broadcasting and Television Station, Xian, Shaanxi, People's Republic of China.

YURKOVICH, Richard; b. 8 June 1947, Neillsville, WI, USA. Musician (accordion). m. Gabrielle Reyzer, 2 s. *Education:* Private accordion lessons. *Career:* Weekly Radio Show; Guest Appearances on Local Television; 2 Musican Tours; Owner, Manager, RY Recording Studio. *Recordings:* 20 Folk Albums. *Membership:* BMI. *Current Management:* RY Productions, N10060 Fisher Ave, Willard, WI 54493, USA.

Z

Z FACTOR. See: **LEE, Dave.**

ZABALA, Fernando; b. 19 April 1962, Madrid, Spain. Promoter; Musician (saxophone). *Education:* Lawyer. *Career:* Promoter in Spain for: U2; Bruce Springsteen; Whitney Houston; REM; Michael Jackson; Pink Floyd; Tina Turner; Bryan Adams; Bon Jovi; Mike Oldfield; Paul McCartney; Dire Straits; Joe Cocker; Simply Red; Keith Richards; Red Hot Chili Peppers; Cirque Du Soliel; David Copperfield; Current manager of Radio Tarifa, Joaquin Ruiz. *Publications:* Guiá de la Música, El Pais, Año de Rock. *Membership:* APCI (International Concert Promoters Asscn). *Address:* Sold Out, Alcalá 114–6B, 28009 Madrid, Spain.

ZAMFIR, Gheorghe; b. 6 April 1941, Găeşti, nr Bucharest, Romania. Musician (pan-pipes). *Education:* Bucharest Acad. of Music, studied under Fănică Luca; Conducting, Ciprian Porumbescu Conservatory, Bucharest, 1968. *Career:* Toured numerous countries in Europe as student and won first prize in many international competitions; Conductor of 'Ciocirlia' Folk Ensemble, Bucharest, 1969; Prof. of pan-pipes, 1970; Formed own orchestra, 1970; Recording artist, traditional folk music, pan-pipe versions of pop, classical and religious tunes, 1974–; Numerous trips to Europe, Australia, South America, Canada and USA. *Recordings:* Numerous albums include: L'Alouette, 1978; Impressions, 1978; In Paris, 1981; Zamfir, 1981; Lonely Shepherd, 1982; Music For The Millions, 1983; Romance, 1984; Atlantis, 1985; By Candlelight, 1986; Beautiful Dreams, 1988; Images, 1989; Glorious Pipes; Singles include: Doina De Jale, theme to BBC series, The Light of Experience, 1976; Theme from De Verlaten Mijn, with James Last, 1979. *Address:* Dr Teohari str. 10, Bucharest, Romania.

ZAMORA, Tye; b. 30 May 1977, Artesia, California, USA. Musician (bass guitar). *Career:* Played with local bands NOW, UVOD, The Color Red, Carpet; Stank Toof, Tyemus; Member: Alien Ant Farm, 1996–; Self-financed independent LP released to acclaim, 1999; Signed to Papa Roach's New Noize label; Second album released in conjunction with DreamWorks label, leading to major international breakthrough, 2000–01. *Recordings:* Albums: Greatest Hits, 1999; ANThology, 2001; Singles: $100 EP, 1996; Love Songs EP, 1998; Movies, Smooth Criminal, 2001. *Honours:* L.A. Music Award, Best Independent Album, 1999. *Address:* c/o New Noize, 2022 Cliff Dr., Suite 123, Santa Barbara, CA 93109, USA. *E-mail:* info@newnoize.com. *Website:* www.alienantfarm.com.

ZANDER, Robin; b. 23 Jan. 1953, Rockford, Illinois, USA. Vocalist; Musician (guitar). *Career:* Founder member, singer, guitarist, Cheap Trick, 1969–; Concerts include: California Music Festival, 1979; Reading Festival, 1979; Montreux Rock Festival, 1988; US tour with Robert Plant, 1988; US tour with Kiss, 1988; US tour with Heart, 1990. *Recordings:* Albums: with Cheap Trick: Cheap Trick, 1977; In Color, 1977; Heaven Tonight, 1978; Cheap Trick At Budokan, 1979; Dream Police, 1979; Found All The Parts, 1980; All Shook Up, 1980; One On One, 1982; Next Positions Please, 1983; Standing On The Edge, 1985; The Doctor, 1986; Lap of Luxury, 1988; Busted, 1990; The Greatest Hits, 1991; Gift, 1996; Silver, 2001; Solo: Robin Zander, 1993; with Shudder to Think: First Love, Last Rites, 1998; with Posies: Amazing Disgrace, 1999; Singles include: I Want You To Want Me, 1979; Voices, from film soundtrack Roadie, 1980; Stop This Game, 1980; If You Want My Love, 1982; Mighty Wings, from film soundtrack Top Gun, 1986; Ghost Town, 1988; Never Had A Lot To Lose, 1990; Surrender To Me, duet with Ann Wilson, from film soundtrack Tequila Sunrise, 1990; Can't Stop Falling Into Love, 1990. *Current Management:* Ken Adamany Associates, 1818 Parmenter St, Suite 202, Middleton, WI 53562, USA.

ZANKLAN; b. 22 Aug. 1966, Atchoukpa, Benin. Musician (percussion). *Education:* Benin National Gendarmerie. *Career:* National Television Programme ORIRE, 1998; Television LC2 First Anniversary, 1998; Radio Atlantique FM, 1998; Radio Golfe FM, 1998. *Compositions:* Sotie; Ohovive; Repos; Mi N'Danase; Gbehobada; Sorcier; ata N'De Kuku. *Recordings:* Album, Ohovive. *Honours:* Prize of the Most Experienced Singer in Lomé, 1996. *Membership:* BUBEDRA; UMC. *Address:* PO Box 1135 Porto-Novo, Benin.

ZANNOU, Guy Dossa; b. 15 June 1962, Porto-Novo, Benin. Musician (guitar); Vocalist. m. Blandine Ayi, 2 s., 1 d. *Career:* Appearances on Beninoise radio and TV including Coup de Pouce, Stars' Music; Participated in shows with famous African stars including François Louga, Acha Koné, Aurlus Mabélé, Afia Mala, Gadji Céli; Musical arrangements for Beninoise artists; Band Leader for Suka-Siko. *Compositions:* Corruption; Ce sera la Fête; Time is Money. *Recordings:* Corruption. *Membership:* Local Union of Pop; Musicians' Local Asscn of Artists for Environment; Secretary General, National Federation of Artists' Asscn. *Current Management:* Z Plus Productions. *Address:* 01 PO Box 447, Porto-Novo, Benin.

ZAPPELLINI, Marino; b. 17 May 1955, Bourges, France. Musician (saxophone, flute); Composer; Actor. *Education:* MMus, University of Paris; Jazz Improvisation, Harmony, Berklee School of Music, Boston, USA; Music info and Midi techniques, AFDAS; Electro-acoustic music, GMEN, GRM; Jazz professional, AFDAS; Theatre production, AFDAS. *Career:* Professional musician, 1978–; Leader, Madzano Quartet; Actor, theatre: Du Vent Dans Les Branches De Sassafras; Actor, film: 10 Seconds; Film director and composer, films: Le Onzième Comandment; 10 Seconds; Saxophone improvisation, orchestra, with MJC Marcel Cachin de Romainville, 1988–; Administrator, Artistic director, L'association loi 1901, Big Band Paris Est; Worked with numerous artistes including: Mama Bea Tiekelski; Toure Kunda; Antoine Tome; Urban Sax; Pierre Henri; Bernard Lubat; Gérard Marais; Mico Nissim; Corazon Rebelde; Pajaro Canzani; Salif Keita; Ousmane Kouyate; Kaba Mane; Manfila Kante; Carlos Nascimiento; Gery Burtin; Organizer, tours for artists from: Africa; UK; Spain; Portugal; Italy; Producer, publisher and promoter, recordings; Agent for shows in France and internationally; Administration for Big Band Paris Est; Tours; Mozambique; Antilles; Algeria; Gabon; UK; Spain; Portugal; Switzerland; Numerous European festivals. *Recordings:* Au Printemps de Bourges, Mama Bea; Mandinka Dong, Toure Kunda; L'Amour Titant, Antoine Tome; with Urban Sax: Urban Sax II; Urban Sax III; Les Noces Alchymiques, Pierre Henry; Kunga Kungaké, Kaba Mane; Madzano Live Concert; Corazon Rebelde; Pajaro Canzani; Kabe Mane. *Membership:* Admin, Cultural division, SPEDIDAM; Mem., Jazz Commission, SNAM; Jazz Players Union (UMJ). *Address:* 81 rue Saint Maur, 75011 Paris, France.

ZAWINUL, Joe (Josef Erich); b. 7 July 1932, Vienna, Austria. Jazz Musician (piano, synthesizer); Songwriter. m. Maxine Byars, 1964, 3 s. *Education:* Vienna Conservatory; Berklee College of Music, Boston, 1959; Studied piano under Prof. Valerie Zschörner in Vienna, under Raymond Lewental in New York. *Career:* Local session musician, dance, radio orchestras, 1950s; House pianist for Polydor Records; Played with leading Austrian bands and orchestras throughout Europe, 1947–59; Played and recorded with Hans Koller, Maynard Ferguson, Dinah Washington, Tim Hardin, Eddie Harris, Quincy Jones, Cannonball Adderley, Miles Davis, 1961–71; Formed jazz/rock group Weather Report with Wayne Shorter, working as prod., composer and keyboard instrumentalist, 1970–86; Sol artiste, 1985–; Leader, own groups Weather Update, Zawinul Syndicate, 1985–. *Recordings:* Albums: with Cannonball Adderley Quintet: Mercy Mercy Mercy, 1966; with Miles Davis: Bitches Brew, 1969; In A Silent Way, 1969; Live Evil, 1972; Big Fun, 1974; Circle In The Round, 1979; with Weather Report: Weather Report, 1971; I Sing The Body Electric, 1972; Live In Tokyo, 1972; Sweetnighter, 1973; Mysterious Traveller, 1974; Tail Spinnin', 1975; Black Market, 1976; Heavy Weather, 1977; Mr Gone, 1978; 8:30, 1979; Night Passage, 1980; Weather Report, 1982; Procession, 1983; Domino Theory, 1984; Sportin' Life, 1985; This Is This, 1986; Heavy Weather–The Collection, 1990; Jazz Collection, 2001; with Zawinul Syndicate: The Immigrants, 1988; Black Water, 1989; Lost Tribes, 1992; World Tour Live, 1997; To You with Love, 1998; with Salif Keita: Amen, 1991; with Trilok Gurtu: Crazy Saints, 1993; Solo: Money In The Pocket, 1966; The Rise And Fall Of The Third Stream, 1967; Zawinul, 1971; Dialects, 1985; My People, 1996; Stories Of The Danube, 1996; Mauthausen, 1999; Faces and Places, 2002. *Honours:* Grammy Award for composition of Mercy, Mercy, Mercy, 1967, In a Silent Way, 1967; Birdland (Best Instrumental Composition), 1977; Weather Report named No. 1 Jazz Band, 1972–78; Five of the eight Weather Report albums named Jazz Album of the Year, Downbeat Magazine; Jazz Forum Awards, No. 1 Synthesizer Player for four consecutive years, No. 1 Composer, Weather Report No. 1 Group. *Address:* International Music Network, 278 Main St, Gloucester, MA 01930, USA.

ZÉ, Tom, (Antonio José Santana Martins); b. 11 Oct. 1936, Irará, Bahia, Brazil. Composer; Vocalist; Arranger; Actor. m. Neusa S Martins, 14 July 1970, 1 s. *Education:* University of Bahia, Music School; Higher Course, 1962–67; Studied composition and structure with Ernst Widmer; History of Music with Professor H J Koellreuter; Cello with Piero Bastianel; Counterpoint with Yulo Brandao; Piano and Guitar studies. *Career:* Tropicalist Movement, 1967; MoMA, New York, Latin American Artists 20th Century, Concert, 1993; Opened London International Festival Theatre, Queen Elizabeth Hall, London, England, 1993; Walker Art Center, USA, 1993; Lincoln Center, New York and Avery Fisher Hall, 1996; Jazz Festivals in USA, Canada and Europe; Only Connect, Barbican Centre Festival, London, 2001; Stage acting roles include: Arena Canta Bahia, by Augusto Boal, 1965; Rocky Horror Show, directed by Rubens Correia, 197; Film appearances include: Sábado, by Ugo Giogetti, 1994; Mater Dei, by Vinícius Mainardi, 2001. *Recordings:* Sao Benedito, 1965; Tropicália, 1968; Todosos Olhos, 1973; Estudanddo o Samba, 1976; The Best of Tom Zé, 1990; The Hips of Tradition, 1993; Fabrication Defect, 1999; Enciclopedia Musical Brasiliera, 2000. *Honours:* Festival Composer to Composer, Telluride Institute, USA; Down Beat magazine awards: Third place (Readers Poll),

Fourth place (Critics Poll), for album The Best of Tom Zé, 1991; Billboard Top Alternative Album, 1991; Music Festival, TV Record: First place, Golden Viola and Silver Sabiá (song São São Paulo, Meu Amor), 1968; Fourth place (song 2001); Award for best lyrics; APCA, Best Composer, 1999; Multicultural Estadão (São Paulo) prize, 2001. *Membership:* USA: BMI; RZO; Brazil: Abramus; Fermata; Arlequim; Irará Edições Musicais. *Address:* Rua Dr Homem de Mello 717, 05007–002 São Paulo, SP, Brazil.

ZECIC, Drazen; b. 24 July 1967, Split, Croatia. m. Bozena Poljak, 29 Aug. 1992, 2 d. *Education:* Hotel Management. *Career:* Concerts: Croatia, including Sports Arena, Split, 1993, 1994; Tours: Canada; Australia; USA; Germany; Switzerland; Italy; Television: HTV-Croatia; Local television in Australia and Canada. *Recordings:* Zagrli Me Nocas Jace, 1990; Govore Mi Mnogi Ljudi, 1993; Boem U Dusi, 1995. *Honours:* Spilt Fest Croatia, Composer I Award, 1992; Melodije Jadrana-Cro/Grand Prix, Singer, Composer, 1993; Cardinal Stepinac Fest Croatia, Composer I Award, 1993. *Membership:* Croatian Musicians' Union; HGU. *Address:* Croatia Records, Medugorska 61, 41000 Zagreb, Croatia.

ZELENKA, Karel; b. 27 May 1946, Prague, Czech Republic. Musician (alto and tenor trombone). *Education:* Studied, Prague Conservatory and Academy of Arts, Prague, Graduated, 1976. *Career:* Prague Jazz Club Reduta; Berlin Jazz Club; Lucerna Hall in Prague; Warzsaw Jazz Club, Poland. *Recordings:* Poste Restante, CD; Prague Big Band, Lucerna Hall Roth; Anniversary Concert, CD. *Membership:* The Prague Big Band. *Address:* Cimelicka 960/7, 142 00 Prague 4, Czech Republic.

ZENDER, Stuart; b. 18 March 1974, Philadelphia, Pennsylvania, USA. Musician (bass). 1 c. *Career:* Member, Jamiroquai; Numerous tours and TV appearances; Left band, 1998. *Recordings:* Singles: When You Gonna Learn, 1993; Emergency on Planet Earth, 1994; Space Cowboy EP, 1995; Cosmic Girl, 1996; Light Years, 1996; Alright, 1997; Deeper Underground (No. 1, UK), 1998; High Times, 1998; Albums: Emergency on Planet Earth, 1993; Travelling Without Moving, 1996; Bass on: Best By Far, Omar, 2001. *Honours:* Gold and Platinum albums; Numerous MTV Video Music Awards.

ZEPHANIAH, Benjamin Obadiah Iqbal; b. 15 April 1958, Birmingham, England. Poet; Writer; Dramatist; Musician; Vocalist. m. Amina Iqbal Zephaniah, 17 March 1990. *Career:* Writer-in-Residence, Africa Arts Collective, Liverpool, 1989, Hay-on-Wye Literature Festival, 1991, Memphis State University, Tennessee, 1991–95; Numerous radio performances, acting roles, appearances. *Recordings:* Albums: Rasta, 1983; Us and Dem, 1990; Back To Our Roots, 1995; Belly Of The Beast, 1996; Heading For The Door, 2000. Singles: Dub Ranting (EP), 1982; Big Boys Don't Make Girls Cry, 1984; Free South Africa, 1986; Crisis, 1992; Contributor to: Thin Red Line, 1999; Dancing Tribes (single, with Back To Base), 1999; Illegal (with Swayzak), 2000. *Publications:* Fiction: Face, 1999; Refugee Boy, 2001. Poetry: Pen Rhythm, 1980; The Dread Affair, 1985; Inna Liverpool, 1988; Rasta Time in Palestine, 1990; City Psalms, 1992; Talking Turkeys, 1994; Funky Chickens, 1996; Propa Propaganda, 1996; School's Out, 1997; We Are Britain, 2002; Too Black, Too Strong, 2002; The Little Book of Vegan Poems, 2002. Plays: Playing the Right Tune, 1985; Job Rocking, 1987; Delirium, 1987; Streetwise, 1990; The Trial of Mickey Tekka, 1991. Radio Plays: Hurricane Dub, 1988; Our Teacher's Gone Crazy, 1990; Listen To Your Parents, 2000. Television Play: Dread Poets Society, 1991. *Contributions to:* Periodicals, radio, television, and recordings. *Honours:* BBC Young Playwrights Festival Award, 1988; Hon. Doctorate, University of North London, 1998, University of West of England, 1999. *Membership:* Musicians' Union; Equity; Performing Rights Society; ALCS. *Current Management:* Sandra Boyce Management, 1 Kingsway House, Albion Rd, London N16 0TA, England. *Address:* PO Box 673, East Ham, London E6 3QD, England. *Website:* www.benjaminzephaniah.com.

ZEVON, Warren; b. 24 Jan. 1947, Chicago, Illinois, USA. Vocalist; Musician (guitar, piano); Songwriter. *Career:* Folk singer, 1969; Writer for commercials; Musician with Everly Brothers and Phil Everly, 1970–73; Solo artiste, 1973–; Member, Hindu Love Gods (with members of R.E.M.), 1990. *Compositions include:* When Johnny Strikes Up The Band; Hasten Down The Wind; Werewolves of London; Poor Poor Pitiful Me; Play It All Night Long. *Recordings:* Albums: Zevon – Wanted Dead Or Alive, 1969; Warren Zevon, 1976; Excitable Boy, 1978; Bad Luck Streak In Dancing School, 1980; Stand In The Fire, 1981; The Envoy, 1982; Sentimental Hygiene, 1987; Quiet Normal Life, 1988; Transverse City, 1989; Mr Bad Example, 1991; Learning To Flinch, 1993; Mutineer, 1995; I'll Sleep When I'm Dead, 1996; Life'll Kill Ya, 2000; with Don Henley; I Can't Stand Still, 1982; with Phil Everly: Star Spangled Springer, 1973; Mystic Line, 1975; with Everly Brothers: Stories We Could Tell, 1972; with Hindu Love Gods: Hindu Love Gods, 1990. *Current Management:* Peter Asher Management.

ZGUROVA, Kalinka Kaneva; b. 25 Sept. 1945, Debelt, Bourgas District, Bulgaria. Folk Vocalist. m. Stefan Kanev, 30 Aug. 1976, 1 s. *Career:* Debut, First National Singing Competition, Gramatikovo, 1960; Concert tours in Europe, Asia, America and Africa. *Recordings:* Over 350 recorded songs on Bulgarian National Radio, Bulgarian TV, cassettes and CDs. *Honours:*

Grammy Award, with Mystery of Bulgarian Voices Folk Ensemble; Numerous Bulgarian and international awards and distinctions. *Address:* 27 Belmeken Str, Pavlovo, Sofia, Bulgaria.

ZHAO, Jia-Zi; b. 30 Aug. 1934, Jiangsu, People's Republic of China. Musicologist. m. Si-Jie Xu, March 1959, 1 s., 1 d. *Education:* Shanghai Conservatory of Music, 1956–61. *Career:* Research Scholar, Music University of New Delhi, Indian Art Centre, Chennai Ethnomusicology Research Institute, 1986–88; Head, Institute of Music Research, Shanghai Conservatory of Music; Full-time Supervisor of Doctorate students; Deputy Director, World Ethnomusicological Association; Deputy Director, Oriental Music Association. *Publications:* The Music of Asia; Ethnic Music of Asian Countries; Collection of Writings, Music of Shen Zhi-Bai; Indian Music around the period of Sui and Tang Dynasty; Rabindranath Tagore and his Music; Gamelan Music in Java and Bali; Comparative Study of Indian and Chinese Ancient Music; Comparative Study of Wu Dan-Qi Shen and Qi Tiao Bei. *Membership:* Chinese Musician Asscn; Life Mem., Indian Musicological Society; Singapore Asscn for Asian Studies; Australian-Chinese Writers' Asscn, Queensland Branch; International Council for Traditional Music, USA; Asian-Pacific Society of Ethnomusicology. *Address:* 6 Garden Court, The Avenue, Sunnybank Hills, Brisbane, Qld 4109, Australia.

ZHOU, Vic; Actor; Vocalist. *Career:* Actor, Taiwanese television series, Meteor Garden, based on Japanese cartoon strip, Boys Are Prettier Than Flowers; Mem., boy band, F4 (Flowers 4). *Recordings:* Album: Meteor Rain, 2002. *Address:* Sony Music Entertainment (Taiwan) Ltd, c/o Sony/ATV Music Publishing Asia, Suite 2801-13, 28th Floor, Citic Tower, No. 1 Tim Mei Ave, Admiralty, Hong Kong.

ZHU, Ken; Actor; Vocalist. *Career:* Actor, Taiwanese television series, Meteor Garden, based on Japanese cartoon strip, Boys Are Prettier Than Flowers; Mem., boy band, F4 (Flowers 4). *Recordings:* Album: Meteor Rain, 2002. *Address:* Sony Music Entertainment (Taiwan) Ltd, c/o Sony/ATV Music Publishing Asia, Suite 2801-13, 28th Floor, Citic Tower, No. 1 Tim Mei Ave, Admiralty, Hong Kong.

ZIEGLER, Michael; b. 7 Nov. 1962, Copenhagen, Denmark. Musician. 1 s., 2 d. *Career:* Hotel Hunger released the album This is Where The Fun Starts in the USA and Canada, 1989; Opened the Orange Stage at Roskilde Festival, 1990; EBU Rock Festival, Ireland and Berlin, 1992. *Compositions:* This is Where The Fun Starts, 1989; Waiting For Alice, 1992; Frankie My Dear I Dont Give A Dam, 1994; Mars Needs Guitars, 1995; Happy Hour, 1996. *Recordings:* This is Where The Fun Starts, 1989; Waiting for Alice, 1992; Frankie My Dear I Dont Give a Dam, 1994; Mars Needs Guitars, 1995; Happy Hour, 1996. *Membership:* Danish Artists Union; DPA. *Current Management:* Mardal Management.

ZIEGLER, Pablo; b. 2 Sept. 1944, Buenos Aires, Argentina. Musician (piano); Composer; Arranger. m. Sandra Sicbert, 10 Oct. 1977, 1 s., 1 d. *Education:* Buenos Aires University, not completed; Classical Music, Music Conservatory of Buenos Aires. *Career:* Astor, Piazzolla, New Tango Quintet, Piano Player, 1978–88; Montreaux Jazz Festival, North Sea Jazz Festival and Nice Jazz Festival; Summer Stage Central Park; Solo Performer: Lincoln Center, Saint Martin in the Fields Cathedral. *Compositions:* Milonga in the Wind; La Conexion Portena Album. *Recordings:* with Piazzolla Quintet: Live in Montreaux; Live in Vienna; Be As Zero Hour; Symphonic Tango; Los Tangueros; with Quintet for New Tango: Tango Romance, 1998; Asfalto: Street Tango, 1998; Quintet for New Tango, 1999; Also appears on recordings by: Gary Burton; Ettore Stratta. *Honours:* Arlequin 1992 National Prize; Hon. Citizen of New Orleans City. *Membership:* ASCAP. *Current Management:* Santa Fe World, Music Agency, 609 Onate Pl., Santa Fe, NM 87501, USA. *Address:* Tucuman, 1455 8 C (CP 1050), Buenos Aires, Argentina.

ZIMMER, Hans; b. 12 Sept. 1957, Frankfurt, Germany. Film Composer; Record Prod. 1 d. *Education:* Formal music studies in England. *Career:* Protégé of Stanley Myers; Collaborations with Bryan Adams, John Badham, Barry Levinson, Penny Marshall, Nico Mastorakis, Nicolas Roeg, Ridley Scott, Tony Scott. *Compositions:* Film scores: Moonlighting, 1982; Histoire d'O: Chapitre 2, 1984; Success Is The Best Revenge, 1984; Wild Horses (TV), 1985; Insignificance, 1985; Separate Vacations, 1986; The Wind, 1987; Terminal Exposure, 1987; Twister, 1988; Taffin, 1988; Spies Inc, 1988; The Fruit Machine, 1988; Burning Secret, 1988; A World Apart, 1988; Rain Man, 1988; Wiezien Rio, 1989; Paperhouse, 1989; Driving Miss Daisy, 1989; Dark Obsession, 1989; First Born (TV), 1989; Black Rain, 1989; Nightmare At Noon, 1990; Green Card, 1990; Fools of Fortune, 1990; Chicago Joe And The Showgirl, 1990; Bird On A Wire, 1990; Days Of Thunder, 1990; Pacific Heights, 1990; K2 (European version), 1991; Backdraft, 1991; Thelma & Louise, 1991; Regarding Henry, 1991; White Fang (additional music), 1991; Where Sleeping Dogs Lie, 1992; Millennium (TV), 1992; The Power of One, 1992; A League Of Their Own, 1992; Radio Flyer, 1992; Toys, 1992; Cool Runnings, 1993; Calendar Girl, 1993; Space Rangers (TV), 1993; Sniper (additional music), 1993; Point Of No Return, 1993; True Romance, 1993; The House of the Spirits, 1993; Younger And Younger, 1993; The Lion King, 1994; The Critic (TV theme), 1994; Africa: The Serengeti, 1994; I'll Do Anything,

1994; Renaissance Man, 1994; Monkey Trouble (additional music), 1994; Drop Zone, 1994; Two Deaths, 1995; Crimson Tide, 1995; Beyond Rangoon, 1995; Nine Months, 1995; Something To Talk About, 1995; The Whole Wide World, 1996; The Rock (theme), 1996; Broken Arrow, 1996; High Incident (TV theme), 1996; Muppet Treasure Island, 1996; The Fan, 1996; The Preacher's Wife, 1996; The Peacemaker, 1997; As Good As It Gets, 1997; The Thin Red Line, 1998; The Prince of Egypt, 1998; The Last Days, 1998; Chill Factor, 1999; Die Motorrad-Cops: Hart am Limit (TV), 1999; El Candidato (TV), 1999; The Road To El Dorado, 2000; Gladiator, 2000; Mission: Impossible II, 2000; An Everlasting Piece, 2000; Pearl Harbor, 2001; Hannibal, 2001; Black Hawk Down, 2001; Spirit, 2002. *Recordings:* Numerous soundtrack recordings; Wings Of Film, 2001. *Honours:* Academy Award, The Lion King; Golden Globes, Gladiator, The Lion King; Grammy Award, Crimson Tide. *Membership:* BMI. *Current Management:* Gorfaine/Schwartz Agency Inc, 13245 Riverside Dr., Suite 450, Sherman Oaks, CA 91423, USA.

ZIMMERMANN, André François; b. 19 Jan. 1965, Fort de France, Martinique. Musician (piano); Composer. *Education:* Music school; Conservatory; Sessions. *Career:* Appearances on TV France; Concerts as soloist, duos, trios, big bands include: Bucharest, 1990; with the Big Band de Jazz, Metabetchouan, Canada; International Festival of Brasov, Transylvania, 1990; Festivals at Mulhouse; Nitting; Avoriaz; Piano solo, St Louis, France, 1991; Teacher, School of Music, Sundgau-Alsace. *Compositions:* Theatre: Les Estivants, Gorki, 1986; La Mouette, Chekov, 1990; Derrière les 7 Papiers Peints, Wilfred Grote, with Haute Alsace, 1990; Un Chapeau de Paille d'Italy, Labiche, 1991; Children's pieces (2 selections for piano and orchestra); Music for flute and strings; Composition for regional cinema. *Recordings:* Album: Jazz Conceptions, music for popular songs. *Address:* 22 rue de Spechbach, 68720 Illfurth, France.

ZIMOLKA, Ales; b. 7 April 1963, Jihlava, Czech Republic. Musician (drums). m. Lenka Zimolková, 8 Oct. 1988. *Education:* Business Academy; Piano, guitar, Basic Art School; Private lessons, drums, Prague Conservatory. *Career:* Member, many rock group bands, 1978–89; Member of band, Harley's John, 1990–95; Member of bands, Zoo, TMA, Little Big Company, Los Vobos, 1995–; Many video and studio recordings. *Recordings:* Ballads L, Irish ballads, 1996; Los Vobos: Cerné Diza (Black Hole), 1996; Zoo, 1997; Zome Country albums, 1996–97; Zoo: Good Morning, 1998. *Honours:* Three-times Winner, Czech Radio Top 10, Harleys, 1991. *Address:* Jicínská 29, 130 00 Prague 3, Czech Republic.

ZLOKIC, Jasna; b. 15 March 1955, Vela Luka, Croatia. Economist. m. Boris Zlokic, 25 June 1977, 1 s. *Education:* Guitar lessons. *Career:* First public performance aged 10; Amateur career sustained until first solo album, 1980; Highly successful solo career, 1980–. *Recordings:* Single: Krugovi Na Vodi, 1980; Albums: Pusti Me Da Prodem, 1983; Skitnica, 1984; Ja Sam Ti Jedini Drug, 1985; Vjeruj Mi, 1986; Kad Odu Svi, 1987; Lutajuce Srce, 1988; Vrijeme Je Uz Nas, 1989; Tiho Sviraj Pjesmu Ljubavnu, 1990; Bez Predaha, 1992; Nisam Ti Se Tugo Nadala, 1994; Ja Zivjet Cu Za Dane Radosti, 1995. *Honours:* Zagreb Fest, Grand Prix, 1984, 1988; Split Musical Festival Award, 1982, 1984, 1987, 1993, 1994; MESAM Awards, Female Singer of the Year, 1984, 1988; Sarajevo Festival, 1988; Bratislava Festival, 1985; Madeira Festival, 1988. *Membership:* HGU (Hrvatska Glazbena Unija). *Current Management:* Boris Zlokic. *Address:* Laurenciceva 8A, 41000 Zagreb, Croatia.

ZOLA, (Thuthukani Bonginkosi Dlamini); b. 1976, South Africa. Vocalist. *Education:* Jabulani Technical High, South Africa. *Career:* Stage named after Zola, suburb of Soweto; Early acting roles included youth series Teens On A Tightrope; Starred as Papa Action in TV series Yizo Yizo 2, 2001; Followed by meteoric rise to fame as kwaito/rap/hip hop music artiste; Has own TV talk show Take 5/Zola On 5. *Recordings:* Albums: Umdlwembe (Stray Dog), 2001; Singles: Ghetto Fabulous (from Yizo Yizo OST), 2001. *Honours:* Metro FM Music Awards: Album of the Year; Artist of the Year; Song of the Year, 2001. *Current Management:* Ghetto Ruff. *E-mail:* lance@ghettoruff.co.za.

ZOLOTHUHIN, Adrian Dimitri; b. 22 July 1970, Middlesbrough, Cleveland, England. Musician (guitar); Arranger; Prod. *Education:* BMus (tonmeister), University of Surrey. *Career:* Guitarist, Kabak; Concerts: Ashcroft Theatre; Spencer House; St James' Palace; National Portrait Gallery; Guitarist, World of Leather; Concerts: Marquee; Garage; Subterrania; Borderline; Television: What's That Noise, BBC TV; Radio: BBC GLR, various sessions. *Recordings:* St Mark's Place, World of Leather, 1994; Guitar, producer: Russian Party, World of Leather, 1994; Guitar, arranger, Blow, as solo artiste on album: Bachology, 1995. *Address:* 110 Grove Ave, Hanwell, London W7 3ES, England.

ZORN, John; b. 2 Sept. 1953, New York, NY, USA. Musician (saxophone, keyboards); Composer. *Career:* Associated with the avant garde tradition,

performing with numerous artistes including Wayne Horvitz and David Moss; Works performed world-wide; Compositions commissioned by groups including the New York Philharmonic Orchestra, Brooklyn Philharmonic, Bayerische Staasoper, WDR Orchestra Köln, American Composers Orchestra, Stephen Drury and The Kronos Quartet. *Compositions:* Christabel, 1972; Conquest of Mexico, 1973; Mikhail Zoetrope, 1974; Lacrosse, 1977; Hockey, 1978; Fencing, 1978; The Book of Heads, 1978; Pool, 1979; Archery, 1979; Track and Field, 1980; Locus Solus, 1982; Sebastopol, 1983; Rugby, 1983; Cobra, 1984; Xu Feng, 1985; Godard, 1985; Spillane, 1986; Hu Die, 1986; Ruan Lingyu, 1987; Hwang Chin-ee, 1988; Cat O'Nine Tails, 1988; Qûé Trân, 1988; For Your Eyes Only, 1989; Bézique, 1989; Torture Garden, 1990; Grand Guignol, 1990; Dead Man, 1990; Elegy, 1991; Leng Teh'e, 1991; Carny, 1992; Memento Mori, 1992; Kristallnacht, 1992; Absinthe, 1992; Angelus Novus, 1993; Masada, 1993–97; The Sand's Share, 1994; Redbird, 1995; Dark River, 1995; Aporias, 1995; Music For Children, 1996; Duras, 1996; Kol Nidre, 1996; Orchestra Variations, 1996; Etant Donnés, 1997; Shibboleth, 1997; Cycles du Nord, 1998; Rituals, 1998; Recent. *Recordings include:* Downtown Lullaby, 1998; Circle Maker, 1998; Bribe, 1998; Masada Live in Jerusalem, 1999; The String Quartets, 1999; Lacrosse, 2000; Cartoon S&M, 2000; The Gift, 2001; Love, Madness And Mysticism, 2001; Songs From The Hermetic Theatre, 2001.

ZULFIKARPSIC, Bojan; b. 2 Feb. 1968, Belgrade, Serbia. Musician (piano). m. Marie Chevallier, Aug. 1993, 1 s. *Career:* Played with: Henri Texier; Michel Portal; Leader, Bojan Z Quartet; Concerts include: Banlieues Bleues Festival; Halle That Jazz Festival; London Jazz Festival; Jazz Across The Border, Berlin; Auditorium des Halles, Paris; Radio France, 1995. *Recordings:* with Bojan Z Quartet: Bojan Z Quartet, 1994; with Henri Texier's Azur Quartet: Indian's Week, 1993; Mad Nomad, *Honours:* First prize for composition; Concours de la Defense, 1993. *Current Management:* Laurence Voiturier, Artalent. *Address:* 15 Passage de la Main d'Or, 75011 Paris, France.

ZURBACH, Cyril, (Zebra); b. 24 Aug. 1974, Paris, France. Composer; Musician (guitars, bass); Sound Engineer; Editor. *Education:* School of Filmmaking, Paris; Art and Cinema, Musicology, University of St Denis. *Career:* TV Signature, France Supervision, 1997; Composer and Writer; Sound Designer, films and TV. *Recordings:* Sound Assistant: Quiet Times; Tommy Carpet; J'Attends, J'Apprends, Nicoletta; Epique Epoque, Alain Goldstein. *Membership:* SALEM. *Current Management:* Zebra Production. *Address:* 57 Blvd Soult, 75012 Paris, France.

ZURSTRASSEN, Pirly; b. 15 April 1958, Heusy, Belgium. Musician (piano); Composer. m. Bouhon Janine, 1 s., 1 d. *Education:* Conservatoire De Verviers; Seminaire De Jazz De Liege; Classe D'Improvisation Du Conservatoire Royal De Liege. *Career:* Many Compositions for theatre, television and dance; Teacher, Jazz Harmony, Jazz Composition, Royal Conservatory, Brussels. *Recordings:* 'H' Septet: Hautes Fagnes; 'H' Septet: Horizons Azur; Zurstrassew/Stokart Duo; Septimana, 2001. *Honours:* Saxe Best Young Musician, 1988; Prix Andre Grosjean, 1993. *Membership:* Lundis D'Hortense. *Address:* 4 Wayai, B 4845 Sart, Belgium.

ZWILGMEYER, Kalle; b. 29 Oct. 1937, Porsgrunn, Norway. Folk Vocalist; Songwriter; Translator; Musician (guitar). *Education:* University Degree in History and Geography. *Career:* Programme Leader, numerous folk song programmes, Norwegian radio and TV; Appearances in great many radio and TV programmes, Nordic countries; Many tours in Scandinavia and as Member of Nordic groups: Polarkvartetten; Viser På Vandring; Nordenom Kalmarunionen; Nordiska Visensemblen; 3 Vise-menn and 1 Svenske; Appearances in folk music festivals; Working for connection between folk singers in The Baltic States and the Nordic countries. *Recordings:* Graverende Bevis, 1987; Fra Lofoten Til Arkipelagos, 2001. *Publications:* Vise Og Gitar, 1977; Bli Dus Med Gitaren, 1978; Viser Som Ringer I Vann, 1980; Songtexts published in more than 20 song books. *Honours:* Visprams Storkens Minne (Swedish folk singers prize), 1983; Nordic folk singer prize, Liv, 1989. *Membership:* TONO; NOPA ang Gramart, Norway; DANSK DJBEA, Denmark. *Address:* Foderstofgården 76, 3600 Frederikssund, Denmark. *E-mail:* kallezwilgmeyer@hotmail.com.

ZYKINA, Ludmila Georgiyevna; b. 10 June 1929, Cheremushki, Moscow Region, USSR. Folk Vocalist. *Education:* Ippolitov-Ivanovo School of Music. *Career:* Soloist, Pyatnitsky Folk Choir, 1947–51, Choir of Russian Song, All-Union Radio, 1951–60, Mosconcert, 1960–77; Artistic Dir, Ensemble Russia, 1977–; Pres., Moscow Regional Charity Public Foundation of Peace, 1998; Pres., Russian Acad. of Folk Art; Mem. of Council, Our Home is Russia Movement, 1995–99. *Honours:* Lenin Prize, 1970; Glinka Prize, 1983; Kyril and Methodius Prize, 1998; Ovation Prize, 1998; People's Artist of Russia, Ukraine, Azerbaijan; Hero of Socialist Labour. *Address:* Kotelnicheskaya nab 15, korp. B, Apt 64, Moscow, Russia.

PART TWO

Directory

APPENDIX A: RECORD COMPANIES

Andorra

Limitada de Producciones SL: Ciutat Consuegra 12, 2°, Edif. Orió, Andorra La Vella; tel. and fax (376) 82 82 11; Admin. Joan Deltell Porta.

Argentina

AIM (Arco Iris Musical): Avda Santa Fé 4910, 4°, Of. B, 1425 Buenos Aires; tel. and fax (11) 4775-2343; e-mail aimcontenidos@aol.com; Dir-Gen. Osvaldo Bermolen.

Barca Discos Srl: Avda Santa Fé 1780, 11°, Of. 1102, 1060 Buenos Aires; Dir Elio Barbeito.

BMG Ariola Argentina SA: Talcahuano 750, Sixth Floor, 1013 Buenos Aires.

Clan Dilo Music: Casilla Correo 123 La Plata, 1900 Buenos Aires; tel. (021) 21-5347; fax (021) 25-1991; Pres. Giorgio di Lorenzo.

D Cipa Diaz Colodrero: Avda Paseo Colón 524, Of. 1, 1063 Buenos Aires; tel. 342-8383; Dir-Gen. María Antonia Diaz Colodrero.

Del Cielito Records: Laprida 1898, 4°, Of. B, 1425 Buenos Aires; tel. 805-2981; fax 806-8724; Dir Gustavo Gauvry.

Discos Melopea SA: Jean Jaurés 444, 1215 Buenos Aires; tel. 861-7057; fax 447-6961; Pres. Félix Francisco Nebbia.

Epsa Electrical Products SAIC: México 2833/35, 1223 Buenos Aires; tel. 932-8316; fax 931-3872; Pres. Laura Roma Casella.

Esther M. Soto Ciclo 3: Estados Unidos 629, 1101 Buenos Aires; Contact Esther M. Soto.

Kralendijk Producciones: Sánchez de Bustamente 444, 5°, Dpto 1, 1173 Buenos Aires; Pres. Alejandro Solignac.

Main Records SA: Tucumán 1673, 3° 6, 1050 Buenos Aires; Pres. Alejandro Amadori.

Musidisc Europe Sudamerica SAIC: Güemes 4418, 1° A, 1425 Buenos Aires; tel. and fax 742-2439; Pres. Jimmy Olszevicki.

OM Records Colombia: 1727 Valantín Alsina, 1822 Buenos Aires; Pres. Oscar Meidvilla.

Polygram Discos y Cintas SA: Avda Córdoba 1345, 14°, 1055 Buenos Aires; tel. 815-4890; fax 812-0034; Man. Dir Rubén Aprile.

Rave On SA: Uruguay 546 2 6, 1015 Buenos Aires; tel. 375-1311; fax 371-3611; Pres. Bernado Bergeret.

Sony Music Entertainment (Argentina) SA: Nicaragua 5410, Capital Federal; tel. 4779-7900; fax 4775-6698; website www.sonymusic.com.ar.

Australia

ABC Music: Level 3, John Mellion Bldg, 10A Campbell St, Artamon, NSW 2064; tel. (02) 9950-3996; fax (02) 9950-3989; e-mail hodson.clive@abc.net.au; website www.abc.net.au; Head of Music Clive Hodson.

Acid Jazz Australia Pty Ltd: Suite 73, 380 Wattle St, Ultimo, NSW 2007; Dirs Carolyn Smee, Mark Lovett.

ACMEC Records: PO Box 393, Erindale, ACT 2903; tel. (02) 6292 4550; fax. (02) 6292 6405; e-mail shelley@acmecrecords.com; Contact Shelley Juner.

Akaba Records Pty Ltd: Level 5, 14 Martin Pl., Sydney, NSW 2000; website www.ozemail.com.au/~akabell; Exec. Dir James R. G. Bell.

ALMA Entertainment Group Pty Ltd: PO Box 473, Bowral, NSW 2576; tel. (02) 4861 1616; fax (02) 4861 7616; e-mail mail@almagroup.com.au; website www.almagroup.com.au; Contact: Carlos Villanueva.

Anabasis: PO Box 437, Kew, Vic. 3101; tel. and fax (03) 9898 5051; e-mail anabasis@alphalink.com.au; Man. Gina Luca Veloci.

Artworks Recorded Music: PO Box 115, Chester Hill, NSW 2162; tel. (02) 9645 2685; fax (02) 9645 5552; e-mail enquiries@artworksmusic.com; website www.artworksmusic.com; Contact: Andrew McKeich.

Au-Go-Go: 2 Somerset Place, Melbourne, Vic. 3000; e-mail augogo@augogo.com; website: www.augogo.com; Dirs Greta Moon, Bruce Milne.

Bahool Records: 752 McCallum Creek Rd, Majorca, Vic. 3465; tel. and fax (03) 5464 7208; e-mail bahoolrecords@yahoo.com.au; website www.stormfront.live.com.au; Contact: Keith McNamara.

BIB Productions Pty Ltd: 356 Swan St, Richmond, Vic. 3121; CEO Mike Brady.

Big Rock Pty Ltd: PO Box 273, Dulwich Hill, NSW 2203; A & R Man. Chris Turner.

Bilarm Music Pty Ltd: 21 Fawkner St, St Kilda, Vic. 3182; tel. (03) 9525 5785; e-mail bilarm@bigpond.com; Contact: Bill Armstrong.

Black Market Music: PO Box 4832, Melbourne, Vic. 3001; tel. (03) 9326 8886; fax (03) 9326 8887; e-mail bmmusic@rainbow.net.au; Contact John Durr.

Blah Records Pty Ltd: Level 1, 365 Little Collins St, Melbourne, Vic. 3000; tel. (03) 9534 3955; fax (03) 9670 9920; e-mail blah@blahrecords.com.au; website www.blahrecords.com.au; Contact: David Gagliardi.

BMG Music Pty Ltd (BMG Australia Ltd): 194 Miller St, N Sydney, NSW 2060; tel. (02) 9900-7888; fax (02) 9955-4825; e-mail ed.stjohn@bmg.com.au; website www.bmg.com.au; Man. Dir Ed St John.

Both Barrels: 106 West Coast Dr., Sorrento, WA 6020; tel. (08) 9448 0155; fax (08) 9448 0166; e-mail bothbarr@iinet.net.au; Contact: Dennis Bryant.

Broad Music Pty Ltd: 56 Winborne Rd, Brookvale, NSW 2100; Man. Dir Ken Broad.

CAAMA Music (Central Australian Aboriginal Media Asscn): PO Box 2608, Alice Springs, NT 0871; tel. (08) 8952-9205; fax (08) 8952-9212; e-mail musicmgr@caama.com.au; website www.caama.com.au; Music Man. Gillian Harrison.

Central Station Records: 81 Market St, South Melbourne, Vic. 3205; tel. (02) 9957-2938; fax (02) 9957-2040; e-mail info@centralstationrec.com; website www.centralstationrec.com; Man. Dir Guiseppe Palumbo.

Chatterbox Records: PO Box A1437, Sydney South, NSW 1235; tel. (02) 9264 8477; fax (02) 9283 8307; e-mail nik@chatterboxrecords.com; website www.chatterboxrecords.com; Contact: Nicholas Tropiano.

CMC Australasia Pty Ltd, PO Box 519, Belmont, Vic. 3216; tel. (03) 5241 3288; fax (03) 5241 3290; e-mail inquiries@cmca.com.au; Contact Stuart Duncan.

Colossal Records: 6-8 Wilson Ave, Brunswick, Vic. 3056; tel. (03) 9387-0555; fax (03) 9388-0080; e-mail mail@colossalrecords.com.au; website www.colossalrecords.com.au; Man. Dir Domenic Loprete.

Creative Vibes: 8/40 Victoria St, Potts Point, NSW 2011; tel. (02) 9267 8860; fax (02) 9267 8862; e-mail info@cvibes.com; website www.cvibes.com; Man. Dirs Gordon Henderson, Peter Pasqual, Heidi Pasqual.

dB Records: PO Box 318, Rosebery, NSW 2018; tel. (02) 9544 0077; e-mail dbrecords@ozemail.com.au; Contact Mark Ciric.

Dino Music Pty Ltd: PO Box 242, Purmont, NSW 2009; Man. Dir John Harper.

Diverse System Music: PO Box 1161, Fitzroy North, Vic. 3068; Man. Dir Tony Greene.

Dr Jim's Records: PO Box 45, Clifton Hill, Vic. 3068; tel. (03) 9428 5495; fax (03) 9428 8785; e-mail drjim@ozemail.com.au; Contact Dr Jim Glaspole.

Dog Meat Records: PO Box 2366 V, Melbourne, Vic. 3001; Man. Dir David Laing.

Dolphin Music Group Pty Ltd: 23 Darvall St, Balmain, NSW 2041; Chair. Barry Chapman.

East West Records: 39-47 Albany St, Crows Nest, NSW 2065; Man. Dir Chris Hanlon.

EMI Music Australia Pty Ltd: 98–100 Glover St, Cremorne, NSW 2088; tel. (02) 9908 0777; fax (02) 9908 0666; e-mail tony.harlow@emimusic.com; website www.emimusic.com.au; Contact: Tony Harlow.

Emily Records: PO Box 405, Hamilton, Brisbane, Qld 4007; Label Man. Mark Hanlon.

Empire Records & Publishing: 23–25A Johnston St, Collingwood, Vic. 3066; tel. (03) 9417-7707; fax (03) 9417-5294; e-mail info@empirerecords.com.au; website www.empirerecords.com.au; Label Man. Paul Higgins.

Fellaheen: PO Box A537, Sydney South, NSW 2000; A & R and Asst Man. Dir Adam Yee.

Festival Mushroom Records Pty Ltd: 63-79 Miller St, Pyrmont, NSW 2009; tel. (02) 9395 8000; fax (02) 9395 8001; website www.fmrecords.com.au; Chair. Allan Hely.

Funky Ink t/as Sweet & Sour Music: PO Box 6268, St Kilda Rd Central, Melbourne, Vic. 8008; tel. (03) 8361 9669; e-mail carlocaiazzo@hotmail.com; Contact Carlo Caiazzo.

Global Grooves: PO Box 169, Sutherland, NSW 1499; tel. (02) 9543 1079; fax (02) 9543 1366; e-mail globalgrooves@globalnetwork.com.au; website www.globalnetwork.com.au; Contact Vicki Hansen.

Gotham Records: Suite 1, 663 Victoria St, Abbotsford, Vic. 3067; tel. (03) 9428 0400; fax (03) 9428 4188; e-mail info@gothamrecords.com.au; website www.gothamrecords.com.au; Contact Ross Fraser.

Half A Cow Records: PO Box 1100, Strawberry Hills, NSW 2012; tel. (02) 6345-3235; fax (02) 6345-3298; e-mail haclabel@mpx.com.au; website www.halfacow.com.au; Owner Nic Dalton.

Image Music Group Pty Ltd: 19 Johnston St, Port Melbourne, Vic. 3207; Man. Dir John McDonald.

Integrity Music Pty Ltd: PO Box 1955, Toowoomba, Qld 4350; tel. (07) 4633 0777; fax. (07) 4633 0888; e-mail kayleenw@integritymusic.com.au; website www.integritymusic.com.au; Gen. Man. Jim Watson.

J. Albert & Son P/L Albert Productions: 9 Rangers Rd, Neutral Bay, NSW 2089; Gen. Man. Fifa Riccobono.

Kriminal Rekords: Suite 314, Prudential Bldg, 2 Queen St, Brisbane, Qld 4000; CEO Alan Maddams.

Larrakin Entertainment Pty Ltd: Unit 4, 809-821 Botany Rd, Rosebery, NSW 2018; Man. Dir Warren Fahey.

Lavender Music: 5/159 Arthurton Rd, Northcote, Vic. 3070; Partners Madelen Rayner, Barbara Young.

MCA Music Entertainment Inc (Australia): PO Box 899, Crows Nest, NSW 2065; Man. Dir Paul Krige.

Mint Records Pty Ltd: PO Box 210, Blackheath, NSW 2785; Contact Charles L. Naudi.

Modern Invasion Music: Unit 2, 14 Spink St, Gardenvale, Vic. 3185; Man. Daniel Janecka.

MRA Group Pty Ltd: PO Box 703, Mt Gravatt, Qld 4122; tel. (07) 3849 6020; fax (07) 3349 8806; e-mail mail@mragroup.com.au; website www.mragroup.com.au; Man. Dir Ray Hartley.

Mushroom Exports Pty Ltd: 55 Danks St, Port Melbourne, Vic. 3207; Man. Dir Scott Murphy.

Mushroom Records Pty Ltd: 9 Dundas Lane, Albert Park, Vic. 3206; Chair. Michael Gudinski.

Music World: PO Box 1462, Milton Centre 4064; Man. Dir Hoghton Hughes.

Natural Symphonies: 10 Broughton St, Camden, NSW 2570; Creative Dir Ian O'Hare.

New World Productions: 151 Boundary St, Bardon, Qld 4065; Man. Dir Andrew Watson.

Newmarket Music: 393–395 Macaulay Rd, Kensington, Vic. 3031; National Sales Man. Len McQualter.

Odessa-Mama Records: 557A North Rd, Ormond, Vic. 3204; Man. Dir David Faiman.

One Movement Records: Suite 335, 410 Elizabeth St, Surry Hills, NSW 2010; Label Man. Matt Hayward.

Opulent Music Entertainment: PO Box 270, 48 David Cres., Bundoora, Vic. 3083; Man. Dir Anthony Chidiac.

ORIGIN Recordings: PO Box 1235, Sydney, NSW 2001; tel. (02) 9518 4600; fax (02) 9518 4611; e-mail philipm@originmusic.com; Man. Dir Philip Mortlock.

Outlaw Records: 62 Thompson St, Darlinghurst, NSW 2010; Dir David Caplice.

Phonogram/Polygram Records Australia: Unit C, 110 McEvoy St, Alexandria, NSW 2015; Man. Dir Tim Delaney.

Pickwick Australia Pty Ltd: 2/111 Queensbridge St, South Melbourne, Vic. 3205; Publicity Man. Louise Bedford.

Pinewood Records and Promotions: 3 Hessel Pl., Emu Heights, NSW 2750; tel. (02) 6742-1543; fax (02) 6742-0249; e-mail ianb@pinewoodrecords.com.au; website www.pinewoodrecords.com.au; Man. Dir Ian B. MacLeod.

Possum Music Pty Ltd: 2/27 Wongala Cres., Beecroft, NSW 2119; Man. Dir Philip Israel.

Rascal Records Pty Ltd: PO Box 146, Glenside, SA 5064; Dir Carolyn Combe.

Ravenswood/Foghorn Records: 64 Wattle St, Ultimo, NSW 2007; Man. Dir Bob Armstrong.

Republic Records: 9 Knox St, Chippendale, NSW 2008; Man. Dir Vicki Gordon.

Request Records: 15 High Peak Pl., Lesmurdie, WA 6076; Proprietor John Green.

Roadrunner Records (Australasia) Pty Ltd, 10–12 Rosser St, Brunswick, Vic. 3056; tel. (03) 9388 2533; fax (03) 9388 2544; e-mail jon_satterley@roadrunnerrecords.com.au; website www.metalshop.com.au; Contact Jon Satterley.

Round Records: 42 Breaker St, St Morris, SA 5068; Contact Terry Bradford.

Rubber Records (Australia) Pty Ltd: 441 Spencer St, West Melbourne, Vic. 3003; tel. (03) 9699 2018; fax (03) 9348 9346; e-mail info@rubberrecords.com.au; website www.rubberrecords.com.au; Man. Dir David Vodicka.

Rufus Records: Unit 6, 264A Bridge Rd, Forrest Lodge, NSW 2037; tel. (02) 9566 1775; fax (02) 9552 3141; e-mail president@rufusrecords.com.au; website www.rufusrecords.com.au; Pres. Tim Dunn.

Sandstock Music Pty Ltd: PO Box 557, Charlestown, NSW 2290; Man. Dir Jill Gartrell.

Servant Communications: PO Box 2020, Launceston, Tasmania 7250; Pres. Kevin N. Hooper.

Shock Records Pty Ltd: 200 Beavers Rd, Northcote, Vic. 3070; tel. (03) 9482 3666; fax (03) 9482 3873; e-mail charles@shock.com.au; website www.shock.com.au; Contact Charles Caldas.

Sirius Music: 70 Toorak Rd, South Yarra, Vic. 3141; Dirs Stephen Robinson, Adrian Marchesani.

Sonart Meca Pty Ltd: PO Box 691, Brookvale, NSW 2100; tel. (02) 9948 1811; fax (02) 9948 5085; e-mail music@sonart.com.au; website www.sonart.com.au; Man. Dir Les Hodge.

Sony Music Entertainment (Australia) Ltd: 11 Hargrave St, East Sydney, NSW 2010; tel. (02) 9383 6200; fax (02) 9331 1377; website www.sonymusic.com.au; Man. Dir Denis Handlin.

Terra Australia Records: Suite 223, 161 Military Rd, Neutral Bay, NSW 2089; Contact Alex Svencis.

Time-Life Australia Pty Ltd: PO Box 3814, Sydney, NSW 2001; tel. (02) 8925 3825; fax (02) 9957 4227; e-mail tl_service@timeinc.com; Contact: Robert Klein.

Universal Music Australia Ltd: 3 Munn Reserve, Millers Point, NSW 2008; tel. (02) 9207 0500; fax (02) 9207 0599; e-mail peter.bond@umusic.com; website www.universal-australia.com.au; Contact: Peter Bond.

Vampire Records: PO Box 669, Epping, NSW 1710; tel. (02) 9876-3239; fax (02) 9617-0199; e-mail vampire@vampire.com.au; website www.vampire.com.au; Man. Dir Danny Kaleda.

Vicious Vinyl: 7B Baxter St, Frankston, Vic. 3199; International Affairs Andy Van.

Virgin Records Australia Pty Ltd: 98–100 Glover St, Cremorne, NSW 2090; Dir of Operations Michael Manos.

Warner Music Australia Pty Ltd: 39-47 Albany St, Crows Nest, NSW 2065; tel. (02) 9950 1500; fax (02) 9950 1510; e-mail shaun.james@warnermusic.com; website www.warnermusic.com.au; Contact: Shaun James.

Word Australia: 142 Canterbury Rd, Kilsyth, Vic. 3137; Product & Marketing Man. Wendy Moulton.

Zomba Records Australia Pty Ltd: PO Box 2327, Richmond South, Vic. 3121; tel. (03) 9429 4599; fax (03) 9429 2957; e-mail info@zra.com.au; website www.zra.com.au; Contact: Paul Paoliello.

Austria

Aardvarks Music: Nachtigallenstr 18, 5023 Salzburg; Man. Dir Michael Wagner.

ATS Records: Breitenau 7, 4591 Molln; tel. (0) 7584-2454; fax (0) 7584-2424; e-mail office@ats-records.com; website www.ats-records.com; Man. Dir Reinhard Brunner.

Banananas Records: Pebalstrasse 31/1, 8700 Leoben; Man. Dir Klaus Katzianka.

Bellaphon Records Schallplatten-Vertriebs GmbH: Grundsteing 5-7, 1160 Vienna; tel. (1) 406-6122.

BMG Ariola Austria GmbH: Erlachgasse 134–140, 1100 Vienna; tel. (1) 601540; fax (1) 6023612; website www.in2sound.at; Promotion Philipp Urban.

Buchgemeinschaft Donauland Kremayr & Scheriau: Niederhofstr 37, 1120 Vienna; tel. (1) 811020.

Cactus Records: Nibelungering 1A, 3423 St Andrä-Wördern; tel. 2242 33-519; fax 2242 33-019; Man. Dir Hans Hartel.

Christmas Records: Reinhard-Machold str 47/3, 8075 Graz; Dir Alexander Rehak.

Doremi Records: Spundag 5/6, 1210 Vienna; Dir Emad Sayyah.

Echo/ZYX Music GmbH: Plüddermanng 54, 8010 Graz; tel. 0316-423000.

Edel Records Austria GmbH: Wallenmahd 53, 6850 Dornbirn; tel. 05572-23494.

Edition Rossori/Pate Records: Hietzinger Hauptstr 94, 1130 Vienna; tel. (1) 8762400; fax (1) 8795464; e-mail office@poppate.com; website www.paterecords.com; Man. Dir Mario Rossori.

EMI Austria GmbH: Webgasse 43, 1060 Vienna; tel. (1) 59989-0; fax (1) 59989-106; website www.emimusic.at; Man. Dir Albert Manzinger.

EMP: Weinitzenstr 1, 8045 Graz; Man. Dir Egon Hinz.

European Music Project: Reinhard-Machold str 47/3, 8075 Hart/Graz; Dir Alexander Rehak.

Extraplatte GmbH: 46 Wahringerstrasse, 1090 Vienna; tel. (1) 310-1084; fax (1) 310-0324; e-mail info@extraplatte.at; website www.extraplatte.at; Man. Dir Harald Quendler.

FIPS Records: Schöpfergasse 3, 1120 Vienna; tel. (1) 8122189; fax (1) 8136878; e-mail fips.records@aon.at; Gen. Man. Gunther Pfeiffer.

Frizzey Records: Hauptstr 13, 6522 Prutz; Man. Dir Friedrich Greif.

Gash: Raaberbahngasse 21/4/5, 1100 Vienna; tel. (1) 4057355; fax (1) 6072616; Man. Dir Edi Ehn.

Gig Records: Fuehrichgasse 8, 1010 Vienna; tel. (1) 5129337; fax (1) 5137646; Man. Dir Marcus Spiegel.

Goblin Records: Dr Theodor Kornerstr, 3100 St Polte; Label Man. Ingrid Mangold.

Honk Music and Records: Hormayrgasse 3/25, 1170 Vienna; tel. and fax (1) 486-4287; website www.sra.at/sr/comps/7196.htm; Man. Dir Jivi Honk.

Koch International Aktiengesellschaft: Gewerbegebiet, 6600 Höfen; tel. 05672 606.

Musica Schallplatten Vertrieb GmbH: Webgasse 43, 1060 Vienna; tel. (1) 597-5646.

Operator: Brauhausgasse 14, 3003 Gablitz; Man. Dir Erwin Kiennaust.

PolyGram GmbH: Edelsinnstr 4, PO Box 85, 1120 Vienna; Asst Man. Dir Ulla Pfeiffer.

Reverso Musik Productions GmbH: Führichg 8, 1010 Vienna; tel. (1) 512-2491.

SBF Records: Molln 129, 4591 Molln; tel. 75844000; fax 75844000; e-mail sbf@stn.at; Man. Dir Manfred Prentner.

Sony Music Entertainment (Austria) GmbH: Erlachgasse 134–140, 1100 Vienna; tel. (1) 60157-0; fax (1) 6023615; e-mail office@sonymusic.at; website www.sonymusic.at; Man. Dir Martin Pammer.

Ton Art: Hietzinger Hauptstr 130, 1130 Vienna; tel. (1) 8771733; e-mail sonic.west@aon.at; Man. Dir Alexander Munkas.

TP Records: Reinhard-Machold str 47/3, 8075 Hart/Graz; Dir Alexander Rehak.

Universal Music GmbH: Edelsinnstrasse 4, 1120 Vienna; tel. (1) 81121-0; fax (1) 8131300; e-mail Bogdan.Roscic@umusic.com; Gen. Man. Bogdan Roscic.

Video & Tontechnik: Hoechsterstr 47, 6850 Dornbirn; Man. Dir Manfred Mäser.

Virgin Records Austria: 109/3/Top 20 Mariahilfer Strasse, 1060 Vienna; tel. (1) 5972710-0; fax (1) 5972710-20; e-mail heidi.list@virginmusic.com; Head: Heidi List.

Warner Music Austria GmbH: Erlachgasse 134–140, 1100 Vienna; tel. (1) 60159-0; fax (1) 6023-623; Man. Dir Manfred Lappe.

Zomba Records GmbH: Zieglergasse 73/1/7, 1070 Vienna; tel. (1) 5247500; fax (1) 5247500-20; e-mail georg.rosa@zomba.co.at; Gen. Man. Silvia Schauer.

Belarus

Beloton Records: Shrader str 8-15, Vitebsk 210015; Dir Vladimir Sartchenko.

Belgium

3Rioart Vzw Maoisch Theater Productions: Juliaandillenstr 22, 2018 Antwerp; Dir Sandy Nys.

A L C Productions: Ave Eugène Ysaye 47, 1070 Brussels; tel. and fax (2) 523-9530; e-mail alcproductions@skynet.be; Label Man. Alexander Louvet.

Alora Music: Brandekensweg 9, 2627 Schelle; tel. (3) 844-8200; Man. Dir Bert Burm.

AMC: Victor Oudart St 3/5, 1030 Brussels; tel. (2) 735-2035; fax (2) 735-2732; website www.amcrecords.com; Contact Jean-Marie Sohie.

AMD: Brabant St 230, 1030 Brussels; tel. (2) 245-1960; fax (2) 245-5881; e-mail elbazi_ahmed@hotmail.com; Contact Ahmed Elbazi.

Amor Et Psyche Productions: Allee du Cloître 43, 1050 Brussels; Man. Laurent Jadot.

Antler-Subway Records: Avenue L. Grosjeanlaan 79, 1140 Brussels; e-mail info@antler-subway.be; website www.antler-subway.be; Contact Roland Beelen.

ARS Productions: Single 5, 2550 Kontich; tel. (3) 457 5859; fax (3) 457 5883; e-mail info@arsproductions.com; website www.arsproductions.be; Man. Dir Patrick Busschots.

Baltic NV: Rederijkersstraat 82, 2610 Wilrijk-Antwerp; tel. (3) 828-4084; fax (3) 829-1068; e-mail info@baltic.be; website www.baltic.be; Man. Dir Ben Gyselinck.

Big Time International: Kloosterstraat 54, 3900 Overpelt; website www.bigtimeinternational.com; Man. Dir Jos Borremans.

Blue Chick Records: Predikherenrei 12, Box 6, 8000 Brugge; tel. (0) 473 344200; fax (0) 50491067; e-mail info@bluechickrecords.com; website www.bluechickrecords.com; Gen. Man. Nicolas Dezeure.

BMG Ariola Belgium NV/SA: J. B. Vandendriesschstraat 12, 1082 Brussels; tel. (2) 482-3800; fax (2) 482-3899; website www.click2music.be; Man. Dir Derk Jolink; Contact Bart Brusseleers.

Boom! Bergensesteenweg: 19, 1500 Halle; tel. (2) 360-2851; fax (2) 361-5678; website www.jpvan.be; Man. Dir J. P. Van.

Byte Records: Paulus Beyestraat 39, 2100 Deurne; tel. (3) 327-3060; e-mail info@byte.be; website www.byte.be; Man. Dir Jean-Paul De Coster.

Caracol Music Sprl Group: 5 rue du Cheneau, 6120 Ham-sur-Heure; Gen. Man. Timothy Hagelstein.

Carbon 7 Records: 23 Ave Général Eisenhower, 1030 Brussels; tel. (2) 242-9703; fax (2) 245-3885; e-mail 100257.214@compuserve.com; Dir Guy Segers.

Clip Records: Rozemarijnstraat 12, 9300 Aalst; Man. Dir Joe Bogart.

Coda bvba: Meistraat 18, 3510 Kremt; tel. (1) 185-8480; fax (1) 185-8489; e-mail be@codaex.com; Contact Dirk de Greef.

Commedia VZW: Fonteinstraat 19, 8000 Bruges; Man. Dir Cherry Deryoke.

Crammed Records: Rue de Général Patton 43, 1050 Brussels; tel. (2) 640-7914; fax (2) 648-8369; e-mail crammed@crammed.be; website www.crammed.be; Man. Dir Marc Hollander.

Culture Records: Gentseteenweg 40, 9230 Wetteren; tel. (9) 365-4000; fax (9) 365-4005; website www.culturerecords.be; Contact Jan Hublau.

Dexon Sprl: 41 rue Cité de L'Enfance, 6001 Marcinelle; Man. Delfosse Pierre.

Disques du Crepuscle: 15 Galerie du Roi, 1000 Brussels; Man. Dir Michel Duval.

DK Music Productions: Rue Souverain Pre 50, 4130 Esneux; tel. (4) 380-3615; fax (4) 380-5015; e-mail dkmusic@skynet.be.

Domomusic-Talent Records: Letterkundestraat 24, 2610 Wilrijk; tel. (3) 827-7087.

Emergency! Records: Rue Ferdinand Bernier 38, 1060 Brussels; Man. Dir Marc Debouvier.

EMI Music Belgium: Kolonel Bourgstraat 128, 1140 Brussels; tel. (2) 702-2411; fax (2) 702-2400; website www.emigroup.com; Man. Dir Guy Brulez; Contact Erwin Goegebeur.

Eva Belgium: Eugene Plasky Ave 179, 1030 Brussels; tel. (2) 456-0590; fax (2) 456-0599; e-mail erik.vervloet.@evamusic.be; Contact Erik Vervloet.

Franc'Amour: Rue Paul Emile Janson 9, 1050 Brussels; Man. Dir Christine Jottard.

Hautregard Recording Sc: 119 Route De Veaviers, 4650 Herue; Public Relations Thieray Steinbrecher.

HKM Records: Broekstraat 10, 1730 Kobbegem; tel. (2) 452-7203; fax (2) 452-3425; e-mail info@kusters.be; Contact Hans Kusters.

Insane Music: 2 Grand rue, 6183 Trazegnies; Contact Alain Neffe.

I Scream Records: Broekstraat 10, 1730 Kobbegem; tel. (2) 452-6775; fax (2) 452-3986; e-mail isr@iscreamrecords.com; website www.iscreamrecords.com; Head of Promotion: Max De Veseleer.

Lightning Records NV: Herentalsebaan 355, 2100 Deurne-Antwerp; tel. (3) 320-8070; fax (3) 366-1135; e-mail labels@lightningrecords.be; Contact Christian Pieters.

Loft Records: Kloosterstraat 54, 3900 Overpelt; Man. Dir Jos Borremans.

Madagascar Records: Krijgsbaan 240, 2070 Zwyndrecht; tel. (3) 253-1480; fax (3) 253-1496; e-mail madagascar@pandora.be; website www.kkrecords.be; Man. Dir Josef Verbruggen.

Mag SA: Ave Louise 65, 1050 Brussels; Man. Dir Pierre Piront.

Mixz Productions: Berchemlei 198, 2140 Borgerhout; Man. Dir Koen Tillic.

MMD SA: Rue Fernand Bernier 38, 1060 Brussels; Man. Dir Plastic Bertrand.

Music & Words Belgium: Europalaan 7, 8970 Poperinge; Pres. Hans Peters.

Myron Records: Bergstraat 13, 1560 Hoeilaart; Man. Dir Leon Lamal.

Parsifal bvba: Gulden Vlieslaan 67, 8000 Bruges; Contact Nico A. Mertens.

Play It Again Sam (PIAS): Rue de Veeweyde 90, 1070 Brussels; tel. (2) 558-5811; fax (2) 558-5886; website www.pias.com; Contact Leo Vanschaick.

Play That Beat: Rue Fernand Bernier 38, 1060 Brussels; Man. Dir Marc Debouvier.

PolyGram Belgium: Roodebeek Ave 30, 1040 Brussels; Man. Dir Bert Cloeckaert.

Private Life/Noise Records: 13 rue Villegas de Clercamp, 1853 Strombeek-Bever; Man. Dir Olivier Verhaeghe.

Punch: Rue de Lausanne 37, 1060 Brussels; Man. Dir Alexandre Saboundjian.

R&S Records: Leiekaai 25, 9000 Gent; fax (9) 216-8999; e-mail rs@macbel.be.

Rainbow Records & Music: Herentaesesteenweg 20A, 2220 Heist-Op-Den Berg; tel. (0) 1524-4950; fax (0) 1524-1470; Contact Kathleen Gossens.

Rainland: 9 rue Paul-Emile Janson, 1050 Brussels; Man. Dir Christine Jottard.

Roadrunner Arcade Music: Rue de Wand 209–213, 1020 Brussels; tel. (2) 264-9910; fax (2) 264-9959; website www.roadrunnerrecords.com; Contact Bert Burm.

Rox Records: Marie Henrieet Laan 71, 1700 Dilbeck; Man. Dir Mario Gucci.

Sawdust Alley: Ave Circulaire 144B, 1180 Brussels; Man. Dir Calvin Owens.

Selection & B Sharp Records: 24 Gachardstreet, 1050 Brussels; Gen. Man. Pierre Pletinckx.

Silver Recordings: Karel Geersstraat 33/3, 2140 Borgerhout; tel. and fax (3) 235-0339; e-mail koen@silverrec.com; website www.silverrec.com.

Smash Productions/Now Discs: Charles Quint 34B-5, 1080 Brussels; Man. Dir Michel Nachtergaele.

Sony Music Entertainment (Belgium) SA: Evenepoelstraat 9, 1030 Brussels; tel. (2) 705-7020; fax (2) 705-6412; e-mail info@sonymusic.be; website www.sonymusic.be; Man. Dir Patrick Decam.

Stargate Records: Gansbroekstraat 50, 2870 Ruisbroek; tel. (3) 886-9678.

Target Records: Oordegemsesteenweg, 1050 Brussels; Contact Claudine Sarlet.

Team for Action (T4A): Ave Oscar van Goibtsnoven 45B, 1180 Brussels; Man. Dir Claude Martin.

Tempo (Top Entertainment Editions): Krijgslaan 61, 9000 Gent; Gen. Man. Luc Standaert.

Tessa Records Rock Label: Dennenlaan 13, 9160 Lokeren; tel. and fax (09) 3489836; Pres. and Owner Marc De Block.

Universal Music: Woluwe ave 34 B1, 1200 Brussels; tel. (2) 775-8140; fax (2) 770-5006; website www.umusic.com; Contact Dirk de Clippeleir.

V2 Records: Hooikaai 33–35, 1000 Brussels; tel. (2) 742-9280; fax (2) 742-9281; website www.v2music.com; Contact Billy Torney.

Virgin Belgium: Plasky ave 179, 1030 Brussels; tel. (2) 743-4242; fax (2) 743-4252; e-mail erwin.goegebeur@emimusic.com; website www.virginmusic.be; Contact Erwin Goegebeur.

Warner Music Benelux: Romeinsesteenweg 468/6, 1853 Grimbergen; tel. (2) 263-0300; fax (2) 263-0330; website www.warner.com; Contact E. Vink.

Witlof: Leernsesteenweg 168, 9800 Deinze; Dir Jean Tant.

Zomba Distribution: Bergensesteenweg 602, 1070 Brussels; tel. (2) 217-6288; fax (2) 217-9452; website www.zomba.be; Contact Filip van den Bosch.

Bolivia

Discolandia Dueri & Cia Ltda: Potosí 920, 1°, 422 La Paz; Proprietor Miriam Dueri.

Producciones Gum Prodisco: Plaza Alonso de Mendoza 500, Edif. Santa Anita Of. 8, 13733 La Paz; Dir-Gen. Germán Urquidi Navric.

Brazil

Abril Music: Rua Dr Mario Ferraz 414, Jardim Paulistano, São Paulo 01453-011; tel. and fax (11) 3046-2400.

Amazon Records: Rua Marilena Machado 200, sala 2, São Paulo, SP 4811-080; fax (11) 5660-7836; e-mail amazonr@uol.com.br.

BMG Brasil Ltda: Avda des Americas 500, Bloco 12/parte, 22640-100 Barra de Tijuca, Rio de Janeiro, RJ; tel. (21) 2483-3000; website www.click2music.com.br.

Caipirapirs Produçoes Artisticas Ltda: Avda das Aguas Marinhas 157 Pg Petrópolis, 07600-00 São Paulo, SP; Gen. Man. Pablo Ossipoff.

Century Media: Caixa Postal 1240, São Paulo, SP 01059-970; tel. (11) 3097-8117; fax (11) 3816-1195; e-mail latina@centurymedia.com.br; website www.centurymedia.com.br.

Estudio Eldorado Ltda: Rua Pires da Mota 820-830, Aclimação 01529, São Paulo, SP; tel. (11) 3274-6800; website www.eldoradodiscos.com.br; Exec. Dir João Lara Mesquita.

Indies Records: Rua Lauro Muller 116, Sala 1906, Botafogo, Rio de Janeiro, RJ 22290-160; tel. (21) 2543-6868.

MCD World Music: Rua Itambé 341, Casa 9, Higienopolis, São Paulo, SP 01239-001; tel. (11) 3257-9744.

Natasha Records: Rua Dias de Barros 43A, Santa Teresa, Rio de Janeiro, 20241-020; tel. (21) 529-0700; fax (21) 529-0722; e-mail natasharec@natasha.com.br.

Paradox Music: Rua Dr Pinto Ferraz 58, Vila Mariana, 04117-040 São Paulo, SP; Dir Silvio Arnaldo Caligaris.

Planet Music: Avda Rebouças 2315, 04501-30 São Paulo, SP; Pres. Carlos Branco.

Sony Music Entertainment Ind. e Com.: Praia de Botafogo 300, 12 andar Botafogo, Rio de Janeiro, RJ 21530-040; tel. (21) 2559-5200; fax (21) 2553-1777; website www.sonymusic.com.

Universal Music: Avda Erico Verissimo 918, Barra da Tijuca, Rio de Janeiro, RJ 22621-180; tel. (21) 3389-7676; website www.universalmusic.com.br.

Warner Music: R. Marques de São Vicente 99, 7 andar Gávea, Rio de Janeiro, RJ 22451-041; tel. (21) 2512-8672; website www.warnermusic.com.br.

Bulgaria

Ara Audio-Video (BMG): 18 Veslec str, Sofia; tel. (2) 981-6020; fax (2) 981-6020; e-mail araavpr@mail.bol.bg; Contact Anton Andreev.

AVA Records: 10/83 Bassanovitch str, 9010 Varna; Man. Dir Anatoly Vapirov.

Balkanton Records: 6 Haidoushka Polyana str, 1612 Sofia; tel. (2) 952-0373; fax (2) 952-6090; e-mail balkanton@yahoo.com; Man. Dir Ventsislav Bozhinov.

Denis Records: 25 Shipka str, 1504 Sofia; Man. Dir Daniel Rizov.

DS Music: 17 Mizia str, 1124 Sofia; Dirs Lubomir Velev, Ivan Vulkov.

Gega New: 1 Acacia str, 1421 Sofia; tel. (2) 650028; fax (2) 9633243; Contact Juliana Marinova.

KA Music: Blvd 10E Motopista, 1404 Sofia; tel. (2) 586191; fax (2) 9581747; e-mail kamen@kamusic.com; website www.kamusic.com; Exclusive partner of EMI International Group, Virgin and ToCo International in Bulgaria; Contact Kamen Spassov.

Kings Records: 37 Hristo Botev Blvd, 1000 Sofia; Man. Dir Valentin Markov.

Kuker Music: 103 Blvd Arsenalski, 1421 Sofia; tel. (8) 870-5280; e-mail kuker-music@gmx.net; website www.kuker-music.com; Contact Ivo Hristov.

Mega Music Ltd: 2 Trapezitza str, 1000 Sofia; tel. (2) 980-9331; fax (2) 980-9344; Man. Dir Dora Tchernkva.

PolySound Inc: 13A Major Gortalov str, 1618 Sofia; tel. (2) 955-9169; fax (2) 955-9760; e-mail polysound@usa.net; Contact Darina Oreshkova.

Riva Sound Records Ltd: Fl 3, 103 Maria Luisa Blvd, 1202 Sofia; tel. (2) 310060; fax (2) 317128; e-mail office@rivasound.com; website www.rivasound.com; Man. Dir Rumen Bonchev; Contact Vassil Serafimov.

Canada

A&M/Island Records: 1345 Denison St, Markham, ON L3R 5V2; tel. (905) 415-1993; fax (905) 415-0850; Pres. and CEO John Rein; Promotion Randy Wells.

Alert Music Inc: Suite 305, 41 Britain St, Toronto, ON M5A 1R7; tel. (416) 364-4200; fax (416) 364-8632; e-mail contact@alertmusic.com; website www.alertmusic.com; Pres. Tom Berry; Promotion Kathy Meisler.

Ambassador Music: DVPO 43029, Calgary, AB T2J 5C6; A & R Man. Wayne Chaulk.

Anthem Records: 189 Carleton St, Toronto, ON M5A 2K7; tel. (416) 923-5855; fax (416) 923-1041; Pres. Ray Danniels.

Aporia Records: 203-411 Parliament St, Toronto, ON M5A 3A1; tel. (416) 944-8034; fax (416) 483-5454; e-mail info@aporia-records.com; website www.aporia-records.com.

Attic Music Group: 102 Atlantic Ave, Toronto, ON M6K 1X9; Pres. Alexander Mair.

Audiogram: 355 Sainte-Catherine ouest, bureau 600, Montréal, QC H3B 1A5; tel. (514) 285-4453; fax (514) 285-4413; e-mail info@audiogram.com; website www.audiogram.com; Chair. Michel Belanger.

BMG Music Canada Inc: 150 John St, Sixth Floor, Toronto, ON M5V 3C3; tel. (416) 586-0022; fax (416) 586-0454; website www.bmg.com; Pres. Paul Aloss; Contact David Bendeth.

Boomtown Music: PO Box 265, Station C, Toronto, ON M6S 3P4; Head of A & R Kevin Leflar.

Borealis Recording Co Ltd: 225 Sterling Rd, Unit 19, Toronto, ON M6R 2B2; tel. (416) 530-4288; fax (416) 530-0461; e-mail info@borealisrecords.com; website www.borealisrecords.com.

Botany Park Records & Music Publishing Co: 361 Walter Dr., Keswick, ON L4P 3A8; Pres. Marlaine Rennocks.

Chacra Alternative Music Inc: 3155 Halpern, St Laurent, QC H4S 1P5; tel. (514) 335-0245; fax (514) 335-5037; e-mail info@chacramusic.com; website www.chacramusic.com; Pres. Bob Chacra.

Contagious Records: PO Box 183, 905 Croydon Ave, Winnipeg, MB R3M 3S7; Contact Roman Panchyshyn.

Current/Rage Records and Management: 4 Bowden St, Toronto, ON M4K 2X2; Pres. Gerry Young.

Distribution Fusion III: 5455 Paré #101, Montréal, QC H4P 1P7; National Promotions Nadine Campbell.

DMT Records: Suite 11714, 113th Ave, Edmonton, AB T5G 0J8; Pres. Danny Makarm.

Duke Street Records: 238 Davenport Rd, Suite 344, Toronto, ON M5R 1J6; tel. (416) 923-5599; fax (416) 923-6595; e-mail dukest@interlog.com; Public Relations Andy Hermant.

Ed Preston Enterprises Inc: 192 Tweedsdale Cres., Oakville, ON L6L 4P7; tel. (905) 827-8095; fax (905) 827-8095; Pres. & Gen. Man. Ed Preston.

EMC Records of Canada: 189 Scugog St, Bowmanville, ON L1C 3J9; Contact Paul Andrew Smith.

EMI Music Canada: 3109 American Dr., Mississauga, ON L4V 1B2; tel. (905) 677-5050; fax (905) 677-1651; Pres. Deane Cameron; Public Relations Liz McElheran.

Festival Distribution: 1351 Grant St, Vancouver, BC V5L 2X7; tel. (604) 253-2662; fax (604) 253-2634; e-mail fd@festival.bc.ca; website www.festival.bc.ca; Public Relations Valdine Ciwko.

Forte Records and Productions Inc: 320 Spadina Rd, Toronto, ON M5R 2V6; Contact Dawna Zeeman.

Fringe Product: PO Box 670, Station A, Toronto, ON M5W 1G2; Gen. Man. Angus MacKay.

Heaven Bent Music Corp: 11 Hopewell Cres., Hamilton, ON L8J 1P3; Gen. Man. Kathie Pietron.

Heritage Music: 1111 Davis Dr., Unit 1, Suite 247, Newmarket, ON L34 7V1; tel. (416) 989-0372; fax (416) 989-0414; Contact Jack Boswell.

Hi-Bias Records Inc: 49 Beckett Ave, Toronto, ON M6L 2B3; Dir Nick Fiorucci.

Hypnotic Records: 96 Spadina Ave, Ninth Floor, Toronto, ON M5V 2J6; Contact Daryn Barry.

Icedrum Records: PO Box 2310, Station A, Sudbury, ON P3A 4S8; Contact James Hunt.

Inner Music: 65 Front St W, Units 116–165, Toronto, ON M5J 1E6; Contact Steve Holt.

Intrepid Music: 93 Hazelton Ave, Third Floor, Toronto, ON M5R 2E1; Public Relations Andy McLean.

Jericho Beach Music: 1351 Grant St, Vancouver, BC V5L 1X7; tel. (604) 253-2662; e-mail fdi@festival.bc.ca.

Joe-Radio: Suite 8, 299 Lesmill Rd, Toronto, ON M3B 2U1; Contact Christine Rodway.

John H. Lennon Music Ltd: 1235 Bay St, Suite 400, Toronto, ON M5R 3K4; Pres. John Lennon; Man. Dir Lenny Moore.

Justin Time Records Inc: 5455 Paré #101, Montréal, QC H4P 1P7; tel. (514) 738-9533; fax (514) 737-9780; e-mail info@justin-time.com; website www.justin-time.com; National Promotions Nadine Campbell.

KSM Records: 2305 Vista Court, Coquitlam, BC V3J 6W2; Pres. David London.

LA Records: PO Box 1096 Hudson, QC J0P 1V0; tel. (450) 458-2819; e-mail la_records@excite.com; website www.radiofreedom.com; Prod. Michael Lengies.

Les Disques Passeport Inc: PO Box 529, Succursale Beaubien, Montréal, QC H2G 3E2; Public Relations Marc Racine.

Les Disques Rubicon: 835 A Querbes, Outremont, QC H2V 3X1; Contact Gilles Bedard.

Magnum Records: 8607 128 Ave, Edmonton, AB T5E 0G3; tel. (780) 476-8230; fax (780) 472-2584; Contact Bill Maxim.

Margaree Sound: 225 The Lake Driveway, West Ajax, ON L1S 5A3; Pres. & CEO Russell Daige.

Master Factory: Suite 11714, 113th Ave, Edmonton, AB T5G 0J8; Pres. Gerry Dere.

MCA Records Canada: 2450 Victoria Park Ave, Willowdale, ON M2J 4A2; tel. (416) 491-3000; fax (416) 490-8206; Promotion Bill Banham.

Murder Records: 1588 Grandville St, Halifax, NS B3J 1X1; Promotion Colin MacKenzie.

MUSINFO Publishing Group Inc: 2504 Mayfair Ave, Montréal, QC H4B 2C8; tel. (514) 484-5419; fax (514) 484-9948; e-mail musinfo@musinfo.com; website www.musinfo.com; Pres. and Owner Jehan V. Valiquet.

Nettwerk Productions: 1650 W Second Ave, Vancouver, BC V6J 4R3; tel. (604) 654-2929; fax (604) 654-1993; e-mail info@nettwerk.com; website www.Nettwerk.com.

Nightlife Records: 2533A Yonge St, Toronto, ON M4P 2H9; Contact Joey Cee.

Oasis Productions Ltd: 76 Cadorna Ave, Toronto, ON M4J 3X1; Vice-Pres. Ron Korb.

PolyGram Records of Canada: 1345 Denison St, Markham, ON L3R 5V2; tel. (905) 415-9900; fax (905) 415-0850; Contact Bob Ansell.

Quantum Records: 170A Baldwin St, Toronto, ON M5T 1L8; Contact Mike Alyanak.

Quinlan Road Ltd: PO Box 933, Stratford, ON N5A 7M3; Controller Bill Bruce; Contact Loreena McKennit.

RDR Music Group: 299 Lesmill Rd, Suite 8, Toronto, ON M3B 2U1; Pres. Joe Wood.

Record Peddler Distribution: 621 Yonge St, Toronto, ON M4Y 1Z5; Pres. Ben Hoffman.

Resort Records: 14 Sumach St, Toronto, ON M5A 1J4; Pres. Joe Bamford.

Roto Noto: 148 Erin Ave, Hamilton, ON L8K 4W3; Promotion Elaine Domsy.

Sam Cat Records: 8 Woodlands Rd, St Albert, AB T8N 3L9; tel. and fax (780) 460-7460; e-mail fun@peterandmary.net; Also organizes the Earth Day Festival; Contact Peter Jansen.

Savannah Music Inc: 123 Applefield Dr., Scarborough, ON M1P 3Y5; Dir of Canadian Operations Bill Carruthers.

Scratch Records: PO Box 5381, Whitehorse, YK Y1A 4Z2; Prod. Daniel Janke.

Skylark Records: 3964 W 18th Ave, Vancouver, BC V6S 1B7; Contact George Laverock.

Slak Productions: 9 Hector Ave, Toronto, ON M6G 3G2; tel. (416) 588-6751; fax (416) 588-6751; e-mail akussin@sympatico.ca; Pres. Al Kussin.

Sony Music Entertainment (Canada) Inc: 1121 Leslie St, North York, ON M3C 2J9; tel. (416) 391-3311; fax (416) 447-6973; Pres. Richard Camilleri; Imports Man. John Ellis Thomson.

Sound Solutions: 5905 Thimens, St Laurent, QC H4S 1V8; Public Relations/Promotion Frank Trimarchi.

Sparwood Music Productions: PO Box 270, Bentley, AB T0C 0J0; Man. Dick Damron.

Spinner Music Group Inc: 1610 Powell St, Vancouver, BC V5L 1H4; tel. (604) 687-2184; fax (604) 687-2185; e-mail spinner@lightspeed.bc.ca; Pres. Ken Spence; Man. Dir Wolfgang Burandt.

Stony Plain Records: PO Box 861, Edmonton, AB T5J 2I8; tel. (780) 468-6423; fax (780) 465-8941; e-mail info@stonyplainrecords.com; website www.stonyplainrecords.com; Pres. Holger Peterson.

Sunnydays Records: 6263 28th Ave, Rosemont, Montréal, QC H1T 3H8; Talent Search Man. Fadel Chidiac.

Tembo Music Canada Inc: 284 Church St, Oakville, ON L6J 7N2; Contact J. Edward Preston.

The Sunshine Group: 275 Selkirk Ave, Winnipeg, MB R2W 2L5; Man. Ness Michaels.

Third Wave Productions Ltd: PO Box 563, Gander, NF A1V 2E1; Pres. R. Archibald Bonnell.

Unidisc Music Inc: 57B Hymus Blvd, Pointe Claire, QC H9R 4T2; Pres. George Cucuzzella.

Virgin Music Canada: Rundle House, 514 Jarvis St, Toronto, ON M4Y 2H6; tel. (416) 961-8863; fax (416) 961-8950; Public Relations Carole MacDonald.

Warner Music Canada: 1810 Birchmount Rd, Scarborough, ON M1P 2J1; tel. (416) 291-2515; fax (416) 291-9253; Promotion Randy Stark.

Windchime Records: 99 Ivy St, Toronto, ON M4L 2H8; Contact Terry Watada.

Chile

Alerce Producciones Fonográficas SA: Jorge Washington 380 Nuñoa, Santiago; tel. (562) 2239216; fax (562) 2042486; website www.alercelaotramusica.cl; Gen. Man. Gloria Trumper.

BMG Chile SA: Avda 11 de Septiembre 2353, 3°, Providencia, Santiago; tel. (562) 2232740; fax (562) 2332742; Gen. Man. Edgardo Larrazabal.

Bolchevique Records: Alberto Decombe #1242, Providencia, Santiago; fax (562) 4218574; e-mail info@bolchevique.com; website www.bolchevique.com.

EMI Odeon Chilena SA: Carlos Antunez 1959, Las Condes, Santiago; tel. (562) 3411313; fax (562) 3415456.

Mundovivo Records: Casilla 188-T, Correo Tajamar, Santiago; tel. and fax (562) 2692779; e-mail mundovivo@scd.cl; website www.mundovivo.cl.

Sony Music Entertainment Chile LTDA: Avda Suecia 2323, Providencia, Santiago; tel. (562) 2008400; fax (562) 2090513; website www.sonymusic.cl.

Universal Music: Cruz del Sur 133 Of. 901, Las Condes, Santiago; tel. (562) 2066362; fax (562) 2066268; website www.universalmusic.cl.

Warner Music Chile SA: Carmen Sylva 2449, Providencia, Santiago; tel. (562) 2315581; fax (562) 2311951.

Colombia

Ava Limitada: Carrera 54, 75-45, PO Box 50-804, Barranquilla; Proprietor Tony Fortou.

BMG/Ariola de Colombia SA: Calle 67, 7-94, 12°, Santafé de Bogotá, DC; Dir-Gen. Francisco Villanueva.

Compañía Colombiana de Discos SA (Codiscos): Carrera 67, 1, Sur 92 Guayabal, 1428 Medellín; Pres. César Vallejo.

Discos Dago: C/ 33AA, 81-25, Medellín; Pres. Dario Gómez Zapata.

Discos Fuentes, International Division: Carrera 51 #13 -223, Apdo Aereo 1960, Medellin; tel. (574) 2657938; fax (574) 3558288; e-mail patri@DiscosFuentes.com; website www.DiscosFuentes.com.

Discos Philips: Calle 13, 51-39, 4282 Santafé de Bogotá, DC; Commercial Man. Martín Wowgemunt.

G&M es Música: Calle 114, 6A-92, Of. 419, Zona D Cundinamarca, Santafé de Bogotá, DC; Gen. Man. Javier Garcia M.

Costa Rica

BMG Centro America: PO Box 1675, 1002 Urbanización Montealegre, Del ITAN, 100m E, 100m S, Zapote San Jose, Costa Rica.

Croatia

Adam Records: Anke Butorac 12, 52000 Pula; e-mail adam.records@hdu.hr; Man. Dir Dario Matosevic.

Crno Bijeli Svijet: Avenija Marina Drzica BB, 41000 Zagreb; e-mail crno.bijeli.svijet@hdu.hr; Man. Dir Branko Paic.

Croatia Records: Medjugorska 61, 10000 Zagreb; Dir of International Business Affairs Djordje Kekic.

Denyken Music: Senoina 1, 41000 Zagreb; Man. Dir Denis Mujavdzic.

Earwing Records: Zedno Uho, PP 970, 10001 Zagreb; tel. and fax (385 1) 614 3204; e-mail info@earwingrecords.com; website www.earwingrecords.com.

Esnaf: Gunduliceva 29, 41000 Zagreb; Man. Dir Husein Hasanefendic.

Jazzette Records: Teslina 7, HR-10000, Zagreb; tel. (385 1) 425-520; fax (385 1) 6110-610; Vice-Pres. Kolya Petrovic.

Koncept VD: Trg Bana Josipa Jelacica 5, 41000 Zagreb; Man. Zvonmir Bencic.

Skalinada: Dubrovacka 23, 58000 Split; Dir Zdenko Runjic.

TRIP: Argentinska 3, 10000 Zagreb; A & R Man. Aleksandar Dragas.

Tutico: Veprinacka 16, 10000 Zagreb; website www.tutico.com; Dir Zrinko Tutic.

Cuba

Artex SA: Quinta Ave, No. 8010 esq. A 82, Miramar, Havana; tel. (537) 242741; fax (537) 242033; Gen. Man. Tony Pinelli.

Bis Music: tel. (537) 204 5261; fax (537) 204 4934; e-mail bismusic@columbus.cu; Gen. Man. Belkis Vilaragut Villanueva; Sales Man. Domingo Novo Zaldivar.

Caribe Productions Inc: Avda 17, 18401 Municipio Playa, Havana; Pres. Federico García Antonio.

Egrem: Avda 3, No. 1008, entre 10 y 12, Miramar, Havana; tel. (537) 331925; fax (537) 338043; Dir Gen. Julio Ballester Guzman.

Czech Republic

BMG Ariola CR/s.r.o.: Heleny Malirove 472/3, 160 00, Prague 6; tel. (220) 513680; website www.bmg.cz; Man. Dir Cap Petr.

Indies Records: Stefanikova 8, 602 00 Brno; tel. and fax (549) 245610; website www.indiesrec.cz; Man. Dir Pales Milan.

Marco Music Box: Sokolskà 8, 702 00 Ostrava; tel. (596) 125503; fax (596) 125503; Man. Dir Krasny Denek.

Monitor-EMI Ltd: Kova'rova 39, 155 00 Prague 5, Stodulky; tel. (257) 115111; fax (235) 518331; website www.monitor-emi.cz; Man. Dir Vladimir Kocandrle.

Popron Music s.r.o.: Jeremiasova 947, 155 00 Prague 5; tel. (251) 613301; fax (251) 610384; website www.popron.cz; Man. Dir Alynsky Zdenek.

Sony Music/Bonton s.r.o.: Palackeho 1, 112 99 Prague 1; tel. (246) 086150; fax (246) 086 116; website www.sonymusicbonton.cz; e-mail info@sonymusicbonton.cz.

Universal Music s.r.o.: Velvarska 7/1652, PO Box 35, 160 00 Prague 6; tel. (233) 029902; fax (233) 029909; website www.universal.cz; Contact Filip Tomas.

Warner Music Czech Republic s.r.o.: Blanicka 20, 120 00 Prague 2; tel. (222) 013222; fax (222) 253622; e-mail lucie.mullerova@warnermusic.com; website www.wmintl.com; Contact Lucie Mullerova.

Denmark

Air Chrysalis: PO Box 110, 1004 Copenhagen K; tel. (45) 3555-2636; e-mail david.rowley@air-Chrysalis.se; website www.chrysalis.com; Man. Dir David Rowley.

BMG Ariola Denmark SA: Overgaden Neden Vandet 17, 1414 Copenhagen K; tel. (45) 3269-9700; fax (45) 3269-9799; e-mail bmg@bmg.dk; website www.click2music.dk; Man. Dir Freddie de Wall.

Classico/Olufsen Records: Uraniavej 12, 1878 Frederiksberg C; tel. (45) 3323-4540; fax (45) 3321-4502; Man. Dir Peter Olufsen.

Cloudland: Skt Jørgens Allé 7 O, G6 1th, 1615 Copenhagen; Man. Dir Simon Sheika.

Cope Records: Oehlenschlaegersgade 28, 1663 Copenhagen V; tel. 7020-0037; e-mail sales@coperecords.com; website www.coperecords.com.

Edel Records: Gronnegade 3, DK 1107 Copenhagen K; tel. (45) 3332-3342; fax 3332-3341; e-mail edel_denmark@edel.com; website www.edel.com; Gen. Man. Jakob Deichmann.

ELAP Music A/S: Bransagervej 2-10, 9490 Pandrup; tel. (45) 9973-4000; fax (45) 9824-6045; e-mail elap@elap.dk; website www.elapmusic.dk; Admin. Dir Svend Jensen; Promotion Steffen Lund Nielsen.

EMI-Medley A/S: Vognmagergade 10, 1120 Copenhagen K; tel. (45) 3393-5222; fax (45) 3393-5221; e-mail ulla.bagge@emimusic.com; website www.emi-medley.dk; Man. Dir Michael Ritto.

Foenix Music APS: Sonder Alle 12, 8000 Aarhus C; tel. (45) 8619-5811; fax (45) 8619-5101; e-mail fonix@fonix.dk; website www.fonix.dk; Man. Dir Ole Kjaer.

Forlaget Kragen (Craw Records): Christians Brygge 3, 1219 Copenhagen K; tel. 3313-5800; fax 3313-5804; e-mail sun@dafo.dk; Admin. Dir Svend Nielsen.

Iceberg Records A/S: Frederiksberggade 23, 8600 Silkeborg; tel. (45) 8720-6600; fax (45) 8682-7733; e-mail iceberg@iceberg-records.com; website www.iceberg-records.com; Man. Dir Manfred Zähringer.

Kavan A/S: Klokkestobervef 39, 8800 Viborg; tel. (45) 8928-2800; fax (45) 8661-4343; e-mail kavan@scanbox.dk; website www.scanbox.dk; Man. Karl Aage Jensen.

Kick Music ApS: Energivej 42 B, 2750 Ballerup; tel. (45) 3345-4750; fax (45) 3345-4751; e-mail kick@kick.dk; website www.kick.dk; Man. Dir Michael Quvang.

Klepto Records & Publishing: Langdries 4, 9450 Haaltert; Man. Dir Wilfried Brits.

Mega Scandinavia A/S: Indiakaj 1, 2100 Copenhagen Ø; tel. (45) 3525-6666; fax (45) 3525-6665; e-mail mega-records@mega-records.dk; website www.mega-records.com; Pres. Kjeld Wennick; Vice-Pres. Cai Leitner; Dir of A & R and Marketing Jesper Ban.

Olafssongs: c/o Warner Chappell Music Denmark, Anker Heegaards Gade 2, 1572 Copenhagen; tel. (45) 3313-3315; fax (45) 3313-3330; e-mail mailbox@warner-chappell.dk; Pres. Finn Olafsson.

Olga Musik ApS: Boleetvej 4, 8680 Ry; tel. (45) 8689-2428; fax (45) 8689-0033; e-mail olgamusik@vip.cybercity.dk; Man. Dir Birger Hansen.

Pineapple Records ApS: Frodesgade 20, 6823 Ansager; tel. (45) 7529-7400; fax (45) 7529-7550; e-mail mail@pineapple.dk; website www.pineapple.dk; Man. Dir Helge Engelbrecht.

Rock Owl Records: Tagensvej 204, 2400 Copenhagen; Man. Dir Kim Kofod.

Sony Music A/S: Vognmagergade 7, 1120 Copenhagen; tel. (45) 3376 0300; fax (45) 3376 0333; website www.sonymusic.dk; Man. Dir Jan Degner.

SteepleChase: PO Box 35, Slots Aleen 16, 2930 Klampenborg; tel. (45) 3964-4244; fax (45) 3964-5044; website www.steeplechase.dk; Man. Dir Nils Winther.

Storyville: Dortheavej 39, 2400 Copenhagen NV; tel. (45) 3819-8259; fax (45) 2819-0110; e-mail storyville@post8.dk; Man. Dir Karl Emil Knudsen.

Street Dance Records ApS: Vestergade 17, 1456 Copenhagen K; tel. (45) 3315-9070; fax (45) 3393-9070; e-mail webmaster@streetdance.com; website www.streetdance.com; Dir Claus Hojlund.

Sundance/The Scandinavian Music Co ApS: Havnegade 41, 1058 Copenhagen K; tel. (45) 3333-8720; fax (45) 3333-8730; e-mail sundance@sundance.dk; website www.sundance.dk; Man. Dirs Peter Littauer, Dietmar Schmidt.

Universal Music A/S: Amaliegade 45, 1256 Copenhagen K; tel. (45) 3391-2110; fax (45) 3391-3110; website www.umusic.com; Gen. Man. Jens-Otto Paludan.

Virgin Records Denmark A/S: Ny Vestergade 7 B, 1471 Copenhagen K; tel. (45) 3313-2666; fax (45) 3332-2449; website www.virgin.dk; Man. Dir Henriette Blix.

Warner Music Denmark A/S: Antoinettevej 2, 2500 Valby/Copenhagen; tel. (45) 3616 6888; fax (45) 3617 0077; e-mail kontakt@warnermusic.com; website www.warnermusic.dk; Man. Dir Finn Work.

Zing Zing Music Production: Kirkegaardsstraede 3, 9000 Aalborg; Man. Dir Birgitte Rode.

Ecuador

Fabrica Ecuatoriana de Discos SA: Km 7.5, Via a la Costa, 09018 56 Guayaquil; Pres. Francisco Feraud Aroca.

Estonia

Forte: PO Box 472, 0090 Tallinn; Man. Dir Mart Maripuu.

Salumusik: Tondi 17A, Tallinn; Man. Dir Madis Salum.

Fiji

Procera Music Co Ltd: PO Box 10272, Suva; Man. Dir Anilesh Chandra.

South Pacific Recordings Ltd: PO Box 17, Nadi; tel. 670-0478; fax 670-2193; e-mail spr@is.com.fj; website www.sprfiji.com; Man. Dir Ravindra Patel.

Finland

Aani Records: Aholantie 43, 03150, Huhmari; Man. Dir Tapani Rinne.

Amigo Musik Finland: Cygnaeuksenkatu 12, 00100 Helsinki; Man. Dir Martti Heikkinen.

Bad Vagum: PO Box 362, 90101 Oulu; Man. Dir Kari Heikonen.

Bluebird Music: Arinatie 8, 00370 Helsinki; Man. Dir Niko Nordström.

Bluelight Records: PO Box 153, 00171 Helsinki; tel. (9) 757-1728; fax (9) 777-2127; e-mail bluelight.records@co.inet.fi; Man. Dir Mika Myyryläinen.

BMG Finland OY: Vattuniemenranta 2, 00210 Helsinki; Man. Dir Kuusi Maija.

EMI Finland: Arinatie 6 E, PO Box 28, 00371 Helsinki; website www.emi.fi; Man. Dir H. Puhakka.

Evidence/Dig It/Fazer Records: PO Box 169, 02101 Espoo; Label Man. Pia Louhivuori.

Gaga Goodies: PO Box 47, 13211 Hämeenlinna; Man. Dir Kari Helenius.

Goofin' Records: PO Box 63, 01601 Vantaa; e-mail info@goofinrecords.com; website www.goofinrecords.com; Man. Dir Pete Hakonen.

Hiljaiset Levyt Records: PO Box 211, 33201 Tampere; e-mail hiljaiset@hiljaiset.sci.fi; website www.hiljaiset.com; Man. Dir Jukka Junttila.

Megamania Music: Hämeentie 6 A 1, 00530 Helsinki; Man. Dir Atte Blom.

MIPU Music: PO Box 15, 82300 Rääkkylä; Man. Dir Heikki Kempainen.

Olarin Musiikki Oy: PO Box 20, 02211 Espoo; tel. (9) 881-3227; e-mail olarinmusiikki@olarinmusiikki.fi; website www.olarinmusiikki.fi; Man. Dir Timo Närväinen.

Poko Records: PO Box 483, 33101 Tampere; Man. Pertti Palkoaho.

Polarvox: Arinatie 2 A, 00370 Helsinki; Man. Dir Leena Juuranto.

PolyGram Finland: Vattuniemenranta 2, PO Box 172, 00211 Helsinki; Man. Dir Gugi Kokljuschkin.

Pro Records: P Hesperiankatu 9 A 7, 00260 Helsinki; Contact Eero Koivistoinen.

Real Art: Pursimiehenkatu 26 i, 00150 Helsinki; Man. Dir Pasi Ervi.

Rockadillo Production: Ilmarinkatu 12 A 2, 33500 Tampere; tel. (3) 2131260; fax (3) 2131297; e-mail records@rockadillo.fi; website www.rockadillo.fi; Man. Dir Tapio Korjus.

Sähkö Recordings: Perämiehenkatu 11, 00150, Helsinki; Contact Tommi Grönlund.

Siboney/Love Records: Hämeentie 6 A 1, 00530 Helsinki; Man. Dir Sini Perho.

Sony Music Entertainment (Finland) Oy: Ahventie 4B, 02170 Espoo; tel. (09) 856 600; fax (09) 8566 0100; e-mail palaute@sonymusic.fi; website www.sonymusic.fi; Gen. Man. Hans Rautio.

Spinefarm Records: PO Box 212, 00181 Helsinki; tel. (9) 4542710; fax (9) 45427133; e-mail info@spinefarm.fi; website www.spinefarm.net; Man. Dir Riku Paakkonen.

Strawberry Records: PO Box 17, 01351 Vantaa; Man. Dir Pasi Kostiainen.

Stupido Twins Records: PO Box 301, 00121 Helsinki; Head of Public Relations Joose Berglund.

Syrene Music: Saarnitie 14A, 00780 Helsinki; tel. (9) 385-7939; fax (9) 385-7349; e-mail jukka.linkola@syrenemusic.fi; website www.fimic.fi; Contact Jukka Linkola; Man. Dir Marita Linkola.

WEA/Warner Music Finland: Melkonkatu 28 E, 00210 Helsinki; website www.warnermusic.fi; Man. Dir Marita Kaasalainen.

Zen Garden: PO Box 76, 00501 Helsinki; tel. (0) 505535597; fax (09) 6949657; e-mail kari@zengarden.fi; website www.zengarden.fi; Man. Dir Kari Hynninen.

France

AB Disques: 144 Ave du Pdt Wilson, 93210 La Plaine St Denis; Chair. Jean-Michel Fava.

Airplay Records: 39 rue de la Rochefoucauld, 92100 Boulogne; Head of Marketing Jean-Michel Doue.

Ariola: 2 rue des Quatre Fils, 75003, Paris; Label Man. Nathalie Mercenier.

Atoll Music: 18/20 rue du Borrego, 75020 Paris; Chair. Charles Ibgui.

Auvidis: PO Box 21, 47 Ave Paul Vaillant Couturier, 94251 Genitilly Cédex; Chair. Louis Bricard.

AYAA Disques: PO Box 167, 51056 Reims Cédex; Owner Denis Thieblemont.

Baya: 18 rue de Reuilly, 75012 Paris; Man. Dir Françis Kertekian.

Black Et Noir Records: 4 rue Valdemaine, 49100 Angers.

BMG France: 4–6 place de la Bourse, 75002 Paris; tel. (1) 4488 6700; fax (1) 4488 6900; website www.ecoutezvous.fr.

Boucherie Productions: 15 Bis rue du Plateau, 75019 Paris; Dir Natali Luc.

Carrere Music: 27 rue de Suresne, 75008 Paris; Gen. Man. Michael Wijnen.

Celine Music: 44 rue de Miromesnil, 75008 Paris; Contact Vline Buggy.

Celluloid/Melodie: 50 rue Stendahl, 75020 Paris; tel. (1) 4349 5900; fax (1) 4358 6226; website www.melodie.fr; Contact Gilbert Castro.

Chrysalis Music: 25 Blvd Berthier, 75017 Paris; tel. (1) 5679 5053; e-mail sbarret@club-internet.fr; website www.chrysalis.com; Man. Dir Stéphane Barret.

Cobalt: 145 rue de Ménilmontant, 75020 Paris; tel. (1) 47 97 69 99; fax (1) 47 97 65 44; e-mail cobalt@africolor.com; website www.africolor.com; Man. Dir Philippe Conrath.

Columbia/Epic Records: 131 Ave de Wagram, 75017 Paris; Dirs Olivier Montfort, Laurence Le Ny.

Crepuscule: 123 rue du Fbg, Poissoniere, 75009 Paris; tel. (1) 5320 2456; fax (1) 5320 0206.

Declic Communication: 45 rue St Sebastein, 75011 Paris; Chair. Eric Basset.

Delabel: 3 rue des Minimes, 75003 Paris; tel. (1) 4478 5551; fax (1) 4478 5568; website www.delabel.com; Chair. Emmanuel de Buretel.

Delphine Productions: 150 Bvd Haussman, 75008 Paris; tel. (1) 4562 6062; fax (1) 4562 1334; Chair. Paul De Senneville.

Dixie Frog: 218 rue du Faubourg St Denis, 75010 Paris; Chair. Philippe Langlois.

Edel Records: 48 rue de Laborde, 75008 Paris; tel. (1) 5343 1353; fax (1) 5343 1351; website www.edel.com.

EMI Music: 43 rue Camille Desmoulins, 92133 Issy Les Moulineaux; tel. (1) 4629 2020; fax (1) 4629 2121; website www.emimusic.fr; Chair. Gilbert Ohayon.

EPM: 188 Blvd Voltaire, 75011 Paris; tel. (1) 4024 0103; fax (1) 4024 0427; website www.epm.fr; Chair. François Dacla.

Eric Taffoureau Productions/Valotte Records International: 138 rue Nationale, PO Box 46, 75013 Paris; tel. (1) 45 83 45 00; fax (1) 45 83 45 00; website www.francemp3.com; Dir Eric Taffoureau.

F Communications: 20-22 rue Richer, 75009 Paris; tel. (1) 4770 7898; fax (1) 4770 7606; website www.fcom.fr; Dir Eric Norand.

FGL: 25 Blvd Arago, 75013 Paris; Man. Dir Thierry Wolf.

Francis Dreyfus Music: 18 rue de Tilsitt, 75017 Paris; tel. (1) 5381 4000; fax (1) 5381 4030; website www.dreyfusrecords.com; Chair. Francis Dreyfus.

Groupe Virgin France: 11 Pl. des Vosges, 75004 Paris; tel. (1) 4454 6474; fax (1) 4454 6496; website www.virgin.fr; Chair. Emmanuel de Buretel.

GRRR: 134 rue d'Estienne d'Orves, 92140 Clamart, France; Contact Jean-Jacques Birge.

Happy Music: 38 rue Voltaire, 92800 Puteaux; Label Man. Frédérick Giteau.

Island/Barclay: 16 rue des Fossés St Jacques, 75005 Paris; Man. Dir Pascal Negre.

Karmel Music: 73 rue de Turbigo, 75003 Paris; Gen. Dir Edward Aprahamian.

Larsen Records & Fanzine: 116 rue Du Crey, 73230 St Alban Leysse; tel. (4) 79 70 14 64; fax (4) 79 70 14 64; e-mail slushyruin@larsen.asso.fr; website www.larsen.asso.fr; Contact Denis Oliveres.

Made In Heaven: 6 rue Rémy de Gourmont, 75019 Paris; Label Man. Mathias Jeannin.

Mango: 20 rue Des Fossés St Jacques, 75005 Paris; Chair. Philippe Constantin.

MCA Music Entertainment SA: 65 rue D'Anjou, 75008 Paris; Asst to the Pres. Vicki Rummler.

MSI SA: Baudrin, Labastide Castel Amouroux, 47250 Bouglon; Contact Pierre-Emmanuel Gilbert.

Musea: 68 La Tinchotte, 57117 Retonfey; Pres. Bernard Gueffier.

Musidisc: PO Box 190, 3/5 ave de Vatimesnil, 92300 Nanterre; tel. (1) 4758 1290; fax (1) 4758 6748; Chair. François Grandchamp.

Mute France: 17 rue Soyer, 92200 Neuilly; Public Relations Helene Lemoine.

Ness Music: 35 rue Petit, 75019 Paris; Dir Nessim Saroussi.

PEM Claude Martinez: 59 Blvd Exelmans, 75016 Paris; tel. (1) 4651 0629; fax (1) 4651 0235; Chair. Claude Martinez.

Play It Again Sam (PIAS): 14 rue Milton, 75009 Paris; tel. (1) 4453 7133; fax (1) 4463 0717.

RCA Records: 17 rue Soyer, 92200 Neuilly; Gen. Man. Antoine Chouchani.

Remark Records: 89 rue de la Boétie, 75008 Paris; Chair. Marc Lumbroso.

Roadrunner: 3-5 rue de Albert Vatimesnil, 92300 Levallois-Perret; Label Man. Stéphane Saunier.

Rosebud Records: 16 rue des Fosses Saint-Jacques, 75235 Paris Cédex 05; tel. (1) 4441 9598; fax (1) 4441 9544; Chair. Alan Gac.

Rose Selavy: PO Box 521, 35006 Rennes Cédex; Co Sec. Olivier Mellano.

Scorpio Music: 12 Ave Georges V, 75008 Paris; tel. (1) 4720 4395; fax (1) 4952 0378; website www.scorpiomusic.fr; Pres. Henri Belolo.

Sephora-La Musique de la Vie (Dept of Gam International SA): 6 Pl. Jean-Paul Sartre, 51170 Fismes; Man. Marc Brunet.

Sidonie: 31 rue François 1er, 75008 Paris; Chair. Christain Dulcy.

Skydog/Kind of Groove: 32 Ave Claude Vellefaux, 75010 Paris; tel. (1) 4249 8073; fax (1) 4240 3442; PDG Marc Zermati.

Sony Music France: 131 rue Ave de Wagram, 75017 Paris; tel. (1) 4440 6060; fax (1) 4440 6666; website www.sonymusic.fr; Chair. Paul-René Albertini.

Source: Hotel Chatillon, 13 rue payenne, 75003 Paris; tel. (1) 4478 8278; fax (1) 4478 8279; website www.sourcelab.net.

Top Records: 17 Ave du Président Wilson, 75116 Paris; Label Man. Alain Belolo.

Topomic Music: 26 rue L. M. Nordmann, 92250 La Garenne-Colombes; Pres. Pierre Jaubert.

Universal Music: 20 rue des Fosses Saint Jacques, 75005 Paris; tel. (1) 4441 9191; fax (1) 4441 9190; website www.universalmusic.fr.

V2 Music: 17 rue Bouchardon, 75010 Paris; tel. (1) 5338 1515; fax (1) 5338 1505; website www.v2.fr.

Vinilkosmo: c/o Eurokka, Esperanto Rok Asocio, 31450 Donneville; Dir Floreal Martorell.

Vogue: 2 rue des Quatre Fils, 75003 Paris; Chair. Fabrice Nataf.

Warner Music: 29 ave MacMahon, 75890 Paris cédex 17; tel. (1) 5660 4000; fax (1) 5660 4050; website www.warnermusic.fr; Chair. Marco-Antonio Bignotti.

XIII Bis Music Group: 34 rue Eugene Flachat, 75017 Paris; tel. (1) 4212 5202; fax (1) 4212 5283; Man. Dir Laurent Dreux-Leblanc; Music Dir Brian Rawling.

Zomba Records Paris: 3 rue Clairaut, 75017 Paris; tel. (1) 5306 1111.

Germany

Arcade Deutschland: Kaiser Wilhelm Ring 17, 40505 Düsseldorf; Man. Dir Sylvian Jonkergow.

Ata Tak Records: Kölner str 226 F, 40227 Düsseldorf; tel. (211) 782-2329; website www.atatak.com; Dir Frank Fenstermacher.

Bellaphon Records GmbH & Co KG: Mainzer Landstr 87–89, 60329 Frankfurt; tel. (069) 242-7120; fax (069) 2427117; e-mail bellaphon@bellaphon.de; website www.bellaphon.de; Chair. Jutta Zizanovic-Riedel.

BMG Ariola GmbH: Wittelshbacher str 18, 10707 Berlin; website www.bmg.de; Man. Dir Thomas Stein.

Century Media Records: Schaferstr 33a, 44147 Dortmund; tel. (492) 318-2970; fax (492) 318-297101; e-mail dortmund@centurymedia.com; website www.centurymedia.de; Man. Dir Robert Kampf.

CMP Records: PO Box 1129, 52368 Kreuzau; Man. Dir Ulrich Kurt Rattay.

Comma Records & Tapes: PO Box 2148, 63243 Neu-Isenburg; Dir Roland Bauer.

Crosscut Records: PO Box 10 65 24, 28195 Bremen; tel. (421) 168020; fax (421) 168021; e-mail blues@crosscut.de; website www.crosscut.de; Man. Dir Detevv Hoegen.

Delta Music GmbH: Am Eekenhoff 21, 26345 Steinhausen; tel. (453) 998969; fax (453) 998904; e-mail petra.hausjell@deltamusic.de; website www.delta-music.de.

EastWest Records GmbH: Postfach 106524, 20044 Hamburg; website www.eastwest.de; Artist Marketing Dir Boris Loehe.

ECM Records: Pasinger Str. 94, 82166 Gräfelfing.

Edel Records GmbH: Neumühlen 17, 22763 Hamburg; e-mail info@edel.de; website www.edel.de.

EMI Music GmbH & Co KG: PO Box 30 03 29, 50773 Cologne; e-mail info-emi@emimusic.de; website www.emimusic.de; Labels incl. Capitol, Mute, Virgin; Man. Dir Helmut Fest.

Enemy Productions Inc: #2 Edward Schmid str 28, 81541 Munich; Pres. Michael Knuth.

Exile Records: Lintuperstr 39, 12305 Berlin; Man. Dir Ted Baxter.

Garbitowski: Metzer str 30, 50677 Cologne; Owner & Dir Jürgen Garbitowski.

Global Records: Frundsbergstr 33, 80634 München; e-mail info@globe-art-group.de; website www.globalmusicgroup.de; Man. Dir Peter Kirsten.

Grover Records: PO Box 3072, 48016 Münster; e-mail info@grover.de; website www.grover.de; Man. Asst Reinhild Sander; Contact Oswald Münnig.

Hammer Musik GmbH: Christophstr 38, 70180 Stuttgart; e-mail hammer_musik@t-online.de.

Hansa Musik Produktion: Wittelbachstr 18, 10707 Berlin; Man. Dir Andre Selleneit.

Harthouse/UCMG: PO Box 1458, 69142 Neckargemund; tel. (622) 392060; fax (622) 3920622; e-mail info@harthouse.com; website www.harthouse.com.

Hyperium Records GmbH: PO Box 910127, 90259 Nürnberg; Gen. Man. Oliver Rösch.

Intercord: Aixhiemer str 26, 70619 Stuttgart; International Label Man. Peter Cadera.

Island-Mercury Label Group: Stralauer Allee 1, 10245 Berlin; Labels incl. 4th & Broadway, Antilles, Bludgeon Riffola, Blue Mountain, Capricorn, Casablanca, Def Jam, Fontana, Island, Jambco, Mango, Mercury, Philips, Precious, Quango, Roadrunner, Rocket, Subsonic, Star Club; website www.islandmercury.de.

Jaro Medien GmbH: Bismarckstr 83, 28203 Bremen; tel. (421) 78080; fax (421) 74066; e-mail mail@jaro.de; website www.jaro.de; Man. Dir Ulrich Balss.

Jupiter Records: Irmgardstr 1, 81479 München; e-mail jupiter-records@writeme.com; website www.jupiter-records.de; Man. Dir Joachim Neubauer.

Logic Records: Strahlenbergerstr 125A, 63067 Offenbach; Man. Dir Matthias Martinsohn.

M A D Fuesgen/Nickel GBR: Hagelberger str 48, 10965 Berlin; Owner Ute Fuesgen.

Media Records GmbH: Walderdorffer Hof, Fahrgasse 5, 65549 Limburg; website www.mediarec.de.

Messidor Musik GmbH: Kleine Bockenheimer str 10-12, 60313 Frankfurt; Man. Dir Goetz Woerner.

Modern Music: Kurfuersten str 23, 10785 Berlin; International Man. Birgit Nielsen.

Motor Music: Stralauer Allee 1, 10245 Berlin; Labels incl. Dreamworks, Geffen, Hot Action, Interscope, MCA, Motor, Stockholm Records; website www.motor.de.

Obsession Records: Mosel str 24, 50674 Cologne; Pres. Cordula Schütten.

Orgasm Records: Obertor str 6, 35792 Löhnberg; Label Man. Erich Knodt.

Perfect Beat: Industriestr 37, 33034 Brakel; Man. Dir Dieter Schubert.

PIAS (Play It Again Sam) Recordings GmbH: Zippelhaus 5A, 20457 Hamburg; e-mail info@piasrecordings.de; Man. Dir Mark Chung.

Polydor: Stralauer Allee 1, 10245 Berlin; Labels incl. Decca, Delphine, Go! Beat, Musik fur Dich, Perspective, Polar, Polydor, Russi, Zeitgeist; website www.polydor.de.

Rough Trade Germany: Eickeler str 25, 44561 Herne; Contact Carsten Stricker.

Sanctuary Records GmbH: Hardenbergstr 9A, 10623 Berlin; e-mail info@sanctuarygroup.de; website www.sanctuarygroup.de.

Sony Music Entertainment GmbH & Co KG: Bellevuestr. 3, 10785 Berlin; tel. (30) 13880; fax (30) 13888-7440; e-mail info@sonymusic.de; website www.sonymusic.de; Labels incl. Columbia, Epic, Sony Classical; Man. Rüdiger Fliege.

SPV GmbH: Brüsseler str 14, 30539 Hannover; Gen. Man. Manfred Schutz.

Sub Pop Germany: Gruener Weg 25, 37688 Beverungen; Man. Dir Reinhard Holstein.

Subway Records: Vohwinkeler str 154, 42329 Wuppertal; Man. Dir Michael Schuster.

Synthetic Product Records: PO Box 690441, 30613 Hanover; Contact Lorenz Macke.

TGM Musikverlag Nietsch, Green, Kleinhammer: Max Beer str 25, 10119 Berlin; CEO Tim Green.

TRITT Records: Siegener str 6, 65936 Frankfurt; Owner Nils Selzer.

TRIXX Musikproduktion GmbH: Prinzessinnen str 16, 10969 Berlin; Studio Man. Klaus Knapp.

Urban-Def Jam Label Group: Stralauer Allee 1, 10245 Berlin; Labels incl. Sound of Barclay, Interscope, Manifesto, MCA, Motown, Universal International; website www.universalrecords.de.

Universal Music: Stralauer Allee 1, 10245 Berlin; Associated companies: Island-Mercury, Jazz, Koch Universal, Polydor, Urban, Universal Classics & Jazz; website www.universalrecords.de.

Vielklang Musikproduktion GmbH: Forster str 4/5, 10999 Berlin; e-mail info@vielklang.de.

V2 Records GmbH: Leuschnerdamm 31, 10999 Berlin.

Virgin Germany: Herzogstr 64, 80803 Munich; International Label Man. Michael Bindernagel.

Warner Music Germany GmbH: Postfach 10 65 24, 20044 Hamburg; e-mail info@warnermusic.de; website www.warnermusic.de; Man. Hans Barth.

Westpark Music: PO Box 260 227, Rathenauplatz 4, 50515 Cologne; tel. (221) 247-644; fax (221) 231-819; e-mail westparkmusic@aop.com; website www.westparkmusic.com; Pres. Ulli Hetscher.

Zomba Records GmbH: Eickleler str 25, 44651 Herne; website www.zomba.de.

Greece

Akti: 311 Mesogheion St, 15231 Athens; Head of Promotion Eleni Mavrovounioti.

Ano Kato Records: PP Germanou St 19, 54622 Salonica; Man. Dir George Tsakalides.

BMG Greece SA: Mesogheion 230 & Perikleous 1, Holargos, 15561 Athens; Man. Dir Miltos Karatzas.

Hitch Hyke Records: Kosma Balanou St 5, 11636 Athens; Man. Dir Hannelore Thospann.

Iptamenoi Diski (Flying Discs): 24 Korytsas St, Papagou, 15669 Athens; Man. Dir Theo Manikas.

Lyra: Zalokosta St 4, 10671 Athens; Man. Dir Panagiotis Maravelias.

Minos-EMI: 245-247 Mesogheion Ave, 15451 Athens; Chair. Makis Matsas.

Pegasus Records: Odiseos Androutsou St 3–5, 15772 Athens; Man. Dir Petros Koutsoumbas.

Penguin Ltd: 58 Lambrou Katsuni St, 11471 Athens; Gen. Man. P. Stavroski.

Polygram Greece: Mesogheion Ave 296, 15510 Athens; Man. Dir Vicotr Antippas.

Sony Music Entertainment: 311 Mesogheion St, 15231 Athens; tel. (10) 6796500; website www.sonymusic.gr; Man. Dir Dimitris Yarmenitis.

Virgin Records Greece: 557 Mesogheion Ave, 15344 Athens; Man. Dir Yannis Petridis.

WEA Greece: 319 Mesogheion Ave, 15231 Athens; Man. Dir Ion Stamboulis.

Wipe Out Records: PO Box 80512, 18510 Piraeus; tel. and fax (10) 494-4488; e-mail wipeout@atenet.gr; website www.wipeout.gr; Man. Dir Theo Kritharis.

Greenland

ULO-Greenlandic Music: PO Box 184, 3911 Sisimiut; Production Man. Karsten Sommer.

Guatemala

Warner Music Latina Inc: Discos de Centroamerica, SA, PO Box 50-F, Guatemala City.

Hong Kong
Special Administrative Region, People's Republic of China

Avex Trax: Room 3608-10, Windsor House, 311 Gloucester Rd, Causeway Bay.

BMG Hong Kong Ltd: 11/F One Harbourfront, 18 Tak Fung St, Hunghorn, Kowloon; Contact Steve Beaver.

HNH International Ltd: 8/F Kai It Bldg, 58 Pak Tai St, Tokwawan, Kowloon; Man. Dir Klaus Heymann.

Polygram Records Ltd: 1503 Garley Bldg, 233–239 Nathan Rd, Kowloon; Man. Dir Douglas Chan.

Rock In Music Ltd: Room A, 24/F Haven Commercial Bldg, 8 Tsing Fung St, Causeway Bay; tel. 2807-1297; fax 2806-3204; Gen. Man. Keith Yip.

Schtung Records Ltd: Top Floor, 2 Kennedy Rd; Man. Dir Morton Wilson.

Sony Music Entertainment (Hong Kong) Ltd: 4/F Acme Bldg, 22–28 Nanking St, Kowloon; Contact Peter Chiu.

Virgin/EMI (Hong Kong) Ltd: Room 3201-7 Shell Tower, Times Sq., 1 Matheson St, Causeway Bay; Man. Dir Herman Ho.

Warner Music Hong Kong Ltd: 12/f Peninsula Office Tower, 18 Middle Rd, Tsimshatsui, Kowloon; Man. Dir Paco Wong.

Wing Hang Record Trading Co Ltd: Flat A, 21/F, Lung Shing Industrial Centre, 142–148 Texaco Rd, Tsuen Wan; NT Man. Dir Tang Ping Hang; Chief Marketing Exec. Winnie Tang.

Hungary

Alt Product: 5002 Szolnok, PO Box 76; Man. Dir Bela Pap.

Bahia Records: Ulloi ut 23, 1091 Budapest; tel. 217-4302; fax 217-4354; website www.bahia.hu; A & R Man. Csaba Hajnoczy.

BMG Ariola Hungary/Bertelsmann Media KFT: Level utca. 4, 1023 Budapest; Man. Dir Jànos Kallus.

EMI-Quint Records: Terez krt 19, 1067 Budapest; Man. Dir Jenö Bors.

HMK Records: Lovag u 2, 1075 Budapest; Man. Dir Vojislav Nesic.

Hungaroton Gong: Vörösmarty tér 1, 1051 Budapest; website www.hungaroton.hu; A & R Mans Laszlo Benkö, Attila Hoth.

LP Records: Bajscy Zsilinsky u 62, 1054 Budapest; Man. Dir Norbert Lapis.

Newsis Records: Villàlyi ùt 107, 1118 Budapest; Man. Dir Robert Mandel.

Polygram Hungary Ltd: Steindl Imre u 12, 1054 Budapest; Man. Dir Laszlo Kegeous.

Record Express Ltd: Kunigunda ut 41/B, 1037 Budapest; tel. (1) 437-1800; fax (1) 437-1899; e-mail meszaros@recordexpress.hu; website www.recordexpress.hu; Man. Dir Attila Schneider; International Affairs Barbara Mészaros.

Rosza Records: Maros u 29, 1122 Budapest; Man. Dir Istvan Rosza.

Sony Music Entertainment (Hungary) KFT: Tusnadi Utca 5/a, 1125 Budapest; tel. 355-5688; fax 355-0213; website www.sonymusic.hu; Man. Dir Malcolm Carruthers.

T3 Records: PO Box 8, 1922 Budapest; Man. Dir Peter György.

Trottel Records: Hunyadi 4, 1011 Budapest; Man. Dir Tamàs Rupaszov.

Warner Music Hungary: Hüvösvölgyi ùt 54 III EP, 1021 Budapest; Man. Dir Istvan Jooz.

Iceland

Bo Haldorson Productions: PO Box 5445, Pverholt 26, 105 Reykjavik; Man. Dir Bo Haldorson.

Platonic: Skeifan 17, 108 Reykjavik; Man. Dir Hilmar Örn Hilmarsson.

Skifan HF: Skeifan 17, 108 Reykjavík; Man. Dir Thorvaldur Thorsteinsson.

Smekkleysa/Bad Taste: PO Box 710, 121 Reykjavík; tel. 5513730; fax 5513737; e-mail asi@smekkleysa.net; website www.smekkleysa.net; Man. Dir Asmundur Jonsson.

Spor HF: Nýbýlavegur 4, PO Box 320, 202 Kópavogur; Man. Dir Steinar Berg Isleifsson.

Thule Musik: Aegisgata 7, 101 Rejkjavik; tel. 5621986; fax 5621973; e-mail thule@thulemusik.com; website www.thulemusik.com.

India

Sony Music Entertainment India Pvt. Ltd: Span Centre, South Ave, Santacruz (w), Mumbai, 400054; tel. (9122) 26461600; fax (9122) 26491723; website www.sonymusic.co.in.

Indonesia

BMG Music Indonesia: Wisma Aldiron Dirgantara, LT GF Unit 107–108, JL Jend. Gatot Subr Kav. 72, Jakarta 12780.

Jeka Records: Jalan Jembatan Tiga, 38 Blok B-13, Jakarta 14440; Dir Sofyan Ali.

Metro Utama Raya Electronics Industry: PO Box 4920/JKTF, Jakarta 11049; Export Man. Miss Lisnawati.

Mythoz Records: Jl. Muara Karang Blok, M4 Barat No. 7; Jakarta 14450; tel. (21) 6617058; fax (21) 6490866; e-mail info@mythozrecords.com; website www.mythozrecords.com; Man. Rosni Chiras.

Polygram Records: PT Suara Sentral Sejati Kapuk Utara 89, Jakarta 14460; Man. Dir Anthony Shih.

RIS Music Wijaya International (BMG): Mangga Dua Plaza, Komplex Agung Sedaya Blok D/11, Jakarta 10730; Man. Dir Effendy Widjaja.

Sony Music Indonesia: PO Box 1818, JKP 10018; website www.sonymusic.co.id; Dir Dr Suntono.

Tira Wahari Lestari (BASF): Tira Bldg Fifth Floor, Jl Hr Rasuna Said Kav, B-3 Jakarta Selatan; Sales Man. Johannes Hardiman.

Ireland

Ainm Music: 5–6 Lombard St E, Dublin 2; tel. (1) 677-8701; fax (1) 671-0042; e-mail fstubbs@ainm-music.com; website www.ainm-music.com; CEO Frank Stubbs.

Aquarhythms Ltd: 15 Upper Mount St, Dublin 2; Label Man. Ann Pomerant.

AX-S Records: 26 Mount Eagle View, Leopardstown Heights, Dublin 18; Man. Dir Peter Jones.

Beaumex: Unit B7-B8, Calmount Park, Calmount Rd, Walkinstown, Dublin 12; tel. (1) 419-1100; fax (1) 450-2513; e-mail beaumex@indigo.ie; Dir Cathal Tully.

Beautiful Records: Ballyloughan, Bagnelstown, Co Carlow; Man. Dir Kieran Connors.

BMG Ireland: Grafton Bldgs, 34 Grafton St, Dublin 2; tel. (1) 677-9006; fax (1) 677-9204; website www.click2music.ie; Man. Dir Freddie Middleton; Marketing Man. Kathryn Mason.

Celtic Heartbeat Ltd: 30/32 Sir John Rogerson's Quay, Dublin 2; Label Man. Aisling Meehan.

Chart Records Ltd: 5 Lombard St E, Westland Row, Dublin 2; tel. (1) 671-3426; fax (1) 671-0237; e-mail imw@iol.ie.

Claddagh Records: Dame House, Dame St, Dublin 2; tel. and fax (1) 679-3664; e-mail claddagh@crl.ie; website www.claddaghrecords.com; Production Man. Tom Sherlock.

CMR Ltd: 28 Molesworth St, Dublin 2; tel. (1) 676-6718; fax (1) 676-6482; e-mail cmrecords@eircom.net.

Cog Communications: 12 Lower Pembroke St, Dublin 2; tel. (1) 662-0737; fax (1) 662-0732; e-mail kgoss@indigo.ie.

Crashed Records Ltd: 162 Church Rd, East Wall, Dublin 3; tel. (1) 888-1188; fax (1) 856-1122; e-mail info@crashedmusic.com; website www.crashedmusic.com.

Cross Border Media Ltd: 10 Deer Park, Ashbourne, Co Meath; Contact Oliver Sweeney.

Dabble Music: The Elms, Richmond Ave S, Dartry, Dublin 6; CEO Peter Blackbyrne.

Danceline Records: 267 Crodaun Forest Park, Celbridge, Co Kildare; Contact Peter McCluskey.

Dara Records/Dolphin Records: Unit 4, Great Ship St, Dublin 8; tel. (1) 478-1891; fax (1) 872-0405; e-mail info@dolphin-dara.ie; website www.dolphin-dara.ie; Man. Dirs Joe O'Reilly, Paul O'Reilly.

Dino Entertainment: Dino House, 12 Malborough Ct, Malborough St, Dublin 1; A & R Man. Susan Dunne.

EMI Records (Ireland) Ltd: EMI House, 1 Ailesbury Rd, Ballsbridge, Dublin 4; tel. (1) 269-3344; fax (1) 269-6341; website www.emirecords.ie; Man. Dir Willie Kavanagh.

Goya Records: Thompson House, McCurtain St, Cork City; PRO Paul McDermott.

Grapevine/Solid Records: Alexandra House, Earlsfort Centre, Earlsfort Terrace, Dublin 2; Man. Dir Peter Kenny; Label Man. Janine Nallen.

Green Linnet Records: 17 Lower Baggot St, Dublin 2; Contact Amy Garvey.

Harmac Music Ltd: 67 Amiens St, Dublin 1; Man. Dir Brendan Harvey.

Hazel Music: Dublin Rd, Monasterevin, Co Kildare; Man. Dir John Kelly.

Hummingbird Records: 27 Lower Leeson St, Dublin 2; tel. (1) 676-2232; e-mail topfloor@indigo.ie; website www.hummingbirdrecords.com.

Independent Records: The Factory, 35A Barrow St, Dublin 4; Contact Dave O'Grady.

Kila Records: Charlemont House, 33 Charlemont St, Dublin 2; tel. and fax (1) 476-0627; e-mail info@kilarecords.com; website www.kila.ie.

K-Tel Ireland Ltd/Celtic Collections: 30–32 Sir John Rogerson's Quay, Dublin 2; tel. (1) 679-0667; fax (1) 679-0668; e-mail celticc@indigo.ie; website www.celtic-collections.com; CEO Sharon Browne.

Lodge Records: Ballinclea Rd, Co Dublin; International Man. Pat Dempsey.

Lunar/Unicorn Records: 5–6 Lombard St E, Dublin 2; tel. (1) 677-4229; fax (1) 671-0421; Contact Brian Molloy, Judy Cardiff; Marketing Man. Graham Molloy.

MCA Records Ireland: 30–32 Sir John Rogerson's Quay, Dublin 2; Gen. Man. Dave Pennefather.

Mother Records: 30–32 Sir John Rogerson's Quay, Dublin 2; Contact Elva Tarpey.

Polygram Records Ireland: 9 Whitefriars, Aungiers St, Dublin 2; Man. Dir Paul Keogh.

Preplay Records: c/o The Galway Arts Centre, 47 Dominick St, Galway; Man. Dir Philip Gray.

Rivervalley Records Ltd: Shruthaun, Baltinglass, Co Wicklow; Man. Dir Fiona Joyce.

Round Tower Music: 48 Downside, Skerries, Co Dublin; Dir Clive Hudson.

RSE Records: 11–13 Station Rd, Raheny, Dublin 5; Dirs Raymond J. Smyth, Breide P. Smyth.

Rut Records: c/o The Galway Arts Centre, 47 Dominick St, Galway; Man. Dir Philip Gray.

Sony Music Ireland: Embassy House, Ballsbridge, Dublin 4, Ireland; tel. (1) 647-3405; fax (1) 647-3430; website www.sonymusic.ie; Man. Dir John Sheehan.

Tara Music Co Ltd: 8 Herbert Lane, Dublin 2; tel. (1) 678-7871; fax (1) 678-7873; e-mail info@taramusic.com; website www.taramusic.com; Man. Dir John Cook.

Universal Music (Ireland) Ltd: 9 Whitefriars, Aungier St, Dublin 2; tel. (1) 402-2600; fax (1) 475-7860; website www.umusic.com.

V2 Music Ireland: 30–32 Sir John Rogerson's Quay, Dublin 2; tel. (1) 671-4280; fax (1) 670-3164; website www.v2music.com.

Virgin Records Ireland: EMI House, 1 Ailesbury Rd, Ballsbridge, Dublin 4; tel. (1) 269-3344; fax (1) 269-6341; e-mail kathryn.walsh@virgin.com; website www.vmg.co.uk; Public Relations Josephine Nestor; Contact Kathryn Walsh.

Warner Music: Alexandra House, Earlsfort Centre, Earlsfort Terrace, Dublin 2; tel. (1) 676-2022; fax (1) 676-2602; websites www.wmg.com, www.warnermusic.co.uk; Man. Dir Dennis Woods.

Whirling Discs Ltd: Cairns Hill, Aughamore, Co Sligo; Man. Dir Brian McDonagh.

Zomba Records: 30–32 Sir John Rogerson's Quay, Dublin 2; tel. (1) 671-4151; fax (1) 671-4041.

Italy

A Tempo Srl: Via Filipo Turati 12, 50136 Florence; Man. Dir Piero Borri.

Abraxas Srl: Via Guglielmo Marconi 106, 50131 Florence; Man. Dir Simone Fringuelli.

Ala Bianca Group Srl: Via Emilia E 1646/c; 41100 Moderna; tel. (059) 284977; fax (059) 284913; e-mail alabianca@alabianca.it; website www.alabianca.com; Gen. Man. Toni Verona.

AND Recommended Records: Italia Via Decembrio 26, 20137 Milan; Man. Dir Alberto Crosta.

Artis/Cramps Records: Via False 33, 36050 Monteviale (Vicenze); Man. Dir Alfredo Tisocco.

Azzurra Music Srl: Via Tione 19, 37010 Pastrengo (VR); tel. (045) 6770495; fax (045) 677-0497; website www.azzurramusic.it.

Baby Records: Via Timavo 34, 20124 Milan; Man. Dir Monica Dahl.

Blindness Inc: Rain 10, 39040 Cortaccia; Man. Dir Giovannetti Reinhold.

Blu Bus: Via Consolata 5, 11100 Aosta; Man. Dir Sergio Milani.

BMG Ricordi S.P.A. (Rome): Via Mascagni 160, 00199 Rome; tel. (06) 865111-02; fax (06) 86511474; website www.bmgricordi.it; Man. Dir Franco Reali.

Cave Canem/Spray Records: Via Saline 8/C, 65013 Marina di Citta San Angelo; Man. Dir Belfino de Leonardis.

C.G.D. East West SPA: Via Ugo Foscolo 1, 20121 Milan; tel. (02) 721281; fax (02) 72128336; website www.warnermusic.it.

Clac Records: Via Salvatore di Giacomo 73, 00142 Rome; Mans Massimo Calabrese, Piero Calabrese.

Contempo Records: Corso de'Tintori 6/18r, 50122 Florence; International Label Man. Sebastian Koch.

Edel Italia Srl: Via Montebello 25, 20121 Milan; tel. (02) 625441; fax (02) 62544200; website www.edel.it.

EMI Music Italy SPA: Piazza San Babila 3, 20122 Milan; tel. (02) 777971; fax (02) 77797410; website www.emimusic.it; International Man. Nico Spinosa.

Energy Productions Srl: Viale G. Mazzini 140, 00195 Rome; tel. (06) 37516950; fax (06) 3700542; website www.energy-prod.it.

Flying Records: Via R. Ruggiero 16D, 80125 Naples; Man. Dir Flavio Rossi.

FMA Edizioni Musicali E Discografiche Srl: Via Boccaccio N 47, 20123 Milan; Pres. Mario Allione.

I Soulzionisti: Largo dell'Olgiata, 15-1s 59 3/2, 00123 Rome; Man. Dir Stefano Bonagura.

Interbeat: Via A Straedella 174, 00124 Rome; International Label Man. Luigi Fedele.

Kaleidoscopic Music Srl: Viale Manzoni 52, Cerveteri, 00052 Rome; Contact Robbie Zee.

Kindergarten Records: Via Panicale 9, 50123 Florence; Man. Dir Fabrizio Federighi.

Klang Records: Via Valle Viola 35, 00141 Rome; Man. Dir Massimo Bernardi.

L. M. Records: Crotalo Ed Mus Via Del Pino 71, 48100; Man. Dir Luigi Mazzesi.

Materiali Sonori: Via Trieste 35, 52027 San Giovanni Valdarno; International Label Man. Arlo Bigazzi.

Minus Habens Records: Via Giustino Fortunato 8/N, 70125 Bari; tel. (80) 5010950; e-mail info@minushabens.com; website www.minushabens.com; Owner Ivan Iusco.

Musica Maxima Magnetica: PO Box 2280, 50110 Florence; tel. (0571) 559000; fax (0571) 959745; e-mail mmm@penteres.it; website www.musicamaximamagnetica.com; Man. Dir Luciano Dari.

New Tone Records: Via Principi d' Acaia 28, 10138 Turin; International Label Man. Bepe Grepi.

Nuova Durium Srl: Piazza Mirabello 1, 20121 Milan; Asst Man. Francesco Piccarreda.

Polygram Italia: Via Carlo Tenca 2, 20124 Milan; Man. Dir Stefano Senardi.

Recordthings Zona Archives: Box 1486, 50122 Florence.

Reform Records: Via Cosenza 5, 20137 Milan; Label Man. Alberto Lapris; A & R International Fran Siccardi.

Robi Droli Snc: Strada Roncaglia 16, 15040 San Germano (AL); Man. Dir Beppe Greppi.

Sentemo Records: Via Calstorta Vecchia 21 A, 31040 Cessalto (Treviso); International Label Man. Paolo Boarato.

Sony Music Entertainment Italy: Via Amedei 9, 20123 Milan; tel. (02) 85361; fax (02) 860175; website www.sonymusic.it; Man. Dir Franco Cabrini.

Studiotianta-Fortuna Records: Via Cernaia 3, 14031 Calliano; Gen. Man. Massimo Visentin.

Universal Music: Via Dante 15, 20123 Milan; tel. (02) 802821; fax (02) 80282170; website www.universalmusic.it.

V2 Records Srl: Via Besana 11, 20122 Milan; tel. (02) 5796971; fax (02) 57969730; website www.v2music.com.

Virgin Italy: Via Porpora 26, 20131 Milan; Man. Dir Luigi Mantovani.

Vizio Records: Via Festaz 52, 11100 Aoste; Man. Dir Francseco Battisti.

Vox Pop/Crazy Mannequin: Via Bergognone 31, 20144 Milan; Man. Dir Carlo Albertoli.

Warner Music/WEA Italiana: Via Milani 16, 20090 Redecescio di Segrate (Milan); tel. (02) 21681; fax (02) 2168299; website www.music.warnerbros.com; Man. Dir Marco Antonio Bignotti.

Zion: Via Latini 5, 24032 Calalziocorte (BG); Man. Dir Cameroni Slivia.

Zomba Records Italia Srl: Corso Concordia 11, 20129 Milan; tel. (02) 7625551; fax (02) 76255532.

Japan

BMG Funhouse Inc: 1-3-9 Shibuya, Shibuya-ku, Tokyo 150-8350; tel. (813) 3797-9020; Pres. Osamu Sato.

East West Japan: 3-1-2 Kita-Aoyama, Minato-ku, Tokyo 107; Pres. Takashi Kamide.

JVC Victor Entertainment Inc: 26-18 Jingu-Mae, 4-Chome, Shibuya-ku, Tokyo 150; Pres. Jun Deguchi.

MCA Victor Inc: 9F JBP Oval, 5-52-2 Jingu-Mae, Shibuya-ku, Tokyo 150; Pres. Hiroyuki Iwata.

Nippon Columbia Co Ltd (Denon): 14-14-4 Chome, Akasaka, Minato-ku, Tokyo 107; Dir Toshikiko Hirahara.

Nippon Crown Co Ltd: 28 Fuji Bldg, 2-7-26 Kita-Aoyama, Minato-ku, Tokyo 107-8405; tel. (813) 5572-4841.

Nippon Phonogram Co Ltd: Wako Bldg, 4-8-5 Roppongi, Minato-ku, Tokyo 106; CEO Alex Abramoff.

Polydor/Polygram K. K.: 1-8-4 Ohashi 1-Chome, Meguro-ku, Tokyo 153; Pres. Takeo Kasahara.

Pony Canyon Inc: 2-5-10 Toranomon, Minato-ku, Tokyo 105-8487; tel. (813) 5521-8000; Gen. Man. of International A & R Tatsuo Ozu; Asst Gen. Man. Kaz Saito.

Seven Gods Productions: Suite 403, Mejidori Bldg, 2-3-21 Kabukicho Shimjulou-lou, Tokyo 160-0021; tel. (3) 5292-5551; fax (3) 5292-5552; e-mail benten@jk9.so-net.no.jp; website www.sister.co.jp; Pres. Hiroshi Asada.

Shinko Music Publishing Co Ltd: 2-1 Ogawamachi, Kanda, Chiyoda-ku, Tokyo 101; Pres. Shoichi Kusano.

Sony Music Entertainment (Japan) Inc: 1-4 Ichigaya-tamachi Shinjuku-ku, Tokyo 162-8715; website www.sonymusic.co.jp; Pres. Shugo Matsuo.

Toshiba-EMI Ltd: 2-2-17 Akasaka, Minato-ku, Tokyo 107-8510; tel. (813) 5512-1700.

Universal Music K.K.: 1-8-4 Ohashi, Meguro-ku, Tokyo 153-0044; tel. (813) 3780-8501.

Victor Entertainment Inc (JVC): Palacion Tower, 3-6-7 Kita-Aoyama, Minato-ku, Tokyo 107-0061; tel. (813) 5467-5401; International Operations Aya Ohi.

Warner Music Japan Inc: 3-1-2 Kita-Aoyama, Minato-ku, Tokyo 107-8639; tel. (813) 5412-3111; Chair. Ryuzo Kosugi.

Republic of Korea

BMG Music Korea Co Ltd: 2/F PyungWon Bldg, 830-40 Yeoksam-dong, Kangnam-ku, Seoul, 135 080; Man. Dir Seung Doo Park.

Columbia/Epic Music (Korea) Inc: Second Floor, Doosung Bldg, 77-2 Sadang-dong, Dongjak-ku, Seoul 156 090; Man. Dir Yeouel Yoon.

EMI-Kemongsa Music Ltd: Ninth Floor, Kemongmunhwa Centre Bldg, 772 Yuksam-dong, Kangnam-ku, Seoul 135 080; Pres. Lee Kwan-Choi.

Korea Music Co: 724-43 Yuksam-dong, Kangnam-ku, Seoul 135 080; Contact Duk-Joo Lee.

Nices A & R International Entertainment: Business Division, Samsung Electronics 19th Floor, Ahtae Bldg, 1337-20, Seocho 2-dong, Seocho-Ku, Seoul 137-072; Man. Kwang Woo Nam.

Polygram Ltd: Third Floor, Sungsoo Bldg, 284-9 2-ka Sungsoo-dong, Sungdong-ku, Seoul; Man. Dir David Lee.

Seoul Music Inc: 3F Jung-Nam Bldg, 721-39 Yuksam-dong, Kang-Nam-Ku, Seoul; Pres. Yong-Il Lee.

Seoul Records Inc: Second Floor, Hankook Glass Bldg, 45-1 Yoido-dong, Youngdeungpo-ku, Seoul 150 010; Contact Hong-Kyun Shin.

Sony Music: 98519 Bangbae-dong, Seocho-ku, Seoul; website www.sonymusic.co.kr; Contact Yun Yeo Ul.

Warner Music Korea Ltd: Fifth Floor, Eunsung Bldg, 601-18 Yuksum-dong, Kangnam-Ku, Seoul 135-080; Man. Dir Jonathan S. Park.

Lithuania

Blue Baltic Records: Arhcitektu 79, 2049 Vilnius; Man. Dir Algis Pigaga.

BNA Music: Gedimino Ave 2, 2001 Vilnius; Pres. Arturas Zuokas.

Bomba: Zygimantu 6, 2001 Vilnius; Gen. Dir Rimas Alisauskas.

Zona Records: Seskines 79, 2010 Vilnius; Man. Dir Giedrus Klimkevicus.

Luxembourg

Intercommunication: 275 Rote d'Arlon, 8001 Strassen; Man. Alex Felten.

Joybringer: 27 rue Victor Hugo, 4583 Differdange; Contact Andre Depienne.

Malaysia

BMG Music (Malaysia) Sdn Bhd: 19/F, Block B, Wisma Semantan, 12 Jalan Gelenggang, Bukit Damansara, 50490 Kuala Lumpur; Man. Dir Frankie Cheah.

EMI (Malaysia) Sdn Bhd: Suite 10.01 10th Floor, Exchange Sq., Off Jalem Semantan, Damansara Heights, 50490 Kuala Lumpur; Man. Dir Beh Suat Pheng.

Musico Sdn Bhd: Rm 3901, China Insurance Bldg, 174 Jalan Tuanku Abdul Rahman, Kuala Lumpur; Pres. Bob Weiss.

Noize Records: 17 Jalan Yap Kwan Seng, Kuala Lumpur 50450; Contact George Lourdes.

Polygram Malaysia Records Sdn Bhd: 83–87 Jalan Kampung Pandan, Taman Maluri, Kuala Lumpur 55100; Man. Dir Eric Yeo.

Sony Music Entertainment (Malaysia): C16 & C17 Jalan Ampang, Utama 1/1, Taman Ampang Utama, 68000 Ampang; tel. (3) 4252-3233; fax (3) 4252-2235; e-mail rickloh@sonymusic.com.my; website www.sonymusic.com.my; Man. Dir Rick Loh.

Warner Music Malaysia: Ninth Floor, Mui Plaza, Jalan P. Ramlee, 50250 Kuala Lumpur; Man. Dir Anthony F. Fernandes.

Mexico

Compañia Fonográfica Internacional SA/IM Discos & Cassettes: Sanctorum 86-B Col. Argentina, 11230 México, DF; tel. (55) 5399-2434; fax (55) 5399-2630; e-mail jmorales@imdiscos.com; website www.imdiscos.com; Dir-Gen. José I. Morales Betancourt.

Discos Continental: Poniente 75, 160 Col. 16 de Septiembre, 11810 México, DF; Pres. Marco Antonio Luga.

EMI Music Mexico: Rio Tigris, 33 Col. Cuauhtémac, 06500 México, DF; Pres. Mario Ruiz.

Maple Audiosistemas: Priv. Alberto Barocio, 3 Circuito Ingeniero, 53100 México, DF; Pres. David Rojas de Avila.

Música de Mexico: Ignacio Esteva 26-A, 11850 México, DF; Proprietor Dario Antonio Zorzano.

Organización Latino Internacional: Avda Insurgentes Sur 953-202, Col. Nápoles, 03810 México, DF; Dir-Gen. Tony Méndez.

Polygram Discos SA: Avda Miguel Angel de Quevedo 531, Col. Romero de Torreros, 04310 México, DF; Dir-Gen. Francisco Bestard.

Producciones Fonográficas: Adolfo Prieto 1649, 1°, Col. del Valle-Benito Juárez, 03100 México, DF; Dir-Gen. Bernado Yancelson.

Suite Sync de México: Prolongación Tajin, 900 Col. Emperadores, 03320 México, DF; Dir Gerardo Suárez.

Netherlands

Ala Bianca Benelux: Zonnelaan 13, 1217 ND Hilversum; Man. Dir H. Lessing.

Artists and Business: PO Box 64, 1200 AB Hilversum; Man. Dir Boudewyn Van Bavel.

Basic Beat: Nieuwe Binnenweg 19, 3014 GB Rotterdam; tel. (10) 436-7937; fax (10) 436-2217; e-mail ron@basic-beat.nl; website www.basic-beat.nl; Man. Dir Ron Hofland.

BMG Nederland BV: PO Box 752, 1200 at Hilversum; Man. Dir D. Sturm.

Brinker Media: PO Box 1276, 1400 Bussum; tel. (35) 603-5368; fax (35) 693-4877; e-mail studio@brinkermedia.com; website www.brinkermedia.com; Man. Dir Eric Van Den Brink.

Brinkman Records BV: Vlietberg 5-45, 6576 JB Ooy; Man. Dir Fred Maessen.

CNR Music Holland: Brinklaan 109, 1404 GA Bussum; Gen. Man. Leon Ten Hengel.

Corazong Records: Langeweid 7, 1831 BL Koedyk; tel. and fax (72) 561-5857; e-mail info@corazong.com; website www.corazong.com. Pres. Evert Wilbrink.

Count Orlok Music: PO Box 2738, 3000 CS Rotterdam; Contact Johnny Zuidhof.

Djax Records: PO Box 2408, 5600 CK Eindhoven; tel. (40) 211-5547; fax (40) 2115004; e-mail box@djax.nl; website www.djax.nl; Man. Dir Saskia Slegers.

EMI Music Netherlands BV: Marathon 11, 1213 PG, Hilversum; tel. (35) 6885900; fax (35) 6852979; e-mail info@emimusic.nl; website www.emimusic.nl; Man. Dir Hennie Van Kuijeren.

Essential Dance Music BV: Nieuwe Binnenweg 19, 3014 GB Rotterdam; Man. Dirs P. Boertje, P. Vriends.

Hotsound: Pleinweg 242 A-d, 3083 EZ Rotterdam; Man. Dir Erik Van Vliet.

Lana Lane Records: Faas Eliaslaan 13, 3742 AR Baarn; Man. Dir Gerry Van Der Zwaard.

Lower East Side Records: Govert Flickstraat 285, 1073 CA Amsterdam; Man. Dir Jeroen Flamman.

Mascot Records: PO Box 231, 2650 AE Berkel; e-mail mail@mascotrecords.com; website www.mascot-provogue.com; Man. Dir Ed Van Zijl.

MMS Group of Companies: PO Box 55559, 1007 NB Amsterdam; Vice-Pres. of A & R Jelle Bakker.

Music & Words: PO Box 1160, 3430 BD Nieuwegein; tel. (30) 606-7674; fax (30) 606-7225; e-mail info@musicwords.nl; website www.musicwords.nl; Pres Hans Peters, Liesbeth Puts.

Play It Again Sam BV: Ampèrestraat 10, 1221 GJ Hilversum; tel. (35) 646-3030; fax (35) 646-3035; e-mail play.it@pias.nl; website www.pias.com; Man. Dir Leo van Schaick.

Replay Records: Herenweg 9, 2465 AA Rijnsaterwoude; tel. (172) 507450; fax (172) 507642; e-mail info@catmusic.nl; website www.catmusic.nl; Man. Dir Aart Mol.

Roadrunner Records: Bijdorp 2, 1181 MZ Amstelveen; Man. Dir Cees Wessels.

Semaphore: PO Box 213, 1740 AE Schagen; Label Man. Marcel Pauvort.

Sony Music Entertainment (Holland) BV: Heuvellaan 50, 1217 JN Hilversum; tel. (35) 629-8298; fax (35) 629-8249; e-mail info@sonymusic.nl; website www.sonymusic.nl; Label Man. Gerard Rutte.

Staalplaat: PO Box 11453, 1001 GC Amsterdam; Man. Dir Geent Jan Hobijn.

Via Records: PO Box 2277, 1200 JV Hilversum; Label Man. Jos Haijer.

Virgin Benelux: Melkpad 29, 1217 KA Hilversum; Label Man. Remmelt Van Beyersbergen.

Warner Music Netherlands BV: Noorderweg 68, 1221 AB Hilversum; International Man. Michiel Ten Veen.

Windham Hill Europe: Oude Enghweg 24, 1217 JD Hilversum; Gen. Man. Frank Van Houten.

Zodiac Records: Rozengracht 228, 1016 SZ Amsterdam; Man. Dir Gert Van Veen.

New Zealand

BMG New Zealand Ltd: Level 4, Young & Rubicam Bldg, Corner Augustus Terrace & Parnell Rd, Parnell, Auckland; tel. (09) 378-0491; fax (09) 378-0496; Contact Micheal Bradshaw.

Deepgrooves Entertainment: PO Box 5404, Wellesley St, Auckland; Contact Kane Massey.

EMI Music NZ Ltd: Ninth Floor, Baycorp House, 15 Hopetoun St, Ponsonby, Auckland; tel. (09) 356-1570; fax (09) 366-7221; website www.emimusic.co.nz; Man. Dir Chris Caddick.

Festival Mushroom Records NZ: 41–45 Ireland St, Freeman's Bay, Auckland; tel. (09) 361-0223; fax (09) 376-1859; Contact Mark Ashbridge.

Flying Nun Records Ltd & Flying In Distribution: PO Box 677, Auckland; website www.flyingnun.co.nz; Gen. Man. Lesley Parrs.

Gateway Productions: PO Box 6735, Wellesley St, Auckland; Man. Greg Henwood.

Gecko Records: 38A Glenmall Pl., Glen Eden, Auckland; Man. Andrew Dixon.

Hark Records: 564 Victoria St, Hamilton; Man. Dir Grant Hislop.

Kiwi Pacific Records Ltd: First Floor, Rainger House, 6 Broomhedge St, Newton; tel. (04) 389-6394; fax (04) 389-6521; Production Man. Murray F. Vincent.

Metro Marketing Ltd: 45 Mackelvie St, Ponsonby, Auckland; Man. Dir Graeme Pethig.

Mushroom Records: Second Floor, ASB Chambers, 138 Queen St, Auckland; Contact Sandii Riches.

Onset Offset: Cashel Chambers, 224 Cashel St, Christchurch; Contact Emilie Dobinson.

Pagan Records: PO Box 47-290, Ponsonby, Auckland; Dirs Trevor Reekie, Sheryl Morris.

Rattle Records: PO Box 4187, Auckland; Man. Dir Keith Hill.

Someone Up There Records: 39A Paunui Rd, St Helliers, Auckland; tel. and fax (09) 575-5946; e-mail some1up@attglobal.net; Dirs Kevin Adair, Darlene Adair; Contact John Burrand.

Sony Music Entertainment (New Zealand) Ltd: Level One, 103 Carlton Gore Rd, Newmarket, Auckland; tel. (9) 979-5330; fax (9) 979-5337; website www.sonymusic.co.nz; Man. Dir Michael Glading.

Sun Pacific Music Co: 49 Murdoch Rd, Grey Lynn; Mans Michael Donnelly, Bernard Griffin.

Tangata Records: PO Box 3679, Shortland St, Auckland; A & R Dir Neil Cruickshank.

Universal Music Ltd: Site 3, Stables Bldg, 30 St Benedicts St, Newton, Auckland; tel. (09) 375-7575; fax (09) 375-7576; Contact Adam Holt.

Virgin Records New Zealand: Ninth Floor, Baycorp House, 15 Hopetoun St, Ponsonby, Auckland; tel. (9) 356-1580; fax (9) 379-9964; website www.virginmusic.co.nz; Man. Dir Chris Caddick.

Warner Music New Zealand Ltd: Seventh Floor, Baycorp House, 15 Hopetoun St, Ponsonby, Auckland; tel. (09) 377-1699; fax (09) 317-0917; Contact James Southgate.

Yellow Bike Records: PO Box 586, Palmerston North; Co-ordinators Claire Pannell, Dave White.

Yellow Eye Music: PO Box 6173, Dunedin North; tel. 3473-9426; fax 3473-9700; e-mail simon@yelloweye.co.nz; website www.yelloweye.co.nz; Partner Simon Vare.

Zomba Records NZ Ltd: Level 4, Young & Rubicam, Cnr Augustus Tce & Parnell Rise, Parnell, Auckland; tel. (09) 302-8444; fax (09) 302-8440; Contact George Spence.

Norway

Air Chrysalis: PO Box 8910, Youngstorget, 0028 Oslo; tel. (47) 2247-8123; e-mail terje.engen@air-chrysalis.no; website www.chrysalis.com; Man. Dir Terje Engen.

Arne Bendiksen Records AS: Jornstadsvn. 62, 1360 Nesbru; tel. 6678-4778; fax 6679-0630; e-mail arnebend@online.no; Man. Dir Arne Bendiksen.

Blue Wolf Productions: PO Box 98, 3671 Notodden; Man. Dir Arild Reinertsen.

BMG Norway AS: PO Box 7030, Homansbyen, 0306 Oslo; tel. 2260-6100; website www.bmg.no.

Busk Records: Fredbo Alle 14, PO Box 471, 3903 Porsgrunn; Man. Dir Terje Welle Busk.

CIA Productions: Waldemar Thranesgate 55 B, 0173 Oslo; Admin. Dir Caroline Asplin.

CNR NonStop AS: Sandakervn. 24C, 0401 Oslo; Man. Dir Ole Vidar Lien.

Continental Records AS: PO Box 110, Smestad, 0309 Oslo; tel. 2206-2770; website www.continentalmusic.net; Man. Dir Barry Matheson.

Crema AS: Nedre Vollgt 3, 0158 Oslo; Man. Dir Arve Sigvaldsen.

Curling Legs Productions DA: PO Box 5298, Majorstua, 0303 Oslo; tel. 2327-0500; fax 2327-0501; e-mail info@curlinglegs.no; website www.curlinglegs.no; Man. Knut Vaernes.

DAT O/S: 9520 Guovdageaidnu; tel. 7848-6772; fax 7848-6788; e-mail dat@dat.net; website www.dat.net; Contact Per L. Boine.

dBut Records: Brennerivn, 9C, 0182 Oslo; tel. 2220-0908; fax 2220-1325; e-mail dbut@dubut.no; website www.dbut.no; Dir Per Platow.

EMI Recorded Music Norway AS: PO Box 492 Sentrum, 0105 Oslo; tel. 2205-2700; website www.emi.no; Man. Dir Jan Ostli.

Enjoy Records: Tidemansgt. 1, 0266 Oslo; Man. Dir Jimmy James.

Gemini Records AS: PO Box 96, 1361 Vettre; tel. 66904499; fax 66904489; e-mail gemini@gemini-records.no; website www.gemini-records.no; Man. Dir Bjorn Petersen.

Grammofon AS: Electra St Halvardsgt. 33, 0192 Oslo; Man. Dir Oyvind Dalsrud.

Grappa Musikkforlag AS: Akersgata 7, 0158 Oslo; tel. 2335-8000; fax 2335-8001; e-mail info@grappa.no; website www.grappa.no; Man. Dir Helge Westbye.

Heilo: PO Box 2645 Solli, 0302 Oslo; Man. Halvard Kvale.

Hot Club Records: PO Box 5202, Majorstua, 0302 Oslo; tel. 2250-1978; e-mail hotclub@c2i.net; website www.hotclub.no; Man. Dir and Prod. Jon Larsen.

Hypertonia World Enterprises: PO Box 4307 Nygardstangen, 5028 Bergen; Man. Jan Bruun.

Idut: Iggaldas, 9710 Inore, Billefjord; Gen. Man. Åge Persen.

Jeps AS: Mandalsgt. 5, 0190 Oslo; Man. Dir Havard Hansteen.

LA Music AS: Skolebakken 14, 1435 Krakstad; Man. Dir Lillian Askeland.

Lynor AS: Bergtorasvn. 74, PO Box 4086 Kongsgard, 4602 Kristiansand S; Man. Dir Livar Holland.

Majorselskapet: Rosenborggt. 19, PO Box 5949 Majorstua, 0308 Oslo; International Label Man. Trond Amlie.

MCA Music Entertainment Norway AS: Parkvn. Blvd, PO Box 2702 Solli, 0204 Oslo; Gen. Man. Petter Singsaas.

MTG Productions: PO Box 2500, 3003 Drammen; tel. 2411-8470; e-mail mtg@mtg.as; website www.mtg.as; Man. Dir Larry Bringssord.

Nidelven Grammofon AS: Hogreina 432, 7079 Flatasen; Man. Dir Per Adlofsen.

Nor Wave/Norsk Gram: PO Box 4603, Valentinlyst., 7002 Trondheim; Man. Dir Gunnar Nordvik.

Nor-CD: Kongens gate 16, 0153 Oslo; tel. 2233-4144; fax 2233-4143; e-mail norcd@norcd.no; website www.norcd.no; Man. Dir Karl Seglem.

Norsk Lyd & Bilde/Norwegian Sound & Vision: Rute 598, 2760 Brandbu; Dirs Odd Erik, Eli Kristin Hagen.

Notabene Records AS: Bogstanvn. 31 B, 0366 Oslo; Man. Dir Ole A. Sorli.

Odin: Tollbugt. 28, 0157 Oslo; tel. 2335-8180; fax 2335-8181; e-mail norsk@jazzforum.no; website www.jazzforum.no; Man. Dir Tone Martinsen.

Origo Sound: Ospelia 8, 1900 Fetsund; Man. Dir Harald Lervik.

Oslo Records: Harald Romckes Vei 37, 0286 Oslo; Man. Lars Borke.

Polygram Norway: PO Box 2645 Solli, Drammensvn 82 B, 0203 Oslo; International Label Man. Petter Singsaas.

Prima Music AS: Storgt. 38, PO Box 4697 Sofienberg, 0506 Oslo; Man. Dir Bjorn Skjennum.

Progress Records: Gregusgt. 9, 7002 Trondheim; Man. Dir Jens Petter Wiig.

Rage Records: PO Box 4721 Sofienberg, 0506 Oslo; Man. Dir Rino Frostad.

Rec 90: PO Box 1291, 5001 Bergen; tel. 5532-3410; fax 5531-1875; e-mail rec90@rec90.com; website www.rec90.com; Man. Dir Torfinn Andersen.

Revolution Records: PO Box 6005, 7003 Trondheim; Man. Dir Diesel Dahl.

Scandinavian Records: Dronningensgt. 8B, PO Box 517 Sentrum, 0105 Oslo; Man. Dir Kai Roger Ottesen.

Sonet Distribution: Drammensvg. 88 B, PO Box 2645 Solli, 0203 Oslo; tel. 2254-1400; fax 2243-0570; e-mail gronn.rune@umusic.com; Distribution Man. Rune Gronn.

Sony Music Entertainment AS: PO Box 134, Okern, 0509 Oslo; tel. 2288-0000; fax 2264-4133; e-mail firmapost@sonymusic.no; website www.sonymusic.no; Man. Dir Rune Hagberg.

Spesial Laboratoriet: Braavallagt. 25 B, 5500 Haugesund; Dir Torgrim Eide.

Truels Brodtkorb: PO Box 2645 Solli, 0271 Oslo; Head of Marketing Truels Brodtkorb.

Tvers Forlag AS: Hasselvn. 47 Ottestad, 2301 Hamar; Man. Dir Arnold Borud.

Universal Music: PO Box 2645, Solli, 0203 Oslo; tel. 2254-1400; website www.universalmusic.no.

V2 Records: Radhugst. 30, 0151 Oslo; tel. 2242-7488; website www.v2music.com.

Virgin Records Norway AS: PO Box 338, Sentrum, 0101 Oslo; tel. 2205-2750; website www.virgin.no; Man. Dir Gyro Leira.

Voices of Wonder: Thv. Meyersgt. 33, 0555 Oslo; Contacts Per Thomas Lund, Ketil Sveen.

Warner Music Norway AS: PO Box 4494, Torshov, 0403 Oslo; tel. 2237-4520; website www.warnermusic.no; Label Mans Steen Brodtkrob, Jonny Styve.

Peru

Discos Hispanos del Peru SA: Esquilache, 179 San Isidro, Lima 27; Gen. Man. Javier Castañeda.

Discos Independientes SA: Avda Arenales 2586, Lima 14; Pres. Samir Giha.

El Virrey Industrias Musicales SA: Avda República de Panamá, 355 San Isidro, Lima 1; Dir Wilan Kafka.

Iempsa SA: Avda Guillermo Dansey 1247, PO Box 67, Lima 1; e-mail arodrich@iempsa.com; website www.iempsa.com; Dir Nilo Marchand.

Philippines

A&W Records: Second Floor, Vergel de Dios Bldg, 530 Evangelista St, Quiapo, Manila; Gen. Man. Willie J. Villar.

BMG Records (Philippines) Inc: 3F, Equitable Bank Bldg, 898 Aurora Blvd, corner Stanford Sts, Cubao, Quezon City, Metro Milano; Man. Dir Rudy Y. Tee.

DD International Recording Corpn: 363 P. Casal St, Quiapo, Manila 1001; Chair. & Pres. Demy A. Quirino Jr.

Ivory Records: 2/F Quadstar Bldg, Ortigas Ave, Greenhills, San Juan, Metro Manila; Pres. Antonio Ocampo.

Platinum Records: Unit 15, Town & Country Arcade, Marcos Highway, Cainta, Rizal; Pres. Eli Balboa.

Solar Records Inc: Second Floor, Roman Santos Bdlg, Plaza Lacson, Santa Cruz, Manila; Pres. Mauro Manalangsang.

Universal Records: 135 P, Sevilla St, Corner Third Ave, Grace Park, Kalookan City, Metro Manila; Vice-Pres. Ramon Chuaying.

Warner Music Philippines Inc: Fourth Floor, Ma. Danile Bldg, 470 MH Del Pilar Corner, San Andres St, Malate, Manila; Man. Dir Ma-an Hontiveros.

Poland

Abrakadabra SA: Sportoaw 5 M 36, 05-400 Otwock; Chair. Antoni Roszczuk.

Artson: Nowogrodzka 49, 00-695 Warsaw; Man. Dir Marek Pioro.

BMG Poland Sp. z.o.o.: ul.: Wiertnicza 94, 02-952 Warsaw; Man. Dir Poitr Naglowski.

Digiton: Aleje Jerozolimskie 29, Apt 3, 00-508 Warsaw; Man. Dir Lyszard Marciniak.

Elbo Phonographic Enterprise: Ul. Moniuszki 10 m 54, 00-009 Warsaw; Man. Dir Boguslaw Borysiuk.

Inter Sonus: Al 3 Maja 2 m 5, 00-391 Warsaw; Man. Dir Rygzard Adamus.

Lion Records: Rejtana 3, 01-800 Warsaw; Man. Dir Piotr Gryglewicz.

Loud Out Records: U. Zielna 45/30, 00-108 Warsaw; Man. Dir Andrzej Mackiewicz.

MJM Music: Ul. Grochowska 341 bud 28, 03-822 Warsaw; Man. Dir Grzegorz Stabeusz.

Polmark: Konrada 30, 01-922 Warsaw; Man. Dir Tadeusz Krasnodebski.

Polonia Records Ltd: Ul. Jana Pawla II 18m 13, 00-116 Warsaw; Man. Dir Stanislaw Sobola.

Polskie Nagrania: Goleszowska 6, 01-249 Warsaw: Man. Dir Aleksander Olaszewski.

Polton Music Distribution: Ul Dantyszka 8, 02-054 Warsaw; Pres. Jan Choonauci.

PUP Metal Mind Productions: Sleligiewicza 8/21, 40-044 Katowice; Man. Dir Tomasz Dziubinski.

Selles Records: Ul Jagielska 43, 02-886 Warsaw; Owner and Man. Dir Tomasz Bielski.

SONIC sp.200: Mscislawska 6, 01-647 Warsaw; tel. (22) 833-3782; fax (22) 833-5784; e-mail sonic@sonicrecords.pl; Man. Dir Marek Proniewicz.

Sony Music Entertainment Polska Sp z.o.o.: ul. Choralna 14, 02-879 Warsaw; tel. (22) 737-6363; fax (22) 737-6300; website www.sonymusic.pl.

Sound Pol: Bitny Warsawskiej, 1920 R 14/88, 02-366 Warsaw; Man. Dir Kajetan Slonina.

SPV Poland: Ul. Twardowska 3, 01-810 Warsaw; Man. Dir Igor Kuronski.

Veriton Records: Bobrowiecka 1, 00-278 Warsaw; Dir Grazyna Solinska.

Zic-Zac Music Co: Sulkowskiego 9, 01-602 Warsaw; Man. Dir Marek Koscikiewicz.

ZPR Inc-United Entertainment Enterprises Inc: Senatorska 13/15, 00 075 Warsaw; Pres. and CEO Zbigniew Benbenek; Artists & Marketing Man. Anna Karolicka.

Portugal

Ama Romanta: R. Coelho da Rocha 46, 1 Dto, 1200 Lisbon; Man. Dir Joao Peste.

Ananana: PO Box 21671, 1137 Lisbon; Man. Dir Fred Sonsen.

Andante-Discos Musica E Som Lda: Avda da Boavista, 1471 Loja 8, 4100 Porto; Pres. Jean Pierre Jongenelen.

BMG Portugal Lda: Edificio Infante D. Henrique, Rua Joao Chagas 53 A-1 Alges, Lisbon 1495-072; Man. Dir Toze Brito.

Dark Records: PO Box 142, 2830 Barreiro Codex; Man. Dir Pedro Cruz.

Discos Belter Lda: Constituiça 74, 4200 Porto: Contact Antonio Figueiredo.

Discossete: Rua Dr Faria Vasconcolos 4A, 1900 Lisbon; Man. Dir Helena Cardinalli.

Edisom: Rua Manuel F. Andrade 6B, 1500 Lisbon; Man. Dir Carlos Ferreira.

Eltatu Editor: R. Rodrigo Da Fonseca, 182 4E, 1070 Lisbon; Dir Antonio Dos Santos; Label Man. Marta Ferreira.

EMI Portugal: Rua de Cruz dos Poias 111, 1200 Lisbon; Man. Dir David Ferreira.

Farol Musica: Alto do Couto, Arnazéns I, 2735 Cacém; Dirs Antonio Guimaráes, Fernando Júrice.

Fast 'N' Loud: PO Box 13037, 1019 Lisbon Codex; Commercial Dir Filipe Marques.

Independent Records: Rua do Jardim, 598-4405 Valadares, Porto; Dir Francisco Pinho.

Johnny Blue: Rua da Madalena 90 3°, 1100 Lisbon; Dir Miguel Santos.

Megamusica Representação e Distribuição Lda: PO Box 13, 2775 Carcavelos; tel. (21) 446-1400; fax (21) 446-1409; e-mail megamusica@mail.telepac.pt; Man. Dir José Eduardo Santos.

Monasterium Records: PO Box 1078, 2670 Santo Antonio Dos Cavaleiros; Man. Dir Duarte Picoto.

Morgana Records: PO Box 845, 2840 Seixal; Man. Dir Duarte Dionisio.

MTM: PO Box 30072, 1321 Lisbon Codex; Man. Dir Hugo Moutinho.

Musica Alternativa: Rua da Republica da Bolivia 75B, 1500-545 Lisbon; tel. (21) 711-2530; fax (21) 711-2531; e-mail company@musicaalternativa.com; website www.musicaalternativa.com; Man. Dir Samuel Lopes.

Polygram Portugal: Rua Prof Reinaldo dos Santos, 12-D, 1500 Lisbon; Man. Dir Rodrigo Marin.

Sony Musica Portugal: Rua Juliao Quintinha 11, 1500 Lisbon; www.sonymusic.com.pt; Head of Public Relations Paolo Bismark.

Strauss Musica e Video SA: Rua Adelaide Cabete 3A, 1500 Lisbon; Admin. Armando Martins.

Vidisco: Ave Bombeiros Voluntarios 13, 1D, 1675 Pontinha, Lisbon; Man. Dir Artur Antunes.

Warner Music Portugal Lda: Rua D. Constantino de Bragança, 26 1400 Lisbon; International Product Co-ordinator Xana Taylor.

Romania

Astra: 22 Adv Ag Str Turda 122, BL 39, ScA, Et 6, Ap 30, Sector 1, Bucharest; Pres. Vertan Adriana.

Electrecord SA: Blvd Timisoara 94, Sector 6, 78702 Bucharest; Gen. Dir Grigore Petreanu.

Romagram Music Ltd: 8 Aviator Mircea Zorileanu str, Sector 1, 70242 Bucharest; Chair. Joey De Alvare.

Roton: 59-61 Str Traian, sect. 3, Bucharest; e-mail info@roton.ro; website www.roton.ro.

Tilt and Partners: 202 A Splaiul Independentei str, Sector 6, 77208 Bucharest; Man. Dir Guiseppe Rossi.

Toji Productions: 9 Piata Romana, C/40, Sector 1, 70167 Bucharest; Man. Dir Nicu Alifantis.

Russia

Alien Records: Bolshaya Serpukhovskaya 44, Moscow; Man. Dir Oleg Kurbatkin.

Aprelevka Sound Inc: Arbat 44, 121 002 Moscow; Man. Dir Grigory Figlin.

BMG Russia: V Maslovka Str. 27/11, 25083 Moscow.

Feelee Record Co: 27 Novozavadskaya str, 121 309 Moscow; website www.feelee.ru; Man. Dir Igor Tonkikh.

Gala Records: Staraya Basmannaya 27-22, 121 309 Moscow; Dir Boris Tzigman.

Lad Records: Dimitrova 39, 117 040 Moscow; Chair. Felix Perepelov.

Russky Disc: Stankevicha 8, 103 009 Moscow; Man. Dir Jury Parol.

SNC Records: Krymsky Val 9, 117 049 Moscow; Man. Dir Alexey Ugrinovitch.

St Petersburg Label B: Sampsoniyevsky Pr. 57, 194 044 St Petersburg; Dir Lydia Cobrina.

Syntex: B. Spasskaya 33-10, 129 010 Moscow; Chair. Alexander Kutikov.

Tau Product: PO Box 377, 117 333 Moscow; Chair. Andrei Bogdanov.

Vist: Triokhprudny Per. 4, 103 031 Moscow; Gen. Man. Vladimir Oletsky.

Zolotaya Dolina Co: Ismaelovsky Proiezd 14/1/34, 105 037 Moscow; Contact Eugeni Grekhov.

Singapore

BMG Singapore Pte. Ltd: No 1, Jalan Kilang, 02-02 Dynasty Industrial Bldg, Singapore 159402; tel. 6278-8388; fax 6353-1771.

EMI (Singapore): 213 Henderson Rd, 04–06 Henderson Industrial Park, Singapore 159553; tel. 6272-8080; fax 6270-3368; Man. Dir David Wee.

Form Pte Ltd: Block 994, Bendemeer Rd 02-01, Singapore; Co Dir Ang Choon Beng.

Hype Records Pte Ltd: 221 Henderson Rd, Suite 02–04 Henderson Bldg, Singapore 159557; tel. 6375-3787; fax 6275-2757; e-mail hype@hyperecords.com; website www.hyperecords.com; Admin. Man. Melvis Yip.

Polygram Records Pte Ltd/Universal Music Pte Ltd: 118 Lor, Geylang SCN, Industrial Bldg 03, Singapore 388402; tel. 6741-2220; fax 6741-0500; Man. Dir Eric Yeo.

Sony Music Entertainment (S) Pte Ltd: 10 Upper Aljunied Link, 03-08, Singapore 367904; tel. 6282-1266; fax 6286-1266; website www.sonymusic.com.sg; Man. Dir Terence Phung.

Warner Music Singapore Pte Ltd: 10 Anson Rd, No. 12-06/07/08, International Plaza, Singapore 079903; tel. 6223-1688; fax 6225-7830; Man. Dir Peter Lau.

White Cloud Record Pte Ltd: 246 MacPherson Rd, #05-01, Betime Bldg, Singapore 348578; tel. 6741-7178; fax 6741-9233; e-mail whitecloud@pacific.net.sg; Man. Dir Heng Ser Piah.

Zomba Records Pte Ltd: SWAT House, 32 Bukit Pasoh Rd, Singapore 089846; tel. 6536-4111; fax 6323-7133.

Slovenia

Dallas: Kersnikova 4, 61000 Ljubljana; Man. Dir Goran Lisica.

Front Rock: PO Box 48, 62000 Maribor; Man. Dujan Hedl.

Matrix Music: Hranilniska 6, 61000 Ljubljana; Man. Dir Primoz Pecounik.

RTV Slovenia Records & Tapes: Dalmatinova 10, 61000 Ljubljana; Label Man. Ivo Umek.

SKUC-AFK: Kersnikova 4, 61000 Ljubljana; Man. Dir Mitja Prezelj.

Zavod Za Umetnisko in Kulturno Produkcijo: Kersnikova 4, 61000 Ljubljana; Man. Dir Monika Skaberne.

South Africa

Ahoy Records: PO Box 5984, Johannesburg 2000; Contact Blondie Makhene.

BMG Records Africa (Pty) Ltd: 26 Cedar Ave, Richmond, Johannesburg 2092; tel. (001) 242-3000; fax (001) 242-3030; website click2music.co.sa; Man. Dir of Records Keith Lister; Man. Dir of Publishing Peter Vee.

Brettian Productions: PO Box 96395, Brixton 2019; Contact Clive Risko.

Cap Records: 134 Unie Ave, Lyttelton 0157; Contact Graham Abrahams.

CCP Record Co (Pty) Ltd: PO Box 83159, 32 Steel St, South Hills, Steeledale 2136; tel. (011) 406-4000; fax (011) 406-4112; Contact Sean Watson.

Cornerstone Records: 175 Nicolette St, Meyerspark 0184; Contact Andrew Cartwright.

CSR Records: PO Box 758, First Floor, Cramerview, Sportron Park, 3 Main View, Bryanston 2021; tel. (011) 463-6485; fax (011) 463-5117; e-mail panhale@csrrecords.co.za; Contact Dave Panhale.

David Gresham Record Co (Pty) Ltd: PO Box 46020, Orange Grove 2119; tel. (011) 444-2630; fax (011) 444-1932; e-mail dgresham@mweb.co.za; website www.greshamrecords.co.za; Owner David Gresham.

Eagle Records: PO Box 11112, Marine Parade 4056; Contact Jean Snyman.

EMI (SA) (Pty) Ltd: PO Box 11254, Johannesburg 2000; tel. (011) 406-4000; fax (011) 623-1731; Contact Irving Schlosberg.

Gazania Records: PO Box 569, Vredendal 8160; Contact H. C. Visser.

Gold Dust Records (Pty) Ltd: 9 Ninth Ave, Houghton 2198; Contact Phil Hollis.

Hit City Records: PO Box 78187, Sandton 2146; tel. (011) 486-0751; fax (011) 646-3717; e-mail jillnorm@iafrica.com; Contact Jill Galankis.

Inhouse Records: PO Box 1072, Fontainebleu 2032; tel. (11) 326-1929; fax (11) 886-3060; e-mail inhouserecords@syrex.co.za; website www.inhouse-records.co.za; Contact Phillip Nel.

Kalawa Records: PO Box 11762, Midrand; tel. (011) 312-1451; fax (011) 315-1438; e-mail kalawjaz@mweb.co.za; Contact Don Laka.

Maranatha Record Co CC: PO Box 32823, Glenstantia 0010; tel. (012) 348-1891; fax (012) 348-1898; e-mail lukiec@mweb.co.za; Contact Lukie Carleson.

Mike Fuller Music Records (Pty) Ltd: PO Box 28292, Kensington 2094; tel. (011) 616-6507-09-11; fax (011) 616-3507; e-mail fullers@netactive.co.za; Proprietor Mike Fuller.

Natal Records: 20B Church Rd, Westville, Durban 3630; Contact Don Clarke.

Phase 2 Records: PO Box 48321, Roosevelt Park, Blackheath; tel. (011) 476-3910; fax (011) 678-4544; e-mail phase2@global.co.za; Contact Terry Fairweather.

Rampant Records: PO Box 661, Ferndale 2160; tel. (011) 462-0150; e-mail gregn@wwe.co.za; Contact Greg Nefdt.

RPM Record Co (Pty) Ltd: PO Box 2807, Johannesburg; tel. (011) 788-0519; fax (011) 442-5962; Contact Charles Kuhn.

Shifty Records: PO Box 93203, Yeoville 2143; e-mail llloyd@yebo.co.za; Contact Lloyd Ross.

Sony Music Entertainment SA (Pty) Ltd: PO Box 411463, Craighall 2024; tel. (011) 328-8500; fax (011) 447-7179; e-mail lazarus_serobe@sz.sonymusic.com; website www.sonymusic.co.za.

Stave Record Productions: PO Box 1854, Pinegowrie 2123; Contact Robert Schroder. .

Tequila Records: PO Box 391405, Bramley, Johannesburg 2018; tel. (011) 448-1133; fax (011) 444-2275; e-mail music@tequila.co.za; Contact David Alexander.

To The Edge Records: PO Box 5012, Weltevreden Park 1715; Exec. Prod. Leon Retief.

Trio Records (Pty) Ltd: PO Box 33283, Jeppsetown 2042; tel. (011) 873-1139; fax (011) 873-1273; e-mail triorecords@worldonline.co.za; Contact Gavin Gibb.

TSOP Record Co: 84 Retief St, Pretoria West 0183; Contact M. M. Mpye.

Universal Music: PO Box 651860, Benmore, Wierda Valley, Sandton; tel. (011) 722-0500; fax (011) 883-2184; Contact Harry Voerman.

Universal Sound & Music Co: PO Box 48782, Roosevelt Park, Johannesburg; tel. (011) 782-6337; fax (011) 782-6338; Contacts Jack Lance Nathan, Nieel Paul Laver.

Uthuli Music CC: PO Box 27149, Sunny Side, Pretoria 0132; fax (012) 341-5825; Contact Thulani Ntuli.

Virgin Records: PO Box 11254, Johannesburg; tel. (011) 406-4000; fax (011) 406-4001; Contact Irving Schlosberg.

Vusa Records: PO Box 423, Milnerton 7435; Contact Mynie Grove.

Spain

Alleluia Records: Rambla Catalunya 10, 08006 Barcelona; Man. Dir Reyes Torio.

Avispa SL: c/o Jeronima Llorente 74, 28039 Madrid; International Dept Margarita Abrante Guerra.

AZ Productions: Riera de Argentona, s/n, 08300 Nataro (Barcelona); International Dept Pere-Lluis Pont.

Bat Discos, SA: Sagunto 2, 28010 Madrid; Gen. Man. Jorge E. Gomez Diaz.

B-Core: Marques de Sentmenat 72, interior 3a, 08029 Barcelona; tel. and fax (9) 3419-7883; e-mail bcore@bcoredisc.com; website www.bcoredisc.com; Man. Dir Jordi Llansama.

BMG Spain: Avda de los Madronos 27, 28043 Madrid.

CDR Praktik: Alcade Mostoles 41, 08026 Barcelona; Man. Dir Ernest Casal.

ChrysalisClip SL: Via Agusta no. 125, Third Floor, 08006 Barcelona; tel. (93) 240-0520; e-mail juliojr@clippersmusic.com; website www.chrysalis.com; Pres Julio Gulu Marquina.

Crab Ediciones Musicales SA: Sagunto 2, 28010 Madrid; Gen. Man. Jorge E. Gomez Diaz.

Disc Medi: Argentona 3–5 Bajos, 08024 Barcelona; Dir Alex Eslava.

Elefant Records: PO Box 331, 28203 Las Rozas, Madrid; tel. (91) 636-0771; fax (91) 710-3543; e-mail elefant@elefant.com; website www.elefant.com; Man. Dir Luis Calvo.

Esese & Co: Llacuna 162, 08018 Barcelona; Man. Dir Sergi Solis.

Fábrica Magnética: Dr Fourquet 31, 28012 Madrid; Man. Dir Servando Carballar.

Fonomusic Distrimusic: Garcia de Paredes 12, 28010 Madrid; Contact Valentin Ladredo.

Goo Records: Bailen 3 1, 48003 Bilbao; Man. Dir Estibaliz Hernandez.

GSG—Grup de Serveis Guilleries: Granja Baró, Ctra de la Guixa, km 2, 08500 Barcelona; Admin. Jordi Costa; Management Ignasi Pla; Production Joan Capdevila.

Lakota SA: Guadalmina Alta, Calle 21 Casa 631, San Pedro de Alcantara, Marbella, 29670 Malaga; Man. Dir Carlo Cavicchi.

Liquid Records: Gomis 42, 08023 Barcelona; Man. Dir Peter Eichenberg.

More Discos/Boy Records: Industria 132, 08025 Barcelona; Man. Dir Ana Moran.

New Music Ediciones Musicales SA: PO Box 9.046, 28060 Madrid; Gen. Man. Gerhard Haltermann.

On The Rock—Caroline: Rossello 336, 08025 Barcelona; Man. Dir Enric Padascoll.

PDI: Passeig de Gracia 74 3 1, 08008 Barcelona; International Label Man. Gerhard Haltermann.

Polygram Iberica: Suero de Quinones 38, 28002 Madrid; Contact Elena Gorostiza, Enrique Prieto.

Por Caridad Producciones: La Palma 72 3, 28015 Madrid; Man. Dir M. José Martin.

Radiation Records: Nicolas Alicorta 2, 48080 Bilbao; Man. Dir Undi Fresnedo.

Salseta Discos: Diputacio 180 5C, 08011 Barcelona; Man. Dir Salvador Escriva.

Siesta Records: Apdo Correos 8117, 28080 Madrid; fax (91) 548-1141; e-mail info@siesta.es; website www.siesta.es; International Man. Joaquin Garcia.

Sony Music: Paseo de la Castellana 93-9a, 28046 Madrid; tel. (91) 596-8474; fax (91) 596-8477; website www.sonymusic.es.

Subterfuge Records: Augusto Figueroa 21 4, 28080 Madrid; Man. Dir Carlos Galan.

Tram Cat: Amigo 26 4, 08021 Barcelona; Man. Dir Toni Oro.

Urantia Records: Rossello 227, 08008 Barcelona; Man. Dir Ramon Bertran.

Victoria Ediciones Musicales SA: Narvaez 14, 28009 Madrid; Man. Dir Gerhard Haltermann.

Walkaria Records: Pl. Morron 16, 10002 Caceres; Man. Dir Victor Guillen.

Warner Music Spain: Aribau 282–284 5 4, 08006 Barcelona; Head of Promotion Lucas Holten.

Sweden

Air Chrysalis Scandinavia: PO Box 10220, 10055 Stockholm; tel. (8) 663-0720; e-mail lars.wiggman@air-chrysalis.se; website www.chrysalis.com; Man. Dir Lars Wiggman.

Amalthea Records: PO Box 271, 18523 Waxholm; Man. Dir Torgny Sjöö.

Atlantis Grammofon AB: Karlbergsvagen 57, 11335 Stockholm; Man. and Owner Jan Hansson.

Birdsnest Records: Kolsvagatan 4, 73133 Köping; Man. Dir Per Granberg.

Blitz Records AB: PO Box 347, 10126 Stockholm 1; Man. Dir Wolfgang Jedliczka.

BMG Sweden AB: Norra Bancogrand 2, PO Box 2082, 103 13 Stockholm; tel. (08) 412-1700; fax (08) 411-1770; website www.bmg.se; Man. Dir Hans Breitholz.

Borderline: Gamlestadsvägen 1, 41502 Gothenburg; Man. Dir Pår Malmstedt.

BORG Music International: PO Box 6082, 20011 Malmö; Chair. Björn Gårdsby.

Burning Heart: Kolsvagatan 4, 73133 Köping; Man. Dir Peter Ahlquist.

Business Record Concept (BRC): PO Box 7083, 63007 Eskilstuna; Dir Peter Rozenbachs.

Caprice Records: Nybrokajen 11, 11148 Stockholm; tel. (08) 407-1600; fax (08) 407-1648; website www.caprice.rikskonserter.se; Man. Dir Kjell Söderqvist.

dB Productions: PO Box 60252, 21609 Malmö; tel. and fax (040) 153996; website www.db-productions.se.

Einnicken Records: Eskilsgatan 11A, 63356 Eskilstuna; tel. 1612-1553; e-mail einnicken@spray.se; Financial Man. Stefan Wistrand.

EMI Svenska AB: PO Box 24058, 10450 Stockholm; tel. (08) 5271-5000; fax (08) 5271-5097; website www.emi.se; Label Man. Per Erik Hotti.

Empire Records: Vintergatan 2, 17230 Sundbyberg; Man. Dir Christer Wedin.

Energy Rekords AB: PO Box 147, SE-343 22 Almhult; fax (04) 7610025; e-mail info@energy-rekords.se; website www.energy-rekords.se; Contact Å. Ehrnst.

Fifty/Fifty Records: PO Box 14096, 63014 Eskilstuna; A & R Peter Torsén.

Four Leaf Clover Records: PO Box 1231, 17224 Sundbyberg; tel. (08) 628-8205; fax (08) 628-8206; e-mail flc@flc.se; website www.flc.se; Dir Lars Samuelson.

Frequent Frenzy Records: PO Box 6009, 10231 Stockholm; Man. Dir Daggan Stamenkovic.

Gazell Music AB: PO Box 10041, 10055 Stockholm; tel. (08) 660-0715; fax (08) 663-7910; e-mail info@gazell.net; website www.gazellmusic.se; Dir Dag Haeggqvist.

Gothenburg Records: Gammlestan 2, 41507 Gothenburg; Man. Dir John Ballard.

H Lime Records: Kvangärdesgatan 36 B, 63355 Eskilstuna; International Man. Magnus Bäckström.

Hawk Records: PO Box 8061, 10420 Stockholm; Man. Dir Björn Håkanson.

House of Kicks Distribution: PO Box 2140, 10314 Stockholm; Dir Roger Reinhold.

HSM Records: PO Box 1122, 22104 Lund; Man. Dir Ulf Lundwall.

Last Buzz Record Co: Husargatanis, 41122 Gothenburg; Prod. Håkan Forshult.

Lush Records: Landsvägsgatan 11, 41304 Gothenburg; Owner Ralph Stern-Pettersson.

M & A Music Art: Simrishamnsgatan 20A, 21423 Malmö; Man. Dir Andreas Larsson.

Mega Records: Ske Pargatan 8, 11452 Stockholm; tel. (08) 663-3660; fax (080) 663-3696; Head of Promotion Brita Jungberg.

MNW Record Group AB: Textilvagen 7, 12030 Stockholm; tel. (08) 630-3600; fax (08) 630-3601; website www.mnw.se; Asst Dir Tomas Sunmo.

MVG Records: PO Box 271, 18523 Waxholm; International Man. Lina Beckmann.

Noble Art Records: PO Box 78, 445 22 Bohus; A & R Man. Magnus Cornelius.

NonStop Records: PO Box 7273, 40235 Gothenburg; Man. Dir Peter Kagerland.

Nordic Soundlab: PO Box 31, 53221 Skara; Man. Dir Lasse Holm.

North of No South (NONS) Records: Sotiehemsv 45, 90738 Umeå; Man. Dir Robert Norsten.

Planet Records: Torggatan 15, 17154 Solna; Chair. Mats Olsson.

Polar AB: PO Box 55777, 11483 Stockholm; tel. (08) 629-5370; fax (08) 764-5383.

Polygram AB: PO Box 55777, 11483 Stockholm; tel. (08) 629-5300; fax (08) 764-5688; Man. Dir Lenart Backman.

Rainbow Music: Höstvägen 5, 17140 Solna/Stockholm; Man. Dir Sture Hallberg.

Real Time Music: Wennerbergsgatan 1, 11258 Stockholm; Man. Allan Gutheim.

Roligan Records: Gotabergsgatan 2, PO Box 53045, 40014 Gothenburg; Man. Dir Jasper Kumberg.

Sidelake: Trädgardstan 23, 85172 Sundsvall; Man. Dir Anders Melin.

Silence: Naved, 67041 Koppom; tel. (5) 711-5050; fax (5) 711-5070; e-mail office@silence.se; website www.silence.se; Man. Dir Eva Wilke.

Sonet Music: PO Box 20105, 16102 Bromma; Man. Dir Börge Engen.

Sony Music Sweden: Kungsholmsgatan 23, PO Box 12745, S-11294 Stockholm; tel. (08) 617 7100; fax (08) 617 7199; e-mail info@sonymusic.se; website www.sonymusic.se; Man. Dir Stefan Klinteberg.

Step One: Katrinebergsvgen 2, 10074 Stockholm; Man. Dir Jörgen Sigfridsson.

Stockholm Records AB: PO Box 55757, 11483 Stockholm; tel. (08) 629-6800; fax (08) 662-8160; website www.stockholmrecords.com; Deputy MD Eric Hasselqvist.

Strawberry Songs: PO Box 157, 63103 Eskilstuna; Man. Dir Hans Lindell.

Swedish Prime Time Records: PO Box 250 32, 75025 Upsala; Man. Dir Dag Carlsson.

Tempo Records: PO Box 231 49, 10435 Stockholm; Man. Dir Peter Hartzell.

Triple/Lionheart Records: Södermannag 38B, 11640 Stockholm; tel. (08) 714-9514; fax (08) 714-9397; Man. Dir Robert Ljunggren.

Universal Music AB: PO Box 55757, 11483 Stockholm; tel. (08) 629-5300; fax (08) 764-5688; website www.umusic.com.

V2 Music Scandinavia AB: Lilla Nygatan 19, 11128 Stockholm; tel. (08) 440-4570; fax (08) 440-4580.

Virgin Records AB: PO Box 6531, 11383 Stockholm; tel. (08) 674-1050; fax (08) 674-1060; website www.virgin.se; Man. Dir Anders Hjelmstorp.

Warner Music Sweden: PO Box 1228, 16428 Kista; tel. (08) 752-2600; fax (08) 752-9650; website www.warnermusic.se; Man. Marten Aglander.

Zakana Records: Skolgatan 73A, 90330 Umeå; Man. Dir Mikael Reinholdsson.

Zomba Records: PO Box 12185, 10225 Stockholm; tel. (08) 545-70800; fax (08) 545-70810.

Switzerland

150 BPM Records: Steinhauserstr 21, 6330 Cham; A & R Man. Hans Raymondaz.

Atina Records GmbH: Hafnarstr 23, 8005 Zürich; Owner and Man. Dir Anita Tiziani.

Black Cat: Faellendenstrase 20, 8124 Maur; Man. Dir Hili Heilinger.

BMG Ariola (Schweiz) AG: Letzigraben 89, 8047 Zürich; Dir Guido Vendramini.

Brambus Records: PO Box 44, 7000 Chur; tel. and fax (55) 614-1077; e-mail info@brambus.com; website www.brambus.com; Dir Paul Rostetter.

Dircom: Fausses-Brayes 19, 2000 Neuchatel; Pres. Joel Desaules.

Dirty Alternative Beat: Rue de O'Ale 35, PO Box 225, 1000 Lausanne 17; Contact T. Leresche.

Disques Cellier: Aiguemont 26, rue du Bourg de Plait, 1605 Chexbres; Dirs Marcel Cellier, Catherine Cellier.

Doublecity: c/o Zumsteg & Partner Ltd, Carmenstrasse 12, 8032 Zürich; tel. (1) 265-5600; fax (1) 265-5684; e-mail pz@doublecity.com; website www.doublecity.com; Contact Peter Zumsteg.

Editions Cellier: Aiguemont 26, rue de Bourg de Plait, 1071 Chexbres; tel. (21) 946-1649; fax (21) 946-3533; e-mail ccellier@merging.com; website ulliherkenhoff.freepage.de/cellier.html; Contacts Marcel Cellier, Catherine Cellier.

EMI Records AG: Buckhauserstr 24, 8048 Zürich; tel. 405-1515; fax 493-2255; e-mail info@emi.ch; website www.emi.ch.

Face Music: Dorfstr 29/1, 8800 Thalwil; e-mail face.music@bluewin.ch; website www.music.ch/face/; Dir Albi Wethli.

Grooveline AG: Laubenhof, 6300 Zug; Man. Dir Ermin Trevisan.

Lux-Noise: PO Box 3212, 5001 Aarau; Man. Dir Michael Hediger.

Noise Product Switzerland: CP 363, 1213 Petit Lancy 1; Label Man. Alban Chaperon.

NSS Records: Fahrweidstr 81 A, 8651 Fahrweid; Contact Michel F. Huwiler.

Off Course Records: PO Box 241, 8025 Zürich; Man. Dir Urs Steiger.

Phonag Records AG: PO Box 322, 8406 Winterthur; tel. (52) 209-0560; fax (52) 209-0561; e-mail info@phonag.ch; website www.phonag.ch; Man. Dir Peter Frei.

Pick Records: Brunnwiesenstr 26, 8049 Zürich; Chair. Anton Peterer.

Sony Music Switzerland: Oberneuhofstr 6, 6341 Baar; website www.sonymusic.ch; Man. Mirco Vaiz.

Steinblatt Music: Via Vicari 18, 6900 Lugano; Man. Dir Marco Antognini.

Turicaphon AG: Turicaphonstr 31, 8616 Riedikon; Man. Dir Hans Oestreicher.

Viteka Music Production: PO Box 173, Ringstr 14, 8600 Dübendorf/Zürich; Chair. Willy Viteka.

Warner Music Switzerland: Ave Chilton 70, 1820 Montreux; Man. Dir Charles Nobs.

Taiwan

BMG Music Taiwan Inc: 9F, No. 100, Sec. 2, An Ho Rd, Taipei 106; tel. (2) 2708-1830; fax (2) 2755-0821; website www.click2music.com.tw; Man. Dir Ren Ren; CEO Kate Su.

Chiang Huat Co/Around The World Music: 3/F 278 Chung Hsiao East Rd, Section 4, Taipei; tel. (886) 2752 4994; fax (886) 2778 6016; Prod. Ms Hsiu Hua Ho.

Decca Records Taiwan Ltd: 12/Fl No. 112 Chung Hsiao East Rd, Section 1, Taipei; tel. (886) 2394 1828; fax (886) 2396 9795; Man. Dir Denver Chang.

EMI (Taiwan) Ltd: Second Floor, No. 12, 10 Alley 321 Lane, Hsing-Ming Rd, Taipei; website www.emimusic.com.tw; Man. Dir Hung Tik.

Hsin Yao Recordings: 6F-4 No. 410, Sec. 5, Chunghsiao E Rd, Taipei; tel. 287883196; fax 387883264.

K & D Music Entertainment Inc: 6F No. 63, Po-Ai Rd, Taipei; Sr Man. Dir Tom Uend.

Polygram Records Ltd: 5F 99 Nankang Rd, Section 3, Nankang District, Taipei; Man. Dir Michael Hwang.

Renaissance Records Co Ltd: No. 12, Lane 13, Kwang Fu South Rd, Taipei; Pres. Bob Chen.

Rock Records and Tapes: 5F, No. 3, Lane 240, Kwang Fu S Rd, Taipei; tel. 227415062; Pres. Sam C. T. Duann.

Sony Music Entertainment (Taiwan) Ltd: Eighth Floor, No. 35, Lane 11, Kwang-Fu North Rd, Taipei; website www.sonymusic.com.tw; Man. Dir Matthew Allison.

Wind Records Co Ltd: 5F, 14 Lane 130, Minchuan E Rd, Taipei; tel. 222185881.

Thailand

BMG (Thailand) Ltd: 18/F Vanissa Bldg, 29 Soi Chidlom, Plaeoanchit Rd, Patumwan, Bangkok 10330; Man. Dir Steven Tan.

EMI (Thailand) Ltd: 1091/183 New Petchburi Rd, Makkasa, Phayathai, Bangkok 10400; Gen. Man. Vichart Jirathiyut.

Giant Records: 61/123 Taveemit Soi 9, Rama IX Rd, Asoke-Din Daeng, Huay-Kwang, Bangkok 10310; Contact Kraisak Ochareon.

Grammy Records: 59/1 Soi Prom Pong, Sukhumvit 39, Sukhumvit Rd, Prakanong, Bangkok 10110; Man. Dir Paiboon Damrong Chaitam.

Michael Record Co Ltd: 52/17-18 Moo 8, Orn-Nuch Rd, Suanluang, Bangkok 10250; Man. Dir Chokechai Jaruwatee.

Polygram (Far East Bangkok Enterprises): 21 115–116 Royal City Ave, Rama IX Rd, Huay Kwang, Bangkok 10310; Man. Dir Jerry Sim.

Sony Music Entertainment (Thailand) Ltd: 1091/184–5 New Petchburi Rd, Payathai, Bangkok 10400; website www.sonymusic.co.th; Gen. Man. Peter Gan.

Warner Music Thailand: 143 Sukhumvit 62/1, Sukhumvit Rd, Prakhanong, Bangkok 10250; Man. Dir Wasana Silpikul.

Turkey

Hades Records: Gazi cd, Reisul Kuttap Sk, Peken Ap 50/B, 81160 Baglarbasi, Istanbul; Dir Volkan Olgun.

Jazz Records & Publishing: Atlamatasi Caddesi 5, Serilen, 34470 Unkapani, Istanbul; Pres. Yasar Demirturk.

MMY: IMC 6, Blok 6437, 34470 Unkapani, Istanbul; Pres. Yesil Giresunlu.

RKD Ltd: Ferah Sok Ferah Apt 1, 19-9 Nisantasi, Istanbul; tel. (212) 241-3411; fax (212) 231-9673; e-mail rkdltd@lxir.com; website www.akustamusic.com; Man. Dir Armagan Ak.

Sony Music Turkey: Mesrutiyet cd. 163/5, Tepebasi, Istanbul 80050; tel. (212) 251-2744; fax (212) 251-3803; website www.sonymusic.com.tr.

Ukraine

Audio Ukraine Laboratory: Provulok 7A, 252 133 Kiev; Man. Dir Yuri Goncharuk.

Komora: Dav 22, NEC, Hlushkova Ave 1, 252 085 Kiev; Interpreter Ivan Chuigouk.

Leva: Kostyushka str 18, 290 000 Lviv; Man. Dir Igor Krytovitch.

NAC: Gorkok str 47, 252 005 Kiev; Man. Dir Volodymyr Lagodny.

United Arab Emirates

BMG Middle East/North Africa: PO Box 29079, Dubai.

United Kingdom

A&M Records: 136–140 New Kings Rd, London SW6 4LZ; Man. Dir Osman Erlap.

Abbey Records: 4 Newtec Pl., Magdalen Rd, Oxford, Oxfordshire OX4 1RE; Press Officer Peter Bromley.

Ace Records: 42–50 Steele Rd, London NW10 7AS; tel. (20) 8453-1311; fax (20) 8961-8725; e-mail sales@acerecords.co.uk; Man. Dir Ted Caroll.

Acid Jazz Records: 11 Greek St, London WC1V 5LE; Man. Dir Edward Piller.

Active Records: Rockfield Studios, Amberley Ct, Monmouth, Gwent NP5 4ET; tel. (1600) 712449; fax (1600) 714421; e-mail rockfieldstudios@compuserve.com; website www.rockfieldstudios.com; Dir Kingsley Ward.

AKR Records: Waterside Penthouse, 156 High St, Brentford, Middlesex TW8 8JA; Man. Dir Kevin Moran.

All Around The World (AATW) Productions Ltd: 9–13 Penny St, Blackburn BB1 6HJ; tel. (1254) 264120; fax (1254) 693768; e-mail info@aatw.com.

Almo Sounds: 3 Heathmans Rd, London SW6 4TJ; Contact Mercedes Luis Fuentes.

Alphabet Records: 253 Camberwell New Rd, London SE5 0TH; Contact Mark Walmesley.

Alternative Tentacles Records: 64 Mountgrove Rd, London N5 2LT; Label Man. Bridget Clay.

Anagram Records: Bishops Park House, 25–29 Fulham High St, London SW6 3JH; Label Man. Adam Velasco.

Anxious: Devonshire House, 2/4 The Broadway, London N8 9SN; Man. Dir Tony Quinn.

Arista Records: Cavendish House, 423 New Kings Rd, London SW6 4RN; Gen. Man. Mark Williams.

Ariwa Sounds Ltd: 34 Whitehorse Lane, South Norwood, London SE25 6RE; tel. (20) 8653-7744; fax (20) 8771-1911; e-mail info@ariwa.com; Man. Dir Neil Fraser.

Arrival Records: 39 Leyton Rd, Harpenden, Hertfordshire AL5 2JB; Man. Dir David Blaylock.

Astranova: Unit 306, Canalot Production Studios, 222 Kensal Rd, London W10 5BN; Dir Scott Hill.

Atomic Records: 32 Neal St, London WC2H 9PS; Contact Mick Newton.

Avex UK: 22 Soho Sq., London W1V 5FJ; Dir Phil France.

Awesome Records: 59 Moore Park Rd, London SW6 2HA; Man. Dir Falcon Stuart.

Bad Habits Music Group: PO Box 111, London W13 0ZH; Man. Dir John S. Rushton.

BBC Music: Room A2039, Woodlands, 80 Wood Lane, London W12 0TT; tel. (20) 8433-1701; fax (20) 8433-1741; e-mail simon.sudbury@bbc.co.uk; Contact Simon Sudbury.

Bearcat Records: PO Box 94, Derby DE22 1XA; Contact Chris Hall.

Beat Goes On (BGO) Records: 7 St Andrews St North, Bury St Edmunds, Suffolk IP33 1TZ; tel. (1284) 724406; fax (1284) 762245; e-mail mike@bgo-records.com; Label Man. Michael Gott.

Beatfarm Recordings: Studio C, Chelsea Studios, 416 Fulham Rd, London SW6 1HP; Owner Marco Perry.

Beechwood Music Ltd: Littleton House, Littleton Rd, Ashford, Middlesex TW15 1UU; tel. (1784) 423214; fax (1784) 251245; e-mail info@beechwoodmusic.co.uk; website www.beechwoodmusic.co.uk; Contact Chet Selwood.

Beggars Group: 17–19 Alma Rd, London SW18 1AA; tel. (20) 8870-9912; fax (20) 8871-1766; e-mail beggars@beggars.com; website www.beggars.com; Labels incl. 4AD, Beggars Banquet, Mantra, Mo' Wax, Nation, Situation Two, Too Pure, Wiiija, XL-Recordings.

Big Bear Music: PO Box 944, Edgbaston, Birmingham B16 8UT; tel. (121) 4547020; fax (121) 4549996; e-mail admin@bigbearmusic.com; website www.bigbearmusic.com; Man. Dir Jim Simpson.

Big Cat (UK) Records Ltd: 131–133 Holland Park Ave, London W11 4UT; tel. (20) 7471-3000; Label Man. Tim Vass.

Big Life Records: 15 Little Portland St, London W1N 5DE; Chair. Jazz Summers.

Blackout Records: 253 Camberwell New Rd, London SE5 0TH; Contact Mark Walmesley.

Blanco y Negro: 66 Golborne Rd, London W10 5PS; tel. (20) 8960-9888; fax (20) 8968-6715; e-mail james@roughtraderecords.com; website www.roughtraderecords.com; Man. Dir Geoff Travis.

Blueprint: PO Box 5, Derwentside, Co Durham DH9 7HR; Label Man. Rob Ayling.

BMG Entertainment UK & Ireland Ltd: Bedford House, 69–79 Fulham High St, London SW6 3JW; tel. (20) 7384-7500; fax (20) 7371-9298; e-mail john.preston@bmg.com; Labels incl. 19, Arista, Camden, Cheeky, dB, Deconstruction, Dedicated, First Avenue, Global TV, Indolent, LaFace, Logic, RCA, S Records, Survival; Chair. John Preston.

Bobb Records: 12 Waterford Rd, Ashley, New Milton, Hants BH25 5BH; tel. (1425) 618286; Dirs Mike Preston, Andrea Preston.

Brilliant Records: 19 Ford Sq., London E1 2HS; tel. (20) 7265-8891; fax (20) 7790-7206; Man. Dir Frazer Henry.

BSC Records: 23 Corbyn St, London N4 3BY; Dirs Andy Monoyos, Gordon Ellington.

Bulldog Records: PO Box 130, Hove, East Sussex BN3 6QU; tel. (1273) 550088; Dir of International Operations Steve Lewis.

Buzz Records: 14 Corsiehill Rd, Perth PH2 7BZ; tel. and fax (1738) 638140; e-mail dave@radiotones.com; Man. Dir Dave Arcari.

Caritas Records: 28 Dalrymple Cres., Edinburgh EH9 2NX; tel. (131) 6673633; fax (131) 6673633; e-mail caritas-records@caritas-music.co.uk; website www.caritas-music.co.uk; Man. Dir James Douglas.

Carlton Records: The Waterfront, Elstree Rd, Elstree, Hertfordshire WD6 3BS; A & R Dir John Howard.

Carrera Recordings Ltd: Elwy Valley Studios, Tan-Y-Clogwyn, Llangernyw, North Wales LL22 8RH; tel. (1745) 860652; fax (1745) 860485; Contact Paul White.

Castle Communications: Unit 29, Barwell Business Park, Leatherhead Rd, Chessington, Surrey KT9 2NY; Chair. Terry Shand.

Charley Records Ltd: 156–166 Ilderton Rd, London SE15 1NT; Founder Jean Luc Young; Dir Jan Friedmann.

Check Records: Stewart House, Hillbottom Rd, Sands Industrial Estate, High Wycombe, Buckinghamshire HP12 4HJ; A & R Copyright Dept Catherine Lee.

Chemikal Underground: PO Box 3609, Glasgow G42 9TP; website www.chemikal.co.uk.

Cherry Red Records: Unit 17, Elysium Gate West, 126–128 New Kings Rd, London SW6 4LZ; tel. (20) 7371-5844; fax (20) 7384-1854; e-mail iain@cherryred.co.uk.

Chimera Records Ltd: 41 Rosebank, Holyport Rd, London SW6 6LQ; tel. (20) 7385-5724; fax (20) 7386-0701; Man. Dir Sadia Sadia.

China Records: Electric Lighting Station, 46 Kensington Ct, London W8 5DA; tel. (20) 7938-5630; fax (20) 7368-4903; Contact Rachel Speers.

Chrysalis Music UK: The Chrysalis Bldg, Bramley Rd, London W10 6SP; tel. (20) 7221-2213; fax (20) 7229-4498; e-mail enquiries@ chrysalis.com; website www.chrysalis.com; Labels incl. Chrysalis, Echo, The Hit Label, Lasgo, Papillon; Chair Chris Wright; Chief Exec. Jeremy Lascelles.

Circle Sound Services: Circle House, 14 Waveney Close, Bicester, Oxfordshire OX6 8GP; Proprietor John Willett.

Columbia Records: 10 Great Marlborough St, London W1V 2LP; Man. Dir Kip Krones.

Confidential Records: The Bungalow, Cadman Lane (off Pontefract Rd), Snaith, East Yorkshire DN14 9JR; tel. and fax (1924) 277508; e-mail conrec@usound.freeserve.co.uk; Dir Nev Barker.

Cooking Vinyl: PO Box 1845, London W3 0ZA; tel. (20) 8600-9200; fax (20) 8743-7448; e-mail info@cookingvinyl.com; website www.cookingvinyl.com; A & R Neil Armstrong.

Deconstruction: Bedford House, 69–79 Fulham High St, London SW6 3JW; Man. Dirs Keith Blackhurst, Pete Hadfield.

Dedicated Records: 36A Notting Hill Gate, London W11 3JQ; Part of BMG; Man. Dir Doug D'Arcy.

Demi Monde Records & Publishing: Foel Studio, Llanfair, Caereinion, Powys SY21 0DS; tel. (1938) 810758; fax (1938) 810758; e-mail dave.anderson@dial.pipex.com; website www.demimonde.co.uk; Man. Dir Dave Anderson.

Dick Bros Record Co Ltd: The Main House, Spittalrig Farm, Nr Haddington EH41 3SU; tel. (62) 082 6150; fax (62) 082 6144; Contact Jeremy Lawson.

Digital Hardcore Recordings (DHR): PO Box 35019, London NW1 9YT; e-mail 6666@digitalhardcore.com; website www.digitalhardcore.com.

Direct Heat Records: PO Box 1345, Worthing, West Sussex BN14 7FB; tel. and fax (1903) 202426; e-mail dhm@happyvibes.co.uk; website www.happyvibes.co.uk; Man. Dir Mike Pailthorpe.

Disky Communications Ltd: Connaught House, 112–120 High Rd, Loughton, Essex IG10 4HJ; tel. (20) 8508-3723; fax (20) 8508-0432; e-mail Disky_uk@disky.nl.

Domino Record Co: 3 Podmore Rd, London SW18 1AJ; tel. (20) 8875-1390; fax (20) 8875-1391; Man. Dir Laurence Bell.

Dorado Records Ltd: 76 Brewer St, London W1R 3PH; tel. (20) 7287-1689; fax (20) 7287-1684; e-mail info@dorado.net; Man. Dir Ollie Buckwell.

Down To Jam Records: 112A-B Westbourne Grove, Chepstow Rd, London W2 5RU; Man. Dir Paul Moore.

Earache Records: PO Box 144, Nottingham NG3 4GE; e-mail mail@earache.com; website www.earache.com; Founder and Man. Dir Digby Pearson.

East West Records: Electric Lighting Station, 46 Kensington Ct, London W8 5DP; tel. (20) 7938-5500; fax (20) 7368-4910; website www.eastwest.co.uk; Man. Dir Christian Tattersfield.

The Echo Label: The Chrysalis Bldg, 13 Bramley Rd, London W10 6SP; tel. (20) 7221-2213; fax (20) 7792-1299; e-mail john.chuter@chrysalis.com; website www.echo.co.uk; Man. Dir John Chuter.

Edel (UK) Records Ltd: 12 Oval Rd, London NW1 7DH; tel. (20) 7482-4848; fax (20) 7482-4846; e-mail info@edel.co.uk.

Ember Records: PO Box 130, Hove, East Sussex BN3 6QU; tel. (1273) 550088; fax (1273) 540969; e-mail jskruger@tkogroup.com; website www.tkogroup.com; Chair. of the Board Jeffrey Kruger.

EMI Records (UK): EMI House, 43 Brook Green, London W6 7EF; tel. (20) 7605-5000; fax (20) 7605-5050; Labels incl. Apple, Astralwerks, Blue Note, Capitol, Caroline, Charisma, Chrysalis, Circa, Compulsion, Cooltempo, DEP International, EG, Ensign, Food, Harvest, HMV, Hut Recordings, Innocent, IRS, Linn, Mute, Parlophone, Pepper, Pointblank, Positiva, Real World, Regal Recordings, Source, Ten, Virgin; Contact David Hughes, Carolyn Crowley.

Engine Records: 253 Camberwell New Rd, London SE5 0TH; Contact Mark Walmesley.

Epic Records: 10 Great Marlborough St, London W1V 2LP; Man. Dir Rob Stringer.

Equity Records: 112A-B Westbourne Grove, Chepstow Rd, London W2 5RU; Man. Dir Paul Moore.

Esprit Music Ltd: Unit 306, Canalot Production Studios, 222 Kensal Rd, London W10 5BN; tel. (20) 8968-0889; fax (20) 8960-8907; Dir Tony Warren.

Fair Oaks Entertainment: PO Box 19, Ulverston, Cumbria CA12 9TF; Proprietor and Man. J. G. Livingstone.

Fat Boy Records: PO Box 130, Hove, East Sussex BN3 6QU; Operations Man. Peter Hazledine.

Fellside Recordings: PO Box 40, Workington, Cumbria CA14 3EW; tel. (1900) 61556; fax (1900) 61585; e-mail info@fellside.com; Partner Paul Adams.

Fiction Records Ltd: 4 Tottenham Mews, London W1P 9PJ; tel. (20) 7323-5555; fax (20) 7323-5323.

Fierce Panda Records Ltd: 39 Tollington Rd, London N7 6PB; tel. (20) 7509-2789; fax (20) 7609-8034; website www.fiercepanda.co.uk; Contact Ian Ballard.

Fire Records: 21A Maury Rd, London N16 7BP; A & R Dept Dave Barker, Jon Eydmann.

First Avenue Records: The Courtyard, 42 Colwith Rd, London W6 9EY; tel. (20) 8741-1419; fax (20) 8741-3289; Contact Oliver Smallman.

Food Records/Parlophone: 172A Arlington Rd, London NW1 7HL; Part of EMI; Contact Ellie O'Ready.

4AD: 15 Alma Rd, London SW18 1AA; Man. Dir Ivor Watts-Russell.

Funki Dred Records Ltd: 36/38 Rochester Pl., London NW1 9JX; tel. (20) 7284-0393; fax (20) 7284-0166; A & R H. Browne.

Go Beat Records: The Fulham Palace, Bishops Ave, London SW6 6EA.

Go! Discs: 72 Black Lion Lane, London W6 9BE; tel. (20) 8910-4600; fax (20) 8741-2184; Man. Dir Andy McDonald; Contact John Kellett.

Grand Records: 107A High St, Canvey Island, Essex SS8 7RF; tel. (1268) 694888; fax (1268) 695009; e-mail grandrecords@aol.com; Contact Ann Adley.

Grasmere Records: 59 Marlpit Lane, Coulsdon, Surrey CR5 2HF; tel. (20) 7584-9765; fax (20) 7823-7100; Man. Dir Bob Barratt.

Greensleeves Records Ltd: Unit 14, Metro Centre, St John's Rd, Isleworth TW7 6NJ; tel. (20) 8758-0564; fax (20) 8758-0811; e-mail mail@greensleeves.net.

Greentrax Recordings Ltd: Cockenzie Business Centre, Edinburgh Rd, Cockenzie, East Lothian EH32 0XL; tel. (1875) 814155; fax (1875) 813545; e-mail iangtrax@aol.com; website www.greentrax.com; Proprietor Ian D. Green.

Grenquille Records: Stewart House, Hill Bottom Rd, Sands Industrial Estate, High Wycombe, Buckinghamshire HP12 4HJ; International A & R Copyright Lawyer Keith R. Phillips.

GRP Records International: 33 Broadwick St, London W1V 1FR; Contact Frank Hendricks.

Gut Records Ltd: Byron House, 112A Shirland Rd, London W9 2EQ; tel. (20) 7266-0777; fax (20) 7266-7734; e-mail gut-intermedia.com.

Handle Records: Handle House, 1 Albion Pl., Galena Rd, Hammersmith, London W6 0QT; Chair. David Walker.

Harbourtown Records: PO Box 25, Ulverston, Cumbria LA12 7UN; tel. (1229) 580577; Man. Dir Gordon Jones.

Hawk Records Ltd: 123–137 York St, Belfast BT15 1AB, Northern Ireland; tel. (1232) 325225; fax (1232) 439069; Man. Dir Charlie Tosh.

Headscope Records: St End Lane, Broadoak, Heathfield, East Sussex TN21 8TU; tel. (1435) 863994; fax (1435) 867027; e-mail ron@geesin.demon.co.uk; website www.rongeesin.com; Partner Ron Geesin.

The Hit Label/Papillon Records: The Chrysalis Bldg, 13 Bramley Rd, London W10 6SP; tel. (20) 7221-2213; website www.papillonrecords.co.uk.

Hotshot Records: 29 St Michaels Rd, Leeds LS6 3BG; Man. Dirs D. Foster, Clio Bradbury.

Hut Records: Kensal House, 553–579 Harrow Rd, London W10 4RH; Part of EMI; Contact David Boyd.

Independiente Ltd: The Drill Hall, 3 Heathfield Terrace, London W4 4JE; tel. (20) 8747-5111; fax (20) 8747-5113; e-mail info@independiente.co.uk; website www.independiente.co.uk; Founder Andy MacDonald.

Indigo Records: Second Floor, Twyman House, 31–39 Camden Rd, London NW1 9LF; Contact Colin Newman.

Inky Blackness: PO Box 32089, Camden, London NW1 0NX; Man. Dir Ian Tregoning.

Innocent Records: Kensal House, 553–579 Harrow Rd, London W10 4RH.

Iona Records: 27–29 Carnoustie Pl., Scotland St, Glasgow G5 8PH; tel. (141) 4201881; fax (141) 4201892; e-mail lismor@lismor.com; website www.lismor.com; Man. Dir Ronnie Simpson.

IRS Records: EMI House, 443 Brook Green, London W6 7EF; Part of EMI; Label Man. Richard Breeden.

Island Records: 22 St Peter's Sq., London W6 9NW; tel. (20) 8910-3333; fax (20) 8913-4541; Man. Dir Marc Marot.

Jeepster Recordings Ltd: PO Box 1359, Croydon, Surrey CR9 5WL; tel. (20) 8405-0090; fax (20) 8686-9831; e-mail mark@jeepster.co.uk; website www.jeepster.co.uk; Dir Mark Jones.

Kickin Music Ltd: 8 Acklam Workshops, 10 Acklam Rd, London W10 5QZ; tel. (20) 8964-3300; fax (20) 8964-4400; e-mail info@kickinmusic.com.

Kinetix: Spirepark, Hall Farm, West Clayton, Chorleywood WD3 5EX; tel. (1923) 285285; fax (1923) 285286; e-mail info@kinetix.ltd.uk; Chair. Jon Sharp.

Kitchenware: 7 The Stables, St Thomas St, Newcastle upon Tyne, Tyne and Wear NE1 4LE; Man. Dir Keith Armstrong.

Klub Records Ltd (KRL): 9 Watt Rd, Hillington, Glasgow G52 4RY; tel. (141) 882 9060; fax (141) 883 3686; e-mail krl@krl.co.uk; Man. Dir Gus McDonald.

Kufe Records Ltd: 154 Rucklidge Ave, Harlesden, London NW10 4PR; tel. (20) 8533-1879; fax (20) 8986-8649; e-mail lindel@kuferecords.com; website www.kuferecords.com; Man. Dir Lindel Lewis.

L'attitude Ltd: First Floor, Ducie House, 37 Ducie St, Manchester M1 2JW; Part of Universal; Dirs Andy Dodd, Elliot Rashman.

Lena Davis, John Bishop Assocs: Cotton's Farmhouse, Whiston Rd, Cogenhoe, Northants NN7 1NL; tel. (1604) 891487; fax (1604) 890405; Dir John Bishop.

Linn Records: 257 Drakemire Dr., Castlemilk, Glasgow G45 9SZ; tel. (141) 303 5189; fax (141) 644 4262; e-mail records@linn.co.uk; Label Man. Philip Hobbs.

Lismor Recordings Ltd: 27–29 Carnoustie Pl., Scotland St, Glasgow G5 8PH; tel. (141) 420-1881; fax (141) 420-1892; e-mail lismor@lismor.com; website www.lismor.com; Man. Dir Ronnie Simpson.

Liverpool Music House Ltd: 51–55 Highfield St, Liverpool L3 6AA; Dir Colin Hall.

Logic/BMG: Bedford House, 69–79 Fulham High St, London SW6 3JW; tel. (20) 7384-7500; fax (20) 7384-7880; Contact Tony Piercy.

London Records: PO Box 1422, Chancellors House, Chancellors Rd, London W6 9SG; Man. Dir Colin Bell.

Luna Park: 81 Harley House, Marylebone Rd, London NW1 5HT; Contact Russell Vaught.

MCA Records Ltd: 139 Piccadilly, London W1V 0AX; Part of Universal; Deputy Man. Dir Jeff Colembo.

Medium Productions Ltd: 74 Saint Lawrence Rd, Upminster, Essex RM14 2UW; tel. (1708) 228016; fax (1708) 640291; e-mail info@mediumproductions.co.uk; website www.mediumproductions.co.uk; Co-Dir Debi Zornes.

Mel Bush Organization Ltd: Tanglewood, Arrowsmith Rd, Wimborne, Dorset BHZ1 3BG; tel. (1202) 691891; fax (1202) 691896; e-mail mbobmth@aol.com; Man. Dir Mel Bush.

Mercury: 136–144 New King's Rd, London SW6 4LE; tel. (20) 7705-4200; fax (20) 7705-4201; Man. Dir Howard Berman.

Metro Music Productions: Metro Radio Ltd, Longriggs, Swalwell, Gateshead, Tyne and Wear NE99 1BB; Dir of Music Production Jon Craig.

Midnight Rock: Grays Farm Barns, Marshside, Kent CT3 4EL; tel. (1227) 860638; fax (1227) 860627; e-mail rockindave@midnightrock.demon.co.uk; website www.midnightrock.demon.co.uk; Contact Dave Taylor.

Millennium Records: 6 Water Lane, Kentish Town Rd, Camden, London NW1 8NZ; tel. (20) 7482-0272; fax (20) 7267-4908; Man. Dir Ralph Ruppert.

Milltown Productions Ltd: 26 East Parade, Bradford, West Yorkshire BD1 5HD; tel. (1274) 776657; fax (1274) 394817; Prod. Ian Smith.

Moksha: Unit 258, Stratford Workshops, Burford Rd, Stratford, London E15 2SP; tel. (20) 8555-5423; fax (20) 8519-6834; Man. Dir Charles Colm.

Moving Shadow Records: 10 Unity Wharf, Mill St, London SE1 2BH; tel. (20) 7252-2661; fax (1462) 835199; e-mail gav@movingshadow.com; Label Co-ordinator Caroline Butler; Contact Gavin Johnson.

Mrs Casey Music: PO Box 296, Aylesbury, Buckinghamshire HP19 3TL; Dir Steve Heap.

Mushroom Records UK Ltd: NISCO, PO Box 151, Peterborough, PE1 1UB; tel. (1733) 555333; fax (1733) 563148; website www.mushroomuk.com; Man. Dir Korda Marshall.

Music For Nations: Electron House, Cray Ave, St Mary Cray, Orpington, Kent; tel. (1689) 870622; fax (1689) 836906; e-mail mfn@music-for-nations.co.uk; website www.music-for-nations.co.uk; Man. Dir Andy Black.

Music of Life/Living Beat Records: 20 Hanway St, London W1P 9DD; Man. Dir Chris France.

Musidisc UK: 32 Queensdale Rd, Holland Park, London W11 4SB; tel. (20) 7602-1124; fax (20) 7602-0704; Label Man. Judith Fisher.

Mute Records: 429 Harrow Rd, London W10 4RE; Part of EMI; Man. Dir Daniel Miller.

Nation Records Ltd: 19 All Saints Rd, Notting Hill, London W11 1HE; tel. (20) 7729-4604; fax (20) 7792-2854; e-mail aki@nationrecords.co.uk; website www.nationrecords.co.uk; Man. Dir Aki Nawaz.

Nettwerk Productions UK: 108b Regents Park Rd, London NW1 8UR; tel. (20) 7586-8511; fax (20) 7586-8539; e-mail gary@nettwerk.com.

NIKT Records: Cadillac Ranch, Pencraig Uchaf, Cwm Bach, Whiland, Dyfed SA3 40DT; tel. (1994) 484466; fax (1994) 484294; e-mail cadillac_ranch@telco4u.net; website www.nikturner.com; A & R Nik Turner.

Now and Then: Unit 29, Empress Industrial Estate, Anderson Sreet, Wigan, Lancashire WN2 2BG; Label Man. Mark Ashton.

NRG Records: 49 High St, Kingston-upon-Thames, Surrey KT1 1LQ; Man. Dir Robert Jones.

Nude Records: 6 Warren Mews, London W1P 5DJ; tel. (20) 7388-5300; fax (20) 7388-6500; Man. Dir Saul Galpern.

One Little Indian Records: 34 Trinity Cres., London SW17 7AE; tel. (20) 8772-7600; fax (20) 8772-7603; e-mail db@indian.co.uk; website www.indian.co.uk; Man. Dir Derek Birkett.

Outburst Music Ltd: 71 High St E, Wallsend, Tyne and Wear NE28 7RJ; tel. (191) 2624999; fax (191) 2637082; e-mail mdwood33@aol.com; website www.geordiestuff.co.uk; Man. Dir Dave Wood.

Palace of Fun: 16 Elm View, Huddersfield Rd, Halifax, Yorkshire HX3 0AE; Man. Dir Bill Byford.

Park Records: PO Box 651, Oxford OX2 9RB; tel. (1865) 241717; fax (1865) 204556; Man. Dir John Dagnell.

Parlophone Records: 43 Brook Green, London W6 7EF.

Perfecto Records: Electric Lighting Station, 46 Kensington Ct, London W8 5DP; Contact Spencer Baldwin.

Performance Equities Ltd: 112 A & B Westbourne Grove, Chepstow Rd, London W2 5RU; Man. Dir Paul Moore.

Permanent Records: 22–23 Brook Mews, London W2 3BW; Man. Dir J. Lennard.

PHAB: High Notes, Sheerwater Ave, Woodham, Weybridge, Surrey KT15 3SD; Contact Philip H. A. Bailey.

Pinnacle Entertainment: Electron House, Cray Ave, St Mary Cray, Orpington, Kent BR5 3NP; tel. (1689) 870622; fax (1689) 821741; Labels incl. Music For Nations, Strange Fruit.

Planet 4: Sun House, 2–4 Little Peter St, Manchester M15 4PS; tel. (161) 834 4406; fax (161) 834 4408; Man. Dir Chris Joyce.

Plankton Records: Sandcastle Productions, PO Box 13533, London E7 0SG; tel. (20) 8534-8500; e-mail plankton.records@virgin.net; Sr Partner Simon Law.

Play It Again Sam (UK): 338A Ladbroke Grove, London W10 5AH; tel. (20) 8324-2411; fax (20) 8324-0017; Gen. Man. Peter Dodge.

Plutonium Records: Stanley House, 15/17 Ladybridge Rd, Cheadle Hulme, Greater Manchester SK8 5BL; tel. (161) 485 6519; fax (161) 488 4399; Press & Promotions Zoey Faulkner.

Pogo Records: Stewart House, Sands Industrial Estate, High Wycombe, Buckinghamshire HP12 4HJ; A & R Xavier Lee.

Pollytone Music: PO Box 124, Ruislip, Middlesex HA4 9BB; tel. (20) 8963-0352; fax (20) 8963-1170; e-mail val@pollyton.demon.co.uk; website www.pollytone.com; Dir Valerie Bird.

Polydor (UK): 72 Black Lion Lane, London W6 9BE.

PolyGram UK: PO Box 1420, 1 Sussex Pl., London W6 9XS; Part of Universal; CEO Roger Aimes.

Positiva: 43 Brook Green, London W6 7EF; tel. (20) 7605-5157; fax (20) 7605-5186; website www.positivarecords.com; Part of EMI; Head of A & R Jason Ellis.

President Records Ltd: Units 6–7, 11 Wyfold Rd, Fulham, London SW6 6SE; tel. (20) 7385-7700; fax (20) 7385-3402; e-mail dkassner@president-records.co.uk; Man. Dir David Kassner.

Priory Records: 3 Eden Ct, Eden Way, Leighton Buzzard, Bedfordshire LU7 8FY; tel. (1525) 377566; fax (1525) 371477; e-mail sales@priory.org.uk; Proprietor Neil Collier.

Profile Records Ltd: 4 Mirabel House, 117 Wandsworth Bridge Rd, London SW6 2TP; tel. (20) 7736-3345; fax (20) 7384-0165; e-mail aj@smilecom.co.uk; Dir Jon Sharp.

PWL International: 222–224 Borough High St, London SE1 1JX; Man. Dir Peter Price.

Quinlan Road (UK): 1 Heathgate Pl., 75/87 Agincourt Rd, London NW3 2NT; Gen. Man. Ian Blackaby.

R & B Division Ltd: 34 Salisbury St, London NW8 8QE; tel. (20) 7402-9111; fax (20) 7723-3064; Man. Dir Eliot M. Cohen.

Red Bus Records Ltd: 34 Salisbury St, London NW8 8QE; tel. (20) 7402-9111; fax (20) 7723-3064; e-mail eliot@amimedia.co.uk; website www.amimedia.co.uk; Man. Dir Eliot M. Cohen.

Red Lightnin' Ltd: The White House, The Street, North Lopham, Diss, Norfolk IP22 2LU; tel. (1379) 687693; fax (1379) 687559; e-mail peter@redlightnin.com; website www.redlightnin.com; Blues specialist; Dir Peter Shertser.

Revolver Music Ltd: 152 Goldthorn Hill, Penn, Wolverhampton, West Midlands WV2 3JA; tel. (1902) 345345; fax (1902) 345155; e-mail paul.birch@revolver-e.com; Contact Paul Birch.

Riddle Records: Cadillac Ranch, Pencraig Uchaf, Cum Bach, Whitland, Dyfed SA34 0DT; e-mail cadillac-ranch@telco4u.net; website www.nikturner.com; A & R M. Menendes, Christy French.

Roadrunner Records: Suite A, Tech West House, Warple Way, London W3 0UE; tel. (20) 8749-2984; fax (20) 8968-8388; e-mail rrguest@roadrunnerrecords.co.uk; Gen. Man. Mark Palmer.

Rock 'n' Roll Enterprises: 16 Grove Pl., Penarth CF64 2ND; tel. (2920) 704279; fax (2920) 709989; e-mail barrett.rocknroll@aimserve.net; Dir Paul Barrett.

Rollover Productions: 29 Beethoven St, London W10 4LJ; Man. Dir Seamus Morley.

Ronnie Scott's Jazz House: Magnum House, High St, Lane End, High Wycombe, Buckinghamshire HP14 3JG; Man. Dir Derek Everett.

RooArt Europe: 22a Lambolle Pl., London NW3 4HP; Contact Paul Craig.

Rough Trade Records: 250 York Rd, London SW11 3SJ; tel. (20) 7924-1661; fax (20) 7924-4274; e-mail james@roughtraderecords.com; website www.roughtraderecords.com; Man. Dir Geoff Travis.

RTL Music: Stewart House, Hill Bottom Rd, Sands Industrial Estate, High Wycombe, Buckinghamshire HP12 4HJ; Owner and Prod. Ron Lee.

Rykodisc Ltd: 78 Stanley Gardens, London W3 7SN; Man. Dir Ian Moss.

Sadia Sadia: 41 Rosebank, Holyport Rd, London SW6 6LQ.

Sain: Caolfan Sain, Llandwrog, Caernarfon, Gwynedd LL54 5TG; tel. (1286) 831111; fax (1286) 831497; Man. Dir Dafydd Iwan.

Sambawamba: 6 Handel St, Nottingham NG3 1JE.

Sanctuary Records Group Ltd: 45/53 Sinclair Rd, London W14 0NS; tel. (20) 7602-6351; fax (20) 7603-5941; e-mail info@sanctuaryrecords.co.uk.

Saxology Records: 49E St Paul's Rd, London N1 2LT; tel. (20) 7354-2595; fax (20) 7354-5094; Man. Dir Mike Tanousis.

Saydisc Records: Chipping Manor, The Chipping, Wotton-Under-Edge, Gloucestershire GL12 7AD; tel. (1453) 845036; fax (1453) 521056; Partner Gef Lucena.

Scotdisc Music & Video: BGS Productions Ltd, Newtown St, Kilsyth, Glasgow G65 0JX; Marketing Dir Dougie Stevenson.

Secret Records Ltd: Regent House, 1 Pratt Mews, London NW1 0AD; tel. (20) 7267-6899; fax (20) 7267-6746; e-mail colin@secretrecordslimited.co.uk.

Seriously Groovy Music Ltd: Third Floor, 28 D'Arblay St, Soho, London W1F 8EW; tel. (20) 7439-1947; fax (20) 7734-7540; e-mail seriously.groovy@virgin.net; website www.seriouslygroovy.com; Dir Lorraine Snape.

Setanta Records: 174 Camden Rd, London NW1 7HJ; tel. (20) 7284-4677; fax (20) 7284-4577; e-mail info@setantarecords.com; Contact Keith Cullen.

Sidestep Records Ltd: 9A Dallington St, London EC1V 0BQ; Joint Man. Dir Heddi Greenwood.

Sony Music Entertainment (UK and European Regional Office): 10 Great Marlborough St, London W1F 7LP; tel. (20) 7911-8200; fax (20) 7911-8600; e-mail info@sonymusic.co.uk; website www.sonymusic.co.uk; Labels incl. Columbia, Disques Dreyfus, Epic, 550 Music, Hard Hands, Immortal, INCredible, MJJ, Monument, Okeh, Relativity, Ruthless, Sony Classical; Sony Soho Square (S²); Chair. Paul Burger; A&R, Ricardo Fernandez.

Sony Soho Square (S²): 10 Great Marlborough St, London W1V 2LP; Part of Sony Music Entertainment; Man. Dir Muff Winwood.

Stamina Management: 47 Prout Grove, London NW10 1PU; Man. Dir Peter Gage.

Stephen W. Tayler: 41 Rosebank, Holyport Rd, London SW6 6LQ; Contact Stephen W. Tayler.

Stone Tiger Records: PO Box 4464, London SW19 6XT; Owner Les Rowley.

Strange Fruit Records: Electron House, Cray Ave, Orpington, Kent BR5 3PN; tel. (20) 8964-9544; fax (20) 8964-5460; e-mail sfm@strange-fruit-music.co.uk; website www.strangefruitrecords.com.

Stress Records: PO Box 89, Slough, Berkshire SL1 8NA; Man. Nick Gordon Brown.

Swoop Records: Stewart House, Hillbottom Rd, Sands Industrial Estate, High Wycombe, Buckinghamshire HP12 4HJ; A & R Katherine Le Matt.

SYME International-Hengest Records: 81 Park Rd, Wath-Upon-Dearne, Rotherham, South Yorkshire S63 7LE; tel. (1709) 877920; fax (1709) 873119; e-mail admin@hengest.com; website www.hengest.com; Product Man. Patsy Prince.

Taurus Records: 23 Blackheath Rise, Lewisham, London SE13 7PN; Contact Beverley Miller.

Telstar Records PLC: Prospect Studios, Barnes High St, London SW13 9LE; tel. (20) 8392-6859; fax (20) 8392-8359.

Tembo Entertainments: PO Box 1655, London W8 5HZ; tel. (20) 7937-1040; Contact Howard Elson.

The Brothers Organisation: 74 The Archway, Station Approach, Ranelagh Gardens, London SW6 3UH; Dirs Ian Titchener, Nick Titchener.

Theobald Dickson Productions Ltd: The Coach House, Swinhope Hall, Swinhope, Lincolnshire LN3 6HT; tel. (1472) 399011; fax (1472) 399025; Man. Dir Bernard Theobald.

3MV: Third Floor, 7 Holyrood St, London SE1 2EL; tel. (20) 7378-8866; fax (20) 7378-8855; e-mail info@3mv.com.

Timbre Records Ltd: PO Box 3698, London NW2 6ZA; tel. (20) 8450-9087; fax (20) 7691-7632; Man. Dir Diane M. Hinds.

TKO Licensing Ltd: PO Box 130, Hove, East Sussex BN3 6QU; tel. (1273) 550088; fax (1273) 540969; e-mail warren@tkogroup.com; website www.tkogroup.com; Head of Licensing Warren Heal.

TKO Magnum Music Ltd: Unit 5, Pilot Trading Estate, West Wycombe Rd, High Wycombe, Buckinghamshire HP12 3AB; tel. (1494) 450606; fax (1494) 450230; e-mail music@tkomagnum.co.uk; website www.tkomagnum.co.uk; Joint CEO Nigel Molden.

Too Pure: 3A Highbury Cres., London N5 1RN.

Trim Top Records: 13 Winton Park, Edinburgh EH10 7EX; tel. (1314) 451687; e-mail gerryford@madasafish.com; website www.gerryford.co.uk; Owner Gerry Ford.

Triple Earth: 24 Foley St, London W1P 7LA; tel. and fax (20) 7636-5443; Partner Iain Scott.

Unexploded Persons Bureau: PO Box 6414, London N1 3SA; Co-ordinator Russell Willes.

Unity Records: John Henry Bldg, 16/24 Brewery Rd, London N7 9NH; tel. (20) 7609-9187; fax (20) 7636-7040; Sales & Retail Man. Pepin Clout.

Universal Music Group UK: PO Box 1420, 1 Sussex Pl., London W6 9XS; tel. (20) 8910-5000; fax (20) 8741-4901; e-mail forename.surname@umusic.com; Labels incl. A&M, Ark 21, Decca, Dreamworks, Go! Discs, GRP, Hip-O, Interscope, Island, Karussell, Mercury, Polydor, PolyGram UK.

Upbeat Management and Recordings: Sutton Business Centre, Rastmor Way, Wallington, Surrey SM6 7AH; tel. (20) 8773-1223; fax (20) 8669-6752; e-mail beryl@upbeat.co.uk; website www.upbeat.co.uk; Contact Beryl Korman.

Upbeat Recordings Ltd: PO Box 63, Wallington, Surrey SM6 7AH; tel. (20) 8773-1223; fax (20) 8669-6752; e-mail liz@upbeat.co.uk; Contact Beryl Korman.

Vinyl Japan (UK) Ltd: 98 Camden Rd, London NW1 9EA; tel. (20) 7284-0359; Man. Patrick James.

Vinyl Solution: 231 Portobello Rd, London W11 1LT; Contacts Rob Tennant, Alain de la Mata, Nick Brown.

Virgin Records Ltd: Kensal House, 553–579 Harrow Rd, London W10 4RH; tel. (20) 8968-6688; fax (20) 8968-6533; Chair. Ken Berry.

Vision Discs: PO Box 92, Gloucester GL4 8HW; Contact Vic Coppersmith.

Vital Distribution Ltd: 338a Ladbroke Grove, London W10 5AH; tel. (20) 8324-2400; fax (20) 8324-0001; e-mail info@vitaluk.com.

V2 Music Ltd: 131 Holland Park Ave, London W11 4UT; tel. (20) 7471-3000; fax (20) 7603-4796.

Warner Music (UK)/WEA Records: The Warner Bldg, 28 Kensington Church St, London W8 4EP; tel. (20) 7368-2500; fax (20) 7368-2760; Labels incl. Atco, Atlantic, blanco y negro, Centredate, China, Coalition Recordings International, Dead Dead Good, Death Row, Duck, EastWest, Elektra, Eternal, Face Value, ffrr, Giant, London, Magnet, Maverick, Nonesuch, Qwest, Reprise, Rhino, Sire, Slash, Sub Pop, Walt Disney, Warner Bros, warner.esp, ZTT; Chair. Rob Dickins.

Warp Records Ltd: Spectrum House, 32–34 Gordon House Rd, London NW5 1LP; tel. (20) 7284-8357; fax (20) 7284-8360; website www.warprecords.com.

Wolf Records: 83 Brixton Water Lane, London SW2 1PH; tel. (20) 7733-8088; fax (20) 7326-4016; Man. Dir Dominique Brethes.

X-Factor Music Group International: PO Box 52, Ilford, Essex IG1 3JT; tel. and fax (20) 8252-1007; e-mail xsquad_uk@yahoo.co.uk; Dir and Prod. Ramesh Kansara.

XL-Recordings: 17–19 Alma Rd, London SW18 1AA; Admin. Man. Elise Theuma.

Young Guns Productions: 95 Carshalton Park Rd, Carshalton Beeches, Surrey SM5 3SJ; Owner Tom Jennings.

Zarg Records: Stewart House, Hillbottom Rd, High Wycombe, Buckinghamshire HP12 4HJ; A & R Writer and Prod. Ron Dickson.

Zomba Records Ltd: Zomba House, 165–167 Willesden High Rd, London NW10 2SG; tel. (20) 8459-9759; fax (20) 8459-9837; e-mail cheryl.goddard@zomba.co.uk; Labels incl. Jive, Pepper, Silvertone, Unity; Gen. Man. Andy Richmond; Contact Cheryl Goddard.

Zoo Bee Records: Suite 6, 1 Cranbourn Alley, Cranbourn St, London WC2H 7AN; Prod. Tim Rabjohns.

ZTT Records Ltd: The Blue Bldg, 42–46 St Lukes Mews, London W11 1DG; tel. (20) 7221-5101; fax (20) 7221-3374; Contact Claire Leadbitter.

United States of America

A & E Music Inc: 13644 S W 142 Ave, Suite D, Miami, FL 33186; Pres. Joe Granda.

A & M Records Inc: 595 Madison Ave, New York, NY 10022.

A & R Records: 900 19th Ave S, Suite 207, Nashville, TN 37212; Owner Ruth Steele.

A&M Records: 1416 N La Brea Ave, Hollywood, CA 90028; Pres. Al Cafaro.

Aarrow Records: 900 19th Ave S, Suite 207, Nashville, TN 37212; Owner Kelli Steele; A & R Dir Ruth Steele.

Airtrax: 273 Chippewa Dr., Columbia, SC 29210-6508.

Alcazar Productions: PO Box 429 South, Main St, Waterbury, VT 05676; Vice-Pres. Jennifer Harwood.

Alexandria House: 3310 West End Ave, Fifth Floor, Nashville, TN 37203; Marketing Co-ordinator Michelle Gust.

All American Music Group: 808 Wilshire Blvd, Santa Monica, CA 90405; Dir National Publicity Sheryl Northrop.

American Music: 1206 Decatur St, New Orleans, LA 70116; Pres. George H. Buck Jr.

American Recordings: 3500 W Olive Ave, Suite 1550, Burbank, CA 91505.

Anti-Inc: 2798 Sunset Blvd, Los Angeles, CA 90026.

Antithesis Records: 273 Chippewa Dr., Columbia, SC 29210-6508.

Arista Records: 6 W 57th St, New York, NY 10019; tel. (212) 489-7400; website www.arista.com; Pres. Clive Davis.

Artan Records: PO Box 5672, Buena Park, CA 90622-5672; Man. Carmen Ortiz.

Ash Music: 116 NE 136 Ave, Portland, OR 97230; A & R Jason Charles.

Asil Records: PO Box 790576, Middle Village, NY 11379-0576; Pres. Dan Karpf.

Astralwerks Records: 104 W 29th St, Fourth Floor, New York, NY 10001.

Atlantic Records: 75 Rockefeller Plaza, New York, NY 10019-6907; website www.atlantic-records.com; Co-Chairs Ahmet Ertegun, Doug Morris.

Audiophile: 1206 Decatur St, New Orleans, LA 70116; Pres. George H. Buck Jr.

Axbar Records: PO Box 12353, San Antonio, TX 78212; tel. (210) 829-1909; e-mail contact@axbarmusic.com; website www.axbarmusic.com; Prod. and Gen. Man. Joe Scates.

Baker Productions: 311 Second Ave SW, Cullman, AL 35055; tel. (256) 739-0388; fax (256) 739-7196; e-mail cbaker@bakerproductions.com; website www.bakerproductions.com; Labels incl. Homefront, New Beginnings; Pres. Charles Baker.

Bar/None Records: PO Box 1704, Hoboken, NJ 07030; tel. (201) 770-9090; fax (201) 770-9290; e-mail info@bar-none.com; website www.bar-none.com; Pres. Tom Prendergast.

Bell Records International: PO Box 725, Daytona Beach, FL 32115-0725; Vice-Pres. Charles Vickers.

Benson Music Group Inc: 365 Great Circle Rd, Nashville, TN 37228; International Sales Janice Cuttler.

Black & Blue Records: Suite 152, 400 D. Putnam Pike, Smithfield, RI 02917; Pres. Peter Yarmouth.

Blaster-Boxx Hits: 519 N Halifax Ave, Dayton Beach, FL 32118; tel. and fax (386) 252-0381; e-mail blasterboxxhits@aol.com; website www.blasterboxxhits.com; CEO Bobby Lee Cude.

Blix Street Records: 4704 35th St NW, Gig Harbor, WA 98335; tel. (253) 851-5810; fax (253) 851-8210; e-mail blixstreet@aol.com; website www.blixstreet.com.

Blowin' Smoke Records: 7438 Shoshone Ave, Van Nuys, CA 91406-2340; tel. (818) 881-9888; fax (818) 881-0555; e-mail blowinsmokeband.com; website www.blowinsmokeband.com; Pres. Larry Weisberg.

Blue Note Records: 304 Park Avenue S, Third Floor, New York, NY 10010; website www.bluenote.com.

BME Records: PO Box 76507, Washington, DC 20013; Pres. Carl Bentley.

BMG Entertainment: 1540 Broadway, New York, NY 10036; tel. (212) 930-4000; e-mail info@bmg.com; website www.bmg.com; Labels incl. Arista, Buddah, J Records, Jive, LaFace, Logic, RCA, RCA Red Seal, RCA Victor, Windham Hill, Zomba Entertainment; Pres. and CEO Pete Jones.

Bob Scott Frick Enterprises: 404 Bluegrass Ave, Madison, TN 37115; tel. (615) 865-6380; e-mail bfrick@att.net; Pres. Bob Frick.

Broken Rekids: PO Box 460402, San Francsico, CA 94146-0402, USA; tel. and fax (415) 552-4757; e-mail jay@brokenrekids.com; website www.brokenrekids.com; Pres. JayDid.

BSW Records: PO Box 2297, Universal City, TX 78148; tel. (210) 599-0022; fax (210) 653-3989; e-mail bswr18@txdirect.net; website www.bswrecords.com; Pres. and CEO Frank Willson.

C & S Productions: PO Box 91492, Anchorage, AK 99509-1492; tel. (907) 522-3228; Partner Tim R. Crawford.

C E R Records: 7400 N Adams Rd, North Adams, MI 49262; tel. (517) 287-4421; Pres. Claude E. Reed.

Cadence Jazz Records: Cadence Bldg, Redwood, NY 13679; tel. (315) 287-2852; fax (315) 287-2860; e-mail cjr@cadencebuilding.com; website www.cadencebuilding.com; Prod. Bob Rusch.

Camaraderie Music Co: 238 Austin St, Boston, MA 02136-1844; Contact Curt Naihersey.

Canyon Records: 3131 W Clarendon Ave, Phoenix, AZ 85017; tel. (800) 268-1141; fax (602) 279-9233; e-mail canyon@canyonrecords.com; website www.canyonrecords.com.

Capitol Records: 1750 N Vine St, Hollywood, CA 90028; website www.hollywoodandvine.com; Labels incl. Angel Records, Blue Note, Capitol Nashville, Freeworld Entertainment, Grand Royal, Java, Mosaic, Neurodisc, Odeon, Priority, The Right Stuff, S-Curve, Virgin; Pres. Gary Gersh.

Caprice International Records: PO Box 808, Lititz, PA 17543; Pres. Joey Welz.

Case Entertainment Group Inc (R): 102 E Pikes Peak Ave, Suite 200, Colorado Springs, CO 80903; Contact Robert A. Case.

Cat's Voice Productions: PO Box 1361, Sanford, ME 04073-7361; Owner Tom Reeves.

Century Media Records: 2323 W El Segundo Blvd, Hawthorne, CA 90250; tel. (323) 418-1400; fax (323) 418-0118; e-mail mail@centurymedia.com; website www.centurymedia.com; Vice-Pres. and Gen. Man. Marco Barbieri.

Cerebral Records: 1236 Laguna Dr., Carlsbad, CA 92008; Pres. Lincoln Kroll; Publicist Carol Leno.

Chapel Music Group Inc: 2021 Richard Jones Rd, Suite 180, Nashville, TN 37215; Dir of Marketing Heather Campbell.

Chemistry Records Ltd: PO Box 68, Las Vegas, NM 87701; website www.chemistryrecords.com; Pres. Robert John Jones.

Circle: 1206 Decatur St, New Orleans, LA 70116; Pres. George H. Buck Jr.

Clarity Recordings: PO Box 411407, San Francisco, CA 94141-1407; Pres. Ed Woods.

Confidential Records: 1013 Evelyn Ave, Albany, CA 94706; Pres. Joel Brandwein.

Convenience: PO Box 66461, AMC O'Hare, IL 60666; Dir John Maz.

Cosmotone Records: 3350 Highway 6 S, PMB 412, Sugar Land, TX 77478; e-mail marianland@earthlink.net; website www.marianland.com/music02.html; Pres. Rafael Brom.

Creative Improvised Music Projects: Cadence Bldg, Redwood, NY 13679; tel. (315) 287-2852; fax (315) 287-2860; Prod. Bob Rusch.

CSP Records MC: PO Box 69646, Los Angeles, CA 90096; Dir Larry Kleno.

Cude & Pickens Music: 519 N Halifax Ave, Daytona Beach, FL 32118; tel. and fax (386) 252-0381; e-mail cudepickenspub@aol.com; website www.broadwayusa.us; CEO Bobby Lee Cude.

Curb Records Inc: 47 Music Sq. E, Nashville, TN 37203; tel. (615) 321-5080; website www.curb.com.

Cybortravik Recording & Video Group: 8927 Claycott Dr., Dallas, TX 75243; CEO David C. May.

DanceFloor Distribution/Echo USA: 95 Cedar Lane, Englewood, NJ 07631; Pres. Jeffrey Collins.

Def Jam Records: 2220 Colorado Ave, Santa Monica, CA 90404.

Del-Fi Records Inc: PO Box 69188, Los Angeles, CA 90069; Owner & Pres. Bob Keane.

Delicious Vinyl Records: 6607 Sunset Blvd, Los Angeles, CA 90028; tel. (323) 465-2700; fax (323) 465-8926; e-mail dvinyl@earthlink.net; website www.deliciousvinyl.com.

Diva Entertainment World: 853 Broadway #1516, New York, NY 10003; Man. Dir Marc Krasnow.

DreamWorks Records: 9268 W Third St, Beverly Hills, CA 90210; website www.dreamworksrecords.com.

E & J Records: 1505 Elvis Presley Blvd, Memphis, TN 38106; Exec. Asst Linda Lloyd.

East West Records America: 75 Rockefeller Plaza, New York, NY 10019-6907; CEO Sylvia Rhone.

Edensong: PO Box 34, Days Creek, OR 97429; Owner Rick Foster.

Elastic Records: PO Box 17598, Anaheim, CA 92817-7598; tel. and fax (310) 659-9214; e-mail aminighashghai@worldnet.att.net; website www.elasticrecords.com; Owner Amin Ghashghai.

Elektra Records: 75 Rockefeller Plaza, New York, NY 10019-6907; website www.elektra.com; Chair. Bob Krasnow.

Ember Records: 4501 Connecticut Ave, NW, Suite 905, Washington, DC 20008; CEO Michael Cohn.

EMI Records Group: 1290 Sixth Ave, New York, NY 10104; website www.emigroup.com; CEO Charles Koppelman.

Enemy Records: 234 Sixth Ave, Brooklyn, NY 11215; e-mail info@enemy.com; website www.enemy.com; Pres. Michael Knuth.

Epic Records: 550 Madison Ave, New York, NY 10022-3211.

Epitaph Records: 2798 Sunset Blvd, Los Angeles, CA 90026.

Ernie Bivens Productions: 203 Gates Dr., Hendersonville, TN 37075-4961; Owner and Prod. Ernie Bivens.

The Eternal Song Agency: 6326 E Livingston Ave, Reynoldsburg, OH 43068; Pres. Leopold Xavier Crawford.

FAME Recording Studios: PO Box 2527, Muscle Shoals, AL 35662; Studio Man. Rodney Hall.

Feather Records: PO Box 132, Astor Station, Boston, MA 02123-0132; Co-Owner L. Pass.

(510) Records: 5299 College Ave, Suite E, Oakland, CA 94618; Pres. Elliot Cahn.

Five Roses Music Group: 34A Lanier Rd, Studio 1, Jekyll Island, GA 31527; Pres. Sammie Lee Marler.

Flying Heart Records: 4026 NE 12th Ave, Portland, OR 97212; website home.teleport.com/~flyheart; Owner Jan Celt.

Fox Records: PO Box 1027, Neenah, WI 54957-1027; Pres. Tony Ansems.

Frank Russell Productions: PO Box 453, Totowa, NJ 07511; Prod. Frank Russell.

GBS Records: 203 Gates Dr., Hendersonville, TN 37075-4961; Owner and Prod. Ernie Bivens.

Geffen/DGC Records: 9130 Sunset Blvd, Los Angeles, CA 90069-6197; Chair. David Geffen.

Genius Records: PO Box 481052, Los Angeles, CA 90048; Contact Marcy Blaustein.

GHB: 1206 Decatur St, New Orleans, LA 70116; Pres. George H. Buck Jr.

Giant Records: 8900 Wilshire Blvd, Suite 200, Beverly Hills, CA 90211; Owner Irving Azoff.

Glide Records: PO Box 8243, Calabasas, CA 91372; tel. (818) 883-8407; Proprietor Cho Paquet.

Gotee Records: 227 Third Ave N, Franklin, TN 37064; Admin. Asst Claudia Tapia.

Gramophone Records: PO Box 910, Beverly Hills, CA 90213; tel. (310) 557-0534; Gen. Man. Lionel Holland.

Gray Dot Records: 1080 Creatwood Circle, Smyrna, GA 30080; website www.graydot.com; CEO Marty Bush.

Greco Holdings Inc: Market St Sq., 33 Wilkes Barre Blvd, Wilkes Barre, PA 18701; Pres. and CEO Thom Greco.

Green Linnet Records: 43 Beaver Brook Rd, Danbury, CT 06810; tel. (203) 730-6333; fax (203) 778-4443; website www.greenlinnet.com; Owner and Creative Dir Wendy Newton.

Greener Pastures Records: 70 N 202, Peterborough, NH 03458-1107; Pres. Wayner Green.

Group Productions: 1515 Cascade Ave, Box 481, Loveland, CO 80538; tel. (970) 669-3836; website www.grouppublishing.com; Contact Brenda Kraft.

GRP Records: 555 W 57th St, New York, NY 10019; Pres. Larry Rosen.

Grrr Records: 920 W Wilson Ave, Chicago, IL 60640; Publicity and Retail Man. Shelley Needham; Booking Man. Diane Borden.

Hammerhead Records Inc: 41 E University Ave, Champaign, IL 61820; tel. (847) 870-8525; e-mail hammerhd@shout.net; website www.shout.net@~hammerhd; Pres. Todd Thorstenson.

Hard Hat Records: 519 N Halifax Ave, Daytona Beach, FL 32118; tel. and fax (386) 252-0381; e-mail hardhatrecords@aol.com; website www.hardhatrecords.com; CEO Bobby Lee Cude.

Heartwrite Music: PO Box 1739, Texarkana, AR 75504; Pres. David Patillo.

High Kite Productions & Publishing: 1245 Elizabeth St, Denver, CO 80206; Prod., Owner and Pres. Henry Broz Rowland.

Higher Octave Music Inc: 23852 Pacific Coast Highway, Suite 2C, Malibu, CA 90265; tel. (310) 589-1515; fax (310) 589-1525; e-mail info@higheroctave.com; website www.higheroctave.com; Sr Vice-Pres. Scott Bergstein.

Hollywood Records: 500 S Buena Vista St, Burbank, CA 91521; tel. (818) 560 5670; e-mail website www.hollywoodrecords.go.com; CEO Wesley Hein.

IKON Records: 212 N 12th St, Suite 3, Philadelphia, PA 19107; Pres. A & R Vincent Krishner.

Imaginary Records: PO Box 66, Whites Creek, TN 37189; e-mail jazz@imaginaryrecords.com; website www.imaginaryrecords.com; production, manufacture, promotion and distribution of jazz recordings; Proprietor Lloyd E. Townsend Jr.

Imago Recording Co: 152 W 57th St, 44th Floor, New York, NY 10019; Pres. Terry Ellis.

Inferno Records: PO Box 28743, Kansas City, MO 64118; Dir of A & R Mark Murtha.

Immortal Records: 12200 Olympic Blvd, Suite 400, W Los Angeles, CA 90064; tel. (310) 582-8300; website www.immortalrecords.com.

Interscope Records: 2220 Colorado Ave, Santa Monica, CA 90404; e-mail feedback@igamail.com; website www.amrecords.com; Assoc. labels incl. A&M, Geffen; Label Man. Ted Field.

Island Records: 825 Eighth Ave, New York, NY 10019; e-mail info@islandrecords.com; website www.islandrecords.com; Chair. Chris Blackwell.

Jay Jay Records: 35 NE 62nd St, Miami, FL 33138; Pres. Walter E. Jagiello.

Jazzology: 61 French Market Pl., New Orleans, LA 70116; tel. (504) 525-5000; fax (504) 525-1776; e-mail info@jazzology.com; website www.jazzology.com; Labels incl. American Music, Audiophile, Black Swan, Circle, GHB, Progressive, Solo Art, Southland; Pres. George H. Buck Jr.

Jin: PO Drawer 10, 238 E Main St, Ville Platte, LA 70586; Pres. Floyd Soileau.

Jive Records: Zomba Recording Corpn, 137–139 W 25th St, New York, NY 10001.

Justice Music Corpn: 11586 Blix St, North Hollywood, CA 91602; Exec. Vice-Pres. Monte R. Thomas.

Ketter Entertainment: PO Box 740702, San Diego, CA 92174-0702; Pres. and CEO Al Ketter.

King of Kings: PO Box 725, Daytona Beach, FL 32115-0725; Vice-Pres. Charles Vickers.

Krypton Records: PO Box 372, Highland, MI 48357; Pres. Dennis Cyporyn.

K-Tel International (USA) Inc: 2605 Fernbrook Lane N, Minneapolis, MN 55447-4736; Pres. & CEO Mickey Elfenbein.

L & A Records: PO Box 296, 324 Godwin Ave, Midland Park, NJ 07432; Pres. Tony Loeffler.

LA International: PO Box 725, Daytona Beach, FL 32115-0725; Vice-Pres. Charles Vickers.

LaFace Records: 1 Capital City Plaza, 3350 Peachtree Rd, Suite 1500, Atlanta, GA 30326.

Landmark Communications Group: PO Box 1444, Hendersonville, TN 37077; Pres. Bill Anderson Jr.

Lanor Records: PO Box 233, 329 N Main St, Church Point, LA 70525; Owner Lee Lavergne.

Liberty Records: 3322 West End Ave, Nashville, TN 37203; Pres. Jimmy Bowen.

Lifesong Records: PO Box 5807, Englewood, NJ 07631; tel. (201) 969-9990; fax (201) 969-9955; e-mail plcagent@aol.com; Pres. Philip S. Kurnit.

Light Records: 1207 17th Ave S, #103, Nashville, TN 37212; Gen. Man. Rob Woolsey.

Loud Cry Records: PO Box 210270, Nashville, TN 37221-0270; Owner and Pres. Don Sanders.

Maiden Music: PO Box 777, Trevilians, VA 23170; Pres. Michael D. Moore.

Mail Order Jazz: 601 Virginia Ave, Tiften, GA 31794; Owner Gus P. Statiras.

Maison de Soul: PO Drawer 10, 238 E Main St, Ville Platte, LA 70586; Pres. Floyd Soileau.

Map The Planet Records: 228 W Fifth St, Kansas City, MO 64105; Project Co-ordinator Joe Comparato.

Maverick Recording Co: 9348 Civic Center Dr., Beverly Hills, CA 90210.

MCA Records: 2220 Colorado Ave, Santa Monica, CA 90404; Chair. Al Teller.

Mel Carter: PO Box 69646, Los Angeles, CA 90069; tel. and fax (323) 934-4122; e-mail red@mel-carter.com; website www.mel-carter.com; Owner Larry Kleno.

Melankolic Records: 104 W 29th St, Fourth Floor, New York, NY 10001; Part of Astralwerks Records.

Mercury Records: Worldwide Plaza, 825 Eighth Ave, New York, NY 10019; Pres. Ed Eckstine.

Metal Blade Records Inc: 2345 Erringer Rd, Suite 108, Simi Valley, CA 93065; Office Man. and Mechanical Licensing Kim Kelly.

Mirror Records Inc: 645 Titus Ave, Rochester, NY 14617; Pres. Armand Schaubroeck.

Mobile Fidelity International: PO Box 8359, Incline Village, NV 89452-8359; Pres. & Exec. Prod. Brad S. Miller.

Monster Music: 455 Valley Dr., Brisbane, CA 94005; tel. (415) 840-2000; fax (415) 468-0204; e-mail monstermusic@monstercable.com; website www.monstermusic.com; Gen. Man. Thad Wharton.

Motown Records: 6255 W Sunset Blvd, 17th Floor, Los Angeles, CA 90028; CEO Jheryl Busby.

NAIL Inc: 231 Commercial St, NE, Salem, OR 97301-3411; Pres. Mike Jones.

Nonesuch Records: Time Warner, 75 Rockefeller Plaza, New York, NY 10019.

Planet Dallas Studios Inc: 3515 Dickason, Dallas, TX 75219; Gen. Man. Debb Rooney.

Platinum Gold Productions: 9200 Sunset Blvd, Suite 1220, Los Angeles, CA 90069; Partner Steve Cohen.

Plug Productions: 273 Chippewa Dr., Columbia, SC 29210-6508; Dir John Mack; Contact Ron Sparks.

Polydor/Atlas: 1416 N La Brea Ave, Los Angeles, CA 90028; Exec. Asst Deana J. Smart.

PolyGram Group: Worldwide Plaza, 825 Eighth Ave, New York, NY 10019; Pres. Rick Dobbis.

PPL-MCI Entertainment Group: 10 Universal Plaza, PO Box 8442, Universal City, CA 91618; tel. (818) 506-8533; fax (818) 506-8534; e-mail pplzmi@aol.com; website www.pplzmi.com; CEO Jaeson St James Jarrett; Man. Dir Maxx Diamond.

Pravda Records Inc: 3823 N Southport, Chicago, IL 60613; Man. Dir Kenneth Goodman.

Primitech Releases: PO Box 210330, San Francisco, CA 94121; Owner and Label Man. Victor Krag.

Progressive: 1206 Decatur St, New Orleans, LA 70116; Pres. George H. Buck Jr.

Projekt Records: PO Box 9140, Long Island City, NY 11103; website www.projekt.com; Dir Sam Rosenthal.

Pulse Records: PO Box 294, Westerville, OH 43086-0294; Pres. and Owner Randy Kettering.

Punk Metal Rock Records: PO Box 410099, San Francisco, CA 94141-0099; A & R Head Stash Ravine.

Quango Music Group Inc: 9744 Wilshire Blvd, Suite 305, Beverly Hills, CA 90212; Pres. George Ghiz.

Rainforest Records Inc: 8855 SW Holly Lane, Suite 110, Wilsonville, OR 97070; Prod. & CEO Ray Woods.

Rambunctious Records Inc: c/o Power, Weiss & Kurnit, LLP, 600 Madison Ave, 22nd Floor, New York, NY 10022-1615; Pres. Philip S. Kurnit.

Randolf Productions Inc: 23181 Verdugo Dr., Suite 106, Laguna Hills, CA 92653; Pres. Randy Ray.

RCA Records: 1540 Broadway, New York, NY 10036.

RCA Victor Group: 1540 Roadway, New York, NY 10036.

Relativity Records: 187-07 Henderson Ave, Hollis, NY 11423; Pres. Barry Korbin.

Rhino Entertainment: 10635 Santa Monica Blvd, Los Angeles, CA 90025; Pres. Richard Foos.

Rhythms Productions/Tom Thumb Music: PO Box 34485, Los Angeles, CA 90034-0485; Pres. Ruth White.

Rising Son Records: PO Box 620, Stockbridge, MA 01262; tel. (413) 445-6403; website www.risingson.com; Asst Dawn Mitchell.

Rising Star Records: 52 Executive Park S, Suite 5203, Atlanta, GA 30329; Owner Barbara Taylor.

Roadrunner Records Inc: 902 Broadway, Eighth Floor, New York, NY 10010; tel. (212) 274-7500; fax (212) 505-7469; e-mail roadrunner@roadrunnerrecords.com; website www.roadrunnerrecords.com.

Rock Dog Records: PO Box 3687, Hollywood, CA 90028; Vice-Pres. of A & R Gerry North.

Rodell Records Inc: PO Box 93457, Hollywood, CA 90093; Pres. Adam S. Rodell.

Rosebud Records: 1030 Villa Pl., Nashville, TN 37212; Pres. and Record Prod. Fate Vanderpool.

Rotten Records: PO Box 2157, Montclair, CA 91763; A & R Dir Dick Shitelmeyer.

Rounder Records Corpn: 1 Camp St, Cambridge, MA 02140; website www.rounder.com.

RRRecords: 151 Paige St, Lowell, MA 01852; Owner Ron.

Rustron-Whimsong Music Productions: c/o The Whimsy, 1156 Park Lane, West Palm Beach, FL 33417; tel. and fax (561) 478-8315; e-mail safehavenwpb@yahoo.com; Exec. Dir and Owner Rusty Gordon.

Rykodisc/Earful: PO Box 141, Gloucester, MA 01931; tel. (888) 232-7385; e-mail earful@rykodisc.com; website.rykodisc.com.

Sabre Productions: PO Box 10147, San Antonio, TX 78210; Prod. E. J. Henke.

Salexo Music Co: PO Box 18093, Charlotte, NC 28218-0093; Pres. Samuel Obie.

Schizophonic Records: 231 Commercial St NE, Salem, OR 97301-3411; Pres. Mike Jones.

Scooter Records/Scootertunes Inc: PO Box 610166, Dallas, TX 75261; tel. (972) 986-5582; fax (972) 986-5582; e-mail scootune@gte.net; website www.scootertunes.com; Pres. Janett Bellamy; Vice-Pres. Gina Bellamy.

Scotti Bros Records: 2114 Pico Blvd, Santa Monica, CA 90405; Pres. Myron Roth.

Shiro Records Inc: 8228 Sunset Blvd, Suite 108, Los Angeles, CA 90046; Pres. Shiro Gutzie.

Sikio Marika Records: 6840 N Maple #157, Fresno, CA 93710; Label Head Tyrone White.

Silent Records: 340 Bryant St, Third Floor, San Francisco, CA 94107; Pres. Kim Cascone.

Songchild Productions: 117 Manor Circle, Myrtle Beach, SC 29575-7201; Artist Paul Skyland.

Sony Music Entertainment Inc: 550 Madison Ave, New York, NY 10022-3211; website www.sonymusic.com; Labels incl. Aware Records, Columbia, Epic, Legacy, Loud, Music World, Sony Classical, Sony Nashville, So So Def.

Southland: 1206 Decatur St, New Orleans, LA 70116; Pres. George H. Buck Jr.

Sovereign Records: 11 Manor House Dr., Dobbs Ferry, NY 10522; tel. and fax (212) 730-4848; e-mail aloftmusic@aol.com; website www.songandstorypress.com; Pres. Ruby Fisher.

Springhollow Records: PO Box 294, Westerville, OH 43086-0294; Owner and Pres. Randy Kettering.

Sub Pop Records: 2514 Fourth Ave, Seattle, WA 98121; tel. (206) 441-8441; fax (206) 441-8245; e-mail info@subpop.com; website www.subpop.com.

Sunset Promotions of Chicago Inc: 9359 S Kedzie Ave, PO Box 42807, Evergreen Park, IL 60805; tel. (773) 586-1800; fax (773) 586-1855; e-mail sunsetpromogip@inetmail.att.net; Pres. Neil J. Cacciottolo.

Swallow: PO Drawer 10, 238 E Main St, Ville Platte, LA 70586; Pres. Floyd Soileau.

Syntonic Research Inc: 3405 Barranos Circle, Austin, TX 78731-5711; Sales Man. Michael Kron.

Tar Heel Records: PO Box 1557, West Caldwell, NJ 07007-1557; Pres. Tar Heel Pete; Vice-Pres. Tony Ansems.

Tedesco Tunes: 16020 Lahey St, Granada Hills, CA 91344; Pres. Dale T. Tedesco.

Temple Productions Ltd: 310 E Chicago St, Elgin, IL 60120; Pres. Caesar F. Kalinowski.

Terra Nova Recording Co: 853 Broadway, #1516, New York, NY 10003; Pres. Marc Krasnow; CEO Robert Mangovleff.

Times Square Fantasy Theatre: 519 N Halifax Ave, Daytona Beach, FL 32118; tel. and fax (386) 252-0381; e-mail timessqfntsythtr@aol.com; website www.timessqfantasytheatre.com; CEO Bobby Lee Cude.

TKO Records: 4501 Connecticut Ave, NW, Suite 905, Washington, DC 20008; CEO Michael Cohn.

Tranquil Technology Music: PO Box 20463, Oakland, CA 94620; Prod. Michael Mantra.

Tropicana Records: PO Box 910, Beverly Hills, CA 90213; tel. (310) 557-0534; Gen. Man. G. O. Hernandez.

Universal Music Group: 2220 Colorado Ave, Santa Monica, CA 90404; tel. (310) 865-5000; website www.umusic.com; Labels incl. Interscope, Geffen, A&M Records, Island, Def Jam, Lost Highway, MCA Nashville, MCA, Mercury, Motown, Universal, Verve Music Group, Universal Classics.

Virgin Records America Inc: 338 N Foothill Rd, Beverly Hills, CA 90210; website www.virginrecords.com; Labels incl. Astralwerks, Immortal, Luaka Bop, Pointblank, Rap-A-Lot, Real World, S-Curve, Pres. Phil Quartararo.

Vokes Music, Record & Promotion Co: PO Box 12, New Kensington, PA 15068-0012; tel. (724) 335-2775 Pres. and Owner Howard Vokes.

Warner Music Group: 3300 Warner Blvd, Burbank, CA 91510; tel. (818) 846-9090; website www.warnerbrosrecords.com; Labels incl. Atlantic, Elektra, Maverick, Reprise, Rhino Entertainment, Ruffnation, Warner Bros., WB Nashville, Word; Chair. Mo Ostin.

WEA Latina: 5201 Blue Lagoon Dr., Suite 200, Miami, FL 33126.

WEA Records: Time Warner, 75 Rockefeller Plaza, New York, NY 10019.

Woodrich Enterprises Inc: PO Box 38, Lexington, AL 35648; e-mail mernee@msn.com; Pres. Woody Richardson.

Worship & Praise Records Inc: PO Box 593, Times Sq. Station, New York, NY 10108; Pres., CEO and Exec. Prod. Minister Maharold Peoples Jr.

Zero Hour Records: 1600 Broadway, No. 701, New York, NY 10019; Contact Serge Zero.

Zippah Recording Studio: PO Box 1790, Brookline, MA 02146; Co-Owner and Prod. Peter Weiss.

Zomba Recording Corpn: 137–139 W 25th St, New York, NY 10001; Includes Jive label; Sr Vice-Pres. and Gen. Man. David Renzer.

Venezuela

Discorona CA: Río a Puente Soublette, Edif. Fonodisco, PO Box 5995, 1010 Caracas; Pres. Evelio Cortés.

Inversiones Rodven CA: Centro Comercial Concresa, 2°, Of. 422 Prado del Este, 1080 Caracas; Pres. Rodolfo Rodríguez.

Manoca Records Venezuela SA: Avda San Martin, PB Local 5-6, Resid. Metroplace, 1020 Caracas; Gen. Man. Angelo Nigro.

APPENDIX B: MANAGEMENT COMPANIES

Andorra

Espectacles del Principat: Ctra de l'Aldosa, Botiga 2, La Massana; Dir Joan M. Armengal.

Limitada de Producciones SL: Ciutat Consuegra 12, 2°, Edif. Orió, Andorra La Vella; tel. and fax (376) 82 82 11; Admin. Joan Deltell Porta.

RIAL Andorra: Avda de Tarragona 24, Andorra La Vella; tel. 860686; fax 866286; e-mail rial@andorra.ad; Man. Pascal Lair.

Argentina

Abraxas Producciones Internacionales: Avda Callao 875, 4° H, 1023 Buenos Aires; Dir-Gen. Carlos Pity Yñurrigarro.

Argentina Producciones: Avda Corrientes 1628, 11°G, Of. B, 1042 Buenos Aires; Dir Norberto Horacio Baccon.

CDN Producciones Iberoamericanas: Loyola 1530, 1414 Buenos Aires; Dir-Gen. Esteba Mellino.

Data Pop Rock Comunicación: 25 de Mayo 758, 5°, Of. E, 1002 Buenos Aires; Pres. Juan Carlos Kohan.

Esther M. Soto Ciclo 3: Estados Unidos 629, 1101 Buenos Aires; Contact Esther M. Soto.

Hector Cavallero Producciones SA: Hipólito Irigoyen 1994, PB 4, 1089 Buenos Aires; Pres. Fernando Cavallero; Contact Hector Cavallero.

JC Producciones Srl: Rivadavia 86, 4°, Of. 6, 8300 Neuquen; Pres. Juan Carlos Allende.

Juan Carlos Baglieto: Fragata Pte, Sarmiento 1663, Buenos Aires; Man. Eduardo Hagopian.

Matt Hungo Srl: Tucumán 1455, 5°, Of. A–B, 1050 Buenos Aires; Gen. Man. Omar Alberto Lauria.

Mediavilla Producciones Srl: Colombia, 1727 Valetin Alsina, 1822 Buenos Aires; Pres. Oscar Mediavilla.

Ohanian Producciones: Aguilar 2073, 1428 Buenos Aires; tel. (11) 4788-4605; Dir Alberto Ohanian.

Poggini & Asociados Srl: Pasteur 250, 1°, Of. C, 1028 Buenos Aires; tel. (11) 4952-5088; fax (11) 4954-1477; e-mail info@poggini.com.ar; website www.poggini.com.ar; Contacts Rodolfo Poggini, Claudio Poggin.

Australia

Alan James Management: PO Box 2727, Darwin, NT 0801; fax (8) 8941-1088; e-mail yothuyindi@yothuyindi.com; website www.yothuyindi.com; Man. Alan James.

Andrew Dinwoodie Management: PO Box 5052, Victoria Point, Qld 4165; tel. (7) 3207-0502; e-mail adinwoodie@redland.net.au.

Andrew McManus Management: Suite 1, 3 Smail St, Ultimo, NSW 2007; Man. Dir Andrew McManus.

B & S Promotions: PO Box 1481, Frankston, Vic. 3199; Partners Bill Dettmer, Sally Dettmer.

Bernie Stahl Entertainments: Parkrise, Fifth Floor, 3 Alison St, Surfers Paradise, Qld 4217; Man. Dir Bernie Stahl; Dir Suzanne Stahl.

Cranium Management: PO Box 240, Annadale, NSW 2038; e-mail cranium@internet.com.au.

Entertainment Plus: Gordon Pl., Suite 15/24 Little Bourke St, Melbourne, Vic. 3000; Man. Andrew Malouf.

Feel Management & Tour Co-ordination: 2/54 Bronte Rd, Bondi Junction, NSW 2022; Dir Tim Pittman.

Gary Morris Management: PO Box 21, Hawks Nest, NSW 2324; e-mail oils@ozemail.com.au; website www.midnightoil.com; Contact Gary Morris.

Grant Thomas Management: PO Box 176, Potts Point, NSW 2011; Principal Grant Thomas.

Harbour Agency Pty Ltd: 135 Forbes St, Woolloomooloo, NSW 2011; tel. (612) 9331 5888; fax (612) 9331 2296; website www.theharbouragency.com; Man. Dir Sam Righi.

Ideal Management P/C: PO Box 1037, Caulfield North, Melbourne, Vic. 3161; Man. Dir/CEO Nathan D. Brenner.

International Management Group: 281 Clarence St, Sydney, NSW 2000; Dir of Arts & Entertainment Stephen Flint Wood.

International Profile Management: Entertainment Pl., PO Box 4, Broadway, Qld 4006; Dir Darren Clark.

Isaac Apel Management: 46 Caroline St, South Yarra, Vic. 3141; tel. (3) 9820-9081; fax (3) 9820-5448; e-mail kj@iam.com.au; Dir Kim Jacobi.

Jaybee's Entertainment Agency: PO Box 37, Sanctuary Pl., NSW 2540; tel. (612) 4443 3422; fax (612) 4443 9968; e-mail jaybees@jaybees.com.au; website www.jaybees.com.au; Man. Narrell M. Brown.

Julie Hickson Management: 25 Overend St, Brunswick, Vic. 3056; Man. Julie Hickson.

Kevin Jacobsen Management: Level 1, 98 Glebe Point Rd, Glebe, NSW 2037; Man. Dir Kevin Jacobsen.

Lighthouse Promotions: First Floor, Cherry Tree, 53 Balmain St, Sandringham Vic. 3121; Dir Linda Gebar.

Loud & Clear Management Pty Ltd: PO Box 276, Albert Park, Vic. 3206; Man. Dir Michael Roberts.

Management Only: PO Box 1289, North Sydney, NSW 2059; Man. Dir Gary Grant.

Mark Bishop Management Pty Ltd: PO Box 123, Kensington, Vic. 3031; Man. Mark Bishop.

McLean's Artist Management: Suite 8, 4 Jacques Ave, Bondi Beach, NSW 2026; Man. Dir Calum McLean.

Melke (Artist Representation & Media Co-ordination): 158 Raglan St, Mosman, Sydney, NSW 2088; Dir Sue Melke.

Melody Management: PO Box 598, Coogee, NSW 2034; Dirs Michael McMartin, Elizabeth McMartin.

MGM (Michael Gudinski Management): 9 Dundas Lane, Albert Park, Vic. 3206; Man. Dir Michael Gudinski.

Michael Long Management: PO Box 494, Double Bay, NSW 2028; Man. Michael Long.

Mighty Management: 21 Castle St, Randwick, Sydney, NSW 2031; Man. Mick Mazzone.

MMA Management International: 351 Crown St, Surry Hills, NSW 2010; Man. Sam Evans.

Mr Walker's Co: 13 Victoria Ave, Albert Park, Vic. 3206; tel. (613) 9645-7300; fax (613) 9645-7311; e-mail mrwalkersco@peg.apc.org; Contact Andrew Walker.

Oz Artist Management: PO Box 4074, Doncaster Heights, Vic. 3109; Man. John Perosa.

Oz-X-Press Music: 400 N Rocks Rd, Carlingford, NSW 2118; Man. Trudi Nicholls.

Painters & Dockers Management: PO Box 69, Burnley, Melbourne, Vic. 3121; Man. Colin Buckler.

Paisley Management: PO Box 2227, Rose Bay N, NSW 2030; Man. Dir Kent Paisley.

Paul Cussen Management: Suite 1, Level 2, 41 Oxford St, Darlinghurst, NSW 2010; Proprietor Paul Cussen.

Peter Rix Management Pty Ltd: PO Box 957, Crows Nest, NSW 1585; tel. (2) 9966-5511; fax (2) 9966-5444; e-mail info@rixman.com.au; Man. Dir Peter Rix.

Phill Shute Management Pty Ltd: PO Box 273, Dulwich Hill, NSW 2203; Man. Dir Phill Shute.

Ralph Carr Management: c/o RCM International Group, 29 Balmain St, Richmond, Vic. 1321; Man. Dir Ralph Carr.

Richard East Management Pty Ltd: 20 Leila St, Prahran, Vic. 3181; Man. Dir Richard East.

RPM Management Services Pty Ltd: 205 Commonwealth St, Surry Hills, Sydney, NSW; tel. (612) 9281-9500; fax (612) 9281-0439; e-mail rpm@zip.com.au.

Russell J. White Management: PO Box 325, South Melbourne, Vic. 3205; Man. Dir Russell White.

Servant Communications: PO Box 2020, Launceston, Tasmania 7250; Pres. Kevin N. Hooper.

Smartartists Management: PO Box 2093, St Kilda West, Vic. 3182; Man. Michael Lynch.

Talentworks Pty Ltd: Suite 1A, 663 Victoria St, Abbotsford, Vic. 3067; tel. (3) 9429-6933; fax (3) 9428-7433; e-mail mail@talentworks.com.au; Man. Dir Glenn Wheatley.

Terry Blamey Management: 329 Monatgue St, Albert Park, Vic. 3206; Dir Terry Blamey.

The Neil Clugston Organization: PO Box 387, Glebe, NSW 2037; tel. (2) 9552-3277; fax (2) 9552-3713; e-mail neil@nco.com.au; website www.nco.com.au; Man. Dir Neil Clugson.

Vicki Watson Management: PO Box 9, Balmain, Sydney, NSW 2041; Dir Vicki Watson.

Woodruff Management: 128 Bourke St, Woolloomooloo, NSW 2011; Dir John Woodruff.

WPA Management: First Floor, 411 George St, Fitzroy, Vic. 3065; Gen. Man. Petula Bier.

Yothu Yindi Music Pty Ltd: PO Box 2727, Darwin, NT 0801; fax (8) 8941-1088; e-mail yothuyindi@yothuyindi.com; website www.yothuyindi.com; Man. Alan James.

Austria

FF Arts and Media Consultants: Kienmayergasse 47, 1140 Vienna; tel. (1) 923-990-230; fax (1) 923-990-211; e-mail harald.buechel@aon.at; Man. Dir Harald Th Buechel.

Georg Leitner Productions: Hütteldorfstr 259/14, 1140 Vienna; Proprietor Georg Leitner.

Hämmerle Barbara & Werner: Harderstr 14, 6972 Fussach; Man. Dirs Barbara Hämmerle, Werner Hämmerle.

Milica: Liebhartstalstr 15/5, 1160 Vienna; Contact Milica.

RATZ Promotions: Vorachstr 65, 6890 Lustenau; Contact Thomas Radovan.

RGG Management: Favoritstr 52.2.6.18, 1100 Vienna; tel. and fax (1) 604-3940; Man. Peter Steinbach.

Rock Promotion: Hietzinger Hauptstr 36A, 1130 Vienna; Contact Peter Fröstl.

Stein Music Wien: Bernardgasse 39/33, 1070 Vienna; tel. (1) 526-7871; fax (1) 523-9891; e-mail stein.music@techno.at; Man. Dir Regine Steinmetz.

WOM: PO Box 20, 3105 St Pölten; Contact Albin Wegerbauer.

Belgium

Aril Private Studio: Rue de Coron 1, 7040 Bougnies; Man. Dir Marylin Leleu.

ARS Management: Singel 5, 2550 Kontich; Man. Dir Patrick Busschots.

Baard & Kale: Brederodestraat 40, 2018 Antwerp; Man. Dir Bob Campenaerts.

Backline: Kammerstraat 19, 9000 Ghent; Man. Robert Van Yper; Bookings Agents Sandra Heylen, Lawrence Van Den Eede.

Commedia VZW: Fonteinstraat 19, 8000 Bruges; Man. Dir Cherry Deryoke.

Foundation VZW: Fruithoflaan 124, PO Box 11, 2600 Berchem/Antwerp; Dirs Peter Verstraeven, Bert Van Roy.

Klepto Management: Hullaertstraat 7, 9880 Aalter; e-mail wilfried.brits@yucom.be; Man. Dir Wilfried Brits.

Kras Artists: Leernsesteenweg 168, 9800 Deinze; Dir Jean Tant.

L&S Agency: PO Box 5, 3800 Sint-Truiden 2; tel. 11671701; fax 11673331; e-mail lsagency@belgacom.net; website www.lsagency.be; Man. Dir Mark Strauven.

Merlijn: Gulden Vlieslaan 67, 8000 Bruges; Contact Nico A. Mertens.

Music BaM: Lelielaan 11, 2460 Lichtaart; Man. Dir Gert Van Dingenen; Asst Man. Dir Tom van Dingenen.

Paperwork: Aarschotsesteenweg 245, 3012 Wilsele; Man. Johan P. Berckmans.

Pyramid International Music: Lepelhoekstraat 26, 9100 Sint-Niklaas; tel. (3) 778-1854; fax (3) 766-8441; e-mail marc@marcdecoen.be; website www.marcdecoen.be; Man. Dir Marc De Coen.

Swing Promotions: Beukenlaan 3, 2970 Schilde; Man. Wim Groos.

Team for Action (T4A): Ave Oscar van Goibtsnoven 45B, 1180 Brussels; Man. Dir Claude Martin.

Tempo (Top Entertainment Editions): Krijgslaan 61, 9000 Gent; Gen. Man. Luc Standaert.

Tour de Force: Rue des Archers 19–21, 1080 Brussels; Man. Dir Ton Van Draanen.

TTT: Vriesenhof 22/5, 3000 Leuven; Mans Rick Tubbax, Johan P. Berckmans.

UBU: Rue Van Obberghen 92, 1140 Brussels; Dir Patrick DuBucq.

Western Productions: Kammerstraat 19, 9000 Ghent; Man. Robert Van Yper.

Bolivia

Chelo Music: Tarbo, 118 Santa Cruz, Santa Cruz de la Sierra; Dir Sergio Serrale Justiniano.

HR Producciones: Loayza 349, 15°, Dpto 1503, Edif. Loayza, La Paz; Gen. Man. Nestor Horacio Rasgido.

Brazil

Carlindo Soares Promoçoes Artisticas: Rua Castro Menezes 51, Rio de Janiero, RJ; Contact Carlindo Soares.

Fred Rossi Eventos e Produçoes: Rua Augusta 2516, Cj 121 Cerqueira César, 01412 100 São Paulo, SP; Dir Fred Rossi.

MR Comunicaçao Produçao Ltda: PO Box 16692, 03197-970, São Paulo, SP; Dir Mário Ronco.

Bulgaria

Berti: 14 A Skobelevska str, 5300 Gabrovo; Man. Dir Plamen Tolev.

Factor TC: 2 Krakra str, 1504 Sofia; Man. Dir Veselin Todorov.

Mega Music Ltd: 2 Trapezitza str, 1000 Sofia; Man. Dir Dora Tchernkva.

New Music Agency: Nadejda Bl 634, Apt 14, 1231 Sofia; tel. 9825-6509; fax 2934-4297; e-mail christ@newmusic.bg; website www.newmusic.bg; Pres. Christo Roussanov.

Canada

Amok Artist Agency: PO Box 21, Fergus, ON N1M 2W7; tel. (519) 787-1100; fax (519) 787-0084; website www.amokmusic.ca; Contact Lorenz Eppinger.

Artistic Canadian Entertainers Management Asscn: 4544 Dufferin St #24, Downsview, ON M3H 5X2; Pres./Consultant Raymond A. Sare.

Balmur Ltd: 2400–4950 Yonge St, Toronto, ON M2N 6K1; Contact Tinti Moffat.

Bamford Group: 14 Sumach St, Toronto, ON M5A 1J4; Pres. Joe Bamford.

Brass Ring Productions/Manford Music Inc: PO Box 1266 Station A, Kelowna, BC V1Y 7V8; tel. and fax (250) 763-5502; e-mail manford@telus.net; Pres. Becky Chapman.

Bruce Allen Talent: 500-425 Carrall St, Vancouver, BC V6B 6E3; tel. (604) 688-7274; fax (604) 688-7118; e-mail info@bruceallen.com; website www.bruceallen.com; Contact Kim Blake.

Current/Rage Records and Management: 4 Bowden St, Toronto, ON M4K 2X2; Pres. Gerry Young.

Donna Kay Music Inc: Ministikwan Lake, PO Box 451, Pierceland, SK S0M 2K0; Contact Paul S. Pospisil.

Double A Productions: 64 Desbrisay Dr., Bridgewater, NS B4V 3H6; Man. Ken Alexander.

Early Morning Productions: 1365 Yonge St #207, Toronto, ON M4T 2P7; Contact Barry Harvey.

Feeling Productions Inc: 2540 blvd Daniel-Johnson, bur. 755, Laval, QC H7T 2S3; tel. (450) 978-9555; fax (450) 978-1055; Man. Rene Angelil.

Finkelstein Management Co Ltd: 301-151 John St, Toronto, ON M5V 2T2; Contact J. Languedoc.

Forte Records and Productions Inc: 320 Spadina Rd, Toronto, ON M5R 2V6; tel. (416) 323-3864; fax (416) 323-0649; e-mail ForteRecords@attcanada.net; Contact Dawna Zeeman.

Gino Empry Entertainment: Suite 1508, 130 Carlton St, Toronto, ON M5A 4K3; tel. (416) 928-1044; fax (416) 928-1415; Owner Gino Empry.

Ground Swell Records: PO Box 245, Station Central, Halifax, NS B3J 2N7; tel. (902) 492-0447; Pres. Ian McKinnon.

Jones & Co: 1819 Granville St, Fourth Floor, Halifax, NS B3J 3R1; Pres. Sheri Jones.

Latitude 45/Arts Promotion Inc: 109 St Joseph Blvd W, Montréal, QC H2T 2P7.

Lazy J Management: PO Box 8085, Saskatoon, SK S7K 4R7; tel. (306) 955-4976; fax (306) 955-4978; e-mail info@oiem.net; website www.oiem.net; Man. Louis O'Reilly.

LCDM Entertainment: #79 564-1995 Weston Rd, Toronto, ON M9N 3W9;:PR Officer L. C. Di Marco.

Lou Blair Management Inc: 407-68 Water St, Vancouver, BC V6B 1A4; tel. (604) 689-7070; Contact Lou Blair.

Management Trust Ltd: 219 Dufferin St, Suite 309B, Toronto, ON M6K 3J1; Contact Sarah Barker-Tonge.

Mary Bailey Management: PO Box 546, 4 Al Wende Ave, ON P2N 3J5; Pres. Mary Bailey.

MBH Music Management: PO Box 1096, Hudson, QC J0P 1H0; tel. (613) 780-1163; e-mail larecord@total.net; website www.radiofreedom.com.

Pandyamonium/William Tenn Artist Management: 67 Mowat #431, Toronto, ON M6K 3E3; Contact Sandy Pandya, William Tenn.

Paquin Entertainment Group: 395 Notre Dame Ave, Winnipeg, MB R3B 1R2; tel. (204) 988-1120; fax (204) 988-1135; e-mail info@paquinentertainment.com; website www.paquinentertainment.com; Pres. Gilles Paquin.

Popas Management Corpn (PMC): 1407 Mount Pleasant Rd, Toronto, ON M4N 2T9; Man. Steve Propas.

Pro Arts Management: Suite 3, 3611 Mavis Rd, Mississauga, ON L5C 1T7; Contact Gil Moore.

Productions Martin Leclerc Inc: 2220 rue Notre-Dame Ouest, Suite 201, Montréal, QC H3J 2V4; Man. Martin Leclerc.

Quinlan Road Ltd: PO Box 933, Stratford, ON N5A 7M3; tel. (519) 273-4491; fax (519) 273-1948; Controller Bill Bruce; Contact Loreena McKennit.

Radius International: PO Box 81, 260 Adelaide St E, Toronto, ON M5A 1N1; tel. (416) 979-5822; fax (416) 979-9886; e-mail radius@interlog.com; Gen. Man. Bob Stevens; artistic management; music festival consultant.

Regal Recordings Ltd: 2421 Hammond Rd, Mississauga, ON L5K 1T3; Vice-Pres. Doreen M. Davey.

Robert Luhtala Management: 99 Victor Ave, Toronto, ON M4K 1A7; tel. (416) 406-2825; fax (416) 406-2945; e-mail liquid@liquidrecords.com; Man. Robert Luhtala.

Savannah Music Inc: 123 Applefield Dr., Scarborough, ON M1P 3Y5; Dir of Canadian Operations Bill Carruthers.

SEG Productions: 3611 Mavis Rd, Mississauga, ON L5C 1T7; Contact Cliff Hunt.

Showcana Corpn: PO Box #4689, Station C, Calgary, AB T2T 5P1; Pres. Robert James Chin.

SL Feldman & Assocs: 1505 W Second Ave, Suite 200, Vancouver, BC V6H 3Y4; tel. (604) 734-5945; fax (604) 732-0922; e-mail feldman@slfa.com; website www.slfa.com; Proprietor Sam L. Feldman; Sr Vice-Pres. Shaw Saltzberg.

SRO Management: 189 Carlton St, Toronto, ON M5A 2K7; Contact Bob Roper.

Star Rise International: 6263 28th Ave, Rosemont, Montréal, QC H1T 3H8; Talent Search/Man. Fadel Chidiac.

Swell Management: 181 Clinton St, Toronto, ON M6G 2Y4; Contact Jeff Rogers, Sandy Rogers.

TKO Entertainment Corpn: 1406-1288 Alberni St, Vancouver, BC V5J 3L2; tel. (604) 331-0110; fax (604) 331-0109; Contact Peter Karroll.

United Artist Productions Worldwide: 224 Beaverbrook St, Winnipeg, MB R3N 1M8; tel. (204) 489-3933; e-mail uartistw@shaw.co; Contact Warren Brown.

Val Haas: Suite 1002, 5 Rowntree Rd, Etobicoke, ON M9V 5G9; Man. Val Haas.

Vocal Image Productions: 192 Kensington Rd, Charlottetown, PEI C1A 7S3; Man. Berni Wood.

Ways and Means Committee: 1971 Sprice Hill Rd, Pickering, ON L1V 1S6; Contact Michael White.

William Seip Management: 1615 Highland Rd, Kitchener, ON N2G 3W5; Contact William Seip.

Chile

Calipso: Thompson 3450, Estación Central, Santiago; Man. Hugo Ascueta Norambuena.

Galo Producciones: Hernando de Aguirre 944, Santiago; tel. (562) 234-3292; fax (562) 231-2656; e-mail galoprod@ia.cl; Gen. Man. Alfredo Saint-Jean.

Producciones Macondo Chile Ltda: Alvarez 58 L-6, Viña Del Mar; Man. Alfredo Troncoso.

Providencia Television: Pedro de Valivia 3128 Nuñoa, Santiago; Exec. Dir Luis Venegas.

Ricardo Suarez Daud Y Cia Ltda: La Concepción 81, Of. 405, Providencia, Santiago; Man. Ricardo Suárez Daud.

Romero & Campbell Producciones: Bombero Nuñez, 385 Barrio Bellavista, Santiago; Dir Carmen Romero Quero.

Croatia

Crno Bijeli Svijet: Avenija Marina Drzica BB, 41000 Zagreb; Man. Dir Branko Paic.

Music Time: Petreticev Trg 4, 41000 Zagreb; Man. Dir Branko Knezevic.

Suput DOO: Novska 41, 41000 Zagreb; Man. Dir Boris Suput.

Tutico: Veprinacka 16, 10000 Zagreb; Dir Zrinko Tutic.

Cuba

Agencia Promusic: Avda 3, 1008, Entre 10 y 12 Miramar, 11300 Municipio Playa, Havana; Dir-Gen. Julio Ballester Guzmán.

Oficina de Pablo Lilanes: Calle 11, 257 Entre J y I Vedado, Havana; Dir-Gen. Orlando Hecahvarría.

Denmark

Buks Booking International: Gunløgsgade 15, 2300 Copenhagen; tel. (45) 3296-1092; fax (45) 3295-9491; Dir Thomas H. Hansen.

Hanne Wilhelm Hansen: Gothersgade 11, 1123 Copenhagen K; Contact Hanne Wilhelm Hansen.

JP Management: Jernbanevej 22, 8660 Skanderborg; Man. Dir J. P. Andersen.

Mega Scandinavia A/S: Indiakaj 1, 2100 Copenhagen Ø; Vice-Pres. Cai Leitner; Dir of A & R and Marketing Jesper Ban.

PDH Dansk Musik Formidling ApS: Ny Vestergade 7, 1471 Copenhagen K; tel. (45) 3311-2200; fax (45) 3333-0020; Man Dir Henrik Seifert.

TG Management: Badehusvej 1, 9000 Aalborg; tel. (45) 3375-0400; fax (45) 3375-0375; e-mail tg-management@tg-management.dk; Man. John Aagaard.

Dominican Republic

July Mateo y Assocs: Jos Coluene, 10 Alma Rosa, Santo Domingo; Contact July Mateo.

Televisa Talents SA: Lea de Castro, 153 Gazcue, Santo Domingo; Dir-Gen. Luis Medrano.

Estonia

Eesti Kontsert: Estonia pst 4, 0001 Tallinn; Dir E. Mattisen.

Estonian Jazz Foundation: PO Box 3641, Viru str 16, 0090 Tallinn; Dir Tiit Lauk.

Makaroy Muusik Management: Regati PST 1-6K, 0019 Tallinn; Man. Martti Kitsing.

Finland

NEM: PO Box 220, 33201 Tampere; Man. Dir Harri Karvinen.

Piikkikasvi Agency: PO Box 145, 00531 Helsinki; Man. Dir Kari Pössi.

Rockadillo: Ilmarisenkatu 12 A2, 33500 Tampere; tel. (358) 3213-1260; fax (358) 3213-1297; e-mail records@rock.pp.fi; website www.rockadillo.fi; Man. Dir Tapio Korjus.

France

3 Comm: 16 Bis rue d'Odessa, 75014 Paris; Dir Jean-Pierre Lenoir.

Africa Music International: 15 rue Charles Gounod, 56100 Lorient; tel. and fax 2 97 83 38 75; Vice-Chair. & Sec. Gaëlla Tonjé-Tonjé.

Agence Kathoche: 16 rue de Marignan, 75008 Paris; Agent/Dir Catherine Poensin.

Agence Sylvie Dupuy: 27 rue Auguste Delaune, 94800 Villejuif; tel. (1) 4726-7171; Man. Sylvie Dupuy.

Alpha Bravo: 64 Ave Jean Jaurès, 93500 Pantin; tel. (1) 4843-8023; Contact Daniel Bornet.

Bistro Production: 31 rue St Sébastien, 75011 Paris; Man. Patrice Eskenazy.

Corida: 120 Blvd, Rochechojart, 75018 Paris; Man. Assaad Debs.

Daniel Bornet Management: 64 Ave Jean Jaurès, 93500 Pantin; Dir Daniel Bornet.

Do Si La Ba: 159 Chemin Lanusse, 31200 Toulouse; Man. Lawrence Larrouy.

Etienne Vanke: 94 Blvd Chaumin, 49000 Angers; Contact Etienne Vanke.

Fiesta Latina Homero Cardoso: 51 rue Mirabeau, 94200 Ivry Sur Seine; Promoter Homero Cardoso.

Gafaiti Production: 31 rue de la Haie Coq, 93300 Aubervilliers; tel. (1) 4352-2829; Man. Nourredine Gafaiti.

Genevieve Peygrene: 62 rue des Rondeaux, 75020 Paris; Dir Genevieve Peygrene.

Infernal: 102 Blvd Henri Barbusse, 93100 Montreuil; Man. Laurent Lefebvre.

IPS Management: 11/13 rue Montlouis, 75001 Paris; Man. André Gnimagnon.

Le Haut de L'Affiche: 2 Bis rue Hiche, 94130 Nogent Sur Marne; Chair. Claude Abihssira.

Made In Heaven: 6 rue Rémy de Gourmont, 75019 Paris; Label Man. Mathias Jeannin.

Marouani, Charley and Maurice: 37 rue Marbeuf, 75008 Paris; Mans Charley Marouani, Maurice Marouani.

Martine Palmé Management: 33 Bis rue Doudeauville, 75018 Paris; Artist Man. Martine Palmé.

Meyer Productions: 13 rue Dautancourt, 75017 Paris; tel. (1) 5306-6600; fax (1) 5306-6599; e-mail meyer-productions@imaginet.fr; Mans Olivia Meyer, Christian Meyer.

Mondial Management: 64 Bis rue de Paris, 93230 Romainville; Mans Georges Lancry, Lisette Obydol.

Musicomedia: 21 Ave d'Italie, 75013 Paris; Man. Gladys Gabison.

RA Production: 471 Ave Victor Hugo, 26000 Valence; Man. Frédéric Loison.

Robert Bialek Conseils: 33 rue des Jeuneurs, 75002 Paris; Contact Robert Bialek.

Salam Aleikum Amusements: 2 rue Carpeaux, 75018 Paris; Dir Stephane Benhamou.

Sixieme Sens: 2 rue du Chemin Vert, 14000 Caen; Contact Jean Michel Lebigot.

Talent Sorcier Productions: Parc d'Activité Activa, 14 rue Batterie, 67118 Geispolsheim/Strasbourg; tel. (3) 8867-3923; Man. Richard Walter.

Tourrillon Sarl: 1/233 rue Barberaisse, 59000 Lille; Agent Xavier Collin.

Utopia Spectacles: 1 rue Niece, 75014 Paris; Dir Jacques Fichelle.

VMA: 40 rue François 1er, 75008 Paris; Dir Rose Leandri.

XIII Bis Music Group: 34 rue Eugene Flachat, 75017 Paris; Man. Dir Laurent Dreux-Leblanc; Music Dir Brian Rawling.

Germany

Blue Star Promotion Konzertagentur GmbH: Goebenstr 3, 28209 Bremen; Public Relations Michael K. Grusche.

Castor Promotions: Dragonerstr 21, 30163 Hanover; tel. (511) 961620; fax (511) 392553; e-mail elke@castor-promotions.de; Contact Elke Fleing.

Commissioned Music: Hauptstr 30, 10827 Berlin; tel. (30) 280-7095; e-mail info@blixa-bargeld.com; website www.blitza-bargeld.com; Man. Dir Blixa Bargeld.

Double Trouble: Haupstr 30, 10437 Berlin; Man. Dir Petra Hammerer.

Falkland Musik Management: Herderstr 16, 44147 Dortmund; Man. Dir Thomas Falke.

Freestyle eV: Morgensternsweg 7, 22305 Hamburg; Contact Helmut Heuer; Music festival and event organizers.

Fun Factory! GmbH: Hermannstadtweg 9, 48151 Münster; tel. (251) 78321; fax (251) 78322; e-mail info@funfactory.org; website www.funfactory.org; Label Mans Axel Seitz, John Fryer.

Kick Musikverlag: Burgunder str 8, 50677 Cologne; Man. Dir Goetz Elbertzhagen; International Man. Lynda Hill.

Künstlersekretariat Ott: Moltkestr 18, 79098 Freiburg; Contact Dieter Ott.

Line Up Co: Linden str 52, 50674 Cologne Centrum.

Meduse Live Events: Karlsruher Ring 1A, 76297 Stutensee; tel. (7249) 94650; fax (7249) 952199; e-mail info@medusa-online.de; website www.medusa-online.de; Contact Reinhard Neroth.

Music Arts Network: Fichtestr 16, 60316 Frankfurt; Gen. Man. Robert Lyng.

Paradise Management International: PO Box 2180, 63243 Neu-Isenburg; Man. Dir Ralf Klug.

Partysanen Music: Skalitzer str 68, 10997 Berlin; Man. Dir Roma Casley.

Playtime Management: Weidengasse 56, 50668 Cologne; Chair. Jochen Sperber.

Rudy Holzhauer Management: Bramfelder Chaussee 238C, 22177 Hamburg; Artist Man. Rudy Holzhauer.

That's Entertainment!: Orleanstr 76, 31135 Hildesheim; Man. Dirs Felix Almstadt, Joachim Friedmann.

Thomann Künstler Management GmbH: PO Box 1, 96136 Burgebrach; tel. (9576) 94490; fax (9576) 6844; e-mail info@tkm-arts.de; website www.tkm-arts.de; Contact Joseph Thomann.

Triple M Management: Schaefflerstr 5, 80333 Munich; Man. Dir Mario Mendrycki.

Greece

Neo Revma: 8 Ainianos str, 10434 Athens; Man. Dir Dimitris Helmis.

Rock Management: PO Box 21526, 55236 Panorama, Thessaloniki; Man. Dir Christos Terzides.

Show Productions: 318 Sygrou Ave, 17673 Kalithea, Athens; Man. Dir Konstantinos Arvanitis; Public Relations Anta Arvanti.

Hong Kong
Special Administrative Region, People's Republic of China

Aural Fidelity: 3B Cambridge Villa, 8–10 Chancery Lane, Central Hong Kong; Man. Dir John Powter.

Paciwood Music and Entertainment Ltd: 8 King Tung St, Hammer Hill Rd, Ngau Chi Wan, Kowloon.

Spraylot Music Ltd: Suite A, 15th Floor, Ritz Plaza, 122 Austin Rd, Tsim Sha Tsui, Kowloon; Publishing Exec. Peggy Yu.

Hungary

OB Art Management/Alt Product: PO Box 76, 5002 Szolnok; Man. Dir Bela Pap.

Iceland

Bo Haldorson Productions: PO Box 5445, Pverholt 26, 105 Reykjavík; Man. Dir Bo Haldorson.

Spor HF: Nýbýlavegur 4, PO Box 320, 202 Kópavogur; Man. Dir Steinar Berg Isleifsson.

Ireland

Bluemedia Ltd: 7 Willow Cres., Riverbank, Anacotty, Limerick; tel. (61) 331276; fax (61) 331277; e-mail bluemedia@eircom.net; website www.bluemedia.ie; Man. Dir Joe Clarke.

Brian Molloy: 5–6 Lombard St E, Dublin 2; Contact Brian Molloy; Marketing Man. Graham Molloy.

Connie Lynch: 11 Stockton Green, Castleknock, Dublin 15; Man. Connie Lynch.

Dabble Music: The Elms, Richmond Ave S, Dartry, Dublin 6; CEO Peter Blackbyrne.

Denis Desmond Promotions: Top House, Clontarf St, Cork 1; Man. Dir Denis Desmond.

Elite Music Management: Oakdale, Roscrea Rd, Templemore, Co Tipperary; Man. Tony O'Toole.

Excellent Management: 137 Carrigwood, Firhouse, Dublin 24; Dir Neil O'Shea.

Fifty-Seventh Street Ltd: 24 Upper Mount St, Dublin 2; Contacts Maurice Cassidy, Elizabeth Reeves.

HARMONY Music Management Ltd: The Grange, Carbury, Co Kildare; tel. (405) 53005; fax (405) 53224; e-mail infocus@eircom.net; website www.infocus.ie; Man. Dir John H. Pickering.

Icebreaker Promotions: Emyvale, Co Monaghan; Contact P. J. McKenna.

Joe McFadden Promotions: 19 Stockton Green, Castleknock, Dublin 15; Man. Dir Joe McFadden.

Mister T Productions: 141 Parnell St, Dublin 1; tel. and fax (1) 878-7623; e-mail mistert@ireland.com; Dir Tonie Walsh.

Muchwood Management: 1 Killiney Ct, Seafield Rd, Killiney, Co Dublin; Man. David O'Reilly.

Pat Egan Sound Ltd: Merchant's Ct, 24 Merchant's Quay, Dublin 8; Man. Dir Pat Egan.

Principle Management: 30–32 Sir John Rogerson's Quay, Dublin 2; tel. (1) 677-7330; fax (1) 677-7276; Man. Dir Paul McGuinness; Contact Sheila Roche.

Real Good Management Ltd: 17 Dame Ct, Dublin 2; Dir Gerard Keenan.

RSE Promotions: 11–13 Station Rd, Raheny, Dublin 5; Dir Raymond J. Smyth.

Ryan Management: 6 Danieli Dr., Artane, Dublin 5; Mans Nicky Ryan, Roma Ryan.

TTMAR: Rear 22 St Stephens Green, Dublin 2; Man. Dir Dermot McEvoy.

Underscore Management: Pellestown House, Ashtown Gate, Ashtown, Dublin 15; Man. Columb Farrelly.

Upfront Management: 4 Windmill Lane, Dublin 2; tel. (1) 671-4344; fax (1) 671-4151; Man. Dir David Kavanagh.

Westland Entertainment: 35 Westland Sq., Dublin 2; Contact Lucy McColgan.

Whirling Music Agency: Cairns Hill, Aughamore, Co Sligo; Man. Brian McDonagh.

Italy

Arci Pisa: Borgo Stretto 72, 56100 Pisa; Man. Dir Nicola Zaccardi.

Casi Umani: Piazza Luigi di Savoia 28, 20124 Milan; Man. Dir Marco Conforti.

City Medial Two: Via Premuda 30, 42100 Reggio Emilia; Man. Dir Roberto Meglioli.

Dell'Amore Management: Via Zeffirino Re 2, 47023 Cesena; Art Dir Franco Dell'Amore.

Duende Management: Via Vanchiglia 9, 10124 Turin; Man. Ettore Carette.

Giancarlo Passarella: Via Salutati 7, 50126, Florence; Contact Giancarlo Passarella.

IRA Transeuropa Management: Via Landucci 38, 50100 Florence; Man. Dir Anne-Marie Pourcet.

Lion Snc: Via Goldoni 42/A, 30174 Mestre, Venezia; Gen. Man. Luciano Trevisan.

Massimo Maggioni Management: Villoresi 24, 20143 Milan; Man. Massimo Maggioni.

Mela Di Odessa: Via Gioberti 119, 58015 Orbetello (Grosseto); Man. Dir Lora Palmerini.

Soggiorno Obbligato Management: Via Delle Viole 17, Vialfiorta, 37020 S, Maria di Negrar (VR); Man. Dir Diego Alvera.

Vitola Dino Management: Via I, Goiran 8, 00195 Rome; Man. Dir Leonardo Vitola.

Vu Balle' Vu Management: Via Andreini 2, 40126 Bologna; Man. Dir Giovanni Vinci.

Japan

International Management Group: Fourth Floor, Moto-Akasaka Kikutei Bldg, 7-18 Moto Akasaka 1-Chome, Minato-ku, Tokyo 107; Contact Kazuo Kondo.

Seven Gods Productions: Suite 403, Mejidori Bldg, 2-3-21 Kabukicho Shimjulou-lou, Tokyo 160-0021; tel. (3) 5292-5551; fax (3) 5292-5552; e-mail benten@jk9.so-net.no.jp; website www.sister.co.jp; Pres. Hiroshi Asada.

Shinko Music Publishing Co Ltd: 2-1 Ogawamachi, Kanda, Chiyoda-ku, Tokyo 101; Pres. Shoichi Kusano.

Malaysia

Public Performance (Malaysia): Second Floor, Wisma Hiap Lee, Jln Segambut, Kuala Lumpur 51200; tel. (3) 6252-5588; fax (3) 6252-1818; e-mail nftan@ppm.org.my; website www.ppm.org.my; CEO Tan Ngiap Foo.

Mexico

AG Ediciones Musicales SA: Peter 117, Col. Narvate, 03020 México, DF; Man. Gerado Fojo.

Arrabal y Compañia SA: Insurgentes Sur 2388, 5° San Angle, 01000 México, DF; Contact Felipe Vega Puentes.

Organización Latino Internacional: Avda Insurgentes Sur 953-202, Col. Nápoles, 03810 México, DF; Dir-Gen. Tony Méndez.

Producciones Enrique Guzmán SA: Avda San Bernabé 781, Col. San Jerónimo, 10200 México, DF; Pres. Enrique Guzmán.

Producciones Música y Equipos SC: Manuel Acuña 3359-B, Fracc, Monraz Guadalajara, 44670 Jalisco; tel. (33) 3642-6511; fax (33) 642-5360; e-mail roxanadrexel@megared.net.mx; website www.mana.com.mx; Man. J. Ulises Calleros Ramos.

Promesa: Camino a Santa Teresa, 13 Toresa 5-1804, 14110 México, DF; Dir-Gen. Ignacio Rodríguez Martínez.

RAC Producciones SA: Sierra Gorda 30, 11010 México, DF; tel. (55) 5202-1313; fax (55) 5202-1980; Dir-Gen. Alejandro Garza.

Netherlands

ACT: Van Leeuwenhoeksingel 69, 2611 AE Delft; Contact A. C. Raven.

Hans Van Pol Management: PO Box 9010, 1006 AA Amsterdam; tel. (20) 610-8281; fax (20) 610-6941.

Home Management: Faas Eliaslaan 13, 3742 AR Baarn; Mans Eric Van Eerdenburg, Geert Van Itallie.

JB Management: Boterstraat 73, 3082 SP Schiedam; Man. Dir Jan Beunk, Rien Rietveld.

Mega Management: PO Box 9242, 1006 AE Amsterdam.

Mojo Management: PO Box 3121, 2601 DC Delft; Man. Dir Paul Van Melis.

Moonshine Management: Langeweid 7, 1831 BL Koedyk; tel. and fax (72) 561-5857; e-mail wilbrink@yahoo.com; website www.moonshine-management.com; Pres. Evert Wilbrink.

Music World Management: PO Box 55 55 9, 1007 NB Amsterdam; Man. Dir Paul Coops.

Ray Derkzen: Zoutstraat 2, 5612 HW Eindhoven; Man. Dir Ray Derkzen.

Supersonic Management: PO Box 339, 3500 AH Utrecht; Man. Dir Lizet Hobeyn.

VIP Promotions: Looievsgracht 38, 1016 VS Amsterdam; PD G. Bezuijen.

New Zealand

Jude Walcott Management: PO Box 55, Paekakariki, Kapiti Coast; Contact Jude Walcott.

McCook Management: 7 Verel St, 2001 Hamilton; Man. Dir Jeannie McCook.

Showcase Management Ltd: 140 Vanguard St, Nelson; Dir Mike Duffield.

Spasim Music Management: PO Box 2901, Christchurch; Contacts Jeff Sim, Karen Neill.

Spirit Management: Lister Bldg, 9 Victoria St E, Auckland; Man. Daniel Keighley.

York Street Management: PO Box 6884, Wellesley St, Auckland; Contact Tanya Moore.

Norway

Continental AS: PO Box 110, Smestad, 0309 Oslo; tel. 2206-2770; fax 2206-2771; website www.continentalmusic.net; Man. Dir Barry Matheson.

dbut internautics: PO Box 9415 Valerenga, 0610 Oslo; Dir Per Platow.

Groovy Management: PO Box 1291, 5001 Bergen; Man. Dir Torfinn Andersen.

Ha-Ha Management: Mandalsgt. 5, 0190 Oslo; Man. Dir Haavard Hansteen.

Petter Sandberg A/S: Cort Adelersgt 2, 0254 Oslo; Contact Jan Sollien.

Rage Management: PO Box 4721, 0506 Oslo; Man. Dir Tord Naess.

Ramalama Management and Productions: Bispegt 12, 0191 Oslo; Man. Dir Steinar Vikan.

Stageway Management AS: Skuteviksboder 11, 5035 Bergen-Sandviken; Man. Woll Steinar.

TS Artist Byra: PO Box 1683, 7002 Trondheim; Man. Dir Terje Storli.

Viggo Lund Management: Akersgt. 7, 0158 Oslo; Man. Dir Viggo Lund.

Wildlife Productions: Ammerudhellinga 74, 0959 Oslo; Man. Dir Oyvind Borgso.

Peru

Acordes EIRL: Los Paujiles 285 D, Lima 34; Proprietor Julie Freundt López.

Mapa Producciones SA: Jr. Mayta Capac 1380, Jesús María; Man. Alfredo Samaniego.

Pro Art SA: Diez Canseco 236, Of. 403, Miraflores, Lima 18; Dir-Gen. Jorge Ferrand Lanciotti.

Poland

Dzem Agency: PO Box 580, Katowice 2; Contact Ena Otolinsua.

Polish Radio Artists Management: Woronicza 17, 00-999 Warsaw; Dir Andrzej Haluch.

Warsaw Artists Management Ltd: Kazimierzowska 47/5, 02-572 Warsaw; Pres. Andrzej Haluch.

ZPR Inc-United Entertainment Enterprises Inc: Senatorska 13/15, 00 075 Warsaw; Pres./CEO Zbigniew Benbenek; Artists & Marketing Man. Anna Karolicka.

Portugal

Companhia das Ideas: Ave Roma 49 5D, 1700 Lisbon; Dir Antonio Avelar Pinho.

Contacto: PO Box 29, 2840 Seixal; Man. Dir Dionisio Duarte.

Dimas Mario Management: Rua Serpa Pinto 4A, 2800 Almada; Public Relations Isabel Silva.

Encore: Rua S. João da Praça 114 1, 1100 Lisbon; Man. Dir Rui Simoes.

MS Management: Rua General c. da Silva 10 7, 1500 Lisbon; Man. Dir Manuel Moura Dos Santos.

MTM: PO Box 30072, 1321 Lisbon Codex; Man. Dir Hugo Moutinho.

Regiespectáculo: Alto do Coutão, Armazem I, 2735 Cacém; CEO António Guimarães.

Sociedade Portuguesa de Autores: Avda Duque de Loulé, 31, 1050 Lisbon; tel. (21) 2394400; fax (21) 3157236; e-mail administacao@spautores.pt; website www.spautores.pt; Pres. Luiz Francisco Rebello.

Terra de Musica: Rua Casimiero Freire 19RC, 1900 Lisbon; Dir Francisco Morgado.

Uniao Lisbon: Rua B Sabrosa 84 2C, 1900 Lisbon; Dir Antonio Cunha.

Puerto Rico

Producciones Norma Pujals: Ave Condado 57, PO Box 7a, Condado Vilomar, 00907 Condado; Man. Norma Pujals.

Producciones Tropical: PO Box 11673, Fernandez Juncos, 00910 San Juan; tel. (787) 728-7428; fax (787) 268-5112; Pres. Angie Garcia.

TS Entertainment: PO Box 12004, 00922-2004 San Juan; Dirs Lynn Santiago, Rafael Tirado.

Romania

AMMA: Scara B, Apt 73, Calea Victorei 48/50, Sector 1, 70102 Bucharest; Man. Aurel Mitran.

Cartianu Ltd: 58 Aviator Traian Vasile str, Sector 1, 78336 Bucharest; Chair. Radu Cartianu.

Russia

M&L Art: PO Box 28, 630 011 Novosibirisk; Man. Dir Sergey Bugeyev.

Rock-Azia: Pupova 96-268, Barnaul, 656062 Siberia; Contact Eugene Kolbashev.

SNC Management: Krymsky Val 9, 103 045 Moscow; Man. Dir Stas Namin.

Singapore

Limelite Management Services: 38B Geylang Lorong 23, Singapore 1438; Operations Man. Ernest Cheong.

Slovakia

Martin Sarvas Productions: Jakubovo nám 14, 81109 Bratislava; tel. 2529-25287; fax 2529-21015; e-mail sarvas@hapri.sk; website www.martinsarvas.sk; Dir Martin Sarvas.

Slovenia

Buba Promotion: 40 A Moskriceva, 61000 Ljubljana; Man. Dir David Krzisnik.

FV-Zavod Za Umetnisko in Kulturno Produkcijo: Kersnikova 4, 61000 Ljubljana; Man. Dir Skaberne Mónika.

SKUC-AFK: Kersnikova 4, 61000 Ljubljana; Man. Dir Mitja Prezelj.

Spain

Attraction Management: Santa Barbara 1, Torrelaguna, 28010 Madrid; tel. (91) 843-0298; fax (91) 848-5508; e-mail attraction@attraction-management.com; website www.attraction-management.com; Man. Dir Paco Lopez.

AYA Producciones y Management: Dante 75 Bajos, 08032 Barcelona; Man. Dir Joaquin Ascon.

AZ Music & Management: Riera Argentona Sin, 08300 Mataro; tel. (93) 741-2828; fax (93) 757-6034; e-mail info@az-records.com; Man. Dir Braulio Paz Simon.

Blac Management: Corcega 257, 08036 Barcelona; Man. Dir Julio Cano.

BM Management: Méjico 17, 4-4A, 08004 Barcelona; Chair. Monica Gutierrez.

Caturla & Navarro: Angela de la Cruz 24, 28020 Madrid; Dirs José Caturla, J. Emilio Navarro.

Chihuahua Management: Sancho Davila, 1 Entreplanta, 28028 Madrid; tel. (91) 469-5251; fax (91) 469-8801; e-mail chihuahua@logiccontrol.es; website www.chihuahuamanag.com; Man. Dir Flor Madrid.

Chusto Producciones Artísticas: Apdo de Correos 462, 03501 Benidorm, Alicante; tel. (96) 681-1176; fax (96) 681-3574; e-mail chusto@teleline.es.

Crab Ediciones Musicales SA: Sagunto 2, 28010 Madrid; Gen. Man. Jorge E. Gomez Diaz.

Diez Management: Martinez Corrochano 3, 28007 Madrid; Chair. Mercedes Martin.

EMC Management: Carlos Latorre 13, 28039 Madrid; Dir Joan A. Serra.

GSG-Grup de Serveis Guilleries: Granja Baró, Ctra de la Guixa, km 2, 08500 VIC (Barcelona); Administration Jordi Costa; Management Ignasi Pla; Production Joan Capdevila.

Madma S L: Calle Major, 5 Urb. La Rosaleda, 08727 Sant Fuitos de Bages (Barcelona); Contact Felix Camprubi i Santamans.

MCM Management: Modesto Lafuento 46 6B, 28003 Madrid; Chair. Isabel Burgos.

Oniria International S L: Alzines 3, St Quirze Parc, 08192 St Quirze Del Vallès, Barcelona; Pres. Michel Huygen; Man. Antoni Brunet.

Pino Sagliocco Presenta SL: Calle Quintana 2, 7° 9a, 28008 Madrid; Chair. Pino Sagliocco.

Posto Nove: Muntaner 494 5B, 08022 Barcelona; Contact Alejandro Navarro.

RLM Producciones: Jose Maria Cavero 9, Ch A, 28027 Madrid; Man. Dir Rosa Lagarrigue.

Sauma & Tumbao: Gral Oraa 37 4, 28006 Madrid; Dir Saul Rodriguez.

Store Music: Gran Via 28, 3C, 18010 Granada; Man. Dir Carmen Carnicero.

WOM Music: Dusai 6, 07001 Palma de Mallorca; Dir Juanjo Arzubialde.

Sweden

AMP: Karlsgatan 9, 252 24 Helsingborg; Man. Dir Hasse Jönsson.

Feedback Management: PO Box 558, 631 07 Eskilstuna; Man. Dir Mats Olsson.

Luger Production: Fredriksgatan 35, 811 33 Sandviken; Man. Dir/Agent Ola Broquist; Agents Patrick Fredriksson, Morgan Johansson.

Madhouse: PO Box 103 30, 100 55 Stockholm; Man. Dir Jon Gray.

MPA Musicart: Simrishamnsgatan 20A, 214 23 Malmö; Man. Dir Andreas Larsson.

Projektbyrån: Kungsgatan 34, 972 41 Luleå; Man. Dir Tomas Lind.

RMP Management AB: PO Box 17180, 104 62 Stockholm; Man. Dir Stefan Liga.

Siljemark Production: Gärdsvagen 2, 171 52 Solna; Man. Jonas Siljemark; Contact Lasse Karlsson.

Stockhouse: PO Box 74, 182 71 Stocksund; tel. (8) 856800; Man. Dir Mats Bokström.

Ton Art: PL 8007, 441 91 Alingås; Man. Klas Johansson.

XTC Productions AB: Ripsavägen 59, 124 51 Bandhagen; Man. Dir Ulf Wahlberg.

Switzerland

Artways Productions: Rue des-deux-Gares 6B, PO Box 30, 1800 Vevey; Man. Fabrice La Luc.

Choc Auditif Management: Route de Genève 17, Le Flon, 1003 Lausanne; Man. Dominique Rottet.

Its Time To Management: PO Box 1344, 5610 Wohlen; Man. Jean-Luc Itten.

Just Two Management: Hagenbuchstr 31, 9000 St Gallen; Contact Christoph Harzenmoser.

Migration: PO Box 431, 1800 Vevey; tel. (21) 923-6363; fax (21) 923-6362; e-mail hdill@bluewin.ch; website www.farafina.com; Contact Heinz Dill.

VIP AG Productions: Schützengasse 30, 8001 Zürich; Man. Dir Urs Peter Keller.

Taiwan

Formosa Artist Management: 11F, 215 Fu-Hsin South Rd Sec. 1, Taipei; Gen. Man. Carlos Yung-Hui Lee.

United Kingdom

140dB Management: The Fan Club 133, Kilburn Lane, London W10 4AN; tel. (20) 8354-2900; fax (20) 8354-2091; e-mail enquiries@140dB.co.uk; website www.140dB.co.uk; Contact Katrina Berry, Justin Pritchard.

Acker's International Jazz Agency: 53 Cambridge Mansions, Cambridge Rd, London SW11 4RX; tel. (20) 7978-5885; fax (20) 7978-5882; e-mail pamela@ackersmusicagency.co.uk; website www.ackersmusicagency.co.uk; Owner Pamela Frances Sutton.

Acorn Entertainments: Winterfold House, 46 Woodfield Rd, Kings Heath, Birmingham, B13 9UJ; tel. (121) 444-7258; fax (121) 443-4677; Man. Dir Jim McPhee.

Adrian Boss Promotions: PO Box 21252, London W9 3FD; Contact Adrian Boss.

AGM UK: 145A Ladbroke Grove, London W10 6HJ; Contact Tony Meilandt.

ARC Management Ltd: Prince Georges Ave, London SW20 8BH; tel. (20) 8540-3163; Contact Alex Ruheman.

Arctic King Management: Bank Chambers, 4–6 Church St, Wilmslow, Cheshire SK9 1AU; Contact John King.

Artist Management Group: 11/13 Broad Ct, Covent Garden, London WC2B 5QN; tel. (20) 7240-5052; fax (20) 7240-4956.

Asgard Management: 125 Parkway, London NW1 7PS; tel. (20) 7387-5090; fax (20) 7387-8740; e-mail pl@asgard.uk.com; Contact Paul Charles.

Atomic Management: 32 Neal St, London WC2H 9PS; tel. (20) 7379-3010; fax (20) 7379-5583; Contact Mick Newton.

Avalon Management Group Ltd: 4a Exmoor St, London W12 6BD; tel. (20) 7598 8000; Co Admin. Marc Goodson.

BA Music Management: PO Box 34351, London NW6 7ZW; tel. (20) 7372-6648; fax (20) 7372-6673; e-mail enquiries@bjornagain.com; website www.bjornagain.com; Dirs John Tyrrell, Rod Leissle.

Bad Habits Music Group: PO Box 111, London W13 0ZH; tel. (20) 8357-2337; Man. Dir John S. Rushton.

Bamn Management: 136–144 New Kings Rd, London SW6 4LZ; tel. (20) 7705-4258; fax (20) 7705-4335; Man. Dir Steve Finan.

Basement Music: 6 Pembridge Rd, London W11 3HL; Man. Dir John Telfer.

BDA—Brian Durkin Assocs Ltd: Bryson House, Chiltern Rd, Culcheth, Warrington WA3 4LL; tel. (1925) 766655; fax (1925) 765577; e-mail bda@exl.co.uk; Man. Dir Brian Durkin.

Bedlam Management (UK) Ltd: Third Floor, Devonshire House, 14 Barley Mow Passage, London W4 4ZN; tel. (20) 8942-8755; fax (20) 8942-8755; Contact Tim Vass.

Bernard Lee Management: 1 Heathside Pl., Epsom, Surrey; tel. and fax (1737) 354777; Man. Dir Bernard Lee.

Big Advance Management: 12 Oval Rd, London NW1 7DH; Contact Paddy Prendergast.

Big Bear Music: PO Box 944, Edgbaston, Birmingham B16 8UT; tel. (121) 4547020; fax (121) 4549996; e-mail bigbearmusic@compuserve.com; website www.bigbearmusic.com; Man. Dir Jim Simpson.

Big Life Management: 15 Little Portland St, London W1N 5DE; Contact Jazz Summers.

Black Magic Management Ltd: 296 Earls Court Rd, London SW5 9BA; tel. (20) 7373-3849; fax (20) 7385-5447; Man. Dir Mataya Clifford.

Blaylock Management Ltd: 39 Leyton Rd, Harpenden, Hertfordshire AL5 2JB: Man. Dir David Blaylock.

Blitz: Edgwarebury Farm, Edgwarebury Lane, Edgware, Middlesex HA8 8QX; Partners Sue Harris, Claire Powell.

Blueprint Management: 134 Lots Rd, London SW10 0RJ; tel. (20) 7351-4333; fax (20) 7352-4652; Dirs John Glover, Matt Glover.

BPR: 36 Como St, Romford, Essex RM7 7DR; tel. (1708) 725330; fax (1708) 725322; website www.bprmusic.com; Man. Brian Theobald.

Brave Management: 15 Nottingham Rd, Wandsworth, London SW17 7EA; tel. (20) 8672-2212; fax (20) 8672-0064; Man. Dir Netty Walker.

Braw Music Management: 76 Pentland Pl., Edinburgh EH10 6HS; Contact Kenny MacDonald.

Brian Gannon Management: PO Box 106, Rochdale, Lancashire OL16 4HW; tel. (1706) 860400; fax (1706) 860406; Man. Dir Brian Gannon.

Brian Reza Management: 416 High Rd, Harrow Weald, Middlesex HA3 6HJ; tel. (20) 8954-3428; fax (20) 8954-3239; Owner Brian Reza.

Brian Yeates Assocs: London Rd, Canwell, Sutton Coldfield, West Midlands B75 5SH; tel. (121) 323-2200; fax (121) 323-2313; e-mail ash@cyberphile.co.uk; website www.ukacts.com/agency/brian-yeates.

Brilliant Artistes: 253 Camberwell New Rd, London SE5 0TH; Contact Mark Walmesley.

Brilliant Management: 20 Stamford Brook Ave, London W6 0YD; Contact Dee Harrington.

Bruno Brookes Media and Management Ltd: Denford Mill House, Lower Derford, Hungerford, Berkshire RE17 0UN; Man. Dir Bruno Brookes.

Buzz Records: 192 Glasgow Rd, Perth PH2 0NA, Scotland; Man. Dir Dave Arcari.

By Eleven: 12 Tideway Yard, 125 Mortlake High St, London SW14 8SN; Man. Jill Taylor.

Caromac Music Management: Unit 104, Ducie House, 37 Ducie St, Manchester M1 2JW; tel. (161) 237-3403; fax (161) 236-4268; Man. Caroline Elleray.

Century Music Entertainment: PO Box 1008, London W3 8ZW; Pres. James Little.

Chapter 22 Music/Sanctuary Music Management (Birmingham): Suite 114, The Custard Factory, Gibb St, Birmingham B9 4AA; tel. (121) 693-5454; fax (121) 693-5424; e-mail rod.thomson@sanctuarygroup.com; Contact Rod Thomson.

Charmenko: 46 Spencer Rd, London SE24 0NR; tel. (20) 7274-6618; fax (20) 7737-4712; e-mail nick@charmenko.net; website www.charmenko.net; Contact Nick Hobbs.

Clive Banks Ltd: 1 Glenthorne Mews, 115A Glenthorne Rd, London W6 0LT; tel. (20) 8748-5036; fax (20) 8748-3356; e-mail mail@clivebanks.com; Man. Dir Clive Banks; Contacts Sharon Wheeler, Caroline Stewart.

CMC Management: First Floor, 50 Bonnington Sq., London SW8 1TQ; tel. (20) 7582-8900; fax (20) 7582-8900; Man. Dir Chris Molloy.

CMO Management (International) Ltd: Unit 32 Ransomes Dock, 35/37 Parkgate Rd, London SW11 4NP; tel. (20) 7228-4000; Man. Dir Chris Morrison.

Congo Music Ltd: 17A Craven Park Rd, Harlesden, London NW10 8SE; Dirs Byron Lye-Fook, Root Jackson.

Courtyard Management: 21 The Nursery, Sutton Courtenay, Abingdon, Oxfordshire OX14 4UA; tel. (1235) 845800; fax (1235) 847692; Mans Bryce Edge, Chris Hufford.

Cromwell Management: 4–5 High St, Huntingdon, Cambridgeshire PE29 3TE; tel. (1480) 435600; fax (1480) 356250; e-mail tricvic@lineone.net; Man. Partner Vic Gibbons.

Cut Throat Management: 267 Coventry Rd, Exhall, Coventry, West Midlands CV1 4BG; tel. (1203) 312985; fax (1203) 318586; Contact Simon Lawler.

Damage Management: 16 Lambton Pl., London W11 2SH; tel. (20) 7229-2292; Man. Dir Ed Bicknell.

David Aspden Management: The Coach House, Capel Leyse, South Holmwood, Dorking, Surrey RH5 4LJ; Proprietor David Aspden.

David Harper Management: c/o DEP, 1 Andover St, Digbeth, Birmingham B5 5RG; tel. (121) 633-4742; fax (121) 643-4904; Contact David Harper.

David Jaymes Assocs/D-Management: Suite 223A, Canalot Studios, 222 Kensal Rd, London W10 5BN; Contact David Jaymes.

The Deluxe Corpn: 13 Charnhill Cres., Bristol BS16 9JU; tel. (117) 970-2712; fax (117) 970-2713; e-mail info@volumerecords.co.uk; website www.volumerecords.co.uk; Admin. Man. Helen Hawken.

Derek Block Artistes Agency Ltd: Promotions: Douglas House, 3 Richmond Bldgs, London W1V 5AE; tel. (20) 7434 2100; fax (20) 7434 0200; e-mail dbaa@derekblock.demon.co.uk; Man. Dir Derek Block.

Diamond Sounds Music Management: The Fox and Punchbowl, Burfield Rd, Old Windsor, Berkshire SL4 2RD; tel. (1753) 855420; fax (1753) 855420; e-mail samueldsm@aol.com; Man. Dir Julie Samuel.

Direct Heat Management: 20 Lafranc Rd, Worthing, Sussex BN14 7ER; tel. (1903) 202426; fax (1903) 238250; e-mail dhm@happyvibes.co.uk; website www.happyvibes.co.uk; Man. Dir Mike Pailthorpe.

Eastonia Entertainments: Eastonia House, 174 Lisnafin Park, Strabane, Co Tyrene, Northern Ireland; Contact Gerry Harding.

EC1: 1 Cowcross St, London EC1 6DE; Contact Alex Nightingale.

EG Management: 63A Kings Rd, London SW3 4NT; Chair. Sam Adler.

Eleventh Hour Arts: 113 Cheesemans Terrace, Star Rd, London W14 9XH; Man. Dir Debbie Golt.

Emka Productions Ltd: 43 Portland Rd, London W11 4LJ; tel. (20) 7221-2046; e-mail emka@emkaproductions.com; Contact S. O'Rourke.

Empire Artists Management: 21 Denmark St, London WC2H 8NA; tel. (20) 7379-0038.

Equator Music Ltd: 17 Hereford Mansions, Hereford Rd, London W2 5BA; tel. (20) 7727-5858; fax (20) 7229-5934; Contact Ernest Chapman.

Eternal Management: 55 Lark St, Liverpool L17 8UW; Contact Jill Thompson.

Europa Jazz Live: 6 Belgrove, Tunbridge Wells, Kent TN1 1YN; tel. (1892) 516722; fax (1892) 536080; e-mail jazz@davidjacobs.f9.co.uk; website www.tinamay.com; Dir David E. Jacobs.

Excellent Management: 50A Waldron Rd, London SW18 3TD; Contact Mark Wood.

Falcon Stuart Management: 59 Moore Park Rd, London SW6 2HH; tel. (20) 7731-0022; fax (20) 7731-1715; Man. Dir Falcon Stuart.

Fexborough Ltd: 195 Sandycombe Rd, Kew, Surrey TW9 2EW; tel. (20) 8948-7600; fax (20) 8940-0280; Man. John Kalinowski.

Firebirds: 11 Chavenage, Kingswood, Bristol BS15 4LA; tel. (117) 967-8277; Dir Craig Dunn.

First Avenue Management: The Courtyard, 42 Colwith Rd, London W6 9EY; Contact Oliver Smallman.

Firstars/Talent Bank Management: Bugle House, 21A Noel St, London W1V 3PD; Contact Tony Brinsley.

Forward Management: 132 Liverpool Rd, London N1 1LA; tel. (20) 7609-9900; fax (20) 7609-8300; Man. Dir Rob Challice.

Friars Management Ltd: 33 Alexander Rd, Aylesbury, Buckinghamshire HP20 2NR; tel. (1296) 434731; fax (1296) 22530; Man. Dir David R. Stopps.

Fruit Management: Unit 104, Saga Centre, 326 Kensal Rd, London W10 5BZ; Mans Caroline Killoury, Debbie Swainson.

Gailforce Management Ltd: 30 Ives St, London SW3 2ND; tel. (20) 7581-0261; fax (20) 7584-5774; Man. Dir Gail Colson; Co-ordinator Norma Bishop.

Ganeshe Management: Ganeshe House, Ingleby Dr., Harrow, Middlesex HA1 3LE; Man. Dir Harvey Frost.

Genius Management: 89A High Rd, London N22 6BB; Contact Bruce Ruffin.

Gloria Butler Management: PO Box 2686, Knowle B94 5NQ; Man. Gloria Butler.

GR Management Ltd: 974 Pollokshaws Rd, Shawlands, Glasgow G41 2HA, Scotland; tel. (141) 632-1111; fax (141) 649-0042; Admin. Man. Alan Connell.

Hal Carter Organization: 101 Hazelwood Lane, Palmers Green, London N13 5HQ; tel. (20) 8886 2801; fax (20) 8882 7380; e-mail halcarterorg@ic24.net; Man. Dir Hal Carter.

Hall or Nothing: 8 Poplar Mews, Uxbridge Rd, London W12 7JS; tel. (20) 8740-6288; fax (20) 8749-5982; Contact Martin Hall.

Handle Artists Management: Handle House, 1 Albion Pl., Galena Rd, Hammersmith, London W6 0QT; Chair. David Walker.

Harvey Lisberg Assocs: Kennedy House, 31 Stamford St, Altrincham, Cheshire WA14 1ES; tel. (161) 941-4560; fax (161) 941-4199; Contacts Harvey Lisberg, Philip Lisberg.

Heavenly Ltd: 72 Wardour St, London W1V 3HP; tel. (20) 7437-3350; fax (20) 7437-3317.

Hit & Run Music Ltd: 25 Ives St, London SW3 2ND; tel. (20) 7581-0261; fax (20) 7584-5774; e-mail tony@hit-and-run.com; website www.genesis-music.com; Chair. & Man. Dir Tony Smith.

Holland-Ford's: 103 Lydyett Lane, Barnton, Northwich, Cheshire CW8 4JT; tel. (1606) 76960; Proprietor Bob Holland-Ford.

Hopscotch Media Management Group Ltd: 46 Broadwick St, London W1V 1FF; tel. (20) 7277 1038; Dir/Partner Alfie Dosoo.

Huge and Jolly Management: 56–60 Islington Park St, London N1 1PX; tel. (20) 7704 0213; Dir Jolyon Burnham.

Hyperactive Music Management: 1 Glenthorne Mews, 115A Glenthorne Rd, Hammersmith, London W6 0LJ; Asst Man. Fiona Riddick.

IE Music Ltd: 111 Frithville Gdns, London W12 7JQ; tel. (20) 8600-3400; fax (20) 8600-3401; e-mail info@iemusic.co.uk; website www.iemusic.co.uk; Dirs Tim Clark, David Enthoven.

Ignition Management: 8A Wyndham Pl., London W1H 1PP; Contacts Marcus Russell, Alec McKinney.

Interaction: 21 Douglas Rd, London NW6 7RN; tel. (20) 7328-6288; fax (20) 7328-6368; Contact Joan Marindin.

Interceptor Enterprises: The Greenhouse, 34–38 Provost St, London N1 7NG; Man. Charlie Charlton.

Interface Management: 37 Oxford Gdns, London W4 3BN; tel. (20) 8994-4398; fax (20) 8742-7794; Contact Douglas Kean.

Invasion Group: 17 Gosfield St, London W1P 7HE; Contact Mike Hedge.

Jack Bruce Music: PO Box 2440, Bures, Suffolk CO8 5HY; tel. (1787) 269402; fax (1787) 269473; e-mail margrit@spotsmusic.co.uk; website www.jackbruce.com; Man. Margrit Seyffer.

Jackie Khan Management: Monroe Studios, 103–105 Holloway Rd, London N7 8LT; Man. Dir Jackie Khan.

Jam X Management: PO Box 3836, London NW3 4XF; tel. (1726) 844466; fax (1726) 844608; e-mail julian.able@jamx.co.uk; website www.jamx.co.uk; Dir Julian Able.

James Joseph Music Management: 15 Cicada Rd, Wandsworth, London SW18 2PA; tel. (20) 8874-8647; fax (20) 8877-9783; Man. Dir James Joseph.

Jef Hanlon Management: 1 York St, London W1P 1PZ; tel. (20) 7487-2558; fax (20) 7487-2584; e-mail jhanlon@agents-uk.com; Man. Dir Jef Hanlon; Dir Alice Hanlon.

JFD Management: 106 Dalling Rd, London W6 0JA; tel. (20) 8748-0244; fax (20) 8748-0759; Contact Jasmine Daines.

John Ford Promotions: Bradford Ct, Bradford St, Digbeth, Birmingham B12 0NS; tel. (121) 693 9911; fax (121) 693 7799; Owner John Ford.

John Henry Management: The John Henry Bldg, 16/24 Brewery Rd, London N7 4NH; Sales & Retail Man. Pepin Clout.

John Osborne Management: PO Box 173, New Malden, Surrey KT3 3YR; tel. (20) 8949-7730; fax (20) 8949-7798; e-mail john.osb1@btinternet.com; website www.vibeuk.co.uk; Contact John Osborne.

Johnny Lawes Management: 18 All Saints Rd, Unit 8, London W11 1HH; Man. Dir Johnny Lawes.

JPR Management: The Power House, 70 Chiswick High Rd, London W4 1SY; tel. (20) 8742-0052; fax (20) 8742-0051; Contact John Reid.

Jukes Productions Ltd: PO Box 13995, London W9 2FL; tel. (20) 7286-9532; fax (20) 7286-4739; e-mail jukes@easynet.co.uk; website www.jukesproductions.co.uk; Contact Geoff Jukes.

Kasevin Rodell: 6 Bowling Green Rd, Cranfield, Bedfordshire MK43 0ET; Partner Diana Rodell.

Kayam: Laurels Farm, Worstead, Norfolk NR28 9RW; tel. (1692) 536025; fax (1692) 535456; e-mail richard@kayam.co.uk; website www.kayam.co.uk; Contact Richard Abel.

Ken Spencer Personal Management: 138 Sandy Hill Rd, London, SE18 7BA; tel. and fax (20) 8854-2558; e-mail pagandferret@hotmail.com; Dir Ken Spencer; Admin. Paul Griffith.

Kitchenware: 7 The Stables, St Thomas St, Newcastle upon Tyne, Tyne & Wear NE1 4LE; tel. (191) 232-4895; fax (191) 232-0262; Man. Dir Keith Armstrong.

Lena Davis, John Bishop Assocs: Cotton's Farmhouse, Whiston Rd, Cogenhoe, Northants NN7 1NL; tel. (1604) 891487; fax (1604) 890405; Dir John Bishop.

Les Johnson Management: 55 Rockford Close, Oakenshaw South, Redditch, Worcestershire B98 7SZ; Contact Les Johnson.

LJE: 32 Willesden Lane, London NW6 7ST; Contact Laurie Jay.

M D O: The Dawn, Northwood Lane, Bewdley, Worcestershire DY12 1AS; tel. (1299) 404579; fax (1299) 405079; e-mail themick.mdo@btinternet.com; Contact Mick Owen.

M Management: 45A Longley Rd, London SW17 9LA; Man. Dir Mort Marrinan.

Management Connection: Flat 3, Haversham Lodge, Melrose Ave, Willesden Green, London NW2 4JS; tel. (20) 8450-8882; fax (20) 8202-4219; e-mail sharon@thepublicityconnection.com; website www.thepublicityconnection.com; Man. Dir Sharon Chevin.

Mark Dean: Electric Lighting Station, 48 Kensington Church St, London W8 5DP; Man. Mark Dean.

Maverick Management: The Old Manor House, Station Rd, Thames Ditton, Surrey KT7 0NU; Man. Stein.

Medium Productions Ltd: 74 Saint Lawrence Rd, Upminster, Essex RM14 2UW; tel. (7939) 080524; fax (1708) 640291; e-mail info@mediumproductions.co.uk; website www.mediumproductions.co.uk; Co-Dir Debi Zornes.

Mercenary Music Services: 143 Turks Rd, Radcliffe, Manchester M26 3WW; Production Man. Paul Naylor.

Midnight Rock: Grays Farm Barns, Marshside, Kent CT3 4EL; tel. (1227) 860638; fax (1227) 860627; e-mail rockindave@midnightrock.demon.co.uk; website www.midnightrock.demon.co.uk; Contact Dave Taylor.

Milltown Productions Ltd: 26 East Parade, Bradford, West Yorkshire BD1 5HD; Prod. Ian Smith.

Mission Control Management Ltd: Unit 3, Brunel Lock Devt, Cumberland Basin, Bristol BS1 6SE; Man. Dir Richard Hutchison.

Modernwood Management: Cambridge House, Card Hill, Forest Row RH18 5BA; Dirs Mark Wood, Mickey Modern.

MoHoHo: 149 Gibson Gdns, London N16 7HH; Man. Ray Hogan.

Moksha: PO Box 102, London E15 2HH; Man. Dir Charles Colm.

Money Talks Management: Cadillac Ranch, Pencraig Uchaf, Cwm Bach, Whitland, Dyfed SA34 0DT, Wales; tel. (1994) 484466; fax (1994) 484294; e-mail cadillac-ranch@telco4u.net; website www.nikturner.com; Man. M. Magoon.

Motley Music Ltd: 132 Liverpool Rd, Islington, London N1 1LA; Man. Debbie Rawlings.

Muirhead Management: Michelin House, 81 Fulham Rd, Chelsea, London SW3 6RD; tel. (20) 7351-5167; fax (870) 1363878; e-mail info@muirheadmanagement.co.uk; website www.muirheadmanagement.co.uk; CEO Dennis Muirhead.

NE Music Management: Priory House, 55 Lawe Rd, South Sheilds, Tyne & Wear NE33 2AL; tel. (191) 427-6207; fax (191) 427-6323; e-mail dave@nemproductions.com; website www.nemproductions.com; Contact Dave Smith.

Negus-Fancey Co: 78 Portland Rd, London W11 4LQ; Contact Charles Negus-Fancey.

Nettwerk Management: 1098 Regents Park Rd, London NW1 8UR; tel. (20) 7586 8511; fax (20) 7586 8539; e-mail nettmanagement@nettwerk.com; website www.nettmanagement.com.

Nigel Martin-Smith Management Ltd: 41 South King St, Manchester M2 6DE; tel. (161) 832-8080; fax (161) 832-1613; Man. Dir Nigel Martin-Smith.

19 Management Ltd: Unit 32, Ransomes Dock, 35–37 Parkgate Rd, London SW11 4NP; tel. (20) 7738-1919; fax (20) 7738-1819; website www.19.co.uk; Man. Dir Simon Fuller.

Northern Music Co: Cheapside Chambers, 43 Cheapside, Bradford, West Yorkshire BO1 4HP; Man. Dir Andy Farrow.

One Fifteen: 1 Prince of Orange Lane, Greenwich, London SE10 8JQ; tel. (20) 8293-0999; fax (20) 8293-9525; e-mail mail@onefifteen.com; website www.onefifteen.com; Man. Paul Loasby.

One Management: 43 St Alban's Ave, London W4 5JS; Man. Dir Karin Clayton.

Opal Ltd: 4 Pembridge Mews, London W11 3EQ; Contact Catherine Dempsey.

Opium (Arts): 49 Portland Rd, London W11 4LJ; tel. (20) 7229-5080; fax (20) 7229-4841; Man. Dir Richard Chadwick.

Palace of Fun: 16 Elm View, Huddersfield Rd, Halifax, Yorkshire HX3 0AE; Man. Dir Bill Byford.

Park Promotions: PO Box 651, Oxford OX2 9RB; tel. (1865) 241717; fax (1865) 204556; website www.parkrecords.com; Man. Dir John Dagnell.

Part Rock Management: Suite 318, 535 Kings Rd, London SW10 0SZ; Contact Stewart Young.

Paul Crockford Management: 56–60 Islington Park St, London N1; Contact Paul Crockford.

Pet Shop Boys Partnership: 8 Pembridge Studios, 27A Pembridge Villas, London W11 3EP; tel. (20) 7221-3355; fax (20) 7229-9651; Contact Jill Wall.

Pete Hawkins Management: 54 The Ave, West Wickham, Kent BR4 0DY; tel. (20) 8777-9959; fax (20) 8777-9330; e-mail petervhawkins@aol.com; Man. Dir Pete Hawkins.

PHAB: High Notes, Sheerwater Ave, Woodham, Weybridge, Surrey KT15 3SD; Contact Philip H. A. Bailey.

Planet 4: Sun House, 2–4 Little Peter St, Manchester M15 4PS; Man. Dir Chris Joyce.

PNG/Worldwide: Westminster Ct, 10 Park Rd N, Birmingham, B6 5UJ; Man. John Slater.

Polar Union: 45–53 Sinclair Rd, London W14 0NS; Contact Sarah Thorp.

Pure Management: 39 Bolton Gdns, London SW5 0AQ; Contact Steve Fargnoli.

Purple Palace: 34A Flower Lane, Mill Hill, London NW7 2JE; Contact Stephanie Kays.

PWL Management: 4–7 The Vineyard, off Sanctuary St, London SE1 1QL; tel. (20) 7403-0007; Gen. Man. Sally Atkins.

Queen Productions: 46 Pembridge Rd, London W11 3HN; tel. (20) 7727-5641; fax (20) 7221-6173; Contact Jim Beach.

Quickfire Management: Basement, 19 All Saints Rd, London W11 1HE; tel. (20) 7792-8167; fax (20) 7792-2854; Proprietor Katherine Canoville.

Quinlan Road (UK): 1 Heathgate Pl., 75/87 Agincourt Rd, London NW3 2NT; Gen. Man. Ian Blackaby.

Raymond Coffer Management Ltd: Suite 1, Hadleigh House, 96 High St, Bushey, Hertfordshire WD2 3DE; Man. Dir Raymond Coffer.

Real Life: 122 Holland Park Ave, London W11 4UA; Contact Paul Lilly.

Ricochet: 5 Old Garden Rd, The Lanterns, Bridge Lane, London SW11 3AD; tel. (20) 7924-2255; Man. Dir Stephen King.

Riviera Global: 20 Cromwell Mews, London SW7 2JY; Contact Jake Riviera.

Roger Forrester Management: 18 Harley House, London NW1 5HE; tel. (20) 7486-8056; fax (20) 7487-5663; Man. Dir Roger Forrester.

Rollover Productions: 29 Beethoven St, London W10 4LJ; Man. Dir Seamus Morley.

Rough Trade Management: 66 Golborne Rd, London W10 5PS; tel. (20) 8960 9888; fax (20) 8968 6715; e-mail info@rough-trade.com; website www.rough-trade.com; Man. Dir Geoff Travis.

Running Dog Management: Minka, Lower Hampton Rd, Sunbury, Middlesex TW16 5PR; Management Co-ordinator Rachel Male.

Rupert Loewenstein: 2 King St, London SW1Y 6QL; Dir Clare Turner.

Salamander & Son Music Ltd: 23 Longman Dr., Inverness IV1 1SU, Scotland; tel. (1463) 710464; Contact Heather Bunting.

Sanctuary Music (Overseas): First Floor Suite, The Colonnades, 82 Bishops Bridge Rd, London W2 6BB; tel. (20) 7243-0640; Contact Rod Smallwood.

Sandcastle Productions: 236 Sebert Rd, Forest Gate, London E7 0NP; Sr Partner Simon Law.

Seb Shelton Management: 13 Lynton Rd, London N8 8SR; Contact Seb Shelton.

Serious Speakout: 42 Old Compton St, London W1V 5PB; Partners John Cumming, John Ellson, David Jones.

Shamrock Music Ltd: 9 Thornton Pl., London W1H 1FG; tel. (20) 7935-9719; fax (20) 7935-0241; e-mail lindy@celtus.demon.co.uk; website www.folking.com/celtus/; Man. Dir Lindy Benson.

Sincere Management: Flat B, 6 Bravington Rd, London W9 3AH; tel. (20) 8960-4438; fax (20) 8968-8458; e-mail office@sinman.co.uk; Contacts Peter Jenner, Mushi Jenner.

So What Arts: First Floor, Ducie House, 37 Ducie St, Manchester M1 2JW; Contact Andy Dodd.

Solid Bond Management: Nomis Studios, 45–53 Sinclair Rd, London W14 0NS; Man. John Weller.

SOS Management: 106 Cleveland St, London W1Y 5DP; Contact Meredith Cork.

Sound Management Assocs: 22A Lambolle Pl., London NW3 4HP; Man. Dir Paul Craig.

Soundtrack Music Management: 22 Ives St, London SW3 2ND; Dirs Olaf Wyper, Carolynne Wyper.

Southwestern Management: 13 Portland Rd, St, Somerset BA16 9PX; tel. (1458) 445186; fax (1458) 841186; e-mail info@sw-management.co.uk; website www.sw-management.co.uk; Dir Chris Hannam.

Splash Management & Promotions: 328 Gray's Inn Rd, King's Cross, London WC1X 8BZ; Man. Dir Nick Moore.

Stamina Management: 47 Prout Grove, London NW10 1PU; Man. Dir Peter Gage.

Startrack Studio & Artist Management: 108B North Western St, Manchester M1 2WS; Studio Man. Royston.

Stephen Budd Management Ltd: 109B Regents Park Rd, Primrose Hill, London NW1 8UR; tel. (20) 7916-3303; fax (20) 7916-3302; e-mail info@record-producers.com; website www.record-producers.com; Man. Dir Stephen Budd.

Sylvantone Promotions: 17 Allerton Grange Way, Leeds LS17 6LP; tel. (113) 268-7788; fax (113) 266 0220; e-mail tonygoodacre@hotmail.com; Proprietor Tony Goodacre.

SYME International-Hengest Records: 81 Park Rd, Wath-Upon-Dearne, Rotherham, South Yorkshire S63 7LE; tel. (1709) 877920; fax (1709) 873119; e-mail admin@hengest.com; website www.hengest.com; Product Man. Patsy Prince.

Taurus Records: 23 Blackheath Rise, Lewisham, London SE13 7PN; Contact Beverley Miller.

Tender Prey Management: 50 Werter Rd, Putney, London SW15 2LJ; tel. (20) 8788-9600; fax (20) 8788-4600; e-mail tanya.rayner@tenderprey.com; Contact Rayner Jesson, Tanya Bushnell.

Theobald Dickson Productions Ltd: The Coach House, Swinhope Hall, Swinhope, Lincolnshire LN3 6HT; Man. Dir Bernard Theobald.

TKO Management: PO Box 130, Hove, East Sussex BN3 6QU; tel. (1273) 550088; fax (1273) 540969; e-mail management@tkogroup.com; website www.tkogroup.com; Contact Howard Kruger.

Tony Denton Promotions Ltd: 19 South Molton Lane, Mayfair, London W1Y 1AQ; tel. (20) 7629 4666; fax (20) 7629 4777; e-mail mail@tdpromo.com; website www.tdpromo.com; Contact Simon Nicholls.

Tracy Carter Management Ltd: WT House, Pilling, Preston, Lancashire PR3 6SJ; Owner William Tracy Carter.

Trinifold Management: 22 Harley House, Marylebone Rd, London NW1 4PR; Man. Dir Bill Curbishley.

TYGER: c/o 19A Bedford Rd, London N15 4HA; Head of Music Tim Noyce.

UK/LA Management: Bugle House, 21A Noel St, London W1V 3PD; Contact Michael Cox.

Value Added Talent (VAT): 1–2 Purley Pl., London N1 1QA; Man. Dir Dan Silver.

Van Walsum Management Ltd: 4 Addison Bridge Pl., London W14 8XP.

Voodoo Productions: 21 Ruckholt Close, Leyton, London E10 5NX; Contact Rita Campbell.

Waveeffect Ltd: 34 Salisbury St, London NW8 8QE; tel. (20) 7402-9111; fax (20) 7723-3064; e-mail satellite_artists@hotmail com; Man. Dir Eliot M. Cohen.

Wedge Music: 63 Grosvenor St, London W1X 9DA; Contact Tony Gordon.

Wilcox Zodiac Organisation: 1099A Finchley Rd, London NW11 0QB; Artist Man. Bert Wilcox.

Wildlife Management: Unit F, 21 Heathmans Rd, London SW6 4TJ; tel. (20) 7371-7008; fax (20) 7371-7708; Man. Dir Ian McAndrew.

William Tracey-Carter Management: WT House, Pilling, Preston, Lancs PR3 6SJ; Contact William Tracey-Carter.

Wolfgang Kuhle Artist Management: PO Box 425, London SW6 3TX; Contact Wolfgang Kuhle.

Worldchief Ltd: 132 Liverpool Rd, London N1 1LA; Dir Steve Baker; Asst Susie Blyth.

X-Factor Music Group International: PO Box 52, Ilford, Essex IG1 3JT; tel. and fax (20) 8252-1007; e-mail xsquad_uk@yahoo.co.uk; Dir/Prod. Ramesh Kansara.

XL Talent: Studio 7, 27A Pembridge Villas, London W11 3EP; tel. (20) 7938-1917; fax (20) 7229-7511; Contact Ian Wright.

United States of America

A Train Management: PO Box 29242, Oakland, CA 94604; tel. (510) 893-4705; fax (510) 893-4807; e-mail postmaster@a-train.com; Contact Al Evers.

Ace Productions: PO Box 428, Portland, TN 37148-0428; Pres. Jim Case.

Addis, Wechsler & Assocs: 955 S Carrillo Dr., Los Angeles, CA 90048; Contact Nick Wechsler.

AEG Management: 1025 16th Ave S, Suite 401, Nashville, TN 37212; CEO Marc Oswald.

AFG Entertainment: 30 W 21st St, Seventh Floor, New York, NY 10010-6905; Contact Ronald Fierstein.

Aggressive Entertainment: 130 W 57th St, Suite 5A, New York, NY 10019; Man. Nick Moyle.

Al Bunetta Management: Suite 102A, 33 Music Sq. W, Nashville, TN 37203; Man. Al Bunetta.

Al Embry International: PO Box 23162, Nashville, TN 37202; tel. (615) 327-4074; fax (615) 329-4777; e-mail alembry@alembryinternational.com; website www.alembryinternational.com; Owner/Pres. Al Embry.

All Access Entertainment: 425 Madison Ave, Ste 802, New York, NY 10017; Mans Brian Doyle, Richard Flynn, Amy McFarland.

Alliance Artists Ltd: Suite 220, 3423 Piedmont Rd NE, Atlanta, GA 30305; Contact Charlie Brusco.

Allman Brothers Band: 18 Tamworth Rd, Waban, MA 02168; Man. Bert Holman.

Ambassador Artist Agency: PO Box 50358, Nashville, TN 37205; tel. (615) 370-4700; fax (615) 661-4344; e-mail wes@ambassadoragency.com; website www.ambassadoragency.com; Pres. Wes Yoder.

American Band Management: PO Box 840607, Houston, TX 77284-0607; Pres. John Blomstrom Sr.

Amethyst Group Ltd: 273 Chippewa Dr., Columbia, SC 29210-6508; Chair. C. G. Butler.

Andon Artists: 79 Farview Farm Rd, W Redding, CT 06896; Owner/Man. Arma Andon.

Angelus Entertainment: 9016 Wilshire Blvd, Suite 346, Beverly Hills, CA 90211; Man. Pete Angelus.

Art Collins Management: PO Box 561, Pine Bush, NY 12566; Man. Art Collins.

Artists International Management—AIM: PO Box 2146, Morristown, NJ 07962-2146; tel. (973) 538-0302; fax (973) 734-1737; e-mail aimartists@aol.com; Exec. Dir Birgit Schmid-Salm.

Artist Representation & Management: 1257 Arcade St, St Paul, MN 55106; tel. (651) 483-8754; fax (651) 776-6338; e-mail ra@armentertainment.com; website www.armentertainment.com; Office Man./Agent Roger Anderson.

Atomic Communications Group: 10553 W Jefferson Blvd, Culver City, CA 90232; CEO Gabriel LeConte.

Barron Entertainment: 209 10th Ave S, Suite 232, Nashville, TN 37203; Contact Jay Barron.

Barry Bergman Management: 350 E 30th St, Ste 4D, New York, NY 10016; Man. Barry Bergman.

Baruck/Consolo Management: 15003 Greenleaf St, Sherman Oaks, CA 91403; Contact John Baruck, Tom Consolo.

Bet-Car Management: 307 Lake St, San Francisco, CA 94118; Contact Ora Harris.

Big FD Entertainment: 10801 National Blvd, Suite 530, Los Angeles, CA 90064; Pres. Doug Goldstein.

Bill Graham Management: PO Box 429094, San Francisco, CA 94142-9094; Owner Bill Graham.

Bill Sammeth Organization: PO Box 960, Beverly Hills, CA 90213; Pres. Bill Sammeth.

Bill Thompson Management: 2051 Third St, San Francisco, CA 94107; Man. Bill Thompson.

BJM: 250 W 57th St, Suite 603–5, New York, NY 10107; Man. Paul Korzilius.

Blanton/Harrell Entertainment: 2910 Poston Ave, Nashville, TN 37203; Mans Michael Blanton, Dan Harrell.

Blowin' Smoke Management & Bookings: 7438 Shoshone Ave, Van Nuys, CA 91406-2340; tel. (818) 881-9888; fax (818) 881-0555; e-mail blowinsmokeband.com; website www.blowinsmokeband.com; Pres. Larry Weisberg.

BMP Artist Management: PO Box 1703, La Mirada, CA 90637; Contact Brian A. Mayes.

Bobby Roberts Co: PO Box 1547, Goodlettsville, TN 37070-1547; tel. (615) 859-8899; fax (615) 859-2200; e-mail info@bobbyroberts.com; Pres. Bobby Roberts.

Borman Entertainment: 9220 Sunset Blvd, Suite 320, Los Angeles, CA 90069; Pres. Gary Borman.

Brock & Assocs Management: 201 Seaboard Lane, Franklin, TN 37067; Pres. Darlene Brock.

Brokaw Co: 9255 Sunset Blvds, Suite 804, Los Angeles, CA 90069; Mans David Brokaw, Sandy Brokaw, Joel Brokaw.

Brothers Productions: 141 Dunbar Ave, Fords, NJ 08863; tel. (908) 738-0880; fax (908) 738-0970.

BTB Management Group: PO Box 3509, Westport, CT 06880; Contact Dee Anthony, Joshua Simons.

Budd Carr Co Inc: 9320 Wilshire Blvd, Suite 200, Beverly Hills, CA 90212; Contact Marni Feenberg.

Bullet Entertainment: 120 N Victory, Suite 102, Burbank, CA 91052; Contacts Karmen Beck, Gary Bird.

Bust It Management: 80 Swan Way, Suite 130, Oakland, CA 94621; CEO Louis Burrell.

C & M Productions Management Group: 5114 Albert Dr., Brentwood, TN 37027; tel. (615) 371-5098; fax (615) 371-5317; e-mail rwcotton@mindspring.com; website www.c-m-production.com; Pres. Ronald Cotton.

C M S Management: 627 Main St, Simpson, PA 18407; Vice-Pres. Carl Candy.

C. Winston Simone Management: 1790 Broadway, 10th Floor, New York, NY 10019; CEO C. Winston Simone.

Carr-Sharpe Entertainment Services: 9320 Wilshire Blvd, Suite 200, Beverly Hills, CA 90212; Partners Budd Carr, Wil Sharpe.

Class Act Entertainment: PO Box 160236, Nashville, TN 37216; tel. (615) 262-6886.

Columbia Artists Management: 165 W 57th St, New York, NY 10019; tel. (212) 841-9686; fax (212) 841-9500; Chair. Ronald Wilford.

Concrete Management: 301 W 53rd St, Suite 11D, New York, NY 10019; Contact Andy Gould.

Courage Management: 2899 Agoura Rd, Suite 562, Westlake, CA 91361; Man. John Courage.

Craig H. Berlin CPA: 1650 Broadway, Suite 510, New York, NY 10019; Principal C. Berlin.

Crossfire Productions: 1209 Baylor St, Austin, TX 78703-4123; Pres. Vicky Moerbe.

Curtis Management: 417 Denny Way, Second Floor, Seattle, WA 98109-4934; Contact Kelly Curtis.

DAS Communications: 83 Riverside Dr., New York, NY 10024; Contacts David Sonenberg, Bernard Alexander.

David Lefkowitz Management: 3470 19th St, San Francisco, CA 94110; Owner David Lefkowitz.

Depth of Field Management: 1501 Broadway, Suite 1304, New York, NY 10036; Pres. Darryl Pitt.

Diamondback-Great Pyramid (Musics): PO Box 170040, San Francisco, CA 94117; Owner Joseph Buchwald.

Dream Street Management: 1460 Fourth St, Suite 205, Santa Monica, CA 90401; Man. Ed Gerrard.

Dynamic Productions Inc: 11410 W Wisconsin Ave, Wauwatosa, WI 53226; Vice-Pres. Arthur Greinke.

Earth Tracks Artists: 4809 Ave N, Suite 286, Brooklyn, NY 11234; Man. Dir David Krinsky.

East End Management: 8209 Melrose Ave, Second Floor, Los Angeles, CA 90046; Man. Tony Dimitriades.

Endangered Species Artists Management: PO Box 20469, Columbus Circle Station, New York, NY 10023-1485; Pres. Fred Porter.

Erv Woolsey Co: 1000 18th Ave S, Nashville, TN 37212; tel. (615) 329-2402; fax (615) 327-4917; e-mail erv@ervwoolsey.com; CEO Erv Woolsey.

ESP Management: 888 Seventh Ave, Suite 2904, New York, NY 10106-0001; Pres. Bud Prager.

Famous Artist Agency: 1700 Broadway, Fifth Floor, New York, NY 10019; tel. (212) 245-3939; Pres. Jerry Ade; Man. David Zedeck.

Firstars: 3520 Hayden Ave, Culver City, CA 90232; Man. Miles Copeland.

Fitzgerald-Hartley Co: 50 W Main St, Ventura, CA 93001; Mans Larry Fitzgerlad, Mark Hartley.

Gallin-Morey Assocs: 345 N Maple Dr., Suite 300, Beverly Hills, CA 90210; Chair. Sandy Gallin; Pres. Jim Morey.

Gold Mountain Entertainment: Suite 450, 3575 Cahuenga Blvd W, Los Angeles, CA 90068; Pres. Ron Stone.

Greco Holdings Inc: Market St Sq., 33 Wilkes Barre Blvd, Wilkes Barre, PA 18701; Pres./CEO Thom Greco.

Grrr Records: 920 W Wilson Ave, Chicago, IL 60640; Publicity/Retail Man. Shelley Needham; Booking Man. Diane Borden.

Hallmark Direction Co: 1905 Broadway, Nashville, TN 37203; Artist Co-ordinator Donna Hysmith.

Hard To Handle Management: 640 Lee Rd, Suite 106, Wayne, PA 19087; Contact Steve Barnett.

Heart Music Inc: PO Box 160326, Austin, TX 78716-0326; Promotion Dir Karen Biller.

Heartwrite Music: PO Box 1739, Texarkana, AR 75504; Pres. David Patillo.

Herbie Herbert Management: 2051 Third St, San Francisco, CA 94107; Contact Herbie Herbert.

HK Management: 8900 Wilshire Blvd, Suite 300, Beverly Hills, CA 90211; Man. Howard Kaufman.

Imani Entertainment Inc: PO Box 150-139, Brooklyn, NY 11215; Dir Guy Anglade.

Industrial Management: 3450 Third St, 2A Suite 300, San Francisco, CA 94124-1402; Pres. Chris Coyle.

J & D Music Services Ltd: 38 W 21st St, Fifth Floor, New York, NY 10010-6906; Pres. Jerome Hershman.

Jerry Kravat Entertainment Services (JKES) Inc: 404 Park Ave, New York, NY 10016; Contact Stan Scottland.

Joe Granda Management: 13644 SW 142nd Ave, Suite D, Miami, FL 33186; Pres. Joe Granda.

Joseph Buchwald: PO Box 347008, San Francisco, CA 94134; Contact Joseph Buchwald.

Ken Adamany Assocs: 1818 Parmenter St, Suite 202, Middleton, WI 53562; Contact Ken Adamany.

Kragen & Co: 1112 N Sherbourne Dr., Los Angeles, CA 90069; Contact Ken Kragen.

Kurfirst/Blackwell Entertainment: 601 W 26th St, 11th Floor, New York, NY 10001; tel. (212) 320-3680; fax (212) 320-3689; website www.kurfirst-blackwellentertainment.com; Pres. Gary Kurfirst.

Landmark Communications Group: PO Box 1444, Hendersonville, TN 37077; Pres. Bill Anderson Jr.

Legend Artists: 120 W 44th St, Suite 404, New York, NY 10036; Pres. Joe Boyland.

Lippman Entertainment: 8900 Wilshire Blvd, Suite 340, Beverly Hills, CA 90211-1906; Contact Michael Lippman, Terry Lippman.

Lone Wolf Management: PO Box 163390, Austin, TX 78716; Pres. Bill Ham.

Lookout Management: 2644 30th St, First Floor, Santa Monica, CA 90405; Contact Frank Gironda, Elliot Roberts.

Louis Levin Management: 130 W 57th St, Suite 10B, New York, NY 10019; Pres. Louis Levin.

Madhouse Management: PO Box 15108, Ann Arbor, MI 48106; Contact Doug Banker.

Management By Jaffe: 1560 Broadway, Suite 1103, New York, NY 10036; tel. (212) 869-6912; fax (212) 869-7102; e-mail jerjaf@aol.com; website www.jocymcintyre.com; Pres. Jerry Jaffe.

Management Network: 19430 Ventura Blvd, Suite 205, Sherman Oaks, CA 91403; Contact Gerry Tolman.

Mark A. Abbattista: 1875 Century Park E, Seventh Floor, Los Angeles, CA 90067; Contact Mark 'Abba' Abbattista.

Mark Alan Agency: PO Box 21323, St Paul, MN 55121; Pres. Mark Alan.

Maxine S. Harvard Unlimited: Commerce Center, 2227 US Highway 1, #251, N Brunswick, NJ 08902; Man. Maxine S. Harvard.

McFadden Artists: 818 18th Ave S, Nashville, TN 37203; Chairs Jack McFadden, Jo McFadden.

McCraw Management: 1830 E Kane Pl., Suite 3, Milwaukee, WI 53202; Man. Mark McCraw.

Metropolitan Entertainment: 7 N Mountain Ave, Montclair, NJ 07042; Contact Robert Kos.

Mirkin Management: 906½ Congress Ave, Austin, TX 78701; tel. (512) 472-1818; fax (512) 472-6915; Owner Jan Mirkin.

Moress Nanas Entertainment: 12424 Wilshire Blvd, Suite 840, Los Angeles, CA 90025; Partner Herb Nanas.

Music Man Productions: 568 Snelling Ave N, Suite 106, St Paul, MN 55104; Owners Paul Manske, Steve York.

Music Umbrella: PO Box 1067, Santa Monica, CA 90406; Pres./CEO Glenn H. Friedman.

Nettwerk Management: (Los Angeles) Suite 304, 8730 Wilshire Blvd, Beverly Hills, CA 90211; tel. (310) 855-0643; fax (310) 855-0658; (New York) 345 Seventh Ave, 24th Floor, New York, NY 10001; tel. (212) 760-1540; fax (212) 760-9719; website www.nettmanagement.com.

Niji Management: Suite 307, 18653 Ventura Blvd, Tarzana, CA 91356; Pres. Wendy Dio.

Nippy Inc: 2160 N Central Rd, Fort Lee, NJ 07024-7547; CEO John Houston.

Oasis Management: 3010 E Bloomfield, Phoenix, AZ 85032; Man. Gloria Cavalera.

Open Door Management: 15327 Sunset Blvd, Suite 365, Pacific Palisades, CA 90272; Pres. Bill Traut.

Panacea Entertainment: 2705 Glendower Ave, Los Angeles, CA 90027; Chair./CEO Eric Garoner.

Peter Asher Management: 644 N Doheny Dr., Los Angeles, CA 90069; Pres. Ira Koslow.

Pilot Management Co: PO Box 23203, Nashville, TN 37202; Pres. Johnson Bell.

Platinum Gold Productions: 9200 Sunset Blvd, Suite 1220, Los Angeles, CA 90069; Partner Steve Cohen.

PPL-MCI Entertainment Group: 10 Universal Plaza, PO Box 8442, Universal City, CA 91618; tel. (818) 506-8533; fax (818) 506-8534; e-mail pplzmi@aol.com; website www.pplzmi.com; CEO Jaeson St James Jarrett; Man. Dir Maxx Diamond.

Precision Management: 825 N King St, Suite A-1, Hampton, VA 23669-2814; Operations Man. Cappriccieo M. Scates.

Premier Artist Services: 1401 University Dr., Suite 305, Coral Springs, FL 33071; Pres. Eliot H. Weisman.

Premier Productions: 1909 N Spruce, Wichita, KS 67214; Owner Anthony Welch.

Production Group International: 2200 Wilson Blvd, Suite 200, Arlington, VA 22201; Pres. Ed Yoe.

Q-Prime Inc: 729 Seventh Ave, 14th Floor, New York, NY 10019; Co-Pres Cliff Burnstein, Peter Mensch.

Quango Music Group Inc: 9744 Wilshire Blvd, Suite 305, Beverly Hills, CA 90212; Pres. George Ghiz.

Quiet Storm Inc: 103 Westward Dr., Miami Springs, FL 33166; Contact Carl C. Valldejuli.

Ralph Mercado Management: 568 Broadway, Suite 806, New York, NY 10012; Pres. Ralph Mercado.

REM/Athens Ltd: PO Box 8032, Athens, GA 30603; Contact Bertis E. Downs, W. Jefferson Holt.

Remington Management Inc: 6602 Harbor Town, Suite 501, Houston, TX 77036; Pres. Janice D. Hayes.

Rick Levy Management: 1881 S Kirkman Rd, 715, Orlando, FL 32811; Pres. Rick Levy.

Roger Davies Management: 15030 Ventura Blvd, Suite 772, Sherman Oaks, CA 91403; Man. Roger Davies.

Ron Weisner Entertainment: 9200 Sunset Blvd, PH 15, Los Angeles, CA 90069; Man. Ron Weisner.

Rosebud Agency: PO Box 170429, San Francisco, CA 94117; tel. (415) 386-3456; fax (415) 386-0599; e-mail info@rosebudus.com; website www.rosebudus.com; Pres. Mike Kappus.

Rustron-Whimsong Music Productions: c/o The Whimsy, 1156 Park Lane, West Palm Beach, FL 33417; tel. and fax (561) 478-8315; e-mail safehavenwpb@yahoo.com; Exec. Dir/Owner Rusty Gordon.

Ruth Blakely Management: 610 Players Ct, Nashville, TN 37211; CEO Ruth Blakely.

Siddons & Assocs: 584 N Larchmont Blvd, Los Angeles, CA 90004; Pres. Bill Siddons.

Slatus Management: 208 E 51st St, New York, NY 10022; Man. Teddy Slater.

SRO Artists Inc: 6629 University Ave, Suite 206, Middleton, WI 53562; Pres. Jeff Laramie.

Stiefel Phillips Entertainment: 9720 Wilshire Blvd, Fourth Floor, Beverly Hills, CA 90212; Mans Arnold Stiefel, Randy Phillips.

Stilleto Entertainment: 5443 Beethoven St, Los Angeles, CA 90066; Partners Edna Collison, Garry Kief, Steve Wax.

Surface Entertainment & Management: PO Box 2935, Church St Station, New York, NY 10008; website www.surfacemgmt.com; Contact Pam Beninon.

Susan Silver Management: 207½ First Ave S, Suite 300, Seattle, WA 98104; Owner Susan Silver.

Suzi Reynolds & Assocs: 200 Rector Pl., Suite 7H, New York, NY 10280; Dir Suzi Reynolds.

Talent House: 7211 Santa Monica, Suite 200, Los Angeles, CA 90046; Pres. Staci Slater.

Ted Kurland Assocs: 173 Brighton Ave, Boston, MA 02134; tel. (617) 254-0007; fax (617) 782-3524; e-mail ted@tedkurland.com; website www.tedkurland.com; Pres. Ted Kurland.

Ten Ten Management: 33 Music Sq. W, Suite 110, Nashville, TN 37203; Pres. Barry Coburn.

Thames Talent: 45 E Putnam Ave, Greenwich, CT 06830; Man. Bruce Payne.

Third Rail Entertainment: 9169 Sunset Blvd, Los Angeles, CA 90069; Contact Bob Cavallo.

Top Rock Development Corpn: 6399 Wilshire Blvd, Suite 1001, Los Angeles, CA 90049; Mans Doug Thaler, Stephanie Gurevitz.

Troubadour Entertainment: 5305 Barton Vale Ct, Nashville, TN 37211-8404; Pres. Tony Lee.

Turi's Music: 103 Westward Dr., Miami Springs, FL 33166; Contact Carl C. Valldejuli.

Umpire Entertainment Enterprises: 1507 Scenic Dr., Longview, TX 75604; Pres. Jerry Haymes.

Up Front Management: 1906 Seward Dr., Pittsburg, CA 94565; CEO Charles Coke; Vice-Pres. Terry Pitts.

Vector Management: PO Box 128037, Nashville, TN 37212; Man. Ken Levitan.

Warren Entner Management: 5550 Wilshire Blvd, Suite 302, Los Angeles, CA 90036; Pres. Warren Entner.

Westwood Entertainment Group: 1115 Inman Ave, Suite 330, Edison, NJ 08820-1132; Gen. Man. Elena Petillo.

Wolgemath & Hyatt Inc: 8012 Brooks Chapel Rd, Suite 243, Brentwood, TN 37027; Artist Man. John Mallory.

Woodrich Enterprises Inc: PO Box 38, Lexington, AL 35648; e-mail mernee@msn.com; Pres. Woody Richardson.

Zane Management: The Land Title Bldg, 100 S Broad St, Suite 630, Philadelphia, PA 19110; tel. (215) 640-9770; fax (215) 640-9769; e-mail lzr@remick-martone.com; website www.zanemanagement.com; Pres., CEO Lloyd Zane Remick.

Uruguay

ABT Producciones: 25 de Mayo 544, 2°, Montevideo; Dir Adolfo Brun Thielman.

Edmundo Klinger-Garcia Rial Asscn: Avda Garibaldi 2748, PO Box 203, Montevideo; Dir Edmundo Klinger.

San Martín Producciones: José Enrique Rodó 1661, PO Box 401, 11200 Montevideo; Dir Eduardo San Martín.

Venezuela

Carlos Cassina: Avda Lecuna, Edif. El Tjar 3, PO Box E Parque Central, Caracas; Contact Carlos Cassina.

Fonart SA: Avda Caurimare, Ctro Caroní MA, Of. A-26, Col. del Bello Monte, 1041 Caracas; Vice-Pres. Antonio Sánchez G.

Producciones Maria Gómez: PO Box 50 158, 1050 A, Caracas; Dir Maria Gómez.

Representaciones Billo SA: Avda Paez, Res. Verónica 7°, PO Box C, El Paraíso, Caracas; Pres. Amable Frómente.

Sonia Guedez: Multicentro Empresarial del Este, Edif. Miranda Nucleo A, 4, Of. 47-A, Caracas; Contact Sonia Guedez

APPENDIX C: BOOKING AGENTS AND PROMOTERS

Andorra

RIAL Andorra: Avda de Tarragona 24, Andorra La Vella; tel. 860686; fax 866286; e-mail rial@andorra.ad; Man. Pascal Lair.

Argentina

Abraxas Producciones Internacionales: Avda Callao 875, 4° H, 1023 Buenos Aires; Dir-Gen. Carlos Pity Yñurrigarro.

Aisenberg & Asociados: Juncal 3361, 6°, Of. C, 1425 Buenos Aires; Dir Chiche Aisenberg.

Dario Arellano Producciones: San Gerónimo 2005, 3000 Santa Fe; Dir Dario Arellano.

Felix Marín & Asociados: Talcahuano 68, 6°, Of. D, 1013 Buenos Aires; Dir Felix Marín.

Fernando Moya Producciones: Heredia 1425, 1427 Buenos Aires; Dir Fernando Moya.

Hector Cavallero Producciones SA: Hipólito Irigoyen 1994, PB 4, 1089 Buenos Aires; Pres. Fernando Cavallero; Contact Hector Cavallero.

Kralendijk Producciones: Sánchez de Bustamente 444, 5°, Dpto 1, 1173 Buenos Aires; Pres. Alejandro Solignac.

Matt Hungo Srl: Tucumán 1455, 5°, Of. A–B, 1050 Buenos Aires; Gen. Man. Omar Alberto Lauria.

Ohanian Producciones: Aguilar 2073, 1428 Buenos Aires; tel. (11) 4788-4605; Dir Alberto Ohanian.

Poggini & Asociados: Pasteur 250, 1°, Of. C, 1028 Buenos Aires; tel. (11) 4952-5088; fax (11) 4954-1477; e-mail info@poggini.com.ar; website www.poggini.com.ar; Contacts Rodolfo Poggini, Claudio Poggin.

Rock & Pop Internacional: Zapiola 1625, 1427 Buenos Aires; Dir Daniel Grinbank.

TM Producciones: Nicaragua 4994, 1425 Buenos Aires; Dir Raúl Fernández.

Australia

A R E The Entertainment Co: 186 Glen Osmond Rd, Fullarton, SA 5063; Dir Mark Draper.

Abracadabra Event Co: 186 Glen Osmond Rd, Fullarton, SA 5063; Dir Brian Gleeson.

Adrian Bohm Presents Pty Ltd: 44 Fourth Ave, St Peters, SA 5069; tel. (8) 8363-0212; fax (8) 8363-1231; e-mail promoter@abpresents.com.au; Dir Adrian Bohm.

Andrew Dinwoodie Management: PO Box 5052, Victoria Point, Qld 4165; tel. (7) 3207-0502; e-mail adinwoodie@redland.net.au.

ATA Allstar Artists Pty Ltd: 98 Glebe Point, Glebe, NSW 2037; tel. (612) 9660 3466; fax (612) 9552 3027; Dirs Tony Brady, Kevin Jacobsen.

Australian Variety Artists: PO Box 300, Kings Cross, NSW 2011; Agents Dez Dalton, Suzanne Terry.

B & S Promotions: PO Box 1481, Frankston, Vic. 3199; Partners Bill Dettmer, Sally Dettmer.

Cheersquad: PO Box 4153, East Richmond, Vic. 3121; Contact Wally Kempton.

Chevy's Entertainment Booking Agency: PO Box 380W, Smithfield West, NSW 2164; tel. and fax (612) 9822-9105; e-mail chevys@zeta.org.au; Man. Mario J. Borg.

Class Entertainment Organization Pty Ltd: PO Box 169, Sutherland, NSW 2232; Man. Dir Ron Ragel.

Cranium Management: PO Box 240, Annadale, NSW 2038; e-mail cranium@internet.com.au.

Entertainers Pty Ltd: 48 Millswood Cr, Millswood, SA 5034; Man. Dir Ivan Tanner.

Feel Management & Tour Co-ordination: 2/54 Bronte Rd, Bondi Junction, NSW 2022; Dir Tim Pittman.

Harbour Agency Pty Ltd: 135 Forbes St, Woolloomooloo, NSW 2011; tel. (612) 9331 5888; fax (612) 9331 2296; website www.theharbouragency.com; Man. Dir Sam Righi.

Heart Beat Promotions: 10 Raggatt St, Alice Springs, NT 0870; Man. Matthew Guggisberg.

International Management Group: 281 Clarence St, Sydney, NSW 2000; Dir of Arts & Entertainment Stephen Flint Wood.

Jaybee's Entertainment Agency: PO Box 37, Sanctuary Pl., NSW 2540; tel. (612) 4443 3422; fax (612) 4443 9968; e-mail jaybees@jaybees.com.au; website www.jaybees.com.au; Man. Narrell M. Brown.

Lynne James & Assocs: PO Box 511, Lane Cove, Sydney, NSW 2066; tel. (612) 9419 7822; fax (612) 9419 2265; website www.lynnejames.com.au; Man. Dir Lynne James.

Mario Maicho Promotions Pty Ltd: PO Box 572, North Adelaide, SA 5006; Sec./Tour Co-ordinator Margaret Rudge.

Melke (Artist Representation & Media Co-ordination): 158 Raglan St, Mosman, Sydney, NSW 2088; Dir Sue Melke.

Michael Coppel Presents: 716–718 High St, Armadale, Vic. 3143; tel. (613) 9509 7666; website www.coppel.com.au; Man. Dir Michael Coppel.

Mr Walker's Co: 13 Victoria Ave, Albert Park, Vic. 3206; tel. (613) 9645-7300; fax (613) 9645-7311; e-mail mrwalkersco@peg.apc.org.

Opulent Music Entertainment: PO Box 270, 48 David Cres., Bundoora, Vic. 3083; Man. Dir Anthony Chidiac.

Paul Cussen Management: Suite 1, Level 2, 41 Oxford St, Darlinghurst, NSW 2010; Proprietor Paul Cussen.

Pegasus Event Management Pty Ltd: The Hills Centre, Carrington Rd, Castle Hill, NSW 2154; Man. Dir Christopher Rix.

Phill Shute Management Pty Ltd: PO Box 273, Dulwich Hill, NSW 2203; Man. Dir Phill Shute.

Pinewood Records and Promotions: 3 Hessel Pl., Emu Heights, NSW 2750; tel. (2) 6742-1543; fax (2) 6742-0249; e-mail ianb@pinewoodrecords.com.au; website www.pinewoodrecords.com.au; Man. Dir Ian B. MacLeod.

Premier Artists Pty Ltd: 9 Dundas Lane, Albert Park, Vic. 3206; Man. Dir Frank Stivala.

RPM Management Services Pty Ltd: 205 Commonwealth St, Surry Hills, Sydney, NSW; tel. (612) 9281-9500; fax (612) 9281-0439; e-mail rpm@zip.com.au.

Servant Communications: PO Box 2020, Launceston, Tasmania 7250; Pres. Kevin N. Hooper.

Shawthing Entertainment: Entertainment Pl., PO Box 4, Broadway, Qld 4006; Man. John Maher.

Sphere Organization: Suite 15, 835 Pennant Hills Rd, Carlingford, NSW 2118; tel. (2) 9872-4144; fax (2) 9872-3992; e-mail sphere@sphereorg.com.au; website www.sphereorg.com.au; Dir and Man. Eric 'Chubby' Carlini.

Sun Promotions: PO Box 192, West Ryde, Sydney, NSW 2114; Reggae Promoter/Venue Consultant Ted Vassell.

Trading Post Entertainments Agency: PO Box 124, Round Corner, Sydney, NSW 2158; Man. Dir/Booking Agent Owen Orford.

Austria

Austrian International Artist Agency: M. Felder str 5, 6900 Bregenz; Man. Dir Viktor Pamminger.

Live Performance Service: Esteplatz 3/13, 1030 Vienna; Pres. Fritz Thom.

Memphis Music Concerts: Sleveringerstr 194, 1190 Vienna; Man. Dir Wolfgang Bergelt.

Milica: Liebhartstalstr 15/5, 1160 Vienna; Contact Milica.

RATZ Promotions: Vorachstr 65, 6890 Lustenau; Contact Thomas Radovan.

Rock Produktion West: Bregenzerstr 73, 6900 Bregenz; Man. Dir Alex Nussbaumer.

RoCo Management: Huetteldorfer str 257C, 1140 Vienna; Owner Roland Colerus.

Stein Music Wien: Bernardgasse 39/33, 1070 Vienna; Man. Dir Regine Steinmetz.

Wien Concerts: Margaretenstr 78, 1050 Vienna; Man. Dir Jeff Maxian.

Belarus

Beloton Records: Shrader str 8-15, Vitebsk 210015; Dir Vladimir Sartchenko.

Belgium

AALN International: PO Box 15, Antwerpen 17, 2018 Antwerp; Man. Dir Luc Nuitten; Jazz, blues and world music events.

ArteFacts: Bosweg 4A, 2220 Heist-op-den-Berg; tel. (320) 1524-8896; fax (320) 1525-1708; e-mail artefacts@pandora.be.

Backline: Kammerstraat 19, 9000 Ghent; Man. Robert Van Yper; Bookings Agents Sandra Heylen, Lawrence Van Den Eede.

Boom!: Bergensesteenweg 19, 1500 Halle; tel. 2360-2851; website www.jpvan.be; Man. Dir J. P. Van.

Centre Culturel de la Communaute Francaise: Wallonie Bruxelles le Botanique, rue Royale 236, 1210 Brussels; Contact Paul-Henri Wauters.

CPA (Country Programmers' Asscn): St Pieterstraat 34/2, 2400 Mol; Pres. Eric Van De Mert.

Euro Promo Music: 5 Sq. de Noville, 1080 Brussels; Chair. Hans Piccini.

Flinter Music: PO Box 15, Antwerp 17, 2018 Antwerp; tel. (320) 3248-0376; fax (320) 3248-3186; e-mail FlinterM@www.dma.be; website www.dma.be.

Foundation VZW: Fruithoflaan 124, PO Box 11, 2600 Berchem/Antwerp; Dirs Peter Verstraeven, Bert Van Roy.

Kras Artists: Leernsesteenweg 168, 9800 Deinze; Dir Jean Tant.

L&S Agency: PO Box 5, 3800 Sint-Truiden 2; tel. 11671701; fax 11673331; e-mail lsagency@belgacom.net; website www.lsagency.be; Man. Dir Mark Strauven.

Les Fruits de la Passion Asbl: Pl. du Nord 3, 4000 Liege; tel. 495546089; fax 42234848; Man. Dir Bernard Hemblenne; Concert promotor.

Merlijn: Gulden Vlieslaan 67, 8000 Brugge; Contact Nico A. Mertens.

Music BaM: Lelielaan 11, 2460 Lichtaart; Man. Dir Gert Van Dingenen; Asst Man. Dir Tom van Dingenen.

Paperwork: Aarschotsesteenweg 245, 3012 Wilsele; Man. Johan P. Berckmans.

Pyramid International Music: Lepelhoekstraat 26, 9100 Sint-Niklaas; tel. (3) 778-1854; fax (3) 766-8441; e-mail marc@marcdecoen.be; website www.marcdecoen.be; Man. Dir Marc De Coen.

Rainbow Records & Music: Herentaesesteenweg 20A, 2220 Heist-Op-Den Berg; tel. 1524-4950; fax 1524-1470; Contact Kathleen Gossens.

Show Organisation: Drève du Prophète 23A, 7000 Mons; Man. Dir George Hayes.

Swing Promotions: Beukenlaan 3, 2970 Schilde; Man. Wim Groos.

Tour de Force: Rue des Archers 19–21, 1080 Brussels; Man. Dir Ton Van Draanen.

Tsahara Productions: Vijverstraat 111, 1040 Brussels; tel. (2) 513-7599; fax (2) 513-3526.

TTT: Vriesenhof 22/5, 3000 Leuven; Mans Rick Tubbax, Johan P. Berckmans.

Witlof: Leernsesteenweg 168, 9800 Deinze; Dir Jean Tant.

Zig Zag World: Rue P. E. Janson 9, 1050 Brussels; tel. (2) 537-2525; fax (2) 538-1117; e-mail zzworld@pophost.eunet.be.

Bolivia

HR Producciones: Loayza 349, 15°, Dpto 1503, Edif. Loayza, La Paz; Gen. Man. Nestor Horacio Rasgido.

Brazil

Ciranda Productions: Rua Lagoa dos Gatos 511, Janga-Paulista-PE, 53437, Olinda, PE; tel. (83) 9302-4222; e-mail iran.gomes@berlin.de; Contacts Iran Gomes, Regina del Papa.

Bulgaria

Arsis Productions: 15 Tsarigradsko Chausse Blvd, 1220 Sofia; Chair. Velizar Sokolov.

Mega Music Ltd: 2 Trapezitza str, 1000 Sofia; Man. Dir Dora Tchernkva.

New Music Agency: Nadejda Bl 634, Apt 14, 1231 Sofia; tel. 9825-6509; fax 2934-4297; e-mail christ@newmusic.bg; website www.newmusic.bg; Pres. Christo Roussanov.

Sofia Music Enterprise: 15 Ivan Rilski str, 1000 Sofia; Man. Dir Dimitur Kovachev.

Sofiaconcert Artistic Agency: Volov 3, 1527 Sofia; Man. Jeanna Mollova.

Canada

Alert Music Inc: 41 Britain St, Suite 305, Toronto, ON M5A 1R7; tel. (416) 364-4200; fax (416) 364-8632; e-mail alert@inforamp.net.

Am-Can International Talent Inc: 9615 Macleod Trail S, Calgary, AB T2J 0P6; Vice-Pres. Dir of Sales Frank Scott.

Amok Artist Agency: PO Box 21, Fergus, ON N1M 2W7; tel. (519) 787-1100; fax (519) 787-0084; website www.amokmusic.ca; Contact Lorenz Eppinger.

August Music: 4 Maple Lead Lane, Aberfoyle, ON N1H 6H9; Gen. Man. Paul Embro.

Bandstand (International Entertainment Agency): PO Box 1010, Simcoe, ON N3Y 5B3; tel. (519) 426-0000; fax (519) 426-3799; e-mail elliot@simcom.on.ca; website www.netaccess.on.ca/-Kellis; Pres. Wayne Elliot.

Big Time Productions Ltd: 54 Duncombe Dr, Lower Level, Hamilton, ON L9A 2G2; tel. (905) 389-4265; e-mail JohnyB@pathcom.com; Pres. and CEO John Balogh Jr.

BWL Entertainment Connection: 19 Acadia Cres., St Catharines, ON L2P 1H7; Contact Bruce Lilley.

Community Box Offices: 1234 W Hastings St, Vancouver, BC V6E 2M4.

Entercom: 372 Richmond St W, Suite 205, ON M5V 1X6; tel. (416) 598-3330; fax (416) 598-5428.

ESP-Elwood Saracuse Productions: 144 Holcolm Rd, Toronto, ON M2N 2E2; tel. (416) 222-5515; fax (416) 730-8973; website www.espentertainment.com; Pres. Elwood Saracuse.

Festival City Folk Guild: 508 Brunswick St, Stratford, ON N5A 3N6; Dir Beth Beech.

Firestar Promotions Inc: PO Box 165, 1896 W Broadway, Vancouver, BC V6J 1Y9.

Gino Empry Entertainment: 315-120 Carlton St, Toronto, ON M5A 4K2; Owner Gino Empry.

MBH Music Management: PO Box 1096, Hudson, QC J0P 1H0; tel. (613) 780-1163; e-mail larecord@total.net; website www.radiofreedom.com.

Joanne Smale Productions Ltd: 51 Bulwer St, Main Level, Toronto, ON M5T 1A1; Pres. Joanne Smale.

KISS Talent Referrals: 19695, 56th Ave, Langley, BC, V3A 3X7; Man./ Agent Shannon M. Myers.

Lenthall & Assocs: Falcon Ave, Suite 2-2447, Ottawa, ON K1V 8C8; tel. (613) 738-2373; fax (613) 523-7941.

Magnum Music Corpn Ltd: 8607-128 Ave, Edmonton, AB T5E 0G3; tel. (403) 476-8230; fax (403) 472-2584.

More Than Booking: 1819 Granville St, Fourth Floor, Halifax, NS B3J 3R1; Pres. Wayne O'Connor.

Multi-Media Entertainment: 1111 E Victoria Ave, Thunder Bay, ON P7C 1B7; tel. (807) 622-0104; fax (807) 622-3961.

Music Co Entertainment: 31 Hamlet Rd, SW, Calgary, AB T2V 3C9; Pres. Fred Thoutenhoofd.

Nat Raider Productions Inc: 5799 Eldriege Ave, Montréal, QC H4W 2E3; Pres. Nat Raider.

Noteable Entertainment Ltd: 940 Brunette Ave, Coquitlam, BC V3K 1C9; Dir, Country Division Don Buchanan.

Phil's Entertainment Agency Ltd: 889 Smyth Rd, Ottawa, ON K1G 1P4; tel. (613) 731-8983.

Productions Martin Leclerc Inc: 2220 rue Notre-Dame Ouest, Suite 201, Montréal, QC H3J 2V4; Man. Martin Leclerc.

Regal Recordings Ltd: 2421 Hammond Rd, Mississauga, ON L5K 1T3; Vice-Pres. Doreen M. Davey.

RGK Entertainment Group: PO Box 243, Station C, Toronto, ON M6J 3P4; tel. (416) 345-8891; fax (416) 345-8879; e-mail rgkent@netcom.ca.

Rose Concert Productions Inc: PO Box 23053, London, ON N6A 5N9; Promoter David Rose.

Sheldon Kagan International: 35 McConnell Dorval, Québec, QC H9S 5L9; tel. (514) 631-2160; fax (514) 631-4430; e-mail sheldon@sheldonkagan.com; website www.sheldonkagan.com.

Showcana Corpn: PO Box 4689, Station C, Calgary, AB T2T 5P1; Pres. Robert James Chin.

Siegel Entertainment Ltd: 101-1648 W Seventh Ave, Vancouver, BC V6J 1S5; tel. (604) 736-3896; fax (604) 736-3464; e-mail siegelent@telus.net; website www.siegelent.com; Pres. Robert Siegel.

Silverhawk Publishing: 3073 Cedarbank Rd, Rural Route 11, Peterborough, ON K9J 6Y3; Pres. Jim Freake.

SL Feldman & Assocs: 1505 W Second Ave, Suite 200, Vancouver, BC V6H 3Y4; tel. (604) 734-5945; fax (604) 732-0922; e-mail feldman@slfa.com; website www.slfa.com; Proprietor Sam L. Feldman; Sr Vice-Pres. Shaw Saltzberg.

Sphere Entertainment: 22 Bainsford Rd, Toronto, ON M4L 3N4; Pres. Patricia Silver.

Stella Black Live Music: PO Box 23, St Anne de Belle, QC H9X 3L4; Pres. Stella Black.

Strictly Forbidden Artists: 595 St Clair W, Suite 1, Toronto, ON M6C 1A3; tel. (416) 656-0085; fax (416) 654-9436.

Tiger Entertainment & Promotions: 453 Drew St, Woostock, ON N4S 4V4; tel. and fax (519) 536-9193.

Trick Or Treat Entertainment: 1971 Spruce Hill Rd, Pickering, ON L1V 1S6; Contact Kay White.

Vocal Image Productions: 192 Kensington Rd, Charlottetown, PEI C1A 7S3; Man. Berni Wood.

William Tenn Artist Management: 431-67 Mowat Ave, Toronto, ON M6K 3E3; tel. (416) 534-7763; fax (416) 534-9726; e-mail pmwtm@io.org.

Chile

Galo Producciones: Alameda 171, Of. 807, Santiago; Gen. Man. Alfredo Saint-Jean.

Geomúsica: Paseo Poniente, 4593 El Portal de la Viña, Santiago; Dir Claudio Cáceras.

Prodin Chile SA: Tomas Andrews 089, Comuna de Providencia, Santiago; Exec. Dir Ernesto Claveria.

Producciones Macondo Chile Ltda: Alvarez 58 L-6, Viña Del Mar; Man. Alfredo Troncoso.

Ricardo Suarez Daud y Cia Ltda: La Concepción 81, Of. 405, Providencia, Santiago; Man. Ricardo Suárez Daud.

Romero & Campbell Producciones: Bombero Nuñez, 385 Barrio Bellavista, Santiago; Dir Carmen Romero Quero.

Colombia

Champeta Criolla Internacional: Manuel Reyes Bolanos, Conjunto Residencial La Plazuela, Apt 304b, Cartagena; tel. (575) 660-2488; e-mail champetacriolla@hotmail.com.

Croatia

Best: Jarunska 88, 41000 Zagreb; Man. Dir Mirko Kramaric.

BJ Promotions: D Cesarica 11, 41000 Zagreb; Man. Dir Borislav Jankovic.

Croatian Music Art: Trg S, Radica 4, 41000 Zagreb; Man. Dir Damir Gostl.

Jazzette: Avenija Vukovar 35, 41000 Zagreb Man. Kolja Petrovic.

Promomedia Ltd: Kralja Zvonimira 82, 10 000 Zabreb; Man. Dir Marijan Crnaric.

T R I P: Argentinska 3, 10000 Zagreb; A & R Man. Aleksandar Dragas.

Urban Concert: K Tomislava 30, 42300 Cakovec; Dir Toni Sabol.

Denmark

Arte Booking: Hvidkildevej 64, 2400 Copenhagen NV; tel. (45) 3888-5555; fax (45) 3833-2083; Man. Dir Fimm Thorkildsen.

Basement Productions: PO Box 394, 8900 Randers; tel. (45) 8640-1400; fax (45) 8640-4999; Man. Dir Peter Astrup.

Buks Booking International: Gunløgsgade 15, 2300 Copenhagen; tel. (45) 3296-1092; fax (45) 3295-9491; Dir Thomas H. Hansen.

DKB Concertpromotion Aps: Vester Soegade 44, 1601 Copenhagen V; tel. (45) 3311-8181; fax (45) 3391-2412; Man. Dir Flemming Schmidt.

ET Promotion: Skindergade 8, 1159 Copenhagen K; Man. Dir Ole Dreyer.

International Concert Organization: Rosenborggade 1, 1130 Copenhagen K; tel. 3312-2000; fax 3393-2290; e-mail arne@concerts.dk; website www.concerts.dk; Man. Dir Arne Worsoe.

Musicline: Livjægergade, 2100 Copenhagen O; Contact Niels Christensen.

PDH Dansk Musik Formidling ApS: Ny Vestergade 7, 1471 Copenhagen K; tel. (45) 3311-2200; fax (45) 3333-0020; Man Dir Henrik Seifert.

Rock On International ApS: Rosenorns Alle 6, 4tv, 1634 Copenhagen K; tel. (45) 3537-8100; fax (45) 3537-8111; Man Dir Niels Lindgren.

Soren Hojberg Booking (SHB) ApS: Frodesgade 74, 6700 Esbjerg; e-mail shb@shb-denmark.dk; website www.shb-denmark.dk; Man. Dir Soren Hojberg.

TG Management: Badehusvej 1, 9000 Aalborg; tel. (45) 3375-0400; fax (45) 3375-0375; e-mail tg-management@tg-management.dk; Man. John Aagaard.

Ecuador

William's Convention Center: Los Rios, 920 Y Hurtado, 11692 Guayquil; Gen. Man. William San Andrés.

Estonia

Estonian Jazz Foundation: PO Box 3641, Viru str 16, 0090 Tallinn; Dir Tiit Lauk.

Raivo Pihlak: 2061 Purtse; Owner Raivo Pihlak.

Tallinn Rock Club: Sopruse Pst 219-68, 13414 Tallin; tel. 652-4345; fax 656-3157; Man. Dir Anatoly Belov.

Tartu Jazzclub: Laulupeo 25, 2400 Tartu; Man. Aadu Birnbaum.

Fiji

Communications Fiji Ltd: 23 Stewart St, Suva; Man. Dir William Parkinson.

Finland

Hoedown: Laivurinrinne 2, 00120 Helsinki; tel. (358) 9622-4804; e-mail pap@hoedown.com.

NEM: PO Box 220, 33201 Tampere; Man. Dir Harri Karvinen.

Piikkikasvi Agency: PO Box 145, 00531 Helsinki; Man. Dir Kari Pössi.

Rockadillo: Ilmarisenkatu 12 A2, 33500 Tampere; tel. (358) 3213-1260; fax (358) 3213-1297; e-mail records@rock.pp.fi; website www.rockadillo.fi; Man. Dir Tapio Korjus.

France

Agence Kathoche: 16 rue de Marignan, 75008 Paris; Agent/Dir Catherine Poensin.

Alias: 17 Ave Trudaine, 75009 Paris; Chair. Dominique Revert.

Aquitania Editions—Stars: Domaine de Barry, 33690 Sigalens; Dir Pryl on Lataste.

Atefact: 13 rue du Howald, 67000 Strasbourg; Dir Patrick Schneider.

Blue Line Productions: 5 rue Leon, Giraud, 75019 Paris; tel. (5) 6527-1515; fax (1) 4848-1742; e-mail blueline@wanadoo.fr; website www.blueline.fr; Dir Michel Vautrot.

Caramba! Productions: 7 Pl. de Seoul, 75014 Paris; Dir Luc Gaurichon.

Diogene Productions: Le Grand Kerven, 29200 Brest; Dir Jacques Abalain.

Do Si La Ba: 159 Chemin Lanusse, 31200 Toulouse; Man. Lawrence Larrouy.

Encore Productions: 8 rue de Mont-Thabor, 75001 Paris; Dir Pascal Bernardin.

Festirock Organisation: Parl Tertiaire Dijon Est, 2 bis rue du Cap Vert, 21800 Quetigny; Pres. G. Gras.

Fiesta Latina Homero Cardoso: 51 rue Mirabeau, 94200 Ivry Sur Seine; Promoter Homero Cardoso.

Francophonie Diffusion: 33 rue du Faubourg, Saint-Antoine, 75011 Paris; tel. (1) 5333-3375; fax (1) 4344-3560; e-mail francodiff@francodiff.org; website www.francodiff.org; Dir Marie Christine Bloch.

Leon: 23 rue des Manguiers, 34070 Montpellier; Mans Philippe Maurizi, Sean Herve Michel.

LPI/Isotope Agency: 23 rue Gravette, 31300 Toulouse; Man. Jean Philippe Morer.

L'Usine: 115 rue Lesage, 51100 Reims; Pres. Alain Boucheron.

Meyer Productions: 13 rue Dautancourt, 75017 Paris; tel. (1) 5306-6600; fax (1) 5306-6599; e-mail meyer-productions@imaginet.fr; Mans Olivia Meyer, Christian Meyer.

Noumatrouff/Fédération Hiéro: 57 rue de la Mertzav, 68100 Mulhouse; tel. (3) 8932-9410; fax (3) 8942-0596; e-mail hiero@fede-hiero.com; website www.fede-hiero.com; Dir Lodet-Boisse Simon.

Ripost-Le Bocal Asscn Ripost: 23 Route de Villeflanzy, 41000 Villebarou-Blois; Pres. Denis Tradeau.

Salam Aleikum Amusements: 2 rue Carpeaux, 75018 Paris; Dir Stephane Benhamou.

VMA: 40 rue François 1er; 75008 Paris; Dir Rose Leandri.

Germany

Alba Kultur: Justinianstr. 16, 50679 Cologne; tel. (221) 813211; fax (221) 811053; e-mail albakultur@yalla.de; website www.yalla.de/alba.

Art Concerts GmbH: Widenmayer str 41, 80538 Munich; Dir Franz Abraham.

ASS Concert & Promotion GmbH: PO Box 730225, 22122 Hamburg; Pres Michael Bisping, Diekr Schubert.

Bizarre Productions GmbH: Buelaustr 8, 20099 Hamburg; Man. Dir Christopher Brosch.

Blue Star Promotion Konzertagentur GmbH: Goebenstr 3, 28209 Bremen; Public Relations Michael K. Grusche.

Castor Promotions: Dragonerstr 21, 30163 Hanover; Contact Elke Fleing.

Freestyle eV: Morgensternsweg 7, 22305 Hamburg; Contact Helmut Heuer; Music festival and event organizers.

Freibank: Ditmar-Koel str 26, 20459 Hamburg; Dirs Mark Chung, Klaus Maeck.

Harde & Partner: Unter de Linde 20, 80939 Munich; Owner Jasmine Harde.

Harry Fox: Steinstr 53, 81667 Munich; Contact Harry Fox.

Hello Concerts GmbH: Philippine-Welser str 6, Rathausplatz, 86150 Augsburg; tel. (821) 154027; fax (821) 154020; e-mail mail@helloconcerts.de; website www.helloconcerts.de; Contacts Walter Czermak, Lothar Schlessmann.

Karsten Jahnke Konzertdirektion GmbH: PO Box 130553, Oberstr 14b, 20144 Hamburg; tel. (40) 414-788; fax (40) 443-597; e-mail info@karsten-jahnke.de; website www.karsten-jahnke.de; Man. and Owner Karsten Jahnke.

Kick Musikverlag: Burgunder str 8, 50677 Cologne; Man. Dir Goetz Elbertzhagen; International Man. Lynda Hill.

Kultur in Der Landschaft: Brückstr 16, 76703 Kraichtal; tel. 7251-69471; fax 7251-61571; website www.kultur-i-d-landschaft.de; Contact Bruno Wallisch.

Künstlersekretariat Ott: Moltkestr 18, 79098 Freiburg; Contact Dieter Ott.

M A D Fuesgen/Nickel GBR: Hagelberger str 48, 10965 Berlin; Owner Ute Fuesgen.

Moskito Promotion: PO Box 3072, 48016 Münster; e-mail info@grover.de; website www.grover.de; Man. Dir Oswald Münnig.

Music Box GmbH: Rahlstedter str 65, 22149 Hamburg; Man. Dir Hubertus Branzko.

Music Contact: Saastr 8, 72070 Tubingen; tel. 7073-2250; fax 7073-2134; e-mail zellner@musiccontact.com; website www.musiccontact.com.

Musik Komh GmbH: Rottscheidter str 6, 42329 Wuppertal; Head of PR Dept Andrea Zech.

Piranha Kultur & Medien Produktion GmbH: Carmer str 11, 10623 Berlin; tel. (30) 318-6140; fax (30) 3186-1410; e-mail womex@womex.com; website www.womex.com; Man. Dir Borkowsky Akbar.

Synthetic Product Records: PO Box 690441, 30613 Hanover; Contact Lorenz Macke.

Thomann Künstler Management GmbH: PO Box 1, 96136 Burgebrach; tel. (9546) 9449; fax (9546) 6844; e-mail info@thomann-music.de; website www.thomann-music.de; Contact Joseph Thomann.

Greece

Anosi: 20 Zan Moreas St, 15232 Halandri, Athens; Man. Dir Nick Hassid.

Rock Management: PO Box 21526, 55236 Panorama, Thessaloniki; Man. Dir Christos Terzides.

Show Productions: 318 Sygrou Ave, 17673 Kalithea, Athens; Man. Dir Konstantinos Arvanitis; Public Relations Anta Arvanti.

Sound & Vision Music: Militiadou str 9, 10560 Athens; Man. Dir Dozi Panagiotopoulou.

Hong Kong Special Administrative Region, People's Republic of China

Arena Group Ltd: 602 California Tower, 30–32 D'Aguilar St, Central Hong Kong; Contact Allen Japp.

International Management Group: 12/F Sunning Plaza, 10 Hysan Ave, Causeway Bay; Dir Mark Cowley.

Hungary

Darshan Court Cultural Centre: Krudy Gy u 7, 1088 Budapest; tel. 1266-6139; e-mail darshan@axelero.hu; Contact Karoly Csonkics.

Krokodil Kft: Parisi u 6B, 1052 Budapest; Man. Dir Laszlo Besnyö.

Multimedia Ltd: Steindl Imre 4 12, 1054 Budapest; Man. Dir Laszlo Hegedus.

OB Art Management/Alt Product: PO Box 76, 5002 Szolnok; Man. Dir Bela Pap.

PG Productions: PO Box 8, 5002 Szolnok; Man. Dir Peter Pap.

Purple Concerts: Menyelske u. 11 F/1, 1112 Budapest; Man. Dir Marton Brady.

Iceland

Bo Haldorson Productions: PO Box 5445, Pverholt 26, 105 Reykjavík; Man. Dir Bo Haldorson.

Smekkleysa/Bad Taste: PO Box 710, 121 Reykjavík; tel. 5513730; fax 5513737; e-mail asi@smekkleysa.net; website www.smekkleysa.net; Man. Dir Asmundur Jonsson.

Spor HF: Nýbýlavegur 4, PO Box 320, 202 Kópavogur; Man. Dir Steinar Berg Isleifsson.

Indonesia

Art Circle Network: Jl Cut Meutia 5, Jakarta-Pusat; Marketing Dir Gumilang Ramadhan.

JEF Production: Jl Setiabudi Tengah 29, Jakarta-Pusat; Contact Sofyan Ali.

Ono Artists Promotion: Jalan Tebet Barat 1, No. 23, Jakarta 12810; Dir Rinny Noor.

Ireland

Ackland Productions: 35 Rehoboth Pl., Dublin 8; Dir Jody Ackland.

AX-S Records: 26 Mount Eagle View, Leopardstown Heights, Dublin 18; Man. Dir Peter Jones.

Bluemedia Ltd: 7 Willow Cres., Riverbank, Anacotty, Limerick; tel. (61) 331276; fax (61) 331277; e-mail bluemedia@eircom.net; website www.bluemedia.ie; Man. Dir Joe Clarke.

Denis Desmond Promotions: Top House, Clontarf St, Cork 1; Man. Dir Denis Desmond.

Fifty-Seventh Street Ltd: 24 Upper Mount St, Dublin 2; Contacts Maurice Cassidy, Elizabeth Reeves.

Frontline Promotions: Thompson House, MacCurtain St, Cork City; PRO Paul McDermott.

HARMONY Music Management Ltd: The Grange, Carbury, Co Kildare; tel. (405) 53005; fax (405) 53224; e-mail infocus@eircom.net; website www.infocus.ie; Man. Dir John H. Pickering.

Joe McFadden Promotions: 19 Stockton Green, Castleknock, Dublin 15; Man. Dir Joe McFadden.

Kieran Cavanagh Promotions: 56 Fitzwilliam Sq., Dublin 2; Man. Dir Kieran Cavanagh.

Mister T Productions: 141 Parnell St, Dublin 1; tel. and fax (1) 878-7623; e-mail mistert@ireland.com; Dir Tonie Walsh.

Pat Egan Sound Ltd: Merchant's Ct, 24 Merchant's Quay, Dublin 8; Man. Dir Pat Egan.

Project Arts Centre: 39 E Essex St, Dublin 2; Contacts Jody Ackland, Ann Marie Walsh.

RSE Promotions: 11–13 Station Rd, Raheny, Dublin 5; Dir Raymond J. Smyth.

Italy

Azelea Promotion: Via Gelio Cassi 36/a, 33053 Latisana (UD); Man. Dir Ivan Tramontin.

Big Mama: Vicolo S Francesco & Ripa, 18 00153 Rome; Man. Marco Tiriemmi.

Circuito Giovani Artisti Italiani: Via Assarotti 2, 10122 Torino; Network Sec. Luigi Ratclif.

City Medial Two: Via Premuda 30, 42100 Reggio Emilia; Man. Dir Roberto Meglioli.

Giancarlo Passarella: Via Salutati 7, 50126 Florence; Contact Giancarlo Passarella.

Lion Snc: Via Goldoni 42/A, 30174 Mestre, Venezia; Gen. Man. Luciano Trevisan.

Made In Italy Productions: Piazale Clodio 8, 00195 Rome; Man. Dir Gepino Afeltra.

Manhattan Agency: F cnr 15, 30015 Chioggia, Venice; e-mail info@manhattanagency.com; website www.manhattanagency.com.

Rock Alliance Productions: Via Marrone 20, 33170 Pordenone; Dir Corrado Rizzotto.

Skip Agency: Via Sivori 16-23, 16136 Genova; Man. Dir Roberto Saracco.

Solid Rock: Passarella Giancarlo, Via Salutati 7, 50126 Florence.

Zard Iniziative: Viale Mazzini 6, 00195 Rome; Chair. David Zard.

Japan

Global Enterprise Co Ltd: 1-15-3 Dogenzaka, Primera Dogenzaka Ste 816, Shibuya-ku, Tokyo 150; Contact Ohno.

Hayashi International Promotion: Aoyama Nozu Bldg 4F, 3-31-20 Jingumae, Shibuya-ku, Tokyo 150; Contact Massy Hayashi.

Min-On Concert Asscn: 1-32-13 Kita-Shinjuku, Shinjuku-ku, Tokyo 169; Contact Teruo Nakamura.

Republic of Korea

Big CI Event: 901 Dongbuk Bldg, 45-14 Youido-dong, Youngdeungpo-ku, Seoul 150 010; Contact Won Bock Choi.

Cosmos Event Promotion: 401 Seongwon Bldg, 3-1 Pil-dong, 1-ga, Jung-ku, Seoul; Contact Sun Chul Kang.

Seoul Promotions: UN Mansion, Ste 2 B2, 1035 Shinsa-dong, Yongsan-ku, Seoul; Contact Tae-Hyun Lee.

Luxembourg

Folk Clupp Letzerverg A S B L: PO Box 2745, 1027; Pres. Marco Uhres.

Promotion 4: PO Box 728, 2017 Luxembourg; Chair. Mike Koedinger.

Real Music: 27 rue Victor Hugo, 4583 Differdange; Contact Andre Depienne.

Malaysia

Asia Entertainment Network: 2768-2769 Jalan Changkat Permata, Taman Permata, Ulu Kelang, Kuala Lumpur 53300; Exec. Chair. Mike Bernie.

Music City Entertainment Corpn: 20 Jalan 20/101, Taman Desa Aman, Cheras, Kuala Lumpur 56100; Man. Dir John Chacko.

Netherlands

ACT: Van Leeuwenhoeksingel 69, 2611 AE Delft; Contact A. C. Raven.

Buro Gogo: PO Box 7092, 9701 JB Groningen; tel. (50) 314-4110; (50) 314-0174; e-mail info@burogogo.nl; Agent Igor Mönnink.

DIBA International Concerts: PO Box 37, Westersingel 46, 8600 AA Sneek; tel. (515) 420510; fax (515) 423606; e-mail bauke@diba.nl; website www.diba.nl; Man. Dir Bauke Algera.

Earth Beat Entertainment: Kloveniersburgwal 47, 1011 JX Amsterdam; tel. (20) 627-9518; fax (20) 620-8500; e-mail dirk@earthbeat.nl; website www.earthbeat.nl.

Hans Van Pol Management: PO Box 9010, 1006 AA Amsterdam; tel. (20) 610-8281; fax (20) 610-6941.

Moonstruck Music Promotion: Jacob van Lennepkade 24, 1053 MK Amsterdam; tel. (20) 616-4218; fax (20) 616-9196; e-mail info@moonstruck.nl; www.moonstruck.nl.

Music World Management: PO Box 55 55 9, 1007 NB Amsterdam; Man. Dir Paul Coops.

Orange Artist Promotion: Bezuidenhoutseweg 106, 2594 AZ Den Haag; Man. Dir Dido Smit.

Paperclip Agency: PO Box 1519, 6501 BM Nymegen; tel. (24) 323-9322; fax (24) 323-2762; e-mail info@paperclip-agency.com; website www.paperclip-agency.com; Proprietor Rob Berends.

Varke International Promotions: Looiersgracht 38, 1016 VS Amsterdam; Man. Gerrie Bezuijen.

New Zealand

Benny Levin Promotions Ltd: PO Box 5564, Auckland; Contact Louise Hunter.

Chamber Music New Zealand: PO Box 6238, Wellington; Gen. Man. Elisabeth Airey.

Entertainment Venues of New Zealand (EVANZ): Private Bag 3029, Rotorua; tel. (7) 347-2751; fax (7) 347-2816; e-mail nick.dallimore@rdc.gout.nz; website www.evanz.co.nz; Pres. Nick Dallimore.

Pacific Region Entertainment Services: PO Box 25275, Auckland 5; Contact Gary Bartlett, Keith Gosling.

Real Groovy Promotions: 438 Queen St, Auckland; Promotions Man. Paul Rose.

Shawthing Entertainment NZ Ltd: 18 Steyne Ave, Plimmerton, Wellington; Man. Dir Philippa Browne.

Sons of Thunder: PO Box 509, 4 Dellys Grove, Levin 5500; Man. Dir Regan Cunliffe.

Norway

Major Artist: Rosenborggaten 19, 0308 Oslo 8; Man. Jan Paulsen.

Norsk Lyd & Bilde/Norwegian Sound & Vision: Rute 598, 2760 Brandbu; Dirs Odd Erik, Eli Kristin Hagen.

Petter Sandberg A/S: Cort Adelersgt 2, 0254 Oslo; Contact Jan Sollien.

WAPL: Gamle Kongev 16, 0743 Trondheim; Man. Dir Kenneth Nygard.

Panama

Ache Booking Agency: Calle 2, Casa 213, Zona 5, Nuevo Reparto Panamá, 6373 Panamá; Pres. Pablo Yanes.

Peru

Acordes EIRL: Los Paujiles 285 D, Lima 34; Proprietor Julie Freundt López.

In & Out Artists: Avda Larco 930, Of. 702 Miraflores, Lima 18; Pres. Roberto Beaumont Frañowsky.

Pro Art SA: Diez Canseco 236, Of. 403, Miraflores, Lima 18; Dir-Gen. Jorge Ferrand Lanciotti.

Philippines

GR Creative Management Services: 7 Washington St, Midland Park Manor II, Greenhills, San Juan, Metro Manilla; Pres. Gerlie Rodis.

Octoarts Entertainments: 108 Panay Ave, Quezon City, Metro Manila; Man. Dir Orly Ilacad.

Poland

Dzem Agency: PO Box 580, Katowice 2; Contact Ena Otolinsua.

Interart Ltd: Ul. Pugeta 6, 51-628 Wroclaw; Contact Margaret Szablowska.

Kantaro Art Agency: Ul. Polistancov W Ucp 20, 70-110 Szczecin; Owner Witold Tanczynski.

Metal Mind Productions Sp Z 00: Szeligiewicza 8/21, 40-044 Katowice; Man. Dir Tomasz Drivbinski.

Tomasz Bielski Agency: Ul. Krucza 49, 00509 Warsaw; Gen. Man. Tomasz Bielski; Man. Dir Krzysztof Wotowiec.

Warsaw Artists Management Ltd: Kazimierzowska 47/5, 02-572 Warsaw; Pres. Andrzej Haluch.

ZPR Inc-United Entertainment Enterprises Inc: Senatorska 13/15, 00 075 Warsaw; Pres./CEO Zbigniew Benbenek; Artists & Marketing Man. Anna Karolicka.

Portugal

Concertos de Portugal: Lote 23, Sub Cave Esq, Quinta de so Miguel das Encostas, 2775 Carcavelos/Parede; Contact Afonso Gomes.

MTM: PO Box 30072, 1321 Lisbon Codex; Man. Dir Hugo Moutinho.

Regiespectáculo: Alto do Coutão, Armazem I, 2735 Cacém; CEO António Guimaräes.

Romania

AMMA: Scara B, Apt 73, Calea Victoriei 48/50, Sector 1, 70102 Bucharest; Man. Aurel Mitran.

Artexim: 155 Calea Victoriei, Bl D1, Scara 8, Et 2, 71102 Bucharest; Gen. Man. Mihai Constantinescu.

Cartianu Ltd: 58 Aviator Traian Vasile str, Sector 1, 78336 Bucharest; Chair. Radu Cartianu.

Holograf Productions Srl: 26 SF Elefterie str, Sector 5, Bucharest; Man. Dir Horia Moculescu.

Russia

Biz Enterprises: Bolshaya Serpukhovskaya 27, 129 010 Moscow; Man. Dir Sergey Chistoprudov.

Fee Lee Promotion: 27 Novozavodskaya str, 121 309 Moscow; Man. Dir Igor Tonkikh.

Rock-Azia: Pupova 96-268, Barnaul, 656062 Siberia; Contact Eugene Kolbashev.

SAV Entertainment: Milyutinsky Per 15/24, 101 000 Moscow; tel. (95) 925-6422; fax (95) 923-7665; e-mail saven@col.ru; Chair. Nadia Solovieva.

Singapore

Hype Records Pte Ltd: 221 Henderson Rd, Suite 02–04 Henderson Bldg, Singapore 159557; tel. 6375-3787; fax 6275-2757; e-mail hype@hyperecords.com; website www.hyperecords.com; Admin. Man. Melvis Yip.

International Management Group: 50 Cuscaden Rd, 05-02 HPL House, Singapore 1024; Contact Bart Collins.

Jasper Productions: Unit 157A, First Floor, Thomson Rd, Singapore 1130; Contact Jimmy Loh.

Top Ten Entertainment: 400 Orchard Rd, 05-18A Orchard Towers, Singapore 0923; Man. Dir Peter Bader.

Slovenia

BUBA Booking and Promotion: PO Box 38, 40A Moskriceva, 1110 Ljubljana; tel. and fax (1) 542-4411; e-mail buba@moj.net; website www.ljudmila.org/buba/; Contact Irena Povse.

FV-Zavod Za Umetnisko in Kulturno Produkcijo: Kersnikova 4, 61000 Ljubljana; Man. Dir Skaberne Mónika.

Radio Student: Cesta 27, Aprila 31, Blou 8, 61000 Ljubljana; Music Ed. Igor Basin.

SKUC-AFK: Kersnikova 4, 61000 Ljubljana; Man. Dir Mitja Prezelj.

South Africa

Makinv Music Artist Agency: 38 Dorp St, Cape Town 8100; tel. (21) 426-0399; fax (21) 426-0199; e-mail csyren@music.org.za; website www.music.org.za/mmp/mmp_agency.htm.

Spain

Artcelona: Regomir 3, 08002 Barcelona; tel. (93) 315-2698; fax (93) 315-2050; e-mail agnes.blot@artcelona.com; website www.artcelona.com; Dir Angel Domínguez.

AZ Productions: Riera de Argentona, s/n, 08300 Nataro (Barcelona); International Dept Pere-Lluis Pont.

Batall: Balmes, 25 Baixos 3, Apdo de correos 45, 43800 Valls; tel. (97) 761-3339; fax (97) 761-3134; e-mail batall@batall.com; website www.batall.com.

Colectivo Promocion de Jazz: Navarro Reverter 22, 46004 Valencia; Contact Julio Martin.

Diez Management: Martinez Corrochano 3, 28007 Madrid; Chair. Mercedes Martin.

GSG-Grup de Serveis Guilleries: Granja Baró, Ctra de la Guixa, km 2, 08500 Victoria (Barcelona); Admin. Jordi Costa; Man. Ignasi Pla; Production Joan Capdevila.

Munster Tourin-Espárrago Rock Productions SL: Calle Reyes Catdlicos 25 Of. 2°, 18001 Granada; Promotion Dir Javier Gonzalez.

Nox Producciones: Gran Via 40, 7-2, 28013 Madrid; Man. Gloria Parra.

Pino Sagliocco Presenta SL: Calle Quintana 2, 7° 9a, 28008 Madrid; Chair. Pino Sagliocco.

Posto Nove: Muntaner 494 5B, 08022 Barcelona; Contact Alejandro Navarro.

Producciones Gonart Cultura y Ocio: Urb. La Roca 36, 39110 Sancibrian, Cantabria; tel. (62) 941-6693; e-mail gonzaloarranz@yahoo.es.

RLM Producciones: Jose Maria Cavero 9, Ch A, 28027 Madrid; Man. Dir Rosa Lagarrigue.

Showcase—Producciones Ibericas: Calle Joaquin Loriga 22 5C, 36203 Vigo/Pontevedra; tel. and fax (98) 642-1319; e-mail showcase@topmail.com.

Store Music: Gran Via 28, 3C, 18010 Granada; Man. Dir Carmen Carnicero.

UADR Marketing: Residencial Coruna 21, Casa 5, 28230 Las Rozas; Dir Carlos Lopez.

Sweden

Ema Telstar: PO Box 1018, 181 21 Lidingö; Man. Dir Thomas Johansson.

Energy Records AB: Vastergatan 23, 21121 Malmö; Contact Håkan Ehrnst.

Export Music Sweden (ExMS): PO Box 27 327, 102 54 Stockholm; tel. 8783-8800; fax 8783-9510; e-mail christer@exms.com; website www.exms.com; Gen. Man. Christer Lundblad.

Fritid & Nöjen: Sandgatan 2, 223 50 Lund; Pres. Julius Malmström.

Headlne Productions: PO Box 5948, Vasatorget 1, 700 05 Örebro; Man. Dir Dennis Karlsson.

Luger Production: Fredriksgatan 35, 811 33 Sandviken; Man. Dir/Agent Ola Broquist; Agents Patrick Fredriksson, Morgan Johansson.

M & A Music Art: Simrishamnsgatan 20A, 214 23 Malmö; Man. Dir Andreas Larsson.

Projektbyrån: Kungsgatan 34, 972 41 Luleå; Man. Dir Tomas Lind.

Release Musik & Media: PO Box 7144, 402 33 Gothenburg; Man. Dir Lotta Jansson.

RMP Management AB: PO Box 17180, 104 62 Stockholm; Man. Dir Stefan Liga.

Siljemark Production: Gärdsvagen 2, 171 52 Solna; Man. Jonas Siljemark; Contact Lasse Karlsson.

Storsjöyran: Storgatan 28, 831 30 Ostersund; Man. Dir Stefan Kauppi.

United Stage Production AB: PO Box 9174, 200 39 Malmö; Man. Dir Anders Larsson.

Switzerland

Artways Productions: Rue des-deux-Gares 6B, PO Box 30, 1800 Vevey; Man. Fabrice La Luc.

BAROCK Enterprises: Waldheimstr 17, 3604 Thun; tel. and fax (33) 335-3530; e-mail barock@bluewin.ch; website www.barock.ch; Contact Beat Aegler.

Jazz Willisau: PO Box, 6130 Willisau; tel. (41) 970-2731; fax (41) 970-3231; e-mail troxler@centralnet.ch; website www.jazzwillisau.ch; Dir Niklaus Troxler; Festival of jazz.

Joker System Agency: PO Box 325, 1000 Lausanne 17; Man. Dir Marc Lambelet.

L'Agence Marcel Schiess: 12 rue du Premier Mars, 2300 La-Chaux-de-Fonds; Contact Marcel Schiess.

Music Service: Adi Weiss AG Buhlweg 5, PO Box 265, 3072 Ostermandiga 2; tel. (31) 930-1010; fax (31) 930-1015; e-mail roli.roethlisberger@musicservice.ch; website www.musicservice.ch; Pres. Roland Röthlisberger.

Panagency: PO Box 39, 3280 Murten; tel. (26) 670-6103; fax (76) 366-2611; e-mail beat@panagency.ch; website www.panagency.ch.

Rocking Chair: PO Box 4, 1800 Vevey 2; Contact Nicola De Pinto.

SOFA Agency: PO Box 101, 1707 Fribourg; Contact Pascal Hunkeler, Jacques Schouwey.

Swiss Music Edition: PO Box 7851, 6000 Luzern 7; tel. and fax (41) 210-6070; e-mail mail@musicedition.ch; Sec. Peter Bitterli.

VIP AG Productions: Schützengasse 30, 8001 Zürich; Man. Dir Urs Peter Keller.

Thailand

Music Train: 186 Soi Samarnmitr, Ramkhamhaeng Rd, Prakanong, Bangkok 10250; Man. Dir Mr Raya.

Nititad Entertainment: 1/79-80 Moo-Baan, Shinnaket Soi 10, Ngamwongwarn Rd, Bangken, Bangkok 10210; Man. Dir Vichian Usvisessivakul.

Soco Entertainment: 21/9 Saladaeng 1 Silom, Bangkok 10500; Chair. Sam Armenio.

Turkey

Imaj Entertainment: Haci Adil Sokak, 4 Aralik No. 2, 80630 Levent, Istanbul; Dir Hale Diceli Yamanoglu.

Major Musical Productions: Ihlamurdere Cad Misirli Sk, Arda Apt, 80690 Besiktas, Istanbul; Man. Dir Eyup Iblag.

Most Production: Yildizcicegi Sok 7, Etiler, Istanbul; Chair. Mustafa Oguz.

Pozitif: Istiklal Caddesi 1, Baro Han 611-612, 80080 Beyoglu, Istanbul; Pres. Cem Yegul.

United Kingdom

Acker's International Jazz Agency: 53 Cambridge Mansions, Cambridge Rd, London SW11 4RX; tel. (20) 7978-5885; fax (20) 7978-5882; e-mail pamela@ackersmusicagency.co.uk; website www.ackersmusicagency.co.uk; Owner Pamela Frances Sutton.

Adastra: 2 Star Row, North Dalton, Driffield, East Yorkshire YO25 9UR; tel. (1377) 217662; fax (1377) 217754; e-mail adastra@adastey.demon.co.uk; website www.adastra-music.co.uk; Owner Chris Wade.

Aiken Promotions Ltd: Marlborough House, 348 Lisburn Rd, Belfast BT9 6GH, Northern Ireland; tel. (2890) 381047; fax (2890) 682091; e-mail office@aikenpromotions.com; website www.aikenpromotions.com; Contact Peter Aiken.

Alan James Public Relations: 253 Camberwell New Rd, London SE5 0TH; Man. Dir Alan James.

Andrew Storr Entertainments: 2 Burn Grange Cottage, Doncaster Rd, Burn Nr Selby, North Yorkshire YO8 8LA; Partner Phil Storr.

Asgard Management: 125 Parkway, London NW1 7PS; tel. (20) 7387-5090; fax (20) 7387-8740; e-mail pl@asgard.uk.com; Contact Paul Charles.

Asgard Promotions Ltd: 125 Parkway, London NW1 7PS; tel. (20) 7387-5090; fax (20) 7387-8740; e-mail info@asgard-uk.com; Joint Man. Dirs Paul Fenn, Paul Charles.

Autonomous Talent Booking: PO Box 7, Ware, Herts; tel. (1920) 467780; fax (1920) 466077; e-mail hincdom@aol.com; Contact Mike Hinc.

Barry Collings Entertainments: 21A Clifftown Rd, Southend-on-Sea, Essex SS1 1AB; tel. (1702) 330005; fax (1702) 333309; e-mail bcollent@aol.com; website www.barrycollings.co.uk; Man. Dir Barry Collings.

BDA—Brian Durkin Assocs Ltd: Bryson House, Chiltern Rd, Culcheth, Warrington WA3 4LL; tel. (1925) 766655; fax (1925) 765577; e-mail bda@exl.co.uk; Man. Dir Brian Durkin.

Bernard Lee Management: 1 Heathside Pl., Epsom, Surrey; tel. and fax (1737) 354777; Man. Dir Bernard Lee.

Big Bear Music: PO Box 944, Edgbaston, Birmingham B16 8UT; tel. (121) 4547020; fax (121) 4549996; e-mail bigbearmusic@compuserve.com; website www.bigbearmusic.com; Man. Dir Jim Simpson.

Black Magic Management Ltd: 296 Earls Court Rd, London SW5 9BA; Man. Dir Mataya Clifford.

Blitz: Edgwarebury Farm, Edgwarebury Lane, Edgware, Middlesex HA8 8QX; Partners Sue Harris, Claire Powell.

BPR: 36 Como St, Romford, Essex RM7 7DR; tel. (1708) 725330; fax (1708) 725322; website www.bprmusic.com; Man. Brian Theobald.

Brian Rix & Assocs: PO Box 100, Ashford, Kent TN24 8AR; Operations Man. Simon Grant.

Brian Yeates Assocs: London Rd, Canwell, Sutton Coldfield, West Midlands B75 5SH; tel. (121) 323-2200; fax (121) 323-2313; e-mail ash@cyberphile.co.uk; website www.ukacts.com/agency/brian-yeates.

Burniston Cooke Productions: 69 MacFarlane Rd, London W12 7JY; Contact Simon Cooke.

Buzz Records: 192 Glasgow Rd, Perth PH2 0NA, Scotland; Man. Dir Dave Arcari.

Cadillac Promotions: Cadillac Ranch, Pencraig Uchaf, Cwm Bach, Whitland, Dyfed SA34 0DT; tel. (1994) 484466; fax (1994) 484294; e-mail cadillac_ranch@telco4u.net; website www.nikturner.com; Man. M. Magoon.

Clear Channel Entertainment (Music) UK Ltd: First Floor, Regent Arcade House, 252–260 Regent St, London W1B 3BX; tel. (20) 7009-3333; fax (8707) 493191; e-mail music@clearchannel.co.uk; website www.uk.cc.com; Man. Dir Tim Parsons.

Concorde International Artistes: Concorde House, 101 Shepherds Bush Rd, London W6 7CP; Man. Dir Louis Parker.

Creeme Entertainments: East Lynne, Harper Green Rd, Doe Hey, Farnworth, Bolton BL4 7HT; tel. (1204) 793441; fax (1204) 792655; e-mail info@creeme.co.uk; website www.creeme.co.uk; Partners Tom Ivers, Lynne Ivers, Anthony Ivers.

Cromwell Management: 4–5 High St, Huntingdon, Cambs PE29 3TE; tel. (1480) 435600; fax (1480) 356250; e-mail tricvic@lineone.net; Man. Partner Vic Gibbons.

D. F. Concerts Ltd: 272 St Vincent St, Glasgow G2 5RL, Scotland: tel. (141) 566-4998; e-mail admin@dfconcerts.co.uk; website www.gigsinscotland.com; Dir Geoff Ellis.

Dark Blues Management Ltd: 30 Stamford Brook Rd, London W6 0XH; tel. (20) 8743 3292; fax (20) 8740 5520; Dir of Business Devt Kate Martin.

Dax Entertainments: 48 Fernside Rd, Poole, Dorset BH15 2JJ; tel. (1202) 773103; fax (1202) 681419; e-mail dave.dacosta@ukonline.co.uk; Man. Dir Dave Dacosta.

Derek Block Artistes Agency Ltd: Douglas House, 3 Richmond Bldgs, London W1V 5AE; tel. (20) 7434 2100; fax (20) 7434 0200; e-mail dbaa@derekblock.demon.co.uk; Man. Dir Derek Block.

Deri Promotions: 8 Wick Lane, Felpham, Bognor Regis, West Sussex PO22 8QG; Proprietor R. W. Cooper.

Devenish Entertainments Ltd: 8 Forthill Rd, Enniskillen, Co Fermanagh BT74 6AW, Northern Ireland; Contact Sean McGrade.

Entertainment Agency Group: 7 Northumberland St, Huddersfield HD1 1RL; Entertainment Exec. Lenny Phillip.

Europa Jazz Live: 6 Belgrove, Tunbridge Wells, Kent TN1 1YN; tel. (1892) 516722; fax (1892) 536080; e-mail jazz@davidjacobs.f9.co.uk; website www.tinamay.com; Dir David E. Jacobs.

Fadermusic: Perth Rd, Wood Green, London N22 5QP; Gen. Man. Bengi F-B.

Fair Oaks Entertainment: PO Box 19, Ulverston, Cumbria CA12 9TF; Proprietor/Man. J. G. Livingstone.

Fanfare 3000: The Folly, Pinner Hill Rd, Pinner, Middlesex HA5 3YQ; tel. (20) 8429 3000; fax (20) 8868 6497; e-mail entertainment@fanfare.co.uk; website www.fanfare.co.uk; Partners Peter Richardson, Paul Baxter.

Fish Krish: 6 Carlton House, 319 West End Lane, London NW6 1RN; Contact Fish Krish.

Fiveash & Hill Publicity and Promotions: 106 Great Portland St, London W1N 5PE; Partner Graeme Hill.

Focus Marketing Communications: HMA House, 78 Durham Rd, Wimbledon, London SW20 0TL; Man. Dir Brian Oliver.

Forward Agency Booking: 132 Liverpool Rd, London N1 1LA; Man. Dir Rob Challice.

Garry Brown Assocs (International) Ltd: 27 Downs Side, Cheam, Surrey SM2 7EH; tel. (20) 8643-3991; fax (20) 8770-7241; e-mail gbaltd@compuserve.com; Chair. Garry Brown.

Gordon Poole Agency Ltd: The Limes, Brockley, Bristol BS48 3BB; tel. (1275) 463222; fax (1275) 462252; e-mail agents@gordonpoole.com; website www.gordonpoole.com; Man. Dir Gordon Poole.

Greig Clifford Promotions: 23 Harsfold Rd, Rustington, West Sussex BN16 2QE; Proprietor Grieg Clifford.

Grosvenor Productions: 14 Tavistock St, London; tel. (20) 7379 9111; fax (20) 7379 3478; e-mail cruise@grosvenor-productions.com; website www.grosvenor-productions.com.

Hal Carter Organization: 101 Hazelwood Lane, Palmers Green, London N13 5HQ; tel. (20) 8886 2801; fax (20) 8882 7380; e-mail halcarterorg@ic24.net; Man. Dir Hal Carter.

Harvey Goldsmith Entertainments: The Glassworks, 3–4 Ashland Pl., London W1M 3JH; Man. Dir Harvey Goldsmith.

Helter Skelter (Agency) Ltd: The Plaza, 535 Kings Rd, London SW10 0SZ; tel. (20) 7376-8501; fax (20) 7376-8336; e-mail johnjackson@helterskelter.co.uk; website www.fwwt.com; Pres. John Jackson.

Holland-Ford's: 103 Lydyett Lane, Barnton, Northwich, Cheshire CW8 4JT; tel. (1606) 76960; Proprietor Bob Holland-Ford.

Hopscotch Media Management: 46 Broadwick St, London W1V 1FF; Dir/Partner Alfie Dosoo.

Houndog Music Entertainment Agency: 49 Arthurton Rd, Spixworth, Norwich NR10 3QU; tel. and fax (1603) 897789; Proprietor Graham John Bailey.

I. A. Entertainment: 44 Top Llan, Glan Conwy, Colwyn Bay, Clwyd LL28 5ND, Wales; Proprietor Andrew Boggie.

International Talent Booking (ITB): 27A Floral St, Covent Garden, London WC2E 9DQ; e-mail barry@itb.co.uk; Man. Dir Barry Dickens.

Jean Mills Entertainments: Cox Park Cottage, Cox Park, Gunnislake, Cornwall PL18 9BB; tel. and fax (1822) 832791; e-mail jmillsents@aol.com; Proprietor Jean Mills.

Jef Hanlon Management: 1 York St, London W1P 1PZ; tel. (20) 7487-2558; fax (20) 7487-2584; e-mail jhanlon@agents-uk.com; Man. Dir Jef Hanlon; Dir Alice Hanlon.

John Boddy Agency: 10 Southfield Gdns, Twickenham, Middlesex; tel. (20) 8892 0133; fax (20) 8892 4283.

John Ford Promotions: Bradford Court, Bradford St, Digbeth, Birmingham B12 0NS; tel. (121) 693 9911; fax (121) 693 7799; Owner John Ford.

John Martin Promotions Ltd: 29 Hartfield Rd, London SW19 3SG; Man. Dir John Martin.

Kasevin Rodell: 6 Bowling Green Rd, Cranfield, Bedfordshire MK43 0ET; Partner Diana Rodell.

Kennedy Street Management: Kennedy House, 31 Stamford St, Altrincham, Cheshire WA14 1ES; tel. (161) 941-5151; fax (161) 928-9491; e-mail kse@kennedystreet.com; Dir Danny Betesh; Production Man. Jim Colson.

Latin Touch Entertainments: Fatima Community Centre, Commonwealth Ave, London W12 7QR; tel. (20) 8740-9020; fax (20) 8740-8903; e-mail sales@latintouch.com; website www.latintouch.com; Man. Dir Orlando Rincon P.

M D O: The Dawn, Northwood Lane, Bewdley, Worcs DY12 1AS; tel. (1299) 404579; fax (1299) 405079; e-mail themick.mdo@btinternet.com; Contact Mick Owen.

Matters Musical Ltd: The Loft, rear of 8 West St, Dorking, Surrey RH4 1BL; Dir Victoria Burns.

Max Clifford Assocs Ltd: Top Floor, 109 New Bond St, London W1Y 9AA; Man. Dir Max Clifford.

Mean Fiddler: 24–28A High St, Harlseden, London NW10 4LX; Man. Dir Vince Power.

Mel Bush Organization: 20–22 Wellington Rd, Bournemouth; tel. (1202) 293093; fax (1202) 293080; e-mail mbobmth@aol.com; Man. Dir Mel Bush.

Mercenary Music Services: 143 Turks Rd, Radcliffe, Manchester M26 3WW; Production Man. Paul Naylor.

Midland Entertainment & Management Agency: PO Box 259, Coventry CV5 8YU; tel. and fax (2476) 715544; e-mail chrissy@midland-entertainment.com; website www.midland-entertainment.com; Proprietor Chrissy Price.

Miracle Prestige International Ltd: Bugle House, 21A Noel St, London W1V 3PD; Man. Dir Steve Parker.

Mission Control Agency: 63 Lant St, London SE1 1QN; Dir Guy Anderson.

Money Talks Agency: Cadillac Ranch, Pencraig Uchaf, Cwm Bach, Whitland, Dyfed SA34 0DT, Wales; tel. (1994) 484466; fax (1994) 484294; e-mail cadillac-ranch@telco4u.net; website www.nikturner.com; Man. M. Magoon.

Mrs Casey Music: PO Box 296, Aylesbury, Buckinghamshire HP19 3TL; Dir Steve Heap.

NE Music Management: Priory House, 55 Lawe Rd, South Sheilds, Tyne & Wear NE33 2AL; tel. (191) 427-6207; fax (191) 427-6323; e-mail dave@nemproductions.com; website www.nemproductions.com; Contact Dave Smith.

Norman Jackson Entertainment Agency: 2 Dawlish Rd, Leyton, London E10 6QY; tel. (20) 556-3222; fax (20) 556-3223; Dir Ray Gould.

NVB Entertainments: 80 Holywell Rd, Studham, Dunstable, Bedfordshire LU6 2PD; tel. (1582) 873623; fax (1582) 873618; e-mail nvb_entertainments@hotmail.com; Contact Henri Harrison.

Park Promotions: PO Box 651, Oxford OX2 9RB; tel. (1865) 241717; fax (1865) 204556; website www.parkrecords.com; Man. Dir John Dagnell.

Paul Barrett Rock 'n' Roll Enterprises: 16 Grove Pl., Penarth, South Glamorgan CF64 2ND, Wales; tel. (2920) 704279; fax (2920) 709989; e-mail barrett.rocknroll@aimserve.net; Dir Paul Barrett.

Paul Dainty Corpn (UK) Ltd: 4 Yeomans Row, Knightsbridge, London SW3 2AH; Vice-Pres. Peter Lyster-Todd.

Pendle Borough Council: Bank House, 61 Albert Rd, Colne, Lancashire BB8 0PB; Arts & Entertainment Man. Gary Hood.

Phil McIntyre Promotions: 15 Riversway Business Village, Navigation Way, Preston PR2 2YP; Man. Dir Phil McIntyre.

Pollytone Music: PO Box 124, Ruislip, Middlesex HA4 9BB; tel. (1895) 638584; fax (1895) 624793; e-mail val@pollyton.demon.co.uk; website www.pollytone.com; Dir Valerie Bird.

Pomona: 14 Oxford Pl., Rochdale OL16 5LU; Man. Dir Mark Jones.

Primary Talent International Ltd: Africa House, 64–78 Kingsway, London WC2B 6PR; Contact Peter Maloney.

Prime Time: 28 Yonge Park, London N4 3NT; Dir Maggie O'Connor.

Profile Artists Agency: 141 Railton Rd, London SE24 0LT; Agent Serena Parsons.

Prostar: 106 Hillcrest Ave, Toftwood, Dereham, Norfolk NR19 1TD; Proprietor Malcolm Cook.

Public Eye Communications: Greyhound House, 16 Greyhound Rd, London W6 8NX; New Business Dir Elaine Robertson.

Purple Palace: 34A Flower Lane, Mill Hill, London NW7 2JE; Contact Stephanie Kays.

Raymond Gubbay Ltd: 176a High St, Barnet, Hertfordshire EN5 5SZ; Man. Dir Raymond Gubbay.

Real Time: 16/18 Ramillies St, London W1V 1DL; PR Man. Charlie Inskip.

Rock 'n' Roll Enterprises: 16 Grove Plce, Penarth CF64 2ND, Wales; tel. (2920) 704279; fax (2920) 709989; e-mail barrett.rocknroll@aimserve.net; Dir Paul Barrett.

Roger James Management: 10A Margaret Rd, Barnet, Hertfordshire EN4 9NP; tel. (20) 8440 9788.

Rush Release Ltd: 74 The Archway, Station Approach, Ranelagh Gdns, London SW6 3UH; Gen. Man. Jo Underwood.

Serious Speakout: 42 Old Compton St, London W1V 5PB; Partners John Cumming, John Ellson, David Jones.

Sharp End Promotions Ltd: Grafton House, 2–3 Golden Sq., London W1R 3AD; Dir Robert Lemon.

Solo: Regent Arcade House, 252–260 Regent St, London W1B 3BX; tel. (20) 7009-3361; fax (870) 7493174; e-mail solo@solo.uk.com; website www.solo.uk.com; Man. Dir John Giddings.

Sound & Light Productions: Kerrison Hall, 28 Kerrison Rd, London W5 5NW; Dir Jan Goodwin.

Splash Management & Promotions: 328 Gray's Inn Rd, King's Cross, London WC1X 8BZ; Man. Dir Nick Moore.

Square Deal Promotions: 56 Kilmuir Rd, Inverness IV3 8EP, Scotland; tel. (1463) 221268; fax (1463) 221268; Proprietor Ann Carmody.

Steve Allen Entertainments: 60 Broadway, Peterborough, Cambridgeshire PE1 1SU; tel. (1733) 569589; fax (1733) 561854; e-mail steve@sallenent.co.uk; website www.sallenent.co.uk; Proprietor Steve Allen.

Stoneyport Agency: 39 Shandon Cres., Edinburgh EH11 1QF, Scotland; tel. (131) 346-8237; fax (131) 313-2083; e-mail jb@stoneyport.demon.co.uk; website www.stoneyport.demon.co.uk; Contact John Barrow.

Swamp Agency: PO Box 94, Derby DE22 1XA; tel. and fax (1332) 332336; e-mail Chrishall@swampmusic.demon.co.uk; Contact Chris Hall.

Sylvantone Promotions: 17 Allerton Grange Way, Leeds LS17 6LP; tel. (113) 268-7788; fax (113) 266 0220; e-mail tonygoodacre@hotmail.com; Proprietor Tony Goodacre.

Talk Loud PR: 90–92 Great Portland St, London W1N 5PB.

Taurus Records: 23 Blackheath Rise, Lewisham, London SE13 7PN; Contact Beverley Miller.

The Life Organisation: 62 Argyle St, Birkenhead, Merseyside L41 6AF; Dir J. O'Connor.

TKO Promotions Ltd: PO Box 130, Hove, East Sussex BN3 6QU; Creative Dir Howard Kruger.

Tony Denton Promotions Ltd: 19 South Molton Lane, Mayfair, London W1Y 1AQ; tel. (20) 7629 4666; fax (20) 7629 4777; e-mail mail@tdpromo.com; website www.tdpromo.com; Contact Simon Nicholls.

Upbeat Management and Recordings: Sutton Business Centre, Rastmor Way, Wallington, Surrey SM6 7AH; tel. (20) 8773-1223; fax (20) 8669-6752; e-mail beryl@upbeat.co.uk; website www.upbeat.co.uk; Contact Beryl Korman.

Vinyl Japan (UK) Ltd: 281 Camden High St, London NW1 7BX; Man. Patrick James.

WOMAD: The Malt House, Mill Lane, Box, Wiltshire SN14 9PN; Man. Dir Thomas Brooman.

Work Hard PR: 19d Pinfold Rd, London SW16 2SL; tel. (20) 8677-8466; fax (20) 8677-5374; e-mail enquiries@workhardpr.com; website www.workhardpr.com; Owner Roland Hyams.

United States of America

A & R European/US Radio Record Promotions: 900 19th Ave S, Suite 207, Nashville, TN 37212; Owners Ruth Steele, David Steele.

Aarrow Artist/Writer Development: 900 19th Ave S, Suite 207, Nashville, TN 37212; Owner Kelli Steele; A & R Dir Ruth Steele.

Abby Hoffer Enterprises: 223½ E 48th St, New York, NY 10017-1538; tel. (212) 935-6350; fax (212) 758-4987; Pres Abby Hoffer, Paul Hoffer.

Al Embry International: PO Box 23162, Nashville, TN 37202; tel. (615) 327-4074; fax (615) 329-4777; e-mail alembry@alembryinternational.com; website www.alembryinternational.com; Owner/Pres. Al Embry.

Ambassadors of Praise: PO Box 369, Pearland, TX 77588-0369; Pres. Patricia Nedbalek.

American Band Management: PO Box 840607, Houston, TX 77284-0607; Pres. John Blomstrom Sr.

American Famous Talent: 816 W Evergreen, Chicago, IL 60622; Pres. Ric Bricamontes.

AristoMedia Group: PO Box 22765, Nashville, TN 37202; tel. (615) 269-7071; Pres./Owner Jeff Walker.

Artist Representation & Management: 1257 Arcade St, St Paul, MN 55106; tel. (651) 483-8754; fax (651) 776-6338; e-mail ra@armentertainment.com; website www.armentertainment.com; Office Man./Agent Roger Anderson.

Barry Agency: PO Box 1414, Maple Grove, MN 55311; e-mail info@thebarryagency.com; Pres. Lisa A. Barry.

Bay Concerts/Up Front Management: 1906 Seward Dr., Pittsburg, CA 94565; tel. and fax (510) 427-7210; CEO/Pres. Charles Coke; Vice-Pres. Terry Pitts.

Bennett Morgan & Assocs Ltd: 1022 Route 370, Wappingers Falls, NY 12590; tel. (845) 227-6065; fax (845) 227-4002; website www.bennettmorgan.com; Pres. Bennett Morgan.

Berkeley Agency: 2608 Ninth St, #301, Berkeley, CA 94710; tel. (510) 843-4902; fax (510) 843-7271; e-mail mail@berkeleyagency.com; Agent Jim Cassell.

Bill Hollingshead Productions Inc: 1720 N Ross St, Santa Ana, CA 92706; tel. (714) 543-4894; fax (714) 542-3460; e-mail bhptalent@aol.com; Pres. Bill Hollingshead.

Blowin' Smoke Management & Bookings: 7438 Shoshone Ave, Van Nuys, CA 91406-2340; tel. (818) 881-9888; fax (818) 881-0555; e-mail blowinsmokeband.com; website www.blowinsmokeband.com; Pres. Larry Weisberg.

BMI (Butler Music International): 273 Chippewa Dr., Columbia, SC 29210-6508.

Bobby Roberts Co: PO Box 1547, Goodlettsville, TN 37070-1547; tel. (615) 859-8899; fax (615) 859-2200; e-mail info@bobbyroberts.com; Pres. Bobby Roberts.

Brad Simon Organization: 122 E 57th St, New York, NY 10022; Pres. Brad Simon.

Brentwood Music Publishing Inc: One Maryland Farms, Brentwood, TN 37027; Vice-Pres. of Publishing Dale Mathews.

Brothers Productions: 141 Dunbar Ave, Fords, NJ 08863; tel. (908) 738-0880; fax (908) 738-0970.

Buddy Lee Attractions: 38 Music Sq. E, Suite 300, Nashville, TN 37203; tel. (615) 244-4336; fax (615) 726-0429; e-mail tconway@blanash.com; website www.buddyleeattractions.com; Pres. Tony Conway.

Captain Telegram Special Event: 2890 N Andrews Ave, Fort Lauderdale, FL 33311-2514; Pres. Roger Hughes.

Cardenas/Fernandez & Assocs: 850 W Jackson, Suite 750, Chicago, IL 60607; tel. (312) 421-5272; fax (312) 421-4878; e-mail esotomayor@cfevents.com; website www.cfevents.com; Pres. Henry Cardenas; Account Exec. Elena Sotomayor.

Cerebral Records: 1236 Laguna Dr., Carlsbad, CA 92008; Pres. Lincoln Kroll; Publicist Carol Leno.

Competitive Edge Public Relations: 9 Music Sq., Suite 240, Nashville, TN 37203; Contact Debbie McClure.

Concerted Efforts Inc: PO Box 99, Newtonville, MA 02160; tel. (617) 969-0810; fax (617) 969-6761; Dir Paul Kahn.

Creative Artists Agency (CAA): 3310 West End Ave, Fifth Floor, Nashville, TN 37203; tel. (615) 383-8787; fax (615) 383-4937; www.caa.com; Contact Ron Baird.

Creative Artists Agency: 9830 Wilshire Blvd, Beverly Hills, CA 90212; tel. (310) 288-4545; fax (310) 288-4800; website www.caa.com.

De Leon Artists: 4031 Panama Ct, Piedmont, CA 94611; tel. (510) 655-2500; fax (510) 655-5208; Agent Lupe De Leon; Contacts Ross Locke, Max Cooperstein.

DMR Booking Agency: Suite 250, The Galleries of Syracuse, Syracuse, NY 13202; tel. (315) 475-2500; fax (315) 475-0752; Owner David Rezak.

Dynamic Directions Inc: 11410 W Wisconsin Ave, Wauwatosa, WI 53226; Vice-Pres. Arthur Greinke.

Events International Inc: PO Box 1560, Honolulu, HI 96806; Pres. David Booth.

Famous Artist Agency: 1700 Broadway, Fifth Floor, New York, NY 10019; tel. (212) 245-3939; Pres. Jerry Ade; Man. David Zedeck.

Fate's House of Music: 1030 Villa Pl., Nashville, TN 37212; Pres. Fate Vanderpool.

Five Roses Music Group: 34A Lanier Rd, Studio 1, Jekyll Island, GA 31527; Pres. Sammie Lee Marler.

Folklore Inc: 1671 Appian Way, Santa Monica, CA 90401; tel. (310) 451-0767; fax (310) 458-6005; Contact Mitch Greenhill.

General Broadcasting Service: 203 Gates Dr., Hendersonville, TN 37075-4961; Owner Ernie Bivens.

Geoffrey Blumenauer Artists (GBA): 11846 Balboa Ave, Suite 204, Granada Hills, CA 91344; tel. (818) 366-8117; fax (818) 366-2890; e-mail gbatalent@aol.com; Pres. Geoffrey Blumenauer.

Grelo Holdings Inc: Market St Sq., 33 Wilkes Barre Blvd, Wilkes Barre, PA 18701; Pres./CEO Thom Grelo.

International Creative Management (ICM): 8943 Wilshire Blvd, Beverly Hills, CA 90211; tel. (310) 550-4000; fax (310) 550-4108; 40 W 57th St, New York, NY 10019; tel. (212) 556-5600; fax (212) 556-5665.

Jackie Paul Entertainment Group Inc: 559 Wanamaker Rd, Jenkintown, PA 19046; CEO Jackie Paul.

Keith Case & Assocs: 59 Music Sq. W, Nashville, TN 37203; Owner Keith Case.

Landmark Communications Group: PO Box 1444, Hendersonville, TN 37077; Pres. Bill Anderson Jr.

Laura Grüb Enterprises: 235-4 Lucas Lane, Voorhees, NJ 08043; Pres. Laura Grüb-Geschwindt.

Living Rock Ministries: 1225 Atlantic Ave, Suite 3, Rochester, NY 14609; Programme & Music Dir Pastor Samme Palermo.

Loud Cry Productions: PO Box 210270, Nashville, TN 37221-0270; Owner/Pres. Don Sanders.

Marco Music Group: 1620 16th Ave S, Nashville, TN 37212; Pres./Owner Jeff Walker.

Mark Alan Agency: PO Box 21323, St Paul, MN 55121; Pres. Mark Alan.

Mazur Publications: PO Box 360, East Windsor, NJ 08520; Publicist Michael Mazur.

Mia Mind Music: 5001/2 E 84th St, Suite 4B, New York, NY 10028-7368; CEO Steven Bentzel.

Mirkin Management: 9061/2 Congress Ave, Austin, TX 78701; tel. (512) 472-1818; fax (512) 472-6915; Owner Jan Mirkin.

Music & Entertainment Division: 2200 Wilson Blvd, Suite 200, Arlington, VA 22201; Pres., Music & Entertainment Division Ed Yoe.

Music Man Productions: 568 Snelling Ave N, Suite 106, St Paul, MN 55104; Owners Paul Manske, Steve York.

Nancy Carlin Assocs: 411 Ferry St, Ste 4, Martinez, CA 94553; tel. (510) 372-4260; fax (510) 372-3762; Agent Nancy Carlin.

Nancy Fly Agency: PO Box 90306, Austin, TX 78709-0306; Dir Nancy Fly.

Only New Age Music Inc: 8033 Sunset Blvd, Suite #472, Los Angeles, CA 90046; Pres. Suzanne Doucet; Vice-Pres. James Bell.

Pal Productions Co: PO Box 80691, Baton Rouge, LA 70898; Pres. Johnny R. Palazzotto.

Plug Productions: 273 Chippewa Dr., Columbia, SC 29210-6508; Dir John Mack; Contact Ron Sparks.

PPL-MCI Entertainment Group: 10 Universal Plaza, PO Box 8442, Universal City, CA 91618; tel. (818) 506-8533; fax (818) 506-8534; e-mail pplzmi@aol.com; website www.pplzmi.com; CEO Jaeson St James Jarrett; Man. Dir Maxx Diamond.

Precision Management: 825 N King St, Suite A-1, Hampton, VA 23669-2814; Operations Man. Cappriccieo M. Scates.

Premier Productions: 1909 N Spruce, Wichita, KS 67214; Owner Anthony Welch.

Prince/SF Productions: 1135 Francisco St, Suite 7, San Francisco, CA 94109-1087; tel. (415) 775-9627; Pres. Ken Malucelli.

Punk Metal Rock Records: PO Box 410099, San Francisco, CA 94141-0099; A & R Head Stash Ravine.

Remington Management Inc: 6602 Harbor Town, Suite 501, Houston, TX 77036; Pres. Janice D. Hayes.

Rock Dog Records: PO Box 3687, Hollywood, CA 90028; Vice-Pres. of A & R Gerry North.

Ron Rainey & Assocs: 315 S Beverly Dr., Suite 206, Beverly Hills, CA 90212; Man. Ron Rainey.

Rosebud Agency: PO Box 170429, San Francisco, CA 94117; tel. (415) 386-3456; fax (415) 386-0599; e-mail info@rosebudus.com; website www.rosebudus.com; Pres. Mike Kappus.

S T A R S Productions: 1 Professional Quadrangle, Second Floor Suite, Sparta, NJ 07871; tel. (201) 729-7242; fax (201) 729-2979; Pres. Stephen Tarkanish.

Silver Star Productions Inc/Gulf Artists: 1800 Amberwood Dr., Riverview, FL 33569; tel. (813) 689-3944; fax (813) 685-6899; e-mail marstarrr@aol.com; Pres. Margorie Sexton.

Southeastern Attractions: 120 Vulcan Rd. Birmingham, AL 35209; tel. (205) 942-6600; fax (205) 942-7700. .

Squad 16: 2632 Boston Rd, PO Box 65, Wilbraham, MA 01095; Contact Tom Najemy.

SRO Entertainment Inc: PO Box 10161, Honolulu, HI 96816; Pres. Ken Rosene.

SRO Productions Inc: 821 Marquette Ave S, Suite 1815, Minneapolis, MN 55402; Pres. Lawrence H. Berle.

St John Artists: PO Box 619, Neenah, WI 54957-0619; Owner Jon St John.

Stardate Concerts Inc: 10430 Shady Trail, Suite 104, Dallas, TX 75220; tel. (940) 497-2200; fax (940) 497-6677; e-mail starconkw@cs.com; Pres. Randy Shelton.

Surface Entertainment & Management: PO Box 2935, Church St Station, New York, NY 10008; website www.surfacemgmt.com; Contact Pam Beninon.

Terrace Entertainment Corpn: PO Box 68, Las Vegas, NM 87701; Pres. Robert John Jones.

Tone Zone Booking Agency: 939 W Wilson Ave, Chicago, IL 60610; Booking Man. Diane Borden.

Triage International: 302 Butler St, Third Floor, Brooklyn, NY 11217; tel. (718) 243-9962; fax (718) 243-9961; e-mail info@triagemusic.com; Man. Bob Weyersberg.

Triangle Talent Inc: 10424 Watterson Trail, Louisville, KY 40299; tel. (502) 267-5466; fax (502) 267-8244; website triangletalent.com; Agent Gary Deusner.

Umpire Entertainment Enterprises: 1507 Scenic Dr., Longview, TX 75604; Pres. Jerry Haymes.

Vokes Music, Record & Promotion Co: PO Box 12, New Kensington, PA 15068-0012; tel. (724) 335-2775; Pres./Owner Howard Vokes.

William Morris Agency: (New York Office) 1325 Avenue of the Americas, New York, NY 10019; tel. (212) 586-5100; fax (212) 246-3583; (Beverly Hills Office) 1 William Morris Pl., Beverly Hills, CA 90212; tel. (310) 859-4000; fax (310) 859-4462; (Nashville Office) 2100 West End Ave, Nashville, TN 37203; tel. (615) 963-3000; fax (615) 963-3090; website www.wma.com.

Work Horse Productions: PO Box 1001, Kapaa, Kauai, HI 96746; tel. (808) 822-0933; fax (808) 822-7737; e-mail whp@aloha.net; Owner Michael Gregg

APPENDIX D: MUSIC PUBLISHERS

Andorra

RIAL Andorra: Avda de Tarragona 24, Andorra La Vella; tel. 860686; fax 866286; e-mail rial@andorra.ad; Man. Pascal Lair.

Argentina

AIM (Arco Iris Musical): Avda Santa Fé 4910, 4°, Of. B, 1425 Buenos Aires; tel. and fax (11) 4775-2343; e-mail aimcontenidos@aol.com; Dir-Gen. Osvaldo Bermolen.

BMG Ariola Argentina: Talcahuano 750, 6°, 1013 Capital Federal; tel. (11) 4373-4051; fax (11) 4814-2415; e-mail bmgargentina@bmge.com.

Clan Dilo Music: Casilla Correo 123 La Plata, 1900 Buenos Aires; tel. (0221) 482-2546; fax (0221) 425-1991; e-mail clandilo@clandilo.com; Pres. Giorgio di Lorenzo.

EMI Music Publishing Argentina: Avda Callao 289, 1°, 1022 Buenos Aires; tel. (11) 4372-9740; fax (11) 4372-6837; e-mail Ncasonu@emimusicpub.com; Man. Dir Nestor E. Casonu.

Musidisc Europe Sudamerica SAIC: Güemes 4418, 1° A, 1425 Buenos Aires; Pres. Jimmy Olszevicki.

Peermusic Argentina Ediciones y Producciones SA: Rivadavia 5012, 6°, 1424 Buenos Aires; Pres. Elsa Villar.

Sony/ATV Music Publishing: Bartolome Mitre 1984/86, 1039 Capital Federal, Buenos Aires; tel. (11) 4959-8516; fax (11) 4959-8517; e-mail Marta_Zega@ar.sonymusic.com; Contact Marta Zega.

Universal Music Publishing SA: Valentin Gomez 3530, 1055 Buenos Aires; tel. (11) 4867-7070; fax (11) 4812-0034; e-mail daniel.retondano@umusic.com; Contact Daniel Retondano.

Australia

Australian Music Publishers Pty Ltd: Level 5, 83 Mount St, North Sydney, NSW 2060; tel. (2) 9925-0765; fax (2) 9925-0521; e-mail srhanson@ozmusicpub.com; Man. Dir Stephen Hanson.

Black Pig Publishing: PO Box 2093, St Kilda West, Vic. 3182; Man. Dir Michael Lynch.

Boosey & Hawkes (Australia) Pty Ltd: Unit 12/6, Campbell St, Artarmon, NSW 2064; Man. Dir Richard Mackie.

Bright Spark Songs Pty Ltd: 20 Leila St, Prahran, Vic. 3181; Contact Tony Moran.

Central Australian Aboriginal Media Assocs Music: 99–101 Todd St, Alice Springs, NT 0871; Gen. Man. Owen Cole.

EMI Music Publishing: Level 1, 1 Gurrigal St, Mosman, NSW 2088; tel. (612) 9960 5400; fax (612) 9960-5122; e-mail australia@emimusicpub.com; Man. Dir John Anderson.

Festival Music Publishing Group: 63–79 Miller St, Pyrmont, NSW 2009; tel. (02) 9660 5218; fax (02) 9692 8058; Copyright Man. Vilma West.

Grundy Music Pty Ltd: Locked Bag 526, Frenchs Forest, NSW 2086; Sr Consultant Business Affairs J. M. Fowler.

Ideal Management P/C: PO Box 1037, Caulfield North, Melbourne, Vic. 3161; Man. Dir and CEO Nathan D. Brenner.

Image Music Group Pty Ltd: 19 Johnston St, Port Melbourne, Vic. 3207; Man. Dir John McDonald.

Immedia!: PO Box 2977, Sydney, NSW 2001; Man. Partner Phil Tripp.

J. Albert & Son P/L Albert Productions: 9 Rangers Rd, Neutral Bay, NSW 2089; Gen. Man. Fifa Riccobono.

Leosong Music Pty Ltd: Level 6, 350 Kent St, Sydney, NSW 2000; tel. (02) 9299 5966; fax (02) 9299 3059; e-mail origin@wr.com.au; Contacts Philip Walker, Sue Boylan.

Mana Music: 117 Rouse St, Port Melbourne, Vic. 3207; tel. (03) 9646 4303; fax (03) 9646 6336.

MCA Music Pty Ltd: 23 Pelican St, Darlinghurst, NSW 2031; tel. (02) 9267 6088; fax (02) 9264 6543; Man. Dir Peter Hebbes.

MMA Music: 26 Bayswater Rd, Kings Cross, NSW 2010; tel. (02) 9326 9599; fax (02) 9326 9641; e-mail office@rooart.com.au; CEO C. M. Murphy.

Mushroom Music: 9 Dundas Lane, Albert Park, Vic. 3206; tel. (03) 9690 3399; fax (03) 9695 7819; Chair. Michael Gudinski.

Polygram Music Publishing (Australia) Pty Ltd: 122 McEvoy St, Alexandria, NSW 2015; Man. Dir Roger Grierson.

Rondor Music: 78 Chandos St, St Leonards, NSW 2065; Man. Dir Bob Aird.

Shock Music Publishing Pty Ltd: 24 High St, Northcote, Vic. 3070; tel. (03) 9482 3666; fax (03) 9482 3873; Publishing Man. Sally Galwey.

Sony Music Publishing Australia: 11–19 Hargrave St, East Sydney, NSW 2010; tel. (02) 9383 6481; fax (02) 9360-2973; e-mail publishing_au@sonymusic.com.au; Gen. Man. Damian Trotter.

Southern: 304/10–12 Clarke St, Crows Nest, NSW 2065; tel. (02) 9436 0799; fax (02) 9437 5980.

Universal Music Publishing Pty Ltd: 3 Munn Reserve, Millers Point, NSW 2000; tel. (02) 9207-0500; fax (02) 9252-0503; e-mail contact.umpaustralia@umusic.com; Man. Dir Bob Aird.

Warner Chappell Music Pty Ltd: 3 Talavera Rd, North Ryde, NSW 2113; tel. (02) 9855 4000; fax (02) 9855 4099; Man. Dir John Bromell.

Zomba Production Music (Australia) Pty Ltd: 25 Burton St, Glebe, NSW 2037; Man. Dir Stuart Livingston.

Austria

ATS Records: Breitenau 7, 4591 Molln; tel. (0) 7584-2454; fax (0) 7584-2424; e-mail office@ats-records.com; website www.ats-records.com; Man. Dir Reinhard Brunner.

Edition Helbing: Kaplanstr 9, 6063 Rum; Man. Dir Elvira Harm-Dematte.

Edition Musica Musikverlag: Webgasse 43, PO Box 451, 1060 Vienna; Man. Dir Franz Wallner.

Edition Rossori/Pate Records: Hietzinger Hauptstr 94, 1130 Vienna; tel. (1) 8762400; fax (1) 8795464; e-mail office@poppate.com; website www.paterecords.com; Man. Dir Mario Rossori.

Honk Music and Records: Hormayrgasse 3/25, 1170 Vienna; tel. and fax (1) 486-4287; website www.sra.at/sr/comps/7196.htm; Man. Dir Jivi Honk.

International Society for Jazz Research: Leonhardstr 15, 8010 Graz; tel. (0) 389-3160; fax (0) 389-3161; e-mail gertrand.steinserger@kug.ac.at; website www.jazzresearch.org; Promotes jazz research; Contact Gertrand Steinserger.

Koch Music Publishing: Gewerbegebeit, PO Box 24, 6600 Höfen; Man. Dir Franz Koch.

Meltemi Music: Hirschstettner str 26/H 13, 1220 Vienna; tel. (1) 203-2272; e-mail meltemi@aon.at; Man. Dir Horst Bichler.

Polygram/Antenna Musikverlag Austria: PO Box 85, Edelsinnstr 4, 1122 Vienna; Chair. Adolf Hoffmann.

Shamrock: Altwaidhofen 37, 3830 Waidhofen/Thaya; Man. Dir Uwe Kranner.

Stein Music Wien: Bernardgasse 39/33, 1070 Vienna; Man. Dir Regine Steinmetz.

Universal Music Publishing GmbH: PO Box 85, 1122 Vienna; fax (1) 813-1300; e-mail petra.heinrich@umusic.com; Gen. Man. Petra Heinrich.

Warner/Chappell Musikverlag GmbH: Diefenbachgasse 35, 1150 Vienna; Man. Dir Peter Gruber.

Belgium

ALC Productions: Ave Eugène Ysaye 47, 1070 Brussels; Label Man. Alexander Louvet.

Baltic NV: Rederijkersstraat 82, 2610 Wilrijk-Antwerp; tel. (3) 828-4084; fax (3) 829-1068; e-mail info@baltic.be; website www.baltic.be; Gen. Man. Koen Bogaerts.

Boom!: Bergensesteenweg 19, 1500 Halle; tel. (0) 2360-2851; website www.jpvan.be; Man. Dir J. P. Van.

Caracol Music Sprl Group: 5 rue du Cheneau, 6120 Ham-sur-Heure; Gen. Man. Timothy Hagelstein.

Carbon 7: 23 Ave Général Eisenhower, 1030 Brussels; tel. (2) 242-9703; fax (2) 245-3885; e-mail carbon7records@compuserve.com; Dir Guy Segers.

Dexon Sprl: 41 rue Cité de L'Enfance, 6001 Marcinelle; Man. Delfosse Pierre.

Editions Confidentielles: 90 rue de Veeweyde, 1070 Brussels; Professional Man. Piet Bekaert.

EMI Music Publishing Belgium SA/NV: Albert Giraudlaan 95, 1030 Brussels; tel. (2) 245-0320; fax (2) 245-3455; Man. Guy Van Handenhove.

MMD SA: Rue Fernand Bernier 38, 1060 Brussels; Man. Dir Plastic Bertrand.

Multi Sound Music Publishing: 24 Gachardstreet, 1050 Brussels; Gen. Man. Pierre Pletinckx.

Prestation Music: 24 Gachardstreet, 1050 Brussels; Gen. Man. Pierre Pletinckx.

Pyramid International Music: Lepelhoekstraat 26, 9100 Sint-Niklaas; tel. (3) 778-1854; fax (3) 766-8441; e-mail marc@marcdecoen.be; website www.marcdecoen.be; Man. Dir Marc De Coen.

RVY Music Publishing: Kammerstraat 19, 9000 Ghent; Man. Robert Van Yper.

Sony/ATV Music Publishing SA: Rue H. Evenepoelstraat 9, 1030 Brussels; tel. (2) 702-9754; fax (2) 726-1357; e-mail Stefan_Robbrecht@be.sonymusic.com; website www.sonyatv.be; Junior Creative Man. Stefan Robbrecht.

T & B Music: Gulden Vlieslaan 67, 8000 Brugge; Contact Nico A. Mertens.

Team for Action (T4A): Ave Oscar van Goibtsnoven 45B, 1180 Brussels; Man. Dir Claude Martin.

Tempo (Top Entertainment Editions): Krijgslaan 61, 9000 Gent; Gen. Man. Luc Standaert.

Tessa Records Rock Label: Dennenlaan 13, 9160 Lokeren; tel. and fax (09) 3489836; Pres. and Owner Marc de Block.

Universal Music Publishing NV: Woluwedal 34, PO Box 6, 1200 Brussels; tel. (2) 775-8188; fax (2) 775-5006; e-mail luc.standaert@umusic.com; Gen. Man. Luc Standaert.

Witlof: Leernsesteenweg 168, 9800 Deinze; Dir Jean Tant.

Brazil

Caipirapirs Produçoes Artisticas Ltda: Avda das Aguas Marinhas 157 Pg Petrópolis, 07600-00 São Paulo, SP; Gen. Man. Pablo Ossipoff.

EMI Music Publishing Brazil: Praia do Flamengo 200, 15°, Flamengo 22210-030, Rio de Janeiro; tel. (21) 2558-7080; fax (21) 2588-7333; Man. Dir Jose Antonio Perdomo.

Estudio Eldorado Ltda: Rua Pires da Mota 820–830, 01529 São Paulo, SP; Exec. Dir João Lara Mesquita.

Paradox Music: Rua Dr Pinto Ferraz 58, Vila Mariana, 04117-040 São Paulo, SP; Dir Silvio Arnaldo Caligaris.

Sony Music Edicoes Musicais Ltda: Edif. Caemi (PB300), Praia de Botafogo 300, 12 andar, Botagofo 22259-900, Rio de Janeiro; tel. (21) 2559-5200; fax (21) 2553-1777; e-mail sampbrazil@br.sonymusic.com; Contact Andrea Tournillon.

Universal Music Publishing Ltda: Avda Erico Verissimo 918, Barra de Tijuca, 22621-180 Rio de Janeiro; tel. (21) 3389-7667; fax (21) 2495-1223; e-mail jose.anchieta@umusic.com; Publishing Man. Jose Cosme Anchieta.

Bulgaria

Arsis Publishing: 15 Tsarigradsko Chausse Blvd, 1220 Sofia; Chair. Borislav Ivanchev.

Balkanton Music Publishing: 6 Haidoushka Polyana str, 1612 Sofia; tel. (2) 952-0373; fax (2) 952-6090; e-mail balkanton@yahoo.com; Man. Dir Ventsislav Bozhinov; Vice-Pres. Ani Pavlova.

Mega Music Ltd: 2 Trapezitza str, 1000 Sofia; Man. Dir Dora Tchernkva.

Union Media Ltd Record Co: 71A Evlogi Georgiev Blvd, Fourth Floor, 1142 Sofia; Pres. Martin Zachariev.

Union of Bulgarian Composers (UBC): 2 Ivan Vazov St, 1000 Sofia; tel. (2) 988-1560; fax (2) 987-4378; e-mail ubc@mail.bol.bg; website www.ubc-bg.com; Pres. Victor Chuchkov.

Virginia Records Publishing: 60 Khan Asparuch St, 1000 Sofia; tel. (2) 980-9024.

Canada

Attic Music Group: 102 Atlantic Ave, Toronto, ON M6K 1X9; Pres. Alexander Mair.

BMG Music Publishing Canada Inc: 150 John St, Sixth Floor, Toronto, ON M5V 3C3.

Botany Park Records & Music Publishing Co: 361 Walter Dr., Keswick, ON L4P 3A8; Pres. Marlaine Rennocks.

Brass Ring Productions/Manford Music Inc: PO Box 1266, Station A, Kelowna, BC V1Y 7V8; tel. and fax (250) 763-5502; e-mail manford@telus.net; Pres. Becky Chapman.

EMI Music Publishing Canada: 119 Spadina Ave, Suite 604, Toronto, ON M5V 2L1; tel. (416) 340 9277; fax (416) 340 9286; Pres. Michael McCarty.

G Man Music: 4 Bowden St, Toronto, ON, M4K 2X2; Pres. Gerry Young.

G String Publishing: PO Box 1096, Hudson, QC J0P 1V0; tel. (450) 458-2819; e-mail la_records@excite.com; website www.radiofreedom.com; Man. Maka Hanna.

Heaven Bent Music Corpn: 11 Hopewell Cres., Hamilton, ON L8J 1P3; Gen. Man. Kathie Pietron.

John H. Lennon Music Ltd: 1235 Bay St, Suite 400, Toronto, ON M5R 3K4; Pres. John Lennon; Man. Dir Lenny Moore.

Montina Music: PO Box 702, Snowdon Station, Montréal, QC H3X 3X8; Professional Gen. Man. D. Leonard.

Morning Music Ltd: 5200 Dixie Rd, Suite 203, Mississauga, ON L4W 1E4; Pres. Mark Altman.

MUSINFO Publishing Group Inc: 2504 Mayfair Ave, Montréal, QC H4B 2C8; tel. (514) 484-5419; fax (514) 484-9948; e-mail musinfo@musinfo.com; website www.musinfo.com; Pres. and Owner Jehan V. Valiquet.

PolyGram Music Publishing: 1345 Denison St, Markham, ON L3R 5V2; Vice-Pres. and Gen. Man. John Redmond.

Savannah Music Inc: 123 Applefield Dr., Scarborough, ON M1P 3Y5; Dir of Canadian Operations Bill Carruthers.

Sony/ATV Music Publishing: 1121 Leslie St, Don Mills, ON M3C 2J9; tel. (416) 391-7661; fax (416) 391-7997; e-mail sonyatvmusicpublishingcanada@sonymusic.com; Pres. Gary Furniss.

Sparwood Music Productions: PO Box 270, Bentley, AB T0C 0J0; Man. Dick Damron.

Spinner Music Group Inc: Third Floor, 68 Water St, Vancouver, BC V6B 1A4; Pres. Ken Spence; Man. Dir Wolfgang Burandt.

Third Wave Productions Ltd: PO Box 563, Gander, NF A1V 2E1; Pres. R. Archibald Bonnell.

TMP—The Music Publisher: Suite 300, 1670 Bayview Ave, Toronto, ON M4G 3C2; Pres. Frank Davies.

Universal Music Publishing: 2450 Victoria Park Ave, Willowdale, ON M2J 4A2; tel. (416) 718-4000; fax (416) 718-4224; e-mail jodie.ferneyhough@umusic.com; Creative Dir Jodie Ferneyhough.

Warner/Chappell Music Canada Ltd: 85 Scarsdale Rd, Unit 101, Don Mills, ON M3B 2R2; Pres. Jerry Renewych; Creative Man. Anne-Marie Smith.

Chile

Ediciones Musicales Fermata Ltda: Ebro 2751, Of. 609, Las Condes 41, Santiago; Gen. Man. Eliana Cisternas.

EMI Music Publishing Chile: Alfredo Barros Errazuriz 1954, Of. 203, Providencia, Santiago; tel. (2) 209-1009; fax (2) 209-5440; Man. Dir Nestor E. Casonu.

PolyGram Music Chile Ltda: Cruz del Sur No. 133, 9°, Las Condes, Santiago; tel. (2) 246-5069; fax (2) 248-1540; e-mail carmen.valencia@umusic.com; Gen. Man. Carmen Valencia.

Sony/ATV Music Publishing SA: Avda Suecia 2323, Providencia, Santiago; tel. (2) 200-8400; fax (2) 274-3216; e-mail Luis_Garay@cl.sonymusic.com; Contact Luis Garay.

Colombia

BMG Ariola de Colombia SA: Calle 67, 7-94, 12°, Santafé de Bogotá, DC; Dir Francisco Villanueva.

Compañia Colombiana de Discos SA (Codiscos): Carrera 67, 1, Sur 92 Guayabal, 1428 Medellín; Pres. César Vallejo.

Edisdago Ltda: C / 33AA, 81-25, Medellín; Pres. Dario Gómez Zapata.

Promotora Colombiana de Musica Ltda: Carrera 67, 1 Sur 92, Medellín; Man. Sylvia N. Arango.

Sony/ATV Music Publishing: Calle 94A, No. 11A-50, Santafé de Bogotá, DC; tel. (1) 621-9151; fax (1) 621-9393; e-mail Gisela_Forero@co.sonymusic.com; Contact Gisela Forero.

Universal Music Publishing Colombia SA: 103 No. 21-60, 3°, Santafé de Bogotá, DC; tel. (1) 218-5114; fax (1) 257-2261; e-mail claudia.tellez@umusic.com; Copyright Man. Claudia Tellez.

Costa Rica

Universal Music Publishing de Centro America SA: De la agencia de autos Subaru, 150m norte, Barrio Dent, San Jose; tel. (506) 283-9063; fax (506) 253-8861; e-mail lilliana.hernandez@umusic.com; Contact Lilliana Hernandez.

Croatia

Kinel Music: Vinogradska Cesta 3, 41000 Zagreb; Man. Dir Mario Kinel.

Melody: Rubesi 139 A, 51215 Kastav; Dir Andrej Basa.

Skalinada: Dubrovacka 23, 58000 Split; Dir Zdenko Runjic.

Tutico: Veprinacka 16, 10000 Zagreb; Dir Zrinko Tutic.

Czech Republic

Czech Music Information Centre: Besední 3, 118 00 Prague 1; tel. (2) 5731-7424; fax (2) 5731-7424; e-mail his@vol.cz; website www.musica.cz; Dir Miroslav Pudlak.

EMI Music Publishing Czech Republic, a.s.: Kovarova 39, 155 00 Prague 5 - Stodulky; tel. (2) 5711-5115; fax (2) 3551-8331; e-mail jzemanova@emimusicpub.com; Man. Dir Jolana Zemanova.

Universal Music Publishing SRO: Velvarska 7, 160 00 Prague 6 - Dejvice; tel. (2) 3302-9902; fax (2) 3302-9909; e-mail jirina.erlebachov@umusic.com; Publishing Man. Jirina Erlebachova.

Denmark

Cloudland: Skt Jørgens Allé 7 O, G6 1th, 1615 Copenhagen; Man. Dir Simon Sheika.

ELAP Music A/S: Bransagervej 2-10, 9490 Pandrup; tel. (45) 9973-4000; fax (45) 9824-6045; e-mail elap@elap.dk; website www.elapmusic.dk; Promotion Steffen Lund Nielsen.

EMI Music Publishing Denmark A/S: PO Box 1094, 1008 Copenhagen K; tel. (45) 3393-5231; fax (45) 3393-5232; e-mail thoehne@emimusicpub.com; Gen. Man. Thomas Hoehne.

Great Dane Music: c/o Replay Records, Frederikssundvej 60 C, 2400 NV Copenhagen; Man. Dir Henrik Boetcher.

Iceberg Music: Ronne Alie 78A, 8600 Silkeborg; Man. Dir Manfred Zähringer.

Inhouse Publishing: Vognmagergade 10, 1120 Copenhagen K.

Klepto Records & Publishing: Langdries 4, 9450 Haaltert; Man. Dir Wilfried Brits.

Mega Scandinavia A/S: Indiakaj 1, 2100 Copenhagen Ø; tel. (45) 3525-6666; fax (45) 3525-6665; e-mail mega-records@mega-records.dk; website www.mega-records.com; Vice-Pres. Cai Leitner; Dir of A & R and Marketing Jesper Ban.

Olafssongs: c/o Warner Chappell Music Denmark, Anker Heegaards, Gade 2, 1572 Copenhagen V; tel. (45) 3313-3315; fax (45) 3313-3330; e-mail mailbox@warner-chappell.dk; Pres. Finn Olafsson.

Pineapple Publishing ApS: Sondergade 20, 6823 Ansager; tel. (45) 7529-7400; fax (45) 7529-7550; e-mail mail@pineapple.dk; website www.pineapple.dk; Man. Dir Helge Engelbrecht.

Sundance/Stunt Records: Havnegade 41, 1050 Copenhagen K; tel. 3333-8720; fax 3333-8730; e-mail sundance@sundance.dk; website www.sundance.dk; Man. Dir Peter Littauer.

Warner Chappell Music Denmark A/S: Antoinettevej 2, 2500 Valby; tel. (45) 3616-6888; fax (45) 3617-0077; website www.warnermusic.dk; Man. Dir Finn Work.

Finland

Bluebird Music: Henrikities 5 C, 00370 Helsinki; Man. Dir Niko Nordström.

BMG Music Publishing: PL 173, 00211 Helsinki; tel. (9) 613-201; fax (9) 613-20299; e-mail mail@bmg.fi.

EMI Finland OY: Tallberginkatu 2A, 00180 Helsinki; tel. (9) 348-426; fax (9) 3484-2797; e-mail veikko.koivumaki@emimusic.com.

Flamingo Music: Vapaalantie 2, 01650 Vantaa; Man. Dir Vexi Salmi.

Love Music Publishing: Hämeentie 6 A 4, 00530 Helsinki; tel. (9) 4176-6600; fax (9) 4176-6650; e-mail sini.perho@lovemusic.fi; website www.lovemusic.fi; Man. Dir Sini Perho.

Polarvox Music Publishing OY: PL 9, 00371 Helsinki; tel. (9) 2252-1340; fax (9) 2252-1310; e-mail olavi@finnvox.fi; Man. Dir Leena Juuranto.

Poplandia Music: PO Box 483, 33101 Tampere; tel. (3) 2136-800; fax (3) 2133-732; e-mail poplandia@poko.fi; Man. Dir Kari Helenius.

Taurus Music: PO Box 33, 02431 Masala; Man. Dir Antero Päiväänen.

Universal Music OY: PL 172, 00211 Helsinki; tel. (9) 6154-677; fax (9) 6154-6700; e-mail antti.lehtinen@umusic.com; website www.universalmusic.fi.

Warner Chappell Music Finland OY: PO Box 126, 00521 Helsinki; tel. (9) 229-560; fax (9) 2295-6600; e-mail tom.frisk@warnerchappell.com; website www.warnerchappell.com; A & R Tom Frisk.

Zen Master Publishing: Ilmarinkatu 12, 33500 Tampere; tel. (3) 2131-260; fax (3) 2131-297; e-mail zenmaster@rock.pp.fi; Man. Dir Tapio Korjus.

France

Alpha Bravo: 64 Ave Jean Jaurès, 93500 Pantin; tel. (1) 4843-8023; Contact Daniel Bornet.

BMG Music Publishing: France 10 rue Duphot, 75001 Paris; Dir Stéphane Berlow.

Boucherie Productions: 15 Bis rue du Plateau, 75019 Paris; Dir Natali Luc.

Caravage: 130 rue Marius Aufan, 92300 Levallois-Perret; Gen. Man. Jean-Paul Smets.

Editions Essex: 5 rue Lincoln, 75008 Paris; Man. Dir René Boyer.

Editions Fortin: 4 Cité Chaptal, 75009 Paris; tel. (1) 4874-2821; fax (1) 4023-9867; e-mail editions_fortin@club-internet.fr; website www.editionsmusicalesfortin.com; Contact Multrier Fortin.

EMI Music Publishing France SA: 20 rue Molitor, 75016 Paris; tel. (1) 4071-3200; fax (1) 4071-6180; e-mail InfoFrance@emimusicpub.com; Man. Dir Fabrice Nataf.

Fairplay (Fair and Square Publishing): 41 rue Emile Zola, 93100 Montreuil; tel. (1) 4172-0830; fax (1) 4172-0839; e-mail fairplay@wanadoo.fr; Dir Fabrice Absil.

FKO Music: 18 rue de Revilly, 25012 Paris; Man. Dir Francis Kertekian; International Dept Grace Casta.

Made In Heaven: 6 rue Rémy de Gourmont, 75019 Paris; Label Man. Mathias Jeannin.

MCA Caravelle France: 35 Blvd Malesherbes, 75008 Paris; Chair. Tom Arena.

Metisse Music Sarl: 1 Villa Juge, 75015 Paris; Man. Dir Petra Gehrmann.

Nouvelles Editions Meridian: 5 rue Lincoln, 75008 Paris; Man. Dir Rene Boyer.

Peermusic: 5 rue Lincoln, 75008 Paris; tel. (1) 5383-9250; fax (1) 5383-9255; website www.peermusic.com; Man. Dir Rene Boyer.

Polygram Music: 14 rue Curie, 75005 Paris; Chair. Philippe Lerichomme.

Promo Sonor International: 30 rue de Saussure, 75017 Paris; Man. Dir Jo Pucheu.

Rondor Music: 32 rue Etienne Marcel, 75002 Paris; Dir Halit Uman.

Salam Aleikum Amusements: 2 rue Carpeaux, 75018 Paris; Dir Stephane Benhamou.

Scorpio Music: 12 Ave George V, 75008 Paris; tel. (1) 4720-4395; fax (1) 4952-0134; website www.scorpiomusic.fr; Pres. Henri Belolo.

Skydog/Kind of Groove: 32 Ave Claude Vellefaux, 75010 Paris; PDG Marc Zermati.

Société d'Editions Musicales Internationales: 5 rue Lincoln, 75008 Paris; Man. Dir René Boyer.

Sony/ATV Music Publishing: 131 ave de Wagram, 75838 Paris; tel. (1) 4440-6060; fax (1) 4440-6688; e-mail Frsonyatv_serviceartistique@fr.sonymusic.com; Dir Nicolas Galibert.

Topomic Music: 26 rue L. M. Nordmann, 92250 La Garenne-Colombes; tel. (1) 4769-9807; fax (1) 4119-0903; e-mail topomic@worldonline.fr; Pres. Pierre Jaubert.

Universal Music Publishing SA: 20/22 rue des Fosses Saint-Jacques, 75005 Paris; tel. (1) 4441-9400; fax (1) 4441-9401; e-mail umpfrance@umusic.com.

Warner Music Distribution: 14 ave Albert Einstein, 93150 Le Blanc Mesnil; tel. (1) 4814-5000; fax (1) 4814-5050.

XIII Bis Music Group: 34 rue Eugene Flachat, 75017 Paris; Man. Dir Laurent Dreux-Leblanc; Music Dir Brian Rawling.

Germany

AlphaTon Publishing GmbH: Am Haidberg 4, 21465 Wentorf; Contacts Joe Rudolph, Gerd Gerdes.

Ata Tak Records: Kölner str 226 F, 40227 Düsseldorf; tel. (211) 782-2329; website www.atatak.com; Dir Frank Fenstermacher.

Blanko Musik: Schongauerstrasse 13, 81377 Munich; e-mail info@blankomusik.de; website www.blankomusik.de; Man. Dir Hage Hein; Asst Man. Dir Gerhild Malorny.

Castor Promotions: Dragonerstr 21, 30163 Hanover; Contact Elke Fleing.

Edition Metromania/Warner Chappell Germany: Osterstr 36, 30159 Hanover; Man. Dir Frank Bornemann.

Edition Partysanen Publishing: Skalitzer str 68, 10997 Berlin; Man. Dir Rona Casley.

EMI Music Publishing Germany GmbH & Co, KG: Alsterufer 1, 20354 Hamburg; e-mail germany@emimusicpub.com; Dir Andreas Kiel.

Freibank: Ditmar-Koel str 26, 20459 Hamburg; e-mail info@freibank.com; website www.freibank.com; Dirs Mark Chung, Klaus Maeck.

Fun Factory! GmbH: Hermannstadtweg 9, 48151 Münster; tel. (251) 78321; fax (251) 78322; e-mail info@funfactory.org; website www.funfactory.org; Label Mans Axel Seitz, John Fryer.

Garbitowski: Metzer str 30, 50677 Cologne; Owner & Dir Jürgen Garbitowski.

Heartpunch Music Publishing & Promotion: Vohwinkeler str 154, 42329 Wuppertal; Man. Dir Michael Schuster.

Kick Musikverlag: Burgunder str 8, 50677 Cologne; Man. Dir Goetz Elbertzhagen; International Man. Lynda Hill.

Mainhattan Music Production: Friedrich-Ebert str 48, 63179 Obertshausen; Man. Uwe Block.

Moderne Welt Musikproduktions & Vennoskfungs GmbH: Marienbaden str 6/1, 70372 Stuttgart; Man. Dir Henning Tögel.

Music Box GmbH: Rahlstedter str 65, 22149 Hamburg; Man. Dir Hubertus Branzko.

Musikverlag Progressive GmbH: Bramfelder Chaussee 238c, 22177 Hamburg; e-mail office@progressive-mv.de; Contact Rudy Holzhauer.

Polygram Songs Musikverlag Germany: Glockengiesserwall 3, 20095 Hamburg; Man. Dir Os Van Joost.

Rolf Budde Musikverlag GmbH: Hohenzollerdamm 54 A, 14199 Berlin; tel. (30) 823-4015; fax (30) 823-7076; e-mail budde@buddemusic.de; website www.buddemusic.de; Man. Dir Dr Rolf Budde.

t'Bwana Sound/Big Easy: Schleswigerstr 19, 44145 Dortmund; Contact Helmut Philipps.

Sony/ATV Publishing GmbH: Bellevustrasse 3, Berlin 10785; tel. (30) 2575-1300; fax (30) 2575-1301; e-mail Georg_Claus@de.sonymusic.com; Contact Georg Claus.

Thomann Künstler Management GmbH: PO Box 1, 96136 Burgebrach; tel. (9546) 9449; fax (9546) 6844; e-mail info@thomann-music.de; website www.thomann-music.de; Contact Joseph Thomann.

Universal Music Publishing GmbH: Stralauer Allee 1, 10245 Berlin; e-mail bettina.moritz@umusic.com; website www.universal-music-publishing.de; Contact Bettina Moritz.

Vielklang Musikproduktion GmbH: Forster str 4/5, 10999 Berlin; tel. (30) 6126068; fax (30) 6189382; Man. Dir Matthias Bröckel.

Westpark Music: PO Box 260 227, Rathenauplatz 4, 50515 Cologne; tel. (221) 247-644; fax (221) 231-819; e-mail westparkmusic@aop.com; website www.westparkmusic.com; Pres. Ulli Hetscher.

Greece

EMI Music Publishing (Greece) LLC: 259 Messoghion Ave, 15451 N Psychiko, Athens; tel. (210) 6714626; fax (210) 6714628; e-mail mkaridi@emimusicpub.com; Man. Dir Maria Karidi.

Filippos Nakas Mousikos Oikos: 13 Navarinoy St, 10680 Athens; Man. Dir G. Nakas.

General Publishing Co SA: 11 Kriezotou St, 10671 Athens; Man. Dir Panayiotis Maravelias.

Sony/ATV Music Publishing: Messoghion 311, 15231 Halandri, Athens; tel. (301) 674-6491; e-mail martha_konstandinidou@gr.sonymusic.com; Contact Martha Konstandinidou.

Universal Music Publishing LLC: PO Box 66017, 15510 Cholorgos, Athens; tel. (301) 6595200; fax (301) 6561143; e-mail umgreece@umusic.com.

Greenland

ULO-Greenlandic Music: PO Box 184, 3911 Sisimiut; Production Man. Karsten Sommer.

Hong Kong Special Administrative Region, People's Republic of China

Blue Max Productions: First Floor, Kingsfield Mansion, 457–459 King's Rd, North Point; Man. Partner Ralph Lister.

BMG Music Publishing Hong Kong Ltd: 11th Floor, Peninsula Office Tower, 18 Middle Rd, Tsimshatsui, Kowloon; Gen. Man. Irene Ho.

Cinepoly Music Publishing Co Ltd: 8/F 100 Canton Rd, Tsimshatsui, Kowloon; Publishing Exec. Sandy Sun.

EMI Music Publishing Hong Kong: Suite 616, AIA Tower, New World Centre, 20 Salisbury Rd, Tsimshatsui, Kowloon; tel. (852) 2956-5400; fax (852) 2506-1007; Gen. Man. Teresa Yiu.

Polygram Music Publishing Hong Kong Ltd: 8F 100 Canton Rd, Kowloon; Pres. Norman Cheng.

Sony/ATV Music Publishing: Suite 2801-13, 28th Floor, CITIC Tower, 1 Tim Mei Ave, Admirality; tel. (852) 2863-1700; fax (2864) 6279; e-mail SAMPHK@sonymusic.com; Gen. Man. Angela Hon.

Universal Music Publishing Ltd: Unit 1805, 18/F, Railway Plaza, 39 Chatham Rd S, Tsimshatsui, Kowloon; tel. (852) 2317-5155; fax (852) 2735-9308; e-mail tony.yapp@umusic.com; Regional Dir Tony Yapp.

Warner Music Publishing Hong Kong Ltd: Rooms 301–303, Corporation Sq., 8 Lam Lok St, Kowloon Bay, Kowloon; Man. Dir Paco Wong.

Hungary

Edito Musica: Vörösmarty tér 1, 1051 Budapest; Man. Dir Istvan Homolya.

EMI Music Publishing Hungary: Bajor Center, Konyves Kalman krt 5, 1097 Budapest; e-mail hungary@emimusicpub.com; Man. Dir Peter Gyorgy.

Joker: Florian ter 4–5, 1033 Budapest; Man. Dir Peter Rado.

PG Publishing: PO Box 8, 1922 Budapest.

Record Express Ltd: Kunigunda ut 41/B, 1037 Budapest; tel. (1) 437-1800; fax (1) 437-1899; e-mail meszaros@recordexpress.hu; website www.recordexpress.hu; Man. Dir Attila Schneider; International Affairs Barbara Mészaros.

Sonic Boom: Iskola U 1, Szentendre; Man. Dir Ditmar Lupfer.

Universal Music Publishing Kft: Steindl Imre U 12, 1054 Budapest; tel. and fax (1) 269-1140; e-mail szilvia.tisler@umusic.com; Contact Szilvia Tisler.

Iceland

Skifan HF: Skiefan 17, 108 Reykjavík; Chair. Jon Olafsson.

Spor HF: Nýbýlavegur 4, PO Box 320, 202 Kópavogur; Man. Dir Steinar Berg Isleifsson.

India

Universal Music India Pvt Ltd: Samir Complex, St Andrews Rd, Bandra, Mumbai 400-050; tel. (22) 655-3241; fax (22) 655-6030; e-mail Rakesh.nigam@umusic.com; Gen. Man. Rakesh Nigam.

Indonesia

PT Suara Publisindo: Midplaza 2, 19th Floor, Jl. Jendral Sudirman Kav. 10–11, Jakarta 10220; tel. (21) 571-1777; fax (21) 574-2091; e-mail damayanti.ariandini@umusic.com; Publishing Officer Damayanti Ariandini.

Sony/ATV Music Publishing: Jl. Johar 13, Menteng, Jakarta 10350; tel. (21) 390-1268; fax (21) 325-739; e-mail Ike_Indah@sonymusic.com; Contact Ike Indah.

Ireland

Acorn Music Ltd: Roncalli, Claremont Pines, Carrickmines, Dublin 18; tel. (1) 289-6628; fax (1) 289-5597; Dir Brendan Graham.

Aigle Music: 6 Danieli Dr., Artane, Dublin 5; Contacts Nicky Ryan, Roma Ryan.

Ainm Music: 5–6 Lombard St E, Dublin 2; tel. and fax (1) 677-8701; e-mail fstubbs@ainm-music.com; website www.ainm-music.com; CEO Frank Stubbs.

Asdee Music: Glenageary Office Park, Glenageary, Co Dublin; Admin. Peter Bardon.

Bardis Music Co Ltd: Glenageary Office Park, Glenageary, Co Dublin; tel. (1) 285-8711; fax (1) 289-5597; Man. Dir Peter Bardon.

Beann Eadair Music: 48 Downside, Skerries, Co Dublin; Dir Clive Hudson.

Blue Dandelion Publishing: 21 Vernon St, Dublin 8; tel. and fax (1) 473-0502; Contact Fran Coleman.

Brian Molloy: 5–6 Lombard St E, Dublin 2; Contact Brian Molloy; Marketing Man. Graham Molloy.

Bright-Child Productions: The Elms, Richmond Ave S, Dartry, Dublin 6; tel. (1) 496-0970; fax (1) 497-9411; e-mail info@bright-child.com; website www.bright-child.com; CEO Peter Blackbyrne; Dir Rosaleen Durkin.

Clannad Music: Film House, 4 Windmill Lane, Dublin 2; Man. Dir David Kavanagh.

Cló Iar—Chonnachta: Indreabhán, Conamara, Co na Gaillimhe; tel. (91) 593307; fax (91) 593362; e-mail cic@iol.ie; website www.cic.ie; Marketing & Sales Man. Deirdre O'Toole.

Coyle and Coyle: 30 Lower Leeson St, Dublin 2; Dir James Coyle.

Danceline Music: 267 Crodaun Forest Park, Celbridge, Co Kildare; tel. (1) 627-1900; Dir Peter McCluskey.

Emma Music Ltd: 5/6 Lombard St, Dublin 2; tel. (1) 677-9244; Dir Michael O'Riordan.

Evolving Music Co Ltd: Alexandra House, Earlsfort Centre, Earlsfort Terrace, Dublin 2; Contact Denis Desmond, John J. Lappin.

Foxrock Music Productions: Alexandra House, Earlsfort Centre, Earlsfort Terrace, Dublin 2; Man. Dir John John Lappin.

Gael Linn: 26–27 Merrion Sq., Dublin 2; tel. (1) 676-7283; fax (1) 676-7030; e-mail eolas@gaellinn.iol.ie; Contact Michael Ward.

Hazel Records: Dublin Rd, Monasterevin, Co Kildare; Man. Dir John Kelly.

Jump Music: 19 Stockton Green, Castleknock, Dublin 15; Man. Dir Joe McFadden.

Lunar/Unicorn Records: 5–6 Lombard St E, Dublin 2; Contacts Brian Molloy, Judy Cardiff; Marketing Man. Graham Molloy.

McGuinness/Whelan Music Publishers: 30/32 Sir John Rogerson's Quay, Dublin 2; tel. (1) 677-7330; fax (1) 677-7276; Man. Dir Barbara Galavan.

Mother Music Ltd: 30–32 Sir John Rogerson's Quay, Dublin 2; tel. (1) 677-7330; fax (1) 677-7276; Man. Dir Barbara Galavan.

Mulligan Music Ltd: 75 Sweetmount Ave, Dundrum, Co Dublin; tel. (1) 405-9026; Man. Dir Brian O'Neill.

Music Network: The Coach House, Dublin Castle, Dublin 2; tel. (1) 671-9429; fax (1) 671-9430; e-mail info@musicnetwork.ie; website www.musicnetwork.ie; Information Man. Seamus O'Reilly.

Peer Music Ireland Ltd: The Peer Suite, 12 Lower Pembroke St, Dublin 2; tel. (1) 662-9337; fax (1) 662-9339; Contact Darragh Kettle.

Raglan Music: Glenageary Office Park, Glenageary, Co Dublin; Admin. Peter Bardon.

Rosette Music Ltd: 5–6 Lombard St, Dublin 2; tel. (1) 677-9244; fax (1) 677-9386; Dir Michael O'Riordan.

RSE Music Publishing: 11–13 Station Rd, Raheny, Dublin 5; Dirs Raymond J. Smyth, Breide P. Smyth.

Third Floor Ltd: 70 Lower Baggot St, Dublin 2; Man. Dir Maurice Cassidy.

Woodtown Music: Dame House, Dame St, Dublin 2; tel. and fax (1) 679-3664; Man. Dir Jane Bolton.

Israel

Helicon Songs Ltd: 7 Hamerkava St, Industrial Zone B, Holon 58851; tel. (3) 556-2212; fax (3) 556-0938; e-mail heliconsongs@helicon.co.il.

Sony/ATV Music Publishing: NMC Music Ltd, PO Box 5225, Rishon Le Zion 75150; tel. (3) 953-2532; fax (3) 952-2050; e-mail Mayer.Paz@NMC; Contact Mayer Paz.

Italy

Ala Bianca Group Srl: Via Emilia Est 1646/c, 41100 Modena; (059) 284913; e-mail alabianca@tin.it; Gen. Man. Toni Verona.

BMG Italy: Via di S Alessandro 7, 00131 Rome; Man. Dir Mario Cantini.

Crotalo Ed Mus: Via del Corniolo 24, 48100 Ravenna; tel. (0544) 470289; e-mail crotalo@linknet.it; website www.romagna.com/crotalo; Man. Dir Luigi Mazzesi.

EMI Music Publishing Italia: Via C Ravizza 43–45, 20148 Milan; tel. (02) 4801-0216; fax (02) 4801-0046; Man. Dir Antonio Marrapodi.

FMA Edizioni Musicali e Discografiche Srl: Via Boccaccio N 47, 20123 Milan; tel. (02) 435093; fax (02) 48194098; Pres. Mario Allione.

General Rock: Viale Manzoni 52, Cerveteri, 00052 Rome; Contact Robbie Zee.

Lion Snc: Via Goldoni 42/A, 30174 Mestre, Venezia; Gen. Man. Luciano Trevisan.

Nuova Durium Srl: Piazza Mirabello 1, 20121 Milan; tel. (02) 2900-3733; fax (02) 2900-3498; Asst Man. Francesco Piccarreda.

Polygram Italia Edizioni: Via Carlo Tenca 2, 20124 Milan; Man. Dir Gianfranco Rebulla.

Sony Music Publishing (Italy): Via Amedei 9, 20123 Milan; e-mail Lorenzo_Grignani@it.sonymusic.com; Chair. Franco Cabrini.

Sugar Music Group: Via Quintiliano 40, 20138 Milan; International Business Affairs Monica Dahl.

Universal Music Publishing SRL: Via Dante 15, Fifth Floor, 20124 Milan; e-mail umpitaly@umusic.com.

Virgin Dicshi Edizioni Musicali: Via Porpora 26, 20131 Milan; Man. Dir Luigi Montovani.

Warner Chappell Music Italiana: Corso Buenos Aires 79, 20124 Milan; Man. Luigi Bartolotta.

Japan

Columbia Music Publishing Co: 4-14-14 Akasaka, Minato-ku, Tokyo 107; Man. Haijime Ogura.

EMI Music Publishing Japan Ltd: 3-3-5 Kita Aoyama, Minato-ku, Tokyo 107-0061; tel. (3) 3796-8603; fax (3) 3796-0153; Man. Dir Namahiko Sasaki.

MCA Panasonic Music Co Ltd: KFI Bdlg 8F, 3-6-20 Kita-Aoyama, Minato-ku, Tokyo 107; Pres. Nobu Yoshinari.

Shinko Music Publishing Co Ltd: 2-1 Ogawamachi, Kanda, Chiyoda-ku, Tokyo 101; Pres. Shoichi Kusano.

Sony Music Publishing Inc: Seizan Bldg, 2F, 2-12-28 Kita-Aoyama, Minato-ku, Tokyo 107-0061; tel. (3) 5775-3910; fax (3) 3796-7027; e-mail smpj@smjp.co.jp; website www.smpj.co.jp.

Sunkyo Music Co Ltd: 87-6 Torocho 2-Chome, Omiya-City 330; Dir Youichi Takeuchi.

Universal Music Publishing KK: 8-5-30 Akasaka, Minato-ku, Tokyo 107-0052; tel. (3) 6406-3070; fax (3) 6406-3167; e-mail takatoshi.matsui@umusic.com; Senior Dir Takatoshi Matsui.

Warner Chappell Music Japan KK: Nichion Inc, Akasaka Media Bldg, 3-6 Akasaka 5-Chome, Minato-ku, Tokyo 107; Man. Dir Manmoru Murakami.

Republic of Korea

EMI Music Publishing Korea: 2F Samha B/D, 145 Samsung-Dong, Kangnam-Gu, Seoul; tel. 822) 560-9700; fax (822) 566-9710.

Korea Music Publishing: 325 Nakwon Arcade, 286-4 Nakwon-dong, Jongro-ku, Seoul; Contact Eun-Sik Lee.

Sony Music Entertainment (Korea) Inc: 985-19 Bangbae-dong, Seochu-ku, Seoul; Finance Man. Tae Hwan Chung.

Time Recording Inc: 620 Daeha Bldg, 14-11 Yoido-dong, Youngdungpo-ku, Seoul; Pres. N. W. Cho.

Universal Music Publishing Ltd: 649-4 Shinsa-dong, Kangnam-ku, Seoul; 135-120; tel. (822) 106-2000; fax (822) 547-0352; e-mail hakjun.jung@umusic.com; Gen. Man. Hakjun Jung.

Luxembourg

Joybringer: 27 rue Victor Hugo, 4583 Differdange; Contact Andre Depienne.

Promotion 4: PO Box 728, 2017 Luxembourg; Chair. Mike Koedinger.

Radio Music International: Villa Louvigny, 2825 Luxembourg-Ville; Man. Dir Ray Van Cant.

Malaysia

BMG Music Publishing Sdn Bhd: 133-1 Jalan Seganmbut, Kuala Lumpur 51200; Man. Dir Frankie Cheah.

EMI Music Publishing Malaysia SDN BHD: C-6-1, Sixth Floor, Block C, The Mines Waterfront Business Park, 3 Jalan Tasik, The Mines Resort City, 43300 Seri Kembangan, Selangor Darul Ehsan; e-mail cchan@emimusicpub.com;Gen. Man. Carol Chan.

Polygram Records Sdn Bhd: 83–87 Jalan Kampung Pandan, Taman Maluri, Kuala Lumpur 55100; Man. Dir Eric Yeo.

Pustaka Muzik EMI (Malaysia): Suite 10.01, 10th Floor, Exchange Sq., off Jln Semantan, Damansara Heights, Kuala Lumpur 50490; Publishing Man. LimCheng Hoo.

Sony Music Entertainment (Malaysia): C16 & C17 Jalan Ampang, Utama 1/1, Taman Ampang Utama, 68000 Ampang; tel. (3) 4252-3233; fax (3) 4252-2235; e-mail rickloh@sonymusic.com.my; website www.sonymusic.com.my; Man. Dir Rick Loh.

Universal Music Publishing Sdn: 102 Block C, Phileo Damansara 1, Jalan 16/11, 46350 Petaling Jaya, Selangor Darul Ehsan; tel. (3) 7958-7433; fax (3) 754-6198; e-mail jack.teo@umusic.com; Publishing Man. Jack Teo.

Mexico

Beechwood de Mexico SA: Río Tigris 33, 06500 México, DF; Dir-Gen. Antonio Fritz.

Compañía Fonográfica Internacional SA/IM: Discos & Cassettes Sanctorum 86-B Col. Argentina, 11230 México, DF; tel. (55) 5399-2434; fax (55) 5399-2630; e-mail jmorales@imdiscos.com; website www.imdiscos.com; Dir-Gen. José I. Morales Betancourt.

Editorial Musical Juventa: Ignacio Esteva 26A, 11850 México, DF; Proprietor Dario Antonio Zorzano.

EMI Music Publishing Mexico: Blvd Manuel Avila Camacho 76, 5°, Col. Lomas de Chapultepec, Del. Miguel Hidalgo, Mexico DF 11000; tel. (55) 5540-7930; fax (55) 5540-7929; e-mail Ncasonu@emimusicpub.com; Man. Dir Nestor E. Casonu.

Galaxia Musical SA: Leibnitz 130, 11590 México, DF; tel. (55) 5250-0378; fax (55) 5254-5790; website www.galaxiamusical.com; Dir-Gen. José G. Cruz Ayala.

Organización Latino Internacional: Avda Insurgentess Sur 953-202, Col. Nápoles, 03810 México, DF; Dir-Gen. Tony Méndez.

Polygram Discos SA: Avda Miguel Angel de Quevedo 531, Col. Romero de Torreros, 04310 México, DF; Dir-Gen. Francisco Bestard.

Produciones Fonograficas SA: Adolfo Prieto 1649, 1°, Col. del Valle, 03100 Benito Juárez, México, DF; Dir-Gen. Bernardo Yancelson.

Sony/ATV Music Publishing: CP 54030, Ave Henry Ford 3, Fraccionamiento Industrial San Nicolas, Tlalnepantla, Estado de Mexico; tel. (52) 5227-0266; fax (52) 5311-4508; e-mail Felipe_S_Carbajal@sonymusic.com; Contact Felipe Saiz Carbajal.

Universal Music Publishing: CP 11580, Hegel 721, Col. Bosques de Chapultepec, Mexico DF; tel. (55) 5263-5200.

Warner Chappell Music Mexico SA: Avda Ejercito Nacional 209, 3°, Col. Verónica Anzures, 11300 México, DF; Dir-Gen. Jesús Pérez Martín.

Netherlands

Best Music: Wilhelminaplein 20, 5171 KX Kaatsheuvel; tel. (416) 273270; fax (416) 273270; Man. Dir Peter van Best.

Blue & White Songs: Utrechtseweg 3g B, 1381 9S Weesp; Pres. Hans W. Van Pol.

Brinker Media: PO Box 1276, 1400 Bussum; tel. (35) 603-5368; fax (35) 693-4877; e-mail studio@brinkermedia.com; website www.brinkermedia.com; Man. Dir Eric Van Den Brink.

CM Songs: Herenweg 9, 2465 AA Rijnsaterwoude; tel. (172) 509853; fax (172) 507642; e-mail info@catmusic.nl; website www.catmusic.nl; Man. Dir Aart Mol.

Conamus Foundation: PO Box 929, Vaartweg 32, 1200 AX Hilversum; tel. (35) 621-8748; fax (35) 621-2750; e-mail info@conamus.nl; website www.conamus.nl; Man. Dir Jerney Kaagman.

Dutchy Publishing: Pampuslaan 45, 1382 JM Weesp; Man. Dir Xavier Pilgrims de Bigard.

EMI Music Publishing BV: Groest 91-93, 1211 EB Hilversum; tel. (35) 646-2000; fax (35) 646-2019; Man. Dir Arjen Witte.

Moonshine Management: Langeweid 7, 1831 BL Koedyk; tel. and fax (72) 561-5857; e-mail wilbrink@yahoo.com; website www.moonshine-management.com; Pres. Evert Wilbrink.

Narada Media: J. Penhyweg 2, 1217 JH Hilversum; Dir of European Marketing Jaap Hoitingh.

Peermusic Holland bv: Larenseweg 159, 1221 CL Hilversum; Man. Dir J. H. M. G. van Dÿl.

Pennies From Heaven: PO Box 3121, 2601 DC Delft; Vice-Pres. Paul van Meelis.

Royal Society for Music History of the Netherlands (KVNM): PO Box 1514, 3500 BM Utrecht; tel. (38) 3323067; fax (30) 2967807; e-mail kunm@planet.nl; website www.kunm.nl; Pres. Prof. Dr E. Wennekes; Sec. Dr F. D. Zeiler.

Strengholt Music Group: Flevolaan 41, 1411 KC Naarden; tel. (35) 695-8580; fax (35) 694-0362; e-mail info@strengholt.com; website www.strengholt.com; Gen. Man. Mark Wgnstekers.

Universal Songs Publishing International BV: PO Box 2305, 1200 CH Hilversum; tel. (35) 548-9206; fax (35) 542-1702; Man. Dir Bram Keizer.

VIP Promotions: Looievsgracht 38, 1016 VS Amsterdam; PD G. Bezuijen.

New Zealand

Jayrem Music: PO Box 3101, Ohope, Woorl, 110 Symonds St, Auckland; Gen. Man. Paul Ellis.

South Pacific Music Asscs Ltd: PO Box 47-088, Ponsonby, Auckland; Man. Clare Chambers.

Yellow Eye Music: 33 Fortune St, Dalmore, Dunedin; tel. 3473-9426; fax 3473-9700; e-mail simon@yelloweye.co.nz; website www.yelloweye.co.nz; Partner Simon Vare.

Norway

EMI Music Publishing Norway A/S: Osterdalsgaten 1b, 0658 Oslo; tel. (47) 2407-1500; fax (47) 2407-1501; e-mail kaartun@emimusicpub.com; Gen. Man. Kristian Aartun.

Frost Music A/S: PO Box 118, Skoyen, 0212 Oslo; tel. (47) 2327-0186; fax (47) 2327-0187; Man. Dir Philip Kevse.

Late Night Music: PO Box 44, Aserudun 2 Strommen, 2014 Blystadlia; Man. Dir Tom Sennerud.

Musikk Produksion AS: Kjelsasvn 139 D, 0491 Oslo; Man. Dir Harald Fjeld.

Norsk Musikkforlag A/S: PO Box 1499, Vika, 0116 Oslo; tel. (47) 2242-7709; fax (47) 2242-4435; e-mail leif.dramstad@musikforlaget.no; Dir Leif Dramstad.

Norwegian Songs: PO Box 4329 Torshov, Sandakaervn 24C, 0402 Oslo; Man. Dir Audun Tylden.

Polygram Publishing Norway: PO Box 2645 Solli, Drammensvn 82B, 0203 Oslo; Man. Dir Stein G. Johnsen.

Rec 90: PO Box 1291, 5001 Bergen; Man. Dir Torfinn Andersen.

Sonet Music Norway: PO Box 26 45 Solli, Drammensvn 88 B, 0403 Oslo; Man. Dir Terje Engen.

Universal Music Publishing Norway: PO Box 2645, Solli, 0203 Oslo; tel. (47) 2254-1400; fax (47) 2243-4430; e-mail helge.barra@umusic.com.

Warner Chappell Music Norway AS: PO Box 4523, Torshov, 0404 Oslo; tel. (47) 2258-0966; fax (47) 2223-2396; e-mail storyteller@oslo.online.no; Contact Jon Johannessen.

Peru

Ediciones Musicales Hispanas: Esquilache 179, Lima 27; Gen. Man. Carlos Renjipo Mercado.

Sony/ATV Music Publishing: Casimiro Ulloa #346, Miraflores, Lima 18; tel. (511) 242-1080; fax (511) 446-2777; e-mail Cesar_Ochoa@sonymusic.com; Contact Cesar Ochoa.

Philippines

BAMI (Bayanihan Music Philippines Inc): PO Box AC 270, 782 Aurora Blvd, Cubao, Quezon City, Manila; Pres. Florendo Garcia.

BMG Music Philippines: 3/F Equitable Banking Corpn Bldg, 898 Aurora Blvd, Cubao, Quezon City, Manila; Contact Nathaniel Tan.

DD International Recording Corpn: 363 P. Casal St, Quiapo, Manila 1001; Chair. & Pres. Demy A. Quirino Jr.

EMI (Eligardi Music Inc): 6/F NIDC Bldg, 259–263 Sen Gil J, Puyat Ave, Makati, Metro Manila; Pres. Eli Gardiner.

Sony/ATV Music Publishing: GDC 1-A Bldg, 750 Shaw Blvd, Mandaluyong City 1552; tel. (632) 636-3721; fax (632) 5225; e-mail Gloria_Dionisio@sonymusic.com; Contact Gloria Dionisio.

Universal Music Publishing: 28 Manga Rd, Brgy. Kaunlaran, Cubao, Quezon City 1104; tel. (632) 727-4011; fax (632) 726-2851; e-mail racquel.dacillo@umusic.com; Publishing Admin. Racquel Dacillo.

Poland

EMI Music Publishing Polska Sp z.o.o.: Osmanska 11, 02-823 Warsaw; fax (22) 549-1809; e-mail jawdziejczyk@emimusicpub.com; Man. Dir Joanna Awdziejczyk.

Polonia Records Ltd: Ul. Jana Pawla II 18m 13, 00-116 Warsaw; Man. Dir Stanislaw Sobola.

Polskie Nagrania: Goleszowska 6, 01-249 Warsaw; Man. Dir Aleksander Olaszewski.

Polskie Wydawnictwo Muzyczne (PWM): Al Krasinskiego 11A, 31-111 Krakow; Man. Dir Jan Betkowski.

Universal Music Publishing Sp. z.o.o.: ul Jagiellonska 78, 03-301 Warsaw; tel. (22) 811-8061; fax (22) 675-7278; e-mail Beata.Olechowska@umusic.com; Contact Beata Olechowska.

Portugal

BMG Ariola Portugal: Edif. Infante D. Henrique, Rua Joao Chagas 53 A, 1495 Lisbon; Man. Dir Toze Brito.

Concertos de Portugal Ltda: PO Box 13, 2775 Carcavelos; Dir José Silva.

EMI Songs Portugal: Praca Nuno Rodrigues do Santos 7, 1600 Lisbon; tel. (21) 7269-011; fax (21) 7270-233; Gen. Man. Jan Van Dijck.

Farol Musica: Alto do Couto, Arnazéns I, 2735 Cacém; Dirs Antonio Guimaráes, Fernando Júrice.

Polygram Discos SA: Rua Prof. Reinaldo dos Santos 12-D, 1500 Lisbon; Man. Dir Rodrigo Marin.

Sony Music Portugal: Rua Juliao Quintinha 11, 1500 Lisbon.

Universal Music Publishing: Rua Prof. Reinaldo dos Santos 12-D; 1549-006 Lisbon; tel. (21) 771-0410; fax (21) 778-0212; e-mail carla.lisboa@umusic.com; Creative Publishin Man. Carla Lisboa.

Vidisco: Avda Bombeiros Voluntarios 13, 1D, 1675 Pontinha, Lisbon; Man. Dir Artur Antunes.

Warner Chappell Portugal: Rua Dr Constantino de Braganca 26A, 1400 Lisbon.

Romania

Contera AV: Str Turda 122, BL 39, SCA, Et 6 Ap 30, Sect 1 Bucharest; Pres. Iordachescu Octavian.

Russia

Mezhdunarodnaya Kniga: Dimitrova 39, 117 049 Moscow; Man. Dir Stanislav Ostapishin.

Muzyka Publishers: Neglinnaya 14, 103 031 Moscow; Man. Dir L. Sidelnikov.

S.B.A. Music Publishing Ltd: 32 Staraya Basmannaya St, 107066 Moscow; tel. (095) 787-5670; fax (095) 267-2848; e-mail btsigman@galarec.ru; Dir-Gen. Boris Tsigman.

Universal Music Publishing: 14A Kastanaevskaya Ulitsa, Moscow 121006; tel. (095) 737-0090; fax (095) 737-3655; e-mail publishing@umusic.ru.

Singapore

EMI Music Publishing Singapore Pte Ltd: 213 Henderson Rd, 04-05 Henderson Industrial Estate, Singapore 0315; tel. (65) 6270-9636; fax (65) 6270-5987; CEO David Wee.

Fox Agency International Inc: 391 B, Orchard Rd, Suite 09-10, Tower B, Ngee Ann City, Singapore 0923; Regional Dir Fabian Lek.

Polygram Music Publishing Pte Ltd: 23 Genting Rd, 04-01 Chevalier House, Singapore 1334; Man. Karen Sim.

Sony Music Publishing (Pte) Ltd: 601 Sims Dr., 02-07, Singapore 1438; Gen. Man. Terence Phung.

Universal Music Publishing Pte Ltd: 118 Lorong 23 Geylang, #03-01/02/03/04, SCN Industrial Bldg, 388402 Singapore; tel. (65) 6741-2220; fax (65) 6741-0500/1266; e-mail karen.sim@umusic.com; Publishing Man. Karen Sim.

Warner/Chappell Music Singapore Pte Ltd: 10 Anson Rd #12-06/07/08, International Plaza, Singapore 079903; Publishing Man. Liz Cheam.

Slovakia

CS Music: Votrubova 2, 82109 Bratislava; Man. Dir Dusan Tlolka.

DMC Disco: PO Box Ruzinovska 28, 82101 Bratislava; Man. Dir Ivan Malovec.

EMI/Monitor Slovakia: Radvanska 1, 81101 Bratislava; Man. Dir Pavol Hammel.

Musica: Palisady 36, 81632 Bratislava; Man. Dir F. J. Walner.

Polygram Slovakia: Pribinova 25, 81109 Bratislava; Man. Dir Peter Riava.

Slovenia

Multipublishing: Peske 7, 10C Tzrin; tel. (0) 1568-0353; fax (0) 1568-0361; e-mail igor@multimedia-rec.si; Man. Dir Igor Ivanic.

SKUC-AFK: Kersnikova 4, 61000 Ljubljana; Man. Dir Mitja Prezelj.

South Africa

BMG Records Africa (Pty) Ltd: PO Box 5894 Johannesburg 2000; tel. (001) 242-3000; fax (001) 242-3030; website click2music.co.sa; Man. Dir of Records Keith Lister; Man. Dir of Publishing Peter Vee.

EMI Music Publishing South Africa (Pty) Ltd: Riverwoods Office Park, Senderwood 2145, Johannesburg; tel. (1) 453-3463; fax (1) 453-1012; e-mail rkallenbach@emimusicpub.com; Man. Dir Robbie Kallenbach.

Sony/ATV Music Publishing: PO Box 411463, Craighall 2024; tel. (11) 328-8500; fax (11) 327-0251; e-mail Lazarus_Serobe@sonymusic.com; Contact Lazarus Serobe.

Universal Music Publishing (Pty) Ltd: PO Box 2660, Cape Town 8000; tel. (21) 424-5374; fax (21) 424-5101; e-mail john.fishlock@umusic.com; Man. Dir John Fishlock.

Spain

B-Core: Marques de Sentmenat 72, Interior 3a, 08029 Barcelona; tel. and fax (9) 3419-7883; e-mail bcore@bcoredisc.com; website www.bcore.com; Man. Dir Jordi Llansama.

Blanco Y Negro: Amigo 14–16, 08021 Barcelona; Man. Dir Sito Manovent.

Canciones del Mundo: Magallanes 25, 28015 Madrid; Man. Dir Luis Regatero.

Crab Ediciones Musicales SA: Sagunto 2, 28010 Madrid; Gen. Man. Jorge E. Gomez Diaz.

Doctor Music Publishing: Alcala 114-6B, 28009 Madrid; Dir Lucia Cardenes.

Ediciones Musicales Warner Bros SA: Lopez de Hoyos 42, 28006 Madrid; Man. Dir Inigo Zabala.

EMI Music Publishing Spain SA: C/Gran Via, 39-7°, Madrid 28013; tel. (9) 1523-9940; fax (9) 1521-1344.

Epoca Music: Joanot Martorell 15, 08203 Barcelona; Man. Dir Len Roy Carvalho.

GSG—Grup de Serveis Guilleries: Granja Baró, Ctra de la Guixa, km 2, 08500 Barcelona; Admin Jordi Costa; Man. Ignasi Pla; Production Joan Capdevila.

Huygen Corpn: Alzines 3, St Quirze Parc, 08192 St Quirze del Vallès, Barcelona; Contact Michel Huygen.

Neuronium Music: Calle Alzines 3, St Quirze Parc, 08192 St Quirze del Vallès, Barcelona; Contact Michel Huygen.

New Music Ediciones Musicales SA: PO Box 9.046, 28060 Madrid; Gen. Man. Gerhard Haltermann.

RLM Producciones: Jose Maria Cavero 9, Ch A, 28027 Madrid; Man. Dir Rosa Lagarrigue.

Sintonía, SA: Abdón Terradas 5, 28015 Madrid; tel. (91) 549-2350; fax (91) 543-9690; e-mail clif@sintonia.es; Publisher Clifton J. Williams.

Sonifolk Arpafolk: Fernando el Catalico 58, 28015 Madrid; Man. Dir Jose de la Fuente.

Sony/ATV Music Publishing LLC: Paseo de la Castellana 93-9, 28046 Madrid; tel. (91) 596-8474; fax (91) 596-8477; e-mail Pedro_Barranco@es.sonymusic.com; Contact Pedro Barranco.

Universal Music Publishing SA: c/o Torrelaguna, 64 Fifth Floor, 28043 Madrid; tel. (91) 744-5656; fax (91) 744-5664; e-mail spain.publishing@umusic.com.

Victoria: Narvaez 14-1A, 28009 Madrid; Gen. Man. Gerhard Haltermann.

Vortex Music: Magallanes 25, 28015 Madrid; Man. Dir Luis Regatero.

Sweden

BMG Music Publishing Scandinavia: PO Box 2176, 10314 Stockholm; tel. (8) 412-1780; fax (8) 412-1799; Man. Dir Lars Karlsson.

EMI Music Publishing Scandinavia AB: Kungsholmsgatan 21, PO Box 12701, 11294 Stockholm; tel. (8) 5879-5500; fax (8) 5879-9555; e-mail sweden@emimusicpub.com; Contact Nina Schrijvershof.

Energy Records AB: Vastergatan 23, 21121 Malmö; Contact Håkan Ehrnst.

Gazell Music AB: PO Box 10041, 10055 Stockholm; tel. (8) 660-0715; fax (8) 663-7910; e-mail info@gazellmusic.se; website www.gazellmusic.se; Dir Dag Haeggqvist.

MCA Music Sweden: PO Box 55 505, Riddargatan 23 4, 10204 Stockholm.

Misty Music AB: PO Box 10 149, 10055 Stockholm; tel. (8) 660-7755; fax (8) 661-0115; e-mail moren@misty.se; Man. Dir Anders Moren.

Mixturen: Frijyrkliga Studieförbundet, PO Box 479, 10129 Stockholm; Ed. Torgny Erséus.

Out Of Time Music: Husargatan 15, 41122 Gothenburg; Prod. Håkan Forshult.

Real Time Music: Wennerbergsgatan 1, 11258 Stockholm; Man. Allan Gutheim.

Sonet Music AB: PO Box 20504, Mariehällsvägen 35, 16103 Bromma; Man. Dir Ingermar Bergman.

Sony/ATV Music Publishing Scandinavia AB: PO Box 12745, 11294 Stockholm; tel. (8) 617-7150; fax (8) 617-7199; e-mail Anette_Hokengren@se.sonymusic.com; Contact Anette Hokengren.

Stockholm Records: PO Box 20504, 16102 Bromma; Gen. Man. Eric Hasselqvist.

Universal Music Publishing AB: PO Box 55755, 11483 Stockholm; tel. (8) 629-5370; fax (8) 662-7850; e-mail pub.scand@umusic.com.

Warner Chappell Music Scandinavia AB: PO Box 533, Vendevägen 85 B, 18215 Danderyd; tel. (8) 622-0900; fax (8) 755-1596; website www.warnerchappell.com; Man. Dir Hans Desmond.

Switzerland

Check Point Music: Rainweg 6, 8967 Widen; Man. Dir Martin Scheiss.

Dinemec Productions SA: Blvd Helvétique 17, PO Box 893, 1211 Geneva; Man. Dir Paul Sutin.

Edition Helbing AG: Pfeaffikerstr 6, 8604 Volgetswil; Man. Dir Willy Vogt.

Edition Melodie: Brunnwiesenstr 26, 8049 Zürich; Chair. Anton Peterer.

Editions Cellier: Aiguemont 26, rue du Bourg de Plait, 1071 Chexbres; tel. (21) 946-1649; fax (21) 946-3533; e-mail ccellier@merging.com; website ulliherkenhoff.freepage.de/cellier.html; Contacts Marcel Cellier, Catherine Cellier.

Global Music Swiss: Im Hauel 15, 4147 Aesch; Public Relations Sonja Schmidt-Montfort.

Hyper Music: Domberweg 12, 4423 Hersberg; Man. Dir P. J. Waserman.

Marion Caravatti Music (MCM): Hochwachstr 27A, 8400 Winterthur; Chair. Marion Caravatti.

Migration: PO Box 431, 1800 Vevey; tel. (21) 923-6363; fax (21) 923-6362; e-mail hdill@bluewin.ch; website www.farafina.com; Contact Heinz Dill.

Turicaphon AG: Turicaphonstr 31, 8616 Riedikon; Man. Dir Hans Oestreicher.

VIP AG Productions: Schützengasse 30, 8001 Zürich; Man. Dir Urs Peter Keller.

Viteka Music Production: PO Box 173, Ringstr 14, 8600 Dübendorf/Zürich; Chair. Willy Viteka.

Taiwan

EMI Music Publishing China: Room 313, Towercrest Plaza, 3 Maizidian W Rd, Chao Yang District, Beijing; tel. (8610) 6467-2018; fax (8610) 8458-0899.

Polygram Music Publishing Ltd: 5F 99 Nankang Rd, Section 3, Nankang District, Taipei; Contact Yvette Tung.

Sony/ATV Music Publishing: Sixth Floor, No. 35, Lane 11, Kwang-Fu North Rd, Taipei; tel. (8862) 2766-8900; fax (8862) 2747-3639; e-mail Belinda_Ho@sonymusic.com; Contact Belinda Ho.

Universal Music Publishing Ltd: 2F 2 Min Sheng E Rd, Section 3, Taipei; tel. (8862) 2502-4546; fax (8862) 2518-3545; e-mail serena.ma@umusic.com; Contact Serena Ma.

Thailand

BMG Music: 18/F Vanissa Bldg, Soi Chidlom, Pleonchit Rd, Patumwam, Bangkok 10110; Man. Dir Steven Tan.

Song Music Publishing: 1091, 185-5 New Petchburi Rd, Payathai, Bangkok 10400; Gen. Man. Peter Gan.

Sony/ATV Music Publishing: Q-house Ploenjit Bldg, 598 15th Floor, Lumpinee, Pathumwan, Bangkok 10330; tel. (662) 650-9797; fax (662) 253-2061; e-mail Lynda_Wangvanich@sonymusic.com; Contact Lynda Wangvanich.

Universal Music Publishing: 540 Mercury Tower 11F, Ploenchit Rd, Lumpinee, Pathumwan, Bangkok 10330; tel. (662) 658-6244; e-mail nadda.buranasiri@umusic.com; Contact Nadda Buranasiri.

Turkey

Jazz Records & Publishing: Atlamatasi Caddesi 5, Serilen, 34470 Unkapani, Istanbul; Pres. Yasar Demirturk.

Muzikotek Ltd: 4 Gazeteciler Sitesi A-17/4, Levent, 80620 Istanbul; tel. (212) 269-5610; fax (212) 282-8195; e-mail muzikotek@muzikotek.com.tr; website www.muzikotek.com.tr.

Topkapi Music: Mesrutiyet Caddesi 113, Ece Han Kat 2, 80050 Tepebasi, Istanbul; Dir Mehmet Arman.

Universal Music Turkey: Gumussuyu Is Merkezi, Zafer Tunaya Sok 14, Third Floor, 80090 Istanbul; tel. (212) 249-7570; fax (212) 292-4092; e-mail mustafa.pehlivan@umusic.com; Contact Mustafa Pehlivan.

Ukraine

Muzychna Ukraina: Pushkinska St 32, 252 004 Kiev; Man. Dir Mykola Lynnyk.

Ukrainian Musical Information Centre: Richkova St 4, 252 135 Kiev; Man. Dir Sergiy Galuzin.

United Kingdom

Acuff-Rose Music Ltd: 13 Great Marlborough St, London W1V 2LP; tel. (20) 7911 8200; fax (20) 7911 8600; Gen. Man. Tony Peters.

Amphonic Music Ltd: Kerchesters, Waterhouse Lane, Kingswood, Tadworth, Surrey KT20 6HT; tel. (1737) 832837; fax (1737) 833812; Dir Erica Dale.

Associated Music International Ltd: 34 Salisbury St, London NW8 8QE; tel. (20) 7402-9111; fax (20) 7723-3064; e-mail admin@amimedia.co.uk; website www.amimedia.co.uk; Man. Dir Eliot M. Cohen.

Bad Habits Music Group: PO Box 111, London W13 0ZH; tel. (20) 8991 1516; fax (20) 8566 7215; Man. Dir John S. Rushton.

Barn Dance Publications Ltd: 62 Beechwood Rd, South Croydon, Surrey CR2 0AA; tel. (20) 8657 2813; fax (20) 8651 6080; Man. Dir Derek Jones.

Barry Collings Music: 21A Clifftown Rd, Southend-on-Sea, Essex SS1 1AB; tel. (1702) 330005; fax (1702) 333309; e-mail bcollent@aol.com; website www.barrycollings.co.uk; Man. Dir Barry Collings.

Big Bear Music: PO Box 944, Edgbaston, Birmingham B16 8UT; tel. (121) 4547020; fax (121) 4549996; e-mail admin@bigbearmusic.com; website www.bigbearmusic.com; Man. Dir Jim Simpson.

Black Magic Management Ltd: 296 Earls Court Rd, London SW5 9BA; Man. Dir Mataya Clifford.

BMG Music Publishing Ltd: Bedford House, 69–79 Fulham High St, London SW6 3JN; tel. (20) 7384 7600; fax (20) 7973 0337; Man. Dir Paul Curran.

Boosey & Hawkes Music Publishers: 295 Regents St, London W1R 8JH; tel. (20) 7580 2060; fax (20) 7291 7101; Man. Dir R. A. Fell.

Brilliant Music: 19 Ford Sq., London E1 2HS; Man. Dir Frazer Henry.

Brothers Organization: 74 The Archway, Station Approach, Ranelagh Gardens, London SW6 3UH; Dirs Ian Titchener, Nick Titchener.

Bucks Music Ltd: Onward House, 11 Uxbridge St, London W8 7TQ; tel. (20) 7221-4275; fax (20) 7229-6893; e-mail info@bucksmusicgroup.co.uk; website www.bucksmusicgroup.com; Man. Dir Simon Platz.

Bulk Music Ltd: 9 Watt Rd, Hillington Industrial Estate, Hillington, Glasgow G52 4RY, Scotland; tel. (141) 882 9060; fax (141) 883 3686; Dir Isobel Waugh.

Bushranger Music: 86 Rayleigh Rd, Hutton, Brentwood, Essex CM13 1BH; tel. (1277) 222095; Man. Dir Kathy Lister.

Campbell Connelly & Co Ltd: 8–9 Frith St, London W1V 5TZ; tel. (20) 7434 0066; fax (20) 7439 2848; Head of Copyright Kevin White.

Carlin Music Corpn: Ironbridge House, 3 Bridge Approach, London NW1 8BD; tel. (20) 7734-3251; fax (20) 7439-2391; e-mail daisie@carlinmusic.com; CEO David Japp.

Charley Publishing Ltd: 156–166 Ilderton Rd, London SE15 1NT; Founder Jean Luc Young; Dir Jan Friedmann.

Chrysalis Music Ltd: The Chrysalis Bldg, 13 Barmley Rd, London W10 6SP; tel. (20) 7465-6169; fax (20) 7465 6231; e-mail jeremy.lascelles@chrysalis.com; website www.chrysalis.com; CEO Jeremy Lascelles.

Congo Music Ltd: 17A Craven Park Rd, Harlesden, London NW10 8SE; tel. and fax (20) 8961 5461; Dirs Byron Lye-Fook, Root Jackson.

Cornish Legend Music: 153 Vauxhall St, The Barbican, Plymouth PL4 0DF, Devon; Partner Nick Strachan.

Cramer Music: 23 Garrick St, London WC2E 8AX; tel. (20) 7240 1612; fax (20) 7240 2639; Contact Peter Maxwell.

Cwmni Cyhoeddi Gwynn Cyf: Y Gerlan Heol Y Dwr, Penygroes, Caernarfon, Gwynedd LL54 6LR, Wales; tel. (1286) 881797; fax (1286) 882634; Contact Wendy Jones.

Dance Music: 7 Mornington Terrace, Camden Town, London NW1 7RR; fax (20) 7387 7962; Man. Dir Ian Tregoning.

Demi Monde Records & Publishing: Foel Studio, Llanfair, Caereinion, Powys SY21 0DS, Wales; tel. (1938) 810758; fax (1938) 810758; e-mail dave.anderson@dial.pipex.com; website www.demimonde.co.uk; Man. Dir Dave Anderson.

Decentric Music Ltd: 12 Tideway Yard, 125 Mortlake High St, London SW14 8SN; tel. and fax (20) 8977 4616.

EMI Music Publishing: 127 Charing Cross Rd, London WC2H 0EA; tel. (20) 7434 2131; fax (20) 7434 3531; Man. Dir Peter Reichardt.

Endomorph Music Publishing: 29 St Michaels Rd, Leeds LS6 3BG; Man. Dir Dave Fostin.

Equity Records: 112A-B Westbourne Grove, Chepstow Rd, London W2 5RU; Man. Dir Paul Moore.

Eschenbach Editions: 28 Dalrymple Cres., Edinburgh EH9 2NX, Scotland; tel. (131) 6673633; fax (131) 6673633; e-mail eschenbach@caritas-music.co.uk; website www.caritas-music.co.uk; Man. Dir James Douglas.

Express Music UK Ltd: Matlock, Brady Rd, Lyminge, Folkestone, Kent CT18 8HA; tel. and fax (1303) 863185; Man. Dir S. Jackson.

Fair Oaks Entertainment: PO Box 19, Ulverston, Cumbria CA12 9TF; Proprietor/Man. J. G. Livingstone.

Friendly Overtures Ltd: Walker Cottage, 26 Aston Lane, Henley-on-Thames, Oxfordshire RG9 3EJ; tel. (1491) 547745; Creative Dir Michael Batory.

Global Chrysalis Music Publishing Co Ltd: The Chrysalis Bldg, 13 Bramley Rd, London W10 6SP; tel. (20) 7465-6203; fax (20) 7465-6318; website www.chrysalis.com; Gen. Man. Peter Knight Jr.

Grade One Music: 34 Salisbury St, London NW8 8QE; tel. (20) 7402-9111; fax (20) 7723-3064; Man. Dir Eliot Cohen.

Gramavision: 329 Latimer Rd, London W10 6RA; tel. (20) 8960-3311; fax (20) 8960-4334; Gen. Man. Andy Childs.

Grian Music: Cockenzie Business Centre, Edinburgh Rd, Cockenzie, East Lothian EH32 0XL, Scotland; tel. (1875) 815888; fax (1875) 813545; e-mail iangtrax@aol.com; website www.greentrax.com; Proprietor Ian D. Green.

Harbourtown Music: PO Box 25, Ulverston, Cumbria LA12 7UN; tel. and fax (1229) 580577; Man. Dir Gordon Jones.

Hit & Run Music Ltd: c/o EMI Music Publishing Ltd, 127 Charing Cross Rd, London WC2H 0EA; tel. (20) 7434 2131; fax (20) 7584 5774; Chair. & Man. Dir Tony Smith.

Howard Jones Music Ltd: 33 Alexander Rd, Aylesbury, Buckinghamshire HP20 2NR; Admin. David R. Stopps.

Jermaine Springer Publishing: PO Box 8969, London SE9 4ZB; Dir Jermaine Springer.

John Fiddy Music: Unit 3, Moorgate Business Centre, South Green, Dereham, Norfolk NR19 1PT; Admin. Cheryl Kenny.

Josef Weinberger Ltd: 12–14 Mortimer St, London W1T 3JJ; tel. (20) 7580 2827; fax (20) 7436 9616; Promotion & Marketing Sean Gray.

Kassner Assoc. Publishers Ltd: Units 6–7, 11 Wyfold Rd, Fulham, London SW6 6SE; Man. Dir David Kassner.

Kinetix: 32 Lexington St, London W1F 0LQ; tel. (20) 7255 8777; Chair. Jon Sharp.

Lee Music: Stewart House, Hillbottom Rd, Sands Industrial Estate, High Wycombe, Buckinghamshire HP12 4HJ; International A & R and Co Lawyer Keith Phillips.

Maecenas Europe Publishers: 5 Bushey Close, Old Barn Lane, Kenley, Surrey CR8 5AU; Sales Man. Alan Kirk.

Maran Steele Music: Ellemford Farmhouse, Duns TD11 3SG, Scotland; Man. Dir Hunter Steele.

MCA Music Ltd: Universal Music Ltd, Bond House, 347–353 Chiswick High Rd, London W4 4HS; tel. (20) 8742 5600; fax (20) 8742 5667; Man. Dir Paul Connolly.

Mcasso Music Productions Ltd: 9 Carnaby St, London W1V 1PG; Prod. Lisa McCaffery.

Metro Music Publishers Ltd: Longriggs, Swalwell, Gateshead, Tyne & Wear NE99 1BB; Dir of Music Production Jon Craig.

Moggie Music Ltd: 101 Hazelwood Lane, Palmers Green, London N13 5HQ; Man. Dir Hal Carter.

Moksha: PO Box 102, London E15 2HH; Man. Dir Charles Colm.

Moving Shadow Music Ltd: PO Box 2251, London SE1 2FH; tel. (20) 7252 2661; Label Co-ordinator Caroline Butler.

Muirhead Music: Michelin House, 81 Fulham Rd, Chelsea, London SW3 6RD; tel. (20) 7351-5167; fax (870) 1363878; e-mail info@muirheadmanagement.co.uk; website www.muirheadmanagement.co.uk; CEO Dennis Muirhead.

Music Collection International Ltd: 36–38 Caxton Way, Watford, Hertfordshire WD1 8UF; Marketing Dir Danny Keene.

Music Copyright Solutions PLC: 32 Lexington St, London W1F 0LQ; tel. (20) 7255-8777; fax (20) 7255-8778; e-mail info@mcs.music.com; website www.mcsmusic.com; CEO Brian Scholfield.

Notting Hill Music UK Ltd: Bedford House, 8b Berkeley Gdns, London W8 4AP; tel. (20) 7243 2921; fax (20) 7243 2894.

Park Records: PO Box 651, Oxford OX2 9RB; Man. Dir John Dagnell.

Peermusic (UK) Ltd: Peer House, 8–14 Verulam St, London WC1X 8LZ; tel. (20) 7404 7200; fax (20) 7404 7004; Man. Dir Nigel Elderton.

Performance Equities Ltd: 112 A & B Westbourne Grove, Chepstow Rd, London W2 5RU; Man. Dir Paul Moore.

Phantom Publishing: 59 Moore Park Rd, London SW6 2HA; Man. Dir Falcon Stuart.

Pink Floyd Music Publishers: 27 Noel St, London W1V 3RD; Dir Peter Barnes.

Pollytone Music: PO Box 124, Ruislip, Middlesex HA4 9BB; tel. (1895) 638584; fax (1895) 624793; e-mail val@pollyton.demon.co.uk; website www.pollytone.com; Dir Valerie Bird.

PolyGram International Music Publishing: 8 St James Sq., London SW1Y 4JU; CEO David Hockman.

R. T. L. Music: Stewart House, Hill Bottom Rd, Sands Industrial Estate, High Wycombe HP12 4HJ; Owner & Prod. Ron Lee.

Rive Droite UK Ltd: Home Park House, Hampton Court Rd, Kingston-upon-Thames, Surrey KT1 4AE; tel. (20) 8977 0666; fax (20) 8977 0660; Music Dir Brian Rawling.

Robert Kingston (Music) Ltd: c/o Music Sales, 8–9 Frith St, London W1V 5TZ; tel. (20) 7434 0066; fax (20) 7439 2848.

Rondor Music (London) Ltd: c/o Universal Music Ltd, Bond House, 347–353 Chiswick High Rd, London W4 4HS; tel. (20) 8742 5600; fax (20) 8742 5667; Man. Dir Stuart Hornall.

Rykomusic Ltd: 329 Latimer Rd, London W10 6RA; tel. (20) 8960-3311; fax (20) 8960-4334; Gen. Man. Paul Lambden.

S. W. Music (UK): 48 Fernside Rd, Poole, Dorset BH15 2JJ; tel. (1202) 773103; fax (1202) 681419; e-mail dave.dacosta@ukonline.co.uk; Man. Dir Dave Dacosta.

Satellite Music Ltd: 34 Salisbury St, London NW8 8QE; tel. (20) 7402-9111; fax (20) 7723-3064; e-mail satellite_artists@hotmail.com; Man. Dir Eliot M. Cohen.

Scotford Music: 13 Winton Park, Edinburgh EH10 7EX, Scotland; tel. (1314) 451687; e-mail gerryford@madasafish.com; website www.gerryford.co.uk; Proprietor Gerry Ford.

Sea Dream Music: 236 Sebert Rd, Forest Gate, London E7 0NP; Sr Partner Simon Law.

Seriously Groovy Music Ltd: Third Floor, 28 D'Arblay St, Soho, London W1F 8EW; tel. (20) 7439-1947; fax (20) 7734-7540; e-mail seriously.groovy@virgin.net; website www.seriouslygroovy.com; Dir Lorraine Snape.

Songs for Today Inc: PO Box 130, Hove, East Sussex BN3 6QU; tel. (1273) 550088; fax (1273) 540969; e-mail publishing@tkogroup.com; website www.tkogroup.com; Dir of Admin Roland Rogers.

Sony/ATV Music Publishing (UK) Ltd: 13 Great Marlborough St, London W1V 2LP; tel. (20) 7911 8200; fax (20) 7911 8600; Man. Dir Blair McDonald.

Soundtrack Music Publishing: 22 Ives St, London SW3 2ND; Contact Olaf Wyper.

Studio G Ltd: Ridgway House, Great Brington, Northampton NN7 4JA; tel. (1604) 770511; fax (1604) 770022; e-mail library@studiog.co.uk; website www.studiog.co.uk; Man. Dir John Gale.

Sylvantone Music: 17 Allerton Grange Way, Leeds LS17 6LP; tel. (113) 2687788; fax (709) 2359333; e-mail sylvantore@hotmail.com; Proprietor Tony Goodacre.

TKO Music Publishing Ltd: PO Box 130, Hove, East Sussex BN3 6QU; tel. (1273) 550088; fax (1273) 540969; e-mail publishing@tkogroup.com; website www.tkogroup.com; Dir of Admin Roland Rogers.

Tonecolor Ltd: Matlock, Brady Farm, Lyminge, Folkestone, Kent CT18 8HA; tel. and fax (1303) 863185; Man. Dir S. Jackson.

Unity Music Publishing: John Henry Bldg, 16/24 Brewery Rd, London N7 9NH; Sales & Retail Man. Pepin Clout.

Universal Edition (Ldn) Ltd: 48 Gt Marlborough St, London W1F 7BB; tel. (20) 7437 5203; fax (20) 7437 6115.

Universal Music Publishing Ltd: Bond House, 347–353 Chiswick High Rd, London W4 4HS; tel. (20) 8742 5600; fax (20) 8742 5667.

Universal Music Publishing Ltd: Elsinore House, 77 Fulham Palace Rd, London W6 8JA; tel. (20) 8752 2600; fax (20) 8752 2601; e-mail ukpublishing@umusic.com.

Universal Songs Ltd: 14 Montpelier Villas, Brighton BN1 3DG; tel. (1273) 771488; e-mail ptubbs@naeamar.co.uk; website www.pierretubbs.uk; Contact Pierre Tubbs.

Vinyl Japan (UK) Ltd: 281 Camden High St, London NW1 7BX; Man. Patrick James.

Warlock Music Ltd: 329 Latimer Rd, London W10 6RA; tel. (20) 8960-3311; fax (20) 8960-4334; Gen. Man. Paul Lambdon.

Warner Chappell Music: Griffin House, 161 Hammersmith Rd, London W6 8BS; tel. (20) 8563 5800; fax (20) 8563 5801; Man. Dir Ed Heine.

Whole Armor/Full Armor: PO Box 130, Hove, East Sussex BN3 6QU; tel. (1273) 550088; fax (1273) 540969; e-mail publishing@tkogroup.com; website www.tkogroup.com; Dir of Admin Roland Rogers.

Windswept Pacific Music (London) Ltd: Hope House, 40 St Peter's Rd, Hammersmith, London W6 9BD; tel. (20) 8237 8400; fax (20) 8741 0825; Contact Debbie Miles.

Wolf Records: 83 Brixton Water Lane, London SW2 1PH; tel. (20) 7733-8088; fax (20) 7326-4016; Man. Dir Dominique Brethes.

Wot Films & Music: Suite 3, 44 Mortimer St, London W1N 7DG; Prod. Jackie Thomas.

Zomba Music Publishers: Unit 22–27, Quadrant Business Centre, 135 Salisbury Rd, Queens Park, London NW6 6RJ; tel. (20) 7604 2600; fax (20) 7604 2601; Man. Dir Steven Howard.

United States of America

ABKCO Music Inc: 1700 Broadway, New York, NY 10019; tel. (212) 399-0300; fax (212) 582-5090; e-mail ikeitel@abkco.com; Contact Iris Keitel.

Acuff-Rose Music Publishing Inc: 65 Music Sq., West Nashville, TN 37203; tel. (615) 321-5000; fax (615) 327-0560; Contact Peggy Lamb.

Another Amethyst Song: 273 Chippewa, Columbia, SC 29210-6508; tel. (803) 750-5391; Contact C. G. Butler.

Arista Music Publishing: 8370 Wilshire Blvd, Third Floor, Beverly Hills, CA 90211; Contact Judy Hicks.

Ashleigh Publishing: PO Box 76507, Washington, DC 20013; Pres. Carl Bentley.

Axbar Records: PO Box 12353, San Antonio, TX 78212; tel. (210) 829-1909; e-mail axbar@stic.net; website www.axbarmusic.com; Prod. and Gen. Man. Joe Scates.

Bekool Music Group: 23 Music Sq. E, Suite 101, Nashville, TN 37203; Pres. Pat McKool.

Benson Music Group Inc: 365 Great Circle Rd, Nashville, TN 37228; International Sales Janice Cuttler.

Betty Jane/Josie Jane Music Publishing Co: 7400 N Adams Rd, North Adams, MI 49262; Pres. Claude E. Reed.

Bivens Music: 203 Gates Dr., Hendersonville, TN 37075-4961; Owner Ernie Bivens.

Bloozy Publishing: 542 Prospect Ave, #1, Brooklyn, NY 11215; Contact Michael Stevens.

BMG Music Publishing: 1 Music Circle N, Nashville, TN 37203; Contact Henry Hurt.

BMG Music Publishing, Licensing: 8750 Wilshire Blvd, Beverly Hills, CA 90211; tel. (310) 358-4700; Contact Maribeth Ackerman.

Bob Scott Frick Enterprises: 404 Bluegrass Ave, Madison, TN 37115; tel. (615) 865-6380; e-mail bfrick@att.net; Pres. Bob Frick.

Bob White Music Inc: 212 Morrison St, McMinnville, TN 37110; Pres. & CEO Thomas B. Vaughn.

Bourne Co Music Publishing: 5 W 37th St, New York, NY 10018; tel. (212) 391-4300; fax (212) 391-4306; e-mail bournemusic@worldnet.att.net; website www.bournemusic.com; Contact Beebe Bourne.

Brentwood-Benson Music Publishing Inc: 741 Cool Springs Blvd, Franklin, TN 37067; tel. (615) 261-3300; fax (615) 261-3386; e-mail custom@providentmusicgroup.com; website www.brentwood-bensonmusic.com.

Bug Music Inc: 6777 Hollywood Blvd, Hollywood, CA 90028; e-mail danb@bugmusic.com; website www.bugmusic.com; Contact Daniel Bourgoise.

Cactus & Winnebago Music Publishing: PO Box 1027, Neenah, WI 54957-1027; Pres. Tony Ansems.

Carl Fischer, LLC: 65 Bleecker St, New York, NY 10012; tel. (212) 777-0900; fax (212) 477-6996; e-mail cf-info@carlfischer.com; website www.carlfischer.com; Contact Lauren Keiser.

Cat's Voice Productions: PO Box 1361, Sanford, ME 04073-7361; Owner Tom Reeves.

Cavet-Vanderpool Publishing/BMI: 1030 Villa Pl., Nashville, TN 37212; Pres. Vera Cavet Vanderpool.

Center for the Queen of Peace: 3350 Highway 6 S, Suite 412, Sugar Land, TX 77478; website www.marianland.com; Dir Rafael Brom.

Cerebral Records: 1236 Laguna Dr., Carlsbad, CA 92008; Pres. Lincoln Kroll; Publicist Carol Leno.

Chapel Music Group Inc: 2021 Richard Jones Rd, Suite 180, Nashville, TN 37215; Dir of Marketing Heather Campbell.

Charisma Music Publishing Co Inc: 1841 Broadway, Suite 411, New York, NY 10023; Pres. Julie Lipsivs.

Cherry Lane Music Co: 6 E 32nd St, 11th Floor, New York, NY 10016; tel. (212) 561-3000; fax (212) 683-2040; e-mail agurwicz@cherrylane.com; website www.cherrylane.com; Contact Aida Gurwicz.

Christmas and Holiday Music: 3517 Warner Blvd, Suite 4, Burbank, CA 91505-4636; Pres. Justin Wilde.

Chrysalis Music Group: 8500 Melrose Ave, Suite 207, Los Angeles, CA 90069; tel. (310) 652-0066; fax (310) 652-2024; e-mail mail@chrysalismusic.com; Contact Carrie Villines.

Cosmotone Records: 3350 Highway 6 S, PMB 412, Sugar Land, TX 77478; website www.marianland.com/music02.html; Pres. Rafael Brom.

CPP/Belwin Music: 15800 NW 48th Ave, Miami, FL 33014; tel. (305) 620-1500; fax (305) 625-3480; Contact David Olsen.

Cude & Pickens Music: 519 N Halifax Ave, Daytona Beach, FL 32118; tel. and fax (386) 252-0381; e-mail cudepickenspub@aol.com; website www.broadwayusa.us; CEO Bobby Lee Cude.

DanceFloor Distribution/Echo USA: 95 Cedar Lane, Englewood, NJ 07631; Pres. Jeffrey Collins.

De Stijl Music (BMI): PO Box 170206, San Francisco, CA 94117-0206.

Disney Music Publishing Group: 500 S Buena Vista St, Burbank, CA 91521; tel. (818) 569-3241; fax (818) 845-9705; Vice-Pres. Susan Borgeson.

Diva Entertainment World: 853 Broadway #1516, New York, NY 10003; Man. Dir Marc Krasnow.

Edensong: PO Box 34, Days Creek, OR 97429; Owner Rick Foster.

EMI/Virgin Music: 827 N Hilldale Ave, West Hollywood, CA 90069; Vice-Pres. Susan Collins.

Energy Productions Inc: 234 Sixth Ave, Brooklyn, NY 11215; Pres. Michael Knuth.

Eternal Song Agency: 6326 E Livingston Ave, Reynoldsburg, OH 43068; Pres. Leopold Xavier Crawford.

FAME Recording Studios: PO Box 2527, Muscle Shoals, AL 35662; Studio Man. Rodney Hall.

Famous Music Publishing: 1633 Broadway, 11th Floor, New York, NY 10019; tel. (212) 654-7407; fax (212) 654-4774; Contact Irwin Z. Robinson.

Faniork Music BMI: 23797 Via Irana Valencia, CA 91355; Owner Don Lee.

Fiesta City Publishers: PO Box 5861, Santa Barbara, CA 93150-5861; Pres. Frank E. Cooke.

Five Roses Music Group: 34A Lanier Rd, Studio 1, Jekyll Island, GA 31527; Pres. Sammie Lee Marler.

Five Star Music Inc: 40 Music Sq. E, Nashville, TN 37203; Contact Guy Parker.

Flat Town Music Co: PO Drawer 10, 238 E Main St, Ville Platte, LA 70586; tel. (318) 363-2177; fax (318) 363-2094; website www.flattownmusic.com; Pres. Floyd Soileau.

Folklore Music: 1671 Appian Way, Santa Monica, CA 90401; tel. (310) 451-0767; fax (310) 458-6005; e-mail mitchg@folkloreproductions.com; website folkloreproductions.com; Contact Mitch Greenhill.

GBS Music: 203 Gates Dr., Hendersonville, TN 37075-4961; Owner Ernie Bivens.

Gramophone Music Co: PO Box 921, Beverly Hills, CA 90213; Gen. Man. O. Berliner.

Group Productions: 1515 Cascade Ave, PO Box 481, Loveland, CO 80538; tel. (970) 669-3836; website www.grouppublishing.com; Contact Brenda Kraft.

Hall of Fame Music Co: PO Box 921, Beverly Hills, CA 90213; Gen. Man. O. Berliner.

Heartwrite Music: PO Box 1739, Texarkana, AR 75504; Pres. David Patillo.

Hidden Pun Music Inc: 1841 Broadway, Suite 411, New York, NY 10023; Pres. Julie Lipsivs.

High Kite Productions & Publishing: 1245 Elizabeth St, Denver, CO 80206; Prod. (Owner and Pres.) Henry Broz Rowland.

Island Music/Ackee Music Inc: 8920 Sunset Blvd, Second Floor, Los Angeles, CA 90069; tel. (213) 276-4500; fax (213) 276-0029; Contact Jan Lettick.

Jobete Music Co Inc: 6255 Sunset Blvd, Hollywood, CA 90028; tel. (213) 856-3507; fax (213) 461-2785.

Jon Music, BMI: PO Box 233, 329 N Main St, Church Point, LA 70525; Owner Lee Lavergne.

Justice Music Corpn: 11586 Blix St, North Hollywood, CA 91602; Exec. Vice-Pres. Monte R. Thomas.

Ketter Enterprises Inc: PO Box 740702, San Diego, CA 92174-0702; tel. (619) 479-5040; Pres. and CEO Al Ketter.

Leiber & Stoller Music Publishers: 9000 Sunset Blvd, Suite 1107, Los Angeles, CA 90069; tel. (310) 273-6401; fax (310) 273-1591; Gen. Man. Randy Poe.

Lipservices: 9 Prospect Park W, Room 14B, Brooklyn, NY 11215-1741; tel. (718) 638-2815; fax (718) 638-0842; e-mail ezclear@mindspring.com; Pres. Julie Lipsivs.

Little Big Town Music: 803 18th Ave S, Nashville, TN 37203; Pres. Wendy Bomar.

Loud Cry Music Publishing Co: PO Box 210270, Nashville, TN 37221-0270; Owner and Pres. Don Sanders.

MCA Music Publishing: 1755 Broadway, Eighth Floor, New York, NY 10019; tel. (212) 841-8000; fax (212) 582-7340; Contact Gail Wooten.

Metrostar Music/Blendingwell Music Inc: PO Box 5807, Englewood, NJ 07631; tel. (201) 969-9990; fax (201) 969-9955; e-mail plcagent@aol.com; Gen. Man. Philip S. Kurnit; Contact Norma Dubon.

MNM Music Group Inc: 1410 Second St, Suite 300, Santa Monica, CA 90401; Pres. Nick Martinelli.

Moller Digital Publishing: 17176 Grand Ave, Lake Elsinore, CA 92530; Sales Man. Irma Moller.

More Brand Music Publishing, BMI: PO Box 1027, Neenah, WI 54957-1027; Pres. Rita Ansems.

Music Sales Corpn: 257 Park Ave S, 20th Floor, New York, NY 10010; tel. (212) 254-2100; fax (212) 254-2013; e-mail dm@musicsales.com; website www.schirmer.com/msg.html; Pres. Barrie Edwards; Contact Denise Maurin.

Namax Music Publishing: PO Box 24162, Richmond, VA 23224; e-mail namaxmusic@aol.com; Pres. Nanette Brown.

Pal Productions Co: PO Box 80691, Baton Rouge, LA 70898; Pres. Johnny R. Palazzotto.

Pathway Music dba: PO Box 2250, Cleveland, TN 37320-2250; Co-ordinator of Music Charles Towler; Copyright Supervisor Connie Caldwell.

Peermusic: 8159 Hollywood Blvd, Los Angeles, CA 90069; 810 Seventh Ave, New York, NY 10019; COO/Sr Vice-Pres. Kathy Spanberger.

PKM Music: PO Box 5807, Englewood, NJ 07631; tel. (201) 969-9990; fax (201) 969-9955; e-mail plcagent@aol.com; Partner Philip S. Kurnit.

Platinum Gold Productions: 9200 Sunset Blvd, Suite 1220, Los Angeles, CA 90069; Partner Steve Cohen.

PolyGram Music Publishing Group: Worldwide Plaza, 825 Eighth Ave, New York, NY 10019; Creative Dirs Randy Sabiston, Dwayne Alexander.

PPL-MCI Entertainment Group: 10 Universal Plaza, PO Box 8442, Universal City, CA 91618; tel. (818) 506-8533; fax (818) 506-8534; e-mail pplzmi@aol.com; website www.pplzmi.com; CEO Jaeson St James Jarrett; Man. Dir Maxx Diamond.

Pravda Records Inc: 3823 N Southport, Chicago, IL 60613; Man. Dir Kenneth Goodman.

Quango Music Group Inc: 9744 Wilshire Blvd, Suite 305, Beverly Hills, CA 90212; Pres. George Ghiz.

Rising Star Music Publishers: 52 Executive Park S, Suite 5203, Atlanta, GA 30329; Ed. Pat Nugent.

Rondor Music International: 360 N La Cienega Blvd, Los Angeles, CA 90048; tel. (310) 289-3500; fax (310) 289-4000; Man. Candi Brown; Contact Randall Rumage.

Rustron Music Publishers: c/o The Whimsy, 1156 Park Lane, West Palm Beach, FL 33417; tel. (561) 686-1354; e-mail safehavenwpb@yahoo.com; Exec. Dir Rusty Gordon.

Set A Record Publishing: 720 North Roosevelt St, Cherokee, IA 51012; Man. Frank Gallagher.

Shapiro, Bernstein & Co Inc: 640 Fifth Ave, New York, NY 10019-6172; tel. (212) 957-0802; fax (212) 397-4638; website www.shapirobernstein.com; Contact Michael Brettler.

Shawnee Press Inc: 49 Waring Dr., Delaware Water Gap, PA 18327; tel. (570) 476-0550; fax (570) 476-5247; e-mail shawneepress@noln.com; website www.shawneepress.com; Dir of Sales Dennis Bell.

Sikio Marika Records: 6840 N Maple #157, Fresno, CA 93710; Label Head Tyrone White.

Single Kick Music: PO Box 8243, Calabasas, CA 91372; tel. (818) 883-8407; Proprietor Cho Paquet.

Songs for Today: 15 Rolling Way, New York, NY 10956-6912; tel. (845) 634-8282; fax (845) 634-5888; e-mail publishing@tkogroup.com; CEO Michael Cohn.

Sony Music Publishing: 666 Fifth Ave, PO Box 4451, New York, NY 10101-4451; Dir of Creative Affairs Pati deVries.

Sony/ATV Music Publishing LLC: 2100 Colorado Ave, Santa Monica, CA 90404; tel. (310) 449-2100; fax (310) 449-2544; e-mail info@sonyatv.com.

Spencer Ministries: 2225 Amoy West Rd, Mansfield, OH 44903; Exec. Dir David Conner.

Sublime Music: 15 Rolling Way, New York, NY 10956-6912; tel. (202) 966-3280; fax (202) 364-1367; e-mail publishing@tkogroup.com; website www.tkogroup.com; CEO Michael Cohn.

Sunset Promotions of Chicago Inc: 9359 S Kedzie Ave, PO Box 42807, Evergreen Park, IL 60805; tel. (773) 586-1800; fax (773) 586-1855; e-mail sunsetpromogip@inetmail.att.net; Pres. Neil J. Cacciottolo.

Tedesco Tunes: 16020 Lahey St, Granada Hills, CA 91344; Pres. Dale T. Tedesco.

Terra Nova Recording Co: 853 Broadway, #1516, New York, NY 10003; Pres. Marc Krasnow; CEO Robert Mangovleff.

The Music Umbrella: PO Box 1067, Santa Monica, CA 90406; Pres. and CEO Glenn H. Friedman.

TKO Publishing Inc: 15 Rolling Way, New York, NY 10956-6912; tel. (845) 634-8282; fax (845) 634-5888; e-mail publishing@tkogroup.com; Admin. M. A. Cohn.

Tranquil Technology Music: PO Box 20463, Oakland, CA 94620; Prod. Michael Mantra.

TurnerSong: 4263 San Jose Blvd, Jacksonville, FL 32207-6342; Partner Lee Turner.

Universal Music Publishing Group: 2440 Sepulveda Blvd, Suite 100, Los Angeles, CA 90064; tel. (310) 235-4700; fax (310) 235-4900; e-mail umpg.newmedia@umusic.com.

ViRay Publishing, BMI/Kerryray Publishing: 22432 Bayberry, Mission Viejo, CA 92692; Pres. Randy Ray.

Warner Chappell Music Inc: 10585 Santa Monica Blvd, Los Angeles, CA 90025-4950; tel. (310) 441-8600; fax (310) 441-1448; website www.warnerchappell.com; Sr Vice-Pres. Rick Shoemaker.

Westwood Entertainment Group: 1115 Inman Ave, Suite 330, Edison, NJ 08820-1132; Gen. Man. Elena Petillo.

Wilcom Publishing: PO Box 4456, West Hills, CA 91308; tel. and fax (661) 285-8032; e-mail info@wilcompublishing.com; website www.wilcompublishing.com; Owner William Clark.

Windswept Holdings LLC: 9320 Wilshire Blvd, Suite 200, Beverly Hills, CA 90212; tel. (310) 550-1500; fax (310) 247-0195; e-mail mail@windsweptpacific.com; website www.windsweptpacific.com; CEO Evan R. Medow.

Woodrich Enterprises Inc: PO Box 38, Lexington, AL 35648; e-mail mernee@msn.com; Pres. Woody Richardson.

Xmas Music: PO Box 828, Hollywood, CA 90028; Pres. Randall Paul.

Zettitalia Music International: PO Box 8442, Universal City, CA 91618; tel. (818) 506-8533; fax (818) 506-8534; e-mail zettworks@aol.com; website www.pplzmi.com; Pres. and CEO Suzette Cuseo-Jarrett.

Zomba Enterprises Inc: 137–139 W 25th St, New York, NY 10001; Sr Vice-Pres. and Gen. Man. David Renzer.

Venezuela

Distribuidora Sonografica CA: Dolores a Pte Soublette, Edif. Centro Empresarial Sur 4, Qta. Crespo, Caracas; Gen. Man. Guillermo Urbano Mijares.

Sony/ATV Music Publishing SA: Avda Blandin, Centro San Ignacio, Torre Copernico, 8°, La Castellana, Caracas 1067; tel. (212) 264-6564; fax (212) 264-7645; e-mail Publishing_Venezuela@ve.sonymusic.com; Contact Elikar Ortega.

Universal Music Publishing SA: Edif. Centro Colonasa, Avda San Felipe, entre 2da. Transversal y Calle Jose Angel Lamas, 5°, Oficinas 54–56, La Castellana, Caracas 1060; tel. (212) 201-9090; fax (212) 201-9091; e-mail miriam.gonzalez@umusic.com; Gen. Man. Miriam Gonzalez

APPENDIX E: MUSIC FESTIVALS AND EVENTS

Australia

Adelaide Fringe Festival: Lion Arts Centre, Cnr N Terrace & Morphett St, Adelaide, SA 5000; tel. (8) 8100-2000; fax(8) 8100-2020; e-mail buzz@adelaidefringe.com.au; website www.adelaidefringe.com.au; Australia's largest fringe festival, held Feb.–March; Artistic Dir Karen Hadfield.

Big Day Out: 212 Palmer St, East Sydney, NSW 2010; website www.bigdayout.com; National alternative music event, held annually in Jan.

Brisbane Biennial International Music Festival: Level 2, 75 Grey St, South Brisbane, Qld 4101; Next festival will take place from May to June; CEO Nicholas Heyward.

Brisbane's World of Music Festival: 120 Main St, Kangaroo Point, Qld 4169; World Music festival, Held at end of Oct.; Dir Christopher Bowen.

East Coast Blues Festival: PO Box 97, Byron Bay, NSW 2481; Festival of Blues & Roots music held each Easter; Dir Co Prod. Keven Oxford.

Festival of Perth: 3 Crawley Ave, Crawley, WA 6009; Multi-arts festival held Feb.-March; Dir David Blenkinsop.

Highfield Music Festival: c/o B & S Promotions, Bears Choice Music & Entertainment, PO Box 1481 Frankston, Vic. 3199; Festival co-ordinators providing live to music to venues; Partners Bill Dettmer, Sally Dettmer.

Melbourne Music Festival: 62-74 Pickles St, S Melbourne, Vic. 3205; Australia's largest contemporary music festival; held in Feb.; Exec. Prod. Dobe Newton.

Moomba Festival: 117 Sturt St, S Melbourne, Vic. 3205; Australia's largest outdoor festival; held annually in mid-March; Dirs Bob Burton, Maria Katsonis.

Port Fairy Folk Festival: PO Box 1252, Geelong, Vic. 3220; tel. (3) 5225-1232; fax (3) 5225-1211; e-mail pfff@portfairyfolkfestival.com; website www.portfairyfolkfestival.com; Nation's premier world and folk music event; Festival Dir Jamie McKew.

Splendour In The Grass: Byron Bay, Australia; e-mail information@splendourinthegrass.com; website www.splendourinthegrass.com; held in July; f. 2001.

Sydney Festival: 18 Hickson Rd, The Rocks, NSW 2000; tel. (2) 8248-6500; fax (2) 8248-6599; website www.sydneyfestival.org.au; Festival Dir Anthony Steel.

Tamworth Country Music Festival: Tamworth City Council, PO Box 555, Tamworth, NSW 2340; Annual Country Music festival held in Jan., incorporating the Golden Guitar Awards.

WOMADelaide: c/o Arts Projects Australia, 12 King William Rd, Unley SA 5061; tel. (8) 8271-1488; fax (8) 8271-9905; e-mail apadmin@artsprojects.com.au; website www.artsprojectsaustralia.com.au; Biennial three-day music festival; part of international World of Music, Arts and Dance, WOMAD, network; Event Dir Ian Scobie.

Austria

Artclub Festival Imst: PO Box 9, 6460 Imst; Open air rock festival; A & R Man. Arin Schrott.

Rock At The Border: Weitaer str 104, 3950 Gmünd; Open-air rock festival held in the second week of Aug.; Chair. Gerard Simon.

Summer Rock Festival: Hauptstr 140, 7203 Wiesen; Open-air pop and indie music festival, held on last weekend of July; Chair. Ewald Tartar.

Sunsplash Festival: Hauptstr 140, 7203 Wiesen; Open-air reggae festival held on the last weekend of Aug.; Chair. Ewald Tartar.

Transmitter: ImSohl 1, 6845 Hohenems; Avant-garde festival held in the first week of July; Dir Bernhard Amann.

Belgium

AALN International: PO Box 15, Antwerpen 17, 2018 Antwerp; Jazz, blues and world music events; Man. Dir Luc Nuitten.

Belga Jazz Festival: c/o Jazzronaute, 34 rue Africaine, 1050 Brussels; Jazz and blues festival held Oct.-Nov.; Man. Jean-Michel de Bie.

Belgium Rhythm 'N' Blues Festival: c/o Breakaway Vzw, Deusterstraat 11A, PO Box 2, 3990 Peer; tel. (11) 611125; fax (11) 611126; e-mail brbf@break-away.be; R & B festival held in July; Man. Dir Louis Vanhoef.

Boogietown Festival: Fruithoflaan 124, PO Box 11, 2600 Berchem, Antwerp; Blues Festival held in May every year; Dirs Peter Verstraelen, Frederic Marechal.

Dour Music Festival: 10 rue du Marché, 7370 Dour; Pop music festival featuring rock, pop and rap; Man. Dir Carlo di Antonio.

European Forum of World-wide Music Festivals: Jan Frans Willemsstraat 10, 2530 Boechout; Sec. Patrick de Groote.

Jazz A Liege: 18 Blvd d'Avroy, 4000 Liege; Jazz festival held in May; Chair. Jean-Marie Peterken.

Leffinge Leuren: c/o Leernsestwg 168, 9800 Deimze; International festival featuring all styles of music, held in Sept.; Dir Jean Tant.

Marktrock: PO Box 21, 3000 Louvain 1; e-mail info@marktrock.be; Festival of rock, pop and blues music with 10 stages; Held August; Man. Dir Omer Hoyelaerts.

Nandrin Rock Festival: 10 rue de Fort, 1060 Brussels; Chair. Pilippe Decoster.

On The Rox: Kleine Gentstraat 46, 9051 Ghent SDW; International rock festival; Man. Dir Chris Verleyen.

Schrikkelpop Festival: Fruithoflaan 12G, Bus 11, 2600 Berchem, Antwerp; Alternative Music festival held in early Aug.; Dirs Peter Verstraelen, Johan Pelgrims.

Sfinks Festival: Jan Frans Willemsstr 10a, 2530 Boechout; tel. (3) 455-6944; fax (3) 454-1162; e-mail info@sfinks.be; website www.sfinks.be; Annual world-wide music festival; held in July; Dir Patrick de Groote.

Torhout-Werchter: Beverlaat 3, 3118 Werchter; International rock festival held on the first weekend of July; Chair. Herman Schueremans.

Bulgaria

Bourgas Blues Festival: Leten Teater, Studio Goresht Piasak, 8000 Bourgas; Open-air blues festival held in Aug.; Dir Roumen Yanev.

Country Festival Society 'Costar': 23 Metodi Popov str, 1113 Sofia; Pres. Constantin Baharov.

Sofia Country Festival: 23 Metodi Popov str, 1113 Sofia; Leading International Country Music festival; Man. Decho Taralezhkov.

Varna Jazz Festival: Varna Municipality, Culture Dept, 43 Osmi Primorski Polk, Varna 9000; International Jazz Festival; held July-Aug.

Canada

Beaches International Jazz Festival: 1976A Queen St E, Toronto, ON M4L 1H8; tel. (416) 698-2152; fax (416) 698-2064; e-mail beachesjazz@rogers.com; website www.beachesjazz.com; Week long festival held in July; Pres. Lido Chilelli.

Big Valley Jamboree: 1042 Winnipeg St, Regina, SK S4R 8P8; Country Music festival; Exec. Prod. Alan Vinet.

Calgary International Jazz Festival: PO Box 2735 Station M, Calgary, AB T2P 3C2; Two-day outdoor event.

Canadian Music Festival: c/o Chart Toppers, 106-5397 Eglinton Ave W, Toronto ON M9C 5K6; Event featuring Canadian artists.

Du Maurier Ltd Downtown Jazz Festival: 366 Adelaide St E, Suite #230, Toronto, ON M5A 3X9; Annual jazz festival held in June-July; Dir of Marketing & Communications Bob McCullough.

Edmonton Folk Festival: PO Box 4130, Edmonton, AB T6E 4T2; tel. (780) 429-1899; fax (780) 424-1132; Four-day music festival held annually in Aug.

Festival International de Jazz de Montréal: 822 Sherbrook E, Montréal, QC H2L 1K4; Largest Jazz festival in North America, held in July.

Folk on the Rocks: PO Box 326, Yellowknife, NWT X1A 2N7; tel. (867) 920-7806; fax (867) 873-6535; e-mail fotr@ssimicro.com; website www.folkontherocks.com; Annual four-day summer music festival held on the third weekend in July; Exec. Festival Dir Tracey Bryant.

JUNO Awards: c/o CARAS, 124 Merton St, 3rd Floor, Toronto, ON M4S 2Z2; Annual awards for outstanding Canadian achievement in the field of recorded music.

Mariposa Folk Festival: 786 Dundas St E, Toronto, ON M4M 1R1; website www.mariposafolkfestival.com; Traditional and contemporary Folk festival; Held in July.

Mill Race Festival of Traditional Folk Music: PO Box 22148, Galt Central PO, Cambridge, ON N1R 8E3; tel. (519) 621-7135; e-mail mill_race@yahoo.com; website www.millracefolksociety.com; Festival of traditional folk music and dance; Chair/Artistic Dir Brad McEwen.

Music West: Suite 306, 21 Water St, Vancouver, BC V6B 1A1; Annual music conference and festival held in May; Prod. Maureen Jack.

Musicfest Canada: Suite 200, 1400 1st St, SW, Calgary, AB T2R 0V8; National music festival; Exec. Dir Jim Howard.

Ottawa International Jazz Festival: PO Box 3104 Station D, Ottawa, ON K1P 6H7; Jazz festival with emphasis on Canadian talent.

Sam Cat Records: 8 Woodlands Rd, St Albert, AB T8N 3L9; tel. and fax (780) 460-7460; e-mail fun@peterandmary.net; Also organizes the Earth Day Festival; Contact Peter Jansen.

St Jean-Baptiste Festival: Sociétè des mélomanes (Canada) Inc, 1056 Burnaby St, Suite 201, Vancouver, BC V6E 1N7; Dir Eugéne Evans.

Summerfolk Music & Crafts Festival: PO Box 521, Oven Sound, ON N4K 5R1; Festival held the third weekend of Aug. every year; Promotion Co-ordinator Linda Ashley.

Under The Volcano Festival of Art & Social Change: #21552, 1850 Commercial Dr., Vancouver, BC V5N 4A0; Annual music and arts event held since 1990; Co-ordinating Collective Member Irwin Oostindie.

Vancouver Folk Music Festival: PO Box 381, 916 W Broadway, Vancouver, BC V5Z 1K7; tel. (604) 602-9798; fax (604) 602-9790; e-mail info@thefestival.bc.ca; Four-day folk/world music festival held in Jericho Beach Park; Gen. Man. Brent Gibson.

Winnipeg Folk Festival: 203-211 Bannatyne Ave, Winnipeg, MB R3B 1B7; tel. (204) 231-0096; fax (204) 231-0076; e-mail info@winnipegfolkfestival.ca; website www.winnipegfolkfestival.ca; Folk music festival takes place during second weekend in July; Artistic Dir Rick Fenton.

Wye Marsh Festival: Music Committee, Wye Marsh Wildlife Centre, PO Box 100, Midland, ON L4R 4K6; Annual wildlife festival which includes a folk music component.

Croatia

B P Club Jazz Festivals: Teslina 7, Zagreb; Two annual jazz festivals; Contact Boško Petrovic.

Croatian Festival of Pop Music-Split: c/o Dalmaciakoncert, Trg Republike 1/11, 58000 Split; Pop Festival held in July; Man. Dir Ivica Vrkic.

HTF: c/o Croatian Television, Prisavlje 3, 10000 Zagreb; tel. 9822-7652; fax 1634-3646; e-mail a.kostadinov@hrt.hr; National contest for Eurovision Song Contest and music shows; Prod. Aleksandar Kostadinov.

ZagrebFest: c/o Alta, Berislaviceva 9, HDS, 41000 Zagreb; Pop Festival held in mid-Dec.; Man. Dir Drago Diklic.

Denmark

Aarhus International Jazz Festival: Thomas Jensens Alle, 8000 C Aarhus; tel. 8940-9191; fax 8940-9199; e-mail mail@aarhusfestival.dk; website www.aarhusfestival.dk; Festival held at the end of Aug. or beginning of Sept.; Head of Programmes Section Annita Hornslet.

Copenhagen Jazz Festival: Kjled Langes Gade 4A, 1367 K Copenhagen; e-mail info@jazzfestival.dk; website www.jazzfestival.dk; Festival of Jazz, Blues and World Music held in July; Man. Bodil Jacobsen.

Esbjerg 60's Festival: SHB-Soeren Hoejberg Booking ApS, Frodesgade 74, 6700 Esbjerg; One-day festival taking place in Spring; Man. Dir Soeren Hoejberg.

Esbjerg Open Air: SHB-Soeren Hoejberg Booking ApS, Frodesgade 74, 6700 Esbjerg; One-day open air festival held in Aug.; Man. Dir Soeren Hoejberg.

Esbjerg Rock Festival: SHB-Soeren Hoejberg Booking ApS, Frodesgade 74, 6700 Esbjerg; Open air festival held on the first weekend of June; Man. Dir Soeren Hoejberg.

Midtfyns Festival: Laessoegade 78 st, 5230 M Odense; Rock, Pop and Folk Music festival held in June-July; Man. Dir Nina Faergeremann.

Roskilde Festival: Havsteensvej 11, 4000 Roskilde; tel. 4636-6613; fax 4632-1499; e-mail info@roskilde-festival.dk; website www.roskilde-festival.dk; Four-day music festival; Held late June; Gen. Man. Leif Skov.

Skagen Festival: PO Box 33, 9990 Skagen; tel. 9844-4969; fax 9844-6377; e-mail peer.andersen@wanadoo.dk; website www.skagenfestival.dk; Held late June; Programme Dir Peer Løgsted Andersen.

Skanderborg Festival: c/o J P Management, Jernbanevej 22, 8660 Skanderborg; Festival of Folk, Pop, Jazz and Rock music held in Aug.; Man. Dir J P Andersen.

Tivoli Festival: Vesterbrogade 3, DK 1630 Copenhagen V.

Tønder Festival: Foundation Vestergade 80, 6270 Tønder Festival; Folk music festival since 1975; Dir Carsten Panduro.

Estonia

Ollefestival: PO Box 2907, Tallina Peapostkontor, Tatari 23, 0090 Tallinn; Pop Music festival held late June-early July; Promoter Lauri Viikna.

Pärnu Jazz: Papiniidu 50, 3600 Pärnu; International beachtown summer festival held in July; Festival Dir Tiit Lauk.

Rock Summer Festival: PO Box 3333, Regati Pst 1-6K, 0019 Tallinn; Rock festival, held in July; Man. Martti Kitsing.

Tartu Jazz: Laulupeo 25, 2400 Tartu Festival Arena; International outdoor festival of traditional and modern jazz held in mid-July; Man. Aadu Birnbaum.

Tartu Rock Festival: Laulupeo 25, 2400 Tartu Festival Arena; Outdoor festival, mainly Estonian artists with some foreign guest musicians; Man. Aadu Birnbaum.

Tudengijazz: PO Box 3641, 0090 Tallinn; International student jazz festival held in Feb.; Man. Reimo Unt.

Finland

April Jazz Espoo: Ahertajantie 6 B, 02100 Espoo; International indoors jazz festival, with special focus on vocal and big band jazz; held in April; Contact Martti Lappaiainen.

Baltic Jazz: Kålabacksvågen 1, 25900 Taalintehdas; National and international swing and traditional jazz event held in July; Contact Magi Kulla.

EloJazz&Blues: Kaislatie 9 M 2, 90160 Oulu; National outdoors and indoors jazz festival held in late July, covering all styles; Contact Kari Kesti.

Finnish National Jazz Days: PO Box 54, 00101 Helsinki; Annual national jazz festival involving all styles; held in a different town each year (recently held in Helsinki and Jyväskylä); held in Nov.; Contact Finnish Jazz Federation.

Global Music Centre: Mikkolantie 17, 00640 Helsinki; Dir Anu Laakkonen.

Helsinki Festival: Rauhankatu 7 E, 00170 Helsinki; Festival of Jazz, Pop, Rock and Ethnic music; held Aug.-Sept.; Artistic Dir Esa-Pekka Salonen.

Imatra Big Band Festival: PO Box 22, 55101 Imatra; National and international outdoors/indoors festival of all jazz styles, with special interest in big band music; held June-July.

Jazz at the Market Place: Vesijärvenkatu 20, 15140 Lahti; National outdoor jazz festival held in mid-Aug.; Contact Martti Peippo.

Jazz on the Beach: Kauppakatu 23, 92100 Raahe; National and international outdoors/indoors festival featuring all jazz styles; held late July; Contact Pertti Kinnunen.

KaamosJazz (Jazz Under Northern Lights): 99695 Tankavaara; tel. (16) 626-158; fax (16) 626-261; National indoors jazz festival held in late Nov.; Contact Kauko Lainonen.

Kainuu Jazz Spring: Kalliokatu 7, 87100 Kajaani; International indoors event with all jazz styles, held in May; Contact Unto Tomiainen.

Kaustinen Folk Music Festival: Kaustinen; Held in July; Contact Jyrki Heiskanen.

Keitele Jazz: Humpinkatu 4 A, 44120 Äänekoski; All jazz styles featured in a national and international event held in July; Contact Kalevi Plattonen.

Kerava Jazz: Asemantie 4, 04200 Kerava; tel. (9) 2949-2005; fax (9) 2949-2082; e-mail mavno.kahranaho@pp.inet.fi; website personal.inet.fi/yhdistys/keravajazz/; International modern and contemporary jazz festival; held in early June; Contact Kerava City Cultural Bureau.

Nummirock: 61910 Nummijärvi; Rock festival held midsummer.

Pori International Jazz Festival: Pohjoisranta 11, 28100 Pori; tel. (2) 626-2200; fax (2) 626-2225; e-mail jyrki.kangas@porijazz.fi; website www.porijazz.fi; International open-air event held in July; all jazz, rhythm 'n' blues and rock styles; Contact Jyrki Kangas.

Provinssirock: PO Box 180, 60101 Seinäjoki; tel. (6) 421-2700; fax (6) 414-8622; e-mail info@provinssirock.fi; website www.provinssirock.fi; Rock festival held in early June.

Ruisrock: Uudenmaankatu 1, 20500 Turku; Rock festival staged by the sea in Turku and has attendance figures close to 25,000; held in mid-summer; Contact Turku Music Festival Foundation.

Ruska-Swing: Oy Yleisradio Ab, PL 64, 98101 Kemijärvi; National swing and traditional jazz event held in Sept.; Contact Pekka Lintula.

Tampere Jazz Happening: Tullikamarinaukio 2, 33100 Tampere; tel. (3) 3146-6136; fax (3) 223-0121; e-mail music@tampere.fi; website www.tampere.fi/jazz/; International contemporary and modern jazz indoor festival held in Oct.-Nov.; Contact Annamaija Saarela.

Turku Jazz Festival: Uudenmaankatu 1, 20500 Turku; National and international festival, with mainly contemporary jazz styles, held in March; Contact Rainer Koski.

Ylläs Jazz Blues: 95970 Äkäslompolo; All jazz and rhythm 'n' blues styles; national and international acts featured; held in Feb.; Contact Pirkko Hietaniemi.

France

Africolor: 145 rue de Ménilmontant, 75020 Paris; tel. 1 47 97 69 99; fax 1 47 97 65 44; e-mail africolor@africolor.com; website www.africolor.com; Music festival focused on music from Western Africa and Indian Ocean; held in Dec.; Artistic Dir Philippe Conrath.

Banlieues Blues: 9 Ave Berlioz, 93270 Sevran; Jazz and blues events throughout Paris in March and April; Dir Jacques Pornon.

Carnavalorock: 9 rue Galis Bizoin, 22000 St Brieuc; Festival held in April-May; Chair. Sam Burlot.

Festival 'Synthèse' International Festival of Electronic Music and Creations of Bourges: Institut International de Musique Electroacoustique, PO Box 39, 18001 Bourges Cédex; tel. 2 48 20 41 87; fax 2 48 20 45 51; e-mail administration@ime-bourges.org; website www.gmeb.fr; Artistic Dirs Françoise Barriere Christian Clozier.

Festival d'Ete de Nantes/Musique Sur L'ile: rue de l'évêché, 44000 Nantes; tel. 2 40 08 01 00; fax 2 40 48 12 64; e-mail contact@festival-ete-nantes.asso.fr; website www.festival-ete-nantes.asso.fr; Festival of world music; held in July; Contact Bertrand de Laporte.

Festival International de Guitares de Vittel: PO Box 698, Porte de la Craffe, 54043 Nancy; Guitar festival held in June; Contact Marc Leonard.

Festival International de Jazz Antibes: Office du Tourisme, 11 Pl. de Gaulle, 06000 Antibes; Open-air Jazz festival held in July; Dir Jean-Pierre González.

Festival National de Blues: c/o Asscn Clin d'Oreille, Hotel de Ville, 71200 Le Creusot; Annual festival held in July in Burgundy; Pres. Renee Cerruti; Artistic Dir Emilio Armilles.

Fiesta des Suds: Latinissimo, PO Box 121, 13473 Marseille; Dir Florence Chastanier.

Jazz A Manosque: Service Culturel, Hotel de Ville, 04100 Manosque; Ten-day festival held in the second fortnight in July; Dir M Gerard Ollivier.

Le Lieu Unique-CRDC: PO Box 21304, 2 rue de la Biscuiterie, 44013 Nantes Cédex 01; tel. 2 51 82 15 00; fax 2 40 20 20 12; e-mail info@lelieuunique.com; website www.lelieuunique.com; popular music and video events and festivals; Dir Jean Blaise; Musical Curator Kitty Hartl.

Les 24 Heures de l'Insa: Amicale des élèves INSA, Bâtiment B2, Ave de Rangueil, 31077 Toulouse; tel. 5 62 17 00 79; fax 5 62 17 75 97; e-mail amicale@etud.insa-tlse.fr; Annual student festival held in May; Contact Renaud Poincloux.

Nice Jazz Festival: c/o Nice Jazz Productions, 7 Pl. de Seoul, 75014 Paris; Annual Jazz festival held in July; Dir Luc Gavrichon.

Octob'rock: 115 reu Lesage, 5110 Reims; Organizer and Promoter of concerts including the Rock Festival held in Oct.; Pres. Alain Boucheron.

Projazz: 10 ave des 27 Martyrs, 78400 Chatou; tel. (1) 39 52 70 05; fax (1) 34 80 96 55; jazz promoter; Pres. Pierre Dieuzey.

Rock 'n' Solex: c/o Amicale de Eleves INSA, 20 Ave des Buttes de Coësmes, 35043 Rennes Cédex; Organizer of the Rennes two-day rock festival; Pres. Nicolas Orhon.

Germany

Alandia Jazz: c/o Nachtigallensteg 3, 23611 Bad Schwartau; tel. 451-27705; fax 451-26491; e-mail alandia.jazz@aland.net; website www.alandiajazz.aland.fi; National and international jazz festival; held in July; Contact Christer Mörn.

Berlin Independence Days: Köpenicker str 6, 10997 Berlin; Held in Oct.; Contact Michael Betz.

Freestyle eV: Morgensternsweg 7, 22305 Hamburg; Music festival and event organizers; Contact Helmut Heuer.

Heimatklänge: Berlin; Held in July-Aug.; Contact Borkowksy Akbar.

Leipziger Rockfestival: Tollweg 42, 04289 Leipzig; Annual rock festival held in June; Man. Dir Edgar Bergmann.

Music Factory: Rottscheidter str 6, 42329 Wuppertal; Organizer of music fairs; Head PR Dept Andrea Zech.

Musikmesse/Pro Light and Sound: Messe Frankfurt GmbH, Ludwig-Erhard-Anlage 1, 60327 Frankfurt; tel. (69) 7575-6452; fax (69) 7575-6613; e-mail wilhelm-p.hosenseidl@messefrankfurt.com; International trade fairs for musical instruments and sheet music, light, sound and event technology; Brand Devt Man. Wilhelm-Peter Hosenseidl.

Popkomm: Rottscheidter str 6, 42329 Wuppertal; Organizer of music fairs; Head of PR Dept Andrea Zech.

Rheinkultur: PO Box 201303, Moltkestr. 41, 53173 Bonn; Germany's largest open-air festival, held in late June-early July; Prod. Sabine Funk.

Tanz & Folkfest: Stadt Rudolstadt, Kulturburo, Markt 7, 07407 Rudolstadt; tel. (3672) 412-651; fax (3672) 412-796; e-mail tffrudolstadt@saale-net.de; website www.rudolstadt.de; Held on the first weekend in July; Contact Peter Uhlmann.

Greece

Athens Festival: Voukourestiou 1, 10564 Athens; International festival held in July-Aug.; Man. Dir Dimos Vratsanos.

Mediterranean Music Festival: 2 Kritis St, 15562 Holargos, Athens; World Music festival held every two years; Public Relations Marilena Koussoulou.

Hungary

Diaksziget: Lonyay u 18/B, 1093 Budapest; International festival held in July-Aug.; A & R Man. Karly Gerendai.

Island Festival: c/o Sziget Kulturális Szervezö Iroda, Ul 18/B Lónyay, 1093 Budapest; Festival held in the third week of Aug. each year; Foreign Affairs Man. Matthew Braghini.

Kalaka Folk Festival: Miskolo; Held in July; Contact Csaba Lökös.

Taban Bem: Rakpart 6, 1014 Budapest; Rock, folk and blues festival; Contact Aranka Marka.

Womufe: Villanyi ut 107, 1118 Budapest; World music event held in May-June in Budapest; Contact Robert Mandel.

Ireland

Bacardi Plugged Band Competition: Hot Press, 13 Trinity St, Dublin 2; tel. (1) 241-1500; fax (1) 241-1538; e-mail jachay@iol.ie; website www.hotpress.com; National band competition; Project Co-ordinator Jackie Hayden.

Boyle Arts Festival: Great Meadow, Boyle, Co Roscommon; Held in last week of July to first week in Aug. each year; Co-ordinator Fergus D Ahern.

Cork Jazz Festival: 18 Stephen's Lane, Upper Mount St, Dublin 2; website www.corkjazzfestival.com; Jazz festival with Irish and international acts held in Oct.; Contact Jack McGouran.

Drogheda Samba Festival: The Droichead Arts Centre, Drogheda, Co Louth; Festival of Afro-Brazilian music including performances, workshops and carnival; held in July each year; Contact Kieran Gallagher.

Feakle Traditional Music Week: Maghera, Caher, Feakle, Co Clare; Festival of traditional music, song and dance from East Clare; Chair. Pat Hayes.

Feile Seamus: Ennis Finglas Art Centre, Art Squad, Unit 14B Main Shopping Centre, Finglas, Dublin 11; Workshops and summer school promoting artists past and present in traditional music; Chair. Mary McDermott.

Galway Arts Festival: Black Box Theatre, Galway; tel. (91) 509700; fax (91) 562655; e-mail info@gaf.iol.ie; website www.galwayartsfestival.ie; Arts Festival held in July; Man. Fergal McGrath.

Hot Press Music Seminars: 13 Trinity St, Dublin 2; tel. (1) 241-1500; fax (1) 241-1538; e-mail jachay@iol.ie; website www.hotpress.com; A series of seminars explaining the basic of the music industry to musicians etc.; Seminar Co-ordinator Jackie Hayden.

Mary From Dungloe International Festival: Festival Office, Main St, Dungloe, Co Donegal; 10 music festivals held late July to early Aug. each year; various concerts during the year; Festival Dir Colm Croffy.

Monaghan Rhythm & Blues Festival: The Arts Office, Market House, Monaghan; tel. (47) 71114; fax (47) 71113; e-mail harvestblues@eircom.net; website www.harvestblues.net; Annual rhythm and blues festival held on the first weekend of Sept.; other annual concerts of popular music; Contact Samhairle Mac Conghail.

Sligo Arts Festival: Model Arts, The Mall, Sligo; Arts festival held at the end of May, with world music, street events and theatre; Contact Danny Kirrane.

Israel

Israel Festival: PO Box 4409, Jerusalem 91044; Festival of performing arts including music, dance and theatre; held in May-June.

Italy

Arezzo Wave: via Masaccio 14, 52100 Arezzo; tel. (0575) 911005, fax (0575) 911038; e-mail info@arezzowave.com; website www.arezzowave.com; European rock festival held in the first week of July; Man. Dir Mauro Valenti.

Bassano Jazz: Via Sonda 21, 36061 Bassano del Grapa; Jazz and progressive music; Man. Dir Giovanni Mayer.

Corridonia Jazz Festival: Antonello Andreaniu di Coop Ephemeria P'zza 30 Aprile, 62100 Macerata; Jazz festival held in July.

Cremona Rock: c/o Centro Musicale Il Cascinetto, Via Maffi 2, 26100 Cremona; Annual Italian rock festival in early June.

Festambiente: Via Tripoli 27, 58100 Grosseto; Ecological festival Cultural Section Resp Michela Presta.

Magna Grecia Rock: Via Cavour, 96100 Siracuse; International festival held annually in Sicily.

Rockin' Umbria: Via Della Viola 1, 06100 Perugia; International music festival; Man. Dir Sergio Piazzoli.

Voci E Suoni Del Mediterraneo: Gibellina; Held Aug.-Sept.; Contact Pompeo Benincasa.

World Music Festival: Rome; Held in Aug.; Contact Pietro Carli.

Japan

Fuji Rock Festival: Naeba Ski Resort, Japan; website www.fujirockers.org; held in July.

Netherlands

12th Music Meeting: Nijmegen; Held in Nov.; Contact Wim Westerveld

Befrydings Festival: Grote Kerkstraat 14, Dg11E6 Leeuwarden Festival programming and production; Contact Sjoerd Cuperus.

Dunya Festival: Rotterdam; Held 1-2 June; Contact Martin Van Ginkel

Dynamo Open Air Festival: Juliusstraat 45, 5621 GC Rotterdam Largest heavy rock festival in Europe; Man. Dir M. Kanters.

Frysk Festival: Grote Kerkstraat 14, DG 1146 Leeuwarden; Contact Sjoerd Cuperus.

Metropolis Festival: PO Box 131, 3000 AC Rotterdam; Pop festival for young up-and-coming bands; held in early July; Man. Dir Corinne Lampen.

Music and Harmony: Oude Enghweg 24, 1217 JD Hilversum; Organizer of international musical instruments fair in Jaarbeurs-Utrecht; held at the beginning of Sept.; Contact P. M. Dooren.

North Sea Jazz Festival: PO Box 3325, 2601 DH Delft; tel. (15) 214-8900; fax (15) 214-8393; e-mail tejo@northseajazz.nl; website www.northseajazz.nl; Largest indoor Jazz festival in Europe; Festival Dir T. van den Hoek.

PinkPop: PO Box 117, 6160 AC Geleen; International pop festival Contact Jan Smeets.

World Roots Festival: Amsterdam; Held in June; Contact Frans Goossens.

New Zealand

Bay of Islands Country Rock Festival: PO Box 355 Kerikeri Bay of Islands; tel. (9) 404-1063; fax (9) 404-1065; e-mail maysplace@actrix.co.nz website www.country-rock.co.nz; Annual country music festival held on the second weekend in May; Contact Shirley May.

Bay of Islands Jazz & Blues Festival: PO Box 355 Kerikeri Bay of Islands; tel. (9) 404-1063; fax (9) 404-1065; e-mail maysplace@actrix.co.nz Annual jazz and blues event, held on second weekend in Aug.; Contact Shirley May.

Fringe Festival: 6 Majoribanks St, Mt Victoria; New Zealand's largest open-access fringe festival; Dir Tracy Medland.

International Music Expo: PO Box 25046, St Heliers, Auckland Annual trade event held in Sept.; Contact Rob Eady.

New Zealand International Festival of the Arts: PO Box 10113, Wellington; Largest arts event in the country, held alternate years; Exec. Dir Carla Van Zon.

Tarankai Festival of the Arts: PO Box 4251, New Plymouth; Three week long festival held on alternate years in March; Festival Dir Roger King.

Norway

Førde Folk Music Festival: PO Box 395, 6801 Førde; tel. 5772-1940; fax 5772-1941; e-mail info@fordefestival.no; website www.fordefestival.no; Held in July; Contact Hilde Bjørkum.

Glopperock: PO Box 222, 6860 Sandane; Rock festival held in June; Man. Dir Remi Tystad.

Kalvöyafestivalen: Karl Johansgaten 8, 0154 Oslo 1; International festival held at the end of June; Man. Paul Karlsen.

Molde International Jazz Festival: PO Box 211, 3671 Notodden; e-mail post@moldejazz.no; website www.moldejazz.no; Major Jazz festival in July; Man. Dir Einar Gjendem.

Notodden Blues Festival: PO Box 211, 3671 Notodden; Blues festival; held in early Aug.; Promoter Espen Fjelle.

Poland

Folk Blues Fair: Poznan; Held in early March; Contact Dionizy Piatkowski.

Jazz on Odra Festival: c/o Interart Ltd, ul. Pugeta 6, 51-628 Wroclaw; Contact Margaret Szablowska.

Odjazdy: ALMA-ART, ul. Teatralna 9, 40-003 Katowice; Festival of rock and independent music; held in mid- Nov. at Spodek Hall; Dir Bogdan Marcinkowski.

Piknik Country: Grojecka 75, 01 094 Warsaw; Country Music festival held in July; Man. Ewa Dabrowska.

Sopot International Music Festival: Ul. Kosciuzki 61, 81703 Sopot; International Song Contest; Contact Wojciech Korzeniewski.

Stage Song Festival: Arts and Culture Centre, Rynek-Ratusz 24, 50-101 Wroclaw; Presentation of Polish musical theatre highlights of the season; promoting young actors through competition; concerts by prominent guest performers from abroad; Artistic Dir Roman Kolakowski.

Warsaw Summer Jazz Days: E Plater 49, 0125 Warsaw; Jazz event held in June; Contact Mariusz Adamiak.

Winter Rock Festival: ALMA-ART, ul. Teatralna 9, 40-003 Katowice; Rock music festival for Polish and foreign bands; 23 Feb. at Spodek Hall; Dir Bogdan Marcinkowski.

Romania

Golden Stag: Etaj 4, cam 412, Calea Dorobanti 101, Sector 1, Bucharest; International music festival; Gen. Man. Dumitri Morosanu.

Slovakia

Rock Pop Bratislava: Jakubovo nam 12, 81499 Bratislava; Major rock and pop festival; Dir Pavel Danek.

Slovenia

Druga Godba: Ljubljana; Held in early June; Contact Bogdan Benigar.

Festival Ljubljana: Trg Francoske Revolucije 1-2, 61000 Ljubljana; Open-air event from June to Sept.; Man. Dir Vladimir Vajda.

No Border Jam Festival: Front Rock, PO Box 48, 62000 Marilor; tel. (41) 832736; fax (26) 476381; e-mail frontrock@iname.com; Annual international punk, rock, pop, ethno, garage festivals held in June and Oct.; Man. Dusan Hedl.

Spain

Barcelona Jazz Festival: Ronda Sant Pere, 33 Principal, 08010 Barcelona; tel. (934) 817040; fax (934) 817041; e-mail theproject@the-project.net; website www.the-project.net; Jazz festival in Oct.-Nov.; Man. Dir Tito Ramoneda.

Espárrago Rock Festival: c/o Reyes, Catolicos 25, Of. 2 Planta, 18001 Granada; Promotion Dir Javier Gonzalez.

Guitar Festival of Cordoba: Avda Gran Capitan, No. 3, 14008 Córdoba; Concerts of Classical, Flamenco, Pop, Rock and Antique music; Production Man. Ana Linares Bueno.

Madrid Jazz Festival: Navarro Reverter 22, 46004 Valencia; Jazz festival held in June and July; A & R Julio Martin.

Pirineos Sur: Huesca; Held July-Aug.; Contact Luis Calvo.

Sweden

Dala Rock: PO Box 12, 77621 Hedemora; Festival held in July, featuring Swedish and international artists; Man. Dir Putte Brolund.

Falun Folk Music Festival: Falun; Held in July; Contact Magnus Bäckström.

Festival Sjöslaget: c/o Projektbyrån, Kungsgatan 34, 97241 Luleå; Man. Dir Tomas Lind.

Gothenburg All Star Festival: World Trade Centre, Box 5264, 40225 Gothenburg; Major rock festival with international acts; A & R Man. Magnus Erikson.

Hultsfred Festival: PO Box 170, 57724 Hultsfred; tel. 4956-9500; fax 4956-9550; e-mail gunnar.lagerman@rockparty.se; website www.rockparty.se; Man. Dir Gunnar Lagerman.

Kalott Jazz & Blues: Tornio City Cultural Bureau, Hallituskatu 9, 95400 Tornio-Haaparanta; National and international festival of all jazz styles and blues; held late June.

Re Orient Festival: Stockholm; Held in June; Contact Jonas Elverstig.

The Arvika Festival: PO Box 99, 671 23 Arvika; tel. 5701-2199; fax 5701-2112; e-mail arvikafestivalen@galaxen.se; website www.galaxen.se; Rock and indie music festival held in July; Mans Björn Serrander, Tomas Fändriks.

Switzerland

Caribana Festival: Rue de la combe 4, 1260 Nyon; Music festival over four days covering rock, folk, tropical, rap and acid jazz; Co-ordinator Tony Lerch.

Estival Jazz: Lugano 6992 Vernate; e-mail info@estivaljazz.ch; website www.estivaljazz.ch; Free open air jazz festival; Man. Andreas Wyden.

Jazz Willisau: PO Box, 6130 Willisau; tel. (41) 970-2731; fax (41) 970-3231; e-mail troxler@centralnet.ch; website www.jazzwillisau.ch; Festival of jazz; Dir Niklaus Troxler.

Montreux Jazz Festival: CP 126, CH 1820 Montreux-Territet; Annual festival held in July consisting of jazz, pop, rock, blues, and soul; 2 halls and 5 off-stages; Workshops; Artistic Dir Claude Nobs.

Turkey

Istanbul International Jazz Festival: Istiklal Caddesi 146, Luvr Apt Beyoglu, 80070 Istanbul; Jazz festival held June-July.

Ukraine

Beatlesmania Music Festival: Independent Artist's Agency, Ljubchenko & Co, Room 7, Mietrostrojevskaja St 5, 320128 Dnipropetrovsk; Annual music festival; Dir Valeri Ljubchenko.

Dirate of the All-Ukrainian Festival of Independent Music: Alternative Culture Foundation, Lesva Kur-Basa str 4, 290007 Lviv; Held in Sept.; Dir Youry Grekh; Vice Dir Ruslan Koshiv.

Kharkiv Assemblies International Music Festival: Institute of Musicology, Soviet Ukraine Sq. 20 #9, 310003 Kharkiv; Dir Grigory Hansburg.

Musica Pura Europae Festival: R Eideman str 2-16, 310112 Kharkiv; International music festival dealing with European neofolk and independent rock music; Man. Sergey Myasoedev.

Rock Fest Bee: c/o Independent Artists Agency Ljubchenko & Co, Room 7, Mietrostrojevskaja St 5, 320128 Dnipropetrovsk; Annual music festival; Dir Valeri Ljubchenko.

'Tavria Games' International Festival: 36V, Lesi Ukrainki Blvd, 252133, Kiev; Organizers of the Tavria Games International Festival since 1992; Gen. Dir Nikolay Bagraev.

Teenwave: c/o Independent Artist Agency Ljubchenko & Co, Room 7, Mietrostrojevskaja St 5, 320128 Dnipropetrovsk; International teenage song festival; Dir Valeri Ljubchenko.

United Kingdom

Aberdeen Alternative Festival: 10 Belmont St, Aberdeen AB1 1JE, Scotland; Annual arts festival held each Oct., combining culture of north-east Scotland with international music, comedy, drama and dance; Dir Duncan Hendry.

Appalachian and Bluegrass Music Festival: Ulster-American Folk Park, Castletown, Omagh, Co Tyrone BT78 5QY; tel. (2882) 243292; held early September; Head of Museum Services John A. Walsh.

Bath International Music Festival: Linley House, 1 Pierrepont Pl., Bath BA1 1JY; Held May-June; Artistic Dir Tim Joss.

Belfast Folk Festival: Students Union, University Rd, Belfast BT17 1PR, Northern Ireland; Irish and international festival; Contact Noel Devlin.

Beverley & East Riding Folk Festival: 2 Star Row, N Dalton, Driffield, E Yorks YO25 9UR; tel. (1377) 217569; fax (1377) 217754; e-mail chris@adastey.demon.co.uk; website www.adastey.demon.co.uk; Annual festival specialising in folk, roots and related music; held third weekend in June; Dir Chris Wade.

Birkenhead Guitar Festival of Great Britain: Dept Leisure Services and Tourism, Westminster House, Birkenhead, Wirral L41 5FN; Held 9-17 Nov.; Festival Dir Ron Smith.

Birmingham International Jazz Festival: PO Box 944, Edgbaston, Birmingham B16 8UT; tel. (121) 454-7020; fax (121) 454-9996; e-mail festival@bigbearmusic.com; website www.bigbearmusic.com; Held in early July; Dir Jim Simpson.

Bracknell Festival: South Hill Park, Ringmead, Bracknell, Berks RG12 7PA; tel. (1344) 484858; fax (1344) 411427; e-mail festival@southhillpark.org.uk; website www.southhillpark.org.uk; Music and arts festival; Festival Dir Simon Chatterton.

Brecon Jazz: Theatr Brycheiniog, Canal Wharf, Brecon, Powys LD3 7EU; tel. (1874) 611622; website www.breconjazz.co.uk; Held in Aug.; Festival Co-ordinator Deborah Parry.

Cambridge Folk Festival: The Guildhall, Cambridge CB2 3QJ; tel. (1223) 457512; fax (1223) 457529; e-mail eddieb@cambridge.gov.uk; website www.cam-folkfest.co.uk; Folk festival with programme including folk, blues and country; Held late July/early August; Promotions Officer Eddie Barcan.

Carling Weekend Leeds Festival: Mean Fiddler Music Group, 16 High St, Harlesden, London NW10 4LX; tel. (20) 8963-0940; website www.leedsfestival.com; British rock and pop festival, held over three days in Aug., in Reading and Leeds; Chair. Vince Power; Man. Dir Melvin Benn.

Carling Weekend Reading Festival: Mean Fiddler Music Group, 16 High St, Harlesden, London NW10 4LX; tel. (20) 8963-0940; website www.readingfestival.com; British rock and pop festival, held over three days in Aug., in Reading and Leeds; Chair. Vince Power; Man. Dir Melvin Benn.

Cheltenham International Festival of Music: Town Hall, Imperial Sq., Cheltenham, Glos GL50 1QA; Held during July; Festival Organizer Kim Sargeant.

City of London Festival: Bishopsgate Hall, 230 Bishopsgate, London EC2M 4HW; tel. (20) 7377-0540; fax (20) 7377-1972; e-mail admin@colf.org; website www.colf.org; Arts Festival; Held in June-July; Gen. Man. Kathryn McDowell.

Cropredy Music Festival: c/o Fairport Convention, PO Box 37, Banbury, Oxon OX16 8YN; website www.faircrop.co.uk; Organizers of the Cropredy Music Festival; Contact David Pegg.

Cross Rhythms: PO Box 183, Plymouth, PL3 4YN; Annual festival; Admin. Jonathan Bellamy.

Edinburgh International Festival: 21 Market St, Edinburgh EH1 1BW, Scotland; tel. (131) 473 2001; website www.eif.co.uk; International Arts Festival of music, theatre and dance; Man. Dir Mike Hart.

Fleadh: 18 High St, Harlesden, London NW10 4LP; tel. (20) 8961-5490; fax (20) 8961-5743; website www.meanfiddler.com; Irish and Scottish folk festival held in Finsbury Park; Chair. Vince Power; Man. Dir Melvin Benn.

Galway Arts Festival: Black Box Theatre, Galway; tel. (91) 509700; fax (91) 562655; e-mail info@gaf.iol.ie; website www.galwayartsfestival.ie; arts festival held in July; Man. Fergal McGrath.

Glasgow International Jazz Festival: 18 Albion St, Merchant City, Glasgow G1 1LH, Scotland; 10-day jazz festival; held late June-early July; Festival Dir Derek Gorman.

Glastonbury Festival: Worthy Farm, Pilton, Shepton Mallet, Somerset; website www.glastonburyfestivals.co.uk; One of the UK's leading international music events; held in June; Man. Dir Michael Eavis.

Great British Rhythm and Blues Festival: Bank House, 61 Albert Rd, Colne, Lancashire BB8 0PB; Arts & Entertainment Man. Gary Hood.

Greenbelt Festival: The Greenhouse, Hillmarton Rd, London N7 9JE; International festival held in Aug.; Contact Martin Evans.

Greenwich Festival: Festival Office, 6 College Approach, Greenwich, London SE10 9HY; Held May-June; Festival Co-ordinator Sophie Elliott.

Heineken Music Big Top: Toll House Studios, Cambridge Cottages, Kew Gardens, Surrey TW9 3AY; International events held in various British cities throughout the summer; Man. Dir Mike Eddowes.

Homelands: Mean Fiddler Music Group, 16 High St, Harlesden, London NW10 4LX; website www.homelands.co.uk; dance music festival held at The Bowl, Matterley Estate, near Winchester, Hampshire, in May/June.

Isle of Wight Festival: Wight Leisure, 17 Quay St, Newport, Isle of Wight PO33 2HY; tel. (1983) 823828; e-mail info@wightleisure.com; website www.isleofwightfestival.com.

Jersey Jazz Festival: 131 Quennevais Park, St Brelade, Jersey; Held in April; Contact Ernie Roscouet.

London Cajun Music Festival: 41 Gillam Way, Rainham, Essex RM13 7HS; Festival of Cajun music and dance; Chair. Erling Hagland.

London Jazz Festival: c/o Serious Speakout, 42 Old Compton St, London W1V 5PB; Annual jazz festival held in May; Contacts David Jones, John Cumming, John Ellson.

Monsters of Rock Festival: 16 Birmingham Rd, Walsall, West Midlands WS1 2NA; The United Kingdom's leading Heavy Metal festival, held annually in Aug.; Man. Dir Maurice Jones.

North Wales Bluegrass Festival: Woodstock, Llanrwst Rd, Glan Conwy, Conwy LL28 5SR, Wales; tel. and fax (1492) 580454; e-mail northwalesbluegrass@hotmail.com; website www.northwalesbluegrass.co.uk; Three-day international bluegrass music festival; held in the first week of July; Festival Organizers John Les, Gill Williams.

Notting Hill Carnival: 332 Ladbroke Grove, London W10 5AH; Street carnival and international music event, held in Aug.; Man. Dir Elaine Spencer.

Oliver Cromwell Jazz Festival: 125 Sandwell St, Highgate, Walsall, West Midlands WS1 3EG; Largest traditional three-day Jazz Festival in the United Kingdom; held last weekend in June; Festival Organizer Alan Buckley.

Phoenix Festival: PO Box 1707, London NW10; International indie music festival, held in Stratford in July; Man. Dir Vince Power.

Portobello Jazz Week: c/o Eleventh Hour Arts, 113 Cheesemans Terrace, Star Rd, London W14 9XH; Man. Dir Debbie Golt.

Pyramid Productions: Cadillac Ranch, Pencraig Uchaf, Cwm Bach, Whitland, Dyfed SA34 0DT; tel. (1994) 484466; fax (1994) 484294; e-mail cadillac_ranch@telco4u.net; website www.nikturner.com; Dir S. M. Stein.

Sidmouth International Festival: PO Box 296, Matlock, Derbyshire DE4 3XU; tel. (1629) 760888; fax (1629) 760777; e-mail info@sidmouthfestival.com; website www.sidmouthfestival.com; Held early August; Contact Steve Heap.

Soho Jazz Festival: 29 Romily St, London W1V 6HP; Held in first week of Oct.; Artistic Dir Peter Boize Oates.

Stanford in the Vale Folk Festival: 1 Membury Way, Grove, Wantage, Oxon OX12 0BP.

T-in-the-Park Festival: Big Day Out Ltd, 272 St Vincent St, Glasgow G2 5RL, Scotland; tel. (141) 566-4998; e-mail admin@dfconcerts.co.uk; website www.tinthepark.com; Dir Geoff Ellis.

V-Festival: The Cake Group, The Mission Hall, 9–11 North End Rd, London W14 8ST; e-mail info@vfestival.com; website www.vfestival.com; held at Hylands Park, Chelmsford and Weston Park, Staffordshire, in Aug.

Warwick Folk Festival: 13 Styvechale Ave, Earlsdon, Coventry CV5 6DW; Annual festival providing concerts, dances, workshops, crafts, displays of traditional and contemporary folk arts; Admin. Frances Dixon.

Winchester Folk Festival: 44 Peverells Wood Ave, Chandlers Ford, Hampshire SO53 3BW; Annual festival of traditional dance, music and song held on the last weekend in April; Press Officer Anne Sutherland.

Woburn Festival: Kilnside, Harvest Hill, Bourne End, Bucks SL8 5JJ; Jazz Festival; Held throughout Oct.; Sec. Kate Booth.

WOMAD: Mill Side, Mill Lane, Box, Wiltshire SN13 8PN; tel. (1225) 743188; fax (1225) 743481; e-mail thomas.brooman@realworld.co.uk; website www.womad.org; World-wide festival co-ordination and production; festival held in July; Artistic Dir Thomas Brooman.

United States of America

American Classic Music Festivals: 4243 E Piedras Dr. Ste. 155, San Antonio, TX 78228; Festival Organizer Rick Dillard.

CMJ Music Marathon: 11 Middle Neck Rd, Suite 400, Great Neck, NY 11021; website www.cmj.com/marathon; three days and four nights of panels, workshops and live music showcases promoting the discovery and development of new music; Exec. Prod. Joanne Abbot Green.

Cultural Initiative Inc: PO Box 1672, Washington, DC 20013-1672; Annual Hip-hop music conference; Dir Timothy Jones.

Foundations Forum Inc: 1133 Broadway, Suite 1220, New York, NY 10010; Annual music event since 1988 of showcases, exhibits, screenings, parties etc.; Vice-Pres. Kevin Keenan.

Independent Label Festival: 600 South Michigan Ave, Chicago, IL 60605; A music industry convention featuring panels, workshops, trade show and showcases; held in late July; Exec. Dir Leopoldo Lastre.

Independent Music Seminar: PO Box 99090, San Diego, CA 92169; Annual independent music event.

Jazz Times Convention: 7961 Eastern Ave, #303, Silver Spring, MD 20910; Music industry convention; Assoc. Publisher Lee Mergner.

Mobile Jazz Festival: 555 Broadcast Dr., Mobile, AL 36606; Festival Organizer: Bob Spielmann.

MusicFest: 231 Harrison Dr., Denver, CO 80206; Songwriters trade event and conference.

NAIRD Convention: 1000 Maplewood Dr., Suite 211, Maple Shade, NJ 08052; Convention for Independent record labels held in May; Contact Holly Cass.

New Music Seminar: 632 Broadway, 9th Floor, New York, NY 10012; International music business convention; Contact Mark Josephson.

New Orleans Jazz & Heritage Festival: 1205 N Rampart St, New Orleans, LA 70116.

Ravinia Jazz Festival: Chicago Symphony Center, 400 Iris Lane, Highland Park, IL 60035; tel. (847) 266-5143; fax (847) 432-3758; e-mail jzzz5@aol.com; website www.ravinia.org; Festival Organizer Penny Tyler.

Songwriters Expo: PO Box 93759, Hollywood, CA 90093; Annual Songwriters conference; Contact Dan Kimpel.

South by Southwest Music and Media Conference: PO Box 4999, Austin, TX 78765; Annual conference held in March for members of the music industry; Man. Dir Roland Swenson.

Talent Search America: 273 Chippewa Dr., Columbia, SC 29210-6508; International songwriting and lyric writing contests.

Tri-C Jazz Festival: Cuyahoga Community College, 2900 Community College Ave, Cleveland, OH 44115; Festival Organizer Dr Thomas Horning.

Undercurrents: PO Box 94040, Cleveland, OH 44101-6040; tel. (216) 571-4141; e-mail music@undercurrents.com; website www.undercurrents.com; Annual international music conference, trade shows and showcase; Dir John Latimer.

Wichita Jazz Festival Inc: PO Box 47231, Wichita, KS 67201; Festival Dir Dee Starkey

APPENDIX F: MUSIC ORGANIZATIONS

Argentina

Asociación Argentina de Interpretes (AADI): Viamonte 1665, 1088 Buenos Aires; tel. 4811-3421.

Asociación de Representantes Artisticos (ADRA): Sarmiento 1848, 1°C, 1044 Buenos Aires; tel. 4371-1197.

Camara Argentina de la Música: Tucumán 1748, 2°, Of. 4, 1050 Buenos Aires.

Camara Argentina de Productores e Indus de Fonogramas y sus Reproduc (CAPIF): Avda Corrientes 1628, 5°H, 1042 Buenos Aires.

Consejo Argentino de la Música: Casilla de Correo 5532, Correo Central, 1000 Buenos Aires.

Fundación Encuentros Internacionales de Música Contemporánea: Casilla de Correo 1008, Correo Central, 100 Buenos Aires.

Sindicato Argentino de Músicos (SADEM): Avda Belgrano 3655, 1210 Buenos Aires; tel. 4957-3522.

Sociedad Argentina de Autores y Compositores de Música (SADAIC): Lavalle 1547, 1048 Buenos Aires; tel. 4379-8600.

Sociedad General de Autores de la Argentina (ARGENTORES): Pacheco de Melo 1820, 1126 Buenos Aires.

Sociedad General de Autores y Editores (SGAE): Uruguay 775, 4° A, 1015 Buenos Aires.

Australia

Australasian Christian Broadcasters: PO Box 2020, Launceston, Tasmania 7250; Pres. Kevin N. Hooper.

Australasian Mechanical Copyright Owners Society Ltd (AMCOS): Locked Bag 3456, St Leonards, NSW 2065; tel. (2) 9935-7700; fax (2) 9935-7709; e-mail info@amcos.com.au; website www.amcos.com.au; Co Sec. Britten Sutcliffe.

Australasian Performing Rights Asscn (APRA) Ltd: 6–12 Atchison St, St Leonards, NSW 2065; tel. (2) 9935-7900; fax (2) 9935-7999; e-mail apra@apra.com.au; website www.apra.com.au; CEO Brett Cottle.

Australian Contemporary Music Development Co Ltd (AUSMUSIC): PO Box 307, Port Melbourne, Vic. 3207; tel. (3) 9696-2422; fax (3) 9696-2879; e-mail info@ausmusic.org.au; website www.ausmusic.org.au; Contact Sue Gillard.

Australian Copyright Council: 3/245 Chalmers St, Redfern, NSW 2016; CEO Libby Baulch.

Australian Entertainment Industry Asscn Ltd: PO Box 423, Crows Nest, NSW 2065; Pres. Nigel Lampe.

Australian Music Asscn Inc: PO Box 6306, St Kilda Rd, Melbourne, Vic. 3004; CEO Rob Walker.

Australian Music Examinations Board: Fifth Floor, 175 Flinders Lane, Melbourne 3000; tel. (3) 9650-2833; fax (3) 9650-6954; e-mail ceo@ameb.net; website www.ameb.edu.au; CEO Kate Lewis.

Australian Music Manager's Forum (AMMF): PO Box 109, Surry Hills, NSW 2010; Co-Chairpersons Michael McMartin, John Woodruff.

Australian Music Publishers Asscn Ltd: 56 Berry St, 14th Floor, North Sydney, NSW 2060.

Australian Music Retailers Asscn (AMRA): PO Box W333, Warringah Mall, NSW 2100; Chair. Barry Bull.

Australian Record Industry Asscn (ARIA) Ltd: Eighth Floor, 263 Clarence St, Sydney, NSW 2000; tel. (2) 9267-7996; fax (2) 9267-7962; e-mail aria@aria.com.au; website www.aria.com.au; CEO Stephen Peach.

Australian Songwriters Asscn: PO Box 123, Surry Hills, Vic. 3127; Pres. Mike Bowen.

Australian Women's Contemporary Music Inc: 9 Knox St, Chippendale, NSW 2008; Pres. Vicki Gordon.

Central Australian Aboriginal Media Assocs Music: 99–101 Todd St, Alice Springs, NT 0871; Gen. Man. Owen Cole.

Country Music Asscn of Australia (CMA): PO Box 298, Tamworth, NSW 2340; tel. (2) 6766 1577; fax (2) 6766-7314; e-mail cmaa@northnet.com.au; Contact Meryl Gross.

Export Music Australia (EMA) Ltd: Ninth Floor, 263 Clarence St, Sydney NSW 2000; Co-ordinator Donna Chapman.

International Society for Contemporary Music (Australian Section): c/o University of Sydney Music Dept, Sydney, NSW 2006.

Music Industry Advisory Council: PO Box 9839, Canberra, ACT 2601; Contact Ian James.

Musicians' Union of Australia: Suite 506, 3 Smail St, Ultimo, NSW 2007; Federal Sec. John McAuliffe.

Musicological Society of Australia Inc: PO Box 2404, Canberra, ACT 2601; National Sec. Jaki Kane.

National Indigenous Arts Advocacy Asscn Inc (NIAAA): Suite 401, Level 4, 60–62 Foveaux St, Surry Hills, NSW 2010; Exec. Dir Bronwyn Bancroft.

Phonographic Performance Co of Australia (PPCA) Ltd: Ninth Floor, 263 Clarence St, Sydney, NSW 2000; tel. (2) 9267-7877; fax (2) 9264-5589; e-mail ppca@ppca.com.au; website www.ppca.com.au; CEO Stephen Peach.

Push Inc: 66 Cecil St, Fitzroy 3065; Exec. Dir Paul Sladdin.

Society of Australian Songwriters Inc: PO Box 290, Leichardt, NSW 2040; Pres. Thomas Poland.

Songwriters, Composers and Lyricists Asscn Inc (SCALA): PO Box 228, Kensington Park, SA 5068; tel. (8) 8431-4063; fax (8) 8332-1013; e-mail scala@senet.com.au/~scala; Contact Jane Childs.

Tasmusic: Level 2, 34 Brisbane St, Launceston, TAS 7250; tel. (3) 6331-4470; fax (3) 6331-0227; e-mail info@tasmusic.com.au; website www.tasmusic.com.au; Man. Martin Stuart.

Venue Management Asscn: PO Box 2080, Richmond S, Vic. 3121; tel. and fax (3) 9486-4123; e-mail vma@ozemail.com.au; website www.vma.org.au; Contact Sally Greaves.

Austria

AIM: Seitenberggasse 50–54, 1160 Vienna; Chair. Frank Golischewski.

AKM: Baumannstr 8–10, 1030 Vienna; tel. (1) 71714; e-mail Direktion@akm.co.at; website www.akm.co.at; Chair. Gerhard Wimberger.

Art Institut Wien: PO Box 101, 1043 Vienna; Chair. Gregor Jasch.

Austria Top 30: Habsburgergasse 6-8/18, 1010 Vienna; Man. Dir Franz Medwenitsch.

Austrian Music Producers (AMP): PO Box 2, 1094 Vienna; Pres. Guenter Menschik.

Austro-Mechana: Baumannstr 8–10, 1030 Vienna; tel. (1) 71787; fax (1) 712-7136; e-mail office@aume.at; Chair. Dieter Kaufmann; Gen. Man. Helmut Steinmetz.

IFPI Austria: Schreyvogelgasse 2/5, 1010 Vienna; tel. (1) 535-6035; fax (1) 535-5191; e-mail ifpi@ifpi.at; website www.ifpi.at; Chair. Franz Medwenitsch.

IGV: Siebenbrunnengasse 20/1, 1050 Vienna; Chair. Andreas Egger.

International Music Centre (IMZ): Lothringerstr 20, 130 Vienna; Chair. Avril MacRory.

LSG: Habsburgergasse 6-8/18, 101 Vienna; Man. Dir Paul Fürst.

Musiker-Komponisten Autorengilde (MKAG): Gartengasse 22, 1050 Vienna; tel. (1) 544-5599; fax (1) 545-6510; e-mail info@musikergilde.at; website www.musikergilde.at; musicians' union; Chair. Peter Paul Skrepek.

Musikverleger Union: Baumannstr 8–10, 1030 Vienna; Chair. Johann Juranek.

Österreichischer Komponistenbund (ÖKM): Ungargasse 9/2, 1030 Vienna.

Österreichishe Tonmeistervereinigung: Natterergasse 4, 2361 Laxenburg; Pres. Wolfgang Fritz.

Verwertungsgesellschaft Bild Und Ton (VBT): Schreyvogelgasse 2/5, 1010 Vienna; tel. (1) 535-6035; fax (1) 535-5191; e-mail ifpi@ifpi.at; Man. Dir Franz Medwenitsch.

Belgium

ACOD Cultuur/Sector Musiek: Fontainasplein 9–11, 1000 Brussels; Sec. Laurette Muylaert.

Artist Service Vzw/ASBL: PO Box 1, 8460 Oudenburg; tel. (59) 332116; fax (59) 331672; e-mail artist-service@village.uunet.be; website gallery.uunet.be/artist-service/; Pres. Jean-Paul Steenmans.

Asscn Belge du Spectacle: Ave Bel Air 36, 1180 Brussels; Pres. Michel Halliwell.

Asscn Diffusion Musique Belge (ADIBUMEL): Rue d'Arlon 75–77, 1040 Brussels; Contact Franz Constant.

Ateliers Chanson: Rue PE Janson 9, 1050 Brussels; Chair. Michel Van Muylem.

Belgian Asscn of Recording Studios: Rue Moorslede 77, 1020 Brussels; Chair. Erwin Veraecke.

Belgian Music Publishers Asscn: Fernand Neuraystraat 8, 1060 Brussels; Pres. Roland Kruger.

Beroepsvereniging Van Belgische Impresario's (BVBI): Kammerstraat 19, 9000 Ghent; Sec. Robert Van Yder.

CMCFB: Local 4 M 24, Blvd Reyers 52, 1044 Brussels; Chair. Robert Wangermee.

Country and Western Asscn Belgium: Nutstraat 18, 3830 Wellen; Chair. William Magnani.

De Bazuin Vzw: Pauwenlaan 23, 3583 Paal-Beringen; tel. (11) 431778; Pres. Louis Tielens.

European Forum of Worldwide Music Festivals: Jan Frans Willemsstraat 10, 2530 Boechout; Sec. Patrick de Groote.

European Music Office: 126 rue Franklin, 1040 Brussels; Gen. Sec. J. F. Michel.

Flanders Music Service: Stationsteenweg 238B, 2560 Nijlen; Man. Dir Francis Thijs.

SABAM: Rue d'Arlon 75–77, 1040 Brussels; website www.sabam.be; Chair. Victor Legley.

SIMIM: Pl. de l'Alma 3 B5, 1200 Brussels; tel. (2) 7758210; fax (2) 7758211; e-mail simim@simim.be; defence of music producers' rights; Man. Dir Vincent Van Néle.

Union Professionelle des Producteurs Independants (UPPI): Rue Gachard 24, 1050 Brussels; Pres. Pierre Platinckx.

Union Royale des Editeurs de Musique: Fernand Neuraystraat 8, 1060 Brussels; Pres. Roland Kruger.

URADEX: Rue d'Arlon 75–77, 1040 Brussels.

Wallonie-Bruxelles Musique: Rue Marche aux Herbes 61, 4 etage, 1000 Brussels; Co-ordinator Patrick Printz.

Bolivia

Asociación Boliviana de Radiodifusoras (ASBORA): Avda Sánchez Lima, 2278 Casilla 5324, La Paz.

Educación Radiofónica de Bolivia (ERBOL): Ballivia, 1323, 4° Casilla 5946, La Paz.

Brazil

Associação Brasileira de Emissoras de Radio e Televisao (ABERT): Mezanino do Hotel Nacional Salas 5–8, 04280, 70322 Brasília, DF.

Associação Brasileira dos Produtores de Discos: Rua Sao José 90, Gr 1406/10, 22021 Rio de Janeiro, RJ.

Instituto Brasileiro de Arte e Cultura: Rua de Imprensa 16, 20030 Rio de Janeiro, RJ.

Sindicato dos Músicos Profissionals do Estado de São Paulo: Largo Paissandu, São Paulo, SP.

Sindicato Nac. de Empresas de Agenciamiento Produção de Eventos (SINAPREM): Avda Iparanga, 877, 13°, 01039 São Paulo, SP.

Sociedada Brasileira de Música Contemporânea: SQS 105, Bloco B, Apt 506, 70344-020 Brasília, DF.

Sociedada Independente de Compositores e Autores Musicals: Largo Paissandú 51, 10th, 11th and 16th Floors, 01034 São Paulo, SP.

Uniao Brasileira de Compositores (UBC): Rua Visconde de Inhaúma 107, 20091 Rio de Janeiro, RJ; website www.ubc.com.br.

Uniao dos Músicos do Brasil: Avda Rio Branco 185, Rio de Janeiro, RJ.

Bulgaria

BAZI: 15 Tsarigradsko Chausse Blvd, 1220 Sofia; Man. Dora Cherneva.

Jusautor: Pl. Bulgaria 1, 1463 Sofia; Dir-Gen. Jana Markova.

Musicautor: 6 Rajcho Dimchev, 1000 Sofia; Chair. Konstantin Dragnev.

Podkrepa: 2 Angel Kunchev str, 1000 Sofia; Chair. Asen Gargov.

Pop-Rock Federation: Liulin Blvd 210, Vh A, 1343 Sofia; Chair. Chavdar Chendov.

Union of Bulgarian Composers (UBC): 2 Ivan Vazov St, 1000 Sofia; tel. (2) 988-1560; fax (2) 987-4378; e-mail ubc@mail.bol.bg; website www.ubc-bg.com; Pres. Victor Chuchkov.

Canada

Alberta Recording Industries Asscn: #208, 10136-100 St, Edmonton, AB T5J 0P1; Exec. Asst Charlotte Bowman.

American Federation of Musicians of the United States and Canada, Canadian Office: 75 The Donway West, Suite 1010, Don Mills, ON M3C 2E9; tel. (416) 391-5161; fax (416) 391-5165; e-mail afmcan@afm.org; website www.afm.org; Vice-Pres. (Canada) David J. Jandrisch.

BCCMA (BC Country Music Asscn): 177 W Seventh Ave, Fourth Floor, Vancouver BC V5Y 1L8; tel. (604) 876-4110; fax (604) 876-4104; e-mail mail@bccountry.com; website www.bccountry.com; Pres. Richard Niddrie.

Black Music Asscn of Canada (BMAC): 59 Chester Hill Rd, Toronto, ON M4K 1X4; tel. (416) 463-8880; e-mail cheer@icon.net; Pres. Daniel Caudeiron.

Caledonia Folk Club: 23 Buchanan Dr., Caledonia, ON N3W 1H1; Organizer Bill Crawford.

Canadian Academy of Recording Arts and Sciences (CARAS): 124 Merton St, Third Floor, Toronto, ON M4S 2Z2; tel. (416) 485-3135; fax (416) 485-4978; e-mail caras@juno-awards.ca; website www.juno-awards.com; Exec. Dir Daisy Falle.

Canadian Amateur Musicians: PO Box 353, Westmount, QC H3Z 2T5; Dir-Gen. Barry Crago.

Canadian Asscn for Music Therapy: c/o Wilfrid Laurier University, 75 University Ave W, Waterloo, ON N2L 3C5; tel. (519) 884-1970; fax (519) 884-8853; e-mail camt@wlu.ca; website www.musictherapy.ca; Admin. Co-ordinator Lynda Tracy.

Canadian Asscn of Artists' Managers: 117 Ava Rd, Toronto, ON M6C 1W2.

Canadian Country Music Asscn (CCMA): 127-3800 Steeles Ave W, Woadbridge, ON L4L 4G9; Exec. Dir Sheila Hamilton.

Canadian Disc Jockey Asscn Inc: National Office, 3148 Kingston Rd, Suite 209–300, Scarborough, ON M1M 1P4; National Pres. & CEO Dennis E. Hampson.

Canadian Independent Record Producers Asscn (CIRPA): 114 Front St W, Suite 202, Toronto, ON M5J 2L7; Exec. Dir Brian Chater.

Canadian Music Centre: 20 St Joseph St, Toronto, ON M4Y 1J9.

Canadian Music Publishers Asscn (CMPA): 320-56 Wellesley St W, Toronto, ON M5S 2S3; tel. (416) 926-1966; fax (416) 926-7521; website www.canadamusic.org; Contact David Basskin.

Canadian Musical Reproduction Rights Agency (CMRRA) Ltd: 56 Wellesley St W, Suite 320, Toronto, ON M5S 2S4; tel. (416) 926-1966; fax (416) 926-7521; website www.cmrra.ca; Contact David Basskin.

Canadian Recording Industry Asscn: 1255 Yonge St, Suite 300, Toronto, ON M4T 1W6; Pres. Brian Robertson.

Canadian Society for Traditional Music: PO Box 4232, Sta C, Calgary, AB T2T 5N1; Membership Co-Sec. John Leeder.

Coastal Jazz and Blues Society: 435 West Hastings St, Vancouver, BC V6B 1L4; Exec. Dir Robert Kerr.

Country Music Foundation of Canada: 8607 128 Ave, Edmonton, AB T5E 0G3; tel. (780) 476-8230; fax (780) 472-2584; museum of country music; Contact Bill Maxim.

Foundation to Assist Canadian Talent on Records: 125 George St, Second Floor, Toronto, ON M5A 2N4; Exec. Dir Heather Sym.

Georgian Bay Folk Society: PO Box 521, Owen Sound, ON N4K 5R1; Promotion Co-ordinator Linda Ashley.

Music Industries Asscn of Canada (MIAC): 33 Medhurst Rd, Toronto, ON M4B 1B2; tel. (416) 490-1871; fax (416) 490-0369; e-mail info@miac.net; website www.miac.net; Contact Al Kowalenko.

Northern Praise Ministries Inc: PO Box 61015, Oakville, ON L6J 7P5; Founder/Admin. Michelle Sim.

Pacific Music Industry Asscn (PMIA): 400-177 W Seventh Ave, Vancouver, BC V5Y 1L8; tel. (604) 873-1914; fax (604) 876-4104; e-mail info@pmia.org; website www.pmia.org; Exec. Dir Ellie O'Day.

Photo-Connect: 244–423 King St W, Hamilton, ON L8P 4Y1; Pres. & CEO Kirby Ellis.

Sociétè des Mélomanes (Canada) Inc: 1056 Burnaby St, Suite 201, Vancouver, BC V6E 1N7; Dir Factotum Eugène Evans.

Society for Reproduction Rights of Authors, Composers and Publishers in Canada (SODRAC): 759 Victoria Sq., Suite 420, Montréal, QC H2Y 2J7; tel. (514) 845-3268; fax (514) 845-3401; e-mail sodrac@sodrac.com; website www.sodrac.com; Gen. Man. Claudette Fortier.

Society of Composers, Authors & Music Publishers in Canada (SOCAN): 41 Valleybrook Dr., Don Mills, ON M3B 2S6; tel. (416) 445-8700; fax (416) 445-7108; e-mail socan@socan.ca; website www.socan.ca.

Toronto Downtown Jazz Society: 366 Adelaide St SE, Suite 230, Toronto, ON M5A 3X9; Dir of Marketing & Communications Barb McCullaugh.

Toronto Musicians' Asscn: 101 Thorncliffe Park Dr., Toronto, ON M4H 1M2; Sec. Mark Tetreault.

Chile

Asociación de Radiodifusores de Chile (ARCHI): Pasaje Matte, 957, Of. 801, Santiago de Chile.

Asociación Nacional de Compositores: Almirante Moritt 453, Santiago de Chile.

Instituto de Música: Universidad Católica de Chile, Jaime Guzman E 3 300, Santiago de Chile.

Sociedad Chilena del Derecho de Autor (SCD): Dpto Internacional, Condell 346 (Providencia), Santiago de Chile; tel. (2) 3708731; fax (2) 3708030; e-mail rpujol@scd.cl; website www.scd.cl.

Colombia

Asociación Colombiana de Músicos Profesionales: Calles 17, 10–16, Of. 607, Santafé de Bogotá, DC.

Asociación des Artistas de Colombia: Calle 13, 9-63, Interior 104, PO Box 24627, Santafé de Bogotá, DC.

Centro de Documentación Musical-Instituto Colombiano de Cultura: Calle 11, 5-51, Second Floor, Santafé de Bogotá, DC.

Instituto Colombiano de Cultura—Colcultura: Calle 11, 5-51, Second Floor, Santafé de Bogotá, DC.

Sociedad de Autores y Compositores de Colombia: Carrera 19, 40-72, PO Box 6482, Santafé de Bogotá, DC.

Croatia

Croatian Authors Agency: Preradoviceva 25, 41000 Zagreb; Man. Zeljka Modrusac-Ranogajec.

Croatian Composers Society: Berislaviceva 9, 41000 Zagreb; Man. Dir Ozren Kanceljak.

Croatian Musicians Union: PP 560, Gruška 10, 41001 Zagreb; Chair. Paolo Sfeci; Sec.-Gen. Siniša Doronjga.

Music Information Centre: Kneza Mislava 18, 41000 Zagreb; Man. Dir Jagoda Martincevic.

Cuba

Centro de Información y Promoción de la Música Cubana: Odilio Urfé Calle 17 esq. a E, Vedado, Havana.

Centro de Investigación y Desarrollo de la Música Cubana: Calle G, No. 505 e/21 y 23, Vedado, Havana.

Centro Nacional de Derecho de Autor: Calle Línea No. 365 (altos), esp a G, Vedado, Havana.

Centro Nacional de Música de Concierto: Calle Línea No. 365, esq a G, Vedado, Havana.

Centro Nacional de Música Popular: Avda 1 ra. e/10 y 12, Playa, Havana.

Editora Musical de Cuba: San Rafael No. 104, esq a Consulado, Centro Habana, Havana.

Empresa de Grabaciones y Ediciones Musicales: Campanario No. 315, e/Neptuno y San Miguel, Centro Habana, Havana.

Instituto Cubano de la Música: Calle 15 No. 452, esq a F Vedado, Havana.

Unión de Escritores y Artistas de Cuba (Music Section): Calle 17 No. 351, esq a H, Vedado, Havana.

Czech Republic

Asscn of Musicians and Musicologists: Maltézské nám. 1, 118 00 Prague 1.

Authors Asscn of Protection for Rights on Musical Works: Cs. armády 20, 160 56 Prague 6.

Czech Music Fund: Besední 3, 118 00 Prague 1.

Czech Music Information Centre: Besední 3, 118 00 Prague 1; tel. (2) 5731-7424; fax (2) 5731-7424; e-mail his@vol.cz; website www.musica.cz; Dir Miroslav Pudlak.

Czech Music Society: Radlická 99, Smíchov, 150 00 Prague 5; tel. (2) 5155-2382; fax (2) 5155-2453; e-mail czechmusiksoc@hotmail.com; Pres. Mila Smetácková.

Guild of Czech Composers and Concert Artists: Valdstejnske nam. 1, 100 00 Prague 1; Pres. Jan Seidel.

IFPI CR: Senovazne nam 23, 112 82 Prague 1; Sec. & CEO Vratislav Safar.

International Federation of Phonogram and Videogram Producers (Czech Section): Gorkého nam. 23, 112 82 Prague 1.

International Music Council (National Committee): Valdstejnske nám. 1, Prague 1.

International Society for Contemporary Music (Czechoslovak Section): Na Brezince 22, 150 00 Prague 5.

Ochranny Svaz Autorsky (OSA): Cs. Armady 20, 160 56 Prague 6; Pres. Petr Janda.

Society for Jazz: Janáckovo nábr. 59, Smíchov, 150 00 Prague 5.

Union of Authors and Interpreters: Skroupova nám 9, 130 00 Prague 3.

Denmark

Asscn of Rock/Jazz Clubs in Denmark (SAMSPIL): Graven 25 A, 8000 Aarhus C; Chair. Palle Skov; Sec. Leader Rikke Sinding.

Danish Asscn of Jazz and Rock Amateurs (FAJABEFA): Musiskkens Hus, Enghavavej 40 sal, 1674 Copenhagen V; Contact Jacob Kragh.

Danish Jazz Asscn: Kjeld Langesgade 4A, 1367 Copenhagen K; Chair. Frans Bak.

Danish Jazz Federation: Nytorv 3, 3, 1450 Copenhagen K; tel. 3345-4300; fax 3345-4311; e-mail info@dkjazz.dk; website www.dkjazz.dk.

Danish Music Council: Vesterbrogade 24 4, 1620 Copenhagen V; Chair. Lars Grunth.

Danish Music Information Centre: Gräbrødretorv 16, 1154 Copenhagen K; Chair. Jorgen Arnsted.

Danish Rock Council (ROSA): Karetmagergaarden, Graven 25 A, 8000 Aarhus C; Chair. Gunnar Madsen.

Dansk Folkemindesamling (Danish Folklore Archives): Christians Brygge 3, 1219 Copenhagen K; Admin. Dir Svend Nielsen.

Danske Jazz Beat Og Folkemusik Autorer (DJBFA): Gräbrødretrov 16, 1154 Copenhagen K; Chair. Torben Kjaer.

Den Rytmiske Konsulentitjeneste: Kjeld Langesgade 4A, 1367 Copenhagen K; Chair. Niller Wischmann.

Foreningen Danmarks Folkeminder (Danish Folklore Society): Christians Brygge 3, 1219 Copenhagen K; Admin. Dir Svend Nielsen.

GRAMEX: GI, Kongevej 11–13, 2., 1610 Copenhagen V; tel. (45) 3385-3200; fax (45) 3385-3215; e-mail gramex@gramex.dk; website www.gramex.dk; Dir Bjorn Juell-Sundbye.

IFPI Denmark: Store Strandstraede 20 st, 1255 Copenhagen K; Chair. Stefan Fryland.

Jazz Centret/Jazzkontakten: Borupvej 66, 4683 Rönnede; tel. 5671-1749; e-mail jazzpar@mail.tele.dk; website www.jazzpar.dk; awards the annual international JAZZPAR Prize; Man. Dir Cim Meyer.

KIM (Women In Music): c/o Conservatory of Music, Niels Brocksgade 1, 1574 Copenhagen V; Chair. Tove Krag.

KODA: Landemaerket 23-25, 1016 Copenhagen K; tel. (45) 3330-6300; fax (45) 3330-6330; e-mail info@koda.dk; website www.koda.dk; Man. Dir Niels Bak.

MXP-Danish Music Export and Promotion: Sondervej 56, 5700 Svendborg; Music Consultant/CEO Mikael Højris.

Nordisk Copyright Bureau (NCB): PO Box 3064, 1021 Copenhagen K; tel. (45) 3312-8700; fax (45) 3312-4262; e-mail ncb@ncb.dk; website www.ncb.dk; Man. Dir Thorkil Emborg.

Rhythmic Music Conservatory: Dr Priemesvej 3, 1854 Frederiksberg C; Dir Erik Moseholm.

Estonia

Estonian Jazz Foundation: PO Box 3641, Viru str 16, 0090 Tallinn; Dir Tiit Lauk.

Tallinn Zeppelin Club: PO Box 3526, Tallinn 0090; Club Consultant Peter Zeluiko.

VAAP: Toompuiestee 7, 0101 Tallinn.

Fiji

Fiji Composers Asscn: PO Box 2371, Government Bldgs, Suva; Vice-Pres. Seru Serevi.

Fiji Musicans' Asscn: PO Box 364, Loutoka; Vice-Pres. Danny Costello Jr.

Fiji Performing Right Asscn Ltd: PO Box 15061, 170 Renwick Rd, Suva; Chair. Saimone Vuatalevu.

Finland

AFRB: Italahdenkatu 22 BC, 00210 Helsinki.

Finnish Big Band Asscn: Makslahdenkatu 1 C, 02140 Espoo; Contact Risto Oinaala.

Finnish Folk and Country Music Society: PO Box 181, 00531 Helsinki; Contact Jihani Aalto.

Finnish Jazz and Pop Archive: Rajasampaanranta 2, 00560 Helsinki.

Finnish Jazz Archives: Pihlajatie 43 A, 00270 Helsinki.

Finnish Jazz Federation: PO Box 54, 00101 Helsinki; tel. (9) 757-2077; fax (9) 757-2067; e-mail info@jazzfin.com; website www.jazzfin.com; Exec. Man. Timo Vahasilta.

Finnish Music Information Centre: Lauttasaarentie 1, 00200 Helsinki; tel. (9) 6810-1313; fax (9) 682-0770; e-mail info@mic.teosto.fi; website www.fimic.fi; Contact Jari Muikku.

Finnish Music Publishers Asscn: Lastenkodinkatu 7, 00180 Helsinki; tel. (9) 5860-870; fax (9) 5860-8755; e-mail info@musiikkikustantajat.fi; website www.musiikkikustantajat.fi; Man. Dir Pekka Sipilä.

Finnish Musicians' Union: Pieni Roobertinkatu 16, 00120 Helsinki; tel. (9) 6803-4073; fax (9) 6803-4087; e-mail raimo.vikstrom@ musicfinland.com; website www.musicfinland.com/sml/; Pres. Raimo Vikstrom.

Global Music Centre: Mikkolantie 17, 00640 Helsinki; Dir Anu Laakkonen.

GRAMEX: Hietaniemenkatu 15/A/12, 00100 Helsinki; Dir Jukka Niskanen.

Musikkikustantajatorg: Hietaniemenkatu 2, 00100 Helsinki; Man. Dir Minna Aalto-Setälä.

Rock Musicians Asscn: Uudenmaankatu 36/F/34, 00120 Helsinki; Chair. Nissila Pekka.

Society of Finnish Composers: Runeberginkatu 15/A/11, 00100 Helsinki.

Teosto: Lauttasaarentie 1, 00200 Helsinki; website www.teosto.fi; Man. Dir Jaakko Fredman.

France

ADAMI: 10A rue de la Paix, 75002 Paris; website www.adami.fr; Contact Marie-Jeanne Peraldi.

ANARLP: PO Box 174, 10005 Troyes Cédex; Pres. Guy Capet.

BIEM: 56 Ave Kleber, 75116 Paris; Pres. Jean Loup Tournier.

Bureau Export de la Musique Française: 27 rue du Docteur Lancereaux, 75008 Paris; Exec. Dir Marie Agnes Beau.

Centre Information et Ressources pour les Musiques Actuelles (IRMA): 22 rue Soleillet, 75020 Paris Cédex 20; tel. 1 43 15 11 11; fax 1 43 15 11 10; e-mail info@irma.asso.fr; website www.irma.asso.fr; Dir Bernard Batzen.

Centre Musical et Creatif de Nancy: 92 Grande rue, PO Box 698, 54063 Nancy Cédex; Teaching Dir Hans J. Kullock.

Centre National d'Action Musicale (CENAM): 11–13 rue de l'Escaut, 75019 Paris; Dir Dominque Ponsard.

CISAC: 1 rue Keppler, 75116 Paris; Sec.-Gen. Jean Alexis Ziegler.

Collectif HASK: 9 Ave Pasteur, 93100 Montreuil; Contact Hubert Dupont.

Comite National de la Musique (CNM): 91 rue Jouffroy d'Abbans, 75017 Paris; tel. and fax 1 42 27 07 31; Gen. Sec. J. Masson Forestier.

Concours de Piano Jazz Martial Solal: Acanthes-Concours Internationaux de la Ville de Paris, 3 rue des Couronnes, 75020 Paris; tel. 1 40 33 45 35; fax 1 40 33 45 38; e-mail civp@acanthes.com; website www.civp.com; international jazz piano competition held in late Sept.; first prize of 70,000 French francs and engagements at a number of festivals; Gen. Delegate Claude Samuel.

CSDEM: 62 rue Blanche, 75009 Paris; Pres. Jean Davoust.

Eurokka (Esperanto-Rok-Asocio): 31450 Donneville; Dir Floréal Martorell.

Ferarock: PO Box 4015, 31028 Toulouse Cédex; Pres. Françoise Duval.

FNAMU: 41 Bis Quai de la Loire, 75019 Paris; Man. Dir Catherine Lesage.

Fondation Pour La Creation Musicale (FCM): 141 rue Lafayette, 75010 Paris; Dir Bruno Rony.

French Studios Asscn (ASF): 30 rue Henri Barbusse, 75005 Paris; Dir Jean Louis Rizet.

Institut du Monde Arabe: 1 rue des Fosses Saint-Bernard, 75236 Paris; Programme Dir for Music, Dance & Theatre Mohamed Metalsi.

Institut International de Musique Electroacoustique: PO Box 39 18001 Bourges Cédex; Dirs Françoise Barriére, Christian Clozier; Sec.-Gen. Catharina Kroling.

International Confederation of Music Publishers: 47 rue de Turbigo, 75003 Paris; tel. 1 42 72 38 99; fax 1 42 72 38 05; e-mail 101374.25@compuserve.com; website www.icmp-ciem.org; Contact Jenny Vacher.

Le Lieu Unique-CRDC: PO Box 21304, 2 rue de la Biscuiterie, 44013 Nantes Cédex 01; tel. 2 51 82 15 00; fax 2 40 20 20 12; e-mail info@lelieuunique.com; website www.lelieuunique.com; popular music and video events and festivals; Dir Jean Blaise; Musical Curator Kitty Hartl.

MIDEM Organization: 179 Ave Victor Hugo, 75116 Paris; website www.midem.com; CEO Xavier Roy.

SACEM/SDRM: 225 Ave Charles de Gaulle, 92521 Neuilly-sur-Seine Cédex; tel. (1) 4715-4715; website www.sacem.fr; Pres. Gerard Calvi.

SCPP: 159 Charles de Gaulle, 92200 Neuilly-sur-Seine; Pres. Rene Guittan.

SIPLACDA: 255 rue Saint-Honoré, 75001 Paris; Pres. Joëlle Feauveau.

SNAAL: 17 rue Brey, 75017 Paris; Pres. Roland Bertin.

SPEDIDAM: 8 rue Bremontier, 75017 Paris; Pres. Maurice Husson.

Syndicat Français des Artistes-Interpretes (SFA): 21 bis rue Victor Masse, 75009 Paris; Exec. Dir François Parrot.

Syndicat National de L'Edition Phonographique (SNEP): 27 rue du Docteur Lancereaux, 75008 Paris; Man. Herve Rony.

Syndicat National des Artistes Musiciens (SNAM): 14–16 rue des Lilas, 75019 Paris; tel. 1 42 02 30 80; fax 1 42 02 34 01; e-mail snamf@free.fr; Pres. Raymond Silvand.

Syndicat National des Auteurs et Compositeurs (SNAC): 80 rue Taitbout, 75442 Paris Cédex 9; Pres. Antoine Duhamel.

Germany

Bundesverband Der Phonographischen Wirtschaft eV (BPW): Grelckstr 36, 20257 Hamburg 1; Contact Petra Denzen.

Deutsche Bibliothek/Deutsches Musikarchiv Berlin: PO Box 4502 29, 12172 Berlin; Library Dir Dr Heinz Lanske.

Deutsche Disc Jockey Organisation: Kaiser Friedrich Allee 1–3, 52074 Aachen; Contact Klaus Quirini.

Deutsche Landesgruppe der IFPI eV: Grelckstr 36, 22529 Hamburg; Head of Public Relations Elmar Kruse.

Deutsche Phono-Akademie: Grelckstr 36, 22529 Hamburg; Contact Hartmuth Bender.

Deutscher Musikverleger Verband (DMV): Freidrich Wilhelm str 31, 53113 Bonn; Pres. Maja Maria Reis.

Deutscher Rock und Pop Musikerverband eV: Kolberger str 30, 21339 Luenburg; tel. (4131) 233-030; fax (4131) 233-0315; e-mail info@drmv.de; website www.drmv.de; Chair. Ole Seelenmeyer.

Deutscher Tonkunstlerverband eV (DTKV): Linprunstr, 16 Rgb 80335 Munchen.

European Asscn of Concert Agents: Sülzgürtel 86, 50937 Cologne; Contact Andreas Braun.

Gesellschaft für musikalische Aufführungs und mechanische Vervielfältigungsrechte (GEMA): (Berlin) Postfach 30 12 40, 10722 Berlin; tel. (30) 212-4500; fax (30) 212-45950; e-mail gema@gema.de; (Munich) Postfach 80 07 67, 81607 Munich; tel. (89) 480-0300; fax (89) 480-03969; e-mail gema@gema.de; website www.gema.de; Dir of Communications Dr Hans-Herwig Geyer.

GVL: Heimhuder str 5, 20148 Hamburg; tel. (40) 411-7070; fax (40) 410-3866; e-mail kontakt@gvl.de; Man. Dir Rolf Duennwald.

IDKV (German Concert Promoter and Artists Agents Asscn): PO Box 202364, 20216 Hamburg; Pres. & Gen. Man. Jens Michow.

Internationaler Arbeitskries für Musik eV: PO Box 410236, 34064 Kassel.

MusikKomm GmbH: Rottscheider str 6, 42329 Wuppertal; Man. Dir Uli Grossmass.

Verband der Deutschen Konzertdirekionen eV: Liebigstr 39, 80538 Munich.

Warehouse: Linden str 52, 50674 Cologne.

Zentrum für Musik & Kommunikations—Tech.: Rottscheider str 6, 42329 Wuppertal; Man. Dir Dieter Gorny.

Greece

AEPI: Deligani 14, 106 83 Athens; Pres. Mimis Traiforis.

IFPI Greece: Aghia Paraskevi 63, 152 34 Halandri, Athens; Sec. Miltos Karadsas.

International Music Council (Greek Section): Mitropoleos 38, 105 63 Athens; Pres. Demetre Michaelides.

Panhellenic Musicians' Union: 10 Sapfous str, 10553 Athens; Pres. T. Athineos; Gen. Sec. G. Lambrianidis.

Hong Kong Special Administrative Region, People's Republic of China

Composers and Authors Society of Hong Kong (CASH) Ltd: 18/F Universal Trade Centre, 3 Arbuthnot Rd, Central Hong Kong; Contact Leslie Ching.

Hong Kong Composers Guild: c/o Music Dept, Chung Chi College, Chinese University, Shatin, New Territories; Contact Chan Wing Wah.

IFPI (Hong Kong Group): 22/F Gitic Centre, 28 Queen's Rd E, Wanchai, Hong Kong; Chief Sec. Patrick Wong.

Music Publishers Asscn: 11/F Peninsula Office Tower, 18 Middle Rd, Kowloon; Contact David Loiterton.

Hungary

Gewerkschaft für Musik und Tanzkünstler: Gorkij Fasor 38, PO Box 8, 1406 Budapest; Sec. László Gyimesi.

Hungarian Music Council: PO Box 47, 1364 Budapest.

Hungarian Music Society: Vörösmarty tér 1, 1051 Budapest; Pres. Zsolt Durkó.

Institute for Musicology of the Hungarian Academy of Sciences: Táncsics Mihály utca 7, 1014 Budapest; Asst Dir Tibor Tallián.

Mahasz (IFPI): Regiposta u 13, 1052 Budapest; Man. Dir Agnes Musinger.

Musicians Trade Union: Gorkij Fasor 38, 1068 Budapest; Pres. Sanor Solyom Nagy.

Society of Hungarian Commercial Radios: Steindl Ihre u 12, 1054 Budapest; Pres. Laszlo Hegeous.

Iceland

Asscn of Light Composers and Songwriters: Háteigsvegur 28, 105 Reykjavík.

Iceland Music Information Centre: Sidumuli 34, 108 Reykjavík; Man. Asta Hrönn.

Icelandic Composers Society: Laufásvegur 40, 101 Reykjavík.

Icelandic Musicians' Union: Laufásvegur 40, Reykjavík; Gen. Sec. Asgeir H. Steingrimsson.

IFPI Iceland: Kringlan 4, PO Box 3360, 123 Reykjavík; Chair. Steinar Berg Isleifsson.

International Society for Contemporary Music: Laufásvegur 40, 101 Reykjavík.

Jazzvakning: PO Box 31, 121 Reykjavík.

Reykjavík Music Society: Garoastraeti 17, 101 Reykjavík.

Society of Icelandic Musicians: Dalsel 8, Reykjavík.

STEF: Laufásvegur 40, 101 Reykjavík; tel. (354) 561-6173; fax (354) 562-6273; e-mail stef@stef.is; Gen. Man. Eirekur Tomasson.

Union of Authors and Copyright Owners: Laufásvegur 40, 101 Reykjavík.

Indonesia

Indonesian Society of Composers and Arrangers: Komp Mangga Dua Plaza, Blok J, no. 30, Jl Mangga Dua raya, Jakarta Utara; Chair. Sakikin Zuchra.

Ireland

An Chomhairle Ealaíon (The Arts Council): 70 Merrion Sq., Dublin 2; tel. (1) 618-0200; fax (1) 676-1302; e-mail dermot@artscouncil.ie; Artform Dir Dermot McLaughlin.

Asscn of Independent Record Retailers: 5 Cope St, Dublin 2; Pres. Brian O'Kelly.

Asscn of Irish Composers: Copyright House, Pembroke Row, Lower Baggot St, Dublin 2; Contact Maura Eaton.

Asscn of Irish Festival Events (AOIFE): Administration Office, Rear 32 Upper Main St, Arklow, Co Wicklow; National Sec. Victor Ryan.

British Institute of Jazz Studies: 17 The Chase, Crowthorne, Berkshire RG45 6HT; Sec. Graham Langley.

Cork Music Resource Co-Op: Unit 12, Thompson's Bldg, McCurtain St, Cork; Admin. Dir Angela Dorcran.

Federation of Music Collectives: The Temple Bar Music Centre, Cyred St North, Temple Bar, Dublin 2; Contact Angela Dorgan.

Folk Music Society of Ireland: 15 Henrietta St, Dublin 1.

IFPI Ireland: 26 Merrion Sq., Dublin 2; Chair. Paul Keogh.

Independent Radio and Television Commission (IRTC): Marine House, Clanwilliam Pl., Dublin 2; Contact Lynne Scanlan.

International Songwriters' Asscn (ISA): PO Box 46, Limerick City, Limerick; Man. Dir James Liddane.

Irish Asscn of Songwriters and Composers (IASC): Ballinclea Lodge, Ballinclea Rd, Killiney, Co Dublin; Chair. Keith Donald.

Irish Bluegrass Music Club: 86 Barton Rd E, Dublin 14; Contact Carol Hawkins.

Irish Federation of Musicians and Associated Professions: 63 Lower Gardiner St, Dublin 1; Pres. Richard Glynn.

Irish Federation of the Phonographic Industry (IFPI): 9 Whitefriars, Aungier St, Dublin 2; Chair. Paul Keogh; Sec. Riobaird MacGorian.

Irish Music Rights Organisation Ltd (IMRO): Copyright House, Pembroke Row, Lower Baggot St, Dublin 2; tel. (1) 661-4844; fax (1) 661-3789; e-mail info@imro.ie; website www.imro.ie; CEO Hugh Duffy.

Irish Recorded Music Asscn (IRMA): IRMA House, 1 Corrig Ave, Dun Laoghaire, Co Dublin; tel. (1) 280-6571; fax (1) 280-6579; e-mail info@irma.ie; website www.irma.ie.

Irish Traditional Music Archive: 63 Merrion Sq., Dublin 2; tel. (1) 661-9699; fax (1) 662-4585; website www.itma.ie Dir Nicholas Carolan.

Mechanical Copyright Protection Society (Ireland) Ltd (MCPS): Copyright House, Pembroke Row, Lower Baggot St, Dublin 2; Gen. Man. Victor Finn.

Music Base: 44 E Essex St, Dublin 2; Youth Arts Devt Officer Greg McAteer.

Music Network: The Coach House, Dublin Castle, Dublin 2; tel. (1) 671-9429; fax (1) 671-9430; e-mail info@musicnetwork.ie; website www.musicnetwork.ie; Information Man. Seamus O'Reilly.

Music Publishers Asscn of Ireland (MPAI): Copyright House, Pembroke Row, Lower Baggot St, Dublin 2; tel. (1) 676-6940; fax (1) 661-1316; Pres. Michael O'Riordan; Sec. John Lappin.

Music Retailers of Ireland: 5 Cope St, Dublin 2; Exec. Mem. Brian O. Kelly.

Oifig an Cheoil (The Music Office): Teo Cuilin, Dingle, Co. Kerry; Contact Joan Maguire.

Performing Rights Society: Copyright House, Pembroke Row, Lower Baggot St, Dublin 2; Contact Paula McDermott.

Phonographic Performance (Ireland) Ltd (PPI): PPI House, 1 Corrig Ave, Dun Laoghaire, Co Dublin; tel. (1) 280-5977; fax (1) 280-6579; CEO Dick Doyle.

Recorded Artists and Performers Ltd (RAAP): Arena House, 4 Glenville Terrace, Main St, Dundrum, Dublin 14; tel. (1) 296-0258; fax (1) 296-2888; e-mail info@raap.ie; website www.raap.ie.

Republic of Ireland Music Publishers Asscn (RIMPA): Copyright House, Pembroke Row, Lower Baggot St, Dublin 2; Sec. John J. Lappin.

Israel

Independent Musicians Union: 6 Malkei Yisrael Sq., 64591 Tel-Aviv; tel. (3) 695-9355; fax (3) 696-3528; e-mail eilam@netvision.net.il; Chair. Dany Gottfried.

International Music Council (Israeli Section): Ministry of Science, Culture and Sport, Kanfei nesharim 22, 91342 Jerusalem; tel. (2) 560-1741; fax (2) 560-1568; e-mail raaya@most.gov.il; website www.most.gov.il; Chief Officer, Music Dept Raaya Simran.

International Society for Contemporary Music (Israeli Section): c/o Israel Composers' League, PO Box 45068, 61450 Tel-Aviv.

Israel Composers' League: PO Box 45068, 61450 Tel-Aviv; Chair. Manachem Zur.

Israel Music Institute (IMI): PO Box 3004, 61030 Tel-Aviv; tel. (3) 524-4645; fax (3) 524-5276; e-mail musicinst@bezeqint.net; Dir Paul Landau.

Jerusalem Music Centre: Mishkanot Sha'ananim, Jerusalem; Dir Benny Gal-Ed.

Jeunesses Musicales Israel: 19 Achad Ha'am St, Tel-Aviv 65151.

Music Information Centre of Israel: PO Box 3004, 61030 Tel-Aviv; tel. (3) 524-6475; fax (3) 524-5276; e-mail musicinst@bexeqint.net; Dir Paul Landau.

National Council for Culture and Arts: 16 Hanatziv St, 67018 Tel-Aviv; Chief Officer David Sinai.

Society of Authors, Composers and Music Publishers in Israel (ACUM): 9 Tuval St, PO Box 1704, Ramatgan 52117; tel. (3) 611-3400; fax (3) 612-2629; e-mail acum@acum.org.il; Chair. Naomi Shemer.

Union of Musicians: Histradut Bldg, 93 Arlozorof St, 62098 Tel-Aviv; Gen. Sec. Aryeh Levanon.

Italy

AMI: Via Montenapoleone 20, 20121 Milan; Chair. Roberto de Luca.

Associazione dei Fonografici Italiani (AFI): Via Vittor Pisani 10, 20124 Milan; Pres. Guido Rignano.

Associazione di Informatica Musicale Italiana (AIMI): c/o La Biennale di Venezia, Settore Musica, San Marco, Ca Giustinian, 30124 Venice.

Associazione Italiana Degli Editori di Musica (AIDEM): Via Enrico Toti 4, 20123 Milan; Pres. Maurizio Corecha.

Associazione Italiana Operatori Musicali (ASSIOM): c/o Centro di Ricerca e Sperimentazione per la Didattica Musicale, Villa La Torraccia, via delle Fontanelle 24, 50016 San Domenico di Fiesolo (FI).

Associazione Nazionale Musicisti di Jazz (ANMJ): Via Vallerozzi 77, 53100 Sienna; Chair. Giorgio Gaslini.

Bluegrass & Country Music Asscn of Italy: PO Box 1733, 20101 Milan; Pres. Maurizio Faulisi.

CIDIM-National Music Committee of Italy (IMC-UNESCO): Via Vittoria Colonna 18, 00193 Rome.

Editori Musicali Associati (EMA): Piazza del Liberty 2, 20121 Milan; Pres. Adriano Solaro.

Federazione Industria Musicale Italiana (FIMI): Largo Augusto 3, 20122 Milan; Pres. Franco Reali.

Federazione Italiana dei Compositori de Musica Contemporanea: Via Cavalieri di Vittorio Veneto 34, 56121 Cascina (PI).

Federazione Italiana della Musica (FEDERMUSICA): Via Vittor Piasni 10, 20124 Milan.

FILIS: Piazza Sallustio 24, 00187 Rome; Gen. Sec. Massimo Bordini.

IMAIE: Via Piave 66, 00187 Rome; tel. (6) 4200-2682; fax (6) 4200-2696; website www.imaie.it; Chair. Angeli Otello.

International Asscn for the Study of Popular Music (IASPM), Italian Section: c/o Il Giornale della Musica, corso Vittorio Emanuelle II n 198 bis, 10138 Turin.

International Dance Organization (IDO): Via Bronzino 117, 50142 Florence.

Istituto Italiano per la Storia della Musica: Via Vittoria 6, 00187 Rome.

Italian Braodcasting Asscn: Via della Moscova 38A, 20121 Milan; Pres. Riccardo Fausone.

Laboratorio Musicale Periferico: Via Pratese 48/a, 50145 Firenze; Pres. Roberto Buoni.

SIAE: Viale della Letteratura 30, 00144 Rome; tel. (6) 59901; website www.siae.it; Pres. Roman Vlad.

Sindacato Nazionale Musicisti (SNM): Via Pinelli 100, 10144 Turin.

Società Italiana Musica Contemporanea (SIMC): Via F. Juvara 11, 21029 Milan.

UNCLA: Galleria del Corso 4, 20122 Milan; Sec.-Gen. Armando Carnadelli.

Unione Editori di Musica Italiani (UNEMI): Via Teulada 52, 00195 Rome; Pres. Luciano Villeville Bideri.

Unione Nazionale Editori di Musica Italiani (UNEMI): Via Teulada 52, 00195 Rome.

Japan

Concert Managers' Asscn of Japan: Mitoko Bldg, 6-2-4 Akasaka, Minato-ku, Tokyo 107; Chair. Naoyasu Kajimoto.

Federation of Music Producers Japan: Jingumae Wada Bdlg, Shibuya-ku, Tokyo 150; Pres. Takeshi Hosokawa.

Japan Asscn of Music Enterprises: 4F Koyanagi Bldg 1-7 Ginza, Chuo-ku, Toyko 104; Contact Akitomo Tanabe.

Japan Audio Society: 3F Mori Bldg, 1-14-34 Jingumae, Shibuya-ku, Tokyo 150; Chair. Heitaro Nakajima.

Japan Council of Performers Organizations (Geidankyo): 11F Tokyo Opera City Tower, 3-20-2 Nishishinjuku, Shinjuku-ku, Tokyo 163-14; PR Samuel Shu. Masuyama.

Japan International League of Artists: 2-3-16-607 Shinjuku, Shinkjku-ku, Tokyo 160; Chief Officer Kazuhiko Hattori.

Japanese Composers Society: Ogawa Bldg, 3-7-15 Akasaka, Minato-ku, Tokyo 107.

Japanese Society for Rights of Authors, Composers & Publishers (JASRAC): 1-7-13 Nishishimbashi, Minato-ku, Tokyo 105; Pres. Ray Nakanishi.

Music Publishers Asscn of Japan: 7F Daiichi Nanou Bldg, 2-21-2 Nishi Shinbashi, Minato-ku, Tokyo 105; Pres. Misa Watanabe.

Musicians' Union of Japan: Showa Bldg, Second Floor, 4-8 Udagawa-cho, Shibuya-ku, Tokyo 150; Sec.-Gen. Kazuharu Sato.

Recording Industry Asscn of Japan (RIAJ): 2F Kobiki Bldg, 7-16-3 Giaza, Chao-ku 104; tel. (3) 3541-4411; fax (3) 3541-4460; website www.riaj.or.jp; Chair. Isamu Tomitsuka.

Union of Tokyo Music Business People: 3F Diar Inoue Bldg, 1-6-6 Akasaka, Mianto-ku, Tokyo 107; Chair. Masakasu Sunadoi.

Republic of Korea

Asian Composers' League (Korean Committee): PO Box 874, Seoul 110 062; Dir Sung-Jae Lee.

IFPI: Fifth Floor, Kumseok Bldg, 1574-14 Seocho-dong, Seocho-ku, Seoul 137 070; Contact Kim Seh Won.

Korea Music Copyright Asscn (KOMCA): 2-4F, Samjeon Bldg, 236-3 Nonhyeon-dong, Kangnam-ku, Seoul 135 010; Pres. Seog-Wan Gim.

Korea Performers' Asscn: Sixth Floor, Yeil B/D, 60 Chungshin-dong, Chongro-ku, Seoul; Contact Yun Tong Woong.

Music Asscn of Korea: 1-117 Dongsoong-dong, Chongro-ku, Seoul; Pres. Sang-Hyun Cho.

Luxembourg

SACEM: 46 rue Goethe, 1637 Luxembourg; Contact Pierre Neuen.

Malaysia

IFPI: 137-1/139-1 First Floor, Wisma Hiap Lee, Jln Segambut, Kuala Lumpur 51200; Gen. Man. Tan Ngiap Foo.

Mexico

AMPROFON: Francisco Petrarca 223-503, Chapultepec Morales, 11560 México, DF.

Cámara Nacional de la Industria de Radio y Television (CIRT): Avda Horacio, 1013 Col. Polanco, 11550 México, DF; Pres. Raul Arechina Espinoza; Gen. Man. César Hernández Espejo.

Dirección de Normas de Radiodifusión: Eugenia, 197, 1°, Col. Vértiz Narvarte, 03020 México, DF; Dir Alfonso Amilpas.

Dirección General de Telecomunicaciones: Lázaro Cárdenas, 567, 11°, ala norte Navarte, 03020 México, DF; Dir Carlos Lara Sumano.

National Traditional Country Music Asscn of Mexico: Esq. Américas, Fracc, Reforma, Veracruz.

Sociedad de Autores y Compositores de Música (SACM): Mayorazgo 129, 03330 México, DF; tel. (525) 604-7733; fax (525) 604-7923; e-mail sacm@sacm.org.mx; website www.sacm.org.mx.

Netherlands

BUMA (Composers Rights Society): PO Box 725, 1180 AS Amstelveen; website www.bumastemra.nl; Chair. Gerard Van Laar.

BVPOP: PO Box 63107, 1005 LC Amsterdam; Chair. Andrea Steinmetz.

Conamus Foundation: PO Box 929, Vaartweg 32, 1200 AX Hilversum; tel. (35) 621-8748; fax (35) 621-2750; e-mail info@conamus.nl; website www.conamus.nl; Man. Dir Jerney Kaagman.

Genootschap van Nederlandse Componisten (GENECO): PO Box 16463, 1001 RN, Amsterdam; tel. and fax (20) 622-7022; e-mail info@geneco.nl; website www.geneco.nl; Sec. C. H. Mackay.

Gong: Kerkweg 41, 3603 CL Maarssen; Contact Michael Lambrechsten.

Hard Disc (Asscn of Hard Rock DJs): Arkplein 103, 1826 DM Alkmaar; Pres. Gus Van Suntenmaartensdijk.

International Federation of Popular Music Publishers (IFPMP): Eikbosserweg 181, 1213 RX Hilversum; Sec.-Gen. Cor Smit.

Mega Top 50: PO Box 483, 1200 AL Hilversum; Man. Dir Sieb Kroeske.

Nederlandse Toonkunstenaarsbond (NTB): Herengracht 272, 1016 BW Amsterdam; Chair. Michiel de Sterke.

Nederlandse Vereniging van Producenten en Importeurs (NVPI): Albertus Perkstraat 36, 1217 NT Hilversum; tel. (35) 625-4411; fax (35) 625-4410; e-mail info@nupi.nl; website www.nupi.nl; Man. Dir P. R. C. Solleveld.

NVGD: Die Noord 3, 1452 PS Ilpendam; Chair. J. F. T. Hotzenbosch.

Osgood and Morley Clip/Music Video Production: Utrechtseweg 39 B, 1301 gs Weesp; Prod. Hans W. Van Pol.

PALM: Vaartweg 32, 1217 SV Hilversum; Chair. Cees Schrama.

SENA: PO Box 113, 1200 AC Hilversum; tel. (35) 625-1700; fax (35) 628-0971; e-mail sena@sena.nl; website www.sena.nl; Man. of International Affairs Natalie Loop.

STEMRA (Mechanical Rights Society): PO Box 725, 1180 AS Amstelveen; website www.bumastemra.nl; Chair. Gerard Van Laar.

UNIM: Eikbosserweg 181, 1213 JE Hilversum; Chair. Guus Jansen Jr.

Vecta: PO Box 49, 1394 ZG Nederhorst Den Berg; Chair. M. Hanson.

New Zealand

Australasian Mechanical Copyright Owners Society Ltd (New Zealand Branch Officer) (AMCOS): PO Box 36795, Parnell, Auckland; Gen. Man. (NZ) Janice Giles.

Composers Asscn of New Zealand (CANZ): PO Box 4065, Wellington; Pres. Denise Hulford.

Independent Music Producers and Performers Asscns (IMPPA): PO Box 68-593, Newton, Auckland; Chair. Jeff Clarkson.

New Zealand Composers Foundation Ltd: 11–13 Broderick Rd, Johnsonville, Wellington; Chair. Ashley Heenan.

New Zealand Country Music Asscn: PO Box 602, Wakatane; Sec. Linda Mita.

New Zealand Jazz Foundation: 18 Motueka St, Ngaio, Wellington; Pres. John Crawford.

New Zealand Music Centre: 15 Brandon St, Wellington; Chair. Merwyn Norrish.

New Zealand Music Information Bureau Inc: Carnegie Centre, 110 Moray Pl., Dunedin; Man. Dir John Kitto.

New Zealand Musicians' Union: Private Bag 68-914, Newton, Auckland; tel. (9) 834-3382; fax (9) 834-5897; e-mail peter@sfwu.org.nz; website www.sfwu.org.nz; Sec. Peter Shannon.

NZ On Air: PO Box 9744, Wellington; tel. (4) 382-9524; fax (4) 382-9546; e-mail kiwihits@nzonair.govt.nz; website www.nzonair.govt.nz; Music Man. Brendan Smyth.

Phonographic Performances (NZ) Ltd (PPNZ): Sixth Floor, Courtenay Chambers Bldg, 15 Courtenay Pl., Wellington; Chair. Terence O'Neill-Joyce.

Recording Industry Asscn of New Zealand (RAINZ): PO Box 37442, Parnell, Auckland; tel. (9) 308-0510; fax (9) 306-4977; e-mail music@rianz.org.nz; website www.rianz.org.nz; Chair. Terence O'Neill-Joyce.

Norway

DENIF: PO Box 365, 1701 Sarpsborg; Chair. Per Langsholt.

Foreningen Norskeplateselkaper (FONO): PO Box 5949, Majorstua, 0308 Oslo; tel. (47) 2327-1830; fax (47) 2327-1834; e-mail fono@fono.no; website www.fono.no; Chair. Jan Paulsen.

Gramo: Osterhaus 6T, 27, 0183 Oslo; Exec. Dir Jon Martin Gran.

IFPI: Norge Sandakervelen 52, 0477 Oslo; tel. 2222-1788; fax 2222-1768; e-mail ifpi.sekretariat@ifpi.no; website www.ifpi.no; Dir Saemund Fiskvik.

Norsk Forening For Opphavsrett: PO Box 9171, 0134 Oslo.

Norsk Jazzarkiv: Toftesgate 69, 0552 Oslo; Dir Finn Kramer-Johansen.

Norsk Musiker Og Musikkpedagogforening (NMM): PO Box 210, 4301 Sandnes; Man. Harald Bjørgan.

Norsk Musikerforbund: Youngsgate 11, 0181 Oslo; Man. Dir Tore Nordvik.

Norsk Rockforbund/Norwegian Rock Asscn: PO Box 8892 Youngstorget, 0028 Oslo; Man. Dir Øystein Ronander.

Norske Populaerautorer (NOPA): Toyenbekken 21, PO Box 9171 Gronland, 0134 Oslo; Chair. Sigurd Jansen.

Norwegian Jazz Asscn: Tollbugt. 28, 0157 Oslo; tel. 2335-8180; fax 2335-8181; e-mail norsk@jazzforum.no; website www.jazzforum.no; Man. Tone Martinsen.

Norwegian Music Information Centre: Toftesgate 69, 0552 Oslo; Contact Hilde Holback Hanssen.

Norwegian Society of Composers: PO Box 9171 Gronland, 0134 Oslo; Chair. Hakon Berge.

Tono: PO Box 9171, Gronland, 0134 Oslo; tel. 2205-7200; fax 2205-7250; e-mail tono@tono.no; website www.tono.no; Man. Cato Ström.

Philippines

Filipino Society of Composers, Authors and Publishers Inc (FILSCAP): 1365 E Rodriguez Sr Ave, Quezon City, Metro Manila; tel. (2) 721-3903; fax (2) 722-9450; website www.filscap.com.ph; Chair. George Canseco.

Philippine Asscn of the Recording Industry: 1020 Soliven Bldg, EDSA, San Juan, Metro Manila; tel. (2) 722-8014; fax (2) 725-0786; Pres. Danilo Olivares.

Poland

Asscn of Polish Musicians (SPAM): Ul. Krucza 24–26, 00 526 Warsaw; Pres. Eugeniusz Sasiadek.

Country Music Asscn of Poland: Ul. Grójecka 75, 02 094 Warsaw; Vice-Pres. Jerzy Gluszyk; Contact Ewa Dabrowska.

IFPI Poland: Ul. Czarnieckiego 5/2, 01 511 Warsaw; Dir Bianka Kortlan.

Polish Composers Union (ZKP): Rynek Starego Miasta 27, 00-272 Warsaw; Pres. Andrzej Chodkowski.

Polish Jazz Society: Ul. Chmielna 20, 00 020 Warsaw; Chair. Henryk Majewski.

Polish Music Centre: Fredry 8, 00-097 Warsaw; Man. Barbara Zwolska-Steszewska.

Society of Authors (ZAIKS): Hipoteczna 2, 00 950 Warsaw; Chair. Tadeusz Maklakiewicz.

Stomur/Asscn of Entertainment Musicians: Ul. Lwowska 13, 00 660 Warsaw; Chair. Maciej Czarnecki.

Union of Lyric Writers and Composers of Light Music (ZAKR): Hipoteczna 2, 00 950 Warsaw; Chair. Tadeusz Maklakiewicz.

Zwiazek Producentow Audio-Video/Polish Society of the Phonographic Industry (ZPAV): Ul. Kruczkowskiego 12m 2, 00-380 Warsaw; tel. (22) 622-9219; fax (22) 625-1661; e-mail biuro@2pav.pl; website www.zpav.pl; Man. Dir Marek Staszewski.

Portugal

Associação Fonografica Portuguesa (AFP): Augusto das Santos, 2/2, 1000 Lisbon; Pres. Daniel de Sousa.

Conselho Portugues da Musica: Rua Rosa Araújo, 6, 3°, 1200 Lisbon.

Instituto de Comunicacoes de Portugal (ICP): Avda José Malhoa, Lote 1683, 1000 Lisbon; Chair. Fernando Mendes.

Sindicato dos Musicos: Avda D Carlos I 72-2°, 1200 Lisbon; Pres. José Tristão Nunes Nogueira.

Romania

Institut de Etnografie Si Folclor C Brailoiu: Str Al Obregria Nr 3, Bloc M2, Apt 73, Sector 4, 75571 Bucharest; Contact Constanta Cristescu.

National Complex Astra Museum: 11 Piata Mica, Sibiu 2400; tel. (69) 218-195; fax (69) 218-060; e-mail astra@sbx.logicnet.ro; website www.romquest.com/astra; museum of traditional and folk music; Gen. Dir Corneliu Bucur.

Union des Musiciens Professionnels: Str Franklin Nr1, Sect 1, 70149 Bucharest; Contact Stefan Gheorghiu.

Union of Composers and Musicians: Calea Victorei 141, Sect 1, 70149 Bucharest; Chair. Adrain Iorgulescu.

Russia

International Music Council: Ul. Nyezhdanova str 8, 103 009 Moscow; Contact Boris Dimentman.

International Union of Musicians: Ul. Gertsena 14/2, 103 009 Moscow; Pres. Irina Arkhipova.

Moscow Jazz Agency (MJA): Ul. Nyezhdanova str 8–10, 103 009 Moscow; Chair. Yurii Saulsky.

Russian Phonographic Asscn: Krymsky Val 7, 117 418 Moscow; Man. Alexey Ugrinovich.

Union of Composers of Russia: Ul. Nyezhdanova 8, 103 009 Moscow; Contact Yevgeni Krivojev.

VAAP (Copyright Agency): Bolshaya Bronnaya 6A, 103 670 Moscow; Chair. Nikolaj Tchetverkiov.

Singapore

Composers and Authors Society of Singapore Ltd (COMPASS): 11-A Bukit Pasoh Rd, Singapore 089825; Gen. Man. Edmund Lam.

IFPI (South East Asia Ltd): 1 Marine Parade Central, #12-01 Parkway Builders' Centre, Singapore 1544; Deputy Regional Dir, S E Asia Leong May Seey.

Music Publishers (S) Ltd: 1 Marine Parade Central, #12-01 Parkway Builders' Centre, Singapore 1544; Admin. Exec. Laraine Soh.

Musicians & Singers Asscn: Block 3, 03-628 Rochor Centre, Rochor Rd, Singapore 0718; Chief Officer Stephen Gomez.

Singapore Phonogram & Videogram Asscn (SPVA): 1 Marine Parade Central, #12-01 Parkway Builders' Centre, Singapore 1544; Admin. Exec. Laraine Soh.

Slovakia

Asscn of Country Music: Jakubovo nam 12, 81109 Bratislava; Chair. Peter Gaspar.

Disco Club Mix (DMC): Klincova 12, 821-08 Bratislava; Man. Igor Malovec.

Slovak Jazz Society: Jakubovo nam 12, 81109 Bratislava; Contact Peter Lipa.

Slovensky Ochranny Zvaz Autorsky (SOZA): Kollarovo nam 20, 81327 Bratislava; Pres. Julius Kincek.

Union of Authors and Interpreters: Jakubovo nam 12, 81109 Bratislava; Dir Jan Balaz.

South Africa

Asscn of the South African Music Industry (RISA): PO Box 367, Randburg 2125, Johannesburg; tel. (11) 886-1342; CEO Des Dubery.

Dramatic, Artistic and Literary Rights Organization Ltd (DALRO): PO Box 9292, Johannnesburg; Man. Dir Gideon Ross.

Foundation for the Creative Arts: PO Box 91122, Auckland Park 2006; Exec. Man. Herman Van Niekerk.

South African Music Rights Organization Ltd (SAMRO): PO Box 9292, Johannesburg 2000; Man. Dir Gideon Ross.

South African Musicians Union: PO Box 5837, Johannesburg 2000; Pres. Howard Belling.

South African Recording Rights Asscn Ltd (SARRAL): PO Box 4378, Johannesburg 2000; Chief Officer George Hardie.

South African Society of Music Teachers: PO Box 5318, Walmer 6065.

Spain

AEDEM: Paseo de la Castellana 93, 28046 Madrid; Pres. Juan Marquez.

AFYVE/IFPI Spain: Pintor Juan Gris 4, 28020 Madrid; tel. (91) 555-8196; fax (91) 555-9592; Dir-Gen. Carlos Grande.

AIE: Calle Principe de Vergara 9, bajo derecha, 28001 Madrid; Pres. Luis Cobos.

Associacio Musics de Jazz: Gran Via 410-4, 08015 Barcelona; Sec. Angel Periera.

Centro para la Difusión de la Música Contemporánea (CDMC): Santa Isabel 52, 28012 Madrid.

Instituto de Bibliografica Musical: Penulas 12, 12p 28071 Madrid; Pres. Jacinto Torres Mulas.

Sindicato Profesional de Músicos Españoles (SPME): Calle Veneras 9-1°, 28013 Madrid; Gen. Sec. Jacinto Berzosa Arroyo.

Sociedad de Conciertos: Atlamira 3, 03002 Alicante; Dir Margarita Berenger.

Sociedad Española de Musicologica (SEM): Canos del Peral 7, 28013 Madrid; Pres. Ismael Fernandez de la Cuesta.

Sociedad General de Autores de España (SGAE): Fernando VI 4, 28004 Madrid; tel. (902) 119711; Pres. Manuel Gutierrez Aragón.

Sweden

DMC Sweden: PO Box 295, 101 25 Stockholm; Contact Per Stavborg.

Folkparkenas Nöjesservice: PO Box 171 94, 104 62 Stockholm; Chair. Björn Eriksson.

Föreningen Svenska Kompositörer Ave Populärmusik (SKAP): Sandhamnsgatan 79, PO Box 27327, 10254 Stockholm; Chair. Haakan Elmguist; Contact Ingered Lindberg.

Föreningen Svenska Tonsättare (FST): PO Box 27 237, 102 54 Stockholm; Chair. Sten Hanson.

IFPI Sweden: PO Box 1008, 171 21 Solna; Chair. Eddie Landquist.

Nordic Music Committee (NOMUS): Nybrokajen 11, 111 48 Stockholm; tel. 8407-1600; e-mail gen.secr@novens.org; Sec.-Gen. Bo Bydberg.

Rockfile Sweden HB: PO Box 558, 631 07 Eskilstuna; Man. Dir Hans Lindell.

Society of Swedish Composers: PO Box 27 327, 102 54 Stockholm.

Svensk Impressarieförening (SVIMP): Villawagen 25A, 19146 Sollentuna; tel. 8661-3800; fax 8665-1795; e-mail knut.rutenborg@ema.se; website www.ema.se; Chair. Asa Ingman.

Svensk Musik/Swedish Music Information Centre: PO Box 27 327, 102 54 Stockholm; Chair. Roland Sandberg.

Swedish Artists' and Musicians' Interest Organization (SAMI): Döbelnsgatan 3, 111 40 Stockholm; tel. 8453-3400; fax 8453-3440; e-mail hans.sami.se; website www.sami.se; Man. Dir Hans Lindström.

Swedish Music Publishers Asscn (SMFF): PO Box 27 327, 102 54 Stockholm; tel. (8) 783-8965; fax (8) 663-4963; e-mail carl.lindencrona@smff.se; website www.smff.sc; Man. Dir Carl Lindencicna.

Swedish Musicians Union/Svenska Musiker Förbundet: PO Box 43, Tegneratan 4, 101 20 Stockholm; Contact Hakan Hillerström.

Swedish Performing Rights Society (STIM): PO Box 27 327, 102 54 Stockholm; tel. (8) 783-8800; fax (8) 662-6275; e-mail info@stim.se; website www.stim.se; Gen. Man. Gunnar Petri.

Switzerland

Asscn of Swiss Concert Agents: 7 rue de la Fontaine, 1211 Geneva; Pres. Jack Yfar.

Asscn of Swiss Musicians: Ave du Grammont 11 bis, Case Postale 177, 1000 Lausanne 13; Gen. Sec. Hélène Petitpierre.

European Asscn of Music Festivals: c/o Centre Européen de la Culture Villa Moynier, 122 rue de Lausanne, 1211 Geneva; Sec. Dr Henry Siegwart.

Federation of International Music Competitions: 104 rue de Carouge, 1205 Geneva.

Fondation Suisa Pour la Musique: Rue de l'Hôpital 22, PO Box 2331, 2001 Neuchatel; tel. (32) 725-2536; fax (32) 724-0472; e-mail info@fondation-suisa.ch; website www.fondation-suisa.ch; Pres. Jean Balissat; Dir Claude Delley.

IFPI Switzerland: Toblerstr 76a, 8044 Zurich; tel. (1) 252-5866; fax (1) 252-6167; website www.ifpi-schwiez.ch; Dir Peter Vosseler.

International Society for Contemporary Music: c/o Asscn of Swiss Musicians, Ave du Grammont 11 bis, Case Postale 177, 1000 Lausanne 13.

Schweizer Zentralband Musikhandels (SZM): Zeughausgasse 9, PO Box 238, 6301 Zug; Pres. Erika Hug.

Schweizerischer Musikverband (SMV): Hotelgasse 1, 300 Bern 7; Pres. Heinz Marti.

Suisa (Performing Rights Society of Switzerland): Bellariastr 82, 8038 Zürich; tel. (1) 485-6666; fax (1) 482-4333; website www.suisa.ch; Man. Fabio Hugel.

Suisa Music Foundation (Music Information Centre): Passage Maxmililien-de-Meuron 4, PO Box 409, 2001 Neuchâtel; Man. Dir P. Liechti.

SVMM: PO Box, 8616 Riedikon /Uster; Pres. Willy Viteka.

Swiss Asscn of Professional Musicians: Elisabethenstr 2, 4051 Basel.

Swiss Society for Musical Research: PO Box 231, 4020 Basel.

Swiss Society for Popular Music: c/o SUISA, Bellariastr 82, 8038 Zürich.

VSM: Zeughausgasse 9, PO Box 238, 6301 Zug; Pres. Edmund Schoenberger.

VSSF: Zeughausgasse 9, PO Box 238, 6301 Zug; Pres. Daniel Baer.

Taiwan

ARCO—Asscn of Recording Copyright Owners of ROC: 3F, No. 95, Sec 4, Nanking E Rd, Taipei; Exec. Dir Robin Lee.

IFPI Members Foundation in Taiwan: 3F, No. 95, Sec 4, Nanking E Rd, Taipei; Sec.-Gen. Robin Lee.

Thailand

Thai Composers Asscn (TCA): 107–108 Siripong Rd, Sao Chingcha, Samranrat, Bangkok 10200.

Turkey

MESAM: Kuyulu Bostan Sokak Kristal Plas Apt, Nisantasi, Istanbul.

MUYAP (Muzik Yapimlari Dernegi): IMC 6, Blok 6437, 34470 Unkapani, Istanbul; Contact Yasar Kekeva.

Ukraine

Broken Barricades: Tchernovoarmiyska 17B, 252 003 Kiev; Man. Sergiy Kalyta.

Dirate of the All-Ukrainian Festival of Independent Music: Alternative Culture Foundation, Lesva Kur-Basa str 4, 290007 Lviv; held in Sept.; Dir Youry Grekh; Vice-Dir Ruslan Koshiv.

Independent Artist's Agency 'Ljubchenko & Co': Room 7, Mietrostrojevskaja St 5, 320128 Dnipropetrovsk; Dir Valeri Ljubchenko.

Institute of Musicology: Soviet Ukraine Sq., 20 # 9, 310003 Kharkiv; Dir Grigory Hansburg.

Musical Information Agency IRA: PO Box 83, 326 840 Novoya Kakhovka/Kherson; Man. Iryna Tsygipa.

Producers Centre Rock Academy: Khreschatyk 6, 252 001 Kiev; Man. Dir Mykola Drik.

United Kingdom

Agents' Asscn (GB): 54 Keyes House, Dolphin Sq., London SW1V 3NA; Gen. Sec. Ivan Birchall.

Alchemea—The London College of Professional Audio Engineering and Production: The Windsor Centre, 2–18 Britannia Row, The Angel Islington, London N1 8QH; College Dir Claude Camilleri.

American Society of Composers, Authors and Publishers (ASCAP): 8 Cork St, London W1X 1PB; Contact Karen Crowley.

Asscn of Music Industry Accountants (AMIA): Becket House, 1 Lambeth Rd, London SE1 7EU; Sec. Nicki Davies.

Asscn of Professional Recording Services Ltd (APRS): 2 Windsor Sq., Reading, Berkshire RG1 2TH; CEO Mark Broad.

Asscn of United Recording Artists (Aura): 7 Russell Gdns, London W14 8EZ; tel. (20) 7602 5985; fax (20) 7603 4411; e-mail info@aurauk.com; website www.aurauk.com; Contact Peter Jenner.

Belfast Jazz Society: 18 Lyndhurst Dr., Belfast B13 3PA, Northern Ireland; Admin. George Chambers.

Black Music Industry Asscn: 146 Manor Park Rd, Harlesden, London NW10 4JP; Contact Kwaku Lutterfoot.

British Academy of Composers and Songwriters (BAC&S): British Music House, 26 Berners St, London W1T 3LR; e-mail info@britishacademy.com; website www.britishacademy.com; formerly the Asscn of Professional Composers (APC), the British Acad. of Songwriters, Composers & Authors (BASCA), and the Composers' Guild of Great Britain; changed name as above, 1999.

British Archive of Country Music: 163 The Gateway, Marine Parade, Dover CT16 1LS, Kent; Man. Dir David Barnes.

British Asscn of Concert Agents: 26 Wadham Rd, London SW15 2LR; Pres. David Sigall.

British Asscn of Record Dealers (BARD): Premier House, Hinton Rd, Bournemouth, Dorset BH1 2EF; Dir-Gen. Bob Lewis.

British Country Music Asscn: PO Box 240, Harrow, Middlesex HA3 7PH; tel. (1273) 559750; fax (1273) 559750; e-mail thebcma@yahoo.com; Chair. Jim Marshall.

British Music Rights: British Music House, 26 Berners St, London W1T 3LR; tel. (20) 7306 4446; fax (20) 7306 4449; e-mail britishmusic@bmr.org; website www.bmr.org.uk.

British Phonographic Industry (BPI): Riverside Bldg, County Hall, Westminster Bridge Rd, London SE1 7JA; tel. (20) 7803 1300; fax (20) 7803 1310; e-mail general@bpi.co.uk; website www.bpi.co.uk; Dir-Gen. John Deacon; Gen. Man. Peter Scaping.

Broadcast Music, Inc (BMI): 84 Harley House, Marylebone Rd, London NW1 5HN; tel. (20) 7486-2036; website www.bmi.com; Dir (UK) Christian Ulf-Hansen.

Celfyddydau Mari: Arts Studio 4, Model House Craft and Design Centre, The Bullring, Llantrisant, Rhondda Cynon Taf, Wales CF72 8EB; Co-ordinator Mick Tems.

Christian Copyright Licensing Ltd: PO Box 1339, Eastbourne, East Sussex BN21 4YF; UK Church & Schools Representative Chris Williams.

Club Gwerin: Llantrisant Folk Club 1 Ty Clwyta Cottages, Cross Inn, Llantrisant, Rhondda Cynon Taf, Wales CF72 8AZ; tel. and fax (1443) 226892; e-mail folkclub@folkwales.org.uk; website www.folkwales.org.uk; Sec. Mick Tems.

Commercial Radio Companies Asscn (CRCA): 77 Shaftesbury Ave, London W1V 7AD; tel. (20) 7306-2603; fax (20) 7470-0062; e-mail info@crea.co.uk; website www.crea.co.uk; CEO Paul Brown.

Country Music Asscn (CMA): Third Floor, 18 Golden Sq., London W1R 3AG; European Operations Co-ordinator Bobbi Boyce; Dir (UK/Ireland) David Bower.

C-Thru Music Ltd: 6 Pleasant Row, Woodford, Northamptonshire NN14 4HP; tel. (1832) 733214; website www.c-thru-music.com; Contact Andrew Llewellyn.

Friends of the Upton Jazz Festival: Court Cottage, Lockeridge Lane, Upton-Upon-Severn WR8 0RP; tel. (1684) 593794; Sec. Paul Lawrence.

Guild of International Songwriters and Composers (GISC): Sovereign House, 12 Trewartha Rd, Parr Sands, Penzance, Cornwall TR20 9ST; tel. (1736) 762826; fax (1736) 763328; e-mail songmag@aol.com; website www.songwriters-guild.co.uk; Gen. Sec. Carole A. Jones.

Guild of Recording Producers, Dirs and Engineers (Re-Pro): 68 Cleveland Gdns, Barnes, London SW13 0AH; Contact Jackie DaCosta.

Incorporated Society of Musicians: 10 Stratford Pl., London W1C 1AA; tel. (20) 7629-4413; fax (20) 7408-1538; e-mail membership@ism.org; website www.ism.org; CEO Neil Hoyle.

International Artist Managers' Asscn (IAMA): 4 Addison Bridge Pl., London W14 8XP.

International Federation of the Phonographic Industry (IFPI): 54 Regent St, London W1R 5PJ; Chair. David Fine; Dir-Gen. Nic Garnett.

International Managers Forum (IMF): 134 Lots Rd, London SW10 0RJ; Gen. Sec. James Fisher.

International Music Markets (IMM) Ltd: 245 Old Marylebone Rd, London NW1 5QT; Gen. Man. Phil Graham.

International Society of European Songwriters and Composers (SESAC): Gresham House, 53 Clarendon Rd, Watford, Herts WD1 1LA; Chair. Wayne Bickerton.

Jazz Action: 1 Portrush Close, Darlington, Co Durham DL1 3HU; Devt Officer Adrian Tilbrook.

Jazz Educaton Trust: 1 Fox Glove Close, Ringmer, East Sussex BN8 5PB; Dir Adrian Kendon.

Jazz North West: 2A Church St, Malpas, Cheshire SY14 8NZ; Dir Nick Purnell.

Jazz Services: First Floor, 132 Southwark St, London SE1 0SW; tel. (20) 7928-9089; fax (20) 7401-6870; e-mail admin@jazzservices.org.uk; website www.jazzservices.org.uk; Contact Celia Wood.

Mechanical Copyright Protection Society Ltd (MCPS): Elgar House, 41 Streatham High Rd, London SW16 1ER; website www.mcps.co.uk; CEO John Hutchinson.

Millward Brown Market Research Ltd: Olympus Ave, Tachbrook Park, Warwick CV34 6RJ; Charts Dir Bob Barnes.

Music Industry Human Rights Asscn: 192 Chiswick Village, London W4 3DG.

Music Industry Research Organization (MIRO): Eighth Floor, Ludgate House, 245 Blackfriars Rd, London SE1 9UR; Ed. Lee Fisher.

Music Publishers Asscn (MPA): Third Floor, Strandgate, 18–20 York Bldgs, London WC2 6JU; CEO Sarah Foulder.

Musicians Benevolent Fund: 16 Ogle St, London W1P 8JB; Sec. to the Fund Helen Faulkner.

Musicians' Union (MU): 60–62 Clapham Rd, London SW9 0JJ; Gen. Sec. Dennis Scard.

National Entertainment Agents Council: PO Box 112, Seaford, East Sussex BN25 2DQ; tel. (1323) 492488; fax (1323) 492234; e-mail info@neac.org.uk; website www.neac.org.uk; Gen. Sec. Chris Bray.

Nordoff Robbins Music Therapy: 55 Fulham High St, London SW6 3JJ; Chair. Andrew Miller.

North West Composers' Asscn: Stanway Rd, Whitefield, Manchester M45 8EG; tel. (161) 766-5950; Treasurer Geoffrey Kimpton; Sec. Colin Bayliss.

Northern Ireland Musicians' Asscn: 525 Antrim Rd, Belfast BT15 3BS; Gen. Sec. Henry C. Hamilton.

North-West Musicians' Collective: 6C Shipquay St, Derry, Northern Ireland BT48 6DN; Co-ordinators John O'Neill, Sean Pemberton.

OVC Ltd: 34 Salisbury St, London NW8 8QE; tel. (20) 7402-9111; fax (20) 7723-3064; e-mail ovcmedia@hotmail.com; website www.ovcmedia.com; Man. Dirs Joanne Cohen, Peter Sullivan.

Performing Artists Media Rights Asscn (PAMRA): Third Floor, 161 Borough High St, London SE1 1HR; tel. (20) 7940 0400; fax (20) 7407 2008; e-mail office@pamra.org.uk; website www.pamra.org.uk; CEO Ann Rawcliffe-King; Dir Benny Gallagher.

Performing Rights Society (PRS): 29–33 Berners St, London W1P 4AA; tel. (20) 7580 5544; fax (20) 7306 4455; CEO John Hutchinson; Membership Dir John Sweeney.

Phonographic Performance Ltd (PPL): 1 Upper James St, London W1R 3HG; website www.ppluk.com; CEO Charles Andrews; Man. Dir John Love.

Publicity Connection: Flat 3, Haversham Lodge, Melrose Ave, Willesden Green, London NW2 4JS; tel. (20) 8450-8882; fax (20) 8202-4219; e-mail sharon@thepublicityconnection.com; website www.thepublicityconnection.com; Man. Dir Sharon Chevin.

Radio Academy: 5 Marklet Pl., London W1N 7AH; tel. (20) 7255-2010; fax (20) 7255-2029; e-mail info@radioacademy.org; website www.radioacademy.org; CEO John Bradford.

Radio Advertising Bureau (RAB): 77 Shaftesbury Ave, London W1V 7AD; Dir Douglas McArthur.

Radio Authority: Holbrook House, 14 Great Queen St, London WC2B 5DG; Chair. Sir Peter Gibbings; Contact Marion Shelley.

Red Bus Music (International) Ltd: 34 Salisbury St, London NW8 8QE; tel. (20) 7402-9111; fax (20) 7723-3064; website www.amimedia.co.uk; Man. Dir Eliot M. Cohen.

Regional Promoters Asscn (RPA): The Leadmill, 6–7 Leadmill Rd, Sheffield S1 4SE; tel. (114) 2212860; fax (114) 2212848; e-mail rupert@leadmill.co.uk; website www.leadmill.co.uk; Contact Rupert Dell.

Scottish Music Information Centre: 1 Bowmont Gardens, Glasgow G12 9LR.

South West Jazz: Exeter and Devon Arts Centre, Bradninch Pl., Gandy St, Exeter EX4 3LS; Regional Devt Officer Kevin Buckland.

The Official UK Charts Co: Third Floor, Century House, 100 Oxford St, London W1N 9LD; tel. (20) 7436-3000; fax (20) 7436-8000; e-mail info@theofficialcharts.com; website www.theofficialcharts.com; Chart Dir Omar Maskatiya.

Variety and Light Entertainment Council: 54 Keyes House, Dolphin Sq., London SW1V 3NA; tel. (20) 7834-0515; fax (20) 7821-0261; e-mail association@agents-uk.com; website www.agents-uk.com; Joint Secretaries Kenneth Earle, Christine Payne.

Video Performance Ltd (VPL): 1 Upper James St, London W1R 3HG; CEO Charles Andrews.

Vocem Electric Voice Theatre: 39 Birnam Rd, London N4 3LJ.

Welsh Jazz Society Ltd: 26 The Balcony, Castle Arcade, Cardiff, South Glamorgan CF10 1BY; tel. (2920) 340591; fax (2920) 665160; e-mail jazzwale@cs.com; website www.jazzwales.org.uk; Dir Brian Hennessey.

Whistlebinkies: 13 Lawrence St, Glasgow G11 5HH; Contact Eddie McGuire.

Women in Music: BAC, Lavender Hill, Battersea, London SW11 5TF; Admin. Dir Lolita Ratchford.

United States of America

Academy of Country Music (ACM): 6255 Sunset Blvd, Suite 923, Hollywood, CA 90028; Pres. Fred Reiser.

Affiliated Independent Record Companies (AIRC): PO Box 241648, Los Angeles, CA 90024; Pres. M. Wilkes.

American Federation of Musicians: 1501 Broadway, Suite 600, New York, NY 10036; Pres. Mark Massagli.

American Federation of Television and Radio Artists (AFTRA): 260 Madison Ave, New York, NY 10016; Exec. Dir Bruce York.

American Mechanical Rights Agency Inc (AMRA): c/o Sindee Levin, 150 S Barrington Ave, Suite 1, Los Angeles, CA 90049; tel. (310) 440-8778; fax (310) 440-0059; website www.amra.com; Chief Officer Patricia Bente.

American Musicians' Union: 8 Tobin Ct, Dumont, NJ 07628; Pres. Ben Intorre.

American Society of Composers, Authors and Publishers (ASCAP): ASCAP Bldg, 1 Lincoln Plaza, New York, NY 10023; website www.ascap.com; Pres. Marilyn Bergman.

American Society of Music Arrangers & Composers (ASMAC): PO Box 17840, Encino, CA 91416; tel. (818) 994-4661; fax (818) 994-6181; e-mail properimage2000@earthlink.net; website www.asmac.org; Pres. John Clayton; Sec. Bonnie Janofsky.

Audio Engineering Society (AES): 60 E 42nd St, Lincoln Bldg, Room 2520, New York, NY 10165; tel. (212) 661-8528; fax (212) 682-0477; e-mail hq@aes.org; website www.aes.org; Dir Donald Plunkett.

Black Rock Coalition: PO Box 1054, Cooper Station, New York, NY 10276; Pres. Bruce Mack.

Broadcast Music Inc (BMI): 320 W 57th St, New York, NY 10019; tel. (212) 586-2000; website www.bmi.com; Pres. Frances Preston.

Chorus America: 1156 15th St, NW Suite 310, Washington, DC 20005; Exec. Dir Maurice Staples.

Company of Fifers and Drummers: PO Box 525, Ivoryton, CT 06443; Archivist Ed Olson.

Composers Guild: PO Box 586, Framington, UT 84025; Pres. Ruth Gatrell.

Concerts for the Environment: 126 N Third St, Suite 305, Minneapolis, MN 55401; Exec. Dir Michael Martin.

Country Music Asscn (CMA): 4 Music Circle S, Nashville, TN 37203; Exec. Dir Ed Benson.

CSP Records MC: PO Box 69646, Los Angeles, CA 90096; Dir Larry Kleno.

GAVIN: 140 Second St, Second Floor, San Francisco, CA 94105; CEO David Dalton.

Gospel Music Asscn: 7 Music Circle N, Nashville, TN 37203; Exec. Dir Bruce Koblish.

Guitar and Accessories Marketing Asscn: 38 W 21st St, Fifth Floor, New York, NY 10010-6906; Pres. Jerome Hershman.

Guitar Foundation of America: PO Box 1240, Calremont, CA 91711; e-mail gunnar@cyberg8t.com; website www.guitarfoundation.org; Exec. Dir Gunnar Eisel.

Harry Fox Agency (HFA): 711 Third Ave, New York, NY 10017; tel. (212) 370-5330; fax (212) 953-2384; website www.hfa.com.

Hawaiian Academy of Recording Arts (HARA): PO Box 821, Honolulu, HI 96808; Contact Bonni Ryder.

Independent Music Asscn: 10 Spruce Rd, Saddle River, NJ 07456; Contact Don Kulak.

Independent Network: (East Coast Office) PO Box 609, Ringwood, NJ 07456; (West Coast Office) PO Box 241648 Los Angeles, CA 90024; CEO M. Wilkins.

Institute of Recording Arts & Sciences: PO Box 22653, Nashville, TN 37202; Founder & Admin. David Mathes.

International Asscn of Electronic Keyboard Manufacturers: 38 W 21st St, Fifth Floor, New York, NY 10010-6906; Pres. Jerome Hershman.

International Bluegrass Music Asscn (IBMA): 207 E Second St, Owensboro, KY 42303.

Jazz Foundation of America: 1200 Broadway, Suite 7D, New York, NY 10001; Promotions Dir Russ Dantzler.

Long Island Songwriters' Asscn Inc (LISA): PO Box 395, Holbrook, NY 11741; Pres./Exec. Dir Erwin K. Cochran.

Mel Carter: PO Box 69646, Los Angeles, CA 90069; tel. and fax (323) 934-4122; e-mail red@mel-carter.com; website www.mel-carter.com; Artist/Owner Larry Kleno.

Mexican Network International: 235-4 Lucas Lane, Voorhees, NJ 08043; Pres./Founder Laura Grüb-Geschwindt.

Music Asscn of America: 224 King St, Englewood, NJ 07631; Exec. Dir George Strum.

Music Distributors Asscn: 38 W 21st St, Fifth Floor, New York, NY 10010-6906; Pres. Jerome Hershman.

Music Educators National Conference: 1806 Robert Fulton Dr., Reston, VA 22091-4348; Exec. Dir John J. Mahlmann.

Music Publishers' Asscn of the United States: 711 Third Ave, New York, NY 10017.

Musicians Contact Service: 7315 Sunset Blvd D, Hollywood, CA 90046; Contact Sterling Haug.

NAIRD: 1000 Maplewood Dr., Suite 211, Maple Shade, NJ 08052; Exec. Dir Holly Cass.

Nashville Entertainment Asscn: PO Box 121948, Nashville, TN 37212-1948; Exec. Dir Sherry Bond.

Nashville Songwriters Asscn International (NSAI): 15 Music Sq. W, Nashville, TN 37203; Exec. Dir Pat Rogers.

Nashville Songwriters' Foundation: PO Box 121775, Nashville, TN 37212-1775.

National Academy of Popular Music: 885 Second Ave, 26th Floor, New York, NY 10017-2201; Dir Bob Leone.

National Academy of Recording Arts & Sciences Inc (NARAS): 2 Music Circle S, Nashville, TN 37203.

National Academy of Songwriters (NAS): 6381 Hollywood Blvd, Suite 780, Hollywood, CA 90028; Exec. Dir Dan Kirkpatrick.

National Asscn of Band Instrument Manufacturers: 38 W 21st St, Fifth Floor, New York, NY 10010-6906; Pres. Jerome Hershman.

National Asscn of Recording Merchandisers (NARM): 11 Eves Dr., Suite 140, Marlton, NJ 08053; Exec. Vice-Pres. Pam Horowitz.

National Coalition Against Censorship: 275 Seventh Ave, New York, NY 10001; Exec. Dir Leanne Katz.

National Council of Music Importers and Exporters: 38 W 21st St, Fifth Floor, New York, NY 10010-6906; Pres. Jerome Hershman.

National Music Publishers' Asscn (NMPA): 475 Park Ave S, 29th Floor, New York, NY 10016; tel. (646) 742-1651; fax (646) 742-1779; website www.nmpa.com; Public Relations Man. Margaret O'Keeffe.

Northern California Songwriters Asscn: 855 Oak Grove Ave, Suite 211, Menlo Park, CA 94025; Exec. Dir Ian Crombie.

Publishers' Licensing Corpn: PO Box 5807, Englewood, NJ 07631; tel. (201) 969-9990; fax (201) 969-9955; e-mail plcagent@aol.com; Pres. Philip S. Kurnit.

Recording Industry Asscn of America (RIAA): 1330 Connecticut Ave NW, Suite 300, Washington, DC 20036; tel. (202) 775-0101; fax (202) 775-7253; website www.riaa.com; Vice-Pres., Member Services John H. Ganoe.

Rhythm and Blues Rock and Roll Society Inc: PO Box 1949, New Haven, CT 06510; tel. (203) 924-1079; Dir Bill Nolan.

Rock and Roll Hall of Fame: 1290 Sixth Ave, New York, NY 10104; Exec. Dir Susan Evans.

Rock Out Censorship (ROC): PO Box 147, Jewett, OH 43986; Co-Founder/Ed. John Woods.

SESAC: 55 Music Sq. E, Nashville, TN 37203; tel. (615) 320-0055; fax (615) 329-9627; website www.sesac.com.

Songwriters Guild of America: 6430 Sunset Blvd, Suite 705, Hollywood, CA 90028; tel. (323) 462-1108; fax (323) 462-5430; e-mail lasga@aol.com; website www.songwriters.org; West Coast Dir B. Aaron Meza.

Songwriters of Wisconsin International—SOWI: PO Box 1027, Neenah, WI 54957-1027; tel. (920) 725-5129; fax (920) 720-0195; e-mail sowtoner@aol.com; Pres. Tony Ansems.

Talent Search America: 273 Chippewa Dr., Columbia, SC 29210-6508; international songwriting and lyric-writing contests.

Tennessee Film, Entertainment and Music Commission: Rachel Jackson Bldg, 320 Sixth Ave, Nashville, TN 37243-0790; Exec. Dir Marsha Blackburn.

Tennessee Songwriters Asscn (TSA): PO Box 2664, Hendersonville, TN 37075; Contact Jim Sylvis.

Texas Music Office: Office of the Governor, PO Box 13246, Austin, TX 78711; Dir Casey Monahan.

Women in Music Business Asscn: 20 Music Sq. W, Suite 200, Nashville, TN 37203; Dir Catherine Masters.

Women in Music National Network: 31121 Mission Blvd, Suite 123, Hayward, CA 94544; Chair. Karen Jackson.

Uruguay

Asociación General de Autores del Uruguay (AGADU): Canelones, 1122, 11100 Montevideo; Pres. Antonio Italiano.

Asociación Uruguay de Músicos: Calle Maldonado 983, CP 11100, Montevideo; Pres. Alfonso Coronel.

Sociedad Uruguay de Interpretes: Canelones 1090, Montevideo; Pres. José Maria Lorenzo.

Sociedad Uruguay de Música Contemporánea: Casilla de Correo 1328, Montevideo; Pres. Diego Legrand.

Venezuela

Sociedad de Autores y Compositores de Venezuela: Edif. Vam, Entrada Oeste 9°, Avda Andrés Bello, Caracas